W9-BKL-742

Oxford American Dictionary and Thesaurus

Oxford American Dictionary and Thesaurus

SECOND EDITION

UNIVERSITY PRESS

OXFORD
UNIVERSITY PRESS

Oxford University Press, Inc., publishes works that further Oxford University's objective of excellence in research, scholarship, and education.

Oxford New York

Auckland Cape Town Dar es Salaam Hong Kong Karachi Kuala Lumpur Madrid Melbourne Mexico City Nairobi New Delhi Shanghai Taipei Toronto

With offices in

Argentina Austria Brazil Chile Czech Republic France Greece Guatemala Hungary Italy Japan Poland Portugal Singapore South Korea Switzerland Thailand Turkey Ukraine Vietnam

Copyright © 2009 by Oxford University Press

First edition 2003
Second edition 2009

Dictionary text first published as the *Pocket Oxford American Dictionary* 2nd edition, published 2008; thesaurus text adapted from the *Oxford Mini Thesaurus*, 4th edition, published 2007

Published by Oxford University Press, Inc.
198 Madison Avenue, New York, NY 10016
www.oup.com

Oxford is a registered trademark of Oxford University Press

All rights reserved. No part of this publication may be reproduced, stored in a retrieval system, or transmitted, in any form or by any means, electronic, mechanical, photocopying, recording, or otherwise, without the prior permission of Oxford University Press.

The Library of Congress Cataloging-in-Publication Data

Data available

ISBN 978-0-19-538465-9

1 3 5 7 9 8 6 4 2

Printed in the United States of America
on acid-free paper

Contents

Contributors

For the Oxford American Dictionary and Thesaurus

Project Manager/Editor
Charlotte Buxton

Editor
Christine A. Lindberg

Associate Editor
Sarah Hilliard

For the Pocket Oxford American Dictionary

Project Manager
Maurice Waite

Senior Editor
Christine A. Lindberg

Editor
Benjamin G. Zimmer

Lexicographers
Orin Hargraves
Sue Ellen Thompson

Preface

This new edition of the *Oxford American Dictionary and Thesaurus* is the ideal reference resource. The text provides dictionary definitions for all of the words you need to know, as well as useful synonyms, in a clear, easy-to-use form. Both dictionary and thesaurus information is provided in fully integrated, multi-purpose entries. Whether you want to check the meaning of a word or find a range of alternative terms with the same meaning, you need only look at one main entry.

The book has been designed to be as user-friendly as possible, with clear definitions, straightforward grammatical information, and pronunciations shown using easily understandable respellings. Both core vocabulary and a wide range of technical terms are covered, combined with thousands of synonyms to help you enrich your writing and express yourself more effectively.

Throughout the text you'll also find a range of boxed features, offering helpful advice on language use and choosing the right word from groups of similar synonyms (such as *replace*, *displace*, *supersede*, and *supplant*). At the center of the book there's a Language Guide, giving in-depth information on aspects of language that often cause problems – such as grammar, spelling, and punctuation. There's also a Wordfinder section containing lists of words that are not normally found as synonyms in a thesaurus. The lists are grouped into thematic categories, such as Animals, Science, and Sports, making them interesting to browse, as well as extremely useful for word puzzles such as crosswords. Finally, there is a handy reference section, containing lists of US Presidents, US States, and Countries of the World.

In all its aspects, the *Oxford American Dictionary and Thesaurus* draws on the expertise of lexicographers based in the US as well as the worldwide resources of Oxford University Press. In particular, it has been compiled using information provided by the Oxford English Corpus, a two-billion word database of many different types of English, and the database of the Oxford Reading Program, so you can be confident in the authenticity and authority of the entire text.

Trademarks
This dictionary includes some words that have, or are asserted to have, proprietary status as trademarks or otherwise. Their inclusion does not imply that they have acquired for legal purposes a nonproprietary or general significance, nor any other judgment concerning their legal status. In cases where the editorial staff have some evidence that a word has proprietary status, this is indicated in the entry for that word by the label trademark, but no judgment concerning the legal status of such words is made or implied thereby.

Guide to the Dictionary and Thesaurus

1. Structure of entries

Here are examples of the major types of information in entries:

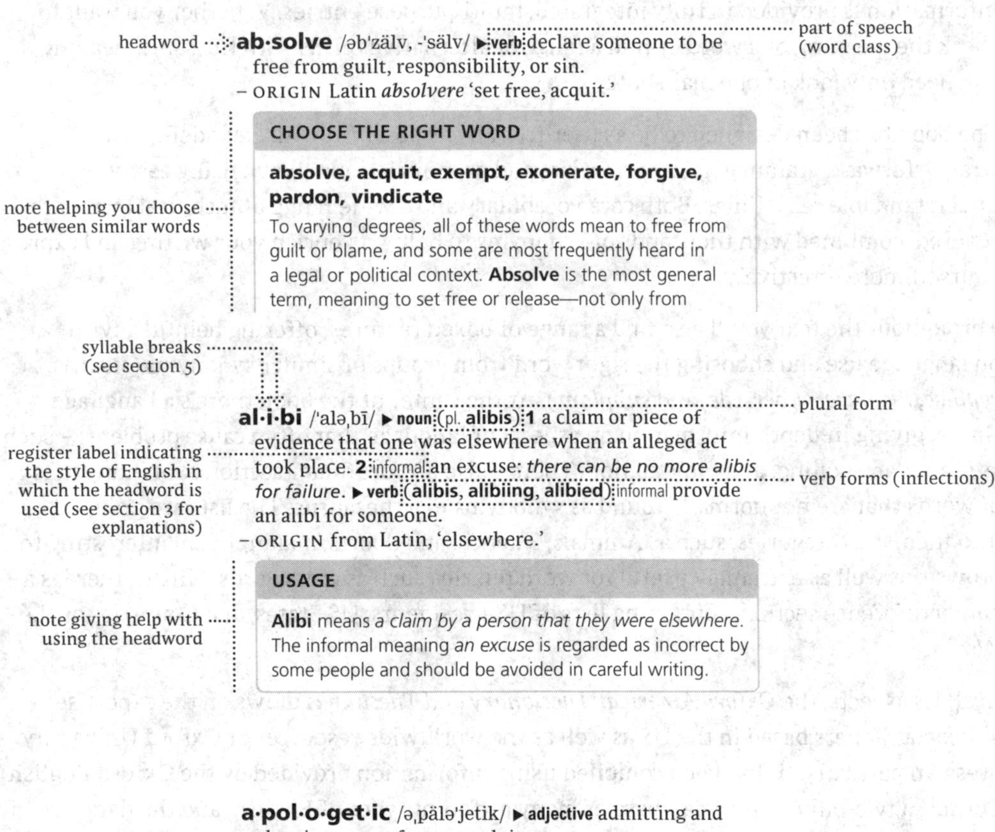

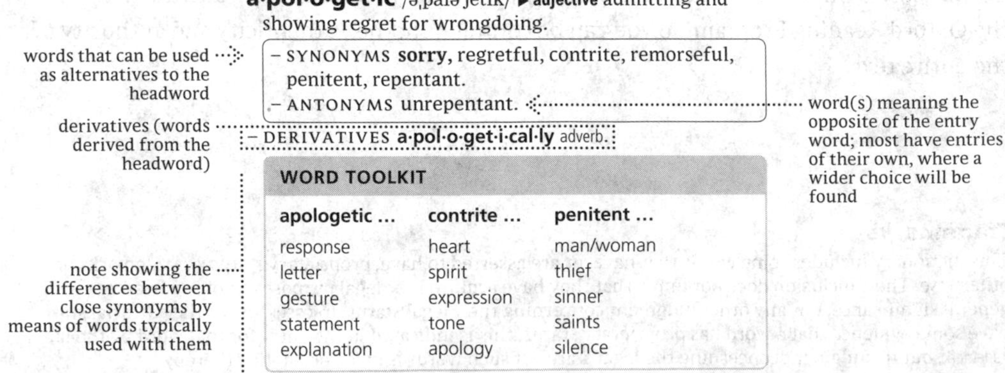

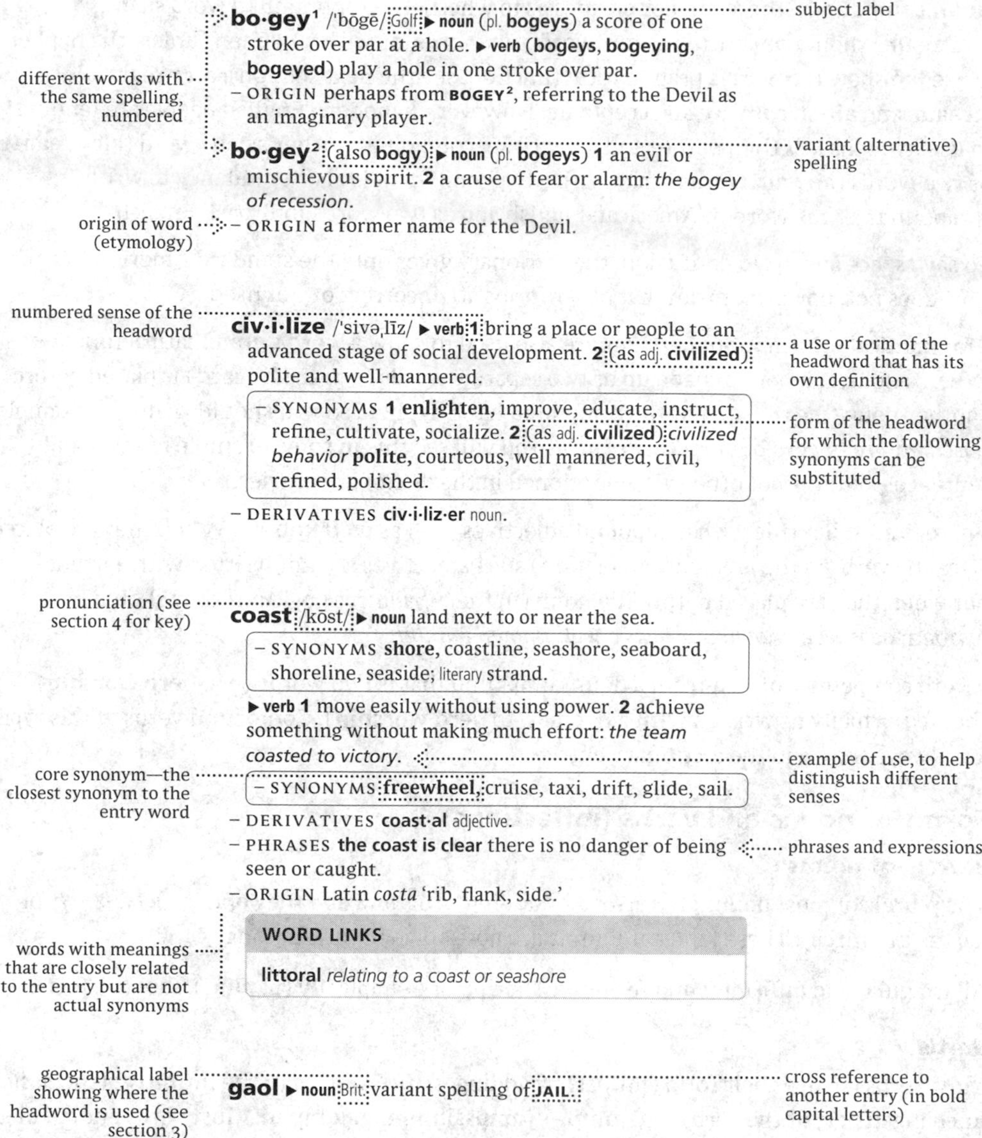

2. Spelling and forms of nouns and verbs

Alternative spellings

The main form of each word given in the dictionary is the accepted American spelling. Although there is only one way that most words can be spelled, sometimes other spellings (called *variants*) are also acceptable. Such spellings are given after the headword, e.g., **adaptor** (also **adapter**), or before a particular sense if the spelling variant is only used in that sense. In all such cases the spelling given as the headword is the one that most people use. The label Brit. shows spellings that are used in British English, e.g. **color** (Brit. **colour**).

Hyphenation

Although standard spelling in English is fixed, the use of hyphens is not. There are a few general rules that should be followed, and these are outlined below.

Noun compounds: there are no set rules as to whether a compound (a word such as **airstream**) should be written as one word, two words, or with a hyphen (unless the hyphen is used to show the word's grammatical function; see the next section): **airstream**, **air stream**, and **air-stream** are all acceptable. However, in modern English people are tending to use hyphens less than before and are writing compounds either as one word (**airstream**) or two words (**air raid**) rather than with a hyphen. There is also a tendency to write compounds as one word in American English and as two words in British English.

To save space and avoid confusion, the dictionary gives only the standard American form. This does not, however, mean that other forms are incorrect or not used.

Grammatical information: hyphens are also used to show a word's grammatical function. When a noun compound made up of two separate words (e.g. **credit card**) is placed before another noun, the rule is that the compound has a hyphen, so you should write, for example, *I used my credit card* but *credit-card debt*. You will see this in some example phrases and sentences, but it is not otherwise mentioned in the dictionary entries.

There is a similar rule with compound adjectives such as **well known**. When they are placed after the verb (in the *predicative* position) such adjectives are not written with a hyphen, but when they are placed before the noun (in the *attributive* position) they should have a hyphen: *he is well known* but *he is a well-known painter*.

A verb compound formed from a noun compound that is two words (e.g. **hero worship**) should normally be written with a hyphen (to **hero-worship**). Compound verbs of this type are always shown in the dictionary entries.

Forms of nouns and verbs (inflections)

Plurals of nouns

The plurals of most nouns are formed by adding *-s*, or *-es* when they end in *-s*, *-x*, *-z*, *-sh*, or *-ch* (as in *church*). These kinds of plurals are not shown in the dictionary.

All irregular and difficult plural forms are shown, for example: **fly** (pl. **flies**), **foot** (pl. **feet**).

Verbs

Most verbs change their form (inflect) by adding *-s*, *-ing*, and *-ed* to the infinitive (the basic unchanged part of the verb), e.g. **jump → jumps, jumping, jumped**. Most verbs ending in *-e* add *-s*, *-ing* (dropping the *-e*), and *-d*, e.g., **bake → bakes, baking, baked.**

Neither of the above patterns of verb forms is shown in the dictionary.

Irregular and difficult verb forms are shown, e.g., **sing** (past **sang**; past part. **sung**), **bat** (**bats**, **batting**, **batted**).

Adjectives

Most adjectives form their comparatives and superlatives in the following ways, and these are not shown in the dictionary:

- words of one syllable adding *-er* and *-est*, e.g., **great → greater, greatest**
- words of one syllable ending in silent (unspoken) *-e*, which drop the *-e* and add *-er* and *-est*, e.g., **brave → braver, bravest**
- words that form the comparative and superlative by adding "more" and "most," e.g., *more beautiful, most beautiful.*

In all other cases the forms are shown in the dictionary, e.g., **hot** (**hotter**, **hottest**), **happy** (**happier**, **happiest**).

3. Labels

The majority of the words and senses in this dictionary are part of standard English, which means that they are the kinds of words we use in every type of situation, whether at home, with friends, or in a formal work situation. Some words, however, are suitable only for certain situations or are found only in certain types of writing, and where this is the case a label (or a combination of labels) is used.

Register labels

Register labels refer to the particular level of use in the language—indicating whether a term is informal, formal, historical, and so on.

- **formal:** normally used only in writing, such as in official documents (e.g., **missive**)
- **informal:** normally used only in speaking or writing to friends (e.g., **cornball**)
- **dated:** no longer used by most English speakers, but still used by older people or to give a humorous or other effect (e.g., **domestic science**)
- **old use:** old-fashioned language, not in ordinary use today, though sometimes used to give an old-fashioned or humorous effect and also found in the literature of the past (e.g., **damsel**)
- **historical:** only used today to refer to something that is no longer part of modern life (e.g., **blunderbuss**)
- **literary:** found only or mainly in literature (e.g., **foe**)
- **technical:** normally used only in technical language, though not restricted to a particular subject field (e.g., **dorsal**)
- **humorous:** used to sound funny or playful (e.g., **beauty sleep**)
- **euphemistic:** used instead of a more direct or rude term (e.g., **powder room** instead of "women's toilet")
- **dialect:** only used in certain local regions of the English-speaking world (e.g., **bide**)
- **derogatory:** deliberately intended to express a low opinion or insult someone else (e.g., **bimbo**)
- **offensive:** likely to cause offence, especially racial offence, whether the person using it means to or not
- **vulgar slang:** very informal language, usually relating to sexual activity or bodily functions, which most people regard as taboo and which may cause offence.

Geographical labels

English is spoken throughout the world, and while most of the words used in American English will be the same as those used in, say, Canadian or British English, there are some words which are only found in one type of English. For example, the normal word in British English for a sidewalk is **pavement**. This dictionary includes a selection of words of this kind with geographical labels. The label Brit. means that the word is found typically in British English but is not found in American English, though it may be found in other varieties such as Australian English.

Subject labels

Subject labels are used to show that a word or sense is associated with a particular subject field or specialist activity, such as Music, Chemistry, or Baseball.

4. Pronunciations

This dictionary uses a simple respelling system to show how entries are pronounced, using the symbols listed below. If two or more identical headwords are pronounced identically, only the first has a pronunciation given. Where a derivative simply adds a common suffix such as **-less**, **-ness**, or **-ly** to the headword, the derivative may not have a pronunciation shown unless some other element of the pronunciation also changes.

Symbol	Example	Symbol	Example	Symbol	Example
a	**hat** /hat/	i	**fit** /fit/	ou	**mouse** /mous/
ā	**day** /dā/	ī	**time** /tīm/	p	**put** /po͝ot/, **cap** /kap/
ä	**lot** /lät/	i(ə)r	**beer** /bi(ə)r/	r	**run** /rən/, **fur** /fər/
b	**big** /big/	j	**judge** /jəj/	s	**sit** /sit/
CH	**church** /CHərCH/	k	**cut** /kət/	SH	**shut** /SHət/
d	**dog** /dôg/	l	**lap** /lap/	t	**top** /täp/
e	**men** /men/	m	**main** /mān/	TH	**thin** /THin/
ē	**feet** /fēt/	n	**need** /nēd/	T͟H	**then** /T͟Hen/
e(ə)r	**care** /ke(ə)r/	NG	**sing** /siNG/, **anger** /'aNGgr/	v	**very** /'verē/
ə	**about** /ə'bout/, **curt** /kərt/	ō	**go** /gō/	w	**wait** /wāt/
f	**free** /frē/	ô	**law** /lô/	y	**yet** /yet/, **accuse** /ə'kyo͞oz/
g	**get** /get/	oi	**boy** /boi/	z	**zipper** /'zipər/
h	**her** /hər/	o͝o	**wood** /wo͝od/, **sure** /SHo͝or/	ZH	**measure** /'meZHər/
(h)w	**when** /(h)wen/	o͞o	**food** /fo͞od/		

Foreign Sounds

KH **Bach** /bäKH/ A "guttural" consonant pronounced with the tongue in the same position as for /k/, as in German *Buch*, or Scottish *loch*.

N **en route** /äN 'ro͞ot/, **Sauvignon** /'sōvin'yôN/ The /N/ does not represent a separate sound: it indicates that the preceding vowel is nasalized, as in French *bon*.

œ **hors d'oeuvre** /ôr 'dœvrə/, **adieu** /ä'dyœ/ A vowel made by rounding the lips as with /ô/ while saying /e/, as in French *feu* or German *Höhle*.

Y **mot juste** /ˌmō 'ZHYst/, **Übermensch** /'Ybərˌmench/ A vowel made by rounding the lips as with /o͞o/ while saying /i/, as in French *rue* or German *fühlen*.

Stress Marks

Stress (or accent) is indicated by the mark ' before the syllable with the heaviest stress, and by ˌ before a syllable with weaker stress, e.g., **oversee** /ˌōvər'sē/.

Variant Pronunciations

There are several ways in which variant pronunciations are indicated in the respellings.

Some respellings show a pronunciation symbol within parentheses to indicate a possible variation in pronunciation; for example, in **sandwich** /'san(d)wiCH/ sometimes the /d/ is pronounced, while sometimes it is not.

Variant pronunciations may be respelled in full, separated by semicolons. The more common pronunciation is listed first, if this can be determined, but it many cases it cannot.

Variant pronunciations may be indicated by respelling only the part of the word that changes; then a hyphen replaces the part of the pronunciation that remains the same, as in **quasiparticle** /ˌkwāzī'pärtikəl; ˌkwäzē-/.

A partial respelling for a derivative refers back to the headword respelling, not the preceding derivative, as in **annotate** /ˈanəˌtāt/... ■ **annotation** /ˌanəˈtāsʜən/ **annotator** /-ˌtātər/.

A hyphen is sometimes used to separate syllables because the respelling might otherwise look confusing, as in **allowedly** /əˈlou-idlē/.

5. Syllable breaks

Syllable breaks are shown for headwords and derivatives, e.g. **de·flect**, **de·flec·tion**. They can be used as a guide for dividing words at the end of lines, but it is best **not** to divide:

- a word of five or fewer letters, e.g., **mor·al**
- a proper name, e.g., **Al·ex·an·der**
- a contraction, e.g., **could·n't**
- after the first letter of a word, e.g., **a·float**
- before the last letter of a word, e.g., **catch·y**
- anywhere other than at the hyphen in a word that is already hyphenated, e.g., **arm-twist·ing**
- if the result would be misleading or distracting, e.g., **leg·end**

6. Abbreviations used in the dictionary and thesaurus

abbr.	abbreviation	Brit.	British	prep.	preposition
adj.	adjective	fem.	feminine	pronunc.	pronunciation
adv.	adverb	n.	noun	sing.	singular
Austral.	Australian	pl.	plural	usu.	usually

Abbreviations in general use (such as e.g., cm, and UK) are explained in their own entries.

Aa

A¹ (also a) ▸ **noun** (pl. **As** or **A's**) **1** the first letter of the alphabet. **2** indicating the first, best, or most important in a set. **3** Music the sixth note of the scale of C major.
– PHRASES **from A to B** from one place to another. **from A to Z** covering or including the entire range or scope of something.

A² ▸ **abbreviation 1** ampere(s). **2** (Å) angstrom(s). **3** answer.

a¹ /ā, ə/ (**an** before a vowel sound) ▸ **determiner 1** used when mentioning someone or something for the first time; the indefinite article. **2** one single: *a hundred.* **3** per: *typing 60 words a minute.* **4** someone like (the name specified): *you're no better than a Hitler.*
– ORIGIN Old English.

a² ▸ **abbreviation 1** (in travel timetables) arrives. **2** (used before a date) before.
– ORIGIN Latin *ante.*

a- (often **an-** before a vowel) ▸ **prefix** not; without: *atheistic.*
– ORIGIN from Greek.

@ /at/ ▸ **symbol** 'at,' used. **1** to indicate cost or rate per unit. **2** in Internet addresses between the user's name and the domain name: *john.smith@oup.com.*

A1 ▸ **adjective** informal excellent.

A4 ▸ **noun** a standard European size of paper, 297 × 210 mm.

AA ▸ **abbreviation 1** Alcoholics Anonymous. **2** antiaircraft. **3** administrative assistant. **4** Associate of Arts. **5** /ˌdubəl ˈā/a dry cell battery of a size commonly used in digital cameras.

AAA /ˌtripəl ˈā/ ▸ **abbreviation 1** American Automobile Association. **2** a dry cell battery of a size commonly used in TV remote controls.

aard·vark /ˈärdˌvärk/ ▸ **noun** an African mammal with a tubular snout and a long tongue, feeding on ants and termites.
– ORIGIN South African Dutch, 'earth pig.'

AB ▸ **abbreviation 1** able seaman. **2** Alberta.

a·back /əˈbak/ ▸ **adverb** (in phrase **take someone aback**) shock or surprise someone: *I was taken aback by the question.*
– ORIGIN Old English.

ab·a·cus /ˈabəkəs/ ▸ **noun** (pl. **abacuses**) a frame with rows of wires or dowels along which beads are slid, used for counting.
– ORIGIN Greek *abax* 'slab, drawing board.'

a·baft /əˈbaft/ ▸ **adverb & preposition** Nautical in or behind the stern of a ship.
– ORIGIN from the old word *baft* 'in the rear.'

ab·a·lo·ne /ˌabəˈlōnē, ˈabəˌlōnē/ ▸ **noun** an edible sea creature that has a shell lined with mother-of-pearl.
– ORIGIN from an American Indian language.

a·ban·don /əˈbandən/ ▸ **verb 1** desert or leave permanently: *he abandoned his family and moved to London.* **2** give up a course of action completely. **3** (**abandon oneself to**) make no attempt to resist something: *she abandoned herself to his kiss.*

> – SYNONYMS **1** *he abandoned his wife* **desert,** leave, turn one's back on, cast aside, finish with, jilt, throw over; informal walk/run out on, dump, ditch; literary forsake. **2** *she had abandoned painting* **give up,** stop, have done with; informal pack in, quit. **3** *they abandoned the car* **leave (behind),** vacate, dump, quit, evacuate, discard, jettison. **4** *the party abandoned those policies* **renounce,** relinquish, dispense with, discard, give up, drop; informal ditch, scrap, junk; formal forswear.
> – ANTONYMS keep.

▸ **noun** complete lack of self-control or self-consciousness: *dancers swung their bodies with wild abandon.*

> – SYNONYMS **uninhibitedness,** recklessness, lack of restraint, lack of inhibition.
> – ANTONYMS self-control.

– DERIVATIVES **a·ban·don·ment** noun.
– ORIGIN Old French *abandoner.*

> **CHOOSE THE RIGHT WORD**
>
> See **RELINQUISH**.

a·ban·doned /əˈbandənd/ ▸ **adjective** wild and uninhibited.

a·base /əˈbās/ ▸ **verb** (**abase oneself**) behave in a way that is demeaning or degrading.
– DERIVATIVES **a·base·ment** noun.
– ORIGIN Old French *abaissier* 'to lower.'

a·bashed /əˈbasht/ ▸ **adjective** embarrassed or ashamed.
– ORIGIN from Old French *esbair* 'utterly astound.'

a·bate /əˈbāt/ ▸ **verb** (of something bad) become less severe or widespread: *the epidemic showed no sign of abating.*

> – SYNONYMS **subside,** die down/away/out, lessen, ease (off/up), let up, decrease, diminish, fade, weaken.
> – ANTONYMS intensify.

– DERIVATIVES **a·bate·ment** noun.
– ORIGIN Old French *abatre* 'to fell.'

> **CHOOSE THE RIGHT WORD**
>
> See **ALLEVIATE**.

ab·at·toir /ˈabəˌtwär/ ▸ **noun** Brit. a slaughterhouse.
– ORIGIN French, from *abattre* 'to fell.'

ab·bé /aˈbā/ ▸ **noun** (in France) an abbot or other clergyman.

ab·bess /ˈabis/ ▸ **noun** a woman who is the head of an abbey of nuns.

ab·bey /ˈabē/ ▶ **noun** (pl. **abbeys**) a building occupied by a community of monks or nuns.
– ORIGIN Old French *abbeie*.

ab·bot /ˈabət/ ▶ **noun** a man who is the head of an abbey of monks.
– ORIGIN Greek *abbas* 'father.'

ab·bre·vi·ate /əˈbrēvēˌāt/ ▶ **verb** shorten a word, phrase, or text.

– SYNONYMS **shorten,** reduce, cut, contract, condense, compress, abridge, summarize, précis.
– ANTONYMS lengthen, expand.

– ORIGIN Latin *abbreviare*, from *brevis* 'short.'

ab·bre·vi·a·tion /əˌbrēvēˈāshən/ ▶ **noun** a shortened form of a word or phrase.

– SYNONYMS **short form,** contraction, acronym, initialism.

ABC ▶ **noun 1** the alphabet. **2** an alphabetical guide to something. **3** the basic facts of a subject.

ab·di·cate /ˈabdiˌkāt/ ▶ **verb 1** (of a king or queen) give up the throne. **2** fail to fulfill or carry out a duty or responsibility.

– SYNONYMS **resign,** retire, stand down, step down, renounce the throne.

– DERIVATIVES **ab·di·ca·tion** /ˌabdiˈkāshən/ noun.
– ORIGIN Latin *abdicare*.

ab·do·men /ˈabdəmən, abˈdōmən/ ▶ **noun 1** the part of the body that contains the stomach, intestines, and reproductive organs. **2** the rear part of the body of an insect, spider, or crustacean.

– SYNONYMS **stomach,** belly, gut, middle; informal tummy, guts.

– ORIGIN Latin.

WORD LINKS

abdominal, **ventral** *relating to the abdomen*

ab·dom·i·nal /abˈdämənl/ ▶ **adjective** relating to the abdomen.

– SYNONYMS *abdominal pains* **gastric,** intestinal, stomach, duodenal, visceral, celiac, ventral.

– DERIVATIVES **ab·dom·i·nal·ly** adverb.

ab·duct /abˈdəkt/ ▶ **verb** take someone away, typically using force to do so.

– SYNONYMS **kidnap,** carry off, seize, capture, run away/off with, take hostage; informal snatch.

– DERIVATIVES **ab·duct·ee** noun **ab·duc·tion** noun **ab·duc·tor** noun.
– ORIGIN Latin *abducere*.

a·beam /əˈbēm/ ▶ **adverb** at right angles to a ship's or an aircraft's length.

a·bed /əˈbed/ ▶ **adverb** old use in bed.

ab·er·rant /ˈabərənt, əˈber-/ ▶ **adjective** not normal or acceptable: *his aberrant behavior*.

ab·er·ra·tion /ˌabəˈrāshən/ ▶ **noun 1** an action, event, or way of behaving that is not normal or acceptable. **2** a temporary failure of judgment or concentration: *a mental aberration*.

– SYNONYMS **anomaly,** deviation, abnormality, irregularity, variation, freak, oddity, peculiarity, curiosity, mistake.

– ORIGIN Latin, from *aberrare* 'to stray.'

a·bet /əˈbet/ ▶ **verb** (**abets, abetting, abetted**) (usu. in phrase **aid and abet**) encourage or assist someone to do something wrong, in particular to commit a crime.
– DERIVATIVES **a·bet·ment** noun **a·bet·tor** (also **abetter**) noun.
– ORIGIN from Old French *beter* 'hound, urge on.'

a·bey·ance /əˈbāəns/ ▶ **noun** (in phrase **in/into abeyance**) temporarily suspended or not in use.
– ORIGIN Old French *abeer* 'aspire after.'

ab·hor /abˈhôr/ ▶ **verb** (**abhors, abhorring, abhorred**) hate or detest: *he abhorred sexism*.

– SYNONYMS **hate,** detest, loathe, despise, shudder at; formal abominate.
– ANTONYMS love, admire.

– ORIGIN from Latin *horrere* 'to shudder.'

CHOOSE THE RIGHT WORD

See **DESPISE**.

ab·hor·rent /abˈhôrənt, -ˈhär-/ ▶ **adjective** disgusting or hateful.

– SYNONYMS **hateful,** detestable, loathsome, abominable, repellent, repugnant, repulsive, revolting, vile, odious, disgusting, horrible, horrid, horrifying, awful, heinous.
– ANTONYMS admirable.

– DERIVATIVES **ab·hor·rence** noun.

a·bide /əˈbīd/ ▶ **verb 1** (**abide by**) accept or obey a rule or decision. **2** (**cannot abide**) dislike very much. **3** (of a feeling or memory) last for a long time. **4** old use live in a place.

– SYNONYMS **1** (**abide by**) **comply with,** obey, observe, follow, keep to, adhere to, stick to, go along with, heed, accept. **2** (**cannot abide**) *I cannot abide smoke* **stand,** bear, tolerate; formal brook. **3** *one memory will abide* **continue,** remain, survive, last, persist, live on.

– ORIGIN Old English, 'wait.'

a·bid·ing /əˈbīdiNG/ ▶ **adjective** lasting a long time; enduring: *an abiding love of the countryside*.

– SYNONYMS **enduring,** lasting, everlasting, perpetual, eternal, unending, permanent.

– DERIVATIVES **a·bid·ing·ly** adverb.

a·bil·i·ty /əˈbilitē/ ▶ **noun** (pl. **abilities**) **1** the power or capacity to do something. **2** skill or talent.

– SYNONYMS **1 capacity,** capability, power, potential, faculty, facility, wherewithal, means. **2 talent,** skill, aptitude, expertise, savoir faire, prowess, accomplishment, competence, proficiency, flair, gift, knack, genius; informal know-how.
– ANTONYMS inability.

– ORIGIN Latin *habilitas*.

ab·ject /ˈabˌjekt, abˈjekt/ ▶ **adjective 1** very unpleasant and degrading: *families living in abject poverty*. **2** completely without pride or dignity: *an abject apology*.
– DERIVATIVES **ab·ject·ly** adverb.
– ORIGIN Latin *abjectus* 'rejected.'

ab·jure /abˈjo͝or/ ▶ **verb** formal swear to give up a belief or claim.
– ORIGIN Latin *abjurare*.

ab·la·tion /əˈblāshən/ ▶ **noun 1** the surgical removal of body tissue. **2** the loss of solid material such as ice or rock by melting, evaporation, or erosion.
– ORIGIN Latin.

ab·la·tive /ˈablətiv/ ▶ **adjective** Grammar (of a case) indicating an agent, instrument, or source, expressed by 'by,' 'with,' or 'from' in English.

a·blaze /əˈblāz/ ▶ **adjective** burning fiercely.

a·ble /ˈābəl/ ▶ **adjective** (**abler, ablest**) **1** having the power, skill, or means to do something. **2** skillful and competent: *a very able public speaker*.

– SYNONYMS **intelligent,** clever, talented, skillful, skilled, expert, accomplished, gifted, proficient, apt, adroit, adept, capable, competent.
– ANTONYMS incompetent.

– DERIVATIVES **a·bly** adverb.
– ORIGIN Latin *habilis* 'handy.'

a·ble-bod·ied /ˈābəl,bädēd, ˌābəlˈbädēd/ ▶ **adjective** physically fit and healthy.

ab·lu·tions /əˈblo͞osHənz/ ▶ **plural noun** formal or humorous the process of washing oneself.
– ORIGIN Latin, from *abluere* 'wash away.'

ABM ▶ **abbreviation** antiballistic missile.

ab·ne·ga·tion /ˌabniˈgāsHən/ ▶ **noun** formal the giving up of something that is valuable or desired.
– DERIVATIVES **ab·ne·gate** /ˈabni,gāt/ verb.
– ORIGIN from Latin *negare* 'deny.'

CHOOSE THE RIGHT WORD

See **ABSTINENCE**.

ab·nor·mal /abˈnôrməl/ ▶ **adjective** differing from what is normal or typical.

– SYNONYMS **unusual,** uncommon, atypical, untypical, unexpected, unrepresentative, irregular, anomalous, deviant, aberrant, freak, strange, odd, peculiar, eccentric, bizarre, weird, unnatural, perverted, twisted, warped; informal funny, freaky, kinky.
– ANTONYMS normal.

– DERIVATIVES **ab·nor·mal·ly** adverb.
– ORIGIN Greek *anōmalos* 'uneven.'

ab·nor·mal·i·ty /ˌabnôrˈmalitē/ ▶ **noun** (pl. **abnormalities**) **1** a feature or event that is not normal: *babies with congenital abnormalities*. **2** the state of being abnormal.

– SYNONYMS **deformity,** defect, malformation, oddity, strangeness, irregularity, anomaly, deviation, aberration.

A·bo /ˈabō/ ▶ **noun** (pl. **Abos**) Austral. informal, offensive an Aboriginal.

a·board /əˈbôrd/ ▶ **adverb & preposition** on or into a ship, train, or other vehicle.

a·bode /əˈbōd/ ▶ **noun** formal or literary a person's house or home.
– ORIGIN from **ABIDE**.

a·bol·ish /əˈbälisH/ ▶ **verb** officially put an end to a system, law, or practice.

– SYNONYMS **put an end to,** get rid of, scrap, cancel, end, remove, dissolve, stop, ban; informal do away with, ax, ditch.

– ORIGIN Latin *abolere* 'destroy.'

ab·o·li·tion /ˌabəˈlisHən/ ▶ **noun** the official ending of a system, law, or practice: *the abolition of the death penalty*.

ab·o·li·tion·ist /ˌabəˈlisHənist/ ▶ **noun** a person who supports the abolition of something, especially capital punishment or (in the past) slavery.
– DERIVATIVES **ab·o·li·tion·ism** noun.

A-bomb ▶ **noun** an atom bomb.

a·bom·i·na·ble /əˈbäm(ə)nəbəl/ ▶ **adjective 1** very unpleasant and causing disgust: *an abominable crime*. **2** informal very bad; terrible.

– SYNONYMS **loathsome,** detestable, hateful, obnoxious, despicable, contemptible, disgusting, revolting, repellent, repulsive, repugnant, abhorrent, reprehensible, atrocious, execrable, foul, vile, wretched, horrible, awful, dreadful, appalling, nauseating; informal terrible, shocking, God-awful, beastly.
– ANTONYMS good, admirable.

– DERIVATIVES **a·bom·i·na·bly** adverb.
– ORIGIN Latin *abominabilis*.

A·bom·i·na·ble Snow·man ▶ **noun** the yeti.

a·bom·i·nate /əˈbämə,nāt/ ▶ **verb** formal detest something or someone.

a·bom·i·na·tion /əˌbäməˈnāsHən/ ▶ **noun 1** a thing that causes disgust or hatred. **2** a feeling of hatred.

ab·o·rig·i·nal /ˌabəˈrijənl/ ▶ **adjective 1** inhabiting or existing in a land from the earliest times or from before the arrival of colonists. **2** (**Aboriginal**) relating to the Australian Aboriginals. ▶ **noun 1** a person who has inhabited a land from the earliest times. **2** (**Aboriginal**) a member of one of the original peoples of Australia.

ab·o·rig·i·ne /ˌabəˈrijənē/ ▶ **noun** an original inhabitant of a land, especially (**Aborigine**) an Australian Aboriginal.
– ORIGIN from Latin *ab origine* 'from the beginning.'

a·bort /əˈbôrt/ ▶ **verb 1** carry out the abortion of a fetus. **2** (of a pregnant woman or female animal) have a miscarriage. **3** bring to a premature end because of a problem or fault: *the helicopter was forced to abort its mission owing to a blizzard*.

– SYNONYMS *the crew aborted the takeoff* **halt,** stop, end, call off, abandon, discontinue, terminate; informal pull the plug on.

– ORIGIN Latin *aboriri* 'miscarry.'

a·bor·ti·fa·cient /ə,bôrtəˈfāsHənt/ Medicine ▶ **adjective** (of a drug) causing an abortion. ▶ **noun** a drug that causes an abortion.

a·bor·tion /əˈbôrsHən/ ▶ **noun 1** a surgical operation in which a human pregnancy is deliberately brought to an end. **2** the natural ending of a pregnancy before the fetus is able to survive on its own.

a·bor·tion·ist /əˈbôrsHənist/ ▶ **noun** derogatory a person who carries out abortions.

a·bor·tive /əˈbôrtiv/ ▶ **adjective** (of an action) failing to achieve the intended result; unsuccessful: *an abortive military coup*.

– SYNONYMS **unsuccessful,** failed, vain, ineffective, ineffectual, unproductive, futile, useless, unavailing.
– ANTONYMS successful.

a·bound /əˈbound/ ▶ **verb 1** exist in large numbers or amounts. **2** (**abound in/with**) have in large numbers or amounts: *woodlands abounding with spring flowers*.

– SYNONYMS **be plentiful,** be abundant, be numerous, be thick on the ground; informal grow on trees, be a dime a dozen.

– ORIGIN Latin *abundare* 'overflow.'

a·bout /ə'bout/ ▶ **preposition & adverb 1** on the subject of; concerning. **2** used to indicate movement within an area or location in a place; around: *she looked about the room.* **3** approximately.

– SYNONYMS **1** *a book about needlecraft* **regarding,** concerning, referring to, with regard to, with respect to, relating to, on, dealing with, on the subject of. **2** *two hundred people were milling about the room* **around,** round, throughout, over, through, on every side of. **3** *the explosion caused about $15,000 worth of damage* **approximately,** roughly, around, round about, in the region of, circa, of/on the order of, something like; or so, or thereabouts, there or thereabouts, more or less, give or take a few, not far off; informal in the ballpark of.

– PHRASES **be about to** be on the point of.
– ORIGIN Old English.

a·bout-face (also Brit. **about-turn**) ▶ **noun 1** a complete change of opinion or policy. **2** Military a turn made so as to face the opposite direction.

a·bove /ə'bəv/ ▶ **preposition & adverb 1** at a higher level than. **2** rather or more than: *he valued safety above comfort.* **3** (**above all**) more so than anything else: *he was concerned above all to speak the truth.* **4** (in printed text) mentioned earlier.

– SYNONYMS **1** *a tiny window above the door* **over,** higher (up) than; on top of, atop, on, upon. **2** *those above the rank of colonel* **superior to,** senior to, over, higher (up) than, more powerful than; in charge of, commanding. **3** *in the darkness above, something moved* **overhead,** on/at the top, high up, on high, up above, (up) in the sky. **4** *they valued pearls above gold* **more than,** over, before, rather than, in preference to, instead of. **5** (**above all**) **most importantly,** most of all, chiefly, primarily, first and foremost, essentially, in essence, at bottom; informal at the end of the day, when all is said and done. **6** *the two cases described above* **earlier,** previously, before, formerly.
– ANTONYMS below.

– PHRASES **above oneself** having too high an opinion of oneself. **not be above** be capable of doing something dishonest or dishonorable.
– ORIGIN Old English.

a·bove·board /ə'bəvˌbôrd/ ▶ **adjective** legitimate, honest, and open. ▶ **adverb** legitimately, honestly, and openly: *the accountants acted completely aboveboard.*

ab·ra·ca·dab·ra /ˌabrəkə'dabrə/ ▶ **exclamation** a word said by magicians when performing a trick.
– ORIGIN Latin.

a·brade /ə'brād/ ▶ **verb** scrape or wear away the surface of something.
– ORIGIN Latin *abradere.*

a·bra·sion /ə'brāzʜən/ ▶ **noun 1** a patch of skin that has been damaged by being scraped. **2** the scraping or wearing away of the surface of something.

– SYNONYMS **1 graze,** cut, scrape, scratch, gash, laceration. **2 erosion,** wearing away/down.

a·bra·sive /ə'brāsiv, -ziv/ ▶ **adjective 1** able to polish or clean a hard surface by rubbing or grinding. **2** showing little concern for the feelings of other people; harsh or unkind: *a politician renowned for his abrasive manner.*

– SYNONYMS **1 rough,** coarse, harsh, scratchy, chafing. **2 curt,** brusque, sharp, harsh, caustic, grating.
– ANTONYMS gentle.

▶ **noun** a substance used for cleaning or polishing hard surfaces.
– DERIVATIVES **a·bra·sive·ly** adverb **a·bra·sive·ness** noun.

a·breast /ə'brest/ ▶ **adverb 1** side by side and facing the same way. **2** (**abreast of**) up to date with: *I shall keep you abreast of any developments.*

a·bridge /ə'brij/ ▶ **verb** shorten a text or filmed production.

– SYNONYMS **shorten,** cut (down), edit, abbreviate, condense, compress, truncate, prune, summarize, précis, synopsize; (**abridged**) concise.
– ANTONYMS extend.

– ORIGIN Old French *abregier.*

a·bridg·ment /ə'brijmənt/ (also **abridgement**) ▶ **noun** a shortened version of a larger work.

– SYNONYMS **summary,** synopsis, précis, abstract, outline, résumé, digest, cut-down version.

a·broad /ə'brôd/ ▶ **adverb 1** in or to a foreign country or countries. **2** felt or talked about by many people: *there was a new mood abroad.* **3** over a wide area: *millions of seeds are scattered abroad.* **4** old use out of doors.

– SYNONYMS **overseas,** out of the country, to/in foreign parts, to/in a foreign country/land.

ab·ro·gate /'abrəˌgāt/ ▶ **verb** formal cancel or end a law or agreement.
– DERIVATIVES **ab·ro·ga·tion** /ˌabrə'gāsʜən/ noun.
– ORIGIN Latin *abrogare.*

ab·rupt /ə'brəpt/ ▶ **adjective 1** sudden and unexpected: *the car came to an abrupt halt.* **2** brief to the point of rudeness: *an unnecessarily abrupt response.*

– SYNONYMS **1 sudden,** rapid, quick, hasty, unexpected, unanticipated, unforeseen, precipitate. **2 curt,** brusque, blunt, short, rude, sharp, terse, brisk, unceremonious.
– ANTONYMS gradual, gentle.

– DERIVATIVES **ab·rupt·ly** adverb **ab·rupt·ness** noun.
– ORIGIN Latin *abruptus* 'broken off, steep.'

ABS ▶ **abbreviation** antilock braking system.

abs /abz/ ▶ **plural noun** informal the abdominal muscles.

ab·scess /'abˌses/ ▶ **noun** a swelling on the skin or in the body, containing pus.
– ORIGIN Latin *abscessus.*

ab·scis·sa /ab'sisə/ ▶ **noun** (pl. **abscissae** /-'sisē/ or **abscissas**) Mathematics the distance from a point on a graph to the vertical or *y*-axis; the *x*-coordinate.
– ORIGIN from Latin *abscissa linea* 'cut-off line.'

ab·scond /ab'skänd/ ▶ **verb** leave a place hurriedly and secretly to escape from custody or avoid arrest.

– SYNONYMS **run away,** run off, escape, bolt, flee, make off, take flight, take off, decamp; informal vamoose.

– DERIVATIVES **ab·scond·er** noun.
– ORIGIN Latin *abscondere* 'hide.'

ab·sence /'absəns/ ▶ **noun 1** the state of being away from a place or person. **2** (**absence of**) the nonexistence or lack of: *the absence of reliable information.*

– SYNONYMS **1 nonattendance,** absenteeism, truancy, leave, vacation, sabbatical. **2 lack,** want, nonexistence, unavailability, scarcity, shortage, dearth.
– ANTONYMS presence.

ab·sent ▸ **adjective** /ˈabsənt/ **1** not present: *the number of students absent from school.* **2** showing that someone is not paying attention: *an absent expression.*

– SYNONYMS **1 away,** off, out, elsewhere, off duty, on leave, playing truant; informal AWOL. **2 nonexistent,** lacking, missing. **3 distracted,** preoccupied, inattentive, vague, absorbed, dreamy, faraway, blank, empty, vacant.
– ANTONYMS present.

▸ **verb** /abˈsent/ (**absent oneself**) leave or stay away from somewhere.

– SYNONYMS *Rose* ***absented herself*** *from the occasion* **stay away,** be absent, go away, leave, withdraw.

– DERIVATIVES **ab·sent·ly** /ˈabsəntlē/ adverb.
– ORIGIN from Latin *abesse* 'to be away.'

ab·sen·tee /ˌabsənˈtē/ ▸ **noun** a person who is absent.

ab·sen·tee·ism /ˌabsənˈtēˌizəm/ ▸ **noun** frequent absences from work or school without good reason.

ab·sent·mind·ed /ˈabsəntˌmīndid/ ▸ **adjective** forgetful or tending not to pay attention.

– SYNONYMS **forgetful,** distracted, scatterbrained, preoccupied, inattentive, vague; informal with a mind/memory like a sieve.

– DERIVATIVES **ab·sent·mind·ed·ly** adverb **ab·sent·mind·ed·ness** noun.

ab·sinthe /ˈabˌsinTH/ ▸ **noun** a green anise-flavored liqueur, formerly made with wormwood.
– ORIGIN French.

ab·so·lute /ˈabsəˌlo͞ot, ˌabsəˈlo͞ot/ ▸ **adjective 1** not qualified or reduced in any way; total: *absolute silence.* **2** having unlimited power: *an absolute ruler.* **3** not related or compared to anything else: *absolute moral principles.* **4** Law (of a decree) final.

– SYNONYMS **1** *absolute silence | an absolute disgrace* **complete,** total, utter, out-and-out, outright, perfect, pure, thorough, unqualified, unreserved, downright, unmitigated, sheer, unadulterated. **2** *absolute power* **unlimited,** unrestricted, unrestrained, infinite, total, supreme, unconditional. **3** *an absolute ruler* **autocratic,** dictatorial, all-powerful, omnipotent, supreme.
– ANTONYMS partial, qualified, limited.

▸ **noun** Philosophy a value or principle that is universally valid or that can be viewed without relation to other things.
– ORIGIN Latin *absolutus* 'freed, unrestricted.'

ab·so·lute·ly /ˌabsəˈlo͞otlē/ ▸ **adverb 1** completely; entirely: *she trusted him absolutely.* **2** used for emphasis or to express agreement.

– SYNONYMS **completely,** totally, utterly, perfectly, entirely, wholly, fully, quite, thoroughly, unreservedly, definitely, certainly, unquestionably, undoubtedly, without (a) doubt, without question, in every way/respect, one hundred percent.

ab·so·lute ma·jor·i·ty ▸ **noun** a majority over all rivals or opposition considered as a group; more than half.

ab·so·lute pitch ▸ **noun** Music **1** perfect pitch. **2** pitch according to a fixed standard defined by the frequency of the sound vibration.

ab·so·lute tem·per·a·ture ▸ **noun** a temperature measured from absolute zero in kelvins.

ab·so·lute ze·ro ▸ **noun** the lowest temperature theoretically possible (zero kelvins, −273.15°C, −459.67.15°F).

ab·so·lu·tion /ˌabsəˈlo͞oSHən/ ▸ **noun** formal forgiveness of a person's sins.
– ORIGIN Latin.

ab·so·lut·ism /ˈabsəlo͞oˌtizəm/ ▸ **noun** the political principle that a ruler or government should have unlimited power.
– DERIVATIVES **ab·so·lut·ist** noun & adjective.

ab·solve /əbˈzälv, -ˈsälv/ ▸ **verb** declare someone to be free from guilt, responsibility, or sin.
– ORIGIN Latin *absolvere* 'set free, acquit.'

CHOOSE THE RIGHT WORD

absolve, acquit, exempt, exonerate, forgive, pardon, vindicate

To varying degrees, all of these words mean to free from guilt or blame, and some are most frequently heard in a legal or political context. **Absolve** is the most general term, meaning to set free or release—not only from guilt or blame, but from a duty or obligation (*absolved from her promise to serve on the committee*) or from the penalties for their violation. **Pardon** is usually associated with the actions of a government or military official (*President Gerald Ford pardoned Richard Nixon following his resignation in the wake of the Watergate scandal*) and specifically refers to a release from prosecution or punishment. It is usually a legal official who decides to **acquit** someone—that is, release someone from a specific and formal accusation of wrongdoing (*the court acquitted the accused due to lack of evidence*). **Exonerate** suggests relief (its origin suggests the lifting of a burden), often in a moral sense, from a definite charge so that not even the suspicion of wrongdoing remains (*completely exonerated from the accusation of cheating*). A person who is **vindicated** is also off the hook, usually due to the examination of evidence (*she vindicated herself by producing the missing documents*). **Exempt** has less to do with guilt and punishment and more to do with duty and obligation (*exempt from paying taxes*). To **forgive**, however, is the most magnanimous act of all: It implies not only giving up on the idea that an offense should be punished, but also relinquishing any feelings of resentment or vengefulness (*"To err is human; to forgive divine"*).

ab·sorb /əbˈzôrb, -ˈsôrb/ ▸ **verb 1** take in or soak up liquid or another substance. **2** understand information fully. **3** incorporate something smaller or less powerful: *the family firm was absorbed into a larger group.* **4** use up time or resources. **5** reduce the effect or strength of sound or an impact. **6** interest someone and hold their attention completely: *she was absorbed in her work.*

– SYNONYMS **1 soak up,** suck up, draw up/in, take up/in, mop up. **2 engross,** captivate, occupy, preoccupy, engage, rivet, grip, hold, immerse, involve, enthrall, spellbind, fascinate.

– DERIVATIVES **ab·sorb·a·ble** adjective **ab·sorb·er** noun.
– ORIGIN Latin *absorbere* 'suck in.'

ab·sorb·ent /əbˈzôrbənt, -ˈsôr-/ ▸ **adjective** able to soak up liquid easily.

– SYNONYMS **spongy,** spongelike, porous, permeable.

– DERIVATIVES **ab·sorb·en·cy** noun.

ab·sorb·ing /əbˈzôrbiNG, -ˈsôr-/ ▸ **adjective** holding someone's interest completely; very interesting.

– SYNONYMS **fascinating,** interesting, captivating, gripping, engrossing, compelling, compulsive, enthralling, riveting, spellbinding; informal unputdownable.
– ANTONYMS boring.

ab·sorp·tion /əbˈzôrpsʜən, -ˈsôrp-/ ▸ noun **1** the process by which one thing absorbs or is absorbed by another. **2** the state of being engrossed in something.

– SYNONYMS **1 soaking up,** sucking up. **2 involvement,** immersion, raptness, preoccupation, captivation, fascination, enthrallment.

– DERIVATIVES **ab·sorp·tive** adjective.

ab·stain /abˈstān/ ▸ verb **1** restrain oneself from doing or enjoying the pleasure of something: *they abstained from alcohol for two months.* **2** formally choose not to vote.

– SYNONYMS **refrain,** desist, forbear, give up, renounce, avoid, eschew, forgo, go/do without, refuse, decline; informal cut out.

– DERIVATIVES **ab·stain·er** noun.
– ORIGIN Latin *abstinere* 'hold from.'

ab·ste·mi·ous /abˈstēmēəs/ ▸ adjective deliberately limiting one's consumption of food or alcohol.

– SYNONYMS **moderate,** restrained, temperate, self-disciplined, self-restrained, self-denying, sober, austere, ascetic, puritanical, spartan.
– ANTONYMS self-indulgent.

– DERIVATIVES **ab·ste·mi·ous·ly** adverb **ab·ste·mi·ous·ness** noun.
– ORIGIN Latin *abstemius.*

ab·sten·tion /abˈstensʜən/ ▸ noun **1** a deliberate decision not to vote. **2** abstinence.

ab·sti·nence /ˈabstənəns/ ▸ noun the avoidance of something enjoyable, such as food or alcohol.

– SYNONYMS **self-denial,** self-restraint, teetotalism, temperance, sobriety, abstemiousness.

– DERIVATIVES **ab·sti·nent** adjective.
– ORIGIN Latin *abstinentia.*

CHOOSE THE RIGHT WORD

abstinence, abnegation, abstemiousness, continence, forbearance, moderation, temperance

Abstinence implies voluntary self-denial and is usually associated with the non-indulgence of an appetite (*total abstinence from cigarettes and alcohol*). **Abstemiousness** is the quality or habit of being abstinent; an abstemious person would be one who is moderate when it comes to eating and drinking. **Continence**, **temperance**, and **moderation** all imply various forms of self-restraint or self-denial: *moderation* is the avoidance of extremes or excesses (*he drank in moderation*); *temperance* is habitual moderation, or even total abstinence, particularly with regard to alcohol (*the nineteenth-century temperance movement*); and *continence* (in this regard) refers to self-restraint with regard to sexual activity. **Forbearance** is self-control, the patient endurance that characterizes deliberately holding back from action or response. **Abnegation** is the rejection or renunciation of something that is generally held in high esteem (*abnegation of the Christian Church*), although it can also mean to refuse or deny oneself a particular right, claim, or convenience (*abnegation of worldly goods*).

ab·stract ▸ adjective /abˈstrakt, ˈabˌstrakt/ **1** relating to ideas or qualities rather than physical things. **2** (of art) using color and shapes to create an effect rather than attempting to represent reality accurately.

– SYNONYMS **theoretical,** conceptual, intellectual, metaphysical, philosophical, academic.
– ANTONYMS actual, concrete.

▸ verb /abˈstrakt/ take out or remove something.

▸ noun /ˈabˌstrakt/ **1** a summary of a book or article. **2** an abstract work of art.

– SYNONYMS **summary,** synopsis, précis, résumé, outline, abridgment, wrap-up.

– DERIVATIVES **ab·stract·ly** adverb.
– ORIGIN from Latin *abstrahere* 'draw away.'

ab·stract·ed /abˈstraktid/ ▸ adjective not concentrating on what is happening; preoccupied.
– DERIVATIVES **ab·stract·ed·ly** adverb.

ab·strac·tion /abˈstraksʜən/ ▸ noun **1** the quality of being abstract. **2** something that exists only as an idea. **3** a preoccupied state of mind. **4** the action of removing something.

ab·struse /abˈstro͞os/ ▸ adjective difficult to understand: *an abstruse philosophical controversy.*

– SYNONYMS **obscure,** arcane, esoteric, rarefied, recondite, difficult, hard, cryptic, over/above one's head, incomprehensible, unfathomable, impenetrable.

– ORIGIN Latin *abstrusus* 'concealed.'

ab·surd /əbˈsərd, -ˈzərd/ ▸ adjective completely unreasonable or illogical; ridiculous.

– SYNONYMS **irrational,** illogical, inappropriate, ridiculous, ludicrous, farcical, comical, stupid, idiotic, asinine, harebrained, foolish, silly, pointless, senseless, preposterous; informal crazy, cockeyed, daft.
– ANTONYMS sensible.

– DERIVATIVES **ab·surd·i·ty** noun **ab·surd·ly** adverb.
– ORIGIN Latin *absurdus* 'out of tune.'

a·bun·dance /əˈbəndəns/ ▸ noun **1** a very large quantity of something. **2** the state of having a very large quantity of something: *vines grew in abundance.*

– SYNONYMS **plenty,** plentifulness, plethora, profusion, exuberance, riot, cornucopia, superabundance.
– ANTONYMS scarcity.

– ORIGIN from Latin *abundare* 'to overflow.'

a·bun·dant /əˈbəndənt/ ▸ adjective **1** existing or available in large quantities; plentiful. **2** (**abundant in**) having plenty of: *riverbanks abundant in beautiful wild plants.*

– SYNONYMS **plentiful,** copious, ample, profuse, large, huge, great, bumper, prolific, overflowing, teeming, superabundant; informal galore.
– ANTONYMS scarce.

CHOOSE THE RIGHT WORD

See **PREVALENT**.

a·bun·dant·ly /əˈbəndəntlē/ ▸ adverb **1** in large quantities; plentifully. **2** extremely: *he made it abundantly clear that he would not tolerate racism.*

a·buse ▸ verb /əˈbyo͞oz/ **1** use badly or wrongly: *he had abused his position as a doctor.* **2** treat a person or animal with cruelty or violence. **3** speak to someone in an insulting and offensive way.

– SYNONYMS **1 misuse,** exploit, take advantage of. **2 mistreat,** maltreat, ill-treat, hurt, harm, beat, molest, interfere with. **3 insult,** be rude to, swear at, shout at, vilify, curse.

▸ noun /əˈbyo͞os/ **1** the wrong use of something: *an abuse of public funds.* **2** cruel and violent treatment of a person or animal. **3** insulting and offensive language.

– SYNONYMS **1 misuse,** exploitation. **2 mistreatment,** maltreatment, ill-treatment, molestation. **3 insults,** expletives, swear words, swearing, name-calling, invective, vilification, curses.

– DERIVATIVES **a·bus·er** noun.
– ORIGIN Latin *abuti* 'misuse.'

a·bu·sive /ə'byo͞osiv, -ziv/ ▸ **adjective 1** very offensive and insulting. **2** involving cruelty and violence: *an abusive relationship.*

– SYNONYMS **1 insulting,** rude, offensive, derogatory, defamatory, slanderous, libelous. **2 violent,** brutal, cruel, harsh, oppressive.
– ANTONYMS polite.

– DERIVATIVES **a·bu·sive·ly** adverb.

a·but /ə'bət/ ▸ **verb** (**abuts, abutting, abutted**) be next to or touching: *the states that abut the Great Lakes.*
– ORIGIN Old French *abouter.*

a·bu·ti·lon /ə'byo͞otl,än/ ▸ **noun** an herbaceous plant or shrub with showy yellow, red, or mauve flowers.
– ORIGIN Latin.

a·but·ment /ə'bətmənt/ ▸ **noun** a structure supporting the side of an arch, especially at the end of a bridge.

a·buzz /ə'bəz/ ▸ **adjective** filled with talk or activity: *the city was abuzz with rumors.*

a·bys·mal /ə'bizməl/ ▸ **adjective 1** extremely bad. **2** literary very deep.

– SYNONYMS **terrible,** dreadful, awful, appalling, frightful, atrocious, disgraceful, deplorable, lamentable; informal rotten, pathetic, pitiful, woeful, useless, lousy, shocking, dire, the pits.

– DERIVATIVES **a·bys·mal·ly** adverb.

a·byss /ə'bis/ ▸ **noun** a very deep chasm or hole.

– SYNONYMS **chasm,** crevasse, gulf, pit, void.

– ORIGIN from Greek *abussos* 'bottomless.'

a·byss·al /ə'bisəl/ ▸ **adjective** relating to the depths of the ocean.

Ab·ys·sin·i·an /,abə'sinēən/ historical ▸ **adjective** relating to Abyssinia (the former name of Ethiopia). ▸ **noun** a person from Abyssinia.

AC ▸ **abbreviation 1** alternating current. **2** air conditioning. **3** athletic club.

Ac ▸ **symbol** the chemical element actinium.

a/c ▸ **abbreviation 1** account. **2** (also **A/C**) air conditioning.

a·ca·cia /ə'kāshə/ ▸ **noun** a tree or shrub with yellow or white flowers, found in warm climates.
– ORIGIN Greek *akakia.*

ac·a·deme /,akə'dēm, 'akə,dēm/ ▸ **noun** (often in phrase **the groves of academe**) literary academia.

ac·a·de·mi·a /,akə'dēmēə/ ▸ **noun** the world of teaching and research conducted at universities and colleges or the people involved in it.

ac·a·dem·ic /,akə'demik/ ▸ **adjective 1** relating to education and scholarship. **2** not connected to a real situation; of theoretical interest only.

– SYNONYMS **1 educational,** scholastic. **2 scholarly,** learned, literary, intellectual, erudite, highbrow, bookish, studious. **3 theoretical,** hypothetical, notional, speculative, conjectural, irrelevant, beside the point.

▸ **noun** a teacher or scholar in a college or university.

– SYNONYMS **scholar,** intellectual, professor, man/woman of letters, thinker; informal egghead.

– DERIVATIVES **ac·a·dem·i·cal·ly** adverb.

ac·a·de·mi·cian /,akədə'mishən, ə,kadə-/ ▸ **noun 1** an academic. **2** a member of an academy.

ac·a·dem·i·cism /,akə'demə,sizəm/ ▸ **noun** the practice of keeping to formal or conventional rules and traditions in art or literature.

a·cad·e·my /ə'kadəmē/ ▸ **noun** (pl. **academies**) **1** a place of study or training in a special field. **2** a society or institution of distinguished scholars, artists, or scientists. **3** a secondary school.

– SYNONYMS **school,** college, university, institute.

– ORIGIN Greek, from *Akadēmos*, the name of the garden where Plato taught.

A·cad·e·my A·ward ▸ **noun** an award given by the Academy of Motion Picture Arts and Sciences for achievement in the motion-picture industry; an Oscar.

A·ca·di·an /ə'kādēən/ ▸ **adjective** relating to the former French colony of Acadia (now Nova Scotia) or its people. ▸ **noun 1** a person from Acadia. **2** a descendant of the Acadians deported to Louisiana in the 18th century; a Cajun.

a·can·thus /ə'kanthəs/ ▸ **noun** a plant or shrub with spiny decorative leaves.
– ORIGIN Greek, from *akantha* 'thorn.'

a cap·pel·la /,ä kə'pelə/ ▸ **adjective & adverb** (of music) sung without instrumental accompaniment.
– ORIGIN Italian, 'in chapel style.'

ac·cede /ak'sēd/ ▸ **verb** (usu. **accede to**) formal **1** agree to a demand or request. **2** take up an office or position: *he acceded to the throne in 1972.*
– ORIGIN Latin *accedere* 'come to.'

ac·cel·er·an·do /äk,selə'rändō, ak-, ä,chelə-/ ▸ **adverb & adjective** Music with a gradual increase of speed.
– ORIGIN Italian.

ac·cel·er·ant /ak'selərənt/ ▸ **noun** a substance used to help fire spread.

ac·cel·er·ate /ak'selə,rāt/ ▸ **verb 1** begin to move more quickly. **2** increase in rate, amount, or extent: *inflation started to accelerate.*

– SYNONYMS **1 speed up,** go faster, gain momentum, increase speed, pick up speed, gather speed. **2 hasten,** quicken, speed up, further, advance, expedite; informal crank up.
– ANTONYMS decelerate, delay.

– ORIGIN Latin *accelerare*, from *celer* 'swift.'

ac·cel·er·a·tion /ak,selə'rāshən/ ▸ **noun 1** the rate at which a vehicle increases speed. **2** an increase in the rate, amount, or extent of something: *the acceleration of economic reform.*

ac·cel·er·a·tor /ak'selə,rātər/ ▸ **noun 1** a foot pedal that controls the speed of a vehicle. **2** Physics a piece of equipment that causes charged particles to move at high speeds.

ac·cel·er·om·e·ter /ak,selə'rämitər/ ▸ **noun** an instrument for measuring the acceleration of a moving vehicle.

ac·cent ▸ **noun** /'ak,sent/ **1** a distinctive way of pronouncing a language, associated with a country, area, or social background. **2** an emphasis given to a syllable, word, or note. **3** a mark on a letter or word showing how a sound is pronounced or stressed. **4** a special importance, value, or prominence: *the accent is on participation.*

– SYNONYMS **1 pronunciation,** intonation, enunciation, articulation, inflection. **2 emphasis,** stress, priority, importance, prominence.

▸ **verb** /ˈakˌsent, akˈsent/ **1** (as adj. **accented**) spoken with a foreign accent: *he spoke heavily accented English.* **2** stress or emphasize something.

– ORIGIN Latin *accentus* 'tone, signal, or intensity.'

ac·cen·tu·ate /akˈsenCHo͞oˌāt/ ▸ **verb** make more noticeable or prominent: *a deep tan that accentuated his blue eyes.*

– SYNONYMS **focus attention on,** draw attention to, point up, underline, underscore, accent, highlight, spotlight, foreground, bring to the fore, emphasize, stress.

– DERIVATIVES **ac·cen·tu·a·tion** noun.

ac·cept /akˈsept/ ▸ **verb 1** agree to receive or do something offered. **2** believe to be valid or correct. **3** admit responsibility or blame for something. **4** make someone welcome. **5** come to terms with an unwelcome situation: *she had to accept the fact that he might not return.*

– SYNONYMS **1 receive,** take, get, obtain, acquire, pick up. **2** *we have agreed to accept his decision* **agree to,** consent to, acquiesce in, concur with, comply with, go along with, defer to, acknowledge. **3** *the committee accepted his explanation* **believe,** trust, credit, be convinced of, have faith in; informal buy, swallow. **4** (as adj. **accepted**) *he wasn't handsome in the accepted sense* **recognized,** acknowledged, established, traditional, orthodox, agreed, approved, customary, normal, standard.
– ANTONYMS reject.

– DERIVATIVES **ac·cep·tor** noun.
– ORIGIN Latin *acceptare.*

USAGE

Do not confuse **accept** with **except**. **Accept** means 'agree to receive or do something' (*she accepted the job*), whereas **except** means 'not including; apart from' (*I work every day except Sunday*).

ac·cept·a·ble /akˈseptəbəl/ ▸ **adjective 1** able to be accepted. **2** good enough; adequate: *the food was just about acceptable.*

– SYNONYMS **satisfactory,** adequate, reasonable, fair, good enough, sufficient, tolerable, passable.

– DERIVATIVES **ac·cept·a·bil·i·ty** /akˌseptəˈbilitē/ noun **ac·cept·a·bly** adverb.

ac·cept·ance /akˈseptəns/ ▸ **noun** the action of accepting something.

– SYNONYMS **1** *the acceptance of an award* **receipt,** receiving, taking. **2** *their acceptance of the ruling* **compliance,** acquiescence, agreement, consent, assent, acknowledgment, respect.

ac·cess /ˈakˌses/ ▸ **noun 1** the means or opportunity to approach or enter a place. **2** the right or opportunity to use something or see someone: *do you have access to a computer?* **3** the process of obtaining information stored in a computer's memory. **4** literary an attack or outburst of an emotion: *an access of rage.*

– SYNONYMS **1** *a side access* **entrance,** entry, approach, path, drive, way in. **2** *they were denied access* **admission,** admittance, entry.

▸ **verb 1** enter a place. **2** obtain data stored in a computer.
– ORIGIN from Latin *accedere* 'come to.'

ac·ces·si·ble /akˈsesəbəl/ ▸ **adjective 1** able to be reached or used. **2** friendly and easy to talk to. **3** easily understood or enjoyed: *her writing is straightforward and very accessible.*

– SYNONYMS **approachable,** attainable, reachable, obtainable, available, understandable, comprehensible, intelligible; informal get-at-able.

– DERIVATIVES **ac·ces·si·bil·i·ty** /-ˌsesəˈbilitē/ noun **ac·ces·si·bly** adverb.

ac·ces·sion /akˈseSHən/ ▸ **noun 1** the gaining of an important position or rank: *her accession to the throne.* **2** the process of formally joining a group or organization. **3** a new item added to a library or museum collection.

ac·ces·so·rize /akˈsesəˌrīz/ ▸ **verb** add a fashion accessory to a garment.

ac·ces·so·ry /akˈses(ə)rē/ ▸ **noun** (pl. **accessories**) **1** a thing that can be added to something else to make it more useful or attractive. **2** a small article carried or worn to improve the look of a garment. **3** Law a person who helps someone commit a crime without taking part in it.

– SYNONYMS **1 extra,** add-on, addition, supplement, attachment, fitment. **2 accomplice,** abetter, collaborator, co-conspirator, henchman, associate.

– ORIGIN Latin *accessorius* 'additional thing.'

ac·ci·dent /ˈaksidənt/ ▸ **noun 1** an unexpected and unpleasant event. **2** an event that is unforeseen or has no apparent cause.

– SYNONYMS **1 mishap,** misadventure, disaster, tragedy, catastrophe, calamity. **2 crash,** collision, wreck, smash, bump, derailment; informal smash-up, pile-up. **3 chance,** fate, fortune, luck, good luck, fluke, coincidence.

– PHRASES **by accident** in a way that is not planned or organized.
– ORIGIN from Latin *accidere* 'to fall or happen.'

ac·ci·den·tal /ˌaksiˈdentl/ ▸ **adjective** happening by accident: *a verdict of accidental death.*

– SYNONYMS **1 chance,** coincidental, unexpected, incidental, fortuitous, serendipitous.
2 unintentional, unintended, unplanned, inadvertent, unwitting, unpremeditated.
– ANTONYMS intentional.

▸ **noun** a sign attached to a musical note indicating a momentary departure from the key signature.
– DERIVATIVES **ac·ci·den·tal·ly** adverb.

CHOOSE THE RIGHT WORD

accidental, adventitious, casual, contingent, fortuitous, incidental

Things don't always go as planned, but there are many ways to describe the role that chance plays. **Accidental** applies to events that occur entirely by chance (*an accidental encounter with the candidate outside the men's room*) ; but it is so strongly influenced by the noun "accident" that it carries connotations of undesirable or possibly disastrous results (*an accidental miscalculation of the distance he had to jump*). A **casual** act or event is one that is random or unpremeditated (*a casual conversation with her son's teacher in the grocery store*), in which the role that chance plays is not always clear. Something that is **incidental** may or may not involve chance; it typically refers to what is secondary or nonessential (*incidental expenses in the budget*) or what occurs without design or regularity (*incidental lighting throughout the garden*).

Adventitious also implies the lack of an essential relationship, referring to something that is a mere random occurrence (*adventitious circumstances that led to victory*). In contrast, **contingent** points to something that is entirely dependent on an uncertain event for its existence or occurrence (*travel plans that are contingent upon the weather*). **Fortuitous** refers to chance events of a fortunate nature; it is about as far as one can get from *accidental* (*a fortuitous meeting with the candidate outside the men's room just before the press conference*).

ac·ci·dent-prone ▶ **adjective** tending to be involved in a greater than average number of accidents.

ac·claim /ə'klām/ ▶ **verb** praise enthusiastically and publicly: *the car was acclaimed as the best in its class.*

– SYNONYMS **praise,** applaud, cheer, commend, approve, welcome, hail, celebrate, eulogize; formal laud.
– ANTONYMS criticize.

▶ **noun** enthusiastic public praise.

– SYNONYMS **praise,** applause, tributes, plaudits, approval, admiration, congratulations, commendation, eulogies.
– ANTONYMS criticism.

– ORIGIN Latin *acclamare*.

ac·cla·ma·tion /ˌakləˈmāsʜən/ ▶ **noun** loud and enthusiastic approval or praise.

ac·cli·ma·tize /ə'klīməˌtīz/ ▶ **verb** adapt to a new climate or new conditions.

– SYNONYMS **adjust,** adapt, acclimate, get used, familiarize oneself, find one's feet, get one's bearings.

– DERIVATIVES **ac·cli·ma·ti·za·tion** /əˌklīmətəˈzāsʜən/ noun.
– ORIGIN French *acclimater*.

ac·co·lade /'akəˌlād, -ˌläd/ ▶ **noun** something given as a special honor or as a reward for excellence.

– SYNONYMS **tribute,** honor, compliment, prize.

– ORIGIN first meaning 'a touch on a person's shoulders with a sword when knighting them': from Provençal *acolada* 'embrace around the neck.'

ac·com·mo·date /ə'käməˌdāt/ ▶ **verb 1** provide lodging or space for: *the boat accommodates 40 passengers.* **2** adapt to or fit in with: *they tried hard to accommodate the children's needs.*

– SYNONYMS **1** *refugees were accommodated in army camps* **lodge,** house, put up, billet, board. **2** *the cottages accommodate six people* **hold,** take, have room for, sleep, seat. **3** *we tried to accommodate her* **help,** assist, oblige, cater for, fit in with, satisfy, meet the needs of.

– ORIGIN Latin *accommodare*.

ac·com·mo·dat·ing /ə'käməˌdātiɴɢ/ ▶ **adjective** willing to help or fit in with someone's wishes.

– SYNONYMS **obliging,** cooperative, helpful, amenable, hospitable, flexible.

ac·com·mo·da·tion /əˌkäməˈdāsʜən/ ▶ **noun** **1** (**accommodations**) a place where someone may live or stay. **2** (**accommodations**) lodging; room and board. **3** an action of accommodating or the process of being accommodated. **4** a settlement or compromise.

– SYNONYMS (**accommodations**) **housing,** homes, lodging(s), (living) quarters, rooms, billet, shelter, a roof over one's head; informal digs, pad; formal residence, dwelling, abode.

ac·com·pa·ni·ment /ə'kəmp(ə)nimənt/ ▶ **noun 1** a musical part played to support a voice, group, or other instrument. **2** something that adds to or improves something else: *the sauce is a perfect accompaniment to all fish dishes.*

– SYNONYMS **1** *a musical accompaniment* **backing,** support, background, soundtrack. **2** *wine is a good accompaniment to cheese* **complement,** addition, adjunct, accessory, companion.

ac·com·pa·nist /ə'kəmpənist/ ▶ **noun** a person who plays a musical accompaniment.

ac·com·pa·ny /ə'kəmp(ə)nē/ ▶ **verb** (**accompanies, accompanying, accompanied**) **1** go somewhere with someone. **2** be present or occur at the same time as: *violent winds accompanied by rain, hail, or snow.* **3** play musical support or backing for a voice, group, or other instrument.

– SYNONYMS **1 escort,** go with, travel with, keep someone company, chaperone, partner, show, see, usher, conduct. **2 occur with,** go along with, go together with, attend, be linked with, go hand in hand with. **3** *he accompanied the choir on the piano* **back,** play along with, support.

– ORIGIN Old French *accompagner*.

ac·com·plice /ə'kämplis/ ▶ **noun** a person who helps another commit a crime.

– SYNONYMS **partner in crime,** abetter, accessory, collaborator, co-conspirator, henchman, associate; informal sidekick.

– ORIGIN from Latin *complex* 'allied.'

ac·com·plish /ə'kämplisʜ/ ▶ **verb** achieve or complete something successfully.

– SYNONYMS **achieve,** succeed in, realize, attain, manage, bring off, carry through, execute, effect, perform, complete.

– ORIGIN Old French *acomplir*.

ac·com·plished /ə'kämplisʜt/ ▶ **adjective** highly skilled: *an accomplished musician.*

– SYNONYMS **expert,** skilled, skillful, masterly, virtuoso, master, proficient, polished, practiced, consummate, talented, gifted, able, capable; informal crack, ace.

ac·com·plish·ment /ə'kämplisʜmənt/ ▶ **noun** **1** something that has been achieved successfully: *his military accomplishments.* **2** a skill or special ability. **3** the successful achievement of a task.

– SYNONYMS **1 achievement,** success, act, deed, exploit, effort, feat, coup. **2 talent,** skill, gift, ability.

ac·cord /ə'kôrd/ ▶ **verb 1** give power or status to someone. **2** (**accord with**) be in agreement or consistent with: *his views accorded with those of Harris.*

– SYNONYMS **1 give,** grant, present, award, confer on, bestow on. **2 correspond,** agree, tally, match, concur, be in harmony, be in tune.
– ANTONYMS disagree, differ.

▶ **noun 1** an official agreement or treaty. **2** agreement in opinion or feeling: *we are in accord on all points.*

– SYNONYMS **1** *a peace accord* **pact,** treaty, agreement, settlement, deal, entente, protocol. **2** *the two sides failed to reach accord* **agreement,** consensus, unanimity, harmony.
– ANTONYMS disagreement.

– PHRASES **of one's own accord** willingly. **with one**

accord in a united way.
– ORIGIN Old French *acorder* 'reconcile, be of one mind.'

ac·cord·ance /ə'kôrdns/ ▶ **noun** (in phrase **in accordance with**) in a way conforming with: *a ballot held in accordance with union rules.*

ac·cord·ing /ə'kôrdiNG/ ▶ **adverb** (**according to**) **1** as stated by someone. **2** following or agreeing with: *the event did not go according to plan.*

ac·cord·ing·ly /ə'kôrdiNGlē/ ▶ **adverb 1** in a way that is appropriate. **2** therefore.

ac·cor·di·on /ə'kôrdēən/ ▶ **noun** a musical instrument played by stretching and squeezing with the hands to work a bellows, the notes being sounded by buttons or keys.
– DERIVATIVES **ac·cor·di·on·ist** noun.
– ORIGIN from Italian *accordare* 'to tune.'

ac·cost /ə'kôst, ə'käst/ ▶ **verb** approach someone and speak to them, especially in a rude or aggressive way.

– SYNONYMS **confront,** approach, stop, detain, speak to; informal buttonhole, collar.

– ORIGIN French *accoster*.

ac·count /ə'kount/ ▶ **noun 1** a description of an event or experience. **2** a record of money spent and received. **3** a service through a bank or firm by which funds are held on behalf of a customer, or goods or services are supplied on credit. **4** importance: *money was of no account to her.*

– SYNONYMS **1 description,** report, version, story, statement, explanation, tale, chronicle, narrative, history, record, log. **2 financial record,** ledger, balance sheet, financial statement; (**accounts**) books. **3** *his background is of no account* **importance,** import, significance, consequence, value.

▶ **verb** regard in a particular way: *her visit could not be accounted a complete success.*
– PHRASES **account for 1** supply or form a particular amount or part of: *the industry accounts for 11 percent of the US economy.* **2** give a satisfactory explanation of. **call someone to account** ask someone to explain a mistake or bad performance. **on someone's account** for someone's benefit: *don't trouble yourself on my account.* **on account of** because of. **on no account** under no circumstances. **take account of** take something into consideration. **turn something to (good) account** turn something to one's advantage.
– ORIGIN Old French *acont*, from *conter* 'to count.'

ac·count·a·ble /ə'kountəbəl/ ▶ **adjective** responsible for one's actions and expected to explain them.

– SYNONYMS **responsible,** liable, answerable, to blame.

– DERIVATIVES **ac·count·a·bil·i·ty** /əˌkountə'bilitē/ noun.

ac·count·ant /ə'kount(ə)nt/ ▶ **noun** a person who keeps or checks financial accounts.
– DERIVATIVES **ac·count·an·cy** noun.

ac·count·ing /ə'kountiNG/ ▶ **noun** the keeping of financial accounts.

ac·cou·tered /ə'ko͞otərd/ (Brit. **accoutred**) ▶ **adjective** clothed or equipped.
– ORIGIN from French *accoutrer*.

ac·cou·ter·ment /ə'ko͞otərmənt, -trə-/ (Brit. **accoutrement**) ▶ **noun** an item of clothing or equipment required for a particular activity.

ac·cred·it /ə'kredit/ ▶ **verb** (**accredits, accrediting, accredited**) **1** (**accredit something to**) attribute something to someone. **2** give official authorization to someone or something. **3** send a diplomat or journalist to a particular place or post.
– DERIVATIVES **ac·cred·i·ta·tion** /əˌkredi'tāSHən/ noun.
– ORIGIN French *accréditer*.

ac·crete /ə'krēt/ ▶ **verb** grow or be formed by a gradual buildup of new layers.
– ORIGIN Latin *accrescere* 'grow.'

ac·cre·tion /ə'krēSHən/ ▶ **noun 1** the process of growing or increasing in size as the result of a gradual buildup of new layers of something. **2** a thing formed or added in this way.

ac·crue /ə'kro͞o/ ▶ **verb** (**accrues, accruing, accrued**) **1** (of money) be received in regular or increasing amounts. **2** collect or receive payments or benefits.
– DERIVATIVES **ac·cru·al** noun.
– ORIGIN Old French *acreistre* 'increase.'

ac·cul·tur·ate /ə'kəlCHəˌrāt/ ▶ **verb** successfully absorb someone or something into a different culture or social group.
– DERIVATIVES **ac·cul·tur·a·tion** /əˌkəlCHə'rāSHən/ noun.

ac·cu·mu·late /ə'kyo͞omyəˌlāt/ ▶ **verb 1** gather together a number or quantity of something. **2** increase in number or quantity: *very large debts accumulated.*

– SYNONYMS **gather,** collect, amass, stockpile, pile up, build up, store (up), hoard, lay in/up, increase, accrue, run up.
– ANTONYMS disperse.

– DERIVATIVES **ac·cu·mu·la·tive** /ə'kyo͞omyələtiv, -ˌlātiv/ adjective.
– ORIGIN Latin *accumulare* 'heap up.'

ac·cu·mu·la·tion /əˌkyo͞omyə'lāSHən/ ▶ **noun 1** the gradual gathering of something. **2** a mass of something that has gradually gathered or been acquired.

– SYNONYMS **1** *the accumulation of illegal funds* amassing, gathering, cumulation, accrual, accretion. **2** *an accumulation of debris* **mass,** buildup, pile, collection, stock, store, stockpile, hoard.

ac·cu·mu·la·tor /ə'kyo͞omyəˌlātər/ ▶ **noun 1** a person or thing that accumulates things. **2** Computing a register used to contain the results of an arithmetical or logical operation. **3** Brit. a large rechargeable electric cell.

ac·cu·ra·cy /'akyərəsē/ ▶ **noun** the quality or state of being correct or precise.

– SYNONYMS **correctness,** precision, exactness, fidelity, truth, truthfulness, authenticity, realism.

ac·cu·rate /'akyərit/ ▶ **adjective 1** correct in all details: *an accurate description.* **2** reaching an intended target: *an accurate shot.*

– SYNONYMS **1 correct,** precise, exact, right, factual, literal, faithful, true, truthful, on the mark, authentic, realistic. informal on the money, on the button, on the nose. **2 well aimed,** on target, unerring, deadly, true.

– DERIVATIVES **ac·cu·rate·ly** adverb.
– ORIGIN from Latin *accurare* 'do with care.'

USAGE

On the distinction between **accurate** and **precise**, see the note at **PRECISE**.

ac·curs·ed /ə'kərst, ə'kərsid/ ▶ **adjective 1** literary under a curse. **2** informal horrible.

ac·cu·sa·tion /ˌakyə'zāsʜən, ˌakyo͞o-/ ▶ **noun** a claim that someone has done something illegal or wrong.

– SYNONYMS **allegation,** charge, indictment, impeachment, claim, assertion, imputation.

ac·cu·sa·tive /ə'kyo͞ozətiv/ ▶ **noun** a grammatical case used for the object of a verb.
– ORIGIN from Latin *casus accusativus* 'the case showing cause.'

ac·cu·sa·to·ry /ə'kyo͞ozəˌtôrē/ ▶ **adjective** suggesting that one believes a person has done something wrong: *an accusatory stare.*

ac·cuse /ə'kyo͞oz/ ▶ **verb** claim that someone has committed a crime or done something wrong: *he was accused of attempted murder.*

– SYNONYMS **1 charge,** indict, impeach, prefer charges against, arraign. **2 blame,** hold responsible, condemn, criticize, denounce; informal point the finger at.

– DERIVATIVES **ac·cus·er** noun.
– ORIGIN Latin *accusare* 'call to account.'

ac·cus·tom /ə'kəstəm/ ▶ **verb 1** (**accustom someone/thing to**) make someone or something used to. **2** (**be accustomed to**) be used to.

– SYNONYMS **adapt,** adjust, acclimate, acclimatize, habituate, familiarize, become reconciled, get used to, come to terms with, learn to live with.

– ORIGIN Old French *acostumer.*

ac·cus·tomed /ə'kəstəmd/ ▶ **adjective** customary; usual: *his accustomed route.*

– SYNONYMS **customary,** established, habitual, usual, normal, regular, routine; literary wonted.

AC/DC ▶ **adjective 1** alternating current/direct current. **2** informal bisexual.

ace /ās/ ▶ **noun 1** a playing card with a single spot on it, the highest card in its suit in most games. **2** informal a person who is very good at a particular activity: *a snowboarding ace.* **3** a war pilot who has shot down many enemy aircraft. **4** Tennis a service that an opponent is unable to return. **5** Golf, informal a hole in one. ▶ **adjective** informal very good.
– PHRASES **ace up one's sleeve** a plan or piece of information kept secret until needed.
– ORIGIN Latin *as* 'unity, a unit.'

a·cel·lu·lar /ā'selyələr/ ▶ **adjective** Biology **1** not divided into or containing cells. **2** consisting of one cell only.

a·cer /'āsər/ ▶ **noun** a maple or related tree, having leaves with five lobes.
– ORIGIN Latin.

a·cer·bic /ə'sərbik/ ▶ **adjective** (of a person or their remarks) sharply critical and forthright.
– DERIVATIVES **a·cer·bi·cal·ly** adverb **a·cer·bi·ty** /-bitē/ noun.
– ORIGIN Latin *acerbus* 'sour-tasting.'

a·ce·ta·min·o·phen /əˌsētə'minəfən/ ▶ **noun** a drug used to relieve pain and reduce fever.

ac·e·tate /'asiˌtāt/ ▶ **noun 1** Chemistry a salt or ester of acetic acid. **2** fiber or plastic made of a substance produced from cellulose.

a·ce·tic ac·id /ə'sētik/ ▶ **noun** the acid that gives vinegar its characteristic taste.
– ORIGIN Latin *acetum* 'vinegar.'

ac·e·tone /'asiˌtōn/ ▶ **noun** a colorless liquid used as a solvent.
– ORIGIN from ACETIC ACID.

a·ce·tyl·cho·line /əˌsētl'kōˌlēn, ˌasitl-/ ▶ **noun** Biochemistry a compound that occurs throughout the nervous system, in which it functions as a neurotransmitter.

a·cet·y·lene /ə'setlən, -ˌēn/ ▶ **noun** a gas that burns with a bright flame, used in welding.
– ORIGIN from ACETIC ACID.

ACH ▶ **abbreviation** Automated Clearinghouse, the system in the US that handles check transactions between banks.

ache /āk/ ▶ **noun** a continuous or long-lasting dull pain.

– SYNONYMS **pain,** twinge, pang, soreness, tenderness, irritation, discomfort, burning, throbbing, cramp.

▶ **verb 1** suffer from an ache. **2** (**ache for/to do**) feel great desire for or to do: *he ached to see her again.*

– SYNONYMS **hurt,** be sore, be painful, be tender, burn, be in pain, throb.

– DERIVATIVES **ach·ing** adjective.
– ORIGIN Old English.

a·chieve /ə'cʜēv/ ▶ **verb** succeed in doing something by effort, skill, or courage.

– SYNONYMS **attain,** reach, realize, bring off, pull off, accomplish, carry through, fulfill, complete, succeed in, manage, effect; informal wrap up, swing.

– DERIVATIVES **a·chiev·a·ble** adjective **a·chiev·er** noun.
– ORIGIN Old French *achever* 'come or bring to a head.'

a·chieve·ment /ə'cʜēvmənt/ ▶ **noun 1** a thing that is done successfully: *the government's greatest economic achievement.* **2** the process of achieving something.

– SYNONYMS **1 attainment,** realization, accomplishment, fulfillment, implementation, completion. **2 feat,** exploit, triumph, coup, accomplishment, act, action, deed, effort, work, handiwork.

Achil·les heel /ə'kilēz/ ▶ **noun** a weak or vulnerable point.
– ORIGIN from *Achilles*, a hero in Greek myth whose mother plunged him into the River Styx when he was a baby to make his body safe from harm or injury; only the heel by which she held him was untouched by the water.

Achil·les ten·don /ə'kilēz/ ▶ **noun** the tendon that connects the calf muscles to the heel.

a·chon·dro·pla·sia /āˌkändrə'plāzʜ(ē)ə/ ▶ **noun** a hereditary condition in which the bones of the arms and legs fail to grow to the normal size.
– ORIGIN from A- + Greek *khondros* 'cartilage' + *plasis* 'molding.'

ach·ro·mat·ic /ˌakrə'matik, ˌākrə-/ ▶ **adjective 1** transmitting light without separating it into its constituent colors. **2** without color.

ach·y /'ākē/ (also **achey**) ▶ **adjective** (**achier**, **achiest**) suffering from an ache or aches.

ac·id /'asid/ ▶ **noun 1** a substance with chemical properties that include turning litmus red, neutralizing alkalis, and dissolving some metals. **2** informal the drug LSD. ▶ **adjective 1** having the properties of an acid; having a pH of less than 7. **2** sharp-tasting or sour. **3** (of a remark) bitter or cutting.

– SYNONYMS **1 sour,** acidic, tart, sharp, vinegary. **2 sharp,** sharp-tongued, catty, sarcastic, scathing, cutting, biting, stinging, caustic; informal bitchy.
– ANTONYMS sweet.

– DERIVATIVES **ac·id·ly** adverb **ac·id·y** adjective.
– ORIGIN Latin *acidus*.

ac·id house ▸ noun a kind of fast, repetitive synthesized dance music.

a·cid·ic /ə'sidik/ ▸ adjective **1** containing acid. **2** having a sour taste.

a·cid·i·fy /ə'sidə,fī/ ▸ verb (**acidifies, acidifying, acidified**) make or become acid.
– DERIVATIVES **a·cid·i·fi·ca·tion** /ə,sidəfi'kāshən/ noun.

a·cid·i·ty /ə'siditē/ ▸ noun **1** the level of acid in something. **2** bitterness or sharpness in a person's remarks or tone.

ac·id jazz ▸ noun a kind of dance music incorporating elements of jazz, funk, soul, and hip-hop.

ac·i·doph·i·lus /,asi'däfələs/ ▸ noun a bacterium used to make yogurt.
– ORIGIN Latin.

ac·id rain ▸ noun rainfall made acidic by atmospheric pollution resulting from the burning of coal or oil in factories.

ac·id re·flux ▸ noun a condition in which gastric acid is regurgitated.

ac·id test ▸ noun a conclusive test of the success, truth, or value of something.
– ORIGIN from the use of nitric acid to test whether or not a metal is gold.

a·cid·u·late /ə'sijə,lāt/ ▸ verb make something slightly acidic.

a·cid·u·lous /ə'sijələs/ ▸ adjective (of a remark) cutting; bitter.

ack-ack /'ak ,ak/ ▸ noun Military, informal antiaircraft gunfire or guns.
– ORIGIN signalers' former name for the letters *AA*.

ac·kee ▸ noun variant spelling of **AKEE**.

ac·knowl·edge /ak'nälij/ ▸ verb **1** accept or admit that something exists or is true: *he acknowledged that he had made mistakes.* **2** confirm that one has received or is grateful for: *please acknowledge receipt of this letter.* **3** show that one has noticed someone by making a gesture of greeting.

> – SYNONYMS **1 admit,** accept, grant, agree, own, allow, concede, confess, recognize. **2 greet,** salute, address, nod to, wave to, say hello to. **3 answer,** reply to, respond to.
> – ANTONYMS deny, ignore.

– ORIGIN from the former verb *knowledge* (in the same sense).

ac·knowl·edg·ment /ak'nälijmənt/ (also chiefly Brit. **acknowledgement**) ▸ noun **1** the action of acknowledging something or someone. **2** something done or given to express gratitude.

ACLU ▸ abbreviation American Civil Liberties Union, a nonprofit advocacy organization.

ac·me /'akmē/ ▸ noun the point at which something is at its best or most highly developed.
– ORIGIN Greek *akmē* 'highest point.'

ac·ne /'aknē/ ▸ noun a skin condition causing many red pimples on the face.
– ORIGIN Greek *aknas*.

ac·o·lyte /'akə,līt/ ▸ noun **1** an assistant or follower. **2** a person helping a priest in a religious service.
– ORIGIN Latin *acolytus*.

ac·o·nite /'akə,nīt/ ▸ noun **1** a poisonous plant with pink or purple flowers. **2** (also **winter aconite**) a small spring-flowering plant with yellow flowers.
– ORIGIN Greek *akoniton*.

a·corn /'ā,kôrn/ ▸ noun the fruit of the oak tree, a smooth oval nut in a cuplike base.
– ORIGIN Old English.

a·cous·tic /ə'ko͞ostik/ ▸ adjective **1** relating to sound or hearing. **2** not having electrical amplification: *an acoustic guitar.* ▸ noun (**acoustics**) **1** the features of a room or building that affect how it transmits sound. **2** the branch of physics concerned with the properties of sound.
– DERIVATIVES **a·cous·ti·cal** adjective **a·cous·ti·cal·ly** adverb.
– ORIGIN Greek *akoustikos*.

ac·quaint /ə'kwānt/ ▸ verb **1** (**acquaint someone with**) make someone aware of or familiar with: *take time to acquaint yourself with your new surroundings.* **2** (**be acquainted**) know someone personally.

> – SYNONYMS *our job is to **acquaint** you **with** the facts* **familiarize with,** make aware of, inform of, advise of, brief on; informal fill in on, clue in on.

– ORIGIN Latin *accognitare*.

ac·quaint·ance /ə'kwāntns/ ▸ noun **1** a person one knows slightly. **2** familiarity with or knowledge of someone or something.

> – SYNONYMS **1** *a business acquaintance* **contact,** associate, colleague. **2** *my acquaintance with George* **association,** relationship. **3** *some **acquaintance with** the language* **familiarity with,** knowledge of, experience with/of, awareness of, understanding of, grasp of.

ac·qui·esce /,akwē'es/ ▸ verb accept something without protest.
– ORIGIN Latin *acquiescere*.

ac·qui·es·cent /,akwē'esənt/ ▸ adjective ready to accept or do something without protest.
– DERIVATIVES **ac·qui·es·cence** noun.

ac·quire /ə'kwī(ə)r/ ▸ verb **1** come to have; obtain: *I managed to acquire a copy of the tape.* **2** learn or develop a quality or skill: *he acquired a taste for whiskey.*

> – SYNONYMS **get,** obtain, come by, receive, collect, gain, buy, earn, win, come into, secure, pick up, procure; informal get one's hands on, get hold of, land, bag, score.
> – ANTONYMS lose.

– DERIVATIVES **ac·quire·ment** noun **ac·quir·er** noun.
– ORIGIN Latin *acquirere* 'get in addition.'

> **CHOOSE THE RIGHT WORD**
>
> See **GET**.

ac·quired taste ▸ noun a thing that one at first dislikes but comes to like over time.

ac·qui·si·tion /,akwə'zishən/ ▸ noun **1** an object that has recently been obtained. **2** the action of acquiring or obtaining something.

> – SYNONYMS **purchase,** addition, investment, possession, accession; informal buy.

ac·quis·i·tive /ə'kwizitiv/ ▸ adjective too interested in obtaining money or possessions.
– DERIVATIVES **ac·quis·i·tive·ly** adverb **ac·quis·i·tive·ness** noun.

CHOOSE THE RIGHT WORD

See **GREEDY**.

ac·quit /ə'kwit/ ▶ **verb** (**acquits, acquitting, acquitted**) **1** formally declare that someone is not guilty of a criminal charge. **2** (**acquit oneself**) behave or perform in a particular way: *he acquitted himself very well on his debut.*

– SYNONYMS **1 clear,** exonerate, find innocent, absolve, discharge, free, release; informal let off (the hook). **2** *the boys* ***acquitted themselves*** *well* **behave oneself,** conduct oneself, perform, act.
– ANTONYMS convict.

– ORIGIN Latin *acquitare* 'pay a debt.'

CHOOSE THE RIGHT WORD

See **ABSOLVE**.

ac·quit·tal /ə'kwitl/ ▶ **noun** an official judgment that a person is not guilty of the crime with which they have been charged.

a·cre /'äkrə, 'äkər, 'ākər/ ▶ **noun** a unit of land area equal to 4,840 square yards (0.405 hectare).
– ORIGIN Old English, originally referring to the amount of land a pair of oxen could plow in a day.

a·cre·age /'āk(ə)rij/ ▶ **noun** an area of land, typically when used for agricultural purposes, but not necessarily measured in acres.

ac·rid /'akrid/ ▶ **adjective** having an unpleasantly strong and bitter smell or taste.

– SYNONYMS **pungent,** bitter, sharp, harsh, stinging, burning.

– ORIGIN from Latin *acer*.

ac·ri·mo·ni·ous /ˌakrə'mōnēəs/ ▶ **adjective** angry and bitter: *a long and acrimonious debate.*

– SYNONYMS **bitter,** angry, rancorous, harsh, vicious, nasty, bad-tempered, ill-natured.

ac·ri·mo·ny /'akrəˌmōnē/ ▶ **noun** feelings of anger and bitterness.
– ORIGIN Latin *acrimonia*.

ac·ro·bat /'akrəˌbat/ ▶ **noun** an entertainer who performs spectacular gymnastic feats.
– ORIGIN from Greek *akrobatos* 'walking on tiptoe.'

ac·ro·bat·ic /ˌakrə'batik/ ▶ **adjective** involving or performing spectacular gymnastic feats. ▶ **noun** (**acrobatics**) spectacular gymnastic feats.
– DERIVATIVES **ac·ro·bat·i·cal·ly** adverb.

ac·ro·nym /'akrəˌnim/ ▶ **noun** a word formed from the initial letters of other words (e.g., *laser*).
– ORIGIN from Greek *akron* 'end' + *onoma* 'name.'

ac·ro·pho·bi·a /ˌakrə'fōbēə/ ▶ **noun** extreme fear of heights.
– DERIVATIVES **ac·ro·pho·bic** /-'fōbik/ adjective.
– ORIGIN Greek *akron* 'summit.'

a·crop·o·lis /ə'kräpəlis/ ▶ **noun** the citadel of an ancient Greek city, built on high ground.
– ORIGIN Greek, from *akron* 'summit' + *polis* 'city.'

a·cross /ə'krôs, ə'kräs/ ▶ **preposition & adverb** from one side to the other of something.
– PHRASES **across the board** affecting or applying to everyone or everything.
– ORIGIN from Old French *a croix, en croix* 'in or on a cross.'

a·cros·tic /ə'krôstik, ə'kräs-/ ▶ **noun** a poem or puzzle in which certain letters in each line form a word or words.
– ORIGIN from Greek *akron* 'end' + *stikhos* 'row, line of verse.'

a·cryl·ic /ə'krilik/ ▶ **adjective** (of a synthetic fabric, plastic, or paint) made from acrylic acid.
– ORIGIN from Latin *acer* 'pungent' + *oleum* 'oil.'

a·cryl·ic ac·id ▶ **noun** Chemistry a strong-smelling liquid organic acid.

ACT ▶ **abbreviation** American College Test.

act /akt/ ▶ **verb 1** take action; do something. **2** take effect or have a particular effect: *a substance that acts on nerves in the digestive system.* **3** behave in a particular way: *he acts as if he owns the place.* **4** (**act as**) fulfill the function of: *she often acted as an interpreter.* **5** (**act for/on behalf of**) represent the interests of someone. **6** (as adj. **acting**) temporarily doing the duties of another person: *the acting president.* **7** perform a role in a play, movie, or television production.

– SYNONYMS **1 take action,** take steps, take measures, move. **2 behave,** conduct oneself, react. **3** *I'll act as lookout* **function,** work, serve, operate. **4** (as adj. **acting**) **temporary,** interim, caretaker, pro tem, provisional, stopgap; informal pinch-hitting. **5 perform,** play, appear; informal tread the boards.

▶ **noun 1** a thing done. **2** a law passed formally by a parliament. **3** a way of behaving that is not genuine or sincere: *she's putting on an act.* **4** a main division of a play, ballet, or opera. **5** a short piece of entertainment in a show: *a comedy act.* **6** a performer or performing group.

– SYNONYMS **1 deed,** action, step, move, gesture, feat, exploit. **2 law,** decree, statute, bill, edict, ruling, order. **3 performance,** turn, routine, number, sketch. **4 pretense,** show, front, facade, masquerade, charade, pose; informal put-on.

– PHRASES **act of God** an event caused by natural forces beyond human control. **act up** informal behave badly. **get in on the act** informal become involved in an activity to share its benefits.
– ORIGIN Latin *actus* 'event, thing done.'

ac·ti·nide /'aktəˌnīd/ ▶ **noun** any of the series of fifteen radioactive metallic elements from actinium to lawrencium in the periodic table.

ac·tin·i·um /ak'tinēəm/ ▶ **noun** a rare radioactive metallic chemical element found in uranium ores.
– ORIGIN Greek *aktis* 'ray.'

ac·tion /'aksʜən/ ▶ **noun 1** the process of doing something to achieve an aim. **2** a thing done. **3** the effect or influence of something such as a chemical. **4** a lawsuit. **5** armed conflict: *servicemen missing in action.* **6** the way in which something works or moves. **7** informal exciting activity: *a preview of the weekend's sporting action.*

– SYNONYMS **1 deed,** act, undertaking, feat, exploit, behavior, conduct, activity. **2 measures,** steps, initiatives, activism, campaigning, pressure. **3 operation,** working, effect, influence, process, power. **4 battle,** combat, hostilities, fighting, conflict, active service. **5 lawsuit,** suit, case, prosecution, litigation, proceedings.

▶ **verb** deal with something: *your request will be actioned.*
– PHRASES **in action** performing an activity; in operation. **out of action** not working.

ac·tion·a·ble /'aksʜənəbəl/ ▶ **adjective** Law giving someone grounds to take legal action.

ac·ti·vate /ˈaktəˌvāt/ ▶ **verb** make something act or start working: *the security alarms had been activated.*

– SYNONYMS **start (up),** switch on, turn on, set going, trigger (off), set off, energize.

– DERIVATIVES **ac·ti·va·tion** /ˌaktəˈvāsʜən/ noun **ac·ti·va·tor** noun.

ac·ti·vat·ed car·bon (also **activated charcoal**) ▶ **noun** charcoal that has been treated to increase its ability to absorb gases and dissolved substances.

ac·tive /ˈaktiv/ ▶ **adjective 1** moving or tending to move about often or energetically. **2** (of a person's mind) alert and lively. **3** doing something regularly: *sexually active adults.* **4** functioning: *the watermill was active until 1960.* **5** (of a volcano) erupting or having erupted in the recent past. **6** having a chemical or biological effect: *salicylic acid is the active ingredient in aspirin.* **7** Grammar referring to verbs in which the subject is the person or thing performing the action and which can take a direct object (e.g., *she loved him* as opposed to the passive form *he was loved*).

– SYNONYMS **1 busy,** lively, dynamic, vigorous, sprightly, spry, mobile; informal on the go, full of beans. **2 hard-working,** industrious, tireless, energetic, diligent, enthusiastic, keen, committed, devoted, zealous. **3 working,** operative, functioning, operational, in action, in operation, in force; informal (up and) running.
– ANTONYMS inactive.

– DERIVATIVES **ac·tive·ly** adverb.
– ORIGIN Latin *activus*.

ac·tive serv·ice ▶ **noun** direct involvement in military operations as a member of the armed forces.

ac·tiv·ist /ˈaktəˌvist/ ▶ **noun** a person who campaigns for political or social change.
– DERIVATIVES **ac·tiv·ism** /ˈaktəˌvizəm/ noun.

ac·tiv·i·ty /akˈtivitē/ ▶ **noun** (pl. **activities**) **1** a situation in which things are happening or being done. **2** busy or energetic action or movement. **3** a thing that a person or group does or has done: *sporting and social activities.*

– SYNONYMS **1 action,** bustle, movement, life, hurly-burly; informal comings and goings. **2 pursuit,** occupation, hobby, pastime, recreation, diversion, venture, undertaking, enterprise, project, scheme.

ac·tor /ˈaktər/ ▶ **noun** a person whose profession is acting.

– SYNONYMS **performer,** player, thespian, star, starlet.

– DERIVATIVES **ac·tor·ish** adjective.

ac·tress /ˈaktris/ ▶ **noun** a female actor.

– SYNONYMS **performer,** player, thespian, star, starlet.

– DERIVATIVES **ac·tress·y** adjective.

ac·tu·al /ˈakcʜo͞oəl/ ▶ **adjective 1** existing in fact: *those were his actual words.* **2** existing now; current: *actual income.*

– SYNONYMS **real,** true, genuine, authentic, bona fide, confirmed, definite, hard, concrete; informal real live.
– ANTONYMS imaginary.

– ORIGIN Latin *actualis*.

ac·tu·al·i·ty /ˌakcʜo͞oˈalitē/ ▶ **noun** (pl. **actualities**) **1** the state of existing in fact; reality: *the $100 mentioned was in actuality $100,000.* **2** (**actualities**) existing conditions or facts.

ac·tu·al·ize /ˈakcʜo͞oəˌlīz/ ▶ **verb** make something real.
– DERIVATIVES **ac·tu·al·i·za·tion** /ˌakcʜo͞oələˈzāsʜən/ noun.

ac·tu·al·ly /ˈakcʜo͞oəlē/ ▶ **adverb 1** in reality. **2** used to emphasize or contradict something: *he actually expected me to be pleased!*

– SYNONYMS **really,** in (actual) fact, in point of fact, as a matter of fact, in reality, in truth, if truth be told, to tell the truth.

ac·tu·ar·y /ˈakcʜo͞oˌerē/ ▶ **noun** (pl. **actuaries**) a person who compiles and analyzes statistics in order to calculate insurance risks and premiums.
– DERIVATIVES **ac·tu·ar·i·al** /ˌakcʜo͞oˈe(ə)rēəl/ adjective.
– ORIGIN Latin *actuarius* 'bookkeeper.'

ac·tu·ate /ˈakcʜo͞oˌāt/ ▶ **verb 1** cause a machine to operate. **2** motivate someone to act: *they were actuated by malice.*
– DERIVATIVES **ac·tu·a·tion** /ˌakcʜo͞oˈāsʜən/ noun **ac·tu·a·tor** noun.

a·cu·i·ty /əˈkyo͞oitē/ ▶ **noun** keenness of thought, vision, or hearing.
– ORIGIN Latin *acuitas*.

a·cu·men /əˈkyo͞omən, ˈakyə-/ ▶ **noun** the ability to make good judgments and quick decisions.

– SYNONYMS **astuteness,** shrewdness, acuity, sharpness, smartness, brains; judgment, canniness, insight; informal savvy, know-how, smarts; formal perspicuity.

– ORIGIN Latin, 'sharpness, point.'

ac·u·pres·sure /ˈakyəˌpresʜər/ ▶ **noun** a form of alternative therapy related to acupuncture in which specific points of the body are pressed to stimulate the flow of energy.

ac·u·punc·ture /ˈakyəˌpəngkcʜər/ ▶ **noun** a system of complementary medicine in which fine needles are inserted in the skin at specific points along supposed lines of energy.
– DERIVATIVES **ac·u·punc·tur·ist** noun.
– ORIGIN from Latin *acu* 'with a needle' + **PUNCTURE**.

a·cute /əˈkyo͞ot/ ▶ **adjective 1** (of something bad) serious or severe: *an acute housing shortage.* **2** (of an illness) coming sharply to a crisis. Often contrasted with **CHRONIC**. **3** showing or having insight; perceptive. **4** (of a sense) highly developed: *an acute sense of smell.* **5** (of an angle) less than 90°.

– SYNONYMS **1 severe,** dire, terrible, grave, serious, desperate, urgent, pressing. **2 excruciating,** sharp, severe, stabbing, agonizing, racking, searing. **3 quick,** astute, shrewd, sharp, keen, penetrating, razor-sharp, quick-witted, agile, nimble, intelligent, canny, discerning, perceptive.
– ANTONYMS mild, dull.

– DERIVATIVES **a·cute·ly** adverb **a·cute·ness** noun.
– ORIGIN Latin *acutus* 'sharpened.'

CHOOSE THE RIGHT WORD

See **KEEN**[1].

a·cute ac·cent ▶ **noun** a mark (´) placed over certain letters in some languages to indicate pronunciation (e.g., in *fiancée*).

AD ▶ **abbreviation** Anno Domini (used to show that a date comes the specified number of years after the traditional date of Jesus's birth).
– ORIGIN Latin, 'in the year of the Lord.'

USAGE

AD is normally written in small capitals and should be placed **before** the numerals, as in AD *375*. However, when the date is spelled out, you should write *the third century* AD.

ad /ad/ ▶ **noun** informal an advertisement.

ad·age /'adij/ ▶ **noun** a popular saying expressing a widely accepted truth.
– ORIGIN Latin *adagium*.

a·da·gio /ə'däjō, ə'däzнē,ō/ Music ▶ **adverb & adjective** in slow time. ▶ **noun** (pl. **adagios**) a passage in slow time.
– ORIGIN from Italian *ad agio* 'at ease.'

ad·a·mant /'adəmənt/ ▶ **adjective** refusing to be persuaded or to change one's mind: *he is adamant that he is not going to resign.*

– SYNONYMS **unshakable,** unwavering, unswerving, immovable, resolute, resolved, determined, firm, dead set.

– DERIVATIVES **ad·a·mant·ly** adverb.
– ORIGIN Greek *adamas* 'invincible.'

ad·a·man·tine /,adə'man,tīn, -tin-, -,tēn/ ▶ **adjective** literary unable to be broken.

Ad·am's ap·ple /'adəmz/ ▶ **noun** a projection at the front of the neck formed by the thyroid cartilage.
– ORIGIN from the belief that a piece of the forbidden fruit became lodged in Adam's throat.

a·dapt /ə'dapt/ ▶ **verb 1** make something suitable for a new use or purpose. **2** become adjusted to new conditions: *older workers are struggling to adapt to change.*

– SYNONYMS **1** *the policy can be adapted* **modify,** alter, change, adjust, remodel, reorganize, customize, tailor; informal tweak. **2** *he adapts well to new surroundings* **adjust,** conform, acclimatize, accommodate, get used, get accustomed, habituate oneself.

– DERIVATIVES **a·dap·tive** adjective.
– ORIGIN Latin *adaptare*.

a·dapt·a·ble /ə'daptəbəl/ ▶ **adjective** able to adjust to or be altered for new conditions or uses.
– DERIVATIVES **a·dapt·a·bil·i·ty** /ə,daptə'bilitē/ noun.

ad·ap·ta·tion /,adap'tāsнən, ,adəp-/ (also **adaption**) ▶ **noun 1** the action of adapting. **2** a movie or play adapted from a written work.

a·dapt·o·gen /ə'daptəjən/ ▶ **noun** (in herbal medicine) a natural substance believed to help the body adapt to stress.
– DERIVATIVES **a·dapt·o·gen·ic** /ə,daptə'jenik/ adjective.

a·dap·tor /ə'daptər/ (also **adapter**) ▶ **noun 1** a device for connecting pieces of equipment. **2** a device for connecting several electric plugs to one socket.

ad·bot /'ad,bät/ ▶ **noun** a computer program that caches advertising on personal computers and then displays the advertising when certain linked programs are being used.
– ORIGIN blend of *advertising* and *robot*.

ADC ▶ **abbreviation 1** aide-de-camp. **2** analog-to-digital converter.

ADD ▶ **abbreviation 1** attention deficit disorder. **2** analog digital, indicating that a music recording was made in analog format before being mastered and stored digitally.

add /ad/ ▶ **verb 1** join to or put with something else: *a new wing was added to the building.* **2** put together two or more numbers or amounts to calculate their total value. **3** (**add up**) increase in amount, number, or degree: *watch those air miles add up!* **4** say something as a further remark. **5** (**add up**) informal make sense.

– SYNONYMS **1 attach,** append, tack on, join on. **2** *her decision just* ***added to*** *his woe* **increase,** augment, magnify, amplify, enhance, intensify, heighten, deepen, exacerbate, aggravate, compound, reinforce. **3** *they added the figures up* **total,** count (up), reckon up, tally. **4** *the subsidies* ***added up to*** *$1,700* **amount to,** come to, run to, make, total, equal, number.
– ANTONYMS subtract.

– ORIGIN Latin *addere*.

ad·den·dum /ə'dendəm/ ▶ **noun** (pl. **addenda** /-də/) an extra item added at the end of a book or other publication.
– ORIGIN Latin, 'that which is to be added.'

ad·der /'adər/ ▶ **noun** a poisonous snake with a dark zigzag pattern on its back.
– ORIGIN Old English *nædre* 'serpent, adder.'

ad·dict /'adikt/ ▶ **noun** a person who is addicted to something.

– SYNONYMS **1 abuser;** informal junkie, druggie, -head, freak, hophead. **2 enthusiast,** fan, lover, devotee, aficionado; informal buff, freak, nut, fanatic.

ad·dict·ed /ə'diktid/ ▶ **adjective 1** physically dependent on a particular substance. **2** devoted to a particular interest or activity: *I'm addicted to crime novels.*

– SYNONYMS *they seem* ***addicted to*** *their cell phones* **dependent on,** obsessed with, fixated on, fanatical about, passionate about, a slave to; informal hooked on.

– ORIGIN from Latin *addicere* 'assign.'

ad·dic·tion /ə'diksнən/ ▶ **noun** the fact or condition of being addicted to something.

– SYNONYMS **dependency,** dependence, habit, obsession, infatuation, passion, love, mania, enslavement.

ad·dic·tive /ə'diktiv/ ▶ **adjective 1** (of a substance or activity) causing someone to become addicted to it. **2** relating or prone to addiction.

– SYNONYMS **habit-forming,** addicting, compulsive.

– DERIVATIVES **ad·dic·tive·ly** adverb.

ad·di·tion /ə'disнən/ ▶ **noun 1** the action of adding. **2** a person or thing that is added: *the mirror would make a handsome addition to a bathroom.*

– SYNONYMS **1 adding,** inclusion, incorporation, introduction. **2 add-on,** extra, adjunct, appendage, supplement, rider, addendum, postscript, appendix.
– ANTONYMS subtraction.

ad·di·tion·al /ə'disнənl/ ▶ **adjective** extra to what is already present or available: *we need additional information.*

– SYNONYMS **extra,** added, supplementary, further, more, spare, other, new, fresh.

ad·di·tion·al·ly /ə'disнənl-ē/ ▶ **adverb** as an extra factor or circumstance.

– SYNONYMS **also,** in addition, besides, too, as well, on top (of that), furthermore, moreover, into the bargain, to boot, to say nothing of.

ad·di·tive /'aditiv/ ▶ **noun** a substance added to something to improve or preserve it.

ad·dle /'adl/ ▶ **verb 1** confuse someone. **2** (as adj. **addled**) (of an egg) rotten.

– SYNONYMS *being in love must have addled your brain* **muddle,** confuse, befuddle, daze, disorient, bewilder.

▶ **adjective** (in combination) not clear; muddled: *an addle-brained adolescent.*
– ORIGIN from Old English, 'liquid filth.'

ad·dress /ə'dres, 'aˌdres/ ▶ **noun 1** the details of the place where someone lives or an organization is situated. **2** a formal speech. **3** a number identifying a location in a data storage system or computer memory. **4** a string of characters that identifies a destination for email messages.

– SYNONYMS **1 house,** home, apartment, location, whereabouts; formal residence, dwelling, domicile. **2 speech,** lecture, talk, presentation, dissertation, sermon, oration.

▶ **verb 1** write a name and address on an envelope or parcel. **2** formal speak to someone. **3** think about and begin to deal with: *the computer industry has started to address the problem.*

– SYNONYMS **speak to,** talk to, give a talk to, lecture, make a speech to, hold forth to.

– DERIVATIVES **ad·dress·a·ble** adjective **ad·dress·er** noun.
– ORIGIN from Latin *ad-* 'toward' + *directus* 'direct.'

ad·dress·ee /ˌadre'sē, əˌdre'sē/ ▶ **noun** the person to whom something is addressed.

ad·duce /ə'd(y)o͞os/ ▶ **verb** refer to something as evidence.
– ORIGIN Latin *adducere.*

ad·dy /'adē/ ▶ **noun** (pl. **addies**) informal an address, especially an email address.

ad·e·nine /'adnˌēn, -ˌīn/ ▶ **noun** Biochemistry a compound that is one of the four constituent bases of nucleic acids.

ad·e·noids /'adnˌoidz/ ▶ **plural noun** a mass of tissue between the back of the nose and the throat, sometimes hindering speaking or breathing in children.
– DERIVATIVES **ad·e·noi·dal** /ˌadn'oidl/ adjective.
– ORIGIN from Greek *adēn* 'gland.'

a·dept ▶ **adjective** /ə'dept/ very good at doing something; skilled: *I became adept at inventing excuses.*

– SYNONYMS **expert,** proficient, accomplished, skillful, practiced, masterly, consummate.
– ANTONYMS inept.

▶ **noun** /'adept, ə'dept/ a person who is skilled at doing something.
– DERIVATIVES **a·dept·ly** adverb **a·dept·ness** noun.
– ORIGIN from Latin *adipisci* 'obtain, attain.'

ad·e·quate /'adikwit/ ▶ **adjective** satisfactory or acceptable in quality or quantity: *an adequate supply of fuel.*

– SYNONYMS **1** *he has adequate financial resources* **sufficient,** enough. **2** *an adequate service* **satisfactory,** acceptable, passable, reasonable, tolerable, fair, average, not bad, all right, middling; informal OK.
– ANTONYMS insufficient, inadequate.

– DERIVATIVES **ad·e·qua·cy** /-kwəsē/ noun **ad·e·quate·ly** adverb.
– ORIGIN from Latin *adaequare* 'make equal to.'

à deux /ä 'dœ/ ▶ **adverb** for or involving two people: *dinner à deux.*
– ORIGIN French.

ADHD ▶ **abbreviation** attention deficit hyperactivity disorder.

ad·here /ad'hi(ə)r/ ▶ **verb** (**adhere to**) **1** stick firmly to something. **2** follow, observe, or support: *members must adhere to a code of practice.* **3** represent something truthfully.

– SYNONYMS **1 stick,** cling, bond, hold. **2 abide by,** stick to, hold to, comply with, conform to, follow, obey, heed, observe, respect, uphold, fulfill.

– DERIVATIVES **ad·her·ence** noun.
– ORIGIN Latin *adhaerere.*

ad·her·ent /ad'hi(ə)rənt, -'her-/ ▶ **noun** a person who supports a particular party, person, or set of ideas.

– SYNONYMS **follower,** supporter, upholder, defender, advocate, disciple, devotee, member.
– ANTONYMS opponent.

▶ **adjective** sticking firmly to something.

ad·he·sion /ad'hēzʜən/ ▶ **noun 1** the action of adhering to something. **2** Medicine an abnormal joining of surfaces in the body as a result of inflammation or injury.

ad·he·sive /ad'hēsiv, -ziv/ ▶ **noun** a substance used for sticking things together. ▶ **adjective** able to stick to something; sticky.
– DERIVATIVES **ad·he·sive·ly** adverb **ad·he·sive·ness** noun.

ad hoc /ad 'häk, 'hōk/ ▶ **adjective & adverb** formed or done for a particular purpose only: *an ad hoc committee.*
– ORIGIN Latin, 'to this.'

ad ho·mi·nem /'ad 'hämənəm/ ▶ **adverb & adjective** (of an argument) personal rather than objective.
– ORIGIN Latin, 'to the person.'

a·dieu /ə'd(y)o͞o, ä'dyœ/ ▶ **exclamation** chiefly literary goodbye.
– ORIGIN Old French.

ad in·fi·ni·tum /ˌad infə'nītəm/ ▶ **adverb** forever in the same way: *I could quote Dylan lyrics ad infinitum.*
– ORIGIN Latin, 'to infinity.'

ad·i·os /ˌädē'ōs, ˌadē-/ ▶ **exclamation** (in Spanish-speaking countries) goodbye.
– ORIGIN Spanish.

ad·i·pose /'adəˌpōs/ ▶ **adjective** technical (of body tissue) used for storing fat.
– ORIGIN from Latin *adeps* 'fat.'

ad·it /'adit/ ▶ **noun** a horizontal access or drainage passage in a mine.
– ORIGIN Latin *aditus* 'approach, entrance.'

ad·ja·cent /ə'jāsənt/ ▶ **adjective** next to or adjoining something else.

– SYNONYMS **1** *adjacent rooms* **adjoining,** neighboring, next-door, abutting; formal contiguous. **2** *a patio* ***adjacent to*** *the greenhouse* **next to,** by the side of, bordering on, beside, alongside, touching.

– DERIVATIVES **ad·ja·cen·cy** noun.
– ORIGIN from Latin *adjacere* 'lie near to.'

ad·jec·tive /'ajiktiv/ ▶ **noun** a word used to describe a noun, such as *sweet, red,* or *technical.*
– DERIVATIVES **ad·jec·ti·val** /ˌajik'tīvəl/ adjective.
– ORIGIN Old French *adjectif.*

ad·join /ə'join/ ▶ **verb** be next to and joined with: *the dining room adjoins a conservatory.*

– SYNONYMS (as adj. **adjoining**) *adjoining hotel rooms* **connecting,** connected, interconnecting, bordering, abutting, attached, adjacent, neighboring, next-door.

– ORIGIN from Latin *adjungere* 'join to.'

ad·journ /ə'jərn/ ▶ **verb 1** break off a meeting or legal case with the intention of resuming it later. **2** postpone a judicial sentence. **3** (of a group) go to another room or place, especially to relax: *they adjourned to the local bar*.

– SYNONYMS **suspend,** break off, discontinue, interrupt, recess, postpone, put off/back, defer, delay, hold over.

– DERIVATIVES **ad·journ·ment** noun.
– ORIGIN Old French *ajorner*, from *a jorn nome* 'to an appointed day.'

CHOOSE THE RIGHT WORD

See **POSTPONE**.

ad·judge /ə'jəj/ ▶ **verb** (especially of an authority) make a decision about someone or something: *she was adjudged guilty*.
– ORIGIN Latin *adjudicare*.

ad·ju·di·cate /ə'jo͞odi,kāt/ ▶ **verb 1** make a formal judgment on a disputed matter. **2** judge a competition.
– DERIVATIVES **ad·ju·di·ca·tion** /ə,jo͞odi'kāsʜən/ noun **ad·ju·di·ca·tor** /-,kātər/ noun.
– ORIGIN Latin *adjudicare* 'adjudge.'

ad·junct /'ajənɢkt/ ▶ **noun** an additional and supplementary part: *computer technology is an adjunct to learning*.
– DERIVATIVES **ad·junc·tive** /ə'jənɢ(k)tiv/ adjective.
– ORIGIN from Latin *adjungere* 'adjoin.'

ad·jure /ə'jo͝or/ ▶ **verb** formal solemnly urge someone to do something.
– ORIGIN Latin *adjurare*.

ad·just /ə'jəst/ ▶ **verb 1** alter something slightly so as to achieve a desired result: *he adjusted his tie*. **2** become used to a new situation. **3** assess loss or damages when settling an insurance claim.

– SYNONYMS **1 modify,** alter, regulate, tune, fine-tune, balance, tailor, customize, rearrange, change, reshape; informal tweak. **2** *she* ***adjusted to*** *her new life* **adapt to,** become accustomed to, get used to, accommodate oneself to, acclimate to, acclimatize to, habituate oneself to, assimilate to, come to terms with, fit in with.

– DERIVATIVES **ad·just·a·bil·i·ty** /ə,jəstə'bilitē/ noun **ad·just·a·ble** adjective **ad·just·er** noun.
– ORIGIN Old French *ajoster* 'to approximate.'

ad·just·ment /ə,jəstmənt/ ▶ **noun 1** a minor change made so as to correct or improve something: *the company will make adjustments to its packaging*. **2** the action of adjusting.

ad·ju·tant /'ajətənt/ ▶ **noun** a military officer acting as an administrative assistant to a senior officer.
– ORIGIN from Latin *adjutare* 'be of service to.'

ad·ju·vant /'ajəvənt/ ▶ **adjective** (of medical treatment) applied after initial treatment for cancer to prevent secondary tumors. ▶ **noun** a substance that improves the body's immune response to an infection or foreign body.
– ORIGIN from Latin *adjuvare* 'help toward.'

ad-lib /'ad'lib/ ▶ **verb** (**ad-libs, ad-libbing, ad-libbed**) speak or perform in public without preparing beforehand. ▶ **adverb & adjective 1** spoken without previous preparation. **2** as much and as often as required: *the price includes meals and drinks ad lib*. ▶ **noun** an unprepared remark or speech.
– ORIGIN abbreviation of Latin *ad libitum* 'according to pleasure.'

ad li·tem /ad 'lītəm/ ▶ **adjective** Law acting in a lawsuit on behalf of people who cannot represent themselves.
– ORIGIN Latin, 'for the lawsuit.'

ad·man /'ad,man/ ▶ **noun** (pl. **admen**) informal a person who works in advertising.

ad·min /'ad,min/ ▶ **noun** informal administration.

ad·min·is·ter /əd'minəstər/ ▶ **verb 1** manage or put into effect: *the abatement program is administered by the EPA*. **2** give out a drug or remedy.

– SYNONYMS **1 manage,** direct, control, operate, regulate, coordinate, conduct, handle, run, organize, govern, steer. **2 dispense,** issue, give out, provide, apply, offer, distribute, deliver, hand out, deal out, dole out.

– ORIGIN Latin *administrare*.

ad·min·is·trate /əd'minə,strāt/ ▶ **verb** manage an organization.

ad·min·is·tra·tion /əd,minə'strāsʜən/ ▶ **noun 1** the organization and running of a business or system. **2** the action of giving out or applying something. **3** the government in power.

– SYNONYMS **1 management,** direction, control, conduct, operation, running, coordination, governance, supervision, regulation. **2 government,** regime, executive, cabinet, authority, directorate, council, leadership, management, incumbency, term of office.

ad·min·is·tra·tive /əd'mini,strātiv, -strətiv/ ▶ **adjective** relating to the running of a business, organization, etc.

– SYNONYMS **managerial,** executive, operational, organizational, supervisory, directorial, governmental, regulatory.

– DERIVATIVES **ad·min·is·tra·tive·ly** adverb.

ad·min·is·tra·tor /əd'minə,strātər/ ▶ **noun** a person responsible for managing an organization.

– SYNONYMS **manager,** director, executive, controller, official, coordinator, supervisor.

ad·mi·ra·ble /'admərəbəl/ ▶ **adjective** deserving respect and approval.

– SYNONYMS **commendable,** praiseworthy, laudable, creditable, exemplary, worthy, deserving, respectable, worthwhile, good, sterling, fine, excellent.
– ANTONYMS deplorable.

– DERIVATIVES **ad·mi·ra·bly** adverb.

ad·mi·ral /'admərəl/ ▶ **noun 1** the most senior commander of a fleet or navy. **2** a naval or coast guard officer of the second most senior rank, ranking above a vice admiral.
– ORIGIN from an Arabic word meaning 'commander.'

Ad·mi·ral·ty /'admərəltē/ ▶ **noun** (pl. **Admiralties**) (in the UK) the government department formerly in charge of the Royal Navy.

ad·mi·ra·tion /,admə'rāsʜən/ ▶ **noun** respect and warm approval.

– SYNONYMS *their* ***admiration*** *for each other was genuine* **respect,** approval, appreciation, (high) regard, esteem, veneration.
– ANTONYMS scorn.

ad·mire /əd'mī(ə)r/ ▶ **verb 1** regard with respect or approval: *I admire your courage*. **2** look at something with pleasure.

– SYNONYMS **1 respect,** think highly of, look up to, have a high opinion of, hold in high regard, rate highly, esteem, prize, approve of. **2 adore,** love, worship, be taken with, be attracted to, idolize, hero-worship; informal carry a torch for, have a thing about.
– ANTONYMS despise.

– DERIVATIVES **ad·mir·ing** /əd'mī(ə)riNG/ adjective.
– ORIGIN Latin *admirari* 'wonder at.'

CHOOSE THE RIGHT WORD
See **REVERE**.

ad·mir·er /əd'mī(ə)rər/ ▶ **noun** someone who has a particular regard for someone or something.

– SYNONYMS **fan,** devotee, enthusiast, aficionado, supporter, adherent, follower, disciple.

ad·mis·si·ble /'misəbəl/ ▶ **adjective 1** acceptable or valid. **2** having the right to be admitted to a place.
– DERIVATIVES **ad·mis·si·bil·i·ty** /əd,misə'bilitē/ noun.

ad·mis·sion /əd'misHən/ ▶ **noun 1** entry to or permission to enter a place or organization: *many victims are refused admission to the shelter.* **2** a confession. **3** a person admitted to a hospital for treatment.

– SYNONYMS **1 confession,** acknowledgment, acceptance, concession, disclosure, divulgence. **2 admittance,** entry, entrance, access, entrée, acceptance, initiation.

ad·mit /əd'mit/ ▶ **verb** (**admits, admitting, admitted**) **1** confess to be true or to be the case: *I admit that I was relieved when he went.* **2** allow someone to enter a place or organization. **3** accept someone into a hospital for treatment. **4** accept something as valid. **5** (**admit of**) allow the possibility of: *the narrative can admit of no deviation.*

– SYNONYMS **1** *Paul admitted that he was angry* **confess,** acknowledge, concede, grant, accept, allow, own, reveal, disclose, divulge. **2** *he admitted the offense* **confess (to),** plead guilty to, own up to. **3 let in,** accept, receive, initiate, take on.
– ANTONYMS deny.

– ORIGIN Latin *admittere* 'let into.'

ad·mit·tance /əd'mitns/ ▶ **noun** the process of entering or the fact of being allowed to enter: *we were unable to gain admittance to the hall.*

– SYNONYMS **entry,** admission, entrance, access, entrée.
– ANTONYMS exclusion.

ad·mix·ture /ad'miksCHər/ ▶ **noun** technical a mixture.
– DERIVATIVES **ad·mix** /ad'miks/ verb.

ad·mon·ish /əd'mänisH/ ▶ **verb 1** reprimand someone firmly. **2** earnestly urge or warn someone.

– SYNONYMS **reprimand,** rebuke, scold, reprove, reproach, upbraid, chastise, chide, berate, criticize, take to task, read the Riot Act to, haul over the coals; informal tell off, dress down, bawl out, rap over the knuckles, give hell, chew out. formal castigate.

– DERIVATIVES **ad·mon·ish·ment** noun **ad·mo·ni·tion** /,admə'nisHən/ noun.
– ORIGIN Latin *admonere*.

CHOOSE THE RIGHT WORD
See **REBUKE**.

ad·mon·i·to·ry /əd'mänə,tôrē/ ▶ **adjective** giving or expressing a warning or reprimand: *she lifted an admonitory finger.*

ad nau·se·am /ad 'nôzēəm/ ▶ **adverb** to an annoyingly excessive extent: *they recycle one idea ad nauseam.*
– ORIGIN Latin, 'to sickness.'

a·do /ə'dōō/ ▶ **noun** trouble; fuss: *I left without further ado.*
– ORIGIN from northern dialect *at do* 'to do.'

a·do·be /ə'dōbē/ ▶ **noun** a kind of clay used to make sun-dried bricks.
– ORIGIN from Spanish *adobar* 'to plaster.'

ad·o·les·cent /,adl'esənt/ ▶ **adjective** in the process of developing from a child into an adult.

– SYNONYMS **teenage,** young, pubescent, immature, childish, juvenile, infantile, puerile; informal teen.
– ANTONYMS mature.

▶ **noun** an adolescent boy or girl.

– SYNONYMS **teenager,** youth, juvenile; informal teen, teeny-bopper.

– DERIVATIVES **ad·o·les·cence** noun.
– ORIGIN from Latin *adolescere* 'to mature.'

A·don·is /ə'dänis/ ▶ **noun** a very handsome young man.
– ORIGIN the name of a beautiful youth in Greek mythology.

a·dopt /ə'däpt/ ▶ **verb 1** legally take another person's child and bring it up as one's own. **2** choose an option or course of action. **3** take on an attitude or position: *he adopted a patronizing tone.* **4** formally approve or accept someone or something.

– SYNONYMS **take on,** embrace, take up, espouse, assume, follow, choose, endorse, approve.
– ANTONYMS abandon.

– DERIVATIVES **a·dopt·a·ble** adjective **a·dopt·ee** /ədäpt'tē/ noun **a·dopt·er** noun **a·dop·tion** noun.
– ORIGIN Latin *adoptare*.

a·dop·tive /ə'däptiv/ ▶ **adjective 1** (of a child or parent) in that relationship by adoption. **2** (of a place) chosen by a person as their permanent place of residence.

a·dor·a·ble /ə'dôrəbəl/ ▶ **adjective** very lovable or charming.

– SYNONYMS **lovable,** appealing, charming, cute, sweet, enchanting, bewitching, captivating, engaging, endearing, dear, delightful, lovely, beautiful, attractive, gorgeous, winsome, winning, fetching; Scottish bonny.
– ANTONYMS repulsive, hateful.

– DERIVATIVES **a·dor·a·bly** adverb.

a·dore /ə'dôr/ ▶ **verb 1** love and respect someone greatly. **2** informal like very much: *she adores Mexican cuisine.*

– SYNONYMS **love,** be devoted to, dote on, cherish, treasure, prize, think the world of, admire, look up to, revere, worship.
– ANTONYMS hate.

– DERIVATIVES **ad·o·ra·tion** /,adə'rāsHən/ noun **a·dor·er** noun **a·dor·ing** adjective.
– ORIGIN Latin *adorare* 'to worship.'

CHOOSE THE RIGHT WORD
See **REVERE**.

a·dorn /ə'dôrn/ ▶ **verb** make something more attractive or beautiful.

– SYNONYMS **decorate,** embellish, array, ornament, bedeck, trim, enhance.
– ANTONYMS disfigure.

– DERIVATIVES **a·dorn·ment** noun.
– ORIGIN Latin *adornare*.

ADP ▶ **abbreviation 1** Biochemistry adenosine diphosphate, a compound involved in metabolic energy transfer. **2** automatic data processing.

ad·re·nal /ə'drēnl/ ▶ **adjective** relating to a pair of glands above the kidneys that produce adrenaline and other hormones.

a·dren·al·ine /ə'drenl-in/ (also **adrenalin**) ▶ **noun** a hormone produced by the adrenal glands that increases rates of blood circulation, breathing, and carbohydrate metabolism.

a·dre·nal·ized /ə'drēnl,īzd/ ▶ **adjective** excited, tense, or highly charged.

A·dri·at·ic /,ādrē'atik/ ▶ **adjective** relating to the region of the Adriatic Sea, between Italy and the Balkans.

a·drift /ə'drift/ ▶ **adjective & adverb 1** (of a boat) drifting without control. **2** no longer fixed in position. **3** lost and confused; without purpose or guidance.

– SYNONYMS *the band has been adrift ever since her departure* **lost,** off course, drifting, disorientated, confused, (all) at sea, rootless, unsettled.

a·droit /ə'droit/ ▶ **adjective** clever or skillful: *an adroit administrator*.

– SYNONYMS **skillful,** adept, dexterous, deft, nimble, able, capable, skilled, expert, masterly, masterful, practiced, polished, slick, proficient, accomplished, gifted, talented; quick-witted, quick-thinking, clever, smart, sharp, cunning, wily, resourceful, astute, shrewd, canny; informal nifty.
– ANTONYMS inept, clumsy.

– ORIGIN from French *à droit* 'according to right, properly.'

ad·sorb /ad'zôrb, -'sôrb/ ▶ **verb** (of a solid) hold molecules of a gas, liquid, or dissolved substance in a layer on its surface.
– DERIVATIVES **ad·sorb·ent** adjective & noun **ad·sorp·tion** noun.

ad·u·la·tion /,ajə'lāsʜən/ ▶ **noun** excessive admiration.
– DERIVATIVES **ad·u·late** /'ajə,lāt/ verb **ad·u·la·to·ry** /'ajələ,tôrē/ adjective.
– ORIGIN from Latin *adulari* 'fawn on.'

a·dult /ə'dəlt, 'ad,əlt/ ▶ **noun 1** a person who is fully grown and developed. **2** Law a person who has reached the age of majority. ▶ **adjective 1** fully grown and developed. **2** for or typical of adults: *adult education*.

– SYNONYMS **mature,** grown-up, fully grown, fully developed, of age.
– ANTONYMS immature.

– DERIVATIVES **a·dult·hood** noun.
– ORIGIN Latin *adultus*.

a·dul·ter·ate /ə'dəltə,rāt/ ▶ **verb** make something poorer in quality by adding another substance.
– DERIVATIVES **a·dul·ter·ant** /ə'dəltərənt/ adjective **a·dul·ter·a·tion** /ə,dəltə'rāsʜən/ noun.
– ORIGIN Latin *adulterare* 'to corrupt.'

a·dul·ter·er /ə'dəltərər/ ▶ **noun** (fem. **adulteress**) a person who has committed adultery.
– ORIGIN from Latin *adulterare* 'to corrupt.'

a·dul·ter·y /ə'dəlt(ə)rē/ ▶ **noun** sexual intercourse between a married person and a person who is not their spouse.
– DERIVATIVES **a·dul·ter·ous** adjective.

ad·um·brate /'adəm,brāt, ə'dəm-/ ▶ **verb** formal **1** give a general idea of; outline: *his essay developed the arguments adumbrated in his earlier message*. **2** be a warning of a future event.
– DERIVATIVES **ad·um·bra·tion** /,adəm'brāsʜən/ noun.
– ORIGIN Latin *adumbrare* 'shade, overshadow.'

ad·vance /əd'vans/ ▶ **verb 1** move forward. **2** make progress. **3** put forward a theory or suggestion. **4** hand over payment to someone as a loan or before it is due: *he advanced me a month's salary*.

– SYNONYMS **1 move forward,** press on, push on, attack, make progress, make headway, gain ground, forge ahead. **2** *the move advanced his career* **promote,** further, forward, help, aid, assist, boost. **3** *technology has advanced* **progress,** develop, evolve, make strides, move forward (in leaps and bounds), move on. **4 lend,** loan, put up, come up with.
– ANTONYMS retreat.

▶ **noun 1** a forward movement. **2** a development or improvement. **3** an amount of money advanced to someone. **4** (**advances**) approaches made to someone with the aim of starting a sexual or romantic relationship.

– SYNONYMS **1 progress,** (forward) movement, attack. **2 breakthrough,** development, step forward, (quantum) leap.

▶ **adjective** done, sent, or supplied beforehand.

– SYNONYMS **early,** prior.

– ORIGIN Old French *avancer*.

ad·vanced /əd'vanst/ ▶ **adjective 1** far on in development or progress: *an advanced computer network*. **2** complex; not basic.

– SYNONYMS **1 state-of-the-art,** modern, sophisticated, up to date, up to the minute, cutting-edge, new, the latest, pioneering, innovative, progressive, trendsetting. **2 higher-level,** higher, tertiary.
– ANTONYMS primitive, elementary.

ad·vance·ment /əd'vansmənt/ ▶ **noun 1** the promotion of a cause or plan: *the advancement of science*. **2** the promotion of a person in rank or status. **3** a development or improvement.

ad·van·tage /əd'vantij/ ▶ **noun 1** a condition or factor that puts one in a more favorable position: *our technology will help you build a competitive advantage*. **2** Tennis a score marking a point between deuce and winning the game.

– SYNONYMS **1 upper hand,** edge, lead, sway, whip hand, superiority, dominance, supremacy. **2 benefit,** value, good/strong point, asset, plus, bonus, boon, blessing, virtue, profit, good.
– ANTONYMS disadvantage.

– PHRASES **take advantage of 1** make unfair use of something for one's own benefit. **2** make good use of the opportunities offered by something.
– ORIGIN Old French *avantage*.

ad·van·ta·geous /,advən'tājəs, -van-/ ▶ **adjective** good or useful in a particular situation.

– SYNONYMS **1 superior,** dominant, powerful, fortunate, lucky, favorable. **2 beneficial,** of benefit, helpful, of assistance, useful, of value, profitable, in someone's interests.
– ANTONYMS disadvantageous.

– DERIVATIVES **ad·van·ta·geous·ly** adverb.

ad·vent /ˈadˌvent/ ▶ **noun 1** the arrival of an important person or thing: *the days before the advent of air conditioning*. **2** (**Advent**) (in Christian belief) the coming or second coming of Jesus. **3** (**Advent**) the first season of the Church year, leading up to Christmas.
– ORIGIN Latin *adventus* 'arrival.'

Ad·vent·ist /ˈadˌventist/ ▶ **noun** a member of a Christian sect who believes that the second coming of Jesus is about to happen.
– DERIVATIVES **Ad·vent·ism** noun.

ad·ven·ti·tious /ˌadvenˈtisHəs/ ▶ **adjective 1** happening by chance. **2** (of roots) growing directly from the stem or other upper part of a plant.
– ORIGIN Latin *adventicius* 'coming to us from abroad.'

> **CHOOSE THE RIGHT WORD**
>
> See **ACCIDENTAL**.

ad·ven·ture /adˈvencHər, əd-/ ▶ **noun 1** an unusual, exciting, and daring experience. **2** excitement arising from danger or risk: *she traveled the world in search of adventure*.

> – SYNONYMS **1 exploit,** escapade, undertaking, experience, incident. **2 excitement,** thrills, action, stimulation, risk, danger.

– DERIVATIVES **ad·ven·ture·some** adjective.
– ORIGIN from Latin *adventurus* 'about to happen.'

ad·ven·tur·er /adˈvencHərər, əd-/ ▶ **noun** (fem. **adventuress**) **1** a person willing to take risks or use dishonest methods to gain wealth or power: *a political adventurer*. **2** a person who enjoys or looks for adventure.

ad·ven·tur·ism /adˈvencHəˌrizəm, əd-/ ▶ **noun** willingness to take risks in business or politics.
– DERIVATIVES **ad·ven·tur·ist** noun & adjective.

ad·ven·tur·ous /adˈvencHərəs, əd-/ ▶ **adjective** open to or involving new or daring methods or experiences: *an adventurous cook*.

> – SYNONYMS **1 intrepid,** daring, daredevil, bold, fearless, brave; informal gutsy. **2 risky,** dangerous, perilous, hazardous, exciting.
> – ANTONYMS cautious, safe.

– DERIVATIVES **ad·ven·tur·ous·ly** adverb **ad·ven·tur·ous·ness** noun.

ad·verb /ˈadˌvərb/ ▶ **noun** a word or phrase that gives more information about an adjective, verb, other adverb, or a sentence (e.g., *gently*, *very*, *fortunately*).
– DERIVATIVES **ad·ver·bi·al** /adˈvərbēəl/ adjective & noun.
– ORIGIN Latin *adverbium*.

ad·ver·sar·i·al /ˌadvərˈse(ə)rēəl/ ▶ **adjective** involving conflict or opposition: *the media's adversarial attitude toward the military*.

ad·ver·sar·y /ˈadvərˌserē/ ▶ **noun** (pl. **adversaries**) an opponent in a contest, dispute, or conflict.

> – SYNONYMS **opponent,** rival, enemy, antagonist, challenger, contender, competitor, opposition, competition; literary foe.
> – ANTONYMS ally.

– ORIGIN Latin *adversarius* 'opposed, opponent.'

ad·verse /adˈvərs, ˈadvərs/ ▶ **adjective** preventing success or progress; harmful or unfavorable.

> – SYNONYMS **1** *adverse weather* **unfavorable,** inclement, bad, poor, untoward, inauspicious, unpropitious. **2** *adverse side effects* **harmful,** dangerous, injurious, detrimental, deleterious, inimical. **3** *an adverse response* **hostile,** unfavorable, antagonistic, unfriendly, negative.
> – ANTONYMS favorable, beneficial.

– DERIVATIVES **ad·verse·ly** adverb.
– ORIGIN Latin *adversus* 'against, opposite.'

> **USAGE**
>
> Do not confuse **adverse** with **averse**. **Adverse** means *harmful* or *unfavorable* (*adverse publicity*), whereas **averse** means *strongly disliking* or *opposed* (*I am not averse to helping out*).

> **CHOOSE THE RIGHT WORD**
>
> See **HOSTILE**.

ad·ver·si·ty /adˈvərsitē/ ▶ **noun** (pl. **adversities**) a difficult or unpleasant situation.

> – SYNONYMS **misfortune,** bad luck, trouble, difficulty, hardship, disaster, suffering, sorrow, misery, woe, trials and tribulations.

ad·vert /adˈvərt, ədˈvərt/ ▶ **verb** (**advert to**) formal refer to something.
– ORIGIN Latin *advertere* 'turn to.'

ad·ver·tise /ˈadvərˌtīz/ ▶ **verb 1** present or describe a product, service, or event in the media so as to promote sales. **2** publicize information about a job vacancy. **3** make a quality or fact known: *she coughed to advertise her presence*.

> – SYNONYMS **publicize,** make public, announce, broadcast, proclaim, trumpet, promote, market; informal push, plug, hype, ballyhoo.

– DERIVATIVES **ad·ver·tis·er** noun **ad·ver·tis·ing** noun.
– ORIGIN from Latin *advertere* 'turn to.'

ad·ver·tise·ment /ˈadvərˌtīzmənt, adˈvərtiz-/ ▶ **noun** a notice or display advertising something.

> – SYNONYMS **announcement,** commercial, promotion, blurb, write-up; informal ad, push, plug.

ad·ver·to·ri·al /ˌadvərˈtôrēəl/ ▶ **noun** an advertisement in the style of an editorial or objective journalistic article.

ad·vice /ədˈvīs/ ▶ **noun 1** guidance or recommendations about what someone should do. **2** a formal notice of a financial transaction.

> – SYNONYMS **guidance,** counseling, counsel, help, direction, recommendations, guidelines, suggestions, hints, tips, pointers.

– ORIGIN Old French *avis*.

> **USAGE**
>
> Do not confuse **advice** with **advise**. **Advice** means *recommendations about what someone should do* (*your doctor can give you advice on diet*), whereas **advise** means *recommend that someone should do something* (*I advised him to leave*).

ad·vis·a·ble /ədˈvīzəbəl/ ▶ **adjective** to be recommended; sensible: *it's advisable to book in advance*.

> – SYNONYMS **wise,** sensible, prudent, expedient, politic, in one's (best) interests.

– DERIVATIVES **ad·vis·a·bil·i·ty** /-ˌvīzəˈbilitē/ noun.

ad·vise /ədˈvīz/ ▶ **verb 1** recommend that someone should do something; offer advice: *I advised him to* *go home.* **2** inform someone formally about a fact or situation.

– SYNONYMS **1 counsel,** give guidance, guide, offer suggestions, give hints/tips/pointers. **2 recommend,** advocate, suggest, urge. **3 inform,** notify, give notice, apprise, warn.

– ORIGIN Old French *aviser.*

USAGE

On the confusion of **advise** and **advice**, see the note at **ADVICE**.

ad·vised /əd'vīzd/ ▶ **adjective** behaving as someone would recommend; sensible.
– DERIVATIVES **ad·vis·ed·ly** adverb.

ad·vis·er /əd'vīzər/ (also **advisor**) ▶ **noun** a person who gives advice.

– SYNONYMS **counselor,** mentor, guide, consultant, confidant, confidante, guru.

ad·vi·so·ry /əd'vīzərē/ ▶ **adjective** having the power to make recommendations but not to ensure that they are carried out.

ad·vo·caat /'advəˌkärt, 'advəˌkär/ ▶ **noun** a liqueur made with eggs, sugar, and brandy.
– ORIGIN Dutch, 'advocate.'

ad·vo·cate ▶ **noun** /'advəkit/ **1** a person who publicly supports or recommends a particular cause or policy: *he was an untiring advocate of reform.* **2** a person who pleads a case on someone else's behalf. **3** Scottish term for **BARRISTER**.

– SYNONYMS **champion,** upholder, supporter, apologist, backer, promoter, booster, proponent, campaigner, lobbyist.
– ANTONYMS critic.

▶ **verb** /'advəˌkāt/ publicly recommend or support something.

– SYNONYMS **recommend,** champion, uphold, support, back, promote, campaign for, urge, subscribe to, speak for, argue for, lobby for.
– ANTONYMS oppose.

– DERIVATIVES **ad·vo·ca·cy** /'advəkəsē/ noun.
– ORIGIN Latin *advocare* 'call (to one's aid).'

adz /adz/ (also **adze**) ▶ **noun** a tool similar to an ax, with an arched blade at right angles to the handle.
– ORIGIN Old English.

Ae·ge·an /i'jēən/ ▶ **adjective** relating to the region of the Aegean Sea, between Greece and Turkey.

ae·gis /'ējis/ ▶ **noun** the protection, backing, or support of someone: *the negotiations were conducted under the aegis of the UN.*
– ORIGIN Greek *aigis* 'shield of Zeus.'

ae·on /'ēən, 'ēˌän/ ▶ **noun** chiefly British spelling of **EON**.

aer·ate /'e(ə)rāt/ ▶ **verb** introduce air into something.
– DERIVATIVES **aer·a·tion** /e(ə)r'āshən/ noun **aer·a·tor** noun.
– ORIGIN from Latin *aer* 'air.'

aer·at·ed /'e(ə)rātid/ ▶ **adjective** (of a liquid) made fizzy by being charged with carbon dioxide.

aer·i·al /'e(ə)rēəl/ ▶ **noun** a structure that sends or receives radio or television signals. ▶ **adjective 1** existing or taking place in the air. **2** involving the use of aircraft.
– ORIGIN from Greek *aēr* 'air.'

aer·i·al·ist /'e(ə)rēəlist/ ▶ **noun** a person who performs acrobatics on a tightrope or trapezes.

aer·ie /'e(ə)rē, 'i(ə)rē/ (also **eyrie**) ▶ **noun** a large nest of an eagle or other bird of prey, typically built high in a tree or on a cliff.
– ORIGIN probably from Old French *aire.*

aero- ▶ **combining form 1** relating to air: *aerobic.* **2** relating to aviation: *aeronautics.*
– ORIGIN from Greek *aēr* 'air.'

aer·o·bat·ics /ˌe(ə)rə'batiks/ ▶ **plural noun** (treated as sing. or pl.) skillful and exciting movements performed in an aircraft for entertainment.
– DERIVATIVES **aer·o·bat·ic** adjective.

aer·o·bic /ə'rōbik, e(ə)'rō-/ ▶ **adjective 1** relating to physical exercise intended to improve the intake of oxygen and its movement around the body. **2** Biology using oxygen from the air: *aerobic bacteria.*
– DERIVATIVES **aer·o·bi·cal·ly** adverb.
– ORIGIN from **AERO-** + Greek *bios* 'life.'

aer·o·bics /ə'rōbiks, e(ə)'rō-/ ▶ **plural noun** (treated as sing. or pl.) aerobic exercises.

aer·o·drome /'e(ə)rəˌdrōm/ ▶ **noun** Brit. a small airport or airfield.

aer·o·dy·nam·ic /ˌe(ə)rōdī'namik/ ▶ **adjective 1** relating to aerodynamics. **2** (of an object) having a shape that reduces the drag from air moving past.
– DERIVATIVES **aer·o·dy·nam·i·cal·ly** adverb.

aer·o·dy·nam·ics /ˌe(ə)rōdī'namiks/ ▶ **plural noun 1** (treated as sing.) the branch of science concerned with the movement of solid bodies through the air. **2** (treated as pl.) the aspects of an object that make it aerodynamic.
– DERIVATIVES **aer·o·dy·nam·i·cist** /-'naməsist/ noun.

aer·o·nau·tics /ˌe(ə)rə'nôtiks/ ▶ **plural noun** (usu. treated as sing.) the study or practice of travel through the air.
– DERIVATIVES **aer·o·nau·tic** adjective **aer·o·nau·ti·cal** adjective.
– ORIGIN from Greek *aēr* 'air' + *nautēs* 'sailor.'

aer·o·plane /'e(ə)rəˌplān/ ▶ **noun** Brit. an airplane.
– ORIGIN from French *aéro-* 'air' + Greek *-planos* 'wandering.'

ae·ro·pon·ics /ˌe(ə)rə'päniks/ ▶ **noun** a plant-growing technique in which the roots of a plant hang suspended in air and nutrient solution is delivered to them in the form of a fine mist.

aer·o·sol /'erəˌsôl, -ˌsäl/ ▶ **noun** a substance sealed in a container under pressure and released as a fine spray.
– ORIGIN from **AERO-** + **SOL**[2].

aer·o·space /'e(ə)rōˌspās/ ▶ **noun** the branch of technology and industry concerned with aviation and space flight.

aes·thete /'esˌthēt/ (also **esthete**) ▶ **noun** a person who is appreciative of art and beauty.

aes·thet·ic /es'thetik/ (also **esthetic**) ▶ **adjective 1** concerned with beauty or the appreciation of beauty. **2** having a pleasant appearance. ▶ **noun** a set of principles underlying the work of a particular artist or artistic movement.
– DERIVATIVES **aes·thet·i·cal·ly** adverb **aes·thet·i·cism** noun.
– ORIGIN from Greek *aisthesthai* 'perceive.'

aes·thet·ics /es'thetiks/ (also **esthetics**) ▶ **plural noun** (usu. treated as sing.) **1** a set of principles concerned with the nature of beauty, especially in art. **2** the branch of philosophy that deals with questions of beauty and artistic taste.

a·far /'äˌfär/ ▶ **adverb** literary at or to a distance.

AFB ▶ **abbreviation** Air Force Base.

AFC ▶ **abbreviation 1** American Football Conference. **2** automatic frequency control, a system in radios and television that keeps them tuned to an incoming signal.

af·fa·ble /ˈafəbəl/ ▶ **adjective** good-natured and sociable.

– SYNONYMS **friendly,** amiable, genial, congenial, cordial, warm, pleasant, nice, likable, personable, charming, agreeable, sympathetic, good-humored, good-natured, kindly, kind, approachable, accessible, amenable, sociable, outgoing, gregarious, neighborly, welcoming, hospitable, obliging.
– ANTONYMS unfriendly.

– DERIVATIVES **af·fa·bil·i·ty** /ˌafəˈbilitē/ noun **af·fa·bly** adverb.
– ORIGIN Latin *affabilis*.

af·fair /əˈfe(ə)r/ ▶ **noun 1** an event of a specified kind or that has previously been referred to: *I want the wedding to be a family affair*. **2** a matter that a person is responsible for. **3** a love affair. **4** (**affairs**) business and financial dealings. **5** (**affairs**) matters of public interest.

– SYNONYMS **1 event,** incident, episode, case, matter, business. **2 business,** concern, matter, responsibility, problem. **3 relationship,** romance, fling, dalliance, liaison, involvement, amour; informal hanky-panky. **4** (**affairs**) **transactions,** activities, dealings, undertakings, ventures, business.

– ORIGIN from Old French *à faire* 'to do.'

af·fect[1] /əˈfekt/ ▶ **verb 1** make a difference to: *the mold has affected my health*. **2** move someone emotionally.

– SYNONYMS **1 influence,** have an effect on, have an impact on, act on, change, alter, modify. **2 move,** touch, hit (hard), make an impression on, upset, trouble, distress, disturb, shake (up).

– DERIVATIVES **af·fect·ing** adjective.
– ORIGIN Latin *afficere*.

USAGE

Affect and **effect** are often confused. **Affect** is a verb meaning *make a difference to* (*the mold has affected my health*). **Effect** is used both as a noun meaning *a result* (*the substance has a painkilling effect*) and as a verb meaning *bring about a result* (*I effected a cost-cutting exercise*).

af·fect[2] ▶ **verb 1** pretend to have or feel something. **2** use or wear in an artificial way or so as to impress: *he'd affected a British accent*.

– SYNONYMS **put on,** assume, take on, adopt, feign.

– ORIGIN Latin *affectare* 'aim at.'

af·fec·ta·tion /ˌafekˈtāsʜən/ ▶ **noun** behavior, speech, or writing that is artificial and designed to impress.

– SYNONYMS **pretension,** pretentiousness, affectedness, artificiality, posturing, airs (and graces).

af·fect·ed /əˈfektid/ ▶ **adjective** artificial and designed to impress.
– DERIVATIVES **af·fect·ed·ly** adverb.

af·fec·tion /əˈfeksʜən/ ▶ **noun** a feeling of fondness or liking.

– SYNONYMS **fondness,** love, liking, soft spot, tenderness, warmth, devotion, caring, attachment, friendship.

af·fec·tion·ate /əˈfeksʜənit/ ▶ **adjective** readily showing affection.

– SYNONYMS **fond,** loving, adoring, devoted, caring, tender, warm, friendly, demonstrative; informal touchy-feely, lovey-dovey.
– ANTONYMS cold.

– DERIVATIVES **af·fec·tion·ate·ly** adverb.

af·fec·tive /əˈfektiv/ ▶ **adjective** Psychology relating to moods, feelings, and attitudes.

af·fi·ance /əˈfīəns/ ▶ **verb** (**be affianced**) literary be engaged to marry.
– ORIGIN Old French *afiancer*.

af·fi·da·vit /ˌafiˈdāvit/ ▶ **noun** Law a written statement for use as evidence in court, sworn on oath to be true.
– ORIGIN Latin, 'he has stated on oath.'

af·fil·i·ate ▶ **verb** /əˈfilēˌāt/ officially link a person or group to an organization.

– SYNONYMS **associate,** unite, combine, join (up), join forces, link up, ally, align, amalgamate, merge.

▶ **noun** /-it/ a person or group linked to a larger organization.
– DERIVATIVES **af·fil·i·a·tion** /əˌfilēˈāsʜən/ noun.
– ORIGIN Latin *affiliare* 'adopt as a son.'

af·fin·i·ty /əˈfinitē/ ▶ **noun** (pl. **affinities**) **1** a natural liking or sympathy for someone or something. **2** close similarity in structure, qualities, or origin: *there is a stylistic affinity between the mosaics*. **3** the tendency of a substance to combine with another.

– SYNONYMS **empathy,** rapport, sympathy, accord, harmony, similarity, relationship, bond, closeness, understanding; informal chemistry.
– ANTONYMS aversion.

– ORIGIN from Latin *affinis* 'related.'

CHOOSE THE RIGHT WORD

See **LIKENESS**.

af·firm /əˈfərm/ ▶ **verb** state something firmly or publicly.

– SYNONYMS **declare,** state, assert, proclaim, pronounce, attest, swear, maintain, avow.
– ANTONYMS deny.

– ORIGIN Latin *affirmare*.

af·firm·a·tion /ˌafərˈmāsʜən/ ▶ **noun 1** the action or process of affirming or being affirmed. **2** Law a formal declaration by a person who declines to take an oath for reasons of conscience.

af·firm·a·tive /əˈfərmətiv/ ▶ **adjective** agreeing with a statement or to a request: *an affirmative answer*.

– SYNONYMS **positive,** assenting, consenting, approving, favorable.
– ANTONYMS negative.

▶ **noun** a statement or word indicating agreement.
▶ **exclamation** yes.
– DERIVATIVES **af·firm·a·tive·ly** adverb.

af·firm·a·tive ac·tion ▶ **noun** action favoring people who are often discriminated against.

af·fix ▶ **verb** /əˈfiks/ attach or fasten something to something else. ▶ **noun** /ˈaˌfiks/ Grammar a letter or letters added to a word in order to alter its meaning or create a new word.
– DERIVATIVES **af·fix·a·tion** /ˌafikˈsāsʜən/ noun.
– ORIGIN Latin *affixare*.

af·flict /əˈflikt/ ▶ **verb** cause pain or trouble to: *the problems that afflict inner-city communities*.

– SYNONYMS **trouble,** burden, distress, beset, harass, worry, oppress, torment, plague, bedevil.

– ORIGIN from Latin *affligere* 'knock down, weaken.'

af·flic·tion /ə'fliksHən/ ▸ **noun 1** something that causes pain or suffering: *a crippling affliction of the nervous system.* **2** pain or suffering.

af·flu·ent /'aflo͞oənt, ə'flo͞o-/ ▸ **adjective** having a great deal of money; wealthy.

– SYNONYMS **wealthy,** rich, prosperous, well off, well-to-do, of means; informal well heeled, rolling in it, made of money, loaded.
– ANTONYMS poor.

– DERIVATIVES **af·flu·ence** noun.
– ORIGIN from Latin *affluere* 'flow freely.'

af·ford /ə'fôrd/ ▸ **verb 1** (**can/could afford**) have enough money, time, or other resources for something. **2** provide or supply: *the rooftop terrace affords beautiful views.*

– SYNONYMS **1 pay for,** find the money for, run to, stretch to, stand, manage, spare. **2 give,** offer, supply, provide, furnish, yield.

– ORIGIN Old English, 'promote, perform.'

CHOOSE THE RIGHT WORD

See **GIVE**.

af·ford·a·ble /ə'fôrdəbəl/ ▸ **adjective** reasonably priced; not expensive.
– DERIVATIVES **af·ford·a·bil·i·ty** /ə,fôrdə'bilitē/ noun **af·ford·a·bly** adverb.

af·for·est·a·tion /ə,fôrə'stāsHən, ə,fär-/ ▸ **noun** the process of planting trees on an area of land in order to form a forest.

af·fray /ə'frā/ ▸ **noun** Law, dated a breach of the peace by fighting in a public place.
– ORIGIN from Old French *afrayer* 'disturb, startle.'

af·front /ə'frənt/ ▸ **noun** an action or remark that causes offense.

– SYNONYMS *an affront to public morality* **insult,** offense, slight, snub, put-down, provocation, injury; outrage, atrocity, scandal; informal slap in the face, kick in the teeth.

▸ **verb** offend or insult: *she was affronted by his familiarity.*

– SYNONYMS *she was affronted by his familiarity* **insult,** offend, provoke, pique, wound, hurt; put out, irk, displease, bother, rankle, vex, gall; outrage, scandalize; informal needle.

– ORIGIN from Old French *afronter* 'to slap in the face, insult.'

Af·ghan /'af,gan/ ▸ **noun** a person from Afghanistan. ▸ **adjective** relating to Afghanistan.
– ORIGIN Pashto.

Af·ghan hound ▸ **noun** a silky-haired breed of dog used for hunting.

af·ghan·i /af'ganē, -'gä-/ ▸ **noun** (pl. **afghanis**) the basic monetary unit of Afghanistan.
– ORIGIN Pashto.

a·fi·ci·o·na·do /ə,fisH(ē)ə'nädō, ə,fisyə-/ ▸ **noun** (pl. **aficionados**) a person who is very knowledgeable and enthusiastic about an activity or subject.

– SYNONYMS **connoisseur,** expert, authority, specialist, pundit; enthusiast, devotee; informal **buff,** freak, nut, fiend, maniac, fanatic, addict.

– ORIGIN Spanish, 'amateur.'

a·field /ə'fēld/ ▸ **adverb** to or at a distance.

a·fire /ə'fī(ə)r/ ▸ **adjective & adverb** chiefly literary on fire; burning.

a·flame /ə'flām/ ▸ **adjective** in flames.

a·float /ə'flōt/ ▸ **adjective & adverb 1** floating in water. **2** on board a ship or boat. **3** out of debt or difficulty: *he takes odd jobs to keep afloat.*

a·flut·ter /ə'flətər/ ▸ **adjective** in a state of agitated excitement.

a·foot /ə'fo͝ot/ ▸ **adverb & adjective 1** happening or in preparation: *plans are afoot for a festival.* **2** on foot.

a·fore /ə'fôr/ ▸ **preposition** old use or dialect before.

afore- ▸ **prefix** before; previously: *aforementioned.*

a·fore·men·tioned /ə'fôr,mensHənd/ (also **aforesaid** /ə'fôr,sed/) ▸ **adjective** referring to a thing or person previously mentioned.

a·fore·thought /ə'fôr,THôt/ ▸ **adjective** see **MALICE AFORETHOUGHT**.

a for·ti·o·ri /'ä ,fôrtē'ôrē, 'ā ,fôrtē'ôrī/ ▸ **adverb** for an even stronger reason.
– ORIGIN from Latin *a fortiori argumento* 'from stronger argument.'

a·foul /ə'foul/ ▸ **adverb** (in phrase **run/fall afoul of**) come into conflict or difficulty with: *he ran afoul of the boss and resigned.*

a·fraid /ə'frād/ ▸ **adjective** feeling fear or anxiety.

– SYNONYMS **1 frightened,** scared, terrified, fearful, nervous, petrified, intimidated, cowardly, faint-hearted; informal scared stiff, chicken, spooked. **2 reluctant,** hesitant, unwilling, slow, shy. **3** *I'm afraid I'm late* **sorry**.
– ANTONYMS brave, confident.

– PHRASES **I'm afraid** expressing polite regret.
– ORIGIN from Old French *afrayer* 'disturb, startle.'

a·fresh /ə'fresH/ ▸ **adverb** in a new or different way.

Af·ri·can /'afrikən/ ▸ **noun 1** a person from Africa, especially a black person. **2** a person descended from black African people. ▸ **adjective** relating to Africa or Africans.
– DERIVATIVES **Af·ri·can·ize** /'afrikə,nīz/ verb.

Af·ri·can A·mer·i·can ▸ **noun** an American of African origin, especially one descended from slaves.
– DERIVATIVES **Af·ri·can-A·mer·i·can** adjective.

Af·ri·can vi·o·let ▸ **noun** a small East African plant with velvety leaves and violet, pink, or white flowers.

Af·ri·kaans /,afri'känz/ ▸ **noun** a language derived from Dutch, one of the official languages of South Africa.
– ORIGIN Dutch, 'African.'

Af·ri·ka·ner /,afri'känər/ ▸ **noun** an Afrikaans-speaking white person in South Africa.
– DERIVATIVES **Af·ri·ka·ner·dom** noun.

Af·ro /'afrō/ ▸ **noun** (pl. **Afros**) a hairstyle consisting of a mass of very tight curls all around the head.

Afro- ▸ **combining form** African: *Afro-American.*

Af·ro-A·mer·i·can ▸ **adjective & noun** another term for **AFRICAN AMERICAN**.

Af·ro·beat /'afrō͵bēt/ ▶ **noun** a style of popular music incorporating elements of African music and jazz, soul, and funk.

Af·ro-Car·ib·be·an ▶ **noun** a person descended from African people who lives in or comes from the Caribbean. ▶ **adjective** relating to Afro-Caribbeans.

aft /aft/ ▶ **adverb & adjective** at, near, or toward the stern of a ship or tail of an aircraft.
– ORIGIN probably related to **ABAFT**.

af·ter /'aftər/ ▶ **preposition 1** in the time following an event or another period of time. **2** next to and following something in order or importance. **3** behind someone. **4** so as to have, get, or find: *most of them are after money*. **5** in reference to: *he was named after his grandfather*.

– SYNONYMS **following,** subsequent to, at the end of, in the wake of.

▶ **conjunction & adverb** in the time following an event. ▶ **adjective** nearer the stern of a ship.
– PHRASES **after all** in spite of any suggestion otherwise. **after hours** after normal working or opening hours.
– ORIGIN Old English.

af·ter·birth /'aftər͵bərTH/ ▶ **noun** the placenta and other material that is discharged from the uterus after a birth.

af·ter·burn·er /'aftər͵bərnər/ ▶ **noun** an auxiliary burner in the exhaust of a jet engine.

af·ter·care /'aftər͵ke(ə)r/ ▶ **noun** care of a person after a stay in a hospital or on release from prison.

af·ter·ef·fect /'aftəri͵fekt/ ▶ **noun** an effect that follows some time after its cause.

af·ter·glow /'aftər͵glō/ ▶ **noun 1** light remaining in the sky after the sun has set. **2** good feelings remaining after a pleasant experience: *basking in the afterglow of victory*.

af·ter·im·age /'aftər͵imij/ ▶ **noun** an impression of a vivid sensation (especially a visual image) retained after the stimulus has ceased.

af·ter·life /'aftər͵līf/ ▶ **noun** (in some religions) life after death.

af·ter·mar·ket /'aftər͵märkit/ ▶ **noun 1** the market for spare parts, accessories, and components, especially for motor vehicles. **2** Stock Market the market for shares and bonds after their original issue.

af·ter·math /'aftər͵maTH/ ▶ **noun** the results of an unpleasant or important event: *prices soared in the aftermath of the drought*.

– SYNONYMS **consequences,** after-effects, results, repercussions, upshot.

– ORIGIN from **AFTER** + dialect *math* 'mowing.'

af·ter·noon /͵aftər'no͞on/ ▶ **noun** the time from noon or lunchtime to evening.

af·ter·shave /'aftər͵SHāv/ ▶ **noun** a scented lotion for putting on a man's face after shaving.

af·ter·shock /'aftər͵SHäk/ ▶ **noun** a smaller earthquake following the main shock of a large earthquake.

af·ter·taste /'aftər͵tāst/ ▶ **noun** a strong or unpleasant taste lingering in the mouth after eating or drinking.

af·ter-tax ▶ **adjective** relating to income that remains after the deduction of taxes due.

af·ter·thought /'aftər͵THôt/ ▶ **noun** something thought of or added later.

af·ter·ward /'aftərwərd/ (also **afterwards** /'aftərwərdz/) ▶ **adverb** at a later or future time.

– SYNONYMS **later,** later on, subsequently, then, next, after this/that, in due course.

af·ter·word /'aftər͵wərd/ ▶ **noun** a section at the end of a book.

af·ter·world /'aftər͵wərld/ ▶ **noun** a world that a person enters after death.

AG ▶ **abbreviation 1** adjutant general. **2** attorney general.

Ag ▶ **symbol** the chemical element silver.
– ORIGIN from Latin *argentum*.

a·gain /ə'gen, ə'gān/ ▶ **adverb 1** once more. **2** returning to a previous position or condition: *he closed the locker and sat down again*. **3** in addition to what has already been mentioned.

– SYNONYMS **once more,** another time, afresh, anew.

– ORIGIN Old English.

a·gainst /ə'genst, ə'gānst/ ▶ **preposition 1** opposing or disagreeing with. **2** close to or touching. **3** so as to anticipate and prepare for a difficulty. **4** as protection from: *I turned up my collar against the wind*. **5** in contrast to: *the benefits must be weighed against the costs*. **6** so as to reduce, cancel, or secure money owed, due, or lent. **7** (in betting) in anticipation of the failure of: *the odds were 5–1 against England*.

– SYNONYMS **opposed to,** in opposition to, hostile to, antagonistic toward, unsympathetic to, at odds with, in disagreement with; informal anti.

– PHRASES **have something against someone** dislike or bear a grudge against someone.

a·gape /ə'gāp/ ▶ **adjective** (of a person's mouth) wide open.

a·gar /'ä͵gär, 'ā͵gär/ (also **agar-agar**) ▶ **noun** a jellylike substance obtained from seaweed, used as a thickener in foods and in biological cultures.
– ORIGIN Malay.

ag·a·ric /'agərik, ə'gar-/ ▶ **noun** a fungus with gills on the underside of the cap, e.g., a mushroom.
– ORIGIN Greek *agarikon* 'tree fungus.'

ag·ate /'agit/ ▶ **noun** a semiprecious variety of quartz with a striped appearance.
– ORIGIN Greek *akhatēs*.

a·ga·ve /ə'gävē/ ▶ **noun** an American plant with narrow spiny leaves and tall flower stems.
– ORIGIN from Greek *Agauē*, one of the daughters of Cadmus in Greek mythology.

age /āj/ ▶ **noun 1** the length of time that a person or thing has existed. **2** a particular stage in someone's life: *children of elementary school age*. **3** old age. **4** a distinct period of history: *the Elizabethan age*.

– SYNONYMS **1 old age,** maturity, advancing years, elderliness, seniority, senescence. **2 era,** epoch, period, time, generation.

▶ **verb** (**ages, aging** or **ageing, aged**) **1** grow or cause to appear old or older: *some foods may protect your eyes as you age*. **2** (of an alcoholic drink, cheese, etc.) mature.

– SYNONYMS **1 mature,** mellow, ripen, soften, season, weather. **2 grow old,** decline, wither, fade.

– PHRASES **come of age** be legally recognized as an adult (in US law at 18).
– ORIGIN from Latin *aevum*.

CHOOSE THE RIGHT WORD

See **MATURE**.

aged ▶ **adjective 1** /ājd/ of a specified age: *the driver, aged 42, was taken into custody.* **2** /'ājid/ having lived or existed for a long time; old.

age·ism /'āj,izəm/ ▶ **noun** prejudice or discrimination on the grounds of a person's age.
– DERIVATIVES **age·ist** adjective & noun.

age·less /'ājlis/ ▶ **adjective** not aging or appearing to age.

a·gen·cy /'ājənsē/ ▶ **noun 1** an organization or government department providing a particular service: *an advertising agency.* **2** action or intervention producing a result: *channels carved by the agency of running water.*

– SYNONYMS **business,** organization, company, firm, office, bureau.

a·gen·da /ə'jendə/ ▶ **noun 1** a list of items to be discussed at a meeting. **2** a list of matters to be dealt with. **3** the underlying intentions or motives of a particular person or group. **4** a diary for listing appointments.

– SYNONYMS **program,** schedule, to-do list, timetable, plan.

– ORIGIN Latin, 'things to be done.'

a·gent /'ājənt/ ▶ **noun 1** a person who provides a service, typically by organizing dealings between two other parties: *a travel agent.* **2** a spy. **3** a person or thing that takes an active role or produces a particular effect: *bleaching agents.*

– SYNONYMS **1 representative,** intermediary, middleman, negotiator, go-between, proxy, broker, emissary, envoy, spokesperson, delegate; informal rep. **2 spy,** secret agent, operative, mole; informal G-man.

– ORIGIN from Latin *agere* 'to do.'

a·gent pro·vo·ca·teur /ä,zhän(t) prə,väkə'tər/ ▶ **noun** (pl. **agents provocateurs** pronunc. same) a person employed to tempt others to break the law and therefore be convicted.
– ORIGIN French, 'provocative agent.'

age of con·sent ▶ **noun** the age at which a person's consent to sexual intercourse is legally valid.

age-old /'āj,ōld/ ▶ **adjective** very old.

ag·glom·er·ate ▶ **verb** /ə'glämə,rāt/ collect or form into a mass. ▶ **noun** /-rit/ a mass or collection of things.
– DERIVATIVES **ag·glom·er·a·tion** /ə,glämə'rāshən/ noun.
– ORIGIN Latin *agglomerare* 'add to.'

ag·glu·ti·nate /ə'glo͞otn,āt/ ▶ **verb** firmly stick together to form a mass.
– DERIVATIVES **ag·glu·ti·na·tion** /ə,glo͞otn'āshən/ noun.
– ORIGIN Latin *agglutinare* 'cause to adhere.'

ag·gran·dize /ə'gran,dīz/ ▶ **verb** increase the power or importance of: *the description "subediting" aggrandizes the nature of my task.*
– DERIVATIVES **ag·gran·dize·ment** /-,dīzmənt, -diz-/ noun.
– ORIGIN French *agrandir*, from Latin *grandis* 'large.'

ag·gra·vate /'agrə,vāt/ ▶ **verb 1** make worse: *military action would only aggravate the situation.* **2** informal annoy someone.

– SYNONYMS **1 worsen,** make worse, exacerbate, inflame, compound. **2 annoy,** antagonize, irritate, exasperate, nettle, provoke, get on someone's nerves, rub the wrong way; informal needle, tick off, get someone's goat.
– ANTONYMS alleviate, improve.

– DERIVATIVES **ag·gra·va·ting** adjective **ag·gra·va·tion** /,agrə'vāshən/ noun.
– ORIGIN Latin *aggravare* 'make heavy.'

USAGE

Some people think that it is incorrect to use **aggravate** to mean 'annoy someone.' However, this sense dates back to the 17th century and is widely used in modern English.

ag·gra·vat·ed /'agrə,vātid/ ▶ **adjective** Law (of an offense) made more serious by related circumstances.

ag·gre·gate ▶ **noun** /'agrigit/ a whole formed by combining several different elements: *the council is an aggregate of three regional assemblies.*

– SYNONYMS **total,** sum, grand total, combined score.

▶ **verb** /-,gāt/ combine into a whole.
▶ **adjective** /'agrigit/ formed or calculated by combining many separate items.
– DERIVATIVES **ag·gre·ga·tion** /,agri'gāshən/ noun.
– ORIGIN from Latin *aggregare* 'herd together.'

ag·gre·ga·tor /'agri,gātər/ ▶ **noun** Computing an Internet company that collects information about competing products and services and distributes it through a single website.

ag·gres·sion /ə'greshən/ ▶ **noun** hostile or violent behavior or attitudes: *a link between extensive TV viewing and aggression in children.*

– SYNONYMS **hostility,** belligerence, force, violence, attack.

– ORIGIN from Latin *aggredi* 'to attack.'

ag·gres·sive /ə'gresiv/ ▶ **adjective 1** very hostile or angry. **2** determined and forceful: *an aggressive campaign to reduce energy use.*

– SYNONYMS **1** *aggressive behavior* **violent,** confrontational, antagonistic, combative, pugnacious. **2** *aggressive foreign policy* **warmongering,** warlike, warring, belligerent, bellicose, hawkish, militaristic, expansionist; informal gung-ho. **3** *an aggressive campaign* **assertive,** forceful, pushy, vigorous, energetic, dynamic, audacious; informal in-your-face, feisty.
– ANTONYMS peaceable, peaceful.

– DERIVATIVES **ag·gres·sive·ly** adverb **ag·gres·sive·ness** noun.

CHOOSE THE RIGHT WORD

See **BOLD**.

ag·gres·sor /ə'gresər/ ▶ **noun** a person or country that attacks without being provoked.

ag·grieved /ə'grēvd/ ▶ **adjective** resentful because of unfair treatment.
– ORIGIN from Latin *aggravare* (see **AGGRAVATE**).

a·ghast /ə'gast/ ▶ **adjective** filled with horror or shock: *he looked aghast at the blood on his blazer.*

– SYNONYMS **horrified,** appalled, dismayed, thunderstruck, stunned, shocked, staggered; informal flabbergasted.

– ORIGIN from former *gast* 'frighten.'

ag·ile /'ajəl/ ▶ **adjective 1** able to move quickly and easily. **2** quick-witted or shrewd.

– SYNONYMS **1 nimble,** lithe, supple, graceful, fit, acrobatic, sprightly, spry. **2 alert,** sharp, acute, shrewd, astute, perceptive, quick.
– ANTONYMS clumsy.

– DERIVATIVES **ag·ile·ly** adverb **a·gil·i·ty** /ə'jilitē/ noun.
– ORIGIN Latin *agilis*.

ag·ing /'ājiNG/ (also **ageing**) ▶ **noun 1** growing old. **2** change in a material over a period, either spontaneous or caused deliberately. ▶ **adjective 1** (of a person) growing old; elderly. **2** (of a thing) reaching the end of its useful life: *the world's aging fleet of oil tankers.*

ag·i·tate /'aji,tāt/ ▶ **verb 1** make someone troubled or nervous. **2** campaign to arouse public concern about something: *they have begun to agitate for better living conditions.* **3** stir or disturb a liquid briskly.

– SYNONYMS **1 upset,** fluster, ruffle, disconcert, unnerve, disquiet, disturb, distress, unsettle, worry, perturb, trouble; informal rattle, faze. **2 shake,** whisk, beat, stir.

– ORIGIN Latin *agitare* 'agitate, drive.'

ag·i·ta·tion /,aji'tāSHən/ ▶ **noun 1** a state of anxiety or nervous excitement. **2** the action of agitating to arouse concern about something.

ag·i·ta·tor /'aji,tātər/ ▶ **noun** a person who urges others to protest or rebel.

ag·it·prop /'ajit,präp/ ▶ **noun** political propaganda, especially in the arts.
– ORIGIN Russian.

ag·let /'aglit/ ▶ **noun** a metal or plastic tube fixed around each end of a shoelace.
– ORIGIN French *aiguillette* 'small needle.'

a·glow /ə'glō/ ▶ **adjective** glowing.

AGM ▶ **abbreviation** air-to-ground missile.

ag·nos·tic /ag'nästik/ ▶ **noun** a person who believes that one cannot know whether or not God exists.
– DERIVATIVES **ag·nos·ti·cism** /-tə,sizəm/ noun.

a·go /ə'gō/ ▶ **adverb** before the present (used with a measurement of time).
– ORIGIN from the former verb *ago* 'to pass.'

USAGE

When **ago** is followed by a clause, you should use **that** rather than **since**, e.g., *it was ten years ago that I left home* (not *it was ten years ago since I left home*).

a·gog /ə'gäg/ ▶ **adjective** very eager to hear or see something: *I was agog with curiosity.*
– ORIGIN from Old French *en* 'in' + *gogue* 'fun.'

ag·o·nist /'agənist/ ▶ **noun 1** Biochemistry a substance that initiates a physiological response when combined with a receptor. **2** Anatomy a muscle whose contraction moves a part of the body directly.
– ORIGIN from Greek *agōnistēs* 'contestant.'

ag·o·nize /'agə,nīz/ ▶ **verb 1** worry greatly: *I didn't agonize over the problem.* **2** (often as adj. **agonizing**) cause great pain to: *an agonizing death.*

– SYNONYMS (as adj. **agonizing**) **excruciating,** painful, acute, searing, severe, harrowing, torturous.

ag·o·ny /'agənē/ ▶ **noun** (pl. **agonies**) great pain or distress.

– SYNONYMS **suffering,** torture, pain, torment, anguish.

– ORIGIN Greek *agōnia*.

ag·o·ra /ə'gôrə, ,ägô'rä/ ▶ **noun** (pl. **agorot** /ə'gôrōt, ,ägô'rōt/ or **agoroth** /ə'gôrōt, ,ägô'rōt/) a unit of money of Israel, equal to one hundredth of a shekel.
– ORIGIN Hebrew, 'small coin.'

ag·o·ra·pho·bi·a /,agərə'fōbēə/ ▶ **noun** irrational fear of open or public places.
– DERIVATIVES **ag·o·ra·pho·bic** adjective & noun.
– ORIGIN from Greek *agora* 'marketplace.'

a·grar·i·an /ə'gre(ə)rēən/ ▶ **adjective** relating to agriculture.
– ORIGIN from Latin *ager* 'field.'

a·gree /ə'grē/ ▶ **verb** (**agrees, agreeing, agreed**) **1** have the same opinion as another person or people. **2** (**agree to/to do**) be willing to do something suggested by another person. **3** (of two or more people) decide on something. **4** (**agree with**) be consistent with: *your body language doesn't agree with what you're saying.* **5** (**agree with**) be good for: *he ate something that didn't agree with him.*

– SYNONYMS **1 concur,** see eye to eye, be in sympathy, be as one, be unanimous. **2** *they* ***agreed to*** *a ceasefire* **consent to,** assent to, acquiesce to, allow, approve; formal accede to. **3 match (up),** correspond, conform, coincide, fit, tally, be consistent; informal square. **4** *can we* ***agree on*** *a price?* **decide on,** settle on, arrive at, negotiate, shake hands on.
– ANTONYMS disagree.

– ORIGIN Old French *agreer*.

a·gree·a·ble /ə'grēəbəl/ ▶ **adjective 1** enjoyable or pleasant. **2** willing to agree to something. **3** able to be agreed on; acceptable: *a compromise that is agreeable to both employers and unions.*

– SYNONYMS **1** *an agreeable atmosphere* **pleasant,** pleasing, enjoyable, pleasurable, nice, appealing, relaxing, friendly, congenial. **2** *an agreeable man* **likable,** amiable, affable, pleasant, nice, friendly, good-natured, sociable, genial. **3 willing,** amenable, in agreement.
– ANTONYMS unpleasant.

– DERIVATIVES **a·gree·a·ble·ness** noun **a·gree·a·bly** adverb.

a·gree·ment /ə'grēmənt/ ▶ **noun 1** the act of agreeing or the state of being agreed: *we failed to reach agreement.* **2** an arrangement or contract agreed between people, typically one that is legally binding.

– SYNONYMS **1 accord,** concurrence, consensus, assent, acceptance, consent, acquiescence. **2 contract,** treaty, pact, concordat, accord, settlement, understanding, bargain. **3 correspondence,** consistency, compatibility, accord, similarity, resemblance, likeness.
– ANTONYMS discord, dissimilarity.

ag·ri·busi·ness /'agrə,biznis/ ▶ **noun 1** agriculture run on strictly commercial principles. **2** the group of industries concerned with agricultural produce and services.

ag·ri·cul·ture /'agri,kəlCHər/ ▶ **noun** the science or practice of farming, including the rearing of crops and animals.

– SYNONYMS **farming,** cultivation, husbandry, agribusiness, agronomy.

– DERIVATIVES **ag·ri·cul·tur·al** /,agri'kəlCHərəl/ adjective **ag·ri·cul·tur·al·ist** /,agri'kəlCHərəlist/ noun **ag·ri·cul·tur·al·ly** /,agri'kəlCHərəlē/ adverb **ag·ri·cul·tur·ist** /'agri,kəlCHərist/ noun.
– ORIGIN from Latin *ager* 'field' + *cultura* 'cultivation.'

WORD LINKS

agrarian *relating to agriculture*

ag·ri·mo·ny /ˈagrəˌmōnē/ ▸ **noun** a plant with slender stalks of yellow flowers.
– ORIGIN Greek *argemōnē* 'poppy.'

ag·ri·tour·ism /ˌagriˈto͝orizəm/ ▸ **noun** tourism in which farms are open to the public for agricultural activities and as lodgings for vacationers.

ag·ro·chem·i·cal /ˌagrōˈkemikəl/ ▸ **noun** a chemical used in agriculture.

a·gron·o·my /əˈgränəmē/ ▸ **noun** the science of soil management and crop production.
– DERIVATIVES **ag·ro·nom·ic** /ˌagrəˈnämik/ adjective **a·gron·o·mist** noun.
– ORIGIN from Greek *agros* 'field' + *-nomos* 'arranging.'

a·ground /əˈground/ ▸ **adjective & adverb** (with reference to a ship) on or onto the bottom in shallow water.

a·gue /ˈāˌgyo͞o/ ▸ **noun** old use malaria or another illness involving fever and shivering.
– ORIGIN from Latin *acuta febris* 'acute fever.'

ah /ä/ ▸ **exclamation** used to express a range of emotions including surprise, pleasure, sympathy, and realization.

a·ha /äˈhä/ ▸ **exclamation** used to express satisfaction, triumph, or surprise.

a·head /əˈhed/ ▸ **adverb 1** farther forward in space or time: *we should plan ahead.* **2** in the lead.
– PHRASES **ahead of 1** in front of; before. **2** earlier than.

a·hem /əˈhem, əˈhm/ ▸ **exclamation** used to represent the noise made when clearing the throat, typically to attract attention or express disapproval or embarrassment.

a·him·sa /əˈhimˌsä/ ▸ **noun** (in the Hindu, Buddhist, and Jain tradition) the principle of nonviolence toward all living things.
– ORIGIN Sanskrit.

a·his·tor·i·cal /ˌāhiˈstôrikəl, -ˈstär-/ ▸ **adjective** lacking historical perspective; not historical.

a·hoy /əˈhoi/ ▸ **exclamation** Nautical a call to attract attention.

AI ▸ **abbreviation** artificial intelligence.

AID ▸ **abbreviation 1** Agency for International Development. **2** artificial insemination by donor.

aid /ād/ ▸ **noun 1** help or support. **2** money or resources given to help a country in need.

– SYNONYMS **1** *with the aid of his colleagues* **assistance,** support, help, backing, cooperation, a helping hand. **2** *humanitarian aid* **relief,** assistance, support, subsidy, funding, donations, grants; historical alms.
– ANTONYMS hindrance.

▸ **verb** help or support: *women, aided by their children, cleaned the fish.*

– SYNONYMS **help,** assist, be of service, support, encourage, further, boost, promote, facilitate.
– ANTONYMS hinder.

– PHRASES **in aid of** in support of.
– ORIGIN from Latin *juvare* 'help.'

aide /ād/ ▸ **noun** an assistant to a political leader.

– SYNONYMS **assistant,** helper, adviser, supporter, right-hand man/woman, adjutant, deputy, second (in command), lieutenant.

aide-de-camp /ˈād də ˈkamp/ ▸ **noun** (pl. **aides-de-camp** pronunc. same) a military officer acting as a personal assistant to a senior officer.
– ORIGIN French.

aide-me·moire /ˈād memˈwär/ ▸ **noun** (pl. **aides-memoires** or **aides-memoire** pronunc. same) **1** a note or book used to help one remember something. **2** an informal diplomatic message.
– ORIGIN French.

AIDS /ādz/ ▸ **noun** a disease, caused by the HIV virus and transmitted in body fluids, in which the sufferer's natural defenses against infection are destroyed.
– ORIGIN from the initial letters of *acquired immune deficiency syndrome*.

ai·ki·do /ˌīkēˈdō, īˈkēdō/ ▸ **noun** a Japanese martial art that uses locks, holds, throws, and the opponent's own movements.
– ORIGIN Japanese, 'way of adapting the spirit.'

ail /āl/ ▸ **verb** old use cause suffering or trouble to someone.
– ORIGIN Old English.

ai·ler·on /ˈāləˌrän/ ▸ **noun** a hinged part on the back of an aircraft's wing, used to control the balance of the aircraft.
– ORIGIN French, 'small wing.'

ail·ing /ˈāliNG/ ▸ **adjective** in poor health or condition: *the country's ailing economy.*

– SYNONYMS **1 ill,** sick, unwell, sickly, poorly, weak, in poor/bad health, infirm. **2 failing,** weak, poor, fragile, unstable.
– ANTONYMS healthy.

ail·ment /ˈālmənt/ ▸ **noun** a minor illness.

– SYNONYMS **illness,** disease, disorder, affliction, malady, complaint, infirmity; informal bug, virus.

aim /ām/ ▸ **verb 1** point a weapon or camera at a target. **2** direct something at someone or something: *the program is aimed at a wide audience.* **3** try to achieve something.

– SYNONYMS **1** *he aimed the rifle* **point,** direct, train, sight, line up. **2** *she* ***aimed at*** *the target* **take aim at,** fix on, zero in on, draw a bead on. **3** *this food is* ***aimed at*** *children* **target at,** intend for, direct at, design for, tailor for, market to, pitch to/at. **4 intend,** mean, hope, want, plan, propose.

▸ **noun 1** a purpose or intention. **2** the aiming of a weapon or missile.

– SYNONYMS **objective,** object, goal, end, target, design, desire, intention, intent, plan, purpose, ambition, aspiration, wish, dream, hope.

– PHRASES **take aim** point a weapon at a target.
– ORIGIN from Latin *aestimare* 'estimate.'

CHOOSE THE RIGHT WORD

See **INTEND**.

aim·less /ˈāmlis/ ▸ **adjective** without purpose or direction: *aimless wandering.*

– SYNONYMS **purposeless,** pointless, directionless, undirected, random.
– ANTONYMS purposeful.

– DERIVATIVES **aim·less·ly** adverb **aim·less·ness** noun.

ain't /ānt/ ▸ **contraction** informal **1** am not; are not; is not. **2** has not; have not.

USAGE

The use of **ain't** was widespread in the 18th century and is still perfectly normal in many dialects and informal contexts in both North America and Britain. Today, however, it does not form part of standard English and should not be used in formal contexts.

air /e(ə)r/ ▶ **noun 1** the invisible mixture of gases surrounding the earth, mainly oxygen and nitrogen. **2** the open space above the earth's surface: *I threw the ball up in the air.* **3** the earth's atmosphere as a medium for transmitting radio waves. **4** (**an air of**) an impression of: *there was an air of sadness about her.* **5** (**airs**) an affected and condescending manner. **6** a tune or short song.

– SYNONYMS **1 breeze,** draft, wind, gust/puff of wind; literary zephyr. **2** *an air of defiance* **look,** appearance, impression, aspect, manner, tone, feel, atmosphere, mood.

▶ **adjective** using aircraft: *air travel.*

▶ **verb 1** express an opinion or complaint publicly. **2** broadcast a program on radio or television. **3** expose a room or washed laundry to fresh or warm air.

– SYNONYMS **1 express,** voice, make public, articulate, give vent to, state, declare. **2 ventilate,** freshen, refresh, cool.

– PHRASES **on** (or **off**) **the air** being (or not being) broadcast on radio or television. **up in the air** (of an issue) still to be settled. **walk on air** feel very happy or pleased.

– ORIGIN Greek *aēr.*

WORD LINKS

aerial *relating to air*

air·bag /ˈe(ə)rˌbag/ ▶ **noun** a safety device that inflates rapidly when there is a sudden impact, so protecting a vehicle's occupants in a collision.

air·base /ˈe(ə)rˌbās/ ▶ **noun** a base for military aircraft.

air·borne /ˈe(ə)rˌbôrn/ ▶ **adjective 1** carried through the air. **2** (of an aircraft) flying.

air brake /ˈe(ə)rˌbrāk/ ▶ **noun** a vehicle brake worked by air pressure.

air·brush /ˈe(ə)rˌbrəsʜ/ ▶ **noun** an artist's device for spraying paint by means of compressed air. ▶ **verb 1** paint a picture or alter a photograph with an airbrush. **2** alter or remove undesirable elements or people to present an improved version of reality: *the failures are airbrushed from history.*

air con·di·tion·ing ▶ **noun** a system for controlling the humidity, ventilation, and temperature in a building or vehicle.

– DERIVATIVES **air-con·di·tion·ed** adjective **air con·di·tion·er** noun.

air cor·ri·dor ▶ **noun** a route over a foreign country that aircraft must take.

air·craft /ˈe(ə)rˌkraft/ ▶ **noun** (pl. same) an airplane, helicopter, or other machine capable of flight.

air·craft car·ri·er /ˈe(ə)rˌkraftˈkarēər/ ▶ **noun** a large warship from which aircraft can take off and land.

air·crew /ˈe(ə)rˌkro͞o/ ▶ **noun** (pl. **aircrews**) (treated as sing. or pl.) the crew of an aircraft.

air cush·ion ▶ **noun** the layer of air supporting a hovercraft or similar vehicle.

air·drop /ˈe(ə)rˌdräp/ ▶ **noun** an act of dropping supplies, troops, or equipment by parachute.

Aire·dale /ˈe(ə)rˌdāl/ ▶ **noun** a large rough-coated black-and-tan breed of terrier.

– ORIGIN from *Airedale,* a district in Yorkshire, England.

air·fare /ˈe(ə)rˌfe(ə)r/ ▶ **noun** the price to be paid by an aircraft passenger for a journey.

air·field /ˈe(ə)rˌfēld/ ▶ **noun** an area of land set aside for the takeoff, landing, and maintenance of aircraft.

air·flow /ˈe(ə)rˌflō/ ▶ **noun** the flow of air, especially that encountered by a moving aircraft or vehicle.

air·foil /ˈe(ə)rˌfoil/ ▶ **noun** a curved structure, such as a wing, designed to give an aircraft lift in flight.

air force /ˈe(ə)rˌfôrs/ ▶ **noun** a branch of the armed forces concerned with fighting or defense in the air.

air·frame /ˈe(ə)rˌfrām/ ▶ **noun** the body of an aircraft as distinct from its engine.

air·freight /ˈe(ə)rˌfrāt/ ▶ **noun** the carriage of goods by aircraft.

air fresh·en·er ▶ **noun** a scented substance or device for disguising unpleasant smells in a room, automobile, etc.

air gun /ˈe(ə)rˌgən/ ▶ **noun 1** a gun that uses compressed air to fire pellets. **2** a tool using very hot air to strip paint.

air·head /ˈe(ə)rˌhed/ ▶ **noun** informal a stupid person.

air·ing /ˈe(ə)rɪɴɢ/ ▶ **noun 1** an act of exposing laundry or a place to warm or fresh air. **2** a public expression of an opinion or discussion of a subject.

air kiss /ˈe(ə)rkis/ ▶ **noun** a kiss close to a person's face, but without making contact.

air·less /ˈe(ə)rlis/ ▶ **adjective** stuffy; not ventilated.

– SYNONYMS **stuffy,** close, muggy, humid, stifling, suffocating, oppressive, unventilated.
– ANTONYMS airy.

air·lift /ˈe(ə)rˌlift/ ▶ **noun** an act of transporting supplies by aircraft, typically in an emergency.

air·line /ˈe(ə)rˌlīn/ ▶ **noun 1** an organization providing a regular passenger air service. **2** (**air line**) a pipe supplying air.

air·lin·er /ˈe(ə)rˌlīnər/ ▶ **noun** a large passenger aircraft.

air·lock /ˈe(ə)rˌläk/ ▶ **noun 1** a stoppage of the flow in a pump or pipe, caused by an air bubble. **2** a compartment with controlled pressure and airtight doors at each end, to allow people to move between areas at different pressures.

air·mail /ˈe(ə)rˌmāl/ ▶ **noun** a system of transporting mail by air.

air·man /ˈe(ə)rmən/ (or **airwoman** /ˈe(ə)rˌwo͝omən/) ▶ **noun** (pl. **airmen** or **airwomen**) **1** a pilot or member of the crew of an aircraft in an air force. **2** a member of the US Air Force of the lowest rank, below sergeant.

air mat·tress ▶ **noun** an inflatable mattress.

air mile ▶ **noun 1** a nautical mile used as a measure of distance flown by aircraft. **2** (**Air Miles**) trademark points (equivalent to miles of free air travel) collected by buyers of airline tickets and other products.

air pis·tol ▶ **noun** a pistol that uses compressed air to fire pellets.

air·plane /ˈe(ə)rˌplān/ ▸ **noun** a fixed-wing powered flying vehicle that is heavier than the air.

air plant /ˈe(ə)rˌplant/ ▸ **noun** a tropical American plant that grows on trees, with long narrow leaves that absorb water and nutrients from the atmosphere.

air·play /ˈe(ə)rˌplā/ ▸ **noun** broadcasting time devoted to a particular recording, performer, or type of music.

air pock·et /ˈe(ə)rˌpäkət/ ▸ **noun 1** a hollow space containing air. **2** a region of low pressure causing an aircraft to lose height suddenly.

air·port /ˈe(ə)rˌpôrt/ ▸ **noun** a complex of runways and buildings for the takeoff, landing, and maintenance of civil aircraft, with facilities for passengers.

air pow·er ▸ **noun** airborne military forces.

air pump /ˈe(ə)rˌpəmp/ ▸ **noun** a device for pumping air into or out of an enclosed space.

air qual·i·ty ▸ **noun** the degree to which the air in a place is pollution-free.

air raid /ˈe(ə)rˌrād/ ▸ **noun** an attack in which bombs are dropped from aircraft onto a ground target.

air ri·fle ▸ **noun** a rifle that uses compressed air to fire pellets.

air-sea res·cue ▸ **noun** a rescue from the sea using aircraft.

air·ship /ˈe(ə)rˌsHip/ ▸ **noun** a power-driven aircraft kept aloft by a body of gas (usually helium) that is lighter than air.

air·sick /ˈe(ə)rˌsik/ ▸ **adjective** feeling sick due to air travel.

air·side /ˈe(ə)rˌsīd/ ▸ **noun** the area beyond passport and customs control in an airport terminal.

air·space /ˈe(ə)rˌspās/ ▸ **noun** the part of the air above and subject to the laws of a particular country.

air·speed /ˈe(ə)rˌspēd/ ▸ **noun** the speed of an aircraft relative to the air through which it is moving.

air·stream /ˈe(ə)rˌstrēm/ ▸ **noun** a current of air.

air·strip /ˈe(ə)rˌstrip/ ▸ **noun** a strip of ground for the takeoff and landing of aircraft.

air·tight /ˈe(ə)rˌtīt/ ▸ **adjective 1** not allowing air to escape or pass through. **2** having no weaknesses: *an airtight alibi.*

air·time /ˈe(ə)rˌtīm/ ▸ **noun 1** the time during which a broadcast is being transmitted. **2** the time during which a cell phone is in use.

air traf·fic con·trol ▸ **noun** the ground-based staff and equipment concerned with controlling air traffic within a particular area.
– DERIVATIVES **air traf·fic con·troll·er** noun.

air·waves /ˈe(ə)rˌwāvz/ ▸ **plural noun** the radio frequencies used for broadcasting.

air·way /ˈeərˌwā/ ▸ **noun 1** the passage by which air reaches the lungs. **2** a tube for supplying air to the lungs in an emergency. **3** a recognized route followed by aircraft.

air·wor·thy /ˈe(ə)rˌwərTHē/ ▸ **adjective** (of an aircraft) safe to fly.
– DERIVATIVES **air·wor·thi·ness** noun.

air·y /ˈe(ə)rē/ ▸ **adjective** (**airier, airiest**) **1** (of a room or building) spacious and well ventilated. **2** not treating something as important; casual: *her airy unconcern for economy.*

> – SYNONYMS **spacious,** uncluttered, light, bright, well ventilated, fresh.
> – ANTONYMS airless, stuffy.

– DERIVATIVES **air·i·ly** adverb **air·i·ness** noun.

air·y-fair·y /ˌe(ə)rēˈfe(ə)rē/ ▸ **adjective** informal, chiefly Brit. vague and unrealistic.

aisle /īl/ ▸ **noun 1** a passage between rows of seats in a public building, aircraft, or train. **2** a passage between sets of shelves in a store.

> – SYNONYMS **passage,** passageway, lane, path, gangway, walkway.

– DERIVATIVES **aisled** adjective.
– ORIGIN Latin *ala* 'wing.'

aitch /āCH/ ▸ **noun** the letter H.
– PHRASES **drop one's aitches** fail to pronounce the letter *h* at the beginning of words.
– ORIGIN Old French *ache.*

aitch·bone /ˈāCHˌbōn/ ▸ **noun 1** the buttock or rump bone of cattle. **2** a cut of beef lying over the rump bone.
– ORIGIN from Latin *natis* 'buttock', + **BONE**.

a·jar /əˈjär/ ▸ **adverb & adjective** (of a door or window) slightly open.
– ORIGIN from Old English, 'a turn.'

AK ▸ **abbreviation** Alaska.

aka ▸ **abbreviation** also known as.

AKC ▸ **abbreviation** American Kennel Club.

a·kee /aˈkē, ˈakē/ (also **ackee**) ▸ **noun** the fruit of a West African tree, eaten as a vegetable.
– ORIGIN from Kru (a West African language).

a·kim·bo /əˈkimbō/ ▸ **adverb** with hands on the hips and elbows turned outward.
– ORIGIN probably from Old Norse.

a·kin /əˈkin/ ▸ **adjective** similar in nature or type: *a road more akin to an army assault course.*

> – SYNONYMS **similar,** related, close, near, comparable, equivalent, connected, alike, analogous.
> – ANTONYMS unlike.

– ORIGIN from *of kin.*

AL ▸ **abbreviation** Alabama.

Al ▸ **symbol** the chemical element aluminum.

à la /ˈä ˌlä, ˈä lə/ ▸ **preposition** in the style or manner of: *a publicity stunt à la Joan Crawford.*
– ORIGIN French.

al·a·bas·ter /ˈaləˌbastər/ ▸ **noun** a white, semitransparent form of the mineral gypsum, often carved into ornaments. ▸ **adjective** literary smooth and white: *pale, alabaster skin.*
– ORIGIN Greek *alabastos, alabastros.*

à la carte /ˌä lä ˈkärt, lə/ ▸ **adjective** (of a menu) listing dishes that can be ordered as separate items, rather than part of a set meal.
– ORIGIN French, 'according to the card.'

a·lac·ri·ty /əˈlakritē/ ▸ **noun** brisk eagerness or enthusiasm: *she accepted the invitation with alacrity.*
– ORIGIN from Latin *alacer* 'brisk.'

A·lad·din's lamp /əˈladnz/ ▸ **noun** an object that brings its holder the promise of having a wish fulfilled.
– ORIGIN from the story of *Aladdin* in the *Arabian Nights,* in which a genie is summoned by rubbing an old oil lamp.

à la mode /ˌä lä ˈmōd/ ▶ **adverb & adjective** up to date; fashionable.
– ORIGIN French.

a·larm /əˈlärm/ ▶ **noun 1** anxious or frightened awareness of danger. **2** a warning of danger: *I hammered on the door to raise the alarm.* **3** a warning sound or device.

– SYNONYMS **1 fear,** anxiety, apprehension, distress, agitation, consternation, fright, panic, trepidation. **2 warning,** danger signal, siren, bell, detector, sensor.
– ANTONYMS calmness, composure.

▶ **verb 1** frighten or disturb someone or something. **2** (**be alarmed**) be fitted or protected with an alarm.

– SYNONYMS **frighten,** scare, panic, unnerve, distress, agitate, upset, disconcert, shock, disturb; informal rattle, spook.

– ORIGIN from Italian *all' arme!* 'to arms!'

a·larm clock ▶ **noun** a clock that can be set to sound an alarm at a particular time, used to wake someone up.

a·larm·ist /əˈlärmist/ ▶ **noun** a person who exaggerates a danger, so causing needless alarm. ▶ **adjective** creating needless alarm.
– DERIVATIVES **a·larm·ism** /-ˌmizəm/ noun.

a·las /əˈlas/ ▶ **exclamation** literary or humorous an expression of grief, pity, or regret: *I, alas, am dieting.*
– ORIGIN Old French *a las*, from Latin *lassus* 'weary.'

alb /alb/ ▶ **noun** a long white robe worn by clergy and servers in some Christian Churches.
– ORIGIN from Latin *tunica alba* 'white garment.'

al·ba·core /ˈalbəˌkôr/ ▶ **noun** a tuna of warm seas that is an important food fish.
– ORIGIN Arabic.

Al·ba·ni·an /alˈbānēən, ôl-/ ▶ **noun 1** a person from Albania. **2** the language of Albania. ▶ **adjective** relating to Albania.

al·ba·tross /ˈalbəˌtrôs, -ˌträs/ ▶ **noun** (pl. **albatrosses**) **1** a very large seabird with long narrow wings, found chiefly in the southern oceans. **2** a burden: *the radioactive albatross around the nuclear power industry's neck.*
– ORIGIN Arabic, 'the diver.'

al·be·do /alˈbēdō/ ▶ **noun** (pl. **albedos**) the proportion of the incident light or radiation that is reflected by a surface, typically that of the earth, the moon, or some other celestial object.
– ORIGIN Latin *albus* 'white.'

al·be·it /ôlˈbē-it, al-/ ▶ **conjunction** although: *I got up, albeit rather groggily.*
– ORIGIN from *all be it.*

al·bi·no /alˈbīnō/ ▶ **noun** (pl. **albinos**) a person or animal born without pigment in the skin and hair (which are white) and the eyes (which are usually pink).
– DERIVATIVES **al·bi·nism** /ˈalbəˌnizəm/ noun.
– ORIGIN from Latin *albus* 'white.'

Al·bi·on /ˈalbēən/ ▶ **noun** literary Britain or England.
– ORIGIN Latin.

al·bum /ˈalbəm/ ▶ **noun 1** a blank book in which photographs, stamps, or other items can be kept. **2** a collection of musical recordings issued as a single item.
– ORIGIN Latin, 'blank tablet.'

al·bu·men /alˈbyo͞omən/ ▶ **noun** egg white, or the protein contained in it.
– ORIGIN from Latin *albus* 'white.'

al·bu·min /alˈbyo͞omən/ ▶ **noun** a form of protein that is soluble in water and is found especially in blood serum and egg white.

al·che·my /ˈalkəmē/ ▶ **noun 1** the medieval forerunner of chemistry, concerned particularly with attempts to convert common metals into gold. **2** a seemingly magical or mysterious process: *watching the great chef create culinary alchemy.*
– DERIVATIVES **al·chem·i·cal** /alˈkemikəl/ adjective **al·che·mist** noun.
– ORIGIN from Greek *khēmia, khēmeia* 'art of transmuting metals.'

al·co·hol /ˈalkəˌhôl, -ˌhäl/ ▶ **noun 1** a colorless volatile liquid that is the intoxicating ingredient in drinks such as wine, beer, and liquor. **2** drink containing alcohol. **3** Chemistry any organic compound containing a hydroxyl group –OH: *propyl alcohol.*
– ORIGIN Arabic, 'the kohl.'

al·co·hol·ic /ˌalkəˈhôlik, -ˈhäl-/ ▶ **adjective 1** relating to alcohol. **2** affected by alcoholism.

– SYNONYMS **intoxicating,** strong, hard, stiff, fermented, brewed, distilled.

▶ **noun** a person affected by alcoholism.

– SYNONYMS **drunkard,** dipsomaniac, drunk, heavy drinker, problem drinker, alcohol abuser; informal lush, alky, dipso, wino.

al·co·hol·ism /ˈalkəhôˌlizəm, -hä-/ ▶ **noun** addiction to alcoholic drink.

al·cove /ˈalˌkōv/ ▶ **noun** a recess in the wall of a room.
– ORIGIN Arabic, 'the vault.'

al·de·hyde /ˈaldəˌhīd/ ▶ **noun** Chemistry an organic compound formed by the oxidation of an alcohol.
– ORIGIN from Latin *alcohol dehydrogenatum* 'alcohol deprived of hydrogen.'

al den·te /äl ˈdentā, al/ ▶ **adjective & adverb** (of food) cooked so as to be still firm when bitten.
– ORIGIN Italian, 'to the tooth.'

al·der /ˈôldər/ ▶ **noun** a tree of the birch family that bears catkins and has toothed leaves.
– ORIGIN Old English.

al·der·man /ˈôldərmən/ ▶ **noun** (pl. **aldermen**) **1** (or **alderwoman**) an elected member of a city council. **2** historical a member of an English county or borough council, next in status to the mayor.
– ORIGIN Old English, 'chief, patriarch.'

ale /āl/ ▶ **noun 1** a type of beer with a bitter flavor and a higher alcoholic content. **2** chiefly Brit. beer, other than lager, stout, or porter.
– ORIGIN Old English.

a·le·a·to·ry /ˈālēəˌtôrē, ˈal-/ (also **aleatoric** /ˌālēəˈtôrik, ˌal-/) ▶ **adjective** depending on the throw of a dice or on chance.
– ORIGIN from Latin *aleator* 'dice player.'

ale·house /ˈālˌhous/ ▶ **noun** dated an inn or tavern.

a·lem·bic /əˈlembik/ ▶ **noun** a container with a long, downward-sloping spout leading from the top, formerly used in distilling.
– ORIGIN from Greek *ambix* 'cup.'

a·lert /əˈlərt/ ▶ **adjective 1** quick to notice and respond to danger or possible problems: *be alert to early signs of stress.* **2** quick-thinking; intelligent.

– SYNONYMS **1 vigilant,** watchful, attentive, observant, wide awake, on the lookout, on one's

guard/toes; informal keeping one's eyes open/peeled. **2 quick-witted,** sharp, bright, quick, perceptive, on one's toes; informal on the ball, quick on the uptake, all there, with it.
– ANTONYMS inattentive.

▶ **noun 1** the state of being watchful for danger or possible problems: *we should be on the alert for terrorists*. **2** a warning of danger.

– SYNONYMS **1 vigilance,** watchfulness, attentiveness, alertness. **2 warning,** notification, notice, siren, alarm, signal.

▶ **verb** warn someone about a danger or problem.

– SYNONYMS **warn,** notify, inform, apprise, forewarn, put on one's guard; informal tip off.

– DERIVATIVES **a·lert·ly** adverb **a·lert·ness** noun.
– ORIGIN from Italian *all' erta* 'to the watchtower.'

Al·ex·an·der tech·nique /ˌaligˈzandər/ ▶ **noun** a system designed to promote well-being through retraining one's habits of posture.
– ORIGIN named after the Australian-born actor Frederick Matthias *Alexander*.

al·ex·an·drine /ˌaligˈzandrin, -ˌdrēn/ ▶ **adjective** (of a line of verse) having six iambic feet. ▶ **noun** an alexandrine line.
– ORIGIN French, from Alexander the Great, the subject of an Old French poem in alexandrines.

al·fal·fa /alˈfalfə/ ▶ **noun** a plant with cloverlike leaves and bluish flowers, grown in warm climates for fodder.
– ORIGIN Arabic, 'green fodder.'

al·fres·co /alˈfreskō, äl-/ ▶ **adverb & adjective** in the open air: *an alfresco meal*.
– ORIGIN Italian *al fresco*.

al·ga /ˈalgə/ ▶ **noun** (pl. **algae** /-jē/) a simple plant of a large group that contain chlorophyll but lack true stems, roots, and leaves, e.g., seaweed.
– DERIVATIVES **al·gal** /-gəl/ adjective.
– ORIGIN Latin, 'seaweed.'

al·ge·bra /ˈaljəbrə/ ▶ **noun** the branch of mathematics in which letters and other symbols are used to represent numbers and quantities.
– DERIVATIVES **al·ge·bra·ic** /ˌaljəˈbrā-ik/ adjective **al·ge·bra·ist** /-ˌbrā-ist/ noun.
– ORIGIN Arabic, 'the reunion of broken parts.'

Al·ge·ri·an /alˈji(ə)rēən/ ▶ **noun** a person from Algeria. ▶ **adjective** relating to Algeria.

-algia ▶ **combining form** used to form nouns referring to pain in a specified part of the body: *neuralgia*.
– DERIVATIVES **-algic** combining form.
– ORIGIN from Greek *algos* 'pain.'

Al·gon·qui·an /alˈgäNGk(w)ēən/ (also **Algonkian** /-kēən/) ▶ **noun 1** a large family of North American Indian languages, including Cree, Blackfoot, and Cheyenne. **2** a speaker of Algonquian. ▶ **adjective** relating to Algonquian.

Al·gon·quin /alˈgäNGk(w)in/ (also **Algonkin** /-kin/) ▶ **noun 1** a member of an American Indian people living in Canada along and westward of the Ottawa River. **2** the language of the Algonquins. ▶ **adjective** relating to the Algonquins.
– ORIGIN Micmac, 'at the place of spearing fish and eels.'

al·go·rithm /ˈalgəˌriT͟Həm/ ▶ **noun** a process or set of rules used in calculations or other problem-solving operations.
– DERIVATIVES **al·go·rith·mic** /ˌalgəˈriT͟Hmik/ adjective.
– ORIGIN Arabic, 'the man of Ḵwārizm' (referring to a 9th-century mathematician).

a·li·as /ˈālēəs/ ▶ **adverb** also known as: *Eric Blair, alias George Orwell*. ▶ **noun 1** a false identity. **2** an identifying label used to access a computer file, command, or address.
– ORIGIN Latin, 'at another time, otherwise.'

a·li·as·ing /ˈālēəsiNG/ ▶ **noun 1** Physics & Telecommunications the misidentification of a signal frequency, introducing distortion or error. **2** the use of aliases to identify computer files, commands, etc.

al·i·bi /ˈaləˌbī/ ▶ **noun** (pl. **alibis**) **1** a claim or piece of evidence that one was elsewhere when an alleged act took place. **2** informal an excuse: *there can be no more alibis for failure*. ▶ **verb** (**alibis, alibiing, alibied**) informal provide an alibi for someone.
– ORIGIN from Latin, 'elsewhere.'

USAGE

Alibi means *a claim by a person that they were elsewhere*. The informal meaning *an excuse* is regarded as incorrect by some people and should be avoided in careful writing.

a·li·en /ˈālyən, ˈālēən/ ▶ **adjective 1** belonging to a foreign country. **2** unfamiliar or unacceptable: *extravagance is alien to his measured approach to life*. **3** relating to beings from other worlds.

– SYNONYMS **foreign,** unfamiliar, unknown, peculiar, exotic, strange.
– ANTONYMS native, familiar.

▶ **noun 1** a foreigner. **2** a being from another world.

– SYNONYMS **1 foreigner,** non-native, immigrant, émigré, stranger. **2 extraterrestrial,** ET; informal little green man.

– DERIVATIVES **al·ien·ness** noun.
– ORIGIN Latin *alienus*.

al·ien·a·ble /ˈālēənəbəl, ˈālyənə-/ ▶ **adjective** Law able to be transferred to new ownership.

al·ien·ate /ˈālēəˌnāt, ˈālyə-/ ▶ **verb 1** make someone feel isolated or estranged. **2** lose the support or sympathy of: *I wanted to keep the friends I had and not alienate any of them*.

– SYNONYMS **isolate,** distance, estrange, cut off, turn away, drive apart, set at variance/odds, drive a wedge between.

– DERIVATIVES **al·ien·a·tion** /ˌālēəˈnāSHən, ˌālyə-/ noun.
– ORIGIN Latin *alienare*.

a·light[1] /əˈlīt/ ▶ **verb 1** (**alight on**) (of a bird) land or settle on something. **2** formal get off a train or bus. **3** (**alight on**) happen to notice something.
– ORIGIN Old English.

a·light[2] ▶ **adverb & adjective 1** on fire. **2** shining brightly.

– SYNONYMS **burning,** ablaze, on fire, in flames, blazing, lit.

a·lign /əˈlīn/ ▶ **verb 1** put things in a straight line or in the correct position in relation to something else. **2** (**align oneself with**) give support to: *newspapers align themselves with certain political parties*.

– SYNONYMS **1 line up,** range, rank, straighten, even up, arrange, coordinate. **2** *he aligned himself with the workers* **ally,** affiliate, associate, side, join forces, team up, band together, throw in one's lot.

– DERIVATIVES **a·lign·ment** noun.
– ORIGIN from French *à ligne* 'into line.'

a·like /əˈlīk/ ▶ **adjective** similar to each other: *the brothers were very much alike*.

– SYNONYMS **similar,** (much) the same, analogous, corresponding, indistinguishable, identical, uniform, interchangeable.
– ANTONYMS different.

▶ **adverb** in a similar way.

– SYNONYMS *great minds think alike* **similarly,** the same, correspondingly, analogously, identically.
– ANTONYMS differently.

– ORIGIN Old English.

al·i·men·ta·ry /ˌaləˈment(ə)rē/ ▶ **adjective** relating to food or nutrition.
– ORIGIN from Latin *alimentum* 'nourishment.'

al·i·men·ta·ry ca·nal ▶ **noun** the whole passage along which food passes through the body during digestion.

al·i·mo·ny /ˈaləˌmōnē/ ▶ **noun** court-ordered financial support for a spouse after separation or divorce.
– ORIGIN from Latin *alimonia* 'nutriment.'

A-line /ˈā ˌlīn/ ▶ **adjective** (of a garment) slightly flared from a narrow waist or shoulders.

al·i·quot /ˈalikwət/ ▶ **noun 1** technical a portion or sample taken for analysis or treatment. **2** (also **aliquot part** or **portion**) Mathematics a quantity that divides into another a whole number of times.
– ORIGIN Latin, 'some, so many.'

A-list /ˈā ˌlist/ (or **B-list**) ▶ **noun** a list of the most (or second most) famous or sought-after people, especially in show business.

a·live /əˈlīv/ ▶ **adjective 1** living; not dead. **2** continuing in existence or use: *keeping hope alive.* **3** alert and active. **4** (**alive to**) aware of and willing to respond to: *I am very alive to the challenges we face.* **5** (**alive with**) teeming with something.

– SYNONYMS **1 active,** in existence, functioning, in operation, operative, on the map. **2 alert,** awake, aware, conscious, mindful, heedful, sensitive.
– ANTONYMS dead, unaware.

al·ka·li /ˈalkəˌlī/ ▶ **noun** (pl. **alkalis**) a compound, such as lime, with particular chemical properties including turning litmus blue and neutralizing or effervescing with acids.
– ORIGIN first referring to a saline substance obtained from the ashes of plants: from Arabic, 'fry, roast.'

al·ka·line /ˈalkəlin, -ˌlīn/ ▶ **adjective** containing an alkali or having the properties of an alkali; having a pH greater than 7.
– DERIVATIVES **al·ka·lin·i·ty** /ˌalkəˈlinitē/ noun.

al·ka·loid /ˈalkəˌloid/ ▶ **noun** Chemistry any of a class of organic compounds containing nitrogen that have significant physiological effects on humans.

al·kane /ˈalˌkān/ ▶ **noun** Chemistry any of the series of saturated hydrocarbons whose simplest members are methane and ethane.
– ORIGIN from **ALKYL**.

al·kene /ˈalˌkēn/ ▶ **noun** Chemistry any of the series of unsaturated hydrocarbons containing a double bond, of which the simplest member is ethylene.
– ORIGIN from **ALKYL**.

al·kyl /ˈalkəl/ ▶ **noun** Chemistry a hydrocarbon radical derived from an alkane by removal of a hydrogen atom.
– ORIGIN German *Alkohol* 'alcohol.'

all /ôl/ ▶ **predeterminer & determiner 1** the whole quantity or extent of. **2** any whatever: *he denied all knowledge.* **3** the greatest possible. ▶ **pronoun** everything or everyone. ▶ **adverb 1** completely. **2** used to show an equal score: *one-all.*
– PHRASES **all along** from the beginning. **all and sundry** everyone or everything. **all around** (also chiefly Brit. **all round**) **1** in all respects: *all around, I think it's a good idea.* **2** for or by each person: *drinks all around.* **all but** very nearly. **all for** informal strongly in favor of. **all in** informal exhausted. **all in all** on the whole. **all out** using every effort. **all over the place** informal **1** everywhere. **2** in a disordered state. **all told** in total. **at all** in any way. **in all** in total. **on all fours** on hands and knees. **one's all** one's greatest effort.
– ORIGIN Old English.

Al·lah /ˈälə, ˈalə/ ▶ **noun** the name of God among Muslims (and Arab Christians).
– ORIGIN Arabic.

all-A·mer·i·can ▶ **adjective 1** possessing qualities characteristic of American ideals, such as honesty, industriousness, and health: *his all-American wholesomeness.* **2** having members or contents drawn only from the Americas or the US: *an all-American anthology.* **3** (of an athlete) honored as one of the best amateur competitors in the US: *an all-American wrestler.* ▶ **noun** an athlete honored as one of the best amateurs in the US.

all-a·round /ˈôləˌround/ (also chiefly Brit. **all-round** /ˈôlˌround/) ▶ **adjective 1** having a wide range of abilities or uses. **2** in many or all respects: *his all-around excellence.*

al·lay /əˈlā/ ▶ **verb** reduce or end fear, concern, or difficulty.

– SYNONYMS **reduce,** diminish, decrease, lessen, alleviate, assuage, ease, relieve, soothe, soften, calm.
– ANTONYMS increase, intensify.

– ORIGIN Old English, 'lay down or aside.'

CHOOSE THE RIGHT WORD

See **ALLEVIATE**.

all-clear ▶ **noun** a signal that danger or difficulty is over.

al·le·ga·tion /ˌaliˈgāshən/ ▶ **noun** an unproven claim that someone has done something illegal or wrong.

– SYNONYMS **claim,** assertion, charge, accusation, contention.

al·lege /əˈlej/ ▶ **verb** claim that someone has done something illegal or wrong: *he alleged that he'd been assaulted.*

– SYNONYMS **claim,** assert, accuse, contend, state, declare, maintain.

– ORIGIN Old French *esligier*, from Latin *lis* 'lawsuit.'

al·leged /əˈlejd/ ▶ **adjective** declared but not proved.

– SYNONYMS *the alleged conspirators* **reported,** supposed, so-called, claimed, professed, purported, ostensible, unproven.
– ANTONYMS confirmed.

– DERIVATIVES **al·leg·ed·ly** /-idlē/ adverb.

al·le·giance /əˈlējəns/ ▶ **noun** loyalty or commitment to a superior person or to a group or cause: *I have no allegiance to any political party.*

– SYNONYMS **loyalty,** faithfulness, fidelity, obedience, adherence, devotion; historical fealty.
– ANTONYMS disloyalty, treachery.

– ORIGIN Old French *ligeance*.

al·le·go·rize /ˈaligəˌrīz/ ▶ **verb** interpret or represent something symbolically.

al·le·go·ry /ˈaləˌgôrē/ ▸ **noun** (pl. **allegories**) a story, poem, or picture that contains a hidden symbolic meaning.
– DERIVATIVES **al·le·gor·i·cal** /ˌaliˈgôrikəl, -ˈgär-/ adjective **al·le·gor·i·cal·ly** /ˌaliˈgôrikəlē, -ˈgär-/ adverb **al·le·go·rist** noun.
– ORIGIN Greek *allēgoria*.

al·le·gret·to /ˌaliˈgretō/ ▸ **adverb & adjective** Music at a fairly brisk speed.
– ORIGIN Italian.

al·le·gro /əˈlegrō/ Music ▸ **adverb & adjective** at a brisk speed. ▸ **noun** (pl. **allegros**) a piece of music to be performed at a brisk speed.
– ORIGIN Italian, 'lively.'

al·lele /əˈlēl/ ▸ **noun** each of two or more alternative forms of a gene that arise by mutation and are found at the same place on a chromosome.
– DERIVATIVES **al·lel·ic** /əˈlēlik, əˈlel-/ adjective.
– ORIGIN from Greek *allēl-* 'one another.'

al·le·lu·ia /ˌaləˈlo͞oyə/ ▸ **exclamation** variant spelling of **HALLELUJAH.**

Al·len wrench /ˈalən/ ▸ **noun** a wrench designed to fit into and turn an **Allen screw** (one with a hexagonal socket in the head).
– ORIGIN formerly a trademark of the *Allen* Manufacturing Company in Connecticut.

al·ler·gen /ˈalərjən/ ▸ **noun** a substance that causes an allergic reaction.

al·ler·gen·ic /ˌalərˈjenik/ ▸ **adjective** likely to cause an allergic reaction.

al·ler·gic /əˈlərjik/ ▸ **adjective 1** caused by or relating to an allergy. **2** having an allergy.

al·ler·gy /ˈalərjē/ ▸ **noun** (pl. **allergies**) a medical condition in which the body reacts badly when it comes into contact with a particular substance.
– DERIVATIVES **al·ler·gist** noun.
– ORIGIN from Greek *allos* 'other.'

al·le·vi·ate /əˈlēvēˌāt/ ▸ **verb** make pain or a problem less severe: *yoga can help alleviate insomnia.*

– SYNONYMS **ease,** relieve, take the edge off, deaden, dull, lessen, reduce, moderate, allay, assuage, soothe, help, soften.
– ANTONYMS aggravate.

– DERIVATIVES **al·le·vi·a·tion** /əˌlēvēˈāsʜən/ noun.
– ORIGIN Latin *alleviare* 'lighten.'

CHOOSE THE RIGHT WORD

alleviate, abate, allay, assuage, mitigate, relieve, temper

To **alleviate** is to make something easier to endure (*alleviate the pain following surgery*) ; **allay** is often used interchangeably, but it also means to put to rest, to quiet or calm (*to allay their suspicions*). **Assuage** and *allay* both suggest the calming or satisfying of a desire or appetite, but *assuage* implies a more complete or permanent satisfaction (*we allay our hunger by nibbling hors d'oeuvres, but a huge dinner assuages our appetite*). To **relieve** implies reducing the misery or discomfort to the point where something is bearable (*relieve the monotony of the cross-country bus trip*) and **mitigate**, which comes from a Latin word meaning to soften, usually means to lessen in force or intensity (*mitigate the storm's impact*). **Abate** suggests a progressive lessening in degree or intensity (*her fever was abating*). To **temper** is to soften or moderate (*to temper justice with mercy*), but it can also mean the exact opposite: to harden or toughen something (*tempering steel; a body tempered by lifting weights*).

al·ley /ˈalē/ ▸ **noun** (pl. **alleys**) **1** a narrow passageway between or behind buildings. **2** a long, narrow area in which games such as bowling are played. **3** a path in a park or garden.

– SYNONYMS **passage,** passageway, alleyway, backstreet, lane, path, pathway, walk.

– PHRASES **up** (or **right up**) **one's alley** informal well suited to one's interests or abilities.
– ORIGIN Old French *alee* 'walking or passage.'

al·ley·way /ˈalēˌwā/ ▸ **noun** an alley between or behind buildings.

al·li·ance /əˈlīəns/ ▸ **noun 1** a relationship established between countries or organizations for a joint purpose: *Saudi Arabia's alliance with the United States.* **2** the state of being joined or associated.

– SYNONYMS **association,** union, league, confederation, federation, syndicate, consortium, cartel, coalition, partnership, relationship, marriage, cooperation.

al·lied /əˈlīd, ˈalˌīd/ ▸ **adjective 1** relating to or part of an alliance. **2** (**Allied**) relating to the US and its allies in World Wars I and II, and in global military actions since. **3** (**allied to/with**) combined or together with: *skilled craftsmanship allied to technology.*

– SYNONYMS **associated,** united, related, connected, interconnected, linked, cooperating, in league, affiliated, combined, coupled, married.
– ANTONYMS unrelated, independent.

al·li·ga·tor /ˈaliˌgātər/ ▸ **noun** a large reptile similar to a crocodile but with a broader and shorter head.
– ORIGIN from Spanish *el lagarto* 'the lizard.'

al·li·ga·tor pear ▸ **noun** an avocado.

all-in·clu·sive ▸ **adjective 1** including everything or everyone. **2** relating to a vacation or resort in which all or most meals, drinks, and activities are included in the overall price.

all-in-one ▸ **adjective** combining two or more items or uses in a single unit.

al·lit·er·a·tion /əˌlitəˈrāsʜən/ ▸ **noun** the occurrence of the same letter or sound at the beginning of words that are close together, as in *sing a song of sixpence*.
– DERIVATIVES **al·lit·er·a·tive** /əˈlitərətiv, -ˌrātiv/ adjective.
– ORIGIN from Latin *littera* 'letter.'

al·li·um /ˈalēəm/ ▸ **noun** (pl. **alliums**) a plant of a genus that includes onions, leeks, and garlic.
– ORIGIN Latin, 'garlic.'

al·lo·cate /ˈaləˌkāt/ ▸ **verb** give or distribute something: *all the tickets have been allocated to tour operators.*

– SYNONYMS **allot,** assign, set aside, earmark, consign, distribute, apportion, share out, dole out, give out.

– DERIVATIVES **al·lo·ca·ble** /-kəbəl/ adjective **al·lo·ca·tor** /-ˌkātər/ noun.
– ORIGIN Latin *allocare*.

al·lo·ca·tion /ˌaləˈkāsʜən/ ▸ **noun 1** the action of allocating something. **2** an amount of a resource given to someone.

– SYNONYMS **1 allotment,** assignment, distribution, sharing out, doling out, giving out. **2 allowance,** allotment, consignment, quota, share, ration; informal cut.

al·lop·a·thy /əˈläpəᴛʜē/ ▸ **noun** the conventional treatment of disease, using drugs that have effects

opposite to the symptoms.
– DERIVATIVES **al·lo·path** /'alə,paTH/ noun **al·lo·path·ic** /,alə'paTHik/ adjective.

al·lot /ə'lät/ ▸ **verb** (**allots, allotting, allotted**) give or share out something: *equal time was allotted to each task.*
– ORIGIN from Latin *loter* 'divide into lots.'

al·lot·ment /ə'lätmənt/ ▸ **noun 1** an amount allotted to someone. **2** the action of allotting something. **3** historical a plot of land deeded by the government to an American Indian. **4** Brit. a plot of land rented by a person from a local authority, for growing vegetables or flowers.

al·lo·trope /'alə,trōp/ ▸ **noun** Chemistry each of two or more different physical forms in which an element can exist (e.g., graphite, charcoal, and diamond as forms of carbon).
– DERIVATIVES **al·lo·trop·ic** /,alə'träpik, -'trō-/ adjective.
– ORIGIN from Greek *allotropos* 'of another form.'

al·low /ə'lou/ ▸ **verb 1** let someone have or do something. **2** decide that something is legal or acceptable. **3** provide or set aside: *allow an hour or so for driving.* **4** (**allow for**) take into consideration: *income rose by 11 percent allowing for inflation.* **5** accept that something is true.

> – SYNONYMS **1 permit,** let, enable, authorize, give leave, license, entitle, consent to, assent to, acquiesce in, agree to, approve; informal give the go-ahead to, give the thumbs up to, OK, give the green light to; formal accede to. **2 set aside,** allocate, allot, earmark, designate, reserve.
> – ANTONYMS prevent, forbid.

– DERIVATIVES **al·low·a·ble** adjective **al·low·ed·ly** /ə'lou-idlē/ adverb.
– ORIGIN from Latin *allaudare* 'to praise.'

> **USAGE**
>
> On the confusion of **allowed** and **aloud**, see the note at **ALOUD**.

al·low·ance /ə'lou-əns/ ▸ **noun 1** the amount of something allowed: *the recommended daily allowance of 1,300 mg calcium.* **2** a sum of money paid regularly to a person.

> – SYNONYMS **1 allocation,** allotment, quota, share, ration, grant, limit. **2 payment,** contribution, grant, handout, subsidy, maintenance.

– PHRASES **make allowances for 1** take something into consideration. **2** treat someone less harshly because of their difficult circumstances.

al·loy ▸ **noun** /'a,loi/ **1** a mixture of two or more metals. **2** an inferior metal mixed with a precious one. ▸ **verb** /'a,loi, ə'loi/ mix metals to make an alloy.
– ORIGIN from Latin *alligare* 'bind.'

all-pur·pose ▸ **adjective** having many uses, especially all that might be expected from something of its type: *an all-purpose kitchen knife.*

all right ▸ **adjective 1** satisfactory; acceptable. **2** able to be done or to happen; allowable.

> – SYNONYMS **1 satisfactory,** acceptable, adequate, passable, reasonable; informal so-so, OK. **2 unhurt,** uninjured, unharmed, in one piece, safe (and sound), alive and well; informal OK. **3 permissible,** permitted, allowed, acceptable, legal, lawful, authorized, approved, in order; informal OK, legit, cool.
> – ANTONYMS unsatisfactory.

▸ **adverb** fairly well.

> – SYNONYMS **satisfactorily,** adequately, fairly well, passably, acceptably, reasonably, well, fine; informal OK.

▸ **exclamation** expressing or asking for agreement or acceptance.

All Saints' Day ▸ **noun** a Christian festival in honor of all the saints, held on November 1.

All Souls' Day ▸ **noun** a Catholic festival with prayers for the souls of the dead in purgatory, held on November 2.

all·spice /'ôl,spīs/ ▸ **noun** the dried fruit of a Caribbean tree, used as a spice in cooking.

all-star ▸ **adjective** composed wholly of outstanding performers or players: *an all-star cast.* ▸ **noun** a member of such a group or team.

all-ter·rain ve·hi·cle ▸ **noun** a motorcycle with four wheels and large tires, for off-road use.

all-time /'ôl,tīm/ ▸ **adjective** not bettered or surpassed: *the all-time record.*

al·lude /ə'lo͞od/ ▸ **verb** (**allude to**) **1** mention briefly: *offering no evidence, he alluded airily to 'scientific findings'* **2** refer to someone or something in an indirect way.

> – SYNONYMS *I have **alluded to** that possibility* **refer to,** touch on, suggest, hint at, imply, make an allusion to, mention (in passing), intimate.

– ORIGIN Latin *alludere.*

al·lure /ə'lo͝or/ ▸ **noun** powerful attractiveness or charm. ▸ **verb** (often as adj. **alluring**) strongly attract or charm: *the alluring scent of lemon.*

> – SYNONYMS (as adj. **alluring**) **enticing,** tempting, attractive, appealing, inviting, captivating, seductive; enchanting, charming, fascinating.

– DERIVATIVES **al·lure·ment** noun **al·lur·ing·ly** adverb.
– ORIGIN from Latin *luere* 'a lure.'

> **CHOOSE THE RIGHT WORD**
>
> See **TEMPT**.

al·lu·sion /ə'lo͞oZHən/ ▸ **noun** an indirect reference to something.

> – SYNONYMS **reference,** mention, suggestion, intimation, hint.

– ORIGIN from Latin *alludere* 'allude.'

al·lu·sive /ə'lo͞osiv/ ▸ **adjective** using or containing indirect references to something: *elaborate, allusive prose.*
– DERIVATIVES **al·lu·sive·ly** adverb **al·lu·sive·ness** noun.

al·lu·vi·um /ə'lo͞ovēəm/ ▸ **noun** a fertile deposit of clay, silt, and sand left by floodwater.
– DERIVATIVES **al·lu·vi·al** adjective.
– ORIGIN Latin.

al·ly ▸ **noun** /'alī/ (pl. **allies**) **1** a person, organization, or country that cooperates with another. **2** (**the Allies**) the countries that fought with the US in World Wars I and II.

> – SYNONYMS **associate,** colleague, friend, confederate, partner, supporter.
> – ANTONYMS enemy, opponent.

▸ **verb** /ə'lī/ (**allies, allying, allied**) **1** (**ally something to/with**) combine a resource or quality with another in a way that benefits both: *he allied his racing experience* *with his father's business skill.* **2** (**ally oneself with**) side with or support something.

> – SYNONYMS **unite,** combine, join (up), join forces, band together, team up, collaborate, side, align oneself.

– ORIGIN from Latin *alligare* 'bind together.'

-ally ▶ **suffix** forming adverbs from adjectives ending in *-al* (such as *radically* from *radical*).

al·ma ma·ter /ˈälmə ˈmätər, ˈalmə/ ▶ **noun** the school, college, or university that one once attended.
– ORIGIN Latin, 'bountiful mother.'

al·ma·nac /ˈôlməˌnak, ˈal-/ (also **almanack**) ▶ **noun** **1** a calendar giving important dates and information, such as the phases of the moon. **2** an annual handbook containing information of general or special interest.
– ORIGIN Greek *almenikhiaka.*

al·might·y /ôlˈmītē/ ▶ **adjective** **1** having complete or very great power: *an almighty army.* **2** informal very big; enormous. ▶ **noun** (**the Almighty**) a name or title for God.

al·mond /ˈä(l)mənd, ˈa(l)-/ ▶ **noun** the oval edible nutlike seed (kernel) of the almond tree.
– ORIGIN from Greek *amugdalē.*

al·mond paste ▶ **noun** marzipan.

al·most /ôlˈmōst, ˈôlˌmōst/ ▶ **adverb** very nearly.

> – SYNONYMS **nearly,** (just) about, practically, virtually, all but, as good as, close to, not quite; informal pretty nearly/much/well; literary well nigh, nigh on.

– ORIGIN Old English.

alms /ä(l)mz/ ▶ **plural noun** old use money or food given to poor people.
– ORIGIN from Greek *eleēmosunē* 'compassion.'

alms·house /ˈä(l)mzˌhous/ ▶ **noun** historical a house founded by charity, offering accommodations for poor people.

al·oe /ˈalō/ ▶ **noun** **1** a succulent tropical plant with thick tapering leaves. **2** (**aloes** or **bitter aloes**) a strong laxative obtained from the bitter juice of some kinds of aloe.
– ORIGIN Greek *aloē.*

al·oe ver·a /ˈalō ˈverə, ˈvi(ə)rə/ ▶ **noun** a jellylike substance obtained from a kind of aloe, used to soothe the skin.
– ORIGIN Latin, 'true aloe.'

a·loft /əˈlôft/ ▶ **adjective & adverb** up in or into the air.
– ORIGIN Old Norse.

a·lo·ha /əˈlōˌhä/ ▶ **exclamation & noun** a Hawaiian word used when greeting or parting from someone.

a·lone /əˈlōn/ ▶ **adjective & adverb** **1** on one's own; by oneself. **2** isolated and lonely. **3** only; exclusively: *it was a smile for him alone.*

> – SYNONYMS **by oneself,** on one's own, unaccompanied, solo, single, isolated, solitary, lonely, deserted, abandoned, friendless.
> – ANTONYMS accompanied.

– DERIVATIVES **a·lone·ness** /əˈlōn(n)əs/ noun.
– PHRASES **leave** (or **let**) **someone/thing alone** **1** abandon someone or something. **2** stop interfering with someone or something.
– ORIGIN from **ALL** + **ONE**.

a·long /əˈlôNG, əˈläNG/ ▶ **preposition & adverb** **1** moving forward on. **2** extending in a horizontal line on. **3** in or into company with other people: *she'd brought along a friend.*
– PHRASES **along with** together with or at the same time as. **be** (or **come**) **along** arrive.
– ORIGIN Old English.

a·long·side /əˈlôNGˈsīd, əˈläNG-/ (often **alongside of**) ▶ **preposition** **1** close to the side of; next to. **2** at the same time as.

a·loof /əˈlo͞of/ ▶ **adjective** cool and distant: *they were polite but faintly aloof.*

> – SYNONYMS **distant,** detached, unfriendly, remote, unapproachable, reserved, unforthcoming, uncommunicative; informal standoffish.
> – ANTONYMS friendly.

– DERIVATIVES **a·loof·ly** adverb **a·loof·ness** noun.
– ORIGIN from **LUFF**; originally meaning 'away and to windward!' (with the ship kept away from a lee shore or other hazard).

al·o·pe·ci·a /ˌaləˈpēSH(ē)ə/ ▶ **noun** Medicine abnormal loss of hair; baldness.
– ORIGIN Greek *alōpekia* 'fox mange.'

a·loud /əˈloud/ ▶ **adverb** out loud; so as to be heard.

> **USAGE**
>
> Do not confuse **aloud** with **allowed**. **Aloud** means *out loud* (*I read the letter aloud*), whereas **allowed** means *permitted* (*smoking is not allowed in the office*).

alp /alp/ ▶ **noun** **1** a high mountain. **2** (**the Alps**) a high range of mountains in Switzerland and adjoining countries.
– ORIGIN Greek *Alpeis.*

al·pac·a /alˈpakə/ ▶ **noun** (pl. same or **alpacas**) **1** a long-haired domesticated South American mammal related to the llama. **2** the wool of the alpaca.
– ORIGIN Spanish.

al·pen·stock /ˈalpənˌstäk/ ▶ **noun** a long iron-tipped stick used by walkers in hilly country.
– ORIGIN German, 'Alp stick.'

al·pha /ˈalfə/ ▶ **noun** the first letter of the Greek alphabet (□, □), represented as 'a'. ▶ **adjective** referring to the dominant animal or person in a group: *an alpha male.*
– PHRASES **alpha and omega** the beginning and the end.

al·pha·bet /ˈalfəˌbet, -bit/ ▶ **noun** an ordered set of letters or symbols used to represent the basic speech sounds of a language.
– ORIGIN from Greek *alpha* and *bēta*, the first two letters of the Greek alphabet.

al·pha·bet·i·cal /ˌalfəˈbetikəl/ ▶ **adjective** in the order of the letters of the alphabet.
– DERIVATIVES **al·pha·bet·ic** adjective **al·pha·bet·i·cal·ly** adverb.

al·pha·bet·ize /ˈalfəbiˌtīz/ ▶ **verb** arrange words in alphabetical order.

al·pha·nu·mer·ic /ˌalfən(y)o͞oˈmerik/ ▶ **adjective** made up of or using both letters and numerals.

al·pha par·ti·cle ▶ **noun** Physics a helium nucleus, especially as given out by some radioactive substances.

al·pine /ˈalˌpīn/ ▶ **adjective** **1** relating to or found on high mountains. **2** (**Alpine**) relating to the Alps. ▶ **noun** a plant that grows on high mountains.

al·read·y /ôlˈredē/ ▶ **adverb** **1** before the time in question. **2** as surprisingly soon or early as this: *you aren't leaving already?*

al·right /ôl'rīt/ ▶ **adjective, adverb, & exclamation** variant spelling of **ALL RIGHT**.

USAGE

Many people consider the spelling **alright** (rather than **all right**) to be unacceptable in formal writing, even though other single-word forms such as **altogether** have long been accepted as standard.

Al·sa·tian /al'sāsHən/ ▶ **noun** Brit. a German shepherd dog.
– ORIGIN Latin, 'Alsace,' a region of NE France.

al·so /'ôlsō/ ▶ **adverb** in addition.

– SYNONYMS **too,** as well, besides, in addition, additionally, furthermore, further, moreover, into the bargain, on top (of that), what's more, to boot.

– ORIGIN Old English.

al·so-ran ▶ **noun** a person who is unsuccessful in a race or contest.

alt. /alt/ ▶ **prefix** referring to a version of something that is intended as a challenge to the traditional version: *an alt.country band.*
– ORIGIN abbreviation of **ALTERNATIVE**, influenced by the *alt.*prefix of some Usenet newsgroups.

al·tar /'ôltər/ ▶ **noun 1** the table in a Christian church at which the bread and wine are consecrated in communion services. **2** a table or other structure on which religious offerings are made.
– ORIGIN Latin, from *altus* 'high.'

al·tar boy ▶ **noun** a boy who assists a priest during a service.

al·tar·piece /'ôltər,pēs/ ▶ **noun** a painting or other work of art set above and behind an altar.

al·ter /'ôltər/ ▶ **verb** make or become different: *she had to alter her vacation plans.*

– SYNONYMS **change,** make/become different, adjust, adapt, amend, modify, revise, rework, redo, transform; informal tweak.

– ORIGIN from Latin *alter* 'other.'

al·ter·a·tion /,ôltə'rāsHən/ ▶ **noun** a change or modification.

– SYNONYMS **change,** adjustment, adaptation, modification, amendment, transformation.

al·ter·ca·tion /,ôltər'kāsHən/ ▶ **noun** a noisy disagreement.
– ORIGIN Latin.

al·ter e·go /'altər 'ēgō, 'ôltər 'ēgō/ ▶ **noun 1** another side to someone's normal personality. **2** a close friend who is very like oneself.
– ORIGIN Latin, 'other self.'

al·ter·nate ▶ **verb** /'ôltər,nāt/ **1** occur or do in turn repeatedly: *the narrative alternates personal observation with historical fact.* **2** change repeatedly between two contrasting states: *his mood alternated between aggression and morose despair.*

– SYNONYMS **1 be interspersed,** follow one another, take turns, take it in turns, oscillate, seesaw. **2 rotate,** swap, exchange, interchange.

▶ **adjective** /'ôltərnit/ **1** every other: *the service runs on alternate days.* **2** (of two things) each following and succeeded by the other in a regular pattern: *put alternate layers of potatoes and fish in the casserole.* **3** another term for **ALTERNATIVE**.

– SYNONYMS **every other,** every second, alternating.

– DERIVATIVES **al·ter·nate·ly** /-nitlē/ adverb **al·ter·na·tion** /,ôltər'nāsHən/ noun.
– ORIGIN Latin *alternare* 'do by turns.'

USAGE

The use of **alternate** to mean **alternative** (as in *we will need to find alternate sources of fuel*) is common in American English, although it is still regarded as incorrect by many people in Britain.

al·ter·nate an·gles ▶ **plural noun** two equal angles on opposite sides of a line crossing two parallel lines.

al·ter·nat·ing cur·rent ▶ **noun** an electric current that reverses its direction many times a second. Compare with **DIRECT CURRENT**.

al·ter·na·tive /ôl'tərnətiv/ ▶ **adjective 1** (of one or more things) available as another possibility. **2** differing from the usual or traditional form of something: *people attracted to alternative lifestyles.*

– SYNONYMS **1 different,** other, second, substitute, alternate, replacement, standby, emergency, reserve, backup, auxiliary, fallback. **2 unorthodox,** unconventional, nonconformist, radical, revolutionary, avant-garde; informal offbeat, way-out.

▶ **noun** one of two or more available possibilities.

– SYNONYMS **(other) option,** (other) choice, substitute, replacement.

– DERIVATIVES **al·ter·na·tive·ly** adverb.

USAGE

Some people say that you can have a maximum of only two alternatives (because the word **alternative** comes from Latin *alter* 'other of two'). References to more than two alternatives are, however, normal in modern standard English.

al·ter·na·tive en·er·gy ▶ **noun** energy produced in ways that do not use up natural resources or harm the environment.

al·ter·na·tive med·i·cine ▶ **noun** medical treatment that does not follow the usual practices of Western medicine, e.g., herbalism.

al·ter·na·tor /'ôltər,nātər/ ▶ **noun** a dynamo that generates an alternating current.

al·though /ôl'<u>TH</u>ō/ ▶ **conjunction 1** in spite of the fact that. **2** however; but.

al·tim·e·ter /al'timitər/ ▶ **noun** an instrument that indicates the altitude reached by something, especially an aircraft.

al·ti·pla·no /alti'plänō/ ▶ **noun** (pl. **altiplanos**) a broad, high, level region in central South America.
– ORIGIN Spanish.

al·ti·tude /'alti,t(y)o͞od/ ▶ **noun** the height of an object or point above sea level or ground level.
– ORIGIN from Latin *altus* 'high.'

al·ti·tude sick·ness ▶ **noun** illness resulting from a shortage of oxygen in places that are high above sea or ground level.

al·to /'altō/ ▶ **noun** (pl. **altos**) the highest adult male or lowest female singing voice. ▶ **adjective** referring to the second or third highest of a family of instruments: *an alto sax.*
– ORIGIN from Italian *alto canto* 'high song.'

al·to·geth·er /ˌôltəˈgeT͟Hər/ ▸ **adverb 1** completely. **2** in total. **3** on the whole.

– SYNONYMS **1 completely,** totally, entirely, absolutely, wholly, fully, thoroughly, utterly, perfectly, one hundred percent, in all respects. **2 in all,** all told, in total.

– PHRASES **in the altogether** informal naked.

USAGE

Note that **altogether** and **all together** do not mean the same thing. **Altogether** means *in total* (*there are six bedrooms altogether*), whereas **all together** means *all in one place* (*it was good to have a group of friends all together*) or *all at once* (*they came in all together*).

al·tru·ism /ˈaltro͞oˌizəm/ ▸ **noun** unselfish concern for the needs and well-being of other people.
– DERIVATIVES **al·tru·ist** noun **al·tru·is·tic** /ˌaltro͞oˈistik/ adjective **al·tru·is·ti·cal·ly** /ˌaltro͞oˈistikəlē/ adverb.
– ORIGIN from Italian *altrui* 'somebody else.'

a·lum /ˈaləm/ ▸ **noun** a crystalline compound of aluminum and potassium, used in dyeing and tanning animal skin.
– ORIGIN Latin *alumen.*

a·lu·mi·na /əˈlo͞omənə/ ▸ **noun** aluminum oxide, a chemical compound found in many types of rock.
– ORIGIN Latin *alumen* 'alum.'

a·lu·mi·nize /əˈlo͞oməˌnīz/ ▸ **verb** coat something with aluminum.

al·u·mi·num /əˈlo͞omənəm/ (Brit **aluminium** /ˌalyəˈminēəm/) ▸ **noun** a lightweight silvery-gray metallic element that is resistant to rust and corrosion.

a·lum·nus /əˈləmnəs/ ▸ **noun** (pl. **alumni** /-nī, -nē/; fem. **alumna** /əˈləmnə/, pl. **alumnae** /-nī, -nē/) a former student of a particular school, college, or university.
– ORIGIN Latin, 'pupil.'

al·ve·o·lus /alˈvēələs/ ▸ **noun** (pl. **alveoli** /-ˌlī/) **1** any of the many tiny air sacs in the lungs. **2** the bony socket for the root of a tooth.
– DERIVATIVES **al·ve·o·lar** /alˈvēələr/ adjective.
– ORIGIN Latin, 'small cavity.'

al·ways /ˈôlˌwāz, -wēz/ ▸ **adverb 1** on all occasions; at all times. **2** forever. **3** repeatedly. **4** failing all else.

– SYNONYMS **1** *he's always late* **every time,** all the time, without fail, consistently, invariably, regularly, habitually, unfailingly. **2** *she's always complaining* **continually,** continuously, constantly, forever, all the time, day and night; informal 24-7. **3** *the place will always be dear to me* **forever,** for good, for evermore, for ever and ever, until the end of time, eternally.
– ANTONYMS never, seldom.

a·lys·sum /əˈlisəm/ ▸ **noun** (pl. **alyssums**) a plant with small flowers, most commonly white.
– ORIGIN Greek *alusson.*

Alz·hei·mer's dis·ease /ˈältsˌhīmərz, ˈôlts-, ˈälz-, ˈôlz-/ ▸ **noun** a disorder that causes progressive mental deterioration, typically affecting older people.
– ORIGIN named after the German neurologist Alois *Alzheimer.*

AM ▸ **abbreviation** amplitude modulation.

Am ▸ **symbol** the chemical element americium.

am /am/ first person singular present of **BE**.

a.m. ▸ **abbreviation** before noon.
– ORIGIN from Latin *ante meridiem.*

AMA ▸ **abbreviation** American Medical Association.

a·mal·gam /əˈmalgəm/ ▸ **noun 1** a mixture or blend. **2** an alloy of mercury with another metal, especially one used for dental fillings.
– ORIGIN Greek *malagma* 'an emollient.'

a·mal·ga·mate /əˈmalgəˌmāt/ ▸ **verb 1** combine or unite to form one organization or structure: *the paper later amalgamated with other publications.* **2** mix a metal with mercury to make an alloy.

– SYNONYMS **combine,** merge, unite, join, fuse, blend, meld, mix, incorporate.
– ANTONYMS separate.

– DERIVATIVES **a·mal·ga·ma·tion** /əˌmalgəˈmāSHən/ noun.

a·man·u·en·sis /əˌmanyo͞oˈensis/ ▸ **noun** (pl. **amanuenses** /-ˌsēz/) a writer's assistant.
– ORIGIN Latin, from *servus a manu* 'slave at handwriting, secretary.'

am·a·ranth /ˈaməˌranTH/ ▸ **noun** a plant of a family that includes love-lies-bleeding.
– ORIGIN from Greek *amarantos* 'not fading.'

am·a·ret·to /ˌaməˈretō, ˌäm-/ ▸ **noun** a brown almond-flavored Italian liqueur.

am·a·ryl·lis /ˌaməˈrilis/ ▸ **noun** a plant with large trumpet-shaped flowers.
– ORIGIN Greek *Amarullis,* a name for a country girl in pastoral poetry.

a·mass /əˈmas/ ▸ **verb** build up over time: *he amassed a fortune of more than $13 million.*

– SYNONYMS **gather,** collect, assemble, accumulate, stockpile, hoard.

– ORIGIN Latin *amassare.*

am·a·teur /ˈamətər, -ˌtər, -ˌCHo͝or, -CHər/ ▸ **noun 1** a person who takes part in a sport or other activity for pleasure, rather than as a profession or job. **2** a person who is not skilled at a particular activity.

– SYNONYMS **nonprofessional,** nonspecialist, layman, layperson, dilettante, dabbler.

▸ **adjective 1** nonprofessional: *an amateur photographer.* **2** done in an unskillful way.

– SYNONYMS **nonprofessional,** unpaid, nonspecialist, lay, unqualified, inexperienced.
– ANTONYMS professional, expert.

– DERIVATIVES **am·a·teur·ism** noun.
– ORIGIN French, 'lover.'

am·a·teur·ish /ˌaməˈtərisH, -ˈt(y)o͝or-, -ˈCHo͝or-/ ▸ **adjective** not done or made skillfully.

– SYNONYMS **incompetent,** inept, inexpert, unprofessional, amateur, clumsy, crude, second-rate.

am·a·to·ry /ˈaməˌtôrē/ ▸ **adjective** relating to sexual love or desire.
– ORIGIN from Latin *amare* 'to love.'

a·maze /əˈmāz/ ▸ **verb** surprise someone very much.

– SYNONYMS **1 astonish,** astound, surprise, stun, stagger, nonplus, shock, startle, stop someone in their tracks, leave open-mouthed, dumbfound; informal bowl over, flabbergast. **2** (as adj. **amazed**) thunderstruck, at a loss for words, speechless.

– ORIGIN Old English.

a·maze·ment /əˈmāzmənt/ ▸ **noun** a feeling of great surprise or wonder.

– SYNONYMS **astonishment,** surprise, shock, speechlessness, awe, wonder.

a·maz·ing /ə'māziNG/ ▶ **adjective 1** very surprising: *it's amazing how quickly she adapted.* **2** informal very good or impressive.

– SYNONYMS **astonishing,** astounding, surprising, stunning, staggering, breathtaking, awesome, awe-inspiring, sensational, remarkable, spectacular, stupendous, phenomenal, extraordinary, incredible, unbelievable; informal mind-blowing; literary wondrous.

– DERIVATIVES **a·maz·ing·ly** adverb.

Am·a·zon /'amə,zän, -zən/ ▶ **noun 1** (in Greek mythology) a member of a race of female warriors. **2** a very tall, strong woman.
– ORIGIN Greek *Amazōn.*

Am·a·zo·ni·an /,amə'zōnēən/ ▶ **adjective 1** relating to the Amazon River. **2** (of a woman) very tall and strong.

am·bas·sa·dor /am'basədər, -,dôr/ ▶ **noun 1** a diplomat sent by a government as its permanent representative in a foreign country. **2** a person who represents or promotes something: *he is a great ambassador for football.*

– SYNONYMS **envoy,** emissary, representative, diplomat, minister, consul, attaché.

– DERIVATIVES **am·bas·sa·do·ri·al** /am,basə'dôrēəl/ adjective.
– ORIGIN Italian *ambasciator.*

am·ber /'ambər/ ▶ **noun 1** a hard translucent yellowish substance formed from the fossilized resin of certain ancient trees, used in jewelry. **2** a honey-yellow color.
– ORIGIN Old French *ambre.*

am·ber·gris /'ambər,gris, -,grē(s)/ ▶ **noun** a waxy substance produced by sperm whales, used in perfume manufacture.
– ORIGIN from Old French *ambre gris* 'gray amber.'

am·bi·dex·trous /,ambi'dekst(ə)rəs/ ▶ **adjective** able to use the right and left hands equally well.
– ORIGIN from Latin *ambi-* 'on both sides' + *dexter* 'right-handed.'

am·bi·ence /'ambēəns/ (also **ambiance**) ▶ **noun** the character and atmosphere of a place: *the gentle color scheme creates a relaxing ambience.*

– SYNONYMS **atmosphere,** air, aura, climate, mood, feel, feeling, vibrations, character, quality, impression, flavor, look, tone; informal vibe(s).

am·bi·ent /'ambēənt/ ▶ **adjective 1** relating to the surrounding area: *the ambient temperature.* **2** referring to a style of electronic instrumental music with no persistent beat, used to create a relaxed atmosphere.
– ORIGIN Latin, from *ambire* 'go around.'

am·bi·gu·i·ty /,ambi'gyo͞o-itē/ ▶ **noun** (pl. **ambiguities**) the quality of having more than one possible meaning or interpretation.

am·big·u·ous /am'bigyo͞oəs/ ▶ **adjective 1** (of language) having more than one possible meaning. **2** not clear or decided: *a European nation whose position had long been ambiguous.*

– SYNONYMS **vague,** unclear, ambivalent, double-edged, equivocal, inconclusive, enigmatic, cryptic.
– ANTONYMS clear.

– DERIVATIVES **am·big·u·ous·ly** adverb.
– ORIGIN Latin *ambiguus* 'doubtful.'

am·bit /'ambit/ ▶ **noun** the scope or extent of something: *the need to bring the activity within the ambit of federal law.*
– ORIGIN Latin *ambitus* 'circuit.'

am·bi·tion /am'bisHən/ ▶ **noun 1** a strong desire to do or achieve something: *her burning ambition was to be world champion.* **2** the desire or determination to become successful or rich.

– SYNONYMS **1 drive,** determination, enterprise, initiative, eagerness, motivation, a sense of purpose; informal get-up-and-go. **2 aspiration,** desire, dream, intention, goal, aim, objective, plan.

– ORIGIN from Latin *ambire* 'go around (canvassing for votes).'

am·bi·tious /am'bisHəs/ ▶ **adjective 1** having or showing a determination to succeed. **2** requiring a great deal of effort, time, or money to succeed: *an ambitious six-year development plan.*

– SYNONYMS **1 aspiring,** determined, motivated, energetic, committed, purposeful, power-hungry; informal go-ahead, go-getting. **2 challenging,** exacting, demanding, formidable, difficult, hard, tough.

– DERIVATIVES **am·bi·tious·ly** adverb.

am·biv·a·lent /am'bivələnt/ ▶ **adjective** having mixed feelings about something or someone.
– DERIVATIVES **am·biv·a·lence** noun **am·biv·a·lent·ly** adverb.
– ORIGIN from Latin *ambi-* 'on both sides' + *valere* 'be worth.'

am·ble /'ambəl/ ▶ **verb** walk at a leisurely pace. ▶ **noun** a leisurely walk.
– ORIGIN Latin *ambulare* 'to walk.'

am·bro·sia /am'brōzH(ē)ə/ ▶ **noun 1** Greek & Roman Mythology the food of the gods. **2** something that tastes or smells very pleasant.
– DERIVATIVES **am·bro·sial** adjective.
– ORIGIN Greek, 'elixir of life.'

am·bu·lance /'ambyələns/ ▶ **noun** a vehicle equipped for taking sick or injured people to and from a hospital.
– ORIGIN French, from Latin *ambulare* 'walk.'

am·bu·lance chas·er ▶ **noun** derogatory a lawyer who encourages accident victims to make claims for damages in a court of law.

am·bu·lant /'ambyələnt/ ▶ **adjective** Medicine able to walk around; not confined to bed.

am·bu·la·to·ry /'ambyələ,tôrē/ ▶ **adjective 1** relating to walking or able to walk: *ambulatory patients.* **2** movable; mobile: *an ambulatory data recorder.* ▶ **noun** (pl. **ambulatories**) an aisle or cloister in a church or monastery.

am·bush /'am,bo͝osH/ ▶ **noun** a surprise attack made by people lying in wait in a concealed position. ▶ **verb** attack a person or group of people from a concealed position.

– SYNONYMS **surprise,** waylay, trap, ensnare, attack, jump on, pounce on, bushwhack.

– ORIGIN Old French *embusche,* from a Latin word meaning 'to place in a wood.'

a·me·ba /ə'mēbə/ (also chiefly Brit. **amoeba**) ▶ **noun** (pl. **amebas** or **amebae**) a single-celled animal that catches food and moves by extending fingerlike projections of protoplasm.
– DERIVATIVES **a·me·bic** /-bik/ adjective **a·me·boid** /-boid/ adjective.
– ORIGIN from Greek *amoibē* 'change, alternation.'

a·me·lio·rate /ə'mēlyə,rāt, ə'mēlēə-/ ▶ **verb** formal make something that is bad or unsatisfactory better.
– DERIVATIVES **a·me·lio·ra·tion** /ə,mēlyə'rāsHən/ noun.
– ORIGIN Latin *meliorare.*

a·men /ä'men, ā'men/ ▶ **exclamation** said at the end of a prayer or hymn, meaning 'so be it'.
– ORIGIN Greek, from a Hebrew word meaning 'truth, certainty.'

a·me·na·ble /ə'mēnəbəl, ə'men-/ ▶ **adjective 1** willing to cooperate or be persuaded to do something. **2** (**amenable to**) able to be affected by: *conditions that are amenable to medical intervention.*
– DERIVATIVES **a·me·na·bil·i·ty** /ə,mēnə'bilitē, ə,men-/ noun.
– ORIGIN Old French *amener* 'bring to.'

a·mend /ə'mend/ ▶ **verb** make small changes or improvements to a document, proposal, etc.

– SYNONYMS **revise,** alter, change, modify, adapt, adjust, edit, rewrite, redraft, rephrase, reword.

– ORIGIN Latin *emendare* 'to correct.'

a·mend·ment /ə'men(d)mənt/ ▶ **noun 1** a small change or improvement made to a document, proposal, etc. **2** (**Amendment**) an article added to the US Constitution.

a·mends /ə'mendz/ ▶ **plural noun** (in phrase **make amends**) do something to show that one regrets a wrong or unfair action.

– SYNONYMS **1** *he's obviously trying to* ***make amends for*** *what he's done* **make up for,** atone for, pay for, make good. **2** *it's up to you to* ***make amends to*** *those you've hurt* **compensate,** recompense, indemnify, make it up to.

a·men·i·ty /ə'menitē, ə'mē-/ ▶ **noun** (pl. **amenities**) a useful or desirable feature of a place: *a convenient location, close to all local amenities.*

– SYNONYMS **facility,** service, resource, convenience, comfort.

– ORIGIN from Latin *amoenus* 'pleasant.'

a·men·or·rhe·a /ā,menə'rēə/ ▶ **noun** the abnormal absence of menstrual periods.
– ORIGIN Latin, from Greek *men* 'month' and *rhein* 'flow.'

Am·er·a·sian /,amər'āzʜən/ ▶ **adjective** having one American and one Asian parent. ▶ **noun** an Amerasian person.

A·mer·i·can /ə'merikən/ ▶ **adjective** relating to the US or to the continents of America. ▶ **noun** a person from the US or any of the countries of North, South, or Central America.
– DERIVATIVES **A·mer·i·can·ize** /ə'merikə,nīz/ verb.

A·mer·i·ca·na /ə,meri'känə, -'kanə/ ▶ **plural noun** things associated with the US.

A·mer·i·can dream ▶ **noun** the ideal of equality of opportunity associated with the US.

A·mer·i·can In·di·an ▶ **noun** a member of the native peoples of America.

USAGE

American Indian has been steadily replaced by the term **Native American**, especially in official contexts. However, **American Indian** is still widespread in general use and is generally acceptable to American Indians themselves.

A·mer·i·can·ism /ə'merikə,nizəm/ ▶ **noun** a word or phrase used or originating in the US.

am·er·i·ci·um /amə'risʜēəm/ ▶ **noun** a radioactive metallic chemical element made by high-energy atomic collisions.
– ORIGIN from *America*, where it was first made.

Am·er·in·di·an /,amə'rindēən/ (also **Amerind** /'amərind/) ▶ **noun & adjective** another term for **AMERICAN INDIAN**.

am·e·thyst /'aməTʜəst/ ▶ **noun** a precious stone consisting of a violet or purple variety of quartz.
– ORIGIN Greek *amethustos* 'not drunken' (because the stone was believed to prevent drunkenness).

Am·har·ic /am'harik/ ▶ **noun** the Semitic official language of Ethiopia.
– ORIGIN from *Amhara*, a region of Ethiopia.

a·mi·a·ble /'āmēəbəl/ ▶ **adjective** friendly and pleasant.

– SYNONYMS **friendly,** affable, amicable, cordial, good-natured, nice, pleasant, agreeable, likable, genial, good-humored, companionable.
– ANTONYMS unfriendly, disagreeable.

– DERIVATIVES **a·mi·a·bil·i·ty** /,āmēə'bilitē/ noun **a·mi·a·bly** adverb.
– ORIGIN Old French.

am·i·ca·ble /'amikəbəl/ ▶ **adjective** friendly and without disagreement or dispute: *an amicable working relationship.*
– DERIVATIVES **am·i·ca·bly** adverb.
– ORIGIN from Latin *amicus* 'friend.'

am·ice /'amis/ ▶ **noun** a white cloth worn on the neck and shoulders by a priest celebrating Holy Communion.
– ORIGIN Latin.

a·mi·cus (in full **amicus curiae** /'kyo͝orē,ī, -ē,ē/) ▶ **noun** (pl. **amici** /ə'mēkē, ə'mīkī/, **amici curiae**) an impartial adviser, often voluntary, to a court of law in a particular case.
– ORIGIN from Latin *amicus curiae* 'friend of the court.'

a·mid /ə'mid/ (or **amidst**) ▶ **preposition** surrounded by; in the middle of.

am·ide /'amīd, -id/ ▶ **noun** Chemistry **1** an organic compound containing the group $-C(O)NH_2$. **2** a saltlike compound containing the anion NH_2^-.
– ORIGIN from **AMMONIA**.

a·mid·ships /ə'mid,sʜips/ ▶ **adverb & adjective** in the middle of a ship.

a·mi·go /ə'mēgō/ ▶ **noun** (pl. **amigos**) informal a friend.
– ORIGIN Spanish.

a·mine /ə'mēn, 'amēn/ ▶ **noun** Chemistry an organic compound obtained from ammonia.

a·mi·no ac·id /ə'mēnō/ ▶ **noun** any of about twenty organic compounds that form the basic constituents of proteins.

a·mir /ə'mi(ə)r/ ▶ **noun** variant spelling of **EMIR**.

A·mish /'ämisʜ/ ▶ **plural noun** a strict Protestant sect living mainly in the US states of Pennsylvania and Ohio.
– ORIGIN from the name of the Swiss preacher Jakob *Amman.*

a·miss /ə'mis/ ▶ **adjective** not quite right: *he didn't notice that anything was amiss.* ▶ **adverb** wrongly or badly: *everything had gone amiss.*
– PHRASES **take something amiss** be offended by something that is said.
– ORIGIN probably from Old Norse, 'so as to miss.'

am·i·ty /'amitē/ ▶ **noun** formal friendly relations between people or countries.
– ORIGIN Old French *amitie*, from Latin *amicus* 'friend.'

am·me·ter /'a(m),mētər/ ▶ **noun** an instrument for measuring electric current in amperes.

am·mo /'amō/ ▶ **noun** informal ammunition.

am·mo·nia /ə'mōnyə, -nēə/ ▶ **noun** a colorless, strong-smelling gas that forms an alkaline solution in water, and that is used as a cleaning fluid.
– ORIGIN from *sal ammoniac*, a substance obtained near the temple of Jupiter *Ammon* in Egypt.

am·mo·nite /'amə͵nīt/ ▶ **noun** an extinct sea creature with a spiral shell, found as a fossil.
– ORIGIN from Latin *cornu Ammonis* 'horn of Ammon,' from the fossil's resemblance to the ram's horn associated with the god Jupiter Ammon.

am·mo·ni·um /ə'mōnēəm/ ▶ **noun** Chemistry the ion NH_4^+, present in solutions of ammonia and in salts obtained from ammonia.

am·mo·noid /'amə͵noid/ ▶ **noun** an extinct cephalopod mollusk with a flat-coiled spiral shell, found commonly as a fossil in marine deposits.

am·mu·ni·tion /͵amyə'nisʜən/ ▶ **noun** **1** a supply of bullets and shells. **2** points used to support one's case in an argument or debate: *the analysis provided vital ammunition to anti-nuclear campaigners*.
– ORIGIN from French *la munition* 'the fortification.'

am·ne·sia /am'nēzʜə/ ▶ **noun** loss of memory.
– DERIVATIVES **am·ne·si·ac** /am'nēzē͵ak, -zʜē͵ak/ noun & adjective.
– ORIGIN Greek, 'forgetfulness.'

am·nes·ty /'amnistē/ ▶ **noun** (pl. **amnesties**) **1** an official pardon given to people convicted of political offenses. **2** a period during which people admitting to particular offenses are not punished: *there will be no amnesty for people who have not paid the tax*.

– SYNONYMS **pardon,** reprieve, forgiveness, release, discharge; informal let-off.

– ORIGIN Greek *amnēstia* 'forgetfulness.'

am·ni·o·cen·te·sis /͵amnē-ōsen'tēsis/ ▶ **noun** (pl. **amniocenteses** /-sēz/) a medical procedure in which a sample of amniotic fluid is taken from a pregnant woman's uterus in order to check for abnormalities in the fetus.
– ORIGIN from **AMNION** + Greek *kentēsis* 'pricking.'

am·ni·on /'amnē͵än, -ən/ ▶ **noun** (pl. **amnions** or **amnia**) the innermost membrane surrounding an embryo.
– DERIVATIVES **am·ni·ot·ic** /͵amnē'ätik/ adjective.
– ORIGIN Greek, 'caul.'

am·ni·ot·ic flu·id /͵amnē'ätik/ ▶ **noun** the fluid surrounding a fetus before birth.

a·moe·ba, etc. /ə'mēbə/ ▶ **noun** (pl. **amoebas** or **amoebae** /-bē/) chiefly British spelling of **AMEBA**, etc.

a·mok /ə'mək, ə'mäk/ (also **amuck**) ▶ **adverb** (in phrase **run amok**) behave in an uncontrolled and disorderly way.
– ORIGIN Malay, 'rushing in a frenzy.'

a·mong /ə'məɴɢ/ (chiefly Brit. also **amongst**) ▶ **preposition** **1** surrounded by; in the middle of. **2** included or occurring in. **3** shared by; between.
– ORIGIN Old English.

a·mon·til·la·do /ə͵mäntl'ädō, -tə'yädō/ ▶ **noun** (pl. **amontillados**) a medium dry sherry.
– ORIGIN Spanish, from *Montilla*, a town in southern Spain.

a·mor·al /ā'môrəl/ ▶ **adjective** without morals; not concerned about right or wrong.
– DERIVATIVES **a·mo·ral·i·ty** /͵āmə'ralitē/ noun.

USAGE

Amoral does not mean the same as **immoral**: while **immoral** means 'not following accepted standards of morality,' **amoral** means 'without morals'.

am·o·rous /'amərəs/ ▶ **adjective** showing or feeling sexual desire.

– SYNONYMS **lustful,** sexual, erotic, amatory, ardent, passionate, impassioned; in love, enamored, lovesick; informal lovey-dovey, kissy, smoochy, hot.
– ANTONYMS unloving.

– DERIVATIVES **am·o·rous·ly** adverb.
– ORIGIN from Latin *amor* 'love.'

a·mor·phous /ə'môrfəs/ ▶ **adjective** without a definite shape or form.
– ORIGIN Greek *amorphos*.

am·or·tize /'amər͵tīz/ ▶ **verb** Finance gradually pay off a debt.
– DERIVATIVES **am·or·ti·za·tion** /͵amərti'zāsʜən, ə͵môrti-/ noun.
– ORIGIN Old French *amortir*.

a·mount /ə'mount/ ▶ **noun** **1** the total number, size, or value of something. **2** a quantity: *add a small amount of water*.

– SYNONYMS **quantity,** number, total, aggregate, sum, quota, size, mass, weight, volume.

▶ **verb** (**amount to**) **1** add up to a total. **2** be the equivalent of: *a degree of carelessness that amounted to gross negligence*.

– SYNONYMS **1 add up to,** come to, run to. **2 constitute,** comprise, be tantamount to.

– ORIGIN from Old French *amont* 'upward.'

a·mour /ə'mo͝or, ä'mo͝or/ ▶ **noun** a secret love affair.
– ORIGIN from Latin *amor* 'love.'

amp¹ /amp/ ▶ **noun** short for **AMPERE**.

amp² ▶ **noun** informal short for **AMPLIFIER**. ▶ **verb** (**amp up**) informal **1** make a quality, feeling, etc., more intense. **2** make a person very excited or energetic through, or as if through, the consumption of amphetamines or another stimulant.

am·per·age /'amp(ə)rij/ ▶ **noun** the strength of an electric current, measured in amperes.

am·pere /'am͵pi(ə)r/ ▶ **noun** the base unit of electric current in the SI system.
– ORIGIN named after the French physicist André-Marie *Ampère*.

am·per·sand /'ampər͵sand/ ▶ **noun** the sign &, standing for *and*.
– ORIGIN from *and per se and*, '& by itself is *and*,' chanted as an aid to learning the sign.

am·phet·a·mine /am'fetə͵mēn, -min/ ▶ **noun** a drug used illegally as a stimulant.
– ORIGIN from its chemical name.

am·phib·i·an /am'fibēən/ ▶ **noun** a cold-blooded animal such as a frog or toad that lives in water when young and on land as an adult.
– ORIGIN from Greek *amphi* 'both' + *bios* 'life.'

am·phib·i·ous /am'fibēəs/ ▶ **adjective** **1** living in or suited for both land and water. **2** (of a military operation) involving forces landing at a place from the sea.

am·phi·the·a·ter /'amfə͵ᴛʜēətər/ (also **amphitheatre**) ▶ **noun** a round building consisting of tiers of seats

surrounding a central space for dramatic or sporting events.
– ORIGIN from Greek *amphi* 'on both sides' + *theatron* 'theater.'

am·pho·ra /'amfərə/ ▸ **noun** (pl. **amphorae** /-ˌrē/ or **amphoras**) an ancient Greek or Roman jar with two handles and a narrow neck.
– ORIGIN Latin, from Greek *amphi-* 'on both sides' + *phoreus* 'bearer.'

am·pi·cil·lin /ˌampi'silin/ ▸ **noun** Medicine a semisynthetic form of penicillin used chiefly to treat infections of the urinary and respiratory tracts.

am·ple /'ampəl/ ▸ **adjective 1** enough or more than enough; plentiful: *there was ample room for storage.* **2** large: *her ample bosom.*

– SYNONYMS **1 enough,** sufficient, adequate, plenty of, more than enough, abundant, copious, profuse, lavish, liberal, generous; informal galore. **2 spacious,** full, capacious, roomy, voluminous, loose-fitting, baggy, sloppy.
– ANTONYMS insufficient.

– DERIVATIVES **am·ply** /-p(ə)lē/ adverb.
– ORIGIN Latin *amplus*.

am·pli·fi·er /'ampləˌfīər/ ▸ **noun** an electronic device for increasing the strength of electrical signals.

am·pli·fy /'ampləˌfī/ ▸ **verb** (**amplifies, amplifying, amplified**) **1** increase the strength of sound or electrical signals. **2** add details to a story or statement.

– SYNONYMS **1 make louder,** turn up, increase, raise. **2 expand,** enlarge on, elaborate on, develop, flesh out.

– DERIVATIVES **am·pli·fi·ca·tion** /ˌampləfi'kāsʜən/ noun.
– ORIGIN Latin *amplificare*.

am·pli·tude /'ampliˌt(y)o͞od/ ▸ **noun 1** Physics the maximum amount by which an alternating current or electromagnetic wave can vary from its average level. **2** great size or extent.

am·pli·tude mod·u·la·tion ▸ **noun** the modification of a radio wave by varying its amplitude, used as a method of broadcasting an audio signal.

am·poule /'amˌp(y)o͞ol/ (also **ampule** or **ampul**) ▸ **noun** a small sealed glass capsule that contains a measured quantity of liquid ready for an injection.
– ORIGIN Latin *ampulla* 'flask.'

am·pul·la /am'po͝olə, -'pələ/ ▸ **noun** (pl. **ampullae** /-lē/) **1** a roughly spherical ancient Roman flask with two handles. **2** a flask holding the consecrated oil in a church.
– ORIGIN Latin.

am·pu·tate /'ampyəˌtāt/ ▸ **verb** cut off a limb in a surgical operation.
– DERIVATIVES **am·pu·ta·tion** /ˌampyə'tāsʜən/ noun.
– ORIGIN Latin *amputare*.

am·pu·tee /ˌampyə'tē/ ▸ **noun** a person who has had a limb amputated.

Am·trak /'amˌtrak/ ▸ **noun** trademark the national passenger railroad service in the US, a government-subsidized corporation.

a·muck /ə'mək/ ▸ **adverb** variant spelling of **AMOK**.

am·u·let /'amyəlit/ ▸ **noun** an ornament or small piece of jewelry worn as protection against evil, illness, or danger.
– ORIGIN Latin *amuletum*.

a·muse /ə'myo͞oz/ ▸ **verb 1** make someone laugh or smile. **2** provide someone with an enjoyable or interesting activity: *he amused himself by writing poetry.*

– SYNONYMS **1 make someone laugh,** entertain, delight, divert, cheer (up), please, charm, tickle; informal crack up. **2 occupy,** engage, busy, absorb, engross, entertain.
– ANTONYMS bore.

– DERIVATIVES **a·mused** adjective.
– ORIGIN Old French *amuser* 'entertain, deceive.'

a·muse·ment /ə'myo͞ozmənt/ ▸ **noun 1** the state or experience of finding something funny. **2** something that causes laughter or provides entertainment.

– SYNONYMS **1 mirth,** merriment, hilarity, glee, delight. **2 entertainment,** pleasure, leisure, relaxation, fun, enjoyment, interest. **3 activity,** entertainment, diversion, pastime, recreation, game, sport.

a·muse·ment park ▸ **noun** a large outdoor area with fairground rides and other entertainments.

a·mus·ing /ə'myo͞ozɪɴɢ/ ▸ **adjective** causing laughter or providing entertainment.

– SYNONYMS **funny,** comical, humorous, lighthearted, jocular, witty, droll, entertaining, diverting.

am·yl·ase /'aməˌlās, -ˌlāz/ ▸ **noun** Biochemistry an enzyme found in saliva that converts starch into sugars.

am·yl ni·trite /'aməl 'nītrīt/ ▸ **noun** a liquid used in medicine to expand blood vessels and sometimes inhaled for its stimulant effect on the body.

an /an/ ▸ **determiner** the form of the indefinite article 'a' used before words beginning with a vowel sound.

USAGE

It is better to use **a** rather than **an** before words beginning with an initial **h** that is sounded, such as *historical* and *hotel*. **An** was common in the 18th and 19th centuries because the initial **h** in such words was then often not pronounced.

an- ▸ **prefix** variant spelling of **A-** before a vowel (as in *anemia*).

An·a·bap·tist /ˌanə'bapˌtist/ ▸ **noun** a member of a Protestant religious group believing that only adults should be baptized.
– ORIGIN from Greek *ana-* 'again' + *baptismos* 'baptism.'

an·a·bol·ic ste·roid /ˌanə'bälik/ ▸ **noun** a synthetic hormone taken illegally to improve a competitor's performance in a sport.

a·nab·o·lism /ə'nabəˌlizəm/ ▸ **noun** a metabolic process in which complex molecules are formed from simpler ones and energy is stored. The opposite of **CATABOLISM**.
– DERIVATIVES **an·a·bol·ic** /ˌanə'bälik/ adjective.
– ORIGIN Greek *anabolē* 'ascent.'

a·nach·ro·nism /ə'nakrəˌnizəm/ ▸ **noun** a thing that belongs or is appropriate to a period of time other than the one in which it exists or is placed: *such lavish houses seemed anachronisms, relics of a long-gone era.*
– DERIVATIVES **a·nach·ro·nis·tic** /əˌnakrə'nistik/ adjective **a·nach·ro·nis·ti·cal·ly** /-'nistik(ə)lē/ adverb.
– ORIGIN from Greek *ana-* 'backward' + *khronos* 'time.'

an·a·con·da /ˌanə'kändə/ ▸ **noun** a very large snake of the boa family, found in tropical South America.
– ORIGIN Sinhalese, 'whip snake.'

a·nae·mi·a, etc. /əˈnēmēə/ ▶ **noun** British spelling of **ANEMIA**, etc.

an·aer·o·bic /ˌane(ə)ˈrōbik, ˌanə-/ ▶ **adjective** Biology not using oxygen from the air.
– DERIVATIVES **an·aer·o·bi·cal·ly** adverb.

an·aes·the·sia, etc. /ˌanəsˈᴛʜēzʜə/ ▶ **noun** British spelling of **ANESTHESIA**, etc.

an·a·gram /ˈanəˌgram/ ▶ **noun** a word or phrase formed by rearranging the letters of another.
– ORIGIN from Greek *ana-* 'back, anew' + *gramma* 'letter.'

a·nal /ˈānl/ ▶ **adjective 1** relating to the anus. **2** fussily concerned about minor details and orderliness.
– DERIVATIVES **a·nal·ly** adverb.

an·al·ge·si·a /ˌanlˈjēzēə, -zʜə/ ▶ **noun** Medicine the loss of sensitivity to pain.
– ORIGIN from Greek *an-* 'not' + *algein* 'feel pain.'

an·al·ge·sic /ˌanlˈjēzik, -sik/ ▶ **noun** a pain-relieving drug. ▶ **adjective** having a pain-relieving effect.

an·a·log /ˈanlˌôg, -ˌäg/ (also **analogue**) ▶ **adjective** relating to electronic information or signals represented by a varying physical effect (e.g., voltage or the position of a pointer) rather than by a digital display. ▶ **noun** a person or thing that is like or comparable to another.

a·nal·o·gous /əˈnaləgəs/ ▶ **adjective** alike or comparable in certain ways: *an analogous situation.*
– ORIGIN Greek *analogos* 'proportionate.'

a·nal·o·gy /əˈnaləjē/ ▶ **noun** (pl. **analogies**) **1** a way of explaining or clarifying something by comparing it to something else: *an analogy between the workings of nature and those of human societies.* **2** a partial similarity.

> – SYNONYMS **similarity,** parallel, correspondence, likeness, resemblance, correlation, relation, comparison.
> – ANTONYMS dissimilarity.

– DERIVATIVES **an·a·log·i·cal** /ˌanəˈläjikəl/ adjective.

> **CHOOSE THE RIGHT WORD**
>
> See **LIKENESS**.

a·nal-re·ten·tive ▶ **adjective** Psychoanalysis excessively fussy and concerned with orderliness (supposedly because of problems with toilet-training in infancy).

a·nal·y·sand /əˈnaləˌsand, -ˌzand/ ▶ **noun** a person who is undergoing psychoanalysis.

a·nal·y·sis /əˈnaləsis/ ▶ **noun** (pl. **analyses** /-ˌsēz/) **1** a detailed examination of the features or structure of something: *an analysis of the causes of unemployment.* **2** the separation of something into its component parts. **3** psychoanalysis.

> – SYNONYMS **examination,** inspection, study, scrutiny, breakdown, investigation, exploration, evaluation.

– ORIGIN from Greek *analuein* 'unloose.'

an·a·lyst /ˈanl-ist/ ▶ **noun 1** a person who carries out an analysis. **2** a psychoanalyst.

an·a·lyt·i·cal /ˌanlˈitikəl/ (also **analytic** /ˌanlˈitik/) ▶ **adjective** relating to or using analysis.

> – SYNONYMS **systematic,** logical, scientific, methodical, precise, meticulous, rigorous, investigative, inquiring.

– DERIVATIVES **an·a·lyt·i·cal·ly** adverb.

an·a·lyze /ˈanlˌīz/ (Brit. **analyse**) ▶ **verb 1** examine something in detail in order to explain it or discover its structure or composition. **2** psychoanalyze someone.

> – SYNONYMS **examine,** inspect, survey, study, scrutinize, investigate, probe, explore, evaluate, break down.

a·naph·o·ra /əˈnafərə/ ▶ **noun** the repetition of a word or phrase at the beginning of successive statements, used for rhetorical effect.
– ORIGIN Greek, 'repetition.'

an·a·phy·lac·tic shock /ˌanəfəˈlaktik/ ▶ **noun** Medicine a severe allergic reaction to something that the body has become extremely sensitive to.
– ORIGIN from Greek *ana-* 'again' + *phulaxis* 'guarding.'

an·ar·chic /aˈnärkik/ ▶ **adjective** having no controlling rules or principles.

an·ar·chist /ˈanərkist/ ▶ **noun** a person who believes that all forms of government should be abolished.
– DERIVATIVES **an·ar·chism** /ˈanərˌkizəm/ noun **an·ar·chis·tic** /ˌanərˈkistik/ adjective.

an·ar·chy /ˈanərkē/ ▶ **noun** a state of disorder due to the lack of any form of government or control.

> – SYNONYMS **lawlessness,** disorder, chaos, pandemonium, mayhem, riot, revolution.
> – ANTONYMS order.

– ORIGIN from Greek *an-* 'without' + *arkhos* 'chief, ruler.'

A·na·sa·zi /ˌanəˈsäzē/ ▶ **noun** (pl. same or **Anasazis**) a member of an ancient American Indian people of the Southwest who flourished between *c.*200 BC and AD1500. The present day Pueblo culture developed from their later stage.

a·nath·e·ma /əˈnaᴛʜəmə/ ▶ **noun** something that one detests: *racism was anathema to her.*
– ORIGIN Greek, 'thing devoted to evil.'

a·nath·e·ma·tize /əˈnaᴛʜəməˌtīz/ ▶ **verb** curse or condemn: *a church council anathematized those who refused to conform.*

a·nat·o·mize /əˈnatəˌmīz/ ▶ **verb** examine and analyze in detail: *successful comedy is notoriously difficult to anatomize.*

a·nat·o·my /əˈnatəmē/ ▶ **noun** (pl. **anatomies**) **1** the scientific study of bodily structure. **2** the bodily structure of a person, animal, or plant. **3** a detailed examination or analysis: *an anatomy of the disaster.*

> – SYNONYMS **structure,** makeup, composition, constitution, form, body, physique.

– DERIVATIVES **an·a·tom·i·cal** /əˈnatəmē/ adjective **an·a·tom·i·cal·ly** adverb **a·nat·o·mist** noun.
– ORIGIN from Greek *ana-* 'up' + *tomia* 'cutting.'

ANC ▶ **abbreviation** African National Congress.

an·ces·tor /ˈanˌsestər/ ▶ **noun 1** a person from whom one is descended. **2** something from which a later species or version has developed: *an ancestor of the horse.*

> – SYNONYMS **forefather,** forebear, predecessor, antecedent, progenitor, parent, grandparent.
> – ANTONYMS descendant.

– ORIGIN from Latin *antecedere* 'go before.'

an·ces·tral /anˈsestrəl/ ▶ **adjective** relating to or inherited from a person's ancestor or ancestors: *his ancestral home.*

an·ces·try /ˈanˌsestrē/ ▶ **noun** (pl. **ancestries**) a person's ancestors or the people from which they are descended: *her Irish ancestry.*

– SYNONYMS **ancestors,** forebears, forefathers, progenitors, antecedents, family tree, lineage, genealogy, parentage, blood.

an·chor /ˈaNGkər/ ▶ **noun** a heavy metal object used to moor a ship to the sea bottom. ▶ **verb 1** moor a ship with an anchor. **2** fix firmly in position: *the rope was anchored to the rocks.*
– ORIGIN Greek *ankura.*

an·chor·age /ˈaNGk(ə)rij/ ▶ **noun** a place where ships may be anchored safely.

an·cho·rite /ˈaNGkəˌrīt/ ▶ **noun** historical a person who lives in isolation from others for religious reasons.
– ORIGIN from Greek *anakhōrein* 'retire.'

an·chor·man /ˈaNGkərˌman/ (or **anchorwoman** /ˈaNGkərˌwo͝omən/) ▶ **noun** (pl. **anchormen** or **anchorwomen**) a person who presents a live television or radio program and coordinates the contributions of participants.

an·cho·vy /ˈanˌCHōvē, anˈCHōvē/ ▶ **noun** (pl. **anchovies**) a small fish of the herring family, with a strong flavor.
– ORIGIN Spanish and Portuguese *anchova.*

an·cien ré·gime /äNˈsyaN rāˈZHēm/ ▶ **noun** (pl. **anciens régimes** pronunc. same) a political or social system that has been replaced by a more modern one.
– ORIGIN French, 'old rule.'

an·cient /ˈānCHənt/ ▶ **adjective 1** belonging to or dating from the very distant past: *an ancient civilization.* **2** very old: *an ancient pair of jeans.*

– SYNONYMS **1** *ancient civilizations* **early,** prehistoric, primeval, primordial, primitive, bygone. **2** *an ancient custom* **old,** age-old, venerable, time-worn, time-honored, archaic, antique, obsolete. **3** *I feel ancient* **antiquated,** antediluvian, geriatric; informal as old as the hills.
– ANTONYMS contemporary, recent.

▶ **noun** (**the ancients**) the people of ancient times.
– DERIVATIVES **an·cient·ly** adverb.
– ORIGIN Old French *ancien,* from Latin *ante* 'before.'

WORD TOOLKIT

See **PREHISTORIC**.

an·cil·lar·y /ˈansəˌlerē/ ▶ **adjective 1** providing support to the main activities of an organization: *ancillary staff.* **2** additional; extra: *ancillary accommodations.*
– ORIGIN from Latin *ancilla* 'maidservant.'

and /and/ ▶ **conjunction 1** used to connect words, clauses, or sentences. **2** used to connect two identical words to show gradual change, continuing action, or great extent: *getting better and better.* **3** (connecting two numbers) plus. **4** informal (after a verb) to: *try and do it.*
– ORIGIN Old English.

USAGE

Some verbs, especially **try**, **come**, and **go**, can be followed by **and** rather than **to** in sentences like *we should try and help them.* The use with **and** is very common but in formal writing or speech it is best to say **to**: *we should try to help them.*

Many people think that **and**, together with other conjunctions such as **but** and **because**, should not be used to start a sentence, the argument being that such a sentence expresses an incomplete thought. However, **and** has long been used in this way in both written and spoken English, and it is quite acceptable to do so.

an·dan·te /änˈdänˌtā/ Music ▶ **adverb & adjective** in a moderately slow tempo. ▶ **noun** a passage to be performed at a moderately slow tempo.
– ORIGIN Italian, 'going.'

An·de·an /ˈandēən, anˈdē-/ ▶ **adjective** relating to the Andes mountains of South America.

and·i·ron /ˈanˌdīərn/ ▶ **noun** either of a pair of metal stands used to support wood burning in a fireplace.
– ORIGIN Old French *andier.*

An·dor·ran /anˈdôrən/ ▶ **noun** a person from Andorra, a small self-governing principality in the southern Pyrenees. ▶ **adjective** relating to Andorra.

an·dro·gen /ˈandrəjən/ ▶ **noun** a male sex hormone, such as testosterone.
– ORIGIN from Greek *anēr* 'man' + *genēs* '-born, of a specified kind.'

an·drog·y·nous /anˈdräjənəs/ ▶ **adjective** partly male and partly female.
– DERIVATIVES **an·drog·y·ny** /-nē/ noun.
– ORIGIN from Greek *anēr* 'man' + *gunē* 'woman.'

an·droid /ˈanˌdroid/ ▶ **noun** (in science fiction) a robot with a human appearance.
– ORIGIN from Greek *anēr* 'man.'

an·ec·do·tal /ˌanikˈdōtl/ ▶ **adjective** (of a story) not necessarily true because based on someone's personal account of an event rather than on facts.
– DERIVATIVES **an·ec·do·tal·ly** adverb.

an·ec·dote /ˈanikˌdōt/ ▶ **noun** a short entertaining story about a real incident or person.

– SYNONYMS **story,** tale, urban myth, narrative, reminiscence; informal yarn.

– ORIGIN from Greek *anekdota* 'things unpublished.'

a·ne·mi·a /əˈnēmēə/ (Brit. **anaemia**) ▶ **noun** deficiency of red blood cells or of hemoglobin in the blood, resulting in weariness.
– ORIGIN from Greek *an-* 'without' + *haima* 'blood.'

a·ne·mic /əˈnēmik/ ▶ **adjective 1** suffering from anemia. **2** not lively or exciting: *an anemic performance.*

an·e·mom·e·ter /ˌanəˈmämitər/ ▶ **noun** an instrument for measuring the speed of the wind.
– ORIGIN Greek *anemos* 'wind.'

a·nem·o·ne /əˈnemənē/ ▶ **noun** a plant having brightly colored flowers with dark centers.
– ORIGIN Greek, 'windflower.'

an·er·oid ba·rom·e·ter /ˈanəˌroid/ ▶ **noun** a barometer that measures air pressure by the action of air on the flexible lid of a box containing a vacuum.
– ORIGIN from Greek *a-* 'without' + *nēros* 'water.'

an·es·the·sia /ˌanəsˈTHēZHə/ (Brit. **anaesthesia**) ▶ **noun** insensitivity to pain, especially as artificially induced by the administration of gases or the injection of drugs before surgical operations.
– ORIGIN from Greek *an-* 'without' + *aisthēsis* 'sensation.'

an·es·the·si·ol·o·gy /ˌanəsˌTHēzēˈäləjē/ ▶ **noun** the branch of medicine concerned with anesthesia and anesthetics.
– DERIVATIVES **an·es·the·si·ol·o·gist** /-jist/ noun.

an·es·thet·ic /ˌanəsˈTHetik/ (Brit. **anaesthetic**) ▶ **noun** a drug or gas that makes one unable to feel pain.

an·es·the·tize /əˈnesTHiˌtīz/ (Brit. **anaesthetize**) ▶ **verb** give an anesthetic to a patient.
– DERIVATIVES **an·es·the·ti·za·tion** /-THitəˈzāSHən/ noun.

an·eu·rysm /ˈanyəˌrizəm/ (also **aneurism**) ▶ **noun** Medicine an excessive swelling of the wall of an artery.
– ORIGIN Greek *aneurusma* 'widening.'

a·new /əˈn(y)o͞o/ ▶ **adverb 1** in a new or different way. **2** once more; again.

an·gel /ˈānjəl/ ▶ **noun 1** a spiritual being acting as an attendant or messenger of God, represented as being of human form with wings. **2** a very beautiful, kind, or good person. **3** informal a person who gives financial backing to a theatrical production.
– ORIGIN Greek *angelos* 'messenger.'

an·gel dust ▶ **noun** informal the hallucinogenic drug phencyclidine hydrochloride.

an·gel·fish /ˈānjəlˌfisʜ/ ▶ **noun** (pl. same or **angelfishes**) a tropical fish with large fins, often vividly colored or patterned.

an·gel food cake ▶ **noun** a very light, pale sponge cake made with no egg yolks.

an·gel hair ▶ **noun** a type of pasta consisting of very fine long strands.

an·gel·ic /anˈjelik/ ▶ **adjective 1** relating to angels. **2** very beautiful, innocent, or kind: *his small, angelic face.*

– SYNONYMS **innocent,** pure, virtuous, saintly, cherubic, adorable.

– DERIVATIVES **an·gel·i·cal·ly** adverb.

WORD TOOLKIT

See **HEAVENLY**.

an·gel·i·ca /anˈjelikə/ ▶ **noun** the stalks of a sweet-smelling plant, preserved in sugar and used in cake decoration.
– ORIGIN from Latin *herba angelica* 'angelic herb' (it was believed to be effective against poisoning and disease).

an·ge·lus /ˈanjələs/ ▶ **noun 1** a Roman Catholic prayer commemorating the Incarnation of Jesus, said at morning, noon, and sunset. **2** a ringing of bells to signal the times of the angelus.
– ORIGIN from Latin *Angelus domini* 'the angel of the Lord,' the opening words of the prayer.

an·ger /ˈaɴɢgər/ ▶ **noun** a strong feeling of extreme displeasure.

– SYNONYMS **annoyance,** vexation, temper, indignation, rage, fury, wrath, outrage; literary ire.

▶ **verb** make someone angry.

– SYNONYMS **annoy,** irk, vex, enrage, incense, infuriate, rile, provoke, outrage.
– ANTONYMS pacify, placate.

– ORIGIN Old Norse, 'grief.'

an·gi·na /anˈjīnə/ (also **angina pectoris** /ˈpektəris/) ▶ **noun** a condition marked by severe pain in the chest, caused by an inadequate supply of blood to the heart.
– ORIGIN from Greek *ankhonē* 'strangling' + Latin *pectoris* 'of the chest.'

an·gi·o·gram /ˈanj(ē)əˌgram/ ▶ **noun** an X-ray photograph of blood or lymph vessels, made after injection of a marking substance.

an·gi·o·plas·ty /ˈanjēəˌplastē/ ▶ **noun** (pl. **angioplasties**) a surgical operation to repair or unblock a blood vessel, especially an artery in the heart.

an·gi·o·sperm /ˈanjēəˌspərm/ ▶ **noun** a plant of a large group that have flowers and produce seeds enclosed in a carpel, including herbaceous plants, shrubs, grasses, and most trees.
– ORIGIN from Greek *angeion* 'container.'

An·gle /ˈaɴɢgəl/ ▶ **noun** a member of an ancient Germanic people who founded kingdoms in the north and east of England in the 5th century AD.
– ORIGIN Latin *Anglus* 'inhabitant of *Angul*' (in northern Germany); related to **ENGLISH**.

an·gle[1] /ˈaɴɢgəl/ ▶ **noun 1** the space between two intersecting lines or surfaces at or close to the point where they meet. **2** a position from which someone or something is viewed: *the camera angle shifted from side view to a full-face closeup.* **3** a particular way of considering something: *let's look at the issue from a different angle.*

– SYNONYMS **1 gradient,** slope, slant, inclination.
2 corner, point, fork, nook, crook, edge.
3 perspective, point of view, viewpoint, standpoint, position, aspect, slant, direction, approach, tack.

▶ **verb 1** move or place something in a slanting position. **2** present information from a particular point of view: *angle your answer so that it is relevant to the job for which you are applying.*

– SYNONYMS **tilt,** slant, twist, swivel, lean, tip, turn.

– DERIVATIVES **an·gled** adjective.
– ORIGIN Latin *angulus* 'corner.'

an·gle[2] ▶ **verb 1** fish with a rod and line. **2** try to get something by indirectly prompting someone to offer it: *she was angling for sympathy.*
– DERIVATIVES **an·gler** noun **an·gling** noun.
– ORIGIN Old English.

an·gle brack·et ▶ **noun** either of a pair of marks in the form<>, used to enclose words or figures so as to separate them from their context.

an·gle grind·er ▶ **noun** a device with a rotating abrasive disk, used to grind, polish, or cut metal and other materials.

an·gle i·ron ▶ **noun** a building material consisting of pieces of iron or steel with an L-shaped cross section, able to be bolted together.

an·gler·fish /ˈaɴɢglərˌfisʜ/ ▶ **noun** (pl. same or **anglerfishes**) a marine fish that lures prey within reach of its mouth with a fleshy filament projecting from its snout.

An·gli·can /ˈaɴɢglikən/ ▶ **adjective** relating to the Church of England or any Church associated with it. ▶ **noun** a member of the Anglican Church.
– DERIVATIVES **An·gli·can·ism** noun.
– ORIGIN Latin *Anglicanus*, from *Anglus* 'Angle.'

An·gli·cism /ˈaɴɢgləˌsizəm/ ▶ **noun** a word or phrase that is peculiar to British English.

an·gli·cize /ˈaɴɢgləˌsīz/ ▶ **verb** make English in form or character: *he anglicized his name from Gutman to Goodman.*
– DERIVATIVES **an·gli·ci·za·tion** /ˌaɴɢgləsəˈzāsʜən/ noun.

An·glo /ˈaɴɢglō/ ▶ **noun** (pl. **Anglos**) a white, English-speaking American as distinct from a Hispanic American.

Anglo- /ˌaɴɢglō-/ ▶ **combining form 1** English: *anglophone.* **2** English or British and ...: *Anglo-Latin.*
– ORIGIN from Latin *Anglus* 'English.'

An·glo-Cath·o·lic ▶ **adjective** a member of a section of the Church of England that is close to Catholicism in its beliefs and worship.
– DERIVATIVES **An·glo-Ca·thol·i·cism** noun.

An·glo·cen·tric /ˌanɡglō'sentrik/ ▶ **adjective** considered in terms of England or Britain; seeing English or British culture as most important.

An·glo-In·di·an ▶ **adjective 1** relating to or involving both Britain and India. **2** of mixed British and Indian parentage. **3** chiefly historical of British descent or birth but having lived for a long time in India. ▶ **noun** an Anglo-Indian person.

An·glo-I·rish ▶ **adjective 1** relating to both Britain and Ireland (or specifically the Republic of Ireland). **2** of mixed English and Irish parentage. **3** of English descent but born or living in Ireland.

An·glo·phile /'anɡglə,fīl/ ▶ **noun** a person who likes or greatly admires England or Britain.
– DERIVATIVES **An·glo·phil·ia** noun.

an·glo·phone /'anɡglə,fōn/ ▶ **adjective** English-speaking.

An·glo-Sax·on ▶ **noun 1** a Germanic inhabitant of England between the 5th century and the Norman Conquest. **2** an English person. **3** a white, English-speaking person. **4** the Old English language.

An·glo·sphere /'anɡglō,sfi(ə)r/ ▶ **noun** the group of countries where English is the main native language.

An·go·lan /anɡ'gōlən, an'gōlən/ ▶ **noun** a person from Angola, a country in SW Africa. ▶ **adjective** relating to Angola.

an·go·ra /anɡ'gôrə/ ▶ **noun 1** a cat, goat, or rabbit of a long-haired breed. **2** a fabric made from the hair of the angora goat or rabbit.
– ORIGIN from *Angora* (now Ankara) in Turkey.

an·gos·tu·ra /ˌanɡgə'st(y)o͝orə/ ▶ **noun 1** a bitter bark from a South American tree, used as a flavoring. **2** (also **Angostura bitters** trademark) a kind of tonic.
– ORIGIN from *Angostura* (now Ciudad Bolívar) in Venezuela.

an·gry /'anɡgrē/ ▶ **adjective** (**angrier, angriest**) **1** feeling or showing anger. **2** (of a wound or sore) red and inflamed.

– SYNONYMS **furious,** irate, vexed, wrathful, irked, enraged, incensed, seething, infuriated, in a temper, fuming, apoplectic, outraged, cross; informal (hopping) mad, up in arms, foaming at the mouth, steamed, sore.
– ANTONYMS pleased.

– DERIVATIVES **an·gri·ly** adverb.

angst /anɡ(k)st, änɡ(k)st/ ▶ **noun** a strong feeling of anxiety about life in general.

– SYNONYMS **anxiety,** fear, worry, trepidation, malaise, disquiet, unease, anguish.

– DERIVATIVES **angst·y** adjective.
– ORIGIN German, 'fear.'

ang·strom /'anɡstrəm/ ▶ **noun** Physics a unit of length equal to one hundred-millionth of a centimeter, 10^{-10} meter.
– ORIGIN named after the Swedish physicist A. J. *Ångström*.

an·guish /'anɡgwish/ ▶ **noun** severe pain or distress.

– SYNONYMS **agony,** pain, torment, torture, suffering, distress, woe, misery, sorrow, heartache.
– ANTONYMS happiness.

▶ **verb** be very distressed: *I was anguishing about whether I'd made the right decision.*
– ORIGIN Latin *angustia* 'tightness.'

an·guished /'anɡgwisht/ ▶ **adjective** feeling or expressing severe pain or distress.

an·gu·lar /'anɡgyələr/ ▶ **adjective 1** having angles or sharp corners. **2** (of a person) lean and bony. **3** Physics measured by means of an angle.
– DERIVATIVES **an·gu·lar·i·ty** noun **an·gu·lar·ly** adverb.

an·hy·drous /an'hīdrəs/ ▶ **adjective** Chemistry containing no water.
– ORIGIN from Greek *an-* 'without' + *hudōr* 'water.'

an·i·line /'anl-in/ ▶ **noun** an oily liquid used in making dyes, drugs, and plastics.
– ORIGIN from Arabic, 'indigo' (from which it was originally obtained).

an·i·mad·vert /ˌanəmad'vərt/ ▶ **verb** (**animadvert on/against**) formal speak out against or criticize someone or something.
– DERIVATIVES **an·i·mad·ver·sion** /ˌanəmad'vərzhən/ noun.
– ORIGIN from Latin *animus* 'mind' + *advertere* 'to turn.'

an·i·mal /'anəməl/ ▶ **noun 1** a living organism that can move about of its own accord and has specialized sense organs and nervous system. **2** a mammal, as opposed to a bird, reptile, fish, or insect. **3** a brutal or uncivilized person. **4** a particular type of person or thing: *she's a political animal.*

– SYNONYMS **1 creature,** beast, (living) thing; (**animals**) wildlife, fauna. **2** *the man was an animal* **beast,** brute, monster, devil, fiend; informal swine, bastard, pig.

▶ **adjective** physical rather than spiritual or intellectual: *animal lust.*
– ORIGIN from Latin *animalis* 'having breath.'

WORD LINKS

zoological *relating to animals*
zoology *study of animals*

an·i·mal·cule /ˌanə'malˌkyo͞ol/ ▶ **noun** chiefly literary a microscopic animal.

an·i·mal·ism /'anəməˌlizəm/ ▶ **noun** physical and instinctive behavior; animality.
– DERIVATIVES **an·i·mal·is·tic** /ˌanəmə'listik/ adjective.

an·i·mal mag·net·ism ▶ **noun** a quality of powerful sexual attractiveness.

an·i·mate ▶ **verb** /'anəˌmāt/ **1** bring life or new vigor to: *Christianity animated a society and reshaped it.* **2** give a movie or television show, or a character, the appearance of movement using animation.

– SYNONYMS **enliven,** energize, invigorate, liven up, inspire, fire, rouse, stir, galvanize, stimulate, excite, move, revitalize, revive, rejuvenate.

▶ **adjective** /-mit/ alive; having life.

– SYNONYMS **living,** alive, live, breathing, sentient.
– ANTONYMS inanimate.

– DERIVATIVES **an·i·ma·tor** /'anəˌmātər/ noun.
– ORIGIN from Latin *anima* 'life, soul.'

an·i·mat·ed /'anəˌmātid/ ▶ **adjective 1** full of interest or energy; lively: *an animated conversation.* **2** (of a movie or television show) made using animation.

– SYNONYMS **lively,** spirited, energetic, full of life, excited, enthusiastic, eager, alive, vigorous, vibrant, vivacious, exuberant, ebullient, bouncy, bubbly, perky; informal bright-eyed and bushy-tailed, full of beans, bright and breezy, chirpy, chipper.
– ANTONYMS lethargic, lifeless.

– DERIVATIVES **an·i·mat·ed·ly** adverb.

an·i·ma·tion /ˌanəˈmāSHən/ ▶ **noun 1** the state of being full of life or energy; liveliness. **2** the technique of filming a sequence of drawings or positions of models to create the appearance of movement. **3** (also **computer animation**) the creation of moving images by means of a computer.

an·i·ma·tron·ics /ˌanəməˈtrāniks/ ▶ **plural noun** (treated as sing.) the creation and operation of lifelike robots, especially for use in movies.
– DERIVATIVES **an·i·ma·tron·ic** adjective.

an·i·me /ˈanəˌmā/ ▶ **noun** Japanese animated films, typically having a science fiction theme.
– ORIGIN Japanese.

an·i·mism /ˈanəˌmizəm/ ▶ **noun** the belief that all things in nature, such as plants and hills, have a soul.
– DERIVATIVES **an·i·mist** /ˈanəmist/ noun **an·i·mis·tic** /ˌanəˈmistik/ adjective.
– ORIGIN from Latin *anima* 'life, soul.'

an·i·mos·i·ty /ˌanəˈmäsitē/ ▶ **noun** (pl. **animosities**) strong hostility; hatred.

– SYNONYMS **hostility,** antipathy, antagonism, rancor, enmity, resentment, hatred, loathing, ill feeling/will, dislike, bad blood, animus.
– ANTONYMS goodwill, friendship.

– ORIGIN Latin *animositas*.

an·i·mus /ˈanəməs/ ▶ **noun** hatred or hostility.
– ORIGIN Latin, 'spirit, mind.'

an·i·on /ˈanˌīən/ ▶ **noun** Chemistry an ion with a negative charge. The opposite of **CATION**.
– DERIVATIVES **an·i·on·ic** /ˌanīˈänik/ adjective.
– ORIGIN from **ANODE** + **ION**.

an·ise /ˈanis/ ▶ **noun 1** a plant grown for its aromatic seeds (aniseed). **2** the flavoring extracted from aniseed: *a light glaze with a hint of anise.*
– ORIGIN Greek *anison* 'anise, dill.'

an·i·seed /ˈanə(s)ˌsēd/ ▶ **noun** the seed, or seeds, of the plant anise, used as a flavoring.

ankh /äNGk/ ▶ **noun** an ancient Egyptian symbol of life in the shape of a cross with a loop instead of the top arm.
– ORIGIN Egyptian, 'life, soul.'

an·kle /ˈaNGkəl/ ▶ **noun 1** the joint connecting the foot with the leg. **2** the narrow part of the leg between the ankle joint and the calf.
– ORIGIN Old English.

an·klet /ˈaNGklit/ ▶ **noun** a chain or band worn around the ankle.

an·na /ˈanə/ ▶ **noun** a former unit of money of India and Pakistan, equal to one sixteenth of a rupee.
– ORIGIN Hindi.

an·nal /ˈanl/ ▶ **noun 1** (**annals**) a historical record of events year by year. **2** a record of the events of one year.
– DERIVATIVES **an·nal·ist** noun.
– ORIGIN from Latin *annales libri* 'yearly books.'

an·nat·to /əˈnätō/ ▶ **noun** an orange-red dye obtained from a tropical fruit, used for coloring foods.
– ORIGIN Carib.

an·neal /əˈnēl/ ▶ **verb** heat metal or glass and allow it to cool slowly, to remove internal stresses.
– ORIGIN Old English, 'set on fire.'

an·ne·lid /ˈanlˌid/ ▶ **noun** a worm with a body made up of segments, such as an earthworm.
– ORIGIN from Latin *annelus* 'small ring.'

an·nex ▶ **verb** /əˈneks, ˈaneks/ **1** seize territory and add it to one's own. **2** (usu. as adj. **annexed**) add or attach something: *the annexed document.* ▶ **noun** /ˈaneks, -iks/ (chiefly Brit. also **annexe**) (pl. **annexes**) **1** a building attached or near to a main building, used for additional space. **2** an addition to a document.
– DERIVATIVES **an·nex·a·tion** /ˌanekˈsāSHən, ˌanik-/ noun.
– ORIGIN Latin *annectere* 'connect.'

an·ni·hi·late /əˈnī-əˌlāt/ ▶ **verb 1** destroy completely: *this bomb could annihilate them all.* **2** defeat someone completely.

– SYNONYMS **destroy,** obliterate, eradicate, wipe out, wipe off the face of the earth; informal rub out, snuff out.
– ANTONYMS create.

– DERIVATIVES **an·ni·hi·la·tion** /əˌnīəˈlāSHən/ noun **an·ni·hi·la·tor** /-ˌlātər/ noun.
– ORIGIN Latin *annihilare* 'reduce to nothing.'

CHOOSE THE RIGHT WORD

See **DESTROY**.

an·ni·ver·sa·ry /ˌanəˈvərsərē/ ▶ **noun** (pl. **anniversaries**) the date on which an event took place in a previous year.
– ORIGIN from Latin *anniversarius* 'returning yearly.'

An·no Dom·i·ni /ˈanō ˈdämənē, -nī, ˈänō/ ▶ **adverb** full form of **AD**.

an·no·tate /ˈanəˌtāt/ ▶ **verb** add explanatory notes to a piece of writing.
– DERIVATIVES **an·no·ta·tion** /ˌanəˈtāSHən/ noun **an·no·ta·tor** /-ˌtātər/ noun.
– ORIGIN Latin *annotare* 'to mark.'

an·nounce /əˈnouns/ ▶ **verb 1** make a public statement about something. **2** be a sign of: *lilies announce the arrival of summer.*

– SYNONYMS **make public,** make known, report, declare, state, publicize, broadcast, publish, advertise, circulate, proclaim, release, disclose, divulge.

– ORIGIN from Latin *nuntius* 'messenger.'

CHOOSE THE RIGHT WORD

announce, blazon, declare, proclaim, promulgate, publish

When you **announce** something, you communicate it in a formal and public manner, often for the first time (*to announce the arrival of the guest of honor*). But just how you go about announcing something depends on what you're trying to convey. If you want to make sure no one misses your message, use **blazon** (*signs along the highway blazoned the local farmers' complaints*). If you plan to make your views known to the general public through the medium of writing, use **publish** (*to publish a story on drunk driving in the local newspaper*). Use **proclaim** if you have something of great importance that you want to announce very formally and officially (*proclaim a national day of mourning*). Although **declare** also implies a very formal announcement (*declare war*), it can refer to any clear and explicit statement (*declare one's love*). **Promulgate** is usually associated with the communication of a creed, doctrine, or law (*promulgate the views of the Democratic Party*).

an·nounce·ment /əˈnounsmənt/ ▶ **noun 1** a public statement. **2** the action of announcing something.

– SYNONYMS **1 statement,** declaration, proclamation, pronouncement, bulletin, advisory, communiqué. **2 declaration,** notification, reporting, publishing, broadcasting, disclosure.

an·nounc·er /ə'nounsər/ ▶ **noun** a person who announces something, especially someone who introduces or gives information about programs on radio or television.

an·noy /ə'noi/ ▶ **verb** make someone slightly angry.

– SYNONYMS **irritate,** bother, vex, make cross, exasperate, irk, anger, antagonize, nettle, rankle with, rub the wrong way; informal aggravate, peeve, miff, rile, needle, get (to), bug, tee off, tick off.
– ANTONYMS please.

– DERIVATIVES **an·noyed** adjective.
– ORIGIN from Latin *mihi in odio est* 'it is hateful to me.'

an·noy·ance /ə'noi-əns/ ▶ **noun 1** the feeling or state of being annoyed. **2** a thing that annoys someone.

– SYNONYMS **irritation,** exasperation, vexation, indignation, anger, displeasure, chagrin.

an·noy·ing /ə'noi-iNG/ ▶ **adjective** causing irritation or annoyance.

– SYNONYMS **irritating,** infuriating, exasperating, maddening, trying, tiresome, troublesome, irksome, vexing, galling; informal aggravating.

– DERIVATIVES **an·noy·ing·ly** adverb.

an·nu·al /'anyo͞oəl/ ▶ **adjective 1** happening once a year. **2** calculated over or covering a year: *annual income*. **3** (of a plant) living for a year or less.

– SYNONYMS **yearly,** once-a-year, year-long, twelve-month.

▶ **noun 1** a book published once a year under the same title but with different contents. **2** an annual plant.
– DERIVATIVES **an·nu·al·ly** adverb.
– ORIGIN from Latin *annus* 'year.'

an·nu·al·ized /'anyo͞oəˌlīzd/ ▶ **adjective** (of a rate of interest, inflation, or return on investment) recalculated as an annual rate.

an·nu·i·ty /ə'n(y)o͞oitē/ ▶ **noun** (pl. **annuities**) a fixed sum of money paid to someone each year.
– ORIGIN from Latin *annuus* 'yearly.'

an·nul /ə'nəl/ ▶ **verb** (**annuls, annulling, annulled**) declare a law, marriage, or other legal contract to be invalid.

– SYNONYMS **declare invalid,** declare null and void, nullify, invalidate, void, repeal, revoke.

– DERIVATIVES **an·nul·ment** noun.
– ORIGIN from Latin *nullum* 'nothing.'

an·nu·lar /'anyələr/ ▶ **adjective** technical ring-shaped.
– ORIGIN from Latin *anulus* 'small ring.'

WORD TOOLKIT

See **CIRCULAR**.

an·nun·ci·a·tion /əˌnənsē'āSHən/ ▶ **noun 1** (**the Annunciation**) the announcement by the angel Gabriel to the Virgin Mary that she was to be the mother of Jesus. **2** a Church festival commemorating the Annunciation, held on March 25.
– ORIGIN from Latin *annuntiare* 'announce.'

an·nus hor·ri·bi·lis /'anəs hə'ribəlis/ ▶ **noun** a disastrous or unlucky year for someone or something.
– ORIGIN Latin.

an·ode /'anōd/ ▶ **noun** an electrode with a positive charge. The opposite of **CATHODE**.
– ORIGIN Greek *anodos* 'way up.'

an·o·dized /'anəˌdīzd/ ▶ **adjective** (of metal, especially aluminum) coated with a protective oxide layer by electrolysis.

an·o·dyne /'anəˌdīn/ ▶ **adjective** unlikely to cause offense or disagreement; bland: *anodyne tales of small-town life*. ▶ **noun** a painkilling drug or medicine.
– ORIGIN Greek *anōdunos* 'painless.'

a·noint /ə'noint/ ▶ **verb 1** smear or rub someone with oil, especially as part of a religious ceremony. **2** choose someone to replace another in a job or role: *he's been anointed country rock's poster boy*.
– ORIGIN from Latin *inungere*.

a·nom·a·lous /ə'nämələs/ ▶ **adjective** differing from what is standard or normal: *anomalous results*.
– DERIVATIVES **a·nom·a·lous·ly** adverb.
– ORIGIN from Greek *an-* 'not' + *homalos* 'even.'

a·nom·a·ly /ə'näməlē/ ▶ **noun** (pl. **anomalies**) something that differs from what is standard or normal.

– SYNONYMS **oddity,** peculiarity, abnormality, irregularity, inconsistency, aberration, quirk.

an·o·mie /'anəˌmē/ ▶ **noun** lack of the usual standards of expected or good behavior.
– ORIGIN from Greek *anomos* 'lawless.'

a·non /ə'nän/ ▶ **adverb** old use or informal soon; shortly.
– ORIGIN Old English, 'in or into one.'

anon. ▶ **abbreviation** anonymous.

a·non·y·mous /ə'nänəməs/ ▶ **adjective 1** with a name that is not known or made known: *an anonymous letter*. **2** having no outstanding or individual features: *an anonymous building on an anonymous street*.

– SYNONYMS **unnamed,** nameless, unidentified, unknown, incognito, unsigned.

– DERIVATIVES **an·o·nym·i·ty** /ˌanə'nimitē/ noun **a·non·y·mous·ly** adverb.
– ORIGIN Greek *anōnumos* 'nameless.'

a·noph·e·les /ə'näfəˌlēz/ ▶ **noun** a mosquito of a genus that is particularly common in warmer countries and includes the mosquitoes that transmit the malarial parasite to humans.
– ORIGIN from Greek *anōphelēs* 'unprofitable, useless.'

an·o·rak /'anəˌrak/ ▶ **noun** a waterproof cold-weather jacket with a hood.
– ORIGIN Greenland Eskimo.

an·o·rex·i·a /ˌanə'reksēə/ (also **anorexia nervosa** /nər'vōsə/) ▶ **noun** a psychological disorder in which a person refuses to eat because they are afraid of becoming fat.
– ORIGIN from Greek *an-* 'without' + *orexis* 'appetite.'

an·o·rex·ic /ˌanə'reksik/ (also **anorectic** /ˌanə'rektik/) ▶ **adjective 1** relating to anorexia. **2** informal very thin. ▶ **noun** a person with anorexia.

an·oth·er /ə'nəT͟Hər/ ▶ **determiner & pronoun 1** one more. **2** different from the one already mentioned.

an·ox·i·a /a'näksēə/ ▶ **noun 1** an absence of oxygen. **2** Medicine an absence or deficiency of oxygen reaching the tissues; severe hypoxia.
– DERIVATIVES **an·ox·ic** /-sik/ adjective.

an·swer /'ansər/ ▶ **noun 1** something said or written in reaction to a question or statement. **2** a solution to a problem: *the hormone has been touted as the answer to aging*.

– SYNONYMS **1 reply,** response, rejoinder, reaction, retort, riposte; informal comeback. **2 solution,** remedy,

way out, explanation.
– ANTONYMS question.

▶ **verb 1** give an answer. **2** (**answer for**) be responsible or to blame for: *Larry has got a lot to answer for.* **3** (**answer back**) give an insolent reply. **4** satisfy a need. **5** (**answer to**) be responsible to someone. **6** defend oneself against an accusation.

– SYNONYMS **1 reply,** respond, rejoin, retort, riposte. **2** *the government has a lot to answer for* **be accountable,** be responsible, be liable, take the blame; informal take the rap.

– DERIVATIVES **an·swer·er** noun.
– ORIGIN Old English.

an·swer·a·ble /ˈansərəbəl/ ▶ **adjective 1** (**answerable to**) responsible to someone. **2** (**answerable for**) responsible for something.

– SYNONYMS **accountable,** responsible, liable.

an·swer·ing ma·chine ▶ **noun** a machine that gives a recorded answer to a telephone call and can record a message from the caller.

an·swer phone ▶ **noun** Brit. an answering machine; voicemail.

ant /ant/ ▶ **noun** a small insect, usually wingless, living with many others in a highly organized group.
– ORIGIN Old English.

ant·ac·id /antˈasid/ ▶ **adjective** (of a medicine) preventing excess stomach acid.

an·tag·o·nism /anˈtagəˌnizəm/ ▶ **noun** open hostility or opposition.

an·tag·o·nist /anˈtagənist/ ▶ **noun** an open opponent or enemy of someone or something.
– ORIGIN from Greek *antagōnizesthai* 'struggle against.'

an·tag·o·nis·tic /anˌtagəˈnistik/ ▶ **adjective** showing or feeling opposition or hostility.

– SYNONYMS **hostile,** opposed, antipathetic, ill-disposed, resistant, in disagreement; informal anti.

an·tag·o·nize /anˈtagəˌnīz/ ▶ **verb** make hostile: *Louis had no wish to antagonize his parents.*

– SYNONYMS **provoke,** intimidate, alienate, anger, annoy, irritate.
– ANTONYMS pacify.

Ant·arc·tic /antˈär(k)tik/ ▶ **adjective** relating to the region surrounding the South Pole.
– ORIGIN Greek *antarktikos* 'opposite to the north.'

an·te /ˈantē/ ▶ **noun** a stake put up by a player in poker and similar games before receiving cards. ▶ **verb** (**antes, anteing, anted**) (**ante up**) put up an amount as an ante in poker and similar games.
– PHRASES **up** (or **raise**) **the ante** increase what is at stake or under discussion.
– ORIGIN Latin, 'before.'

ante- ▶ **prefix** before; preceding: *antecedent.*

ant·eat·er /ˈantˌētər/ ▶ **noun** a mammal with a long snout, feeding on ants and termites.

an·te·bel·lum /ˌantēˈbeləm/ ▶ **adjective** occurring or existing before a war, especially the US Civil War.
– ORIGIN from Latin *ante* 'before' and *bellum* 'war.'

an·te·ced·ent /ˌantəˈsēdnt/ ▶ **noun 1** a thing that occurs or exists before another: *the antecedents to aggressive actions.* **2** (**antecedents**) a person's ancestors and social background. **3** Grammar an earlier word, phrase, or clause to which a following pronoun refers back. ▶ **adjective** coming before in time or order.
– ORIGIN from Latin *antecedere* 'go before.'

an·te·cham·ber /ˈantēˌchāmbər/ ▶ **noun** a small room leading to a main one.

an·te·date /ˈantiˌdāt/ ▶ **verb 1** come before something in time. **2** indicate that a document or event belongs to an earlier date.

an·te·di·lu·vi·an /ˌantēdəˈlo͞ovēən/ ▶ **adjective 1** belonging to the time before the biblical Flood. **2** ridiculously old-fashioned: *antediluvian video games.*
– ORIGIN from **ANTE-** + Latin *diluvium* 'deluge.'

an·te·lope /ˈantlˌōp/ ▶ **noun 1** a swift deerlike animal with upward-pointing horns, native to Africa and Asia. **2** (also **pronghorn antelope**) inaccurate term for **PRONGHORN**.
– ORIGIN Greek *antholops*.

an·te·na·tal /ˌantēˈnātl/ ▶ **adjective** Brit. during pregnancy; before birth.

an·ten·na /anˈtenə/ ▶ **noun** (pl. **antennae** /-ˈtenē/) **1** each of a pair of long, thin parts on the heads of some insects, shellfish, etc., used for feeling. **2** (pl. also **antennas**) an aerial.
– ORIGIN Latin *antemna* 'yard' (of a ship's mast).

an·te·pe·nul·ti·mate /ˌantēpəˈnəltəmit/ ▶ **adjective** last but two in a series.

an·te·ri·or /anˈti(ə)rēər/ ▶ **adjective** technical at or nearer the front. The opposite of **POSTERIOR**.
– ORIGIN Latin.

an·te·room /ˈantēˌro͞om, -ˌro͝om/ ▶ **noun** a small room leading to a larger one.

an·them /ˈanTHəm/ ▶ **noun 1** an uplifting song associated with a group or cause, especially one chosen by a country to express patriotic feelings. **2** a musical setting of a religious text to be sung by a choir during a church service.

– SYNONYMS **hymn,** song, chorale, chant, psalm, canticle.

– DERIVATIVES **an·the·mic** /anˈTHēmik, -ˈTHemik/ adjective.
– ORIGIN from Latin *antiphona* 'antiphon.'

an·ther /ˈanTHər/ ▶ **noun** the part of a flower's stamen that contains the pollen.
– ORIGIN Greek *anthos* 'flower.'

ant·hill /ˈantˌhil/ ▶ **noun** a mound-shaped nest built by ants or termites.

an·thol·o·gy /anˈTHäləjē/ ▶ **noun** (pl. **anthologies**) a collection of poems or other pieces of writing or music.

– SYNONYMS **collection,** selection, compendium, compilation, miscellany, treasury.

– DERIVATIVES **an·thol·o·gist** noun **an·thol·o·gize** verb.
– ORIGIN from Greek *anthos* 'flower' + *-logia* 'collection.'

an·thra·cite /ˈanTHrəˌsīt/ ▶ **noun** hard coal that burns with little flame and smoke.
– ORIGIN from Greek *anthrax* 'coal.'

an·thrax /ˈanˌTHraks/ ▶ **noun** a serious disease of sheep and cattle, caused by a bacterium and able to be transmitted to humans.
– ORIGIN Greek *anthrax* 'coal, boil.'

an·thro·po·cen·tric /ˌanTHrəpōˈsentrik/ ▶ **adjective** regarding humankind as the most important element of existence.
– DERIVATIVES **an·thro·po·cen·trism** /-ˌtrizəm/ noun.

an·thro·poid /ˈanTHrəˌpoid/ ▶ **adjective** referring to the higher primate mammals, including monkeys, apes, and humans.
– ORIGIN from Greek *anthrōpos* 'human being.'

an·thro·pol·o·gy /ˌanTHrəˈpäləjē/ ▶ **noun** the study of societies, cultures, and human origins.
– DERIVATIVES **an·thro·po·log·i·cal** /-pəˈläjikəl/ adjective **an·thro·pol·o·gist** noun.
– ORIGIN from Greek *anthrōpos* 'human being.'

an·thro·po·mor·phic /ˌanTHrəpəˈmôrfik/ ▶ **adjective** treating a god, animal, or object as if they were human.
– DERIVATIVES **an·thro·po·mor·phism** /ˌanTHrəpəˈmôrˌfizəm/ noun.

an·thro·poph·a·gy /ˌanTHrəˈpäfəjē/ ▶ **noun** the eating of human flesh by other humans; cannibalism.
– ORIGIN from Greek *anthrōpophagos* 'man-eating.'

an·ti /ˈanˌtī, ˈantē/ ▶ **preposition** opposed to; against.

anti- ▶ **prefix 1** opposed to; against: *antiaircraft*. **2** preventing or relieving: *antibacterial*. **3** the opposite of: *anticlimax*.
– ORIGIN Greek.

an·ti·air·craft /ˌantēˈerˌkraft, ˌantī-/ ▶ **adjective** (especially of a gun or missile) used to attack enemy aircraft.

an·ti·bac·te·ri·al /ˌantēbakˈti(ə)rēəl, ˌantī-/ ▶ **adjective** active against bacteria.

an·ti·bi·ot·ic /ˌantēbīˈätik, ˌantī-/ ▶ **noun** a medicine that destroys bacteria or slows their growth.
– ORIGIN from Greek *biōtikos* 'fit for life.'

an·ti·bod·y /ˈantiˌbädē/ ▶ **noun** (pl. **antibodies**) a protein produced in the blood to destroy an antigen (harmful substance).

An·ti·christ /ˈantēˌkrīst, ˈantī-/ ▶ **noun** an enemy of Jesus believed by the early Church to appear before the end of the world.

an·tic·i·pate /anˈtisəˌpāt/ ▶ **verb 1** be aware of a future event and prepare for it. **2** regard as probable: *she anticipated scorn on her return to acting*. **3** look forward to something. **4** happen or do something before: *he anticipated Bates's theories on mimicry*.

> – SYNONYMS **1 expect,** foresee, predict, be prepared for, bargain on, reckon on; informal figure on. **2 look forward to,** await, long for, can't wait for.

– DERIVATIVES **an·tic·i·pa·tor** /-ˌpātər/ noun **an·tic·i·pa·to·ry** /anˈtisəpəˌtôrē/ adjective.
– ORIGIN Latin *anticipare*.

an·tic·i·pa·tion /anˌtisəˈpāSHən/ ▶ **noun** the action of anticipating something.

> – SYNONYMS **expectation,** expectancy, prediction, hope, excitement, suspense.

an·ti·cli·max /ˌantēˈklīˌmaks, ˌantī-/ ▶ **noun** a disappointing end to an exciting series of events.

> – SYNONYMS **letdown,** disappointment, comedown, nonevent, disillusionment. informal washout; literary bathos.

– DERIVATIVES **an·ti·cli·mac·tic** /ˌantēklīˈmaktik/ adjective.

an·ti·cline /ˈantēˌklīn, ˈantī-/ ▶ **noun** a ridge or fold of rock in which the strata slope downward from the crest. Compare with **SYNCLINE**.
– ORIGIN from **ANTI-** + Greek *klinein* 'lean.'

an·ti·clock·wise /ˌantēˈkläkˌwīz, ˌantī-/ ▶ **adverb & adjective** British term for **COUNTERCLOCKWISE**.

an·ti·co·ag·u·lant /ˌantēkōˈagyələnt, ˌantī-/ ▶ **noun** a substance that prevents the blood from clotting.

an·ti·con·vul·sant /ˌantēkənˈvəlsənt, ˌantī-/ ▶ **noun** a drug that prevents or reduces the severity of epileptic fits or other convulsions.

an·tics /ˈantiks/ ▶ **plural noun** foolish, outrageous, or amusing behavior.

> – SYNONYMS **capers,** pranks, larks, high jinks, skylarking, horseplay, clowning; informal monkey business.

– ORIGIN from Italian *antico* 'antique,' also 'grotesque.'

an·ti·cy·clone /ˌantēˈsīklōn, ˌantī-/ ▶ **noun** an area of high atmospheric pressure around which air slowly circulates, usually resulting in calm, fine weather.
– DERIVATIVES **an·ti·cy·clon·ic** /-sīˈklänik/ adjective.

an·ti·de·pres·sant /ˌantēdəˈpresnt, ˌantī-/ ▶ **noun** a drug used to relieve depression.

an·ti·dote /ˈantiˌdōt/ ▶ **noun 1** a medicine taken to counteract a poison. **2** something that counteracts an unpleasant feeling or situation: *laughter is a good antidote to stress*.

> – SYNONYMS **remedy,** cure, solution, countermeasure, corrective.

– ORIGIN Greek *antidoton*.

an·ti·freeze /ˈantiˌfrēz/ ▶ **noun** a liquid added to water to prevent it from freezing, used in the radiator of a motor vehicle.

an·ti·gen /ˈantijən/ ▶ **noun** a harmful substance that causes the body to produce antibodies.
– DERIVATIVES **an·ti·gen·ic** /ˌantiˈjenik/ adjective.

an·ti·glob·al·i·za·tion /ˌantēˌglōbələˈzāSHən, ˌantī-/ ▶ **noun** opposition to the agendas and actions of groups perceived to favor globalization.

An·ti·guan /anˈtēgwən, -ˈtigwən/ ▶ **noun** a person from Antigua, or the country of Antigua and Barbuda, in the West Indies. ▶ **adjective** relating to Antigua or Antigua and Barbuda.

an·ti·he·ro /ˈantēˌhi(ə)rō, ˈantī-/ (or **antiheroine** /ˈantēˌherōin, ˈantī-/) ▶ **noun** a central character in a story who lacks typical heroic qualities.

an·ti·his·ta·mine /ˌantēˈhistəmin, -mēn/ ▶ **noun** a drug that counteracts the effects of histamine, used in treating allergies.

an·ti·in·flam·ma·to·ry /ˌantēinˈflaməˌtôrē, ˌantī-/ ▶ **adjective** (of a drug) used to reduce inflammation.

an·ti·lock /ˌantēˈläk, ˌantī-/ ▶ **adjective** (of brakes) designed so as to prevent the wheels from locking and the vehicle from skidding if applied suddenly.

an·ti·log·a·rithm /ˌantēˈlôgəˌriTHəm, -ˈläg-, ˌantī-/ ▶ **noun** Mathematics the number of which a given number is the logarithm.

an·ti·ma·cas·sar /ˌantēməˈkasər/ ▶ **noun** a cloth put over the back of a chair to protect it from grease and dirt.
– ORIGIN from **ANTI-** + *Macassar*, a kind of hair oil formerly used by men.

an·ti·ma·lar·i·al /ˌantēməˈle(ə)rēəl, ˌantī-/ ▶ **adjective** used to prevent malaria. ▶ **noun** an antimalarial drug.

an·ti·mat·ter /ˈantēˌmatər, ˈantī-/ ▶ **noun** Physics matter consisting of the antiparticles of the particles that make up normal matter.

an·ti·mi·cro·bi·al /ˌantēmīˈkrōbēəl, ˌantī-/ ▶ **adjective** active against microbes. ▶ **noun** a substance that acts against microbes.

an·ti·mo·ny /ˈantəˌmōnē/ ▶ **noun** a brittle silvery-white metallic element.
– ORIGIN Latin *antimonium*.

an·ti·no·mi·an /ˌantiˈnōmēən/ ▶ **adjective** believing that Christians are released by grace from obeying moral laws. ▶ **noun** a person with such a belief.
– DERIVATIVES **an·ti·no·mi·an·ism** /-ˌnizəm/ noun.
– ORIGIN from Greek *anti-* 'against' + *nomos* 'law.'

an·tin·o·my /anˈtinəmē/ ▶ **noun** (pl. **antinomies**) formal a contradiction between two beliefs or conclusions that are reasonable in themselves; a paradox.
– ORIGIN from Greek *anti* 'against' + *nomos* 'law.'

an·ti·ox·i·dant /ˌantēˈäksidənt, ˌantī-/ ▶ **noun** a substance that counteracts oxidation.

an·ti·par·ti·cle /ˈantēˌpärtikəl, ˈantī-/ ▶ **noun** Physics a subatomic particle with the same mass as a given particle but an opposite electric charge or magnetic effect.

an·ti·pas·to /ˌantēˈpästō, ˌän-/ ▶ **noun** (pl. **antipasti** /-ˈpästē/) an Italian appetizer, usually including an assortment of olives, cheeses, and meats.
– ORIGIN from Italian *anti-* 'before' + *pasto* 'food.'

an·tip·a·thy /anˈtipəTHē/ ▶ **noun** (pl. **antipathies**) a strong feeling of dislike.

– SYNONYMS **hostility,** antagonism, animosity, aversion, animus, distaste, dislike, hatred, abhorrence, loathing.
– ANTONYMS affinity, liking.

– DERIVATIVES **an·ti·pa·thet·ic** /anˌtipəˈTHetik/ adjective.
– ORIGIN from Greek *anti-* 'against' + *pathos* 'feeling.'

an·ti·per·son·nel /ˌantēˌpərsəˈnel, ˌantī-/ ▶ **adjective** (of weapons) designed to kill or injure people rather than to damage buildings or equipment.

an·ti·per·spi·rant /ˌantiˈpərspərənt/ ▶ **noun** a substance applied to the skin to prevent or reduce sweating.

an·ti·phon /ˈantəˌfän/ ▶ **noun** (in the Christian Church) a short chant sung before or after a psalm or canticle.
– ORIGIN from Greek *antiphōna* 'harmonies.'

an·tiph·o·nal /anˈtifənl/ ▶ **adjective** sung or recited alternately between two groups.

An·tip·o·des /anˈtipədēz/ ▶ **plural noun** (**the Antipodes**) Australia and New Zealand (in relation to the northern hemisphere).
– DERIVATIVES **An·tip·o·de·an** /anˌtipəˈdēən/ adjective & noun.
– ORIGIN from Greek *antipodes* 'having the feet opposite.'

an·ti·psy·chot·ic /ˌantēsīˈkätik, ˌantī-/ ▶ **noun** a drug used to treat psychotic disorders.

an·ti·py·ret·ic /ˌantēˌpīˈretik, ˌantī-/ ▶ **adjective** (of a drug) used to prevent or reduce fever.

an·ti·quar·i·an /ˌantiˈkwe(ə)rēən/ ▶ **adjective** relating to the collection or study of antiques, rare books, or antiquities. ▶ **noun** (also **antiquary** /ˈantiˌkwerē/) a person who studies or collects antiquarian items.
– DERIVATIVES **an·ti·quar·i·an·ism** /-ˌnizəm/ noun.

an·ti·quat·ed /ˈantiˌkwātid/ ▶ **adjective** old-fashioned or outdated.

– SYNONYMS **outdated,** outmoded, outworn, behind the times, old, old-fashioned, anachronistic, antediluvian; informal out of the ark, superannuated.
– ANTONYMS modern.

an·tique /anˈtēk/ ▶ **noun** a decorative object or piece of furniture that is valuable because of its age.

– SYNONYMS **collector's item,** museum piece, period piece, antiquity.

▶ **adjective 1** (of an object) valuable because of its age. **2** old-fashioned or outdated.

– SYNONYMS **antiquarian,** old, collectable, vintage, classic.
– ANTONYMS modern.

– ORIGIN Latin *antiquus* 'former, ancient.'

an·tiq·ui·ty /anˈtikwitē/ ▶ **noun** (pl. **antiquities**) **1** the distant past, especially before the Middle Ages. **2** an object from the distant past. **3** great age: *a church of great antiquity.*

– SYNONYMS **1** *the civilizations of antiquity* **long ago,** the past, prehistory, classical/ancient times. **2** *Inuit antiquities* **antique,** artifact, treasure, object, collector's piece.

an·ti·re·tro·vi·ral /ˌantēˌretrōˈvīrəl, ˌantī-/ ▶ **adjective** working against or targeted against retroviruses, especially HIV: *antiretroviral therapy.* ▶ **noun** an antiretroviral drug.

an·tir·rhi·num /ˌantiˈrīnəm/ ▶ **noun** (pl. **antirrhinums**) a snapdragon.
– ORIGIN from Greek *anti-* 'imitating' + *rhis* 'nose' (from the flower's resemblance to an animal's snout).

an·ti-Sem·i·tism ▶ **noun** hostility to or prejudice against Jews.
– DERIVATIVES **an·ti-Sem·ite** noun **an·ti-Se·mit·ic** adjective.

an·ti·sep·tic /ˌantiˈseptik/ ▶ **adjective 1** preventing the growth of microorganisms that cause disease or infection. **2** so clean or pure as to lack character: *the antiseptic modernity of a conference center.* ▶ **noun** an antiseptic substance.

CHOOSE THE RIGHT WORD

See **SANITARY**.

an·ti·se·rum /ˈantiˌsi(ə)rəm/ ▶ **noun** (pl. **antisera** /-ˌsi(ə)rə/) a blood serum containing antibodies against specific antigens (harmful substances).

an·ti·so·cial /ˌantēˈsōSHəl, ˌantī-/ ▶ **adjective 1** (especially of behavior) conflicting with accepted standards and causing annoyance. **2** not wanting to mix with other people.

– SYNONYMS **1** *antisocial behavior* **objectionable,** offensive, unacceptable, disruptive, rowdy. **2** *I'm feeling a bit antisocial* **unsociable,** unfriendly, uncommunicative, reclusive, misanthropic.
– ANTONYMS acceptable, sociable.

– DERIVATIVES **an·ti·so·cial·ly** adverb.

an·ti·ter·ror·ism /ˌantēˈterəˌrizəm, ˌantī-/ ▶ **noun** activities or measures designed to prevent or thwart terrorism.
– DERIVATIVES **an·ti·ter·ror·ist** adjective.

an·tith·e·sis /anˈtiTHəsis/ ▶ **noun** (pl. **antitheses** /-ˌsēz/) **1** a person or thing that is the direct opposite of another. **2** the putting together of contrasting ideas or words to produce an effect in speaking or writing.
– ORIGIN from Greek *antitithenai* 'set against.'

an·ti·thet·i·cal /ˌantəˈTHetikəl/ ▶ **adjective** opposed to or incompatible with each other: *those whose religious beliefs are antithetical to mine.*

CHOOSE THE RIGHT WORD

See **OPPOSITE**.

an·ti·tox·in /ˌantēˈtäksin/ ▸ **noun** an antibody that counteracts a toxin.

an·ti·trust /ˌantēˈtrəst, ˌantī-/ ▸ **adjective** (of laws) preventing or controlling monopolies, so assisting fair competition.

an·ti·tus·sive /ˌantēˈtəsiv/ ▸ **noun** a drug or other preparation that cures or relieves a cough.

an·ti·ven·in /ˌantēˈvenin, ˌantī-/ ▸ **noun** an antiserum containing antibodies against poisons in the venom of snakes.

an·ti·vi·ral /ˌantēˈvīrəl, ˌantī-/ ▸ **adjective** (of a drug or treatment) effective against viruses.

an·ti·viv·i·sec·tion·ist /ˌantēˌviviˈsekshənist, ˌantī-/ ▸ **noun** a person who is opposed to the use of live animals for scientific research.

ant·ler /ˈantlər/ ▸ **noun** each of a pair of branched horns on the head of an adult male deer.
– ORIGIN Old French *antoillier*.

an·to·nym /ˈantəˌnim/ ▸ **noun** a word opposite in meaning to another (e.g., *bad* and *good*).
– ORIGIN from Greek *anti-* 'against' + *onoma* 'a name.'

ant·sy /ˈantsē/ ▸ **adjective** agitated, impatient, or restless: *he was too antsy to stay in one place for long*.

a·nus /ˈānəs/ ▸ **noun** the opening at the end of the digestive system through which solid waste leaves the body.
– ORIGIN Latin.

an·vil /ˈanvil/ ▸ **noun** a heavy iron block on which metal can be hammered and shaped.
– ORIGIN Old English.

anx·i·e·ty /angˈzī-itē/ ▸ **noun** (pl. **anxieties**) **1** a feeling of unease or worry. **2** strong concern or eagerness: *the housekeeper's anxiety to please*.

– SYNONYMS **worry,** concern, apprehension, unease, fear, disquiet, doubts, nervousness, nerves, tension, stress, angst; informal butterflies (in one's stomach), the jitters.

anx·ious /ˈang(k)shəs/ ▸ **adjective 1** feeling or causing worry or unease: *she became anxious about his debts*. **2** very eager and concerned to do something.

– SYNONYMS **1 worried,** concerned, apprehensive, fearful, uneasy, disturbed, fretful, agitated, nervous, on edge, worked up, jumpy, tense, distraught; informal uptight, with butterflies in one's stomach, jittery, twitchy, antsy. **2** *she was anxious for news* **eager,** keen, itching, impatient, desperate.
– ANTONYMS unconcerned.

– DERIVATIVES **anx·ious·ly** adverb **anx·ious·ness** noun.
– ORIGIN Latin *anxius*.

an·y /ˈenē/ ▸ **determiner & pronoun 1** one or some of a thing or things, no matter how much or how many. **2** whichever or whatever one chooses. ▸ **adverb** at all.
– ORIGIN Old English.

USAGE

When used as a pronoun **any** can be used with either a singular or a plural verb, depending on the rest of the sentence: *we needed more sugar but there wasn't any left* (singular verb, to match *sugar*) or *are any of the new videos available?* (plural verb, to match *videos*).

an·y·bod·y /ˈenēˌbädē, -ˌbədē/ ▸ **pronoun** anyone.

an·y·how /ˈenēˌhou/ ▸ **adverb 1** anyway. **2** in a careless or haphazard way.

an·y·more /ˌenēˈmôr/ ▸ **adverb** to any further extent; any longer: *she refused to listen anymore*.

an·y·one /ˈenēˌwən/ ▸ **pronoun** any person or people.

an·y·place /ˈenēˌplās/ ▸ **adverb** informal term for **ANYWHERE**.

an·y·thing /ˈenēˌthing/ ▸ **pronoun** a thing of any kind, no matter what.
– PHRASES **anything but** not at all.

an·y time (also **anytime**) ▸ **adverb 1** at whatever time: *she can come any time*. **2** without exception or doubt: *I can handle a shrimp like him anytime*.

an·y·way /ˈenēˌwā/ ▸ **adverb 1** used to emphasize something just said or to change the subject. **2** nevertheless.

an·y·where /ˈenēˌ(h)we(ə)r/ ▸ **adverb** in or to any place. ▸ **pronoun** any place.

An·zac /ˈanˌzak/ ▸ **noun** a soldier in the Australian and New Zealand Army Corps (1914–18).

A-OK informal ▸ **noun** in good order or condition; all right. ▸ **adverb** in a good manner or way; all right: *we hit it off A-OK*.

a·or·ta /āˈôrtə/ ▸ **noun** the main artery supplying blood from the heart to the rest of the body.
– DERIVATIVES **a·or·tic** adjective.
– ORIGIN Greek *aortē*.

a·pace /əˈpās/ ▸ **adverb** literary quickly: *sales are growing apace*.
– ORIGIN from Old French *a pas* 'at (a considerable) pace.'

A·pach·e /əˈpachē/ ▸ **noun** (pl. same or **Apaches**) a member of an American Indian people living chiefly in New Mexico and Arizona.
– ORIGIN probably from an American Indian word meaning 'enemy.'

a·part /əˈpärt/ ▸ **adverb 1** separated by a distance in time or space. **2** having distinctive qualities: *wrestlers were a breed apart*. **3** into pieces.
– PHRASES **apart from 1** except for. **2** as well as.
– ORIGIN from Latin *a parte* 'at the side.'

a·part·heid /əˈpärtˌ(h)āt, -ˌ(h)īt/ ▸ **noun** the official system of segregation or discrimination on racial grounds formerly in force in South Africa.
– ORIGIN Afrikaans, 'separateness.'

a·part·ment /əˈpärtmənt/ ▸ **noun 1** a set of rooms forming an individual home within a larger building. **2** (**apartments**) a private suite of rooms in a very large house.

– SYNONYMS **1** flat, efficiency (unit), loft, studio apartment, walk-up, penthouse; informal pad. **2 suite (of rooms),** rooms, quarters, accommodations.

– ORIGIN from Italian *appartare* 'to separate.'

ap·a·thet·ic /ˌapəˈthetik/ ▸ **adjective** not interested or enthusiastic.

– SYNONYMS **uninterested,** indifferent, unenthusiastic, unconcerned, unmoved, uninvolved, unemotional, lukewarm, half-hearted, unresponsive, lethargic; informal couldn't-care-less.
– ANTONYMS enthusiastic.

– DERIVATIVES **ap·a·thet·i·cal·ly** adverb.

ap·a·thy /'apəTHē/ ▸ **noun** lack of interest or enthusiasm: *the task of overcoming voter apathy.*
– ORIGIN from Greek *apathēs* 'without feeling.'

ap·a·to·sau·rus /ˌapətō'sôrəs/ ▸ **noun** a huge plant-eating dinosaur with a long neck and tail; a brontosaurus.
– ORIGIN from Greek *apatē* 'deceit' + *sauros* 'lizard.'

APC ▸ **abbreviation** armored personnel carrier.

ape /āp/ ▸ **noun 1** an animal similar to a monkey but without a tail, such as a gorilla or chimpanzee. **2** informal a stupid or clumsy person. ▸ **verb** imitate in an absurd or unthinking way: *his sons aped those who were more westernized.*
– ORIGIN Old English.

> **CHOOSE THE RIGHT WORD**
>
> See **IMITATE**.

a·per·çu /äper'so͞o/ ▸ **noun** (pl. **aperçus** pronunc. same) a comment that makes a clever or entertaining point.
– ORIGIN French, 'thing perceived.'

a·pe·ri·tif /äˌperi'tēf, -əˌper-/ ▸ **noun** a drink of alcohol taken before a meal.
– ORIGIN French.

ap·er·ture /'apərˌCHər/ ▸ **noun 1** an opening, hole, or gap. **2** the variable opening by which light enters a camera.

> – SYNONYMS **opening,** hole, gap, slit, slot, vent, crevice, chink, crack; technical orifice.

– ORIGIN from Latin *aperire* 'to open.'

A·pex /'āpeks/ (also **APEX**) ▸ **noun** a system of reduced fares for air or rail journeys booked in advance.
– ORIGIN from *A*dvance *P*urchase *Ex*cursion.

a·pex /'āpeks/ ▸ **noun** (pl. **apexes** or **apices** /'āpəˌsēz, 'apə-/) the top or highest point: *the paper was regarded as the apex of journalism.*
– ORIGIN Latin, 'peak, tip.'

a·pha·sia /ə'fāZHə/ ▸ **noun** the inability to understand or produce speech, as a result of brain damage.
– DERIVATIVES **a·pha·sic** /-zik/ adjective & noun.
– ORIGIN from Greek *aphatos* 'speechless.'

a·phe·li·on /ə'fēlyən, ə'fēlēən/ ▸ **noun** (pl. **aphelia** /əfēlyə, ə'fēlēə/) the point in the orbit of a planet, asteroid, or comet at which it is farthest from the sun. The opposite of **PERIHELION**.
– ORIGIN from Greek *aph' hēlion* 'from the sun.'

a·phid /'āfid, 'af-/ ▸ **noun** a greenfly or similar small insect feeding on the sap of plants.
– ORIGIN Greek *aphis*.

aph·o·rism /'afəˌrizəm/ ▸ **noun** a short clever phrase that states something true.
– DERIVATIVES **aph·o·ris·tic** /ˌafə'ristik/ adjective.
– ORIGIN Greek *aphorismos* 'definition.'

> **CHOOSE THE RIGHT WORD**
>
> See **SAYING**.

aph·ro·dis·i·ac /ˌafrə'dizēˌak, -'dēzē-, -'dēZHē-/ ▸ **noun** a food, drink, or other thing that arouses sexual desire. ▸ **adjective** acting as an aphrodisiac: *the root of the plant is said to have aphrodisiac properties.*
– ORIGIN from *Aphrodite*, the Greek goddess of love.

a·pi·ar·y /'āpēˌerē/ ▸ **noun** (pl. **apiaries**) a place where bees are kept.
– DERIVATIVES **a·pi·a·rist** noun.
– ORIGIN from Latin *apis* 'bee.'

a·pi·cal /'āpikəl, 'ap-/ ▸ **adjective** technical relating to or forming an apex.
– ORIGIN from Latin *apex* 'peak, tip.'

a·pi·ces /'āpəˌsēz, 'apə-/ plural of **APEX**.

a·pi·cul·ture /'āpiˌkəlCHər/ ▸ **noun** technical beekeeping.
– ORIGIN from Latin *apis* 'bee.'

a·piece /ə'pēs/ ▸ **adverb** to, for, or by each one; each.

a·plen·ty /ə'plentē/ ▸ **adjective** in abundance: *he has work aplenty.*

a·plomb /ə'pläm, ə'pləm/ ▸ **noun** calm self-confidence: *he took the penalty with aplomb.*
– ORIGIN from French *à plomb* 'straight as a plumb line.'

ap·ne·a /'apnēə, ap'nēə/ ▸ **noun** a medical condition in which a person temporarily stops breathing, especially during sleep.
– ORIGIN from Greek *apnous* 'breathless.'

APO ▸ **abbreviation** Army Post Office.

a·poc·a·lypse /ə'päkəˌlips/ ▸ **noun 1** an event involving great and widespread destruction. **2** (**the Apocalypse**) the final destruction of the world, as described in the biblical book of Revelation.
– ORIGIN from Greek *apokaluptein* 'reveal.'

a·poc·a·lyp·tic /əˌpäkə'liptik/ ▸ **adjective** relating to or resembling the destruction of the world: *an apocalyptic war.*
– DERIVATIVES **a·poc·a·lyp·ti·cal·ly** adverb.

A·poc·ry·pha /ə'päkrəfə/ ▸ **plural noun** (treated as sing. or pl.) those books of the Old Testament not accepted as part of Hebrew scripture and excluded from the Protestant Bible at the Reformation.
– ORIGIN from Latin *apocrypha scripta* 'hidden writings.'

a·poc·ry·phal /ə'päkrəfəl/ ▸ **adjective 1** widely known but unlikely to be true: *an apocryphal story.* **2** relating to the Apocrypha.

ap·o·gee /'apəjē/ ▸ **noun 1** the highest point in the development of something: *they regarded Alexandria as the apogee of civilization.* **2** the point in the orbit of the moon or a satellite at which it is farthest from the earth. The opposite of **PERIGEE**.
– ORIGIN from Greek *apogaion diastēma*, 'distance away from earth.'

a·po·lit·i·cal /ˌāpə'litikəl/ ▸ **adjective** not interested or involved in politics.

a·pol·o·get·ic /əˌpälə'jetik/ ▸ **adjective** admitting and showing regret for wrongdoing.

> – SYNONYMS **sorry,** regretful, contrite, remorseful, penitent, repentant.
> – ANTONYMS unrepentant.

– DERIVATIVES **a·pol·o·get·i·cal·ly** adverb.

WORD TOOLKIT

apologetic ...	contrite ...	penitent ...
response	heart	man/woman
letter	spirit	thief
gesture	expression	sinner
statement	tone	saints
explanation	apology	silence

a·pol·o·get·ics /əˌpälə'jetiks/ ▸ **plural noun** (treated as sing. or pl.) reasoned arguments defending a theory or doctrine.

ap·o·lo·gi·a /ˌapəˈlōj(ē)ə/ ▶ **noun** a formal written statement defending one's opinions or behavior.
– ORIGIN Latin, 'apology.'

a·pol·o·gist /əˈpäləjist/ ▶ **noun** a person who offers an argument in defense of something controversial: *an apologist for fascism.*

a·pol·o·gize /əˈpäləˌjīz/ ▶ **verb** say sorry for something that one has done wrong: *we apologize for any inaccuracy.*

– SYNONYMS **say (one is) sorry,** express regret, ask forgiveness, ask for pardon, eat humble pie.

a·pol·o·gy /əˈpäləjē/ ▶ **noun** (pl. **apologies**) **1** an expression of regret for a wrongdoing. **2** (**an apology for**) a very poor example of.

– SYNONYMS **1 regrets,** expression of regret. **2** (**an apology for**) *it's an apology for a bridge, built of leftover stones* **travesty of,** poor imitation of, poor substitute for, (pale) shadow of; informal (poor) excuse for.

– ORIGIN Greek *apologia* 'a speech in one's own defense.'

ap·o·phthegm ▶ **noun** British spelling of **APOTHEGM**.

ap·o·plec·tic /ˌapəˈplektik/ ▶ **adjective 1** overcome with anger. **2** dated relating to apoplexy (stroke).

ap·o·plex·y /ˈapəˌpleksē/ ▶ **noun** (pl. **apoplexies**) **1** extreme anger. **2** dated unconsciousness or inability to move or feel, caused by a stroke.
– ORIGIN from Greek *apoplēssein* 'disable by a stroke.'

ap·op·to·sis /ˌapə(p)ˈtōsis/ ▶ **noun** Physiology the death of cells that occurs as a normal and controlled part of an organism's growth or development.
– ORIGIN from Greek *apoptōsis* 'falling off.'

a·pos·ta·sy /əˈpästəsē/ ▶ **noun** the abandonment of a belief or principle.
– ORIGIN Greek *apostasis* 'desertion.'

a·pos·tate /əˈpäsˌtāt, -tit/ ▶ **noun** a person who abandons a belief or principle.

a pos·te·ri·o·ri /ˈā päˌsti(ə)rēˈôrˌē, -ˈôrˌī/ ▶ **adjective & adverb** involving reasoning based on known facts to deduce causes.
– ORIGIN Latin, 'from what comes after.'

a·pos·tle /əˈpäsəl/ ▶ **noun 1** (**Apostle**) each of the twelve chief disciples of Jesus. **2** a pioneering advocate or enthusiastic supporter of an idea or cause: *he's an apostle of positive thinking.*
– ORIGIN Greek *apostolos* 'messenger.'

a·pos·to·late /əˈpästəˌlāt, -lit/ ▶ **noun 1** the position or authority of a religious leader. **2** evangelistic activity.

ap·os·tol·ic /ˌapəˈstälik/ ▶ **adjective 1** relating to the Apostles. **2** relating to the Pope, regarded as the successor to St. Peter.

a·pos·tro·phe /əˈpästrəfē/ ▶ **noun 1** a punctuation mark (') used to show either possession or the omission of letters or numbers. **2** a passage in a speech or poem that turns away from the subject to address an absent person or thing.
– ORIGIN from Greek *apostrephein* 'turn away.'

USAGE

The apostrophe should be used to show that a person or thing relates or belongs to someone or something (*Sue's cat, yesterday's weather*) or that letters or numbers have been omitted (*he's gone; the winter of '99*). Do not use an apostrophe to form the plural of ordinary words, as in *apple's*, or in the possessive pronouns **its**, **hers**, **yours**, or **theirs**.

a·pos·tro·phize /əˈpästrəˌfīz/ ▶ **verb 1** punctuate a word with an apostrophe. **2** address a separate passage in a speech or poem to an absent person or thing.

a·poth·e·car·y /əˈpäTHiˌkerē/ ▶ **noun** (pl. **apothecaries**) old use a person who prepared and sold medicines.
– ORIGIN from Greek *apothēkē* 'storehouse.'

ap·o·thegm /ˈapəˌTHem/ (Brit. **apophthegm**) ▶ **noun** a short phrase stating a general truth.
– ORIGIN from Greek *apophthengesthai* 'speak out.'

a·poth·e·o·sis /əˌpäTHēˈōsis, ˌapəˈTHēəsis/ ▶ **noun** (pl. **apotheoses** /-ˌsēz/) **1** the highest point: *science is the apotheosis of the intellect.* **2** the raising of someone to the rank of a god.
– DERIVATIVES **a·poth·e·o·size** /əˈpäTHēəˌsīz, ˌapəˈTHēə-/ verb.
– ORIGIN from Greek *apotheoun* 'make a god of.'

ap·pall /əˈpôl/ (Brit. **appal**) ▶ **verb 1** cause great shock or dismay to: *I am appalled at his lack of understanding.* **2** (as adj. **appalling**) informal shockingly bad.

– SYNONYMS **1 horrify,** shock, dismay, distress, outrage, scandalize, disgust, revolt, sicken, nauseate, offend, make someone's blood run cold. **2** (as adj. **appalling**) *an appalling crime* **horrific,** shocking, horrible, terrible, awful, dreadful, ghastly, hideous, horrendous, frightful, atrocious, abominable, outrageous. **3** (as adj. **appalling**) *your schoolwork is appalling* **dreadful,** terrible, atrocious, deplorable, hopeless, lamentable; informal rotten, crummy, woeful, useless, lousy, abysmal, dire, shocking.

– DERIVATIVES **ap·pall·ing·ly** /əˈpôliNGlē/ adverb.
– ORIGIN Old French *apalir* 'grow pale.'

Ap·pa·loo·sa /ˌapəˈlo͞osə/ ▶ **noun** a horse of a North American breed having dark spots on a light background.
– ORIGIN from *Opelousas* in Louisiana, or *Palouse*, a river in Idaho.

ap·pa·rat·chik /ˌäpəˈräCHik/ ▶ **noun 1** chiefly derogatory an official in a large political organization. **2** chiefly historical a member of the administrative system of a communist party.
– ORIGIN Russian.

ap·pa·rat·us /ˌapəˈratəs, -ˈrātəs/ ▶ **noun** (pl. **apparatuses**) **1** the equipment needed for a particular activity or purpose. **2** the complex structure of an organization: *the apparatus of government.*

– SYNONYMS **equipment,** gear, tackle, mechanism, appliance, device, instrument, machine, tool.

– ORIGIN Latin.

CHOOSE THE RIGHT WORD

See **TOOL**.

ap·par·el /əˈparəl/ ▶ **noun** formal clothing. ▶ **verb** (**apparels, appareling, appareled**) old use clothe someone.
– ORIGIN Old French *apareillier.*

ap·par·ent /əˈparənt, əˈpe(ə)r-/ ▶ **adjective 1** clearly seen or understood; obvious. **2** seeming real, but not necessarily so: *his apparent lack of concern.*

– SYNONYMS **1 evident,** plain, obvious, clear, manifest, visible, discernible, noticeable, perceptible, unmistakable, patent. **2 seeming,**

ostensible, outward, superficial.
– ANTONYMS unclear, real.

– DERIVATIVES **ap·par·ent·ly** adverb.
– ORIGIN from Latin *apparere* 'appear.'

ap·pa·ri·tion /ˌapəˈrisʜən/ ▶ **noun** a remarkable thing that makes a sudden appearance, especially a ghost.

– SYNONYMS **ghost,** phantom, specter, spirit, wraith; informal spook; literary phantasm.

ap·peal /əˈpēl/ ▶ **verb 1** make a serious or earnest request. **2** be attractive or interesting. **3** ask a higher court of law to reverse the decision of a lower court. **4** (in sports) call on an umpire or referee to rule on a completed play or move.

– SYNONYMS **1 ask,** request, call, petition, plead, entreat, beg, implore, beseech. **2** *activities that appeal to all* **attract,** interest, fascinate, please, tempt, lure, draw; informal float someone's boat.

▶ **noun 1** an act of appealing. **2** the quality of being attractive or interesting: *the popular appeal of football.*

– SYNONYMS **1 plea,** request, petition, entreaty, cry, call, cri de coeur. **2 attraction,** allure, charm, fascination, magnetism, pull.

– ORIGIN Latin *appellare* 'to address.'

ap·peal·ing /əˈpēlinɢ/ ▶ **adjective** attractive or interesting.

– SYNONYMS **attractive,** engaging, alluring, enchanting, captivating, bewitching, fascinating, tempting, enticing, irresistible, charming.

– DERIVATIVES **ap·peal·ing·ly** adverb.

WORD TOOLKIT

See **ENCHANTING**.

ap·pear /əˈpi(ə)r/ ▶ **verb 1** come into sight or existence: *Pat appeared at the door.* **2** give a particular impression; seem: *she appeared antisocial.* **3** perform in a movie, play, etc. **4** present oneself formally in a court of law. **5** be published.

– SYNONYMS **1 become visible,** come into view, materialize, turn up, show up. **2** *differences were beginning to appear* **be revealed,** emerge, surface, manifest itself, become apparent/evident, come to light, arrive, arise, crop up, show up. **3** *they appeared completely devoted* **seem,** look, give the impression of being, come across as, strike someone as.
– ANTONYMS vanish.

– ORIGIN from Latin *parere* 'come into view.'

ap·pear·ance /əˈpi(ə)rəns/ ▶ **noun 1** the way that someone or something looks or seems: *you can improve your appearance with makeup.* **2** an act of appearing.

– SYNONYMS **1** *her disheveled appearance* **look,** air, aspect, looks, mien, expression, behavior. **2** *an appearance of respectability* **impression,** air, (outward) show, semblance, illusion, facade, front, pretense. **3 occurrence,** manifestation, emergence, arrival, development, materialization.

– PHRASES **keep up appearances** keep up an impression of wealth or well-being.

ap·pease /əˈpēz/ ▶ **verb** make someone calmer or less hostile by agreeing to their demands.

– SYNONYMS **placate,** conciliate, pacify, mollify, reconcile, win over; informal sweeten.
– ANTONYMS provoke.

– DERIVATIVES **ap·pease·ment** noun **ap·peas·er** noun.
– ORIGIN Old French *apaisier.*

CHOOSE THE RIGHT WORD

See **PACIFY**.

ap·pel·lant /əˈpelənt/ ▶ **noun** Law a person who appeals to a higher court to reverse the decision of a lower court.

ap·pel·late /əˈpelit/ ▶ **adjective** Law (of a court) dealing with appeals.

ap·pel·la·tion /ˌapəˈlāsʜən/ ▶ **noun** formal a name or title.
– ORIGIN from Latin *appellare* 'to address.'

ap·pend /əˈpend/ ▶ **verb** add something to the end of a document or piece of writing.
– ORIGIN Latin *appendere* 'hang on.'

ap·pend·age /əˈpendij/ ▶ **noun** a thing attached to or projecting from something larger or more important.

ap·pen·dec·to·my /ˌapənˈdektəmē/ (Brit. also **appendicectomy** /əˌpendəˈsektəmē/) ▶ **noun** (pl. **appendectomies**) a surgical operation to remove the appendix.

ap·pen·di·ci·tis /əˌpendəˈsītis/ ▶ **noun** inflammation of the appendix.

ap·pen·dix /əˈpendiks/ ▶ **noun** (pl. **appendices** /-diˌsēz/ or **appendixes**) **1** a small tube of tissue attached to the lower end of the large intestine. **2** a section of additional information at the end of a book.

– SYNONYMS **supplement,** addendum, postscript, codicil, coda, epilogue, afterword, tailpiece.

– ORIGIN from Latin *appendere* 'hang on.'

ap·per·tain /ˌapərˈtān/ ▶ **verb** (**appertain to**) formal relate to: *the law appertaining to businesses is rather different.*
– ORIGIN Latin *appertinere.*

ap·pe·tite /ˈapiˌtīt/ ▶ **noun 1** a natural desire to satisfy a bodily need, especially for food. **2** a liking or inclination: *the nation's growing appetite for the Internet.*

– SYNONYMS **1 hunger,** taste, palate, stomach. **2** *my appetite for learning* **desire,** liking, hunger, thirst, longing, yearning, passion, enthusiasm, keenness, eagerness; informal yen.

– DERIVATIVES **ap·pe·ti·tive** /ˈapiˌtītiv/ adjective.
– ORIGIN Latin *appetitus* 'desire for.'

ap·pe·tiz·er /ˈapiˌtīzər/ ▶ **noun** a small dish of food or a drink taken before a meal to stimulate the appetite.

ap·pe·tiz·ing /ˈapiˌtīzinɢ/ ▶ **adjective** causing a pleasant feeling of hunger.

– SYNONYMS **mouthwatering,** inviting, tempting, tasty, delicious, flavorsome, toothsome, delectable; informal scrumptious, scrummy, yummy.

ap·plaud /əˈplôd/ ▶ **verb 1** show approval by clapping. **2** express approval of: *the world applauded his courage.*

– SYNONYMS **1 clap,** give a standing ovation, put one's hands together; informal give someone a big hand. **2 praise,** congratulate, commend, salute, welcome, celebrate, approve of.
– ANTONYMS boo, criticize.

– ORIGIN from Latin *plaudere* 'to clap.'

ap·plause /əˈplôz/ ▶ **noun** approval shown by clapping.

ap·ple /ˈapəl/ ▶ **noun** the round fruit of a tree of the rose family, with green or red skin and crisp flesh.
– DERIVATIVES **ap·pley** adjective.
– PHRASES **the apple of one's eye** a person of whom one is extremely fond and proud. [first referring to the pupil

of the eye.] **a rotten** (or **bad**) **apple** informal a corrupt person in a group, likely to have a bad influence on the others. **upset the apple cart** spoil a plan.
– ORIGIN Old English.

ap·ple-pie or·der ▶ **noun** perfect neatness or order.

ap·plet /ˈaplit/ ▶ **noun** Computing a small application running within a larger program.

ap·pli·ance /əˈplīəns/ ▶ **noun** a device designed to perform a specific task: *a gas appliance*.

– SYNONYMS **device,** machine, instrument, gadget, tool, contraption, apparatus, mechanism, contrivance, labor-saving device; informal gizmo.

CHOOSE THE RIGHT WORD

See **TOOL**.

ap·pli·ca·ble /ˈaplikəbəl, əˈplik-/ ▶ **adjective** relevant or appropriate: *most of the book is applicable to any country*.

– SYNONYMS **relevant,** appropriate, pertinent, apposite, material, fitting, suitable, apt.
– ANTONYMS inappropriate, irrelevant.

– DERIVATIVES **ap·pli·ca·bil·i·ty** /ˌaplikəˈbilitē/ noun.

ap·pli·cant /ˈaplikənt/ ▶ **noun** a person who applies for something.

– SYNONYMS **candidate,** interviewee, contender, entrant, claimant, petitioner, prospective student/ employee, job-seeker.

ap·pli·ca·tion /ˌapliˈkāsʜən/ ▶ **noun** **1** a formal request to an authority. **2** the action of applying something. **3** practical use or relevance: *this principle has no application to the present case*. **4** sustained effort; hard work. **5** a computer program designed to fulfill a particular purpose.

– SYNONYMS **1 request,** appeal, petition, approach, claim, demand. **2 implementation,** use, exercise, employment, execution, enactment. **3 hard work,** diligence, industry, effort, commitment, dedication, devotion, perseverance, persistence, concentration.

ap·pli·ca·tor /ˈapliˌkātər/ ▶ **noun** a device for inserting or applying something.

ap·plied /əˈplīd/ ▶ **adjective** practical rather than theoretical: *applied chemistry*.

ap·pli·qué /ˌapliˈkā/ ▶ **noun** decorative needlework in which fabric shapes are sewn or fixed onto a fabric background.
– DERIVATIVES **ap·pli·quéd** adjective.
– ORIGIN French, 'applied.'

ap·ply /əˈplī/ ▶ **verb** (**applies, applying, applied**) **1** make a formal request: *he applied for a job as a plumber*. **2** bring something into operation or use. **3** be relevant: *the regulations apply to all member nations*. **4** put a substance on a surface. **5** (**apply oneself**) put all one's efforts into a task.

– SYNONYMS **1** *300 people **applied for** the job* **put in,** bid for, try (out) for, audition for, seek, solicit (for), claim, request, ask for, petition for, make a bid for. **2** *the law does not **apply to** to students* **be relevant to,** pertain to, appertain to, relate to, concern, affect, involve, cover, touch, deal with, have a bearing on. **3 implement,** put into practice, introduce. **4 put on,** rub in/on, work in, spread, smear on, slap on. **5 exert,** administer, use, exercise, employ, utilize, bring to bear. **6** (**apply oneself**) **work hard,** exert oneself, make an effort, be industrious, show dedication, buckle down, persevere, persist, concentrate; informal put one's back into it, knuckle down.

– ORIGIN Latin *applicare* 'fold, fasten to.'

ap·point /əˈpoint/ ▶ **verb** **1** give a job or role to someone. **2** decide on a time or place.

– SYNONYMS **nominate,** name, designate, install, commission, engage, co-opt, select, choose, elect, vote in.

– DERIVATIVES **ap·point·ee** /əˌpoinˈtē/ noun.
– ORIGIN Old French *apointer*.

ap·point·ed /əˈpointid/ ▶ **adjective** **1** (of a time or place) prearranged. **2** equipped or furnished: *a luxuriously appointed lounge*.

– SYNONYMS **1 scheduled,** arranged, prearranged, specified, agreed, designated, set, allotted, fixed. **2 furnished,** decorated, fitted out, supplied.

ap·point·ment /əˈpointmənt/ ▶ **noun** **1** an arrangement to meet someone. **2** a job or position. **3** the action of appointing someone to a job. **4** (**appointments**) the furniture or fittings in a room.

– SYNONYMS **1 meeting,** engagement, interview, consultation, rendezvous, date, assignation; literary tryst. **2 nomination,** naming, designation, installation, commissioning, engagement, co-option, selection, election. **3 job,** post, position, situation, place, office.

ap·por·tion /əˈpôrsʜən/ ▶ **verb** share something out.
– DERIVATIVES **ap·por·tion·ment** noun.
– ORIGIN from Latin *portionare* 'divide into portions.'

ap·po·site /ˈapəzit/ ▶ **adjective** very appropriate; apt.
– ORIGIN from Latin *apponere* 'apply.'

ap·po·si·tion /ˌapəˈzisʜən/ ▶ **noun** **1** chiefly technical the positioning of things next to each other. **2** Grammar a relationship in which a word or phrase is placed next to another in order to qualify or explain it (e.g., *my friend Sue*).

ap·prais·al /əˈprāzəl/ ▶ **noun** **1** an act of assessing someone or something. **2** a formal assessment of an employee's performance.

– SYNONYMS **assessment,** evaluation, estimation, judgment, summing-up, consideration.

ap·praise /əˈprāz/ ▶ **verb** **1** assess the quality or nature of: *she appraised the damage and groaned*. **2** give an employee an appraisal. **3** (of an official valuer) set a price on something.
– DERIVATIVES **ap·prais·ee** /əˌprāzˈē/ noun **ap·prais·er** noun.
– ORIGIN alteration of **APPRISE**.

USAGE

Appraise is often confused with **apprise**. **Appraise** means *assess someone or something,* whereas **apprise** means *inform someone* (*psychiatrists were apprised of his condition*).

ap·pre·ci·a·ble /əˈprēsʜ(ē)əbəl/ ▶ **adjective** large or important enough to be noticed.

– SYNONYMS **considerable,** substantial, significant, sizable, goodly, fair, reasonable, marked; perceptible, noticeable, visible; informal tidy.
– ANTONYMS negligible.

– DERIVATIVES **ap·pre·ci·a·bly** adverb.

WORD TOOLKIT

See **PERCEPTIBLE**.

ap·pre·ci·ate /ə'prēsHē,āt/ ▶ **verb 1** recognize the worth of: *that's a son who appreciates his mother.* **2** understand a situation fully. **3** be grateful for something. **4** rise in value or price.

– SYNONYMS **1 value,** admire, respect, think highly of, think much of, be grateful for, be glad of. **2 recognize,** realize, know, be aware of, be conscious of, be sensitive to, understand, sympathize with. **3 increase,** gain, grow, rise, go up, soar.
– ANTONYMS disparage, depreciate.

– DERIVATIVES **ap·pre·ci·a·tor** noun.
– ORIGIN Latin *appretiare* 'appraise.'

ap·pre·ci·a·tion /ə,prēsHē'āsHən/ ▶ **noun 1** recognition of the worth of something. **2** gratitude. **3** a favorable written assessment of a person or their work. **4** increase in value.

– SYNONYMS **1 acknowledgment,** recognition, realization, knowledge, awareness, consciousness, understanding. **2 knowledge,** awareness, enjoyment, love, feeling, discrimination, sensitivity. **3 gratitude,** thanks, gratefulness. **4 review,** critique, criticism, assessment, evaluation, judgment. **5 increase,** gain, growth, rise, inflation, escalation.
– ANTONYMS ingratitude, depreciation.

ap·pre·cia·tive /ə'prēsH(ē)ətiv/ ▶ **adjective** feeling or showing gratitude or pleasure.

– SYNONYMS **1** *we are* ***appreciative of*** *your support* **grateful for,** thankful for, obliged for, indebted for. **2** *an appreciative audience* **admiring,** enthusiastic, approving, complimentary.

– DERIVATIVES **ap·pre·cia·tive·ly** adverb **ap·pre·cia·tive·ness** /ə'prēsH(ē)ətiv,nəs/ noun.

ap·pre·hend /,apri'hend/ ▶ **verb 1** seize or arrest someone for a crime. **2** understand something.

– SYNONYMS **1** *the thieves were apprehended* **arrest,** catch, capture, seize; take prisoner, take into custody; informal collar, nab, nail, run in, bust, pick up, pull in. **2** *they are slow to apprehend danger* **appreciate,** recognize, discern, perceive, grasp, understand, comprehend; informal get the picture.

– ORIGIN from Latin *prehendere* 'lay hold of.'

ap·pre·hen·sion /,apri'hensHən/ ▶ **noun 1** worry or fear about what might happen. **2** understanding. **3** the action of arresting someone.

– SYNONYMS **1 anxiety,** worry, unease, nervousness, nerves, misgivings, disquiet, concern, trepidation. **2 arrest,** capture, seizure, detention.
– ANTONYMS confidence.

WORD TOOLKIT

apprehensive ...	tense ...	neurotic ...
knock	situation	behavior
expression	silence	disorder
glance	atmosphere	passion
face	relationship	tendencies
voice	game	personality
parents	standoff	individuals
approach	encounter	patterns
steps	drama	obsession

ap·pre·hen·sive /,apri'hensiv/ ▶ **adjective** worried or afraid about what might happen: *she was apprehensive about attending classes.*

– SYNONYMS **anxious,** worried, uneasy, nervous, concerned, fearful.
– ANTONYMS confident.

– DERIVATIVES **ap·pre·hen·sive·ly** adverb.

ap·pren·tice /ə'prentis/ ▶ **noun** a person learning a skilled practical profession from an employer.

– SYNONYMS **trainee,** learner, probationer, novice, beginner, tyro, student, pupil; informal rookie, tenderfoot, greenhorn.
– ANTONYMS veteran.

▶ **verb** employ someone as an apprentice.
– DERIVATIVES **ap·pren·tice·ship** /-,sHip/ noun.
– ORIGIN from Old French *apprendre* 'learn.'

CHOOSE THE RIGHT WORD

See **NOVICE**.

ap·prise /ə'prīz/ ▶ **verb** inform or tell: *I had better apprise you of the situation.*
– ORIGIN French *apprendre* 'learn, teach.'

USAGE

On the confusion of **apprise** and **appraise**, see the note at **APPRAISE**.

ap·proach /ə'prōcH/ ▶ **verb 1** come near to someone or something in distance, time, or standard. **2** go to someone with a proposal or request. **3** start to deal with in a particular way: *one must approach the matter with caution.*

– SYNONYMS **1 move toward,** near, come near, close in on, close with, gain on. **2 speak to,** talk to, sound out, make a proposal to, proposition, appeal to. **3 tackle,** address, manage, set about, go about, start work on.
– ANTONYMS leave.

▶ **noun 1** a way of dealing with something. **2** an initial proposal or request. **3** the action of approaching. **4** a way leading to a place.

– SYNONYMS **1 method,** procedure, technique, modus operandi, style, way, strategy, tactic, system, means, line of action. **2 proposal,** submission, application, appeal, plea, request, overture, proposition. **3 advance,** arrival, appearance. **4 driveway,** road, path, entry, way.

– ORIGIN from Latin *appropiare* 'draw near.'

ap·proach·a·ble /ə'prōcHəbəl/ ▶ **adjective 1** friendly and easy to talk to. **2** able to be reached from a particular direction or by a particular means: *the peak is approachable via a six-mile hike.*

– SYNONYMS **1 friendly,** welcoming, pleasant, agreeable, affable, sympathetic, congenial. **2 accessible,** reachable, attainable; informal get-at-able.
– ANTONYMS aloof, inaccessible.

– DERIVATIVES **ap·proach·a·bil·i·ty** /ə,prōcHə'bilitē/ noun.

ap·pro·ba·tion /,aprə'bāsHən/ ▶ **noun** approval; praise.
– ORIGIN from Latin *approbare* 'approve.'

ap·pro·pri·ate ▶ **adjective** /ə'prōprē-it/ suitable or proper in the circumstances: *there is an appropriate time for training.*

– SYNONYMS **suitable,** proper, fitting, seemly, apt, right, convenient, opportune, relevant, apposite.
– ANTONYMS inappropriate.

▶ **verb** /-ˌāt/ **1** take something for one's own use without permission. **2** allocate money for a special purpose.

– SYNONYMS **seize,** commandeer, requisition, expropriate, usurp, take over, hijack, steal; informal swipe, nab.

– DERIVATIVES **ap·pro·pri·ate·ly** /-itlē/ adverb **ap·pro·pri·ate·ness** /-itnis/ noun **ap·pro·pri·a·tion** /-ˈāshən/ noun **ap·pro·pri·a·tor** /-ˌātər/ noun.
– ORIGIN Latin *appropriare* 'make one's own.'

ap·prov·al /əˈpro͞ovəl/ ▶ **noun 1** the belief that someone or something is good. **2** official acceptance that something is satisfactory.

– SYNONYMS **1 acceptance,** agreement, consent, assent, permission, rubber stamp, sanction, blessing, endorsement, ratification, authorization; informal the go-ahead, the green light, the OK, the thumbs up. **2 favor,** liking, appreciation, admiration, regard, esteem, respect.
– ANTONYMS refusal, disapproval.

– PHRASES **on approval** (of goods) able to be returned to a supplier if unsatisfactory.

ap·prove /əˈpro͞ov/ ▶ **verb 1** believe that someone or something is good or acceptable: *I don't approve of romance*. **2** officially accept something as satisfactory.

– SYNONYMS **1** *his boss doesn't* ***approve of*** *his lifestyle* **agree with,** hold with, endorse, support, be in favor of, favor, think well of, like, take kindly to, admire. **2** *the government approved the proposals* **agree to,** accept, consent to, assent to, give one's blessing to, bless, ratify, sanction, endorse, authorize, validate, pass, rubber-stamp; informal give the go-ahead to, give the green light to, give the OK to, give the thumbs up to.
– ANTONYMS refuse.

– ORIGIN from Latin *approbare*.

ap·prox·i·mate ▶ **adjective** /əˈpräksəmit/ almost but not completely accurate.

– SYNONYMS **estimated,** rough, imprecise, inexact, broad, loose; informal ballpark.
– ANTONYMS precise.

▶ **verb** /-ˌmāt/ **1** come close in nature or quantity to: *shoppers can create a computer image that approximates their body shape*. **2** estimate something fairly accurately.
– ORIGIN Latin *approximatus*.

ap·prox·i·mate·ly /əˈpräksəmitlē/ ▶ **adverb** near to but not exactly.

– SYNONYMS **roughly,** about, around, circa, round/around about, more or less, nearly, almost, approaching. informal pushing, in the ballpark of.

ap·prox·i·ma·tion /əˌpräksəˈmāshən/ ▶ **noun 1** an approximate figure or result. **2** the action of estimating something fairly accurately.

ap·pur·te·nan·ces /əˈpərtn-ənsiz/ ▶ **plural noun** formal accessories associated with a particular activity.
– ORIGIN from Latin *appertinere* 'belong to.'

APR ▶ **abbreviation** annual (or annualized) percentage rate.

a·près-ski /ˌäprā ˈskē/ ▶ **noun** social activities following a day's skiing.
– ORIGIN French, 'after skiing.'

ap·ri·cot /ˈapriˌkät, ˈāpri-/ ▶ **noun** an orange-yellow fruit resembling a small peach.
– ORIGIN from Latin *praecox* 'early-ripe.'

A·pril /ˈāprəl/ ▶ **noun** the fourth month of the year.
– ORIGIN Latin *Aprilis*.

A·pril Fool's Day ▶ **noun** April 1, traditionally an occasion for playing practical jokes.

a pri·o·ri /ˈä prēˈôrē, prīˈôrī, ˈā/ ▶ **adjective & adverb** based on theoretical reasoning rather than actual observation.
– ORIGIN Latin, 'from what is before.'

a·pron /ˈāprən/ ▶ **noun 1** a protective garment covering the front of one's clothes and tied at the back. **2** an area on an airfield used for maneuvering or parking aircraft. **3** (also **apron stage**) a strip of stage projecting in front of the curtain.
– PHRASES **tied to someone's apron strings** dominated or excessively influenced by someone, especially one's mother.
– ORIGIN from Old French *naperon* 'small tablecloth.'

ap·ro·pos /ˌaprəˈpō/ ▶ **preposition** with reference to: *she kept smiling down at her plate, apropos of nothing*.
▶ **adjective** very appropriate.
– ORIGIN French *à propos*.

apse /aps/ ▶ **noun** a large recess with a domed or arched roof at the eastern end of a church.
– DERIVATIVES **ap·si·dal** /ˈapsidl/ adjective.
– ORIGIN Greek *apsis* 'arch, vault.'

apt /apt/ ▶ **adjective 1** appropriate; suitable. **2** having a tendency to: *junior recruits are most apt to have low morale*. **3** quick to learn.

– SYNONYMS **1 suitable,** fitting, appropriate, relevant, apposite, felicitous. **2 inclined,** given, likely, liable, prone. **3 clever,** quick, bright, sharp, smart, able, gifted, talented.
– ANTONYMS inappropriate.

– DERIVATIVES **apt·ly** adverb **apt·ness** noun.
– ORIGIN Latin *aptus* 'fitted.'

ap·ti·tude /ˈaptiˌt(y)o͞od/ ▶ **noun** a natural ability or tendency: *a youth with a remarkable aptitude for math*.

– SYNONYMS **talent,** gift, flair, bent, skill, knack, facility, ability, capability, potential, capacity, faculty.

– ORIGIN from Latin *aptus* 'fitted.'

aq·ua /ˈäkwə, ˈak-/ ▶ **noun** a light bluish-green color; aquamarine.

aqua- ▶ **combining form** relating to water: *aqualung*.
– ORIGIN Latin *aqua* 'water.'

aq·ua·cul·ture /ˈäkwəˌkəlchər, ˈak-/ ▶ **noun** the rearing of aquatic animals or the cultivation of aquatic plants for food.

aq·ua·lung /ˈäkwəˌləng, ˈak-/ ▶ **noun** another term for **SCUBA**.

aq·ua·ma·rine /ˌäkwəməˈrēn, ˌak-/ ▶ **noun 1** a precious stone consisting of a light bluish-green variety of beryl. **2** a light bluish-green color.
– ORIGIN from Latin *aqua marina* 'seawater.'

aq·ua·naut /ˈäkwəˌnôt, ˈak-/ ▶ **noun** a diver.
– ORIGIN from Latin *aqua* 'water' + Greek *nautēs* 'sailor.'

aq·ua·plane /ˈäkwəˌplān, ˈak-/ ▶ **verb 1** (of a vehicle) slide uncontrollably on a wet surface. **2** ride on an aquaplane. ▶ **noun** a board for riding on water, pulled by a speedboat.
– ORIGIN from Latin *aqua* 'water' + **PLANE**[1].

aq·ua re·gi·a /ˈäkwə ˈrejēə, ˈak-/ ▶ **noun** a highly corrosive mixture of concentrated nitric and hydrochloric acids.
– ORIGIN Latin, 'royal water' (because it is able to dissolve gold).

aq·ua·relle /ˌäkwəˈrel, ˌak-/ ▶ **noun** the technique of painting with thin, transparent watercolors.
– ORIGIN from Italian *acquarella* 'watercolor.'

a·quar·ist /əˈkwe(ə)rist/ ▶ **noun** a person who keeps an aquarium.

a·quar·i·um /əˈkwe(ə)rēəm/ ▶ **noun** (pl. **aquariums** or **aquaria** /-ēə/) a water-filled glass tank for keeping fish and other water creatures and plants.
– ORIGIN Latin.

A·quar·i·us /əˈkwe(ə)rēəs/ ▶ **noun 1** a constellation and the eleventh sign of the zodiac (the Water Carrier), which the sun enters about January 21. **2** (**an Aquarius**) a person born when the sun is in this sign.
– DERIVATIVES **A·quar·i·an** /əˈkwe(ə)rēən/ noun & adjective.

a·quat·ic /əˈkwätik, əˈkwat-/ ▶ **adjective 1** relating to water. **2** living in or near water. ▶ **noun** an aquatic plant or animal.

aq·ua·tint /ˈäkwəˌtint, ˈak-/ ▶ **noun** a print resembling a watercolor, made using a copper plate etched with acid.
– ORIGIN from Italian *acqua tinta* 'colored water.'

aq·ua·vit /ˈäkwəˌvēt, ˈak-/ ▶ **noun** an alcoholic spirit made from potatoes.
– ORIGIN from Norwegian, Swedish, and Danish *akvavit* 'water of life.'

aq·ue·duct /ˈäkwəˌdəkt, ˈak-/ ▶ **noun** a long channel or raised bridgelike structure, used for carrying water across country.
– ORIGIN from Latin *aquae ductus* 'conduit.'

a·que·ous /ˈākwēəs, ˈak-/ ▶ **adjective** relating to or containing water.
– ORIGIN from Latin *aqua* 'water.'

a·que·ous hu·mor ▶ **noun** the clear fluid in the eyeball in front of the lens.

aq·ui·fer /ˈäkwəfər, ˈak-/ ▶ **noun** a body of rock that holds water or through which water flows.
– ORIGIN from Latin *aqua* 'water' and *-fer* 'bearing.'

aq·ui·le·gi·a /ˌakwəˈlēj(ē)ə/ ▶ **noun** a garden plant bearing showy flowers with backward-pointing spurs; columbine.
– ORIGIN probably from Latin *aquilegus* 'water-collecting.'

aq·ui·line /ˈakwəˌlīn, -lin/ ▶ **adjective 1** (of a nose) curved like an eagle's beak. **2** like an eagle.
– ORIGIN from Latin *aquila* 'eagle.'

AR ▶ **abbreviation** Arkansas.

Ar ▶ **symbol** the chemical element argon.

Ar·ab /ˈarəb/ ▶ **noun 1** a member of a Semitic people inhabiting much of the Middle East and North Africa. **2** a breed of horse originating in Arabia.
– DERIVATIVES **Ar·ab·ize** /ˈarəˌbīz/ verb.
– ORIGIN Arabic.

ar·a·besque /ˌarəˈbesk/ ▶ **noun 1** a ballet posture in which one leg is extended horizontally backward and the arms are outstretched. **2** an ornamental design consisting of intertwined flowing lines. **3** a musical passage with a highly ornamented melody.
– ORIGIN from Italian *arabesco* 'in the Arabic style.'

A·ra·bi·an /əˈrābēən/ ▶ **adjective** relating to Arabia or its people. ▶ **noun** historical an Arab.

Ar·a·bic /ˈarəbik/ ▶ **noun** the Semitic language of the Arabs, written from right to left. ▶ **adjective** relating to the Arabs or Arabic.

a·rab·i·ca /əˈrabikə/ ▶ **noun** a type of coffee bean widely grown in tropical Asia and Africa.
– ORIGIN Latin, 'Arabic.'

Ar·a·bic nu·mer·al ▶ **noun** any of the numerals 0, 1, 2, 3, 4, 5, 6, 7, 8, and 9.

Ar·ab·ism /ˈarəˌbizəm/ ▶ **noun 1** Arab culture or identity. **2** an Arabic word or phrase.
– DERIVATIVES **Ar·ab·ist** noun & adjective.

ar·a·ble /ˈarəbəl/ ▶ **adjective 1** (of land) used or suitable for growing crops. **2** (of crops) able to be grown on arable land.
– ORIGIN from Latin *arare* 'to plow.'

a·rach·nid /əˈraknid/ ▶ **noun** an invertebrate animal of a class including spiders, scorpions, mites, and ticks.
– ORIGIN from Greek *arakhnē* 'spider.'

a·rach·no·pho·bi·a /əˌraknəˈfōbēə/ ▶ **noun** extreme fear of spiders.
– DERIVATIVES **a·rach·no·phobe** /əˈraknəˌfōb/ noun.
– ORIGIN from Greek *arakhnē* 'spider.'

ar·ak ▶ **noun** variant spelling of **ARRACK**.

Ar·a·ma·ic /ˌarəˈmāik/ ▶ **noun** an ancient Semitic language still spoken in parts of the Middle East. ▶ **adjective** relating to Aramaic.
– ORIGIN Greek *Aramaios* 'of *Aram*' (the biblical name of Syria).

Ar·an /ˈarən/ ▶ **adjective** (of knitwear) featuring patterns of cable stitch and diamond designs, as made traditionally in the Aran Islands off the west coast of Ireland.

A·rap·a·ho /əˈrapəˌhō/ ▶ **noun** (pl. same or **Arapahos**) **1** a member of a North American Indian people living on the Great Plains. **2** the language of the Arapaho.
– ORIGIN from an American Indian word meaning 'many tattoo marks.'

Ar·a·wak /ˈarəˌwäk/ ▶ **noun** (pl. same or **Arawaks**) **1** a member of a group of native peoples of the Greater Antilles and northern and western South America. **2** any of the languages of the Arawak.
– ORIGIN Carib.

ar·bi·ter /ˈärbitər/ ▶ **noun 1** a person who settles a dispute. **2** a person who has influence in a particular area: *an arbiter of taste*.
– ORIGIN Latin, 'judge, supreme ruler.'

ar·bi·trage /ˈärbiˌträzh/ ▶ **noun** the buying and selling of assets at the same time in different markets or in derivative forms, taking advantage of the differing prices.
– DERIVATIVES **ar·bi·tra·geur** /ˌärbiträˈzhər, ˈärbiˌträzhər/ noun.
– ORIGIN from French *arbitrer* 'give judgment.'

ar·bi·trar·y /ˈärbiˌtrerē/ ▶ **adjective 1** not appearing to be based on any reason or system: *an arbitrary decision*. **2** (of power or authority) used without restraint.

> – SYNONYMS **random,** unpredictable, capricious, subjective, whimsical, wanton, motiveless, irrational, groundless, unjustified.

– DERIVATIVES **ar·bi·trar·i·ly** /ˌärbiˈtre(ə)rəlē/ adverb **ar·bi·trar·i·ness** noun.
– ORIGIN from Latin *arbiter* 'judge, supreme ruler.'

ar·bi·trate /ˈärbiˌtrāt/ ▶ **verb** (of an independent person or body) officially settle a dispute.
– ORIGIN from Latin *arbiter* 'judge, supreme ruler.'

ar·bi·tra·tion /ˌärbiˈtrāshən/ ▶ **noun** the use of an arbitrator to settle a dispute.

– SYNONYMS *the council called for arbitration to settle the dispute* **adjudication,** judgment, mediation, conciliation, intervention.

ar·bi·tra·tor /ˈärbiˌtrātər/ ▶ **noun** an independent person or body officially appointed to settle a dispute.

– SYNONYMS **adjudicator,** arbiter, judge, referee, umpire, mediator, go-between.

ar·bor¹ /ˈärbər/ (Brit. **arbour**) ▶ **noun** a garden shelter formed by trees or climbing plants trained over a framework.
– ORIGIN from Latin *herba* 'grass, herb,' influenced by *arbor* 'tree.'

ar·bor² ▶ **noun 1** an axle on which something revolves. **2** a device holding a tool in a lathe.
– ORIGIN French *arbre* 'tree, axis.'

Ar·bor Day ▶ **noun** a day dedicated annually to public tree-planting in the US, Australia, and other countries. It is usually observed in late April or early May.

ar·bo·re·al /ärˈbôrēəl/ ▶ **adjective 1** living in trees. **2** relating to trees.
– ORIGIN from Latin *arbor* 'tree.'

ar·bo·re·tum /ˌärbəˈrētəm/ ▶ **noun** (pl. **arboretums** or **arboreta**) a botanical garden devoted to trees.
– ORIGIN from Latin *arbor* 'tree.'

ar·bor·i·cul·ture /ˈärbəriˌkəlCHər, ärˈbôri-/ ▶ **noun** the cultivation of trees and shrubs.

ar·bour, etc. ▶ **noun** British spelling of **ARBOR¹**, etc.

ARC ▶ **abbreviation 1** AIDS-related complex. **2** American Red Cross.

arc /ärk/ ▶ **noun 1** a curve forming part of the circumference of a circle. **2** a curving passage of something in the air: *he swung his torch in a wide arc.* **3** a luminous electrical discharge between two points.

– SYNONYMS **curve,** arch, bow, curl, crescent, semicircle, half-moon.

▶ **verb** (**arcs, arcing, arced**) **1** move in an arc: *the ball arced over the goal.* **2** (as n. **arcing**) the forming of an electric arc.
– ORIGIN Latin *arcus* 'bow, curve.'

ar·cade /ärˈkād/ ▶ **noun 1** a covered passage with arches along one or both sides. **2** a covered walk with stores along one or both sides. **3** Architecture a series of arches supporting a wall.
– DERIVATIVES **ar·cad·ing** noun.
– ORIGIN from Latin *arcus* 'bow, curve.'

Ar·ca·di·an /ärˈkādēən/ ▶ **adjective** literary rural in an unrealistically pleasant way.
– ORIGIN from *Arcadia*, a region of southern Greece.

ar·ca·na /ärˈkānə/ ▶ **plural noun** (sing. **arcanum** /-nəm/) mysteries or secrets.
– ORIGIN Latin.

ar·cane /ärˈkān/ ▶ **adjective** understood by few people; mysterious: *arcane arguments about economics.*
– DERIVATIVES **ar·cane·ly** adverb.
– ORIGIN from Latin *arcere* 'shut up.'

WORD TOOLKIT

See **SECRET**.

arch¹ /ärCH/ ▶ **noun 1** a curved structure spanning an opening or supporting the weight of a bridge, roof, or wall. **2** the inner side of the foot.

– SYNONYMS **archway,** vault, span.

▶ **verb** form or make a curved shape.

– SYNONYMS **curve,** arc, bend, bow, crook, hunch.

– DERIVATIVES **arched** adjective.
– ORIGIN from Latin *arcus* 'bow.'

arch² ▶ **adjective** self-consciously playful or teasing.
– DERIVATIVES **arch·ly** adverb **arch·ness** noun.
– ORIGIN from **ARCH-**, by association with the sense 'rogue' in words such as *arch-scoundrel*.

arch- ▶ **combining form 1** chief; main: *archbishop*. **2** foremost: *archenemy*.
– ORIGIN from Greek *arkhos* 'chief.'

Ar·chae·an /ärˈkēən/ ▶ **adjective** British spelling of **ARCHEAN**.

ar·chae·ol·o·gy /ˌärkēˈäləjē/ (also **archeology**) ▶ **noun** the study of human history and prehistory through the excavation of sites and the analysis of objects found in them.
– DERIVATIVES **ar·chae·o·log·ic** /-əˈläjik/ adjective **ar·chae·o·log·i·cal** /-əˈläjikəl/ adjective **ar·chae·ol·o·gist** /-ˈäləjist/ noun.
– ORIGIN from Greek *arkhaios* 'ancient.'

ar·chae·op·ter·yx /ˌärkēˈäptəriks/ ▶ **noun** the oldest known fossil bird, of the late Jurassic period, which had feathers and wings like a bird, but teeth and a bony tail like a dinosaur.
– ORIGIN from Greek *arkhaios* 'ancient' + *pterux* 'wing.'

ar·cha·ic /ärˈkāik/ ▶ **adjective 1** very old or old-fashioned. **2** belonging to former or ancient times.
– DERIVATIVES **ar·cha·i·cal·ly** adverb.
– ORIGIN Greek *arkhaios* 'ancient.'

ar·cha·ism /ˈärkēˌizəm, ˈärkā-/ ▶ **noun 1** an old or old-fashioned word or style of art or language. **2** the use of old or old-fashioned features or styles in language or art.

arch·an·gel /ˈärkˌānjəl/ ▶ **noun** an angel of a high rank.

arch·bish·op /ˈärCHˈbiSHəp/ ▶ **noun** the chief bishop responsible for a large district.

arch·dea·con /ˈärCHˈdēkən/ ▶ **noun** a senior Christian priest ranking immediately below an archbishop.

arch·di·o·cese /ˌärCHˈdīəsis, -ˌsēz/ ▶ **noun** the district for which an archbishop is responsible.
– DERIVATIVES **arch·di·oc·e·san** /ˌärCHdīˈäsəsən/ adjective.

arch·duke /ˈärCHˈd(y)o͞ok/ ▶ **noun 1** a chief duke. **2** historical a son of the emperor of Austria.

Ar·che·an /ärˈkēən/ (Brit. **Archaean**) ▶ **adjective** relating to the earlier part of the Precambrian eon (before about 2,500 million years ago).
– ORIGIN from Greek *arkhaios* 'ancient.'

arch·en·e·my /ˈärCHˈenəmē/ ▶ **noun** a chief enemy.

ar·che·ol·o·gy ▶ **noun** variant spelling of **ARCHAEOLOGY**.

arch·er /ˈärCHər/ ▶ **noun** a person who shoots with a bow and arrows.
– ORIGIN from Latin *arcus* 'bow.'

ar·cher·y /ˈärCHərē/ ▶ **noun** the activity or sport of shooting with a bow and arrows.

ar·che·type /ˈärk(i)ˌtīp/ ▶ **noun 1** a very typical example: *she's the archetype of the single American female.* **2** an original model from which other forms are developed. **3** a recurrent symbol in literature or art.
– DERIVATIVES **ar·che·typ·al** /ˌärk(i)ˈtīpəl/ adjective **ar·che·typ·i·cal** /ˌärk(i)ˈtipikəl/ adjective **ar·che·typ·i·cal·ly**

/ˌärk(i)ˈtipikəlē/ adverb.
– ORIGIN from Greek *arkhe-* 'primitive' + *tupos* 'a model.'

ar·chi·e·pis·co·pal /ˌärkēəˈpiskəpəl/ ▶ **adjective** relating to an archbishop.

Ar·chi·me·des' prin·ci·ple /ˌärkəˈmēdēz/ ▶ **noun** Physics a law discovered by the Greek mathematician Archimedes (*c.*287–212 BC), stating that a body immersed in a fluid is subject to an upward force equal to the weight of fluid the body displaces.

ar·chi·pel·a·go /ˌärkəˈpeləˌgō/ ▶ **noun** (pl. **archipelagos** or **archipelagoes**) a group of many islands.
– ORIGIN from Greek *arkhi-* 'chief' + *pelagos* 'sea.'

ar·chi·tect /ˈärkiˌtekt/ ▶ **noun 1** a person who designs buildings and supervises their construction. **2** a person who originates or realizes an idea or project: *the architects of the green revolution.*

– SYNONYMS **designer,** planner, originator, author, creator, founder, inventor.

– ORIGIN Greek *arkhitektōn* 'chief builder.'

ar·chi·tec·ton·ic /ˌärkitekˈtänik/ ▶ **adjective 1** relating to architecture or architects. **2** having a clearly defined and artistically pleasing structure: *architectonic cheekbones.* ▶ **noun** (**architectonics**) (treated as sing.) the scientific study of architecture.

ar·chi·tec·ture /ˈärkiˌtekCHər/ ▶ **noun 1** the art or practice of designing and constructing buildings. **2** the style in which a building is designed and constructed: *Gothic architecture.* **3** the complex structure of something.

– SYNONYMS **building,** planning, design, construction.

– DERIVATIVES **ar·chi·tec·tur·al** /ˌärkiˈtekCHərəl/ adjective.

ar·chi·trave /ˈärkiˌtrāv/ ▶ **noun 1** (in classical architecture) a main beam resting across the tops of columns. **2** the frame around a doorway or window.
– ORIGIN from Latin *trabs* 'a beam.'

ar·chive /ˈärˌkīv/ ▶ **noun 1** a collection of historical documents or records. **2** a complete record of the data in a computer system, stored on a less frequently used medium.

– SYNONYMS **1** *the family archives* **records,** papers, documents, files, annals, chronicles, history. **2** *the Institute's archive* **record office,** registry, repository, museum, library.

▶ **verb** place or store something in an archive.

– SYNONYMS **file,** log, catalog, document, record, register, store.

– DERIVATIVES **ar·chi·val** /ärˈkīvəl/ adjective.
– ORIGIN from Greek *arkheia* 'public records.'

ar·chi·vist /ˈärkəvist, -ˌkī-/ ▶ **noun** a person who is in charge of archives.

arch·ri·val ▶ **noun** the chief rival of a person, team, or organization.

arch·way /ˈärCHˌwā/ ▶ **noun** a curved structure forming a passage or entrance.

arc lamp (also **arc light**) ▶ **noun** a light source using an electric arc.

Arc·tic /ˈärktik, ˈärtik/ ▶ **adjective 1** relating to the regions around the North Pole. **2** living or growing in the regions around the North Pole. **3** (**arctic**) informal (of weather) very cold. ▶ **noun** (**the Arctic**) the regions around the North Pole.
– ORIGIN from Greek *arktos* 'bear, Ursa Major, polestar.'

ar·cu·ate /ˈärkyo͞oit, -ˌāt/ ▶ **adjective** technical curved.
– ORIGIN from Latin *arcus* 'bow, curve.'

ar·dent /ˈärdnt/ ▶ **adjective 1** very enthusiastic; passionate: *an ardent supporter of organic agriculture.* **2** old use burning or glowing.

– SYNONYMS **passionate,** fervent, zealous, wholehearted, intense, fierce, enthusiastic, keen, eager, avid, committed, dedicated.
– ANTONYMS apathetic.

– DERIVATIVES **ar·dent·ly** adverb.
– ORIGIN from Latin *ardere* 'to burn.'

ar·dor /ˈärdər/ (Brit. **ardour**) ▶ **noun** great enthusiasm; passion.
– ORIGIN from Latin *ardere* 'to burn.'

ar·du·ous /ˈärjo͞oəs/ ▶ **adjective** difficult and tiring.

– SYNONYMS **tough,** difficult, hard, heavy, laborious, onerous, taxing, strenuous, back-breaking, demanding, challenging, punishing, grueling; informal killing.
– ANTONYMS easy.

– DERIVATIVES **ar·du·ous·ly** adverb **ar·du·ous·ness** noun.
– ORIGIN Latin *arduus* 'steep, difficult.'

WORD TOOLKIT

arduous ...	challenging ...	onerous ...
journey	problem	responsibility
process	task	regulations
training	question	tax
climb	environment	debt

are /är/ second person singular present and first, second, third person plural present of **BE**.

ar·e·a /ˈe(ə)rēə/ ▶ **noun 1** a part of a place, object, or surface. **2** the extent or measurement of a surface. **3** a space allocated for a specific use: *a picnic area.* **4** a subject or range of activity.

– SYNONYMS **1 district,** zone, region, sector, quarter, locality, neighborhood; informal neck of the woods, turf. **2** *the dining area* **space,** section, part, place, room. **3** *specific areas of knowledge* **field,** sphere, realm, domain, sector, province, territory.

– DERIVATIVES **ar·e·al** adjective.
– ORIGIN Latin, 'piece of level ground.'

ar·e·a code ▶ **noun** a telephone dialing code.

a·re·na /əˈrēnə/ ▶ **noun 1** a level area surrounded by seating, in which sports and other public events are held. **2** an area of activity: *conflicts within the political arena.*

– SYNONYMS **1 stadium,** amphitheater, ground, field, ring, rink, court, bowl, park. **2 scene,** sphere, realm, province, domain, forum, territory, world.

– ORIGIN Latin *harena, arena* 'sand, sand-covered place of combat.'

aren't /är(ə)nt/ ▶ **contraction 1** are not. **2** am not (only used in questions): *I'm right, aren't I?*

a·re·o·la /əˈrēələ/ ▶ **noun** (pl. **areolae** /-ˌlē/) Anatomy a small circular area, especially the darker skin surrounding a human nipple.
– ORIGIN Latin, 'small open space.'

a·rête /əˈrāt/ ▶ **noun** a sharp mountain ridge.
– ORIGIN French.

ar·gent /ˈärjənt/ ▶ **adjective & noun** literary & Heraldry silver.
– ORIGIN Latin *argentum* 'silver.'

Ar·gen·tin·i·an /ˌärjənˈtinēən/ (also **Argentine** /ˈärjənˌtīn, -ˌtēn/) ▶ **noun** a person from Argentina. ▶ **adjective** relating to Argentina.

ar·gon /ˈärˌgän/ ▶ **noun** an inert gaseous chemical element, present in small amounts in the air.
– ORIGIN from Greek *argos* 'idle.'

ar·go·sy /ˈärgəsē/ ▶ **noun** (pl. **argosies**) literary a large merchant ship, originally one from Ragusa (now Dubrovnik) or Venice.
– ORIGIN from Italian *Ragusea nave* 'vessel of *Ragusa*.'

ar·got /ˈärgō, -gət/ ▶ **noun** the jargon or slang of a particular group or area of activity: *the argot of city planning.*
– ORIGIN French.

ar·gu·a·ble /ˈärgyo͞oəbəl/ ▶ **adjective 1** able to be argued or asserted: *it is arguable that the company was already experiencing problems.* **2** open to disagreement.
– DERIVATIVES **ar·gu·a·bly** adverb.

ar·gue /ˈärgyo͞o/ ▶ **verb** (**argues, arguing, argued**) **1** exchange conflicting views heatedly. **2** give reasons or evidence in support of something.

> – SYNONYMS **1 claim,** maintain, insist, contend, assert, hold, reason, allege. **2 quarrel,** disagree, dispute, squabble, bicker, have words, cross swords, fight, wrangle, row.

– DERIVATIVES **ar·gu·er** noun.
– ORIGIN Latin *arguere* 'prove, accuse.'

ar·gu·ment /ˈärgyəmənt/ ▶ **noun 1** a heated exchange of conflicting views. **2** a set of reasons given in support of something.

> – SYNONYMS **1 quarrel,** disagreement, difference of opinion, squabble, dispute, altercation, fight, wrangle, row; informal tiff, set-to. **2 reasoning,** justification, explanation, case, defense, vindication, evidence, reasons, grounds.

ar·gu·men·ta·tion /ˌärgyəmənˈtāsʜən/ ▶ **noun** systematic reasoning in support of something.

ar·gu·men·ta·tive /ˌärgyəˈmentətiv/ ▶ **adjective** apt to argue.

ar·gyle /ˈärˌgīl/ ▶ **noun** a pattern used in knitwear, consisting of colored diamonds on a plain background.
– ORIGIN from *Argyll,* the Scottish clan on whose tartan the pattern is based.

a·ri·a /ˈärēə/ ▶ **noun** a long accompanied song for a solo voice in an opera or oratorio.
– ORIGIN Italian.

ar·id /ˈarid/ ▶ **adjective 1** very dry because having little or no rain. **2** uninteresting; unsatisfying.

> – SYNONYMS **dry,** waterless, parched, scorched, desiccated, desert, barren, infertile.
> – ANTONYMS wet, fertile.

– DERIVATIVES **a·rid·i·ty** /əˈriditē/ noun.
– ORIGIN from Latin *arere* 'be dry or parched.'

> **CHOOSE THE RIGHT WORD**
>
> See **DRY**.

Ar·ies /ˈe(ə)rēz, ˈe(ə)rē-ēz/ ▶ **noun 1** a constellation and the first sign of the zodiac (the Ram), which the sun enters about March 20. **2** (**an Aries**) a person born when the sun is in this sign.
– DERIVATIVES **Ar·i·an** /ˈe(ə)rēən/ noun & adjective.
– ORIGIN Latin.

a·right /əˈrīt/ ▶ **adverb** dialect correctly; properly.
– ORIGIN Old English.

a·rise /əˈrīz/ ▶ **verb** (past **arose** /əˈrōz/; past part. **arisen** /əˈrizən/) **1** come into being or come to notice: *new difficulties had arisen.* **2** (**arise from/out of**) occur as a result of: *back pain can arise from a multitude of problems.* **3** formal get or stand up.

> – SYNONYMS **1** *many problems arose* **come about,** happen, occur, come into being, emerge, crop up, come to light, become apparent, appear, turn up, surface, spring up. **2** *injuries arising from defective products* **result,** stem, originate, proceed, follow, ensue, be caused by.

– ORIGIN Old English.

ar·is·toc·ra·cy /ˌariˈstäkrəsē/ ▶ **noun** (pl. **aristocracies**) the highest social class, consisting of people of noble birth with hereditary titles.
– ORIGIN from Greek *aristos* 'best' + *-kratia* 'power.'

a·ris·to·crat /əˈristəˌkrat/ ▶ **noun** a member of the aristocracy.

> – SYNONYMS **nobleman,** noblewoman, lord, lady, peer (of the realm), patrician.
> – ANTONYMS commoner.

a·ris·to·crat·ic /əˌristəˈkratik/ ▶ **adjective** relating to or typical of the aristocracy.

> – SYNONYMS **noble,** titled, upper-class, blue-blooded, high-born, patrician; informal upper crust, top drawer; Brit. informal posh.
> – ANTONYMS common.

– DERIVATIVES **a·ris·to·crat·i·cal·ly** adverb.

Ar·is·to·te·lian /əˌristəˈtēlyən, ˌaristə-, -lēən/ ▶ **adjective** relating to the theories of the Greek philosopher Aristotle (384–322 BC). ▶ **noun** a student or follower of Aristotle or his philosophy.

a·rith·me·tic ▶ **noun** /əˈriᴛʜməˌtik/ **1** the branch of mathematics concerned with the properties and manipulation of numbers. **2** the use of numbers in counting and calculation. ▶ **adjective** /ˌariᴛʜˈmetik/ relating to arithmetic.
– DERIVATIVES **ar·ith·met·i·cal** /ˌariᴛʜˈmetikəl/ adjective **ar·ith·met·i·cal·ly** /ˌariᴛʜˈmetikəlē/ adverb **a·rith·me·ti·cian** /əˌriᴛʜməˈtisʜən/ noun.
– ORIGIN from Greek *arithmētikē tekhnē* 'art of counting.'

ar·ith·met·ic pro·gres·sion /ˌariᴛʜˈmetik/ (also **arithmetic series**) ▶ **noun** a sequence of numbers in which each differs from the preceding one by a constant quantity (e.g., 9, 7, 5, 3, etc.).

ark /ärk/ ▶ **noun 1** (in the Bible) the ship built by Noah to save his family and two of every kind of animal from the Flood. **2** (also **Holy Ark**) a chest or cupboard housing the Torah scrolls in a synagogue. **3** (**Ark of the Covenant**) the chest that contained the laws of the ancient Israelites.
– ORIGIN Latin *arca* 'chest.'

ARM ▶ **abbreviation** adjustable rate mortgage.

arm[1] /ärm/ ▶ **noun 1** each of the two upper limbs of the human body from the shoulder to the hand. **2** a side part of a chair supporting a sitter's arm. **3** a narrow strip of water or land projecting from a larger area. **4** a branch or division of an organization.
– DERIVATIVES **arm·ful** noun **arm·less** adjective **arm·load** /ˈärmˌlōd/ noun.
– PHRASES **arm in arm** with arms linked. **cost an arm and a leg** informal be very expensive. **keep someone/thing**

at arm's length avoid close contact with someone or something. **with open arms** with great affection or enthusiasm.
– ORIGIN Old English.

arm² ▶ **verb 1** supply someone with weapons. **2** provide with essential equipment or information: *we were armed with all sorts of statistics.* **3** activate the fuse of a bomb or missile so that it is ready to explode.

– SYNONYMS **equip,** provide, supply, furnish, issue, fit out.

– ORIGIN from Latin *arma* 'armor, arms.'

ar·ma·da /är'mädə/ ▶ **noun** a fleet of warships.
– ORIGIN Spanish, from Latin *armare* 'to arm.'

ar·ma·dil·lo /ˌärmə'dilō/ ▶ **noun** (pl. **armadillos**) an insect-eating mammal of Central and South America, with a body covered in bony plates.
– ORIGIN Spanish, 'little armed man.'

Ar·ma·ged·don /ˌärmə'gedn/ ▶ **noun 1** (in the New Testament) the last battle between good and evil before the Day of Judgment. **2** a catastrophic conflict or event: *the threat of nuclear Armageddon.*
– ORIGIN Hebrew, 'hill of Megiddo' (Book of Revelation, chapter 16).

Ar·mag·nac /ˌärmən'yak, -'yäk/ ▶ **noun** a type of brandy made in Aquitaine in SW France.
– ORIGIN the former name of a district in Aquitaine.

ar·ma·ment /'ärməmənt/ ▶ **noun 1** (also **armaments**) military weapons and equipment. **2** the equipping of military forces for war.

– SYNONYMS (**armaments**) **arms,** weapons, weaponry, firearms, guns, ordnance, artillery, munitions, materiel.

– ORIGIN from Latin *armare* 'to arm.'

ar·ma·ture /'ärməCHər, -ˌCHŏŏr/ ▶ **noun 1** the rotating coil of a dynamo or electric motor. **2** any moving part of an electrical machine in which a voltage is induced by a magnetic field. **3** a piece of iron placed across the poles of a magnet to preserve its power. **4** the protective covering of an animal or plant.
– ORIGIN Latin *armatura* 'armor.'

arm·band /'ärmˌband/ ▶ **noun 1** a band worn around the upper arm to indicate something, such as a person's role or identity. **2** an inflatable plastic band worn around the upper arm as a swimming aid.

arm·chair /'ärmˌCHe(ə)r/ ▶ **noun** an upholstered chair with side supports for the sitter's arms. ▶ **adjective** experiencing something through reading, television, etc., rather than doing it: *an armchair traveler.*

armed /ärmd/ ▶ **adjective** equipped with or involving a firearm.

armed forc·es ▶ **plural noun** a country's army, navy, and air force.

Ar·me·ni·an /är'mēnēən, -yən/ ▶ **noun 1** a person from Armenia. **2** the language of Armenia. ▶ **adjective** relating to Armenia.

arm·hole /'ärmˌhōl/ ▶ **noun** each of two openings in a garment through which the wearer puts their arms.

ar·mi·stice /'ärməstis/ ▶ **noun** a truce.

– SYNONYMS **truce,** ceasefire, peace, suspension of hostilities.

– ORIGIN from Latin *arma* 'arms' + *-stitium* 'stoppage.'

arm·let /'ärmlit/ ▶ **noun** a bracelet worn around the upper arm.

arm·lock /'ärmˌläk/ ▶ **noun** a method of restraining someone by holding their arm bent tightly behind their back.

ar·moire /ärm'wär, 'ärmˌwär/ ▶ **noun** a large cabinet used especially for storing clothes; a wardrobe.
– ORIGIN French.

ar·mor /'ärmər/ (Brit. **armour**) ▶ **noun 1** the metal coverings formerly worn to protect the body in battle. **2** (also **armor plate**) the tough metal layer covering a military vehicle or ship. **3** military vehicles as a whole. **4** the protective layer or shell of some animals and plants.
– ORIGIN from Latin *arma* 'armor, arms.'

ar·mored /'ärmərd/ ▶ **adjective** covered with armor.

– SYNONYMS **armor-plated,** steel-plated, ironclad, bulletproof, bombproof, reinforced, toughened.

ar·mor·er /'ärmərər/ ▶ **noun 1** a maker or supplier of weapons or armor. **2** an official in charge of the arms of a warship or regiment.

ar·mo·ri·al /är'môrēəl/ ▶ **adjective** relating to heraldry or coats of arms.

ar·mor-plat·ed ▶ **adjective** covered with armor plate.

ar·mor·y /'ärmərē/ ▶ **noun** (pl. **armories**) **1** a store or supply of arms. **2** a set of resources available for a purpose: *their armory of tax-gathering methods.*

ar·mour, etc. /'ärmər/ ▶ **noun** British spelling of **ARMOR**, etc.

arm·pit /'ärmˌpit/ ▶ **noun** a hollow under the arm at the shoulder.

arm·rest /'ärmˌrest/ ▶ **noun** an arm of a chair.

arms /ärmz/ ▶ **plural noun 1** guns and other weapons. **2** the heraldic emblems on a coat of arms.

– SYNONYMS **weapons,** weaponry, firearms, guns, ordnance, artillery, armaments, munitions.

– PHRASES **a call to arms** a call to prepare for conflict. **up in arms** strongly opposed to and protesting about something.
– ORIGIN Latin *arma.*

arms con·trol ▶ **noun** international agreement to limit the production and accumulation of arms.

arms race ▶ **noun** a situation in which nations compete for superiority in developing and stockpiling weapons.

arm-twist·ing ▶ **noun** informal persuasion by the use of physical force or moral pressure: *eight years of arguing and diplomatic arm-twisting.*
– DERIVATIVES **arm-twist** verb.

arm-wres·tling ▶ **noun** a contest in which two seated people clasp hands and try to force each other's arm down onto a surface.

ar·my /'ärmē/ ▶ **noun** (pl. **armies**) **1** an organized military force equipped for fighting on land. **2** a large number of similar people or things: *an army of cleaners.*

– SYNONYMS **1 armed force,** military force, land force(s), military, soldiery, infantry, militia, troops, soldiers. **2** *an army of tourists* **crowd,** swarm, horde, mob, gang, throng, mass, flock, herd, pack.

– ORIGIN from Latin *armare* 'to arm.'

WORD LINKS

military, **martial** *relating to armies*

ar·ni·ca /'ärnikə/ ▶ **noun** a plant with yellow daisylike flowers, used for the treatment of bruises.
– ORIGIN Latin.

a·ro·ma /ə'rōmə/ ▶ **noun 1** a pleasant and distinctive smell. **2** a particular quality or atmosphere: *the aroma of officialdom.*

– SYNONYMS **smell,** odor, fragrance, scent, perfume, bouquet, nose.

– ORIGIN Greek, 'spice.'

a·ro·ma·ther·a·py /ə,rōmə'THerəpē/ ▶ **noun** the use of aromatic oils obtained from plants for healing or to promote well-being.
– DERIVATIVES **a·ro·ma·ther·a·peu·tic** /-,THerə'pyo͞otik/ adjective **a·ro·ma·ther·a·pist** noun.

ar·o·mat·ic /,arə'matik/ ▶ **adjective 1** having a pleasant and distinctive smell. **2** (of an organic compound such as benzene) containing a flat ring of atoms in its molecule.

– SYNONYMS **fragrant,** scented, perfumed, fragranced.

▶ **noun** an aromatic plant, substance, or compound.
– DERIVATIVES **ar·o·mat·i·cal·ly** adverb.

WORD TOOLKIT

See **PUNGENT**.

a·rose /ə'rōz/ past of **ARISE**.

a·round /ə'round/ ▶ **adverb 1** with circular movement; so as to rotate. **2** so as to cover the whole area surrounding a particular center: *she glanced around admiringly at the decor.* **3** so as to turn and face in the opposite direction. **4** used in describing the relative position of something: *the pieces are the wrong way around.* **5** on every side; so as to surround or give support. **6** in or to many places throughout. **7** so as to reach a new place or position. **8** available or present. **9** approximately. ▶ **preposition 1** on every side of. **2** in or to many places throughout. **3** so as to encircle or surround. **4** following a circular route. **5** from or on the other side of. **6** so as to cover the whole area of.

– SYNONYMS **1 surrounding,** enclosing, on all sides of. **2 approximately,** about, around about, circa, roughly, more or less, nearly, almost, approaching. informal in the ballpark of.

a·rouse /ə'rouz/ ▶ **verb 1** bring about a feeling or response: *the invitation had aroused my curiosity.* **2** excite someone sexually. **3** awaken someone from sleep.

– SYNONYMS **1 provoke,** trigger, stir up, engender, cause, whip up, rouse, inflame, agitate, incite, galvanize, electrify, stimulate, inspire, fire up. **2 wake (up),** awaken, bring to/around, rouse.
– ANTONYMS allay.

– DERIVATIVES **a·rous·al** noun.
– ORIGIN from **ROUSE**.

ar·peg·gi·o /är'pejē,ō/ ▶ **noun** (pl. **arpeggios**) the notes of a musical chord played in rapid succession.
– ORIGIN Italian.

arr. ▶ **abbreviation 1** (of a piece of music) arranged by. **2** (with reference to the arrival time of a bus, train, or airplane) arrives.

ar·rab·bi·a·ta /ə,räbē'ätə/ ▶ **noun** a spicy pasta sauce made with tomatoes and chili peppers.

ar·rack /'arək, ə'rak/ (also **arak**) ▶ **noun** an alcoholic spirit made in Eastern countries from the sap of the coconut palm or from rice.
– ORIGIN Arabic, 'sweat.'

ar·raign /ə'rān/ ▶ **verb** call someone before a court to answer a criminal charge.
– DERIVATIVES **ar·raign·ment** noun.
– ORIGIN Old French *araisnier.*

ar·range /ə'rānj/ ▶ **verb 1** put tidily or in a particular order: *the columns are arranged in rows.* **2** organize or plan for something. **3** adapt a musical composition for performance with instruments or voices other than those originally specified.

– SYNONYMS **1 set out,** (put in) order, lay out, align, position, present, display, exhibit, group, sort, organize, tidy. **2 organize,** fix (up), plan, schedule, contrive, determine, agree. **3** *he arranged the piece for a full orchestra* **adapt,** set, score, orchestrate.

– DERIVATIVES **ar·range·a·ble** adjective **ar·rang·er** noun.
– ORIGIN Old French *arangier.*

ar·range·ment /ə'rānjmənt/ ▶ **noun 1** a plan for a future event: *I made arrangements to meet him.* **2** an agreement to do something. **3** something made up of items placed in an attractive or ordered way: *a flower arrangement.* **4** an arranged musical composition.

– SYNONYMS **1 positioning,** presentation, grouping, organization, alignment. **2 preparation,** plan, provision, planning. **3 agreement,** deal, understanding, bargain, settlement, pact. **4** *an arrangement of Beethoven's symphonies* **adaptation,** orchestration, scoring, interpretation.

ar·rant /'arənt/ ▶ **adjective** utter; complete: *what arrant nonsense!*
– ORIGIN variant of **ERRANT**, originally in phrases such as *arrant thief*, meaning 'outlawed, roving thief.'

ar·ras /ä'räs, 'arəs/ ▶ **noun** a tapestry wall hanging.
– ORIGIN named after the French town of *Arras.*

ar·ray /ə'rā/ ▶ **noun 1** an impressive display or range: *a bewildering array of choices.* **2** an ordered arrangement of troops. **3** literary elaborate or beautiful clothing.

– SYNONYMS **range,** collection, selection, assortment, variety, arrangement, lineup, display, exhibition.

▶ **verb 1** display or arrange in a neat or impressive way: *bottled waters are arrayed on crushed ice.* **2** (**be arrayed in**) be elaborately clothed in something.

– SYNONYMS **arrange,** assemble, group, order, range, place, position, set out, lay out, spread out, display, exhibit.

– ORIGIN Old French *arei.*

ar·rears /ə'ri(ə)rz/ ▶ **plural noun** money owed that should already have been paid.
– PHRASES **in arrears 1** behind with paying money that is owed. **2** (of wages or rent) paid at the end of each period of work or occupation.
– ORIGIN Old French *arere.*

ar·rest /ə'rest/ ▶ **verb 1** seize someone by legal authority and take them into custody. **2** stop or delay progress or a process: *the spread of the disease can be arrested.* **3** (as adj. **arresting**) attracting attention.

– SYNONYMS **1 detain,** apprehend, seize, capture, take into custody; informal pick up, pull in, collar; informal nab. **2 stop,** halt, check, block, curb, prevent,

obstruct, stem, slow, interrupt, delay. **3** (as adj. **arresting**) **striking,** eye-catching, conspicuous, impressive, imposing, spectacular, dramatic, breathtaking, stunning, awe-inspiring.
– ANTONYMS release.

▶ **noun 1** an act of arresting someone. **2** a sudden stop.

– SYNONYMS **detention,** apprehension, seizure, capture.

– DERIVATIVES **ar·rest·ing·ly** adverb.
– ORIGIN Latin *restare* 'remain, stop.'

ar·rhyth·mi·a /ā'riᴛʜmēə, ə'riᴛʜ-/ ▶ **noun** a medical condition in which the heart beats with an irregular or abnormal rhythm.
– DERIVATIVES **ar·rhyth·mic** /ə'riᴛʜmik/ adjective.
– ORIGIN Greek *arruthmia* 'lack of rhythm.'

ar·ri·val /ə'rīvəl/ ▶ **noun 1** the action of arriving. **2** a person or thing that has just arrived or appeared.

– SYNONYMS **coming,** appearance, entrance, entry, approach, advent.
– ANTONYMS departure.

ar·rive /ə'rīv/ ▶ **verb 1** reach a destination. **2** be brought or delivered. **3** (of a moment or event) happen: *spring has finally arrived.* **4** (**arrive at**) reach a conclusion or decision. **5** informal become successful and well known.

– SYNONYMS **come,** turn up, get here/there, make it, appear; informal show (up), roll in/up, blow in.
– ANTONYMS depart, leave.

– ORIGIN Old French *ariver*, from Latin *ripa* 'shore.'

ar·ri·vi·der·ci /ˌarivə'dərcнi/ ▶ **exclamation** goodbye until we meet again.
– ORIGIN Italian, 'to the seeing again.'

ar·ri·viste /ˌärē'vēst/ ▶ **noun** often derogatory a person who has recently become wealthy or risen in social status or is ambitious to do so.
– ORIGIN French.

ar·ro·gant /'arəgənt/ ▶ **adjective** having an exaggerated sense of one's own importance or abilities.

– SYNONYMS **haughty,** conceited, self-important, cocky, supercilious, condescending, full of oneself, overbearing, imperious, proud; informal high and mighty, too big for one's boots/britches.
– ANTONYMS modest.

– DERIVATIVES **ar·ro·gance** noun **ar·ro·gant·ly** adverb.
– ORIGIN from Latin *arrogare* 'claim for oneself.'

CHOOSE THE RIGHT WORD

See **PRIDE**.

ar·ro·gate /'arəˌgāt/ ▶ **verb** take or claim something for oneself without justification.
– DERIVATIVES **ar·ro·ga·tion** /ˌarə'gāsнən/ noun.
– ORIGIN Latin *arrogare*.

ar·ron·disse·ment /ə'rändismənt, ä'ränDēsˌmäN/ ▶ **noun 1** (in France) a subdivision of a local government department. **2** an administrative district of Paris.
– ORIGIN French.

ar·row /'arō/ ▶ **noun 1** a stick with a sharp pointed head, designed to be shot from a bow. **2** a symbol resembling an arrow, used to show direction or position.
– DERIVATIVES **ar·rowed** adjective.
– ORIGIN Old Norse.

ar·row·head /'arōˌhed/ ▶ **noun 1** the pointed end of an arrow, typically wedge-shaped. **2** a decorative device resembling an arrowhead. **3** an aquatic or semiaquatic plant with arrow-shaped leaves and three-petaled white flowers.

ar·row·root /'arōˌro͞ot, -ˌro͞ot/ ▶ **noun** a plant that yields a fine-grained starch used in cooking and medicine.
– ORIGIN Arawak, 'meal of meals,' altered by association with **ARROW** and **ROOT**[1], the plant's tubers being used to absorb poison from arrow wounds.

ar·roy·o /ə'roiˌō/ ▶ **noun** (pl. **arroyos**) a deep gully cut by the action of fast-flowing water in an arid area.
– ORIGIN Spanish.

arse /ärs/ ▶ **noun** British form of **ASS**[2].

ar·se·nal /'ärs(ə)-nl/ ▶ **noun** a store of weapons and ammunition.
– ORIGIN Arabic, 'house of industry.'

ar·se·nic /'ärs(ə)nik/ ▶ **noun** a brittle steel-gray chemical element with poisonous compounds.
– DERIVATIVES **ar·sen·i·cal** /är'senikəl/ adjective **ar·se·nide** /'ärs(ə)ˌnīd/ noun.
– ORIGIN Greek *arsenikon.*

ar·son /'ärsən/ ▶ **noun** the criminal act of deliberately setting fire to property.
– DERIVATIVES **ar·son·ist** noun.
– ORIGIN from Latin *ardere* 'to burn.'

art[1] /ärt/ ▶ **noun 1** the expression of creative skill in a visual form such as painting or sculpture. **2** paintings, drawings, and sculpture as a whole. **3** (**the arts**) the branches of creative activity, such as painting, music, and drama. **4** (**arts**) subjects of study mainly concerned with human culture (as contrasted with scientific or technical subjects). **5** a skill: *the art of conversation.*

– SYNONYMS **1 fine art,** design, artwork, aesthetics. **2 skill,** craft, technique, knack, facility, aptitude, talent, flair, mastery, expertise.

– ORIGIN Latin *ars.*

art[2] old-fashioned or dialect second person singular present of **BE**.

art dec·o /'dekō/ ▶ **noun** a decorative art style of the 1920s and 1930s, characterized by geometric shapes.
– ORIGIN French *art décoratif* 'decorative art.'

ar·te·fact /'ärtəˌfakt/ ▶ **noun** British spelling of **ARTIFACT**.

ar·te·ri·al /är'ti(ə)rēəl/ ▶ **adjective 1** relating to an artery or arteries. **2** relating to an important transport route.

ar·te·ri·o·scle·ro·sis /ärˌti(ə)rēōsklə'rōsis/ ▶ **noun** thickening and hardening of the walls of the arteries.

ar·ter·y /'ärtərē/ ▶ **noun** (pl. **arteries**) **1** any of the tubes through which blood flows from the heart around the body. **2** an important transport route.
– ORIGIN Greek *artēria.*

ar·te·sian well /är'tēzнən/ ▶ **noun** a well bored vertically into a layer of water-bearing rock that is lying at an angle, the water coming to the surface by natural pressure.
– ORIGIN from *Artois*, a region in France.

art·ful /'ärtfəl/ ▶ **adjective** clever, especially in a cunning way.
– DERIVATIVES **art·ful·ly** adverb **art·ful·ness** noun.

art house ▶ **noun** a movie theater that shows independently made artistic or experimental films.

ar·thri·tis /är'тнrītis/ ▶ **noun** painful inflammation and stiffness of the joints.
– DERIVATIVES **ar·thrit·ic** /-'тнritik/ adjective & noun.
– ORIGIN from Greek *arthron* 'joint.'

ar·thro·pod /'ärᴛʜrəˌpäd/ ▶ **noun** an invertebrate animal with a body divided into segments and an external skeleton, such as an insect, spider, or crab.
– ORIGIN from Greek *arthron* 'joint' + *pous* 'foot.'

ar·thro·scope /'ärᴛʜrəˌskōp/ ▶ **noun** Medicine an instrument through which the interior of a joint may be inspected or operated on.
– DERIVATIVES **ar·thro·scop·ic** /ˌärᴛʜrə'skäpik/ adjective **ar·thros·co·py** /är'ᴛʜräskəpē/ noun.

Ar·thu·ri·an /är'ᴛʜo͝orēən/ ▶ **adjective** relating to the reign of the legendary King Arthur of Britain.

ar·ti·choke /'ärtiˌᴄʜōk/ ▶ **noun** (also **globe artichoke**) a vegetable consisting of the unopened flowerhead of a thistlelike plant.
– ORIGIN from Arabic.

ar·ti·cle /'ärtikəl/ ▶ **noun 1** a particular object. **2** a piece of writing in a newspaper or magazine. **3** a separate clause or paragraph of a legal document. **4** Brit. (**articles**) a period of professional training as a solicitor, architect, surveyor, or accountant.

> – SYNONYMS **1 object,** thing, item, piece, artifact, device, implement. **2 report,** account, story, essay, feature, item, piece (of writing), column. **3 clause,** section, paragraph, point, item.

▶ **verb** Brit. (**be articled**) (of a solicitor, architect, etc.) be employed under contract as a trainee.
– PHRASES **article of faith** a firmly held belief.
– ORIGIN Latin *articulus* 'small connecting part.'

ar·tic·u·lar /är'tikyələr/ ▶ **adjective** Anatomy relating to a joint.

ar·tic·u·late ▶ **adjective** /är'tikyəlit/ **1** able to speak fluently and clearly. **2** having joints or jointed segments.

> – SYNONYMS **eloquent,** fluent, effective, persuasive, lucid, expressive, silver-tongued, clear, coherent.
> – ANTONYMS unintelligible.

▶ **verb** /-ˌlāt/ **1** pronounce words distinctly. **2** clearly express in words: *the president articulated the feelings of the vast majority*. **3** form a joint. **4** (as adj. **articulated**) having sections connected by a flexible joint.

> – SYNONYMS **express,** voice, vocalize, put in words, communicate, state.

– DERIVATIVES **ar·tic·u·la·cy** /-ləsē/ noun **ar·tic·u·late·ly** adverb **ar·tic·u·late·ness** noun **ar·tic·u·la·tor** /-ˌlātər/ noun.
– ORIGIN from Latin *articulus* 'small connecting part.'

ar·tic·u·la·tion /ärˌtikyə'lāsʜən/ ▶ **noun 1** the expression of an idea or feeling in words. **2** the formation of distinct sounds in speech. **3** the state of being jointed.

ar·ti·fact /'ärtəˌfakt/ (Brit. **artefact**) ▶ **noun** a useful or decorative man-made object.
– ORIGIN from Latin *arte* 'using art' + *factum* 'something made.'

ar·ti·fice /'ärtəfis/ ▶ **noun** the use of skill or cunning in order to trick or deceive: *the writing is deliberately free of artifice*.
– ORIGIN from Latin *ars* 'art' + *facere* 'make.'

ar·ti·fi·cial /ˌärtə'fisʜəl/ ▶ **adjective 1** made as a copy of something natural: *artificial flowers*. **2** not sincere; affected.

> – SYNONYMS **1 synthetic,** fake, imitation, mock, ersatz, man-made, manufactured, plastic, simulated, faux; informal pretend. **2 insincere,** feigned, false, unnatural, contrived, put-on, forced, labored, hollow; informal pretend, phony.
> – ANTONYMS natural, genuine.

– DERIVATIVES **ar·ti·fi·ci·al·i·ty** /-ˌfisʜē'alitē/ noun **ar·ti·fi·cial·ly** adverb.
– ORIGIN from Latin *ars* 'art' + *facere* 'make.'

WORD TOOLKIT

artificial ...	synthetic ...	man-made ...
intelligence	chemical	structure
chromosome	hormone	lake
reef	peptide	canal
turf	fiber	waterfall
sweetener	rubber	disaster
limb	dye	catastrophe
heart	fertilizer	warming
flowers	pesticide	pollutant
nails	pyrethroid	emission

ar·ti·fi·cial in·sem·i·na·tion ▶ **noun** the injection of semen into the vagina or uterus of a woman or female animal, as a medical method of fertilizing an egg.

ar·ti·fi·cial in·tel·li·gence ▶ **noun** the performance by computers of tasks normally requiring human intelligence.

ar·ti·fi·cial res·pi·ra·tion ▶ **noun** the forcing of air into and out of a person's lungs to make them begin breathing again.

ar·til·ler·y /är'tilərē/ ▶ **noun 1** large-caliber guns used in warfare on land. **2** a branch of the armed forces trained to use artillery.
– ORIGIN from Old French *atillier* 'equip, arm.'

ar·ti·san /'ärtizən/ ▶ **noun** a skilled worker who makes things by hand.
– DERIVATIVES **ar·ti·san·al** adjective.
– ORIGIN from Latin *artire* 'instruct in the arts.'

art·ist /'ärtist/ ▶ **noun 1** a person who paints or draws as a profession or hobby. **2** a person who practices or performs any of the creative arts. **3** informal a person who practices a particular activity: *a con artist*.
– ORIGIN from Latin *ars* 'art.'

ar·tiste /är'tēst/ ▶ **noun** a professional singer or dancer.
– ORIGIN French, 'artist.'

ar·tis·tic /är'tistik/ ▶ **adjective 1** having creative skill. **2** relating to or characteristic of art or artists: *an artistic temperament*. **3** pleasing to look at: *artistic designs*.

> – SYNONYMS **1 creative,** imaginative, inventive, sensitive, perceptive, discerning. **2 attractive,** aesthetic, beautiful, stylish, ornamental, decorative, graceful, subtle, expressive.

– DERIVATIVES **ar·tis·ti·cal·ly** adverb.

art·ist·ry /'ärtistrē/ ▶ **noun** creative skill or ability: *the artistry of the pianist*.

art·less /'ärtlis/ ▶ **adjective 1** sincere, straightforward, or unpretentious: *an artless, naive girl*. **2** without skill; clumsy.
– DERIVATIVES **art·less·ly** adverb.

art nou·veau /är(t) no͞o'vō/ ▶ **noun** a style of art and architecture of the late 19th and early 20th centuries, having intricate linear designs and flowing curves.
– ORIGIN French, 'new art.'

art·sy /'ärtsē/ (also **arty** /'ärtē/) ▶ **adjective** (**artsier, artsiest**) informal interested or involved in the arts in an affected way.
– DERIVATIVES **art·si·ness** noun.

art·work /'ärtˌwərk/ ▶ **noun** illustrations for inclusion in a publication.

a·ru·gu·la /ə'rōōgələ/ ▶ **noun** an edible Mediterranean plant eaten in salads.
– ORIGIN Italian dialect *arucula*.

ar·um /'arəm/ ▶ **noun** jack-in-the-pulpit or a related plant.
– ORIGIN Greek *aron*.

ar·um lil·y ▶ **noun** a tall lilylike African plant of the arum family.

Ar·y·an /'e(ə)rēən, 'ar-, -yən/ ▶ **noun 1** a member of a people speaking an Indo-European language who spread into northern India in the 2nd millennium BC. **2** the language of the ancient Aryans. **3** (in Nazi ideology) a non-Jewish person of Caucasian race. ▶ **adjective** relating to the Aryan people.
– ORIGIN from Sanskrit, 'noble.'

As ▶ **symbol** the chemical element arsenic.

as /az/ ▶ **adverb** used in comparisons to refer to the extent or amount of something. ▶ **conjunction 1** while. **2** in the way that. **3** because. **4** even though. ▶ **preposition 1** in the role of; being: *a job as a cook*. **2** while; when.
– PHRASES **as for** with regard to. **as yet** until now or that time.
– ORIGIN Old English, 'similarly.'

USAGE

Some people think that you should say *he's not as shy as I* (rather than *he's not as shy as me*), but this sounds stilted and is now rarely used in normal speech. For more information, see the note at **PERSONAL PRONOUN**.

a·sa·fet·i·da /ˌasə'fetidə/ (Brit. **asafoetida**) ▶ **noun** an unpleasant-smelling gum obtained from the roots of a plant, used in herbal medicine and Indian cooking.
– ORIGIN from Latin *asa* 'mastic' + *foetida* 'stinking.'

a·sa·na /'äsənə/ ▶ **noun** a posture adopted in hatha yoga.
– ORIGIN from Sanskrit *āsana*.

ASAP ▶ **abbreviation** as soon as possible.

as·bes·tos /as'bestəs, az-/ ▶ **noun** a fibrous silicate mineral used in fire-resistant and insulating materials.
– ORIGIN from Greek, 'unquenchable.'

as·bes·to·sis /ˌasbes'tōsis, ˌaz-/ ▶ **noun** a serious lung disease, often accompanied by cancer, resulting from breathing asbestos dust.

as·cend /ə'send/ ▶ **verb 1** go up; rise or climb: *I ascended the stairs*. **2** move up in rank or status.
– DERIVATIVES **as·cend·er** noun.
– ORIGIN Latin *ascendere*.

as·cend·ant /ə'sendənt/ ▶ **adjective 1** rising in power or influence. **2** Astrology (of a planet or sign of the zodiac) just above the eastern horizon.
– DERIVATIVES **as·cend·an·cy** noun.
– PHRASES **in the ascendant** rising in power or influence.

as·cen·sion /ə'sensʜən/ ▶ **noun 1** the action of rising in status. **2** (**Ascension**) the ascent of Jesus into heaven after the Resurrection.

as·cent /ə'sent/ ▶ **noun 1** an act of ascending something: *the first ascent of the Matterhorn*. **2** an upward slope.

– SYNONYMS **1** *the ascent of the Matterhorn* **climbing,** scaling, conquest. **2** *the ascent grew steeper* **slope,** incline, gradient, grade, hill, climb.
– ANTONYMS descent, drop.

as·cer·tain /ˌasər'tān/ ▶ **verb** find out for certain: *an investigation to ascertain the cause of the accident*.

– SYNONYMS **find out,** discover, get to know, work out, make out, fathom (out), learn, deduce, divine, establish, determine; informal figure out.

– DERIVATIVES **as·cer·tain·a·ble** adjective **as·cer·tain·ment** noun.
– ORIGIN Old French *acertener*, from Latin *certus* 'settled, sure.'

as·cet·ic /ə'setik/ ▶ **adjective** strictly self-disciplined and avoiding any pleasures or luxuries. ▶ **noun** an ascetic person.
– DERIVATIVES **as·cet·i·cism** /-ˌsizəm/ noun.
– ORIGIN from Greek *askētēs* 'monk.'

CHOOSE THE RIGHT WORD

See **SEVERE**.

ASCII /'askē/ ▶ **abbreviation** Computing American Standard Code for Information Interchange.

a·scor·bic ac·id /ə'skôrbik/ ▶ **noun** vitamin C.
– ORIGIN from Latin *scorbutus* 'scurvy.'

as·cot /'asˌkät, -kət/ ▶ **noun** a man's broad silk necktie.
– ORIGIN from the place name *Ascot* in the UK, by association with formal dress at horse races held there.

as·cribe /ə'skrīb/ ▶ **verb** (**ascribe something to**) **1** consider something to be caused by: *he ascribed his fits of depression to the divorce*. **2** consider that a particular quality belongs to someone or something: *those who ascribe great importance to his theories*.
– DERIVATIVES **as·crip·tion** noun.
– ORIGIN from Latin *scribere* 'write.'

ASEAN /'äsēˌän, 'as-/ ▶ **abbreviation** Association of Southeast Asian Nations.

a·sep·tic /ā'septik/ ▶ **adjective** free from harmful bacteria, viruses, and other microorganisms.

a·sex·u·al /ā'seksʜōōəl/ ▶ **adjective 1** not having sexual feelings or associations. **2** (of reproduction) not involving sexual activity. **3** not having sexual organs.
– DERIVATIVES **a·sex·u·al·ly** adverb.

ash[1] /asʜ/ ▶ **noun 1** the powder remaining after something has been burned. **2** (**ashes**) the remains of a human body after cremation.
– DERIVATIVES **ash·y** adjective.
– ORIGIN Old English.

ash[2] ▶ **noun** a tree with winged fruits and hard pale wood.
– ORIGIN Old English.

a·shamed /ə'sʜāmd/ ▶ **adjective** feeling embarrassed or guilty.

– SYNONYMS **1 sorry,** shamefaced, sheepish, guilty, contrite, remorseful, regretful, apologetic, mortified, red-faced, repentant, penitent, rueful, chagrined. **2 reluctant,** loath, unwilling, afraid, embarrassed.
– ANTONYMS proud.

– ORIGIN Old English.

A·shan·ti /ə'sʜäntē, ə'sʜantē/ (also **Asante** /ə'säntē, ə'santē/) ▶ **noun** (pl. same) a member of a people of south central Ghana.
– ORIGIN the name in Akan (an African language).

ash blonde (also **ash blond**) ▶ **adjective** very pale blond.

ash·en /'asʜən/ ▶ **adjective** very pale as a result of shock, fear, or illness.

Ash·ke·naz·i /ˌasʜkə'nazē, ˌäsʜkə'näzē/ ▶ **noun** (pl. **Ashkenazim** /-'nazim, -'näzim/) a Jew of central or

eastern European descent. Compare with **SEPHARDI**.
– ORIGIN from *Ashkenaz*, a grandson of Noah.

ash·lar /ˈasHlər/ ▶ **noun** large square-cut stones used as the surface layer of a wall.
– ORIGIN Old French *aisselier*.

a·shore /əˈsHôr/ ▶ **adverb** to or on the shore or land.

ash·ram /ˈäsHrəm/ ▶ **noun** a Hindu religious retreat or community.
– ORIGIN Sanskrit, 'hermitage.'

ash·tang·a /äsHˈtäNGə/ ▶ **noun** a type of yoga based on eight principles and consisting of a series of poses performed in rapid succession, combined with deep, controlled breathing.
– ORIGIN from a Sanskrit word meaning 'eight.'

ash·tray /ˈasH,trā/ ▶ **noun** a small receptacle for tobacco ash and cigarette butts.

Ash Wednes·day ▶ **noun** the first day of Lent in the Christian Church.
– ORIGIN from the custom of marking the foreheads of penitents with ashes on that day.

A·sian /ˈāzHən/ ▶ **noun** a person from Asia or a person of Asian descent. ▶ **adjective** relating to Asia.

A·si·at·ic /,āzHēˈatik, ,āzē-/ ▶ **adjective** relating to Asia.

USAGE

Although it is standard in scientific and technical use, **Asiatic** can be offensive when used of individual people: use **Asian** instead.

a·side /əˈsīd/ ▶ **adverb 1** to one side; out of the way. **2** in reserve. ▶ **noun 1** an actor's remark spoken to the audience rather than the other characters. **2** a remark that is not directly related to the main subject of discussion.
– PHRASES **aside from** apart from.

A-side ▶ **noun** the side of a pop single regarded as the main one.

as·i·nine /ˈasə,nīn/ ▶ **adjective** extremely stupid or foolish.
– ORIGIN Latin *asinus* 'ass.'

CHOOSE THE RIGHT WORD

See **STUPID**.

-asis (also **-iasis**) ▶ **suffix** forming the names of diseases: *psoriasis.*
– ORIGIN Greek.

ask /ask/ ▶ **verb 1** say something in order to get an answer or some information. **2** say that one wants someone to do, give, or allow something: *she asked me to help her.* **3** (**ask for**) request to speak to someone. **4** expect or demand something from someone: *you are asking too much of her.* **5** invite someone to a social occasion. **6** (**ask someone out**) invite someone out on a date. **7** (**ask after**) chiefly Brit. make polite inquiries about someone's health or well-being.

– SYNONYMS **1 enquire,** want to know, question, interrogate, quiz. **2** *they'll ask a few questions* **put (forward),** pose, raise, submit. **3 request,** demand, seek, solicit, apply, petition, call, appeal.
– ANTONYMS answer.

– PHRASES **for the asking** for little or no effort or cost: *the job was his for the asking.*
– ORIGIN Old English.

a·skance /əˈskans/ ▶ **adverb** with a suspicious or disapproving look.
– ORIGIN unknown.

a·skew /əˈskyōō/ ▶ **adverb & adjective** not straight or level.

ask·ing price ▶ **noun** the price at which something is offered for sale.

a·slant /əˈslant/ ▶ **adverb & preposition** at or across at a slant.

a·sleep /əˈslēp/ ▶ **adjective & adverb** in or into a state of sleep.

– SYNONYMS **sleeping,** napping, dozing, drowsing; informal snoozing, dead to the world; humorous in the land of Nod.
– ANTONYMS awake.

a·so·cial /āˈsōsHəl/ ▶ **adjective** avoiding social interaction; inconsiderate of or hostile to others.

asp /asp/ ▶ **noun 1** a small viper with an upturned snout. **2** the Egyptian cobra.
– ORIGIN Greek *aspis*.

as·par·a·gus /əˈsparəgəs/ ▶ **noun** a vegetable consisting of the tender young shoots of a tall plant.
– ORIGIN Greek *asparagos*.

as·par·tame /ˈaspär,tām/ ▶ **noun** a low-calorie artificial sweetener.
– ORIGIN from *aspartic acid*, a related chemical named after *asparagus*.

ASPCA ▶ **abbreviation** American Society for the Prevention of Cruelty to Animals.

as·pect /ˈaspekt/ ▶ **noun 1** a particular part or feature of something: *a training course covering all aspects of the business.* **2** a particular appearance or quality: *the black eyepatch gave his face a sinister aspect.* **3** the side of a building facing a particular direction.

– SYNONYMS **1 feature,** facet, side, characteristic, particular, detail. **2 point of view,** position, standpoint, viewpoint, perspective, angle, slant. **3** *his face had a sinister aspect* **appearance,** look, air, mien, demeanor, expression.

– ORIGIN Latin *aspectus*, from *aspicere* 'look at.'

as·pect ra·tio ▶ **noun** the ratio of the width to the height of an image on a television screen.

as·pen /ˈaspən/ ▶ **noun** a poplar tree with small rounded leaves.
– ORIGIN dialect.

As·per·ger's syn·drome /ˈaspərgərz/ ▶ **noun** a mild form of autism.
– ORIGIN named after the Austrian psychiatrist Hans *Asperger*.

as·per·i·ty /əˈsperitē/ ▶ **noun** harshness of tone or manner.
– ORIGIN from Latin *asper* 'rough.'

as·per·sions /əˈspərzHən/ ▶ **plural noun** (in phrase **cast aspersions on**) make critical or unpleasant remarks about: *no one is casting aspersions on you or your officers.*
– ORIGIN from Latin *aspergere* 'sprinkle.'

as·phalt /ˈasfôlt/ ▶ **noun** a dark tarlike substance used in surfacing roads or waterproofing buildings.
– ORIGIN Greek *asphalton*.

as·pho·del /ˈasfə,del/ ▶ **noun** a plant of the lily family with clusters of yellow or white flowers on a long stem.
– ORIGIN Greek *asphodelos*.

as·phyx·i·a /as'fiksēə/ ▶ **noun** a condition arising when the body is deprived of oxygen, causing unconsciousness or death.
– ORIGIN Greek *asphuxia*, from *a-* 'without' + *sphuxis* 'pulse.'

as·phyx·i·ate /as'fiksē,āt/ ▶ **verb 1** kill someone by depriving them of oxygen. **2** die as a result of a lack of oxygen.
– DERIVATIVES **as·phyx·i·a·tion** /as,fiksē'āsʜən/ noun.

as·pic /'aspik/ ▶ **noun** a savory jelly made with meat stock.
– ORIGIN French, 'asp,' the colors of the jelly being compared with those of the snake.

as·pi·dis·tra /,aspi'distrə/ ▶ **noun** a plant of the lily family with broad tapering leaves.
– ORIGIN Greek *aspis* 'shield.'

as·pir·ant /'aspərənt, ə'spī-/ ▶ **noun** a person with strong ambitions to do or be something.

as·pi·rate ▶ **verb** /'aspə,rāt/ **1** pronounce a word with the sound of the letter *h* at the start. **2** remove fluid from a part of the body using suction. **3** technical inhale. ▶ **noun** /'asp(ə)rit/ the sound of the letter *h*.
– ORIGIN Latin *aspirare*.

as·pi·ra·tion /,aspə'rāsʜən/ ▶ **noun** a strong desire to do or have something; an ambition: *he never showed any aspirations for political office*.

– SYNONYMS **desire,** hope, dream, wish, longing, yearning, aim, ambition, expectation, goal, target.

as·pi·ra·tion·al /,aspə'rāsʜənl/ ▶ **adjective 1** having a strong desire to do or have something: *young, aspirational women*. **2** referring or relating to something that people strongly desire to do or have: *an aspirational lifestyle*.

as·pi·ra·tor /'aspə,rātər/ ▶ **noun** an instrument or device for removing fluid from a part of the body by suction.

as·pire /ə'spī(ə)r/ ▶ **verb** have strong ambitions to be or do something.

– SYNONYMS **1** *she* ***aspired to*** *study at Cambridge* **desire,** aim for, hope for, dream of, long for, yearn for, set one's heart on, wish for, want, seek, set one's sights on. **2** (as adj. **aspiring**) *an aspiring journalist* **would-be,** hopeful, budding, potential, prospective; informal wannabe.

– ORIGIN Latin *aspirare*.

as·pi·rin /'asp(ə)rin/ ▶ **noun** (pl. same or **aspirins**) a medicine used in tablet form to relieve pain and reduce fever and inflammation.
– ORIGIN from its chemical name.

ass[1] /as/ ▶ **noun 1** a donkey or related small wild horse. **2** informal a stupid person.
– ORIGIN Latin *asinus*.

ass[2] ▶ **noun** vulgar slang **1** a person's buttocks or anus. **2** a stupid, irritating, or contemptible person. **3** women regarded as a source of sexual gratification.

as·sail /ə'sāl/ ▶ **verb 1** attack someone or something violently. **2** (of an unpleasant feeling) come upon someone suddenly and strongly: *she was assailed by doubts and regrets*.
– ORIGIN Latin *assalire*, from *salire* 'to leap.'

CHOOSE THE RIGHT WORD

See **ATTACK**.

as·sail·ant /ə'sālənt/ ▶ **noun** an attacker.

as·sas·sin /ə'sasin/ ▶ **noun** a person who assassinates someone.

– SYNONYMS **murderer,** killer, gunman, executioner; informal hit man.

– ORIGIN Arabic, 'hashish eater' (referring to a fanatical Muslim sect at the time of the Crusades who were said to use hashish before murder missions).

as·sas·si·nate /ə'sasə,nāt/ ▶ **verb** murder an important person for political or religious reasons.

– SYNONYMS **murder,** kill, eliminate, liquidate, execute, terminate; informal hit, whack.

– DERIVATIVES **as·sas·si·na·tion** /ə,sasə'nāsʜən/ noun.

as·sault /ə'sôlt/ ▶ **noun 1** a violent attack. **2** Law an act that threatens physical harm to a person. **3** a determined attempt to do something difficult: *a winter assault on Mt. Everest*.

– SYNONYMS **1 violence,** battery, (grievous) bodily harm. **2 attack,** strike, onslaught, offensive, charge, push, thrust, raid.

▶ **verb** attack someone violently.

– SYNONYMS **attack,** hit, strike, beat up; informal lay into, rough up, do over.

– ORIGIN Old French *assauter*, from Latin *saltare* 'to leap.'

CHOOSE THE RIGHT WORD

See **ATTACK**.

as·sault and bat·ter·y ▶ **noun** Law the action of threatening a person together with making physical contact with them.

as·sault ri·fle ▶ **noun** a lightweight rifle that may be set to fire automatically or semiautomatically.

as·say /'a,sā, a'sā/ ▶ **noun** the process of testing a metal or ore to establish its composition or purity. ▶ **verb 1** test a metal or ore to establish its composition or purity. **2** old use attempt.
– ORIGIN Old French *assai, essai* 'trial.'

as·sem·blage /ə'semblij/ ▶ **noun 1** a collection or gathering of things or people: *a rich assemblage of 16th-century paintings*. **2** something made of pieces fitted together.

as·sem·ble /ə'sembəl/ ▶ **verb 1** come or bring together: *a crowd assembled outside the gates*. **2** fit together the component parts of: *supplied in flat-pack form, the shed is easily assembled*.

– SYNONYMS **1 gather,** collect, get together, congregate, convene, meet, muster, rally, round up, marshal. **2 construct,** build, erect, set up, make, manufacture, fabricate, put together, connect.
– ANTONYMS disperse, dismantle.

– ORIGIN Old French *asembler*.

as·sem·bler /ə'semblər/ ▶ **noun 1** a person who assembles a machine or its parts. **2** Computing a program for converting instructions written in low-level symbolic code into machine code.

as·sem·bly /ə'semblē/ ▶ **noun** (pl. **assemblies**) **1** a group of people gathered together. **2** a body of people with powers to make decisions and laws. **3** a regular gathering of teachers and students in a school. **4** the action of assembling the component parts of something.

– SYNONYMS **1 gathering,** meeting, congregation, convention, council, rally, group, crowd; informal get-together. **2 construction,** manufacture, building, fabrication, erection.

as·sem·bly line ▶ **noun** a series of workers and machines in a factory that assemble the component parts of identical products in successive stages.

as·sent /ə'sent/ ▶ **noun** approval or agreement. ▶ **verb** agree to a request or suggestion: *both parties assented to the terms of the agreement.*
– ORIGIN Latin *assentire.*

as·sert /ə'sərt/ ▶ **verb 1** state a fact or belief confidently and firmly: *he asserted that he had no intention of stepping down.* **2** make other people recognize something by behaving confidently and forcefully: *a young woman seeking to assert her independence.* **3** (**assert oneself**) behave in a confident and forceful way.

– SYNONYMS **1 declare,** state, maintain, contend, argue, claim, insist. **2** *you should assert your rights* **insist on,** stand up for, uphold, defend, press/push for.

– ORIGIN Latin *asserere* 'claim, affirm.'

as·ser·tion /ə'sərsʜən/ ▶ **noun 1** a confident and forceful statement. **2** the action of asserting something.

– SYNONYMS **declaration,** contention, statement, claim, opinion, protestation.

as·ser·tive /ə'sərtiv/ ▶ **adjective** having or showing a confident and forceful personality.

– SYNONYMS **confident,** self-confident, bold, decisive, forceful, insistent, emphatic, determined, strong-willed, commanding, pushy; informal feisty.
– ANTONYMS timid.

– DERIVATIVES **as·ser·tive·ly** adverb **as·ser·tive·ness** noun.

as·ses /'asiz/ plural of **ASS**[1], **ASS**[2].

as·sess /ə'ses/ ▶ **verb 1** calculate or estimate the value, importance, or quality of: *a survey to assess the damage caused by the oil spill.* **2** set the value of a tax for a person or property.

– SYNONYMS **evaluate,** judge, gauge, rate, estimate, appraise, weigh up, calculate, value, work out, determine; informal size up.

– DERIVATIVES **as·sess·ment** noun **as·ses·sor** noun.
– ORIGIN Latin *assidere* 'sit by' (later 'levy tax').

as·set /'aset/ ▶ **noun 1** a useful or valuable thing or person. **2** (**assets**) the property owned by a person or company.

– SYNONYMS **1 benefit,** advantage, blessing, good/strong point, strength, forte, virtue, recommendation, attraction, resource. **2** *the seizure of all their assets* **property,** resources, estate, holdings, funds, valuables, possessions, effects, belongings.
– ANTONYMS liability.

– ORIGIN Old French *asez* 'enough.'

as·set-strip·ping ▶ **noun** the practice of taking over a company that is in financial difficulty and then selling its assets separately at a profit.

as·sev·er·a·tion /ə͵sevə'rāsʜən/ ▶ **noun** formal a solemn or emphatic declaration or statement.
– DERIVATIVES **as·sev·er·ate** /ə'sevə͵rāt/ verb.
– ORIGIN Latin, from *asseverare.*

ass·hole /'as͵hōl/ ▶ **noun** vulgar slang **1** the anus. **2** an irritating or contemptible person.

as·sid·u·ous /ə'sijəwəs/ ▶ **adjective** showing or done with great care and thoroughness: *he was assiduous in his duties.*
– DERIVATIVES **as·si·du·i·ty** /͵asi'd(y)o͞oitē/ noun **as·sid·u·ous·ly** adverb.
– ORIGIN Latin *assiduus.*

CHOOSE THE RIGHT WORD

See **BUSY**.

as·sign /ə'sīn/ ▶ **verb 1** give a task or duty to someone: *work duties were assigned at the beginning of the shift.* **2** give someone a job or task: *she had been assigned to a new post.* **3** regard something as belonging to or being caused by: *a mosaic assigned to the late third century* BC.

– SYNONYMS **1 allocate,** give, set, charge with, entrust with. **2 appoint,** promote, delegate, nominate, commission, post, co-opt; Military detail. **3 earmark,** designate, set aside, reserve, appropriate, allot, allocate.

– ORIGIN Latin *assignare.*

as·sig·na·tion /͵asig'nāsʜən/ ▶ **noun** a secret meeting, especially one between lovers.

– SYNONYMS **rendezvous,** date, appointment, meeting; literary tryst.

as·sign·ee /ə͵sī'nē/ ▶ **noun** chiefly Law **1** a person to whom a right or liability is legally transferred. **2** a person appointed to act for another.

as·sign·ment /ə'sīnmənt/ ▶ **noun 1** a task allocated to someone as part of a job or course of study. **2** the assigning of a job or task to someone.

– SYNONYMS **task,** job, duty, responsibility, mission, errand, undertaking, commission.

as·sim·i·late /ə'simə͵lāt/ ▶ **verb 1** take in and understand information or ideas. **2** absorb and integrate people or ideas into a wider society or culture: *they were assimilated into mainstream American society.* **3** absorb and digest food or nutrients.
– DERIVATIVES **as·sim·i·la·ble** /-ləbəl/ adjective **as·sim·i·la·tion** /ə͵simə'lāsʜən/ noun.
– ORIGIN Latin *assimilare.*

as·sist /ə'sist/ ▶ **verb** give help or support to someone.

– SYNONYMS **1 help,** aid, lend a (helping) hand to, support, back (up), work with, cooperate with. **2** *the aim was to assist cashflow* **facilitate,** aid, ease, promote, boost, speed, benefit, encourage, further.
– ANTONYMS hinder.

– ORIGIN Latin *assistere* 'stand by.'

as·sis·tance /ə'sistəns/ ▶ **noun** help or support.

– SYNONYMS **help,** aid, a (helping) hand, support, backing, reinforcement.
– ANTONYMS hindrance.

as·sis·tant /ə'sistənt/ ▶ **noun 1** a person who ranks below a senior person. **2** a person who provides help in a particular role or type of work: *an administrative assistant.*

– SYNONYMS **helper,** aide, deputy, second (in command), number two, right-hand man/woman, personal assistant, PA, auxiliary, attendant, henchman; informal sidekick, gofer.

as·size /ə'sīz/ (also **assizes**) ▶ **noun** historical a court that sat at intervals in each county of England and Wales.
– ORIGIN Old French *assise.*

ass-kick·ing informal ▶ **noun** forceful or aggressive behavior; an instance of this; a beating. ▶ **adjective** dominant or powerful, especially exceptionally so: *she makes an ass-kicking hot sauce.*

as·so·ci·ate ▶ **verb** /ə'sōsēˌāt, -shē-/ **1** connect in one's mind: *I associated wealth with freedom.* **2** frequently meet or have dealings with: *she began associating with Marxists.* **3** (**be associated with** or **associate oneself with**) be involved with.

> – SYNONYMS **1 link,** connect, relate, bracket, identify, equate. **2 mix,** keep company, mingle, socialize, go around, have dealings; informal **hobnob,** hang out/around.
> – ANTONYMS avoid.

▶ **noun** /-it/ a work partner or colleague.

> – SYNONYMS **partner,** colleague, coworker, workmate, collaborator, comrade, ally; informal crony.

▶ **adjective** /-it/ **1** connected with an organization or business. **2** belonging to an organization but not having full membership.
– ORIGIN Latin *associare.*

as·so·ci·at·ed /ə'sōsēˌātid, -shē-/ ▶ **adjective** (of a person or thing) connected with something else: *two associated events.*

> – SYNONYMS **related,** connected, linked, similar, corresponding, attendant, accompanying, incidental.
> – ANTONYMS unrelated.

as·so·ci·a·tion /əˌsōsē'āshən, -shē-/ ▶ **noun 1** a group of people organized for a joint purpose. **2** a connection or relationship: *his close association with the university.* **3** an idea, memory, or feeling that is connected to someone or something: *the name had unpleasant associations for him.*

> – SYNONYMS **1 alliance,** consortium, coalition, union, league, guild, syndicate, federation, confederation, cartel, cooperative, partnership. **2 relationship,** relation, interrelation, connection, interconnection, interdependence, link, bond.

as·so·ci·a·tive /ə'sōsēˌātiv, -shē-, -sēətiv, -shətiv/ ▶ **adjective 1** relating to or involving association. **2** Mathematics producing the same result however quantities are grouped, as long as their order remains the same, as in the equation $(a \times b) \times c = a \times (b \times c)$.

as·so·nance /'asənəns/ ▶ **noun** the rhyming of vowels only (e.g., *hide, line*) or of consonants but not vowels (e.g., *cold, killed*).
– ORIGIN Latin *assonare* 'respond to.'

as·sort·ed /ə'sôrtid/ ▶ **adjective** of various different sorts put together: *a plate of assorted vegetables.*

> – SYNONYMS **various,** miscellaneous, mixed, varied, diverse, different, sundry.
> – ANTONYMS uniform.

– ORIGIN Old French *assorter.*

as·sort·ment /ə'sôrtmənt/ ▶ **noun** a collection of different things: *an assortment of boots and shoes.*

> – SYNONYMS **variety,** mixture, array, mix, miscellany, selection, medley, melange, ragbag, potpourri.

as·suage /ə'swāj/ ▶ **verb 1** make an unpleasant feeling less intense: *his letter assuaged the fears of most members.* **2** satisfy an appetite or desire.
– ORIGIN Old French *assouagier,* from Latin *suavis* 'sweet.'

> **CHOOSE THE RIGHT WORD**
>
> See **ALLEVIATE**.

as·sume /ə'so͞om/ ▶ **verb 1** accept as true or being the case without having proof: *he assumed she was married.* **2** take responsibility or control. **3** begin to have: *foreign trade has assumed greater importance in recent years.* **4** pretend to have: *he assumed an air of indifference* | (as adj. **assumed**) *a man living under an assumed name.*

> – SYNONYMS **1 presume,** suppose, take it (as given), take for granted, take as read, conclude, infer, think, fancy, imagine, surmise, believe, understand, gather, suspect, figure. **2 accept,** shoulder, bear, undertake, take on/up. **3 seize,** take (over), appropriate, wrest, usurp. **4 affect,** adopt, put on. **5** (as adj. **assumed**) **false,** fictitious, fake, bogus, invented, made-up; informal pretend, phony.

– ORIGIN Latin *assumere.*

as·sum·ing /ə'so͞omiNG/ ▶ **conjunction** based on the assumption that.

as·sump·tion /ə'səm(p)shən/ ▶ **noun 1** a thing that is assumed to be true. **2** the assuming of responsibility or control. **3** (**Assumption**) the taking up of the Virgin Mary into heaven, according to Roman Catholic doctrine.

> – SYNONYMS **supposition,** presumption, inference, conjecture, belief, surmise, hypothesis, theory, suspicion, guess.

as·sur·ance /ə'sho͝orəns/ ▶ **noun 1** a statement or promise intended to give someone confidence. **2** confidence in one's own abilities. **3** chiefly Brit. life insurance.

> – SYNONYMS **1 promise,** word (of honor), pledge, vow, oath, undertaking, guarantee, commitment. **2 confidence,** self-confidence, self-assurance, self-possession, nerve, poise; informal cool. **3 insurance,** indemnity, protection, security, cover.

as·sure /ə'sho͝or/ ▶ **verb 1** tell someone that something is definitely true or will be the case: *she assured him that everything was under control.* **2** make something certain to happen: *victory would assure their promotion.* **3** Brit. insure a person's life.

> – SYNONYMS **1 reassure,** convince, satisfy, persuade. **2 promise,** guarantee, swear, confirm, certify, vow, give one's word. **3 ensure,** secure, guarantee, seal, clinch; informal sew up.

– ORIGIN Old French *assurer.*

as·sured /ə'sho͝ord/ ▶ **adjective 1** having or showing confidence: *her calm, assured voice.* **2** protected against change or ending: *an assured tenancy.*

> – SYNONYMS **1 confident,** self-confident, self-assured, self-possessed, poised, composed, imperturbable, unruffled; informal unflappable, together. **2 guaranteed,** certain, sure, secure, reliable, dependable; informal sure-fire.
> – ANTONYMS nervous, uncertain.

– DERIVATIVES **as·sur·ed·ly** /ə'sho͝oridlē/ adverb.

As·syr·i·an /ə'si(ə)rēən/ ▶ **noun** an inhabitant of Assyria, an ancient country in what is now Iraq.

as·ta·tine /'astəˌtēn, -tin/ ▶ **noun** a very unstable radioactive chemical element belonging to the halogen group.
– ORIGIN Greek *astatos* 'unstable.'

as·ter /'astər/ ▶ **noun** a garden plant of the daisy family, typically having purple or pink flowers.
– ORIGIN Greek, 'star.'

as·ter·isk /'astə,risk/ ▶ **noun** a symbol (*) used in text as a pointer to a note elsewhere.
– ORIGIN Greek *asteriskos* 'small star.'

a·stern /ə'stərn/ ▶ **adverb** behind or toward the rear of a ship or aircraft.

as·ter·oid /'astə,roid/ ▶ **noun** a small rocky planet orbiting the sun.
– ORIGIN Greek *asteroeidēs* 'starlike.'

asth·ma /'azmə/ ▶ **noun** a medical condition causing difficulty in breathing.
– DERIVATIVES **asth·mat·ic** /az'matik/ adjective & noun.
– ORIGIN Greek, from *azein* 'breathe hard.'

a·stig·ma·tism /ə'stigmə,tizəm/ ▶ **noun** a defect in an eye or lens that prevents it from focusing properly.
– DERIVATIVES **as·tig·mat·ic** /,astig'matik/ adjective.
– ORIGIN Greek *stigma* 'point.'

a·stil·be /ə'stilbē/ ▶ **noun** a plant with plumes of tiny white, pink, or red flowers.
– ORIGIN Latin.

a·stir /ə'stər/ ▶ **adjective 1** in a state of excited movement. **2** awake and out of bed.

as·ton·ish /ə'stänisн/ ▶ **verb** surprise or impress someone greatly.

– SYNONYMS **amaze,** astound, stagger, startle, stun, surprise, confound, dumbfound, nonplus, take aback, leave open-mouthed; informal flabbergast, bowl over, blow away, floor, throw/knock for a loop.

– DERIVATIVES **as·ton·ished** adjective **as·ton·ish·ment** noun.
– ORIGIN Old French *estoner* 'stun,' from Latin *tonare* 'to thunder.'

as·ton·ish·ing /ə'stänisнiNG/ ▶ **adjective** extremely surprising.

– SYNONYMS **amazing,** astounding, staggering, surprising, breathtaking, remarkable, extraordinary, incredible, unbelievable, phenomenal; informal mind-boggling.
– ANTONYMS unremarkable.

as·tound /ə'stound/ ▶ **verb** shock or greatly surprise someone.

– SYNONYMS **amaze,** astonish, stagger, surprise, startle, stun, confound, dumbfound, take aback, leave open-mouthed; informal flabbergast, bowl over, blow away, floor, throw/knock for a loop.

– DERIVATIVES **as·tound·ed** adjective.
– ORIGIN related to **ASTONISH**.

as·tound·ing /ə'stoundiNG/ ▶ **adjective** surprisingly impressive or notable.

– SYNONYMS **amazing,** astonishing, staggering, surprising, breathtaking, remarkable, extraordinary, incredible, unbelievable, phenomenal; informal mind-boggling.
– ANTONYMS unremarkable.

as·tral /'astrəl/ ▶ **adjective** relating to the stars.
– ORIGIN Latin *astrum* 'star.'

a·stray /ə'strā/ ▶ **adverb** away from the right path or direction.
– ORIGIN from Old French *estraie*.

a·stride /ə'strīd/ ▶ **preposition & adverb 1** with a leg on each side of something. **2** (as adv.) (of a person's legs) wide apart.

as·trin·gent /ə'strinjənt/ ▶ **adjective 1** (of a substance) making body tissue contract. **2** harsh or severe in manner or style: *her astringent comments.* ▶ **noun** an astringent lotion used medically or as a cosmetic.
– DERIVATIVES **as·trin·gen·cy** noun **as·trin·gent·ly** adverb.
– ORIGIN Latin *astringere* 'pull tight.'

astro- ▶ **combining form** relating to the stars or to outer space: *astronaut*.
– ORIGIN Greek *astron* 'star.'

as·tro·bi·o·lo·gy /,astrōbī'äləjē/ ▶ **noun** the branch of biology concerned with the discovery or study of life on other planets or in space.
– DERIVATIVES **as·tro·bi·o·lo·gist** noun.

as·tro·labe /'astrə,lāb/ ▶ **noun** an instrument formerly used for measuring the altitudes of stars and calculating latitude in navigation.
– ORIGIN Greek *astrolabos* 'star-taking.'

as·trol·o·gy /ə'sträləjē/ ▶ **noun** the study of the supposed influence of stars and planets on human affairs.
– DERIVATIVES **as·trol·o·ger** noun **as·tro·log·i·cal** /,astrə'läjikəl/ adjective **as·tro·log·i·cal·ly** /,astrə'läjik(ə)lē/ adverb.

as·tro·naut /'astrə,nôt/ ▶ **noun** a person trained to travel in a spacecraft.
– ORIGIN from Greek *astron* 'star' + *nautēs* 'sailor.'

as·tro·nau·tics /,astrə'nôtiks/ ▶ **plural noun** (treated as sing.) the science and technology of space travel and exploration.

as·tro·nom·i·cal /,astrə'nämikəl/ ▶ **adjective 1** relating to astronomy. **2** informal extremely large: *astronomical fees*.
– DERIVATIVES **as·tro·nom·ic** adjective **as·tro·nom·i·cal·ly** /-ik(ə)lē/ adverb.

as·tro·nom·i·cal u·nit ▶ **noun** a unit of measurement equal to the mean distance from the earth to the sun, 149.6 million kilometers.

as·tron·o·my /ə'stränəmē/ ▶ **noun** the science of stars, planets, and the universe.
– DERIVATIVES **as·tron·o·mer** noun.

as·tro·phys·ics /,astrō'fiziks/ ▶ **plural noun** (treated as sing.) the branch of astronomy concerned with the physical nature of stars and planets.
– DERIVATIVES **as·tro·phys·i·cal** adjective **as·tro·phys·i·cist** /-isist/ noun.

As·tro·Turf /'astrō,tərf/ ▶ **noun** trademark an artificial grass surface, used for sports fields.

as·tute /ə'st(y)o͞ot/ ▶ **adjective** good at making accurate judgments; shrewd.

– SYNONYMS **shrewd,** sharp, acute, quick, clever, intelligent, bright, smart, canny, perceptive, perspicacious; informal quick on the uptake.
– ANTONYMS stupid.

– DERIVATIVES **as·tute·ly** adverb **as·tute·ness** noun.
– ORIGIN Latin *astutus*.

CHOOSE THE RIGHT WORD

See **KEEN**[1].

a·sun·der /ə'səndər/ ▶ **adverb** literary apart.
– ORIGIN Old English.

a·sy·lum /ə'sīləm/ ▶ **noun 1** protection from danger, especially for people who leave their own country as a result of suffering persecution for their political beliefs. **2** dated an institution for the care of people who are mentally ill.

– SYNONYMS **refuge,** sanctuary, shelter, protection, immunity, a safe haven.

– ORIGIN Greek *asulon* 'refuge.'

a·sym·met·ri·cal /ˌāsəˈmetrikəl/ ▶ **adjective** having sides or parts that do not correspond in size, shape, or arrangement; lacking symmetry.
– DERIVATIVES **a·sym·met·ric** adjective **a·sym·met·ri·cal·ly** adverb.

a·sym·me·try /āˈsimitrē/ ▶ **noun** (pl. **asymmetries**) lack of symmetry between the sides or parts of something.

a·symp·to·mat·ic /ˌāsim(p)təˈmatik/ ▶ **adjective** producing or showing no symptoms of a disease or condition.

a·syn·chro·nous /āˈsiNGkrənəs/ ▶ **adjective** not existing or occurring at the same time.
– DERIVATIVES **a·syn·chro·nous·ly** adverb **a·syn·chro·ny** noun.

At ▶ **symbol** the chemical element astatine.

at /at/ ▶ **preposition** (used to express:) **1** location, arrival, or time. **2** a value, rate, or point on a scale. **3** a state or condition. **4** the object or target of a look, shot, action, or plan.
– PHRASES **at that** in addition; furthermore.
– ORIGIN Old English.

at·a·vis·tic /ˌatəˈvistik/ ▶ **adjective** related or reverting to the feelings or behavior of the earliest humans: *an atavistic fear of the dark.*
– DERIVATIVES **at·a·vism** /ˈatəˌvizəm/ noun **at·a·vis·ti·cal·ly** /-tik(ə)lē/ adverb.
– ORIGIN Latin *atavus* 'forefather.'

a·tax·i·a /əˈtaksēə/ ▶ **noun** Medicine the loss of the ability to control or coordinate one's movements.
– ORIGIN Greek, 'disorder.'

ATC ▶ **abbreviation 1** air traffic control or controller. **2** Air Training Corps.

ate /āt/ past of **EAT**.

at·el·ier /ˌatlˈyā/ ▶ **noun** a workshop or studio used by an artist or designer.
– ORIGIN French.

a·the·ism /ˈāTHēˌizəm/ ▶ **noun** disbelief in the existence of a god or gods.
– DERIVATIVES **a·the·ist** noun **a·the·is·tic** /ˌāTHēˈistik/ adjective.
– ORIGIN from Greek *a-* 'without' + *theos* 'god.'

A·the·ni·an /əˈTHēnēən/ ▶ **noun** a person from Athens in Greece. ▶ **adjective** relating to Athens.

ath·er·o·scle·ro·sis /ˌaTHərōskləˈrōsis/ ▶ **noun** a disease of the arteries in which fatty material is deposited on their inner walls.
– DERIVATIVES **ath·er·o·scle·rot·ic** /-ˈrätik/ adjective.
– ORIGIN from Greek *athērē* 'groats' + *sklērōsis* 'hardening.'

ath·lete /ˈaTHˌlēt/ ▶ **noun 1** a person who is good at sports. **2** a person who competes in track and field events.
– ORIGIN Greek *athlētēs*, from *athlon* 'prize.'

ath·lete's foot ▶ **noun** a contagious fungal infection affecting the skin between the toes.

ath·let·ic /aTHˈletik/ ▶ **adjective 1** fit and active; good at sports. **2** relating to athletes or athletics.

– SYNONYMS **muscular,** fit, strapping, well built, strong, sturdy, powerful, brawny, burly.

– DERIVATIVES **ath·let·i·cal·ly** /-ik(ə)lē/ adverb **ath·let·i·cism** /-ˌsizəm/ noun.

ath·let·ics /aTHˈletiks/ ▶ **plural noun** (usu. treated as sing.) **1** physical sports and games of any kind. **2** chiefly Brit. the sport of competing in track and field events.

a·thwart /əˈTHwôrt/ ▶ **preposition & adverb** from side to side of something; across.
– ORIGIN from an old sense of **THWART**, meaning 'across.'

At·kins di·et /ˈatkinz/ ▶ **noun** trademark a high-protein, high-fat diet in which carbohydrates are severely restricted.
– ORIGIN named after the American cardiologist R. C. *Atkins*.

At·lan·tic /ətˈlantik, at-/ ▶ **adjective** relating to the Atlantic Ocean.
– ORIGIN first referring to Mount Atlas in Libya; named after the god *Atlas* (see **ATLAS**).

at·las /ˈatləs/ ▶ **noun** a book of maps or charts.
– ORIGIN named after the Greek god *Atlas*, shown on early atlases as supporting the pillars of the universe.

ATM ▶ **abbreviation** automated teller machine.

at·mos·phere /ˈatməsˌfi(ə)r/ ▶ **noun 1** the gases surrounding the earth or another planet. **2** the quality of the air in a place: *the smoky atmosphere of an industrial town.* **3** an overall tone or mood: *a hotel with a friendly, relaxed atmosphere.* **4** a unit of pressure equal to the pressure of the atmosphere at sea level, 101,325 pascals (roughly 14.7 pounds per square inch).

– SYNONYMS **1 air,** sky; literary the heavens, the ether. **2** *a relaxed atmosphere* **ambience,** spirit, air, mood, feel, feeling, character, tone, aura, quality, environment, climate; informal vibe.

– ORIGIN from Greek *atmos* 'vapor' + *sphaira* 'globe.'

WORD LINKS

meteorology *study of the atmosphere*

at·mos·pher·ic /ˌatməsˈfi(ə)rik, -ˈferik/ ▶ **adjective 1** relating to the atmosphere of the earth or another planet. **2** creating a distinctive mood, especially one of romance, nostalgia, or excitement: *a very atmospheric location.*
– DERIVATIVES **at·mos·pher·i·cal·ly** adverb.

at·mos·pher·ics /ˌatməsˈfi(ə)riks, -ˈferiks/ ▶ **plural noun** electrical disturbances in the atmosphere that interfere with telecommunications.

at·oll /ˈatˌôl, ˈatˌäl, ˈāˌtôl, ˈāˌtäl/ ▶ **noun** a ring-shaped coral reef or chain of islands.
– ORIGIN Maldivian.

at·om /ˈatəm/ ▶ **noun 1** the smallest particle of a chemical element that can exist. **2** an extremely small amount: *she did not have an atom of strength left.*
– ORIGIN Greek *atomos* 'indivisible.'

at·om bomb ▶ **noun** (also **atomic bomb**) a bomb whose explosive power comes from the fission (splitting) of the nuclei of atoms.

a·tom·ic /əˈtämik/ ▶ **adjective 1** relating to an atom or atoms. **2** relating to nuclear energy or weapons.

a·tom·ic mass u·nit ▶ **noun** a unit of mass used to express atomic and molecular weights, equal to one twelfth of the mass of an atom of carbon-12.

a·tom·ic num·ber ▶ **noun** the number of protons in the nucleus of a chemical element's atom, which determines its place in the periodic table.

a·tom·ic the·o·ry ▶ **noun** the theory that all matter is made up of tiny indivisible particles (atoms).

a·tom·ic weight ▶ **noun** another term for **RELATIVE ATOMIC MASS**.

at·om·ize /ˈatəˌmīz/ ▶ **verb** convert a substance into very fine particles or droplets.
– DERIVATIVES **at·om·i·za·tion** /ˌatəməˈzāSHən/ noun.

at·om·iz·er /ˈatəˌmīzər/ ▶ **noun** a device for sending out water, perfume, or other liquids as a fine spray.

a·ton·al /āˈtōnl/ ▶ **adjective** not written in any musical key.
– DERIVATIVES **a·to·nal·i·ty** /ˌātōˈnalitē/ noun.

a·tone /əˈtōn/ ▶ **verb** (**atone for**) make amends for a sin, crime, or other wrongdoing.
– ORIGIN from *at one*.

a·tone·ment /əˈtōnmənt/ ▶ **noun 1** the action of making amends for a sin, crime, or other wrongdoing. **2** (**the Atonement**) the reconciliation of God and humankind brought about through the death of Jesus.

a·top /əˈtäp/ ▶ **preposition** on the top of.

ATP ▶ **abbreviation** Biochemistry adenosine triphosphate.

at-risk ▶ **adjective** vulnerable, especially to abuse or delinquency: *a church-run school for the most at-risk children*.

a·tri·um /ˈātrēəm/ ▶ **noun** (pl. **atria** /ˈātrēə/ or **atriums**) **1** a central hall rising through several stories and having a glazed roof. **2** an open area in the center of an ancient Roman house. **3** each of the two upper cavities of the heart.
– DERIVATIVES **a·tri·al** /ˈātrēəl/ adjective.
– ORIGIN Latin.

a·tro·cious /əˈtrōSHəs/ ▶ **adjective 1** horrifyingly cruel or wicked. **2** extremely bad or unpleasant.

> – SYNONYMS **1 wicked,** cruel, brutal, barbaric, vicious, monstrous, vile, inhuman, fiendish. **2 appalling,** awful, dreadful, terrible, miserable; informal abysmal, dire, shocking, rotten, lousy.
> – ANTONYMS admirable, superb.

– DERIVATIVES **a·tro·cious·ly** adverb.
– ORIGIN Latin *atrox* 'cruel.'

a·troc·i·ty /əˈträsitē/ ▶ **noun** (pl. **atrocities**) an extremely cruel or wicked act.

> – SYNONYMS **1** *a number of atrocities* **outrage,** horror, violation, abuse, crime. **2** *scenes of hardship and atrocity* **wickedness,** cruelty, brutality, barbarity, viciousness, savagery, inhumanity.

at·ro·phy /ˈatrəfē/ ▶ **verb** (**atrophies, atrophying, atrophied**) **1** (of body tissue or an organ) waste away. **2** gradually become weaker: *the local shipbuilding industry had atrophied*. ▶ **noun** the condition or process of atrophying.
– ORIGIN from Greek *atrophia* 'lack of food.'

at·ro·pine /ˈatrəˌpēn/ ▶ **noun** a poisonous compound found in deadly nightshade.
– ORIGIN from *Atropos*, one of the Fates in Greek mythology.

at·tach /əˈtaCH/ ▶ **verb 1** fasten or join one thing to another. **2** include a condition as part of an agreement. **3** attribute importance or value to: *they attached great importance to this research*. **4** appoint someone for special or temporary duties: *I was attached to another working group*.

> – SYNONYMS **1 fasten,** fix, affix, join, secure, stick, connect, tie, link, couple, pin, hitch. **2** *they attach importance to research* **ascribe,** assign, attribute, accredit, impute. **3** *the medical officer attached to HQ* **assign,** appoint, allocate, second.
> – ANTONYMS detach.

– DERIVATIVES **at·tach·a·ble** adjective.
– ORIGIN Old French *atachier*.

at·ta·ché /ˌatəˈSHā, ˌata-/ ▶ **noun** a person on an ambassador's staff who has a specific responsibility or works in a particular area of activity: *a military attaché*.
– ORIGIN French, 'attached.'

at·ta·ché case ▶ **noun** a small, flat briefcase for carrying documents.

at·tached /əˈtaCHt/ ▶ **adjective** very fond of someone.

> – SYNONYMS *Mark became increasingly attached to Tara* **fond of,** devoted to, keen on; informal mad about, crazy about.

at·tach·ment /əˈtaCHmənt/ ▶ **noun 1** an extra part attached to something in order to perform a particular function: *a detachable roof rack with attachments for carrying bikes*. **2** a computer file sent with an email. **3** the action of attaching one thing to another. **4** affection or fondness.

> – SYNONYMS **1 bond,** closeness, devotion, loyalty, fondness for, love for, affection for, feeling for, sympathy for. **2 accessory,** fitting, extension, add-on.

at·tack /əˈtak/ ▶ **verb 1** take violent action against someone or something. **2** (of a disease, chemical, etc.) act harmfully on: *meningitis attacks the brain*. **3** criticize fiercely and publicly: *he attacked the government's defense policy*. **4** begin to deal with a problem or task in a determined way. **5** (in sports) attempt to score goals or points.

> – SYNONYMS **1 assault,** beat up, set upon, mug, charge, pounce on, raid, rush, storm; informal lay into, do over, work over, rough up. **2 criticize,** censure, condemn, denounce, revile, vilify, impugn, disparage; informal knock, slam, lay into.
> – ANTONYMS defend, praise.

▶ **noun 1** an act of attacking someone or something. **2** a sudden short period of an illness: *a bad attack of the flu*. **3** the players in a team whose role is to attack.

> – SYNONYMS **1 assault,** onslaught, offensive, strike, blitz, raid, incursion, sortie, foray, charge, invasion. **2 criticism,** censure, condemnation, vilification, disparagement. **3 fit,** seizure, spasm, convulsion, paroxysm, bout, episode.
> – ANTONYMS defense, praise.

– ORIGIN Italian *attaccare* 'join battle.'

CHOOSE THE RIGHT WORD

attack, assail, assault, beset, besiege, bombard, charge, molest, storm

There is no shortage of "fighting words." **Attack** is the most general verb, meaning to set upon someone or something in a violent, forceful, or aggressive way (*the rebels attacked at dawn*); but it can also be used figuratively (*attack the government's policy*). **Assault** implies a greater degree of violence or viciousness and the infliction of more damage. As part of the legal term "assault and battery," it suggests an attempt or threat to injure someone physically. **Molest** is another word meaning to *attack* and is used today almost exclusively of sexual molestation (*she had been molested as a child*). **Charge** and **storm** are primarily military words, both suggesting a forceful assault on a fixed position. To *charge* is to make a violent onslaught (*the infantry charged the enemy camp*) and is often used as a command (*"Charge!" the general cried*). To *storm* means to take by force, with all the momentum and fury of a storm (*after days of planning, the soldiers stormed the castle*), but there is often the suggestion of a last-ditch, all-out effort to end a long siege or avoid defeat. To **assail** is to attack with repeated thrusts or blows, implying that victory depends not so much on force as on persistence. To **bombard** is to assail continuously with bombs or shells (*they bombarded the city without mercy for days*). **Besiege** means to surround with an armed force (*to besiege the capital city*). When used figuratively, its meaning comes close to that of *assail*, but with an emphasis on being hemmed in and enclosed rather than punished repeatedly (*besieged with fears*). **Beset** also means to attack on all sides (*beset by enemies*), but it is also used frequently in other contexts to mean set or placed upon (*a bracelet beset with diamonds*).

at·tack·er /ə'takər/ ▶ **noun** a person that attacks someone or something.

– SYNONYMS **assailant,** assaulter, mugger, aggressor, raider, invader.
– ANTONYMS victim.

at·tain /ə'tān/ ▶ **verb 1** succeed in achieving something one has worked for: *he attained the rank of brigadier.* **2** reach a particular age, size, or level: *the cheetah can attain speeds of 68 mph.*

– SYNONYMS **achieve,** accomplish, reach, obtain, gain, secure, get, win, earn, realize, fulfill; informal clinch, bag, wrap up.

– DERIVATIVES **at·tain·a·ble** adjective.
– ORIGIN Latin *attingere*.

CHOOSE THE RIGHT WORD

See **GET**.

at·tain·der /ə'tāndər/ ▶ **noun** historical the forfeiting of land and civil rights as a result of being sentenced to death.
– PHRASES **bill of attainder** a piece of legislation inflicting attainder without judicial process.
– ORIGIN Old French *ateindre* 'accomplish, bring to justice.'

at·tain·ment /ə'tānmənt/ ▶ **noun 1** the achieving of something. **2** something that one has achieved: *his educational attainments.*

at·tar /'atər/ ▶ **noun** a sweet-smelling oil made from rose petals.
– ORIGIN Arabic, 'perfume, essence.'

at·tempt /ə'tem(p)t/ ▶ **verb** make an effort to do something.

– SYNONYMS **try,** strive, aim, venture, endeavor, seek, have a go.

▶ **noun** an effort to do something.

– SYNONYMS **try,** effort, endeavor, venture, bid, go; informal crack, shot, stab.

– ORIGIN Latin *attemptare*.

at·tend /ə'tend/ ▶ **verb 1** be present at an event. **2** go regularly to a school, church, etc. **3** (**attend to**) deal with or pay attention to. **4** occur at the same time as or as a result of: *the unfortunate events that attended their arrival.* **5** escort and assist an important person.

– SYNONYMS **1 be present at,** sit in on, take part in, appear at, turn up at, visit, go to; informal show up at. **2** *he had not attended to the regulations* **pay attention,** listen, be attentive, concentrate. **3** *he had important business to* **attend to deal with,** see to, look after, manage, organize, sort out, handle, take care of, tackle. **4** *the wounded were* **attended to** *nearby* **care for,** look after, minister to, see to, tend, treat, help.

– DERIVATIVES **at·tend·ee** /ə,ten'dē, ,aten-/ noun **at·tend·er** noun.
– ORIGIN Latin *attendere*.

at·tend·ance /ə'tendəns/ ▶ **noun 1** the action of attending a place or event: *her infrequent attendance at church.* **2** the number of people present at a particular occasion.

– SYNONYMS **1 presence,** appearance, attention. **2 audience,** turnout, house, gate, crowd.
– ANTONYMS absence.

at·tend·ant /ə'tendənt/ ▶ **noun 1** a person employed to provide a service to the public: *a museum attendant.* **2** an assistant to an important person.

– SYNONYMS **assistant,** aide, companion, escort, steward, equerry, servant, retainer, valet, maid.

▶ **adjective** occurring at the same time or as a result of: *obesity and its attendant health problems.*

– SYNONYMS **accompanying,** associated, concomitant, related, connected, resulting, consequent.

at·ten·tion /ə'tensнən/ ▶ **noun 1** the mental faculty of considering or taking notice of someone or something: *he turned his attention to the educational system.* **2** special care or consideration: *a child in need of medical attention.* **3** (**attentions**) things done to express an interest in or please someone: *she was flattered by his attentions.* **4** an erect position taken by a soldier, with the feet together and the arms straight down the sides of the body.

– SYNONYMS **1 consideration,** contemplation, deliberation, thought, study, observation, mind, investigation, action. **2 awareness,** notice, scrutiny, eye, gaze. **3** *medical attention* **care,** ministrations, treatment, therapy, relief, aid, assistance.

at·ten·tion def·i·cit dis·or·der ▶ **noun** a condition found in children, marked by hyperactivity, poor concentration, and learning difficulties.

at·ten·tive /ə'tentiv/ ▶ **adjective 1** paying close attention to something: *an attentive audience.* **2** considerate and helpful: *the staff were friendly and attentive.*

– SYNONYMS **1** *an attentive student* **alert,** perceptive, observant, acute, aware, heedful, focused, studious, diligent, conscientious, earnest. **2** *the most attentive of husbands* **considerate,** conscientious, thoughtful, kind, caring, solicitous, understanding, sympathetic.
– ANTONYMS inattentive.

– DERIVATIVES **at·ten·tive·ly** adverb **at·ten·tive·ness** noun.

at·ten·u·ate /ə'tenyoo͞,āt/ ▶ **verb 1** make something weaker or less effective. **2** make someone or something thin or thinner.
– DERIVATIVES **at·ten·u·a·tion** /ə,tenyoo͞'āsнən/ noun.
– ORIGIN Latin *attenuare* 'make slender.'

at·test /ə'test/ ▶ **verb 1** provide or act as clear evidence of: *the collection attests to his interest in mythology.* **2** declare that something is true or is the case.

– DERIVATIVES **at·tes·ta·tion** /ˌateˈstāsʜən/ noun.
– ORIGIN Latin *attestari*.

At·tic /ˈatik/ ▸ **adjective** relating to Attica in Greece, or to ancient Athens.

at·tic /ˈatik/ ▸ **noun** a space or room inside the roof of a building.

– SYNONYMS **loft**, roof space, garret.

– ORIGIN Latin *Atticus* 'Attic.'

at·tire /əˈtī(ə)r/ formal or literary ▸ **noun** clothes of a particular kind: *formal evening attire.* ▸ **verb** (**be attired**) be dressed in clothes of a particular kind: *he was attired in a dark suit.*
– ORIGIN Old French *atirer* 'equip.'

at·ti·tude /ˈatiˌt(y)o͞od/ ▸ **noun 1** a way of thinking or feeling: *his attitude to the job had changed.* **2** a position of the body. **3** informal self-confident or uncooperative behavior.

– SYNONYMS **1 view,** viewpoint, outlook, perspective, stance, standpoint, position, frame of mind, approach, opinion. **2** *an attitude of prayer* **posture,** position, pose, stance.

– DERIVATIVES **at·ti·tu·di·nal** /ˌatiˈt(y)o͞odn-əl/ adjective.
– ORIGIN Italian *attitudine* 'suitability.'

at·ti·tu·di·nize /ˌatiˈt(y)o͞odnˌīz/ ▸ **verb** adopt or express an attitude for effect.

at·tor·ney /əˈtərnē/ ▸ **noun** (pl. **attorneys**) **1** a person appointed to act for another in legal matters. **2** a lawyer.
– ORIGIN Old French *atorner* 'assign.'

at·tor·ney gen·er·al ▸ **noun** (pl. **attorneys general**) the most senior legal officer in some countries or states.

at·tract /əˈtrakt/ ▸ **verb 1** cause someone to come to a place or event or participate in an undertaking. **2** cause a particular reaction: *the decision attracted widespread criticism.* **3** cause someone to have a liking for or interest in: *many men were attracted to her.* **4** draw something closer by exerting a force on it.

– SYNONYMS **1 appeal to,** fascinate, charm, captivate, interest, tempt, entice, lure, bewitch, beguile, seduce. **2 draw,** pull, magnetize.
– ANTONYMS repel.

– DERIVATIVES **at·trac·tor** noun.
– ORIGIN Latin *attrahere* 'draw near.'

at·tract·ant /əˈtraktənt/ ▸ **noun** a substance that attracts something.

at·trac·tion /əˈtraksʜən/ ▸ **noun 1** the action or power of attracting someone or something. **2** an interesting or appealing feature or quality: *the apartment's main attraction is the large pool.* **3** Physics a force under the influence of which objects tend to move toward each other.

– SYNONYMS **1 appeal,** attractiveness, pull, desirability, fascination, allure, charisma, charm. **2** *the town's main attractions* **entertainment,** activity, diversion, amenity, service. **3** *magnetic attraction* **pull,** draw, force.
– ANTONYMS repulsion.

at·trac·tive /əˈtraktiv/ ▸ **adjective 1** pleasing in appearance: *a very attractive man.* **2** having features or qualities that arouse interest: *an attractive investment proposition.* **3** relating to attraction between physical objects.

– SYNONYMS **1 good-looking,** beautiful, pretty, handsome, lovely, stunning, striking, desirable, gorgeous, prepossessing, fetching; Scottish bonny; informal cute, drop-dead gorgeous, hunky. old use comely. **2 appealing,** inviting, tempting, pleasing, interesting.
– ANTONYMS unattractive, ugly.

– DERIVATIVES **at·trac·tive·ly** adverb **at·trac·tive·ness** noun.

at·trib·ute ▸ **verb** /əˈtriˌbyo͞ot/ (**attribute something to**) regard something as belonging to, made, or being caused by: *he attributed his success to his parents' unwavering support.*

– SYNONYMS **ascribe,** assign, accredit, credit, put down, chalk up, pin on.

▸ **noun** /ˈatrəˌbyo͞ot/ **1** a characteristic quality or feature: *she has the key attributes of any journalist.* **2** an object that is traditionally associated with a person or thing: *the hourglass is an attribute of Father Time.*

– SYNONYMS **quality,** characteristic, trait, feature, element, aspect, property, sign, hallmark, mark.

– DERIVATIVES **at·trib·ut·a·ble** /əˈtribyətəbəl/ adjective **at·tri·bu·tion** /ˌatrəˈbyo͞osʜən/ noun.
– ORIGIN Latin *attribuere* 'assign to.'

CHOOSE THE RIGHT WORD

See **EMBLEM**.

at·trib·u·tive /əˈtribyətiv/ ▸ **adjective** Grammar (of an adjective) coming before the word that it describes, as *old* in *the old dog*. Contrasted with **PREDICATIVE**.
– DERIVATIVES **at·trib·u·tive·ly** adverb.

at·tri·tion /əˈtrisʜən/ ▸ **noun 1** the gradual reduction of something's strength or effectiveness through prolonged attack or pressure. **2** the wearing away of something by friction.
– DERIVATIVES **at·tri·tion·al** adjective.
– ORIGIN Latin *atterere* 'to rub.'

at·tune /əˈt(y)o͞on/ ▸ **verb** (**be attuned**) be receptive to and able to understand someone or something: *a royal family more attuned to the feelings of the public.*

Atty. ▸ **abbreviation** attorney.

ATV ▸ **abbreviation** all-terrain vehicle.

a·typ·i·cal /āˈtipikəl/ ▸ **adjective** not representative of a type, group, or class.
– DERIVATIVES **a·typ·i·cal·ly** adverb.

Au ▸ **symbol** the chemical element gold.
– ORIGIN Latin *aurum*.

au·ber·gine /ˈōbərˌzʜēn/ ▸ **noun** chiefly Brit. term for **EGGPLANT**.
– ORIGIN French.

au·bre·ti·a /ôˈbrēsʜ(ē)ə/ (also **aubrietia**) ▸ **noun** a trailing plant with purple, pink, or white flowers, commonly grown in rock gardens.
– ORIGIN named after the French botanist Claude *Aubriet*.

au·burn /ˈôbərn/ ▸ **noun** a reddish-brown color.
– ORIGIN Old French *auborne*.

auc·tion /ˈôksʜən/ ▸ **noun** a public sale in which goods or property are sold to the highest bidder. ▸ **verb** sell an item or items at an auction.
– ORIGIN Latin, 'increase, auction.'

auc·tion·eer /ˌôksʜəˈni(ə)r/ ▸ **noun** a person who conducts auctions.

au·da·cious /ôˈdāsʜəs/ ▸ **adjective 1** willing to take daring risks. **2** showing a lack of respect; rude or impudent.

– DERIVATIVES **au·da·cious·ly** adverb **au·da·cious·ness** noun.
– ORIGIN Latin *audax* 'bold.'

CHOOSE THE RIGHT WORD

See **BOLD**.

au·dac·i·ty /ô'dasitē/ ▶ **noun 1** the willingness to take risks: *a traveler of extraordinary audacity*. **2** rude or disrespectful behavior: *he had the audacity to contradict me*.

– SYNONYMS **1 boldness,** daring, pluck; recklessness; spirit; informal guts, gutsiness, spunk, moxie. **2 impudence,** impertinence, insolence, presumption, cheek, effrontery, nerve, gall, defiance, temerity; informal brass, chutzpah.

au·di·ble /'ôdəbəl/ ▶ **adjective** able to be heard.

– SYNONYMS **perceptible,** discernible, detectable, distinct, clear.
– ANTONYMS inaudible, faint.

– DERIVATIVES **au·di·bil·i·ty** /ˌôdə'bilitē/ noun **au·di·bly** adverb.
– ORIGIN Latin *audire* 'hear.'

au·di·ence /'ôdēəns/ ▶ **noun 1** the people gathered to see or listen to a play, concert, movie, etc. **2** a formal interview with a person in authority.

– SYNONYMS **1 spectators, listeners,** viewers, onlookers, crowd, throng, gallery, congregation, turnout. **2 meeting,** interview, consultation, conference, hearing, reception.

– ORIGIN Latin *audire* 'hear.'

au·di·o /'ôdēˌō/ ▶ **adjective** relating to sound, especially when recorded, transmitted, or reproduced: *audio equipment*.

audio- ▶ **combining form** relating to hearing or sound: *audiovisual*.
– ORIGIN Latin *audire* 'hear.'

au·di·o fre·quen·cy /'ôdēˌō/ ▶ **noun** a frequency capable of being perceived by the human ear, generally between 20 and 20,000 hertz.

au·di·ol·o·gy /ˌôdē'äləjē/ ▶ **noun** the branch of science and medicine concerned with the sense of hearing.
– DERIVATIVES **au·di·o·log·i·cal** /-ə'läjikəl/ adjective **au·di·ol·o·gist** /-jist/ noun.

au·di·o·phile /'ôdē-ōˌfīl/ ▶ **noun** an enthusiast of recorded music.

au·di·o·tape /'ôdē-ōˌtāp/ ▶ **noun** magnetic tape on which sound can be recorded.

au·di·o·vis·u·al /ˌôdē-ō'vizHo͞oəl/ ▶ **adjective** using both sight and sound.

au·dit /'ôdit/ ▶ **noun** an official examination of an organization's accounts. ▶ **verb** (**audits, auditing, audited**) make an official examination of an organization's accounts.
– ORIGIN from Latin *audire* 'hear' (because an audit was originally presented orally).

au·di·tion /ô'disHən/ ▶ **noun** an interview for an actor, singer, etc., in which they give a practical demonstration of their skill. ▶ **verb** assess or be assessed by means of an audition.

au·di·tor /'ôditər/ ▶ **noun 1** a person who carries an audit of an organization's accounts. **2** a listener.

au·di·to·ri·um /ˌôdi'tôrēəm/ ▶ **noun** (pl. **auditoriums** or **auditoria** /-'tôrēə/) **1** the part of a theater or hall in which the audience sits. **2** a large hall or room used for public gatherings, especially at a school.
– ORIGIN Latin.

au·di·to·ry /'ôdiˌtôrē/ ▶ **adjective** relating to the sense of hearing.

au fait /ˌō 'fe/ ▶ **adjective** (**au fait with**) having a good or detailed knowledge of something: *she was au fait with all the latest technology*.
– ORIGIN French, 'to the point.'

au·ger /'ôgər/ ▶ **noun** a tool resembling a large corkscrew, for boring holes.
– ORIGIN Old English.

USAGE

On the confusion of **auger** and **augur**, see the note at **AUGUR**.

aught[1] /awt/ (also **ought**) ▶ **pronoun** old use anything at all.
– ORIGIN Old English.

aught[2] ▶ **noun 1** the digit 0; zero. **2** (**the aughts**) informal the years from 2000 to 2009, or corresponding years in another century.

aug·ment /ôg'ment/ ▶ **verb** increase the amount, size, or value of: *many people work overtime to augment their income*.

– SYNONYMS **increase,** add to, supplement, enhance, build up, raise, boost, up, hike up, enlarge, swell, expand, extend.
– ANTONYMS decrease, reduce.

– DERIVATIVES **aug·men·ta·tion** /ˌôgmen'tāsHən/ noun.
– ORIGIN Latin *augmentare*.

au grat·in /ˌō 'grätn, 'gratn, gra'taN/ ▶ **adjective** sprinkled with breadcrumbs and/or grated cheese and browned: *ratatouille au gratin*.
– ORIGIN French, 'by grating.'

au·gur /'ôgər/ ▶ **verb** (**augur well/badly**) be a sign of a good or bad outcome: *the announcement does not augur well for the economy*.
– ORIGIN Latin, 'person who interprets omens.'

USAGE

Do not confuse the verb **augur**, meaning 'be a sign of a good or bad outcome,' with the noun **auger**, which is a tool for boring holes.

au·gu·ry /'ôgyərē/ ▶ **noun** (pl. **auguries**) a sign of what will happen in the future; an omen.

CHOOSE THE RIGHT WORD

See **SIGN**.

Au·gust /'ôgəst/ ▶ **noun** the eighth month of the year.
– ORIGIN named after the Roman emperor *Augustus* Caesar.

au·gust /ô'gəst/ ▶ **adjective** inspiring respect and admiration.

– SYNONYMS **distinguished,** respected, eminent, venerable, illustrious, prestigious, renowned, celebrated, honored, acclaimed, esteemed.

– ORIGIN Latin *augustus* 'venerable.'

Au·gus·tan /ô'gəstən/ ▶ **adjective 1** relating to or written during the reign of the Roman emperor Augustus.

2 relating to a classical style of 17th- and 18th-century English literature.

auk /ôk/ ▶ **noun** a black and white seabird with short wings.
– ORIGIN Old Norse.

auld lang syne /ôld laNG 'zīn/ ▶ **noun** times long past.
– ORIGIN Scots, 'old long since.'

au na·tu·rel /,ō ,naCHə'rel/ ▶ **adjective & adverb 1** in the most simple or natural way. **2** humorous naked.
– ORIGIN French.

aunt /ant, änt/ ▶ **noun** the sister of one's father or mother or the wife of one's uncle.
– ORIGIN Old French *ante*.

aunt·ie /'antē, 'än-/ (also **aunty**) ▶ **noun** (pl. **aunties**) informal a person's aunt.

au pair /,ō 'pe(ə)r/ ▶ **noun** a foreign girl employed to look after children and help with housework in exchange for room and board.
– ORIGIN French, 'on equal terms.'

au·ra /'ôrə/ ▶ **noun** (pl. **auras**) **1** the distinctive atmosphere or quality associated with someone or something: *the hotel had an aura of glamour and excitement.* **2** a supposed invisible force surrounding a living creature.

– SYNONYMS **atmosphere,** ambience, air, quality, character, mood, feeling; informal vibe.

– ORIGIN Greek, 'breeze, breath.'

au·ral /'ôrəl/ ▶ **adjective** relating to the ears or the sense of hearing.
– DERIVATIVES **au·ral·ly** adverb.
– ORIGIN Latin *auris* 'ear.'

USAGE

Do not confuse **aural** with **oral**. **Aural** means 'relating to the ears or sense of hearing' (*her new album provides pure aural pleasure*), whereas **oral** means 'spoken' or 'relating to the mouth' (*oral communication*).

au·re·ate /'ôrē-it, -,āt/ ▶ **adjective** made of or having the color of gold.
– ORIGIN from Latin *aurum* 'gold.'

au·re·ole /'ôrē,ōl/ ▶ **noun 1** (in paintings) a bright circle surrounding a person to indicate that they are holy. **2** a circle of light around the sun or moon.
– ORIGIN from Latin *aureola corona* 'golden crown.'

au re·voir /,ō rəv'wär/ ▶ **exclamation** goodbye.
– ORIGIN French, 'to the seeing again.'

au·ri·cle /'ôrikəl/ ▶ **noun 1** the external part of the ear. **2** an upper cavity of the heart.
– ORIGIN Latin *auricula* 'little ear.'

au·rochs /'ouräks, 'ô,räks/ ▶ **noun** (pl. same) a large extinct European wild ox.
– ORIGIN German.

au·ro·ra /ə'rôrə, ô'rôrə/ ▶ **noun** a phenomenon characterized by streamers of colored light in the sky near the earth's magnetic poles, known as the Northern Lights (**aurora borealis**) near the North Pole and the Southern Lights (**aurora australis**) near the South Pole.
– ORIGIN Latin, 'dawn, goddess of the dawn.'

aus·cul·ta·tion /,ôskəl'tāSHən/ ▶ **noun** listening to sounds from the heart, lungs, or other organs with a stethoscope.
– ORIGIN Latin, from *auscultare* 'listen to.'

aus·pice /'ôspis/ ▶ **noun** (in phrase **under the auspices of**) with the support or protection of: *elections held under the auspices of the United Nations.*
– ORIGIN first meaning 'an omen,' from Latin *auspicium*.

aus·pi·cious /ô'spiSHəs/ ▶ **adjective** suggesting that there is a good chance of success: *his new assignment has not had an auspicious start.*

– SYNONYMS **favorable,** promising, encouraging, fortunate, opportune, timely, advantageous, good.
– ANTONYMS inauspicious, unfavorable.

– DERIVATIVES **aus·pi·cious·ly** adverb.

Aus·sie /'ôsē/ (also **Ozzie**) ▶ **noun** (pl. **Aussies**) & **adjective** informal Australia or Australian.

aus·tere /ô'sti(ə)r/ ▶ **adjective 1** severe or strict in appearance or manner. **2** without comforts or luxuries: *their austere living conditions.*

– SYNONYMS **1 severe,** stern, strict, harsh, dour, grim, cold, frosty, unfriendly. **2 spartan,** frugal, ascetic, puritanical, abstemious, strict, simple, hard. **3** *an austere building* **plain,** simple, basic, functional, unadorned, bleak, bare, clinical.
– ANTONYMS easygoing, ornate.

– DERIVATIVES **aus·tere·ly** adverb.
– ORIGIN Greek *austēros*.

CHOOSE THE RIGHT WORD

See **SEVERE**.

aus·ter·i·ty /ô'steritē/ ▶ **noun** (pl. **austerities**) **1** strictness or severity of appearance or manner. **2** difficult economic conditions resulting from a cut in public spending.

aus·tral /'ôstrəl/ ▶ **adjective** technical of the southern hemisphere.
– ORIGIN Latin *australis*.

Aus·tral·a·sian /,ôstrə'lāZHən/ ▶ **adjective** relating to Australasia, a region made up of Australia, New Zealand, and islands of the SW Pacific.

Aus·tral·ian /ô'strālyən/ ▶ **noun** a person from Australia. ▶ **adjective** relating to Australia.
– ORIGIN from Latin *Terra Australis* 'the southern land.'

Aus·tral·ian Rules ▶ **plural noun** (treated as sing.) a form of football played on an oval field with teams of eighteen players.

Aus·tri·an /'ôstrēən/ ▶ **noun** a person from Austria. ▶ **adjective** relating to Austria.

au·tar·chy /'ô,tärkē/ ▶ **noun** (pl. **autarchies**) **1** another term for **AUTOCRACY**. **2** variant spelling of **AUTARKY**.

au·tar·ky /'ô,tärkē/ (also **autarchy**) ▶ **noun** (pl. **autarkies**) **1** economic independence or self-sufficiency. **2** an economically independent country, state, or society.
– DERIVATIVES **au·tar·kic** /ô'tärkik/ adjective.
– ORIGIN from Greek *autarkēs*.

au·teur /ô'tər/ ▶ **noun** a movie director regarded as the author of their movies.
– ORIGIN French, 'author.'

au·then·tic /ô'THentik/ ▶ **adjective 1** of undisputed origin; genuine: *the letter is now accepted as an authentic document.* **2** based on facts; accurate.

– SYNONYMS **1 genuine,** real, bona fide, true, legitimate; informal kosher. **2 accurate,** factual, true, truthful, reliable, trustworthy, honest, faithful.
– ANTONYMS fake, unreliable.

– DERIVATIVES **au·then·ti·cal·ly** /-ik(ə)lē/ adverb **au·then·tic·i·ty** /ˌôTHen'tisitē/ noun.
– ORIGIN Greek *authentikos*.

au·then·ti·cate /ô'THentiˌkāt/ ▶ **verb** prove or show something to be genuine.

– SYNONYMS **verify,** validate, prove, substantiate, corroborate, confirm, support, back up.
– ANTONYMS disprove.

– DERIVATIVES **au·then·ti·ca·tion** /ôˌTHenti'kāSHən/ noun **au·then·ti·ca·tor** /-ˌkātər/ noun.

au·thor /'ôTHər/ ▶ **noun 1** a writer of a book or article. **2** a person who thinks of a plan or idea.

– SYNONYMS **1 writer,** novelist, poet, playwright, dramatist, columnist, reporter, wordsmith; informal scribe, scribbler. **2 creator,** originator, founder, father, architect, designer, producer.

– DERIVATIVES **au·thor·ess** /'ôTHəris/ noun **au·tho·ri·al** /ô'THôrēəl/ adjective **au·thor·ship** /'ôTHərˌSHip/ noun.
– ORIGIN Latin *auctor*.

au·thor·i·tar·i·an /əˌTHôri'te(ə)rēən, ôˌTHär-/ ▶ **adjective** in favor of or demanding strict obedience to authority.

– SYNONYMS **strict,** autocratic, dictatorial, despotic, tyrannical, domineering, imperious, illiberal, undemocratic; informal bossy.
– ANTONYMS democratic, liberal.

▶ **noun** an authoritarian person.

– SYNONYMS **disciplinarian,** autocrat, dictator, despot, tyrant.
– ANTONYMS democrat, liberal.

– DERIVATIVES **au·thor·i·tar·i·an·ism** noun.

au·thor·i·ta·tive /ə'THôriˌtātiv, ə'THär-/ ▶ **adjective 1** true or accurate and so able to be trusted: *authoritative information*. **2** commanding and self-confident; likely to be respected and obeyed: *his quiet but authoritative voice*. **3** coming from an official source.

– SYNONYMS **1 reliable,** dependable, trustworthy, accurate, authentic, valid, definitive, classic. **2 commanding,** masterful, assertive, self-assured, self-confident.
– ANTONYMS unreliable.

– DERIVATIVES **au·thor·i·ta·tive·ly** adverb **au·thor·i·ta·tive·ness** noun.

au·thor·i·ty /ə'THôritē, ô'THär-/ ▶ **noun** (pl. **authorities**) **1** the power to give orders to other people and enforce their obedience. **2** a person or organization with official power. **3** official permission to do something. **4** a person with expert knowledge of a particular subject. **5** recognized knowledge about or expertise in something.

– SYNONYMS **1** *a rebellion against those in authority* **power,** command, control, charge, dominance, jurisdiction, rule; informal clout. **2** (**authorities**) *they failed to report the theft to the authorities* **officials,** officialdom, government, administration, establishment, police; informal the powers that be. **3** *the authority to arrest drug traffickers* **right,** authorization, power, mandate, prerogative, license. **4** *they need congressional authority* **permission,** authorization, consent, sanction, assent, agreement, approval, clearance; informal the go-ahead. **5** *he was an authority on the stock market* **expert,** specialist, professional, master, connoisseur, pundit, doyen/doyenne, guru.

– ORIGIN Old French *autorite*.

CHOOSE THE RIGHT WORD

See **JURISDICTION**.

au·thor·ize /'ôTHəˌrīz/ ▶ **verb** give official permission for.

– SYNONYMS **1** *they authorized further action* **permit,** sanction, allow, approve, consent to, assent to; informal give the go-ahead to, OK. **2** *the troops were authorized to fire* **empower,** give authority, mandate, commission, entitle. **3** (as adj. **authorized**) *an authorized dealer* **approved,** sanctioned, accredited, recognized, licensed, certified, official, legal, legitimate.
– ANTONYMS forbid.

– DERIVATIVES **au·thor·i·za·tion** /ˌôTHərə'zāSHən/ noun.

Au·thor·ized Ver·sion ▶ **noun** an English translation of the Bible made in 1611.

au·tism /'ôˌtizəm/ ▶ **noun** a mental condition in which a person has great difficulty in communicating with others.
– DERIVATIVES **au·tis·tic** /ô'tistik/ adjective.
– ORIGIN Greek *autos* 'self.'

au·to /'ôtō/ ▶ **adjective & noun 1** short for **AUTOMOBILE**. **2** short for **AUTOMATIC**.

Au·to·bahn /'ôtəˌbän/ ▶ **noun** a German expressway.
– ORIGIN German, from *Auto* 'car' + *Bahn* 'road.'

au·to·bi·og·ra·phy /ˌôtəbī'ägrəfē/ ▶ **noun** (pl. **autobiographies**) an account of a person's life written by that person.
– DERIVATIVES **au·to·bi·og·ra·pher** noun **au·to·bi·o·graph·i·cal** /ˌôtəbīə'grafikəl/ adjective.

au·toch·tho·nous /ô'täkTHənəs/ ▶ **adjective** inhabiting a place from the earliest times; indigenous.

au·to·clave /'ôtəˌklāv/ ▶ **noun** a strong heated container used for processes using high pressures and temperatures, e.g., steam sterilization.
– ORIGIN from Greek *auto-* 'self' + Latin *clavis* 'key' (because it is self-fastening).

au·toc·ra·cy /ô'täkrəsē/ ▶ **noun** (pl. **autocracies**) **1** a system of government in which one person has total power. **2** a country, state, or society governed by a person with total power.
– ORIGIN from Greek *autos* 'self' + *kratos* 'power.'

au·to·crat /'ôtəˌkrat/ ▶ **noun 1** a ruler who has total power. **2** a person who insists on complete obedience from others.

au·to·crat·ic /ˌôtə'kratik/ ▶ **adjective 1** relating to a ruler who has total power. **2** taking no account of other people's wishes and insisting on complete obedience: *his autocratic management style*.
– DERIVATIVES **au·to·crat·i·cal·ly** adverb.

au·to-da-fé /'ôtō də 'fā/ ▶ **noun** (pl. **autos-da-fé** pronunc. same) the burning of a heretic by the Spanish Inquisition.
– ORIGIN Portuguese, 'act of the faith.'

au·to·di·al /'ôtōˌdī(ə)l/ ▶ **verb** (**autodials, autodialing, autodialed**) Computing (of a modem) automatically dial a telephone number or establish a connection with a computer.

au·to·di·dact /ˌôtō'dīˌdakt/ ▶ **noun** a self-taught person.
– ORIGIN Greek.

au·to·fo·cus /'ôtōˌfōkəs/ ▶ **noun** a device focusing a camera or other device automatically.

au·to·gi·ro /ˌôtōˈjīrō/ (also **autogyro**) ▶ **noun** (pl. **autogiros**) a form of aircraft with unpowered freely rotating horizontal blades and a propeller.
– ORIGIN Spanish, from *auto-* 'self' + *giro* 'gyration.'

au·to·graph /ˈôtəˌgraf/ ▶ **noun 1** a celebrity's signature written for a fan or admirer. **2** a manuscript or musical score in an author's or composer's own handwriting. ▶ **verb** write one's signature on something.
– ORIGIN Greek *autographos* 'written with one's own hand.'

au·to·im·mune /ˌôtōəˈmyo͞on/ ▶ **adjective** (of disease) caused by antibodies or lymphocytes produced by the body to counteract substances naturally present in it.

au·to·mate /ˈôtəˌmāt/ ▶ **verb** convert a process or facility so that it can be operated by automatic equipment.

au·to·mat·ed tell·er ma·chine ▶ **noun** a machine that provides cash and other banking services when a special card is inserted.

au·to·mat·ic /ˌôtəˈmatik/ ▶ **adjective 1** operating by itself without human control. **2** (of a firearm) able to load bullets automatically and fire continuously. **3** done or occurring without conscious thought or as a matter of course: *an automatic decision*. **4** enforced without question because of a fixed rule: *murder carries an automatic life sentence*.

– SYNONYMS **1 mechanized,** powered, mechanical, automated, computerized, electronic, robotic. **2 instinctive,** involuntary, unconscious, reflex, knee-jerk, subconscious, spontaneous, impulsive, unthinking, mechanical; informal gut. **3 inevitable,** unavoidable, inescapable, certain.
– ANTONYMS manual, conscious, deliberate.

▶ **noun** an automatic machine.
– DERIVATIVES **au·to·mat·i·cal·ly** /-ik(ə)lē/ adverb **au·to·ma·tic·i·ty** /-məˈtisitē/ noun.
– ORIGIN Greek *automatos* 'acting by itself.'

au·to·mat·ic pi·lot ▶ **noun** a device for keeping an aircraft on a set course.
– PHRASES **on automatic pilot** doing something out of habit and without thinking.

au·to·ma·tion /ˌôtəˈmāsʜən/ ▶ **noun** the use of automatic equipment in manufacturing or similar processes.

au·tom·a·tism /ôˈtäməˌtizəm/ ▶ **noun** action that does not involve conscious thought or intention.

au·tom·a·ton /ôˈtämətən, -ˌtän/ ▶ **noun** (pl. **automata** /-tə/ or **automatons**) **1** a moving mechanical device resembling a human being. **2** a machine that operates according to coded instructions.
– ORIGIN from Greek *automatos* 'acting of itself.'

au·to·mo·bile /ˌôtəmōˈbēl/ ▶ **noun** a powered road vehicle designed to carry a small number of people.

au·to·mo·tive /ˌôtəˈmōtiv/ ▶ **adjective** relating to motor vehicles.

au·to·nom·ic /ˌôtəˈnämik/ ▶ **adjective** relating to the part of the nervous system that controls involuntary bodily functions such as digestion.

au·ton·o·mous /ôˈtänəməs/ ▶ **adjective** self-governing or independent.

– SYNONYMS **self-governing,** independent, sovereign, free.
– ANTONYMS dependent.

– DERIVATIVES **au·ton·o·mous·ly** adverb.

au·ton·o·my /ôˈtänəmē/ ▶ **noun 1** the possession or right of self-government. **2** freedom of action: *a structure that gives greater autonomy to employees*.

– SYNONYMS **self-government,** self-rule, home rule, self-determination, independence, sovereignty, freedom.
– ANTONYMS dependence.

– ORIGIN from Greek *autonomos* 'having its own laws.'

au·to·pi·lot /ˈôtōˌpīlət/ ▶ **noun** short for **AUTOMATIC PILOT**.

au·top·sy /ˈôˌtäpsē/ ▶ **noun** (pl. **autopsies**) an examination of a dead body to discover the cause of death.
– ORIGIN from Greek *autoptēs* 'eyewitness.'

au·to·sug·ges·tion /ˌôtōsə(g)ˈjescʜən/ ▶ **noun** the hypnotic or subconscious adoption of an idea that one has originated oneself.

au·tumn /ˈôtəm/ ▶ **noun** the season after summer and before winter; fall.
– DERIVATIVES **au·tum·nal** /ôˈtəmnəl/ adjective.
– ORIGIN Latin *autumnus*.

aux·il·ia·ry /ôgˈzilyərē, -ˈzil(ə)rē/ ▶ **adjective** providing extra help and support.

– SYNONYMS **additional,** supplementary, extra, reserve, backup, emergency, fallback, second.

▶ **noun** (pl. **auxiliaries**) a person or thing that provides extra help or support.
– ORIGIN from Latin *auxilium* 'help.'

aux·il·ia·ry verb ▶ **noun** a verb used in forming the tenses, moods, and voices of other verbs (e.g., *be*, *do*, and *have*).

AV ▶ **abbreviation 1** audiovisual. **2** Authorized Version.

a·vail /əˈvāl/ ▶ **verb 1** (**avail oneself of**) formal use or take advantage of: *she did not avail herself of my advice*. **2** help or benefit someone. ▶ **noun** use or benefit: *his protests were to little avail*.
– ORIGIN Latin *valere* 'be strong, be of value.'

a·vail·a·ble /əˈvāləbəl/ ▶ **adjective 1** able to be used or obtained. **2** free to do something: *the nurse is only available in the mornings*.

– SYNONYMS **obtainable,** accessible, at hand, to be had, on sale, untaken, unsold, free, vacant, unoccupied; informal up for grabs, on tap.

– DERIVATIVES **a·vail·a·bil·i·ty** /əˌvāləˈbilitē/ noun.

av·a·lanche /ˈavəˌlancʜ/ ▶ **noun 1** a mass of snow and ice falling rapidly down a mountainside. **2** an overwhelming amount: *an avalanche of gifts*.

– SYNONYMS *an avalanche of inquiries* **barrage,** flood, deluge, torrent, wave, onslaught.

– ORIGIN French.

a·vant-garde /ˈavänt ˈgärd, ˌavän/ ▶ **adjective** (in the arts) new and experimental.

– SYNONYMS **experimental,** modern, cutting-edge, progressive, unorthodox, unconventional; informal edgy, offbeat, way-out.
– ANTONYMS conservative, traditional.

▶ **noun** (**the avant-garde**) new and experimental ideas or artists.
– DERIVATIVES **a·vant-gard·ism** /-ˌdizəm/ noun **a·vant-gard·ist** /-dist/ noun.
– ORIGIN French, 'vanguard.'

av·a·rice /ˈavəris/ ▶ **noun** extreme greed for wealth or material things.

– SYNONYMS **greed,** acquisitiveness, covetousness, materialism.
– ANTONYMS generosity.

– ORIGIN from Latin *avarus* 'greedy.'

CHOOSE THE RIGHT WORD

See **GREEDY**.

av·a·ri·cious /ˌavəˈrisHəs/ ▶ **adjective** very greedy for wealth or material things.

a·vast /əˈvast/ ▶ **exclamation** Nautical stop; cease.
– ORIGIN Dutch *hou'vast* 'hold fast!'

av·a·tar /ˈavəˌtär/ ▶ **noun** Hinduism **1** a god or goddess appearing in bodily form on earth. **2** Computing a two- or three-dimensional on-screen graphic that represents an Internet user.
– ORIGIN Sanskrit, 'descent.'

A·ve Ma·ri·a /ˈävā məˈrēə/ ▶ **noun** a prayer to the Virgin Mary used in Catholic worship.
– ORIGIN the opening words of the prayer in Latin, 'hail, Mary!'

a·venge /əˈvenj/ ▶ **verb** punish or harm someone in return for a wrong.

– SYNONYMS **requite,** punish, repay, pay back, take revenge for, get even for.

– DERIVATIVES **a·veng·er** noun.
– ORIGIN from Latin *vindicare* 'vindicate.'

av·e·nue /ˈavəˌn(y)o͞o/ ▶ **noun 1** a broad road or path. **2** a way of approaching or achieving something: *the discovery has opened up new avenues of research.*
– ORIGIN from French *avenir* 'arrive, approach.'

a·ver /əˈvər/ ▶ **verb** (**avers, averring, averred**) formal declare something to be the case.
– ORIGIN from Latin *verus* 'true.'

av·er·age /ˈav(ə)rij/ ▶ **noun 1** the result obtained by adding several amounts together and then dividing the total by the number of amounts. **2** a usual amount or level.

– SYNONYMS **mean,** median, mode, norm, standard, rule, par.

▶ **adjective 1** being an average. **2** usual or ordinary. **3** not very good; mediocre.

– SYNONYMS **1** *the average temperature* **mean,** median. **2** *a woman of average height* **normal,** standard, typical, ordinary, common, regular.
– ANTONYMS abnormal, unusual.

▶ **verb 1** amount to or achieve as an average: *her website averaged 30,000 hits a day.* **2** calculate the average of something.
– DERIVATIVES **av·er·age·ly** adverb **av·er·age·ness** noun.
– ORIGIN French *avarie* 'damage to ship or cargo'; the modern sense came from the sharing of the costs of things lost at sea between the owners of the ship and of the cargo.

a·verse /əˈvərs/ ▶ **adjective** (**averse to**) strongly disliking or opposed to: *he's not averse to change.*

– SYNONYMS **opposed,** hostile, antagonistic, resistant, disinclined, reluctant, loath; informal anti.
– ANTONYMS keen.

– ORIGIN from Latin *avertere* (see **AVERT**).

USAGE

On the confusion of **averse** and **adverse**, see the note at **ADVERSE**.

a·ver·sion /əˈvərZHən/ ▶ **noun** strong opposition or dislike.

– SYNONYMS **dislike,** hatred, loathing, abhorrence, distaste, antipathy, hostility, reluctance, disinclination.
– ANTONYMS liking.

– DERIVATIVES **a·ver·sive** /-siv, -ziv/ adjective.

a·vert /əˈvərt/ ▶ **verb 1** turn away one's eyes. **2** prevent an undesirable event.

– SYNONYMS **1 turn aside,** turn away, shift, redirect. **2 prevent,** avoid, stave off, ward off, head off, forestall.

– ORIGIN from Latin *vertere* 'to turn.'

a·vi·an /ˈāvēən/ ▶ **adjective** relating to birds.
– ORIGIN from Latin *avis* 'bird.'

a·vi·an flu ▶ **noun** formal term for **BIRD FLU**.

a·vi·ar·y /ˈāvēˌerē/ ▶ **noun** (pl. **aviaries**) a large enclosure for keeping birds in.

a·vi·a·tion /ˌāvēˈāsHən/ ▶ **noun** the activity of operating and flying aircraft.
– ORIGIN from Latin *avis* 'bird.'

a·vi·a·tor /ˈāvēˌātər/ ▶ **noun** a pilot.

a·vi·cul·ture /ˈāviˌkəlcHər, ˈavi-/ ▶ **noun** the breeding of birds.
– DERIVATIVES **a·vi·cul·tur·al** /ˌāviˈkəlcHərəl, ˌavi-/ adjective **a·vi·cul·tur·ist** /-rist/ noun.

av·id /ˈavid/ ▶ **adjective** keenly interested or enthusiastic: *avid baseball fans.*

– SYNONYMS **keen,** eager, enthusiastic, ardent, passionate, zealous, devoted.
– ANTONYMS apathetic.

– DERIVATIVES **a·vid·i·ty** /ˈəviditē/ noun **av·id·ly** adverb.
– ORIGIN from Latin *avere* 'crave.'

a·vi·on·ics /ˌāvēˈäniks/ ▶ **plural noun** (usu. treated as sing.) electronics used in aviation.

av·o·ca·do /ˌavəˈkädō, ˌävə-/ ▶ **noun** (pl. **avocados**) a pear-shaped fruit with a rough dark green skin, pale green flesh, and a large stone.
– ORIGIN Spanish.

av·o·ca·tion /ˌavəˈkāsHən/ ▶ **noun** formal a hobby or minor occupation.
– ORIGIN from Latin *avocare* 'call away.'

av·o·cet /ˈavəˌset/ ▶ **noun** a long-legged wading bird with an upturned bill.
– ORIGIN Italian *avosetta.*

a·void /əˈvoid/ ▶ **verb 1** keep away from or stop oneself from doing something. **2** prevent from happening: *book early to avoid disappointment.*

– SYNONYMS **1 keep away from,** steer clear of, give a wide berth to. **2 evade,** dodge, sidestep, escape, run away from; informal duck, wriggle out of, get out of. **3** *book early to avoid disappointment* **prevent,** preclude, stave off, forestall, head off, ward off. **4** *avoid alcohol* **refrain from,** abstain from, desist from, steer clear of, eschew.
– ANTONYMS confront, face.

– DERIVATIVES **a·void·a·ble** /əˈvoidəbəl/ adjective **a·void·a·bly** /əˈvoidəblē/ adverb **a·void·ance** /əˈvoidns/ noun.
– ORIGIN Old French *evuider* 'clear out, get rid of.'

av·oir·du·pois /ˌävərdəˈpoiz/ ▶ **noun** a system of weights based on a pound of 16 ounces or 7,000 grains. Compare with **TROY**.
– ORIGIN from Old French *aveir de peis* 'goods of weight.'

a·vow /əˈvou/ ▶ **verb** declare or confess something openly.
– DERIVATIVES **a·vow·al** /əˈvouəl/ noun **a·vowed** adjective.
– ORIGIN from Latin *advocare* 'summon in defense.'

a·vun·cu·lar /əˈvəNGkyələr/ ▶ **adjective** (of a man) friendly and kind toward a younger person.
– ORIGIN from Latin *avunculus* 'maternal uncle.'

AWACS /ˈāˌwaks/ ▶ **abbreviation** airborne warning and control system.

a·wait /əˈwāt/ ▶ **verb 1** wait for an event. **2** be in store for: *many dangers await them.*

– SYNONYMS **1 wait for,** expect, look forward to, anticipate. **2 be in store for,** lie ahead of, be waiting for, be (right/just) around the corner.

a·wake /əˈwāk/ ▶ **verb** (past **awoke** /əˈwōk/; past part. **awoken** /əˈwōkən/) **1** stop sleeping. **2** make or become active again.

– SYNONYMS **wake up,** wake, awaken, waken, stir, come to, come around, rouse, call.

▶ **adjective** not asleep.

– SYNONYMS **1 sleepless,** wide awake, restless, insomniac. **2** *too few are* **awake to** *the dangers* **aware of,** conscious of, mindful of, alert to.
– ANTONYMS asleep, oblivious.

a·wak·en /əˈwākən/ ▶ **verb 1** stop sleeping; awake. **2** stir up a feeling.

– SYNONYMS **1** see **AWAKE**. **2 arouse,** kindle, bring out, trigger, stir up, stimulate, revive.

– DERIVATIVES **a·wak·en·ing** noun & adjective.

a·ward /əˈwôrd/ ▶ **verb** give something officially as a prize, payment, or reward.

– SYNONYMS **give,** grant, accord, confer on, bestow on, present to, decorate with.

▶ **noun 1** a payment, prize, or honor given to someone. **2** the giving of an award.

– SYNONYMS **1 prize,** trophy, medal, decoration, reward; informal gong. **2 grant,** scholarship, endowment.

– ORIGIN Old French *esguarder* 'consider, ordain.'

CHOOSE THE RIGHT WORD

See **GIVE**.

a·ware /əˈwe(ə)r/ ▶ **adjective** having knowledge of a situation or fact: *everyone is aware of aging.*

– SYNONYMS **1** *she is* **aware of** *the dangers* **conscious of,** mindful of, informed about, acquainted with, familiar with, alive to, alert to; informal wise to, in the know about. **2** *environmentally* **aware sensitive,** enlightened, knowledgeable, (well) informed; informal clued in.
– ANTONYMS ignorant.

– DERIVATIVES **a·ware·ness** noun.
– ORIGIN Old English.

a·wash /əˈwôsH, əˈwäsH/ ▶ **adjective** covered or flooded with water.

a·way /əˈwā/ ▶ **adverb 1** to or at a distance. **2** into a place for storage. **3** until disappearing: *the sound died away.* **4** continuously or persistently.

– SYNONYMS **elsewhere,** abroad, gone, off, out, absent, on vacation.

▶ **adjective** (of a sports contest) played at the opponents' park: *this is the Twins' last away game of the season.*
– ORIGIN Old English.

awe /ô/ ▶ **noun** a feeling of great respect mixed with fear.

– SYNONYMS **wonder,** wonderment, admiration, reverence, respect, fear, dread.

▶ **verb** fill someone with awe.
– ORIGIN Old English.

a·weigh /əˈwā/ ▶ **adjective** (of a ship's anchor) raised just clear of the seabed.

awe·some /ˈôsəm/ ▶ **adjective 1** very impressive or daunting: *the awesome power of the sea.* **2** informal excellent.

– SYNONYMS **breathtaking,** awe-inspiring, magnificent, amazing, stunning, staggering, imposing, formidable, intimidating; informal mind-boggling, mind-blowing, brilliant.
– ANTONYMS unimpressive.

awe·struck /ˈôˌstrək/ ▶ **adjective** filled with awe.

aw·ful /ˈôfəl/ ▶ **adjective 1** very bad or unpleasant. **2** used for emphasis: *an awful lot.* **3** old use causing awe.

– SYNONYMS **1** *the place smells* **awful disgusting,** terrible, dreadful, ghastly, horrible, vile, foul, revolting, repulsive, repugnant, sickening, nauseating; informal gross. **2** *an* **awful** *book* **dreadful,** terrible, frightful, atrocious, lamentable; informal crummy, pathetic, rotten, woeful, lousy, appalling, abysmal, dismal, dire. **3** *I feel* **awful ill,** unwell, sick, nauseous, poorly.
– ANTONYMS delightful, excellent, well.

– DERIVATIVES **aw·ful·ness** noun.

aw·ful·ly /ˈôf(ə)lē/ ▶ **adverb 1** informal very or very much. **2** very badly or unpleasantly.

– SYNONYMS **1** *an* **awfully** *nice man* **very,** extremely, really, immensely, exceedingly, thoroughly, dreadfully, terrifically, terribly, exceptionally, remarkably, extraordinarily; informal real, mighty, seriously; dated frightfully. **2** *we played* **awfully terribly,** dreadfully, atrociously, appallingly; informal abysmally.

a·while /əˈ(h)wīl/ ▶ **adverb** for a short time.

awk·ward /ˈôkwərd/ ▶ **adjective 1** hard to do or deal with: *awkward questions.* **2** causing embarrassment or inconvenience. **3** feeling embarrassed. **4** not graceful; clumsy.

– SYNONYMS **1 difficult,** tricky, cumbersome, unwieldy. **2 unreasonable,** uncooperative, unhelpful, difficult, obstructive, contrary, perverse, obstinate, stubborn. informal balky. **3** *an* **awkward** *time* **inconvenient,** inappropriate, inopportune, difficult. **4** *he put her in an* **awkward** *position* **embarrassing,** uncomfortable, unenviable, delicate, tricky, problematic, troublesome, humiliating, compromising; informal sticky. **5** *she felt* **awkward uncomfortable,** uneasy, tense, nervous, edgy, self-conscious, embarrassed. **6** *his* **awkward** *movements* **clumsy,** ungainly, uncoordinated, graceless, inelegant, gauche, gawky, stiff, unskillful, inept, blundering; informal all thumbs, ham-fisted, cack-handed.
– ANTONYMS easy, amenable, convenient, graceful.

– DERIVATIVES **awk·ward·ly** adverb **awk·ward·ness** noun.
– ORIGIN from Old Norse.

awl /ôl/ ▶ **noun** a small pointed tool used for piercing holes.
– ORIGIN Old English.

awn /ôn/ ▶ **noun** a stiff bristle growing from the ear or flower of barley, rye, and grasses.
– ORIGIN Old Norse.

awn·ing /ˈôniNG/ ▶ **noun** a sheet of canvas stretched on a frame, used for shelter.
– ORIGIN unknown.

a·woke /əˈwōk/ past of **AWAKE**.

a·wo·ken /əˈwōkən/ past participle of **AWAKE**.

AWOL /ˈāˌwôl/ ▶ **adjective** Military absent but without intent to desert.
– ORIGIN from *absent without (official) leave*.

a·wry /əˈrī/ ▶ **adverb & adjective** away from the expected course or position.
– ORIGIN from **WRY**.

ax /aks/ (also **axe**) ▶ **noun 1** a tool with a heavy blade, used for chopping wood. **2** (**the ax**) severe cost-cutting action: *thirty workers are facing the ax.*

– SYNONYMS **hatchet,** chopper, cleaver; historical battleax.

▶ **verb 1** cancel or reduce something by a large amount. **2** dismiss someone ruthlessly.

– SYNONYMS **1 cancel,** withdraw, drop, scrap, cut, discontinue, end; informal ditch, dump, pull the plug on. **2 dismiss,** lay off, get rid of; informal sack, fire, can.

– PHRASES **have an ax to grind** have a private reason for doing something.
– ORIGIN Old English.

ax·el /ˈaksəl/ ▶ **noun** Figure Skating a jump with a forward takeoff from the forward outside edge of one skate to the backward outside edge of the other, with one and a half turns in the air.
– ORIGIN named after *Axel* R. Paulsen (1885–1938), Norwegian skater.

ax·es /ˈakˌsēz/ plural of **AXIS**.

ax·i·al /ˈaksēəl/ ▶ **adjective** relating to or forming an axis.
– DERIVATIVES **ax·i·al·ly** adverb.

ax·il /ˈaksəl/ ▶ **noun** the upper angle where a leaf joins a stem.
– ORIGIN Latin *axilla* 'armpit.'

ax·i·om /ˈaksēəm/ ▶ **noun** a statement regarded as accepted or obviously true.
– DERIVATIVES **ax·i·o·mat·ic** /ˌaksēəˈmatik/ adjective.
– ORIGIN Greek *axiōma* 'what is thought fitting.'

ax·is /ˈaksis/ ▶ **noun** (pl. **axes** /ˈaksēz/) **1** an imaginary line through a body, about which it rotates. **2** an imaginary line about which a regular figure is symmetrically arranged. **3** Mathematics a fixed reference line for the measurement of coordinates.
– ORIGIN Latin, 'axle, pivot.'

ax·le /ˈaksəl/ ▶ **noun** a rod passing through the center of a wheel or group of wheels.

– SYNONYMS **shaft,** spindle, rod.

– ORIGIN Old Norse.

ax·on /ˈakˌsän/ ▶ **noun** the long threadlike part of a nerve cell.
– ORIGIN Greek, 'axis.'

a·yah /ˈäyə/ ▶ **noun** a nanny employed by Europeans in India or another former British territory.
– ORIGIN Portuguese *aia* 'nurse.'

a·ya·tol·lah /ˌäyəˈtōlə/ ▶ **noun** a Shiite religious leader in Iran.
– ORIGIN from Arabic, 'token of God.'

aye /ī/ (also **ay**) ▶ **exclamation** old use or dialect yes. ▶ **noun** a vote in favor of a proposal.
– ORIGIN probably from *I*, first person personal pronoun.

A·yur·ve·da /ˌäyərˈvādə, -ˈvēdə/ ▶ **noun** the traditional Hindu system of medicine, using diet, herbal treatment, and yogic breathing.
– DERIVATIVES **A·yur·ve·dic** /-ˈvedik/ adjective.
– ORIGIN from Sanskrit *āyus* 'life' + *veda* '(sacred) knowledge.'

AZ ▶ **abbreviation** Arizona.

a·zal·ea /əˈzālyə/ ▶ **noun** a shrub with brightly colored flowers.
– ORIGIN from Greek *azaleos* 'dry' (because the shrubs flourish in dry soil).

A·zer·bai·ja·ni /ˌazərbīˈjänē, ˌäzər-/ ▶ **noun** (pl. **Azerbaijanis**) a person from Azerbaijan. ▶ **adjective** relating to Azerbaijan or Azerbaijanis.

az·i·muth /ˈazəməTH/ ▶ **noun** Astronomy the horizontal direction of a celestial object, measured from the north or south point of the horizon.
– DERIVATIVES **az·i·muth·al** /ˌazəˈməTHəl/ adjective.
– ORIGIN Arabic, 'the way, direction.'

Az·tec /ˈazˌtek/ ▶ **noun** a member of the American Indian people dominant in Mexico before the Spanish conquest.
– ORIGIN Nahuatl, 'person of Aztlan,' their legendary place of origin.

az·ure /ˈaZHər/ ▶ **noun** a bright blue color.
– ORIGIN from Persian, 'lapis lazuli.'

Bb

B[1] (also **b**) ▶ **noun** (pl. **Bs** or **B's**) **1** the second letter of the alphabet. **2** Music the seventh note of the scale of C major.

B[2] ▶ **abbreviation** **1** (in chess) bishop. **2** black (used in describing grades of pencil lead). ▶ **symbol** the chemical element boron.

b ▶ **abbreviation** **1** (**b.**) born. **2** billion.

B. & B. ▶ **abbreviation** bed and breakfast.

B2B ▶ **abbreviation** business-to-business, referring to trade carried out via the Internet between businesses.

BA ▶ **abbreviation** **1** Bachelor of Arts. **2** Baseball batting average.

Ba ▶ **symbol** the chemical element barium.

baa /bä/ ▶ **verb** (**baas, baaing, baaed**) (of a sheep or lamb) bleat. ▶ **noun** the cry of a sheep or lamb.
– ORIGIN imitating the sound.

bab·ble /'babəl/ ▶ **verb** **1** talk rapidly in a foolish or confused way. **2** (of a stream) flow with a continuous murmur.

> – SYNONYMS **prattle,** rattle on, gabble, chatter, jabber, twitter, burble, blather; informal yatter, blabber, jaw, gas, shoot one's mouth off.

▶ **noun** **1** foolish or confused talk. **2** a babbling sound.
– DERIVATIVES **bab·bler** noun.
– ORIGIN German *babbelen.*

babe /bāb/ ▶ **noun** **1** literary a baby. **2** informal an attractive young woman. **3** informal an affectionate form of address for a lover.

ba·bel /'babəl, 'bā-/ ▶ **noun** a confused noise made by a number of voices.
– ORIGIN from the Tower of *Babel* in the Bible, where God confused the languages of the builders.

ba·boon /ba'bo͞on/ ▶ **noun** a large monkey with a long snout, large teeth, and a pink rump.
– ORIGIN from Old French *babuin* or Latin *babewynus.*

ba·bush·ka /bə'bo͝oshkə/ ▶ **noun** (in Russia) an old woman or grandmother.
– ORIGIN Russian, 'grandmother.'

ba·by /'bābē/ ▶ **noun** (pl. **babies**) **1** a child or animal that is newly or recently born. **2** a timid or childish person. **3** informal a person's lover. **4** (**one's baby**) one's particular responsibility or concern.

> – SYNONYMS **infant,** newborn, child. technical neonate; informal tot; literary babe.

▶ **adjective** small or immature in comparison with others of the same kind: *baby carrots.*

> – SYNONYMS **miniature,** mini, little, toy, pocket, midget, dwarf, vest-pocket; Scottish wee; informal teeny, teensy, tiddly, bite-sized.

▶ **verb** (**babies, babying, babied**) treat someone too protectively.
– DERIVATIVES **ba·by·hood** noun.
– PHRASES **throw the baby out with the bathwater** discard something valuable while getting rid of the inessential or unwanted.
– ORIGIN probably imitating a child's first attempts at speech.

ba·by boom ▶ **noun** informal a temporary marked increase in the birth rate, especially the one following World War II.
– DERIVATIVES **ba·by boom·er** noun.

ba·by bug·gy ▶ **noun** a baby carriage.

ba·by car·riage ▶ **noun** a four-wheeled carriage for a baby, typically with a retractable hood and pushed by a person on foot.

ba·by-doll ▶ **adjective** referring to a style of women's clothing resembling that traditionally worn by a young child.

bab·y fat ▶ **noun** fat on a child's body which disappears around adolescence.

ba·by grand ▶ **noun** the smallest size of grand piano, about 4.5 feet (1.5 m) long.

ba·by·ish /'bābē-ish/ ▶ **adjective** childish and immature.

> – SYNONYMS **childish,** infantile, juvenile, puerile, immature.
> – ANTONYMS mature.

Bab·y·lo·ni·an /ˌbabə'lōnēən/ ▶ **noun** a person from Babylon or Babylonia, an ancient city and kingdom in Mesopotamia (part of what is now Iraq). ▶ **adjective** relating to Babylon or Babylonia.

ba·by·sit /'bābēˌsit/ ▶ **verb** (**babysits, babysitting, babysat**) look after a child or children while the parents are out.
– DERIVATIVES **ba·by·sit·ter** noun.

bac·ca·lau·re·ate /ˌbakə'lôrēit/ ▶ **noun** **1** an exam that qualifies candidates for higher education. **2** a bachelor's degree.
– ORIGIN from Latin *baccalaureus* 'bachelor.'

bac·ca·rat /'bäkəˌrä, ˌbakə'rä/ ▶ **noun** a gambling card game in which players bet against a banker.
– ORIGIN French *baccara.*

bac·cha·nal /ˌbäkə'näl, ˌbak-, 'bakənl/ ▶ **noun** chiefly literary a wild and drunken party or celebration.
– ORIGIN from *Bacchus*, the Greek or Roman god of wine.

Bac·cha·na·li·a /ˌbakə'nālyə, ˌbäk-/ ▶ **plural noun** (also treated as sing.) **1** the ancient Roman festival of the god Bacchus. **2** (**bacchanalia**) drunken celebrations.
– DERIVATIVES **bac·cha·na·li·an** adjective.

ba·cha·ta /bä'chätä/ ▶ **noun** a style of romantic music originating in the Dominican Republic.
– ORIGIN Caribbean Spanish, 'party, good time.'

bach·e·lor /'bach(ə)lər/ ▶ **noun** **1** a man who has never been married. **2** a person who holds an undergraduate degree from a college or university.

– DERIVATIVES **bach·e·lor·hood** noun.
– ORIGIN Old French *bacheler* 'a young man wishing to become a knight.'

bach·e·lor·ette /ˌbacн(ə)ləˈret/ ▶ **noun** a young unmarried woman.

Bach flow·er rem·e·dies /bäкн, bäk/ ▶ **plural noun** preparations of the flowers of various plants used in a system of complementary medicine.
– ORIGIN named after the British physician Edward *Bach*.

ba·cil·lus /bəˈsiləs/ ▶ **noun** (pl. **bacilli** /-ˈsilī/) a rod-shaped bacterium.
– DERIVATIVES **bac·il·lar·y** /ˈbasəˌlerē/ adjective.
– ORIGIN Latin, 'little stick.'

back /bak/ ▶ **noun 1** the rear surface of a person's body from the shoulders to the hips. **2** the upper surface of an animal's body, equivalent to a person's back. **3** the side or part of something that is farthest from the front or that is not normally seen or used. **4** a player in a team game who plays in a defensive position behind the front line.

– SYNONYMS **1 spine,** backbone, spinal column, vertebrae, vertebral column. **2 rear,** end, rear end, tail end; Nautical stern. **3 reverse,** other side, underside; informal flip side.
– ANTONYMS front.

▶ **adverb 1** in the opposite direction from that in which one is facing or traveling. **2** so as to return to an earlier or normal position or state. **3** into the past. **4** in return.
▶ **verb 1** give support to: *the scheme is backed by the education secretary*. **2** walk or drive backward. **3** bet money on a person or animal winning a race or contest. **4** (**back on/onto**) (of a building or other structure) have its back facing or adjacent to something. **5** cover the back of an object. **6** provide musical accompaniment to a singer or musician. **7** (of the wind) change direction counterclockwise around the points of the compass.

– SYNONYMS **1** *the government backed the initiative with $4 million* **sponsor,** finance, fund, subsidize, underwrite; informal pick up the bill for. **2** *most people backed the idea* **support,** endorse, sanction, approve of, give one's blessing to, smile on, favor, advocate, promote, champion; informal throw one's weight behind. **3** *he backed into the yard* **reverse,** draw back, step back, pull back, retreat, withdraw. **4** *he backed the horse at 33–1* **bet on,** gamble on, stake money on.
– ANTONYMS oppose, advance.

▶ **adjective 1** of or at the back. **2** in a remote or less important position. **3** relating to the past.

– SYNONYMS **1** *the back seats* **rear,** rearmost, hind, hindmost, posterior. **2** *a back copy* **past,** old, previous, earlier.
– ANTONYMS front, future.

– DERIVATIVES **back·less** adjective.
– PHRASES **back and forth** to and fro. **the back of beyond** a very remote place. **back down** admit defeat. **back off** draw back from confrontation. **back out** withdraw from a commitment. **back to front** Brit. with the back at the front and the front at the back. **back something up** Computing make a spare copy of data or a disk. **behind someone's back** without a person's knowledge. **get** (or **put**) **someone's back up** annoy someone. **put one's back into** tackle a task in a determined and energetic way. **turn one's back on** ignore; reject. **with one's back to** (or **up against**) **the wall** in a desperate situation.
– ORIGIN Old English.

WORD LINKS

dorsal, **lumbar** *relating to the back*
supine *lying on one's back*

back·ache /ˈbakˌāk/ ▶ **noun** prolonged pain in one's back.

back·beat /ˈbakˌbēt/ ▶ **noun** Music a strong accent on one of the normally unaccented beats of the bar.

back·bench·er /ˈbakˈbencнər/ ▶ **noun** (in the UK) a member of parliament who does not hold a government or opposition post and who sits behind the front benches in the House of Commons.
– DERIVATIVES **back·bench** adjective.

back·bit·ing /ˈbakˌbītiNG/ ▶ **noun** spiteful talk about a person who is not present.

back·board /ˈbakˌbôrd/ ▶ **noun 1** a board placed at or forming the back of something, such as a collage or piece of electronic equipment. **2** Basketball an upright board behind the basket, off which the ball may rebound.

back·bone /ˈbakˌbōn/ ▶ **noun 1** the spine. **2** the chief support of a system or organization: *small customers are the backbone of a profitable business.* **3** strength of character.

– SYNONYMS **1 spine,** spinal column, vertebrae, vertebral column. **2 mainstay,** cornerstone, foundation. **3 strength of character,** strength of will, firmness, resolution, resolve, grit, determination, fortitude, mettle, spirit.

back-break·ing ▶ **adjective** (of manual labor) physically demanding.

back burn·er ▶ **noun** (in phrase **on the back burner**) set aside because low priority.

back cat·a·log ▶ **noun** all the works previously produced by a recording artist, record company, or movie director.

back·coun·try /ˈbakˌkəntrē/ ▶ **noun** sparsely inhabited rural areas; wilderness.

back·cross /ˈbakˌkrôs/ Genetics ▶ **verb** cross a hybrid with one of its parents or an organism with the same genetic characteristics as one of the parents. ▶ **noun 1** an instance of backcrossing. **2** the product of such a cross.

back·date /ˈbakˌdāt/ ▶ **verb 1** make something valid from an earlier date. **2** put an earlier date on a document than the actual one.

back·door /ˈbakˌdôr/ ▶ **adjective** underhanded or secret.

back·drop /ˈbakˌdräp/ ▶ **noun 1** a painted cloth hung at the back of a theater stage as part of the scenery. **2** the setting or background for an event.

back·er /ˈbakər/ ▶ **noun** a person, institution, or country that supports something, especially financially.

– SYNONYMS **1** *$3 million was provided by the project's backers* **sponsor,** investor, underwriter, financier, patron, benefactor; informal angel. **2** *the backers of the proposition* **supporter,** defender, advocate, promoter, booster.

back·field /ˈbakˌfēld/ ▶ **noun** Football the area of play behind either the offensive or defensive line.

back·fill /ˈbakˌfil/ ▶ **verb** refill an excavated hole with the material dug out of it.

back·fire /ˈbakˌfī(ə)r/ ▶ **verb 1** (of a vehicle or its engine) undergo a mistimed explosion in the cylinder or exhaust. **2** produce the opposite effect to what was intended: *his trick backfired on him.*

– SYNONYMS **rebound,** boomerang, come back, fail; informal blow up in someone's face.

back·gam·mon /'bak,gamən/ ▶ **noun** a board game in which two players move their pieces around triangular points according to the throw of dice.
– ORIGIN from **BACK** + an Old English word meaning 'game.'

back·ground /'bak,ground/ ▶ **noun 1** part of a picture, scene, or description that forms a setting for the main figures or events. **2** information or circumstances that influence or explain something: *the historical background to the rebellion.* **3** a person's education, experience, and social circumstances. **4** a persistent low level of radioactivity, noise, etc., present in a particular environment.

– SYNONYMS **1 backdrop,** backcloth, surrounding(s), setting, scene, framework. **2 social circumstances,** family circumstances, environment, class, culture, tradition. **3 experience,** record, history, past, training, education.
– ANTONYMS foreground.

▶ **verb** form a background to something.

back·hand /'bak,hand/ ▶ **noun** (in racket sports) a stroke played with the back of the hand facing in the direction of the stroke. ▶ **verb** strike someone or something with a backhanded blow or stroke.

back·hand·ed /'bak,handid/ ▶ **adjective 1** made with the back of the hand facing in the direction of movement. **2** expressed in an indirect or ambiguous way: *a backhanded compliment.*

back·hand·er /'bak,handər/ ▶ **noun 1** a backhand stroke or blow. **2** Brit. informal a bribe.

back·hoe /'bak,hō/ (Brit. also **backhoe loader**) ▶ **noun** a mechanical digger with a bucket attached to a hinged boom.

back·ing /'bakiɴɢ/ ▶ **noun 1** help or support. **2** a layer of material that forms or strengthens the back of something. **3** (especially in popular music) music or vocals accompanying the main singer.

– SYNONYMS **1 support,** endorsement, approval, blessing, assistance, aid, help. **2 sponsorship,** finance, funding, subsidy, patronage.

back·ing track ▶ **noun** a recorded musical accompaniment.

back·lash /'bak,lash/ ▶ **noun 1** a strong and adverse reaction by a large number of people: *the backlash against conservatism.* **2** recoil between parts of a mechanism.

– SYNONYMS **adverse reaction,** counterblast, repercussion, comeback, retaliation, reprisal.

back·list /'bak,list/ ▶ **noun** a publisher's list of books published before the current season and still in print.

back·lit /'bak,lit/ ▶ **adjective** illuminated from behind.

back·log /'bak,lôg, -,läg/ ▶ **noun** a buildup of matters needing to be dealt with.

back·lot /'bak,lät/ ▶ **noun** an outdoor area in a movie studio where large sets are made and some outside scenes are filmed.

back·pack /'bak,pak/ ▶ **noun** a bag with shoulder straps that allow it to be carried on someone's back. ▶ **verb** travel carrying one's belongings in a backpack.
– DERIVATIVES **back·pack·er** noun.

back·ped·al /'bak,pedl/ ▶ **verb 1** reverse a previous action or opinion. **2** move the pedals of a bicycle backward (formerly so as to brake).

back·room /'bak,ro͞om/ ▶ **adjective** relating to secret work or planning.

back·seat driv·er /'bak'sēt/ ▶ **noun** informal a passenger in a car who gives the driver unwanted advice.

back·side /'bak,sīd/ ▶ **noun** informal a person's buttocks.

back·slap·ping /'bak,slapiɴɢ/ ▶ **noun** the offering of hearty congratulations or praise.

back·slash /'bak,slash/ ▶ **noun** a backward-sloping diagonal line (\).

back·slide /'bak,slīd/ ▶ **verb** (past and past part. **backslid**) return to bad ways.
– DERIVATIVES **back·slid·er** noun **back·slid·ing** noun.

back·space /'bak,spās/ ▶ **noun** a key on a typewriter or computer keyboard used to move the carriage or cursor backward. ▶ **verb** move a typewriter carriage or computer cursor backward.

back·spin /'bak,spin/ ▶ **noun** a backward spin given to a moving ball, causing it to stop more quickly or rebound at a steeper angle.

back·splash /'bak,splash/ ▶ **noun** a panel behind a sink or stove that protects the wall from splashes.

back·stab·bing /'bak,stabiɴɢ/ ▶ **noun** the action of criticizing someone while pretending to be friendly.

back·stage /'bak'stāj/ ▶ **adverb & adjective** behind the stage in a theater.

back·stairs /'bak'ste(ə)rz/ ▶ **adjective** secret or underhanded: *backstairs deals.*

back·stitch /'bak,stich/ ▶ **noun** a method of sewing with overlapping stitches.

back·stop /'bak,stäp/ ▶ **noun 1** a person or thing placed at the rear of or behind something as a barrier, support, or reinforcement. **2** Baseball a high fence or similar structure behind the home plate area. **3** informal Baseball a catcher.

back·sto·ry /'bak,stôrē/ ▶ **noun** (pl. **backstories**) a history or background created for a fictional character in a movie or television program.

back·street /'bak,strēt/ ▶ **noun** a minor street. ▶ **adjective** acting or done secretly and typically illegally: *backstreet abortions.*

back·stroke /'bak,strōk/ ▶ **noun** a swimming stroke in which the swimmer lies on their back and lifts their arms alternately out of the water in a backward circular movement.

back·swing /'bak,swiɴɢ/ ▶ **noun** a backward swing, especially of an arm or of a golf club when about to hit a ball.

back·talk /'bak ,tôk/ ▶ **noun** informal rude or impertinent remarks made in reply to someone in authority.

back-to-back ▶ **adjective** following one after the other. ▶ **adverb** (**back to back**) **1** (of two people) facing in opposite directions with backs touching. **2** in succession.

back·track /'bak,trak/ ▶ **verb 1** retrace one's steps. **2** reverse one's previous opinion or position: *he denied that he was backtracking on his promise.*

back·up /'bak,əp/ ▶ **noun 1** help or support. **2** a person or thing kept ready to be used if necessary.

– SYNONYMS **help,** support, assistance, aid, reserve, reinforcements.

back·ward /ˈbakwərd/ ▸ **adjective 1** directed toward the back. **2** having made less progress than is normal or expected.

– SYNONYMS **1 rearward,** toward the rear, behind you, reverse. **2 retrograde,** regressive, for the worse, in the wrong direction, downhill, negative. **3 underdeveloped,** undeveloped, primitive. **4 hesitant,** reticent, reluctant, shy, diffident, timid, self-effacing, unassertive.
– ANTONYMS forward, advanced.

▸ **adverb** (also **backwards**) **1** toward one's back. **2** back toward the starting point. **3** opposite to the usual direction or order.

– SYNONYMS **backwards,** toward the rear, rearward, behind you.
– ANTONYMS forward.

– PHRASES **bend over backward** informal try one's hardest to be fair or helpful. **know something backward and forward** be completely familiar with something.
– DERIVATIVES **back·ward·ly** adverb **back·ward·ness** noun.

back·wash /ˈbakˌwôsн, -ˌwäsн/ ▸ **noun** waves flowing outward behind a ship.

back·wa·ter /ˈbakˌwôtər, -ˌwätər/ ▸ **noun 1** a stretch of stagnant water on a river. **2** a place or state in which no development is happening: *the country remains an economic backwater*.

back·woods /ˈbakˈwo͝odz/ ▸ **plural noun 1** remote uncleared forest land. **2** a region that is remote or has few inhabitants.
– DERIVATIVES **back·woods·man** noun (pl. **backwoodsmen**).

back·yard /ˈbakˈyärd/ ▸ **noun** a yard at the back of a house or building.
– PHRASES **in one's (own) backyard** informal the area close to where one lives.

ba·con /ˈbākən/ ▸ **noun** salted or smoked meat from the back or sides of a pig.
– PHRASES **bring home the bacon** informal make money or achieve success.
– ORIGIN Old French.

bac·te·ri·a /bakˈti(ə)rēə/ plural of **BACTERIUM**.

bac·te·ri·o·log·i·cal /bakˌti(ə)rēəˈläjikəl/ ▸ **adjective 1** relating to bacteriology or bacteria. **2** relating to germ warfare.

bac·te·ri·ol·o·gy /bakˌti(ə)rēˈäləjē/ ▸ **noun** the study of bacteria.
– DERIVATIVES **bac·te·ri·ol·o·gist** noun.

bac·te·ri·um /bakˈti(ə)rēəm/ ▸ **noun** (pl. **bacteria**) a member of a large group of microscopic single-celled organisms, many of which can cause disease.
– DERIVATIVES **bac·te·ri·al** /-ˈti(ə)rēəl/ adjective **bac·te·ri·al·ly** /-ˈti(ə)rēəlē/ adverb.
– ORIGIN from Greek *baktērion* 'little rod.'

USAGE

Bacteria is the plural form of **bacterium** and should always be used with the plural form of the verb: *the bacteria are killed by thorough cooking*.

Bac·tri·an cam·el /ˈbaktrēən/ ▸ **noun** a camel with two humps, native to central Asia.
– ORIGIN named after the ancient empire of *Bactria* in central Asia.

bad /bad/ ▸ **adjective** (**worse, worst**) **1** of poor quality or a low standard. **2** unwelcome or unpleasant: *bad news*. **3** severe or serious. **4** wicked or evil. **5** (**bad for**) harmful to: *fatty food is bad for you*. **6** injured, ill, or diseased. **7** (of food) decayed. **8** (**badder, baddest**) informal excellent.

– SYNONYMS **1** *bad workmanship* **unsatisfactory,** substandard, poor, inferior, second-rate, second-class, inadequate, deficient, imperfect, defective, faulty, shoddy, negligent, disgraceful, awful, terrible, appalling, dreadful, frightful, atrocious, abysmal; informal crummy, rotten, pathetic, useless, woeful, lousy. **2** *the alcohol had a bad effect* **harmful,** damaging, detrimental, injurious, hurtful, destructive, deleterious, inimical. **3** *the bad guys* **wicked,** evil, sinful, criminal, immoral, corrupt, villainous; informal crooked. **4** *you bad girl!* **naughty,** badly behaved, disobedient, wayward, willful, defiant, unruly, undisciplined. **5** *bad news* **unpleasant,** disagreeable, unwelcome, unfavorable, unfortunate, grim, distressing, gloomy. **6** *a bad time to arrive* **unfavorable,** inauspicious, unpropitious, inopportune, unfortunate, disadvantageous, inappropriate, unsuitable. **7** *a bad accident* **serious,** severe, grave, critical, acute. **8** *the meat's bad* **rotten,** decayed, putrid, rancid, curdled, sour, moldy, off. **9** *a bad knee* **injured,** wounded, diseased; dated game.
– ANTONYMS good, beneficial, virtuous, favorable.

– DERIVATIVES **bad·ness** noun.
– PHRASES **too bad** informal regrettable but unable to be changed.
– ORIGIN perhaps from Old English, 'womanish man.'

bad blood ▸ **noun** hostility or hatred between people.

bad debt ▸ **noun** a debt that will not be repaid.

bad·dy /ˈbadē/ (also **baddie**) ▸ **noun** (pl. **baddies**) informal a wicked or evil person in a book, movie, or play.

bade /bad, bād/ past of **BID**².

bad faith ▸ **noun** intention to deceive: *they were accused of negotiating in bad faith*.

bad form ▸ **noun** an offense against accepted behavior.

badge /baj/ ▸ **noun** a small flat object worn by a person to show who they are or what they do.

– SYNONYMS **1 brooch,** pin, button, emblem, crest, insignia. **2** *a badge of success* **sign,** symbol, indication, signal, mark, hallmark, trademark.

– ORIGIN unknown.

badg·er /ˈbajər/ ▸ **noun** a heavily built mammal with a gray and black coat and a white-striped head that lives underground. ▸ **verb** pester someone to do something.

– SYNONYMS **pester,** harass, hound, harry, nag, bother, go on at; informal hassle, bug.

– ORIGIN perhaps from **BADGE**, because of the animal's head markings.

bad hair day ▸ **noun** informal a day on which everything goes wrong.

bad·i·nage /ˌbadnˈäzн/ ▸ **noun** witty conversation.
– ORIGIN French.

bad·lands /ˈbadˌlandz/ ▸ **plural noun** poor land with very little soil.

bad·ly /ˈbadlē/ ▸ **adverb** (**worse, worst**) **1** in a way that is not acceptable or satisfactory. **2** severely; seriously. **3** very much.

– SYNONYMS **1 poorly,** unsatisfactorily, inadequately, incorrectly, faultily, defectively, shoddily, amateurishly, carelessly, incompetently, inexpertly. **2 unfavorably,** ill, critically, disapprovingly. **3 naughtily,** disobediently, willfully, mischievously. **4 cruelly,** wickedly, unkindly, harshly, shamefully, unfairly, unjustly, wrongly. **5 unfavorably,** unsuccessfully, adversely, unfortunately. **6 severely,** seriously, gravely, acutely, critically.
– ANTONYMS well.

– PHRASES **badly off** not wealthy; poor.

bad·min·ton /ˈbadmintn/ ▶ **noun** a game with rackets in which a shuttlecock is hit back and forth across a net.
– ORIGIN named after *Badminton* in SW England.

bad-mouth ▶ **verb** informal criticize someone.

bad-tem·pered ▶ **adjective** easily angered or annoyed.

– SYNONYMS **irritable,** irascible, tetchy, testy, grumpy, grouchy, crotchety, in a (bad) mood, cantankerous, curmudgeonly, ill-tempered, ill-humored, peevish, cross, fractious, petulant, pettish, crabby, quarrelsome, dyspeptic; informal cranky, ornery, on a short fuse.
– ANTONYMS good-humored, affable.

baf·fle /ˈbafəl/ ▶ **verb** make someone feel bewildered or puzzled.

– SYNONYMS **puzzle,** perplex, bewilder, mystify, confuse; informal flummox, stump.

▶ **noun** a device for controlling or stopping the flow of sound, light, gas, or a fluid.
– DERIVATIVES **baf·fle·ment** noun **baf·fling** adjective.
– ORIGIN perhaps related to French *bafouer* 'ridicule.'

CHOOSE THE RIGHT WORD

See **THWART**.

bag /bag/ ▶ **noun 1** a flexible container with an opening at the top. **2** (**bags**) loose folds of skin under a person's eyes. **3** (**bags of**) informal, chiefly Brit. plenty of. **4** informal, derogatory an unpleasant or unattractive woman.

– SYNONYMS **suitcase,** case, valise, carryall, grip, rucksack, haversack, satchel, handbag.

▶ **verb** (**bags, bagging, bagged**) **1** put something in a bag. **2** succeed in getting: *get there early to bag a seat.* **3** succeed in killing or catching an animal. **4** (of clothes) form loose bulges.

– SYNONYMS **1 catch,** land, capture, trap, net, snare. **2 get,** secure, obtain, acquire, pick up, win, achieve; informal land, net.

– DERIVATIVES **bag·ful** noun **bag·ger** noun.
– PHRASES **in the bag** informal sure to be gained.
– ORIGIN perhaps from Old Norse.

bag·a·telle /ˌbagəˈtel/ ▶ **noun 1** a game in which small balls are hit into numbered holes on a board. **2** something unimportant.
– ORIGIN Italian *bagatella.*

ba·gel /ˈbāgəl/ ▶ **noun** a ring-shaped bread roll with a heavy texture.
– ORIGIN Yiddish.

bag·gage /ˈbagij/ ▶ **noun 1** luggage packed with belongings for traveling. **2** past experiences or long-held attitudes regarded as having an undesirable influence: *emotional baggage.* **3** dated a disagreeable girl or woman.

– SYNONYMS **luggage,** suitcases, cases, bags, belongings.

– ORIGIN Old French *bagage.*

bag·gy /ˈbagē/ ▶ **adjective** (**baggier, baggiest**) loose and hanging in bulges or folds.

– SYNONYMS **loose,** roomy, generously cut, sloppy, voluminous, full.
– ANTONYMS tight.

– DERIVATIVES **bag·gi·ness** noun.

bag la·dy ▶ **noun** informal a homeless woman who carries her possessions in shopping bags.

bag·man /ˈbagˌman, -mən/ ▶ **noun** (pl. **bagmen**) informal an agent who collects or distributes the proceeds of illicit activities.

bag·pipe /ˈbagˌpīp/ (also **bagpipes**) ▶ **noun** a musical instrument with pipes that are sounded by wind squeezed from a bag.
– DERIVATIVES **bag·pip·er** noun.

ba·guette /baˈget/ ▶ **noun** a long, narrow loaf of French bread.
– ORIGIN French.

bah /bä/ ▶ **exclamation** an expression of contempt.

Ba·ha·'i /bəˈhī/ (also **Bahai**) ▶ **noun** (pl. **Baha'is**) **1** a religion founded in Persia, emphasizing that there is one god and that humankind and all religions are essentially one. **2** a follower of the Baha'i faith.
– ORIGIN from Arabic, 'splendor.'

Ba·ha·mi·an /bəˈhāmēən, -ˈhäm-/ ▶ **noun** a person from the Bahamas. ▶ **adjective** relating to the Bahamas.

Bah·rain·i /bäˈrānē/ ▶ **noun** (pl. **Bahrainis**) a person from Bahrain. ▶ **adjective** relating to Bahrain.

baht /bät/ ▶ **noun** (pl. same) the basic unit of money of Thailand.
– ORIGIN Thai.

Ba·hu·tu /bäˈho͞oˌto͞o/ plural of **HUTU**.

bail[1] /bāl/ ▶ **noun 1** the temporary release of an accused person before they are tried, often on condition that a sum of money is promised to the court to ensure they attend the trial. **2** money paid to a court for this reason.

– SYNONYMS **surety,** security, indemnity, bond, guarantee, pledge.

▶ **verb** release an accused person on payment of bail.
– PHRASES **jump bail** informal fail to appear for trial after being released on bail. **post bail** provide bail money for an accused person.
– ORIGIN Old French, 'custody, jurisdiction.'

bail[2] ▶ **noun 1** a bar on a typewriter or computer printer that holds the paper steady. **2** a bar separating horses in an open stable. **3** an arched handle.
– ORIGIN Old French *baile* 'palisade, enclosure.'

bail[3] (Brit. also **bale**) ▶ **verb 1** scoop water out of a ship or boat. **2** (**bail out**) make an emergency parachute descent from an aircraft. **3** (**bail someone/thing out**) rescue from a difficulty: *the state will not bail out loss-making enterprises.*

– SYNONYMS **1** (**bail out**) **eject,** parachute to safety. **2** (**bail someone/thing out**) **rescue,** save, relieve, finance, help (out), aid.

– ORIGIN from French *baille* 'bucket.'

bai·ley /ˈbālē/ ▶ **noun** (pl. **baileys**) the outer wall of a castle.
– ORIGIN probably from Old French *baile* 'palisade, enclosure.'

bail·iff /ˈbālif/ ▸ **noun** an official in a court of law who keeps order, looks after prisoners, etc.
– ORIGIN Old French *baillif*.

bail·i·wick /ˈbāləˌwik/ ▸ **noun 1** (**one's bailiwick**) one's area of activity or interest: *after the war, the Middle East remained his bailiwick.* **2** Law a district over which a bailiff has authority.
– ORIGIN from **BAILIFF** + Old English *wick* 'dwelling place.'

bail·out /ˈbālˌout/ ▸ **noun** informal an act of giving financial assistance to a failing business or economy to save it from collapse.

bain-ma·rie /ˌban məˈrē/ ▸ **noun** (pl. **bains-marie** or **bain-maries** pronunc. same) a pan of hot water in which a cooking container is placed for slow cooking.
– ORIGIN French, 'bath of Maria,' said to be the name of an alchemist.

bait /bāt/ ▸ **noun** food put on a hook or in a trap to attract fish or other animals.

> – SYNONYMS **enticement,** lure, decoy, snare, trap, inducement, siren, carrot, attraction; informal come-on.

▸ **verb 1** taunt or tease someone. **2** set dogs on an animal that is trapped or tied up. **3** put bait on a hook or in a trap or net.

> – SYNONYMS **taunt,** tease, goad, pick on, torment, persecute, harass; informal needle.

– PHRASES **rise to the bait** react to taunting or temptation exactly as someone intended.
– ORIGIN Old Norse, 'pasture, food.'

baize /bāz/ ▸ **noun** a green feltlike material, used for covering billiard and card tables.
– ORIGIN from French *bai* 'chestnut-colored.'

bake /bāk/ ▸ **verb 1** cook food by dry heat in an oven. **2** heat something so as to dry or harden it. **3** informal be or become very hot in hot weather. ▸ **noun** a social gathering at which baked food is eaten: *a lobster bake.*
– ORIGIN Old English.

baked beans ▸ **plural noun** haricot beans cooked in a sauce.

Ba·ke·lite /ˈbāk(ə)ˌlīt/ ▸ **noun** trademark an early brittle form of plastic.
– ORIGIN named after the Belgian-born chemist Leo H. *Baekeland*, who invented it.

bak·er /ˈbākər/ ▸ **noun** a person who makes bread and cakes.
– DERIVATIVES **bak·er·y** noun (pl. **bakeries**).
– PHRASES **baker's dozen** a group of thirteen. [from the former bakers' custom of adding an extra loaf to a dozen sold to a retailer, this being the retailer's profit.]

bak·ing pow·der ▸ **noun** a mixture of sodium bicarbonate and cream of tartar, used in baking to make cakes rise.

bak·ing so·da ▸ **noun** sodium bicarbonate.

ba·kla·va /ˌbākləˈvä/ ▸ **noun** a Middle Eastern dessert made of filo pastry filled with chopped nuts and soaked in honey.
– ORIGIN Turkish.

bak·sheesh /ˈbakSHēSH, bakˈSHēSH/ ▸ **noun** (in India and some eastern countries) a small sum of money given as charity, a tip, or a bribe.
– ORIGIN Persian.

bal·a·cla·va /ˌbaləˈklävə/ ▸ **noun** a close-fitting woolen hat covering the whole head and neck except for the face.
– ORIGIN first worn by soldiers in the Crimean War and named after *Balaclava*, site of a battle in that war.

bal·a·fon /ˈbaləˌfōn/ ▸ **noun** a large xylophone with hollow gourds as resonators, used in West African music.
– ORIGIN from a West African language.

bal·a·lai·ka /ˌbaləˈlīkə/ ▸ **noun** a Russian musical instrument like a guitar with a triangular body and three strings.
– ORIGIN Russian.

bal·ance /ˈbaləns/ ▸ **noun 1** a state in which weight is distributed evenly, enabling a person or thing to remain steady and upright. **2** a situation in which different elements are equal or in the correct proportions: *elections left the political balance almost unchanged.* **3** mental or emotional stability. **4** a device for weighing. **5** a predominating amount: *the balance of opinion was that work was important.* **6** an amount that is the difference between money received and money spent in an account: *a healthy bank balance.* **7** an amount still owed when part of a debt has been paid.

> – SYNONYMS **1 stability,** equilibrium, steadiness, footing. **2 fairness,** justice, impartiality, parity, equity, evenness, uniformity, comparability. **3 remainder,** outstanding amount, rest, residue, difference.
> – ANTONYMS instability, bias.

▸ **verb 1** be or put in a steady position. **2** compare the value of one thing with another. **3** establish a balance of proportions or elements in: *she manages to balance work and family life.* **4** compare sums of money owed and paid to an account to ensure that they are equal.

> – SYNONYMS **1 steady,** stabilize, poise, level. **2 counterbalance,** balance out, offset, counteract, compensate for, make up for. **3 correspond,** agree, tally, match up, coincide. **4 weigh (up),** compare, evaluate, consider, assess.

– DERIVATIVES **bal·anc·er** noun.
– PHRASES **balance of payments** the difference in total value between payments into and out of a country over a period. **balance of power 1** a situation in which nations of the world have roughly equal power. **2** the power held by a small group when larger groups are of equal strength. **balance of trade** the difference in value between a country's imports and exports. **be** (or **hang**) **in the balance** be in an uncertain state. **on balance** when everything is considered.
– ORIGIN from Latin *libra bilanx* 'balance having two scale pans.'

bal·ance sheet ▸ **noun** a written statement detailing what a business owns and what it owes at a particular point in time.

bal·bo·a /balˈbōə/ ▸ **noun** the basic unit of money of Panama.
– ORIGIN named after the Spanish explorer Vasco Núñez de *Balboa*.

bal·co·ny /ˈbalkənē/ ▸ **noun** (pl. **balconies**) **1** an enclosed platform projecting from the outside of a building. **2** the highest tier of seats in a theater or movie theater.
– DERIVATIVES **bal·co·nied** adjective.
– ORIGIN Italian *balcone*.

bald /bôld/ ▸ **adjective 1** having very little or no hair on the head. **2** (of an animal) not covered by the usual fur, hair, or feathers. **3** (of a tire) having the tread worn away. **4** without any extra detail or explanation: *the bald facts.*

– SYNONYMS **1 hairless,** smooth, shaven, depilated. **2 plain,** simple, direct, blunt, unadorned, unvarnished, unembellished, stark; informal upfront.
– ANTONYMS hairy.

– DERIVATIVES **bald·ing** adjective **bald·ish** adjective **bald·ly** adverb **bald·ness** noun.
– ORIGIN probably from a former word meaning 'white patch.'

CHOOSE THE RIGHT WORD

See **NAKED**.

bal·da·chin /'bôldəkin/ (also **baldaquin** pronunc. same) ▶ **noun** a ceremonial canopy over an altar, throne, or doorway.
– ORIGIN first referring to a rich brocade from Baghdad: from Italian *Baldacco* 'Baghdad.'

bald ea·gle ▶ **noun** a white-headed North American eagle; it is the national emblem of the US.

bal·der·dash /'bôldər,dasн/ ▶ **noun** senseless talk or writing; nonsense.
– ORIGIN unknown.

bale[1] /bāl/ ▶ **noun** a large wrapped or bound bundle of paper, hay, or cotton. ▶ **verb** make up paper, hay, or cotton into bales.
– DERIVATIVES **bal·er** noun.
– ORIGIN probably from Dutch.

bale[2] ▶ **verb** Brit. variant spelling of **BAIL**[3].

ba·leen /bə'lēn/ ▶ **noun** whalebone.
– ORIGIN Latin *balaena* 'whale.'

ba·leen whale ▶ **noun** any of the kinds of whale that have plates of whalebone in the mouth for straining plankton from the water.

bale·ful /'bālfəl/ ▶ **adjective** causing or threatening to cause harm: *she watched him with baleful eyes.*
– DERIVATIVES **bale·ful·ly** adverb.
– ORIGIN Old English, 'evil.'

Ba·li·nese /,bälə'nēz, ,bal-, -'nēs/ ▶ **noun** (pl. same) a person from Bali. ▶ **adjective** relating to Bali.

balk /bôk/ (Brit. also **baulk**) ▶ **verb 1** (**balk at**) hesitate to accept an idea. **2** thwart or hinder a plan or person. ▶ **noun** a roughly squared timber beam.
– ORIGIN from Old Norse, 'partition.'

CHOOSE THE RIGHT WORD

See **THWART**.

Bal·kan /'bôlkən/ ▶ **adjective** relating to the countries on the peninsula in SE Europe surrounded by the Adriatic, Ionian, Aegean, and Black Seas. ▶ **noun** (**the Balkans** /'bôlkənz/) the Balkan countries.

Bal·kan·ize /'bôlkə,nīz/ ▶ **verb** divide a region or organization into smaller states or groups who oppose each other.
– DERIVATIVES **Bal·kan·i·za·tion** /,bôlkənə'zāsнən/ noun.

ball[1] /bôl/ ▶ **noun 1** a rounded object that is kicked, thrown, or hit in a game. **2** a single throw or kick of the ball in a game. **3** a rounded part or thing: *the ball of the foot.*

– SYNONYMS **sphere,** globe, orb, globule, spheroid.

▶ **verb 1** squeeze or form something into a ball. **2** (**ball something up**) bungle something.
– PHRASES **the ball is in your court** it is up to you to make the next move. **keep one's eye on** (or **take one's eye off**) **the ball** keep (or fail to keep) one's attention focused on the matter in hand. **on the ball** alert to new ideas or methods. **play ball** informal cooperate. **start** (or **get** or **set**) **the ball rolling** make a start.
– ORIGIN Old Norse.

ball[2] ▶ **noun** a formal social gathering for dancing.
– PHRASES **have a ball** informal enjoy oneself very much.
– ORIGIN from Latin *ballare* 'to dance.'

bal·lad /'baləd/ ▶ **noun 1** a poem or song telling a popular story. **2** a slow sentimental or romantic song.
– DERIVATIVES **bal·lad·eer** /,balə'di(ə)r/ noun **bal·lad·ry** /'balədrē/ noun.
– ORIGIN from Latin *ballare* 'to dance.'

bal·lade /bə'läd/ ▶ **noun 1** a poem with three eight-line stanzas, each ending with the same line, and a short stanza (envoy) in conclusion. **2** a short, lyrical piece of music, especially one for piano.
– ORIGIN earlier spelling of **BALLAD**.

ball-and-sock·et joint ▶ **noun** a joint in which a rounded end lies in a socket, allowing movement in all directions.

bal·last /'baləst/ ▶ **noun 1** a heavy substance carried by a ship or hot-air balloon to keep it stable. **2** gravel or coarse stone used to form the base of a railroad track or road.
– ORIGIN probably German or Scandinavian.

ball bear·ing ▶ **noun 1** a bearing in which the parts are separated by a ring of small metal balls that reduce friction. **2** a ball used in such a bearing.

ball·boy /'bôl,boi/ (or **ballgirl** /'bôl,gərl/) ▶ **noun** a boy (or girl) who retrieves balls that go out of play during a game such as tennis or baseball.

ball·cock /'bôl,käk/ ▶ **noun** a valve that automatically fills up a tank when liquid is drawn from it.

bal·le·ri·na /,balə'rēnə/ ▶ **noun** a female ballet dancer.
– ORIGIN from Italian *ballerino* 'dancing master.'

bal·let /ba'lā/ ▶ **noun 1** an artistic form of dancing performed to music, using set steps and gestures. **2** a creative work of this form.
– DERIVATIVES **bal·let·ic** /ba'letik, bə-/ adjective.
– ORIGIN Italian *balletto* 'a little dance.'

bal·let·o·mane /bə'letə,mān, ba-/ ▶ **noun** a ballet enthusiast.

ball game ▶ **noun** a game played with a ball.
– PHRASES **a different** (or **whole new**) **ball game** informal a situation that is completely different from a previous one.

bal·lis·tic /bə'listik/ ▶ **adjective 1** relating to projectiles or their flight through the air. **2** moving under the force of gravity only.
– PHRASES **go ballistic** informal fly into a rage.
– ORIGIN from Greek *ballein* 'to throw.'

bal·lis·tic mis·sile ▶ **noun** a missile that is initially powered and guided but falls under gravity onto its target.

bal·lis·tics /bə'listiks/ ▶ **plural noun** (treated as sing.) the science of projectiles and firearms.

bal·loon /bə'lo͞on/ ▶ **noun 1** a small rubber bag that is inflated and used as a toy or a decoration. **2** (also **hot-air balloon**) a large bag filled with hot air or gas to make it rise in the air, with a basket for passengers hanging from it. **3** a rounded outline containing the words or thoughts of characters in a comic strip. ▶ **verb 1** swell outward. **2** increase rapidly: *the company's debt*

ballooned in the last five years. **3** (usu. as n. **ballooning**) travel by hot-air balloon.
– DERIVATIVES **bal·loon·ist** noun.
– ORIGIN French *ballon* or Italian *ballone* 'large ball.'

bal·lot /'balət/ ▶ **noun 1** a way of voting secretly on something, usually by placing paper slips in a box. **2** (**the ballot**) the total number of votes cast in such a way.

– SYNONYMS **vote,** poll, election, referendum, show of hands, plebiscite.

▶ **verb** (**ballots, balloting, balloted**) **1** obtain a secret vote from members. **2** cast one's vote on an issue.
– ORIGIN Italian *ballotta* 'little ball' (from the former practice of voting by placing a ball in a container).

ball·park /'bôl,pärk/ ▶ **noun 1** a baseball field or stadium. **2** informal an area or range within which an estimate is likely to be correct. ▶ **adjective** informal approximate: *a ballpark figure.*

ball·point pen /'bôl,point/ ▶ **noun** a pen with a tiny ball as its writing point.

ball·room /'bôl,rōōm, -,rŏŏm/ ▶ **noun** a large room for formal dancing.

ball·room danc·ing ▶ **noun** formal social dancing in couples.

balls /'bôlz/ vulgar slang ▶ **plural noun 1** testicles. **2** courage; nerve.

balls-out ▶ **adjective** informal without moderation or restraint.

balls·y /'bôlzē/ ▶ **adjective** (**ballsier, ballsiest**) informal bold and confident.

ball valve ▶ **noun** a one-way valve opened and closed by pressure on a ball that fits into a cup-shaped opening.

bal·ly·hoo /'balē,hōō/ ▶ **noun** informal excessive publicity or fuss.
– ORIGIN unknown.

balm /bä(l)m/ ▶ **noun 1** a fragrant ointment used to heal or soothe the skin. **2** something that soothes or heals: *the story was balm to American hearts.*
– ORIGIN from Latin *balsamum* 'balsam.'

balm·y /'bä(l)mē/ ▶ **adjective** (**balmier, balmiest**) **1** (of the weather or a period of time) pleasantly warm. **2** informal mad or foolish.

ba·lo·ney /bə'lōnē/ ▶ **noun** informal nonsense.
– ORIGIN perhaps from *bologna*, a type of smoked sausage.

bal·sa /'bôlsə/ (also **balsa wood**) ▶ **noun** very lightweight wood from a tropical American tree, used for making models.
– ORIGIN Spanish, 'raft.'

bal·sam /'bôlsəm/ ▶ **noun 1** a scented resin obtained from certain trees and shrubs, used in perfumes and medicines. **2** a plant grown for its pink or purple flowers.
– DERIVATIVES **bal·sam·ic** /bôl'samik/ adjective.
– ORIGIN Greek *balsamon.*

bal·sam·ic vin·e·gar ▶ **noun** dark, sweet Italian vinegar that has been matured in wooden barrels.

Bal·tic /'bôltik/ ▶ **adjective** relating to the Baltic Sea or the countries on its eastern shores.

bal·us·ter /'baləstər/ ▶ **noun** a short pillar forming part of a series supporting a rail.
– ORIGIN French *balustre.*

bal·us·trade /'balə,strād/ ▶ **noun** a railing supported by balusters.
– DERIVATIVES **bal·us·trad·ed** adjective.

bam·bi·no /bam'bēnō/ ▶ **noun** (pl. **bambini** /-nē/ or **bambinos**) a baby or young child.
– ORIGIN Italian, 'little silly.'

bam·boo /,bam'bōō/ ▶ **noun** a giant tropical grass with hollow woody stems.
– ORIGIN Malay.

bam·boo shoot ▶ **noun** a young shoot of bamboo, eaten as a vegetable.

bam·boo·zle /bam'bōōzəl/ ▶ **verb** informal cheat or deceive someone.
– ORIGIN unknown.

ban[1] /ban/ ▶ **verb** (**bans, banning, banned**) officially forbid something or prevent someone from doing something.

– SYNONYMS **prohibit,** forbid, veto, proscribe, outlaw, make illegal, bar, debar, prevent, exclude, banish.
– ANTONYMS permit, admit.

▶ **noun** an official order forbidding something.

– SYNONYMS **prohibition,** embargo, veto, boycott, bar, proscription, moratorium, injunction.

– ORIGIN Old English, 'summon by a public proclamation.'

CHOOSE THE RIGHT WORD

See **PROHIBIT**.

ban[2] /bän/ ▶ **noun** (pl. **bani** /'bänē/) a unit of money of Romania, equal to one hundredth of a leu.
– ORIGIN Romanian.

ba·nal /'bānl, bə'nal, -'näl/ ▶ **adjective** very ordinary and unoriginal: *songs with banal, repeated words.*

– SYNONYMS **unoriginal,** unimaginative, uninspired, trite, hackneyed, clichéd, platitudinous, commonplace, stereotyped, overused, stale, boring, dull, obvious, predictable, tired, pedestrian; informal corny, old hat.
– ANTONYMS original.

– DERIVATIVES **ba·nal·i·ty** /bə'nalitē/ noun (pl. **banalities**) **ba·nal·ly** adverb.
– ORIGIN first meaning 'compulsory': from French *ban* 'summons.'

ba·nan·a /bə'nanə/ ▶ **noun** a long curved fruit of a tropical or subtropical treelike grass, with yellow skin and soft flesh.
– PHRASES **go bananas** informal become (or be) insane or angry.
– ORIGIN from an African language.

ba·nan·a re·pub·lic ▶ **noun** derogatory a small country that is politically unstable because its economy is dominated by a single export controlled by foreign businesses.

ba·nan·a split ▶ **noun** a dessert made with bananas cut down the middle and filled with ice cream, sauce, whipped cream, and nuts.

band[1] /band/ ▶ **noun 1** a flat, thin strip or loop of material used as a fastener, for reinforcement, or as decoration. **2** a stripe or strip of a different color or nature from its surroundings: *a band of cloud.* **3** a range of frequencies or wavelengths in a spectrum: *the UHF band.*

– SYNONYMS **1 loop,** wristband, headband, ring, hoop, circlet, belt, sash, girdle, strap, strip, tape, circle. **2 stripe,** strip, line, belt, bar, streak, border, swath.

▶ **verb 1** fit a band on or around something. **2** mark something with a stripe or stripes.
– DERIVATIVES **band·ing** noun.
– ORIGIN Old English.

band² ▶ **noun 1** a small group of musicians and singers who play pop, jazz, or rock music. **2** a group of musicians who play brass, wind, or percussion instruments. **3** a group of people with a shared interest or purpose.

– SYNONYMS **1 (musical) group,** pop group, rock group, ensemble, orchestra; informal combo. **2 gang,** group, mob, pack, troop, troupe, company, set, party, crew, body, team; informal bunch.

▶ **verb** form a group to achieve the same aim: *people banded together to help each other.*
– ORIGIN Old French *bande.*

band·age /ˈbandij/ ▶ **noun** a strip of material used to bind up a wound or to protect an injury.

– SYNONYMS **dressing,** covering, plaster, compress, gauze, lint.

▶ **verb** bind a wound or part of the body with a bandage.

– SYNONYMS **bind,** dress, cover, strap (up).

– ORIGIN French.

Band-Aid /ˈband ˌād/ ▶ **noun** trademark **1** an adhesive bandage with a gauze pad in the center, used to cover minor wounds. **2** a makeshift or temporary solution.

ban·dan·na /banˈdanə/ (also **bandana**) ▶ **noun** a square of brightly colored fabric worn on the head or around the neck.
– ORIGIN Hindi.

band·box /ˈbandˌbäks/ ▶ **noun** a circular cardboard box for carrying hats.

ban·deau /banˈdō/ ▶ **noun** (pl. **bandeaux** /-ˈdōz/) **1** a narrow band worn around the head to hold the hair in position. **2** a woman's strapless top consisting of a band of fabric fitting around the bust.
– ORIGIN Old French *bandel* 'small band.'

ban·di·coot /ˈbandiˌko͞ot/ ▶ **noun** an insect-eating marsupial of Australia and New Guinea.
– ORIGIN from a word in an Indian language meaning 'pig-rat.'

ban·dit /ˈbandit/ ▶ **noun** a member of a gang of armed robbers.

– SYNONYMS **robber,** thief, raider, mugger, pirate, outlaw, hijacker, looter, marauder, gangster; literary brigand; historical rustler, highwayman, footpad.

– DERIVATIVES **ban·dit·ry** noun.
– ORIGIN from Italian *bandito* 'banned.'

band·lead·er /ˈbandˌlēdər/ ▶ **noun** a player at the head of a musical band.

ban·do·lier /ˌbandəˈli(ə)r/ (also **bandoleer**) ▶ **noun** a shoulder belt with loops or pockets for cartridges.
– ORIGIN French *bandoulière.*

band·saw /ˈbandˌsô/ ▶ **noun** a power saw consisting of an endless moving steel belt with a serrated edge.

band·stand /ˈbandˌstand/ ▶ **noun** a platform for a band to play on, covered if out of doors.

band·wag·on /ˈbandˌwagən/ ▶ **noun** an activity or cause that has suddenly become fashionable or popular: *the company is jumping on the Green bandwagon.*

band·width /ˈbandˌwidTH/ ▶ **noun 1** a range of frequencies used in telecommunications. **2** the ability of a computer network or other telecommunication system to transmit signals.

ban·dy¹ /ˈbandē/ ▶ **adjective** (**bandier, bandiest**) (of a person's legs) curved outward so that the knees are wide apart.
– ORIGIN perhaps from former *bandy* 'curved hockey stick.'

ban·dy² ▶ **verb** (**bandies, bandying, bandied**) pass on or discuss an idea, rumor, or name in a casual or uninformed way: *$40,000 is the figure that has been bandied about.*
– PHRASES **bandy words** exchange angry remarks.
– ORIGIN perhaps from French *bander* 'take sides at tennis.'

bane /bān/ ▶ **noun** a cause of great distress or annoyance: *the phone was the bane of my existence.*
– ORIGIN Old English, 'thing causing death, poison.'

bang /baNG/ ▶ **noun 1** a sudden loud sharp noise. **2** a sudden painful blow. **3** (**bangs**) a fringe of hair cut straight across the forehead.

– SYNONYMS **1 crash,** crack, thud, thump, bump, boom, blast, clap, report, explosion. **2 blow,** bump, knock, hit, smack, crack, thump; informal bash, whack.

▶ **verb 1** hit or put down something forcefully and noisily. **2** make or cause to make a bang. **3** vulgar slang (of a man) have sex with someone.

– SYNONYMS **1 hit,** strike, beat, thump, hammer, knock, rap, pound, thud, punch, bump, smack, crack, slap, slam; informal bash, whack, clobber, clout, wallop. **2 crash,** boom, pound, explode, detonate, burst, blow up.

▶ **adverb** informal, chiefly Brit. exactly: *bang in the middle of town.*
– PHRASES **bang for one's** (or **the**) **buck** value or performance for cost: *get more bang for your buck by ordering the three-course lunch menu for $21.* **with a bang** suddenly or impressively.
– ORIGIN imitating the sound.

bang·er /ˈbaNGər/ ▶ **noun** Brit. informal **1** a sausage. **2** an old car. **3** a loud explosive firework.

Bang·la·desh·i /ˌbäNGgləˈdeSHē, ˌbaNGglə-/ ▶ **noun** (pl. **Bangladeshis**) a person from Bangladesh. ▶ **adjective** relating to Bangladesh.

ban·gle /ˈbaNGgəl/ ▶ **noun** a rigid bracelet worn around the arm.
– ORIGIN Hindi.

bang-up ▶ **adjective** informal excellent: *for a novice, he has done a bang-up job.*

ba·ni /ˈbänē/ plural of **BAN²**.

ban·ish /ˈbaniSH/ ▶ **verb 1** make someone leave a place as an official punishment. **2** get rid of: *I banished the thought from my mind.*

– SYNONYMS **1 exile,** expel, deport, eject, repatriate, transport, extradite, evict, throw out, exclude, shut out, ban. **2 dispel,** dismiss, disperse, scatter, dissipate, drive away, chase away, shut out.

– DERIVATIVES **ban·ish·ment** noun.
– ORIGIN Old French *banir.*

ban·is·ter /ˈbanəstər/ (also **bannister**) ▶ **noun 1** (also **banisters**) the uprights and handrail at the side of a staircase. **2** a single upright at the side of a staircase.
– ORIGIN from **BALUSTER**.

ban·jo /ˈbanjō/ ▶ **noun** (pl. **banjos** or **banjoes**) a musical instrument like a guitar, with a circular body and a long neck.
– DERIVATIVES **ban·jo·ist** /-ist/ noun.
– ORIGIN from *bandore*, a kind of lute.

bank[1] /baNGk/ ▶ **noun 1** the land alongside a river or lake. **2** a long, high slope, mound, or mass: *mud banks*. **3** a set of similar things grouped together in rows.

– SYNONYMS **1 edge,** shore, side, embankment, levee, margin, verge, brink. **2 slope,** rise, incline, gradient, grade, ramp, mound, pile, heap, ridge, hillock, knoll, bar, shoal, mass, drift. **3 array,** row, line, tier, group, series.

▶ **verb 1** heap or form a substance into a mass or mound. **2** (of an aircraft or vehicle) tilt sideways in making a turn. **3** build a road, railroad, or sports track higher at the outer edge of a bend.

– SYNONYMS **1 pile up,** heap up, stack up, amass. **2 tilt,** lean, tip, slant, incline, angle, list, camber, pitch.

– ORIGIN Old Norse.

bank[2] ▶ **noun 1** an organization offering financial services, especially loans and the safekeeping of customers' money. **2** a stock or supply available for use: *a blood bank*. **3** a place where something may be safely kept: *the computer's memory bank*. **4** (**the bank**) the store of money or tokens held by the banker in some gambling or board games.

– SYNONYMS **1 financial institution,** merchant bank, savings bank, finance company, trust company, credit union. **2 store,** reserve, stock, stockpile, supply, pool, fund, cache, hoard, deposit.

▶ **verb 1** deposit money or valuables in a bank. **2** have an account at a bank. **3** (**bank on**) rely on confidently: *he can't bank on their support*.

– SYNONYMS **1 deposit,** pay in, save. **2** (**bank on**) **rely on,** depend on, count on, place reliance on, bargain on, plan on; anticipate, expect; be confident of, be sure of, pin one's hopes/faith on, figure on.

– PHRASES **break the bank** informal cost more than one can afford.
– ORIGIN first meaning a money dealer's table: from Latin *banca* 'bench.'

bank·a·ble /ˈbaNGkəbəl/ ▶ **adjective** certain to bring profit and success.
– DERIVATIVES **bank·a·bil·i·ty** /ˌbaNGkəˈbilitē/ noun.

bank card ▶ **noun** a credit card, debit card, or ATM card issued by a bank.

bank·er /ˈbaNGkər/ ▶ **noun 1** a person who manages or owns a bank. **2** the person who keeps the bank in some gambling or board games.

bank hol·i·day ▶ **noun** Brit. a public holiday, when banks are officially closed.

bank·ing /ˈbaNGkiNG/ ▶ **noun** the business activity of a bank.

bank·note /ˈbaNGkˌnōt/ ▶ **noun** a piece of paper money issued by a central bank.

bank rate ▶ **noun** the rate of discount set by a central bank.

bank·roll /ˈbaNGkˌrōl/ ▶ **noun 1** a roll of banknotes. **2** available funds. ▶ **verb** informal support someone or something financially.

bank·rupt /ˈbaNGkˌrəpt, -rəpt/ ▶ **adjective 1** declared in law as unable to pay one's debts. **2** completely lacking in a particular good quality or value: *their cause is morally bankrupt*.

– SYNONYMS **insolvent,** ruined, in receivership. informal bust, broke, belly up, wiped out.
– ANTONYMS solvent.

▶ **noun** a person judged by a court to be bankrupt.
▶ **verb** make a person or organization bankrupt.
– DERIVATIVES **bank·rupt·cy** /ˈbaNGkˌrəp(t)sē, -rəp(t)sē/ noun (pl. **bankruptcies**).
– ORIGIN from Italian *banca rotta* 'broken bench.'

bank swal·low ▶ **noun** another term for **SAND MARTIN**.

ban·ner /ˈbanər/ ▶ **noun 1** a long strip of cloth bearing a slogan or design, hung up or carried on poles. **2** an advertisement on a website in the form of a bar, column, or box.

– SYNONYMS **1 placard,** sign, poster, notice. **2 flag,** standard, ensign, color(s), pennant, pennon, banderole.

▶ **adjective** excellent; outstanding: *a banner year*.
– ORIGIN Old French *baniere*.

ban·nis·ter /ˈbanəstər/ ▶ **noun** variant spelling of **BANISTER**.

banns /banz/ ▶ **plural noun** a public announcement of an intended marriage read out in a parish church.
– ORIGIN plural of **BAN**[1].

ban·quet /ˈbaNGkwit/ ▶ **noun** an elaborate and formal meal for many people.

– SYNONYMS **feast,** dinner; informal spread, blowout.

▶ **verb** (**banquets, banqueting, banqueted**) give or take part in a banquet.
– ORIGIN French, 'little bench.'

ban·quette /baNGˈket/ ▶ **noun** an upholstered bench along a wall.
– ORIGIN French.

ban·shee /ˈbanSHē/ ▶ **noun** (in Irish legend) a female spirit whose wailing warns of an impending death in a house.
– ORIGIN from Old Irish *ben síde* 'woman of the fairies.'

ban·tam /ˈbantəm/ ▶ **noun** a chicken of a small breed.
– ORIGIN probably named after the province of *Bantam* in Java.

ban·tam·weight /ˈbantəmˌwāt/ ▶ **noun** a weight in boxing and other sports between flyweight and featherweight.

ban·ter /ˈbantər/ ▶ **noun** the good-humored exchange of teasing remarks.

– SYNONYMS **repartee,** witty conversation, raillery, wordplay, cut and thrust, badinage, persiflage.

▶ **verb** exchange remarks in a good-humored teasing way.

– SYNONYMS **joke,** jest; informal josh, wisecrack.

– ORIGIN unknown.

Ban·tu /ˈbantoo͞/ ▶ **noun** (pl. same or **Bantus**) **1** a member of a large group of peoples of central and southern Africa. **2** the group of languages spoken by the Bantu.
– ORIGIN Bantu, 'people.'

USAGE

Bantu is a strongly offensive word in South African English, especially when used to refer to individual black people.

ban·yan /ˈbanyən/ (also **banian** pronunc. same) ▶ **noun** an Indian fig tree with spreading branches from which

roots grow downward to the ground and form new trunks.
– ORIGIN from Gujarati, 'trader' (because first used by Europeans to refer to a tree under which traders had built a pagoda).

ban·zai /ˈbanˈzī/ ▶ **exclamation** a cry used by the Japanese when going into battle or in greeting their emperor.
– ORIGIN Japanese, 'ten thousand years (of life to you).'

ba·o·bab /ˈbāōˌbab, ˈbä-ō-/ ▶ **noun** a short African tree with a very thick trunk and large edible fruit.
– ORIGIN probably from an African language.

bap·tism /ˈbapˌtizəm/ ▶ **noun** the Christian rite of sprinkling a person with water or dipping them in it, as a sign that they have been cleansed of sin and have entered the Church.
– DERIVATIVES **bap·tis·mal** /bapˈtizməl/ adjective.
– PHRASES **baptism of fire** a difficult new experience.
– ORIGIN from Greek *baptizein* 'immerse, baptize.'

Bap·tist /ˈbaptist/ ▶ **noun** a member of a Protestant group believing that only adults should be baptized and that this should be by total immersion in water.

bap·tis·tery /ˈbaptəstrē/ (also **baptistry**) ▶ **noun** (pl. **baptisteries**) a building or part of a church used for baptism.

bap·tize /ˈbapˌtīz, bapˈtīz/ ▶ **verb 1** admit someone to the Christian Church by the rite of baptism. **2** give a name or nickname to: *the media baptized the murderer 'The Babysitter'*

– SYNONYMS **1 christen. 2** *they were baptized into the church* **admit,** initiate, enroll, recruit. **3 name,** call, dub.

– ORIGIN Greek *baptizein* 'immerse, baptize.'

bar[1] /bär/ ▶ **noun 1** a long rigid piece of wood, metal, etc. **2** a counter, room, or place where alcoholic drinks or refreshments are served. **3** a small shop or counter serving refreshments or providing a service: *a snack bar*. **4** a barrier or obstacle: *her humble beginnings were no bar to becoming head of state*. **5** any of the short units into which a piece of music is divided, shown on a score by vertical lines. **6** (**the bar**) the place in a courtroom where an accused person stands during a trial. **7** (**the Bar**) the legal profession. **8** (**the Bar**) lawyers as a group.

– SYNONYMS **1 rod,** stick, pole, batten, shaft, rail, spar, strut, crosspiece, beam. **2 block,** slab, cake, tablet, wedge, ingot. **3 counter,** table, buffet. **4 tavern,** barroom, taproom, pub, club, sports bar, cocktail lounge, lounge, roadhouse, saloon; informal watering hole, nineteenth hole. **5 obstacle,** impediment, hindrance, obstruction, block, hurdle, barrier.
– ANTONYMS aid.

▶ **verb** (**bars, barring, barred**) **1** fasten something with a bar or bars. **2** forbid from doing something or prevent from going somewhere: *they were barred from entering the room*.

– SYNONYMS **1 bolt,** lock, fasten, secure, block, barricade, obstruct. **2 prohibit,** debar, preclude, forbid, ban, exclude, obstruct, prevent, hinder, block, stop.

▶ **preposition** chiefly Brit. except for.
– DERIVATIVES **barred** adjective.
– PHRASES **bar none** with no exceptions. **behind bars** in prison.
– ORIGIN Old French *barre*.

bar[2] ▶ **noun** a unit of pressure equivalent to a hundred thousand newtons per square meter.
– ORIGIN Greek *baros* 'weight.'

bar·a·the·a /ˌbarəˈᴛʜēə/ ▶ **noun** a fine woolen cloth.
– ORIGIN unknown.

barb /bärb/ ▶ **noun 1** a sharp backward-pointing part of the head of an arrow, a fishhook, etc., that makes it difficult to remove from something it has pierced. **2** a spiteful remark. **3** a barbel at the mouth of some fish.
– DERIVATIVES **barb·less** adjective.
– ORIGIN from Latin *barba* 'beard.'

Bar·ba·di·an /bärˈbādēən/ ▶ **noun** a person from Barbados. ▶ **adjective** relating to Barbados.

bar·bar·i·an /bärˈbe(ə)rēən/ ▶ **noun 1** (in ancient times) a member of a people not belonging to the Greek, Roman, or Christian civilizations. **2** an uncivilized or cruel person.

– SYNONYMS **savage,** heathen, brute, beast, philistine, boor, yahoo, oaf, lout, vandal.

▶ **adjective** uncivilized or cruel.
– ORIGIN from Greek *barbaros* 'foreign.'

bar·bar·ic /bärˈbarik/ ▶ **adjective 1** savagely cruel. **2** lacking sophistication; primitive.

– SYNONYMS **1 cruel,** brutal, barbarous, brutish, savage, vicious, wicked, ruthless, vile, inhuman. **2 uncultured,** uncivilized, barbarian, philistine, boorish, loutish.
– ANTONYMS civilized.

– DERIVATIVES **bar·bar·i·cal·ly** adverb.

bar·ba·rism /ˈbärbəˌrizəm/ ▶ **noun 1** extreme cruelty. **2** an uncivilized or primitive state. **3** a word or expression that is badly formed according to traditional rules, e.g., the word *television*, which is formed from two different languages.

bar·bar·i·ty /bärˈbaritē/ ▶ **noun** (pl. **barbarities**) **1** extreme cruelty. **2** lack of culture and civilization.

bar·ba·rous /ˈbärbərəs/ ▶ **adjective 1** extremely cruel. **2** primitive; uncivilized.
– DERIVATIVES **bar·ba·rous·ly** adverb.

bar·be·cue /ˈbärbiˌkyo͞o/ ▶ **noun 1** an outdoor meal or party at which food is grilled over an open fire. **2** a structure or device for grilling food outdoors. ▶ **verb** (**barbecues, barbecuing, barbecued**) cook on a barbecue.
– ORIGIN from Spanish *barbacoa* 'wooden frame.'

bar·be·cue sauce ▶ **noun** a spicy sauce made from tomatoes, chilies, etc.

barbed /bärbd/ ▶ **adjective 1** having a barb or barbs. **2** (of a remark) spiteful.

WORD TOOLKIT

See **SPIKY**.

barbed wire ▶ **noun** wire with clusters of short, sharp spikes along it.

bar·bel /ˈbärbəl/ ▶ **noun 1** a long, thin growth hanging from the mouth or snout of certain fish. **2** a large freshwater fish with barbels hanging from the mouth.
– ORIGIN Latin *barbellus* 'small barbel.'

bar·bell /ˈbärˌbel/ ▶ **noun** a long metal bar to which discs of varying weights are attached at each end, used for weightlifting.

bar·ber /ˈbärbər/ ▶ **noun** a person who cuts men's hair and shaves or trims beards as an occupation. ▶ **verb** cut or trim a man's hair.
– ORIGIN Old French *barbe* 'beard.'

bar·ber·ry /ˈbärˌberē, -bərē/ ▶ **noun** (pl. **barberries**) another term for **BERBERIS**.
– ORIGIN Old French *berberis*.

bar·ber·shop /ˈbärbərˌSHäp/ ▶ **noun** a style of singing in which four men sing in close harmony without musical accompaniment.

bar·bi·can /ˈbärbikən/ ▶ **noun** a double tower above a gate or drawbridge of a castle or fortified city.
– ORIGIN Old French *barbacane*.

bar·bi·tu·rate /bärˈbiCHərit, -əˌrāt/ ▶ **noun** a kind of sedative drug derived from a synthetic compound (**barbituric acid** /ˌbärbiˈCHo͝orik/).
– ORIGIN from German *Barbitursäure*.

barb·wire /ˈbärbˈwīr/ ▶ **noun** barbed wire.

bar code ▶ **noun** a set of stripes printed on a product, able to be read by a computer to provide information on prices and quantities in stock.

bard /bärd/ ▶ **noun 1** old use or literary a poet. **2** (**the Bard**) Shakespeare. **3** (**Bard**) the winner of a prize for Welsh verse at an eisteddfod.
– DERIVATIVES **bard·ic** adjective.
– ORIGIN Celtic.

bare /be(ə)r/ ▶ **adjective 1** not clothed or covered. **2** without the appropriate or usual covering or contents: *a big, bare room*. **3** without detail; basic. **4** only just enough: *a bare majority*.

– SYNONYMS **1 naked,** unclothed, undressed, uncovered, stripped, with nothing on, nude; informal without a stitch on, in the altogether, buck naked, in one's birthday suit. **2 empty,** unfurnished, clear, undecorated, unadorned, bleak, austere. **3 basic,** essential, fundamental, plain, straightforward, simple, unembellished, pure, stark, bald, cold, hard.
– ANTONYMS dressed.

▶ **verb** uncover or reveal: *the dog bared its teeth*.
– DERIVATIVES **bare·ness** noun.
– PHRASES **with one's bare hands** without using tools or weapons.
– ORIGIN Old English.

USAGE

On the confusion of **bare** and **bear**, see the note at **BEAR**[1].

CHOOSE THE RIGHT WORD

See **NAKED**.

bare·back /ˈbe(ə)rˌbak/ ▶ **adverb & adjective** on a horse without a saddle.

bare·boat /ˈbe(ə)rˌbōt/ ▶ **adjective** (of a boat or ship) hired without a crew.

bare·faced /ˈbe(ə)rˌfāst/ ▶ **adjective** shameless and undisguised: *a barefaced lie*.

bare·foot /ˈbe(ə)rˌfo͝ot/ (also **barefooted** /-ˌfo͝otid/) ▶ **adjective & adverb** wearing nothing on one's feet.

bare·head·ed /ˈbe(ə)rˌhedid/ ▶ **adjective & adverb** without a covering for one's head.

bare·ly /ˈbe(ə)rlē/ ▶ **adverb 1** only just; almost not: *she nodded, barely able to speak*. **2** only a short time before: *they had barely sat down when forty policemen swarmed in*. **3** in a simple and sparse way: *their barely furnished house*.

– SYNONYMS **hardly,** scarcely, only just, narrowly, by the skin of one's teeth, by a hair's breadth; informal by a whisker.

barf /bärf/ ▶ **verb** informal vomit.
– ORIGIN unknown.

bar·fly /ˈbärˌflī/ ▶ **noun** (pl. **barflies**) informal a person who spends much time drinking in bars.

bar·gain /ˈbärgən/ ▶ **noun 1** a thing offered for sale or bought for a low price. **2** an agreement made between people as to what each will do for the other.

– SYNONYMS **1 good buy,** (good) value for the money; informal steal, giveaway. **2 agreement,** arrangement, understanding, deal, contract, pact.

▶ **verb 1** negotiate the terms of an agreement. **2** (**bargain for/on**) expect: *I got more information than I'd bargained for*.

– SYNONYMS **1 haggle,** negotiate, discuss terms, deal, barter. **2** (**bargain for/on**) **expect,** anticipate, be prepared for, allow for, plan for, envisage, foresee, predict, count on, reckon on; informal figure on.

– DERIVATIVES **bar·gain·er** noun.
– PHRASES **drive a hard bargain** press hard for a deal in one's favor. **into the bargain** in addition.
– ORIGIN Old French *bargaine*.

bar·gain base·ment ▶ **noun** a part of a store where goods are sold cheaply, typically because they are old or imperfect: *investors snapped up shares at bargain-basement prices*.

barge /bärj/ ▶ **noun 1** a long flat-bottomed boat for carrying freight on canals and rivers. **2** a large ornamental boat used for pleasure or on ceremonial occasions. ▶ **verb 1** move forcefully or roughly: *she barged into the room and accosted him*. **2** (**barge in**) intrude or interrupt rudely or awkwardly.
– ORIGIN Old French.

bar graph (also **bar chart**) ▶ **noun** a diagram in which different quantities are represented by rectangles of varying height.

ba·ri·sta /bəˈrēstə/ ▶ **noun** a person who serves in a coffee bar.
– ORIGIN Italian, 'barman.'

bar·i·tone /ˈbariˌtōn/ ▶ **noun** an adult male singing voice between tenor and bass. ▶ **adjective** referring to an instrument that is second lowest in pitch in its family: *a baritone sax*.
– ORIGIN from Greek *barus* 'heavy' + *tonos* 'tone.'

bar·i·um /ˈbe(ə)rēəm, ˈbar-/ ▶ **noun** a soft, reactive metallic chemical element.
– ORIGIN from Greek *barus* 'heavy.'

bark[1] /bärk/ ▶ **noun** the sharp sudden cry of a dog, fox, or seal. ▶ **verb 1** give a bark. **2** shout something in a fierce or abrupt way.

– SYNONYMS **1 woof,** yap, yelp, bay. **2** *"Get out!" he barked* **shout,** snap, bawl, yell, roar, bellow, thunder; informal holler.
– ANTONYMS whisper.

– PHRASES **one's bark is worse than one's bite** one is not as fierce as one seems. **be barking up the wrong tree** informal be pursuing a mistaken idea or course of action.
– ORIGIN Old English.

bark[2] ▶ **noun** the tough protective outer covering of the trunk and branches of a tree.

– SYNONYMS **rind,** skin, peel, covering.

▶ **verb** scrape the skin off one's shin by accidentally hitting it.
– ORIGIN Old Norse.

bark[3] ▶ **noun** (also **barque**) old use or literary a ship or boat.
– ORIGIN variant of **BARQUE**.

bar·keep·er /ˈbärˌkēpər/ ▶ **noun** a person who owns or serves drinks in a bar.

bark·er /ˈbärkər/ ▶ **noun** informal a person at a fair who calls out to passersby to persuade them to visit a sideshow.

bar·ley /ˈbärlē/ ▶ **noun** a cereal plant with bristly heads, the grains of which are used in brewing and animal feed.
– ORIGIN Old English.

bar·maid /ˈbärˌmād/ ▶ **noun** a woman who serves drinks in a bar.

bar·man /ˈbärmən/ ▶ **noun** (pl. **barmen**) chiefly Brit. a man who serves drinks in a bar.

bar mitz·vah /ˌbär ˈmitsvə/ ▶ **noun** a religious ceremony in which a Jewish boy aged 13 takes on adult responsibilities under Jewish law.
– ORIGIN Hebrew, 'son of the commandment.'

barn /bärn/ ▶ **noun** a large farm building used for storage or for housing livestock.
– ORIGIN Old English, 'barley house.'

bar·na·cle /ˈbärnəkəl/ ▶ **noun** a small shellfish that attaches itself permanently to underwater surfaces.
– DERIVATIVES **bar·na·cled** adjective.
– ORIGIN Latin *bernaca*.

barn dance ▶ **noun** a party with country dancing.

barn owl ▶ **noun** a pale-colored owl with a heart-shaped face.

barn·storm /ˈbärnˌstôrm/ ▶ **verb 1** tour rural districts putting on shows or giving flying displays. **2** make a rapid tour as part of a political campaign.

barn·yard /ˈbärnˌyärd/ ▶ **noun** a farmyard.

bar·o·graph /ˈbarəˌgraf/ ▶ **noun** a barometer that records its readings on a moving chart.

ba·rom·e·ter /bəˈrämitər/ ▶ **noun 1** an instrument that measures atmospheric pressure, used in forecasting the weather. **2** an indicator of change: *furniture is a barometer of changing tastes.*
– DERIVATIVES **bar·o·met·ric** adjective.
– ORIGIN from Greek *baros* 'weight.'

bar·on /ˈbarən/ ▶ **noun 1** a man belonging to the lowest rank of the British nobility. **2** historical a man who held lands or property from the sovereign or an overlord. **3** a powerful person in business or industry: *a press baron.*
– DERIVATIVES **ba·ro·ni·al** /bəˈrōnēəl/ adjective.
– ORIGIN Latin *baro* 'man, warrior.'

bar·on·ess /ˈbarənis/ ▶ **noun 1** the wife or widow of a baron. **2** a woman holding the rank of baron.

bar·on·et /ˈbarənit, ˌbarəˈnet/ ▶ **noun** a man who holds a title below that of baron, with the status of a commoner.
– DERIVATIVES **bar·on·et·cy** noun.

bar·o·ny /ˈbarənē/ ▶ **noun** (pl. **baronies**) the rank and estates of a baron.

ba·roque /bəˈrōk/ ▶ **adjective 1** relating to a highly decorated style of European architecture, art, and music of the 17th and 18th centuries. **2** very elaborate or showy. ▶ **noun** the baroque style or period.
– ORIGIN from Portuguese *barroco* 'irregularly shaped pearl.'

ba·rouche /bəˈro͞osн/ ▶ **noun** historical a four-wheeled horse-drawn carriage with a collapsible hood over the rear half.
– ORIGIN Italian *baroccio* 'two-wheeled carriage.'

barque /bärk/ ▶ **noun 1** a sailing ship with three masts, one of which is rigged fore-and-aft while the others are square-rigged. **2** literary a boat.
– ORIGIN Latin *barca* 'ship's boat.'

bar·rack /ˈbarək/ ▶ **verb** provide soldiers with accommodations.

bar·racks /ˈbarəks/ ▶ **plural noun** (often treated as sing.) a large building or group of buildings for housing soldiers.

> – SYNONYMS **garrison,** camp, encampment, depot, billet, quarters, fort, cantonment.

– ORIGIN Italian *baracca* or Spanish *barraca* 'soldier's tent.'

bar·ra·cu·da /ˌbarəˈko͞odə/ ▶ **noun** (pl. same or **barracudas**) a large, slender predatory fish of tropical seas.
– ORIGIN unknown.

bar·rage /bəˈräzн/ ▶ **noun 1** a continuous artillery bombardment over a wide area. **2** an overwhelming number of things coming in rapid succession: *a barrage of questions.* **3** a barrier built across a river to control the water level.

> – SYNONYMS **1 bombardment,** gunfire, shelling, salvo, volley, fusillade; historical broadside. **2 deluge,** stream, storm, torrent, onslaught, flood, spate, tide, avalanche, hail, blaze. **3 dam,** barrier, weir, dike, embankment, wall.

▶ **verb** bombard someone with questions or complaints.
– ORIGIN from French *barrer* 'to bar.'

barre /bär/ ▶ **noun** a horizontal bar at waist level used by ballet dancers as a support during exercises.
– ORIGIN French.

bar·rel /ˈbarəl/ ▶ **noun 1** a large cylindrical container bulging out in the middle and with flat ends. **2** a measure of capacity for oil and beer (36 imperial gallons for beer and 35 for oil). **3** a tube forming part of an object such as a gun or a pen.

> – SYNONYMS **cask,** keg, butt, vat, tun, drum, hogshead, firkin.

▶ **verb** (**barrels, barreling, barreled**) **1** put something into a barrel or barrels. **2** informal drive or move very fast.
– PHRASES **over a barrel** informal at a great disadvantage.
– ORIGIN Latin *barriclus* 'small cask.'

> **WORD LINKS**
>
> **cooper** *person who makes barrels*

bar·rel or·gan ▶ **noun** a small pipe organ that plays a preset tune when a handle is turned.

bar·rel vault ▶ **noun** a vault in a roof forming a half cylinder.

bar·ren /ˈbarən/ ▶ **adjective 1** (of land) too poor to produce vegetation. **2** (of a female animal) unable to bear young. **3** bleak and lifeless: *huge barren rooms.* **4** lacking meaning or value: *heads stuffed with barren facts.*

> – SYNONYMS **unproductive,** infertile, unfruitful, sterile, arid, desert, waste, lifeless, empty.
> – ANTONYMS fertile.

– DERIVATIVES **bar·ren·ness** noun.
– ORIGIN Old French *barhaine*.

> **CHOOSE THE RIGHT WORD**
>
> See **NAKED**.

bar·rette /bəˈret/ ▸ **noun** a hair clip.
– ORIGIN French, 'small bar.'

bar·ri·cade /ˈbariˌkād/ ▸ **noun** a makeshift barrier erected to block a road or entrance.

– SYNONYMS **barrier,** roadblock, blockade, obstacle, obstruction.

▸ **verb** block or defend something with a barricade.

– SYNONYMS **seal up,** close up, block off, shut off/up, defend, protect, fortify, occupy.

– ORIGIN from Spanish *barrica* 'cask' (barrels often being used to build barricades).

bar·ri·er /ˈbarēər/ ▸ **noun 1** an obstacle that prevents movement or access. **2** something that prevents or hinders communication or progress: *a language barrier.*

– SYNONYMS **1 fence,** railing, barricade, hurdle, bar, blockade, roadblock. **2** *a barrier to international trade* **obstacle,** obstruction, hurdle, stumbling block, bar, impediment, hindrance, curb.

– ORIGIN Old French *barriere.*

bar·ri·er meth·od ▸ **noun** contraception using a device or preparation that prevents sperm from reaching an ovum.

bar·ri·er reef ▸ **noun** a coral reef close to the shore but separated from it by a channel of deep water.

bar·ring /ˈbäriNG/ ▸ **preposition** except for; if not for.

bar·ri·o /ˈbärēˌō/ ▸ **noun** (pl. **barrios**) **1** (in a Spanish-speaking country) a district of a town. **2** (in the US) the Spanish-speaking quarter of a town or city.
– ORIGIN Spanish.

bar·ris·ter /ˈbarəstər/ ▸ **noun** chiefly Brit. a lawyer qualified to argue a case in court, especially in the higher courts. Compare with **SOLICITOR**.
– ORIGIN from **BAR**[1].

bar·room /ˈbärˌro͞om, -ˌro͝om/ ▸ **noun** a room where alcoholic drinks are served over a counter.

bar·row[1] /ˈbarō/ ▸ **noun 1** a metal frame with two wheels used to carry objects such as luggage. **2** a wheelbarrow.
– ORIGIN Old English, 'stretcher, bier.'

bar·row[2] ▸ **noun** an ancient burial mound.
– ORIGIN Old English.

bar·tend·er /ˈbärˌtendər/ ▸ **noun** a person serving drinks at a bar.
– DERIVATIVES **bar·tend·ing** noun.

bar·ter /ˈbärtər/ ▸ **verb** exchange goods or services for other goods or services.

– SYNONYMS **1 swap,** trade, exchange, sell. **2 haggle,** bargain, negotiate, deal.

▸ **noun** trading by bartering.
– ORIGIN probably from Old French *barater* 'deceive.'

bar·y·on /ˈbarēˌän/ ▸ **noun** Physics a subatomic particle with a mass equal to or greater than that of a proton.
– ORIGIN from Greek *barus* 'heavy.'

ba·sal /ˈbāsəl, -zəl/ ▸ **adjective** chiefly technical forming or belonging to a bottom layer or base.

ba·sal met·a·bol·ic rate ▸ **noun** the rate at which the body uses energy while at rest to maintain vital functions such as breathing.

ba·salt /bəˈsôlt/ ▸ **noun** a dark fine-grained volcanic rock.
– DERIVATIVES **ba·sal·tic** /-tik/ adjective.
– ORIGIN from Greek *basanos* 'touchstone.'

bas·cule bridge /ˈbaskyo͞ol/ ▸ **noun** a type of bridge with a section that can be raised and lowered using counterweights.
– ORIGIN French *bascule* 'seesaw.'

base[1] /bās/ ▸ **noun 1** the lowest or supporting part of something. **2** a foundation, support, or starting point: *the town's economic base collapsed.* **3** the main place where a person works or stays. **4** a center of operations: *a military base.* **5** a main element or ingredient to which others are added. **6** Chemistry a substance capable of reacting with an acid to form a salt and water. **7** Mathematics the number on which a system of counting is based, e.g., 10 in conventional notation. **8** Baseball each of the four stations that must be reached in turn to score a run.

– SYNONYMS **1 foundation,** bottom, foot, support, stand, pedestal, plinth, rest. **2 basis,** foundation, bedrock, starting point, source, origin, root(s), core, key component. **3 headquarters,** camp, site, station, settlement, post, center.
– ANTONYMS top.

▸ **verb 1** use something as the foundation for: *the film is based on a novel.* **2** situate something at a center of operations.

– SYNONYMS **1 found,** build, construct, form, ground; (**be based on**) derive from, spring from, stem from, depend on. **2 locate,** situate, position, install, station, site.

– DERIVATIVES **based** adjective.
– PHRASES **touch base** informal briefly make or renew contact.
– ORIGIN Greek *basis* 'base, pedestal.'

base[2] ▸ **adjective 1** without moral principles: *the baser instincts of greed and selfishness.* **2** old use of low social class.

– SYNONYMS **sordid,** ignoble, low, mean, immoral, unscrupulous, unprincipled, dishonest, dishonorable, shameful, shabby, contemptible, despicable.
– ANTONYMS noble.

– DERIVATIVES **base·ness** noun.
– ORIGIN Latin *bassus* 'short.'

base·ball /ˈbāsˌbôl/ ▸ **noun** a team game played with a bat and ball on a diamond-shaped circuit of four bases, to all of which in turn a batter must run to score.

base·ball cap ▸ **noun** a cotton cap with a large bill.

base·board /ˈbāsˌbôrd/ ▸ **noun** a narrow wooden board running along the base of an interior wall.

base hit ▸ **noun** Baseball a fair ball hit such that the batter can advance safely to first base without aid of an error committed by the fielding team or a fielder's choice.

base jump ▸ **noun** a parachute jump from a fixed point, e.g., a high building.
– ORIGIN from *b*uilding, *a*ntenna-tower, *s*pan, *e*arth (referring to the types of structure used).

base·less /ˈbāslis/ ▸ **adjective** not based on fact; untrue.

base·line /ˈbāsˌlīn/ ▸ **noun 1** a minimum or starting point used for comparisons. **2** (in tennis, volleyball, etc.) the line marking each end of a court. **3** Baseball the line between bases, which a runner must stay close to.

base·man /ˈbāsmən/ ▸ **noun** (pl. **basemen**) Baseball a fielder designated to cover first, second, or third base.

base·ment /ˈbāsmənt/ ▸ **noun** a room or floor below ground level.
– ORIGIN probably from former Dutch, 'foundation.'

base met·al ▶ noun a common nonprecious metal such as copper, tin, or zinc.

base on balls ▶ noun Baseball another term for WALK (sense 5 of the noun).

ba·ses /ˈbāsēz/ plural of BASE[1] and BASIS.

bash /basʜ/ informal ▶ verb **1** hit someone or something hard. **2** (**bash something out**) produce something rapidly and carelessly. ▶ noun **1** a heavy blow. **2** a party.
– DERIVATIVES **ba·sher** noun.
– ORIGIN perhaps from BANG and SMASH.

bash·ful /ˈbasʜfəl/ ▶ adjective shy and easily embarrassed.

– SYNONYMS **shy,** reserved, diffident, inhibited, retiring, reticent, reluctant, shrinking, self-effacing, unassertive, timid, nervous, self-conscious.
– ANTONYMS bold, confident.

– DERIVATIVES **bash·ful·ly** adverb **bash·ful·ness** noun.
– ORIGIN from ABASHED.

BASIC /ˈbāsik/ ▶ noun a simple high-level computer programming language.
– ORIGIN from *Beginners' All-purpose Symbolic Instruction Code*.

ba·sic /ˈbāsik/ ▶ adjective **1** forming an essential foundation; fundamental: *certain basic rules must be obeyed*. **2** consisting of the minimum required or offered: *a basic wage*. **3** Chemistry containing or having the properties of a base; alkaline.

– SYNONYMS **1 fundamental,** essential, vital, primary, principal, cardinal, elementary, intrinsic, central, pivotal, critical, key, focal. **2 plain,** simple, unsophisticated, straightforward, adequate, spartan, stark, severe, austere, limited, meager, rudimentary, patchy, sketchy, minimal, crude, makeshift.
– ANTONYMS unimportant, luxurious.

▶ noun (**basics**) essential facts or principles of a subject.

– SYNONYMS **fundamentals,** essentials, first principles, foundations, preliminaries, groundwork, essence, basis, core; informal nitty-gritty, brass tacks, nuts and bolts, ABCs.

ba·si·cal·ly /ˈbāsik(ə)lē/ ▶ adverb **1** in the most fundamental respects. **2** used to sum up a more complex situation: *I basically did the same thing*.

– SYNONYMS **fundamentally,** essentially, first and foremost, primarily, at heart, intrinsically, inherently, principally, chiefly, above all, mostly, mainly, on the whole, by and large; informal at the end of the day.

bas·il /ˈbāzəl, ˈbazəl/ ▶ noun an herb of the mint family, used in cooking.
– ORIGIN from Greek *basilikos* 'royal.'

ba·sil·i·ca /bəˈsilikə/ ▶ noun **1** (in ancient Rome) a large oblong public building with two rows of columns and a domed recess at one end. **2** a Christian church of a similar design.
– ORIGIN from Greek *basilikos* 'royal.'

bas·i·lisk /ˈbasəˌlisk, ˈbaz-/ ▶ noun **1** a mythical reptile whose gaze or breath could kill. **2** a long, slender Central American lizard.
– ORIGIN Greek *basiliskos* 'little king, serpent.'

ba·sin /ˈbāsən/ ▶ noun **1** a large bowl or open container for preparing food or holding liquid. **2** a circular valley or natural depression. **3** an area drained by a river and its tributaries. **4** an enclosed area of water for mooring boats.

– SYNONYMS **bowl,** dish, pan, container, receptacle, vessel.

– ORIGIN Latin *bacinus*.

ba·sis /ˈbāsis/ ▶ noun (pl. **bases** /-sēz/) **1** the underlying support for an idea or process. **2** the principles according to which an activity is carried on: *she needed coaching on a regular basis*.

– SYNONYMS **1** *the basis of his method* **foundation,** support, base, reasoning, rationale, defense, reason, grounds, justification. **2** *the basis of discussion* **starting point,** base, point of departure, beginning, premise, fundamental point/principle, cornerstone, core, heart. **3** *on a part-time basis* **footing,** condition, status, position, arrangement.

– ORIGIN Greek, 'step, pedestal.'

bask /bask/ ▶ verb **1** lie in warmth and sunlight for pleasure. **2** (**bask in**) take great pleasure in: *he was basking in the glory of his first book*.

– SYNONYMS **1 laze,** lie, lounge, relax, sprawl, loll, luxuriate. **2 revel,** wallow, delight, take pleasure, enjoy, relish, savor.

– ORIGIN perhaps related to Old Norse, 'bathe.'

bas·ket /ˈbaskit/ ▶ noun **1** a container for holding or carrying things, made from interwoven strips of cane or wire. **2** Basketball a net fixed on a hoop, used as the goal. **3** Basketball a goal scored. **4** a group or range of currencies or investments.
– ORIGIN Old French.

bas·ket·ball /ˈbaskitˌbôl/ ▶ noun a team game in which goals are scored by throwing a ball through a net fixed on a hoop.

bas·ket case ▶ noun informal a useless person or thing.
– ORIGIN first referring to a soldier who had lost all four limbs.

bas·ket·ry /ˈbaskitrē/ ▶ noun **1** the craft of basketmaking. **2** baskets as a whole.

bas·ket·work /ˈbaskitˌwərk/ ▶ noun material woven in the style of a basket.

bask·ing shark ▶ noun a large shark that feeds on plankton and swims slowly close to the surface.

bas·ma·ti rice /bäsˈmätē/ ▶ noun a kind of long-grain Indian rice with a delicate aroma.
– ORIGIN Hindi, 'fragrant.'

Basque /bask/ ▶ noun **1** a member of a people living in the western Pyrenees in France and Spain. **2** the language of the Basques.
– ORIGIN Latin *Vasco* 'inhabitant of Vasconia' (the Latin name also of Gascony in SW France).

bas-re·lief /ˌbä rəˈlēf/ ▶ noun Art low relief.
– ORIGIN Italian *basso-rilievo*.

bass[1] /bās/ ▶ noun **1** the lowest adult male singing voice. **2** informal a bass guitar or double bass. **3** the low-frequency output of transmitted or reproduced sound. ▶ adjective referring to an instrument that is lowest in pitch in its family: *a bass clarinet*.

– SYNONYMS **low,** deep, resonant, sonorous, rumbling, booming, resounding.
– ANTONYMS high.

– DERIVATIVES **bass·ist** noun.
– ORIGIN alteration of BASE[2].

bass[2] /bas/ ▶ noun (pl. same or **basses**) **1** the common European freshwater perch (fish). **2** an American fish of the freshwater sunfish family. **3** a sea bass.
– ORIGIN Germanic.

bass clef /bās klef/ ▶ **noun** Music a clef placing F below middle C on the second-highest line of the staff.

bas·set /'basit/ (also **basset hound**) ▶ **noun** a breed of hunting dog with a long body, short legs, and long ears.
– ORIGIN from French *bas* 'low.'

bas·si·net /ˌbasə'net/ ▶ **noun** a child's wicker cradle.
– ORIGIN French, 'little basin.'

bas·so /'basō, bä-/ ▶ **noun** (pl. **bassos** or **bassi** /'bäsē/) a bass voice or vocal part.
– ORIGIN Italian, 'low.'

bas·soon /bə'so͞on, ba-/ ▶ **noun** a large bass woodwind instrument of the oboe family.
– DERIVATIVES **bas·soon·ist** noun.
– ORIGIN from Italian *basso* 'low.'

bas·so pro·fun·do /'basō prō'fəndō, 'bäsō/ ▶ **noun** (pl. **bassos profundos** or **bassi profundi** /'bäsē prō'fəndē/) a bass singer with an exceptionally low range.

bass·wood /'basˌwo͝od/ ▶ **noun** any of the linden trees native to North America.

bas·tard /'bastərd/ ▶ **noun 1** old use or derogatory a person born to parents who are not married to each other. **2** informal an unpleasant person. **3** informal a person of a specified kind: *the poor bastard.* ▶ **adjective** no longer in a pure or original form: *a bastard language.*
– ORIGIN Latin *bastardus.*

bas·tard·ize /'bastərˌdīz/ ▶ **verb** (often as adj. **bastardized**) make something impure by adding new elements: *a bastardized form of French.*
– DERIVATIVES **bas·tard·i·za·tion** /ˌbastərdi'zāsʜən/ noun.

bas·tar·dy /'bastərdē/ ▶ **noun** old use illegitimacy.

baste[1] /bāst/ ▶ **verb** pour fat or juices over meat during cooking.
– DERIVATIVES **ba·ster** noun.
– ORIGIN unknown.

baste[2] ▶ **verb** sew something with long, loose stitches in preparation for permanent sewing.
– ORIGIN Old French *bastir* 'sew lightly.'

bas·ti·na·do /ˌbastə'nādō, -'nädō/ ▶ **noun** chiefly historical a form of punishment or torture that involves caning the soles of someone's feet.
– ORIGIN from Spanish *bastón* 'stick, cudgel.'

bas·tion /'bascʜən/ ▶ **noun 1** a projecting part of a fortification allowing an increased angle of fire. **2** something that preserves particular principles or activities: *the town was a bastion of conservatism.*
– ORIGIN Italian *bastione.*

bat[1] /bat/ ▶ **noun** an implement with a handle and a solid surface, used in sports for hitting the ball. ▶ **verb** (**bats**, **batting**, **batted**) **1** (in sports) take the role of hitting rather than fielding the ball. **2** hit someone or something with the flat of one's hand. **3** (**bat something around/about**) informal casually discuss an idea.
– PHRASES **bat a thousand** informal produce consistently favorable outcomes; be consistently correct about something or a series of things. **go to bat for** informal support.
– ORIGIN Old English, 'club, stick, staff.'

bat[2] ▶ **noun 1** a flying mammal with wings that extend between the fingers and limbs, active at night. **2** (**old bat**) informal an unattractive and unpleasant woman.
– PHRASES **have bats in the belfry** informal be eccentric or crazy.
– ORIGIN Scandinavian; sense 2 is from an old slang term for 'prostitute' or from BATTLEAX.

bat[3] ▶ **verb** (**bats**, **batting**, **batted**) flutter one's eyelashes.
– PHRASES **not bat an eyelid** informal show no surprise or concern.
– ORIGIN from Old French *batre* 'to beat.'

batch /bacʜ/ ▶ **noun 1** a quantity of goods produced or dispatched at one time. **2** a group of people or things. **3** Computing a group of records processed as a single unit.

– SYNONYMS **group**, quantity, lot, bunch, cluster, raft, set, collection, bundle, pack, consignment, shipment.

▶ **verb** arrange things in batches.
– ORIGIN first meaning 'quantity baked at one time': from Old English.

bat·ed /'bātid/ ▶ **adjective** (in phrase **with bated breath**) in great suspense.
– ORIGIN from ABATE.

USAGE

The correct spelling is **with bated breath** (not *baited*).

bath /baᴛʜ, bäᴛʜ/ ▶ **noun 1** a large tub that is filled with water for washing one's body. **2** an act of washing in a bath. **3** (also **baths**) Brit. a building containing a public swimming pool or washing facilities. **4** a container holding a liquid in which an object is immersed in chemical processing. ▶ **verb** Brit. wash someone in a bath.
– ORIGIN Old English.

bathe /bā_ᴛʜ_/ ▶ **verb 1** wash by immersing one's body in water. **2** chiefly Brit. take a swim. **3** soak or wipe something gently with liquid to clean or soothe it. **4** fill with or envelop in something: *my desk is bathed in sunlight.*

– SYNONYMS **1 swim**, take a dip. **2 clean**, wash, rinse, wet, soak, steep. **3 envelop**, cover, flood, fill, wash, pervade, suffuse.

▶ **noun** Brit. a swim.
– DERIVATIVES **bath·er** noun.
– ORIGIN Old English.

bath·house /'baᴛʜˌhous/ ▶ **noun 1** a building with baths for communal use. **2** a building where swimmers change clothes.

bath·ing suit (Brit. also **bathing costume**) ▶ **noun** a swimsuit.

ba·thos /'bāᴛʜäs/ ▶ **noun** (in literature) an unintentional change in mood from the important and serious to the trivial or ridiculous.
– DERIVATIVES **ba·thet·ic** /bə'ᴛʜetik/ adjective.
– ORIGIN Greek, 'depth.'

bath·robe /'baᴛʜˌrōb/ ▶ **noun** a robe, typically made of terrycloth.

bath·room /'baᴛʜˌro͞om, -ˌro͝om/ ▶ **noun 1** a room containing a bathtub or shower and usually also a washbasin and toilet. **2** a room containing a toilet.

– SYNONYMS **restroom**, washroom, toilet, men's/ladies' room, powder room, lavatory, comfort station, urinal. Military latrine, head; informal facilities, little boys'/girls' room, can, john; Brit. informal WC, loo, the Ladies/Gents; old use commode, privy, outhouse.

bath salts ▶ **plural noun** crystals that are dissolved in bathwater to soften or perfume it.

bath·tub /'baᴛʜˌtəb/ ▶ **noun** a tub in which to bathe.

bath·y·sphere /'baᴛʜəˌsfir/ ▶ **noun** a manned spherical vessel for deep-sea observation.
– ORIGIN from Greek *bathus* 'deep.'

ba·tik /bəˈtēk/ ▸ **noun** a method of producing colored designs on cloth by waxing the parts not to be dyed.
– ORIGIN from Javanese, 'painted.'

ba·tiste /bəˈtēst/ ▸ **noun** a fine linen or cotton fabric.
– ORIGIN French.

bat mitz·vah /bät ˈmitsvə/ ▸ **noun** a religious ceremony in which a Jewish girl aged twelve years and a day takes on adult responsibilities under Jewish law.
– ORIGIN Hebrew, 'daughter of commandment.'

ba·ton /bəˈtän/ ▸ **noun 1** a thin stick used to conduct an orchestra or choir. **2** a short stick passed from runner to runner in a relay race. **3** a stick carried and twirled by a drum major. **4** a police officer's club.

– SYNONYMS **stick,** rod, staff, wand, truncheon, club, mace.

– ORIGIN from Latin *bastum* 'stick.'

bats·man /ˈbatsmən/ ▸ **noun** (pl. **batsmen**) a player who bats in cricket.

bat·tal·ion /bəˈtalyən/ ▸ **noun** a large body of troops, forming part of a brigade.
– ORIGIN French *bataillon.*

bat·ten¹ /ˈbatn/ ▸ **noun** a long wooden or metal strip for strengthening or securing something. ▸ **verb** strengthen or fasten something with battens.
– PHRASES **batten down the hatches 1** secure a ship's tarpaulins. **2** prepare for a difficult situation.
– ORIGIN Old French *batant.*

bat·ten² ▸ **verb** (**batten on**) thrive or prosper at the expense of: *multinational monopolies batten on the working classes.*
– ORIGIN Old Norse, 'get better.'

bat·ter¹ /ˈbatər/ ▸ **verb 1** hit someone or something hard and repeatedly. **2** damage or harm: *the space program has been battered by bureaucratic wrangling.*

– SYNONYMS **beat up,** hit repeatedly, pummel, pound, rain blows on, buffet, belabor, thrash; informal knock about/around, lay into, do over.

– DERIVATIVES **bat·ter·er** noun.
– ORIGIN Old French *batre* 'to beat.'

bat·ter² ▸ **noun** a mixture of flour, egg, and milk or water, used for making pancakes or coating food before frying.
– DERIVATIVES **bat·tered** adjective.
– ORIGIN from Old French *batre* 'to beat.'

bat·ter³ ▸ **noun** a player who bats in baseball.

bat·ter·ing ram ▸ **noun** a heavy object swung or rammed against a door to break it down.

bat·ter·y /ˈbatərē/ ▸ **noun** (pl. **batteries**) **1** a device containing one or more electrical cells, for use as a source of power. **2** an extensive series: *a battery of tests.* **3** Law unlawful physical contact with another person. **4** a group of heavy guns.
– ORIGIN first meaning 'metal articles made by hammering': from Latin *battuere* 'to beat.'

bat·ting or·der ▸ **noun** Baseball the fixed order in which batters take their turn at bat.

bat·tle /ˈbatl/ ▸ **noun 1** a prolonged fight between organized armed forces. **2** a long and difficult struggle or conflict: *a battle of wits.*

– SYNONYMS **1** *he was killed in the battle* **fight,** engagement, armed conflict, clash, struggle, skirmish, fray, war, campaign, crusade, warfare, combat, action, hostilities; informal scrap, dogfight, shoot-out. **2** *a legal battle* **conflict,** clash, struggle, disagreement, argument, dispute, tussle.

▸ **verb** fight or struggle with determination: *the city's two tabloids are battling for survival.*

– SYNONYMS **fight,** combat, contend with, resist, withstand, stand up to, confront, war, feud, struggle, strive, work.

– DERIVATIVES **bat·tler** noun.
– PHRASES **battle royal** a fierce fight or dispute.
– ORIGIN from Latin *battuere* 'to beat.'

battle·ax /ˈbatl,aks/ (also **battleaxe**) ▸ **noun 1** a large ax used in ancient warfare. **2** informal an aggressive older woman.

bat·tle·dress /ˈbatl,dres/ ▸ **noun** combat uniform worn by soldiers.

bat·tle·field /ˈbatl,fēld/ (also **battleground**) ▸ **noun** the piece of ground on which a battle is fought.

– SYNONYMS **battleground,** field of battle, field of operations, combat zone, lines, front, theater of war.

bat·tle·ment /ˈbatlmənt/ ▸ **noun** a parapet at the top of a wall with gaps for firing from, forming part of a fortification.
– DERIVATIVES **bat·tle·ment·ed** adjective.
– ORIGIN from Old French *bataillier* 'fortify with movable turrets.'

bat·tle·ship /ˈbatl,sʜip/ ▸ **noun** a heavily armored warship with large-caliber guns.

bat·ty /ˈbatē/ ▸ **adjective** (**battier, battiest**) informal crazy.
– DERIVATIVES **bat·ti·ness** noun.
– ORIGIN from **BAT²**.

bat·wing /ˈbat,wɪɴɢ/ ▸ **adjective** (of a sleeve) having a deep armhole and a tight cuff.

bau·ble /ˈbôbəl/ ▸ **noun** a small, showy trinket or decoration.
– ORIGIN Old French *baubel* 'child's toy.'

baud /bôd/ ▸ **noun** (pl. same or **bauds**) Computing a unit of transmission speed for electronic signals, corresponding to one information unit or event per second.
– ORIGIN named after the French engineer Jean M. E. *Baudot.*

baulk ▸ **verb & noun** chiefly British spelling of **BALK**.

baux·ite /ˈbôksīt/ ▸ **noun** a claylike rock from which aluminum is obtained.
– ORIGIN from the French village of *Les Baux,* where it was first found.

bawd·y /ˈbôdē/ ▸ **adjective** (**bawdier, bawdiest**) dealing with sex in a comical way.

– SYNONYMS **ribald,** indecent, risqué, racy, earthy, rude, suggestive, titillating, naughty, improper, indelicate, vulgar, crude, smutty; informal raunchy.

– DERIVATIVES **bawd·i·ness** noun.
– ORIGIN from Old French *baude* 'shameless.'

bawd·y house ▸ **noun** old use a brothel.

bawl /bôl/ ▸ **verb 1** shout out noisily. **2** (**bawl someone out**) reprimand someone angrily. **3** weep noisily.

– SYNONYMS **1 shout,** yell, roar, bellow, screech, scream, shriek, bark, thunder; informal yammer, holler. **2 cry,** sob, weep, wail, whine, howl.
– ANTONYMS whisper.

▸ **noun** a loud shout.
– ORIGIN imitating the sound.

bay¹ /bā/ ▸ **noun** a broad curved inlet of the sea.

– SYNONYMS **cove,** inlet, gulf, sound, bight, basin, fjord.

– ORIGIN Old French *baie*.

bay² (also **bay laurel** or **sweet bay**) ▶ **noun** an evergreen Mediterranean shrub with aromatic leaves that are used in cooking.
– ORIGIN from Latin *baca* 'berry.'

bay³ ▶ **noun 1** a window area that projects outward from a wall. **2** an area allocated for a purpose: *a loading bay*. **3** a compartment with a particular function in an aircraft, motor vehicle, or ship: *a bomb bay*.

– SYNONYMS **alcove,** recess, niche, nook, opening, inglenook.

– ORIGIN from Latin *batare* 'to gape.'

bay⁴ ▶ **adjective** (of a horse) reddish-brown with black points. ▶ **noun** a bay horse.
– ORIGIN from Latin *badius*.

bay⁵ ▶ **verb** (of a dog) howl loudly.

– SYNONYMS *coyotes baying at the moon* **howl,** bark, yelp, yap, cry, bellow, roar.

▶ **noun** the sound of baying.
– PHRASES **at bay** trapped or cornered. **hold** (or **keep**) **someone/thing at bay** prevent someone or something from approaching or having an effect.
– ORIGIN Old French *abaiier* 'to bark.'

bay·ber·ry /ˈbāˌberē/ ▶ **noun** (pl. **bayberries**) a North American shrub with aromatic leathery leaves and waxy berries.

bay leaf ▶ **noun** the aromatic, usually dried, leaf of a bay, used in cooking.

bay·o·net /ˈbāənit, ˌbāəˈnet/ ▶ **noun** a long blade fixed to the muzzle of a rifle for hand-to-hand fighting. ▶ **verb** (**bayonets, bayoneting, bayoneted**) stab someone with a bayonet. ▶ **adjective** referring to a type of fitting for a light bulb that is pushed into a socket and then twisted into place.
– ORIGIN French *baïonnette* 'dagger,' named after the French town of *Bayonne*, where the daggers were made.

bay·ou /ˈbīo͞o, ˈbīō/ ▶ **noun** (pl. **bayous**) (in the southern US) a marshy outlet of a lake or river.
– ORIGIN Louisiana French.

bay rum ▶ **noun** a perfume for the hair, distilled originally from rum and bayberry leaves.

bay win·dow ▶ **noun** a window built to project outward from a wall.

ba·zaar /bəˈzär/ ▶ **noun 1** a market in a Middle Eastern country. **2** a sale of goods to raise funds for charity.

– SYNONYMS **1 market,** marketplace, mart. **2 fete,** fair, fund-raiser, rummage sale, tag sale, flea market.

– ORIGIN Persian, 'market.'

ba·zoo·ka /bəˈzo͞okə/ ▶ **noun** a short-range rocket launcher used against tanks.
– ORIGIN probably from US slang *bazoo* 'kazoo.'

BB ▶ **noun** a lead pellet of a standard size, used in air rifles.

BBC ▶ **abbreviation** British Broadcasting Corporation.

BBQ ▶ **abbreviation** barbecue.

BC ▶ **abbreviation 1** before Christ (used to show that a date comes the specified number of years before the traditional date of Jesus's birth). **2** British Columbia.

USAGE

BC is normally written in small capitals and placed **after** the numerals, as in *72* BC.

bcc ▶ **abbreviation** blind carbon copy.

BCE ▶ **abbreviation** before the Common Era (indicating dates before the Christian era).

BCG ▶ **abbreviation** Bacillus Calmette-Guérin, an anti-tuberculosis vaccine.

BD ▶ **abbreviation** Bachelor of Divinity.

BDSM ▶ **abbreviation** bondage, domination, sadism, masochism.

BE ▶ **abbreviation 1** Bachelor of Education. **2** Bachelor of Engineering.

Be ▶ **symbol** the chemical element beryllium.

be /bē/ ▶ **verb** (sing. present **am; are; is;** pl. present **are;** 1st and 3rd sing. past **was;** 2nd sing. past and pl. past **were;** present subjunctive **be;** past subjunctive **were;** present part. **being;** past part. **been**) **1** (usu. **there is/are**) exist; be present. **2** take place. **3** have the specified state, nature, or role: *the floor was uneven*. **4** come; go; visit.

– SYNONYMS **1** *there was once a king* **exist,** live, be alive, breathe, be extant. **2** *the trial is tomorrow* **occur,** happen, take place, come about, arise, fall; literary come to pass, befall, betide. **3** *the bed is over there* **be situated,** be located, be found, be present, be set, be positioned, be placed, be installed, sit, lie. **4** *it has been like this for hours* **remain,** stay, last, continue, persist.

▶ **auxiliary verb 1** used with a present participle to form continuous tenses: *they are coming*. **2** used with a past participle to form the passive voice. **3** used to indicate something that is due to, may, or should happen.
– PHRASES **the be-all and end-all** informal the most important aspect. **-to-be** of the future: *his bride-to-be*.
– ORIGIN Old English.

be- ▶ **prefix** forming verbs. **1** all over; all around: *bespatter*. **2** thoroughly; excessively: *bewilder*. **3** expressing transitive action: *bemoan*. **4** affect with or cause to be: *becalm*. **5** (forming adjectives ending in *-ed*) having; covered with: *bejeweled*.
– ORIGIN Old English.

beach /bēCH/ ▶ **noun** a pebbly or sandy shore at the edge of the sea or a lake.

– SYNONYMS **sands,** seaside, seashore, coast; literary strand, littoral.

▶ **verb 1** bring or come onto a beach from the water. **2** (as adj. **beached**) cause (a whale or similar animal) to become stranded out of the water.

– SYNONYMS **1 land,** ground, strand, run ashore. **2** (as adj. **beached**) **stranded,** run aground, ashore, marooned, high and dry, stuck.

– ORIGIN perhaps related to Old English, 'brook.'

beach ball ▶ **noun** a large, light inflatable ball used for playing games on the beach.

beach·comb·er /ˈbēCHˌkōmər/ ▶ **noun** a person who searches beaches for articles of interest or value.

beach·head /ˈbēCHˌhed/ ▶ **noun** a defended position on a beach taken from the enemy by landing forces.

beach·wear /ˈbēCHˌwe(ə)r/ ▶ **noun** clothing suitable for wearing on the beach.

bea·con /ˈbēkən/ ▶ **noun 1** a fire lit on the top of a hill as a signal. **2** a signal light for ships or aircraft. **3** a radio transmitter signaling the position of a ship or aircraft.

– SYNONYMS **signal,** light, fire, danger signal, bonfire, lighthouse.

– ORIGIN Old English, 'sign, portent, ensign.'

bead /bēd/ ▶ **noun 1** a small piece of glass, stone, etc., threaded in a string with others to make a necklace or rosary. **2** a drop of a liquid on a surface. **3** a small knob forming the front sight of a gun. **4** the reinforced inner edge of a tire.

– SYNONYMS **1 ball,** pellet, pill, globule, sphere, spheroid, orb, round; (**beads**) necklace, rosary, chaplet. **2** *beads of sweat* **droplet,** drop, drip, blob, pearl, dot.

▶ **verb** (often as adj. **beaded**) decorate or cover with beads: *a beaded bag.*

– ORIGIN Old English, 'prayer' (each bead on a rosary representing a prayer).

bead·y /'bēdē/ ▶ **adjective** (of a person's eyes) small, round, and observing things clearly.

– DERIVATIVES **bead·i·ly** adverb.

bea·gle /'bēgəl/ ▶ **noun** a small, short-legged breed of hound.

– ORIGIN perhaps from Old French *beegueule* 'open-mouthed.'

beak /bēk/ ▶ **noun** a bird's horny projecting jaws; a bill.

– SYNONYMS **bill,** nib, mandible; Scottish neb.

– DERIVATIVES **beaked** adjective **beak·y** adjective.

– ORIGIN Latin *beccus.*

beak·er /'bēkər/ ▶ **noun** a cylindrical glass container used in laboratories.

– SYNONYMS **cup,** tumbler, glass, mug, drinking vessel.

– ORIGIN Old Norse.

beam /bēm/ ▶ **noun 1** a long piece of timber or metal used as a support in building. **2** a narrow horizontal length of timber for balancing on in gymnastics. **3** a ray or shaft of light or particles. **4** a radiant smile. **5** a ship's breadth at its widest point.

– SYNONYMS **1 plank,** timber, joist, rafter, lintel, spar, girder, support. **2 ray,** shaft, stream, streak, pencil, flash, gleam, glint. **3 grin,** smile.
– ANTONYMS frown.

▶ **verb 1** transmit a radio signal or broadcast. **2** shine brightly. **3** smile radiantly.

– SYNONYMS **1 broadcast,** transmit, relay, disseminate, direct, send, aim. **2 shine,** radiate, glare, gleam. **3 grin,** smile.
– ANTONYMS frown.

– PHRASES **off beam** informal on the wrong track; mistaken.

– ORIGIN Old English, 'tree, beam.'

bean /bēn/ ▶ **noun 1** an edible seed growing in long pods on certain plants. **2** the hard seed of a coffee or cocoa plant. **3** informal a very small amount or nothing at all: *there is not a bean of truth in the report.*

– PHRASES **full of beans** informal lively; in high spirits. **old bean** Brit. informal, dated a friendly form of address to a man.

– ORIGIN Old English.

bean·bag /'bēn,bag/ ▶ **noun 1** a small bag filled with dried beans and used in children's games. **2** a large cushion filled with polystyrene beads, used as a seat.

bean count·er ▶ **noun** informal an accountant or bureaucrat who is excessively concerned with controlling expenditure.

bean curd ▶ **noun** another term for TOFU.

bean·ie /'bēnē/ ▶ **noun** (pl. **beanies**) a small close-fitting hat worn on the back of the head.

– ORIGIN perhaps from BEAN (in the old-fashioned sense 'head').

bean·pole /'bēn,pōl/ ▶ **noun** informal a tall, thin person.

bean sprouts ▶ **plural noun** the edible sprouting seeds of certain beans.

bear[1] /be(ə)r/ ▶ **verb** (past **bore**; past part. **borne**) **1** carry someone or something. **2** have something as a quality or visible mark. **3** support a weight. **4** manage to tolerate: *the grief was more than he could bear.* **5** (**cannot bear**) strongly dislike someone or something. **6** give birth to a child. **7** (of a tree or plant) produce fruit or flowers. **8** (**bear oneself**) behave in a specified way: *she bore herself with dignity.* **9** turn and go in a specified direction: *bear left.*

– SYNONYMS **1** *I come bearing gifts* **carry,** bring, transport, move, convey, take, fetch; informal tote. **2** *the bag bore my name* **display,** be marked with, show, carry, exhibit. **3** *will it bear his weight?* **withstand,** support, sustain, stand, take, carry, hold up, cope with, handle. **4** *I can't bear his arrogance* **endure,** tolerate, put up with, stand, abide, countenance, stomach; informal hack, swallow. formal brook. **5** *she bore a son* **give birth to,** bring forth, deliver, have, produce, spawn. **6** *a shrub that bears yellow berries* **produce,** yield, give, provide, supply.

– PHRASES **bear down on** approach in a purposeful or threatening way. **bear fruit** have good results. **bear someone a grudge** feel resentment against someone. **bear something in mind** remember something and take it into account. **bear on** be relevant to. **bear something out** support or confirm something. **bear up** stay cheerful in difficult circumstances. **bear with** be patient or tolerant with. **bear witness** (or **testimony**) **to** provide evidence of.

– ORIGIN Old English.

USAGE

Do not confuse **bear** with **bare**. **Bear** means *carry* (*he was bearing a tray of food*) or *tolerate,* whereas **bare** is an adjective that means *naked* or a verb meaning *uncover or reveal* (*he bared his chest*).

bear[2] ▶ **noun 1** a large, heavy mammal with thick fur and a very short tail. **2** Stock Exchange a person who sells shares hoping to buy them back later at a lower price. Often contrasted with BULL[1].

– PHRASES **loaded for bear** informal fully prepared for a confrontation or challenge.

– ORIGIN Old English.

WORD LINKS

ursine *relating to bears*

bear·a·ble /'be(ə)rəbəl/ ▶ **adjective** able to be endured.

– SYNONYMS **tolerable,** endurable, supportable, sustainable.

– DERIVATIVES **bear·a·bly** adverb.

bear-bait·ing ▶ **noun** historical a form of entertainment that involved setting dogs to attack a captive bear.

bear claw ▶ **noun** a semicircular sweet pastry, usually flavored with almond and often containing raisins.

beard /bi(ə)rd/ ▶ **noun 1** a growth of hair on the chin and lower cheeks of a man's face. **2** a tuft of hairs or bristles

on certain animals or plants. ▶ **verb** boldly confront or challenge someone daunting.
– DERIVATIVES **beard·ed** adjective **beard·less** adjective.
– ORIGIN Old English.

bear·er /ˈbe(ə)rər/ ▶ **noun 1** a person or thing that carries something. **2** a person who presents a check or other order to pay money.

– SYNONYMS **1 carrier,** porter. **2 bringer,** messenger, agent, conveyor, emissary.

bear hug ▶ **noun** a rough, tight embrace.

bear·ing /ˈbe(ə)riNG/ ▶ **noun 1** a person's way of standing, moving, or behaving: *a man of dignified bearing.* **2** the way in which something is related to or influences something else: *past accidents can have a bearing on back problems.* **3** (usu. **bearings**) a part of a machine that allows one part to rotate or move in contact with another. **4** direction or position relative to a fixed point. **5** (**one's bearings**) awareness of one's position in relation to one's surroundings: *I checked my map to get my bearings.* **6** a heraldic emblem.

– SYNONYMS **1 posture,** stance, carriage, gait, demeanor, deportment, manner, mien, air, aspect, attitude, style. **2** *this has no bearing on the matter* **relevance,** pertinence, connection, relation, relationship, import, significance, application. **3 direction,** orientation, course, trajectory, heading, tack, path. **4** *I lost my* ***bearings*** **orientation,** sense of direction, whereabouts, location, position.
– ANTONYMS irrelevance.

bear·ish /ˈbe(ə)risH/ ▶ **adjective** resembling a bear, especially in being surly or clumsy.

bear mar·ket ▶ **noun** Stock Exchange a market in which share prices are falling.

Bé·ar·naise sauce /ˌberˈnāz/ ▶ **noun** a rich sauce thickened with egg yolks and flavored with tarragon.
– ORIGIN named after the French region of *Béarn.*

bear·skin /ˈbe(ə)rˌskin/ ▶ **noun** a tall cap of black fur worn ceremonially by certain troops.

beast /bēst/ ▶ **noun 1** an animal, especially a large or dangerous mammal. **2** a very cruel or wicked person.

– SYNONYMS **1 creature,** animal; informal critter. **2 monster,** brute, savage, barbarian, animal, swine, ogre, fiend, sadist, demon, devil.

– ORIGIN Latin *bestia.*

beast·ie /ˈbēstē/ ▶ **noun** (pl. **beasties**) Scottish or humorous a small animal or insect.

beast·ly /ˈbēstlē/ ▶ **adjective** informal very unpleasant.
– DERIVATIVES **beast·li·ness** noun.

beast of bur·den ▶ **noun** an animal used for carrying loads.

beat /bēt/ ▶ **verb** (past **beat**; past part. **beaten**) **1** hit someone repeatedly and violently. **2** hit something repeatedly to flatten it or make a noise. **3** defeat someone or overcome something. **4** do or be better than: *he beat his own world record.* **5** (of the heart) throb. **6** (of a bird) move the wings up and down. **7** stir cooking ingredients vigorously. **8** informal baffle someone. **9** move across land striking at the vegetation to raise game birds for shooting.

– SYNONYMS **1 hit,** strike, batter, thump, bang, hammer, punch, knock, thrash, pound, pummel, slap, rain blows on, assault; informal wallop, belt, bash, whack, clout, clobber. **2** *she beat him easily at chess* **defeat,** conquer, vanquish, trounce, rout, overpower, overcome; informal lick, thrash, whip. **3** *he beat the record* **exceed,** surpass, better, improve on, eclipse, transcend, top, trump, cap. **4** *her heart was still beating* **throb,** pulse, pulsate, pump, palpitate, pound, thump, thud, hammer, drum. **5** *the eagle beat its wings* **flap,** flutter, thrash, wave, vibrate. **6** *beat the cream into the mixture* **whisk,** mix, blend, whip.

▶ **noun 1** a main accent in music or poetry. **2** a throb of the heart. **3** a movement of a bird's wings. **4** an area patrolled by a police officer. **5** a brief pause.

– SYNONYMS **1** *the song has a good beat* **rhythm,** pulse, meter, time, measure, cadence, stress, accent. **2** *the beat of hooves* **pounding,** banging, thumping, thudding, hammering, crashing. **3** *the beat of her heart* **pulse,** pulsation, vibration, throb, palpitation, reverberation, pounding, thump, thud, hammering, drumming. **4** *a cop on his beat* **circuit,** round, route, path.

▶ **adjective** informal completely exhausted.
– DERIVATIVES **beat·a·ble** adjective **beat·er** noun.
– PHRASES **beat around** (or **about**) **the bush** discuss a matter without coming to the point. **beat a dead horse** waste energy on something that can never be successful. **beat down** shine very brightly. **beat someone down** force someone to reduce the price of something. **beat it** informal leave. **beat someone up** attack someone and hit them repeatedly. **beat a retreat** withdraw quickly to avoid something. **off the beaten track** isolated.
– ORIGIN Old English.

beat·box /ˈbētˌbäks/ ▶ **noun** informal **1** a drum machine. **2** a radio or radio cassette player for playing loud music, especially rap.

beat gen·er·a·tion ▶ **noun** a movement of young people in the 1950s and early 1960s who rejected conventional society.

be·a·tif·ic /ˌbēəˈtifik/ ▶ **adjective 1** feeling or expressing intense happiness. **2** (in the Christian Church) bestowing spiritual blessedness.
– DERIVATIVES **be·a·tif·i·cal·ly** adverb.

be·at·i·fy /bēˈatəˌfī/ ▶ **verb** (**beatifies, beatifying, beatified**) (in the Roman Catholic Church) announce that a dead person is in a state of spiritual bliss, the first step toward making them a saint.
– DERIVATIVES **be·at·i·fi·ca·tion** /bēˌatəfiˈkāsHən/ noun.
– ORIGIN from Latin *beatus* 'blessed.'

be·at·i·tude /bēˈatiˌt(y)o͞od/ ▶ **noun** very great happiness or blessedness.

beat·nik /ˈbētnik/ ▶ **noun** a young person associated with the beat generation.

beat-up ▶ **adjective** informal worn out by overuse.

beau /bō/ ▶ **noun** (pl. **beaux** /bōz/ or **beaus** /bōz/) dated **1** a boyfriend or male admirer. **2** a dandy.
– ORIGIN French, 'handsome.'

Beau·fort scale /ˈbōfərt/ ▶ **noun** a scale of wind speed ranging from force 0 to force 12.
– ORIGIN named after the English admiral Sir Francis *Beaufort.*

Beau·jo·lais /ˌbōzHəˈlā/ ▶ **noun** a light red wine produced in the Beaujolais district of SE France.

beau monde /ˌbō ˈmônd/ ▶ **noun** fashionable society.
– ORIGIN French, 'fine world.'

beau·te·ous /ˈbyo͞otēəs/ ▶ **adjective** literary beautiful.

beau·ti·cian /byo͞o'tisʜən/ ▶ **noun** a person whose job is to give beauty treatments.

beau·ti·ful /'byo͞otəfəl/ ▶ **adjective 1** very pleasing to the senses or to the mind. **2** of a very high standard; excellent.

– SYNONYMS **attractive,** pretty, handsome, good-looking, fetching, lovely, charming, graceful, elegant, appealing, winsome, ravishing, gorgeous, stunning, glamorous; Scottish bonny; informal knockout, drop-dead gorgeous, cute, foxy. old use comely.
– ANTONYMS ugly.

– DERIVATIVES **beau·ti·ful·ly** adverb.

beau·ti·fy /'byo͞otə,fī/ ▶ **verb** (**beautifies, beautifying, beautified**) make someone or something beautiful.

– SYNONYMS **adorn,** embellish, enhance, decorate, ornament, prettify, glamorize; informal do up, spruce up.

– DERIVATIVES **beau·ti·fi·ca·tion** /,byo͞otəfi'kāsʜən/ noun.

beau·ty /'byo͞otē/ ▶ **noun** (pl. **beauties**) **1** a combination of qualities that is very pleasing to the senses or to the mind. **2** a beautiful woman. **3** an excellent example of something. **4** an attractive feature or advantage.

– SYNONYMS **1 attractiveness,** prettiness, good looks, loveliness, appeal, winsomeness, charm, grace, elegance, exquisiteness, glamour; literary pulchritude. **2 belle,** vision, goddess, picture, Venus; informal babe, looker, lovely, stunner, knockout, bombshell.
– ANTONYMS ugliness.

▶ **adjective** intended to make someone more attractive: *beauty treatment.*
– ORIGIN Latin *bellus* 'beautiful, fine.'

beau·ty con·test ▶ **noun** a contest in which the winner is the woman judged the most beautiful.

beau·ty mark (also **beauty spot**) ▶ **noun** a dark facial mole, especially one near a woman's upper lip, or an artificial mole applied to the face.

beau·ty queen ▶ **noun** the winner of a beauty contest.

beau·ty sa·lon (also **beauty parlour**) ▶ **noun** an establishment in which hairdressing and beauty treatments are carried out.

beau·ty sleep ▶ **noun** humorous sleep that helps one remain young and attractive.

beaux /bōz/ plural of **BEAU**.

bea·ver /'bēvər/ ▶ **noun** (pl. same or **beavers**) **1** a large rodent with a broad tail and strong teeth that lives partly in water. **2** a hat made of beaver fur. **3** a very hard-working person. ▶ **verb** informal work hard: *she beavered away to keep things running smoothly.*
– ORIGIN Old English.

be·bop /'bē,bäp/ ▶ **noun** a type of jazz characterized by complex harmony and rhythms.
– ORIGIN imitating the rhythm.

be·calm /bi'kä(l)m/ ▶ **verb** (**be becalmed**) (of a sailing ship) be unable to move through lack of wind.

be·came /bi'kām/ past of **BECOME**.

be·cause /bi'kôz, -'kəz/ ▶ **conjunction** for the reason that; since.

– SYNONYMS **since,** as, seeing that, in view of the fact that, in that.

– PHRASES **because of** by reason of.
– ORIGIN from *by cause.*

USAGE

Confusion can arise when **because** follows a negative such as *not*. For example, the sentence *he didn't go because he was ill* could mean either 'the reason he didn't go was that he was ill' or 'being ill wasn't the reason for him going; there was another reason.' Use a comma when the first meaning is intended (*he didn't go, because he was ill*), or avoid using **because** after a negative altogether.

On starting a sentence with **because**, see the note at **AND**.

bé·cha·mel /,bāsʜə'mel/ ▶ **noun** a rich white sauce flavored with herbs and other seasonings.
– ORIGIN named after the Marquis Louis de *Béchamel.*

beck /bek/ ▶ **noun** (in phrase **at someone's beck and call**) always having to be ready to obey someone's orders.
– ORIGIN from **BECKON**.

beck·on /'bekən/ ▶ **verb 1** make a gesture to encourage or instruct someone to approach or follow. **2** seem appealing or inviting: *the wide-open spaces of Australia beckoned.*

– SYNONYMS **1 gesture,** signal, wave, gesticulate, motion. **2 entice,** invite, tempt, lure, charm, attract, draw, call.

– ORIGIN Old English.

be·come /bi'kəm/ ▶ **verb** (past **became** /bi'kām/; past part. **become**) **1** begin to be. **2** develop into: *the child will become an adult.* **3** (**become of**) happen to: *what would become of her now?* **4** suit or be appropriate to: *celebrity status did not become him.*

– SYNONYMS **1** *she became rich* **grow,** get, turn, come to be, get to be. **2** *he became foreign secretary* **be appointed,** be assigned as, be nominated, be elected. **3** *he became a tyrant* **turn into,** change into, be transformed into, be converted into. **4** (**become of**) **happen to,** be the fate of, be the lot of, overtake. **5 suit,** flatter, look good on, set off; informal do something for.

– ORIGIN Old English.

CHOOSE THE RIGHT WORD

See **HAPPEN**.

be·com·ing /bi'kəmiɴɢ/ ▶ **adjective 1** (of clothing) looking good on someone. **2** appropriate or suitable.

– SYNONYMS **flattering,** fetching, attractive, pretty, elegant, handsome, well chosen, stylish, fashionable, tasteful.

– DERIVATIVES **be·com·ing·ly** adverb.

bec·que·rel /,bek(ə)'rel/ ▶ **noun** Physics a unit of radioactivity in the SI system.
– ORIGIN named after the French physicist A-H. *Becquerel.*

BEd /,bē 'ed/ ▶ **abbreviation** Bachelor of Education.

bed /bed/ ▶ **noun 1** a piece of furniture for sleeping on. **2** an area of ground where flowers and plants are grown. **3** a part or layer on which something rests or is supported: *roast chicken on a bed of herbs.* **4** a layer of rock. **5** the bottom of the sea or a lake or river. **6** informal a bed as a place for sexual activity.

– SYNONYMS **1 cot,** bunk bed, futon, daybed, sofa bed, four-poster, berth, crib, cradle; informal the sack. **2** *a flower bed* **patch,** plot, border, strip. **3 base,** foundation, footing, support, basis.

▶ verb (**beds, bedding, bedded**) **1** fix something firmly. **2** provide someone with or settle in sleeping accommodations. **3** informal have sex with someone. **4** (**bed something out**) transfer a plant from a pot to the ground.

– SYNONYMS **embed,** set, fix, insert, inlay, implant, bury, plant.

– DERIVATIVES **bed·ded** adjective.
– PHRASES **a bed of roses** (usu. with negative) a comfortable or easy situation or activity.
– ORIGIN Old English.

bed and board ▶ **noun** lodging and food.

bed and break·fast ▶ **noun 1** sleeping accommodations and breakfast in a guest house or hotel. **2** a guest house.

be·daz·zle /bi'dazəl/ ▶ **verb** greatly impress someone with brilliance or skill.

bed·bug /'bed,bəg/ ▶ **noun** a wingless bug that sucks the blood of sleeping humans.

bed·cham·ber /'bed,CHāmbər/ ▶ **noun** old use a bedroom.

bed·clothes /'bed,klō(TH)z/ ▶ **plural noun** coverings for a bed, such as sheets and blankets.

bed·ding /'bediNG/ ▶ **noun 1** bedclothes. **2** straw or similar material for animals to sleep on.

bed·ding plant ▶ **noun** an annual plant produced for planting in a garden in spring.

be·deck /bi'dek/ ▶ **verb** decorate lavishly: *the town was bedecked with flags.*

be·dev·il /bi'devəl/ ▶ **verb** (**bedevils, bedeviling, bedeviled**) cause continual trouble to: *the devices were bedeviled by mechanical failures.*

bed·fel·low /'bed,felō/ ▶ **noun 1** a person or thing closely associated with another: *laughter and tragedy are not such strange bedfellows.* **2** a person sharing a bed with another.

bed head ▶ **noun** informal a casual hairstyle resulting from failure to comb or arrange the hair after sleep.

be·di·zen /bi'dīzən/ ▶ **verb** literary decorate someone or something gaudily.
– ORIGIN from former *dizen* 'deck out.'

bed·lam /'bedləm/ ▶ **noun** a scene of uproar and confusion.
– ORIGIN from the name of the mental hospital of St. Mary of *Bethlehem* in London.

bed linen ▶ **noun** sheets and pillowcases.

Bed·ou·in /'bed(ə)win/ (also **Beduin**) ▶ **noun** (pl. same) an Arab living as a nomad in the desert.
– ORIGIN Arabic, 'dwellers in the desert.'

bed·pan /'bed,pan/ ▶ **noun** a container used as a toilet by a bedridden patient.

bed·post /'bed,pōst/ ▶ **noun** any of the four upright supports of a bedstead.

be·drag·gled /bi'dragəld/ ▶ **adjective** untidy or disheveled.

– SYNONYMS **disheveled,** disordered, untidy, unkempt, tousled; informal mussed.
– ANTONYMS neat.

bed·rid·den /'bed,ridn/ ▶ **adjective** having to stay in bed because of sickness or old age.

bed·rock /'bed,räk/ ▶ **noun 1** solid rock underlying loose deposits such as soil. **2** underlying or basic principles: *self-sufficiency was the bedrock of the regime.*

bed·roll /'bed,rōl/ ▶ **noun** a sleeping bag or other bedding rolled into a bundle.

bed·room /'bed,ro͝om, -,ro͞om/ ▶ **noun** a room for sleeping in.

bed·side man·ner /'bed,sīd/ ▶ **noun** a doctor's approach to a patient.

bed·sore /'bed,sôr/ ▶ **noun** a sore caused by lying in bed in one position for a long time.

bed·spread /'bed,spred/ ▶ **noun** a decorative cloth used to cover a bed.

bed·stead /'bed,sted/ ▶ **noun** the framework of a bed.

bed·straw /'bed,strô/ ▶ **noun** a plant with small flowers and slender leaves, formerly used for stuffing mattresses.

bed·time /'bed,tīm/ ▶ **noun** the usual time when someone goes to bed.

bed-wet·ting ▶ **noun** urinating unintentionally while asleep.

bee /bē/ ▶ **noun 1** a stinging winged insect that collects nectar and pollen and produces wax and honey. **2** a meeting for communal work or amusement: *a sewing bee.*
– PHRASES **the bee's knees** informal an outstandingly good person or thing. **have a bee in one's bonnet** informal be obsessed with something.
– ORIGIN Old English.

beech /bēCH/ ▶ **noun** a large tree with gray bark and hard, pale wood.
– ORIGIN Old English.

bee-eat·er ▶ **noun** a brightly colored insect-eating Old World bird with a curved bill and a long tail.

beef /bēf/ ▶ **noun 1** the flesh of a cow, bull, or ox, used as food. **2** informal strength or power: *he was brought in to give the team more beef.* **3** informal flesh with well-developed muscle. **4** (pl. **beefs**) informal a complaint or grievance. ▶ **verb** informal **1** (**beef something up**) make stronger or more substantial: *rifles were supplied to the police to beef up security.* **2** complain about someone or something.
– ORIGIN Old French *boef.*

beef·cake /'bēf,kāk/ ▶ **noun** informal men with well-developed muscles.

beef·eat·er /'bēf,ētər/ ▶ **noun** a Yeoman Warder or Yeoman of the Guard in the Tower of London.
– ORIGIN formerly a derogatory term for a well-fed servant.

beef·steak /'bēf,stāk/ ▶ **noun** a thick slice of steak, especially rump steak.

beef·steak to·ma·to ▶ **noun** a large, firm variety of tomato.

beef·y /'bēfē/ ▶ **adjective** (**beefier, beefiest**) **1** informal muscular or powerful. **2** tasting like beef.

bee·hive /'bē,hīv/ ▶ **noun 1** a structure in which bees are kept. **2** a woman's domed and lacquered hairstyle popular in the 1960s.

bee·keep·ing /'bē,kēpiNG/ ▶ **noun** the occupation of owning and breeding bees for their honey.
– DERIVATIVES **bee·keep·er** noun.

bee·line /'bē,līn/ ▶ **noun** (in phrase **make a beeline for**) hurry directly to.

– ORIGIN a bee is said to take a straight line instinctively when returning to the hive.

Be·el·ze·bub /bē'elzə,bəb/ ▶ **noun** the Devil.
– ORIGIN Hebrew, 'lord of flies.'

been /bin/ past participle of **BE**.

beep /bēp/ ▶ **noun** a short, high-pitched sound made by electronic equipment or a vehicle horn. ▶ **verb** produce a beep.
– ORIGIN imitating the sound.

beep·er /'bēpər/ ▶ **noun** another term for **PAGER**.

beer /bi(ə)r/ ▶ **noun** an alcoholic drink made from fermented malt flavored with hops.
– ORIGIN from Latin *biber* 'a drink.'

beer bel·ly (also **beer gut**) ▶ **noun** informal a man's fat belly caused by excessive beer-drinking.

beer gar·den ▶ **noun** a yard next to a bar or tavern, where drinks are served.

beer·y /'bi(ə)rē/ ▶ **adjective** informal **1** smelling or tasting of beer. **2** influenced by the drinking of beer: *a burst of beery laughter*.

bee-stung ▶ **adjective** informal (of a woman's lips) full and red.

bees·wax /'bēz,waks/ ▶ **noun 1** wax produced by bees to make honeycombs, used for wood polishes and candles. **2** informal a person's concern or business.

beet /bēt/ ▶ **noun** a plant with a fleshy root, grown for food and for processing into sugar.
– ORIGIN Latin *beta*.

bee·tle[1] /'bētl/ ▶ **noun** an insect with the forewings modified into a hard case that covers the hind wings and abdomen. ▶ **verb** informal make one's way hurriedly.
– ORIGIN Old English, 'biter.'

bee·tle[2] ▶ **noun** a very heavy mallet.
– ORIGIN Old English.

bee·tle[3] ▶ **verb** (usu. as adj. **beetling**) project or overhang: *his beetling brows*.

beet·root /'bēt,ro͞ot/ ▶ **noun** chiefly Brit. the edible dark-red root of a variety of beet.

BEF ▶ **abbreviation** British Expeditionary Force.

be·fall /bi'fôl/ ▶ **verb** (past **befell**; past part. **befallen**) literary (especially of something bad) happen to: *a terrible tragedy befell him*.

be·fit /bi'fit/ ▶ **verb** (**befits**, **befitting**, **befitted**) be appropriate for: *as befits a Quaker, he was a humane man*.
– DERIVATIVES **be·fit·ting** adjective.

be·fore /bi'fôr/ ▶ **preposition, conjunction, & adverb 1** during the time preceding. **2** in front of. **3** rather than.

> – SYNONYMS **1 prior to,** previous to, earlier than, preparatory to, in advance of, ahead of, pre-. **2 in front of,** in the presence of. **3 in preference to,** rather than, sooner than.
> – ANTONYMS after.

– ORIGIN Old English, from **BY** + **FORE**.

be·fore·hand /bi'fôr,hand/ ▶ **adverb** in advance.

> – SYNONYMS **in advance,** in readiness, ahead of time, before, before now/then, earlier (on), previously, already, sooner.
> – ANTONYMS afterward.

be·friend /bi'frend/ ▶ **verb** become a friend to someone.

be·fud·dle /bi'fədl/ ▶ **verb** (often as adj. **befuddled**) muddle or confuse someone.
– DERIVATIVES **be·fud·dle·ment** noun.

beg /beg/ ▶ **verb** (**begs**, **begging**, **begged**) **1** ask someone earnestly or humbly for something. **2** ask for food or money as charity. **3** (**beg off**) withdraw from something planned or promised: *they went to see the fireworks—I begged off*.

> – SYNONYMS **1 ask for money,** seek charity; informal sponge, cadge, scrounge, bum. **2** *we* ***begged for*** *mercy* **plead for,** request, ask for, appeal for, call for, sue for, solicit, seek. **3** *he begged her not to go* **implore,** entreat, plead with, appeal to, pray to, call on, petition; literary beseech.

– PHRASES **beg the question 1** invite an obvious question. **2** assume the truth of something without arguing it. **go begging** be available because unwanted by others.
– ORIGIN probably Old English.

be·gan /bi'gan/ past of **BEGIN**.

be·gat /bi'gat/ old-fashioned past of **BEGET**.

be·get /bi'get/ ▶ **verb** (**begets**, **begetting**, **begot** /bi'gät/; past part. **begotten** /bi'gätn/) literary **1** cause: *vengeance begets vengeance*. **2** produce a child.
– DERIVATIVES **be·get·ter** noun.
– ORIGIN Old English, 'get, obtain by effort.'

beg·gar /'begər/ ▶ **noun 1** a person who lives by begging for food or money. **2** informal a person of a particular type: *lucky beggar!*

> – SYNONYMS **tramp,** hobo, vagrant, vagabond, mendicant; informal scrounger, sponger, freeloader, bum.

▶ **verb** make someone very poor.
– PHRASES **beggar belief** (or **description**) be too extraordinary to be believed or described.

beg·gar·ly /'begərlē/ ▶ **adjective 1** very small in amount. **2** very poor.

beg·gar·y /'begərē/ ▶ **noun** a state of extreme poverty.

be·gin /bi'gin/ ▶ **verb** (**begins**, **beginning**, **began** /-'gan/; past part. **begun** /-'gən/) **1** perform or undergo the first part of an action or activity. **2** come into being. **3** have as its starting point: *the track begins at the village*. **4** (**begin on**) set to work on something. **5** informal have any chance of doing: *I can't begin to describe my confusion*.

> – SYNONYMS **1 start,** commence, set about, go about, embark on, launch into, get down to, take up, initiate, set in motion, get going, get off the ground, lead off, institute, inaugurate, open; informal get cracking on, kick off. **2 appear,** arise, become apparent, spring up, crop up, turn up, come into existence, originate, start, commence, develop.
> – ANTONYMS finish, end.

– ORIGIN Old English.

be·gin·ner /bi'ginər/ ▶ **noun** a person just starting to learn a skill or take part in an activity.

> – SYNONYMS **novice,** learner, starter, (raw) recruit, newcomer, tyro, probationer, apprentice, trainee; informal rookie, new kid (on the block), tenderfoot, greenhorn.
> – ANTONYMS expert, veteran.

be·gin·ning /bi'giniNG/ ▶ **noun 1** the time or place at which something begins. **2** the first or earliest part.

> – SYNONYMS **1** *the beginning of modern science* **start,** commencement, creation, birth, inception,

conception, origination, origin, genesis, germ, emergence, rise, dawn, launch, onset, outset, day one; informal kickoff. **2** *the beginning of the article* **opening**, start, commencement, first part, introduction, preamble.
– ANTONYMS end, conclusion.

be·gone /bi'gôn, -'gän/ ▶ **exclamation** old use go away at once.

be·go·nia /bi'gōnyə, -nēə/ ▶ **noun** a garden or house plant with brightly colored flowers.
– ORIGIN named after the French botanist Michel *Bégon*.

be·got /bi'gät/ past of **BEGET**.

be·got·ten /bi'gätn/ past participle of **BEGET**.

be·grudge /bi'grəj/ ▶ **verb 1** feel envious that someone possesses or enjoys something: *I've never begrudged my father his achievements.* **2** give something reluctantly or resentfully.

– SYNONYMS **envy,** resent, grudge, be jealous of, be envious of, mind, object to.

be·guile /bi'gīl/ ▶ **verb 1** charm or trick someone. **2** literary help time pass pleasantly.
– DERIVATIVES **be·guil·ing** adjective.

CHOOSE THE RIGHT WORD

See **TEMPT**.

be·guine /'begēn, 'bāˌgēn, bə'gēn/ ▶ **noun** a popular dance of Caribbean origin, similar to the foxtrot.
– ORIGIN from French *béguin* 'infatuation.'

be·gum /'bāgəm, 'bē-/ ▶ **noun** Indian **1** a Muslim woman of high rank. **2** (**Begum**) the title of a married Muslim woman.
– ORIGIN Turkish, 'princess.'

be·gun /bi'gən/ past participle of **BEGIN**.

be·half /bi'haf/ ▶ **noun** (in phrase **on behalf of** or **on someone's behalf**) **1** in the interests of a person, group, or principle. **2** as a representative of someone.

– SYNONYMS **1** *a campaign* **on behalf of** *recycling* **in the interests of,** in support of, for, for the benefit of, for the good of, for the sake of. **2** *I am writing* **on behalf of** *my client* **representing,** as a representative of, as a spokesperson for, for, in the name of, in place of, on the authority of.

– ORIGIN from former *on his halve* and *bihalve him*, both meaning 'on his side.'

be·have /bi'hāv/ ▶ **verb 1** act or operate in a specified way: *he always behaved like a gentleman.* **2** (also **behave oneself**) act in a polite or proper way.

– SYNONYMS **1** *she behaved badly* **act,** conduct oneself, acquit oneself. **2** *the children behaved themselves* **act correctly,** be good, be well behaved, mind one's manners; informal mind one's Ps and Qs.
– ANTONYMS misbehave.

– ORIGIN from **BE-** + **HAVE** in the sense 'bear oneself in a particular way.'

be·haved /bi'hāvd/ ▶ **adjective** acting in a specified way: *a well-behaved child.*

be·hav·ior /bi'hāvyər/ (Brit. **behaviour**) ▶ **noun** the way in which someone or something behaves: *he was shocked by the behavior of the fans.*

– SYNONYMS **functioning,** action, performance, operation, working, reaction, response.

– DERIVATIVES **be·hav·ior·al** adjective.

be·hav·ior·ism /bi'hāvyəˌrizəm/ ▶ **noun** the theory that behavior can be explained in terms of conditioning, and that psychological disorders are best treated by altering behavior patterns.
– DERIVATIVES **be·hav·ior·ist** noun & adjective.

be·head /bi'hed/ ▶ **verb** execute someone by cutting off their head.

be·held /bi'held/ past and past participle of **BEHOLD**.

be·he·moth /bi'hēməTH, 'bēəməTH/ ▶ **noun 1** a huge creature. **2** something very large, especially an organization.
– ORIGIN Hebrew, 'monstrous beast.'

be·hest /bi'hest/ ▶ **noun** (in phrase **at the behest of**) literary at the request or command of.
– ORIGIN Old English, 'a vow.'

be·hind /bi'hīnd/ ▶ **preposition & adverb 1** at or to the back or far side of. **2** farther back than other members of a group. **3** in support of. **4** responsible for an event or plan. **5** less advanced than. **6** late in achieving or paying something. **7** remaining after the departure or death of.

– SYNONYMS **1 at the back of,** at the rear of, in back of, beyond, on the far side of. **2 after,** following, at the back/rear of, hard on the heels of, in the wake of. **3 responsible for,** at the bottom of, the cause of, the perpetrator of, the organizer of, to blame for, guilty of. **4 supporting,** backing, for, on the side of, in agreement with; informal rooting for.

▶ **noun** informal a person's buttocks.
– ORIGIN Old English.

be·hold /bi'hōld/ ▶ **verb** (past and past part. **beheld**) old use or literary see or observe someone or something.
– DERIVATIVES **be·hold·er** noun.
– ORIGIN Old English.

be·hold·en /bi'hōldən/ ▶ **adjective** owing a debt of thanks to someone in return for a favor: *they don't want to be beholden to anyone.*

be·hoove /bi'ho͞ov/ ▶ **verb** (**it behooves someone to do**) formal it is necessary or appropriate for someone to do something: *if my brother is ill, then it behooves me to see him.*
– ORIGIN Old English.

beige /bāZH/ ▶ **noun** a pale whitish-brown color.
– ORIGIN French.

be·ing /'bēiNG/ ▶ **noun 1** the state of existing; existence: *the town came into being because there was gold nearby.* **2** the nature of a person. **3** a living creature: *alien beings.*

– SYNONYMS **1 existence,** living, life, reality, lifeblood, vital force. **2 soul,** spirit, nature, essence, psyche, heart, bosom, breast. **3 creature,** life form, organism, living thing, individual, person, human.

be·jew·eled /bi'jo͞oəld/ ▶ **adjective** decorated with jewels.

be·la·bor /bi'lābər/ ▶ **verb 1** attack someone physically or verbally. **2** argue or discuss in excessive detail: *there's no need to belabor the point.*

Be·la·rus·ian /ˌbelə'ro͞osiən, ˌbā-/ (also **Belarussian** /ˌbelə'rəSHən/) ▶ **noun 1** a person from Belarus in eastern Europe. **2** the Slavic language of Belarus. ▶ **adjective** relating to Belarus.

be·lat·ed /bi'lātid/ ▶ **adjective** coming or happening late or too late: *a belated birthday present.*

– SYNONYMS **late,** overdue, behindhand, delayed, tardy, unpunctual.
– ANTONYMS early.

– DERIVATIVES **be·lat·ed·ly** adverb **be·lat·ed·ness** noun.

be·lay /bi'lā/ ▶ **verb 1** fix a rope around a rock, pin, or other object to secure it. **2** nautical slang stop! ▶ **noun** an act of belaying.

bel can·to /bel 'käntō, 'kan-/ ▶ **noun** a style of operatic singing using a full, rich, broad tone.
– ORIGIN Italian, 'fine song.'

belch /belCH/ ▶ **verb 1** noisily expel wind from the stomach through the mouth. **2** give out smoke or flames with great force. ▶ **noun** an act of belching.
– ORIGIN Old English.

be·lea·guered /bi'lēgərd/ ▶ **adjective 1** in difficulties: *the beleaguered telecom industry.* **2** (of a place) under siege.

– SYNONYMS **1 besieged,** blockaded, surrounded, encircled, hemmed in, under attack. **2 troubled,** harassed, hard-pressed, in difficulties, under pressure, in a tight corner; informal up against it.

– ORIGIN from Dutch *belegeren* 'camp round.'

bel·em·nite /'beləm,nīt/ ▶ **noun** a type of extinct marine mollusk with a bullet-shaped internal shell, found as a fossil.
– ORIGIN from Greek *belemnon* 'dart.'

bel·fry /'belfrē/ ▶ **noun** (pl. **belfries**) the place in a bell tower or steeple in which bells are housed.
– ORIGIN Old French *belfrei.*

Bel·gian /'beljən/ ▶ **noun** a person from Belgium. ▶ **adjective** relating to Belgium.

Be·li·al /'bēlēəl/ ▶ **noun** the Devil.
– ORIGIN Hebrew, 'worthlessness.'

be·lie /bi'lī/ ▶ **verb** (**belies, belying, belied**) **1** fail to give a true idea of: *her fast reflexes belied her age.* **2** show something to be untrue or unjustified.
– ORIGIN Old English, 'deceive by lying.'

be·lief /bi'lēf/ ▶ **noun 1** a feeling that something exists or is true, especially one without proof. **2** a firmly held opinion. **3** (**belief in**) trust or confidence in: *we must have belief in our own capabilities.* **4** religious faith.

– SYNONYMS **1 opinion,** view, conviction, judgment, thinking, idea, theory, thought, feeling. **2 faith,** trust, reliance, confidence, credence. **3 ideology,** principle, ethic, tenet, doctrine, teaching, dogma, creed, credo.
– ANTONYMS disbelief, doubt.

– PHRASES **beyond belief** astonishing; incredible.
– ORIGIN Old English.

CHOOSE THE RIGHT WORD

See **OPINION**.

be·lieve /bi'lēv/ ▶ **verb 1** accept that something is true or someone is telling the truth. **2** think that something is the case: *I believe we've already met.* **3** (**believe in**) feel certain that someone or something exists. **4** have religious faith.

– SYNONYMS **1** *I don't believe you* **trust,** have confidence in, consider honest, consider truthful. **2** *do you believe that story?* **accept,** be convinced by, give credence to, credit, trust, put confidence in; informal swallow, buy, go for. **3 think,** be of the opinion that, have an idea that, imagine, assume, presume, take it, understand, gather; informal reckon, figure. **4** (**believe in**) **have faith in,** trust in, have every confidence in, cling to, set (great) store by, value, be convinced by, be persuaded by; informal swear by.
– ANTONYMS doubt.

– DERIVATIVES **be·liev·a·bil·i·ty** /bi,lēvə'bilitē/ noun **be·liev·a·ble** /bi'lēvəbəl/ adjective **be·liev·a·bly** adverb.

be·liev·er /bi'lēvər/ ▶ **noun 1** a person who believes in the truth or existence of something. **2** someone with religious faith.

– SYNONYMS **disciple,** follower, supporter, adherent, devotee, upholder, worshiper.
– ANTONYMS infidel, skeptic.

be·lit·tle /bi'litl/ ▶ **verb** dismiss someone or something as unimportant.

– SYNONYMS **disparage,** denigrate, run down, deprecate, play down, trivialize, minimize; informal pooh-pooh.

Be·li·ze·an /bə'lēzēən/ (also **Belizian**) ▶ **noun** a person from Belize, a country in Central America. ▶ **adjective** relating to Belize.

bell /bel/ ▶ **noun 1** a metal cup-shaped object that sounds a clear musical note when struck. **2** a device that buzzes or rings to give a signal. **3** a bell-shaped thing. **4** (**bells**) a musical instrument consisting of a set of metal tubes, played by being struck. **5** Nautical the time as indicated every half-hour of a watch by the striking of the ship's bell one to eight times. ▶ **verb** spread or flare outward like the lip of a bell.
– PHRASES **bells and whistles** attractive additional features or trimmings. **ring a bell** informal sound vaguely familiar.
– ORIGIN Old English.

bel·la·don·na /,belə'dänə/ ▶ **noun 1** deadly nightshade. **2** a drug made from deadly nightshade.
– ORIGIN from Italian *bella donna* 'beautiful lady.'

bell-bot·toms ▶ **plural noun** pants with a marked flare below the knee.

bell·boy /'bel,boi/ (also **bellhop**) ▶ **noun** a porter in a hotel.

belle /bel/ ▶ **noun** a beautiful girl or woman.
– ORIGIN French.

belle é·poque /,bel ā'pôk/ ▶ **noun** the period of settled and comfortable life before World War I.
– ORIGIN French, 'fine period.'

belles-let·tres /,bel 'letrə/ ▶ **plural noun** literary essays written and read for their elegant style.
– ORIGIN French, 'fine letters.'

bell·flow·er /'bel,flou(-ə)r/ ▶ **noun** a plant with blue, purple, or white bell-shaped flowers.

bell·hop /'bel,häp/ ▶ **noun** an attendant in a hotel who performs services such as carrying guests' luggage; a bellboy.

bel·li·cose /'beli,kōs/ ▶ **adjective** aggressive and ready to fight.
– DERIVATIVES **bel·li·cos·i·ty** /,belə'käsitē/ noun.
– ORIGIN from Latin *bellum* 'war.'

CHOOSE THE RIGHT WORD

See **HOSTILE**.

bel·lig·er·ence /bə'lijərəns/ (also **belligerency**) ▶ **noun** aggressive or warlike behavior.

bel·lig·er·ent /bə'lijərənt/ ▶ **adjective 1** hostile and aggressive. **2** engaged in a war or conflict.

– SYNONYMS **1 hostile,** aggressive, threatening, antagonistic, pugnacious, bellicose, truculent, confrontational, contentious, militant, combative, argumentative; informal scrappy, spoiling for a fight. **2** *the belligerent states* **warring,** combatant, fighting, battling.
– ANTONYMS peaceable.

▶ **noun** a nation or person engaged in war or conflict.
– DERIVATIVES **bel·lig·er·ent·ly** adverb.
– ORIGIN from Latin *belligerare* 'wage war.'

CHOOSE THE RIGHT WORD

See **HOSTILE**.

Bel·li·ni /bə'lēnē/ ▶ **noun** (pl. **Bellinis**) a cocktail consisting of peach juice mixed with champagne.
– ORIGIN named after the Venetian painter Giovanni *Bellini.*

bell jar ▶ **noun** a bell-shaped glass cover used in a laboratory.

bel·low /'belō/ ▶ **verb 1** give a loud, deep roar of pain or anger. **2** shout or sing something very loudly.

– SYNONYMS **roar,** shout, bawl, thunder, boom, bark, yell, shriek, howl, scream; informal holler.
– ANTONYMS whisper.

▶ **noun** a loud, deep shout or sound.
– ORIGIN perhaps from Old English.

bel·lows /'belōz/ ▶ **plural noun 1** a device consisting of a bag with two handles, used for blowing air into a fire. **2** an object or device with folded sides that allow it to expand and contract.
– ORIGIN probably from Old English, 'belly.'

bell-ring·ing ▶ **noun** the activity or pastime of ringing church bells or handbells.
– DERIVATIVES **bell-ring·er** noun.

Bell's pal·sy /belz/ ▶ **noun** paralysis of the facial nerve, causing muscular weakness in one side of the face.
– ORIGIN named after the Scottish anatomist Sir Charles *Bell.*

bell·weth·er /'bel,weTHər/ ▶ **noun 1** the leading sheep of a flock, with a bell on its neck. **2** a leader or indicator: *university campuses are often the bellwether of change.*

bel·ly /'belē/ ▶ **noun** (pl. **bellies**) **1** the front part of the human body below the ribs, containing the stomach and bowels. **2** a person's stomach. **3** the rounded underside of a ship or aircraft. **4** the top surface of a violin or similar instrument, over which the strings are placed.

– SYNONYMS **stomach,** abdomen, paunch, middle, midriff, girth; informal tummy, gut, insides.

▶ **verb** (**bellies, bellying, bellied**) swell or bulge: *the sails bellied out in the breeze.*
– DERIVATIVES **bel·lied** adjective.
– PHRASES **go belly up** informal go bankrupt.
– ORIGIN Old English, 'bag.'

bel·ly·ache /'belē,āk/ informal ▶ **noun** a stomach pain. ▶ **verb** complain noisily or persistently.

bel·ly but·ton ▶ **noun** informal a person's navel.

bel·ly dance ▶ **noun** a dance originating in the Middle East, typically performed by a woman and involving undulating movements of the belly and rapid gyration of the hips.
– DERIVATIVES **bel·ly danc·er** noun **bel·ly danc·ing** noun.

bel·ly·flop /'belē,fläp/ ▶ **noun** informal a dive into water, landing flat on one's front.

bel·ly·ful /'belē,fo͝ol/ ▶ **noun** a sufficient amount to eat.
– PHRASES **have a bellyful of** informal have more than enough of something.

bel·ly laugh ▶ **noun** a loud unrestrained laugh.

be·long /bi'lôNG/ ▶ **verb 1** (**belong to**) be the property of someone. **2** (**belong to**) be a member of a group or organization. **3** be rightly put into a particular position or category: *I put the chair back where it belonged.* **4** feel at ease in a particular place or with a particular group.

– SYNONYMS **1 be owned by,** be the property of, be held by, be in the hands of. **2 be a member of,** be in, be affiliated to, be allied to, be associated with. **3 be part of,** be attached to, go with. **4 fit in,** be suited to; informal go, click.

be·long·ings /bi'lôNGiNGz/ ▶ **plural noun** a person's movable possessions.

– SYNONYMS **possessions,** effects, worldly goods, chattels, property; informal gear, tackle, things, stuff, bits and pieces.

Be·lo·rus·sian /,belō'rəSHən/ ▶ **adjective** of or relating to Belarus, its people, or its language. ▶ **noun 1** a person from Belarus. **2** the East Slavic language of Belarus.

be·lov·ed /bi'ləv(i)d/ ▶ **adjective** dearly loved.

– SYNONYMS **darling,** dear, precious, adored, cherished, treasured, prized, valued, idolized.

▶ **noun** a much loved person.

– SYNONYMS **sweetheart,** love, darling, dearest, lover, girlfriend, boyfriend; informal steady, baby, angel, honey, pet.

be·low /bi'lō/ ▶ **preposition & adverb 1** at a lower level than. **2** mentioned further on in a piece of writing.

– SYNONYMS **1** *the water rushed below them* **beneath,** under, underneath, further down than, lower than. **2** *the result is below average* **less than,** lower than, under, not as much as, smaller than. **3** *a captain is below a major* **inferior to,** subordinate to, under, beneath. **4** *I could see what was happening below* **further down,** lower down, in a lower position, underneath, beneath. **5** *the statements below* **underneath,** following, further on, at a later point.
– ANTONYMS above, over.

belt /belt/ ▶ **noun 1** a strip of leather or other material worn around the waist to support or hold in clothes or to carry weapons. **2** a continuous band in machinery that transfers motion from one wheel to another. **3** a strip or encircling area: *the asteroid belt.* **4** informal a heavy blow. **5** informal a gulp or shot of liquor.

– SYNONYMS **1 sash,** girdle, band, strap, cummerbund. **2 region,** strip, stretch, zone, area, district, sector, territory.

▶ **verb 1** fasten or secure something with a belt. **2** hit someone or something very hard. **3** (**belt something out**) informal sing or play something loudly and forcefully. **4** informal rush or dash. **5** gulp a drink quickly.
– DERIVATIVES **belt·ed** adjective.
– PHRASES **below the belt** disregarding the rules; unfair. [from the idea of an illegal blow in boxing.] **tighten**

one's belt cut one's spending. **under one's belt** safely or satisfactorily achieved or acquired.
– ORIGIN Latin *balteus* 'girdle.'

belt·way /'belt,wā/ ▶ **noun** a highway encircling an urban area.

be·lu·ga /bə'lo͞ogə/ ▶ **noun** (pl. same or **belugas**) **1** a small white toothed whale of Arctic waters. **2** a very large sturgeon from which caviar is obtained.
– ORIGIN from Russian, 'white.'

bel·ve·dere /'belvi,di(ə)r/ ▶ **noun** a summer house or open-sided gallery positioned to command a fine view.
– ORIGIN Italian, 'beautiful sight.'

be·ly·ing /bi'lī-iNG/ present participle of **BELIE**.

be·moan /bi'mōn/ ▶ **verb** express discontent or sorrow about something.

> **CHOOSE THE RIGHT WORD**
>
> See **MOURN**.

be·muse /bi'myo͞oz/ ▶ **verb** (usu. as adj. **bemused**) confuse or bewilder someone.

> – SYNONYMS *her bemused expression* **bewildered,** confused, puzzled, perplexed, baffled, mystified, nonplussed, dumbfounded, at sea, at a loss; informal flummoxed, bamboozled, fazed.

– DERIVATIVES **be·muse·ment** noun.

bench /benCH/ ▶ **noun 1** a long seat for more than one person. **2** a long worktable in a workshop or laboratory. **3** (**the bench**) the office of judge or magistrate. **4** (**the bench**) a seat at the side of a sports field for coaches and players not taking part in a game.

> – SYNONYMS **1 seat,** form, pew, stall, settle. **2 workbench,** worktop, counter.

– ORIGIN Old English.

bench·mark /'benCH,märk/ ▶ **noun 1** a standard against which things may be compared: *champagne will remain the quality benchmark for all sparkling wines.* **2** a surveyor's mark cut in a wall and used as a reference point in measuring altitudes.

> – SYNONYMS **standard,** point of reference, guide, guideline, norm, touchstone, yardstick, barometer, model, gauge, criterion, specification.

bench press ▶ **noun** an exercise in which one lies on a bench with feet on the floor and raises a weight with both arms.

bench test ▶ **noun** a test carried out on a product before it is released.

bend[1] /bend/ ▶ **verb** (past and past part. **bent** /bent/) **1** give or have a curved or angled shape, form, or course: *the road bends right and then left.* **2** lean or curve the body downward. **3** force or be forced to give in: *a refusal to bend to mob rule.* **4** interpret or modify a rule to suit someone. **5** direct one's attention or energies to a task.

> – SYNONYMS **1 curve,** crook, flex, angle, hook, bow, arch, buckle, warp, contort, distort, deform, twist. **2 turn,** curve, incline, swing, veer, fork, change course, curl, loop. **3 stoop,** bow, crouch, hunch, lean down/over.
> – ANTONYMS straighten.

▶ **noun 1** a curved or angled part or course. **2** a kind of knot used to join two ropes together, or one rope to another object. **3** (**the bends**) (treated as sing.) decompression sickness.

> – SYNONYMS **curve,** turn, corner, kink, angle, arc, twist.

– DERIVATIVES **bend·a·ble** adjective.
– PHRASES **bend someone's ear** informal talk to someone at length or to ask a favor. **around the bend** informal crazy.
– ORIGIN Old English, 'put in bonds, tension a bow.'

bend[2] ▶ **noun** Heraldry a broad diagonal stripe from top left to bottom right of a shield.
– ORIGIN Old French *bende* 'flat strip.'

bend·er /'bendər/ ▶ **noun** informal a drinking session.

bend sin·is·ter ▶ **noun** Heraldry a broad diagonal stripe from top right to bottom left of a shield (a supposed sign of illegitimacy).

bend·y /'bendē/ ▶ **adjective** (**bendier, bendiest**) **1** capable of bending; flexible. **2** having many bends: *bendy country roads.*

be·neath /bi'nēTH/ ▶ **preposition & adverb** extending or directly underneath.

> – SYNONYMS **1** *we sat beneath the trees* **under,** underneath, below, at the foot of, at the bottom of, lower than. **2** *sand with rock beneath* **underneath,** below, further down, lower down.
> – ANTONYMS above.

▶ **preposition** of lower status or worth than.

> – SYNONYMS **1** *the rank beneath theirs* **inferior to,** below, lower than, subordinate to. **2** *such an attitude was beneath her* **unworthy of,** unbecoming to, degrading to.
> – ANTONYMS above.

– ORIGIN Old English.

Ben·e·dic·tine /,beni'dik,tēn, -tin/ ▶ **noun 1** a monk or nun of a Christian religious order following the rule of St. Benedict. **2** trademark a liqueur based on brandy, originally made by Benedictine monks in France.
▶ **adjective** relating to St. Benedict or the Benedictines.

ben·e·dic·tion /,beni'dikSHən/ ▶ **noun 1** the speaking of a blessing. **2** the state of being blessed.
– ORIGIN from Latin *benedicere* 'bless.'

ben·e·fac·tion /,benə'fakSHən/ ▶ **noun** formal a donation or gift.
– ORIGIN from Latin *bene facere* 'do good (to).'

ben·e·fac·tor /'benə,faktər, ,benə'faktər/ ▶ **noun** a person who gives money or other help.

> – SYNONYMS **patron,** supporter, backer, sponsor, donor, contributor, subscriber; informal angel.

– DERIVATIVES **ben·e·fac·tress** /'benə,faktris, ,benə'faktris/ noun.

ben·e·fice /'benəfis/ ▶ **noun** (in the Christian Church) an office whereby a member of the clergy receives accommodations and income in return for their duties.
– ORIGIN Latin *beneficium* 'favor, support.'

be·nef·i·cent /bə'nefəsənt/ ▶ **adjective** doing or resulting in good: *a beneficent democracy.*
– DERIVATIVES **be·nef·i·cence** noun.

ben·e·fi·cial /,benə'fiSHəl/ ▶ **adjective** having a good effect; favorable.

> – SYNONYMS **advantageous,** favorable, helpful, useful, of assistance, valuable, salutary, worthwhile, fruitful, productive, profitable, rewarding, gainful.
> – ANTONYMS disadvantageous.

– DERIVATIVES **ben·e·fi·cial·ly** adverb.

ben·e·fi·ci·ar·y /ˌbenəˈfisHēˌerē/ ▶ **noun** (pl. **beneficiaries**) a person who benefits from something, especially a trust or will.

– SYNONYMS **recipient,** payee, heir, heiress, inheritor.

ben·e·fit /ˈbenəfit/ ▶ **noun 1** advantage or profit gained from something: *the benefits of a private education.* **2** a payment made by the government or an insurance company to someone entitled to receive it. **3** a public performance to raise money for a charity.

– SYNONYMS **1 good,** sake, welfare, well-being, advantage, comfort, ease, convenience, help, aid, assistance, service. **2 advantage,** profit, plus point, boon, blessing, reward; informal perk. **3 social security payment,** welfare, charity; informal the dole.
– ANTONYMS detriment, disadvantage.

▶ **verb** (**benefits, benefiting** or **benefitting, benefited** or **benefitted**) **1** receive an advantage: *areas that would benefit from regeneration.* **2** bring advantage to someone or something.

– SYNONYMS **1 help,** be advantageous to, be beneficial to, profit, do good to, be of service to, serve, be useful to, be helpful to, aid, assist. **2 profit,** gain, reap reward, make the most of, exploit, turn to one's advantage, put to good use.
– ANTONYMS disadvantage, harm.

– PHRASES **the benefit of the doubt** an acceptance that a person is truthful or innocent if the opposite cannot be proved.
– ORIGIN Latin *benefactum* 'good deed.'

be·nev·o·lent /bəˈnevələnt/ ▶ **adjective 1** well meaning and kindly. **2** (of an organization) charitable rather than profit-making.

– SYNONYMS **kind,** kindly, kind-hearted, good-natured, compassionate, caring, altruistic, humanitarian, philanthropic, beneficent, well meaning, benign.
– ANTONYMS unkind.

– DERIVATIVES **be·nev·o·lence** noun **be·nev·o·lent·ly** adverb.
– ORIGIN from Latin *bene* 'well' + *velle* 'to wish.'

WORD TOOLKIT

See **GENEROUS**.

Ben·ga·li /ˌbeNGˈgälē/ ▶ **noun** (pl. **Bengalis**) **1** a person from Bengal in the northeast of the Indian subcontinent. **2** the language of Bangladesh and West Bengal. ▶ **adjective** relating to Bengal.
– ORIGIN Hindi.

be·night·ed /biˈnītid/ ▶ **adjective 1** lacking understanding of cultural, intellectual, or moral matters: *you're a provincial, benighted fool.* **2** old use unable to travel further because night has fallen.

be·nign /biˈnīn/ ▶ **adjective 1** kind and gentle. **2** not harmful or harsh; favorable: *Spain's benign climate.* **3** (of a tumor) not malignant.

– SYNONYMS **1 kindly,** kind, warmhearted, good-natured, friendly, genial, tenderhearted, gentle, sympathetic, compassionate, caring, well disposed, benevolent. **2 mild,** temperate, gentle, balmy, soft, pleasant, favorable, healthy. **3** *a benign tumor* **harmless,** nonmalignant, noncancerous.
– ANTONYMS unkind, malignant.

– DERIVATIVES **be·nig·ni·ty** /biˈnignitē/ noun **be·nign·ly** adverb.
– ORIGIN Latin *benignus.*

WORD TOOLKIT

See **HARMLESS**.

be·nig·nant /biˈnignənt/ ▶ **adjective** less common term for **BENIGN**.

Be·ni·nese /ˌbenəˈnēz, -ˈnēs/ ▶ **noun** a person from Benin, a country in West Africa. ▶ **adjective** relating to Benin.

ben·i·son /ˈbenəsən, -zən/ ▶ **noun** literary a blessing.
– ORIGIN Old French *beneiçun.*

bent /bent/ past and past participle of **BEND**[1] ▶ **adjective 1** having an angle or sharp curve. **2** (**bent on**) determined to do or have something.

– SYNONYMS **1 twisted,** crooked, warped, contorted, deformed, misshapen, out of shape, bowed, arched, curved, angled, hooked, kinked; informal pretzeled. **2** (**bent on**) **intent on,** determined on, set on, insistent on, resolved on.
– ANTONYMS straight.

▶ **noun** a natural talent or inclination: *a man of a religious bent.*

– SYNONYMS **inclination,** leaning, tendency, talent, gift, flair, aptitude, facility, skill.

bent·wood /ˈbentˌwŏŏd/ ▶ **noun** wood that is artificially shaped for making furniture.

be·numb /biˈnəm/ ▶ **verb** deprive someone of feeling.

ben·zene /ˈbenˌzēn, benˈzēn/ ▶ **noun** a volatile liquid hydrocarbon present in coal tar and petroleum.
– ORIGIN from French *benjoin,* referring to a resin obtained from an East Asian tree.

ben·zine /ˈbenˌzēn, benˈzēn/ (also **benzin** /ˈbenzin/) ▶ **noun** a mixture of liquid hydrocarbons obtained from petroleum.

ben·zo·di·az·e·pine /ˌbenzōˌdīˈazəˌpēn/ ▶ **noun** any of a class of organic compounds used as tranquilizers, such as Valium.

be·queath /biˈkwēTH, -ˈkwēTH/ ▶ **verb 1** leave property to someone by a will. **2** pass on: *he ditched the unpopular policies bequeathed to him.*

– SYNONYMS **leave,** will, hand down, pass on, entrust, make over, grant, transfer, give, bestow on, confer on.

– ORIGIN Old English.

be·quest /biˈkwest/ ▶ **noun 1** a legacy bequeathed to someone. **2** the action of bequeathing something.

– SYNONYMS **legacy,** estate, inheritance, endowment, settlement.

be·rate /biˈrāt/ ▶ **verb** scold or criticize someone angrily.

– SYNONYMS **scold,** rebuke, reprimand, reproach, reprove, admonish, chide, criticize, upbraid, take to task; informal tell off, give someone a talking-to, read someone the riot act, give someone a dressing-down, bawl out, come down on, tear into, chew out, ream (out), blast. formal castigate.
– ANTONYMS praise.

CHOOSE THE RIGHT WORD

See **SCOLD**.

Ber·ber /ˈbərbər/ ▶ **noun** a member of a people native to North Africa.

ber·be·ris /ˈbərbəris/ ▶ **noun** a spiny shrub with yellow flowers and red berries.
– ORIGIN Latin *barbaris*.

be·reave /biˈrēv/ ▶ **verb** (**be bereaved**) be deprived of a close relation or friend through their death.
– DERIVATIVES **be·reave·ment** noun.
– ORIGIN Old English.

be·reft /biˈreft/ ▶ **adjective 1** (**bereft of**) deprived of or lacking: *her room was bereft of color.* **2** sad and lonely because someone has died or gone away.

– SYNONYMS **deprived,** robbed, stripped, devoid, bankrupt; (**bereft of**) wanting, in need of, lacking, without; informal minus, clean out of; literary sans.

– ORIGIN from **BEREAVE**.

be·ret /bəˈrā/ ▶ **noun** a flat round cap of felt or cloth.
– ORIGIN French, 'Basque cap.'

ber·ga·mot /ˈbərgəˌmät/ ▶ **noun 1** an oily substance extracted from Seville oranges, used as flavoring in Earl Grey tea. **2** an herb of the mint family.
– ORIGIN named after *Bergamo* in Italy.

ber·i·ber·i /ˈberēˈberē/ ▶ **noun** a disease causing inflammation of the nerves and heart failure, due to a deficiency of vitamin B_1.
– ORIGIN Sinhalese.

ber·ke·li·um /bərˈkēlēəm/ ▶ **noun** a radioactive metallic chemical element.
– ORIGIN named after the University of California, *Berkeley*.

berm /bərm/ ▶ **noun** a raised bank or flat strip of land on the edge of a river, canal, or road.
– ORIGIN French *berme*.

Ber·mu·dan /bərˈmyo͞odn/ (also **Bermudian** /bərˈmyo͞odēən/) ▶ **noun** a person from Bermuda.
▶ **adjective** relating to Bermuda.

Ber·mu·da shorts /bərˈmyo͞odə/ ▶ **plural noun** casual knee-length shorts.

ber·ry /ˈberē/ ▶ **noun** (pl. **berries**) **1** a small round juicy fruit without a stone. **2** Botany a fruit that has its seeds enclosed in a fleshy pulp, e.g., a banana or tomato.
– ORIGIN Old English.

ber·serk /bərˈzərk, -ˈsərk/ ▶ **adjective** out of control with anger or excitement: *the crowd went berserk.*

– SYNONYMS **mad,** crazy, insane, out of one's mind, hysterical, frenzied, crazed, demented, maniacal, manic, frantic, raving, wild, out of control, amok, on the rampage; informal off the deep end, ape, bananas, bonkers, postal.

– ORIGIN Old Norse.

berth /bərTH/ ▶ **noun 1** a place for a ship to moor at a wharf or harbor. **2** a bunk on a ship or train.

– SYNONYMS **1 bunk,** bed, cot, couch, hammock. **2 mooring,** dock, pier, jetty, quay.

▶ **verb** moor a ship in a berth.

– SYNONYMS **dock,** moor, land, tie up, make fast.

– PHRASES **give someone/thing a wide berth** stay well away from someone or something.
– ORIGIN probably from a nautical use of **BEAR**[1].

ber·yl /ˈberəl/ ▶ **noun** a transparent pale green, blue, or yellow mineral used as a gemstone.
– ORIGIN Greek *bērullos*.

be·ryl·li·um /bəˈrilēəm/ ▶ **noun** a hard, gray, lightweight metallic chemical element.

be·seech /biˈsēCH/ ▶ **verb** (past and past part. **besought** /biˈsôt/ or **beseeched**) literary ask someone urgently or pleadingly to do or give something: *they beseeched him to stay.*

– SYNONYMS **implore,** beg, entreat, plead with, appeal to, call on, importune, pray to, ask, petition.

– ORIGIN Old English.

be·set /biˈset/ ▶ **verb** (**besetting**; past and past part. **beset**) (of an unwelcome or unpleasant situation) affect or trouble someone or something: *the consortium has been beset by financial difficulties.*
– ORIGIN Old English.

CHOOSE THE RIGHT WORD

See **ATTACK**.

be·side /biˈsīd/ ▶ **preposition 1** at the side of; next to. **2** compared with. **3** in addition to; apart from.

– SYNONYMS **alongside,** by/at the side of, next to, parallel to, abreast of, adjacent to, next door to, neighboring.

– PHRASES **beside oneself** frantic with worry. **beside the point** irrelevant.

be·sides /biˈsīdz/ ▶ **preposition** in addition to; apart from.

– SYNONYMS **in addition to,** as well as, over and above, on top of, apart from, other than, aside from, not counting, excluding, leaving aside; informal outside of.

▶ **adverb** in addition; as well.

– SYNONYMS **1** *there's a lot more besides* **in addition,** as well, too, also, into the bargain, on top of that, to boot. **2** *besides, he's a man* **furthermore,** moreover, further; informal what's more.

be·siege /biˈsēj/ ▶ **verb 1** surround a place with armed forces in order to force it to surrender. **2** crowd around someone oppressively: *she was besieged by newsmen.* **3** overwhelm with requests or complaints: *the radio station was besieged with calls.*

– SYNONYMS **1 lay siege to,** beleaguer, blockade. **2 surround,** mob, harass, pester, badger. **3 overwhelm,** bombard, inundate, deluge, flood, swamp, snow under.

– DERIVATIVES **be·sieg·er** noun.
– ORIGIN Old French *asegier*.

be·smirch /biˈsmərCH/ ▶ **verb** damage someone's reputation.

be·som /ˈbēzəm/ ▶ **noun** a broom made of twigs tied around a stick.
– ORIGIN Old English.

be·sot·ted /biˈsätid/ ▶ **adjective** completely infatuated with someone.
– ORIGIN from **SOT**.

be·sought /biˈsôt/ past and past participle of **BESEECH**.

be·spat·ter /biˈspatər/ ▶ **verb** splash something with liquid: *his shoes were bespattered with mud.*

be·speak /biˈspēk/ ▶ **verb** (past **bespoke** /biˈspōk/; past part. **bespoken** /biˈspōkən/) formal **1** be evidence of: *the attractive tree-lined road bespoke money.* **2** order something in advance.

be·spec·ta·cled /biˈspektəkəld/ ▶ **adjective** wearing eyeglasses.

best /best/ ▶ **adjective 1** of the highest quality. **2** most suitable or sensible.

– SYNONYMS **finest,** premier, greatest, top, foremost, leading, preeminent, supreme, superlative, unrivaled, second to none, without equal, unsurpassed, unparalleled, unbeatable, optimum, ultimate, incomparable, record-breaking; informal star, number-one, a cut above the rest, top-drawer.

▶ **adverb 1** to the highest degree or standard; most. **2** most suitably or sensibly.

– SYNONYMS **1** *the best-dressed man* **to the highest standard,** in the best way. **2** *the food he liked best* **most,** to the highest/greatest degree. **3** *this is best done at home* **most appropriately,** most suitably, most fittingly, most usefully, most advantageously, most sensibly, most prudently, most wisely.
– ANTONYMS worst, least.

▶ **noun 1** (**the best**) that which is of the highest quality. **2** (**one's best**) the highest standard one can reach.

– SYNONYMS *only the best will do* **finest,** choicest, top, cream, choice, prime, elite, crème de la crème, flower, jewel in the crown; informal tops, pick of the litter.
– ANTONYMS worst.

▶ **verb** informal outwit or defeat someone.
– PHRASES **at best** taking the most optimistic view of a situation. **the best of three** (or **five**, etc.) victory achieved by winning the majority of a specified odd number of games. **the best part of** most of. **get the best of** overcome: *the disease almost got the best of her.* **had best** find it most sensible to do something: *I'd best be going.* **make the best of** get what limited advantage one can from a situation.
– ORIGIN Old English.

best boy ▶ **noun** the assistant to the chief electrician of a movie crew.

bes·tial /ˈbēsCHəl, ˈbes-/ ▶ **adjective 1** relating to or like an animal or beast. **2** savagely cruel: *bestial and barbaric acts.*
– DERIVATIVES **bes·tial·ly** adverb.
– ORIGIN Latin *bestia* 'beast.'

bes·ti·al·i·ty /ˌbēsCHēˈalitē, ˌbes-/ ▶ **noun 1** savagely cruel behavior. **2** sexual intercourse between a person and an animal.

bes·ti·ar·y /ˈbēsCHēˌerē, ˈbes-/ ▶ **noun** (pl. **bestiaries**) a medieval collection of descriptions of various kinds of animals.

be·stir /biˈstər/ ▶ **verb** (**bestirs, bestirring, bestirred**) (**bestir oneself**) make a physical or mental effort; rouse oneself to activity.

best man ▶ **noun** a man chosen by a bridegroom to assist him at his wedding.

be·stow /biˈstō/ ▶ **verb** award an honor, right, or gift to someone: *he wore the medals bestowed upon him by the president.*

– SYNONYMS **confer on,** grant, accord, afford, endow with, present, award, give, donate, entrust with, vouchsafe.

– DERIVATIVES **be·stow·al** noun.
– ORIGIN Old English.

CHOOSE THE RIGHT WORD

See **GIVE**.

be·stride /biˈstrīd/ ▶ **verb** (past **bestrode** /biˈstrōd/; past part. **bestridden** /biˈstridən/) have a leg on either side of something.

best·sell·er /ˌbestˈselər/ ▶ **noun** a book or other product that sells in very large numbers.
– DERIVATIVES **best·sell·ing** adjective.

be·suit·ed /biˈso͞otid/ ▶ **adjective** (of a man) wearing a suit.

bet /bet/ ▶ **verb** (**bets, betting;** past and past part. **bet** or **betted**) **1** risk money or property against someone else's on the outcome of an unpredictable event such as a race. **2** informal feel sure: *I bet she made it all up.*

– SYNONYMS **1 wager,** gamble, stake, risk, venture, hazard, chance. **2 be certain,** be sure, be convinced, be confident, expect, predict, guess.

▶ **noun 1** an act of betting money on something. **2** an amount of money bet: *a $10 bet.* **3** informal an option: *your best bet is to go early.* **4** (**one's bet**) informal one's opinion: *my bet is that she'll stay.*

– SYNONYMS **1 wager,** gamble, stake, ante. **2** *your best bet is to go early* **option,** choice, alternative, course of action, plan.

– DERIVATIVES **bet·tor** (also **better**) noun.
– PHRASES **you bet** informal of course; certainly.
– ORIGIN perhaps from a former word meaning 'abetting.'

be·ta /ˈbātə/ ▶ **noun 1** the second letter of the Greek alphabet (Β, β), represented as 'b'. **2** short for **BETA TEST**.

be·ta block·er ▶ **noun** a drug used to treat angina and reduce high blood pressure.

be·take /biˈtāk/ ▶ **verb** (past **betook** /biˈto͝ok/; past part. **betaken**) (**betake oneself to**) literary go to a place.

be·ta par·ti·cle (also **beta ray**) ▶ **noun** Physics a fast-moving electron given off by some radioactive substances.

be·ta test ▶ **noun** a trial of machinery, software, etc., in the final stages of its development, carried out by people not connected with its development.
▶ **verb** (**beta-test**) subject a product to such a test.

be·tel /ˈbētl/ ▶ **noun** the leaf of an Asian plant, chewed as a mild stimulant.
– ORIGIN Portuguese.

be·tel nut ▶ **noun** the seed of a tropical areca palm tree, often chewed with betel leaves.

bête noire /ˌbāt ˈnwär, ˌbet/ ▶ **noun** (pl. **bêtes noires** pronunc. same) (**one's bête noire**) a person or thing that one particularly dislikes.
– ORIGIN French, 'black beast.'

be·think /biˈTHiNGk/ ▶ **verb** (past and past part. **bethought** /biˈTHôt/) (**bethink oneself**) formal come to think about something.

be·tide /biˈtīd/ ▶ **verb** literary happen, or happen to someone.

be·times /biˈtīmz/ ▶ **adverb** literary in good time; early.

be·to·ken /biˈtōkən/ ▶ **verb** literary be a warning or sign of: *the blue sky betokened a day of good weather.*

bet·o·ny /ˈbetn-ē/ ▶ **noun** (pl. **betonies**) a plant of the mint family with purple flowers.
– ORIGIN Latin.

be·took /biˈto͝ok/ past of **BETAKE**.

be·tray /biˈtrā/ ▶ **verb 1** endanger one's country, a person, or group of people by treacherously helping an enemy. **2** be disloyal to: *many of the unemployed felt betrayed by the government.* **3** unintentionally reveal something: *Lou's heightened color betrayed her embarrassment.*

– SYNONYMS **1 be disloyal to,** be unfaithful to, break faith with, inform on/against, give away, denounce, sell out, stab in the back; informal rat on/out, snitch on, finger, sell down the river. **2 reveal,** disclose, divulge, tell, give away, leak, bring out into the open.

– DERIVATIVES **be·tray·er** noun.
– ORIGIN from Latin *tradere* 'hand over.'

be·tray·al /bi'trāəl/ ▶ **noun** the act of being disloyal.

– SYNONYMS **disloyalty,** treachery, bad faith, breach of faith, breach of trust, faithlessness, duplicity, deception, double-dealing, stab in the back, double-cross, sellout.
– ANTONYMS loyalty.

be·trothed /bə'trōT͟Hd, -'trôTHd/ formal ▶ **adjective** engaged to be married. ▶ **noun** (**one's betrothed**) the person to whom one is engaged to be married.
– DERIVATIVES **be·troth·al** /bə'trōT͟Həl, -'trôTHəl/ noun.
– ORIGIN from **TRUTH**.

bet·ter /'betər/ ▶ **adjective 1** more satisfactory or effective. **2** partly or fully recovered from an illness or injury.

– SYNONYMS **1 superior,** finer, of higher quality, preferable; informal a cut above, head and shoulders above, ahead of the pack/field. **2 healthier,** fitter, stronger, well again, cured, healed, recovered, recovering, on the road to recovery, on the mend.
– ANTONYMS worse, inferior.

▶ **adverb 1** in a more satisfactory or effective way. **2** to a greater degree; more.

– SYNONYMS **1 to a higher standard,** in a superior way, more effectively. **2** *this may suit you better* **more,** to a greater degree/extent. **3** *the money could be better spent* **more wisely,** more sensibly, more suitably, more fittingly, more advantageously, more usefully.

▶ **noun 1** something that is better. **2** (**one's betters**) dated or humorous people who are superior to oneself in social status.
▶ **verb 1** improve on: *a record bettered by only one other nonleague team.* **2** (**better oneself**) improve one's social status.

– SYNONYMS **1 surpass,** improve on, beat, exceed, top, cap, trump, eclipse. **2 improve,** ameliorate, raise, advance, further, lift, upgrade, enhance.
– ANTONYMS worsen.

– PHRASES **better off** in a more favorable position, especially financially. **the better part of** most of. **get the better of** defeat or overcome: *no one had ever gotten the better of her.* **had better** ought to do something: *I'd better get on with my work.*
– ORIGIN Old English.

USAGE

In the phrase **had better do something** the word **had** is often dropped in informal speech, as in *you better not come tonight.* In writing, the **had** may be shortened to **'d** but it should not be dropped altogether (*you'd better not come tonight*).

bet·ter half ▶ **noun** informal a person's husband, wife, or partner.

bet·ter·ment /'betərmənt/ ▶ **noun** the improvement of someone or something: *the betterment of society.*

be·tween /bi'twēn/ ▶ **preposition & adverb 1** at, into, or across the space separating two things. **2** in the period separating two points in time.

– SYNONYMS *Philip stood between his parents* **in the middle of,** with one on either side; old use betwixt.

▶ **preposition 1** indicating a connection or relationship. **2** by combining the resources or actions of two or more parties.

– SYNONYMS *the bond between Amy and her mother* **connecting,** linking, joining, uniting, allying.

– PHRASES **between you and me** (or **between ourselves**) in confidence.
– ORIGIN Old English.

USAGE

A preposition such as **between** takes the object case and is correctly followed by object pronouns such as **me** rather than subject pronouns such as **I**. It is therefore correct to say **between you and me** rather than **between you and I**.

be·twixt /bi'twikst/ ▶ **preposition & adverb** old use between.
– PHRASES **betwixt and between** informal neither one thing nor the other.
– ORIGIN Old English.

bev·el /'bevəl/ ▶ **noun 1** (in carpentry) a sloping surface or edge. **2** (also **bevel square**) a tool for marking angles in carpentry and stonework. ▶ **verb** (**bevels, beveling, beveled**) cut a sloping edge on an object.
– ORIGIN Old French, from *baif* 'open-mouthed.'

bev·er·age /'bev(ə)rij/ ▶ **noun** a drink other than water.
– ORIGIN Old French *bevrage.*

bev·y /'bevē/ ▶ **noun** (pl. **bevies**) a large group of people or things: *a bevy of children.*
– ORIGIN unknown.

be·wail /bi'wāl/ ▶ **verb** express great regret or sorrow over: *she wept copiously and bewailed her bad luck.*

be·ware /bi'we(ə)r/ ▶ **verb** be cautious and alert to risks or dangers: *beware of pickpockets at the train and bus stations.*

– SYNONYMS **watch out,** look out, mind out, be alert, be on one's guard, keep one's eyes open/peeled, keep an eye out, take care, be careful, be cautious, watch one's step, guard against.

– ORIGIN from *be ware* 'be aware.'

be·wil·der /bi'wildər/ ▶ **verb** puzzle or confuse someone.

– SYNONYMS **baffle,** mystify, bemuse, perplex, puzzle, confuse; informal flummox, faze, stump, beat.

– DERIVATIVES **be·wil·der·ing** adjective **be·wil·der·ment** noun.
– ORIGIN from the old word *wilder,* meaning 'lead or go astray.'

be·witch /bi'wicH/ ▶ **verb 1** cast a spell over someone. **2** enchant and delight someone.

– SYNONYMS **captivate,** enchant, entrance, enrapture, charm, beguile, delight, fascinate, enthrall, cast a spell on.

– DERIVATIVES **be·witch·ing** adjective **be·witch·ment** noun.
– ORIGIN from **WITCH**.

bey /bā/ ▶ **noun** (pl. **beys**) historical the governor of a province in the Ottoman Empire.
– ORIGIN Turkish *beg* 'prince, governor.'

be·yond /bē'änd, bi'yänd/ ▶ **preposition & adverb 1** at or to the farther side of. **2** outside the range or limits of. **3** to or in a state where something is impossible: *the engine* *was beyond repair.* **4** happening or continuing after. **5** apart from.

– SYNONYMS **1 on the far side of,** on the other side of, further away than, behind, past, after. **2 later than,** past, after. **3 greater than,** more than, exceeding, in excess of, above, upwards of.

– ORIGIN Old English.

bez·el /'bezəl/ ▸ **noun** a groove holding a gemstone or the glass cover of a watch in position.
– ORIGIN Old French.

be·zique /bə'zēk/ ▸ **noun** a card game for two players, played with a double deck of 64 cards.
– ORIGIN French *bésigue.*

Bh ▸ **symbol** the chemical element bohrium.

bha·ji /'bäjē/ (also **bhajia** /'bäjēə/) ▸ **noun** (pl. **bhajis, bhajia**) (in Indian cooking) a small flat cake or ball of vegetables, fried in batter.
– ORIGIN Hindi.

bhan·gra /'bäNGgrə/ ▸ **noun** a type of popular music combining Punjabi folk traditions with Western pop music.
– ORIGIN Punjabi.

b.h.p. ▸ **abbreviation** brake horsepower.

Bhu·tan·ese /ˌbo͞otn'ēz, -'ēs/ ▸ **noun** a person from Bhutan, a small kingdom in the Himalayas. ▸ **adjective** relating to Bhutan.

Bi ▸ **symbol** the chemical element bismuth.

bi /bī/ ▸ **adjective** informal bisexual.

bi- ▸ **combining form 1** two; having two: *biathlon.* **2** occurring twice in every one or once in every two: *bicentennial.* **3** lasting for two: *biennial.*
– ORIGIN Latin.

bi·an·nu·al /bī'anyo͞oəl/ ▸ **adjective** occurring twice a year.
– DERIVATIVES **bi·an·nu·al·ly** adverb.

bi·as /'bīəs/ ▸ **noun 1** an inclination or prejudice in favor of or against a particular person or thing: *some people alleged there was a bias toward the Democrats.* **2** a slanting direction across the grain of a fabric. **3** the tendency of a ball in the game of lawn bowling to swerve because of the way it is weighted. **4** Electronics a steady voltage, applied to an electronic device, that can be adjusted to change the way the device operates.

– SYNONYMS **prejudice,** partiality, favoritism, partisanship, unfairness, one-sidedness, discrimination, leaning, tendency, inclination.
– ANTONYMS impartiality.

▸ **verb** (**biases, biasing, biased** or **biassing, biassed**) cause someone to have an opinion or prejudice in favor of or against.

– SYNONYMS **1** *he claimed the judge was biased against him* **prejudice,** influence, color, sway, predispose, distort, skew, slant. **2** (as adj. **biased**) *a biased view of the situation* **prejudiced,** partial, partisan, one-sided, bigoted, discriminatory, distorted, warped, twisted, skewed.

– ORIGIN French *biais.*

bi·ath·lon /bī'aTHlän/ ▸ **noun** a sporting event combining cross-country skiing and rifle shooting.
– ORIGIN from Greek *athlon* 'contest.'

bib /bib/ ▸ **noun 1** a piece of cloth or plastic fastened under a child's chin to keep its clothes clean while it is eating. **2** the part of an apron or pair of dungarees that covers the chest.
– PHRASES **one's best bib and tucker** informal one's smartest clothes.
– ORIGIN probably from Latin *bibere* 'to drink.'

bi·be·lot /'bib(ə)ˌlō/ ▸ **noun** a small ornament or trinket.
– ORIGIN French.

Bi·ble /'bībəl/ ▸ **noun 1** the Christian scriptures, consisting of the Old and New Testaments. **2** the Jewish scriptures. **3** (**bible**) informal a book regarded as giving comprehensive and reliable information about something: *the professional electrician's bible.*
– ORIGIN Greek *biblion* 'book.'

Bi·ble Belt ▸ **noun** the areas of the southern and midwestern US and western Canada where many Protestants believe in a literal interpretation of the Bible.

bib·li·cal /'biblikəl/ ▸ **adjective** relating to or found in the Bible.
– DERIVATIVES **bib·li·cal·ly** adverb.

bib·li·og·ra·phy /ˌbiblē'ägrəfē/ ▸ **noun** (pl. **bibliographies**) **1** a list of the books or articles referred to in a scholarly work. **2** a list of books on a particular subject or by a particular author. **3** the study of books and their production.
– DERIVATIVES **bib·li·og·ra·pher** noun **bib·li·o·graph·ic** /ˌbiblēə'grafik/ adjective.
– ORIGIN from Greek *biblion* 'book.'

bib·li·o·phile /'biblēəˌfīl/ ▸ **noun** a person who collects or loves books.

bib·u·lous /'bibyələs/ ▸ **adjective** formal very fond of drinking alcohol.
– ORIGIN from Latin *bibere* 'to drink.'

bi·cam·er·al /bī'kamərəl/ ▸ **adjective** (of a parliament or other legislative body) having two chambers.
– ORIGIN from Latin *camera* 'chamber.'

bi·car·bo·nate /bī'kärbəˌnāt, -nit/ ▸ **noun 1** Chemistry a compound containing HCO_3 negative ions together with a metallic element. **2** (also **bicarbonate of soda**) sodium bicarbonate.

bi·cen·ten·ar·y /ˌbīsen'tenərē/ ▸ **noun** another name for **BICENTENNIAL.**

bi·cen·ten·ni·al /ˌbīsen'tenēəl/ ▸ **noun** the two-hundredth anniversary of an event.

bi·ceps /'bīˌseps/ ▸ **noun** (pl. same) a large muscle in the upper arm that flexes the arm and forearm.
– ORIGIN Latin, 'two-headed' (because the muscle has two points of attachment).

bi·chon frise /'bēsHän 'frēz/ ▸ **noun** a breed of toy dog with a curly white coat.
– ORIGIN from French *barbichon* 'little water spaniel' + *frisé* 'curly-haired.'

bick·er /'bikər/ ▸ **verb** argue about unimportant things.
– ORIGIN unknown.

bi·cus·pid /bī'kəspid/ ▸ **noun** a tooth with two cusps or points. ▸ **adjective** having two cusps or points.
– ORIGIN from Latin *cuspis* 'sharp point.'

bi·cy·cle /'bīsikəl/ ▸ **noun** a vehicle with two wheels held in a frame one behind the other, propelled by pedals. ▸ **verb** ride a bicycle.
– DERIVATIVES **bi·cy·clist** noun.
– ORIGIN from Greek *kuklos* 'wheel.'

bid[1] /bid/ ▸ **verb** (**bids, bidding;** past and past part. **bid**) **1** offer a price for something, especially at an auction.

2 (**bid for**) offer to do work or supply goods for a stated price. **3** try to get or achieve: *the two boys are bidding for places on the swim team.*

– SYNONYMS **offer,** put up, tender, proffer, propose.

▶ **noun 1** an offer to buy something. **2** an offer to do work or supply goods at a stated price. **3** an effort to get or achieve something: *a bid for power.*

– SYNONYMS **1 offer,** tender, proposal. **2 attempt,** effort, endeavor, try; informal crack, go, shot, stab.

– DERIVATIVES **bid·der** noun.
– ORIGIN Old English.

bid[2] ▶ **verb** (**bids, bidding**; past **bid** or **bade** /bad, bād/; past part. **bid**) **1** utter a greeting or farewell to someone. **2** old use order someone to do something.
– ORIGIN Old English, 'ask.'

bid·da·ble /'bidəbəl/ ▶ **adjective** meekly ready to obey instructions.

bid·den /'bidn/ old-fashioned past participle of **BID**[2].

bid·ding /'bidiNG/ ▶ **noun** an authoritative instruction to do something.

– SYNONYMS *let's make it clear that I am not here at your bidding* **command,** order, direction, instruction, decree, injunction, demand, beck and call.

bid·dy /'bidē/ ▶ **noun** (pl. **biddies**) informal an old woman.
– ORIGIN unknown.

bide /bīd/ ▶ **verb** old use or dialect remain or stay in a place.
– PHRASES **bide one's time** wait patiently for a good opportunity to do something.
– ORIGIN Old English.

bi·det /bi'dā/ ▶ **noun** a low basin used for washing one's genital and anal area.
– ORIGIN French, 'pony.'

bi·en·ni·al /bī'enēəl/ ▶ **adjective 1** taking place every other year. Compare with **BIANNUAL**. **2** (of a plant) living for two years. ▶ **noun 1** a biennial plant. **2** an event celebrated or taking place every two years.
– DERIVATIVES **bi·en·ni·al·ly** adverb.
– ORIGIN from Latin *annus* 'year.'

bi·en·ni·um /bī'enēəm/ ▶ **noun** (pl. **bienniums** or **biennia** /-'enēə/) a specified period of two years.

bier /bi(ə)r/ ▶ **noun** a movable platform on which a coffin or dead body is placed before burial.
– ORIGIN Old English.

biff /bif/ informal ▶ **verb** hit someone or something hard with the fist. ▶ **noun** a sharp blow with the fist.
– ORIGIN probably imitating the sound.

bi·fid /'bīfid/ ▶ **adjective** technical (of a part of a plant or animal) divided into two parts by a deep cleft or notch.
– ORIGIN Latin *bifidus*.

bi·fo·cal /'bī,fōkəl/ ▶ **adjective** (of a lens) made in two sections, one with a focus for seeing distant things and one for seeing things that are close. ▶ **noun** (**bifocals**) a pair of glasses with bifocal lenses.

bi·fur·cate /'bīfər,kāt/ ▶ **verb** (of a road, river, etc.) divide into two branches or forks.
– DERIVATIVES **bi·fur·ca·tion** /,bīfər'kāSHən/ noun.
– ORIGIN from Latin *furca* 'a fork.'

big /big/ ▶ **adjective** (**bigger, biggest**) **1** of great size, power, or extent. **2** very important or serious: *a big decision.* **3** older or grown-up: *my big sister.* **4** informal very popular: *fast food isn't big in Iceland.*

– SYNONYMS **1 large,** sizable, substantial, considerable, great, huge, immense, enormous, extensive, colossal, massive, mammoth, vast, gigantic, giant, spacious; informal jumbo, whopping, bumper, mega, ginormous. formal commodious. **2 well built,** sturdy, brawny, burly, broad-shouldered, muscular, bulky, hulking, strapping, hefty, tall, huge, fat, stout; informal hunky, beefy. **3 elder,** older, grown-up, adult, mature, grown. **4 important,** significant, major, momentous, weighty, far-reaching, key, vital, crucial. **5** *that was big of you* **generous,** kind, kindly, caring, compassionate, loving.
– ANTONYMS small, minor.

– DERIVATIVES **big·gish** adjective **big·ness** noun.
– PHRASES **be big with child** old use be in a late stage of pregnancy. **the Big Apple** informal New York City. **the big screen** informal the cinema. **think big** informal be ambitious. **too big for one's britches** informal conceited.
– ORIGIN unknown.

big·a·my /'bigəmē/ ▶ **noun** the crime of marrying someone while already married to another person.
– DERIVATIVES **big·a·mist** noun **big·a·mous** adjective.
– ORIGIN from **BI-** + Greek *-gamos* 'married.'

big band ▶ **noun** a large group of musicians playing jazz or swing music.

Big Bang ▶ **noun** the rapid expansion of extremely dense matter that, according to current cosmological theories, marked the origin of the universe.

big box ▶ **noun** (also **big-box store**) a superstore. ▶ **adjective** relating to or functioning as a superstore: *big-box retailers will dominate the landscape.*

Big Broth·er ▶ **noun** a person or organization exercising total control over people's lives.
– ORIGIN from the name of the fictitious head of state in George Orwell's novel *Nineteen Eighty-Four*.

Big·foot /'big,fo͝ot/ ▶ **noun** (pl. same) a large, hairy apelike creature, supposedly found in NW America.

big game ▶ **noun** large animals hunted for sport.

big·head /'big,hed/ ▶ **noun** informal a conceited person.
– DERIVATIVES **big·head·ed** adjective.

big hit·ter ▶ **noun** another term for **HEAVY HITTER**.

big·horn /'big,hôrn/ ▶ **noun** a stocky brown North American wild sheep, found in the Rocky Mountains and other western ranges.

bight /bīt/ ▶ **noun 1** a long inward curve in a coastline. **2** a loop of rope.
– ORIGIN Old English.

big mouth ▶ **noun** informal a person who boasts, or one who cannot keep secrets.

big·ot /'bigət/ ▶ **noun** a person with strong and prejudiced views who will not listen to the opinions of others.
– DERIVATIVES **big·ot·ry** noun.
– ORIGIN French.

big·ot·ed /'bigətid/ ▶ **adjective** unreasonably intolerant.

– SYNONYMS **prejudiced,** biased, partial, one-sided, sectarian, discriminatory, opinionated, dogmatic, intolerant, narrow-minded, blinkered, illiberal.
– ANTONYMS open-minded.

big shot (also **big noise**) ▶ **noun** informal an important person.

big top ▶ **noun** the main tent in a circus.

big wheel ▶ **noun** another term for **BIGWIG**.

big·wig /'big,wig/ ▶ **noun** informal an important person.

bi·jou /'bēzHōō/ ▶ **adjective** small and elegant: *a bijou apartment.*
– ORIGIN French, 'jewel.'

bike /bīk/ informal ▶ **noun** a bicycle or motorcycle. ▶ **verb** ride a bicycle or motorcycle.
– DERIVATIVES **bik·er** noun.

bi·ki·ni /bi'kēnē/ ▶ **noun** (pl. **bikinis**) a women's two-piece swimsuit.
– ORIGIN named after *Bikini* atoll in the western Pacific, where an atom bomb was exploded in 1946 (because of the garment's devastating effect).

bi·ki·ni line ▶ **noun** the area of skin around the pubic mound as revealed by the high-cut legs of a bikini.

bi·lat·er·al /bī'latərəl/ ▶ **adjective 1** having two sides. **2** involving two parties: *bilateral discussions.*
– DERIVATIVES **bi·lat·er·al·ly** adverb.

bil·ber·ry /'bil,berē/ ▶ **noun** (pl. **bilberries**) the small blue edible berry of a shrub closely related to the blueberry.
– ORIGIN probably Scandinavian.

Bil·dungs·ro·man /'bildōōnGzrō,män, 'bēldōōnGks-/ ▶ **noun** a novel about one person's formative years or spiritual education.
– ORIGIN German, from *Bildung* 'education' + *Roman* 'a novel.'

bile /bīl/ ▶ **noun 1** a bitter fluid that helps digestion, produced by the liver and stored in the gall bladder. **2** anger or irritability.
– ORIGIN Latin *bilis.*

bile duct ▶ **noun** the tube that conveys bile from the liver and the gall bladder to the duodenum.

bilge /bilj/ ▶ **noun 1** the bottom of a ship's hull. **2** (also **bilge water**) dirty water that collects in the bilge. **3** informal nonsense.
– ORIGIN probably from **BULGE**.

bil·har·zi·a /bil'härzēə/ ▶ **noun** a disease caused by infestation of the body with a type of parasitic flatworm.
– ORIGIN named after the German physician T. *Bilharz*, who discovered the parasite.

bi·lin·gual /bī'linGgwəl/ ▶ **adjective 1** speaking two languages fluently. **2** expressed in or using two languages: *a bilingual dictionary.*
– DERIVATIVES **bi·lin·gual·ism** noun **bi·lin·gual·ly** adverb.

bil·ious /'bilyəs/ ▶ **adjective 1** affected by nausea or vomiting. **2** relating to bile. **3** spiteful or bad-tempered.
– DERIVATIVES **bil·ious·ly** adverb **bil·ious·ness** noun.

bil·i·ru·bin /'bili,rōōbin/ ▶ **noun** Biochemistry an orange-yellow pigment formed in the liver by the breakdown of hemoglobin and excreted in bile.

bilk /bilk/ ▶ **verb** informal cheat or defraud someone.
– ORIGIN perhaps a variant of **BALK**.

bill[1] /bil/ ▶ **noun 1** a printed or written statement of the money owed for goods or services. **2** a draft of a proposed law presented to a legislature for discussion. **3** a program of entertainment at a theater or movie theater. **4** a banknote. **5** an advertising poster.

– SYNONYMS **1 invoice,** account, statement, check, list of charges; humorous damage; informal tab. **2 draft law,** proposal, measure. **3 program,** lineup, playbill. **4** *Jefferson is on the $2 bill* **banknote,** note; informal greenback. **5 poster,** advertisement, notice, announcement, flyer, leaflet, handbill; informal ad.

▶ **verb 1** list a person or event in a program of entertainment. **2** (**bill someone/thing as**) describe someone or something as: *the vehicle has been billed as the car of the future.* **3** send a statement of charges to a person or organization.

– SYNONYMS **1 invoice,** charge, debit. **2 advertise,** announce, schedule, program, slate. **3** *he was billed as the new Sean Connery* **describe,** call, style, label, dub, promote, talk up; informal hype.

– DERIVATIVES **bill·ing** noun.
– PHRASES **a clean bill of health** a statement confirming that someone is in good health or that something is in good condition. **fit the bill** be suitable for a particular purpose.
– ORIGIN Old French *bille.*

bill[2] ▶ **noun 1** the beak of a bird. **2** a stiff brim at the front of a cap.
– PHRASES **bill and coo** informal behave or talk in a loving and sentimental way.
– ORIGIN Old English.

bill·a·ble /'biləbəl/ ▶ **adjective** (of activities or time devoted to them) chargeable to an account or customer: *billable hours.*

bil·la·bong /'bilə,bônG/ ▶ **noun** Austral. a branch of a river forming a backwater or stagnant pool.
– ORIGIN from an Aboriginal language.

bill·board /'bil,bôrd/ ▶ **noun** a large outdoor board used to display advertisements.

bil·let[1] /'bilit/ ▶ **noun** a civilian house where soldiers live temporarily. ▶ **verb** (**billets, billeting, billeted**) provide soldiers with temporary accommodations in a civilian house.
– ORIGIN Old French *billette* 'small document.'

bil·let[2] ▶ **noun 1** a thick piece of wood. **2** a small bar of metal.
– ORIGIN Old French *billette* and *billot* 'little tree trunk.'

bil·let-doux /'bilā 'dōō, 'bēyā-/ ▶ **noun** (pl. **billets-doux** /-'dōōz/) chiefly humorous a love letter.
– ORIGIN French, 'sweet note.'

bill·fold /'bil,fōld/ ▶ **noun** a man's wallet.

bill·hook /'bil,hŏŏk/ ▶ **noun** a tool with a curved blade, used for pruning.

bil·liards /'bilyərdz/ ▶ **plural noun** (treated as sing.) a game for two people, played on a rectangular cloth-covered table with three balls.
– ORIGIN French *billard.*

bil·lion /'bilyən/ ▶ **cardinal number** (pl. **billions** or (with numeral or quantifying word) same) **1** a thousand million; 1,000,000,000 or 10^9. **2** (**billions**) informal a very large number or amount: *billions of tiny sea creatures.*
– DERIVATIVES **bil·lionth** ordinal number.
– ORIGIN French.

bil·lion·aire /'bilyə,ne(ə)r/ ▶ **noun** a person owning money and property worth at least a billion dollars (or pounds, etc.).

bill of at·tain·der ▶ **noun** Law an item of legislation (prohibited by the US Constitution) that inflicts attainder without judicial process.

bill of ex·change ▶ **noun** a document instructing a person to pay a stated sum of money to someone on a particular date.

bill of fare ▸ **noun** dated a menu.

bill of goods ▸ **noun** a consignment of merchandise.
– PHRASES **sell someone a bill of goods** deceive someone, usually by persuading them to accept something untrue or undesirable: *she was sold a bill of goods about that dog's pedigree.*

bill of lad·ing ▸ **noun** a document giving full details of a ship's cargo.

bill of rights ▸ **noun** a written statement of the basic rights of a country's citizens.

bil·low /ˈbilō/ ▸ **verb 1** (of smoke, cloud, or steam) roll outward: *smoke was billowing from the chimney.* **2** (of fabric or a garment) fill with air and swell out: *her dress billowed out around her.*

– SYNONYMS **1 puff out,** balloon (out), swell, fill (out). **2 swirl,** spiral, roll, undulate, eddy, pour, flow.

▸ **noun 1** a large rolling mass of cloud, smoke, or steam. **2** old use a large wave.

– SYNONYMS **cloud,** mass.

– DERIVATIVES **bil·low·y** adjective.
– ORIGIN Old Norse.

bil·ly /ˈbilē/ ▸ **noun** (pl. **billies**) **1** short for BILLY GOAT. **2** (also **billy club**) a truncheon; a cudgel.

bil·ly goat ▸ **noun** a male goat.
– ORIGIN *Billy*, familiar form of the man's name *William*.

bim·bo /ˈbimbō/ ▸ **noun** (pl. **bimbos**) informal, derogatory an attractive but unintelligent young woman.
– DERIVATIVES **bim·bette** /bimˈbet/ noun.
– ORIGIN Italian, 'little child.'

bi·me·tal·lic /ˌbīməˈtalik/ ▸ **adjective** made or consisting of two metals.

bi·month·ly /bīˈmənTHlē/ ▸ **adjective & adverb** appearing or taking place twice a month or every two months.

bin /bin/ ▸ **noun 1** a large storage container: *a bread bin.* **2** a partitioned stand or case for storing bottles of wine. ▸ **verb** (**bins, binning, binned**) place something in a bin.
– ORIGIN Old English.

bi·na·ry /ˈbīˌnerē, -nərē/ ▸ **adjective 1** composed of or involving two things. **2** using or relating to a system of numbers with two as its base, using the digits 0 and 1. ▸ **noun** (pl. **binaries**) **1** the binary system of notation. **2** Astronomy a system of two stars revolving around their common center.
– ORIGIN Latin *binarius*.

bind /bīnd/ ▸ **verb** (past and past part. **bound**) **1** tie or fasten something tightly together. **2** restrain someone by tying their hands and feet: *he was bound and gagged.* **3** wrap or encircle tightly: *her blond hair was bound with a scarf.* **4** stick together in a single mass: *mix the flour with the coconut and enough egg white to bind them.* **5** hold together as a united group: *the religious and social rituals that bind people together.* **6** require someone to do something by law or because of a contract. **7** (**bind someone over**) (of a court of law) require someone to do something: *he was bound over to keep the peace.* **8** fix together and enclose the pages of a book in a cover. **9** trim the edge of a piece of material with a fabric strip.

– SYNONYMS **1 tie up,** fasten together, secure, make fast, attach, rope, lash, tether. **2 bandage,** dress, cover, wrap, strap up, tape up. **3 trim,** hem, edge, border, fringe.
– ANTONYMS untie.

▸ **noun** informal an annoying or difficult situation.
– ORIGIN Old English.

bind·er /ˈbīndər/ ▸ **noun 1** a cover for holding magazines or loose papers together. **2** a reaping machine that binds grain into sheaves. **3** a bookbinder.

bind·er·y /ˈbīndərē/ ▸ **noun** (pl. **binderies**) a workshop or factory in which books are bound.

bin·di /ˈbindē/ ▸ **noun** (pl. **bindis**) a decorative mark worn in the middle of the forehead by Indian women.
– ORIGIN Hindi.

bind·ing /ˈbīndiNG/ ▸ **noun 1** a strong covering holding the pages of a book together. **2** fabric cut or woven in a strip, used for binding the edges of a piece of material. ▸ **adjective** (of an agreement) putting someone under a legal obligation.

– SYNONYMS **irrevocable,** unalterable, inescapable, unbreakable, contractual, compulsory, obligatory, mandatory, incumbent.

bind·weed /ˈbīndˌwēd/ ▸ **noun** a plant with trumpet-shaped flowers that twines itself around things.

binge /binj/ informal ▸ **noun** a short period of uncontrolled indulgence in an activity, especially eating or drinking.

– SYNONYMS **bout,** spell, fling, spree, orgy, drinking bout; informal bender, session, jag.

▸ **verb** (**binges, bingeing** or **binging, binged**) do something, especially eat, without being able to control oneself.
– DERIVATIVES **bing·er** noun.
– ORIGIN unknown.

bin·go /ˈbiNGgō/ ▸ **noun** a game in which players mark off randomly called numbers on printed cards, the winner being the first to mark off all their numbers. ▸ **exclamation 1** a call by someone who wins a game of bingo. **2** said to express satisfaction at a sudden good event.
– ORIGIN unknown.

bin·na·cle /ˈbinəkəl/ ▸ **noun** a casing for holding a ship's compass.
– ORIGIN Spanish *bitácula, bitácora* or Portuguese *bitacola*.

bin·oc·u·lar /biˈnäkyələr/ ▸ **adjective** adapted for or using both eyes.
– ORIGIN from Latin *bini* 'two together' + *oculus* 'eye.'

bin·oc·u·lars /biˈnäkyələrz/ ▸ **plural noun** an instrument with a separate lens for each eye, used for viewing distant objects.

bi·no·mi·al /bīˈnōmēəl/ ▸ **noun** Mathematics an algebraic expression consisting of two terms linked by a plus or minus sign. ▸ **adjective** consisting of two terms.
– ORIGIN from Latin *bi-* 'having two' + Greek *nomos* 'part.'

bi·o /ˈbīō/ ▸ **noun** (pl. **bios**) informal **1** biology. **2** biography.

bio- ▸ **combining form 1** relating to life or living beings: *biosynthesis.* **2** biological; relating to biology: *biohazard.*
– ORIGIN from Greek *bios* 'human life.'

bi·o·ac·tive /ˌbīōˈaktiv/ ▸ **adjective** (of a substance) having a biological effect.
– DERIVATIVES **bi·o·ac·tiv·i·ty** /-akˈtivitē/ noun.

bi·o·chem·is·try /ˌbīōˈkeməstrē/ ▸ **noun** the branch of science concerned with the chemical processes that occur within living organisms.
– DERIVATIVES **bi·o·chem·i·cal** /ˌbīōˈkemikəl/ adjective **bi·o·chem·ist** noun.

bi·o·cide /ˈbīəˌsīd/ ▸ **noun** a substance that is poisonous to living organisms, such as a pesticide.

bi·o·de·grad·a·ble /ˌbīōdiˈgrādəbəl/ ▶ **adjective** (of a substance or object) capable of being decomposed by bacteria or other living organisms.
– DERIVATIVES **bi·o·de·grad·a·bil·i·ty** /-ˌgrādəˈbilitē/ noun **bi·o·deg·ra·da·tion** /ˌbīōdegrəˈdāshən/ noun **bi·o·de·grade** /ˌbīōdiˈgrād/ verb.

bi·o·die·sel /ˈbīōˌdēzəl, -səl/ ▶ **noun** a biofuel intended as a substitute for diesel.

bi·o·di·ver·si·ty /ˌbīōdiˈvərsitē/ ▶ **noun** the variety of plant and animal life in the world or in a particular habitat.

bi·o·en·gi·neer·ing /ˌbīōˌenjəˈni(ə)riNG/ ▶ **noun** **1** genetic engineering. **2** the use of artificial tissues or organs in the body. **3** the use of organisms or biological processes in industry.
– DERIVATIVES **bi·o·en·gi·neer** noun & verb.

bi·o·eth·ics /ˌbīōˈeTHiks/ ▶ **plural noun** (treated as sing.) the ethics of medical and biological research.
– DERIVATIVES **bi·o·eth·i·cal** /-ˈeTHikəl/ adjective **bi·o·eth·i·cist** /-ˈeTHəsist/ noun.

bi·o·feed·back /ˌbīōˈfēdˌbak/ ▶ **noun** the electronic monitoring of a normally automatic bodily function in order to train someone to control that function of their own accord.

bi·o·fla·vo·noid /ˌbīōˈflāvəˌnoid/ ▶ **noun** any of a group of compounds occurring mainly in citrus fruits and black currants, sometimes regarded as vitamins.

bi·o·fu·el /ˈbīōˌfyo͞oəl/ ▶ **noun** fuel obtained directly from living matter.

bi·o·gas /ˈbīōˌgas/ ▶ **noun** gaseous fuel, especially methane, produced by the fermentation of organic matter.

bi·o·gen·e·sis /ˌbīōˈjenəsis/ ▶ **noun** the synthesis of substances by living organisms.
– DERIVATIVES **bi·o·ge·net·ic** /-jəˈnetik/ adjective.

bi·o·graph·i·cal /ˌbīəˈgrafikəl/ ▶ **adjective** relating to or dealing with a particular person's life: *detailed biographical information.*

bi·og·ra·phy /bīˈägrəfē/ ▶ **noun** (pl. **biographies**) an account of a person's life written by someone else.
– DERIVATIVES **bi·og·ra·pher** noun.

bi·o·haz·ard /ˈbīōˌhazərd/ ▶ **noun** a risk to human health or the environment resulting from biological research.

bi·o·in·for·mat·ics /ˌbīōˌinfərˈmatiks/ ▶ **plural noun** (treated as sing.) the science of collecting and analyzing complex biological data such as genetic codes.

bi·o·log·i·cal /ˌbīəˈläjikəl/ ▶ **adjective** **1** relating to biology or living organisms. **2** (of a parent or child) related by blood. **3** relating to the use of harmful microorganisms as weapons of war. **4** (of a detergent) containing enzymes to help in the removal of stains.
– DERIVATIVES **bi·o·log·i·cal·ly** adverb.

WORD TOOLKIT

See **ORGANIC**.

bi·o·log·i·cal clock ▶ **noun** a natural mechanism that controls certain regularly recurring physical processes in an animal or plant, such as sleeping.

bi·o·log·i·cal con·trol ▶ **noun** the control of a pest by nonchemical means, by bringing a natural enemy or predator of the pest into the environment.

bi·ol·o·gy /bīˈäləjē/ ▶ **noun** **1** the scientific study of living organisms. **2** the features of a particular organism or class of organisms: *the biology of marine plants.*
– DERIVATIVES **bi·ol·o·gist** noun.

bi·o·lu·mi·nes·cence /ˌbīōˌlo͞oməˈnesəns/ ▶ **noun** the production of light by living creatures such as fireflies and deep-sea fishes.
– DERIVATIVES **bi·o·lu·mi·nes·cent** adjective.

bi·o·mark·er /ˈbīōˌmärkər/ ▶ **noun** a measurable substance in an organism whose presence indicates disease, infection, or environmental exposure.

bi·o·mass /ˈbīōˌmas/ ▶ **noun** **1** the total quantity of organisms in a given area. **2** organic matter used as a fuel, especially in the production of electricity.

bi·o·ma·ter·i·al /ˌbīōməˈti(ə)rēəl/ ▶ **noun** synthetic or natural material that can be used in constructing artificial organs and prostheses or to replace bone or tissue.

bi·ome /ˈbīˌōm/ ▶ **noun** a large community of plants and animals occupying a major habitat, such as forest or tundra.

bi·o·me·chan·ics /ˌbīōməˈkaniks/ ▶ **noun** (treated as sing.) the study of the mechanical laws relating to the movement or structure of living organisms.

bi·o·met·rics /ˌbīōˈmetriks/ ▶ **noun** the application of statistical analysis to biological data.
– DERIVATIVES **bi·o·met·ric** /ˌbīōˈmetrik/ adjective **bi·o·met·ri·cal** /ˌbīōˈmetrikəl/ adjective **bi·o·me·tri·cian** /ˌbīōməˈtrisHən/ noun.

bi·o·mi·met·ics /ˌbīōməˈmetiks/ (also **biomimicry**) ▶ **noun** the design and production of materials, structures, and systems that are modeled on biological entities and processes.
– DERIVATIVES **bi·o·mi·met·ic** adjective.

bi·o·morph /ˈbīōˌmôrf/ ▶ **noun** a design or decorative form resembling or representing a living organism.
– DERIVATIVES **bi·o·mor·phic** /ˌbīōˈmôrfik/ adjective.

bi·on·ic /bīˈänik/ ▶ **adjective** **1** relating to the use of electrically powered artificial body parts. **2** informal having ordinary physical powers increased by the use of such artificial body parts.

bi·o·pharm·a·ceut·i·cal /ˌbīōˌfärməˈso͞otikəl/ ▶ **noun** a pharmaceutical substance, especially a protein or peptide, produced by biotechnology.

bi·o·pic /ˈbīōˌpik/ ▶ **noun** informal a movie about the life of a particular person.

bi·op·sy /ˈbīˌäpsē/ ▶ **noun** (pl. **biopsies**) an examination of tissue taken from the body, to discover the presence, cause, or extent of a disease.
– ORIGIN from Greek *bios* 'life' + *opsis* 'sight.'

bi·o·rhythm /ˈbīōˌriT͟Həm/ ▶ **noun** a recurring cycle in the physiology or functioning of the body, such as the daily cycle of sleeping and waking.

bi·o·se·cur·i·ty /ˌbīōsiˈkyo͝oritē/ ▶ **noun** procedures intended to protect humans or animals against disease or harmful substances.

bi·o·sphere /ˈbīəˌsfi(ə)r/ ▶ **noun** the parts of the earth's surface and atmosphere that are inhabited by living things.

bi·o·syn·the·sis /ˌbīōˈsinTHəsis/ ▶ **noun** the production of complex molecules within living organisms or cells.
– DERIVATIVES **bi·o·syn·thet·ic** /-ˌsinˈTHetik/ adjective.

bi·o·ta /bīˈōtə/ ▶ **noun** the animal and plant life of a particular region, habitat, or geological period.
– ORIGIN Greek *biotē* 'life.'

bi·o·tech /ˌbīō'tek, 'bīōˌtek/ ▸ **noun** informal biotechnology.

bi·o·tech·nol·o·gy /ˌbīōtek'näləjē/ ▸ **noun** the use of microorganisms in industry and medicine for the production of antibiotics, hormones, etc.
– DERIVATIVES **bi·o·tech·no·lo·gi·cal** /ˌbīōˌteknə'läjikəl/ adjective **bi·o·tech·nol·o·gist** noun.

bi·o·ter·ror·ism /ˌbīō'terəˌrizəm/ ▸ **noun** the use of harmful biological or biochemical substances as weapons of terrorism.
– DERIVATIVES **bi·o·ter·ror·ist** /ˌbīō'terəˌrist/ noun.

bi·o·ther·a·py /ˌbīō'THerəpē/ ▸ **noun** (pl. **biotherapies**) the treatment of disease using substances obtained or derived from living organisms.

bi·ot·ic /bī'ätik/ ▸ **adjective** relating to living things and the effect they have on each other.
– ORIGIN from Greek *bios* 'life.'

bi·o·tin /'bīətin/ ▸ **noun** a vitamin of the B complex, found in egg yolk, liver, and yeast.
– ORIGIN from Greek *bios* 'life.'

bi·o·war·fare /ˌbīō'wôrˌfe(ə)r/ ▸ **noun** biological warfare.

bi·o·weap·on /'bīōˌwepən/ ▸ **noun** a harmful organism or biological substance used as a weapon of war.

bi·par·ti·san /bī'pärtəzən/ ▸ **adjective** involving the agreement or cooperation of two political parties.
– DERIVATIVES **bi·par·ti·san·ship** /-ˌSHip/ noun.

bi·par·tite /bī'pärˌtīt/ ▸ **adjective 1** involving two separate parties: *a bipartite agreement.* **2** technical consisting of two parts.

bi·ped /'bīped/ ▸ **noun** an animal that walks on two feet.
– DERIVATIVES **bi·ped·al** /bī'pedl/ adjective.
– ORIGIN from Latin *bi-* 'having two' + *pes* 'foot.'

bi·plane /'bīˌplān/ ▸ **noun** an early type of aircraft with two pairs of wings, one above the other.

bi·po·lar /bī'pōlər/ ▸ **adjective 1** (especially of an electronic device) having two poles. **2** having two opposite extremes: *a bipolar view of the world.*
– DERIVATIVES **bi·po·lar·i·ty** /ˌbīpō'laritē, -pə-/ noun.

bi·po·lar dis·or·der ▸ **noun** a mental disorder marked by alternating periods of elation and depression.

birch /bərCH/ ▸ **noun 1** a slender tree with thin peeling bark and hard fine-grained wood. **2** (**the birch**) historical a punishment in which a person was beaten with a bundle of birch twigs.
– ORIGIN Old English.

bird /bərd/ ▸ **noun 1** a warm-blooded egg-laying animal that has feathers, wings, and a beak, and typically is able to fly. **2** informal a person of a particular kind: *she's a sharp old bird.*

– SYNONYMS fowl, chick, fledgling, nestling.

– PHRASES **the birds and the bees** informal basic facts about sex, as told to a child.
– ORIGIN Old English.

WORD LINKS

avian *relating to birds*
ornithology *study of birds*

bird·brain /'bərdˌbrān/ ▸ **noun** informal a stupid person.

bird·cage /'bərdˌkāj/ ▸ **noun** a cage for pet birds.

bird·er /'bərdər/ ▸ **noun** informal a birdwatcher.
– DERIVATIVES **bird·ing** noun.

bird flu ▸ **noun** an often fatal flu virus of birds that is transmissible from them to humans, in whom it may also prove fatal.

bird·ie /'bərdē/ ▸ **noun** (pl. **birdies**) **1** informal a little bird. **2** Golf a score of one stroke under par at a hole. ▸ **verb** (**birdies, birdying, birdied**) Golf play a hole with a score of one stroke under par.
– ORIGIN the golf term is from US slang *bird,* meaning any first-rate thing.

bird of par·a·dise ▸ **noun** (pl. **birds of paradise**) a tropical bird, the male of which has brightly colored plumage.

bird of prey ▸ **noun** (pl. **birds of prey**) a bird that feeds on animal flesh, such as an eagle, hawk, or owl.

bird·seed /'bərdˌsēd/ ▸ **noun** a blend of seeds for feeding birds.

bird's-eye view ▸ **noun** a general view of something from a high position above it.

bird's nest soup ▸ **noun** (in Chinese cooking) a soup made from the dried gelatinous coating of the nests of swifts and other birds.

bird·song /'bərdˌsôNG/ ▸ **noun** the musical sounds made by birds.

bird·watch·ing /'bərdˌwäCHiNG/ ▸ **noun** the hobby of observing birds in their natural environment.
– DERIVATIVES **bird·watch·er** noun.

bi·ret·ta /bə'retə/ ▸ **noun** a square cap with three flat projections on top, worn by Roman Catholic clergymen.
– ORIGIN Italian *berretta* or Spanish *birreta.*

birth /bərTH/ ▸ **noun 1** the emergence of a baby or other young from the body of its mother. **2** the beginning of something: *the birth of modern jazz.* **3** a person's origin or ancestry: *he is of noble birth.*

– SYNONYMS **1 childbirth,** delivery, nativity. **2 beginning(s),** emergence, genesis, dawn, dawning, rise, start. **3 ancestry,** lineage, blood, descent, parentage, family, extraction, origin, stock.
– ANTONYMS death, end.

– DERIVATIVES **birth·ing** noun.
– PHRASES **give birth** produce a child or young animal.
– ORIGIN Old Norse.

WORD LINKS

antenatal *before birth*
postnatal *after birth*
obstetrics *branch of medicine concerned with birth*

birth cer·tif·i·cate ▸ **noun** an official document recording a person's name, their place and date of birth, and the names of their parents.

birth con·trol ▸ **noun** the prevention of unwanted pregnancies, especially through the use of contraception.

birth·date /'bərTHˌdāt/ ▸ **noun** the date on which a person is born.

birth·day /'bərTHˌdā/ ▸ **noun** the annual anniversary of the day on which a person was born.

birth de·fect ▸ **noun** a physical or biochemical abnormality that is present at birth and that may be inherited or the result of environmental influence.

birth·mark /'bərTHˌmärk/ ▸ **noun** an unusual, typically permanent, mark on the body that is there from birth.

birth moth·er ▸ **noun** a woman who has given birth to a child, as opposed to an adoptive mother.

birth·place /ˈbərTH,plās/ ▶ **noun 1** the place where a person was born. **2** the place where something began or originated: *the birthplace of feminism*.

birth rate ▶ **noun** the number of live births per thousand of population per year.

birth·right /ˈbərTH,rīt/ ▶ **noun 1** a right or privilege that a person has as a result of being born into a particular family, social class, or place. **2** a natural or basic right possessed by all people: *a college education should be regarded as everyone's birthright*.

birth·stone /ˈbərTH,stōn/ ▶ **noun** a gemstone popularly associated with the month or astrological sign of a person's birth.

bi·ry·a·ni /,birēˈänē/ (also **biriani**) ▶ **noun** an Indian dish made with highly seasoned rice and meat, fish, or vegetables.
– ORIGIN Urdu.

bis·cuit /ˈbiskit/ ▶ **noun 1** a small, round cake of bread leavened with baking powder or soda. **2** a light brown color. **3** porcelain or other pottery that has been fired but not glazed.
– DERIVATIVES **bis·cuit·y** adjective.
– ORIGIN from Latin *bis* 'twice' + *coquere* 'to cook' (because biscuits were originally cooked in a twofold process: first baked and then dried out in a slow oven).

bi·sect /bīˈsekt, ˈbī,sekt/ ▶ **verb** divide something into two parts.
– DERIVATIVES **bi·sec·tion** noun **bi·sec·tor** noun.
– ORIGIN from Latin *secare* 'to cut.'

bi·sex·u·al /bīˈsekSHo͞oəl/ ▶ **adjective 1** sexually attracted to both men and women. **2** Biology having characteristics of both sexes. ▶ **noun** a person who is sexually attracted to both men and women.
– DERIVATIVES **bi·sex·u·al·i·ty** /,bīsekSHo͞oˈalitē/ noun.

bish·op /ˈbisHəp/ ▶ **noun 1** a senior member of the Christian clergy, usually in charge of a diocese. **2** a chess piece with a top shaped like a miter, that can move diagonally in any direction.
– ORIGIN Greek *episkopos* 'overseer.'

bish·op·ric /ˈbisHəprik/ ▶ **noun** the position or diocese of a bishop.

bis·muth /ˈbizməTH/ ▶ **noun** a brittle reddish-gray metallic element resembling lead.
– ORIGIN from German *Wismut*.

bi·son /ˈbīsən, -zən/ ▶ **noun** (pl. same) a shaggy-haired wild ox with a humped back.
– ORIGIN Latin.

bisque[1] /bisk/ ▶ **noun** a rich soup made from lobster or other shellfish.
– ORIGIN French.

bisque[2] ▶ **noun** another term for **BISCUIT** (sense 3).

bis·tro /ˈbistrō, ˈbē-/ ▶ **noun** (pl. **bistros**) a small, inexpensive restaurant.
– ORIGIN French.

bit[1] /bit/ ▶ **noun 1** a small piece or quantity of something. **2** (**a bit**) a short time or distance.

> – SYNONYMS **piece,** portion, section, part, chunk, lump, hunk, fragment, scrap, shred, crumb, grain, speck, spot, drop, pinch, dash, morsel, mouthful, bite, sample, iota, jot, whit, atom, particle, trace, touch, suggestion, hint, tinge; informal smidgen, tad.

– PHRASES **a bit** rather; slightly: *you're a bit late*. **bit by bit** gradually. **do one's bit** informal make a useful contribution to a task or enterprise. **to bits 1** into pieces. **2** informal very much: *he was thrilled to bits*.
– ORIGIN Old English, 'bite, mouthful.'

bit[2] past of **BITE**.

bit[3] ▶ **noun 1** a metal mouthpiece attached to a bridle, used to control a horse. **2** a tool or part of a tool for boring or drilling. **3** the part of a key that engages with the lock lever.
– PHRASES **get the bit between one's teeth** begin to tackle a task with determination.
– ORIGIN Old English, 'biting, a bite.'

bit[4] ▶ **noun** Computing a unit of information expressed as either a 0 or 1 in binary notation.
– ORIGIN from **BINARY** and **DIGIT**.

bitch /biCH/ ▶ **noun 1** a female dog, wolf, fox, or otter. **2** informal a spiteful or unpleasant woman. **3** (**a bitch**) informal a difficult or unpleasant thing or situation: *working the night shift is a bitch*. ▶ **verb** informal make spiteful comments.
– ORIGIN Old English.

bitch·y /ˈbiCHē/ ▶ **adjective** (**bitchier**, **bitchiest**) informal spiteful.
– DERIVATIVES **bitch·i·ly** adverb **bitch·i·ness** noun.

bite /bīt/ ▶ **verb** (past **bit**; past part. **bitten**) **1** cut into something with the teeth. **2** (of a snake, insect, or spider) wound someone or something with a sting, pincers, or fangs. **3** (of a fish) take the bait or lure on the end of a fishing line into the mouth. **4** (of a tool, tire, etc.) grip a surface. **5** (of a policy or situation) take effect, with unpleasant consequences: *in hospitals, the strike action was beginning to bite*. **6** (**bite something back**) stop oneself saying something.

> – SYNONYMS **1 chew,** sink one's teeth into, munch, crunch, chomp, champ. **2 grip,** hold, get a purchase on. **3 take effect,** work, act, have results.

▶ **noun 1** an act of biting. **2** a piece of food bitten off. **3** Dentistry the bringing together of the teeth when the jaws are closed. **4** informal a quick snack. **5** a sharpness or strength of flavor: *chicory leaves add color and bite to a salad*. **6** a feeling of cold in the air.

> – SYNONYMS **1 chew,** munch, nibble, gnaw, nip. **2 mouthful,** piece, bit, morsel, snack. **3 piquancy,** pungency, spiciness, tang, zest; informal kick, punch, zing.

– DERIVATIVES **bit·er** noun.
– PHRASES **bite the bullet** make oneself do something difficult or unpleasant that can no longer be avoided. [from the old custom of giving wounded soldiers a bullet to bite on when undergoing surgery without anaesthetic.] **bite the dust** informal die or be killed. **bite the hand that feeds one** deliberately hurt or offend a person who is trying to help. **bite off more than one can chew** take on a commitment one cannot fulfill. **bite one's tongue** make a desperate effort to avoid saying something.
– ORIGIN Old English.

bit·ing /ˈbītiNG/ ▶ **adjective 1** (of a wind) very cold and unpleasant. **2** harshly critical: *a biting commentary on contemporary society*.

> – SYNONYMS **1 vicious,** harsh, cruel, savage, cutting, sharp, bitter, scathing, caustic, acerbic, acid, acrimonious, spiteful, venomous, vitriolic; informal bitchy, catty. **2 freezing,** icy, arctic, bitter, piercing, penetrating, raw.
> – ANTONYMS mild.

– DERIVATIVES **bit·ing·ly** adverb.

bit·map /ˈbit,map/ ▶ **noun** the information used to control an image or display on a computer screen, in which each item corresponds to one or more bits of information.

bit part ▸ noun a small acting role in a play or movie.

bit·ten /'bitn/ past participle of **BITE**.

bit·ter /'bitər/ ▸ adjective **1** having a sharp taste or smell; not sweet. **2** causing pain or unhappiness: *the decision came as a bitter blow*. **3** feeling anger, hurt, and resentment. **4** (of a conflict) intense and full of hatred: *a long and bitter dispute*. **5** (of wind or weather) intensely cold.

– SYNONYMS **1 sharp,** acid, acrid, tart, sour, vinegary. **2 acrimonious,** hostile, angry, rancorous, spiteful, vicious, vitriolic, savage, ferocious, nasty. **3 resentful,** embittered, aggrieved, spiteful, jaundiced, sullen, sour. **4 freezing,** icy, arctic, biting, piercing, penetrating, raw.
– ANTONYMS sweet, mild.

▸ noun **1** Brit. bitter-tasting beer that is strongly flavored with hops. **2** (**bitters**) (treated as sing.) alcohol flavored with bitter plant extracts, used as an ingredient in cocktails.
– DERIVATIVES **bit·ter·ly** adverb **bit·ter·ness** noun.
– PHRASES **to the bitter end** to the very end, in spite of severe difficulties.
– ORIGIN Old English.

bit·tern /'bitərn/ ▸ noun a marshland bird of the heron family, noted for the male's deep booming call.
– ORIGIN Old French *butor*.

bit·ter or·ange ▸ noun another term for **SEVILLE ORANGE**.

bit·ter·sweet /'bitər,swēt/ ▸ adjective **1** sweet with a bitter aftertaste. **2** bringing pleasure mixed with a touch of sadness.

bit·ty /'bitē/ ▸ adjective (**bittier, bittiest**) tiny.

bi·tu·men /bi't(y)o͞omən, bī-/ ▸ noun a black sticky substance obtained naturally or from petroleum, used for road surfacing.
– DERIVATIVES **bi·tu·mi·nous** /bi't(y)o͞omənəs, bī-/ adjective.
– ORIGIN Latin.

bi·tu·mi·nous coal ▸ noun a type of black coal that burns with a characteristically bright smoky flame.

bi·valve /'bī,valv/ ▸ noun a mollusk that lives in water and has a hinged double shell, such as an oyster, mussel, or scallop. ▸ adjective (also **bivalved**) having a hinged double shell.

biv·ou·ac /'bivo͞o,ak, 'bivwak/ ▸ noun a temporary camp without tents, used especially by soldiers or mountaineers. ▸ verb (**bivouacks, bivouacking, bivouacked**) stay in a bivouac.
– ORIGIN French.

bi·week·ly /bī'wēklē/ ▸ adjective & adverb appearing or taking place every two weeks or twice a week.

biz /biz/ ▸ noun informal business.

bi·zarre /bi'zär/ ▸ adjective very strange or unusual.

– SYNONYMS **strange,** peculiar, odd, funny, fantastic, extraordinary, curious, outlandish, eccentric, unconventional, unorthodox, weird, outré, surreal; informal wacky, wacko, oddball, way out, freaky.
– ANTONYMS normal.

– DERIVATIVES **bi·zarre·ly** adverb **bi·zarre·ness** noun.
– ORIGIN from Italian *bizzarro* 'angry.'

WORD TOOLKIT

See **ECCENTRIC**.

Bk ▸ symbol the chemical element berkelium.

blab /blab/ ▸ verb (**blabs, blabbing, blabbed**) informal reveal information that should have been kept secret.

blab·ber /'blabər/ ▸ verb informal talk at length about foolish or unimportant things.

blab·ber·mouth /'blabər,mouTH/ ▸ noun informal a person who reveals secrets or talks too much.

black /blak/ ▸ adjective **1** of the very darkest color. **2** marked by tragedy, disaster, or despair: *the blackest day of the war*. **3** (of humor) presenting tragic or distressing situations in comic terms. **4** full of anger or hatred: *he threw me a black look*. **5** (of coffee or tea) served without milk. **6** relating to the human group having dark-colored skin.

– SYNONYMS **1 dark,** pitch-black, coal-black, jet-black, ebony, inky, sable. **2** *a black day* **tragic,** dark, disastrous, calamitous, catastrophic, cataclysmic, fateful. **3** *a black mood* **miserable,** unhappy, sad, wretched, heartbroken, grief-stricken, sorrowful, anguished, desolate, despairing, disconsolate, downcast, dejected, gloomy; informal blue. **4 macabre,** cynical, unhealthy, ghoulish, weird, morbid, gruesome; informal sick.
– ANTONYMS white, bright.

▸ noun **1** black color. **2** a member of a dark-skinned people.
▸ verb make something black, especially by applying black polish or makeup.
– DERIVATIVES **black·ish** adjective **black·ly** adverb **black·ness** noun.
– PHRASES **black out** lose consciousness; faint. **black something out** make a room or building dark by switching off all the lights and covering the windows. **in the black** not owing any money.
– ORIGIN Old English.

USAGE

Black, designating Americans of African heritage, became the most widely used and accepted term in the 1960s and 1970s, replacing **Negro**. It is not usually capitalized: *black Americans*. Through the 1980s, the more formal **African American** replaced **black** in much usage, but both are now generally acceptable.

black and white ▸ adjective (of a situation or debate) involving clear-cut opposing opinions or issues.

black art (also **black arts**) ▸ noun black magic.

black·ball /'blak,bôl/ ▸ verb reject a candidate applying to become a member of a private club.
– ORIGIN from the practice of voting against something by placing a black ball in a ballot box.

black bean ▸ noun a cultivated variety of soybean.

black belt ▸ noun a black belt worn by an expert in judo, karate, and other martial arts.

Black·Ber·ry /'blak,berē/ ▸ noun trademark a hand-held wireless electronic device that provides Internet access along with email, telephone, and text messaging services.

black·ber·ry /'blak,berē/ ▸ noun (pl. **blackberries**) the purple-black edible fruit of a prickly climbing shrub.

black·ber·ry·ing /'blak,bərēiNG, 'blak,brēiNG/ ▸ noun the activity of picking blackberries.

black bile ▸ noun (in medieval science and medicine) one of the four bodily humors, believed to be associated with a melancholy temperament.

– ORIGIN translation of Greek *melankholia* (see MELANCHOLY).

black·bird /ˈblak͵bərd/ ▶ **noun** an American songbird, the male of which has black plumage that is iridescent or has patches of red or yellow.

black·board /ˈblak͵bôrd/ ▶ **noun** a large board with a dark surface for writing on with chalk.

black box ▶ **noun** a flight recorder in an aircraft.

black cur·rant ▶ **noun** the small round edible black berry of a shrub.

black e·con·o·my ▶ **noun** the part of a country's economic activity that is not recorded or taxed by its government.

black·en /ˈblakən/ ▶ **verb 1** become or make black or dark. **2** damage or destroy someone's reputation.

black eye ▶ **noun 1** an area of bruised skin around the eye caused by a blow. **2** a mark or source of dishonor or shame.

black-eyed pea ▶ **noun** a plant of the pea family native to the Old World tropics. It is an important forage and human food crop.

black·fly /ˈblak͵flī/ ▶ **noun** (pl. **blackflies**) a small black fly that sucks blood and can transmit diseases.

Black·foot /ˈblak͵fo͝ot/ ▶ **noun** (pl. same or **Blackfeet**) a member of an allied group of North American Indian peoples of the northwestern plains.

black·guard /ˈblagərd, ˈblak͵gärd/ ▶ **noun** dated a man who behaves in a dishonorable or dishonest way.
– ORIGIN first referring to a group of kitchen servants.

black·head /ˈblak͵hed/ ▶ **noun** a lump of oily matter blocking a hair follicle.

black hole ▶ **noun** a region of space that has a gravitational field so intense that no matter or radiation can escape from it.

black ice ▶ **noun** a transparent layer of ice on a road surface.

black·ing /ˈblakiNG/ ▶ **noun** black paste or polish.

black·jack /ˈblak͵jak/ ▶ **noun 1** a gambling card game in which players try to acquire cards with a face value as close as possible to 21 without going over. **2** a flexible lead-filled club.

black light ▶ **noun** ultraviolet or infrared radiation, invisible to the eye.

black·list /ˈblak͵list/ ▶ **noun** a list of people or groups seen as unacceptable or untrustworthy. ▶ **verb** put the name of a person or group on a blacklist: *the author was blacklisted for his political beliefs.*

> – SYNONYMS **boycott,** ostracize, avoid, embargo, ignore, refuse to employ.

black mag·ic ▶ **noun** a type of magic that involves the summoning of evil spirits.

black·mail /ˈblak͵māl/ ▶ **noun 1** the crime of demanding money from someone in return for not revealing information that could disgrace them. **2** the use of threats or other pressure in an attempt to persuade someone to do something they do not want to do: *she resorted to emotional blackmail.*

> – SYNONYMS **extortion,** threats, intimidation.

▶ **verb 1** demand money from someone in return for not revealing information that could disgrace them. **2** force someone to do something by using threats or other pressure: *he blackmailed her into marrying him.*

> – SYNONYMS **1 extort money from,** threaten, hold for ransom, intimidate. **2 coerce,** pressure, force, dragoon; informal lean on, twist someone's arm.

– DERIVATIVES **black·mail·er** noun.
– ORIGIN Old Norse, 'speech, agreement.'

Black Ma·ri·a /məˈrīə/ ▶ **noun** informal a police vehicle for transporting prisoners.
– ORIGIN said to be named after *Maria* Lee, a black woman who kept a Boston boarding house and helped police take drunk and disorderly customers to jail.

black mark ▶ **noun** informal a record of the fact that someone has done something that is disapproved of by others.

black mar·ket ▶ **noun** the illegal buying and selling of goods that are officially controlled or hard to obtain.
– DERIVATIVES **black mar·ke·teer** noun.

black mass ▶ **noun** an imitation of the Roman Catholic Mass, performed in worship of the Devil.

Black Mus·lim ▶ **noun** a member of the Nation of Islam.

black·out /ˈblak͵out/ ▶ **noun 1** a period when all lights must be turned off during an enemy air raid. **2** a sudden failure of an electrical power supply. **3** a temporary loss of consciousness. **4** an official suppression of information: *a total news blackout.*

Black Pan·ther ▶ **noun** a member of a militant political organization set up in the US in 1966 to fight for black rights.

black sheep ▶ **noun** informal a member of a family or group who is regarded by the other members as a source of shame or embarrassment.

black·shirt /ˈblak͵SHərt/ ▶ **noun** a member of a Fascist organization.
– ORIGIN so named because of the black uniforms worn by the Italian Fascists before and during World War II.

black·smith /ˈblak͵smiTH/ ▶ **noun 1** a person who makes and repairs things in iron by hand. **2** a person who shoes horses; a farrier.

black·thorn /ˈblak͵THôrn/ ▶ **noun** a thorny shrub with white flowers and blue-black fruits (sloes).

black tie ▶ **noun** men's formal evening clothes, specifically a black bow tie worn with a dinner jacket.

black·top /ˈblak͵täp/ ▶ **noun 1** asphalt or other black material used for surfacing roads. **2** a road or area surfaced with such material.

black wid·ow ▶ **noun** a highly poisonous American spider having a black body with red markings.

blad·der /ˈbladər/ ▶ **noun 1** a sac in the abdomen that receives urine from the kidneys and stores it for excretion. **2** an inflated or hollow flexible bag.
– ORIGIN Old English.

blad·der·wort /ˈbladər͵wərt, -͵wôrt/ ▶ **noun** a water plant with small air-filled sacs that keep it afloat.

blad·der·wrack /ˈbladər͵rak/ ▶ **noun** a type of seaweed with long, flat brown fronds that contain sacs filled with air.

blade /blād/ ▶ **noun 1** the flat part of a knife or other tool or weapon that has a sharp edge for cutting. **2** the broad flat part of an oar, leaf, or other object. **3** a long narrow leaf of grass. **4** informal, dated a dashing young man.
– ORIGIN Old English.

blame /blām/ ▸ **verb** feel or state that someone or something is responsible for a bad or unfortunate act, situation, or occurrence: *he blamed Francis for his mother's death.*

– SYNONYMS **1 hold responsible,** hold accountable, condemn, accuse, find/consider guilty. **2** *they* ***blame*** *the economic decline* ***on*** *this administration* **attribute to,** ascribe to, impute to, lay at the door of, put down to; informal pin on.
– ANTONYMS absolve.

▸ **noun** responsibility for a bad or unfortunate act, situation, or occurrence: *she's trying to put the blame on me.*

– SYNONYMS **responsibility,** guilt, accountability, liability, culpability, fault.

– DERIVATIVES **blame·wor·thy** /ˈblām,wərT͟Hē/ adjective.
– PHRASES **be to blame** be responsible for a bad or unfortunate act, situation, or occurrence.
– ORIGIN Old French *blasmer.*

blame game ▸ **noun** the act of individuals or groups assigning blame to one another rather than taking a constructive position: *we should all stop this blame game and start the negotiations process.*

blame·less /ˈblāmlis/ ▸ **adjective** free from responsibility for any bad or unfortunate act, situation, or occurrence.

– SYNONYMS **innocent,** guiltless, above reproach, irreproachable, unimpeachable, in the clear, exemplary, impeccable, unblemished; informal squeaky clean.
– ANTONYMS guilty.

blanch /blanCH/ ▸ **verb 1** make or become white or pale. **2** prepare vegetables by plunging them briefly in boiling water. **3** peel almonds by scalding them.
– ORIGIN from Old French *blanc* 'white.'

blanc·mange /bləˈmänj, -ˈmänZH/ ▸ **noun** Brit. a sweet jellylike dessert made with cornstarch and milk.
– ORIGIN from Old French *blanc* 'white' + *mangier* 'eat.'

bland /bland/ ▸ **adjective 1** lacking strong qualities and therefore uninteresting: *bland, mass-produced pop music.* **2** showing little emotion: *his bland expression.*

– SYNONYMS **1 uninteresting,** dull, boring, tedious, monotonous, ordinary, run-of-the-mill, drab, dreary, unexciting, lackluster, flat, stale, trite. **2 tasteless,** flavorless, plain, insipid, weak, watery, thin, wishy-washy.
– ANTONYMS interesting, tangy.

– DERIVATIVES **bland·ly** adverb **bland·ness** noun.
– ORIGIN Latin *blandus* 'soft, smooth.'

bland·ish·ments /ˈblandiSHmənts/ ▸ **plural noun** flattering remarks intended to persuade someone to do something.

blank /blaNGk/ ▸ **adjective 1** not marked or decorated; bare or plain: *a blank piece of paper.* **2** not understanding or reacting: *he gave me a blank look.* **3** complete; absolute: *a blank refusal.*

– SYNONYMS **1 empty,** unmarked, unused, clear, free, bare, clean, plain. **2 expressionless,** deadpan, wooden, stony, impassive, inscrutable, glazed, fixed, lifeless.
– ANTONYMS expressive.

▸ **noun 1** a space left to be filled in a document. **2** a cartridge containing gunpowder but no bullet. **3** an empty space or period of time.

– SYNONYMS **space,** gap, void.

▸ **verb 1** hide or cover: *the sun had gone, blanked out by the smoke.* **2** defeat (a sports opponent) without allowing the opposition to score: *Baltimore blanked Toronto in a 7-0 victory.*
– DERIVATIVES **blank·ly** adverb **blank·ness** noun.
– PHRASES **draw a blank** get no response or result.
– ORIGIN Old French *blanc* 'white.'

blank check ▸ **noun 1** a signed check with the amount left for the person cashing it to fill in. **2** complete freedom of action.

blan·ket /ˈblaNGkit/ ▸ **noun 1** a large piece of woolen or similar material used as a warm covering. **2** a thick mass or layer of something: *a blanket of cloud.*

– SYNONYMS *a blanket of cloud* **covering,** layer, coating, carpet, cloak, mantle, veil, pall, shroud.

▸ **adjective** covering all cases; total: *a blanket ban on tobacco advertising.*

▸ **verb** (**blankets, blanketing, blanketed**) cover completely with a thick layer: *the countryside was blanketed with snow.*

– SYNONYMS **cover,** coat, carpet, cloak, shroud, swathe, envelop.

– DERIVATIVES **blan·ket·ing** noun.
– ORIGIN Old French *blanc* 'white.'

blank verse ▸ **noun** poetry written in iambic pentameter that does not rhyme.

blare /ble(ə)r/ ▸ **verb** sound loudly and harshly: *a police car with its siren blaring.* ▸ **noun** a loud, harsh sound.
– ORIGIN Dutch or German *blaren.*

blar·ney /ˈblärnē/ ▸ **noun** talk intended to be charming, flattering, or persuasive.
– ORIGIN named after the *Blarney* Stone in Ireland, said to give the gift of persuasive speech to anyone who kisses it.

bla·sé /bläˈzā/ ▸ **adjective** unimpressed with or indifferent to something because one has seen or experienced it many times before.

– SYNONYMS **indifferent,** unconcerned, casual, nonchalant, offhand, uninterested, unimpressed, unmoved, uncaring; informal laid-back.

– ORIGIN French.

blas·pheme /blasˈfēm, ˈblas,fēm/ ▸ **verb** speak disrespectfully about God or sacred things.
– DERIVATIVES **blas·phem·er** noun.
– ORIGIN from Greek *blasphēmos* 'evil-speaking.'

blas·phe·mous /ˈblasfəməs/ ▸ **adjective** disrespectful toward God or sacred things.

– SYNONYMS **sacrilegious,** profane, irreligious, irreverent, impious, ungodly, godless.
– ANTONYMS reverent.

– DERIVATIVES **blas·phe·mous·ly** adverb.

blas·phe·my /ˈblasfəmē/ ▸ **noun** (pl. **blasphemies**) disrespectful talk about God or sacred things.

– SYNONYMS **profanity,** sacrilege, irreligion, irreverence, taking the Lord's name in vain, impiety, desecration.
– ANTONYMS reverence.

blast /blast/ ▸ **noun 1** an explosion, or the destructive wave of air spreading outward from it. **2** a strong gust of wind or air. **3** a single loud note of a horn or whistle. **4** informal an enjoyable experience.

– SYNONYMS **1 explosion,** detonation, discharge, burst. **2 gust,** rush, gale, squall, flurry. **3** *the shrill* *blast of the trumpets* **blare,** wail, roar, screech, shriek, hoot, honk, beep.

▶ **verb 1** blow something up with explosives. **2** (**blast off**) (of a rocket or spacecraft) take off. **3** produce loud music or noise. **4** strike a ball hard. **5** informal criticize someone or something fiercely.

– SYNONYMS **1 blow up,** bomb, blow (to pieces), dynamite, explode, fire, shoot, blaze, let fly, discharge. **2 blare,** boom, roar, thunder, bellow, shriek, screech.

▶ **exclamation** Brit. informal expressing annoyance.
– DERIVATIVES **blast·er** noun.
– PHRASES **(at) full blast** at maximum power or volume.
– ORIGIN Old English.

blast·ed /'blastid/ ▶ **adjective 1** informal used to express annoyance: *make your own blasted coffee!* **2** informal drunk.

blast fur·nace ▶ **noun** a smelting furnace using blasts of hot compressed air.

blast-off /'blast,ôf, -,äf/ ▶ **noun** the launch of a rocket or spacecraft.

bla·tant /'blā̄tnt/ ▶ **adjective** (of an act considered to be bad) done in an open, obvious, and unashamed way: *a blatant abuse of human rights.*

– SYNONYMS **flagrant,** glaring, obvious, undisguised, open, overt, outright, naked, shameless, barefaced, unashamed, brazen.
– ANTONYMS discreet, inconspicuous.

– DERIVATIVES **bla·tan·cy** /'blātnsē/ noun **bla·tant·ly** adverb.
– ORIGIN first used by the poet Edmund Spenser; perhaps from Scots *blatand* 'bleating.'

blath·er /'blaT͟Hər/ (also **blither**) ▶ **verb** talk at length without making much sense.

– SYNONYMS **prattle,** babble, chatter, twitter, prate, go on, run on, rattle on, yap, ramble, drivel; informal yak, yatter.

▶ **noun** rambling talk.
– ORIGIN Old Norse.

blaze /blāz/ ▶ **noun 1** a very large or fiercely burning fire. **2** a very bright light or display of color. **3** a conspicuous display or outburst of something: *a blaze of publicity.* **4** a white stripe down the face of a horse or other animal. **5** (**blazes**) informal a euphemism for 'hell': *go to blazes!*

– SYNONYMS **1 fire,** flames, conflagration, inferno, holocaust. **2** *a blaze of light* **glare,** flash, burst, flare, streak, radiance, brilliance, beam, glitter.

▶ **verb 1** burn or shine fiercely or brightly. **2** (of guns) be fired repeatedly or wildly. **3** informal achieve something in an impressive manner.

– SYNONYMS **1 burn,** be alight, be on fire, be in flames. **2 shine,** flash, flare, glare, gleam, glitter, glisten. **3 fire,** shoot, blast, let fly.

– DERIVATIVES **blaz·ing** adjective.
– PHRASES **blaze a trail 1** mark out a path or route. **2** be the first to do something.
– ORIGIN Old English; sense 3 of the verb is from German or Dutch *blāzen* 'to blow.'

blaz·er /'blāzər/ ▶ **noun 1** a jacket worn by schoolchildren or team members as part of a uniform. **2** a man's sports jacket that does not form part of a suit.

bla·zon /'blāzən/ ▶ **verb 1** display or describe prominently or vividly: *his name was blazoned all over the newspapers.* **2** Heraldry depict a coat of arms. ▶ **noun** old use a coat of arms.
– ORIGIN Old French *blason* 'shield.'

CHOOSE THE RIGHT WORD

See **ANNOUNCE**.

bleach /blēCH/ ▶ **verb 1** make something white or lighter by the use of chemicals or by exposing it to sunlight. **2** clean or sterilize a drain, sink, etc., with bleach.

– SYNONYMS **turn white,** whiten, turn pale, blanch, lighten, fade.
– ANTONYMS darken.

▶ **noun** a chemical used to lighten things and also to sterilize drains, sinks, etc.
– ORIGIN Old English.

bleach·er /'blēCHər/ ▶ **noun** (usu. **bleachers**) a cheap bench seat in an uncovered part of a sports arena.

bleak /blēk/ ▶ **adjective 1** bare and exposed to the weather: *the bleak snow-covered hillside.* **2** empty or unwelcoming; without pleasant features: *a bleak room in a grimy hotel.* **3** (of a situation) not hopeful or encouraging: *HIV patients in the town face a bleak future.*

– SYNONYMS **1 bare,** exposed, desolate, stark, desert, lunar, open, empty, windswept. **2 unpromising,** unfavorable, dim, gloomy, black, grim, discouraging, disheartening, depressing, dismal.
– ANTONYMS lush, promising.

– DERIVATIVES **bleak·ly** adverb **bleak·ness** noun.
– ORIGIN Old English or Old Norse, 'white, shining.'

WORD TOOLKIT

See **DISMAL**.

blear·y /'bli(ə)rē/ ▶ **adjective** (**blearier, bleariest**) (of a person's eyes) dull and not focusing properly, especially as a result of tiredness.

– SYNONYMS **blurry,** unfocused, fogged, clouded, misty, watery, rheumy.
– ANTONYMS clear.

– DERIVATIVES **blear·i·ly** adverb.
– ORIGIN probably from German *blerre* 'blurred vision.'

bleat /blēt/ ▶ **verb 1** (of a sheep or goat) make a weak, wavering cry. **2** speak or complain in a weak or petulant way. ▶ **noun** a bleating sound.
– ORIGIN Old English.

bleed /blēd/ ▶ **verb** (past and past part. **bled** /bled/) **1** lose blood from the body. **2** take blood from someone as a former method of medical treatment. **3** (of dye or color) seep into an adjoining color or area. **4** informal deprive of money or resources. **5** allow fluid or gas to escape from a closed system through a valve.

– SYNONYMS **1 lose blood,** hemorrhage. **2** *one color bled into another* **flow,** run, seep, filter, percolate, leach. **3** *the country was* ***bled dry*** *by poachers* **drain,** sap, deplete, milk (dry), exhaust.

▶ **noun** an instance of losing blood from a part of the body.
– ORIGIN Old English.

bleed·ing /'blēdiNG/ ▶ **adjective** Brit. informal used for emphasis or to express annoyance.

bleed·ing heart ▶ **noun** informal, derogatory a person considered to be too softhearted or liberal.

bleep /blēp/ ▶ **noun** a short high-pitched sound made by an electronic device. ▶ **verb 1** make a bleep. **2** substitute a bleep or bleeps for (a censored word or phrase).
– ORIGIN imitating the sound.

blem·ish /ˈblemisʜ/ ▶ **noun 1** a small mark or flaw that spoils the appearance of something. **2** a fault or failing.

– SYNONYMS **imperfection,** flaw, defect, fault, discoloration, stain, scar, mark, spot.

▶ **verb** spoil the appearance of something.

– SYNONYMS **mar,** spoil, impair, disfigure, deface, mark, stain, scar, blight, tarnish.
– ANTONYMS enhance.

– ORIGIN Old French *blesmir* 'make pale, injure.'

blench /blencʜ/ ▶ **verb** flinch suddenly through fear or pain.
– ORIGIN Old English, 'deceive.'

blend /blend/ ▶ **verb 1** mix a substance with another substance so that they combine together. **2** combine with something in an attractive or harmonious way: *costumes, music, and lighting all blend together*. **3** be an unobtrusive or attractive part of something by being similar in appearance or behavior: *a tourist resort designed to blend in with the natural surroundings*.

– SYNONYMS **1 mix,** mingle, combine, merge, fuse, amalgamate, stir, whisk, fold in. **2 harmonize,** go (well), fit (in), be in tune, be compatible, coordinate, match, complement, suit.

▶ **noun** a mixture of different things or people.

– SYNONYMS **mixture,** mix, melange, combination, synthesis, compound, amalgam, fusion, alloy.

– ORIGIN probably Scandinavian.

blend·er /ˈblendər/ ▶ **noun** an electric device used for liquidizing or chopping food.

blen·ny /ˈblenē/ ▶ **noun** (pl. **blennies**) a small sea fish with spiny fins and a scaleless skin.
– ORIGIN from Greek *blennos* 'mucus' (because the fish is covered with mucus).

bless /bles/ ▶ **verb 1** ask God to protect someone or something: *may God bless you and keep you*. **2** make holy by performing a religious rite: *the priest had broken the bread and blessed the wine*. **3** praise God. **4** (**be blessed with**) have or be given something that is greatly wished for: *we have been blessed with a baby boy*.

– SYNONYMS **1 consecrate,** sanctify, dedicate to God, make holy; formal hallow. **2 endow,** bestow, furnish, give, favor, confer on. **3 sanction,** consent to, endorse, agree to, approve, back, support; informal give the green light to, OK.
– ANTONYMS curse, oppose.

– PHRASES **bless you!** said to a person who has just sneezed.
– ORIGIN Old English.

bless·ed /blest, ˈblesid/ ▶ **adjective 1** made holy. **2** protected by God. **3** bringing welcome pleasure or relief: *blessed sleep*. **4** informal used in mild expressions of exasperation.

– SYNONYMS **holy,** sacred, hallowed, consecrated, sanctified, ordained, canonized, beatified.
– ANTONYMS cursed.

– DERIVATIVES **bless·ed·ly** /ˈblesidlē/ adverb **bless·ed·ness** /ˈblesidnis/ noun.

bless·ing /ˈblesiɴɢ/ ▶ **noun 1** God's favor and protection. **2** a prayer asking for this. **3** something for which one is very grateful: *it's a blessing we're alive*. **4** a person's approval or support: *he gave the plan his blessing*.

– SYNONYMS **1 benediction,** dedication, consecration, grace, invocation, intercession. **2 sanction,** endorsement, approval, consent, assent, agreement, backing, support; informal the green light, OK. **3 advantage,** godsend, boon, benefit, help, bonus, plus, stroke of luck, windfall.
– ANTONYMS condemnation.

– PHRASES **a blessing in disguise** something that at first seems unfortunate but eventually has good results.

blew /blo͞o/ past of **BLOW**[1].

blight /blīt/ ▶ **noun 1** a plant disease, especially one caused by fungi. **2** a thing that spoils or damages something: *an ugly building that is a blight on the landscape*. **3** ugly or neglected urban landscape.

– SYNONYMS **1** *potato blight* **disease,** canker, infestation, fungus, mildew, mold. **2** *the blight of aircraft noise* **curse,** scourge, affliction, plague, menace, misfortune, bane, trouble, nuisance, pest.

▶ **verb 1** infect plants with blight. **2** spoil or destroy: *lives blighted by economic hardship*.

– SYNONYMS **ruin,** wreck, spoil, mar, frustrate, disrupt, undo, scotch, destroy, shatter, devastate, demolish; informal mess up, foul up, put paid to, put the kibosh on, stymie; Brit. informal scupper.

– ORIGIN unknown.

bli·mey /ˈblīmē/ ▶ **exclamation** Brit. informal expressing surprise or alarm.
– ORIGIN altered form of *Godblind* (or *blame*) *me!*

blimp /blimp/ ▶ **noun 1** a small nonrigid airship. **2** informal an obese person.
– DERIVATIVES **blimp·ish** adjective.
– ORIGIN of unknown origin.

blind /blīnd/ ▶ **adjective 1** not able to see. **2** done without being able to see or without having certain information: *a blind tasting of eight wines*. **3** not noticing or realizing something: *I am not blind to her shortcomings*. **4** not controlled by reason: *they left in blind panic*. **5** (of a corner or bend in a road) impossible to see around.

– SYNONYMS **1 sightless,** unsighted, visually impaired, unseeing. **2 uncritical,** unreasoned, unthinking, unquestioning, mindless, undiscerning, indiscriminate. **3** *blind to the realities of the situation* **unaware of,** oblivious to, ignorant of, unmindful of, heedless of, insensible to, indifferent to.

▶ **verb 1** make someone or something blind. **2** make someone no longer able to think clearly or sensibly: *they were blinded by hatred*. **3** (**blind someone with**) confuse or overawe someone with something they do not understand: *a manual that does not blind you with computer science*.
▶ **noun 1** a screen for a window. **2** something designed to conceal one's real intentions.

– SYNONYMS **screen,** shade, sunshade, curtain, awning, canopy, louver, jalousie, shutter.

▶ **adverb** without being able to see clearly.
– DERIVATIVES **blind·ness** noun.
– PHRASES **blind drunk** informal extremely drunk. **turn a blind eye** pretend not to notice.
– ORIGIN Old English.

blind al·ley ▶ **noun 1** a cul-de-sac. **2** a course of action that does not produce useful results.

blind date ▶ **noun** a meeting with a person one has not met before, with the aim of developing a romantic relationship.

blind·ers /ˈblīndərz/ ▶ **plural noun 1** a pair of small pieces of leather attached to a horse's bridle to prevent the horse seeing sideways. **2** something that prevents someone from fully understanding a situation.

blind·fold /ˈblīndˌfōld/ ▸ **noun** a piece of cloth tied around the head to cover someone's eyes. ▸ **verb** put a blindfold on someone so that they cannot see. ▸ **adverb** with a blindfold covering the eyes: *I could find my way around the place blindfold.*
– ORIGIN Old English.

blind·ing /ˈblīndiNG/ ▸ **adjective** **1** (of light) very bright. **2** (of pain) very intense: *a blinding headache.* **3** informal very skillful and exciting: *a blinding performance.*
– DERIVATIVES **blind·ing·ly** adverb.

blind·ly /ˈblīndlē/ ▸ **adverb** **1** as if blind. **2** without reasoning or questioning.

– SYNONYMS *solutions must be assessed, not blindly accepted* **uncritically,** unquestioningly, unthinkingly, mindlessly, indiscriminately.

blind man's buff (also **blind man's bluff**) ▸ **noun** a children's game in which a blindfolded player tries to catch others while being pushed around by them.
– ORIGIN from *buff* 'a blow,' from Old French.

blind side ▸ **noun** a direction in which a person has a poor view of approaching traffic or danger.

blind spot ▸ **noun** **1** a small area of the retina in the eye that is insensitive to light. **2** an area where a person's view is obstructed. **3** an area or subject about which a person lacks understanding or impartiality: *he has a blind spot where his daughter is concerned.*

blind·worm /ˈblīndˌwərm/ ▸ **noun** another term for **SLOW-WORM**.

bling-bling /ˈbliNG ˌbliNG/ (also **bling**) ▸ **noun & adjective** informal used to refer to expensive, showy clothing and jewelry, or the style or attitudes associated with them.
– ORIGIN perhaps in imitation of light reflecting off jewelry.

blin·i /ˈblinē, ˈblē-/ (also **blinis**) ▸ **plural noun** pancakes made from buckwheat flour.
– ORIGIN Russian.

blink /bliNGk/ ▸ **verb** **1** shut and open the eyes quickly. **2** (of a light) flash on and off. ▸ **noun** an act of blinking the eyes.
– PHRASES **on the blink** informal out of order.
– ORIGIN Scots variant of **BLENCH**.

blink·er /ˈbliNGkər/ ▸ **noun** **1** a device that blinks, especially a vehicle's turn signal. **2** (**blinkers**) another term for **BLINDERS**. ▸ **verb** put blinders on a horse.

blink·ered /ˈbliNGkərd/ ▸ **adjective** **1** (of a horse) wearing blinders. **2** having or showing a narrow or limited outlook or point of view: *a small-minded, blinkered approach.*

blip /blip/ ▸ **noun** **1** a very short high-pitched sound made by an electronic device. **2** a small flashing point of light on a radar screen. **3** an unexpected and usually temporary change in the pattern of a situation or process: *a blip in what has otherwise been a successful career.* ▸ **verb** (**blips, blipping, blipped**) (of an electronic device) make a blip.
– ORIGIN imitating the sound.

bliss /blis/ ▸ **noun** **1** a state or feeling of perfect happiness. **2** a state of spiritual blessedness.

– SYNONYMS **joy,** happiness, pleasure, delight, ecstasy, elation, rapture, euphoria, seventh heaven.
– ANTONYMS misery.

– ORIGIN Old English.

CHOOSE THE RIGHT WORD

See **RAPTURE**.

bliss·ful /ˈblisfəl/ ▸ **adjective** extremely happy.
– DERIVATIVES **bliss·ful·ly** adverb.

B-list ▸ **noun** see **A-LIST**.

blis·ter /ˈblistər/ ▸ **noun** **1** a small bubble on the skin filled with watery liquid, typically caused when the skin is rubbed against another surface or by burning. **2** a similar swelling, filled with air or fluid, on the surface of painted wood, heated metal, etc. ▸ **verb** form or cause to form blisters: *his skin was beginning to blister with the heat.*
– ORIGIN perhaps from Old French *blestre* 'swelling, pimple.'

blis·ter·ing /ˈblistəriNG/ ▸ **adjective** **1** (of heat) intense. **2** (of criticism) very forceful: *a blistering attack on the government.* **3** extremely fast, energetic, or impressive: *he set a blistering pace.*
– DERIVATIVES **blis·ter·ing·ly** adverb.

blithe /blīTH, blīTH/ ▸ **adjective** **1** showing a casual lack of concern about something: *a blithe disregard for the rules of the road.* **2** literary happy.

– SYNONYMS **casual,** indifferent, unconcerned, unworried, untroubled, uncaring, careless, heedless, thoughtless; nonchalant, blasé.
– ANTONYMS thoughtful.

– DERIVATIVES **blithe·ly** adverb **blithe·ness** noun.
– ORIGIN Old English.

blith·er·ing /ˈbliTHəriNG/ ▸ **adjective** informal complete: *you blithering idiot.*

blitz /blits/ ▸ **noun** **1** an intensive or sudden military attack. **2** (**the Blitz**) the German air raids on Britain in 1940–41. **3** informal a sudden and concentrated effort to deal with something: *the Department launched a blitz on drunk drivers.*

– SYNONYMS **bombing,** air raid, air strike, bombardment, barrage, attack, assault.

▸ **verb** attack or seriously damage a place in a blitz.
– ORIGIN abbreviation of **BLITZKRIEG**.

blitz·krieg /ˈblitsˌkrēg/ ▸ **noun** an intense military campaign intended to bring about a rapid victory.
– ORIGIN German, 'lightning war.'

bliz·zard /ˈblizərd/ ▸ **noun** a severe snowstorm with high winds.
– ORIGIN unknown.

bloat /blōt/ ▸ **verb** swell or cause to swell with fluid or gas.
– ORIGIN perhaps from an Old Norse word meaning 'soft.'

bloat·ed /ˈblōtid/ ▸ **adjective** swollen with fluid or gas.

– SYNONYMS **swollen,** distended, bulging, puffed out, inflated, dilated.

blob /bläb/ ▸ **noun** **1** a drop of a thick liquid or sticky substance. **2** a roundish mass or shape.

– SYNONYMS **drop,** droplet, globule, bead, bubble, spot, dab, blotch, blot, dot, smudge.

– DERIVATIVES **blob·by** adjective.

bloc /bläk/ ▸ **noun** a group of countries or political parties who have formed an alliance.

– SYNONYMS **group,** alliance, coalition, federation, confederation, league, union, axis, association.

– ORIGIN French, 'block.'

block /bläk/ ▸ **noun** **1** a large piece of a solid material with flat surfaces on each side. **2** a building, usually part of a complex, used for a particular purpose: *a cell block.*

3 a group of buildings with streets on all four sides. **4** a large quantity of things regarded as a unit: *a block of shares.* **5** a thing that makes movement or progress difficult: *a block to career advancement.* **6** a solid area of color on a surface. **7** (also **cylinder block** or **engine block**) a large metal molding containing the cylinders of an internal-combustion engine. **8** a pulley or system of pulleys mounted in a case.

– SYNONYMS **1 chunk,** hunk, lump, wedge, cube, brick, ingot, slab, piece. **2 building,** complex, structure, development. **3 obstacle,** bar, barrier, impediment, hindrance, check, hurdle.

▶ **verb 1** prevent movement or flow in a road, passage, pipe, etc.: *all three lanes were blocked with traffic.* **2** hinder or prevent: *unions threatened to block the deal.*

– SYNONYMS **1 clog,** stop up, choke, plug, bung up, obstruct, gum up, dam up, congest, jam. **2 hinder,** hamper, obstruct, impede, inhibit, halt, stop, bar, check, prevent, fend off, hold off, repel.
– ANTONYMS clear, aid.

– DERIVATIVES **block·er** noun.
– PHRASES **block something out** exclude something unpleasant from one's thoughts or memory. **knock someone's block off** informal hit someone on the head. **put one's head** (or **neck**) **on the block** informal put one's position or reputation at risk by doing or saying something.
– ORIGIN Dutch.

block·ade /blä'kād/ ▶ **noun** an act of sealing off a place to prevent goods or people from entering or leaving. ▶ **verb** seal off a place to prevent goods or people from entering or leaving.

block·age /'bläkij/ ▶ **noun** an obstruction that makes movement or flow difficult or impossible.

– SYNONYMS **obstruction,** stoppage, block, jam, congestion, bottleneck.

block and tack·le ▶ **noun** a lifting mechanism consisting of ropes, a pulley block, and a hook.

block·bust·er /'bläk,bəstər/ ▶ **noun** informal a movie or book that is a great commercial success.
– DERIVATIVES **block·bust·ing** adjective.

block cap·i·tals ▶ **plural noun** plain capital letters.

block·head /'bläk,hed/ ▶ **noun** informal a very stupid person.

block·house /'bläk,hous/ ▶ **noun** a reinforced concrete shelter used as an observation point.

block let·ters ▶ **plural noun** block capitals.

blog /bläg/ ▶ **noun** a personal website on which someone regularly records their opinions or experiences and creates links to other sites. ▶ **verb** (**blogs, blogging, blogged**) (usu. as n. **blogging**) regularly update a blog.
– DERIVATIVES **blog·ger** noun.

blog·o·sphere /'blägə,sfi(ə)r/ ▶ **noun** the world of weblogs.

blog·roll /'bläg,rōl/ ▶ **noun** (on a weblog) a list of hyperlinks to other weblogs.

bloke /blōk/ ▶ **noun** Brit. informal a man.
– ORIGIN Shelta.

blond /bländ/ ▶ **adjective** (also **blonde**) **1** (of hair) fair or pale yellow. **2** having fair hair and a light complexion.

– SYNONYMS **fair,** light, yellow, flaxen, golden.
– ANTONYMS dark.

▶ **noun** a person with fair hair.
– ORIGIN French.

blood /bləd/ ▶ **noun 1** the red liquid that circulates in the arteries and veins, carrying oxygen and carbon dioxide. **2** a person's family background: *she must have Irish blood.* **3** dated a fashionable and dashing young man.

– SYNONYMS **1 lifeblood,** gore, vital fluid. **2 ancestry,** lineage, descent, parentage, family, birth, extraction, origin, stock.

▶ **verb** initiate someone in an activity: *clubs are too slow in blooding young players.*
– PHRASES **be** (or **run**) **in one's blood** be a natural or fundamental part of one's character and, typically, of the character of other family members: *writing is in her blood.* **blood, sweat, and tears** extremely hard work. **first blood 1** the first shedding of blood in a fight. **2** the first point or advantage gained in a contest. **have blood on one's hands** be responsible for someone's death. **make someone's blood boil** informal make someone extremely angry. **make someone's blood run cold** horrify someone. **new** (or **fresh** or **young**) **blood** new (or younger) members of a group or organization, especially those seen as having new and invigorating ideas or skills. **someone's blood is up** someone is angry and in a fighting mood.
– ORIGIN Old English.

WORD LINKS

hematology *branch of medicine concerned with blood*

blood bank ▶ **noun** a place where supplies of blood or plasma for transfusion are stored.

blood·bath /'bləd,baTH/ ▶ **noun** an event in which many people are killed violently.

blood broth·er ▶ **noun** a man who has sworn to treat another man as a brother.

blood count ▶ **noun** a calculation of the number of corpuscles (red and white blood cells) in a particular quantity of blood.

blood·cur·dling /'bləd,kərd(ə)liNG/ ▶ **adjective** horrifying; extremely frightening.

blood feud ▶ **noun** a lengthy conflict between families involving a cycle of revenge killings.

blood group ▶ **noun** any of the various types into which human blood is classified for medical purposes.

blood·hound /'bləd,hound/ ▶ **noun** a large hound with a very keen sense of smell, used in tracking.

blood·less /'blədlis/ ▶ **adjective 1** without violence or killing: *a bloodless coup.* **2** (of the skin) looking very pale; drained of color. **3** lacking emotion or vitality: *a pedantic, bloodless character.*
– DERIVATIVES **blood·less·ly** adverb.

blood·let·ting /'bləd,letiNG/ ▶ **noun 1** historical the surgical removal of some of a patient's blood for medical purposes. **2** violence during a war or conflict.

blood·line /'bləd,līn/ ▶ **noun** a pedigree, set of ancestors, or line of descent.

blood mon·ey ▶ **noun 1** money paid to compensate the family of a murdered person. **2** money paid to a hired killer.

blood or·ange ▶ **noun** an orange of a variety with red flesh.

blood poi·soning ▶ **noun** a serious illness that occurs when harmful microorganisms have infected the blood.

blood pres·sure ▸ noun the pressure of the blood in the circulatory system, which is closely related to the force and rate of the heartbeat.

blood re·la·tion (also **blood relative**) ▸ noun a person who is related to another by birth.

blood sau·sage (also **blood pudding**) ▸ noun sausage made from pork and dried pig's blood.

blood·shed /ˈbləd,sʜed/ ▸ noun the killing or wounding of people.

– SYNONYMS **slaughter,** massacre, killing, wounding, carnage, butchery, bloodletting, bloodbath.

blood·shot /ˈbləd,sʜät/ ▸ adjective (of the eyes) having the whites tinged with blood.

blood sport ▸ noun a sport involving the hunting, wounding, or killing of animals.

blood·stain /ˈbləd,stān/ ▸ noun a stain or a spot caused by blood.
– DERIVATIVES **blood·stained** adjective.

blood·stock /ˈbləd,stäk/ ▸ noun thoroughbred horses.

blood·stream /ˈbləd,strēm/ ▸ noun the blood circulating through the body.

blood·suck·er /ˈbləd,səkər/ ▸ noun **1** an animal or insect that sucks blood. **2** informal a person who extorts money from other people.
– DERIVATIVES **blood·suck·ing** adjective.

blood sug·ar ▸ noun the concentration of glucose in the blood.

blood·thirst·y /ˈbləd,ᴛʜərstē/ ▸ adjective taking great pleasure in violence and killing.

– SYNONYMS **murderous,** homicidal, violent, vicious, barbarous, barbaric, savage, brutal, cutthroat.

blood ves·sel ▸ noun a vein, artery, or capillary carrying blood through the body.

blood·y /ˈblədē/ ▸ adjective (**bloodier, bloodiest**) **1** covered with or containing blood. **2** involving much violence or cruelty: *a bloody military coup.* **3** informal, chiefly Brit. used to express anger or shock, or for emphasis.

– SYNONYMS **1 bloodstained,** blood-soaked, gory, bleeding. **2 vicious,** ferocious, savage, fierce, brutal, cruel, murderous.

▸ verb (**bloodies, bloodying, bloodied**) cover or stain something with blood.
– DERIVATIVES **blood·i·ly** /ˈblədəlē/ adverb **blood·i·ness** noun.

Blood·y Mar·y ▸ noun (pl. **Bloody Marys**) a drink consisting of vodka and tomato juice.

bloom /blo͞om/ ▸ verb **1** produce flowers; be in flower. **2** be or become very healthy: *she had bloomed during her pregnancy.*

– SYNONYMS **1 flower,** blossom, open, mature. **2 flourish,** thrive, prosper, progress, burgeon; informal be in the pink.
– ANTONYMS wither, decline.

▸ noun **1** a flower. **2** the state or period of blooming: *the apple trees were in bloom.* **3** a youthful or healthy glow in a person's complexion: *the rosy bloom in her cheeks.* **4** a delicate powdery deposit on the surface of fruits or leaves.
– ORIGIN Old Norse.

bloom·er /ˈblo͞omər/ ▸ noun **1** a plant that flowers at a specified time. **2** a person who matures or flourishes at a specified time: *he was a late bloomer.*
– ORIGIN unknown.

bloo·mers /ˈblo͞omərz/ ▸ plural noun **1** women's loose-fitting knee-length underpants. **2** historical women's loose-fitting trousers, gathered at the knee or ankle.
– ORIGIN named after the American social reformer Mrs Amelia J. *Bloomer.*

bloom·ing /ˈblo͞omiɴɢ/ ▸ adjective Brit. informal used to express annoyance or for emphasis: *of all the blooming nerve!*

bloop·er /ˈblo͞opər/ ▸ noun informal an embarrassing mistake.
– ORIGIN first referring to an electronic device which made a loud, howling sound.

blos·som /ˈbläsəm/ ▸ noun **1** a flower or a mass of flowers on a tree or bush. **2** the state or period of flowering: *the cherry trees are in blossom.*

– SYNONYMS **flower,** bloom, bud.

▸ verb **1** (of a tree or bush) produce flowers. **2** develop in a promising or healthy way: *their friendship blossomed into romance.*

– SYNONYMS **1 bloom,** flower, open, mature. **2 develop,** grow, mature, progress, evolve, burgeon, flourish, thrive, prosper, bloom.
– ANTONYMS wither, decline.

– ORIGIN Old English.

blot /blät/ ▸ noun **1** a mark or stain, especially one made by ink. **2** a thing that spoils something that is otherwise good or attractive: *the only blot on his dazzling career.*

– SYNONYMS **1 patch,** dab, smudge, blotch, mark, dot, spot. **2 blemish,** taint, stain, blight, flaw, fault. **3** *a blot on the landscape* **eyesore,** monstrosity, mess; informal sight.

▸ verb (**blots, blotting, blotted**) **1** dry a wet surface or substance with an absorbent material. **2** mark, stain, or spoil: *the eyesores that have blotted our cityscapes.* **3** (**blot something out**) cover or hide something from view. **4** (**blot something out**) try to keep an unpleasant memory or thought from one's mind.

– SYNONYMS **1** (**blot something out**) *clouds were starting to blot out the stars* **conceal,** hide, obscure, exclude, obliterate, shadow, eclipse. **2** (**blot something out**) *he tried to blot out the image of Helen's sad face* **wipe out,** erase, blank out, eradicate.

– ORIGIN probably Scandinavian.

blotch /bläcʜ/ ▸ noun a large irregular mark.
– DERIVATIVES **blotched** adjective **blotch·y** adjective.
– ORIGIN from **BLOT** and **BOTCH**.

blot·ter /ˈblätər/ ▸ noun a sheet or pad of blotting paper kept on a desk.

blot·ting pa·per ▸ noun absorbent paper used for soaking up excess ink when writing.

blot·to /ˈblätō/ ▸ adjective informal extremely drunk.

blouse /blous, blouz/ ▸ noun **1** a garment like a shirt, worn by women. **2** a type of jacket worn as part of a military uniform. ▸ verb make a garment hang in full, loose folds.
– ORIGIN French.

blous·on /ˈblou,sän, -,zän/ ▸ noun a short loose-fitting jacket.
– ORIGIN French.

blo·vi·ate /ˈblōvēāt/ ▸ verb talk at length, especially using inflated or empty rhetoric.

blow[1] /blō/ ▸ **verb** (past **blew**; past part. **blown**) **1** (of wind) move, creating a current or air. **2** carry or be carried by the wind: *my tent had blown away.* **3** send out air through pursed lips. **4** force air through the mouth into a musical instrument. **5** sound the horn of a vehicle. **6** (of an explosion) force something out of place: *the blast blew out the windows.* **7** burst or burn out through pressure or overheating: *the fuse in the plug had blown.* **8** shape molten glass by forcing air into it through a tube. **9** informal spend money recklessly. **10** informal waste an opportunity: *they blew their championship chances.* **11** informal reveal or expose something: *one mistake could blow his cover.*

– SYNONYMS **1 gust,** puff, flurry, blast, roar, bluster, rush, storm. **2 sweep,** carry, toss, drive, push, force, drift, flutter, waft, float, glide, whirl. **3** *he blew the trumpet* **sound,** blast, toot, play, pipe, trumpet.

▸ **noun 1** an act of blowing something. **2** a strong wind.
– PHRASES **blow a fuse** (or **gasket**) informal lose one's temper. **blow hot and cold** keep changing one's mind. **blow someone's mind** informal impress or affect someone very strongly. **blow one's nose** clear one's nose of mucus by blowing through it. **blow over** (of trouble) fade away without having any serious effects. **blow one's top** informal lose one's temper. **blow up 1** explode. **2** lose one's temper. **3** develop suddenly and violently: *a crisis blew up between the two countries in 1967.* **blow something up 1** make something explode. **2** inflate something.
– ORIGIN Old English.

blow[2] ▸ **noun 1** a powerful stroke with a hand or weapon. **2** a sudden shock or disappointment: *the news came as a crushing blow.*

– SYNONYMS **1 stroke,** knock, bang, hit, punch, thump, smack, crack, rap; informal whack, bash, clout, wallop. **2 upset,** disaster, setback, misfortune, disappointment, calamity, catastrophe, thunderbolt, bombshell, shock, surprise, jolt.

– PHRASES **come to blows** start fighting after a disagreement.
– ORIGIN unknown.

blow-by-blow ▸ **adjective** (of a description of an event) giving all the details in the order in which they happened.

blow-dry ▸ **verb** dry the hair with a hand-held dryer, arranging it into a particular style.

blow·er /ˈblōər/ ▸ **noun** a device that creates a current of air to dry or heat something.

blow·fish /ˈblō,fisн/ ▸ **noun** (pl. same or **blowfishes**) a fish that is able to inflate its body when it is alarmed.

blow·fly /ˈblō,flī/ ▸ **noun** (pl. **blowflies**) a bluebottle or similar large fly that lays its eggs on meat and carcasses.

blow·hard /ˈblō,härd/ ▸ **noun** informal a boastful or pompous person.

blow·hole /ˈblō,hōl/ ▸ **noun 1** the nostril of a whale or dolphin, on the top of its head. **2** a hole in ice for breathing or fishing through. **3** a vent for air or smoke in a tunnel.

blow job ▸ **noun** vulgar slang an act of fellatio.

blown /blōn/ past participle of BLOW[1].

blow·out /ˈblō,out/ ▸ **noun 1** an occasion when a vehicle tire bursts or an electric fuse melts. **2** informal a large meal or social gathering.

blow·pipe /ˈblō,pīp/ ▸ **noun 1** a weapon consisting of a long tube through which an arrow or dart is blown. **2** a long tube used for blowing glass.

blows·y /ˈblouzē/ (also **blowzy**) ▸ **adjective** (of a woman) red-faced and untidy in appearance.
– ORIGIN from an old word meaning 'a beggar's female companion.'

blow·torch /ˈblō,tôrcн/ ▸ **noun** a portable device producing a very hot flame, used to burn paint off a surface.

blow·up /ˈblō,əp/ ▸ **noun 1** an enlargement of a photograph. **2** informal an outburst of anger. ▸ **adjective** inflatable: *a blowup neck pillow.*

BLT ▸ **noun** a sandwich filled with bacon, lettuce, and tomato.

blub·ber[1] /ˈbləbər/ ▸ **noun** the fat of sea mammals, especially whales and seals.
– DERIVATIVES **blub·ber·y** adjective.
– ORIGIN first referring to foam on the sea.

blub·ber[2] ▸ **verb** informal sob noisily.
– ORIGIN probably imitating the sound.

bludg·eon /ˈbləjən/ ▸ **noun** a thick stick with a heavy end, used as a weapon.

– SYNONYMS **cudgel,** club, stick, truncheon, nightstick, blackjack, baton.

▸ **verb 1** hit someone repeatedly with a bludgeon or other heavy object. **2** bully into doing something: *he bludgeoned Congress into approving the measures.*

– SYNONYMS **1 batter,** cudgel, club, beat, thrash; informal clobber. **2 coerce,** force, compel, pressurize, pressure, bully, browbeat, hector, dragoon, steamroller; informal strong-arm, railroad.

– ORIGIN unknown.

blue /blo͞o/ ▸ **adjective** (**bluer**, **bluest**) **1** of the color of the sky on a sunny day. **2** informal sad or depressed. **3** informal having sexual or pornographic content: *a blue movie.*

– SYNONYMS azure, cobalt, sapphire, navy, indigo, sky-blue, ultramarine, aquamarine, turquoise, cyan.

▸ **noun 1** blue color or material. **2** (**the blue**) literary the sky or sea; the unknown.
– DERIVATIVES **blue·ness** noun.
– PHRASES **blue on blue** Military referring to an attack made by one's own side that accidentally harms one's own forces. [from the use of blue to indicate friendly forces in military exercises.] **once in a blue moon** informal very rarely. **out of the blue** informal unexpectedly.
– ORIGIN Old French *bleu.*

blue ba·by ▸ **noun** a baby born with bluish skin as the result of a lack of oxygen in the blood.

blue·bell /ˈblo͞o,bel/ ▸ **noun** a woodland plant with clusters of blue bell-shaped flowers.

blue·ber·ry /ˈblo͞o,berē/ ▸ **noun** (pl. **blueberries**) the dark blue edible berry of a North American shrub.

blue·bird /ˈblo͞o,bərd/ ▸ **noun** an American songbird, the male of which has a blue head, back, and wings.

blue blood ▸ **noun 1** noble birth: *blue blood is no guarantee of any particular merit, competence, or expertise.* **2** a person of noble birth.
– DERIVATIVES **blue-blood·ed** adjective.

blue book ▸ **noun 1** a listing of socially prominent people. **2** a reference book listing the prices of used cars. **3** a blank book used for written examinations in high school and college.

blue·bot·tle /ˈblo͞oˌbätl/ ▸ **noun** a large fly with a metallic-blue body.

blue cheese ▸ **noun** cheese containing veins of blue mold, such as Stilton.

blue-chip ▸ **adjective** (of a company or shares) considered to be a reliable investment.
– ORIGIN from the *blue chip* used in gambling games, which usually has a high value.

blue-col·lar ▸ **adjective** relating to manual work or workers.

blue crab ▸ **noun** a large edible swimming crab of the Atlantic coast of North America.

blue-eyed boy ▸ **noun** informal, chiefly derogatory a person who is held in high regard by someone else and treated with special favor.

blue·grass /ˈblo͞oˌgras/ ▸ **noun 1** (also **Kentucky bluegrass**) a meadow grass grown for fodder in North America. **2** a kind of traditional American country music played on banjos and guitars.

blue-green al·gae ▸ **plural noun** cyanobacteria.

blue·ish /ˈblo͞oisʜ/ ▸ **adjective** variant spelling of **BLUISH**.

blue jay ▸ **noun** a common North American jay with a blue crest, back, wings, and tail.

blue·print /ˈblo͞oˌprint/ ▸ **noun 1** a design plan or other technical drawing. **2** something that acts as a plan or model: *a blueprint for an integrated transport system*.

– SYNONYMS **plan,** design, diagram, drawing, sketch, layout, model, template, pattern, example, guide, prototype, pilot.

– ORIGIN from the original process in which prints were composed of white lines on a blue ground or of blue lines on a white ground.

blue rib·bon ▸ **noun** a blue silk ribbon given to the winner of a competition or as a mark of great distinction. ▸ **adjective** (**blue-ribbon**) of the highest quality; first-class.

blues /blo͞oz/ ▸ **plural noun 1** (treated as sing. or pl.) a type of mainly slow, sad music that originated among black Americans in the southern US. **2** (**the blues**) informal feelings of sadness or depression.
– DERIVATIVES **blues·y** adjective.
– ORIGIN from *blue devils* 'depression.'

blue-sky ▸ **adjective** informal creative or visionary and not yet having a practical use or application: *blue-sky research*.

blues·man /ˈblo͞ozmən/ ▸ **noun** (pl. **bluesmen**) a male performer of blues music.

blue state ▸ **noun** a US state that has or is thought to have more Democratic than Republican voters.

blue·stock·ing /ˈblo͞oˌstäkiNG/ ▸ **noun** often derogatory an intellectual or literary woman.
– ORIGIN in reference to literary parties held in 18th-century London by three society ladies, where some of the men wore blue worsted stockings (as opposed to the more formal black silk ones).

blue whale ▸ **noun** a bluish-gray whale that is the largest living animal.

blu·ey /ˈblo͞oē/ ▸ **adjective** almost or partly blue.

bluff¹ /bləf/ ▸ **noun** an attempt to deceive someone into believing that one knows or will do something.

– SYNONYMS **trick,** deception, fraud, ruse, pretense, sham, fake, hoax, charade; informal put-on.

▸ **verb** try to deceive someone about what one knows, or about what one can or is going to do: *she knew him well enough to suspect that he was bluffing*.

– SYNONYMS **pretend,** sham, fake, feign, lie, deceive, delude, mislead, trick, fool, hoodwink, dupe, hoax; informal con, kid, put on.

– DERIVATIVES **bluff·er** noun.
– PHRASES **call someone's bluff** challenge someone to do what they are threatening to do, in the belief that they will not in fact be able to.
– ORIGIN Dutch *bluffen* 'brag.'

bluff² ▸ **adjective** (of a person or their manner) frank and direct but in a good-natured way.

– SYNONYMS **plain-spoken,** straightforward, blunt, direct, no-nonsense, frank, open, candid, forthright, unequivocal; informal upfront.
– ANTONYMS guarded.

– DERIVATIVES **bluff·ness** noun.
– ORIGIN from **BLUFF³**.

CHOOSE THE RIGHT WORD

See **BRUSQUE**.

bluff³ ▸ **noun** a steep bank or slope.

– SYNONYMS **cliff,** promontory, headland, crag, bank, peak, escarpment, scarp.

– ORIGIN unknown.

blu·ish /ˈblo͞oisʜ/ (also **blueish**) ▸ **adjective** having a blue tinge.

blun·der /ˈbləndər/ ▸ **noun** a stupid or careless mistake.

– SYNONYMS **mistake,** error, gaffe, slip, oversight, faux pas; informal slip-up, boo-boo, blooper.

▸ **verb 1** make a blunder. **2** move clumsily or as if unable to see.

– SYNONYMS **1 make a mistake,** err, miscalculate, bungle, trip up; informal slip up, screw up, blow it, goof; Brit. informal boob. **2 stumble,** lurch, stagger, flounder, grope.

– ORIGIN probably Scandinavian.

CHOOSE THE RIGHT WORD

See **MISTAKE**.

blun·der·buss /ˈbləndərˌbəs/ ▸ **noun** historical a gun with a short, wide barrel, firing balls or lead bullets.
– ORIGIN Dutch *donderbus* 'thunder gun.'

blunt /blənt/ ▸ **adjective 1** lacking a sharp edge or point. **2** very frank and direct: *a blunt statement of fact*.

– SYNONYMS **1** *a blunt knife* **dull,** worn. **2** *a broad leaf with a blunt tip* **rounded,** flat, stubby. **3 straightforward,** frank, plain-spoken, candid, direct, bluff, forthright, unequivocal, brusque, abrupt, curt, bald, brutal, harsh, stark; informal upfront.
– ANTONYMS sharp, subtle.

▸ **verb 1** make or become blunt. **2** make weaker or less effective: *this coming and going between home and school blunted his alertness*.

– SYNONYMS **dull,** deaden, dampen, numb, take the edge off, weaken, allay, diminish, lessen.
– ANTONYMS intensify.

– DERIVATIVES **blunt·ly** adverb **blunt·ness** noun.
– ORIGIN perhaps Scandinavian.

CHOOSE THE RIGHT WORD

See **BRUSQUE**.

blur /blər/ ▶ **verb** (**blurs**, **blurring**, **blurred**) make or become unclear or less distinct.

– SYNONYMS **1** *tears blurred her vision* **cloud,** fog, obscure, dim, make hazy, make fuzzy, soften, dull, numb, deaden, mute. **2** (as adj. **blurred**) *a blurred photograph* **indistinct,** fuzzy, hazy, misty, foggy, clouded, cloudy, faint, unclear, vague, indefinite, unfocused.

▶ **noun** something that cannot be seen, heard, or recalled clearly.
– DERIVATIVES **blur·ry** adjective (**blurrier**, **blurriest**).
– ORIGIN perhaps from **BLEARY**.

blurb /blərb/ ▶ **noun** informal a short description written to promote a book, movie, or other product.
– ORIGIN coined by the American humorist Gelett Burgess.

blurt /blərt/ ▶ **verb** say something suddenly and without careful thought.

– SYNONYMS *he* ***blurted out*** *his story* **burst out with,** exclaim, call out, divulge, disclose, reveal, betray, let slip, give away; informal blab, spill the beans.

– ORIGIN probably imitating the sound.

blush /bləsʜ/ ▶ **verb** become red in the face through shyness or embarrassment.

– SYNONYMS **redden,** go pink, go red, flush, color, burn up.

▶ **noun 1** an instance of blushing. **2** literary a pink tinge. **3** blusher.

– SYNONYMS **flush,** rosiness, redness, pinkness, bloom, glow.

– DERIVATIVES **blush·ing** adjective.
– ORIGIN Old English.

blush·er /ˈbləsʜər/ ▶ **noun** a cosmetic used to give a warm color to the cheeks.

blus·ter /ˈbləstər/ ▶ **verb 1** talk in a loud or aggressive way with little effect. **2** (of wind or rain) blow or beat fiercely and noisily. ▶ **noun** loud and empty talk.
– DERIVATIVES **blus·ter·er** noun.
– ORIGIN imitating the sound.

blus·ter·y /ˈbləstərē/ ▶ **adjective** (of weather) characterized by strong winds.

– SYNONYMS **stormy,** gusty, blowy, windy, squally, wild.
– ANTONYMS calm.

blvd. ▶ **abbreviation** boulevard.

BMI ▶ **abbreviation** body mass index, a measure of whether someone is over- or underweight calculated by dividing their weight in kilograms by the square of their height in meters.

B-mov·ie ▶ **noun** a low-budget movie, especially one supporting the main attraction in a double feature.

BMX ▶ **abbreviation** bicycle motocross (referring to bicycles designed for cross-country racing).

bo·a /ˈbōə/ ▶ **noun 1** a large snake that winds itself around its prey and crushes it to death. **2** a long, thin stole of feathers or fur worn around a woman's neck.
– ORIGIN Latin.

boar /bôr/ ▶ **noun** (pl. same or **boars**) **1** (also **wild boar**) a wild pig with tusks. **2** an uncastrated domestic male pig.
– ORIGIN Old English.

board /bôrd/ ▶ **noun 1** a long, thin, flat piece of wood used in building. **2** a thin, flat, rectangular piece of stiff material used for various purposes. **3** a group of people who control an organization. **4** the provision of regular meals in return for payment: *room and board*.

– SYNONYMS **1 plank,** beam, panel, slat, batten, timber. **2 committee,** council, panel, directorate, commission.

▶ **verb 1** get on or into a ship, aircraft, or other vehicle. **2** receive meals and accommodations in return for payment. **3** (of a student) live at school during the semester. **4** (**board something up/over**) cover or seal something with pieces of wood.

– SYNONYMS **1 get on,** go on board, go aboard, enter, mount, ascend, embark, catch. **2 lodge,** live, reside, stay, room, be housed. **3 accommodate,** take in, put up, house, keep, billet.

– PHRASES **go by the board** (of a plan or principle) be abandoned or rejected. [from nautical use meaning 'fall overboard.'.] **on board** on or in a ship, aircraft, or other vehicle. **take something on board** informal fully consider or accept a new idea or situation. **tread the boards** informal appear on stage as an actor.
– ORIGIN Old English.

board·er /ˈbôrdər/ ▶ **noun 1** a student who lives at school during the semester. **2** a person who receives regular meals and lodging in return for payment.

board game ▶ **noun** a game that involves the movement of pieces around a board.

board·ing house ▶ **noun** a private house providing food and lodging for paying guests.

board·ing school ▶ **noun** a school at which the students live during the semester.

board·room /ˈbôrdˌro͞om/ ▶ **noun** a room in which a board of directors meets regularly.

board·sail·ing /ˈbôrdˌsālinɢ/ ▶ **noun** another term for **WINDSURFING**.
– DERIVATIVES **board·sail·or** /-ˌsālər/ noun.

board·walk /ˈbôrdˌwôk/ ▶ **noun 1** a wooden walkway across sand or marshy ground. **2** a promenade along a beach or waterfront.

boast /bōst/ ▶ **verb 1** talk about oneself with excessive pride. **2** possess an impressive or admirable feature: *the resort complex boasts ten pools*.

– SYNONYMS **1 brag,** crow, swagger, swank, show off, blow one's own horn, sing one's own praises; informal talk big, lay it on thick. **2** *the hotel boasts a fine restaurant* **have,** possess, own, enjoy, pride oneself/itself on, offer.

▶ **noun** an act of boasting.

– SYNONYMS **1 brag,** exaggeration, overstatement. **2 pride,** joy, pride and joy, apple of someone's eye, wonder, delight.

– DERIVATIVES **boast·er** noun.
– ORIGIN unknown.

boast·ful /ˈbōstfəl/ ▶ **adjective** showing excessive pride in oneself.

– SYNONYMS **bragging,** swaggering, bumptious, swell-headed, swollen-headed, puffed up, full of oneself, cocky, conceited, arrogant; informal swanky, bigheaded.
– ANTONYMS modest.

– DERIVATIVES **boast·ful·ly** adverb **boast·ful·ness** noun.

boat /bōt/ ▶ **noun** a vessel for traveling on water.

– SYNONYMS **vessel,** craft, watercraft, ship; literary keel, barque.

▶ **verb** travel in a boat for pleasure.

– SYNONYMS **sail,** yacht, cruise.

– DERIVATIVES **boat·ing** noun **boat·load** noun.
– PHRASES **be in the same boat** informal be in the same difficult situation as others. **rock the boat** informal disturb an existing situation.
– ORIGIN Old English.

boat·er /ˈbōtər/ ▶ **noun 1** a flat-topped straw hat with a brim. **2** a person who travels in a boat.

boat·house /ˈbōtˌhous/ ▶ **noun** a shed at the edge of a river or lake used for housing boats.

boat·man /ˈbōtmən/ ▶ **noun** (pl. **boatmen**) a person who provides transport by boat.

boat peo·ple ▶ **plural noun** refugees who have left a country by sea.

boat·swain /ˈbōsən/ (also **bo'sun** or **bosun** pronunc. same) ▶ **noun** a ship's officer in charge of equipment and the crew.
– ORIGIN from **BOAT** + **SWAIN**.

boat train ▶ **noun** a train scheduled to connect with the arrival or departure of a boat.

boat·yard /ˈbōtˌyärd/ ▶ **noun** a place where boats are built, maintained, or stored.

bob[1] /bäb/ ▶ **verb** (**bobs, bobbing, bobbed**) **1** make or cause to make a quick, short movement up and down. **2** curtsy briefly.

– SYNONYMS **move up and down,** bounce, toss, skip, dance, wobble, jiggle, joggle, jolt, jerk.

▶ **noun** a quick, short movement up and down.
– ORIGIN unknown.

bob[2] ▶ **noun 1** a short hairstyle hanging evenly all around. **2** a weight on a pendulum, plumb line, or kite-tail. **3** a bobsled. ▶ **verb** (**bobs, bobbing, bobbed**) cut hair in a bob.
– ORIGIN unknown.

bob[3] ▶ **noun** (pl. same) Brit. informal a shilling.
– ORIGIN unknown.

bob·bin /ˈbäbin/ ▶ **noun** a cylinder, cone, or reel holding thread.
– ORIGIN French *bobine*.

bob·ble[1] /ˈbäbəl/ ▶ **verb 1** informal move with an irregular bouncing motion. **2** mishandle (a ball).
– ORIGIN from **BOB**[1].

bob·ble[2] ▶ **noun** chiefly Brit. a small ball made of strands of wool; a pom-pom.
– DERIVATIVES **bob·bly** adjective.
– ORIGIN from **BOB**[2].

bob·by /ˈbäbē/ ▶ **noun** (pl. **bobbies**) Brit. informal a police officer.
– ORIGIN after Sir *Robert* Peel, the British Prime Minister who established the Metropolitan Police.

bob·by pin ▶ **noun** a sprung hairpin or small clip.
– ORIGIN from **BOB**[2].

bob·cat /ˈbäbˌkat/ ▶ **noun** a small North American lynx with a striped and spotted coat and a short tail.
– ORIGIN from **BOBCAT**.

bob·sled /ˈbäbˌsled/ ▶ **noun** a sled with brakes and a steering mechanism, used for racing down an ice-covered run.
– DERIVATIVES **bob·sled·ding** noun.

bob·tail /ˈbäbˌtāl/ ▶ **noun** a docked tail of a horse or dog.

bod /bäd/ ▶ **noun** informal a body.

bo·da·cious /bōˈdāsʜəs/ ▶ **adjective** informal excellent, admirable, or attractive.
– ORIGIN perhaps a blend of **BOLD** and **AUDACIOUS**.

bode /bōd/ ▶ **verb** (**bode well/ill**) be a sign of a good or bad outcome: *recent sales trends bode well for the coming year.*
– ORIGIN Old English, 'proclaim, foretell.'

bo·de·ga /bōˈdāgə/ ▶ **noun** (in Spanish-speaking countries) a grocery store.
– ORIGIN Spanish.

bo·dhi tree /ˈbōdē/ ▶ **noun** a fig tree native to India and SE Asia, regarded as sacred by Buddhists because it was under such a tree that Buddha's enlightenment took place.

bod·ice /ˈbädis/ ▶ **noun 1** the part of a woman's dress that is above the waist. **2** a woman's sleeveless undergarment, often laced at the front.
– ORIGIN formerly *bodies*, plural of **BODY**.

bod·ice-rip·per ▶ **noun** informal, humorous a sexually explicit historical novel or movie.

bod·i·ly /ˈbädl-ē/ ▶ **adjective** relating to the body.

– SYNONYMS **physical,** corporeal, corporal, mortal, material, tangible, concrete, real, actual, incarnate.
– ANTONYMS spiritual, mental.

▶ **adverb** by taking hold of a person's body with force: *the blast lifted me bodily off the floor.*

– SYNONYMS **forcefully,** forcibly, violently, completely, entirely.

bod·kin /ˈbädkin/ ▶ **noun** a thick, blunt needle with a large eye, used for drawing tape or cord through a hem.
– ORIGIN perhaps Celtic.

bod·y /ˈbädē/ ▶ **noun** (pl. **bodies**) **1** the whole physical structure of a person or an animal. **2** the trunk of the body. **3** a corpse. **4** the main or central part: *the body of the plane filled with smoke.* **5** a mass or collection. **6** an organized group of people with a common function: *a regulatory body.* **7** technical an object: *the path taken by the falling body.* **8** a full flavor in wine. **9** fullness of a person's hair.

– SYNONYMS **1 figure,** frame, form, physique, anatomy, skeleton. **2 torso,** trunk. **3 corpse,** carcass, skeleton, remains; informal stiff; Medicine cadaver. **4 main part,** core, heart, hub. **5 association,** organization, assembly, delegation, committee, executive, company, society, corporation, group.

▶ **verb** (**bodies, bodying, bodied**) (**body something forth**) formal give physical form to something abstract.
– DERIVATIVES **bod·ied** adjective.
– PHRASES **keep body and soul together** stay alive in difficult circumstances.
– ORIGIN Old English.

WORD LINKS

corporal, **corporeal** *relating to the body*

CHOOSE THE RIGHT WORD

body, cadaver, carcass, corpse, cremains, remains

The problem of what to call the human **body** after it has departed this life is a delicate one. Although a *body* can be either dead or alive, human or animal, a **corpse** is most definitely a dead human body and a **carcass** is the body of a dead animal. The issue has been confused, of course, by the figurative use of *carcass* as a term of contempt (*"Get your carcass out of bed and come down here!"*). While *carcass* is often used humorously, there's nothing funny about *corpse*, a no-nonsense term for a lifeless physical body (*the battlefield was littered with corpses*). A funeral director is likely to prefer the term **remains**, which is a euphemism for the body of the deceased (*he had his wife's remains shipped home for burial*), or **cremains**, if the body has been cremated. A medical student, on the other hand, is much more likely to use the term **cadaver**, which is a corpse that is dissected in a laboratory for scientific study.

bod·y bag ▶ **noun** a bag used for carrying a corpse from a battlefield, accident, or the scene of a crime.

bod·y blow ▶ **noun** **1** a heavy punch to the body. **2** a severe setback.

bod·y·board /ˈbädēˌbôrd/ ▶ **noun** a short, light surfboard ridden in a prone position.
– DERIVATIVES **bod·y·board·er** noun **bod·y·board·ing** noun.

bod·y·build·er /ˈbädēˌbildər/ ▶ **noun** a person who strengthens and enlarges their muscles through exercise such as weightlifting.

bod·y clock ▶ **noun** a person's biological clock.

bod·y dou·ble ▶ **noun** a stand-in for a movie actor during stunt or nude scenes.

bod·y·guard /ˈbädēˌgärd/ ▶ **noun** a person employed to protect an important or famous person.

bod·y lan·guage ▶ **noun** the communication of one's feelings by the movement or position of one's body.

bod·y pol·i·tic ▶ **noun** the people of a nation or society considered as an organized group of citizens.

bod·y shop ▶ **noun** a garage where repairs to the bodies of vehicles are carried out.

bod·y·snatch·er /ˈbädēˌsnaCHər/ ▶ **noun** historical a person who illegally dug up corpses for dissection.

bod·y stock·ing ▶ **noun** a woman's one-piece undergarment covering the torso and legs.

bod·y·suit /ˈbädēˌso͞ot/ ▶ **noun** a close-fitting one-piece stretch garment for women, typically worn for sports or exercise.

bod·y·surf /ˈbädēˌsərf/ ▶ **verb** surf without using a board.

bod·y·work /ˈbädēˌwərk/ ▶ **noun** **1** repairs done to the bodies of motor vehicles. **2** the metal outer shell of a vehicle.

Boer /bôr, bo͝or/ ▶ **noun** an early Dutch or Huguenot settler of southern Africa. ▶ **adjective** relating to the Boers.
– ORIGIN Dutch, 'farmer.'

boff /bäf/ informal ▶ **verb** have sex with someone. ▶ **noun** an act of sexual intercourse.

bog /bäg, bôg/ ▶ **noun** an area of soft, wet, muddy ground.

– SYNONYMS **marsh,** swamp, mire, quagmire, morass, slough, fen, wetland.

▶ **verb** (**be/get bogged down**) **1** be or become stuck in mud. **2** be prevented from progressing: *we are hopelessly bogged down in bureaucracy.*

– SYNONYMS **mire,** stick, entangle, ensnare, embroil, hamper, hinder, impede, obstruct, swamp, overwhelm.

– DERIVATIVES **bog·gi·ness** noun **bog·gy** adjective.
– ORIGIN Irish or Scottish Gaelic *bogach.*

bo·gey[1] /ˈbōgē/ Golf ▶ **noun** (pl. **bogeys**) a score of one stroke over par at a hole. ▶ **verb** (**bogeys, bogeying, bogeyed**) play a hole in one stroke over par.
– ORIGIN perhaps from BOGEY[2], referring to the Devil as an imaginary player.

bo·gey[2] (also **bogy**) ▶ **noun** (pl. **bogeys**) **1** an evil or mischievous spirit. **2** a cause of fear or alarm: *the bogey of recession.*
– ORIGIN a former name for the Devil.

bo·gey·man /ˈbo͝ogēˌman, ˈbō-/ (also **bogyman**) ▶ **noun** (pl. **bogeymen**) an evil spirit.

bog·gle /ˈbägəl/ ▶ **verb** informal **1** be astonished or baffled: *the mind boggles at the spectacle.* **2** (**boggle at**) hesitate to do something.
– ORIGIN probably related to BOGEY[2].

bo·gus /ˈbōgəs/ ▶ **adjective** not genuine or true: *a bogus police officer.*

– SYNONYMS **fake,** spurious, false, fraudulent, sham, counterfeit, forged, feigned; informal phony, pretend.
– ANTONYMS genuine.

– ORIGIN unknown.

bo·gy /ˈbōgē, ˈbo͝ogē/ ▶ **noun** (pl. **bogies**) variant spelling of BOGEY[2].

Bo·he·mi·an /bōˈhēmēən/ ▶ **noun** **1** (also **bohemian**) a person, especially an artist or writer, who does not follow accepted standards of behavior. **2** a person from Bohemia, a region of the Czech Republic.

– SYNONYMS **nonconformist,** avant-gardist, free spirit, dropout; hippie, beatnik.
– ANTONYMS conservative.

▶ **adjective** **1** (also **bohemian**) unconventional. **2** relating to Bohemia.

– SYNONYMS *a bohemian student life* **unconventional,** nonconformist, unorthodox, avant-garde, irregular, alternative; artistic; informal artsy-fartsy, way-out, offbeat.
– ANTONYMS conventional.

– DERIVATIVES **Bo·he·mi·an·ism** noun.
– ORIGIN sense 1 is from French *bohémien* 'Gypsy' (because Gypsies were thought to come from Bohemia).

bo·ho /ˈbōˌhō/ ▶ **noun** (pl. **bohos**) & **adjective** informal term for **BOHEMIAN** (sense 1 of the noun).

bohr·i·um /ˈbôrēəm/ ▶ **noun** a very unstable chemical element made by high-energy atomic collisions.
– ORIGIN named after the Danish physicist Niels *Bohr.*

boil[1] /boil/ ▶ **verb** **1** (with reference to a liquid) reach or cause to reach the temperature at which it bubbles and turns to vapor. **2** cook or be cooked in boiling water: *boil the potatoes for 20 minutes.* **3** seethe or bubble; be turbulent. **4** (of a person or emotion) be stirred up. **5** (**boil down to**) amount to: *everything boils down to money in the end.*

– SYNONYMS **simmer,** bubble, stew, seethe, froth, foam.

▶ **noun** **1** the action of boiling; boiling point. **2** a state of great activity or excitement: *the housing market has gone off the boil.*
– ORIGIN from Latin *bullire* 'to bubble.'

boil[2] ▶ **noun** an inflamed pus-filled swelling on the skin.

– SYNONYMS **swelling,** spot, pimple, blister, gathering, pustule, carbuncle, abscess.

– ORIGIN Old English.

boil·er /'boilər/ ▶ **noun** a fuel-burning device for heating water.

boil·er·plate /'boilər,plāt/ ▶ **noun 1** rolled steel plates for making boilers. **2** standardized pieces of writing for use as clauses in contracts. **3** stereotyped or clichéd writing.

boil·ing /'boiliNG/ ▶ **adjective 1** at or near boiling point. **2** informal extremely hot. **3** (of an emotion) intense.

boil·ing point ▶ **noun** the temperature at which a liquid boils.

bois·ter·ous /'boist(ə)rəs/ ▶ **adjective 1** noisy, lively, and high-spirited: *boisterous gangs of youths.* **2** literary (of weather or water) wild or stormy.

– SYNONYMS **lively,** animated, exuberant, spirited, noisy, loud, rowdy, unruly, wild, uproarious, unrestrained, uninhibited, uncontrolled, rough, disorderly, riotous; informal rumbustious.
– ANTONYMS restrained.

– DERIVATIVES **bois·ter·ous·ly** adverb **bois·ter·ous·ness** noun.
– ORIGIN unknown.

WORD TOOLKIT

See **ROWDY**.

bok choy /,bäk 'CHoi/ ▶ **noun** a variety of Chinese cabbage with smooth-edged tapering leaves.
– ORIGIN Chinese, 'white vegetable.'

bo·la /'bōlə/ (also **bolas**) ▶ **noun** (especially in South America) a missile consisting of a number of balls connected by cord, thrown to entangle the limbs of animals.
– ORIGIN Spanish and Portuguese, 'ball.'

bold /bōld/ ▶ **adjective 1** confident and brave: *the company's bold new approach.* **2** (of a color or design) strong or vivid. **3** dated lacking respect; impudent. **4** (of type) having thick strokes.

– SYNONYMS **1 daring,** intrepid, brave, courageous, valiant, valorous, fearless, dauntless, audacious, daredevil, adventurous, heroic, plucky; informal gutsy, spunky. **2 striking,** vivid, bright, strong, eye-catching, prominent, gaudy, lurid, garish.
– ANTONYMS timid, faint.

▶ **noun** a bold typeface.
– DERIVATIVES **bold·ly** adverb **bold·ness** noun.
– PHRASES **as bold as brass** so confident as to be disrespectful.
– ORIGIN Old English.

CHOOSE THE RIGHT WORD

bold, aggressive, audacious, bumptious, brazen, intrepid, presumptuous

Is walking up to an attractive stranger and asking him or her to have dinner with you tonight a **bold** move or merely an **aggressive** one? Both words suggest assertive, confident behavior that is a little on the shameless side, but *bold* has a wider range of application. It can suggest self-confidence that borders on impudence (*to be so bold as to call the president by his first name*), but it can also be used to describe a daring temperament that is either courageous or defiant (*a bold investigator who would not give up*). *Aggressive* behavior, on the other hand, usually falls within a narrower range, somewhere between menacing (*aggressive attacks on innocent villagers*) and just plain pushy (*an aggressive salesperson*). **Brazen** implies a defiant lack of modesty (*a brazen stare*), and **presumptuous** goes even further, suggesting over-confidence to the point of causing offense (*a presumptuous request for money*). **Bumptious** behavior can also be offensive, but it is usually associated with the kind of cockiness that can't be helped (*a bumptious young upstart*). An **audacious** individual is bold to the point of recklessness (*an audacious explorer*), which brings it very close in meaning to **intrepid**, suggesting fearlessness in the face of the unknown (*the intrepid settlers of the Great Plains*).

bole /bōl/ ▶ **noun** a tree trunk.
– ORIGIN Old Norse.

bo·le·ro /bə'le(ə)rō/ ▶ **noun** (pl. **boleros**) **1** a Spanish dance in simple triple time. **2** a woman's short open jacket.
– ORIGIN Spanish.

bo·le·tus /bō'lētəs/ (also **bolete** /bō'lēt/) ▶ **noun** (pl. **boletuses** /bō'lētəsəz/) a toadstool with pores rather than gills on the underside of the cap.
– ORIGIN Greek *bōlitēs*.

bol·i·var /bə'lē,vär, 'bälәvәr/ ▶ **noun** the basic unit of money of Venezuela.
– ORIGIN named after Simon *Bolívar*, who liberated Venezuela from the Spanish.

Bo·liv·i·an /bə'livēən/ ▶ **noun** a person from Bolivia. ▶ **adjective** relating to Bolivia.

boll /bōl/ ▶ **noun** the rounded seed capsule of plants such as cotton.
– ORIGIN Dutch *bolle* 'rounded object.'

bol·lard /'bälərd/ ▶ **noun 1** a short post on a ship or wharf for securing a rope. **2** Brit. a short post used to prevent traffic from entering an area.
– ORIGIN perhaps from Old Norse, 'bole.'

bol·locks /'bäləks/ (also **ballocks**) ▶ **plural noun** Brit. vulgar slang **1** the testicles. **2** (treated as sing.) nonsense; rubbish.
– ORIGIN related to **BALL**[1].

Bol·ly·wood /'bälē,wo͝od/ ▶ **noun** the Indian movie industry, based in Bombay (now Mumbai).
– ORIGIN blend of *Bombay* and *Hollywood*.

bo·lo·gna /bə'lōnē/ ▶ **noun** a large smoked, seasoned sausage made of various meats, especially beef and pork.

bo·lo tie /'bōlō/ ▶ **noun** a tie consisting of a cord around the neck with a large ornamental fastening at the throat.
– ORIGIN alteration of *bola tie*, from its resemblance to the **BOLA**.

Bol·she·vik /'bōlSHə,vik/ ▶ **noun** historical **1** a member of the majority group within the Russian Social Democratic Party, which seized power in the Revolution of 1917. **2** a person with revolutionary or politically radical views.
– DERIVATIVES **Bol·she·vism** /-,vizəm/ noun **Bol·she·vist** /-vist/ noun.
– ORIGIN from Russian *bol'she* 'greater.'

bol·ster /'bōlstər/ ▶ **noun 1** a long, firm pillow. **2** a part in a tool, vehicle, or structure providing support or reducing friction. ▶ **verb** support or strengthen: *the conservation zones should help to bolster tourism.*

– SYNONYMS **strengthen,** reinforce, boost, fortify, support, prop up, buoy up, shore up, buttress, maintain, help, augment, increase.

– DERIVATIVES **bol·ster·er** noun.
– ORIGIN Old English.

bolt[1] /bōlt/ ▶ **noun 1** a long metal pin with a head that screws into a nut, used to fasten things together. **2** a bar that slides into a socket to fasten a door or window. **3** a flash of lightning. **4** a short, heavy arrow shot from a crossbow. **5** the sliding piece of the breech mechanism of a rifle.

– SYNONYMS **1** *the bolt on the door* **bar,** lock, catch, latch, fastener. **2** *nuts and bolts* **pin,** rivet, peg, screw.

▶ **verb 1** fasten something with a bolt. **2** run away suddenly: *they bolted down the stairs.* **3** eat food quickly. **4** (of a plant) grow quickly upward and stop flowering as seeds develop.

– SYNONYMS **1** *he bolted the door* **lock,** bar, latch, fasten, secure. **2** *the lid was bolted down* **pin,** rivet, peg, screw, fasten, fix. **3 dash,** dart, run, sprint, hurtle, rush, fly, shoot; informal tear, scoot. **4 gobble,** gulp, wolf, guzzle, devour; informal demolish, polish off, scarf (down), shovel in.

– DERIVATIVES **bolt·er** noun.
– PHRASES **a bolt from** (or **out of**) **the blue** a sudden and unexpected event. **bolt upright** with the back very straight. **have shot one's bolt** informal have done everything possible but still not succeeded. **make a bolt for** try to escape by running suddenly toward something.
– ORIGIN Old English.

bolt[2] ▶ **noun** a roll of fabric, originally as a measure.
– ORIGIN from **BOLT**[1].

bo·lus /ˈbōləs/ ▶ **noun** (pl. **boluses**) **1** a small rounded mass of something, especially of food being swallowed. **2** a large pill used in veterinary medicine. **3** a single dose of a medicinal drug given all at once.
– ORIGIN Greek *bōlos* 'clod.'

bomb /bäm/ ▶ **noun 1** a container of material capable of exploding or causing a fire. **2** (**the bomb**) nuclear weapons as a whole. **3** (**da** (or **the**) **bomb**) informal an outstandingly good person or thing.

– SYNONYMS **explosive,** incendiary (device), missile, projectile.

▶ **verb 1** attack someone or something with a bomb or bombs. **2** informal fail badly: *the film bombed, losing ten million dollars.*

– SYNONYMS **blow up,** blast, shell, blitz, strafe, pound, bombard, attack, assault, destroy, demolish.

– PHRASES **it looks like a bomb hit it** (or **went off**) informal used to describe a place that is extremely messy or untidy in appearance.
– ORIGIN Italian *bomba.*

bom·bard ▶ **verb** /bämˈbärd/ **1** attack someone or something continuously with bombs or other missiles. **2** direct a continuous flow of questions or information at: *they were bombarded with complaints.* **3** Physics direct a stream of high-speed particles at a substance.

– SYNONYMS **1 shell,** pound, blitz, strafe, bomb, batter, blast, pelt. **2 swamp,** inundate, flood, deluge, snow under, overwhelm.

▶ **noun** /ˈbämˌbärd/ an early form of cannon, which fired a stone ball.
– DERIVATIVES **bom·bard·ment** /bämˈbärdmənt/ noun.
– ORIGIN from Old French *bombarde* 'a cannon' or French *bombarder.*

CHOOSE THE RIGHT WORD

See **ATTACK**.

bom·bar·dier /ˌbämbə(r)ˈdi(ə)r/ ▶ **noun 1** a rank of noncommissioned officer in certain Canadian and British artillery regiments, equivalent to corporal. **2** a member of a bomber crew in the US Air Force responsible for aiming and releasing bombs.
– ORIGIN French.

bom·bast /ˈbämbast/ ▶ **noun** language that sounds impressive but has little meaning.
– ORIGIN Old French *bombace* 'cotton used as padding.'

bom·bas·tic /bämˈbastik/ ▶ **adjective** using inflated language.

– SYNONYMS **pompous,** blustering, turgid, verbose, orotund, high-flown, high-sounding, overwrought, pretentious, ostentatious, grandiloquent; informal highfalutin.

– DERIVATIVES **bom·bas·ti·cal·ly** /bämˈbastik(ə)lē/ adverb.

bombe /bäm(b)/ ▶ **noun** a frozen dome-shaped dessert.
– ORIGIN French, 'bomb.'

bombed /bämd/ ▶ **adjective** informal intoxicated by drink or drugs.

bomb·er /ˈbämər/ ▶ **noun 1** an aircraft that drops bombs. **2** a person who plants bombs, especially as a terrorist.

bomb·er jack·et ▶ **noun** a short jacket, usually leather, gathered at the waist and cuffs by elasticized bands and having a zipper front.

bomb·shell /ˈbämˌsʜel/ ▶ **noun 1** something that comes as a great surprise or shock. **2** informal a very attractive woman.

bo·na fide /ˈbōnə ˌfīd, ˈbänə/ ▶ **adjective** genuine; real: *she was a bona fide expert.*

– SYNONYMS **authentic,** genuine, real, true, actual; legal, legitimate, lawful, valid, proper; informal legit, the real thing, the real McCoy, the genuine article.
– ANTONYMS bogus.

▶ **adverb** chiefly Law without intention to deceive.
– ORIGIN Latin, 'with good faith.'

bo·na fi·des /ˈbōnə ˌfīdz, ˈfīdēz, ˈbänə/ ▶ **noun** (treated as pl.) evidence proving that a person is what they claim to be; credentials.
– ORIGIN Latin, 'good faith.'

bo·nan·za /bəˈnanzə/ ▶ **noun 1** a situation creating an increase in wealth, profit, or good luck: *a natural gas bonanza.* **2** a large amount of something desirable.

– SYNONYMS **windfall,** godsend, blessing, bonus, stroke of luck; informal jackpot.

– ORIGIN Spanish, 'good weather, prosperity.'

bon ap·pé·tit /ˈbōn ˌapəˈtē/ ▶ **exclamation** used to wish someone an enjoyable meal.
– ORIGIN French, 'good appetite.'

bon·bon /ˈbänˌbän/ ▶ **noun** a piece of candy.
– ORIGIN from French *bon* 'good.'

bond /bänd/ ▶ **noun 1** a thing used to tie or fasten things together. **2** (**bonds**) ropes or chains used to hold someone prisoner. **3** a force or feeling that unites people: *the bonds between mother and daughter.* **4** an agreement with legal force. **5** a certificate issued by a government or a public company promising to repay borrowed money at a fixed rate of interest and at a specified time. **6** a sum of money paid as bail. **7** (also **chemical bond**) a strong force of attraction holding atoms together in a molecule.

– SYNONYMS **1 friendship,** relationship, fellowship, partnership, association, affiliation, alliance, attachment, tie, connection, link. **2 promise,** pledge, vow, oath, word (of honor), guarantee, assurance, agreement, contract, pact, deal.

▶ **verb 1** join or be joined securely to something else. **2** form a relationship based on shared feelings or experiences: *you naturally bond with people in that sort of situation.*

– SYNONYMS **join,** fasten, fix, affix, attach, secure, bind, stick, fuse.

– PHRASES **in bond** (of goods) stored by customs until the importer pays the duty owing.
– ORIGIN variant of **BAND**[1].

bond·age /ˈbändij/ ▶ **noun 1** the state of being a slave. **2** sexual practice that involves the tying up of one partner.
– ORIGIN from Old Norse *bóndi* 'tiller of the soil'; influenced by **BOND**.

bond·ed /ˈbändid/ ▶ **adjective 1** joined securely together. **2** bound by a legal agreement.

bond pa·per ▶ **noun** high-quality writing paper.

bonds·man /ˈbändzmən/ ▶ **noun** (pl. **bondsmen**) **1** a person who takes responsibility for the payment of a bond. **2** old use a slave.

bone /bōn/ ▶ **noun 1** any of the pieces of hard, whitish tissue making up the skeleton in vertebrates. **2** the hard material of which bones consist. **3** a thing made or formerly made of bone, such as a strip of stiffening for an undergarment. ▶ **verb 1** remove the bones from meat or fish before cooking. **2** (**bone up on**) informal study a subject intensively.
– DERIVATIVES **bone·less** adjective.
– PHRASES **bone of contention** a subject over which there is continuing disagreement. **close to the bone 1** (of a remark) accurate to the point of causing discomfort. **2** (of a joke or story) near the limit of decency. **have a bone to pick with someone** informal have reason to quarrel or be annoyed with someone. **in one's bones** felt or believed deeply or instinctively. **make no bones about** be straightforward in stating or dealing with something. **work one's fingers to the bone** work very hard.
– ORIGIN Old English.

bone chi·na ▶ **noun** white porcelain containing the mineral residue of burned bones.

bone dry ▶ **adjective** very or completely dry.

bone·head /ˈbōnˌhed/ ▶ **noun** informal a stupid person.

bone·meal /ˈbōnˌmēl/ ▶ **noun** ground bones used as a fertilizer.

bon·er /ˈbōnər/ ▶ **noun 1** informal a stupid mistake. **2** vulgar slang an erection of the penis.

bon·fire /ˈbänˌfīr/ ▶ **noun** an open-air fire lit to burn trash or as a celebration.
– ORIGIN first referring to a fire on which bones were burned.

Bon·fire Night ▶ **noun** (in the UK) November 5, on which fireworks are set off, bonfires lit, and figures representing Guy Fawkes burned, in memory of the Gunpowder Plot of 1605.

bong /bäng/ ▶ **noun** a water pipe used for smoking marijuana or other drugs.
– ORIGIN from Thai *baung*, literally 'wooden tube.'

bon·go /ˈbänggō, ˈbông-/ ▶ **noun** (pl. **bongos**) each of a pair of small drums, held between the knees and played with the fingers.
– ORIGIN Latin American Spanish *bongó*.

bon·ho·mie /ˈbänəˌmē, ˌbänəˈmē/ ▶ **noun** good-natured friendliness.
– DERIVATIVES **bon·ho·mous** adjective.
– ORIGIN French.

bo·ni·to /bəˈnētō/ ▶ **noun** (pl. **bonitos**) a small tuna with dark stripes.
– ORIGIN Spanish.

bonk /bängk/ informal ▶ **verb 1** hit someone or something. **2** have sex. ▶ **noun 1** an act or sound of hitting someone or something. **2** an act of sexual intercourse.
– ORIGIN imitating the sound of hitting.

bon·kers /ˈbängkərz/ ▶ **adjective** informal mad; crazy.
– ORIGIN unknown.

bon mot /ˈbän ˈmō, ˌbôn ˈmō/ ▶ **noun** (pl. **bons mots** pronunc. same or /ˈmōz/) a clever or witty remark.
– ORIGIN French, 'good word.'

bon·net /ˈbänit/ ▶ **noun 1** a woman's or child's hat tied under the chin and with a brim framing the face. **2** (also **war bonnet**) the ceremonial feathered headdress of an American Indian.
– DERIVATIVES **bon·net·ed** adjective.
– ORIGIN Old French *bonet*.

bon·sai /bänˈsī, ˈbänsī/ ▶ **noun** the art of growing ornamental trees or shrubs kept very small by pruning.
– ORIGIN Japanese, 'tray planting.'

bo·nus /ˈbōnəs/ ▶ **noun 1** a sum of money added to a person's wages for good performance. **2** an unexpected and extra benefit: *as an added bonus, prizewinners will have their adventures videotaped.*

– SYNONYMS **1 advantage,** plus, benefit, extra, boon, blessing, godsend, stroke of luck, attraction. **2 gratuity,** handout, gift, present, reward, prize, incentive; informal perk, sweetener.
– ANTONYMS disadvantage.

– ORIGIN Latin, 'good.'

CHOOSE THE RIGHT WORD

See **PRESENT**[3].

bon vi·vant /ˈbän vēˈvänt, ˌbôn vēˈvän/ ▶ **noun** (pl. **bon vivants** or **bons vivants** pronunc. same) a person who enjoys a sociable and luxurious lifestyle.
– ORIGIN French, 'person living well.'

bon vi·veur /ˈbän vēˈvər, ˌbôn vēˈvœr/ ▶ **noun** (pl. **bon viveurs** or **bons viveurs** pronunc. same) another term for **BON VIVANT**.
– ORIGIN from French *bon* 'good' and *viveur* 'a living person.'

bon vo·yage /ˈbän voiˈäzh, ˈbōn, bôn/ ▶ **exclamation** have a good journey.
– ORIGIN French, 'good journey.'

bon·y /ˈbōnē/ ▶ **adjective** (**bonier**, **boniest**) **1** relating to or containing bones. **2** so thin that the bones can be seen.

– SYNONYMS **skinny,** thin, lean, gaunt, scrawny, spare, skin and bones, skeletal, emaciated, underweight.
– ANTONYMS plump.

– DERIVATIVES **bon·i·ness** noun.

bon·y fish ▶ **noun** a fish with a skeleton of bone rather than cartilage.

boo /bo͞o/ ▶ **exclamation 1** said suddenly to surprise someone. **2** said to show disapproval or contempt. ▶ **verb** (**boos, booing, booed**) say 'boo' to show disapproval.
– ORIGIN imitating the lowing of oxen.

boob[1] /bo͞ob/ informal ▸ **noun** a foolish or stupid person. ▸ **verb** make an embarrassing mistake.
– ORIGIN from **BOOBY**[1].

boob[2] ▸ **noun** informal a woman's breast.
– ORIGIN from **BOOBY**[2].

boo-boo ▸ **noun 1** informal a mistake. **2** informal a minor injury.
– ORIGIN from **BOOB**[1].

boob tube ▸ **noun** informal television; a television set.

boo·by[1] /ˈbo͞obē/ ▸ **noun** (pl. **boobies**) **1** informal a stupid person. **2** a large tropical seabird of the gannet family.
– ORIGIN probably from Spanish *bobo*.

booby[2] ▸ **noun** (pl. **boobies**) informal a woman's breast.
– ORIGIN from dialect *bubby*.

boo·by prize ▸ **noun** a prize given to the person who comes last in a contest.

boo·by trap ▸ **noun** an object containing a hidden device that is designed to explode when someone touches it. ▸ **verb** (**booby-trap**) place a booby trap in or on an object or area.

boog·ie /ˈbo͝ogē/ ▸ **noun** (also **boogie-woogie** /-ˈwo͝ogē/) (pl. **boogies**) **1** a style of blues played on the piano with a strong, fast beat. **2** informal a dance to pop or rock music. ▸ **verb** (**boogies, boogieing, boogied**) informal dance to pop or rock music.
– ORIGIN unknown.

boog·ie board ▸ **noun** a short, light surfboard ridden in a prone position.

book /bo͝ok/ ▸ **noun 1** a written or printed work consisting of pages fastened together along one side and bound in covers. **2** a main division of a literary work or of the Bible. **3** a bound set of blank pages for writing in: *an exercise book*. **4** (**books**) a set of records or accounts. **5** a set of tickets, stamps, matches, etc., bound together. **6** a bookmaker's record of bets accepted and money paid out.

> – SYNONYMS **1 volume,** tome, publication, title, novel, treatise, manual. **2 notepad,** notebook, pad, scratch pad, exercise book, logbook, ledger, journal, diary.

▸ **verb 1** reserve accommodations, a ticket, etc. **2** engage a performer or guest for an event. **3** (**be booked up**) have all places or dates reserved. **4** make an official note of the details of someone who has broken a law or rule.

> – SYNONYMS **reserve,** prearrange, order.

– DERIVATIVES **book·a·ble** adjective **book·er** noun **book·ing** noun.
– PHRASES **bring someone to book** officially ask someone to explain their behavior. **by the book** strictly according to the rules. **on the books** contained in a book of laws or records. **take a leaf out of someone's book** imitate someone in a particular way. **throw the book at someone** informal charge or punish someone as severely as possible.
– ORIGIN Old English, 'to grant by charter.'

> **WORD LINKS**
>
> **bibliography** *list of books*
> **bibliophile** *a person who collects or loves books*

book·bind·er /ˈbo͝ok,bīndər/ ▸ **noun** a person skilled in the craft of binding books.
– DERIVATIVES **book·bind·ing** noun.

book·case /ˈbo͝ok,kās/ ▸ **noun** an open cabinet containing shelves on which to keep books.

book club ▸ **noun** an organization that sells its members selected books at reduced prices.

book·end /ˈbo͝ok,end/ ▸ **noun** a support placed at the end of a row of books to keep them upright.

book·ie /ˈbo͝okē/ ▸ **noun** (pl. **bookies**) informal a bookmaker.

book·ish /ˈbo͝okisн/ ▸ **adjective 1** devoted to reading and studying: *a bookish, intellectual young man*. **2** (of language) literary in style.

book·keep·ing /ˈbo͝ok,kēpiɴɢ/ ▸ **noun** the activity of keeping records of financial dealings.
– DERIVATIVES **book·keep·er** /-,kēpər/ noun.

book learn·ing ▸ **noun** knowledge gained from books or study; mere theory.

book·let /ˈbo͝oklit/ ▸ **noun** a small, thin book with paper covers.

> – SYNONYMS **pamphlet,** brochure, folder, mailer, leaflet, tract.

book·mak·er /ˈbo͝ok,mākər/ ▸ **noun** a person whose job is to take bets, calculate odds, and pay out winnings.

book·mark /ˈbo͝ok,märk/ ▸ **noun 1** a strip of leather or cardboard used to mark a place in a book. **2** a record of the address of a computer file, Internet page, etc., enabling quick access by a user. ▸ **verb** record the address of a computer file, Internet page, etc., for quick access.

book·sell·er /ˈbo͝ok,selər/ ▸ **noun** a person who sells books, especially as the owner or manager of a bookstore.

book·shelf /ˈbo͝ok,sнelf/ ▸ **noun** (pl. **bookshelves** /-sнelvz/) a shelf on which books can be stored.

book·store /ˈbo͝ok,stôr/ ▸ **noun** a store that sells new or used books.

book val·ue ▸ **noun** the value of a security or asset as entered in a company's books. Often contrasted with **MARKET VALUE**.

book·worm /ˈbo͝ok,wərm/ ▸ **noun** informal a person who greatly enjoys reading.

Bool·e·an /ˈbo͞olēən/ ▸ **adjective** (of a system of notation) used to represent logical operations by means of the binary digits 0 (false) and 1 (true), especially in computing and electronics.
– ORIGIN named after the English mathematician George *Boole*.

boom[1] /bo͞om/ ▸ **noun 1** a loud, deep, resonant sound. **2** a period of great prosperity or rapid economic growth.

> – SYNONYMS **1 roar,** rumble, thunder, crashing, drumming, pounding, echoing, resonance, reverberation. **2 increase,** growth, advance, boost, escalation, improvement, upsurge, upturn.
> – ANTONYMS slump.

▸ **verb 1** make a loud, deep, resonant sound. **2** experience a period of rapid economic growth: *business is booming*.

> – SYNONYMS **1 roar,** rumble, thunder, crash, roll, clap, explode, bang, resound, blare, echo, resonate, reverberate. **2 shout,** yell, bellow, roar, thunder, bawl; informal holler. **3 flourish,** thrive, prosper, burgeon, progress, improve, pick up, expand.

– DERIVATIVES **boom·y** adjective.
– ORIGIN imitating the sound.

boom[2] ▸ **noun 1** a pivoted spar to which the foot of a vessel's sail is attached. **2** a movable arm carrying a microphone or movie camera. **3** a floating beam used to

contain oil spills or to form a barrier across the mouth of a harbor.
– ORIGIN Dutch, 'beam, tree, pole.'

boo·mer·ang /ˈbo͞omə,raNG/ ▶ **noun** a curved flat piece of wood that can be thrown so as to return to the thrower, used by Australian Aboriginals as a hunting weapon.
– ORIGIN from an Aboriginal language.

boom·town /ˈbo͞om,toun/ ▶ **noun** a town undergoing rapid growth due to sudden prosperity: *a former mining boomtown.*

boon /bo͞on/ ▶ **noun 1** something that is helpful or beneficial: *the detailed information is a boon to researchers.* **2** old use a favor or request.

> – SYNONYMS **blessing,** godsend, bonus, plus, benefit, advantage, help, aid, asset; stroke of luck; informal perk; formal perquisite.
> – ANTONYMS curse.

– ORIGIN Old Norse.

boon·docks /ˈbo͞on,däks/ ▶ **plural noun** (**the boondocks**) informal rough or isolated country.
– ORIGIN Tagalog, 'mountain.'

boon·dog·gle /ˈbo͞on,dägəl, -,dôgəl/ ▶ **noun** informal an unnecessary, wasteful, or fraudulent project.
– ORIGIN unknown.

boon·ies /ˈbo͞onēz/ ▶ **plural noun** short for BOONDOCKS.

boor /bo͝or/ ▶ **noun** a rude, ill-mannered person.

> – SYNONYMS **lout,** oaf, ruffian, thug, barbarian, Neanderthal, brute, beast; informal yahoo, clod, roughneck, pig.

– ORIGIN German *būr* or Dutch *boer* 'farmer.'

boor·ish /ˈbo͝orisH/ ▶ **adjective** rude and ill-mannered.

> – SYNONYMS **coarse,** uncouth, rude, vulgar, uncivilized, unrefined, oafish, ignorant, uncultured, philistine, rough, thuggish, loutish, Neanderthal.
> – ANTONYMS refined.

– DERIVATIVES **boor·ish·ly** adverb **boor·ish·ness** noun.

boost /bo͞ost/ ▶ **verb 1** help or encourage to increase or improve: *praise certainly boosts confidence.* **2** push someone from below.

> – SYNONYMS **increase,** raise, escalate, improve, strengthen, inflate, push up, promote, advance, foster, stimulate, encourage, facilitate, help, assist, aid; informal hike, bump up.
> – ANTONYMS decrease.

▶ **noun 1** a source of help or encouragement. **2** an increase. **3** a push from below.

> – SYNONYMS **1** *a boost to your morale* **uplift,** lift, spur, encouragement, help, inspiration, stimulus, fillip; informal shot in the arm. **2** *a boost in sales* **increase,** expansion, upturn, upsurge, rise, escalation, improvement, advance, growth, boom; informal hike.
> – ANTONYMS decrease.

– ORIGIN unknown.

boost·er /ˈbo͞ostər/ ▶ **noun 1** a source of help or encouragement: *the rodeo is a morale booster for employees.* **2** a dose of a vaccine that increases or renews the effect of an earlier one. **3** the part of a rocket or spacecraft used to give acceleration after liftoff. **4** a device for increasing electrical voltage or signal strength.

boot[1] /bo͞ot/ ▶ **noun 1** an item of footwear covering the foot and ankle, and sometimes the lower leg. **2** short for DENVER BOOT. **3** informal a hard kick. **4** Brit. an automobile's trunk. ▶ **verb 1** kick something hard. **2** (**boot someone out**) informal force someone to leave. **3** start a computer and put it into a state of readiness for operation.

> – SYNONYMS **kick,** punt, tap, propel, drive, knock.

– DERIVATIVES **boot·a·ble** adjective **boot·ed** adjective.
– PHRASES **give someone** (or **get**) **the boot** informal dismiss someone (or be dismissed) from a job.
– ORIGIN Old Norse, or Old French *bote.*

boot[2] ▶ **noun** (in phrase **to boot**) as well.
– ORIGIN Old English, 'advantage, remedy.'

boot·black /ˈbo͞ot,blak/ ▶ **noun** a person who makes a living by polishing boots and shoes.

boot camp ▶ **noun 1** a military training camp with very harsh discipline. **2** a military-style prison for young offenders.

boot-cut ▶ **adjective** (of jeans or other pants) flared very slightly below the knee, so as to be worn over boots.

booth /bo͞oTH/ ▶ **noun 1** an enclosed compartment allowing privacy when telephoning, voting, etc. **2** a small temporary structure used for selling goods or staging shows at a market or fair.

> – SYNONYMS **1 stall,** stand, kiosk. **2** *a phone booth* **cubicle,** kiosk, box, compartment, enclosure, cabin.

– ORIGIN from Old Norse, 'dwell.'

boot·ie /ˈbo͞otē, bo͞oˈtē/ (also **bootee**) ▶ **noun 1** a baby's soft shoe. **2** a woman's short boot.

boot·lace /ˈbo͞ot,lās/ ▶ **noun** a cord or leather strip for lacing boots.

boot·leg /ˈbo͞ot,leg/ ▶ **adjective** (of liquor, computer software, or a recording) made or distributed illegally. ▶ **verb** (**bootlegs, bootlegging, bootlegged**) make or distribute illicit goods. ▶ **noun** an illegal musical recording.
– DERIVATIVES **boot·leg·ger** noun.
– ORIGIN from the smugglers' practice of hiding bottles in their boots.

boot·less /ˈbo͞otlis/ ▶ **adjective** old use (of an action) not successful or useful.
– ORIGIN Old English, 'not able to be compensated for by payment.'

boot·lick·er /ˈbo͞ot,likər/ ▶ **noun** informal a person who tries to gain favor by servile behavior.

boot·strap /ˈbo͞ot,strap/ ▶ **noun** a loop at the back of a boot, used to pull it on.
– PHRASES **pull oneself up by one's bootstraps** improve one's position by one's own efforts.

boo·ty[1] /ˈbo͞otē/ ▶ **noun** valuable stolen goods.

> – SYNONYMS **loot,** plunder, haul, spoils, ill-gotten gains, pickings; informal swag.

– ORIGIN German *būte, buite* 'exchange, distribution.'

boo·ty[2] ▶ **noun** informal a person's buttocks.

boo·ty·li·cious /,bo͞otlˈisHəs/ ▶ **adjective** informal sexually attractive.

booze /bo͞oz/ informal ▶ **noun** alcohol, especially hard liquor. ▶ **verb** drink large quantities of alcohol.
– DERIVATIVES **booz·y** (**boozier, booziest**) adjective.
– ORIGIN from Dutch *būsen* 'drink to excess.'

booz·er /ˈbo͞ozər/ ▶ **noun** informal a person who drinks large quantities of alcohol.

bop[1] /bäp/ informal ▶ **noun 1** a dance to pop music. **2** a social occasion with dancing. ▶ **verb** (**bops, bopping, bopped**) dance to pop music.
– DERIVATIVES **bop·per** noun.
– ORIGIN shortening of **BEBOP**.

bop[2] informal ▶ **verb** (**bops, bopping, bopped**) hit or punch someone quickly. ▶ **noun** a quick blow or punch.
– ORIGIN imitating the sound.

bo·rac·ic /bəˈrasik/ ▶ **adjective** consisting of or containing boric acid.

bor·age /ˈbôrij, ˈbär-/ ▶ **noun** a plant with bright blue flowers and hairy leaves.
– ORIGIN Latin *borrago.*

bo·rax /ˈbôraks/ ▶ **noun** a white mineral that is a compound of boron, used in making glass and as a flux in soldering or smelting.
– ORIGIN Latin.

Bor·deaux /bôrˈdō/ ▶ **noun** (pl. same /bôrˈdōz/) a wine from the Bordeaux region of SW France.

bor·del·lo /bôrˈdelō/ ▶ **noun** (pl. **bordellos**) literary a brothel.

– SYNONYMS **brothel,** whorehouse. informal cathouse; euphemistic massage parlor; old use bawdy house, house of ill repute.

– ORIGIN Italian.

bor·der /ˈbôrdər/ ▶ **noun 1** a boundary between two countries or other areas. **2** a decorative band around the edge of something. **3** a strip of ground along the edge of a lawn for planting flowers or shrubs.

– SYNONYMS **1 edge,** margin, perimeter, circumference, periphery, rim, fringe, verge, sides. **2 frontier,** boundary, borderline, perimeter.

▶ **verb 1** form a border around or along. **2** (of a country or area) be next to another. **3** (**border on**) come close to being.

– SYNONYMS **1** *a pool bordered by palm trees* **surround,** enclose, encircle, edge, fringe, bound, flank. **2** *the straps are bordered with gold braid* **edge,** fringe, hem, trim, pipe, finish. **3 adjoin,** abut, be next to, be adjacent to, touch. **4** (**border on**) *his tone bordered on contempt* **verge on,** approach, come close to, be comparable to, approximate to, be tantamount to.

– ORIGIN Old French *bordeure.*

CHOOSE THE RIGHT WORD

border, brim, brink, edge, margin, rim, verge

A **border** is the part of a surface that is nearest to its boundary (*a rug with a flowered border*)—although it may also refer to the boundary line itself (*the border between Vermont and New Hampshire*). A **margin** is a *border* of a definite width that is usually distinct in appearance from what it encloses; but unlike *border*, it usually refers to the blankness or emptiness that surrounds something (*the margin on a printed page*). While *border* and *margin* usually refer to something that is circumscribed, **edge** may refer to only a part of the perimeter (*the edge of the lawn*) or the line where two planes or surfaces converge (*the edge of the table*). *Edge* can also connote sharpness (*the edge of a knife*) and can be used metaphorically to suggest tension, harshness, or keenness (*there was an edge in her voice; take the edge off their nervousness*). **Verge** may also be used metaphorically to describe the extreme limit of something (*on the verge of a nervous breakdown*), but in a more literal sense, it sometimes is used of the line or narrow space that marks the limit or termination of something (*the verge of a desert or forest*). **Brink** denotes the edge of something very steep or an abrupt division between land and water (*the brink of the river*), or metaphorically the very final limit before an abrupt change (*on the brink of disaster*). **Rim** and **brim** apply only to things that are circular or curving. But while *rim* describes the edge or lip of a rounded or cylindrical shape (*the rim of a glass*), *brim* refers to the inner side of the rim when the container is completely full (*a cup filled to the brim with steaming coffee*). However, when one speaks of the *brim* of a hat, it comes closer to the meaning of *margin* or *border*.

bord·er·line /ˈbôrdərˌlīn/ ▶ **noun** a boundary.

– SYNONYMS **dividing line,** division, line, cutoff point; threshold, margin, border, boundary.

▶ **adjective** on the boundary between two states or categories: *references may be requested in borderline cases.*

– SYNONYMS *borderline cases* **marginal,** uncertain, indefinite, unsettled, undecided, doubtful, indeterminate, unclassifiable, equivocal; questionable, debatable, controversial, contentious, problematic; informal iffy.

bore[1] /bôr/ ▶ **verb 1** make a hole in something with a drill or other tool. **2** hollow out a gun barrel or other tube.

– SYNONYMS **drill,** pierce, perforate, puncture, punch, tunnel, burrow, mine, dig, gouge, sink.

▶ **noun 1** the hollow part inside a gun barrel or other tube. **2** the diameter of a bore: *a small-bore rifle.*
– ORIGIN Old English.

bore[2] ▶ **noun** a dull and uninteresting person or activity.

– SYNONYMS **tedious person/thing,** tiresome person/thing, bother, nuisance, pest, annoyance, trial, thorn in one's flesh/side; informal drag, pain (in the neck), headache, hassle.

▶ **verb** make someone feel tired and uninterested by dull talk or behavior.

– SYNONYMS **weary,** pall on, tire, fatigue, send to sleep, leave cold; informal turn off.
– ANTONYMS interest.

– ORIGIN unknown.

bore[3] (also **tidal bore**) ▶ **noun** a steep-fronted wave caused by the meeting of two tides or by a tide rushing up a narrow estuary.
– ORIGIN perhaps from Old Norse.

bore[4] past of **BEAR**[1].

bo·re·al /ˈbôrēəl/ ▶ **adjective** chiefly technical of the North or northern regions.
– ORIGIN from Latin *Boreas*, the god of the north wind.

bored /bôrd/ ▶ **adjective** feeling tired and impatient because one is doing something dull or one has nothing to do.

USAGE

You should use **bored by** or **bored with** rather than **bored of**. Although **bored of** is often used informally, it is not acceptable in standard written English.

bore·dom /ˈbôrdəm/ ▶ **noun** the state of being bored.

– SYNONYMS **tedium,** ennui, apathy, weariness, dullness, monotony, repetitiveness, flatness, dreariness.
– ANTONYMS interest, excitement.

bore·hole /ˈbôrˌhōl/ ▶ **noun** a deep, narrow hole in the ground made to find water or oil.

bor·er /ˈbôrər/ ▶ **noun 1** a worm, mollusk, insect, or insect larva that bores into wood, other plant material, or rock: *a squash vine borer*. **2** a tool for boring.

bo·ric /ˈbôrik/ ▶ **adjective** Chemistry of boron.

bo·ric ac·id ▶ **noun** a compound derived from borax, used as a mild antiseptic.

Bo·ri·cua /bôˈrēkwə/ ▶ **noun** informal a Puerto Rican, especially one living in the US.

bor·ing /ˈbôriNG/ ▶ **adjective** dull and uninteresting.

– SYNONYMS **tedious,** dull, dreary, monotonous, repetitive, uneventful, unimaginative, characterless, featureless, colorless, lifeless, uninteresting, unexciting, lackluster, humdrum, mind-numbing, soul-destroying, wearisome, tiresome; informal deadly, dullsville.
– ANTONYMS interesting, exciting.

born /bôrn/ ▶ **adjective 1** existing as a result of birth. **2** (**-born**) having a particular nationality: *a German-born philosopher*. **3** having a natural ability to do a particular job: *a born engineer*. **4** (**born of**) existing as a result of: *a confidence born of success*.
– PHRASES **born and bred** by birth and upbringing. **in all one's born days** throughout one's life (used for emphasis). **I** (or **she**, etc.) **wasn't born yesterday** I am (or she, etc., is) not foolish or easily deceived.
– ORIGIN Old English, past participle of **BEAR**[1].

USAGE

Do not confuse **born**, which means *existing as a result of birth* (*she was born in New Jersey*) with **borne**, which is the past participle of **bear** and means *carried* (*the coffin was borne by eight soldiers*; *soil-borne bacteria*).

born-a·gain ▶ **adjective 1** (of a person) newly converted to a personal faith in Jesus. **2** newly converted to and very enthusiastic about a cause: *born-again environmentalists*.

borne /bôrn/ past participle of **BEAR**[1] ▶ **adjective** (**-borne**) carried by the thing specified: *soil-borne bacteria*.

Bor·ne·an /ˈbôrnēən/ ▶ **noun** a person from Borneo. ▶ **adjective** relating to Borneo.

bo·ron /ˈbôrän/ ▶ **noun** a crystalline chemical element used in making alloy steel and in nuclear reactors.
– ORIGIN from **BORAX**.

bor·ough /ˈbərō/ ▶ **noun 1** an administrative division of London or of New York City. **2** a municipal corporation in certain US states.
– ORIGIN Old English, 'fortress, citadel.'

bor·row /ˈbärō, ˈbôrō/ ▶ **verb 1** take and use something belonging to someone else with the intention of returning it. **2** have money on loan from a person or bank. **3** take and use a word or idea from another language or person.

– SYNONYMS **1 loan,** lease, hire; informal mooch, cadge, scrounge, bum, hit someone up for. **2 adopt,** take on, acquire, embrace, copy, imitate.
– ANTONYMS lend.

– DERIVATIVES **bor·row·er** noun.
– PHRASES **be** (**living**) **on borrowed time** be surviving beyond the time that one was expected to do so.
– ORIGIN Old English.

USAGE

On the confusion of **borrow** and **lend**, see the note at **LEND**.

borscht /bôrsHt/ (also **borsch** /bôrsH/) ▶ **noun** a Russian or Polish soup made with beets and served with sour cream.
– ORIGIN Russian *borshch*.

bor·zoi /ˈbôrzoi/ ▶ **noun** (pl. **borzois**) a breed of large Russian wolfhound with a narrow head and silky coat.
– ORIGIN from Russian *borzyĭ* 'swift.'

Bos·ni·an /ˈbäznēən/ ▶ **noun** a person from Bosnia. ▶ **adjective** relating to Bosnia.

bos·om /ˈbo͝ozəm/ ▶ **noun 1** a woman's breasts or chest. **2** loving care or protection: *he went home to the bosom of his family*.

– SYNONYMS **1 bust,** chest; breasts; informal boobs, knockers, bazooms. **2 heart,** breast, soul, core, spirit.

▶ **adjective** (of a friend) very close.

– SYNONYMS *bosom friends* **close,** boon, intimate, inseparable, faithful, constant, devoted; good, best, firm, favorite.

– DERIVATIVES **bos·om·y** adjective.
– ORIGIN Old English.

boss[1] /bôs, bäs/ informal ▶ **noun** a person who is in charge of a worker or organization.

– SYNONYMS **head,** chief, principal, director, president, chief executive, chair, manager, supervisor, foreman, overseer, controller, employer, owner, proprietor. informal head honcho.

▶ **verb** give orders in a domineering way: *now you're an adult I can't boss you around*.

– SYNONYMS **order around,** dictate to, bully, push around/about, call the shots, lay down the law; informal bulldoze, walk all over, railroad.

▶ **adjective** excellent.
– ORIGIN Dutch *baas* 'master.'

boss[2] ▶ **noun 1** a projecting knob or stud, especially on the center of a shield. **2** an ornamental carving at the point where the ribs in a ceiling cross.
– ORIGIN Old French *boce*.

bos·sa no·va /ˈbäsə ˈnōvə, ˈbô-/ ▶ **noun 1** a Brazilian dance like the samba. **2** music composed for this dance.
– ORIGIN Portuguese, 'new tendency.'

boss·y /ˈbôsē, ˈbäs-/ ▶ **adjective** (**bossier, bossiest**) informal fond of giving orders; domineering.

– SYNONYMS **domineering,** pushy, overbearing, imperious, officious, high-handed, authoritarian, dictatorial, autocratic; informal high and mighty.
– ANTONYMS submissive.

– DERIVATIVES **boss·i·ly** adverb **boss·i·ness** noun.

Bos·ton baked beans /ˈbôstən/ ▶ **plural noun** a dish of baked beans with salt pork and molasses.

bo·sun (also **bo'sun**) ▶ **noun** variant spelling of **BOATSWAIN**.

bot /bät/ ▶ **noun** an autonomous program on a computer network that can interact with systems or users.
– ORIGIN from **ROBOT**.

bo·tan·i·cal /bəˈtanikəl/ ▶ **adjective** relating to botany. ▶ **noun** a substance obtained from a plant and used in cosmetic and medicinal products.
– DERIVATIVES **bo·tan·i·cal·ly** adverb.

bo·tan·i·cal gar·den (also **botanic garden**) ▶ **noun** a place where plants are grown for scientific study and display to the public.

bot·a·ny /ˈbätn-ē/ ▶ **noun** the scientific study of plants.

– DERIVATIVES **bo·tan·ic** /bəˈtanik/ adjective **bot·a·nist** noun.
– ORIGIN from Greek *botanē* 'plant.'

botch /bäcH/ informal ▶ **verb** perform an action or task badly or carelessly. ▶ **noun** (also **botch-up**) a badly performed action or task.
– DERIVATIVES **botch·er** noun.
– ORIGIN unknown.

both /bōTH/ ▶ **predeterminer, determiner, & pronoun** two people or things, regarded together. ▶ **adverb** applying equally to each of two alternatives.
– PHRASES **have it both ways** benefit from two conflicting ways of thinking or behaving.
– ORIGIN Old Norse.

USAGE

When **both** is used with **and**, the structures following the two words should be symmetrical: *both at home and at work* is better than *both at home and work*.

both·er /ˈbäT͟Hər/ ▶ **verb 1** take the trouble to do something. **2** worry, disturb, or upset someone. **3** (**bother with/about**) feel concern about or interest in: *she has never bothered about boys before*.

– SYNONYMS **1** *no one bothered her* **disturb,** trouble, inconvenience, pester, badger, harass, molest, plague; informal hassle, bug, ride. **2** *don't bother about me* **concern oneself,** worry, trouble oneself, care. **3** *something was bothering him* **worry,** trouble, concern, perturb, disturb, disquiet; informal rattle.

▶ **noun 1** trouble or effort. **2** (**a bother**) a cause of trouble or annoyance.

– SYNONYMS **1 trouble,** effort, exertion, inconvenience, fuss, pains; informal hassle. **2 nuisance,** pest, palaver, rigmarole, trial, bore, drag, inconvenience, trouble; informal hassle, headache, pain (in the neck). **3** *a spot of bother in the public bar* **disorder,** fighting, trouble, disturbance, commotion, uproar; informal hoo-ha, aggro, argy-bargy, kerfuffle.

▶ **exclamation** Brit. used to express mild irritation.
– ORIGIN Anglo-Irish.

both·er·some /ˈbäT͟Hərsəm/ ▶ **adjective** troublesome; annoying.

Bo·tox /ˈbōˌtäks/ ▶ **noun** trademark a drug prepared from botulin (the toxin involved in botulism), used cosmetically to remove wrinkles by temporarily paralyzing the muscles of the face.
– DERIVATIVES **Bo·toxed** adjective.
– ORIGIN from *bo(tulinum) tox(in)*.

Bot·swa·nan /bätˈswänən/ ▶ **noun** a person from Botswana, a country of southern Africa. ▶ **adjective** relating to Botswana.

bot·tle /ˈbätl/ ▶ **noun 1** a container with a narrow neck, used for storing liquids. **2** the contents of such a container: *he managed to put away a bottle of wine*.

– SYNONYMS **flask,** carafe, decanter, pitcher, flagon, magnum, demijohn, vial.

▶ **verb 1** put liquid in bottles. **2** (**bottle something up**) repress or hide one's feelings.

– SYNONYMS (**bottle something up**) *don't bottle up your emotions* **suppress,** repress, restrain, hold in, smother, contain, conceal, hide; informal keep a lid on.

– PHRASES **hit the bottle** informal start to drink alcohol heavily.
– ORIGIN from Latin *butticula* 'small cask.'

bot·tle-feed ▶ **verb** (**bottle-feeds, bottle-feeding, bottle-fed**) feed a baby with milk from a bottle.

bot·tle green ▶ **adjective** dark green.

bot·tle·neck /ˈbätlˌnek/ ▶ **noun 1** a narrow section of road where traffic flow is restricted. **2** a cause of delay in a process or system.

– SYNONYMS **1 traffic jam,** congestion, holdup, gridlock, bumper-to-bumper traffic; informal snarl-up. **2** constriction, narrowing, restriction, obstruction, blockage.

bot·tom /ˈbätəm/ ▶ **noun 1** the lowest point or part. **2** the farthest point or part. **3** the lowest position in a competition or ranking: *life at the bottom of society*. **4** a person's buttocks. **5** (also **bottoms**) the lower half of a two-piece garment.

– SYNONYMS **1 foot,** lowest part, base, foundation. **2 underside,** underneath, undersurface, underbelly. **3 floor,** bed, depths. **4 farthest point,** extremity, far end. **5 buttocks,** rear (end), rump, seat, derrière; informal behind, backside, butt, fanny. humorous posterior.
– ANTONYMS top, surface.

▶ **adjective** in the lowest or farthest position.

– SYNONYMS **lowest,** last, bottommost.
– ANTONYMS top.

▶ **verb 1** (**bottom out**) reach the lowest point before stabilizing or improving: *the real estate market has probably bottomed out*. **2** (of a ship) touch the bottom of the sea.
– DERIVATIVES **bot·tom·less** adjective **bot·tom·most** /-ˌmōst/ adjective.
– PHRASES **at bottom** basically. **be at the bottom of** be the basic cause of something. **the bottom falls** (or **drops**) **out** something suddenly fails or collapses. **bottoms up!** informal said as a toast before drinking. **get to the bottom of** find an explanation for a mystery.
– ORIGIN Old English.

bot·tom feed·er ▶ **noun 1** any marine creature that lives on the seabed and feeds by scavenging. **2** informal a member of a group of very low social status who survives by any means possible.

bot·tom line ▶ **noun** informal **1** the final total of an account or balance sheet. **2** the basic and most important factor: *the bottom line is that the economy is recovering*.

bot·u·lism /ˈbäcHəˌlizəm/ ▶ **noun** food poisoning caused by a bacterium growing on preserved foods that have not been properly sterilized.
– ORIGIN German *Botulismus*, originally 'sausage poisoning.'

bou·clé /ˌbo͞oˈklā/ ▶ **noun** yarn with a looped or curled strand.
– ORIGIN French, 'buckled, curled.'

bou·doir /ˈbo͞oˌdwär/ ▶ **noun** a woman's bedroom or small private room.
– ORIGIN French, 'sulking place.'

bouf·fant /bo͞oˈfänt/ ▶ **adjective** (of hair) styled so as to stand out from the head in a rounded shape. ▶ **noun** a bouffant hairstyle.
– ORIGIN French, 'swelling.'

bou·gain·vil·le·a /ˌbo͞ogənˈvilyə, -ˈvēə, ˌbō-/ (also **bougainvillaea**) ▶ **noun** a tropical climbing plant with brightly colored modified leaves (bracts) surrounding the flowers.
– ORIGIN named after the French explorer L. A. de *Bougainville*.

bough /bou/ ▶ **noun** a main branch of a tree.
– ORIGIN Old English.

bought /bôt/ past and past participle of **BUY**.

> **USAGE**
>
> On the confusion of **bought** and **brought**, see the note at **BROUGHT**.

bouil·la·baisse /ˌbo͞o(l)yəˈbās, ˈbo͞o(l)yəˌbās/ ▶ **noun** a rich fish stew or soup, as made originally in Provence.
– ORIGIN French.

bouil·lon /ˈbo͝olyən, -yän/ ▶ **noun** thin soup or stock made by stewing meat, fish, or vegetables.
– ORIGIN from French *bouillir* 'to boil.'

boul·der /ˈbōldər/ ▶ **noun** a large rock.
– DERIVATIVES **boul·der·y** adjective.
– ORIGIN Scandinavian.

bou·le /bo͞ol/ (also **boules** pronunc. same) ▶ **noun** a French game similar to lawn bowling, played with metal balls.
– ORIGIN French, 'bowl.'

boul·e·vard /ˈbo͝oləˌvärd/ ▶ **noun** a wide street, typically one lined with trees.
– ORIGIN French, 'rampart,' later 'a promenade on the site of a rampart.'

bou·le·var·dier /ˌbo͝oləvärˈdi(ə)r/ ▶ **noun** a wealthy, fashionable person who is fond of social activities.
– ORIGIN French, 'person who frequents boulevards.'

bounce /bouns/ ▶ **verb** **1** move quickly up or away from a surface after hitting it. **2** move or jump up and down repeatedly. **3** (**bounce back**) recover well after a setback. **4** informal (of a check) be returned by a bank when there is not enough money in an account for it to be paid. **5** eject (from a nightclub or similar establishment) a troublemaker.

> – SYNONYMS **1 rebound,** spring back, ricochet, carom. **2 bound,** leap, jump, spring, bob, hop, skip, gambol, trip, prance.

▶ **noun** **1** an act of bouncing. **2** energy or self-confidence: *the bounce was back in Jane's step*. **3** health and body in a person's hair.

> – SYNONYMS **1 springiness,** resilience, elasticity, give. **2 vitality,** vigor, energy, vivacity, liveliness, animation, sparkle, verve, spirit; informal get-up-and-go, pep, zing.

– ORIGIN perhaps from German *bunsen* 'beat' or Dutch *bons* 'a thump.'

bounc·er /ˈbounsər/ ▶ **noun** a person employed by a nightclub, etc., to prevent troublemakers entering or to remove them from the building.

bounc·ing /ˈbounsiNG/ ▶ **adjective** (of a baby) lively and healthy.

bounc·y /ˈbounsē/ ▶ **adjective** (**bouncier**, **bounciest**) **1** able to bounce or making something bounce: *a bouncy ball*. **2** confident and lively.

> – SYNONYMS **1 springy,** flexible, resilient, elastic, stretchy, rubbery. **2** *a bouncy ride* **bumpy,** jolting, jerky, jumpy, jarring, rough. **3 lively,** energetic, perky, frisky, jaunty, dynamic, vital, vigorous, vibrant, animated, spirited, buoyant, bubbly, sparkling, vivacious; enthusiastic, upbeat; informal peppy, zingy, chirpy.

– DERIVATIVES **bounc·i·ly** adverb **bounc·i·ness** noun.

bound[1] /bound/ ▶ **verb** walk or run with leaping strides.

> – SYNONYMS **leap,** jump, spring, vault, bounce, hop, skip, dance, prance, gambol, gallop.

▶ **noun** a leaping movement toward or over something.
– ORIGIN French *bondir* 'resound,' later 'rebound.'

bound[2] ▶ **noun** a boundary or limit: *her grief knew no bounds*. ▶ **verb** **1** form the boundary of something. **2** place something within limits.

> – SYNONYMS **1 limit,** restrict, confine, circumscribe, demarcate, delimit. **2 enclose,** surround, encircle, circle, border, close in/off, hem in.

– PHRASES **out of bounds 1** (in sports) beyond the field of play. **2** beyond permitted limits.
– ORIGIN from Latin *bodina*.

bound[3] ▶ **adjective** going toward somewhere: *a train bound for New York City*.
– ORIGIN from Old Norse, 'get ready.'

bound[4] past and past participle of **BIND** ▶ **adjective** **1** (**-bound**) restricted to a place or by a situation: *his job kept him city-bound*. **2** certain to be, do, or have: *there's bound to be a bar open somewhere*. **3** obliged to do something.

> – SYNONYMS **1 tied,** restrained, fixed, fastened, secured. **2 certain,** sure, very likely, destined. **3** *bound by secrecy* **constrained,** obliged, compelled, required, obligated. **4** *religion and morality are bound up with one another* **connected,** linked, tied, united, allied, interdependent.
> – ANTONYMS free.

bound·a·ry /ˈbound(ə)rē/ ▶ **noun** (pl. **boundaries**) **1** a line marking the limits of an area. **2** a limit, especially of a subject or area of activity.

> – SYNONYMS **1 border,** frontier, borderline, partition, dividing line. **2** *the boundary of his estate* **limits,** confines, bounds, margins, edges, fringes, border, periphery, perimeter.

– ORIGIN from **BOUND**[2].

bound·en /ˈboundən/ ▶ **adjective** (in phrase **one's bounden duty**) a responsibility that cannot be ignored; something one feels morally obliged to do.
– ORIGIN old-fashioned past participle of **BIND**.

bound·less /ˈboundlis/ ▶ **adjective** unlimited or immense: *a man of boundless enthusiasm*.

> – SYNONYMS **limitless,** untold, immeasurable, abundant, inexhaustible, endless, infinite, interminable, unfailing, ceaseless, everlasting.
> – ANTONYMS limited.

boun·te·ous /ˈbountēəs/ ▶ **adjective** old use bountiful.
– ORIGIN from Old French *bontif* 'benevolent.'

boun·ti·ful /ˈbountəfəl/ ▶ **adjective** **1** large in quantity; abundant: *bountiful crops*. **2** giving generously.

> – SYNONYMS **1 generous,** magnanimous, munificent, open-handed, unselfish, unstinting, lavish; benevolent, beneficent, charitable. **2 abundant,** plentiful, ample, copious, bumper, superabundant, inexhaustible, prolific, profuse; lavish, generous, handsome, rich; informal whopping; literary plenteous.
> – ANTONYMS mean, meager.

– DERIVATIVES **boun·ti·ful·ly** adverb.

boun·ty /ˈbountē/ ▶ **noun** (pl. **bounties**) **1** literary something given or occurring in generous amounts. **2** literary generosity: *people along the Nile depend on its bounty*. **3** a reward paid for killing or capturing a person or animal. **4** historical a sum paid by the government to encourage trade.

> – SYNONYMS **reward,** prize, award, commission, premium, dividend, bonus, gratuity, tip, donation,

handout; incentive, inducement; informal perk, sweetener; formal perquisite.

– ORIGIN Old French *bonte* 'goodness.'

boun·ty hunt·er ▶ **noun** a person who pursues a criminal for a reward.

bou·quet /bō'kā, bo͞o-/ ▶ **noun 1** a bunch of flowers. **2** the characteristic scent of a wine or perfume.

– SYNONYMS **1 posy,** nosegay, spray, corsage, buttonhole, garland, wreath, arrangement. **2 aroma,** nose, smell, fragrance, perfume, scent, odor.

– ORIGIN French.

bou·quet gar·ni /bō'kā gär'nē, bo͞o-/ ▶ **noun** (pl. **bouquets garnis**) a bunch of herbs used for flavoring a stew or soup.

– ORIGIN French, 'garnished bouquet.'

bour·bon /'bərbən/ ▶ **noun** an American whiskey distilled from corn and rye.

– ORIGIN named after *Bourbon* County, Kentucky.

bour·geois /bo͝or'zhwä, 'bo͝orzhwä/ (also **bourgeoise** /bo͝or'zhwäz, 'bo͝orzhwäz/) ▶ **adjective 1** belonging to or characteristic of the middle class, especially in being materialistic or conventional: *they are the epitome of bourgeois complacency.* **2** (in Marxism) capitalist.

– SYNONYMS **middle-class,** conservative, conformist, conventional, propertied, provincial, suburban, small-town.

– ANTONYMS proletarian.

▶ **noun** (pl. same) a bourgeois person.

– ORIGIN French, from Latin *burgus* 'castle, fortified town.'

bour·geoi·sie /ˌbo͝orzhwä'zē/ ▶ **noun** (treated as sing. or pl.) **1** the middle class. **2** (in Marxism) the capitalist class.

– ORIGIN French.

bourn /bôrn, bo͝orn/ (also **bourne**) ▶ **noun** literary a boundary or limit.

– ORIGIN French *borne*.

bourse /bo͝ors/ ▶ **noun** a stock market in a non-English-speaking country, especially France.

– ORIGIN French, 'purse.'

bout /bout/ ▶ **noun 1** a short period of illness or intense activity. **2** a wrestling or boxing match.

– SYNONYMS **1 spell,** period, stretch, stint, session, burst, flurry, spurt. **2 attack,** fit, spasm. **3 contest,** fight, match, round, competition, meeting, encounter.

– ORIGIN from dialect *bought* 'bend, loop.'

bou·tique /bo͞o'tēk/ ▶ **noun** a small store selling fashionable clothes.

– ORIGIN French.

bou·tique ho·tel ▶ **noun** a small stylish hotel situated in a fashionable location in a town or city.

bou·zou·ki /bo͝o'zo͞okē/ ▶ **noun** (pl. **bouzoukis**) a long-necked Greek form of mandolin.

– ORIGIN modern Greek *mpouzouki*.

bo·vine /'bōvīn, -vēn/ ▶ **adjective 1** relating to cattle. **2** sluggish or stupid: *a look of bovine contentment.* ▶ **noun** an animal of the cattle group, which also includes buffaloes and bison.

– DERIVATIVES **bo·vine·ly** adverb.

– ORIGIN Latin *bovinus*.

bo·vine spon·gi·form en·ceph·a·lop·a·thy ▶ **noun** see **BSE**.

bow[1] /bō/ ▶ **noun 1** a knot tied with two loops and two loose ends. **2** a weapon for shooting arrows, made of curved wood joined at both ends by a taut string. **3** a rod with horsehair stretched along its length, used for playing some stringed instruments. ▶ **verb** play a stringed instrument using a bow.

– ORIGIN Old English, 'bend, bow, arch.'

bow[2] /bou/ ▶ **verb 1** bend the head or upper body as a sign of respect, greeting, or shame. **2** bend with age or under a heavy weight. **3** give in to pressure: *the company bowed to public pressure and withdrew its product.* **4** (**bow out**) withdraw or retire from an activity.

– SYNONYMS **1 incline one's head,** bend, stoop, bob, curtsy, kneel, genuflect. **2** *the mast bowed in the wind* **bend,** buckle, curve, flex. **3** *they bowed to foreign pressure* **give in,** submit, yield, surrender, succumb, capitulate.

▶ **noun** an act of bowing.

– SYNONYMS **nod,** bob, obeisance, curtsy, genuflection, salaam.

– PHRASES **bow and scrape** behave in a servile way. **take a bow** acknowledge applause by bowing.

– ORIGIN Old English, 'bend, stoop.'

bow[3] /bou/ (also **bows**) ▶ **noun** the front end of a ship.

– SYNONYMS **prow,** front, stem, nose, head.

– ORIGIN German *boog* or Dutch *boeg* 'shoulder or ship's bow.'

bowd·ler·ize /'bōdləˌrīz, 'boud-/ ▶ **verb** remove indecent or offensive material from a written work.

– ORIGIN from the name of Dr Thomas *Bowdler*, who published a censored edition of Shakespeare.

bow·el /'bou(ə)l/ ▶ **noun 1** the intestine. **2** (**bowels**) the deepest inner parts of something.

– SYNONYMS **1** *a disorder of the bowels* **intestines,** entrails, viscera, innards, digestive system; Medicine gut; informal guts, insides. **2** *the bowels of the ship* **interior,** inside, core, belly, depths, recesses; informal innards.

– ORIGIN Latin *botellus* 'little sausage.'

bow·el move·ment ▶ **noun** an act of defecation.

bow·er /'bou(-ə)r/ ▶ **noun 1** a pleasant shady place under climbing plants or trees. **2** literary a woman's private room.

– ORIGIN Old English.

bow·er·bird /'bou(-ə)rˌbərd/ ▶ **noun** an Australasian bird noted for the male's habit of building an elaborate structure to attract the female.

bow·head /'bōˌhed/ ▶ **noun** a black Arctic right whale that feeds by skimming the surface for plankton.

bow·ie knife /'bo͞oē, 'bōē/ ▶ **noun** a long knife with a blade double-edged at the point.

– ORIGIN named after the American frontiersman Jim *Bowie*.

bowl[1] /bōl/ ▶ **noun 1** a round, deep dish or basin. **2** a rounded, hollow part of an object. **3** a hollow or depression in the landscape. **4** a stadium for sporting or musical events.

– SYNONYMS **dish,** basin, pot, crock, vessel, receptacle.

– ORIGIN Old English.

bowl[2] ▶ **verb 1** roll a round object along the ground. **2** move rapidly and smoothly: *we bowled along the country roads.* **3** (**bowl someone over**) knock someone down. **4** (**bowl someone over**) informal greatly impress or overwhelm someone. **5** play a game of tenpin bowling.

– SYNONYMS **throw,** pitch, hurl, toss, lob, fling, roll, launch, propel; informal chuck, sling.

▶ **noun** a large heavy ball used in tenpin bowling, lawn bowling, or skittles.
– ORIGIN from Latin *bulla* 'bubble.'

bow·leg·ged ▶ **adjective** having legs that curve outward at the knee.

bowl·er[1] /ˈbōlər/ ▶ **noun** a player at tenpin bowling, lawn bowling, or skittles.

bowl·er[2] ▶ **noun** a man's hard felt hat with a round dome-shaped crown.
– ORIGIN named after the English hatter William *Bowler*.

bow·line /ˈbōlin, ˈbōˌlīn/ ▶ **noun 1** a simple knot for forming a nonslipping loop at the end of a rope. **2** a rope attaching the windward side of a square sail to a ship's bow.

bowl·ing /ˈbōliNG/ ▶ **noun** the game of tenpin bowling, lawn bowling, or skittles.

bowl·ing al·ley ▶ **noun** a building containing lanes for bowling.

bowl·ing green ▶ **noun** an area of closely mown grass on which the game of lawn bowling is played.

bowls /bōlz/ ▶ **plural noun** (treated as sing.) British name for **LAWN BOWLING**.

bow·man /ˈbōmən/ ▶ **noun** (pl. **bowmen**) an archer.

bow·sprit /ˈbouˌsprit, ˈbō-/ ▶ **noun** a pole projecting from a ship's bow, to which the ropes supporting the front mast are fastened.

bow·string /ˈbōˌstriNG/ ▶ **noun** the string of an archer's bow. ▶ **verb** (past and past participle **bowstrung**) historical strangle with a bowstring (a former Turkish method of execution).

bow tie /bō/ ▶ **noun** a necktie in the form of a bow.

bow win·dow /bō/ ▶ **noun** a curved bay window.

box[1] /bäks/ ▶ **noun 1** a container with a flat base and sides and a lid. **2** an area enclosed within straight lines on a page or computer screen. **3** an enclosed area reserved for a group of people in a theater or sports ground, or for witnesses or the jury in a court of law. **4** a mailbox at a post office, newspaper office, or other facility for keeping letters until collected. **5** (**the box**) Soccer the penalty area. **6** (**the batter's box**) Baseball the rectangular area occupied by the batter.

– SYNONYMS **1 carton,** pack, packet, case, crate, chest, coffer, casket. **2** *a telephone box* **booth,** kiosk, cubicle, compartment, cabin, hut.

▶ **verb 1** put something in a box. **2** (**box someone in**) restrict or confine someone.

– SYNONYMS **pack,** package, parcel, encase, bundle, crate.

– PHRASES **think outside the box** informal have original or creative ideas.
– ORIGIN Old English.

box[2] ▶ **verb** fight an opponent with the fists in padded gloves as a sport.

– SYNONYMS **fight,** spar, battle, brawl; informal scrap.

▶ **noun** a slap on the side of a person's head.
– DERIVATIVES **box·ing** noun.
– PHRASES **box someone's ears** slap someone on the side of the head.
– ORIGIN unknown.

box[3] ▶ **noun** an evergreen shrub with small glossy leaves and hard wood.
– ORIGIN Greek *puxos*.

box·car /ˈbäksˌkär/ ▶ **noun** an enclosed railroad freight car.

box·er /ˈbäksər/ ▶ **noun 1** a person who boxes as a sport. **2** a medium-sized breed of dog with a smooth brown coat and puglike face. **3** (**boxers**) another term for **BOXER SHORTS**.

– SYNONYMS **fighter,** pugilist, prizefighter; informal bruiser, scrapper.

box·er shorts ▶ **plural noun** men's loose-fitting underpants resembling shorts.

Box·ing Day ▶ **noun** Brit. (in Canada and the UK) a public holiday on the first day after Christmas Day.
– ORIGIN from the former custom of giving tradespeople a Christmas box (gift) on this day.

box of·fice ▶ **noun 1** a place at a theater or other arts establishment where tickets are sold. **2** (often as adj. **box-office**) used to refer to the commercial success of a play, movie, or actor: *the movie was a huge box-office hit.*

box score ▶ **noun** the tabulated results of a baseball game or other sporting event, with statistics given for each player's performance.

box seat ▶ **noun** a seat in a box in a theater or sports stadium.

box spring ▶ **noun** each of a set of vertical springs housed in a frame in a mattress or upholstered chair base.

box·y /ˈbäksē/ ▶ **adjective** (**boxier, boxiest**) **1** squarish in shape. **2** (of a room or space) cramped.

boy /boi/ ▶ **noun 1** a male child or youth. **2** a man, especially one who comes from a particular place or who does a particular job: *the inspector was a local boy.* **3** (**boys**) informal men who mix socially or belong to a particular group.

– SYNONYMS **lad,** youth, young man, stripling; Scottish laddie.

▶ **exclamation** used to express admiration, surprise, etc.
– DERIVATIVES **boy·hood** noun **boy·ish** adjective.
– ORIGIN unknown.

bo·yar /bōˈyär/ ▶ **noun** a member of the old aristocracy in Russia, next in rank to a prince.
– ORIGIN Russian *boyarin* 'grandee.'

boy·cott /ˈboiˌkät/ ▶ **verb** refuse to deal with a person, organization, or country as a punishment or protest.

– SYNONYMS **shun,** snub, spurn, avoid, ostracize, blacklist, blackball, reject, veto.

▶ **noun** an act of boycotting.

– SYNONYMS **ban,** veto, embargo, prohibition, moratorium, sanction, restriction, avoidance, rejection.

– ORIGIN from Captain Charles C. *Boycott*, an Irish land agent so treated in 1880 in an attempt to get rents reduced.

boy·friend /ˈboiˌfrend/ ▶ **noun** a person's regular male companion in a romantic or sexual relationship.

– SYNONYMS **lover,** sweetheart, beloved, darling, partner; informal fella, (main) squeeze; dated beau; literary swain.

Boyle's law /boilz/ ▸ **noun** Chemistry a law stating that the pressure of a given mass of an ideal gas is inversely proportional to its volume at a constant temperature.
– ORIGIN named after the English scientist Robert *Boyle*.

Boy Scout ▸ **noun 1** a member of the Boy Scouts of America. **2** an honest, friendly, and typically naive man.

boy·sen·ber·ry /'boizən,berē/ ▸ **noun** (pl. **boysenberries**) a large red edible blackberrylike fruit.
– ORIGIN named after the American horticulturalist Robert *Boysen*.

bo·zo /'bōzō/ ▸ **noun** (pl. **bozos**) informal a stupid or insignificant man.
– ORIGIN unknown.

BP ▸ **abbreviation 1** before the present (era). **2** blood pressure.

bp ▸ **abbreviation 1** Biochemistry base pair(s), as a unit of length in nucleic acid chains. **2** Finance basis point(s).

bps ▸ **abbreviation** Computing bits per second.

Bq ▸ **abbreviation** becquerel.

Br ▸ **symbol** the chemical element bromine.

Br. ▸ **abbreviation 1** British. **2** (in religious orders) Brother.

bra /brä/ ▸ **noun** a woman's undergarment worn to support the breasts.
– DERIVATIVES **bra·less** adjective.
– ORIGIN short for **BRASSIERE**.

brace /brās/ ▸ **noun 1** a strengthening or supporting device or part. **2** (**braces**) a wire device fitted in the mouth to straighten the teeth. **3** (pl. same) a pair of things: *a brace of grouse*. **4** either of two connecting marks, { and }, used in printing and music. **5** (also **brace and bit**) a drilling tool with a crank handle and a socket to hold a bit.

– SYNONYMS **prop,** strut, stay, support, bracket.

▸ **verb 1** make something stronger or firmer with a brace. **2** press one's body firmly against something to stay balanced. **3** prepare for something demanding or unpleasant: *he braced himself for the interview*.

– SYNONYMS **1 support,** shore up, prop up, hold up, buttress, reinforce. **2 steady,** secure, stabilize, poise, fix. **3** *brace yourself for disappointment* **prepare,** get ready, gear up, nerve, steel, fortify; informal psych (oneself) up.

– ORIGIN from Latin *bracchium* 'arm.'

brace·let /'brāslit/ ▸ **noun** an ornamental band or chain worn on the wrist or arm.
– ORIGIN from Old French *bras* 'arm.'

bra·chi·al /'brākēəl, 'brak-/ ▸ **adjective** Anatomy of or relating to the arm, specifically the upper arm, or an armlike structure: *the brachial artery*.
– ORIGIN from Latin *brac(c)hium* 'arm.'

bra·chi·o·pod /'brākēə,päd, 'brak-/ ▸ **noun** an invertebrate sea creature with two hinged shells and tentacles used for filter-feeding.
– ORIGIN from Greek *brakhiōn* 'arm' + *pous* 'foot.'

bra·chi·o·sau·rus /,brākēə'sôrəs, ,brak-/ ▸ **noun** a huge plant-eating dinosaur with forelegs much longer than the hind legs.
– ORIGIN from Greek *brakhiōn* 'arm' + *sauros* 'lizard.'

brac·ing /'brāsiNG/ ▸ **adjective** refreshing; invigorating: *bracing winds*.

– SYNONYMS **invigorating,** refreshing, stimulating, energizing, exhilarating, restorative, rejuvenating.

– DERIVATIVES **brac·ing·ly** adverb.

WORD TOOLKIT

bracing ...	stimulating ...	exhilarating ...
walk	environment	feeling
cold air	conversation	ride
wind	discussion	performance
climate	work	rush
drink	reading	speed
tonic	material	sport
swim	challenge	adventure
slap	activity	victory

brack·en /'brakən/ ▸ **noun** a tall fern with coarse fronds.
– ORIGIN Scandinavian.

brack·et /'brakit/ ▸ **noun 1** each of a pair of marks, [and], used to enclose words or figures. **2** a category of similar people or things: *a high income bracket*. **3** a right-angled support projecting from a wall.

– SYNONYMS **1 support,** prop, stay, batten, rest, mounting, rack, frame. **2 group,** category, grade, classification, division.

▸ **verb** (**brackets, bracketing, bracketed**) **1** enclose words or figures in brackets. **2** place in the same category: *being bracketed with the world's greatest movie director was thrill enough*. **3** hold or attach something by means of a bracket.
– ORIGIN from Latin *bracae* 'breeches.'

brack·ish /'brakiSH/ ▸ **adjective** (of water) slightly salty.
– ORIGIN from German, Dutch *brac*.

bract /brakt/ ▸ **noun** a modified leaf with a flower in the angle where it meets the stem.
– ORIGIN Latin *bractea* 'thin metal plate.'

brad /brad/ ▸ **noun** a nail with a rectangular cross section and a small head.
– ORIGIN Old Norse.

brad·y·car·di·a /,bradi'kärdēə/ ▸ **noun** Medicine abnormally slow heart action.
– ORIGIN from Greek *bradus* 'slow' + *kardia* 'heart.'

brag /brag/ ▸ **verb** (**brags, bragging, bragged**) say something boastfully.

– SYNONYMS **boast,** crow, swagger, swank, show off, blow one's own horn, sing one's own praises; informal talk big.

▸ **noun 1** a boastful statement. **2** a simplified form of poker.
– ORIGIN unknown.

brag book ▸ **noun** informal an album of photographs intended to show the subjects, especially one's family, to others in an admiring way.

brag·ga·do·ci·o /,bragə'dōSHē,ō/ ▸ **noun** boastful or arrogant behavior.
– ORIGIN from *Braggadocchio*, a boastful character in Spenser's *The Faerie Queene*.

brag·gart /'bragərt/ ▸ **noun** a person who boasts about their achievements or possessions.
– ORIGIN from French *braguer* 'to brag.'

Brah·man /'brämən/ ▸ **noun** (pl. **Brahmans**) **1** (also **Brahmin** /-min/) a member of the highest Hindu caste, that of the priesthood. **2** (also **Brahma**) (in Hinduism) the ultimate reality underlying all phenomena.
– ORIGIN Sanskrit.

Brah·min /'brämin/ ▸ **noun 1** variant spelling of **BRAHMAN** (sense 1). **2** a socially or culturally superior person.
– DERIVATIVES **Brah·min·i·cal** /brä'minikəl/ adjective.

braid /brād/ ▶ **noun 1** threads woven into a decorative band for trimming garments. **2** a length of hair made up of three or more interlaced strands. ▶ **verb 1** interlace three or more strands of (hair or other flexible material) to form a length. **2** edge or trim a garment with braid.
– ORIGIN Old English, 'make a sudden movement' or 'interweave.'

Braille /brāl/ ▶ **noun** a written language for the blind, in which characters are represented by patterns of raised dots.
– ORIGIN named after the blind French educationist Louis *Braille*.

brain /brān/ ▶ **noun 1** an organ of soft nervous tissue inside the skull, functioning as the coordinating center of the nervous system. **2** the ability to use one's intelligence: *she's got brains, that child.* **3** (**the brains**) informal a clever person who is the main organizer in a group.

– SYNONYMS **intelligence,** intellect, brainpower, cleverness, wit(s), reasoning, wisdom, judgment, understanding, sense; informal nous, gray matter, smarts.

▶ **verb** informal hit someone hard on the head with an object.
– PHRASES **have something on the brain** informal be obsessed with something.
– ORIGIN Old English.

WORD LINKS

cerebral *relating to the brain*

brain·child /'brān,CHīld/ ▶ **noun** (pl. **brainchildren**) informal an idea or invention originated by a particular person.

brain-dead ▶ **adjective 1** having suffered brain death. **2** informal very stupid.

brain death ▶ **noun** irreversible brain damage causing the end of independent breathing.

brain drain ▶ **noun** informal the emigration of highly skilled or qualified people from a country.

brain·less /'brānlis/ ▶ **adjective** stupid; very foolish.

brain·pow·er /'brān,pouər/ ▶ **noun** mental ability; intelligence.

brain·stem /'brān,stem/ ▶ **noun** the central trunk of the brain, consisting of the medulla oblongata, pons, and midbrain.

brain·storm /'brān,stôrm/ ▶ **noun 1** informal a moment in which one is suddenly unable to think clearly. **2** a group discussion to produce ideas. ▶ **verb** have a group discussion to produce ideas.

brain·teas·er ▶ **noun** informal a problem or puzzle.

brain·wash /'brān,wôSH, -,wäSH/ ▶ **verb** force someone to accept an idea or belief by using mental pressure, constant repetition, etc.

– SYNONYMS **indoctrinate,** condition, re-educate, persuade, influence.

brain·wave /'brān,wāv/ ▶ **noun 1** an electrical impulse in the brain. **2** informal a sudden clever idea.

brain·y /'brānē/ ▶ **adjective** (**brainier, brainiest**) informal intelligent; clever.
– DERIVATIVES **brain·i·ness** noun.

braise /brāz/ ▶ **verb** fry food lightly and then stew it slowly in a closed container.
– ORIGIN from French *braise* 'live coals.'

brake[1] /brāk/ ▶ **noun** a device for slowing or stopping a moving vehicle.

– SYNONYMS **curb,** check, restraint, constraint, control, limit.

▶ **verb** slow or stop a vehicle with a brake.

– SYNONYMS **slow (down),** decelerate, reduce speed.
– ANTONYMS accelerate.

– ORIGIN unknown.

USAGE

Do not confuse **brake** with **break**. **Brake** means *a device for slowing or stopping a vehicle* or *slow or stop a vehicle* (*I had to brake hard*), whereas **break** mainly means *separate into pieces* or *a pause or interruption* (*a coffee break*).

brake[2] ▶ **noun** historical an open horse-drawn carriage with four wheels.
– ORIGIN unknown.

brake[3] ▶ **noun** a thicket.
– ORIGIN Old English.

brake drum ▶ **noun** a broad, short cylinder attached to a wheel, against which the brake shoes press to cause braking.

brake horse·pow·er ▶ **noun** an imperial unit equal to one horsepower, used in expressing the power available at the shaft of an engine.

brake shoe ▶ **noun** a long curved block that presses on a brake drum.

bram·ble /'brambəl/ ▶ **noun 1** a prickly shrub of the rose family, especially a blackberry. **2** any rough, prickly vine or shrub.
– ORIGIN Old English.

bran /bran/ ▶ **noun** pieces of grain husk separated from flour after milling.
– ORIGIN Old French.

branch /branCH/ ▶ **noun 1** a part of a tree that grows out from the trunk or a bough. **2** a river, road, or railroad extending out from a main one. **3** a division of a large organization, subject, etc.

– SYNONYMS **1 bough,** limb, arm, offshoot, twig. **2 division,** subdivision, section, subsection, department, unit, sector, wing, office, bureau, agency, subsidiary.

▶ **verb 1** divide into one or more branches. **2** (**branch out**) extend one's activities in a new direction: *the company is branching out into Europe.*

– SYNONYMS **1 fork,** divide, split, bifurcate. **2** *narrow paths* ***branched off*** *the road* **diverge from,** deviate from, split off from, fan out from, radiate from.

– ORIGIN from Latin *branca* 'paw.'

brand /brand/ ▶ **noun 1** a type of product manufactured by a company under a particular name. **2** a brand name. **3** an identifying mark burned on livestock with a heated iron. **4** a piece of burning wood.

– SYNONYMS **1 make,** line, label, marque, trademark, trade name, proprietary name. **2 type,** kind, sort, variety, class, category, genre, style, ilk, stripe.

▶ **verb 1** mark livestock with a branding iron. **2** mark out as having a particular shameful quality: *she was branded a liar.* **3** give a brand name to a product.

– SYNONYMS **1 mark,** stamp, burn, sear. **2 stigmatize,** characterize, label, mark out, denounce, discredit, vilify.

– ORIGIN Old English, 'burning.'

bran·dish /ˈbrandisн/ ▶ **verb** wave or flourish something as a threat or in anger or excitement.

– SYNONYMS **flourish,** wave, shake, wield, swing, swish.

– ORIGIN Old French *brandir*.

brand name ▶ **noun** a name given by the maker to a product or range of products.

brand new ▶ **adjective** completely new.
– ORIGIN with the idea of a brand of wood being 'straight from the fire.'

bran·dy /ˈbrandē/ ▶ **noun** (pl. **brandies**) a strong alcoholic spirit distilled from wine or fermented fruit juice.
– ORIGIN from Dutch *branden* 'burn, distil' + *wijn* 'wine.'

brash /brasн/ ▶ **adjective 1** self-assertive in a rude, noisy, or overbearing way. **2** showy or tasteless in appearance: *the cafe was a brash new building.*

– SYNONYMS **1 self-assertive,** pushy, cocky, self-confident, arrogant, bold, audacious, brazen. **2 garish,** gaudy, loud, flamboyant, showy, tasteless; informal flashy, tacky.
– ANTONYMS meek.

– DERIVATIVES **brash·ly** adverb **brash·ness** noun.
– ORIGIN perhaps from **RASH**[1].

brass /bras/ ▶ **noun 1** a yellow alloy of copper and zinc. **2** a brass memorial plaque in the wall or floor of a church. **3** brass wind instruments forming a band or section of an orchestra. **4** (also **top brass**) informal people in authority.
– PHRASES **get down to brass tacks** informal start to consider the basic facts.
– ORIGIN Old English.

brass band ▶ **noun** a group of musicians playing brass instruments.

bras·se·rie /ˌbrasəˈrē/ ▶ **noun** (pl. **brasseries**) an inexpensive French or French-style restaurant.
– ORIGIN French, 'brewery.'

bras·si·ca /ˈbrasikə/ ▶ **noun** a plant of a family that includes cabbage, turnip, and Brussels sprouts.
– ORIGIN Latin, 'cabbage.'

bras·siere /brəˈzi(ə)r/ ▶ **noun** full form of **BRA**.
– ORIGIN French, 'bodice, child's vest.'

brass knuck·les ▶ **noun** a metal guard worn over the knuckles in fighting, especially to increase the effect of the blows.

brass rub·bing ▶ **noun** the copying of the design on an engraved brass by rubbing crayon or chalk over paper laid on it.

brass·y /ˈbrasē/ ▶ **adjective** (**brassier, brassiest**) **1** bright or harsh yellow. **2** tastelessly showy or loud: *a tawdry, brassy woman.* **3** harsh or blaring like a brass instrument.

brat /brat/ ▶ **noun** derogatory or humorous a badly behaved child.

– SYNONYMS **spoiled child,** scamp, rascal, imp. informal monster, horror, hellion, whippersnapper, rotten kid.

– DERIVATIVES **brat·tish** adjective.
– ORIGIN perhaps from Old French *brachet* 'hound, bitch.'

brat·wurst /ˈbrätˌwərst/ ▶ **noun** a type of fine German pork sausage.
– ORIGIN from German *Brat* 'a spit' + *Wurst* 'sausage.'

bra·va·do /brəˈvädō/ ▶ **noun** confidence or a show of confidence that is intended to impress.

– SYNONYMS **boldness,** swaggering, bluster; machismo; boasting, bragging, bombast, braggadocio; informal showing off.

– ORIGIN from Spanish *bravo* 'brave.'

brave /brāv/ ▶ **adjective** ready to face and endure danger, pain, or difficulty.

– SYNONYMS **courageous,** intrepid, bold, plucky, heroic, fearless, daring, audacious, dauntless, valiant, valorous, doughty, indomitable, stouthearted; informal game, gutsy.
– ANTONYMS cowardly.

▶ **noun** dated an American Indian warrior.
▶ **verb** endure or face unpleasant conditions with courage: *more than 1,000 visitors braved a downpour to get in.*

– SYNONYMS **endure,** put up with, bear, withstand, weather, suffer, face, confront, defy.

– DERIVATIVES **brave·ly** adverb.
– ORIGIN Italian or Spanish *bravo* 'bold, untamed.'

brav·er·y /ˈbrāv(ə)rē/ ▶ **noun** courageous behavior or character.

– SYNONYMS **courage,** boldness, heroism, intrepidity, nerve, daring, fearlessness, audacity, pluck, mettle, valor; informal guts.

bra·vo[1] /bräˈvō/ ▶ **exclamation** shouted to express approval for a performer.
– ORIGIN Italian, 'bold.'

bra·vo[2] /ˈbrävō/ ▶ **noun** (pl. **bravos** or **bravoes**) dated a thug or hired assassin.
– ORIGIN Italian, 'bold (one).'

bra·vu·ra /brəˈv(y)o͝orə/ ▶ **noun 1** great skill and brilliance, typically shown in a performance. **2** the display of great daring.
– ORIGIN Italian.

brawl /brôl/ ▶ **noun** a rough or noisy fight or quarrel.

– SYNONYMS **fight,** skirmish, scuffle, tussle, fray, melee, fracas, fisticuffs; informal scrap, set-to.

▶ **verb** fight or quarrel in a rough or noisy way.
– DERIVATIVES **brawl·er** noun.
– ORIGIN perhaps related to **BRAY**.

brawn /brôn/ ▶ **noun** physical strength as opposed to intelligence.
– ORIGIN Old French *braon* 'fleshy part of the leg.'

brawn·y /ˈbrônē/ ▶ **adjective** physically strong; muscular.

– SYNONYMS **strong,** muscular, muscly, well built, powerful, strapping, burly, sturdy; informal beefy, hulking.
– ANTONYMS puny, weak.

bray /brā/ ▶ **verb 1** (of a donkey) make a loud, harsh cry. **2** (of a person) speak or laugh loudly and harshly. ▶ **noun** a loud, harsh cry of a donkey.
– ORIGIN from Old French *braire* 'to cry.'

braze /brāz/ ▶ **verb** solder something with an alloy of copper and zinc.
– ORIGIN French *braser* 'solder.'

bra·zen /ˈbrāzən/ ▶ **adjective 1** bold and shameless. **2** old use made of brass.

– SYNONYMS **bold,** shameless, unashamed, unrepentant, unabashed, defiant, impudent, impertinent, cheeky, barefaced, blatant, flagrant.

▶ **verb** (**brazen it out**) endure a difficult situation with apparent confidence and lack of shame.

– DERIVATIVES **bra·zen·ly** adverb.
– ORIGIN Old English.

CHOOSE THE RIGHT WORD

See **BOLD**.

bra·zier¹ /ˈbrāzhər/ ▸ **noun** a portable heater holding lighted coals.
– ORIGIN from French *braise* 'hot coals.'

bra·zier² ▸ **noun** a person who works in brass.

Bra·zil·ian /brəˈzilēən/ ▸ **noun** a person from Brazil. ▸ **adjective** relating to Brazil.

Bra·zil nut ▸ **noun** the large three-sided nut of a South American tree.

breach /brēch/ ▸ **verb 1** make a gap or hole in something. **2** break a law, rule, or agreement.

– SYNONYMS **1 break (through),** burst, rupture. **2 contravene,** break, violate, infringe, defy, disobey, flout.

▸ **noun 1** a gap made in a wall or barrier. **2** an act of breaking a rule or agreement. **3** a break in relations: *a sudden breach between father and son.*

– SYNONYMS **1 contravention,** violation, infringement, infraction, transgression. **2 break,** rupture, split, crack, fracture, opening, gap, hole, fissure. **3 rift,** severance, estrangement, parting, parting of the ways, split, falling-out, schism.

– PHRASES **breach of the peace** public disturbance, or an act considered likely to cause one. **step into the breach** replace someone who is suddenly unable to do a job.
– ORIGIN Old French *breche.*

bread /bred/ ▸ **noun 1** food made of flour, water, and yeast mixed together and baked. **2** informal money.
– PHRASES **bread and butter** a person's main source of income. **break bread** celebrate Holy Communion. **know which side one's bread is buttered (on)** informal know where one's advantage lies.
– ORIGIN Old English.

bread·bas·ket /ˈbred,baskit/ ▸ **noun 1** a part of a region that produces cereals for the rest of it. **2** informal a person's stomach, considered as the target for a blow.

bread·crumb /ˈbred,krəm/ ▸ **noun** a small fragment of bread.

bread·ed /ˈbredid/ ▸ **adjective** (of food) coated with breadcrumbs and fried.

bread·fruit /ˈbred,fro͞ot/ ▸ **noun** a large round starchy fruit of a tropical tree, used as a vegetable.

bread·line /ˈbred,līn/ ▸ **noun** a line of people waiting to receive free food.

bread·stick /ˈbred,stik/ ▸ **noun** a crisp stick of baked dough.

breadth /bredth/ ▸ **noun 1** the distance or measurement from side to side of something. **2** wide range: *they have talent but no breadth of vision.*

– SYNONYMS **1 width,** broadness, thickness, span, diameter. **2 range,** extent, scope, depth, reach, compass, scale.

– ORIGIN related to **BROAD.**

bread·win·ner /ˈbred,winər/ ▸ **noun** a person who supports their family with the money they earn.

break /brāk/ ▸ **verb** (past **broke**; past part. **broken**) **1** separate into pieces as a result of a blow, shock, or strain. **2** make or become unable to function: *you've broken the stereo.* **3** fail to observe a law, regulation, or agreement. **4** crush the spirit of someone. **5** beat a record. **6** decipher a code. **7** suddenly make or become public: *once the news broke, emails circulated worldwide.* **8** (of a person's voice) falter and change tone. **9** (of a boy's voice) change in tone and register at puberty. **10** make a rush or dash. **11** lessen the impact of a fall. **12** interrupt a sequence or course. **13** (of the weather) change suddenly, especially after a fine spell. **14** (of a storm, dawn, or day) begin. **15** use a bill to pay for something and receive change.

– SYNONYMS **1** *the mirror broke* **shatter,** smash, crack, snap, fracture, fragment, splinter, split, burst; informal bust. **2** *the coffee machine has broken* **stop working,** break down, give out, go wrong, malfunction, crash; informal go kaput, conk out. **3** *employers who break the law will be prosecuted* **violate,** contravene, infringe, breach, defy, flout, disobey. **4** *the strategies used to break the union* **destroy,** crush, quash, defeat, vanquish, overcome, overpower, overwhelm, suppress, cripple; weaken, subdue, cow, undermine. **5** *the movie broke box-office records* **beat,** surpass, exceed, better, cap, top, outdo, outstrip. **6** *he broke the encryption code* **decipher,** decode, decrypt, unravel, work out; informal figure out. **7** *he tried to break the news gently* **reveal,** disclose, divulge, impart, tell, announce, release. **8** *her voice broke as she relived the experience* **falter,** quaver, quiver, tremble, shake.
– ANTONYMS repair, obey.

▸ **noun 1** an interruption, pause, or gap. **2** a short rest or vacation. **3** an instance of breaking, or the point where something is broken. **4** a sudden rush or dash: *she made a break for the door.* **5** informal an opportunity or chance. **6** (also **break of serve** or **service break**) Tennis the winning of a game against an opponent's serve. **7** make the first stroke at the beginning of a game of pool, snooker, or billiards.

– SYNONYMS **1 interval,** interruption, gap, disruption, stoppage, cessation, halt, stop. **2 rest,** respite, recess, pause, intermission; informal breather, time out. **3 gap,** opening, space, hole, breach, chink, crack, fracture, fissure, tear, split.

– DERIVATIVES **break·a·ble** adjective & noun.
– PHRASES **break away** escape from someone's control or influence. **break the back of** accomplish the main or hardest part of something. **break cover** (of people or animals being hunted) suddenly leave shelter. **break down 1** suddenly fail or stop functioning. **2** lose control of one's emotions when upset. **break even** reach a point in a business when the profits are equal to the costs. **break in 1** force entry to a building. **2** interrupt with a remark. **break something in 1** make a horse used to being ridden. **2** make new shoes comfortable by wearing them. **break into** burst into laughter, song, or faster movement. **break of day** dawn. **break something off** suddenly stop or end something. **break out 1** (of something unwelcome) start suddenly. **2** escape from confinement. **break something out** informal open and start using something. **break out in** be suddenly affected by: *I broke out in a rash.* **break someone's serve** win a game in a tennis match against an opponent's service. **break up** (of a gathering or relationship) end or part. **break wind** release gas from the anus. **break with someone/thing 1** quarrel with someone. **2** go against a custom or tradition. **give someone a break** informal stop putting pressure on someone.
– ORIGIN Old English.

USAGE

On the confusion of **break** and **brake**, see the note at **BRAKE**[1].

break·age /ˈbrākij/ ▶ **noun** the action of breaking something or the fact of being broken.

break·a·way /ˈbrākəˌwā/ ▶ **noun 1** a departure from something established or long-standing. **2** (in sports) a sudden attack or forward movement. ▶ **adjective** having separated from a larger group or country: *a breakaway republic.*

break·beat /ˈbrākˌbēt/ ▶ **noun** a sampled electronic drumbeat repeated to form a rhythm used as a basis for dance music or hip-hop.

break·dan·cing ▶ **noun** an energetic and acrobatic style of street dancing.

break·down /ˈbrākˌdoun/ ▶ **noun 1** a failure or collapse. **2** an explanatory analysis of figures or costs.

– SYNONYMS **1 failure,** collapse, disintegration, foundering. **2 nervous breakdown,** collapse. **3 malfunction,** failure, crash. **4 analysis,** itemization, classification, examination, investigation, explanation.

break·er /ˈbrākər/ ▶ **noun 1** a heavy sea wave that breaks on the shore. **2** a person who breaks or breaks up something.

break·fast /ˈbrekfəst/ ▶ **noun** a meal eaten in the morning, the first of the day. ▶ **verb** eat breakfast.
– ORIGIN from **BREAK** + **FAST**[2].

break-in ▶ **noun** an illegal forced entry in order to steal something.

– SYNONYMS **burglary,** robbery, theft, raid, breaking and entering.

break·ing point ▶ **noun** the moment of greatest strain at which someone or something gives way.

break·neck /ˈbrākˌnek/ ▶ **adjective** dangerously fast.

break·out /ˈbrākˌout/ ▶ **noun 1** a forcible escape, especially from prison. **2** an outbreak.

break point ▶ **noun 1** a place or time at which an interruption or change is made. **2** Tennis the state of a game when the side receiving service needs only one more point to win the game. **3** Tennis a point of this nature. **4** Computing a place in a computer program where the sequence of instructions is interrupted.

break·through /ˈbrākˌTHro͞o/ ▶ **noun** a sudden important development or success.

– SYNONYMS **advance,** development, step forward, success, improvement, discovery, innovation, revolution, quantum leap.
– ANTONYMS setback.

break-up ▶ **noun 1** the breaking up of something into several parts. **2** an end to a relationship.

break·wa·ter /ˈbrākˌwôtər, -ˌwätər/ ▶ **noun** a barrier built out into the sea to protect a coast or harbor from the force of waves.

bream /brim, brēm/ ▶ **noun** (pl. same) a deep-bodied greenish-bronze freshwater fish.
– ORIGIN Old French *bresme.*

breast /brest/ ▶ **noun 1** either of the two protruding organs on a woman's chest that produce milk after childbirth. **2** a person's or animal's chest region.

– SYNONYMS **chest,** bosom, bust; informal boobs, knockers, hooters.

▶ **verb 1** face and move forward against or through: *I watched him breast the wave.* **2** reach the top of a hill.
– DERIVATIVES **breast·ed** adjective.
– ORIGIN Old English.

breast·bone /ˈbrestˌbōn/ ▶ **noun** a thin, flat bone running down the center of the chest, to which the ribs are attached; the sternum.

breast·feed /ˈbrestˌfēd/ ▶ **verb** (**breastfeeds, breastfeeding, breastfed** /ˈbrestˌfed/) feed a baby with milk from the breast.

breast·plate /ˈbrestˌplāt/ ▶ **noun** a piece of armor covering the chest.

breast·stroke /ˈbrestˌstrōk/ ▶ **noun** a style of swimming in which the arms are pushed forward and then swept back while the legs are tucked in and then kicked out.

breast·work /ˈbrestˌwərk/ ▶ **noun** a low temporary defense or parapet.

breath /breTH/ ▶ **noun 1** air taken into or sent out of the lungs. **2** an instance of breathing in or out. **3** a slight movement of air. **4** a hint or suggestion: *he avoided the slightest breath of scandal.*

– SYNONYMS **inhalation,** exhalation, gulp of air, puff, gasp; Medicine respiration.

– PHRASES **breath of fresh air** a refreshing change. **hold one's breath** stop breathing temporarily. **out of breath** gasping for air. **take someone's breath away** astonish or inspire someone. **under one's breath** in a very quiet voice.
– ORIGIN Old English, 'smell, scent.'

breath·a·ble /ˈbrēT͟Həbəl/ ▶ **adjective 1** (of air) fit to breathe. **2** (of clothing or material) allowing air to the skin so that sweat may evaporate.
– DERIVATIVES **breath·a·bi·li·ty** noun.

breath·a·lyz·er /ˈbreTHəˌlīzər/ ▶ **noun** trademark a device used by police for measuring the amount of alcohol in a driver's breath.
– DERIVATIVES **breath·a·lyze** verb.

breathe /brēT͟H/ ▶ **verb 1** take air into the lungs and send it out again as a regular process. **2** say something quietly. **3** let air or moisture in or out. **4** give an impression of: *the room breathed an air of efficiency.*

– SYNONYMS **1 inhale,** exhale, respire, draw breath, puff, pant, blow, gasp, wheeze; Medicine inspire, expire. **2 whisper,** murmur, purr, sigh.

– PHRASES **breathe down someone's neck 1** follow closely behind someone. **2** constantly check up on someone.

WORD LINKS

respiratory *relating to breathing*

breath·er /ˈbrēT͟Hər/ ▶ **noun** informal a brief pause for rest.

breath·ing space ▶ **noun** an opportunity to pause, relax, or decide what to do next.

breath·less /ˈbreTHlis/ ▶ **adjective 1** gasping for breath. **2** feeling or causing great excitement, fear, etc.: *breathless enthusiasm.*

– SYNONYMS **1 out of breath,** panting, puffing, gasping, wheezing, winded; informal out of wind. **2 eager,** agog, open-mouthed, excited, on the edge of one's seat, on tenterhooks.

– DERIVATIVES **breath·less·ly** adverb **breath·less·ness** noun.

breath·tak·ing /'breTH,tākiNG/ ▶ **adjective** astonishing or awe-inspiring.

– SYNONYMS **spectacular,** magnificent, awe-inspiring, awesome, astonishing, amazing, stunning, thrilling; informal sensational, out of this world.

– DERIVATIVES **breath·tak·ing·ly** adverb.

breath test ▶ **noun** a test in which a driver is made to blow into a breathalyzer.

breath·y /'breTHē/ ▶ **adjective** (of a voice) having an audible sound of breathing.
– DERIVATIVES **breath·i·ly** adverb.

brec·ci·a /'brecHēə, 'bresH-/ ▶ **noun** rock consisting of angular fragments cemented by finer chalky material.
– ORIGIN Italian, 'gravel.'

bred /bred/ past and past participle of **BREED**.

breech /brēCH/ ▶ **noun** the back part of a rifle or gun barrel.
– ORIGIN Old English, 'garment covering the loins and thighs.'

breech birth ▶ **noun** a birth in which the baby's buttocks or feet are delivered first.

breech·es /'bricHiz, 'brē-/ ▶ **plural noun** short trousers fastened just below the knee, now worn for riding or as part of ceremonial dress.

breed /brēd/ ▶ **verb** (past and past part. **bred**) **1** (of animals) mate and then produce offspring. **2** keep animals to produce offspring. **3** bring up in a particular way: *Penny had been beautifully bred.* **4** develop a variety of plant. **5** produce or lead to.

– SYNONYMS **1 reproduce,** produce offspring, procreate, multiply, mate. **2 bring up,** rear, raise, nurture. **3 cause,** produce, bring about, give rise to, occasion, arouse, stir up, generate, foster.

▶ **noun 1** a distinctive type within a species of animals or plants, especially one deliberately developed. **2** a sort or kind: *a new breed of executive.*

– SYNONYMS **1** *a breed of cow* **variety,** stock, strain, race, species. **2** *a new breed of journalist* **type,** kind, sort, variety, class, genre, generation.

– DERIVATIVES **breed·er** noun.
– ORIGIN Old English.

breed·ing /'brēdiNG/ ▶ **noun** upper-class good manners regarded as being passed on from one generation to another.

– SYNONYMS **(good) manners,** gentility, refinement, cultivation, polish, urbanity; informal class.

breeze /brēz/ ▶ **noun 1** a gentle wind. **2** informal a thing that is easy to do.

– SYNONYMS **gentle wind,** gust, draft; literary zephyr.

▶ **verb** informal **1** come or go in a casual way. **2** (**breeze through**) deal with or accomplish something with ease.
– ORIGIN probably from Old Spanish and Portuguese *briza*.

breez·y /'brēzē/ ▶ **adjective** (**breezier, breeziest**) **1** pleasantly windy. **2** relaxed and cheerily brisk.

– SYNONYMS **1 windy,** fresh, brisk, blowy, blustery, gusty. **2 jaunty,** cheerful, cheery, brisk, carefree, easy, casual, relaxed, informal, lighthearted, upbeat.

– DERIVATIVES **breez·i·ly** adverb **breez·i·ness** noun.

bre·sao·la /bre'sōlə, bri'zō-/ ▶ **noun** an Italian dish of sliced raw beef that has been cured by salting and air-drying.
– ORIGIN Italian, from *brasare* 'braise.'

breth·ren /'breTH(ə)rin/ old-fashioned plural of **BROTHER** ▶ **plural noun** fellow Christians or members of a group: *their baseball brethren.*

Bret·on /'bretn/ ▶ **noun 1** a person from Brittany. **2** the Celtic language of Brittany.
– ORIGIN Old French, 'Briton.'

breve /brēv, brev/ ▶ **noun 1** Music a note twice as long as a whole note. **2** a written or printed mark (˘) indicating a short or unstressed vowel.
– ORIGIN variant of **BRIEF**.

bre·vi·ar·y /'brēvē,erē, 'brev-/ ▶ **noun** (pl. **breviaries**) a book containing the service for each day, used in the Roman Catholic Church.
– ORIGIN Latin *breviarium* 'summary.'

brev·i·ty /'brevitē/ ▶ **noun 1** concise and exact use of words. **2** shortness of time.

– SYNONYMS **conciseness,** concision, succinctness, pithiness, incisiveness, shortness, compactness.

– ORIGIN from Latin *brevis* 'brief.'

brew /broo/ ▶ **verb 1** make beer by soaking, boiling, and fermentation. **2** make tea or coffee by mixing it with hot water. **3** begin to develop: *a real crisis is brewing.*

– SYNONYMS **1 ferment,** make, prepare, infuse, steep. **2 develop,** loom, be imminent, be on the horizon, be in the offing, be just around the corner.

▶ **noun 1** a drink that has been brewed. **2** a mixture of different things: *her smell was a powerful brew of cheap perfume and mothballs.*

– SYNONYMS **1** *home brew* **beer,** ale. **2** *a hot brew* **drink,** beverage, infusion. **3 mixture,** mix, blend, combination, amalgam, cocktail.

– DERIVATIVES **brew·er** noun.
– ORIGIN Old English.

brew·er·y /'brooərē/ ▶ **noun** (pl. **breweries**) a place where beer is made.

bri·ar[1] /'brī(ə)r/ (also **brier**) ▶ **noun** a prickly shrub, especially a wild rose.
– ORIGIN Old English.

bri·ar[2] (also **briar pipe, brier**) ▶ **noun** a tobacco pipe made from the woody nodules of a shrub of the heather family.
– ORIGIN French *bruyère* 'heath, heather.'

bribe /brīb/ ▶ **verb** dishonestly persuade someone to act in one's favor, especially by giving them money.

– SYNONYMS **buy off,** pay off, suborn; informal grease someone's palm.

▶ **noun** something offered or given to bribe someone.

– SYNONYMS **inducement**; informal payoff, kickback, sweetener.

– ORIGIN Old French *briber, brimber* 'to beg.'

brib·er·y /'brīb(ə)rē/ ▶ **noun** the giving or offering of a bribe: *he was convicted of racketeering and bribery.*

– SYNONYMS **corruption,** payola; informal palm-greasing, graft, hush money.

bric-a-brac /'brik ə ,brak/ ▶ **noun** various objects and ornaments of little value.
– ORIGIN from former French *à bric et à brac* 'at random.'

brick /brik/ ▶ **noun 1** a small rectangular block of fired or sun-dried clay, used in building. **2** informal, dated a helpful and reliable person. ▶ **verb** block or enclose something with a wall of bricks.

– PHRASES **bricks and mor·tar** buildings, especially housing.
– ORIGIN German, Dutch *bricke, brike*.

brick·bat /ˈbrikˌbat/ ▸ **noun 1** a critical remark. **2** a piece of brick used as a missile.

brick·lay·er /ˈbrikˌlāər/ ▸ **noun** a person whose job is to build structures with bricks.
– DERIVATIVES **brick·lay·ing** noun.

brick red ▸ **noun** a deep brownish red.

brick·work /ˈbrikˌwərk/ ▸ **noun** the bricks in a wall or building.

brick·yard /ˈbrikˌyärd/ ▸ **noun** a place where bricks are made.

bri·co·lage /ˌbrēkōˈläzʜ, ˌbrikə-/ ▸ **noun** (in art or literature) the creation of something from a diverse range of available things.
– ORIGIN French.

brid·al /ˈbrīdl/ ▸ **adjective** relating to a bride or a newly married couple.
– ORIGIN from Old English, 'wedding feast.'

bride /brīd/ ▸ **noun** a woman on her wedding day or just before and after the event.
– ORIGIN Old English.

bride·groom /ˈbrīdˌgro͞om/ ▸ **noun** a man on his wedding day or just before and after the event.
– ORIGIN Old English, 'bride man.'

brides·maid /ˈbrīdzˌmād/ ▸ **noun** a girl or woman who accompanies a bride on her wedding day.

bridge[1] /brij/ ▸ **noun 1** a structure carrying a route or railroad across a river, road, or other obstacle. **2** the platform on a ship from which the captain and officers direct its course. **3** the upper bony part of a person's nose. **4** a false tooth or teeth supported by natural teeth on either side. **5** the part on a stringed instrument over which the strings are stretched.

– SYNONYMS **1 viaduct,** flyover, overpass, aqueduct. **2 link,** connection, bond, tie.

▸ **verb 1** be or make a bridge over or between something. **2** make a difference or gap between two groups or things less significant: *how do we bridge the gap between politicians and people?*

– SYNONYMS **span,** cross (over), extend across, traverse, arch over, straddle.

– ORIGIN Old English.

WORD LINKS

pontine *relating to bridges*

bridge[2] ▸ **noun** a card game related to whist, played by two partnerships of two players.
– ORIGIN unknown.

bridge-and-tun·nel ▸ **adjective** (of a person) living in the suburbs and perceived as unsophisticated.
– ORIGIN with reference to the means used to commute into New York.

bridge·head /ˈbrijˌhed/ ▸ **noun** a strong position secured by an army inside enemy territory.

bridge loan ▸ **noun** a sum of money lent by a bank to cover the period of time between the buying of one thing and the selling of another.

bri·dle /ˈbrīdl/ ▸ **noun** the headgear used to control a horse, consisting of buckled straps to which a bit and reins are attached. ▸ **verb 1** put a bridle on a horse. **2** bring something under control. **3** show resentment or anger: *she bridled at being given an order*.
– ORIGIN Old English.

bri·dle path ▸ **noun** a path or track along which horses are ridden.

Brie /brē/ ▸ **noun** a kind of soft, mild, creamy cheese.
– ORIGIN named after *Brie* in northern France.

brief /brēf/ ▸ **adjective 1** lasting a short time. **2** using few words; concise. **3** (of clothing) not covering much of the body.

– SYNONYMS **1 concise,** succinct, short, pithy, compact, thumbnail, potted, condensed, to the point, terse, summary. **2 short,** flying, fleeting, hasty, hurried, quick, cursory, perfunctory, temporary, short-lived, ephemeral, transient, transitory.
– ANTONYMS long.

▸ **noun 1** a set of instructions about a task. **2** a summary of the facts in a case, filed by an attorney before arguing the case in court. **3** a letter from the Pope on a matter of discipline.

– SYNONYMS **1 instructions,** directions, directive, remit, mandate. **2** *a lawyer's brief* **case,** summary, argument, contention, dossier.

▸ **verb** give someone information so as to prepare them to deal with something.

– SYNONYMS **inform,** tell, update, notify, advise, prepare, prime, instruct; informal fill in, put in the picture.

– ORIGIN from Latin *brevis* 'short.'

brief·case /ˈbrēfˌkās/ ▸ **noun** a flat rectangular case for carrying books and documents.

brief·ing /ˈbrēfiɴɢ/ ▸ **noun** a meeting for giving information or instructions.

brief·ly /brēflē/ ▸ **adverb 1** for a short time. **2** in a few words.

– SYNONYMS **1** *Henry paused briefly* **momentarily,** temporarily, fleetingly. **2** *briefly, the plot is as follows* **in short,** to make a long story short, in brief, in a word, in a nutshell, in essence.

briefs /brēfs/ ▸ **plural noun** short, close-fitting underpants.

– SYNONYMS **underpants,** underwear, shorts, bikini briefs; Brit. knickers; informal panties.

bri·er[1] ▸ **noun** variant spelling of **BRIAR**[1].

bri·er[2] ▸ **noun** variant spelling of **BRIAR**[2].

brig /brig/ ▸ **noun 1** a two-masted square-rigged ship. **2** informal a prison on a warship.
– ORIGIN short for **BRIGANTINE**.

Brig. ▸ **abbreviation 1** brigade. **2** brigadier.

bri·gade /briˈgād/ ▸ **noun 1** a subdivision of an army, typically consisting of a small number of battalions and forming part of a division. **2** informal, often derogatory a particular group of people: *the anti-smoking brigade*.

– SYNONYMS **squad,** team, group, band, party, crew, force, outfit.

– ORIGIN from Italian *brigata* 'company.'

brig·a·dier /ˌbrigəˈdi(ə)r, ˈbrigəˌdi(ə)r/ ▸ **noun** a rank of officer in the British army, above colonel and below major general.

brig·a·dier gen·er·al ▸ **noun** a rank of officer in the US Army, Air Force, and Marine Corps, above colonel and below major general.

brig·and /ˈbrigənd/ ▶ **noun** a member of a gang of bandits.
– DERIVATIVES **brig·and·age** noun.
– ORIGIN Italian *brigante* '(person) contending.'

brig·an·tine /ˈbrigənˌtēn/ ▶ **noun** a two-masted sailing ship, with the foremast square-rigged and the mainmast fore-and-aft rigged.
– ORIGIN Italian *brigantino.*

bright /brīt/ ▶ **adjective 1** giving out or filled with light. **2** (of color) vivid and bold. **3** intelligent and quick-witted. **4** cheerful and lively. **5** (of future prospects) good.

– SYNONYMS **1 shining,** brilliant, dazzling, glaring, sparkling, flashing, glittering, gleaming, glistening, shimmering, radiant, glowing, luminous, shiny, glossy, lustrous. **2 sunny,** cloudless, clear, fair, fine. **3** *bright colors* **vivid,** brilliant, intense, strong, vibrant, bold, gaudy, lurid, garish. **4 clever,** intelligent, quick-witted, smart, canny, astute, perceptive, ingenious; informal brainy.
– ANTONYMS dull, cloudy, dark, stupid.

– DERIVATIVES **bright·ly** adverb **bright·ness** noun.
– ORIGIN Old English.

CHOOSE THE RIGHT WORD

bright, brilliant, effulgent, luminous, lustrous, radiant, refulgent, resplendent, shining

Looking for just the right word to capture the quality of the light on a moonlit night or a summer day? All of these adjectives describe an intense, steady light emanating (or appearing to emanate) from a source. **Bright** is the most general term, applied to something that gives forth, reflects, or is filled with light (*a bright and sunny day* ; *a bright star*). **Brilliant** light is even more intense or dazzling (*the brilliant diamond on her finger*), and **resplendent** is a slightly more formal, even poetic, way of describing a striking brilliance (*the sky was resplendent with stars*). Poets also prefer adjectives like **effulgent** and **refulgent**, both of which can be applied to an intense, pervading light, sometimes from an unseen source (*her effulgent loveliness*) ; but *refulgent* specifically refers to reflected light (*a chandelier of refulgent crystal pendants*). **Radiant** is used to describe the power of giving off light, either literally or metaphorically (*a radiant June day* ; *the bride's radiant face*) ; it describes a steady, warm light that is emitted in all directions. Like *radiant*, **luminous** suggests sending forth light, but light of the glow-in-the-dark variety (*the luminous face of the alarm clock*). While diamonds are known for being *brilliant*, fabrics like satin and surfaces like polished wood, which reflect light and take on a gloss or sheen, are often called **lustrous**. If none of these words captures the exact quality of the light you're trying to describe, you can always join the masses and use **shining**, a word that has been overworked to the point of cliché (*my knight in shining armor*).

bright·en /ˈbrītn/ ▶ **verb 1** make or become brighter. **2** make or become happier and more cheerful.

– SYNONYMS **1 illuminate,** light up, lighten. **2 cheer up,** perk up, liven up, rally, feel heartened; informal buck up.

brill /bril/ ▶ **noun** a European flatfish similar to the turbot.
– ORIGIN unknown.

bril·liance /ˈbrilyəns/ (also **brilliancy** /-sē/) ▶ **noun 1** intense brightness of light. **2** exceptional talent or intelligence.

– SYNONYMS **1** *the brilliance of the sunshine* **brightness,** vividness, intensity, sparkle, glitter, blaze, luminosity, radiance. **2** *a philosopher of great brilliance* **genius,** intelligence, talent, ability, prowess, skill, expertise, aptitude, flair, wisdom, intellect.
– ANTONYMS dullness, stupidity.

bril·liant /ˈbrilyənt/ ▶ **adjective 1** (of light or color) very bright or vivid. **2** exceptionally clever or talented. **3** Brit. informal excellent; marvelous.

– SYNONYMS **1 bright,** shining, sparkling, blazing, dazzling, vivid, intense, glaring, luminous, radiant. **2 clever,** bright, intelligent, smart, able, talented, gifted, skillful, astute; informal brainy. **3** *her brilliant career* **superb,** glorious, illustrious, successful, impressive, remarkable, exceptional, excellent, outstanding, distinguished.
– ANTONYMS dim, stupid, undistinguished.

– DERIVATIVES **bril·liant·ly** adverb.
– ORIGIN from French *briller* 'to shine.'

CHOOSE THE RIGHT WORD

See **BRIGHT**.

brim /brim/ ▶ **noun 1** the projecting edge around the bottom of a hat. **2** the lip of a cup, bowl, or other container.

– SYNONYMS **1** peak, visor, shield. **2 rim,** lip, brink, edge.

▶ **verb** (**brims, brimming, brimmed**) fill or be full to the point of overflowing: *he's brimming with ideas.*

– SYNONYMS **be full (up),** overflow, run over, well over.

– DERIVATIVES **brim·ful** adjective.
– ORIGIN perhaps related to German *Bräme* 'trimming.'

CHOOSE THE RIGHT WORD

See **BORDER**.

brim·stone /ˈbrimˌstōn/ ▶ **noun 1** a large bright yellow or greenish-white butterfly. **2** old use sulfur.
– ORIGIN Old English.

brin·dle /ˈbrindl/ (also **brindled**) ▶ **adjective** (of a domestic animal) brownish or tawny with streaks of other color.
– ORIGIN probably Scandinavian.

brine /brīn/ ▶ **noun** water containing dissolved salt.
– ORIGIN Old English.

bring /briNG/ ▶ **verb** (past and past part. **brought**) **1** take or go with someone or something to a place. **2** cause to be in a particular position or state: *the agreement brought an end to hostilities.* **3** cause someone to receive money as income or profit. **4** (**bring oneself to do**) force oneself to do something unpleasant. **5** begin legal action.

– SYNONYMS **1** *he brought a tray* **fetch,** carry, bear, take, convey, transport, shift. **2** *she brought Luke home from the hospital* **escort,** conduct, guide, lead, usher. **3** *the wind changed and brought rain* **cause,** produce, create, bring about, generate, precipitate, occasion, provoke, lead to, give rise to, result in.

– DERIVATIVES **bring·er** noun.
– PHRASES **bring something about** cause something to happen. **bring someone along** encourage or help someone to develop or improve. **bring someone around 1** cause an unconscious person to become

conscious. **2** persuade someone to agree to something. **bring something forward 1** move something planned to an earlier time. **2** propose an idea for consideration. **bring something on** cause something unpleasant to happen. **bring something out 1** produce and launch a new product or publication. **2** emphasize something. **bring the house down** make an audience laugh or applaud very enthusiastically. **bring someone to** cause an unconscious person to become conscious. **bring something to bear** use influence or pressure to achieve a result. **bring something to pass** chiefly literary cause something to happen. **bring to the table** (or **party**) contribute something of value to a discussion, project, etc. **bring someone/thing up 1** look after a child until it is an adult. **2** raise a matter for discussion.
– ORIGIN Old English.

brink /briNGk/ ▶ **noun 1** the extreme edge of land before a steep slope or a body of water. **2** the point at which a new or unwelcome situation is about to begin: *companies on the brink of bankruptcy.*

– SYNONYMS **1 edge,** verge, margin, rim, lip, border, boundary. **2** *on the brink of war* **verge,** threshold, point, edge.

– ORIGIN Scandinavian.

CHOOSE THE RIGHT WORD

See **BORDER**.

brink·man·ship /ˈbriNGkmən,SHip/ (also **brinksmanship**) ▶ **noun** the pursuit of a dangerous policy to the limits of safety before stopping.

brin·y /ˈbrīnē/ ▶ **adjective** relating to brine; salty. ▶ **noun** (**the briny**) Brit. informal the sea.

bri·o /ˈbrēō/ ▶ **noun** energy or liveliness.
– ORIGIN Italian.

bri·oche /brēˈōSH, -ˈôSH/ ▶ **noun** a small, round, sweet French roll.
– ORIGIN French.

bri·quette /briˈket/ (also **briquet**) ▶ **noun** a block of compressed coal dust or peat used as fuel.
– ORIGIN French, 'small brick.'

brisk /brisk/ ▶ **adjective 1** quick, active, or lively. **2** practical and efficient: *a brisk, businesslike tone.* **3** (of wind or the weather) cold but refreshing.

– SYNONYMS **1 quick,** rapid, fast, swift, speedy, hurried, energetic, lively; informal nippy. **2 no-nonsense,** businesslike, decisive, brusque, abrupt, short, sharp, curt, blunt, terse; informal snappy.
– ANTONYMS leisurely.

– DERIVATIVES **brisk·ly** adverb **brisk·ness** noun.
– ORIGIN probably from French *brusque* 'lively, fierce.'

bris·ket /ˈbriskit/ ▶ **noun** meat from the breast of a cow.
– ORIGIN perhaps from Old Norse, 'cartilage, gristle.'

bris·ling /ˈbrizliNG, ˈbris-/ ▶ **noun** (pl. same or **brislings**) a sprat, typically one smoked and canned.
– ORIGIN Norwegian and Danish.

bris·tle /ˈbrisəl/ ▶ **noun 1** a short, stiff hair on an animal's skin or a man's face. **2** a stiff animal or artificial hair, used to make a brush.

– SYNONYMS **1 hair,** whisker; (**bristles**) stubble, five o'clock shadow. **2 spine,** prickle, quill, barb.

▶ **verb 1** (of hair or fur) stand upright away from the skin. **2** react angrily or defensively. **3** (**bristle with**) be covered with or full of.

– SYNONYMS **1 rise,** stand up, stand on end. **2 take offense,** bridle, take umbrage, be offended. **3** *the island **bristles with** forts* **be crowded,** be full, be packed, be jammed, be covered, overflow; informal be thick, be chock-full.

– DERIVATIVES **bris·tly** adjective.
– ORIGIN Old English.

Brit /brit/ ▶ **noun** informal a British person.

Bri·tan·ni·a /briˈtanyə, -ˈtanēə/ ▶ **noun** a woman wearing a helmet and carrying a shield and trident, used to represent Britain.
– ORIGIN the Latin name for Britain.

Bri·tan·nic /briˈtanik/ ▶ **adjective** dated relating to Britain or the British Empire.

Brit·ish /ˈbritiSH/ ▶ **adjective** relating to Great Britain or the United Kingdom.
– DERIVATIVES **Brit·ish·ness** noun.
– ORIGIN Old English.

Brit·ish·er /ˈbritiSHər/ ▶ **noun** informal (especially in North America) a British person.

Brit·ish ther·mal u·nit ▶ **noun** a unit of heat equal to the amount of heat needed to raise 1 lb of water at maximum density through one degree Fahrenheit.

Brit·on /ˈbritn/ ▶ **noun 1** a British person. **2** a Celtic inhabitant of southern Britain before and during Roman times.
– ORIGIN Old French *Breton*.

brit·tle /ˈbritl/ ▶ **adjective 1** hard but likely to break or shatter easily. **2** sharp or artificial and showing signs of nervousness: *a brittle laugh.*

– SYNONYMS **breakable,** fragile, crisp, crumbly, delicate.
– ANTONYMS flexible.

– DERIVATIVES **brit·tle·ness** noun.
– ORIGIN related to an Old English word meaning 'break up.'

brit·tle bone dis·ease ▶ **noun** a disease in which the bones become brittle, especially osteoporosis.

bro /brō/ ▶ **noun** informal short for **BROTHER**.

broach /brōCH/ ▶ **verb 1** raise a subject for discussion. **2** pierce or open a cask or container to draw out liquid.

– SYNONYMS **bring up,** raise, introduce, mention, touch on, air.

– ORIGIN Old French *brochier*.

broad /brôd/ ▶ **adjective 1** having a distance larger than usual from side to side; wide. **2** of a particular distance wide. **3** large in area or range: *a broad expanse of water.* **4** without detail; general: *a broad outline.* **5** (of a hint) clear and unmistakable. **6** (of a regional accent) very strong.

– SYNONYMS **1 wide,** extensive, vast, immense, great, spacious, expansive, sizable, sweeping. **2 comprehensive,** inclusive, extensive, wide, all-embracing, unlimited. **3** *a broad outline* **general,** nonspecific, rough, approximate, basic, loose, vague.
– ANTONYMS narrow, limited.

▶ **noun** informal a woman.
– DERIVATIVES **broad·ly** adverb **broad·ness** noun.
– PHRASES **broad daylight** full daylight; day.
– ORIGIN Old English.

broad·band /ˈbrôd,band/ ▶ **noun** a high-capacity telecommunications technique that uses a wide range of frequencies, enabling messages to be sent simultaneously.

broad bean ▸ noun a large flat green bean.

broad-brush ▸ adjective dealing with something in a general way; lacking in detail: *a broad-brush approach to the problem*.

broad·cast /ˈbrôdˌkast/ ▸ verb (past **broadcast**; past part. **broadcast** or **broadcasted**) **1** transmit a program or information by radio or television. **2** tell something to many people. **3** scatter seeds rather than placing them in rows.

– SYNONYMS **1 transmit,** relay, air, beam, show, televise, screen. **2 report,** announce, publicize, advertise, make public, proclaim, spread, circulate, promulgate.

▸ noun a radio or television transmission.

– SYNONYMS **transmission,** program, show, telecast, production.

– DERIVATIVES **broad·cast·er** noun.

CHOOSE THE RIGHT WORD

See **SCATTER**.

broad·cloth /ˈbrôdˌklôTH/ ▸ noun a fine wool or cotton cloth.

broad·en /ˈbrôdn/ ▸ verb make or become broader.

– SYNONYMS **1** *her smile broadened* **widen,** expand, stretch (out), spread. **2** *the government tried to broaden its political base* **expand,** enlarge, extend, widen, swell, increase, add to, develop.
– ANTONYMS narrow, restrict.

broad gauge ▸ noun a railroad gauge that is wider than the standard gauge of 4 ft. 8½ in. (1.435 m.).

broad·leaved /ˈbrôdˌlēvd/ (also **broadleaf** /ˈbrôdˌlēf/) ▸ adjective (of trees or herbaceous plants) having relatively wide flat leaves, as opposed to conifers or grasses.

broad·loom /ˈbrôdˌlo͞om/ ▸ noun carpet woven in wide widths.

broad-mind·ed ▸ adjective tolerant of views or behavior different from one's own; not easily offended.

– SYNONYMS **liberal,** tolerant, freethinking, indulgent, progressive, permissive, unshockable, unprejudiced, unbiased.
– ANTONYMS intolerant.

broad·sheet /ˈbrôdˌSHēt/ ▸ noun **1** a newspaper with a large format. **2** another term for **BROADSIDE**.

broad·side /ˈbrôdˌsīd/ ▸ noun **1** a strongly worded critical attack. **2** historical a firing of all the guns from one side of a warship. **3** the side of a ship above the water between the bow and quarter. **4** a large sheet of paper printed on one side only.
– PHRASES **broadside on** sideways on.

broad-spec·trum ▸ adjective referring to antibiotics, pesticides, etc., effective against a large variety of organisms.

broad·sword /ˈbrôdˌsôrd/ ▸ noun a sword with a wide blade, used for cutting rather than thrusting.

Brob·ding·nag·i·an /ˌbräbdiNGˈnagēən/ ▸ adjective gigantic.
– ORIGIN from *Brobdingnag*, a land in *Gulliver's Travels* where everything is of huge size.

bro·cade /brōˈkād/ ▸ noun a rich fabric woven with a raised pattern, usually with gold or silver thread.
– DERIVATIVES **bro·cad·ed** adjective.
– ORIGIN Spanish and Portuguese *brocado*.

broc·co·li /ˈbräk(ə)lē/ ▸ noun a vegetable with heads of small green or purplish flower buds.
– ORIGIN Italian.

bro·chette /brōˈSHet/ ▸ noun a dish of meat or fish chunks barbecued, grilled, or roasted on a skewer.
– ORIGIN French, 'little skewer.'

bro·chure /brōˈSHo͝or/ ▸ noun a small book or pamphlet containing pictures and information about a product or service.

– SYNONYMS **booklet,** prospectus, catalog, pamphlet, leaflet, circular, mailer.

– ORIGIN French, 'something stitched.'

bro·de·rie an·glaise /ˌbrōdəˈrē äNGˈglez, -ˈglāz/ ▸ noun open embroidery on fine white cotton or linen.
– ORIGIN French, 'English embroidery.'

brogue /brōg/ ▸ noun **1** a strong outdoor shoe with perforated patterns in the leather. **2** a noticeable accent, especially Irish or Scottish, when speaking English.
– ORIGIN Scottish Gaelic and Irish *bróg*.

broil /broil/ ▸ verb cook meat or fish using direct heat, especially heat that radiates downward.
– ORIGIN Old French *bruler* 'to burn.'

broil·er /ˈbroilər/ ▸ noun **1** a young chicken suitable for roasting, broiling, or barbecuing. **2** a frame or device used for cooking meat or fish with direct radiant heat, especially the broiling unit in an oven.

broke /brōk/ past (and old-fashioned past participle) of **BREAK** ▸ adjective informal having no money.
– PHRASES **go for broke** informal risk everything in one determined effort.

bro·ken /ˈbrōkən/ past participle of **BREAK** ▸ adjective (of a language) spoken hesitantly and with many mistakes, as by a foreigner.

– SYNONYMS **1 smashed,** shattered, fragmented, splintered, crushed, snapped, in bits, in pieces, cracked, split, fractured; informal in smithereens. **2 faulty,** damaged, defective, not working, malfunctioning, out of order, broken down, down; informal kaput, bust, acting up. **3 interrupted,** disturbed, fitful, disrupted, discontinuous, intermittent. **4 halting,** hesitating, disjointed, faltering, imperfect.

– DERIVATIVES **bro·ken·ly** adverb **bro·ken·ness** noun.

bro·ken-down ▸ adjective **1** worn out and in a bad condition. **2** not working.

bro·ken-heart·ed ▸ adjective overwhelmed by grief or disappointment.

– SYNONYMS **heartbroken,** grief-stricken, desolate, devastated, inconsolable, miserable, wretched, forlorn, heavy-hearted, woeful.
– ANTONYMS overjoyed.

bro·ken home ▸ noun a family in which the parents are divorced or separated.

bro·ker /ˈbrōkər/ ▸ noun a person who buys and sells goods or assets for other people.

– SYNONYMS **dealer,** agent, middleman, intermediary, mediator, factor, liaison, stockbroker.

▸ verb arrange or negotiate a deal or plan.

– SYNONYMS **arrange,** organize, orchestrate, work out, settle, clinch, negotiate, mediate.

– DERIVATIVES **bro·ker·age** noun.
– ORIGIN Old French *brocour.*

bro·me·li·ad /brō'mēlē,ad/ ▶ **noun** a member of a family of tropical American plants.
– ORIGIN named after the Swedish botanist Olaf *Bromel.*

bro·mide /'brōmīd/ ▶ **noun 1** a compound of bromine with another chemical element or group. **2** dated a preparation containing potassium bromide, used as a sedative. **3** an unoriginal idea or remark.

bro·mine /'brōmēn/ ▶ **noun** a dark red liquid chemical element of the halogen group, with a strong, irritating smell.
– ORIGIN from Greek *brōmos* 'a stink.'

bron·chi /'bränGkī, -kē/ plural of **BRONCHUS**.

bron·chi·al /'bränGkēəl/ ▶ **adjective** relating to the bronchi or bronchioles.

bron·chi·ole /'bränGkē,ōl/ ▶ **noun** any of the minute branches into which the bronchi in the lungs divide.
– ORIGIN Latin *bronchiolus.*

bron·chi·tis /bräNG'kītis/ ▶ **noun** inflammation of the mucous membrane in the bronchial tubes.
– DERIVATIVES **bron·chit·ic** /bräNG'kitik/ adjective & noun.

bron·chus /'bränGkəs/ ▶ **noun** (pl. **bronchi** /-kī, -kē/) any of the major air passages of the lungs that spread out from the windpipe.
– ORIGIN Greek *bronkhos* 'windpipe.'

bron·co /'bränGkō/ ▶ **noun** (pl. **broncos**) a wild or half-tamed horse of the western US.
– ORIGIN from Spanish, 'rough, rude.'

bron·to·sau·rus /,bräntə'sôrəs/ ▶ **noun** former term for **APATOSAURUS**.
– ORIGIN from Greek *brontē* 'thunder' + *sauros* 'lizard.'

bronze /bränz/ ▶ **noun 1** a yellowish-brown alloy of copper and tin. **2** a yellowish-brown color. **3** an object made of bronze. ▶ **verb** make a person or part of the body suntanned.
– DERIVATIVES **bronz·y** adjective.
– ORIGIN Italian *bronzo.*

Bronze Age ▶ **noun** a historical period that followed the Stone Age and preceded the Iron Age, when tools were made of bronze.

bronze med·al ▶ **noun** a medal made of or colored bronze, awarded for third place in a race or competition.

brooch /brōCH, brōōCH/ ▶ **noun** an ornament fastened to clothing with a hinged pin and catch.
– ORIGIN Old French *broche* 'spit for roasting.'

brood /brōōd/ ▶ **noun 1** a family of young animals produced at one hatching or birth. **2** informal all the children in a family.

– SYNONYMS **offspring,** young, family, litter, clutch, progeny.

▶ **verb 1** think deeply about an unpleasant subject. **2** (as adj. **brooding**) mysterious or menacing: *the dark, brooding atmosphere.* **3** (of a bird) sit on eggs to hatch them.

– SYNONYMS **think,** ponder, contemplate, meditate, ruminate, muse, worry, dwell on, fret, agonize.

▶ **adjective** (of an animal) kept for breeding: *a brood mare.*
– ORIGIN Old English.

brood·y /'brōōdē/ ▶ **adjective** (**broodier, broodiest**) **1** (of a hen) wanting to lay or sit on eggs. **2** informal (of a woman) wanting very much to have a baby. **3** thoughtful and unhappy.
– DERIVATIVES **brood·i·ly** adverb **brood·i·ness** noun.

brook[1] /brŏŏk/ ▶ **noun** a small stream.

– SYNONYMS **stream,** creek, streamlet, rivulet, rill.

– ORIGIN Old English.

brook[2] ▶ **verb** formal tolerate or allow: *she would brook no criticism.*

– SYNONYMS **tolerate,** allow, stand, bear, abide, put up with, endure; accept, permit, countenance; informal stomach, hack.

– ORIGIN Old English 'use, possess' (later 'digest, stomach').

brook trout ▶ **noun** a freshwater fish of the salmon family, common throughout much of N America and popular with anglers.

broom /brōōm, brŏŏm/ ▶ **noun 1** a long-handled brush used for sweeping. **2** a shrub with many yellow flowers and small or few leaves.
– ORIGIN Old English.

broom·stick /'brōōm,stik, 'brŏŏm-/ ▶ **noun** a brush with twigs at one end and a long handle, on which witches are said to fly.

Bros. ▶ **plural noun** brothers (in names of companies).

broth /bräTH, brôTH/ ▶ **noun** soup made from meat or vegetables cooked in stock.
– ORIGIN Old English.

broth·el /'bräTHəl, 'brôTHəl/ ▶ **noun** a house where men visit prostitutes.

– SYNONYMS **whorehouse,** bordello. informal cathouse; euphemistic massage parlor. old use bawdy house, house of ill repute.

– ORIGIN related to an Old English word meaning 'deteriorate.'

broth·er /'brəTHər/ ▶ **noun 1** a man or boy in relation to other children of his parents. **2** a male associate or fellow member of an organization. **3** (pl. also **brethren**) a (male) fellow Christian. **4** a member of a religious order of men: *a Benedictine brother.*
– ORIGIN Old English.

broth·er·hood /'brəTHər,hŏŏd/ ▶ **noun 1** the relationship between brothers. **2** a feeling of fellowship and understanding. **3** a group of people linked by a shared interest or belief: *a religious brotherhood.*

broth·er-in-law ▶ **noun** (pl. **brothers-in-law**) **1** the brother of one's wife or husband. **2** the husband of one's sister or sister-in-law.

broth·er·ly /'brəTHərlē/ ▶ **adjective 1** relating to a brother. **2** kind and affectionate.

– SYNONYMS **1** *brotherly rivalry* **fraternal,** sibling. **2** *brotherly love* **friendly,** comradely, affectionate, amicable, kind, devoted, loyal.

brought /brôt/ past and past participle of **BRING**.

USAGE

Do not confuse **bought** and **brought**. **Bought** is the past tense and past participle of **buy** (*she bought a bar of chocolate*), whereas **brought** is the past tense and past participle of **bring** (*the article brought a massive response*).

brou·ha·ha /ˈbro͞ohäˌhä, bro͞oˈhähä/ ▶ **noun** a noisy and overexcited reaction.
– ORIGIN French.

brow /brou/ ▶ **noun 1** a person's forehead. **2** an eyebrow. **3** the summit of a hill or pass.

– SYNONYMS **1 forehead,** temple. **2 summit,** peak, top, crest, crown, head, pinnacle, apex.

– ORIGIN Old English.

brow·beat /ˈbrouˌbēt/ ▶ **verb** (past **browbeat**; past part. **browbeaten**) bully or intimidate someone by using stern or abusive words.

– SYNONYMS **bully,** intimidate, force, coerce, compel, dragoon, bludgeon, pressure, pressurize, tyrannize, terrorize; informal bulldoze, railroad.

brown /broun/ ▶ **adjective 1** of a color produced by mixing red, yellow, and blue, as of dark wood or rich soil. **2** dark-skinned or suntanned.

– SYNONYMS **1** hazel, chestnut, chocolate, coffee, brunette, sepia, mahogany, tan, café au lait, caramel. **2 tanned,** suntanned, bronzed, swarthy.

▶ **noun** brown color or material.
▶ **verb** make or become brown by cooking.

– SYNONYMS **grill,** toast, singe, sear, barbecue, sauté.

– DERIVATIVES **brown·ish** adjective **brown·y** adjective.
– ORIGIN Old English.

brown bear ▶ **noun** a large bear with a coat color ranging from cream to black.

brown belt ▶ **noun** a brown belt marking a level of skill below that of a black belt in judo, karate, or other martial arts.

brown coal ▶ **noun** lignite.

brown dwarf ▶ **noun** Astronomy a celestial object midway in size between a large planet and a small star.

brown·field /ˈbrounˌfēld/ ▶ **adjective** (of an urban site) having been previously built on. Compare with **GREENFIELD**.

brown goods ▶ **plural noun** television sets, audio equipment, and similar household appliances. Compare with **WHITE GOODS**.

Brown·i·an mo·tion /ˈbrounēən/ ▶ **noun** Physics the erratic movement of microscopic particles in a fluid, as a result of collisions with the surrounding molecules.
– ORIGIN named after the Scottish botanist Robert *Brown*.

Brown·ie /ˈbrounē/ ▶ **noun** (pl. **Brownies**) **1** a member of the junior branch of the Girl Scouts. **2** (**brownie**) a small square of rich chocolate cake. **3** (**brownie**) a kind elf that supposedly does housework secretly.
– PHRASES **brownie point** informal an imaginary good mark given for an attempt to please someone.

brown-nose ▶ **noun** (also **brown-noser**) informal a person who behaves in a very servile or ingratiating way toward someone in an attempt to gain their approval.

brown·out /ˈbrounˌout/ ▶ **noun** a partial blackout.

brown rice ▶ **noun** unpolished rice with only the husk of the grain removed.

Brown·shirt /ˈbrounˌsʜərt/ ▶ **noun** a member of a Nazi military force founded by Hitler in 1921 and suppressed in 1934, with brown uniforms.

brown·stone /ˈbrounˌstōn/ ▶ **noun 1** a kind of reddish-brown sandstone used for building. **2** a building faced with this kind of sandstone.

brown sug·ar ▶ **noun** unrefined or partially refined sugar.

brown trout ▶ **noun** (pl. same) the common trout of European lakes and rivers, typically with dark spotted skin.

browse /brouz/ ▶ **verb 1** look at goods or text in a leisurely way. **2** read or look at computer files via a network. **3** (of an animal) feed on leaves, twigs, etc.

– SYNONYMS ***browsing through** the want ads* **look through,** scan (through), skim (through), glance through, peruse, thumb through, leaf through, flick through, dip into.

▶ **noun** an act of browsing.
– DERIVATIVES **brows·a·ble** adjective.
– ORIGIN from Old French *brost* 'young shoot.'

brows·er /ˈbrouzər/ ▶ **noun 1** a person or animal that browses. **2** a computer program used to navigate the World Wide Web.

bru·cel·lo·sis /ˌbro͞osəˈlōsis/ ▶ **noun** a disease caused by a bacterium, which chiefly affects cattle.
– ORIGIN from *Brucella*, the name of the bacterium responsible.

bruise /bro͞oz/ ▶ **noun 1** an area of discolored skin on the body, caused by a blow or impact that bursts underlying blood vessels. **2** a similar area of damage on a fruit, vegetable, or plant.

– SYNONYMS **contusion,** bump, swelling, lump, mark, injury, welt.

▶ **verb 1** inflict a bruise on someone or something. **2** develop a bruise.

– SYNONYMS **contuse,** injure, mark, discolor, make black and blue, blemish, damage, spoil.

– ORIGIN Old English.

bruis·er /ˈbro͞ozər/ ▶ **noun** informal, derogatory a tough, aggressive person.

bruis·ing /ˈbro͞oziɴɢ/ ▶ **adjective** conducted in an aggressive way and likely to be stressful: *a bruising cabinet battle over public spending.* ▶ **noun** bruises on the skin.

bruit /bro͞ot/ ▶ **verb** spread a story or rumor widely.
– ORIGIN Old French *bruire* 'to roar.'

brume /bro͞om/ ▶ **noun** literary mist or fog.
– ORIGIN French, from Latin *bruma* 'winter.'

brunch /brənʜ/ ▶ **noun** a late morning meal eaten instead of breakfast and lunch.

Bru·nei·an /bro͞oˈnīən/ ▶ **noun** a person from the sultanate of Brunei. ▶ **adjective** relating to Brunei.

bru·nette /bro͞oˈnet/ (also **brunet**) ▶ **noun** a woman or girl with dark brown hair.
– ORIGIN from French *brun* 'brown.'

brunt /brənt/ ▶ **noun** the chief impact of something bad or unwelcome: *the island bore the brunt of the storm.*
– ORIGIN unknown.

bru·schet·ta /bro͞oˈsketə/ ▶ **noun** toasted Italian bread drizzled with olive oil and often topped with tomatoes or other ingredients.
– ORIGIN Italian.

brush[1] /brəsʜ/ ▶ **noun 1** an implement with a handle and a block of bristles, hair, or wire, used especially for cleaning, smoothing, or painting. **2** an act of brushing. **3** a brief encounter with something bad or unwelcome:

a brush with death. **4** the bushy tail of a fox. **5** a piece of carbon or metal serving as an electrical contact with a moving part in a motor or alternator.

– SYNONYMS **1** hairbrush, toothbrush, paintbrush, scrub brush, whisk broom. **2** *give it a brush* **sweep,** wipe, dust. **3** *a brush with the law* **encounter,** clash, confrontation, conflict, altercation, incident; informal run-in, to-do.

▶ **verb 1** clean, smooth, or apply with a brush. **2** touch something lightly. **3** (**brush someone/thing off** (or **aside**)) dismiss someone or something in an abrupt way: *he brushed aside their questions.* **4** (**brush up on something**) work to improve a skill that has not been used for some time.

– SYNONYMS **1** *brush your hair* **groom,** comb, neaten, tidy, smooth, arrange. **2** *his lips brushed her cheek* **touch,** stroke, caress, skim, sweep, graze, contact, kiss. **3** (**brush someone/thing off** (or **aside**)) **disregard,** ignore, dismiss, shrug off, wave aside, reject, spurn, laugh off, make light of; informal pooh-pooh. **4** (**brush up on something**) **relearn,** read up on, go over, study, improve, polish up, refine, hone, perfect; informal bone up on.

– ORIGIN Old French *broisse.*

brush² ▶ **noun** undergrowth, small trees, and shrubs.

– SYNONYMS **undergrowth,** scrub, underbrush, chaparral, brushwood, shrubs, bushes.

– ORIGIN Old French *broce.*

brushed /brəsʜt/ ▶ **adjective 1** (of fabric) having a soft raised nap. **2** (of metal) finished with a nonreflective surface.

brush-off ▶ **noun** informal a rejection or dismissal.

brush·stroke /ˈbəsʜˌstrōk/ ▶ **noun** a mark made by a paintbrush drawn across a surface.

brush·wood /ˈbrəsʜˌwo͝od/ ▶ **noun** undergrowth, twigs, and small branches.

brush·work /ˈbrəsʜˌwərk/ ▶ **noun** the way in which a painter uses a brush.

brusque /brəsk/ ▶ **adjective** abrupt or offhand in manner or speech.

– SYNONYMS **curt,** abrupt, blunt, short, sharp, brisk, peremptory, gruff, discourteous, impolite, rude.
– ANTONYMS polite.

– DERIVATIVES **brusque·ly** adverb **brusque·ness** noun.
– ORIGIN French, 'lively, fierce,' from Italian *brusco* 'sour.'

CHOOSE THE RIGHT WORD

brusque, blunt, bluff, curt, gruff, surly

Brusque, which comes from an Italian word meaning rude, describes an abruptness of speech or manner that is not necessarily meant to be rude (*a brusque handshake ; a brusque reply*). **Curt** is more deliberately unfriendly, suggesting brevity and coldness of manner (*a curt dismissal*). There's nothing wrong with being **blunt**, although it implies an honesty and directness that can border on tactlessness (*a blunt reply to his question about where the money went*). Someone who is **bluff** is usually more likable, possessing a frank, hearty manner that may be a little too outspoken but is seldom offensive (*a bluff man who rarely minced words*). Exhibiting **gruff** or **surly** behavior will not win friends, since both words suggest bad temper if not rudeness. But *gruff* is used to describe a rough or grouchy disposition and, like *bluff*, is applied more often to a man. Anyone who has had to deal with an overworked store clerk while shopping during the holidays knows the meaning of *surly*, which is worse than *gruff*. It describes not only a sour disposition but an outright hostility toward people, and it can apply to someone of either sex (*that surly woman at the customer service desk*).

Brus·sels sprout /ˈbrəsəlz/ (also **Brussel sprout** /ˈbrəsəl/) ▶ **noun** the bud of a variety of cabbage, eaten as a vegetable.

brut /bro͞ot/ ▶ **adjective** (of sparkling wine) very dry.
– ORIGIN French, 'raw, rough.'

bru·tal /ˈbro͞otl/ ▶ **adjective 1** savagely violent. **2** not attempting to disguise something unpleasant: *he replied with brutal honesty.*

– SYNONYMS **savage,** violent, cruel, vicious, ferocious, barbaric, wicked, murderous, bloodthirsty, cold-blooded, callous, ruthless, heartless, merciless, sadistic, inhuman.
– ANTONYMS gentle.

– DERIVATIVES **bru·tal·i·ty** /bro͞oˈtalitē/ noun **bru·tal·ly** adverb.

bru·tal·ism /ˈbro͞otlˌizəm/ ▶ **noun 1** cruelty and savagery. **2** a stark style of architecture that makes use of massive blocks of steel and concrete.

bru·tal·ize /ˈbro͞otlˌīz/ ▶ **verb 1** make someone cruel, violent, or callous by repeatedly exposing them to violence. **2** treat someone in a violent way.
– DERIVATIVES **bru·tal·i·za·tion** /ˈbro͞otliˈzāsʜən/ noun.

brute /bro͞ot/ ▶ **noun 1** a violent or savage person or animal. **2** informal a cruel or insensitive person.

– SYNONYMS **1 savage,** beast, monster, animal, barbarian, fiend, ogre; sadist; thug, lout, ruffian; informal swine, pig. **2** *the Alsatian was a vicious-looking brute* **animal,** beast, creature; N. Amer. informal critter.

▶ **adjective 1** involving physical strength alone, rather than thought or intelligence: *brute force.* **2** unpleasant and inescapable: *the brute facts of the human condition.*

– SYNONYMS *brute strength* **physical,** bodily; crude, violent.

– DERIVATIVES **brut·ish** adjective.
– ORIGIN Latin *brutus* 'dull, stupid.'

bry·o·ny /ˈbrīənē/ ▶ **noun** (pl. **bryonies**) a climbing plant with red berries.
– ORIGIN Greek *bruōnia.*

bry·o·phyte /ˈbrīəˌfīt/ ▶ **noun** any of a division of small, simple plants that comprises the mosses and liverworts.
– ORIGIN from Greek *bruon* 'moss' + *phuta* 'plants.'

bry·o·zo·an /ˌbrīəˈzōən/ ▶ **noun** any of a group of sedentary aquatic invertebrates.
– ORIGIN from Greek *bruon* 'moss' + *zōia* 'animals.'

BS ▶ **abbreviation 1** Bachelor of Science. **2** vulgar slang bullshit.

BSE ▶ **abbreviation** bovine spongiform encephalopathy, a fatal disease of cattle that affects the central nervous system and is believed to be related to Creutzfeldt–Jakob disease in humans.

B-side ▶ **noun** the side of a pop single regarded as the less important one.

Btu (also **BTU**) ▶ **abbreviation** British thermal unit(s).

btw ▶ **abbreviation** by the way.

bub·ble /ˈbəbəl/ ▶ **noun 1** a thin sphere of liquid enclosing air or another gas. **2** an air- or gas-filled spherical cavity in a liquid or a solidified liquid such as glass. **3** a transparent cover or enclosure in the shape of

a dome. ▶ **verb 1** (of a liquid) contain rising bubbles of air or gas. **2** (**bubble with**) be filled with an irrepressible feeling: *she was bubbling with excitement.*
– ORIGIN imitating the sound of bubbling.

bub·ble bath ▶ **noun** sweet-smelling liquid added to bathwater to make it foam.

bub·ble·gum /ˈbəbəlˌgəm/ ▶ **noun** chewing gum that can be blown into bubbles.

bub·ble wrap ▶ **noun** trademark protective plastic packaging in the form of sheets containing numerous small air pockets.

bub·bly /ˈbəb(ə)lē/ ▶ **adjective** (**bubblier, bubbliest**) **1** containing bubbles. **2** cheerful and high-spirited.

> – SYNONYMS **1 fizzy,** sparkling, effervescent, gassy, aerated, carbonated, frothy, foamy. **2 vivacious,** animated, ebullient, lively, high-spirited, bouncy, merry, happy, cheerful, sunny; informal chirpy.
> – ANTONYMS still.

▶ **noun** informal champagne.

bu·bo /ˈb(y)o͞obō/ ▶ **noun** (pl. **buboes**) a swollen inflamed lymph node in the armpit or groin.
– DERIVATIVES **bu·bon·ic** /b(y)o͞oˈbänik/ adjective.
– ORIGIN Greek *boubōn.*

bu·bon·ic plague ▶ **noun** a form of plague transmitted by rat fleas, causing swellings (buboes) in the groin or armpits.

buc·cal /ˈbəkəl/ ▶ **adjective** technical relating to the cheek or mouth.
– ORIGIN from Latin *bucca* 'cheek.'

buc·ca·neer /ˌbəkəˈni(ə)r/ ▶ **noun 1** historical a pirate, originally one operating in the Caribbean. **2** a recklessly adventurous and unscrupulous person.
– DERIVATIVES **buc·ca·neer·ing** adjective.
– ORIGIN French *boucanier.*

buck[1] /bək/ ▶ **noun 1** the male of some animals, e.g., deer and rabbits. **2** a vertical jump performed by a horse, with the back arched and the back legs thrown out behind. **3** old use a fashionable young man. ▶ **verb 1** (of a horse) perform a buck. **2** resist or go against: *utility shares bucked the trend and rallied.* **3** (**buck someone up** or **buck up**) informal make or become more cheerful.
– ORIGIN Old English.

buck[2] ▶ **noun** informal a dollar.
– ORIGIN unknown.

buck[3] ▶ **noun** an object placed in front of a poker player whose turn it is to deal.
– PHRASES **the buck stops here** informal the responsibility for something cannot be avoided. **pass the buck** informal shift responsibility to someone else.
– ORIGIN unknown.

buck·a·roo /ˌbəkəˈro͞o/ ▶ **noun** dated or humorous a cowboy.
– ORIGIN alteration of **VAQUERO**.

buck·board /ˈbəkˌbôrd/ ▶ **noun** an open horse-drawn carriage with four wheels and seating that is attached to a plank between the front and rear axles.
– ORIGIN from *buck* 'body of a cart' + **BOARD**.

buck·et /ˈbəkit/ ▶ **noun 1** a cylindrical open container with a handle, used to carry liquids. **2** (**buckets**) informal large quantities of liquid. **3** a scoop on a dredger, or one attached to the front of a digger or tractor. ▶ **verb** (**buckets, bucketing, bucketed**) (**bucket down**) Brit. informal rain heavily.
– DERIVATIVES **buck·et·ful** noun.
– ORIGIN Old French *buquet.*

buck·et·load /ˈbəkitˌlōd/ ▶ **noun** informal a large amount or number.

buck·et seat ▶ **noun** a vehicle seat with a rounded back to fit one person.

buck·eye /ˈbəkˌī/ ▶ **noun 1** a North American tree or shrub related to the horse chestnut, with showy yellow, red, or white flowers. **2** (**Buckeye**) a native of Ohio.

buck·le /ˈbəkəl/ ▶ **noun** a flat frame with a hinged pin, used for fastening a belt or strap.

> – SYNONYMS **clasp,** clip, catch, hasp, fastener.

▶ **verb 1** fasten a belt or strap with a buckle. **2** bend and give way under pressure. **3** (**buckle down**) tackle a task with determination.

> – SYNONYMS **1 fasten,** do up, hook, secure, clasp, clip. **2 bend,** warp, twist, distort, contort, deform, crumple, collapse, give way.

– ORIGIN Latin *buccula* 'cheek strap of a helmet'; sense 2 is from French *boucler* 'to bulge.'

buck na·ked ▶ **adjective** informal completely naked.

buck·ram /ˈbəkrəm/ ▶ **noun** coarse linen or other cloth stiffened with paste, used in bookbinding.
– ORIGIN Old French *boquerant.*

buck·shot /ˈbəkˌsʜät/ ▶ **noun** coarse lead shot used in shotgun shells.

buck·skin /ˈbəkˌskin/ ▶ **noun 1** soft leather made from the skin of deer or sheep. **2** (**buckskins**) clothes or shoes made from buckskin. **3** thick smooth cotton or woolen fabric.

buck teeth ▶ **plural noun** upper teeth that project over the lower lip.
– DERIVATIVES **buck-toothed** adjective.

buck·thorn /ˈbəkˌᴛʜôrn/ ▶ **noun** a thorny shrub or small tree that bears black berries.

buck·wheat /ˈbəkˌ(h)wēt/ ▶ **noun** a plant producing starchy seeds used for animal fodder or milled into flour.
– ORIGIN Dutch *boecweite* 'beech wheat,' its grains being shaped like the nuts of the beech tree.

bu·col·ic /byo͞oˈkälik/ ▶ **adjective** relating to country life.
– ORIGIN from Greek *boukolos* 'herdsman.'

bud[1] /bəd/ ▶ **noun 1** a growth on a plant that develops into a leaf, flower, or shoot. **2** Biology an outgrowth from an organism that separates to form a new individual without sexual reproduction taking place. ▶ **verb** (**buds, budding, budded**) form a bud or buds.
– ORIGIN unknown.

bud[2] ▶ **noun** informal a companion or friend: *Johnson and Rooney are buds.*
– ORIGIN abbreviation of *buddy.*

Bud·dhism /ˈbo͞odizəm, ˈbo͝od-/ ▶ **noun** a religion or philosophy, founded by Siddartha Gautama (Buddha; *c.*563–*c.*483 BC), that teaches that enlightenment may be reached by the elimination of earthly desires.
– DERIVATIVES **Bud·dhist** noun & adjective.

bud·ding /ˈbədiɴɢ/ ▶ **adjective** beginning to develop and showing signs of promise or success: *their budding relationship.*

> – SYNONYMS **promising,** up-and-coming, rising, in the making, aspiring, future, fledgling, developing.

bud·dle·ia /ˈbədlēə, bədˈlēə/ ▶ **noun** a shrub with clusters of lilac, white, or yellow flowers.
– ORIGIN named after the English botanist Adam *Buddle.*

bud·dy /'bədē/ ▶ **noun** (pl. **buddies**) informal a close friend.
– ORIGIN perhaps an alteration of **BROTHER**.

budge /bəj/ ▶ **verb** **1** make or cause to make the slightest movement. **2** change or cause to change an opinion.

– SYNONYMS **1 move,** shift, stir, go. **2 persuade,** convince, influence, sway, bend.

– ORIGIN French *bouger* 'to stir.'

budg·et /'bəjit/ ▶ **noun** **1** an estimate of income and expenditure for a set period of time. **2** the amount of money needed or available for a particular purpose: *a $1 million advertising budget.* **3** a regular estimate of national or state income and expenditure put forward by a government.

– SYNONYMS **1 financial plan,** forecast. **2** *the defense budget* **allowance,** allocation, quota, funds, resources, capital.

▶ **verb** (**budgets, budgeting, budgeted**) allow for in a budget: *they budgeted for a new roof.*

– SYNONYMS **allocate,** allot, allow, earmark, designate, set aside.

▶ **adjective** inexpensive.
– DERIVATIVES **budg·et·ar·y** adjective.
– ORIGIN Old French *bougette* 'little leather bag'; the word first referred to a pouch or wallet, and in the UK in the 18th century the Chancellor of the Exchequer, in presenting his annual statement, was said 'to open the budget.'

bu·do /'bo͞odō, 'bo͝odō/ ▶ **noun** Japanese martial arts, or the code on which they are based.
– ORIGIN Japanese.

buff[1] /bəf/ ▶ **noun** **1** a yellowish-beige color. **2** a dull yellow leather with a velvety surface. ▶ **verb** **1** polish something. **2** give a velvety finish to leather.

– SYNONYMS **polish,** burnish, shine, smooth, rub.

– PHRASES **in the buff** informal naked.
– ORIGIN probably from French *buffle* 'buffalo.'

buff[2] ▶ **noun** informal a person who is interested in and very knowledgeable about a particular subject: *a movie buff.*

– SYNONYMS **enthusiast,** fan, devotee, lover, admirer, expert, aficionado, authority; freak, nut, addict.

– ORIGIN from **BUFF**[1], first referring to enthusiastic spectators of fires in New York City, because of the firemen's buff-colored uniforms.

buf·fa·lo /'bəfə,lō/ ▶ **noun** (pl. same or **buffaloes**) **1** a heavily built wild ox with backward-curving horns. **2** the North American bison.
– ORIGIN Latin *bufalus.*

buff·er[1] /'bəfər/ ▶ **noun** **1** a person or thing that lessens the impact of something harmful or forms a barrier between adversaries: *she often had to act as a buffer between father and son.* **2** (also **buffer solution**) Chemistry a solution that resists changes in pH when acid or alkali is added to it. **3** Computing a temporary memory area or queue used when creating or editing text, or when transferring data.

– SYNONYMS **cushion,** bulwark, shield, barrier, guard, safeguard.

– ORIGIN probably from the former verb *buff* 'deaden the force of something.'

buff·er[2] ▶ **noun** Brit. informal a foolish or incompetent elderly man.
– ORIGIN probably from the former verb *buff* (see **BUFFER**[1]), or from dialect *buff* 'stutter, splutter.'

buff·er zone ▶ **noun** a neutral area serving to separate hostile forces or nations.

buf·fet[1] /bə'fā/ ▶ **noun** **1** a meal consisting of several dishes from which guests serve themselves. **2** a room or counter selling light meals or snacks. **3** a cabinet with shelves and drawers for keeping dinnerware and table linens.

– SYNONYMS **1 smorgasbord,** self-service meal, spread. **2 sideboard,** cabinet, cupboard.

– ORIGIN Old French *bufet* 'stool.'

buf·fet[2] /'bəfit/ ▶ **verb** (**buffets, buffeting, buffeted**) (especially of wind or waves) strike or push someone or something repeatedly and violently.

– SYNONYMS **batter,** pound, lash, strike, hit, beat.

▶ **noun** dated a blow.
– ORIGIN Old French *buffeter.*

buf·foon /bə'fo͞on/ ▶ **noun** a ridiculous but amusing person.
– DERIVATIVES **buf·foon·er·y** noun **buf·foon·ish** adjective.
– ORIGIN from Latin *buffo* 'clown.'

bug /bəg/ ▶ **noun** **1** a small insect. **2** informal a harmful microorganism or an illness caused by a microorganism. **3** informal an enthusiasm for something: *they caught the sailing bug.* **4** a microphone used for secret recording. **5** an error in a computer program or system.

– SYNONYMS **1 insect,** arachnid; informal creepy-crawly. **2 illness,** disease, sickness, disorder, upset, ailment, infection, virus. **3 listening device,** hidden microphone, wire, wiretap, tap. **4 fault,** error, defect, flaw, virus; informal glitch, gremlin.

▶ **verb** (**bugs, bugging, bugged**) **1** conceal a microphone in a room or telephone. **2** informal annoy or bother someone.

– SYNONYMS **eavesdrop on,** spy on, wiretap, tap, monitor.

– ORIGIN unknown.

bug·a·boo /'bəgə,bo͞o/ ▶ **noun** a cause of fear.
– ORIGIN probably Celtic.

bug·bear /'bəg,be(ə)r/ ▶ **noun** a cause of anxiety or irritation.
– ORIGIN probably from the old word *bug* 'evil spirit' + **BEAR**[2].

bug-eyed ▶ **adjective** with bulging eyes.

bug·ger /'bəgər, 'bo͝og-/ vulgar slang, chiefly Brit. ▶ **noun** **1** a person regarded with contempt or pity. **2** an annoying or awkward thing. **3** derogatory a person who commits buggery. ▶ **verb** **1** (**bugger off**) go away. **2** cause serious harm or trouble to someone or something. **3** have anal intercourse with someone. ▶ **exclamation** used to express annoyance.
– ORIGIN Old French *bougre* 'heretic.'

bug·ger·y /'bəgərē, 'bo͝og-/ ▶ **noun** anal intercourse.

bug·gy[1] /'bəgē/ ▶ **noun** (pl. **buggies**) **1** historical a light horse-drawn vehicle for one or two people. **2** short for **BABY BUGGY**. **3** a small motor vehicle with an open top; a motorized cart.
– ORIGIN unknown.

bug·gy[2] ▶ **adjective** **1** infested with bugs. **2** (of a computer program or system) faulty in operation.

bu·gle[1] /'byo͞ogəl/ ▶ **noun** a brass instrument like a small trumpet with no valves, traditionally used for military signals.
– DERIVATIVES **bu·gler** noun.

– ORIGIN Latin *buculus* 'little ox,' from *bos* 'ox': the horn of an ox was used to give signals.

bu·gle² ▶ **noun** a creeping plant with blue flowers on upright stems.
– ORIGIN Latin *bugula*.

bu·gloss /'byo͞oglôs, -läs/ ▶ **noun** a bristly plant with bright blue flowers.
– ORIGIN Greek *bouglōssos* 'ox-tongued.'

build /bild/ ▶ **verb** (past and past part. **built**) **1** construct something by putting parts or materials together. **2** (often **build up**) increase in size or intensity over time. **3** (**build on**) use something as a basis for further progress or development. **4** (**build something in/into**) incorporate something as a permanent part of a larger structure.

> – SYNONYMS **1 construct,** erect, put up, assemble, make, create, fashion, model, shape. **2** *the traffic continues to* ***build up*** **increase,** grow, mount up, intensify, strengthen. **3** *she* ***built up*** *her stamina* **boost,** strengthen, increase, improve, augment, raise, enhance, swell. **4** *I have* ***built up*** *a collection of prints* **accumulate,** amass, collect, gather.
> – ANTONYMS demolish, dismantle.

▶ **noun** the size and shape of a person's or animal's body: *a man of stocky build.*

> – SYNONYMS **physique,** frame, body, figure, form, shape, stature, proportions; informal vital statistics.

– DERIVATIVES **build·er** noun.
– ORIGIN Old English.

build·ing /'bildiNG/ ▶ **noun 1** a structure with a roof and walls. **2** the process or profession of building houses and other structures.

> – SYNONYMS **structure,** construction, edifice, pile, property, premises, establishment.

WORD LINKS

architectural *relating to building*

build·out /'bild,out/ ▶ **noun 1** the growth, development, or expansion of something: *the rapid buildout of digital technology.* **2** the state of maximum development as permitted by a plan or regulations: *concerns about water as the community approaches its buildout.* **3** the execution of a building or community development plan.

build·up /'bild,əp/ ▶ **noun 1** a gradual increase in something over a period of time. **2** a period of excitement and preparation before an event.

> – SYNONYMS **increase,** growth, expansion, enlargement, escalation, accumulation, development.

built /bilt/ past and past participle of **BUILD** ▶ **adjective** of a particular physical build: *a slightly built woman.*

built-in ▶ **adjective** included as part of a larger structure.

built-up ▶ **adjective** (of an area) covered by many buildings.

bulb /bəlb/ ▶ **noun 1** the rounded underground base of the stem of some plants, from which the roots grow. **2** a light bulb. **3** an expanded or rounded part at the end of something such as a thermometer.
– ORIGIN Greek *bolbos* 'onion.'

bul·bous /'bəlbəs/ ▶ **adjective 1** round or bulging in shape. **2** (of a plant) growing from a bulb.

> – SYNONYMS **bulging,** round, fat, rotund, swollen, distended, bloated.

Bul·gar·i·an /,bəl'ge(ə)rēən, ,bo͝ol-/ ▶ **noun 1** a person from Bulgaria. **2** the Slavic language spoken in Bulgaria. ▶ **adjective** relating to Bulgaria.

bulge /bəlj/ ▶ **noun 1** a rounded swelling on a flat surface. **2** informal a temporary increase: *a bulge in the birth rate.*

> – SYNONYMS **swelling,** bump, lump, hump, protrusion, protuberance.

▶ **verb 1** swell or stick out. **2** be full of: *a bag bulging with papers and letters.*

> – SYNONYMS **swell,** stick out, project, protrude, stand out, puff out, balloon (out), fill out, distend.

– DERIVATIVES **bulg·y** adjective.
– ORIGIN Latin *bulga* 'leather bag.'

CHOOSE THE RIGHT WORD

bulge, project, protrude, protuberate

While all of these verbs mean to extend outward, beyond the normal line or surface of something, it is almost impossible not to associate the word **bulge** with the human body (*a stomach that bulges over a waistband, muscles that bulge beneath a shirt*). *Bulge* suggests a swelling out that is quite noticeable or even abnormal, and that may be the result of internal pressure, although a brick wall can *bulge*, as can a bicep muscle. **Protuberate** is a less common word meaning to swell or stick out, but it does not necessarily imply that anything is abnormal or radically wrong (*he was so thin that his knees protuberated*). To **protrude** is to thrust forth in an unexpected way or to stick out in a way that is abnormal or disfiguring (*her eyes protruded from her skull*). **Project** is the least upsetting of all these words, probably because it is used less often with reference to the human body. Anything that juts out abruptly beyond the rest of a surface is said to *project* (*the balcony projected from the south side of the house*).

bul·gur /'bəlgər/ ▶ **noun** (also **bulgar**) a cereal food made from whole wheat partially boiled and then dried.
– ORIGIN Turkish *bulgur* 'bruised grain.'

bu·lim·i·a /bo͞o'limēə, 'lē-/ (also **bulimia nervosa** /nər'vōsə/) ▶ **noun** an emotional disorder that causes bouts of overeating, followed by fasting or self-induced vomiting.
– DERIVATIVES **bu·lim·ic** /-'limik, 'lē-/ adjective & noun.
– ORIGIN Greek *boulimia* 'ravenous hunger,' from *bous* 'ox' + *limos* 'hunger.'

bulk /bəlk/ ▶ **noun 1** the mass or size of something large. **2** the greater part of something: *the bulk of the club's supporters are well behaved.* **3** a large mass or shape. **4** roughage in food.

> – SYNONYMS **1 size,** volume, dimensions, proportions, mass, scale. **2 majority,** mass, generality, main part, lion's share, preponderance.

▶ **adjective** large in quantity: *bulk orders.*
▶ **verb** (**bulk something up/out**) treat a product so that its quantity appears greater than it really is.
– PHRASES **in bulk** (of goods) in large quantities.
– ORIGIN probably from an Old Norse word meaning 'cargo.'

bulk·head /'bəlk,hed/ ▶ **noun** a barrier between separate compartments inside a ship or aircraft.

bulk·y /'bəlkē/ ▶ **adjective** (**bulkier**, **bulkiest**) large and awkward to handle.

> – SYNONYMS **unwieldy,** cumbersome, unmanageable, awkward, ponderous, outsize, oversized; informal hulking.

WORD TOOLKIT

See **BURLY**.

bull[1] /'bo͝ol/ ▸ **noun 1** an uncastrated male animal of the cattle family. **2** a large male animal, e.g., a whale or elephant. **3** Stock Exchange a person who buys shares hoping to sell them at a higher price later. Often contrasted with **BEAR**[2].
– PHRASES **like a bull in a china shop** behaving clumsily in a delicate situation. **take the bull by the horns** deal decisively with a difficult situation.
– ORIGIN Old Norse.

bull[2] ▸ **noun** an order or announcement issued by the Pope.
– ORIGIN Latin *bulla* 'bubble,' later 'seal or sealed document.'

bull[3] ▸ **noun** informal nonsense.
– ORIGIN unknown.

bull·dog /'bo͝ol,dôg/ ▸ **noun** a breed of dog with a protruding lower jaw, a flat wrinkled face, and a broad chest.

bulldog clip ▸ **noun** trademark a metal device with two flat plates held together by a spring, used to hold papers together.

bull·doze /'bo͝ol,dōz/ ▸ **verb 1** clear ground or destroy buildings with a bulldozer. **2** informal use force to do something or deal with someone: *he bulldozed his way to his first Formula One victory.*
– ORIGIN from **BULL**[1] + *-doze*, an alteration of the noun **DOSE**.

bull·doz·er /'bo͝ol,dōzər/ ▸ **noun** a tractor with a broad curved blade at the front for clearing ground.

bul·let /'bo͝olit/ ▸ **noun 1** a projectile fired from a small firearm. **2** a solid circle printed before each item in a list.

– SYNONYMS **ball,** shot, pellet; informal slug; (**bullets**) lead.

– ORIGIN French *boulet* 'small ball.'

bul·le·tin /'bo͝olitn, -,tin/ ▸ **noun 1** a short official statement or summary of news. **2** a regular newsletter or report.

– SYNONYMS **1 report,** dispatch, story, newsflash, statement, announcement, message, communication, communiqué. **2 newsletter,** proceedings, newspaper, magazine, gazette, review.

– ORIGIN Italian *bullettino* 'little passport.'

bul·le·tin board ▸ **noun 1** a site on a computer system where users can read or download files supplied by others and add their own files. **2** a board, typically made of cork, for displaying notices, posters, etc.

bul·let·proof /'bo͝olit,pro͞of/ ▸ **adjective** able to resist the penetration of bullets.

bull·fight·ing /'bo͝ol,fītiNG/ ▸ **noun** the sport of baiting and killing a bull for public entertainment.
– DERIVATIVES **bull·fight** noun **bull·fight·er** noun.

bull·finch /'bo͝ol,finCH/ ▸ **noun** a Eurasian finch with mainly gray and black plumage, the male having a pink breast.

bull·frog /'bo͝ol,frôg, -,fräg/ ▸ **noun** a very large frog with a deep croak.

bull·head·ed /'bo͝ol,hedid/ ▸ **adjective** determined and obstinate.

bull·horn /'bo͝ol,hôrn/ ▸ **noun** a megaphone.

bul·lion /'bo͝olyən/ ▸ **noun** gold or silver in bulk before being made into coins.
– ORIGIN Old French *bouillon*.

bull·ish /'bo͝oliSH/ ▸ **adjective 1** aggressively confident and self-assertive. **2** Stock Exchange characterized or influenced by rising share prices.
– DERIVATIVES **bull·ish·ly** adverb **bull·ish·ness** noun.

bull mar·ket ▸ **noun** Stock Exchange a market in which share prices are rising.

bull-necked ▸ **adjective** (of a man) having a thick neck.

bul·lock /'bo͝olək/ ▸ **noun** a castrated male animal of the cattle family, raised for beef.
– ORIGIN Old English.

bull·pen /'bo͝ol,pen/ ▸ **noun 1** an enclosure for bulls. **2** a warm-up area for baseball pitchers. **3** the relief pitchers on a baseball team.

bull·ring /'bo͝ol,riNG/ ▸ **noun** an arena where bullfights are held.

bulls·eye /'bo͝olz,ī/ (also **bull's-eye**) ▸ **noun** the center of the target in sports such as archery and darts.

bull·shit /'bo͝ol,SHit/ vulgar slang ▸ **noun** nonsense. ▸ **verb** (**bullshits, bullshitting, bullshitted**) talk nonsense in an attempt to deceive someone.
– DERIVATIVES **bull·shit·ter** noun.

bull ter·ri·er ▸ **noun** a dog that is a crossbreed of bulldog and terrier.

bul·ly[1] /'bo͝olē/ ▸ **noun** (pl. **bullies**) a person who intimidates or persecutes weaker people.

– SYNONYMS **persecutor,** oppressor, tyrant, tormentor, intimidator, thug.

▸ **verb** (**bullies, bullying, bullied**) intimidate or persecute someone.

– SYNONYMS **1** *the others bully him* **persecute,** oppress, tyrannize, browbeat, intimidate, dominate, terrorize; informal push around/about. **2** *she was bullied into helping* **coerce,** pressure, press, push, prod, browbeat, dragoon, strong-arm; informal bulldoze, railroad, lean on.

– ORIGIN probably from Dutch *boele* 'lover.'

bul·ly[2] ▸ **noun** (pl. **bullies**) (also **bully off**) the start of play in field hockey, in which two opponents strike each other's sticks three times and then go for the ball.
– ORIGIN unknown.

bul·ly[3] ▸ **adjective** informal very good; first-rate. ▸ **exclamation** (**bully for**) an expression of admiration or approval: *he got away—bully for him.*
– ORIGIN originally of a person meaning 'admirable, gallant, jolly.'

bul·ly boy ▸ **noun** a tough or aggressive man.

bul·ly pul·pit ▸ **noun** a public office or position of authority that provides its occupant with an opportunity to speak out on any issue.
– ORIGIN apparently originally used of the presidency by Theodore Roosevelt.

bul·rush /'bo͝ol,rəSH/ (also **bullrush**) ▸ **noun** a tall waterside plant with a long brown head.
– ORIGIN probably from **BULL**[1] in the sense 'large, coarse.'

bul·wark /'bo͝ol,wərk/ ▸ **noun 1** a defensive wall. **2** a person or thing that acts as a defense: *a bulwark against fascism.* **3** an extension of a ship's sides above deck level.
– ORIGIN German and Dutch *bolwerk*.

bum[1] /bəm/ informal ▸ **noun 1** a homeless person or beggar. **2** a lazy or worthless person. ▸ **verb** (**bums, bumming, bummed**) **1** get something by asking or begging for it: *I bummed a cigarette off him.* **2** (**bum around**) travel or spend one's time with no particular aim or plan. ▸ **adjective** bad; wrong: *the first bum note she'd played all evening.*
– ORIGIN probably from **BUMMER**.

bum[2] ▸ **noun** Brit. informal a person's buttocks.
– ORIGIN unknown.

bum·ble /'bəmbəl/ ▸ **verb** move or speak in an awkward or confused way.
– ORIGIN from **BOOM**[1].

bum·ble·bee /'bəmbəl,bē/ ▸ **noun** a large hairy bee with a loud hum.

bum·mer /'bəmər/ ▸ **noun** informal an annoying or disappointing thing.
– ORIGIN perhaps from German *bummeln* 'stroll, loaf about.'

bump /bəmp/ ▸ **noun 1** a light blow or collision. **2** a hump or swelling on a level surface.

> – SYNONYMS **1 jolt,** crash, smash, smack, crack, bang, thud, thump, clang, knock, clunk, boom; informal whack, wallop. **2 swelling,** lump, bulge, injury, contusion, hump, knob.

▸ **verb 1** knock or run into someone or something with a jolt. **2** travel with a jolting movement: *the car bumped along the rutted track.* **3** (**bump into**) meet someone by chance. **4** (**bump someone off**) informal murder someone. **5** (**bump something up**) informal increase or raise something: *the company bumped up the prices.*

> – SYNONYMS **1** *their car* ***bumped into*** *our mailbox* **hit,** crash into, smash into, slam into, bang (into), knock (into), run into, plow into, ram (into), collide with, strike. **2** *a cart bumping along the road* **bounce,** jolt, jerk, rattle, shake. **3** (**bump into**) *you'll never guess who we* ***bumped into*** *at the theater* **meet,** meet by chance, encounter, run into/across, come across, happen on/upon, chance on/upon.

– ORIGIN perhaps Scandinavian.

bump·er /'bəmpər/ ▸ **noun** a horizontal bar fixed across the front or back of a motor vehicle to reduce damage in a collision. ▸ **adjective** exceptionally large or successful: *a bumper crop.*

> – SYNONYMS **exceptional,** large, abundant, rich, bountiful, good, plentiful, record, successful; informal whopping.
> – ANTONYMS meager.

bump·er car ▸ **noun** a small electrically powered car with rubber bumpers, driven within an enclosure at an amusement park with the aim of bumping other such cars.

bump·er stick·er ▸ **noun** an adhesive label carrying a slogan or advertisement, made to go on a vehicle's bumper.

bump·kin /'bəmpkin/ ▸ **noun** an unsophisticated person from the countryside.
– ORIGIN perhaps from Dutch *boomken* 'little tree' or *bommekijn* 'little barrel.'

bump·tious /'bəmpsHəs/ ▸ **adjective** irritatingly confident or self-important.
– DERIVATIVES **bump·tious·ly** adverb **bump·tious·ness** noun.
– ORIGIN from **BUMP**.

> **CHOOSE THE RIGHT WORD**
>
> See **BOLD**.

bump·y /'bəmpē/ ▸ **adjective** (**bumpier, bumpiest**) **1** (of a surface) uneven. **2** (of a journey) involving sudden jolts and jerks.

> – SYNONYMS **1** *a bumpy road* **uneven,** rough, rutted, pitted, potholed, lumpy, rocky. **2** *a bumpy ride* **bouncy,** rough, uncomfortable, jolting, lurching, jerky, jarring, bone-shaking.
> – ANTONYMS smooth.

bum rap ▸ **noun** informal a false charge or unfair criticism.

bun /bən/ ▸ **noun 1** a bread roll of various shapes and flavorings. **2** a hairstyle in which the hair is drawn into a tight coil at the back of the head. **3** (**buns**) informal a person's buttocks.
– PHRASES **have a bun in the oven** informal be pregnant.
– ORIGIN unknown.

bunch /bənCH/ ▸ **noun 1** a number of things growing or fastened together. **2** informal a group of people. **3** informal a lot.

> – SYNONYMS **1 bouquet,** posy, nosegay, spray, wreath, garland. **2 cluster,** clump, knot, group, bundle.

▸ **verb** collect or form into a bunch.

> – SYNONYMS **cluster,** huddle, gather, congregate, collect, amass, group, crowd.

– ORIGIN unknown.

bun·dle /'bəndl/ ▸ **noun 1** a collection of things or quantity of material tied or wrapped up together. **2** a set of nerve, muscle, or other fibers that run parallel to each other. **3** informal a large amount of money.

> – SYNONYMS **collection,** roll, clump, wad, parcel, sheaf, bale, pile, stack, heap, mass, bunch; informal load.

▸ **verb 1** tie or roll something up in a bundle. **2** (**be bundled up**) be dressed in many warm clothes. **3** informal push or carry forcibly: *they bundled him into a van.*

> – SYNONYMS **1 tie,** parcel, wrap, swathe, roll, fold, bind, pack. **2** *he was bundled into a van* **push,** shove, thrust, throw, propel, jostle, manhandle.

– ORIGIN perhaps from Old English.

Bundt cake /'bənt/ ▸ **noun** trademark a ring-shaped cake made in a fluted tube pan, called a **Bundt pan**.

bung /bəNG/ ▸ **noun** a stopper for a hole in a container. ▸ **verb 1** close a container with a bung. **2** (**bung something up**) block something up.
– ORIGIN Dutch *bonghe*.

bun·ga·low /'bəNGgə,lō/ ▸ **noun** a house with only one story.
– ORIGIN Hindi, 'belonging to Bengal.'

bun·gee /'bənjē/ (also **bungee cord** or **rope**) ▸ **noun** a long rubber band encased in nylon, used for securing luggage and in bungee jumping.
– ORIGIN unknown.

bun·gee jump·ing ▸ **noun** the sport of leaping from a high place, held by a bungee around the ankles.
– DERIVATIVES **bun·gee jump** noun **bun·gee jump·er** noun.

bun·gle /'bəNGgəl/ ▸ **verb 1** perform a task clumsily or incompetently. **2** (as adj. **bungling**) tending to make many mistakes.

> – SYNONYMS **1 mishandle,** mismanage, mess up, spoil, ruin; informal blow, botch, fluff, make a mess of, screw up, goof up. **2** (as adj. **bungling**) **incompetent,** blundering, amateurish, inept, unskillful, clumsy, awkward, bumbling; informal ham-fisted.

▸ **noun** a mistake or failure.
– DERIVATIVES **bun·gler** noun.
– ORIGIN unknown.

bun·ion /ˈbənyən/ ▸ **noun** a painful swelling on the big toe.
– ORIGIN Old French *buignon.*

bunk[1] /bəNGk/ ▸ **noun** a narrow shelflike bed.
– ORIGIN unknown.

bunk[2] ▸ **noun** informal, dated nonsense.
– ORIGIN abbreviation of **BUNKUM**.

bunk bed ▸ **noun** a piece of furniture consisting of two beds, one above the other.

bun·ker /ˈbəNGkər/ ▸ **noun 1** a large container for storing fuel. **2** an underground shelter for use in wartime. **3** a hollow filled with sand, forming an obstacle on a golf course.
– ORIGIN Scots, 'seat or bench.'

bunk·house /ˈbəNGkˌhous/ ▸ **noun** a building with sleeping accommodations for workers.

bun·kum /ˈbəNGkəm/ ▸ **noun** informal nonsense.
– ORIGIN named after *Buncombe* County in North Carolina, mentioned in a speech made by its congressman with the sole intention of pleasing his constituents (*c.*1820).

bun·ny /ˈbənē/ ▸ **noun** (pl. **bunnies**) (also **bunny rabbit**) informal a child's term for a rabbit.
– ORIGIN dialect *bun* 'squirrel, rabbit.'

Bun·sen burn·er /ˈbənsən/ ▸ **noun** a small adjustable gas burner used in laboratories.
– ORIGIN named after the German chemist Robert *Bunsen.*

bunt[1] /bənt/ ▸ **verb 1** Baseball (of a batter) gently tap a pitched ball without swinging in an attempt to make it more difficult to field. **2** (of a batter) help a base runner to progress to a further base by tapping a ball in such a way: *he bunted Davis to third.* **3** (of a person or animal) butt with the head or horns. ▸ **noun 1** Baseball an act or result of tapping a pitched ball in such a way. **2** an act of flying an aircraft in part of an outside loop.
– ORIGIN probably related to the noun **BUTT[1]**.

bunt[2] ▸ **noun** a disease of wheat caused by a smut fungus, the spores of which give off a smell of rotten fish.
– ORIGIN of unknown origin.

bunt·ing[1] /ˈbəntiNG/ ▸ **noun** a songbird with brown streaked plumage and a boldly marked head.
– ORIGIN unknown.

bunt·ing[2] ▸ **noun** flags and streamers used as decorations.
– ORIGIN unknown.

bu·oy /ˈbo͞o-ē, boi/ ▸ **noun** a floating object anchored to the seabed that marks safe navigation channels for boats.

– SYNONYMS **float,** marker, beacon.

▸ **verb 1** keep someone or something afloat. **2** make or remain cheerful and confident: *he was buoyed up by his success.*
– ORIGIN probably from Dutch *boye, boeie*; the verb is from Spanish *boyar* 'to float.'

buoy·ant /ˈboi-ənt, ˈbo͞oyənt/ ▸ **adjective 1** able to keep afloat. **2** cheerful and optimistic. **3** (of an economy or market) involved in much successful trade or activity.

– SYNONYMS **1 floating,** floatable. **2 cheerful,** cheery, happy, lighthearted, carefree, joyful, bubbly, bouncy, sunny, upbeat.
– ANTONYMS gloomy.

– DERIVATIVES **buoy·an·cy** /ˈboi-ənsē, ˈbo͞oyənsē/ noun **buoy·ant·ly** adverb.

bur /bər/ ▸ **noun** see **BURR**.

bur·ble /ˈbərbəl/ ▸ **verb 1** make a continuous murmuring noise. **2** speak at length in a way that is difficult to understand. ▸ **noun** a continuous murmuring noise.
– ORIGIN imitating the sound.

bur·bot /ˈbərbət/ ▸ **noun** a fish that is the only freshwater member of the cod family.
– ORIGIN Old French *borbete.*

bur·den /ˈbərdn/ ▸ **noun 1** a heavy load. **2** a cause of hardship, worry, or grief: *the tax burden on low-income families.* **3** the main responsibility for a task. **4** the main theme of a speech, book, or argument.

– SYNONYMS **responsibility,** onus, obligation, duty, liability, trouble, care, problem, difficulty, worry, strain.

▸ **verb 1** load someone or something heavily. **2** cause someone worry, hardship, or grief: *I don't want to burden you with my problems.*

– SYNONYMS **oppress,** trouble, worry, weigh down, overload, encumber, saddle, tax, afflict.

– PHRASES **burden of proof** the obligation to prove that something is true.
– ORIGIN Old English.

bur·den·some /ˈbərdnˈsəm/ ▸ **adjective** causing worry or difficulty.

bur·dock /ˈbərdäk/ ▸ **noun** a plant of the daisy family, with large leaves and prickly flowers.

bu·reau /ˈbyo͝orō/ ▸ **noun** (pl. **bureaux** or **bureaus** /ˈbyo͝orōz/) **1** a chest of drawers. **2** an office that carries out a particular type of business: *a news bureau.* **3** a government department. **4** Brit. a slant top desk.

– SYNONYMS **1 dresser,** chest of drawers, tallboy, highboy, cabinet. **2 department,** agency, office, division, branch, section, station, unit.

– ORIGIN French.

bu·reauc·ra·cy /byo͝oˈräkrəsē/ ▸ **noun** (pl. **bureaucracies**) **1** a system of government in which most decisions are made by bureaus and officials rather than by elected representatives. **2** administrative procedures that are too complicated.

– SYNONYMS **1 red tape,** rules and regulations, protocol, officialdom, paperwork. **2 civil service,** government, administration, establishment, system, powers that be, authorities.

bu·reau·crat /ˈbyo͝orəˌkrat/ ▸ **noun** an official in an organization or government department who is seen as being too concerned with following administrative guidelines.

– SYNONYMS **official,** administrator, civil servant, minister, functionary, mandarin; derogatory apparatchik.

– DERIVATIVES **bu·reau·crat·ic** /ˌbyo͝orəˈkratik/ adjective.

bu·reauc·ra·tize /byo͝oˈräkrəˌtīz/ ▸ **verb** run a government or organization by implementing or following administrative procedures that are too complicated.
– DERIVATIVES **bu·reauc·ra·ti·za·tion** /-ˌräkrətiˈzāSHən/ noun.

bu·reau de change /ˈbyo͝orō də ˈSHänZH/ ▸ **noun** (pl. **bureaux de change** pronunc. same) a place where foreign money can be exchanged.
– ORIGIN French, 'office of exchange.'

bu·rette /byo͝o'ret/ (also **buret**) ▶ **noun** a glass tube with measurements on it and a tap at one end, for delivering known amounts of a liquid.
– ORIGIN French.

burg /bərg/ ▶ **noun 1** informal a town or city: *a bucolic burg framed by snowcapped mountains*. **2** an ancient or medieval fortress or walled town.
– ORIGIN from German *Burg* 'castle, city.'

bur·geon /'bərjən/ ▶ **verb** grow or increase rapidly.

– SYNONYMS **grow,** increase, rocket, mushroom, expand, escalate, swell, boom, flourish, thrive, prosper.

– ORIGIN Old French *bourgeonner* 'put out buds.'

burg·er /'bərgər/ ▶ **noun** a hamburger.

bur·gess /'bərjis/ ▶ **noun** chiefly historical a person with municipal authority or privileges, such as a member of the assembly of colonial Maryland or Virginia.
– ORIGIN Old French *burgeis*.

burgh·er /'bərgər/ ▶ **noun** old use a citizen of a town or city.

bur·glar /'bərglər/ ▶ **noun** a person who commits burglary.

– SYNONYMS **robber,** thief, intruder, housebreaker, raider, looter, cat burglar.

– ORIGIN Old French *burgier* 'pillage.'

bur·glar·ize /'bərglə,rīz/ ▶ **verb** enter a building illegally with the intention of committing a crime.

bur·gla·ry /'bərglərē/ ▶ **noun** (pl. **burglaries**) the crime of entering a building illegally with the intent of stealing something inside.

– SYNONYMS **housebreaking,** breaking and entering, break-in, theft, raid, stealing, robbery, larceny, looting. informal heist.

bur·gle /'bərgəl/ ▶ **verb** chiefly Brit. burglarize.

– SYNONYMS **rob,** loot, steal from, raid.

bur·gun·dy /'bərgəndē/ ▶ **noun** (pl. **burgundies**) **1** a red wine from Burgundy, a region of east central France. **2** a deep red color.

bur·i·al /'berēəl/ ▶ **noun** the burying of a dead body.

– SYNONYMS **funeral,** interment, committal, inhumation, entombment, obsequies, exequies.
– ANTONYMS exhumation.

– ORIGIN Old English.

bu·rin /'byo͝orin/ ▶ **noun 1** a steel tool used for engraving. **2** Archaeology a flint tool with a chisel point.
– ORIGIN French.

bur·ka /'bo͝orkə/ (also **burkha** or **burqa**) ▶ **noun** a long, loose garment covering the whole body, worn in public by some Muslim women.
– ORIGIN Urdu and Persian.

Bur·ki·nan /bər'kēnən/ ▶ **noun** a person from Burkina, a country in western Africa. ▶ **adjective** relating to Burkina or its people.

burl /bərl/ ▶ **noun** a rounded knotty growth on a tree, often polished and used for handcrafted objects and veneers.

bur·lap /'bərlap/ ▶ **noun** coarse canvas woven from jute or hemp, used to make sacks.
– ORIGIN unknown.

bur·lesque /bər'lesk/ ▶ **noun 1** a performance or piece of writing that makes fun of something by representing it in a comically exaggerated way. **2** a variety show, typically including bawdy humor and striptease. ▶ **verb** (**burlesques, burlesquing, burlesqued**) make fun of someone or something by representing them in a comically exaggerated way.
– ORIGIN French.

CHOOSE THE RIGHT WORD

See **CARICATURE**.

bur·ly /'bərlē/ ▶ **adjective** (**burlier, burliest**) (of a person) large and strong.

– SYNONYMS **strapping,** well built, strong, muscular, muscly, hefty, sturdy, brawny; informal hunky, beefy.
– ANTONYMS puny.

– DERIVATIVES **bur·li·ness** noun.
– ORIGIN probably from an Old English word meaning 'stately.'

WORD TOOLKIT

burly ...	sturdy ...	bulky ...
guy	boots	sweater
security guard	legs	jacket
soldier	branch	equipment
bouncer	construction	backpack
policeman	cardboard	package
quarterback	chair	shape

Bur·man /'bərmən/ ▶ **noun** (pl. **Burmans**) & **adjective** another term for **BURMESE**.

Bur·mese /bər'mēz, -'mēs/ ▶ **noun** (pl. same) **1** a member of the largest ethnic group of Burma (now Myanmar) in SE Asia. **2** a person from Burma. **3** (also **Burmese cat**) a cat of a short-coated breed that originated in Asia. ▶ **adjective** relating to Burma or the Burmese.

burn[1] /bərn/ ▶ **verb** (past and past part. **burned** or chiefly Brit. **burnt**) **1** (of a fire) flame or glow while using up a fuel. **2** be or cause to be harmed or destroyed by fire. **3** use a fuel as a source of heat or energy. **4** (of the skin) become red and painful as a result of exposure to the sun. **5** (**be burning with**) experience a very strong desire or emotion: *she was burning with curiosity*. **6** (**burn out**) become exhausted through overwork. **7** produce a CD by copying from an original or master copy.

– SYNONYMS **1 be on fire,** be alight, blaze, go up in flames/smoke, be in flames, smolder, glow. **2 set fire to,** set alight, kindle, ignite, touch off, incinerate, cremate; informal torch. **3 scorch,** singe, sear, char, blacken, brand.

▶ **noun** an injury caused by burning.
– PHRASES **burn one's bridges** do something that makes it impossible to return to the previous situation. **burn the candle at both ends** go to bed late and get up early. **burn the midnight oil** work late into the night.
– ORIGIN Old English.

burn[2] ▶ **noun** Scottish & N. English a small stream.
– ORIGIN Old English.

burn·er /'bərnər/ ▶ **noun 1** a part of a stove, lamp, etc., that gives out a flame. **2** a heating element on a stovetop. **3** a device for burning something. **4** short for **CD BURNER**.

burn·ing /'bərniNG/ ▶ **adjective 1** very strong or deeply felt: *her burning ambition to win*. **2** of great interest and importance; requiring immediate action or attention: *the burning issues of the day*.

– SYNONYMS **1 on fire,** blazing, flaming, fiery, glowing, red-hot, smoldering. **2** *a burning desire* **intense,** passionate, deep-seated, profound, strong, ardent, fervent, urgent, fierce, consuming. **3** *burning issues* **important,** crucial, critical, vital, essential, pivotal, urgent, pressing, compelling.

– DERIVATIVES **burn·ing·ly** adverb.

bur·nish /ˈbərnisʜ/ ▶ **verb** polish something by rubbing it. ▶ **noun** the shine on a polished surface.
– ORIGIN Old French *brunir* 'make brown.'

bur·noose /bərˈnōōs/ ▶ **noun** a long hooded cloak worn by Arabs.
– ORIGIN Arabic.

burn·out /ˈbərnˌout/ ▶ **noun 1** physical or mental collapse. **2** overheating of an electrical device or component.

burn rate ▶ **noun** the rate at which an enterprise spends money, especially venture capital, in excess of income.

burnt /bərnt/ chiefly Brit. past and past participle of **BURN**[1]

burp /bərp/ informal ▶ **verb 1** belch. **2** make a baby belch after feeding. ▶ **noun** a belch.
– ORIGIN imitating the sound.

bur·qa /ˈbo͝orkə/ ▶ **noun** variant spelling of **BURKA**.

burr /bər/ ▶ **noun 1** a whirring sound. **2** a rough pronunciation of the letter *r*, as in some regional accents. **3** (also **bur**) a prickly seed case or flowerhead that clings to clothing and animal fur. **4** (also **bur**) a rough edge left on a metal object by the action of a tool. ▶ **verb** make a whirring sound.
– ORIGIN probably Scandinavian.

bur·ri·to /bəˈrētō/ ▶ **noun** (pl. **burritos**) a Mexican dish consisting of a tortilla rolled around a filling of beans or chopped or shredded beef.
– ORIGIN Latin American Spanish.

bur·ro /ˈbərō, ˈbo͝orō/ ▶ **noun** (pl. **burros**) a small donkey used as a pack animal.
– ORIGIN Spanish.

bur·row /ˈbərō/ ▶ **noun** a hole or tunnel dug by a small animal as a home.

– SYNONYMS **hole,** tunnel, warren, dugout, lair, set, den, earth.

▶ **verb 1** dig a hole or tunnel. **2** hide underneath or nestle into something. **3** search for something: *he was burrowing among his files.*

– SYNONYMS **tunnel,** dig, excavate, mine, bore, channel.

– DERIVATIVES **bur·row·er** noun.
– ORIGIN variant of **BOROUGH**.

bur·sar /ˈbərsər/ ▶ **noun** a person who manages the financial affairs of a college or university.
– ORIGIN from Latin *bursa* 'bag, purse.'

bur·si·tis /bərˈsītis/ ▶ **noun** inflammation of a bursa (fluid-filled sac), typically in a shoulder joint.
– ORIGIN from Latin *bursa* 'bag, purse.'

burst /bərst/ ▶ **verb** (past and past part. **burst**) **1** break suddenly and violently apart. **2** be very full: *her closet was bursting with clothes.* **3** move or be opened suddenly and forcibly. **4** (**be bursting with**) feel a very strong emotion or impulse. **5** suddenly begin doing or producing something: *she burst into tears.*

– SYNONYMS **1** *one balloon burst* **split (open),** rupture, break, tear. **2** *a shell burst* **explode,** blow up, detonate, go off. **3** *smoke burst through the hole* **gush,** erupt, surge, rush, stream, flow, pour, spurt, jet. **4** *he burst into the room* **charge,** plunge, barge, plow, hurtle, career, rush, dash, tear.

▶ **noun 1** an instance of bursting. **2** a sudden brief outbreak: *a burst of activity.* **3** a period of continuous effort.

– SYNONYMS **1 rupture,** puncture, breach, split, blowout. **2 explosion,** detonation, blast, eruption, bang. **3** *a burst of gunfire* **volley,** salvo, barrage, hail, rain. **4** *a burst of activity* **outbreak,** eruption, flare-up, blaze, attack, fit, rush, storm, surge, spurt.

– ORIGIN Old English.

Bu·run·di·an /bəˈro͝ondēən/ ▶ **noun** a person from Burundi, a country in central Africa. ▶ **adjective** relating to Burundi.

bur·y /ˈberē/ ▶ **verb** (**buries, burying, buried**) **1** put or hide something underground. **2** place a dead body in the earth or a tomb. **3** cover someone or something completely. **4** hide or try to ignore something: *I buried the memories for years.* **5** (**bury oneself**) involve oneself deeply in something.

– SYNONYMS **1 inter,** lay to rest, entomb. **2 hide,** conceal, cover, enfold, sink. **3** *the bullet buried itself in the wood* **embed,** sink, implant, submerge, lodge.
– ANTONYMS exhume.

– PHRASES **bury one's head in the sand** ignore unpleasant realities.
– ORIGIN Old English.

bus /bəs/ ▶ **noun** (pl. **buses** or **busses**) **1** a large motor vehicle carrying customers along a fixed route. **2** a distinct set of conductors within a computer system, to which pieces of equipment may be connected in parallel. ▶ **verb** (**buses, busing, bused**; or **busses, bussing, bussed**) **1** transport or travel in a bus. **2** clear dirty dishes in a restaurant or cafeteria.
– DERIVATIVES **bus·load** noun.
– ORIGIN shortening of **OMNIBUS**.

bus·boy /ˈbəsˌboi/ ▶ **noun** a young man who clears tables in a restaurant or cafeteria.

bus·by /ˈbəzbē/ ▶ **noun** (pl. **busbies**) a tall fur hat worn by certain military regiments.
– ORIGIN unknown.

bush /bo͝osʜ/ ▶ **noun 1** a shrub or clump of shrubs with stems of moderate length. **2** (**the bush**) (in Australia and Africa) wild or uncultivated country. **3** a thick growth of hair.

– SYNONYMS **1 shrub,** thicket; (**bushes**) undergrowth, shrubbery. **2** (**the bush**) **wilds,** wilderness, backwoods, backcountry; Austral. outback; informal boondocks, boonies.

– ORIGIN Old French *bois* 'wood.'

bush·ba·by /ˈbo͝osʜˌbābē/ ▶ **noun** (pl. **bushbabies**) a small African mammal with very large eyes.

bushed /bo͝osʜt/ ▶ **adjective** informal very tired; exhausted.

bush·el /ˈbo͝osʜəl/ ▶ **noun 1** a measure of capacity equal to 64 US pints (35.2 liters). **2** Brit. a measure of capacity equal to 8 gallons (36.4 liters).
– ORIGIN Old French *boissel*.

bu·shi·do /ˈbo͞osʜēdō/ ▶ **noun** the code of honor and morals of the Japanese samurai.
– ORIGIN Japanese.

bush·ing /ˈbo͝osʜiɴɢ/ ▶ **noun 1** a metal lining for a hole in which something fits or revolves. **2** a sleeve that protects an electric cable.

Bush·man /ˈbo͝oshmən/ ▶ **noun** (pl. **Bushmen**) **1** a member of any of several aboriginal peoples of southern Africa. **2** (**bushman**) a person who lives or travels in the Australian bush.

bush·whack /ˈbo͝osh,(h)wak/ ▶ **verb 1** live or travel in wild or uncultivated country. **2** work clearing scrub and felling trees. **3** ambush someone.
– DERIVATIVES **bush·whack·er** noun.

bush·y /ˈbo͝oshē/ ▶ **adjective** (**bushier, bushiest**) **1** growing thickly. **2** covered with bush or bushes.

– SYNONYMS **thick,** shaggy, curly, fuzzy, bristly, fluffy, woolly.

– DERIVATIVES **bush·i·ly** adverb **bush·i·ness** noun.

busi·ness /ˈbiznis/ ▶ **noun 1** a person's regular occupation or profession. **2** commercial activity. **3** a commercial organization. **4** work to be done or matters to be attended to. **5** a person's concern: *that's none of your business*. **6** informal a difficult matter. **7** (**the business**) informal harsh verbal criticism.

– SYNONYMS **1 work,** occupation, profession, career, employment, job, position. **2 trade,** commerce, dealing, traffic, dealings, transactions, negotiations. **3 firm,** company, concern, enterprise, venture, organization, operation, undertaking; informal outfit. **4** *it's none of your business* **concern,** affair, responsibility, duty. **5** *an odd business* **affair,** matter, case, circumstance, situation, event, incident.

– PHRASES **in business** (of a commercial organization) operating. **mind one's own business** avoid interfering in other people's affairs.
– ORIGIN Old English, 'anxiety' (from **BUSY** + **-NESS**).

busi·ness end ▶ **noun** informal the functional part of a tool or device.

busi·ness·like /ˈbiznis,līk/ ▶ **adjective** efficient and practical.

– SYNONYMS **professional,** efficient, organized, slick, methodical, systematic, orderly, structured, disciplined, practical, pragmatic.

busi·ness·man /ˈbiznis,man, -mən/ (or **businesswoman**) ▶ **noun** (pl. **businessmen** or **businesswomen**) a person who works in commerce, especially at an executive level.

– SYNONYMS **executive,** entrepreneur, industrialist, merchant, dealer, trader, manufacturer, tycoon, employer, broker, buyer, seller, tradesman, retailer, supplier.

busi·ness mod·el ▶ **noun** a design for the successful operation of a business, identifying revenue sources, customer base, products, and details of financing.

busk /bəsk/ ▶ **verb** play music in the street in order to be given money by passersby.
– DERIVATIVES **busk·er** noun.
– ORIGIN from former French *busquer* 'seek.'

bus·man's hol·i·day /ˈbəsmən/ ▶ **noun** leisure time spent doing the same thing that one does at work.

bust[1] /bəst/ ▶ **noun 1** a woman's breasts. **2** a sculpture of a person's head, shoulders, and chest.

– SYNONYMS **1 bosom,** breasts, chest. **2 sculpture,** carving, effigy, statue, head and shoulders.

– ORIGIN from Latin *bustum* 'tomb, tomb monument.'

bust[2] informal ▶ **verb** (past and past part. **busted** or **bust**) **1** break, split, or burst. **2** hit someone hard. **3** (of the police) raid or search a building. **4** arrest someone.
▶ **noun 1** a period of economic difficulty. **2** a police raid.
▶ **adjective** bankrupt.
– ORIGIN variant of **BURST**.

bus·tard /ˈbəstərd/ ▶ **noun** a large swift-running bird found in open country.
– ORIGIN perhaps from Old French *bistarde* and *oustarde*, from Latin *avis tarda* 'slow bird.'

bust·er /ˈbəstər/ ▶ **noun** informal **1** a form of address to a man or boy. **2** a person or thing that stops a specified thing: *a crime-buster*.

bus·tier /bo͞osˈtyā/ ▶ **noun** a woman's close-fitting strapless top.
– ORIGIN French.

bus·tle[1] /ˈbəsəl/ ▶ **verb 1** move in an energetic and busy way. **2** (often as adj. **bustling**) (of a place) be full of activity.

– SYNONYMS **1 rush,** dash, hurry, scurry, scuttle, scamper, scramble; informal scoot, beetle, buzz. **2** (as adj. **bustling**) **busy,** crowded, swarming, teeming, humming, buzzing, hectic, lively.

▶ **noun** excited activity and movement.

– SYNONYMS **activity,** action, liveliness, excitement, tumult, commotion, hubbub, hurly-burly, whirl.

– ORIGIN perhaps from former *busk* 'prepare.'

bus·tle[2] ▶ **noun** historical a pad or frame worn under a skirt to puff it out behind.
– ORIGIN unknown.

bust-up ▶ **noun** informal a serious quarrel or fight.

bust·y /ˈbəstē/ ▶ **adjective** (**bustier, bustiest**) informal having large breasts.

bus·y /ˈbizē/ ▶ **adjective** (**busier, busiest**) **1** having a great deal to do. **2** currently occupied with an activity. **3** full of activity: *busy streets*. **4** excessively detailed or decorated.

– SYNONYMS **1** *I'm very busy* **hard at work,** involved, hard-pressed; informal on the go, hard at it. **2** *I'm sorry, she's busy* **unavailable,** engaged, occupied, absorbed, engrossed, immersed, preoccupied, working; informal tied up. **3** *a busy day* **hectic,** active, lively, full, eventful, energetic, tiring.
– ANTONYMS idle, free, quiet.

▶ **verb** (**busies, busying, busied**) (**busy oneself**) keep oneself occupied.

– SYNONYMS **occupy,** involve, engage, concern, absorb, engross, immerse, distract.

– DERIVATIVES **bus·i·ly** adverb **bus·y·ness** noun.
– ORIGIN Old English.

CHOOSE THE RIGHT WORD

busy, assiduous, diligent, engaged, industrious, sedulous

There are varying degrees of busyness. **Busy** implies actively and attentively involved in work or a pastime (*too busy to come to the phone*). It can also be used to describe intensive activity of any kind (*a busy intersection* ; *a busy day*). Someone who is **engaged** is also *busy*, but in a more focused way (*engaged in compiling a dictionary*). **Diligent** is used to describe earnest and constant effort, and it often connotes enjoyment of or dedication to what one is doing (*diligent efforts to rescue injured animals*). To be **industrious** is to be more focused still, often with a definite goal in mind (*an industrious employee working for a promotion*). **Sedulous** also applies to goal-oriented activity, but it suggests more close care and perseverance than *industrious* does (*a sedulous investigation of the accident*). The award for concentrated effort goes to the person who is **assiduous**, which suggests painstaking preoccupation with a specific task (*an assiduous student is the one most likely to win his or her teacher's favor*).

bus·y·bod·y /ˈbizēˌbädē/ ▶ **noun** (pl. **busybodies**) an interfering or nosy person.

– SYNONYMS **meddler,** interferer, troublemaker; gossip, scandalmonger; eavesdropper, gawker; informal snoop, buttinsky.

bus·y sig·nal ▶ **noun** a sound indicating that a telephone line is in use, typically a repeated single bleep.

but /bət/ ▶ **conjunction 1** in spite of that; nevertheless. **2** on the contrary. **3** (with negative or in questions) other than; otherwise than. **4** (with negative) old use without it being the case that.

– SYNONYMS **1** *he stumbled but didn't fall* **yet,** nevertheless, nonetheless, even so, however, still. **2** *that one's expensive, but this one isn't* **whereas,** conversely, but then, then again, on the other hand, by/in contrast, on the contrary.

▶ **preposition** except; apart from.

– SYNONYMS *everyone but him* **except (for),** apart from, other than, besides, aside from, with the exception of, bar.

▶ **adverb** no more than; only.

▶ **noun** an objection.

– PHRASES **but for 1** except for. **2** if it were not for. **but then** on the other hand.

– ORIGIN Old English, 'outside, without, except.'

USAGE

On starting a sentence with **but**, see the note at **AND**.

bu·tane /ˈbyo͞oˌtān/ ▶ **noun** a flammable hydrocarbon gas present in petroleum and natural gas and used as a fuel.

– ORIGIN from Latin *butyrum* 'butter.'

butch /bo͝ocн/ ▶ **adjective** informal masculine in a conspicuous or aggressive way.

– ORIGIN perhaps an abbreviation of **BUTCHER**.

butch·er /ˈbo͝ocнər/ ▶ **noun 1** a person who cuts up and sells meat as a profession. **2** a person who slaughters animals for food. **3** a person who kills brutally. ▶ **verb 1** slaughter or cut up an animal for food. **2** kill someone brutally. **3** spoil something by doing it badly.

– DERIVATIVES **butch·er·y** noun (pl. **butcheries**).

– ORIGIN Old French *bochier*.

but·ler /ˈbətlər/ ▶ **noun** the chief manservant of a house.

– ORIGIN Old French *bouteillier* 'cup-bearer.'

butt[1] /bət/ ▶ **verb 1** hit someone or something with the head or horns. **2** (**butt in**) interrupt a conversation or activity.

– SYNONYMS **1 ram,** headbutt, bump, poke, prod, push, shove, thrust. **2** (**butt in**) **interrupt,** intrude, break in, cut in, interfere; informal poke one's nose in.

▶ **noun** a rough push with the head.

– ORIGIN Old French *boter*.

butt[2] ▶ **noun 1** a person or thing that is the target of criticism or ridicule. **2** a target or range in archery or shooting.

– SYNONYMS **target,** victim, object, dupe, laughingstock.

– ORIGIN Old French *but*.

butt[3] ▶ **noun 1** the thicker end of a tool or a weapon. **2** the stub of a cigar or a cigarette. **3** informal a person's buttocks.

– SYNONYMS **1 stock,** end, handle, hilt, haft. **2 stub,** end, stump.

▶ **verb 1** adjoin or meet end to end. **2** join pieces of wood or other building materials with the ends or sides flat against each other.

– SYNONYMS *the shop butts up against the house* **adjoin,** abut, be next to, be adjacent to, border (on), neighbor.

– PHRASES **butt naked** informal completely naked.

– ORIGIN from Dutch *bot* 'stumpy.'

butt[4] ▶ **noun** a cask used for wine, ale, or water.

– ORIGIN Latin *buttis*.

butte /byo͞ot/ ▶ **noun** technical an isolated hill with steep sides and a flat top.

– ORIGIN French, 'mound.'

but·ter /ˈbətər/ ▶ **noun** a pale yellow fatty substance made by churning cream. ▶ **verb 1** spread something with butter. **2** (**butter someone up**) informal flatter someone.

– PHRASES **look as if butter wouldn't melt in one's mouth** informal appear innocent while being the opposite.

– ORIGIN from Greek *bouturon*.

but·ter bean ▶ **noun** a large flat white edible bean.

but·ter·cream /ˈbətərˌkrēm/ ▶ **noun** a mixture of butter and powdered sugar used as a filling or topping for a cake.

but·ter·cup /ˈbətərˌkəp/ ▶ **noun** a plant with bright yellow cup-shaped flowers.

but·ter·fat /ˈbətərˌfat/ ▶ **noun** the natural fat contained in milk and dairy products.

but·ter·fin·gers /ˈbətərˌfiNGgərz/ ▶ **noun** informal a person who often drops things.

but·ter·fly /ˈbətərˌflī/ ▶ **noun** (pl. **butterflies**) **1** an insect with two pairs of large wings that feeds on nectar and is active by day. **2** a showy or frivolous person: *a social butterfly*. **3** (**butterflies**) informal a fluttering sensation felt in the stomach when one is nervous. **4** a stroke in swimming in which both arms are raised out of the water and lifted forward together.

– ORIGIN Old English.

but·ter·milk /ˈbətərˌmilk/ ▶ **noun** the slightly sour liquid left after butter has been churned.

but·ter·nut /ˈbətərˌnət/ ▶ **noun 1** a North American walnut tree valued for its nuts and its light-colored wood. **2** the edible, oblong, sticky fruit of this tree.

but·ter·nut squash ▶ **noun** a pear-shaped variety of winter squash with light yellowish-brown rind and orange flesh.

but·ter·scotch /ˈbətərˌskäcн/ ▶ **noun** a candy or syrup made with melted butter and brown sugar.

but·ter·y[1] /ˈbətərē/ ▶ **adjective** containing, tasting like, or covered with butter.

but·ter·y[2] ▶ **noun** (pl. **butteries**) a room for storing wine and liquor.

– ORIGIN Old French *boterie* 'cask store.'

but·tock /ˈbətək/ ▶ **noun** either of the two round fleshy parts that form the lower rear area of a human trunk.

– SYNONYMS (**buttocks**) **rear (end),** rump, seat, bottom, derrière, cheeks; informal behind, backside, butt, fanny, ass; Brit. informal bum; humorous posterior.

– ORIGIN Old English.

but·ton /ˈbətn/ ▸ **noun 1** a small disk or knob sewn onto a garment to fasten it by being pushed through a buttonhole. **2** a knob on an electrical or electronic device that is pressed to operate it. **3** a decorative badge pinned to clothing. **4** an object placed in front of a poker player whose turn it is to deal. ▸ **verb 1** fasten or be fastened with buttons. **2** (**button something up**) informal complete something satisfactorily.
– DERIVATIVES **but·toned** adjective.
– PHRASES **button one's lip** informal stop or refrain from talking. **buttoned-up** informal conservative or inhibited. **on the button** informal precisely.
– ORIGIN Old French *bouton*.

but·ton·hole /ˈbətn,hōl/ ▸ **noun** a slit made in a garment to receive a button for fastening. ▸ **verb** informal stop someone so as to begin a conversation.

but·ton mush·room ▸ **noun** a young unopened mushroom.

but·tress /ˈbətris/ ▸ **noun 1** a projecting support built against a wall. **2** a projecting portion of a hill or mountain. ▸ **verb 1** support something with buttresses. **2** support or reinforce: *I was hoping that facts would buttress my point of view.*

– SYNONYMS **strengthen,** shore up, reinforce, fortify, support, bolster, underpin, cement, uphold, defend, back up.

– ORIGIN from Old French *ars bouterez* 'thrusting arch.'

bu·tyl /ˈbyo͞otl/ ▸ **noun** Chemistry the radical $-C_4H_9$, derived from butane.

bux·om /ˈbəksəm/ ▸ **adjective** (of a woman) attractively plump and large-breasted.

– SYNONYMS **large-breasted,** bosomy, big-bosomed; shapely, ample, plump, rounded, full-figured, voluptuous, curvaceous, Rubenesque; informal busty, chesty, well endowed, curvy.

– ORIGIN first meaning 'compliant': from Old English, 'to bend.'

buy /bī/ ▸ **verb** (**buys, buying, bought**) **1** obtain something in exchange for payment. **2** get by sacrifice or great effort: *greatness is dearly bought.* **3** informal accept the truth of: *I don't buy the claim that the ends justify the means.*

– SYNONYMS **purchase,** acquire, obtain, get, pick up, snap up, invest in; informal get hold of, score.
– ANTONYMS sell.

▸ **noun** informal something bought; a purchase.

– SYNONYMS **purchase,** deal, bargain, investment, acquisition.

– PHRASES **buy someone out** pay someone to give up an interest or share in something. **buy time** delay an event so as to have longer to improve one's own position. **have bought it** informal be killed.
– ORIGIN Old English.

USAGE

For an explanation of the difference between **brought** and **bought**, see the note at **BROUGHT**.

buy·er /ˈbīər/ ▸ **noun 1** a person who buys something. **2** a person employed to buy stock for a retail or manufacturing business.

– SYNONYMS **purchaser,** customer, consumer, shopper, investor; (**buyers**) clientele, market.

buy·er's mar·ket ▸ **noun** an economic situation in which goods or shares are plentiful and buyers can keep prices down.

buy·out /ˈbī,out/ ▸ **noun** the purchase of a controlling share in a company.

buzz /bəz/ ▸ **noun 1** a low, continuous humming or murmuring sound. **2** the sound of a buzzer or telephone. **3** an atmosphere of excitement and activity. **4** informal a thrill.

– SYNONYMS **hum,** murmur, drone, whirr.

▸ **verb 1** make a humming sound. **2** call someone with a buzzer. **3** move quickly. **4** (**buzz off**) informal go away. **5** be full of excitement or activity: *the department was buzzing with the news.* **6** informal (of an aircraft) fly very close to something at high speed.
– ORIGIN imitating the sound.

buz·zard /ˈbəzərd/ ▸ **noun 1** a large bird of prey that soars in wide circles. **2** a vulture.
– ORIGIN Old French *busard*.

buzz cut ▸ **noun** a very short haircut in which the hair is clipped close to the head.

buzz·er /ˈbəzər/ ▸ **noun** an electrical device that makes a buzzing noise to attract attention.

buzz·word /ˈbəz,wərd/ ▸ **noun** informal a technical word or phrase that has become fashionable.

buzz·y /ˈbəzē/ ▸ **adjective** informal (of a place or atmosphere) lively and exciting.

bwa·na /ˈbwänə/ ▸ **noun** (in East Africa) a form of address for a boss or master.
– ORIGIN Swahili.

by /bī/ ▸ **preposition 1** indicating the person or thing performing an action or the means of achieving something. **2** indicating a quantity or amount, or the size of a margin. **3** expressing multiplication, especially in dimensions. **4** indicating the end of a time period. **5** near to; beside. **6** past and beyond. **7** during. **8** according to. ▸ **adverb** so as to go past. ▸ **noun** (pl. **byes**) variant spelling of **BYE**[1].
– PHRASES **by and by** before long. **by the by** (or **by the bye**) incidentally. **by and large** on the whole. [first describing the handling of a ship both to the wind and off it.]
– ORIGIN Old English.

by- (also **bye-**) ▸ **prefix** less important; secondary: *by-election.*

bye[1] /bī/ (also **by**) ▸ **noun** the transfer of a competitor directly to the next round of a competition because they have no opponent assigned to them.
– PHRASES **by the bye** variant spelling of **BY THE BY** (see **BY**).
– ORIGIN from **BY**.

bye[2] (also **bye-bye**) ▸ **exclamation** informal goodbye.

by·gone /ˈbī,gôn/ ▸ **adjective** belonging to an earlier time.
– PHRASES **let bygones be bygones** forget past disagreements and be reconciled.

by·law /ˈbī,lô/ ▸ **noun 1** a rule made by a company or society to regulate the actions of its members. **2** a regulation made by a local authority; an ordinance.

by·line /ˈbī,līn/ ▸ **noun** a line in a newspaper naming the writer of an article.

by·pass /ˈbī,pas/ ▸ **noun 1** a road passing around a town for through traffic. **2** a secondary channel or connection to allow a flow when the main one is closed or blocked.

3 a surgical operation to make an alternative passage to aid the circulation of blood.

– SYNONYMS **detour,** alternate route, diversion, shortcut.

▶ **verb 1** go past or around something. **2** avoid a problem or obstacle.

– SYNONYMS **1 go around,** go past, make a detour around, avoid. **2 avoid,** sidestep, evade, escape, elude, skirt, dodge, circumvent, get around, pass over, ignore; informal duck.

by·play /ˈbīˌplā/ ▶ **noun** secondary action in a play or movie.

by·prod·uct /ˈbīˌprädəkt/ ▶ **noun 1** an incidental or secondary product made in the manufacture of something else. **2** an unintended but unavoidable secondary result.

by·road /ˈbīˌrōd/ ▶ **noun** a minor road.

By·ron·ic /bīˈränik/ ▶ **adjective 1** characteristic of Lord Byron (1788–1824) or his poetry. **2** (of a man) attractively mysterious and moody.

by·stand·er /ˈbīˌstandər/ ▶ **noun** a person who is present at an event but does not take part.

– SYNONYMS **onlooker,** passerby, observer, spectator, eyewitness.

byte /bīt/ ▶ **noun** a unit of information stored in a computer, equal to eight bits.

– ORIGIN from **BIT**[4] and **BITE**.

by·way /ˈbīˌwā/ ▶ **noun** a minor road or path.

by·word /ˈbīˌwərd/ ▶ **noun 1** a notable example: *his name became a byword for luxury.* **2** a proverb or saying.

Byz·an·tine /ˈbizənˌtēn, bəˈzan-, -ˌtīn/ ▶ **adjective 1** relating to Byzantium (now Istanbul), the Byzantine Empire, or the Eastern Orthodox Church. **2** excessively complicated. **3** very crafty or underhanded. ▶ **noun** a citizen of Byzantium or the Byzantine Empire.

Cc

C[1] (also **c**) ▶ **noun** (pl. **Cs** or **C's**) **1** the third letter of the alphabet. **2** indicating the third item in a set. **3** Music the first note of the scale of C major. **4** the Roman numeral for 100.

C[2] ▶ **abbreviation 1** (**C.**) (on maps) Cape. **2** Celsius or centigrade. **3** (©) copyright. **4** a dry cell battery of a size commonly used in flashlights and toys. **5** Physics coulomb(s). ▶ **symbol** the chemical element carbon.

c ▶ **abbreviation 1** cent(s). **2** (preceding a date or amount) circa. **3** (**c.**) century or centuries. ▶ **symbol** Physics the speed of light in a vacuum.

CA ▶ **abbreviation** California.

Ca ▶ **symbol** the chemical element calcium.

ca. ▶ **abbreviation** (preceding a date or amount) circa.

cab /kab/ ▶ **noun 1** (also **taxi cab**) a taxi. **2** the driver's compartment in a truck, bus, or train. **3** historical a horse-drawn vehicle for public hire.

– SYNONYMS **taxi,** taxicab, hack; pedicab.

– ORIGIN abbreviation of **CABRIOLET**.

ca·bal /kə'bäl, -'bal/ ▶ **noun** a small group of people who plot secretly to gain political power.
– ORIGIN Latin *cabala* 'Kabbalah.'

CHOOSE THE RIGHT WORD

See **PLOT**.

Cab·a·la /kə'bälə, 'kabələ/ ▶ **noun** variant spelling of **KABBALAH**.

ca·ban·a /kə'ban(y)ə/ ▶ **noun** a cabin, hut, or shelter, especially one at a beach or swimming pool.
– ORIGIN from Spanish *cabaña*.

cab·a·ret /ˌkabə'rā, 'kabəˌrā/ ▶ **noun 1** entertainment held in a nightclub or restaurant while the audience sits at tables. **2** a nightclub or restaurant where cabaret is performed.
– ORIGIN Old French, 'wooden structure, inn.'

cab·bage /'kabij/ ▶ **noun** a vegetable with thick green or purple leaves surrounding a heart or head of young leaves.
– ORIGIN Old French *caboche* 'head.'

cab·bage white ▶ **noun** a white butterfly whose caterpillars are pests of cabbages and related plants.

Cab·ba·la /kə'bälə, 'kabələ/ ▶ **noun** variant spelling of **KABBALAH**.

cabb·a·lis·tic /ˌkabə'listik/ ▶ **adjective** relating to or associated with the Kabbalah.
– ORIGIN variant of **KABBALISTIC** (see **KABBALAH**).

cab·by /'kabē/ (also **cabbie**) ▶ **noun** (pl. **cabbies**) informal a taxi driver.

Ca·ber·net Sau·vi·gnon /ˌkabər'nā ˌsōvin'yôN, -vē'nyôN/ ▶ **noun** a variety of black wine grape originally from the Bordeaux area of France.
– ORIGIN French.

cab·in /'kabən/ ▶ **noun 1** a private room on a ship. **2** the passenger compartment in an aircraft. **3** a small wooden shelter or house.

– SYNONYMS **1 cottage,** log cabin, shanty, hut, shack; chalet; cabana. **2 berth,** stateroom, compartment.

– ORIGIN from Latin *capanna*.

cab·in boy ▶ **noun** chiefly historical a boy employed to wait on a ship's officers or passengers.

cab·in cruis·er ▶ **noun** a motorboat with living accommodations.

cab·i·net /'kabənit/ ▶ **noun 1** a cupboard with drawers or shelves for storing or displaying articles. **2** a wooden box or piece of furniture housing a radio, television, or speaker. **3** a body of advisers to the president.

– SYNONYMS **1 cupboard,** wall unit, bookcase; china cabinet, file cabinet, medicine cabinet; sideboard, credenza, buffet. **2 council,** administration, ministry.

– DERIVATIVES **cab·i·net·ry** /'kabənitrē/ noun.
– ORIGIN from **CABIN**; sense 3 derives from the former sense 'small private room.'

cab·i·net·mak·er /'kabənitˌmākər/ ▶ **noun** a skilled joiner who makes furniture or similar high-quality woodwork.

cab·in fe·ver ▶ **noun** informal depression and irritability resulting from long confinement indoors during the winter.

ca·ble /'kābəl/ ▶ **noun 1** a thick rope of wire or hemp. **2** an insulated wire or wires for transmitting electricity or telecommunication signals. **3** a cablegram. **4** Nautical a length of 200 yards (182.9 m) or (in the US) 240 yards (219.4 m).

– SYNONYMS **1** *a thick cable moored the ship* **rope,** cord, line, guy; Nautical hawser. **2** *electric cables* **wire,** lead, cord, power line.

▶ **verb** dated send a cablegram to someone.
– ORIGIN from Latin *capulum* 'halter.'

ca·ble car ▶ **noun** a small car suspended on a moving cable and typically traveling up and down a mountainside.

ca·ble·gram /'kābəlˌgram/ ▶ **noun** historical a telegraph message sent by cable.

ca·ble-knit ▶ **adjective** (of an item of clothing) knitted using cable stitch.

ca·ble mo·dem ▶ **noun** a modem that uses a cable television connection to provide high-speed Internet service.

ca·ble stitch ▶ **noun** a combination of knitted stitches resembling twisted rope.

ca·ble tel·e·vi·sion ▶ **noun** a system in which television programs are transmitted to subscribers by cable.

cab·o·chon /'kabə,SHän/ ▶ **noun** a gem that is polished but not cut in facets.
– ORIGIN French, 'small head.'

ca·boo·dle /kə'bo͞odl/ ▶ **noun** (in phrase **the whole caboodle** or **the whole kit and caboodle**) informal the whole number or quantity of people or things in question.
– ORIGIN uncertain.

ca·boose /kə'bo͞os/ ▶ **noun 1** a railroad car with accommodations for the crew, typically at the end of a train. **2** informal a person's buttocks.
– ORIGIN Dutch *kabuis* 'kitchen on a ship's deck.'

cab·ri·o·let /,kabrēə'lā/ ▶ **noun 1** a car with a roof that folds down. **2** historical a light two-wheeled carriage with a hood, drawn by one horse.
– ORIGIN from French *cabriole* 'light leap' (because of the carriage's motion).

ca·ca·o /kə'kou, kə'kāō/ ▶ **noun** the beanlike seeds of a tropical American tree, from which cocoa and chocolate are made.
– ORIGIN Nahuatl.

ca·cha·ca /kə'SHäsə/ ▶ **noun** a Brazilian white rum made from sugarcane.
– ORIGIN Portuguese *cacaça*.

cache /kaSH/ ▶ **noun 1** a hidden store of things. **2** Computing an auxiliary memory from which high-speed retrieval is possible.

– SYNONYMS **hoard,** store, stockpile, stock, supply, reserve, arsenal; informal **stash.**

▶ **verb** store something in a cache.
– ORIGIN from French *cacher* 'to hide.'

ca·chet /ka'SHā/ ▶ **noun 1** the state of being respected or admired; prestige: *he would miss the cachet of working at one of the world's best companies.* **2** a distinguishing mark or seal.
– ORIGIN French.

ca·chex·i·a /kə'keksēə/ ▶ **noun** Medicine weakness and wasting of the body.
– ORIGIN Greek *kakhexia*.

ca·cique /kə'sēk/ ▶ **noun 1** (in Latin America or the Spanish-speaking Caribbean) a native chief. **2** (in Spain or Latin America) a local political boss.
– ORIGIN from Taino (an extinct Caribbean language).

cack·le /'kakəl/ ▶ **verb 1** laugh in a noisy, harsh way. **2** (of a hen or goose) make a noisy clucking cry. ▶ **noun** a noisy clucking cry or laugh.
– ORIGIN probably from German *kākelen*.

ca·coph·o·ny /kə'käfənē/ ▶ **noun** (pl. **cacophonies**) a mixture of loud and unpleasant sounds.
– DERIVATIVES **ca·coph·o·nous** /-nəs/ adjective.
– ORIGIN Greek *kakophōnia*.

cac·tus /'kaktəs/ ▶ **noun** (pl. **cacti** /-tī, -tē/ or **cactuses**) a succulent plant with a thick fleshy stem bearing spines but no leaves.
– ORIGIN Greek *kaktos* 'cardoon.'

CAD /kad/ ▶ **abbreviation** computer-aided design.

cad /kad/ ▶ **noun** dated or humorous a man who behaves dishonorably, especially toward a woman.
– DERIVATIVES **cad·dish** adjective.
– ORIGIN abbreviation of CADDIE or CADET.

ca·dav·er /kə'davər/ ▶ **noun** Medicine or literary a corpse.
– ORIGIN from Latin *cadere* 'to fall.'

CHOOSE THE RIGHT WORD

See **BODY**.

ca·dav·er·ous /kə'davərəs/ ▶ **adjective** very pale, thin, or bony.

cad·die /'kadē/ (also **caddy**) ▶ **noun** (pl. **caddies**) a person who carries a golfer's clubs and provides other assistance during a match. ▶ **verb** (**caddies, caddying, caddied**) work as a caddie.
– ORIGIN French *cadet* (see CADET).

cad·dis·fly /'kadis,flī/ ▶ **noun** (pl. **caddisflies**) a small winged insect having larvae that live in water and build cases of sticks, stones, etc.
– ORIGIN unknown.

cad·dy /'kadē/ ▶ **noun** (pl. **caddies**) a small storage container, especially for tea.
– ORIGIN Malay, referring to a unit of weight of 1⅓ lb (0.61 kg).

ca·dence /'kādns/ ▶ **noun 1** the rise and fall in pitch of a person's voice. **2** a sequence of notes or chords making up the end of a musical phrase.

– SYNONYMS **modulation,** intonation, inflection, lilt; rhythm, tempo, meter, beat, pulse.

– DERIVATIVES **ca·denced** adjective.
– ORIGIN Italian *cadenza*.

ca·den·za /kə'denzə/ ▶ **noun** a difficult solo passage in a concerto or other musical work, typically near the end.
– ORIGIN Italian.

ca·det /kə'det/ ▶ **noun 1** a young trainee in the armed services or police. **2** formal or old use a younger son or daughter.
– DERIVATIVES **ca·det·ship** /-,SHip/ noun.
– ORIGIN French.

cadge /kaj/ ▶ **verb** informal ask for or get something without giving anything in return.
– DERIVATIVES **cadg·er** noun.
– ORIGIN from northern English and Scots *cadger* 'traveling dealer.'

cad·mi·um /'kadmēəm/ ▶ **noun** a silvery-white metallic chemical element resembling zinc.
– ORIGIN from Latin *cadmia* 'calamine' (it is found with calamine in zinc ore).

ca·dre /'kadrē, 'käd-, ,rā/ ▶ **noun 1** a small group of people trained for a particular purpose or profession. **2** a group of activists in a revolutionary organization.
– ORIGIN French.

ca·du·ce·us /kə'd(y)o͞osēəs, -SHəs/ ▶ **noun** (pl. **caducei** /-sē,ī, -SHē,ī/) an ancient Greek or Roman herald's wand, typically one with two serpents twined around it, carried by the messenger god Hermes or Mercury.
– ORIGIN Latin.

cae·cum ▶ **noun** (pl. **caeca**) British spelling of CECUM.

Caer·phil·ly /kär'filē/ ▶ **noun** a kind of mild white cheese, originally made in Caerphilly in Wales.

Cae·sar /'sēzər/ ▶ **noun** a title of Roman emperors, especially those from Augustus to Hadrian.
– ORIGIN family name of the Roman statesman Gaius Julius *Caesar*.

cae·sar·e·an ▶ **noun** variant spelling of CESAREAN.

Cae·sar sal·ad ▶ **noun** a salad consisting of romaine lettuce and croutons served with a dressing of olive oil, lemon juice, raw egg, and Worcestershire sauce.

– ORIGIN named after *Caesar* Cardini, the Mexican restaurateur who invented it.

cae·su·ra /si'zHo͞orə, -'zo͞orə/ ▶ **noun** a pause near the middle of a line of verse.
– ORIGIN Latin.

ca·fe /ka'fā, kə-/ (also **café**) ▶ **noun** a small restaurant selling light meals and drinks.

> – SYNONYMS **bistro,** restaurant, coffee shop, tea room; diner, snack bar, cafeteria, lunchroom.

– ORIGIN French, 'coffee or coffee house.'

ca·fe so·ci·e·ty ▶ **noun** people who spend a lot of time in fashionable restaurants and nightclubs.

caf·e·te·ri·a /ˌkafi'ti(ə)rēə/ ▶ **noun** a self-service restaurant.

> – SYNONYMS **lunchroom,** canteen, luncheonette, buffet, cafe, snack bar, mess hall; informal **caf.**

– ORIGIN Latin American Spanish, 'coffee shop.'

caf·feine /ka'fēn, 'kafˌēn/ ▶ **noun** a substance found in tea, coffee, and other plants that stimulates the central nervous system.
– DERIVATIVES **caf·fein·at·ed** /'kafəˌnātid/ adjective.
– ORIGIN French *caféine.*

caf·tan ▶ **noun** variant spelling of **KAFTAN**.

cage /kāj/ ▶ **noun 1** a structure of bars or wires in which birds or other animals are confined. **2** any similar structure, especially the compartment in an elevator.

> – SYNONYMS **enclosure,** pen, pound, coop, hutch, birdcage, aviary.

▶ **verb** confine someone or something in a cage.

> – SYNONYMS **confine,** shut in/up, fence in, pen, coop up, enclose, impound.

– ORIGIN Old French.

cag·ey /'kājē/ ▶ **adjective** (**cagier, cagiest**) informal cautiously reluctant to give information: *airlines are cagey about their policy on free upgrades to business class.*

> – SYNONYMS **secretive,** guarded, tight-lipped, reticent, evasive; informal playing one's cards close to one's chest.

– DERIVATIVES **cag·i·ly** /'kājilē/ adverb **cag·i·ness** (also **cageyness**) noun.
– ORIGIN unknown.

ca·hoots /kə'ho͞ots/ ▶ **plural noun** (in phrase **in cahoots**) informal secretly working to achieve something dishonest or underhanded with others.
– ORIGIN unknown.

cai·man /'kāmən/ (also **cayman**) ▶ **noun** a tropical American reptile similar to an alligator.
– ORIGIN Carib.

Cain /kān/ ▶ **noun** (in phrase **raise Cain**) informal create trouble or a commotion.
– ORIGIN from *Cain,* eldest son of Adam and Eve and murderer of his brother Abel (Genesis 4).

ca·ique /kä'ēk, kīk/ ▶ **noun 1** a light rowboat used on the Bosporus. **2** a small eastern Mediterranean sailing ship.
– ORIGIN Turkish *kayık.*

cairn /ke(ə)rn/ ▶ **noun 1** a mound of rough stones built as a memorial or landmark. **2** (also **cairn terrier**) a small breed of terrier with a shaggy coat.
– ORIGIN Scottish Gaelic *carn.*

cais·son /'kāˌsän, 'kāsən/ ▶ **noun 1** a large watertight chamber in which underwater construction work may be carried out. **2** a vessel or structure used as a gate across the entrance of a dry dock or basin.
– ORIGIN French, 'large chest.'

ca·jole /kə'jōl/ ▶ **verb** persuade someone to do something by coaxing or flattery.

> – SYNONYMS **persuade,** wheedle, coax, talk into, prevail on; informal sweet-talk, soft-soap.

– DERIVATIVES **ca·jol·er·y** noun.
– ORIGIN French *cajoler.*

Ca·jun /'kājən/ ▶ **noun** a member of a French-speaking community in areas of southern Louisiana, descended from French Canadians. ▶ **adjective** relating to the Cajuns.
– ORIGIN alteration of *Acadian* 'relating to Acadia,' a former French colony in Canada.

cake /kāk/ ▶ **noun 1** an item of soft sweet food made from baking a mixture of flour, shortening, eggs, and sugar. **2** a flat round item of savory food that is baked or fried. **3** a block or brick of soap, etc.

> – SYNONYMS **1** *chocolate cake* gateau, torte, layer cake, sheet cake, petit four. **2** *a cake of soap* **bar,** brick, block, slab, lump.

▶ **verb** (of a thick or sticky substance) cover and form a hard layer on something: *my clothes were caked with mud.*

> – SYNONYMS *boots caked with mud* **coat,** encrust, plaster, cover.

– DERIVATIVES **ca·key** adjective (informal).
– PHRASES **a piece of cake** informal something easily achieved. **sell like hot cakes** informal be sold quickly and in large quantities. **take the cake** surpass or exceed all others.
– ORIGIN Scandinavian.

cakehole ▶ **noun** chiefly Brit. informal a person's mouth: *shut your cakehole.*

cake·walk /'kākˌwôk/ ▶ **noun** informal a very easy task.
– ORIGIN first referring to an American black contest in graceful walking that had a cake as a prize.

Cal ▶ **abbreviation** large calorie(s).

cal ▶ **abbreviation** small calorie(s).

cal·a·bash /'kaləˌbasH/ ▶ **noun** a water container, tobacco pipe, or other object made from the dried shell of a gourd.
– ORIGIN Spanish *calabaza.*

cal·a·brese /'kaləˌbrēz/ ▶ **noun** a bright green variety of broccoli.
– ORIGIN Italian, 'Calabrian' (*Calabria* is a region of SW Italy).

cal·a·mine /'kaləˌmīn/ ▶ **noun** a pink powder consisting of zinc carbonate and ferric oxide, used to make a soothing lotion.
– ORIGIN Latin *calamina.*

ca·lam·i·ty /kə'lamitē/ ▶ **noun** (pl. **calamities**) a sudden event causing great damage or distress.

> – SYNONYMS **disaster,** catastrophe, tragedy, cataclysm, accident, misfortune, misadventure.

– DERIVATIVES **ca·lam·i·tous** /-itəs/ adjective **ca·lam·i·tous·ly** adverb.
– ORIGIN Latin *calamitas.*

cal·car·e·ous /kal'ke(ə)rēəs/ ▶ **adjective** containing calcium carbonate; chalky.
– ORIGIN from Latin *calx* 'lime.'

cal·cif·er·ol /kal'sifəˌrôl, -ˌrōl/ ▶ **noun** vitamin D_2, essential for the deposition of calcium in bones.

cal·cif·er·ous /kal'sifərəs/ ▶ **adjective** containing or producing calcium salts, especially calcium carbonate.

cal·ci·fy /ˈkalsəˌfī/ ▶ **verb** (**calcifies, calcifying, calcified**) harden something by a deposit of calcium salts.
– DERIVATIVES **cal·ci·fi·ca·tion** /ˌkalsəfiˈkāSHən/ noun.

cal·cine /ˈkalˌsīn/ ▶ **verb** reduce, oxidize, or dry a substance by exposure to strong heat.
– DERIVATIVES **cal·ci·na·tion** /kalsəˈnāSHən/ noun.
– ORIGIN Latin *calcinare*.

cal·cite /ˈkalˌsīt/ ▶ **noun** a white or colorless mineral consisting of calcium carbonate.
– ORIGIN German *Calcit*.

cal·ci·um /ˈkalsēəm/ ▶ **noun** a soft gray reactive metallic chemical element.
– ORIGIN from Latin *calx* 'lime.'

cal·ci·um car·bon·ate ▶ **noun** a white insoluble compound occurring naturally as chalk, limestone, marble, and calcite.

cal·cu·late /ˈkalkyəˌlāt/ ▶ **verb 1** determine the amount or number of something mathematically. **2** intend an action to have a particular effect: *his words were calculated to hurt her*. **3** (**calculate on**) include something as an essential element in one's plans.

– SYNONYMS **1 compute,** work out, reckon, figure, add up/together, count up, tally, total, tote, tot up. **2 intend,** mean, design.

– DERIVATIVES **cal·cu·la·ble** /ˈkalkyələbəl/ adjective.
– ORIGIN Latin *calculare* 'count.'

cal·cu·lat·ed /ˈkalkyəˌlātid/ ▶ **adjective** done with awareness of the likely consequences: *a calculated act of terrorism*.

– SYNONYMS **deliberate,** premeditated, planned, preplanned, preconceived, intentional, intended.
– ANTONYMS unintentional.

– DERIVATIVES **cal·cu·lat·ed·ly** adverb.

cal·cu·lat·ing /ˈkalkyəˌlātiNG/ ▶ **adjective** shrewdly planning things so as to benefit oneself.

– SYNONYMS **cunning,** crafty, wily, sly, scheming, devious, disingenuous.

cal·cu·la·tion /ˌkalkyəˈlāSHən/ ▶ **noun 1** an act of calculating the amount or number of something mathematically. **2** an assessment of the effects of a course of action.

– SYNONYMS **1 computation,** reckoning, adding up, counting up, working out. **2 assessment,** judgment, forecast, projection, prediction.

cal·cu·la·tor /ˈkalkyəˌlātər/ ▶ **noun** something used for making mathematical calculations, in particular a small electronic device.

cal·cu·lus /ˈkalkyələs/ ▶ **noun 1** (pl. **calculuses**) the branch of mathematics concerned with problems involving rates of variation. **2** (pl. **calculi** /-ˌlī, -ˌlē/) a hard mass formed by minerals in the kidney, gall bladder, or other organ of the body.
– ORIGIN Latin, 'small pebble' (as used on an abacus).

cal·de·ra /kalˈderə, kôl-, -ˈdi(ə)rə/ ▶ **noun** a large volcanic crater, especially one formed by the collapse of the volcano's mouth.
– ORIGIN from Latin *caldaria* 'boiling pot.'

cal·dron ▶ **noun** variant spelling of **CAULDRON**.

Cal·e·do·ni·an /ˌkaləˈdōnēən/ ▶ **adjective** relating to Scotland or the Scottish Highlands.
– ORIGIN from *Caledonia*, the Latin name for northern Britain.

cal·en·dar /ˈkaləndər/ ▶ **noun 1** a chart or series of pages showing the days, weeks, and months of a particular year. **2** a system by which the beginning, length, and subdivisions of the year are fixed. **3** a list of special days, events, or activities.

– SYNONYMS **schedule,** agenda, timetable, diary, program.

– DERIVATIVES **ca·len·dri·cal** /kəˈlendrikəl/ adjective.
– ORIGIN from Latin *kalendae* (see **CALENDS**).

cal·en·der /ˈkaləndər/ ▶ **noun** a machine in which cloth or paper is pressed by rollers to glaze or smooth it.
– ORIGIN French *calendre*.

cal·ends /ˈkaləndz, ˈkā-/ (also **kalends**) ▶ **plural noun** the first day of the month in the ancient Roman calendar.
– ORIGIN Latin *kalendae, calendae*.

ca·len·du·la /kəˈlenjələ/ ▶ **noun** a plant of a family that includes the common marigold.
– ORIGIN from Latin *calendae* (see **CALENDS**); perhaps because it flowers for most of the year.

calf[1] /kaf/ ▶ **noun** (pl. **calves**) **1** a domestic cow or bull in its first year. **2** the young of some other large mammals, such as elephants.
– ORIGIN Old English.

calf[2] ▶ **noun** (pl. **calves**) the fleshy part at the back of a person's leg below the knee.
– ORIGIN Old Norse.

calf·skin /ˈkafˌskin/ ▶ **noun** leather made from the hide or skin of a calf.

cal·i·ber /ˈkaləbər/ (Brit. **calibre**) ▶ **noun 1** the quality of something, especially a person's ability: *scholars of the highest caliber*. **2** the diameter of the inside of a gun barrel, or of a bullet or shell.

– SYNONYMS **1 quality,** standard, level, merit, distinction, stature, excellence, ability, expertise, talent, capability. **2 bore,** diameter, gauge.

– ORIGIN French.

cal·i·brate /ˈkaləˌbrāt/ ▶ **verb 1** mark a gauge or instrument with a standard scale of readings. **2** compare the readings of an instrument with those of a standard.
– DERIVATIVES **cal·i·bra·tion** /kaləˈbrāSHən/ noun **cal·i·bra·tor** /-brātər/ noun.
– ORIGIN from **CALIBER**.

cal·i·co /ˈkaliˌkō/ ▶ **noun** (pl. **calicoes** or **calicos**) printed cotton fabric. ▶ **adjective** (of a cat) multicolored.
– ORIGIN from *Calicut*, a seaport in India where the fabric originated.

cal·i·for·ni·um /ˌkaləˈfôrnēəm/ ▶ **noun** an unstable, artificially made radioactive metallic chemical element.
– ORIGIN named after the *University of California* (where it was first made).

cal·i·per /ˈkaləpər/ (also **calliper**) ▶ **noun 1** (also **calipers**) a measuring instrument with two hinged legs and in-turned or out-turned points. **2** a motor-vehicle or bicycle brake consisting of two or more hinged components. **3** a metal support for a person's leg.
– ORIGIN probably from **CALIBER**.

ca·liph /ˈkālif, ˈkal-/ ▶ **noun** historical the chief Muslim civil and religious ruler, regarded as the successor of Muhammad.
– DERIVATIVES **cal·iph·ate** /ˈkāləˌfāt, ˈkal-, -fit/ noun.
– ORIGIN Arabic, 'deputy of God.'

cal·is·then·ics /ˌkaləsˈTHeniks/ (Brit. **callisthenics**) ▶ **plural noun** gymnastic exercises to achieve bodily fitness and grace of movement.
– ORIGIN from Greek *kallos* 'beauty' + *sthenos* 'strength.'

calk ▸ **noun & verb** variant spelling of CAULK.

call /kôl/ ▸ **verb** **1** cry out to someone so as to summon them or attract their attention. **2** telephone someone. **3** order or ask someone to go or come somewhere. **4** pay a brief visit. **5** give a specified name or description to. **6** fix a date or time for a meeting, election, or strike. **7** predict the outcome of a future event. **8** (of a bird or animal) make its typical cry. **9** inspire or urge someone to do something.

– SYNONYMS **1 cry,** cry out, shout, yell, sing out, exclaim, shriek, scream, roar; informal holler. **2 phone,** telephone, give someone a call; informal call up, give someone a ring, give someone a buzz. **3** *dinner's ready—call the kids* **summon,** send for, order. **4** *I might **call on** her later* **pay a visit to,** visit, drop in on, look in on, drop/stop by, pop in on. **5** *they called their son David* **name,** christen, baptize, designate, style, term, dub. **6** *yes, I would call him a friend* **describe as,** regard as, look on as, think of as, consider to be. **7** *the vice president called a meeting* **convene,** summon, assemble.

▸ **noun** **1** an act or instance of calling. **2** the typical cry of a bird or animal. **3** a brief visit. **4** (**call for**) demand or need for. **5** a vocation: *his call to be a disciple*.

– SYNONYMS **1 cry,** shout, yell, exclamation, shriek, scream, roar; informal holler. **2** *the call of the barn owl* **cry,** song. **3** *a call for party unity* **appeal,** plea, request. **4** *there's no **call for** that kind of language* **need,** necessity, reason, justification, excuse. **5** *there is little **call for** antique furniture* **demand,** desire, market.

– DERIVATIVES **call·er** noun.
– PHRASES **call for** require; demand. **call something in** require payment of a loan. **call something off** cancel an event or agreement. **call on/upon** turn to someone as a source of help. **call of nature** euphemistic a need to go to the bathroom. **call the shots** (or **tune**) take the initiative in deciding how something should be done. **call someone/thing up 1** summon someone to serve in the army or to play in a team. **2** bring something stored into use. **on call** available to provide a professional service if necessary.
– ORIGIN Old Norse.

cal·la /ˈkalə/ ▸ **noun** a plant of the arum family with a showy white spathe.

call cen·ter ▸ **noun** an office in which telephone calls are handled for an organization.

call girl ▸ **noun** a female prostitute who accepts appointments by telephone.

cal·lig·ra·phy /kəˈligrəfē/ ▸ **noun** decorative handwriting or handwritten lettering.
– DERIVATIVES **cal·lig·ra·pher** noun **cal·li·graph·ic** /ˌkaliˈgrafik/ adjective.
– ORIGIN from Greek *kalligraphos* 'person who writes beautifully.'

call-in ▸ **noun** a radio or television program during which listeners or viewers can make comments or ask questions by telephoning the studio.

call·ing /ˈkôliNG/ ▸ **noun** **1** a profession or occupation. **2** a vocation.

– SYNONYMS **profession,** occupation, job, vocation, career, métier, work, line of work, employment, trade, craft.

call·ing card ▸ **noun** **1** a visiting card or business card. **2** a prepaid card allowing the user to make calls from a public telephone.

cal·li·o·pe /kəˈlīəpē/ ▸ **noun** chiefly historical an American keyboard instrument resembling an organ but with the notes produced by steam whistles.
– ORIGIN from *Calliope*, the Greek Muse of epic poetry.

call·i·per ▸ **noun** variant spelling of CALIPER.

call op·tion ▸ **noun** Stock Market an option to buy assets at an agreed price on or before a particular date.

cal·los·i·ty /kəˈläsitē/ ▸ **noun** (pl. **callosities**) technical a thickened and hardened part of the skin; a callus.

cal·lous /ˈkaləs/ ▸ **adjective** insensitive and cruel.

– SYNONYMS **heartless,** unfeeling, uncaring, cold, cold-hearted, hard, hardbitten, as hard as nails, hard-hearted, insensitive, unsympathetic.
– ANTONYMS kind, compassionate.

– DERIVATIVES **cal·lous·ly** adverb **cal·lous·ness** noun.
– ORIGIN Latin *callosus* 'hard-skinned.'

cal·loused /ˈkaləst/ (also **callused**) ▸ **adjective** having hardened skin.

cal·low /ˈkalō/ ▸ **adjective** (of a young person) inexperienced and immature.

– SYNONYMS **immature,** inexperienced, naive, green, raw, untried, unworldly, unsophisticated; informal wet behind the ears.
– ANTONYMS mature.

– ORIGIN Old English, 'bald.'

CHOOSE THE RIGHT WORD

See GULLIBLE.

call sign (also **call signal**) ▸ **noun** a message or tune that is broadcast by radio to identify the broadcaster or transmitter.

call-up ▸ **noun** **1** an act of summoning someone or of being summoned to serve in the armed forces or on a sports team. **2** a person so summoned: *De La Rosa was a surprise call-up after the injury to Cabrera*.

cal·lus /ˈkaləs/ ▸ **noun** a thickened and hardened part of the skin or soft tissue.
– ORIGIN Latin, 'hardened skin.'

calm /kä(l)m/ ▸ **adjective** **1** not showing or feeling nervousness, anger, or other emotions. **2** peaceful, quiet, or undisturbed: *the comfortable, calm atmosphere of my home*. **3** (of the weather) without wind.

– SYNONYMS **1 relaxed,** composed, self-possessed, serene, tranquil, unruffled, unperturbed, unflustered, untroubled, unexcitable, levelheaded, unemotional, phlegmatic, imperturbable; informal unflappable, laid-back. **2 windless,** still, quiet, tranquil, smooth.
– ANTONYMS excited, nervous, stormy.

▸ **noun** a calm state or period.

– SYNONYMS **1** *his usual calm deserted him* **composure,** coolness, calmness, self-possession, sangfroid, serenity, tranquility; informal cool, unflappability. **2** *calm prevailed* **tranquility,** stillness, quiet, peace.

▸ **verb** make or become tranquil and quiet.

– SYNONYMS **1** *I tried to **calm** her **down*** **soothe,** pacify, placate, mollify. **2** *she forced herself to **calm down*** **compose yourself,** regain your composure, control yourself, pull yourself together, simmer down, cool down/off, take it easy; informal get a grip, chill (out), keep your shirt on, cool your jets, decompress.

– DERIVATIVES **calm·ly** adverb **calm·ness** noun.
– ORIGIN from Greek *kauma* 'heat of the day.'

calm·a·tive /'kä(l)mətiv/ ▶ **adjective** (of a drug) having a sedative effect.

ca·lor·ic /kə'lôrik, -'lär-/ ▶ **adjective** technical relating to heat or calories; calorific.

cal·o·rie /'kal(ə)rē/ ▶ **noun** (pl. **calories**) **1** (also **large calorie**) a unit of energy equal to the energy needed to raise the temperature of 1 kilogram of water through 1°C (4.1868 kilojoules). **2** (also **small calorie**) a unit of energy equal to one-thousandth of a large calorie.
– ORIGIN from Latin *calor* 'heat.'

cal·o·rif·ic /ˌkalə'rifik/ ▶ **adjective 1** relating to the amount of energy contained in food or fuel. **2** (of food or drink) high in calories.

cal·o·rim·e·ter /ˌkalə'rimitər/ ▶ **noun** a device for measuring the amount of heat involved in a chemical reaction or other process.
– DERIVATIVES **cal·o·ri·met·ric** /ˌkalərə'metrik/ adjective **cal·o·rim·e·try** /-'rimitrē/ noun.

ca·lum·ni·ate /kə'ləmnēˌāt/ ▶ **verb** formal make false and defamatory statements about someone.
– DERIVATIVES **ca·lum·ni·a·tor** /-ˌātər/ noun.

cal·um·ny /'kaləmnē/ ▶ **noun** (pl. **calumnies**) the making of false statements about someone in order to damage their reputation.
– DERIVATIVES **ca·lum·ni·ous** /kə'ləmnēəs/ adjective.
– ORIGIN Latin *calumnia*.

Cal·va·dos /ˌkalvə'dōs/ ▶ **noun** apple brandy, traditionally made in the Calvados region of Normandy.

calve /kav/ ▶ **verb 1** give birth to a calf. **2** (of a mass of ice) split off from an iceberg or glacier.
– ORIGIN Old English.

calves /kavz/ plural of CALF[1], CALF[2].

Cal·vin·ism /'kalvəˌnizəm/ ▶ **noun** the form of Protestantism of John Calvin (1509–64), centering on the belief that God has decided everything that happens in advance.
– DERIVATIVES **Cal·vin·ist** noun **Cal·vin·is·tic** /ˌkalvə'nistik/ adjective.

ca·lyp·so /kə'lipsō/ ▶ **noun** (pl. **calypsos**) a kind of West Indian music or song, typically with improvised words on a topical theme.
– ORIGIN unknown.

ca·lyx /'kāliks, 'kal-/ ▶ **noun** (pl. **calyces** /'kāləˌsēz, 'kal-/ or **calyxes**) the sepals of a flower, forming a protective layer around a flower in bud.
– ORIGIN Greek *kalux* 'case of a bud, husk.'

cal·zo·ne /kal'zōn(ē)/, ▶ **noun** (pl. **calzoni** /-'zōnē/ or **calzones**) a type of pizza that is folded in half before cooking to contain a filling.
– ORIGIN Italian dialect, probably a special use of *calzone* 'trouser leg.'

CAM /kam/ ▶ **abbreviation** computer-aided manufacturing.

cam /kam/ ▶ **noun 1** a projecting part on a wheel or shaft, designed to come into contact with another part while rotating and cause it to move. **2** a camshaft.
– ORIGIN Dutch *kam* 'comb.'

ca·ma·ra·de·rie /ˌkäm(ə)'rädərē, ˌkam-, -'rad-/ ▶ **noun** trust and friendship between people.
– ORIGIN French.

cam·ber /'kambər/ ▶ **noun 1** a slightly convex or arched shape of a road or other horizontal surface. **2** the slight sideways inclination of the front wheels of a motor vehicle.
– DERIVATIVES **cam·bered** adjective.
– ORIGIN from Old French *chambre* 'arched.'

cam·bi·um /'kambēəm/ ▶ **noun** (pl. **cambia** /-bēə/ or **cambiums**) a layer of cells in a plant stem, from which new tissue grows by the division of cells.
– ORIGIN Latin, 'change, exchange.'

Cam·bo·di·an /kam'bōdēən/ ▶ **noun 1** a person from Cambodia. **2** the Khmer language. ▶ **adjective** relating to Cambodia.

Cam·bri·an /'kambrēən, 'kām-/ ▶ **adjective 1** Welsh. **2** Geology relating to the first period in the Paleozoic era, about 570 to 510 million years ago.
– ORIGIN from Latin *Cambria*.

cam·bric /'kāmbrik/ ▶ **noun** a lightweight, closely woven white linen or cotton fabric.
– ORIGIN named after the town of *Cambrai* in northern France.

cam·cord·er /'kamˌkôrdər/ ▶ **noun** a portable combined video camera and video recorder.

came /kām/ past tense of COME.

cam·el /'kaməl/ ▶ **noun** a large mammal of arid country, with a long neck and either one or two humps on the back.
– ORIGIN Greek *kamēlos*.

cam·el hair ▶ **noun 1** a fabric made from the hair of a camel. **2** fine, soft hair from a squirrel's tail, used in artists' brushes.

ca·mel·lia /kə'mēlyə/ ▶ **noun** an evergreen shrub with showy flowers and shiny leaves.
– ORIGIN named after the Moravian botanist Joseph *Kamel*.

Cam·em·bert /'kaməmˌbe(ə)r/ ▶ **noun** a kind of rich, soft, creamy cheese originally made near Camembert in Normandy.

cam·e·o /'kamēˌō/ ▶ **noun** (pl. **cameos**) **1** a piece of jewelry consisting of a carving of a head shown in profile against a background of a different color. **2** a short descriptive written sketch. **3** a small part in a play or movie for a distinguished actor.
– ORIGIN Latin *cammaeus*.

cam·er·a /'kam(ə)rə/ ▶ **noun** a device for taking photographs or recording moving images.
– DERIVATIVES **cam·er·a·man** noun (pl. **cameramen**).
– PHRASES **in cam·er·a** chiefly Law in private, in particular in the private rooms of a judge. [Latin, 'in the chamber.']
– ORIGIN Latin, 'vault, arched chamber.'

cam·er·a ob·scu·ra /əb'skyo͝orə/ ▶ **noun** a darkened box or building with a lens or opening for projecting the image of an external object onto a screen inside.
– ORIGIN Latin, 'dark chamber.'

cam·er·a-read·y ▶ **adjective** (of material to be printed) in the right form to be reproduced photographically onto a printing plate.

Cam·e·roon·i·an /ˌkamə'ro͞onēən/ ▶ **noun** a person from Cameroon, a country on the west coast of Africa. ▶ **adjective** relating to Cameroon.

cam·i·sole /'kaməˌsōl/ ▶ **noun** a woman's loose-fitting undergarment for the upper body.
– ORIGIN French.

cam·o·mile /'kaməˌmēl, -ˌmīl/ ▶ **noun** variant spelling of CHAMOMILE.

cam·ou·flage /ˈkaməˌfläzʜ, -ˌfläj/ ▶ **noun 1** the disguising of military forces and equipment by painting or covering them to make them blend in with their surroundings. **2** clothing or materials used as camouflage. **3** the natural coloring or form of an animal that enables it to blend in with its surroundings.

– SYNONYMS **disguise,** mask, screen, cover, cloak, front, facade, blind, concealment, subterfuge.

▶ **verb** hide or disguise someone or something by means of camouflage.

– SYNONYMS **disguise,** hide, conceal, mask, screen, cover (up).

– ORIGIN French *camoufler* 'to disguise.'

camp[1] /kamp/ ▶ **noun 1** a place with temporary accommodations of tents, huts, etc., for soldiers, refugees, or travelers. **2** a recreational facility with outdoor activities, sports, crafts, etc., and rustic overnight accommodations. **3** the supporters of a particular party or set of beliefs: *the liberal and conservative camps.*

– SYNONYMS **1 campsite,** encampment, camping ground, bivouac, base, settlement. **2 faction,** wing, group, lobby, caucus, bloc.

▶ **verb** stay in a tent or camper while on vacation.
– PHRASES **break camp** take down a tent or the tents of an encampment ready to leave.
– ORIGIN Latin *campus* 'level ground.'

camp[2] informal ▶ **adjective 1** (of a man) effeminate in an exaggerated or flamboyant way. **2** deliberately exaggerated and theatrical in style. ▶ **noun** camp behavior or style. ▶ **verb** (usu. **camp it up**) behave in a camp way.
– DERIVATIVES **camp·y** adjective.
– ORIGIN unknown.

cam·paign /kamˈpān/ ▶ **noun 1** a series of military operations intended to achieve an objective in a particular area. **2** an organized course of action to achieve a goal.

– SYNONYMS **1** *Napoleon's Russian campaign* **operation(s),** maneuver(s), offensive, attack, war, battle, crusade. **2** *the campaign to reduce vehicle emissions* **effort,** drive, push, struggle, movement, crusade, operation, strategy.

▶ **verb** work in an organized way toward a goal: *groups that campaigned for cheaper anti-AIDS drugs.*

– SYNONYMS **fight,** battle, push, press, strive, struggle, lobby, agitate.

– DERIVATIVES **cam·paign·er** noun.
– ORIGIN French *campagne* 'open country,' from Latin *campus* 'level ground.'

cam·pa·ni·le /ˌkampəˈnēlē, -ˈnēl/ ▶ **noun** a bell tower, especially one that is separate from a church or other building.
– ORIGIN Italian.

cam·pa·nol·o·gy /ˌkampəˈnäləjē/ ▶ **noun** the art or practice of bell-ringing.
– DERIVATIVES **cam·pa·nol·o·gist** noun.
– ORIGIN from Latin *campana* 'bell.'

cam·pan·u·la /kamˈpanyələ/ ▶ **noun** another term for **BELLFLOWER**.
– ORIGIN from Latin *campana* 'bell.'

camp·er /ˈkampər/ ▶ **noun 1** a person who spends a vacation in a tent or camp. **2** a large motor vehicle with facilities for sleeping and cooking while camping.
– PHRASES **happy camper** a comfortable, contented person.

cam·pe·si·no /ˌkampəˈsēnō, ˌkäm-/ ▶ **noun** (pl. **campesinos**) (in Spanish-speaking countries) a peasant farmer.
– ORIGIN Spanish.

camp·fire /ˈkampˌfī(ə)r/ ▶ **noun** an open-air fire in a camp.

camp fol·low·er ▶ **noun 1** a civilian working in or attached to a military camp. **2** a person who associates with a group without making a full contribution to its activities.

camp·ground /ˈkampˌground/ ▶ **noun** a place used for camping, especially one with some common facilities for campers.

cam·phor /ˈkamfər/ ▶ **noun** a white substance with an aromatic smell and bitter taste, used in insect repellents.
– ORIGIN Latin *camphora.*

cam·pi·on /ˈkampēən/ ▶ **noun** a plant of the pink family, typically having pink or white flowers with notched petals.
– ORIGIN uncertain.

camp·site /ˈkampˌsīt/ ▶ **noun** a place used for camping, especially one equipped for vacationers.

cam·pus /ˈkampəs/ ▶ **noun** (pl. **campuses**) **1** the grounds and buildings of a college or university. **2** a branch or area of a university away from the main site.
– ORIGIN Latin, 'level ground.'

cam·py·lo·bac·ter /ˈkampələˌbaktər, kamˈpilə-/ ▶ **noun** a genus of bacterium that sometimes causes food poisoning in humans and abortion in animals.
– ORIGIN from Greek *kampulos* 'bent' + **BACTERIUM**.

cam·shaft /ˈkamˌsʜaft/ ▶ **noun** a shaft with one or more cams attached to it, especially one operating the valves in an internal-combustion engine.

can[1] /kan/ ▶ **modal verb** (3rd sing. present **can**; past **could** /ko͝od/) **1** be able to. **2** used to express doubt or surprise: *he can't have finished.* **3** used to indicate that something is typically the case: *he could be very moody.* **4** be permitted to.
– ORIGIN Old English, 'know.'

USAGE

The verb **can** is chiefly used to mean 'be able to,' as in *can he move?* (i.e. is he physically able to move?). Although it is not wrong to use **can** when requesting permission, it is more polite to say **may** (i.e. *may we leave now?* rather than *can we leave now?*).

can[2] ▶ **noun 1** a cylindrical metal container, in particular one in which food or drink is sealed for long-term storage. **2** (**the can**) informal prison. **3** (**the can**) informal the toilet. ▶ **verb** (**cans, canning, canned**) **1** preserve food in a can. **2** informal dismiss (someone) from their job.
– DERIVATIVES **can·ner** noun.
– PHRASES **a can of worms** a complex matter that is full of possible problems. **in the can** informal on tape or film and ready to be broadcast or released.
– ORIGIN Old English.

Can·a·da goose /ˈkanədə/ ▶ **noun** a common brownish-gray North American goose with a black head and neck and a loud trumpeting call.

Ca·na·di·an /kəˈnādēən/ ▶ **noun** a person from Canada. ▶ **adjective** relating to Canada.
– DERIVATIVES **Ca·na·di·an·ism** /kəˈnādēəˌnizəm/ noun.

ca·nal /kəˈnal/ ▶ **noun 1** a waterway cut through land for the passage of boats or for conveying water for

irrigation. **2** a tubular passage in a plant or animal conveying food, liquid, or air.
– ORIGIN Latin *canalis* 'pipe, channel.'

can·al·ize /ˈkanəlˌīz/ ▶ **verb 1** convert a river into a canal. **2** convey something through a duct or channel.
– DERIVATIVES **ca·nal·i·za·tion** /ˌkanl-əˈzāSHən/ noun.

can·a·pé /ˈkanəˌpā, -pē/ ▶ **noun** a small piece of bread or pastry with a savory topping, often served with drinks.
– ORIGIN French, 'sofa, couch.'

ca·nard /kəˈnär(d)/ ▶ **noun** an unfounded rumor or story.
– ORIGIN French, 'duck,' also 'hoax.'

ca·nar·y /kəˈne(ə)rē/ ▶ **noun** (pl. **canaries**) **1** a bright yellow finch with a tuneful song, popular as a cage bird. **2** (also **canary yellow**) a bright yellow color.
– ORIGIN from the *Canary* Islands, to which one species of the bird is native.

ca·nas·ta /kəˈnastə/ ▶ **noun** a card game resembling rummy, using two packs and usually played by two pairs of partners.
– ORIGIN Spanish, 'basket.'

can·can /ˈkanˌkan/ ▶ **noun** a lively, high-kicking stage dance originating in 19th-century Parisian music halls.
– ORIGIN French.

can·cel /ˈkansəl/ ▶ **verb** (**cancels, canceling, canceled**) **1** decide that a planned event will not take place. **2** withdraw from or end a formal arrangement. **3** (**cancel something out**) have an equal but opposite effect on: *the heat given off by the fan motor probably cancels out any cooling effect.* **4** mark a stamp, ticket, etc., to show that it has been used and is no longer valid.

> – SYNONYMS **1 call off,** abandon, scrap, drop, ax; informal scrub, nix, redline. **2** *his visa has been canceled* **annul,** invalidate, declare null and void, void, revoke, rescind, retract, withdraw. **3** (**cancel something out**) **nullify,** negate, neutralize, wipe out, balance (out), make up for, compensate for, offset.

– DERIVATIVES **can·cel·la·tion** /ˌkansəˈlāSHən/ noun **can·cel·ler** /ˈkansələr/ noun.
– ORIGIN Latin *cancellare.*

Can·cer /ˈkansər/ ▶ **noun 1** a constellation and the fourth sign of the zodiac (the Crab), which the sun enters about June 21. **2** (**a Cancer**) a person born when the sun is in this sign.
– DERIVATIVES **Can·cer·i·an** /kanˈsərēən, -ˈsi(ə)r-/ noun & adjective.
– ORIGIN Latin, 'crab.'

can·cer /ˈkansər/ ▶ **noun 1** a disease caused by an uncontrolled division of abnormal cells in a part of the body. **2** a malignant growth or tumor resulting from an uncontrolled division of cells. **3** something evil or destructive that is hard to contain or destroy: *the cancer of racism.*

> – SYNONYMS **(malignant) growth,** tumor, malignancy; technical carcinoma, sarcoma.

– DERIVATIVES **can·cer·ous** adjective.
– ORIGIN Latin, 'crab, creeping ulcer.'

> **WORD LINKS**
>
> **carcinogenic** *causing cancer*
> **oncology** *branch of medicine concerned with cancer*

can·de·la /kanˈdēlə, -ˈdelə/ ▶ **noun** Physics the SI unit of luminous intensity.
– ORIGIN Latin, 'candle.'

can·de·la·brum /ˌkandəˈläbrəm, -ˈlab-/ ▶ **noun** (pl. **candelabra** /-ˈläbrə, -ˈlabrə/) a large candlestick or other holder for several candles or lights.
– ORIGIN Latin.

> **USAGE**
>
> **Candelabrum** is a Latin word, and the correct plural is **candelabra**, but people often incorrectly think that the singular form is **candelabra** and therefore its plural is **candelabras**.

can·did /ˈkandid/ ▶ **adjective** truthful and straightforward; frank.

> – SYNONYMS **frank,** forthright, direct, blunt, outspoken, plain-spoken, open, honest, truthful, sincere; informal upfront, on the up and up.
> – ANTONYMS guarded.

– DERIVATIVES **can·did·ly** adverb.
– ORIGIN from Latin *candidus* 'white.'

can·di·da /ˈkandidə/ ▶ **noun** a yeastlike parasitic fungus that sometimes causes thrush.
– ORIGIN from Latin *candidus* 'white.'

can·di·date /ˈkandiˌdāt, -dit/ ▶ **noun 1** a person who applies for a job or is nominated for election. **2** a person or thing regarded as suitable for something or likely to experience a particular fate: *she was the perfect candidate for a biography.*

> – SYNONYMS **applicant,** interviewee, examinee; contender, competitor, nominee, entrant, hopeful.

– DERIVATIVES **can·di·da·cy** /ˈkandidəsē/ noun.
– ORIGIN from Latin *candidatus* 'white-robed,' also referring to a candidate for office (who wore a white toga).

can·di·di·a·sis /ˌkandiˈdīəsis/ ▶ **noun** infection with candida, especially as causing oral or vaginal thrush.

can·died /ˈkandēd/ ▶ **adjective** (of fruit) preserved in a sugar syrup.

can·dle /ˈkandl/ ▶ **noun** a stick or block of wax or tallow with a central wick that is lit to produce light as it burns.
– PHRASES **cannot hold a candle to** informal be not nearly as good as: *the song can't hold a candle to James Taylor's 'Fire and Rain.'*
– ORIGIN Latin *candela.*

can·dle·light /ˈkandlˌlīt/ ▶ **noun** dim light provided by a candle or candles.
– DERIVATIVES **can·dle·lit** /ˈkandlˌlit/ adjective.

Can·dle·mas /ˈkandlməs/ ▶ **noun** a Christian festival held on February 2 to commemorate the purification of the Virgin Mary and the presentation of Jesus in the Temple.

can·dle·pow·er /ˈkandlˌpou(ə)r/ ▶ **noun** the illuminating power of a light source, expressed in candelas (formerly candles).

can·dle·stick /ˈkandlˌstik/ ▶ **noun** a support or holder for a candle.

can·dle·wick /ˈkandlˌwik/ ▶ **noun** a thick, soft cotton fabric with a raised, tufted pattern.

can·dor /ˈkandər, -ˌdôr/ ▶ **noun** the quality of being open and honest.

> – SYNONYMS **frankness,** openness, honesty, candidness, truthfulness, sincerity, forthrightness, directness, bluntness; informal telling it like it is.

– ORIGIN Latin *candor* 'whiteness, purity.'

can·dy /ˈkandē/ ▸ **noun** (pl. **candies**) a sweet food made with sugar or syrup combined with fruit, chocolate, or nuts.
– ORIGIN from French *sucre candi* 'crystallized sugar.'

can·dy ap·ple ▸ **noun 1** an apple coated with a thin layer of cooked sugar or caramel and fixed on a stick. **2** (also **candy-apple red**) a bright red color.

can·dy-striped ▸ **adjective** patterned with alternating stripes of white and another color, typically pink.

can·dy-strip·er /ˈstrīpər/ ▸ **noun** informal a teenage girl who does volunteer nursing in a hospital.
– ORIGIN so named because of the candy-striped uniforms worn by such nurses.

can·dy·tuft /ˈkandēˌtəft/ ▸ **noun** a plant with small heads of white, pink, or purple flowers.
– ORIGIN from *Candia*, the former name of Crete.

cane /kān/ ▸ **noun 1** the hollow jointed stem of tall reeds, grasses, etc., especially bamboo. **2** the slender, flexible stem of plants such as rattan. **3** a woody stem of a raspberry or related plant. **4** a length of cane or a stick used as a support for plants, a walking stick, or for hitting someone as a punishment. ▸ **verb** hit someone with a cane as a punishment.
– DERIVATIVES **can·er** noun.
– ORIGIN Greek *kanna, kannē*.

caned /kānd/ ▸ **adjective** (of furniture) made or repaired with cane.

can·id /ˈkanid, ˈkā-/ ▸ **noun** Zoology a mammal of the dog family; a canine.

ca·nine /ˈkāˌnīn/ ▸ **adjective** relating to or resembling a dog or dogs. ▸ **noun 1** a dog or other animal of the dog family. **2** (also **canine tooth**) a pointed tooth between the incisors and premolars.
– ORIGIN from Latin *canis* 'dog.'

can·is·ter /ˈkanəstər/ ▸ **noun** a round or cylindrical container.
– ORIGIN Greek *kanastron* 'wicker basket.'

can·ker /ˈkaNGkər/ ▸ **noun 1** a destructive fungal disease of trees that results in damage to the bark. **2** a condition in animals that causes open sores. **3** an evil or corrupting influence: *you're tainted with the canker of rebellion*. ▸ **verb** become infected with canker.
– ORIGIN Latin *cancer* 'crab, creeping ulcer.'

can·na /ˈkanə/ ▸ **noun** a lilylike tropical American plant with bright flowers and ornamental leaves.
– ORIGIN Latin.

can·na·bis /ˈkanəbəs/ ▸ **noun** a drug obtained from the hemp plant.
– ORIGIN Greek *kannabis*.

canned /kand/ ▸ **adjective 1** preserved in a sealed can. **2** informal, chiefly derogatory (of music, applause, or laughter) prerecorded.

can·nel·li·ni bean /ˌkanlˈēnē/ ▸ **noun** a kidney-shaped bean of a creamy-white variety.
– ORIGIN Italian *cannellini*, 'small tubes.'

can·nel·lo·ni /ˌkanlˈōnē/ ▸ **plural noun** rolls of pasta stuffed with a meat or vegetable mixture, typically cooked in a cheese sauce.
– ORIGIN Italian, 'large tubes.'

can·ner·y /ˈkanərē/ ▸ **noun** (pl. **canneries**) a factory where food is canned.

can·ni·bal /ˈkanəbəl/ ▸ **noun** a person who eats the flesh of other human beings.
– DERIVATIVES **can·ni·bal·ism** /-ˌlizəm/ noun **can·ni·bal·is·tic** /ˌkanəbəˈlistik/ adjective.
– ORIGIN Spanish *Canibales*, a variant of *Caribes*, a West Indian people said to eat humans.

can·ni·bal·ize /ˈkanəbəˌlīz/ ▸ **verb 1** use a machine as a source of spare parts for another machine. **2** (of an animal) eat an animal of its own kind.
– DERIVATIVES **can·ni·bal·i·za·tion** /ˌkanəbələˈzāSHən/ noun.

can·no·li /kəˈnōlē/ ▸ **plural noun** Italian pastries in the form of tubular shells filled with sweetened ricotta cheese and often containing nuts, citron, or chocolate bits.

can·non /ˈkanən/ ▸ **noun** (pl. usu. same) **1** a large, heavy gun formerly used in warfare. **2** a heavy automatic gun that fires shells from an aircraft or tank. ▸ **verb** chiefly Brit. (**cannon into/off**) collide with forcefully or at an angle: *the couple behind almost cannoned into us*.
– ORIGIN Italian *cannone* 'large tube.'

can·non·ade /ˌkanəˈnād/ ▸ **noun** a period of continuous heavy gunfire.

can·non·ball /ˈkanənˌbôl/ ▸ **noun** a metal or stone ball fired from a cannon.

can·non fod·der ▸ **noun** soldiers regarded only as a resource to be used up in war.

can·not /kəˈnät, ˈkanˌät/ ▸ **contraction** can not.

can·nu·la /ˈkanyələ/ ▸ **noun** (pl. **cannulae** /-lē, -lī/ or **cannulas**) a thin tube put into the body to administer medication, drain off fluid, or insert a surgical instrument.
– ORIGIN Latin, 'small reed.'

can·ny /ˈkanē/ ▸ **adjective** (**cannier**, **canniest**) shrewd, especially in financial or business matters.

– SYNONYMS **shrewd**, astute, smart, sharp, discerning, discriminating, perceptive, clever, judicious, wise.
– ANTONYMS foolish.

– DERIVATIVES **can·ni·ly** adverb **can·ni·ness** noun.
– ORIGIN from **CAN**[1], in the former sense 'know.'

ca·noe /kəˈnōō/ ▸ **noun** a narrow shallow boat with pointed ends, propelled by a paddle or paddles. ▸ **verb** (**canoes**, **canoeing**, **canoed**) travel in or paddle a canoe.
– DERIVATIVES **ca·no·er** noun **ca·noe·ist** noun.
– ORIGIN Spanish *canoa*.

can·o·la /kəˈnōlə/ ▸ **noun** oilseed rape of a variety developed in Canada and grown in North America. It yields a valuable cooking oil.
– ORIGIN from *Canada* + *-ola* (based on Latin *oleum* 'oil').

can·on[1] /ˈkanən/ ▸ **noun 1** a general rule or principle by which something is judged: *his designs break the canons of fashion*. **2** the works of a particular author or artist that are recognized as genuine. **3** a list of literary works considered to be permanently established as being of the highest quality. **4** a Church decree or law. **5** a piece of music in which a theme is taken up by two or more parts that overlap.
– ORIGIN Greek *kanōn* 'rule.'

can·on[2] ▸ **noun 1** a member of the clergy on the staff of a cathedral. **2** (also **canon regular** or **regular canon**) (fem. **canoness**) a member of certain orders of Roman Catholic clergy that live communally like monks or nuns.
– ORIGIN from Latin *canonicus* 'according to rule.'

ca·non·ic /kəˈnänik/ ▸ **adjective 1** in the form of a musical canon. **2** another term for **CANONICAL**.
– DERIVATIVES **can·on·ic·i·ty** /ˌkanəˈnisitē/ noun.

ca·non·i·cal /kəˈnänikəl/ ▸ **adjective** **1** accepted as being authentic or established as a standard: *the canonical works of science fiction.* **2** according to the laws of the Christian Church.
– DERIVATIVES **ca·non·i·cal·ly** adverb.

can·on·ize /ˈkanəˌnīz/ ▸ **verb** (in the Roman Catholic Church) officially declare a dead person to be a saint.
– DERIVATIVES **can·on·i·za·tion** /ˌkanənəˈzāsʜən/ noun.
– ORIGIN Latin *canonizare* 'admit as authoritative.'

can·on law ▸ **noun** the laws of the Christian Church.

ca·noo·dle /kəˈno͞odl/ ▸ **verb** informal kiss and cuddle amorously.
– ORIGIN unknown.

can·o·py /ˈkanəpē/ ▸ **noun** (pl. **canopies**) **1** a cloth covering hung or held up over a throne or bed. **2** a rooflike projection or shelter. **3** the part of a parachute that opens. **4** the top branches of the trees in a forest, forming an almost continuous layer of foliage.

– SYNONYMS **awning,** shade, sunshade, covering.

– DERIVATIVES **can·o·pied** adjective.
– ORIGIN Latin *conopeum* 'mosquito net over a bed.'

cant¹ /kant/ ▸ **noun** **1** insincere talk about moral or religious matters. **2** derogatory the language specific to a particular group: *thieves' cant.*
– ORIGIN probably from Latin *cantare* 'to sing.'

cant² ▸ **verb** be or cause to be in a slanting position; tilt. ▸ **noun** a slope or tilt.
– ORIGIN German *kant, kante* or Dutch *cant* 'point, side, edge.'

can't /kant/ ▸ **contraction** cannot.

can·ta·bi·le /känˈtäbəˌlā/ ▸ **adverb & adjective** Music in a smooth singing style.
– ORIGIN Italian, 'singable.'

can·ta·loupe /ˈkantlˌōp/ ▸ **noun** a small round variety of melon with orange flesh and ribbed skin.
– ORIGIN from the villa of *Cantaluppi* near Rome.

can·tan·ker·ous /kanˈtaɴɢkərəs/ ▸ **adjective** bad-tempered, argumentative, and uncooperative.

– SYNONYMS **grumpy,** grouchy, irritable, crotchety, testy, curmudgeonly, ill-tempered, ill-humored, crabby; cranky, ornery.
– ANTONYMS affable.

– DERIVATIVES **can·tan·ker·ous·ly** adverb **can·tan·ker·ous·ness** noun.
– ORIGIN perhaps from Anglo-Irish *cant* 'auction' and *rancorous.*

can·ta·ta /kənˈtätə/ ▸ **noun** a narrative or descriptive piece of accompanied vocal music, typically for solos, chorus, and orchestra.
– ORIGIN from Italian *cantata aria* 'sung air.'

can·teen /kanˈtēn/ ▸ **noun** **1** a restaurant in a military camp, workplace, school, or factory. **2** a small water bottle, as used by soldiers or campers.
– ORIGIN Italian *cantina* 'cellar.'

can·ter /ˈkantər/ ▸ **noun** a pace of a horse between a trot and a gallop, with not less than one foot on the ground at any time. ▸ **verb** move at a canter.
– ORIGIN short for *Canterbury pace,* the easy pace at which medieval pilgrims were said to travel to Canterbury.

Can·ter·bur·y bell /ˈkantərˌberē, -bərē/ ▸ **noun** a tall cultivated bellflower with large pale blue flowers.
– ORIGIN named after the bells on Canterbury pilgrims' horses.

can·ti·cle /ˈkantikəl/ ▸ **noun** a hymn or chant forming a regular part of a church service.
– ORIGIN Latin *canticulum* 'little song.'

can·ti·le·ver /ˈkantlˌēvər, -ˌevər/ ▸ **noun** **1** a long projecting beam or girder fixed at only one end, used in bridge construction. **2** a bracket or beam projecting from a wall to support a balcony, cornice, etc. ▸ **verb** support something by a cantilever or cantilevers.
– ORIGIN unknown.

can·to /ˈkanˌtō/ ▸ **noun** (pl. **cantos**) one of the sections into which some long poems are divided.
– ORIGIN Italian, 'song.'

can·ton /ˈkantn, ˈkanˌtän/ ▸ **noun** a political or administrative subdivision of a country, especially in Switzerland.
– ORIGIN Old French, 'corner.'

Can·ton·ese /ˌkantnˈēz, -ˈēs/ ▸ **noun** (pl. same) **1** a person from Canton (another name for Guangzhou), a city in China. **2** a form of Chinese spoken mainly in SE China and Hong Kong. ▸ **adjective** relating to Canton or Cantonese.

can·ton·ment /kanˈtōnmənt, -ˈtän-/ ▸ **noun** (especially in the Indian subcontinent) a military garrison or camp.
– ORIGIN French *cantonnement.*

can·tor /ˈkantər/ ▸ **noun** **1** an official who sings liturgical music and leads prayer in a Jewish synagogue. **2** a person who sings solo verses to which the choir or congregation in a Christian service responds.
– ORIGIN Latin, 'singer.'

Ca·nuck /kəˈnək/ ▸ **noun** informal, often derogatory in the US a Canadian, especially a French Canadian.
– ORIGIN apparently from *Canada.*

can·vas /ˈkanvəs/ ▸ **noun** (pl. **canvases** or **canvasses**) **1** a strong, coarse unbleached cloth used to make sails, tents, etc., and as a surface for oil painting. **2** an oil painting on canvas. **3** (**the canvas**) the floor of a boxing or wrestling ring, having a canvas covering. **4** either of the tapering ends of a rowboat used in racing.
– PHRASES **under canvas** in a tent or tents.
– ORIGIN Old French *canevas,* from Latin *cannabis* 'hemp.'

can·vas·back /ˈkanvəsˌbak/ ▸ **noun** a North American diving duck with a long, sloping black bill and a light gray back.

can·vass /ˈkanvəs/ ▸ **verb** **1** visit someone to seek their vote in an election. **2** question someone to find out their opinion.

– SYNONYMS **1 campaign,** electioneer. **2 poll,** question, survey, interview, consult.

▸ **noun** an act of canvassing.
– DERIVATIVES **can·vass·er** noun.
– ORIGIN first meaning 'toss someone in a canvas sheet' (as a sport or punishment).

can·yon /ˈkanyən/ ▸ **noun** a deep gorge, especially one with a river flowing through it.

– SYNONYMS **ravine,** gorge, gully, chasm, abyss, gulf, gulch, coulee.

– ORIGIN Spanish *cañón* 'tube.'

can·yon·ing /ˈkanyəniɴɢ/ ▸ **noun** (also **canyoneering**) the sport of following the stream down a canyon by means of such techniques as climbing, rappelling, jumping, and swimming.

CAP ▸ **abbreviation** Civil Air Patrol.

cap¹ /kap/ ▸ **noun** **1** a soft, flat hat with a peak. **2** a soft, close-fitting head covering worn for a particular purpose: *a shower cap*. **3** a lid or cover for a bottle, pen, etc. **4** the broad upper part of a mushroom or toadstool. **5** an upper limit imposed on spending or borrowing. **6** (also **percussion cap**) a small amount of explosive powder in a metal or paper case that explodes when struck.

– SYNONYMS **1 hat,** baseball cap, ski cap, stocking cap, beanie, yarmulke; mortarboard. **2 lid,** top, stopper, cork, bung, stopple. **3 limit,** ceiling, curb, check.

▶ **verb** (**caps, capping, capped**) **1** put or form a cap, lid, or cover on something. **2** provide a fitting climax to: *she capped a phenomenal year with three Oscar nominations*. **3** place a limit on prices or expenditure.

– SYNONYMS **1 top,** crown, cover, coat, tip. **2 limit,** restrict, curb, control, peg.

– DERIVATIVES **cap·ful** noun **cap·per** noun.
– PHRASES **cap in hand** humbly asking for a favor. **set one's cap at someone** dated (of a woman) try to attract a man.
– ORIGIN Latin *cappa*.

cap² /kap/ ▶ **noun** Finance short for **CAPITALIZATION**: *mid-cap companies*.

ca·pa·bil·i·ty /ˌkāpəˈbilitē/ ▶ **noun** (pl. **capabilities**) the power or ability to do something.

– SYNONYMS **ability,** capacity, power, potential, competence, aptitude, faculty, skill, talent, flair; informal know-how.
– ANTONYMS inability.

ca·pa·ble /ˈkāpəbəl/ ▶ **adjective 1** (**capable of**) having the ability or quality necessary to do: *I'm quite capable of taking care of myself*. **2** able to achieve whatever one has to do; competent.

– SYNONYMS **able,** competent, effective, proficient, accomplished, experienced, skillful, talented, gifted; informal useful.
– ANTONYMS incapable, incompetent.

– DERIVATIVES **ca·pa·bly** /-blē/ adverb.
– ORIGIN from Latin *capere* 'take or hold.'

ca·pa·cious /kəˈpāsнəs/ ▶ **adjective** having a lot of space inside; roomy.
– ORIGIN from Latin *capax* 'capable.'

ca·pac·i·tance /kəˈpasitəns/ ▶ **noun** the ability of a system to store electric charge, equivalent to the ratio of the change in electric charge to the corresponding change in electric potential.

ca·pac·i·tor /kəˈpasitər/ ▶ **noun** a device used to store electric charge.

ca·pac·i·ty /kəˈpasitē/ ▶ **noun** (pl. **capacities**) **1** the maximum amount that something can contain or produce: *the room was filled to capacity*. **2** the ability or power to do something. **3** a specified role or position: *I was engaged in a voluntary capacity*.

– SYNONYMS **1 volume,** size, dimensions, measurements, proportions. **2 ability,** capability, power, potential, competence, aptitude, faculty, skill, talent, flair. **3 role,** function, position, post, job, office.

▶ **adjective** fully occupying the available space: *a capacity crowd*.
– ORIGIN from Latin *capere* 'take or hold.'

ca·par·i·son /kəˈparəsən/ ▶ **verb** (**be caparisoned**) be dressed in rich decorative coverings or clothes.
– ORIGIN Spanish *caparazón* 'saddlecloth.'

cape¹ /kāp/ ▶ **noun** a short cloak.

– SYNONYMS **cloak,** mantle, shawl, poncho, pashmina.

– DERIVATIVES **caped** adjective.
– ORIGIN from Latin *cappa* 'covering for the head.'

cape² ▶ **noun** a piece of land that projects into the sea; a headland.

– SYNONYMS **headland,** promontory, point, head, horn, mull, peninsula.

– ORIGIN Latin *caput* 'head.'

Cape goose·ber·ry ▶ **noun** the edible yellow berry of a tropical South American plant, enclosed in a lantern-shaped husk.

cap·e·lin /ˈkap(ə)lən/ ▶ **noun** a small food fish of the smelt family, found in North Atlantic coastal waters.
– ORIGIN French.

cap·el·li·ni /ˌkapəˈlēnē/ ▶ **plural noun** pasta in the form of very thin strands.
– ORIGIN Italian, 'small hairs.'

ca·per¹ /ˈkāpər/ ▶ **verb** skip or dance around in a lively or playful way. ▶ **noun 1** a playful skipping movement. **2** informal a lighthearted or illicit activity, or a movie or novel portraying one: *a futuristic crime caper*.
– DERIVATIVES **ca·per·er** noun.
– ORIGIN from Latin *capreolus* 'little goat.'

ca·per² ▶ **noun** a pickled flower bud of a southern European shrub, used in sauces and as a garnish.
– ORIGIN Greek *kapparis*.

cap·er·cail·lie /ˌkapərˈkāl(y)ē/ ▶ **noun** (pl. **capercaillies**) a large turkeylike grouse of pine forests in northern Europe.
– ORIGIN from Scottish Gaelic *capull coille*, 'horse of the wood.'

cap·il·lar·i·ty /kapəˈlaritē/ ▶ **noun** the tendency of a liquid in a narrow tube or absorbent material to rise or fall as a result of surface tension.

cap·il·lar·y /ˈkapəˌlerē/ ▶ **noun** (pl. **capillaries**) **1** any of the fine branching blood vessels that form a network between the arteries and veins. **2** (also **capillary tube**) a tube with an internal diameter of hairlike thinness.
– ORIGIN from Latin *capillus* 'hair.'

cap·il·lar·y ac·tion ▶ **noun** another term for **CAPILLARITY**.

cap·i·tal¹ /ˈkapitl/ ▶ **noun 1** the main city or town of a country or region, typically where the government is based. **2** wealth owned by a person or organization or invested, lent, or borrowed. **3** the amount by which a company's assets exceeds its liabilities. **4** a capital letter.

– SYNONYMS **money,** finance(s), funds, cash, wherewithal, means, assets, wealth, resources.

▶ **adjective 1** (of an offense) punishable by death. **2** (of a letter of the alphabet) large in size and of the form used to begin sentences and names. **3** informal, dated excellent.
– PHRASES **make capital out of** use something to one's advantage.
– ORIGIN from Latin *caput* 'head.'

cap·i·tal² ▶ **noun** the top part of a pillar or column.
– ORIGIN Latin *capitellum* 'little head.'

cap·i·tal gain ▶ **noun** a profit from the sale of property or an investment.

cap·i·tal goods ▶ **plural noun** goods that are used in producing other goods, rather than being bought by consumers.

cap·i·tal·ism /'kapətl,izəm/ ▶ **noun** an economic and political system in which a country's trade and industry are controlled by private owners for profit.

– SYNONYMS **private enterprise,** free enterprise, the free market, private ownership.
– ANTONYMS communism.

– DERIVATIVES **cap·i·tal·ist** /'kapətlist/ noun & adjective **cap·i·tal·is·tic** /,kapətl'istik/ adjective.

cap·i·tal·ize /'kapətl,īz/ ▶ **verb 1** (**capitalize on**) take advantage of: *the software lets you capitalize on new customer opportunities.* **2** provide a company with financial capital. **3** convert income into financial capital. **4** write or print a word or letter in capital letters or with an initial capital.

– SYNONYMS (**capitalize on**) **take advantage of,** profit from, make the most of, exploit, develop; informal cash in on.

– DERIVATIVES **cap·i·tal·i·za·tion** /,kapətl-ə'zāsʜən/ noun.

cap·i·tal pun·ish·ment ▶ **noun** the punishment of a crime by death.

cap·i·tal sum ▶ **noun** a lump sum of money payable to an insured person or paid as an initial fee or investment.

cap·i·ta·tion /,kapi'tāsʜən/ ▶ **noun** the payment of a fee or grant to a doctor, school, etc., the amount being determined by the number of people that are served.
– ORIGIN from Latin *caput* 'head.'

cap·i·tol /'kapitl/ ▶ **noun 1** a building housing a legislative assembly. **2** (**the Capitol**) the seat of the US Congress in Washington DC.
– ORIGIN from Latin *caput* 'head.'

ca·pit·u·late /kə'picʜə,lāt/ ▶ **verb** give in to an opponent or an unwelcome demand.

– SYNONYMS **surrender,** give in, yield, concede defeat, give up (the struggle), submit, lay down one's arms, throw in the towel.
– ANTONYMS resist.

– DERIVATIVES **ca·pit·u·la·tion** noun **ca·pit·u·la·tor** noun.
– ORIGIN from Latin *capitulare* 'draw up under headings.'

cap'n /'kapn/ ▶ **noun** informal contraction of captain, used in representing speech.

ca·po[1] /'kāpō, 'käpō/ ▶ **noun** (pl. **capos**) a clamp fastened across all the strings of a guitar or similar instrument to raise their tuning.
– ORIGIN from Italian *capo tasto* 'head stop.'

ca·po[2] ▶ **noun** (pl. **capos**) the head of a branch of the Mafia.
– ORIGIN Italian.

ca·po·ei·ra /,käpōō'ārə/ ▶ **noun** a martial art and dance form originating among Angolan slaves in Brazil.
– ORIGIN Portuguese.

ca·pon /'kā,pän, -pən/ ▶ **noun** a domestic cock that has been castrated and fattened for eating.
– ORIGIN Latin *capo.*

cap·puc·ci·no /,käpə'cʜēnō, ,kap-/ ▶ **noun** (pl. **cappuccinos**) coffee made with milk that has been frothed up with pressurized steam.
– ORIGIN Italian, 'Capuchin' (because the color resembles that of a Capuchin monk's habit).

ca·pric·ci·o /kə'prēcʜē,ō, -cʜō/ ▶ **noun** (pl. **capriccios**) **1** a lively piece of music, typically one that is short and free in form. **2** a painting or other work of art representing a fantasy or a mixture of real and imaginary features.
– ORIGIN from Italian, literally 'head with the hair standing on end.'

ca·price /kə'prēs/ ▶ **noun** a sudden change of mood or behavior.
– ORIGIN Italian *capriccio* 'sudden start.'

ca·pri·cious /kə'prisʜəs, -'prē-/ ▶ **adjective** prone to sudden changes of mood or behavior.

– SYNONYMS **fickle,** volatile, unpredictable, temperamental, mercurial, impulsive, changeable, unreliable, erratic, wayward, whimsical, flighty.
– ANTONYMS consistent.

– DERIVATIVES **ca·pri·cious·ly** adverb **ca·pri·cious·ness** noun.

Cap·ri·corn /'kapri,kôrn/ ▶ **noun 1** a constellation and the tenth sign of the zodiac (the Goat), which the sun enters about December 21. **2** (**a Capricorn**) a person born when the sun is in this sign.
– DERIVATIVES **Cap·ri·corn·i·an** /,kapri'kôrnēən/noun & adjective.
– ORIGIN Latin *capricornus.*

cap·rine /'kap,rīn/ ▶ **adjective** relating to or resembling a goat or goats.
– ORIGIN from Latin *caper* 'goat.'

ca·pri pants /kə'prē/ (also **capris**) ▶ **plural noun** close-fitting calf-length tapered pants for women.
– ORIGIN named after the Italian island of *Capri.*

caps /kaps/ ▶ **abbreviation** capital letters.

cap·si·cum /'kapsikəm/ ▶ **noun** (pl. **capsicums**) a sweet pepper or chili pepper.
– ORIGIN Latin.

cap·size /'kap,sīz, kap'sīz/ ▶ **verb** (of a boat) be overturned in the water.

– SYNONYMS **overturn,** turn over, turn upside down, upend, flip/tip over, keel over, turn turtle.

– ORIGIN perhaps from Spanish *capuzar* 'sink a ship by the head.'

cap sleeve ▶ **noun** a sleeve that extends a short distance from the shoulder and tapers to nothing under the arm.

cap·stan /'kapstən/ ▶ **noun** a broad revolving cylinder with a vertical axis, used for winding a rope or cable.
– ORIGIN Provençal *cabestan.*

cap·stone /'kap,stōn/ ▶ **noun** a stone fixed on top of a wall or prehistoric tomb.

cap·sule /'kapsəl, 'kap,sōōl/ ▶ **noun 1** a small case or container. **2** a small case of gelatin containing a dose of medicine, which dissolves after it is swallowed. **3** Botany a dry fruit that releases its seeds by bursting open when ripe.

– SYNONYMS **1 pill,** tablet, lozenge, pastille; informal tab. **2 module,** craft, probe.

▶ **adjective** brief, condensed, or compact: *a capsule review of the movie.*
– DERIVATIVES **cap·su·lar** adjective.
– ORIGIN Latin *capsula.*

cap·sul·ize /'kapsə,līz/ ▶ **verb** put information in compact form.

Capt. ▶ **abbreviation** captain.

cap·tain /'kaptən/ ▶ **noun 1** the person in command of a ship or civil aircraft. **2** a rank of naval officer above commander and below commodore. **3** a rank of officer in the US Army, Marine Corps, or Air Force above lieutenant and below major. **4** the leader of a team, especially in sports. **5** a police officer in charge of a precinct.

– SYNONYMS **1** *the ship's captain* **commander,** master; informal skipper. **2** *the team captain* **leader,** head, chief; informal boss, skipper.

▶ **verb** be the captain of a ship, aircraft, or team.
– DERIVATIVES **cap·tain·cy** /-tənsē/ noun.
– ORIGIN Old French *capitain* 'chief.'

cap·tion /'kapsʜən/ ▶ **noun 1** a title or brief explanation accompanying an illustration or cartoon. **2** a piece of text appearing on screen as part of a movie or television broadcast.

– SYNONYMS **title,** heading, legend, description.

▶ **verb** provide an illustration with a title or explanation.
– ORIGIN Latin, 'capture, seizing.'

cap·tious /'kapsʜəs/ ▶ **adjective** formal tending to find fault or raise petty objections.
– ORIGIN Old French *captieux.*

cap·ti·vate /'kaptə,vāt/ ▶ **verb** attract and hold the interest of someone; charm.

– SYNONYMS **enthrall,** charm, enchant, bewitch, fascinate, beguile, entrance, delight, attract, allure.
– ANTONYMS bore.

– DERIVATIVES **cap·ti·vat·ing** adjective **cap·ti·va·tion** /,kaptə'vāsʜən/ noun.
– ORIGIN Latin *captivare* 'take captive.'

cap·tive /'kaptiv/ ▶ **noun** a person who has been taken prisoner or held in confinement.

– SYNONYMS **prisoner,** convict, detainee, hostage, prisoner of war, internee.

▶ **adjective 1** imprisoned or confined. **2** not free to choose an alternative: *a captive audience.*

– SYNONYMS **confined,** caged, incarcerated, locked up, jailed, imprisoned, interned, detained.
– ANTONYMS free.

– ORIGIN Latin *captivus.*

cap·tiv·i·ty /kap'tivitē/ ▶ **noun** the condition of being imprisoned or confined.

– SYNONYMS **imprisonment,** incarceration, confinement, detention, internment.
– ANTONYMS freedom.

cap·tor /'kaptər, -,tôr/ ▶ **noun** a person who captures or confines another.

cap·ture /'kapcʜər/ ▶ **verb 1** take control of something by force. **2** take someone prisoner. **3** record accurately in words or pictures: *the illustrations capture the dogs' antics.* **4** cause data to be stored in a computer.

– SYNONYMS **1 catch,** apprehend, seize, arrest, take prisoner, take into custody, detain. **2 occupy,** invade, conquer, seize, take.
– ANTONYMS release, liberate.

▶ **noun** the action of capturing or the state of being captured.

– SYNONYMS **arrest,** apprehension, detention, seizure.

– DERIVATIVES **cap·tur·er** noun.
– ORIGIN from Latin *capere* 'seize, take.'

Cap·u·chin /'kap(y)əsʜən, kə'p(y)o͞o-/ ▶ **noun 1** a friar belonging to a strict branch of the Franciscan order. **2** (**capuchin**) a South American monkey with a hoodlike cap of hair on the head.
– ORIGIN from Italian *cappuccino* 'small hood.'

cap·y·ba·ra /'kapə,berə, -,bärə/ ▶ **noun** (pl. same or **capybaras**) a large South American rodent resembling a long-legged guinea pig.
– ORIGIN Tupi, 'grass eater.'

car /kär/ ▶ **noun 1** an automobile. **2** a vehicle that runs on rails, especially one that is part of a train.

– SYNONYMS **1 automobile,** motor vehicle, vehicle; dated or Brit. motorcar; informal auto, wheels, jalopy. **2** *the dining car* **railroad car,** coach, carriage.

– ORIGIN Latin *carrus* 'two-wheeled vehicle.'

car·a·bi·ner /,karə'bēnər/ ▶ **noun** variant spelling of **KARABINER.**

ca·ra·bi·nie·re /,karəbən'ye(ə)rē/ ▶ **noun** (pl. **carabinieri** pronunc. same) a member of the Italian paramilitary police.
– ORIGIN Italian, 'soldier armed with a carbine.'

car·a·cal /'karə,kal/ ▶ **noun** a brown lynxlike cat with black tufted ears, native to Africa and western Asia.
– ORIGIN from Turkish *kara* 'black' + *kulak* 'ear.'

car·a·cul ▶ **noun** variant spelling of **KARAKUL.**

ca·rafe /kə'raf, -'räf/ ▶ **noun** an open-topped glass flask used for serving wine or water in a restaurant.
– ORIGIN French.

ca·ram·bo·la /,karəm'bōlə/ ▶ **noun** a golden-yellow fruit with a star-shaped cross section; starfruit.
– ORIGIN Portuguese.

car·a·mel /'karəməl, -,mel, 'kärməl/ ▶ **noun 1** a soft toffee made with sugar and butter. **2** sugar or syrup heated until it turns brown, used as a flavoring or coloring for food.
– DERIVATIVES **car·a·mel·ize** /'karəmə,līz, 'kärmə-/ verb.
– ORIGIN Spanish *caramelo.*

car·a·pace /'karə,pās/ ▶ **noun** the hard upper shell of a tortoise, lobster, or other animal.
– ORIGIN Spanish *carapacho.*

car·at /'karət/ ▶ **noun 1** a unit of weight for precious stones and pearls, equivalent to 200 milligrams. **2** chiefly British spelling of **KARAT.**
– ORIGIN Greek *keration* 'carob fruit' (also referring to a unit of weight).

car·a·van /'karə,van/ ▶ **noun 1** a group of people traveling together. **2** Brit. a recreational vehicle or camper; a travel trailer.
– DERIVATIVES **car·a·van·ner** noun **car·a·van·ning** noun.
– ORIGIN Persian.

car·a·van·sa·ry /,karə'vansərē/ (chiefly Brit. also **caravanserai** /-sə,rī/) ▶ **noun** (pl. **caravansaries** or **caravanserais**) **1** a group of people traveling together; a caravan. **2** historical an inn with a central courtyard in the deserts of Asia or North Africa.
– ORIGIN Persian, 'caravan palace.'

car·a·vel /'karə,vel, -vəl/ (also **carvel** /'kärvel/) ▶ **noun** a small, fast Spanish or Portuguese sailing ship of the 15th–17th centuries.
– ORIGIN Portuguese *caravela.*

car·a·way /'karə,wā/ ▶ **noun** the seeds of a plant of the parsley family, used for flavoring.
– ORIGIN Latin *carui.*

car·bide /'kär,bīd/ ▶ **noun** a compound of carbon with a metal or other element.

car·bine /'kär,bīn, -,bēn/ ▶ **noun 1** a light automatic rifle. **2** historical a short rifle or musket used by cavalry.
– ORIGIN French *carabine.*

car·bo·hy·drate /,kärbə'hī,drāt/ ▶ **noun** any of a large group of compounds (including sugars, starch, and cellulose) that contain carbon, hydrogen, and oxygen, found in food and used to give energy.

car·bol·ic ac·id /kär'bälik/ (also **carbolic**) ▶ **noun** phenol, used as a disinfectant.

carbo-load /'kärbō,lōd/ ▶ **verb** eat large amounts of carbohydrates, especially in preparation for athletic endurance.

car·bon /'kärbən/ ▶ **noun 1** a nonmetallic chemical element that has two main forms (diamond and graphite) and is present in all organic compounds. **2** carbon dioxide or other gaseous substances released into the atmosphere.
– ORIGIN Latin *carbo* 'coal, charcoal.'

car·bo·na·ceous /,kärbə'nāsHəs/ ▶ **adjective** consisting of or containing carbon or its compounds.

car·bo·na·ra /,kärbə'närə, -'narə/ ▶ **noun** a pasta sauce made with bacon or ham, egg, and cream.
– ORIGIN Italian, 'charcoal kiln.'

car·bo·nate /'kärbənət, -,nāt/ ▶ **noun** a compound containing CO_3 negative ions together with a metallic element.
– DERIVATIVES **car·bo·na·tion** /,kärbə'nāsHən/ noun.

car·bo·nat·ed /'kärbə,nātid/ ▶ **adjective** (of a drink) containing dissolved carbon dioxide and therefore fizzy.

car·bon black ▶ **noun** a fine carbon powder used as a pigment.

car·bon cop·y ▶ **noun 1** a copy made with carbon paper. **2** a person or thing identical to another.

car·bon dat·ing (also **radiocarbon dating**) ▶ **noun** a method of determining the age of an organic object by measuring the amount of radioactive carbon-14 that it contains.

car·bon di·ox·ide ▶ **noun** a colorless, odorless gas produced by burning carbon and organic compounds and by breathing, and absorbed by plants in photosynthesis.

car·bon fi·ber ▶ **noun** a material consisting of thin, strong crystalline filaments of carbon.

car·bon foot·print ▶ **noun** the amount of carbon dioxide emitted due to the the consumption of fossil fuels by a particular person or group.

car·bon·ic /kär'bänik/ ▶ **adjective** relating to carbon or carbon dioxide.

car·bon·ic ac·id ▶ **noun** a very weak acid formed when carbon dioxide dissolves in water.

Car·bon·if·er·ous /,kärbə'nifərəs/ ▶ **adjective** Geology relating to the fifth period of the Paleozoic era (about 363 to 290 million years ago), when extensive coal-bearing strata were formed.

car·bon·ize /'kärbə,nīz/ ▶ **verb** convert something into carbon, typically by heating or burning.
– DERIVATIVES **car·bon·i·za·tion** /,kärbənə'zāsHən/ noun.

car·bon mon·ox·ide ▶ **noun** an odorless toxic flammable gas formed by incomplete burning of carbon.

car·bon-neu·tral ▶ **adjective** making no net release of carbon dioxide to the atmosphere, especially through offsetting emissions by planting trees.

car·bon off·set·ting ▶ **noun** the counteracting of carbon dioxide emissions by doing something that reduces carbon dioxide in the atmosphere by an equivalent amount, e.g., planting trees.

car·bon pa·per ▶ **noun** thin paper coated with carbon, used for making a copy as a document is being written or typed.

car·bon sink ▶ **noun** a forest, ocean, or other natural environment viewed in terms of its ability to absorb carbon dioxide from the atmosphere.

car·bon steel ▶ **noun** steel in which the main alloying element is carbon.

car·bon tax ▶ **noun** a tax on gasoline and other fossil fuels.

car·bon tra·ding ▶ **noun** another term for **EMISSIONS TRADING**.

car·bon·yl /'kärbə,nil/ ▶ **noun** Chemistry a radical consisting of a carbon atom linked to an oxygen atom, present in aldehydes and many other organic compounds.

car·bo·run·dum /,kärbə'rəndəm/ ▶ **noun** a very hard black solid consisting of silicon and carbon, used for grinding, smoothing, and polishing.
– ORIGIN blend of **CARBON** and **CORUNDUM**.

car·box·yl /kär'bäksəl/ ▶ **noun** Chemistry a radical consisting of a carbon atom linked to an oxygen atom and a hydroxyl group, present in organic acids.

car·box·yl·ic ac·id /'kärbäk'silik/ ▶ **noun** an acid containing a carboxyl group, such as formic and acetic acids.

car·boy /'kär,boi/ ▶ **noun** a large globular glass bottle with a narrow neck, used for holding acids.
– ORIGIN Persian, 'large glass flagon.'

carbs /kärbz/ ▶ **plural noun** informal dietary carbohydrates.

car·bun·cle /'kär,bəNGkəl/ ▶ **noun 1** a severe abscess or multiple boil in the skin. **2** a polished garnet (gem).
– DERIVATIVES **car·bun·cu·lar** /kär'bəNGkyələr/ adjective.
– ORIGIN Latin *carbunculus* 'small coal.'

car·bu·re·tor /'kärb(y)ə,rātər/ ▶ **noun** a device in an internal combustion engine for mixing air with a fine spray of liquid fuel.
– ORIGIN from former *carburet* 'combine or fill with carbon.'

car·cass /'kärkəs/ (Brit. also **carcase**) ▶ **noun 1** the dead body of an animal, especially one prepared for cutting up as meat. **2** the remains of a cooked bird after all the edible parts have been removed. **3** the structural framework of a building, ship, or piece of furniture.

– SYNONYMS **corpse,** dead body, remains; Medicine cadaver; informal stiff.

– ORIGIN Old French *charcois*.

CHOOSE THE RIGHT WORD

See **BODY**.

car·cin·o·gen /kär'sinəjən, 'kärsənə,jen/ ▶ **noun** a substance that can cause cancer.
– DERIVATIVES **car·cin·o·gen·ic** /,kärsənə'jenik/ adjective.
– ORIGIN from **CARCINOMA**.

car·ci·no·ma /,kärsə'nōmə/ ▶ **noun** (pl. **carcinomas** or **carcinomata** /-'nōmətə/) a cancer arising in the tissues of the skin or of the lining of the internal organs.
– ORIGIN from Greek *karkinos* 'crab.'

card[1] /kärd/ ▶ **noun 1** thick, stiff paper or thin cardboard. **2** a piece of card for writing on or printed with information. **3** a small rectangular piece of plastic containing personal data in a form that can be read by a computer: *a credit card*. **4** a playing card. **5** (**cards**) a game played with playing cards. **6** informal, dated an odd or amusing person.

– PHRASES **in the cards** informal possible or likely. **play the —— card** exploit a particular issue, especially for political advantage: *he played the race card to win votes.* **play one's cards right** make the best use of one's assets and opportunities. **put** (or **lay**) **one's cards on the table** state one's intentions openly.
– ORIGIN Greek *khartēs* 'papyrus leaf.'

card² ▶ **verb** comb and clean raw wool or similar material with a sharp-toothed instrument to disentangle the fibers before spinning. ▶ **noun** a toothed implement or machine for combing and cleaning wool.
– DERIVATIVES **card·er** noun.
– ORIGIN from Latin *carduus* 'thistle.'

car·da·mom /'kärdəməm/ ▶ **noun** the seeds of a SE Asian plant, used as a spice.
– ORIGIN from Greek *kardamon* 'cress' + *amōmon*, a kind of spice plant.

card·board /'kärd,bôrd/ ▶ **noun** thin board made from layers of paper pasted together or from paper pulp. ▶ **adjective** (of a fictional character) not realistic.

card-car·ry·ing ▶ **adjective** **1** registered as a member of a political party or labor union. **2** informal confirmed in or dedicated to a specified pursuit or outlook: *a card-carrying pessimist.*

car·di·ac /'kärdē,ak/ ▶ **adjective** relating to the heart.
– ORIGIN from Greek *kardia* 'heart.'

car·di·gan /'kärdigən/ ▶ **noun** a knitted long-sleeved sweater that fastens down the front.
– ORIGIN named after the 7th Earl of *Cardigan*, whose troops first wore such garments in the Crimean War.

car·di·nal /'kärd-nl, 'kärdn-əl/ ▶ **noun** **1** a leading Roman Catholic clergyman, nominated by and having the power to elect the Pope. **2** a deep scarlet color like that of a cardinal's robes. **3** a New World songbird of the bunting family, with a stout bill and typically with a conspicuous crest. The male is mostly red in color. ▶ **adjective** of the greatest importance; fundamental.
– ORIGIN Latin *cardinalis*, from *cardo* 'hinge.'

car·di·nal hu·mor ▶ **noun** see **HUMOR** (sense 3 of the noun).

car·di·nal num·ber ▶ **noun** a number expressing quantity (one, two, three, etc.) rather than order (first, second, third, etc.).

car·di·nal point ▶ **noun** each of the four main points of the compass (north, south, east, and west).

car·di·nal sin ▶ **noun** **1** (in Christian tradition) any of the seven deadly sins. **2** a serious error of judgment.

car·di·nal vir·tue ▶ **noun** each of the chief moral virtues in medieval philosophy: justice, prudence, temperance, and fortitude.

card in·dex ▶ **noun** a catalog in which each item is entered on a separate card.

car·di·o·gram /'kärdēə,gram/ ▶ **noun** a record of muscle activity within the heart made by a cardiograph.

car·di·o·graph /'kärdēə,graf/ ▶ **noun** an instrument for recording heart muscle activity.
– DERIVATIVES **car·di·og·ra·pher** /,kärdē'ägrəfər/ noun **car·di·og·ra·phy** /-'ägrəfē/ noun.
– ORIGIN from Greek *kardia* 'heart.'

car·di·ol·o·gy /,kärdē'äləjē/ ▶ **noun** the branch of medicine concerned with the heart.
– DERIVATIVES **car·di·o·log·i·cal** adjective **car·di·ol·o·gist** noun.
– ORIGIN from Greek *kardia* 'heart.'

car·di·o·pul·mo·nar·y /,kärdēō'pŏŏlmə,nerē, -'pəl-/ ▶ **adjective** relating to the heart and the lungs.

car·di·o·vas·cu·lar /,kärdēō'vaskyələr/ ▶ **adjective** relating to the heart and blood vessels.

car·doon /kär'dōōn/ ▶ **noun** a tall thistlelike plant related to the globe artichoke, with edible leaves and roots.
– ORIGIN Latin *carduus* 'thistle, artichoke.'

card sharp (also **card sharper** or **card shark**) ▶ **noun** a person who cheats at cards.

CARE /ke(ə)r/ ▶ **abbreviation** Cooperative for American Relief Everywhere, a large private organization that provides emergency and long-term assistance.

care /ke(ə)r/ ▶ **noun** **1** the provision of welfare and protection. **2** serious attention applied to avoid damage, risk, or error: *handle with care.* **3** a feeling of or cause for anxiety.

> – SYNONYMS **1 safekeeping,** supervision, custody, charge, protection, responsibility, guardianship. **2 discretion,** caution, sensitivity, thought, regard, consideration. **3 worry,** anxiety, trouble, concern, stress, pressure, strain.
> – ANTONYMS neglect, carelessness.

▶ **verb** **1** feel concern or interest. **2** feel affection or liking. **3** (**care for**) look after and provide for the needs of someone or something. **4** (**care for/to do**) like to have or be willing to do: *would you care for some tea?*

> – SYNONYMS **1 be concerned,** worry (oneself), trouble/concern oneself, bother, mind, be interested; informal give a damn/hoot. **2** *you care very deeply for him* **love,** be fond of, be devoted to, treasure, adore, dote on, think the world of, worship. **3** *he has numerous animals to care for* **look after,** take care of, tend, attend to, minister to, nurse.

– DERIVATIVES **car·ing** noun & adjective.
– PHRASES **care of** at the address of. **take care 1** be careful. **2** make sure to do something. **take care of someone/thing 1** keep someone or something safe and provided for. **2** deal with something.
– ORIGIN Old English.

ca·reen /kə'rēn/ ▶ **verb** **1** tilt a ship on its side for cleaning or repair. **2** move quickly and in an uncontrolled way.
– ORIGIN from Latin *carina* 'a keel.'

ca·reer /kə'ri(ə)r/ ▶ **noun** an occupation undertaken for a significant period of a person's life, usually with opportunities for progress.

> – SYNONYMS **profession,** occupation, vocation, calling, life's work, employment.

▶ **adjective** **1** (of a woman) choosing to pursue a profession rather than devoting herself to childcare or housekeeping. **2** working with long-term commitment in a particular profession: *a career diplomat.*
▶ **verb** move swiftly and in an uncontrolled way: *I careered across the desert at 150 mph.*

> – SYNONYMS **hurtle,** rush, shoot, race, speed, charge, fly; informal belt, tear.

– ORIGIN French *carrière* 'racecourse.'

ca·reer·ist /kə'ri(ə)rist/ ▶ **noun** a person whose main concern is to progress in their profession.
– DERIVATIVES **ca·reer·ism** /-,izəm/ noun.

care·free /'ke(ə)r,frē/ ▶ **adjective** free from anxiety or responsibility.

> – SYNONYMS **unworried,** untroubled, blithe, nonchalant, happy-go-lucky, free and easy, easygoing, relaxed; informal laid-back.
> – ANTONYMS troubled.

care·ful /ˈke(ə)rfəl/ ▶ **adjective 1** taking care to avoid harm or trouble; cautious. **2** sensible in the use of something: *he'd always been careful with money*. **3** done with or showing thought and attention.

– SYNONYMS **1** *be careful on the stairs* **cautious,** alert, attentive, watchful, vigilant, wary, on one's guard, circumspect. **2** *careful with money* **prudent,** thrifty, economical, sparing, frugal. **3** *careful consideration of the facts* **attentive,** conscientious, painstaking, meticulous, diligent, assiduous, scrupulous, methodical.
– ANTONYMS careless.

– DERIVATIVES **care·ful·ly** adverb **care·ful·ness** noun.

care·giv·er /ˈke(ə)rˌgivər/ ▶ **noun** a family member or paid helper who regularly looks after a child or a sick, elderly, or disabled person.
– DERIVATIVES **care·giv·ing** noun & adjective.

care·less /ˈkerlis/ ▶ **adjective 1** not giving sufficient attention or thought to avoiding harm or mistakes. **2** (**careless of/about**) not concerned or worried about: *he was careless of the truth*. **3** showing no interest or effort.

– SYNONYMS **1** *careless drivers* **inattentive,** negligent, heedless, irresponsible, impetuous, reckless. **2** *careless work* **shoddy,** slapdash, slipshod, scrappy, slovenly, sloppy, negligent, lax, slack, disorganized, hasty, hurried. **3** *a careless remark* **thoughtless,** insensitive, indiscreet, unguarded, incautious, inadvertent.
– ANTONYMS careful.

– DERIVATIVES **care·less·ly** adverb **care·less·ness** noun.

CARE pack·age ▶ **noun 1** a box of food and relief supplies sent by CARE. **2** (**care package**) a box of small gifts for a relative or friend, typically of something not readily available: *convince Aunt Alice to send me a care package full of homemade goodies*.

ca·ress /kəˈres/ ▶ **verb** touch or stroke someone or something lovingly.

– SYNONYMS **stroke,** touch, fondle, brush, feel, skim.

▶ **noun** a gentle or loving touch.
– DERIVATIVES **ca·ress·ing** adjective **ca·ress·ing·ly** adverb.
– ORIGIN French *caresser*.

car·et /ˈkarit/ ▶ **noun** a mark (^, ʎ) placed below or in a line of text to indicate an insertion.
– ORIGIN Latin, 'is lacking.'

care·tak·er /ˈke(ə)rˌtākər/ ▶ **noun** a person employed to look after a public building or a house in the owner's absence.

– SYNONYMS **custodian,** janitor, maintenance man/woman, superintendent; curator; attendant, porter, concierge; informal super.

▶ **adjective** holding power temporarily: *a caretaker government*.

– SYNONYMS **temporary,** acting, provisional, substitute, interim, stand-in, fill-in, stopgap; N. Amer. informal pinch-hitting.

care·worn /ˈke(ə)rˌwôrn/ ▶ **adjective** tired and unhappy because of prolonged worry.

car·go /ˈkärgō/ ▶ **noun** (pl. **cargoes** or **cargos**) freight carried on a ship, aircraft, or motor vehicle.

– SYNONYMS **freight,** load, haul, consignment, delivery, shipment, goods, merchandise.

– ORIGIN Spanish.

car·go pants ▶ **plural noun** loose-fitting casual cotton pants with large patch pockets halfway down each leg.

Car·ib /ˈkarib/ ▶ **noun 1** a member of a South American people living mainly in coastal regions of French Guiana, Suriname, Guyana, and Venezuela. **2** the language of the Carib.
– ORIGIN Spanish *caribe*.

Car·ib·be·an /ˌkarəˈbēən, kəˈribēən/ ▶ **adjective** relating to the region consisting of the Caribbean Sea, its islands, and the surrounding coasts.

car·i·bou /ˈkarəˌbo͞o/ ▶ **noun** (pl. same) a large North American reindeer.
– ORIGIN Canadian French.

car·i·ca·ture /ˈkarikəCHər, -ˌCHo͝or/ ▶ **noun** a picture or description in which a person's distinctive features are exaggerated for comic effect.

– SYNONYMS **cartoon,** parody, satire, lampoon, burlesque; informal sendup, takeoff.

▶ **verb** make a caricature of someone.

– SYNONYMS **parody,** satirize, lampoon, make fun of, mock, ridicule; informal send up, take off.

– DERIVATIVES **car·i·ca·tur·al** /ˌkarikəˈCHo͝orəl/ adjective **car·i·ca·tur·ist** /-ˌCHo͝orist/ noun.
– ORIGIN Italian *caricatura*.

CHOOSE THE RIGHT WORD

caricature, burlesque, lampoon, mimicry, parody, travesty

Skilled writers and artists who want to poke fun at someone or something have a number of weapons at their disposal. An artist might come up with a **caricature**, which is a drawing or written piece that exaggerates its subject's distinguishing features or peculiarities (*the cartoonist's caricature of the presidential candidate*). A **parody** is similar to a caricature in purpose, but is used of written work, or performances that ridicule an author or performer's work by imitating its language and style for comic effect (*a parody of the scene between Romeo and Juliet*). While a *parody* concentrates on distorting the content of the original work, a **travesty** retains the subject matter but imitates the style in a grotesque or absurd way (*their version of the Greek tragedy was a travesty*). A **lampoon** is a strongly satirical piece of writing that attacks or ridicules an individual or an institution; it is more commonly used as a verb (*to lampoon the government in a local newspaper*). While a *caricature*, a *parody*, and a *travesty* must have an original to imitate, a **burlesque** can be an independent creation or composition; it is a comic or satiric imitation, often a theatrical one, that treats a serious subject lightly or a trivial subject with mock seriousness (*the play was a burlesque of Homer's great epic*). **Mimicry** is something you don't have to be an artist, a writer, or an actor to be good at. Anyone who successfully imitates another person's speech or gestures is a good mimic or impressionist, whether the intent is playful or mocking (*he showed an early talent for mimicry*; *entertaining his parents with imitations of their friends*).

car·ies /ˈkerēz/ ▶ **noun** decay and crumbling of a tooth or bone.
– DERIVATIVES **car·i·ous** /ˈkarēəs/ adjective.
– ORIGIN Latin.

car·il·lon /ˈkarəˌlän, -lən/ ▶ **noun** a set of bells sounded from a keyboard or by an automatic mechanism.
– ORIGIN Old French *quarregnon* 'peal of four bells.'

car·jack·ing /ˈkärˌjakiNG/ ▶ **noun** the action of stealing a car after violently ejecting its driver.

car·load /ˈkärˌlōd/ ▶ **noun 1** the number of people that can travel in an automobile. **2** the quantity of goods that can be carried in a railroad freight car.

Car·mel·ite /ˈkärməˌlīt/ ▶ **noun** a friar or nun of an order founded at Mount Carmel in Israel during the Crusades (*c.*1154). ▶ **adjective** relating to the Carmelites.

car·min·a·tive /kärˈminətiv, ˈkärməˌnātiv/ ▶ **noun** a drug that relieves flatulence.
– ORIGIN from Latin *carminare* 'heal by incantation.'

car·mine /ˈkärmən, -ˌmīn/ ▶ **noun** a vivid crimson color.
– ORIGIN French *carmin.*

car·nage /ˈkärnij/ ▶ **noun** the killing of a large number of people.

– SYNONYMS **slaughter,** massacre, murder, butchery, bloodbath, bloodletting, holocaust.

– ORIGIN from Latin *caro* 'flesh.'

car·nal /ˈkärnl/ ▶ **adjective** relating to physical, especially sexual, needs and activities.
– DERIVATIVES **car·nal·i·ty** /kärˈnalitē/ noun **car·nal·ly** adverb.
– ORIGIN from Latin *caro* 'flesh.'

car·nal know·ledge ▶ **noun** dated, chiefly Law sexual intercourse.

car·na·tion /kärˈnāsʜən/ ▶ **noun** a cultivated variety of pink, with double pink, white, or red flowers.
– ORIGIN perhaps based on a misreading of an Arabic word.

car·nel·ian /kärˈnēlyən/ (also **cornelian**) ▶ **noun** a dull red or pink semiprecious variety of chalcedony (a form of quartz).
– ORIGIN Old French *corneline.*

car·ni·val /ˈkärnəvəl/ ▶ **noun 1** an annual public festivity involving processions, music, and dancing. **2** a traveling amusement show or circus.

– SYNONYMS **festival,** fiesta, fete, fair, gala, Mardi Gras.

– DERIVATIVES **car·ni·val·esque** /ˌkärnəvəˈlesk/ adjective.
– ORIGIN Italian *carnevale*, from Latin *carnelevamen* 'Shrovetide,' from *caro* 'flesh' + *levare* 'put away.'

car·ni·vore /ˈkärnəˌvôr/ ▶ **noun** an animal that feeds on meat.

car·niv·o·rous /kärˈnivərəs/ ▶ **adjective** (of an animal) feeding on meat.
– ORIGIN from Latin *caro* 'flesh.'

car·ob /ˈkarəb/ ▶ **noun** the edible brownish-purple pod of an Arabian tree, from which a substitute for chocolate is made.
– ORIGIN Old French *carobe.*

car·ol /ˈkarəl/ ▶ **noun** a religious song or popular hymn sung at Christmas. ▶ **verb** (**carols, caroling, caroled**) **1** (**go caroling**) sing carols in the streets. **2** sing or say something happily.
– DERIVATIVES **car·ol·er** noun.
– ORIGIN Old French *carole.*

Car·o·lin·gi·an /ˌkarəˈlinj(ē)ən/ ▶ **adjective** relating to the dynasty founded by Charlemagne's father, which ruled in western Europe from 750 to 987.
– ORIGIN alteration of earlier *Carlovingian.*

car·om /ˈkarəm/ ▶ **noun 1** Billiards a stroke in which the cue ball strikes two balls successively. **2** any of the billiard games played on a table without pockets. ▶ **verb** make a carom; strike and rebound.

car·o·tene /ˈkarəˌtēn/ ▶ **noun** an orange or red substance found in carrots and many other plants, important in the formation of vitamin A.
– ORIGIN from Latin *carota* 'carrot.'

ca·rot·e·noid /kəˈrätnˌoid/ ▶ **noun** any of a group of mainly yellow, orange, or red pigments, including carotene, that give color to plant parts such as ripe tomatoes and autumn leaves.

ca·rot·id /kəˈrätid/ ▶ **adjective** relating to the two main arteries carrying blood to the head and neck.
– ORIGIN from Greek *karōtis* 'drowsiness, stupor' (because compression of these arteries was thought to cause unconsciousness).

ca·rouse /kəˈrouz/ ▶ **verb** drink alcohol and enjoy oneself with others in a noisy, lively way.

– SYNONYMS **revel,** celebrate, roister; drink and make merry, go on a drinking bout/spree; informal booze (it up), go boozing, paint the town red, party, whoop it up.

– DERIVATIVES **ca·rous·al** noun **ca·rous·er** noun.
– ORIGIN from German *gar aus trinken.*

car·ou·sel /ˌkarəˈsel, ˈkarəˌsel/ ▶ **noun 1** a merry-go-round at a fair. **2** a conveyor system at an airport from which arriving passengers collect their luggage.
– ORIGIN Italian *carosello* 'tournament for knights on horseback.'

carp[1] /kärp/ ▶ **noun** (pl. same) a freshwater fish, often kept in ponds and sometimes farmed for food.
– ORIGIN Latin *carpa.*

carp[2] ▶ **verb** complain about something continually.

– SYNONYMS **complain,** find fault, quibble, grumble, grouse, whine; informal nitpick, gripe, moan, bitch; Brit. informal whinge.

– DERIVATIVES **carp·er** noun.
– ORIGIN Old Norse, 'brag.'

car·pac·cio /kärˈpäcʜ(ē)ō/ ▶ **noun** an Italian hors d'oeuvre consisting of thin slices of raw beef or fish served with a sauce.
– ORIGIN named after the Italian painter Vittore *Carpaccio*, from his use of red pigments.

car·pal /ˈkärpəl/ ▶ **adjective** relating to the bones in the wrist. ▶ **noun** a bone in the wrist.
– ORIGIN from **CARPUS**.

car·pal tun·nel syn·drome ▶ **noun** a painful condition of the hand and fingers caused by compression of a major nerve where it passes over the bones in the wrist.

car park ▶ **noun** Brit. a parking lot or parking garage.

car·pe di·em /ˌkärpā ˈdēˌem/ ▶ **exclamation** make the most of the present time.
– ORIGIN Latin, 'seize the day!'

car·pel /ˈkärpəl/ ▶ **noun** the female reproductive organ of a flower, consisting of an ovary, a stigma, and usually a style.
– ORIGIN Greek *karpos* 'fruit.'

car·pen·ter /ˈkärpəntər/ ▶ **noun** a person who makes wooden objects and structures.

– SYNONYMS **woodworker,** cabinetmaker; dated joiner.

– DERIVATIVES **car·pen·try** /ˈkärpəntrē/ noun.
– ORIGIN from Latin *carpentarius artifex* 'carriage-maker.'

car·pet /ˈkärpit/ ▶ **noun 1** a floor covering made from thick woven fabric. **2** a large rug. **3** a thick or soft expanse or layer of something: *a carpet of snow and ice.* ▶ **verb** (**carpets, carpeting, carpeted**) **1** cover a floor with a carpet. **2** figurative cover with a thick or soft expanse or layer of something.

– PHRASES **on the carpet** informal being reprimanded by someone in authority. **sweep something under the carpet** conceal or ignore a problem in the hope that it will be forgotten.
– ORIGIN Old French *carpite* or Latin *carpita* 'woolen covering for a table or bed.'

car·pet·bag /'kärpit,bag/ ▶ **noun** a traveling bag of a kind originally made of thick carpetlike fabric.

car·pet·bag·ger /'kärpit,bagər/ ▶ **noun** informal, derogatory **1** a politician who tries to get elected in an area where they have no local connections. **2** historical a person from the northern states who went to the South after the Civil War to profit from Reconstruction.
– ORIGIN first referring to a person from the northern states of the US who went to the South after the Civil War to make money.

car·pet-bomb ▶ **verb** bomb an area intensively.

car·pet·ing /'kärpitiNG/ ▶ **noun** material for making carpets or carpets in general.

car·pet slip·per ▶ **noun** a soft slipper with an upper of wool or thick cloth.

car·pool /'kär,po͞ol/ ▶ **noun 1** an arrangement among people to make a regular trip in a single vehicle, typically with each person taking turns to drive the others. **2** a group of people with such an arrangement. ▶ **verb** form or participate in a carpool.

car·port /'kär,pôrt/ ▶ **noun** an open-sided shelter for a car, projecting from the side of a house.

car·pus /'kärpəs/ ▶ **noun** (pl. **carpi** /-,pī, -,pē/) the group of small bones in the wrist.
– ORIGIN Greek *karpos* 'wrist.'

car·ra·geen /'karə,gēn/ ▶ **noun** an edible red seaweed with flattened branching fronds.
– ORIGIN Irish.

car·rel /kä'rel/ ▶ **noun 1** a small cubicle with a desk for a reader in a library. **2** historical a small enclosure or study in a cloister.
– ORIGIN apparently related to **CAROL** in the former sense 'a ring or enclosure.'

car·riage /'karij/ ▶ **noun 1** a four-wheeled passenger vehicle pulled by two or more horses. **2** a baby carriage. **3** a person's way of standing or moving. **4** a moving part of a machine that carries other parts into the required position. **5** a wheeled support for moving a heavy object such as a gun.
– ORIGIN Old French *cariage*.

car·ri·er /'karēər/ ▶ **noun 1** a person or thing that carries or holds something. **2** a company that transports goods or people for payment. **3** a person or animal that transmits a disease to others without suffering from it themselves.

car·ri·er pig·eon ▶ **noun** a homing pigeon trained to carry messages.

car·ri·on /'karēən/ ▶ **noun** the decaying flesh of dead animals.
– ORIGIN Old French *caroine, charoigne*.

car·ri·on crow ▶ **noun** a common black crow.

car·rot /'karət/ ▶ **noun 1** the tapering orange root of a plant of the parsley family, eaten as a vegetable. **2** something tempting offered to someone as a means of persuasion: *training that relies more on the carrot than on the stick*.
– ORIGIN Greek *karōton*.

car·rot·y /'karətē/ ▶ **adjective** (of a person's hair) orange-red.

car·ry /'karē/ ▶ **verb** (**carries, carrying, carried**) **1** move or take someone or something from one place to another. **2** have on one's person: *he is believed to be carrying a gun*. **3** support the weight of someone or something. **4** take or accept responsibility or blame. **5** have as a feature or result: *a crime that carries a maximum penalty of 20 years*. **6** take or develop an idea or activity to a particular point: *he carried the criticism much further*. **7** approve a proposal by a majority of votes: *the motion was carried by one vote*. **8** publish or broadcast something. **9** (of a sound or voice) travel. **10** (**carry oneself**) stand and move in a particular way. **11** be pregnant with: *she was carrying twins*.

> – SYNONYMS **1** *she carried the box into the kitchen* **convey,** transfer, transport, move, haul, take, bring, bear, fetch; informal cart, lug. **2** *satellites carry the signal across the country* **transmit,** conduct, relay, communicate, convey, beam, send. **3** *a resolution was carried* **approve,** pass, accept, endorse, ratify. **4** *his voice carried across the field* **be audible,** travel, reach, be heard.

– PHRASES **be/get carried away** lose one's self-control. **carry the day** be victorious or successful. **carry something forward** transfer figures to a new page or account. **carry someone off 1** take someone away by force. **2** (of a disease) kill someone. **carry something off** succeed in doing something. **carry on 1** continue. **2** informal be engaged in a love affair. **carry something on** take part in something: *it's difficult to carry on a conversation with him*. **carry something out** perform a task. **carry something over 1** keep something to use or deal with in a new context. **2** postpone an event. **carry something through** bring a project to completion. **carry weight** be influential.
– ORIGIN Old French *carier*, from Latin *carrus* 'wheeled vehicle.'

car·ry-on ▶ **noun 1** a bag or suitcase suitable for taking onto an aircraft as hand-held luggage. **2** (also **carryings-on**) improper behavior.

car·ry-out ▶ **noun** another term for **TAKEOUT**.

car·sick /'kär,sik/ ▶ **adjective** feeling sick as a result of traveling in a car.

cart /kärt/ ▶ **noun 1** an open horse-drawn vehicle with two or four wheels, used for carrying loads or passengers. **2** a shallow open container on wheels, pulled or pushed by hand. ▶ **verb 1** carry something in a cart or similar vehicle. **2** informal carry a large, heavy, or unwieldy object somewhere with difficulty. **3** take someone somewhere roughly: *the demonstrators were carted off by the police*.
– PHRASES **put the cart before the horse** do things in the wrong order.
– ORIGIN Old Norse.

carte blanche /'kärt 'blänsh, 'blänch/ ▶ **noun** complete freedom to do whatever one wants to do.
– ORIGIN French, 'blank paper.'

car·tel /kär'tel/ ▶ **noun** an association of manufacturers or suppliers formed to keep prices high and restrict competition.
– ORIGIN German *Kartell*.

Car·te·sian /kär'tēzhən/ ▶ **adjective** relating to the French philosopher René Descartes (1596–1650) and his ideas.
– DERIVATIVES **Car·te·sian·ism** /-,nizəm/ noun.
– ORIGIN from *Cartesius*, Latin form of *Descartes*.

Car·te·sian co·or·di·nates ▶ **plural noun** a system for locating a point by reference to its distance from axes intersecting at right angles.

Car·tha·gin·i·an /ˌkärTHəˈjinēən/ ▶ **noun** a person from the ancient city of Carthage on the coast of North Africa. ▶ **adjective** relating to Carthage or its people.

Car·thu·sian /kärˈTH(y)o͞ozHən/ ▶ **noun** a monk or nun of a strict order founded at Chartreuse in France in 1084. ▶ **adjective** relating to this order.
– ORIGIN from *Carthusia*, the Latin name for *Chartreuse*.

car·ti·lage /ˈkärtl-ij/ ▶ **noun** firm, flexible tissue that covers the ends of joints and forms structures such as the larynx and the external ear.
– DERIVATIVES **car·ti·lag·i·nous** /ˌkärtlˈajənəs/ adjective.
– ORIGIN Latin *cartilago*.

car·ti·lag·i·nous fish ▶ **noun** a fish with a skeleton of cartilage rather than bone, e.g., a shark or ray.

car·tog·ra·phy /kärˈtägrəfē/ ▶ **noun** the science or practice of drawing maps.
– DERIVATIVES **car·tog·ra·pher** noun **car·to·graph·ic** /ˌkärtəˈgrafik/ adjective.
– ORIGIN French *carte* 'card, map.'

car·ton /ˈkärtn/ ▶ **noun** a light cardboard box or container.

> – SYNONYMS **box,** package, cardboard box, case, container, pack, packet.

– ORIGIN French, from Italian *cartone* 'cartoon.'

car·toon /kärˈto͞on/ ▶ **noun 1** a humorous or satirical drawing in a newspaper or magazine. **2** (also **cartoon strip**) a comic strip. **3** a film made from a sequence of drawings, using animation techniques to give the appearance of movement. **4** a full-size drawing made as a preliminary design for a painting or other work of art.

> – SYNONYMS **1 animation,** animated film, comic strip, graphic novel. **2 caricature,** parody, lampoon, satire; informal takeoff, sendup.

– DERIVATIVES **car·toon·ist** noun.
– ORIGIN Italian *cartone*, from Latin *carta, charta* 'card, map.'

car·touche /kärˈto͞osH/ ▶ **noun 1** a carved decoration or drawing in the form of a scroll with rolled-up ends. **2** an oval or oblong containing Egyptian hieroglyphs that represent the name and title of a monarch.
– ORIGIN French.

car·tridge /ˈkärtrij/ ▶ **noun 1** a container holding a spool of film, a quantity of ink, or other item or substance, to be inserted into a mechanism. **2** a casing containing a charge and a bullet or shot for a gun.

> – SYNONYMS **cassette,** magazine, canister, case, container.

– ORIGIN variant of **CARTOUCHE**.

cart·wheel /ˈkärtˌ(h)wēl/ ▶ **noun** a circular sideways handspring with the arms and legs extended. ▶ **verb** perform cartwheels.

carve /kärv/ ▶ **verb 1** cut into or shape a hard material to produce an object or design: *the tools used to carve marble*. **2** produce a design or object by carving: *I carved my initials on the tree*. **3** cut cooked meat into slices for eating. **4** (**carve something up**) divide something ruthlessly into separate parts or areas. **5** (**carve something out**) develop a career, reputation, etc., through great effort.

> – SYNONYMS **1 sculpt,** cut, hew, whittle, chisel, shape, fashion. **2 engrave,** incise, score, cut. **3 slice,** cut up, chop. **4** (**carve something up**) **divide,** break up, partition, apportion, subdivide, split up, share out.

– ORIGIN Old English.

car·vel /ˈkärvel/ ▶ **noun** variant spelling of **CARAVEL**.

car·ver /ˈkärvər/ ▶ **noun** a person or tool that carves.

car·ver·y /ˈkärvərē/ ▶ **noun** (pl. **carveries**) a buffet or restaurant where cooked roasts of meat are carved as required.

carv·ing /ˈkärviNG/ ▶ **noun** an object or design carved from wood or stone as a work of art.

car wash ▶ **noun** a structure containing equipment for washing vehicles automatically.

car·y·at·id /ˌkarēˈatid, ˈkarēəˌtid/ ▶ **noun** Architecture a supporting pillar in the form of a clothed female figure.
– ORIGIN Greek *karuatides* 'priestesses of Artemis at Caryae,' from *Karuai* (Caryae) in Laconia.

Cas·a·no·va /ˌkazəˈnōvə, ˌkasə-/ ▶ **noun** a man notorious for seducing women.
– ORIGIN from the name of the Italian adventurer Giovanni Jacopo *Casanova*.

cas·bah /ˈkasˌbä/ ▶ **noun** variant spelling of **KASBAH**.

cas·cade /kasˈkād/ ▶ **noun 1** a small waterfall, especially one in a series. **2** a mass of something that falls, hangs, or occurs in large quantities: *a cascade of raindrops*. **3** a succession of devices or stages in a process, each of which triggers the next.

> – SYNONYMS **waterfall,** cataract, falls, rapids, whitewater, flood, torrent.

▶ **verb** pour downward rapidly and in large quantities.

> – SYNONYMS **pour,** gush, surge, spill, stream, flow, issue, spurt, jet.

– ORIGIN from Italian *cascare* 'to fall.'

cas·car·a /kasˈkarə/ (also **cascara sagrada** /səˈgrädə/) ▶ **noun** a laxative made from the dried bark of a North American shrub.
– ORIGIN Spanish, '(sacred) bark.'

case[1] /kās/ ▶ **noun 1** an instance of a particular situation: *a case of mistaken identity*. **2** an instance of a disease, injury, or problem: *1,000 new cases of cancer*. **3** an incident being investigated by the police. **4** a legal action that is to be or has been decided in a court of law. **5** a set of facts or arguments supporting one side of a debate or lawsuit. **6** a person or problem requiring or receiving the attention of a doctor, social worker, etc. **7** Grammar a form of a noun, adjective, or pronoun expressing the relationship of the word to other words in the sentence: *the possessive case*.

> – SYNONYMS **1** *a classic case of overreaction* **instance,** example, occurrence, occasion, demonstration, illustration. **2** *is that the case?* **situation,** position, state of affairs, circumstances, conditions, facts; informal score. **3 assignment,** job, project, investigation, exercise. **4** *he lost his case* **lawsuit,** legal action, trial, legal proceedings, litigation. **5** *the case against animal testing* **argument,** defense, justification, vindication, exposition, thesis.

– PHRASES **be the case** be so. **in case** so as to allow for the possibility of something happening or being true.
– ORIGIN Latin *casus* 'fall, occurrence, chance.'

case[2] ▶ **noun 1** a container or protective covering. **2** Brit. a suitcase. **3** a box containing twelve bottles of wine or other drink, sold as a unit.

> – SYNONYMS **1 container,** box, carton, canister, holder. **2 casing,** cover, sheath, envelope, sleeve, jacket, shell. **3 suitcase,** travel bag, valise; (**cases**) luggage, baggage. **4** *a glass display case* **cabinet,** cupboard, buffet.

▸ **verb 1** enclose something within a case. **2** informal look around a place before carrying out a robbery.
– ORIGIN Latin *capsa* 'box.'

case·book /'kās,bo͝ok/ ▸ **noun** a book containing a selection of source materials on a particular subject.

case-hard·ened ▸ **adjective** made callous or tough by experience: *a case-hardened politician.*

case his·to·ry ▸ **noun** a record of a person's background or medical history kept by a doctor or social worker.

ca·sein /kā'sēn, 'kāsēən/ ▸ **noun** the main protein present in milk and (in coagulated form) in cheese.
– ORIGIN from Latin *caseus* 'cheese.'

case law ▸ **noun** the law as established by the outcome of former cases rather than by legislation.

case·load /'kās,lōd/ ▸ **noun** the number of cases being dealt with by a doctor, lawyer, or social worker at one time.

case·ment /'kāsmənt/ ▸ **noun** a window set on a vertical hinge so that it opens like a door.
– ORIGIN Latin *cassimentum.*

case-sen·si·tive ▸ **adjective** Computing **1** (of a program or function) differentiating between capital and lowercase letters. **2** (of input) treated differently depending on whether it is in capitals or lowercase text.

case stud·y ▸ **noun 1** a detailed study of the development of a particular person, group, or situation over a period of time. **2** a particular instance of something used or analyzed to illustrate a theory or principle.

case·work /'kās,wərk/ ▸ **noun** social work involving the study of a particular person's family history and personal circumstances.
– DERIVATIVES **case·work·er** noun.

cash /kash/ ▸ **noun 1** money in the form of coins or bills. **2** money in any form: *he was always short of cash.*

– SYNONYMS **1 money,** currency, banknotes, bills, coins, change; informal dough, loot, dinero, moolah, bucks, bread. **2 finance,** money, resources, funds, assets, means, wherewithal.

▸ **verb 1** give or get bills or coins for a check or money order. **2** (**cash something in**) convert an insurance policy, savings account, etc., into money. **3** (**cash in on**) informal take advantage of a situation.
– DERIVATIVES **cash·less** adjective.
– PHRASES **cash in hand** payment in cash rather than by check or other means.
– ORIGIN Old French *casse* 'box for money,' from Latin *capsa* 'box, receptacle.'

cash and car·ry ▸ **noun** a system of wholesale trading in which goods are paid for in full and taken away by the buyer.

cash·back /'kash,bak/ ▸ **noun 1** a service offered by a store by which a customer may withdraw cash when buying goods with a debit card. **2** a cash refund offered as an incentive to buyers of certain products.

cash book ▸ **noun** a book in which amounts of money paid and received are recorded.

cash cow ▸ **noun** informal a business or investment that provides a steady income or profit.

cash crop ▸ **noun** a crop produced for selling rather than for use by the grower.

cash·ew /'kash,o͞o, kə'sho͞o/ ▸ **noun** (also **cashew nut**) the edible kidney-shaped nut of a tropical American tree.
– ORIGIN Tupi.

cash flow ▸ **noun** the total amount of money passing into and out of a business.

cash·ier[1] /ka'shi(ə)r/ ▸ **noun** a person whose job is to pay out and receive money in a store, bank, or business.

– SYNONYMS **clerk,** teller, banker, treasurer, bursar, purser.

– ORIGIN French *caissier.*

cash·ier[2] ▸ **verb** dismiss someone from the armed forces because of a serious wrongdoing.
– ORIGIN French *casser* 'revoke, dismiss.'

cash·mere /'kazh,mi(ə)r, 'kash-/ ▸ **noun** fine soft wool, originally that obtained from a breed of Himalayan goat.
– ORIGIN an early spelling of *Kashmir,* a region on the border of India and NE Pakistan.

cash reg·is·ter ▸ **noun** a machine used in stores for adding up and recording the amount of each sale and storing the money received.

cash-strapped ▸ **adjective** informal very short of money.

cas·ing /'kāsing/ ▸ **noun 1** a cover or shell that protects or encloses something. **2** the frame around a door or window.

ca·si·no /kə'sēnō/ ▸ **noun** (pl. **casinos**) a public building or room for gambling.
– ORIGIN Italian, 'little house.'

cask /kask/ ▸ **noun** a large barrel for storing alcoholic drinks.

– SYNONYMS **barrel,** keg, butt, tun, vat, drum, hogshead; historical firkin.

– ORIGIN French *casque* or Spanish *casco* 'helmet.'

cas·ket /'kaskit/ ▸ **noun 1** a small ornamental box or chest for holding valuable objects. **2** a coffin.
– ORIGIN perhaps a variant of Old French *cassette* 'little box.'

Cas·san·dra /kə'sandrə/ ▸ **noun** a person who makes pessimistic predictions.
– ORIGIN from *Cassandra* in Greek mythology, whose prophecies, though true, were not believed.

cas·sa·va /kə'sävə/ ▸ **noun** the starchy root of a tropical American tree, used as food.
– ORIGIN from Taino (an extinct Caribbean language).

cas·se·role /'kasə,rōl/ ▸ **noun 1** a large dish with a lid, used for cooking food slowly in an oven. **2** a kind of stew cooked slowly in an oven. ▸ **verb** cook food slowly in a casserole.
– ORIGIN French.

cas·sette /kə'set/ ▸ **noun** a sealed plastic case containing audiotape, videotape, film, etc., to be inserted into a recorder, camera, or other device.
– ORIGIN French, 'little box.'

cas·sia /'kashə/ ▸ **noun 1** a tree or plant of warm climates from which senna (a mild laxative) is obtained. **2** the bark of an East Asian tree, from which an inferior kind of cinnamon is obtained.
– ORIGIN Latin.

cas·sis /ka'sēs/ (also **crème de cassis** /,krem də ka'sēs/) ▸ **noun** a syrupy black currant liqueur.
– ORIGIN French, 'blackcurrant.'

cas·sock /'kasək/ ▸ **noun** a long garment worn by some Christian clergy and members of church choirs.
– ORIGIN Italian *casacca* 'riding coat.'

cas·sou·let /ˌkasəˈlā/ ▶ **noun** a stew made with meat and beans.
– ORIGIN French, 'small stew pan.'

cas·so·war·y /ˈkasəˌwerē/ ▶ **noun** (pl. **cassowaries**) a very large flightless bird related to the emu, native mainly to New Guinea.
– ORIGIN Malay.

cast /kast/ ▶ **verb** (past and past part. **cast**) **1** throw something forcefully. **2** cause light or shadow to appear on a surface. **3** direct one's eyes or thoughts toward something. **4** express: *journalists cast doubt on this account.* **5** register a vote. **6** give a part to an actor or allocate parts in a play, movie, or television show. **7** leave aside: *he jumped in, casting caution to the winds.* **8** throw the hooked and baited end of a fishing line out into the water. **9** shape metal or other material by pouring it into a mold while molten. **10** produce an object by casting metal: *a figure cast in bronze.* **11** describe or present in a particular way: *he cast himself as the embodiment of the American dream.* **12** cause a magic spell to take effect.

– SYNONYMS **1 throw,** toss, fling, pitch, hurl, lob; informal chuck, sling. **2 direct,** shoot, throw, fling, send. **3** *cast your vote* **register,** record, enter, file. **4 emit,** give off, throw, send out, radiate. **5 mold,** fashion, form, shape, forge.

▶ **noun 1** the actors taking part in a play, movie, or television show. **2** an object made by casting metal or other material. **3** (also **plaster cast**) a bandage stiffened with plaster of Paris, molded to support and protect a broken limb. **4** the appearance or nature of someone or something: *minds of a philosophical cast.* **5** a slight squint.

– SYNONYMS **1 actors,** performers, players, company, troupe, dramatis personae, characters. **2 mold,** die, matrix, shape, casting, model.

– PHRASES **be cast away** be stranded after a shipwreck. **be cast down** feel depressed. **cast about** (or **around**) search far and wide. **cast off** Knitting take the stitches off the needle by looping each over the next. **cast something off** release a boat or ship from its moorings. **cast on** Knitting make the first row of loops on the needle.
– ORIGIN Old Norse.

cas·ta·nets /ˌkastəˈnets/ ▶ **plural noun** a pair of small curved pieces of wood, ivory, or plastic, clicked together by the fingers as an accompaniment to Spanish dancing.
– ORIGIN Spanish *castañeta* 'little chestnut.'

cast·a·way /ˈkastəˌwā/ ▶ **noun** a person who has been shipwrecked and stranded in an isolated place.

caste /kast/ ▶ **noun** each of the hereditary classes of Hindu society.

– SYNONYMS **class,** rank, level, order, stratum, echelon, status.

– ORIGIN Spanish and Portuguese *casta* 'lineage, breed.'

cas·tel·lat·ed /ˈkastəˌlātid/ ▶ **adjective** having battlements.
– DERIVATIVES **cas·tel·la·tion** /ˌkastəˈlāsʜən/ noun.
– ORIGIN from Latin *castellum* 'little fort.'

cast·er /ˈkastər/ ▶ **noun 1** each of a set of small swiveling wheels fixed to the legs or base of a piece of furniture. **2** a small container with holes in the top, used for sprinkling salt, sugar, etc.

cas·ti·gate /ˈkastəˌgāt/ ▶ **verb** reprimand someone severely.
– DERIVATIVES **cas·ti·ga·tion** /ˌkastəˈgāsʜən/ noun.
– ORIGIN Latin *castigare.*

Cas·til·ian /kəˈstilyən/ ▶ **noun 1** a person from the Spanish region of Castile. **2** the language of Castile, the standard form of both spoken and literary Spanish. ▶ **adjective** relating to Castile or Castilian.

cast·ing /ˈkastiɴɢ/ ▶ **noun** an object made by casting molten metal or other material.

cast·ing vote ▶ **noun** an extra vote used by a chairperson to decide an issue when votes on each side are equal.

cast i·ron ▶ **noun** a hard alloy of iron and carbon that can be readily cast in a mold. ▶ **adjective** firm and unchangeable: *a cast-iron guarantee.*

cas·tle /ˈkasəl/ ▶ **noun 1** a large fortified building or group of buildings constructed during medieval times. **2** Chess, informal old-fashioned term for **ROOK**[2].

– SYNONYMS **fortress,** fort, stronghold, fortification, keep, citadel, palace, chateau, tower.

– PHRASES **castles in the air** (or **in Spain**) plans or dreams that are never likely to be achieved or fulfilled.
– ORIGIN Latin *castellum* 'little fort.'

cast·off /ˈkastˌôf/ ▶ **adjective** no longer wanted; abandoned or discarded. ▶ **noun** a garment that is no longer wanted.

cas·tor /ˈkastər/ ▶ **noun** variant spelling of **CASTER**.

cas·tor oil ▶ **noun** an oil obtained from the seeds of an African shrub, used as a laxative.
– ORIGIN Greek *kastōr* 'beaver': perhaps because an oily substance produced by beavers was formerly used as a laxative.

cas·trate /ˈkasˌtrāt/ ▶ **verb 1** remove the testicles of a male animal or person. **2** deprive someone or something of power or vitality.
– DERIVATIVES **cas·tra·tion** /kaˈstrāsʜən/ noun **cas·tra·tor** /-ˌtrātər/ noun.
– ORIGIN Latin *castrare.*

cas·tra·to /kasˈträˌtō/ ▶ **noun** (pl. **castrati** /-tē/) historical a male singer castrated before puberty so that he kept a soprano or alto voice.
– ORIGIN Italian.

ca·su·al /ˈkazʜo͞oəl/ ▶ **adjective 1** relaxed and unconcerned. **2** done or made without much thought: *a casual remark.* **3** not regular or firmly established; occasional or temporary: *casual jobs.* **4** happening by chance; accidental. **5** (of clothes) suitable for informal everyday wear: *a casual short-sleeved shirt.*

– SYNONYMS **1** *a casual attitude* **unconcerned,** uncaring, indifferent, lackadaisical, nonchalant, offhand, flippant, easy-going, free and easy, blithe, carefree, devil-may-care; informal laid-back. **2** *a casual remark* **offhand,** spontaneous, unthinking, unconsidered, impromptu, throwaway, unguarded; informal off-the-cuff. **3** *a casual glance* **cursory,** perfunctory, superficial, passing, fleeting. **4** *casual work* **temporary,** freelance, irregular, occasional. **5** *a casual meeting* **chance,** accidental, unplanned, unintended, unexpected, unforeseen. **6** *a casual atmosphere* **relaxed,** friendly, informal, easygoing, free and easy; informal laid-back.
– ANTONYMS serious, deliberate, formal.

▶ **noun 1** a person who does something irregularly, especially a temporary worker. **2** (**casuals**) clothes or shoes suitable for informal everyday wear.
– DERIVATIVES **cas·u·al·ly** adverb **cas·u·al·ness** noun.
– ORIGIN Latin *casualis.*

CHOOSE THE RIGHT WORD

See **ACCIDENTAL**.

cas·u·al·ty /ˈkazH(o͞o)əltē/ ▸ **noun** (pl. **casualties**) **1** a person killed or injured in a war or accident. **2** a person or thing badly affected by an event or situation: *the firm was one of the casualties of the recession.*

– SYNONYMS **victim,** sufferer, fatality, death, loss, wounded person, injured person.

cas·u·ist·ry /ˈkazHo͞oəstrē/ ▸ **noun** the use of clever but false reasoning.
– DERIVATIVES **cas·u·ist** /ˈkazHo͞oist/ noun **cas·u·is·tic** /ˌkazHo͞oˈistik/ adjective **cas·u·is·ti·cal** /ˌkazHo͞oˈistikəl/ adjective.
– ORIGIN from Latin *casus* 'fall, chance.'

CAT /ˈkat/ ▸ **abbreviation** Medicine computerized axial tomography.

cat /ˈkat/ ▸ **noun 1** a small domesticated mammal with soft fur. **2** a wild animal related to or resembling this, e.g., a lion or tiger.

– SYNONYMS **feline,** tomcat, tom, kitten; informal pussy (cat), puss, kitty.

– DERIVATIVES **cat·like** adjective.
– PHRASES **the cat's meow** (or **pajamas** or **whiskers**) informal an excellent person or thing. **let the cat out of the bag** informal reveal a secret by mistake. **like a cat on a hot tin roof** informal very agitated or anxious.
– ORIGIN Old English.

WORD LINKS

feline *relating to cats*

ca·tab·o·lism /kəˈtabəˌlizəm/ ▸ **noun** a metabolic process in which complex molecules are broken down to form simpler ones and energy is released. The opposite of **ANABOLISM**.
– DERIVATIVES **cat·a·bol·ic** /ˌkatəˈbälik/ adjective.
– ORIGIN Greek *katabolē* 'throwing down.'

cat·a·clysm /ˈkatəˌklizəm/ ▸ **noun** a violent upheaval or disaster.
– DERIVATIVES **cat·a·clys·mic** /ˌkatəˈklizmik/ adjective **cat·a·clys·mi·cal·ly** /-mik(ə)lē/ adverb.
– ORIGIN Greek *kataklusmos* 'deluge.'

cat·a·comb /ˈkatəˌkōm/ ▸ **noun** an underground cemetery consisting of tunnels with recesses for tombs.
– ORIGIN Latin *catacumbas*, the name of an underground cemetery near Rome.

cat·a·falque /ˈkatəˌfô(l)k, -ˌfalk/ ▸ **noun** a decorated wooden framework used to support a coffin.
– ORIGIN Italian *catafalco.*

Cat·a·lan /ˈkatlˌan, ˈkatl-ən/ ▸ **noun 1** a person from Catalonia in NE Spain. **2** the language of Catalonia. ▸ **adjective** relating to Catalonia.
– ORIGIN Spanish.

cat·a·lep·sy /ˈkatlˌepsē/ ▸ **noun** a medical condition in which a person suffers a loss of consciousness and their body becomes rigid.
– DERIVATIVES **cat·a·lep·tic** /ˌkatlˈeptik/ adjective & noun.
– ORIGIN from Greek *katalambanein* 'seize upon.'

cat·a·log /ˈkatlˌôg, -ˌäg/ (also **catalogue**) ▸ **noun 1** a complete list of items arranged in alphabetical or other systematic order. **2** a publication containing details of items for sale. **3** a series of bad things: *a catalog of disasters.*

– SYNONYMS **1 directory,** register, index, list, listing, record, schedule, archive, inventory. **2 brochure,** mailer, magazine, wish book.

▸ **verb** (**catalogs, cataloging, cataloged**; also **catalogues, cataloguing, catalogued**) list an item or items in a catalog.

– SYNONYMS **classify,** categorize, index, list, archive, record, itemize.

– DERIVATIVES **cat·a·log·er, cat·a·log·uer** noun.
– ORIGIN Greek *katalogos.*

Cat·a·lo·ni·an /ˌkatlˈōnēən/ ▸ **adjective & noun** another term for **CATALAN**.

ca·tal·pa /kəˈtalpə/ ▸ **noun** a tree with heart-shaped leaves, native to North America and east Asia.
– ORIGIN from an American Indian language.

ca·tal·y·sis /kəˈtaləsis/ ▸ **noun** the speeding up of a chemical reaction by a catalyst.
– DERIVATIVES **cat·a·lyt·ic** /ˌkatlˈitik/ adjective.
– ORIGIN Greek *katalusis* 'dissolution.'

cat·a·lyst /ˈkatl-ist/ ▸ **noun 1** a substance that increases the speed of a chemical reaction without undergoing any permanent chemical change itself. **2** a person or thing that causes something to happen: *his speech had acted as a catalyst for debate.*

cat·a·lyt·ic con·vert·er ▸ **noun** a device in the exhaust system of a motor vehicle, containing a catalyst for converting pollutant gases into less harmful ones.

cat·a·lyze /ˈkatlˌīz/ (Brit. **catalyse**) ▸ **verb** cause or speed up a reaction by acting as a catalyst.
– DERIVATIVES **cat·a·lyz·er** noun.

cat·a·ma·ran /ˌkatəməˈran, ˈkatəməˌran/ ▸ **noun** a sailboat or other boat with twin parallel hulls.
– ORIGIN Tamil, 'tied wood.'

cat·a·mite /ˈkatəˌmīt/ ▸ **noun** old use a boy kept by an older man as a homosexual partner.
– ORIGIN Latin *catamitus.*

cat·a·plex·y /ˈkatəˌpleksē/ ▸ **noun** a medical condition in which strong emotion or laughter causes a person to experience sudden weakness in the muscles.
– ORIGIN Greek *kataplēxis* 'stupefaction.'

cat·a·pult /ˈkatəˌpəlt, -ˌpo͝olt/ ▸ **noun 1** historical a military machine for hurling large stones or other missiles. **2** a mechanical device for launching a glider or aircraft. ▸ **verb 1** throw something forcefully. **2** move suddenly or very fast.
– ORIGIN Latin *catapulta.*

cat·a·ract /ˈkatəˌrakt/ ▸ **noun 1** a large waterfall. **2** a medical condition in which the lens of the eye becomes opaque, resulting in blurred vision.
– ORIGIN from Greek *kataraktēs* 'down-rushing.'

ca·tarrh /kəˈtär/ ▸ **noun** excessive mucus in the nose or throat.
– DERIVATIVES **ca·tarrh·al** adjective.
– ORIGIN from Greek *katarrhein* 'flow down.'

ca·tas·tro·phe /kəˈtastrəfē/ ▸ **noun** an event causing great damage or suffering.

– SYNONYMS **disaster,** calamity, cataclysm, ruin, tragedy, fiasco, debacle.

– DERIVATIVES **cat·a·stroph·ic** /ˌkatəˈsträfik/ adjective **cat·a·stroph·i·cal·ly** /-ik(ə)lē/ adverb.
– ORIGIN Greek *katastrophē* 'overturning, sudden turn.'

cat·a·to·ni·a /ˌkatəˈtōnēə/ ▸ **noun** a condition resulting from schizophrenia or another mental disorder,

in which a person experiences both periods of unconsciousness and overactivity.
– ORIGIN from Greek *tonos* 'tone or tension.'

cat·a·ton·ic /ˌkatəˈtänik/ ▶ adjective **1** suffering from catatonia. **2** informal inert or completely unresponsive.

cat·bird /ˈkatˌbərd/ ▶ noun a long-tailed American songbird of the mockingbird family, with mainly gray plumage and catlike calls.
– PHRASES **in the catbird seat** informal in a superior or advantageous position. [said to be an allusion to a baseball player in the fortunate position of having no strikes and therefore three balls still to play (a reference made in James Thurber's short story *The Catbird Seat*).]

cat bur·glar ▶ noun a thief who enters a building by climbing to an upper story.

cat·call /ˈkatˌkôl/ ▶ noun a shrill whistle or shout of mockery or disapproval. ▶ verb make a catcall.

catch /kach, kech/ ▶ verb (past and past part. **caught**) **1** seize and take hold of a moving object. **2** capture a person or animal. **3** entangle or become entangled. **4** surprise someone in the act of doing something wrong or embarrassing. **5** become infected with an illness. **6** be in time to board a train, bus, etc., or to see a person or event. **7** (**be caught in**) unexpectedly find oneself in an unwelcome situation. **8** see, hear, or understand: *I couldn't catch what he said.* **9** gain a person's interest or attention. **10** hit someone or something: *she fell and caught her head on the hearth.* **11** start burning.

– SYNONYMS **1 seize,** grab, snatch, grasp, grip, clutch, intercept, trap, receive, get. **2 capture,** apprehend, seize, arrest, take prisoner, trap, snare, net; informal nab, collar. **3** *her heel caught in a hole* **become trapped,** become entangled, snag, jam, wedge, lodge, get stuck. **4** *she caught him flirting with another woman* **discover,** find, come across, stumble on, chance on, surprise. **5** *he caught malaria* **contract,** go/come down with, be taken ill with, develop, pick up, succumb to.
– ANTONYMS drop, release.

▶ noun **1** an act of catching something. **2** a device for fastening a door, window, etc. **3** a hidden problem. **4** an amount of fish caught. **5** a break in a person's voice caused by emotion. **6** informal a person thought of as being desirable or suitable as a husband or wife.

– SYNONYMS **1** *the window catch was rusty* **latch,** lock, fastener, clasp, hasp. **2** *it looks great, but there's a catch* **snag,** disadvantage, drawback, stumbling block, hitch, complication, problem, trap, trick. **3** *a catch of fish* **haul,** net, bag, yield.

– PHRASES **catch one's breath 1** breathe in sharply as a result of a strong emotion. **2** recover one's breath after exercise. **catch someone's eye 1** be noticed by someone. **2** attract someone's attention by making eye contact. **catch on** informal **1** become popular. **2** understand what is meant. **catch up 1** do tasks that one should have done earlier. **2** (**be/get caught up in**) become involved in. **catch someone up** succeed in reaching a person ahead.
– ORIGIN from Latin *captare* 'try to catch.'

catch-22 /ˌtwentēˈto͞o/ ▶ noun a difficult situation from which there is no escape because it involves situations that conflict with or are dependent on each other.
– ORIGIN title of a novel by Joseph Heller (1961).

catch-all ▶ noun a term or category intended to cover all possibilities.

catch·er /ˈkachər, ˈkech-/ ▶ noun Baseball a fielder positioned behind home plate to catch pitches not hit by the batter and to execute other defensive plays.

catch·ing /ˈkaching, ˈkech-/ ▶ adjective (of a disease) infectious.

– SYNONYMS **infectious,** contagious, communicable; dated infective.

catch·ment /ˈkachmənt, ˈkech-/ ▶ noun **1** the action of collecting water, especially the collection of rainfall over a natural drainage area. **2** the area from which rainfall flows into a river, lake, or reservoir. **3** the activity of collecting something in a place it gathers. **4** (also **catchment area**) the area of a city, town, etc., from which a hospital's patients or school's students are drawn.

catch·pen·ny /ˈkachˌpenē, ˈkech-/ ▶ adjective having a superficially attractive appearance so as to sell quickly.

catch·phrase /ˈkachˌfrāz, ˈkech-/ ▶ noun a well-known sentence or phrase.

catch-up ▶ noun informal an instance of catching up to someone in a particular activity.
– PHRASES **play catch-up 1** fall behind continually with work or financial matters: *I'm always playing catch-up with my homework.* **2** try to equal a competitor in a sport or game.

catch·word /ˈkachˌwərd, ˈkech-/ ▶ noun a frequently used word or phrase that is associated with or encapsulates a particular thing: *perestroika was the catchword of the Gorbachev era.*

catch·y /ˈkachē, ˈkechē/ ▶ adjective (**catchier, catchiest**) (of a tune or phrase) instantly appealing and easy to remember.

– SYNONYMS **memorable,** unforgettable, haunting, appealing, popular.
– ANTONYMS forgettable.

– DERIVATIVES **catch·i·ness** noun.

cat door ▶ noun a small hinged flap in an outer door through which a cat may pass in and out.

cat·e·che·sis /ˌkatəˈkēsis/ ▶ noun religious instruction given to prepare someone for Christian baptism or confirmation.
– ORIGIN Greek *katēkhēsis* 'oral instruction.'

cat·e·chism /ˈkatəˌkizəm/ ▶ noun a summary of the principles of the Christian religion in the form of questions and answers, used for teaching.

cat·e·chist /ˈkatəkist/ ▶ noun a Christian teacher, especially one using a catechism.

cat·e·chize /ˈkatəˌkīz/ ▶ verb teach someone about the principles of the Christian religion by means of question and answer, especially by using a catechism.
– ORIGIN from Greek *katēkhein* 'teach orally.'

cat·e·go·ri·cal /ˌkatəˈgôrikəl/ (also **categoric**) ▶ adjective completely explicit and direct.

– SYNONYMS **unqualified,** unconditional, unequivocal, absolute, explicit, unambiguous, definite, direct, emphatic, positive, out-and-out.

– DERIVATIVES **cat·e·gor·i·cal·ly** /-ik(ə)lē/ adverb.

cat·e·go·rize /ˈkatəgəˌrīz/ ▶ verb place someone or something in a particular category: *the population is categorized according to age, sex, and socioeconomic group.*
– DERIVATIVES **cat·e·go·ri·za·tion** /ˌkatəgərəˈzāshən/ noun.

cat·e·go·ry /ˈkatəˌgôrē/ ▶ noun (pl. **categories**) a class or group of people or things with shared characteristics.

– SYNONYMS **class,** classification, group, grouping, bracket, heading, set, type, sort, kind, grade, order, rank.

– ORIGIN Greek *katēgoria* 'statement.'

cat·e·nar·y /ˈkatəˌnerē, ˈkatnˌerē/ ▶ **noun** (pl. **catenaries**) a curve formed by a wire, chain, etc., hanging from two points on the same horizontal level. ▶ **adjective** involving or referring to a curve of this type.
– ORIGIN Latin *catena* 'chain.'

ca·ter /ˈkātər/ ▶ **verb 1** provide food and drink at a social event. **2** (**cater to**) provide with what is needed or required. **3** (**cater to**) satisfy a need or demand.

> – SYNONYMS **1** *we cater for vegetarians* **provide (food) for,** feed, serve, cook for. **2** (**cater to**) *a resort catering to the rich* **serve,** provide for, meet the needs/wants of, accommodate. **3** (**cater to**) *we cater to all tastes* **take into account,** take into consideration, allow for, consider, bear in mind, make provision for, have regard for.

– DERIVATIVES **ca·ter·er** noun.
– ORIGIN Old French *acater* 'buy,' from Latin *captare* 'seize.'

cat·er·cor·nered /ˈkatē ˌkôrnərd, ˈkatər/ (also **kitty-corner**) ▶ **adjective & adverb** situated diagonally opposite someone or something.
– ORIGIN from dialect *cater* 'diagonally.'

cat·er·pil·lar /ˈkatə(r)ˌpilər/ ▶ **noun 1** the larva of a butterfly or moth. **2** (also **caterpillar track** or **tread**) trademark a segmented steel band passing around the wheels of a vehicle for travel on rough ground.
– ORIGIN perhaps from Old French *chatepelose* 'hairy cat.'

cat·er·waul /ˈkatərˌwôl/ ▶ **verb** make a shrill howling or wailing noise.

cat·fight /ˈkatˌfīt/ ▶ **noun** informal a fight between women.
– DERIVATIVES **cat·fight·ing** noun.

cat·fish /ˈkatˌfisн/ ▶ **noun** (pl. same or **catfishes**) a freshwater or sea fish with whiskerlike growths around the mouth.

cat·gut /ˈkatˌgət/ ▶ **noun** material used for the strings of musical instruments and formerly for surgical sutures, made of the dried intestines of sheep or horses (but not cats).
– ORIGIN the association with **CAT** is uncertain.

Cath. ▶ **abbreviation 1** Cathedral. **2** Catholic.

ca·thar·sis /kəˈтнärsis/ ▶ **noun** the process of releasing strong but repressed emotions so as to be relieved of them.
– ORIGIN from Greek *kathairein* 'cleanse.'

ca·thar·tic /kəˈтнärtik/ ▶ **adjective** providing psychological relief through the expression of strong but previously repressed emotions: *writing the book was a very cathartic experience.*

ca·the·dral /kəˈтнēdrəl/ ▶ **noun** the principal church of a diocese.
– ORIGIN from Greek *kathedra* 'seat.'

cath·e·ter /ˈkaтнətər/ ▶ **noun** a flexible tube inserted into the bladder or another body cavity to remove fluid.
– ORIGIN from Greek *kathienai* 'send or let down.'

cath·e·ter·ize /ˈkaтнitəˌrīz/ ▶ **verb** Medicine insert a catheter into (a patient or body cavity).
– DERIVATIVES **cath·e·ter·i·za·tion** /ˌkaтнitərəˈzāsнən/ noun.

cath·ode /ˈkaтнˌōd/ ▶ **noun** an electrode with a negative charge. The opposite of **ANODE**.
– ORIGIN Greek *kathodos* 'way down.'

cath·ode ray ▶ **noun** a beam of electrons sent out from the cathode of a vacuum tube.

cath·ode ray tube ▶ **noun** a high-vacuum tube in which cathode rays produce a luminous image on a fluorescent screen, used in televisions and visual display units.

cath·o·lic /ˈkaтн(ə)lik/ ▶ **adjective 1** including a wide variety of things: *catholic tastes.* **2** (**Catholic**) Roman Catholic. **3** (**Catholic**) of or including all Christians. ▶ **noun** (**Catholic**) a Roman Catholic.
– DERIVATIVES **Ca·thol·i·cism** /kəˈтнäləˌsizəm/ noun **cath·o·lic·i·ty** /ˌkaтн(ə)ˈlisətē/ noun.
– ORIGIN Greek *katholikos* 'universal.'

cat·i·on /ˈkatˌīən, -ˌīän/ ▶ **noun** Chemistry an ion with a positive charge. The opposite of **ANION**.
– DERIVATIVES **cat·i·on·ic** /ˌkatīˈänik/ adjective.
– ORIGIN from **CATHODE** + **ION**.

cat·kin /ˈkatkin/ ▶ **noun** a spike of small soft flowers hanging from trees such as willow and hazel.
– ORIGIN the former Dutch word *katteken* 'kitten.'

cat lit·ter ▶ **noun** see **LITTER** (sense 4 of the noun).

cat·nap /ˈkatˌnap/ ▶ **noun** a short sleep during the day. ▶ **verb** (**catnaps, catnapping, catnapped**) have a catnap.

cat·nip /ˈkatˌnip/ ▶ **noun** a plant with a strong smell that is very attractive to cats.

cat-o'-nine-tails ▶ **noun** historical a whip consisting of a rope made from nine knotted cords, used for flogging people.

cat's cra·dle ▶ **noun** a child's game in which patterns are formed in a loop of string held between the fingers of each hand.

cats·eye /ˈkatsˌī/ ▶ **noun** a semiprecious stone, especially chalcedony or chrysoberyl.

cat's paw ▶ **noun** a person used by someone else to carry out an unpleasant task on their behalf.

cat·suit /ˈkatˌso͞ot/ ▶ **noun** a woman's close-fitting jumpsuit that covers the body from the neck to the feet.

cat·sup /ˈkecнəp, ˈkacнəp, ˈkatsəp/ ▶ **noun** another term for **KETCHUP**.

cat·tail /ˈkatˌtāl/ ▶ **noun** a tall, reedlike marsh plant with straplike leaves and a dark brown, velvety cylindrical head of numerous tiny flowers.

cat·tle /ˈkatl/ ▶ **plural noun** large domesticated animals with horns and cloven hoofs; cows, bulls, and oxen.

> – SYNONYMS **cows,** oxen, herd, livestock.

– ORIGIN Old French *chatel* 'chattel.'

> **WORD LINKS**
>
> **bovine** *relating to cattle*

cat·tle guard ▶ **noun** a metal grid covering a trench across a road, allowing vehicles and pedestrians to cross but not animals.

cat·tle·man /ˈkatlmən, -ˌman/ ▶ **noun** (pl. **cattlemen**) a person who tends or rears cattle.

cat·ty /ˈkatē/ ▶ **adjective** (**cattier, cattiest**) spiteful.
– DERIVATIVES **cat·ti·ly** adverb.

CATV ▶ **abbreviation** community antenna television (cable television).

cat·walk /ˈkatˌwôk/ ▶ **noun 1** a narrow platform along which models walk to display clothes. **2** a raised narrow walkway or open bridge.

Cau·ca·sian /kôˈkāzнən/ ▶ **adjective 1** relating to a division of humankind covering peoples from Europe, western Asia, and parts of India and North Africa. **2** white-skinned; of European origin. ▶ **noun** a Caucasian person.

cau·cus /ˈkôkəs/ ▶ **noun** (pl. **caucuses**) **1** a meeting of a policy-making committee of a political party. **2** a group of people with shared concerns within a larger organization.
– ORIGIN perhaps from an American Indian word meaning 'adviser.'

cau·dal /ˈkôdl/ ▶ **adjective** of, at, or near the tail or the rear part of an animal's body.
– DERIVATIVES **cau·dal·ly** adverb.
– ORIGIN Latin *cauda* 'tail.'

cau·dil·lo /kôˈdēlyō, -ˈdēō, kouˈdē,(y)ō/ ▶ **noun** (pl. **caudillos**) (in Spanish-speaking regions) a military or political leader.
– ORIGIN Spanish.

caught /kôt/ past and past participle of **CATCH**.

caul /kôl/ ▶ **noun** the membrane enclosing a fetus, part of which is sometimes found on a baby's head at birth.
– ORIGIN perhaps from Old French *cale* 'head covering.'

caul·dron /ˈkôldrən/ (also **caldron**) ▶ **noun** a large metal pot, used for cooking over an open fire.
– ORIGIN Old French *caudron*, from Latin *caldarium* 'hot bath.'

cau·li·flow·er /ˈkôli,flou(-ə)r, ˈkäli-/ ▶ **noun** a variety of cabbage with a large flowerhead of small creamy-white flower buds.
– ORIGIN from former French *chou fleuri* 'flowered cabbage.'

cau·li·flow·er ear ▶ **noun** a person's ear that has become thickened or deformed as a result of repeated blows.

caulk /kôk/ (also **calk**) ▶ **noun** a waterproof substance used in building work to fill cracks and seal joints. ▶ **verb** **1** seal something with caulk. **2** make a boat or its seams watertight.
– ORIGIN Latin *calcare* 'to tread.'

caus·al /ˈkôzəl/ ▶ **adjective** relating to or being a cause of something: *a causal connection between smoking and lung cancer.*
– DERIVATIVES **caus·al·ly** adverb.

cau·sal·i·ty /kôˈzalətē/ ▶ **noun** the relationship between something that happens and the effect it produces.

cau·sa·tion /kôˈzāsʜən/ ▶ **noun** **1** the action of causing something. **2** another term for **CAUSALITY**.

caus·a·tive /ˈkôzətiv/ ▶ **adjective** acting as a cause of something.

cause /kôz/ ▶ **noun** **1** a person or thing that produces an effect. **2** good reason for thinking or doing something: *there is no cause for concern.* **3** a principle, aim, etc., that one is prepared to support or fight for: *the socialist cause.* **4** a lawsuit.

> – SYNONYMS **1** *the cause of the fire* **source,** root, origin, beginning(s), starting point, originator, author, creator, agent. **2** *there is no cause for alarm* **reason,** grounds, justification, call, need, necessity, occasion, excuse. **3** *raising money for good causes* **principle,** ideal, belief, conviction, object, aim, objective, purpose, charity.

▶ **verb** make something, especially something bad, happen.

> – SYNONYMS **bring about,** give rise to, lead to, result in, create, produce, generate, engender, spawn, bring on, precipitate, prompt, provoke, trigger, make happen, induce, inspire, promote, foster.

– PHRASES **cause and effect** the relationship between an action or event and the effect it produces.
– ORIGIN Latin *causa*.

cause cé·lè·bre /ˈkôz səˈleb(rə), ˈkōz/ ▶ **noun** (pl. **causes célèbres** pronunc. same) a controversial issue arousing great public interest.
– ORIGIN French, 'famous case.'

cause·way /ˈkôz,wā/ ▶ **noun** a raised road or track across low or wet ground.
– ORIGIN Old French *causee*.

caus·tic /ˈkôstik/ ▶ **adjective** **1** able to burn or corrode living tissue by chemical action. **2** bitterly critical or sarcastic.

> – SYNONYMS **1 corrosive,** acid, burning. **2 sarcastic,** cutting, biting, mordant, sharp, scathing, sardonic, scornful, trenchant, acerbic, vitriolic.

– DERIVATIVES **caus·ti·cal·ly** /-ik(ə)lē/ adverb.
– ORIGIN from Greek *kaustos* 'combustible.'

caus·tic so·da ▶ **noun** sodium hydroxide.

cau·ter·ize /ˈkôtə,rīz/ ▶ **verb** burn the skin or flesh of a wound to stop bleeding or prevent infection.
– DERIVATIVES **cau·ter·i·za·tion** /,kôtərəˈzāsʜən/ noun.
– ORIGIN from Greek *kautērion* 'branding iron.'

cau·tion /ˈkôsʜən/ ▶ **noun** **1** care taken to avoid danger or mistakes. **2** warning: *advisers sounded a note of caution.*

> – SYNONYMS **care,** attention, attentiveness, vigilance, carefulness, alertness, circumspection, discretion, prudence.

▶ **verb** warn or advise: *economic advisers cautioned against a tax increase.*

> – SYNONYMS **advise,** warn, counsel; admonish, exhort.

– PHRASES **throw caution to the wind** (or **winds**) act in a reckless way.
– ORIGIN Latin, from *cavere* 'take heed.'

cau·tion·ar·y /ˈkôsʜə,nerē/ ▶ **adjective** acting as a warning.

cau·tious /ˈkôsʜəs/ ▶ **adjective** careful to avoid possible problems or dangers.

> – SYNONYMS **careful,** attentive, alert, judicious, circumspect, prudent, tentative, guarded.
> – ANTONYMS reckless.

– DERIVATIVES **cau·tious·ly** adverb **cau·tious·ness** noun.

ca·va /ˈkävə/ ▶ **noun** a Spanish sparkling wine made in the same way as champagne.
– ORIGIN Spanish.

cav·al·cade /,kavəlˈkād/ ▶ **noun** a procession of vehicles or people on horseback.
– ORIGIN Italian *cavalcare* 'to ride.'

cav·a·lier /,kavəˈli(ə)r/ ▶ **noun** (**Cavalier**) historical a supporter of King Charles I in the English Civil War. ▶ **adjective** showing a lack of proper concern: *the president's cavalier attitude to America's international obligations.*
– DERIVATIVES **cav·a·lier·ly** adverb.
– ORIGIN Italian *cavaliere* 'knight, gentleman,' from Latin *caballus* 'horse.'

cav·al·ry /ˈkavəlrē/ ▶ **noun** (pl. **cavalries**) (usu. treated as pl.) soldiers who formerly fought on horseback, but who now use armored vehicles.
– DERIVATIVES **cav·al·ry·man** /-mən/ noun (pl. **cavalrymen**).

– ORIGIN Italian *cavallo* 'horse.'

cave /kāv/ ▶ **noun** a large natural hollow in the side of a hill or cliff, or underground.

– SYNONYMS **cavern,** grotto, underground chamber.

▶ **verb** (**cave in**) **1** give way or collapse. **2** finally agree to someone's demands: *the bank caved in to pressure from local community groups.*

– SYNONYMS **1 collapse,** fall in/down, give, give way, crumble. **2 yield,** capitulate, surrender, give in, back down, submit.

– ORIGIN from Latin *cavus* 'hollow.'

WORD LINKS

speleology, **spelunking** *exploration of caves*

ca·ve·at /'kavē,ät, 'käv-/ ▶ **noun** a warning that certain conditions or provisos need to be taken into account.
– ORIGIN Latin, 'let a person beware.'

ca·ve·at emp·tor /'emp,tôr/ ▶ **noun** the principle that the buyer is responsible for checking the quality and suitability of goods before buying them.
– ORIGIN Latin, 'let the buyer beware.'

cave-in ▶ **noun 1** a collapse of a roof or similar structure, typically underground. **2** an instance of yielding or submitting under pressure: *the government's cave-in to industry pressure.*

cave·man /'kāv,man/ (or **cavewoman**) ▶ **noun** (pl. **cavemen** or **cavewomen**) a prehistoric person who lived in caves.

cav·ern /'kavərn/ ▶ **noun** a large cave, or chamber in a cave.
– ORIGIN Latin *caverna.*

cav·ern·ous /'kavərnəs/ ▶ **adjective** (of a room or space) like a cavern in being very large and empty or dark.

cav·i·ar /'kavē,är/ (also **caviare**) ▶ **noun** the pickled roe of the sturgeon (a large fish), eaten as a delicacy.
– ORIGIN French.

cav·il /'kavəl/ ▶ **verb** (**cavils, caviling, caviled**) make trivial complaints or objections. ▶ **noun** a trivial complaint or objection.
– ORIGIN Latin *cavillari.*

cav·ing /'kāviNG/ ▶ **noun** another term for **SPELUNKING**.
– DERIVATIVES **cav·er** noun.

cav·i·ta·tion /,kavə'tāSHən/ ▶ **noun** the formation of bubbles in a liquid.

cav·i·ty /'kavitē/ ▶ **noun** (pl. **cavities**) **1** a hollow space within a solid object. **2** a decayed part of a tooth.

– SYNONYMS **space,** chamber, hollow, hole, pocket, gap, crater, pit.

– ORIGIN Latin *cavitas,* from *cavus* 'hollow.'

cav·i·ty wall ▶ **noun** a wall formed from two layers of bricks with a space between them.

cav·ort /kə'vôrt/ ▶ **verb** jump or dance around excitedly.

ca·vy /'kāvē/ ▶ **noun** (pl. **cavies**) a guinea pig or related South American rodent.
– ORIGIN Latin *cavia.*

caw /kô/ ▶ **noun** the harsh cry of a crow, rook, or similar bird. ▶ **verb** (of a crow, rook, or similar bird) make a harsh cry.
– ORIGIN imitating the sound.

cay /kē, kā/ ▶ **noun** a low bank or reef of coral, rock, or sand.

cay·enne /kī'en, kā'en/ (also **cayenne pepper**) ▶ **noun** a hot-tasting red powder prepared from dried chilies.
– ORIGIN Tupi.

cay·man ▶ **noun** variant spelling of **CAIMAN**.

CB ▶ **abbreviation** Citizens' Band (radio frequencies).

CC ▶ **abbreviation 1** closed-captioned. **2** Cape Cod.

cc (also **c.c.**) ▶ **abbreviation 1** carbon copy (an indication that a duplicate has been or should be sent to another person). **2** cubic centimeter(s).

CCTV ▶ **abbreviation** closed-circuit television.

CCU ▶ **abbreviation 1** cardiac care unit. **2** coronary care unit. **3** critical care unit.

CD ▶ **abbreviation 1** compact disc. **2** certificate of deposit.

Cd ▶ **symbol** the chemical element cadmium.

cd ▶ **abbreviation** candela.

CD burner ▶ **noun** a device for producing a compact disc by copying from an original or master copy.

CDC ▶ **abbreviation** Centers for Disease Control.

CD-R ▶ **abbreviation** compact disc recordable, a CD that can be recorded on once only.

CD-ROM /,sē ,dē 'räm/ ▶ **noun** a compact disc used in a computer as a read-only device for displaying data.
– ORIGIN from *compact disc read-only memory.*

CD-RW ▶ **abbreviation** compact disc rewritable, a CD on which recordings can be made and erased a number of times.

CDT ▶ **abbreviation** Central Daylight Time.

CE ▶ **abbreviation 1** Church of England. **2** Common Era. **3** Corps of Engineers.

Ce ▶ **symbol** the chemical element cerium.

ce·a·no·thus /,sēə'nōTHəs/ ▶ **noun** a North American shrub with dense clusters of small blue flowers.
– ORIGIN Greek *keanōthos,* a kind of thistle.

cease /sēs/ ▶ **verb** come or bring to an end; stop.

– SYNONYMS **stop,** come/bring to an end, come/bring to a halt, end, halt, conclude, terminate, finish, wind up, discontinue, suspend, break off.
– ANTONYMS start, continue.

– PHRASES **without cease** without stopping.
– ORIGIN Latin *cessare.*

cease·fire /'sēs,fīr/ ▶ **noun** a temporary period when fighting is stopped.

cease·less /'sēslis/ ▶ **adjective** constant; never stopping.

– SYNONYMS **continual,** constant, continuous, incessant, unending, endless, never-ending, interminable, nonstop, unremitting, relentless, unrelenting, sustained, persistent, eternal, perpetual.
– ANTONYMS intermittent.

– DERIVATIVES **cease·less·ly** adverb.

ce·cum /'sēkəm/ (Brit. **caecum**) ▶ **noun** (pl. **ceca** /-kə/) a pouch connected to the junction of the small and large intestines.
– DERIVATIVES **ce·cal** /-kəl/ adjective.
– ORIGIN from Latin *intestinum caecum* 'blind gut.'

ce·dar /'sēdər/ ▶ **noun** a tall coniferous tree with hard, sweet-smelling wood.
– ORIGIN Greek *kedros.*

cede /sēd/ ▶ **verb** give up power or territory.
– ORIGIN Latin *cedere.*

CHOOSE THE RIGHT WORD

See **RELINQUISH**.

ce·dil·la /sə'dilə/ ▶ **noun** a mark (¸) written under the letter *c*, especially in French, to show that it is pronounced like an *s* (e.g., *soupçon*).
– ORIGIN Spanish *zedilla* 'little z.'

cei·lidh /'kālē/ ▶ **noun** a social event with Scottish or Irish folk music and singing, traditional dancing, and storytelling.
– ORIGIN Old Irish *céilide* 'visit, visiting.'

ceil·ing /'sēliNG/ ▶ **noun 1** the upper inside surface of a room. **2** an upper limit set on prices, wages, or spending. **3** the maximum altitude to which an aircraft can climb.
– ORIGIN from former *ceil* 'line or plaster the roof of a building.'

cel·an·dine /'selən,dīn, -,dēn/ ▶ **noun** a yellow-flowered plant of the buttercup family.
– ORIGIN from Greek *khelidōn* 'swallow' (because the flowering of the plant was associated with the arrival of migrating swallows).

ce·leb /sə'leb/ ▶ **noun** informal a celebrity.

cel·e·brant /'seləbrənt/ ▶ **noun 1** a person who performs a religious ceremony, especially a priest who leads the service of Holy Communion. **2** a person who celebrates something.

cel·e·brate /'selə,brāt/ ▶ **verb 1** mark an important occasion with a social gathering or enjoyable activity. **2** (often as adj. **celebrated**) honor or praise publicly: *a celebrated mathematician.* **3** perform a religious ceremony, in particular the Christian service of Holy Communion.

– SYNONYMS **1 have a party,** make merry, enjoy yourself, have fun, have a good time; informal party, whoop it up, have a ball, step out. **2 commemorate,** observe, mark, keep, honor, remember. **3** (as adj. **celebrated**) **acclaimed,** admired, highly rated, esteemed, exalted, vaunted, eminent, great, distinguished, prestigious, illustrious, notable. **4 perform,** observe, officiate at, preside at.

– DERIVATIVES **cel·e·bra·tor** /-,brātər/ noun **cel·e·bra·to·ry** /sə'lebrə,tôrē, 'seləbrə-/ adjective.
– ORIGIN Latin *celebrare*.

cel·e·bra·tion /,selə'brāSHən/ ▶ **noun 1** the action of celebrating. **2** a social gathering held to celebrate something.

– SYNONYMS **1** *the celebration of his 50th birthday* **commemoration,** observance, marking, keeping; officiation, solemnization. **2** *a birthday celebration* **party,** merrymaking, festivities, revelry, festival, fete, carnival, jamboree; informal do, bash, partying.

ce·leb·ri·ty /sə'lebrətē/ ▶ **noun** (pl. **celebrities**) **1** a famous person. **2** the state of being famous.

– SYNONYMS **1 famous person,** VIP, personality, big name, household name, star, superstar; informal celeb, megastar. **2 fame,** prominence, renown, stardom, popularity, distinction, prestige, stature, repute, reputation.
– ANTONYMS obscurity.

ce·ler·i·ac /sə'lerē,ak/ ▶ **noun** a variety of celery that forms a large edible root.
– ORIGIN from **CELERY**.

ce·ler·i·ty /sə'leritē/ ▶ **noun** old use or literary speed of movement.
– ORIGIN from Latin *celer* 'swift.'

cel·er·y /'sel(ə)rē/ ▶ **noun** a plant with crisp juicy stalks, eaten in salads or as a vegetable.
– ORIGIN from Greek *selinon* 'parsley.'

ce·les·ta /sə'lestə/ (also **celeste** /sə'lest/) ▶ **noun** a small keyboard instrument in which felt-covered hammers strike a row of steel plates.
– ORIGIN from French *céleste* 'heavenly' (with reference to the instrument's light, delicate sound).

ce·les·tial /sə'lesCHəl/ ▶ **adjective 1** belonging or relating to heaven. **2** positioned in or relating to the sky or outer space.

– SYNONYMS **1 (in) space,** heavenly, astronomical, extraterrestrial, stellar, planetary. **2 heavenly,** holy, saintly, divine, godly, godlike, ethereal, angelic.

– DERIVATIVES **ce·les·tial·ly** adverb.
– ORIGIN from Latin *caelum* 'heaven.'

ce·les·tial e·qua·tor ▶ **noun** the projection into space of the earth's equator.

ce·les·tial pole ▶ **noun** Astronomy the point on the celestial sphere directly above either of the earth's geographic poles, around which the stars appear to rotate.

ce·les·tial sphere ▶ **noun** an imaginary sphere of which the observer is the center and on which all celestial objects are considered to lie.

ce·li·ac dis·ease /'sēlē,ak/ ▶ **noun** a condition in which the small intestine fails to digest and absorb food, caused by excessive sensitivity to gluten.
– ORIGIN from Greek *koilia* 'belly.'

cel·i·bate /'seləbət/ ▶ **adjective 1** not marrying or having sex, especially for religious reasons. **2** not having or involving a sexual relationship.

– SYNONYMS **unmarried,** single, chaste, pure, virginal.

▶ **noun** a person who is celibate.
– DERIVATIVES **cel·i·ba·cy** /-bəsē/ noun.
– ORIGIN Latin *caelibatus* 'unmarried state.'

cell /sel/ ▶ **noun 1** a small room for a prisoner, monk, or nun. **2** the smallest unit of a living organism that is able to reproduce and perform other functions. **3** a small compartment in a larger structure such as a honeycomb. **4** a small group of people working as part of a larger political organization, usually in secret: *a terrorist cell.* **5** a device or unit in which electricity is produced using chemical energy or light, or in which electrolysis takes place.

– SYNONYMS **1 room,** cubicle, chamber, dungeon, compartment, lockup. **2 unit,** squad, detachment, group.

– ORIGIN Latin *cella* 'storeroom or chamber.'

cel·lar /'selər/ ▶ **noun 1** a storage space or room below ground level in a building. **2** a stock of wine.

– SYNONYMS **basement,** vault, crypt.

– ORIGIN Latin *cellarium* 'storehouse.'

cell·mate /'sel,māt/ ▶ **noun** a person with whom one shares a cell.

cel·lo /'CHelō/ ▶ **noun** (pl. **cellos**) a large instrument of the violin family, held upright on the floor between the legs of the seated player.
– DERIVATIVES **cel·list** noun.
– ORIGIN shortening of **VIOLONCELLO**.

cel·lo·phane /'selə,fān/ ▶ **noun** trademark a thin transparent wrapping material made from viscose.

– ORIGIN from **CELLULOSE**.

cell phone (also **cellular phone**) ▶ **noun** a portable telephone using a cellular radio system.

cel·lu·lar /ˈselyələr/ ▶ **adjective 1** relating to or made up of living cells. **2** relating to a mobile telephone system that uses a number of short-range radio stations to cover the area it serves. **3** (of fabric) woven so as to form holes or hollows that trap air and provide extra insulation. **4** consisting of small compartments or rooms.
– ORIGIN Latin *cellularis*.

cel·lu·lite /ˈselyəˌlīt/ ▶ **noun** fat that accumulates under the skin, causing a dimpled effect.
– ORIGIN French.

cel·lu·loid /ˈselyəˌloid/ ▶ **noun 1** a transparent plastic formerly used for movie film. **2** motion pictures considered as a type of art.

cel·lu·lose /ˈselyəˌlōs, -ˌlōz/ ▶ **noun** a substance found in all plant tissues, used in making paint, plastics, and artificial fibers.
– DERIVATIVES **cel·lu·lo·sic** /ˌselyəˈlōsik, -ˈlōzik/ adjective.
– ORIGIN French.

Cel·si·us /ˈselsēəs, ˈselsHəs/ ▶ **adjective** relating to a scale of temperature on which water freezes at 0° and boils at 100°.
– ORIGIN named after the Swedish astronomer Anders *Celsius*.

USAGE

Celsius rather than **centigrade** is the standard accepted term when giving temperatures.

Celt /kelt, selt/ ▶ **noun 1** a member of a group of peoples inhabiting much of Europe and the western peninsula of Asia in pre-Roman times. **2** a native of a modern region in which a Celtic language is (or was) spoken.
– ORIGIN Greek *Keltoi* 'Celts.'

Celt·ic /ˈkeltik, ˈsel-/ ▶ **noun** a group of languages including Irish, Scottish Gaelic, Welsh, Breton, Manx, and Cornish. ▶ **adjective** relating to Celtic or to the Celts.

Celt·ic cross ▶ **noun** a Latin cross with a circle around the center.

ce·ment /siˈment/ ▶ **noun 1** a powdery substance made by strongly heating lime and clay, used in making mortar and concrete. **2** a soft glue that hardens on setting.

– SYNONYMS **adhesive**, glue, fixative, gum, paste.

▶ **verb 1** fix something with cement. **2** establish firmly: *the occasion cemented our friendship*.
– DERIVATIVES **ce·men·ta·tion** /ˌsēˌmenˈtāsHən/ noun.
– ORIGIN Latin *caementum* 'quarry stone.'

cem·e·ter·y /ˈseməˌterē/ ▶ **noun** (pl. **cemeteries**) a large burial ground.

– SYNONYMS **graveyard**, churchyard, burial ground, necropolis, memorial park; informal boneyard; historical potter's field; archaic God's acre.

– ORIGIN Greek *koimētērion* 'dormitory.'

ce·no·taph /ˈsenəˌtaf/ ▶ **noun** a monument to members of the armed forces killed in a war.
– ORIGIN from Greek *kenos* 'empty' + *taphos* 'tomb.'

Ce·no·zo·ic /ˌsenəˈzōik/ (also **Cainozoic** /ˌkīnə-/) ▶ **adjective** Geology relating to the era following the Mesozoic era (from about 65 million years ago to the present).
– ORIGIN from Greek *kainos* 'new' + *zōion* 'animal.'

cen·ser /ˈsensər/ ▶ **noun** a container in which incense is burned during a religious ceremony.
– ORIGIN from Old French *encens* 'incense.'

cen·sor /ˈsensər/ ▶ **noun** an official who examines material that is to be published and suppresses parts considered offensive or a threat to security. ▶ **verb** officially suppress unacceptable parts of a book, movie, etc.

– SYNONYMS **cut**, edit, expurgate, sanitize, clean up, ban, delete.

– DERIVATIVES **cen·sor·ship** noun.
– ORIGIN from Latin *censere* 'assess.'

cen·so·ri·ous /senˈsôrēəs/ ▶ **adjective** severely critical.

– SYNONYMS **critical**, overcritical, hypercritical, disapproving, condemnatory, judgmental, moralistic, fault-finding, reproachful.

cen·sure /ˈsensHər/ ▶ **verb** criticize someone or something severely.

– SYNONYMS **condemn**, criticize, attack, reprimand, rebuke, admonish, upbraid, reproach.
– ANTONYMS defend, praise.

▶ **noun** strong disapproval or criticism.

– SYNONYMS **condemnation**, criticism, attack, reprimand, rebuke, admonishment, reproof, disapproval, reproach.
– ANTONYMS approval, praise.

– ORIGIN from Latin *censura* 'judgment.'

USAGE

Censure and **censor** are often confused. **Censure** means 'criticize severely' (*the country was censured for human rights abuses*) or 'strong disapproval,' while **censor** means 'officially suppress unacceptable parts of a book, movie, or similar work' or 'an official who censors books and other material'.

CHOOSE THE RIGHT WORD

See **REBUKE**.

cen·sus /ˈsensəs/ ▶ **noun** (pl. **censuses**) an official count or survey of a population.
– ORIGIN Latin.

cent /sent/ ▶ **noun** a unit of money equal to one hundredth of a dollar, euro, or other decimal currency unit.
– ORIGIN from Latin *centum* 'hundred.'

cen·taur /ˈsenˌtôr/ ▶ **noun** Greek Mythology a creature with the head, arms, and torso of a man and the body and legs of a horse.
– ORIGIN Greek *kentauros*, referring to a people of Thessaly who were expert horsemen.

cen·ta·vo /senˈtävō/ ▶ **noun** (pl. **centavos**) a unit of money of Mexico, Brazil, and certain other countries, equal to one hundredth of the basic unit.
– ORIGIN Spanish and Portuguese.

cen·te·nar·i·an /ˌsentnˈe(ə)rēən/ ▶ **noun** a person who is a hundred or more years old.

cen·ten·ar·y /senˈtenərē, ˈsentnˌerē/ ▶ **noun** (pl. **centenaries**) Brit. the hundredth anniversary of an event.
– ORIGIN from Latin *centenarius* 'containing a hundred.'

cen·ten·ni·al /senˈtenēəl/ ▶ **adjective** relating to a hundredth anniversary. ▶ **noun** a hundredth anniversary.
– ORIGIN from Latin *centum* 'a hundred.'

cen·ter /ˈsentər/ (Brit. **centre**) ▶ **noun 1** a point or part in the middle of something. **2** a place devoted to a specified activity: *a conference center*. **3** a point from which something spreads or to which something is directed: *the city was a center of discontent*. **4** the middle player in some team games.

– SYNONYMS **middle,** nucleus, heart, core, hub.
– ANTONYMS edge.

▶ **verb 1** place something in the center. **2** (**center on/around**) have as a major concern or theme: *several questions center on funding*.

– SYNONYMS **focus,** concentrate, pivot, revolve, be based.

– PHRASES **center of gravity** the central point in an object, around which its mass is evenly balanced.
– ORIGIN Latin *centrum*.

cen·ter back ▶ **noun** a player in the middle of the back line of some sports, such as volleyball.

cen·ter·board /ˈsentərˌbôrd/ ▶ **noun** a board lowered through the hull of a sailboat to reduce sideways movement.

cen·ter field ▶ **noun** Baseball **1** the central part of the outfield, behind second base. **2** the position of an outfielder in this area.
– DERIVATIVES **cen·ter field·er** noun.

cen·ter·fold /ˈsentərˌfōld/ ▶ **noun 1** the two middle pages of a magazine, often containing a single illustration or feature. **2** an illustration on such pages, typically a picture of a naked or scantily clad model.

cen·ter for·ward ▶ **noun** Soccer & Field Hockey an attacker who plays in the middle of the field.

cen·ter half ▶ **noun** Soccer a center back.

cen·ter·piece /ˈsentərˌpēs/ ▶ **noun 1** an object or item that is intended to be a focus of attention: *the centerpiece of the project is the construction of a new theater*. **2** a decorative piece or display placed in the middle of a dining or serving table.

cen·ter stage ▶ **noun** the most prominent position.
▶ **adverb** in or toward the most prominent position.

cen·tes·i·mal /senˈtesəməl/ ▶ **adjective** relating to division into hundredths.
– ORIGIN from Latin *centesimus* 'hundredth.'

centi- ▶ **combining form 1** one hundredth: *centiliter*. **2** hundred: *centipede*.
– ORIGIN from Latin *centum* 'hundred.'

cen·ti·grade /ˈsentəˌgrād/ ▶ **adjective** relating to the Celsius scale of temperature.
– ORIGIN from Latin *centum* 'a hundred' + *gradus* 'step.'

USAGE

On using **centigrade** or **Celsius**, see the note at **CELSIUS**.

cen·ti·gram /ˈsentəˌgram/ ▶ **noun** a metric unit of mass equal to one hundredth of a gram.

cen·ti·li·ter /ˈsentəˌlētər/ (Brit. **centilitre**) ▶ **noun** a metric unit of capacity equal to one hundredth of a liter.

cen·time /ˈsänˌtēm, ˈsent-/ ▶ **noun** a unit of money equal to one hundredth of a franc or some other decimal currency units (used in France, Belgium, and Luxembourg until the introduction of the euro in 2002).
– ORIGIN from Latin *centesimus* 'hundredth.'

cen·ti·me·ter /ˈsentəˌmētər, ˈsän-/ (Brit. **centimetre**) ▶ **noun** a metric unit of length equal to one hundredth of a meter.

cen·ti·mo /ˈsentəmō/ ▶ **noun** (pl. **centimos**) a unit of money of a number of Latin American countries (and formerly of Spain), equal to one hundredth of the basic unit.
– ORIGIN Spanish.

cen·ti·pede /ˈsentəˌpēd/ ▶ **noun** an insectlike creature with a long body composed of many segments, most of which have a pair of legs.
– ORIGIN from Latin *centum* 'a hundred' + *pes* 'foot.'

cen·tral /ˈsentrəl/ ▶ **adjective 1** in or near the center. **2** very important; essential.

– SYNONYMS **1 middle,** center, halfway, midway, mid; inner, innermost. **2 main,** chief, principal, primary, foremost, key, crucial, vital, essential, basic, fundamental, core; informal number-one.
– ANTONYMS side, outer.

– DERIVATIVES **cen·tral·i·ty** /senˈtralətē/ noun **cen·tral·ly** adverb.

cen·tral bank ▶ **noun** a national bank that provides services for its country's government and commercial banking system and issues currency.

cen·tral heat·ing ▶ **noun** a system for warming a building by heating water or air in one place and circulating it through pipes and radiators or vents.

cen·tral·ize /ˈsentrəˌlīz/ ▶ **verb** bring something under the control of a central authority.

– SYNONYMS **concentrate,** consolidate, amalgamate, condense, unify, focus.
– ANTONYMS devolve.

– DERIVATIVES **cen·tral·ism** /ˈsentrəˌlizəm/ noun **cen·tral·ist** /ˈsentrəˌlist/ noun & adjective **cen·tral·i·za·tion** /ˌsentrələˈzāsʜən/ noun.

cen·tral nerv·ous sys·tem ▶ **noun** the complex of nerve tissues that controls the activities of the body.

cen·tral proc·ess·ing u·nit (also **central processor**) ▶ **noun** the part of a computer in which operations are controlled and executed.

Cen·tral time ▶ **noun** the standard time in a zone that includes the central states of the US and parts of central Canada.

cen·tre, etc. ▶ **noun** British spelling of **CENTER**, etc.

-centric ▶ **combining form 1** having a specified center: *geocentric*. **2** originating from a specified viewpoint: *Eurocentric*.
– DERIVATIVES **-centricity** combining form.
– ORIGIN from Greek *kentrikos*.

cen·trif·u·gal /senˈtrif(y)əgəl/ ▶ **adjective** Physics moving away from a center.
– DERIVATIVES **cen·trif·u·gal·ly** adverb.
– ORIGIN from Latin *centrum* 'center' + *-fugus* 'fleeing.'

cen·trif·u·gal force ▶ **noun** Physics a force that appears to cause a body traveling around a central point to fly outward from its circular path.

cen·tri·fuge /ˈsentrəˌfyo͞oj/ ▶ **noun** a machine with a rapidly rotating container, used to separate liquids from solids.

cen·trip·e·tal /senˈtripətl/ ▶ **adjective** Physics pulling toward a center.
– DERIVATIVES **cen·trip·e·tal·ly** adverb.
– ORIGIN from Latin *centrum* 'center' + *-petus* 'seeking.'

cen·trip·e·tal force ▶ **noun** Physics a force that causes a body traveling around a central point to maintain its circular path.

cen·trist /ˈsentrəst/ ▶ **noun** a person having moderate political views or policies.
– DERIVATIVES **cen·trism** /-ˌtrizəm/ noun.

cen·tu·ri·on /senˈt(y)o͝orēən/ ▶ **noun** the commander of a hundred men in the ancient Roman army.
– ORIGIN from Latin *centuria* 'century.'

cen·tu·ry /ˈsenCH(ə)rē/ ▶ **noun** (pl. **centuries**) **1** a period of one hundred years. **2** a company of a hundred men in the ancient Roman army.
– ORIGIN Latin *centuria*.

USAGE

Strictly speaking, centuries run from 01 to 100, meaning that the new century begins on the first day of the year 01 (e.g. January 1, 2001). In practice and in popular belief, however, the new century is regarded as beginning when the significant digits in the date change, e.g. on January 1, 2000, when 1999 became 2000.

CEO ▶ **abbreviation** chief executive officer.

cep /sep/ ▶ **noun** an edible mushroom with a smooth brown cap.
– ORIGIN French *cèpe*.

ce·phal·ic /səˈfalik/ ▶ **adjective** technical relating to the head.
– ORIGIN from Greek *kephalē* 'head.'

ceph·a·lo·pod /ˈsefələˌpäd/ ▶ **noun** a mollusk of a class including octopuses and squids.
– ORIGIN from Greek *kephalē* 'head' + *pous* 'foot.'

ce·ram·ic /səˈramik/ ▶ **adjective** made of clay that is permanently hardened by heat. ▶ **noun** (**ceramics**) **1** ceramic articles. **2** (usu. treated as sing.) the art of making ceramic articles.
– DERIVATIVES **ce·ram·i·cist** /səˈraməsist/ noun.
– ORIGIN from Greek *keramos* 'pottery.'

ce·re·al /ˈsi(ə)rēəl/ ▶ **noun** **1** a grain used for food, for example wheat, oats, or corn. **2** a grass producing a cereal grain. **3** a breakfast food made from a cereal grain or grains.
– ORIGIN from *Ceres*, the Roman goddess of agriculture.

cer·e·bel·lum /ˌserəˈbeləm/ ▶ **noun** (pl. **cerebellums** or **cerebella** /-ˈbelə/) the part of the brain at the back of the skull that coordinates muscular activity.
– DERIVATIVES **cer·e·bel·lar** adjective.
– ORIGIN Latin, 'little brain.'

ce·re·bral /səˈrēbrəl, ˈserəbrəl/ ▶ **adjective** **1** relating to the cerebrum of the brain. **2** intellectual rather than emotional or physical.
– DERIVATIVES **ce·re·bral·ly** adverb.

ce·re·bral pal·sy ▶ **noun** a condition in which a person has difficulty in controlling or moving their muscles, caused by brain damage before or at birth.

cer·e·bra·tion /ˌserəˈbrāSHən/ ▶ **noun** chiefly formal the working of the brain; thinking.

ce·re·bro·spi·nal /səˌrēbrōˈspīnl, ˌserəbrō-/ ▶ **adjective** relating to the brain and spine.

ce·re·bro·spi·nal flu·id ▶ **noun** the clear watery fluid that fills the space between membranes in the brain and the spinal chord.

ce·re·bro·vas·cu·lar /səˌrēbrōˈvaskyələr, ˌserəbrō-/ ▶ **adjective** relating to the brain and its blood vessels.

ce·re·brum /səˈrēbrəm, ˈserə-/ ▶ **noun** (pl. **cerebra** /-brə/) the main part of the brain, located in the front of the skull.
– ORIGIN Latin, 'brain.'

cer·e·mo·ni·al /ˌserəˈmōnēəl/ ▶ **adjective** **1** relating to or used for ceremonies. **2** (of a position or role) in name only; without real authority or power.

– SYNONYMS **formal,** official, state, public, ritual, ritualistic, stately, solemn.
– ANTONYMS informal.

▶ **noun** another term for **CEREMONY**.
– DERIVATIVES **cer·e·mo·ni·al·ly** adverb.

cer·e·mo·ni·ous /ˌserəˈmōnēəs/ ▶ **adjective** relating or appropriate to grand and formal occasions.
– DERIVATIVES **cer·e·mo·ni·ous·ly** adverb.

cer·e·mo·ny /ˈserəˌmōnē/ ▶ **noun** (pl. **ceremonies**) **1** a formal religious or public occasion, typically celebrating a particular event. **2** the set procedures performed at grand and formal occasions: *the new president was welcomed with due ceremony.*

– SYNONYMS **1 rite,** ritual, observance, service, event, function. **2 pomp,** protocol, formality, formalities, niceties, decorum, etiquette, pageantry, ceremonial.

– PHRASES **stand on ceremony** insist on formal behavior.
– ORIGIN Latin *caerimonia* 'religious worship.'

ce·rise /səˈrēs, -ˈrēz/ ▶ **noun** a light, clear red color.
– ORIGIN French, 'cherry.'

ce·ri·um /ˈsi(ə)rēəm/ ▶ **noun** a silvery-white metallic chemical element.
– ORIGIN named after the asteroid *Ceres*.

cert. ▶ **abbreviation** **1** certificate. **2** certified. **3** Law certiorari.

cer·tain /ˈsərtn/ ▶ **adjective** **1** able to be relied on to happen or be the case: *it's certain that more changes are in the offing.* **2** completely sure that something is the case. **3** specific but not actually stated: *he raised certain personal problems.*

– SYNONYMS **1** *I'm certain he's guilty* **sure,** confident, positive, convinced, in no doubt, satisfied. **2** *it is certain that more changes are in the offing* **unquestionable,** sure, definite, beyond question, indubitable, undeniable, indisputable. **3** *they are certain to win* **sure,** bound, destined. **4** *certain defeat* **inevitable,** assured, unavoidable, inescapable, inexorable. **5** *there is no certain cure* **reliable,** dependable, foolproof, guaranteed, sure, infallible; informal sure-fire.
– ANTONYMS doubtful, unlikely, possible.

▶ **pronoun** (**certain of**) some but not all.
– ORIGIN Latin *certus* 'settled, sure.'

cer·tain·ly /ˈsərtnlē/ ▶ **adverb** **1** without doubt; definitely. **2** yes; by all means.

– SYNONYMS **definitely,** surely, assuredly, unquestionably, beyond/without question, undoubtedly, without doubt, indubitably, undeniably, irrefutably, indisputably.

cer·tain·ty /ˈsərtntē/ ▶ **noun** (pl. **certainties**) **1** the quality or state of being certain or sure. **2** a fact that is true or an event that is definitely going to take place.

– SYNONYMS **1 confidence,** sureness, conviction, assurance. **2 inevitability,** foregone conclusion; informal sure thing.
– ANTONYMS doubt, possibility.

cer·ti·fi·a·ble /ˌsərtəˈfīəbəl/ ▶ **adjective** **1** able or needing to be officially confirmed or recorded. **2** officially recognized as needing treatment for a mental disorder.
– DERIVATIVES **cer·ti·fi·a·bly** adverb.

cer·tif·i·cate /sər'tifikit/ ▶ **noun 1** an official document recording a particular fact, event, or achievement. **2** a document attesting ownership of a certain item.

– SYNONYMS **guarantee,** document, authorization, authentication, accreditation, credentials, testimonial.

– DERIVATIVES **cer·ti·fi·ca·tion** /ˌsərtəfi'kāsʜən/ noun.

cer·tif·i·cate of de·pos·it (abbr.: **CD**) ▶ **noun** a certificate issued by a bank to a person depositing money for a specified length of time.

cer·ti·fied pub·lic ac·count·ant /'sərtəˌfīd/ (abbr.: **CPA**) ▶ **noun** a member of an officially accredited professional body of accountants.

cer·ti·fy /'sərtəˌfī/ ▶ **verb** (**certifies, certifying, certified**) **1** confirm or state something in a formal document. **2** officially recognize that someone or something meets certain standards. **3** officially declare someone insane.

– SYNONYMS **1 verify,** guarantee, attest, validate, confirm, endorse. **2 accredit,** recognize, license, authorize, approve.

– DERIVATIVES **cer·ti·fi·er** noun.
– ORIGIN Latin *certificare*.

cer·ti·o·ra·ri /ˌsersʜ(ē)ə'rärē, -'re(ə)rī/ ▶ **noun** Law a writ or order by which a higher court reviews a decision of a lower court.
– ORIGIN from Latin 'to be informed.'

cer·ti·tude /'sərtəˌt(y)o͞od/ ▶ **noun** a feeling of absolute certainty.
– ORIGIN Latin *certitudo*.

ce·ru·le·an /sə'ro͞olēən/ ▶ **adjective** deep blue in color.
– ORIGIN from Latin *caelum* 'sky.'

cer·vi·cal /'sərvikəl/ ▶ **adjective 1** relating to the neck of the uterus. **2** relating to the neck: *the fifth cervical vertebra*.
– ORIGIN from Latin *cervix* 'neck.'

cer·vix /'sərviks/ ▶ **noun** (pl. **cervices** /-vəˌsēz/) the narrow necklike passage forming the lower end of the uterus.
– ORIGIN Latin.

ce·sar·e·an /si'ze(ə)rēən/ (also **caesarean**) ▶ **noun** a cesarean section.

ce·sar·e·an sec·tion ▶ **noun** a surgical operation for delivering a child by cutting through the wall of the mother's abdomen.
– ORIGIN from the story that Julius Caesar was delivered by this method.

ce·si·um /'sēzēəm/ (Brit. **caesium**) ▶ **noun** a soft, silvery, extremely reactive metallic chemical element.
– ORIGIN from Latin *caesius* 'grayish-blue.'

ces·sa·tion /se'sāsʜən/ ▶ **noun** the ending of something.

– SYNONYMS **end,** termination, halt, finish, stoppage, conclusion, winding up, pause, suspension.
– ANTONYMS start, resumption.

– ORIGIN from Latin *cessare* 'cease.'

ces·sion /'sesʜən/ ▶ **noun** the formal giving up of rights, power, or territory by a country or state.
– ORIGIN from Latin *cedere* 'cede.'

cess·pool /'sesˌpo͞ol/ (also **cesspit** /'sesˌpit/) ▶ **noun** an underground tank or covered pit where liquid waste and sewage are stored before disposal.
– ORIGIN probably from Old French *souspirail* 'air hole.'

c'est la vie /ˌsā lä 'vē/ ▶ **exclamation** expressing resigned acceptance of an undesirable situation.
– ORIGIN French, 'that's life.'

ce·ta·cean /si'tāsʜən/ ▶ **noun** a sea mammal of an order including whales and dolphins.
– ORIGIN from Greek *kētos* 'whale.'

ce·vi·che /sə'vēcʜā, -cʜē/ (also **seviche**) ▶ **noun** a South American dish of marinaded raw fish or seafood.
– ORIGIN Latin American Spanish.

CF ▶ **abbreviation 1** cystic fibrosis. **2** center field(er).

Cf ▶ **symbol** the chemical element californium.

cf. ▶ **abbreviation** compare with.
– ORIGIN from Latin *confer* 'compare.'

CFA ▶ **abbreviation 1** chartered (or certified) financial analyst. **2** Consumer Federation of America.

CFC ▶ **abbreviation** chlorofluorocarbon, a gas that is a compound of carbon, hydrogen, chlorine, and fluorine, used in refrigerators and aerosols and harmful to the ozone layer.

CFS ▶ **abbreviation** chronic fatigue syndrome.

CGI ▶ **abbreviation 1** computer-generated imagery. **2** Computing common gateway interface.

ch. ▶ **abbreviation** chapter.

Cha·blis /sʜa'blē, sʜə-, sʜä-/ ▶ **noun** a dry white burgundy wine from Chablis in France.

cha-cha /'cʜä ˌcʜä/ ▶ **noun** a ballroom dance with swaying hip movements, performed to a Latin American rhythm.
– ORIGIN Latin American Spanish.

cha·conne /sʜä'kôn, -'kän, -'kən/ ▶ **noun 1** a musical composition in a series of varying sections in slow triple time. **2** a stately dance performed to a chaconne.
– ORIGIN French.

Chad·i·an /'cʜadēən/ ▶ **noun** a person from Chad in central Africa. ▶ **adjective** relating to Chad or Chadians.

chad·or /'cʜədər, 'cʜädˌôr/ (also **chadar** or **chuddar**) ▶ **noun** a piece of dark cloth worn by Muslim women around the head and upper body, so that only part of the face can be seen.
– ORIGIN Persian, 'sheet or veil.'

chafe /cʜāf/ ▶ **verb 1** make or become sore or worn by rubbing against something. **2** rub a part of the body to warm it. **3** become impatient because of a restriction or disadvantage: *the women chafed at earning less than the men*.
– ORIGIN Old French *chaufer* 'make hot.'

chaf·er /'cʜāfər/ ▶ **noun** a large flying beetle of a group including the Japanese beetle.
– ORIGIN Old English.

chaff[1] /cʜaf/ ▶ **noun 1** the husks of grain separated from the seed by winnowing or threshing. **2** chopped hay and straw used as cattle fodder.
– PHRASES **separate the wheat from the chaff** distinguish valuable people or things from worthless ones.
– ORIGIN Old English.

chaff[2] ▶ **noun** light-hearted joking. ▶ **verb** tease someone.
– ORIGIN perhaps from **CHAFE**.

chaf·finch /'cʜafˌincʜ/ ▶ **noun** a finch, the male of which has a bluish head, pink underparts, and dark wings.
– ORIGIN Old English.

chaf·ing dish /'cʜāfiɴɢ/ ▶ **noun 1** a cooking pot with an outer pan of hot water, used for keeping food warm. **2** a metal pan with a heating device below it, used for cooking at the table.
– ORIGIN from the original sense of **CHAFE** 'become warm, warm up.'

cha·grin /sʜə'grin/ ▶ **noun** annoyance or shame at having failed. ▶ **verb** (**be chagrined**) feel annoyed or ashamed.
– ORIGIN French, 'rough skin, shagreen.'

chain /cʜān/ ▶ **noun 1** a connected series of metal links used for fastening or pulling something, or as jewelry. **2** a connected series, set, or sequence: *a chain of restaurants*. **3** a part of a molecule consisting of a number of atoms bonded together in a series. **4** a measure of length equal to 66 ft.

– SYNONYMS **1 fetters,** shackles, irons, manacles, handcuffs; informal cuffs, bracelets. **2 series,** succession, string, sequence, train, course.

▶ **verb 1** fasten or confine someone or something with a chain. **2** restrict or limit to a situation or place: *the chef was chained to his stove six days a week*.

– SYNONYMS **secure,** fasten, tie, tether, hitch, restrain, shackle, fetter, manacle, handcuff.

– ORIGIN Old French *chaine*.

chain gang ▶ **noun** a group of convicts chained together while working outside the prison.

chain let·ter ▶ **noun** a letter sent to a number of people, all of whom are asked to make copies and send these to other people, who then do the same.

chain-link ▶ **adjective** made of wire in a diamond-shaped mesh: *a chain-link fence*.

chain mail ▶ **noun** historical armor made of small metal rings linked together.

chain re·ac·tion ▶ **noun 1** a series of events, each caused by the previous one. **2** a chemical reaction in which the products of the reaction cause other changes.

chain·saw /'cʜān,sô/ ▶ **noun** a power-driven saw with teeth set on a moving chain.

chain-smoke ▶ **verb** smoke cigarettes one after the other.

chain store ▶ **noun** one of a group of stores owned by the same company and selling the same goods.

chair /cʜe(ə)r/ ▶ **noun 1** a separate seat for one person, with a back and four legs. **2** the person in charge of a meeting or an organization. **3** a professorship. **4** (**the chair**) the electric chair. ▶ **verb** act as chairperson of a meeting or organization.
– ORIGIN from Greek *kathedra*.

chair·lift /'cʜe(ə)r,lift/ ▶ **noun** a series of chairs hung from a moving cable, used for carrying passengers up and down a mountain.

chair·man /'cʜe(ə)rmən/ (or **chairwoman** /'cʜe(ə)r,wo͝omən/) ▶ **noun** (pl. **chairmen** or **chairwomen**) a person in charge of a meeting or organization.

– SYNONYMS **chair,** chairperson, president, chief executive, leader, master of ceremonies, emcee, MC.

chair·per·son /'cʜe(ə)r,pərsən/ ▶ **noun** a chairman or chairwoman.

chaise /sʜāz/ ▶ **noun 1** chiefly historical a two-wheeled horse-drawn carriage for one or two people. **2** a chaise longue.
– ORIGIN French.

chaise longue /'sʜāz 'lôɴɢ/ (also **chaise lounge** /'sʜāz 'lounj, 'cʜās/) ▶ **noun** (pl. **chaises longues** pronunc. same) a sofa with a backrest at only one end.
– ORIGIN French, 'long chair.'

chak·ra /'cʜäkrə/ ▶ **noun** (in Indian thought) each of seven centers of spiritual power in the human body.
– ORIGIN Sanskrit, 'wheel or circle.'

chal·ced·o·ny /kal'sedn,ē, cʜal-, 'kalsə,dōnē, 'cʜalsə-/ ▶ **noun** (pl. **chalcedonies**) a type of quartz with very small crystals, such as onyx.
– ORIGIN Greek *khalkēdōn*.

cha·let /sʜa'lā, 'sʜa,lā/ ▶ **noun 1** a wooden house with overhanging eaves, typically in the Swiss Alps. **2** a similar building used as a ski lodge.
– ORIGIN Old French *chasel* 'farmstead.'

chal·ice /'cʜaləs/ ▶ **noun 1** historical a goblet. **2** the wine cup used in Holy Communion.
– ORIGIN Latin *calix* 'cup.'

chalk /cʜôk/ ▶ **noun 1** a white soft limestone formed from the skeletal remains of sea creatures. **2** a similar substance made into sticks and used for drawing or writing. ▶ **verb 1** draw or write something with chalk. **2** (**chalk something up**) achieve something noteworthy. **3** (**chalk something up**) ascribe something to a particular cause.
– DERIVATIVES **chalk·y** adjective.
– ORIGIN Latin *calx* 'lime.'

chalk·board /'cʜôk,bôrd/ ▶ **noun** another term for **BLACKBOARD**.

chal·lah /'hälə, 'ᴋʜälə/ ▶ **noun** (pl. **challahs**) a braided loaf of white bread, traditionally baked to celebrate the Jewish sabbath.
– ORIGIN Hebrew *ḥallah*.

chal·lenge /'cʜalənj/ ▶ **noun 1** a demanding task or situation. **2** a call to someone to participate in a contest. **3** an action or statement that calls something into question: *a legal challenge to the ruling failed in the High Court*. **4** an attempt to win a contest or championship in a sport.

– SYNONYMS **1 dare,** provocation, offer. **2 problem,** difficult task, test, trial.

▶ **verb 1** raise doubt as to whether something is true or genuine. **2** invite someone to do something demanding or take part in a fight. **3** (of a sentry) call on someone to prove their identity. **4** Law object to a jury member.

– SYNONYMS **1 question,** dispute, take issue with, call into question, protest against, oppose. **2 dare,** defy, invite, throw down the gauntlet to. **3 test,** tax, strain, make demands on, stretch.

– DERIVATIVES **chal·leng·er** noun.
– ORIGIN Old French *chalenge*.

chal·lenged /'cʜalənjd/ ▶ **adjective 1** euphemistic having a particular disability or impairment: *physically challenged*. **2** humorous lacking in a specified respect: *vertically challenged*.

chal·leng·ing /'cʜalənjiɴɢ/ ▶ **adjective** presenting a test of one's abilities: *a challenging job*.

– SYNONYMS **demanding,** testing, taxing, exacting, hard, difficult, stimulating.
– ANTONYMS easy.

WORD TOOLKIT

See **ARDUOUS**.

chal·lis /'sʜalē/ ▶ **noun** a lightweight soft clothing fabric made from silk and worsted.
– ORIGIN uncertain.

cham·ber /'cʜāmbər/ ▶ **noun 1** a large room used for formal or public events. **2** one of the parts of a lawmaking body. **3** (**chambers**) Law rooms used by a judge or judges. **4** old use a private room, especially a bedroom. **5** an enclosed space or cavity. **6** a cavity in the

body, an organ, or a plant. **7** the part of a gun bore that contains the charge. ▶ **adjective** relating to or for a small group of musical instruments: *a chamber orchestra*.
– DERIVATIVES **cham·bered** adjective.
– ORIGIN from Latin *camera* 'vault, arched chamber.'

cham·ber·lain /ˈCHāmbərlən/ ▶ **noun** historical an officer who managed the household of a monarch or noble.
– ORIGIN Old French.

cham·ber·maid /ˈCHāmbərˌmād/ ▶ **noun** a woman who cleans rooms in a hotel.

cham·ber mu·sic ▶ **noun** instrumental music played by a small ensemble, such as a string quartet.

cham·ber of com·merce ▶ **noun** a local association to promote the interests of the business community.

cham·ber pot ▶ **noun** a bowl kept in a bedroom and used as a toilet.

cham·bray /ˈSHamˌbrā, -brē/ ▶ **noun** a cloth with a white weft and a colored warp.
– ORIGIN from *Cambrai* (see **CAMBRIC**).

cha·me·le·on /kəˈmēlyən, -lēən/ (also **chamaeleon**) ▶ **noun** a small lizard that can change color according to its surroundings.
– DERIVATIVES **cha·me·le·on·ic** /kəˌmēlēˈänik/ adjective.
– ORIGIN from Greek *khamai* 'on the ground' + *leōn* 'lion.'

cham·fer /ˈCHamfər/ ▶ **verb** Carpentry cut away a right-angled edge or corner to make a symmetrical sloping edge.
– ORIGIN French *chamfrain*.

cham·ois /ˈSHamē/ ▶ **noun** (pl. same, pronounced /ˈSHamēz/) **1** an agile goat-antelope found in mountainous areas of southern Europe. **2** (also **chamois leather**) soft pliable leather made from the skin of sheep, goats, or deer.
– ORIGIN French.

cham·o·mile /ˈkaməˌmēl, -ˌmīl/ (also **camomile**) ▶ **noun** a plant with white and yellow flowers, used in herbal medicine.
– ORIGIN Greek *khamaimēlon* 'earth-apple' (because of the apple-like smell of its flowers).

champ[1] /CHamp/ ▶ **verb 1** munch noisily. **2** fret impatiently.
– PHRASES **champ at the bit** be very impatient to start doing something.
– ORIGIN probably imitating the sound.

champ[2] ▶ **noun** informal a champion.

cham·pagne /SHamˈpān/ ▶ **noun** a white sparkling wine from the Champagne region of France.

cham·pi·on /ˈCHampēən/ ▶ **noun 1** a person who has won a sporting contest or other competition. **2** a person who actively supports or defends another person or cause.

> – SYNONYMS **1 winner,** title-holder, gold medalist, prizewinner; informal champ, number one. **2 advocate,** proponent, promoter, supporter, defender, upholder, backer, booster.

▶ **verb** actively support: *priests who championed human rights*.

> – SYNONYMS **advocate,** promote, defend, uphold, support, espouse, stand up for, campaign for, lobby for, fight for.
> – ANTONYMS oppose.

▶ **adjective** Brit. informal or dialect excellent.
– ORIGIN Latin *campion* 'fighter.'

cham·pi·on·ship /ˈCHampēənˌSHip/ ▶ **noun 1** a contest for the position of champion in a sport. **2** the active support of a person or cause.

chance /CHans/ ▶ **noun 1** a possibility of something happening. **2** an opportunity. **3** (**chances**) the probability of something happening: *spelling errors could jeopardize your chances of promotion*. **4** the way in which things happen without any obvious plan or cause.

> – SYNONYMS **1 possibility,** prospect, probability, likelihood, risk, threat, danger. **2** *I gave her a chance to answer* **opportunity,** opening, occasion, window. **3** *he took an awful chance* **risk,** gamble, leap in the dark. **4** *they met* **by chance** *at a youth hostel* **by accident,** fortuitously, accidentally, coincidentally, unintentionally, inadvertently.
> – ANTONYMS certainty.

▶ **adjective** fortuitous; accidental.

> – SYNONYMS *a chance discovery* **accidental,** fortuitous, fluky, coincidental.

▶ **verb 1** do something by accident. **2** informal do something even though it is risky.
– PHRASES **on the (off) chance** just in case. **stand a chance** have a likelihood of success. **take a chance** (or **chances**) take a risk.
– ORIGIN from Old French *cheoir* 'fall, befall.'

> **CHOOSE THE RIGHT WORD**
>
> See **HAPPEN**.

chan·cel /ˈCHansəl/ ▶ **noun** the part of a church near the altar, reserved for the clergy and choir.
– ORIGIN from Latin *cancelli* 'crossbars.'

chan·cel·ler·y /ˈCHans(ə)lərē/ ▶ **noun** (pl. **chancelleries**) the post or department of a chancellor.

chan·cel·lor /ˈCHans(ə)lər/ ▶ **noun 1** a senior government or legal official of various kinds. **2** the president or chief administrative officer of a college or university. **3** (**Chancellor**) the head of the government in some European countries.
– DERIVATIVES **chan·cel·lor·ship** /-ˌSHip/ noun.
– ORIGIN Latin *cancellarius* 'porter, secretary.'

Chan·cel·lor of the Ex·cheq·uer ▶ **noun** the chief finance minister of the United Kingdom.

Chan·cer·y /ˈCHans(ə)rē/ (also **Chancery Division**) ▶ **noun** (pl. **Chanceries**) (in the UK) the Lord Chancellor's court, a division of the High Court of Justice.
– ORIGIN from **CHANCELLERY**.

chan·cre /ˈkaNGkər, ˈSHaNG-/ ▶ **noun** a painless ulcer, especially one developing on the genitals in syphilis.
– ORIGIN Latin *cancer* 'creeping ulcer.'

chanc·y /ˈCHansē/ ▶ **adjective** (**chancier, chanciest**) informal uncertain; risky.

chan·de·lier /ˌSHandəˈli(ə)r/ ▶ **noun** a large hanging light with branches for several light bulbs or candles.
– ORIGIN French.

chan·dler /ˈCHan(d)lər/ (also **ship chandler**) ▶ **noun** a dealer in supplies and equipment for ships.
– DERIVATIVES **chan·dler·y** noun (pl. **chandleries**).
– ORIGIN Old French *chandelier* 'candle-maker, candle-seller.'

change /CHānj/ ▶ **verb 1** make or become different. **2** exchange something for another: *he scarcely knew how to change a spark plug*. **3** move from one to another: *I had to change trains*. **4** (**change over**) move from one system or situation to another. **5** exchange a sum of money for the same sum in a different currency or denomination.

– SYNONYMS **1 alter,** make/become different, adjust, adapt, amend, modify, revise, vary, transform, metamorphose, evolve. **2 exchange,** substitute, swap, switch, replace, alternate.

▸ noun **1** the action of changing. **2** a different experience: *heated pools make a welcome change from a chilly beach.* **3** money returned to someone as the balance of the sum paid. **4** money given in exchange for the same sum in larger units. **5** coins as opposed to paper currency. **6** a clean set of clothes. **7** an order in which a peal of bells can be rung.

– SYNONYMS **1 alteration,** modification, variation, revision, amendment, adjustment, adaptation, metamorphosis, transformation, evolution. **2 replacement,** exchange, substitution, swap, switch.

– DERIVATIVES **change·less** adjective **chang·er** noun.

– PHRASES **change hands** pass to a different owner. **change one's tune** express a very different attitude. **ring the changes** vary the ways of doing something.

– ORIGIN Old French *changer.*

change·a·ble /ˈCHānjəbəl/ ▸ adjective **1** likely to change in an unpredictable way. **2** able to be changed.

– SYNONYMS **variable,** varying, changing, fluctuating, irregular, erratic, inconsistent, unstable, unsettled, inconstant, fickle, capricious, temperamental, volatile, mercurial, unpredictable.
– ANTONYMS constant.

– DERIVATIVES **change·a·bil·i·ty** /ˌCHānjəˈbilətē/ noun.

change·ling /ˈCHānjliNG/ ▸ noun a child believed to have been secretly substituted by fairies for the parents' real child.

change·o·ver /ˈCHānjˌōvər/ ▸ noun a change from one system or situation to another.

chan·nel /ˈCHanl/ ▸ noun **1** a band of frequencies used in radio and television transmission, or a station using such a band. **2** a means of communication: *apply through the proper channels.* **3** a passage along which liquid or a watercourse may flow. **4** a wide stretch of water joining two seas. **5** a passage that boats can use in a stretch of water that is otherwise unsafe. **6** an electric circuit that acts as a path for a signal.

– SYNONYMS **1 strait(s),** sound, narrows, passage. **2 duct,** gutter, conduit, trough, sluice, drain. **3 means,** medium, instrument, mechanism, agency, vehicle, route, avenue.

▸ verb (**channels, channeling, channeled**) **1** direct toward a particular purpose: *the money has been channeled into the establishment of DNA banks.* **2** pass something along or through a specified route or medium.

– SYNONYMS **convey,** transmit, conduct, direct, relay, pass on, transfer.

– ORIGIN Latin *canalis* 'pipe, channel.'

chan·nel-surf ▸ verb informal change frequently from one television channel to another.

chant /CHant/ ▸ noun **1** a repeated rhythmic phrase that is shouted or sung together by a group. **2** a tune to which the words of psalms or other works with irregular rhythm are fitted by singing several syllables or words to the same note.

– SYNONYMS **shout,** cry, call, slogan, chorus, refrain.

▸ verb say, shout, or sing in a chant.

– SYNONYMS **shout,** chorus, repeat, call.

– ORIGIN Old French *chanter* 'sing.'

chant·er /ˈCHantər/ ▸ noun the pipe of a bagpipe with finger holes, on which the melody is played.

chan·te·relle /ˌSHantəˈrel, ˌSHänt-/ ▸ noun an edible woodland mushroom with a yellow funnel-shaped cap.

– ORIGIN Latin *cantharellus.*

chan·teuse /ˌSHänˈto͞oz, ˈtœz/ ▸ noun a female singer of popular songs.

– ORIGIN French.

chant·ey /ˈSHantē/ (also **chanty, shanty,** or **sea chantey**) ▸ noun a song in which a solo part alternates with a chorus, sung by sailors when working together.

– ORIGIN probably from French *chantez!* 'sing!'

chan·try /ˈCHantrē/ ▸ noun (pl. **chantries**) a chapel or other part of a church established by an endowment in order for masses to be said for the donor's soul.

– ORIGIN from Old French *chanter* 'to sing.'

chant·y ▸ noun (pl. **chanties**) variant spelling of **CHANTEY**.

Cha·nuk·kah /ˈKHänəkə, ˈhänəkə/ ▸ noun variant spelling of **HANUKKAH**.

cha·os /ˈkāˌäs/ ▸ noun **1** complete disorder and confusion. **2** the formless matter supposed to have existed before the creation of the universe.

– SYNONYMS **disorder,** disorganization, confusion, mayhem, bedlam, pandemonium, havoc, turmoil, a shambles, anarchy, lawlessness; informal all hell broken loose.
– ANTONYMS order.

– ORIGIN Greek *khaos* 'vast chasm, void.'

cha·os the·o·ry ▸ noun the branch of science concerned with the behavior of complex systems in which tiny changes can have major effects.

cha·ot·ic /kāˈätik/ ▸ adjective in a state of complete confusion and disorder.

– SYNONYMS **disorderly,** disorganized, in confusion, in turmoil, topsy-turvy, anarchic, lawless.

– DERIVATIVES **cha·ot·i·cal·ly** adverb.

WORD TOOLKIT

See **MESSY**.

chap[1] /CHap/ ▸ verb (**chaps, chapping, chapped**) **1** (of the skin) crack and become sore through exposure to cold weather. **2** (as adj. **chapped**) (of the skin) cracked and sore through exposure to cold weather.

– ORIGIN unknown.

chap[2] ▸ noun Brit. informal a man.

– ORIGIN from former *chapman* 'pedlar.'

chap·ar·ral /ˌSHapəˈral/ ▸ noun vegetation consisting of tangled shrubs and thorny bushes.

– ORIGIN Spanish.

cha·pat·ti /CHəˈpätē/ ▸ noun (pl. **chapattis**) (in Indian cooking) a flat cake of wholemeal bread cooked on a griddle.

– ORIGIN Hindi.

chap·el /ˈCHapəl/ ▸ noun **1** a small building or room for Christian worship in an institution or large private house. **2** a part of a large church with its own altar.

– ORIGIN Old French *chapele.*

chap·er·one /ˈSHapəˌrōn/ ▸ noun **1** a person who accompanies and looks after another person or people. **2** dated an older woman who accompanies and supervises

an unmarried girl at social occasions. ▶ **verb** accompany and supervise someone.
– ORIGIN French.

chap·lain /ˈCHaplən/ ▶ **noun** a member of the clergy attached to a chapel in a private house or an institution, or to a military unit.
– DERIVATIVES **chap·lain·cy** noun.
– ORIGIN Old French *chapelain*.

chap·let /ˈCHaplət/ ▶ **noun** a decorative circular band worn on the head.
– ORIGIN Old French *chapelet* 'little hat.'

chaps /CHaps, SHaps/ ▶ **plural noun** leather pants without a seat, worn by a cowboy over ordinary pants to protect the legs.
– ORIGIN short for *chaparajos*, from Mexican Spanish *chaparreras*.

chap·ter /ˈCHaptər/ ▶ **noun 1** a main division of a book. **2** a particular period in history or in a person's life. **3** the governing body of a cathedral or other religious community. **4** a local branch of a society.

> – SYNONYMS **1 section,** part, division, topic, stage, episode. **2 period,** phase, page, stage, epoch, era.

– PHRASES **chapter and verse** an exact reference or authority.
– ORIGIN Old French *chapitre*.

char[1] /CHär/ ▶ **verb** (**chars, charring, charred**) partially burn something so as to blacken the surface.
– ORIGIN probably from CHARCOAL.

char[2] ▶ **noun** variant spelling of CHARR.

char[3] Brit. informal , dated ▶ **noun** a charwoman. ▶ **verb** (**chars, charring, charred**) work as a charwoman.

char·ac·ter /ˈkariktər/ ▶ **noun 1** the qualities that make a person different from others. **2** the particular nature of something: *the picturesque character of the village*. **3** strength and originality in a person's nature. **4** a person's good reputation. **5** a person in a novel, play, movie, or television show. **6** informal an eccentric or amusing person. **7** a printed or written letter or symbol.

> – SYNONYMS **1 personality,** nature, quality, disposition, temperament, mentality, makeup, spirit, identity, tone, feel. **2 integrity,** honor, moral strength/fiber, strength, backbone, resolve, grit, will power; informal guts; Brit. informal bottle. **3 reputation,** (good) name, standing, position, status. **4 eccentric,** oddity, crank, original, individualist, madcap, nonconformist; informal oddball. **5 person,** man, woman, soul, creature, individual, customer; informal guy. **6 letter,** figure, symbol, mark, device, sign, hieroglyph.

– DERIVATIVES **char·ac·ter·ful** /-fəl/ adjective **char·ac·ter·less** adjective.
– ORIGIN from Greek *kharaktēr* 'a stamping tool.'

char·ac·ter ac·tor ▶ **noun** an actor who specializes in playing unusual people rather than leading roles.

char·ac·ter·is·tic /ˌkariktəˈristik/ ▶ **noun** a feature or quality typical of a person, place, or thing.

> – SYNONYMS **attribute,** feature, quality, property, trait, aspect, idiosyncrasy, peculiarity, quirk.

▶ **adjective** typical of a particular person, place, or thing: *the characteristic tilt of her head*.

> – SYNONYMS **typical,** usual, normal, distinctive, representative, particular, special, peculiar, idiosyncratic.
> – ANTONYMS abnormal.

– DERIVATIVES **char·ac·ter·is·ti·cal·ly** adverb.

char·ac·ter·ize /ˈkariktəˌrīz/ ▶ **verb 1** describe the character of someone or something. **2** be typical of: *the rugged hills that characterize New England*.

> – SYNONYMS **1 distinguish,** mark, typify, set apart. **2 portray,** depict, present, represent, describe, categorize, class, brand.

– DERIVATIVES **char·ac·ter·i·za·tion** /ˌkariktərəˈzāSHən/ noun.

cha·rade /SHəˈrād/ ▶ **noun 1** an absurd pretense. **2** (**charades**) a game of guessing a word or phrase from written or acted clues.

> – SYNONYMS **pretense,** act, masquerade, show, facade, pantomime, farce, travesty, mockery, parody.

– ORIGIN Provençal *charrado* 'conversation.'

char·broil /ˈCHärˌbroil/ ▶ **verb** grill food, especially meat on a rack over charcoal.

char·coal /ˈCHärˌkōl/ ▶ **noun 1** a black form of carbon obtained when wood is heated in the absence of air. **2** a dark gray color.
– ORIGIN probably related to COAL.

char·cu·te·rie /SHärˌkoōtəˈrē, -ˈkoōtərē/ ▶ **noun** (pl. **charcuteries**) **1** cold cooked meats. **2** a store selling cold cooked meats.
– ORIGIN French.

chard /CHärd/ (also **Swiss chard**) ▶ **noun** a variety of beet with edible, slightly bitter, broadly ribbed leaves.
– ORIGIN French *carde*.

Char·don·nay /ˌSHärdnˈā/ ▶ **noun** a white wine made from a variety of grape used for making champagne and other wines.
– ORIGIN French.

char·ette /SHəˈret/ ▶ **noun** a meeting or conference devoted to a concerted effort to solve a problem or plan something.

charge /CHärj/ ▶ **verb 1** ask an amount of money as a price for goods or a service. **2** formally accuse someone of something. **3** rush forward so as to attack someone or something. **4** rush in a particular direction: *he charged up the stairs*. **5** entrust someone with a task. **6** store electrical energy in a battery. **7** load or fill a container, gun, etc. **8** fill with a quality or emotion: *the air was charged with menace*.

> – SYNONYMS **1 ask,** demand, bill, invoice. **2 accuse,** indict, arraign, prosecute, try, put on trial, impeach. **3 entrust,** burden, encumber, saddle, tax. **4 attack,** storm, assault, assail, descend on; informal lay into, tear into. **5 rush,** storm, stampede, push, plow, go headlong; informal barrel, steam. **6** *charge your glasses!* **fill (up),** top up, load (up), arm.

▶ **noun 1** a price asked. **2** a formal accusation made against a prisoner brought to trial. **3** responsibility for care or control: *she felt out of touch with the youngsters in her charge*. **4** a person or thing entrusted to someone's care. **5** a headlong rush forward. **6** the property of matter that is responsible for electrical phenomena, existing in a positive or negative form. **7** energy stored chemically in a battery for conversion into electricity. **8** a quantity of explosive to be detonated in order to fire a gun or similar weapon.

> – SYNONYMS **1 fee,** payment, price, rate, tariff, fare, levy. **2 accusation,** allegation, indictment, impeachment, arraignment. **3 attack,** assault, offensive, onslaught, drive, push. **4** *the child was in her charge* **care,** protection, safekeeping, control, custody, hands.

– DERIVATIVES **charge·a·ble** adjective **charged** adjective.
– PHRASES **press charges** accuse someone formally of a crime so that they can be brought to trial.
– ORIGIN Old French *charger.*

CHOOSE THE RIGHT WORD

See **ATTACK**.

charge·back /'cHärj,bak/ ▶ **noun 1** a demand by a credit-card provider for a retailer to make good the loss on a fraudulent or disputed transaction. **2** an act or policy of allocating the cost of an organization's centrally located resources to the individuals or departments that use them.

charge card ▶ **noun** a credit card issued by a chain store or bank.

char·gé d'af·faires /sHär,zHā dä'fer/ (also **chargé**) ▶ **noun** (pl. **chargés d'affaires** pronunc. same) **1** an ambassador's deputy. **2** a government's diplomatic representative in a country to which an ambassador has not been sent.
– ORIGIN French, 'a person in charge of affairs.'

charg·er[1] /'cHärjər/ ▶ **noun 1** a device for charging a battery. **2** historical a horse ridden by a knight or cavalryman.

charg·er[2] ▶ **noun** old use a large flat dish.
– ORIGIN Old French *chargeour.*

char·i·ot /'cHarēət/ ▶ **noun** a two-wheeled vehicle drawn by horses, used in ancient warfare and racing.
– DERIVATIVES **char·i·ot·eer** /,cHarēə'ti(ə)r/ noun.
– ORIGIN Old French.

cha·ris·ma /kə'rizmə/ ▶ **noun 1** attractiveness or charm that can inspire admiration or enthusiasm in other people. **2** (pl. **charismata** /-,mətə/) (in Christian belief) a special gift given by God.

– SYNONYMS **charm,** presence, (force of) personality, strength of character, (animal) magnetism, appeal, allure.

– ORIGIN Greek *kharisma.*

char·is·mat·ic /,kariz'matik/ ▶ **adjective 1** having a charm that can inspire admiration in other people. **2** relating to a Christian movement that emphasizes special gifts from God, such as the healing of the sick.

– SYNONYMS **charming,** magnetic, compelling, inspiring, captivating, mesmerizing, appealing, alluring, glamorous.

– DERIVATIVES **char·is·mat·i·cal·ly** adverb.

char·i·ta·ble /'cHaritəbəl/ ▶ **adjective 1** relating to the assistance of people in need. **2** not judging others too severely; tolerant.

– SYNONYMS **1 philanthropic,** generous, open-handed, giving, munificent, benevolent, altruistic, unselfish, public-spirited, humanitarian, non-profit-making. **2 magnanimous,** generous, liberal, tolerant, sympathetic, understanding, lenient, indulgent, forgiving.
– ANTONYMS commercial, mean.

– DERIVATIVES **char·i·ta·bly** adverb.

char·i·ty /'cHaritē/ ▶ **noun** (pl. **charities**) **1** an organization set up to help people in need. **2** the voluntary giving of money or other help to people in need. **3** help or money given to people in need. **4** tolerance in judging others.

– SYNONYMS **1 nonprofit organization,** charitable institution, fund, trust, foundation. **2 aid,** financial assistance, welfare, relief, donations, handouts, gifts, largesse; historical alms. **3 philanthropy,** humanitarianism, altruism, public-spiritedness, social conscience, benevolence. **4 goodwill,** compassion, consideration, concern, kindness, sympathy, indulgence, tolerance, leniency.

– ORIGIN Latin *caritas.*

char·la·tan /'sHärlətən, 'sHärlətn/ ▶ **noun** a person who falsely claims to have a particular skill.

– SYNONYMS **quack,** sham, fraud, fake, impostor, hoodwinker, double-dealer, swindler, fraudster; informal phony, shark, con man/artist, bunco artist, chiseler.

– DERIVATIVES **char·la·tan·ism** /-lətə,nizəm, -lətn,izəm/ noun **char·la·tan·ry** noun.
– ORIGIN from Italian *ciarlare* 'to babble.'

CHOOSE THE RIGHT WORD

See **QUACK**[2].

Charles's law /cHärlz, cHärlziz/ ▶ **noun** a law stating that the volume of an ideal gas at constant pressure is directly proportional to the absolute temperature.
– ORIGIN named after the French physicist Jacques A. C. *Charles.*

charles·ton /'cHärlstən/ ▶ **noun** a lively dance of the 1920s that involved turning the knees inward and kicking out the lower legs.
– ORIGIN named after the city of *Charleston* in South Carolina, US.

char·lotte /'sHärlət/ ▶ **noun** a pudding made of stewed fruit with a casing or covering of bread, sponge cake, or cookies.
– ORIGIN French, from the woman's name *Charlotte.*

charm /cHärm/ ▶ **noun 1** the power or quality of delighting or fascinating others. **2** a small ornament worn on a necklace or bracelet. **3** an object, act, or saying believed to have magic power.

– SYNONYMS **1 appeal,** attraction, fascination, beauty, loveliness, allure, seductiveness, magnetism, charisma; informal pulling power. **2 spell,** incantation, formula; mojo, hex. **3 talisman,** trinket, amulet, mascot, fetish.

▶ **verb 1** delight greatly: *she charmed me with her intelligence.* **2** use one's charm in order to influence someone.

– SYNONYMS **1 delight,** please, win (over), attract, captivate, lure, fascinate, enchant, beguile. **2 coax,** cajole, wheedle; informal sweet-talk, soft-soap.

– DERIVATIVES **charm·er** noun **charm·less** adjective.
– ORIGIN from Latin *carmen* 'song, verse.'

charmed /cHärmd/ ▶ **adjective** (of a person's life) unusually lucky as though protected by magic.
▶ **exclamation** dated expressing polite pleasure at an introduction.

charm·ing /'cHärmiNG/ ▶ **adjective 1** delightful; attractive. **2** very polite, friendly, and likable.

– SYNONYMS **delightful,** pleasing, endearing, lovely, adorable, appealing, attractive, good-looking, alluring, winning, fetching, captivating, enchanting, entrancing.

▶ **exclamation** used as an ironic expression of displeasure.
– DERIVATIVES **charm·ing·ly** adverb.

charm of·fen·sive ▶ **noun** a campaign of flattery and friendliness designed to achieve the support of others.

char·nel house /ˈCHärnl/ ▸ **noun** historical a building or vault in which corpses or bones were piled.
– ORIGIN from Latin *carnalis* 'relating to flesh.'

Cha·ro·lais /ˌSHarəˈlā/ ▸ **noun** (pl. same) an animal of a breed of large white beef cattle.
– ORIGIN named after the *Monts du Charollais*, hills in eastern France.

charr /CHär/ (also **char**) ▸ **noun** (pl. same) a troutlike northern freshwater or sea fish.
– ORIGIN perhaps Celtic.

chart /CHärt/ ▸ **noun 1** a sheet of information in the form of a table, graph, or diagram. **2** a geographical map, especially one used for navigation by sea or air. **3** (**the charts**) a weekly listing of the current best-selling pop records.

– SYNONYMS **graph,** table, diagram, plan, map; Computing **graphic.**

▸ **verb 1** make a map of an area. **2** plot or record something on a chart.

– SYNONYMS **1 plot,** tabulate, graph, record, register, represent. **2 follow,** trace, outline, describe, detail, record, document.

– ORIGIN from Greek *khartēs* 'papyrus leaf.'

char·ter /ˈCHärtər/ ▸ **noun 1** a document granted by a ruler or government, by which an institution such as a university is created or its rights are defined. **2** a written constitution or description of an organization's functions. **3** the hiring of an aircraft, ship, or motor vehicle.

– SYNONYMS **1** *a royal charter* **authority,** authorization, sanction, dispensation, permit, license, warrant. **2** *the UN Charter* **constitution,** code, principles.

▸ **verb 1** hire an aircraft, ship, or motor vehicle. **2** grant a charter to a university or organization.

– SYNONYMS **hire,** lease, rent, book.

– DERIVATIVES **char·ter·er** noun.
– ORIGIN Latin *chartula* 'little paper.'

char·ter flight ▸ **noun** a flight by an aircraft chartered for a specific journey, not part of an airline's regular schedule.

char·ter mem·ber ▸ **noun** an original or founding member of an organization.

Chart·ism /ˈCHärtˌizəm/ ▸ **noun** a UK movement (1837–48) for social and legislative reform, the principles of which were set out in *The People's Charter*.
– DERIVATIVES **Chart·ist** /ˈCHärtəst/ noun & adjective.

char·treuse /SHärˈtro͞oz, -ˈtro͞os/ ▸ **noun** a pale green or yellow liqueur made from brandy.
– ORIGIN named after *La Grande Chartreuse*, a monastery near Grenoble where the liqueur was first made.

char·wom·an /ˈCHärˌwo͝omən/ ▸ **noun** (pl. **charwomen**) Brit. dated a woman employed as a cleaner in a house or office.
– ORIGIN from former *char* or *chare* 'a chore.'

char·y /ˈCHe(ə)rē/ ▸ **adjective** cautiously reluctant: *leaders are chary of reform.*
– ORIGIN Old English, 'sorrowful, anxious.'

chase¹ /CHās/ ▸ **verb 1** pursue someone or something so as to catch them. **2** hurry or cause to hurry somewhere: *she chased him out of the house.* **3** try to obtain something owed or required.

– SYNONYMS **1 pursue,** run after, follow, hunt, track, trail; informal tail. **2** *she chased away the dogs* **drive,** send, scare; informal send packing. **3** *she chased away all thoughts of him* **dispel,** banish, dismiss, drive away, shut out, put out of one's mind.

▸ **noun 1** an act of chasing. **2** (**the chase**) hunting as a sport.

– SYNONYMS **pursuit,** hunt, trail.

– PHRASES **give chase** pursue someone or something so as to catch them.
– ORIGIN Old French *chacier*.

chase² ▸ **verb** engrave metal or a design on metal.
– ORIGIN probably from Old French *enchasser* 'enclose.'

chas·er /ˈCHāsər/ ▸ **noun 1** a person or thing that chases someone or something. **2** informal a weak alcoholic drink taken after a stronger one.

chasm /ˈkazəm/ ▸ **noun 1** a deep crack or opening in the earth. **2** a marked difference between people, opinions, or feelings: *the chasm between rich and poor.*

– SYNONYMS **1** *a deep chasm* **gorge,** abyss, canyon, ravine, gully, gulch, gulf, crevasse, fissure, crevice. **2** *the chasm between their views* **breach,** gulf, rift; difference, separation, division, schism.

– ORIGIN Greek *khasma* 'gaping hollow.'

chas·sis /ˈCHasē, ˈSHasē/ ▸ **noun** (pl. same /-sēz/) the base frame of a car or other wheeled vehicle.
– ORIGIN French, 'frame.'

chaste /CHāst/ ▸ **adjective 1** refraining from all sex, or from sex outside marriage. **2** without unnecessary decoration; simple.
– ORIGIN Latin *castus* 'morally pure.'

chas·ten /ˈCHāsən/ ▸ **verb** (often as adj. **chastened**) make someone feel ashamed or sorry: *you walk like a chastened but defiant kid.*
– ORIGIN Old French *chastier*.

chas·tise /CHasˈtīz/ ▸ **verb** reprimand someone severely.
– DERIVATIVES **chas·tise·ment** /CHasˈtīzmənt, ˈCHastəz-/ noun.

chas·ti·ty /ˈCHastətē/ ▸ **noun** the practice of refraining from all sex, or from sex outside marriage.

chas·ti·ty belt ▸ **noun** historical a garment or device designed to prevent the woman wearing it from having sex.

chas·u·ble /ˈCHazəbəl, ˈCHazH-, ˈCHas-/ ▸ **noun** a sleeveless outer garment worn by a Christian priest when celebrating Mass.
– ORIGIN from Latin *casula* 'hooded cloak, little cottage.'

chat /CHat/ ▸ **verb** (**chats, chatting, chatted**) **1** talk in an informal way. **2** (**chat someone up**) informal talk to someone flirtatiously.

– SYNONYMS **talk,** gossip; informal jaw, yammer, chew the fat, shoot the breeze.

▸ **noun** an informal conversation.

– SYNONYMS **talk,** conversation, gossip; informal rap/bull session, confab, chinwag.

– ORIGIN shortening of **CHATTER**.

CHOOSE THE RIGHT WORD

See **CONVERSATION**.

cha·teau /SHaˈtō/ ▸ **noun** (pl. **chateaux** or **chateaus** pronunc. same or /-ˈtō(z)/) a large French country house or castle.
– ORIGIN French.

chat·e·laine /ˈSHatlˌān/ ▸ **noun** dated a woman in charge of a large house.
– ORIGIN French.

chat room ▶ **noun** an area on the Internet or other computer network where users can communicate.

chat·tel /ˈCHatl/ ▶ **noun** a personal possession.
– ORIGIN Old French *chatel*.

chat·ter /ˈCHatər/ ▶ **verb 1** talk informally about minor matters. **2** (of a bird or monkey) make a series of quick high-pitched sounds. **3** (of a person's teeth) click repeatedly together from cold or fear.

– SYNONYMS **blather,** prattle, chat, gossip, jabber, babble; informal yatter.

▶ **noun 1** informal talk. **2** a series of quick high-pitched sounds.

– SYNONYMS **prattle,** chat, gossip, patter, jabber, babble; informal chitchat, yammering, yattering.

– DERIVATIVES **chat·ter·er** noun.
– PHRASES **the chattering classes** derogatory educated people considered as a social group prone to expressing liberal opinions.
– ORIGIN imitating the sound.

chat·ter·box /ˈCHatər,bäks/ ▶ **noun** informal a person who talks too much, especially about trivial matters.

chat·ty /ˈCHatē/ ▶ **adjective** (**chattier**, **chattiest**) **1** fond of chatting. **2** (of a letter) informal and lively.

– SYNONYMS **talkative,** communicative, effusive, gossipy, loquacious, voluble; informal mouthy, gabby.
– ANTONYMS taciturn.

– DERIVATIVES **chat·ti·ly** adverb **chat·ti·ness** noun.

chauf·feur /ˈSHōfər, SHōˈfər/ ▶ **noun** a person employed to drive a car. ▶ **verb** drive a car or a passenger in a car, especially as one's job.
– ORIGIN French, 'stoker' (by association with steam engines).

chau·vin·ism /ˈSHōvə,nizəm/ ▶ **noun 1** extreme or aggressive support for one's own country or group. **2** the belief held by some men that men are superior to women.
– DERIVATIVES **chau·vin·ist** /ˈSHōvənist/ noun & adjective **chau·vin·is·tic** /,SHōvəˈnistik/ adjective.
– ORIGIN named after Nicolas *Chauvin*, a French soldier noted for his extreme patriotism.

Ch.E. ▶ **abbreviation** chemical engineer.

cheap /CHēp/ ▶ **adjective 1** low in price. **2** charging low prices. **3** low in price and of poor quality. **4** having no value because achieved in a regrettable way: *her moment of cheap triumph.*

– SYNONYMS **1 inexpensive,** low-priced, low-cost, economical, competitive, affordable, reasonable, budget, economy, bargain, reduced, discounted; informal dirt cheap. **2 poor-quality,** second-rate, substandard, inferior, vulgar, shoddy, trashy, tawdry; informal tacky. **3 despicable,** contemptible, immoral, unscrupulous, unprincipled, cynical.
– ANTONYMS expensive.

▶ **adverb** at or for a low price.
– DERIVATIVES **cheap·ly** adverb **cheap·ness** noun.
– ORIGIN Old English 'bargaining, trade.'

cheap·en /ˈCHēpən/ ▶ **verb 1** lower the price of something. **2** reduce the worth of someone or something.

cheap·jack /ˈCHēp,jak/ ▶ **adjective** of inferior quality.

cheap·skate /ˈCHēp,skāt/ ▶ **noun** informal a stingy person.
– ORIGIN from *skate* 'a disreputable or unpleasant person.'

cheat /CHēt/ ▶ **verb 1** act dishonestly or unfairly in order to gain an advantage. **2** deprive someone of something by dishonest or unfair means. **3** manage to avoid something bad or unwelcome: *he cheated death after falling 20 feet to the pavement.*

– SYNONYMS **swindle,** defraud, deceive, trick, dupe, hoodwink, double-cross, gull; informal rip off, con, pull a fast one on, sucker.

▶ **noun 1** a person who cheats. **2** an act of cheating.

– SYNONYMS **swindler,** fraudster, confidence trickster, double-dealer, double-crosser, fraud, fake, charlatan; informal con artist.

– ORIGIN shortening of **ESCHEAT**.

Che·chen /ˈCHeCHən/ ▶ **noun** (pl. same or **Chechens**) a person from Chechnya, a self-governing republic in SW Russia.
– ORIGIN Russian.

check[1] /CHek/ ▶ **verb 1** examine the accuracy, quality, or condition of something. **2** make sure that something is the case: *I checked that all the doors were secure.* **3** stop or slow the progress of: *measures to check the growth in crime and violence.* **4** Chess move a piece or pawn to a square where it directly attacks the opposing king.

– SYNONYMS **1 examine,** inspect, look at/over, scrutinize, study, investigate, probe, look into, inquire into; informal check out, give something a/the once-over. **2 make sure,** confirm, verify. **3 halt,** stop, arrest, bar, obstruct, foil, thwart, curb, block.

▶ **noun 1** an act of checking the accuracy, quality, or condition of something. **2** a means of controlling or restraining something. **3** Chess a position in which a king is directly threatened. **4** the bill in a restaurant.

– SYNONYMS **1 examination,** inspection, scrutiny, perusal, study, investigation, test, checkup; informal once-over. **2 control,** restraint, constraint, curb, limitation.

– PHRASES **check in** register at a hotel or airport. **check out** settle one's hotel bill before leaving. **check something out** investigate or find out about something. **check up on** investigate something. **in check 1** under control. **2** Chess (of a king) directly attacked by an opponent's piece or pawn.
– ORIGIN from a Persian word meaning 'king.'

check[2] ▶ **noun** a pattern of small squares. ▶ **adjective** (also **checked**) having a pattern of small squares.
– ORIGIN probably from **CHEQUER**.

check[3] /CHek/ (Brit. **cheque**) ▶ **noun** a written order to a bank to pay a stated sum from an account to a particular person.
– ORIGIN variant of **CHECK**[1], in the former sense 'device for checking the amount of an item.'

check·book /ˈCHek,bo͝ok/ ▶ **noun** a book of blank checks with a register for recording the checks written.

check·er[1] /ˈCHekər/ ▶ **noun 1** a person or thing that verifies or examines something. **2** a cashier in a store or supermarket.

check·er[2] (Brit. **chequer**) ▶ **noun 1** (often **checkers**) a pattern of squares, typically alternately colored: *a geometric shape bordered by checkers.* **2** (**checkers**) (treated as sing.) a game for two players, with twelve pieces each, played on a checkerboard. **3** a round flat piece, usually red or black, used to play checkers.

check·er·board /ˈCHekər,bôrd/ ▶ **noun 1** a board for playing checkers and similar games, having a regular checkered pattern in black and white. **2** a pattern resembling such a board.

check·ered /ˈCHekərd/ ▶ **adjective 1** having a pattern of alternating squares of different colors. **2** marked by periods of varied fortune or discreditable incidents: *his checkered past might hurt his electability.*

check·ered flag ▶ **noun** a flag with a black-and-white checkered pattern, shown to racing drivers at the end of a race.

check-in ▶ **noun** the place at an airport where a passenger registers before departure.

check·ing ac·count ▶ **noun** an account at a bank against which checks can be drawn by the account holder.

check·list /ˈchekˌlist/ ▶ **noun** a list of items required or things to be done or considered.

check mark ▶ **noun** a mark (✓) used to indicate that a written item is correct or has been chosen or verified.

check·mate /ˈchekˌmāt/ Chess ▶ **noun** a position of check from which a king cannot escape. ▶ **verb** put a king into checkmate.
– ORIGIN from Persian, 'the king is dead.'

check·out /ˈchekˌout/ ▶ **noun 1** a place where goods are paid for in a supermarket or similar store. **2** the procedure followed when a guest leaves a hotel at the end of a stay.

check·point /ˈchekˌpoint/ ▶ **noun** a barrier where security checks are carried out on travelers.

check·up /ˈchekˌəp/ ▶ **noun** a thorough examination to detect any problems, especially medical or mechanical ones.

ched·dar /ˈchedər/ ▶ **noun** a kind of firm, smooth cheese originally made in Cheddar in SW England.

cheek /chēk/ ▶ **noun 1** either side of the face below the eye. **2** either of the buttocks. **3** remarks or behavior seen as rude or disrespectful. ▶ **verb** informal speak rudely or disrespectfully to someone.
– PHRASES **cheek by jowl** close together. **turn the other cheek** choose not to retaliate after one has been attacked or insulted. [from the Gospel of Matthew, chapter 5.]
– ORIGIN Old English.

cheek·bone /ˈchēkˌbōn/ ▶ **noun** the bone below the eye.

cheek·y /ˈchēkē/ ▶ **adjective** (**cheekier**, **cheekiest**) showing a lack of respect, often in an amusing way.
– DERIVATIVES **cheek·i·ly** adverb **cheek·i·ness** noun.

cheep /chēp/ ▶ **noun** a shrill, squeaky cry made by a young bird. ▶ **verb** make a cheep.
– ORIGIN imitating the sound.

cheer /chi(ə)r/ ▶ **verb 1** shout for joy or in praise or encouragement. **2** praise or encourage a person, team, etc., with shouts. **3** (**cheer up** or **cheer someone up**) become or make less miserable. **4** give comfort or support to someone.

> – SYNONYMS **1 applaud,** hail, salute, shout for, clap, put one's hands together for, bring the house down; informal holler for, give someone a big hand, ballyhoo. **2** *he* ***cheered up*** *at the sight of the food* **perk up,** brighten up, rally, revive, bounce back, take heart; informal buck up. **3** *the bad weather did little to cheer me* **please,** raise/lift someone's spirits, brighten, buoy up, hearten, gladden, perk up, encourage; informal buck up.
> – ANTONYMS boo, depress.

▶ **noun 1** a shout of joy, encouragement, or praise. **2** (also **good cheer**) a feeling of happiness or optimism.

> – SYNONYMS **hurrah,** hurray, whoop, bravo, shout; (**cheers**) acclaim, applause, ovation.
> – ANTONYMS boo.

– ORIGIN Old French *chiere* 'face' (first meaning 'face, expression, mood.')

cheer·ful /ˈchi(ə)rfəl/ ▶ **adjective 1** noticeably happy and optimistic. **2** bright and pleasant: *cheerful colors.*

> – SYNONYMS **1 happy,** jolly, merry, bright, sunny, joyful, in good/high spirits, buoyant, cheery, animated, smiling, good-humored; informal chipper, chirpy, full of beans. **2 pleasant,** agreeable, bright, sunny, friendly, welcoming.
> – ANTONYMS sad, gloomy.

– DERIVATIVES **cheer·ful·ly** adverb **cheer·ful·ness** noun.

cheer·i·o /ˌchi(ə)rēˈō/ ▶ **exclamation** Brit. informal goodbye.

cheer·lead·er /ˈchi(ə)rˌlēdər/ ▶ **noun 1** a person belonging to a group that performs organized chanting and dancing in support of a team at a sports event. **2** an enthusiastic and vocal supporter.

cheer·less /ˈchi(ə)rlis/ ▶ **adjective** gloomy and depressing.

> – SYNONYMS **gloomy,** dreary, dull, dismal, bleak, drab, somber, dark, dim, dingy, funereal, austere, stark, unwelcoming, uninviting, depressing.

cheers /chi(ə)rz/ ▶ **exclamation** informal **1** expressing good wishes before drinking. **2** chiefly Brit. said to express thanks or on parting.

cheer·y /ˈchi(ə)rē/ ▶ **adjective** (**cheerier**, **cheeriest**) happy and optimistic.
– DERIVATIVES **cheer·i·ly** adverb **cheer·i·ness** noun.

cheese[1] /chēz/ ▶ **noun** a food made from the pressed curds of milk, either firm or soft in texture.
– ORIGIN Latin *caseus.*

cheese[2] (also **big cheese**) ▶ **noun** informal an important person: *he was a big cheese in the business world.*
– ORIGIN probably from Persian *č īz* 'thing.'

cheese[3] ▶ (**be cheesed off**) chiefly Brit. informal be irritated or bored.
– ORIGIN unknown.

cheese·burg·er /ˈchēzˌbərgər/ ▶ **noun** a hamburger with a slice of cheese on it.

cheese·cake /ˈchēzˌkāk/ ▶ **noun 1** a rich sweet cake made with cream and soft cheese on a cookie or pastry crust. **2** informal pictures of scantily dressed women posing in a sexually attractive way.

cheese·cloth /ˈchēzˌklôth/ ▶ **noun** thin, loosely woven cotton cloth.

cheese·steak /ˈchēzˌstāk/ ▶ **noun** (also **Philly cheesesteak**) a submarine sandwich containing thin-sliced sautéed beef, melted cheese, and sautéed onions.

chees·y /ˈchēzē/ ▶ **adjective** (**cheesier**, **cheesiest**) **1** like cheese in taste, smell, or consistency. **2** informal cheap and low in quality. **3** informal unoriginal or sentimental: *an album of cheesy pop hits.*
– DERIVATIVES **chees·i·ly** adverb **chees·i·ness** noun.

chee·tah /ˈchētə/ ▶ **noun** a large fast-running spotted cat found in Africa and parts of Asia.
– ORIGIN Hindi.

chef /shef/ ▶ **noun** a professional cook, especially the chief cook in a restaurant or hotel.
– ORIGIN French, 'head.'

chef-d'œu·vre /shā ˈdœv(rə), ˈdə(r)v/ ▶ **noun** (pl. **chefs-d'œuvre** pronunc. same) a masterpiece.
– ORIGIN French, 'chief work.'

chem. ▶ **abbreviation 1** chemical. **2** chemistry.

chem·i·cal /'kemikəl/ ▶ **adjective** relating to chemistry or chemicals. ▶ **noun** a compound or substance that has been artificially prepared or purified.
– DERIVATIVES **chem·i·cal·ly** adverb.
– ORIGIN French *chimique*.

chem·i·cal en·gi·neer·ing ▶ **noun** the branch of engineering concerned with the design and operation of industrial chemical plants.

che·mise /SHə'mēz, -'mēs/ ▶ **noun 1** a dress hanging straight from the shoulders, popular in the 1920s. **2** a woman's loose-fitting petticoat or nightdress.
– ORIGIN from Latin *camisia* 'shirt or nightgown.'

chem·ist /'kemist/ ▶ **noun 1** a person engaged in chemical research. **2** Brit. a person who is authorized to dispense medicinal drugs. **3** Brit. a drugstore.
– ORIGIN Latin *alchimista* 'alchemist.'

chem·is·try /'keməstrē/ ▶ **noun** (pl. **chemistries**) **1** the branch of science concerned with the nature and properties of substances and how they react with each other. **2** the chemical properties of a particular substance: *the patient's blood chemistry was monitored regularly*. **3** the interaction between two people, especially when experienced as a strong mutual attraction: *sexual chemistry*.

che·mo /'kēmō/ ▶ **noun** informal chemotherapy.

che·mo·ther·a·py /,kēmō'THerəpē, ,kemō-/ ▶ **noun** the treatment of disease, especially cancer, by the use of chemical substances.

che·nille /SHə'nēl/ ▶ **noun** fabric with a long velvety pile.
– ORIGIN French, 'hairy caterpillar.'

Che·nin blanc /'SHenan 'bläNGk, 'SHenan / (also **Chenin**) ▶ **noun** a white wine made from a variety of grape native to the Loire valley in France.
– ORIGIN French.

cheong·sam /'CHôNG,säm/ ▶ **noun** a straight, close-fitting silk dress with a high neck, worn by Chinese and Indonesian women.
– ORIGIN Chinese.

cheque ▶ **noun** British spelling of CHECK[3].

cheq·uer ▶ **noun** British spelling of CHECKER[2].

cher·ish /'CHeriSH/ ▶ **verb 1** protect and care for someone or something lovingly. **2** keep in one's mind: *he had long cherished a secret fantasy about his future*.

– SYNONYMS **1 adore,** love, dote on, be devoted to, revere, think the world of, care for, look after, protect, keep safe. **2 treasure,** prize, hold dear. **3 harbor,** entertain, nurse, cling to, foster.
– ANTONYMS hate.

– ORIGIN Old French *cherir*, from *cher* 'dear.'

Cher·o·kee /'CHerəkē/ ▶ **noun** (pl. same or **Cherokees**) a member of an American Indian people formerly living in much of the southern US.
– ORIGIN the Cherokees' name for themselves.

che·root /SHə'ro͞ot/ ▶ **noun** a cigar that has both ends open.
– ORIGIN from a Tamil word meaning 'roll of tobacco.'

cher·ry /'CHerē/ ▶ **noun** (pl. **cherries**) **1** a small, round bright or dark red fruit with a stone. **2** a bright, deep red color.
– PHRASES **a bowl of cherries** a pleasant or enjoyable situation or experience.
– ORIGIN from Greek *kerasos*.

cher·ry-pick ▶ **verb** selectively choose the best things or people from those available.

cher·ry to·ma·to ▶ **noun** a miniature tomato.

cher·ub /'CHerəb/ ▶ **noun 1** (pl. **cherubim** /'CHer(y)əbim/ or **cherubs**) a type of angel, represented in art as a chubby child with wings. **2** (pl. **cherubs**) a beautiful or innocent-looking child.
– DERIVATIVES **che·ru·bic** /CHə'ro͞obik/ adjective **che·ru·bi·cal·ly** /-bik(ə)lē/ adverb.
– ORIGIN Hebrew.

cher·vil /'CHərvəl/ ▶ **noun** an herb with an anise flavor, used in cooking.
– ORIGIN Greek *khairephullon*.

Chesh·ire /'CHeSHər, 'CHeSH,ir/ ▶ **noun** a kind of firm, crumbly cheese, originally made in Cheshire, England.

Chesh·ire cat ▶ **noun** a cat with a broad fixed grin, as described in Lewis Carroll's *Alice's Adventures in Wonderland* (1865).
– ORIGIN uncertain, but it is said that *Cheshire* cheeses used to be marked with the face of a smiling cat.

chess /CHes/ ▶ **noun** a board game for two players, the object of which is to put the opponent's king under a direct attack, leading to checkmate.
– ORIGIN from a Persian word meaning 'king.'

chess·board /'CHes,bôrd/ ▶ **noun** a square board divided into sixty-four checkered squares, used for playing chess or checkers.

chest /CHest/ ▶ **noun 1** the front surface of a person's body between the neck and the stomach. **2** a large strong box in which things may be stored or transported.

– SYNONYMS **1 breast,** upper body, torso, trunk, front. **2 box,** case, crate, trunk, coffer, strongbox, casket.

– DERIVATIVES **chest·ed** adjective.
– PHRASES **get something off one's chest** informal say something that one has wanted to say for a long time. **keep** (or **play**) **one's cards close to one's chest** informal be extremely secretive about one's plans.
– ORIGIN Greek *kistē* 'box.'

WORD LINKS

pectoral, thoracic *relating to the chest*

ches·ter·field /'CHestər,fēld/ ▶ **noun** a sofa whose back and outward-curving arms are padded and of the same height.
– ORIGIN named after a 19th-century Earl of *Chesterfield*.

chest·nut /'CHes(t),nət/ ▶ **noun 1** a shiny brown edible nut that develops within a bristly case. **2** (also **sweet chestnut** or **Spanish chestnut**) the large tree that produces chestnuts. **3** a deep reddish-brown color. **4** a reddish-brown horse. **5** (**old chestnut**) a joke or story that has become uninteresting because it has been repeated too often.
– ORIGIN from Greek *kastanea* + NUT.

chest of drawers ▶ **noun** a piece of furniture consisting of an upright frame fitted with a set of drawers.

chest·y /'CHestē/ ▶ **adjective 1** informal (of a woman) having large or prominent breasts. **2** produced deep in the chest. **3** conceited and arrogant.
– DERIVATIVES **chest·i·ness** noun.

che·val glass /SHə'val/ (also **cheval mirror**) ▶ **noun** a tall mirror fitted at its middle to an upright frame so that it can be tilted.
– ORIGIN French *cheval* 'horse, frame.'

chev·a·lier /sHə'val,yā, sHəval'yā/ ▶ **noun 1** historical a knight. **2** a member of the French Legion of Honor.
– ORIGIN Old French.

chè·vre /'sHev(rə)/ ▶ **noun** French cheese made with goat's milk.
– ORIGIN French, 'goat.'

chev·ron /'sHevrən/ ▶ **noun 1** a V-shaped line or stripe, especially one on the sleeve of a soldier's or police officer's uniform to show their rank. **2** Heraldry a broad upside-down V-shape.
– ORIGIN Old French.

chew /CHōō/ ▶ **verb 1** bite and work food in the mouth to make it easier to swallow. **2** (**chew something over**) discuss or consider something at length.

– SYNONYMS **munch,** champ, chomp, crunch, gnaw, bite, masticate.

▶ **noun 1** an act of chewing something. **2** something other than food that is meant for chewing: *a dog chew.*
– DERIVATIVES **chew·a·ble** adjective **chew·er** noun.
– PHRASES **chew the fat** informal chat in a leisurely way. **chew the scenery** see **SCENERY**.
– ORIGIN Old English.

chew·ing gum ▶ **noun** a flavored gum that is chewed but not swallowed.

chew·y /'CHōōē/ ▶ **adjective** (**chewier, chewiest**) (of food) needing much chewing before it can be swallowed.
– DERIVATIVES **chew·i·ness** noun.

Chey·enne /sHī'an, sHī'en/ ▶ **noun** (pl. same or **Cheyennes**) a member of an American Indian people formerly living between the Missouri and Arkansas Rivers.
– ORIGIN from Dakota (an American Indian language), 'speak incoherently.'

chez /sHā/ ▶ **preposition** chiefly humorous at the home of.
– ORIGIN French.

chi /CHē/ (also **qi** or **ki** pronunc. same) ▶ **noun** the circulating life force whose existence and properties are the basis of much Chinese philosophy and medicine.
– ORIGIN Chinese, 'air, breath.'

Chi·an·ti /kē'äntē, -'antē/ ▶ **noun** (pl. **Chiantis**) a dry red Italian wine.
– ORIGIN named after the *Chianti* Mountains in Tuscany.

chi·a·ro·scu·ro /kē,ärə'sk(y)ŏŏrō, kē,arə-/ ▶ **noun** the treatment of light and shade in drawing and painting.
– ORIGIN Italian, from *chiaro* 'clear, bright' + *oscuro* 'dark, obscure.'

chic /sHēk/ ▶ **adjective** (**chicer, chicest**) elegant and stylish.

– SYNONYMS **stylish,** smart, elegant, sophisticated, fashionable; informal trendy, kicky, tony; Brit. informal swish.
– ANTONYMS unfashionable.

▶ **noun** elegance and stylishness.
– DERIVATIVES **chic·ly** adverb.
– ORIGIN French.

chi·cane /sHi'kān, CHi-/ ▶ **noun** a sharp double bend created to form an obstacle on an auto-racing course.
– ORIGIN French *chicaner* 'quibble.'

chi·can·er·y /sHi'kānərē, CHi-/ ▶ **noun** trickery or deception.

Chi·ca·no /CHi'känō, sHi-/ ▶ **noun** (pl. **Chicanos**; fem. **Chicana** /CHi'känə, sHi-/, pl. **Chicanas**) (in North America) a person of Mexican origin or descent.
– ORIGIN Spanish *mejicano* 'Mexican.'

chi·chi /'sHēsHē, 'CHēCHē/ ▶ **adjective** intended to be stylish or elegant but seeming over-elaborate or artificial.
– ORIGIN French.

chick /CHik/ ▶ **noun 1** a young bird, especially one newly hatched. **2** informal a young woman.
– ORIGIN abbreviation of **CHICKEN**.

chick·a·dee /'CHikədē/ ▶ **noun** a North American titmouse with a black head and white breast, widely distributed in the US and Canada.

chick·en /'CHikən/ ▶ **noun 1** a domestic fowl kept for its eggs or meat. **2** informal a coward. ▶ **adjective** informal cowardly. ▶ **verb** (**chicken out**) informal be too scared to do something.
– PHRASES **chicken-and-egg** referring to a situation in which each of two things appears to be necessary to the other.
– ORIGIN Old English.

chick·en feed ▶ **noun** informal a very small sum of money.

chick·en·pox /'CHikən,päks/ ▶ **noun** an infectious disease causing a mild fever and a rash of itchy inflamed pimples.
– ORIGIN probably so named because of its mildness, in comparison with smallpox.

chick·en wire ▶ **noun** wire netting with a hexagonal mesh.

chick·pea /'CHik,pē/ ▶ **noun** a yellowish seed cooked and eaten as a vegetable.
– ORIGIN Latin *cicer*.

chick·weed /'CHik,wēd/ ▶ **noun** a small white-flowered plant, often growing as a garden weed.

chic·le /'CHikəl, 'CHiklē/ ▶ **noun** the milky latex of the sapodilla tree, used to make chewing gum.
– ORIGIN Nahuatl.

chic·o·ry /'CHikərē/ ▶ **noun** (pl. **chicories**) **1** a blue-flowered plant with edible leaves and a root that can be used as an additive to or substitute for coffee. **2** another term for **ENDIVE** (sense 1).
– ORIGIN Greek *kikhorion*.

chide /CHīd/ ▶ **verb** (past **chided** or **chid**; past part. **chided**) scold or rebuke someone.
– ORIGIN Old English.

CHOOSE THE RIGHT WORD

See **SCOLD**.

chief /CHēf/ ▶ **noun 1** a leader or ruler of a people. **2** the head of an organization.

– SYNONYMS **1** *an Iroquois chief* **leader,** chieftain, head, ruler, master, commander. **2** *the chief of the central bank* **head,** chief executive, chief executive officer, CEO, president, chairman, chairwoman, principal, governor, director, manager; informal boss, (head) honcho.

▶ **adjective 1** having the highest rank or authority. **2** most important: *the chief reason.*

– SYNONYMS **1 head,** leading, principal, premier, highest, supreme, arch. **2 main,** principal, primary, prime, first, cardinal, central, key, crucial, essential; informal number-one.
– ANTONYMS subordinate, minor.

– DERIVATIVES **chief·dom** noun.
– ORIGIN Old French.

chief·ly /'CHēflē/ ▶ **adverb** mainly; mostly.

– SYNONYMS **mainly,** in the main, primarily, principally, predominantly, mostly, for the most part, usually, typically, commonly, generally, on the whole, largely.

chief of staff ▶ **noun** the senior staff officer of an armed service or command.

chief·tain /ˈCHēftən/ ▶ **noun** the leader of a people or clan.
– DERIVATIVES **chief·tain·cy** /-sē/ noun (pl. **chieftaincies**) **chief·tain·ship** /-ˌSHip/ noun.
– ORIGIN Old French *chevetaine.*

chif·fon /SHiˈfän, ˈSHifˌän/ ▶ **noun** a light, transparent silk or nylon fabric.
– ORIGIN French, from *chiffe* 'rag.'

chif·fo·nier /ˌSHifəˈni(ə)r/ ▶ **noun** a tall chest of drawers.
– ORIGIN French.

chig·ger /ˈCHigər/ (also **jigger** /ˈjigər/) ▶ **noun** a tropical flea, the female of which lays eggs beneath the host's skin, causing painful sores.
– ORIGIN variant of **CHIGOE**.

chi·gnon /ˈSHēnˌyän, SHēnˈyän/ ▶ **noun** a knot or coil of hair arranged on the back of a woman's head.
– ORIGIN French, 'nape of the neck.'

chig·oe /ˈCHigō, ˈCHē-/ ▶ **noun** another term for **CHIGGER**.
– ORIGIN French *chique.*

chi·hua·hua /CHəˈwäwə, SHə-/ ▶ **noun** a very small breed of dog with smooth hair and large eyes.
– ORIGIN named after *Chihuahua* in northern Mexico.

chil·blain /ˈCHilˌblān/ ▶ **noun** a painful, itching swelling on a hand or foot caused by poor circulation in the skin during exposure to cold weather.
– ORIGIN from **CHILL** + an Old English word meaning 'inflamed swelling or sore.'

child /CHīld/ ▶ **noun** (pl. **children**) **1** a young human being below the age of full physical development. **2** a son or daughter of any age. **3** (**children**) old use the descendants of a family or people.

– SYNONYMS **youngster,** baby, infant, toddler, minor, juvenile, junior, descendant. informal kid, kiddie, nipper, rugrat, tyke, tot; derogatory brat.

– DERIVATIVES **child·less** adjective.
– PHRASES **child's play** an easy task. **with child** old use pregnant.
– ORIGIN Old English.

WORD LINKS

pediatrics *branch of medicine concerned with children*

child·bed /ˈCHīldˌbed/ ▶ **noun** old use childbirth.

child·birth /ˈCHīldˌbərTH/ ▶ **noun** the action of giving birth to a child.

– SYNONYMS **labor,** delivery, birthing; formal parturition; old use confinement.

child·care /ˈCHīldˌke(ə)r/ ▶ **noun** the care of children while the parents are working.

child·hood /ˈCHīldˌho͝od/ ▶ **noun** the state or period of being a child.

– SYNONYMS **youth,** early years/life, infancy, babyhood, boyhood, girlhood, minority.
– ANTONYMS adulthood.

child·ish /ˈCHīldiSH/ ▶ **adjective 1** like or appropriate to a child. **2** silly and immature.

– SYNONYMS **immature,** babyish, infantile, juvenile, puerile, silly.
– ANTONYMS mature.

– DERIVATIVES **child·ish·ly** adverb **child·ish·ness** noun.

child·like /ˈCHīldˌlīk/ ▶ **adjective** (of an adult) having the good qualities associated with a child, such as innocence.

– SYNONYMS **youthful,** innocent, unsophisticated, naive, trusting, artless, unaffected, uninhibited, natural, spontaneous.
– ANTONYMS adult.

child·proof /ˈCHīldˌpro͞of/ ▶ **adjective** designed to prevent children from injuring themselves or doing damage.

chil·dren /ˈCHildrən/ plural of **CHILD**.

Chil·e·an /ˈCHilēən, CHəˈlāən/ ▶ **noun** a person from Chile. ▶ **adjective** relating to Chile.

chil·i /ˈCHilē/ (also **chile**, Brit. **chili**) ▶ **noun** (pl. **chilies, chiles,** or Brit. **chillies**) **1** a small hot-tasting kind of pepper, used in cooking and as a spice. **2** chili con carne.
– ORIGIN Nahuatl.

chil·i con car·ne /kän ˈkärnē, kən/ ▶ **noun** a stew of ground beef and beans flavored with chili.
– ORIGIN Spanish *chile con carne* 'chilli pepper with meat.'

chil·i pow·der ▶ **noun** a mixture of ground dried red chilies and other spices.

chill /CHil/ ▶ **noun 1** an unpleasant feeling of coldness. **2** a feverish cold.

– SYNONYMS **1 coldness,** chilliness, coolness, nip. **2 cold,** dose of flu, fever. **3 shiver,** frisson.
– ANTONYMS warmth.

▶ **verb 1** make someone or something cold. **2** horrify or frighten someone. **3** (usu. **chill out**) informal calm down and relax.

– SYNONYMS **scare,** frighten, petrify, terrify, alarm, make someone's blood run cold; informal scare the pants off.

▶ **adjective** chilly.

– SYNONYMS **cold,** chilly, cool, fresh, wintry, frosty, icy, arctic, bitter, freezing; informal nippy.
– ANTONYMS warm.

– PHRASES **take a chill pill** informal calm down; relax.
– ORIGIN Old English.

chill·er /ˈCHilər/ ▶ **noun** a cold cabinet or refrigerator for keeping stored food a few degrees above freezing.

chill·i ▶ **noun** British spelling of **CHILI**.

chill·y /ˈCHilē/ ▶ **adjective** (**chillier, chilliest**) **1** unpleasantly cold. **2** unfriendly.

– SYNONYMS **1 cold,** cool, crisp, fresh, wintry, frosty, icy; informal nippy. **2 unfriendly,** unwelcoming, cold, cool, frosty; informal standoffish.
– ANTONYMS warm.

– DERIVATIVES **chill·i·ness** noun.

chi·mae·ra ▶ **noun** variant spelling of **CHIMERA**.

chime /CHīm/ ▶ **noun 1** a tuneful ringing sound. **2** a bell or a metal bar or tube used in a set to produce chimes when struck. ▶ **verb 1** (of a bell or clock) make a tuneful ringing sound. **2** (**chime in**) interrupt a conversation with a remark.
– ORIGIN probably from **CYMBAL** (interpreted as *chime bell*).

chi·me·ne·a /ˌSHimiˈnēə/ (also **chiminea**) ▸ **noun** an earthenware outdoor fireplace shaped like a light bulb, with the bulbous lower part housing the fire and typically supported by a wrought-iron stand.

chi·me·ra /kīˈmi(ə)rə, kə-/ (also **chimaera**) ▸ **noun 1** an unrealistic hope or idea. **2** Greek Mythology a fire-breathing female monster with a lion's head, a goat's body, and a serpent's tail.
– ORIGIN Greek *khimaira*.

chi·mer·i·cal /kīˈmi(ə)rikəl, kə-/ ▸ **adjective** impossible to achieve; unrealistic.

chim·ney /ˈCHimnē/ ▸ **noun** (pl. **chimneys**) **1** a vertical channel or pipe that takes smoke and gases up from a fire or furnace. **2** a steep, narrow cleft by which a rock face may be climbed.
– ORIGIN Old French *cheminee*, from Greek *kaminos* 'oven.'

chim·ney pot ▸ **noun** an earthenware or metal pipe at the top of a chimney.

chim·ney stack ▸ **noun** the part of a chimney that sticks up above a roof.

chim·ney sweep ▸ **noun** a person whose job is cleaning out the soot from chimneys.

chimp /CHimp/ ▸ **noun** informal a chimpanzee.

chim·pan·zee /ˌCHimˌpanˈzē, -panˈzē, -ˈpanzē/ ▸ **noun** an ape native to west and central Africa.
– ORIGIN Kikongo (a language of the Congo and surrounding areas).

chin /CHin/ ▸ **noun** the part of the face below the mouth.
– PHRASES **keep one's chin up** informal remain cheerful in difficult circumstances. **take it on the chin** informal accept a difficult or unpleasant situation without complaining.
– ORIGIN Old English.

chi·na /ˈCHīnə/ ▸ **noun 1** a fine white ceramic material. **2** household objects made from china.

– SYNONYMS **dishes,** plates, cups and saucers, tableware, porcelain, dinnerware, dinner service, tea service; Brit. crockery.

– ORIGIN from Persian, 'relating to China.'

chi·na clay ▸ **noun** another term for **KAOLIN**.

Chi·na·man /ˈCHīnəmən/ ▸ **noun** (pl. **Chinamen**) chiefly old use or derogatory a native of China.

Chi·na syn·drome ▸ **noun** a hypothetical chain of events following the meltdown of a nuclear reactor, in which the core melts deep into the earth.
– ORIGIN so named because China is on the opposite side of the earth from a reactor in the US.

Chi·na tea ▸ **noun** tea made from a type of tea plant grown in China, often smoked or with flower petals added.

Chi·na·town /ˈCHīnəˌtoun/ ▸ **noun** a district of a non-Chinese town in which the majority of the population is of Chinese origin.

chinch bug /CHinCH/ ▸ **noun** a plant-eating ground bug that forms large swarms on grasses and rushes.
– ORIGIN from Spanish *chinche*.

chin·chil·la /CHinˈCHilə/ ▸ **noun 1** a small South American rodent with soft gray fur and a long bushy tail. **2** a breed of cat or rabbit with silver-gray or gray fur.
– ORIGIN Aymara or Quechua (South American Indian languages).

chine¹ /CHīn/ ▸ **noun** the backbone of an animal, or a cut of meat containing part of it.
– ORIGIN Old French *eschine*.

chine² ▸ **noun** the angle where the planks or plates at the bottom of a boat or ship meet the side.
– ORIGIN Old English.

Chi·nese /CHīˈnēz, -ˈnēs/ ▸ **noun** (pl. same) **1** the language of China. **2** a person from China. ▸ **adjective** relating to China.

Chi·nese check·ers ▸ **plural noun** (treated as sing.) a board game in which players attempt to move marbles or counters from one corner to the opposite one on a star-shaped board.

Chi·nese lan·tern ▸ **noun 1** a collapsible paper lantern. **2** a plant with white flowers and round orange fruits enclosed in a papery orange-red calyx.

Chi·nese puz·zle ▸ **noun** an intricate puzzle consisting of many interlocking pieces.

Chi·nese wall ▸ **noun** something that prevents information passing from one person or group to another.

Chink /CHiNGk/ ▸ **noun** informal, offensive a Chinese person.
– DERIVATIVES **Chink·y** adjective.

chink¹ /CHiNGk/ ▸ **noun 1** a narrow opening or crack. **2** a beam of light entering through a chink.

– SYNONYMS **gap,** crack, space, hole, aperture, fissure, cranny, cleft, split, slit.

– ORIGIN Old English.

chink² ▸ **verb** make a light, high-pitched ringing sound, like that of glasses or coins striking each other. ▸ **noun** a high-pitched ringing sound.
– ORIGIN imitating the sound.

chin·less /ˈCHinlis/ ▸ **adjective 1** (of a man) having a very small chin. **2** informal having a weak character.

chi·no /ˈCHēnō/ ▸ **noun 1** a cotton twill fabric. **2** (**chinos**) casual cotton pants, originally made from this fabric.
– ORIGIN Latin American Spanish, 'toasted' (referring to the typical color of the fabric).

chi·noi·se·rie /ˌSHēnˌwäz(ə)ˈrē, ˌSHēnˈwäzərē/ ▸ **noun 1** the use of Chinese images and styles in Western art, furniture, and architecture. **2** objects or decorations made in this style.
– ORIGIN French.

Chi·nook /SHəˈnŏŏk, CHə-/ ▸ **noun** (pl. same or **Chinooks**) a member of an American Indian people originally living in Oregon.
– ORIGIN Salish.

chi·nook /SHəˈnŏŏk, CHə-/ ▸ **noun 1** a warm, dry wind that blows down the east side of the Rocky Mountains at the end of winter. **2** a large North Pacific salmon that is an important food fish.

chintz /CHints/ ▸ **noun** multicolored cotton fabric with a shiny finish, used for curtains and upholstery.
– ORIGIN Hindi, 'spattering, stain.'

chintz·y /ˈCHintsē/ ▸ **adjective** (**chintzier, chintziest**) **1** decorated with or resembling chintz. **2** decorated in a colorful but gaudy and tasteless way: *a chintzy little hotel*.

chin·wag /ˈCHinˌwag/ ▸ **noun** chiefly Brit. informal a chat.

chip /CHip/ ▸ **noun 1** a small, thin piece cut or broken off from a hard material. **2** a mark left by the removal of such a piece. **3** a thin slice of food made crisp by being fried, baked, or dried and typically eaten as a snack. **4** a microchip. **5** a counter used in certain gambling games to represent money. **6** (in soccer or golf) a short, high kick or shot.

– SYNONYMS **1 fragment,** sliver, splinter, shaving, shard, flake. **2 nick,** crack, scratch. **3 counter,** token.

▶ **verb** (**chips, chipping, chipped**) **1** cut or break a small piece from a hard material. **2** break at the edge or on the surface. **3** (**chip away**) gradually and relentlessly make something smaller or weaker: *rival firms are chipping away at their market share.* **4** (in soccer or golf) strike the ball to produce a short, high shot or pass.

– SYNONYMS **1 nick,** crack, scratch. **2** *chip off the old plaster* **cut,** hack, chisel, carve, hew, whittle.

– PHRASES **chip in** contribute money to a joint fund. **a chip off the old block** informal someone who resembles their mother or father in character. **a chip on one's shoulder** informal a long-held grievance. **when the chips are down** informal when a very serious situation occurs.
– ORIGIN from an Old English word meaning 'cut off.'

chip·board /'CHip,bôrd/ ▶ **noun** material made from compressed wood chips and resin.

chip·mak·er /'CHip,mākər/ ▶ **noun** a company that manufactures microchips.

chip·munk /'CHip,məNGk/ ▶ **noun** a burrowing ground squirrel with light and dark stripes running down the body.
– ORIGIN Ojibwa (an American Indian language).

chi·pot·le /CHi'pōtlā/ ▶ **noun** a smoked hot chili pepper used especially in Mexican cooking.
– ORIGIN Nahuatl.

Chip·pen·dale /'CHipən,dāl/ ▶ **adjective** (of furniture) designed by or in the style of the English furniture-maker Thomas Chippendale (1718–79).

chip·per¹ /'CHipər/ ▶ **adjective** informal cheerful and lively.
– ORIGIN perhaps from northern English dialect *kipper* 'lively.'

chip·per² ▶ **noun 1** a machine for chipping the trunks and limbs of trees. **2** a person or device that produces chips.

chip·py /'CHipē/ (also **chippie**) ▶ **noun** (pl. **chippies**) informal a promiscuous young woman, especially a prostitute.

chip·set /'CHip,set/ ▶ **noun** a collection of integrated circuits that form the set needed to make an electronic device.

chi·rop·o·dy /kə'räpədē, SHə-/ ▶ **noun** the medical treatment of the feet.
– DERIVATIVES **chi·rop·o·dist** noun.
– ORIGIN from Greek *kheir* 'hand' + *pous* 'foot.'

chi·ro·prac·tic /,kīrə'praktik/ ▶ **noun** a system of complementary medicine based on the manipulation of the joints, especially those of the spinal column.
– DERIVATIVES **chi·ro·prac·tor** /'kīrə,praktər/ noun.
– ORIGIN from Greek *kheir* 'hand' + *praktikos* 'practical.'

chirp /CHərp/ ▶ **verb 1** (of a small bird) make a short, sharp, high-pitched sound. **2** say something in a lively and cheerful way. ▶ **noun** a chirping sound.
– ORIGIN imitating the sound.

chirp·y /'CHərpē/ ▶ **adjective** (**chirpier, chirpiest**) informal cheerful and lively.
– DERIVATIVES **chirp·i·ly** adverb **chirp·i·ness** noun.

chirr /CHər/ (also **churr**) ▶ **verb** (of a bird or insect) make a low trilling sound. ▶ **noun** a low trilling sound.
– ORIGIN imitating the sound.

chir·rup /'CHi(ə)rəp, 'CHərəp/ ▶ **verb** (**chirrups, chirruping, chirruped**) (of a small bird) make repeated short high-pitched sounds. ▶ **noun** a chirruping sound.
– ORIGIN alteration of **CHIRP**.

chis·el /'CHizəl/ ▶ **noun** a hand tool with a long blade and a beveled cutting edge, used to cut or shape wood, stone, or metal. ▶ **verb** (**chisels, chiseling, chiseled**) **1** cut or shape wood, stone, or metal with a chisel. **2** informal swindle: *do you think you can chisel me out of a fortune?*
– ORIGIN Old French.

chit¹ /CHit/ ▶ **noun** derogatory a rude or impudent young woman.
– ORIGIN perhaps related to a dialect word meaning 'sprout.'

chit² ▶ **noun** a short official note recording a sum of money owed.
– ORIGIN Hindi, 'note, pass.'

chitchat informal ▶ **noun** conversation about unimportant things. ▶ **verb** talk about unimportant things.

chi·tin /'kītn/ ▶ **noun** a tough substance that forms the external covering of the bodies of arthropods.
– DERIVATIVES **chi·tin·ous** /'kītn-əs/ adjective.
– ORIGIN Greek *khitōn* (see **CHITON**).

chi·ton /'kītn, 'kī,tän/ ▶ **noun 1** a long woolen tunic worn in ancient Greece. **2** a marine mollusk that has a shell of overlapping plates.
– ORIGIN Greek *khitōn* 'tunic.'

chit·ter /'CHitər/ ▶ **verb** make a twittering or chattering sound.
– ORIGIN imitating the sound.

chit·ter·lings /'CHitlənz/ ▶ **plural noun** the smaller intestines of a pig, cooked for food.
– ORIGIN uncertain.

chiv·al·rous /'SHivəlrəs/ ▶ **adjective** (of a man) polite and gallant, especially toward women.

– SYNONYMS **gallant,** gentlemanly, honorable, respectful, considerate, courteous, polite, gracious, well mannered.
– ANTONYMS rude.

– DERIVATIVES **chiv·al·rous·ly** adverb.

chiv·al·ry /'SHivəlrē/ ▶ **noun 1** (in medieval times) the religious, moral, and social code of behavior that a knight was expected to follow. **2** polite behavior, especially that of a man toward women.
– DERIVATIVES **chi·val·ric** /SHə'valrik/ adjective.
– ORIGIN Old French *chevalerie*, from Latin *caballarius* 'horseman.'

chives /CHīvz/ ▶ **plural noun** an herb with long tubular leaves, used in cooking.
– ORIGIN Old French.

chla·myd·i·a /klə'midēə/ ▶ **noun** (pl. same) a very small parasitic bacterium that can cause various diseases.
– ORIGIN Greek *khlamus* 'cloak.'

chlo·ral /'klôrəl/ ▶ **noun** a colorless liquid used as a sedative.
– ORIGIN French.

chlo·rate /'klôr,āt/ ▶ **noun** Chemistry a salt containing ClO_3 negative ions together with a metallic element: *sodium chlorate.*

chlo·ride /'klôr,īd/ ▶ **noun** a compound of chlorine with another element or group.

chlo·ri·nate /'klôrə,nāt/ ▶ **verb** put chlorine in something.
– DERIVATIVES **chlo·ri·na·tion** /,klôrə'nāSHən/ noun.

chlo·rine /'klôr,ēn/ ▶ **noun** a poisonous pale green gaseous chemical element that may be added to water as a disinfectant.
– ORIGIN Greek *khlōros* 'green.'

chlo·ro·fluor·o·car·bon /ˌklôrōˌfloŏrō'kärbən/ ▶ **noun** see **CFC**.

chlo·ro·form /'klôrəˌfôrm/ ▶ **noun** a sweet-smelling liquid used as a solvent and formerly as a general anesthetic.
– ORIGIN from **CHLORINE** + **FORMIC ACID**.

chlo·ro·phyll /'klôrəˌfil/ ▶ **noun** a green pigment that enables plants to absorb light so as to provide energy for photosynthesis.
– ORIGIN from Greek *khlōros* 'green' + *phullon* 'leaf.'

chlo·ro·plast /'klôrəˌplast/ ▶ **noun** a structure in green plant cells that contains chlorophyll and in which photosynthesis takes place.
– ORIGIN from Greek *khlōros* 'green' + *plastos* 'formed.'

chlo·ro·sis /klô'rōsəs/ ▶ **noun** Botany abnormal reduction or loss of the normal green coloration of leaves of plants, typically caused by mineral deficiency, disease, or lack of light.

choc·a·hol·ic ▶ **noun** variant spelling of **CHOCOHOLIC**.

chock /CHäk/ ▶ **noun** a wedge or block placed against a wheel to prevent it from moving.
– ORIGIN Old French *çoche*.

chock-a-block ▶ **adjective** informal completely full of people or things pressed close together.
– ORIGIN first in nautical use, with reference to tackle having two blocks (pulleys) running close together.

chock-full /'CHäk 'fŏŏl, 'CHək-/ ▶ **adjective** informal filled to overflowing.
– ORIGIN unknown.

choc·o·hol·ic /ˌCHäkə'hôlik, ˌCHô-, -'hälik/ (also **chocaholic**) ▶ **noun** informal a person who is very fond of chocolate.

choc·o·late /'CHäk(ə)lit, 'CHôk-/ ▶ **noun 1** a food made from roasted and ground cacao seeds, eaten as a candy or mixed with milk and water to make a drink. **2** a candy made of or covered with chocolate. **3** a deep brown color.
– DERIVATIVES **choc·o·lat·ey** (also **chocolaty**) adjective.
– ORIGIN Nahuatl.

cho·co·la·tier /ˌCHôk(ə)lə'ti(ə)r, ˌSHôkəlä'tyā/ ▶ **noun** (pl. pronounced same) a person who makes or sells chocolate.
– ORIGIN French.

choice /CHois/ ▶ **noun 1** an act of choosing. **2** the right or ability to choose. **3** a range from which to choose: *a menu offering a wide choice of dishes.* **4** a person or thing that has or can be chosen: *this disk drive is the perfect choice for your computer.*

> – SYNONYMS **1** *freedom of choice* **selection,** choosing, picking, pick, preference, decision, say, vote. **2** *you have no other choice* **option,** alternative, course of action. **3** *an extensive choice* **range,** variety, selection, assortment.

▶ **adjective 1** of very good quality. **2** (of language) rude and abusive.

> – SYNONYMS **superior,** first-class, first-rate, prime, premier, grade A, best, finest, select, quality, top, top-quality, high-grade, prize; informal A1, top-notch.
> – ANTONYMS inferior.

– PHRASES **of choice** chosen as one's favorite or the best: *champagne was his drink of choice.*
– ORIGIN Old French *chois*.

choir /'kwīr/ ▶ **noun 1** an organized group of singers, especially one that takes part in church services. **2** the part of a large church between the altar and the nave, used by the choir and clergy.
– ORIGIN Old French *quer*, from Latin *chorus*.

choir·boy /'kwīrˌboi/ (or **choirgirl** /'kwīrˌgərl/) ▶ **noun** a boy (or girl) who sings in a church or cathedral choir.

choke /CHōk/ ▶ **verb 1** prevent someone from breathing by squeezing or blocking their throat or depriving them of air. **2** have trouble breathing. **3** fill a space so as to make movement difficult or impossible: *the roads were choked with traffic.* **4** (**choke something back**) suppress a strong emotion: *she choked back tears of rage.* **5** (**choke up** or **be choked up**) feel tearful or very upset.

> – SYNONYMS **1 suffocate,** asphyxiate, smother, stifle, strangle, throttle; informal strangulate. **2 gag,** retch, cough, fight for breath. **3 clog (up),** bung up, stop up, block, obstruct.

▶ **noun** a valve in the carburetor of a gasoline engine used to reduce the amount of air in the fuel mixture.
– ORIGIN Old English.

chok·er /'CHōkər/ ▶ **noun** a necklace or band of fabric that fits closely around the neck.

chok·y /'CHōkē/ ▶ **adjective 1** having or causing difficulty in breathing. **2** having difficulty speaking as a result of strong emotion.

cho·le·cal·cif·er·ol /ˌkōləˌkal'sifəˌrôl, -ˌrōl/ ▶ **noun** a form of vitamin D (vitamin D_3), produced naturally in the skin by the action of sunlight.
– ORIGIN from Greek *kholē* 'gall, bile' + **CALCIFEROL**.

chol·er /'kälər/ ▶ **noun 1** (in medieval science and medicine) one of the four bodily humors, believed to be associated with an irritable temperament. **2** old use anger or bad temper.
– ORIGIN from Greek *kholē* 'bile.'

chol·er·a /'kälərə/ ▶ **noun** an infectious disease of the small intestine that causes severe vomiting and diarrhea.
– ORIGIN Latin, 'diarrhea, bile.'

chol·er·ic /'kälərik, kə'lerik/ ▶ **adjective** bad-tempered or irritable.

cho·les·ter·ol /kə'lestəˌrôl, -ˌrōl/ ▶ **noun** a compound that occurs normally in most body tissues and is believed to lead to disease of the arteries if present in high concentrations in the blood (e.g., as a result of a diet high in animal fat).
– ORIGIN from Greek *kholē* 'bile' + *stereos* 'stiff.'

cho·line /'kōˌlēn/ ▶ **noun** Biochemistry a strongly basic compound occurring widely in living tissues and important in the synthesis and transport of lipids.
– ORIGIN from Greek *kholē* 'bile.'

chomp /CHämp, CHômp/ ▶ **verb** munch or chew food noisily or vigorously.
– ORIGIN imitating the sound.

choose /CHōōz/ ▶ **verb** (past **chose**; past part. **chosen**) **1** pick someone or something out as being the best of two or more alternatives. **2** decide on a course of action: *the men chose to ignore his orders.*

> – SYNONYMS **1 select,** pick (out), opt for, settle on, prefer, decide on, fix on, elect, adopt. **2 wish,** want, desire, please, like.

– ORIGIN Old English.

choos·y /'CHōōzē/ ▶ **adjective** (**choosier**, **choosiest**) informal very careful when making a choice and so hard to please.

> – SYNONYMS **fussy,** finicky, fastidious, overparticular, hard to please; informal picky, persnickety.

– DERIVATIVES **choos·i·ness** noun.

chop /CHäp/ ▶ **verb** (**chops, chopping, chopped**) **1** cut something into pieces with repeated sharp, heavy blows of an ax or knife. **2** strike something with a short, heavy blow. **3** get rid of something or reduce it by a large amount: *the share price was chopped from $10 to $7.*

– SYNONYMS **1** *chop the potatoes into small pieces* **cut (up)**, cube, dice, hash, hew, split, fell. **2** *four fingers were* ***chopped off*** **cut off**, sever, lop, shear.

▶ **noun 1** a thick slice of meat, especially pork or lamb, next to and usually including a rib. **2** a downward cutting blow or movement. **3** the broken motion of water, typically due to the action of the wind against the tide.
– ORIGIN variant of **CHAP**[1].

chop·per /ˈCHäpər/ ▶ **noun 1** a short ax with a large blade. **2** informal a helicopter. **3** (**choppers**) informal teeth. **4** informal a type of motorcycle with high handlebars.

chop·py /ˈCHäpē/ ▶ **adjective** (**choppier, choppiest**) (of the sea) having many small waves.

– SYNONYMS **rough,** turbulent, heavy, heaving, stormy, tempestuous, squally.
– ANTONYMS calm.

– DERIVATIVES **chop·pi·ness** noun.

chops /CHäps/ ▶ **plural noun** informal a person's or animal's mouth, jaws, or cheeks.
– ORIGIN unknown.

chop·stick /ˈCHäpˌstik/ ▶ **noun** each of a pair of thin, tapered sticks held in one hand and used as eating utensils by the Chinese and Japanese.
– ORIGIN pidgin English, from a Chinese dialect word meaning 'nimble ones.'

chop su·ey /ˌCHäp ˈso͞oē/ ▶ **noun** a Chinese-style dish of meat with bean sprouts, bamboo shoots, and onions.
– ORIGIN Chinese, 'mixed bits.'

cho·ral /ˈkôrəl/ ▶ **adjective** relating to or sung by a choir or chorus.
– DERIVATIVES **cho·ral·ly** adverb.

cho·rale /kəˈral, -ˈräl/ ▶ **noun** a simple, stately hymn tune for a choir or chorus.
– ORIGIN from Latin *cantus choralis.*

chord[1] /kôrd/ ▶ **noun** a group of three or more musical notes sounded together in harmony.
– DERIVATIVES **chord·al** adjective.
– ORIGIN from **ACCORD**.

USAGE

Do not confuse **chord** with **cord**. **Chord** means 'a group of musical notes' (*an E major chord*), whereas **cord** means 'thin string or rope' or 'a part of the body resembling string or rope' (*the spinal cord*).

chord[2] ▶ **noun** a straight line joining the ends of an arc.
– PHRASES **strike** (or **touch**) **a chord** say or do something that arouses sympathy, enthusiasm, etc., in others.
– ORIGIN a later spelling of **CORD**.

chor·date /ˈkôrdət, -ˌdāt/ ▶ **noun** an animal of a large group, including all the vertebrates, with a skeletal rod of cartilage supporting the body.
– ORIGIN from Latin *chorda* 'rope.'

chore /CHôr/ ▶ **noun** a routine or boring task, especially a household one.

– SYNONYMS **task,** job, duty, errand, burden; informal hassle.

– ORIGIN from former *char* or *chare* 'an odd job.'

cho·re·a /kəˈrēə/ ▶ **noun** a disorder of the nervous system characterized by uncontrollable jerky movements.
– ORIGIN Greek *khoreia* 'dancing together.'

cho·re·o·graph /ˈkôrēəˌgraf/ ▶ **verb** compose the sequence of steps and moves for a ballet or other dance.

cho·re·og·ra·pher /ˌkôrēˈägrəfər/ ▶ **noun** a person who designs the steps and movements for a ballet or other dance.

cho·re·og·ra·phy /ˌkôrēˈägrəfē/ ▶ **noun 1** the sequence of steps and movements in a ballet or other dance. **2** the art of designing such sequences.
– DERIVATIVES **cho·re·o·graph·ic** /ˌkôrēəˈgrafik/ adjective.
– ORIGIN from Greek *khoreia* 'dancing together.'

cho·rine /ˈkôrˌēn/ ▶ **noun** a chorus girl.

chor·is·ter /ˈkôrəstər, ˈkär-/ ▶ **noun** a member of a church choir.
– ORIGIN Old French *cueriste.*

cho·ri·zo /CHəˈrēzō, -sō/ ▶ **noun** (pl. **chorizos**) a spicy Spanish pork sausage.
– ORIGIN Spanish.

chor·tle /ˈCHôrtl/ ▶ **verb** laugh loudly with pleasure or amusement. ▶ **noun** a loud laugh of pleasure or amusement.
– ORIGIN coined by Lewis Carroll in *Through the Looking-Glass*; probably a blend of **CHUCKLE** and **SNORT**.

cho·rus /ˈkôrəs/ ▶ **noun** (pl. **choruses**) **1** a part of a song that is repeated after each verse. **2** a piece of choral music, especially one forming part of an opera or oratorio. **3** a large group of singers performing with an orchestra. **4** a group of singers or dancers in a musical or an opera. **5** (in ancient Greek tragedy) a group of performers who comment on the main action of the play. **6** something said at the same time by many people.
▶ **verb** (**choruses, chorusing, chorused**) (of a group of people) say the same thing at the same time.
– ORIGIN Latin, from Greek *khoros.*

cho·rus girl ▶ **noun** a young woman who sings or dances in the chorus of a musical.

chose /CHōz/ past of **CHOOSE**.

cho·sen /ˈCHōzən/ past participle of **CHOOSE**.

chough /CHəf/ ▶ **noun** a black Old World bird of the crow family with a red or yellow bill.
– ORIGIN probably imitating its call.

choux past·ry /SHo͞o/ ▶ **noun** very light pastry made with egg, used for eclairs and profiteroles.
– ORIGIN from French *chou* 'cabbage, rosette.'

chow /CHou/ ▶ **noun 1** informal food. **2** (also **chow chow**) a Chinese breed of dog with a tail curled over its back, a bluish-black tongue, and a thick coat.
– ORIGIN from pidgin English *chow chow* 'mixed pickle.'

chow·der /ˈCHoudər/ ▶ **noun** a rich soup containing fish, clams, or corn with potatoes and onions.
– ORIGIN perhaps from French *chaudière* 'stew pot.'

chow mein /ˈCHou ˈmān/ ▶ **noun** a Chinese-style dish of fried noodles with shredded meat or seafood and vegetables.
– ORIGIN Chinese, 'stir-fried noodles.'

chrism /ˈkrizəm/ ▶ **noun** a consecrated oil used for anointing in rites such as baptism in the Catholic, Orthodox, and Anglican Churches.
– ORIGIN Greek *khrisma* 'anointing.'

Christ /krīst/ ▶ **noun** the title given to Jesus. ▶ **exclamation** used to express irritation, dismay, or surprise.

– DERIVATIVES **Christ·like** adjective **Christ·ly** adjective.
– ORIGIN Greek *Khristos* 'anointed one.'

chris·ten /'krisən/ ▶ verb **1** name a baby at baptism as a sign of admission to a Christian Church. **2** informal use something for the first time.

– SYNONYMS **1** *she was christened Sara* **baptize,** name, give the name of, call. **2** *a group christened "The Magic Circle"* **call,** name, dub, style, term, label, nickname.

– DERIVATIVES **chris·ten·ing** /'kris(ə)niNG/ noun.
– ORIGIN Old English, 'make Christian.'

Chris·ten·dom /'krisəndəm/ ▶ noun literary the worldwide body of Christians.

Chris·tian /'krisCHən/ ▶ adjective relating to or believing in Christianity or its teachings. ▶ noun a person who has received Christian baptism or is a believer in Christianity.
– DERIVATIVES **Chris·tian·ize** /-ˌnīz/ (or **Christianise**) verb.

Chris·tian e·ra ▶ noun the era beginning with the traditional date of Jesus's birth.

Chris·ti·an·i·ty /ˌkrisCHē'anitē/ ▶ noun the religion based on the teachings and works of Jesus.

Chris·tian name ▶ noun a first name, especially one given at baptism.

Chris·tian Sci·ence ▶ noun the beliefs and practices of the Church of Christ Scientist, a Christian sect.
– DERIVATIVES **Chris·tian Sci·en·tist** noun.

Christ·mas /'krisməs/ ▶ noun (pl. **Christmases**) **1** (also **Christmas Day**) the annual Christian festival celebrating Jesus's birth, held on December 25. **2** the period immediately before and after December 25.
– ORIGIN Old English, 'Mass of Christ.'

Christ·mas cac·tus ▶ noun a succulent South American plant with red, pink, or white flowers.
– ORIGIN because it flowers at about the northern midwinter.

Christ·mas rose ▶ noun a small white-flowered winter-blooming hellebore.

Christ·mas tree ▶ noun an evergreen or artificial tree decorated with lights and ornaments at Christmas.

chro·ma /'krōmə/ ▶ noun purity or intensity of color.

chro·mate /'krōˌmāt/ ▶ noun Chemistry a salt in which the anion contains both chromium and oxygen.

chro·mat·ic /krō'matik/ ▶ adjective **1** relating or referring to a musical scale that rises or falls by half steps. **2** relating to or produced by color.
– ORIGIN from Greek *khrōma* 'color, chromatic scale.'

chro·ma·tin /'krōmətən/ ▶ noun Biology the material of which nonbacterial chromosomes are composed, consisting of DNA and protein (and RNA at certain times).

chro·ma·tog·ra·phy /ˌkrōmə'tägrəfē/ ▶ noun Chemistry a technique for separating and analyzing a mixture by passing it through a medium in which the components move at different rates.
– DERIVATIVES **chro·mat·o·gram** /krō'matəˌgram/ noun **chro·mat·o·graph** /krō'matəˌgraf/ noun **chro·mat·o·graph·ic** /krōˌmatə'grafik/ adjective.
– ORIGIN from Greek *khrōma* 'color' (early separations being displayed as colored bands or spots).

chrome /krōm/ ▶ noun a hard shiny metal coating made from chromium. ▶ adjective referring to compounds or alloys of chromium: *chrome steel.*
– DERIVATIVES **chromed** adjective.
– ORIGIN Greek *khrōma* 'color.'

chro·mite /'krōˌmīt/ ▶ noun the main ore of chromium, a brownish-black oxide of chromium and iron.

chro·mi·um /'krōmēəm/ ▶ noun a hard white metallic chemical element used in stainless steel and other alloys.

chro·mo·some /'krōməˌsōm/ ▶ noun a threadlike structure in a cell nucleus, carrying the genes.
– DERIVATIVES **chro·mo·so·mal** /ˌkrōmə'sōməl/ adjective.
– ORIGIN from Greek *khrōma* 'color' + *sōma* 'body.'

chron·ic /'kränik/ ▶ adjective **1** (of an illness or problem) lasting for a long time. **2** having a bad habit: *a chronic liar.*

– SYNONYMS **1** *a chronic illness* **persistent,** long-standing, long-term, incurable. **2** *chronic economic problems* **constant,** continuing, persistent, long-lasting, severe, serious, acute, grave, dire. **3** *a chronic liar* **inveterate,** hardened, dyed-in-the-wool, incorrigible, compulsive; informal pathological.
– ANTONYMS acute, temporary.

– DERIVATIVES **chron·i·cal·ly** /-ik(ə)lē/ adverb.
– ORIGIN Greek *khronikos* 'of time.'

chron·ic fa·tigue syn·drome ▶ noun a medical condition of unknown cause, with fever, aching, and prolonged tiredness and depression.

chron·i·cle /'kränikəl/ ▶ noun a written account of historical events in the order of their occurrence.

– SYNONYMS **record,** account, history, annals, archive(s), log, diary, journal.

▶ verb record a series of events in a factual way.

– SYNONYMS **record,** write down, set down, document, report.

– DERIVATIVES **chron·i·cler** noun.
– ORIGIN Greek *khronika* 'annals.'

chron·o·graph /'kränəˌgraf, 'krō-/ ▶ noun an instrument for recording time with great accuracy.

chron·o·log·i·cal /ˌkränl'äjikəl/ ▶ adjective **1** (of a record of events) following the order in which they occurred: *the video shows all his goals in chronological order.* **2** relating to the establishment of the dates of past events.
– DERIVATIVES **chron·o·log·i·cal·ly** /-ik(ə)lē/ adverb.

chro·nol·o·gy /krə'näləjē/ ▶ noun (pl. **chronologies**) **1** the arrangement of events in the order of their occurrence. **2** the study of records to establish the dates of past events. **3** a list of events or dates in chronological order.
– DERIVATIVES **chro·nol·o·gist** /-jist/ noun.
– ORIGIN from Greek *khronos* 'time.'

chro·nom·e·ter /krə'nämətər/ ▶ noun an instrument for measuring time accurately in spite of motion or varying conditions.

chrys·a·lis /'krisələs/ ▶ noun (pl. **chrysalises**) **1** a dormant insect pupa, especially of a butterfly or moth. **2** the hard outer case enclosing an insect pupa.
– ORIGIN from Greek *khrusos* 'gold' (because of the metallic sheen of some pupae).

chry·san·the·mum /kri'sanTHəməm/ ▶ noun (pl. **chrysanthemums**) a garden plant of the daisy family with brightly colored flowers.
– ORIGIN from Greek *khrusos* 'gold' + *anthemon* 'flower.'

chthon·ic /'THänik/ (also **chthonian** /'THōnēən/) ▶ adjective literary relating to or inhabiting the underworld.

– ORIGIN from Greek *khthōn* 'earth.'

chub /CHəb/ ▶ **noun** (pl. same or **chubs**) a thick-bodied river fish with a gray-green back and white underparts.
– ORIGIN unknown.

chub·by /'CHəbē/ ▶ **adjective** (**chubbier, chubbiest**) plump and rounded.

> – SYNONYMS **plump,** tubby, flabby, rotund, portly, chunky. informal zaftig, corn-fed.
> – ANTONYMS skinny.

– DERIVATIVES **chub·bi·ness** noun.
– ORIGIN from **CHUB**.

chuck[1] /CHək/ ▶ **verb** informal **1** throw something carelessly or casually. **2** (**chuck something away/out**) throw something away. **3** (**chuck someone out**) force someone to leave a building. **4** give up suddenly: *he chucked his history course*. **5** break off a relationship with (a partner): *Mary chucked him for another guy*.

> – SYNONYMS **1 throw,** toss, fling, hurl, pitch, cast, lob. **2 throw away,** throw out, discard, dispose of, get rid of, dump, bin, jettison; informal ditch, trash, junk. **3 give up,** leave, resign from; informal quit, pack in. **4 jilt,** finish with, break off with, leave; informal dump, ditch, give someone the brush-off.

– DERIVATIVES **chuck·er** noun.
– ORIGIN from **CHUCK**[2].

chuck[2] ▶ **verb** touch someone playfully under the chin.
▶ **noun** a playful touch under the chin.
– ORIGIN probably from Old French *chuquer* 'to knock, bump.'

chuck[3] ▶ **noun 1** a device for holding a workpiece in a lathe or a tool in a drill. **2** (also **chuck steak**) a cut of beef extending from the neck to the ribs.
– ORIGIN variant of **CHOCK**.

chuck[4] ▶ **noun** food or provisions.
– ORIGIN alteration of **CHICK**.

chuck·le /'CHəkəl/ ▶ **verb** laugh quietly or inwardly.

> – SYNONYMS **laugh,** chortle, giggle, titter, snigger.

▶ **noun** a quiet laugh.
– ORIGIN from former *chuck* 'to cluck.'

chuck·le·head /'CHəkəl,hed/ ▶ **noun** informal a stupid person.
– ORIGIN from former *chuckle* 'big and clumsy.'

chuck wag·on ▶ **noun** a wagon or other vehicle with cooking facilities providing food on a ranch, worksite, or campsite.

chuff /CHəf/ ▶ **verb** (of a steam engine) move with a regular puffing sound.
– ORIGIN imitating the sound.

chug[1] /CHəg/ ▶ **verb** (**chugs, chugging, chugged**) move with a series of muffled explosive sounds, as of an engine running slowly.
– ORIGIN imitating the sound.

chug[2] (also **chugalug** or **chug-a-lug** /'CHəgə,ləg/) ▶ **verb** informal consume a drink in large gulps without pausing.
– ORIGIN imitative.

chuk·ker /'CHəkər/ (also **chukka**) ▶ **noun** each of a number of periods into which a game of polo is divided.
– ORIGIN Sanskrit, 'circle or wheel.'

chum[1] /CHəm/ informal ▶ **noun** a close friend.

> – SYNONYMS **friend,** companion, playmate, classmate, schoolmate, workmate; informal pal, crony, buddy, bud.
> – ANTONYMS enemy.

▶ **verb** (**chums, chumming, chummed**) form a friendship with someone: *they started chumming around in high school*.
– DERIVATIVES **chum·my** adjective.
– ORIGIN Oxford University slang for a roommate: probably short for *chamber-fellow*.

chum[2] ▶ **noun** chopped fish and other material thrown overboard as angling bait.
– ORIGIN unknown.

chump /CHəmp/ ▶ **noun** informal a foolish or easily deceived person.
– ORIGIN probably a blend of **CHUNK**[1] and **LUMP**[1] or **STUMP**.

chunk[1] /CHəNGk/ ▶ **noun 1** a thick, solid piece. **2** a large amount.

> – SYNONYMS **lump,** hunk, wedge, block, slab, square, nugget, brick, cube; informal gob.

– ORIGIN probably from **CHUCK**[3].

chunk[2] ▶ **verb** make a muffled, metallic sound.
– ORIGIN imitating the sound.

chunk·y /'CHəNGkē/ ▶ **adjective** (**chunkier, chunkiest**) **1** (of a person) short and sturdy. **2** bulky and thick. **3** containing chunks.
– DERIVATIVES **chunk·i·ly** /-kəlē/ adverb **chunk·i·ness** noun.

church /CHərCH/ ▶ **noun 1** a building used for public Christian worship. **2** (**Church**) a particular Christian organization: *the Catholic Church*. **3** the Christian religion as an institution with political or social influence: *the separation of church and state*.
– ORIGIN from Greek *kuriakon dōma* 'Lord's house.'

church·go·er /'CHərCH,gōər/ ▶ **noun** a person who attends church services regularly.

church·man /'CHərCHmən/ (or **churchwoman** /'CHərCH,wo͝omən/) ▶ **noun** (pl. **churchmen** or **churchwomen**) a member of the Christian clergy or of a Church.

Church of Eng·land ▶ **noun** the English branch of the Western Christian Church, which has the king or queen as its head.

Church of Scot·land ▶ **noun** the national (Presbyterian) Christian Church in Scotland.

church·ward·en /'CHərCH,wôrdn/ ▶ **noun** either of two people who are elected by an Anglican congregation to take care of church property and keep order.

church·y /'CHərCHē/ ▶ **adjective 1** excessively pious. **2** resembling a church.

church·yard /'CHərCH,yärd/ ▶ **noun** an enclosed area surrounding a church, especially as used for burials.

churl /CHərl/ ▶ **noun 1** a rude and surly person. **2** old use a peasant.
– ORIGIN Old English.

churl·ish /'CHərlisH/ ▶ **adjective** rude and surly.

> – SYNONYMS **rude,** ill-mannered, discourteous, ungracious, impolite, inconsiderate, surly, sullen.
> – ANTONYMS polite.

– DERIVATIVES **churl·ish·ly** adverb **churl·ish·ness** noun.

churn /CHərn/ ▶ **verb 1** (of liquid) move about vigorously: *the water churned and foamed*. **2** (**churn something up**) break up the surface of an area of ground. **3** (**churn something out**) produce something in large quantities and without much thought. **4** (as adj. **churned up**) upset or nervous. **5** shake milk or cream in a churn to produce butter.

> – SYNONYMS **disturb,** stir up, agitate, beat.

▸ noun a machine for making butter by shaking milk or cream.
– ORIGIN Old English.

chur·ro /ˈCHo͝orō/ ▸ noun a Spanish sweet snack consisting of a strip of fried dough dusted with sugar or cinnamon.

chute[1] /SHo͞ot/ (also **shoot**) ▸ noun **1** a sloping channel for conveying things to a lower level. **2** a water slide into a swimming pool.
– ORIGIN French, 'fall' (of water or rocks).

chute[2] ▸ noun informal a parachute.

chut·ney /ˈCHətnē/ ▸ noun (pl. **chutneys**) a spicy condiment made of fruits or vegetables with vinegar, spices, and sugar.
– ORIGIN Hindi.

chutz·pah /ˈho͝otspə, ˈKHo͝otspə, -spä/ ▸ noun informal extreme self-confidence or audacity.
– ORIGIN Yiddish.

chyle /kīl/ ▸ noun a milky fluid that drains from the small intestine into the lymphatic system during digestion.
– ORIGIN Greek *khūlos* 'juice.'

chyme /kīm/ ▸ noun the fluid that passes from the stomach to the small intestine, consisting of gastric juices and partly digested food.
– ORIGIN Greek *khūmos* 'juice.'

Ci ▸ abbreviation curie.

CIA ▸ abbreviation Central Intelligence Agency.

cia·bat·ta /CHəˈbätə/ ▸ noun a flattish Italian bread made with olive oil.
– ORIGIN Italian, 'slipper' (from its shape).

ciao /CHou/ ▸ exclamation informal hello or goodbye.
– ORIGIN Italian.

ci·ca·da /səˈkādə, səˈkädə/ ▸ noun a large insect with long wings that makes a shrill droning noise after dark.
– ORIGIN Latin.

cic·a·trix /ˈsikəˌtriks/ (also **cicatrice** /-ˌtris/) ▸ noun (pl. **cicatrices** /ˌsikəˈtrīsēz, səˈkātrəˌsēz/) a scar.
– ORIGIN Latin.

cic·a·trize /ˈsikəˌtrīz/ ▸ verb heal a wound by scar formation.

cic·e·ly /ˈsisilē/ (also **sweet cicely**) ▸ noun (pl. **cicelies**) a white-flowered plant with fernlike leaves.
– ORIGIN Greek *seselis*.

cic·e·ro·ne /ˌsisəˈrōnē, ˌCHēCHə-/ ▸ noun (pl. **ciceroni** pronunc. same) a guide who gives information to sightseers.
– ORIGIN Italian, from the Roman writer *Cicero*, probably comparing the guides' knowledge to his learning.

cich·lid /ˈsiklid/ ▸ noun a perchlike freshwater fish of a large family.
– ORIGIN Greek *kikhlē*.

-cide ▸ combining form **1** referring to a person or substance that kills: *insecticide*. **2** referring to an act of killing: *suicide*.
– ORIGIN from Latin *-cida*, *-cidium*.

ci·der /ˈsīdər/ ▸ noun **1** (also **sweet cider**) an unfermented drink made from crushed apples. **2** (also **hard cider**) an alcoholic drink made from fermented crushed apples.
– ORIGIN Old French *sidre*.

cig /sig/ ▸ noun informal a cigarette.

ci·gar /siˈgär/ ▸ noun a cylinder of tobacco rolled in tobacco leaves for smoking.
– ORIGIN French *cigare*.

cig·a·rette /ˌsigəˈret, ˈsigəˌret/ ▸ noun a cylinder of finely cut tobacco rolled in paper for smoking.
– ORIGIN French, 'little cigar.'

cig·a·ril·lo /ˌsigəˈrilō, -ˈrē(y)ō/ ▸ noun (pl. **cigarillos**) a small cigar.
– ORIGIN Spanish.

cil·i·um /ˈsilēəm/ ▸ noun (pl. **cilia** /ˈsilēə/) Biology a microscopic hairlike vibrating structure, occurring on the surface of certain cells.
– DERIVATIVES **cil·i·ar·y** /ˈsilēˌerē/ adjective.
– ORIGIN Latin.

cim·ba·lom /ˈsimbələm/ ▸ noun a large Hungarian dulcimer (musical instrument).
– ORIGIN from Latin *cymbalum* 'cymbal.'

CINC ▸ abbreviation Commander in Chief.

C. in C. ▸ abbreviation Commander in Chief.

cinch /sinCH/ ▸ noun informal **1** a very easy task. **2** a certainty.
– ORIGIN from Spanish *cincha* 'girth.'

cin·cho·na /siNGˈkōnə, sinˈCHōnə/ ▸ noun a medicinal drug obtained from the bark of a South American tree, containing quinine.
– ORIGIN named after the Countess of *Chinchón*, who brought the drug to Spain.

cin·der /ˈsindər/ ▸ noun a small piece of partly burned coal or wood.
– DERIVATIVES **cin·der·y** adjective.
– ORIGIN Old English.

cin·der block ▸ noun a lightweight building brick made from small cinders mixed with sand and cement.

Cin·der·el·la /ˌsindəˈrelə/ ▸ noun a person or thing that is undeservedly neglected.
– ORIGIN from the fairy story of *Cinderella*, whose family treat her as a servant but who eventually marries Prince Charming.

cin·e /ˈsinē/ ▸ adjective chiefly Brit relating to filmmaking: *a cine camera*.

cin·e·aste /ˈsinēˌast/ ▸ noun a person who is fond of or knowledgeable about movies or filmmaking.
– ORIGIN French.

cin·e·ma /ˈsinəmə/ ▸ noun **1** the production of movies as an art or industry. **2** Brit. a movie theater.
– DERIVATIVES **cin·e·mat·ic** /ˌsinəˈmatik/ adjective **cin·e·mat·i·cal·ly** /-ik(ə)lē/ adverb.
– ORIGIN Greek *kinēma* 'movement.'

cin·e·mat·o·graph /ˌsinəˈmatəgraf/ ▸ noun historical, chiefly Brit. an early movie projector.

cin·e·ma·tog·ra·phy /ˌsinəməˈtägrəfē/ ▸ noun the art of making motion pictures.
– DERIVATIVES **cin·e·ma·tog·ra·pher** /-fər/ noun **cin·e·mat·o·graph·ic** /-ˌmatəˈgrafik/ adjective.

cin·e·phile /ˈsiniˌfīl/ ▸ noun a movie enthusiast.

cin·e·plex /ˈsiniˌpleks/ ▸ noun trademark a movie theater with several separate screens; a multiplex.

cin·e·rar·i·a /ˌsinəˈre(ə)rēə/ ▸ noun a winter-flowering plant of the daisy family.
– ORIGIN from Latin *cinerarius* 'of ashes' (from the ash-colored down on the leaves).

cin·e·rar·y urn /ˈsinəˌrerē/ ▸ noun an urn for holding a person's ashes after cremation.
– ORIGIN from Latin *cinerarius* 'of ashes.'

cin·na·bar /'sinə,bär/ ▶ **noun 1** a bright red mineral consisting of mercury sulfide. **2** (also **cinnabar moth**) a moth with black and red wings.
– ORIGIN Greek *kinnabari.*

cin·na·mon /'sinəmən/ ▶ **noun 1** a spice made from the dried bark of an Asian tree. **2** a reddish- or yellowish-brown color.
– ORIGIN Greek *kinnamōmon.*

cinque·foil /'siNGk,foil, 'saNGk-/ ▶ **noun 1** a plant with leaves made up of five leaflets and five-petaled yellow flowers. **2** a decorative design of five arcs arranged inside a circle.
– ORIGIN from Latin *quinque* 'five' + *folium* 'leaf.'

ci·pher /'sīfər/ (also **cypher**) ▶ **noun 1** a code, especially one in which a set of letters or symbols is used to represent others. **2** a key to a code. **3** an unimportant person. **4** dated a zero. ▶ **verb** put a message into code.
– ORIGIN from Arabic, 'zero.'

cir·ca /'sərkə/ ▶ **preposition** approximately.

– SYNONYMS **approximately,** about, around, in the region of, roughly, something like, or so, or thereabouts, more or less. informal in the ballpark of.
– ANTONYMS exactly.

– ORIGIN Latin.

cir·ca·di·an /sər'kādēən/ ▶ **adjective** (of biological processes) recurring on a twenty-four-hour cycle.
– ORIGIN from Latin *circa* 'about' + *dies* 'day.'

cir·cle /'sərkəl/ ▶ **noun 1** a round plane figure whose boundary consists of points at an equal distance from the center. **2** a thing or group of people or things shaped like a circle. **3** a curved upper tier of seats in a theater. **4** a group of people with a shared profession, interests, or friends.

– SYNONYMS **1 ring,** band, hoop, circlet, halo, disk/disc. **2 group,** set, crowd, band, company, clique, coterie, club, society; informal gang, bunch.

▶ **verb 1** move or be situated all the way around: *the cat circled the room twice.* **2** draw a line around something.

– SYNONYMS **1** *seagulls circled above* **wheel,** revolve, rotate, whirl, spiral. **2** *satellites circling the earth* **go around,** travel around, circumnavigate, orbit. **3** *the abbey was circled by a wall* **surround,** encircle, ring, enclose.

– PHRASES **come** (or **turn**) **full circle** return to a previous position or situation.
– ORIGIN Latin *circulus* 'small ring.'

cir·clet /'sərklət/ ▶ **noun** an ornamental circular band worn on the head.

cir·cuit /'sərkət/ ▶ **noun 1** a roughly circular line, route, or movement. **2** a system of conductors and components forming a complete path for an electric current. **3** an established series of sporting events or entertainments: *the comedy circuit.* **4** a series of physical exercises performed in one training session. **5** a regular journey by a judge around a district to hear court cases.

– SYNONYMS *two circuits of the track* **lap,** turn, round, circle.

▶ **verb** move all the way around something.
– ORIGIN Latin *circuitus.*

cir·cuit board ▶ **noun** a thin rigid board containing an electric circuit; a printed circuit.

cir·cuit break·er ▶ **noun** an automatic safety device for stopping the flow of current in an electric circuit.

cir·cu·i·tous /sər'kyo͞oətəs/ ▶ **adjective** (of a route) longer than the most direct way.

– SYNONYMS **roundabout,** indirect, winding, meandering, twisting, tortuous.
– ANTONYMS direct.

cir·cuit·ry /'sərkətrē/ ▶ **noun** (pl. **circuitries**) a system of electric circuits.

cir·cu·lar /'sərkyələr/ ▶ **adjective 1** having the form of a circle. **2** (of an argument) false because it uses as evidence the point that is to be proved. **3** (of a letter or advertisement) for distribution to a large number of people.

– SYNONYMS **round,** ring-shaped.

▶ **noun** a circular letter or advertisement.

– SYNONYMS **leaflet,** pamphlet, handbill, flyer, advertisement, notice.

– DERIVATIVES **cir·cu·lar·i·ty** /,sərkyə'laritē/ noun **cir·cu·lar·ly** adverb.

WORD TOOLKIT

circular ...	round ...	annular ...
motion	table	eclipse
orbit	face	lesion
room	hole	rings
route	ball	disk
path	corners	eruption
driveway	belly	rim

cir·cu·lar·ize /'sərkyələ,rīz/ ▶ **verb** distribute circulars to a large number of people.

cir·cu·lar saw ▶ **noun** a power saw with a rapidly rotating toothed disk.

cir·cu·late /'sərkyə,lāt/ ▶ **verb 1** move continuously through a closed system or area: *antibodies circulate in the bloodstream.* **2** pass from place to place or person to person. **3** move around a social function and talk to many people.

– SYNONYMS **1 spread,** communicate, disseminate, make known, make public, broadcast, publicize, distribute. **2 socialize,** mingle, mix, wander, stroll.

– DERIVATIVES **cir·cu·la·tor** /-,lātər/ noun.

cir·cu·la·tion /,sərkyə'lāsHən/ ▶ **noun 1** movement around something. **2** the continuous motion of blood around the body. **3** the public availability of something: *a large number of counterfeit tickets are in circulation.* **4** the number of copies sold of a newspaper or magazine.
– DERIVATIVES **cir·cu·la·to·ry** /'sərkyələ,tôrē/ adjective.
– PHRASES **in** (or **out of**) **circulation** (of a person) seen (or not seen) in public.

circum- ▶ **prefix** about; around: *circumambulate.*
– ORIGIN from Latin *circum* 'around.'

cir·cum·am·bu·late /,sərkəm'ambyə,lāt/ ▶ **verb** formal walk all the way around something.
– DERIVATIVES **cir·cum·am·bu·la·tion** /-,ambyə'lāsHən/ noun.

cir·cum·cise /'sərkəm,sīz/ ▶ **verb 1** cut off the foreskin of a young boy or man as a Jewish or Islamic rite. **2** cut off the clitoris, and sometimes the labia, of a girl or young woman.
– DERIVATIVES **cir·cum·ci·sion** /,sərkəm'sizHən, 'sərkəm,sizHən/ noun.
– ORIGIN Latin *circumcidere* 'cut around.'

cir·cum·fer·ence /sər'kəmf(ə)rəns/ ▶ **noun 1** the boundary that encloses a circle. **2** the distance around something.

– DERIVATIVES **cir·cum·fer·en·tial** /sər,kəmfə'renCHəl/ adjective.
– ORIGIN from Latin *circum* 'around' + *ferre* 'carry.'

cir·cum·flex /'sərkəm,fleks/ ▸ **noun** a mark (^) placed over a vowel in some languages to indicate a change in the way it is pronounced.
– ORIGIN from Latin *circum* 'around' + *flectere* 'to bend.'

cir·cum·lo·cu·tion /,sərkəm,lō'kyo͞oSHən/ ▸ **noun** the use of many words where fewer would do.
– DERIVATIVES **cir·cum·loc·u·to·ry** /-'läkyə,tôrē/ adjective.
– ORIGIN from Latin *circum* 'around' + *loqui* 'speak.'

cir·cum·nav·i·gate /,sərkəm'navə,gāt/ ▸ **verb** go all the way around something, especially by sail.
– DERIVATIVES **cir·cum·nav·i·ga·tion** /-,navə'gāSHən/ noun.

cir·cum·po·lar /,sərkəm'pōlər/ ▸ **adjective** situated or occurring around one of the earth's poles.

cir·cum·scribe /'sərkəm,skrīb/ ▸ **verb 1** put limits on; restrict: *the joys of country life were circumscribed by foot-and-mouth disease.* **2** Geometry draw a figure around another, touching it at points but not cutting it.
– DERIVATIVES **cir·cum·scrip·tion** /,sərkəm'skripSHən/ noun.
– ORIGIN from Latin *circum* 'around' + *scribere* 'write.'

cir·cum·spect /'sərkəm,spekt/ ▸ **adjective** wary and unwilling to take risks; cautious.

> – SYNONYMS **cautious,** wary, careful, chary, guarded, on one's guard; informal cagey.
> – ANTONYMS unguarded.

– DERIVATIVES **cir·cum·spec·tion** /,sərkəm'spekSHən/ noun **cir·cum·spect·ly** adverb.
– ORIGIN from Latin *circumspicere* 'look around.'

> **WORD TOOLKIT**
>
> See **WARY**.

cir·cum·stance /'sərkəm,stans, -stəns/ ▸ **noun 1** a fact or condition connected with an event or action. **2** unforeseen and influential events that are outside one's control: *a victim of circumstance.* **3** (**circumstances**) a person's financial or personal situation. **4** old use ceremony and public display: *pomp and circumstance.*

> – SYNONYMS (**circumstances**) **situation,** conditions, state of affairs, position, the lay of the land, (turn of) events, factors, facts, background, environment, context.

– ORIGIN from Latin *circumstare* 'encircle.'

cir·cum·stan·tial /,sərkəm'stanCHəl/ ▸ **adjective 1** (of evidence) strongly suggesting something, but not proving it conclusively. **2** related to the particular circumstances of something: *a circumstantial log of our travels.*
– DERIVATIVES **cir·cum·stan·ti·al·i·ty** /-,stanSHē'alətē/ noun **cir·cum·stan·tial·ly** adverb.

cir·cum·vent /,sərkəm'vent/ ▸ **verb** find a way of avoiding a problem, regulation, or obstacle.
– DERIVATIVES **cir·cum·ven·tion** /-'venCHən/ noun.
– ORIGIN Latin *circumvenire.*

cir·cus /'sərkəs/ ▸ **noun** (pl. **circuses**) **1** a traveling company of acrobats, trained animals, and clowns. **2** informal a scene of hectic activity: *a media circus.* **3** (in ancient Rome) a circular sports arena lined with seats.
– ORIGIN Latin, 'ring or circus.'

cirque /sərk/ ▸ **noun** a steep-sided hollow at the head of a valley or on a mountainside.
– ORIGIN French.

cir·rho·sis /sə'rōsəs/ ▸ **noun** a chronic liver disease typically caused by alcoholism or hepatitis.
– DERIVATIVES **cir·rhot·ic** /sə'rätik/ adjective.
– ORIGIN from Greek *kirrhos* 'tawny' (often the color of the liver).

cir·ro·cu·mu·lus /,sirō'kyo͞omyələs/ ▸ **noun** cloud forming a broken layer of small fleecy clouds at high altitude.

cir·ro·stra·tus /,sirō'stratəs, -'strātəs/ ▸ **noun** cloud forming a thin, uniform layer at high altitude.

cir·rus /'sirəs/ ▸ **noun** (pl. **cirri** /'sir,ī, 'sirē/) **1** cloud forming wispy streaks at high altitude. **2** Zoology & Botany a slender tendril or filament.
– ORIGIN Latin, 'a curl.'

CIS ▸ **abbreviation** Commonwealth of Independent States.

cis·co /'siskō/ ▸ **noun** (pl. **ciscoes**) a northern freshwater whitefish, important as a food fish.
– ORIGIN unknown.

Cis·ter·cian /sis'tərSHən/ ▸ **noun** a monk or nun of an order that is a stricter branch of the Benedictines. ▸ **adjective** relating to the Cistercians.
– ORIGIN from *Cîteaux* in France, where the order was founded.

cis·tern /'sistərn/ ▸ **noun** a water storage tank, especially as part of a flushing toilet.
– ORIGIN Latin *cisterna.*

cistus /'sistəs/ ▸ **noun** a shrub with large white or red flowers.
– ORIGIN Greek *kistos.*

cit·a·del /'sitədl, -,del/ ▸ **noun** a fortress protecting or overlooking a city.
– ORIGIN French *citadelle* or Italian *cittadella.*

ci·ta·tion /sī'tāSHən/ ▸ **noun 1** a quotation from or reference to a book or author. **2** a mention of a praiseworthy act in an official report. **3** a note accompanying an award, giving reasons for it.

cite /sīt/ ▸ **verb 1** quote a book or author as evidence for an argument. **2** praise someone for a courageous act in an official report. **3** summon someone to appear in court.

> – SYNONYMS **quote,** mention, refer to, allude to, instance, specify, name.

– ORIGIN Latin *citare.*

cit·i·fied /'siti,fīd/ ▸ **adjective** chiefly derogatory characteristic of a city: *the obligations of citified life.*

cit·i·zen /'sitizən, -sən/ ▸ **noun 1** a person who is legally recognized as a subject or national of a country. **2** an inhabitant of a town or city.

> – SYNONYMS **1** *a US citizen* **subject,** national, passport holder. **2** *the citizens of Juneau* **inhabitant,** resident, native, townsman, townswoman, townsperson, taxpayer; formal denizen.

– DERIVATIVES **cit·i·zen·ry** /-rē/ noun **cit·i·zen·ship** /-,SHip/ noun.
– ORIGIN Old French *citezein.*

cit·i·zen's ar·rest ▸ **noun** an arrest by an ordinary person without a warrant, allowable in certain cases.

Cit·i·zens' Band ▸ **noun** a range of radio frequencies that are allocated for local communication by private individuals.

cit·rate /'si,trāt/ ▸ **noun** a salt or ester of citric acid.

cit·ric /'sitrik/ ▸ **adjective** related to citrus fruit: *a sharp, citric flavor.*

– ORIGIN from Latin *citrus* 'citron tree.'

cit·ric ac·id ▶ **noun** a sharp-tasting acid present in the juice of lemons and other sour fruits.

cit·ron /'sitrən/ ▶ **noun** the large, lemonlike fruit of an Asian tree.
– ORIGIN Latin *citrus* 'citron tree.'

cit·ron·el·la /ˌsitrə'nelə/ ▶ **noun** a fragrant oil obtained from a South Asian grass, used as an insect repellent and in perfume.

cit·rus /'sitrəs/ (also **citrus fruit**) ▶ **noun** (pl. **citruses**) a fruit of a group that includes lemons, limes, oranges, and grapefruit.
– DERIVATIVES **cit·rus·y** adjective.
– ORIGIN Latin, 'citron tree.'

cit·y /'sitē/ ▶ **noun** (pl. **cities**) **1** a large town. **2** an incorporated municipal center.

– SYNONYMS **town,** municipality, metropolis, megapolis, megacity, conurbation, urban area, borough, township. informal burg.

– ORIGIN Latin *civitas.*

WORD LINKS

urban, civic, metropolitan *relating to cities*

cit·y fa·ther ▶ **noun** a person concerned with the administration of a city.

cit·y hall ▶ **noun** municipal offices or officers.

cit·y·scape /'sitēˌskāp/ ▶ **noun** a city landscape.

cit·y slick·er /'slikər/ ▶ **noun** informal, derogatory a person with the sophisticated tastes or values associated with people who live in cities.

cit·y-state ▶ **noun** chiefly historical a city and surrounding territory that forms an independent state.

cit·y·wide /'sitēˌwīd/ ▶ **adjective & adverb** extending throughout a city.

civ·et /'sivət/ ▶ **noun 1** a slender cat native to Africa and Asia. **2** a strong musky perfume obtained from the scent glands of the civet.
– ORIGIN Arabic.

civ·ic /'sivik/ ▶ **adjective** relating to a city or town or to the duties or activities of its citizens.

– SYNONYMS **municipal,** city, town, urban, metropolitan, public, community.

– DERIVATIVES **civ·i·cal·ly** /-ik(ə)lē/ adverb.
– ORIGIN Latin *civicus.*

civ·ic cen·ter ▶ **noun** a municipal building or building complex consisting of government or other public-use buildings.

civ·ics /'siviks/ ▶ **plural noun** (treated as sing.) the study of the rights and duties of citizenship.

civ·il /'sivəl/ ▶ **adjective 1** relating to ordinary citizens, as distinct from military or church matters. **2** Law noncriminal: *a civil court.* **3** courteous and polite.

– SYNONYMS **1 secular,** nonreligious, lay. **2 nonmilitary,** civilian. **3 polite,** courteous, well mannered, gentlemanly, chivalrous, ladylike.
– ANTONYMS religious, military, rude.

– DERIVATIVES **civ·il·ly** adverb.
– ORIGIN Latin *civilis.*

civ·il de·fense ▶ **noun** the organization and training of civilians for their protection during wartime.

civ·il dis·o·be·di·ence ▶ **noun** the refusal to obey certain laws as a political protest.

civ·il en·gi·neer ▶ **noun** an engineer who designs roads, bridges, dams, and similar structures.

ci·vil·ian /sə'vilyən/ ▶ **noun** a person not in the armed services or the police force. ▶ **adjective** relating to a civilian.
– ORIGIN from Old French *droit civilien* 'civil law.'

ci·vil·i·ty /sə'vilətē/ ▶ **noun** (pl. **civilities**) **1** politeness and courtesy. **2** (**civilities**) polite remarks used in formal conversation.

civ·i·li·za·tion /ˌsivələ'zāsнən/ ▶ **noun 1** an advanced stage or system of human social development: *the Victorians equated the railroads with progress and civilization.* **2** the process of achieving a civilized stage of human development. **3** a civilized nation or region.

– SYNONYMS **1 human development,** advancement, progress, enlightenment, culture, refinement, sophistication. **2 culture,** society, nation, people.

civ·i·lize /'sivəˌlīz/ ▶ **verb 1** bring a place or people to an advanced stage of social development. **2** (as adj. **civilized**) polite and well-mannered.

– SYNONYMS **1 enlighten,** improve, educate, instruct, refine, cultivate, socialize. **2** (as adj. **civilized**) *civilized behavior* **polite,** courteous, well mannered, civil, refined, polished.

– DERIVATIVES **civ·i·liz·er** noun.

civ·il law ▶ **noun 1** law concerned with ordinary citizens, rather than criminal, military, or religious affairs. **2** the system of law predominant on the European continent, influenced by that of ancient Rome.

civ·il lib·er·ty ▶ **noun 1** freedom of action and speech subject to laws established for the good of the community. **2** (**civil liberties**) a person's right to be subject only to laws established for the good of the community.
– DERIVATIVES **civ·il lib·er·tar·i·an** noun.

civ·il mar·riage ▶ **noun** a marriage solemnized without a religious ceremony.

civ·il rights ▶ **plural noun** the rights of citizens to political and social freedom and equality.

civ·il serv·ant ▶ **noun** a member of the civil service.

civ·il serv·ice ▶ **noun** the branches of government administration, excluding military and judicial branches and elected politicians.

civ·il u·ni·on ▶ **noun** (in some countries and in some US states) a legally recognized union of a couple of the same sex, with rights similar to those of marriage.

civ·il war ▶ **noun** a war between citizens of the same country.

civ·vy /'sivē/ ▶ **noun** (pl. **civvies**) informal **1** a civilian. **2** (**civvies**) civilian clothes, as distinct from uniform.

CJD ▶ **abbreviation** Creutzfeldt–Jakob disease.

Cl ▶ **symbol** the chemical element chlorine.

cl ▶ **abbreviation** centiliter.

clack /klak/ ▶ **verb** make a sharp sound as of a hard object striking another. ▶ **noun** a clacking sound.
– ORIGIN imitating the sound.

clad /klad/ old-fashioned or literary past participle of CLOTHE ▶ **adjective 1** clothed: *leather-clad boys.* **2** covered with cladding.

clad·ding /ˈkladiNG/ ▶ **noun** a covering or coating on a structure or material.

clade /klād/ ▶ **noun** a group of organisms comprising all the evolutionary descendants of a common ancestor.
– ORIGIN Greek *klados* 'branch.'

cla·dis·tics /kləˈdistiks/ ▶ **plural noun** (treated as sing.) a method of classifying animals and plants based on only those shared characteristics that can be deduced to have originated in the common ancestor of a group of species during evolution.
– DERIVATIVES **cla·dis·tic** adjective.

claim /klām/ ▶ **verb** **1** state that something is the case, without being able to give proof. **2** ask for something that one has a right to have: *she went to Germany, where she claimed asylum.* **3** cause the loss of someone's life. **4** request money under the terms of an insurance policy. **5** call for someone's attention.

– SYNONYMS **1 assert,** declare, profess, protest, maintain, insist, contend, allege. **2 request,** ask for, apply for, demand.

▶ **noun** **1** a statement that something is the case. **2** a demand for something to which one has a right. **3** a request for compensation under the terms of an insurance policy.

– SYNONYMS **1 assertion,** declaration, profession, protestation, insistence, contention, allegation. **2 application,** request, demand.

– DERIVATIVES **claim·a·ble** adjective **claim·ant** noun.
– ORIGIN Latin *clamare* 'call out.'

claims ad·just·er ▶ **noun** an insurance agent who assesses the amount of compensation that should be paid to a person making a claim.

clair·voy·ance /kle(ə)rˈvoiəns/ ▶ **noun** the supposed ability of being able to see future events or to communicate with people who are dead or far away.
– ORIGIN from French *clair* 'clear' + *voir* 'to see.'

clair·voy·ant /kle(ə)rˈvoiənt/ ▶ **noun** a person claiming to be able to predict the future or communicate with the dead. ▶ **adjective** able to predict the future.

clam /klam/ ▶ **noun** a large shellfish with two shells of equal size. ▶ **verb** (**clams, clamming, clammed**) (**clam up**) informal stop talking abruptly.
– ORIGIN Old English, 'a bond or bondage.'

clam·bake /ˈklamˌbāk/ ▶ **noun** an outdoor social gathering at which clams and other seafood are baked or steamed.

clam·ber /ˈklambər, ˈklamər/ ▶ **verb** climb or move in an awkward and laborious way: *Saul clambered into the back of the truck.* ▶ **noun** an act of clambering.
– ORIGIN probably from CLIMB.

clam·dig·gers /ˈklamˌdigərz/ ▶ **plural noun** close-fitting calf-length pants for women.

clam·my /ˈklamē/ ▶ **adjective** (**clammier, clammiest**) **1** unpleasantly damp and sticky. **2** (of air) cold and damp.
– DERIVATIVES **clam·mi·ly** adverb **clam·mi·ness** noun.
– ORIGIN from dialect *clam* 'be sticky.'

clam·or /ˈklamər/ (Brit. **clamour**) ▶ **noun** **1** a loud and confused noise. **2** a strong protest or demand.

– SYNONYMS **noise,** din, racket, rumpus, uproar, shouting, commotion, hubbub; Brit. row; informal hullabaloo.

▶ **verb** (of a group) shout or demand loudly: *the surging crowds clamored for attention.*
– DERIVATIVES **clam·or·ous** /-ərəs/ adjective.
– ORIGIN from Latin *clamare* 'cry out.'

clamp /klamp/ ▶ **noun** a brace, band, or clasp for strengthening or holding things together. ▶ **verb** **1** fasten a thing or things in place or together with a clamp. **2** (**clamp down**) take firm or harsh action to prevent something: *a plan to clamp down on smuggling.*

– SYNONYMS **fasten,** secure, fix, attach, clench, grip, hold, press, clasp, screw, bolt.

– DERIVATIVES **clamp·er** noun.
– ORIGIN probably Dutch.

clamp·down /ˈklampˌdoun/ ▶ **noun** informal a firm or harsh attempt to prevent something.

clan /klan/ ▶ **noun** **1** a close-knit group of related families, especially in the Scottish Highlands. **2** a group with a shared interest or characteristic: *a clan of born-again Christians.*

– SYNONYMS **family,** house, dynasty, tribe.

– ORIGIN Scottish Gaelic, 'offspring, family.'

clan·des·tine /klanˈdestən, -ˌtīn, -ˌtēn, ˈklandəs-/ ▶ **adjective** kept secret or done secretively.

– SYNONYMS **secret,** covert, furtive, surreptitious, stealthy, cloak-and-dagger, underhanded/underhand; informal hush-hush.

– DERIVATIVES **clan·des·tine·ly** adverb **clan·des·tin·i·ty** /ˌklandesˈtinitē/ noun.
– ORIGIN Latin *clandestinus*.

clang /klaNG/ ▶ **noun** a loud metallic sound. ▶ **verb** make a clang.
– ORIGIN influenced by Latin *clangere* 'resound.'

clang·or /ˈklaNGər/ (Brit. **clangour**) ▶ **noun** a continuous clanging sound.
– DERIVATIVES **clang·or·ous** /ˈklaNGərəs/ adjective.
– ORIGIN from Latin *clangere* 'resound.'

clank /klaNGk/ ▶ **noun** a loud, sharp metallic sound. ▶ **verb** make a clank.
– ORIGIN imitating the sound.

clan·nish /ˈklanisH/ ▶ **adjective** (of a group) tending to exclude others outside the group.
– DERIVATIVES **clan·nish·ness** noun.

clans·man /ˈklanzmən/ (or **clanswoman** /ˈklanzˌwo͝omən/) ▶ **noun** (pl. **clansmen** or **clanswomen**) a member of a clan.

clap[1] /klap/ ▶ **verb** (**claps, clapping, clapped**) **1** strike the palms of one's hands together repeatedly, especially to applaud. **2** slap someone encouragingly on the back. **3** put someone or something somewhere quickly or suddenly: *he clapped a hand to his forehead.*

– SYNONYMS **applaud,** give someone a round of applause, put one's hands together; informal give someone a (big) hand, give it up (for someone).

▶ **noun** **1** an act of clapping. **2** a sudden loud noise, especially of thunder.

– SYNONYMS **1 round of applause,** handclap; informal hand. **2 crack,** peal, crash, bang, boom.

– PHRASES **clap someone in jail** (or **irons**) put someone in prison (or in chains).
– ORIGIN Old English, 'throb, beat.'

clap[2] ▶ **noun** informal a sexually transmitted disease, especially gonorrhea.
– ORIGIN Old French *clapoir*.

clap·board /ˈklabərd, ˈklapˌbôrd/ ▶ **noun** one of a series of planks of wood with edges horizontally overlapping,

used to cover the outer walls of buildings.
– ORIGIN German *klappholt* 'barrel stave.'

clap·per /'klapər/ ▶ **noun** the free-swinging metal piece inside a bell that strikes the bell to produce the sound.

clap·per·board /'klapərˌbôrd/ ▶ **noun** hinged boards that are struck together at the beginning of filming to enable the picture and sound to be synchronized during editing.

clap·trap /'klapˌtrap/ ▶ **noun** nonsense: *feminist claptrap.*
– ORIGIN first referring to something designed to make people applaud.

claque /klak/ ▶ **noun 1** a group of people who follow someone in an obsequious way. **2** a group of people hired to applaud or heckle a performer.
– ORIGIN from French *claquer* 'to clap.'

clar·et /'klarit/ ▶ **noun 1** a red wine, especially from Bordeaux. **2** a deep purplish red color.
– ORIGIN from Latin *claratum vinum* 'clarified wine.'

clar·i·fy /'klarəˌfī/ ▶ **verb** (**clarifies, clarifying, clarified**) **1** make easier to understand: *the judges' ruling had clarified the law of rape.* **2** melt butter to separate out the impurities.

> – SYNONYMS **make clear,** shed/throw light on, illuminate, elucidate, explain, interpret, spell out, clear up.
> – ANTONYMS confuse.

– DERIVATIVES **clar·i·fi·ca·tion** /ˌklarəfi'kāsʜən/ noun **clar·i·fi·er** noun.
– ORIGIN Old French *clarifier.*

> **CHOOSE THE RIGHT WORD**
>
> **clarify, construe, elucidate, explain, explicate, interpret**
>
> When a biology teacher gets up in front of a class and tries to **explain** how two brown-eyed parents can produce a blue-eyed child, the purpose is to make an entire process or sequence of events understandable. In a less formal sense, to *explain* is to make a verbal attempt to justify certain actions or to make them understood (*she tried to explain why she was so late*). That same teacher might **clarify** a particular exam question that almost everyone in the class got wrong—a word that means to make an earlier event, situation, or statement clear. **Elucidate** is a more formal word meaning to *clarify,* but where the root of the latter refers to clearness, the root of the former refers to light; to *elucidate* is to shed light on something through explanation, illustration, etc. (*the principal's comments were an attempt to elucidate the school's policy on cheating*). A teacher who **explicates** something discusses a complex subject in a point-by-point manner (*to explicate a poem*). If a personal judgment is inserted in making such an explication, the correct word is **interpret** (*to interpret a poem's symbolic meanings*). To **construe** is to make a careful interpretation of something, especially where the meaning is ambiguous. For example, when a class misbehaves in front of a visitor, the teacher is likely to *construe* that behavior as an attempt to cause embarrassment or ridicule.

clar·i·net /ˌklarə'net/ ▶ **noun** a woodwind instrument with holes stopped by keys and a mouthpiece with a single reed.
– DERIVATIVES **clar·i·net·ist** /-'netist/ noun.
– ORIGIN French *clarinette.*

clar·i·on /'klarēən/ ▶ **adjective** literary loud and clear. ▶ **noun** historical a shrill war trumpet.
– PHRASES **clarion call** a strongly expressed demand for action.
– ORIGIN Latin.

clar·i·ty /'klaritē/ ▶ **noun 1** the state or quality of being easy to understand, see, or hear: *she analyzes the pros and cons with admirable clarity.* **2** transparency or purity.

> – SYNONYMS **1** *the clarity of his explanation* **lucidity,** precision, coherence, transparency, simplicity. **2** *the clarity of the image* **sharpness,** clearness, crispness, definition. **3** *the clarity of the water* **transparency,** clearness, limpidity, translucence.

– ORIGIN Latin *clarus* 'clear.'

clash /klasʜ/ ▶ **noun 1** a conflict or disagreement. **2** an inconvenient occurrence of dates or events at the same time. **3** a loud discordant sound.

> – SYNONYMS **1 fight,** battle, confrontation, skirmish, engagement, encounter, conflict. **2 argument,** altercation, confrontation, quarrel, disagreement, dispute; informal run-in. **3 crash,** clang, bang, clatter, clangor.

▶ **verb 1** (of opposing groups) come into conflict. **2** disagree or be at odds: *Shanghai's decadent culture once clashed with Maoist principles.* **3** (of colors) appear discordant when placed together. **4** (of dates or events) occur inconveniently at the same time: *he was invited to a dinner party, but it clashed with one of his seminars.* **5** strike cymbals together, producing a loud discordant sound.

> – SYNONYMS **1 fight,** battle, confront, skirmish, contend, come to blows. **2 disagree,** differ, wrangle, dispute, cross swords, lock horns, be at loggerheads. **3 conflict,** coincide, overlap. **4 bang,** strike, clang, crash.

– ORIGIN imitating the sound.

clasp /klasp/ ▶ **verb 1** grasp something tightly with one's hand. **2** place one's arms tightly around someone or something. **3** fasten something with a clasp.

> – SYNONYMS **grasp,** grip, clutch, hold, squeeze, seize, grab, embrace, hug.

▶ **noun 1** a device with interlocking parts used for fastening. **2** an act of embracing or grasping.

> – SYNONYMS **1 fastener,** catch, clip, pin, buckle. **2 grasp,** grip, squeeze, embrace, hug.

– ORIGIN unknown.

class /klas/ ▶ **noun 1** a set or category of people or things having a common characteristic: *a new class of antibiotics.* **2** a system that divides members of a society into sets based on social or economic status. **3** a social division based on social or economic status: *the ruling class.* **4** a group of students who are taught together. **5** a lesson. **6** informal impressive stylishness. **7** Biology a principal category into which animals and plants are divided, ranking below phylum or division.

> – SYNONYMS **1 kind,** sort, type, variety, genre, category, grade, rating, classification. **2 group,** grouping, rank, stratum, level, echelon, status, caste.

▶ **verb** put someone or something in a particular category.

> – SYNONYMS **classify,** categorize, group, grade, order, rate, bracket, designate, label, rank.

▶ **adjective** informal showing stylish excellence: *a class player.*
– ORIGIN Latin *classis* 'division of the Roman people, class.'

class ac·tion ▶ **noun** Law a lawsuit filed or defended by an individual acting on behalf of a group.

clas·sic /ˈklasik/ ▸ **adjective 1** judged over time to be of the highest quality. **2** typical: *the classic symptoms of flu.* **3** (of a garment or design) simple and elegant.

– SYNONYMS **1 definitive,** authoritative, outstanding, first-rate, first-class, best, finest, excellent, superior, masterly. **2 typical,** archetypal, quintessential, model, representative, perfect, prime, textbook. **3 timeless,** traditional, simple, elegant, understated.

▸ **noun 1** a work of art that is recognized as being of high quality. **2** a thing that is an excellent example of its kind: *tomorrow's game should be a classic.* **3** (**Classics**) the study of ancient Greek and Latin literature, philosophy, and history. **4** (**the classics**) the works of ancient Greek and Latin writers.

– SYNONYMS **definitive example,** model, epitome, paradigm, exemplar, masterpiece, masterwork.

– ORIGIN Latin *classicus* 'belonging to a class.'

clas·si·cal /ˈklasikəl/ ▸ **adjective 1** relating to ancient Greek or Latin literature, art, or culture. **2** (of a form of art or a language) representing the highest standard within a long-established form. **3** (of music) of long-established form or style or (more specifically) written in the European tradition between approximately 1750 and 1830. **4** relating to the first significant period of an area of study: *classical Marxism.*

– DERIVATIVES **clas·si·cal·ly** /-ik(ə)lē/ adverb.

clas·sic car ▸ **noun** an old car, generally one built before 1948 and in good condition.

clas·si·cism /ˈklasəˌsizəm/ ▸ **noun** the following of ancient Greek or Roman principles and style in art and literature, generally associated with harmony and restraint.

clas·si·cist /ˈklasəsist/ ▸ **noun 1** a person who studies Classics. **2** a follower of classicism.

clas·si·ciz·ing /ˈklasəˌsīziNG/ ▸ **adjective** imitating a classical style.

clas·si·fi·ca·tion /ˌklasəfəˈkāSHən/ ▸ **noun 1** the action of classifying something. **2** a category into which something is put.

– SYNONYMS **categorization,** classifying, grouping, grading, ranking, organization, sorting, codification.

– DERIVATIVES **clas·si·fi·ca·to·ry** /ˈklasəfikəˌtôrē/ adjective.

clas·si·fied /ˈklasəˌfīd/ ▸ **adjective 1** (of newspaper or magazine advertisements) organized in categories. **2** (of information or documents) officially classed as secret. ▸ **noun** (**classifieds**) classified advertisements.

clas·si·fy /ˈklasəˌfī/ ▸ **verb** (**classifies, classifying, classified**) **1** arrange a group in classes according to shared characteristics. **2** put in a particular class or category: *it's the only French winery classified as a National Monument.* **3** categorize documents or information as officially secret.

– SYNONYMS **categorize,** group, grade, rank, order, organize, sort, type, codify, bracket.

– DERIVATIVES **clas·si·fi·a·ble** /ˌklasəˈfīəbəl/ adjective **clas·si·fi·er** noun.

class·less /ˈklasləs/ ▸ **adjective 1** (of a society) not divided into social classes. **2** not showing characteristics of a particular social class.

– DERIVATIVES **class·less·ness** noun.

class·mate /ˈklasˌmāt/ ▸ **noun** a fellow member of one's school or college class.

class·room /ˈklasˌro͞om, -ˌro͝om/ ▸ **noun** a room in which a class of students is taught.

class·y /ˈklasē/ ▸ **adjective** (**classier, classiest**) informal stylish and sophisticated.

– SYNONYMS **stylish,** high-class, superior, exclusive, chic, elegant, smart, sophisticated, upscale, high-toned. informal posh, ritzy, plush, swanky.

– DERIVATIVES **class·i·ly** adverb **class·i·ness** noun.

clat·ter /ˈklatər/ ▸ **noun** a loud rattling sound as of hard objects striking each other. ▸ **verb** make or move with a clatter.

– ORIGIN Old English.

clause /klôz/ ▸ **noun 1** a group of words that includes a subject and a verb, forming a sentence or part of a sentence. **2** a particular and separate item of a treaty, bill, or contract.

– SYNONYMS **section,** paragraph, article, passage, subsection, chapter, condition, proviso, rider.

– DERIVATIVES **claus·al** adjective.

– ORIGIN from Latin *claudere* 'close.'

claus·tro·pho·bi·a /ˌklôstrəˈfōbēə/ ▸ **noun** extreme or irrational fear of being in an enclosed place.

– DERIVATIVES **claus·tro·pho·bic** /ˌklôstrəˈfōbik/ adjective.

– ORIGIN from Latin *claustrum* 'lock, bolt.'

clav·i·chord /ˈklavəˌkôrd/ ▸ **noun** a small early keyboard instrument with a soft tone.

– ORIGIN from Latin *clavis* 'key' + *chorda* 'string.'

clav·i·cle /ˈklavikəl/ ▸ **noun** technical term for **COLLARBONE**.

– ORIGIN Latin *clavicula* 'small key.'

claw /klô/ ▸ **noun 1** a curved pointed nail on each digit of the foot in birds, lizards, and some mammals. **2** the pincer of a crab, scorpion, or similar creature.

– SYNONYMS **talon,** nail, pincer.

▸ **verb 1** (usu. **claw at**) scratch or tear something with the claws or fingernails. **2** (**claw something back**) regain or recover money or power with difficulty.

– SYNONYMS **scratch,** lacerate, tear, rip, scrape, dig into.

– DERIVATIVES **clawed** adjective.

– ORIGIN Old English.

claw ham·mer ▸ **noun** a hammer with one side of the head split and curved, used for extracting nails.

clay /klā/ ▸ **noun 1** a heavy sticky earth that can be molded when wet and baked to make bricks and pottery. **2** literary the substance of the human body: *this lifeless clay.*

– DERIVATIVES **clay·ey** adjective.

– ORIGIN Old English.

clay pig·eon ▸ **noun** a saucer-shaped piece of baked clay or other material thrown up in the air as a target for shooting.

clean /klēn/ ▸ **adjective 1** free from dirt, stains, or harmful substances. **2** maintaining good personal hygiene. **3** not immoral or obscene: *good clean fun.* **4** showing or having no record of offenses or crimes: *a clean driving license.* **5** done according to the rules: *a good clean fight.* **6** free from irregularities; smooth. **7** (of an action) smoothly and skillfully done.

– SYNONYMS **1 washed,** scrubbed, cleansed, cleaned, laundered, spotless, unstained, unsullied, unblemished, immaculate, pristine, disinfected, sterilized, sterile, aseptic, decontaminated. **2 blank,** empty, clear, plain, unused, new, pristine, fresh, unmarked. **3 pure,** clear, fresh, unpolluted, uncontaminated.
– ANTONYMS dirty, polluted.

▶ **verb 1** make someone or something clean. **2** (**clean someone out**) informal use up or take all someone's money. **3** (**clean up**) informal make a substantial gain or profit.

– SYNONYMS **wash,** cleanse, wipe, sponge, scrub, mop, rinse, scour, swab, shampoo, launder, dry-clean.
– ANTONYMS dirty.

▶ **adverb 1** so as to be free from dirt. **2** informal completely: *I clean forgot her birthday.*
▶ **noun** an act of cleaning.
– DERIVATIVES **clean·a·ble** adjective **clean·ness** noun.
– PHRASES **clean and jerk** a weightlifting exercise in which a weight is raised above the head following an initial lift to shoulder level. **a clean slate** an absence of existing restraints or commitments. **come clean** (or **make a clean breast of it**) informal fully confess something. **keep one's hands clean** remain uninvolved in something immoral or illegal. **make a clean sweep 1** remove all unwanted people or things ready to start afresh. **2** win all of a group of related sports contests.
– ORIGIN Old English.

clean-cut ▶ **adjective 1** (of a person, especially a man) neat and respectable. **2** sharply outlined.

clean·er /'klēnər/ ▶ **noun 1** a person or thing that cleans something. **2** (**the cleaners**) a place of business where clothes and fabrics are dry-cleaned.
– PHRASES **take someone to the cleaners** informal cheat or defraud someone of all their money or possessions.

clean·ly /'klēnlē/ ▶ **adverb** in a clean way.
– DERIVATIVES **clean·li·ness** /'klenlēnis/ noun.

cleanse /klenz/ ▶ **verb 1** make something thoroughly clean. **2** remove something unpleasant or unwanted from: *he wanted to cleanse the town of immorality.*

– SYNONYMS **1 clean (up),** wash, bathe, rinse, disinfect. **2** *cleansing the environment of traces of lead* **rid,** clear, free, purify, purge.

▶ **noun** an act of cleansing.
– ORIGIN Old English.

cleans·er /'klenzər/ ▶ **noun 1** a powder or liquid for scouring sinks, toilets, and bathtubs. **2** a cosmetic product for cleansing the skin.

clean-shav·en ▶ **adjective** (of a man) without a beard or mustache.

clean·up /'klēn,əp/ ▶ **noun 1** an act of cleaning a place. **2** an act of removing or putting an end to disorder, immorality, or crime. **3** Baseball the fourth position in a team's batting order, typically reserved for a power hitter likely to clear the bases by enabling any runners to score.

clear /'kli(ə)r/ ▶ **adjective 1** easy to see, hear, or understand. **2** leaving or feeling no doubt. **3** transparent: *a stream of clear water.* **4** free of obstructions or unwanted objects. **5** (of a period of time) free of commitments. **6** free from disease or guilt. **7** (**clear of**) not touching; away from. **8** complete: *seven clear days' notice.* **9** (of a sum of money) net: *a clear profit of $1,100.*

– SYNONYMS **1 understandable,** comprehensible, intelligible, plain, uncomplicated, explicit, lucid, coherent, simple, straightforward, unambiguous, clear-cut. **2 obvious,** evident, plain, sure, definite, unmistakable, manifest, indisputable, unambiguous, patent, incontrovertible, visible, conspicuous, overt, blatant, glaring. **3 transparent,** limpid, translucent, crystal clear, pellucid. **4** *a clear blue sky* **bright,** cloudless, unclouded, blue, sunny, starry. **5 unobstructed,** passable, open, unrestricted, unhindered.
– ANTONYMS incoherent, vague, cloudy.

▶ **adverb 1** so as to be out of the way of or uncluttered by. **2** with clarity.
▶ **verb 1** make or become clear. **2** get past or over something safely or without touching it. **3** show or declare someone to be innocent. **4** cause people to leave a building or place. **5** give official approval to; authorize: *I cleared him to return to his squadron.* **6** (of a check) pass through a clearinghouse so that the money enters a person's account. **7** earn an amount of money as a net profit. **8** pay off a debt.

– SYNONYMS **1** *the drizzle had cleared* **disappear,** go away, stop, die away, fade, wear off, lift, settle, evaporate, dissipate, decrease, lessen, shift.
2 *clearing drains* **unblock,** unstop, clean out.
3 *I cleared the bar on my first attempt* **go over,** pass over, sail over, jump (over), vault (over), leap (over). **4** *he was cleared by an appeals court* **acquit,** declare innocent, find not guilty, absolve, exonerate; informal let off (the hook). **5** *staff cleared the building* **evacuate,** vacate, empty, leave.

– DERIVATIVES **clear·ness** noun.
– PHRASES **clear the air 1** make the air less humid. **2** defuse a tense situation by frank discussion. **clear the decks** prepare for something by dealing with possible obstacles to progress. **clear off** (or **out**) informal go away. **clear something out** informal empty something. **clear up 1** (of an illness or other medical condition) become cured. **2** (of the weather) become fine and dry. **clear something up 1** tidy something by removing unwanted items. **2** solve or explain something. **in the clear** no longer in danger or under suspicion.
– ORIGIN Latin *clarus.*

clear·ance /'kli(ə)rəns/ ▶ **noun 1** the action of clearing. **2** official authorization for something. **3** clear space allowed for a thing to move past or under another.

– SYNONYMS **1 removal,** clearing, demolition. **2 authorization,** permission, consent, approval, leave, sanction, license, dispensation; informal the go-ahead. **3 space,** room (to spare), headroom, margin, leeway.

clear-cut ▶ **adjective** easy to see or understand.

– SYNONYMS **definite,** distinct, precise, specific, explicit, unambiguous, unequivocal, black and white.
– ANTONYMS vague.

clear·ing /'kli(ə)riNG/ ▶ **noun** an open space in a forest.

clear·ing·house /'kli(ə)riNG,hous/ ▶ **noun 1** a bankers' establishment where checks and bills from member banks are exchanged. **2** an agency that collects and distributes information.

clear·ly /'kli(ə)rlē/ ▶ **adverb 1** in a clear way. **2** without doubt; obviously.

– SYNONYMS **1 intelligibly,** plainly, distinctly, comprehensibly, legibly, audibly. **2 obviously,** evidently, patently, unquestionably, undoubtedly, without doubt, plainly, undeniably.

clear-sight·ed ▶ **adjective** thinking clearly.

cleat /klēt/ ▶ **noun 1** a T-shaped projection to which a rope may be attached. **2** a projecting piece of metal or rubber on the sole of a shoe, to prevent a person from slipping.
– DERIVATIVES **cleat·ed** adjective.
– ORIGIN Germanic.

cleav·age /ˈklēvij/ ▶ **noun 1** the space between a woman's breasts. **2** a marked difference or division between people. **3** cell division, especially of a fertilized egg cell.

cleave[1] /klēv/ ▶ **verb** (**cleaves, cleaving, clove** /klōv/ or **cleft** /kleft/ or **cleaved**; past part. **cloven** /ˈklōvən/ or **cleft** or **cleaved** /klēvd/) **1** split something along a natural grain or line. **2** move forcefully through: *they watched a coot cleave the smooth water.*
– ORIGIN Old English.

cleave[2] ▶ **verb** (**cleave to**) literary **1** stick fast to. **2** become strongly involved with or emotionally attached to: *sport was something he could cleave to.*
– ORIGIN Old English.

cleav·er /ˈklēvər/ ▶ **noun** a tool with a heavy broad blade, used for chopping meat.

clef /klef/ ▶ **noun** Music any of several symbols placed on a stave, indicating the pitch of the notes written on the stave.
– ORIGIN French.

cleft /kleft/ past and past participle of CLEAVE[1] ▶ **adjective** split, divided, or partially divided into two. ▶ **noun 1** a crack or split in rock or the ground. **2** a narrow vertical indentation in the chin or other part of the body.

– SYNONYMS **split,** crack, fissure, crevice.

cleft lip ▶ **noun** a split in the upper lip on one or both sides of the center, present from birth.

cleft pal·ate ▶ **noun** a split in the roof of the mouth that is present from birth.

clem·a·tis /ˈklemətəs, kləˈmatəs/ ▶ **noun** a climbing plant with white, pink, or purple flowers.
– ORIGIN Greek *klēmatis.*

clem·en·cy /ˈklemənsē/ ▶ **noun** the quality of being clement or merciful.

clem·ent /ˈklemənt/ ▶ **adjective 1** (of weather) mild. **2** showing mercy.
– ORIGIN Latin *clemens.*

clem·en·tine /ˈklemənˌtīn, -ˌtēn/ ▶ **noun** a deep orange-red variety of tangerine.
– ORIGIN French, from the man's name *Clément.*

clench /klench/ ▶ **verb 1** close or press one's teeth or fists together tightly, as a reaction to stress or anger. **2** contract a set of muscles sharply. **3** hold something tightly: *he clenched the steering wheel.*

– SYNONYMS **grip,** grasp, grab, clutch, clasp, clamp, hold tightly, seize, squeeze.

– ORIGIN Old English; related to CLING.

clere·sto·ry /ˈkli(ə)rˌstôrē/ (also **clearstory**) ▶ **noun** (pl. **clerestories**) the upper part of the nave, choir, and transepts of a large church, with a series of windows that allow light into the central parts of the building.
– ORIGIN from CLEAR + STORY[2].

cler·gy /ˈklərjē/ ▶ **noun** (pl. **clergies**) (usu. treated as pl.) the people ordained for religious duties considered as a group, especially those in the Christian Church.
– ORIGIN Latin *clericus* 'clergyman.'

cler·gy·man /ˈklərjēmən/ (or **clergywoman** /ˈklərjēˌwo͝omən/) ▶ **noun** (pl. **clergymen** or **clergywomen**) a Christian priest or minister.

– SYNONYMS **priest,** cleric, minister, preacher, chaplain, padre, father, pastor, vicar, rector, parson, curate.

cler·ic /ˈklerik/ ▶ **noun** a priest or religious leader.
– ORIGIN Latin *clericus.*

cler·i·cal /ˈklerikəl/ ▶ **adjective 1** relating to the routine work of an office clerk. **2** relating to the clergy.

– SYNONYMS **1 office,** desk, administrative, secretarial, white-collar. **2 ecclesiastical,** church, priestly, religious, spiritual, holy.

– DERIVATIVES **cler·i·cal·ly** adverb.

cler·i·cal col·lar ▶ **noun** a stiff upright white collar that fastens at the back, worn by the clergy in some Christian churches.

cler·i·cal er·ror ▶ **noun** a mistake made in copying or writing out a document.

cler·i·hew /ˈklerəˌhyo͞o/ ▶ **noun** a short comic verse consisting of two rhyming couplets, usually referring to a famous person.
– ORIGIN named after Edmund *Clerihew* Bentley, the English writer who invented it.

clerk /klərk/ ▶ **noun 1** a person employed in an office or bank to keep records or accounts and to carry out other routine administrative duties. **2** a person in charge of the records of a local council or court. **3** (also **desk clerk**) a receptionist in a hotel. **4** (also **sales clerk**) an assistant in a store.
– DERIVATIVES **clerk·ly** adjective.
– ORIGIN Latin *clericus* 'clergyman.'

clev·er /ˈklevər/ ▶ **adjective** (**cleverer, cleverest**) **1** quick to understand and learn things. **2** skilled at doing something: *he's very clever with his hands.*

– SYNONYMS **1 intelligent,** bright, smart, astute, quick-witted, shrewd, talented, gifted, capable, able, competent; informal brainy. **2** *a clever scheme* **ingenious,** canny, cunning, crafty, artful, slick, neat. **3** *she was clever with her hands* **skillful,** dexterous, adroit, adept, deft, nimble, handy, skilled, talented, gifted.
– ANTONYMS stupid.

– DERIVATIVES **clev·er·ly** adverb **clev·er·ness** noun.
– ORIGIN perhaps from Dutch or German.

WORD TOOLKIT

See WITTY.

clew /klo͞o/ ▶ **noun** the lower corner of a sail or that nearest the stern of the boat.
– ORIGIN related to CLUE.

cli·ché /klēˈshā, kli-, ˈklēˌshā/ (also **cliche**) ▶ **noun** a phrase or idea that has been used so often that it is no longer interesting or effective.

– SYNONYMS **platitude,** hackneyed phrase, commonplace, banality, truism, stock phrase; informal old chestnut.

– DERIVATIVES **cli·chéd** adjective.
– ORIGIN French.

click /klik/ ▶ **noun 1** a short, sharp sound. **2** Computing an act of pressing one of the buttons on a mouse. ▶ **verb 1** make or cause to make a click: *the cameras started clicking.* **2** Computing press a mouse button. **3** informal become suddenly clear or understandable. **4** informal (of two people) become friends, especially at the first meeting.

– SYNONYMS **1 clack,** snap, pop, tick, clink. **2 become clear,** fall into place, make sense, dawn on someone, register, get through, sink in. **3 take to each other,** get along, be compatible, be like-minded, see eye to eye, be on the same wavelength; informal hit it off.

4 **go down well,** prove popular, be a hit, succeed, resonate, work, take off.

– DERIVATIVES **click·a·ble** adjective.
– ORIGIN imitating the sound.

cli·ent /ˈklīənt/ ▸ **noun** a person using the services of a professional person or organization.

– SYNONYMS **customer,** buyer, purchaser, shopper, patient, patron.

– ORIGIN Latin *cliens*.

cli·en·tele /ˌklīənˈtel, ˌklē-/ ▸ **noun** all the clients or customers of a particular store, restaurant, or other business.
– ORIGIN French.

cli·ent-serv·er ▸ **adjective** Computing referring to a computer system in which a central server provides data to a number of networked workstations.

cliff /klif/ ▸ **noun** a steep rock face, especially at the edge of the sea.

– SYNONYMS **precipice,** rock face, crag, bluff, ridge, escarpment, scar, scarp.

– ORIGIN Old English.

cliff·hang·er /ˈklifˌhaNGər/ ▸ **noun 1** a dramatic ending to an episode of a serial drama, leaving the audience in suspense. **2** an exciting situation in which the outcome is uncertain.

cli·mac·ter·ic /klīˈmaktərik, ˌklīmakˈterik/ ▸ **noun 1** the period of life when fertility is in decline; (in women) menopause. **2** a critical period or event.
– ORIGIN Greek *klimaktēr*.

cli·mac·tic /klīˈmaktik, klə-/ ▸ **adjective** forming an exciting climax.
– DERIVATIVES **cli·mac·ti·cal·ly** /-ik(ə)lē/ adverb.

USAGE

Do not confuse **climactic** with **climatic**. **Climactic** means 'forming a climax' (*the thrilling climactic scene*), whereas **climatic** means 'relating to climate' (*climatic and environmental change*).

cli·mate /ˈklīmit/ ▸ **noun 1** the general weather conditions in an area over a long period. **2** a general trend, attitude, or situation: *the current economic climate*.

– SYNONYMS **1 (weather) conditions,** weather. **2 atmosphere,** mood, spirit, ethos, feeling, ambience, environment.

– DERIVATIVES **cli·ma·tol·o·gy** /ˌklīməˈtäləjē/ noun **cli·ma·to·log·i·cal** /ˌklīmətlˈläjikəl/ adjective.
– ORIGIN Greek *klima* 'slope, zone.'

cli·mate change ▸ **noun** long-term, significant change in the climate of an area or of the earth, usually seen as resulting from human activity.

cli·mat·ic /klīˈmatik/ ▸ **adjective** relating to climate.
– DERIVATIVES **cli·mat·i·cal·ly** /klīˈmatik(ə)lē/ adverb.

cli·max /ˈklīˌmaks/ ▸ **noun 1** the most intense, exciting, or important point of something. **2** an orgasm.

– SYNONYMS **peak,** pinnacle, height, high point, top, zenith, culmination.
– ANTONYMS anticlimax, nadir.

▸ **verb** reach a climax.
– ORIGIN Greek *klimax* 'ladder, climax.'

climb /klīm/ ▸ **verb 1** go or come up to a higher position. **2** go up a hill, rock face, etc. **3** (**climb down**) withdraw from a position taken up in an argument or negotiation; admit that one was wrong. **4** move somewhere, especially with effort or difficulty: *he climbed out through the kitchen window*. **5** (of a plant) grow up a supporting structure by clinging to or twining around it. **6** increase in amount, value, or power: *the shares climbed more than $3*.

– SYNONYMS **1 rise,** ascend, go up, gain height, soar, rocket. **2** *the road climbs steeply* **slope (upward),** rise, go uphill, incline. **3 ascend,** mount, scale, scramble up, clamber up, shinny up, conquer.
4 (climb down) back down, retreat, give in, backtrack, eat your words, eat humble pie, do a U-turn; N. Amer. informal eat crow.
– ANTONYMS descend.

▸ **noun 1** an act of climbing. **2** a route up a mountain or cliff.
– DERIVATIVES **climb·a·ble** adjective.
– ORIGIN Old English.

climb·er /ˈklīmər/ ▸ **noun** a person who climbs rocks or mountains as a sport.

climb·ing wall ▸ **noun** a wall at a sports center or in a gymnasium fitted with attachments to simulate a rock face for climbing practice.

clime /klīm/ ▸ **noun** chiefly literary a region with a particular climate: *people leaving the Northwest for sunnier climes*.
– ORIGIN Greek *klima* 'slope, zone.'

clinch /klinCH/ ▸ **verb 1** succeed in achieving or winning: *he clinched a $5 million sponsorship deal*. **2** settle an argument or debate.

– SYNONYMS **1** *he clinched the deal* **secure,** settle, conclude, close, confirm, seal, finalize, wrap up; informal sew up. **2** *these findings clinched the matter* **settle,** decide, determine, resolve.

▸ **noun 1** an act of grappling at close quarters in a fight. **2** informal an embrace.
– ORIGIN from CLENCH.

clinch·er /ˈklinCHər/ ▸ **noun** informal a fact, argument, or event that settles something decisively.

cline /klīn/ ▸ **noun** a continuum with an infinite number of gradations from one extreme to the other.
– DERIVATIVES **clin·al** /ˈklīnl/ adjective.
– ORIGIN from Greek *klinein* 'to slope.'

cling /kliNG/ ▸ **verb** (past and past part. **clung** /kləNG/) (**cling to/on to**) **1** hold on tightly to. **2** stick to: *her hair clung to her damp skin*. **3** be unwilling to give up a belief or hope: *she clung to her convictions*. **4** be emotionally dependent on someone.

– SYNONYMS **1 hold on,** clutch, grip, grasp, clasp, hang on, embrace, hug. **2 stick,** adhere, hold.

– ORIGIN Old English.

cling·y /ˈkliNGē/ ▸ **adjective** (**clingier, clingiest**) **1** (of a garment) clinging to the body. **2** (of a person) too emotionally dependent on someone else.
– DERIVATIVES **cling·i·ness** noun.

clin·ic /ˈklinik/ ▸ **noun 1** a place where or time when specialized medical treatment or advice is given. **2** an occasion at which advice and training in a particular subject or activity is given: *a tennis clinic*.
– ORIGIN from Greek *klinē* 'bed.'

clin·i·cal /ˈklinikəl/ ▸ **adjective 1** relating to the observation and treatment of patients (rather than theoretical studies). **2** without feeling or sympathy: *she looked at him with clinical detachment*. **3** (of a place) very clean and plain.

– SYNONYMS **1 detached,** impersonal, dispassionate, indifferent, uninvolved, distant, remote, aloof, cold. **2 plain,** stark, austere, spartan, bleak, bare, functional, basic, institutional.
– ANTONYMS emotional.

– DERIVATIVES **clin·i·cal·ly** /ˈklinik(ə)lē/ adverb.

clin·i·cal psy·chol·o·gy ▶ **noun** the branch of psychology concerned with the assessment and treatment of mental illness and behavioral problems.

cli·ni·cian /kləˈnisʜən/ ▶ **noun** a doctor having direct contact with and responsibility for treating patients, rather than one involved with theoretical studies.

clink[1] /klinɢk/ ▶ **noun** a sharp ringing sound, like that made when metal or glass is struck. ▶ **verb** make or cause to make a clink.
– ORIGIN Dutch *klinken.*

clink[2] ▶ **noun** informal prison.
– ORIGIN unknown.

clink·er[1] /ˈklinɢkər/ ▶ **noun** the stony remains from burned coal or from a furnace.
– ORIGIN Dutch *klinken* 'to clink.'

clink·er[2] ▶ **noun** informal something that is unsatisfactory, of poor quality, or a failure: *marketing couldn't save such clinkers as these films.*
– ORIGIN originally referring to a person or thing that clinks.

clip[1] /klip/ ▶ **noun 1** a flexible or spring-loaded device for holding an object or objects together or in place. **2** a piece of jewelry that can be fastened onto a garment with a clip. **3** a metal holder containing cartridges for an automatic firearm.

– SYNONYMS **fastener,** clasp, hasp, catch, hook, buckle, lock.

▶ **verb** (**clips, clipping, clipped**) fasten something with a clip or clips.

– SYNONYMS **fasten,** attach, fix, join, pin, staple, tack.

– ORIGIN Old English.

clip[2] ▶ **verb** (**clips, clipping, clipped**) **1** cut or trim something, or cut something out with shears or scissors. **2** trim an animal's hair or wool. **3** strike someone or something with a sharp blow.

– SYNONYMS **1 trim,** prune, cut, snip, crop, shear, lop. **2 hit,** strike, graze, glance off, nudge, scrape.

▶ **noun 1** an act of clipping something. **2** a short sequence taken from a movie or broadcast. **3** informal a sharp blow. **4** informal a rapid speed: *they went by at a fast clip.*

– SYNONYMS **1 trim,** cut, crop, haircut. **2 extract,** excerpt, snippet, fragment, trailer.

– ORIGIN Old Norse.

clip art ▶ **noun** digital pictures and symbols provided with word-processing software.

clip·board /ˈklipˌbôrd/ ▶ **noun** a small board with a spring clip at the top, used for holding papers and providing support for writing.

clip joint ▶ **noun** informal a nightclub or bar that charges extremely high prices.

clipped /klipt/ ▶ **adjective** (of speech) having short, sharp vowel sounds and clear pronunciation.

clip·per /ˈklipər/ ▶ **noun 1** (**clippers**) an instrument for clipping. **2** a fast sailing ship of the 19th century.

clip·ping /ˈklipiɴɢ/ ▶ **noun 1** a small piece trimmed from something: *grass clippings.* **2** an article cut out of a newspaper or magazine.

clique /klēk, klik/ ▶ **noun** a small group of people who spend time together and are unwilling to allow others to join them.

– SYNONYMS **coterie,** set, circle, ring, in-crowd, group, gang, fraternity.

– DERIVATIVES **cli·quey** adjective **cli·quish** adjective.
– ORIGIN French.

clit·o·ris /ˈklitərəs/ ▶ **noun** a small sensitive organ at the front end of the female external genitals.
– DERIVATIVES **clit·o·ral** /ˈklitərəl/ adjective.
– ORIGIN Greek *kleitoris.*

clo·a·ca /klōˈākə/ ▶ **noun** (in some animals) a cavity at the end of the digestive tract into which the urinary and reproductive systems also open, leading to a single opening in the body.
– ORIGIN Latin, 'sewer.'

cloak /klōk/ ▶ **noun 1** an outer garment that hangs loosely from the shoulders over the arms to the knees or ankles. **2** something that hides or covers: *a cloak of secrecy.*

– SYNONYMS **1 cape,** robe, wrap, mantle. **2** *a cloak of secrecy* **cover,** veil, mantle, shroud, screen, blanket.

▶ **verb 1** hide or cover: *the summit was cloaked in thick mist.* **2** (as adj. **cloaked**) wearing a cloak.

– SYNONYMS **conceal,** hide, cover, veil, shroud, mask, obscure, cloud, envelop, swathe, surround.

– ORIGIN Old French *cloke.*

cloak-and-dag·ger ▶ **adjective** involving intrigue and secrecy.

cloak·room /ˈklōkˌro͞om, -ˌro͝om/ ▶ **noun** a room in a public building where outdoor clothes and bags may be left.

clob·ber /ˈklābər/ ▶ **verb 1** hit someone hard. **2** defeat a person or team heavily. ▶ **noun** Brit. clothing and personal belongings.
– ORIGIN unknown.

cloche /klōsʜ/ ▶ **noun 1** a small glass or plastic cover for protecting outdoor plants or making them develop faster than usual. **2** (also **cloche hat**) a woman's close-fitting bell-shaped hat.
– ORIGIN French, 'bell.'

clock /kläk/ ▶ **noun 1** an instrument that measures and indicates the time by means of a dial or a digital display. **2** informal a measuring device resembling a clock, such as a speedometer. ▶ **verb 1** reach or achieve a particular time, distance, or speed. **2** (**clock in/out**) record the time of one's arrival at or departure from work, especially by inserting a card in a special clock. **3** informal, chiefly Brit. hit someone on the head.
– PHRASES **around the clock** all day and all night. **turn back the clock** return to the past or to a previous way of doing things.
– ORIGIN Latin *clocca* 'bell.'

clock-watch·er ▶ **noun** a person who constantly checks the time to make sure that they do not work longer than they are supposed to.

clock·wise /ˈkläkˌwīz/ ▶ **adverb & adjective** in the direction of the movement of the hands of a clock.

clock·work /ˈkläkˌwərk/ ▶ **noun** a mechanism with a spring and toothed gearwheels, used to drive a mechanical clock, toy, or other device.
– PHRASES **like clockwork** very smoothly and easily.

clod /kläd/ ▶ **noun 1** a lump of earth. **2** informal a stupid person.

– ORIGIN variant of **CLOT**.

clod·dish /ˈklädisн/ ▶ **adjective** foolish, awkward, or clumsy.

clod·hop·per /ˈkläd,häpər/ ▶ **noun** informal **1** a large, heavy shoe. **2** a foolish, awkward, or clumsy person.

clog /kläg, klôg/ ▶ **noun** a shoe with a thick wooden sole. ▶ **verb** (**clogs, clogging, clogged**) block or become blocked: *the gutters were clogged with leaves.*

– SYNONYMS **block,** obstruct, congest, jam, choke, bung up, plug, stop up.

– ORIGIN unknown.

cloi·son·né /,kloizəˈnā, ,klwäz-/ ▶ **noun** enamel work in which the different colors in the design are separated by strips of flattened wire placed on a metal backing.
– ORIGIN French, 'partitioned.'

clois·ter /ˈkloistər/ ▶ **noun 1** a covered passage around an open courtyard in a convent, monastery, college, or cathedral, usually having a row of columns on the inner side. **2** (**the cloister**) the secluded life of a monk or nun.
– ORIGIN Old French *cloistre*, from Latin *claustrum* 'lock, enclosed place.'

clois·tered /ˈkloistərd/ ▶ **adjective 1** having or enclosed by a cloister: *a cloistered walkway.* **2** protected from the problems of ordinary life.

clomp /klämp, klômp/ ▶ **verb** walk heavily.
– ORIGIN imitating the sound.

clone /klōn/ ▶ **noun 1** an animal or plant produced from the cells of another, to which it is genetically identical. **2** a person or thing regarded as an exact copy of another. ▶ **verb 1** create an animal or plant as a clone. **2** make an identical copy of something.
– ORIGIN Greek *klōn* 'twig.'

clonk /klängk, kbôngk/ ▶ **noun** a loud sound made by heavy things hitting each other. ▶ **verb 1** move with or make a clonk. **2** informal hit.
– ORIGIN imitating the sound.

clop /kläp/ ▶ **noun** a sound made by a horse's hooves on a hard surface. ▶ **verb** (**clops, clopping, clopped**) move with such a sound.

close¹ /klōs/ ▶ **adjective 1** only a short distance away or apart in space or time. **2** (**close to**) almost doing or being something: *she was close to tears.* **3** (of a connection or resemblance) strong. **4** (of a person) part of someone's immediate family: *a close relative.* **5** (of a relationship or the people in it) very affectionate or intimate. **6** (of observation or examination) done in a careful and thorough way. **7** uncomfortably humid or airless.

– SYNONYMS **1 near,** nearby, adjacent, neighboring, adjoining, abutting, at hand. **2 neck and neck,** even, nip and tuck. **3 intimate,** dear, bosom, close-knit, inseparable, devoted, faithful, special, firm. **4** *a close resemblance* **noticeable,** marked, distinct, pronounced, strong. **5 careful,** detailed, thorough, minute, searching, painstaking, meticulous, rigorous. **6 humid,** muggy, stuffy, airless, heavy, sticky, sultry, stifling.
– ANTONYMS far, distant.

▶ **adverb** so as to be very near.
▶ **noun** Brit. **1** a residential street from which there is no access to other streets. **2** the grounds surrounding a cathedral.
– DERIVATIVES **close·ly** adverb **close·ness** noun.
– PHRASES **at close quarters** (or **range**) very near to someone or something. **close-knit** (of a group of people) united by strong relationships and common interests. **close-run** (of a contest) won or lost by a very small amount. **close shave** (also **close call**) informal a narrow escape from danger or disaster.
– ORIGIN Old French *clos*, from Latin *claudere* 'close, shut.'

close² /klōz/ ▶ **verb 1** move something so as to cover an opening. **2** bring two parts of something together: *she closed the book.* **3** (**close on/in on**) gradually get nearer to or surround someone or something. **4** (**close in**) (of bad weather or darkness) gradually surround someone. **5** (**close in**) (of days) get successively shorter with the approach of the winter solstice. **6** (**close around/over**) encircle and hold. **7** bring or come to an end. **8** finish speaking or writing. **9** (often **close down/up**) (with reference to a business or other organization) stop or cause to stop trading or operating. **10** bring to a conclusion: *he closed a deal with one of the supermarkets.*

– SYNONYMS **1** *she closed the door* **shut,** pull (shut), push (shut), slam. **2** *close the hole* **block,** stop up, plug, seal, bung up, clog up, choke, obstruct. **3 end,** conclude, finish, terminate, wind up. **4 shut down,** close down, cease production, cease trading, be wound up, go out of business; informal fold, go to the wall, go bust. **5 clinch,** settle, secure, seal, confirm, pull off, conclude, finalize; informal wrap up.
– ANTONYMS open, start.

▶ **noun** the end of an event or of a period of time or activity.

– SYNONYMS **end,** finish, conclusion.
– ANTONYMS beginning.

– ORIGIN Old French *clore*, from Latin *claudere.*

closed /klōzd/ ▶ **adjective 1** not open or allowing access. **2** not communicating with or influenced by others: *a closed society.*
– PHRASES **behind closed doors** in private. **a closed book** a subject or person about which one knows nothing.

closed cap·tion ▶ **noun** one of a series of subtitles to a television program, accessible through a decoder.
– DERIVATIVES **closed-cap·tion·ing** noun.

closed-cir·cuit tel·e·vi·sion ▶ **noun** a television system in which the signals are transmitted from one or more cameras by cable to a restricted set of monitors.

closed shop ▶ **noun** a place of work where all employees must belong to a particular labor union.

close har·mo·ny /klōs/ ▶ **noun** Music harmony in which the notes of the chord are close together, typically in vocal music.

close-mouthed /ˈklōs ˈmouthd, ˈmoutht/ ▶ **noun** reticent; not communicating freely: *the candidates have been close-mouthed about their fund-raising goals.*

clos·et /ˈkläzit/ ▶ **noun 1** a tall cupboard or wardrobe. **2** a small room. **3** old use a toilet.

– SYNONYMS **cupboard,** wardrobe, cabinet, locker.

▶ **adjective** secret: *a closet socialist.*

– SYNONYMS **secret,** covert, private, surreptitious, clandestine.

▶ **verb** (**closets, closeting, closeted**) **1** shut oneself away in private to talk to someone or to be alone: *he closeted himself in his room.* **2** (as adj. **closeted**) keeping the fact of being homosexual secret.

– SYNONYMS **shut away,** sequester, seclude, cloister, confine, isolate.

– PHRASES **in** (or **out of**) **the closet** not admitting (or admitting) that one is homosexual.
– ORIGIN Old French.

close-up /ˈklōs ˌəp/ ▶ **noun** a photograph, movie, or video taken at close range.

clo·sure /ˈklōZHər/ ▶ **noun** **1** an act or process of closing something. **2** a device that closes or seals something. **3** (in a parliament) a procedure for ending a debate and taking a vote. **4** a feeling that an emotional or upsetting experience has been resolved.
– ORIGIN from Latin *claudere* 'to close.'

clot /klät/ ▶ **noun** a thick semisolid mass formed from a liquid substance, especially blood.

– SYNONYMS **lump,** clump, mass, thrombosis; informal glob.

▶ **verb** (**clots, clotting, clotted**) form into clots.

– SYNONYMS **coagulate,** set, congeal, thicken, solidify.

– ORIGIN Old English.

cloth /klôTH/ ▶ **noun** (pl. **cloths**) **1** fabric made by weaving or knitting a soft fiber such as wool or cotton. **2** a piece of cloth used for a particular purpose. **3** (**the cloth**) Christian priests as a group.

– SYNONYMS **1 fabric,** material, textile(s), stuff. **2 rag,** wipe, duster, flannel.

– ORIGIN Old English.

clothe /klō<u>TH</u>/ ▶ **verb** (past and past part. **clothed** or old use or literary **clad** /klad/) **1** provide someone with clothes. **2** (**be clothed in**) be dressed in.

– SYNONYMS **dress,** attire, robe, garb, costume, swathe, deck (out), turn out, fit out, rig (out); informal get up.

– ORIGIN Old English.

clothes /klō(<u>TH</u>)z/ ▶ **plural noun** things worn to cover the body.

– SYNONYMS **clothing,** garments, attire, garb, dress, wear, costume, wardrobe; informal gear, togs, threads, getup. formal apparel.

WORD LINKS

sartorial *relating to clothes*
clothier, couturier, tailor *person who sells or makes clothes*

clothes horse ▶ **noun** **1** a frame on which washed clothes are hung to dry. **2** informal a person who models or is over-concerned with wearing fashionable clothes.

clothes·line /ˈklō(<u>TH</u>)zˌlīn/ ▶ **noun** a rope or wire on which washed clothes are hung to dry.

clothes moth ▶ **noun** a small brown moth whose larvae can damage fabric, especially wool.

clothes·pin /ˈklō(<u>TH</u>)zˌpin/ ▶ **noun** a wooden or plastic clip for securing clothes to a clothesline.

cloth·ier /ˈklō<u>TH</u>yər, -<u>TH</u>ēər/ ▶ **noun** a person who makes or sells clothes or cloth.

cloth·ing /ˈklō<u>TH</u>iNG/ ▶ **noun** clothes.

clot·ted cream ▶ **noun** chiefly Brit. thick cream made by heating milk slowly and then allowing it to cool while the cream rises to the top in lumps.

clo·ture /ˈklōCHər/ ▶ **noun** (in a legislature) a procedure for ending a debate and taking a vote.

cloud /kloud/ ▶ **noun** **1** a white or gray mass of condensed watery vapor floating in the atmosphere. **2** a mass of smoke, dust, etc. **3** a large number of insects or birds moving together. **4** a state or cause of gloom or anxiety: *injury worries cast a cloud over the team's preparations.*

– SYNONYMS *a cloud of exhaust smoke* **mass,** billow, mantle, blanket, pall.

▶ **verb** **1** (**cloud over**) (of the sky) become full of clouds. **2** make or become less clear: *all sorts of doubts clouded my mind.* **3** (of someone's face or eyes) show sadness, anxiety, or anger.

– SYNONYMS **confuse,** muddle, obscure.

– DERIVATIVES **cloud·less** adjective.
– PHRASES **have one's head in the clouds** be full of idealistic dreams. **on cloud nine** extremely happy. **under a cloud** under suspicion of having done wrong.
– ORIGIN Old English, 'mass of rock or earth.'

cloud·burst /ˈkloudˌbərst/ ▶ **noun** a sudden violent rainstorm.

cloud·y /ˈkloudē/ ▶ **adjective** **1** covered with clouds; having many clouds. **2** (of a liquid) not clear or transparent.

– SYNONYMS **1 overcast,** dark, gray, black, leaden, murky, gloomy, sunless, starless. **2 murky,** muddy, milky, dirty, turbid.
– ANTONYMS clear, sunny.

– DERIVATIVES **cloud·i·ness** noun.

clout /klout/ informal ▶ **noun** **1** a heavy blow. **2** influence or power. ▶ **verb** hit someone hard.
– ORIGIN Old English, 'a patch or metal plate.'

clove[1] /klōv/ ▶ **noun** **1** the dried flower bud of a tropical tree, used as a spice. **2** (**oil of cloves**) a strong-smelling oil extracted from these flower buds and used for the relief of toothache.
– ORIGIN from Old French *clou de girofle* 'nail of gillyflower' (from the shape of the flower buds), gillyflower being originally the name of the spice.

clove[2] ▶ **noun** any of the small bulbs making up a compound bulb of garlic.
– ORIGIN Old English.

clove[3] past of CLEAVE[1].

clove hitch ▶ **noun** a knot used to fasten a rope to a spar or another rope.
– ORIGIN *clove,* past tense of CLEAVE[1] (because the rope appears as separate parallel lines at the back of the knot).

clo·ven /ˈklōvən/ past participle of CLEAVE[1].

clo·ven hoof (also **cloven foot**) ▶ **noun** the divided hoof or foot of animals such as cattle, sheep, goats, and deer.

clo·ver /ˈklōvər/ ▶ **noun** a plant with round white or deep pink flowerheads and leaves with three rounded parts.
– PHRASES **in clover** living a comfortable life with plenty of money.
– ORIGIN Old English.

clo·ver·leaf /ˈklōvərˌlēf/ ▶ **noun** a junction of roads intersecting at different levels with connecting sections forming the pattern of a four-leaf clover. ▶ **adjective** having a shape or pattern resembling a leaf of clover, especially a four-leaf clover.

clown /kloun/ ▶ **noun** **1** a comic entertainer, especially one in a circus, wearing a traditional costume and exaggerated makeup. **2** a playful and amusing person. **3** a foolish or incompetent person.

– SYNONYMS **1 joker,** comedian, comic, wag, wit, jester. **2 fool,** idiot, buffoon, dolt, ignoramus; informal moron, ass, numbskull, halfwit, fathead, twerp; Brit. informal twit.

▶ **verb** behave in a silly or playful way.
– DERIVATIVES **clown·ish** adjective.
– ORIGIN perhaps German.

cloy·ing /kloi-ING/ ▶ **adjective** so sweet or sentimental as to be unpleasant.
– DERIVATIVES **cloy·ing·ly** adverb.
– ORIGIN from Old French *encloyer* 'drive a nail into.'

club[1] /kləb/ ▶ **noun 1** an association of people who meet regularly to take part in a particular activity. **2** an organization where members can meet, eat meals, and stay overnight. **3** a nightclub with dance music.

> – SYNONYMS **1 society,** association, group, circle, league, guild, union. **2 team,** squad, side. **3 nightclub,** bar, discotheque, disco.

▶ **verb** (**clubs, clubbing, clubbed**) informal go out to nightclubs.
– DERIVATIVES **club·ber** noun.
– ORIGIN from CLUB[2].

club[2] ▶ **noun 1** a heavy stick with a thick end, used as a weapon. **2** (also **golf club**) a club used to hit the ball in golf, with a heavy wooden or metal head on a slender shaft. **3** (**clubs**) one of the four suits in a conventional deck of playing cards, represented by a design of three black leaves on a short stem.

> – SYNONYMS **stick,** cudgel, truncheon, bludgeon, baton, mace, bat, blackjack, nightstick.

▶ **verb** (**clubs, clubbing, clubbed**) beat someone or something with a club or similar object.

> – SYNONYMS **hit,** beat, strike, cudgel, bludgeon, batter; informal clout, clobber.

– ORIGIN Old Norse.

club·by /'kləbē/ ▶ **adjective** (**clubbier, clubbiest**) informal friendly and sociable with fellow members of a group or organization but not with outsiders.

club foot ▶ **noun** a deformed foot that is twisted so that the sole cannot be placed flat on the ground.

club·house /'kləbˌhous/ ▶ **noun** a building having a bar and other facilities for the members of a club.

club·moss /'kləbˌmos, -ˌmän/ ▶ **noun** a low-growing flowerless plant.

club·root /'kləbˌro͞ot, -ˌro͝ot/ ▶ **noun** a disease of cabbages, turnips, etc., in which the root becomes swollen and distorted.

club sand·wich ▶ **noun** a sandwich consisting typically of ham, turkey, or chicken and bacon, tomato, and lettuce, layered between three slices of bread.

club so·da ▶ **noun** another term for SODA (sense 2).

cluck /klək/ ▶ **verb 1** (of a hen) make a short, low sound. **2** (**cluck over/around**) express fussy concern about someone. ▶ **noun** the short, low sound made by a hen.
– ORIGIN imitating the sound.

clue /klo͞o/ ▶ **noun** a fact or piece of evidence that helps to clear up a mystery or solve a problem.

> – SYNONYMS **hint,** indication, sign, signal, pointer, lead, tip, evidence.

▶ **verb** (**clues, clueing, clued**) (**clue someone in**) informal inform someone about something.
– PHRASES **not have a clue** informal not know about something, or about how to do something.
– ORIGIN first meaning a ball of thread, as used to guide a person out of a maze.

clue·less /'klo͞oləs/ ▶ **adjective** informal having no knowledge, understanding, or ability.
– DERIVATIVES **clue·less·ness** noun.

clump /kləmp/ ▶ **noun 1** a small group of trees or plants growing closely together. **2** a mass or lump of something. **3** the sound of heavy footsteps.

> – SYNONYMS **1** *a clump of trees* **cluster,** thicket, group, bunch. **2** *a clump of earth* **lump,** clod, mass, chunk.

▶ **verb 1** form into a clump or mass. **2** walk or tread heavily.
– ORIGIN from CLUB[2].

clump·y /'kləmpē/ ▶ **adjective 1** containing or tending to form clumps. **2** (of shoes or boots) heavy and clumsy-looking.

clum·sy /'kləmzē/ ▶ **adjective** (**clumsier, clumsiest**) **1** not smooth or graceful in movement or action. **2** difficult to handle or use. **3** tactless.

> – SYNONYMS **1 awkward,** uncoordinated, ungainly, graceless, lumbering, inelegant, inept, unskillful, accident-prone, all fingers and thumbs; informal klutzy, having two left feet, ham-fisted, butterfingered. **2 unwieldy,** cumbersome, bulky, awkward.
> – ANTONYMS graceful.

– DERIVATIVES **clum·si·ly** /-zəlē/ adverb **clum·si·ness** noun.
– ORIGIN probably Scandinavian.

clung /kləNG/ past and past participle of CLING.

clunk /kləNGk/ ▶ **noun** a dull, heavy sound like that made by thick pieces of metal striking together. ▶ **verb** move with or make a clunk.
– ORIGIN imitating the sound.

clunk·y /'kləNGkē/ ▶ **adjective** (**clunkier, clunkiest**) informal **1** solid, heavy, and old-fashioned. **2** making a clunking sound.

clus·ter /'kləstər/ ▶ **noun** a group of similar things positioned or occurring closely together.

> – SYNONYMS **bunch,** clump, mass, knot, group, clutch, huddle, crowd.

▶ **verb** form a cluster.

> – SYNONYMS **congregate,** gather, collect, group, assemble, huddle, crowd.

– ORIGIN Old English.

clus·ter bomb ▶ **noun** a bomb that releases a number of smaller bombs when it explodes.

clutch[1] /kləCH/ ▶ **verb** grasp something tightly.

> – SYNONYMS **grip,** grasp, clasp, cling to, hang on to, clench, hold, grab, snatch.

▶ **noun 1** a tight grasp. **2** (**clutches**) power or control: *he had fallen into her clutches.* **3** a mechanism for connecting and disconnecting the engine and the transmission system in a vehicle.
– ORIGIN Old English.

clutch[2] ▶ **noun 1** a group of eggs fertilized at the same time and laid in a single session. **2** a brood of chicks. **3** a small group of people or things.
– ORIGIN Old Norse.

clutch bag ▶ **noun** a slim, flat handbag without handles or a strap.

clut·ter /'klətər/ ▶ **verb** cover or fill something with an untidy collection of things.

> – SYNONYMS **litter,** mess up, be strewn, be scattered, cover, bury.

▶ **noun 1** things lying around untidily. **2** an untidy state.

– SYNONYMS **disorder,** chaos, mess, disarray, untidiness, confusion, litter, rubbish, junk.

– ORIGIN variant of dialect *clotter* 'to clot.'

Cm ▶ **symbol** the chemical element curium.

cm ▶ **abbreviation** centimeter or centimeters.

Cmdr. ▶ **abbreviation** commander.

Cmdre. ▶ **abbreviation** Commodore.

CNN ▶ **abbreviation** Cable News Network.

CO ▶ **abbreviation 1** Colorado. **2** Commanding Officer.

Co ▶ **symbol** the chemical element cobalt.

Co. ▶ **abbreviation 1** company. **2** county.

co- ▶ **prefix 1** (forming nouns) joint; mutual; common: *co-driver*. **2** (forming adjectives) jointly; mutually: *coequal*. **3** (forming verbs) together with another or others: *co-produce*.
– ORIGIN Latin.

c/o ▶ **abbreviation** care of.

coach[1] /kōCH/ ▶ **noun 1** a closed horse-drawn carriage. **2** a railroad car. **3** Brit. a bus with comfortable seats, used for longer journeys.
– ORIGIN French *coche*, from *Kocs*, a town in Hungary where horse-drawn carriages were made.

coach[2] ▶ **noun 1** an athletic instructor or trainer. **2** a tutor who gives private or specialized teaching.

– SYNONYMS **instructor,** trainer, teacher, tutor, mentor, guru.

▶ **verb** train or teach someone as a coach.

– SYNONYMS **instruct,** teach, tutor, school, educate, drill, train.

– ORIGIN from COACH[1].

coach·man /'kōCHmən/ ▶ **noun** (pl. **coachmen**) a driver of a horse-drawn carriage.

co·ag·u·lant /kō'agyələnt/ ▶ **noun** a substance that causes a fluid to coagulate.

co·ag·u·late /kō'agyə,lāt/ ▶ **verb** (of a fluid, especially blood) change to a solid or semisolid state.

– SYNONYMS **congeal,** clot, thicken, solidify, harden, set, dry.

– DERIVATIVES **co·ag·u·la·tion** /kō,agyə'lāSHən/ noun.
– ORIGIN Latin *coagulare* 'curdle.'

coal /kōl/ ▶ **noun 1** a black rock consisting mainly of carbon formed from the remains of ancient trees and other vegetation and used as fuel. **2** a red-hot piece of coal or other material in a fire.
– ORIGIN Old English.

co·a·lesce /,kōə'les/ ▶ **verb** come or bring together to form one mass or whole.
– DERIVATIVES **co·a·les·cence** noun.
– ORIGIN Latin *coalescere*.

coal·face /'kōl,fās/ ▶ **noun** an exposed area of coal in a mine.

coal·field /'kōl,fēld/ ▶ **noun** a large area rich in underground coal.

co·a·li·tion /,kōə'liSHən/ ▶ **noun** a temporary alliance, especially of political parties forming a government.

– SYNONYMS **alliance,** union, partnership, bloc, federation, league, association, confederation, consortium, syndicate, amalgamation, merger.

– DERIVATIVES **co·a·li·tion·ist** noun.
– ORIGIN Latin, from *coalescere* 'coalesce.'

coal tar ▶ **noun** a thick black liquid distilled from coal, containing various organic chemicals.

coam·ing /'kōmiNG/ (also **coamings**) ▶ **noun** a raised border around the cockpit or hatch of a boat to keep out water.
– ORIGIN unknown.

coarse /kôrs/ ▶ **adjective 1** rough or harsh in texture. **2** consisting of large grains or particles. **3** rude or vulgar in behavior or speech.

– SYNONYMS **1 rough,** scratchy, prickly, wiry, harsh. **2** *coarse manners* **uncouth,** oafish, loutish, boorish, rude, impolite, ill-mannered, vulgar, common, rough. **3** *a coarse remark* **vulgar,** crude, rude, off color, lewd, smutty, indelicate.
– ANTONYMS soft, refined, polite.

– DERIVATIVES **coarse·ly** adverb **coarse·ness** noun.
– ORIGIN perhaps related to COURSE.

coars·en /'kôrsən/ ▶ **verb** make or become coarse.

coast /kōst/ ▶ **noun** land next to or near the sea.

– SYNONYMS **shore,** coastline, seashore, seaboard, shoreline, seaside; literary strand.

▶ **verb 1** move easily without using power. **2** achieve something without making much effort: *the team coasted to victory*.

– SYNONYMS **freewheel,** cruise, taxi, drift, glide, sail.

– DERIVATIVES **coast·al** adjective.
– PHRASES **the coast is clear** there is no danger of being seen or caught.
– ORIGIN Latin *costa* 'rib, flank, side.'

WORD LINKS

littoral *relating to a coast or seashore*

coast·er /'kōstər/ ▶ **noun 1** a small mat for a glass. **2** a ship carrying cargo along the coast from port to port.

coast guard ▶ **noun 1** (**Coast Guard**) a branch of the US armed forces responsible for the enforcement of maritime law and for the protection of life and property at sea. **2** a civilian or volunteer organization keeping watch on the sea near a coast in order to assist people or ships in danger and to prevent smuggling.

coast·line /'kōst,līn/ ▶ **noun** a stretch of coast: *a rugged coastline*.

coat /kōt/ ▶ **noun 1** a full-length outer garment with sleeves. **2** an animal's covering of fur or hair. **3** an enclosing or covering layer or structure. **4** a single application of paint or similar substance.

– SYNONYMS **1 fur,** hair, wool, fleece, hide, pelt, skin. **2 layer,** covering, coating, skin, film, deposit.

▶ **verb** provide with or form a layer or covering: *vanilla ice cream coated with chocolate*.

– SYNONYMS **cover,** surface, plate, spread, daub, smear, plaster, cake.

– ORIGIN Old French *cote*.

co·a·ti /kō'ätē/ ▶ **noun** (pl. **coatis**) a raccoonlike animal found in Central and South America, with a long flexible snout and a tail with circular stripes.
– ORIGIN Spanish and Portuguese.

co·a·ti·mun·di /kō,äti'məndē/ ▶ **noun** (pl. **coatimundis**) another term for COATI.
– ORIGIN Portuguese.

coat·ing /ˈkōtiNG/ ▶ **noun** a thin layer or covering of something.

coat of arms ▶ **noun** the distinctive heraldic design or shield of a person, family, corporation, or country.

coat of mail ▶ **noun** historical a jacket made of metal rings or plates, used as armor.

coat·tail /ˈkōtˌtāl/ ▶ **noun** each of the flaps formed by the back of a tailcoat.
– PHRASES **on someone's coattails** benefiting from someone else's success.

coax[1] /kōks/ ▶ **verb 1** gradually or gently persuade someone to do something. **2** manipulate something carefully into a particular situation or position.

– SYNONYMS **persuade,** wheedle, cajole, get around, inveigle, maneuver; informal sweet-talk, soft-soap, twist someone's arm.

– ORIGIN from the old word *cokes*, 'simpleton.'

coax[2] /ˈkō-aks, kōˈaks/ ▶ **noun** informal coaxial cable.

co·ax·i·al /kōˈaksēəl/ ▶ **adjective 1** having a common axis. **2** (of a cable or line) transmitting by means of two concentric conductors separated by an insulator.

cob /käb/ ▶ **noun 1** a corncob. **2** (also **cobnut**) a hazelnut or filbert. **3** a powerfully built, short-legged horse. **4** a male swan.
– ORIGIN unknown.

co·balt /ˈkōˌbôlt/ ▶ **noun** a hard silvery-white metallic chemical element, used in alloys.
– ORIGIN German *Kobalt* 'goblin, demon' (from the belief that cobalt had been placed in silver mines by goblins to cause the miners problems).

co·balt blue ▶ **noun** a deep blue pigment containing cobalt and aluminum oxides.

cob·ble[1] /ˈkäbəl/ ▶ **noun** (also **cobblestone**) a small round stone used to cover road surfaces.
– DERIVATIVES **cob·bled** adjective.
– ORIGIN from **COB**.

cob·ble[2] ▶ **verb** (**cobble something together**) produce something quickly and without great care: *the movie was cobbled together from two separate stories.*
– ORIGIN from **COBBLER**.

cob·bler /ˈkäblər/ ▶ **noun 1** a person whose job is mending shoes. **2** a fruit pie with a rich crust on top.
– ORIGIN unknown.

COBOL /ˈkōˌbôl/ ▶ **noun** a computer programming language designed for use in commerce.
– ORIGIN from *co(mmon) b(usiness) o(riented) l(anguage)*.

co·bra /ˈkōbrə/ ▶ **noun** a highly poisonous snake that spreads the skin of its neck into a hood when disturbed, native to Africa and Asia.
– ORIGIN from Portuguese *cobra de capello* 'snake with hood.'

cob·web /ˈkäbˌweb/ ▶ **noun** a spider's web, especially an old or dusty one.
– DERIVATIVES **cob·webbed** adjective **cob·web·by** adjective.
– ORIGIN from Old English *coppe* 'spider.'

co·ca /ˈkōkə/ ▶ **noun** a tropical American shrub grown for its leaves, which are the source of cocaine.
– ORIGIN Spanish.

Co·ca-Co·la ▶ **noun** trademark a carbonated nonalcoholic drink.

co·caine /kōˈkān, ˈkōˌkān/ ▶ **noun** an addictive drug obtained from coca or prepared synthetically, used as an illegal stimulant and sometimes in medicine as a local anesthetic.
– ORIGIN from **COCA**.

coc·cus /ˈkäkəs/ ▶ **noun** (pl. **cocci** /ˈkäkˌ(s)ī, ˈkäkˌ(s)ē/) Biology any rounded bacterium.
– ORIGIN Greek *kokkos* 'berry.'

coc·cyx /ˈkäksiks/ ▶ **noun** (pl. **coccyges** /ˈkäksəˌjēz/ or **coccyxes** /ˈkäksiksiz/) a small triangular bone at the base of the spinal column in humans and some apes.
– DERIVATIVES **coc·cyg·e·al** /käkˈsijēəl/ adjective.
– ORIGIN Greek *kokkux* 'cuckoo' (because the shape of the human bone resembles a cuckoo's bill).

coch·i·neal /ˈkäCHəˌnēəl, ˈkō-/ ▶ **noun** a scarlet dye used for coloring food, made from the crushed dried bodies of a kind of insect.
– ORIGIN French *cochenille* or Spanish *cochinilla*.

coch·le·a /ˈkōklēə, ˈkäk-/ ▶ **noun** (pl. **cochleae** /-lēˌē, -lēˌī/) the spiral cavity of the inner ear, containing an organ that produces nerve impulses in response to sound vibrations.
– DERIVATIVES **coch·le·ar** adjective.
– ORIGIN Latin, 'snail shell or screw.'

cock /käk/ ▶ **noun 1** a male bird, especially of a domestic fowl. **2** vulgar slang a man's penis. **3** a firing lever in a gun that can be raised to be released by the trigger. ▶ **verb 1** tilt or bend something in a particular direction. **2** raise the cock of a gun to make it ready for firing.
– PHRASES **cock one's ear** (of a dog) raise its ears to an erect position.
– ORIGIN Latin *coccus*.

cock·ade /käˈkād/ ▶ **noun** a rosette or knot of ribbons worn in a hat as a badge of office or as part of a livery.
– DERIVATIVES **cock·ad·ed** adjective.
– ORIGIN French *cocarde*.

cock-a-hoop /ˌkäk ə ˈho͞op, ˈho͝op/ ▶ **adjective** extremely pleased.
– ORIGIN from the phrase *set cock a hoop*, apparently referring to the action of turning on the tap of a cask and allowing alcohol to flow.

cock-a-leek·ie /ˌkäk ə ˈlēkē/ ▶ **noun** a soup traditionally made in Scotland with chicken and leeks.

cock and bull sto·ry ▶ **noun** informal an unbelievable story, especially one used as an excuse.

cock·a·tiel /ˈkäkəˌtēl/ ▶ **noun** a small crested Australian parrot with a mainly gray body and a yellow and orange face.
– ORIGIN Dutch *kaketielje*.

cock·a·too /ˈkäkəˌto͞o/ ▶ **noun** a crested parrot found in Australia and Indonesia.
– ORIGIN Dutch *kaketoe*.

cock·a·trice /ˈkäkətris, -ˌtrīs/ ▶ **noun 1** another term for **BASILISK** (sense 1). **2** Heraldry a mythical animal represented as a two-legged dragon with a cock's head.
– ORIGIN Old French *cocatris*.

cock·chaf·er /ˈkäkˌCHāfər/ ▶ **noun** a large brown flying beetle.
– ORIGIN from **COCK** + **CHAFER**.

cock·crow /ˈkäkˌkrō/ ▶ **noun** literary dawn.

cock·er·el /ˈkäkərəl/ ▶ **noun** a young domestic cock.

cock·er span·iel /ˈkäkər/ ▶ **noun** a small breed of spaniel with a silky coat.
– ORIGIN from **COCK**, because the dog was bred to flush game birds such as woodcock.

cock·eyed /ˈkäkˈīd/ ▸ **adjective** informal **1** crooked or askew; not level. **2** absurd; impractical. **3** drunk.

cock·fight·ing /ˈkäkˌfītiNG/ ▸ **noun** the sport (illegal in some countries) of setting two cocks to fight each other.
– DERIVATIVES **cock·fight** noun.

cock·le /ˈkäkəl/ ▸ **noun 1** an edible shellfish with a strong ribbed shell. **2** (also **cockleshell** /ˈkäkəlˌSHel/) literary a small, shallow boat.
– PHRASES **warm the cockles of one's heart** give one a feeling of contentment.
– ORIGIN Old French *coquille* 'shell.'

cock·ney /ˈkäknē/ ▸ **noun** (pl. **cockneys**) **1** a person from the East End of London, traditionally one born within the sound of Bow Bells. **2** the dialect or accent used in this area.
– ORIGIN uncertain.

cock·pit /ˈkäkˌpit/ ▸ **noun 1** a compartment for the pilot and crew in an aircraft or spacecraft. **2** the driver's compartment in a race car. **3** a place where cockfights are held.
– ORIGIN from **COCK** + **PIT**[1].

cock·roach /ˈkäkˌrōCH/ ▸ **noun** a beetlelike insect with long antennae and legs, some kinds of which are household pests.
– ORIGIN Spanish *cucaracha*.

cocks·comb /ˈkäksˌkōm/ ▸ **noun 1** the crest or comb of a domestic cock. **2** a tropical plant with a showy crest of flowers.

cock·sure /ˈkäkˈSHo͝or/ ▸ **adjective** arrogantly confident.
– ORIGIN from former *cock* (a euphemism for *God*) + **SURE**.

cock·tail /ˈkäkˌtāl/ ▸ **noun 1** an alcoholic drink consisting of a spirit mixed with other ingredients, such as fruit juice. **2** a dish consisting of a mixture of small pieces of food: *shrimp cocktail*. **3** a mixture of different substances or factors, especially when dangerous or unpleasant: *a cocktail of drugs*.
– ORIGIN first meaning a horse with a docked tail.

cock·y /ˈkäkē/ ▸ **adjective** (**cockier, cockiest**) conceited in a bold or impudent way.

> – SYNONYMS **arrogant,** conceited, overconfident, swollen-headed, self-important, full of oneself, egotistical, presumptuous, boastful; informal too big for one's boots.
> – ANTONYMS modest.

– DERIVATIVES **cock·i·ly** adverb **cock·i·ness** noun.
– ORIGIN from **COCK**.

co·coa /ˈkōkō/ ▸ **noun 1** a powder made from roasted and ground cacao seeds. **2** a hot drink made from cocoa powder mixed with milk or water.
– ORIGIN alteration of **CACAO**.

co·coa bean ▸ **noun** a cacao seed.

co·coa but·ter ▸ **noun** a fatty substance obtained from cocoa beans, used in confectionery and cosmetics.

co·co·nut /ˈkōkəˌnət/ ▸ **noun 1** the large brown seed of a tropical palm, consisting of a hard woody husk surrounded by fiber, lined with edible white flesh and containing a clear liquid (**coconut milk**). **2** the edible white flesh of a coconut.
– ORIGIN from Spanish and Portuguese *coco* 'grinning face.'

co·coon /kəˈko͞on/ ▸ **noun 1** a protective silky case spun by the larvae of many insects, in which the pupa develops. **2** a covering that prevents the corrosion of metal equipment. **3** something that envelops someone in a protective or comforting way: *a cocoon of sheets and blankets*. ▸ **verb** envelop in a protective or comforting way: *we were cocooned in our sleeping bags*.
– ORIGIN French *cocon*.

co·cotte /kôˈkôt, kəˈkät/ ▸ **noun** (usu. in phrase **en cocotte** /äN/) a small dish in which individual portions of food can be cooked and served.
– ORIGIN French.

COD ▸ **abbreviation** cash on delivery.

cod /käd/ (also **codfish**) ▸ **noun** (pl. same) a large sea fish that is important as a food fish.
– ORIGIN perhaps from Old English *codd* 'bag.'

co·da /ˈkōdə/ ▸ **noun 1** Music the concluding passage of a piece or movement. **2** a concluding event, remark, or section.
– ORIGIN Italian, from Latin *cauda* 'tail.'

cod·dle /ˈkädl/ ▸ **verb 1** treat someone in an indulgent or overprotective way. **2** cook an egg in water below the boiling point.
– ORIGIN uncertain.

code /kōd/ ▸ **noun 1** a system of words, figures, or symbols used to represent others, especially for the purposes of secrecy. **2** a series of numbers or letters used to classify or identify something. **3** (also **area code**) a sequence of numbers dialed to connect a telephone line with another exchange. **4** Computing program instructions. **5** a set of moral principles or rules of behavior: *a strict code of conduct*. **6** a systematic collection of laws or statutes: *the penal code*.

> – SYNONYMS **1 cipher**. **2 convention,** etiquette, protocol, ethic. **3 law(s),** rules, regulations, constitution, system.

▸ **verb 1** convert the words of a message into a code. **2** (usu. as adj. **coded**) express the meaning of something in an indirect way: *his coded criticism of the prime minister*.
– DERIVATIVES **cod·er** noun.
– ORIGIN Latin *codex* 'block of wood.'

co·deine /ˈkōˌdēn/ ▸ **noun** a painkilling drug obtained from morphine.
– ORIGIN Greek *kōdeia* 'poppy head.'

code name ▸ **noun** a word used for secrecy or convenience instead of the usual name.

co·de·pend·en·cy /ˌkōdəˈpendənsē/ ▸ **noun** the state of being too emotionally or psychologically dependent on a partner, especially one who has an illness or addiction and needs care or support.
– DERIVATIVES **co·de·pend·ence** /-dəns/ noun **co·de·pend·ent** /-dənt/ adjective & noun.

code·share /ˈkōdˌSHe(ə)r/ ▸ **noun 1** a marketing arrangement in which two airlines sell seats on a flight that one of them operates. **2** a flight or aircraft in which such an arrangement is in effect.
– DERIVATIVES **code·shar·ing** noun.

co·dex /ˈkōˌdeks/ ▸ **noun** (pl. **codices** /ˈkōdəˌsēz, ˈkäd-/ or **codexes**) **1** an ancient manuscript in book form. **2** an official list of medicines, chemicals, etc.
– ORIGIN Latin, 'block of wood.'

cod·fish /ˈkädˌfiSH/ ▸ **noun** (pl. same or **codfishes**) another term for **COD**.

codg·er /ˈkäjər/ ▸ **noun** informal, derogatory an elderly man.
– ORIGIN perhaps from **CADGE**.

cod·i·cil /ˈkädəsəl, -ˌsil/ ▸ **noun** an addition or supplement that explains, changes, or cancels a will or part of one.

– ORIGIN from *codex* 'block of wood.'

cod·i·fy /'kädə,fī, 'kōd-/ ▶ **verb** (**codifies, codifying, codified**) organize procedures or rules into a system.
– DERIVATIVES **cod·i·fi·ca·tion** /,kädəfə'kāsʜən, ,kōd-/ noun.

cod·ling /'kädlɪɴɢ/ ▶ **noun** a young cod.

cod·ling moth ▶ **noun** a small grayish moth whose larvae feed on apples.

cod liv·er oil ▶ **noun** oil obtained from the fresh liver of cod, which is rich in vitamins D and A.

co·don /'kō,dän/ ▶ **noun** Biochemistry a sequence of three nucleotides that together form a unit of genetic code in a DNA or RNA molecule.

cod·piece /'käd,pēs/ ▶ **noun** (in the 15th and 16th centuries) a pouch covering the genitals, attached to a pair of man's breeches.
– ORIGIN from former *cod* 'scrotum.'

co·ed /'kō,ed/ ▶ **noun** dated a female student at a co-educational institution. ▶ **adjective** (of an institution or system) co-educational.

co·ed·u·ca·tion /,kō,ejə'kāsʜən/ ▶ **noun** the education of students of both sexes together.
– DERIVATIVES **co·ed·u·ca·tion·al** adjective.

co·ef·fi·cient /,kōə'fisʜənt/ ▶ **noun 1** Mathematics a quantity placed before and multiplying the variable in an algebraic expression (e.g., *4* in $4x^2$). **2** Physics a multiplier or factor that measures a particular property.

coe·la·canth /'sēlə,kanᴛʜ/ ▶ **noun** a large bony sea fish with a tail fin in three rounded parts, known only from fossils until one was found alive in 1938.
– ORIGIN from Greek *koilos* 'hollow' + *akantha* 'spine' (because its fins have hollow spines).

coe·len·ter·ate /si'lentə,rāt, -rət/ ▶ **noun** Zoology a member of a large group of invertebrate sea animals that usually have a tube- or cup-shaped body with a single opening fringed with tentacles, such as jellyfish, corals, and sea anemones.
– ORIGIN from Greek *koilos* 'hollow' + *enteron* 'intestine.'

co·en·zyme /kō'en,zīm/ ▶ **noun** Biochemistry a compound that is essential for the functioning of an enzyme.

co·e·qual /kō'ēkwəl/ ▶ **adjective** (of two or more people or things) having the same rank or importance. ▶ **noun** a person or thing equal with another.

co·erce /kō'ərs/ ▶ **verb** persuade an unwilling person to do something by using force or threats.

> – SYNONYMS **pressure,** press, push, constrain, force, compel, oblige, browbeat, bully, threaten, intimidate, dragoon, twist someone's arm; informal railroad, lean on.

– DERIVATIVES **co·er·cion** /kō'ərzʜən, -sʜən/ noun **co·er·cive** /kō'ərsiv/ adjective.
– ORIGIN Latin *coercere* 'restrain.'

co·e·val /kō'ēvəl/ ▶ **adjective** having the same age or date of origin; contemporary. ▶ **noun** a person of roughly the same age as oneself; a contemporary.
– ORIGIN Latin *coaevus*.

co·ex·ist /,kō-ig'zist/ ▶ **verb 1** exist at the same time or in the same place. **2** exist together in a peaceful or harmonious way.
– DERIVATIVES **co·ex·ist·ence** /-'zistəns/ noun **co·ex·ist·ent** /-'zistənt/ adjective.

co·ex·ten·sive /,kō-ik'stensiv/ ▶ **adjective** formal extending over the same area, extent, or time: *we are not separate from but coextensive with nature.*

cof·fee /'kôfē, 'käfē/ ▶ **noun 1** a hot drink made from the roasted and ground beanlike seeds of a tropical shrub. **2** the seeds used to make this drink.
– ORIGIN Arabic.

cof·fee break ▶ **noun** a short rest from work during which refreshments are usually taken.

cof·fee cake ▶ **noun** a cake, often cinnamon-flavored, with a drizzled white icing or crumb topping and usually eaten with coffee.

cof·fee ta·ble ▶ **noun** a small, low table.

cof·fee-ta·ble book ▶ **noun** a large book with many pictures or photographs.

cof·fer /'kôfər, 'käfər/ ▶ **noun 1** a small chest for holding valuables. **2** (**coffers**) used to refer to the money that a government or organization has available to spend: *the company's coffers have run dry.* **3** a decorative sunken panel in a ceiling.
– ORIGIN Old French *coffre*.

cof·fer·dam /'kôfər,dam, 'käfər,dam/ ▶ **noun** a watertight enclosure pumped dry to allow construction work below the waterline, e.g., when building bridges or repairing a ship.

cof·fin /'kôfən, 'käf-/ ▶ **noun** a long, narrow box in which a dead body is buried or cremated.
– ORIGIN Old French *cofin* 'little basket.'

cog /käg/ ▶ **noun 1** a wheel or bar with a series of projections on its edge, which transfers motion by engaging with projections on another wheel or bar. **2** any one of these projections.
– ORIGIN probably Scandinavian.

co·gent /'kōjənt/ ▶ **adjective** (of an argument or case) clear, logical, and convincing.

> – SYNONYMS **convincing**, persuasive, compelling, strong, forceful, powerful, potent, effective, sound, telling, coherent, clear, lucid, logical, well argued.

– DERIVATIVES **co·gen·cy** /'kōjənsē/ noun **co·gent·ly** adverb.
– ORIGIN Latin *cogere* 'compel.'

cog·i·tate /'käjə,tāt/ ▶ **verb** formal think deeply.
– DERIVATIVES **cog·i·ta·tion** /,käjə'tāsʜən/ noun.
– ORIGIN Latin *cogitare* 'to consider.'

co·gnac /'kōn,yak, 'kän-, 'kôn-/ ▶ **noun** a high-quality brandy made in Cognac in western France.

cog·nate /'käg,nāt/ ▶ **adjective 1** (of a word) having the same original form as another in a different language (e.g., English *father*, German *Vater*, and Latin *pater*). **2** formal related; connected. ▶ **noun** a word that has the same original form as another in a different language.
– ORIGIN Latin *cognatus* 'born together.'

cog·ni·tion /,käg'nisʜən/ ▶ **noun** the process of obtaining knowledge through thought, experience, and the senses.
– ORIGIN from Latin *cognoscere* 'get to know.'

cog·ni·tive /'kägnətiv/ ▶ **adjective** relating to the process of obtaining knowledge through thought, experience, and the senses.
– DERIVATIVES **cog·ni·tive·ly** adverb.

cog·ni·tive ther·a·py ▶ **noun** a type of psychotherapy based on the belief that psychological problems are caused by negative ways of thinking, which can be avoided or changed.

cog·ni·zance /'kägnəzəns/ ▶ **noun** formal knowledge or awareness.
– DERIVATIVES **cog·ni·zant** /'kägnəzənt/ adjective.
– ORIGIN from Latin *cognoscere* 'get to know.'

cog·no·men /käg'nōmən, 'kägnəmən/ ▸ noun **1** a name or nickname. **2** (in ancient Rome) an extra name given to a citizen, functioning rather like a nickname and often passed down from father to son.
– ORIGIN Latin.

co·gno·scen·ti /ˌkänyō'sHentē, ˌkägnə-/ ▸ plural noun people who are well informed about a particular subject.
– ORIGIN Italian, 'people who know.'

cog·wheel /'käg,(h)wēl/ ▸ noun another term for **COG** (sense 1).

co·hab·it /kō'habit/ ▸ verb (**cohabits, cohabiting, cohabited**) **1** live together and have a sexual relationship without being married. **2** coexist.
– DERIVATIVES **co·hab·i·ta·tion** /kō,habə'tāsHən/ noun **co·hab·it·ant** noun **co·hab·it·er** noun.
– ORIGIN Latin *cohabitare.*

co·here /kō'hi(ə)r/ ▸ verb form a unified whole; be logically consistent.
– ORIGIN Latin *cohaerere.*

co·her·ent /kō'hi(ə)rənt/ ▸ adjective **1** (of an argument or theory) logical and consistent. **2** able to speak clearly and logically.

– SYNONYMS **logical,** reasoned, rational, sound, cogent, consistent, clear, lucid, articulate, intelligible.
– ANTONYMS muddled.

– DERIVATIVES **co·her·ence** /kō'hi(ə)rəns/ noun **co·her·ent·ly** adverb.

co·he·sion /kō'hēzHən/ ▸ noun the action or fact of holding together or forming a unified whole.

co·he·sive /kō'hēsiv, -ziv/ ▸ adjective **1** forming a unified whole: *a cohesive group.* **2** causing people or things to form a unified whole: *a cohesive force.*
– DERIVATIVES **co·he·sive·ness** noun.

co·hort /'kō,hôrt/ ▸ noun **1** an ancient Roman military unit equal to one tenth of a legion. **2** a group of people with a shared characteristic: *a cohort of students.* **3** a supporter or companion.
– ORIGIN Latin *cohors* 'yard, retinue.'

co·hosh /'kō,häsH/ ▸ noun a North American plant with medicinal properties.
– ORIGIN from Abnaki.

co-host ▸ noun a person who hosts an event or broadcast with another or others. ▸ verb be the co-host of an event or broadcast.

coif /koif/ ▸ noun **1** a close-fitting cap worn by nuns under a veil. **2** informal coiffure. ▸ verb /kwäf, koif/ (**coifs, coiffing** or **coifing, coiffed** or **coifed**) style or arrange someone's hair.
– ORIGIN Old French *coife* 'headdress.'

coif·feur /kwä'fər/ ▸ noun (fem. **coiffeuse** /kwä'f(y)o͞oz, -'fə(r)z/) a hairdresser.
– ORIGIN French, from *coiffer* 'arrange the hair.'

coif·fure /kwä'fyo͝or/ ▸ noun a person's hairstyle.
– DERIVATIVES **coif·fured** adjective.

coign /koin/ ▸ noun a projecting corner or angle of a wall.
– ORIGIN variant of **COIN**.

coil /koil/ ▸ noun **1** a length of something wound in a joined sequence of loops. **2** a contraceptive device in the form of a coil, placed inside the uterus. **3** an electrical device consisting of a coiled wire, for converting the level of a voltage, producing a magnetic field, or adding inductance to a circuit. ▸ verb arrange or form into a coil.

– SYNONYMS **wind,** loop, twist, curl, spiral, twine, wrap.

– ORIGIN Old French *coillir.*

coin /koin/ ▸ noun a flat disk or piece of metal with an official stamp, used as money. ▸ verb **1** invent a new word or phrase. **2** make coins by stamping metal.

– SYNONYMS **invent,** create, make up, conceive, originate, think up, dream up.

– ORIGIN Old French, 'wedge, corner.'

WORD LINKS

numismatic *relating to coins*

coin·age /'koinij/ ▸ noun **1** coins as a whole. **2** the process of producing coins. **3** a system or type of coins in use. **4** a newly invented word or phrase.

co·in·cide /ˌkōən'sīd, 'kōən,sīd/ ▸ verb **1** happen at the same time or place. **2** be the same or similar.

– SYNONYMS **1 occur simultaneously,** happen together, co-occur, coexist. **2 tally,** correspond, agree, accord, match up, be compatible, dovetail, mesh; informal square.
– ANTONYMS differ.

– ORIGIN Latin *coincidere.*

co·in·ci·dence /kō'insədəns, -ˌdens/ ▸ noun **1** a remarkable concurrence of events or circumstances without apparent connection. **2** the fact of two or more things happening at the same time or being the same.

– SYNONYMS **accident,** chance, providence, happenstance, fate, luck, fortune, fluke.

co·in·ci·dent /kō'insədənt, -ˌdent/ ▸ adjective **1** happening at the same time or in the same place. **2** in agreement or harmony.

co·in·ci·den·tal /kō,insə'dentl/ ▸ adjective resulting from a coincidence; not planned or intentional.

– SYNONYMS **accidental,** chance, fluky, random, fortuitous, unintentional, unplanned.

– DERIVATIVES **co·in·ci·den·tal·ly** adverb.

Coin·treau /kwän'trō/ ▸ noun trademark a colorless orange-flavored liqueur.
– ORIGIN French.

coir /'koi(ə)r/ ▸ noun fiber from the outer husk of the coconut, used in potting compost and for making ropes and matting.
– ORIGIN from a Dravidian word.

co·i·tus /'kōətəs, kō'ētəs/ ▸ noun technical sexual intercourse.
– DERIVATIVES **co·i·tal** /'kōətl, kō'ētl/ adjective.
– ORIGIN Latin, from *coire* 'go together.'

co·i·tus in·ter·rup·tus /intə'rəptəs/ ▸ noun sexual intercourse in which the man withdraws his penis before ejaculation.

Coke /kōk/ ▸ noun trademark short for **COCA-COLA**.

coke[1] /kōk/ ▸ noun **1** a solid fuel made by heating coal in the absence of air. **2** carbon residue left after the incomplete combustion of gasoline or other fuels.
– ORIGIN unknown.

coke[2] ▸ noun informal cocaine.

col /käl/ ▸ noun the lowest point between two peaks of a mountain ridge.
– ORIGIN French, 'neck.'

Col. ▸ abbreviation Colonel.

COLA ▶ abbreviation cost-of-living adjustment, an increase made to wages or Social Security benefits to keep them in line with inflation.

co·la /'kōlə/ ▶ noun **1** a brown carbonated drink flavored with an extract of cola nuts, or with a similar flavoring. **2** (also **kola**) a small tropical evergreen tree whose seed (the **cola nut**) contains caffeine.
– ORIGIN Temne (an African language).

col·an·der /'kələndər, 'käl-/ ▶ noun a bowl with holes in it, used for draining food.
– ORIGIN Latin *colare* 'to strain.'

cold /kōld/ ▶ adjective **1** of or at a low or relatively low temperature. **2** not feeling or showing emotion or affection. **3** not influenced by personal feeling or emotion: objective: *the cold facts.* **4** (of a color) containing pale blue or gray and giving no impression of warmth. **5** (of a scent or trail) no longer fresh and easy to follow. **6** without preparation or rehearsal; unawares: *they went into the test cold.* **7** informal unconscious: *she was out cold.*

– SYNONYMS **1 chilly,** chill, cool, freezing, icy, wintry, frosty, raw, bitter; informal nippy. **2 unfriendly,** inhospitable, unwelcoming, cool, frigid, frosty, distant, formal, stiff.
– ANTONYMS hot, warm.

▶ noun **1** cold weather or surroundings. **2** an infection in which the mucous membrane of the nose and throat becomes inflamed, causing sneezing and a runny nose.
– DERIVATIVES **cold·ly** adverb **cold·ness** noun.
– PHRASES **cold comfort** little or no consolation under the circumstances. **get cold feet** lose one's nerve. **the cold shoulder** deliberate unfriendliness or rejection. **in cold blood** without pity; in a deliberately cruel way.
– ORIGIN Old English.

cold-blood·ed ▶ adjective **1** (of animals, e.g., reptiles and fish) having a body whose temperature varies with that of the environment. **2** without emotion or pity.
– DERIVATIVES **cold-blood·ed·ly** adverb.

cold-call ▶ verb visit or telephone someone without being asked to do so in an attempt to sell them goods or services.

cold chis·el ▶ noun a toughened chisel used for cutting metal.

cold cream ▶ noun a cream for cleansing and softening the skin.

cold cuts /'kōld ˌkəts/ ▶ plural noun slices of cold cooked meats.

cold frame ▶ noun a frame with a glass top in which small plants are grown and protected.

cold fu·sion ▶ noun nuclear fusion supposedly occurring at or close to room temperature.

cold-heart·ed ▶ adjective lacking affection or warmth; unfeeling.

cold snap ▶ noun a brief spell of cold weather.

cold sore ▶ noun an inflamed blister in or near the mouth, caused by a virus.

cold stor·age ▶ noun preservation of something in a refrigerated room.
– PHRASES **in/into cold storage** so as to be postponed temporarily.

cold sweat ▶ noun a state of sweating caused by nervousness or illness.

cold tur·key ▶ noun informal the abrupt withdrawal from a drug to which one is addicted, often accompanied by sweating and nausea.

cold war ▶ noun a state of hostility between the countries allied to the former Soviet Union and the Western powers after World War II.

cole·slaw /'kōlˌslô/ ▶ noun a salad dish of shredded raw cabbage and carrots mixed with mayonnaise.
– ORIGIN Dutch *koolsla.*

co·le·us /'kōlēəs/ ▶ noun a tropical plant with brightly colored variegated leaves.
– ORIGIN Greek *koleos* 'sheath.'

col·ic /'kälik/ ▶ noun severe pain in the abdomen caused by gas or obstruction in the intestines.
– DERIVATIVES **col·ick·y** adjective.
– ORIGIN Latin *colicus.*

col·i·se·um /ˌkälə'sēəm/ (also **colosseum**) ▶ noun (in names) a large theater, movie theater, or stadium.
– ORIGIN from the *Colosseum*, a huge amphitheater in ancient Rome.

co·li·tis /kə'lītis, kō-/ ▶ noun inflammation of the lining of the colon.

col·lab·o·rate /kə'labəˌrāt/ ▶ verb **1** work jointly on an activity or project. **2** betray one's country by cooperating with an enemy.

– SYNONYMS **1 cooperate,** join forces, work together, combine, pool resources. **2 fraternize,** conspire, collude, cooperate, consort.

– DERIVATIVES **col·lab·o·ra·tion** /kəˌlabə'rāsнən/ noun **col·lab·o·ra·tion·ist** /kəˌlabə'rāsнənist/ noun & adjective **col·lab·o·ra·tive** /kə'labərətiv/ adjective.
– ORIGIN Latin *collaborare.*

col·lab·o·ra·tor /kə'labəˌrātər/ ▶ noun **1** a person who works with someone on an activity or project. **2** a person who betrays their country by cooperating with an enemy.

– SYNONYMS **1 coworker,** partner, associate, colleague, confederate, assistant. **2 sympathizer,** traitor, quisling, fifth columnist.

col·lage /kə'läzн, kô-, kō-/ ▶ noun **1** a form of art in which various materials are arranged and stuck to a backing. **2** a combination of various things: *the collage of cultures within our nation.*
– ORIGIN French, 'gluing.'

col·la·gen /'käləjən/ ▶ noun any of a group of proteins that form the main structural component of animal connective tissue.
– ORIGIN from Greek *kolla* 'glue.'

col·lapse /kə'laps/ ▶ verb **1** suddenly fall down or give way. **2** (of a person) fall down as a result of illness or fatigue. **3** fail suddenly and completely: *when he died the family business collapsed.*

– SYNONYMS **1 cave in,** fall in, subside, fall down, give (way), crumple, crumble, disintegrate. **2 faint,** pass out, black out, lose consciousness. **3 go to pieces,** break down, be overcome; informal crack up. **4 fail,** break down, fall through, fold, founder; informal flop, fizzle out.

▶ noun **1** an instance of a structure collapsing. **2** a sudden failure or breakdown.

– SYNONYMS **1 cave-in,** disintegration. **2 breakdown,** failure.

– ORIGIN Latin *collabi.*

col·laps·i·ble /kə'lapsəbəl/ ▶ adjective able to be folded into a small space.

col·lar /'kälər/ ▶ **noun 1** the part around the neck of a garment, either upright or turned over. **2** a band put around the neck of a dog or other domestic animal. **3** a connecting band or pipe in a piece of machinery. ▶ **verb** informal stop or arrest someone.
– DERIVATIVES **col·lar·less** adjective.
– ORIGIN Latin *collare* 'band for the neck.'

col·lar·bone /'kälər,bōn/ ▶ **noun** either of the pair of bones joining the breastbone to the shoulder blades; the clavicle.

col·late /kə'lāt, 'kō,lāt, 'käl,āt/ ▶ **verb 1** collect and combine documents or information. **2** compare and analyze two or more sources of information.
– DERIVATIVES **col·la·tor** noun.
– ORIGIN Latin *collatus* 'brought together.'

col·lat·er·al /kə'latərəl, kə'latrəl/ ▶ **noun** something that is promised to someone if one is not able to repay a loan. ▶ **adjective 1** additional but less important. **2** situated side by side; parallel.
– DERIVATIVES **col·lat·er·al·ly** adverb.
– ORIGIN Latin *collateralis.*

col·lat·er·al dam·age ▶ **noun** unintentional casualties and destruction in civilian areas caused by military operations.

col·la·tion /kə'lāsʜən, kō-, kä-/ ▶ **noun 1** the action of collating something. **2** formal a light informal meal.

col·league /'käl,ēg/ ▶ **noun** a person with whom one works.

> – SYNONYMS **coworker,** fellow worker, workmate, teammate, associate, partner, collaborator, ally, confederate.

– ORIGIN Latin *collega* 'partner in office.'

col·lect¹ /kə'lekt/ ▶ **verb 1** bring or come together: *a crowd collected at the door.* **2** find or buy items of a particular kind as a hobby. **3** call for and take away someone or something. **4** ask for money or receive a prize or award. **5** (**collect oneself**) regain control of oneself.

> – SYNONYMS **1** *he collected the trash* **gather,** accumulate, assemble, amass, stockpile, pile up, heap up, store (up), hoard, save. **2** *a crowd soon collected* **gather,** assemble, meet, muster, congregate, convene, converge. **3 fetch,** pick up, go/come and get, call for.
> – ANTONYMS distribute, disperse.

▶ **adverb & adjective** (of a telephone call) to be paid for by the person receiving it.
– ORIGIN Latin *colligere.*

col·lect² /'käl,ekt, -likt/ ▶ **noun** (in the Christian Church) a short prayer used on a particular day or during a particular period.
– ORIGIN Latin *collecta* 'a gathering.'

col·lect·a·ble /kə'lektəbəl/ (also **collectible**) ▶ **adjective 1** worth collecting; of interest to a collector. **2** able to be collected. ▶ **noun** (usu. **collectibles**) an item valued by collectors.
– DERIVATIVES **col·lect·a·bi·li·ty** /kə,lektə'bilitē/ noun.

col·lect·ed /kə'lektid/ ▶ **adjective 1** calm and self-controlled. **2** (of works) brought together in one volume or edition.

> – SYNONYMS **calm,** cool, self-possessed, self-controlled, composed, poised, serene, tranquil, relaxed; informal laid-back.
> – ANTONYMS excited.

col·lec·tion /kə'leksʜən/ ▶ **noun 1** the action of collecting. **2** a number of things that have been collected. **3** a new range of clothes produced by a designer. **4** a regular removal of mail or garbage.

> – SYNONYMS **1 hoard,** pile, heap, stock, store, stockpile, accumulation, reserve, supply, bank, pool, fund; informal stash. **2 group,** crowd, body, gathering, knot, cluster. **3 anthology,** selection, compendium, compilation, miscellany, treasury. **4 appeal;** informal whip-round.

col·lec·tive /kə'lektiv/ ▶ **adjective 1** done by or involving all the members of a group. **2** taken as a whole: *the collective power of the workforce.*

> – SYNONYMS **common,** shared, joint, combined, mutual, communal, pooled, united, allied, cooperative, collaborative.
> – ANTONYMS individual.

▶ **noun** a business or farm owned or run as a cooperative venture.
– DERIVATIVES **col·lec·tive·ly** adverb **col·lec·tiv·i·ty** /kə,lek'tivitē, ,käl,ek-/ noun.

col·lec·tive bar·gain·ing ▶ **noun** negotiation of wages and other conditions of employment by an organized body of employees.

col·lec·tive farm ▶ **noun** a farm or group of farms owned by the government and run by a group of people.

col·lec·tive noun ▶ **noun** a noun that refers to a group of individuals (e.g., *assembly, family*).

> **USAGE**
>
> In the US, a **collective noun** is usually used with a singular verb (*my family was always hard-working*), while in Britain it is often used with a plural verb (*his family were disappointed in him*). It is important to remember that, if the verb is singular, any following pronouns (words such as 'he,' 'she,' or 'they') must be too: *the government is prepared to act, but not until it knows the outcome of the talks* (not ...*until they know the outcome*...).

col·lec·tiv·ism /kə'lektə,vizəm/ ▶ **noun** the ownership of land, business, and industry by the people or the government.
– DERIVATIVES **col·lec·tiv·ist** adjective & noun **col·lec·ti·vize** /kə'lektə,vīz/ verb.

col·lec·tor /kə'lektər/ ▶ **noun 1** a person who collects things of a specified type. **2** an official who is responsible for collecting money owed.

col·leen /kə'lēn, 'käl,ēn/ ▶ **noun** Irish a girl or young woman.
– ORIGIN Irish *cailín* 'country girl.'

col·lege /'kälij/ ▶ **noun 1** an educational establishment providing higher education or specialized training. **2** any of the independent institutions into which some universities are separated. **3** an organized group of professional people: *the College of Fellows of the Society.*
– ORIGIN Latin *collegium* 'partnership.'

col·le·gi·al /kə'lēj(ē)əl/ ▶ **adjective 1** relating to a college or its students; collegiate. **2** involving shared responsibility.

col·le·gian /kə'lējən/ ▶ **noun** a member of a college.

col·le·giate /kə'lējət/ ▶ **adjective 1** relating to a college or its students. **2** (of a university) composed of different colleges.

col·lide /kə'līd/ ▶ **verb 1** hit by accident when moving. **2** come into conflict: *the culture of the two companies collided.*

– SYNONYMS *they nearly* ***collided with*** *a bus* **crash into,** hit, strike, run into, bump into.

– ORIGIN Latin *collidere*.

col·lie /ˈkälē/ ▶ **noun** (pl. **collies**) a breed of sheepdog with a long, pointed nose and long hair.
– ORIGIN perhaps from **COAL** (the breed originally being black).

col·lier /ˈkälyər/ ▶ **noun** chiefly Brit. **1** a coal miner. **2** a ship carrying coal.

col·lier·y /ˈkälyərē/ ▶ **noun** (pl. **collieries**) a coal mine.

col·lin·e·ar /kəˈlinēər, kä-/ ▶ **adjective** Geometry (of points) lying in the same straight line.

col·li·sion /kəˈlizʜən/ ▶ **noun 1** an instance of a person or object colliding with another. **2** a conflict of ideas, qualities, or groups: *a calculated collision of science and humanity*.

– SYNONYMS **crash,** accident, smash, wreck; informal smash-up, pile-up.

col·lo·cate ▶ **verb** /ˈkäləˌkāt/ (of a word) frequently occur with another: *'maiden' collocates with 'voyage'* ▶ **noun** a word that frequently occurs with another.

col·lo·ca·tion /ˌkäləˈkāsʜən/ ▶ **noun 1** the frequent occurrence of a word with another word or words. **2** a pair or group of words that frequently occur together (e.g., *heavy drinker*).
– ORIGIN from Latin *collocare* 'place together.'

col·loid /ˈkälˌoid/ ▶ **noun** a homogeneous substance consisting of submicroscopic particles of one substance dispersed in another, as in an emulsion or gel.
– DERIVATIVES **col·loi·dal** /kəˈloidl/ adjective.
– ORIGIN from Greek *kolla* 'glue.'

col·lo·qui·al /kəˈlōkwēəl/ ▶ **adjective** (of language) used in ordinary conversation; not formal or literary.

– SYNONYMS **informal,** conversational, everyday, familiar, popular, casual, idiomatic, slangy, vernacular.
– ANTONYMS formal.

– DERIVATIVES **col·lo·qui·al·ly** adverb.
– ORIGIN from Latin *colloquium* 'conversation.'

col·lo·qui·al·ism /kəˈlōkwēəˌlizəm/ ▶ **noun** an informal word or phrase.

col·lo·qui·um /kəˈlōkwēəm/ ▶ **noun** (pl. **colloquiums** or **colloquia** /-kwēə/) an academic conference or seminar.
– ORIGIN Latin.

col·lo·quy /ˈkäləkwē/ ▶ **noun** (pl. **colloquies**) formal a conference or conversation.
– ORIGIN Latin *colloquium*.

col·lude /kəˈlo͞od/ ▶ **verb** cooperate secretly for a dishonest or underhanded purpose: *the president accused his opponents of colluding with foreigners*.
– ORIGIN Latin *colludere* 'have a secret agreement.'

col·lu·sion /kəˈlo͞ozʜən/ ▶ **noun** secret cooperation in order to deceive others.
– DERIVATIVES **col·lu·sive** /-siv, -ziv/ adjective.

col·o·bus /ˈkäləbəs/ ▶ **noun** (pl. same) a slender African monkey with silky fur.
– ORIGIN from Greek *kolobos* 'curtailed' (with reference to its shortened thumbs).

co·logne /kəˈlōn/ ▶ **noun** eau de cologne or other scented toilet water.

Co·lom·bi·an /kəˈləmbēən/ ▶ **noun** a person from Colombia. ▶ **adjective** relating to Colombia.

co·lon¹ /ˈkōlən/ ▶ **noun** a punctuation mark (:) used before a list, a quotation, or an explanation.
– ORIGIN Greek *kōlon* 'limb, clause.'

co·lon² ▶ **noun** the main part of the large intestine, which passes from the cecum to the rectum.
– DERIVATIVES **co·lon·ic** /kōˈlänik, kə-/ adjective.
– ORIGIN Greek *kolon* 'food, meat.'

colo·nel /ˈkərnl/ ▶ **noun** a rank of officer in the US Army, Air Force, and Marine Corps above a lieutenant colonel and below a brigadier or brigadier general.
– DERIVATIVES **colo·nel·cy** noun (pl. **colonelcies**).
– ORIGIN from Italian *colonnello* 'column of soldiers.'

co·lo·ni·al /kəˈlōnyəl, -nēəl/ ▶ **adjective 1** relating to a colony or colonialism. **2** in a neoclassical style characteristic of the period of the British colonies in America before independence. ▶ **noun** a person who lives in a colony.
– DERIVATIVES **co·lo·ni·al·ly** adverb.

co·lo·ni·al·ism /kəˈlōnēəˌlizəm, kəˈlōnyəˌlizəm/ ▶ **noun** the practice of acquiring control over another country, occupying it with settlers, and exploiting it economically.
– DERIVATIVES **co·lo·ni·al·ist** /-list/ noun & adjective.

co·lon·ic ir·ri·ga·tion ▶ **noun** a therapeutic treatment in which water is inserted via the anus to flush out the colon.

col·o·nist /ˈkälənist/ ▶ **noun** an inhabitant of a colony.

col·o·nize /ˈkäləˌnīz/ ▶ **verb 1** establish a colony in a place. **2** take over for one's own use: *his work has colonized the space outside his studio*.

– SYNONYMS **settle (in),** people, populate, occupy, take over, invade.

– DERIVATIVES **col·o·ni·za·tion** /ˌkälənəˈzāsʜən/ noun **col·o·niz·er** noun.

col·on·nade /ˌkäləˈnād/ ▶ **noun** a row of evenly spaced columns supporting a roof or other structure.
– DERIVATIVES **col·on·nad·ed** adjective.
– ORIGIN French.

co·lon·os·co·py /ˌkōləˈnäskəpē/ ▶ **noun** (pl. **colonoscopies**) examination of the colon with a fiber-optic instrument inserted through the anus.

col·o·ny /ˈkälənē/ ▶ **noun** (pl. **colonies**) **1** a country or area under the control of another country and occupied by settlers from that country. **2** a group of people of one nationality or race living in a foreign place. **3** a place where a group of people with the same interest live together: *a nudist colony*. **4** a community of animals or plants of one kind living close together.

– SYNONYMS **territory,** dependency, protectorate, satellite, settlement, outpost, province.

– ORIGIN Latin *colonia* 'settlement, farm.'

col·o·phon /ˈkäləfən, -ˌfän/ ▶ **noun** a publisher's emblem or imprint.
– ORIGIN Greek *kolophōn* 'summit or finishing touch.'

col·or /ˈkələr/ (Brit. **colour**) ▶ **noun 1** the property possessed by an object of producing different sensations on the eye as a result of the way it reflects or emits light. **2** one, or any mixture, of the constituents into which light can be separated: *a rich brown color*. **3** the use of all colors, not only black and white, in photography or television. **4** the shade of the skin as an indication of someone's race. **5** redness of the complexion. **6** interest, excitement, and vitality: *a town full of color and character*. **7** (**colors**) an item or items of a particular color worn for identification in sports. **8** (**colors**) the flag of a regiment or ship.

– SYNONYMS **1 hue,** shade, tint, tone, coloration. **2 paint,** pigment, colorant, dye, stain.

▸ **verb 1** change the color of something. **2** show embarrassment by becoming red; blush. **3** influence, especially in a negative way: *the experience had colored her whole existence.*

– SYNONYMS **1 tint,** dye, stain, tinge. **2 influence,** affect, taint, warp, skew, distort.

– PHRASES **show one's true colors** reveal one's real character or intentions.
– ORIGIN Latin.

WORD LINKS

chromatic *relating to color*

Col·o·rad·o po·ta·to bee·tle /ˌkäləˈrädō, -ˈradō/ ▸ **noun** a yellow- and black-striped beetle whose larvae are highly destructive to potato plants.

col·or·ant /ˈkələrənt/ ▸ **noun** a dye or pigment used to color something.

col·or·a·tion /ˌkələˈrāsʜən/ ▸ **noun 1** the natural coloring of something. **2** character or tone: *he gives each performance its own emotional coloration.*

col·o·ra·tu·ra /ˌkələrəˈto͝orə, ˌkäl-/ ▸ **noun 1** elaborate ornamentation of a vocal melody, especially in opera. **2** a soprano skilled in coloratura singing.
– ORIGIN Italian, 'coloring.'

col·or-blind ▸ **adjective** unable to distinguish certain colors.
– DERIVATIVES **col·or blind·ness** noun.

col·ored /ˈkələrd/ ▸ **adjective 1** having a color or colors. **2** offensive wholly or partly of nonwhite descent. **3** (usu. **Coloured**) S. African historical of mixed ethnic origin. ▸ **noun 1** offensive a person who is wholly or partly of nonwhite descent. **2** (usu. **Coloured**) S. African a person of mixed descent, usually speaking Afrikaans or English as their mother tongue. **3** (**coloreds**) clothes or household linen that are any color but white.

col·or·fast ▸ **adjective** dyed in colors that will not fade or be washed out.

col·or·ful /ˈkələrfəl/ ▸ **adjective 1** having many or varied colors. **2** lively and exciting; vivid.

– SYNONYMS **1 bright,** vivid, vibrant, brilliant, radiant, gaudy, garish, multicolored, psychedelic; informal jazzy. **2** *a colorful account* **vivid,** graphic, lively, animated, dramatic, fascinating, interesting, stimulating, scintillating, evocative.
– ANTONYMS drab, dull.

– DERIVATIVES **col·or·ful·ly** /-f(ə)lē/ adverb.

col·or·ing /ˈkələriɴɢ/ ▸ **noun 1** the process or art of applying color. **2** the appearance of something with regard to its color. **3** the natural colors of a person's skin, hair, and eyes. **4** a substance used to color something, especially food.

col·or·ist /ˈkələrist/ ▸ **noun** an artist or designer who uses color in a special or skillful way.

col·or·is·tic /ˌkələˈristik/ ▸ **adjective 1** showing a special use of color. **2** having a variety of musical expression.

col·or·less /ˈkələrləs/ ▸ **adjective 1** without color. **2** lacking character or interest; dull.

col·or scheme ▸ **noun** an arrangement or combination of colors.

col·or·way /ˈkələrˌwā/ ▸ **noun** any of a range of combinations of colors in which something is available.

co·los·sal /kəˈläsəl/ ▸ **adjective** extremely large.

– SYNONYMS **huge,** massive, enormous, gigantic, giant, mammoth, vast, immense, monumental, mountainous; informal monster, whopping, humongous, ginormous.
– ANTONYMS tiny.

– DERIVATIVES **co·los·sal·ly** adverb.
– ORIGIN from Latin *colossus.*

WORD TOOLKIT

colossal ...	immense ...	giant ...
failure	pressure	step
waste	potential	leap
blunder	importance	screen
explosion	popularity	corporation
disappointment	relief	monster
mess	satisfaction	waves
tragedy	courage	oak

col·os·se·um /ˌkäləˈsēəm/ ▸ **noun** variant spelling of COLISEUM.

co·los·sus /kəˈläsəs/ ▸ **noun** (pl. **colossi** /-ˈläsˌī/) **1** a person or thing of great size or importance. **2** a statue that is much bigger than life size.
– ORIGIN Greek *kolossos.*

co·los·to·my /kəˈlästəmē/ ▸ **noun** (pl. **colostomies**) a surgical operation in which the colon is shortened and the cut end diverted to an opening in the abdominal wall.
– ORIGIN from COLON² + Greek *stoma* 'mouth.'

co·los·trum /kəˈlästrəm/ ▸ **noun** the first fluid produced by the mammary glands after giving birth.
– ORIGIN Latin.

col·our, etc. ▸ **noun & verb** British spelling of COLOR, etc.

col·pos·co·py /kälˈpäskəpē/ ▸ **noun** surgical examination of the vagina and the neck of the uterus.
– ORIGIN from Greek *kolpos* 'womb.'

colt /kōlt/ ▸ **noun** a young uncastrated male horse.
– ORIGIN Old English.

col·ter /ˈkōltər/ ▸ **noun** a vertical cutting blade attached to the front of a plowshare.
– ORIGIN Latin *culter* 'knife or plowshare.'

colt·ish /ˈkōltisʜ/ ▸ **adjective** lively but awkward in one's movements or behavior.

colts·foot /ˈkōltsˌfo͝ot/ ▸ **noun** a plant with yellow flowers and large heart-shaped leaves.

co·lum·bine /ˈkäləmˌbīn/ ▸ **noun** an aquilegia with long-spurred flowers.
– ORIGIN from Latin *columba* 'dove' (from the flower's resemblance to a cluster of doves).

col·umn /ˈkäləm/ ▸ **noun 1** an upright pillar supporting an arch or other structure or standing alone as a monument. **2** a line of people or vehicles moving in the same direction. **3** a vertical division of a page. **4** a regular section of a newspaper or magazine on a particular subject or by a particular person: *a weekly column in a Sunday newspaper.* **5** an upright shaft used for controlling a machine.

– SYNONYMS **1 pillar,** post, support, upright, pier, pile. **2 article,** piece, feature. **3 line,** file, queue, procession, convoy.

– DERIVATIVES **col·um·nar** /kə'ləmnər/ adjective **col·umned** adjective.
– ORIGIN Latin *columna* 'pillar.'

col·um·nist /'käləmnist/ ▶ **noun** a journalist who writes a column in a newspaper or magazine.

com- (also **co-**, **col-**, **con-**, or **cor-**) ▶ **prefix** with; together; altogether: *combine*.
– ORIGIN from Latin *cum* 'with.'

co·ma /'kōmə/ ▶ **noun** a state of prolonged deep unconsciousness.
– ORIGIN Greek *kōma* 'deep sleep.'

Co·man·che /kə'mancHē/ ▶ **noun** (pl. same or **Comanches**) a member of an American Indian people of the southwestern US.
– ORIGIN the Comanches' name for themselves.

com·a·tose /'kōməˌtōs, 'kämə-/ ▶ **adjective 1** relating to or in a state of coma. **2** humorous very tired or lethargic.

comb /kōm/ ▶ **noun 1** an object with a row of narrow teeth, used for untangling or arranging the hair. **2** a device for separating and dressing textile fibers. **3** the red fleshy crest on the head of a domestic fowl, especially a cock. **4** a honeycomb. ▶ **verb 1** untangle or arrange the hair with a comb. **2** search carefully and systematically: *I combed the stores for a leather jacket*. **3** prepare wool, flax, or cotton for manufacture with a comb.

– SYNONYMS **1 groom,** brush, untangle, smooth, straighten, neaten, tidy, arrange. **2 search,** scour, explore, sweep.

– ORIGIN Old English.

com·bat /'kämˌbat/ ▶ **noun** fighting, especially between armed forces.

– SYNONYMS **battle,** fighting, action, hostilities, conflict, war, warfare.

▶ **verb** (**combats, combating, combated**; also **combats, combatting, combatted**) take action to reduce or prevent: *equipping people to combat crime*.

– SYNONYMS **fight,** battle, tackle, attack, counter, resist.

– ORIGIN from Latin *combattere* 'fight with.'

com·bat·ant /kəm'batnt, 'kämbətənt/ ▶ **noun** a person or nation taking part in fighting during a war.

com·bat fa·tigue ▶ **noun 1** psychological disturbance caused by prolonged exposure to active warfare, especially being under bombardment. **2** (**combat fatigues**) a uniform of a type to be worn into combat.

com·bat·ive /kəm'bativ/ ▶ **adjective** ready or eager to fight or argue.

– SYNONYMS **aggressive,** pugnacious, antagonistic, quarrelsome, argumentative, hostile, truculent, belligerent; informal spoiling for a fight.
– ANTONYMS conciliatory.

– DERIVATIVES **com·bat·ive·ly** adverb **com·bat·ive·ness** noun.

comb·er /'kōmər/ ▶ **noun** a long curling sea wave.

com·bi·na·tion /ˌkämbə'nāsHən/ ▶ **noun 1** something made up of distinct elements: *a combination of drama, dance, and music*. **2** the combining of two or more different things. **3** a sequence of numbers or letters used to open a combination lock.

– SYNONYMS **mixture,** mix, blend, fusion, amalgamation, amalgam, merger, marriage, synthesis.

– DERIVATIVES **com·bi·na·tion·al** adjective.

com·bi·na·tion lock ▶ **noun** a lock that is opened by using a specific sequence of letters or numbers.

com·bine ▶ **verb** /kəm'bīn/ **1** join or mix to form a whole. **2** join with others for a common purpose. **3** do at the same time: *an ideal place to combine shopping and sightseeing*. **4** Chemistry unite to form a compound.

– SYNONYMS **1 mix,** blend, fuse, amalgamate, integrate, merge, marry. **2 unite,** collaborate, join forces, get together, team up.

▶ **noun** /'kämˌbīn/ a group of people or companies acting together for a commercial purpose.
– DERIVATIVES **com·bin·er** /kəm'bīnər/ noun.
– ORIGIN Latin *combinare* 'join two by two.'

CHOOSE THE RIGHT WORD

See **JOIN**.

com·bine har·ves·ter ▶ **noun** a machine that reaps, threshes, and cleans a cereal crop in one operation.

com·bin·ing form /kəm'bīniNG/ ▶ **noun** a form of a word used in combination with another element to form a word (e.g., *bio-* 'life' in *biology*).

com·bo /'kämbō/ ▶ **noun** (pl. **combos**) informal **1** a small jazz, rock, or pop band. **2** a combination.

com·bust /kəm'bəst/ ▶ **verb** burn or be burned by fire.
– DERIVATIVES **com·bust·or** noun.
– ORIGIN Latin *comburere* 'burn up.'

com·bus·ti·ble /kəm'bəstəbəl/ ▶ **adjective** able to catch fire and burn easily. ▶ **noun** a substance that is able to catch fire and burn easily.

com·bus·tion /kəm'bəsCHən/ ▶ **noun 1** the process of burning. **2** rapid chemical combination with oxygen, producing heat and light.

come /kəm/ ▶ **verb** (past **came**; past part. **come**) **1** move or reach toward or into a place. **2** arrive at a place. **3** happen; take place. **4** have or achieve a specified position in order or priority: *she came second*. **5** pass into or reach a specified state, situation, or state of mind: *my shirt came undone*. **6** be sold or available in a specified form: *the tops come in three sizes*. **7** (also **come, come**) said to correct, reassure, or urge someone on. **8** informal have an orgasm.

– SYNONYMS **1** *come and listen* **approach,** advance, draw close/closer, draw near/nearer. **2** *they came last night* **arrive,** get here/there, make it, appear, turn up, materialize; informal show (up), roll in/up. **3** *they came to a stream* **reach,** arrive at, get to, come across, run across, happen on, chance on, come upon, stumble on, end up at; informal wind up at. **4** *the attacks came without warning* **happen,** occur, take place, come about, fall, crop up. **5** *she comes from Belgium* **be from,** be a native of, hail from, live in, reside in.
– ANTONYMS go, leave.

▶ **preposition** informal when a specified time is reached or event happens.
– PHRASES **come about 1** take place. **2** (of a ship) change direction. **come across 1** give a specified impression. **2** meet or find someone or something by chance. **come back** respond, especially vigorously. **come by** manage to get something. **come down on** criticize or punish someone harshly. **come down to** be dependent on a factor. **come forward** volunteer for a task or to give evidence. **come from** originate in something. **come in** prove to be: *I'm sure the money will come in handy*. **come in for** receive a negative reaction. **come into** inherit money or property. **come of 1** result from

something. **2** be descended from someone. **come off 1** be accomplished. **2** end up in a specified situation: *he always came off worse in a fight*. **come off it** informal said when expressing strong disbelief. **come on 1** (of a state or condition) start to arrive or happen. **2** (also **come upon**) meet or find someone or something by chance. **come on to** informal make sexual advances toward someone. **come out 1** (of a fact) become known. **2** declare oneself as being for or against something. **3** end up in a specified situation. **4** (of a photograph) be produced satisfactorily or in a specified way. **5** (of the result of a calculation or measurement) emerge at a specified figure. **6** informal openly declare that one is homosexual. **7** dated (of a young upper-class woman) make one's debut in society. **come out with** say something in a sudden or incautious way. **come over** (of a feeling) begin to affect someone. **come around 1** recover consciousness. **2** be converted to another person's opinion. **come to 1** recover consciousness. **2** (of an expense) reach an amount in total. **3** (of a ship) come to a stop. **come to pass** literary happen. **come up 1** (of a situation or problem) occur or arise. **2** (of a time or event) draw near. **come up with** produce something, especially when pressured or challenged. **come upon 1** attack someone by surprise. **2** see **COME** (sense 2 of the verb). **come what may** no matter what happens. **have it coming (to one)** informal be due to face the unpleasant results of one's behavior.
– ORIGIN Old English.

USAGE

On the use of **come** followed by **and**, see the note at **AND**.

come·back /ˈkəmˌbak/ ▸ **noun 1** a return to fame or fashionability. **2** informal a quick reply to a critical remark.

– SYNONYMS **return,** recovery, resurgence, rally, upturn.

co·me·di·an /kəˈmēdēən/ ▸ **noun** (fem. **comedienne**) **1** an entertainer whose act is intended to make people laugh. **2** a comic actor.

– SYNONYMS **1 comic,** comedienne, funny man/woman, humorist, stand-up. **2 joker,** wit, wag, comic, clown; informal laugh, hoot.

come·down /ˈkəmˌdoun/ ▸ **noun** informal **1** a loss of status or importance. **2** a feeling of disappointment or depression.

com·e·dy /ˈkämədē/ ▸ **noun** (pl. **comedies**) **1** entertainment consisting of jokes and sketches intended to make people laugh. **2** an amusing movie, play, or television show. **3** a humorous play in which the characters find happiness after experiencing difficulty.

– SYNONYMS **humor,** fun, hilarity, funny side, laughs, jokes.
– ANTONYMS tragedy.

– DERIVATIVES **co·me·dic** /kəˈmēdik/ adjective.
– ORIGIN Greek *kōmōidia*.

com·e·dy of man·ners ▸ **noun** a play, novel, or movie that satirizes behavior in a particular social group.

come-hith·er ▸ **adjective** informal flirtatious: *a come-hither look*.

come·ly /ˈkəmlē/ ▸ **adjective** (**comelier, comeliest**) old use or humorous pleasant to look at; attractive.
– DERIVATIVES **come·li·ness** noun.
– ORIGIN probably from *becomely* 'fitting, becoming.'

come-on ▸ **noun** informal a gesture or remark intended to attract someone sexually.

com·er /ˈkəmər/ ▸ **noun 1** a person who arrives somewhere: *feeding every comer is still a sacred duty*. **2** informal a person or thing likely to succeed.

co·mes·ti·ble /kəˈmestəbəl/ ▸ **noun** formal or humorous an item of food.
– ORIGIN from Latin *comedere* 'eat up.'

com·et /ˈkämit/ ▸ **noun** an object that moves around the solar system, consisting of a nucleus of ice and dust and, when near the sun, a long tail.
– DERIVATIVES **com·et·ar·y** /ˈkämiˌterē/ adjective.
– ORIGIN Greek *komētēs* 'long-haired star.'

come·up·pance /kəˈməpəns/ ▸ **noun** informal a punishment or fate that someone deserves.

com·fit /ˈkəmfit, ˈkämfit/ ▸ **noun** dated a candy consisting of a nut or other center coated in sugar.
– ORIGIN Old French *confit*.

com·fort /ˈkəmfərt/ ▸ **noun 1** a state of being physically relaxed and free from pain. **2** (**comforts**) things that contribute to physical ease and well-being. **3** relief for unhappiness or worry: *a few words of comfort*.

– SYNONYMS **1 ease,** repose, luxury, prosperity. **2 consolation,** condolence, sympathy, commiseration, support, reassurance, cheer.
– ANTONYMS discomfort.

▸ **verb** make someone feel less unhappy.

– SYNONYMS **console,** support, reassure, soothe, calm, cheer, hearten.
– ANTONYMS distress, depress.

– ORIGIN from Latin *confortare* 'strengthen.'

com·fort·a·ble /ˈkəmfərtəbəl, ˈkəmftərbəl/ ▸ **adjective 1** providing or enjoying physical comfort. **2** free from financial worry. **3** (of a victory) easily achieved.

– SYNONYMS **1 cozy,** snug, warm, pleasant, agreeable, homey, homely; informal comfy. **2 loose,** loose-fitting, roomy, casual; informal comfy. **3 affluent,** prosperous, well-to-do, pleasant, luxurious, opulent.

– DERIVATIVES **com·fort·a·bly** /-blē/ adverb.

com·fort·er /ˈkəmfərtər/ ▸ **noun 1** a warm quilt. **2** a person or thing that provides relief from grief or worry.

com·fort·ing /ˈkəmfərtiNG/ ▸ **adjective** giving comfort: *his comforting presence*.

– SYNONYMS **soothing,** reassuring, calming, heartening, cheering.
– ANTONYMS upsetting.

com·frey /ˈkəmfrē/ ▸ **noun** (pl. **comfreys**) a plant with clusters of purplish or white bell-shaped flowers.
– ORIGIN from Latin *confervere* 'heal.'

com·fy /ˈkəmfē/ ▸ **adjective** (**comfier, comfiest**) informal comfortable: *a comfy chair*.
– DERIVATIVES **com·fi·ly** adverb **com·fi·ness** noun.

com·ic /ˈkämik/ ▸ **adjective 1** causing or meant to cause laughter. **2** relating to or in the style of comedy.

– SYNONYMS **humorous,** funny, amusing, hilarious, comical, zany, witty, droll.
– ANTONYMS serious.

▸ **noun 1** a comedian. **2** a children's magazine containing comic strips.

– SYNONYMS **comedian,** comedienne, funny man/woman, humorist, wit, joker.

– ORIGIN Greek *kōmikos*.

com·i·cal /ˈkämikəl/ ▸ **adjective** causing laughter, especially through being ridiculous.

– SYNONYMS **1 funny,** humorous, droll, witty, comic, amusing, entertaining; informal wacky. **2 absurd,** silly, ridiculous, laughable, ludicrous, preposterous, foolish; informal crazy.
– ANTONYMS serious.

– DERIVATIVES **com·i·cal·ly** /-ik(ə)lē/ adverb.

com·ic op·er·a ▶ **noun** an opera that portrays humorous situations and characters, with much spoken dialogue.

com·ic re·lief ▶ **noun** humorous content in a play or novel that offsets more serious parts.

com·ic strip ▶ **noun** a sequence of drawings in boxes that typically tell an amusing story.

com·ing ▶ **adjective** due to happen or just beginning: *the coming election.*

– SYNONYMS **forthcoming,** imminent, impending, approaching.

▶ **noun** an arrival or an approach: *the coming of spring.*

– SYNONYMS **approach,** advance, advent, arrival, appearance, emergence.

com·i·ty /ˈkämitē/ ▶ **noun** (pl. **comities**) **1** formal polite and considerate behavior toward others. **2** (also **comity of nations**) the mutual recognition by nations of the laws and customs of others.
– ORIGIN from Latin *comis* 'courteous.'

comm. ▶ **abbreviation 1** commercial. **2** commission. **3** committee. **4** communication. **5** community.

com·ma /ˈkämə/ ▶ **noun** a punctuation mark (,) showing a pause between parts of a sentence or separating items in a list.
– ORIGIN Greek *komma* 'piece cut off, short clause.'

com·mand /kəˈmand/ ▶ **verb 1** give an order. **2** be in charge of a military unit. **3** be in a position that gives a good view or control of something: *I climbed up a rocky outcrop commanding a view of the valley.* **4** be in a position to have or secure: *emeralds command a high price.*

– SYNONYMS **1 order,** tell, direct, instruct, call on, require, charge, enjoin, ordain; old use bid. **2 be in charge of,** be in command of, head, lead, control, direct, manage, supervise, oversee; informal head up.

▶ **noun 1** an order. **2** authority, especially over armed forces: *the officer in command.* **3** the ability to use or control something: *her poor command of English.* **4** a group of officers having control over a particular group or operation. **5** an instruction causing a computer to perform one of its basic functions.

– SYNONYMS **1 order,** instruction, direction, directive, injunction, decree, edict, dictate, mandate, commandment, fiat. **2** *he had 160 men under his command* **authority,** control, charge, power, direction, dominion, guidance, leadership, rule, government, management, supervision, jurisdiction. **3 knowledge,** mastery, grasp, comprehension, understanding.

– ORIGIN Latin *commandare.*

com·man·dant /ˈkämən,dant, -,dänt/ ▶ **noun** an officer in charge of a force or institution.

com·mand e·con·o·my ▶ **noun** an economy in which production, investment, prices, and incomes are determined centrally by the government.

com·man·deer /,kämənˈdi(ə)r/ ▶ **verb 1** officially take possession of something for military purposes. **2** seize for one's own purposes: *the men in the family have commandeered my other computer.*
– ORIGIN Dutch *commanderen* 'command.'

com·mand·er /kəˈmandər/ ▶ **noun 1** a person in authority, especially in a military situation. **2** a rank of naval officer next below captain. **3** (in certain metropolitan police departments) the person in charge of a district, precinct, or squad. **4** a member of a higher class in some orders of knighthood.

– SYNONYMS **leader,** head, chief, overseer, director, controller; informal boss, skipper, head honcho.

com·mand·er-in-chief ▶ **noun** (pl. **commanders-in-chief**) an officer in charge of all of the armed forces of a country.

com·mand·ing /kəˈmandiNG/ ▶ **adjective 1** having or expressing authority. **2** possessing or giving superior strength: *a commanding lead.*

– SYNONYMS **dominant,** controlling, superior, powerful, advantageous, favorable.

– DERIVATIVES **com·mand·ing·ly** adverb.

com·mand·ment /kəˈmandmənt/ ▶ **noun** a rule given by God, especially one of the Ten Commandments.

com·man·do /kəˈmandō/ ▶ **noun** (pl. **commandos**) **1** a soldier specially trained for carrying out raids. **2** a unit of commandos.
– ORIGIN Portuguese.

com·mand per·for·mance ▶ **noun** a presentation of a play, concert, or other show at the request of royalty.

com·me·dia dell'ar·te /kəˈmādēə dəl ˈärtē/ ▶ **noun** an Italian kind of improvised comedy popular in the 16th–18th centuries, based on stock characters.
– ORIGIN Italian, 'comedy of art.'

comme il faut /,kôm ēl ˈfō/ ▶ **adjective** correct in behavior or etiquette.
– ORIGIN French, 'as is necessary.'

com·mem·o·rate /kəˈmemə,rāt/ ▶ **verb** take action to honor the memory of: *the town held a silent march to commemorate the dead.*

– SYNONYMS **celebrate,** remember, recognize, acknowledge, observe, mark, pay tribute to, pay homage to, honor, salute.

– DERIVATIVES **com·mem·o·ra·tion** /kə,meməˈrāSHən/ noun.
– ORIGIN Latin *commemorare* 'bring to remembrance.'

com·mem·o·ra·tive /kəˈmem(ə)rətiv, kəˈmemə,rātiv/ ▶ **adjective** acting to honor the memory of an event or person.

com·mence /kəˈmens/ ▶ **verb** start or be started; begin.

– SYNONYMS **begin,** inaugurate, start, initiate, launch into, open, get the ball rolling, get going, get under way, get off the ground, set about, embark on; informal kick off.
– ANTONYMS conclude.

– ORIGIN Old French *commencier.*

com·mence·ment /kəˈmensmənt/ ▶ **noun 1** the beginning of something. **2** a ceremony in which degrees or diplomas are conferred on graduating students.

com·mend /kəˈmend/ ▶ **verb 1** praise someone or something formally. **2** present as suitable or good; recommend: *I commend you to her without reservation.* **3** (**commend someone/thing to**) chiefly old use entrust someone or something to.

– SYNONYMS **1 praise,** compliment, congratulate, applaud, salute, honor, sing the praises of, pay

tribute to. **2 recommend,** endorse, vouch for, speak for, support, back.
– ANTONYMS criticize.

– DERIVATIVES **com·men·da·tion** /ˌkämənˈdāsHən, -ˌen-/ noun.
– ORIGIN Latin *commendare*.

com·mend·a·ble /kəˈmendəbəl/ ▶ **adjective** deserving praise and approval.
– SYNONYMS **admirable,** praiseworthy, creditable, laudable, meritorious, exemplary, honorable, respectable.
– ANTONYMS reprehensible.

– DERIVATIVES **com·mend·a·bly** adverb.

com·men·sal /kəˈmensəl/ ▶ **adjective** Biology (of two organisms) having an association in which one benefits and the other derives neither benefit nor harm.
– ORIGIN from Latin *com-* 'sharing' + *mensa* 'a table.'

com·men·su·ra·ble /kəˈmensərəbəl, kəˈmensHərəbəl/ ▶ **adjective 1** formal measurable by the same standard: *not every chapter is commensurable with every other.* **2** Mathematics (of numbers) in a ratio equal to a ratio of integers.
– ORIGIN Latin *commensurabilis*.

com·men·su·rate /kəˈmensərət, -ˈmensHə-/ ▶ **adjective** corresponding in size or degree; in proportion: *salary will be commensurate with experience.*
– DERIVATIVES **com·men·su·rate·ly** adverb.

com·ment /ˈkämˌent/ ▶ **noun 1** a remark expressing an opinion or reaction. **2** discussion of an issue or event.
– SYNONYMS **1 remark,** observation, statement, pronouncement, judgment, reflection, opinion, view. **2 discussion,** debate, interest. **3 note,** annotation, commentary, footnote, gloss, explanation.

▶ **verb** express an opinion or reaction.
– SYNONYMS **remark,** observe, say, state, note, point out, mention, interject; formal opine.

– ORIGIN Latin *commentum* 'device, interpretation.'

com·men·tar·y /ˈkämənˌterē/ ▶ **noun** (pl. **commentaries**) **1** a broadcast spoken account of an event as it happens. **2** the expression of opinions or offering of explanations about an event: *a piece marrying fact and commentary from the paper's Paris correspondent.* **3** a set of explanatory or critical notes on a written work.
– SYNONYMS **1 narration,** description, report, review, voice-over. **2 explanation,** elucidation, interpretation, analysis, assessment, review, criticism, notes, comments.

com·men·tate /ˈkämənˌtāt/ ▶ **verb** provide a commentary on a sports contest or other event.

com·men·ta·tor /ˈkämənˌtātər/ ▶ **noun 1** a person who comments on events, especially in the media. **2** a person who provides a commentary on a live event.
– SYNONYMS **1 reporter,** narrator, journalist, newscaster. **2 analyst,** pundit, critic, columnist, leader-writer, opinion-former, monitor, observer.

com·merce /ˈkämərs/ ▶ **noun 1** the activity of buying and selling, especially on a large scale. **2** dated social dealings between people.
– SYNONYMS **trade,** trading, business, dealing, buying and selling, traffic, trafficking.

– ORIGIN Latin *commercium* 'trade, trading.'

com·mer·cial /kəˈmərsHəl/ ▶ **adjective 1** concerned with or engaged in commerce. **2** making or intended to make a profit. **3** (of television or radio) funded by broadcast advertisements.
– SYNONYMS **1 trade,** trading, business, mercantile, sales. **2 profit-making,** materialistic, mercenary.

▶ **noun** a television or radio advertisement.
– DERIVATIVES **com·mer·ci·al·i·ty** /kəˌmərsHēˈalitē/ noun **com·mer·cial·ly** adverb.

com·mer·cial·ism /kəˈmərsHəˌlizəm/ ▶ **noun** emphasis on making maximum profit.

com·mer·cial·ize /kəˈmərsHəˌlīz/ ▶ **verb** manage or exploit something in a way designed to make a profit.
– DERIVATIVES **com·mer·cial·i·za·tion** /kəˌmərsHələˈzāsHən/ noun.

com·mer·cial space ▶ **noun** an area rented or sold as business premises.

Com·mie /ˈkämē/ ▶ **noun** (pl. **Commies**) informal, derogatory a communist.

com·min·gle /kəˈmiNGgəl, kä-/ ▶ **verb** literary mix; blend.

com·mi·nut·ed /ˈkäməˌn(y)o͞otəd/ ▶ **adjective** technical reduced to minute particles or fragments.
– DERIVATIVES **com·mi·nu·tion** /ˌkäməˈn(y)o͞osHən/ noun.
– ORIGIN from Latin *comminuere* 'break into pieces.'

com·mis·er·ate /kəˈmizəˌrāt/ ▶ **verb** express sympathy or pity; sympathize.
– DERIVATIVES **com·mis·er·a·tion** /kəˌmizəˈrāsHən/ noun.
– ORIGIN Latin *commiserari*.

com·mis·sar /ˈkäməˌsär, ˌkäməˈsär/ ▶ **noun** a Communist official responsible for political education.
– ORIGIN Russian *komissar*.

com·mis·sar·i·at /ˌkäməˈse(ə)rēit/ ▶ **noun** a military department for the supply of food and equipment.

com·mis·sar·y /ˈkäməˌserē/ ▶ **noun** (pl. **commissaries**) **1** a restaurant or food store in a military base or other institution. **2** a deputy or delegate.

com·mis·sion /kəˈmisHən/ ▶ **noun 1** an instruction, command, or duty. **2** a formal request for something to be designed or made. **3** a group of people given official authority to do something. **4** a sum paid to an agent for selling something: *foreign banks may charge a commission.* **5** a warrant conferring the rank of military officer. **6** the committing of a crime or offense.
– SYNONYMS **1 percentage,** share, premium, fee, bonus, royalty; informal cut, take, slice. **2 contract,** engagement, assignment, booking, job. **3 committee,** board, council, panel, body.

▶ **verb 1** order or authorize the production of: *the council commissioned a study of the issue.* **2** bring something newly produced into working order. **3** appoint someone to the rank of military officer.
– SYNONYMS **1 engage,** contract, book, employ, hire, recruit, take on, retain, appoint. **2 order,** place an order for, pay for.

– PHRASES **in** (or **out of**) **commission** in (or not in) use or working order.
– ORIGIN Latin.

com·mis·sion·er /kəˈmisH(ə)nər/ ▶ **noun 1** a person appointed by, or as a member of, an official commission. **2** a representative of the highest authority in an area. **3** a person appointed to regulate a particular sport: *the baseball commissioner.*

com·mit /kəˈmit/ ▶ **verb** (**commits, committing, committed**) **1** do something wrong, bad, or illegal. **2** dedicate or allocate to a course or use: *the Government should commit more money to training judges.* **3** (**commit**

oneself) promise to do something. **4** (**be committed to**) be in a long-term emotional relationship with someone. **5** (**commit something to**) put something somewhere to preserve it: *she committed each detail to memory.* **6** send someone to prison or a psychiatric hospital, or for trial in a higher court.

– SYNONYMS **1 carry out,** do, perpetrate, engage in, execute, accomplish, be responsible for; informal pull off. **2 entrust,** consign, assign, deliver, hand over. **3 consign,** send, confine.

– ORIGIN Latin *committere* 'join, entrust.'

com·mit·ment /kə'mitmənt/ ▶ **noun 1** dedication to a cause or activity. **2** a promise to do something. **3** an engagement or duty that restricts freedom of action.

– SYNONYMS **1 responsibility,** obligation, duty, liability, engagement, tie. **2 dedication,** devotion, allegiance, loyalty. **3 promise,** vow, pledge, undertaking.

com·mit·tal /kə'mitl/ ▶ **noun 1** the sending of someone to prison or a psychiatric hospital, or for trial. **2** the burial of a corpse.

com·mit·ted /kə'mitid/ ▶ **adjective** dedicated to a cause, activity, job, etc.: *a committed democrat.*

– SYNONYMS **devoted,** dedicated, staunch, loyal, faithful, devout, firm, steadfast, unwavering, passionate, ardent, sworn.
– ANTONYMS apathetic.

com·mit·tee /kə'mitē/ ▶ **noun** (treated as sing. or pl.) a group of people appointed for a specific function by a larger group.

com·mode /kə'mōd/ ▶ **noun 1** a piece of furniture containing a concealed chamber pot. **2** a chest of drawers of a decorative type popular in the 18th century.
– ORIGIN French, 'convenient, suitable.'

com·mod·i·fy /kə'mädə,fī/ ▶ **verb** (**commodifies, commodifying, commodified**) turn into or treat as a mere commodity: *a culture in which sexuality is commodified.*
– DERIVATIVES **com·mod·i·fi·ca·tion** /kə,mädəfə'kāsнən/ noun.

com·mo·di·ous /kə'mōdēəs/ ▶ **adjective** formal roomy and comfortable.
– ORIGIN Latin *commodus* 'convenient.'

com·mod·i·ty /kə'mäditē/ ▶ **noun** (pl. **commodities**) **1** a raw material or agricultural product that can be bought and sold. **2** something useful or valuable.
– ORIGIN from Latin *commodus* 'convenient.'

com·mo·dore /'kämə,dôr/ ▶ **noun 1** a naval rank above captain and below rear admiral. **2** the president of a yacht club.
– ORIGIN probably from Dutch *komandeur* 'commander.'

com·mon /'kämən/ ▶ **adjective** (**commoner, commonest**) **1** occurring, found, or done often; not rare: *remedies for common ailments.* **2** without special qualities or position; ordinary. **3** shared by two or more people or things: *working toward our common goal.* **4** belonging to or affecting the whole of a community: *common land.* **5** showing a lack of taste and refinement supposedly typical of lower-class people; vulgar.

– SYNONYMS **1** *a common occurrence* **frequent,** regular, everyday, normal, usual, ordinary, familiar, standard, commonplace, average, unexceptional, typical. **2** *a common belief* **widespread,** general, universal, popular, mainstream, prevalent, rife, established, conventional, accepted. **3 collective,** communal, shared, community, public, popular, general. **4 uncouth,** vulgar, coarse, rough, uncivilized, unsophisticated, unrefined, inferior, plebeian.
– ANTONYMS unusual, rare.

▶ **noun** a piece of open land for public use.
– DERIVATIVES **com·mon·ness** noun.
– PHRASES **in common** in joint use or possession; shared. **in common with** in the same way as.
– ORIGIN Latin *communis.*

WORD TOOLKIT

See **TYPICAL**.

CHOOSE THE RIGHT WORD

See **PREVALENT**.

com·mon·al·i·ty /'kämən,alitē/ ▶ **noun** (pl. **commonalities**) the sharing of common features: *the commonality of grief.*

com·mon·al·ty /'kämənl-tē/ ▶ **noun** (treated as pl.) (**the commonalty**) chiefly historical people without special rank or position.

com·mon de·nom·i·na·tor ▶ **noun 1** Mathematics a common multiple of the denominators of several fractions. **2** a feature shared by all members of a group.

com·mon·er /'kämənər/ ▶ **noun** one of the ordinary or common people, as opposed to the aristocracy or to royalty.

Com·mon E·ra ▶ **noun** another term for **CHRISTIAN ERA**.

com·mon frac·tion ▶ **noun** a fraction expressed by a numerator and a denominator (numbers above and below the line), not decimally.

com·mon ground ▶ **noun** views shared by each of two or more parties.

com·mon law ▶ **noun** the part of English law that is based on custom and judicial decisions rather than created by Parliament.

com·mon-law hus·band (or **wife**) ▶ **noun** a man or woman who has lived with a person long enough to be recognized as a husband or wife, but has not been married in a civil or religious ceremony.

com·mon·ly /'kämənlē/ ▶ **adverb** very often; frequently.

com·mon mar·ket ▶ **noun 1** a group of countries imposing few or no duties on trade with one another. **2** (**the Common Market**) the European Union.

com·mon noun ▶ **noun** a noun referring to a class of things (e.g., *tree, cat*) as opposed to a particular person or thing. Often contrasted with **PROPER NOUN**.

com·mon·place /'kämən,plās/ ▶ **adjective** not unusual or original; ordinary.

– SYNONYMS see **COMMON**.

▶ **noun 1** a usual or ordinary thing. **2** an unoriginal remark; a cliché.

com·mon room ▶ **noun 1** a room in a school or college for use of students or staff outside teaching hours. **2** a room in a residential facility for the recreational use of all residents.

com·mons /'kämənz/ ▶ **plural noun 1** a dining hall in a residential school or college. **2** (treated as sing.) land or resources belonging to or affecting the whole of a community. **3** a public park of a town or city.

com·mon salt ▶ noun see **SALT**.

com·mon sense ▶ noun good sense and sound judgment in practical matters.

– SYNONYMS **good sense,** native wit, good judgment, levelheadedness, prudence, wisdom; informal horse sense, smarts, savvy, street smarts.
– ANTONYMS stupidity.

com·mon·sen·si·cal /ˌkämən'sensikəl/ ▶ adjective having or showing common sense.

com·mon stock ▶ noun shares entitling their holder to dividends that vary in amount and may even be missed, depending on the fortunes of the company. Compare with **PREFERRED STOCK**.

com·mon time ▶ noun a rhythmic musical pattern in which there are two or four beats in a measure.

com·mon·weal /'kämənˌwēl/ ▶ noun (**the commonweal**) old use the welfare of the public.

com·mon·wealth /'kämənˌwelTH/ ▶ noun **1** an independent country or community. **2** a grouping of countries or other bodies. **3** (**the Commonwealth** or in full **the Commonwealth of Nations**) an association consisting of the UK together with countries that were previously part of the British Empire, and dependencies. **4** the formal title of the US states of Massachusetts, Pennsylvania, Virginia, and Kentucky.

com·mo·tion /kə'mōSHən/ ▶ noun a state of confused and noisy disturbance.

– SYNONYMS **disturbance,** uproar, disorder, confusion, rumpus, fuss, furor, hue and cry, stir, storm, chaos, havoc, pandemonium.

– ORIGIN from Latin *com-* 'altogether' + *motio* 'motion.'

com·mu·nal /kə'myo͞onl/ ▶ adjective **1** shared or done by all members of a community. **2** (of conflict) between different communities, especially those having different religions or ethnic origins.

– SYNONYMS **1** *a communal kitchen* **shared,** joint, common, public, general. **2** *they farm on a communal basis* **collective,** cooperative, community.
– ANTONYMS private, individual.

– DERIVATIVES **com·mu·nal·i·ty** /ˌkämyə'nalitē/ noun **com·mu·nal·ly** adverb.
– ORIGIN Latin *communalis*.

com·mu·nal·ism /kə'myo͞onlˌizəm/ ▶ noun **1** a principle of political organization based on federated communes. **2** the principle or practice of living together and sharing possessions and responsibilities.

com·mu·nard /ˌkämyə'när(d)/ ▶ noun **1** a member of a commune. **2** (**Communard**) historical a supporter of the Paris Commune.

com·mune[1] /'kämˌyo͞on/ ▶ noun **1** a group of people living together and sharing possessions and responsibilities. **2** (in France) the smallest district for administrative purposes. **3** (**the Paris Commune**) the short-lived government elected in Paris in 1871, advocating communal organization of society.
– ORIGIN Latin *communia*.

com·mune[2] /kə'myo͞on/ ▶ verb (**commune with**) share one's intimate thoughts or feelings with: *visitors can stroll the fields and commune with nature*.
– ORIGIN Old French *comuner* 'to share.'

com·mu·ni·ca·ble /kə'myo͞onikəbəl/ ▶ adjective (especially of a disease) able to be communicated to others.

com·mu·ni·cant /kə'myo͞onikənt/ ▶ noun a person who receives Holy Communion.

com·mu·ni·cate /kə'myo͞onəˌkāt/ ▶ verb **1** share or exchange information or ideas. **2** pass on, transmit, or convey an emotion, disease, heat, etc. **3** (as adj. **communicating**) (of two rooms) having a common connecting door. **4** receive Holy Communion.

– SYNONYMS **1 liaise,** be in touch, be in contact, have dealings, talk, speak, interface. **2 convey,** tell, relay, transmit, impart, pass on, report, recount, relate. **3 transmit,** spread, transfer, pass on.

– DERIVATIVES **com·mu·ni·ca·tor** noun.
– ORIGIN Latin *communicare* 'to share.'

com·mu·ni·ca·tion /kəˌmyo͞onə'kāSHən/ ▶ noun **1** the action of communicating. **2** a letter or other message. **3** (**communications**) the means of sending or receiving information, such as telephone lines or computers. **4** (**communications**) means of traveling or of transporting goods, such as roads or railroads.

– SYNONYMS **1 contact,** dealings, relations, connection, correspondence, dialogue, conversation. **2 message,** statement, announcement, report, dispatch, bulletin, disclosure, communiqué, letter, correspondence.

– DERIVATIVES **com·mu·ni·ca·tion·al** adjective.

com·mu·ni·ca·tive /kə'myo͞onəˌkātiv, -nikətiv/ ▶ adjective willing or eager to talk or impart information.

– SYNONYMS **forthcoming,** expansive, expressive, unreserved, vocal, outgoing, frank, open, candid, talkative, chatty.

com·mun·ion /kə'myo͞onyən/ ▶ noun **1** the sharing of intimate thoughts and feelings: *man's mystical communion with the divine*. **2** (also **Holy Communion**) the service of Christian worship at which bread and wine are consecrated and shared; the Eucharist. **3** an allied group of Christian Churches or communities: *the Anglican communion*.

CHOOSE THE RIGHT WORD

See **CONVERSATION**.

com·mu·ni·qué /kəˌmyo͞onə'kā, kə'myo͞onəˌkā/ ▶ noun an official announcement or statement, especially one made to the media.
– ORIGIN French, 'communicated.'

com·mu·nism /'kämyəˌnizəm/ ▶ noun **1** a political and social system whereby all property is owned by the community and each person contributes and receives according to their ability and needs. **2** a system of this kind derived from Marxism, practiced in China and formerly in the Soviet Union.
– DERIVATIVES **com·mu·nist** noun & adjective **com·mu·nis·tic** /ˌkämyə'nistik/ adjective.
– ORIGIN French *communisme*.

com·mu·ni·tar·i·an·ism /kəˌmyo͞oni'te(ə)rēəˌnizəm/ ▶ noun a theory that emphasizes the responsibility of the individual to the community and the importance of the family unit.
– DERIVATIVES **com·mu·ni·tar·i·an** adjective & noun.

com·mu·ni·ty /kə'myo͞onitē/ ▶ noun (pl. **communities**) **1** a group of people living together in one place. **2** (**the community**) the people of an area as a social group; society. **3** a group of people with a common religion, race, or profession: *the scientific community*. **4** the holding of certain attitudes and interests in common: *the sense of community that organized religion can* *provide.* **5** a group of interdependent plants or animals growing or living in the same place.

– SYNONYMS **society,** population, populace, people, public, residents, inhabitants, citizens.

– ORIGIN from Latin *communis* 'common.'

com·mu·ni·ty care ▶ **noun** long-term care for mentally ill, elderly, and disabled people within the community rather than in hospitals or other institutions.

com·mu·ni·ty cen·ter ▶ **noun** a place providing educational or recreational activities for the residents of a particular community.

com·mu·ni·ty col·lege ▶ **noun** a nonresidential junior college offering courses to people living in a particular area.

com·mu·ni·ty serv·ice ▶ **noun 1** voluntary work intended to help people. **2** socially useful work that an offender is required to do instead of going to prison.

com·mu·tate /'kämyə,tāt/ ▶ **verb** regulate or reverse the direction of an alternating electric current, especially to make it a direct current.

– DERIVATIVES **com·mu·ta·tion** /,kämyə'tāsʜən/ noun.

com·mu·ta·tive /'kämyə,tātiv, kə'myōōtətiv/ ▶ **adjective** Mathematics unchanged in result by interchanging the order of quantities, as in the equation $a \times b = b \times a$.

com·mu·ta·tor /'kämyə,tātər/ ▶ **noun** an attachment, connected to the armature of a motor or generator, that ensures the current flows as direct current.

com·mute /kə'myōōt/ ▶ **verb 1** travel some distance between one's home and place of work on a regular basis. **2** reduce a judicial sentence, especially a death sentence, to a less severe one. **3** change one kind of payment or obligation for another.

– DERIVATIVES **com·mut·a·ble** adjective **com·mu·ta·tion** /,kämyə'tāsʜən/ noun **com·mut·er** noun.

– ORIGIN Latin *commutare*; sense 1 is from *commutation ticket*, the US term for a season ticket.

co·mor·bid·i·ty /,kōmôr'biditē/ ▶ **noun** the simultaneous presence of two chronic diseases or conditions in a patient: *the comorbidity of anxiety and depression in Parkinson's disease.*

comp /kämp/ informal ▶ **noun 1** short for a complimentary ticket or voucher. **2** short for composition. **3** short for a comprehensive examination. **4** short for computation. **5** (in real estate) short for a comparable property. ▶ **verb 1** play music as an accompaniment, especially in jazz or blues. **2** give something away free, especially as part of a promotion: *the management graciously comped our wine selection.*

com·pact[1] ▶ **adjective** /kəm'pakt, käm-, 'käm,pakt/ **1** closely and neatly packed together; dense. **2** having all the necessary parts or features fitted into a small space.

– SYNONYMS **1 dense,** tightly packed, compressed, thick, tight, firm, solid. **2 neat,** small, handy, portable. **3 concise,** succinct, condensed, brief, pithy, to the point, short and sweet; informal snappy.
– ANTONYMS loose, bulky, lengthy.

▶ **verb** /kəm'pakt, käm-/ press firmly together; compress: *the waste is compacted and buried.*

– SYNONYMS **compress,** condense, pack down, tamp (down), flatten.

▶ **noun** /'käm,pakt/ **1** a small flat case containing face powder, a mirror, and a powder puff. **2** a compact car.

– DERIVATIVES **com·pac·tion** /kəm'paksʜən/ noun **com·pact·ly** adverb **com·pact·ness** noun **com·pac·tor** /kəm'paktər, käm-, 'käm,paktər/ noun.

– ORIGIN from Latin *compingere* 'fasten together.'

com·pact[2] /'käm,pakt/ ▶ **noun** a formal agreement or contract.

– SYNONYMS **treaty,** pact, accord, agreement, contract, bargain, deal, settlement.

– ORIGIN from Latin *compacisci* 'make a covenant with.'

com·pact car ▶ **noun** a medium-sized car.

com·pact disc ▶ **noun** (also **compact disk**) a small plastic disc on which music or other digital information is stored in a form that can be read by a laser.

com·pa·dre /kəm'pädrā/ ▶ **noun** (pl. **compadres**) informal a friend or companion.

– ORIGIN Spanish, 'godfather.'

com·pan·ion /kəm'panyən/ ▶ **noun 1** a person with whom one spends time or travels. **2** each of a pair of things intended to complement or match each other. **3** (**Companion**) a member of the lowest grade of certain orders of knighthood.

– SYNONYMS **comrade,** fellow, partner, associate, escort, compatriot, confederate, friend; informal pal, buddy, bud, chum, crony; Brit. informal mate.

– DERIVATIVES **com·pan·ion·ship** /kəm'panyən,sʜip/ noun.

– ORIGIN Old French *compaignon* 'person who breaks bread with another.'

com·pan·ion·a·ble /kəm'panyənəbəl/ ▶ **adjective** friendly and sociable.

– DERIVATIVES **com·pan·ion·a·bly** /-blē/ adverb.

com·pan·ion·way /kəm'panyən,wā/ ▶ **noun** a set of steps leading from a ship's deck down to a cabin or lower deck.

– ORIGIN from former Dutch *kompanje* 'quarterdeck.'

com·pa·ny /'kəmpənē/ ▶ **noun** (pl. **companies**) **1** a commercial business. **2** the fact of being with another person or other people: *she is excellent company.* **3** a guest or guests: *we're expecting company.* **4** a gathering of people. **5** a body of soldiers, especially the smallest subdivision of an infantry battalion. **6** a group of actors, singers, or dancers who perform together.

– SYNONYMS **1 firm,** business, corporation, establishment, agency, office, house, institution, concern, enterprise, consortium, syndicate; informal outfit. **2 companionship,** fellowship, society, presence. **3 unit,** section, detachment, corps, squad, platoon.

– PHRASES **in company with** together with. **keep someone company** spend time with someone to prevent them feeling lonely or bored.

– ORIGIN Old French *compainie*.

com·pa·ra·ble /'kämp(ə)rəbəl/ ▶ **adjective 1** able to be compared. **2** similar: *prices online and in the shops are broadly comparable.*

– SYNONYMS **1 similar,** close, near, approximate, equivalent, proportionate. **2** *nobody is comparable with him* **equal to,** as good as, in the same league as, on a level with, a match for.
– ANTONYMS incomparable.

– DERIVATIVES **com·pa·ra·bil·i·ty** /,kämp(ə)rə'bilitē/ noun **com·pa·ra·bly** /-blē/ adverb.

com·par·a·tive /kəm'parətiv/ ▶ **adjective 1** measured or judged by comparing one thing with another; relative: *I returned to the comparative comfort of my own home.* **2** involving comparison between two or more subjects or branches of science. **3** (of an adjective or adverb) expressing a higher degree of a quality, but not the highest possible (e.g., *braver*; *more fiercely*). Contrasted with **POSITIVE, SUPERLATIVE.**

com·par·a·tive·ly /kəmˈparətivlē/ ▶ **adverb** to a moderate degree as compared with something else; relatively.

com·par·a·tor /kəmˈparətər/ ▶ **noun** a device for comparing something measurable with a reference or standard.

com·pare /kəmˈpe(ə)r/ ▶ **verb 1** estimate, measure, or note the similarity or difference between: *revenues will amount to $138 million this year, compared with $147 million last year.* **2** (**compare something to**) describe the resemblances of something with something else. **3** be similar to or have a specified relationship with another thing or person: *salaries compare favorably with those of other professions.*

– SYNONYMS **1 contrast,** balance, set against, weigh up. **2 liken,** equate, class with. **3 be as good as,** be comparable to, bear comparison with, be the equal of, match up to, be on a par with, be in the same league as, come close to, rival.

– PHRASES **beyond** (or **without**) **compare** better than all others of the same kind. **compare notes** exchange ideas or information.
– ORIGIN from Latin *compar* 'like, equal.'

com·par·i·son /kəmˈparəsən/ ▶ **noun 1** an instance of comparing things or people. **2** the quality of being similar or equivalent: *there is no comparison between the two offenses.*

– SYNONYMS **resemblance,** likeness, similarity, correspondence.

com·part·ment /kəmˈpärtmənt/ ▶ **noun 1** a separate section of a structure or container. **2** a division of a railroad car marked by partitions.

– SYNONYMS **bay,** locker, recess, alcove, cell, cubicle, pod, pigeonhole, cubbyhole.

– DERIVATIVES **com·part·men·tal** /kəmˌpärtˈmentl/ adjective.
– ORIGIN French *compartiment.*

com·part·men·tal·ize /kəmˌpärtˈmentlˌīz/ ▶ **verb** divide something into categories or sections.
– DERIVATIVES **com·part·men·tal·i·za·tion** /kəmˌpärtˌmentl-əˈzāsʜən/ noun.

com·pass /ˈkəmpəs/ ▶ **noun 1** an instrument containing a magnetized pointer that shows the direction of magnetic north. **2** (also **pair of compasses**) an instrument for drawing circles and arcs and measuring distances between points, consisting of two arms linked by a movable joint. **3** range or scope: *it would be impossible to bring all the subjects within the compass of a single volume.*

– SYNONYMS **scope,** range, extent, reach, span, breadth, ambit, limits, parameters, bounds.

– ORIGIN Old French *compas.*

CHOOSE THE RIGHT WORD

See **RANGE**.

com·pas·sion /kəmˈpasʜən/ ▶ **noun** sympathetic pity and concern for the sufferings or misfortunes of others.

– SYNONYMS **sympathy,** empathy, understanding, fellow feeling, pity, care, concern, sensitivity, kindness.
– ANTONYMS indifference, cruelty.

– ORIGIN from Latin *compati* 'suffer with.'

com·pas·sion·ate /kəmˈpasʜənət/ ▶ **adjective** feeling or showing sympathy and concern for others.

– SYNONYMS **sympathetic,** understanding, pitying, caring, sensitive, warm, loving, kind.
– ANTONYMS unsympathetic, uncaring.

– DERIVATIVES **com·pas·sion·ate·ly** adverb.

com·pas·sion·ate leave ▶ **noun** leave from work granted to someone as a result of personal circumstances, especially the death of a close relative.

com·pass saw ▶ **noun** a handsaw with a narrow blade for cutting curves.

com·pat·i·ble /kəmˈpatəbəl/ ▶ **adjective 1** able to exist or be used together without problems or conflict: *a contemporary design theme that's compatible with any decor.* **2** (of two people) able to have a good relationship; well suited. **3** consistent or in keeping: *the symptoms were compatible with a peptic ulcer.*

– SYNONYMS **well matched,** (well) suited, like-minded, in tune, in harmony, in keeping, consistent, consonant; informal on the same wavelength.

– DERIVATIVES **com·pat·i·bil·i·ty** /kəmˌpatəˈbilitē/ noun **com·pat·i·bly** adverb.
– ORIGIN Latin *compatibilis.*

com·pa·tri·ot /kəmˈpātrēət/ ▶ **noun** a fellow citizen or national of a country.
– ORIGIN French *compatriote.*

com·pel /kəmˈpel/ ▶ **verb** (**compels, compelling, compelled**) **1** force or oblige someone to do something. **2** cause by force or pressure: *ground troops would be necessary to compel capitulation.*

– SYNONYMS **force,** pressure, coerce, dragoon, press, push, oblige, require, make; informal lean on, railroad, put the screws on.

– ORIGIN Latin *compellere.*

com·pel·ling /kəmˈpeliɴɢ/ ▶ **adjective 1** strongly arousing attention or admiration. **2** not able to be resisted or doubted: *a compelling argument.*

– SYNONYMS **1 enthralling,** captivating, gripping, riveting, spellbinding, mesmerizing, absorbing. **2 convincing,** persuasive, cogent, irresistible, powerful, strong.
– ANTONYMS boring, weak.

– DERIVATIVES **com·pel·ling·ly** adverb.

com·pen·di·ous /kəmˈpendēəs/ ▶ **adjective** formal presenting the essential facts in a detailed but concise way.
– DERIVATIVES **com·pen·di·ous·ly** adverb.
– ORIGIN Latin *compendiosus* 'advantageous, brief.'

com·pen·di·um /kəmˈpendēəm/ ▶ **noun** (pl. **compendiums** or **compendia** /-dēə/) **1** a collection of concise but detailed information about a subject. **2** a collection of similar items.
– ORIGIN Latin, 'profit, saving.'

com·pen·sate /ˈkämpənˌsāt/ ▶ **verb 1** give someone something in recognition of loss, suffering, or injury. **2** (**compensate for**) reduce or counteract something undesirable by having an opposite force or effect.

– SYNONYMS **1 recompense,** repay, pay back, reimburse, remunerate, indemnify. **2 balance (out),** counterbalance, counteract, offset, make up for, cancel out.

– DERIVATIVES **com·pen·sa·tor** /-ˌsātər/ noun **com·pen·sa·to·ry** /kəmˈpensəˌtôrē/ adjective.
– ORIGIN Latin *compensare* 'weigh against.'

com·pen·sa·tion /ˌkämpən'sāsʜən/ ▶ **noun 1** something given to someone to compensate for loss, suffering, or injury. **2** something that makes up for an undesirable situation: *getting older has its compensations.* **3** the action of compensating.

– SYNONYMS **recompense,** repayment, reimbursement, remuneration, redress, amends, damages; informal comp.

com·pete /kəm'pēt/ ▶ **verb 1** try to gain or win something by defeating or being better than others. **2** be able to rival another or others: *in this business no one can compete with Schumacher.*

– SYNONYMS **1 take part,** participate, be a contestant, play, enter, go in for. **2** *they had to compete with other firms* **contend,** vie, battle, jockey, go head to head, pit oneself against, challenge, take on.

– ORIGIN Latin *competere.*

com·pe·tence /'kämpətəns/ (also **competency**) ▶ **noun 1** the ability to do something well. **2** the authority of a court or other body to deal with a particular matter.

– SYNONYMS **1** *my technical competence* **ability,** capability, proficiency, accomplishment, expertise, skill, prowess; informal know-how. **2** *the competence of the system* **adequacy,** suitability, fitness.

com·pe·tent /'kämpətənt/ ▶ **adjective 1** having the necessary skill or knowledge to do something successfully. **2** acceptable and satisfactory: *she spoke quite competent French.* **3** having legal authority to deal with a particular matter.

– SYNONYMS **1 able,** capable, proficient, adept, accomplished, skillful, skilled, expert. **2 fit,** suitable, suited, appropriate, qualified, empowered, authorized.

– DERIVATIVES **com·pe·tent·ly** adverb.

– ORIGIN from Latin *competere* in the sense 'be fit or proper.'

com·pe·ti·tion /ˌkämpə'tisʜən/ ▶ **noun 1** the activity of competing against others. **2** an event or contest in which people compete. **3** the person or people with whom one is competing.

– SYNONYMS **1 contest,** tournament, championship, match, game, heat. **2 rivalry,** competitiveness, conflict; informal keeping up with the Joneses. **3 opposition,** rivals, other side, field, enemy.

com·pet·i·tive /kəm'petətiv/ ▶ **adjective 1** relating to competition. **2** strongly desiring to be more successful than others. **3** as good as or better than others of a similar nature: *we offer prompt service at competitive rates.*

– SYNONYMS **1** *a competitive player* **ambitious,** zealous, keen, combative, aggressive. **2** *a highly competitive industry* **ruthless,** aggressive, fierce, cutthroat; informal dog-eat-dog. **3** *competitive prices* **reasonable,** moderate, keen, low, cheap, budget, bargain, rock-bottom, bargain-basement.

– DERIVATIVES **com·pet·i·tive·ly** adverb **com·pet·i·tive·ness** noun.

com·pet·i·tor /kəm'petətər/ ▶ **noun 1** a person who takes part in an athletic contest. **2** an organization or country that competes with others in business or trade.

– SYNONYMS **1 contestant,** contender, challenger, participant, entrant, player. **2 rival,** challenger, opponent, competition, opposition.

com·pi·la·tion /ˌkämpə'lāsʜən/ ▶ **noun 1** the action of compiling something. **2** a thing, especially a book or record, compiled from different sources.

com·pile /kəm'pīl/ ▶ **verb 1** produce a book, report, etc., by assembling material from other sources. **2** gather material to produce a book, report, etc.

– SYNONYMS **assemble,** put together, make up, collate, compose, organize, arrange, gather, collect.

– ORIGIN Latin *compilare* 'plunder or plagiarize.'

com·pil·er /kəm'pīlər/ ▶ **noun 1** a person who compiles information. **2** a computer program that translates instructions from a high-level language into a form that can be executed by the computer.

com·pla·cent /kəm'plāsənt/ ▶ **adjective** satisfied with oneself in a smug or uncritical way.

– SYNONYMS **smug,** self-satisfied, self-congratulatory, resting on one's laurels, pleased with oneself.

– DERIVATIVES **com·pla·cen·cy** /kəm'plāsənsē/ (also **complacence**) noun **com·pla·cent·ly** adverb.

– ORIGIN Latin *complacere* 'to please.'

USAGE

Do not confuse **complacent** with **complaisant**. **Complacent** means *smugly self-satisfied* (*don't be complacent about security*), whereas **complaisant** means *willing to please* (*the local people were complaisant and cordial*).

com·plain /kəm'plān/ ▶ **verb 1** express dissatisfaction or annoyance about something. **2** (**complain of**) state that one is suffering from a symptom of illness.

– SYNONYMS **protest,** grumble, whine, bleat, carp, cavil, grouse, make a fuss, object, find fault; informal gripe, moan, bitch.

– DERIVATIVES **com·plain·er** noun.

– ORIGIN Latin *complangere* 'bewail.'

com·plain·ant /kəm'plānənt/ ▶ **noun** Law a person who brings a case against another in certain lawsuits.

com·plaint /kəm'plānt/ ▶ **noun 1** an act of complaining. **2** a reason for being dissatisfied with something. **3** the expression of dissatisfaction: *a letter of complaint.* **4** an illness or medical condition, especially a minor one.

– SYNONYMS **1 protest,** objection, grievance, grouse, grumble, criticism; informal gripe. **2 disorder,** disease, illness, sickness, ailment, infection, condition, problem, upset, trouble.

com·plai·sant /kəm'plāsənt/ ▶ **adjective** willing to please others or to accept their behavior without protest.

– DERIVATIVES **com·plai·sance** noun.

– ORIGIN Latin *complacere* 'to please.'

USAGE

On the difference between **complaisant** and **complacent**, see the note at **COMPLACENT**.

com·ple·ment ▶ **noun** /'kämpləmənt/ **1** a thing that contributes extra features to something else so as to improve it. **2** the number or quantity that makes something complete: *we have a full complement of staff.* **3** a word or words used with a verb to complete the meaning of the subject (e.g., *happy* in the sentence *we are happy*). **4** Geometry the amount by which a given angle is less than 90°.

– SYNONYMS **1 accompaniment,** companion, addition, supplement, accessory, finishing touch. **2 amount,** contingent, capacity, allowance, quota.

▸ **verb** /-ˌment, -mənt/ add extra features to someone or something in a way that improves.

– SYNONYMS **accompany,** go with, round off, set off, suit, harmonize with, enhance, complete.

– DERIVATIVES **com·ple·men·ta·tion** /ˌkämpləmenˈtāsʜən/ noun.

– ORIGIN from Latin *complere* 'fill up.'

USAGE

The words **complement** and **compliment** are often confused. As a verb, **complement** means 'add extra features to someone or something in a way that improves' (*a classic blazer complements a look that's smart or casual*), while **compliment** means 'politely congratulate or praise someone or something' (*he complimented Kate on her appearance*).

com·ple·men·tar·i·ty /ˌkämpləmenˈtaritē/ ▸ **noun** (pl. **complementarities**) a situation in which two or more different things improve each other or form a balanced whole.

com·ple·men·ta·ry /ˌkämpləˈment(ə)rē/ ▸ **adjective** **1** combining so as to form a whole or to improve each other: *they have different but complementary skills.* **2** relating to complementary medicine.

– SYNONYMS **harmonious,** compatible, corresponding, matching, reciprocal.

USAGE

On the confusion of **complementary** and **complimentary**, see the note at **COMPLIMENTARY**.

com·ple·men·ta·ry an·gle ▸ **noun** either of two angles whose sum is 90°.

com·ple·men·ta·ry col·or ▸ **noun** either of two colors that, when combined, produce white (in the case of light) or black (in the case of pigments).

com·ple·men·ta·ry med·i·cine ▸ **noun** medical therapy that is not part of scientific medicine but may be used alongside it, e.g., acupuncture.

com·plete /kəmˈplēt/ ▸ **adjective 1** having all the necessary or appropriate parts; entire. **2** having run its full course; finished. **3** to the greatest extent or degree; total: *a complete ban on smoking.* **4** (also **compleat**) chiefly humorous skilled at every aspect of an activity: *the compleat mathematician.* **5** (**complete with**) having something as an additional part or feature.

– SYNONYMS **1 entire,** whole, full, total, uncut, unabridged, unexpurgated. **2 finished,** ended, concluded, completed; informal wrapped up, sewn up. **3 absolute,** utter, out-and-out, total, downright, prize, perfect, unqualified, unmitigated, sheer, full-bore.
– ANTONYMS partial, unfinished.

▸ **verb 1** finish making or doing something. **2** provide with the items necessary to make entire or complete: *quarry tiles complete the look.* **3** write the required information on a form.

– SYNONYMS **1 finish,** end, conclude, finalize, wind up, clinch; informal wrap up. **2 finish off,** round off, top off, crown, cap, add the finishing touch.

– DERIVATIVES **com·plete·ness** noun.

– ORIGIN from Latin *complere* 'fill up, finish.'

com·plete·ly /kəmˈplētlē/ ▸ **adverb** totally; utterly.

– SYNONYMS **totally,** entirely, wholly, thoroughly, fully, utterly, absolutely, perfectly, downright.

com·ple·tion /kəmˈplēsʜən/ ▸ **noun 1** the action of completing something or the state of being completed. **2** Football a successful forward pass.

com·ple·tist /kəmˈplētist/ ▸ **noun** an obsessive, typically indiscriminate, collector or fan.

com·plex ▸ **adjective** /kämˈpleks, kəmˈpleks, ˈkämˌpleks/ **1** consisting of many different and connected parts. **2** difficult to understand; complicated.

– SYNONYMS **1 compound,** composite, multiplex. **2 complicated,** involved, intricate, convoluted, elaborate, difficult.
– ANTONYMS simple.

▸ **noun** /ˈkämˌpleks/ **1** a group of similar buildings or facilities on the same site. **2** an interlinked system; a network. **3** a group of repressed feelings that lead to abnormal mental states or behavior. **4** informal a strong concern or anxiety about something.

– SYNONYMS **1 network,** system, nexus, web. **2 obsession,** fixation, preoccupation, neurosis; informal hang-up, thing.

– DERIVATIVES **com·plex·i·ty** /kəmˈpleksitē/ noun (pl. **complexities**) **com·plex·ly** adverb.

– ORIGIN Latin *complexus*.

WORD TOOLKIT

See **INTRICATE**.

com·plex·ion /kəmˈpleksʜən/ ▸ **noun 1** the natural color and texture of the skin of a person's face. **2** the general character of something: *he can single-handedly change the complexion of a game.*

– SYNONYMS **1 skin,** skin color/tone, coloring. **2 kind,** nature, character, color, persuasion, outlook.

– DERIVATIVES **-com·plex·ioned** adjective.

– ORIGIN Latin, 'combination.'

com·plex num·ber ▸ **noun** Mathematics a number containing both a real and an imaginary part.

com·pli·ance /kəmˈplīəns/ ▸ **noun** the action of obeying an order, rule, or request.

com·pli·ant /kəmˈplīənt/ ▸ **adjective 1** tending to be excessively obedient or ready to accept something. **2** in accordance with rules or standards.

– DERIVATIVES **com·pli·ant·ly** adverb.

com·pli·cate /ˈkämpləˌkāt/ ▸ **verb** make something more intricate or confusing.

– SYNONYMS **make (more) difficult,** make complicated, mix up, confuse, muddle, obscure.
– ANTONYMS simplify.

– ORIGIN Latin *complicare* 'fold together.'

com·pli·cat·ed /ˈkämpləˌkātid/ ▸ **adjective 1** consisting of many interconnecting elements; intricate. **2** involving many confusing aspects.

– SYNONYMS **complex,** involved, intricate, convoluted, elaborate, difficult, knotty, tortuous, labyrinthine, Byzantine.
– ANTONYMS simple, straightforward.

com·pli·ca·tion /ˌkämpləˈkāsʜən/ ▸ **noun 1** a thing that complicates something; a difficulty. **2** an involved or confused state: *companies offering a variety of solutions with a minimum of complication.* **3** a secondary disease or condition that makes an already existing one worse.

– SYNONYMS **difficulty,** problem, obstacle, hurdle, stumbling block, snag, catch, hitch; informal headache, fly in the ointment, monkey wrench in the works.

com·plic·it /kəm'plisit/ ▶ **adjective** involved with others in an unlawful activity: *the militant group may be complicit in ten violent incidents.*

com·plic·i·ty /kəm'plisitē/ ▶ **noun** involvement with others in an unlawful activity.
– ORIGIN from Old French *complice* 'an associate.'

com·pli·ment ▶ **noun** /'kämpləmənt/ **1** a polite expression of praise or admiration. **2** (**compliments**) formal greetings.

– SYNONYMS **tribute,** accolade, commendation, pat on the back; (**compliments**) praise, acclaim, admiration, flattery, congratulations.
– ANTONYMS criticism, insult.

▶ **verb** /'kämplə,ment/ politely congratulate or praise: *he complimented Kate on her appearance.*

– SYNONYMS **praise,** pay tribute to, flatter, commend, acclaim, applaud, salute, congratulate.
– ANTONYMS criticize.

– PHRASES **return the compliment** retaliate or respond in a similar way. **with one's compliments** provided free of charge.
– ORIGIN Italian *complimento* 'fulfillment of the requirements of courtesy.'

USAGE

On the confusion of **compliment** and **complement**, see the note at **COMPLEMENT**.

com·pli·men·ta·ry /,kämplə'mentərē, -'mentrē/ ▶ **adjective 1** praising or approving: *a complimentary remark.* **2** given free of charge.

– SYNONYMS **1 flattering,** appreciative, congratulatory, admiring, approving, favorable, glowing. **2 free (of charge),** gratis; informal on the house.
– ANTONYMS critical.

USAGE

Do not confuse the words **complimentary** and **complementary**. **Complimentary** means 'praising' or 'given free of charge' (*a complimentary breakfast*), whereas **complementary** means 'combining to form a whole or to improve each other' (*they have different but complementary skills*).

com·pline /'kämplin, -,plīn/ ▶ **noun** (in the Roman Catholic and High Anglican Church) an evening service traditionally said before retiring for the night.
– ORIGIN from Old French *complie* 'completed.'

com·ply /kəm'plī/ ▶ **verb** (**complies, complying, complied**) (often **comply with**) **1** act in accordance with a request or order. **2** meet specified standards: *engines designed to comply with state emissions standards.*

– SYNONYMS *I can't* ***comply with*** *those rules* **obey,** observe, abide by, adhere to, conform to, follow, respect, go along with.
– ANTONYMS disobey.

– ORIGIN Latin *complere* 'fulfill, fill up.'

com·po·nent /kəm'pōnənt/ ▶ **noun** a part or element of a larger whole.

– SYNONYMS **part,** piece, bit, element, constituent, ingredient, unit, module.

▶ **adjective** being part of a larger whole.
– ORIGIN from Latin *componere* 'put together.'

com·port /kəm'pôrt/ ▶ **verb** (**comport oneself**) formal behave in a particular way: *students who comported themselves well in television interviews.*
– ORIGIN Latin *comportare.*

com·port·ment /kəm'pôrtmənt/ ▶ **noun** formal a person's behavior or bearing.

com·pose /kəm'pōz/ ▶ **verb 1** make up a whole: *the committee is composed of ten senators.* **2** create a work of art, especially music or poetry. **3** form a whole by arranging parts in an orderly or artistic way. **4** phrase a letter or other piece of writing with care and thought. **5** (often as adj. **composed**) settle one's features or thoughts. **6** prepare a written work for printing by setting up the characters to be printed.

– SYNONYMS **1 write,** devise, make up, think up, produce, invent, pen, author. **2 organize,** arrange, construct, set out. **3 make up,** constitute, form, comprise. **4** *she tried to* ***compose herself*** **calm down,** control oneself, regain one's composure, pull oneself together, steady oneself; informal get a grip. **5** (as adj. **composed**) *she remained composed throughout the ordeal* **calm,** collected, cool (as a cucumber), self-possessed, poised, serene, relaxed, at ease, unruffled, unperturbed; informal unflappable, together, laid-back.

– ORIGIN Latin *componere* 'put together.'

com·pos·er /kəm'pōzər/ ▶ **noun** a person who writes music.

com·pos·ite /kəm'päzət, käm-/ ▶ **adjective 1** made up of various parts. **2** (**Composite**) relating to a classical style of architecture consisting of elements of the Ionic and Corinthian orders. **3** (of a plant) having flowerheads consisting of numerous florets, such as a daisy. ▶ **noun 1** a thing made up of several parts. **2** a motion for debate composed of two or more related resolutions.
– ORIGIN from Latin *componere* 'put together.'

com·po·si·tion /,kämpə'zisʜən/ ▶ **noun 1** the way in which something is made up from different elements: *the molecular composition of cells.* **2** a work of music, literature, or art. **3** a thing made up of various elements. **4** the composing of something. **5** the artistic arrangement of the parts of a picture.

– SYNONYMS **1 makeup,** constitution, configuration, structure, formation, anatomy, organization. **2 work (of art),** creation, opus, piece. **3 writing,** creation, formulation, compilation. **4 essay,** paper, study, piece of writing, theme. **5 arrangement,** layout, proportions, balance, symmetry.

– DERIVATIVES **com·po·si·tion·al** adjective.

com·pos·i·tor /kəm'päzitər/ ▶ **noun** a person who arranges type for printing or who keys text into a composing machine.

com·pos men·tis /,kämpəs 'mentəs/ ▶ **adjective** having full control of one's mind.
– ORIGIN Latin.

com·post /'käm,pōst/ ▶ **noun 1** decayed organic material used as a fertilizer for plants. **2** a mixture of compost with soil used for growing plants. ▶ **verb** make organic matter into compost.
– DERIVATIVES **com·post·er** noun.
– ORIGIN Latin *composita* 'something put together.'

com·po·sure /kəm'pōzHər/ ▶ **noun** the state of being calm and self-controlled.

– SYNONYMS **self-control,** self-possession, calm, equanimity, equilibrium, serenity, tranquility, poise, presence of mind, sangfroid, placidness, impassivity; informal cool.

com·pote /'käm,pōt/ ▶ **noun** fruit preserved or cooked in syrup.
– ORIGIN French.

com·pound[1] ▶ **noun** /'käm,pound/ **1** a thing composed of two or more separate elements. **2** a substance formed from two or more elements chemically united in fixed proportions. **3** a word made up of two or more existing words.

– SYNONYMS **amalgam,** blend, mixture, mix, alloy.

▶ **adjective** /'käm,pound, käm'pound, kəm'pound/ **1** made up or consisting of several elements. **2** (of interest) payable on both capital and the accumulated interest. Compare with **SIMPLE**. **3** (of a leaf, flower, or eye) consisting of two or more simple parts or individuals in combination.

– SYNONYMS **composite,** complex, multiple.
– ANTONYMS simple.

▶ **verb** /kəm'pound, käm'pound, 'käm,pound/ **1** make up a composite whole. **2** mix ingredients to form a whole. **3** make something bad worse.

– SYNONYMS **1 mix,** combine, blend. **2 aggravate,** exacerbate, worsen, add to, augment, intensify, heighten, increase.

– DERIVATIVES **com·pound·er** noun.
– ORIGIN from Latin *componere* 'put together.'

com·pound[2] /'käm,pound/ ▶ **noun** a large open area enclosed by a fence, for example within a prison.
– ORIGIN Malay, 'enclosure, hamlet.'

com·pound eye ▶ **noun** an eye consisting of an array of numerous small visual units, as found in insects and crustaceans.

com·pound frac·ture ▶ **noun** an injury in which a broken bone pierces the skin.

com·pre·hend /,kämpri'hend/ ▶ **verb 1** fully understand something. **2** formal include or encompass: *a divine order comprehending all men.*

– SYNONYMS **understand,** grasp, see, take in, follow, make sense of, fathom; informal work out, figure out, get.

– ORIGIN Latin *comprehendere.*

com·pre·hen·si·ble /,kämpri'hensəbəl/ ▶ **adjective** able to be understood; intelligible.

– SYNONYMS **intelligible,** understandable, lucid, coherent, accessible, self-explanatory, clear, plain, straightforward.
– ANTONYMS incomprehensible.

– DERIVATIVES **com·pre·hen·si·bil·i·ty** /-,hensə'bilitē/ noun.

com·pre·hen·sion /,kämpri'hencHən/ ▶ **noun** the ability to understand something.

– SYNONYMS **understanding,** grasp, mastery, conception, knowledge, awareness.
– ANTONYMS ignorance.

com·pre·hen·sive /,kämpri'hensiv/ ▶ **adjective 1** including or dealing with all or nearly all aspects of something: *a comprehensive guidebook.* **2** (also **comprehensive examination** or **comp**) an examination testing a student's command of a special field of knowledge. **3** (of motor-vehicle insurance) providing cover for most risks.

– SYNONYMS **inclusive,** all-inclusive, complete, full, thorough, extensive, all-embracing, blanket, exhaustive, detailed, sweeping, wholesale, broad, wide-ranging.
– ANTONYMS limited.

▶ **noun** Brit. a comprehensive school.
– DERIVATIVES **com·pre·hen·sive·ly** adverb **com·pre·hen·sive·ness** noun.

com·press ▶ **verb** /kəm'pres/ **1** squeeze or press so as to occupy less space: *the skirt can be compressed into a small bag.* **2** squeeze or press two things together.

– SYNONYMS **1 squeeze,** press, squash, crush, compact. **2 shorten,** abridge, condense, abbreviate, contract, telescope, summarize, précis.
– ANTONYMS expand, pad out.

▶ **noun** /'käm,pres/ a pad of absorbent material pressed onto part of the body to relieve inflammation or stop bleeding.
– DERIVATIVES **com·press·i·bil·i·ty** /kəm,presə'bilitē/ noun **com·press·i·ble** adjective **com·pres·sive** /-'presiv/ adjective.
– ORIGIN from Latin *comprimere* 'press together.'

com·pressed air ▶ **noun** air that is at more than atmospheric pressure.

com·pres·sion /kəm'presHən/ ▶ **noun 1** the action of compressing something. **2** the reduction in volume (causing an increase in pressure) of the fuel mixture in an internal-combustion engine before ignition.
– DERIVATIVES **com·pres·sion·al** adjective.

com·pres·sor /kəm'presər/ ▶ **noun 1** an instrument or device for compressing something. **2** a machine used to supply air or other gas at increased pressure.

com·prise /kəm'prīz/ ▶ **verb 1** be made up of; consist of: *the country comprises twenty states.* **2** (also **be comprised of**) make up a whole: *this breed comprises 50 percent of the Swiss cattle population.*

– SYNONYMS **1** *the country comprises twenty states* **consist of,** be made up of, be composed of, contain. **2** *this breed comprises half the herd* **make up,** constitute, form, account for.

– ORIGIN from French *comprendre* 'comprehend.'

USAGE

Traditionally, **comprise** means 'consist of' and should not be used to mean 'make up a whole.' However, a passive use of **comprise** (as in *the country is comprised of twenty states*) is now becoming part of standard English: this has broadly the same meaning as the traditional active sense (*the country comprises twenty states*).

com·pro·mise /'kämprə,mīz/ ▶ **noun 1** an agreement reached by each side making concessions. **2** something that is halfway between conflicting elements: *a compromise between greed and caution.*

– SYNONYMS **agreement,** understanding, settlement, terms, deal, trade-off, bargain, middle ground.

▶ **verb 1** settle a dispute by each side making concessions. **2** accept standards that are lower than is desirable for practical reasons: *we weren't prepared to compromise on safety.* **3** bring someone into disrepute or danger by reckless behavior.

– SYNONYMS **1 meet each other halfway,** come to an understanding, make a deal, make concessions, find a happy medium, strike a balance. **2 undermine,** weaken, damage, harm, jeopardize, prejudice.

– DERIVATIVES **com·pro·mis·er** noun.
– ORIGIN from Latin *compromittere*.

com·pro·mis·ing /'kämprə,mīzinG/ ▶ **adjective** revealing an embarrassing or incriminating secret.

comp·trol·ler /kən'trōlər, ,käm(p)'trōlər, 'käm(p),trōlər/ ▶ **noun** a controller (used in the title of some financial officers).
– ORIGIN variant of **CONTROLLER**.

com·pul·sion /kəm'pəlsHən/ ▶ **noun** **1** the compelling of someone to do something. **2** an irresistible urge to do something.

> – SYNONYMS **1** *he is under no compulsion to go* **obligation,** pressure, coercion. **2** **urge,** impulse, need, desire, drive, obsession, fixation, addiction.

com·pul·sive /kəm'pəlsiv/ ▶ **adjective** **1** resulting from or acting on an irresistible urge: *compulsive eating*. **2** powerfully interesting or exciting.

> – SYNONYMS **1** *a compulsive desire* **irresistible,** uncontrollable, compelling, overwhelming. **2** *compulsive eating* **obsessive,** obsessional, addictive, uncontrollable. **3** **inveterate,** chronic, incorrigible, incurable, hopeless, persistent, habitual; informal pathological. **4** **fascinating,** compelling, gripping, riveting, engrossing, enthralling, captivating.

– DERIVATIVES **com·pul·sive·ly** adverb **com·pul·sive·ness** noun.

com·pul·so·ry /kəm'pəlsərē/ ▶ **adjective** required by law or a rule; obligatory.

> – SYNONYMS **obligatory,** mandatory, required, requisite, necessary, binding, enforced, prescribed.
> – ANTONYMS optional.

– DERIVATIVES **com·pul·so·ri·ly** /-sərəlē/ adverb.

com·punc·tion /kəm'pəNG(k)sHən/ ▶ **noun** a feeling of guilt that prevents or follows wrongdoing: *he felt no compunction about deceiving them*.
– ORIGIN Latin, from *compungere* 'prick sharply.'

com·pu·ta·tion /,kämpyŏŏ'tāsHən/ ▶ **noun** **1** mathematical calculation. **2** the use of computers, especially as a subject of research or study.
– DERIVATIVES **com·pu·ta·tion·al** /,kämpyŏŏ'tāsHənl/ adjective.

com·pute /kəm'pyōōt/ ▶ **verb** calculate a figure or amount.

> – SYNONYMS **calculate,** work out, reckon, determine, evaluate, add up, total.

– ORIGIN Latin *computare*.

com·put·er /kəm'pyōōtər/ ▶ **noun** an electronic device capable of storing and processing information according to a predetermined set of instructions.

com·put·er·ize /kəm'pyōōtə,rīz/ ▶ **verb** convert something to a system or form that is controlled, stored, or processed by computer.
– DERIVATIVES **com·put·er·i·za·tion** /kəm,pyōōtərə'zāsHən/ noun.

com·put·er-lit·er·ate ▶ **adjective** having enough knowledge and skill to be able to use computers.

com·put·ing /kəm'pyōōtiNG/ ▶ **noun** the use or operation of computers.

com·rade /'käm,rad, 'kämrəd/ ▶ **noun** **1** (among men) a colleague or a fellow member of an organization. **2** (also **comrade-in-arms**) a fellow soldier.

> – SYNONYMS **companion,** friend, colleague, associate, partner, ally; informal **buddy;** Brit. informal **mate.**

– DERIVATIVES **com·rade·ly** adjective **com·rade·ship** /-,sHip/ noun.
– ORIGIN Spanish *camarada* 'room-mate.'

con[1] /kän/ informal ▶ **verb** (**cons, conning, conned**) persuade someone to do or believe something by lying to them. ▶ **noun** an act of deceiving or tricking someone.
– ORIGIN abbreviation of **CONFIDENCE**, as in *confidence trick*.

con[2] ▶ **noun** (usu. in phrase **pros and cons**) a disadvantage of or argument against something.
– ORIGIN from Latin *contra* 'against.'

con[3] ▶ **noun** informal a convict.

con[4] ▶ **verb** variant spelling of **CONN**.

con·cat·e·nate /kən'katn,āt/ ▶ **verb** formal or technical link things together in a chain or series.
– ORIGIN Latin *concatenare* 'link together.'

con·cat·e·na·tion /kən,katn'āsHən/ ▶ **noun** a series of interconnected things: *a concatenation of events that had led to the murder*.

con·cave /kän'kāv, 'kän,kāv/ ▶ **adjective** having an outline or surface that curves inward like the inside of a ball. Compare with **CONVEX**.
– DERIVATIVES **con·cav·i·ty** /kän'kavitē/ noun.
– ORIGIN Latin *concavus*, from *cavus* 'hollow.'

con·ceal /kən'sēl/ ▶ **verb** **1** prevent someone or something from being seen. **2** keep something secret.

> – SYNONYMS **1** *clouds concealed the sun* **hide,** screen, cover, obscure, block out, blot out, mask. **2** *he concealed his true feelings* **keep secret,** hide, disguise, mask, veil, bottle up; informal keep a/the lid on.
> – ANTONYMS reveal, confess.

– DERIVATIVES **con·ceal·er** noun **con·ceal·ment** noun.
– ORIGIN Latin *concelare*, from *celare* 'hide.'

con·cede /kən'sēd/ ▶ **verb** **1** finally admit or agree that something is true. **2** give up a possession, advantage, or right. **3** admit defeat in a match or contest. **4** fail to prevent an opponent scoring a goal or point.

> – SYNONYMS **1** **admit,** acknowledge, accept, allow, grant, recognize, own, confess, agree. **2** **surrender,** yield, give up, relinquish, hand over.
> – ANTONYMS deny.

– ORIGIN Latin *concedere*.

con·ceit /kən'sēt/ ▶ **noun** **1** excessive pride in oneself. **2** an artistic effect or device. **3** a complicated metaphor.

> – SYNONYMS **vanity,** pride, arrogance, egotism, self-importance, narcissism, self-admiration.
> – ANTONYMS humility.

– ORIGIN from **CONCEIVE**.

> **CHOOSE THE RIGHT WORD**
>
> See **PRIDE**.

con·ceit·ed /kən'sētid/ ▶ **adjective** excessively proud of oneself.

> – SYNONYMS **vain,** proud, arrogant, egotistic, self-important, narcissistic, full of oneself, swollen-headed, boastful, cocky, self-satisfied, smug; informal bigheaded, stuck-up.

WORD TOOLKIT

conceited ...	smug ...	condescending ...
jerk	look	tone
bastard	satisfaction	manner
pig	smirk	voice
idiot	superiority	remarks
jackass	confidence	message

con·ceiv·a·ble /kən'sēvəbəl/ ▶ adjective capable of being imagined or understood.

– SYNONYMS **imaginable,** possible, plausible, credible, believable, feasible.

– DERIVATIVES **con·ceiv·a·bly** /-blē/ adverb.

con·ceive /kən'sēv/ ▶ verb **1** become pregnant with a child. **2** form a plan or idea in the mind: *the project was conceived by a Dutch businessman.*

– SYNONYMS **1 think up,** think of, dream up, devise, formulate, design, create, develop; informal cook up. **2 imagine,** envisage, visualize, picture.

– ORIGIN Latin *concipere.*

con·cen·trate /'känsən,trāt/ ▶ verb **1** focus all one's attention on a particular object or activity: *she couldn't concentrate on the movie.* **2** gather together in large numbers or a mass at one point: *resources should be concentrated in areas where unemployment is highest.* **3** increase the strength of a substance or solution.

– SYNONYMS **1** *she **concentrated on** the movie* **focus on,** pay attention to, give one's attention to, put one's mind to, keep one's mind on, be absorbed in, be engrossed in, be immersed in. **2** (as adj. **concentrated**) *a concentrated effort* **strenuous,** concerted, intensive, all-out, intense. **3 collect,** gather, congregate, converge, mass, rally. **4** (as adj. **concentrated**) *concentrated fruit juice* **condensed,** reduced, undiluted, strong.

▶ noun a concentrated substance or solution.

– DERIVATIVES **con·cen·tra·tor** noun.

– ORIGIN from Latin *con-* 'together' + *centrum* 'center.'

con·cen·tra·tion /,känsən'trāsнən/ ▶ noun **1** the action or power of concentrating. **2** a close gathering of people or things. **3** the relative amount of a particular substance within a solution or mixture.

– SYNONYMS **close attention,** attentiveness, application, single-mindedness, absorption.
– ANTONYMS inattention.

con·cen·tra·tion camp ▶ noun a camp for holding political prisoners, especially in Nazi Germany.

con·cen·tric /kən'sentrik, kän-/ ▶ adjective (of circles or arcs) sharing the same center.

– ORIGIN Latin *concentricus.*

con·cept /'kän,sept/ ▶ noun an abstract idea: *the concept of justice.*

– SYNONYMS **idea,** notion, conception, abstraction, theory, hypothesis.

– ORIGIN Latin *conceptum* 'something conceived.'

con·cep·tion /kən'sepsнən/ ▶ noun **1** the process of conceiving a child. **2** the forming of a plan or idea. **3** the way in which something is viewed or regarded: *our conception of democracy.* **4** ability to imagine or understand something: *the administration had no conception of women's problems.*

– SYNONYMS **1 pregnancy,** fertilization, impregnation, insemination. **2 inception,** genesis, origination, creation, invention, beginning, origin. **3 plan,** idea, notion, scheme, project, proposal, intention, aim.

con·cep·tu·al /kən'sepcнo͞oəl/ ▶ adjective relating to ideas or concepts.

– DERIVATIVES **con·cep·tu·al·ly** adverb.

con·cep·tu·al·ize /kən'sepcнo͞oə,līz/ ▶ verb form an idea or concept of something in the mind.

– DERIVATIVES **con·cep·tu·al·i·za·tion** /kən,sepcнo͞oələ'zāsнən/ noun.

con·cern /kən'sərn/ ▶ verb **1** relate to; be about. **2** affect or involve: *stop interfering in matters that don't concern you.* **3** make someone anxious or worried.

– SYNONYMS **1** *the memo concerns health benefits* **be about,** deal with, cover, relate to, pertain to. **2** *does this concern you?* **affect,** involve, be relevant to, apply to, have a bearing on, impact on. **3 worry,** disturb, trouble, bother, perturb, unsettle.

▶ noun **1** worry or anxiety. **2** a matter of interest or importance: *the court's primary concern is her welfare.* **3** a business or company.

– SYNONYMS **1 anxiety,** worry, disquiet, apprehensiveness, unease, misgiving. **2 care,** consideration, solicitude, sympathy. **3 responsibility,** business, affair, duty, job; informal bailiwick. **4** *issues of concern to women* **interest,** importance, relevance, significance. **5 firm,** business, company, enterprise, operation, corporation; informal outfit.
– ANTONYMS indifference.

– ORIGIN Latin *concernere.*

con·cerned /kən'sərnd/ ▶ adjective worried or anxious.

– SYNONYMS **1 worried,** anxious, upset, troubled, uneasy, bothered. **2 interested,** involved, affected, implicated.
– ANTONYMS unconcerned.

con·cern·ing /kən'sərnɪɴɢ/ ▶ preposition about.

– SYNONYMS **about,** regarding, relating to, with reference to, referring to, with regard to, as regards, touching, in connection with, re, apropos.

con·cert /'kän,sərt, 'känsərt/ ▶ noun a musical performance given in public.

– PHRASES **in concert 1** acting together. **2** giving a live public performance.

– ORIGIN from Italian *concertare* 'harmonize.'

con·cert·ed /kən'sərtəd/ ▶ adjective **1** jointly arranged or carried out: *a concerted campaign.* **2** done with great effort or determination.

– SYNONYMS **1** *a concerted effort* **strenuous,** vigorous, intensive, all-out, intense, concentrated. **2** *concerted action* **joint,** united, collaborative, collective, combined, cooperative.

con·cer·ti·na /,känsər'tēnə/ ▶ noun a small musical instrument played by stretching and squeezing a central bellows, each note being sounded by a button. ▶ verb (**concertinas, concertinaing** /,känsər'tēnəɪɴɢ/, **concertinaed** or **concertina'd**) compress something into folds like those of a concertina.

con·cer·to /kən'cнertō/ ▶ noun (pl. **concertos** or **concerti** /-tē/) a musical composition for an orchestra and one or more solo instruments.

– ORIGIN Italian.

con·cert pitch ▶ noun **1** an international standard for the tuning of musical instruments. **2** a state of readiness and keenness.

con·ces·sion /kən'sesHən/ ▸ **noun 1** a thing given up or allowed to settle a dispute: *the union was reluctant to make any concessions.* **2** a reduction in price for a certain kind of person. **3** a commercial operation set up within the premises of a larger business. **4** the right to use land or other property for a particular purpose, granted by a government or other controlling body.

– SYNONYMS **1 compromise,** accommodation, trade-off, sop. **2 reduction,** cut, discount, deduction, rebate; informal break. **3 right,** privilege, license, permit, franchise, warrant.

– DERIVATIVES **con·ces·sion·ar·y** adjective.
– ORIGIN Latin.

con·ces·sion·aire /kən,sesHə'ne(ə)r/ ▸ **noun** someone who holds a concession.

conch /kängk, känch, kôngk/ ▸ **noun** (pl. **conchs** /kängks, kôngks/ or **conches** /'känchiz/) a mollusk of tropical seas, with a spiral shell.
– ORIGIN Greek *konkhē* 'mussel, cockle.'

con·cierge /kôn'syerzh, ,känsē'erzh/ ▸ **noun 1** (especially in France) a resident caretaker of an apartment block or small hotel. **2** a hotel employee who assists guests by booking tours, making theater and restaurant reservations, etc.
– ORIGIN French.

con·cil·i·ate /kən'silē,āt/ ▸ **verb 1** make someone calmer or less angry. **2** act as a mediator in a dispute.
– DERIVATIVES **con·cil·i·a·tion** /kən,silē'āsHən/ noun **con·cil·i·a·tor** /-,ātər/ noun.
– ORIGIN Latin *conciliare* 'combine.'

CHOOSE THE RIGHT WORD

See **PACIFY**.

con·cil·i·a·to·ry /kən'silēə,tôrē/ ▸ **adjective** intended to make someone calmer or less angry: *a conciliatory tone of voice.*

con·cise /kən'sīs/ ▸ **adjective** giving information clearly and in few words.

– SYNONYMS **succinct,** pithy, brief, abridged, condensed, abbreviated, compact.
– ANTONYMS lengthy.

– DERIVATIVES **con·cise·ly** adverb **con·cise·ness** noun **con·ci·sion** /-'sizHən/ noun.
– ORIGIN Latin *concisus* 'cut up, cut down.'

con·clave /'kän,klāv/ ▸ **noun 1** a private meeting. **2** (in the Roman Catholic Church) a meeting of cardinals in order to elect a pope.
– ORIGIN Latin, 'lockable room,' from *clavis* 'key.'

con·clude /kən'klo͞od/ ▸ **verb 1** bring or come to an end. **2** arrive at a judgment or opinion by reasoning: *doctors concluded that she had suffered a stroke.* **3** formally settle or arrange a treaty or agreement.

– SYNONYMS **1 finish,** end, come/bring to an end, draw to a close, close, wind up, terminate, stop, cease; informal wrap up. **2 settle,** clinch, finalize, tie up; informal sew up. **3 deduce,** infer, gather, judge, decide, surmise, figure.
– ANTONYMS begin.

– ORIGIN Latin *concludere.*

con·clu·sion /kən'klo͞ozHən/ ▸ **noun 1** an end or finish. **2** the summing-up of an argument or text. **3** a judgment or decision reached by reasoning: *she came to the conclusion that her husband was right.* **4** the settling of a treaty or agreement.

– SYNONYMS **1 end,** ending, finish, close. **2 settlement,** clinching, completion, arrangement. **3 deduction,** inference, interpretation, judgment, verdict.
– ANTONYMS beginning.

con·clu·sive /kən'klo͞osiv, -ziv/ ▸ **adjective** decisive or convincing: *conclusive evidence.*

– SYNONYMS **incontrovertible,** undeniable, indisputable, irrefutable, unquestionable, convincing, certain, decisive, definitive, definite, positive, categorical, unequivocal.
– ANTONYMS unconvincing.

– DERIVATIVES **con·clu·sive·ly** adverb.

WORD TOOLKIT

See **FINAL**.

con·coct /kən'käkt/ ▸ **verb 1** make a dish or meal by combining different ingredients. **2** invent a story or plan.

– SYNONYMS **make up,** dream up, fabricate, invent, devise, formulate, hatch, brew; informal cook up.

– DERIVATIVES **con·coc·tion** /kən'käksHən/ noun.
– ORIGIN Latin *concoquere* 'cook together.'

con·com·i·tant /kən'kämitənt/ formal ▸ **adjective** occurring or naturally connected with something else: *the Gulf crisis and the concomitant rise in oil prices.* ▸ **noun** a phenomenon that occurs or is naturally connected with something else.
– DERIVATIVES **con·com·i·tant·ly** adverb.
– ORIGIN Latin *concomitari* 'accompany.'

con·cord /'käng,kôrd, 'kän-/ ▸ **noun 1** literary agreement; harmony. **2** a treaty.
– ORIGIN Latin *concordia.*

con·cord·ance /kən'kôrdns/ ▸ **noun 1** an alphabetical list of the important words in a text, usually with quotations from or references to the passages concerned. **2** formal agreement.
– ORIGIN Latin *concordare* 'agree on.'

con·cord·ant /kən'kôrdnt/ ▸ **adjective** in agreement; consistent.

con·cor·dat /kən'kôr,dat/ ▸ **noun** an agreement or treaty, especially one between the Vatican and a government.

con·course /'kän,kôrs, 'käng-/ ▸ **noun 1** a large open area inside or in front of a public building. **2** formal a crowd of people.
– ORIGIN Latin *concursus.*

con·crete /kän'krēt, 'kän,krēt, kən'krēt/ ▸ **adjective 1** existing in a physical form; not abstract. **2** specific; definite: *concrete proof.*

– SYNONYMS **1 solid,** material, real, physical, tangible. **2 definite,** specific, firm, positive, conclusive, definitive.
– ANTONYMS abstract, imaginary.

▸ **noun** a building material made from gravel, sand, cement, and water, forming a stonelike mass when dry. ▸ **verb** cover a surface with concrete.
– DERIVATIVES **con·crete·ly** adverb **con·crete·ness** noun.
– ORIGIN Latin *concretus* 'grown together.'

con·crete jun·gle ▸ **noun** an urban area with many large, unattractive, modern buildings.

con·cre·tion /kən'krēsHən, kän-/ ▸ **noun** a hard solid mass.

con·cu·bine /'kängkyo͝o,bīn/ ▸ **noun 1** chiefly historical (in societies in which a man may have more than one wife)

a woman who lives with a man but has lower status than his wife or wives. **2** old use a man's mistress.
– ORIGIN Latin *concubina*.

con·cu·pis·cence /kän'kyo͞opisəns, kən-/ ▶ **noun** formal lust.
– DERIVATIVES **con·cu·pis·cent** /kän'kyo͞opisənt, kən-/ adjective.
– ORIGIN Latin *concupiscere* 'begin to desire.'

con·cur /kən'kər/ ▶ **verb** (**concurs, concurring, concurred**) **1** agree: *the Council concurred with this decision.* **2** happen at the same time.

– SYNONYMS **agree,** be in agreement, accord, be in sympathy, see eye to eye, be of the same mind, be of the same opinion.
– ANTONYMS disagree.

– ORIGIN Latin *concurrere* 'run together.'

con·cur·rent /kən'kərənt, -'kə-rənt/ ▶ **adjective 1** existing or happening at the same time. **2** Mathematics (of three or more lines) meeting at or approaching one point.
– DERIVATIVES **con·cur·rence** noun **con·cur·rent·ly** adverb.

con·cuss /kən'kəs/ ▶ **verb** hit someone on the head, making them temporarily unconscious or confused.

con·cus·sion /kən'kəsнən/ ▶ **noun 1** temporary unconsciousness or confusion caused by a blow on the head. **2** a violent shock as from a heavy blow.
– ORIGIN Latin.

con·demn /kən'dem/ ▶ **verb 1** express complete disapproval of someone or something. **2** sentence someone to a punishment: *the rebels had been condemned to death.* **3** force someone to endure something unpleasant: *he was condemned to a lifelong struggle with depression.* **4** officially declare something to be unfit for use.

– SYNONYMS **1 censure,** criticize, denounce, deplore, decry; informal slam. **2** *his illness condemned him to a lonely childhood* **doom,** destine, damn, sentence.
– ANTONYMS praise.

– DERIVATIVES **con·dem·na·tion** /ˌkändem'nāsнən, -dəm-/ noun **con·dem·na·to·ry** /-'demnəˌtôrē/ adjective.
– ORIGIN Latin *condemnare*.

con·den·sa·tion /ˌkänˌden'sāsнən, -dən-/ ▶ **noun 1** water from humid air collecting as droplets on a cold surface. **2** the conversion of a vapor or gas to a liquid.

con·dense /kən'dens/ ▶ **verb 1** change from a gas or vapor to a liquid. **2** make something denser or more concentrated. **3** express a piece of writing or speech in fewer words.

– SYNONYMS **abridge,** compress, summarize, shorten, cut, abbreviate, edit.
– ANTONYMS expand.

– ORIGIN Latin *condensare*.

con·densed milk ▶ **noun** milk that has been thickened by evaporation and sweetened.

con·dens·er /kən'densər/ ▶ **noun 1** a piece of equipment for condensing vapor. **2** a lens or system of lenses for collecting and directing light. **3** another term for **CAPACITOR**.

con·de·scend /ˌkändə'send/ ▶ **verb 1** behave as if one is better than other people. **2** do something that one believes to be below one's dignity or level of importance: *he condescended to see me at my hotel.*

– SYNONYMS **1 patronize,** talk down to, look down one's nose at, look down on. **2** *he condescended to see us* **deign,** stoop, lower oneself, demean oneself, consent.

– DERIVATIVES **con·de·scen·sion** /-'sencнən/ noun.
– ORIGIN Latin *condescendere*.

con·de·scend·ing /ˌkändə'sendiNG/ ▶ **adjective** feeling or showing that one thinks one is better than other people.

– SYNONYMS **patronizing,** supercilious, superior, disdainful, lofty, haughty; informal snooty, stuck-up; Brit. informal toffee-nosed.

– DERIVATIVES **con·de·scend·ing·ly** adverb.

WORD TOOLKIT

See **CONCEITED**.

con·dign /kən'dīn/ ▶ **adjective** formal (of punishment) fitting and deserved.
– ORIGIN Latin *condignus*.

con·di·ment /'kändəmənt/ ▶ **noun** a substance such as salt, mustard, or ketchup, used to flavor food.
– ORIGIN Latin *condimentum*.

con·di·tion /kən'disнən/ ▶ **noun 1** the state of something or someone, with regard to appearance, fitness, or working order. **2** (**conditions**) the circumstances affecting something: *the health risks associated with poor living conditions.* **3** a state of affairs that must exist before something else is possible: *for a country to borrow money, three conditions must be met.* **4** an illness or medical problem.

– SYNONYMS **1 state,** shape, order, fitness, health, form. **2 circumstances,** surroundings, environment, situation, state of affairs, position. **3 disorder,** problem, complaint, illness, disease, ailment, malady. **4 stipulation,** constraint, prerequisite, precondition, requirement, term, proviso.

▶ **verb 1** train or accustom to behave in a certain way: *some students may have been conditioned to respond to authority figures.* **2** have a significant influence on or determine something. **3** bring something into a good or desired state or condition. **4** apply conditioner to the hair.

– SYNONYMS **train,** teach, educate, guide, accustom, adapt, habituate, mold.

– PHRASES **on condition that** as long as certain requirements are fulfilled.
– ORIGIN Latin *condicion* 'agreement.'

con·di·tion·al /kən'disнənl/ ▶ **adjective 1** subject to one or more conditions or requirements being fulfilled; depending on other factors: *a conditional offer.* **2** (of a clause, phrase, conjunction, or verb form) expressing a condition.

– SYNONYMS **qualified,** dependent, contingent, with reservations, limited, provisional, provisory.

▶ **noun** the conditional form of a verb, for example *should* in *if I should die*.
– DERIVATIVES **con·di·tion·al·ly** adverb.

con·di·tion·er /kən'disн(ə)nər/ ▶ **noun** a thing used to improve the condition of something, especially a liquid applied to the hair after shampooing.

con·do /'kändō/ ▶ **noun** (pl. **condos**) informal short for **CONDOMINIUM** (sense 1).

con·dole /kən'dōl/ ▶ **verb** (**condole with**) express sympathy for someone.
– ORIGIN Latin *condolere* 'grieve or suffer with.'

con·do·lence /kən'dōləns/ ▸ **noun** an expression of sympathy for someone, especially when a relative or close friend has died.

con·dom /'kändəm, 'kən-/ ▸ **noun** a thin rubber sheath worn on the penis during sex as a contraceptive or to protect against infection.
– ORIGIN unknown.

con·do·min·i·um /ˌkändə'minēəm/ ▸ **noun** (pl. **condominiums**) **1** a building or complex containing a number of individually owned apartments or houses. **2** an apartment or house in a condominium. **3** the joint control of a country's affairs by other countries.
– ORIGIN Latin.

con·done /kən'dōn/ ▸ **verb** overlook or forgive an offense or wrongdoing.

> – SYNONYMS **disregard,** accept, allow, let pass, turn a blind eye to, overlook, forget, forgive, pardon, excuse.
> – ANTONYMS condemn.

– ORIGIN Latin *condonare* 'refrain from punishing.'

con·dor /'känˌdôr, -dər/ ▸ **noun** a very large South American vulture with a bare head and mainly black plumage.
– ORIGIN Spanish.

con·duce /kən'd(y)o͞os/ ▸ **verb** (**conduce to**) formal help to bring something about.
– ORIGIN Latin *conducere* 'bring together.'

con·du·cive /kən'd(y)o͞osiv/ ▸ **adjective** (**conducive to**) contributing to or helping to bring something about: *an environment that is conducive to learning.*

> – SYNONYMS **favorable,** beneficial, advantageous, opportune, encouraging, promising, convenient, good, helpful, instrumental.
> – ANTONYMS unfavorable.

con·duct ▸ **noun** /'känˌdəkt/ **1** the way in which a person behaves. **2** management or direction: *the conduct of foreign affairs.*

> – SYNONYMS **1 behavior,** actions, deeds, doings, exploits. **2 management,** running, direction, control, supervision, regulation, administration, organization, coordination, handling.

▸ **verb** /kən'dəkt/ **1** organize and carry something out. **2** guide someone to or around a place. **3** (**conduct oneself**) behave in a particular way. **4** transmit heat, electricity, etc., by conduction. **5** direct the performance of a piece of music or an orchestra or choir.

> – SYNONYMS **1 manage,** direct, run, administer, organize, coordinate, orchestrate, handle, carry out/on. **2** *he was conducted through the corridors* **escort,** guide, lead, usher, steer. **3** *I am proud of the way they* ***conducted themselves*** **behave,** act, acquit oneself, bear oneself. **4** *aluminum conducts heat* **transmit,** convey, carry, channel.

– ORIGIN Latin *conducere* 'bring together.'

con·duct·ance /kən'dəktəns/ ▸ **noun** the degree to which a material conducts electricity.

con·duc·tion /kən'dəksʜən/ ▸ **noun** the transmission of heat or electricity directly through a substance.
– DERIVATIVES **con·duc·tive** /kən'dəktiv/ adjective.

con·duc·tiv·i·ty /ˌkänˌdək'tivitē, kən-/ ▸ **noun** the degree to which a particular material conducts electricity or heat.

con·duc·tor /kən'dəktər/ ▸ **noun 1** a person who conducts an orchestra or choir. **2** a material or device that conducts heat or electricity. **3** a person who sells tickets and collects fares on a train, streetcar, or other public conveyance.
– DERIVATIVES **con·duc·tress** /kən'dəktrəs/ noun.

con·duit /'känˌd(y)o͞oət, 'känd(w)ət/ ▸ **noun 1** a channel for carrying water or other fluid from one place to another. **2** a tube or trough protecting electric wiring.
– ORIGIN Old French.

cone /kōn/ ▸ **noun 1** an object that tapers from a circular base to a point. **2** (also **traffic cone**) a plastic cone used to separate off sections of a road. **3** the cone-shaped dry fruit of a conifer. **4** a cone-shaped wafer for holding ice cream. **5** one of two types of light-sensitive cell in the retina of the eye, responsible for sharpness of vision and color perception. Compare with **ROD**.
– ORIGIN Greek *kōnos.*

co·ney /'kōnē/ (also **cony**) ▸ **noun** (pl. **coneys**) a rabbit.
– ORIGIN Old French *conin,* from Latin *cuniculus.*

con·fab /'känˌfab, kən'fab/ ▸ **noun** informal an informal conversation or discussion.

con·fab·u·late /kən'fabyəˌlāt/ ▸ **verb** formal have a conversation.
– DERIVATIVES **con·fab·u·la·tion** /-ˌfabyə'lāsʜən/ noun.
– ORIGIN Latin *confabulari.*

con·fect /kən'fekt/ ▸ **verb** formal make something by putting together various elements.
– ORIGIN Latin *conficere* 'put together.'

con·fec·tion /kən'feksʜən/ ▸ **noun 1** an elaborate sweet dish. **2** an elaborately constructed thing: *an extravagant confection of marble and gilt.*

con·fec·tion·er /kən'feksʜənər/ ▸ **noun** a person who makes or sells candy and other sweets.

con·fec·tion·ers' sug·ar (also **confectioner's sugar**) ▸ **noun** finely powdered sugar used to make icing.

con·fec·tion·er·y /kən'feksʜəˌnerē/ ▸ **noun** candy and other sweets.

con·fed·er·a·cy /kən'fedərəsē/ ▸ **noun** (pl. **confederacies**) **1** a league or alliance, especially of confederate states. **2** (**the Confederacy**) the Confederate States of America.

con·fed·er·ate ▸ **adjective** /kən'fedərət/ **1** joined by an agreement or treaty. **2** (**Confederate**) referring to the southern states that separated from the US in 1860–1861. ▸ **noun** /kən'fedərət/ an accomplice or fellow worker. ▸ **verb** /-ˌrāt/ (usu. as adj. **confederated**) bring states or groups of people into an alliance.
– ORIGIN Latin *confoederatus.*

con·fed·er·a·tion /kənˌfedə'rāsʜən/ ▸ **noun 1** an alliance of a number of parties or groups. **2** a union of states with some political power belonging to a central authority.

con·fer /kən'fər/ ▸ **verb** (**confers, conferring, conferred**) **1** grant a title, award, benefit, or right to someone: *an honorary degree was conferred on her.* **2** have discussions.

> – SYNONYMS **1 bestow,** present, grant, award, honor with. **2 consult,** talk, speak, converse, have a chat, deliberate, compare notes.

– DERIVATIVES **con·fer·ment** noun **con·fer·ral** /-'fərəl/ noun.
– ORIGIN Latin *conferre* 'bring together.'

> **CHOOSE THE RIGHT WORD**
>
> See **GIVE**.

con·fer·ee /ˌkänfəˈrē/ ▶ **noun** a person who attends a conference.

con·fer·ence /ˈkänf(ə)rəns/ ▶ **noun** a formal meeting for discussion or debate.

– SYNONYMS **meeting,** congress, convention, seminar, discussion, council, forum, summit.

con·fess /kənˈfes/ ▶ **verb 1** admit to a crime or wrongdoing. **2** acknowledge something reluctantly. **3** declare one's sins formally to a priest.

– SYNONYMS **1 admit,** acknowledge, reveal, disclose, divulge, own up, plead guilty, accept the blame; informal come clean. **2** *I confess I don't know* **acknowledge,** admit, concede, grant, allow, own.
– ANTONYMS deny.

– ORIGIN Old French *confesser*.

con·fes·sion /kənˈfesHən/ ▶ **noun 1** an act of confessing, especially a formal statement admitting to a crime. **2** an account of one's sins given privately to a priest. **3** (also **confession of faith**) a statement setting out essential religious beliefs.

con·fes·sion·al /kənˈfesHənl/ ▶ **noun 1** an enclosed stall in a church, in which a priest sits to hear confessions. **2** a confession. ▶ **adjective 1** referring to speech or writing in which a person admits to private thoughts or incidents in their past. **2** relating to religious confession.

con·fes·sor /kənˈfesər/ ▶ **noun 1** a priest who hears confessions. **2** a person who makes a confession.

con·fet·ti /kənˈfetē/ ▶ **noun** small pieces of colored paper traditionally thrown over a bride and groom after a marriage ceremony.
– ORIGIN Italian, 'sweets' (from the Italian custom of throwing sweets during carnivals).

con·fi·dant /ˈkänfəˌdant, -ˌdänt/ ▶ **noun** (fem. **confidante** pronunc. same) a person in whom one confides.

con·fide /kənˈfīd/ ▶ **verb 1** tell someone about a secret or private matter in confidence: *he decided to confide in Elizabeth*. **2** (**confide something to**) dated entrust something to the care of someone.

– SYNONYMS **reveal,** disclose, divulge, impart, declare, vouchsafe, tell, confess.

– ORIGIN Latin *confidere* 'have full trust.'

con·fi·dence /ˈkänfədəns, -fəˌdens/ ▶ **noun 1** the belief that one can have faith in or rely on someone or something. **2** self-assurance resulting from a belief in one's own ability to achieve things. **3** a feeling of trust that someone will not reveal private information to others: *things I had told her in confidence*. **4** a private matter told to someone under the understanding that they will keep it secret.

– SYNONYMS **1 trust,** belief, faith, credence. **2 self-assurance,** self-confidence, self-possession, assertiveness, self-belief, conviction.
– ANTONYMS distrust, doubt.

– PHRASES **in someone's confidence** in a position of trust with someone.

con·fi·dence game ▶ **noun** an act of cheating someone by gaining their trust.

con·fi·dent /ˈkänfədənt, -fəˌdent/ ▶ **adjective 1** feeling confidence in oneself. **2** feeling certainty about something.

– SYNONYMS **1 sure,** certain, positive, convinced, in no doubt, satisfied. **2 self-assured,** assured, self-confident, positive, assertive, self-possessed.

– DERIVATIVES **con·fi·dent·ly** adverb.

WORD TOOLKIT

confident ...	sanguine ...	optimistic ...
mood	expectation	outlook
smile	attitude	view
voice	temperament	forecast
tone	acceptance	prediction
manner	approach	assessment
assertion	response	estimate
stride	resignation	prognosis
swagger	conclusion	scenario

con·fi·den·tial /ˌkänfəˈdencHəl/ ▶ **adjective 1** intended to be kept secret: *confidential information*. **2** entrusted with private information: *a confidential secretary*.

– SYNONYMS **private,** personal, intimate, quiet, secret, sensitive, classified, restricted; informal **hush-hush.**

– DERIVATIVES **con·fi·den·ti·al·i·ty** /-ˌdencHēˈalitē/ noun **con·fi·den·tial·ly** adverb.

con·fig·u·ra·tion /kənˌfig(y)əˈrāsHən/ ▶ **noun** an arrangement of the parts of something in a particular way.

con·fig·ure /kənˈfigyər/ ▶ **verb 1** arrange something in a particular way. **2** arrange a computer system so that it is able to perform a particular task.
– DERIVATIVES **con·fig·ur·a·ble** adjective.
– ORIGIN Latin *configurare*.

con·fine ▶ **verb** /kənˈfīn/ **1** (**confine someone/thing to**) keep someone or something within certain limits of space, scope, or time. **2** (**be confined to**) be unable to leave one's bed, home, etc., due to illness or disability. **3** (**be confined**) dated (of a woman) remain in bed for a period before, during, and after giving birth.

– SYNONYMS **1 enclose,** incarcerate, imprison, intern, hold captive, cage, lock up, coop up. **2 restrict,** limit.

▶ **noun** /ˈkänˌfīn/ (**confines** /ˈkänˌfīnz/) limits or boundaries.
– ORIGIN from Latin *confinis* 'bordering.'

con·fined /kənˈfīnd/ ▶ **adjective** (of a space) small and enclosed.

con·fine·ment /kənˈfīnmənt/ ▶ **noun 1** the state of being confined. **2** dated the time at which a woman gives birth.

con·firm /kənˈfərm/ ▶ **verb 1** state or show that something is true or correct: *the Stock Exchange confirmed that it was investigating the rumors*. **2** make something definite or formally valid: *hotels usually require a deposit to confirm a booking*. **3** (**confirm someone in**) make someone feel or believe something more strongly: *the experience confirmed her in her decision not to employ a nanny*. **4** administer the religious ceremony of confirmation to someone.

– SYNONYMS **1 corroborate,** verify, prove, substantiate, justify, vindicate, bear out. **2 affirm,** reaffirm, assert, assure someone, repeat. **3 ratify,** approve, endorse, validate, sanction, authorize.
– ANTONYMS contradict, deny.

– DERIVATIVES **con·firm·a·to·ry** /-məˌtôrē/ adjective.
– ORIGIN Latin *confirmare*.

con·fir·ma·tion /ˌkänfərˈmāsHən/ ▶ **noun 1** the action of confirming something. **2** the religious rite at which a baptized person is admitted as a full member of the Christian Church. **3** the Jewish ceremony of bar mitzvah.

con·firmed /kən'fərmd/ ▶ adjective firmly established in a habit, belief, or way of life: *a confirmed bachelor*.

con·fis·cate /'känfəˌskāt/ ▶ verb take or seize property with authority.

– SYNONYMS **impound**, seize, commandeer, requisition, appropriate, expropriate, take, sequestrate.

– DERIVATIVES **con·fis·ca·tion** /ˌkänfə'skāsʜən/ noun.
– ORIGIN Latin *confiscare* 'put away in a chest.'

con·fit /kôɴ'fē/ ▶ noun duck or other meat cooked very slowly in its own fat.
– ORIGIN French, 'conserved.'

con·fla·gra·tion /ˌkänflə'grāsʜən/ ▶ noun a large and destructive fire.
– ORIGIN Latin, from *flagrare* 'to blaze.'

con·flate /kən'flāt/ ▶ verb combine two or more things into one.
– DERIVATIVES **con·fla·tion** /-'flāsʜən/ noun.
– ORIGIN Latin *conflare* 'kindle, fuse.'

con·flict ▶ noun /'känˌflikt/ **1** a serious disagreement or argument. **2** a long-lasting armed struggle. **3** a lack of agreement between opinions, principles, etc.: *a conflict of interests*.

– SYNONYMS **1 dispute,** quarrel, squabble, disagreement, clash, feud, discord, friction, strife, antagonism, hostility. **2 war,** campaign, fighting, engagement, struggle, hostilities, warfare, combat. **3** *a conflict between work and home life* **clash,** incompatibility, friction, mismatch, variance, contradiction.
– ANTONYMS agreement, peace, harmony.

▶ verb /kən'flikt, 'känˌflikt/ be different or in opposition: *his theory conflicted with those generally accepted at the time*.

– SYNONYMS **1 clash,** be incompatible, be at odds, differ, diverge, disagree, collide. **2** (as adj. **conflicting**) *the two suspects gave conflicting stories* **contradictory,** incompatible, inconsistent, irreconcilable, contrary, opposite, opposing, clashing.

– ORIGIN Latin *conflictus*.

con·flu·ence /'känˌflo͞oəns, kən'flo͞oəns/ ▶ noun **1** a place where two rivers join. **2** an act or the process of two or more things merging.
– ORIGIN from Latin *confluere*.

con·form /kən'fôrm/ ▶ verb **1** obey or follow rules, standards, or conventions: *the kitchen does not conform to hygiene regulations*. **2** be similar in form or type: *families that do not conform to the conventional stereotype*.

– SYNONYMS **1** *visitors have to* **conform to** *our rules* **comply with,** abide by, obey, observe, follow, keep to, stick to, adhere to, uphold, heed, accept, go along with. **2 fit in,** behave (oneself), toe the line, obey the rules; informal play by the rules.
– ANTONYMS flout, rebel.

– ORIGIN Latin *conformare*.

con·form·ance /kən'fôrməns/ ▶ noun another term for CONFORMITY.

con·for·ma·tion /ˌkänfôr'māsʜən, -fər-/ ▶ noun the shape or structure of something.

con·form·ist /kən'fôrmist/ ▶ noun a person who behaves or thinks in the same way as most other people, rather than in an original or unconventional way. ▶ adjective conventional.
– DERIVATIVES **con·form·ism** /-ˌmizəm/ noun.

con·form·i·ty /kən'fôrmitē/ ▶ noun **1** the fact of following or obeying conventions, rules, or laws. **2** similarity in form or type.

con·found /kən'found/ ▶ verb **1** surprise or confuse someone. **2** prove a theory or expectation wrong. **3** defeat a plan, aim, or hope.

– SYNONYMS **baffle,** bewilder, mystify, bemuse, perplex, puzzle, confuse, dumbfound, throw; informal flabbergast, flummox.

– ORIGIN Latin *confundere* 'pour together, mix up.'

con·found·ed /kən'foundəd, kän-/ ▶ adjective informal, dated used to express annoyance.
– DERIVATIVES **con·found·ed·ly** adverb.

con·fra·ter·ni·ty /ˌkänfrə'tərnitē/ ▶ noun (pl. **confraternities**) a brotherhood, especially with a religious or charitable purpose.
– ORIGIN Latin *confraternitas*.

con·frère /'känˌfrer, kän'frer, kôɴ'frer/ ▶ noun a fellow member of a profession.
– ORIGIN French, from Latin *frater* 'brother.'

con·front /kən'frənt/ ▶ verb **1** come face to face with someone in a hostile or defiant way: *he was confronted by a police officer*. **2** (of a problem) present itself to someone: *the government was confronted with many difficulties*. **3** face up to and deal with a problem. **4** force someone to face or consider something: *she confronted him with her suspicions*.

– SYNONYMS **1 challenge,** square up to, face (up to), come face to face with, meet, accost, stand up to, tackle. **2 face,** bedevil, beset, plague, bother, trouble, threaten. **3** *they must confront these issues* **tackle,** address, face (up to), come to grips with, grapple with, deal with, sort out.
– ANTONYMS evade.

– ORIGIN Latin *confrontare*.

con·fron·ta·tion /ˌkänfrən'tāsʜən/ ▶ noun a situation of angry disagreement or opposition.

– SYNONYMS **conflict,** clash, fight, battle, encounter, head-to-head; informal set-to, run-in, dust-up, showdown.

– DERIVATIVES **con·fron·ta·tion·al** adjective.

Con·fu·cian /kən'fyo͞osʜən/ ▶ adjective relating to the Chinese philosopher Confucius (551–479 BC) or his philosophy. ▶ noun a follower of Confucius or his philosophy.
– DERIVATIVES **Con·fu·cian·ism** /kən'fyo͞osʜəˌnizəm/ noun **Con·fu·cian·ist** noun & adjective.

con·fuse /kən'fyo͞oz/ ▶ verb **1** make someone unable to think clearly or understand something. **2** make something less easy to understand. **3** mistake one person or thing for another.

– SYNONYMS **1 bewilder,** baffle, mystify, bemuse, perplex, puzzle, nonplus; informal flummox, faze. **2** *the authors have confused the issue* **complicate,** muddle, blur, obscure, cloud. **3** (as adj. **confusing**) *the instructions are confusing* **puzzling,** baffling, perplexing, bewildering, mystifying, ambiguous, misleading, inconsistent, contradictory. **4** *some confuse strokes with heart attacks* **mix up with,** muddle up with, mistake for.
– ANTONYMS enlighten, simplify.

– DERIVATIVES **con·fus·a·ble** adjective.
– ORIGIN from Latin *confusus*.

con·fused /kən'fyo͞ozd/ ▶ **adjective** **1** unable to think clearly or understand something. **2** lacking order and so difficult to understand or make sense of.

– SYNONYMS **1 puzzled,** bemused, bewildered, perplexed, baffled, mystified; informal flummoxed. **2 disorientated,** bewildered, muddled, addled, befuddled, demented, senile. **3** *a confused recollection* **vague,** unclear, indistinct, imprecise, blurred, hazy, dim. **4 disorderly,** disorganized, untidy, jumbled, mixed up, chaotic, topsy-turvy, tangled; informal higgledy-piggledy.
– ANTONYMS clear, lucid.

– DERIVATIVES **con·fus·ed·ly** /-'fyo͞ozədlē/ adverb.

con·fu·sion /kən'fyo͞ozhən/ ▶ **noun** **1** the state of being confused; uncertainty or lack of understanding. **2** a situation or state of panic or disorder. **3** the mistaking of one person or thing for another.

– SYNONYMS **1 bewilderment,** bafflement, perplexity, puzzlement, bemusement, mystification, befuddlement, disorientation, uncertainty. **2 disorder,** disarray, muddle, mess, chaos, mayhem, pandemonium, turmoil; informal shambles.
– ANTONYMS clarity, order.

con·fute /kən'fyo͞ot/ ▶ **verb** formal prove a person or an accusation or assertion to be wrong.
– DERIVATIVES **con·fu·ta·tion** /ˌkänfyo͝o'tāshən/ noun.
– ORIGIN Latin *confutare* 'restrain, answer conclusively.'

CHOOSE THE RIGHT WORD

See **REFUTE**.

con·ga /'käNGgə/ ▶ **noun** **1** a Latin American dance performed by people in single file and consisting of three steps forward followed by a kick. **2** (also **conga drum**) a tall, narrow drum beaten with the hands.
– ORIGIN Spanish, from *congo* 'Congolese.'

con·geal /kən'jēl/ ▶ **verb** (of a liquid substance) become semisolid, especially by cooling.

– SYNONYMS **coagulate,** clot, thicken, cake, set, gel.

– ORIGIN Latin *congelare*, from *gelare* 'freeze.'

con·ge·ner /kən'jēnər/ ▶ **noun** a chemical constituent, especially one that gives a distinctive character to a wine or liquor or is responsible for some of its effects on the body.
– ORIGIN Latin.

con·gen·ial /kən'jēnyəl/ ▶ **adjective** **1** (of a person) pleasant to be with because their qualities or interests are similar to one's own: *congenial company*. **2** pleasant because suited to one's taste or character: *congenial working conditions*.

– SYNONYMS **agreeable,** pleasant, friendly, amicable, amiable, nice.
– ANTONYMS unfriendly, unpleasant.

– DERIVATIVES **con·ge·ni·al·i·ty** /-ˌjēnē'alitē/ noun **con·gen·ial·ly** adverb.

con·gen·i·tal /kən'jenətl/ ▶ **adjective** **1** (of a disease or abnormality) present from birth. **2** having a particular trait as an apparently permanent part of one's character: *a congenital liar*.
– DERIVATIVES **con·gen·i·tal·ly** adverb.
– ORIGIN from Latin *congenitus* 'born together.'

con·ger /'käNGgər/ (also **conger eel**) ▶ **noun** a large eel of coastal waters.
– ORIGIN Greek *gongros*.

con·ge·ries /'känjərēz/ ▶ **noun** (pl. same) a disorderly collection.
– ORIGIN Latin, 'heap, pile.'

con·gest·ed /kən'jestid/ ▶ **adjective** **1** so crowded as to make movement difficult or impossible. **2** abnormally full of blood. **3** blocked with mucus.

– SYNONYMS **blocked,** clogged, choked, jammed, obstructed, crowded, overcrowded, overflowing, packed; informal snarled up, gridlocked.
– ANTONYMS clear.

– ORIGIN Latin *congerere* 'heap up.'

con·ges·tion /kən'jesCHən/ ▶ **noun** the state of being congested: *the new bridge should ease congestion in the area*.

con·ges·tive /kən'jestiv/ ▶ **adjective** Medicine involving or occurring as a result of a part of the body becoming abnormally full of blood.

con·glom·er·ate ▶ **noun** /kən'glämərət/ **1** something consisting of a number of different and distinct things. **2** a large corporation formed by the merging of separate firms. **3** a type of sedimentary rock consisting of rounded fragments cemented together. ▶ **verb** /-ˌrāt/ gather into or form a conglomerate.
– DERIVATIVES **con·glom·er·a·tion** /kənˌglämə'rāshən/ noun.
– ORIGIN Latin *conglomerare* 'roll or heap together.'

Con·go·lese /ˌkäNGgə'lēz, -'lēs/ ▶ **noun** (pl. same) **1** a person from the Congo or the Democratic Republic of Congo (formerly Zaire). **2** any of the languages spoken in the Congo region. ▶ **adjective** relating to the Congo or the Democratic Republic of Congo.

con·grat·u·late /kən'graCHəˌlāt, -'grajə-/ ▶ **verb** **1** express good wishes or praise at the happiness or success of someone. **2** (**congratulate oneself**) think oneself lucky or clever.

– SYNONYMS **compliment,** wish someone happiness, pay tribute to, pat on the back, take one's hat off to, praise, applaud, salute, honor.
– ANTONYMS criticize.

– DERIVATIVES **con·grat·u·la·to·ry** /-ləˌtôrē/ adjective.
– ORIGIN Latin *congratulari*.

con·grat·u·la·tion /kənˌgraCHə'lāshən, -ˌgrajə-/ ▶ **noun** **1** (**congratulations**) praise or good wishes on a special occasion. **2** the action of congratulating someone.

– SYNONYMS (**congratulations**) **best wishes,** compliments, greetings, felicitations.

con·gre·gant /'käNGgrəgənt/ ▶ **noun** a member of a congregation.

con·gre·gate /'käNGgrəˌgāt/ ▶ **verb** gather into a crowd or mass.

– SYNONYMS **assemble,** gather, collect, come together, convene, rally, muster, meet, cluster, group.
– ANTONYMS disperse.

– ORIGIN Latin *congregare*.

con·gre·ga·tion /ˌkäNGgrə'gāshən/ ▶ **noun** **1** a group of people gathered together for religious worship. **2** a gathering of people or things.
– DERIVATIVES **con·gre·ga·tion·al** adjective.

Con·gre·ga·tion·al·ism /ˌkäNGgrə'gāshənlˌizəm/ ▶ **noun** a system of organization among Christian churches in which individual churches are largely self-governing.
– DERIVATIVES **Con·gre·ga·tion·al** adjective **Con·gre·ga·tion·al·ist** noun & adjective.

con·gress /ˈkängɡrəs, ˈkän-/ ▶ **noun 1** a formal meeting or series of meetings between delegates. **2** (**Congress**) the national lawmaking body of the US. **3** formal the action of coming together.
– DERIVATIVES **con·gres·sion·al** /kənˈɡreshənl/ adjective.
– ORIGIN Latin *congressus*.

con·gress·man /ˈkängɡrəsmən, ˈkän-/ (or **congresswoman** /ˈkängɡrəs,wo͝omən, ˈkän-/) ▶ **noun** (pl. **congressmen** or **congresswomen**) a member of the US Congress.

con·gru·ent /kənˈɡro͞oənt, ˈkängɡro͞oənt/ ▶ **adjective 1** in agreement or harmony. **2** Geometry (of figures) identical in form.
– DERIVATIVES **con·gru·ence** noun.
– ORIGIN from Latin *congruere* 'agree.'

con·gru·ous /ˈkängɡro͞oəs/ ▶ **adjective** in agreement or harmony.
– DERIVATIVES **con·gru·i·ty** /kənˈɡro͞oitē/ noun.

con·i·cal /ˈkänikəl/ ▶ **adjective** shaped like a cone.

con·ic sec·tion /ˈkänik/ ▶ **noun** the figure of a circle, ellipse, parabola, or hyperbola formed by the intersection of a plane and a circular cone.

co·ni·fer /ˈkänəfər, kō-/ ▶ **noun** a tree bearing cones and evergreen needlelike or scalelike leaves, e.g., a pine or cypress.
– DERIVATIVES **co·nif·er·ous** /kəˈnifərəs/ adjective.
– ORIGIN Latin, 'cone-bearing.'

con·jec·ture /kənˈjekchər/ ▶ **noun** an opinion or conclusion based on incomplete information; a guess. ▶ **verb** form a conjecture; guess.
– DERIVATIVES **con·jec·tur·al** /kənˈjekchərəl/ adjective.
– ORIGIN Latin *conjectura*.

con·join /kənˈjoin, kän-/ ▶ **verb** formal join; combine.

con·joined twins ▶ **plural noun** technical term for **Siamese twins**.

con·joint /kənˈjoint, kän-/ ▶ **adjective** formal combined or united.

con·ju·gal /ˈkänjəɡəl/ ▶ **adjective** relating to marriage or the relationship between husband and wife.
– ORIGIN Latin *conjugalis*.

con·ju·gate /ˈkänjə,ɡāt/ ▶ **verb** give the different forms of a verb.
– DERIVATIVES **con·ju·ga·tion** /ˌkänjəˈɡāshən/ noun.
– ORIGIN Latin *conjugare* 'yoke together.'

con·junct ▶ **adjective** /kənˈjəngkt, kän-/ joined together, combined, or associated. ▶ **noun** /ˈkänjəngkt/ each of two or more things that are joined or associated.
– ORIGIN from Latin *conjunctus* 'join together.'

con·junc·tion /kənˈjəngkshən/ ▶ **noun 1** a word used to connect words or clauses (e.g., *and*, *if*). **2** an instance of two or more events occurring at the same point in time or space. **3** Astronomy & Astrology an alignment of two planets so that they appear to be in the same place in the sky.
– PHRASES **in conjunction** together.
– ORIGIN Latin.

con·junc·ti·va /ˌkän,jəng(k)ˈtīvə, kən-/ ▶ **noun** (pl. **conjunctivae**) the mucous membrane that covers the front of the eye and lines the inside of the eyelids.
– ORIGIN from Latin *membrana conjunctiva* 'conjunctive membrane.'

con·junc·tive /kənˈjəng(k)tiv/ ▶ **adjective** relating to or forming a conjunction.

con·junc·ti·vi·tis /kən,jəng(k)təˈvītis/ ▶ **noun** inflammation of the conjunctiva.

con·junc·ture /kənˈjəngkchər/ ▶ **noun 1** a combination of events. **2** a state of affairs.

con·jure /ˈkänjər, ˈkən-/ ▶ **verb** (usu. **conjure something up**) **1** cause a spirit or ghost to appear by magic. **2** cause something to appear as if by magic. **3** create an image of something in the mind: *the books conjure up nostalgic memories of Christmases past.*

> – SYNONYMS **1 produce,** magic, summon. **2** *the picture that his words **conjured up*** **bring to mind,** call to mind, evoke, summon up, suggest.

– ORIGIN Latin *conjurare* 'conspire.'

con·jur·ing /ˈkänjəriNG, ˈkən-/ ▶ **noun** a form of entertainment involving apparently magical tricks, typically ones that seem to make objects appear or disappear.

con·ju·ror /ˈkänjərər, ˈkən-/ (also **conjurer**) ▶ **noun** a person who performs conjuring tricks.

conk[1] /kängk, kôngk/ ▶ **verb** (**conk out**) informal **1** (of a machine) break down. **2** faint or go to sleep. **3** die.
– ORIGIN unknown.

conk[2] ▶ **verb** informal hit someone on the head.
– ORIGIN perhaps from **conch**.

con man ▶ **noun** informal a man who cheats people by using a confidence game.

conn /kän/ (also **con**) ▶ **verb** direct the steering of a ship.
– ORIGIN apparently from the old word *cond* 'conduct, guide,' from Old French *conduire*.

con·nect /kəˈnekt/ ▶ **verb 1** bring together so as to establish a link. **2** join together so as to provide access and communication: *the buildings were connected by underground passages.* **3** (**be connected**) be related in some way: *bonuses are connected to the firm's performance.* **4** (of a train, bus, etc.) arrive at its destination just before another leaves so that passengers can transfer.

> – SYNONYMS **1 attach,** join, fasten, fix, link, hook (up), secure, hitch, stick. **2** *rituals **connected with** Easter* **associate with,** link to/with, couple with, identify with, relate to.
> – ANTONYMS detach.

– DERIVATIVES **con·nect·or** noun.
– ORIGIN Latin *connectere*.

> **CHOOSE THE RIGHT WORD**
>
> See **join**.

con·nect·ing rod ▶ **noun** the rod connecting the piston and the crankshaft in an engine.

con·nec·tion /kəˈnekshən/ ▶ **noun 1** a link or relationship. **2** (**connections**) influential people with whom one has contact or to whom one is related. **3** an opportunity for catching a connecting train, bus, etc.

> – SYNONYMS **1 link,** relationship, relation, interconnection, interdependence, association, bond, tie, tie-in, correspondence. **2** *he has the right connections* **contact,** friend, acquaintance, ally, colleague, associate, relation.

– PHRASES **in connection with** concerning.

con·nec·tive /kəˈnektiv/ ▶ **adjective** connecting one thing to another.

con·nec·tive tis·sue ▶ **noun** body tissue that connects, supports, binds, or separates other tissues or organs.

con·nec·tiv·i·ty /kəˌnek'tivitē/ ▶ **noun 1** the state or extent of being connected. **2** Computing capacity for the interconnection of systems, applications, etc.

conn·ing tow·er ▶ **noun** a raised structure on a submarine, containing the periscope.

con·nive /kə'nīv/ ▶ **verb 1** (often **connive with**) conspire. **2** (**connive at/in**) secretly allow a wrongdoing.

– SYNONYMS **1** *he connived with a coworker to steal two million dollars* **conspire,** collude, collaborate, plot, scheme. **2** (as adj. **conniving**) *his conniving brother planned the whole dirty affair* **scheming,** cunning, calculating, devious, wily, sly, artful, manipulative, Machiavellian, deceitful.

– DERIVATIVES **con·niv·ance** /kə'nīvəns/ noun.
– ORIGIN Latin *connivere* 'shut the eyes (to).'

con·nois·seur /ˌkänə'sər, -'so͝or/ ▶ **noun** an expert in matters involving the judgment of beauty, quality, or skill: *a connoisseur of Renaissance art.*
– ORIGIN French, from *connaître* 'know.'

con·no·ta·tion /ˌkänə'tāshən/ ▶ **noun** an idea or feeling suggested by a word in addition to its main or literal meaning.

– SYNONYMS **overtone,** undertone, undercurrent, implication, nuance, hint, echo, association.

con·note /kə'nōt/ ▶ **verb** (of a word or phrase) imply or suggest something in addition to its main or literal meaning (e.g., the word *mother* connotes qualities such as protection and affection).
– ORIGIN Latin *connotare* 'mark in addition.'

con·nu·bi·al /kə'n(y)o͞obēəl/ ▶ **adjective** literary relating to marriage; conjugal.
– ORIGIN Latin *connubialis.*

con·quer /'käNGkər/ ▶ **verb 1** overcome and take control of a territory or its people by military force. **2** successfully overcome a problem or climb a mountain.

– SYNONYMS **1 defeat,** beat, vanquish, triumph over, overcome, overwhelm, overpower, overthrow, subdue, subjugate. **2** *Peru was conquered by Spain* **seize,** take (over), appropriate, capture, occupy, invade, annex, overrun. **3 overcome,** get the better of, control, master, deal with, cope with, rise above; informal lick.

– DERIVATIVES **con·quer·or** noun.
– ORIGIN Latin *conquirere* 'gain, win.'

con·quest /'känˌkwest, 'käNG-/ ▶ **noun 1** the action of conquering a territory or its people. **2** a conquered territory. **3** a person whose affection or favor has been won.

– SYNONYMS **1 defeat,** overthrow, subjugation. **2 seizure,** takeover, capture, occupation, invasion, annexation.

con·quis·ta·dor /kôNG'kēstəˌdôr, kän'k(w)istə-, kən-/ ▶ **noun** (pl. **conquistadores** /-ˌkēstə'dôrēz, -ās, -ˌk(w)istə-/ or **conquistadors**) a Spanish conqueror of Mexico or Peru in the 16th century.
– ORIGIN Spanish.

con·san·guin·i·ty /ˌkänˌsaNG'gwinitē/ ▶ **noun** formal descent from the same ancestor.
– DERIVATIVES **con·san·guin·e·ous** /ˌkänˌsaNG'gwinēəs/ adjective.
– ORIGIN Latin *consanguineus* 'of the same blood.'

con·science /'känCHəns/ ▶ **noun** a person's moral sense of right and wrong, chiefly as it affects their own behavior.

– SYNONYMS **moral sense,** morals, sense of right and wrong, standards, values, principles, ethics, beliefs, scruples, qualms.

– PHRASES **in (good) conscience** by all that is fair.
– ORIGIN Latin *conscientia* 'knowledge within oneself,' from *scire* 'to know.'

con·sci·en·tious /ˌkänCHē'enCHəs/ ▶ **adjective 1** diligent and thorough in carrying out one's work or duty. **2** relating to a person's conscience.

– SYNONYMS **diligent,** industrious, punctilious, painstaking, dedicated, careful, meticulous, thorough, attentive, hard-working, rigorous, scrupulous.
– ANTONYMS casual.

– DERIVATIVES **con·sci·en·tious·ly** adverb **con·sci·en·tious·ness** noun.

con·sci·en·tious ob·jec·tor ▶ **noun** a person who refuses to serve in the armed forces for moral reasons.

con·scious /'känCHəs/ ▶ **adjective 1** aware of and responding to one's surroundings. **2** (usu. **conscious of**) aware of something: *I was very conscious of his disappointment.* **3** deliberate: *a conscious effort.*

– SYNONYMS **1 aware,** awake, responsive; informal with us. **2 deliberate,** purposeful, knowing, considered, calculated, willful, premeditated.
– ANTONYMS unaware, unconscious.

– DERIVATIVES **con·scious·ly** adverb.
– ORIGIN Latin *conscius* 'knowing with others or in oneself.'

con·scious·ness /'känCHəsnəs/ ▶ **noun 1** the state of being conscious. **2** one's awareness or perception of something.

con·script ▶ **verb** /kən'skript/ call someone up for compulsory military service. ▶ **noun** /'känˌskript/ a conscripted person.
– DERIVATIVES **con·scrip·tion** /kən'skripSHən/ noun.
– ORIGIN from Latin *conscriptus.*

con·se·crate /'känsiˌkrāt/ ▶ **verb 1** make or declare something to be holy or sacred. **2** ordain someone to a sacred office, typically that of bishop. **3** (in Christian belief) declare that bread or wine represents or is the body and blood of Jesus.
– DERIVATIVES **con·se·cra·tion** /ˌkänsi'krāSHən/ noun.
– ORIGIN Latin *consecrare.*

con·sec·u·tive /kən'sekyətiv/ ▶ **adjective** following in unbroken sequence.

– SYNONYMS **successive,** succeeding, in succession, running, in a row, straight.

– ORIGIN Latin *consecutivus.*

con·sen·su·al /kən'senCHo͞oəl/ ▶ **adjective** relating to or involving consent or consensus.

con·sen·sus /kən'sensəs/ ▶ **noun** general agreement about something.

– SYNONYMS **1 agreement,** unanimity, harmony, accord, unity, solidarity. **2** *the consensus was that they should act* **general opinion,** common view.
– ANTONYMS disagreement.

– ORIGIN Latin.

con·sent /kən'sent/ ▶ **noun** permission or agreement.

– SYNONYMS **agreement,** assent, acceptance, approval, permission, authorization, sanction; informal go-ahead, green light, OK, okay.
– ANTONYMS dissent.

▶ **verb 1** give permission for something. **2** agree to do something.

> – SYNONYMS *she **consented to** surgery* **agree to,** assent to, submit to, allow, sanction, approve, go along with; informal give the go-ahead, green-light, OK, okay.
> – ANTONYMS forbid, refuse.

– ORIGIN from Latin *consentire* 'agree.'

con·sent·ing a·dult ▶ **noun** an adult who willingly agrees to engage in a sexual act.

con·se·quence /'känsikwəns, -ˌkwens/ ▶ **noun 1** a result or effect, especially one that is unpleasant. **2** importance or relevance: *the past is of no consequence*. **3** dated social distinction.

> – SYNONYMS **1 result,** upshot, outcome, effect, repercussion, ramification, product, end result. **2** *the past is of no consequence* **importance,** import, significance, account, value, concern.
> – ANTONYMS cause.

– ORIGIN Latin *consequentia*.

con·se·quent /'känsikwənt, -ˌkwent/ ▶ **adjective** following as a result or effect of something.

> – SYNONYMS **resulting,** resultant, ensuing, consequential, following, subsequent.

– DERIVATIVES **con·se·quen·tial** /ˌkänsə'kwenCHəl/ adjective.

con·se·quent·ly /'känsikwəntlē, -ˌkwentlē/ ▶ **adverb** as a result: *flexible workers find themselves in great demand, and consequently earn high salaries*.

> – SYNONYMS **as a result,** as a consequence, so, thus, therefore, accordingly, hence, for this/that reason, because of this/that.

con·serv·an·cy /kən'sərvənsē/ ▶ **noun** (pl. **conservancies**) **1** an organization concerned with the preservation of natural resources. **2** the conservation of wildlife and the environment.

con·ser·va·tion /ˌkänsər'vāSHən/ ▶ **noun 1** preservation or restoration of the natural environment and wildlife. **2** preservation and repair of archaeological, historical, and cultural sites and objects. **3** careful use of a resource: *energy conservation*. **4** Physics the principle by which the total value of a quantity (e.g., mass or energy) remains constant in a closed system.

> – SYNONYMS **preservation,** protection, safekeeping, husbandry, upkeep, maintenance, repair, restoration.

– DERIVATIVES **con·ser·va·tion·ist** noun.

con·serv·a·tive /kən'sərvətiv/ ▶ **adjective 1** opposed to change and holding traditional values. **2** (in politics) favoring free enterprise and private ownership. **3** (**Conservative**) relating to the Conservative Party of Great Britain. **4** (of an estimate) deliberately low or high for the sake of caution.

> – SYNONYMS **1 right-wing,** reactionary, traditionalist, old-fashioned, dyed-in-the-wool, hidebound, unadventurous, set in one's ways; informal stick-in-the-mud. **2 conventional,** sober, modest, sensible, restrained; informal square.
> – ANTONYMS socialist, radical.

▶ **noun 1** a conservative person. **2** (**Conservative**) a supporter or member of the Conservative Party.

– DERIVATIVES **con·serv·a·tism** /kən'sərvəˌtizəm/ noun **con·serv·a·tive·ly** adverb.

Con·serv·a·tive Par·ty ▶ **noun** a major British right-wing political party that favors free enterprise and private ownership.

con·ser·va·toire /kən'sərvəˌtwär/ ▶ **noun** a college for the study of classical music.

– ORIGIN French.

con·ser·va·tor /kən'sərvətər, -ˌtôr, 'känsərˌvātər/ ▶ **noun** a person involved in conservation.

con·serv·a·to·ry /kən'sərvəˌtôrē/ ▶ **noun** (pl. **conservatories**) **1** a room with a glass roof and walls, attached to a house and used as a sunroom or greenhouse. **2** a conservatoire.

con·serve /kən'sərv/ ▶ **verb 1** protect something from harm or waste. **2** Physics maintain a quantity at a constant overall total.

> – SYNONYMS **preserve,** protect, save, safeguard, keep, look after, sustain, husband.
> – ANTONYMS squander.

▶ **noun** /'känˌsərv/ jam or marmalade.

– ORIGIN Latin *conservare*.

con·sid·er /kən'sidər/ ▶ **verb 1** think carefully about something. **2** believe or think: *people considered to be at risk of contracting the disease*. **3** take something into account when making a judgment: *his record is even more remarkable when you consider his age*. **4** look attentively at someone or something.

> – SYNONYMS **1 think about,** contemplate, reflect on, mull over, ponder, deliberate on, chew over, meditate on, ruminate on, evaluate, weigh up, appraise, take account of, bear in mind; informal size up. **2 deem,** think, believe, judge, rate, count, find, regard as, hold to be, reckon to be, view as, see as.

– ORIGIN Latin *considerare*.

con·sid·er·a·ble /kən'sidər(ə)bəl, -'sidrəbəl/ ▶ **adjective** great in size, amount, or importance.

> – SYNONYMS **sizable,** substantial, appreciable, significant, plentiful, goodly; informal tidy.
> – ANTONYMS paltry.

con·sid·er·a·bly /kən'sidər(ə)blē, -'sidrəblē/ ▶ **adverb** to a great extent: *alcoholic drinks vary considerably in strength*.

> – SYNONYMS **greatly,** (very) much, a great deal, a lot, lots, significantly, substantially, appreciably, markedly, noticeably; informal plenty.

con·sid·er·ate /kən'sidərət/ ▶ **adjective** careful not to harm or inconvenience others.

> – SYNONYMS **attentive,** thoughtful, solicitous, kind, unselfish, caring, polite, sensitive.

– DERIVATIVES **con·sid·er·ate·ly** adverb.

con·sid·er·a·tion /kənˌsidə'rāSHən/ ▶ **noun 1** careful thought. **2** a fact taken into account when making a decision. **3** thoughtfulness toward others. **4** a payment or reward.

> – SYNONYMS **1 thought,** deliberation, reflection, contemplation, examination, inspection, scrutiny, analysis, discussion, attention. **2 factor,** issue, matter, concern, aspect, feature. **3 attentiveness,** concern, care, thoughtfulness, solicitude, understanding, respect, sensitivity.

– PHRASES **take something into consideration** think about something when making a decision or forming an opinion.

con·sid·er·ing /kən'sidəriNG/ ▶ **preposition & conjunction** taking something into consideration.

– SYNONYMS **bearing in mind,** taking into consideration, taking into account, in view of, in the light of.

▶ **adverb** informal taking everything into account.

con·sign /kən'sīn/ ▶ **verb 1** (**consign someone/thing to**) put someone or something in a place so as to be rid of them. **2** deliver someone or something to someone's possession or care.
– ORIGIN Latin *consignare* 'mark with a seal.'

con·sign·ment /kən'sīnmənt/ ▶ **noun** a batch of goods delivered or sent somewhere.

con·sist /kən'sist/ ▶ **verb 1** (**consist of**) be composed of: *the exhibition consists of 180 drawings.* **2** (**consist in**) have as an essential feature: *poetry consists in the use of emotive language.*

– SYNONYMS (**consist of**) **be composed of,** be made up of, be formed of, comprise, include, contain.

– ORIGIN Latin *consistere* 'stand firm.'

con·sist·en·cy /kən'sistənsē/ (also **consistence**) ▶ **noun** (pl. **consistencies**) **1** the state of being consistent. **2** the degree of thickness of a substance.

con·sist·ent /kən'sistənt/ ▶ **adjective 1** always acting or done in the same way. **2** unchanging over a period of time: *consistent growth in the manufacturing sector of the economy.* **3** in agreement with something: *the results are consistent with other research.*

– SYNONYMS **1 constant,** regular, uniform, steady, stable, even, unchanging. **2** *her injuries were consistent with a knife attack* **compatible with,** in tune with, in line with, corresponding to, conforming to, consonant with.
– ANTONYMS irregular, incompatible.

– DERIVATIVES **con·sist·ent·ly** adverb.

con·sis·to·ry /kən'sistərē/ ▶ **noun** (pl. **consistories**) **1** (in the Roman Catholic Church) the council of cardinals, with or without the Pope. **2** (also **consistory court**) (in the Church of England) a court presided over by a bishop, for the administration of ecclesiastical law in a diocese.
– ORIGIN Latin *consistorium.*

con·so·la·tion /ˌkänsə'lāsʜən/ ▶ **noun 1** comfort received after a loss or disappointment. **2** a person or thing providing such comfort.

– SYNONYMS **comfort,** solace, sympathy, pity, commiseration, relief, encouragement, reassurance.

– DERIVATIVES **con·sol·a·to·ry** /kən'sōləˌtôrē/ adjective.

con·so·la·tion prize ▶ **noun** a prize given to a competitor who narrowly fails to win.

con·sole¹ /kən'sōl/ ▶ **verb** comfort someone in a time of grief or disappointment.

– SYNONYMS **comfort,** sympathize with, commiserate with, show compassion for, help, support, cheer (up), hearten, encourage, reassure, soothe.
– ANTONYMS upset.

– ORIGIN Latin *consolari.*

con·sole² /'känˌsōl/ ▶ **noun 1** a panel or unit containing a set of controls. **2** a cabinet for television or radio equipment. **3** (also **games console**) a small machine for playing computerized video games. **4** the cabinet containing the keyboards, stops, etc., of an organ. **5** an ornamental bracket used to support a structure or fixture on a wall.
– ORIGIN French.

con·sol·i·date /kən'säləˌdāt/ ▶ **verb 1** make something stronger or more stable: *the company consolidated its position in the market.* **2** combine two or more things into a single unit: *arrangements can be made to consolidate your debts.*

– SYNONYMS **1 strengthen,** secure, stabilize, reinforce, fortify. **2 combine,** unite, merge, integrate, amalgamate, fuse, synthesize.

– DERIVATIVES **con·sol·i·da·tion** /-ˌsälə'dāsʜən/ noun **con·sol·i·da·tor** /-ˌdātər/ noun.
– ORIGIN Latin *consolidare,* from *solidus* 'solid.'

CHOOSE THE RIGHT WORD

See **JOIN**.

con·som·mé /ˌkänsə'mā/ ▶ **noun** a clear soup made with concentrated stock.
– ORIGIN French.

con·so·nance /'känsənəns/ ▶ **noun** agreement or compatibility.

con·so·nant /'känsənənt/ ▶ **noun 1** a speech sound in which the breath is at least partly obstructed and which forms a syllable when combined with a vowel. **2** a letter representing such a sound (e.g., *c, t*). ▶ **adjective** (**consonant with**) in agreement or harmony with: *the findings are consonant with recent research.*
– DERIVATIVES **con·so·nan·tal** /ˌkänsə'nantl/ adjective.
– ORIGIN Latin *consonare.*

con·sort¹ ▶ **noun** /'känˌsôrt/ a wife or husband, especially of a reigning monarch. ▶ **verb** /kən'sôrt, 'känˌsôrt/ (**consort with**) regularly associate with someone.

– SYNONYMS *she is now consorting with the in-crowd* **associate,** keep company, mix, socialize, fraternize, have dealings.

– ORIGIN Latin *consors* 'sharing, partner.'

con·sort² /'känˌsôrt/ ▶ **noun** a small group of musicians performing together, typically playing Renaissance music.
– ORIGIN earlier form of **CONCERT**.

con·sor·ti·um /kən'sôrsʜ(ē)əm, -'sôrtēəm/ ▶ **noun** (pl. **consortia** /-tēə, -sʜ(ē)ə/ or **consortiums**) an association of several companies.
– ORIGIN Latin, 'partnership.'

con·spec·tus /kən'spektəs/ ▶ **noun** a summary or overview of a subject.
– ORIGIN Latin, 'a view or survey.'

con·spic·u·ous /kən'spikyo͞oəs/ ▶ **adjective 1** clearly visible. **2** attracting notice; notable: *his conspicuous bravery.*

– SYNONYMS **obvious,** evident, apparent, visible, noticeable, clear, plain, marked, patent, blatant.
– ANTONYMS inconspicuous.

– DERIVATIVES **con·spic·u·ous·ly** adverb.
– ORIGIN from Latin *conspicere* 'look at attentively.'

con·spir·a·cist /kən'spirəsist/ ▶ **noun** a supporter of a conspiracy theory.

con·spir·a·cy /kən'spirəsē/ ▶ **noun** (pl. **conspiracies**) **1** a secret plan by a group to do something unlawful or harmful. **2** the action of conspiring to do something.

– SYNONYMS **plot,** scheme, intrigue, plan, collusion.

CHOOSE THE RIGHT WORD

See **PLOT**.

con·spir·a·cy the·o·ry ▶ **noun** a belief that some secret but influential organization is responsible for an unexplained event.

con·spire /kən'spīr/ ▶ **verb 1** jointly make secret plans to commit a wrongful act. **2** (of circumstances) seem to be acting together to bring about an unfortunate result: *the illness and her failing marriage conspired to make her life intolerable.*

– SYNONYMS **1 plot,** scheme, intrigue, maneuver, plan. **2 combine,** unite, join forces, work together.

– DERIVATIVES **con·spir·a·tor** /kən'spirətər/ noun **con·spir·a·to·ri·al** /kən,spirə'tôrēəl/ adjective **con·spir·a·to·ri·al·ly** /kən,spirə'tôrēəlē/ adverb.
– ORIGIN Latin *conspirare* 'agree, plot.'

con·sta·ble /'känstəbəl/ ▶ **noun 1** a peace officer with limited authority, typically in a small town. **2** Brit. a police officer of the lowest rank.
– ORIGIN from Old French *conestable,* from Latin *comes stabuli* 'head officer of the stable.'

con·stab·u·lar·y /kən'stabyə,lerē/ ▶ **noun** (pl. **constabularies**) the constables of a district.

con·stant /'känstənt/ ▶ **adjective 1** occurring continuously: *a constant stream of visitors.* **2** remaining the same: *a constant speed.* **3** faithful and dependable.

– SYNONYMS **1** *constant noise* **continuous,** persistent, sustained, ceaseless, unceasing, perpetual, incessant, never-ending, eternal, endless, nonstop. **2** *a constant speed* **consistent,** regular, steady, uniform, even, invariable, unvarying, unchanging. **3 faithful,** loyal, devoted, true, fast, firm, unswerving.
– ANTONYMS intermittent, variable, fickle.

▶ **noun 1** an unchanging situation. **2** Mathematics & Physics a number or quantity that does not change its value.
– DERIVATIVES **con·stan·cy** noun **con·stant·ly** adverb.
– ORIGIN Old French, from Latin *constare* 'stand firm.'

con·stel·la·tion /,känstə'lāsHən/ ▶ **noun** a group of stars forming a recognized pattern and typically named after a mythological or other figure.
– ORIGIN Latin, from *stella* 'star.'

con·ster·na·tion /,känstər'nāsHən/ ▶ **noun** a feeling of anxiety or dismay.

– SYNONYMS **dismay,** distress, disquiet, discomposure, surprise, alarm, fear, fright, shock.

– ORIGIN Latin.

con·sti·pat·ed /'känstə,pātid/ ▶ **adjective** suffering from constipation.
– ORIGIN Latin *constipare* 'crowd or press together.'

con·sti·pa·tion /,känstə'pāsHən/ ▶ **noun** the condition of having difficulty in emptying the bowels.

con·stit·u·en·cy /kən'sticHo͞oənsē/ ▶ **noun** (pl. **constituencies**) **1** the group of voters in a particular area who elect a representative to a lawmaking body. **2** the area represented in this way.

con·stit·u·ent /kən'sticHo͞oənt/ ▶ **adjective 1** being a part of a whole: *the constituent republics of the USSR.* **2** having the power to appoint or elect a representative. **3** able to make or change a political constitution. ▶ **noun 1** a voter in a constituency. **2** a component part of something: *the essential constituents of the human diet.*
– ORIGIN Latin, from *constituere* 'establish, appoint.'

con·sti·tute /'känstə,t(y)o͞ot/ ▶ **verb 1** be a part of a whole: *women constitute more than half the workforce.* **2** be or be equivalent to: *his failure to act constituted a breach of duty.* **3** (**be constituted**) be established by law.

– SYNONYMS **1 comprise,** make up, form, account for. **2 amount to,** be tantamount to, be equivalent to, represent. **3 establish,** inaugurate, found, create, set up.

– ORIGIN Latin *constituere* 'establish, appoint.'

con·sti·tu·tion /,känstə't(y)o͞osHən/ ▶ **noun 1** a body of principles according to which a country, state, or organization is governed. **2** the composition or formation of something. **3** a person's physical or mental state.

– SYNONYMS **1 composition,** makeup, structure, construction, arrangement, configuration, formation, anatomy. **2 health,** condition, strength, stamina, build, physique.

con·sti·tu·tion·al /,känstə't(y)o͞osHənl/ ▶ **adjective 1** relating to or according to the principles of a constitution. **2** relating to a person's physical or mental state. ▶ **noun** dated a walk taken regularly to maintain good health.
– DERIVATIVES **con·sti·tu·tion·al·i·ty** /-,t(y)o͞osHə'nalitē/ noun **con·sti·tu·tion·al·ly** adverb.

con·sti·tu·tive /'känstə,t(y)o͞otiv, kən'sticHətiv/ ▶ **adjective 1** having the power to establish something. **2** forming a constituent of something.

con·strain /kən'strān/ ▶ **verb 1** force someone to do something: *he felt constrained to explain.* **2** (as adj. **constrained**) appearing forced or unnatural. **3** severely restrict the scope, extent, or activity of: *most developing countries are constrained by limited resources.*
– ORIGIN Old French *constraindre.*

con·straint /kən'strānt/ ▶ **noun 1** a limitation or restriction: *tight financial constraints.* **2** strict control of one's behavior or repression of one's feelings.

– SYNONYMS **1 restriction,** limitation, curb, check, restraint, control. **2 inhibition,** uneasiness, embarrassment, self-consciousness, awkwardness.
– ANTONYMS freedom, ease.

con·strict /kən'strikt/ ▶ **verb 1** make or become narrower or tighter: *a drug that constricts the blood vessels.* **2** limit or restrict: *political parties constricted by the need to appeal to public opinion.*

– SYNONYMS **narrow,** tighten, compress, contract, squeeze, strangle.
– ANTONYMS expand, dilate.

– DERIVATIVES **con·stric·tion** noun.
– ORIGIN Latin *constringere* 'bind tightly together.'

con·stric·tor /kən'striktər/ ▶ **noun 1** a snake that kills by squeezing and choking its prey, such as a boa or python. **2** a muscle whose contraction narrows a vessel or passage in the body.

con·struct ▶ **verb** /kən'strəkt/ **1** build or make something. **2** form something from different elements: *he constructed his own theory of the universe.*

– SYNONYMS **1 build,** erect, put up, set up, assemble, fabricate. **2 formulate,** create, form, put together, devise, compose, work out, frame.
– ANTONYMS demolish.

▶ **noun** /'kän,strəkt/ **1** an idea or theory containing various elements. **2** a thing that has been built or made.
– DERIVATIVES **con·struc·tor** /kən'strəktər/ noun.
– ORIGIN Latin *construere.*

con·struc·tion /kən'strəksHən/ ▶ **noun 1** the action or process of constructing something. **2** a building or other structure. **3** the industry of erecting buildings or other structures. **4** an interpretation or explanation of something.

– SYNONYMS **1 structure,** building, edifice, work. **2 interpretation,** explanation, analysis, reading, meaning; informal take.

– DERIVATIVES **con·struc·tion·al** adjective.

con·struc·tive /kən'strəktiv/ ▶ **adjective** useful and helpful: *constructive suggestions.*

– SYNONYMS **useful,** helpful, productive, positive, practical, valuable, profitable, worthwhile.

– DERIVATIVES **con·struc·tive·ly** adverb.

con·strue /kən'stro͞o/ ▶ **verb** (**construes, construing, construed**) interpret something in a particular way: *his silence could be construed as an admission of guilt.*

– DERIVATIVES **con·stru·al** noun.

– ORIGIN Latin *construere* 'heap together, build.'

CHOOSE THE RIGHT WORD

See **CLARIFY**.

con·sul /'känsəl/ ▶ **noun 1** a government official living in a foreign city and protecting the government's citizens and interests there. **2** (in ancient Rome) one of two elected chief magistrates who ruled the republic jointly for a year.

– DERIVATIVES **con·su·lar** /'käns(y)ələr/ adjective.

– ORIGIN Latin.

con·su·late /'känsələt/ ▶ **noun 1** the place where a consul works. **2** (in ancient Rome) the period of office of a consul or the system of government by consuls.

con·sult /kən'səlt/ ▶ **verb 1** ask someone for information or advice. **2** discuss something with someone, especially in order to get their approval or permission: *patients are entitled to be consulted about their treatment.* **3** (as adj. **consulting**) acting as a professional adviser to others in the same field.

– SYNONYMS **1 seek advice from,** ask, call (on), turn to; informal pick someone's brains. **2 confer,** talk things over, communicate, deliberate, compare notes. **3 refer to,** look at, check.

– DERIVATIVES **con·sul·ta·tive** /-'səltətiv/ adjective.

– ORIGIN Latin *consultare.*

con·sult·an·cy /kən'səltnsē/ ▶ **noun** (pl. **consultancies**) a company giving expert advice in a particular field.

con·sult·ant /kən'səltnt/ ▶ **noun** a person who provides expert advice professionally.

– SYNONYMS **adviser,** expert, specialist, authority.

con·sul·ta·tion /ˌkänsəl'tāsʜən/ ▶ **noun 1** the process of consulting someone or discussing something. **2** a meeting to discuss something or to get advice or treatment.

– SYNONYMS **1 discussion,** talk(s), dialogue, debate, negotiation, deliberation. **2 meeting,** talk, discussion, interview, audience, hearing.

con·sume /kən'so͞om/ ▶ **verb 1** eat or drink something. **2** use up a resource: *a smaller vehicle that consumes less fuel.* **3** (especially of a fire) completely destroy something. **4** (of a feeling) completely fill the mind of someone: *she was consumed with guilt.*

– SYNONYMS **1 eat,** devour, swallow, gobble up, wolf down, guzzle, drink. **2 use (up),** expend, deplete, exhaust, spend. **3 destroy,** demolish, lay waste, raze, devastate, gut, ruin, wreck. **4 eat up,** devour, grip, overwhelm, absorb, obsess, preoccupy.

– DERIVATIVES **con·sum·a·ble** /kən'so͞oməbəl/ adjective **con·sum·ing** adjective.

– ORIGIN Latin *consumere.*

con·sum·er /kən'so͞omər/ ▶ **noun** a person who buys a product or service for personal use.

– SYNONYMS **buyer,** purchaser, customer, shopper, user.

con·sum·er·ism /kən'so͞oməˌrizəm/ ▶ **noun 1** the preoccupation of society with acquiring goods. **2** the protection of the interests of consumers.

– DERIVATIVES **con·sum·er·ist** adjective & noun.

con·sum·er price in·dex ▶ **noun** an index of the variation in prices paid by typical consumers for retail goods and other items.

con·sum·mate ▶ **verb** /'känsəˌmāt/ **1** make a marriage or relationship complete by having sex. **2** complete a transaction. ▶ **adjective** /'känsəmət, kən'səmət/ showing great skill and flair.

– DERIVATIVES **con·sum·mate·ly** /'känsəmətlē, kən'səmətlē/ adverb **con·sum·ma·tion** /ˌkänsə'māsʜən/ noun.

– ORIGIN Latin *consummare.*

con·sump·tion /kən'səm(p)sʜən/ ▶ **noun 1** the action or process of consuming something. **2** an amount of something that is consumed: *she had managed to reduce her alcohol consumption.* **3** dated a wasting disease, especially tuberculosis.

– DERIVATIVES **con·sump·tive** /kən'səm(p)tiv/ adjective & noun (dated).

cont. ▶ **abbreviation 1** continued. **2** contents.

con·tact ▶ **noun** /'känˌtakt/ **1** the state of touching something. **2** the state of communicating or meeting: *she had lost contact with her son.* **3** a relationship or communication established with someone: *we have good contacts with the local community.* **4** a person who may be asked for information or help. **5** a person who has associated with a patient suffering from a contagious disease. **6** a connection for the passage of an electric current from one thing to another.

– SYNONYMS **1 communication,** correspondence, connection, relations, dealings, touch. **2 connection,** link, acquaintance, associate, friend.

▶ **verb** /'känˌtakt, kən'takt/ get in touch or communication with someone.

– SYNONYMS **get in touch with,** communicate with, approach, notify, speak to, write to, come forward; informal get (a) hold of.

▶ **adjective** /'känˌtakt/ caused by or operating through physical touch: *contact dermatitis.*

– DERIVATIVES **con·tact·a·ble** /'känˌtaktəbəl, kən'tak-/ adjective.

– ORIGIN Latin *contactus,* from *contingere* 'touch, border on.'

con·tact lens ▶ **noun** a thin plastic lens placed directly on the surface of the eye to correct visual defects.

con·tact sport ▶ **noun** a sport in which bodily contact between the participants is a necessary feature.

con·ta·gion /kən'tājən/ ▶ **noun** the passing of disease from one person to another by close contact.

– ORIGIN Latin.

con·ta·gious /kən'tājəs/ ▶ **adjective 1** (of a disease) spread by direct or indirect contact between people or organisms. **2** having a contagious disease. **3** (of an emotion, attitude, etc.) likely to spread to and affect others: *her enthusiasm is contagious.*

– SYNONYMS **infectious,** communicable, transmittable, transmissible; informal catching.

con·tain /kən'tān/ ▶ **verb 1** have or hold within: *a wallet containing cash and credit cards.* **2** control or restrain oneself or a feeling. **3** prevent a problem from becoming worse.

– SYNONYMS **1 hold,** carry, enclose, accommodate, have room for. **2 include,** comprise, incorporate, involve, consist of, be made up of, be composed of. **3 restrain,** control, curb, rein in, suppress, stifle, swallow, bottle up, keep in check.

– DERIVATIVES **con·tain·a·ble** adjective.
– ORIGIN Latin *continere*.

con·tain·er /kən'tānər/ ▶ **noun 1** a box, cylinder, or similar object for holding something. **2** a large metal box for the transport of goods by road, rail, sea, or air.

– SYNONYMS **receptacle,** vessel, holder, repository.

con·tain·er·ize /kən'tānə,rīz/ ▶ **verb** pack cargo into containers or transport it in containers.
– DERIVATIVES **con·tain·er·i·za·tion** /-,tānərə'zāsʜən/ noun.

con·tain·ment /kən'tānmənt/ ▶ **noun** the action of keeping something harmful under control.

con·tam·i·nate /kən'tamə,nāt/ ▶ **verb** pollute something by exposing it to or adding a substance that is poisonous or carries disease.

– SYNONYMS **pollute,** taint, poison, stain, adulterate, defile, debase, corrupt.
– ANTONYMS purify.

– DERIVATIVES **con·tam·i·nant** /-'tamənənt/ noun **con·tam·i·na·tion** /-,tamə'nāsʜən/ noun.
– ORIGIN Latin *contaminare*.

con·tem·plate /'käntəm,plāt/ ▶ **verb 1** look at someone or something thoughtfully. **2** think about: *the idea was too awful to contemplate.* **3** think deeply and at length.

– SYNONYMS **1 look at,** gaze at, stare at, view, regard, examine, inspect, observe, survey, study, eye. **2 think about,** ponder, reflect on, consider, mull over, muse on, dwell on, deliberate over, meditate on, ruminate on, chew over. **3 envisage,** consider, think about, have in mind, intend, plan, propose.

– ORIGIN Latin *contemplari*.

con·tem·pla·tion /,käntəm'plāsʜən/ ▶ **noun 1** the process of contemplating something. **2** religious meditation.

con·tem·pla·tive /kən'templətiv/ ▶ **adjective** showing or involving contemplation: *a contemplative mood.*

– SYNONYMS **thoughtful,** pensive, reflective, meditative, ruminative, introspective, brooding, deep/lost in thought.

▶ **noun** a person whose life is devoted to prayer, especially in a monastery or convent.

con·tem·po·ra·ne·ous /kən,tempə'rānēəs/ ▶ **adjective** existing at or occurring in the same period of time.
– DERIVATIVES **con·tem·po·ra·ne·i·ty** /-rə'nēitē, -rə'nāitē/ noun.
– ORIGIN Latin.

con·tem·po·rar·y /kən'tempə,rerē/ ▶ **adjective 1** living, occurring, or originating at the same time: *Greek literature contemporary with the New Testament.* **2** belonging to or occurring in the present. **3** modern in style or design.

– SYNONYMS **1** *contemporary sources* **of the time,** contemporaneous, concurrent, coexisting, coeval. **2** *contemporary society* **modern,** present-day, present, current. **3** *a very contemporary design* **modern,** up to date, up to the minute, fashionable, recent; informal trendy.
– ANTONYMS former, old-fashioned.

▶ **noun** (pl. **contemporaries**) **1** a person or thing existing at the same time as another. **2** a person of roughly the same age as another.
– ORIGIN Latin *contemporarius*, from *tempus* 'time.'

WORD TOOLKIT

See **NEW**.

con·tempt /kən'tem(p)t/ ▶ **noun 1** the feeling that a person or a thing is worthless or deserves no respect at all. **2** (also **contempt of court**) the offense of being disobedient to or disrespectful of a court of law.

– SYNONYMS **scorn,** disdain, derision, disgust, disrespect.
– ANTONYMS respect.

– PHRASES **beneath contempt** utterly worthless. **hold someone/thing in contempt** despise someone or something.
– ORIGIN Latin *contemptus*.

con·tempt·i·ble /kən'tem(p)təbəl/ ▶ **adjective** deserving to be hated or despised: *a display of contemptible cowardice.*

– SYNONYMS **despicable,** detestable, beneath contempt, reprehensible, deplorable, unspeakable, disgraceful, shameful, ignominious, abject, low, mean, cowardly, discreditable, worthless, shabby, cheap.
– ANTONYMS admirable.

– DERIVATIVES **con·tempt·i·bly** adverb.

con·temp·tu·ous /kən'tem(p)cʜo͞oəs/ ▶ **adjective** showing or feeling a lack of respect for someone or something.

– SYNONYMS **scornful,** disdainful, derisive, mocking, sneering, scoffing, condescending, dismissive.
– ANTONYMS respectful.

– DERIVATIVES **con·temp·tu·ous·ly** adverb.

WORD TOOLKIT

See **DISMISSIVE**.

con·tend /kən'tend/ ▶ **verb 1** (**contend with/against**) struggle to deal with a difficulty. **2** struggle or campaign to achieve something. **3** put forward a position in an argument.

– SYNONYMS **1** *the pilot had to contend with torrential rain* **cope with,** struggle with, grapple with, deal with, take on, handle. **2** *three main groups were contending for power* **compete,** vie, battle, tussle, struggle, jostle, strive. **3** *he contends that the judge was wrong* **assert,** maintain, hold, claim, argue, insist, allege.

– DERIVATIVES **con·tend·er** noun.
– ORIGIN Latin *contendere*.

con·tent[1] /kən'tent/ ▶ **adjective** happy and satisfied.

– SYNONYMS **satisfied,** contented, pleased, gratified, fulfilled, happy, glad, cheerful, at ease, at peace, relaxed, comfortable, untroubled.
– ANTONYMS dissatisfied.

▶ **verb 1** satisfy or please someone. **2** (**content oneself with**) accept something as adequate despite wanting something more or better.

– SYNONYMS **satisfy,** comfort, gratify, gladden, please, soothe, placate, appease, mollify.

▶ **noun** a state of happiness or satisfaction.
– PHRASES **to one's heart's content** as much as one wants.
– ORIGIN Latin *contentus*.

con·tent² /ˈkänˌtent/ ▶ **noun 1** (**contents**) the things that are contained in something. **2** the amount of a particular thing occurring in a substance: *soy milk has a low fat content.* **3** the material dealt with in a speech or text as distinct from its form or style. **4** (**contents** or **table of contents**) a list of chapters or sections at the front of a book or periodical.

– SYNONYMS **1 constituents,** ingredients, components. **2 amount,** proportion, level. **3 subject matter,** theme, argument, thesis, message, substance, material, ideas.

– ORIGIN Latin *contentum*.

con·tent·ed /kənˈtentəd/ ▶ **adjective** happy and satisfied.

– SYNONYMS see **CONTENT¹**.

– DERIVATIVES **con·tent·ed·ly** adverb.

con·ten·tion /kənˈtenCHən/ ▶ **noun 1** heated disagreement between people. **2** a point of view expressed or asserted.
– PHRASES **in** (or **out of**) **contention** having (or not having) a good chance of success in a contest.
– ORIGIN Latin.

con·ten·tious /kənˈtenCHəs/ ▶ **adjective 1** causing or likely to cause disagreement or controversy. **2** tending to provoke arguments.

– SYNONYMS **controversial,** debatable, disputed, open to debate, moot, vexed.

con·tent·ment /kənˈtentmənt/ ▶ **noun** a state of happiness and satisfaction.

– SYNONYMS **contentedness,** content, satisfaction, fulfillment, happiness, pleasure, cheerfulness, ease, comfort, well-being, peace.

con·tent pro·vid·er ▶ **noun** a person or organization who supplies information for use on a website.

con·test ▶ **noun** /ˈkänˌtest/ **1** an event in which people compete to try to win something. **2** a struggle to win power or control: *the Republican leadership contest.*

– SYNONYMS **1 competition,** match, tournament, rally, race, game, bout. **2 fight,** battle, tussle, struggle, competition, race.

▶ **verb** /kənˈtest, ˈkänˌtest/ **1** take part in a competition, election, or struggle for a position of power: *one of the first women to contest a parliamentary seat.* **2** challenge or dispute: *he intended to contest his father's will.*

– SYNONYMS **1** *he will contest the seat* **compete for,** contend for, vie for, fight for. **2** *the parties contesting the election* **compete in,** take part in, fight, enter. **3 oppose,** challenge, take issue with, question, call into question, object to.
– ANTONYMS accept.

– DERIVATIVES **con·test·a·ble** /kənˈtestəbəl/ adjective.
– PHRASES **no contest 1** another term for **NOLO CONTENDERE**: *he pleaded no contest to two misdemeanor counts.* **2** a competition, comparison, or choice whose outcome is a foregone conclusion.
– ORIGIN Latin *contestari* 'call upon to witness.'

con·test·ant /kənˈtestənt/ ▶ **noun** a person who takes part in a contest.

– SYNONYMS **competitor,** participant, player, contender, candidate, entrant.

con·text /ˈkänˌtekst/ ▶ **noun 1** the circumstances that form the setting for an event, statement, or idea. **2** the parts that immediately precede and follow a word or passage and make its meaning clear.

– SYNONYMS **circumstances,** conditions, frame of reference, factors, state of affairs, situation, background, scene, setting.

– DERIVATIVES **con·tex·tu·al** /kənˈteksCHo͞oəl/ adjective **con·tex·tu·al·ly** adverb.
– ORIGIN Latin *contextus*.

con·tex·tu·al·ize /kənˈteksCHo͞oəˌlīz/ ▶ **verb** consider something together with the surrounding words or circumstances.

con·tig·u·ous /kənˈtigyo͞oəs/ ▶ **adjective 1** sharing a border. **2** next or together in sequence.
– DERIVATIVES **con·ti·gu·i·ty** /ˌkäntəˈgyo͞oitē/ noun.
– ORIGIN Latin *contiguus* 'touching.'

con·ti·nent¹ /ˈkäntn-ənt, ˈkäntnənt/ ▶ **noun 1** any of the world's main continuous expanses of land (Europe, Asia, Africa, North and South America, Australia, Antarctica). **2** (also **the Continent**) the mainland of Europe as distinct from the British Isles.
– ORIGIN from Latin *terra continens* 'continuous land.'

con·ti·nent² ▶ **adjective 1** able to control the bowels and bladder. **2** self-restrained, especially sexually.
– DERIVATIVES **con·ti·nence** noun.
– ORIGIN from Latin *continere*, from *tenere* 'to hold.'

con·ti·nen·tal /ˌkäntnˈentl/ ▶ **adjective 1** forming or belonging to a continent. **2** (also **Continental**) coming from or typical of mainland Europe. ▶ **noun** (also **Continental**) a person from mainland Europe.

con·ti·nen·tal break·fast ▶ **noun** a light breakfast of coffee and bread rolls.

con·ti·nen·tal cli·mate ▶ **noun** a relatively dry climate with very hot summers and very cold winters, characteristic of the central parts of Asia and North America.

con·ti·nen·tal drift ▶ **noun** the gradual movement of the continents across the earth's surface through geological time.

con·ti·nen·tal shelf ▶ **noun** an area of seabed around a large landmass where the sea is relatively shallow.

con·tin·gen·cy /kənˈtinjənsē/ ▶ **noun** (pl. **contingencies**) **1** a future event or circumstance that is possible but cannot be predicted with certainty. **2** something done in case of a possible event or circumstance occurring: *supplies were kept as a contingency against a blockade.*

– SYNONYMS **eventuality,** possibility, chance event, incident, occurrence, accident, emergency.

con·tin·gent /kənˈtinjənt/ ▶ **noun 1** a group of people with a common feature, forming part of a larger group. **2** a body of troops or police sent to join a larger force. ▶ **adjective 1** (**contingent on**) dependent on something: *the merger is contingent on government approval.* **2** subject to or happening by chance.
– ORIGIN Latin *contingere* 'befall.'

CHOOSE THE RIGHT WORD

See **ACCIDENTAL**.

con·tin·u·al /kənˈtinyo͞oəl/ ▶ **adjective 1** constantly or frequently occurring. **2** having no interruptions:

a continual process of growth.

– SYNONYMS **1** *continual breakdowns* **frequent,** regular, repeated, constant, recurrent, recurring, habitual. **2** *continual pain* **constant,** continuous, unremitting, unrelenting, nonstop, sustained, chronic, uninterrupted, incessant, ceaseless, unceasing, never-ending, unbroken, perpetual.
– ANTONYMS occasional, temporary.

– DERIVATIVES **con·tin·u·al·ly** adverb.

USAGE

On the distinction between **continual** and **continuous**, see the note at **CONTINUOUS**.

con·tin·u·ance /kən'tinyo͞oəns/ ▶ **noun** formal **1** the state of continuing. **2** the time for which a situation or action lasts.

con·tin·u·a·tion /kənˌtinyə'wāshən/ ▶ **noun 1** the action or state of continuing. **2** a part that is attached to and is an extension of something else.

con·tin·ue /kən'tinyo͞o/ ▶ **verb** (**continues, continuing, continued**) **1** keep existing or happening without stopping: *the rain continued to pour down.* **2** carry on with: *he returned to America to continue his work.* **3** carry on traveling in the same direction. **4** start again: *the trial continues tomorrow.*

– SYNONYMS **1 carry on,** go on, keep on, persist, persevere, proceed, pursue, keep at; informal stick at. **2** *we hope to continue this relationship* **maintain,** keep up, sustain, keep going, keep alive, preserve, perpetuate. **3** *his willingness to continue in office* **remain,** stay, carry on, keep going. **4** *we continued our conversation* **resume,** pick up, take up, carry on with, return to, revisit.
– ANTONYMS stop.

– ORIGIN Latin *continuare.*

con·ti·nu·i·ty /ˌkäntn'(y)o͞oətē/ ▶ **noun** (pl. **continuities**) **1** the uninterrupted and unchanged existence or operation of something. **2** a logical connection or smooth line of development between things. **3** the maintaining of continuous action and consistent details in the scenes of a movie or broadcast. **4** the linking of broadcast items by a spoken commentary.

con·tin·u·o /kən'tinyəˌwō/ ▶ **noun** (pl. **continuos**) (in baroque music) an accompanying part that includes a bass line and harmonies, typically played on a keyboard instrument.
– ORIGIN Italian *basso continuo* 'continuous bass.'

con·tin·u·ous /kən'tinyo͞oəs/ ▶ **adjective** forming an unbroken whole or sequence without interruptions or exceptions.

– SYNONYMS **continual,** persistent, sustained, ceaseless, unceasing, unremitting, unrelenting, perpetual, incessant, never-ending, eternal, endless, nonstop, unbroken, uninterrupted.
– ANTONYMS intermittent.

– DERIVATIVES **con·tin·u·ous·ly** adverb.

USAGE

Continuous and **continual** can both mean 'without interruption' (*years of continuous/continual warfare*), but only **continual** can be used to mean 'happening frequently' (*the continual arguments*).

con·tin·u·um /kən'tinyo͞oəm/ ▶ **noun** (pl. **continua** /-yo͞oə/) a continuous sequence in which the elements next to each other are very similar, but the last and the first are very different.
– ORIGIN Latin.

con·tort /kən'tôrt/ ▶ **verb** twist or bend something out of its normal shape.

– SYNONYMS **twist,** bend out of shape, distort, misshape, warp, buckle, deform.

– DERIVATIVES **con·tor·tion** /kən'tôrshən/ noun.
– ORIGIN Latin *contorquere.*

con·tor·tion·ist /kən'tôrshənist/ ▶ **noun** an entertainer who twists and bends their body into strange and unnatural positions.

con·tour /'känˌto͝or/ ▶ **noun 1** an outline of the shape or form of something. **2** (also **contour line**) a line on a map joining points of equal height. ▶ **verb** mold something into a particular shape.
– ORIGIN French.

con·tour line ▶ **noun** a line on a map joining points of equal height above or below sea level.

contra- ▶ **prefix** against; opposite: *contraception.*
– ORIGIN Latin *contra.*

con·tra·band /'käntrəˌband/ ▶ **noun 1** goods that have been imported or exported illegally. **2** trade in smuggled goods.
– ORIGIN Italian *contrabando.*

con·tra·cep·tion /ˌkäntrə'sepshən/ ▶ **noun** the use of contraceptives to prevent pregnancy.

con·tra·cep·tive /ˌkäntrə'septiv/ ▶ **noun** a device or drug used to prevent a woman becoming pregnant. ▶ **adjective 1** preventing pregnancy. **2** relating to contraception.

con·tract ▶ **noun** /'känˌtrakt/ **1** a written or spoken agreement intended to be enforceable by law. **2** informal an arrangement for someone to be killed by a hired assassin.

– SYNONYMS **agreement,** arrangement, commitment, settlement, understanding, compact, covenant, deal, bargain.

▶ **verb 1** decrease in size, number, or range. **2** (of a muscle) become shorter and tighter in order to move part of the body. **3** catch or develop a disease. **4** enter into a legally binding agreement with someone. **5** (**contract something out**) arrange for work to be done by another organization. **6** become liable to pay a debt.

– SYNONYMS **1 shrink,** diminish, reduce, decrease, dwindle, decline. **2 tighten,** tense, flex, constrict, draw in. **3 catch,** pick up, come/go down with, develop. **4 engage,** take on, hire, commission, employ.
– ANTONYMS expand, relax, lengthen.

– DERIVATIVES **con·trac·tu·al** /kən'trakcho͞oəl/ adjective **con·trac·tu·al·ly** adverb.
– ORIGIN Latin *contractus.*

con·tract bridge /'känˌtrakt/ ▶ **noun** the standard form of the card game bridge, in which only tricks bid and won count toward the game.

con·tract·i·ble /kən'traktəbəl/ ▶ **adjective** able to be shrunk or capable of contracting.

con·trac·tile /kən'traktəl, -ˌtīl/ ▶ **adjective** technical able to contract or produce contraction.

con·trac·tion /kən'trakshən/ ▶ **noun 1** the process of contracting. **2** a shortening of the muscles of the uterus occurring at intervals during childbirth. **3** a shortened form of a word or group of words.

– SYNONYMS **1 shrinking,** shrinkage, decline, decrease, diminution, dwindling. **2 tightening,** tensing, flexing. **3 abbreviation,** short form, shortening.

con·trac·tor /'kän,traktər/ ▶ **noun** a person who undertakes a contract to provide materials or labor for a job.

con·tra·dict /,käntrə'dikt/ ▶ **verb** deny the truth of a statement made by someone by saying the opposite.

– SYNONYMS **1 deny,** refute, rebut, dispute, challenge, counter. **2 argue with,** go against, challenge, oppose.
– ANTONYMS confirm, agree with.

– ORIGIN Latin *contradicere* 'speak against.'

con·tra·dic·tion /,käntrə'diksHən/ ▶ **noun 1** an opposition or lack of agreement between statements, ideas, or features. **2** the action of saying the opposite to something that has already been said.

– SYNONYMS **1 conflict,** clash, disagreement, inconsistency, mismatch. **2 denial,** refutation, rebuttal, countering.
– ANTONYMS agreement, confirmation.

– PHRASES **contradiction in terms** a statement containing words or ideas that are incompatible in meaning.

con·tra·dic·to·ry /,käntrə'dikt(ə)rē/ ▶ **adjective 1** opposed or inconsistent. **2** containing opposing or inconsistent elements.

– SYNONYMS **inconsistent,** incompatible, irreconcilable, opposed, opposite, contrary, conflicting, at variance.

CHOOSE THE RIGHT WORD

See **OPPOSITE**.

con·tra·dis·tinc·tion /,käntrədə'stiNGksHən/ ▶ **noun** distinction made by contrasting the different qualities of two things.

con·tra·in·di·cate /,käntrə'ində,kāt/ ▶ **verb** Medicine (of a condition or circumstance) suggest or indicate that a particular technique or drug should not be used.
– DERIVATIVES **con·tra·in·di·ca·tion** /-,ində'kāsHən/ noun.

con·tral·to /kən'traltō/ ▶ **noun** (pl. **contraltos**) the lowest female singing voice.
– ORIGIN Italian.

con·trap·tion /kən'trapsHən/ ▶ **noun** a machine or device that appears strange or unnecessarily complicated.

– SYNONYMS **device,** gadget, apparatus, machine, appliance, mechanism, invention, contrivance; informal gizmo, widget.

– ORIGIN perhaps from **CONTRIVE**, by association with **TRAP**.

con·tra·pun·tal /,käntrə'pəntl/ ▶ **adjective** Music relating to or in counterpoint.
– DERIVATIVES **con·tra·pun·tal·ly** adverb.
– ORIGIN from Italian *contrapunto* 'counterpoint.'

con·trar·i·an /kən'tre(ə)rēən, kän-/ ▶ **noun** a person who opposes or rejects popular opinion.

con·tra·ri·e·ty /,käntrə'rīətē/ ▶ **noun** opposition or inconsistency between two things.

con·trar·i·wise /'kän,trerē,wīz, kən'tre(ə)rē-/ ▶ **adverb 1** in the opposite way. **2** on the other hand.

con·trar·y ▶ **adjective** /'kän,tre(ə)rē/ **1** opposite in nature, direction, or meaning. **2** (of two or more statements, beliefs, etc.) opposed to one another. **3** /kən'tre(ə)rē/ deliberately inclined to do the opposite of what is expected or desired.

– SYNONYMS **1 opposite,** opposing, contradictory, clashing, conflicting, antithetical, incompatible, irreconcilable. **2 perverse,** awkward, difficult, uncooperative, obstinate, pigheaded, intractable. informal balky.
– ANTONYMS compatible, accommodating.

▶ **noun** /'kän,tre(ə)rē/ (**the contrary**) the opposite.

– SYNONYMS **opposite,** reverse, converse, antithesis.

– DERIVATIVES **con·trar·i·ly** /-əlē/ adverb **con·trar·i·ness** noun.
– PHRASES **to the contrary** with the opposite meaning or implication.
– ORIGIN Latin *contrarius*.

CHOOSE THE RIGHT WORD

See **OPPOSITE**.

con·trast ▶ **noun** /'kän,trast/ **1** the state of being noticeably different from something else when put or considered together: *in contrast to karate, tae kwon do is characterized by its high kicks.* **2** a thing or person noticeably different from another. **3** the degree of difference between tones in a television picture, photograph, or other image.

– SYNONYMS **1 difference,** dissimilarity, disparity, divergence, variance, distinction, comparison. **2 opposite,** antithesis, foil, complement.
– ANTONYMS similarity.

▶ **verb** /'kän,trast, kən'trast/ **1** differ noticeably. **2** compare people or things so as to emphasize differences.

– SYNONYMS **1** *a view that **contrasts with** his earlier opinion* **differ from,** be at variance with, be contrary to, conflict with, be at odds with, disagree, clash with. **2** *they **contrasted** her **with** her sister* **compare with/to,** juxtapose with/to, measure against, distinguish from, differentiate from.
– ANTONYMS resemble, liken.

– DERIVATIVES **con·tras·tive** /kən'trastiv, 'kän,tras-/ adjective.
– ORIGIN Latin *contrastare*.

con·tra·vene /,käntrə'vēn/ ▶ **verb 1** commit an act that is not allowed by a law, rule, treaty, etc. **2** conflict with a right or principle.
– DERIVATIVES **con·tra·ven·er** noun **con·tra·ven·tion** /,käntrə'vencHən/ noun.
– ORIGIN Latin *contravenire*.

con·tre·temps /'käntrə,täN, ,kôntrə'täN/ ▶ **noun** (pl. same or /-,täN(z), -'täN(z)/) a minor disagreement.
– ORIGIN French, originally meaning 'motion out of time.'

con·trib·ute /kən'tribyo͞ot, -byət/ ▶ **verb 1** give something in order to help achieve or provide something. **2** (**contribute to**) help to cause: *all of these factors can contribute to depression.* **3** give one's views in a discussion.

– SYNONYMS **1 give,** donate, put up, grant, provide, supply; informal chip in. **2** (**contribute to**) **play a part in,** be instrumental in, have a hand in, be conducive to, make for.

– DERIVATIVES **con·trib·u·tive** /-yətiv/ adjective.
– ORIGIN Latin *contribuere* 'bring together, add.'

con·tri·bu·tion /ˌkäntrəˈbyo͞oshən/ ▸ **noun 1** a gift or payment to a common fund or collection. **2** the part played by a person or thing in causing or advancing something: *his contribution to 20th century music cannot be overstated.* **3** an item that forms part of a journal, book, broadcast, or discussion.

– SYNONYMS **gift,** donation, offering, present, handout, grant, subsidy.

con·trib·u·tor /kənˈtribyətər/ ▸ **noun** a person who contributes something.

– SYNONYMS **donor,** benefactor, supporter, backer, patron, sponsor.

con·trib·u·to·ry /kənˈtribyəˌtôrē/ ▸ **adjective 1** playing a part in bringing something about. **2** (of a pension or insurance scheme) operated by means of a fund into which people pay.

con·trite /kənˈtrīt/ ▸ **adjective** very sorry or regretful for having done wrong.

– SYNONYMS **remorseful,** repentant, penitent, regretful, sorry, apologetic, rueful, sheepish, hangdog, ashamed, shamefaced.

– DERIVATIVES **con·trite·ly** adverb **con·tri·tion** /kənˈtrishən/ noun.
– ORIGIN from Latin *conterere* 'grind down, wear away.'

WORD TOOLKIT

See **APOLOGETIC**.

con·triv·ance /kənˈtrīvəns/ ▸ **noun 1** a clever or inventive device or scheme. **2** the use of skill to create or achieve something.

con·trive /kənˈtrīv/ ▸ **verb 1** plan or achieve something in a clever or skillful way. **2** manage to do something foolish.

– SYNONYMS **1 create,** engineer, manufacture, devise, concoct, construct, fabricate, hatch. **2 manage,** find a way, engineer a way, arrange.
– ANTONYMS fail.

– DERIVATIVES **con·triv·er** noun.
– ORIGIN Old French *controver* 'imagine, invent.'

con·trived /kənˈtrīvd/ ▸ **adjective** deliberately created rather than arising naturally, and typically seeming artificial.

– SYNONYMS **forced,** strained, labored, overdone, unnatural, artificial, false, affected.
– ANTONYMS natural.

con·trol /kənˈtrōl/ ▸ **noun 1** the power to influence people's behavior or the course of events. **2** the restriction of something: *crime control.* **3** a means of limiting or regulating something: *controls on spending.* **4** a device by which a machine is regulated. **5** the place where something is checked or from which an activity is directed: *passport control.* **6** a person or thing used as a standard of comparison for checking the results of a survey or experiment.

– SYNONYMS **1 power,** authority, command, dominance, sway, management, direction, leadership, rule, government, sovereignty, supremacy. **2 limit,** limitation, restriction, restraint, check, curb, regulation. **3 self-control,** self-restraint, composure, calm; informal cool.

▸ **verb (controls, controlling, controlled) 1** have control of; direct or supervise: *she was appointed to control the firm's marketing strategy.* **2** limit or regulate something.

– SYNONYMS **1 run,** manage, direct, preside over, supervise, command, rule, govern, lead, dominate. **2** *she struggled to control her temper* **restrain,** keep in check, curb, hold back, suppress, repress. **3** *public spending was controlled* **limit,** restrict, curb, cap.

– DERIVATIVES **con·trol·la·bil·i·ty** /kənˌtrōləˈbilitē/ noun **con·trol·la·ble** adjective **con·trol·la·bly** /-əblē/ adverb.
– PHRASES **in control** able to direct a situation, person, or activity. **out of control** no longer manageable. **under control** (of a danger or emergency) being dealt with or contained successfully.
– ORIGIN Old French *contreroller* 'keep a copy of a roll of accounts.'

con·trol·ler /kənˈtrōlər/ ▸ **noun** a person in charge of an organization's finances.

con·trol·ling in·ter·est ▸ **noun** the holding by one person or group of a majority of the stock of a business.

con·trol tow·er ▸ **noun** a tall building from which the movements of air traffic are controlled.

con·tro·ver·sial /ˌkäntrəˈvərshəl, -ˈvərsēəl/ ▸ **adjective** causing or likely to cause much debate and conflicting opinions.

– SYNONYMS **disputed,** contentious, moot, debatable, arguable, vexed.

– DERIVATIVES **con·tro·ver·sial·ist** /-list/ noun **con·tro·ver·sial·ly** adverb.

con·tro·ver·sy /ˈkäntrəˌvərsē/ ▸ **noun** (pl. **controversies**) debate about a matter that arouses conflicting opinions.

– SYNONYMS **dispute,** disagreement, argument, debate, contention, quarrel, war of words, storm; Brit. row.

– ORIGIN from Latin *controversus* 'turned against, disputed.'

con·tro·vert /ˈkäntrəˌvərt, ˌkäntrəˈvərt/ ▸ **verb** deny the truth of something.
– ORIGIN from Latin *controversus* 'turned against, disputed.'

con·tu·ma·cious /ˌkänt(y)əˈmāshəs/ ▸ **adjective** old use or Law willfully disobedient to authority.
– DERIVATIVES **con·tu·ma·cy** /kənˈt(y)o͞oməsē, ˈkänt(y)əməsē/ noun.
– ORIGIN from Latin *contumax*.

con·tu·me·ly /kənˈt(y)o͞oməlē, ˈkänt(y)əˌmēlē, ˈkänˌt(y)o͞omlē/ ▸ **noun** (pl. **contumelies**) old use insolent or insulting language or treatment.
– ORIGIN Latin *contumelia*.

con·tu·sion /kənˈto͞ozhən/ ▸ **noun** Medicine a bruise.
– DERIVATIVES **con·tuse** /kənˈto͞oz/ verb.
– ORIGIN from Latin *contundere* 'to bruise, crush.'

co·nun·drum /kəˈnəndrəm/ ▸ **noun** (pl. **conundrums**) **1** a confusing and difficult problem or question. **2** a riddle.
– ORIGIN unknown.

CHOOSE THE RIGHT WORD

See **RIDDLE**[1].

con·ur·ba·tion /ˌkänərˈbāshən/ ▸ **noun** an extended urban area consisting of several towns merging with the suburbs of a central city.
– ORIGIN from Latin *urbs* 'city.'

con·va·lesce /ˌkänvəˈles/ ▸ **verb** gradually recover one's health after an illness or medical treatment.

– SYNONYMS **recuperate,** get better, recover, get well, get back on one's feet.

– ORIGIN Latin *convalescere*.

con·va·les·cent /ˌkänvəˈlesənt/ ▶ **adjective** recovering from an illness or medical treatment. ▶ **noun** a person who is recovering from an illness or medical treatment.
– DERIVATIVES **con·va·les·cence** noun.

con·vec·tion /kənˈvekSHən/ ▶ **noun** transference of mass or heat within a fluid caused by the tendency of warmer and less dense material to rise.
– DERIVATIVES **con·vect** /kənˈvekt/ verb **con·vec·tive** /kənˈvektiv/ adjective.
– ORIGIN from Latin *convehere*.

con·vec·tor /kənˈvektər/ ▶ **noun** a heating appliance that circulates warm air by convection.

con·vene /kənˈvēn/ ▶ **verb** come or bring together for a meeting or activity.

– SYNONYMS **1** *he convened a meeting* **summon,** call, order. **2** *the committee convened* **assemble,** gather, meet, come together; formal foregather.

– ORIGIN Latin *convenire* 'assemble, agree, fit.'

con·ven·er /kənˈvēnər/ (also **convenor**) ▶ **noun** a person who arranges the meetings of a committee.

con·ven·ience /kənˈvēnyəns/ ▶ **noun 1** freedom from effort or difficulty: *food today is more about convenience than nourishment*. **2** a useful or helpful thing. **3** Brit. a public toilet.

– SYNONYMS **1 advantage,** benefit, expedience, suitability. **2 ease of use,** usefulness, utility, accessibility, availability.
– ANTONYMS inconvenience.

– PHRASES **at one's convenience** when or where it suits one. **at one's earliest convenience** as soon as one can without difficulty.
– ORIGIN Latin *convenientia*.

con·ven·ience food ▶ **noun** a food that has been preprepared commercially and so requires little preparation by the consumer.

con·ven·ience store ▶ **noun** a store with extended opening hours and in a convenient location, stocking a limited range of household goods and groceries.

con·ven·ient /kənˈvēnyənt/ ▶ **adjective 1** fitting in well with a person's needs, activities, and plans. **2** involving little trouble or effort.

– SYNONYMS **1 suitable,** favorable, advantageous, appropriate, opportune, timely, expedient. **2 nearby,** handy, well situated, practical, useful, accessible.

– DERIVATIVES **con·ven·ient·ly** adverb.

WORD TOOLKIT

See **NEARBY**.

con·ve·nor ▶ **noun** variant spelling of **CONVENER**.

con·vent /ˈkänˌvent/ ▶ **noun 1** a Christian community of nuns living under monastic vows. **2** (also **convent school**) a school attached to and run by a convent.
– ORIGIN Latin *conventus* 'assembly, company.'

con·ven·tion /kənˈvenCHən/ ▶ **noun 1** a way in which something is usually done: *he is at his best working within the established conventions*. **2** socially acceptable behavior. **3** an agreement between countries. **4** a large meeting or conference. **5** an assembly of the delegates of a political party to select candidates for office. **6** a body set up by agreement to deal with a particular issue.

– SYNONYMS **1 custom,** usage, practice, tradition, etiquette, protocol. **2 agreement,** accord, protocol, pact, treaty. **3 conference,** meeting, congress, assembly, gathering.

– ORIGIN Latin, 'meeting, covenant.'

con·ven·tion·al /kənˈvenCHənl/ ▶ **adjective 1** based on or in accordance with what is generally done or believed. **2** following social conventions; not individual or adventurous. **3** (of weapons or power) nonnuclear.

– SYNONYMS **1 orthodox,** traditional, established, accepted, customary, received, prevailing, normal, standard, regular, ordinary, usual, typical. **2 conservative,** traditional, conformist, old-fashioned; informal square, stick-in-the-mud. **3 unoriginal,** formulaic, predictable, unadventurous, run-of-the-mill, routine, pedestrian.
– ANTONYMS unorthodox, original.

– DERIVATIVES **con·ven·tion·al·i·ty** /-ˌvenCHəˈnalitē/ noun **con·ven·tion·al·ize** /-ˌīz/ verb **con·ven·tion·al·ly** adverb.

con·verge /kənˈvərj/ ▶ **verb 1** come together from different directions so as eventually to meet. **2** (**converge on**) come from different directions and meet at a place.

– SYNONYMS **1 meet,** intersect, cross, connect, link up, join, merge. **2** (**converge on**) **meet at,** arrive at, close in on, bear down on, descend on, approach, move towards.
– ANTONYMS diverge.

– DERIVATIVES **con·ver·gent** adjective.
– ORIGIN Latin *convergere*.

con·ver·sant /kənˈvərsənt/ ▶ **adjective** (**conversant with**) familiar with or knowledgeable about something.

con·ver·sa·tion /ˌkänvərˈsāSHən/ ▶ **noun** an informal spoken exchange of news and ideas between people.

– SYNONYMS **discussion,** talk, chat, gossip, tête-à-tête, exchange, dialogue; informal chinwag.

– DERIVATIVES **con·ver·sa·tion·al** adjective.

CHOOSE THE RIGHT WORD

conversation, chat, colloquy, communion, dialogue, parley, tête-à-tête

It is nearly impossible for most people to get through a day without having a **conversation** with someone, even if it's only a **chat** with the mailman. Although *conversation* can and does take place in all sorts of contexts, both formal and informal, the word usually implies a relaxed, casual exchange. A *chat* is the least formal of all conversations, whether it's a father talking to his son about girls or two women having a **tête-à-tête** (French for "head to head," meaning a confidential conversation) about their wayward husbands. Men, of course, often complain that women don't understand the meaning of **dialogue**, which is a two-way conversation that may involve opposing points of view. Argument is even more likely to play a role in a **parley**, which formally is a discussion between enemies regarding the terms of a truce. A **colloquy** is the most formal of all conversations (*a colloquy on nuclear disarmament*); it can also be used to jocularly describe a guarded exchange (*a brief colloquy with the arresting officer*). **Communion** is a form of conversation as well—one that may take place on such a profound level that no words are necessary (*communion with nature*).

con·ver·sa·tion·al·ist /ˌkänvərˈsāSHənl-ist/ ▶ **noun** a person who is good at or fond of engaging in conversation.

con·verse[1] /kən'vərs/ ▸ **verb** hold a conversation.
– ORIGIN Latin *conversari* 'keep company with.'

con·verse[2] /'kän,vərs/ ▸ **noun** the opposite of a situation, fact, or statement. ▸ **adjective** /'kän,vərs, kən'vərs/ opposite.
– DERIVATIVES **con·verse·ly** /'kän,vərslē, kən'vərslē/ adverb.
– ORIGIN Latin *conversus* 'turned about.'

con·ver·sion /kən'vərzʜən/ ▸ **noun 1** the action of converting someone or something. **2** Football the act of scoring an extra point or points after having scored a touchdown.

– SYNONYMS **change,** transformation, metamorphosis, alteration, adaptation, modification, redevelopment, rebuilding, remodeling.

con·vert ▸ **verb** /kən'vərt/ **1** change in form, character, or function: *grazing lands are being converted to farming.* **2** change money, stocks, or units into others of a different kind. **3** adapt a building for a new purpose. **4** change one's religious faith or other beliefs. **5** Football score extra points after a touchdown.

– SYNONYMS **1 change,** transform, alter, adapt, turn, modify, redevelop, remodel, rebuild, reorganize, metamorphose. **2 win over,** convince, persuade, claim, redeem, save, reform, re-educate, proselytize, evangelize.

▸ **noun** /'kän,vərt/ a person who has changed their religious faith or other beliefs.
– DERIVATIVES **con·vert·er** (also **convertor**) noun.
– ORIGIN Latin *convertere* 'turn about.'

con·vert·i·ble /kən'vərtəbəl/ ▸ **adjective 1** able to be changed in form, character, or function. **2** (of a car) having a folding or detachable roof. ▸ **noun** a car with a folding or detachable roof.
– DERIVATIVES **con·vert·i·bil·i·ty** /-,vərtə'bilitē/ noun.

con·vex /kän'veks, 'kän,veks, kən'veks/ ▸ **adjective** having an outline or surface that curves outward. Compare with CONCAVE.
– DERIVATIVES **con·vex·i·ty** /kän'veksitē, kən-/ noun.
– ORIGIN Latin *convexus* 'vaulted, arched.'

con·vey /kən'vā/ ▸ **verb 1** transport or carry something to a place. **2** communicate an idea, quality, or feeling. **3** Law transfer the title to property.

– SYNONYMS **1 transport,** carry, bring, take, fetch, move. **2 communicate,** pass on, impart, relate, relay, transmit, send. **3 express,** get across/over, put across/over, communicate, indicate.

– DERIVATIVES **con·vey·or** (also **conveyer**) noun.
– ORIGIN Latin *conviare* 'escort.'

con·vey·ance /kən'vāəns/ ▸ **noun 1** the action of conveying something. **2** formal a means of transport. **3** the legal process of transferring property from one owner to another.
– DERIVATIVES **con·vey·anc·er** noun **con·vey·anc·ing** noun.

con·vey·or belt ▸ **noun** a continuous moving belt for transporting objects within a building.

con·vict ▸ **verb** /kən'vikt/ declare someone to be guilty of a criminal offense by the verdict of a jury or the decision of a judge in a court of law.

– SYNONYMS **find guilty,** sentence.
– ANTONYMS acquit.

▸ **noun** /'kän,vikt/ a person found guilty of a criminal offense and serving a sentence of imprisonment.

– SYNONYMS **prisoner,** inmate, criminal, offender, felon; informal jailbird, con.

– ORIGIN from Latin *convictus* 'demonstrated, convicted.'

con·vic·tion /kən'viksʜən/ ▸ **noun 1** an instance of formally being found guilty of a criminal offense in a court of law. **2** a firmly held belief or opinion. **3** the feeling or appearance of being sure in one's belief: *his voice lacked conviction.*

– SYNONYMS **1 beliefs,** opinions, views, persuasion, ideals, position, stance, values. **2 assurance,** confidence, certainty.
– ANTONYMS diffidence.

CHOOSE THE RIGHT WORD

See **OPINION**.

con·vince /kən'vins/ ▸ **verb 1** cause someone to believe firmly in the truth of something: *he tried to convince her that everything would be all right.* **2** persuade someone to do something.

– SYNONYMS **1** *he convinced me I was wrong* **assure,** persuade, satisfy, prove to. **2** *I convinced her to marry me* **persuade,** induce, prevail on, talk into, win over, coax, cajole.

– DERIVATIVES **con·vinc·er** noun.
– ORIGIN Latin *convincere* 'overcome, demonstrate.'

CHOOSE THE RIGHT WORD

convince, persuade

Although it is common to see **convince** and **persuade** used interchangeably, there are distinctions in meaning that careful writers and speakers try to preserve. **Convince** derives from a Latin word meaning 'to conquer, overcome.' **Persuade** derives from a Latin word meaning 'to advise, make appealing, sweeten.' One can **convince** or **persuade** someone with facts or arguments, but, in general, *convincing* is limited to the mind, while *persuasion* results in action (just as *dissuasion* results in nonaction): *the prime minister convinced the council that delay was pointless; the senator persuaded her colleagues to pass the legislation.*

con·vinc·ing /kən'vinsiɴɢ/ ▸ **adjective 1** able to convince. **2** (of a victory or a winner) leaving no margin of doubt.

– SYNONYMS **1 persuasive,** powerful, strong, forceful, compelling, cogent, plausible, irresistible, telling. **2** *a convincing win* **resounding,** emphatic, decisive, conclusive.
– ANTONYMS unconvincing.

– DERIVATIVES **con·vinc·ing·ly** adverb.

con·viv·i·al /kən'vivēəl, kən'vivyəl/ ▸ **adjective 1** (of an atmosphere or event) friendly and lively. **2** cheerful and sociable.

– SYNONYMS **friendly,** genial, affable, amiable, congenial, agreeable, cordial, warm, sociable, outgoing, gregarious, cheerful.

– DERIVATIVES **con·viv·i·al·i·ty** /kən,vivē'alitē/ noun **con·viv·i·al·ly** adverb.
– ORIGIN from Latin *convivium* 'a feast.'

con·vo·ca·tion /,känvə'kāsʜən/ ▸ **noun** a large formal assembly of people.
– ORIGIN Latin.

con·voke /kən'vōk/ ▸ **verb** formal call together an assembly or meeting.
– ORIGIN Latin *convocare*.

con·vo·lut·ed /'känvə,lo͞otid/ ▸ **adjective 1** (of an argument, statement, or story) very complex. **2** twisted or coiled in a complex way.

WORD TOOLKIT

See **INTRICATE**.

con·vo·lu·tion /ˌkänvəˈlo͞oshən/ ▸ **noun 1** a coil or twist. **2** the state of being coiled or twisted. **3** a complex argument, statement, etc.
– DERIVATIVES **con·vo·lu·tion·al** adjective.
– ORIGIN from Latin *convolvere* 'roll together.'

con·vol·vu·lus /kənˈvälvyələs, -ˈvôl-/ ▸ **noun** (pl. **convolvuluses**) a twining plant with trumpet-shaped flowers.
– ORIGIN Latin, 'bindweed.'

con·voy /ˈkänˌvoi/ ▸ **noun** a group of ships or vehicles traveling together under armed protection.

– SYNONYMS **group,** fleet, cavalcade, motorcade, cortège, caravan, line.

▸ **verb** (of a warship or armed troops) accompany a group of ships or vehicles for protection.
– PHRASES **in convoy** traveling as a group.
– ORIGIN from Latin *conviare* 'convey.'

con·vulse /kənˈvəls/ ▸ **verb 1** suffer convulsions. **2** (**be convulsed**) make sudden uncontrollable movements because of emotion, laughter, etc.
– DERIVATIVES **con·vul·sive** /kənˈvəlsiv/ adjective **con·vul·sive·ly** adverb.
– ORIGIN Latin *convellere* 'pull violently.'

con·vul·sion /kənˈvəlshən/ ▸ **noun 1** a sudden irregular movement of the body, caused by the muscles contracting involuntarily. **2** (**convulsions**) uncontrollable laughter. **3** a violent social or natural upheaval.

co·ny ▸ **noun** (pl. **conies**) variant spelling of **CONEY**.

coo /ko͞o/ ▸ **verb** (**coos, cooing, cooed**) **1** (of a pigeon or dove) make a soft murmuring sound. **2** speak in a soft gentle voice. ▸ **noun** a cooing sound.
– ORIGIN imitating the sound.

cook /ko͝ok/ ▸ **verb 1** prepare food or a meal by mixing and heating the ingredients. **2** (of food) be heated so as to reach an edible state. **3** informal alter something dishonestly. **4** (**cook something up**) informal invent a story, excuse, or plan.

– SYNONYMS **prepare,** make, put together; informal fix, rustle up.

▸ **noun** a person who cooks food.
– PHRASES **cook someone's goose** informal spoil someone's plans.
– ORIGIN from Latin *coquus* 'a cook.'

WORD LINKS

culinary *relating to cooking*

cook·book /ˈko͝okˌbo͝ok/ ▸ **noun** a recipe book.

cook·er /ˈko͝okər/ ▸ **noun** Brit. an appliance for cooking food; a kitchen stove.

cook·er·y /ˈko͝okərē/ ▸ **noun** the practice or skill of preparing and cooking food.

cook·house /ˈko͝okˌhous/ ▸ **noun** a building used for cooking, especially on a ranch or military camp.

cook·ie /ˈko͝okē/ ▸ **noun** (pl. **cookies**) **1** a small sweet cake, typically round, flat, and crisp. **2** informal a person of a specified kind: *she's a tough cookie*.
– PHRASES **that's the way the cookie crumbles** informal that's the situation, and it must be accepted, however undesirable.
– ORIGIN Dutch *koekje* 'little cake.'

Cook's tour ▸ **noun** informal a rapid tour of many places.
– ORIGIN named after the English travel agent Thomas *Cook*.

cook·ware /ˈko͝okˌwe(ə)r/ ▸ **noun** pots, pans, or dishes in which food can be cooked.

cool /ko͞ol/ ▸ **adjective 1** fairly cold. **2** keeping one from becoming too hot. **3** not excited, angry, or emotional: *he kept a cool head*. **4** not friendly or enthusiastic. **5** informal fashionably attractive or impressive. **6** informal excellent. **7** informal used to express acceptance or agreement. **8** (**a cool ——**) informal used to emphasize a specified large amount of money: *they pocketed a cool $1 million each*.

– SYNONYMS **1 chilly,** chill, bracing, cold, brisk, crisp, fresh; informal nippy. **2 unenthusiastic,** lukewarm, tepid, indifferent, uninterested, apathetic. **3 unfriendly,** distant, remote, aloof, cold, chilly, frosty, unwelcoming; informal standoffish. **4 calm,** collected, composed, self-possessed, poised, serene, relaxed, at ease, unruffled, unperturbed; informal unflappable, together, laid-back.
– ANTONYMS warm, enthusiastic, friendly.

▸ **noun** (**the cool**) a fairly low temperature, or a fairly cold place or time: *the cool of the day*.

– SYNONYMS **1 chill,** chilliness, coldness, coolness. **2 self-control,** control, composure, self-possession, calmness, aplomb, poise.
– ANTONYMS warmth.

▸ **verb 1** make or become cool. **2** make or become less excited or angry.

– SYNONYMS **chill,** refrigerate, freeze.
– ANTONYMS warm.

– DERIVATIVES **cool·ish** adjective **cool·ly** adverb **cool·ness** noun.
– PHRASES **keep** (or **lose**) **one's cool** informal stay (or fail to stay) calm and controlled.
– ORIGIN Old English.

cool·ant /ˈko͞olənt/ ▸ **noun** a fluid used to cool an engine or other device.

cool·er /ˈko͞olər/ ▸ **noun 1** a device or container for keeping things cool. **2** (**the cooler**) informal prison.

cool·head·ed /ˈko͞olˌhedəd/ ▸ **adjective** not easily worried or excited.

coo·lie /ˈko͞olē/ ▸ **noun** (pl. **coolies**) dated an unskilled native laborer in some Asian countries.
– ORIGIN Hindi, 'day-laborer.'

cool·ing-off pe·ri·od ▸ **noun 1** a period during which the people in a dispute can try to settle their differences before taking further action. **2** a period after a sale contract is agreed upon during which the buyer can decide to cancel without losing any money.

cool·ing tow·er ▸ **noun** an open-topped, cylindrical concrete tower, used for cooling water or condensing steam from an industrial process.

coolth /ko͞olth/ ▸ **noun 1** pleasantly low temperature. **2** informal the quality of being fashionable.

coon /ko͞on/ ▸ **noun 1** short for **RACCOON**. **2** informal, offensive a black person.

coop /ko͞op, ko͝op/ ▸ **noun** a cage or pen for poultry. ▸ **verb** confine in a small space: *I'm sick of being cooped up at home*.
– ORIGIN Latin *cupa* 'cask, tub.'

co-op /ˈkōˌäp, kōˈäp/ ▸ **noun** informal a cooperative organization.

coop·er /'ko͞opər, 'ko͝opər/ ▶ **noun** a person who makes or repairs casks and barrels.
– DERIVATIVES **coop·er·age** /'ko͞opərij, 'ko͝op-/ noun.
– ORIGIN from Latin *cupa* 'cask, tub.'

co·op·er·ate /kō'äpə,rāt/ (also **co-operate**) ▶ **verb** **1** work together to achieve something. **2** do what is requested.

– SYNONYMS **1 collaborate,** work together, pull together, join forces, team up, unite, combine, pool resources. **2 assist,** help, lend a hand, be of service, do one's bit/part; informal play ball.

– DERIVATIVES **co·op·er·a·tor** noun.
– ORIGIN Latin *cooperari*.

co·op·er·a·tion /kō,äpə'rāsʜən/ (also **co-operation**) ▶ **noun** the process of working together to achieve something.

– SYNONYMS **collaboration,** joint action, combined effort, teamwork, give and take, compromise.

co·op·er·a·tive /kō'äp(ə)rətiv/ (also **co-operative**) ▶ **adjective** **1** involving cooperation. **2** willing to help. **3** (of a farm or business) owned and run jointly by its members, with profits or benefits shared among them.

– SYNONYMS **1 collaborative,** collective, combined, joint, shared, united, concerted. **2 helpful,** eager to help, obliging, accommodating, willing.

▶ **noun** an organization owned and run jointly by its members.
– DERIVATIVES **co·op·er·a·tive·ly** adverb.

co-opt /kō'äpt, 'kō,äpt/ ▶ **verb** **1** make someone a member of a committee or other body by invitation of the existing members. **2** divert to a role different from the usual one: *can a government co-opt private industry to promote its policies?* **3** adopt an idea or policy for one's own use.
– DERIVATIVES **co-op·ta·tion** noun **co-op·tion** noun.
– ORIGIN Latin *cooptare*.

co·or·di·nate (also **co-ordinate**) ▶ **verb** /kō'ôrdə,nāt/ **1** bring the different elements of a complex activity or organization into an efficient relationship. **2** (**coordinate with**) negotiate with others in order to work together effectively. **3** match or harmonize attractively.

– SYNONYMS **organize,** arrange, order, synchronize, bring together, orchestrate.

▶ **noun** /kō'ôrdn-ət/ **1** Mathematics each of a group of numbers used to indicate the position of a point, line, or plane. **2** (**coordinates**) matching items of clothing. ▶ **adjective** /kō'ôrdənət/ equal in rank or importance.
– DERIVATIVES **co·or·di·na·tor** /-'ôrdn,ātər/ noun.
– ORIGIN from Latin *ordinare* 'put in order.'

co·or·di·na·tion /kō,ôrdn'āsʜən/ (also **co-ordination**) ▶ **noun** **1** the organization of things so as to work together effectively. **2** the ability to move different parts of the body smoothly and at the same time.

coot /ko͞ot/ ▶ **noun** **1** (pl. same) a black waterbird with a white bill. **2** (usu. **old coot**) informal a foolish person, typically an old man.
– ORIGIN probably Dutch or German.

coot·ie /'ko͞otē/ ▶ **noun** informal a children's term for an imaginary germ or repellent quality transmitted by undesirable or repugnant people.

cop /käp/ informal ▶ **noun** a police officer. ▶ **verb** (**cops, copping, copped**) **1** arrest an offender. **2** experience or receive something unwelcome: *the team's captain copped the blame.* **3** steal. **4** (**cop out**) avoid doing something that one ought to do.
– PHRASES **cop a feel** informal fondle someone sexually. **cop a plea** engage in plea bargaining.
– ORIGIN perhaps from Old French *caper* 'seize.'

co·pal /'kōpəl/ ▶ **noun** resin from certain tropical trees, used to make varnish.
– ORIGIN Spanish.

co-par·ent ▶ **verb** (especially of a separated or unmarried couple) share the duties of bringing up a child. ▶ **noun** a person who co-parents a child.

cope[1] /kōp/ ▶ **verb** deal effectively with something difficult.

– SYNONYMS **1 manage,** survive, look after oneself, fend for oneself, get by/through, hold one's own. **2** *his inability to cope with the situation* **deal with,** handle, manage, address, face (up to), confront, tackle, come to grips with.

– DERIVATIVES **cop·er** noun.
– ORIGIN Old French *coper* 'to strike.'

cope[2] ▶ **noun** a long cloak worn by a priest or bishop on ceremonial occasions. ▶ **verb** (in building) cover a joint or structure with a coping.
– ORIGIN Latin *cappa* 'covering for the head.'

co·peck /'kō,pek/ ▶ **noun** variant spelling of **KOPEK**.

Co·per·ni·can sys·tem /kə'pərnikən/ (also **Copernican theory**) ▶ **noun** the theory proposed by the Polish astronomer Nicolaus Copernicus that the sun is the center of the solar system, with the planets orbiting around it. Compare with **PTOLEMAIC SYSTEM**.

cop·i·er /'käpēər/ ▶ **noun** a machine that makes exact copies of something.

co·pi·lot /'kō,pīlət/ ▶ **noun** a second pilot in an aircraft.

cop·ing /'kōpiɴɢ/ ▶ **noun** the curved or sloping top course of a brick or stone wall.
– ORIGIN from **COPE[2]**.

co·pi·ous /'kōpēəs/ ▶ **adjective** abundant in supply or quantity: *drinking copious amounts of beer.*

– SYNONYMS **abundant,** plentiful, ample, profuse, extensive, generous, lavish, liberal, overflowing, in abundance, numerous, many; informal galore; literary plenteous.
– ANTONYMS sparse.

– DERIVATIVES **co·pi·ous·ly** adverb **co·pi·ous·ness** noun.
– ORIGIN from Latin *copia* 'plenty.'

CHOOSE THE RIGHT WORD

See **PREVALENT**.

co·pol·y·mer /kō'päləmər/ ▶ **noun** Chemistry a polymer made by reaction of two different monomers, with units of more than one kind.

cop-out ▶ **noun** informal an instance of avoiding a commitment or responsibility.

cop·per[1] /'käpər/ ▶ **noun** **1** a red-brown metallic chemical element that is used for electrical wiring and as a component of brass and bronze. **2** (**coppers**) Brit. coins of low value made of copper or bronze. **3** a reddish-brown color. ▶ **verb** cover or coat something with copper.
– DERIVATIVES **cop·per·y** adjective.
– ORIGIN from Latin *cyprium aes* 'Cyprus metal.'

cop·per[2] ▶ **noun** Brit. informal a police officer.
– ORIGIN from **COP**.

cop·per beech ▶ **noun** a variety of beech tree with purplish-brown leaves.

cop·per·head /ˈkäpərˌhed/ ▶ **noun** any of a number of stout-bodied venomous snakes with coppery-pink or reddish-brown coloration, in particular a North American pit viper.

cop·per·plate /ˌkäpərˈplāt, ˈkäpərˌplāt/ ▶ **noun 1** a polished copper plate with a design engraved or etched into it. **2** a neat, looped style of handwriting.

cop·per sul·fate ▶ **noun** a blue crystalline solid used in electroplating and as a fungicide.

cop·pice /ˈkäpəs/ ▶ **noun** an area of woodland in which the trees or shrubs are periodically cut back to ground level to stimulate growth. ▶ **verb** cut back a tree or shrub to ground level.
– ORIGIN Old French *copeiz*.

cop·ra /ˈkäprə/ ▶ **noun** dried coconut kernels, from which oil is obtained.
– ORIGIN Portuguese and Spanish.

co·proc·es·sor /kōˈpräˌsesər, ˌkōˈpräsəsər/ ▶ **noun** Computing a microprocessor designed to supplement the capabilities of the primary processor.

co·pro·duce /ˌkōprəˈd(y)o͞os/ ▶ **verb** produce a theatrical work or a radio or television program jointly.
– DERIVATIVES **co·pro·duc·er** noun **co·pro·duc·tion** /-ˈdəkSHən/ noun.

copse /käps/ ▶ **noun** a small group of trees.
– ORIGIN from **COPPICE**.

Copt /käpt/ ▶ **noun 1** a member of the Coptic Church, the native Christian Church in Egypt. **2** a native Egyptian in the periods of Greek and Roman rule.
– ORIGIN Latin *Coptus*.

cop·ter /ˈkäptər/ ▶ **noun** informal a helicopter.

Cop·tic /ˈkäptik/ ▶ **noun** the language of the ancient Copts, which survives only in the Coptic Church. ▶ **adjective** relating to the Copts or their language.

cop·u·la /ˈkäpyələ/ ▶ **noun** a verb, especially the verb *be*, that links a subject and complement (e.g., *was* in the sentence *I was happy*).
– ORIGIN Latin, 'connection, linking of words.'

cop·u·late /ˈkäpyəˌlāt/ ▶ **verb** have sexual intercourse.
– DERIVATIVES **cop·u·la·tion** /ˌkäpyəˈlāSHən/ noun **cop·u·la·to·ry** /-ləˌtôrē/ adjective.
– ORIGIN Latin *copulare* 'fasten together.'

cop·y /ˈkäpē/ ▶ **noun** (pl. **copies**) **1** a thing made to be similar or identical to another. **2** a single specimen of a particular book, record, etc. **3** material to be printed in a book, newspaper, or magazine. **4** the written part of an advertisement.

> – SYNONYMS **1 duplicate,** facsimile, photocopy; trademark Xerox. **2 replica,** reproduction, imitation, likeness, forgery, fake, counterfeit.

▶ **verb** (**copies, copying, copied**) **1** make a copy of something. **2** imitate the behavior or style of: *this view of leadership is copied from business.*

> – SYNONYMS **1 duplicate,** photocopy, xerox, photostat, reproduce. **2 reproduce,** replicate, forge, fake, counterfeit. **3 imitate,** reproduce, emulate, mimic; informal rip off.

– ORIGIN Latin *copia* 'abundance,' later 'transcript.'

> **CHOOSE THE RIGHT WORD**
>
> See **IMITATE**.

cop·y·book /ˈkäpēˌbo͝ok/ ▶ **noun** a book containing models of handwriting for learners to imitate. ▶ **adjective** exactly in accordance with established standards: *a copybook landing.*

cop·y·cat /ˈkäpēˌkat/ ▶ **noun** informal a person who copies another. ▶ **adjective** (of an action, especially a crime) done in imitation of another: *copycat attacks.*

cop·y-ed·it ▶ **verb** edit written material by checking its consistency and accuracy.
– DERIVATIVES **cop·y ed·i·tor** noun.

cop·y·ist /ˈkäpē-ist/ ▶ **noun 1** a person who makes copies. **2** a person who imitates the styles of others, especially in art.

cop·y·right /ˈkäpēˌrīt/ ▶ **noun** the exclusive legal right, given to the originator for a fixed number of years, to print, publish, perform, film, or record literary, artistic, or musical material.

cop·y·writ·er /ˈkäpiˌrītər/ ▶ **noun** a person who writes advertisements or publicity material.

coq au vin /ˌkōk ō ˈvaN, ˌkäk/ ▶ **noun** a casserole of chicken pieces cooked in red wine.
– ORIGIN French, 'cock in wine.'

co·quette /kōˈket/ ▶ **noun** a woman who flirts.
– DERIVATIVES **co·quet·ry** /ˈkōkətrē, kōˈketrē/ noun **co·quet·tish** adjective **co·quet·tish·ly** adverb.
– ORIGIN French, 'wanton female.'

cor·a·cle /ˈkôrəkəl, ˈkär-/ ▶ **noun** a small, round boat made of wickerwork covered with a watertight material, propelled with a paddle.
– ORIGIN Welsh *corwgl*.

cor·al /ˈkôrəl, ˈkär-/ ▶ **noun 1** a hard stony substance produced by certain sea creatures as an external skeleton, typically forming large reefs. **2** precious red coral, used in jewelry. **3** a pinkish-red color.
– ORIGIN Greek *korallion, kouralion*.

cor·al snake ▶ **noun** a brightly colored venomous snake of the cobra family, typically having conspicuous bands of red, yellow, white, and black.

cor an·glais /ˌkôr ˈäNGlā/ ▶ **noun** (pl. **cors anglais** pronunc. same) a woodwind instrument of the oboe family, sounding a fifth lower than the oboe.
– ORIGIN French, 'English horn.'

cor·bel /ˈkôrbəl/ ▶ **noun** a projection jutting out from a wall to support a structure above it.
– DERIVATIVES **cor·beled** adjective **cor·bel·ing** noun.
– ORIGIN Old French, 'little crow.'

cord /kôrd/ ▶ **noun 1** thin string or rope made from several twisted strands. **2** a length of cord. **3** a structure in the body resembling a cord (e.g., the spinal cord). **4** a flexible insulated cable used for carrying electric current. **5** corduroy. **6** (**cords**) corduroy pants. **7** a measure of cut wood (usually 128 cu. ft., 3.62 cubic meters).

> – SYNONYMS **string,** thread, line, rope, cable, wire, twine, yarn.

– DERIVATIVES **cord·ing** noun.
– ORIGIN Greek *khordē* 'gut, string.'

> **USAGE**
>
> On the confusion of **cord** and **chord**, see the note at **CHORD**[1].

cor·date /ˈkôrˌdāt/ ▶ **adjective** Botany & Zoology heart-shaped.
– ORIGIN Latin *cordatus* 'wise,' later 'heart-shaped.'

cord blood ▶ **noun** blood from the human umbilical cord, a source of stem cells.

cor·dial /'kôrjəl/ ▶ **adjective 1** warm and friendly. **2** strongly felt: *I earned his cordial loathing.* ▶ **noun 1** another term for **LIQUEUR**. **2** a pleasant-tasting medicine.
– DERIVATIVES **cor·dial·i·ty** /ˌkôrjē'alitē/ noun **cor·dial·ly** adverb.
– ORIGIN Latin *cordialis*, from *cor* 'heart.'

cor·dil·le·ra /ˌkôrdl'(y)erə/ ▶ **noun** a system or group of parallel mountain ranges together with the intervening plateaus and other features, especially in the Andes or the Rockies.
– ORIGIN Spanish.

cord·ite /'kôrˌdīt/ ▶ **noun** a smokeless explosive used in ammunition.
– ORIGIN from **CORD**, because of its appearance.

cord·less /'kôrdləs/ ▶ **adjective** (of an electrical appliance) working without connection to a main supply or central unit.

cor·do·ba /'kôrdəbə, -dəvə/ ▶ **noun** the basic unit of money of Nicaragua.
– ORIGIN named after F. Fernández de *Córdoba*, a former Spanish governor of Nicaragua.

cor·don /'kôrdn/ ▶ **noun 1** a line or circle of police, soldiers, or guards forming a barrier. **2** a fruit tree trained to grow as a single ropelike stem.

– SYNONYMS **barrier,** line, chain, ring, circle.

▶ **verb** (**cordon something off**) close somewhere off by surrounding it with police or other guards.

– SYNONYMS **close off,** seal off, fence off, separate off, isolate, enclose, encircle, surround.

– ORIGIN Italian *cordone* and French *cordon*.

cor·don bleu /ˌkôrdôɴ 'blœ/ ▶ **adjective 1** (of a cook or cooking) of the highest class. **2** referring to a dish consisting of veal or chicken rolled, filled with cheese and ham, and then fried in breadcrumbs.
– ORIGIN French, 'blue ribbon' (once signifying the highest order of French chivalry).

cor·don sa·ni·taire /kôrdôɴ ˌsänē'ter/ ▶ **noun** (pl. **cordons sanitaires** pronunc. same) **1** a line of guards positioned around an area infected by disease, preventing anyone from leaving. **2** a measure designed to prevent communication or the spread of undesirable influences.
– ORIGIN French, 'sanitary line.'

cor·du·roy /'kôrdəˌroi/ ▶ **noun** a thick cotton fabric with velvety ribs.
– ORIGIN probably from **CORD** + *duroy*, a former kind of lightweight cloth.

core /kôr/ ▶ **noun 1** the tough central part of various fruits, containing the seeds. **2** the central or most important part: *mysticism was the core of his faith.* **3** the dense metallic or rocky central region of a planet. **4** the central part of a nuclear reactor, which contains the fissile material.

– SYNONYMS **1** *the earth's core* **center,** interior, middle, nucleus. **2** *the core of the argument* **heart,** nucleus, nub, kernel, meat, essence, crux, pith, substance; informal nitty-gritty.

▶ **verb** remove the core from a fruit.
– DERIVATIVES **cor·er** noun.
– ORIGIN unknown.

co·re·op·sis /ˌkôrē'äpsəs/ ▶ **noun** a plant of the daisy family, cultivated for its rayed, typically yellow, flowers.
– ORIGIN from Greek *koris* 'bug' + *opsis* 'appearance' (because of the shape of the seed).

co·re·spond·ent ▶ **noun** a person named in a divorce case as having committed adultery with the husband or wife of the person who wants a divorce.

cor·gi /'kôrgē/ (also **Welsh corgi**) ▶ **noun** (pl. **corgis**) a breed of dog with short legs and a foxlike head.
– ORIGIN from Welsh *cor* 'dwarf' + *ci* 'dog.'

co·ri·an·der /'kôrēˌandər, ˌkôrē'andər/ ▶ **noun** a Mediterranean plant of the parsley family, used as an herb in cooking.
– ORIGIN Greek *koriannon*.

Co·rin·thi·an /kə'rinᴛʜēən/ ▶ **adjective 1** relating to Corinth, a city in southern Greece and a city-state in ancient Greece. **2** relating to an ornate classical style of architecture having flared capitals with rows of acanthus leaves. ▶ **noun** a person from Corinth.

cork /kôrk/ ▶ **noun 1** a buoyant, light brown substance obtained from the bark of a kind of Mediterranean oak tree. **2** a bottle stopper made of cork. ▶ **verb 1** close or seal a bottle with a cork. **2** (as adj. **corked**) (of wine) spoiled by tannin from the cork.
– ORIGIN ultimately from Latin *quercus* 'oak, cork oak.'

cork·age /'kôrkij/ ▶ **noun** a charge made by a restaurant for serving wine that has been brought in by a customer.

cork·er /'kôrkər/ ▶ **noun** informal an excellent person or thing.
– DERIVATIVES **cork·ing** adjective.

cork·screw /'kôrkˌskro͞o/ ▶ **noun** a device with a spiral metal rod, used for pulling corks from bottles. ▶ **verb** move or twist in a spiral.

corm /kôrm/ ▶ **noun** the underground storage organ of plants such as crocuses, consisting of a swollen stem base covered with scale leaves.
– ORIGIN Greek *kormos* 'trunk stripped of its boughs.'

cor·mo·rant /'kôrmərənt/ ▶ **noun** a large diving seabird with a long neck, long hooked bill, and mainly black plumage.
– ORIGIN Old French *cormaran*.

corn[1] /kôrn/ ▶ **noun 1** a North American cereal plant that yields large kernels set in rows on a cob. **2** the grains of this plant. **3** informal something unoriginal or sentimental: *the movie is pure corn.*
– PHRASES **corn on the cob** corn when cooked and eaten straight from the cob.
– ORIGIN Old English.

corn[2] ▶ **noun** a small, painful area of thickened skin on the foot, caused by pressure.
– ORIGIN Latin *cornu* 'horn.'

corn·ball /'kôrnˌbôl/ ▶ **adjective** trite and sentimental: *a cornball movie.* ▶ **noun** a person with trite or sentimental ideas.

corn·bread /'kôrnˌbred/ ▶ **noun** a type of bread made from cornmeal and typically leavened without yeast.

corn·cob /'kôrnˌkäb/ ▶ **noun** the central woody part of an ear of corn, to which the grains are attached.

cor·ne·a /'kôrnēə/ ▶ **noun** the transparent layer forming the front of the eye.
– DERIVATIVES **cor·ne·al** adjective.
– ORIGIN from Latin *cornea tela* 'horny tissue.'

corned beef ▶ **noun** beef brisket cured in brine and boiled, typically served cold.

cor·ner /'kôrnər/ ▶ **noun 1** a place or angle where two or more sides or edges meet. **2** a place where two streets meet. **3** a remote area. **4** a difficult or awkward position: *Mick thought it was a crazy idea, but he was in a corner.*

5 Baseball first or third base on a baseball diamond. **6** Boxing & Wrestling each of the diagonally opposite ends of the ring, where a contestant rests between rounds.

– SYNONYMS **1 bend,** curve, turn, junction, hairpin turn. **2 district,** region, area, quarter; informal neck of the woods.

▸ **verb 1** force into a place or situation from which it is hard to escape: *my landlord cornered me as I was going upstairs.* **2** go around a bend in a road. **3** control a market by dominating the supply of a particular commodity.

– SYNONYMS **1 surround,** trap, hem in, pen in, cut off. **2 gain control of,** take over, dominate, monopolize, capture; informal sew up.

– ORIGIN Latin *cornu* 'horn, tip, corner.'

cor·ner·back /ˈkôrnərˌbak/ ▸ **noun** Football a defensive back positioned to the outside of the linebackers.

cor·ner·stone /ˈkôrnərˌstōn/ ▸ **noun 1** a vital part or basis: *sugar was the cornerstone of the economy.* **2** a stone that forms the base of a corner of a building, joining two walls.

cor·net /kôrˈnet/ ▸ **noun 1** a brass instrument resembling a trumpet but shorter and wider. **2** British term for **ICE CREAM CONE** (sense 1).
– DERIVATIVES **cor·net·ist** /-ˈnetəst/ (also **cornettist**) noun.
– ORIGIN Old French, 'little horn.'

corn·flakes /ˈkôrnˌflāks/ ▸ **plural noun** a breakfast cereal consisting of toasted flakes made from corn.

corn·flow·er /ˈkôrnˌflouər/ ▸ **noun** a plant of the daisy family with deep blue flowers.

cor·nice /ˈkôrnis/ ▸ **noun 1** an ornamental molding around the wall of a room just below the ceiling. **2** a horizontal molded projection crowning a building or structure.
– DERIVATIVES **cor·niced** adjective **cor·nic·ing** noun.
– ORIGIN Italian.

cor·niche /ˈkôrnisн, kôrˈnēsн/ ▸ **noun** a road cut into the edge of a cliff and running along a coastline.
– ORIGIN French, 'cornice.'

Cor·nish /ˈkôrnisн/ ▸ **adjective** relating to Cornwall. ▸ **noun** the ancient Celtic language of Cornwall.

corn·meal /ˈkôrnˌmēl/ ▸ **noun** meal made from ground, dried corn.

corn·rows /ˈkôrnˌrōz/ ▸ **plural noun** (especially among black people) a style of braiding the hair in narrow strips to form geometric patterns on the scalp.

corn sal·ad ▸ **noun** a small plant with soft roundish leaves that are eaten in salads.

corn·starch /ˈkôrnˌstärcн/ ▸ **noun** finely ground corn flour, used for thickening sauces.

cor·nu·co·pi·a /ˌkôrn(y)əˈkōpēə/ ▸ **noun 1** an abundant supply of good things. **2** a symbol of plenty consisting of a goat's horn overflowing with flowers, fruit, and cereals.
– DERIVATIVES **cor·nu·co·pi·an** adjective.
– ORIGIN from Latin *cornu copiae* 'horn of plenty.'

corn·y /ˈkôrnē/ ▸ **adjective (cornier, corniest)** informal unoriginal or very sentimental: *corny jokes.*
– DERIVATIVES **corn·i·ness** noun.
– ORIGIN first meaning 'rustic, appealing to country folk.'

co·rol·la /kəˈrälə, kəˈrōlə/ ▸ **noun** the petals of a flower, typically forming a whorl within the sepals.
– ORIGIN Latin, 'little crown.'

cor·ol·lar·y /ˈkôrəˌlerē, ˈkärə-/ ▸ **noun** (pl. **corollaries**) **1** a direct consequence or result. **2** a logical proposition that follows from one already proved. ▸ **adjective** associated; supplementary.
– ORIGIN Latin *corollarium* 'money paid for a garland or chaplet' (later 'a deduction').

co·ro·na /kəˈrōnə/ ▸ **noun** (pl. **coronae** /-nē, -nī/) **1** the envelope of gas around the sun or another star. **2** a small circle of light seen around the sun or moon. **3** (also **corona discharge**) Physics the glow around a conductor at high potential. **4** a long, straight-sided cigar.
– DERIVATIVES **cor·o·nal** /ˈkôrənl, ˈkär-/ adjective.
– ORIGIN Latin, 'wreath, crown'; sense 4 comes from a proprietary name of a cigar.

cor·o·nar·y /ˈkôrəˌnerē, ˈkär-/ ▸ **adjective** relating to the arteries that surround and supply the heart. ▸ **noun** (pl. **coronaries**) (also **coronary thrombosis**) a blockage of the flow of blood to the heart, caused by a clot in a coronary artery.
– ORIGIN Latin *coronarius* 'resembling or forming a crown.'

cor·o·na·tion /ˌkôrəˈnāsнən, ˌkär-/ ▸ **noun** the ceremony of crowning a sovereign or a sovereign's consort.
– ORIGIN from Latin *coronare* 'to crown.'

cor·o·ner /ˈkôrənər, ˈkär-/ ▸ **noun** an official who holds inquests into violent, sudden, or suspicious deaths.
– ORIGIN Old French *coruner.*

cor·o·net /ˌkôrəˈnet, ˌkär-/ ▸ **noun 1** a small or simple crown. **2** a circular decorative band worn on the head.
– ORIGIN Old French *coronete* 'little crown.'

Corp. ▸ **abbreviation 1** Corporal. **2** Corporation.

cor·po·ra /ˈkôrpərə/ plural of **CORPUS**.

cor·po·ral¹ /ˈkôrp(ə)rəl/ ▸ **noun** a rank of noncommissioned officer in the US Army or Marine Corps, above lance corporal or private first class and below sergeant.
– ORIGIN Italian *caporale.*

cor·po·ral² ▸ **adjective** relating to the human body.
– ORIGIN Latin *corporalis.*

cor·po·ral pun·ish·ment ▸ **noun** physical punishment, such as caning.

cor·po·rate /ˈkôrp(ə)rət/ ▸ **adjective 1** relating to a business corporation. **2** relating to or shared by all members of a group: *corporate responsibility.*
– DERIVATIVES **cor·po·rate·ly** adverb.
– ORIGIN from Latin *corporare* 'form into a body.'

cor·po·rate raid·er ▸ **noun** a financier who makes a practice of making hostile takeover bids for companies, either to control their policies or to resell them for a profit.

cor·po·rate tax ▸ **noun** tax paid by companies on their profits.

cor·po·ra·tion /ˌkôrpəˈrāsнən/ ▸ **noun 1** a large company or group of companies recognized by law as a single unit. **2** (also **municipal corporation**) a group of people elected to govern a city, town, or borough.

– SYNONYMS **company,** firm, business, concern, operation, conglomerate, group, chain, multinational.

cor·po·rat·ism /ˈkôrp(ə)rəˌtizəm/ ▸ **noun** the control of a government or organization by large interest groups.
– DERIVATIVES **cor·po·rat·ist** adjective & noun.

cor·po·re·al /kôrˈpôrēəl/ ▸ **adjective** relating to a person's body; physical rather than spiritual.
– DERIVATIVES **cor·po·re·al·i·ty** /kôrˌpôrēˈalitē/ noun.
– ORIGIN Latin *corporealis.*

corps /kôr/ ▶ **noun** (pl. **corps** /kôrz/) **1** a main subdivision of an army in the field, consisting of two or more divisions. **2** a branch of an army assigned to a particular kind of work. **3** a group of people engaged in a particular activity: *the press corps.*
– ORIGIN French.

corps de bal·let /ˌkôr də baˈlā/ ▶ **noun** (treated as sing. or pl.) **1** the members of a ballet company who dance together as a group. **2** the lowest rank of dancers in a ballet company.

corpse /kôrps/ ▶ **noun** a dead body, especially of a person.

– SYNONYMS **dead body,** carcass, remains; informal stiff; Medicine cadaver.

– ORIGIN Latin *corpus.*

CHOOSE THE RIGHT WORD

See **BODY**.

cor·pu·lent /ˈkôrpyələnt/ ▶ **adjective** (of a person) fat.
– DERIVATIVES **cor·pu·lence** noun.
– ORIGIN Latin *corpulentus.*

cor·pus /ˈkôrpəs/ ▶ **noun** (pl. **corpora** /-pərə/ or **corpuses**) **1** a collection of written works. **2** a collection of written or spoken material in a form that is readable by a computer.
– ORIGIN Latin, 'body.'

Cor·pus Chris·ti /ˌkôrpəs ˈkristē/ ▶ **noun** a Christian feast commemorating the institution of Holy Communion, observed on the Thursday after Trinity Sunday.
– ORIGIN Latin, 'body of Christ.'

cor·pus·cle /ˈkôrˌpəsəl/ ▶ **noun** a red or white blood cell.
– DERIVATIVES **cor·pus·cu·lar** /kôrˈpəskyələr/ adjective.
– ORIGIN Latin *corpusculum* 'small body.'

cor·ral /kəˈral/ ▶ **noun** a pen for livestock on a farm or ranch. ▶ **verb** (**corrals, corralling, corralled**) **1** put or keep livestock in a corral. **2** gather a group together.
– ORIGIN Spanish and Portuguese.

cor·rect /kəˈrekt/ ▶ **adjective 1** free from error; true; right: *they came up with the correct answer.* **2** meeting accepted social standards.

– SYNONYMS **1 right,** accurate, exact, true, perfect; informal spot on. **2 proper,** decent, right, respectable, decorous, seemly, suitable, appropriate, accepted.
– ANTONYMS wrong, improper.

▶ **verb 1** put right an error or fault. **2** mark the errors in written work. **3** tell someone that they are mistaken. **4** adjust a result or reading to allow for departure from standard conditions.

– SYNONYMS **rectify,** right, put right, set right, amend, remedy, repair, reform, cure.

– DERIVATIVES **cor·rect·a·ble** adjective **cor·rect·ly** adverb **cor·rect·ness** noun **cor·rec·tor** noun.
– ORIGIN from Latin *corrigere* 'make straight, amend.'

cor·rec·tion /kəˈrekshən/ ▶ **noun 1** the action of correcting something. **2** a change that puts right an error or inaccuracy.

– SYNONYMS **rectification,** righting, amendment, repair, remedy, cure.

cor·rec·tion·al /kəˈrekshənl/ ▶ **adjective** relating to punishment intended to rectify criminals' behavior: *a correctional institution.*

cor·rec·tive /kəˈrektiv/ ▶ **adjective** designed to put right something undesirable.

cor·re·late /ˈkôrəˌlāt, ˈkär-/ ▶ **verb** have or bring into a relationship in which one thing depends on another and vice versa: *success in the educational system correlates highly with class.* ▶ **noun** each of two or more related or complementary things.

cor·re·la·tion /ˌkôrəˈlāshən/ ▶ **noun 1** a relationship in which one thing depends on another and vice versa. **2** the process of correlating two or more things.

cor·rel·a·tive /kəˈrelətiv/ ▶ **adjective 1** having a relationship in which one thing affects or depends on another. **2** (of words such as *neither* and *nor*) corresponding to each other and regularly used together.
– ORIGIN Latin *correlativus.*

cor·re·spond /ˌkôrəˈspänd, ˌkär-/ ▶ **verb 1** match or agree almost exactly. **2** be comparable or equivalent in character or form: *many companies assign employees numbers that correspond to their date of hire.* **3** communicate by exchanging letters.

– SYNONYMS **1 be consistent,** correlate, agree, accord, coincide, tally, tie in, match; informal square. **2** *a rank corresponding to a British sergeant* **be equivalent,** be analogous, be comparable, equate. **3 exchange letters,** write, communicate.

– ORIGIN Latin *correspondere.*

cor·re·spond·ence /ˌkôrəˈspändəns, ˌkär-/ ▶ **noun 1** a close similarity, link, or equivalence. **2** letters sent or received.

– SYNONYMS **1 correlation,** parallel, agreement, consistency, conformity, similarity, resemblance, comparability. **2 letters,** messages, mail, post, communication.

cor·re·spond·ence course ▶ **noun** a course of study in which student and teachers communicate by mail.

cor·re·spond·ent /ˌkôrəˈspändənt, ˌkär-/ ▶ **noun 1** a journalist reporting on a particular subject or from a particular country: *a White House correspondent.* **2** a person who writes letters on a regular basis.

– SYNONYMS **reporter,** journalist, columnist, writer, contributor, commentator.

cor·ri·da /kôˈrēdə/ ▶ **noun** a bullfight.
– ORIGIN from Spanish *corrida de toros* 'running of bulls.'

cor·ri·dor /ˈkôrədər, ˈkär-, -ˌdôr/ ▶ **noun 1** a passage in a building, with doors leading into rooms. **2** a strip of land linking two other areas or following a road or river.
– PHRASES **the corridors of power** the senior levels of government or administration.
– ORIGIN Italian *corridore,* from *corridoio* 'running-place.'

cor·rob·o·rate /kəˈräbəˌrāt/ ▶ **verb** confirm or give support to a statement or theory.
– DERIVATIVES **cor·rob·o·ra·tion** /kəˌräbəˈrāshən/ noun **cor·rob·o·ra·tive** /-ˈräb(ə)rətiv/ adjective.
– ORIGIN Latin *corroborare* 'strengthen.'

cor·rob·o·ree /kəˈräbərē/ ▶ **noun** an Australian Aboriginal dance ceremony in the form of a sacred ritual or informal gathering.
– ORIGIN from an Aboriginal word.

cor·rode /kəˈrōd/ ▶ **verb 1** (with reference to metal or other hard material) wear or be worn away slowly by chemical action. **2** gradually weaken or destroy: *the criticism corroded his reputation.*
– ORIGIN Latin *corrodere.*

cor·ro·sion /kəˈrōzhən/ ▶ **noun 1** the process of wearing away something. **2** damage caused by this process.

cor·ro·sive /kə'rōsiv, -ziv/ ▶ **adjective** causing corrosion. ▶ **noun** a corrosive substance.

cor·ru·gate /'kôrə,gāt, 'kär-/ ▶ **verb 1** contract into wrinkles or folds: *his brow corrugated in a frown.* **2** (as adj. **corrugated**) shaped into alternate ridges and grooves: *corrugated iron.*
– DERIVATIVES **cor·ru·ga·tion** /,kôrə'gāsʜən, ,kär-/ noun.
– ORIGIN Latin *corrugare* 'to wrinkle.'

cor·rupt /kə'rəpt/ ▶ **adjective 1** willing to act dishonestly in return for money or personal gain. **2** evil or very immoral. **3** (of a written work or computer data) made unreliable by errors or alterations.

> – SYNONYMS **1 dishonest,** unscrupulous, criminal, fraudulent, illegal, unlawful; informal crooked; Brit. informal bent. **2 immoral,** depraved, degenerate, debauched, vice-ridden, perverted, dissolute.
> – ANTONYMS honest, ethical, pure.

▶ **verb 1** make dishonest or depraved: *he was corrupted by power.* **2** introduce errors into a written work or computer data.

> – SYNONYMS **deprave,** pervert, lead astray, debauch, defile, pollute, sully.

– DERIVATIVES **cor·rupt·er** noun **cor·rupt·i·ble** adjective **cor·rup·tive** adjective **cor·rupt·ly** adverb.
– ORIGIN from Latin *corrumpere* 'mar, bribe, destroy.'

> **WORD TOOLKIT**
>
> See **ILLEGAL**.

cor·rup·tion /kə'rəpsʜən/ ▶ **noun 1** dishonest or illegal behavior. **2** the action of corrupting someone or something.

> – SYNONYMS **1 dishonesty,** unscrupulousness, double-dealing, fraud, misconduct, bribery, payola, venality; informal graft, sleaze. **2 immorality,** depravity, vice, degeneracy, perversion, debauchery, wickedness, evil, sin.
> – ANTONYMS honesty, morality.

cor·sage /kôr'säzʜ, -'säj/ ▶ **noun** a spray of flowers worn pinned to a woman's clothes.
– ORIGIN French.

cor·sair /'kôr,se(ə)r/ ▶ **noun 1** old use a pirate. **2** historical a privateer, especially one operating in the Mediterranean in the 17th century.
– ORIGIN French *corsaire.*

cor·set /'kôrsət/ ▶ **noun 1** a woman's tight-fitting undergarment extending from below the chest to the hips, worn to shape the figure. **2** a similar garment worn to support a weak or injured back.
– DERIVATIVES **cor·set·ed** adjective **cor·set·ry** noun.
– ORIGIN Old French, 'little body.'

Cor·si·can /'kôrsikən/ ▶ **noun 1** a person from Corsica. **2** the language of Corsica. ▶ **adjective** relating to Corsica.

cor·tège /kôr'tezʜ, 'kôr,tezʜ/ ▶ **noun** a solemn funeral procession.
– ORIGIN Italian *corteggio* 'entourage or retinue.'

cor·tex /'kôr,teks/ ▶ **noun** (pl. **cortices** /-tə,sēz/) the outer layer of a bodily organ or structure, especially the outer, folded layer of the brain (**cerebral cortex**).
– DERIVATIVES **cor·ti·cal** /'kôrtikəl/ adjective.
– ORIGIN Latin, 'bark.'

cor·ti·co·ster·oid /,kôrtikō'ster,oid, -'sti(ə)r,oid/ ▶ **noun** any of a group of steroid hormones produced by the cortex of the adrenal glands.

cor·ti·sol /'kôrtə,sôl, -,sōl/ ▶ **noun** another name for **HYDROCORTISONE**.

cor·ti·sone /'kôrtə,sōn/ ▶ **noun** a steroid hormone used to treat inflammation and allergies.
– ORIGIN from its chemical name.

co·run·dum /kə'rəndəm/ ▶ **noun** an extremely hard form of aluminum oxide, used as an abrasive.
– ORIGIN Tamil.

cor·us·cate /'kôrə,skāt, 'kär-/ ▶ **verb** literary (usu. as adj. **coruscating**) **1** flash; sparkle. **2** be brilliant or exciting: *a coruscating attack on the rock tradition.*
– DERIVATIVES **cor·us·ca·tion** /,kôrə'skāsʜən/ noun.
– ORIGIN Latin *coruscare* 'glitter.'

cor·vette /kôr'vet/ ▶ **noun** a small warship designed for convoy escort duty.
– ORIGIN French.

cor·vine /'kôr,vīn/ ▶ **adjective** relating to or like a raven or crow.
– ORIGIN from Latin *corvus* 'raven.'

cos[1] /käs, kôs/ (also **cos lettuce**) ▶ **noun** chiefly Brit. another term for **ROMAINE**.
– ORIGIN named after the Greek island of *Cos.*

cos[2] ▶ **abbreviation** cosine.

co·se·cant /kō'sē,kant, -kənt/ ▶ **noun** (in a right triangle) the ratio of the hypotenuse to the side opposite an acute angle.

cosh /käsʜ/ Brit. ▶ **noun** a thick heavy stick or bar used as a weapon. ▶ **verb** hit someone with a cosh.
– ORIGIN unknown.

co·sig·na·to·ry /kō'signə,tôrē/ ▶ **noun** a person or country signing a treaty or other document jointly with others.

co·sine /'kō,sīn/ ▶ **noun** (in a right triangle) the ratio of the side adjacent to a particular acute angle to the hypotenuse.

co-sleep·ing ▶ **noun** the practice of parents allowing a young child to sleep in the same bed as them.
– DERIVATIVES **co-sleep** verb.

cos·met·ic /käz'metik/ ▶ **adjective 1** relating to treatment intended to improve a person's appearance. **2** improving only the appearance of something: *the reforms were merely a cosmetic exercise.*

> – SYNONYMS **superficial,** surface, skin-deep, outward, external.
> – ANTONYMS fundamental.

▶ **noun** (**cosmetics**) substances used to improve the appearance of the face and body.
– DERIVATIVES **cos·met·i·cal·ly** /-(ə)lē/ adverb.
– ORIGIN Greek *kosmein* 'arrange or decorate.'

cos·me·tol·o·gy /,käzmə'täləjē/ ▶ **noun** the professional skill or practice of beautifying the face, hair, and skin.
– DERIVATIVES **cos·me·tol·o·gist** /-jist/ noun.

cos·mic /'käzmik/ ▶ **adjective** relating to the universe or cosmos.
– DERIVATIVES **cos·mi·cal** adjective **cos·mi·cal·ly** /-(ə)lē/ adverb.

cos·mic rays ▶ **plural noun** highly energetic atomic nuclei or other particles traveling through space at a speed approaching that of light.

cos·mog·o·ny /käz'mägənē/ ▶ **noun** (pl. **cosmogonies**) the branch of science concerned with the origin of the universe, especially the solar system.
– DERIVATIVES **cos·mo·gon·ic** /,käzmə'gänik/ adjective

cos·mog·o·nist /-nist/ noun.
– ORIGIN from Greek *kosmos* 'order or world' + *-gonia* '-creating.'

cos·mog·ra·phy /käz'mägrəfē/ ▶ **noun** (pl. **cosmographies**) **1** the branch of science that deals with the general features of the universe, including the earth. **2** a description or representation of the universe or the earth.
– DERIVATIVES **cos·mog·ra·pher** noun **cos·mo·graph·i·cal** /ˌkäzmə'grafikəl/ adjective.

cos·mol·o·gy /käz'mäləjē/ ▶ **noun** (pl. **cosmologies**) **1** the science of the origin and development of the universe. **2** a theory of the origin of the universe.
– DERIVATIVES **cos·mo·log·i·cal** /ˌkäzmə'läjikəl/ adjective **cos·mol·o·gist** noun.

cos·mo·naut /'käzməˌnôt, -ˌnät/ ▶ **noun** a Russian astronaut.
– ORIGIN from **COSMOS**[1], on the pattern of *astronaut* and Russian *kosmonavt*.

cos·mo·pol·i·tan /ˌkäzmə'pälitn/ ▶ **adjective** **1** consisting of people from many different countries and cultures: *Barcelona is a cosmopolitan city.* **2** familiar with and at ease in different countries and cultures.

– SYNONYMS **1 multicultural,** multiracial, international, worldwide, global. **2 sophisticated,** cultivated, cultured, worldly, suave, urbane.

▶ **noun 1** a person who is familiar with different countries and cultures. **2** a cocktail made with Cointreau, vodka, cranberry juice, and lime juice.
– DERIVATIVES **cos·mo·pol·i·tan·ism** /-ˌizəm/ noun.
– ORIGIN from Greek *kosmos* 'world' + *politēs* 'citizen.'

CHOOSE THE RIGHT WORD

See **URBANE**.

cos·mos[1] /'käzməs, -ˌmōs, -ˌmäs/ ▶ **noun** the universe seen as a well-ordered whole.
– ORIGIN Greek *kosmos* 'order or world.'

cos·mos[2] ▶ **noun** an ornamental plant of the daisy family with single dahlialike flowers.
– ORIGIN from Greek *kosmos* in the sense 'ornament.'

Cos·sack /'käsˌak, -ək/ ▶ **noun** a member of a people of southern Russia, Ukraine, and Siberia, noted for their horsemanship and military skill.
– ORIGIN Turkic, 'vagabond, nomad.'

cos·set /'käsət/ ▶ **verb** (**cossets, cosseting, cosseted**) care for and protect someone in an overindulgent way.
– ORIGIN first meaning a lamb brought up by hand: probably from Old English, 'cottar.'

cost /kôst/ ▶ **verb** (past and past part. **cost**) **1** be able to be bought or done for a specific price: *tickets cost $15.* **2** involve the loss of: *his heroism cost him his life.* **3** (past and past part. **costed**) estimate the cost of something.

– SYNONYMS **1 be priced at,** sell for, be valued at, fetch, come to, amount to; informal set someone back, go for. **2 price,** value, put a price/value/figure on.

▶ **noun 1** an amount given or required as payment. **2** the effort or loss necessary to achieve something. **3** (**costs**) legal expenses.

– SYNONYMS **1 price,** fee, tariff, fare, toll, levy, charge, payment, value, rate, outlay; humorous damage. **2 sacrifice,** loss, toll, harm, damage, price. **3** *we need to cover our costs* **expenses,** outgoings, overheads, expenditure, spend, outlay.

– PHRASES **at all costs** (or **at any cost**) regardless of the price or the effort needed. **at cost** without profit to the seller.
– ORIGIN Old French *couster*.

cost ac·count·ing ▶ **noun** the recording of all the costs arising in a business in a way that can be used to improve its management.
– DERIVATIVES **cost ac·count·ant** noun.

co·star /'kōˌstär, kō'stär/ ▶ **noun** a movie or stage star appearing with another or others of equal importance. ▶ **verb 1** appear in a movie or play as a costar. **2** (of a movie or play) include someone as a costar.

Cos·ta Ri·can /ˌkōstə 'rēkən, ˌkôstə, ˌkästə/ ▶ **noun** a person from Costa Rica, a republic in Central America. ▶ **adjective** relating to Costa Rica.

cost-ef·fec·tive (also **cost-efficient**) ▶ **adjective** effective or productive in relation to its cost.

cost·ly /'kôstlē/ ▶ **adjective** (**costlier, costliest**) **1** expensive; not cheap. **2** causing suffering, loss, or disadvantage: *her most costly mistake*.

– SYNONYMS **1 expensive,** dear, high-cost, overpriced; informal steep, pricey. **2 catastrophic,** disastrous, calamitous, ruinous, damaging, harmful, deleterious.
– ANTONYMS cheap.

– DERIVATIVES **cost·li·ness** noun.

cost of liv·ing ▶ **noun** the level of prices relating to a range of everyday items.

cos·tume /'käsˌt(y)o͞om, -təm/ ▶ **noun 1** a set of clothes in a style typical of a particular country or historical period: *authentic Elizabethan costumes.* **2** a set of clothes worn by an actor or performer for a role. **3** a set of clothes, particularly a woman's ensemble, for a particular occasion.

– SYNONYMS **clothes,** garments, outfit, ensemble, dress, clothing, attire, garb, uniform, livery; formal apparel.

▶ **verb** dress someone in a set of clothes.
– ORIGIN Italian, 'custom, fashion, habit.'

cos·tume dra·ma ▶ **noun** a television or movie production set in a historical period.

cos·tume jew·el·ry ▶ **noun** jewelry made with inexpensive materials or imitation gems.

cos·tum·er /'käsˌt(y)o͞omər, käs't(y)o͞o-/ (also chiefly Brit. **costumier** /käs't(y)o͞omēər/) ▶ **noun** a maker or supplier of theatrical or party costumes.

co·sy, etc. ▶ **adjective** British spelling of **COZY**, etc.

cot[1] /kät/ ▶ **noun 1** a portable, collapsible bed. **2** Brit. a baby's crib.
– ORIGIN Hindi, 'bedstead, hammock.'

cot[2] ▶ **noun 1** a small shelter for livestock. **2** old use a small, simple cottage.
– ORIGIN Old English.

cot[3] ▶ **abbreviation** Mathematics cotangent.

co·tan·gent /kō'tanjənt/ ▶ **noun** (in a right triangle) the ratio of the side (other than the hypotenuse) adjacent to a particular acute angle to the side opposite the angle.

cote /kōt, kät/ ▶ **noun** a shelter for mammals or birds, especially pigeons.
– ORIGIN Old English.

co·te·rie /'kōtərē, ˌkōtə'rē/ ▶ **noun** (pl. **coteries**) a small exclusive group of people with shared interests or tastes.
– ORIGIN French.

co·ter·mi·nous /kō'tərmənəs/ ▶ **adjective** having the same boundaries or extent: *on the east the area is coterminous with Sweden.*
– ORIGIN from Latin *terminus* 'boundary.'

co·to·ne·as·ter /kə'tōnē,astər, 'kätn,ēstər/ ▶ **noun** a shrub with bright red berries, often grown as a hedge.
– ORIGIN from Latin *cotoneum* 'quince.'

cot·tage /'kätij/ ▶ **noun** a small house, typically one in the country.

– SYNONYMS **cabin,** lodge, bungalow, country house, chalet, shack, shanty.

– DERIVATIVES **cot·tag·ey** adjective.
– ORIGIN Latin *cotagium.*

cot·tage cheese ▶ **noun** soft, lumpy white cheese made from the curds of skimmed milk.

cot·tage in·dus·try ▶ **noun** a business or manufacturing activity carried on in people's homes.

cot·tag·er /'kätijər/ ▶ **noun** a person living in a cottage.

cot·ter pin /'kätər/ ▶ **noun 1** a metal pin used to fasten two parts of a mechanism together. **2** a split pin that is opened out after being passed through a hole.
– ORIGIN unknown.

cot·ton /'kätn/ ▶ **noun** the soft white fibers that surround the seeds of a tropical and subtropical plant, used to make cloth and thread for sewing. ▶ **verb** informal (**cotton on**) begin to understand or realize: *I cottoned on to what Bill was saying.*
– DERIVATIVES **cot·ton·y** adjective.
– ORIGIN Arabic.

cot·ton ball ▶ **noun** a fluffy soft wad of cotton, used for applying or removing cosmetics or bathing wounds.

cot·ton can·dy ▶ **noun** a mass of artificially colored spun sugar wrapped around a stick.

cot·ton·mouth /'kätn,mouTH/ ▶ **noun** a large, dangerous semiaquatic pit viper that inhabits lowland swamps and waterways of the southeastern US.

cot·ton·tail /'kätn,tāl/ ▶ **noun** a North American rabbit that has a speckled brownish coat and a white underside to the tail.

cot·ton·wood /'kätn,wo͝od/ ▶ **noun** any of several North American poplars with seeds covered in white cottony hairs.

cot·y·le·don /,kätl'ēdn/ ▶ **noun** the first leaf to grow from a germinating seed.
– ORIGIN Greek *kotulēdōn* 'cup-shaped cavity.'

couch[1] /kouCH/ ▶ **noun 1** a long upholstered piece of furniture for several people to sit on. **2** a long seat with a headrest at one end on which a psychoanalyst's subject or doctor's patient lies during treatment.

– SYNONYMS **sofa,** settee, divan, chaise longue, chesterfield, daybed, davenport, love seat, ottoman.

▶ **verb 1** express in language of a specified type: *the announcement was couched in technical language.* **2** literary lie down.

– SYNONYMS **express,** phrase, word, frame, put, formulate, style, convey, say, state, utter.

– ORIGIN Old French *couche.*

couch[2] (also **couch grass**) ▶ **noun** a coarse grass with long creeping roots.
– ORIGIN Old English.

cou·chette /ko͞o'SHet/ ▶ **noun 1** a railroad car with seats convertible into sleeping berths. **2** a berth in a couchette car.
– ORIGIN French, 'small couch.'

couch po·ta·to ▶ **noun** informal a person who spends a great deal of time watching television.

cou·gar /'ko͞ogər/ ▶ **noun** a large American wild cat with a plain tawny to grayish coat.
– ORIGIN French *couguar.*

cough /kôf/ ▶ **verb 1** expel air from the lungs with a sudden sharp sound. **2** (of an engine) make a sudden harsh noise. **3** (**cough something up**) informal give something, especially money, reluctantly.

– SYNONYMS **hack,** hawk, bark, clear one's throat.

▶ **noun 1** an act of coughing. **2** a condition of the throat or lungs causing coughing.

– SYNONYMS **bark,** hack; informal frog in one's throat.

– DERIVATIVES **cough·er** noun.
– ORIGIN imitating the sound.

cough drop ▶ **noun** a medicated lozenge sucked to relieve a cough or sore throat.

could /ko͝od/ ▶ **modal verb** past of CAN[1].

USAGE

For advice on **could have** versus **could of**, see the note at **HAVE.**

could·n't /'ko͝odnt/ ▶ **contraction** could not.

cou·lomb /'ko͞o,läm, -,lōm/ ▶ **noun** the SI unit of electric charge, equal to the quantity of electricity conveyed in one second by a current of one ampere.
– ORIGIN named after the French military engineer Charles-Augustin de *Coulomb.*

coun·cil /'kounsəl/ ▶ **noun 1** an assembly of people that meets regularly to discuss, advise on, or administer something. **2** a group of people elected to manage a city, county, or district.

– SYNONYMS **1** *the town council* **authority,** government, administration, executive, chamber, assembly. **2** *the Student Council* **committee,** board, commission, assembly, panel, synod.

▶ **adjective** Brit. (of housing) provided by a local council.
– ORIGIN Latin *concilium* 'assembly.'

USAGE

Do not confuse **council** with **counsel**. **Council** means 'a group of people who manage an area or advise on something' (*the city council*), whereas **counsel** means 'advice' or 'advise someone' (*we counseled him on estate planning*).

coun·cil·man /'kounsəlmən/ (or **councilwoman** /'kounsəl,wo͝omən/) ▶ **noun** (pl. **councilmen** or **councilwomen**) a member of a council, especially a municipal one.

coun·ci·lor /'kouns(ə)lər/ (Brit. **councillor**) ▶ **noun** a member of a council.

coun·sel /'kounsəl/ ▶ **noun 1** advice given to someone. **2** (pl. same) a lawyer or other legal adviser conducting a case.

– SYNONYMS **1 advice,** guidance, counseling, recommendations, suggestions, direction. **2 lawyer,** attorney, attorney-at-law, counselor, advocate; Brit. barrister.

▶ **verb** (**counsels, counseling, counseled**) **1** give advice to: *we counseled him on estate planning.* **2** give professional help and advice to someone with personal or psychological problems. **3** recommend a course of action.

> – SYNONYMS **advise,** recommend, advocate, encourage, warn, caution, guide.

– PHRASES **keep one's own counsel** not reveal one's plans or opinions.
– ORIGIN Latin *consilium* 'consultation, advice.'

coun·se·lor /'kouns(ə)lər/ (Brit. **counsellor**) ▶ **noun** **1** a person trained to give advice on personal or psychological problems. **2** a person who supervises children at a camp. **3** a senior officer in the diplomatic service. **4** a trial lawyer.

count[1] /kount/ ▶ **verb 1** calculate the total number of a collection of people or things. **2** say numbers in ascending order. **3** include someone or something when calculating a total. **4** regard or be regarded as being: *people she had counted as her friends.* **5** be important; matter: *it's the thought that counts.* **6** (**count on**) rely on someone or something. **7** (**count someone in** or **out**) include (or exclude) someone in a planned activity.

> – SYNONYMS **1 add up,** reckon up, total, tally, calculate, compute. **2 include,** take into account/consideration, take account of, allow for. **3 consider,** think, feel, regard, look on as, view as, hold to be, judge, deem. **4 matter,** be important, be of consequence, be significant, signify, carry weight, rate. **5** (**count on**) **rely on,** depend on, bank on, be sure of, have confidence in, believe in, put your faith in, take for granted, take as read.

▶ **noun 1** an act of counting. **2** the total found by counting. **3** a point for discussion or consideration: *she is unsuitable on every count.* **4** Law each of the charges against an accused person.
– DERIVATIVES **count·a·ble** adjective.
– PHRASES **count the days** (or **hours**) be impatient for time to pass. **keep** (or **lose**) **count** take note of (or forget) the number or amount when counting. **down for the count 1** Boxing defeated by being knocked to the ground and unable to rise within ten seconds. **2** unconscious or sound asleep.
– ORIGIN Latin *computare* 'calculate.'

count[2] ▶ **noun** a European nobleman whose rank corresponds to that of an English earl.
– ORIGIN Old French *conte*.

count·down /'kount,doun/ ▶ **noun 1** an act of counting in reverse order to zero, especially before the launch of a rocket. **2** the final moments before a significant event.

coun·te·nance /'kountn-əns/ ▶ **noun** a person's face or facial expression. ▶ **verb** tolerate or agree to: *his mother would never countenance such a marriage.*
– ORIGIN Old French *contenance* 'bearing, behavior.'

coun·ter[1] /'kountər/ ▶ **noun 1** a long flat fixture over which goods are sold or served or across which business is conducted with customers. **2** a small disk used in board games for keeping the score or as a place marker. **3** a person or thing that counts something. **4** a token representing a coin.
– PHRASES **over the counter** by ordinary sale in a store, with no need for a prescription or license. **under the counter** (or **table**) bought or sold secretly and illegally.
– ORIGIN Old French *conteor*.

coun·ter[2] ▶ **verb 1** speak or act in opposition or response to. **2** Boxing give a return blow while parrying.

> – SYNONYMS **1** *workers countered accusations of dishonesty* **respond to,** parry, hit back at, answer. **2** *the second argument is more difficult to counter* **oppose,** dispute, argue against/with, contradict, challenge, contest.
> – ANTONYMS support.

▶ **adverb** (**counter to**) in the opposite direction or in opposition to.

> – SYNONYMS *nearly all of his proposals are counter to our original agreement* **against,** in opposition to, contrary to, at variance with, in defiance of, in conflict with, at odds with.

▶ **adjective** responding to something of the same kind, especially in opposition: *argument and counter argument.*

▶ **noun** an act that opposes or prevents something else.
– ORIGIN from Latin *contra* 'against.'

coun·ter- ▶ **prefix 1** opposing or done in return: *counterattack.* **2** in the opposite direction: *counterpoise.* **3** corresponding: *counterpart.*
– ORIGIN from Latin *contra* 'against.'

coun·ter·act /'kountər,akt/ ▶ **verb** act against something so as to reduce its force or cancel it out.

> – SYNONYMS **offset,** counterbalance, balance (out), cancel out, work against, countervail, neutralize, nullify, prevent.

– DERIVATIVES **coun·ter·ac·tion** /,kountər'aksHən/ noun **coun·ter·ac·tive** /kountər'aktiv/ adjective.

coun·ter·at·tack /'kountərə,tak/ ▶ **noun** an attack made in response to one by an opponent. ▶ **verb** attack someone in response to an attack.

coun·ter·bal·ance ▶ **noun** /'kountər,baləns/ **1** a weight that balances another. **2** a factor that has the opposite effect to that of another and so balances it out. ▶ **verb** /,kountər'baləns/ have an opposing and balancing effect on: *his steadiness would counterbalance the kid's nervous manner.*

coun·ter·charge /'kountər,CHärj/ ▶ **noun 1** an accusation made in turn by someone against their accuser: *charges and countercharges concerning producers, quotas, and affidavits.* **2** a charge by police or an armed force in response to one made against them.

coun·ter·claim /'kountər,klām/ ▶ **noun** a claim made in response to and opposing a previous claim.

coun·ter·clock·wise /,kountər'kläk,wīz/ ▶ **adverb & adjective** in the opposite direction to the way in which the hands of a clock move around.

coun·ter·cul·ture /'kountər,kəlCHər/ ▶ **noun** a way of life and set of attitudes that are at variance with those accepted by most of society.

coun·ter·es·pi·o·nage /,kountər'espēə,näzH, -,näj/ ▶ **noun** activities designed to prevent or thwart spying by an enemy.

coun·ter·feit /'kountər,fit/ ▶ **adjective** made in exact imitation of something valuable with the intention to deceive or defraud others.

> – SYNONYMS **fake,** pirate, bogus, forged, imitation; informal phony.
> – ANTONYMS genuine.

▶ **noun** a forgery.

> – SYNONYMS **fake,** forgery, copy, reproduction, imitation, fraud, sham; informal phony.
> – ANTONYMS original.

▶ **verb 1** imitate something fraudulently. **2** pretend to feel or possess an emotion or quality.

> – SYNONYMS **fake,** forge, copy, reproduce, imitate, falsify.

– DERIVATIVES **coun·ter·feit·er** noun.
– ORIGIN Old French *contrefait* 'made in opposition.'

coun·ter·in·tel·li·gence /ˌkountərin'teləjəns/ ▸ **noun** activities designed to prevent or thwart spying, intelligence gathering, and sabotage by an enemy or other foreign entity.

coun·ter·in·tu·i·tive /ˌkountərin't(y)o͞oitiv/ ▸ **adjective** at variance with intuition or common-sense expectation.

coun·ter·mand /ˌkountər'mand, 'kountərˌmand/ ▸ **verb** cancel an order.
– ORIGIN Latin *contramandare.*

coun·ter·meas·ure /'kountərˌmezʜər/ ▸ **noun** an action taken to counteract a danger or threat.

coun·ter·of·fen·sive /'kountərəˌfensiv/ ▸ **noun** an attack made in response to one from an enemy, typically on a large scale or for a prolonged period.

coun·ter·pane /'kountərˌpān/ ▸ **noun** a bedspread.
– ORIGIN from Latin *culcitra puncta* 'quilted mattress.'

coun·ter·part /'kountərˌpärt/ ▸ **noun** a person or thing that corresponds to another: *the minister held talks with his French counterpart.*

– SYNONYMS **equivalent,** opposite number, peer, equal, parallel, complement, analog, match, twin, mate, fellow.

coun·ter·point /'kountərˌpoint/ ▸ **noun 1** the technique of writing or playing a melody or melodies together with another, according to fixed rules. **2** a melody played together with another. **3** a pleasing or notable contrast to something: *dill crème fraiche was a nice counterpoint to the fish.* ▸ **verb 1** add counterpoint to a melody. **2** contrast with something.
– ORIGIN Latin *contrapunctum* '(song) marked over against (the original melody).'

coun·ter·poise /'kountərˌpoiz/ ▸ **noun & verb** another term for **COUNTERBALANCE.**

coun·ter·pro·duc·tive /ˌkountərprə'dəktiv/ ▸ **adjective** having the opposite of the desired effect.

Coun·ter-Ref·or·ma·tion ▸ **noun** the reform of the Church of Rome in the 16th and 17th centuries that was stimulated by the Protestant Reformation.

coun·ter·rev·o·lu·tion /'kountərˌrevə'lo͞osʜən/ ▸ **noun** a revolution opposing a former one or reversing its results.
– DERIVATIVES **coun·ter·rev·o·lu·tion·ar·y** /-ˌnerē/ adjective & noun.

coun·ter·sign /'kountərˌsīn/ ▸ **verb** sign a document already signed by another person.

coun·ter·sink /'kountərˌsiɴɢk/ ▸ **verb** (past and past part. **countersunk** /-ˌsəɴɢk/) **1** enlarge the rim of a drilled hole so that a screw or bolt can be inserted level with the surface. **2** drive a screw or bolt into such a hole.

coun·ter·ten·or /'kountərˌtenər/ ▸ **noun** the highest male adult singing voice.

coun·ter·ter·ror·ism /ˌkountər'terəˌrizəm/ ▸ **noun** political or military activities designed to prevent or thwart terrorism.
– DERIVATIVES **coun·ter·ter·ror·ist** /ˌkountər'terərist/ noun.

counter·top /'kountərˌtäp/ ▸ **noun** the flat top of a counter, especially when regarded as a work or storage space: *countertop appliances.*

coun·ter·vail /ˌkountər'vāl/ ▸ **verb** (usu. as adj. **countervailing**) counteract something with something of equal force: *a profusion of countervailing opinions.*
– ORIGIN from Latin *contra valere* 'be of worth against.'

coun·ter·weight /'kountərˌwāt/ ▸ **noun** a weight that counterbalances another.

count·ess /'kountəs/ ▸ **noun 1** the wife or widow of a count or earl. **2** a woman holding the rank of count or earl.

count·ing /'kountiɴɢ/ ▸ **preposition** taking account of; including.

count·less /'kountləs/ ▸ **adjective** too many to be counted; very many.

– SYNONYMS **innumerable,** numerous, untold, legion, numberless, limitless, incalculable; informal umpteen, gazillions of.
– ANTONYMS few.

count noun ▸ **noun** a noun that can form a plural and, in the singular, can be used with *a* (the indefinite article), e.g., *books, a book.* Contrasted with **MASS NOUN.**

coun·tri·fied /'kəntriˌfīd/ (also **countryfied**) ▸ **adjective** characteristic of the country or country life.

coun·try /'kəntrē/ ▸ **noun** (pl. **countries**) **1** a nation with its own government, occupying a particular territory. **2** districts outside large urban areas. **3** an area with regard to its physical features: *hill country.* **4** country music.

– SYNONYMS **1 nation,** (sovereign) state, kingdom, realm, land, territory, province. **2 people,** public, population, populace, citizens, nation; informal John Q. Public. **3 terrain,** land, territory, landscape, countryside, scenery, surroundings, environment. **4 countryside,** provinces, rural areas, backwoods, backcountry, hinterland; Austral./NZ outback, bush; informal sticks, boondocks, boonies.

– PHRASES **across country** not keeping to roads.
– ORIGIN from Latin *contrata terra* 'land lying opposite.'

coun·try and west·ern ▸ **noun** country music.

coun·try club ▸ **noun** a club with sporting and social facilities, set in a suburban area.

coun·try code ▸ **noun** a sequence of numbers prefixed to a telephone number to connect to an exchange in another country.

coun·try cous·in ▸ **noun** an unsophisticated and provincial person.

coun·try dance ▸ **noun** a traditional type of English dance, in particular one performed by couples facing each other in long lines.

coun·try·fied ▸ **adjective** variant spelling of **COUNTRIFIED.**

coun·try·man /'kəntrēmən/ (or **countrywoman**) ▸ **noun** (pl. **countrymen** or **countrywomen**) **1** a person from the same country as someone else. **2** Brit a person living or born in a rural area.

coun·try mu·sic ▸ **noun** a form of popular music originating in the rural southern US, typically featuring ballads and dance tunes accompanied by a guitar.

coun·try rock ▸ **noun** a type of popular music that is a blend of country and rock.

coun·try·side /'kəntrēˌsīd/ ▸ **noun** the land and scenery of a rural area.

– SYNONYMS see **COUNTRY** (sense 3), **COUNTRY** (sense 4).

coun·try·wide /'kəntrē'wīd/ ▸ **adjective & adverb** extending throughout a nation.

coun·ty /'kountē/ ▶ **noun** (pl. **counties**) **1** each of the main areas into which some countries are divided for the purposes of local government. **2** a political and administrative division of a state.

– SYNONYMS **shire,** province, territory, region, district, area.

▶ **adjective** Brit. relating to or typical of upper-class people with an estate in a particular county: *loud county voices.*
– ORIGIN Old French *conte* 'land of a count.'

coun·ty seat ▶ **noun** the town that is the administrative capital of a county.

coup /ko͞o/ ▶ **noun** (pl. **coups** /ko͞oz/) **1** (also **coup d'état** /ˌko͞o dā'tä/) a sudden violent seizure of power from a government. **2** a successful move that achieves something difficult: *the ten-year agreement is a major coup for the company.*

– SYNONYMS **1 takeover,** coup d'état, overthrow, palace revolution, rebellion, uprising. **2 success,** triumph, feat, masterstroke, accomplishment, achievement, scoop.

– ORIGIN French.

coup de grâce /ˌko͞o də 'gräs/ ▶ **noun** (pl. **coups de grâce** pronunc. same) a final blow or shot given to kill a wounded person or animal.
– ORIGIN French, 'stroke of grace.'

coupe /ko͞op/ (also **coupé** /ko͞o'pā/) ▶ **noun** a car with a fixed roof, two doors, and a sloping rear.
– ORIGIN from French *carrosse coupé* 'cut carriage.'

cou·ple /'kəpəl/ ▶ **noun 1** two people or things of the same sort considered together. **2** (treated as sing. or pl.) two people who are married or in a romantic or sexual relationship. **3** informal an indefinite small number.

– SYNONYMS **1 pair,** duo, twosome, two, brace. **2 husband and wife,** twosome, partners, lovers; informal item.

▶ **verb 1** link or combine: *anger control coupled with relaxation therapy significantly lowered blood pressure.* **2** have sex.

– SYNONYMS **1** *the picnic was* ***coupled with*** *a nature walk* **combine with,** accompany with, ally with, mix with, incorporate with, add to, join to. **2 connect,** attach, join, fasten, fix, link, secure, hook (up).
– ANTONYMS detach.

– DERIVATIVES **cou·ple·dom** noun **cou·pler** /'kəp(ə)lər/ noun.
– ORIGIN Latin *copula* 'connection.'

cou·plet /'kəplət/ ▶ **noun** a pair of successive lines of verse, typically rhyming and of the same length.

cou·pling /'kəp(ə)liNG/ ▶ **noun** a device for connecting railroad vehicles or parts of machinery together.

cou·pon /'k(y)o͞oˌpän/ ▶ **noun 1** a voucher entitling the holder to a discount or to buy something. **2** a detachable portion of a bond that is given up in return for a payment of interest.

– SYNONYMS **voucher,** token, ticket, slip.

– ORIGIN French, 'piece cut off.'

cour·age /'kərij, 'kə-rij/ ▶ **noun 1** the ability to do something that frightens one. **2** strength in the face of pain or grief.

– SYNONYMS **bravery,** pluck, valor, fearlessness, nerve, daring, audacity, boldness, grit, heroism, gallantry; informal guts.
– ANTONYMS cowardice.

– PHRASES **have the courage of one's convictions** act on one's beliefs despite danger or disapproval.
– ORIGIN Old French *corage.*

cou·ra·geous /kə'rājəs/ ▶ **adjective** not deterred by danger or pain; brave.

– SYNONYMS **brave,** plucky, fearless, intrepid, valiant, heroic, undaunted, dauntless; informal gutsy.
– ANTONYMS cowardly.

– DERIVATIVES **cou·ra·geous·ly** adverb.

cour·gette /ˌko͝or'ZHet/ ▶ **noun** Brit. a zucchini.
– ORIGIN French, 'little gourd.'

cour·i·er /'ko͝orēər, 'kərēər/ ▶ **noun 1** a person employed to deliver goods or documents quickly. **2** chiefly Brit. a person employed to guide and assist a group of tourists.
▶ **verb** send goods or documents by courier.
– ORIGIN Old French *coreor* or French *courrier.*

course /kôrs/ ▶ **noun 1** a direction taken or intended to be taken. **2** the way in which something progresses or develops: *the course of history.* **3** (also **course of action**) a way of dealing with a situation: *my decision represented the wisest course open to me at the time.* **4** a series of lectures or lessons in a particular subject. **5** a series of repeated treatments or doses of medication. **6** a dish forming one of the stages of a meal. **7** an area of land or water prepared for racing, golf, or another sport. **8** a continuous horizontal layer of brick or stone in a wall.

– SYNONYMS **1 route,** way, track, path, line, trail, trajectory, bearing, heading. **2 procedure,** plan (of action), course of action, practice, approach, technique, policy, strategy, tactic. **3 course of study,** curriculum, syllabus, classes, lectures, studies. **4** *a course of antibiotics* **program,** series, sequence, system, schedule, regime.

▶ **verb 1** (of liquid) flow. **2** (often as n. **coursing**) pursue game, especially hares, with greyhounds using sight rather than scent.

– SYNONYMS **flow,** pour, stream, run, rush, gush, cascade, flood, roll.

– PHRASES **in (the) course of 1** in the process of. **2** during. **of course 1** as expected. **2** certainly; yes.
– ORIGIN Old French *cours.*

cours·er¹ /'kôrsər/ ▶ **noun** literary a swift horse.
– ORIGIN Old French *corsier.*

cours·er² ▶ **noun** a person who goes coursing with greyhounds.

course·work /'kôrsˌwərk/ ▶ **noun** work done during a course of study, usually counting toward a final grade.

court /kôrt/ ▶ **noun 1** (also **court of law**) the judge, jury, and law officers before whom legal cases are heard. **2** the place where a court of law meets. **3** a quadrangular area marked out for ball games such as tennis. **4** a quadrangle surrounded by a building or group of buildings. **5** the residence, councilors, and household of a sovereign.

– SYNONYMS **1 court of law,** bench, bar, tribunal. **2 household,** retinue, entourage, train, courtiers, attendants.

▶ **verb 1** pay special attention to someone to try to win their support. **2** try hard to win favorable attention. **3** behave in a way that makes one vulnerable to: *he has often courted controversy.* **4** dated be involved with someone romantically, especially with a view to marriage. **5** (of a male bird or other animal) try to attract a mate.

– SYNONYMS **1 cultivate,** flatter, curry favor with, wine and dine; informal butter up. **2 seek,** pursue, go after, strive for, solicit. **3 risk,** invite, attract, bring on oneself. **4 woo,** go out with, date, go steady with.

– PHRASES **hold court** be the center of attention. **out of court** before a legal hearing can take place. **pay court to** pay flattering attention to someone.
– ORIGIN Old French *cort.*

WORD LINKS

forensic *relating to a court of law*

cour·te·ous /ˈkərtēəs/ ▶ **adjective** polite, respectful, and considerate.

– SYNONYMS **polite,** well mannered, civil, respectful, well behaved, gracious, obliging, considerate.
– ANTONYMS rude.

– DERIVATIVES **cour·te·ous·ly** adverb **cour·te·ous·ness** noun.
– ORIGIN Old French *corteis* 'having manners fit for a royal court.'

cour·te·san /ˈkôrtəzən, ˈkər-/ ▶ **noun** a prostitute with wealthy or upper-class clients.
– ORIGIN French *courtisane.*

cour·te·sy /ˈkərtəsē/ ▶ **noun** (pl. **courtesies**) **1** polite and considerate behavior. **2** something said or done for politeness in a formal social situation: *there was a ritual exchange of courtesies with the lawyers.*

– SYNONYMS **politeness,** good manners, civility, respect, grace, consideration, thought.

– PHRASES **(by) courtesy of** given or allowed by someone.

cour·te·sy ti·tle ▶ **noun** a title given to someone as a mark of courtesy, such as Mr. or Mrs.

court·house /ˈkôrtˌhous/ ▶ **noun 1** a building in which a court of law meets. **2** a building containing the administrative offices of a county.

cour·ti·er /ˈkôrtēər, ˈkôrCHər/ ▶ **noun** a sovereign's companion or adviser.

court·ly /ˈkôrtlē/ ▶ **adjective** (**courtlier, courtliest**) very polite and dignified.
– DERIVATIVES **court·li·ness** noun.

court mar·tial ▶ **noun** (pl. **courts martial**) a court for trying members of the armed services accused of breaking military law. ▶ **verb** (**court-martial**) (**court-martials, court-martialing, court-martialed**) try a member of the armed services by court martial.

court or·der ▶ **noun** a direction issued by a court or a judge requiring a person to do or not do something.

court re·port·er ▶ **noun** a stenographer who makes a verbatim record and transcription of the proceedings in a court of law.

court·room /ˈkôrtˌro͞om, -ˌro͝om/ ▶ **noun** the room or building in which a court of law meets.

court·ship /ˈkôrtˌSHip/ ▶ **noun 1** a period during which a couple develop a romantic relationship. **2** the courting of a person to win their support. **3** the behavior of male birds and other animals aimed at attracting a mate.

court·yard /ˈkôrtˌyärd/ ▶ **noun** an open area enclosed by walls or buildings, especially in a castle or large house.

cous·cous /ˈko͞os ˌko͞os/ ▶ **noun** a North African dish of steamed or soaked semolina, usually served with spicy meat or vegetables.
– ORIGIN Arabic.

cous·in /ˈkəzən/ ▶ **noun 1** (also **first cousin**) a child of one's uncle or aunt. **2** a person of a similar or related people or nation: *our American cousins.*
– DERIVATIVES **cous·in·ly** adjective **cous·in·ship** /-ˌSHip/ noun.
– PHRASES **second cousin** a child of one's parent's first cousin. **third cousin** a child of one's parent's second cousin.
– ORIGIN Old French *cosin.*

cou·ture /ko͞oˈto͝or, -ˈtYr/ ▶ **noun 1** the design and manufacture of fashionable clothes to a client's specific requirements. **2** fashionable made-to-measure clothes.
– ORIGIN French, 'sewing, dressmaking.'

cou·tu·ri·er /ko͞oˈto͝orēər, -ˈto͝orēˌā/ ▶ **noun** (fem. **couturière** /ko͞oˈto͝orēər, -ˌto͝orēˈe(ə)r/) a person who designs and sells fashionable made-to-measure clothes.

cou·ver·ture /ˌko͞overˈt(y)o͝or/ ▶ **noun** chocolate with extra cocoa butter to give a high gloss, used to cover candies and cakes.
– ORIGIN French, 'covering.'

co·va·lent /ˌkōˈvālənt/ ▶ **adjective** (of a chemical bond) formed by the sharing of electrons between atoms. Often contrasted with **IONIC.**
– DERIVATIVES **co·va·len·cy** noun **co·va·lent·ly** adverb.

cove /kōv/ ▶ **noun 1** a small sheltered bay. **2** a concave arch or arched molding at the junction of a wall with a ceiling.

– SYNONYMS **bay,** inlet, fjord.

– DERIVATIVES **coved** adjective **cov·ing** noun.
– ORIGIN Old English, 'chamber, cave.'

cov·en /ˈkəvən/ ▶ **noun** a group of witches who meet regularly.
– ORIGIN from Latin *convenire* 'come together.'

cov·e·nant /ˈkəvənənt/ ▶ **noun 1** a formal agreement, especially a written contract by which one agrees to make regular payments to a charity. **2** (in Judaism and Christianity) an agreement that brings about a commitment between God and his people. ▶ **verb** agree or pay something by a formal written contract.
– DERIVATIVES **cov·e·nan·tal** /ˌkəvəˈnantl/ adjective.
– ORIGIN Old French, 'agreeing.'

cov·er /ˈkəvər/ ▶ **verb 1** put something over or in front of someone or something so as to protect or hide them. **2** spread or extend over: *the grounds covered eight acres.* **3** deal with or report on: *the course will cover a range of subjects.* **4** travel a specified distance. **5** (of money) be enough to pay for something. **6** (of insurance) protect against a liability, loss, or accident. **7** disguise or hide: *I laughed to cover my embarrassment.* **8** (**cover something up**) try to hide or deny something illegal or wrong. **9** (**cover for**) temporarily take over the job of a colleague. **10** aim a gun at someone to prevent them from moving or escaping. **11** protect an exposed person by shooting at the enemy. **12** (in team games) take up a position ready to defend against an opponent. **13** record or perform a cover version of a song.

– SYNONYMS **1 protect,** shield, shelter, hide, conceal, mask, screen, veil, obscure, spread over, extend over, overlay. **2 cake,** coat, encrust, plaster, smother, blanket, carpet, shroud. **3 deal with,** consider, take in, include, involve, incorporate, embrace.
– ANTONYMS reveal.

▶ **noun 1** something that covers or protects. **2** a thick protective outer part or page of a book or magazine. **3** shelter or protection: *they ran for cover.* **4** military support for someone in danger. **5** a means of concealing an illegal or secret activity: *we are not using science as a cover for commercial whaling.* **6** (also **cover version**) a recording or performance of a song previously recorded by a different artist. **7** a place setting at a table in a restaurant.

– SYNONYMS **1** *a protective cover* **covering,** sleeve, wrapping, wrapper, envelope, sheath, housing, jacket, casing, cowling, canopy. **2** *a manhole cover* **lid,** top, cap. **3** *a book cover* **binding,** jacket, dust jacket, dust cover, wrapper. **4 coating,** coat, covering, layer, carpet, blanket, film, sheet, veneer, crust, skin, cloak, mantle, veil, pall, shroud. **5 shelter,** protection, refuge, sanctuary.

– DERIVATIVES **cov·er·ing** noun.
– PHRASES **cover one's back** informal take steps to avoid attack or criticism. **under cover of 1** concealed by something. **2** while pretending to do something.
– ORIGIN Latin *cooperire*.

cov·er·age /ˈkəv(ə)rij/ ▶ **noun 1** the treatment of a subject by the media. **2** the extent to which something is covered: *eighty transmitters would give nationwide coverage*.

cov·er·all /ˈkəvərˌôl/ ▶ **noun** (also **coveralls**) a full-length protective outer garment.

cov·er charge ▶ **noun** a service charge per person added to the bill in a restaurant.

cov·er girl ▶ **noun** a female whose picture appears on a magazine cover.

cov·er·let /ˈkəvərlət/ ▶ **noun** a bedspread.
– ORIGIN from Old French *covrir* 'to cover' + *lit* 'bed.'

cov·er let·ter ▶ **noun** a letter sent with, and explaining the contents of, another document or a parcel.

co·vert ▶ **adjective** /ˈkōvərt, kōˈvərt, ˈkəvərt/ not done openly; secret.

– SYNONYMS **secret,** furtive, clandestine, surreptitious, stealthy, cloak-and-dagger, backstairs, hidden, concealed, private, undercover, underground; informal hush-hush.
– ANTONYMS overt.

▶ **noun** /ˈkəvər(t), ˈkōvərt/ a thicket in which game can hide.
– DERIVATIVES **co·vert·ly** /ˈkōvərtlē, kōˈvərtlē, ˈkəvərtlē/ adverb.
– ORIGIN Old French, 'covered.'

cov·er-up ▶ **noun** an attempt to conceal a mistake or crime.

cov·et /ˈkəvət/ ▶ **verb** (**covets, coveting, coveted**) long to possess something belonging to someone else.

– SYNONYMS **desire,** yearn for, crave, have one's heart set on, long for, hanker after/for, hunger after/for, thirst for.

– DERIVATIVES **cov·et·a·ble** adjective.
– ORIGIN Old French *cuveitier*.

cov·et·ous /ˈkəvətəs/ ▶ **adjective** longing to possess something.
– DERIVATIVES **cov·et·ous·ly** adverb **cov·et·ous·ness** noun.

CHOOSE THE RIGHT WORD

See **GREEDY**.

cov·ey /ˈkəvē/ ▶ **noun** (pl. **coveys**) a small flock of game birds, especially partridge.
– ORIGIN from Old French *cover* 'sit on, hatch.'

cow¹ /kou/ ▶ **noun 1** a fully grown female animal of a domesticated breed of ox. **2** the female of certain other large animals, such as the elephant. **3** informal, derogatory a disliked or unpleasant woman.
– PHRASES **till the cows come home** informal for an indefinitely long time.
– ORIGIN Old English.

cow² ▶ **verb** frighten someone into giving in to one's wishes.
– ORIGIN probably from Old Norse, 'oppress.'

cow·ard /ˈkou-ərd/ ▶ **noun** a person who is afraid to do dangerous or unpleasant things.

– SYNONYMS **mouse,** baby; informal chicken, scaredy-cat, yellow-belly, sissy, pantywaist, candy-ass.

– ORIGIN Old French *couard*.

cow·ard·ice /ˈkou-ərdəs/ ▶ **noun** lack of courage.

cow·ard·ly /ˈkou-ərdlē/ ▶ **adjective** lacking courage.

– SYNONYMS **faint-hearted,** lily-livered, spineless, craven, timid, timorous, fearful; informal yellow, chicken, gutless, yellow-bellied.
– ANTONYMS brave.

– DERIVATIVES **cow·ard·li·ness** /ˈkou-ərdlēnis/ noun.

cow·bell /ˈkouˌbel/ ▶ **noun** a bell hung around a cow's neck.

cow·boy /ˈkouˌboi/ ▶ **noun 1** a man on horseback who herds cattle, especially in the western US. **2** a reckless or careless person.

cow·boy boot ▶ **noun** a high-heeled boot of a style originally worn by cowboys, typically with a pointed toe.

cow·catch·er /ˈkouˌkachər, -ˌkechər/ ▶ **noun** a metal frame at the front of a locomotive for pushing aside obstacles.

cow·er /ˈkou(-ə)r/ ▶ **verb** shrink back or crouch down in fear.

– SYNONYMS **cringe,** shrink, flinch, crouch, blench.

– ORIGIN German *kūren* 'lie in wait.'

CHOOSE THE RIGHT WORD

See **WINCE**.

cow flop ▶ **noun** informal a cowpat.

cow·hand /ˈkouˌhand/ ▶ **noun** a person employed to tend or ranch cattle.

cow·herd /ˈkouˌhərd/ ▶ **noun** a person who looks after grazing cattle.

cow·hide /ˈkouˌhīd/ ▶ **noun** a cow's hide.

cowl /koul/ ▶ **noun 1** a large loose hood forming part of a monk's habit. **2** a hood-shaped covering for a chimney or ventilation shaft. **3** another term for **COWLING**.
– DERIVATIVES **cowled** adjective.
– ORIGIN Latin *cucullus* 'hood of a cloak.'

cow·lick /ˈkouˌlik/ ▶ **noun** a lock of hair that grows in a direction different from the rest and that resists being combed flat.

cowl·ing /ˈkouliNG/ ▶ **noun** a removable cover for a vehicle or aircraft engine.

cow·pat /ˈkouˌpat/ ▶ **noun** a flat, round piece of cow dung.

cow·pea /ˈkouˌpē/ ▶ **noun** a black-eyed pea, especially when grown as a forage or cover crop.

cow·poke /ˈkouˌpōk/ ▶ **noun** informal a cowboy.

cow·pox /ˈkouˌpäks/ ▶ **noun** a disease of cows' udders spread by a virus, which can be caught by humans and resembles mild smallpox.

cow·rie /ˈkourē/ ▶ **noun** (pl. **cowries**) a sea mollusk having a glossy, domed shell with a long, narrow opening.
– ORIGIN Hindi.

cow·slip /ˈkouˌslip/ ▶ **noun** a wild primula with clusters of yellow flowers in spring.
– ORIGIN Old English, 'cow slime.'

cox /käks/ ▶ **noun** a coxswain. ▶ **verb** act as a coxswain for a racing boat or crew.
– DERIVATIVES **cox·less** adjective.

cox·comb /ˈkäksˌkōm/ ▶ **noun** old use a vain and conceited man; a dandy.
– ORIGIN variant of **COCKSCOMB**.

cox·swain /ˈkäksən/ ▶ **noun** a person who steers a boat.
– ORIGIN from former *cock* 'small boat' + **SWAIN**.

coy /koi/ ▶ **adjective** (**coyer**, **coyest**) **1** pretending to be shy or modest. **2** reluctant to give details about something sensitive: *he's coy about his age*.

– SYNONYMS **demure**, shy, modest, bashful, diffident, self-effacing, shrinking.
– ANTONYMS brazen.

– DERIVATIVES **coy·ly** adverb **coy·ness** noun.
– ORIGIN Old French *coi*.

coy·o·te /ˈkīˌōt, kīˈōtē/ ▶ **noun** (pl. same or **coyotes**) a wolflike wild dog native to North America.
– ORIGIN Nahuatl.

coy·pu /ˈkoiˌpo͞o/ ▶ **noun** (pl. **coypus**) a large beaverlike South American rodent, farmed for its fur.
– ORIGIN from a Chilean language.

coz /kəz/ ▶ **conjunction** informal short for **BECAUSE**.

co·zy /ˈkōzē/ (Brit. **cosy**) ▶ **adjective** (**cozier**, **coziest**) **1** comfortable, warm, and secure. **2** not seeking or offering challenge or difficulty: *the cozy belief that man is master*. **3** (of a transaction or arrangement) working to the mutual advantage of the people involved (used to convey a suspicion of corruption): *a cozy deal*.

– SYNONYMS **1 snug**, comfortable, warm, homey, homely, welcoming, safe, sheltered, secure; informal comfy. **2 intimate**, relaxed, informal, friendly.

▶ **noun** (pl. **cozies**) a cover to keep a teapot or a boiled egg hot.
▶ **verb** (**cozies, cozying, cozied**) informal (**cozy up to**) try to gain the favor of someone.
– DERIVATIVES **co·zi·ly** adverb **co·zi·ness** noun.
– ORIGIN unknown.

CPA ▶ **abbreviation** certified public accountant.

CPI ▶ **abbreviation** consumer price index.

Cpl. ▶ **abbreviation** corporal.

CPR ▶ **abbreviation** cardiopulmonary resuscitation.

cps (also **c.p.s.**) ▶ **abbreviation 1** Computing characters per second. **2** cycles per second.

Cpt. ▶ **abbreviation** captain.

CPU ▶ **abbreviation** Computing central processing unit.

Cr ▶ **symbol** the chemical element chromium.

crab /krab/ ▶ **noun 1** a marine shellfish, some kinds of which are edible, with a broad shell and five pairs of legs, the first of which are modified as pincers. **2** (**crabs**) informal an infestation of crab lice. ▶ **verb** (**crabs, crabbing, crabbed**) **1** move sideways or at an angle. **2** fish for crabs.
– DERIVATIVES **crab·ber** noun **crab·like** /-ˌlīk/ adjective & adverb.
– PHRASES **catch a crab** make a faulty stroke in rowing in which the oar is jammed under the water or misses the water completely.
– ORIGIN Old English.

crab ap·ple ▶ **noun** a small, sour kind of apple.
– ORIGIN probably Scandinavian.

crab·bed /ˈkrabəd/ ▶ **adjective 1** (of writing) very small and hard to read. **2** bad-tempered; crabby.
– ORIGIN from **CRAB**, because of the crab's sideways movement and habit of snapping.

crab·by /ˈkrabē/ ▶ **adjective** (**crabbier, crabbiest**) bad-tempered; irritable.
– DERIVATIVES **crab·bi·ly** adverb **crab·bi·ness** noun.

crab·grass /ˈkrabˌgras/ ▶ **noun** a creeping grass that can become a serious weed.

crab louse ▶ **noun** a louse that infests human body hair.

crab·meat /ˈkrabˌmēt/ ▶ **noun** the flesh of a crab as food.

crack /krak/ ▶ **noun 1** a narrow opening between two parts of something that has split or been broken. **2** a sudden sharp noise. **3** a sharp blow. **4** informal a joke, especially a critical one. **5** informal an attempt to do something: *she's made the most of her first crack at stardom*. **6** (also **crack cocaine**) a very strong form of cocaine broken into small pieces.

– SYNONYMS **1** *a crack in the glass* **split**, break, chip, fracture, rupture. **2** *a crack between two rocks* **space**, gap, crevice, fissure, cleft, cranny, chink. **3 bang**, report, explosion, detonation, clap, crash. **4** *a crack on the head* **blow**, bang, hit, knock, rap, bump, smack, slap; informal bash, whack, clout.

▶ **verb 1** break apart or without complete separation of the parts. **2** give way under pressure or strain. **3** make a sudden sharp sound. **4** hit someone or something hard. **5** (of a person's voice) suddenly change in pitch, especially through strain. **6** informal solve or decipher: *he took less than a day to crack the code*. **7** tell a joke.

– SYNONYMS **1 break**, split, fracture, rupture, snap. **2 break down**, give way, cave in, go to pieces, give in, yield, succumb. **3 hit**, strike, smack, slap, beat, thump, knock, rap; informal bash, whack, clobber, clout, clip. **4 decipher**, interpret, decode, break, solve.

▶ **adjective** very good or skillful: *he is a crack shot*.
– PHRASES **crack down on** informal take strong action against someone or something. **crack of dawn** daybreak. **crack up** informal **1** suffer an emotional breakdown under pressure. **2** burst into laughter. **3** (**be cracked up to be**) informal be claimed to be: *acting isn't as glamorous as it's cracked up to be*. **get cracking** informal begin immediately and work quickly.
– ORIGIN Old English.

crack·brained /ˈkrakˌbrānd/ ▶ **adjective** informal very foolish.

crack·down /ˈkrakˌdoun/ ▶ **noun** a set of severe measures against undesirable or illegal behavior.

cracked /krakt/ ▶ **adjective 1** having cracks. **2** informal insane; crazy.

WORD TOOLKIT

cracked ...	fractured ...	shattered ...
mirror	skull	glass
lips	cheekbone	lives
voice	leg	dreams
sidewalk	pelvis	economy
plaster	rock	nerves

cracked wheat ▶ **noun** grains of wheat that have been crushed into small pieces.

crack·er /ˈkrakər/ ▶ **noun** **1** a thin, crisp wafer. **2** a firework that explodes with a crack. **3** Brit. informal an excellent example of something.

crack·er·jack /ˈkrakərˌjak/ ▶ **noun** exceptionally good: *the actors do a crackerjack job.*

crack·ers /ˈkrakərz/ ▶ **adjective** informal insane; crazy.

crack·le /ˈkrakəl/ ▶ **verb** make a series of slight cracking noises. ▶ **noun** a series of slight cracking noises.
– DERIVATIVES **crack·ly** adjective.

crack·ling /ˈkraklən, -lɪɴɢ/ ▶ **noun** the crisp fatty skin of roast pork.

crack·pot /ˈkrakˌpät/ informal ▶ **noun** an eccentric or foolish person. ▶ **adjective** eccentric; impractical.

-cracy ▶ **combining form** referring to a particular form of government or rule: *democracy.*
– ORIGIN from Greek *-kratia* 'power, rule.'

cra·dle /ˈkrādl/ ▶ **noun** **1** a baby's bed, especially one on rockers. **2** a place in which something originates or flourishes: *the Middle East is believed to be the cradle of agriculture.* **3** a supporting framework, in particular for a boat under repair. **4** the part of a telephone on which the receiver rests when not in use.

– SYNONYMS **1 crib,** bassinet, cot. **2 birthplace,** fount, fountainhead, source, spring, origin.

▶ **verb** hold something gently and protectively.

– SYNONYMS **hold,** support, cushion, pillow, nurse, rest.

– ORIGIN Old English.

cra·dle-rob·ber ▶ **noun** informal, derogatory a person who has a sexual relationship with a much younger person.

craft /kraft/ ▶ **noun** **1** an activity involving skill in making things by hand. **2** the skill needed for one's work: *he learned his craft in Holland.* **3** (**crafts**) things made by hand. **4** skill in deceiving others; cunning. **5** (pl. same) a boat, ship, or aircraft.

– SYNONYMS **1 activity,** occupation, trade, profession, work, line of work, job. **2 cunning,** craftiness, guile, wiliness, artfulness, deviousness, slyness, trickery, duplicity, dishonesty, deceit, deceitfulness, deception, intrigue, subterfuge, wiles, ploys, ruses, schemes, tricks. **3 vessel,** ship, boat, aircraft, spacecraft.

▶ **verb** make something skillfully.
– DERIVATIVES **craft·er** noun.
– ORIGIN Old English.

crafts·man /ˈkraf(t)smən/ (or **craftswoman** /ˈkraf(t)sˌwo͝omən/) ▶ **noun** (pl. **craftsmen** or **craftswomen**) a worker skilled in a particular craft.

– SYNONYMS **artisan,** artist, skilled worker, technician, expert, master.

– DERIVATIVES **crafts·man·ship** /-ˌsʜɪp/ noun.

craft·work /ˈkraftˌwərk/ ▶ **noun** **1** the making of things by hand. **2** items produced by hand.
– DERIVATIVES **craft·work·er** noun.

craft·y /ˈkraftē/ ▶ **adjective** (**craftier, craftiest**) clever at deceiving people; cunning.

– SYNONYMS **cunning,** wily, sly, artful, devious, tricky, scheming, calculating, shrewd, canny, dishonest, deceitful.
– ANTONYMS honest.

– DERIVATIVES **craft·i·ly** adverb **craft·i·ness** noun.
– ORIGIN Old English.

crag /krag/ ▶ **noun** a steep or rugged cliff or rock face.
– ORIGIN Celtic.

crag·gy /ˈkragē/ ▶ **adjective** (**craggier, craggiest**) **1** having many crags. **2** (of a man's face) attractively rugged.

crake /krāk/ ▶ **noun** a bird of the rail family with a short bill, such as the corn crake.
– ORIGIN Old Norse.

cram /kram/ ▶ **verb** (**crams, cramming, crammed**) **1** force too many people or things into a place or container. **2** fill to overflowing: *the hut was crammed with sacks of wheat or corn.* **3** study intensively just before an exam.

– SYNONYMS **1** *closets crammed with clothes* **fill,** stuff, pack, jam, fill to overflowing, overload, crowd, throng. **2** *he crammed his clothes into a case* **push,** thrust, shove, force, ram, jam, stuff, pack, pile, squash, squeeze, compress. **3 study,** review; informal bone up.

– ORIGIN Old English.

cramp /kramp/ ▶ **noun** **1** painful involuntary contraction of a muscle or muscles. **2** a tool for clamping two objects together.

– SYNONYMS **spasm,** pain, shooting pain, twinge, pang, convulsion.

▶ **verb** **1** restrict the development of: *tighter rules will cramp economic growth.* **2** fasten something with a cramp or cramps.

– SYNONYMS **hinder,** impede, inhibit, hamper, constrain, hamstring, interfere with, restrict, limit, slow.

– ORIGIN German and Dutch.

cramped /kram(p)t/ ▶ **adjective** **1** uncomfortably small or crowded. **2** (of handwriting) small and difficult to read.

– SYNONYMS **1 confined,** uncomfortable, restricted, constricted, small, tiny, narrow, crowded, congested. **2** *his cramped signature* **small,** crabbed, illegible, unreadable, indecipherable.
– ANTONYMS spacious.

cram·pon /ˈkramˌpän/ ▶ **noun** a metal plate with spikes, fixed to a boot for climbing on ice or rock.
– ORIGIN Old French.

cran·ber·ry /ˈkranˌberē, -bərē/ ▶ **noun** (pl. **cranberries**) a small sour red berry used in cooking.
– ORIGIN German *Kranbeere* 'crane-berry.'

crane /krān/ ▶ **noun** **1** a tall machine used for moving heavy objects by suspending them from a projecting arm. **2** a gray or white wading bird with long legs and a long neck. ▶ **verb** stretch out one's neck to see something.
– ORIGIN Old English.

crane fly ▶ **noun** a slender fly with very long legs; a daddy longlegs.

cra·ni·al /ˈkrānēəl/ ▶ **adjective** relating to the skull or cranium.

cra·ni·o·sa·cral ther·a·py /ˌkrānēōˈsakrəl, -ˈsākrəl/ ▶ **noun** a system of alternative medicine intended to relieve pain and tension by gentle manipulations of the skull.

cra·ni·um /ˈkrānēəm/ ▶ **noun** (pl. **craniums** or **crania** /ˈkrānēə/) the skull, especially the part enclosing the brain.
– ORIGIN Latin.

crank[1] /kraɴɢk/ ▶ **verb** **1** turn a crankshaft or handle to start an internal combustion engine. **2** (**crank something

up) informal increase the intensity of something. **3** (**crank something out**) informal, derogatory produce something regularly and routinely. ▶ **noun** a right-angled part of an axle or shaft, for converting linear to circular motion or vice versa.
– ORIGIN Old English.

crank² ▶ **noun** an eccentric or obsessive person.
– ORIGIN from **CRANKY**.

crank·case /'kraNGk,kās/ ▶ **noun** a case or covering enclosing a crankshaft.

crank·shaft /'kraNGk,SHaft/ ▶ **noun** a shaft driven by a crank.

crank·y /'kraNGkē/ ▶ **adjective** (**crankier, crankiest**) informal **1** bad-tempered; irritable. **2** Brit. eccentric or odd.
– DERIVATIVES **crank·i·ly** adverb **crank·i·ness** noun.
– ORIGIN perhaps from Dutch or German *krank* 'sick.'

cran·ny /'kranē/ ▶ **noun** (pl. **crannies**) a small, narrow space or opening.
– ORIGIN Latin *crena* 'notch.'

crap¹ /krap/ vulgar slang ▶ **noun 1** something that is of extremely poor quality. **2** excrement. **3** nonsense. **4** clutter; junk. ▶ **verb** (**craps, crapping, crapped**) defecate. ▶ **adjective** Brit. very poor in quality.
– DERIVATIVES **crap·py** adjective.
– ORIGIN related to Dutch *krappe* 'chaff.'

crap² ▶ **noun** a losing throw of 2, 3, or 12 in craps. ▶ **verb** (**crap out**) informal **1** make a losing throw at craps. **2** fail in what one is attempting to do: *the Rams almost crapped out late in the game*. **3** (of a machine) break down: *his laptop crapped out*.

crape /krāp/ ▶ **noun** black silk, formerly used for mourning clothes.
– ORIGIN variant of **CRÊPE**.

craps /kraps/ ▶ **plural noun** (treated as sing.) a gambling game played with two dice.
– ORIGIN perhaps from **CRAB** or *crab's eyes*, referring to a throw of two ones.

crap·shoot /'krap,SHōōt/ ▶ **noun 1** a game of craps. **2** a risky or uncertain matter.

crash /krasH/ ▶ **verb 1** (of a vehicle) collide violently with an obstacle or another vehicle. **2** (of an aircraft) fall from the sky and hit the land or sea. **3** move with force, speed, and sudden loud noise: *the cup crashed to the floor*. **4** make a sudden loud noise. **5** (of shares) fall suddenly in value. **6** (of a computer, system, or software) fail suddenly. **7** informal fall deeply asleep. **8** informal gate-crash a party.

> – SYNONYMS **1** *the car* ***crashed into*** *a tree* **smash into,** collide with, be in collision with, hit, strike, ram, impact, cannon into, plow into, meet head-on. **2** *he crashed his car* **smash,** wreck. informal total. **3 fall,** drop, plummet, plunge, sink, dive, tumble. **4 fail,** fold, collapse, go under, go bankrupt; informal go bust, go broke, go belly up.

▶ **noun** an instance or sound of crashing.

> – SYNONYMS **1 accident,** collision, wreck, smash; informal pile-up. **2 bang,** smash, smack, crack, bump, thud, explosion. **3 failure,** collapse, liquidation, bankruptcy.

▶ **adjective** rapid and concentrated: *a crash course in Italian*.
– ORIGIN imitating the sound.

crash-dive ▶ **verb** (of an aircraft or submarine) dive rapidly or uncontrollably.

crash hel·met ▶ **noun** a helmet worn by a motorcyclist to protect the head.

crash·ing /'krasHiNG/ ▶ **adjective** informal complete; total: *a crashing bore*.
– DERIVATIVES **crash·ing·ly** adverb.

crash-land ▶ **verb** (of an aircraft) land roughly in an emergency.

crash·wor·thi·ness /'krasH,wərTHēnis/ ▶ **noun** the degree to which a vehicle will protect its occupants from the effects of a crash.
– DERIVATIVES **crash·wor·thy** /'krasH,wərTHē/ adjective.

crass /kras/ ▶ **adjective** very thoughtless and stupid.

> – SYNONYMS **stupid,** insensitive, thoughtless, witless, oafish, boorish, coarse, gross, graceless, tasteless, tactless, clumsy, blundering; informal ignorant.
> – ANTONYMS intelligent.

– DERIVATIVES **crass·ly** adverb **crass·ness** noun.
– ORIGIN Latin *crassus* 'solid, thick.'

-crat ▶ **combining form** referring to a member or supporter of a particular form of government or rule: *democrat*.
– ORIGIN from Greek *-kratia* 'power, rule.'

crate /krāt/ ▶ **noun 1** a slatted wooden case for transporting goods. **2** a square container divided into small individual units for holding bottles. **3** informal an old and ramshackle vehicle.

> – SYNONYMS **packing case,** chest, tea chest, box, container.

▶ **verb** pack something in a crate for transportation.
– ORIGIN perhaps related to Dutch *krat* 'tailboard of a wagon.'

cra·ter /'krātər/ ▶ **noun 1** a large hollow forming the mouth of a volcano. **2** a large bowl-shaped hollow caused by an explosion or the impact of a meteorite.

> – SYNONYMS **hollow,** bowl, basin, hole, cavity, depression, dip; Geology caldera.

▶ **verb** form a crater or craters in the ground or a planet.
– ORIGIN Greek *kratēr* 'mixing-bowl.'

-cratic ▶ **combining form** relating to a particular kind of government or rule: *democratic*.

cra·vat /krə'vat/ ▶ **noun** a short, wide strip of fabric worn by men around the neck and tucked inside an open-necked shirt.
– ORIGIN French *cravate*.

crave /krāv/ ▶ **verb 1** feel a powerful desire for something. **2** old use ask for: *I must crave your indulgence*.

> – SYNONYMS **long for,** yearn for, hanker after, desire, want, hunger for, thirst for, pine for; informal be dying for.

– ORIGIN Old English.

cra·ven /'krāvən/ ▶ **adjective** lacking in courage; cowardly.
– DERIVATIVES **cra·ven·ly** adverb.
– ORIGIN perhaps from Old French *cravanter* 'crush, overwhelm.'

crav·ing /'krāviNG/ ▶ **noun** a powerful desire for something.

> – SYNONYMS **longing,** yearning, desire, hankering, hunger, thirst, appetite.

craw /krô/ ▶ **noun** dated the crop (part of the throat) of a bird.
– PHRASES **stick in one's craw** see **STICK**².
– ORIGIN related to Dutch *crāghe* or German *krage* 'neck, throat.'

craw·fish /ˈkrôˌfisʜ/ ▶ **noun** (pl. same or **crawfishes**) a crayfish.
– ORIGIN variant of **CRAYFISH**.

crawl /krôl/ ▶ **verb 1** move forward on the hands and knees or with the body close to the ground. **2** (of an insect or small animal) move slowly along a surface. **3** move along very slowly: *the traffic was crawling along*. **4** (**be crawling with**) be unpleasantly covered or crowded with: *the place was crawling with soldiers*. **5** informal behave in an excessively friendly or submissive way to win someone's favor.

> – SYNONYMS **1 creep,** worm one's way, go on all fours, wriggle, slither, squirm. **2** *the arena was crawling with police* **be full of,** overflow with, teem with, be packed with, be crowded with, be alive with. **3 grovel,** kowtow, pander, toady, bow and scrape, fawn; informal suck up, lick someone's boots.

▶ **noun 1** an act of crawling. **2** a very slow speed. **3** a swimming stroke involving alternate overarm movements and rapid kicks of the legs.
– PHRASES **make one's skin crawl** cause one to feel fear or disgust (likened to something crawling on the skin).
– ORIGIN perhaps related to Swedish *kravla* and Danish *kravle*.

crawl·er /ˈkrôlər/ ▶ **noun** Computing a program that searches the World Wide Web, typically in order to create an index of data.

cray·fish /ˈkrāˌfisʜ/ ▶ **noun** (pl. same or **crayfishes**) a freshwater or sea shellfish resembling a small lobster.
– ORIGIN Old French *crevice*.

cray·on /ˈkrāˌän, ˈkrāən/ ▶ **noun** a stick of colored chalk or wax, used for drawing. ▶ **verb** draw something with a crayon or crayons.
– ORIGIN French.

craze /krāz/ ▶ **noun** a widespread but short-lived enthusiasm for something.

> – SYNONYMS **fad,** fashion, trend, vogue, enthusiasm, mania, passion, rage; informal thing.

▶ **verb** (**be crazed**) (of a surface) be covered with a network of fine cracks.
– DERIVATIVES **cra·zing** noun.
– ORIGIN perhaps Scandinavian.

crazed /krāzd/ ▶ **adjective** (often in combination) behaving in an uncontrolled or insane way: *drug-crazed kids*.

> **WORD TOOLKIT**
>
> See **PSYCHOTIC**.

cra·zy /ˈkrāzē/ ▶ **adjective** (**crazier, craziest**) **1** insane, especially in a wild way. **2** very enthusiastic: *I'm crazy about Cindy*. **3** foolish or absurd: *it was a crazy idea*.

> – SYNONYMS **1 mad,** insane, out of one's mind, deranged, demented, crazed, lunatic, unbalanced, unhinged; informal mental, nuts, nutty, batty, bonkers, cuckoo, loony, loco, off one's rocker, round/around the bend. **2** *a crazy idea* **stupid,** foolish, idiotic, silly, absurd, ridiculous, ludicrous, preposterous, asinine; informal cockeyed, half-baked, daft. **3** *he's crazy about her* **passionate about,** (very) keen on, enamored of, infatuated with, smitten with, enthusiastic about, fanatical about; informal wild, mad, nuts.
> – ANTONYMS sane, sensible.

▶ **noun** (pl. **crazies**) informal an insane person.
– DERIVATIVES **cra·zi·ly** adverb **cra·zi·ness** noun.
– PHRASES **like crazy** to a great degree.

creak /krēk/ ▶ **verb 1** make or move with a scraping or squeaking sound. **2** show weakness under strain: *the system is creaking at the seams*. ▶ **noun** a scraping or squeaking sound.
– DERIVATIVES **creak·y** adjective (**creakier, creakiest**).
– ORIGIN imitating the sound.

cream /krēm/ ▶ **noun 1** the thick fatty liquid that rises to the top when milk is left to stand. **2** a food containing cream or having a creamy consistency. **3** a thick liquid cosmetic or medical substance that is applied to the skin. **4** the very best of a group: *the cream of American society*. **5** a very pale yellow or off-white color: (as adj.) *a cream dress*.

> – SYNONYMS **1 lotion,** ointment, moisturizer, cosmetic, salve, rub. **2 best,** finest, pick, flower, crème de la crème, elite. **3** (as adj.) **off-white,** creamy, ivory.
> – ANTONYMS dregs.

▶ **verb 1** mash a cooked vegetable with milk or cream. **2** work butter to form a smooth soft paste. **3** defeat someone heavily, especially in a sports contest.
– ORIGIN Old French *cresme*.

cream cheese ▶ **noun** soft, rich cheese made from unskimmed milk and cream.

cream·er /ˈkrēmər/ ▶ **noun 1** a cream or milk substitute for adding to coffee or tea. **2** a small pitcher for cream.

cream·er·y /ˈkrēm(ə)rē/ ▶ **noun** (pl. **creameries**) a place where butter and cheese are made.

cream of tar·tar ▶ **noun** an acidic compound produced during the fermentation of wine and used chiefly in baking powder.

cream puff ▶ **noun** a cake made of puff pastry filled with cream.

cream·y /ˈkrēmē/ ▶ **adjective** (**creamier, creamiest**) resembling or containing a lot of cream.

> – SYNONYMS **smooth,** thick, velvety, rich, buttery.

– DERIVATIVES **cream·i·ly** adverb **cream·i·ness** noun.

crease /krēs/ ▶ **noun 1** a line or ridge produced on paper or cloth by folding, pressing, or crushing. **2** a wrinkle or furrow in the skin.

> – SYNONYMS **fold,** line, crinkle, ridge, furrow, groove, corrugation, wrinkle, crow's foot.

▶ **verb 1** make or become crumpled or wrinkled. **2** (of a bullet) graze someone or something, causing little damage.

> – SYNONYMS **crumple,** wrinkle, crinkle, line, scrunch up, rumple, ruck up, pucker.

– ORIGIN probably a variant of **CREST**.

cre·ate /krēˈāt/ ▶ **verb 1** bring something into existence. **2** cause to happen: *divorce creates problems for children*. **3** appoint to a noble title or rank: *he was created a baronet*.

> – SYNONYMS **1 produce,** generate, bring into being, make, fashion, build, construct. **2 establish,** found, initiate, institute, constitute, inaugurate, launch, set up, form. **3 bring about,** give rise to, lead to, result in, cause, breed, generate, engender, produce.
> – ANTONYMS destroy, abolish.

– ORIGIN Latin *creare* 'produce.'

cre·a·tine /ˈkrēəˌtēn, ˈkrēətn/ ▶ **noun** a compound formed in protein metabolism and involved in the supply of energy for contraction of the muscles.
– ORIGIN from Greek *kreas* 'meat.'

cre·a·tion /krēˈāsHən/ ▶ **noun** **1** the action of bringing something into existence. **2** a thing that has been made or invented, especially something showing artistic talent. **3** (**the Creation**) the creating of the universe, regarded as an act of God. **4** (**Creation**) literary the universe.

– SYNONYMS **1 establishment,** formation, foundation, initiation, institution, inauguration, constitution, setting up. **2 work,** work of art, production, opus, oeuvre, achievement, concoction, invention; informal brainchild. **3 the world,** the universe, the cosmos, nature, the natural world.
– ANTONYMS abolition, destruction.

cre·a·tion·ism /krēˈāsHəˌnizəm/ ▶ **noun** the belief that the universe and living creatures were created by God in accordance with the account given in the Old Testament.
– DERIVATIVES **cre·a·tion·ist** noun & adjective.

cre·a·tive /krēˈātiv/ ▶ **adjective** **1** involving the use of the imagination or original ideas in order to create something. **2** having good imagination or original ideas.

– SYNONYMS **inventive,** imaginative, innovative, experimental, original, artistic, inspired, visionary.
– ANTONYMS unimaginative.

– DERIVATIVES **cre·a·tive·ly** adverb **cre·a·tive·ness** noun **cre·a·tiv·i·ty** /ˌkrē-āˈtivitē/ noun.

CHOOSE THE RIGHT WORD

creative, inventive, original, resourceful, imaginative, ingenious

Everyone likes to think that he or she is **creative**, which is used to describe the active, exploratory minds possessed by artists, writers, and inventors (*a creative approach to problem-solving*). Today, however, *creative* has become an advertising buzzword (*creative cooking, creative hair-styling*) that simply means new or different. **Original** is more specific and limited in scope. Someone who is *original* comes up with things that no one else has thought of (*an original approach to constructing a doghouse*), or thinks in an independent and creative way (*a highly original filmmaker*). **Imaginative** implies having an active and creative imagination, which often means that the person visualizes things quite differently than the way they appear in the real world (*imaginative illustrations for a children's book*). The practical side of *imaginative* is **inventive**; the *inventive* person figures out how to make things work (*an inventive solution to the problem of getting a wheelchair into a van*). But where an *inventive* mind tends to come up with solutions to problems it has posed for itself, a **resourceful** mind deals successfully with externally imposed problems or limitations (*A resourceful child can amuse herself with simple wooden blocks*). Someone who is **ingenious** is both *inventive* and *resourceful*, with a dose of cleverness thrown in (*the ingenious idea of using recycled plastic to create a warm, fleecelike fabric*).

cre·a·tive ac·count·ing ▶ **noun** informal the exploitation of loopholes in financial regulation to gain advantage or to present figures in a misleadingly favorable light.

cre·a·tor /krēˈātər/ ▶ **noun** **1** a person or thing that creates something. **2** (**the Creator**) God.

– SYNONYMS **maker,** producer, author, designer, deviser, originator, inventor, architect.

crea·ture /ˈkrēcHər/ ▶ **noun** **1** a living being, in particular an animal as distinct from a person. **2** a person viewed in a particular way: *you heartless creature!*

– SYNONYMS **animal,** beast, brute, living thing, living being; informal critter.

– ORIGIN Latin *creatura*.

crea·ture com·forts ▶ **plural noun** things that contribute to a comfortable life, such as good food and accommodations.

crèche /kresH/ ▶ **noun** a model or tableau representing the scene of Jesus Christ's birth, typically displayed at Christmas.
– ORIGIN French.

cred /kred/ ▶ **noun** informal short for **CREDIBILITY** (sense 2).

cred·al /ˈkrēdl/ (also **creedal**) ▶ **adjective** relating to a statement of Christian or other religious belief.

cre·dence /ˈkrēdns/ ▶ **noun** **1** belief in something as true: *he gave no credence to the witness's statement*. **2** the likelihood of something being true; plausibility.
– ORIGIN from Latin *credere* 'believe.'

cre·den·tial /krəˈdencHəl/ ▶ **noun** (usu. **credentials**) **1** a qualification, achievement, or quality that gives an indication of a person's suitability for something: *her academic credentials cannot be doubted*. **2** a document proving a person's identity or qualifications. **3** a letter of introduction given by a government to an ambassador before a new posting.

– SYNONYMS **1 suitability,** eligibility, attributes, qualifications, record, experience, background. **2 documentation,** documents, ID, proof of identity, passport, testimonial, reference, certification.

cred·i·bil·i·ty /ˌkredəˈbilitē/ ▶ **noun** **1** the quality of being trusted or believable. **2** (also **street credibility**) acceptability among fashionable young urban people.

– SYNONYMS **plausibility,** believability, credence, trustworthiness, reliability, dependability, integrity.

cred·i·bil·i·ty gap ▶ **noun** an apparent difference between what is said or promised and what happens or is true.

cred·i·ble /ˈkredəbəl/ ▶ **adjective** able to be believed; convincing.

– SYNONYMS **believable,** plausible, conceivable, persuasive, convincing, tenable, probable, possible, feasible, reasonable.

– DERIVATIVES **cred·i·bly** adverb.
– ORIGIN from Latin *credere* 'believe.'

cred·it /ˈkredit/ ▶ **noun** **1** an arrangement in which a store or other business enables a customer to pay at a later date for goods or services supplied: *we supply quality cars on credit*. **2** money borrowed or lent under a credit arrangement. **3** public acknowledgment or praise for an achievement or quality. **4** a source of pride: *the fans are a credit to the club*. **5** a written acknowledgment of a contributor's role displayed at the beginning or end of a movie or television program. **6** an entry in an account recording a sum received. **7** a unit of study counting toward a degree or diploma.

– SYNONYMS **praise,** commendation, acclaim, acknowledgment, recognition, kudos, glory, respect, appreciation.

▶ **verb** (**credits, crediting, credited**) **1** believe that someone has done something or has a particular quality. **2** add an amount of money to an account.

– SYNONYMS *we credit our success to one woman* **ascribe,** attribute, assign, put down.

– PHRASES **do someone credit** make someone worthy of

praise or respect.
– ORIGIN Latin *creditum*.

cred·it·a·ble /ˈkreditəbəl/ ▶ **adjective** deserving public acknowledgment and praise.
– DERIVATIVES **cred·it·a·bly** /-blē/ adverb.

cred·it card ▶ **noun** a plastic card allowing the holder to buy things on credit.

cred·it crunch ▶ **noun** a period of economic recession in which credit is difficult to obtain: *many companies will not survive the unfolding credit crunch.*

cred·i·tor /ˈkreditər/ ▶ **noun** a person or company to whom money is owing.

cred·it un·ion ▶ **noun** a nonprofit cooperative whose members can borrow money at low interest rates.

cred·it·worth·y /ˈkreditˌwərt͟hē/ ▶ **adjective** considered suitable to receive financial credit.
– DERIVATIVES **cred·it·wor·thi·ness** noun.

cre·do /ˈkrēdō, ˈkrādō/ ▶ **noun** (pl. **credos**) a statement of a person's beliefs or aims.
– ORIGIN Latin, 'I believe.'

cred·u·lous /ˈkrejələs/ ▶ **adjective** excessively ready to believe things; gullible.

– SYNONYMS **gullible,** naive, easily taken in, impressionable, unsuspecting, unsuspicious, innocent, inexperienced, unsophisticated, wide-eyed.
– ANTONYMS suspicious.

– DERIVATIVES **cre·du·li·ty** /krəˈd(y)o͞olitē/ noun **cred·u·lous·ly** adverb.
– ORIGIN Latin *credulus*.

CHOOSE THE RIGHT WORD

See **GULLIBLE**.

Cree /krē/ ▶ **noun** (pl. same or **Crees**) a member of an American Indian people of central Canada.
– ORIGIN Algonquian.

creed /krēd/ ▶ **noun 1** a system of religious belief; a faith. **2** a statement of beliefs or principles: *nationalism is his creed.*

– SYNONYMS **1** *people of many creeds* **faith,** religion, belief, religious persuasion. **2** *his political creed* **beliefs,** principles, articles of faith, tenets, ideology, credo, doctrines, teachings.

– ORIGIN from Latin *credo* 'I believe.'

creed·al /ˈkrēdl/ ▶ **adjective** variant spelling of **CREDAL**.

creek /krēk/ ▶ **noun 1** a small waterway such as an inlet in a shoreline. **2** a stream or minor tributary of a river.

– SYNONYMS **inlet,** bay, estuary, fjord; Scottish firth.

– PHRASES **up the creek** informal in severe difficulty or trouble.
– ORIGIN Old French *crique* or Old Norse *kriki* 'nook.'

creel /krēl/ ▶ **noun** a large basket for carrying fish.
– ORIGIN unknown.

creep /krēp/ ▶ **verb** (past and past part. **crept**) **1** move slowly and carefully to avoid being noticed. **2** progress or develop gradually: *errors crept into his game.* **3** (as adj. **creeping**) (of a plant) growing along the ground or other surface.

– SYNONYMS **tiptoe,** steal, sneak, slink, edge, inch, skulk, prowl.

▶ **noun 1** informal a contemptible person, especially one who behaves in a servile way to win favor. **2** slow and gradual movement or progress.
– PHRASES **give someone the creeps** informal make someone feel disgust or fear.
– ORIGIN Old English.

creep·er /ˈkrēpər/ ▶ **noun** a plant that grows along the ground or another surface.

creep·y /ˈkrēpē/ ▶ **adjective** (**creepier, creepiest**) informal causing fear or unease.

– SYNONYMS **frightening,** eerie, disturbing, sinister, weird, menacing, threatening; informal spooky, scary.

– DERIVATIVES **creep·i·ly** adverb **creep·i·ness** noun.

creep·y-crawl·y /ˈkrôlē/ ▶ **noun** (pl. **creepy-crawlies**) informal a spider, worm, or other small creature.

cre·ma /ˌkrāmə/ ▶ **noun** a frothy film that forms on the top of freshly made espresso.

cre·mate /ˈkrēˌmāt, kriˈmāt/ ▶ **verb** dispose of a corpse by burning it to ashes.
– DERIVATIVES **cre·ma·tion** /kriˈmāsʜən/ noun.
– ORIGIN Latin *cremare* 'burn.'

cre·ma·to·ri·um /ˌkrēməˈtôrēəm, ˌkrem-/ ▶ **noun** (pl. **crematoria** /-ˈtôrēə/ or **crematoriums**) a building where the dead are cremated.

crème brû·lée /ˌkrem bro͞oˈlā/ ▶ **noun** (pl. **crèmes brûlées** pronunc. same, or **crème brûlées** /bro͞oˈlāz/) a dessert of custard topped with caramelized sugar.
– ORIGIN French, 'burnt cream.'

crème car·a·mel /ˌkrem karəˈmel, ˈkarəˌmel/ ▶ **noun** (pl. **crèmes caramel** pronunc. same, or **crème caramels**) a custard dessert made with whipped cream and eggs and topped with caramel.
– ORIGIN French.

crème de la crème /ˌkrem də lə ˈkrem/ ▶ **noun** the best person or thing of a particular kind.
– ORIGIN French, 'cream of the cream.'

crème de menthe /ˌkrēm də ˈmenтн, ˌkrēm də ˈmint/ ▶ **noun** a green peppermint-flavored liqueur.
– ORIGIN French, 'cream of mint.'

crème fraiche /ˌkrem ˈfresʜ/ ▶ **noun** a type of thick cream with buttermilk, sour cream, or yogurt.
– ORIGIN French, 'fresh cream.'

cren·el·la·ted /ˈkrenlˌātid/ (also **crenelated**) ▶ **adjective** (of a building) having battlements.
– ORIGIN from Latin *crena* 'notch.'

cren·el·la·tions /ˌkrenlˈāsʜənz/ ▶ **plural noun** battlements.

Cre·ole /ˈkrēˌōl/ ▶ **noun 1** a person of mixed European and black descent. **2** a descendant of European settlers in the Caribbean or Central or South America. **3** a white descendant of French settlers in Louisiana. **4** a language formed from a combination of a European language and another language, especially an African language.
– ORIGIN French.

cre·o·sote /ˈkrēəˌsōt/ ▶ **noun** a dark brown oil used as a wood preservative. ▶ **verb** treat something with creosote.
– ORIGIN from Greek *kreas* 'flesh' + *sōtēr* 'preserver.'

crêpe /krāp/ (also **crepe**) ▶ **noun 1** a light, thin fabric with a wrinkled surface. **2** hard-wearing wrinkled rubber used for the soles of shoes. **3** /krāp, krep/a thin pancake.
– DERIVATIVES **crêp·ey** (also **crêpy**) adjective.
– ORIGIN French.

crêpe de Chine /ˌkrāp də ˈsʜēn/ ▶ **noun** a fine crêpe fabric of silk or a similar material.
– ORIGIN French, 'crêpe of China.'

crepe pa·per ▶ **noun** thin, crinkled paper used for making decorations.

crêpe Su·zette /ˌkrāp so͞oˈzet/ ▶ **noun** (pl. **crêpes Suzette** pronunc. same) a thin sweet pancake flamed briefly in alcohol at the table before being served.

crept /krept/ past and past participle of **CREEP**.

cre·pus·cu·lar /krəˈpəskyələr/ ▶ **adjective** chiefly literary resembling or relating to twilight.
– ORIGIN Latin *crepusculum* 'twilight.'

cre·scen·do /krəˈsʜendō/ ▶ **noun 1** (pl. **crescendos** or **crescendi** /-dē/) a gradual increase in loudness in a piece of music. **2** the loudest or climactic point: *the shrieks of laughter reached a crescendo.* ▶ **adverb & adjective** Music gradually becoming louder. ▶ **verb** (**crescendoes, crescendoing, crescendoed**) increase in loudness or intensity.
– ORIGIN Italian.

cres·cent /ˈkresənt/ ▶ **noun** the form of the waxing or waning moon, seen as a narrow curved shape tapering to a point at each end.
– ORIGIN from Latin *crescere* 'grow.'

cress /kres/ ▶ **noun** a plant with pungent, edible leaves, some kinds of which are used in salads.
– ORIGIN Old English.

crest /krest/ ▶ **noun 1** a tuft or growth of feathers, fur, or skin on the head of a bird or other animal. **2** a plume of feathers on a helmet. **3** the top of a ridge, wave, etc. **4** a distinctive heraldic design representing a family or organization.

– SYNONYMS **1 tuft,** comb, plume, crown. **2 summit,** peak, top, ridge, pinnacle, brow, crown, apex. **3 insignia,** emblem, coat of arms, arms, badge, device, regalia.

▶ **verb 1** reach the top of: *he finally crested the hill.* **2** (as adj. **crested**) having a crest.
– ORIGIN from Latin *crista*.

crest·fal·len /ˈkrestˌfôlən/ ▶ **adjective** sad and disappointed.

– SYNONYMS **downhearted,** downcast, despondent, disappointed, disconsolate, disheartened, discouraged, dispirited, dejected, sad, dismayed, unhappy, forlorn.
– ANTONYMS cheerful.

Cre·ta·ceous /krəˈtāsʜəs/ ▶ **adjective** relating to the last period of the Mesozoic era (about 146 to 65 million years ago), at the end of which dinosaurs and many other organisms died out.
– ORIGIN from Latin *creta* 'chalk.'

Cre·tan /ˈkrētn/ ▶ **noun** a person from the Greek island of Crete. ▶ **adjective** relating to Crete.

cre·tin /ˈkrētn/ ▶ **noun 1** a stupid person. **2** Medicine, dated a person who is deformed and has learning difficulties because of a congenital lack of thyroid hormone.
– DERIVATIVES **cre·tin·ism** /-ˌizəm/ noun.
– ORIGIN from Swiss French *crestin* 'Christian,' apparently intended as a reminder that disabled people are human.

cre·tin·ous /ˈkrētnəs/ ▶ **adjective** very stupid.

cre·tonne /ˈkrēˌtän, kriˈtän/ ▶ **noun** a heavy cotton fabric, typically with a floral pattern, used for upholstery.
– ORIGIN French.

Creutz·feldt–Ja·kob dis·ease /ˈkroitsˌfelt ˈyäkôb/ ▶ **noun** a fatal disease that affects nerve cells in the brain, one form of which (**new variant Creutzfeldt–Jakob disease**) is possibly linked to BSE.
– ORIGIN named after the German neurologists H. G. *Creutzfeldt* and A. *Jakob*.

cre·vasse /krəˈvas/ ▶ **noun** a deep open crack in a glacier or ice field.
– ORIGIN Old French *crevace* (see **CREVICE**).

crev·ice /ˈkrevəs/ ▶ **noun** a narrow opening or crack in a rock or wall.

– SYNONYMS **crack,** fissure, interstice, cleft, chink, cranny, slit, split.

– ORIGIN Old French *crevace*, from *crever* 'to burst.'

crew /kro͞o/ ▶ **noun** (treated as sing. or pl.) **1** a group of people who work on and operate a ship, boat, aircraft, or train. **2** a group of such people excluding the officers. **3** informal, often derogatory a group of people associated in some way.

– SYNONYMS **1** *the ship's crew* **company,** complement, sailors, hands. **2** *a film crew* **team,** squad, company, unit, party, gang.

▶ **verb** act as a member of a crew on a ship, boat, aircraft, etc.
– ORIGIN Old French *creue* 'increase.'

crew cut ▶ **noun** a very short haircut for men and boys.
– ORIGIN apparently first adopted by boat crews of Harvard and Yale universities.

crew·el /ˈkro͞oəl/ ▶ **noun** a thin, loosely twisted worsted yarn used for tapestry and embroidery.
– ORIGIN unknown.

crew neck ▶ **noun** a close-fitting round neckline.

crib /krib/ ▶ **noun 1** a child's bed. **2** a rack for animal fodder; a manger. **3** informal a translation of a text for use by students, especially in a surreptitious way. **4** informal a house or apartment. **5** short for **CRIBBAGE**. ▶ **verb** (**cribs, cribbing, cribbed**) informal copy another person's work dishonestly or without acknowledgment.
– ORIGIN Old English.

crib·bage /ˈkribij/ ▶ **noun** a card game for two players, the objective of which is to play cards whose value reaches exactly 15 or 31.
– ORIGIN from **CRIB**.

crib death ▶ **noun** the unexplained death of a baby in its sleep.

crick /krik/ ▶ **noun** a painful stiff feeling in the neck or back. ▶ **verb** twist or strain one's neck or back, causing painful stiffness.
– ORIGIN unknown.

crick·et[1] /ˈkrikit/ ▶ **noun** an open-air game played by two teams of eleven players with a ball, bats, and wickets, the batsmen attempting to score runs by hitting the ball and running between the wickets.
– DERIVATIVES **crick·et·er** noun **crick·et·ing** adjective.
– PHRASES **not cricket** Brit. informal not fair or honorable.
– ORIGIN unknown.

crick·et[2] ▶ **noun** an insect like a grasshopper but with shorter legs, the male of which produces a shrill chirping sound.
– ORIGIN from Old French *criquer* 'to crackle.'

cri de cœur /ˌkrē də ˈkər/ ▶ **noun** (pl. **cris de cœur** pronunc. same) a passionate appeal or complaint.
– ORIGIN French, 'cry from the heart.'

cried /krīd/ past and past participle of **CRY**.

cri·er /ˈkrīər/ ▶ **noun 1** an officer who makes public announcements in a court of law. **2** short for **TOWN CRIER**.

crime /krīm/ ▶ **noun 1** an act or activity that is illegal and can be punished by law. **2** such acts or activities considered as a whole: *the victims of violent crime.* **3** something seen as immoral or shameful: *such a war would be a crime against humanity.*

– SYNONYMS **1 offense,** unlawful act, illegal act, felony, violation, misdemeanor. **2 lawbreaking,** delinquency, wrongdoing, criminality, misconduct, illegality, villainy, vice.

– ORIGIN Latin *crimen* 'judgment, offense.'

CHOOSE THE RIGHT WORD

See **SIN**[1].

crim·i·nal /'krimənl/ ▶ **noun** a person who has committed a crime.

– SYNONYMS **lawbreaker,** felon, offender, malefactor, villain, delinquent, culprit, miscreant, wrongdoer; informal crook.

▶ **adjective 1** relating to crime or a crime. **2** informal disgraceful and shocking: *a criminal waste of taxpayers' money.*

– SYNONYMS **1 unlawful,** illegal, illicit, lawless, delinquent, corrupt, felonious, nefarious; informal crooked. **2 deplorable,** shameful, reprehensible, disgraceful, inexcusable, outrageous, scandalous.
– ANTONYMS lawful.

– DERIVATIVES **crim·i·nal·i·ty** /ˌkrimə'nalitē/ noun **crim·i·nal·ly** adverb.

crim·i·nal·ize /'krimənlˌīz/ ▶ **verb 1** make an activity illegal. **2** turn someone into a criminal by making their activities illegal.
– DERIVATIVES **crim·i·nal·i·za·tion** /ˌkrimənl-ə'zāsʜən/ noun.

crim·i·nol·o·gy /ˌkrimə'näləjē/ ▶ **noun** the scientific study of crime and criminals.
– DERIVATIVES **crim·i·nol·o·gist** noun.

crimp /krimp/ ▶ **verb 1** press something into small folds or ridges. **2** make curls or waves in a person's hair by pressing it with a curling iron or a similar device.
– DERIVATIVES **crimp·er** noun.
– ORIGIN Old English.

crim·son /'krimzən/ ▶ **noun** a rich deep red color. ▶ **verb** (of a person's face) become flushed, especially through embarrassment.
– ORIGIN Arabic.

cringe /krinj/ ▶ **verb** (**cringes, cringing, cringed**) **1** shrink back or cower in fear or in a submissive way. **2** have a sudden feeling of embarrassment or disgust.

– SYNONYMS **1 cower,** shrink, recoil, shy away, flinch, quail, blench, tremble, quiver, quake. **2 wince,** shudder, squirm, feel embarrassed/mortified.

– ORIGIN from an Old English word meaning 'bend, yield, fall in battle.'

CHOOSE THE RIGHT WORD

See **WINCE**.

crin·kle /'krinɢkəl/ ▶ **verb** form small creases or wrinkles. ▶ **noun** a small crease or wrinkle.
– DERIVATIVES **crin·kly** adjective.
– ORIGIN related to **CRINGE**.

crin·o·line /'krinl-in/ ▶ **noun** a stiffened or hooped petticoat formerly worn to give a long skirt a very full and rounded shape.
– ORIGIN French, from Latin *crinis* 'hair' + *linum* 'thread.'

cripes /krīps/ ▶ **exclamation** informal an expression of surprise.
– ORIGIN euphemism for **CHRIST**.

crip·ple /'kripəl/ ▶ **noun** old use or offensive a person who is unable to walk or move properly through disability or injury. ▶ **verb 1** make someone unable to move or walk properly. **2** severely damage or weaken something: *families crippled by mounting debts.*

– SYNONYMS **1 disable,** paralyze, immobilize, incapacitate, handicap. **2 damage,** weaken, hamper, paralyze, ruin, destroy, wipe out, bring to a standstill, put out of action, put out of business.

– ORIGIN Old English.

USAGE

As a noun, the word **cripple** is often regarded as offensive and should be avoided. Terms such as 'disabled person' are preferable.

cri·sis /'krīsis/ ▶ **noun** (pl. **crises**) **1** a time of extreme difficulty or danger: *the current economic crisis.* **2** the time when a problem or difficult situation is at its worst point.

– SYNONYMS **1 emergency,** disaster, catastrophe, calamity, meltdown, predicament, plight, dire straits. **2 critical point,** turning point, crossroads, head, point of no return, moment of truth; informal crunch.

– ORIGIN Greek *krisis* 'decision.'

crisp /krisp/ ▶ **adjective 1** firm, dry, and brittle. **2** (of the weather) cool, fresh, and invigorating. **3** (of a person's way of speaking) brisk and decisive.

– SYNONYMS **1 crunchy,** crispy, brittle, breakable, dry. **2 invigorating,** brisk, cool, fresh, refreshing, exhilarating.
– ANTONYMS soft.

▶ **noun** a dessert of fruit baked with a crunchy topping of brown sugar, butter, and flour.
▶ **verb** give food a crisp surface by cooking it in an oven or under a broiler.
– DERIVATIVES **crisp·ly** adverb **crisp·ness** noun.
– ORIGIN Latin *crispus* 'curled.'

crisp·bread /'krispˌbred/ ▶ **noun** a thin, crisp cracker made from crushed rye or wheat.

crisp·y /'krispē/ ▶ **adjective** (**crispier, crispiest**) firm and brittle; crisp.

criss·cross /'krisˌkrôs/ ▶ **adjective** with a pattern of intersecting lines. ▶ **verb 1** form a crisscross pattern on a place. **2** move or travel around a place by going back and forth repeatedly.

cri·te·ri·on /krī'ti(ə)rēən/ ▶ **noun** (pl. **criteria** /-'ti(ə)rēə/) a principle or standard by which something may be judged or decided.

– SYNONYMS **standard,** measure, gauge, test, benchmark, yardstick, touchstone, barometer.

– ORIGIN Greek *kritērion* 'means of judging.'

USAGE

The singular form is **criterion** and the plural form is **criteria**. Do not use **criteria** as if it were a singular noun: say *a further criterion needs to be considered* not *a further criteria needs to be considered.*

crit·ic /ˈkritik/ ▸ **noun 1** a person who expresses disapproval of someone or something. **2** a person who reviews literary or artistic works.

– SYNONYMS **1 reviewer,** commentator, analyst, judge, pundit, expert. **2 detractor,** attacker, fault-finder.

– ORIGIN from Greek *kritēs* 'a judge.'

crit·i·cal /ˈkritikəl/ ▸ **adjective 1** expressing disapproving comments or judgments: *the judge was very critical of him.* **2** expressing or involving an assessment of a literary or artistic work. **3** at a point of danger or crisis: *the floods were rising and the situation was critical.* **4** extremely ill and at risk of death. **5** having a decisive importance in the success or failure of something; crucial: *confidence has been the critical factor in their success.* **6** Mathematics & Physics relating to a point of transition from one state to another. **7** (of a nuclear reactor or fuel) maintaining a chain reaction that can sustain itself.

– SYNONYMS **1 disapproving,** disparaging, scathing, fault-finding, judgmental, negative, unfavorable, censorious; informal nitpicking, picky. **2 serious,** grave, precarious, touch-and-go, in the balance, desperate, dire, acute, life-and-death. **3 crucial,** vital, essential, all-important, paramount, fundamental, key, pivotal.
– ANTONYMS complimentary.

– DERIVATIVES **crit·i·cal·ly** adverb.

crit·i·cal mass ▸ **noun 1** Physics the minimum amount of fissile material needed to maintain a nuclear chain reaction. **2** the minimum amount of resources required to start a venture or keep it going.

crit·i·cism /ˈkritəˌsizəm/ ▸ **noun 1** the expression of disapproval of someone or something. **2** the assessment of literary or artistic works.

– SYNONYMS **1 fault-finding,** censure, condemnation, disapproval, disparagement; informal flak, bad press, panning. **2 evaluation,** assessment, appraisal, appreciation, analysis, critique, judgment, commentary.
– ANTONYMS praise.

crit·i·cize /ˈkritəˌsīz/ ▸ **verb 1** express disapproval of someone or something. **2** assess a literary or artistic work.

– SYNONYMS **find fault with,** censure, condemn, attack, disparage, denigrate, run down; informal knock, pan, pull to pieces, trash.
– ANTONYMS praise.

cri·tique /kriˈtēk/ ▸ **noun** a detailed analysis and assessment of something. ▸ **verb** (**critiques, critiquing, critiqued**) analyze and assess something in detail.
– ORIGIN French.

crit·ter /ˈkritər/ ▸ **noun** informal or dialect a living creature.

croak /krōk/ ▸ **noun** a characteristic deep hoarse sound made by a frog or a crow. ▸ **verb 1** utter a croak. **2** informal die.
– DERIVATIVES **croak·y** adjective.
– ORIGIN imitating the sound.

croak·er /ˈkrōkər/ ▸ **noun** another name for **DRUM**[2].

Cro·a·tian /krōˈāSHən/ ▸ **noun** (also **Croat** /ˈkrōˌat, ˈkrōˌät, krōt/) **1** a person from Croatia. **2** the language of the Croatians, almost identical to Serbian but written in the Roman alphabet. ▸ **adjective** relating to Croatia or Croatian.

croc /kräk/ ▸ **noun** informal a crocodile.

cro·chet /krōˈSHā/ ▸ **noun** a handicraft in which yarn is looped into a fabric of connected stitches by means of a hooked needle. ▸ **verb** (**crochets** /krōˈSHāz/, **crocheting** /-ˈSHāiNG/, **crocheted** /-ˈSHād/) make a garment or piece of fabric in this way.
– ORIGIN French, 'little hook.'

crock[1] /kräk/ ▸ **noun 1** an earthenware pot or jar. **2** (also vulgar slang **crock of shit**) a thing that is considered to be complete nonsense.
– ORIGIN probably related to **CRACK**.

crock[2] ▸ **noun 1** an earthenware pot or jar. **2** an item of crockery.
– ORIGIN Old English.

crock·er·y /ˈkräkərē/ ▸ **noun** plates, dishes, cups, and similar items made of earthenware or china.
– ORIGIN from the former word *crocker* 'potter.'

croc·o·dile /ˈkräkəˌdīl/ ▸ **noun** a large predatory tropical reptile living partly in water, with long jaws and a long tail.
– ORIGIN from Greek *krokodilos* 'worm of the stones.'

croc·o·dile tears ▸ **plural noun** insincere tears or expressions of sorrow.
– ORIGIN from a belief that crocodiles wept while eating or luring their prey.

cro·cus /ˈkrōkəs/ ▸ **noun** (pl. **crocuses**) a small spring-flowering plant with bright yellow, purple, or white flowers.
– ORIGIN Greek *krokos*.

Croe·sus /ˈkrēsəs/ ▸ **noun** a very wealthy person.
– ORIGIN from the name of a famously wealthy king of Lydia, an ancient region of Asia.

croft /krôft/ Brit. ▸ **noun** a small rented farm in Scotland or northern England. ▸ **verb** farm land as a croft or crofts.
– DERIVATIVES **croft·er** noun.
– ORIGIN Old English.

Crohn's dis·ease /ˈkrōnz/ ▸ **noun** a disease of the intestines, especially the colon and ileum.
– ORIGIN named after the American pathologist Burrill B. *Crohn*.

crois·sant /k(r)wäˈsänt, -ˈsäN/ ▸ **noun** a crescent-shaped roll made of sweet flaky dough.
– ORIGIN French, 'crescent.'

Cro-Mag·non /krō ˈmagnən, ˈmanyən/ ▸ **noun** the earliest form of modern human in Europe, appearing *c.*35,000 years ago.
– ORIGIN the name of a hill in the Dordogne, France.

crone /krōn/ ▸ **noun** an ugly old woman.
– ORIGIN Old French *caroigne* 'carrion.'

cro·ny /ˈkrōnē/ ▸ **noun** (pl. **cronies**) informal, often derogatory a person's close friend or companion.
– ORIGIN Greek *khronios* 'long-lasting.'

cro·ny·ism /ˈkrōnēˌizəm/ (also **croneyism**) ▸ **noun** derogatory the practice of appointing friends and associates to positions of authority, especially when they are not suitably qualified.

crook /kro͝ok/ ▸ **noun 1** a shepherd's hooked staff. **2** a bishop's crozier. **3** a bend, especially at the elbow in a person's arm. **4** informal a criminal or dishonest person.

– SYNONYMS see **CRIMINAL**.

▸ **verb** bend a finger or leg.
▸ **adjective** Austral./NZ informal **1** bad or unwell. **2** dishonest or illegal.
– ORIGIN Old Norse, 'hook.'

crook·ed /ˈkro͝okəd/ ▸ **adjective** **1** bent or twisted out of shape or position. **2** informal dishonest or illegal.

– SYNONYMS **1 winding,** twisting, zigzag, meandering, tortuous, serpentine. **2 bent,** twisted, misshapen, deformed, malformed, contorted, warped, bowed, distorted. **3 lopsided,** askew, awry, off-center, out of true, at an angle, slanting. Brit. informal wonky. **4 dishonest,** criminal, illegal, unlawful, nefarious, fraudulent, corrupt; informal shady.
– ANTONYMS straight.

– DERIVATIVES **crook·ed·ly** adverb **crook·ed·ness** noun.

croon /kro͞on/ ▸ **verb** hum, sing, or speak in a soft, low voice.
– DERIVATIVES **croon·er** noun.
– ORIGIN German and Dutch *krōnen* 'groan, lament.'

crop /kräp/ ▸ **noun** **1** a plant, especially a cereal, fruit, or vegetable, grown for food or other use. **2** an amount of a crop harvested at one time. **3** an amount of people or things appearing at one time: *this new crop of indie bands.* **4** a very short hairstyle. **5** a riding crop. **6** a pouch in a bird's throat where food is stored or prepared for digestion.

– SYNONYMS **harvest,** yield, fruits, produce, vintage.

▸ **verb** (**crops, cropping, cropped**) **1** cut something very short. **2** (of an animal) bite off and eat the tops of plants. **3** (**crop up**) appear or happen unexpectedly. **4** harvest a crop from an area. **5** sow or plant land with plants that will produce a crop.

– SYNONYMS **1 cut,** clip, trim, shear, shave, lop off, chop off, hack off, dock. **2 graze on,** browse on, feed on, nibble, eat. **3** *his name* ***cropped up*** *in the conversation* **happen,** occur, arise, turn up, pop up, emerge, materialize, surface, appear, come to light.

– ORIGIN Old English.

crop cir·cle ▸ **noun** an area of crops that has been flattened in the form of a circle or other pattern by unexplained means.

crop dust·ing ▸ **noun** the spraying of powdered insecticide or fertilizer on crops from the air.

crop·per /ˈkräpər/ ▸ **noun** a plant that yields a particular crop.
– PHRASES **come a cropper** informal **1** fall over heavily. **2** experience a defeat or disaster.

crop top (also **cropped top**) ▸ **noun** a woman's casual garment for the upper body, cut short so that it reveals the stomach.

cro·quet /krōˈkā/ ▸ **noun** a game played on a lawn, in which wooden balls are driven through a series of hoops with a mallet.
– ORIGIN perhaps a dialect form of French *crochet* 'hook.'

cro·quette /krōˈket/ ▸ **noun** a small cake or roll of chopped vegetables, meat, or fish, fried in breadcrumbs.
– ORIGIN French, from *croquer* 'to crunch.'

cro·sier ▸ **noun** variant spelling of CROZIER.

cross /krôs/ ▸ **noun** **1** a mark, object, or figure formed by two short intersecting lines or pieces (+ or ×). **2** an upright post with a bar fixed across it, as used in ancient times for crucifixion. **3** (**the Cross**) the cross on which Christ was crucified. **4** a cross-shaped medal awarded for bravery or showing rank in some orders of knighthood. **5** a thing that is unavoidable and has to be endured: *she's just a cross we have to bear.* **6** an animal or plant resulting from cross-breeding; a hybrid. **7** (**a cross between**) a mixture of two things: *a cross between a bar and a restaurant.* **8** (in soccer) a pass of the ball across the field toward the center close to one's opponents' goal.

– SYNONYMS **1** *we all have our crosses to bear* **burden,** trouble, worry, trial, tribulation, affliction, curse, misfortune, woe; informal hassle, headache. **2** *a cross between a yak and a cow* **mixture,** blend, combination, amalgam, hybrid, crossbreed, mongrel.

▸ **verb** **1** go or extend across or to the other side of: *she crossed the street and walked down the hill.* **2** pass in an opposite or different direction; intersect. **3** oppose or stand in the way of: *no one dared to cross him.* **4** cause an animal of one species, breed, or variety to interbreed with one of another. **5** place crosswise: *Michelle crossed her legs.* **6** draw a line or lines across something. **7** Soccer pass the ball across the field toward the center when attacking.

– SYNONYMS **1 travel across,** traverse, negotiate, navigate, cover. **2 intersect,** meet, join, connect. **3 oppose,** resist, defy, obstruct, contradict, argue with, stand up to. **4 hybridize,** crossbreed, interbreed, cross-fertilize, cross-pollinate.

▸ **adjective** annoyed.

– SYNONYMS **angry,** annoyed, irate, vexed, irritated, in a bad mood, put out, exasperated; informal hot under the collar, sore, ticked off, peeved.
– ANTONYMS pleased.

– DERIVATIVES **cross·ly** adverb **cross·ness** noun.
– PHRASES **at cross purposes** misunderstanding one another. **cross one's fingers** put one finger across another as a sign of hoping for good luck. **cross my heart (and hope to die)** used to emphasize the truthfulness and sincerity of what one is saying. **cross something off** delete an item from a list. **cross oneself** make the sign of the Cross in front of one's chest as a sign of Christian reverence or to call on God for protection. **cross something out/through** delete a word or phrase by drawing a line through it. **cross swords** have an argument or dispute. **get one's wires** (or **lines**) **crossed** have a misunderstanding.
– ORIGIN Old Irish *cros,* from Latin *crux.*

cross·bar /ˈkrôsˌbär/ ▸ **noun** **1** (in sports) a horizontal bar between the two upright posts of a goal. **2** a bar between the handlebars and saddle on a bicycle.

cross·bill /ˈkrôsˌbil/ ▸ **noun** a finch with a beak whose upper and lower parts are crossed, enabling it to extract seeds from the cones of conifers.

cross-bor·der ▸ **adjective** passing, occurring, or performed across a border between two countries.

cross·bow /ˈkrôsˌbō/ ▸ **noun** a medieval bow fixed across a wooden support, having a groove for the bolt and a mechanism for drawing and releasing the string.

cross·breed /ˈkrôsˌbrēd/ ▸ **noun** an animal or plant produced by crossing two different species, breeds, or varieties. ▸ **verb** produce an animal or plant in this way.

cross-check ▸ **verb** check figures or information by using an alternative source or method.

cross-con·tam·i·na·tion ▸ **noun** the process by which bacteria or other microorganisms are unintentionally transferred from one substance or object to another.
– DERIVATIVES **cross-con·tam·i·nate** verb.

cross-coun·try ▸ **adjective** **1** across fields or countryside, rather than keeping to roads or tracks. **2** across a region or country, in particular not keeping to main or direct routes. ▸ **noun** the sport of cross-country running, riding, skiing, or driving.

cross-cul·tur·al ▸ **adjective** of or relating to different cultures or comparison between them.

cross·cur·rent /ˈkrôs,kərənt/ ▸ **noun 1** a current in a river or sea that flows across another. **2** a situation or tendency marked by conflict with another: *political crosscurrents.*

cross·cut /ˈkrôs,kət/ ▸ **verb 1** cut wood or stone across its main grain or axis. **2** alternate one sequence with another when editing a movie.

cross-dres·sing ▸ **noun** the practice of wearing clothing usually worn by the opposite sex.

crosse /krôs/ ▸ **noun** the stick used in lacrosse.
– ORIGIN Old French *croce* 'bishop's crook.'

cross-ex·am·ine ▸ **verb** question a witness called by the other party in a court of law to challenge or extend the testimony that they have already given.
– DERIVATIVES **cross-ex·am·i·na·tion** noun.

cross-eyed ▸ **adjective** having one or both eyes turned inward toward the nose, either temporarily or as a permanent condition.

cross-fer·ti·lize ▸ **verb** fertilize a plant using pollen from another plant of the same species.
– DERIVATIVES **cross-fer·ti·li·za·tion** noun.

cross·fire /ˈkrôs,fīr/ ▸ **noun** gunfire from two or more directions passing through the same area.

cross-grained ▸ **adjective 1** (of timber) having a grain that runs across the regular grain. **2** stubbornly uncooperative or bad-tempered.

cross·hairs /ˈkrôs,he(ə)rz/ ▸ **plural noun** a pair of fine wires crossing at right angles at the focus of an optical instrument or gunsight.

cross·hatch /ˈkrôs,hacн/ ▸ **verb** shade an area with many intersecting parallel lines.

cross·ing /ˈkrôsiNG/ ▸ **noun 1** a place where things, especially roads or railroad lines, cross. **2** a place at which one may safely cross a street or railroad track. **3** a journey across water in a ship.

– SYNONYMS **1 junction,** crossroads, intersection, interchange, grade crossing, railroad crossing. **2 journey,** passage, voyage.

cross-leg·ged /ˈleg(ə)d/ ▸ **adjective & adverb** (of a seated person) with the legs crossed at the ankles and the knees bent outward.

cross·o·ver /ˈkrôs,ōvər/ ▸ **noun 1** a point or place of crossing from one side to the other. **2** the production of work in a new style or combination of styles, especially in popular music: *a rock-funk crossover.*

cross-own·er·ship ▸ **noun** the ownership by one corporation of different companies with related interests or commercial aims.

cross·piece /ˈkrôs,pēs/ ▸ **noun** a beam or bar fixed or placed across something else.

cross-pol·li·nate ▸ **verb** pollinate a flower or plant with pollen from another flower or plant.

cross-post ▸ **verb** send a message to more than one Internet newsgroup at the same time. ▸ **noun** a message that has been cross-posted.

cross-ques·tion ▸ **verb** question someone in great detail.

cross ref·er·ence ▸ **noun** a reference to another text or part of a text, given to provide further information.
– DERIVATIVES **cross-re·fer** verb.

cross·roads /ˈkrôs,rōdz/ ▸ **noun** an intersection of two or more roads.

cross sec·tion ▸ **noun 1** a surface exposed by making a straight cut through a solid object at right angles to its length. **2** a typical or representative sample of a larger group: *a cross-section of society.*

cross stitch ▸ **noun** an embroidery stitch formed of two stitches crossing each other.

cross·talk /ˈkrôs,tôk/ ▸ **noun 1** unwanted transfer of signals between communication channels. **2** witty conversation.

cross·walk /ˈkrôs,wôk/ ▸ **noun** a pedestrian crossing.

cross·wind /ˈkrôs,wind/ ▸ **noun** a wind blowing across one's direction of travel.

cross·wise /ˈkrôs,wīz/ (also **crossways**) ▸ **adverb 1** in the form of a cross. **2** diagonally.

cross·word /ˈkrôswərd/ ▸ **noun** a puzzle consisting of a grid of squares and blanks into which words crossing vertically and horizontally are written according to clues.

crotch /kräcн/ ▸ **noun 1** the part of the human body between the legs where they join the torso. **2** a fork in a tree, road, or river.
– ORIGIN partly a variant of **CRUTCH.**

crotch·et·y /ˈkräcнətē/ ▸ **adjective** irritable.

crouch /kroucн/ ▸ **verb** bend the knees and bring the upper body forward and down.

– SYNONYMS **squat,** bend (down), hunker down, hunch over, stoop, duck, cower.

▸ **noun** a crouching position.
– ORIGIN perhaps from Old French *crochir* 'be bent.'

croup[1] /kro͞op/ ▸ **noun** inflammation of the throat in children, causing coughing and breathing difficulties.
– ORIGIN dialect, 'to croak.'

croup[2] ▸ **noun** the rump or hindquarters of a horse.
– ORIGIN Old French.

croup·i·er /ˈkro͞opē,ā, -pēər/ ▸ **noun** the person in charge of a gambling table, gathering in and paying out money or tokens.
– ORIGIN French.

crou·ton /ˈkro͞o,tän, kro͞oˈtän/ ▸ **noun** a small piece of fried or toasted bread served with soup or used as a garnish.
– ORIGIN French, from *croûte* 'crust.'

crow[1] /krō/ ▸ **noun** a large bird with glossy black plumage, a heavy bill, and a harsh call.
– PHRASES **as the crow flies** in a straight line across country.
– ORIGIN Old English.

crow[2] ▸ **verb** (past **crowed**) **1** (of a cock) make its characteristic loud cry. **2** express pride or triumph in a tone of gloating satisfaction.

– SYNONYMS **boast,** brag, blow one's own trumpet, swagger, swank, gloat.

▸ **noun** the cry of a cock.
– ORIGIN Old English.

crow·bar /ˈkrō,bär/ ▸ **noun** an iron bar with a flattened end, used as a lever.

crowd /kroud/ ▸ **noun 1** a large number of people gathered together. **2** informal, often derogatory a group of people with a shared interest or quality: *a day at the beach with the sailing crowd.*

– SYNONYMS **1 horde,** throng, mass, multitude, host, army, herd, swarm, troop, mob, rabble; informal gaggle. **2** *they're a nice crowd* **group,** set, circle, clique; informal gang, bunch, crew, lot. **3** *a capacity crowd* **audience,** spectators, listeners, viewers, house, turnout, attendance, gate, congregation.

▶ **verb 1** (of a number of people) fill a space almost completely. **2** move or come together as a crowd: *passengers crowded into the train.* **3** move or stand too close to someone. **4** (**crowd someone/thing out**) keep someone or something out by taking their place.

– SYNONYMS **1 cluster,** flock, swarm, mill, throng, huddle, gather, assemble, congregate, converge. **2 surge,** throng, push, jostle, elbow one's way, squeeze, pile, cram.

– ORIGIN Old English, 'press, hasten.'

crowd·ed /'kroudid/ ▶ **adjective** (of a place) filled almost completely by a large number of people.

– SYNONYMS **packed,** full, filled to capacity, full to bursting, congested, overflowing, teeming, swarming, thronged, populous, overpopulated, busy; informal jam-packed, stuffed, chock-a-block, chock-full, bursting at the seams, full to the gunwales, wall-to-wall, mobbed.
– ANTONYMS deserted.

crowd-pleas·er ▶ **noun** a person or thing with great popular appeal.

crow·foot /'krōˌfo͝ot/ ▶ **noun** (pl. **crowfoots**) a water plant with white or yellow flowers.

crown /kroun/ ▶ **noun 1** a circular ornamental headdress worn by a monarch as a symbol of authority. **2** (**the Crown**) the monarchy or reigning monarch. **3** a wreath of leaves or flowers worn as an emblem of victory. **4** an award or distinction gained by a victory or achievement: *the world championship crown.* **5** the top or highest part of something such as a person's head or a hat. **6** the part of a tooth projecting from the gum. **7** an artificial replacement or covering for the upper part of a tooth. **8** a former British coin worth five shillings (or 25 pence).

– SYNONYMS **1 coronet,** diadem, tiara, circlet. **2 monarch,** sovereign, king, queen, emperor, empress, monarchy, royalty. **3 top,** crest, summit, peak, pinnacle, tip, brow, apex.

▶ **verb 1** ceremonially place a crown on the head of someone to invest them as a monarch. **2** rest on or form the top of: *a simple altar crowned by a wooden cross.* **3** be the triumphant conclusion of: *the victory that crowned his career.* **4** fit a crown on a tooth. **5** informal hit someone on the head.

– SYNONYMS *the building is crowned by a balustrade* **top,** cap, tip, head, surmount.

– ORIGIN Latin *corona* 'wreath.'

Crown Col·o·ny ▶ **noun** a British colony controlled by the Crown.

Crown jew·els ▶ **plural noun** the crown and other jewelry worn or carried by the sovereign on state occasions.

crown prince ▶ **noun** (in some countries) a male heir to a throne.

Crown prin·cess ▶ **noun 1** the wife of a crown prince. **2** (in some countries) a female heir to a throne.

crow's feet ▶ **plural noun** wrinkles at the outer corner of a person's eye.

crow's nest ▶ **noun** a platform for a lookout at the masthead of a ship.

cro·zier /'krōzнər/ (also **crosier**) ▶ **noun** a hooked staff carried by a bishop.
– ORIGIN Old French *croisier* 'cross-bearer.'

CRT ▶ **abbreviation** cathode ray tube.

cru·cial /'kro͞osнəl/ ▶ **adjective** of great importance, especially in the success or failure of something: *negotiations were at a crucial stage.*

– SYNONYMS **1 pivotal,** critical, key, decisive, life-and-death. **2 all-important,** of the utmost importance, of the essence, critical, paramount, essential, vital.
– ANTONYMS insignificant, unimportant.

– DERIVATIVES **cru·cial·ly** adverb.
– ORIGIN Latin *crux* 'cross.'

WORD TOOLKIT

See **VITAL**.

cru·ci·ate lig·a·ment /'kro͞osн(ē)ət, -sнēˌāt/ ▶ **noun** either of a pair of ligaments in the knee that cross each other and connect the femur (thigh bone) to the tibia (shinbone).
– ORIGIN Latin *cruciatus* 'cross-shaped.'

cru·ci·ble /'kro͞osəbəl/ ▶ **noun 1** a container in which metals or other substances may be melted or subjected to very high temperatures. **2** a situation in which people or things are severely tested, often interacting to produce something new: *a relationship forged in the crucible of war.*
– ORIGIN Latin *crucibulum.*

cru·cif·er·ous /kro͞o'sifərəs/ ▶ **adjective** (of a plant) belonging to the cabbage family, with four equal petals arranged in a cross.
– ORIGIN from Latin *crux* 'cross' + *-fer* 'bearing.'

cru·ci·fix /'kro͞osəˌfiks/ ▶ **noun** a representation of a cross with a figure of Jesus on it.
– ORIGIN from Latin *cruci fixus* 'fixed to a cross.'

cru·ci·fix·ion /ˌkro͞osə'fiksнən/ ▶ **noun 1** the execution of a person by crucifying them. **2** (**the Crucifixion**) the killing of Jesus in this way.

cru·ci·form /'kro͞osəˌfôrm/ ▶ **adjective** having the shape of a cross.

cru·ci·fy /'kro͞osəˌfī/ ▶ **verb** (**crucifies, crucifying, crucified**) **1** put someone to death by nailing or binding them to a cross. **2** informal criticize someone severely.
– ORIGIN from Latin *crux* 'cross' + *figere* 'fix.'

crud /krəd/ ▶ **noun** informal **1** an unpleasantly dirty or messy substance. **2** nonsense.
– DERIVATIVES **crud·dy** adjective.
– ORIGIN variant of **CURD**.

crude /kro͞od/ ▶ **adjective 1** in a natural or raw state; not yet processed or refined: *crude oil.* **2** simple or makeshift: *crude stone tools.* **3** likely to be only approximately accurate: *a crude index of economic progress.* **4** offensively coarse or vulgar.

– SYNONYMS **1 unrefined,** unpurified, unprocessed, untreated, coarse, raw, natural. **2 primitive,** simple, basic, homespun, rudimentary, rough and ready, makeshift, improvised, unsophisticated. **3 vulgar,** rude, dirty, naughty, smutty, indecent, obscene, coarse; informal blue.
– ANTONYMS refined.

▶ **noun** natural petroleum.

– DERIVATIVES **crude·ly** adverb **crude·ness** noun **cru·di·ty** /ˈkro͞oditē/ noun.
– ORIGIN Latin *crudus* 'raw, rough.'

cru·di·tés /ˌkro͞odəˈtā/ ▶ **plural noun** mixed raw vegetables served with a sauce into which they may be dipped.
– ORIGIN plural of French *crudité* 'rawness.'

cru·el /ˈkro͞oəl/ ▶ **adjective** (**crueler, cruelest**) **1** taking pleasure in the pain or suffering of others. **2** causing pain or suffering.

– SYNONYMS **1** *a cruel man* **brutal,** savage, inhuman, barbaric, vicious, sadistic, monstrous, callous, ruthless, merciless, heartless, pitiless, implacable, unkind, inhumane. **2** *her death was a cruel blow* **harsh,** severe, bitter, heartbreaking, heart-rending, painful, agonizing, traumatic.
– ANTONYMS compassionate.

– DERIVATIVES **cru·el·ly** adverb.
– ORIGIN Latin *crudelis.*

cru·el·ty /ˈkro͞oəltē/ ▶ **noun** (pl. **cruelties**) cruel behavior or attitudes.

– SYNONYMS **brutality,** savagery, inhumanity, barbarity, viciousness, sadism, callousness, ruthlessness.

cru·et /ˈkro͞oət/ ▶ **noun** a small container or set of containers for salt, pepper, oil, or vinegar for use at a dining table.
– ORIGIN Old French, 'small pot.'

cruise /kro͞oz/ ▶ **verb 1** sail, travel, or move slowly around without a definite destination, especially for pleasure. **2** travel smoothly at a moderate or economical speed. **3** easily achieve an objective: *the home team cruised to a 7–2 victory.* **4** informal wander about in search of a sexual partner.

– SYNONYMS **1 sail,** voyage. **2 drive slowly,** drift; informal mosey, tootle.

▶ **noun** a voyage on a ship taken as a vacation and usually calling in at several places.

– SYNONYMS **(boat) trip,** voyage, sail.

– ORIGIN probably from Dutch *kruisen* 'to cross.'

cruise con·trol ▶ **noun** a device in a motor vehicle that maintains a selected constant speed without requiring the driver to use the accelerator pedal.

cruise mis·sile ▶ **noun** a low-flying missile that is guided to its target by an on-board computer.

cruis·er /ˈkro͞ozər/ ▶ **noun 1** a fast warship larger than a destroyer and less heavily armed than a battleship. **2** a yacht or motorboat with passenger accommodations.

crumb /krəm/ ▶ **noun 1** a small fragment of bread, cake, or cookie. **2** a very small amount: *there was only one crumb of comfort.*

– SYNONYMS **fragment,** bit, morsel, particle, speck, scrap, shred, atom, trace, mite, jot, ounce; informal smidgen, tad.

– ORIGIN Old English.

crum·ble /ˈkrəmbəl/ ▶ **verb 1** break or fall apart into small fragments. **2** gradually disintegrate or fail: *the party's fragile unity began to crumble.*

– SYNONYMS **1 disintegrate,** fall apart, fall to pieces, collapse, decompose, break up, decay, become dilapidated, deteriorate, degenerate. **2 break up,** crush, fragment, pulverize.

▶ **noun** a baked dessert made with fruit and a crumbly pastry topping.
– ORIGIN Old English.

crum·bly /ˈkrəmblē/ ▶ **adjective** easily breaking into small fragments.

crum·my /ˈkrəmē/ (also **crumby**) ▶ **adjective** (**crummier, crummiest**) informal bad, unpleasant, or of poor quality.

crum·pet /ˈkrəmpət/ ▶ **noun** a thick, flat cake with a soft, open texture, eaten toasted and buttered.
– ORIGIN unknown.

crum·ple /ˈkrəmpəl/ ▶ **verb 1** crush something so that it becomes creased and wrinkled. **2** suddenly fall or collapse: *she crumpled to the floor.*

– SYNONYMS **1 crush,** scrunch up, screw up, squash, squeeze. **2 crease,** wrinkle, crinkle, rumple. **3 collapse,** give way, cave in, go to pieces, break down, crumble.

– ORIGIN Old English *crump* 'bent, crooked.'

crum·ple zone ▶ **noun** a part of a motor vehicle designed to crumple easily in a crash and absorb the main force of an impact.

crunch /krənCH/ ▶ **verb 1** crush something hard or brittle with the teeth, making a grinding sound. **2** make or move with a grinding sound: *the snow crunched as we walked.*

– SYNONYMS **munch,** chomp, champ, bite into, crush, grind.

▶ **noun 1** a crunching sound. **2** (**the crunch**) informal the crucial point of a situation. **3** a sit-up.
– ORIGIN probably imitating the sound.

crunch·y /ˈkrənCHē/ ▶ **adjective** (**crunchier, crunchiest**) making a crunching noise when bitten or crushed.
– DERIVATIVES **crunch·i·ness** noun.

cru·sade /kro͞oˈsād/ ▶ **noun 1** any of a series of medieval military expeditions made by Europeans to recover the Holy Land from the Muslims. **2** an energetic organized campaign with a political, social, or religious aim: *a crusade against crime.*

– SYNONYMS **campaign,** drive, push, movement, effort, struggle, battle, war, offensive.

▶ **verb** (often as adj. **crusading**) lead or take part in a crusade.

– SYNONYMS **campaign,** fight, battle, do battle, strive, struggle, agitate, lobby.

– DERIVATIVES **cru·sad·er** noun.
– ORIGIN French *croisade,* from *croisée* 'the state of being marked with the Cross.'

crush /krəSH/ ▶ **verb 1** press or squeeze forcefully so as to injure, squash, or break up: *the car was crushed under a truck.* **2** violently subdue or defeat: *troops were used to crush the rebellion.* **3** make someone feel extremely disappointed or embarrassed.

– SYNONYMS **1 squash,** squeeze, press, pulp, mash, mangle, pulverize. **2 crease,** crumple, rumple, wrinkle, scrunch up. **3 suppress,** put down, quell, stamp out, repress, subdue, extinguish. **4 demoralize,** deflate, flatten, squash, devastate, shatter, mortify, humiliate.

▶ **noun 1** a crowd of people pressed closely together. **2** informal a strong, usually short-lived feeling of love for someone; an infatuation. **3** a drink made from the juice of crushed fruit.

– SYNONYMS **crowd,** throng, horde, swarm, press, mob.

– DERIVATIVES **crush·a·ble** adjective **crush·er** noun.
– ORIGIN Old French *cruissir* 'crack.'

crushed vel·vet ▸ **noun** a type of velvet that has its nap pointing in different directions in irregular patches.

crust /krəst/ ▸ **noun 1** the tough outer part of a loaf of bread. **2** a hardened layer or coating on something soft. **3** a layer of pastry covering a pie. **4** the outermost layer of rock of which a planet consists, especially the part of the earth above the mantle. **5** a deposit formed in wine or port aged in the bottle.

– SYNONYMS **covering,** layer, coating, surface, topping, sheet, film, skin, shell, scab.

▸ **verb** form into or cover with a crust.
– ORIGIN Latin *crusta*.

crus·ta·cean /krəˈstāsнən/ ▸ **noun** an animal with a hard outer shell, usually living in water, such as a crab, lobster, or shrimp.
– ORIGIN Latin, from *crusta* 'shell, crust.'

crust·y /ˈkrəstē/ ▸ **adjective** (**crustier, crustiest**) **1** having or consisting of a crust. **2** (of an old person) easily irritated. ▸ **noun** (pl. **crusties**) informal a young person of a group having a shabby appearance and no fixed home.
– DERIVATIVES **crust·i·ness** noun.

crutch /krəcн/ ▸ **noun 1** a long stick with a crosspiece at the top, used as a support by a person who is lame. **2** a person or thing used for support or reassurance. **3** the crotch of the body or a garment.
– ORIGIN Old English.

crux /krəks, kro͝oks/ ▸ **noun** (**the crux**) the most important or difficult part of an issue or problem: *the crux of the matter is whether compensation should be paid.*
– ORIGIN Latin, 'cross.'

cry /krī/ ▸ **verb** (**cries, crying, cried**) **1** shed tears. **2** shout or scream loudly. **3** (of a bird or other animal) make a loud distinctive call. **4** (**cry out for**) be in great need of: *a system that is crying out for fundamental change.*

– SYNONYMS **1 weep,** shed tears, sob, wail, snivel, whimper. informal blubber. **2 call,** shout, exclaim, sing out, yell, bawl, bellow, roar; informal holler.
– ANTONYMS laugh.

▸ **noun** (pl. **cries**) **1** a period of shedding tears. **2** a loud shout or scream. **3** a distinctive call made by a bird or other animal.

– SYNONYMS **call,** shout, exclamation, yell, bawl, bellow, roar; informal holler.

– ORIGIN Old French *crier*.

cry·ba·by /ˈkrī,bābē/ ▸ **noun** (pl. **crybabies**) a person who cries frequently or readily.

cry·ing /ˈkrī-ɪɴɢ/ ▸ **adjective** very great: *it'd be a crying shame if the local bar disappeared.*

cry·o·gen·ics /,krīəˈjeniks/ ▸ **plural noun** (treated as sing.) **1** the branch of physics concerned with the production and effects of very low temperatures. **2** another term for **CRYONICS**.
– DERIVATIVES **cry·o·gen·ic** adjective.
– ORIGIN Greek *kruos* 'frost.'

cry·on·ics /krīˈäniks/ ▸ **plural noun** (treated as sing.) the deep-freezing of the bodies of people who have died of an incurable disease, in the hope of a future cure.
– DERIVATIVES **cry·on·ic** adjective.
– ORIGIN shortened form of **CRYOGENICS**.

cry·o·sur·ger·y /,krīōˈsərjərē/ ▸ **noun** a type of surgery using instruments that freeze and destroy diseased or unwanted tissue.

crypt /kript/ ▸ **noun** an underground room or vault beneath a church, used as a chapel or burial place.

– SYNONYMS **tomb,** vault, burial chamber, sepulcher, catacomb.

– ORIGIN from Greek *kruptos* 'hidden.'

cryp·tic /ˈkriptik/ ▸ **adjective 1** mysterious or obscure in meaning: *a cryptic message.* **2** (of a crossword) having difficult clues that indicate the solutions indirectly. **3** Zoology referring to coloration or markings that camouflage an animal in its natural environment.

– SYNONYMS **enigmatic,** mysterious, mystifying, puzzling, obscure, abstruse, arcane, unintelligible.
– ANTONYMS clear.

– DERIVATIVES **cryp·ti·cal·ly** /-ik(ə)lē/ adverb.
– ORIGIN from Greek *kruptos* 'hidden.'

cryp·to·gram /ˈkriptə,gram/ ▸ **noun** a text written in code.

cryp·tog·ra·phy /kripˈtägrəfē/ ▸ **noun** the art of writing or solving codes.
– DERIVATIVES **cryp·tog·ra·pher** noun **cryp·to·graph·ic** /,kriptəˈgrafik/ adjective.

cryp·tol·o·gy /kripˈtäləjē/ ▸ **noun** the study of codes, or the art of writing and solving them.
– DERIVATIVES **cryp·to·log·i·cal** /,kriptəˈläjikəl/ adjective **cryp·tol·o·gist** noun.

cryp·to·spor·i·di·um /,kriptəspəˈridēəm/ ▸ **noun** (pl. **cryptosporidia** /,kriptəspəˈridēə/) a single-celled parasite found in the intestines of many animals, where it sometimes causes disease.
– ORIGIN from Greek *kruptos* 'hidden' + Latin *sporidium* 'small spore.'

crys·tal /ˈkristl/ ▸ **noun 1** a clear transparent mineral, especially quartz. **2** a piece of a solid substance with a regular internal structure with symmetrically arranged plane faces. **3** very clear glass. ▸ **adjective** clear and transparent: *the crystal waters of the lake.*
– ORIGIN Greek *krustallos* 'ice, crystal.'

crys·tal ball ▸ **noun** a solid globe of glass or rock crystal, used for predicting the future.

crys·tal·line /ˈkristl-in, -tl-,īn, -tl-,ēn/ ▸ **adjective 1** having the structure and form of a crystal. **2** literary very clear.

crys·tal·lize /ˈkristə,līz/ ▸ **verb 1** form crystals. **2** make or become definite and clear: *writing can help to crystallize your thoughts.* **3** (as adj. **crystallized**) (of fruit) coated with and preserved in sugar.
– DERIVATIVES **crys·tal·li·za·tion** /,kristələˈzāsнən/ noun.

crys·tal·log·ra·phy /,kristəˈlägrəfē/ ▸ **noun** the branch of science concerned with the structure and properties of crystals.
– DERIVATIVES **crys·tal·log·ra·pher** noun **crys·tal·lo·graph·ic** /-ləˈgrafik/ adjective.

crys·tal meth /meтн/ ▸ **noun** the crystalline, smokable form of methamphetamine, produced only for illicit use.

Cs ▸ **symbol** the chemical element cesium.

c/s ▸ **abbreviation** cycles per second.

C-sec·tion ▸ **noun** short for **CESAREAN SECTION**.

CS gas ▸ **noun** a powerful form of tear gas used in the control of riots.
– ORIGIN from the initials of the American chemists Ben B. *Corson* and Roger W. *Stoughton*.

CST ▸ **abbreviation** Central Standard Time.

CT ▸ **abbreviation 1** computerized (or computed) tomography. **2** Connecticut.

ct ▸ **abbreviation 1** carat. **2** cent.

CTS ▸ **abbreviation** carpal tunnel syndrome.

Cu ▸ **symbol** the chemical element copper.
– ORIGIN Latin *cuprum*.

cu. ▸ **abbreviation** cubic.

cub /kəb/ ▸ **noun 1** the young of a fox, bear, lion, or other carnivorous mammal. **2** (also **Cub Scout**) a member of the junior branch of the Boy Scouts of America, for boys aged about 7 to 10. ▸ **verb** (**cubs, cubbing, cubbed**) **1** give birth to cubs. **2** hunt fox cubs.
– ORIGIN unknown.

Cu·ban /ˈkyo͞obən/ ▸ **noun** a person from Cuba. ▸ **adjective** relating to Cuba.

cub·by /ˈkəbē/ ▸ **noun** (pl. **cubbies**) a cubbyhole.

cub·by·hole /ˈkəbēˌhōl/ ▸ **noun** a small enclosed space or room.
– ORIGIN from dialect *cub* 'stall, pen, hutch.'

cube /kyo͞ob/ ▸ **noun 1** a symmetrical three-dimensional shape with six equal square faces. **2** the product of a number multiplied by itself twice. ▸ **verb 1** find the cube of a number. **2** cut food into small cube-shaped pieces.
– ORIGIN Greek *kubos*.

cube root ▸ **noun** the number that, when multiplied by itself twice, produces a particular number.

cu·bic /ˈkyo͞obik/ ▸ **adjective 1** having the shape of a cube. **2** referring to a volume equal to that of a cube whose edge is a given unit of length: *a cubic meter*. **3** involving the cube of a number.
– DERIVATIVES **cu·bi·cal** adjective.

cu·bi·cle /ˈkyo͞obikəl/ ▸ **noun** a small area of a room that is partitioned off for privacy.
– ORIGIN Latin *cubiculum* 'bedroom.'

cub·ism /ˈkyo͞oˌbizəm/ ▸ **noun** an early 20th-century style of painting in which objects are represented as being made up of geometric shapes.
– DERIVATIVES **cub·ist** noun & adjective.

cu·bit /ˈkyo͞obit/ ▸ **noun** an ancient measure of length, approximately equal to the length of a forearm.
– ORIGIN Latin *cubitum* 'elbow, forearm.'

cu·boid /ˈkyo͞oˌboid/ ▸ **adjective** having the shape of a cube. ▸ **noun** a solid that has six rectangular faces at right angles to each other.

cub re·port·er ▸ **noun** informal a young or inexperienced newspaper reporter.

cuck·old /ˈkəkəld, -ōld/ ▸ **noun** a man whose wife has committed adultery. ▸ **verb** make a married man a cuckold.
– DERIVATIVES **cuck·old·ry** noun.
– ORIGIN from Old French *cucu* 'cuckoo' (from the cuckoo's habit of laying its egg in another bird's nest).

cuck·oo /ˈko͝oko͞o, ˈko͞oko͞o/ ▸ **noun** a gray or brown bird known for the two-note call of the male and for the habit of laying its eggs in the nests of other birds. ▸ **adjective** informal crazy.
– ORIGIN Old French *cucu*, imitating its call.

cuck·oo clock ▸ **noun** a clock with a mechanical cuckoo that pops out on the hour making a sound like a cuckoo's call.

cuck·oo spit ▸ **noun** whitish froth found in compact masses on leaves and plant stems, produced by the larvae of certain insects.

cu·cum·ber /ˈkyo͞oˌkəmbər/ ▸ **noun** a long green-skinned fruit with watery flesh, eaten raw in salads.
– ORIGIN Latin *cucumis*.

cud /kəd/ ▸ **noun** partly digested food returned from the first stomach of cattle or similar animals to the mouth for further chewing.
– PHRASES **chew the cud** think or talk in a thoughtful way.
– ORIGIN Old English.

cud·dle /ˈkədl/ ▸ **verb 1** hold someone close in one's arms as a way of showing love or affection. **2** (often **cuddle up to**) lie or sit close to someone.

> – SYNONYMS **1 hug,** embrace, clasp, hold in one's arms, caress, pet, fondle; informal canoodle, smooch. **2 snuggle,** nestle, curl, nuzzle.

▸ **noun** an affectionate hug.
– ORIGIN unknown.

cud·dly /ˈkədlē, ˈkədl-ē/ ▸ **adjective** (**cuddlier, cuddliest**) pleasantly soft or plump.

cudg·el /ˈkəjəl/ ▸ **noun** a short thick stick used as a weapon.

> – SYNONYMS **club,** truncheon, bludgeon, mace, blackjack, nightstick, baton; Brit. shillelagh.

▸ **verb** (**cudgels, cudgeling, cudgeled**) beat someone with a cudgel.

> – SYNONYMS **club,** bludgeon, beat, batter, bash.

– PHRASES **take up the cudgels** start to defend or support someone or something strongly.
– ORIGIN Old English.

cue[1] /kyo͞o/ ▸ **noun 1** a signal to an actor to enter or to begin their speech or performance. **2** an action or event that is a signal for someone to do something: *he took her words as a cue to leave*. **3** a facility for playing through an audio or video recording very quickly until a desired point is reached.

> – SYNONYMS **signal,** sign, indication, prompt, reminder.

▸ **verb** (**cues, cueing** or **cuing, cued**) **1** give someone a cue. **2** set a piece of audio or video equipment so that it is ready to play a particular part of a recording.
– PHRASES **on cue** at the right moment.
– ORIGIN unknown.

cue[2] (also **cue stick**) ▸ **noun** a long tapering wooden rod for striking the ball in snooker, billiards, or pool. ▸ **verb** (**cues, cueing** or **cuing, cued**) use a cue to strike the ball.
– ORIGIN variant of **QUEUE**.

cue ball ▸ **noun** the ball that is to be struck with the cue in pool, snooker, billiards, etc.

cue card ▸ **noun** a card held beside a camera for a television broadcaster to read from while appearing to look into the camera.

cuff[1] /kəf/ ▸ **noun 1** the end part of a sleeve, where the material is turned back or a separate band is sewn on. **2** the turned-up end of a trouser leg. **3** (**cuffs**) informal handcuffs.
– PHRASES **off the cuff** informal without previous thought or preparation. [as if from notes jotted on one's shirt cuffs.]
– ORIGIN unknown.

cuff[2] ▸ **verb** hit someone with an open hand, especially on the head. ▸ **noun** a blow given with an open hand.
– ORIGIN unknown.

cuff·link /ˈkəfˌliNGk/ ▸ **noun** a device for fastening together the sides of a shirt cuff.

cui·rass /kwiˈras, kyo͝orˈas/ ▸ **noun** historical a piece of armor covering the chest and the back.
– ORIGIN Old French, from Latin *corium* 'leather.'

cui·sine /kwiˈzēn/ ▶ **noun** a style or method of cooking, especially as characteristic of a particular country or region: *traditional French cuisine*.
– ORIGIN French, 'kitchen.'

cul-de-sac /ˈkəl di ˌsak/ ▶ **noun** (pl. **cul-de-sacs** or **culs-de-sac** pronunc. same) a street or passage closed at one end.
– ORIGIN French, 'bottom of a sack.'

cu·li·nar·y /ˈkələˌnerē, ˈkyo͞olə-/ ▶ **adjective** of or for cooking.
– ORIGIN Latin *culina* 'kitchen.'

cull /kəl/ ▶ **verb 1** slaughter a selected number of a certain kind of animal in order to reduce its population. **2** select or obtain from a large quantity or a variety of sources: *data culled from a number of websites*. ▶ **noun** a selective slaughter of a certain kind of animal: *a seal cull*.
– ORIGIN from Latin *colligere* 'gather together.'

cul·mi·nate /ˈkəlməˌnāt/ ▶ **verb** reach a climax or point of highest development: *the protests culminated in a mass rally at the town hall*.

– SYNONYMS **come to a climax,** come to a head, climax, end, finish, conclude, build up to, lead up to.

– ORIGIN Latin *culminare*, from *culmen* 'summit.'

cul·mi·na·tion /ˌkəlməˈnāshən/ ▶ **noun** the highest or climactic point of something.

– SYNONYMS **climax,** peak, pinnacle, high point, height, summit, zenith, apotheosis, apex, apogee.

cu·lottes /ˈk(y)o͞oˌläts, k(y)o͞oˈläts/ ▶ **plural noun** women's knee-length shorts, cut with very full legs to resemble a skirt.
– ORIGIN French, from *cul* 'rump.'

cul·pa·ble /ˈkəlpəbəl/ ▶ **adjective** deserving blame.

– SYNONYMS **to blame,** guilty, at fault, in the wrong, answerable, accountable, responsible.
– ANTONYMS innocent.

– DERIVATIVES **cul·pa·bil·i·ty** /ˌkəlpəˈbilitē/ noun **cul·pa·bly** /-blē/ adverb.
– ORIGIN from Latin *culpa* 'fault, blame.'

cul·prit /ˈkəlprət, ˈkəlˌprit/ ▶ **noun** a person who is responsible for a crime or offense.

– SYNONYMS **guilty party,** offender, wrongdoer, perpetrator, miscreant, criminal, lawbreaker, felon, delinquent; informal baddy, bad guy, crook, perp.

– ORIGIN perhaps from a misinterpretation of the written abbreviation *cul. prist* for Old French *Culpable: prest d'averrer notre bille* '(You are) guilty: (We are) ready to prove our indictment.'

cult /kəlt/ ▶ **noun 1** a system of religious worship directed toward a particular figure or object. **2** a small religious group regarded by others as strange or as having too great a control over its members. **3** (often before another noun) something popular or fashionable among a particular group of people: *a cult film*.

– SYNONYMS **1 sect,** group, movement. **2 obsession,** fixation, idolization, devotion, worship, veneration.

– DERIVATIVES **cult·ish** adjective **cult·ist** noun.
– ORIGIN Latin *cultus* 'worship.'

cul·ti·var /ˈkəltəˌvär/ ▶ **noun** a plant variety that has been produced by selective breeding.
– ORIGIN blend of **CULTIVATE** and **VARIETY**.

cul·ti·vate /ˈkəltəˌvāt/ ▶ **verb 1** prepare and use land for crops or gardening. **2** grow plants or crops. **3** try to develop or gain a quality or skill: *he cultivated an air of sophistication*. **4** try to win the friendship or support of someone. **5** (as adj. **cultivated**) refined and well educated.

– SYNONYMS **1 farm,** work, till, plow, dig. **2 grow,** raise, rear, tend, plant, sow. **3 woo,** court, curry favor with, ingratiate oneself with; informal get in good with someone. **4 improve,** better, refine, educate, develop, enrich.

– DERIVATIVES **cul·ti·va·ble** /-vəbəl/ adjective **cul·ti·vat·a·ble** /-ˌvātəbəl/ adjective **cul·ti·va·tion** /ˌkəltəˈvāshən/ noun.
– ORIGIN Latin *cultivare*.

cul·ti·va·tor /ˈkəltəˌvātər/ ▶ **noun** a mechanical implement for breaking up the ground.

cul·tur·al /ˈkəlchərəl/ ▶ **adjective 1** relating to the culture of a society. **2** relating to the arts and to intellectual achievements.

– SYNONYMS **1 social,** lifestyle, sociological, anthropological, racial, ethnic. **2 aesthetic,** artistic, intellectual, educational, civilizing.

– DERIVATIVES **cul·tur·al·ly** adverb.

cul·ture /ˈkəlchər/ ▶ **noun 1** the arts and other instances of human intellectual achievement regarded as a whole. **2** a refined understanding or appreciation of this. **3** the art, customs, ideas, and social behavior of a nation, people, or group: *Afro-Caribbean culture*. **4** a preparation of cells or bacteria grown in an artificial medium for scientific study, or the process of growing such cells or bacteria. **5** the growing of plants.

– SYNONYMS **1** *a lover of culture* **the arts,** high art. **2** *a man of culture* **education,** cultivation, enlightenment, discernment, discrimination, taste, refinement, sophistication. **3 civilization,** society, way of life, lifestyle, customs, traditions, heritage, values. **4 philosophy,** ethic, outlook, approach, rationale.

▶ **verb** grow cells or bacteria for scientific study.
– ORIGIN Latin *cultura* 'growing.'

cul·tured /ˈkəlchərd/ ▶ **adjective 1** well educated and able to appreciate art, literature, music, etc. **2** (of a pearl) formed around a foreign body inserted into an oyster.

– SYNONYMS **cultivated,** artistic, enlightened, civilized, educated, well read, learned, discerning, discriminating, refined, sophisticated; informal arty.
– ANTONYMS ignorant.

cul·ture shock ▶ **noun** a feeling of disorientation experienced when someone suddenly comes into contact with an unfamiliar culture or way of life.

cul·ture vul·ture ▶ **noun** informal a person who is very interested in the arts.

cul·vert /ˈkəlvərt/ ▶ **noun** a tunnel carrying a stream or open drain under a road or railroad.
– ORIGIN unknown.

cum /ko͝om, kəm/ ▶ **preposition** combined with; also used as: *a study-cum-bedroom*.
– ORIGIN Latin.

cum·ber·some /ˈkəmbərsəm/ ▶ **adjective 1** large and heavy and so difficult to carry or use. **2** complicated and inefficient or time-consuming: *NATO's cumbersome decision-making processes*.

cum·brous /ˈkəmbrəs/ ▶ **adjective** literary cumbersome.

cum·in /ˈkəmən, ˈk(y)o͞o-/ (also **cummin**) ▶ **noun** the seeds of a plant of the parsley family, used as a spice in cooking.
– ORIGIN Greek *kuminon*.

cum·mer·bund /ˈkəmərˌbənd/ ▶ **noun** a sash worn around the waist, especially as part of a man's formal evening suit.
– ORIGIN Urdu and Persian.

cum·quat /ˈkəmˌkwät/ ▶ **noun** variant spelling of **KUMQUAT**.

cu·mu·late /ˈkyo͞omyəˌlāt/ ▶ **verb** accumulate or be accumulated.
– DERIVATIVES **cu·mu·la·tion** /ˌkyo͞omyəˈlāsʜən/ noun.
– ORIGIN from Latin *cumulus* 'a heap.'

cu·mu·la·tive /ˈkyo͞omyələtiv, -ˌlātiv/ ▶ **adjective** increasing or increased in amount, strength, or effect by successive additions: *the cumulative effect of human activities on the environment.*
– DERIVATIVES **cu·mu·la·tive·ly** adverb.

cu·mu·lo·nim·bus /ˌkyo͞omyəlōˈnimbəs/ ▶ **noun** (pl. **cumulonimbi** /-ˈnimbī, -bē/) cloud forming a towering mass with a flat base, as in thunderstorms.

cu·mu·lus /ˈkyo͞omyələs/ ▶ **noun** (pl. **cumuli** /-ˌlī, -lē/) cloud forming rounded masses heaped on each other above a flat base.
– ORIGIN Latin, 'heap.'

cu·ne·i·form /kyo͞oˈnēəˌfôrm, ˈkyo͞on(ē)ə-/ ▶ **adjective** relating to the wedge-shaped characters used in the ancient writing systems of Mesopotamia, Persia, and Ugarit. ▶ **noun** cuneiform writing.
– ORIGIN from Latin *cuneus* 'wedge.'

cun·ni·lin·gus /ˌkənlˈiɴɢgəs/ ▶ **noun** stimulation of a woman's genitals using the tongue or lips.
– ORIGIN from Latin *cunnus* 'vulva' + *lingere* 'lick.'

cun·ning /ˈkəniɴɢ/ ▶ **adjective 1** skilled in deceiving people to achieve one's aims. **2** ingenious; clever.

> – SYNONYMS **1 crafty,** wily, artful, devious, Machiavellian, sly, scheming, canny, dishonest, deceitful. **2 clever,** shrewd, astute, canny, ingenious, imaginative, enterprising, inventive, resourceful, creative, original, inspired, brilliant.
> – ANTONYMS honest, stupid.

▶ **noun** the ability to achieve things by using deception or cleverness.

> – SYNONYMS **1 guile,** craftiness, deviousness, trickery, duplicity. **2 ingenuity,** imagination, inventiveness, enterprise, resourcefulness.

– DERIVATIVES **cun·ning·ly** adverb.
– ORIGIN perhaps from an Old Norse word meaning 'knowledge.'

cunt /kənt/ ▶ **noun** vulgar slang **1** a woman's genitals. **2** an unpleasant or stupid person.
– ORIGIN Germanic.

cup /kəp/ ▶ **noun 1** a small bowl-shaped container with a handle for drinking from. **2** a cup-shaped trophy with a stem and two handles, awarded as a prize in a contest. **3** a sports contest in which the winner is awarded a cup. **4** a measure of capacity used in cooking, equal to half a US pint (0.237 liter). **5** either of the two parts of a bra shaped to contain or support one breast. **6** a mixed drink made from wine or cider and fruit juice. ▶ **verb** (**cups, cupping, cupped**) **1** form one's hand or hands into the curved shape of a cup. **2** place one's curved hand or hands around something.
– PHRASES **in one's cups** informal drunk. **not one's cup of tea** informal not what one likes or is interested in.
– ORIGIN Latin *cuppa.*

cup·board /ˈkəbərd/ ▶ **noun** a piece of furniture or small recess with a door and usually shelves, used for storage.

cup·cake /ˈkəpˌkāk/ ▶ **noun** a small iced cake baked in a cup-shaped container.

cup·ful /ˈkəpˌfo͝ol/ ▶ **noun 1** the amount held by a cup. **2** (in cooking) the amount a measuring cup will hold: *add two cupfuls of flour.*

Cu·pid /ˈkyo͞opəd/ ▶ **noun 1** Roman Mythology the god of love. **2** (also **cupid**) a picture or statue of a naked winged baby boy with a bow and arrow.

cu·pid·i·ty /kyo͞oˈpiditē/ ▶ **noun** greed for money or possessions.
– ORIGIN from Latin *cupidus* 'desirous.'

Cu·pid's bow ▶ **noun** a pronounced double curve at the top edge of a person's upper lip.

cu·po·la /ˈkyo͞opələ/ ▶ **noun 1** a small rounded dome on or forming a roof. **2** a gun turret.
– ORIGIN Latin *cupula* 'small cask.'

cu·pro·nick·el /ˌk(y)o͞oprōˈnikəl/ ▶ **noun** an alloy of copper and nickel, especially as used in "silver" coins.

cur /kər/ ▶ **noun 1** an aggressive mongrel dog. **2** informal a despicable man.
– ORIGIN perhaps from Old Norse *kurr* 'grumbling.'

cu·ra·çao /ˌk(y)o͝orəˈsō, -ˈsou/ ▶ **noun** (pl. **curaçaos**) a liqueur flavored with bitter oranges.
– ORIGIN named after the Caribbean island of *Curaçao.*

cu·ra·re /k(y)o͝oˈrärē/ ▶ **noun** a paralyzing poison obtained from South American plants.
– ORIGIN Carib.

cu·rate¹ /ˈkyo͝orət, -ˌrāt/ ▶ **noun** a member of the clergy who assists a parish priest.
– ORIGIN from Latin *cura* 'care.'

cu·rate² /ˈkyo͝oˌrāt/ ▶ **verb** select, organize, and look after the items in a collection or exhibition.
– DERIVATIVES **cu·ra·tion** /kyəˈrāsʜən/ noun.
– ORIGIN from **CURATOR**.

cur·a·tive /ˈkyo͝orətiv/ ▶ **adjective** able to cure disease. ▶ **noun** something that is able to cure disease.

cu·ra·tor /ˈkyo͝orˌātər, kyo͝oˈrātər, ˈkyo͝orətər/ ▶ **noun** a keeper of a museum or other collection.

> – SYNONYMS **custodian,** keeper, conservator, guardian, caretaker.

– DERIVATIVES **cu·ra·to·ri·al** /ˌkyo͝orəˈtôrēəl/ adjective.
– ORIGIN from Latin *curare* 'take care of.'

curb /kərb/ ▶ **verb** control or put a limit on: *the new law aims to curb fraud.*

> – SYNONYMS **restrain,** hold back, keep in check, control, rein in, contain; informal keep a lid on.

▶ **noun 1** a stone or concrete edging to a sidewalk or raised path. **2** a control or limit on something. **3** a type of bit with a strap or chain attached that passes under a horse's lower jaw.

> – SYNONYMS **restraint,** restriction, check, brake, control, limit.

– ORIGIN Old French *courber* 'bend.'

curb·side /ˈkərbˌsīd/ ▶ **noun** the side of a road or sidewalk that is nearer to the curb.

curb·stone /ˈkərbˌstōn/ ▶ **noun** a long, narrow stone or concrete block, laid end to end with others to form a curb.

curd /kərd/ (also **curds**) ▶ **noun** a soft, white substance formed when milk coagulates, used to make cheese.
– ORIGIN unknown.

cur·dle /ˈkərdl/ ▶ **verb** (of a liquid) separate into solid and liquid parts.

cure /kyo͝or/ ▶ **verb 1** make a person who is ill well again. **2** end a disease or condition or solve a problem. **3** preserve meat, fish, etc., by salting, drying, or smoking.

– SYNONYMS **1 heal,** restore to health, make well/better. **2 rectify,** remedy, put/set right, right, fix, mend, repair, solve, sort out, eliminate, end. **3 preserve,** smoke, salt, dry, pickle.

▶ **noun 1** something that cures a disease or solves a problem. **2** the healing of a person who is unwell. **3** a Christian minister's area of responsibility.

– SYNONYMS **remedy,** medicine, medication, antidote, treatment, therapy.

– DERIVATIVES **cur·a·ble** adjective **cur·er** noun.
– ORIGIN Latin *cura* 'care.'

cure-all ▶ **noun** a remedy that will supposedly cure any ailment or problem.

cu·ret·tage /ˌkyo͝orəˈtäzн/ ▶ **noun** the use of a curette, especially to scrape material from the lining of the uterus.
– ORIGIN French.

cu·rette /kyo͝oˈret/ ▶ **noun** a small surgical instrument used to scrape away material, especially from the uterus.
– ORIGIN French.

cur·few /ˈkərˌfyo͞o/ ▶ **noun 1** a regulation ordering people to remain indoors between specified hours, typically at night. **2** the time at which a curfew begins.
– ORIGIN first referring to a regulation requiring fires to be put out at a fixed time: from Old French *cuvrir* 'to cover' + *feu* 'fire.'

Cu·ri·a /ˈkyo͝orēə/ ▶ **noun** the papal court at the Vatican, by which the Roman Catholic Church is governed.
– DERIVATIVES **Cu·ri·al** adjective.
– ORIGIN Latin.

cu·rie /kyo͝oˈrē, ˈkyo͝orē/ ▶ **noun** (pl. **curies**) a unit of radioactivity, corresponding to 3.7×10^{10} disintegrations per second.
– ORIGIN named after the French physicists Pierre and Marie *Curie*.

cu·ri·o /ˈkyo͝orēˌō/ ▶ **noun** (pl. **curios**) an object that is interesting because it is rare or unusual.
– ORIGIN from CURIOSITY.

cu·ri·os·i·ty /ˌkyo͝orēˈäsitē/ ▶ **noun** (pl. **curiosities**) **1** a strong desire to know or learn something. **2** an unusual or interesting object or fact.

– SYNONYMS **1 interest,** inquisitiveness, attention, spirit of inquiry; informal nosiness. **2 oddity,** curio, novelty, rarity.

cu·ri·ous /ˈkyo͝orēəs/ ▶ **adjective 1** eager to know or learn something. **2** strange; unusual.

– SYNONYMS **1 intrigued,** interested, eager, inquisitive. **2 strange,** odd, peculiar, funny, unusual, queer, bizarre, weird, eccentric, extraordinary, abnormal, anomalous.
– ANTONYMS uninterested, normal.

– DERIVATIVES **cu·ri·ous·ly** adverb.
– ORIGIN Latin *curiosus* 'careful.'

cu·ri·um /ˈkyo͝orēəm/ ▶ **noun** a radioactive metallic chemical element made by high-energy atomic collisions.
– ORIGIN named after Marie and Pierre *Curie*.

curl /kərl/ ▶ **verb 1** form or cause to form a curved or spiral shape: *her fingers curled around the microphone.* **2** (**curl up**) sit or lie with the knees drawn up. **3** move in a spiral or curved course. **4** play at the game of curling.

– SYNONYMS **spiral,** coil, wreathe, twirl, swirl, wind, curve, twist (and turn), snake, corkscrew, twine, entwine, wrap.

▶ **noun** a thing forming a spiral or coil, especially a lock of hair.

– SYNONYMS **1 ringlet,** corkscrew, kink, lock. **2** *a curl of smoke* **spiral,** coil, twirl, swirl, twist, corkscrew.

– PHRASES **make someone's hair curl** informal shock or horrify someone.
– ORIGIN from Dutch *krul*.

curl·er /ˈkərlər/ ▶ **noun 1** a roller or clasp around which a lock of hair is wrapped to curl it. **2** a player in the game of curling.

cur·lew /ˈkərˌlo͞o, ˈkərlˌyo͞o/ ▶ **noun** (pl. same or **curlews**) a large brown wading bird with a long bill that curves downward.
– ORIGIN Old French *courlieu* (from the bird's call).

curl·i·cue /ˈkərlēˌkyo͞o/ ▶ **noun** a decorative curl or twist.
– ORIGIN from CURLY + CUE[2] (in the sense 'pigtail').

curl·ing /ˈkərlɪɴɢ/ ▶ **noun** a game played on ice, in which large circular flat stones are slid across the surface toward a mark.

curl·ing i·ron ▶ **plural noun** a device incorporating a heated rod around which hair can be wound so as to curl it.

curl·y /ˈkərlē/ ▶ **adjective** (**curlier, curliest**) having curls.

– SYNONYMS **wavy,** curling, curled, frizzy, kinky, corkscrew.
– ANTONYMS straight.

cur·mudg·eon /kərˈməjən/ ▶ **noun** a bad-tempered or surly person.
– DERIVATIVES **cur·mudg·eon·ly** adjective.
– ORIGIN unknown.

cur·rant /ˈkərənt, ˈkə-rənt/ ▶ **noun 1** a dried fruit made from a small seedless variety of grape. **2** a shrub producing small edible black, red, or white berries.
– ORIGIN from Old French *raisins de Corauntz* 'grapes of Corinth.'

cur·ren·cy /ˈkərənsē, ˈkə-rənsē/ ▶ **noun** (pl. **currencies**) **1** a system of money in general use in a country. **2** the fact or quality or period of being accepted or in use: *this minority view has now gained currency.*

– SYNONYMS **1 money,** legal tender, cash, banknotes, notes, bills, coins. **2 popularity,** circulation, exposure, acceptance, prevalence.

cur·rent /ˈkərənt, ˈkə-rənt/ ▶ **adjective 1** happening or being used or done now: *current events.* **2** in common or general use: *the other meaning of the word is still current.*

– SYNONYMS **1 contemporary,** present-day, modern, topical, live, burning. **2 prevalent,** common, accepted, in circulation, popular, widespread. **3 valid,** usable, up to date. **4 incumbent,** present, in office, in power, reigning.
– ANTONYMS past, former.

▶ **noun 1** a body of water or air moving in a definite direction through a surrounding body of water or air. **2** a flow of electrically charged particles.

– SYNONYMS **1 flow,** stream, draft, jet, tide. **2 course,** progress, progression, flow, tide, movement.

– ORIGIN from Latin *currere* 'run.'

USAGE

Do not confuse **current** with **currant**. **Current** means 'happening now' (*current events*) or 'a flow of water, air, or electricity' (*strong ocean currents*), whereas **currant** means 'a dried grape.'

cur·rent as·sets ▸ **plural noun** cash and other assets that are expected to be converted to cash within a year. Compare with **FIXED ASSETS.**

cur·rent·ly /'kərəntlē, 'kə-rəntlē / ▸ **adverb** at the present time.

cur·ric·u·lum /kə'rikyələm/ ▸ **noun** (pl. **curricula** /-lə/ or **curriculums**) the subjects comprising a course of study in a school or college.
– DERIVATIVES **cur·ric·u·lar** /-lər/ adjective.
– ORIGIN Latin, 'course, racing chariot.'

cur·ric·u·lum vi·tae /kə'rik(y)ələm 'vē,tī, 'vītē/ ▸ **noun** (pl. **curricula vitae** /kə'rik(y)ələ/) a résumé.
– ORIGIN Latin, 'course of life.'

cur·ry[1] /'kərē, 'kə-rē/ ▸ **noun** (pl. **curries**) a dish of meat, vegetables, or fish, cooked in a hot, spicy sauce of Indian origin. ▸ **verb** (**curries, currying, curried**) prepare or flavor food with a spicy sauce.
– ORIGIN Tamil.

cur·ry[2] ▸ **verb** (**curries, currying, curried**) **1** groom a horse with a curry comb. **2** historical treat tanned leather to improve its properties.
– PHRASES **curry favor** try to gain favor by flattery and servile behavior. [from the name (*Favel*) of a horse in a medieval French story who became a symbol of cunning; hence 'to rub down Favel' meant to use cunning.]
– ORIGIN Old French *correier*.

cur·ry comb ▸ **noun** a hand-held device with serrated ridges, used for grooming horses.

cur·ry pow·der ▸ **noun** a mixture of finely ground spices, such as turmeric and coriander, used for making curry.

curse /kərs/ ▸ **noun 1** an appeal to a supernatural power to harm someone or something. **2** a cause of harm or misery: *the disease became the curse of cotton workers.* **3** an offensive word or phrase used to express anger or annoyance.

> – SYNONYMS **1 jinx,** malediction, hex; formal imprecation, anathema. **2 affliction,** burden, misery, ordeal, evil, scourge. **3 swear word,** expletive, oath, profanity, four-letter word, dirty word, obscenity; informal cuss word.

▸ **verb 1** use a curse against someone. **2** (**be cursed with**) be continually affected by something bad: *I'm cursed with a slow metabolism*. **3** say offensive words; swear.

> – SYNONYMS **1 afflict,** trouble, plague, bedevil. **2 swear,** take the Lord's name in vain, blaspheme; informal cuss.

– ORIGIN Old English.

curs·ed /'kərsid, kərst/ ▸ **adjective** informal, dated used to express annoyance or irritation.

> – SYNONYMS **damned,** doomed, ill-fated, ill-starred, jinxed.

cur·sive /'kərsiv/ ▸ **adjective** (of writing) written with the characters joined.
– ORIGIN Latin *cursivus*.

cur·sor /'kərsər/ ▸ **noun 1** a movable indicator on a computer screen identifying the point that will be affected by input from the user. **2** the sliding part engraved with a hairline used to locate points on a slide rule.
– ORIGIN Latin, 'runner.'

cur·so·ry /'kərsərē/ ▸ **adjective** hasty and therefore not thorough.

> – SYNONYMS **brief,** hasty, hurried, quick, rapid, passing, perfunctory, desultory, casual.
> – ANTONYMS thorough.

– DERIVATIVES **cur·so·ri·ly** /'kərsərəlē/ adverb.

> **WORD TOOLKIT**
>
> See **INCOMPLETE**.

curt /kərt/ ▸ **adjective** so brief or abrupt as to be rude.

> – SYNONYMS **terse,** brusque, snappish, abrupt, clipped, blunt, short, sharp, rude, ungracious.
> – ANTONYMS expansive.

– DERIVATIVES **curt·ly** adverb **curt·ness** noun.
– ORIGIN Latin *curtus* 'cut short.'

> **CHOOSE THE RIGHT WORD**
>
> See **BRUSQUE**.

cur·tail /kər'tāl/ ▸ **verb** limit or cut short: *we would not wish to curtail freedom of speech.*

> – SYNONYMS **reduce,** shorten, cut, cut down, decrease, trim, restrict, limit, curb, rein in, cut short, truncate; informal slash.
> – ANTONYMS increase, extend.

– DERIVATIVES **cur·tail·ment** noun.
– ORIGIN French *courtault* 'horse with a docked tail.'

cur·tain /'kərtn/ ▸ **noun 1** a piece of material suspended at the top to form a screen, hung at a window in pairs or between the stage and auditorium of a theater. **2** (**the curtain**) the rise or fall of a stage curtain between acts or scenes. **3** (**curtains**) informal a disastrous outcome. ▸ **verb** provide or screen something with a curtain or curtains.
– ORIGIN Latin *cortina*.

cur·tain call ▸ **noun** the appearance of one or more performers on stage after a performance to acknowledge the audience's applause.

cur·tain-rais·er ▸ **noun** an event happening just before a longer or more important one.

cur·tain wall ▸ **noun 1** a fortified wall around a medieval castle, typically one linking towers together. **2** a wall that encloses the space within a building but does not support the roof.

curt·sy /'kərtsē/ (also **curtsey**) ▸ **noun** (pl. **curtsies** or **curtseys**) a woman's or girl's respectful greeting, made by bending the knees with one foot in front of the other. ▸ **verb** (**curtsies, curtsying, curtsied**; also **curtseys, curtseying, curtseyed**) perform a curtsy.
– ORIGIN variant of **COURTESY**.

cur·va·ceous /kər'vāsʜəs/ ▸ **adjective** (especially of a woman or a woman's figure) having an attractively curved shape.

cur·va·ture /'kərvəcʜər, -,cʜo͝or/ ▸ **noun** the fact of being curved or the degree to which something is curved: *at that level the curvature of the earth is visible*.

curve /kərv/ ▸ **noun 1** a line or outline that gradually bends. **2** a line on a graph showing how one quantity varies with respect to another.

> – SYNONYMS **bend,** turn, loop, arc, arch, bow, curvature.

▸ **verb** form or move in a curve: *the path curved around the house.*

> – SYNONYMS **1 bend,** turn, loop, wind, meander, snake, arc, arch. **2** (as adj. **curved**) *birds with long curved bills* **bent,** arched, bowed, rounded, crescent.

– ORIGIN from Latin *curvus* 'bent.'

cur·vi·lin·e·ar /ˌkərvəˈlinēər/ ▶ **adjective** contained by or consisting of a curved line or lines.

curv·y /ˈkərvē/ ▶ **adjective** (**curvier, curviest**) **1** having many curves. **2** informal (of a woman's figure) curvaceous.
– DERIVATIVES **curv·i·ness** noun.

cush·ion /ˈko͝osHən/ ▶ **noun 1** a bag of cloth stuffed with soft material, used as a comfortable support for sitting or leaning on. **2** a means of protection against impact or something unpleasant. **3** the elastic lining of the sides of a billiard table, from which the ball rebounds.

– SYNONYMS *a cushion against inflation* **protection,** buffer, shield, defense, bulwark.

▶ **verb 1** soften the effect of an impact on someone or something. **2** lessen the adverse effects of: *he presented her with a gift to cushion the shock.*

– SYNONYMS **1** *cushioned from the outside world* **protect,** shield, shelter, cocoon. **2** *cushion the blow* **soften,** lessen, diminish, mitigate, alleviate, take the edge off, dull, deaden.

– ORIGIN Old French *cuissin.*

cush·y /ˈko͝osHē/ ▶ **adjective** (**cushier, cushiest**) informal (of a task or situation) easy and undemanding.
– ORIGIN from Urdu, 'pleasure.'

cusp /kəsp/ ▶ **noun 1** a pointed end where two curves meet, such as each of the ends of a crescent moon. **2** a cone-shaped projection on a tooth. **3** the initial point of an astrological sign or house. **4** a point of transition between two different states: *those on the cusp of adulthood.*
– DERIVATIVES **cusped** adjective.
– ORIGIN Latin *cuspis* 'point or apex.'

cuss /kəs/ informal ▶ **noun** an annoying or stubborn person or animal. ▶ **verb** swear or curse.

cuss·ed /ˈkəsəd/ ▶ **adjective** informal awkward; annoying.
– DERIVATIVES **cuss·ed·ness** noun.

cuss word ▶ **noun** a swear word.

cus·tard /ˈkəstərd/ ▶ **noun** a boiled or baked dessert made with milk, eggs, and sugar.
– ORIGIN first referring to a pie containing meat or fruit in a sauce thickened with eggs: from Old French *crouste* 'crust.'

cus·tard ap·ple ▶ **noun** a large fleshy, tropical fruit with a sweet yellow pulp.

cus·tard pie ▶ **noun** an open pie containing cold set custard, or a similar container of foam, as thrown in slapstick comedy.

cus·to·di·an /kəsˈtōdēən/ ▶ **noun 1** a person who has responsibility for or looks after something. **2** a janitor.

cus·to·dy /ˈkəstədē/ ▶ **noun 1** protective care of someone or something. **2** Law parental responsibility, especially as allocated to one of two parents who are getting divorced. **3** imprisonment, especially while waiting for trial.

– SYNONYMS **1 care,** guardianship, charge, supervision, safekeeping, responsibility, protection. **2** *the carjacker is in custody* **imprisonment,** detention, confinement, incarceration.

– DERIVATIVES **cus·to·di·al** /ˌkəˈstōdēəl/ adjective.
– ORIGIN from Latin *custos* 'guardian.'

cus·tom /ˈkəstəm/ ▶ **noun 1** a traditional way of behaving or doing something that is specific to a particular society, place, or time. **2** a thing that a person often does; a habit: *it was my custom to nap for an hour every day.*

– SYNONYMS **1** *local customs* **tradition,** practice, usage, way, convention, formality, ritual, mores. **2** *it was his custom to sleep in a chair* **habit,** practice, routine, way; formal wont.

– ORIGIN Old French *coustume.*

cus·tom·ar·y /ˈkəstəˌmerē/ ▶ **adjective** in accordance with custom; usual.

– SYNONYMS **usual,** traditional, normal, conventional, habitual, familiar, accepted, accustomed, routine, established, time-honored, prevailing.
– ANTONYMS unusual.

– DERIVATIVES **cus·tom·ar·i·ly** adverb.

cus·tom·er /ˈkəstəmər/ ▶ **noun 1** a person who buys goods or services from a store or business. **2** a person of a specified kind that one has to deal with: *he's a tough customer.*

– SYNONYMS **consumer,** buyer, purchaser, patron, client, shopper.

cus·tom house (also **customs house**) ▶ **noun** chiefly historical the office at a port or frontier where customs duty is collected.

cus·tom·ize /ˈkəstəˌmīz/ ▶ **verb** modify to suit a particular person or task: *food manufacturers customize products for restaurant chains.*
– DERIVATIVES **cus·tom·iz·a·ble** adjective **cus·tom·i·za·tion** /ˌkəstəməˈzāsHən/ noun.

cus·tom-made (also **custom-built**) ▶ **adjective** made to a particular customer's order.

cus·toms /ˈkəstəmz/ ▶ **plural noun 1** the duties charged by a government on imported goods. **2** the official department that administers and collects such duties.

cut /kət/ ▶ **verb** (**cuts, cutting, cut**) **1** make an opening, incision, or wound in something with a sharp implement. **2** make, shorten, remove, or divide with a sharp implement: *I cut his photo out of the paper.* **3** (as adj. **cut**) make or design a garment in a particular way: *an impeccably cut suit.* **4** reduce the amount or quantity of something. **5** end or interrupt the provision of a supply. **6** go across or through: *is it illegal to cut across a highway on foot?* **7** stop filming or recording. **8** move to another shot in a movie. **9** make a sound recording. **10** divide a deck of playing cards by lifting a portion from the top. **11** mix an illegal drug with another substance.

– SYNONYMS **1 gash,** slash, lacerate, slit, wound, scratch, graze, nick. **2 slice,** chop, dice, cube, carve, hash. **3 carve,** engrave, incise, etch, score, chisel, whittle. **4 reduce,** cut back/down on, decrease, lessen, mark down, discount, lower; informal slash. **5 shorten,** abridge, condense, abbreviate, truncate, edit, censor. **6 delete,** remove, take out, excise.

▶ **noun 1** an act of cutting. **2** a result of cutting: *a cut on his jaw.* **3** a reduction in amount or size. **4** the style in which a garment or the hair is cut: *the elegant cut of his jacket.* **5** a piece of meat cut from a carcass. **6** informal a share of profits. **7** a version of a movie after editing: *the director's cut.*

– SYNONYMS **1 gash,** slash, laceration, incision, wound, scratch, graze, nick. **2 piece,** joint, fillet, section. **3 share,** portion, quota, percentage; informal slice (of the cake). **4 reduction,** cutback, rollback, decrease, lessening. **5 style,** design, line, fit.

– PHRASES **be cut from the same cloth** be of the same

nature. **be cut out for** (or **to be**) informal have exactly the right qualities for a particular role. **a cut above** informal noticeably better than. **cut and dried** (of a situation) completely settled. **cut and paste** (on a word processor or computer) move an item from one part of a file to another. **cut and run** informal hastily leave a difficult situation rather than deal with it. **cut and thrust** a spirited and rapid interchange of views. **cut both ways** **1** (of a point) serve both sides of an argument. **2** have both good and bad effects. **cut corners** do something with a lack of thoroughness to save time or money. **cut someone dead** completely ignore someone. **cut in** **1** interrupt someone. **2** pull in too closely in front of another vehicle after overtaking. **3** move ahead of one's proper place in a line of people. **4** (of a machine) begin operating automatically. **cut someone in** informal include someone in a deal and give them a share of the profits. **cut it out** informal stop it. **cut the mustard** informal reach the required standard. **cut no ice** informal have no influence or effect. **cut someone/thing off** **1** block the usual means of access to a place. **2** deprive someone of a supply of power, water, etc. **3** break a telephone connection with someone. **4** disinherit someone. **cut out** (of an engine) suddenly stop operating. **cut someone out** exclude someone. **cut one's teeth** gain initial experience of an activity. **cut a tooth** (of a baby) have a tooth appear through the gum. **cut someone up** informal (of a driver) overtake someone and pull in too closely. **make the cut** reach a certain standard, especially one that allows you into the final round of a competition.
– ORIGIN probably Germanic.

cu·ta·ne·ous /kyo͞oˈtānēəs/ ▶ **adjective** relating to or affecting the skin.
– ORIGIN from Latin *cutis* 'skin.'

cut·a·way /ˈkətəˌwā/ ▶ **adjective** **1** (of a coat or jacket) having the front cut away below the waist. **2** (of a diagram of an object) having some external parts left out to reveal the interior.

cut·back /ˈkətˌbak/ ▶ **noun** a reduction, especially in expenditure.

– SYNONYMS **reduction,** cut, rollback, decrease, economy, saving.
– ANTONYMS increase.

cute /kyo͞ot/ ▶ **adjective** **1** attractive in a charming or sweet way. **2** informal sexually attractive. **3** informal clever; shrewd.

– SYNONYMS **endearing,** adorable, lovable, sweet, lovely, appealing, engaging, delightful, dear.

– DERIVATIVES **cute·ly** adverb **cute·ness** noun.
– ORIGIN shortening of ACUTE.

cute·sy /ˈkyo͞otsē/ ▶ **adjective** informal excessively charming or sweet.

cut glass ▶ **noun** glass with decorative patterns cut into it. ▶ **adjective** (of a person's accent) characterized by very precise pronunciation.

cu·ti·cle /ˈkyo͞otikəl/ ▶ **noun** **1** the dead skin at the base of a fingernail or toenail. **2** the outer cellular layer of a hair. **3** the epidermis of the body.
– ORIGIN from Latin *cuticula* 'little skin.'

cut·ie /ˈkyo͞otē/ ▶ **noun** an attractive or endearing person.

cut·lass /ˈkətləs/ ▶ **noun** a short sword with a slightly curved blade, formerly used by sailors.
– ORIGIN Latin *cultellus* 'little knife.'

cut·ler /ˈkətlər/ ▶ **noun** a person who makes or sells cutlery.
– ORIGIN from Latin *cultellus* 'little knife.'

cut·ler·y /ˈkətlərē/ ▶ **noun** knives, forks, and spoons used for eating or serving food.

cut·let /ˈkətlət/ ▶ **noun** **1** a portion of sliced meat, coated in breadcrumbs and served either grilled or fried. **2** a flat cake of chopped meat, covered in breadcrumbs and shaped like a veal chop.
– ORIGIN French *côtelette*.

cut·off /ˈkətˌôf/ ▶ **noun** **1** (usu. before another noun) a point or level marking a limit: *May 21 is the official cutoff date.* **2** a device for interrupting a power or fuel supply. **3** (**cutoffs**) shorts made by cutting off the legs of a pair of jeans.

cut·out /ˈkətˌout/ ▶ **noun** **1** a shape cut out of board or paper. **2** a hole cut for decoration or for something to be inserted. **3** a device that automatically breaks an electric circuit for safety.

cut·purse /ˈkətˌpərs/ ▶ **noun** old use a pickpocket.
– ORIGIN from the former practice of stealing purses by cutting them from a waistband.

cut-rate (also **cut-price**) ▶ **adjective** for sale at a reduced price; cheap.

cut·ter /ˈkətər/ ▶ **noun** **1** a person or thing that cuts something. **2** a light, fast patrol boat or sailboat.

cut·throat /ˈkətˌTHrōt/ ▶ **adjective** fierce and ruthless: *an unforgiving, cutthroat business.* ▶ **noun** dated a murderer or other violent criminal.

cut·ting /ˈkətiNG/ ▶ **noun** **1** a piece cut off from something, such as a piece cut from a plant for propagation. **2** an open passage dug out through higher ground for a railroad, road, or canal.

– SYNONYMS **clipping,** article, piece, column, paragraph.

▶ **adjective** **1** capable of cutting. **2** (of a remark) hurtful.

– SYNONYMS **hurtful,** wounding, barbed, sharp, scathing, caustic, sarcastic, snide, spiteful, malicious, vicious, cruel; informal bitchy.

– DERIVATIVES **cut·ting·ly** adverb.

cut·ting edge ▶ **noun** the latest or most advanced stage; the forefront. ▶ **adjective** (**cutting-edge**) innovative; pioneering.

cut·tle·fish /ˈkətlˌfiSH/ ▶ **noun** (pl. same or **cuttlefishes**) a squidlike marine mollusk that squirts out a black liquid when attacked.
– ORIGIN Old English.

cut up ▶ **adjective** informal (of a person) very distressed: *his girlfriend is dying and he's really cut up about it.* ▶ **noun** **1** a film or sound recording made by cutting and editing material from preexisting recordings. **2** (**cutup**) informal a person who is fond of making jokes or playing pranks.

cut·worm /ˈkətˌwərm/ ▶ **noun** a moth caterpillar that lives in the upper layers of the soil and eats through the stems of young plants at ground level.

cu·vée /k(y)o͞oˈvā/ ▶ **noun** a type, blend, or batch of wine, especially champagne.
– ORIGIN French, 'vatful.'

cuz /kəz/ ▶ **conjunction** informal short for BECAUSE.

CV ▶ **abbreviation** curriculum vitae.

CVS ▶ **abbreviation** chorionic villus sampling, a test made in early pregnancy to detect fetal abnormalities.

cwm /ko͞om/ ▶ **noun** (chiefly in Wales) a steep-sided hollow at the head of a valley or on a mountainside.
– ORIGIN Welsh.

cwt ▸ abbreviation hundredweight.
– ORIGIN from Latin *centum* 'a hundred.'

cy·an /ˈsīˌan, ˈsīən/ ▸ noun a greenish-blue color that is one of the primary colors.
– ORIGIN Greek *kuaneos* 'dark blue.'

cy·a·nide /ˈsīəˌnīd/ ▸ noun a highly poisonous compound containing a metal combined with carbon and nitrogen atoms.

cy·a·no·bac·te·ri·a /ˌsīənōbakˈtirēə, sīˌanō-/ ▸ plural noun microorganisms that are related to bacteria but capable of photosynthesis; blue-green algae.

cy·a·no·co·bal·a·min /ˌsīənōˌkōˈbaləmin, sīˌanō-/ ▸ noun vitamin B_{12}, found in liver, fish, and eggs, a deficiency of which can cause pernicious anemia.
– ORIGIN from Greek *kuanos* 'dark blue' + a blend of **COBALT** and **VITAMIN**.

cy·a·no·gen /sīˈanəjən/ ▸ noun a highly poisonous gas.
– ORIGIN from Greek *kuanos* 'dark blue mineral' (because it is a constituent of Prussian blue).

cy·a·no·sis /ˌsīəˈnōsəs/ ▸ noun a bluish discoloration of the skin due to poor circulation or inadequate oxygenation of the blood.
– DERIVATIVES **cy·a·not·ic** /ˌsīəˈnätik/ adjective.
– ORIGIN Greek *kuanōsis* 'blueness.'

cyber- ▸ combining form relating to information technology, the Internet, and virtual reality: *cyberspace*.
– ORIGIN from **CYBERNETICS**.

cy·ber·ca·fe /ˌsībərkaˈfā/ ▸ noun a cafe where customers can also use computer terminals and access the Internet.

cy·ber·crime /ˈsībərˌkrīm/ ▸ noun criminal activities carried out by means of computers or the Internet.
– DERIVATIVES **cy·ber·crim·i·nal** /ˈsībərˌkrimənl/ noun.

cy·ber·net·ics /ˌsībərˈnetiks/ ▸ plural noun (treated as sing.) the science of communications and automatic control systems in both machines and living things.
– DERIVATIVES **cy·ber·net·ic** adjective.
– ORIGIN from Greek *kubernētēs* 'steersman.'

cy·ber·punk /ˈsībərˌpəNGk/ ▸ noun a type of science fiction set in a lawless subculture of an oppressive society dominated by computer technology.

cy·ber·space /ˈsībərˌspās/ ▸ noun the hypothetical environment in which communication over computer networks occurs.

cy·ber·squat·ting /ˈsībərˌskwätiNG/ ▸ noun the practice of registering an Internet domain name that a company or organization may later want for itself, in the hope of selling it back to them at a profit.
– DERIVATIVES **cy·ber·squat·ter** noun.

cy·ber·stalk·ing /ˈsībərˌstôkiNG/ ▸ noun the repeated use of electronic communications to harass or frighten someone, for example by sending threatening emails.
– DERIVATIVES **cy·ber·stalk·er** noun.

cy·ber·ter·ror·ism /ˌsībərˈterəˌrizəm/ ▸ noun the use of computers to cause severe disruption or widespread fear in the attempt to achieve a political aim.
– DERIVATIVES **cy·ber·ter·ror·ist** noun.

cy·borg /ˈsīˌbôrg/ ▸ noun (in science fiction) a person having mechanical elements built into the body to extend their normal physical abilities.
– ORIGIN blend of **CYBER-** and **ORGANISM**.

cy·brid /ˈsīˌbrid/ ▸ noun Microbiology a hybrid cell produced artificially by the fusion of two cells, one of which lacks a nucleus.

cy·cad /ˈsīkəd, ˈsīˌkad/ ▸ noun a tall, cone-bearing, palmlike plant of warm regions.
– ORIGIN Latin.

cy·cla·men /ˈsīkləmən, ˈsik-/ ▸ noun (pl. same or **cyclamens**) a plant having pink, red, or white flowers with backward-curving petals.
– ORIGIN Greek *kuklaminos*.

cy·cle /ˈsīkəl/ ▸ noun **1** a series of events that are regularly repeated in the same order: *the cycle of growth and harvest*. **2** a complete sequence of changes associated with a recurring phenomenon such as an alternating electric current. **3** a bicycle. **4** a series of musical or literary works composed around a particular theme.

– SYNONYMS **1** *the cycle of birth, death, and rebirth* **circle,** round, pattern, rhythm, loop. **2** *a cycle of three plays* **series,** sequence, set, succession, run.

▸ verb **1** ride a bicycle. **2** follow a repeated sequence of events: *on the laptop this message cycles every few seconds*.
– ORIGIN Greek *kuklos* 'circle.'

cy·clic /ˈsīklik, ˈsik-/ ▸ adjective **1** occurring in cycles: *the cyclic rotation of the earth and moon*. **2** having a molecular structure containing one or more closed rings of atoms.
– DERIVATIVES **cy·cli·cal** adjective **cy·cli·cal·ly** /-ik(ə)lē/ adverb.

cy·clist /ˈsīk(ə)list/ ▸ noun a person who rides a bicycle.

cy·clone /ˈsīˌklōn/ ▸ noun **1** a system of winds rotating inward to an area of low barometric pressure; a depression. **2** a tropical storm.
– DERIVATIVES **cy·clon·ic** /sīˈklänik/ adjective.
– ORIGIN probably from Greek *kuklōma* 'wheel, coil of a snake.'

cy·clo·pe·an /ˌsīkləˈpēən, sīˈklōpēən/ ▸ adjective **1** relating to or resembling a Cyclops. **2** made with massive irregular stone blocks: *cyclopean walls*.

cy·clo·pe·di·a /ˌsīkləˈpēdēə/ (also **cyclopaedia**) ▸ noun (in book titles) an encyclopedia.

Cy·clops /ˈsīˌkläps/ ▸ noun (pl. same) Greek Mythology a member of a race of savage giants with only one eye.
– ORIGIN from Greek *Kuklōps* 'round-eyed.'

cy·clo·tron /ˈsīkləˌträn/ ▸ noun a piece of equipment for accelerating charged atomic and subatomic particles by making them move spirally in a magnetic field.

cyg·net /ˈsignət/ ▸ noun a young swan.
– ORIGIN Greek *kuknos* 'swan.'

cyl·in·der /ˈsiləndər/ ▸ noun **1** a three-dimensional shape with straight parallel sides and a circular or oval cross section. **2** a piston chamber in a steam or internal combustion engine. **3** a cylindrical container for liquefied gas under pressure.
– ORIGIN Greek *kulindros* 'roller.'

cyl·in·der head ▸ noun the end cover of a cylinder in an internal combustion engine, against which the piston compresses the cylinder's contents.

cy·lin·dri·cal /səˈlindrikəl/ ▸ adjective having the shape of a cylinder.
– DERIVATIVES **cy·lin·dri·cal·ly** /səˈlindrik(ə)lē/ adverb.

cym·bal /ˈsimbəl/ ▸ noun a musical instrument consisting of a slightly concave round brass plate that is either struck against another one or hit with a stick.
– ORIGIN Greek *kumbalon*.

cyme /sīm/ ▸ noun a flower cluster with a central stem bearing a single flower on the end that develops first. Compare with **RACEME**.
– ORIGIN Latin *cyma* 'summit.'

Cym·ric /ˈkəmrik/ ▸ **adjective** (of language or culture) Welsh. ▸ **noun** the Welsh language.
– ORIGIN from Welsh *Cymru* 'Wales.'

cyn·ic /ˈsinik/ ▸ **noun 1** a person who believes that people are motivated purely by self-interest. **2** a person who raises doubts about something; a skeptic. **3** (**Cynic**) (in ancient Greece) a member of a school of philosophers who despised wealth and pleasure.

– SYNONYMS **skeptic,** doubter, doubting Thomas, pessimist, prophet of doom.
– ANTONYMS idealist, optimist.

– DERIVATIVES **cyn·i·cism** noun.
– ORIGIN Greek *kunikos.*

cyn·i·cal /ˈsinikəl/ ▸ **adjective 1** believing that people always act from selfish motives. **2** proceeding from self-interest, regardless of accepted standards: *a cynical disregard for safety.* **3** doubtful; skeptical: *young people are very cynical about advertising.* **4** contemptuous; mocking.

– SYNONYMS **skeptical,** doubtful, distrustful, suspicious, disbelieving, pessimistic, negative, world-weary, disillusioned, disenchanted, jaundiced.
– ANTONYMS idealistic, optimistic.

– DERIVATIVES **cyn·i·cal·ly** adverb.

cy·no·sure /ˈsīnəˌsHo͝or, ˈsin-/ ▸ **noun** a person or thing that is the center of attention or admiration.
– ORIGIN Greek *kunosoura* 'dog's tail,' also 'Ursa Minor' (the constellation contains the pole star, used as a guide by sailors).

cy·pher ▸ **noun** variant spelling of **CIPHER**.

cy·press /ˈsīprəs/ ▸ **noun** an evergreen coniferous tree with small dark green leaves.
– ORIGIN Greek *kuparissos.*

Cyp·ri·ot /ˈsiprēət, -ˌät/ ▸ **noun 1** a person from Cyprus. **2** the dialect of Greek used in Cyprus. ▸ **adjective** relating to Cyprus.

Cy·ril·lic /səˈrilik/ ▸ **adjective** referring to the alphabet used for Russian, Ukrainian, Bulgarian, Serbian, and some other Slavic languages. ▸ **noun** the Cyrillic alphabet.
– ORIGIN named after the 9th-century Greek missionary St. *Cyril.*

cyst /sist/ ▸ **noun 1** a thin-walled abnormal sac or cavity in the body, containing fluid. **2** a sac or bladder containing liquid in an animal or plant.
– ORIGIN Greek *kustis* 'bladder.'

cys·tic /ˈsistik/ ▸ **adjective 1** relating to cysts. **2** relating to the urinary bladder or the gallbladder.

cys·tic fi·bro·sis ▸ **noun** an inherited disease in which the production of abnormally thick mucus leads to the blockage of the pancreatic ducts, intestines, and bronchi.

cys·ti·tis /sisˈtītis/ ▸ **noun** inflammation of the urinary bladder, typically caused by infection and accompanied by frequent painful urination.

cy·tol·o·gy /sīˈtäləjē/ ▸ **noun** the branch of biology concerned with the structure and function of plant and animal cells.
– DERIVATIVES **cy·to·log·i·cal** /ˌsītlˈäjikəl/ adjective **cy·tol·o·gist** noun.

cy·to·meg·a·lo·vi·rus /ˌsītəˌmegəlōˈvīrəs/ ▸ **noun** a kind of herpesvirus that usually produces very mild symptoms in an infected person but may cause severe neurological damage in people with weakened immune systems and in the newborn.

cy·to·plasm /ˈsītəˌplazəm/ ▸ **noun** the material or protoplasm within a living cell, excluding the nucleus.
– DERIVATIVES **cy·to·plas·mic** /ˌsītəˈplazmik/ adjective.

czar /zär, (t)sär/ (etc.) ▸ **noun 1** variant spelling of **TSAR**. **2** a person with great authority or power in a particular area: *the government's new drug czar.*

Czech /cHek/ ▸ **noun 1** a person from the Czech Republic or (formerly) Czechoslovakia. **2** the Slavic language spoken in the Czech Republic. ▸ **adjective** relating to the Czech Republic.

Czech·o·slo·vak /ˌcHekəˈslōˌväk, -ˌvak/ (also **Czechoslovakian** /ˌcHekəsləˈväkēən, -ˈvakēən/) ▸ **noun** a person from the former country of Czechoslovakia, now divided between the Czech Republic and Slovakia. ▸ **adjective** relating to the former country of Czechoslovakia.

Dd

D¹ (also **d**) ▶ **noun** (pl. **Ds** or **D's**) **1** the fourth letter of the alphabet. **2** referring to the fourth item in a set. **3** Music the second note of the scale of C major. **4** the Roman numeral for 500.

D² ▶ **abbreviation 1** Democrat or Democratic. **2** depth (in the sense of the dimension of an object from front to back). **3** (with a numeral) dimension(s) or dimensional. **4** a dry cell battery of a size commonly used in flashlights and portable televisions. **5** (in tables of sports results) drawn.

d ▶ **abbreviation 1** (in genealogies) daughter. **2** deci-. **3** (in travel timetables) departs. **4** (**d.**) died (used to indicate a date of death).

'd ▶ **contraction 1** had. **2** would.

D & X ▶ **abbreviation** dilation and extraction, a method of performing late-term abortions.

DA ▶ **abbreviation** district attorney.

D/A ▶ **abbreviation** Electronics digital to analog.

DAB ▶ **abbreviation** digital audio broadcasting.

dab¹ /dab/ ▶ **verb** (**dabs, dabbing, dabbed**) **1** press something lightly with a cloth or sponge. **2** apply a substance with light quick strokes.

– SYNONYMS **pat,** press, touch, blot, swab, daub, wipe.

▶ **noun** a small amount of a substance lightly applied.

– SYNONYMS **drop,** spot, smear, splash, bit.

– ORIGIN representing a light striking movement.

dab² ▶ **noun** a small North Atlantic flatfish.
– ORIGIN unknown.

dab·ble /'dabəl/ ▶ **verb 1** move one's hands or feet around gently in water. **2** take part in an activity in a casual way: *I was a vegetarian and dabbled in yoga.*

– SYNONYMS **toy with,** dip into, flirt with, tinker with, play with.

– DERIVATIVES **dab·bler** noun.
– ORIGIN from former Dutch *dabbelen* or from **DAB¹**.

dab hand ▶ **noun** Brit. informal a person who is very skilled in a particular activity.
– ORIGIN unknown.

da ca·po /dä 'käpō/ ▶ **adverb & adjective** Music repeat or repeated from the beginning.
– ORIGIN Italian, 'from the head.'

dace /dās/ ▶ **noun** (pl. same) a small freshwater fish related to the carp.
– ORIGIN Old French *dars* (see **DART**).

da·cha /'däCHə/ ▶ **noun** (in Russia) a country house or cottage, used as a vacation home.
– ORIGIN Russian.

dachs·hund /'däksənd, 'däks,ho͝ont/ ▶ **noun** a breed of dog with a long body and very short legs.
– ORIGIN German, 'badger dog.'

da·coit /də'koit/ ▶ **noun** a member of a band of armed robbers in India or Myanmar (Burma).
– ORIGIN Hindi, 'robbery by a gang.'

Da·cron /'dā,krän, 'dak,rän/ ▶ **noun** trademark a synthetic polyester (polyethylene terephthalate) with tough, elastic properties, used as a textile fabric.
– ORIGIN an invented name.

dac·tyl /'daktl/ ▶ **noun** Poetry a metrical foot consisting of one stressed syllable followed by two unstressed syllables.
– DERIVATIVES **dac·tyl·ic** /dak'tilik/ adjective.
– ORIGIN Greek *daktulos* 'finger' (the three bones of the finger corresponding to the three syllables).

dad /dad/ ▶ **noun** informal one's father.
– ORIGIN perhaps from a child's first syllables *da, da.*

Da·da /'dädä/ ▶ **noun** an early 20th-century movement in the arts that mocked conventions and emphasized the illogical and absurd.
– DERIVATIVES **Da·da·ism** /-,izəm/ noun **Da·da·ist** noun & adjective.
– ORIGIN French, 'hobby horse,' the title of a review published in Zurich in 1916.

dad·dy /'dadē/ ▶ **noun** (pl. **daddies**) informal one's father.

dad·dy long·legs /'läNG,legz/ ▶ **noun** (pl. same) an arachnid with a globular body and long thin legs, typically living in leaf litter and on tree trunks.

da·do /'dādō/ ▶ **noun** (pl. **dados**) **1** the lower part of the wall of a room, when decorated differently from the upper part. **2** Architecture the part of a pedestal between the base and the cornice.
– ORIGIN Italian, 'dice or cube.'

dae·mon /'dēmən/ ▶ **noun** old-fashioned spelling of **DEMON**.
– DERIVATIVES **dae·mon·ic** /di'mänik/ adjective.
– ORIGIN Greek *daimon.*

daf·fo·dil /'dafə,dil/ ▶ **noun** a plant bearing bright yellow flowers with a long trumpet-shaped center.
– ORIGIN Latin *asphodilus* 'asphodel.'

daf·fy /'dafē/ ▶ **adjective** (**daffier, daffiest**) informal silly or mildly eccentric.
– DERIVATIVES **daf·fi·ness** noun.
– ORIGIN from northern English dialect *daff* 'simpleton.'

daft /daft/ ▶ **adjective** informal silly; foolish.

– SYNONYMS **absurd,** preposterous, ridiculous, ludicrous, idiotic, stupid, foolish, asinine, senseless, inane; informal crazy, cockeyed, half-baked.
– ANTONYMS sensible.

– ORIGIN Old English, 'mild, meek.'

dag·ger /'dagər/ ▶ **noun 1** a short pointed knife, used as a weapon. **2** another term for **OBELUS**.
– PHRASES **be at daggers drawn** (of two people) be bitterly hostile toward each other. **look daggers at** glare angrily at.

– ORIGIN perhaps from former *dag* 'pierce,' influenced by Old French *dague* 'long dagger.'

da·go /'dāgō/ ▸ **noun** (pl. **dagos** or **dagoes**) informal, offensive a Spanish, Portuguese, or Italian-speaking person.
– ORIGIN from the Spanish man's name *Diego* 'James.'

da·guerre·o·type /də'ge(ə)rəˌtīp/ (also **daguerrotype**) ▸ **noun** an early type of photograph produced by means of a silver-coated copper plate and mercury vapor.
– ORIGIN named after L.-J.-M. *Daguerre*, its French inventor.

dahl·ia /'dalyə, 'däl-/ ▸ **noun** a garden plant with brightly colored single or double flowers.
– ORIGIN named after the Swedish botanist Andreas *Dahl*.

dai·kon /'dīˌkän, -kən/ ▸ **noun** a radish with a large slender white root that is typically eaten cooked, especially in Eastern cuisine.
– ORIGIN Japanese.

dai·ly /'dālē/ ▸ **adjective** done, happening, or produced every day or every weekday.

– SYNONYMS **everyday,** day-to-day; formal **quotidian.**

▸ **adverb** every day.

– SYNONYMS **every day,** once a day, day after day.

▸ **noun** (pl. **dailies**) informal a newspaper published every day except Sunday.

dain·ty /'dāntē/ ▸ **adjective** (**daintier, daintiest**) delicately small and pretty: *dainty white snowdrops.*

– SYNONYMS **1 delicate,** fine, elegant, exquisite, graceful. **2 fastidious,** fussy, particular, finicky; informal choosy, picky.
– ANTONYMS unwieldy.

▸ **noun** (pl. **dainties**) a small appetizing item of food.
– DERIVATIVES **dain·ti·ly** adverb **dain·ti·ness** noun.
– ORIGIN from Old French *daintie* 'choice morsel, pleasure.'

dai·qui·ri /'dakərē, 'dīkə-/ ▸ **noun** (pl. **daiquiris**) a cocktail containing rum and lime juice.
– ORIGIN from *Daiquiri*, a rum-producing district in Cuba.

dair·y /'de(ə)rē/ ▸ **noun** (pl. **dairies**) a building where milk and milk products are processed and distributed. ▸ **adjective 1** made from milk. **2** involved in milk production.
– DERIVATIVES **dair·y·ing** noun.
– ORIGIN Old English, 'female servant.'

dair·y·maid /'de(ə)rēˌmād/ ▸ **noun** old use a woman employed in a dairy.

dair·y·man /'de(ə)rēmən, -ˌman/ ▸ **noun** (pl. **dairymen**) a man who works in a dairy or who sells dairy products.

da·is /'dāis, 'dī-/ ▸ **noun** a low platform for a lectern or throne.
– ORIGIN Old French *deis*.

dai·sy /'dāzē/ ▸ **noun** (pl. **daisies**) a small plant having flowers with a yellow center and white petals.
– ORIGIN Old English, 'day's eye' (because the flower opens in the morning and closes at night).

dai·sy chain ▸ **noun** a string of daisies threaded together by their stems.

dai·sy wheel ▸ **noun** a spoked disk carrying printing characters, used in word processors and typewriters.

dal /däl/ (also **dhal**) ▸ **noun** (in Indian cooking) split legumes.
– ORIGIN Hindi.

Da·lai La·ma /'dälī 'lämə/ ▸ **noun** the spiritual head of Tibetan Buddhism.
– ORIGIN Tibetan, 'ocean monk,' because he is regarded as 'the ocean of compassion.'

dale /dāl/ ▸ **noun** a valley, especially in northern England.
– ORIGIN Old English.

dal·li·ance /'dalēəns, 'dalyəns/ ▸ **noun 1** a casual romantic or sexual relationship. **2** a brief or casual involvement with something: *his dalliance with the far right.*

dal·ly /'dalē/ ▸ **verb** (**dallies, dallying, dallied**) **1** act or move slowly. **2** (**dally with**) have a casual sexual relationship with someone. **3** (**dally with**) take a casual interest in: *I dallied with the idea of asking her friend to come, too.*
– ORIGIN Old French *dalier* 'to chat.'

CHOOSE THE RIGHT WORD

See **LOITER**.

Dal·ma·tian /dal'māshən/ ▸ **noun** a breed of large dog with short white hair and dark spots.
– ORIGIN named after *Dalmatia*, a region of Croatia.

dam¹ /dam/ ▸ **noun** a barrier built across a river to hold back water, in order to form a reservoir or prevent flooding.

– SYNONYMS **barrage,** barrier, weir, wall, embankment, barricade, obstruction.

▸ **verb** (**dams, damming, dammed**) build a dam across a river.

– SYNONYMS **block (up),** obstruct, bung up, close, hold back.

– ORIGIN German or Dutch.

dam² ▸ **noun** the female parent of certain mammals, especially horses.
– ORIGIN from **DAME.**

dam·age /'damij/ ▸ **noun 1** physical harm that affects the value, functioning, or usefulness of something. **2** harmful effects: *the damage to his reputation was considerable.* **3** (**damages**) financial compensation for a loss or injury.

– SYNONYMS **1 harm,** destruction, vandalism, injury, ruin, devastation. **2** *she won $4,000 damages* **compensation,** recompense, restitution, redress, reparation(s); informal comp.

▸ **verb** cause harm to; have a bad effect on: *some industrial solvents can damage people's health.*

– SYNONYMS **harm,** injure, deface, spoil, impair, vandalize, ruin, destroy, wreck; informal trash.
– ANTONYMS repair.

– PHRASES **what's the damage?** informal, humorous what does it cost?
– ORIGIN Old French.

dam·ag·ing /'damijiNG/ ▸ **adjective** harmful or undesirable.

– SYNONYMS **harmful,** detrimental, injurious, hurtful, destructive, ruinous, deleterious.
– ANTONYMS beneficial.

dam·a·scened /'daməˌsēnd, ˌdamə'sēnd/ ▸ **adjective 1** (of iron or steel) given a wavy pattern by hammer-welding and repeated heating and forging. **2** (of metal) inlaid with gold or silver.
– ORIGIN from the Syrian city of *Damascus*.

dam·ask /ˈdaməsk/ ▶ **noun** a rich heavy fabric with a pattern woven into it. ▶ **adjective** literary pink or light red.
– ORIGIN from the Syrian city of *Damascus*.

dame /dām/ ▶ **noun 1** (**Dame**) (in the UK) the title of a woman awarded a knighthood, equivalent to *Sir*. **2** informal a woman.
– ORIGIN Old French.

dam·mit /ˈdamit/ ▶ **exclamation** used to express anger and frustration.
– ORIGIN alteration of *damn it*.

damn /dam/ ▶ **verb 1** curse someone or something. **2** criticize strongly: *a company spokesman damned the plan as financially unsound*. **3** (**be damned**) (in Christian belief) be condemned by God to eternal punishment in hell. **4** (**be damned**) be doomed to misfortune or failure.

> – SYNONYMS **condemn,** censure, criticize, attack, denounce.
> – ANTONYMS praise.

▶ **exclamation** informal expressing anger or frustration.
▶ **adjective** informal used to emphasize anger or frustration.
– PHRASES **damn someone/thing with faint praise** praise someone or something so unenthusiastically as to suggest condemnation. **not be worth a damn** informal have no value.
– ORIGIN Latin *dampnare* 'inflict loss on.'

dam·na·ble /ˈdamnəbəl/ ▶ **adjective** very bad or unpleasant.
– DERIVATIVES **dam·na·bly** /-blē/ adverb.

dam·na·tion /damˈnāsʜən/ ▶ **noun** condemnation to eternal punishment in hell. ▶ **exclamation** expressing anger or frustration.

damned /damd/ ▶ **adjective** used to emphasize anger or frustration.
– PHRASES **do** (or **try**) **one's damnedest** do (or try) one's utmost.

damn·ing /ˈdamiɴɢ/ ▶ **adjective** strongly suggestive of guilt: *damning evidence*.

> – SYNONYMS **incriminating,** damaging, condemnatory, conclusive, irrefutable.

damp /damp/ ▶ **adjective** slightly wet.

> – SYNONYMS **moist,** humid, muggy, clammy, sweaty, dank, wet, rainy, drizzly, showery, misty, foggy, dewy.
> – ANTONYMS dry.

▶ **noun** moisture in the air, on a surface, or in a solid substance.

> – SYNONYMS **moisture,** liquid, wet, wetness, dampness, humidity.

▶ **verb 1** make something damp. **2** (**damp something down**) control or restrain a feeling or situation. **3** (**damp something down**) make a fire burn less strongly by reducing its air supply. **4** reduce or stop the vibration of the strings of a musical instrument.
– DERIVATIVES **damp·ish** adjective **damp·ly** adverb **damp·ness** noun.
– ORIGIN Germanic.

> **WORD TOOLKIT**
>
> See **WET**.

damp·en /ˈdampən/ ▶ **verb 1** make something damp. **2** make less strong or intense: *nothing could dampen her enthusiasm*.

> – SYNONYMS **1 moisten,** damp, wet, soak. **2 lessen,** decrease, diminish, reduce, moderate, cool, suppress, stifle, inhibit.
> – ANTONYMS dry, heighten.

– DERIVATIVES **damp·en·er** noun.

damp·er /ˈdampər/ ▶ **noun 1** a pad for silencing a piano string. **2** a device for reducing vibration or oscillation. **3** a movable metal plate used to regulate the air flow in a flue or chimney.
– PHRASES **put a damper on** informal have a subduing or restraining effect on.

dam·sel /ˈdamzəl/ ▶ **noun** old use or humorous a young unmarried woman.
– ORIGIN Old French *dameisele*.

dam·sel·fly /ˈdamzəlˌflī/ ▶ **noun** (pl. **damselflies**) a slender insect related to the dragonflies.

dam·son /ˈdamzən, -sən/ ▶ **noun** a small purple-black plumlike fruit.
– ORIGIN from Latin *damascenum prunum* 'plum of Damascus.'

dan /dan/ ▶ **noun 1** any of ten degrees of advanced proficiency in judo or karate. **2** a person who has achieved a dan.
– ORIGIN Japanese.

dance /dans/ ▶ **verb 1** move rhythmically to music. **2** move in a quick and lively way: *midges danced over the stream*.

> – SYNONYMS **1 trip,** sway, twirl, whirl, pirouette, gyrate, jive; informal bop, get down, trip the light fantastic. **2** *the children danced around me* **caper,** cavort, frolic, skip, prance, gambol, leap, hop, jig, bounce.

▶ **noun 1** a series of steps and movements that match the rhythm of a piece of music. **2** an act of dancing. **3** a social gathering at which people dance. **4** (also **dance music**) pop music for dancing to in clubs.

> – SYNONYMS **ball,** prom, hoedown; informal disco, rave, hop.

– DERIVATIVES **danc·er** noun **danc·ing** noun.
– PHRASES **dance attendance on** try hard to please someone.
– ORIGIN Old French *dancer*.

dance hall ▶ **noun 1** a large public hall or building where people pay to enter and dance. **2** (**dancehall**) a style of dance music derived from reggae.

D and C ▶ **abbreviation** dilatation and curettage.

dan·de·li·on /ˈdandlˌīən/ ▶ **noun** a weed with large bright yellow flowers followed by rounded heads of seeds with downy tufts.
– ORIGIN French *dent-de-lion* 'lion's tooth' (from the shape of the leaves).

dan·der /ˈdandər/ ▶ **noun** (in phrase **get/have one's dander up**) informal lose one's temper.
– ORIGIN unknown.

dan·di·fied /ˈdandiˌfīd/ ▶ **adjective** (of a man) excessively concerned about his clothes and appearance.

dan·dle /ˈdandl/ ▶ **verb** gently bounce a young child on one's knees or in one's arms.
– ORIGIN unknown.

dan·druff /ˈdandrəf/ ▶ **noun** flakes of dead skin on a person's scalp and in the hair.
– ORIGIN uncertain.

dan·dy /ˈdandē/ ▶ **noun** (pl. **dandies**) a man who is excessively concerned with having a stylish and

fashionable appearance. ▶ **adjective** (**dandier, dandiest**) informal excellent.
– DERIVATIVES **dan·dy·ish** adjective.
– ORIGIN a familiar form of the man's name *Andrew*.

Dane /dān/ ▶ **noun** a person from Denmark.
– ORIGIN Old English.

dan·ger /ˈdānjər/ ▶ **noun 1** the possibility of suffering harm: *her life was in danger*. **2** a cause of harm. **3** the possibility of something unpleasant or undesirable happening: *there's no danger of putting on weight in that restaurant*.

– SYNONYMS **1 peril,** hazard, risk, jeopardy, endangerment, menace. **2 possibility,** chance, risk, probability, likelihood, threat.
– ANTONYMS safety.

– PHRASES **in danger of** likely to incur or to suffer from. **out of danger** (of a person who has suffered a serious injury or illness) not expected to die.
– ORIGIN Old French *dangier* 'jurisdiction, power to harm.'

dan·ger·ous /ˈdānjərəs/ ▶ **adjective 1** able or likely to cause harm: *dangerous chemicals like DDT*. **2** likely to cause problems.

– SYNONYMS **1 menacing,** threatening, treacherous. **2 hazardous,** perilous, risky, unsafe, unpredictable, precarious, insecure; informal dicey, hairy.
– ANTONYMS harmless, safe.

– DERIVATIVES **dan·ger·ous·ly** adverb **dan·ger·ous·ness** noun.

dan·gle /ˈdaNGgəl/ ▶ **verb 1** hang so as to swing freely. **2** offer something attractive to someone to persuade them to do something: *one firm is dangling a grand prize of a Porsche for referrals*.

– SYNONYMS **hang,** swing, droop, wave, trail, stream.

– DERIVATIVES **dan·gler** noun **dan·gly** adjective.
– ORIGIN uncertain.

dan·gling par·ti·ci·ple /ˈdaNGg(ə)liNG/ ▶ **noun** Grammar a participle intended to refer to a noun that is not actually present.

USAGE

A **dangling participle** is one that is left 'hanging' because it does not relate to the noun it should. For example, in the sentence *arriving at the station, the sun came out*, the word **arriving** is a dangling participle, because the sentence reads grammatically as if it is **the sun** (the subject of the sentence) that is **arriving**. This is incorrect in standard English.

Dan·ish /ˈdāniSH/ ▶ **adjective** relating to Denmark or the Danes. ▶ **noun** the language of Denmark.

Dan·ish blue ▶ **noun** a strong-flavored blue-veined white cheese.

Dan·ish pas·try ▶ **noun** a pastry of sweetened yeast dough topped with icing and filled with fruit, cheese, or nuts.

dank /daNGk/ ▶ **adjective** damp and cold.

– SYNONYMS **damp,** musty, chilly, clammy.
– ANTONYMS dry.

– ORIGIN probably Scandinavian.

daph·ni·a /ˈdafnēə/ ▶ **noun** (pl. same) a minute semitransparent freshwater crustacean.
– ORIGIN Latin.

dap·per /ˈdapər/ ▶ **adjective** (of a man) neat in dress and appearance.

– SYNONYMS **smart,** spruce, trim, debonair, neat, well dressed, elegant; informal snappy, natty, spiffy, fly.
– ANTONYMS scruffy.

– ORIGIN probably from a German or Dutch word meaning 'strong, stout.'

dap·ple /ˈdapəl/ ▶ **verb** mark with spots or small patches: *a forest clearing dappled with sunlight*. ▶ **noun** a patch of color or light.
– ORIGIN perhaps from Old Norse.

dap·ple gray ▶ **adjective** (of a horse) gray or white with darker ringlike markings.

DAR ▶ **abbreviation** Daughters of the American Revolution.

dare /de(ə)r/ ▶ **verb** (3rd sing. present usu. **dare** before an expressed or implied infinitive without 'to') **1** have the courage to do something. **2** challenge to do something: *he ran his first marathon because his grandchildren dared him to*.

– SYNONYMS **1 be brave enough,** have the courage, venture, have the nerve, risk, take the liberty of. informal stick one's neck out. **2 challenge,** defy, invite, bid, provoke, goad.

▶ **noun** a challenge, especially to prove courage.

– SYNONYMS **challenge,** invitation, wager, bet.

– PHRASES **how dare you** used to express indignation. **I dare say** (or **daresay** /ˌde(ə)rˈsā/) it is probable.
– ORIGIN Old English.

dare·dev·il /ˈde(ə)rˌdevəl/ ▶ **noun** a person who enjoys doing dangerous things.

dar·ing /ˈde(ə)riNG/ ▶ **adjective 1** willing to do dangerous or risky things; bold. **2** involving risk or danger. **3** boldly unconventional: *daring, see-through evening gowns*.

– SYNONYMS **bold,** audacious, intrepid, fearless, brave, heroic, dashing; informal gutsy.
– ANTONYMS cowardly, timid.

▶ **noun** adventurous courage; boldness.

– SYNONYMS **boldness,** audacity, temerity, fearlessness, bravery, courage, pluck; informal nerve, guts, moxie.
– ANTONYMS cowardice.

– DERIVATIVES **dar·ing·ly** adverb.

Dar·jee·ling /därˈjēliNG/ ▶ **noun** a high-quality tea grown in northern India.
– ORIGIN from *Darjeeling*, a hill station in West Bengal.

dark /därk/ ▶ **adjective 1** with little or no light. **2** of a deep color: *dark green*. **3** (of skin, hair, or eyes) brown or black. **4** unpleasant or gloomy: *the dark days of the war*. **5** evil. **6** mysterious: *a dark secret*. **7** (**darkest**) humorous most remote or uncivilized.

– SYNONYMS **1** *a dark room* **dingy,** gloomy, shadowy, murky, gray, poorly lit, inky, black. **2** *dark hair* **brunette,** dark brown, sable, jet-black, ebony. **3** *dark skin* **swarthy,** dusky, olive, black, ebony. **4** *dark thoughts* **gloomy,** dismal, negative, downbeat, bleak, grim, fatalistic, black. **5** *a dark look* **angry,** forbidding, threatening, ominous, moody, brooding, sullen, scowling, glowering. **6** *dark deeds* **evil,** wicked, sinful, bad, iniquitous, ungodly, vile, foul, monstrous; informal dirty, shady, crooked.
– ANTONYMS bright, light, blonde, pale.

▶ **noun 1** (**the dark**) the absence of light. **2** nightfall.

– SYNONYMS **night,** nighttime, nightfall, darkness, blackout.

– DERIVATIVES **dark·ish** adjective **dark·ly** adverb.
– PHRASES **in the dark** in a state of ignorance. **a shot** (or **stab**) **in the dark** a wild guess.
– ORIGIN Old English.

Dark Ag·es ▶ **plural noun** **1** the period in Europe between the fall of the Roman Empire and the Middle Ages, *c.*500–1100, regarded as lacking culture and knowledge. **2** a period characterized by a lack of knowledge or progress: *the dark ages of computing*.

dark·en /'därkən/ ▶ **verb** **1** make or become darker. **2** become unhappy or angry.

– SYNONYMS **grow dark,** make dark, blacken, grow dim, cloud over, lour.
– ANTONYMS lighten.

– PHRASES **never darken someone's door** keep away from someone's home.

dark horse ▶ **noun** a competitor or candidate who has little chance of winning or who wins unexpectedly.

dark·ling /'därkliNG/ ▶ **adjective** literary **1** characterized by darkness. **2** growing darker.

dark mat·ter ▶ **noun** Astronomy nonluminous material believed to exist in space.

dark·ness /'därknis/ ▶ **noun** **1** absence of light. **2** night. **3** wickedness or evil.

– SYNONYMS **1** *lights shone in the darkness* **dark,** blackness, gloom, dimness, murk, shadow, shade, blackout. **2** *darkness fell* **night,** nighttime, dark. **3** *the forces of darkness* **evil,** wickedness, sin, immorality, the Devil.

dark·net /'därk,net/ ▶ **noun** Computing a computer network with restricted access that is used chiefly for illegal peer-to-peer file sharing.

dark·room /'därk,ro͞om, -,ro͝om/ ▶ **noun** a room for developing photographs, from which normal light is excluded.

dar·ling /'därliNG/ ▶ **noun** **1** used as an affectionate form of address. **2** a lovable person. **3** a person popular with a particular group: *she is the darling of the media*.

– SYNONYMS **1 dear,** dearest, love, sweetheart, beloved; informal honey, angel, pet, sweetie, baby. **2 favorite,** idol, hero, heroine; informal blue-eyed boy/girl.

▶ **adjective** **1** beloved. **2** pretty; charming.

– SYNONYMS **1 dear,** dearest, precious, beloved. **2 adorable,** charming, cute, sweet, enchanting, dear, delightful; Scottish bonny.

– ORIGIN Old English, from **DEAR**.

darm·stadt·i·um /därm'statēəm, -'SHtät-/ ▶ **noun** a radioactive chemical element produced artificially.
– ORIGIN named after a laboratory in *Darmstadt*, Germany, where the element was first created.

darn[1] /därn/ ▶ **verb** mend knitted material by interweaving yarn across it.
– DERIVATIVES **darn·ing** noun.
– ORIGIN perhaps from an Old English word meaning 'to hide.'

darn[2] ▶ **verb, adjective, & exclamation** informal euphemism for **DAMN**.

darned /därnd/ ▶ **adjective** informal euphemism for **DAMNED**.

dart /därt/ ▶ **noun** **1** a small pointed missile thrown or fired as a weapon. **2** a small pointed missile used in the game of darts. **3** (**darts**) (usu. treated as sing.) an indoor game in which darts are thrown at a dartboard. **4** a sudden rapid movement. **5** a tapered tuck in a garment.
▶ **verb** move suddenly or rapidly.

– SYNONYMS **1 dash,** rush, tear, shoot, sprint, bound, scurry, scamper; informal scoot, whip. **2 direct,** cast, throw, shoot, send, flash.

– ORIGIN Old French.

dart·board /'därt,bôrd/ ▶ **noun** a circular board used as a target in the game of darts.

Dar·win·ism /'därwə,nizəm/ ▶ **noun** the theory of the evolution of species by natural selection, put forward by the English natural historian Charles Darwin.
– DERIVATIVES **Dar·win·i·an** /där'winēən/ noun & adjective **Dar·win·ist** noun & adjective.

dash /dasH/ ▶ **verb** **1** run or travel in a great hurry. **2** strike or throw something with great force. **3** destroy or frustrate: *his political hopes were dashed*. **4** (**dash something off**) write something hurriedly.

– SYNONYMS **1 rush,** race, run, sprint, career, charge, shoot, hurtle, fly, speed, zoom; informal tear, belt, barrel. **2 hurl,** smash, fling, slam, throw, toss, cast. **3 shatter,** destroy, wreck, ruin, demolish, scotch, frustrate, thwart.
– ANTONYMS dawdle.

▶ **noun** **1** an act of dashing. **2** a small amount added: *whiskey with a dash of soda*. **3** a horizontal stroke in writing, marking a pause or omission. **4** the longer of the signals used in Morse code. **5** a combination of style, enthusiasm, and confidence.

– SYNONYMS **1 rush,** race, run, sprint, bolt, dart, leap, charge, bound. **2 pinch,** touch, sprinkle, taste, spot, drop, dab, splash; informal smidgen, tad.

– ORIGIN probably symbolic of forceful movement.

dash·board /'dasH,bôrd/ ▶ **noun** the panel of instruments and controls facing the driver of a vehicle.
– ORIGIN first meaning a board in front of a carriage, to keep out mud.

da·shi·ki /də'sHēkē/ ▶ **noun** (pl. **dashikis**) a loose, brightly colored shirt, originally from West Africa.
– ORIGIN Yoruba or Hausa (a West African language).

dash·ing /'dasHiNG/ ▶ **adjective** (of a man) attractive, adventurous, and confident.

– SYNONYMS **debonair,** stylish, dapper, devil-may-care, raffish, flamboyant, swashbuckling.

– DERIVATIVES **dash·ing·ly** adverb.

das·tard·ly /'dastərdlē/ ▶ **adjective** dated or humorous wicked and cruel.
– ORIGIN from the old word *dastard* 'despicable person.'

DAT /dat/ ▶ **abbreviation** digital audiotape.

da·ta /'datə, 'dātə/ ▶ **noun** **1** facts and statistics used for reference or analysis. **2** the quantities, characters, or symbols on which operations are performed by a computer.

– SYNONYMS **facts,** figures, statistics, details, particulars, information.

– ORIGIN Latin, plural of **DATUM**.

USAGE

The word **data** is the plural of the Latin word **datum**, and in scientific use it is usually treated as a plural noun, taking a plural verb (e.g. *the data were classified*). In everyday use, however, **data** is often treated as a singular, and sentences such as *data was collected over a number of years* are now generally accepted.

da·ta·bank /ˈdatəˌbaNGk, ˈdā-/ ▸ **noun** a large store of data in a computer.

da·ta·base /ˈdatəˌbās, ˈdā-/ ▸ **noun** a structured set of data held in a computer.

dat·a·ble /ˈdātəbəl/ (also **dateable**) ▸ **adjective 1** able to be dated to a particular time. **2** (of a person) suitable as a companion on a date.

da·ta cap·ture ▸ **noun** the action of gathering data and putting it into a form accessible by computer.

da·ta proc·ess·ing ▸ **noun** any operation performed on data, especially by a computer.

da·ta pro·tec·tion ▸ **noun 1** protection of the integrity of digitally stored data. **2** legal control over access to data stored in computers.

date[1] /dāt/ ▸ **noun 1** the day of the month or year as specified by a number. **2** a day or year when a particular event occurred or will occur. **3** a social or romantic appointment. **4** a musical or theatrical performance, especially as part of a tour.

– SYNONYMS **1 day,** occasion, time, year, age, period, era, epoch. **2 appointment,** meeting, engagement, rendezvous, commitment, assignation; literary tryst. **3 partner,** escort, girlfriend, boyfriend.

▸ **verb 1** establish the date of something. **2** write or print the date on something. **3** (**date from** or **date back to**) start or originate at a particular time in the past. **4** (often as adj. **dated**) appear or cause to appear old-fashioned. **5** informal go on a date or regular dates with someone.

– SYNONYMS **1** (**date from** or **date back to**) **be from,** originate in, come from, belong to, go back to. **2** (as adj. **dated**) *the graphics look somewhat dated* **old-fashioned,** outdated, outmoded, unfashionable, passé, behind the times, archaic, obsolete, antiquated; informal old hat, out of the Dark Ages. **3 go out with,** take out, go with, see; informal go steady with; dated court, woo.

– PHRASES **to date** until now.
– ORIGIN Latin *data*, from *dare* 'give.'

WORD LINKS

chronological *relating to dates*

date[2] ▸ **noun 1** a sweet, dark brown, oval fruit with a hard stone, usually eaten dried. **2** (also **date palm**) a tall palm tree that bears this fruit, native to western Asia and North Africa.
– ORIGIN Greek *daktulos* 'finger' (because of the finger-like shape of the tree's leaves).

date·a·ble ▸ **adjective** variant spelling of DATABLE.

date·book /ˈdātˌbo͝ok/ ▸ **noun** a book with spaces for each day of the year in which one notes appointments or important information.

date·line /ˈdātˌlīn/ ▸ **noun** a line at the head of a dispatch or newspaper article showing the date and place of writing.

date rape ▸ **noun** rape by a person with whom the victim has gone on a date.

dat·ing a·gen·cy ▸ **noun** a service that arranges introductions for people seeking romantic partners or friends.

da·tive /ˈdātiv/ ▸ **noun** (in Latin, Greek, German, etc.) the grammatical case of nouns and pronouns that indicates an indirect object or the person or thing affected by a verb.
– ORIGIN from Latin *casus dativus* 'case of giving.'

da·tum /ˈdātəm, ˈdatəm/ ▸ **noun** (pl. **data** /ˈdatə, ˈdātə/) a piece of information.
– ORIGIN Latin, 'something given.'

da·tu·ra /dəˈt(y)o͝orə/ ▸ **noun** a North American plant whose flowers contain toxic or narcotic substances.
– ORIGIN Hindi.

daub /dôb/ ▸ **verb 1** carelessly coat or smear something with a thick substance. **2** spread a thick substance on a surface. ▸ **noun 1** plaster, clay, or a similar substance, especially when mixed with straw and applied to laths or wattles to form a wall. **2** a patch or smear of a thick substance. **3** a painting done without much skill.
– ORIGIN Old French *dauber*.

daugh·ter /ˈdôtər, ˈdä-/ ▸ **noun 1** a girl or woman in relation to her parents. **2** a female descendant.
– DERIVATIVES **daugh·ter·ly** adjective.
– ORIGIN Old English.

daugh·ter·board /ˈdôtərˌbôrd, ˈdä-/ (also **daughtercard** /ˈdôtərˌkärd, ˈdä-/) ▸ **noun** a small printed circuit board that attaches to a larger one.

daugh·ter-in-law ▸ **noun** (pl. **daughters-in-law**) the wife of one's son.

daunt /dônt, dänt/ ▸ **verb** (usu. **be daunted**) make someone feel intimidated or apprehensive: *wintry conditions did not daunt the runners*.

– SYNONYMS **discourage,** deter, demoralize, put off, dishearten, intimidate, overawe, awe, frighten, scare, unsettle, unnerve.

– DERIVATIVES **daunt·ing** adjective.
– ORIGIN Old French *danter*.

daunt·less /ˈdôntlis, ˈdänt-/ ▸ **adjective** fearless and determined.

dau·phin /ˈdôfin/ ▸ **noun** historical the eldest son of a king of France.
– ORIGIN French.

dav·en·port /ˈdavənˌpôrt/ ▸ **noun** a large upholstered sofa, typically able to be converted into a bed.
– ORIGIN probably a manufacturer's name.

da·vit /ˈdavit, ˈdā-/ ▸ **noun** a small crane on a ship, especially one of a pair for lowering a lifeboat.
– ORIGIN Old French *daviot*.

Da·vy Jones's lock·er /ˌdāvē ˈjōnz(əz)/ ▸ **noun** informal the bottom of the sea, regarded as the grave of people who drown.
– ORIGIN from 18th-century nautical slang *Davy Jones*, referring to the evil spirit of the sea.

daw·dle /ˈdôdl/ ▸ **verb** move slowly; take one's time.

– SYNONYMS **linger,** take one's time, be slow, waste time, dally, amble, stroll, trail, move at a snail's pace; informal dilly-dally.
– ANTONYMS hurry.

– DERIVATIVES **daw·dler** noun.
– ORIGIN related to dialect *daddle*, *doddle* 'dally.'

CHOOSE THE RIGHT WORD

See LOITER.

dawn /dôn, dän/ ▸ **noun 1** the first appearance of light in the sky in the morning. **2** the beginning of something: *the dawn of civilization.*

– SYNONYMS **1 daybreak,** sunrise, sunup, first light, daylight, crack of dawn. **2 beginning,** start, birth, inception, genesis, emergence, advent, appearance, arrival, rise, origin.
– ANTONYMS dusk.

▶ **verb 1** (of a day) begin. **2** come into existence: *a new era had dawned.* **3** (**dawn on**) become obvious to.

– SYNONYMS **1** *Thursday dawned crisp and sunny* **begin,** break, arrive, emerge. **2** *a bright new future has dawned* **begin,** start, commence, be born, appear, arrive, emerge, arise, rise, unfold, develop. **3** *the truth began to* ***dawn on*** *him* **become evident,** register, cross someone's mind, suggest itself, occur to, come to, strike, hit.

– ORIGIN Old English.

dawn cho·rus ▶ **noun** the early-morning singing of birds.

day /dā/ ▶ **noun 1** a period of twenty-four hours, reckoned from midnight to midnight and corresponding to a rotation of the earth on its axis. **2** the time between sunrise and sunset. **3** (usu. **days**) a particular period of the past. **4** (**the day**) the present time or the time in question. **5** (**one's day**) the youthful or successful period of one's life.

– SYNONYMS **1 daytime,** daylight (hours), waking hours. **2 period,** time, date, age, era, generation.
– ANTONYMS night.

▶ **adjective** working or done during the day: *my day job.*
– PHRASES **any day** informal at any time or under any circumstances. **call it a day** decide to stop doing something. **day by day** gradually and steadily. **day in, day out** continuously or repeatedly over a long period. **day-to-day 1** happening on a daily basis. **2** involving the usual tasks or routines of every day: *the day-to-day running of the company.* **that will be the day** informal that is very unlikely. **these days** at present.
– ORIGIN Old English.

WORD LINKS

diurnal *relating to the day*

day·bed /ˈdāˌbed/ ▶ **noun** a couch that can be made into a bed.

day·break /ˈdāˌbrāk/ ▶ **noun** dawn.

day care cen·ter ▶ **noun** a place providing daytime care for children or for elderly or disabled people.

day·dream /ˈdāˌdrēm/ ▶ **noun** a series of pleasant thoughts that distract one's attention from the present.
▶ **verb** have a daydream.
– DERIVATIVES **day·dream·er** noun.

Day-Glo /ˈdā ˌglō/ ▶ **noun** trademark a fluorescent paint or other coloring.

day·light /ˈdāˌlīt/ ▶ **noun 1** the natural light of the day. **2** dawn. **3** visible distance between one person or thing and another.
– PHRASES —— **the living daylights out of someone** do a particular thing to someone very strongly or severely: *you scared the living daylights out of me.*

day·light sav·ing time ▶ **noun** time as adjusted to achieve longer evening daylight by setting the clocks an hour ahead of the standard time.

day off ▶ **noun** (pl. **days off**) a day's vacation from work or school.

day·pack /ˈdāˌpak/ ▶ **noun** a small backpack.

day school ▶ **noun** a school for students who live at home.

day·time /ˈdāˌtīm/ ▶ **noun 1** the time between sunrise and sunset. **2** the period of time corresponding to normal working hours.

day trip ▶ **noun** a journey or excursion completed in one day.
– DERIVATIVES **day trip·per** noun.

daze /dāz/ ▶ **verb** make someone feel stunned or bewildered.

– SYNONYMS **dumbfound,** stupefy, stun, shock, stagger, bewilder, take aback, nonplus; informal flabbergast, knock for a loop.

▶ **noun** a state of stunned confusion or bewilderment.

– SYNONYMS **stupor,** trance, haze, spin, whirl, muddle, jumble.

– DERIVATIVES **daz·ed·ly** /ˈdāzidlē/ adverb.
– ORIGIN Old Norse, 'weary.'

daz·zle /ˈdazəl/ ▶ **verb 1** (of a bright light) blind someone temporarily. **2** impress someone greatly: *I was dazzled by the beauty of the exhibition.*

– SYNONYMS **1 blind,** confuse, disorient. **2 overwhelm,** overcome, impress, move, stir, touch, awe, overawe; informal bowl over, blow away, knock out.

▶ **noun** blinding brightness.
– DERIVATIVES **daz·zle·ment** noun **daz·zler** noun **daz·zling** adjective.
– ORIGIN from DAZE.

Db ▶ **symbol** the chemical element dubnium.

dB ▶ **abbreviation** decibel(s).

DBS ▶ **abbreviation 1** direct broadcasting by satellite. **2** direct-broadcast satellite.

DC ▶ **abbreviation 1** direct current. **2** District of Columbia.

DD ▶ **abbreviation** Doctor of Divinity.

D-Day ▶ **noun 1** the day (June 6, 1944) in World War II on which Allied forces invaded northern France. **2** the day on which something important is to begin.
– ORIGIN from *D* for *day* + DAY.

DDR ▶ **abbreviation** historical German Democratic Republic.
– ORIGIN abbreviation of German *Deutsche Demokratische Republik.*

DDT ▶ **abbreviation** dichlorodiphenyltrichloroethane, a compound used as an insecticide but now banned in many countries.

DE ▶ **abbreviation** Delaware.

de- ▶ **prefix** forming or added to verbs or their derivatives. **1** down; away: *deduct.* **2** completely: *denude.* **3** referring to removal or reversal: *de-ice.*
– ORIGIN from Latin *de* 'off, from' or *dis-*.

dea·con /ˈdēkən/ ▶ **noun 1** (in Catholic, Anglican, and Orthodox Churches) a minister ranking below a priest. **2** (in some Protestant Churches) a lay officer assisting a minister.
– ORIGIN Greek *diakonos* 'servant.'

dea·con·ess /ˈdēkənis/ ▶ **noun** a woman with duties similar to those of a deacon.

de·ac·ti·vate /dēˈaktəvāt/ ▶ **verb** make something inactive by disconnecting or destroying it.
– DERIVATIVES **de·ac·ti·va·tion** /dēˌaktəˈvāshən/ noun.

dead /ded/ ▸ **adjective 1** no longer alive. **2** (of a part of the body) numb. **3** displaying no emotion. **4** no longer relevant or important. **5** without activity or excitement. **6** (of equipment) not working. **7** complete; absolute: *dead silence*.

– SYNONYMS **1 passed on,** passed away, departed, late, lost, perished, fallen, killed, lifeless, extinct; informal six feet under, pushing up daisies; formal deceased. **2 obsolete,** extinct, defunct, disused, abandoned, superseded, vanished, archaic, ancient. **3 not working,** out of order, inoperative, inactive, broken, defective; informal kaput, conked out, on the blink, bust. **4 boring,** uninteresting, unexciting, uninspiring, dull, flat, quiet, sleepy, slow, lifeless; informal one-horse, dullsville.
– ANTONYMS alive, living, lively.

▸ **adverb 1** completely; exactly: *dead on time*. **2** straight; directly: *dead ahead*.

– SYNONYMS **1 completely,** absolutely, totally, utterly, deadly, perfectly, entirely, quite, thoroughly. **2 directly,** exactly, precisely, immediately, right, straight, due.

– DERIVATIVES **dead·ness** noun.
– PHRASES **dead and buried** over; finished. **dead meat** informal in trouble: *if anyone finds out, you're dead meat*. **the dead of night** the quietest, darkest part of the night. **the dead of winter** the coldest part of winter. **dead to the world** informal fast asleep. **from the dead** from being dead; from death.
– ORIGIN Old English.

dead·beat /ˈdedˌbēt/ ▸ **adjective** (**dead beat**) informal completely exhausted. ▸ **noun** informal **1** a lazy or disreputable person. **2** a person who tries to evade paying a debt.

dead·bolt /ˈdedˌbōlt/ ▸ **noun** a bolt secured by turning a knob or key, rather than by spring action.

dead duck ▸ **noun** informal an unsuccessful or useless person or thing.

dead·en /ˈdedn/ ▸ **verb 1** make a noise or sensation less intense. **2** make something numb.

– SYNONYMS **1 numb,** dull, blunt, alleviate, mitigate, diminish, reduce, lessen, ease, soothe, relieve, assuage. **2 muffle,** mute, smother, stifle, damp (down), soften, cushion.
– ANTONYMS intensify, amplify.

dead end ▸ **noun 1** an end of a road or passage from which no exit is possible. **2** a situation in which no further progress can be made.

dead hand ▸ **noun** an undesirable and long-lasting influence.

dead·head /ˈdedˌhed/ ▸ **noun 1** (**Deadhead**) a fan and follower of the rock group The Grateful Dead. **2** a passenger or member of an audience with a free ticket. ▸ **verb** remove dead flowerheads from a plant.

dead heat ▸ **noun** a result in a race in which two or more competitors finish at exactly the same time.

dead let·ter ▸ **noun** a law or treaty that has not been repealed but is no longer applied.

dead·line /ˈdedˌlīn/ ▸ **noun** the latest time or date by which something should be completed.

– SYNONYMS **time limit,** finishing date, target date, cutoff point.

dead·lock /ˈdedˌläk/ ▸ **noun** a situation in which no progress can be made.

– SYNONYMS **stalemate,** impasse, checkmate, standoff, standstill, gridlock.

▸ **verb** (**be deadlocked**) be in a situation in which no progress can be made.

dead loss ▸ **noun** an unproductive or useless person or thing.

dead·ly /ˈdedlē/ ▸ **adjective** (**deadlier, deadliest**) **1** causing or able to cause death. **2** complete; total: *they were deadly enemies*. **3** extremely accurate or effective: *her deadly aim with a tennis ball*. **4** informal extremely boring.

– SYNONYMS **1 fatal,** lethal, mortal, life-threatening, noxious, toxic, poisonous. **2** *deadly enemies* **mortal,** irreconcilable, implacable, bitter, sworn. **3** *his aim is deadly* **unerring,** unfailing, perfect, true, accurate.
– ANTONYMS harmless.

▸ **adverb 1** in a way that resembles or suggests death: *her skin was deadly pale*. **2** extremely: *he was deadly serious*.
– DERIVATIVES **dead·li·ness** noun.

dead·ly night·shade ▸ **noun** a poisonous bushy plant with drooping purple flowers and round black fruit.

dead·ly sin ▸ **noun** (in Christian tradition) a sin regarded as leading to damnation.

dead·pan /ˈdedˌpan/ ▸ **adjective** (of a person's expression) not showing any emotion.

dead reck·on·ing ▸ **noun** the calculation of one's position, especially at sea, by estimating the direction and distance traveled.

dead ring·er ▸ **noun** a person or thing that looks very like another.

dead·weight /ˈdedˌwāt/ ▸ **noun 1** the weight of a person or thing without the strength or ability to move themselves. **2** the total weight of cargo, stores, etc., that a ship can carry.

dead·wood /ˈdedˌwo͝od/ ▸ **noun** useless or unproductive people or things.

dead zone ▸ **noun 1** a place or period in which nothing happens. **2** a place where it is not possible to receive a cell-phone or radio signal.

deaf /def/ ▸ **adjective 1** wholly or partially unable to hear. **2** (**deaf to**) unwilling to listen or respond to: *she was deaf to all advice*.
– DERIVATIVES **deaf·ness** noun.
– PHRASES **fall on deaf ears** be ignored. **turn a deaf ear** refuse to listen or respond.
– ORIGIN Old English.

deaf·en /ˈdefən/ ▸ **verb 1** make someone deaf. **2** (as adj. **deafening**) extremely loud.

– SYNONYMS (as adj. **deafening**) *the deafening noise from the construction site* **ear-splitting,** thunderous, crashing, uproarious, almighty, booming.
– ANTONYMS low, soft.

– DERIVATIVES **deaf·en·ing·ly** /ˈdefəniNGlē/ adverb.

deaf mute ▸ **noun** a person who is deaf and unable to speak.

USAGE

As the noun **deaf mute** may be regarded as offensive, it is advisable to use terms such as **profoundly deaf** instead.

deal[1] /dēl/ ▸ **noun 1** an agreement between two or more parties for their mutual benefit. **2** a particular form of treatment given or received: *working mothers get a bad deal*. **3** the process of distributing cards in a card game.

– SYNONYMS **agreement,** understanding, pact, bargain, covenant, contract, treaty, arrangement, compromise, settlement, terms.

▶ **verb** (past and past part. **dealt** /delt/) **1** (**deal something out**) distribute something. **2** (usu. **deal in**) buy and sell a product or commodity commercially. **3** buy and sell illegal drugs. **4** distribute cards to players for a game or round. **5** (**deal with**) do business with. **6** (**deal with**) take action to put something right. **7** (**deal with**) have something as a subject. **8** (**deal with**) cope with: *a way of helping people deal with loss.*

– SYNONYMS **1 trade in,** buy and sell, purvey, supply, market, traffic in. **2 distribute,** give out, share out, divide out, hand out, pass out, pass around, dispense, allocate. **3** *the article* ***deals with*** *advances in chemistry* **concern,** be about, have to do with, discuss, consider, cover, tackle, explore, investigate, examine. **4** *how to* ***deal with*** *difficult children* **cope with,** handle, manage, treat, take care of, take charge of, take in hand, sort out, tackle, take on, control.

– PHRASES **a big deal** informal an important thing. **deal someone or something a blow** hit or be harmful to someone or something. **a good** (or **great**) **deal 1** a large amount. **2** to a considerable extent: *a good deal better.* **3** an attractive price; a bargain: *she gave me a good deal on her old car.* **a square deal** a fair bargain or treatment.

– ORIGIN Old English.

deal² ▶ **noun** fir or pine wood (as a building material).

– ORIGIN German and Dutch *dele* 'plank.'

deal·er /ˈdēlər/ ▶ **noun 1** a person who buys and sells goods. **2** a person who sells illegal drugs. **3** a player who deals cards in a card game.

– SYNONYMS **trader,** merchant, salesman, saleswoman, seller, vendor, purveyor, peddler, distributor, supplier, shopkeeper, retailer, wholesaler, tradesman, tradesperson.

– DERIVATIVES **deal·er·ship** /-ˌSHip/ noun.

dealer plates ▶ **plural noun** temporary license plates used by car dealers or manufacturers on unlicensed cars.

dealt /delt/ past participle of **DEAL¹**.

dean /dēn/ ▶ **noun 1** the head of the governing body of a cathedral. **2** the head of a university faculty or department or of a medical school. **3** a college official who is responsible for the discipline and welfare of students.

– ORIGIN Old French *deien.*

dean·er·y /ˈdēnərē/ ▶ **noun** (pl. **deaneries**) the official house of a dean.

dear /di(ə)r/ ▶ **adjective 1** regarded with deep affection. **2** used in the polite introduction to a letter. **3** expensive.

– SYNONYMS **1** *a dear friend* **beloved,** precious, close, intimate, bosom. **2** *her pictures were too dear to part with* **precious,** treasured, valued, prized, cherished, special. **3 endearing,** adorable, lovable, appealing, engaging, charming, captivating, lovely, delightful, sweet, darling. **4 expensive,** costly, high-priced, overpriced, exorbitant, extortionate. informal pricey.
– ANTONYMS disagreeable, cheap.

▶ **noun 1** a lovable person. **2** used as an affectionate form of address.

– SYNONYMS **darling,** dearest, love, beloved, sweetheart, precious; informal sweetie, sugar, honey, baby, pet.

▶ **adverb** chiefly Brit. at a high cost.

▶ **exclamation** used in expressions of surprise or dismay.

– ORIGIN Old English.

dear·ly /ˈdi(ə)rlē/ ▶ **adverb 1** very much. **2** at great cost.

– SYNONYMS **very much,** a great deal, greatly, profoundly, deeply.

dearth /dərTH/ ▶ **noun** a lack or inadequate amount of something: *a dearth of reliable information.*

– SYNONYMS **lack,** scarcity, shortage, shortfall, deficiency, insufficiency, inadequacy, absence.
– ANTONYMS surfeit.

– ORIGIN first meaning 'dearness and shortage of food': from **DEAR**.

death /deTH/ ▶ **noun 1** the action or fact of dying. **2** an instance of a person or an animal dying. **3** the state of being dead. **4** the end of something: *the death of communism.*

– SYNONYMS **1 dying,** demise, end, passing, loss of life; formal decease. **2 end,** finish, termination, extinction, extinguishing, collapse, destruction.
– ANTONYMS life, birth.

– DERIVATIVES **death·less** adjective.

– PHRASES **at death's door** so ill that one may die. **catch one's death (of cold)** informal catch a severe cold. **die a death** fail or come to an end. **do something to death** do something so often that it becomes boring. **like death warmed over** informal extremely tired or ill. **put someone to death** execute someone. **to death 1** until dead. **2** used for emphasis: *I'm sick to death of him.*

– ORIGIN Old English.

WORD LINKS

fatal, **lethal**, **mortal** *causing death*

death·bed /ˈdeTHˌbed/ ▶ **noun** the bed where someone is dying or has died.

death camp ▶ **noun** a prison camp in which many people die or are put to death.

death cer·tif·i·cate ▶ **noun** an official statement, signed by a doctor, giving details of a person's death.

death knell ▶ **noun** an event that signals the end of something.

– ORIGIN from the ringing of a bell to mark a person's death.

death·ly /ˈdeTHlē/ ▶ **adjective** (**deathlier, deathliest**) suggesting death: *a deathly silence.*

– SYNONYMS **deathlike,** ghostly, ghastly, ashen, white, pale, pallid.

death mask ▶ **noun** a plaster cast of a person's face, made just after their death.

death pen·al·ty ▶ **noun** punishment by execution.

death rate ▶ **noun** the number of deaths per one thousand people per year.

death rat·tle ▶ **noun** a gurgling sound in a dying person's throat.

death row /rō/ ▶ **noun** a prison block for people sentenced to death.

death toll ▶ **noun** the number of deaths resulting from a particular cause.

death trap ▶ **noun** a dangerous building, vehicle, etc.

death-watch bee·tle ▶ **noun** a beetle whose larvae bore into dead wood and timbers.
– ORIGIN so called because it makes a ticking sound, formerly believed to be an omen of death.

death wish ▶ **noun** an unconscious desire for one's own death.

deb /deb/ ▶ **noun** informal a debutante.

de·ba·cle /di'bakəl, -'bäkəl/ ▶ **noun** a complete failure or disaster.

– SYNONYMS **fiasco,** failure, catastrophe, disaster.

– ORIGIN French, from *débâcler* 'unleash.'

de·bar /dē'bär/ ▶ **verb** (**debars, debarring, debarred**) officially prohibit someone from doing something.
– DERIVATIVES **de·bar·ment** noun.
– ORIGIN Old French *desbarrer* 'unbar.'

de·bark /dē'bärk/ ▶ **verb** leave a ship or aircraft.
– ORIGIN French *débarquer.*

de·base /di'bās/ ▶ **verb** lower the quality, value, or character of someone or something.

– SYNONYMS **degrade,** devalue, demean, cheapen, prostitute, discredit, drag down, tarnish, blacken, disgrace, dishonor, shame.
– ANTONYMS enhance.

– DERIVATIVES **de·base·ment** noun.

de·bat·a·ble /di'bātəbəl/ ▶ **adjective** open to discussion or argument.

– SYNONYMS **arguable,** questionable, open to question, disputable, controversial, contentious, doubtful, dubious, uncertain, borderline, moot.

de·bate /di'bāt/ ▶ **noun 1** a formal discussion in a public meeting or lawmaking body, in which opposing arguments are presented. **2** an argument.

– SYNONYMS **discussion,** argument, dispute, talks.

▶ **verb 1** discuss or argue about something. **2** consider a course of action: *she debated whether or not to go for a swim.*

– SYNONYMS **1 discuss,** talk over/through, talk about, thrash out, argue, dispute. **2 consider,** think over/about, chew over, mull over, weigh up, ponder, deliberate.

– DERIVATIVES **de·bat·er** noun.
– PHRASES **under debate** being discussed.
– ORIGIN Old French, from Latin *battere* 'to fight.'

de·bauched /di'bôcht/ ▶ **adjective** overindulging in sex, alcohol, or drugs.

– SYNONYMS **dissolute,** dissipated, degenerate, decadent, profligate, immoral, lecherous, lewd, licentious.
– ANTONYMS wholesome.

– DERIVATIVES **de·bauch·er·y** /di'bôchərē/ noun.
– ORIGIN from Old French *desbaucher* 'turn away from one's duty.'

de·ben·ture /di'benchər/ ▶ **noun** an unsecured loan certificate issued by a company, backed by general credit rather than by specified assets.
– ORIGIN Latin *debentur* 'are owing.'

de·bil·i·tate /di'bili,tāt, dē-/ ▶ **verb** severely weaken someone or something.
– DERIVATIVES **de·bil·i·ta·tion** /di,bili'tāshən/ noun.
– ORIGIN from Latin *debilis* 'weak.'

de·bil·i·ty /di'bilitē/ ▶ **noun** (pl. **debilities**) physical weakness.

deb·it /'debit/ ▶ **noun 1** an entry in an account recording a sum owed. **2** a payment made or owed. ▶ **verb** (**debits, debiting, debited**) (of a bank) remove money from a customer's account.
– ORIGIN French, from Latin *debitum* 'something owed.'

deb·it card ▶ **noun** a card allowing the holder to remove money from a bank account electronically when making a purchase.

deb·o·nair /,debə'ne(ə)r/ ▶ **adjective** (of a man) confident, stylish, and charming.

– SYNONYMS **suave,** urbane, sophisticated, cultured, self-possessed, self-assured, confident, charming, gracious, courteous, gallant, gentlemanly, refined, polished, well bred, genteel, dignified, courtly, well groomed, elegant, stylish, smart, dashing; informal smooth, sharp.
– ANTONYMS unsophisticated.

– ORIGIN from Old French *de bon aire* 'of good disposition.'

de·bouch /di'bouch, -'bo͞osh/ ▶ **verb** emerge from a confined space into a wide, open area.
– DERIVATIVES **de·bouch·ment** noun.
– ORIGIN French, from *bouche* 'mouth.'

de·brief /dē'brēf/ ▶ **verb** question someone in detail about a completed mission.
– DERIVATIVES **de·brief·ing** noun.

de·bris /də'brē, ,dā-/ ▶ **noun 1** scattered pieces of trash or the remains of something that has been destroyed. **2** loose broken pieces of rock.

– SYNONYMS **ruins,** remains, rubble, wreckage, detritus, refuse, rubbish, waste, scrap, flotsam and jetsam.

– ORIGIN French.

debt /det/ ▶ **noun 1** a sum of money owed. **2** the state of owing money: *he got into debt.* **3** a feeling of gratitude for a favor or service.

– SYNONYMS **1 bill,** account, dues, arrears, charges. **2 indebtedness,** obligation, gratitude, appreciation.

– ORIGIN Latin *debitum* 'something owed.'

debt of hon·or ▶ **noun** a debt whose repayment is not legally binding but depends on a sense of moral obligation.

debt·or /'detər/ ▶ **noun** a person who owes money.

de·bug /dē'bəg/ ▶ **verb** (**debugs, debugging, debugged**) remove errors from computer hardware or software.
– DERIVATIVES **de·bug·ger** noun.

de·bunk /di'bəngk/ ▶ **verb** show that a widely held belief or opinion is false or exaggerated.
– DERIVATIVES **de·bunk·er** noun.

de·burr /dē'bər/ (also **debur**) ▶ **verb** (**deburrs, deburring, deburred**) smooth the rough edges of an object.

de·but /dā'byo͞o/ ▶ **noun 1** a person's first appearance or performance in a capacity or role. **2** dated the first appearance of a debutante in society.

– SYNONYMS **first appearance,** first performance, launch, entrance, premiere, introduction, inception, inauguration; informal kickoff.

▶ **adjective** referring to the first recording or publication of a singer or writer: *her debut album.*
▶ **verb** perform in public for the first time.
– ORIGIN from French *débuter* 'lead off.'

deb·u·tant /'debyo͞o,tänt, 'debyə-/ ▶ **noun** a person making a debut.

deb·u·tante /ˈdebyo͝oˌtänt, ˈdebyə-/ ▸ **noun** a young upper-class woman making her first appearance in society.

Dec. ▸ **abbreviation** December.

dec·ade /ˈdekād/ ▸ **noun** a period of ten years.
– ORIGIN Old French, from Greek *deka* 'ten.'

dec·a·dent /ˈdekədənt/ ▸ **adjective 1** having low moral standards and interested only in pleasure and enjoyment. **2** luxuriously self-indulgent: *a decadent soak in a scented bath.*

– SYNONYMS **dissolute,** dissipated, degenerate, corrupt, depraved, sinful, unprincipled, immoral, amoral, licentious, abandoned, profligate, intemperate, sybaritic, hedonistic, pleasure-seeking, self-indulgent.

– DERIVATIVES **dec·a·dence** noun **dec·a·dent·ly** adverb.
– ORIGIN French, from Latin *decadentia.*

de·caf /ˈdēˌkaf/ ▸ **noun** informal decaffeinated coffee.

de·caf·fein·a·ted /dēˈkafəˌnātəd/ ▸ **adjective** (of tea or coffee) having had most or all of its caffeine removed.

dec·a·gon /ˈdekəˌgän/ ▸ **noun** a plane figure with ten straight sides and angles.

dec·a·he·dron /ˌdekəˈhēdrən/ ▸ **noun** (pl. **decahedra** /-drə/ or **decahedrons**) a solid figure with ten plane faces.

de·cal /ˈdēkal/ ▸ **noun** a design on prepared paper for transferring onto glass, porcelain, etc.
– ORIGIN abbreviation of *decalcomania,* from French *décalquer* 'transfer a tracing' + *-manie* '-mania.'

de·cal·ci·fied /dēˈkalsəˌfīd/ ▸ **adjective** (of rock or bone) containing a reduced quantity of calcium salts.
– DERIVATIVES **de·cal·ci·fi·ca·tion** /dēˌkalsəfiˈkāsʜən/ noun.

dec·a·li·ter /ˈdekəˌlētər/ ▸ **noun** a metric unit of capacity, equal to 10 liters.

Dec·a·logue /ˈdekəˌlôg, -ˌläg/ ▸ **noun** the Ten Commandments.
– ORIGIN from Greek *dekalogos biblos* 'book of the Ten Commandments.'

de·camp /diˈkamp/ ▸ **verb** leave suddenly or secretly.

de·cant /diˈkant/ ▸ **verb 1** pour something from one container into another to separate liquid from sediment. **2** figurative empty out; move as if by pouring.
– ORIGIN Latin *decanthare.*

de·cant·er /diˈkantər/ ▸ **noun** a glass container with a stopper into which wine or liquor is decanted.

de·cap·i·tate /diˈkapiˌtāt/ ▸ **verb** kill someone by cutting off their head.
– DERIVATIVES **de·cap·i·ta·tion** /diˌkapiˈtāsʜən/ noun.
– ORIGIN Latin *decapitare,* from *caput* 'head.'

dec·a·pod /ˈdekəˌpäd/ ▸ **noun** a crustacean with five pairs of walking legs, such as a shrimp.
– ORIGIN from Greek *deka* 'ten' + *pous* 'foot.'

de·car·bon·ize /dēˈkärbəˌnīz/ ▸ **verb** remove carbon deposits from an engine.

de·cath·lon /diˈkaᴛʜ(ə)ˌlän/ ▸ **noun** a track-and-field event in which each competitor takes part in the same ten events.
– DERIVATIVES **de·cath·lete** /-ˈkaᴛʜ(ə)ˌlēt/ noun.
– ORIGIN from Greek *deka* 'ten' + *athlon* 'contest.'

de·cay /diˈkā/ ▸ **verb 1** rot as a result of the action of bacteria and fungi. **2** become progressively worse; deteriorate. **3** Physics (of a radioactive substance, particle, etc.) undergo change to a different form by emitting radiation.

– SYNONYMS **1 decompose,** rot, putrefy, go bad, go off, spoil, fester, perish. **2 deteriorate,** degenerate, decline, go downhill, slump, slide, go to rack and ruin, go to seed; informal go to the dogs.

▸ **noun 1** the state or process of decaying. **2** rotten matter or tissue.

– SYNONYMS **1 decomposition,** putrefaction, rot. **2 deterioration,** degeneration, decline, weakening, crumbling, disintegration, collapse.

– ORIGIN Old French *decair.*

de·cease /diˈsēs/ ▸ **noun** formal or Law death.
– ORIGIN Latin *decessus.*

de·ceased /diˈsēst/ formal or Law ▸ **noun** (**the deceased**) the recently dead person in question. ▸ **adjective** recently dead.

de·ce·dent /diˈsēdnt/ ▸ **noun** Law a person who has died: *questions concerning the decedent's intentions.*

de·ceit /diˈsēt/ ▸ **noun** behavior intended to make someone believe something that is not true.

– SYNONYMS **deception,** deceitfulness, duplicity, double-dealing, deviousness, slyness, lies, fraud, cheating, trickery.
– ANTONYMS honesty.

de·ceit·ful /diˈsētfəl/ ▸ **adjective** deliberately behaving in a way that makes others believe things that are not true.

– SYNONYMS **dishonest,** untruthful, insincere, false, disingenuous, untrustworthy, unscrupulous, unprincipled, two-faced, duplicitous, fraudulent, double-dealing; informal sneaky, tricky, crooked.
– ANTONYMS honest.

– DERIVATIVES **de·ceit·ful·ly** adverb **de·ceit·ful·ness** noun.

de·ceive /diˈsēv/ ▸ **verb 1** deliberately make someone believe something that is not true. **2** (of a thing) give a mistaken impression: *don't be deceived by the book's title.*

– SYNONYMS **trick,** cheat, defraud, swindle, hoodwink, hoax, dupe, take in, mislead, delude, fool; informal con, sucker, pull the wool over someone's eyes.

– DERIVATIVES **de·ceiv·er** noun.
– ORIGIN Old French *deceivre.*

de·cel·er·ate /dēˈseləˌrāt/ ▸ **verb** begin to move more slowly.
– DERIVATIVES **de·cel·er·a·tion** /-ˌseləˈrāsʜən/ noun.

De·cem·ber /diˈsembər/ ▸ **noun** the twelfth month of the year.
– ORIGIN Latin, from *decem* 'ten' (being originally the tenth month of the Roman year).

de·cen·cy /ˈdēsənsē/ ▸ **noun** (pl. **decencies**) **1** behavior that follows generally accepted standards of morality or respectability. **2** (**decencies**) standards of acceptable behavior.

– SYNONYMS **1 propriety,** decorum, good taste, respectability, morality, virtue, modesty. **2 courtesy,** politeness, good manners, civility, consideration, thoughtfulness.

de·cen·ni·al /diˈsenēəl/ ▸ **adjective** lasting for or happening every ten years.
– ORIGIN from Latin *decem* 'ten' + *annus* 'year.'

de·cent /'dēsənt/ ▶ **adjective 1** following generally accepted standards of morality or respectability. **2** of an acceptable standard. **3** informal kind or generous.

– SYNONYMS **1** *a decent burial* **proper,** correct, appropriate, suitable, respectable, decorous, seemly, accepted. **2** *a job with decent pay* **satisfactory,** reasonable, fair, acceptable, adequate, sufficient, not bad, all right, tolerable, passable, suitable; informal OK. **3 kind,** generous, thoughtful, considerate, obliging, courteous, polite, neighborly, hospitable, pleasant, agreeable, amiable.
– ANTONYMS improper, unsatisfactory.

– DERIVATIVES **de·cent·ly** adverb.
– ORIGIN from Latin *decere* 'to be fit.'

de·cen·tral·ize /dē'sentrə,līz/ ▶ **verb** transfer authority from central to local government.
– DERIVATIVES **de·cen·tral·i·za·tion** /dē,sentrəli'zāsʜən/ noun.

de·cep·tion /di'sepsʜən/ ▶ **noun 1** the action of deceiving someone. **2** a thing that deceives others into believing something that is not true.

– SYNONYMS **1 deceit,** duplicity, double-dealing, fraud, cheating, trickery, guile, bluff, lying, pretense, treachery. **2 trick,** sham, fraud, pretense, hoax, ruse, scheme, dodge, cheat, swindle; informal con, setup, scam.

CHOOSE THE RIGHT WORD

See **FICTION**.

de·cep·tive /di'septiv/ ▶ **adjective** giving an impression different from the true one; misleading.

– SYNONYMS **misleading,** confusing, illusory, distorted, ambiguous.

de·cep·tive·ly /di'septivlē/ ▶ **adverb 1** to a lesser extent than appears the case. **2** to a greater extent than appears the case.

USAGE

Deceptively can mean both one thing and also its complete opposite. A *deceptively smooth surface* is one that appears smooth but in fact is not smooth at all, while a *deceptively spacious room* is one that does not look spacious but is in fact **more** spacious than it appears. To avoid confusion, it is often better to reword a sentence rather than use **deceptively**.

deci- ▶ **combining form** one tenth: *deciliter.*
– ORIGIN from Latin *decimus* 'tenth.'

dec·i·bel /'desə,bel, -bəl/ ▶ **noun** a unit of measurement expressing the intensity of a sound or the power of an electrical signal.
– ORIGIN from **DECI-** + *bel*, a unit (= 10 decibels) named after Alexander Graham *Bell*, inventor of the telephone.

de·cide /di'sīd/ ▶ **verb 1** consider something carefully and make a judgment or choice: *she decided to stay at home.* **2** settle an issue or contest: *the game was decided by a penalty shot.* **3** give a judgment concerning a legal case.

– SYNONYMS **1 resolve,** determine, make up one's mind, choose, opt, plan, aim, intend, have in mind. **2 settle,** resolve, determine, work out, answer; informal sort out. **3 adjudicate,** arbitrate, judge, pronounce on, give a verdict on, rule on.

– DERIVATIVES **de·cid·a·ble** adjective **de·cid·ing** adjective.
– ORIGIN Latin *decidere* 'determine.'

de·cid·ed /di'sīdid/ ▶ **adjective** definite; clear: *a decided improvement.*

de·cid·ed·ly /di'sīdidlē/ ▶ **adverb** clearly and distinctly.

– SYNONYMS *they were decidedly hostile to one another* **distinctly,** clearly, markedly, obviously, noticeably, unmistakably, patently, manifestly, definitely, positively.

de·cid·u·ous /di'sijōōəs/ ▶ **adjective 1** (of a tree or shrub) shedding its leaves annually. Contrasted with **EVERGREEN**. **2** (of teeth or horns) shed after a time.
– ORIGIN Latin *deciduus.*

dec·i·li·ter /'desə,lētər/ (Brit. **decilitre**) ▶ **noun** a metric unit of capacity, equal to one tenth of a liter.

dec·i·mal /'des(ə)məl/ ▶ **adjective** relating to a system of numbers based on the number ten. ▶ **noun** a fractional number in the decimal system, written with figures to the right of a decimal point.
– ORIGIN from Latin *decimus* 'tenth.'

dec·i·mal·ize /'desəmə,līz/ ▶ **verb** convert a system of coinage or weights and measures to a decimal system.
– DERIVATIVES **dec·i·mal·i·za·tion** /,des(ə)mələ'zāsʜən/ noun.

dec·i·mal place ▶ **noun** the position of a digit to the right of a decimal point.

dec·i·mal point ▶ **noun** a dot placed after the figure representing units in a decimal fraction.

dec·i·mate /'desə,māt/ ▶ **verb 1** kill or destroy a large proportion of a group. **2** drastically reduce the strength of something.
– DERIVATIVES **dec·i·ma·tion** /,desə'māsʜən/ noun.
– ORIGIN Latin *decimare* 'take as a tenth.'

USAGE

The earliest sense of **decimate** was 'kill one in every ten of a group,' a reference to the ancient Roman practice of killing one in every ten of a group of soldiers as a collective punishment. This has been more or less totally superseded by the sense 'kill or destroy a large proportion of a group,' although some people argue that this later sense is wrong.

dec·i·me·ter /'desə,mētər/ (Brit. **decimetre**) ▶ **noun** a metric unit of length, equal to one tenth of a meter.

de·ci·pher /di'sīfər/ ▶ **verb 1** convert something written in code into normal language. **2** succeed in understanding or interpreting something: *his handwriting was difficult to decipher.*
– DERIVATIVES **de·ci·pher·a·ble** adjective **de·ci·pher·ment** noun.

de·ci·sion /di'sizʜən/ ▶ **noun 1** a choice or judgment made after considering something. **2** the action or process of deciding. **3** decisiveness.

– SYNONYMS **1 resolution,** conclusion, settlement, choice, option, selection. **2 verdict,** finding, ruling, judgment, adjudication, sentence.

de·ci·sive /di'sīsiv/ ▶ **adjective 1** having great importance for the final result of a situation: *a decisive battle.* **2** able to make decisions quickly.

– SYNONYMS **1 deciding,** conclusive, determining, key, pivotal, critical, crucial. **2 resolute,** firm, strong-minded, strong-willed, determined, purposeful.

– DERIVATIVES **de·ci·sive·ly** adverb **de·ci·sive·ness** noun.

deck /dek/ ▶ **noun 1** a floor of a ship, especially the upper level. **2** a floor or platform resembling a ship's deck,

especially one attached to a house. **3** a set of playing cards. **4** a component in sound-reproduction equipment, incorporating a player or recorder for discs or tapes. ▶ **verb 1** decorate or dress someone or something brightly or attractively: *the Morris dancers were decked out in rustic costume.* **2** informal knock someone to the ground with a punch.
– PHRASES **hit the deck** informal fall to the ground.
– ORIGIN Dutch *dec* 'covering, roof.'

deck chair ▶ **noun** a folding chair with a wooden frame and a canvas seat.

deck·hand /'dek,hand/ ▶ **noun** a member of a ship's crew performing cleaning or manual work.

deck·ing /'dekiNG/ ▶ **noun** material used in making a deck.

deck·le /'dekəl/ ▶ **noun** a continuous belt on either side in a paper-making machine, used for controlling the size of paper produced.
– ORIGIN German, 'small covering.'

de·claim /di'klām/ ▶ **verb** speak or recite something in an emphatic or dramatic way.

> – SYNONYMS **make a speech,** give an address, give a lecture, speak, hold forth, orate, preach, lecture, deliver a sermon, sermonize, moralize; informal sound off, spout; speak out, rail, inveigh, fulminate, rage, rant, thunder.

– DERIVATIVES **de·clam·a·to·ry** /-'klamə,tôrē/ adjective.
– ORIGIN Latin *declamare.*

dec·la·ma·tion /,dekləˈmāsHən/ ▶ **noun** the action of declaiming something.

dec·la·ra·tion /,dekləˈrāsHən/ ▶ **noun 1** a formal statement or announcement. **2** an act of declaring something.

> – SYNONYMS **1 announcement,** statement, communication, pronouncement, proclamation, advisory. **2 assertion,** profession, affirmation, acknowledgment, revelation, disclosure, confirmation, testimony, avowal, protestation.

de·clar·a·tive /di'kle(ə)rətiv, -'klar-/ ▶ **adjective 1** making a declaration: *a declarative statement.* **2** (of a sentence or phrase) taking the form of a simple statement.

de·clare /di'kle(ə)r/ ▶ **verb 1** announce something solemnly or officially. **2** (**declare oneself**) reveal one's intentions or identity. **3** (as adj. **declared**) having stated something openly: *a declared atheist.* **4** acknowledge that one has income or goods on which tax or duty should be paid.

> – SYNONYMS **1 announce,** proclaim, state, reveal, air, voice, articulate, express, vent, set forth, publicize, broadcast. **2 assert,** profess, affirm, maintain, state, contend, claim, argue, insist, avow.

– ORIGIN Latin *declarare,* from *clarare* 'make clear.'

> **CHOOSE THE RIGHT WORD**
>
> See **ANNOUNCE**.

dé·clas·sé /,dāklä'sā/ (also **déclassée**) ▶ **adjective** having fallen in social status.
– ORIGIN French.

de·clas·si·fy /dē'klasə,fī/ ▶ **verb** (**declassifies, declassifying, declassified**) officially declare information or documents to be no longer secret.
– DERIVATIVES **de·clas·si·fi·ca·tion** /dē,klasəfi'kāsHən/ noun.

de·clen·sion /di'klensHən/ ▶ **noun** the changes in the form of a noun, pronoun, or adjective that identify its grammatical case, number, and gender.
– ORIGIN from Old French *decliner* 'to decline.'

dec·li·na·tion /,deklə'nāsHən/ ▶ **noun 1** Astronomy the position of a point in the sky equivalent to latitude on the earth. **2** the angular deviation of a compass needle from true north.

de·cline /di'klīn/ ▶ **verb 1** become smaller, weaker, or worse: *the breeding population has declined in recent years.* **2** politely refuse to accept or do something: *he declined to comment on the rumors.* **3** (especially of the sun) move downward. **4** Grammar form a noun, pronoun, or adjective according to case, number, and gender.

> – SYNONYMS **1 turn down,** reject, brush aside, refuse, rebuff, spurn, repulse, dismiss, pass up, say no (to); informal give something a miss. **2 decrease,** reduce, lessen, diminish, dwindle, contract, shrink, fall off, tail off, drop, fall, go down. **3 deteriorate,** degenerate, decay, crumble, collapse, slump, slip, slide, go downhill, worsen; informal go to the dogs.
> – ANTONYMS accept, increase, improve.

▶ **noun** a gradual and continuous loss of strength, numbers, or value.

> – SYNONYMS **1 reduction,** decrease, downturn, downswing, diminution, ebb, drop, slump, plunge. **2 deterioration,** degeneration, degradation, shrinkage, erosion.
> – ANTONYMS rise, improvement.

– ORIGIN Latin *declinare* 'bend down, turn aside.'

de·cliv·i·ty /di'klivitē/ ▶ **noun** (pl. **declivities**) a downward slope.
– ORIGIN Latin *declivitas.*

de·clut·ter /dē'klətər/ ▶ **noun** remove superfluous or unnecessary articles from a house, room, etc.

dec·o /'dekō/ ▶ **noun** short for **ART DECO**.

de·coc·tion /di'käksHən/ ▶ **noun** a concentrated liquid produced by heating or boiling a substance.
– ORIGIN Latin.

de·code /di'kōd/ ▶ **verb 1** convert a coded message into intelligible language. **2** convert audio or video signals from analog to digital.

> – SYNONYMS **decipher,** decrypt, work out, solve, interpret, translate, make sense of, get to the bottom of, unravel, find the key to; informal crack, figure out.

– DERIVATIVES **de·cod·er** noun.

dé·colle·tage /dā,kälə'täzH ,dekələ-/ ▶ **noun 1** a low neckline on a woman's dress or top. **2** a woman's cleavage or breasts as revealed by such a neckline.
– ORIGIN French, from *décolleter* 'expose the neck.'

dé·colle·té /dā,kälə'tā, ,dekələ-/ ▶ **adjective** having a low neckline. ▶ **noun** a décolletage.
– ORIGIN French.

de·col·o·nize /dē'kälə,nīz/ ▶ **verb** withdraw from a colony, leaving it independent.
– DERIVATIVES **de·col·o·ni·za·tion** /-,kälənə'zāsHən/ noun.

de·com·mis·sion /,dēkə'misHən/ ▶ **verb 1** take a ship out of service. **2** dismantle a nuclear reactor or weapon and make it safe.

de·com·pose /,dēkəm'pōz/ ▶ **verb 1** (of organic matter) decay. **2** (of a substance) break down into its component elements.

– SYNONYMS **decay,** rot, putrefy, go bad, go off, spoil, perish, deteriorate, degrade, break down.

– DERIVATIVES **de·com·po·si·tion** /dēˌkämpəˈzisʜən/ noun.

de·com·press /ˌdēkəmˈpres/ ▶ verb **1** expand compressed computer data to its normal size. **2** reduce the air pressure on a person who has been experiencing high pressure while deep-sea diving.
– DERIVATIVES **de·com·pres·sor** noun.

de·com·pres·sion /ˌdēkəmˈpresʜən/ ▶ noun **1** reduction in air pressure. **2** a gradual reduction of air pressure on a person who has been experiencing high pressure while deep-sea diving. **3** the process of decompressing computer data.

de·com·pres·sion cham·ber ▶ noun a small room in which the air pressure can be varied, used to allow deep-sea divers to adjust to normal air pressure.

de·com·pres·sion sick·ness ▶ noun a serious condition that results when too rapid decompression causes nitrogen bubbles to form in the tissues of the body.

de·con·ges·tant /ˌdēkənˈjestənt/ ▶ noun a medicine taken to relieve a stuffy nose.

de·con·struct /ˌdēkənˈstrəkt/ ▶ verb **1** analyze something by the method of deconstruction. **2** reduce something to its constituent parts in order to reinterpret it.
– DERIVATIVES **de·con·struc·tive** adjective.

de·con·struc·tion /ˌdēkənˈstrəksʜən/ ▶ noun a method of literary and cultural analysis that states that something has many different meanings and emphasizes the role of the subject in the production of meaning.
– DERIVATIVES **de·con·struc·tion·ism** /-ˌnizəm/ noun **de·con·struc·tion·ist** /-ist/ adjective & noun.

de·con·tam·i·nate /ˌdēkənˈtaməˌnāt/ ▶ verb remove dangerous substances from an area or object.
– DERIVATIVES **de·con·tam·i·na·tion** /-ˌtaməˈnāsʜən/ noun.

de·con·tex·tu·al·ize /ˌdēkənˈteksᴄʜo͞oəˌlīz/ ▶ verb consider something separately from its context.
– DERIVATIVES **de·con·tex·tu·al·i·za·tion** /-ˌteksᴄʜo͞oələˈzāsʜən/ noun.

de·cor /dāˈkôr, di-/ ▶ noun the furnishing and decoration of a room.

– SYNONYMS **decoration,** furnishing, color scheme.

– ORIGIN French.

dec·o·rate /ˈdekəˌrāt/ ▶ verb **1** make something more attractive by putting extra items in or on it: *the square was decorated with colored lights.* **2** apply paint, wallpaper, etc., to a room or building. **3** give an award or medal to someone.

– SYNONYMS **1 ornament,** adorn, trim, embellish, garnish, furnish, enhance. **2 paint,** wallpaper, paper, refurbish, renovate, redecorate; informal do up, give something a facelift, give something a makeover. **3 give a medal to,** honor, cite, reward.

– ORIGIN Latin *decorare* 'embellish.'

dec·o·ra·tion /ˌdekəˈrāsʜən/ ▶ noun **1** the process or art of decorating something. **2** an object or pattern that makes something look more attractive. **3** the way in which something is decorated. **4** a medal or award conferred as an honor.

– SYNONYMS **1 ornamentation,** adornment, trimming, embellishment, beautification. **2 ornament,** bauble, trinket, knick-knack. **3 medal,** award, prize.

dec·o·ra·tive /ˈdek(ə)rətiv, ˈdekəˌrātiv/ ▶ adjective **1** making something look more attractive: *decorative motifs.* **2** relating to decoration.

– SYNONYMS **ornamental,** fancy, ornate, attractive, pretty, showy.
– ANTONYMS functional.

– DERIVATIVES **dec·o·ra·tive·ly** adverb.

dec·o·ra·tor /ˈdekəˌrātər/ ▶ noun a person whose job it is to design the interior of someone's home, by choosing colors, materials, and furnishings.

dec·o·rous /ˈdekərəs, diˈkôrəs/ ▶ adjective in keeping with good taste; polite and restrained.
– DERIVATIVES **dec·o·rous·ly** adverb **dec·o·rous·ness** noun.
– ORIGIN Latin *decorus* 'seemly.'

de·co·rum /diˈkôrəm/ ▶ noun polite and socially acceptable behavior.

– SYNONYMS **1 propriety,** seemliness, decency, good taste, correctness, politeness, good manners. **2 etiquette,** protocol, good form, custom, convention.
– ANTONYMS impropriety.

– ORIGIN Latin, 'seemly thing.'

de·cou·page /ˌdāko͞oˈpäzʜ/ ▶ noun the decoration of a surface with paper cutouts.
– ORIGIN French, from *découper* 'cut out.'

de·cou·ple /dēˈkəpəl/ ▶ verb separate or disengage one thing from another.

de·coy ▶ noun /ˈdēˌkoi/ **1** a real or imitation bird or mammal used by hunters to lure game. **2** a person or thing used to mislead someone or lure them into a trap. ▶ verb /diˈkoi/ lure a person or animal by means of a decoy.
– ORIGIN from Dutch *de kooi* 'the decoy,' from Latin *cavea* 'cage.'

de·crease ▶ verb /diˈkrēs/ make or become smaller or fewer in size, amount, or strength.

– SYNONYMS **lessen,** reduce, drop, diminish, decline, dwindle, fall off, plummet, plunge.
– ANTONYMS increase.

▶ noun /ˈdēˌkrēs, diˈkrēs/ **1** an instance of decreasing. **2** the process of decreasing.

– SYNONYMS **reduction,** drop, decline, downturn, cut, cutback, diminution.
– ANTONYMS increase.

– ORIGIN Latin *decrescere.*

de·cree /diˈkrē/ ▶ noun **1** an official order from a ruler or government that has the force of law. **2** a judgment or decision made by certain courts of law.

– SYNONYMS **1** *a presidential decree* **order,** command, commandment, edict, proclamation, law, statute, act. **2** *a court decree* **judgment,** verdict, adjudication, finding, ruling, decision.

▶ verb (**decrees, decreeing, decreed**) order something by decree.

– SYNONYMS **order,** direct, command, rule, dictate, pronounce, proclaim, ordain.

– ORIGIN Latin *decretum* 'something decided.'

dec·re·ment /ˈdekrəmənt/ ▶ noun **1** a reduction or diminution: *a decrement in sympathetic nervous activity.* **2** an amount by which something is reduced or diminished: *10 mg weekly decrements.* ▶ verb chiefly

Computing cause a discrete reduction in a numerical quantity: *the instruction decrements the accumulator by one.*

de·crep·it /di'krepit/ ▶ **adjective 1** worn out or ruined because of age or neglect. **2** elderly and infirm.

– SYNONYMS **dilapidated,** rickety, run-down, tumbledown, ramshackle, derelict, ruined, in (a state of) disrepair, gone to rack and ruin, on its last legs, decayed, crumbling.

– DERIVATIVES **de·crep·i·tude** /-ˌt(y)o͞od/ noun.
– ORIGIN Latin *decrepitus,* from *crepare* 'rattle, creak.'

de·crim·i·nal·ize /dē'kriminlˌīz/ ▶ **verb** change the law so that something is no longer illegal or a criminal offense.
– DERIVATIVES **de·crim·i·nal·i·za·tion** /-ˌkriminl-i'zāsʜən/ noun.

de·cry /di'krī/ ▶ **verb** (**decries, decrying, decried**) express strong public disapproval of something.

– SYNONYMS **denounce,** condemn, criticize, censure, attack, rail against, run down, pillory, lambaste, vilify, revile; disparage, deprecate; informal slam, blast, knock.
– ANTONYMS praise.

– ORIGIN French *décrier* 'cry down.'

de·crypt /di'kript/ ▶ **verb** make a coded or unclear message intelligible.
– DERIVATIVES **de·cryp·tion** noun.

ded·i·cate /'dediˌkāt/ ▶ **verb 1** devote time or effort to a particular task, activity, or purpose: *Joan has dedicated her life to animals.* **2** address a book to a person as a sign of respect or affection. **3** hold an official ceremony to mark the fact that something has been built to honor a particular deity, saint, etc.: *the temple is dedicated to Krishna.*

– SYNONYMS **1 commit,** devote, pledge, give (up), sacrifice, set aside. **2 inscribe,** address, offer. **3 devote,** assign, bless, consecrate, sanctify.

– DERIVATIVES **ded·i·ca·tee** /ˌdedikā'tē/ noun **ded·i·ca·tor** noun **ded·i·ca·to·ry** /-kəˌtôrē/ adjective.
– ORIGIN Latin *dedicare* 'devote or consecrate.'

ded·i·cat·ed /'dediˌkātid/ ▶ **adjective 1** devoting much time or effort to a particular task, activity, or purpose: *a dedicated musician.* **2** used or designed for one particular purpose only: *a dedicated high-speed rail link.*

– SYNONYMS **1 committed,** devoted, enthusiastic, keen, staunch, firm, steadfast, loyal, faithful. **2 specialized,** custom-built, customized, purpose-built, exclusive.
– ANTONYMS half-hearted.

ded·i·ca·tion /ˌdedi'kāsʜən/ ▶ **noun 1** the quality of devoting much time or effort to a particular task, activity, or purpose. **2** the action of dedicating a church or other building to a particular deity or saint. **3** the words with which a book is dedicated to someone.

– SYNONYMS **1 commitment,** devotion, loyalty, allegiance, application, resolve, conscientiousness, perseverance, persistence. **2 inscription,** message.
– ANTONYMS apathy.

de·duce /di'd(y)o͞os/ ▶ **verb** form an opinion or conclusion on the basis of the information or evidence available.

– SYNONYMS **conclude,** reason, work out, infer, understand, assume, presume, surmise, reckon; informal figure out, put two and two together.

– DERIVATIVES **de·duc·i·ble** /-səbəl/ adjective.
– ORIGIN Latin *deducere* 'to take or lead away.'

de·duct /di'dəkt/ ▶ **verb** subtract an amount from a total: *the tax is deducted from your earnings.*

– SYNONYMS **subtract,** take away, take off, debit, dock, stop; informal knock off.
– ANTONYMS add.

– ORIGIN Latin *deducere* 'to take or lead away.'

de·duct·i·ble /di'dəktəbəl/ ▶ **adjective** able to be deducted, especially from taxable income.
– DERIVATIVES **de·duct·i·bil·i·ty** /-ˌdəktə'bilitē/ noun.

de·duc·tion /di'dəksʜən/ ▶ **noun 1** the action of deducting an amount from a total. **2** an amount that is or may be deducted. **3** a method of reasoning in which a general rule or principle is used to draw a particular conclusion.

– SYNONYMS **1 subtraction,** removal, debit. **2 stoppage,** tax, expenses, rebate, discount, concession. **3 conclusion,** inference, supposition, hypothesis, assumption, presumption, suspicion.

– DERIVATIVES **de·duc·tive** /di'dəktiv/ adjective.

deed /dēd/ ▶ **noun 1** an action that is performed deliberately. **2** a legal document that is signed and delivered, especially one relating to property ownership or legal rights.

– SYNONYMS **1 act,** action, feat, exploit, achievement, accomplishment, endeavor. **2 document,** contract, instrument.

– ORIGIN Old English.

dee·jay /'dēˌjā/ ▶ **noun** informal a DJ.

deem /dēm/ ▶ **verb** formal regard or consider something in a particular way: *the event was deemed a great success.*

– SYNONYMS **consider,** regard as, judge, hold to be, view as, see as, take for, class as, count, find, esteem, suppose, reckon.

– ORIGIN Old English.

de·em·pha·size /dē'emfəˌsīz/ ▶ **verb** reduce the importance or prominence given to something.

deep /dēp/ ▶ **adjective 1** extending far down or in from the top or surface. **2** extending a particular distance from the top, surface, or outer edge. **3** (of sound) low in pitch and full in tone. **4** (of color) dark: *a deep blue.* **5** very intense or extreme: *a deep sleep.* **6** difficult to understand. **7** (in ball games) far down or across the field.

– SYNONYMS **1 cavernous,** yawning, gaping, huge, extensive, bottomless, fathomless. **2 intense,** heartfelt, wholehearted, deep-seated, sincere, genuine, earnest, enthusiastic, great. **3 profound,** serious, intelligent, intellectual, learned, wise, scholarly. **4** *he was deep in concentration* **rapt,** absorbed, engrossed, preoccupied, intent, immersed, lost, gripped. **5 obscure,** complex, mysterious, unfathomable, opaque, abstruse, esoteric, enigmatic. **6 low-pitched,** low, bass, rich, resonant, booming, sonorous. **7 dark,** intense, rich, strong, vivid.
– ANTONYMS shallow, superficial, high.

▶ **noun 1** (**the deep**) literary the sea. **2** (usu. **deeps**) a deep part of the sea.
▶ **adverb** far down or in; deeply.
– DERIVATIVES **deep·ness** noun.
– PHRASES **go off the deep end** informal give way suddenly to an outburst of emotion. **in deep water** informal in trouble or difficulty. **jump** (or **be thrown**) **in at the**

deep end informal face a difficult situation without much experience.
– ORIGIN Old English.

deep-dyed ▶ **adjective** informal complete: *a deep-dyed conservative.*

deep·en /ˈdēpən/ ▶ **verb** make or become deeper.

deep freeze ▶ **noun** (also **deep freezer**) a freezer. ▶ **verb** (**deep-freeze**) freeze or store food in a deep freeze.

deep-fry ▶ **verb** fry food in enough fat or oil to cover it completely.

deep·ly /ˈdēplē/ ▶ **adverb 1** far down or in. **2** intensely.

– SYNONYMS **profoundly,** greatly, enormously, extremely, very, strongly, intensely, keenly, acutely, thoroughly, completely, entirely, seriously.

deep-root·ed ▶ **adjective 1** firmly embedded in thought, behavior, or culture, and so having a persistent influence: *deep-rooted concern about declining values.* **2** (of a plant) having roots that extend well down into the soil.

deep-seat·ed (also **deep-rooted**) ▶ **adjective** firmly established.

deep space ▶ **noun** outer space.

deep-vein throm·bo·sis ▶ **noun** thrombosis in a vein lying deep below the skin, especially in the legs.

deer /di(ə)r/ ▶ **noun** (pl. same) a hoofed animal, the male of which usually has antlers.
– ORIGIN Old English.

deer·skin /ˈdi(ə)rˌskin/ ▶ **noun** leather made from the skin of a deer.

deer·stalk·er /ˈdi(ə)rˌstôkər/ ▶ **noun** a soft cloth cap, originally worn for hunting, with ear flaps that can be tied together over the top.

de-es·ca·late /dēˈeskəˌlāt/ ▶ **verb** reduce the intensity of a conflict or crisis.
– DERIVATIVES **de-es·ca·la·tion** noun.

de·face /diˈfās/ ▶ **verb** deliberately spoil the appearance of something.

– SYNONYMS **vandalize,** disfigure, spoil, ruin, damage; informal trash.

– DERIVATIVES **de·face·ment** noun.

de fac·to /di ˈfaktō, dā/ ▶ **adverb** existing in fact, whether legally recognized or not. Compare with **DE JURE**. ▶ **adjective** existing in fact but not necessarily legally recognized: *a de facto one-party system.*
– ORIGIN Latin, 'of fact.'

de·fal·ca·tion /ˌdēfalˈkāsʜən, -fôl-/ ▶ **verb** formal the stealing or misuse of funds placed in one's trust or under one's control.
– ORIGIN from Latin *defalcare* 'to lop.'

de·fame /diˈfām/ ▶ **verb** say or write something that damages the reputation of someone or something.

– SYNONYMS **libel,** slander, malign, slur, cast aspersions on, smear, traduce, give someone a bad name, run down, speak ill of, vilify, besmirch, disparage, denigrate, discredit; informal bad-mouth, do a hatchet job on, drag through the mud.
– ANTONYMS compliment.

– DERIVATIVES **def·a·ma·tion** /ˌdefəˈmāsʜən/ noun **de·fam·a·to·ry** /-ˈfaməˌtôrē/ adjective.
– ORIGIN Latin *diffamare* 'spread evil report.'

de·fault /diˈfôlt/ ▶ **noun 1** failure to fulfill an obligation, especially to repay a loan or appear in a court of law. **2** a previously selected option adopted by a computer program or other mechanism when no alternative is specified. ▶ **verb 1** fail to fulfill an obligation, especially to repay a loan or to appear in court. **2** (**default to**) go back automatically to a previously selected option.
– DERIVATIVES **de·fault·er** noun.
– PHRASES **by default** because of a lack of opposition or positive action. **in default of** in the absence of.
– ORIGIN from Old French *defaillir* 'to fail.'

de·feat /diˈfēt/ ▶ **verb 1** win a victory over a person, team, army, etc. **2** prevent someone from achieving an aim or prevent an aim from being achieved. **3** reject or block a proposal or motion.

– SYNONYMS **1 beat,** conquer, win against, triumph over, get the better of, vanquish, rout, trounce, overcome, overpower; informal lick, thrash. **2 thwart,** frustrate, foil, ruin, scotch, derail; informal put paid to, stymie.

▶ **noun** an instance of defeating someone or something or the state of being defeated.

– SYNONYMS **loss,** conquest, rout; informal thrashing, hiding, drubbing, licking.
– ANTONYMS victory.

– ORIGIN Old French *desfaire.*

de·feat·ist /diˈfētist/ ▶ **noun** a person who gives in to failure too readily or who expects to fail. ▶ **adjective** accepting failure too readily; expecting to fail.
– DERIVATIVES **de·feat·ism** /-tizəm/ noun.

def·e·cate /ˈdefiˌkāt/ ▶ **verb** expel waste matter from the bowels.
– DERIVATIVES **def·e·ca·tion** /ˌdefiˈkāsʜən/ noun.
– ORIGIN Latin *defaecare.*

de·fect[1] /ˈdēˌfekt/ ▶ **noun** a fault or imperfection.

– SYNONYMS **fault,** flaw, imperfection, deficiency, deformity, blemish, mistake, error.

– ORIGIN Latin *defectus.*

de·fect[2] /diˈfekt/ ▶ **verb** abandon one's country or cause in favor of an opposing one.
– DERIVATIVES **de·fec·tion** /diˈfeksʜən/ noun **de·fec·tor** /-tər/ noun.
– ORIGIN Latin *deficere.*

de·fec·tive /diˈfektiv/ ▶ **adjective** imperfect or faulty.

– SYNONYMS **faulty,** flawed, imperfect, unsound, inoperative, malfunctioning, out of order, broken; informal on the blink.
– ANTONYMS perfect.

– DERIVATIVES **de·fec·tive·ly** adverb **de·fec·tive·ness** noun.

de·fend /diˈfend/ ▶ **verb 1** protect someone or something from harm or danger. **2** act as the lawyer for the party being accused or sued in a lawsuit. **3** attempt to justify: *he defended his decision to fire the strikers.* **4** compete to hold on to a title or seat in a contest or election. **5** (in sports) protect one's goal rather than attempt to score against one's opponents.

– SYNONYMS **1 protect,** guard, safeguard, secure, shield, fortify, watch over. **2 justify,** vindicate, explain, argue for, support, back, stand by, make a case for, stick up for.
– ANTONYMS attack, criticize.

– DERIVATIVES **de·fend·a·ble** adjective.
– ORIGIN Latin *defendere.*

de·fend·ant /diˈfendənt/ ▶ **noun** a person sued or accused in a court of law. Compare with **PLAINTIFF**.

de·fend·er /di'fendər/ ▶ **noun** a person who defends someone or something.

– SYNONYMS **1** *defenders of the environment* **protector,** guardian, guard, custodian. **2** *a defender of family values* **supporter,** upholder, backer, champion, advocate, apologist.

de·fen·es·tra·tion /dē,fenə'strāsHən/ ▶ **noun** formal or humorous the action of throwing someone out of a window.
– DERIVATIVES **de·fen·es·trate** /-'fenə,strāt/ verb.
– ORIGIN Latin, from *fenestra* 'window.'

de·fense /di'fens, 'dē,fens/ (Brit. **defence**) ▶ **noun** **1** the action of defending something against attack. **2** military measures or resources for protecting a country. **3** (**defenses**) fortifications against attack. **4** the attempted justification of something: *the government's defense of the police action.* **5** the case presented by or on behalf of the party being accused or sued in a lawsuit. **6** (**the defense**) the counsel for the defendant in a lawsuit. **7** (in sports) the action of defending one's goal, or the players on a team who perform this role.

– SYNONYMS **1 protection,** guarding, security, fortification, resistance. **2 armaments,** weapons, weaponry, arms, the military, the armed forces. **3 justification,** vindication, explanation, mitigation, excuse, alibi, denial, rebuttal, plea, pleading, argument, case.
– ANTONYMS attack, prosecution.

de·fense·less /di'fenslis/ ▶ **adjective** without defense or protection; completely vulnerable.

– SYNONYMS **vulnerable,** helpless, powerless, weak, undefended, unprotected, unguarded, unarmed, exposed, open to attack.

de·fense·man /di'fensmən/ ▶ **noun** (pl. **defensemen**) (mainly in ice hockey and lacrosse) a player in a defensive position.

de·fense mech·an·ism ▶ **noun** **1** an automatic reaction of the body against disease-causing organisms. **2** a mental process (e.g., repression or projection) initiated, typically unconsciously, to avoid conscious conflict or anxiety.

de·fen·si·ble /di'fensəbəl/ ▶ **adjective** **1** able to be justified by reasoning or argument. **2** able to be defended or protected.

de·fen·sive /di'fensiv/ ▶ **adjective** **1** used or intended to defend or protect: *troops in defensive positions.* **2** very anxious to defend oneself against or avoid criticism.

– SYNONYMS **1 defending,** protective. **2 self-justifying,** oversensitive, prickly, paranoid, neurotic; informal twitchy.

– DERIVATIVES **de·fen·sive·ly** adverb **de·fen·sive·ness** noun.
– PHRASES **on the defensive** expecting or resisting criticism or attack.

de·fer¹ /di'fər/ ▶ **verb** (**defers, deferring, deferred**) put something off until a later time.

– SYNONYMS **postpone,** put off, table, delay, hold over/off, put back, shelve, suspend; informal put on ice, put on the back burner.

– DERIVATIVES **de·fer·ment** noun **de·fer·ral** /-'fərəl/ noun.
– ORIGIN Latin *differre*.

CHOOSE THE RIGHT WORD

See **POSTPONE**.

de·fer² ▶ **verb** (**defers, deferring, deferred**) (**defer to**) give in to or agree to accept: *he deferred to Tim's superior knowledge.*
– ORIGIN Latin *deferre* 'carry away, refer.'

def·er·ence /'defərəns/ ▶ **noun** polite respect shown toward someone or something.

CHOOSE THE RIGHT WORD

See **HONOR**.

def·er·en·tial /,defə'rencHəl/ ▶ **adjective** showing polite respect.
– DERIVATIVES **def·er·en·tial·ly** adverb.

WORD TOOLKIT

See **HUMBLE**.

de·fi·ance /di'fīəns/ ▶ **noun** open refusal to obey someone or something.

– SYNONYMS **resistance,** opposition, noncompliance, disobedience, insubordination, rebellion, disregard, contempt, insolence.
– ANTONYMS obedience.

– ORIGIN Old French.

de·fi·ant /di'fīənt/ ▶ **adjective** openly refusing to obey someone or something.

– SYNONYMS **disobedient,** resistant, obstinate, uncooperative, noncompliant, recalcitrant, insubordinate.
– ANTONYMS cooperative.

– DERIVATIVES **de·fi·ant·ly** adverb.

WORD TOOLKIT

See **UNRULY**.

de·fib·ril·la·tion /dē,fibrə'lāsHən/ ▶ **noun** Medicine the administration of a controlled electric shock to the heart to stop fibrillation of the muscles and allow the normal rhythm to be resumed.
– DERIVATIVES **de·fib·ril·late** /dē'fibrə,lāt/ verb **de·fib·ril·la·tor** /dē'fibrə,lātər/ noun.

de·fi·cien·cy /di'fisHənsē/ ▶ **noun** (pl. **deficiencies**) **1** a lack or shortage of something. **2** a failing or shortcoming.

– SYNONYMS **1 lack,** insufficiency, shortage, inadequacy, deficit, shortfall, scarcity, dearth. **2 defect,** fault, flaw, failing, weakness, shortcoming, limitation.
– ANTONYMS surplus, strength.

de·fi·cien·cy dis·ease ▶ **noun** a disease caused by the lack of some essential element in the diet, usually a particular vitamin or mineral.

de·fi·cient /di'fisHənt/ ▶ **adjective** **1** not having enough of a particular quality or ingredient: *a diet deficient in vitamin A.* **2** inadequate in amount or quality: *the documentary evidence is deficient.*
– ORIGIN Latin, from *deficere* 'fail.'

def·i·cit /'defəsit/ ▶ **noun** **1** the amount by which something, especially a sum of money, falls short. **2** an excess of money spent over money earned.

– SYNONYMS **shortfall,** deficiency, shortage, debt, arrears, loss.
– ANTONYMS surplus.

– ORIGIN Latin, 'it is lacking.'

de·file[1] /di'fīl/ ▸ verb **1** make something dirty or polluted. **2** treat something holy with a lack of respect.
– DERIVATIVES **de·file·ment** noun **de·fil·er** noun.
– ORIGIN Old French *defouler* 'trample down.'

de·file[2] /di'fīl, 'dē,fīl/ ▸ noun a steep-sided narrow gorge or passage (originally one requiring troops to march in single file).
– ORIGIN French, from *file* 'column, file.'

de·fine /di'fīn/ ▸ verb **1** state or describe the exact nature or scope of: *the contract will seek to define the client's obligations.* **2** give the meaning of a word or phrase. **3** mark out the limits or outline of something.

> – SYNONYMS **1 explain,** give the meaning of, spell out, expound, interpret, describe. **2 determine,** establish, fix, specify, designate, decide, stipulate, set out.

– DERIVATIVES **de·fin·a·ble** adjective.
– ORIGIN Latin *definire.*

def·i·nite /'defənit/ ▸ adjective **1** clearly stated or decided; not vague or doubtful: *a definite answer.* **2** known to be true or real: *we have no definite proof.* **3** (of a person) certain about something. **4** having exact and measurable physical limits.

> – SYNONYMS **specific,** explicit, express, precise, exact, clear, clear-cut, unambiguous, certain, sure, positive, conclusive, decisive, firm, unequivocal, unmistakable, proven, decided, marked, distinct, identifiable.
> – ANTONYMS vague, ambiguous.

– DERIVATIVES **def·i·nite·ness** noun.

def·i·nite ar·ti·cle ▸ noun Grammar the word *the.*

def·i·nite·ly /'defənitlē/ ▸ adverb without doubt; certainly.

> – SYNONYMS **certainly,** surely, for sure, unquestionably, without doubt, undoubtedly, undeniably, clearly, positively, absolutely, unmistakably.

def·i·ni·tion /,defə'nisʜən/ ▸ noun **1** a statement of the exact meaning of a word or the nature or scope of something. **2** the action of defining something. **3** the degree of sharpness in outline of an object or image.

> – SYNONYMS **1 meaning,** sense, interpretation, explanation, description. **2 clarity,** sharpness, focus, crispness, resolution.

– DERIVATIVES **def·i·ni·tion·al** adjective.
– PHRASES **by definition** by its very nature.

de·fin·i·tive /di'finitiv/ ▸ adjective **1** (of a conclusion or agreement) final and not able to be changed. **2** (of a book or other text) the most accurate and trusted of its kind.

> – SYNONYMS **1 conclusive,** final, unqualified, absolute, categorical, positive, definite. **2 authoritative,** best, ultimate, classic, standard, recognized, accepted, exhaustive.

– DERIVATIVES **de·fin·i·tive·ly** adverb.

de·flate /di'flāt/ ▸ verb **1** let air or gas out of a tire, balloon, etc. **2** make someone feel suddenly gloomy or discouraged. **3** reduce price levels in an economy.
– DERIVATIVES **de·fla·tor** noun.

de·fla·tion /di'flāsʜən/ ▸ noun **1** the action or process of deflating or being deflated. **2** reduction of the general level of prices in an economy.
– DERIVATIVES **de·fla·tion·ar·y** /di'flāsʜə,nerē/ adjective.

de·flect /di'flekt/ ▸ verb **1** turn aside from a straight course. **2** prevent something undesirable from being aimed at one: *the mayor has sought to deflect criticism over the issue.* **3** prevent someone from following an intended course of action.

> – SYNONYMS **divert,** turn away, draw away, distract, fend off, parry, stave off.

– DERIVATIVES **de·flec·tion** /di'fleksʜən/ noun **de·flec·tive** adjective **de·flec·tor** noun.
– ORIGIN Latin *deflectere.*

de·flow·er /dē'flou(-ə)r/ ▸ verb dated or literary have sex with a woman who is a virgin.

de·fo·li·ant /dē'fōlēənt/ ▸ noun a chemical used to remove the leaves from trees and plants.

de·fo·li·ate /dē'fōlē,āt/ ▸ verb remove leaves from trees or plants.
– DERIVATIVES **de·fo·li·a·tion** /dē,fōlē'āsʜən/ noun.
– ORIGIN Latin *defoliare.*

de·for·est /dē'fôrist, -'fär-/ ▸ verb clear an area of forest or trees.
– DERIVATIVES **de·for·est·a·tion** /dē,fôrə'stāsʜən, -,fär-/ noun.

de·form /di'fôrm/ ▸ verb change or spoil the usual shape of someone or something.

> – SYNONYMS (as adj. **deformed**) *deformed hands* **misshapen,** distorted, malformed, contorted, out of shape, twisted, crooked, warped, buckled, gnarled, disfigured, mutilated, mangled.

– DERIVATIVES **de·form·a·ble** adjective **de·for·ma·tion** /,dēfôr'māsʜən, ,defər-/ noun.

de·form·i·ty /di'fôrmitē/ ▸ noun (pl. **deformities**) **1** a deformed part, especially of the body. **2** the state of being deformed.

de·frag·ment /,dēfrag'ment/ ▸ verb Computing reduce the fragmentation of a file or set of files by concatenating parts stored in separate locations on a disk.
– DERIVATIVES **de·frag·men·ta·tion** /dē,fragmən'tāsʜən, -,men-/ noun **de·frag·ment·er** noun.

de·fraud /di'frôd/ ▸ verb illegally obtain money from someone by deception.

> – SYNONYMS **swindle,** cheat, rob, deceive, dupe, hoodwink, double-cross, trick; informal con, do, sting, diddle, rip off, shaft, pull a fast one on, put one over on, sucker, snooker, stiff.

– ORIGIN Latin *defraudare.*

de·fray /di'frā/ ▸ verb provide money to pay an expense.
– ORIGIN French *défrayer.*

de·frock /dē'fräk/ ▸ verb officially remove a member of the Christian clergy from their job because of wrongdoing.

de·frost /di'frôst/ ▸ verb **1** free a freezer or refrigerator of ice. **2** thaw frozen food.

deft /deft/ ▸ adjective **1** quick and neatly skillful: *deft athletic moves.* **2** showing cleverness and skill: *a deft comedy.*

> – SYNONYMS **skillful,** adept, adroit, dexterous, agile, nimble, handy, able, capable, skilled, proficient, accomplished, expert, polished, slick, professional.
> – ANTONYMS clumsy.

– DERIVATIVES **deft·ly** adverb **deft·ness** noun.
– ORIGIN from DAFT, in the former sense 'meek.'

de·funct /di'fəngkt/ ▸ adjective no longer existing or functioning.

– SYNONYMS **disused,** inoperative, nonfunctioning, unusable, obsolete, discontinued, no longer existing, extinct; discontinued.
– ANTONYMS working, extant.

– ORIGIN Latin *defunctus* 'dead.'

de·fuse /di'fyo͞oz/ ▶ **verb 1** make a situation less tense or dangerous. **2** remove the fuse from an explosive device so as to prevent it from exploding.

USAGE

Defuse and **diffuse** are often confused. **Defuse** means 'make a situation less tense or dangerous' (*talks were held to defuse the crisis*), while **diffuse** means 'spread over a wide area' (*this early language probably diffused across the world*).

de·fy /di'fī/ ▶ **verb** (**defies, defying, defied**) **1** openly resist or refuse to obey someone or something. **2** be of such a kind that something is almost impossible: *his actions defy belief.* **3** challenge someone to do or prove something.

– SYNONYMS **disobey,** flout, disregard, ignore, break, violate, contravene, breach, challenge, fly in the face of, confront.
– ANTONYMS obey.

– DERIVATIVES **de·fi·er** noun.
– ORIGIN Old French *desfier.*

dé·ga·gé /ˌdāgä'zʜā/ ▶ **adjective** literary not concerned with or involved in something.
– ORIGIN French, 'set free.'

de·gen·er·ate ▶ **verb** /di'jenəˌrāt/ become worse; deteriorate: *the meeting threatened to degenerate into a brawl.*

– SYNONYMS **deteriorate,** decline, worsen, slip, slide, go downhill; informal go to the dogs.
– ANTONYMS improve.

▶ **adjective** /di'jenərit/ having very low moral standards.

– SYNONYMS **corrupt,** perverted, decadent, dissolute, dissipated, debauched, immoral, unprincipled, disreputable.

▶ **noun** /di'jenərit/ a person with very low moral standards.
– DERIVATIVES **de·gen·er·a·cy** /-rəsē/ noun **de·gen·er·a·tion** /diˌjenə'rāsʜən/ noun.
– ORIGIN Latin *degeneratus* 'no longer of its kind.'

de·gen·er·a·tive /di'jenərətiv, -əˌrātiv/ ▶ **adjective** (of a disease) becoming progressively worse, with loss of function in the organs or tissues.

de·glaze /dē'glāz/ ▶ **verb** add liquid to the cooking juices and meat sediments in a pan to make a gravy or sauce.

deg·ra·da·tion /ˌdegrə'dāsʜən/ ▶ **noun 1** the state of being degraded or humiliated. **2** the process of being broken down or made worse.

de·grade /di'grād/ ▶ **verb 1** cause someone to suffer a loss of dignity or self-respect: *viewers want to see reality TV that degrades participants.* **2** lower the quality of something. **3** cause something to break down or deteriorate chemically.

– SYNONYMS **demean,** debase, humiliate, humble, belittle, mortify, dehumanize, brutalize.
– ANTONYMS dignify.

– DERIVATIVES **de·grad·a·ble** adjective **deg·ra·da·tive** /'degrəˌdātiv/ adjective.

de·grad·ing /di'grādiNG/ ▶ **adjective** causing a loss of self-respect; humiliating.

– SYNONYMS **humiliating,** demeaning, shameful, mortifying, ignominious, undignified.

de·gree /di'grē/ ▶ **noun 1** the amount, level, or extent to which something happens or is present: *a degree of caution is wise.* **2** a unit of measurement of angles, equivalent to one ninetieth of a right angle. **3** a unit in a scale of temperature, intensity, hardness, etc. **4** an academic rank awarded by a college or university after examination or completion of a course. **5** each of a set of grades used to classify burns or criminal offenses: *second-degree murder.* **6** old use social or official rank.

– SYNONYMS **level,** standard, grade, stage, mark, amount, extent, measure, intensity, strength, proportion.

– PHRASES **by degrees** gradually. **to a degree** to some extent.
– ORIGIN Old French.

de·gree day ▶ **noun** a unit used to determine the heating requirements of buildings, representing a fall of one degree below a specified average outdoor temperature (usually 18°C or 65°F) for one day.

de·hisce /di'his/ ▶ **verb** technical (especially of a seed case) gape or burst open.
– DERIVATIVES **de·his·cence** /-'hisəns/ noun **de·his·cent** /-'hisənt/ adjective.
– ORIGIN Latin *dehiscere.*

de·hu·man·ize /dē'(h)yo͞oməˌnīz/ ▶ **verb** deprive someone of good human qualities such as compassion or kindness.
– DERIVATIVES **de·hu·man·i·za·tion** /dēˌ(h)yo͞oməni'zāsʜən/ noun.

de·hu·mid·i·fy /ˌdē(h)yo͞o'midəˌfī/ ▶ **verb** (**dehumidifies, dehumidifying, dehumidified**) remove moisture from the air or a gas.
– DERIVATIVES **de·hu·mid·i·fi·ca·tion** /-midəfi'kāsʜən/ noun **de·hu·mid·i·fi·er** noun.

de·hy·drate /dē'hīdrāt/ ▶ **verb 1** cause someone to lose a large amount of water from their body. **2** remove water from food in order to preserve it.
– DERIVATIVES **de·hy·dra·tion** /ˌdēhī'drāsʜən/ noun.
– ORIGIN from Greek *hudros* 'water.'

CHOOSE THE RIGHT WORD

See **DRY**.

de-ice /dē'īs/ ▶ **verb** remove ice from something.
– DERIVATIVES **de-ic·er** noun.

de·i·fy /'dēəˌfī/ ▶ **verb** (**deifies, deifying, deified**) worship or treat someone as a god.
– DERIVATIVES **de·i·fi·ca·tion** /ˌdēəfi'kāsʜən/ noun.
– ORIGIN Latin *deificare.*

deign /dān/ ▶ **verb** do something that one considers to be beneath one's dignity: *celebrities often don't deign to talk to the masses.*

– SYNONYMS **condescend,** stoop, lower oneself, demean oneself, humble oneself, consent.

– ORIGIN Latin *dignare* 'deem worthy.'

de·in·dus·tri·al·i·za·tion /ˌdē-inˌdəstrēəli'zāsʜən/ ▶ **noun** the reduction of industrial activity in a region or economy.

de·ism /'dēizəm/ ▶ **noun** belief in the existence of an all-powerful creator who does not intervene in the universe. Compare with **THEISM**.
– DERIVATIVES **de·ist** noun **de·is·tic** /dē'istik/ adjective.

de·i·ty /ˈdēitē/ ▶ **noun** (pl. **deities**) **1** a god or goddess. **2** the state or quality of being a god or goddess.

– SYNONYMS **god,** goddess, divine being, supreme being, godhead, creator, divinity, immortal.

– ORIGIN Latin *deitas.*

dé·jà vu /ˌdāzнä ˈvo͞o/ ▶ **noun** a feeling of having already experienced the present situation.
– ORIGIN French, 'already seen.'

de·ject·ed /diˈjektəd/ ▶ **adjective** sad and dispirited.

– SYNONYMS **downcast,** downhearted, despondent, disconsolate, dispirited, crestfallen, disheartened, depressed; informal down in the mouth, down in the dumps.
– ANTONYMS cheerful.

– DERIVATIVES **de·ject·ed·ly** adverb.

de·jec·tion /diˈjeksнən/ ▶ **noun** sadness or low spirits.
– ORIGIN from Latin *deicere* 'throw down.'

de ju·re /di ˈjo͝orē, dā ˈjo͝orā/ ▶ **adverb** according to rightful entitlement; by right. Often contrasted with DE FACTO. ▶ **adjective** existing by legal right; rightful.
– ORIGIN Latin, 'of law.'

de·lay /diˈlā/ ▶ **verb 1** make or be late or slow. **2** put off to a later time; postpone: *ministers agreed to delay their decision.*

– SYNONYMS **1 detain,** hold up, make late, slow up/down, bog down, hinder, hamper, impede, obstruct. **2 linger,** drag one's feet, hold back, dawdle, waste time, stall, hesitate, dither, shilly-shally; informal dilly-dally. **3 postpone,** put off, defer, hold over, adjourn, reschedule.
– ANTONYMS hurry, advance.

▶ **noun 1** a period of time by which someone or something is delayed. **2** the action of delaying someone or something.

– SYNONYMS **1 holdup,** wait, interruption, stoppage. **2** *the delay of his trial* **postponement,** deferral, adjournment.

– ORIGIN Old French *delayer.*

CHOOSE THE RIGHT WORD

See POSTPONE.

de·lec·ta·ble /diˈlektəbəl/ ▶ **adjective** delicious or delightful.

– SYNONYMS **1 delicious,** mouthwatering, appetizing, flavorsome, toothsome, succulent, luscious, tasty; informal scrumptious, yummy, nummy. **2 delightful,** lovely, captivating, charming, enchanting, appealing, beguiling; informal divine, heavenly, dreamy.
– ANTONYMS unpalatable, unattractive.

– DERIVATIVES **de·lec·ta·bly** /-blē/ adverb.

de·lec·ta·tion /ˌdēlekˈtāsнən/ ▶ **noun** formal, chiefly humorous pleasure and delight.
– ORIGIN from Latin *delectare* 'to charm.'

del·e·gate ▶ **noun** /ˈdeligit/ **1** a person sent to represent others, in particular at a conference. **2** a member of a committee.

– SYNONYMS **representative,** envoy, emissary, commissioner, agent, deputy.

▶ **verb** /ˈdeləˌgāt/ **1** give a task or responsibility to a less senior person. **2** authorize someone to act as a representative.

– SYNONYMS **assign,** entrust, pass on, hand on/over, turn over, devolve.

– DERIVATIVES **del·e·ga·tor** /-ˌgātər/ noun.
– ORIGIN from Latin *delegare* 'send away, assign.'

del·e·ga·tion /ˌdeliˈgāsнən/ ▶ **noun 1** a group of delegates or representatives. **2** the action of giving one's work or responsibilities to someone else.

– SYNONYMS **deputation,** mission, commission, contingent, legation.

de·lete /diˈlēt/ ▶ **verb 1** remove or cross out written or printed matter. **2** remove data from a computer's memory.

– SYNONYMS **remove,** cut (out), take out, edit out, excise, cancel, cross out, strike out, obliterate, rub out, erase.
– ANTONYMS add.

– DERIVATIVES **de·le·tion** /diˈlēsнən/ noun.
– ORIGIN Latin *delere* 'blot out.'

del·e·te·ri·ous /ˌdeliˈti(ə)rēəs/ ▶ **adjective** formal causing harm or damage.
– ORIGIN Greek *dēlētērios* 'harmful.'

delft /delft/ ▶ **noun** glazed earthenware, typically with blue decoration on a white background.
– ORIGIN named after the town of *Delft* in the Netherlands.

del·i /ˈdelē/ ▶ **noun** (pl. **delis**) informal a delicatessen.

de·lib·er·ate ▶ **adjective** /diˈlibərit/ **1** done on purpose; intentional. **2** careful and unhurried: *a conscientious and deliberate worker.*

– SYNONYMS **1 intentional,** calculated, conscious, intended, planned, willful, premeditated. **2 careful,** cautious, measured, regular, even, steady. **3 methodical,** systematic, careful, painstaking, meticulous, thorough.
– ANTONYMS accidental, hasty.

▶ **verb** /-ˌrāt/ consider carefully and for a long time: *I deliberated over the menu.*

– SYNONYMS **think,** think about/over/on, ponder, consider, contemplate, reflect on, muse on, meditate on, ruminate on, mull over.

– DERIVATIVES **de·lib·er·ate·ness** /-ritnis/ noun.
– ORIGIN Latin *deliberare* 'consider carefully.'

de·lib·er·ate·ly /diˈlibəritlē/ ▶ **adverb 1** intentionally; not accidentally. **2** slowly and carefully.

– SYNONYMS **1** *he deliberately hurt me* **intentionally,** on purpose, purposely, by design, knowingly, wittingly, consciously, willfully. **2** *he walked deliberately down the aisle* **carefully,** cautiously, slowly, steadily, evenly.

de·lib·er·a·tion /diˌlibəˈrāsнən/ ▶ **noun 1** long and careful consideration. **2** carefulness and lack of haste.

– SYNONYMS **thought,** consideration, reflection, contemplation, discussion.

de·lib·er·a·tive /diˈlibərətiv, -əˌrātiv/ ▶ **adjective** relating to consideration or discussion.

del·i·ca·cy /ˈdelikəsē/ ▶ **noun** (pl. **delicacies**) **1** fineness or intricacy: *the delicacy of the palace's architecture.* **2** lack of robustness; fragility. **3** discretion and tact. **4** a delicious or expensive food.

– SYNONYMS **1 fineness,** delicateness, fragility, thinness, lightness, flimsiness. **2 difficulty,** trickiness, sensitivity, ticklishness, awkwardness. **3 care,** sensitivity, tact, discretion, diplomacy, subtlety. **4 treat,** luxury, tidbit, specialty.

del·i·cate /ˈdelikit/ ▶ **adjective 1** very fine or intricate in texture or structure: *a delicate lace shawl*. **2** easily broken or damaged; fragile. **3** tending to become ill easily. **4** requiring or showing tact, sensitivity, or skill: *a delicate issue*. **5** (of a color or flavor) subtle and pleasant.

– SYNONYMS **1** *delicate embroidery* **fine,** intricate, dainty, exquisite, graceful. **2** *a delicate shade of blue* **subtle,** soft, pale, muted, pastel, light. **3** *delicate china cups* **fragile,** dainty. **4** *his wife is very delicate* **sickly,** unhealthy, frail, feeble, weak. **5** *a delicate issue* **difficult,** tricky, sensitive, ticklish, awkward, touchy, embarrassing; informal sticky, dicey. **6** *the matter needs delicate handling* **careful,** sensitive, tactful, diplomatic, discreet, kid-glove, subtle. **7** *a delicate mechanism* **sensitive,** light, precision.
– ANTONYMS coarse, strong, robust.

– DERIVATIVES **del·i·cate·ly** adverb.
– ORIGIN Latin *delicatus* 'delightful, charming.'

del·i·ca·tes·sen /ˌdelikəˈtesən/ ▶ **noun** a store selling cooked meats, cheeses, and unusual or foreign prepared foods.
– ORIGIN German or Dutch.

De·li·cious /diˈlisнəs/ ▶ **noun** a red or yellow variety of eating apple with a sweet flavor and a slightly elongated shape.

de·li·cious /diˈlisнəs/ ▶ **adjective 1** very pleasant to the taste. **2** giving great pleasure; delightful: *a delicious irony*.

– SYNONYMS **delectable,** mouthwatering, appetizing, tasty, flavorsome; informal scrumptious, finger-licking (good).
– ANTONYMS unpalatable.

– DERIVATIVES **de·li·cious·ly** adverb **de·li·cious·ness** noun.
– ORIGIN from Latin *deliciae* 'delight, pleasure.'

de·light /diˈlīt/ ▶ **verb 1** please someone greatly. **2** (**delight in**) take great pleasure in doing something.

– SYNONYMS **1 charm,** enchant, captivate, entrance, thrill, entertain, amuse, divert; informal send, tickle pink, bowl over. **2** *they* ***delight in*** *playing tricks* **love,** relish, savor, adore, lap up, take pleasure in, enjoy, revel in.
– ANTONYMS dismay, disgust.

▶ **noun 1** great pleasure. **2** a cause of great pleasure: *the illustrations are a delight*.

– SYNONYMS **pleasure,** happiness, joy, glee, excitement, amusement, bliss, ecstasy.
– ANTONYMS displeasure.

– ORIGIN Latin *delectare* 'to charm.'

de·light·ed /diˈlītid/ ▶ **adjective** feeling or showing great pleasure.

– SYNONYMS **pleased,** glad, happy, thrilled, overjoyed, ecstatic, elated, on cloud nine, walking on air, in seventh heaven, jumping for joy, gleeful; informal over the moon, tickled pink, as pleased as Punch, on top of the world.

– DERIVATIVES **de·light·ed·ly** adverb.

de·light·ful /diˈlītfəl/ ▶ **adjective** causing delight; very pleasing.

– SYNONYMS **1** *a delightful evening* **lovely,** enjoyable, amusing, entertaining, pleasant, pleasurable. **2** *a delightful girl* **charming,** enchanting, captivating, bewitching, appealing, sweet, endearing, cute, adorable, delectable.

– DERIVATIVES **de·light·ful·ly** adverb.

de·lim·it /diˈlimit/ ▶ **verb** (**delimits, delimiting, delimited**) determine the limits or boundaries of something.
– DERIVATIVES **de·lim·i·ta·tion** /-ˌlimiˈtāsнən/ noun **de·lim·it·er** noun.

de·lin·e·ate /diˈlinēˌāt/ ▶ **verb** describe or indicate something precisely.
– DERIVATIVES **de·lin·e·a·tion** /-ˌlinēˈāsнən/ noun.
– ORIGIN Latin *delineare* 'to outline.'

de·link /dēˈlinɢk/ ▶ **verb** break the connection between two things: *In 1971, the United States government delinked the dollar from gold*.

de·lin·quen·cy /diˈlinɢkwənsē/ ▶ **noun** (pl. **delinquencies**) **1** minor crime, especially that committed by young people. **2** formal neglect of one's duty.

de·lin·quent /diˈlinɢkwənt/ ▶ **adjective 1** (especially of young people) tending to commit crime. **2** formal failing in one's duty.

– SYNONYMS **lawless,** lawbreaking, criminal; errant, badly behaved, troublesome, difficult, unruly, disobedient, uncontrollable.

▶ **noun** a person who tends to commit crime.

– SYNONYMS **offender,** wrongdoer, malefactor, lawbreaker, criminal, hooligan, vandal, ruffian, hoodlum.

– ORIGIN from Latin *delinquere* 'to offend.'

del·i·ques·cent /deliˈkwesənt/ ▶ **adjective** technical or literary becoming or having a tendency to become liquid.
– DERIVATIVES **del·i·ques·cence** noun **del·i·quesce** /ˌdeliˈkwes/ verb.
– ORIGIN Latin *deliquescere* 'dissolve.'

de·lir·i·ous /diˈli(ə)rēəs/ ▶ **adjective 1** in a very disturbed mental state; affected by delirium. **2** very excited or happy.

– SYNONYMS **1 incoherent,** raving, babbling, irrational, deranged, demented, out of one's mind, feverish, frenzied. **2** *the crowd was delirious* **ecstatic,** elated, thrilled, overjoyed, beside oneself, walking on air, on cloud nine, in seventh heaven, transported, rapturous; hysterical, wild, frenzied; informal blissed out, over the moon.
– ANTONYMS lucid.

– DERIVATIVES **de·lir·i·ous·ly** adverb.

de·lir·i·um /diˈli(ə)rēəm/ ▶ **noun** a highly disturbed state of mind characterized by restlessness, illusions, and incoherent thought and speech.
– ORIGIN Latin.

de·lir·i·um tre·mens /diˈli(ə)rēəm ˈtrēmənz/ ▶ **noun** a condition in which alcoholics who are trying to give up alcohol experience tremors and hallucinations.
– ORIGIN Latin, 'trembling delirium.'

de·liv·er /diˈlivər/ ▶ **verb 1** bring and hand over something to the person who is to receive it. **2** provide something promised or expected: *the complex delivers all the usual attractions*. **3** state or present in a formal way: *he delivered a lecture on endangered species*. **4** launch or aim a blow or attack. **5** save or set someone free from something. **6** assist in the birth of a baby. **7** (also **be delivered of**) give birth to a baby.

– SYNONYMS **1 bring,** take, convey, carry, transport, send, distribute, dispatch, ship. **2 state,** utter, give, read, broadcast, pronounce, announce, declare, proclaim, hand down, return. **3 administer,** deal, inflict, give; informal land.

– DERIVATIVES **de·liv·er·a·ble** /diˈlivərəbəl/ adjective **de·liv·er·er** noun.

– PHRASES **deliver the goods** informal provide what is promised or expected.
– ORIGIN Old French *delivrer*.

de·liv·er·ance /di'livərəns/ ▶ **noun 1** the action of being rescued or set free. **2** a formal or authoritative statement.

de·liv·er·y /di'livərē/ ▶ **noun** (pl. **deliveries**) **1** the action of delivering something. **2** the process of giving birth. **3** an act of throwing or bowling a ball, or striking a blow. **4** the way or style of giving a speech: *her delivery was stilted.*

– SYNONYMS **1 conveyance,** carriage, transportation, transport, distribution, dispatch, shipping. **2 consignment,** load, shipment. **3 speech,** pronunciation, enunciation, articulation, elocution.

dell /del/ ▶ **noun** literary a small valley.
– ORIGIN Old English.

Del·phic /'delfik/ ▶ **adjective** deliberately ambiguous or hard to understand: *Delphic utterances.*
– ORIGIN from the ancient Greek oracle at *Delphi*.

del·phin·i·um /del'fīnēəm/ ▶ **noun** (pl. **delphiniums**) a garden plant having tall spikes of blue flowers.
– ORIGIN Greek *delphinion* 'larkspur.'

del·ta /'deltə/ ▶ **noun 1** a triangular area of land at the mouth of a river where it splits into several channels. **2** the fourth letter of the Greek alphabet (Δ, δ), represented as 'd.'

del·ta wing ▶ **noun** a single triangular swept-back wing on some aircraft.

del·toid /'deltoid/ ▶ **noun** (also **deltoid muscle**) a thick triangular muscle covering the shoulder joint. ▶ **adjective** technical triangular.
– ORIGIN Greek *deltoeidēs*.

de·lude /di'lo͞od/ ▶ **verb** persuade someone to believe something that is not true.

– SYNONYMS **mislead,** deceive, fool, take in, trick, dupe, hoodwink, gull, lead on; informal con, pull the wool over someone's eyes, sucker, snooker, lead up the garden path, take for a ride.

– DERIVATIVES **de·lud·ed** adjective.
– ORIGIN Latin *deludere* 'to mock.'

del·uge /'del(y)o͞oj/ ▶ **noun 1** a severe flood or very heavy fall of rain. **2** a great quantity of something arriving at the same time: *a deluge of angry letters.* ▶ **verb 1** overwhelm with a great quantity of something: *they've been deluged with unwanted emails.* **2** flood a place.
– ORIGIN Old French.

de·lu·sion /di'lo͞ozʜən/ ▶ **noun** a false belief or impression about oneself or one's situation: *I must get over this delusion that I know how to type.*

– SYNONYMS **misapprehension,** misconception, false impression, misunderstanding, mistake, error, misconstruction, illusion, fantasy, fancy.

– DERIVATIVES **de·lu·sion·al** /-ʜənl/ adjective **de·lu·sive** /di'lo͞osiv/ adjective **de·lu·so·ry** /di'lo͞osərē, -zərē/ adjective.

de·luxe /di'ləks/ ▶ **adjective** of a higher quality and more expensive than usual.
– ORIGIN French, 'of luxury.'

delve /delv/ ▶ **verb 1** reach inside a receptacle and search for something. **2** investigate something in depth: *any financial company can delve into my private life.* **3** old use dig or excavate.

– SYNONYMS **1 rummage,** search, hunt, scrabble about/around, root about/around, ferret (about/around), fish about/around, dig, rifle through. **2 investigate,** inquire, probe, explore, research, look into, go into.

– ORIGIN Old English.

de·mag·net·ize /dē'magni,tīz/ ▶ **verb** remove magnetic properties from something.
– DERIVATIVES **de·mag·net·i·za·tion** /-,magnitə'zāsʜən/ noun.

dem·a·gogue ▶ **noun** /'demə,gäg/ a political leader who appeals to the desires and prejudices of the general public.
– DERIVATIVES **dem·a·gog·ic** /,demə'gäjik, -'gägik, -'gōjik/ adjective **dem·a·gogu·er·y** /'demə,gägərē/ noun **dem·a·go·gy** /'demə,gäjē, -,gōjē/ noun.
– ORIGIN from Greek *dēmos* 'the people' + *agōgos* 'leading.'

de·mand /di'mand/ ▶ **noun 1** a very firm and forceful request. **2** (**demands**) things that are urgent, necessary, or difficult: *the physical and mental demands of climbing.* **3** the desire of consumers for a particular product or service: *a surge in demand for strong ales.*

– SYNONYMS **1** *I gave in to her demands* **request,** call, command, order, dictate. **2** *the demands of a young family* **requirement,** need, claim, commitment, imposition. **3 market,** call, appetite, desire.

▶ **verb 1** ask or ask for in a firm or forceful way. **2** need a quality, skill, action, etc.: *it was a difficult job that demanded their attention.*

– SYNONYMS **1 call for,** ask for, request, push for, press for, seek, claim, insist on. **2 order,** command, enjoin, require. **3 ask,** inquire, question, query. **4 require,** need, necessitate, call for, involve, entail. **5 insist on,** stipulate, expect, look for.

– PHRASES **in demand** sought after. **on demand** as soon as or whenever required.
– ORIGIN Latin *demandare* 'hand over, entrust.'

de·mand·ing /di'mandiɴɢ/ ▶ **adjective** requiring much skill or effort.

– SYNONYMS **1 difficult,** challenging, taxing, exacting, tough, hard, onerous, formidable, arduous, grueling, back-breaking, punishing. **2 nagging,** trying, tiresome, hard to please, high-maintenance.
– ANTONYMS easy.

de·mar·cate /di'mär,kāt, 'dēmär,kāt/ ▶ **verb** set the boundaries or limits of something.

de·mar·ca·tion /,dēmär'kāsʜən/ ▶ **noun 1** the action of fixing boundaries. **2** a dividing line.
– ORIGIN Spanish *demarcación*.

de·ma·te·ri·al·ize /,dēmə'ti(ə)rēə,līz/ ▶ **verb** become no longer physically present; disappear.
– DERIVATIVES **de·ma·te·ri·al·i·za·tion** /-,ti(ə)rēələ'zāsʜən/ noun.

de·mean /di'mēn/ ▶ **verb 1** cause a loss of dignity or respect for: *much reality TV demeans people for the sake of ratings.* **2** (**demean oneself**) do something that is beneath one's dignity.

– SYNONYMS **discredit,** lower, degrade, debase, devalue, cheapen, abase, humiliate.
– ANTONYMS dignify.

– DERIVATIVES **de·mean·ing** adjective.
– ORIGIN from **DE-** + **MEAN²**.

de·mean·or /di'mēnər/ (Brit. **demeanour**) ▶ **noun** a person's outward behavior or bearing.

– SYNONYMS **manner,** air, attitude, appearance, look, mien, bearing, carriage, behavior, conduct.

– ORIGIN from Old French *demener* 'to lead.'

de·ment·ed /di'mentid/ ▶ **adjective 1** suffering from dementia. **2** informal wild and irrational.

– SYNONYMS **mad,** insane, deranged, out of one's mind, crazed, lunatic, unbalanced, unhinged, disturbed, non compos mentis; informal crazy, mental, raving mad, not all there.
– ANTONYMS sane.

– DERIVATIVES **de·ment·ed·ly** adverb.
– ORIGIN from Latin *demens* 'insane.'

WORD TOOLKIT

See **PSYCHOTIC**.

de·men·tia /di'mensHə/ ▶ **noun** a mental disorder marked by memory failures, personality changes, and impaired reasoning.
– ORIGIN Latin.

dem·e·ra·ra su·gar /ˌdemə're(ə)rə, -'rärə/ ▶ **noun** Brit. light brown cane sugar.
– ORIGIN from the region of *Demerara* in Guyana.

de·mer·it /di'merit/ ▶ **noun** a mark awarded against someone for a fault or offense.

de·mer·sal /di'mərsəl/ ▶ **adjective** living close to the seabed.
– ORIGIN from Latin *demergere* 'submerge.'

de·mesne /di'mān/ ▶ **noun 1** historical land attached to a manor. **2** old use a region or domain.
– ORIGIN from Old French *demeine* 'belonging to a lord.'

demi- ▶ **prefix 1** half: *demisemiquaver*. **2** partially; lesser: *demigod*.
– ORIGIN from Latin *dimidius* 'half.'

dem·i·god /'demēˌgäd/ (or **demigoddess**) ▶ **noun** a partly divine or lesser god (or goddess).

dem·i·john /'demēˌjän/ ▶ **noun** a bulbous narrow-necked bottle holding from 3 to 10 gallons of liquid.
– ORIGIN probably from French *dame-jeanne* 'Lady Jane.'

de·mil·i·ta·rize /dē'militəˌrīz/ ▶ **verb** remove all military forces from an area.
– DERIVATIVES **de·mil·i·ta·ri·za·tion** /-ˌmilitərə'zāsHən/ noun.

dem·i·monde /'demēˌmänd/ ▶ **noun** a group of people on the fringes of respectable society.
– ORIGIN French, 'half-world.'

de·mise /di'mīz/ ▶ **noun 1** a person's death. **2** the end or failure of something.

– SYNONYMS **1 death,** dying, passing, end. **2 end,** break-up, disintegration, fall, downfall, collapse, overthrow.
– ANTONYMS birth.

– ORIGIN Old French.

dem·o /'demō/ informal ▶ **noun** (pl. **demos**) a demonstration recording or piece of software. ▶ **verb** (**demos, demoing, demoed**) demonstrate software or equipment.

de·mo·bi·lize /dē'mōbəˌlīz/ ▶ **verb** take troops out of active service.
– DERIVATIVES **de·mo·bi·li·za·tion** /-ˌmōbəli'zāsHən/ noun.

de·moc·ra·cy /di'mäkrəsē/ ▶ **noun** (pl. **democracies**) **1** a form of government in which the people can vote for representatives to govern the country on their behalf. **2** a country governed by elected representatives. **3** control of a group by the majority of its members.
– ORIGIN from Greek *dēmos* 'the people' + *-kratia* 'power, rule.'

dem·o·crat /'deməˌkrat/ ▶ **noun 1** a supporter of democracy. **2** (**Democrat**) a member of the Democratic Party.

dem·o·crat·ic /ˌdemə'kratik/ ▶ **adjective 1** relating to or supporting democracy. **2** based on the principle that all members of society are equal. **3** (**Democratic**) relating to the Democratic Party.

– SYNONYMS **elected,** representative, parliamentary, popular, egalitarian, self-governing.

– DERIVATIVES **dem·o·crat·i·cal·ly** /-ik(ə)lē/ adverb.

Dem·o·crat·ic Par·ty ▶ **noun** one of the two main US political parties (the other being the Republican Party), which follows a program tending to promote a strong central government and expansive social programs.

de·moc·ra·tize /di'mäkrəˌtīz/ ▶ **verb** introduce a democratic system or principles to something.
– DERIVATIVES **de·moc·ra·ti·za·tion** /-ˌmäkrətə'zāsHən/ noun.

de·mod·u·late /dē'mäjəˌlāt/ ▶ **verb** Electronics extract or separate a modulating signal from its carrier.
– DERIVATIVES **de·mod·u·la·tion** /-ˌmäjə'lāsHən/ noun **de·mod·u·la·tor** noun.

dem·o·graph·ic /ˌdemə'grafik/ ▶ **adjective** relating to the structure of populations. ▶ **noun** a particular sector of a population: *the drink is popular with a young demographic.*
– DERIVATIVES **dem·o·graph·i·cal·ly** /-ik(ə)lē/ adverb.

de·mog·ra·phy /di'mägrəfē/ ▶ **noun** the study of the structure of human populations using statistics of births, deaths, etc.
– DERIVATIVES **de·mog·ra·pher** noun.

dem·oi·selle /ˌdem(w)ə'zel/ ▶ **noun** old use a young woman.
– ORIGIN French.

de·mol·ish /di'mälisH/ ▶ **verb 1** pull or knock down a building. **2** prove wrong or put an end to: *the authors demolish a number of old myths.* **3** informal overwhelmingly defeat someone. **4** humorous eat up food quickly.

– SYNONYMS **1 knock down,** pull down, tear down, destroy, flatten, raze (to the ground), dismantle, level, bulldoze, blow up. **2 destroy,** ruin, wreck, overturn, explode; informal shoot full of holes.
– ANTONYMS build.

– ORIGIN Latin *demoliri*.

CHOOSE THE RIGHT WORD

See **DESTROY**.

dem·o·li·tion /ˌdemə'lisHən/ ▶ **noun** the action of demolishing something.

de·mon /'dēmən/ ▶ **noun 1** an evil spirit or devil. **2** often humorous an evil or destructive person or thing. ▶ **adjective** forceful or skillful: *she's a demon cook.*
– ORIGIN Greek *daimōn* 'deity, spirit.'

de·mon·e·tize ▶ **verb** make a coin or currency no longer valid as money.
– DERIVATIVES **de·mon·e·ti·za·tion** /-ˌmänitə'zāsHən/ noun.
– ORIGIN French *démonétiser*.

de·mo·ni·ac /di'mōnē,ak/ ▸ **adjective** relating to or resembling a demon or demons; demonic.
– DERIVATIVES **de·mo·ni·a·cal** /,dēmə'nīəkəl/ adjective.

de·mon·ic /di'mänik/ ▸ **adjective** relating to or resembling demons or evil spirits.
– DERIVATIVES **de·mon·i·cal·ly** /-ik(ə)lē/ adverb.

de·mon·ize /'dēmə,nīz/ ▸ **verb** portray as wicked or threatening: *he aims to demonize smokers and make them social outcasts.*
– DERIVATIVES **de·mon·i·za·tion** /,dēməni'zāsʜən/ noun.

de·mon·ol·o·gy /,dēmə'näləjē/ ▸ **noun 1** the study of demons or belief in demons. **2** a set of beliefs about a group regarded as harmful or unwelcome.

de·mon·stra·ble /di'mänstrəbəl/ ▸ **adjective** clearly apparent or able to be logically proved.
– DERIVATIVES **de·mon·stra·bly** /-blē/ adverb.

dem·on·strate /'demən,strāt/ ▸ **verb 1** clearly show something by giving proof or evidence: *these results demonstrate our continued strong performance.* **2** show and explain how something works or is done. **3** reveal a feeling or quality by one's actions. **4** take part in a public demonstration.

– SYNONYMS **1 indicate,** prove, show, establish, confirm, verify. **2 reveal,** manifest, indicate, illustrate, signify, signal, denote, show, display, exhibit. **3 protest,** march, parade, picket, strike.

– ORIGIN Latin *demonstrare* 'point out.'

dem·on·stra·tion /,demən'strāsʜən/ ▸ **noun 1** the action of demonstrating or showing something. **2** a public meeting or march protesting against something or expressing views on an issue.

– SYNONYMS **1 exhibition,** presentation, display. **2 manifestation,** indication, sign, mark, proof, testimony. **3 protest,** march, rally, mass lobby, sit-in; informal demo.

de·mon·stra·tive /di'mänstrətiv/ ▸ **adjective 1** tending to show one's feelings openly. **2** serving to show or prove something. **3** Grammar (of a determiner or pronoun) indicating the person or thing referred to (e.g., *this, that, those*).

– SYNONYMS **expressive,** open, forthcoming, communicative, unreserved, emotional, effusive, affectionate, loving, warm, friendly, approachable; informal touchy-feely.
– ANTONYMS reserved.

– DERIVATIVES **de·mon·stra·tive·ly** adverb.

dem·on·stra·tor /'demən,strātər/ ▸ **noun 1** a person who takes part in a public protest meeting or march. **2** a person who shows how a particular piece of equipment works or how a skill or craft is performed. **3** a piece of merchandise that can be tested by potential buyers.

de·mor·al·ize /di'môrə,līz/ ▸ **verb** (usu. as adj. **demoralized**) cause someone to lose confidence or hope.

– SYNONYMS (as adj. **demoralized**) *demoralized employees fearful of losing their jobs* **dispirited,** disheartened, downhearted, dejected, downcast, low, depressed, dismayed, daunted, discouraged.

– DERIVATIVES **de·mor·al·i·za·tion** /-,môrələ'zāsʜən/ noun **de·mor·al·iz·ing** adjective.
– ORIGIN French *démoraliser* 'corrupt, deprave.'

de·mote /di'mōt/ ▸ **verb** move someone to a lower rank or position.

– SYNONYMS **downgrade,** relegate, reduce, depose, unseat, displace, oust; Military cashier.
– ANTONYMS promote.

– DERIVATIVES **de·mo·tion** /di'mōsʜən/ noun.
– ORIGIN from **DE-** + a shortened form of **PROMOTE**.

de·mot·ic /di'mätik/ ▸ **adjective** (of language) used by ordinary people; colloquial. ▸ **noun** ordinary colloquial speech.
– ORIGIN Greek *dēmotikos.*

de·mo·ti·vate /dē'mōtə,vāt/ ▸ **verb** make someone less eager to work or make an effort.
– DERIVATIVES **de·mo·tiv·a·tion** /dē,mōtə'vāsʜən/ noun.

de·mount·a·ble /dē'mountəbəl/ ▸ **adjective** able to be dismantled or removed and readily reassembled or repositioned.

de·mur /di'mər/ ▸ **verb** (**demurs, demurring, demurred**) raise objections or show reluctance.
– DERIVATIVES **de·mur·ral** noun.
– PHRASES **without demur** without objecting or hesitating: *they accepted without demur.*
– ORIGIN Old French *demourer.*

de·mure /di'myo͝or/ ▸ **adjective** (**demurer, demurest**) (of a woman) reserved, modest, and shy.

– SYNONYMS **modest,** reserved, shy, unassuming, decorous, decent, proper.
– ANTONYMS brazen.

– DERIVATIVES **de·mure·ly** adverb **de·mure·ness** noun.
– ORIGIN perhaps from Old French *demourer* 'remain.'

de·mu·tu·al·ize /dē'myo͞ocʜo͞owə,līz/ ▸ **verb** change a mutual organization such as a savings and loan association to one of a different kind.

de·mys·ti·fy /dē'mistə,fī/ ▸ **verb** (**demystifies, demystifying, demystified**) make a subject easier to understand.
– DERIVATIVES **de·mys·ti·fi·ca·tion** /-,mistəfi'kāsʜən/ noun.

de·my·thol·o·gize /,dēmi'ᴛʜälə,jīz/ ▸ **verb** reinterpret a subject so that it is free of mythical elements.

den /den/ ▸ **noun 1** a wild animal's lair or home. **2** informal a small, comfortable room in a house where a person can relax or pursue an activity in private. **3** a place where people meet to do something wrong or forbidden: *a den of vice.*

– SYNONYMS **1 lair,** burrow, hole, shelter, hiding place, hideout. **2 study,** studio, workshop, retreat, sanctuary, hideaway.

– ORIGIN Old English.

de·nar·i·us /di'ne(ə)rēəs/ ▸ **noun** (pl. **denarii** /-'ne(ə)rē,ī/) an ancient Roman silver coin.
– ORIGIN Latin, 'containing ten.'

de·na·tion·al·ize /dē'nasʜənl,īz/ ▸ **verb** transfer a nationalized industry or organization to private ownership.
– DERIVATIVES **de·na·tion·al·i·za·tion** /-,nasʜənlə'zāsʜən/ noun.

de·na·ture /dē'nācʜər/ ▸ **verb 1** alter the natural qualities of: *the scrambler denatured her voice.* **2** make alcohol unfit for drinking by adding poisonous or foul-tasting substances.
– DERIVATIVES **de·na·tur·a·tion** /dē,nācʜə'rāsʜən/ noun.

den·drite /'dendrīt/ ▸ **noun** a short extension of a nerve cell that conducts impulses to the cell body.
– DERIVATIVES **den·drit·ic** /den'dritik/ adjective.
– ORIGIN from Greek *dendritēs* 'tree-like.'

den·gue /ˈdeNGgē, -gā/ (also **dengue fever**) ▶ **noun** a tropical disease transmitted by mosquitoes, causing sudden fever and acute pains in the joints.
– ORIGIN Swahili.

de·ni·a·ble /diˈnīəbəl/ ▶ **adjective** able to be denied.
– DERIVATIVES **de·ni·a·bil·i·ty** /-ˌnīəˈbilitē/ noun.

de·ni·al /diˈnīəl/ ▶ **noun 1** a statement that something is not true. **2** the action of denying something. **3** refusal to accept that something unpleasant or distressing is true: *Tim was initially in denial of his illness.*

– SYNONYMS **1 contradiction,** rebuttal, repudiation, refutation, disclaimer. **2 refusal,** withholding.

de·ni·er /ˈdenēər/ ▶ **noun** a unit by which the fineness of yarn is measured.
– ORIGIN Latin *denarius* (see **DENARIUS**).

den·i·grate /ˈdeniˌgrāt/ ▶ **verb** criticize someone or something in an unfair way.

– SYNONYMS **disparage,** belittle, deprecate, decry, cast aspersions on, criticize, attack, speak ill of, give someone a bad name, defame, slander, slur, libel, run down, abuse, insult, revile, malign, vilify; informal bad-mouth.
– ANTONYMS extol.

– DERIVATIVES **den·i·gra·tion** /ˌdeniˈgrāsHən/ noun **den·i·gra·tor** noun.
– ORIGIN Latin *denigrare* 'blacken, make dark.'

den·im /ˈdenəm/ ▶ **noun 1** a hard-wearing cotton twill fabric. **2** (**denims**) jeans or other clothes made of denim.
– ORIGIN from French *serge de Nîmes*, referring to serge from the town of *Nîmes*.

den·i·zen /ˈdenəzən/ ▶ **noun** formal or humorous an inhabitant or occupant of a particular place.

– SYNONYMS **inhabitant,** resident, townsman, townswoman, native, local, occupant, dweller.

– ORIGIN from Old French *deinz* 'within.'

de·nom·i·nate /diˈnäməˌnāt/ ▶ **verb 1** formal give a name to: *he has denominated her 'Little Mother.'* **2** (**be denominated**) (of sums of money) be expressed in a specified unit of money.
– ORIGIN Latin *denominare*.

de·nom·i·na·tion /diˌnäməˈnāsHən/ ▶ **noun 1** a recognized branch of a church or religion. **2** the face value of a bill, coin, postage stamp, etc. **3** formal a name.

– SYNONYMS **1 religious group,** sect, cult, movement, persuasion, order, creed, school, church. **2 value,** unit, size.

de·nom·i·na·tion·al /diˌnäməˈnāsHənl/ ▶ **adjective** relating to a particular branch of a church or religion.
– DERIVATIVES **de·nom·i·na·tion·al·ism** /-ˌizəm/ noun.

de·nom·i·na·tor /diˈnäməˌnātər/ ▶ **noun** Mathematics the number below the line in a fraction; a divisor.

de·note /diˈnōt/ ▶ **verb 1** be a sign of or indicate something. **2** (of a word or phrase) have as a main or literal meaning (e.g., the word *mother* denotes 'a woman who is a parent').

– SYNONYMS **indicate,** be a mark of, signify, signal, designate, symbolize, represent.

– DERIVATIVES **de·no·ta·tion** /ˌdēnōˈtāsHən/ noun.
– ORIGIN Latin *denotare*.

de·noue·ment /ˌdānōōˈmäN/ (also **dénouement**) ▶ **noun** the final part of a play, movie, or story, in which matters are explained or resolved.
– ORIGIN French.

de·nounce /diˈnouns/ ▶ **verb** publicly declare someone or something to be wrong or evil.

– SYNONYMS **1 condemn,** attack, censure, decry, stigmatize, deprecate, disparage, revile, damn. **2 expose,** betray, inform on, incriminate, implicate, cite, accuse.

– DERIVATIVES **de·nounce·ment** noun.
– ORIGIN Latin *denuntiare* 'give official information.'

de no·vo /dā ˈnōvō, di/ ▶ **adverb & adjective** starting from the beginning; anew.
– ORIGIN Latin, 'from new.'

dense /dens/ ▶ **adjective 1** containing many people or things crowded closely together: *dense jungle.* **2** having a thick or closely packed texture: *dense rye bread.* **3** informal stupid.

– SYNONYMS **1** *a dense forest* **thick,** crowded, compact, solid, tight, overgrown, impenetrable, impassable. **2** *dense smoke* **thick,** heavy, opaque, murky. **3 stupid,** brainless, foolish, slow, simple-minded, empty-headed, obtuse; informal thick, dim, dopey.
– ANTONYMS sparse, thin.

– DERIVATIVES **dense·ly** adverb **dense·ness** noun.
– ORIGIN Latin *densus*.

CHOOSE THE RIGHT WORD

See **STUPID**.

den·si·ty /ˈdensitē/ ▶ **noun** (pl. **densities**) **1** the degree to which a substance is dense; mass per unit volume. **2** the quantity of people or things in a particular area: *areas of low population density.*

– SYNONYMS **solidity,** solidness, denseness, thickness, substance, mass, compactness, tightness, hardness.

dent /dent/ ▶ **noun** a slight hollow in a surface made by a blow or pressure.

– SYNONYMS **knock,** indentation, dint, depression, hollow, crater, pit; informal ding.

▶ **verb 1** mark something with a dent. **2** have an adverse effect on something.

– SYNONYMS **knock,** dint, mark; informal ding.

– ORIGIN variant of **DINT**.

den·tal /ˈdentl/ ▶ **adjective 1** relating to the teeth or to dentistry. **2** Phonetics (of a consonant) pronounced with the tip of the tongue against the upper front teeth (as *th*) or the ridge containing the sockets of the upper teeth (as *n*, *d*, *t*).
– DERIVATIVES **den·tal·ly** adverb.
– ORIGIN Latin *dentalis*.

den·tate /ˈdenˌtāt/ ▶ **adjective** technical having a toothlike or serrated edge.

den·ti·frice /ˈdentəfris/ ▶ **noun** a paste or powder for cleaning the teeth.
– ORIGIN from Latin *dens* 'tooth' + *fricare* 'to rub.'

den·til /ˈdentl, -til/ ▶ **noun** Architecture one of a series of small rectangular blocks used as a decoration under the molding of a cornice.
– ORIGIN Italian *dentello* 'little tooth.'

den·tine /ˈdenˌtēn/ (also **dentin** /ˈdentn/) ▶ **noun** hard dense bony tissue forming the bulk of a tooth.

den·tist /ˈdentist/ ▶ **noun** a person who is qualified to treat the diseases and conditions that affect the teeth and gums.
– DERIVATIVES **den·tist·ry** noun.

den·ti·tion /den'tisHən/ ▸ **noun** the arrangement or condition of the teeth in a particular species.

den·ture /'dencHər/ ▸ **noun** a removable plate or frame holding one or more false teeth.

de·nude /di'n(y)o͞od/ ▸ **verb** strip of covering; make bare: *the land is denuded of trees.*
– DERIVATIVES **den·u·da·tion** /ˌden(y)o͞o'dāsHən/ noun.
– ORIGIN Latin *denudare.*

de·nun·ci·a·tion /diˌnənsē'āsHən/ ▸ **noun** public condemnation of someone or something.
– DERIVATIVES **de·nun·ci·a·to·ry** /-'nənsēəˌtôrē/ adjective.

Den·ver boot ▸ **noun** a clamp placed by the police on the wheel of an illegally parked vehicle to make it immobile.

de·ny /di'nī/ ▸ **verb** (**denies, denying, denied**) **1** state that something is not true. **2** refuse to admit or accept: *they denied all knowledge of the ship's sinking.* **3** refuse to give something requested or desired to someone. **4** (**deny oneself**) go without something that one desires.

– SYNONYMS **1 contradict,** rebut, repudiate, refute, challenge, contest. **2 refuse,** turn down, reject, rebuff, decline, veto, dismiss; informal give the thumbs down to.
– ANTONYMS confirm, allow, accept.

– ORIGIN Old French *deneier.*

CHOOSE THE RIGHT WORD

See **REFUTE**.

de·o·dor·ant /dē'ōdərənt/ ▸ **noun** a substance that removes or conceals bodily smells.
– ORIGIN from Latin *odor* 'smell.'

de·o·dor·ize /dē'ōdəˌrīz/ ▸ **verb** remove or conceal an unpleasant smell in a place.
– DERIVATIVES **de·o·dor·iz·er** noun.

de·ox·y·gen·a·ted /dē'äksijəˌnātid/ ▸ **adjective** having had the oxygen removed.
– DERIVATIVES **de·ox·y·gen·a·tion** /-ˌäksijə'nāsHən/ noun.

de·ox·y·ri·bo·nu·cle·ic ac·id /dēˌäksēˌrībōn(y)o͞o'klēik/ ▸ **noun** see **DNA**.

de·part /di'pärt/ ▸ **verb 1** leave, especially to start a journey. **2** (**depart from**) do something different from a usual course of action.

– SYNONYMS **1 leave,** go away, withdraw, absent oneself, quit, exit, decamp, retreat, retire, make off; informal make tracks, take off, split. **2 deviate,** diverge, digress, stray, veer, differ, vary.
– ANTONYMS arrive.

– ORIGIN Old French *departir.*

de·part·ed /di'pärtid/ ▸ **adjective** dead; deceased.

de·part·ment /di'pärtmənt/ ▸ **noun 1** a division of a business, government, or other large organization, dealing with a specific area of activity. **2** an administrative district, especially in France. **3** (**one's department**) informal an area of special skill or responsibility: *Tiling the floor? That's your department.*

– SYNONYMS **division,** section, sector, unit, branch, wing, office, bureau, agency, ministry.

– DERIVATIVES **de·part·men·tal** /diˌpärt'mentl, ˌdēpärt-/ adjective **de·part·men·tal·ly** /diˌpärt'mentlē, ˌdēpärt-/ adverb.

de·part·ment store ▸ **noun** a large store stocking many types of goods in different departments.

de·par·ture /di'pärcHər/ ▸ **noun 1** the action of leaving. **2** a change from a usual course of action.

– SYNONYMS **1 leaving,** going, leave-taking, withdrawal, exit. **2 deviation,** divergence, digression, shift, variation. **3 change,** innovation, novelty.

de·pend /di'pend/ ▸ **verb** (**depend on**) **1** be controlled or determined by: *differences in earnings depended on a variety of factors.* **2** rely on someone or something.

– SYNONYMS **1 be dependent,** hinge, hang, rest, rely. **2** *my family **depends on** me* **rely on,** lean on, count on, bank on, trust (in), pin one's hopes on.

– ORIGIN Latin *dependere* 'hang down.'

de·pend·a·ble /di'pendəbəl/ ▸ **adjective** trustworthy and reliable.

– SYNONYMS **reliable,** trustworthy, trusty, faithful, loyal, stable, sensible, responsible.

– DERIVATIVES **de·pend·a·bil·i·ty** /-ˌpendə'bilitē/ noun **de·pend·a·bly** /-blē/ adverb.

de·pend·en·cy /di'pendənsē/ ▸ **noun** (pl. **dependencies**) **1** a country or province controlled by another. **2** the state of being dependent on someone or something.

de·pend·ent /di'pendənt/ ▸ **adjective 1** (**dependent on**) determined or influenced by. **2** relying on someone or something for support. **3** (**dependent on**) unable to do without something.

– SYNONYMS **1** *benefits will be **dependent on** length of service* **conditional on,** contingent on, based on, subject to, determined by, influenced by. **2** *he is ill and dependent* **reliant,** needy, helpless, infirm, invalid, incapable, debilitated, disabled. **3** *the army is **dependent on** volunteers* **reliant on,** relying on, counting on, sustained by. **4** *she is **dependent on** drugs* **addicted to,** reliant on; informal hooked on.
– ANTONYMS independent.

▸ **noun** (Brit. **dependant**) a person who relies on another, especially a family member, for financial support.
– DERIVATIVES **de·pend·ence** noun **de·pend·ent·ly** adverb.

de·per·son·al·ize /dē'pərsənəˌlīz/ ▸ **verb** deprive someone or something of human characteristics or individuality.
– DERIVATIVES **de·per·son·al·i·za·tion** /dēˌpərsənələ'zāsHən/ noun.

de·pict /di'pikt/ ▸ **verb 1** represent someone or something by a drawing, painting, or other art form. **2** describe something in words.

– SYNONYMS **1 portray,** show, represent, picture, illustrate, reproduce, render. **2 describe,** detail, relate, present, set forth, set out, outline.

– DERIVATIVES **de·pic·tion** noun.
– ORIGIN Latin *depingere.*

dep·i·late /'depəˌlāt/ ▸ **verb** remove the hair from someone.
– DERIVATIVES **dep·i·la·tion** /ˌdepə'lāsHən/ noun **dep·i·la·tor** /'depəˌlātər/ noun.
– ORIGIN Latin *depilare.*

de·pil·a·to·ry /di'piləˌtôrē/ ▸ **adjective** used to remove unwanted hair. ▸ **noun** (pl. **depilatories**) a cream or lotion for removing unwanted hair.

de·plane /dē'plān/ ▸ **verb** disembark from an aircraft.

de·plete /di'plēt/ ▸ **verb** reduce the number or quantity of: *fish stocks are severely depleted.*

– SYNONYMS **reduce,** decrease, diminish, exhaust, use up, consume, expend, drain, empty.
– ANTONYMS augment.

– DERIVATIVES **de·plet·er** noun.
– ORIGIN Latin *deplere* 'empty out.'

de·plet·ed u·ra·ni·um ▶ **noun** uranium from which most of the fissile isotope uranium-235 has been removed.

de·ple·tion /di'plēsʜən/ ▶ **noun** the action of decreasing something.

– SYNONYMS *the depletion of our natural resources* **exhaustion,** use, consumption, expenditure; reduction, decrease, diminution; impoverishment.

de·plor·a·ble /di'plôrəbəl/ ▶ **adjective** deserving strong condemnation; shockingly bad.

– SYNONYMS **1** *deplorable conduct* **disgraceful,** shameful, inexcusable, unpardonable, atrocious, awful, terrible, dreadful, diabolical, unforgivable, despicable, abominable, contemptible, beyond the pale. **2** *a deplorable state of neglect* **lamentable,** regrettable, unfortunate, wretched, atrocious, awful, terrible, dreadful, sorry, poor; informal appalling, dire, abysmal, woeful, lousy; formal grievous.
– ANTONYMS admirable.

– DERIVATIVES **de·plor·a·bly** adverb.

de·plore /di'plôr/ ▶ **verb** feel or express strong disapproval of something.

– SYNONYMS **1 abhor,** find unacceptable, frown on, disapprove of, take a dim view of, take exception to, condemn, denounce. **2 regret,** lament, mourn, bemoan, bewail, complain about, grieve over, sigh over.
– ANTONYMS applaud.

– ORIGIN Latin *deplorare*.

de·ploy /di'ploi/ ▶ **verb 1** bring or move troops into position for military action. **2** bring into effective action: *the FBI began to deploy an Internet monitoring system*.

– SYNONYMS **1 position,** station, post, place, install, locate, base. **2 use,** utilize, employ, take advantage of, exploit, call on.

– DERIVATIVES **de·ploy·a·ble** adjective **de·ploy·ment** noun.
– ORIGIN French *déployer*.

de·po·lit·i·cize /ˌdēpə'litiˌsīz/ ▶ **verb** remove something from political activity or influence.
– DERIVATIVES **de·po·lit·i·ci·za·tion** /-ˌlitisə'zāsʜən/ noun.

de·po·nent /di'pōnənt/ ▶ **noun** Law a person who gives a sworn statement to be used as evidence.
– ORIGIN from Latin *deponere* 'put down.'

de·pop·u·late /dē'päpyəˌlāt/ ▶ **verb** substantially reduce the population of an area.
– DERIVATIVES **de·pop·u·la·tion** /-ˌpäpyə'lāsʜən/ noun.

de·port /di'pôrt/ ▶ **verb 1** expel a foreigner or immigrant from a country. **2** (**deport oneself**) old use behave in a specified way.

– SYNONYMS **expel,** banish, extradite, repatriate.
– ANTONYMS admit.

– DERIVATIVES **de·por·ta·tion** /ˌdēpôr'tāsʜən/ noun **de·por·tee** /ˌdēpôr'tē/ noun.
– ORIGIN Latin *deportare*.

de·port·ment /di'pôrtmənt/ ▶ **noun 1** the way a person stands and walks. **2** a person's behavior or manners.

de·pose /di'pōz/ ▶ **verb 1** remove someone from office suddenly and forcefully. **2** Law give evidence under oath, especially in writing.

– SYNONYMS **overthrow,** unseat, dethrone, topple, remove, supplant, displace, oust.

– ORIGIN Old French *deposer*.

de·pos·it /di'päzit/ ▶ **noun 1** a sum of money paid into a bank account. **2** a sum payable as a first installment of a larger payment. **3** a returnable sum paid on the rental of something, to cover possible loss or damage. **4** a layer of a substance that has accumulated or been laid down: *mineral deposits*. **5** the action of depositing something.

– SYNONYMS **1 layer,** covering, coating, blanket, accumulation, sediment. **2 seam,** vein, lode, layer, stratum, bed. **3 down payment,** advance payment, prepayment, installment, retainer, security.

▶ **verb** (**deposits, depositing, deposited**) **1** put down in a specific place: *he deposited her at the station*. **2** put something in a place for safekeeping. **3** pay a sum of money as a deposit. **4** (of water or another natural agency) lay down matter as a layer or covering.

– SYNONYMS **1 put down,** place, set down, unload, rest, drop; informal dump, park, plunk, plonk. **2 leave (behind),** precipitate, dump, wash up, cast up. **3 lodge,** bank, house, store, stow.

– DERIVATIVES **de·pos·i·tor** noun.
– ORIGIN Latin *depositum*.

de·pos·i·tar·y /di'päziˌterē/ (also **depository**) ▶ **noun** (pl. **depositaries**) a person to whom something is given for safekeeping.

dep·o·si·tion /ˌdepə'zisʜən/ ▶ **noun 1** the action of removing someone from office. **2** Law a sworn statement to be used as evidence. **3** the action of depositing something.

de·pos·i·tor·y /di'päziˌtôrē/ ▶ **noun** (pl. **depositories**) **1** a place where things are stored. **2** variant spelling of **DEPOSITARY**.

de·pot /'dēpō, 'de-/ ▶ **noun 1** a place for the storage of large quantities of goods. **2** a place where buses, trains, or other vehicles are housed and maintained. **3** a railroad or bus station.

– SYNONYMS **1 terminal,** terminus, station, garage, headquarters, base. **2 storehouse,** warehouse, store, repository, depository, cache, arsenal, armory, dump.

– ORIGIN French.

de·prave /di'prāv/ ▶ **verb** make someone immoral or wicked.
– DERIVATIVES **de·prav·i·ty** /di'pravitē/ noun.
– ORIGIN Latin *depravare*.

de·praved /di'prāvd/ ▶ **adjective** morally corrupt.

– SYNONYMS **corrupt,** perverted, deviant, degenerate, debased, immoral, unprincipled, debauched, dissolute, licentious, lecherous, prurient, indecent, sordid, wicked, sinful, vile, iniquitous, nefarious; informal warped, twisted, sick.

dep·re·cate /'depriˌkāt/ ▶ **verb 1** express disapproval of someone or something. **2** another term for **DEPRECIATE** (sense 2).
– DERIVATIVES **dep·re·ca·tion** /ˌdeprə'kāsʜən/ noun **dep·re·ca·to·ry** /'deprikəˌtôrē/ adjective.
– ORIGIN Latin *deprecari* 'pray to ward off evil.'

de·pre·ci·ate /di'prēsʜēˌāt/ ▶ **verb 1** reduce in value over time: *avoid buying new cars that depreciate quickly*. **2** criticize or dismiss something as unimportant.
– DERIVATIVES **de·pre·ci·a·ble** /di'prēsʜ(ē)əbəl/ adjective **de·pre·ci·a·tion** /diˌprēsʜē'āsʜən/ noun.
– ORIGIN Latin *depreciare* 'lower in price, undervalue.'

dep·re·da·tion /ˌdeprəˈdāsнən/ ▶ **noun** an act that causes harm or damage: *the protection of crops from the depredations of birds.*
– ORIGIN from Latin *depraedari* 'to plunder.'

de·press /diˈpres/ ▶ **verb 1** make someone feel very unhappy or dispirited. **2** reduce the level of activity in a system. **3** push or pull something down.

> – SYNONYMS **1 sadden,** dispirit, cast down, get down, dishearten, demoralize, crush, weigh down on. **2** *new economic policies depressed sales* **slow down,** weaken, impair, inhibit, restrict. **3** *foreign imports will depress domestic prices* **reduce,** lower, cut, cheapen, discount, deflate, diminish, depreciate, devalue. **4 press,** push, hold down.
> – ANTONYMS cheer, boost, raise.

– ORIGIN Latin *depressare.*

de·pres·sant /diˈpresənt/ ▶ **adjective** reducing activity in bodily processes. ▶ **noun** a drug or other agent that reduces activity in bodily processes.

de·pressed /diˈprest/ ▶ **adjective 1** very unhappy and dispirited. **2** suffering from clinical depression. **3** suffering from economic recession: *depressed rural areas.*

> – SYNONYMS **1 sad,** unhappy, miserable, gloomy, dejected, downhearted, downcast, down, despondent, dispirited, low, morose, dismal, desolate; informal blue, down in the dumps, down in the mouth. **2 weak,** inactive, flat, slow, slack, sluggish, stagnant. **3 poverty-stricken,** poor, disadvantaged, deprived, needy, distressed, run-down.
> – ANTONYMS cheerful.

de·press·ing /diˈpresiNG/ ▶ **adjective** causing unhappiness or dejection.

> – SYNONYMS *depressing thoughts* **dismal,** sad, unhappy, somber, gloomy, grave, bleak, black, melancholy, dreary, grim, cheerless.

– DERIVATIVES **de·press·ing·ly** adverb.

de·pres·sion /diˈpresнən/ ▶ **noun 1** severe unhappiness and dejection. **2** a medical condition in which a person experiences severe feelings of hopelessness and inadequacy. **3** a long and severe recession in an economy or market. **4** the action of lowering or depressing something. **5** a sunken place or hollow. **6** an area of low atmospheric pressure that may bring rain.

> – SYNONYMS **1 unhappiness,** sadness, melancholy, melancholia, misery, sorrow, gloom, despondency, low spirits. **2 recession,** slump, decline, downturn. **3 hollow,** indentation, dent, cavity, dip, pit, crater, basin, bowl.

de·pres·sive /diˈpresiv/ ▶ **adjective** tending to cause depression. ▶ **noun** a person who tends to suffer from depression.

de·pres·sur·ize /dēˈpresнəˌrīz/ ▶ **verb** release the pressure inside a compartment or container.
– DERIVATIVES **de·pres·sur·i·za·tion** /-ˌpresнərəˈzāsнən/ noun.

dep·ri·va·tion /ˌdeprəˈvāsнən/ ▶ **noun 1** hardship resulting from the lack of basic necessities. **2** the lack or denial of something necessary: *sleep deprivation.*

> – SYNONYMS **1 poverty,** impoverishment, privation, hardship, destitution, need, want. **2 dispossession,** withholding, withdrawal, removal, seizure.
> – ANTONYMS prosperity.

de·prive /diˈprīv/ ▶ **verb** prevent from having or using something: *the city was deprived of its water supply.*

> – SYNONYMS **dispossess,** strip, divest, relieve, rob, cheat out of.

– ORIGIN Latin *deprivare.*

de·prived /diˈprīvd/ ▶ **adjective** suffering a harmful lack of basic material and cultural necessities.

> – SYNONYMS **disadvantaged,** underprivileged, poverty-stricken, impoverished, poor, dirt poor, destitute, needy.
> – ANTONYMS privileged.

Dept ▶ **abbreviation** Department.

depth /depтн/ ▶ **noun 1** the distance from the top or surface down or from the front to back of something. **2** the quality of being intense, extreme, or complex. **3** extensive and detailed treatment or knowledge: *third-year courses go into more depth.* **4** (**the depths**) the deepest, lowest, or inmost part: *the depths to which morality has sunk.*

> – SYNONYMS **1 deepness,** drop, height. **2 extent,** range, scope, breadth, width. **3 profundity,** wisdom, understanding, intelligence, discernment, penetration, insight, awareness. **4 intensity,** richness, vividness, strength, brilliance.

– DERIVATIVES **depth·less** adjective.
– PHRASES **out of one's depth** in a situation beyond one's ability to cope.
– ORIGIN from **DEEP**.

depth charge ▶ **noun** an explosive charge designed to explode under water, used for attacking submarines.

dep·u·ta·tion /ˌdepyəˈtāsнən/ ▶ **noun** a group of people who are appointed to act on behalf of a larger group.

de·pute ▶ **verb** /diˈpyo͞ot/ appoint someone to perform a task for which one is responsible. ▶ **noun** /ˈdepyo͞ot/ Scottish a deputy.
– ORIGIN Latin *deputare* 'consider to be, assign.'

dep·u·tize /ˈdepyəˌtīz/ ▶ **verb 1** make someone a deputy. **2** temporarily act on behalf of someone else: *you will be required to deputize for the manager in her absence.*

> – SYNONYMS **stand in,** sit in, fill in, cover, substitute, replace, take someone's place, take over, hold the fort, step into the breach.

dep·u·ty /ˈdepyətē/ ▶ **noun** (pl. **deputies**) **1** a person appointed to undertake the duties of a more senior person in that person's absence. **2** a parliamentary representative in certain countries.

> – SYNONYMS **second in command,** number two, assistant, aide, proxy, stand-in, replacement, substitute, representative, reserve.

de·rac·i·nat·ed /diˈrasəˌnātid/ ▶ **adjective** displaced from one's environment.
– DERIVATIVES **de·rac·i·na·tion** /-ˌrasəˈnāsнən/ noun.
– ORIGIN French *déraciner* 'uproot.'

de·rail /dēˈrāl/ ▶ **verb 1** cause a train to leave the tracks. **2** obstruct a process by diverting it from its intended course.
– DERIVATIVES **de·rail·ment** noun.

de·rail·leur /diˈrālər/ ▶ **noun** a bicycle gear that works by lifting the chain from one sprocket wheel to another.
– ORIGIN from French *dérailler* 'derail.'

de·range /diˈrānj/ ▶ **verb 1** (usu as adj. **deranged**) make someone insane. **2** throw something into disorder.

– SYNONYMS (as adj. **deranged**) **insane,** mad, disturbed, unbalanced, unhinged, unstable, irrational, crazed, demented, berserk, frenzied, lunatic, non compos mentis; informal touched, crazy, mental.
– ANTONYMS rational.

– DERIVATIVES **de·range·ment** noun.
– ORIGIN Old French *desrengier* 'move from orderly rows.'

Der·by /'dərbē/ ▶ **noun** (pl. **Derbies**) **1** an annual race at Epsom Downs in England for three-year-old horses, founded by the 12th Earl of Derby. **2** a similar race elsewhere: *the Kentucky Derby*. **3** (**derby**) a bowler hat.

de·reg·u·late /dē'regyə,lāt/ ▶ **verb** remove regulations from something.
– DERIVATIVES **de·reg·u·la·tion** /-,regyə'lāsʜən/ noun **de·reg·u·la·to·ry** /-lə,tôrē/ adjective.

der·e·lict /'derə,likt/ ▶ **adjective 1** in a very poor condition as a result of disuse and neglect. **2** shamefully negligent.

– SYNONYMS **dilapidated,** ramshackle, run-down, tumbledown, in ruins, falling down, disused, abandoned, deserted.

▶ **noun** a person without a home, job, or possessions.

– SYNONYMS **tramp,** vagrant, down and out, homeless person, drifter, beggar; informal bag lady.

– ORIGIN from Latin *derelinquere* 'to abandon.'

WORD TOOLKIT

derelict ...	disintegrating ...	decaying ...
building	marriage	corpse
property	relationship	flesh
area	economy	leaves
mill	world	wood
housing	family	plants
farm	situation	logs
barn	infrastructure	fish
church	society	vegetation

der·e·lic·tion /,derə'liksʜən/ ▶ **noun 1** the state of having been abandoned and become dilapidated. **2** (**dereliction of duty**) shameful failure to fulfill one's obligations.

de·ride /di'rīd/ ▶ **verb** express contempt for someone or something; ridicule.
– ORIGIN Latin *deridere* 'scoff at.'

de ri·gueur /də ri'gər, rē'gœr/ ▶ **adjective** considered necessary for acceptance in fashionable society.
– ORIGIN French, 'in strictness.'

de·ri·sion /di'rizʜən/ ▶ **noun** contemptuous ridicule or mockery.

– SYNONYMS **mockery,** ridicule, jeers, sneers, taunts, disdain, disparagement, denigration, insults.

– ORIGIN Latin.

de·ri·sive /di'rīsiv/ ▶ **adjective** expressing contempt or ridicule.
– DERIVATIVES **de·ri·sive·ly** adverb.

de·ri·so·ry /di'rīsərē, -'rī-/ ▶ **adjective 1** ridiculously small or inadequate: *a derisory pay rise*. **2** expressing derision; derisive.

der·i·va·tion /,derə'vāsʜən/ ▶ **noun 1** the action of obtaining something from a source or origin. **2** the formation of a word from another word.
– DERIVATIVES **der·i·va·tion·al** adjective.

de·riv·a·tive /di'rivətiv/ ▶ **adjective** imitative of the work of another artist, writer, etc., and regarded as unoriginal. ▶ **noun 1** something that is based on or derived from something else: *the new drug is just a derivative of an old antibiotic*. **2** Mathematics an expression representing the rate of change of one quantity in relation to another.

de·rive /di'rīv/ ▶ **verb 1** (**derive something from**) obtain or get something from: *they derived great comfort from this assurance*. **2** (**derive something from**) base something on a modification of something else. **3** (**derive from**) originate or develop from: *the word may derive from Old English*.
– DERIVATIVES **de·riv·a·ble** adjective.
– ORIGIN Latin *derivare* 'draw off water.'

der·ma·ti·tis /,dərmə'tītis/ ▶ **noun** inflammation of the skin as a result of irritation or an allergic reaction.
– ORIGIN from Greek *derma* 'skin.'

der·ma·tol·o·gy /,dərmə'täləjē/ ▶ **noun** the branch of medicine concerned with skin disorders.
– DERIVATIVES **der·ma·to·log·i·cal** /-mətl'äjikəl/ adjective **der·ma·to·log·i·cal·ly** /-mətl'äjik(ə)lē/ adverb **der·ma·tol·o·gist** /-jist/ noun.

der·mis /'dərmis/ ▶ **noun** the thick layer of the skin below the epidermis, consisting of living tissue.
– DERIVATIVES **der·mal** /-məl/ adjective.
– ORIGIN Latin.

der·nier cri /'dernyā 'krē/ ▶ **noun** the very latest fashion: *she's wearing the dernier cri in bohemian chic*.
– ORIGIN French, 'last cry.'

der·o·gate /'derə,gāt/ ▶ **verb** formal **1** (**derogate from**) cause something to seem less valuable or important; detract from. **2** (**derogate from**) deviate from an agreement or rule: *one country derogated from the Rome Convention*. **3** be critical of someone or something.
– DERIVATIVES **der·o·ga·tion** /,derə'gāsʜən/ noun.
– ORIGIN Latin *derogare* 'abrogate.'

de·rog·a·to·ry /di'rägə,tôrē/ ▶ **adjective** showing a critical or disrespectful attitude.

– SYNONYMS **disparaging,** disrespectful, demeaning, critical, pejorative, negative, unfavorable, uncomplimentary, unflattering, insulting, defamatory, slanderous, libelous.
– ANTONYMS complimentary.

– DERIVATIVES **de·rog·a·to·ri·ly** /-,tôrəlē/ adverb.

der·rick /'derik/ ▶ **noun 1** a kind of crane with a movable pivoted arm. **2** the framework over an oil well, holding the drilling machinery.
– ORIGIN from *Derrick*, the surname of a 17th-century hangman.

der·ri·ère /,derē'e(ə)r/ ▶ **noun** euphemistic or humorous a person's buttocks.
– ORIGIN French, 'behind.'

der·ring-do /'deriɴɢ 'do͞o/ ▶ **noun** dated or humorous action displaying heroic courage.
– ORIGIN from the Middle English phrase *dorryng do* 'daring to do.'

der·ris /'deris/ ▶ **noun** an insecticide made from the powdered roots of a tropical plant.
– ORIGIN Greek, 'leather covering' (referring to the plant's pods).

der·vish /'dərvisʜ/ ▶ **noun** a member of a Muslim (specifically Sufi) religious group vowed to poverty, some orders of which are known for their wild rituals.
– ORIGIN Persian, 'religious beggar.'

de·sal·i·nate /dēˈsaləˌnāt/ ▸ **verb** remove salt from seawater.
– DERIVATIVES **de·sal·i·na·tion** /-ˌsaləˈnāsʜən/ noun.

des·cant /ˈdesˌkant/ ▸ **noun** an independent treble melody sung or played above a basic melody.
– ORIGIN Latin *discantus* 'part song, refrain.'

des·cant re·cord·er ▸ **noun** Music the most common size of recorder, with a range of two octaves above the C above middle C.

de·scend /diˈsend/ ▸ **verb 1** move down or downward. **2** slope or lead downward. **3** (**descend on**) make a sudden attack on or unwelcome visit to someone or something. **4** (**descend to**) act in a shameful way that is below one's usual standards: *she began to despise herself for having descended to self-pity*. **5** (**be descended from**) have someone as an ancestor. **6** pass by inheritance: *his lands descended to his eldest son*.

– SYNONYMS **1 go down,** come down, drop, fall, sink, dive, plummet, plunge, nosedive. **2 slope,** dip, slant, go down, fall away. **3** (**descend on**) **flock to,** besiege, surround, take over, invade, swoop on, occupy. **4** (**descend to**) **stoop,** lower oneself, demean oneself, debase oneself; resort, be reduced.
– ANTONYMS climb.

– DERIVATIVES **de·scend·ent** adjective **de·scend·er** noun.
– ORIGIN Latin *descendere* 'climb down.'

de·scend·ant /diˈsendənt/ ▸ **noun 1** a person, animal, or plant that is descended from a particular ancestor. **2** something that has developed from an earlier version of something: *the instrument is a descendant of the lute*.

de·scent /diˈsent/ ▸ **noun 1** the action of descending. **2** a downward slope. **3** a person's origin or nationality.

– SYNONYMS **1 dive,** drop, fall, plunge, nosedive. **2 slope,** incline, dip, drop, gradient. **3 decline,** slide, fall, degeneration, deterioration. **4 ancestry,** parentage, ancestors, family, extraction, origin, derivation, birth, lineage, stock, blood, roots, origins.

de·scribe /diˈskrīb/ ▸ **verb 1** give a detailed account in words of someone or something. **2** mark out or draw a geometrical figure.

– SYNONYMS **1 report,** recount, relate, narrate, tell of, set out, detail, give a rundown of. **2 portray,** depict, paint, define, characterize, call, label, class, brand. **3 mark out,** delineate, outline, trace, draw.

– DERIVATIVES **de·scrib·a·ble** adjective **de·scrib·er** noun.
– ORIGIN Latin *describere* 'write down.'

de·scrip·tion /diˈskripsʜən/ ▸ **noun 1** a spoken or written account. **2** the action of describing someone or something. **3** a sort, kind, or class: *people of any description*.

– SYNONYMS **1 account,** report, narrative, story, portrayal, portrait, sketch, details. **2 designation,** labeling, naming, dubbing, characterization, definition, classification, branding. **3 sort,** variety, kind, type.

de·scrip·tive /diˈskriptiv/ ▸ **adjective 1** describing someone or something; giving a description. **2** describing something in an objective and nonjudgmental way.
– DERIVATIVES **de·scrip·tive·ly** adverb.

de·scrip·tor /diˈskriptər/ ▸ **noun 1** a word or expression used to describe or identify something. **2** Computing a piece of stored data that indicates how other data is stored.

de·scry /diˈskrī/ ▸ **verb** (**descries, descrying, descried**) literary catch sight of someone or something.
– ORIGIN Old French *descrier* 'publish, proclaim.'

CHOOSE THE RIGHT WORD

See **DISTINGUISH**.

des·e·crate /ˈdesiˌkrāt/ ▸ **verb** treat something sacred with violent disrespect.

– SYNONYMS **violate,** profane, defile, debase, degrade, dishonor, vandalize, damage, destroy, deface.

– DERIVATIVES **des·e·cra·tion** /ˌdesiˈkrāsʜən/ noun **des·e·cra·tor** /-ˌkrātər/ noun.
– ORIGIN from **DE-** + a shortened form of **CONSECRATE**.

de·seg·re·gate /dēˈsegriˌgāt/ ▸ **verb** end a policy of racial segregation in a school or similar institution.
– DERIVATIVES **de·seg·re·ga·tion** /dēˌsegriˈgāsʜən/ noun.

de·se·lect /ˌdēsəˈlekt/ ▸ **verb** turn off a selected feature on a list of options on a computer menu.
– DERIVATIVES **de·se·lec·tion** /-ˈleksʜən/ noun.

de·sen·si·tize /dēˈsensiˌtīz/ ▸ **verb 1** make something less sensitive. **2** make someone less likely to be shocked or distressed by cruelty or suffering.
– DERIVATIVES **de·sen·si·ti·za·tion** /dēˌsensitəˈzāsʜən/ noun.

de·sert[1] /dəˈzərt/ ▸ **verb 1** leave in a disloyal or treacherous way; abandon: *her husband deserted her long ago*. **2** (usu. as adj. **deserted**) leave a place, causing it to appear empty. **3** illegally leave the armed forces.

– SYNONYMS **1 abandon,** leave, jilt, leave high and dry, leave in the lurch, leave behind, strand, maroon; informal walk/run out on, dump, ditch; literary forsake. **2** (as adj. **deserted**) *a deserted village* **empty,** uninhabited, unoccupied, abandoned, evacuated, desolate, lonely, godforsaken. **3 abscond,** defect, run away, decamp, flee, turn tail, take French leave; Military go AWOL.

– DERIVATIVES **de·ser·tion** /-ˈzərsʜən/ noun.
– ORIGIN Latin *desertare*.

de·sert[2] /ˈdezərt/ ▸ **noun 1** a waterless area of land with little or no vegetation, typically covered with sand. **2** a situation or area considered dull and uninteresting: *a cultural desert*.

– SYNONYMS **wasteland,** wastes, wilderness, dust bowl.

▸ **adjective** (of a place) like a desert.
– ORIGIN Latin *desertum* 'something left waste.'

de·sert·er /dəˈzərtər/ ▸ **noun** a member of the armed forces who deserts.

de·sert·i·fi·ca·tion /diˌzərtəfiˈkāsʜən/ ▸ **noun** the process by which fertile land becomes desert.

des·ert is·land /ˈdezərt/ ▸ **noun** a remote, uninhabited tropical island.

de·serts /dəˈzərts/ ▸ **plural noun** (usu. in phrase **get** or **receive one's just deserts**) the reward or punishment that a person deserves.
– ORIGIN from Old French *deservir* 'serve well, deserve.'

de·serve /dəˈzərv/ ▸ **verb** do something or show qualities worthy of a reward or punishment: *Amanda deserves a lot of credit*.

– SYNONYMS **1 merit,** earn, warrant, rate, justify, be worthy of, be entitled to. **2** (as adj. **deserved**) *they clinched a deserved victory* **well earned,** merited, warranted, justified, rightful, due, fitting, just, proper.

– DERIVATIVES **de·serv·ed·ly** /-vidlē/ adverb.
– ORIGIN Latin *deservire* 'serve well.'

de·serv·ing /də'zərviNG/ ▶ **adjective** worthy of favorable treatment or assistance.

– SYNONYMS **worthy,** commendable, praiseworthy, admirable, estimable, creditable.

de·sex /dē'seks/ ▶ **verb 1** deprive someone of sexual qualities. **2** castrate or spay an animal.

dés·ha·bil·lé /ˌdezə'bēlā, -'bēā/ (also **dishabille** /ˌdisə'bēl/) ▶ **noun** the state of being only partly clothed.
– ORIGIN French, 'undressed.'

des·ic·cate /'desiˌkāt/ ▶ **verb** (usu. as adj. **desiccated**) remove the moisture from something.
– DERIVATIVES **des·ic·ca·tion** /-'kāSHən/ noun.
– ORIGIN Latin *desiccare* 'make thoroughly dry.'

de·sid·er·a·tum /diˌsidə'rätəm, -'rātəm, -ˌzidə-/ ▶ **noun** (pl. **desiderata** /-tə/) something that is needed or wanted.
– ORIGIN Latin, 'something desired.'

de·sign /də'zīn/ ▶ **noun 1** a plan or drawing produced to show the appearance and workings of something before it is made. **2** the art or action of producing a design. **3** a decorative pattern. **4** underlying purpose or planning: *the appearance of design in the universe.*

– SYNONYMS **1 plan,** blueprint, drawing, sketch, outline, map, plot, diagram, draft. **2 pattern,** motif, device, style, theme, layout.

▶ **verb 1** produce a design for something. **2** plan or intend for a purpose: *the reforms were designed to stimulate economic growth.*

– SYNONYMS **1 invent,** create, think up, come up with, devise, formulate, conceive; informal dream up. **2 intend,** aim, mean.

– PHRASES **by design** on purpose; intentionally. **have designs on** aim to obtain something.
– ORIGIN Latin *designare* 'mark out, designate.'

CHOOSE THE RIGHT WORD

See **INTEND**.

des·ig·nate ▶ **verb** /'dezigˌnāt/ **1** officially give a specified status or name to: *most of the waste is designated as hazardous.* **2** appoint someone to a specified position.

– SYNONYMS **1 appoint,** nominate, delegate, select, choose, pick, elect, name, identify, assign. **2 classify,** class, label, tag, name, call, term, dub.

▶ **adjective** /-nit, -ˌnāt/ (after a noun) appointed to a post but not yet having taken it up: *the Director designate.*
– DERIVATIVES **des·ig·na·tor** /-ˌnātər/ noun.
– ORIGIN Latin *designare* 'mark out, designate.'

des·ig·nat·ed driv·er ▶ **noun** a person who abstains from alcohol in order to drive others home safely.

des·ig·nat·ed hit·ter ▶ **noun** Baseball a nonfielding player named before the start of a game to be in the batting order, typically in place of the pitcher.

des·ig·na·tion /ˌdezig'nāSHən/ ▶ **noun 1** the action of designating or choosing someone or something. **2** an official title or description.

de·sign·ed·ly /də'zīnidlē/ ▶ **adverb** on purpose; intentionally.

de·sign·er /də'zīnər/ ▶ **noun** a person who designs things. ▶ **adjective** made by a famous fashion designer: *designer jeans.*

de·sign·er ba·by ▶ **noun** a baby whose genetic makeup has been selected in order to remove a particular defect, or to ensure that a particular gene is present.

de·sign·er drug ▶ **noun** a synthetic analog of an illegal drug, especially one devised to circumvent drug laws.

de·sign·ing /də'zīniNG/ ▶ **adjective** acting in a calculating, deceitful way.

de·sir·a·ble /də'zī(ə)rəbəl/ ▶ **adjective 1** wished for as being attractive, useful, or necessary: *it is desirable to have a rechargeable battery.* **2** sexually attractive.

– SYNONYMS **1 attractive,** sought-after, in demand, popular, enviable; informal to die for, must-have. **2 advantageous,** advisable, wise, sensible, recommended, beneficial, preferable. **3 (sexually) attractive,** beautiful, pretty, appealing, seductive, alluring, irresistible; informal sexy.
– ANTONYMS unattractive.

– DERIVATIVES **de·sir·a·bil·i·ty** /-ˌzī(ə)rə'bilitē/ noun **de·sir·a·bly** adverb.

de·sire /də'zī(ə)r/ ▶ **noun 1** a strong feeling of wanting to have something or wishing for something to happen: *the desire for fame.* **2** strong sexual feeling or appetite.

– SYNONYMS **1 wish,** want, aspiration, yearning, longing, craving, hankering, hunger; informal yen, itch. **2 lust,** passion, sensuality, sexuality, libido, lasciviousness.

▶ **verb 1** strongly wish for or want something. **2** want someone sexually.

– SYNONYMS **want,** wish for, long for, yearn for, crave, hanker after, be desperate for, be bent on, covet, aspire to.

– ORIGIN Latin *desiderare.*

de·sir·ous /di'zīrəs/ ▶ **adjective** strongly wishing to have: *the pope was desirous of peace.*

de·sist /di'sist/ ▶ **verb** stop doing something; cease.
– ORIGIN Latin *desistere.*

desk /desk/ ▶ **noun 1** a piece of furniture with a flat or sloping surface, for writing or other work. **2** a counter in a hotel, bank, or airport. **3** a specified section of a news organization: *the sports desk.*
– ORIGIN Latin *discus* 'plate' (later 'desk').

de·skill /dē'skil/ ▶ **verb** reduce the level of skill required to carry out a job.

desk·top /'deskˌtäp/ ▶ **noun 1** a microcomputer suitable for use at an ordinary desk. **2** the working area of a computer screen regarded as representing the working surface of a desk.

desk·top pub·lish·ing ▶ **noun** the production of high-quality printed matter by means of a printer linked to a computer, with special software.

des·o·late ▶ **adjective** /'desəlit/ **1** (of a place) empty and bleak. **2** very unhappy or lonely.

– SYNONYMS **1 bleak,** stark, bare, dismal, grim, wild, inhospitable, deserted, uninhabited, empty, abandoned, godforsaken, isolated, remote. **2 miserable,** unhappy, despondent, depressed, disconsolate, devastated, despairing, inconsolable, wretched, broken-hearted.

▶ **verb** /'desəˌlāt/ make someone very unhappy.
– DERIVATIVES **des·o·la·tion** /ˌdesə'lāSHən/ noun.
– ORIGIN from Latin *desolare* 'abandon.'

de·spair /di'spe(ə)r/ ▶ **noun** the complete loss or absence of hope.

– SYNONYMS **desperation,** anguish, unhappiness, despondency, depression, misery, wretchedness, hopelessness.
– ANTONYMS hope, joy.

▶ **verb** lose or be without hope: *he despaired of finding a good restaurant.*

– SYNONYMS **lose hope,** give up, lose heart, be discouraged, be despondent, be demoralized.

– PHRASES **be the despair of** cause someone to lose hope.
– ORIGIN from Latin *desperare.*

des·patch ▶ **verb & noun** variant spelling of **DISPATCH**.

des·per·a·do /ˌdespə'rädō/ ▶ **noun** (pl. **desperadoes** or **desperados**) a desperate or reckless criminal.
– ORIGIN mock Spanish.

des·per·ate /'desp(ə)rit/ ▶ **adjective 1** full of despair; completely without hope. **2** extremely bad or serious: *a desperate shortage.* **3** having a great need or desire for something: *I'm desperate for a drink.* **4** violent or dangerous.

– SYNONYMS **1 despairing,** hopeless, anguished, distressed, wretched, desolate, forlorn, distraught, at one's wits' end. **2 last-ditch,** last-gasp, eleventh-hour, do-or-die, final, frantic, frenzied, wild. **3 grave,** serious, critical, acute, urgent, pressing, drastic, extreme.

– DERIVATIVES **des·per·ate·ly** adverb.
– ORIGIN Latin *desperatus* 'deprived of hope.'

des·per·a·tion /ˌdespə'rāsʜən/ ▶ **noun** a state of despair, especially as resulting in extreme behavior.

– SYNONYMS **hopelessness,** despair, distress, anguish, agony, torment, misery.

des·pi·ca·ble /di'spikəbəl/ ▶ **adjective** deserving hatred and contempt.

– SYNONYMS **contemptible,** loathsome, hateful, detestable, reprehensible, abhorrent, abominable, awful, heinous, odious, vile, low, mean, abject, shameful, ignominious, shabby, ignoble, disreputable, discreditable, unworthy; informal dirty, rotten, low-down.
– ANTONYMS admirable.

– DERIVATIVES **des·pi·ca·bly** /-blē/ adverb.
– ORIGIN from Latin *despicari* 'look down on.'

de·spise /di'spīz/ ▶ **verb** feel hatred or disgust for someone or something.

– SYNONYMS **detest,** hate, loathe, abhor, deplore, scorn, disdain, deride, sneer at, revile, spurn, shun.
– ANTONYMS adore, respect.

– DERIVATIVES **de·spis·er** noun.
– ORIGIN Latin *despicere* 'look down.'

CHOOSE THE RIGHT WORD

despise, abhor, contemn, detest, disdain, loathe, scorn

It's one thing to dislike someone; it's quite another to **despise** or **detest** the person. Both are strong words, used to describe extreme dislike or hatred. *Detest* is probably the purest expression of hatred (*she detested the woman who had raised her, and longed to find her own mother*), while *despise* suggests looking down with great contempt and regarding the person as mean, petty, weak, or worthless (*he despised men whose only concern was their own safety*). **Disdain** carries even stronger connotations of superiority, often combined with self-righteousness (*to disdain anyone lacking a college education*). **Scorn** is a stronger word for *disdain,* and it implies an attitude of not only contempt but of haughty rejection or refusal (*to scorn the woman he'd once loved*). To **loathe** something is to feel utter disgust toward it (*he grew to loathe peanut butter and jelly sandwiches*) and to **abhor** it is to feel a profound, shuddering, repugnance (*she abhorred the very idea of asking her husband for the money*). **Contemn** is a more literary word meaning to treat with disdain, scorn, or contempt.

de·spite /di'spīt/ ▶ **preposition** in spite of.

– SYNONYMS **in spite of,** notwithstanding, regardless of, in the face of, in the teeth of, undeterred by, for all, even with.

– ORIGIN first meaning 'contempt': from Latin *despectus* 'looking down on.'

de·spoil /di'spoil/ ▶ **verb** literary steal valuable possessions from a place.
– DERIVATIVES **de·spoil·er** noun **de·spo·li·a·tion** /-ˌspōlē'āsʜən/ noun.
– ORIGIN Latin *despoliare* 'rob, plunder.'

de·spond·ent /di'spändənt/ ▶ **adjective** in low spirits from loss of hope or courage.

– SYNONYMS **disheartened,** discouraged, dispirited, downhearted, downcast, crestfallen, down, low, disconsolate, despairing, wretched, melancholy, gloomy, morose, dismal, woebegone, miserable, depressed, dejected, sad; informal down in the mouth, down in the dumps.
– ANTONYMS hopeful, cheerful.

– DERIVATIVES **de·spond·en·cy** noun **de·spond·ent·ly** adverb.
– ORIGIN from Latin *despondere* 'give up, abandon.'

des·pot /'despət/ ▶ **noun** a ruler with total power, especially one who uses it in a cruel way.
– DERIVATIVES **des·pot·ism** /'despəˌtizəm/ noun.
– ORIGIN Greek *despotēs* 'master, absolute ruler.'

des·pot·ic /di'spätik/ ▶ **adjective** ruling with absolute power; tyrannical.

– SYNONYMS **autocratic,** dictatorial, totalitarian, absolutist, undemocratic, one-party, tyrannical, tyrannous, oppressive, repressive, draconian, illiberal.
– ANTONYMS democratic.

des·sert /di'zərt/ ▶ **noun** the sweet dish eaten at the end of a meal.
– ORIGIN French.

des·sert wine ▶ **noun** a sweet wine drunk with or following dessert.

de·sta·bi·lize /dē'stābəˌlīz/ ▶ **verb** upset the stability of something.
– DERIVATIVES **de·sta·bi·li·za·tion** /-ˌstābələ'zāsʜən/ noun.

des·ti·na·tion /ˌdestə'nāsʜən/ ▶ **noun** the place to which someone or something is going or being sent.

des·tine /'destin/ ▶ **verb** (**be destined**) **1** be intended for or certain to do something. **2** be bound for a particular destination.

– SYNONYMS **1** *he was destined to be an engineer* **fated,** ordained, predestined, doomed, meant, intended. **2** *computers destined for Pakistan* **heading,** bound, en route, scheduled, headed.

– ORIGIN Latin *destinare* 'make firm, establish.'

des·ti·ny /'destinē/ ▶ **noun** (pl. **destinies**) **1** the events that will happen to a person or thing in the future: *we share* *a common destiny.* **2** the power believed to control the future; fate.

– SYNONYMS **1 future,** fate, fortune, doom, lot. **2 providence,** fate, God, the stars, luck, fortune, chance, karma, kismet.

– ORIGIN from Latin *destinare* 'make firm, establish.'

des·ti·tute /ˈdestiˌt(y)o͞ot/ ▶ **adjective** very poor and lacking the means to provide for oneself.

– SYNONYMS **penniless,** poor, dirt poor, impoverished, poverty-stricken, impecunious, indigent, down and out. informal (flat) broke. formal penurious.
– ANTONYMS rich.

– DERIVATIVES **des·ti·tu·tion** /ˌdestiˈt(y)o͞osHən/ noun.
– ORIGIN from Latin *destituere* 'forsake.'

de·stroy /diˈstroi/ ▶ **verb 1** end the existence of something by attacking or damaging it. **2** kill an animal in a quick and painless way.

– SYNONYMS **1 demolish,** knock down, level, raze (to the ground), fell, blow up. **2 spoil,** ruin, wreck, blight, devastate, wreak havoc on. **3 kill,** put down, put to sleep, slaughter, cull. **4 annihilate,** wipe out, obliterate, eliminate, eradicate, liquidate, exterminate; informal take out, waste.
– ANTONYMS build.

– ORIGIN Latin *destruere.*

CHOOSE THE RIGHT WORD

destroy, annihilate, demolish, eradicate, exterminate, extirpate, raze

If you're interested in getting rid of something, you've got a number of options at your disposal. **Destroy** is a general term covering any force that wrecks, ruins, kills, etc. (*to destroy an ant hill by pouring boiling water on it*). If it's a building, you'll want to **demolish** or **raze** it, two words that are generally applied only to very large things. *Raze* is used almost exclusively with structures; it means to bring something down to the level of the ground (*they razed the apartment building to make way for the new hospital*). *Demolish* implies pulling or smashing something to pieces; when used with regard to buildings, it conjures up a vision of complete wreckage and often a heap of rubble (*their new house was demolished by the first hurricane of the season*). But unlike *raze, demolish* can also be applied to nonmaterial things (*to demolish the theory with a few simple experiments*). If you **eradicate** something, you eliminate it completely, literally or figuratively, pull it out by the roots (*to eradicate smallpox with a vaccine*) and prevent its reappearance. **Extirpate**, like *eradicate*, implies the utter destruction of something (*the species was extirpated from the park by the flooding*). If you're dealing with cockroaches, you'll probably want to **exterminate** them, which means to wipe out or kill in great numbers. Or better yet, you'll want to **annihilate** them, which is the most extreme word in this group and literally means to reduce to nothingness.

de·stroy·er /diˈstroiər/ ▶ **noun 1** a person or thing that destroys something. **2** a small, fast warship.

de·struct·i·ble /diˈstrəktəbəl/ ▶ **adjective** able to be destroyed.

de·struc·tion /diˈstrəksHən/ ▶ **noun 1** the action of destroying something or the state of being destroyed. **2** a cause of someone's ruin: *gambling was his destruction.*

– SYNONYMS **1 devastation,** carnage, ruin, chaos, wreckage. **2** *the destruction of the countryside* **wrecking,** ruining, annihilation, obliteration, elimination, eradication, devastation. **3** *the destruction of cattle* **killing,** slaughter, extermination, culling.
– ANTONYMS preservation.

– ORIGIN Latin.

de·struc·tive /diˈstrəktiv/ ▶ **adjective 1** causing severe damage or destruction. **2** negative and unhelpful: *destructive criticism.*

– SYNONYMS **devastating,** ruinous, damaging, harmful, detrimental, injurious, hurtful, deleterious.

– DERIVATIVES **de·struc·tive·ly** adverb **de·struc·tive·ness** noun.

des·ue·tude /ˈdeswiˌt(y)o͞od/ ▶ **noun** formal a state of disuse.
– ORIGIN Latin *desuetudo.*

des·ul·to·ry /ˈdesəlˌtôrē/ ▶ **adjective 1** lacking purpose or enthusiasm. **2** going from one subject to another in a half-hearted way: *a desultory conversation.*
– DERIVATIVES **des·ul·to·ri·ly** /-ˌtôrəlē/ adverb.
– ORIGIN Latin *desultorius* 'superficial.'

de·tach /diˈtacH/ ▶ **verb 1** disconnect something and remove it. **2** (**detach oneself from**) leave or distance oneself from a group or situation. **3** (**be detached**) (of a group of soldiers) be sent on a separate mission.

– SYNONYMS **disconnect,** separate, unfasten, disengage, uncouple, isolate, remove, loose, unhitch, unhook, free, pull off, cut off, break off, split off, sever.
– ANTONYMS attach, join.

– DERIVATIVES **de·tach·a·ble** adjective.
– ORIGIN French *détacher.*

de·tached /diˈtacHt/ ▶ **adjective 1** separate or disconnected. **2** (of a house) not joined to another on either side. **3** not involved; objective: *a detached, cynical reporter.*

– SYNONYMS **1 disconnected,** separated, separate, unfastened, disengaged, uncoupled, isolated, loosened, unhitched, unhooked, free, severed, cut off. **2 dispassionate,** disinterested, objective, outside, neutral, unbiased, impartial.

de·tach·ment /diˈtacHmənt/ ▶ **noun 1** the state of being objective or aloof. **2** a group of troops, ships, etc., sent on a separate mission. **3** the action of detaching something.

– SYNONYMS **1 objectivity,** dispassion, disinterest, neutrality, impartiality. **2 unit,** squad, detail, troop, contingent, task force, party, platoon.

de·tail /diˈtāl, ˈdētāl/ ▶ **noun 1** a small individual item or fact. **2** small items or facts as a whole: *attention to detail.* **3** a small part of a picture reproduced separately for close study. **4** a small detachment of troops or police officers given a special duty.

– SYNONYMS **1 feature,** respect, particular, characteristic, specific, aspect, fact, point, element. **2 triviality,** technicality, nicety, fine point. **3 unit,** detachment, squad, troop, contingent, outfit, task force, party, platoon.

▶ **verb 1** give full information about something. **2** select someone to undertake a particular task.

– SYNONYMS **describe,** relate, catalog, list, spell out, itemize, identify, specify.

– PHRASES **in detail** as regards every aspect; fully.
– ORIGIN French *détail.*

de·tailed /di'tāld, 'dē,tāld/ ▶ **adjective** having many details.

– SYNONYMS **comprehensive,** full, complete, thorough, exhaustive, all-inclusive, elaborate, minute, precise, itemized, blow-by-blow.
– ANTONYMS general.

de·tail·ing /'dētāliNG/ ▶ **noun** small decorative features on a building, garment, or work of art.

de·tain /di'tān/ ▶ **verb 1** prevent someone from proceeding; delay. **2** keep someone in official custody.

– SYNONYMS **1 hold,** take into custody, confine, imprison, intern, arrest, apprehend, seize; informal pick up. **2 delay,** hold up, make late, keep, slow up/down, hinder.
– ANTONYMS release.

– DERIVATIVES **de·tain·er** noun **de·tain·ment** noun.
– ORIGIN Latin *detinere* 'keep back.'

de·tain·ee /di,tā'nē, ,dētā'nē/ ▶ **noun** a person held in custody, especially for political reasons.

de·tect /di'tekt/ ▶ **verb 1** discover the presence or existence of something. **2** notice something very slight: *I detected a hint of nervousness in him.* **3** discover or investigate a crime.

– SYNONYMS **1 notice,** perceive, discern, become aware of, note, make out, spot, recognize, identify, catch, sense. **2 discover,** uncover, turn up, unearth, dig up, root out, expose. **3 catch,** hunt down, track down, find out, expose, reveal, unmask, smoke out.

– DERIVATIVES **de·tect·a·ble** adjective **de·tect·a·bly** /-əblē/ adverb **de·tec·tion** /di'tekSHən/ noun.
– ORIGIN Latin *detegere* 'uncover.'

de·tec·tive /di'tektiv/ ▶ **noun** a person, especially a police officer, whose occupation is to investigate crimes.

– SYNONYMS **investigator,** police officer; informal private eye, sleuth, gumshoe.

de·tec·tor /di'tektər/ ▶ **noun** a device designed to discover the presence of something and to send out a signal.

dé·tente /dā'tänt/ ▶ **noun** the easing of hostility or strained relations between countries.
– ORIGIN French, 'loosening, relaxation.'

de·ten·tion /di'tensHən/ ▶ **noun 1** the state of being detained in official custody. **2** the punishment of being kept in school after hours.

– SYNONYMS **custody,** imprisonment, incarceration, internment, captivity, remand, arrest, quarantine.
– ANTONYMS release.

de·ten·tion cen·ter ▶ **noun** an institution where people are held in detention for short periods, in particular illegal immigrants, refugees, people awaiting trial or sentence, or youthful offenders.

de·ter /di'tər/ ▶ **verb** (**deters, deterring, deterred**) **1** discourage from doing something, especially by fear of the consequences: *the record heat didn't deter her from her daily run.* **2** prevent something from happening.

– SYNONYMS **1 discourage,** dissuade, put off, scare off, dishearten, demoralize, daunt, intimidate. **2 prevent,** stop, avert, stave off, ward off.
– ANTONYMS encourage.

– ORIGIN Latin *deterrere.*

de·ter·gent /di'tərjənt/ ▶ **noun** a liquid or powder for removing dirt and grease from clothes, dishes, etc.
– ORIGIN from Latin *detergere* 'wipe away.'

de·te·ri·o·rate /di'ti(ə)rēə,rāt/ ▶ **verb** become gradually worse.

– SYNONYMS **worsen,** decline, degenerate, fail, go downhill, wane.
– ANTONYMS improve.

– DERIVATIVES **de·te·ri·o·ra·tion** /-,ti(ə)rēə'rāsHən/ noun.
– ORIGIN Latin *deteriorare.*

de·ter·mi·nant /di'tərminənt/ ▶ **noun 1** a factor that decisively affects the nature or outcome of something: *genetics may be the most important determinant of your weight.* **2** Mathematics a quantity obtained by adding products of the elements of a square matrix according to a given rule.

de·ter·mi·nate /də'tərmənit/ ▶ **adjective** having fixed and definite limits.
– DERIVATIVES **de·ter·mi·na·cy** /-minəsē/ noun.

de·ter·mi·na·tion /di,tərmə'nāsHən/ ▶ **noun 1** the quality of being determined; firmness of purpose. **2** the action of establishing or deciding something.

– SYNONYMS **resolution,** resolve, willpower, strength of character, dedication, single-mindedness, perseverance, persistence, tenacity, staying power, doggedness; informal guts.

de·ter·mine /di'tərmin/ ▶ **verb 1** cause to happen in a particular way or to have a particular nature: *it is biological age that determines our looks.* **2** firmly decide to do something. **3** establish something by research or calculation.

– SYNONYMS **1 control,** decide, regulate, direct, dictate, govern. **2 resolve,** decide, make up one's mind, choose, elect, opt. **3 specify,** set, fix, decide on, settle, establish, ordain, prescribe, decree. **4 ascertain,** find out, discover, learn, establish, calculate, work out; informal figure out.

– DERIVATIVES **de·ter·mi·na·ble** /di'tərminəbəl/ adjective.
– ORIGIN Latin *determinare* 'limit, fix.'

de·ter·mined /di'tərmind/ ▶ **adjective** having firmness of purpose; resolute.

– SYNONYMS **resolute,** purposeful, adamant, single-minded, unswerving, unwavering, persevering, persistent, tenacious, dedicated, dogged.
– ANTONYMS irresolute.

– DERIVATIVES **de·ter·mined·ly** adverb.

WORD TOOLKIT

See **STAUNCH**[1].

de·ter·min·er /di'tərminər/ ▶ **noun 1** a person or thing that determines or decides something. **2** Grammar a word that comes before a noun to show how the noun is being used, for example *a, the, every.*

de·ter·min·ism /di'tərmə,nizəm/ ▶ **noun** the belief that people are not free to do as they wish because their lives are determined by factors outside their control.
– DERIVATIVES **de·ter·min·ist** noun & adjective **de·ter·min·is·tic** /-,tərmə'nistik/ adjective.

de·ter·rent /di'tərənt/ ▶ **noun** a thing that discourages or is intended to discourage someone from doing something.

– SYNONYMS **disincentive,** discouragement, damper, curb, check, restraint, inhibition.
– ANTONYMS incentive.

▶ **adjective** able or intended to deter.
– DERIVATIVES **de·ter·rence** noun.

de·test /di'test/ ▶ **verb** dislike someone or something intensely.

– SYNONYMS **hate,** abhor, loathe, regard with disgust, be unable to bear, have an aversion to, find intolerable, disdain, despise.
– ANTONYMS love.

– ORIGIN Latin *detestari* 'denounce, abhor.'

CHOOSE THE RIGHT WORD

See **DESPISE**.

de·test·a·ble /di'testəbəl/ ▶ **adjective** deserving intense dislike.

de·tes·ta·tion /ˌdēte'stāsʜən/ ▶ **noun** intense dislike.

de·throne /dē'ᴛʜrōn/ ▶ **verb 1** remove a monarch from power. **2** remove someone from a position of authority or dominance.
– DERIVATIVES **de·throne·ment** noun.

det·o·nate /'detnˌāt/ ▶ **verb** explode or cause to explode.
– DERIVATIVES **det·o·na·tion** /ˌdetn'āsʜən/ noun.
– ORIGIN Latin *detonare.*

det·o·na·tor /'detnˌātər/ ▶ **noun** a device or charge used to detonate an explosive.

de·tour /'dēˌto͝or/ ▶ **noun** a long or roundabout route taken to avoid something or to visit something along the way.

– SYNONYMS **diversion,** roundabout route, indirect route, scenic route, bypass, digression, deviation.

▶ **verb** take a detour.
– ORIGIN French, 'change of direction.'

de·tox /'dētäks/ informal ▶ **noun** detoxification. ▶ **verb** detoxify.

de·tox·i·fy /dē'täksəˌfī/ ▶ **verb** (**detoxifies, detoxifying, detoxified**) **1** remove harmful or toxic substances from something. **2** abstain or help to abstain from alcohol or drugs until the bloodstream is free of toxins.
– DERIVATIVES **de·tox·i·fi·ca·tion** /dēˌtäksəfi'kāsʜən/ noun **de·tox·i·fi·er** noun.

de·tract /di'trakt/ ▶ **verb** (**detract from**) cause something to seem less valuable or impressive.

– SYNONYMS **belittle,** take away from, diminish, reduce, lessen, minimize, play down, trivialize, decry, devalue.

– DERIVATIVES **de·trac·tion** /-'traksʜən/ noun.
– ORIGIN Latin *detrahere* 'draw away.'

de·trac·tor /di'traktər/ ▶ **noun** a person who is critical of someone or something.

de·train /dē'trān/ ▶ **verb** leave a train.

det·ri·ment /'detrəmənt/ ▶ **noun** harm or damage: *she fasted to the detriment of her health.*
– ORIGIN Latin *detrimentum.*

det·ri·men·tal /ˌdetrə'mentl/ ▶ **adjective** causing harm or damage.

– SYNONYMS *moving her could have a detrimental effect on her health* **harmful,** damaging, injurious, hurtful, inimical, deleterious, destructive, pernicious, undesirable, unfavorable.
– ANTONYMS beneficial.

– DERIVATIVES **det·ri·men·tal·ly** adjective.

de·tri·tus /di'trītəs/ ▶ **noun** debris or waste material.
– DERIVATIVES **de·tri·tal** /-təl/ adjective.
– ORIGIN Latin.

de·tu·mes·cence /ˌdēt(y)o͞o'mesəns/ ▶ **noun** the process of subsiding from a state of swelling or sexual arousal.
– DERIVATIVES **de·tu·mes·cent** adjective.
– ORIGIN Latin *detumescere.*

de·tune /dē't(y)o͞on/ ▶ **verb 1** cause a musical instrument to become out of tune. **2** reduce the performance of a motor vehicle or engine by adjustment.

deuce[1] /d(y)o͞os/ ▶ **noun 1** Tennis the score of 40 all in a game, at which two consecutive points are needed to win the game. **2** the number two on dice or playing cards.
– ORIGIN Latin *duos* 'two.'

deuce[2] ▶ **noun** (**the deuce**) informal used as a euphemism for 'devil' in exclamations or for emphasis.
– ORIGIN German *duus*, probably related to **DEUCE**[1] (two aces at dice being the worst throw).

de·us ex ma·chi·na /'dāəs eks 'mäkənə, -'mak-/ ▶ **noun** an unexpected event that saves a seemingly hopeless situation.
– ORIGIN Latin, 'god from the machinery' (referring to the actors representing gods suspended above the stage in ancient Greek theater, who intervened in the play's outcome).

deu·te·ri·um /d(y)o͞o'ti(ə)rēəm/ ▶ **noun** Chemistry a stable isotope of hydrogen with a mass approximately twice that of the usual isotope.
– ORIGIN Latin.

Deutsch·mark /'doicʜˌmärk/ ▶ **noun** (until the introduction of the euro in 2002) the basic unit of money of Germany.
– ORIGIN from German *deutsche Mark* 'German mark.'

de·val·ue /dē'valyo͞o/ ▶ **verb** (**devalues, devaluing, devalued**) **1** reduce the worth of: *people seem to devalue my achievement.* **2** reduce the official value of a currency in relation to other currencies.

– SYNONYMS **belittle,** disparage, denigrate, discredit, diminish, trivialize, reduce, undermine.

– DERIVATIVES **de·val·u·a·tion** /ˌdēvalyo͞o'āsʜən/ noun.

dev·as·tate /'devəˌstāt/ ▶ **verb 1** destroy or ruin something. **2** (**be devastated**) be overwhelmed with shock or grief.

– SYNONYMS **1 destroy,** ruin, wreck, lay waste, ravage, demolish, raze (to the ground), level, flatten. **2 shatter,** shock, stun, daze, dumbfound, traumatize, distress; informal knock for a loop, knock sideways.

– DERIVATIVES **dev·as·ta·tor** noun.
– ORIGIN Latin *devastare.*

dev·as·tat·ing /'devəˌstātiɴɢ/ ▶ **adjective 1** highly destructive. **2** very distressing or shocking. **3** informal very impressive or attractive.
– DERIVATIVES **dev·as·tat·ing·ly** adverb.

dev·as·ta·tion /ˌdevə'stāsʜən/ ▶ **noun** the action of destroying something or the state of being destroyed.

– SYNONYMS **1** *the hurricane left a trail of devastation* **destruction,** ruin, desolation, havoc, wreckage; ruins. **2** *the devastation of Prussia* **destruction,** wrecking, ruination; demolition, annihilation. **3** *the devastation you have caused the family* **shock,** trauma, distress, stress, strain, pain, anguish, suffering, upset, agony, misery, heartache.

de·vel·op /di'veləp/ ▶ **verb** (**develops**, **developing**, **developed**) **1** become or make larger or more advanced. **2** start to exist, experience, or possess: *he developed a passionate interest in fitness.* **3** convert land to a new purpose, especially by constructing buildings. **4** treat a photographic film with chemicals to make a visible image.

– SYNONYMS **1 grow,** expand, spread, advance, progress, evolve, mature. **2 initiate,** instigate, set in motion, originate, invent, form. **3 expand,** augment, broaden, supplement, reinforce, enhance, refine, improve, polish, perfect. **4 start,** begin, emerge, erupt, break out, arise, break, unfold.

– DERIVATIVES **de·vel·op·a·ble** /di'veləpəbəl/ adjective **de·vel·op·er** noun.
– ORIGIN French *développer* 'unfold.'

CHOOSE THE RIGHT WORD

See **MATURE**.

de·vel·op·ing coun·try ▶ **noun** a poor agricultural country that is seeking to become more advanced economically and socially.

de·vel·op·ment /di'veləpmənt/ ▶ **noun 1** the action of developing or the state of being developed: *she traces the development of the novel.* **2** a new product or idea. **3** a new stage in a changing situation. **4** an area with new buildings on it.

– SYNONYMS **1 evolution,** growth, expansion, enlargement, spread, progress. **2 event,** change, circumstance, incident, occurrence. **3 estate,** complex, site.

– DERIVATIVES **de·vel·op·men·tal** /di,veləp'mentl/ adjective **de·vel·op·men·tal·ly** adverb.

de·vi·ant /'dēvēənt/ ▶ **adjective** departing from normal standards, especially in social or sexual behavior.

– SYNONYMS **aberrant,** abnormal, atypical, anomalous, irregular, nonstandard; nonconformist, perverse, uncommon, unusual, freakish, strange, warped, perverted, odd, peculiar, bizarre, eccentric, idiosyncratic, unorthodox, exceptional; informal kinky, quirky.
– ANTONYMS normal.

▶ **noun** a person who departs from normal standards.

– SYNONYMS **nonconformist,** eccentric, maverick, outsider, misfit, individualist; informal oddball, screwball, kook, weirdo, freak.

– DERIVATIVES **de·vi·ance** /'dēvēəns/ noun **de·vi·an·cy** /-ənsē/ noun.

de·vi·ate /'dēvē,āt/ ▶ **verb** depart from an established course or from normal standards: *the vet deviated from an accepted standard of care.*

– SYNONYMS **diverge,** digress, drift, stray, veer, swerve, get sidetracked, branch off, differ, vary.

– DERIVATIVES **de·vi·a·tion** /,dēvē'āsʜən/ noun.
– ORIGIN Latin *deviare* 'turn out of the way.'

de·vice /di'vīs/ ▶ **noun 1** a piece of mechanical or electronic equipment made for a particular purpose. **2** a plan or method with a particular aim: *a clever marketing device.* **3** a drawing or design.

– SYNONYMS **1 implement,** gadget, utensil, tool, appliance, apparatus, instrument, machine, mechanism, contrivance, contraption; informal gizmo. **2 ploy,** tactic, move, stratagem, scheme, maneuver, plot, trick, ruse.

– PHRASES **leave someone to their own devices** leave someone to do as they wish.
– ORIGIN Old French *devis* 'device, intention.'

dev·il /'devəl/ ▶ **noun 1** (**the Devil**) (in Christian and Jewish belief) the most powerful evil spirit. **2** an evil spirit. **3** a very wicked or cruel person. **4** a mischievous person. **5** informal a person with specified characteristics: *the poor devil.* **6** (**the devil**) expressing surprise or annoyance.

– SYNONYMS **1 Satan,** Beelzebub, Lucifer, the Prince of Darkness; informal Old Nick. **2 evil spirit,** demon, fiend. **3 brute,** beast, monster, fiend, villain, sadist, barbarian, ogre.

– PHRASES **between the devil and the deep blue sea** caught in a dilemma. **devil-may-care** cheerful and reckless. **the devil to pay** serious trouble to be dealt with. **like the devil** with great speed or energy. **speak** (or **talk**) **of the devil** said when a person appears just after being mentioned.
– ORIGIN Greek *diabolos* 'accuser, slanderer.'

WORD LINKS

diabolical, **diabolic**, **satanic** *relating to the Devil*

dev·iled /'devəld/ ▶ **adjective** cooked with hot seasoning.

dev·il·ish /'devəlisʜ/ ▶ **adjective 1** evil and cruel. **2** mischievous: *a devilish grin.* **3** very difficult to deal with. ▶ **adverb** informal, dated very: *a devilish clever guy.*
– DERIVATIVES **dev·il·ish·ly** adverb **dev·il·ish·ness** noun.

dev·il·ment /'devəlmənt/ ▶ **noun** reckless mischief.

dev·il·ry /'devəlrē/ ▶ **noun 1** wicked activity. **2** reckless mischief.

dev·il's ad·vo·cate ▶ **noun** a person who expresses an unpopular opinion in order to provoke debate.

de·vi·ous /'dēvēəs/ ▶ **adjective 1** skillful in using underhanded tactics. **2** (of a route or journey) indirect.

– SYNONYMS **1 underhanded/underhand,** dishonest, crafty, cunning, conniving, scheming, sneaky, furtive; informal crooked, shady. **2 circuitous,** roundabout, indirect, meandering, tortuous.
– ANTONYMS honest, direct.

– DERIVATIVES **de·vi·ous·ly** adverb **de·vi·ous·ness** noun.
– ORIGIN Latin *devius* 'out of the way.'

de·vise /di'vīz/ ▶ **verb** plan or invent a complex procedure or device.

– SYNONYMS **conceive,** think up, dream up, work out, formulate, concoct, hatch, contrive, design, invent, coin; informal cook up.

– DERIVATIVES **de·vis·er** noun.
– ORIGIN Old French *deviser.*

de·vi·tal·ize /dē'vītl,īz/ ▶ **verb** deprive someone or something of strength and energy.
– DERIVATIVES **de·vi·tal·i·za·tion** /dē,vītlə'zāsʜən/ noun.

de·void /di'void/ ▶ **adjective** (**devoid of**) completely lacking in: *the dancers were devoid of glamour.*

– SYNONYMS **empty of,** free of, bereft of, lacking, deficient in, without, wanting in; informal minus.

– ORIGIN from Old French *devoidier* 'cast out.'

dev·o·lu·tion /,devə'lo͞osʜən/ ▶ **noun** the transfer of power by central government to local or regional governments.
– DERIVATIVES **dev·o·lu·tion·ar·y** /-,nerē/ adjective **dev·o·lu·tion·ist** /-ist/ noun.

de·volve /di'välv/ ▶ **verb** **1** transfer power to a lower level, especially from central to regional government. **2** (**devolve on/upon/to**) (of duties or responsibility) pass to a deputy or successor.
– ORIGIN Latin *devolvere* 'roll down.'

De·vo·ni·an /di'vōnēən/ ▶ **adjective** Geology relating to the fourth period of the Paleozoic era (about 409 to 363 million years ago), when the first amphibians appeared.

de·vo·ré /də'vôrā/ ▶ **noun** a velvet fabric with a pattern formed by burning the pile away with acid.
– ORIGIN French, 'devoured.'

de·vote /di'vōt/ ▶ **verb** (**devote something to**) give time or resources to a person or activity.

– SYNONYMS **dedicate,** allocate, assign, allot, commit, give (over), consign, pledge, set aside, earmark, reserve.

– ORIGIN Latin *devovere* 'consecrate.'

de·vot·ed /di'vōtid/ ▶ **adjective** very loving or loyal.

– SYNONYMS **dedicated,** committed, devout, loyal, faithful, true, staunch, steadfast, fond, loving.

– DERIVATIVES **de·vot·ed·ly** adverb.

dev·o·tee /ˌdevə'tē, -'tā/ ▶ **noun** **1** a person who is very enthusiastic about someone or something. **2** a person with a strong belief in a particular religion or god.

– SYNONYMS **enthusiast,** fan, lover, aficionado, admirer, supporter, disciple; informal buff, freak, nut, fanatic.

de·vo·tion /di'vōsʜən/ ▶ **noun** **1** great love or loyalty. **2** religious worship. **3** (**devotions**) prayers or religious observances.

– SYNONYMS **1 loyalty,** fidelity, commitment, allegiance, dedication, fondness, love, care. **2 piety,** spirituality, godliness, holiness, sanctity.

– DERIVATIVES **de·vo·tion·al** adjective.

de·vour /di'vou(ə)r/ ▶ **verb** **1** eat food greedily. **2** (of fire or a similar force) destroy something completely. **3** read something quickly and eagerly.

– SYNONYMS **1 gobble,** guzzle, gulp down, bolt, wolf; informal polish off, scarf up/down. **2 consume,** engulf, envelop.

– DERIVATIVES **de·vour·er** noun.
– ORIGIN Latin *devorare.*

de·vout /di'vout/ ▶ **adjective** **1** deeply religious. **2** earnestly sincere: *my devout hope.*

– SYNONYMS **dedicated,** devoted, committed, loyal, sincere, fervent, pious, reverent, God-fearing, dutiful, churchgoing.

– DERIVATIVES **de·vout·ly** adverb.
– ORIGIN Latin *devotus* 'devoted.'

dew /d(y)o͞o/ ▶ **noun** tiny drops of moisture that form on cool surfaces at night when water vapor in the air condenses.
– ORIGIN Old English.

dew·ber·ry /'d(y)o͞oˌberē/ ▶ **noun** (pl. **dewberries**) the edible blue-black fruit of a trailing bramble.

dew·drop /'d(y)o͞oˌdräp/ ▶ **noun** a drop of dew.

Dew·ey dec·i·mal clas·si·fi·ca·tion /'d(y)o͞o-ē/ ▶ **noun** a decimal system of library classification that uses a three-figure code from 000 to 999 to represent the major branches of knowledge.
– ORIGIN named after the American librarian Melvil *Dewey.*

dew·lap /'d(y)o͞oˌlap/ ▶ **noun** a fold of loose skin hanging from the neck or throat of an animal such as a cow.

dew point ▶ **noun** the atmospheric temperature (varying according to pressure and humidity) below which water droplets begin to condense and dew can form.

dew·y /'d(y)o͞oē/ ▶ **adjective** wet with dew.

dew·y-eyed ▶ **adjective** naive or sentimental: *dewy-eyed liberals.*

dex·ter /'dekstər/ ▶ **adjective** Heraldry on or toward the bearer's right-hand side of a coat of arms. The opposite of **SINISTER**.
– ORIGIN Latin, 'on the right.'

dex·ter·i·ty /dek'sterité/ ▶ **noun** **1** skill in performing tasks with the hands. **2** the ability to do something skillfully: *mental dexterity.*

– SYNONYMS **deftness,** adeptness, adroitness, agility, ability, talent, skill, proficiency, expertise, experience, efficiency, mastery, finesse.

– ORIGIN from Latin *dexter* 'on the right.'

dex·ter·ous /'dekst(ə)rəs/ (also **dextrous** /'dekstrəs/) ▶ **adjective** showing skill; adroit.
– DERIVATIVES **dex·ter·ous·ly** adverb.

dex·trose /'dekstrōs/ ▶ **noun** a naturally occurring form of glucose.
– ORIGIN from Latin *dexter* 'on the right.'

DH ▶ **abbreviation** **1** Doctor of Humanities. **2** Baseball designated hitter.

dhar·ma /'därmə/ ▶ **noun** (in Indian religion) the eternal law of the universe.
– ORIGIN Sanskrit, 'decree or custom.'

dho·bi /'dōbē/ ▶ **noun** (pl. **dhobis**) (in the Indian subcontinent) a person whose occupation is washing clothes.
– ORIGIN Hindi.

dho·ti /'dōtē/ ▶ **noun** (pl. **dhotis**) a piece of cloth tied around the waist and covering most of the legs, worn by some Indian men.
– ORIGIN Hindi.

dhow /dou/ ▶ **noun** a ship with a lateen sail or sails, used in the Arabian region.
– ORIGIN Arabic.

di- ▶ **combining form** twice; two-; double: *dioxide.*
– ORIGIN from Greek *dis* 'twice.'

dia. ▶ **abbreviation** diameter.

di·a·be·tes /ˌdīə'bētēz, -tis/ ▶ **noun** a disorder of the metabolism in which a lack of the hormone insulin results in a failure to absorb sugar and starch properly.
– ORIGIN Greek, 'siphon.'

di·a·be·tic /ˌdīə'betik/ ▶ **adjective** having or relating to diabetes. ▶ **noun** a person with diabetes.

di·a·bol·i·cal /ˌdīə'bälikəl/ ▶ **adjective** (also **diabolic**) relating to or like the Devil, especially in being evil.

– SYNONYMS *diabolical forces* **devilish,** satanic, demonic, hellish, infernal, evil, wicked, ungodly, unholy.

– DERIVATIVES **di·a·bol·i·cal·ly** /-ik(ə)lē/ adverb.
– ORIGIN from Greek *diabolos* 'accuser, slanderer' (see **DEVIL**).

di·ab·o·lism /dī'abəˌlizəm/ ▶ **noun** worship of the Devil.
– DERIVATIVES **di·ab·o·list** noun.

diachronic /ˌdīəˈkränik/ ▸ **adjective** concerned with the way in which something, especially language, has developed through time. Often contrasted with **SYNCHRONIC**.

di·ac·o·nal /dīˈakənl/ ▸ **adjective** (in the Christian Church) relating to a deacon or deacons.
– ORIGIN from Latin *diaconus* 'deacon.'

di·ac·o·nate /dīˈakənit, -ˌnāt/ ▸ **noun 1** (in the Christian Church) the position of deacon. **2** a group of deacons.

di·a·crit·ic /ˌdīəˈkritik/ ▸ **noun** a sign, such as an accent, written above or below a letter to indicate a difference in pronunciation from the same letter when unmarked.
– DERIVATIVES **di·a·crit·i·cal** adjective.
– ORIGIN from Greek *diakrinein* 'distinguish.'

di·a·dem /ˈdīəˌdem/ ▸ **noun** a jeweled crown or headband worn as a symbol of royalty.
– ORIGIN Greek *diadēma*.

di·ag·nose /ˌdīəgˈnōs/ ▸ **verb 1** identify the nature of an illness or problem by examining the symptoms. **2** identify the medical condition of someone.

– SYNONYMS **identify,** determine, distinguish, recognize, interpret, detect, pinpoint.

– DERIVATIVES **di·ag·nos·a·ble** adjective.

di·ag·no·sis /ˌdīəgˈnōsis/ ▸ **noun** (pl. **diagnoses**) the identification of the nature of an illness or other problem by examination of the symptoms.

– SYNONYMS **1 identification,** detection, recognition, determination, discovery, pinpointing. **2 opinion,** judgment, verdict, conclusion.

– ORIGIN Greek.

di·ag·nos·tic /ˌdīəgˈnästik/ ▸ **adjective** relating to the diagnosis of illness or other problems. ▸ **noun 1** a distinctive symptom or characteristic. **2** (**diagnostics**) (treated as sing. or pl.) the practice or techniques of diagnosis.
– DERIVATIVES **di·ag·nos·ti·cal·ly** /-ik(ə)lē/ adverb **di·ag·nos·ti·cian** /-ˌnäsˈtisнən/ noun.

di·ag·o·nal /dīˈagənl/ ▸ **adjective 1** (of a straight line) joining two opposite corners of a rectangle, square, or other shape. **2** (of a line) straight and at an angle; slanting.

– SYNONYMS **crosswise,** crossways, slanting, slanted, oblique, angled, cornerways, cornerwise.

▸ **noun** a diagonal line.
– DERIVATIVES **di·ag·o·nal·ly** adverb.
– ORIGIN Greek *diagōnios* 'from angle to angle.'

di·a·gram /ˈdīəˌgram/ ▸ **noun** a simplified drawing showing the appearance or structure of something.

– SYNONYMS **drawing,** representation, plan, outline, figure, chart, graph.

– DERIVATIVES **di·a·gram·mat·ic** /ˌdīəgrəˈmatik/ adjective **di·a·gram·mat·i·cal·ly** /ˌdīəgrəˈmatik(ə)lē/ adverb.
– ORIGIN Greek *diagramma*.

di·al /ˈdī(ə)l/ ▸ **noun 1** a disk marked to show the time on a clock or to indicate a measurement by means of a pointer. **2** a disc with numbered holes on a telephone, turned to make a call. **3** a disc turned to select a setting on a radio, washing machine, etc. ▸ **verb** (**dials, dialing, dialed**) call a telephone number by turning a dial or using a keypad.
– DERIVATIVES **di·al·er** noun.
– ORIGIN Latin *diale* 'clock dial.'

di·a·lect /ˈdīəˌlekt/ ▸ **noun** a form of a language that is used in a specific region or by a specific social group: *this novel is written in the dialect of Trinidad.*
– DERIVATIVES **di·a·lec·tal** /ˌdīəˈlektəl/ adjective.
– ORIGIN Greek *dialektos* 'discourse, way of speaking.'

di·a·lec·tic /ˌdīəˈlektik/ (also **dialectics**) ▸ **noun** (usu. treated as sing.) Philosophy **1** the investigation of the truth of opposing opinions by logical discussion. **2** the existence of opposing social forces, concepts, etc.: *union leaders have been hidebound by the dialectic of class war.*
– DERIVATIVES **di·a·lec·ti·cal** /ˌdīəˈlektikəl/ adjective **di·a·lec·ti·cal·ly** /-ik(ə)lē/ adverb.
– ORIGIN from Greek *dialektikē tekhnē* 'art of debate.'

di·a·log box /ˈdīəˌläg, -ˌlôg/ ▸ **noun** a small area on a computer screen in which the user is prompted to provide information or select commands.

di·a·log·ic /ˌdīəˈläjik/ ▸ **adjective** relating to or in the form of dialogue.
– DERIVATIVES **di·a·log·i·cal** adjective.

di·a·logue /ˈdīəˌläg, -ˌlôg/ (also **dialog**) ▸ **noun 1** conversation between two or more people as a feature of a book, play, movie, etc. **2** a discussion intended to explore a subject or resolve a problem.

– SYNONYMS **conversation,** talk, discussion, chat, tête-à-tête, exchange, debate, conference, consultation; informal confab.

– ORIGIN Greek *dialogos*.

CHOOSE THE RIGHT WORD

See **CONVERSATION**.

di·al tone ▸ **noun** a sound produced by a telephone that indicates that a caller may start to dial.

di·al-up ▸ **adjective** (of a computer system or service) used remotely via a telephone line.

di·al·y·sis /dīˈaləsis/ ▸ **noun** (pl. **dialyses** /-sēz/) **1** Chemistry the separation of particles in a liquid on the basis of differences in their ability to pass through a membrane. **2** the purification of blood by dialysis, as a substitute for the normal function of the kidney.
– ORIGIN Greek *dialusis*.

di·a·man·té /ˌdēəmänˈtā/ ▸ **adjective** decorated with glass cut to resemble diamonds.
– ORIGIN French, 'set with diamonds.'

di·am·e·ter /dīˈamitər/ ▸ **noun** a straight line passing from side to side through the center of a circle or sphere.
– ORIGIN from Greek *diametros grammē* 'line measuring across.'

di·a·met·ri·cal /ˌdīəˈmetrikəl/ (also **diametric**) ▸ **adjective 1** (of opposites) completely different: *he's the diametrical opposite of Gabriel.* **2** relating to a diameter.
– DERIVATIVES **di·a·met·ri·cal·ly** adverb.

dia·mond /ˈdī(ə)mənd/ ▸ **noun 1** a precious stone consisting of a clear and colorless crystalline form of pure carbon, the hardest naturally occurring substance. **2** a figure with four straight sides of equal length forming two opposite acute angles and two opposite obtuse angles; a rhombus. **3** a baseball field. **4** (**diamonds**) one of the four suits in a deck of playing cards.
– PHRASES **diamond in the rough 1** an uncut diamond. **2** a good or kind person who is not very polite, stylish, or well educated.
– ORIGIN Old French *diamant*.

dia·mond·back /ˈdī(ə)məndˌbak/ ▸ **noun 1** (also **diamondback rattlesnake**) a large, common North

American rattlesnake with diamond-shaped markings. **2** (also **diamondback terrapin**) another term for TERRAPIN (sense 1).

dia·mond ju·bi·lee ▶ **noun** the sixtieth anniversary of a notable event.

di·a·mor·phine /ˌdīəˈmôrfēn/ ▶ **noun** technical heroin.
– ORIGIN short for *diacetylmorphine* in the same sense.

di·an·thus /dīˈanTHəs/ ▶ **noun** (pl. **dianthuses**) a flowering plant of a group that includes the pinks and carnations.
– ORIGIN from Greek *Dios* 'of Zeus' + *anthos* 'flower.'

di·a·pa·son /ˌdīəˈpāzən, -sən/ ▶ **noun** an organ stop sounding a main set of pipes.
– ORIGIN from Greek *dia pasōn khordōn* 'through all notes.'

dia·per /ˈdī(ə)pər/ ▶ **noun** a piece of material wrapped around a baby's bottom and between its legs to absorb and retain urine and feces.
– ORIGIN from Greek *dia* 'across' + *aspros* 'white.'

di·aph·a·nous /dīˈafənəs/ ▶ **adjective** light, delicate, and translucent.
– ORIGIN Greek *diaphanēs*.

WORD TOOLKIT

diaphanous ...	transparent ...	translucent ...
gown	plastic	skin
veil	wall	paper
wings	crystals	powder
fabric	tape	resin

di·a·phragm /ˈdīəˌfram/ ▶ **noun 1** a muscular partition separating the thorax from the abdomen in mammals. **2** a taut flexible membrane in mechanical or acoustic systems. **3** a thin contraceptive cap fitting over the neck of the uterus. **4** a device for varying the effective aperture of the lens in a camera or other optical system.
– DERIVATIVES **di·a·phrag·mat·ic** /ˌdīəfragˈmatik/ adjective.
– ORIGIN Latin *diaphragma*.

di·a·rist /ˈdīərist/ ▶ **noun** a person who writes a diary.

di·ar·rhe·a /ˌdīəˈrēə/ (Brit. **diarrhoea**) ▶ **noun** an illness in which there are frequent discharges of liquid feces from the bowels.
– DERIVATIVES **di·ar·rhe·al** adjective.
– ORIGIN Greek *diarrhoia*.

di·a·ry /ˈdīərē/ ▶ **noun** (pl. **diaries**) **1** a book in which one keeps a daily record of events and experiences. **2** a book marked with each day's date, in which to note appointments.

– SYNONYMS **1 appointment book,** engagement book, personal organizer. **2 journal,** memoir, chronicle, log, logbook, daybook, history, annal, record, weblog, blog.

– ORIGIN Latin *diarium*.

di·as·po·ra /dīˈaspərə/ ▶ **noun 1** (**the diaspora**) the dispersion of the Jews beyond Israel, chiefly in the 8th to 6th centuries BC. **2** the dispersion of any people from their original homeland.
– ORIGIN Greek.

di·as·to·le /dīˈastl-ē/ ▶ **noun** the phase of the heartbeat when the heart muscle relaxes and the chambers fill with blood. Often contrasted with SYSTOLE.
– DERIVATIVES **di·as·tol·ic** /ˌdīəˈstälik/ adjective.
– ORIGIN Greek, 'separation, expansion.'

di·a·tom /ˈdīəˌtäm/ ▶ **noun** a single-celled alga that has a cell wall of silica.
– DERIVATIVES **di·a·to·ma·ceous** /ˌdīətəˈmāSHəs/ adjective.
– ORIGIN from Greek *diatomos* 'cut in two.'

di·a·tom·ic /ˌdīəˈtämik/ ▶ **adjective** Chemistry consisting of two atoms.

di·a·ton·ic /ˌdīəˈtänik/ ▶ **adjective** Music involving only the notes of the major or minor scale, without additional sharps, flats, etc.
– ORIGIN Greek *diatonikos* 'at intervals of a tone.'

di·a·tribe /ˈdīəˌtrīb/ ▶ **noun** a harsh and forceful verbal attack.

– SYNONYMS **tirade,** harangue, onslaught, attack, polemic, denunciation, broadside, fulmination; informal blast.

– ORIGIN Greek, 'spending of time, discourse.'

di·az·e·pam /dīˈazəˌpam/ ▶ **noun** a tranquilizing drug used to relieve anxiety. Also called **VALIUM** (trademark).

dib·ble /ˈdibəl/ ▶ **noun** a pointed hand tool for making holes in the ground for seeds or young plants.
– ORIGIN uncertain.

dibs /dibz/ (also **first dibs**) ▶ **plural noun** informal a pre-emptive claim or right: *strategists will get first dibs on plumbing the data.*

dice /dīs/ ▶ **noun** (pl. same; sing. also **die** /dī/) a small cube with faces bearing from one to six spots, used in games of chance. See also DIE[2]. ▶ **verb 1** cut food into small cubes. **2** (**dice with**) take great risks with: *he enjoyed dicing with death.*
– ORIGIN Old French *des*, plural of *de*.

dic·ey /ˈdīsē/ ▶ **adjective** (**dicier, diciest**) informal unpredictable and potentially dangerous.

di·chot·o·my /dīˈkätəmē/ ▶ **noun** (pl. **dichotomies**) a separation between two things that are opposed or different: *the dichotomy between good and evil.*
– DERIVATIVES **di·chot·o·mous** adjective.
– ORIGIN Greek *dikhotomia* 'a cutting in two.'

dick[1] /dik/ ▶ **noun** vulgar slang a penis.
– ORIGIN familiar form of the man's name *Richard*.

dick[2] ▶ **noun** informal, dated a detective.
– ORIGIN perhaps a shortening of DETECTIVE, or from Romany *dick* 'look.'

dick·ens /ˈdikənz/ ▶ **noun** informal used to express annoyance or surprise: *what the dickens is going on?*
– ORIGIN a euphemism for 'devil.'

Dick·en·si·an /diˈkenzēən/ ▶ **adjective** like the novels of Charles Dickens, especially in terms of the poverty that they portray.

dick·er /ˈdikər/ ▶ **verb 1** engage in petty argument or bargaining: *she advised him not to dicker over the extra fee.* **2** treat something casually or irresponsibly; toy with something.

dick·ey /ˈdikē/ (also **dicky**) ▶ **noun** (pl. **dickies** or **dickeys**) informal a false shirt front.
– ORIGIN perhaps from *Dicky*, familiar form of the man's name *Richard*.

dick·head /ˈdikˌhed/ ▶ **noun** vulgar slang a stupid or ridiculous man.

di·cot·y·le·don /dīˌkätlˈēdn/ ▶ **noun** a plant with an embryo bearing two cotyledons (leaves growing from a germinating seed).

dic·ta /ˈdiktə/ plural of DICTUM.

dic·tate ▶ **verb** /ˈdikˌtāt/ **1** state or order something authoritatively. **2** control or influence: *choice is often* *dictated by availability.* **3** say or read aloud words to be typed or written down.

– SYNONYMS **1** *the president's attempts to dictate policy* **prescribe,** lay down, impose, set down, order, command, decree, ordain, direct. **2** *you are in no position to **dictate to** me* **give orders to,** order about/around, lord it over; informal boss around, push around. **3 determine,** control, govern, decide, influence, affect.

▸ **noun** /ˌdik'tāt/ an order or principle that must be obeyed: *those who follow the dictates of fashion.*
– DERIVATIVES **dic·ta·tion** /dik'tāsʜən/ noun.
– ORIGIN Latin *dictare.*

dic·ta·tor /'dikˌtātər/ ▸ **noun** a ruler with total power over a country.

– SYNONYMS **autocrat,** despot, tyrant, absolute ruler.
– ANTONYMS democrat.

dic·ta·to·ri·al /ˌdiktə'tôrēəl/ ▸ **adjective 1** relating to or controlled by a dictator. **2** insisting on total obedience; domineering.

– SYNONYMS **domineering,** autocratic, authoritarian, oppressive, imperious, overweening, overbearing, peremptory; informal bossy, high-handed.

– DERIVATIVES **dic·ta·to·ri·al·ly** adverb.

dic·ta·tor·ship /dik'tātərˌsʜip, 'diktātər-/ ▸ **noun 1** government by a dictator. **2** a country governed by a dictator.

dic·tion /'diksʜən/ ▸ **noun 1** the choice and use of words in speech or writing. **2** a person's way of pronouncing words.
– ORIGIN Latin.

dic·tion·ar·y /'diksʜəˌnerē/ ▸ **noun** (pl. **dictionaries**) a book that lists the words of a language and gives their meaning, or their equivalent in a different language.

– SYNONYMS **lexicon,** glossary, vocabulary.

– ORIGIN from Latin *dictionarium manuale* or *dictionarius liber* 'manual or book of words.'

WORD LINKS

lexicography *writing of dictionaries*

dic·tum /'diktəm/ ▸ **noun** (pl. **dicta** /-tə/ or **dictums**) **1** a formal or authoritative statement. **2** a short statement that expresses a general truth.
– ORIGIN Latin, 'something said.'

did /did/ past of DO[1].

di·dac·tic /dī'daktik/ ▸ **adjective** intended to teach or give moral guidance: *a didactic religious novel.*
– DERIVATIVES **di·dac·ti·cal·ly** /-ik(ə)lē/ adverb **di·dac·ti·cism** /-təˌsizəm/ noun.
– ORIGIN from Greek *didaskein* 'teach.'

did·dle /'didl/ ▸ **verb 1** informal cheat or swindle someone. **2** informal pass time aimlessly or unproductively. **3** vulgar slang have sexual intercourse with (someone).
– ORIGIN probably from Jeremy *Diddler*, a character in a farce who constantly borrowed small sums of money.

didg·er·i·doo /ˌdijərē'do͞o/ ▸ **noun** an Australian Aboriginal wind instrument in the form of a long wooden tube, blown to produce a deep resonant sound.
– ORIGIN from an Aboriginal language.

did·n't /'didnt/ ▸ **contraction** did not.

didst /didst/ old-fashioned second person singular past of DO[1].

die[1] /dī/ ▸ **verb** (**dies, dying, died**) **1** stop living. **2** (**die out**) become extinct. **3** become less loud or strong: *the storm had died down by now.* **4** (**be dying for/to do**) informal be very eager to have or to do something.

– SYNONYMS **1 pass away,** pass on, perish; informal give up the ghost, kick the bucket, buy the farm, croak, bite the dust. **2 lessen,** subside, drop, ease (off), let up, moderate, abate, fade, peter out, wane, ebb. **3** *the engine died* **fail,** cut out, give out, break down, stop; informal conk out, go kaput. **4** (as adj. **dying**) *his dying aunt* **terminally ill,** at death's door, on one's deathbed, fading fast, not long for this world, moribund, in extremis. **5** (as adj. **dying**) *a dying art form* **declining,** vanishing, fading, waning; informal on the way out.
– ANTONYMS live.

– PHRASES **die hard** change very slowly: *old habits die hard.* **never say die** do not give up hope. **to die for** informal extremely good or desirable.
– ORIGIN Old Norse.

die[2] ▸ **noun 1** singular form of DICE. **2** (pl. **dies**) a device for cutting or molding metal or for stamping a design onto coins or medals.
– PHRASES **the die is cast** an event has happened that cannot be changed.
– ORIGIN Old French *de.*

die·back /'dīˌbak/ ▸ **noun** a condition in which a tree or shrub begins to die from the tip of its leaves or roots backward.

die-cast ▸ **adjective** (of a metal object) formed by pouring molten metal into a mold.

die·hard /'dīˌhärd/ ▸ **noun** a person who strongly supports something in spite of opposition or changing circumstances: (as adj.) *a diehard hockey fan.*

– SYNONYMS (as adj.) **hard-line,** reactionary, ultraconservative, traditionalist, dyed-in-the-wool, intransigent, inflexible, uncompromising, rigid, staunch, entrenched.

di·e·lec·tric /ˌdīə'lektrik/ Physics ▸ **adjective** that does not conduct electricity; insulating. ▸ **noun** an insulator.

die-off ▸ **noun** the death of a significant proportion of a population: *mass die-offs of staghorn and elkhorn corals.*

di·er·e·sis /dī'erəsis/ ▸ **noun** (pl. **diereses** /-sēz/) a mark (¨) placed over a vowel to indicate that it is sounded separately, as in *naïve.*
– ORIGIN Greek *diairesis* 'separation.'

die·sel /'dēzəl/ ▸ **noun 1** an internal combustion engine in which the heat of compressed air is used to ignite the fuel. **2** (also **diesel oil**) a form of petroleum used to fuel diesel engines.
– ORIGIN named after the German engineer Rudolf *Diesel.*

di·et[1] /'dī-it/ ▸ **noun 1** the kinds of food that a person or animal usually eats. **2** a limited range or amount of food, eaten in order to lose weight or for medical reasons.

– SYNONYMS **1** *a healthy diet* **food,** nutrition, eating habits. **2** *she's on a diet* **dietary regime,** regimen, restricted diet, fast.

▸ **verb** (**diets, dieting, dieted**) eat a limited range or amount of food to lose weight.

– SYNONYMS **be on a diet,** slim, reduce, lose weight, watch one's weight, count calories; informal slenderize.

▸ **adjective** (of food or drink) having a reduced fat or sugar content.

– DERIVATIVES **die·tar·y** /'dī-iˌterē/ adjective **di·et·er** noun.
– ORIGIN Greek *diaita* 'a way of life.'

diet² ▶ **noun 1** a lawmaking assembly in certain countries. **2** historical a regular meeting of the states of a confederation.
– ORIGIN Latin *dieta* 'day's work, meeting of councillors.'

di·e·tet·ics /ˌdī-i'tetiks/ ▶ **plural noun** (treated as sing.) the branch of knowledge concerned with the diet and its effects on health.
– DERIVATIVES **di·e·tet·ic** adjective.

di·e·ti·tian /ˌdī-i'tisʜən/ (also **dietician**) ▶ **noun** an expert on diet and nutrition.

diff /dif/ ▶ **noun** informal **1** difference. **2** different.

dif·fer /'difər/ ▶ **verb 1** be unlike or dissimilar. **2** disagree with someone.

> – SYNONYMS **1** *the second set of data* ***differed from*** *the first* **contrast with,** be different to, vary from, deviate from, conflict with, run counter to, be at odds with, contradict. **2** **disagree,** conflict, be at variance/odds, be in dispute, not see eye to eye.
> – ANTONYMS resemble, agree.

– PHRASES **beg to differ** politely disagree.
– ORIGIN Latin *differre.*

dif·fer·ence /'dif(ə)rəns/ ▶ **noun 1** a way in which people or things are not the same. **2** the state of being unlike: *there's little difference between the two main parties.* **3** a disagreement or quarrel. **4** the remainder left after one value is subtracted from another.

> – SYNONYMS **1** **dissimilarity,** contrast, distinction, differentiation, variance, variation, divergence, disparity, contradiction. **2** **disagreement,** difference of opinion, dispute, argument, quarrel. **3** *I'll pay the difference* **balance,** remainder, rest.
> – ANTONYMS similarity.

dif·fer·ent /'dif(ə)rənt/ ▶ **adjective 1** not the same as another or each other. **2** separate: *he was arrested on two different occasions.* **3** informal new and unusual.

> – SYNONYMS **1** **dissimilar,** unlike, contrasting, differing, varying, disparate, poles apart, incompatible, mismatched; informal like oil and water. **2** **changed,** altered, transformed, new, unfamiliar, unknown, strange. **3** **distinct,** separate, individual, independent. **4** **unusual,** out of the ordinary, unfamiliar, novel, new, fresh, original, unconventional, exotic.
> – ANTONYMS similar, ordinary.

– DERIVATIVES **dif·fer·ent·ly** adverb **dif·fer·ent·ness** noun.

> **USAGE**
>
> In general, **different from** is the construction most often used in the US and Britain, although **different than** (used almost exclusively in North America) is also used, especially in speech. **Different to** is common in Britain, but sounds strange to American ears.

dif·fer·en·ti·a·ble /ˌdifə'rensʜəbəl/ ▶ **adjective** able to be distinguished or differentiated.
– DERIVATIVES **dif·fer·en·ti·a·bil·i·ty** /-ˌrensʜə'bilitē/ noun.

dif·fer·en·tial /ˌdifə'rencʜəl/ ▶ **adjective** relating to or depending on a difference; varying according to circumstances: *intense competition has not eliminated differential pricing.* ▶ **noun 1** a difference in amount. **2** Mathematics an infinitesimal difference between successive values of a variable. **3** a gear allowing a vehicle's driven wheels to revolve at different speeds in cornering.
– DERIVATIVES **dif·fer·en·tial·ly** adverb.

dif·fer·en·tial cal·cu·lus ▶ **noun** Mathematics the part of calculus concerned with the derivatives of functions.

dif·fer·en·tial e·qua·tion ▶ **noun** an equation involving derivatives of a function or functions.

dif·fer·en·ti·ate /ˌdifə'rensʜēˌāt/ ▶ **verb 1** recognize or identify as different; distinguish: *children can differentiate the past from the present.* **2** cause something to appear different or distinct. **3** Mathematics transform a function into its derivative.
– DERIVATIVES **dif·fer·en·ti·a·tion** /-ˌrensʜē'āsʜən/ noun **dif·fer·en·ti·a·tor** /-ˌātər/ noun.

> **CHOOSE THE RIGHT WORD**
>
> See **DISTINGUISH**.

dif·fi·cult /'difikəlt/ ▶ **adjective 1** needing much effort or skill to do or understand: *I had a difficult decision to make.* **2** causing or full of problems: *a difficult economic climate.* **3** not easy to please or satisfy; awkward.

> – SYNONYMS **1** *a difficult job* **laborious,** strenuous, arduous, hard, tough, demanding, punishing, grueling, back-breaking, exhausting, tiring; informal hellish, no picnic. **2** *a difficult problem* **hard,** complicated, complex, puzzling, perplexing, baffling, problematic, thorny, ticklish. **3** *a difficult child* **troublesome,** tiresome, trying, exasperating, awkward, demanding, contrary, recalcitrant, uncooperative, fussy.
> – ANTONYMS easy, simple, cooperative.

dif·fi·cul·ty /'difikəltē/ ▶ **noun** (pl. **difficulties**) **1** the state of being difficult. **2** a problem. **3** a difficult or dangerous situation: *he went for a swim but got into difficulties.*

> – SYNONYMS **1** **strain,** stress, trouble, problems, struggle; informal hassle. **2** **problem,** complication, snag, hitch, obstacle, hurdle, stumbling block, pitfall. informal headache. **3** *he got into* ***difficulties*** **trouble,** a predicament, a plight, hard times; informal a fix, a scrape, a jam.
> – ANTONYMS ease.

– ORIGIN Latin *difficultas.*

dif·fi·dent /'difidənt/ ▶ **adjective** modest or shy because of a lack of self-confidence.

> – SYNONYMS **shy,** bashful, modest, self-effacing, unassuming, meek, unconfident, insecure, unassertive, timid, shrinking, reticent.
> – ANTONYMS confident.

– DERIVATIVES **dif·fi·dence** noun **dif·fi·dent·ly** adverb.
– ORIGIN from Latin *diffidere* 'fail to trust.'

dif·frac·tion /di'fraksʜən/ ▶ **noun** Physics the process by which a beam of light or other system of waves is spread out as a result of passing through a narrow opening or across an edge.
– DERIVATIVES **dif·fract** /di'frakt/ verb **dif·frac·tive** /-tiv/ adjective.
– ORIGIN from Latin *diffringere* 'break into pieces.'

dif·fuse ▶ **verb** /di'fyo͞oz/ **1** spread over a wide area: *this early language probably diffused across the world.* **2** Physics (of a gas or liquid) intermingle with another substance by movement. ▶ **adjective** /di'fyo͞os/ **1** spread out over a large area; not concentrated. **2** not clear or concise.
– DERIVATIVES **dif·fuse·ly** /-'fyo͞oslē/ adverb **dif·fus·er** /di'fyo͞ozər/ (also **diffusor**) noun.
– ORIGIN Latin *diffundere* 'pour out.'

USAGE

On the difference between **diffuse** and **defuse**, see the note at **DEFUSE**.

CHOOSE THE RIGHT WORD

See **SCATTER**.

dif·fu·sion /di'fyo͞ozHən/ ▶ **noun 1** the action of spreading over a wide area. **2** Physics the intermingling of substances by the natural movement of their particles. ▶ **adjective** (of a range of garments) produced for the mass market by a fashion designer: *a revamped diffusion line*.
– DERIVATIVES **dif·fu·sive** /-siv/ adjective.

dig /dig/ ▶ **verb** (**digs, digging**; past and past part. **dug**) **1** break up and turn over or move earth. **2** make a hole by digging. **3** remove from the ground by digging: *workmen dug the cable up*. **4** push or poke sharply. **5** (**dig into/through**) search or rummage in something. **6** (**dig something out/up**) discover facts. **7** (**dig in**) begin eating heartily. **8** informal, dated like or appreciate.

– SYNONYMS **1** *digging the soil* **turn over,** work, break up. **2** *he dug a hole* **excavate,** dig out, quarry, hollow out, scoop out, bore, burrow, mine. **3** *the bodies were hastily* ***dug up*** **exhume,** disinter, unearth. **4** *he dug his hands in his pockets* **poke,** prod, jab, stab, shove, ram, push, thrust, drive, stick. **5** *he'd been* ***digging into*** *my past* **delve,** probe, search, inquire, look, investigate, research.

▶ **noun 1** an act of digging. **2** an archaeological excavation. **3** a sharp push or poke. **4** informal a mocking or critical remark. **5** (**digs**) informal lodgings.

– SYNONYMS **1 poke,** prod, jab, stab, shove, push. **2 snide remark,** cutting remark, jibe, taunt, sneer, insult; informal wisecrack, put-down.

– PHRASES **dig in one's heels** stubbornly refuse to compromise.
– ORIGIN perhaps from Old English, 'ditch.'

di·ge·ra·ti /dijə'rätē/ ▶ **plural noun** informal people with expertise in information technology.
– ORIGIN blend of **DIGITAL** and **LITERATI**.

di·gest ▶ **verb** /di'jest, dī-/ **1** break down food in the stomach and intestines into substances that can be absorbed by the body. **2** reflect on and absorb information.

– SYNONYMS **assimilate,** absorb, take in, understand, comprehend, grasp.

▶ **noun** /'dīˌjest/ a compilation or summary of material or information.

– SYNONYMS **summary,** synopsis, abstract, précis, résumé, summation.

– DERIVATIVES **di·gest·er** noun.
– ORIGIN Latin *digerere* 'distribute, dissolve, digest.'

di·gest·i·ble /di'jestəbəl, dī-/ ▶ **adjective 1** (of food) able to be digested. **2** (of information) easy to understand.
– DERIVATIVES **di·gest·i·bil·i·ty** /-ˌjestə'bilitē/ noun.

di·ges·tif /ˌdējes'tēf/ ▶ **noun** a drink taken before or after a meal in order to help digestion.
– ORIGIN French, 'digestive.'

di·ges·tion /di'jescHən, dī-/ ▶ **noun 1** the process of digesting food. **2** a person's capacity to digest food.

di·ges·tive /di'jestiv, dī-/ ▶ **adjective** relating to the digestion of food. ▶ **noun** a food or medicine that aids the digestion of food.

dig·ger /'digər/ ▶ **noun** a person, animal, or large machine that digs earth.

dig·i·cam /'dijiˌkam/ ▶ **noun** a digital camera.

dig·it /'dijit/ ▶ **noun 1** any of the numerals from 0 to 9. **2** a finger or thumb.
– ORIGIN Latin *digitus* 'finger, toe.'

dig·it·al /'dijitl/ ▶ **adjective 1** relating to information represented as a series of binary digits, as in a computer. **2** relating to computer technology: *the digital revolution*. **3** (of a clock or watch) showing the time by displaying numbers electronically. **4** relating to a finger or fingers.
– DERIVATIVES **dig·it·al·ly** adverb.

dig·it·al au·di·o·tape ▶ **noun** magnetic tape on which sound is recorded digitally.

dig·it·al cam·er·a ▶ **noun** a camera that produces digital images that can be stored in a computer and displayed on screen.

dig·it·al di·vide ▶ **noun** the gulf between those who have ready access to computers and the Internet, and those who do not.

dig·i·tal·is /ˌdiji'talis/ ▶ **noun** a drug prepared from foxglove leaves, containing substances that stimulate the heart muscle.
– ORIGIN from the Latin genus name of the foxglove.

dig·i·tal·ize ▶ **verb** another term for **DIGITIZE**.
– DERIVATIVES **dig·i·tal·i·za·tion** /ˌdijitl-ə'zāsHən/ noun.

dig·it·al sig·na·ture ▶ **noun** a digital code that is attached to an electronically transmitted document to verify its contents and the sender's identity.

dig·i·tize /'dijiˌtīz/ ▶ **verb** convert pictures or sound into a digital form that can be processed by a computer.
– DERIVATIVES **dig·i·ti·za·tion** /ˌdijitə'zāsHən/ noun **dig·i·tiz·er** noun.

dig·ni·fied /'digniˌfīd/ ▶ **adjective** having a serious manner that is worthy of respect.

– SYNONYMS **stately,** noble, majestic, distinguished, regal, imposing, impressive, grand, solemn, formal, ceremonious, decorous, sedate.

dig·ni·fy /'dignəˌfī/ ▶ **verb** (**dignifies, dignifying, dignified**) make something seem impressive or worthy of respect.
– ORIGIN Latin *dignificare*.

dig·ni·tar·y /'digniˌterē/ ▶ **noun** (pl. **dignitaries**) a high-ranking person.

dig·ni·ty /'dignitē/ ▶ **noun** (pl. **dignities**) **1** the state of being worthy of respect: *the dignity of labor*. **2** a calm or serious manner. **3** a sense of self-respect.

– SYNONYMS **1 stateliness,** nobility, majesty, impressiveness, grandeur, magnificence, ceremoniousness, formality, decorum, propriety, respectability, worthiness, integrity, solemnity, gravitas. **2 self-respect,** pride, self-esteem, self-worth.

– ORIGIN Latin *dignitas*.

di·graph /'dīˌgraf/ ▶ **noun** a combination of two letters representing one sound, as in *ph* and *ey*.

di·gress /dī'gres/ ▶ **verb** leave the main subject temporarily in speech or writing.
– DERIVATIVES **di·gres·sion** /-'gresHən/ noun **di·gres·sive** /-'gresiv/ adjective.
– ORIGIN Latin *digredi* 'step away.'

di·he·dral /dīˈhēdrəl/ ▸ **adjective** having or contained by two plane faces.

dike[1] /dīk/ (also **dyke**) ▸ **noun 1** an embankment built to prevent flooding from the sea. **2** an earthwork serving as a boundary or defense: *Offa's Dike*. **3** a ditch or watercourse. **4** Geology an intrusion of igneous rock cutting across existing strata. Compare with **SILL**.

dike[2] ▸ **noun** variant spelling of **DYKE**[2].

dik·tat /dikˈtät/ ▸ **noun** a decree imposed by someone in power without popular consent.
– ORIGIN German.

di·lap·i·dat·ed /diˈlapiˌdātid/ ▸ **adjective** in a state of disrepair or ruin.

> – SYNONYMS **run-down,** tumbledown, ramshackle, in disrepair, shabby, battered, rickety, crumbling, in ruins, ruined, decaying, decrepit, neglected, uncared-for, gone to rack and ruin.

– DERIVATIVES **di·lap·i·da·tion** /diˌlapiˈdāsʜən/ noun.
– ORIGIN from Latin *dilapidare* 'demolish.'

dil·a·ta·tion /ˌdiləˈtāsʜən, ˌdī-/ ▸ **noun** Medicine & Physiology the action of widening a vessel or opening in the body.

di·late /ˈdīˌlāt, dīˈlāt/ ▸ **verb 1** make or become wider, larger, or more open: *her eyes dilated with horror*. **2** (**dilate on**) speak or write at length on a subject.
– DERIVATIVES **di·la·tion** /dīˈlāsʜən/ noun **di·la·tor** /ˈdīˌlātər, dīˈlātər/ noun.
– ORIGIN Latin *dilatare* 'spread out.'

dil·a·to·ry /ˈdiləˌtôrē/ ▸ **adjective 1** slow to act. **2** intended to cause delay: *dilatory tactics*.
– DERIVATIVES **dil·a·to·ri·ness** noun.
– ORIGIN Latin *dilatorius*.

dil·do /ˈdildō/ ▸ **noun** (pl. **dildos** or **dildoes**) an object shaped like an erect penis, used for sexual stimulation.
– ORIGIN unknown.

di·lem·ma /diˈlemə/ ▸ **noun 1** a situation in which a difficult choice has to be made between alternatives that are equally undesirable. **2** informal a difficult situation or problem.

> – SYNONYMS **quandary,** predicament, catch-22, vicious circle, plight, conflict; informal fix, tight spot/corner.

– ORIGIN Greek.

dil·et·tante /ˌdiliˈtänt/ ▸ **noun** (pl. **dilettanti** /-ˈtäntē/ or **dilettantes**) a person who dabbles in a subject for enjoyment but without serious study.

> – SYNONYMS **dabbler,** amateur, nonprofessional, nonspecialist, layman, layperson.

– DERIVATIVES **dil·et·tan·tish** adjective **dil·et·tant·ism** /-ˌtizəm/ noun.
– ORIGIN Italian, 'art-lover.'

dil·i·gent /ˈdiləjənt/ ▸ **adjective** careful and conscientious in carrying out a task or duties.

> – SYNONYMS **industrious,** hard-working, assiduous, conscientious, particular, punctilious, meticulous, painstaking, rigorous, careful, thorough, sedulous.
> – ANTONYMS lazy.

– DERIVATIVES **dil·i·gence** noun **dil·i·gent·ly** adverb.
– ORIGIN from Latin *diligere* 'love, take delight in.'

> **CHOOSE THE RIGHT WORD**
>
> See **BUSY**.

dill /dil/ ▸ **noun** an herb, the leaves and seeds of which are used in cooking or for medicinal purposes.
– ORIGIN Old English.

dil·ly-dal·ly /ˈdilē/ ▸ **verb** (**dilly-dallies, dilly-dallying, dilly-dallied**) informal dawdle or be indecisive.
– ORIGIN from **DALLY**.

di·lute /diˈlo͞ot, dī-/ ▸ **verb 1** make a liquid thinner or weaker by adding water or another solvent. **2** make weaker by modifying or adding other elements: *they rejected any attempt to dilute the law*.

> – SYNONYMS **1** *dilute the bleach with water* **make weaker,** water down, thin, doctor, adulterate; informal cut. **2** *the original plans have been diluted* **tone down,** moderate, weaken, water down, compromise.

▸ **adjective 1** (of a liquid) made thinner or weaker by the addition of a solvent. **2** Chemistry (of a solution) having a relatively low concentration of solute.
– DERIVATIVES **di·lut·er** noun **di·lu·tion** /diˈlo͞osʜən, dī-/ noun **di·lu·tive** /-ˈlo͞otiv/ adjective.
– ORIGIN Latin *diluere* 'wash away, dissolve.'

dim /dim/ ▸ **adjective** (**dimmer, dimmest**) **1** not bright or well lit: *the dim corridors of the building*. **2** made difficult to see by darkness or distance: *dim shapes of men passed to and fro*. **3** (of the eyes) not able to see clearly. **4** not clearly remembered. **5** informal stupid or slow to understand.

> – SYNONYMS **1** *the dim light* **faint,** weak, feeble, soft, pale, dull, subdued, muted. **2** *long dim corridors* **dark,** badly lit, dingy, dismal, gloomy, murky. **3** *a dim figure* **indistinct,** ill-defined, vague, shadowy, nebulous, blurred, fuzzy. **4** *dim memories* **vague,** imprecise, imperfect, unclear, indistinct, sketchy, hazy. **5** see **STUPID**.
> – ANTONYMS bright, distinct, clear.

▸ **verb** (**dims, dimming, dimmed**) make or become dim.

> – SYNONYMS **1 turn down,** lower, soften, subdue. **2 fade,** dwindle, dull.
> – ANTONYMS brighten.

– DERIVATIVES **dim·ly** adverb **dimm·a·ble** adjective **dim·ness** noun.
– PHRASES **take a dim view of** regard with disapproval.
– ORIGIN Old English.

dime /dīm/ ▸ **noun** a ten-cent coin.
– ORIGIN Old French *disme* 'tenth part.'

di·men·sion /diˈmencʜən/ ▸ **noun 1** a measurable extent, such as length, breadth, or height. **2** an aspect or feature: *the story has an international dimension*.

> – SYNONYMS **1 size,** measurements, proportions, extent, length, width, breadth, depth. **2 aspect,** feature, element, angle, facet, side.

– DERIVATIVES **di·men·sion·al** /-cʜənl/ adjective **di·men·sion·al·ly** /-cʜənl-ē/ adverb.
– ORIGIN Latin.

di·mer /ˈdīmər/ ▸ **noun** Chemistry a molecule consisting of two identical molecules linked together.
– ORIGIN from **DI-**, on the pattern of *polymer*.

di·min·ish /diˈminisʜ/ ▸ **verb 1** become or make smaller, weaker, or less. **2** cause to seem less impressive or valuable: *the trial has aged and diminished him*.

> – SYNONYMS **1 subside,** lessen, decline, reduce, decrease, dwindle, fade, slacken off, let up. **2** *new laws diminished the courts' authority* **reduce,** decrease, lessen, curtail, cut, limit, curb.
> – ANTONYMS increase.

– ORIGIN Latin *deminuere* 'lessen.'

di·min·u·en·do /di,minyo͞o'endō/ ▶ **adverb & adjective** Music with a decrease in loudness. ▶ **noun** Music a decrease in loudness.
– ORIGIN Italian, 'diminishing.'

dim·i·nu·tion /,dimə'n(y)o͞osʜən/ ▶ **noun** a reduction in the size, extent, or importance of something.

di·min·u·tive /di'minyətiv/ ▶ **adjective 1** very or unusually small. **2** (of a word, name, or suffix) implying smallness (e.g., *-let* in *booklet*). ▶ **noun** a shortened form of a name, typically used informally.
– ORIGIN Latin *diminutivus*.

> **CHOOSE THE RIGHT WORD**
>
> See **SMALL**.

dim·i·ty /'dimitē/ ▶ **noun** a sheer cotton fabric woven with raised stripes or checks.
– ORIGIN Greek *dimitos*.

dim·mer /'dimər/ (also **dimmer switch**) ▶ **noun** a device for varying the brightness of an electric light.

di·mor·phic /dī'môrfik/ ▶ **adjective** chiefly Biology occurring in or representing two distinct forms.
– DERIVATIVES **di·mor·phism** /-fizəm/ noun.
– ORIGIN from Greek *dimorphos*.

dim·ple /'dimpəl/ ▶ **noun 1** a small depression formed in the fleshy part of the cheeks when one smiles. **2** a slight depression in the surface of an object. ▶ **verb** produce a dimple or dimples on something.
– DERIVATIVES **dim·ply** adjective.
– ORIGIN Germanic.

dim sum /'dim 'səm/ ▶ **noun** a Chinese dish of small dumplings containing various fillings.
– ORIGIN from the Chinese words for 'dot' and 'heart.'

dim·wit /'dim,wit/ ▶ **noun** informal a stupid or silly person.
– DERIVATIVES **dim·wit·ted** adjective.

DIN /din/ ▶ **noun** any of a series of international technical standards, used especially for electrical connections and film speeds.
– ORIGIN from the initial letters of German *Deutsche Industrie-Norm* 'German Industrial Standard.'

din /din/ ▶ **noun** a prolonged loud and unpleasant noise.

> – SYNONYMS **noise,** racket, rumpus, cacophony, hubbub, uproar, ruckus, commotion, clangor, clatter, clamor. informal hullabaloo.
> – ANTONYMS silence.

▶ **verb** (**dins, dinning, dinned**) (**din something into**) put information into someone's mind by constant repetition.
– ORIGIN Old English.

di·nar /di'när/ ▶ **noun 1** the basic unit of money of Bosnia and Serbia. **2** the basic unit of money of certain countries of the Middle East and North Africa.
– ORIGIN Turkish and Serbo-Croat.

dine /dīn/ ▶ **verb 1** eat dinner. **2** (**dine out on**) regularly entertain friends with an interesting or amusing story.

> – SYNONYMS **eat,** have dinner, have lunch.

– ORIGIN Old French *disner*.

din·er /'dīnər/ ▶ **noun 1** a person eating a meal, especially in a restaurant. **2** a dining car on a train. **3** a small roadside restaurant.

di·nette /dī'net/ ▶ **noun 1** a small room or part of a room used for eating meals. **2** a set of table and chairs for such an area.

ding[1] /diɴɢ/ ▶ **verb** make a metallic ringing sound.

ding[2] informal ▶ **noun** a mark or dent on the bodywork of a car, boat, or other vehicle. ▶ **verb 1** dent something. **2** hit someone, especially on the head. **3** criticize, injure, or penalize someone.
– ORIGIN probably of Scandinavian origin.

ding·bat /'diɴɢ,bat/ ▶ **noun** informal a stupid or eccentric person.
– ORIGIN uncertain.

ding-dong /'diɴɢ ,dôɴɢ/ ▶ **noun** informal a silly or foolish person. ▶ **adjective** (of a contest) evenly matched and hard fought.
– ORIGIN from the sound of a bell.

din·ghy /'diɴɢē/ ▶ **noun** (pl. **dinghies**) a small open boat for recreation or racing.
– ORIGIN Hindi, 'rowboat.'

din·go /'diɴɢgō/ ▶ **noun** (pl. **dingoes** or **dingos**) a wild or semi-domesticated Australian dog with a sandy-colored coat.
– ORIGIN from an Aboriginal language.

din·gy /'dinjē/ ▶ **adjective** (**dingier, dingiest**) gloomy and drab.

> – SYNONYMS **gloomy,** dark, dull, dim, dismal, dreary, drab, somber, grim, cheerless, dirty, grimy, shabby, seedy, run-down.
> – ANTONYMS bright.

– DERIVATIVES **din·gi·ly** adverb **din·gi·ness** noun.
– ORIGIN perhaps from an Old English word meaning 'dung.'

din·ing car ▶ **noun** a railroad car equipped as a restaurant.

din·ing room ▶ **noun** a room in a house or hotel in which meals are eaten.

dink·y /'diɴɢkē/ ▶ **adjective** (**dinkier, dinkiest**) informal attractively small and neat.
– ORIGIN from Scots and northern English dialect *dink* 'neat, trim.'

din·ner /'dinər/ ▶ **noun 1** the main meal of the day, taken either around midday or in the evening. **2** a formal evening meal.

> – SYNONYMS **main meal,** lunch, evening meal, supper, feast, banquet.

– ORIGIN from Old French *disner* 'to dine.'

din·ner jack·et ▶ **noun** a man's short jacket without tails, worn with a bow tie for formal evening occasions.

di·no·saur /'dīnə,sôr/ ▶ **noun 1** an extinct reptile of the Mesozoic era, often reaching an enormous size. **2** a thing that is outdated or has become obsolete.
– ORIGIN from Greek *deinos* 'terrible' + *sauros* 'lizard.'

dint /dint/ ▶ **noun** a dent or hollow in a surface.
– PHRASES **by dint of** by means of.
– ORIGIN Old English, 'a blow with a weapon.'

di·o·cese /'dīəsis, -,sēz, -,sēs/ ▶ **noun** (pl. **dioceses** /'dīəsēz/) (in the Christian Church) a district for which a bishop is responsible.
– DERIVATIVES **di·oc·e·san** /dī'äsisən/ adjective.
– ORIGIN Latin *dioecesis* 'governor's jurisdiction, diocese.'

di·ode /'dī,ōd/ ▶ **noun 1** a semiconductor device with two terminals, typically allowing the flow of current in one direction only. **2** a thermionic valve with two electrodes.
– ORIGIN from **DI-** + a shortened form of **ELECTRODE**.

di·oe·cious /dī'ēsʜəs/ ▶ **adjective** (of a plant or invertebrate animal) having the male and female

reproductive organs in separate individuals. Compare with **MONOECIOUS**.
– ORIGIN from **DI-** + Greek *-oikos* 'house.'

Di·o·ny·sian /ˌdīəˈnisHən, -ˈnisēən, -ˈnīsēən/ (also **Dionysiac** /-ˈnisēˌak, -ˈnīsē-/) ▸ **adjective 1** relating to Dionysus, the Greek god of fertility and wine, associated with ecstatic religious rites. **2** wild and uninhibited.

di·op·ter /dīˈäptər/ ▸ **noun** a unit of refractive power, equal to the reciprocal of the focal length (in meters) of a given lens.
– ORIGIN from Greek *di-* 'through' + *optos* 'visible.'

di·op·tric /dīˈäptrik/ ▸ **adjective** relating to the refraction of light.
– DERIVATIVES **di·op·trics** plural noun.

di·o·ram·a /ˌdīəˈramə, -ˈrä-/ ▸ **noun 1** a model representing a scene with three-dimensional figures against a painted background. **2** chiefly historical a scenic painting, viewed through a peephole, in which changes in color and direction of illumination simulate changes in the weather and time of day.
– ORIGIN French.

di·o·rite /ˈdīəˌrīt/ ▸ **noun** a speckled, coarse-grained igneous rock.
– ORIGIN French.

di·ox·ide /dīˈäkˌsīd/ ▸ **noun** Chemistry an oxide with two atoms of oxygen to one of a metal or other element.

di·ox·in /dīˈäksin/ ▸ **noun** a highly toxic organic compound produced as a byproduct in some manufacturing processes.

dip /dip/ ▸ **verb (dips, dipping, dipped) 1 (dip something in/into)** put or lower something briefly in or into liquid. **2** sink, drop, or slope downward: *the sun had dipped below the horizon.* **3** (of a level or amount) temporarily become lower or smaller. **4** move something briefly downward. **5 (dip into)** spend from one's financial resources. **6 (dip into)** reach into a bag or container to take something out.

> – SYNONYMS **1 immerse,** submerge, plunge, dunk, bathe, sink. **2 sink,** set, drop, fall, descend. **3 decrease,** fall, drop, fall off, decline, diminish, dwindle, slump, plummet, plunge. **4 slope down,** descend, go down, drop (away), fall away. **5** *you might have to dip into your savings* **draw on,** use, spend.
> – ANTONYMS rise, increase.

▸ **noun 1** an act of dipping. **2** a brief swim. **3** a brief downward slope followed by an upward one. **4** a thick sauce in which pieces of food are dipped before eating.

> – SYNONYMS **1 decrease,** fall, drop, downturn, decline, falling-off, slump, reduction. **2 swim,** bathe, paddle. **3 slope,** incline, decline, descent, hollow, depression, basin.

– ORIGIN Old English.

Dip. ▸ **abbreviation** diploma.

diph·the·ri·a /difˈTHi(ə)rēə, dip-/ ▸ **noun** a serious contagious disease causing inflammation of the mucous membranes, especially in the throat.
– ORIGIN Greek *diphthera* 'skin, hide' (referring to the false membrane that forms in the throat).

diph·thong /ˈdifˌTHäNG, ˈdip-, -ˌTHÔNG/ ▸ **noun** a sound formed by the combination of two vowels in a single syllable (as in *coin*).
– ORIGIN from Greek *di-* 'twice' + *phthongos* 'sound.'

di·plod·o·cus /diˈplädəkəs/ ▸ **noun** a huge plant-eating dinosaur of the late Jurassic period, with a long slender neck and tail.
– ORIGIN from Greek *diplous* 'double' + *dokos* 'wooden beam.'

dip·loid /ˈdipˌloid/ ▸ **adjective** (of a cell or nucleus) containing two complete sets of chromosomes, one from each parent. Compare with **HAPLOID**.
– ORIGIN from Greek *diplous* 'double.'

di·plo·ma /diˈplōmə/ ▸ **noun** a certificate awarded by a school or college for successfully completing a course of study.
– ORIGIN Greek, 'folded paper.'

di·plo·ma·cy /diˈplōməsē/ ▸ **noun 1** the profession, activity, or skill of managing international relations. **2** skill and tact in dealing with people.

> – SYNONYMS **1 statesmanship,** statecraft, negotiation(s), discussion(s), talks. **2 tact,** tactfulness, sensitivity, discretion.

– ORIGIN French *diplomatie*.

dip·lo·mat /ˈdipləˌmat/ ▸ **noun** an official representing a country abroad.

> – SYNONYMS **ambassador,** attaché, consul, chargé d'affaires, envoy, emissary.

dip·lo·mat·ic /ˌdipləˈmatik/ ▸ **adjective 1** relating to diplomacy. **2** dealing with people in a tactful way.

> – SYNONYMS **tactful,** sensitive, subtle, delicate, polite, discreet, judicious, politic.
> – ANTONYMS tactless.

– DERIVATIVES **dip·lo·mat·i·cal·ly** /-ik(ə)lē/ adverb.

dip·lo·mat·ic im·mu·ni·ty ▸ **noun** exemption from certain laws granted to diplomats by the country in which they are working.

dip·lo·mat·ic pouch ▸ **noun** a container in which official mail is sent to or from an embassy, and which is not subject to customs inspection.

di·pole /ˈdīˌpōl/ ▸ **noun 1** Physics a pair of equal and oppositely charged or magnetized poles separated by a distance. **2** an aerial consisting of a horizontal metal rod with a connecting wire at its center.
– DERIVATIVES **di·po·lar** /dīˈpōlər/ adjective.

dip·per /ˈdipər/ ▸ **noun 1** a songbird that dives into fast-flowing streams to feed. **2** a ladle.

dip·py /ˈdipē/ ▸ **adjective (dippier, dippiest)** informal foolish or eccentric.
– ORIGIN unknown.

dip·so·ma·ni·a /ˌdipsəˈmānēə/ ▸ **noun** alcoholism.
– DERIVATIVES **dip·so·ma·ni·ac** /-nēˌak/ noun.
– ORIGIN from Greek *dipsa* 'thirst.'

dip·stick /ˈdipˌstik/ ▸ **noun** a rod for measuring the depth of a liquid, especially oil in an engine.

dip·tych /ˈdiptik/ ▸ **noun** a painting on two hinged wooden panels, typically forming an altarpiece.
– ORIGIN Greek *diptukha* 'pair of writing tablets.'

dire /dīr/ ▸ **adjective 1** very serious or urgent. **2** (of a threat or warning) portending disaster.

> – SYNONYMS **terrible,** dreadful, appalling, frightful, awful, grim, sore, alarming, acute, grave, serious, urgent, pressing, wretched, desperate, parlous.

– ORIGIN Latin *dirus* 'fearful, threatening.'

di·rect /diˈrekt, dī-/ ▸ **adjective 1** going from one place to another without changing direction or stopping. **2** with nothing or no one in between: *I had no direct* *contact with Mr. Clark.* **3** straightforward; frank. **4** clear; unambiguous. **5** (of descent) proceeding in continuous succession from parent to child.

– SYNONYMS **1 straight,** short, quick. **2 nonstop,** through, unbroken, uninterrupted. **3 frank,** candid, straightforward, open, blunt, plain-spoken, outspoken, forthright, no-nonsense, matter-of-fact; informal upfront.

▶ **adverb** in a direct way or by a direct route.

▶ **verb 1** aim something toward: *he directed his criticism at the media.* **2** control or manage something. **3** supervise and control a movie, play, or other production. **4** tell or show someone the way. **5** give an order to someone.

– SYNONYMS **1 manage,** govern, run, administer, control, conduct, handle, be in charge of, preside over, lead, head, rule. **2 aim,** target, address to, intend for, mean for, design for. **3 give directions,** show the way, point someone in the direction of. **4 instruct,** tell, command, order, require; old use bid.

– DERIVATIVES **di·rect·ness** noun.

– ORIGIN Latin *directus.*

di·rect ac·tion ▶ **noun** the use of strikes or other public forms of protest rather than negotiation to achieve one's aims.

di·rect cur·rent ▶ **noun** an electric current flowing in one direction only. Compare with **ALTERNATING CURRENT**.

di·rec·tion /di'reksʜən, dī-/ ▶ **noun 1** a course along which someone or something moves, or which leads to a destination. **2** a point to or from which a person or thing moves or faces: *a house with views in all directions.* **3** the management or guidance of someone or something. **4** aim or purpose: *his lack of direction in life.* **5** (**directions**) instructions on how to reach a destination or how to do something.

– SYNONYMS **1 way,** route, course, line, bearing, orientation. **2 running,** management, administration, conduct, handling, supervision, superintendence, command, rule, leadership. **3 instruction,** order, command, rule, regulation, requirement.

– DERIVATIVES **di·rec·tion·less** adjective.

di·rec·tion·al /di'reksʜənl/ ▶ **adjective 1** relating to or indicating direction. **2** operating or sending radio signals in one direction only: *a directional microphone.*

di·rec·tive /di'rektiv/ ▶ **noun** an official or authoritative instruction.

– SYNONYMS **instruction,** direction, command, order, injunction, decree, dictum, edict.

di·rect·ly /di'rektlē/ ▶ **adverb 1** in a direct way. **2** exactly in a specified position: *the house directly opposite.* **3** immediately; at once.

– SYNONYMS **1** *they flew directly to New York* **straight,** as the crow flies. **2** *directly after breakfast* **immediately,** right (away), straight, straightaway, without delay, promptly. **3** *the houses directly opposite* **exactly,** right, immediately, diametrically; informal bang. **4 frankly,** candidly, openly, bluntly, forthrightly, without beating around/about the bush.

▶ **conjunction** Brit. as soon as.

di·rect mail ▶ **noun** advertising material mailed to prospective customers without their having asked for it.

di·rect ob·ject ▶ **noun** a noun phrase that refers to a person or thing that is directly affected by the action of a transitive verb (e.g., *the dog* in *she fed the dog*).

di·rec·tor /di'rektər/ ▶ **noun 1** a person who is in charge of a department, organization, or activity. **2** a member of the managing board of a business. **3** a person who directs a movie, play, etc.

– SYNONYMS **manager,** head, chief, principal, leader, governor, president, chair, chief executive; informal boss.

– DERIVATIVES **di·rec·to·ri·al** /di,rek'tôrēəl, ,dīrek-/ adjective **di·rec·tor·ship** /-,sʜip/ noun.

di·rec·to·rate /di'rektərit/ ▶ **noun 1** the board of directors of a company. **2** a section of a government department in charge of a particular activity.

di·rec·tor gen·er·al ▶ **noun** (pl. **directors general**) the chief executive of a large governmental, multinational, or private organization.

di·rec·to·ry /di'rektərē/ ▶ **noun** (pl. **directories**) **1** a book listing individuals or organizations with details such as addresses and telephone numbers. **2** a computer file listing other files.

di·rect speech ▶ **noun** the reporting of speech by repeating the actual words of a speaker, for example *'I'm going,' she said.* Contrasted with **REPORTED SPEECH**.

di·rect tax ▶ **noun** a tax, such as income tax, that is charged on the income or profits of the person who pays it.

dirge /dərj/ ▶ **noun 1** a lament for the dead, especially one forming part of a funeral rite. **2** a mournful song or piece of music.

– ORIGIN from Latin *dirige!* 'direct!,' the first word of a psalm used in service for the dead.

dir·ham /də'ram/ ▶ **noun** the basic unit of money of Morocco and the United Arab Emirates.

– ORIGIN Arabic.

dir·i·gi·ble /'dirijəbəl, də'rijə-/ ▶ **noun** an airship.

– ORIGIN from Latin *dirigere* 'to direct.'

di·ri·gisme /'diri,zʜizəm, ,diri'zʜizəm, ,dērē'zʜēsm(ə)/ ▶ **noun** government control of economic and social matters.

– DERIVATIVES **di·ri·giste** /,diri'zʜēst, ,dirē-/ adjective.

– ORIGIN French.

dirk /dərk/ ▶ **noun** a short dagger of a kind formerly carried by Scottish Highlanders.

– ORIGIN unknown.

dirn·dl /'dərndl/ ▶ **noun 1** (also **dirndl skirt**) a full, wide skirt gathered into a tight waistband. **2** a woman's dress with a dirndl skirt and a close-fitting bodice.

– ORIGIN German dialect, 'little girl.'

dirt /dərt/ ▶ **noun 1** a substance that makes something unclean. **2** soil or earth. **3** informal excrement. **4** informal scandalous or damaging information.

– SYNONYMS **1 grime,** filth, muck, dust, mud, pollution; informal grunge. **2** *a dirt road* **earth,** soil, clay, loam.

– ORIGIN Old Norse, 'excrement.'

dirt·bag /'dərt,bag/ ▶ **noun** informal a physically or morally repulsive person.

dirt bike ▶ **noun** a motorcycle designed for use on rough terrain, especially in scrambling.

dirt cheap ▶ **adjective & adverb** informal very cheap.

dirt poor ▶ **adjective & adverb** very poor.

dirt track ▶ **noun** a racing track made of earth or rolled cinders.

dirt·y /ˈdərtē/ ▸ **adjective** (**dirtier, dirtiest**) **1** covered or marked with dirt; not clean. **2** concerned with sex in a lewd or obscene way: *dirty jokes*. **3** dishonest; dishonorable. **4** (of weather) rough and unpleasant. **5** (of a nuclear weapon) producing considerable radioactive fallout.

> – SYNONYMS **1 soiled,** grimy, grubby, filthy, mucky, stained, unwashed, greasy, muddy, dusty, polluted, contaminated, foul, unhygienic. informal grungy. **2 obscene,** indecent, rude, naughty, vulgar, smutty, coarse, crude, filthy, off color, pornographic, explicit, X-rated; informal blue; euphemistic adult. **3 malevolent,** hostile, angry, disapproving.
> – ANTONYMS clean.

▸ **adverb** Brit. informal used for emphasis: *a dirty great slab of stone*.

▸ **verb** (**dirties, dirtying, dirtied**) make someone or something dirty.

> – SYNONYMS **soil,** stain, muddy, blacken, mess (up), mark, spatter, smudge, smear, splatter, sully, pollute, foul.

– DERIVATIVES **dirt·i·ly** adverb **dirt·i·ness** noun.
– PHRASES **do the dirty on** Brit. informal cheat or betray someone. **play dirty** informal act in a dishonest or unfair way.

WORD TOOLKIT

dirty ...	sordid ...	foul ...
hands	affair	language
habit	details	smell
streets	past	breath
clothes	business	taste

dirt·y bomb ▸ **noun** a conventional bomb that contains radioactive material.

dirt·y look ▸ **noun** informal a look expressing disapproval, disgust, or anger.

dirt·y trick ▸ **noun** **1** a dishonest or unkind act. **2** (**dirty tricks**) underhanded political or commercial activity designed to discredit an opponent or competitor.

dirt·y word ▸ **noun** a thing regarded with dislike: *capitalism is a dirty word for some young people*.

dirt·y work ▸ **noun** unpleasant or dishonest activities that are delegated to someone else.

dis /dis/ (also **diss**) ▸ **verb** (**disses, dissing, dissed**) informal act or speak in a disrespectful way toward.

dis- ▸ **prefix** **1** expressing negation: *disadvantage*. **2** expressing reversal or absence: *dishonor*. **3** expressing removal or separation: *disperse*.
– ORIGIN Latin.

dis·a·bil·i·ty /ˌdisəˈbilitē/ ▸ **noun** (pl. **disabilities**) **1** a physical or mental condition that limits a person's movements, senses, or activities. **2** a disadvantage.

> – SYNONYMS **handicap,** incapacity, impairment, infirmity, defect, abnormality, condition, disorder, affliction.

dis·a·ble /disˈābəl/ ▸ **verb** **1** (of a disease, injury, or accident) limit someone in their movements, senses, or activities. **2** put something out of action.

> – SYNONYMS **1 incapacitate,** put out of action, debilitate, handicap, cripple, lame, maim, immobilize, paralyze. **2 deactivate,** defuse, disarm, make safe.

– DERIVATIVES **dis·a·ble·ment** noun.

dis·a·bled /disˈābəld/ ▸ **adjective** having a physical or mental disability.

> – SYNONYMS **handicapped,** incapacitated, infirm, crippled, lame, paralyzed, immobilized, bedridden; euphemistic physically challenged, differently abled.
> – ANTONYMS able-bodied.

USAGE

Disabled is the standard term for people with physical or mental disabilities, and should be used instead of terms such as **crippled** or **handicapped**, which often cause offense.

dis·a·buse /ˌdisəˈbyo͞oz/ ▸ **verb** persuade someone that an idea or belief is mistaken: *Greg soon disabused her of this idea*.

di·sac·cha·ride /dīˈsakəˌrīd/ ▸ **noun** a sugar whose molecule can be broken down to give two simple sugar molecules.

dis·ad·van·tage /ˌdisədˈvantij/ ▸ **noun** something that causes a problem or that makes success or progress less likely: *women are at a disadvantage in competing for jobs with men*.

> – SYNONYMS **1 drawback,** snag, downside, fly in the ointment, catch, nuisance, handicap, trouble; informal minus. **2 detriment,** prejudice, harm, loss, hurt.
> – ANTONYMS advantage.

▸ **verb** **1** put someone in an unfavorable position. **2** (as adj. **disadvantaged**) having less money and fewer opportunities than the rest of society.
– DERIVATIVES **dis·ad·van·ta·geous** /disˌadvənˈtājəs/ adjective.

dis·af·fect·ed /ˌdisəˈfektid/ ▸ **adjective** discontented through having lost one's feelings of loyalty.
– DERIVATIVES **dis·af·fec·tion** /ˌdisəˈfeksʜən/ noun.

CHOOSE THE RIGHT WORD

See **SOLITUDE**.

dis·a·gree /ˌdisəˈgrē/ ▸ **verb** (**disagrees, disagreeing, disagreed**) **1** have a different opinion. **2** fail to correspond or be consistent: *results that disagree with the findings reported so far*. **3** (**disagree with**) make someone slightly ill.

> – SYNONYMS **1 be of a different opinion,** not see eye to eye, take issue, challenge, contradict, differ, dissent, be in dispute, clash. **2 differ,** be dissimilar, be different, be at variance/odds, vary, contradict each other, conflict. **3** *the food* ***disagreed with*** *her* **make ill,** make unwell, upset, nauseate.
> – ANTONYMS agree.

dis·a·gree·a·ble /ˌdisəˈgrēəbəl/ ▸ **adjective** **1** not pleasant or enjoyable. **2** unfriendly and bad-tempered.

> – SYNONYMS **unpleasant,** distasteful, off-putting, unpalatable, nasty, objectionable, disgusting, horrible, offensive, repulsive, obnoxious, odious, repellent, revolting, vile, foul.
> – ANTONYMS pleasant.

– DERIVATIVES **dis·a·gree·a·bly** adverb.

dis·a·gree·ment /ˌdisəˈgrēmənt/ ▸ **noun** lack of consensus or approval.

> – SYNONYMS **dissent,** difference of opinion, controversy, discord, division, dispute, quarrel.
> – ANTONYMS agreement.

dis·al·low /ˌdisəˈlou/ ▶ **verb** declare something to be invalid.
– DERIVATIVES **dis·al·low·ance** noun.

> **CHOOSE THE RIGHT WORD**
> See **PROHIBIT**.

dis·am·big·u·ate /ˌdisamˈbigyo͞oˌāt/ ▶ **verb** remove uncertainty of meaning from something with more than one possible meaning.
– DERIVATIVES **dis·am·big·u·a·tion** /-ˌbigyo͞oˈāsʜən/ noun.

dis·ap·pear /ˌdisəˈpi(ə)r/ ▶ **verb 1** cease to be visible. **2** cease to exist. **3** be lost or impossible to find.

> – SYNONYMS **1 vanish,** be lost to view/sight, recede, fade away, melt away, clear. **2 die out,** cease to exist, end, go, pass away, pass into oblivion, vanish, perish.
> – ANTONYMS materialize.

– DERIVATIVES **dis·ap·pear·ance** noun.

dis·ap·point /ˌdisəˈpoint/ ▶ **verb 1** fail to fulfill someone's hopes. **2** prevent hopes from becoming a reality.

> – SYNONYMS **let down,** fail, dissatisfy, upset, dismay, sadden, disenchant, disillusion, shatter someone's illusions.

– DERIVATIVES **dis·ap·point·ing** adjective **dis·ap·point·ing·ly** adverb.
– ORIGIN Old French *desappointer* 'deprive of a position.'

dis·ap·point·ed /ˌdisəˈpointid/ ▶ **adjective** sad or displeased because one's hopes have not been fulfilled.

> – SYNONYMS **upset,** saddened, let down, displeased, dissatisfied, disheartened, downhearted, discouraged, crestfallen, disenchanted, disillusioned; informal choked, cut up.
> – ANTONYMS delighted.

– DERIVATIVES **dis·ap·point·ed·ly** adverb.

dis·ap·point·ment /ˌdisəˈpointmənt/ ▶ **noun 1** sadness or displeasure caused by the failure of one's hopes to be fulfilled. **2** a cause of disappointment.

> – SYNONYMS **1 sadness,** sorrow, regret, dismay, displeasure, dissatisfaction, disenchantment, disillusionment. **2 letdown,** nonevent, anticlimax. informal washout.
> – ANTONYMS delight.

dis·ap·pro·ba·tion /disˌaprəˈbāsʜən/ ▶ **noun** formal strong disapproval.

dis·ap·prov·al /ˌdisəˈpro͞ovəl/ ▶ **noun** the possession or expression of an unfavorable opinion.

> – SYNONYMS **disfavor,** objection, dislike, dissatisfaction, distaste, displeasure, criticism, censure, condemnation, denunciation.
> – ANTONYMS approval.

dis·ap·prove /ˌdisəˈpro͞ov/ ▶ **verb** think that someone or something is wrong or bad.

> – SYNONYMS *he* ***disapproved of*** *gamblers* **object to,** have a poor opinion of, take exception to, dislike, take a dim view of, look askance at, frown on, be against, not believe in, deplore, censure, condemn, denounce.

– DERIVATIVES **dis·ap·prov·ing** adjective.

dis·arm /disˈärm/ ▶ **verb 1** take a weapon or weapons away from a person, force, or country. **2** win over a hostile or suspicious person: *her political skills will disarm critics.* **3** remove the fuse from a bomb.

> – SYNONYMS **1 lay down one's arms,** demobilize, disband, demilitarize. **2 defuse,** disable, deactivate, make safe. **3 win over,** charm, persuade, soothe, mollify, appease, placate.
> – ANTONYMS arm, antagonize.

dis·ar·ma·ment /disˈärməmənt/ ▶ **noun** the reduction or withdrawal of military forces and weapons.

> – SYNONYMS **demilitarization,** demobilization, disbandment, decommissioning, arms reduction, arms limitation.

dis·arm·ing /disˈärmiɴɢ/ ▶ **adjective** removing suspicion or hostility, especially through charm.

> – SYNONYMS **winning,** charming, irresistible, persuasive, soothing, conciliatory, mollifying.

– DERIVATIVES **dis·arm·ing·ly** adverb.

dis·ar·range /ˌdisəˈrānj/ ▶ **verb** make something untidy or disordered.

dis·ar·ray /ˌdisəˈrā/ ▶ **noun** a state of disorder or untidiness.

> – SYNONYMS **disorder,** confusion, chaos, untidiness, disorganization, a mess, a muddle, a shambles.
> – ANTONYMS tidiness.

dis·as·sem·ble /ˌdisəˈsembəl/ ▶ **verb** take something to pieces.
– DERIVATIVES **dis·as·sem·bly** noun.

dis·as·so·ci·ate /ˌdisəˈsōsʜēˌāt, -ˈsōsē-/ ▶ **verb** another term for **DISSOCIATE**.
– DERIVATIVES **dis·as·so·ci·a·tion** /ˌdisəˌsōsʜēˈāsʜən, -ˌsōsē-/ noun.

dis·as·ter /diˈzastər/ ▶ **noun 1** a sudden accident or a natural catastrophe that causes great damage or loss of life. **2** an event or situation causing ruin or failure: *the deteriorating dollar is a disaster for the economy.*

> – SYNONYMS **1 catastrophe,** calamity, cataclysm, tragedy, act of God, accident. **2 misfortune,** mishap, misadventure, setback, reversal, stroke of bad luck, blow. **3 failure,** fiasco, catastrophe; informal flop, washout, dead loss.
> – ANTONYMS success.

– ORIGIN Italian *disastro* 'unlucky event.'

dis·as·trous /diˈzastrəs/ ▶ **adjective 1** causing great damage. **2** informal highly unsuccessful.

> – SYNONYMS **catastrophic,** calamitous, cataclysmic, tragic, devastating, ruinous, terrible, awful.

– DERIVATIVES **dis·as·trous·ly** adverb.

dis·a·vow /ˌdisəˈvou/ ▶ **verb** deny any responsibility or support for something.
– DERIVATIVES **dis·a·vow·al** noun.

dis·band /disˈband/ ▶ **verb** stop or cause to stop operating as an organized group.

> – SYNONYMS **break up,** disperse, demobilize, dissolve, scatter, separate, go separate ways, part company.
> – ANTONYMS assemble.

dis·bar /disˈbär/ ▶ **verb** (**disbars, disbarring, disbarred**) expel a lawyer from the Bar.
– DERIVATIVES **dis·bar·ment** /-mənt/ noun.

dis·be·lief /ˌdisbəˈlēf/ ▶ **noun 1** inability or refusal to accept that something is true or real. **2** lack of faith.

> – SYNONYMS **incredulity,** incredulousness, skepticism, doubt, cynicism, suspicion, distrust, mistrust.

dis·be·lieve /ˌdisbəˈlēv/ ▶ **verb** **1** be unable to believe someone or something. **2** have no religious faith.
– DERIVATIVES **dis·be·liev·er** noun.

dis·burse /disˈbərs/ ▶ **verb** pay out money from a fund.
– DERIVATIVES **dis·burse·ment** noun.
– ORIGIN Old French *desbourser*.

disc ▶ **noun** variant spelling of **DISK**.

dis·card ▶ **verb** /disˈkärd/ get rid of something as useless or unwanted.

> – SYNONYMS **dispose of,** throw away/out, get rid of, toss out, jettison, dispense with, scrap, reject, drop; informal ditch, trash, junk.
> – ANTONYMS keep.

▶ **noun** /ˈdisˌkärd/ a discarded item.
– ORIGIN from **DIS-** + **CARD**[1].

disc brake ▶ **noun** a type of vehicle brake employing the friction of pads against a disk attached to the wheel.

dis·cern /diˈsərn/ ▶ **verb** **1** recognize or find something out. **2** see or hear someone or something with difficulty.

> – SYNONYMS **perceive,** make out, pick out, detect, identify, determine, distinguish, recognize, notice, observe, see, spot; literary espy.

– DERIVATIVES **dis·cern·i·ble** adjective.
– ORIGIN Latin *discernere*.

> **CHOOSE THE RIGHT WORD**
>
> See **DISTINGUISH**.

dis·cern·ing /diˈsərniNG/ ▶ **adjective** having or showing good judgment.

> – SYNONYMS **discriminating,** judicious, shrewd, astute, intelligent, sharp, selective, sophisticated, tasteful, sensitive, perceptive, knowing.

– DERIVATIVES **dis·cern·ment** noun.

dis·charge ▶ **verb** /disˈCHärj/ **1** officially tell someone that they can or must leave: *he was discharged from the Air Force*. **2** cause a liquid, gas, or other substance to flow out. **3** fire a gun or missile. **4** do all that is required to fulfill a responsibility. **5** release someone from a contract or obligation. **6** Physics release or neutralize the electric charge of a battery or electric field.

> – SYNONYMS **1 dismiss,** eject, expel, throw out, make redundant, release, let go; Military cashier; informal sack, fire. **2 free,** set free, release, let out, liberate. **3 emit,** give off, let out, send out, exude, leak, secrete, excrete, release. **4 fire,** shoot, let off, set off, trigger, launch. **5 unload,** offload, put off, remove. **6 carry out,** perform, execute, conduct, fulfill, complete.
> – ANTONYMS recruit, imprison.

▶ **noun** /ˈdisˌCHärj/ **1** the action of discharging someone or something. **2** a substance that has been discharged. **3** a flow of electricity through the air or other gas.

> – SYNONYMS **1 dismissal,** release, removal, ejection, expulsion; Military cashiering; informal the sack, the boot. **2 leak,** leakage, emission, secretion, excretion, suppuration, pus. **3 carrying out,** performance, execution, conduct, fulfillment, accomplishment, completion.

– DERIVATIVES **dis·charg·er** /disˈCHärjər/ noun.
– ORIGIN Latin *discarricare* 'unload.'

dis·ci·ple /diˈsīpəl/ ▶ **noun** **1** a follower of Jesus during his life, especially one of the twelve Apostles. **2** a follower or student of a teacher, leader, or philosopher.

> – SYNONYMS **follower,** adherent, believer, admirer, devotee, acolyte, apostle, supporter, advocate.

– DERIVATIVES **dis·ci·ple·ship** /diˈsīpəlˌSHip/ noun.
– ORIGIN Latin *discipulus* 'learner.'

dis·ci·pli·nar·i·an /ˌdisəpləˈnerēən/ ▶ **noun** a person who enforces firm discipline.

dis·ci·pline /ˈdisəplin/ ▶ **noun** **1** the training of people to obey rules or a code of behavior. **2** controlled behavior resulting from such training: *he was able to maintain discipline among his men*. **3** an activity providing mental or physical training: *kung fu is a discipline open to all*. **4** a branch of academic study.

> – SYNONYMS **1 control,** regulation, direction, order, authority, strictness. **2 good behavior,** order, control, obedience. **3 field (of study),** branch of knowledge, subject, area, specialty.

▶ **verb** **1** train someone to be obedient or self-controlled by punishment or imposing rules. **2** formally punish someone for an offense. **3** (as adj. **disciplined**) behaving in a controlled way.

> – SYNONYMS **1 train,** drill, teach, school, coach. **2 punish,** penalize, reprimand, chastise, rebuke; informal throw the book at, call someone on the carpet.

– DERIVATIVES **dis·ci·pli·nar·y** /ˈdisəpləˌnerē/ adjective.
– ORIGIN Latin *disciplina* 'instruction, knowledge.'

disc jock·ey ▶ **noun** (also **disk jockey**) full form of **DJ**.

dis·claim /disˈklām/ ▶ **verb** **1** deny responsibility for or knowledge of something. **2** Law renounce a legal claim to a property or title.

dis·claim·er /disˈklāmər/ ▶ **noun** a statement denying responsibility for something.

dis·close /disˈklōz/ ▶ **verb** **1** make secret or new information known. **2** allow something hidden to be seen.

> – SYNONYMS **reveal,** make known, divulge, tell, impart, communicate, pass on, release, make public, broadcast, publish.
> – ANTONYMS conceal.

dis·clo·sure /disˈklōZHər/ ▶ **noun** **1** the disclosing of new or secret information. **2** a fact that is made known.

> – SYNONYMS **1 revelation,** declaration, announcement, news, report, leak. **2** *the disclosure of official information* **publishing,** broadcasting, leaking, revelation, communication, release, uncovering, unveiling, exposure.

dis·co /ˈdiskō/ ▶ **noun** (pl. **discos**) **1** a club or party at which people dance to pop music. **2** (also **disco music**) soul-influenced, melodic pop music.
– ORIGIN short for **DISCOTHEQUE**.

dis·cog·ra·phy /disˈkägrəfē/ ▶ **noun** (pl. **discographies**) **1** a descriptive catalog of musical recordings. **2** the study of musical recordings and compilation of descriptive catalogs.

dis·coid /ˈdisˌkoid/ ▶ **adjective** technical shaped like a disk.
– DERIVATIVES **dis·coi·dal** /disˈkoidl/ adjective.

dis·col·or /disˈkələr/ ▶ **verb** change to a different, less attractive color.

> – SYNONYMS **stain,** mark, soil, dirty, streak, smear, tarnish, spoil.

– DERIVATIVES **dis·col·or·a·tion** /-ˌkələˈrāSHən/ noun.

dis·com·bob·u·late /ˌdiskəmˈbäbyəˌlāt/ ▶ **verb** humorous disconcert or confuse someone.

dis·com·fit /dis'kəmfit/ ▶ **verb** (**discomfits, discomfiting, discomfited**) make someone uneasy or embarrassed.
– DERIVATIVES **dis·com·fi·ture** /dis'kəmfi,cHo͝or/ noun.
– ORIGIN Old French *desconfire* 'defeat.'

dis·com·fort /dis'kəmfərt/ ▶ **noun 1** slight pain. **2** slight anxiety or embarrassment.

> – SYNONYMS **1 pain,** aches and pains, soreness, aching, twinge, pang, throb, cramp. **2 inconvenience,** difficulty, problem, trial, tribulation, hardship. **3 embarrassment,** discomfiture, unease, awkwardness, discomposure, confusion, nervousness, distress, anxiety.

▶ **verb** cause discomfort to someone.

dis·com·mode /,diskə'mōd/ ▶ **verb** formal cause someone trouble or inconvenience.
– ORIGIN former French *discommoder*.

dis·com·pose /,diskəm'pōz/ ▶ **verb** disturb or agitate someone.
– DERIVATIVES **dis·com·po·sure** /-'pōzHər/ noun.

dis·con·cert /,diskən'sərt/ ▶ **verb** disturb the composure of; unsettle: *Sheila's unexpected appearance disconcerted him.*
– DERIVATIVES **dis·con·cert·ed** adjective.
– ORIGIN former French *desconcerter*.

dis·con·cert·ing /,diskən'sərtiNG/ ▶ **adjective** causing one to feel unsettled.

> – SYNONYMS *the intense scrutiny was disconcerting* **unsettling,** unnerving, discomfiting, disturbing, perturbing, troubling, upsetting, worrying, alarming, confusing, bewildering, perplexing.

dis·con·nect /,diskə'nekt/ ▶ **verb 1** break the connection between two things. **2** detach an electrical device from a power supply.

> – SYNONYMS **1 detach,** disengage, uncouple, unhook, unhitch, undo, unfasten, unyoke. **2 separate,** cut off, divorce, sever, isolate, dissociate, remove. **3 deactivate,** shut off, turn off, switch off, unplug.
> – ANTONYMS attach, connect.

– DERIVATIVES **dis·con·nec·tion** /-'neksHən/ noun.

dis·con·nect·ed /,diskə'nektid/ ▶ **adjective** (of speech, writing, or thought) lacking a logical sequence.

dis·con·so·late /dis'känsəlit/ ▶ **adjective** very unhappy and unable to be comforted.
– DERIVATIVES **dis·con·so·late·ly** adverb.

dis·con·tent /,diskən'tent/ ▶ **noun** lack of contentment or satisfaction.

> – SYNONYMS **dissatisfaction,** disaffection, grievances, unhappiness, displeasure, resentment, envy, restlessness, unrest, unease.
> – ANTONYMS satisfaction.

– DERIVATIVES **dis·con·tent·ment** noun.

dis·con·tent·ed /,diskən'tentid/ ▶ **adjective** dissatisfied, especially with one's circumstances.

> – SYNONYMS **dissatisfied,** disgruntled, disaffected, unhappy, aggrieved, displeased, resentful, envious, restless, frustrated; informal fed up.
> – ANTONYMS satisfied.

dis·con·tin·ue /,diskən'tinyo͞o/ ▶ **verb** (**discontinues, discontinuing, discontinued**) stop doing, providing, or making something.

> – SYNONYMS **stop,** end, terminate, put an end/stop to, wind up, finish, call a halt to, cancel, drop, abandon, dispense with, do away with, get rid of, ax, abolish, suspend, interrupt, break off, withdraw; informal cut, pull the plug on, scrap.

– DERIVATIVES **dis·con·tin·u·a·tion** /-,tinyo͞o'āsHən/ noun.

dis·con·tin·u·ous /,diskən'tinyo͞oəs/ ▶ **adjective** having intervals or gaps; not continuous.
– DERIVATIVES **dis·con·ti·nu·i·ty** /,diskäntn'(y)o͞oitē/ noun (pl. **discontinuities**).

dis·cord /'diskôrd/ ▶ **noun 1** lack of agreement or harmony: *financial difficulties can lead to marital discord.* **2** lack of harmony between musical notes sounding together.

> – SYNONYMS **1 strife,** conflict, friction, hostility, antagonism, antipathy, enmity, bad feeling, ill feeling, bad blood, argument, quarreling, squabbling, bickering, wrangling, feuding, disagreement, dissension, dispute, disunity, division. **2** *the music faded in discord* **dissonance,** discordance, disharmony, cacophony.
> – ANTONYMS accord, harmony.

– ORIGIN from Latin *discors* 'discordant.'

dis·cord·ant /dis'kôrdnt/ ▶ **adjective 1** not in harmony or agreement: *discordant opinions.* **2** (of a sound) harsh and unpleasant.

> – SYNONYMS **tunelesss,** inharmonious, off-key, dissonant, harsh, jarring, grating, jangly, jangling, strident, shrill, cacophonous.
> – ANTONYMS harmonious.

– DERIVATIVES **dis·cord·ance** /-dns/ noun.

di·sco·theque /'diskə,tek/ ▶ **noun** full form of DISCO (sense 1).
– ORIGIN French.

dis·count ▶ **noun** /'diskount/ a deduction from the usual cost of something.

> – SYNONYMS **reduction,** deduction, markdown, price cut, concession, rebate.

▶ **verb** /'diskount, dis'kount/ **1** deduct a discount from the usual price of something. **2** regard something as unworthy of consideration because it seems improbable.

> – SYNONYMS **1 disregard,** pay no attention to, take no notice of, dismiss, ignore, overlook; informal pooh-pooh. **2 reduce,** mark down, cut, lower; informal knock down.

– DERIVATIVES **dis·count·er** noun.

dis·coun·te·nance /dis'kountn-əns/ ▶ **verb 1** refuse to approve something. **2** unsettle someone.

dis·cour·age /dis'kərij, -'kə-rij/ ▶ **verb 1** cause someone to lose confidence or enthusiasm. **2** try to persuade someone not to do something.

> – SYNONYMS **1** *she was discouraged by his hostile tone* **dishearten,** dispirit, demoralize, disappoint, put off, unnerve, daunt, intimidate. **2** (as adj. **discouraged**) *Doug must be feeling pretty discouraged* **disheartened,** dispirited, demoralized, deflated, disappointed, let down, disconsolate, despondent, dejected, cast down, downcast, crestfallen, dismayed, low-spirited, gloomy, glum, unenthusiastic, put off, daunted, intimidated, cowed, crushed; informal down in the mouth, down in the dumps, fed up, unenthused. **3** *we want to* ***discourage*** *children* ***from*** *smoking* **dissuade,** deter, put off, talk out of. **4** *he sought to discourage further conversation* **prevent,** deter, stop, avert, inhibit, curb.
> – ANTONYMS encourage.

– DERIVATIVES **dis·cour·age·ment** noun **dis·cour·ag·ing** adjective.
– ORIGIN Old French *descouragier*.

dis·course ▶ **noun** /ˈdisˌkôrs/ **1** written or spoken communication or debate. **2** a formal written or verbal discussion of a topic.

– SYNONYMS **1 discussion,** conversation, talk, dialogue, conference, debate, consultation, parley, powwow, chat; informal confab; formal confabulation, colloquy. **2 essay,** treatise, dissertation, paper, study, critique, monograph, disquisition, tract, lecture, address, speech, oration, sermon, homily.

▶ **verb** /disˈkôrs/ speak or write about a topic with authority.

– SYNONYMS **1 hold forth,** expatiate, pontificate, talk, give a talk, give a speech, lecture, sermonize, preach; informal spout, sound off. **2 converse,** talk, speak, debate, confer, consult, parley, chat.

– ORIGIN Latin *discursus* 'running to and fro.'

dis·cour·te·ous /disˈkərtēəs/ ▶ **adjective** rude and lacking consideration for others.

– SYNONYMS **rude,** impolite, ill-mannered, bad-mannered, disrespectful, uncivil, ungentlemanly, unladylike, ill-bred, boorish, crass, ungracious, uncouth, insolent, impudent, audacious, presumptuous, curt, brusque, blunt, abrupt, offhand, short, sharp; informal ignorant.
– ANTONYMS polite, courteous.

– DERIVATIVES **dis·cour·te·ous·ly** adverb.

dis·cour·te·sy /disˈkərtəsē/ ▶ **noun** (pl. **discourtesies**) **1** rude and inconsiderate behavior. **2** a rude and inconsiderate act or remark.

dis·cov·er /disˈkəvər/ ▶ **verb 1** find someone or something unexpectedly or during a search. **2** become aware of a fact or situation. **3** be the first to find or observe a place, substance, or scientific phenomenon.

– SYNONYMS **1 find,** locate, come across/upon, stumble on, chance on, uncover, unearth, turn up. **2 find out,** learn, realize, ascertain, work out, recognize; informal figure out.

– DERIVATIVES **dis·cov·er·a·ble** adjective **dis·cov·er·er** noun.

dis·cov·er·y /disˈkəvərē/ ▶ **noun** (pl. **discoveries**) **1** the action of discovering something. **2** a person or thing discovered.

– SYNONYMS **1 finding,** location, uncovering, unearthing. **2 realization,** recognition, revelation, disclosure. **3 breakthrough,** finding, find, innovation.

dis·cred·it /disˈkredit/ ▶ **verb** (**discredits, discrediting, discredited**) **1** damage a person's good reputation. **2** make an idea or account seem false or unreliable.

– SYNONYMS **1 bring into disrepute,** disgrace, dishonor, blacken the name of, put/show in a bad light, compromise, smear, slur, tarnish. **2 disprove,** invalidate, explode, refute; informal debunk.
– ANTONYMS honor, prove.

▶ **noun** loss or lack of respect for someone.

– SYNONYMS **dishonor,** disgrace, shame, humiliation, ignominy.

– DERIVATIVES **dis·cred·it·a·ble** /disˈkreditəbəl/ adjective.

dis·creet /disˈkrēt/ ▶ **adjective** (**discreeter, discreetest**) careful to keep something secret or to avoid undue attention.

– SYNONYMS **tactful,** circumspect, diplomatic, judicious, sensitive, careful, cautious, strategic.

– DERIVATIVES **dis·creet·ly** adverb.
– ORIGIN Latin *discretus* 'separate.'

USAGE

Discrete and **discreet** are often confused. **Discreet** means 'careful to keep something secret or to avoid attention' (*we made some discreet inquiries*), while **discrete** means 'separate' (*products are organized in discrete batches*).

dis·crep·an·cy /disˈkrepənsē/ ▶ **noun** (pl. **discrepancies**) a difference between facts that should be the same.

– SYNONYMS **difference,** disparity, variation, deviation, divergence, disagreement, inconsistency, mismatch, conflict.
– ANTONYMS correspondence.

– DERIVATIVES **dis·crep·ant** /-pənt/ adjective.
– ORIGIN Latin *discrepantia*.

dis·crete /disˈkrēt/ ▶ **adjective** separate and distinct.
– DERIVATIVES **dis·crete·ly** adverb **dis·crete·ness** noun.
– ORIGIN Latin *discretus* 'separate.'

dis·cre·tion /disˈkreshən/ ▶ **noun 1** the quality of being careful not to reveal information or give offense. **2** the freedom to decide what should be done in a particular situation: *you will be offered bribes, which you may accept or decline at your discretion*.

– SYNONYMS **1 tact,** diplomacy, delicacy, sensitivity, good sense, prudence, circumspection. **2** *at the discretion of the council* **choice,** option, preference, disposition, pleasure, will, inclination.

– ORIGIN Latin, 'separation' (later 'discernment').

dis·cre·tion·ar·y /disˈkreshəˌnerē/ ▶ **adjective** done or used according to a person's judgment.

dis·crim·i·nate /disˈkriməˌnāt/ ▶ **verb 1** recognize a difference: *babies can discriminate between different facial expressions*. **2** treat different categories of people unfairly on the grounds of race, sex, or age.

– SYNONYMS **1 differentiate,** distinguish, draw a distinction, tell the difference, tell apart, separate. **2** *policies that* ***discriminate against*** *women* **be biased against,** be prejudiced against, treat differently, treat unfairly, put at a disadvantage, victimize, pick on.

– DERIVATIVES **dis·crim·i·na·tive** /disˈkriməˌnātiv/ adjective **dis·crim·i·na·tor** /disˈkriməˌnātər/ noun.
– ORIGIN Latin *discriminare*.

CHOOSE THE RIGHT WORD

See **DISTINGUISH**.

dis·crim·i·nat·ing /disˈkriməˌnātiNG/ ▶ **adjective** having or showing good taste or judgment.

– SYNONYMS **discerning,** perceptive, judicious, selective, tasteful, refined, sensitive, cultivated, cultured.
– ANTONYMS indiscriminate.

dis·crim·i·na·tion /disˌkriməˈnāshən/ ▶ **noun 1** unfair treatment of different categories of people on the grounds of race, sex, or age. **2** recognition of the difference between one thing and another. **3** good judgment or taste.

– SYNONYMS **1 prejudice,** bias, bigotry, intolerance, favoritism, partisanship. **2 discernment,** judgment, perceptiveness, (good) taste, refinement, sensitivity, cultivation.
– ANTONYMS impartiality.

dis·crim·i·na·to·ry /disˈkrimənəˌtôrē/ ▶ **adjective** showing discrimination or prejudice.

dis·cur·sive /disˈkərsiv/ ▶ **adjective 1** wandering from subject to subject. **2** relating to discourse.
– DERIVATIVES **dis·cur·sive·ly** adverb **dis·cur·sive·ness** noun.
– ORIGIN Latin *discursivus*.

dis·cus /ˈdiskəs/ ▶ **noun** (pl. **discuses**) a heavy disk thrown in athletic contests.
– ORIGIN Greek *diskos*.

dis·cuss /disˈkəs/ ▶ **verb 1** talk about something so as to reach a decision. **2** talk or write about a topic in detail.

– SYNONYMS **1 talk over,** talk about, talk through, debate, confer about. **2 examine,** explore, study, analyze, go into, deal with, consider, tackle.

– DERIVATIVES **dis·cuss·a·ble** adjective.
– ORIGIN Latin *discutere* 'dash to pieces, investigate.'

dis·cus·sant /disˈkəsənt/ ▶ **noun** a person who takes part in a discussion, especially a prearranged one.

dis·cus·sion /disˈkəsʜən/ ▶ **noun 1** the action of discussing something. **2** a debate about or a detailed written treatment of a topic.

– SYNONYMS **1 conversation,** talk, chat, dialogue, conference, debate, exchange of views, consultation, deliberation; informal confab. **2 examination,** exploration, study, analysis, treatment, consideration.

dis·cus·sion board ▶ **noun** Computing another term for **MESSAGE BOARD.**

dis·dain /disˈdān/ ▶ **noun** the feeling that someone or something does not deserve one's consideration or respect.

– SYNONYMS **contempt,** scorn, derision, disrespect, condescension, superciliousness, hauteur, haughtiness.
– ANTONYMS respect.

▶ **verb** consider to be unworthy of respect: *people disdained the go-getters of eighties Wall Street.*

– SYNONYMS **scorn,** deride, regard with contempt, sneer at, look down one's nose at, look down on, despise.

– ORIGIN Old French *desdeign*.

CHOOSE THE RIGHT WORD

See **DESPISE**.

dis·dain·ful /disˈdānfəl/ ▶ **adjective** showing contempt or lack of respect.
– DERIVATIVES **dis·dain·ful·ly** adverb.

dis·ease /diˈzēz/ ▶ **noun** a disorder in a human, animal, or plant, caused by infection, diet, or faulty functioning of a process.

– SYNONYMS **illness,** sickness, ill health, infection, ailment, malady, disorder, condition, problem; informal bug, virus.

– ORIGIN Old French *desaise* 'lack of ease.'

WORD LINKS

pathological *relating to disease*

dis·eased /diˈzēzd/ ▶ **adjective** suffering from disease.

– SYNONYMS **unhealthy,** ill, sick, unwell, ailing, infected, septic, rotten, bad.

dis·e·con·o·my /ˌdisiˈkänəmē/ ▶ **noun** (pl. **diseconomies**) an economic disadvantage such as an increase in cost arising from an increase in the size of an organization.

dis·em·bark /ˌdisemˈbärk/ ▶ **verb** leave a ship, aircraft, or train.
– DERIVATIVES **dis·em·bar·ka·tion** /disˌembärˈkāsʜən/ noun.

dis·em·bod·ied /ˌdisemˈbädēd/ ▶ **adjective 1** separated from or existing without the body. **2** (of a sound) coming from a person who cannot be seen.
– DERIVATIVES **dis·em·bod·i·ment** noun.

dis·em·bow·el /ˌdisemˈbouəl/ ▶ **verb** (**disembowels, disemboweling, disemboweled**) cut open and remove the internal organs of someone or something.
– DERIVATIVES **dis·em·bow·el·ment** noun.

dis·em·pow·er /ˌdisemˈpouər/ ▶ **verb** make someone less powerful or confident.
– DERIVATIVES **dis·em·pow·er·ment** noun.

dis·en·chant /ˌdisenˈcʜant/ ▶ **verb** make someone disillusioned.
– DERIVATIVES **dis·en·chant·ment** noun.

dis·en·fran·chise /ˌdisenˈfrancʜīz/ ▶ **verb** deprive someone of a right, especially the right to vote.
– DERIVATIVES **dis·en·fran·chise·ment** noun.

dis·en·gage /ˌdisenˈgāj/ ▶ **verb 1** release or detach: *he disengaged his arm from hers.* **2** remove troops from an area of conflict. **3** (as adj. **disengaged**) emotionally detached; uninvolved.
– DERIVATIVES **dis·en·gage·ment** noun.

dis·en·tan·gle /ˌdisenˈtaɴɢgəl/ ▶ **verb** free someone or something from something they are entangled with.

dis·e·qui·lib·ri·um /disˌēkwəˈlibrēəm/ ▶ **noun** a loss or lack of equilibrium or stability, especially in relation to supply, demand, and prices.

dis·es·tab·lish /ˌdisiˈstablisʜ/ ▶ **verb** deprive a national Church of its official status.
– DERIVATIVES **dis·es·tab·lish·ment** noun.

dis·es·teem /ˌdisiˈstēm/ ▶ **noun** lack of respect or admiration. ▶ **verb** formal have a low opinion of someone or something.

dis·fa·vor /disˈfāvər/ ▶ **noun 1** disapproval or dislike. **2** the state of being disliked.

dis·fig·ure /disˈfigyər/ ▶ **verb** spoil the appearance of someone or something.

– SYNONYMS **mar,** spoil, deface, scar, blemish, damage, mutilate, deform, maim, ruin; vandalize.
– ANTONYMS adorn.

– DERIVATIVES **dis·fig·u·ra·tion** /-ˌfigyəˈrāsʜən/ noun **dis·fig·ure·ment** noun.

dis·gorge /disˈgôrj/ ▶ **verb 1** pour out; discharge: *a bus disgorged a load of tourists.* **2** vomit food.
– ORIGIN Old French *desgorger*.

dis·grace /disˈgrās/ ▶ **noun 1** loss of the respect of others as the result of unacceptable behavior: *he left office in disgrace.* **2** a shamefully bad person or thing.

– SYNONYMS **1 dishonor,** shame, discredit, ignominy, disrepute, infamy, scandal, stigma, humiliation, loss of face. **2 scandal,** discredit, reproach, stain, blemish, blot, black mark, outrage, affront.
– ANTONYMS honor, credit.

▶ **verb** bring disgrace to someone or something.

– SYNONYMS **shame,** bring shame on, dishonor, discredit, stigmatize, taint, sully, tarnish, stain, blacken.
– ANTONYMS honor.

– ORIGIN Italian *disgrazia*.

dis·grace·ful /dis'grāsfəl/ ▶ **adjective** shockingly unacceptable.

– SYNONYMS **shameful,** scandalous, contemptible, dishonorable, discreditable, disreputable, reprehensible, blameworthy, unworthy, ignoble.
– ANTONYMS admirable.

– DERIVATIVES **dis·grace·ful·ly** adverb.

dis·grun·tled /dis'grəntld/ ▶ **adjective** angry or dissatisfied.

– SYNONYMS **dissatisfied,** discontented, fed up, put out, aggrieved, resentful, displeased, unhappy, disappointed, annoyed. informal sore, ticked off.
– ANTONYMS contented.

– DERIVATIVES **dis·grun·tle·ment** noun.
– ORIGIN from dialect *gruntle* 'utter little grunts, grumble.'

dis·guise /dis'gīz/ ▶ **verb 1** change the appearance or nature of someone or something so as to prevent recognition: *a reporter disguised himself as a delivery man.* **2** hide a feeling or situation.

– SYNONYMS **camouflage,** conceal, hide, cover up, mask, screen, veil, paper over.
– ANTONYMS expose.

▶ **noun 1** a means of concealing one's identity. **2** the state of being disguised: *the troops were rebels in disguise.*
– ORIGIN Old French *desguisier*.

dis·gust /dis'gəst/ ▶ **noun** revulsion or strong disapproval.

– SYNONYMS **revulsion,** repugnance, aversion, distaste, abhorrence, loathing, hatred.
– ANTONYMS delight.

▶ **verb** cause someone to feel revulsion or strong disapproval.

– SYNONYMS **revolt,** repel, repulse, sicken, nauseate, horrify, appal, shock, turn someone's stomach, scandalize, outrage, offend, affront; informal gross out.
– ANTONYMS delight.

– DERIVATIVES **dis·gust·ed** adjective **dis·gust·ed·ly** adverb.
– ORIGIN French *desgoust* or Italian *disgusto*.

dis·gust·ing /dis'gəstiNG/ ▶ **adjective** arousing revulsion or strong disapproval.

– SYNONYMS **1** *the food was disgusting* **revolting,** repulsive, sickening, nauseating, stomach-turning, off-putting. informal gross. **2** *I find racism disgusting* **outrageous,** objectionable, abhorrent, repellent, loathsome, offensive, appalling, shocking, horrifying, scandalous, monstrous, detestable; informal sick.
– ANTONYMS delightful.

– DERIVATIVES **dis·gust·ing·ly** adverb **dis·gust·ing·ness** noun.

dish /disH/ ▶ **noun 1** a shallow container for cooking or serving food. **2** a particular kind of food served as part of a meal: *Thai dishes.* **3** (**the dishes**) all the crockery and utensils used for a meal. **4** a shallow, concave container: *a soap dish.* **5** informal an attractive person.

– SYNONYMS **1 bowl,** plate, platter, salver, serving dish. **2 recipe,** meal, course, fare.

▶ **verb 1** (**dish something out/up**) put food on a plate or plates before a meal. **2** (**dish something out**) distribute in a casual or indiscriminate way: *the company dished out free tickets to all its employees.*

– SYNONYMS **distribute,** dispense, issue, hand out/around, give out, pass around, deal out, dole out, allocate.

– PHRASES **dish the dirt** informal reveal or spread scandal.
– ORIGIN Greek *diskos* 'discus.'

dis·har·mo·ny /dis'härmənē/ ▶ **noun** lack of harmony; disagreement or discord.
– DERIVATIVES **dis·har·mo·ni·ous** /-ˌhär'mōnēəs/ adjective.

dish·cloth /'disHˌklôTH/ (also **dishrag** /'disHˌrag/) ▶ **noun** a cloth for washing dishes.

dis·heart·en /dis'härtn/ ▶ **verb** make someone lose hope or confidence.

– SYNONYMS **discourage,** dispirit, demoralize, cast down, depress, disappoint, dismay, put off, deter, unnerve, daunt.
– ANTONYMS encourage.

– DERIVATIVES **dis·heart·en·ing** adjective.

di·shev·eled /di'sHevəld/ ▶ **adjective** (of a person's hair, clothes, or appearance) unkempt; disordered.

– SYNONYMS **untidy,** unkempt, scruffy, messy, disarranged, rumpled, bedraggled, tousled, tangled, windswept; informal mussed (up).
– ANTONYMS tidy.

– DERIVATIVES **di·shev·el·ment** noun.
– ORIGIN Old French *deschevele*.

dis·hon·est /dis'änist/ ▶ **adjective** not honest, trustworthy, or sincere.

– SYNONYMS **fraudulent,** cheating, underhanded/underhand, devious, treacherous, unfair, dirty, criminal, illegal, unlawful, false, untruthful, deceitful, lying, corrupt, dishonorable, untrustworthy, unscrupulous; informal crooked, shady, sharp.
– ANTONYMS honest.

– DERIVATIVES **dis·hon·est·ly** adverb **dis·hon·es·ty** noun (pl. **dishonesties**).

dis·hon·or /dis'änər/ (Brit. **dishonour**) ▶ **noun** a state of shame or disgrace. ▶ **verb 1** bring shame or disgrace to someone or something. **2** fail to honor an agreement or check.

dis·hon·or·a·ble /dis'änərəbəl/ ▶ **adjective** bringing shame or disgrace.

– SYNONYMS **disgraceful,** shameful, discreditable, ignoble, reprehensible, shabby, shoddy, despicable, contemptible, base, low.

– DERIVATIVES **dis·hon·or·ably** /-blē/ adverb.

dis·hon·or·a·ble dis·charge ▶ **noun** dismissal from the armed forces as a result of criminal or morally unacceptable actions.

dish tow·el ▶ **noun** a cloth for drying washed dishes, glasses, and utensils.

dish·wash·er /'disHˌwôsHər, -ˌwäsH-/ ▶ **noun** a machine for washing dishes automatically.

dish·wa·ter /'disHˌwôtər, -ˌwätər/ ▶ **noun 1** dirty water in which dishes have been washed. **2** insipid drink: *I sipped the barely brown dishwater he passed off as coffee.*

dish·y /'disHē/ ▶ **adjective** (**dishier, dishiest**) informal, chiefly Brit. sexually attractive.

dis·il·lu·sion /ˌdisə'lo͞ozHən/ ▶ **noun** disappointment from discovering that one's beliefs are mistaken or

unrealistic. ▶ verb make someone realize that a belief is mistaken or unrealistic.
– DERIVATIVES **dis·il·lu·sioned** adjective **dis·il·lu·sion·ment** /ˌdisəˈlo͞ozhənmənt/ noun.

dis·in·cen·tive /ˌdisinˈsentiv/ ▶ noun a factor that discourages a particular action: *falling house prices are a disincentive to development.*

dis·in·cli·na·tion /disˌinkləˈnāshən, disˌinGklə-/ ▶ noun a reluctance to do something.

dis·in·clined /ˌdisinˈklīnd/ ▶ adjective reluctant; unwilling.

dis·in·fect /ˌdisinˈfekt/ ▶ verb clean something with a disinfectant in order to destroy bacteria.
– DERIVATIVES **dis·in·fec·tion** /-ˈfekshən/ noun.

dis·in·fect·ant /ˌdisinˈfektənt/ ▶ noun a chemical liquid that destroys bacteria.

dis·in·for·ma·tion /disˌinfərˈmāshən/ ▶ noun information that is intended to mislead.

dis·in·gen·u·ous /ˌdisinˈjenyo͞oəs/ ▶ adjective not candid or sincere, especially in pretending ignorance about something.
– DERIVATIVES **dis·in·gen·u·ous·ly** adverb **dis·in·gen·u·ous·ness** noun.

dis·in·her·it /ˌdisinˈherit/ ▶ verb (**disinherits, disinheriting, disinherited**) prevent a person who was one's heir from inheriting one's property.

dis·in·te·grate /disˈintəˌgrāt/ ▶ verb **1** break up into small parts as a result of impact or decay. **2** become weaker or less united and gradually fail: *I'm afraid that our family is disintegrating.*

– SYNONYMS **break up,** crumble, break apart, fall apart, fall to pieces, collapse, fragment, shatter, splinter.

– DERIVATIVES **dis·in·te·gra·tion** /disˌintəˈgrāshən/ noun **dis·in·te·gra·tor** /-ˌgrātər/ noun.

dis·in·ter /ˌdisinˈtər/ ▶ verb (**disinters, disinterring, disinterred**) dig up something buried.

dis·in·ter·est /disˈint(ə)rist/ ▶ noun **1** the state of being impartial. **2** lack of interest.

dis·in·ter·est·ed /disˈintəˌrestid, -tristid/ ▶ adjective **1** not influenced by personal feelings; impartial. **2** not interested in someone or something.

– SYNONYMS **unbiased,** unprejudiced, impartial, neutral, detached, objective, dispassionate, nonpartisan.

– DERIVATIVES **dis·in·ter·est·ed·ly** adverb **dis·in·ter·est·ed·ness** noun.

USAGE

Strictly speaking, **disinterested** should only be used to mean 'impartial' (*the judgments of disinterested outsiders are likely to be more useful*) and should not be used to mean 'not interested' (in other words, the same as **uninterested**). The second meaning is very common, but should be avoided as it is not accepted by everyone.

dis·in·ter·me·di·a·tion /ˌdisintərˌmēdēˈāshən/ ▶ noun reduction in the use of intermediaries between producers and consumers, e.g., by investing directly in the securities market rather than through a bank.
– DERIVATIVES **dis·in·ter·me·di·ate** /-ˌintərˈmēdēāt/ verb.

dis·in·vest /ˌdisinˈvest/ ▶ verb withdraw or reduce an investment.
– DERIVATIVES **dis·in·vest·ment** noun.

dis·joint·ed /disˈjointid/ ▶ adjective not coherent or connected: *a disjointed, scrappy game.*

dis·junc·tion /disˈjəNGkshən/ ▶ noun a difference or lack of agreement between things expected to be similar.

dis·junc·tive /disˈjəNGktiv/ ▶ adjective lacking connection or consistency.

disk /disk/ (also **disc**) ▶ noun **1** a flat, thin, circular object. **2** an information storage device for a computer, on which data is stored either magnetically or optically. **3** (**disc**) a layer of cartilage separating vertebrae in the spine. **4** (**disc**) dated a phonograph record.
– ORIGIN Greek *diskos* 'discus.'

disk drive ▶ noun a device that allows a computer to read from and write to computer disks.

disk·ette /disˈket/ ▶ noun another term for **FLOPPY**.

disk jockey ▶ noun variant spelling of **DISC JOCKEY**.

dis·like /disˈlīk/ ▶ verb feel distaste for or hostility toward someone or something.

– SYNONYMS **find distasteful,** regard with distaste, be averse to, have an aversion to, disapprove of, object to, take exception to, have no taste for, hate, despise.
– ANTONYMS like.

▶ noun **1** a feeling of distaste or hostility. **2** a thing that is disliked.

– SYNONYMS **distaste,** aversion, disfavor, antipathy, disgust, abhorrence, hatred.
– ANTONYMS liking.

– DERIVATIVES **dis·lik·a·ble** (also **dislikeable**) adjective.

dis·lo·cate /disˈlōkāt, ˈdislōˌkāt/ ▶ verb **1** displace a bone from its proper position in a joint. **2** disrupt something.
– DERIVATIVES **dis·lo·ca·tion** /ˌdislōˈkāshən/ noun.

dis·lodge /disˈläj/ ▶ verb remove something from a fixed position.
– DERIVATIVES **dis·lodge·ment** noun.

dis·loy·al /disˈloiəl/ ▶ adjective not loyal or faithful to someone or something.

– SYNONYMS **unfaithful,** faithless, false, untrue, inconstant, two-faced, double-dealing, double-crossing, deceitful, treacherous, subversive, seditious, unpatriotic; informal backstabbing, two-timing; literary perfidious.

– DERIVATIVES **dis·loy·al·ly** adverb **dis·loy·al·ty** /-tē/ noun.

WORD TOOLKIT

See **UNFAITHFUL**.

dis·mal /ˈdizməl/ ▶ adjective **1** causing or showing gloom or depression. **2** informal disgracefully bad.

– SYNONYMS **1** *a dismal look* **gloomy,** glum, melancholy, morose, doleful, woebegone, forlorn, dejected, downcast. **2** *a dismal hall* **dim,** dingy, dark, gloomy, dreary, drab, dull.
– ANTONYMS cheerful, bright.

– DERIVATIVES **dis·mal·ly** adverb.
– ORIGIN from Latin *dies mali* 'evil days.'

WORD TOOLKIT

dismal ...	dreary ...	bleak ...
performance	existence	outlook
record	landscape	future
failure	weather	picture
year	lives	prospect
rating	months	period

dis·man·tle /disˈmantl/ ▶ verb take something to pieces.

– SYNONYMS **take apart,** take to pieces/bits, pull to pieces, disassemble, break up, strip (down).
– ANTONYMS build.

– DERIVATIVES **dis·man·tle·ment** noun **dis·man·tler** /-t(ə)lər/ noun.
– ORIGIN Old French *desmanteler*.

dis·mast /dis'mast/ ▶ **verb** break or force down the mast or masts of a ship.

dis·may /dis'mā/ ▶ **noun** concern and distress resulting from an unpleasant surprise.

– SYNONYMS **alarm,** distress, concern, surprise, consternation, disquiet.
– ANTONYMS pleasure, relief.

▶ **verb** make someone concerned and upset.

– SYNONYMS **concern,** distress, disturb, worry, alarm, disconcert, take aback, unnerve, unsettle.
– ANTONYMS encourage.

– ORIGIN Old French.

dis·mem·ber /dis'membər/ ▶ **verb 1** cut off the limbs of a person or animal. **2** divide up a territory or organization.
– DERIVATIVES **dis·mem·bered** adjective **dis·mem·ber·ment** noun.
– ORIGIN Old French *desmembrer*.

dis·miss /dis'mis/ ▶ **verb 1** order or allow someone to leave. **2** order an employee to leave a job. **3** treat as unworthy of serious consideration: *his comments were dismissed as a joke by the minister*. **4** refuse to allow a legal case to continue.

– SYNONYMS **1 give someone their notice,** discharge, lay off; informal sack, fire. **2 send away,** let go, release, disband, discharge. **3 banish,** set aside, put out of one's mind, brush aside, reject, repudiate, spurn; informal pooh-pooh.

– DERIVATIVES **dis·miss·a·ble** (also **dismissible**) adjective **dis·miss·al** noun.
– ORIGIN Latin *dimittere* 'send away.'

CHOOSE THE RIGHT WORD

See **EJECT**.

dis·mis·sive /dis'misiv/ ▶ **adjective** suggesting that something is unworthy of serious consideration.
– DERIVATIVES **dis·mis·sive·ly** adverb.

WORD TOOLKIT

dismissive ...	contemptuous ...	snide ...
attitude	look	remark
gesture	sneer	commentary
tone	disregard	innuendo
manner	smirk	sarcasm
shrug	glare	joke

dis·mount /dis'mount/ ▶ **verb** get off or down from a horse or bicycle.

dis·o·be·di·ent /ˌdisə'bēdēənt/ ▶ **adjective** failing or refusing to obey rules or someone in authority.

– SYNONYMS **naughty,** insubordinate, defiant, unruly, wayward, badly behaved, delinquent, rebellious, mutinous, troublesome, willful.
– ANTONYMS obedient.

– DERIVATIVES **dis·o·be·di·ence** noun **dis·o·be·di·ent·ly** adverb.

dis·o·bey /ˌdisə'bā/ ▶ **verb** fail or refuse to obey an order, rule, or person in authority.

– SYNONYMS **defy,** go against, flout, contravene, infringe, transgress, violate, disregard, ignore, pay no heed to.

dis·o·blig·ing /ˌdisə'blījiNG/ ▶ **adjective** unwilling to help or cooperate.

dis·or·der /dis'ôrdər/ ▶ **noun 1** a lack of order; confusion. **2** the breakdown of peaceful and law-abiding behavior. **3** an illness that disrupts normal physical or mental functions: *a skin disorder*.

– SYNONYMS **1 untidiness,** mess, disarray, chaos, confusion, clutter, jumble, a muddle, a shambles. **2 unrest,** disturbance, turmoil, mayhem, violence, fighting, fracas, rioting, lawlessness, anarchy, breach of the peace. **3 disease,** infection, complaint, condition, affliction, malady, sickness, illness, ailment.
– ANTONYMS tidiness, peace.

▶ **verb** (usu. as adj. **disordered**) bring disorder to: *a disordered room*.

dis·or·der·ly /dis'ôrdərlē/ ▶ **adjective 1** not organized or tidy. **2** involving a breakdown of peaceful and law-abiding behavior.

– SYNONYMS **1 untidy,** disorganized, topsy-turvy, at sixes and sevens, messy, jumbled, cluttered, in disarray, chaotic; informal like a bomb's hit it, higgledy-piggledy. **2 unruly,** riotous, disruptive, troublesome, disobedient, lawless.
– ANTONYMS tidy, peaceful.

– DERIVATIVES **dis·or·der·li·ness** noun.

WORD TOOLKIT

See **MESSY**.

dis·or·gan·ized /dis'ôrgəˌnīzd/ ▶ **adjective 1** not properly planned and controlled. **2** not able to plan one's activities efficiently.

– SYNONYMS **unmethodical,** unsystematic, undisciplined, unstructured, haphazard, chaotic, muddled, hit-or-miss, sloppy, slapdash, slipshod.
– ANTONYMS organized.

– DERIVATIVES **dis·or·gan·i·za·tion** /-ˌôrgənə'zāSHən/ noun.

dis·o·ri·ent /dis'ôrēˌent/ ▶ **verb** cause someone to lose their sense of direction or feel confused.
– DERIVATIVES **dis·o·ri·en·ta·tion** /disˌôrēən'tāSHən/ noun.

dis·o·ri·en·tate /dis'ôrēənˌtāt/ ▶ **verb** another term for **DISORIENT**.

dis·own /dis'ōn/ ▶ **verb** refuse to have anything further to do with someone.

– SYNONYMS **reject,** cast off/aside, abandon, renounce, repudiate, deny, turn one's back on, wash one's hands of, disinherit.

dis·par·age /di'sparij/ ▶ **verb** suggest that someone or something is worthless or unimportant.

– SYNONYMS **belittle,** denigrate, deprecate, play down, trivialize, ridicule, deride, mock, scorn, scoff at, sneer at, run down, defame, slur, discredit, speak badly of, cast aspersions on, impugn, vilify, traduce, criticize; informal pick holes in, knock, slam, pan, bad-mouth, pooh-pooh.
– ANTONYMS praise.

– DERIVATIVES **dis·par·age·ment** noun **dis·par·ag·ing** adjective.
– ORIGIN Old French *desparagier* 'marry someone of unequal rank.'

dis·pa·rate /ˈdisparit, diˈsparit/ ▶ **adjective 1** very different from one another: *no small feat, blending such disparate languages into one.* **2** containing elements very different from one another: *a culturally disparate country.*
– ORIGIN from Latin *disparare* 'to separate.'

dis·par·i·ty /diˈsparitē/ ▶ **noun** (pl. **disparities**) a great difference.

– SYNONYMS **discrepancy,** inconsistency, imbalance, variance, variation, divergence, gap, gulf, difference, dissimilarity, contrast.
– ANTONYMS similarity.

dis·pas·sion·ate /disˈpasʜənit/ ▶ **adjective** not influenced by strong emotion; rational and impartial.
– DERIVATIVES **dis·pas·sion** noun **dis·pas·sion·ate·ly** adverb.

dis·patch /disˈpacʜ/ ▶ **verb 1** send someone or something to a destination or for a purpose. **2** deal with a task or opponent quickly and efficiently. **3** kill someone or something.

– SYNONYMS **1 send (off),** post, mail, forward. **2 deal with,** finish, conclude, settle, discharge, perform. **3 kill,** put to death, massacre, wipe out, exterminate, eliminate, murder, assassinate, execute.

▶ **noun 1** the action of dispatching someone or something. **2** an official report on government or military affairs. **3** a report sent to a newspaper by a journalist working abroad. **4** promptness and efficiency: *officials believed the problem would be resolved with dispatch.*

– SYNONYMS **message,** report, communication, communiqué, bulletin, statement, letter, news, intelligence.

– DERIVATIVES **dis·patch·er** noun.
– ORIGIN Italian *dispacciare* or Spanish *despachar* 'expedite.'

dis·pel /disˈpel/ ▶ **verb** (**dispels, dispelling, dispelled**) make a doubt, feeling, or belief disappear.

– SYNONYMS **banish,** drive away/off, chase away, scatter, eliminate, dismiss, allay, ease, quell.

– ORIGIN Latin *dispellere* 'drive apart.'

CHOOSE THE RIGHT WORD

See **SCATTER**.

dis·pen·sa·ble /disˈpensəbəl/ ▶ **adjective** able to be replaced or done without.

dis·pen·sa·ry /disˈpensərē/ ▶ **noun** (pl. **dispensaries**) a room where medicines are prepared and provided.

dis·pen·sa·tion /ˌdispənˈsāsʜən, -pen-/ ▶ **noun 1** permission to be exempt from a rule or usual requirement. **2** the religious or political system of a particular time: *the capitalist dispensation.* **3** the action of dispensing something.
– DERIVATIVES **dis·pen·sa·tion·al** adjective.

dis·pense /disˈpens/ ▶ **verb 1** distribute or supply something to a number of people. **2** (of a pharmacist) supply medicine according to a doctor's prescription. **3** (**dispense with**) get rid of or manage without: *we intend to dispense with a central heating system.*

– SYNONYMS **1 distribute,** pass around, hand out, dole out, dish out, share out. **2 administer,** deliver, issue, deal out, mete out. **3** *dispensing medicines* **prepare,** make up, supply, provide. **4** (**dispense with**) **waive,** omit, drop, leave out, forgo, do away with; informal give something a miss. **5** (**dispense with**) **get rid of,** throw away/out, dispose of, discard; informal ditch, scrap, dump.

– DERIVATIVES **dis·pens·er** noun.
– ORIGIN Latin *dispensare* 'continue to weigh out.'

dis·per·sal /disˈpərsəl/ ▶ **noun 1** the spreading of things or people over a wide area. **2** the action of causing a group to go in different directions.

dis·per·sant /disˈpərsənt/ ▶ **noun** a liquid or gas used to disperse small particles in a medium.

dis·perse /disˈpərs/ ▶ **verb 1** spread something over a wide area. **2** go in different directions: *the crowd dispersed.* **3** Physics divide light into constituents of different wavelengths.

– SYNONYMS **1 break up,** split up, disband, scatter, leave, go their separate ways, drive away/off, chase away. **2 dissipate,** dissolve, melt away, fade away, clear, lift. **3 scatter,** distribute, spread, disseminate.
– ANTONYMS assemble, gather.

– DERIVATIVES **dis·pers·er** noun **dis·pers·i·ble** adjective **dis·per·sive** adjective.
– ORIGIN Latin *dispergere* 'scatter widely.'

CHOOSE THE RIGHT WORD

See **SCATTER**.

dis·per·sion /disˈpərzʜən, -sʜən/ ▶ **noun** the action of dispersing people or things or the state of being dispersed.

dis·pir·it /diˈspirit/ ▶ **verb** cause someone to lose enthusiasm or hope.
– DERIVATIVES **dis·pir·it·ed·ly** adverb **dis·pir·it·ing** adjective.

dis·place /disˈplās/ ▶ **verb 1** move something from its proper or usual position. **2** take over the position or role of: *drama, having been displaced by soap operas a couple of years ago, is back.* **3** (especially of war or natural disaster) force someone to leave their home.

– SYNONYMS **1 dislodge,** dislocate, move out of place/position, shift. **2 replace,** take the place of, supplant, supersede, oust, remove, depose.

CHOOSE THE RIGHT WORD

See **REPLACE**.

dis·placed per·son ▶ **noun** a person who is forced to leave their home country because of war, persecution, or natural disaster; a refugee.

dis·place·ment /disˈplāsmənt/ ▶ **noun 1** the action of displacing someone or something. **2** the amount by which something is moved from its position. **3** the volume or weight of water displaced by a floating ship, used as a measure of the ship's size.

dis·play /disˈplā/ ▶ **verb 1** put something on show in a noticeable and attractive way. **2** clearly show a quality, emotion, or skill. **3** show data or an image on a screen.

– SYNONYMS **1 exhibit,** show, arrange, array, present, lay out, set out. **2 show off,** parade, highlight, reveal, showcase. **3 manifest,** be evidence of, reveal, demonstrate, show.
– ANTONYMS conceal.

▶ **noun 1** a show or other event for public entertainment. **2** an act of showing something: *a public display of affection.* **3** objects, data, or images that are displayed. **4** an electronic device for displaying data.

– SYNONYMS **1 exhibition,** exposition, array, arrangement, presentation, demonstration, spectacle, show, parade. **2 manifestation,** expression, show, proof, demonstration, evidence.

– ORIGIN Latin *displicare* 'scatter, disperse.'

dis·please /dis'plēz/ ▶ **verb** annoy or upset someone.

– SYNONYMS **annoy,** irritate, anger, incense, irk, vex, nettle, put out, upset, exasperate.

– DERIVATIVES **dis·pleased** adjective **dis·pleas·ing** adjective.

dis·pleas·ure /dis'plezhər/ ▶ **noun** a feeling of annoyance or dissatisfaction.

dis·port /dis'pôrt/ ▶ **verb** (**disport oneself**) old use enjoy oneself unrestrainedly; frolic.

– ORIGIN Old French *desporter* 'carry away.'

dis·pos·a·ble /dis'pōzəbəl/ ▶ **adjective 1** (of an article) intended to be used once and then thrown away. **2** (of financial assets) available to be used when required. ▶ **noun** a disposable article.

– DERIVATIVES **dis·pos·a·bil·i·ty** /-ˌpōzə'bilitē/ noun.

dis·pos·a·ble in·come ▶ **noun** income remaining after deduction of taxes and other compulsory charges, available to be spent or saved as one wishes.

dis·pos·al /dis'pōzəl/ ▶ **noun** the action of disposing or getting rid of something.

– PHRASES **at one's disposal** available for one to use whenever or however one wishes.

dis·pose /dis'pōz/ ▶ **verb 1** (**dispose of**) get rid of something by throwing it away or by giving or selling it to someone. **2** (**dispose of**) overcome a rival, problem, or threat. **3** (usu. **be disposed to**) make someone likely to do or think something: *I am not disposed to argue about it.* **4** (as adj. **disposed**) having a specified attitude: *he was never favorably disposed toward the proposals.* **5** arrange people or things in a particular way.

– SYNONYMS (**dispose of**) **throw away,** throw out, get rid of, discard, jettison, scrap; informal dump, trash, junk, ditch.

– DERIVATIVES **dis·pos·er** noun.

– ORIGIN Latin *disponere* 'arrange.'

dis·po·si·tion /ˌdispə'zishən/ ▶ **noun 1** a person's natural qualities of mind and character. **2** an inclination or tendency to do something. **3** the way in which people or things are arranged.

– SYNONYMS **1 temperament,** nature, character, constitution, makeup, mentality. **2 arrangement,** positioning, placement, configuration, setup, lineup, layout.

dis·pos·sess /ˌdispə'zes/ ▶ **verb** deprive someone of land or property.

– DERIVATIVES **dis·pos·ses·sion** noun.

dis·proof /dis'pro͞of/ ▶ **noun** evidence that something is untrue.

dis·pro·por·tion /ˌdisprə'pôrshən/ ▶ **noun** a state of inequality between two things.

– DERIVATIVES **dis·pro·por·tion·al** adjective **dis·pro·por·tion·al·ly** adverb.

dis·pro·por·tion·ate /ˌdisprə'pôrshənit/ ▶ **adjective** too large or too small in comparison with something else.

– DERIVATIVES **dis·pro·por·tion·ate·ly** adverb.

dis·prove /dis'pro͞ov/ ▶ **verb** prove that something is false.

– SYNONYMS **refute,** prove false, rebut, debunk, demolish; informal shoot full of holes, blow out of the water.

dis·put·a·ble /dis'pyo͞otəbəl/ ▶ **adjective** open to question.

dis·pu·ta·tion /ˌdispyo͞o'tāshən/ ▶ **noun** debate or argument.

dis·pu·ta·tious /ˌdispyo͞o'tāshəs/ ▶ **adjective** fond of having arguments.

dis·pute /dis'pyo͞ot/ ▶ **verb 1** argue about something. **2** question whether a statement or fact is true or valid. **3** compete for: *the two drivers crashed while disputing the lead.*

– SYNONYMS **1 debate,** discuss, exchange views, quarrel, argue, disagree, clash, fall out, wrangle, bicker, squabble. **2 challenge,** contest, question, call into question, quibble over, contradict, argue about, disagree with, take issue with.
– ANTONYMS accept.

▶ **noun 1** an argument or disagreement. **2** a disagreement between management and employees that leads to industrial action.

– SYNONYMS **1 debate,** discussion, argument, controversy, disagreement, dissent, conflict. **2 quarrel,** argument, altercation, squabble, falling-out, disagreement, difference of opinion, clash.
– ANTONYMS agreement.

– DERIVATIVES **dis·pu·tant** /-'pyo͞otnt/ noun.

– ORIGIN Latin *disputare* 'to estimate.'

dis·qual·i·fy /dis'kwäləˌfī/ ▶ **verb** (**disqualifies, disqualifying, disqualified**) prevent someone from performing an activity or taking up a job because they have broken a law or rule or are unsuitable: *he was disqualified from being a company director.*

– SYNONYMS **rule out,** bar, exclude, prohibit, debar, preclude.

– DERIVATIVES **dis·qual·i·fi·ca·tion** /disˌkwäləfi'kāshən/ noun.

dis·qui·et /dis'kwī-it/ ▶ **noun** a feeling of worry or unease. ▶ **verb** make someone worried or uneasy.

– DERIVATIVES **dis·qui·et·ing** adjective **dis·qui·e·tude** /dis'kwī-iˌt(y)o͞od/ noun.

dis·qui·si·tion /ˌdiskwə'zishən/ ▶ **noun** a long or complex discussion of a topic in speech or writing.

– ORIGIN Latin, 'investigation.'

dis·re·gard /ˌdisri'gärd/ ▶ **verb** fail to consider or pay attention to someone or something.

– SYNONYMS **ignore,** take no notice of, pay no attention to, discount, overlook, turn a blind eye to, shut one's eyes to, gloss over, brush off/aside, shrug off.
– ANTONYMS heed.

▶ **noun** lack of attention or consideration: *they have shown utter disregard for customers.*

– SYNONYMS **indifference,** nonobservance, inattention, heedlessness, neglect, contempt.
– ANTONYMS attention.

CHOOSE THE RIGHT WORD

See **NEGLECT**.

dis·re·pair /ˌdisri'pe(ə)r/ ▶ **noun** poor condition due to neglect.

dis·rep·u·ta·ble /dis'repyətəbəl/ ▶ **adjective** not respectable in appearance or character.

– SYNONYMS **bad,** unwholesome, villainous, unsavory, slippery, seedy, sleazy; informal crooked, shady, shifty.
– ANTONYMS respectable.

dis·re·pute /ˌdisrəˈpyo͞ot/ ▸ **noun** the state of having a bad reputation: *he was accused of bringing football into disrepute*.

dis·re·spect /ˌdisriˈspekt/ ▸ **noun** lack of respect or courtesy. ▸ **verb** informal show a lack of respect for someone or something.
– DERIVATIVES **dis·re·spect·ful** adjective **dis·re·spect·ful·ly** adverb.

dis·robe /disˈrōb/ ▸ **verb** take off one's clothes.

dis·rupt /disˈrəpt/ ▸ **verb** interrupt the normal operation of an activity or process.

> – SYNONYMS **interrupt,** disturb, interfere with, play havoc with, upset, unsettle, obstruct, impede, hold up, delay.

– DERIVATIVES **dis·rupt·er** (also **disruptor**) noun **dis·rup·tion** /-ˈrəpsʜən/ noun.
– ORIGIN Latin *disrumpere* 'break apart.'

dis·rup·tive /disˈrəptiv/ ▸ **adjective** disturbing or interrupting the normal operation of something.

> – SYNONYMS **troublesome,** disturbing, upsetting, unsettling, unruly, badly behaved, rowdy, disorderly, undisciplined, unmanageable, uncontrollable, uncooperative.
> – ANTONYMS well behaved.

diss ▸ **verb** variant spelling of **DIS**.

dis·sat·is·fac·tion /disˌsatisˈfaksʜən/ ▸ **noun** lack of satisfaction.

dis·sat·is·fied /disˈsatisˌfīd/ ▸ **adjective** not content or happy.

> – SYNONYMS **discontented,** disappointed, disaffected, displeased, disgruntled, aggrieved, unhappy.
> – ANTONYMS contented.

dis·sect /diˈsekt, dī-/ ▸ **verb 1** methodically cut up a body or plant in order to study its internal parts. **2** analyze something in great detail. **3** (as adj. **dissected**) technical divided into separate parts.
– DERIVATIVES **dis·sec·tion** noun **dis·sec·tor** noun.
– ORIGIN Latin *dissecare* 'cut up.'

dis·sem·ble /diˈsembəl/ ▸ **verb** hide or disguise one's true motives or feelings.
– DERIVATIVES **dis·sem·bler** noun.
– ORIGIN Latin *dissimulare* 'disguise, conceal.'

dis·sem·i·nate /diˈseməˌnāt/ ▸ **verb** spread something, especially information, widely.
– DERIVATIVES **dis·sem·i·na·tion** /-ˌseməˈnāsʜən/ noun **dis·sem·i·na·tor** noun.
– ORIGIN Latin *disseminare* 'scatter.'

> **CHOOSE THE RIGHT WORD**
>
> See **SCATTER**.

dis·sen·sion /diˈsensʜən/ ▸ **noun** disagreement that causes trouble within a group.
– ORIGIN from Latin *dissentire* 'differ in sentiment.'

dis·sent /diˈsent/ ▸ **verb 1** express disagreement with an official or widely held view. **2** disagree with the doctrine of an established or orthodox church.

> – SYNONYMS **disagree,** differ, demur, be at variance/odds, take issue, protest, object.
> – ANTONYMS agree, conform.

▸ **noun** disagreement with an official or widely held view.

> – SYNONYMS **disagreement,** difference of opinion, argument, dispute, resistance, objection, protest, opposition.
> – ANTONYMS agreement, conformity.

– ORIGIN Latin *dissentire* 'differ in sentiment.'

dis·sent·er /diˈsentər/ ▸ **noun 1** a person who disagrees with a widely held view. **2** (**Dissenter**) Brit. historical a member of a nonestablished Church; a Nonconformist.

dis·ser·ta·tion /ˌdisərˈtāsʜən/ ▸ **noun** a long essay, especially one written for a university degree.
– ORIGIN from Latin *dissertare* 'continue to discuss.'

dis·serv·ice /disˈsərvis/ ▸ **noun** a harmful action.

dis·si·dent /ˈdisidənt/ ▸ **noun** a person who opposes official policy.

> – SYNONYMS **dissenter,** objector, protester, rebel, revolutionary, subversive, agitator, refusenik.
> – ANTONYMS conformist.

▸ **adjective** opposing official policy.

> – SYNONYMS **dissenting,** opposing, objecting, protesting, rebellious, revolutionary, subversive, nonconformist.
> – ANTONYMS conformist.

– DERIVATIVES **dis·si·dence** /ˈdisidəns/ noun.
– ORIGIN from Latin *dissidere* 'sit apart, disagree.'

dis·sim·i·lar /disˈsimilər/ ▸ **adjective** not similar; different: *two seemingly dissimilar ideas*.

> – SYNONYMS **different,** differing, unalike, variant, diverse, divergent, heterogeneous, disparate, unrelated, distinct, contrasting.

– DERIVATIVES **dis·sim·i·lar·i·ty** /-ˌsiməˈlaritē/ noun.

> **WORD TOOLKIT**
>
> See **DIVERGENT**.

dis·sim·u·late /diˈsimyəˌlāt/ ▸ **verb** hide or disguise one's thoughts or feelings.
– DERIVATIVES **dis·sim·u·la·tion** /-ˌsimyəˈlāsʜən/ noun.
– ORIGIN Latin *dissimulare* 'to conceal.'

dis·si·pate /ˈdisəˌpāt/ ▸ **verb 1** disperse or disappear: *his anger seemed to dissipate*. **2** waste money, energy, or resources.
– DERIVATIVES **dis·si·pa·tive** /-ˌpātiv/ adjective **dis·si·pa·tor** noun.
– ORIGIN Latin *dissipare* 'scatter.'

> **CHOOSE THE RIGHT WORD**
>
> See **SCATTER**.

dis·si·pat·ed /ˈdisəˌpātid/ ▸ **adjective** indulging excessively in sex, drinking alcohol, and similar activities.

dis·si·pa·tion /ˌdisəˈpāsʜən/ ▸ **noun 1** dissipated living. **2** the action of dissipating something.

dis·so·ci·ate /diˈsōsʜēˌāt, -ˈsōsē-/ ▸ **verb 1** disconnect or separate something from something else. **2** (**dissociate oneself from**) declare that one is not connected with someone or something.

> – SYNONYMS **separate,** detach, disconnect, sever, cut off, divorce, isolate, alienate.
> – ANTONYMS associate.

– DERIVATIVES **dis·so·ci·a·tion** /diˌsōsēˈāsʜən/ noun **dis·so·ci·a·tive** /-ˌātiv, -sʜətiv/ adjective.
– ORIGIN Latin *dissociare* 'separate.'

dis·sol·u·ble /di'sälyəbəl/ ▶ **adjective** able to be dissolved, loosened, or disconnected.

dis·so·lute /'disə,lo͞ot/ ▶ **adjective** indulging in immoral activities.
– ORIGIN Latin *dissolutus* 'disconnected, loose.'

dis·so·lu·tion /,disə'lo͞osʜən/ ▶ **noun 1** the formal closing down or ending of an official body or agreement. **2** the action of dissolving or decomposing. **3** immoral living.

dis·solve /di'zälv/ ▶ **verb 1** (of a solid) disperse into a liquid so as to form a solution. **2** close down, dismiss, or end an assembly or agreement. **3** (**dissolve into/in**) give way to strong emotion.

> – SYNONYMS **1 break down,** liquefy, melt, deliquesce, disintegrate. **2 disband,** disperse, bring to an end, end, terminate, discontinue, break up, close down, wind up/down, suspend, adjourn. **3 annul,** nullify, void, invalidate, revoke.

– DERIVATIVES **dis·solv·a·ble** adjective.
– ORIGIN Latin *dissolvere.*

dis·so·nant /'disənənt/ ▶ **adjective** lacking harmony; discordant.

> – SYNONYMS **inharmonious,** discordant, unmelodious, atonal, off-key, cacophonous.
> – ANTONYMS harmonious.

– DERIVATIVES **dis·so·nance** noun.
– ORIGIN from Latin *dissonare* 'be discordant.'

dis·suade /di'swād/ ▶ **verb** (**dissuade someone from**) persuade or advise someone not to do something.

> – SYNONYMS **discourage,** deter, prevent, stop, talk out of, persuade against, advise against, argue out of.
> – ANTONYMS encourage.

– DERIVATIVES **dis·sua·sion** /-'swāzʜən/ noun **dis·sua·sive** /-'swāsiv/ adjective.
– ORIGIN Latin *dissuadere.*

dis·taff /'distaf/ ▶ **noun** a stick or spindle onto which wool or flax is wound for spinning.
– PHRASES **the distaff side** the female side of a family.
– ORIGIN Old English.

dis·tal /'distl/ ▶ **adjective** chiefly Anatomy situated away from the center of the body or from the point of attachment. The opposite of **PROXIMAL**.
– DERIVATIVES **dis·tal·ly** adverb.
– ORIGIN from **DISTANT**.

dis·tance /'distəns/ ▶ **noun 1** the length of the space between two points. **2** the state of being distant or remote: *they are separated by decades and by distance.* **3** a far-off point or place. **4** an interval of time. **5** the full length or time of a race or other contest.

> – SYNONYMS **1 interval,** space, span, gap, extent, length, range, reach. **2 aloofness,** remoteness, detachment, unfriendliness, reserve, reticence, formality; informal standoffishness.
> – ANTONYMS proximity.

▶ **verb 1** make someone or something far off or remote. **2** (**distance oneself from**) declare that one is not connected with someone or something.
– ORIGIN Latin *distantia.*

dis·tance learn·ing ▶ **noun** a method of studying in which lectures are broadcast and lessons are conducted by correspondence or over the Internet.

dis·tant /'distənt/ ▶ **adjective 1** far away in space or time. **2** at a specified distance: *the town lay half a mile distant.* **3** far apart in resemblance or relationship: *a distant acquaintance.* **4** aloof or reserved.

> – SYNONYMS **1 faraway,** far-off, far-flung, remote, out of the way, outlying. **2 bygone,** remote, ancient, prehistoric. **3 vague,** faint, dim, indistinct, sketchy, hazy. **4 aloof,** reserved, remote, detached, unapproachable, unfriendly; informal standoffish. **5 distracted,** absent, faraway, detached, vague.
> – ANTONYMS near, close, recent.

– DERIVATIVES **dis·tant·ly** adverb.

dis·taste /dis'tāst/ ▶ **noun** dislike or mild hostility.

dis·taste·ful /dis'tāst,fəl/ ▶ **adjective** unpleasant or disagreeable.

> – SYNONYMS **unpleasant,** disagreeable, displeasing, undesirable, objectionable, offensive, unsavory, unpalatable.
> – ANTONYMS agreeable.

– DERIVATIVES **dis·taste·ful·ly** adverb **dis·taste·ful·ness** noun.

dis·tem·per /dis'tempər/ ▶ **noun 1** a kind of paint made of powdered pigment mixed with glue or size, used on walls. **2** a disease affecting dogs, causing fever and coughing. ▶ **verb** paint something with distemper.
– ORIGIN from Latin *distemperare* 'soak, mix in the wrong proportions.'

dis·tend /dis'tend/ ▶ **verb** swell because of internal pressure.
– DERIVATIVES **dis·tend·ed** adjective **dis·ten·si·bil·i·ty** /-,tensə'bilitē/ noun **dis·ten·si·ble** /-'tensəbəl/ adjective **dis·ten·sion** /-'tensʜən/ noun.
– ORIGIN Latin *distendere.*

dis·till /dis'til/ (Brit. **distil**) ▶ **verb 1** purify a liquid by heating it so that it vaporizes, then cooling and condensing the vapor and collecting the resulting liquid. **2** make liquor by distilling. **3** extract the most important aspects of: *he distilled their comments into two-page summaries.*
– DERIVATIVES **dis·til·la·tion** /,distə'lāsʜən/ noun **dis·till·er** noun.
– ORIGIN Latin *distillare.*

dis·til·late /'distilit, -,lāt/ ▶ **noun** a substance formed by distillation.

dis·till·er·y /dis'tilərē/ ▶ **noun** (pl. **distilleries**) a place where liquor is manufactured.

dis·tinct /dis'tiɴɢkt/ ▶ **adjective 1** recognizably different. **2** able to be perceived clearly by the senses: *a distinct smell of vinegar.*

> – SYNONYMS **1** *two distinct categories* **discrete,** separate, different, unconnected, distinctive, contrasting. **2** *the tail has distinct black tips* **clear,** well defined, unmistakable, easily distinguishable, recognizable, visible, obvious, pronounced, prominent, striking.
> – ANTONYMS similar.

– DERIVATIVES **dis·tinct·ly** adverb **dis·tinct·ness** noun.
– ORIGIN Latin *distinctus.*

dis·tinc·tion /dis'tiɴɢksʜən/ ▶ **noun 1** a noticeable difference or contrast. **2** the separation of people or things into different groups. **3** outstanding excellence. **4** a special honor or recognition.

> – SYNONYMS **1 difference,** contrast, variation, division, differentiation, discrepancy. **2 merit,** worth, greatness, excellence, quality, repute, renown, honor, credit.
> – ANTONYMS similarity.

dis·tinc·tive /dis'tiNGktiv/ ▶ **adjective** characteristic of a person or thing, so making it different from others: *a coffee with a distinctive caramel flavor.*

– SYNONYMS **distinguishing,** characteristic, typical, individual, particular, peculiar, unique, exclusive, special.
– ANTONYMS common.

– DERIVATIVES **dis·tinc·tive·ly** adverb **dis·tinc·tive·ness** noun.

dis·tin·guish /dis'tiNGgwisH/ ▶ **verb 1** recognize or treat someone or something as different. **2** manage to see or hear something barely perceptible. **3** be a distinctive characteristic of: *what distinguishes sports from games?* **4** (**distinguish oneself**) do something very well.

– SYNONYMS **1 differentiate,** tell apart, discriminate between, tell the difference between. **2 discern,** see, perceive, make out, detect, recognize, identify. **3 separate,** set apart, make distinctive, make different, single out, mark off.

– DERIVATIVES **dis·tin·guish·a·ble** adjective.
– ORIGIN Latin *distinguere.*

CHOOSE THE RIGHT WORD

distinguish, descry, differentiate, discern, discriminate

What we **discern** we see apart from all other objects (*to discern the lighthouse beaming on the far shore*). **Descry** puts even more emphasis on the distant or unclear nature of what we're seeing (*the lookout was barely able to descry a man approaching in the dusk*). To **discriminate** is to perceive the differences between or among things that are very similar; it may suggest that some aesthetic evaluation is involved (*to discriminate between two painters' styles*). **Distinguish** requires making even finer distinctions among things that resemble each other even more closely (*unable to distinguish the shadowy figures moving through the forest*). *Distinguish* can also mean recognizing by some special mark or outward sign (*the sheriff could be distinguished by his silver badge*). **Differentiate**, on the other hand, suggests the ability to perceive differences between things that are easily confused. In contrast to *distinguish, differentiate* suggests subtle differences that must be compared in some detail (*the color of her dress was difficult to differentiate from the color of the chair in which she was seated; it took a sharp eye to distinguish where her skirt ended and the upholstery began*). If you have trouble *differentiating* among these closely related verbs, you're not alone.

dis·tin·guished /dis'tiNGgwisHt/ ▶ **adjective 1** very successful and greatly respected. **2** dignified in appearance.

– SYNONYMS **eminent,** famous, renowned, prominent, well known, great, esteemed, respected, notable, illustrious, acclaimed, celebrated.
– ANTONYMS unknown, obscure.

dis·tort /dis'tôrt/ ▶ **verb 1** pull or twist something out of shape. **2** give a misleading account of something. **3** change the form of an electrical signal or sound wave during transmission or amplification.

– SYNONYMS **1** (as adj. **distorted**) *his face was distorted with rage* **twisted,** warped, contorted, buckled, deformed, malformed, misshapen, disfigured, crooked, out of shape. **2** (as adj. **distorted**) *his report gives a distorted view of the meeting* **misrepresented,** perverted, twisted, falsified, misreported, misstated, garbled, inaccurate, biased, prejudiced.

– DERIVATIVES **dis·tort·ed** adjective **dis·tor·tion** /-'tôrsHən/ noun.
– ORIGIN Latin *distorquere* 'twist apart.'

dis·tract /dis'trakt/ ▶ **verb 1** prevent someone from concentrating on something. **2** divert attention from something.

– SYNONYMS **divert,** sidetrack, draw away, lead astray, disturb, put off.

– DERIVATIVES **dis·tract·ing** adjective.
– ORIGIN Latin *distrahere* 'draw apart.'

dis·tract·ed /dis'traktəd/ ▶ **adjective** unable to concentrate.

– SYNONYMS **preoccupied,** inattentive, vague, abstracted, absentminded, faraway, in a world of one's own, troubled, harassed, worried; informal miles away, not with it.
– ANTONYMS attentive.

dis·trac·tion /dis'traksHən/ ▶ **noun 1** a thing that distracts someone's attention. **2** an activity that provides entertainment. **3** mental agitation: *he loved her to distraction.*

– SYNONYMS **1 diversion,** interruption, disturbance, interference. **2 amusement,** entertainment, diversion, recreation, pastime, leisure pursuit.

dis·trait /dis'trā/ ▶ **adjective** distracted; absentminded.
– ORIGIN French.

dis·traught /dis'trôt/ ▶ **adjective** very worried and upset.

– SYNONYMS **distressed,** frantic, fraught, overcome, overwrought, beside oneself, out of one's mind, desperate, hysterical, worked up, at one's wits' end; informal in a state.
– ANTONYMS calm.

– ORIGIN Latin *distractus* 'pulled apart.'

dis·tress /dis'tres/ ▶ **noun 1** great anxiety, sorrow, or difficulty. **2** the state of a ship or aircraft when in danger or difficulty. **3** a state of physical strain, especially difficulty in breathing.

– SYNONYMS **1 anguish,** suffering, pain, agony, torment, heartache, heartbreak, sorrow, sadness, unhappiness. **2** *a ship in distress* **danger,** peril, difficulty, trouble, jeopardy, risk.
– ANTONYMS happiness.

▶ **verb 1** make someone very worried or upset. **2** give furniture or clothing artificial marks of age and wear.

– SYNONYMS **upset,** pain, trouble, worry, perturb, disturb, disquiet, agitate, torment.
– ANTONYMS comfort.

– DERIVATIVES **dis·tressed** adjective **dis·tress·ful** adjective **dis·tress·ing** adjective.
– ORIGIN Old French *destresce.*

dis·trib·u·tar·y /dis'tribyo͝o͝ˌterē/ ▶ **noun** (pl. **distributaries**) a branch of a river that does not return to the main stream after leaving it, as in a delta.

dis·trib·ute /dis'tribyo͞ot/ ▶ **verb 1** hand out or give shares of something to a number of people. **2** (**be distributed**) be spread over an area. **3** supply goods to retailers.

– SYNONYMS **1 give out,** deal out, pass out/around, dole out, dish out, hand out/around, share out, divide out/up, parcel out, apportion, allocate, allot. **2** *the newsletter is distributed free* **circulate,** issue, deliver, disseminate, publish.
– ANTONYMS collect.

– DERIVATIVES **dis·trib·ut·a·ble** adjective.
– ORIGIN Latin *distribuere* 'divide up.'

dis·tri·bu·tion /ˌdistrəˈbyo͞osʜən/ ▶ noun **1** the action of distributing something. **2** the way in which something is shared among a group or spread over an area: *the uneven distribution of wealth.*

– SYNONYMS **1** *the distribution of aid* **giving out,** dealing out, doling out, handing out/around, issuing, allocation, sharing out, dividing up/out, parceling out. **2** *centers of food distribution* **supply,** delivery, dispersal, transportation.

– DERIVATIVES **dis·tri·bu·tion·al** adjective.

dis·tri·bu·tive /disˈtribyətiv/ ▶ adjective relating to distribution or things that are distributed.

dis·trib·u·tor /disˈtribyətər/ ▶ noun **1** an agent who supplies goods to retailers. **2** a device in a gasoline engine for passing electric current to each spark plug in turn.

dis·trict /ˈdistrikt/ ▶ noun an area of a town or region, regarded as a unit for administrative purposes or because of a particular feature: *the central business district.*

– SYNONYMS **area,** region, quarter, sector, zone, territory, locality, neighborhood, community.

▶ verb divide into districts.
– ORIGIN Latin *districtus* '(territory of) jurisdiction.'

dis·trict at·tor·ney ▶ noun a public official who acts as prosecutor for the government in a particular district.

dis·tro /ˈdistrō/ ▶ noun Computing **1** a distribution, especially of Linux software or of webzines. **2** a particular distributable or distributed version of Linux software.

dis·trust /disˈtrəst/ ▶ noun the feeling that someone or something cannot be relied on.

– SYNONYMS **mistrust,** suspicion, wariness, skepticism, doubt, cynicism, misgivings, qualms.
– ANTONYMS trust.

▶ verb have little trust in someone or something.

– SYNONYMS **mistrust,** be suspicious of, be wary of, be chary of, regard with suspicion, suspect, be skeptical of, doubt, be unsure of/about, have misgivings about.
– ANTONYMS trust.

– DERIVATIVES **dis·trust·ful** adjective **dis·trust·ful·ly** adverb.

dis·turb /disˈtərb/ ▶ verb **1** interfere with the normal arrangement or functioning of something. **2** interrupt the sleep, relaxation, or privacy of someone. **3** make someone anxious.

– SYNONYMS **1 move,** rearrange, mix up, interfere with, mess up. **2 interrupt,** intrude on, butt in on, barge in on, distract, disrupt, bother, trouble, pester, harass. **3 perturb,** trouble, concern, worry, upset, fluster, disconcert, dismay, alarm, distress, unsettle. **4** (as adj. **disturbing**) *he gave us some disturbing information* **worrying,** troubling, upsetting, distressing, discomfiting, disconcerting, disquieting, unsettling, dismaying, alarming, frightening.
– ANTONYMS calm, reassure.

– ORIGIN Latin *disturbare.*

dis·tur·bance /disˈtərbəns/ ▶ noun **1** the interruption or disruption of a settled or normal condition: *precautions can be taken to minimize wildlife disturbance.* **2** a breakdown of peaceful behavior; a riot.

– SYNONYMS **1 disruption,** distraction, interference, inconvenience, upset, annoyance, irritation, intrusion. **2 riot,** fracas, brawl, street fight, free-for-all, commotion, disorder.
– ANTONYMS order.

dis·turbed /disˈtərbd/ ▶ adjective **1** disrupted or broken. **2** having emotional or psychological problems.

– SYNONYMS **1** *disturbed sleep* **disrupted,** interrupted, fitful, intermittent, broken. **2 troubled,** distressed, upset, distraught, unbalanced, unstable, disordered, dysfunctional, maladjusted, neurotic, unhinged; informal screwed up.
– ANTONYMS uninterrupted.

di·sul·fide /dīˈsəlˌfīd/ ▶ noun Chemistry a sulfide containing two atoms of sulfur in its molecule or empirical formula.

dis·un·ion /disˈyo͞onyən/ ▶ noun the breaking up of something such as a federation.

dis·u·nit·ed /ˌdisyo͞oˈnītid/ ▶ adjective lacking unity or agreement.
– DERIVATIVES **dis·u·ni·ty** /disˈyo͞onitē/ noun.

dis·use /disˈyo͞os/ ▶ noun the state of not being used.
– DERIVATIVES **dis·used** /disˈyo͞ozd/ adjective.

di·syl·la·ble /dīˈsiləbəl, di-/ ▶ noun Poetry a word or metrical foot consisting of two syllables.
– DERIVATIVES **di·syl·lab·ic** /ˌdīsiˈlabik, di-/ adjective.
– ORIGIN from Greek *disullabos* 'of two syllables.'

ditch /dicʜ/ ▶ noun a narrow channel dug to hold or carry water.

– SYNONYMS **trench,** trough, channel, dike, drain, gutter, gully, watercourse.

▶ verb **1** informal abandon or get rid of: *she had recently been ditched by her boyfriend.* **2** (with reference to an aircraft) bring or come down in a forced landing on the sea. **3** provide a place with a ditch.
– ORIGIN Old English.

dith·er /ˈdi<u>th</u>ər/ ▶ verb be indecisive. ▶ noun informal a state of agitation or indecision.
– DERIVATIVES **dith·er·er** noun **dith·er·y** adjective.
– ORIGIN variant of dialect *didder* 'tremble.'

dith·y·ramb /ˈdiᴛʜəˌram/ ▶ noun (in ancient Greece) an ecstatic choral hymn dedicated to the god Dionysus.
– DERIVATIVES **dith·y·ram·bic** /ˌdiᴛʜəˈrambik/ adjective.
– ORIGIN Greek *dithurambos.*

dit·to /ˈditō/ ▶ noun **1** the same thing again (used in lists and often indicated by a ditto mark). **2** (also **ditto mark**) a symbol consisting of two apostrophes (") placed under an item to be repeated.
– ORIGIN Italian *detto* 'said.'

dit·ty /ˈditē/ ▶ noun (pl. **ditties**) a short simple song.
– ORIGIN Old French *dite* 'composition.'

ditz /dits/ ▶ noun informal a scatterbrained person.

dit·zy /ˈditsē/ (also **ditsy**) ▶ adjective informal silly or scatterbrained.
– DERIVATIVES **dit·zi·ness** noun.
– ORIGIN unknown.

di·u·ret·ic /ˌdīyəˈretik/ ▶ adjective causing an increase in the flow of urine. ▶ noun a diuretic drug.
– ORIGIN from Greek *diourein* 'urinate.'

di·ur·nal /dīˈərnl/ ▶ adjective **1** of or during the daytime. **2** daily; of each day.
– DERIVATIVES **di·ur·nal·ly** adverb.
– ORIGIN Latin *diurnalis.*

di·va /'dēvə/ ▸ **noun 1** a famous female opera singer. **2** a haughty, spoiled woman.
– ORIGIN Latin, 'goddess.'

Di·va·li ▸ **noun** variant spelling of **Diwali**.

di·van /di'van, 'dī,van/ ▸ **noun** a long, low sofa without a back or arms.
– ORIGIN Persian, 'bench, court.'

dive /dīv/ ▸ **verb** (past and past part. **dived** or **dove** /dōv/) **1** plunge head first and with arms outstretched into water. **2** go to a deeper level in water. **3** swim under water using breathing equipment. **4** plunge steeply downward through the air. **5** move quickly or suddenly: *he dived into the bushes.*

– SYNONYMS **1 plunge,** plummet, nosedive, jump, fall, drop, pitch. **2 leap,** jump, lunge, throw/fling oneself, go headlong.

▸ **noun 1** an act of diving. **2** informal a disreputable nightclub or bar.

– SYNONYMS **1 plunge,** nosedive, jump, fall, drop, swoop. **2 lunge,** spring, jump, leap.

– ORIGIN Old English.

dive-bomb ▸ **verb 1** bomb a target while diving steeply in an aircraft. **2** (of a bird or flying insect) attack something by swooping down on it.
– DERIVATIVES **dive-bomb·er** noun.

div·er /'dīvər/ ▸ **noun 1** a person who dives under water as a sport or as part of their work. **2** a large diving waterbird with a straight pointed bill.

di·verge /di'vərj, dī-/ ▸ **verb 1** (of a road or route) separate from another route and go in a different direction. **2** (of opinions, theories, etc.) be different from one another. **3** (**diverge from**) depart from a particular pattern or standard: *individuals may well diverge from the norm.*

– SYNONYMS **1 separate,** part, fork, divide, split, bifurcate, go in different directions. **2 differ,** be different, be dissimilar, disagree, be at variance/odds, conflict, clash.
– ANTONYMS converge, agree.

– DERIVATIVES **di·ver·gence** noun **di·verg·ing** adjective.
– ORIGIN Latin *divergere*.

di·ver·gent /di'vərjənt, dī-/ ▸ **adjective** different.

WORD TOOLKIT

divergent ...	varying ...	dissimilar ...
views	degrees	materials
sequences	sizes	systems
opinions	levels	characters
paths	ages	elements
interests	lengths	triangles
goals	shades	species

di·vers /'dīvərz/ ▸ **adjective** old use or literary of many different kinds.

di·verse /di'vərs, dī-/ ▸ **adjective** widely varied: *people from diverse backgrounds.*

– SYNONYMS **various,** sundry, varied, varying, miscellaneous, assorted, mixed, diversified, divergent, different, differing, distinct, unlike, dissimilar.
– ANTONYMS similar.

– DERIVATIVES **di·verse·ly** adverb.
– ORIGIN Latin *diversus*.

WORD TOOLKIT

diverse ...	sundry ...	manifold ...
backgrounds	items	problems
population	expenses	sins
cultures	lists	forms
interests	knickknacks	effects
needs	relatives	benefits

di·ver·si·fy /di'vərsi,fī, dī-/ ▸ **verb** (**diversifies, diversifying, diversified**) **1** make or become more varied. **2** (of a company) enlarge or vary its range of products or field of operation.
– DERIVATIVES **di·ver·si·fi·ca·tion** /-,vərsifi'kāshən/ noun.

di·ver·sion /di'vərzhən, dī-/ ▸ **noun 1** an instance of diverting something. **2** something intended to distract attention: *a raid was carried out at the airfield to create a diversion.* **3** a pastime or pleasant activity.

– SYNONYMS **1 detour,** deviation, alternative route, rerouting, redirection. **2 distraction,** disturbance, smokescreen; informal red herring. **3 entertainment,** amusement, pastime, delight, fun, recreation, pleasure.

– DERIVATIVES **di·ver·sion·ar·y** /-,nerē/ adjective.

di·ver·si·ty /di'vərsitē, dī-/ ▸ **noun** (pl. **diversities**) **1** the state of being varied. **2** a variety of things.

– SYNONYMS **variety,** miscellany, assortment, mixture, mix, range, array, multiplicity, variation, difference.
– ANTONYMS uniformity.

di·vert /di'vərt, dī-/ ▸ **verb 1** change the direction or course of: *traffic was diverted from the highway.* **2** distract someone or their attention. **3** amuse or entertain someone.

– SYNONYMS **1 reroute,** redirect, change the course of, deflect, channel. **2 distract,** sidetrack, disturb, draw away, put off. **3 amuse,** entertain, distract, delight, enchant, interest, fascinate, absorb, engross, rivet, grip.

– DERIVATIVES **di·vert·ing** adjective.
– ORIGIN Latin *divertere* 'turn in separate ways.'

di·ver·tic·u·li·tis /,dīvər,tikyə'lītis/ ▸ **noun** inflammation of a diverticulum in the alimentary tract, causing abdominal pain and diarrhea or constipation.

di·ver·tic·u·lum /,dīvər'tikyələm/ ▸ **noun** (pl. **diverticula** /-lə/) an abnormal sac or pouch formed in the wall of the alimentary tract.
– ORIGIN Latin *deverticulum* 'byway.'

di·ver·ti·men·to /di,vərtə'mentō/ ▸ **noun** (pl. **divertimenti** /-'mentē/ or **divertimentos**) a light and entertaining piece of music.
– ORIGIN Italian, 'diversion.'

di·ver·tisse·ment /di'vərtismənt/ ▸ **noun** a minor entertainment.
– ORIGIN French.

di·vest /di'vest, dī-/ ▸ **verb 1** (**divest someone/thing of**) deprive someone or something of: *he was divested of his property.* **2** (**divest oneself of**) remove or get rid of: *he divested himself of his jacket.*
– ORIGIN Old French *desvestir*, from Latin *vestire* 'clothe.'

di·vide /di'vīd/ ▸ **verb 1** separate something into parts. **2** share something out: *the house was sold and the money divided between us.* **3** cause disagreement between people or groups: *the issue has divided the community.* **4** form a boundary between between two areas. **5** find how many times a number contains another. **6** (of a lawmaking assembly) separate into two groups for voting.

– SYNONYMS **1** *he divided his land among his heirs* **split (up),** cut up, carve up, dissect, bisect, halve, quarter. **2** *a curtain divided her cabin from the galley* **separate,** segregate, partition, screen off, section off, split off. **3 diverge,** separate, part, branch (off), fork, split (in two). **4 share,** ration out, parcel out, deal out, dole out, dish out, distribute. **5 disunite,** drive apart, drive a wedge between, break up, split (up), separate, isolate, alienate.
– ANTONYMS unify, converge, unite.

▶ **noun** a wide difference between two groups: *the profound cultural divide between the parties.*
– ORIGIN Latin *dividere* 'force apart, remove.'

div·i·dend /ˈdiviˌdend/ ▶ **noun 1** a sum of money that is divided among a number of people, such as the part of a company's profits paid to its shareholders. **2** (**dividends**) benefits gained from something: *the policy would pay dividends in the future.* **3** Mathematics a number to be divided by another number.
– ORIGIN Latin *dividendum* 'something to be divided.'

di·vid·er /diˈvīdər/ ▶ **noun 1** a screen or piece of furniture that divides a room into two separate parts. **2** (**dividers**) a measuring compass.

div·i·na·tion /ˌdivəˈnāsʜən/ ▶ **noun** the use of supernatural means to find out about the future or the unknown.
– DERIVATIVES **di·vin·a·to·ry** /diˈvinəˌtôrē/ adjective.

di·vine[1] /diˈvīn/ ▶ **adjective** (**diviner, divinest**) **1** relating to, from, or like God or a god. **2** informal excellent.

– SYNONYMS **godly,** angelic, heavenly, celestial, holy, sacred.
– ANTONYMS mortal.

▶ **noun 1** dated a priest, religious leader, or theologian. **2** (**the Divine**) providence or God.
– DERIVATIVES **di·vine·ly** adverb.
– ORIGIN Latin *divinus.*

WORD TOOLKIT

See **HEAVENLY**.

di·vine[2] ▶ **verb 1** discover something by guesswork or intuition. **2** have supernatural insight into the future. **3** search for underground water or minerals using a pointer that is supposedly moved by unseen influences.

– SYNONYMS **guess,** surmise, deduce, infer, discern, discover, perceive; informal **figure (out).**

– DERIVATIVES **di·vin·er** noun.
– ORIGIN Latin *divinare* 'predict.'

div·ing bell ▶ **noun** an open-bottomed chamber supplied with air, in which a person can be let down under water.

div·ing board ▶ **noun** a board projecting over a swimming pool or other body of water, from which people dive or jump in.

div·ing suit ▶ **noun** a watertight suit, typically with a helmet and an air supply, worn for working or exploring deep under water.

di·vin·ing rod ▶ **noun** a forked stick or rod supposed to move when held over ground in which water or minerals can be found.

di·vin·i·ty /diˈvinitē/ ▶ **noun** (pl. **divinities**) **1** the state or quality of being divine. **2** a god or goddess. **3** (**the Divinity**) God. **4** the study of religion; theology.

di·vis·i·ble /diˈvizəbəl/ ▶ **adjective 1** capable of being divided. **2** (of a number) containing another number a number of times without a remainder.
– DERIVATIVES **di·vis·i·bil·i·ty** /-ˌvizəˈbilitē/ noun.

di·vi·sion /diˈvizʜən/ ▶ **noun 1** the action of dividing something or the state of being divided. **2** each of the parts into which something is divided. **3** a major unit or section of an organization. **4** a number of teams or players grouped together in a sport for competitive purposes. **5** a partition that divides two groups or things.

– SYNONYMS **1** *the division of the island* **dividing (up),** breaking up, break-up, carving up, splitting, dissection, partitioning, separation, segregation. **2** *the division of his estates* **dividing up,** sharing, parceling out, dishing out, allocation, allotment, splitting up, carving up. **3 dividing line,** divide, boundary, border, demarcation line, gap, gulf. **4 section,** subsection, subdivision, category, class, group, grouping, set. **5 department,** branch, arm, wing. **6 disunity,** disunion, conflict, discord, disagreement, alienation, isolation.
– ANTONYMS unification.

– DERIVATIVES **di·vi·sion·al** /diˈvizʜənl/ adjective.

di·vi·sion sign ▶ **noun** the sign ÷, placed between two numbers showing that the first is to be divided by the second, as in *6 ÷ 3 = 2.*

di·vi·sive /diˈvīsiv/ ▶ **adjective** causing disagreement or hostility between people or groups.
– DERIVATIVES **di·vi·sive·ness** noun.

di·vi·sor /diˈvīzər/ ▶ **noun** Mathematics a number by which another number is to be divided.

di·vorce /diˈvôrs/ ▶ **noun 1** the legal ending of a marriage. **2** a division or separation.

– SYNONYMS **1 dissolution,** annulment, decree nisi, separation. **2** *the divorce between the church and people* **separation,** division, split, gulf, disunity, alienation, schism.
– ANTONYMS marriage.

▶ **verb 1** legally end one's marriage with one's husband or wife. **2** (**divorce someone/thing from**) detach or separate someone or something from.

– SYNONYMS **1 split up,** get a divorce, separate. **2** *religion cannot be divorced from morality* **separate,** divide, detach, isolate, alienate, set apart, cut off.

– ORIGIN Old French.

di·vor·cée /divôrˈsā, -ˈsē/ ▶ **noun** a divorced woman.
– ORIGIN French *divorcé(e)* 'divorced man (or woman).'

div·ot /ˈdivət/ ▶ **noun** a piece of turf cut out of the ground, especially by a golf club in making a stroke.
– ORIGIN unknown.

di·vulge /diˈvəlj, dī-/ ▶ **verb** reveal information that is meant to be private or secret.

– SYNONYMS **disclose,** reveal, tell, communicate, pass on, publish, give away, let slip.
– ANTONYMS conceal.

– ORIGIN Latin *divulgare* 'publish widely.'

div·vy /ˈdivē/ ▶ **verb** (**divvies, divvying, divvied**) informal divide up and share.

Di·wa·li /diˈwälē/ (also **Divali**) ▶ **noun** a Hindu festival held in October and November and celebrated with lights.
– ORIGIN Sanskrit, 'row of lights.'

Dix·ie /ˈdiksē/ ▶ **noun** an informal name for the southern states of the US.
– ORIGIN unknown.

Dix·ie·land /ˈdiksē,land/ ▶ **noun** a kind of jazz with a strong two-beat rhythm.

diz·zy /ˈdizē/ ▶ **adjective** (**dizzier, dizziest**) **1** having a sensation of spinning around and losing one's balance. **2** informal (of a woman) silly but attractive.

– SYNONYMS **giddy,** lightheaded, faint, unsteady, shaky, muzzy, wobbly; informal woozy.

▶ **verb** (**dizzies, dizzying, dizzied**) make someone feel unsteady, confused, or amazed.
– DERIVATIVES **diz·zi·ly** adverb **diz·zi·ness** noun.
– ORIGIN Old English, 'foolish.'

DJ /ˈdē,jā/ ▶ **noun 1** a person who introduces and plays recorded pop music on the radio or at a nightclub or private party; a disc jockey. **2** a person who uses samples of recorded music to make techno or rap music.
▶ **verb** (**DJ's, DJ'ing, DJ'd**) perform as a DJ.
– ORIGIN short for **DISC JOCKEY**.

djel·la·ba /jəˈläbə/ (also **djellabah** or **jellaba**) ▶ **noun** a loose woolen hooded cloak of a kind traditionally worn by Arabs.
– ORIGIN Arabic.

Dji·bou·ti·an /jəˈbo͞otēən/ ▶ **noun** a person from Djibouti, a country on the northeast coast of Africa.
▶ **adjective** relating to Djibouti.

djinn /jin/ ▶ **noun** (pl. same or **djinns**) (in Arabian and Muslim mythology) an intelligent spirit able to appear in human or animal form.
– ORIGIN Arabic.

DL ▶ **abbreviation 1** Football defensive lineman. **2** disabled list.

dl ▶ **abbreviation** deciliter(s).

DM (also **D-mark**) ▶ **abbreviation** Deutschmark.

dm ▶ **abbreviation** decimeter(s).

DMA ▶ **abbreviation** Computing direct memory access.

DMZ ▶ **abbreviation** demilitarized zone, an area from which warring parties agree to remove their military forces.

DNA ▶ **noun** deoxyribonucleic acid, a substance carrying genetic information that is present in the cell nuclei of nearly all living organisms.

DNA fin·ger·print·ing (also **DNA profiling**) ▶ **noun** another term for **GENETIC FINGERPRINTING**.

do[1] /do͞o/ ▶ **verb** (**does** /dəz/; past **did** /did/; past part. **done** /dən/) **1** carry out or complete an action, duty, or task. **2** act or progress in a particular way: *the team did well.* **3** work on something to bring it to a required state: *she's doing her hair*. **4** have a particular result or effect on: *the walk will do me good*. **5** work at for a living or take as one's subject of study: *what does she do?* **6** make or provide something. **7** be suitable or acceptable: *he'll do*. **8** (**be/have done with**) stop being concerned about someone or something.

– SYNONYMS **1** *she does most of the work* **carry out,** undertake, discharge, execute, perform, accomplish, achieve, bring about, engineer; informal pull off. **2** *they can do as they please* **act,** behave, conduct oneself. **3** *a portrait I am doing* **make,** create, produce, work on, design, manufacture. **4 suffice,** be adequate, be satisfactory, fill/fit the bill, serve.

▶ **auxiliary verb 1** used before a verb in questions and negative statements. **2** used to refer back to a verb already mentioned: *he looks better than he did before*. **3** used in commands, or to give emphasis to a positive verb: *do sit down*.

▶ **noun** (pl. **dos** or **do's**) **1** informal a party or other social event. **2** informal a hairdo.
– DERIVATIVES **do·a·ble** /ˈdo͞oəbəl/ (informal) adjective **do·er** noun.
– PHRASES **can/could do with** would find useful or would like. **do away with** informal put an end to; kill. **do for 1** informal defeat, ruin, or kill. **2** be good enough for. **do someone in** informal kill someone. **dos and don'ts** rules of behavior. **do time** informal spend a period of time in prison. **do something up 1** fasten or wrap something. **2** informal renovate or redecorate a building or room.
– ORIGIN Old English.

do[2] /dō/ ▶ **noun** Music the first note of a major scale, coming before 're'.
– ORIGIN Italian *do.*

DOA ▶ **abbreviation** dead on arrival, used to describe a person who is declared dead immediately upon arrival at a hospital.

Do·ber·man /ˈdōbərmən/ (also **Dobermann** or **Doberman pinscher** /ˈpinCHər/) ▶ **noun** a large breed of dog with powerful jaws, typically black with tan markings.
– ORIGIN named after the German dog breeder Ludwig *Dobermann* (+ German *Pinscher* 'terrier').

doc /däk/ ▶ **abbreviation** informal doctor.

do·cent /ˈdōsənt/ ▶ **noun 1** (in certain colleges and universities) a member of the teaching staff immediately below professor in rank. **2** a guide in a museum, art gallery, or zoo.
– ORIGIN from Latin *docere* 'teach.'

doc·ile /ˈdäsəl/ ▶ **adjective** willing to accept control or instruction; submissive.

– SYNONYMS **compliant,** obedient, pliant, submissive, deferential, unassertive, cooperative, amenable, accommodating, biddable.
– ANTONYMS disobedient, willful.

– DERIVATIVES **doc·ile·ly** adverb **do·cil·i·ty** /däˈsilitē/ noun.
– ORIGIN Latin *docilis*, from *docere* 'teach.'

dock[1] /däk/ ▶ **noun 1** a structure extending alongshore or out from the shore into a body of water, to which boats may be moored. **2** an enclosed area of water in a port for the loading, unloading, and repair of ships. **3** (also **loading dock**) a platform for loading trucks or freight trains.

– SYNONYMS **harbor,** marina, port, wharf, quay, pier, jetty, landing stage.

▶ **verb 1** (with reference to a ship) come or bring into a dock. **2** (of a spacecraft) join with a space station or another spacecraft in space. **3** attach a piece of equipment to another.

– SYNONYMS **moor,** berth, put in, tie up, anchor.

– ORIGIN Dutch or German *docke.*

dock[2] ▶ **noun** the enclosure in a criminal court where a defendant stands or sits.
– ORIGIN probably related to Flemish *dok* 'chicken coop, rabbit hutch.'

dock[3] ▶ **noun** a weed with broad leaves, popularly used to relieve nettle stings.
– ORIGIN Old English.

dock[4] ▶ **verb 1** deduct money or a point in a game. **2** cut an animal's tail short.

– SYNONYMS **1 deduct,** subtract, remove, debit, take off/away; informal knock off. **2 reduce,** cut, decrease. **3 cut off,** cut short, shorten, crop, lop.

– ORIGIN uncertain.

dock·er /ˈdäkər/ ▸ **noun** another term for **LONGSHOREMAN**.

dock·et /ˈdäkit/ ▸ **noun 1** a calendar or list of cases awaiting action in a court. **2** a document or label listing the contents of a package or delivery. ▸ **verb** (**dockets, docketing, docketed**) **1** enter (a case) in a court calendar. **2** mark a package with a label or document listing the contents.
– ORIGIN perhaps from **DOCK**[4].

dock·ing sta·tion ▸ **noun** a device to which a portable computer is connected so that it can be used like a desktop computer.

dock·side /ˈdäkˌsīd/ ▸ **noun** the area immediately next to a dock.

dock·yard /ˈdäkˌyärd/ ▸ **noun** an area with docks and equipment for repairing and maintaining ships.

doc·tor /ˈdäktər/ ▸ **noun 1** a person who is qualified to practice medicine. **2** (**Doctor**) a person who holds the highest university degree.

– SYNONYMS **physician,** medical practitioner, general practitioner, GP, clinician, consultant; informal doc, medic.

▸ **verb 1** change something in order to deceive other people: *the technical data had been doctored.* **2** add a harmful or strong ingredient to food or drink.

– SYNONYMS **1 falsify,** tamper with, interfere with, alter, change, forge, fake. **2 adulterate,** tamper with, lace; informal spike.

– PHRASES **be what the doctor ordered** informal be beneficial or desirable.
– ORIGIN Latin, 'teacher.'

doc·tor·al /ˈdäktərəl/ ▸ **adjective** relating to a doctorate.

doc·tor·ate /ˈdäktərit/ ▸ **noun** the highest degree awarded by a graduate school or other educational institution.

Doc·tor of Phi·los·o·phy ▸ **noun** a person holding a doctorate in any subject except law, medicine, or sometimes theology.

doc·tri·naire /ˌdäktrəˈner/ ▸ **adjective** very strict in applying beliefs or principles.
– ORIGIN French.

doc·trine /ˈdäktrin/ ▸ **noun** a set of beliefs or principles held and taught by a Church, political party, or other group.

– SYNONYMS **creed,** credo, dogma, belief, teaching, ideology, tenet, maxim, canon, principle.

– DERIVATIVES **doc·tri·nal** /ˈdäktrənl/ adjective **doc·tri·nal·ly** adverb.
– ORIGIN Latin *doctrina* 'teaching, learning.'

doc·u·dra·ma /ˈdäkyəˌdrämə/ ▸ **noun** a television movie based on a dramatized version of real events.

doc·u·ment ▸ **noun** /ˈdäkyəmənt/ a piece of written, printed, or electronic matter that provides information or evidence.

– SYNONYMS **paper,** certificate, deed, form, contract, agreement, report, record.

▸ **verb** /ˈdäkyəˌment/ record something in written, photographic, or other form.

– SYNONYMS **record,** register, report, log, chronicle, authenticate, verify.

– ORIGIN Latin *documentum* 'lesson.'

doc·u·men·ta·ry /ˌdäkyəˈmentərē/ ▸ **noun** (pl. **documentaries**) a movie or television or radio program giving a factual account of something, using film, photographs, and sound recordings of real events. ▸ **adjective** consisting of documents and other material providing a factual account of something: *documentary evidence.*

doc·u·men·ta·tion /ˌdäkyəmenˈtāsʜən/ ▸ **noun 1** documents providing official information or evidence. **2** written specifications or instructions.

dod·der /ˈdädər/ ▸ **verb** be slow and unsteady.
– DERIVATIVES **dod·der·er** noun **dod·der·ing** adjective **dod·der·y** adjective.
– ORIGIN related to **DITHER**.

dod·dle /ˈdädl/ ▸ **noun** Brit. informal a very easy task.
– ORIGIN unknown.

do·dec·a·gon /dōˈdekəˌgän/ ▸ **noun** a plane figure with twelve straight sides and angles.
– ORIGIN Greek *dōdekagōnos* 'twelve-angled.'

do·dec·a·he·dron /dōˌdekəˈhēdrən/ ▸ **noun** (pl. **dodecahedra** /-drə/ or **dodecahedrons**) a three-dimensional shape having twelve plane faces.
– ORIGIN from Greek *dōdekaedros* 'twelve-faced.'

dodge /däj/ ▸ **verb 1** avoid someone or something by making a sudden quick movement. **2** cunningly avoid doing or paying something.

– SYNONYMS **1** *he dodged the police* **elude,** evade, avoid, escape, run away from, lose, shake (off); informal give someone the slip. **2** *the minister tried to dodge the debate* **avoid,** evade, get out of, back out of, sidestep; informal duck, wriggle out of. **3 dart,** duck, dive, swerve, veer.

▸ **noun 1** an act of dodging someone or something. **2** informal a cunning trick, especially one used to avoid something.

– SYNONYMS *a clever dodge* | *a tax dodge* **ruse,** scheme, tactic, stratagem, ploy, subterfuge, trick, hoax, cheat, deception, fraud; informal scam.

– ORIGIN unknown.

dodg·er /ˈdäjər/ ▸ **noun** informal a person who avoids doing or paying something: *a tax dodger.*

dodg·y /ˈdäjē/ ▸ **adjective** (**dodgier, dodgiest**) Brit. informal **1** dishonest. **2** risky. **3** not working well or in good condition.

do·do /ˈdōdō/ ▸ **noun** (pl. **dodos** or **dodoes**) **1** a large extinct flightless bird formerly found on Mauritius. **2** informal an old-fashioned or ineffective person or thing.
– ORIGIN Portuguese *doudo* 'simpleton' (because the birds were tame and easy to catch).

DOE ▸ **abbreviation** Department of Energy.

doe /dō/ ▸ **noun 1** a female deer or reindeer. **2** a female hare, rabbit, rat, ferret, or kangaroo.
– ORIGIN Old English.

doe-eyed ▸ **adjective** having large, gentle, dark eyes.

do·er /ˈdo͞oər/ ▸ **noun 1** the person who does something: *the doer of the action.* **2** a person who acts rather than merely talking or thinking.

does /dəz/ third person singular present of **DO**[1].

does·n't /ˈdəzənt/ ▸ **contraction** does not.

doff /däf, dôf/ ▸ **verb** remove an item of clothing, especially a hat.
– ORIGIN shortened form of *do off.*

dog /dôg/ ▸ **noun 1** a domesticated carnivorous mammal kept as a pet or used for work or hunting. **2** any member of the dog family, which includes the wolf, fox, coyote, jackal, and other species. **3** the male of an animal of the dog family. **4** informal, derogatory a woman regarded as unattractive. **5** dated a person of a particular kind: *you lucky dog!*

– SYNONYMS **hound,** canine, man's best friend, mongrel; informal pooch, mutt.

▶ **verb** (**dogs, dogging, dogged**) **1** follow someone closely and persistently. **2** cause continual trouble for: *he was dogged by ill health in later years.*

– SYNONYMS **plague,** beset, bedevil, blight, trouble.

– PHRASES **dog eat dog** used to describe an extremely competitive situation in which people are willing to harm each other in order to succeed. **go to the dogs** informal get into a very bad state.
– ORIGIN Old English.

WORD LINKS

canine *relating to dogs*

dog col·lar ▶ **noun** informal a clerical collar.

dog days ▶ **plural noun** chiefly literary the hottest period of the year (formerly calculated from the first time Sirius, the Dog Star, rose at the same time as the sun).

doge /dōj/ ▶ **noun** historical the chief magistrate of Venice or Genoa.
– ORIGIN Italian *doze*, from Latin *dux* 'leader.'

dog-eared ▶ **adjective** having worn or battered corners.

dog·fight /ˈdôgˌfīt/ ▶ **noun 1** a close combat between military aircraft. **2** a ferocious struggle or fight.
– DERIVATIVES **dog·fight·ing** noun.

dog·fish /ˈdôgˌfisʜ/ ▶ **noun** (pl. same or **dogfishes**) a small shark with a long tail, living close to the seabed.

dog·ged /ˈdôgid/ ▶ **adjective** very persistent.

– SYNONYMS **tenacious,** determined, resolute, stubborn, obstinate, purposeful, persistent, persevering, single-minded, tireless.
– ANTONYMS half-hearted.

– DERIVATIVES **dog·ged·ly** adverb **dog·ged·ness** noun.

CHOOSE THE RIGHT WORD

See **STUBBORN**.

dog·ger·el /ˈdôgərəl, ˈdäg-/ ▶ **noun** badly written poetry, often intended to be amusing.
– ORIGIN apparently from **DOG**.

dog·gie ▶ **noun** variant spelling of **DOGGY**.

dog·gone /ˈdôgˈgôn/ ▶ **adjective** informal used to express surprise, annoyance, or pleasure.
– ORIGIN probably from *dog on it*, euphemism for *God damn it*.

dog·gy /ˈdôgē/ ▶ **adjective 1** relating to or like a dog. **2** fond of dogs. ▶ **noun** (also **doggie**) (pl. **doggies**) a child's word for a dog.

dog·gy bag ▶ **noun** a bag used to take home food left uneaten after a meal in a restaurant.

dog·house /ˈdôgˌhous/ ▶ **noun** a dog's kennel.
– PHRASES **in the doghouse** informal having annoyed or displeased someone.

dog·leg /ˈdôgˌleg/ ▶ **noun 1** a sharp bend in a road. **2** Golf a hole at which the player cannot aim directly at the green from the tee.

dog·ma /ˈdôgmə/ ▶ **noun** a principle or set of principles laid down by an authority and intended to be accepted without question.

– SYNONYMS **teaching,** belief, tenet, principle, precept, maxim, article of faith, canon, creed, credo, doctrine, ideology.

– ORIGIN Greek, 'opinion.'

dog·mat·ic /dôgˈmatik/ ▶ **adjective** forcefully putting forward one's own beliefs or opinions and unwilling to accept those of other people.

– SYNONYMS **opinionated,** assertive, insistent, emphatic, adamant, doctrinaire, authoritarian, imperious, dictatorial, uncompromising.

– DERIVATIVES **dog·mat·i·cal·ly** /-ik(ə)lē/ adverb **dog·ma·tism** /ˈdôgməˌtizəm/ noun **dog·ma·tist** noun.

do-good·er /ˈdo͞o ˌgo͝odər/ ▶ **noun** a well-meaning but unrealistic or interfering person.

dog pad·dle ▶ **noun** a simple swimming stroke resembling that of a dog. ▶ **verb** (**dog-paddle**) swim using this stroke.

dog·sled /ˈdôgˌsled/ ▶ **noun** a sled designed to be pulled by dogs.

Dog Star ▶ **noun** Sirius, the brightest star in the sky.
– ORIGIN so named as it appears to follow at the heels of Orion (the hunter).

dog tag ▶ **noun 1** a metal tag attached to a dog's collar, typically giving its name and owner's address. **2** informal a soldier's metal identity tag, worn on a chain around the neck.

dog-tired ▶ **adjective** extremely tired.

dog·wood /ˈdôgˌwo͝od/ ▶ **noun** a flowering shrub or small tree with hard wood, red stems, and colorful berries.
– ORIGIN so named because the wood was formerly used to make skewers known as 'dogs'

doh ▶ **exclamation** variant spelling of **DUH**.

doi·ly /ˈdoilē/ ▶ **noun** (pl. **doilies**) a small ornamental mat made of lace or paper.
– ORIGIN from *Doiley* or *Doyley*, a London draper.

do·ing /ˈdo͞oiɴɢ/ ▶ **noun 1** (also **doings**) a person's actions or activities. **2** effort: *it would take some doing to calm him down.*

do-it-your·self ▶ **adjective** (of work, especially building, painting, or decorating) done or to be done by an amateur at home.

do·jo /ˈdōjō/ ▶ **noun** (pl. **dojos**) a place in which judo and other martial arts are practiced.
– ORIGIN from the Japanese words for 'way, pursuit' and 'a place.'

Dol·by /ˈdōlbē, ˈdôl-/ ▶ **noun** trademark **1** a noise-reduction system used in tape recording. **2** an electronic system providing stereophonic sound for movie theaters and televisions.
– ORIGIN named after the American engineer Ray M. *Dolby*.

dol·ce vi·ta /ˌdōlcʜā ˈvētə/ ▶ **noun** a life of pleasure and luxury.
– ORIGIN Italian 'sweet life.'

dol·drums /ˈdōldrəmz, ˈdäl-, ˈdôl-/ ▶ **plural noun** (**the doldrums**) **1** a state of inactivity or depression. **2** a region of the Atlantic Ocean with calms, sudden storms, and unpredictable winds.
– ORIGIN perhaps from **DULL**.

dole /dōl/ ▶ **noun** (often in phrase **on the dole**) registered as unemployed and receiving benefits from the government. ▶ **verb** (**dole something out**) distribute something.

– SYNONYMS **deal out,** pass out, share, divide up, allocate, distribute, dispense, hand out, give out, dish out.

– ORIGIN Old English, 'division or share.'

dole·ful /ˈdōlfəl/ ▶ **adjective 1** sorrowful. **2** causing unhappiness or misfortune.
– DERIVATIVES **dole·ful·ly** adverb.
– ORIGIN from Latin *dolere* 'grieve.'

dol·er·ite /ˈdäləˌrīt/ ▶ **noun** a dark igneous rock.
– ORIGIN from Greek *doleros* 'deceptive' (because it resembles diorite).

doll /däl/ ▶ **noun 1** a small model of a human figure, used as a child's toy. **2** informal an attractive young woman. ▶ **verb** (**doll oneself up**) informal dress oneself smartly and attractively.
– ORIGIN from the woman's name *Dorothy*.

dol·lar /ˈdälər/ ▶ **noun** the basic unit of money of the US, Canada, Australia, and various other countries.
– ORIGIN German *Thaler*, referring to a silver coin.

dol·lar sign (also **dollar mark**) ▶ **noun** the sign $, representing a dollar.

doll·house /ˈdälˌhous/ ▶ **noun** a miniature toy house for dolls.

dol·lop /ˈdäləp/ informal ▶ **noun** a shapeless mass or lump, especially of soft food. ▶ **verb** (**dollops, dolloping, dolloped**) add or serve out soft food in a casual or careless way.
– ORIGIN perhaps Scandinavian.

dol·ly /ˈdälē/ ▶ **noun** (pl. **dollies**) **1** a child's word for a doll. **2** informal, dated an attractive young woman. **3** a small platform on wheels for holding or moving heavy objects.

dol·ma·des /dôlˈmäT͟Hes/ ▶ **plural noun** (sing. **dolma** /ˈdôlmə/) a Greek and Turkish dish of spiced rice and meat wrapped in vine or cabbage leaves.
– ORIGIN Turkish, from *dolmak* 'fill, be filled.'

dol·man sleeve /ˈdōlmən/ ▶ **noun** a loose sleeve cut in one piece with the body of a garment.
– ORIGIN *dolman* from Turkish *dolama* 'open robe.'

dol·men /ˈdōlmən, ˈdäl-/ ▶ **noun** a megalithic tomb with a large flat stone laid on upright ones.
– ORIGIN Cornish, 'hole of a stone.'

do·lo·mite /ˈdäləˌmīt, ˈdō-/ ▶ **noun** a mineral or rock consisting chiefly of a carbonate of calcium and magnesium.
– DERIVATIVES **dol·o·mit·ic** /ˌdäləˈmitik/ adjective.
– ORIGIN named after the French geologist M. *Dolomieu*.

do·lor /ˈdōlər/ ▶ **noun** literary a state of great sorrow or distress.
– ORIGIN Latin *dolor* 'pain, grief.'

dol·or·ous /ˈdōlərəs/ ▶ **adjective** literary feeling great sorrow or distress.

dol·phin /ˈdälfin, ˈdôl-/ ▶ **noun** a small whale with a beaklike snout and a curved fin on the back.
– ORIGIN Old French *dauphin*, from Greek *delphin*.

dol·phi·nar·i·um /ˌdälfiˈne(ə)rēəm, ˌdôl-/ ▶ **noun** (pl. **dolphinariums** or **dolphinaria**) an aquarium in which dolphins are kept and trained for public entertainment.

dolt /dōlt/ ▶ **noun** a stupid person.
– DERIVATIVES **dolt·ish** adjective.
– ORIGIN perhaps a variant of *dulled*, from **DULL**.

do·main /dōˈmān/ ▶ **noun 1** an area controlled by a ruler or government. **2** an area of activity or knowledge. **3** a subset of the Internet with addresses all having the same suffix.

– SYNONYMS **1 realm,** kingdom, empire, dominion, province, territory, land. **2 field,** area, sphere, discipline, province, world.

– ORIGIN from Old French *demeine* 'belonging to a lord.'

dome /dōm/ ▶ **noun 1** a rounded vault forming the roof of a building, typically with a circular base. **2** a sports stadium or other building with a domed roof.
– DERIVATIVES **domed** adjective.
– ORIGIN Italian *duomo* 'cathedral, dome.'

do·mes·tic /dəˈmestik/ ▶ **adjective 1** relating to a home or family. **2** of or for use in the home. **3** fond of family life and running a home. **4** (of an animal) tame and kept by humans. **5** existing or occurring within a country; not foreign.

– SYNONYMS **1 family,** home, household. **2 domesticated,** homely, home-loving. **3 tame,** pet, domesticated. **4 national,** state, home, internal.

▶ **noun** a person employed to do household tasks.
– DERIVATIVES **do·mes·ti·cal·ly** /-ik(ə)lē/ adverb.
– ORIGIN Latin *domesticus*, from *domus* 'house.'

do·mes·ti·cate /dəˈmestiˌkāt/ ▶ **verb 1** tame an animal and keep it as a pet or for farm produce. **2** make someone fond of and good at family life and running a home. **3** grow a plant for food.
– DERIVATIVES **do·mes·ti·ca·tion** /-ˌmestiˈkāsʜən/ noun.

do·mes·tic·i·ty /ˌdōmeˈstisitē/ ▶ **noun** home or family life.

do·mes·tic part·ner·ship ▶ **noun** (in some US states) a legally recognized union of a couple who have not been joined in a traditional marriage and whose status may or may not be that of a civil union.

do·mes·tic sci·ence ▶ **noun** dated home economics.

dom·i·cile /ˈdäməˌsīl, ˈdō-, ˈdäməsəl/ ▶ **noun** formal or Law **1** the country in which a person lives permanently. **2** a person's home. ▶ **verb** (**be domiciled**) formal or Law be living in a particular place.
– ORIGIN Latin *domicilium* 'dwelling.'

dom·i·cil·i·ar·y /ˌdäməˈsilēˌerē, ˌdō-/ ▶ **adjective** concerned with or occurring in someone's home.

dom·i·nant /ˈdämənənt/ ▶ **adjective 1** most important, powerful, or influential. **2** (of a gene) appearing in offspring even if a contrary gene is also inherited. Compare with **RECESSIVE**.

– SYNONYMS **1 ruling,** governing, controlling, presiding, commanding. **2 assertive,** authoritative, forceful, domineering, commanding, controlling, pushy. **3 main,** principal, prime, chief, primary, central, key, crucial, core.
– ANTONYMS subservient, subsidiary.

– DERIVATIVES **dom·i·nance** noun **dom·i·nant·ly** adverb.

dom·i·nate /ˈdäməˌnāt/ ▶ **verb 1** have power or influence over: *the economy is dominated by multinational corporations*. **2** be the most important or noticeable person or thing in: *he dominated the race from start to finish*. **3** be the tallest or largest thing in a place.

– SYNONYMS **1 control,** influence, command, be in charge of, rule, govern, direct. **2 overlook,** command, tower above/over, loom over.

– DERIVATIVES **dom·i·na·tor** noun.

– ORIGIN Latin *dominari* 'rule,' from *dominus* 'lord, master.'

dom·i·na·tion /ˌdäməˈnāsʜən/ ▶ **noun** the action of controlling someone or something.

– SYNONYMS **control,** power, command, authority, dominion, rule, supremacy, superiority, ascendancy, sway, mastery.

dom·i·na·trix /ˌdäməˈnātriks/ ▶ **noun** (pl. **dominatrices** /-trəˌsēz/ or **dominatrixes**) a dominating woman, especially in sadomasochistic practices.
– ORIGIN Latin.

dom·i·neer·ing /ˌdäməˈni(ə)rɪɴɢ/ ▶ **adjective** arrogant and overbearing.

– SYNONYMS **overbearing,** authoritarian, imperious, high-handed, peremptory, autocratic, dictatorial, despotic, strict, harsh; informal bossy.

– ORIGIN from Latin *dominari* 'rule.'

Do·min·i·can[1] /dəˈminikən/ ▶ **noun** a member of an order of friars founded by St. Dominic, or of a similar religious order for women. ▶ **adjective** relating to St. Dominic or the Dominicans.

Do·min·i·can[2] ▶ **noun** a person from the Dominican Republic in the Caribbean. ▶ **adjective** relating to the Dominican Republic.

Do·min·i·can[3] ▶ **adjective** of or relating to the island of Dominica or its people.

do·min·ion /dəˈminyən/ ▶ **noun 1** supreme power or control. **2** the territory of a sovereign or government. **3** (**Dominion**) historical a self-governing territory of the British Commonwealth.

– SYNONYMS **supremacy,** ascendancy, dominance, domination, superiority, predominance, preeminence, hegemony, authority, mastery, control, command, power, sway, rule, government, jurisdiction, sovereignty.

– ORIGIN Latin *dominium*, from *dominus* 'lord.'

CHOOSE THE RIGHT WORD

See **JURISDICTION**.

dom·i·no /ˈdäməˌnō/ ▶ **noun** (pl. **dominoes**) **1** any of 28 small oblong pieces marked with 0–6 dots in each half. **2** (**dominoes**) (treated as sing.) the game played with these pieces.
– ORIGIN probably from Latin *dominus* 'lord.'

dom·i·no ef·fect ▶ **noun** a situation in which one event appears to cause a series of similar events to happen elsewhere.

don[1] /dän/ ▶ **noun 1** a university teacher, especially a senior member of a college at Oxford or Cambridge. **2** informal a high-ranking member of the Mafia.
– ORIGIN Spanish, from Latin *dominus* 'lord.'

don[2] ▶ **verb** (**dons, donning, donned**) put on an item of clothing.

– SYNONYMS **put on,** get dressed in, dress (oneself) in, get into, slip into/on, change into.

– ORIGIN shortened form of *do on*.

do·nate /ˈdōnāt, dōˈnāt/ ▶ **verb 1** give money, clothes, etc., to a charity or good cause. **2** allow blood or an organ to be removed from one's body for transfusion or transplantation.

– SYNONYMS **give,** contribute, gift, subscribe, grant, present, endow; informal chip in.

– DERIVATIVES **do·na·tor** noun.
– ORIGIN Latin *donare*.

CHOOSE THE RIGHT WORD

See **GIVE**.

do·na·tion /dōˈnāsʜən/ ▶ **noun 1** something that is given to a charity. **2** the act of donating something.

– SYNONYMS **gift,** contribution, subscription, present, handout, grant, offering.

CHOOSE THE RIGHT WORD

See **PRESENT**[3].

done /dən/ past participle of **DO**[1] ▶ **adjective 1** (of food) cooked thoroughly. **2** no longer happening or existing. **3** informal socially acceptable: *the done thing*. ▶ **exclamation** (in response to an offer) I accept!
– PHRASES **done for** informal in serious trouble. **done in** informal extremely tired.

don·gle /ˈdäɴɢgəl, ˈdôɴɢ-/ ▶ **noun** an electronic device that must be attached to a computer in order for protected software to be used.
– ORIGIN an invented word.

don·jon /ˈdänjən, ˈdən-/ ▶ **noun** the strongest or central tower of a castle.
– ORIGIN from **DUNGEON**.

Don Juan /ˌdän ˈ(h)wän/ ▶ **noun** a man who seduces many women.
– ORIGIN from the name of a legendary Spanish nobleman.

don·key /ˈdôɴɢkē, ˈdäɴɢ-/ ▶ **noun** (pl. **donkeys**) **1** a domesticated mammal of the horse family with long ears and a braying call. **2** informal a foolish person.
– PHRASES **donkey's years** informal a very long time.
– ORIGIN perhaps from **DUN**[1], or from the man's name *Duncan*.

don·nish /ˈdänisʜ/ ▶ **adjective** like a college don; concerned with scholarly rather than practical matters.

do·nor /ˈdōnər/ ▶ **noun 1** a person who donates something. **2** a substance, molecule, etc., that provides electrons for a physical or chemical process.

– SYNONYMS **giver,** contributor, benefactor, benefactress, subscriber, supporter, backer, patron, sponsor.
– ANTONYMS beneficiary.

– ORIGIN from Latin *donare* 'give.'

do·nor card ▶ **noun** a card consenting to the use of one's organs for transplant surgery in the event of one's death.

don't /dōnt/ ▶ **contraction** do not.

do·nut /ˈdōˌnət/ (also **doughnut**) ▶ **noun** a small fried cake or ring of sweetened dough.

doo·dad /ˈdo͞oˌdad/ ▶ **noun** informal **1** an object whose name is not known or has been forgotten. **2** a fancy article or trivial ornament: *there were crystal doodads all over the place*.

doo·dle /ˈdo͞odl/ ▶ **verb** draw or scribble absentmindedly. ▶ **noun** a drawing made absentmindedly.
– DERIVATIVES **doo·dler** noun.
– ORIGIN German *dudeldopp* 'simpleton.'

doo·dle·bug /ˈdo͞odlˌbəg/ ▶ **noun** informal a V-1 flying bomb used by Germany in World War II.

doom /do͞om/ ▶ **noun** death, destruction, or another terrible fate.

– SYNONYMS **destruction,** downfall, ruin, extinction, annihilation, death, nemesis.

▶ **verb** (**be doomed**) be fated to fail or be destroyed.

– SYNONYMS **1** *we were doomed to fail* **destine,** fate, predestine, preordain, mean, condemn, sentence. **2** (as adj. **doomed**) *the moving story of their doomed love affair* **ill-fated,** ill-starred, cursed, jinxed, damned; literary star-crossed.

– DERIVATIVES **doom·y** adjective.
– ORIGIN Old English, 'statute, judgment.'

doom·say·er /ˈdo͞omˌsāər/ ▶ **noun** a person who predicts disaster, especially in politics or economics.
– DERIVATIVES **doom·say·ing** noun.

dooms·day /ˈdo͞omzˌdā/ ▶ **noun 1** the last day of the world's existence. **2** (in religious belief) the day of the Last Judgment.

door /dôr/ ▶ **noun 1** a movable barrier at the entrance to a building, room, or vehicle, or in the framework of a cupboard. **2** the distance from one building in a row to another: *he lived two doors away.*
– PHRASES **lay something at someone's door** blame someone for something. **out of doors** in or into the open air.
– ORIGIN Old English.

door·bell /ˈdôrˌbel/ ▶ **noun** a bell in a building that can be rung by visitors outside.

do-or-die /ˈdo͞o ər ˈdī/ ▶ **adjective** showing or requiring a great determination to succeed.

door·keep·er /ˈdôrˌkēpər/ ▶ **noun** a person on duty at the entrance to a building.

door·knob /ˈdôrˌnäb/ ▶ **noun** a rounded door handle.

door·man /ˈdôrˌman, -mən/ ▶ **noun** (pl. **doormen**) a man who is on duty at the entrance to a large building.

door·mat /ˈdôrˌmat/ ▶ **noun 1** a mat placed in a doorway for wiping the shoes. **2** informal a person who allows others to control them or treat them badly.

door·nail /ˈdôrˌnāl/ ▶ **noun** (in phrase **dead as a doornail**) dead (used for emphasis).

door prize ▶ **noun** a prize awarded by lottery to the holder of a ticket purchased or distributed at a dance, party, or other function.

door·step /ˈdôrˌstep/ ▶ **noun** a step leading up to the outer door of a house. ▶ **verb** (**doorsteps, doorstepping, doorstepped**) Brit. informal (of a journalist) try to get an interview with or photograph of someone by waiting outside their home.
– PHRASES **on one's** (or **the**) **doorstep** situated very close by.

door·stop /ˈdôrˌstäp/ (also **doorstopper**) ▶ **noun** an object that keeps a door open or in place.

door·way /ˈdôrˌwā/ ▶ **noun** an entrance with a door.

doo-wop /ˈdo͞o ˌwäp/ ▶ **noun** a style of pop music involving close harmony vocals and nonsense phrases.
– ORIGIN imitating the sound.

doo·zy /ˈdo͞ozē/ ▶ **noun** (pl. **doozies**) informal something outstanding or unique of its kind.

do·pa·mine /ˈdōpəˌmēn/ ▶ **noun** a compound that exists in the body as a neurotransmitter and from which other substances including adrenaline are formed.
– ORIGIN from *dopa* (a related substance) + **AMINE**.

dope /dōp/ ▶ **noun 1** informal an illegal drug, especially marijuana or heroin. **2** a drug used to improve the performance of an athlete, racehorse, or greyhound. **3** informal a stupid person. **4** informal information. ▶ **verb 1** give a drug to a racehorse, greyhound, or athlete to improve their performance. **2** (**be doped up**) informal be heavily under the influence of drugs.
– ORIGIN Dutch *doop* 'sauce.'

dope·y /ˈdōpē/ (also **dopy**) ▶ **adjective** (**dopier, dopiest**) informal **1** in a semiconscious state from sleep or a drug. **2** stupid.
– DERIVATIVES **dop·i·ly** adverb **dop·i·ness** noun.

dop·pel·gäng·er /ˈdäpəlˌgaNGər/ ▶ **noun** a ghost or double of a living person.
– ORIGIN German, 'double-goer.'

Dop·pler ef·fect /ˈdäplər/ ▶ **noun** Physics an increase (or decrease) in the apparent frequency of sound, light, or other waves as the source and the observer move toward (or away from) each other.
– ORIGIN named after the Austrian physicist Johann Christian *Doppler*.

do·ra·do /dəˈrädō/ ▶ **noun** (pl. **dorados**) a large brightly colored edible fish of warm seas.
– ORIGIN Spanish, 'gilded.'

Dor·ic /ˈdôrik, ˈdär-/ ▶ **adjective** relating to a classical order of architecture characterized by a fluted column with a square slab on top.
– ORIGIN from Greek *Dorios*, referring to a people of ancient Greece.

dork /dôrk/ ▶ **noun** informal a stupid person.
– ORIGIN perhaps a variant of **DICK**[1].

dorm /dôrm/ ▶ **noun** informal a dormitory.

dor·mant /ˈdôrmənt/ ▶ **adjective 1** (of an animal) in or as if in a deep sleep. **2** (of a plant or bud) alive but not growing. **3** (of a volcano) temporarily inactive.

– SYNONYMS **sleeping,** resting, **inactive,** passive, inert, latent, idle, quiescent.
– ANTONYMS awake, active.

– DERIVATIVES **dor·man·cy** noun.
– ORIGIN from Latin *dormire* 'to sleep.'

WORD TOOLKIT

See **LATENT**.

dor·mer /ˈdôrmər/ (also **dormer window**) ▶ **noun** a window set vertically into a sloping roof.
– ORIGIN Old French *dormir* 'to sleep.'

dor·mi·to·ry /ˈdôrmiˌtôrē/ ▶ **noun** (pl. **dormitories**) a bedroom for a number of people in an institution. ▶ **adjective** referring to a small town or suburb from which people travel to work in a nearby city.
– ORIGIN Latin *dormitorium*.

dor·mouse /ˈdôrˌmous/ ▶ **noun** (pl. **dormice**) a small mouselike rodent with a bushy tail.
– ORIGIN unknown.

dor·sal /ˈdôrsəl/ ▶ **adjective** technical on or relating to the upper side or back. Compare with **VENTRAL**.
– DERIVATIVES **dor·sal·ly** adverb.
– ORIGIN from Latin *dorsum* 'back.'

do·ry[1] /ˈdôrē/ ▶ **noun** (pl. **dories**) a narrow sea fish with a large mouth.
– ORIGIN French *dorée* 'gilded.'

do·ry[2] ▶ **noun** (pl. **dories**) a small flat-bottomed rowboat

with a high bow and stern, originally used for fishing in New England.
– ORIGIN perhaps from American Indian *dóri* 'dugout.'

DOS /dôs/ ▶ **abbreviation** Computing disk operating system.

DoS ▶ **abbreviation** Computing denial of service.

dos·age /'dōsij/ ▶ **noun** the size of a dose of medicine or radiation.

dose /dōs/ ▶ **noun 1** a quantity of a medicine or drug taken at one time. **2** an amount of radiation received or absorbed at one time. **3** informal a sexually transmitted infection.

– SYNONYMS **measure,** portion, draft, dosage.

▶ **verb** give someone a medicine or drug.
– ORIGIN Greek *dosis* 'gift.'

do·sha /'dōsHə/ ▶ **noun** (in Ayurvedic medicine) each of three energies believed to circulate in the body and control its activity.
– ORIGIN Sanskrit, literally 'fault, disease.'

do-si-do /'dō sē 'dō/ ▶ **noun** (pl. **do-si-dos**) (in country dancing) a figure in which two dancers pass around each other back to back.
– ORIGIN French *dos-à-dos* 'back to back.'

do·sim·e·ter /dō'simitər/ ▶ **noun** a device used to measure an absorbed dose of radiation.
– DERIVATIVES **do·sim·e·try** noun.

dos·si·er /'dôsē,ā, 'däs-/ ▶ **noun** a collection of documents about a person or subject.
– ORIGIN French.

dost /dəst/ old-fashioned second person singular present of **DO**[1].

DOT ▶ **abbreviation** Department of Transportation.

dot /dät/ ▶ **noun 1** a small round mark or spot. **2** the shorter signal of the two used in Morse code. **3** Music a dot used to indicate the lengthening of a note or rest by half, or to indicate staccato.

– SYNONYMS **spot,** speck, fleck, speckle, period, decimal point.

▶ **verb** (**dots, dotting, dotted**) **1** mark something with a dot or dots. **2** scatter something over an area: *the meadow was dotted with buttercups and daisies.*

– SYNONYMS **1 spot,** fleck, mark, spatter. **2 scatter,** pepper, sprinkle, strew, spread.

– PHRASES **dot the i's and cross the t's** informal ensure that all details are correct. **on the dot** informal exactly on time.
– ORIGIN Old English, 'head of a boil.'

dot·age /'dōtij/ ▶ **noun** the period of life in which a person is old and weak.
– ORIGIN from **DOTE**.

do·tard /'dōtərd/ ▶ **noun** an old person, especially one who is weak or senile.

dot-com (also **dot.com**) ▶ **noun** a company that conducts its business on the Internet.
– ORIGIN from '.com' in an Internet address, indicating a commercial site.

dote /dōt/ ▶ **verb** (**dote on**) be extremely and uncritically fond of: *she's a flirt but he dotes on her.*

– SYNONYMS **adore,** love dearly, be devoted to, idolize, treasure, cherish, worship.

– DERIVATIVES **dot·ing** adjective.
– ORIGIN related to Dutch *doten* 'be silly.'

doth /dəTH/ old-fashioned third person singular present of **DO**[1].

dot ma·trix ▶ **noun** a grid of dots that are filled selectively to produce an image on a screen or on paper.

dot-org (also **dot.org**) ▶ **noun** a nonprofit organization that conducts its business on the Internet.

dot·ted line ▶ **noun** a line made up of dots or dashes (often used in reference to the space left for a signature on a contract).

dot·ter·el /'dätərəl/ ▶ **noun** (pl. same or **dotterels**) a small migratory plover (bird).
– ORIGIN from **DOTE** (because the bird is easily caught).

dot·ty /'dätē/ slightly mad or eccentric.
– DERIVATIVES **dot·ti·ly** adverb **dot·ti·ness** noun.
– ORIGIN perhaps from former *dote* 'fool.'

dou·ble /'dəbəl/ ▶ **adjective 1** consisting of two equal, identical, or similar parts or things. **2** having twice the usual size, quantity, or strength: *a double brandy.* **3** designed to be used by two people. **4** having two different roles or interpretations: *she began a double life.* **5** (of a flower) having more than one circle of petals.

– SYNONYMS **dual,** duplex, twin, binary, duplicate, coupled, matching, twofold, in pairs.
– ANTONYMS single.

▶ **adverb** twice the amount or extent.
▶ **noun 1** a thing that is twice as large as usual or is made up of two parts. **2** a person who looks exactly like another. **3** (**doubles**) a game involving sides made up of two players. **4** Baseball a hit that allows the batter to reach second base safely.

– SYNONYMS **lookalike,** twin, clone, duplicate, exact likeness, replica, copy, facsimile, doppelgänger; informal spitting image, dead ringer.

▶ **pronoun** an amount twice as large as usual.
▶ **verb 1** make or become double. **2** fold or bend over on itself. **3** (**double up**) bend over or curl up with pain or laughter. **4** (**double as**) be used in or play another, different role: *a pocket-sized computer that doubles as a cell phone.* **5** (**double back**) go back in the direction one has come.
– DERIVATIVES **dou·ble·ness** noun **dou·bler** noun **dou·bly** adverb.
– PHRASES **at the double** very fast.
– ORIGIN Latin *duplus*, from *duo* 'two.'

dou·ble a·gent ▶ **noun** an agent who pretends to act as a spy for one country while in fact acting for its enemy.

dou·ble-bar·reled ▶ **adjective 1** (of a gun) having two barrels. **2** having two parts or aspects: *a double-barreled strategy for reducing crime.* **3** more than usually forceful, impressive, or sensational: *John Woo's double-barreled action sequences.*

dou·ble bass /bās/ ▶ **noun** the largest and lowest-pitched instrument of the violin family.

dou·ble bill ▶ **noun** a program of entertainment with two main items.

dou·ble bind ▶ **noun** a dilemma.

dou·ble-blind ▶ **adjective** (of a test or trial) in which information that may influence the behavior of the tester or subject is withheld.

dou·ble boil·er ▶ **noun** a saucepan with an upper compartment heated by boiling water in the lower one.

dou·ble bond ▶ **noun** a chemical bond in which two pairs of electrons are shared between two atoms.

dou·ble-breast·ed ▶ **adjective** (of a jacket or coat) having a large overlap at the front and two rows of buttons.

dou·ble-check ▶ **verb** check something again to make certain.

dou·ble chin ▶ **noun** a roll of flesh below a person's chin.

dou·ble-cross ▶ **verb** betray a person one is supposedly helping.

– SYNONYMS **betray,** cheat, defraud, trick, hoodwink, mislead, deceive, swindle, be disloyal to, be unfaithful to; informal sell down the river.

dou·ble-deal·ing ▶ **noun** deceitful behavior.
▶ **adjective** acting deceitfully.

dou·ble-deck·er ▶ **noun** a vehicle with two floors, one on top of the other.

dou·ble-dig·it ▶ **adjective** (of a number, variable, or percentage) between 10 and 99: *double-digit inflation.*

dou·ble Dutch ▶ **noun** a jump-rope game played with two ropes swung in opposite directions.

dou·ble-edged ▶ **adjective 1** (of a blade) having two cutting edges. **2** having two contrasting aspects or possible outcomes.

dou·ble en·ten·dre /ˈdo͞ob(ə)l änˈtändrə/ ▶ **noun** (pl. **double entendres** pronunc. same) a word or phrase with two possible meanings, one of which is usually risqué or indecent.
– ORIGIN from former French, 'double understanding.'

dou·ble-en·try ▶ **adjective** relating to a system of bookkeeping in which each transaction is entered as a debit in one account and a credit in another.

dou·ble ex·po·sure ▶ **noun** the repeated exposure of a photographic plate or film.

dou·ble fault ▶ **noun** Tennis an instance of two consecutive faults in serving, resulting in the loss of a point.

Dou·ble Glouces·ter ▶ **noun** a hard cheese originally made in Gloucestershire, England.

dou·ble·head·er /ˌdəbəlˈhedər/ ▶ **noun 1** a sporting event in which two games are played in succession at the same venue. **2** a train pulled by two locomotives.

dou·ble he·lix ▶ **noun** a pair of parallel helices intertwined about a common axis, especially that in the structure of DNA.

dou·ble jeop·ard·y ▶ **noun** Law the prosecution or punishment of a person twice for the same offense.

dou·ble-joint·ed ▶ **adjective** (of a person) having unusually flexible joints.

dou·ble neg·a·tive ▶ **noun** Grammar a negative statement containing two negative elements (e.g., *didn't say nothing*), regarded as incorrect in standard English.

USAGE

A **double negative** uses two negative words in the same clause to convey a single negative, such as *I don't know nothing* (rather than *I don't know anything*). The structure is regarded as bad English because the two negative elements cancel each other out to give a positive statement, so that *I don't know nothing* could be taken to mean *I know something.*

dou·ble-park ▶ **verb** park a vehicle alongside one that is already parked.

dou·ble play ▶ **noun** Baseball a defensive play in which two players are put out.

dou·ble pneu·mo·nia ▶ **noun** pneumonia affecting both lungs.

dou·ble·speak /ˈdəbəlˌspēk/ ▶ **noun** language that is deliberately unclear or ambiguous.
– ORIGIN coined by George Orwell (see **DOUBLETHINK**).

dou·ble stand·ard ▶ **noun** a rule or principle applied unfairly in different ways to different people.

dou·blet /ˈdəblət/ ▶ **noun 1** a man's short close-fitting padded jacket, worn from the 14th to the 17th century. **2** a pair of similar things.
– ORIGIN Old French, 'something folded.'

dou·ble take ▶ **noun** a second reaction to something unexpected, immediately after one's first reaction.

dou·ble·think /ˈdəbəlˌTHiNGk/ ▶ **noun** the acceptance of conflicting opinions or beliefs at the same time.
– ORIGIN coined by George Orwell in his novel *Nineteen Eighty-Four.*

dou·ble time ▶ **noun** a rate of pay equal to double the standard rate.

dou·ble vi·sion ▶ **noun** the perception of two overlapping images of a single scene.

dou·ble wham·my ▶ **noun** informal a blow or setback consisting of two separate elements.

dou·bloon /dəˈblo͞on/ ▶ **noun** historical a Spanish gold coin.
– ORIGIN Spanish *doblón.*

doubt /dout/ ▶ **noun** a feeling of uncertainty.

– SYNONYMS **1** *there was some doubt as to the caller's identity* **uncertainty,** indecision, hesitation, irresolution, hesitancy, vacillation, lack of conviction. **2** *there is doubt about their motives* **skepticism,** distrust, mistrust, suspicion, cynicism, wariness, reservations, misgivings, suspicions.
– ANTONYMS certainty, trust.

▶ **verb 1** disbelieve or mistrust: *I have no reason to doubt him.* **2** feel uncertain about something: *I doubt if he makes much money.*

– SYNONYMS **disbelieve,** distrust, mistrust, suspect, be suspicious of, have misgivings about.

– DERIVATIVES **doubt·er** noun **doubt·ing** adjective.
– PHRASES **no doubt 1** certainly. **2** probably.
– ORIGIN from Latin *dubius* 'doubtful.'

CHOOSE THE RIGHT WORD

See **UNCERTAINTY**.

doubt·ful /ˈdoutfəl/ ▶ **adjective 1** feeling uncertain. **2** not known with certainty: *the fire was of doubtful origin.* **3** unlikely: *it's doubtful whether the council will be able to recover the money.*

– SYNONYMS **1 hesitant,** in doubt, unsure, uncertain, in two minds, in a quandary, in a dilemma. **2 in doubt,** uncertain, open to question, unsure, debatable, up in the air, inconclusive, unconfirmed. **3 unlikely,** improbable. **4 distrustful,** mistrustful, skeptical, suspicious, having reservations, wary, chary, leery. **5 questionable,** dubious, suspect, suspicious.
– ANTONYMS confident, certain.

– DERIVATIVES **doubt·ful·ly** adverb.

doubt·ing Thom·as /'täməs/ ▶ **noun** a person who refuses to believe something without proof.
– ORIGIN referring to the apostle Thomas (Gospel of John, Chapter 20).

doubt·less /'doutlis/ ▶ **adverb** very probably.

– SYNONYMS **undoubtedly,** no doubt, unquestionably, indisputably, undeniably, certainly, surely, of course.

– DERIVATIVES **doubt·less·ly** adverb.

douche /do͞osн/ ▶ **noun 1** a shower of water. **2** a jet of liquid applied to part of the body for cleansing or medicinal purposes. **3** a device for washing out the vagina as a contraceptive measure. ▶ **verb** spray or clean someone or something with water.
– ORIGIN French.

dough /dō/ ▶ **noun 1** a thick mixture of flour and liquid, for baking into bread or pastry. **2** informal money.
– DERIVATIVES **dough·y** adjective.
– ORIGIN Old English.

dough·ty /'doutē/ ▶ **adjective** (**doughtier, doughtiest**) brave and determined.
– ORIGIN Old English.

Doug·las fir /'dəgləs/ ▶ **noun** a tall, slender conifer valued for its wood.
– ORIGIN named after the Scottish botanist and explorer David *Douglas*.

dour /do͝or, dou(ə)r/ ▶ **adjective** very severe, stern, or gloomy.

– SYNONYMS **stern,** unsmiling, unfriendly, severe, forbidding, gruff, surly, grim, sullen, solemn, austere, stony.
– ANTONYMS cheerful, friendly.

– DERIVATIVES **dour·ly** adverb **dour·ness** noun.
– ORIGIN probably from Scottish Gaelic, 'dull, obstinate, stupid.'

douse /dous/ (also **dowse**) ▶ **verb 1** drench something with liquid. **2** extinguish a fire or light.

– SYNONYMS **1 drench,** soak, saturate, wet. **2 extinguish,** put out, quench, smother.

– ORIGIN uncertain.

dove¹ /dəv/ ▶ **noun 1** a stocky bird with a small head, short legs, and a cooing voice, very similar to but generally smaller than a pigeon. **2** (in politics) a person who favors a policy of peace and negotiation.
– DERIVATIVES **dov·ish** (also **doveish**) adjective.
– ORIGIN Old Norse.

dove² /dōv/ past and past participle of **DIVE**.

dove·cote /'dəv,kōt/ (also **dovecot**) ▶ **noun** a shelter with nest holes for domesticated pigeons.

dove·tail /'dəv,tāl/ ▶ **verb 1** fit together easily or conveniently: *flights that dovetail with the working day.* **2** join things by means of a dovetail joint. ▶ **noun** a wedge-shaped joint formed by interlocking two pieces of wood.

dow·a·ger /'douəjər/ ▶ **noun 1** a widow who holds a title or property that belonged to her late husband. **2** a dignified elderly woman.
– ORIGIN Old French *douagiere*.

dow·dy /'doudē/ ▶ **adjective** (**dowdier, dowdiest**) (especially of a woman) unfashionable and dull in appearance.

– SYNONYMS **unfashionable,** frumpy, old-fashioned, shabby, frowzy.
– ANTONYMS fashionable.

– DERIVATIVES **dow·di·ly** adverb **dow·di·ness** noun.

dow·el /'douəl/ ▶ **noun** a headless peg used for holding together components. ▶ **verb** (**dowels, doweling, doweled**) fasten things with a dowel.
– ORIGIN perhaps German.

dow·el·ing /'douəliNG/ ▶ **noun** cylindrical rods that are cut into dowels.

dow·er /'dou(-ə)r/ ▶ **noun 1** a widow's share for life of her husband's estate. **2** old use a dowry.
– ORIGIN Old French *douaire*.

Dow Jones In·dus·tri·al Av·er·age /'dou 'jōnz/ ▶ **noun** an index of figures indicating the relative price of shares on the New York Stock Exchange.
– ORIGIN named after the financial news agency *Dow Jones & Co, Inc.*

down¹ /doun/ ▶ **adverb 1** toward or in a lower place or position. **2** to or at a lower level or value. **3** in or into a weaker or worse position, mood, or condition. **4** to a smaller amount or size, or a simpler or more basic state. **5** away from a central place or the north. **6** from an earlier to a later point in time or order. **7** in or into writing. **8** (of a computer system) out of action. ▶ **preposition 1** from a higher to a lower point of. **2** at a point farther along the course of. **3** along the course or extent of. **4** informal at or to a place. ▶ **adjective 1** directed or moving toward a lower place or position. **2** unhappy. **3** (of a computer system) out of action. ▶ **verb** informal **1** knock or bring someone or something to the ground. **2** consume a drink.
– PHRASES **be down on** informal dislike or feel hostile toward someone. **be down to 1** be caused by. **2** be left with: *I'm down to my last few dollars.* **down in the mouth** informal unhappy. **down on one's luck** informal having a period of bad luck.
– ORIGIN Old English.

down² ▶ **noun** fine, soft feathers or hairs.
– ORIGIN Old Norse.

down³ ▶ **noun 1** a gently rolling hill. **2** (**the Downs**) ridges of undulating chalk and limestone hills in southern England.
– ORIGIN Old English.

down and out ▶ **adjective** homeless and having no money; destitute. ▶ **noun** (**down-and-out**) a destitute person.

down-at-the-heels ▶ **adjective** shabby because of a lack of money.

down·beat /'doun,bēt/ ▶ **adjective 1** pessimistic or gloomy. **2** relaxed and understated. ▶ **noun** Music an accented beat, usually the first of the bar.

down·cast /'doun,kast/ ▶ **adjective 1** (of a person's eyes) looking downward. **2** feeling sad or depressed.

down·draft /'doun,draft/ ▶ **noun** a downward current or draft of air, especially one down a chimney into a room.

down·er /'dounər/ ▶ **noun** informal **1** a depressant or tranquilizing drug. **2** a sad or depressing experience.

down·fall /'doun,fôl/ ▶ **noun** a loss of power, wealth, or status.

– SYNONYMS **ruin,** ruination, undoing, defeat, overthrow, destruction, annihilation, end, collapse, fall, crash, failure.
– ANTONYMS rise.

down·field /'doun'fēld/ ▶ **adverb** (in sports) in or to a position nearer to the opponents' end of a field.

down·force /'doun,fôrs/ ▶ **noun** a force acting on a moving vehicle having the effect of pressing it down toward the ground, giving it increased stability.

down·grade /'doun,grād/ ▶ **verb** reduce someone or something to a lower grade, rank, or level of importance.

– SYNONYMS **demote,** reduce, relegate.
– ANTONYMS promote.

down·heart·ed /'doun'härtid/ ▶ **adjective** feeling sad or discouraged.

– SYNONYMS **despondent,** disheartened, discouraged, dispirited, downcast, crestfallen, down, low, disconsolate, wretched, melancholy, gloomy, glum, doleful, dismal, woebegone, miserable, depressed, dejected, sorrowful, sad; informal blue, down in the mouth, down in the dumps.
– ANTONYMS elated.

down·hill /'doun'hil/ ▶ **adverb & adjective 1** toward the bottom of a slope. **2** into a steadily worsening situation: *his career was rapidly going downhill.*

down·link /'doun,lingk/ ▶ **noun** a telecommunications link for signals coming to the earth from a satellite, spacecraft, or aircraft.

down·load /'doun,lōd/ ▶ **verb** copy data from one computer system to another or to a disk. ▶ **noun 1** a downloaded computer file. **2** the process of downloading data.
– DERIVATIVES **down·load·a·ble** adjective.

down·mar·ket /'doun,märkit/ ▶ **adjective & adverb** cheaper and of low quality or status.

down pay·ment ▶ **noun** an initial payment made when buying something on credit.

down·play /'doun,plā/ ▶ **verb** make something appear less important than it really is.

down·pour /'doun,pôr/ ▶ **noun** a heavy fall of rain.

down·right /'doun,rīt/ ▶ **adjective** utter; complete: *a downright lie.*

– SYNONYMS **complete,** total, absolute, utter, thorough, out-and-out, outright, sheer, arrant, pure.

▶ **adverb** extremely: *he was downright rude.*

– SYNONYMS **thoroughly,** utterly, positively, profoundly, really, completely, totally, entirely.

down·riv·er /'doun'rivər/ ▶ **adverb & adjective** toward or situated at a point nearer the mouth of a river.

down·scale /'doun,skāl/ ▶ **verb** reduce the size or extent of something. ▶ **adjective** downmarket.

down·shift /'doun,shift/ ▶ **verb** adopt a simpler and less stressful lifestyle.

down·side /'doun,sīd/ ▶ **noun** the negative aspect of something.

down·size /'doun,sīz/ ▶ **verb** reduce the number of staff employed by a company in order to cut costs.

down·spout /'doun,spout/ ▶ **noun** a pipe to carry rainwater from a roof to a drain or to ground level.

down·stage /'doun'stāj/ ▶ **adjective & adverb** at or toward the front of a stage.

down·stairs /'doun'ste(ə)rz/ ▶ **adverb & adjective** down a flight of stairs; on or to a lower floor. ▶ **noun** the ground floor or lower floors of a building.

down·state /'doun'stāt/ ▶ **adjective & adverb** of, in, or to the southern part of a state.

down·stream /'doun'strēm/ ▶ **adverb & adjective** situated or moving in the direction in which a stream or river flows.

Down syn·drome /dounz/ (also **Down's syndrome**) ▶ **noun** a medical disorder caused by a genetic defect, causing intellectual impairment and physical abnormalities.
– ORIGIN named after the English physician John L. H. *Down.*

down·tem·po /'doun,tempō/ ▶ **adjective** (of music) played at a slow tempo.

down·time /'doun,tīm/ ▶ **noun** time during which a computer or other machine is out of action.

down-to-earth ▶ **adjective** practical and realistic.

down·town /'doun'toun/ ▶ **adjective & adverb** of, in, or toward the central area or main business area of a city. ▶ **noun** a downtown area.
– DERIVATIVES **down·town·er** noun.

down·trend /'doun,trend/ ▶ **noun** a downward tendency, especially in economic matters: *a downtrend in the share price.*

down·trod·den /'doun,trädn/ ▶ **adjective** treated badly by people in power and lacking the energy or ability to resist.

down·turn /'doun,tərn/ ▶ **noun** a decline in economic or other activity.

down un·der informal (also **Down Under**) ▶ **adverb** in or to Australia or New Zealand. ▶ **noun** Australia and New Zealand.

down·ward /'dounwərd/ ▶ **adverb** (also **downwards**) toward a lower point or level. ▶ **adjective** moving toward a lower level.
– DERIVATIVES **down·ward·ly** adverb.

down·wind /'doun'wind/ ▶ **adverb & adjective** in the direction in which the wind is blowing.

down·y /'dounē/ ▶ **adjective** (**downier, downiest**) covered with fine soft hair or feathers.

dow·ry /'dou(ə)rē/ ▶ **noun** (pl. **dowries**) property or money brought by a bride to her husband on their marriage.
– ORIGIN Old French *dowarie.*

dowse[1] /douz/ ▶ **verb** search for underground water or minerals with a pointer that is supposedly moved by unseen influences.
– DERIVATIVES **dows·er** noun.
– ORIGIN unknown.

dowse[2] /dous/ ▶ **verb** variant spelling of **DOUSE**.

dox·ol·o·gy /däk'säləjē/ ▶ **noun** (pl. **doxologies**) a set form of prayer praising God.
– ORIGIN Greek *doxologia.*

doy·en /doi'en, 'doi-en/ ▶ **noun** (fem. **doyenne** /doi'en/) the most respected or prominent person in a particular group or profession: *the doyenne of American poetry.*
– ORIGIN Old French *deien.*

doz. ▶ **abbreviation** dozen.

doze /dōz/ ▶ **verb** sleep lightly. ▶ **noun** a short light sleep.
– ORIGIN perhaps related to Danish *døse* 'make drowsy.'

doz·en /'dəzən/ ▶ **noun** (pl. same) **1** a group or set of twelve. **2** informal a lot.
– DERIVATIVES **doz·enth** /'dəzənth/ adjective.
– ORIGIN Old French *dozeine.*

do·zy /ˈdōzē/ ▸ **adjective** (**dozier, doziest**) feeling drowsy and lazy.
– DERIVATIVES **do·zi·ly** adverb **do·zi·ness** noun.

DP ▸ **abbreviation** **1** data processing. **2** Baseball double play.

DPT ▸ **abbreviation** diphtheria, pertussis (whooping cough), and tetanus, a combined vaccine given to small children.

Dr. ▸ **abbreviation** (as a title) Doctor.

dr. ▸ **abbreviation** **1** drachma(s). **2** dram(s).

drab /drab/ ▸ **adjective** (**drabber, drabbest**) lacking brightness or interest; dull and dreary.

– SYNONYMS **1 colorless,** gray, dull, washed out, dingy, dreary, dismal, cheerless, gloomy, somber. **2 uninteresting,** dull, boring, tedious, monotonous, dry, dreary.
– ANTONYMS bright, interesting.

▸ **noun** a dull light brown color.
– DERIVATIVES **drab·ly** adverb **drab·ness** noun.
– ORIGIN probably from Old French *drap* 'cloth.'

drach·ma /ˈdräkmə/ ▸ **noun** (pl. **drachmas** or **drachmae** /-mē/) **1** (until the introduction of the euro in 2002) the basic unit of money of Greece. **2** a silver coin of ancient Greece.
– ORIGIN Greek *drakhmē*, an ancient weight and coin.

dra·co·ni·an /drəˈkōnēən, drā-/ ▸ **adjective** (of laws or punishments) extremely harsh or severe.
– ORIGIN named after the ancient Athenian legislator *Draco*.

draft /draft/ ▸ **noun** **1** a preliminary version of a piece of writing. **2** a plan or sketch. **3** (Brit. **draught**) a current of cool air in a room or confined space. **4** (Brit. **draught**) a written order requesting a bank to pay a specified sum of money. **5** (Brit. **draught**) a single act of drinking or breathing in. **6** (**the draft**) compulsory recruitment for military service. **7** (Brit. **draught**) the depth of water needed to float a particular ship.

– SYNONYMS **1 version,** sketch, attempt, effort, outline, plan. **2 current of air,** wind, breeze, gust, puff, waft. **3 check,** order, money order, bill of exchange. **4 gulp,** drink, swallow, mouthful; informal swig.

▸ **verb** **1** prepare a preliminary version of a piece of writing. **2** select a person or group and send them somewhere for a purpose: *volunteers were drafted to help with crowd control.* **3** conscript someone for military service.
▸ **adjective** (Brit. **draught**) **1** (of beer) served from a cask rather than from a bottle or can. **2** (of an animal) used for pulling heavy loads.
– DERIVATIVES **draft·er** noun.
– ORIGIN from **DRAUGHT**.

draft·ee /drafˈtē/ ▸ **noun** a person conscripted for military service.

drafts·man /ˈdraftsmən/ (or **draftswoman** /ˈdrafts,wo͝omən/) ▸ **noun** (pl. **draftsmen** or **draftswomen**) **1** a person who makes detailed technical plans or drawings. **2** an artist skilled in drawing. **3** a person who drafts legal documents.
– DERIVATIVES **drafts·man·ship** /-,SHip/ noun.

draft·y /ˈdraftē/ (Brit. **draughty**) ▸ **adjective** (**draftier, draftiest**) (of a room, space, etc.) uncomfortable because drafts of cold air are blowing through it.

drag /drag/ ▸ **verb** (**drags, dragging, dragged**) **1** pull something along forcefully, roughly, or with difficulty. **2** trail along the ground. **3** take someone somewhere, despite their reluctance. **4** move an image across a computer screen using a mouse. **5** (of time) pass slowly. **6** (**drag something out**) prolong something unnecessarily. **7** (**drag something up**) informal deliberately mention something unwelcome. **8** search the bottom of an area of water with grapnels or nets. **9** (**drag on**) informal inhale the smoke from a cigarette.

– SYNONYMS **haul,** pull, tug, heave, lug, draw, trail.

▸ **noun** **1** informal a boring or tiresome person or thing. **2** the force exerted by air or water to slow down a moving object. **3** informal an act of inhaling smoke from a cigarette. **4** the action of dragging.

– SYNONYMS **1 bore,** nuisance, bother, trouble, pest, annoyance, trial; informal pain (in the neck), bind, headache, hassle. **2 pull,** resistance, tug.

– PHRASES **drag one's feet** **1** walk wearily or with difficulty. **2** be slow or reluctant to act. **in drag** (of a man) wearing women's clothes.
– ORIGIN Old English or Old Norse.

drag·gle /ˈdragəl/ ▸ **verb** **1** make something dirty or wet by trailing it on the ground. **2** hang untidily.
– ORIGIN from **DRAG**.

drag·net /ˈdrag,net/ ▸ **noun** **1** a net drawn through water or across ground to trap fish or game. **2** a systematic search for criminals.

drag·o·man /ˈdragəmən/ ▸ **noun** (pl. **dragomans** or **dragomen**) an interpreter or guide in a country speaking Arabic, Turkish, or Persian.
– ORIGIN Arabic, 'interpreter.'

drag·on /ˈdragən/ ▸ **noun** **1** a mythical monster like a giant reptile, typically able to breathe out fire. **2** derogatory a fierce and intimidating woman.
– ORIGIN Greek *drakōn* 'serpent.'

drag·on·fly /ˈdragən,flī/ ▸ **noun** (pl. **dragonflies**) a fast-flying long-bodied insect with two pairs of large transparent wings.

dra·goon /drəˈgo͞on/ ▸ **noun** **1** a member of any of several British cavalry regiments. **2** historical a mounted infantryman armed with a rifle or musket. ▸ **verb** force or persuade someone to do something: *she had been dragooned into helping with the housework.*
– ORIGIN French *dragon* 'dragon.'

drag queen ▸ **noun** informal a man who dresses up in very flamboyant or showy women's clothes.

drag race ▸ **noun** a short race between two cars to see which can accelerate fastest from a standstill.
– DERIVATIVES **drag rac·er** noun **drag rac·ing** noun.

drag·ster /ˈdragstər/ ▸ **noun** a car used in drag races.

drain /drān/ ▸ **verb** **1** make the liquid in something run out: *we drained the swimming pool.* **2** (of liquid) flow away from, out of, or into something: *the river drains into the Pacific.* **3** become dry as liquid runs off. **4** deprive of strength or vitality: *she felt drained of energy.* **5** cause a resource to be lost or used up: *my mother's hospital bills are draining my income.* **6** drink the entire contents of a glass, cup, etc.

– SYNONYMS **1** *a valve for draining the tank* **empty (out),** void, clear (out), evacuate, unload. **2** *drain off any surplus liquid* **draw off,** extract, siphon off, pour out, pour off, bleed, tap, filter, discharge. **3** *the water drained away* **flow,** pour, trickle, stream, run, rush, gush, flood, surge, leak, ooze, seep, dribble. **4 use up,** exhaust, deplete, consume, expend, get through, sap, milk, bleed. **5 drink,** gulp (down),

guzzle, quaff, swallow, finish off, toss off; informal sink, down, swig, swill (down), knock back.
– ANTONYMS fill.

▶ **noun 1** a channel or pipe carrying off surplus liquid. **2** a thing that uses up a resource or one's strength.

– SYNONYMS **1 sewer,** channel, ditch, culvert, duct, pipe, gutter. **2 strain,** pressure, burden, load, demand.

– PHRASES **go down the drain** informal be totally wasted.
– ORIGIN Old English.

drain·age /ˈdrānij/ ▶ **noun 1** the action or process of draining something. **2** a system of drains.

drain·board /ˈdrānˌbôrd/ ▶ **noun** a sloping grooved surface next to a sink, on which dishes are left to drain.

drain·er /ˈdrānər/ ▶ **noun 1** a rack used to hold draining dishes. **2** a drainboard.

drain·pipe /ˈdrānˌpīp/ ▶ **noun** a pipe for carrying off rainwater from a building.

drake /drāk/ ▶ **noun** a male duck.
– ORIGIN Germanic.

DRAM /ˈdēˌram/ ▶ **noun** Electronics a memory chip that depends upon an applied voltage to keep the stored data.
– ORIGIN acronym from *dynamic random-access memory*.

dram /dram/ ▶ **noun 1** historical a unit of weight equivalent to one eighth of an ounce. **2** (also **fluid dram**) historical a liquid measure equivalent to one eighth of a fluid ounce. **3** chiefly Scottish a small drink of liquor.
– ORIGIN Latin *dragma*, from Greek *drakhmē* 'drachma.'

dra·ma /ˈdrämə/ ▶ **noun 1** a play. **2** plays as a literary genre. **3** an exciting series of events.

– SYNONYMS **1 play,** show, piece, theatrical work, stage show, dramatization. **2 acting,** the theater, the stage, dramatic art, stagecraft, dramaturgy. **3 incident,** scene, spectacle, crisis, disturbance, row, commotion, excitement, thrill, sensation, dramatics, theatrics, histrionics.

– ORIGIN Greek.

dra·mat·ic /drəˈmatik/ ▶ **adjective 1** relating to drama. **2** sudden and striking: *a dramatic increase in the prison population.* **3** exciting or impressive. **4** intended to create an effect; theatrical: *he flung out his arms in a dramatic gesture.*

– SYNONYMS **1 theatrical,** thespian, dramaturgical. **2 considerable,** substantial, significant, remarkable, extraordinary, exceptional, phenomenal. **3 exciting,** stirring, action-packed, sensational, spectacular, startling, unexpected, tense, gripping, riveting, thrilling, hair-raising, lively. **4 striking,** impressive, imposing, spectacular, breathtaking, dazzling, sensational, awesome, awe-inspiring, remarkable. **5 exaggerated,** theatrical, ostentatious, actressy, stagy, showy, melodramatic.
– ANTONYMS unremarkable, boring.

– DERIVATIVES **dra·mat·i·cal·ly** /-ik(ə)lē/ adverb.

dra·mat·ics /drəˈmatiks/ ▶ **plural noun 1** the study or practice of acting in and producing plays. **2** theatrically exaggerated behavior.

dram·a·tis per·so·nae /ˈdrämətis pərˈsōnē/ ▶ **plural noun** the characters of a play or novel.
– ORIGIN Latin, 'persons of the drama.'

dram·a·tist /ˈdräməˌtist/ ▶ **noun** a person who writes plays.

dram·a·tize /ˈdräməˌtīz/ ▶ **verb 1** present a novel, event, etc., as a play or movie. **2** exaggerate the excitement or seriousness of something.

– SYNONYMS **1 adapt,** turn into a play/movie. **2 exaggerate,** overdo, overstate, magnify, amplify, inflate, sensationalize, embroider, color, aggrandize, embellish, elaborate; informal blow up (out of all proportion).

– DERIVATIVES **dram·a·ti·za·tion** /ˌdrämətiˈzāsʜən/ noun.

dram·a·turge /ˈdräməˌtərj/ (also **dramaturg**) ▶ **noun 1** a dramatist. **2** a literary editor on the staff of a theater who consults with authors and edits texts.
– ORIGIN from Greek *dramatourgos*.

dram·a·tur·gy /ˈdräməˌtərjē/ ▶ **noun** the theory and practice of writing plays.
– DERIVATIVES **dram·a·tur·gi·cal** /ˌdräməˈtərjikəl/ adjective.

Dram·bu·ie /dramˈbo͞oē/ ▶ **noun** trademark a sweet Scotch whiskey liqueur.
– ORIGIN from Scottish Gaelic *dram buidheach* 'satisfying drink.'

dra·me·dy /ˈdrämədē/ ▶ **noun** (pl. **dramedies**) a television program or movie containing both dramatic and comedic elements.

drank /draɴɢk/ past of **DRINK**.

drape /drāp/ ▶ **verb** arrange cloth or clothing loosely on or around something.

– SYNONYMS **wrap,** cover, envelop, shroud, wind, swathe, festoon, hang.

▶ **noun 1** (**drapes**) long curtains. **2** the way in which a garment or fabric hangs.
– ORIGIN from **DRAPERY**.

drap·er /ˈdrāpər/ ▶ **noun** Brit. dated a person who sells fabrics.

dra·per·y /ˈdrāpərē/ ▶ **noun** (pl. **draperies**) cloth, curtains, or clothing hanging in loose folds.
– ORIGIN from Old French *drap* 'cloth.'

dras·tic /ˈdrastik/ ▶ **adjective** having a strong or far-reaching effect.

– SYNONYMS **extreme,** serious, desperate, radical, far-reaching, momentous, substantial.
– ANTONYMS moderate.

– DERIVATIVES **dras·ti·cal·ly** /-ik(ə)lē/ adverb.
– ORIGIN Greek *drastikos*.

drat /drat/ ▶ **exclamation** used to express mild annoyance.
– DERIVATIVES **drat·ted** adjective.
– ORIGIN shortening of *od rat*, a euphemism for *God rot*.

draught /ˈdraft/ ▶ **noun & adjective** British spelling of certain senses of **DRAFT**.
– ORIGIN Old Norse.

draughts /ˈdraf(t)s/ ▶ **noun** British term for the game of checkers (see **CHECKER[2]**).
– ORIGIN from **DRAUGHT** in the former sense 'move' (in chess).

Dra·vid·i·an /drəˈvidēən/ ▶ **noun 1** a family of languages spoken in southern India and Sri Lanka, including Tamil and Kannada. **2** a member of any of the peoples speaking these languages. ▶ **adjective** relating to Dravidian or Dravidians.
– ORIGIN Sanskrit, 'relating to the Tamils.'

draw /drô/ ▶ **verb** (past **drew**; past part. **drawn**) **1** produce a picture, diagram, etc., by making lines and marks on paper. **2** pull or drag a vehicle so as to make it follow behind. **3** pull or move in a particular direction: *the* *train drew out of the station.* **4** take something from a container or receptacle. **5** attract someone to a place or an event. **6** get or take something from a source: *he draws inspiration from ordinary scenes and places.* **7** pull curtains shut or open. **8** arrive at a point in time: *the campaign drew to a close.* **9** take in a breath. **10** be the cause of a particular response: *his action drew fierce criticism.* **11** persuade someone to reveal or do something: *he refused to be drawn into the argument.* **12** reach a conclusion. **13** finish a contest or game with an even score.

– SYNONYMS **1 sketch,** outline, rough out, illustrate, render, represent, trace, portray, depict. **2 pull,** haul, drag, tug, heave, lug, tow; informal yank. **3 move,** go, come, proceed, progress, pass, drive, inch, roll, glide, cruise, sweep. **4** *he drew his gun* **pull out,** take out, produce, fish out, extract, withdraw, unsheathe. **5** *she was drawing huge audiences* **attract,** win, capture, catch, engage, lure, entice, bring in. **6** *you can always* **draw on** *your carpentry skills* **call on,** have recourse to, turn to, look to, exploit, use, employ, utilize, bring into play.

▶ **noun 1** a game or match that ends with the scores even. **2** a person or thing that is very attractive or interesting. **3** an act of selecting names at random, for prizes, sporting events, etc. **4** an act of inhaling smoke from a cigarette.

– SYNONYMS **1 tie,** dead heat, stalemate. **2 attraction,** lure, allure, pull, appeal, temptation, charm, fascination.

– PHRASES **draw someone's fire** attract hostile criticism away from a more important target. **draw the line at** refuse to do or tolerate something. **draw on 1** (of a period of time) pass by and approach its end. **2** suck smoke from a cigarette or pipe. **draw someone/thing out 1** make something last longer. **2** persuade someone to be more talkative. **draw up** come to a halt. **draw something up** prepare a plan or document.
– ORIGIN Old English.

USAGE

On the confusion of **draw** and **drawer**, see the note at **DRAWER**.

draw·back /ˈdrôˌbak/ ▶ **noun** a disadvantage or problem.

– SYNONYMS **disadvantage,** snag, downside, stumbling block, catch, hitch, pitfall, fly in the ointment, weak spot/point, weakness, imperfection; informal minus.
– ANTONYMS benefit.

draw·bridge /ˈdrôˌbrij/ ▶ **noun** a bridge that is hinged at one end so that it can be raised.

draw·er /ˈdrô(ə)r/ ▶ **noun 1** a storage compartment made to slide horizontally in and out of a desk or chest. **2** (**drawers**) dated or humorous underpants. **3** a person who draws something. **4** the person who writes a check.

USAGE

The word **drawer**, which mainly means 'a sliding storage compartment,' is often spelled incorrectly as **draw** (which, as a noun, chiefly means *an even score at the end of a game,* as in *the match ended in a draw*).

draw·ing /ˈdrô-iNG/ ▶ **noun 1** a picture or diagram made with a pencil, pen, or crayon rather than paint. **2** the art or skill of making drawings.

– SYNONYMS **1 sketch,** picture, illustration, representation, portrayal, depiction, diagram, outline. **2 raffle,** lottery, sweepstake.

WORD LINKS

graphic *relating to drawing*

draw·ing board ▶ **noun** a board on which paper can be spread for artists or designers to work on.
– PHRASES **back to the drawing board** a plan has failed and a new one is needed.

draw·ing room ▶ **noun** a room in a large private house in which guests can be received.
– ORIGIN abbreviation of *withdrawing-room* 'a room to withdraw to.'

drawl /drôl/ ▶ **verb** speak in a slow, lazy way with prolonged vowel sounds. ▶ **noun** a drawling accent.
– ORIGIN from German or Dutch *dralen* 'delay, linger.'

drawn /drôn/ past participle of **DRAW** ▶ **adjective** looking strained from illness or exhaustion.

drawn-out ▶ **adjective** lasting longer than is necessary.

draw·string /ˈdrôˌstriNG/ ▶ **noun** a string in the seam of a garment or bag that can be pulled to tighten or close it.

dray /drā/ ▶ **noun** a low vehicle or cart without sides, for delivering barrels or other heavy loads.
– ORIGIN perhaps from an Old English word meaning 'dragnet.'

dread /dred/ ▶ **verb** anticipate something with great anxiety or fear.

– SYNONYMS **fear,** be afraid of, worry about, be anxious about, shudder at the thought of.

▶ **noun** great anxiety or fear.

– SYNONYMS **fear,** apprehension, trepidation, anxiety, panic, alarm, terror, disquiet, unease.

▶ **adjective** greatly feared; dreadful: *the dread disease.*
– DERIVATIVES **dread·ed** adjective.
– ORIGIN Old English.

dread·ful /ˈdredfəl/ ▶ **adjective 1** extremely bad or serious. **2** used for emphasis: *I'm a dreadful hoarder.*

– SYNONYMS **1** *a dreadful accident* **terrible,** frightful, horrible, grim, awful, horrifying, shocking, distressing, appalling, harrowing, ghastly, gruesome, fearful, horrendous, tragic. **2** *a dreadful meal* **very bad,** frightful, shocking, awful, abysmal, dire, atrocious, disgraceful, deplorable; informal woeful, rotten, lousy, ropy. **3** *a dreadful flirt* **outrageous,** shocking, real, awful, terrible, inordinate, incorrigible.
– ANTONYMS wonderful, excellent.

– DERIVATIVES **dread·ful·ly** adverb.

dread·locks /ˈdredˌläks/ ▶ **plural noun** a Rastafarian hairstyle in which the hair is twisted into tight braids or ringlets.
– DERIVATIVES **dread·locked** adjective.

dread·nought /ˈdredˌnôt/ ▶ **noun** historical a type of battleship of the early 20th century, equipped entirely with large-caliber guns.
– ORIGIN named after Britain's HMS *Dreadnought.*

dream /drēm/ ▶ **noun 1** a series of thoughts, images, and sensations occurring in a person's mind during sleep. **2** a long-held ambition or ideal: *his childhood dream of climbing Everest.* **3** informal a wonderful or perfect person or thing.

– SYNONYMS **1 daydream,** reverie, trance, daze, stupor. **2 ambition,** aspiration, hope, goal, aim, objective, intention, desire, wish, daydream,

fantasy. **3 delight,** joy, marvel, wonder, gem, treasure.
– ANTONYMS nightmare.

▶ **verb** (past and past part. **dreamed** or **dreamt** /dremt/) **1** experience dreams during sleep. **2** indulge in daydreams or fantasies. **3** think of as being possible: *I never dreamed she'd take offense.* **4** (**dream something up**) imagine or invent something.

– SYNONYMS **1 daydream,** be in a trance, be lost in thought, be preoccupied, be abstracted, stare into space, be in la-la land. **2** *I* ***dreamt of*** *making the Olympic team* **fantasize,** daydream, wish, hope, long, yearn, hanker. **3** *I* ***dreamed up*** *some new excuse* **think up,** invent, concoct, devise, hatch, come up with.

– DERIVATIVES **dream·er** noun **dream·less** adjective.
– PHRASES **like a dream** informal very easily or successfully.
– ORIGIN Germanic.

dream·boat /'drēm,bōt/ ▶ **noun** informal a very attractive person, especially a man.

dream·land /'drēm,land/ ▶ **noun 1** sleep regarded as a world of dreams. **2** an imagined and unrealistically ideal world: *there was always in the Cotton Club a certain dreamland aspect.*

dream·scape /'drēm,skāp/ ▶ **noun** a scene with the strangeness characteristic of dreams.

dream·y /'drēmē/ ▶ **adjective** (**dreamier, dreamiest**) **1** tending to daydream, or giving the impression that someone is daydreaming: *she had a dreamy look in her eyes.* **2** having a magical or pleasantly unreal quality.
– DERIVATIVES **dream·i·ly** adverb **dream·i·ness** noun.

drear·y /'dri(ə)rē/ ▶ **adjective** (**drearier, dreariest**) dull, bleak, and depressing.

– SYNONYMS **dull,** uninteresting, tedious, boring, unexciting, unstimulating, uninspiring, soul-destroying, monotonous, uneventful.
– ANTONYMS exciting.

– DERIVATIVES **drear·i·ly** adverb **drear·i·ness** noun.
– ORIGIN Old English, 'gory, cruel, melancholy.'

WORD TOOLKIT

See **DISMAL**.

dreck /drek/ ▶ **noun** informal rubbish.
– ORIGIN Yiddish, 'filth, dregs.'

dredge[1] /drej/ ▶ **verb 1** clean out the bed of a harbor, river, etc., with a dredge. **2** bring something up from a river or seabed with a dredge. **3** (**dredge something up**) mention something unwelcome or unpleasant that has been forgotten. ▶ **noun** a piece of equipment for bringing up objects or mud from a river or seabed by scooping or dragging.
– DERIVATIVES **dredg·er** noun.
– ORIGIN perhaps related to Dutch *dregghe* 'grappling hook.'

dredge[2] ▶ **verb** sprinkle food with sugar or another powdered substance.
– ORIGIN from Old French *dragie.*

dregs /dregz/ ▶ **plural noun 1** the last drops of a liquid left in a container, together with any sediment. **2** the most worthless parts: *the dregs of society.*
– ORIGIN probably Scandinavian.

drench /drench/ ▶ **verb 1** wet someone or something thoroughly. **2** (often as adj. **drenched**) cover with large amounts of something: *a sun-drenched clearing.*

– SYNONYMS **soak,** saturate, wet through, douse, steep, flood, drown.

▶ **noun** a dose of medicine given to an animal.
– ORIGIN Old English.

Dres·den chi·na /'drezdən/ ▶ **noun** porcelain with elaborate decoration and delicate colorings, made originally at Dresden in Germany.

dress /dres/ ▶ **verb 1** (also **get dressed**) put on one's clothes. **2** put clothes on someone else. **3** wear clothes in a particular way or of a particular type: *she dresses well.* **4** decorate or arrange something in an artistic or attractive way. **5** clean, treat, or apply a dressing to a wound. **6** clean and prepare food for cooking or eating. **7** add a dressing to a salad. **8** apply fertilizer to an area of ground or a plant. **9** treat or smooth the surface of leather, fabric, or stone.

– SYNONYMS **1 clothe,** attire, deck out, garb. **2 decorate,** trim, adorn, arrange, prepare. **3 bandage,** cover, bind, wrap.
– ANTONYMS undress.

▶ **noun 1** a one-piece garment for a woman or girl that covers the body and extends down over the legs. **2** clothing of a particular kind: *evening dress.*

– SYNONYMS **1** *a long blue dress* gown, robe, shift, frock. **2** *full evening dress* **clothes,** clothing, garments, garb, attire, costume, outfit; informal getup, gear. formal apparel.

▶ **adjective** (of clothing) formal or ceremonial: *a dress suit.*
– PHRASES **dress down** informal wear informal clothes. **dressed to kill** informal wearing glamorous clothes intended to create a striking impression. **dress up** dress in smart or formal clothes, or in a special costume.
– ORIGIN Old French *dresser* 'arrange, prepare.'

WORD LINKS

sartorial *relating to dress*

dres·sage /drə'säzh/ ▶ **noun** the art of training horses to perform a set of controlled movements at the rider's command.
– ORIGIN French, 'training.'

dress cir·cle ▶ **noun** the first level of seats above the ground floor in a theater.

dress code ▶ **noun** a set of rules specifying the required manner of dress at a school, office, club, restaurant, etc.

dres·ser[1] /'dresər/ ▶ **noun 1** a sideboard with shelves above for storing and displaying dishes. **2** a chest of drawers.
– ORIGIN first referring a sideboard or table on which food was prepared.

dres·ser[2] ▶ **noun 1** a person who dresses in a particular way: *a snappy dresser.* **2** a person who looks after theatrical costumes.

dress·ing /'dresing/ ▶ **noun 1** (also **salad dressing**) a sauce for salads, usually consisting of oil and vinegar with herbs or other flavorings. **2** stuffing. **3** a piece of material placed on a wound to protect it. **4** a layer of fertilizer spread over land.

dress·ing-down ▶ **noun** informal a severe reprimand.

dress·ing gown ▶ **noun** a long, loose robe worn after getting out of bed or having a bath or shower.

dress·ing room ▶ **noun 1** a room in which actors or other performers change clothes. **2** a small room attached to a bedroom for storing clothes.

dress·ing ta·ble ▶ **noun** a table with a mirror and drawers, used while dressing or applying makeup.

dress·mak·er /ˈdres,mākər/ ▶ **noun** a person who makes women's clothes.
– DERIVATIVES **dress·mak·ing** noun.

dress re·hears·al ▶ **noun** a final rehearsal in which everything is done as it would be in a real performance.

dress shirt ▶ **noun** a man's white shirt worn with a bow tie and a dinner jacket on formal occasions.

dress·y /ˈdresē/ ▶ **adjective** (**dressier**, **dressiest**) (of clothes) suitable for a festive or formal occasion.

drew /dro͞o/ past of DRAW.

drib·ble /ˈdribəl/ ▶ **verb 1** (of a liquid) fall slowly in drops or a thin stream. **2** allow saliva to run from the mouth. **3** (in sports) take the ball forward with slight touches or (in basketball) by continuous bouncing.

– SYNONYMS **1 drool,** slaver, slobber. **2 trickle,** drip, roll, run, drizzle, ooze, seep, leak.

▶ **noun 1** a thin stream of liquid. **2** (in sports) an act of dribbling.
– DERIVATIVES **drib·bler** noun **drib·bly** adjective.
– ORIGIN variant of DRIP.

dribs and drabs /ˈdribz and ˈdrabz/ ▶ **plural noun** (in phrase **in dribs and drabs**) informal in small amounts over a period of time.

dried /drīd/ past and past participle of DRY.

dri·er[1] /ˈdrīər/ ▶ **noun** variant spelling of DRYER.

dri·er[2] ▶ **adjective** comparative of DRY.

drift /drift/ ▶ **verb 1** be carried slowly by a current of air or water. **2** walk or move slowly or casually. **3** (of snow, leaves, etc.) be blown into heaps by the wind.

– SYNONYMS **1 be carried,** be borne, float, bob, glide, coast, waft. **2 wander,** meander, stray, stroll, dawdle, float, roam. **3 stray,** digress, wander, deviate, get sidetracked. **4 pile up,** bank up, heap up, accumulate, gather, amass.

▶ **noun 1** a continuous slow movement from one place to another: *the population drift from rural areas to cities.* **2** the general intention or meaning of someone's remarks: *he got her drift.* **3** a large mass of snow, leaves, etc., piled up by the wind. **4** movement away from an intended course or direction because of currents or winds. **5** Geology deposits left by retreating ice sheets.

– SYNONYMS **1 movement,** shift, flow, transfer, gravitation. **2 gist,** meaning, sense, significance, thrust, import, tenor, intention, direction. **3 pile,** heap, bank, mound, mass, accumulation.

– ORIGIN Old Norse, 'snowdrift, something driven.'

drift·er /ˈdriftər/ ▶ **noun 1** a person who is continually moving from place to place, without any fixed home or job. **2** a fishing boat equipped with a drift net.

drift net ▶ **noun** a large fishing net kept upright by weights at the bottom and floats at the top and allowed to drift in the sea.

drift·wood /ˈdrift,wo͝od/ ▶ **noun** pieces of wood floating on the sea or washed ashore.

drill[1] /dril/ ▶ **noun 1** a tool or machine used for boring holes. **2** training in military exercises. **3** instruction by means of repeated exercises. **4** (**the drill**) informal the correct procedure.

– SYNONYMS **1 training,** instruction, coaching, teaching, (physical) exercises. **2 procedure,** routine, practice, program, schedule, method, system.

▶ **verb 1** bore a hole with a drill. **2** subject someone to military training or other intensive instruction. **3** Computing (**drill down**) access data that is in a lower level of a hierarchically structured database.

– SYNONYMS **1 bore,** pierce, puncture, perforate. **2 train,** instruct, coach, teach, discipline, exercise.

– DERIVATIVES **drill·er** noun.
– ORIGIN Dutch *drillen*.

drill[2] ▶ **noun 1** a machine that makes small furrows, sows seed in them, and then covers the sown seed. **2** a small furrow made by such a machine. ▶ **verb** sow seed with a drill.
– ORIGIN perhaps from DRILL[1].

drill[3] ▶ **noun** a strong cotton or linen fabric woven with parallel diagonal lines.
– ORIGIN from Latin *trilix* 'triple-twilled.'

drill·ing rig ▶ **noun** a large structure with equipment for drilling an oil well.

drill press ▶ **noun** a machine tool for drilling holes, set on a fixed stand.

drill ser·geant ▶ **noun** a noncommissioned officer who trains soldiers in basic military skills.

dri·ly /ˈdrīlē/ (also **dryly**) ▶ **adverb** in a matter-of-fact or ironically humorous way.

drink /driNGk/ ▶ **verb** (past **drank**; past part. **drunk**) **1** take a liquid into the mouth and swallow. **2** consume alcohol, especially regularly or in large amounts. **3** (**drink something in**) watch or listen eagerly to something.

– SYNONYMS **1 swallow,** gulp (down), quaff, guzzle, imbibe, sip, drain; informal swig, down, knock back. **2 drink alcohol,** tipple, indulge, carouse; informal hit the bottle, booze.

▶ **noun 1** a liquid for drinking. **2** a quantity of liquid swallowed at one time. **3** alcohol or an alcoholic drink.

– SYNONYMS **1 beverage,** liquid refreshment. **2 alcohol,** intoxicating liquor, spirits; informal booze, the hard stuff, the bottle. **3 swallow,** gulp, mouthful, draft, sip; informal swig, slug.

– DERIVATIVES **drink·a·ble** adjective **drink·er** noun.
– PHRASES **drink someone's health** (or **drink to someone**) express good wishes for someone by raising one's glass and drinking a small amount.
– ORIGIN Old English.

drink·ing foun·tain ▶ **noun** a device producing a small jet of water for drinking.

drip /drip/ ▶ **verb** (**drips**, **dripping**, **dripped**) fall or let fall in small drops of liquid.

– SYNONYMS **drop,** dribble, leak, trickle, run, splash, sprinkle.

▶ **noun 1** a small drop of a liquid. **2** a piece of equipment that slowly passes fluid, nutrients, or drugs into a patient's body through a vein. **3** informal a weak and ineffectual person.

– SYNONYMS **drop,** dribble, spot, trickle, splash, bead.

– ORIGIN Old English.

drip-dry ▶ **adjective** (of an item of clothing) able to dry without forming creases if hung up when wet.

drip-feed ▶ **verb** supply a patient with fluid through a drip.

drip·ping /ˈdripiNG/ ▶ **noun** (**drippings**) fat that has melted and dripped from roasting meat. ▶ **adjective** extremely wet.

drip·py /ˈdripē/ ▶ **adjective** (**drippier, drippiest**) informal weak, ineffectual, or very sentimental.
– DERIVATIVES **drip·pi·ly** adverb **drip·pi·ness** noun.

drive /drīv/ ▶ **verb** (past **drove** /drōv/; past part. **driven**) **1** operate and control a motor vehicle. **2** carry someone or something in a motor vehicle. **3** propel or carry along: *the storm drove the vessel onto the rocks.* **4** urge animals or people to move. **5** make someone act in a particular way: *depression drove him to attempt suicide.* **6** provide the energy to keep an engine or machine in motion. **7** Golf hit a ball from the tee.

> – SYNONYMS **1 operate,** handle, manage, pilot, steer, work. **2 go by car,** motor. **3 run,** chauffeur, give someone a lift, take, ferry, transport, convey. **4 power,** propel, move, push. **5 hammer,** screw, ram, sink, plunge, thrust, knock. **6 force,** compel, prompt, precipitate, oblige, coerce, pressure, spur, prod.

▶ **noun 1** a trip or journey in a car. **2** (also **driveway**) a short private road leading to a house. **3** an inborn desire or urge: *his sex drive.* **4** an organized effort to achieve a particular purpose: *a sales drive.* **5** determination and ambition. **6** the transmission of power to machinery or to the wheels of a vehicle. **7** Golf a shot from the tee.

> – SYNONYMS **1 excursion,** outing, trip, jaunt, tour, ride, run, journey; informal spin. **2 motivation,** ambition, single-mindedness, determination, willpower, dedication, doggedness, tenacity, enthusiasm, zeal, commitment, energy, vigor; informal get-up-and-go. **3 campaign,** crusade, movement, effort, push, initiative.

– DERIVATIVES **driv·a·ble** (also **driveable**) adjective.
– PHRASES **what someone is driving at** the point that someone is trying to make.
– ORIGIN Old English.

drive-by ▶ **adjective 1** (of a shooting or other act) carried out from a passing vehicle: *a drive-by shooting.* **2** informal superficial or casual: *drive-by journalism.* **3** informal (of a medical procedure in a hospital or clinic) involving a brief duration of on-site care for the patient. **4** informal referring to a facility that performs such procedures as a customary practice: *drive-by clinics.*

drive-in ▶ **adjective** (of a movie theater, restaurant, etc.) that one can visit without leaving one's car.

driv·el /ˈdrivəl/ ▶ **noun** silly nonsense.

> – SYNONYMS **nonsense,** twaddle, claptrap, balderdash, gibberish, garbage, rubbish, mumbo-jumbo; informal rot, poppycock, phooey, piffle, tripe, bosh, bull, hogwash, baloney, flapdoodle, bushwa. informal, dated bunkum.

▶ **verb** talk nonsense.

> – SYNONYMS *you always drivel on* **talk nonsense,** talk rubbish, babble, ramble, gibber, blather, blether, prattle, gabble; Brit. informal waffle, witter.

– ORIGIN Old English.

driv·en /ˈdrivən/ past participle of **DRIVE**.

driv·er /ˈdrīvər/ ▶ **noun 1** a person or thing that drives something. **2** a flat-faced golf club used for hitting the ball from the tee.
– PHRASES **in the driver's seat** in control.

driv·er's li·cense ▶ **noun** an official document permitting a person to drive a motor vehicle.

drive·shaft /ˈdrīvˌsHaft/ ▶ **noun** a rotating shaft that transmits torque in an engine.

drive·train /ˈdrīvˌtrān/ ▶ **noun** the system in a motor vehicle that connects the transmission to the drive axles.

drive·way /ˈdrīvˌwā/ ▶ **noun** a short road leading from a public road to a house or garage.

driv·ing /ˈdrīviNG/ ▶ **adjective 1** having a controlling influence: *the driving force behind the plan.* **2** being blown by the wind with great force: *driving rain.*

driv·ing range ▶ **noun** an area where golfers can practice drives.

driz·zle /ˈdrizəl/ ▶ **noun** light rain falling in very fine drops. ▶ **verb 1** (**it drizzles, it is drizzling, it drizzled**) rain lightly. **2** pour a thin stream of a liquid ingredient over food.
– DERIVATIVES **driz·zly** adjective.
– ORIGIN probably from an Old English word meaning 'to fall.'

DRM ▶ **abbreviation** digital rights management; the protection of the interests of owners of copyright on digitally stored data, or technology that facilitates this.

drogue /drōg/ ▶ **noun** a device towed behind a boat or aircraft to reduce speed or improve stability, or as a target for gunnery practice.
– ORIGIN perhaps related to **DRAG**.

droid /droid/ ▶ **noun** (in science fiction) a robot.
– ORIGIN shortening of **ANDROID**.

droit de sei·gneur /ˌdrwä də sānˈyər/ ▶ **noun** the alleged right of a medieval feudal lord to have sex with a vassal's bride on her wedding night.
– ORIGIN French, 'lord's right.'

droll /drōl/ ▶ **adjective** amusing in a strange or unexpected way.

> – SYNONYMS **funny,** humorous, amusing, comic, comical, mirthful, hilarious, jocular, lighthearted, witty, whimsical, wry, tongue-in-cheek, zany, quirky; informal waggish, wacky, side-splitting, rib-tickling.
> – ANTONYMS serious.

– DERIVATIVES **droll·er·y** /ˈdrōlərē/ noun **drol·ly** adverb.
– ORIGIN French.

> **WORD TOOLKIT**
>
> See **WITTY**.

drom·e·dar·y /ˈdräməˌderē/ ▶ **noun** (pl. **dromedaries**) an Arabian camel, with one hump.
– ORIGIN from Latin *dromedarius camelus* 'swift camel,' from Greek *dromas* 'runner.'

drone /drōn/ ▶ **verb 1** make a continuous low humming sound. **2** (**drone on**) speak at length in a boring way. ▶ **noun 1** a low continuous humming sound. **2** a pipe (especially in a set of bagpipes) or string used to sound a continuous low-pitched note. **3** a male bee that does no work in a colony but can fertilize a queen. **4** a lazy person. **5** a remote-controlled aircraft with no pilot.
– ORIGIN Old English, 'male bee.'

drool /dro͞ol/ ▶ **verb 1** drop saliva uncontrollably from the mouth. **2** (often **drool over**) informal show great pleasure or desire. ▶ **noun** saliva falling from the mouth.
– ORIGIN from **DRIVEL**.

droop /dro͞op/ ▶ **verb 1** bend or hang downward limply. **2** sag down as a result of tiredness or low spirits: *the corners of his mouth drooped.*

– SYNONYMS **hang down,** wilt, dangle, sag, flop, sink, slump, drop.

▶ **noun** an act of drooping.
– ORIGIN Old Norse, 'hang the head.'

droop·y /ˈdro͞opē/ ▶ **adjective** (**droopier, droopiest**) **1** hanging down limply; drooping. **2** not having much strength or spirit.
– DERIVATIVES **droop·i·ly** adverb **droop·i·ness** noun.

drop /dräp/ ▶ **verb** (**drops, dropping, dropped**) **1** fall or cause to fall. **2** sink to the ground. **3** make or become lower, weaker, or less: *he dropped his speed.* **4** abandon or discontinue: *the charges against him were dropped.* **5** (often **drop someone off**) set down or unload a passenger or goods. **6** informal collapse from exhaustion. **7** lose a point, game, etc. **8** mention something casually.

– SYNONYMS **1 let fall,** let go of, release. **2 fall,** descend, plunge, plummet, dive, sink, dip, tumble. **3 decrease,** lessen, reduce, fall, decline, dwindle, sink, slump. **4 abandon,** give up, discontinue, finish with, renounce, reject, forgo, relinquish, dispense with, leave out; informal dump, pack in.
– ANTONYMS rise, increase.

▶ **noun 1** a small round or pear-shaped amount of liquid. **2** an instance of falling or dropping. **3** an abrupt fall or slope. **4** a small drink, especially of alcohol. **5** a small candy.

– SYNONYMS **1 droplet,** blob, globule, bead. **2 small amount,** little, bit, dash, spot, dribble, sprinkle, trickle, splash, mouthful; informal smidgen, tad. **3 decrease,** reduction, decline, falloff, downturn, slump. **4 cliff,** precipice, slope, descent, incline.

– PHRASES **at the drop of a hat** informal without hesitation; immediately. **drop back/behind** fall back or get left behind. **drop by/in** pay someone a brief or casual visit. **drop dead** die suddenly and unexpectedly. **drop one's guard** stop being defensive or self-protective. **a drop in the bucket** a very small amount compared with what is needed. **drop someone a line** informal send someone a note or letter. **drop off** fall asleep. **drop out 1** stop participating in something. **2** start living an unconventional lifestyle.
– ORIGIN Old English.

drop cloth ▶ **noun** a sheet for covering furniture or flooring to protect it from dust or while decorating.

drop-dead ▶ **adjective** informal used to emphasize attractiveness: *drop-dead gorgeous.*

drop goal ▶ **noun** Rugby a goal scored by a drop kick of the ball over the crossbar.

drop han·dle·bars ▶ **plural noun** handlebars with the handles bent below the rest of the bar, used especially on racing cycles.

drop-in ▶ **noun 1** visited or visiting on an informal basis without making appointments: *a drop-in center for addicts.* **2** (of an object such as a chair seat) designed to drop into position.

drop kick ▶ **noun** (formerly, in football) a kick for a field goal or conversion made by dropping the ball and kicking it as it bounces.

drop·let /ˈdräplit/ ▶ **noun** a very small drop of a liquid.

drop-off ▶ **noun** a decline or decrease.

drop·out /ˈdräpˌout/ ▶ **noun** a person who has abandoned a course of study or rejected conventional society to pursue an alternative lifestyle.

drop·per /ˈdräpər/ ▶ **noun** a short glass tube with a rubber bulb at one end, for measuring out drops of liquid.

drop·pings /ˈdräpiNGz/ ▶ **plural noun** the excrement of animals.

drop shot ▶ **noun** (in tennis or squash) a softly hit shot that drops abruptly to the ground.

drop·sy /ˈdräpsē/ ▶ **noun** old-fashioned or less technical term for **EDEMA**.
– DERIVATIVES **drop·si·cal** /ˈdräpsikəl/ adjective.
– ORIGIN shortening of former *hydropsy*, from Greek *hudōr* 'water.'

drop waist ▶ **noun** a style of waistline with the seam positioned at the hips rather than the waist.

drop zone ▶ **noun** an area into which troops or supplies are dropped by parachute.

dro·soph·i·la /drəˈsäfələ/ ▶ **noun** a fruit fly of a kind widely used in genetic research.
– ORIGIN from Greek *drosos* 'dew, moisture' + *philos* 'loving.'

dross /drôs, dräs/ ▶ **noun 1** rubbish. **2** scum on the surface of molten metal.
– ORIGIN Old English.

drought /drout/ ▶ **noun** a very long period of abnormally low rainfall, leading to a shortage of water.
– ORIGIN Old English, 'dryness.'

drove[1] /drōv/ past of **DRIVE**.

drove[2] ▶ **noun 1** a flock of animals being driven. **2** a large number of people doing the same thing: *tourists arrived in droves.*
– ORIGIN Old English.

dro·ver /drōvər/ ▶ **noun** historical a person who drove sheep or cattle to market.

drown /droun/ ▶ **verb 1** die as a result of submersion in water, or kill someone in this way. **2** flood an area. **3** (usu. **drown someone/thing out**) make someone or something impossible to hear by making a very loud noise.
– PHRASES **drown one's sorrows** forget one's problems by getting drunk.
– ORIGIN related to an Old Norse word meaning 'be drowned.'

drowse /drouz/ ▶ **verb** be half asleep; doze.

drow·sy /ˈdrouzē/ ▶ **adjective** (**drowsier, drowsiest**) sleepy.

– SYNONYMS **sleepy,** dozy, heavy-eyed, groggy, somnolent, tired, weary, fatigued, exhausted, yawning, nodding, lethargic, sluggish, torpid, listless, languid; informal snoozy, dopey, yawny, dead beat, all in, dog-tired.
– ANTONYMS alert.

– DERIVATIVES **drow·si·ly** adverb **drow·si·ness** noun.
– ORIGIN probably from an Old English word meaning 'be languid or slow.'

drub·bing /ˈdrəbiNG/ ▶ **noun 1** a beating. **2** informal a resounding defeat in a match or contest.
– DERIVATIVES **drub** verb.
– ORIGIN probably from Arabic.

drudge /drəj/ ▶ **noun** a person made to do hard, menial, or dull work.
– ORIGIN unknown.

drudg·er·y /ˈdrəjərē/ ▶ **noun** hard, menial, or dull work.

CHOOSE THE RIGHT WORD

See **LABOR**.

drug /drəg/ ▶ **noun 1** a substance used in the treatment or prevention of disease or infection. **2** an illegal substance taken for its narcotic or stimulant effects.

– SYNONYMS **1 medicine,** medication, remedy, cure, antidote. **2 narcotic,** stimulant, hallucinogen; informal dope, gear.

▶ **verb** (**drugs, drugging, drugged**) give someone a drug, especially in order to make them unconscious.

– SYNONYMS **1 anaesthetize,** poison, knock out; informal dope. **2 tamper with,** lace, poison; informal dope, spike, doctor.

– ORIGIN Old French *drogue*.

drug·gie /ˈdrəgē/ ▶ **noun** informal a drug addict.

drug·gist /ˈdrəgist/ ▶ **noun** a pharmacist or a seller of medicinal drugs.

drug·store /ˈdrəgˌstôr/ ▶ **noun** a pharmacy that also sells toiletries and other articles.

Dru·id /ˈdro͞oid/ ▶ **noun** a priest in the ancient Celtic religion.

– DERIVATIVES **Dru·id·ic** /dro͞oˈidik/ adjective **Dru·id·i·cal** /dro͞oˈidikəl/ adjective **Dru·id·ism** /-ˌizəm/ noun.

– ORIGIN Gaulish (the language of the ancient Gauls).

drum[1] /drəm/ ▶ **noun 1** a percussion instrument with a skin stretched across a rounded frame, sounded by being struck with sticks or the hands. **2** a sound made by or resembling that of a drum. **3** a cylindrical container or part.

– SYNONYMS *a drum of radioactive waste* **canister,** barrel, cylinder, tank, bin, can.

▶ **verb** (**drums, drumming, drummed**) **1** play on a drum. **2** make a continuous rhythmic noise. **3** (**drum something into**) teach someone something by repeating it many times. **4** (**drum something up**) try to get business or support from people. **5** (**drum someone out**) expel someone from somewhere in disgrace.

– SYNONYMS **1 tap,** beat, rap, thud, thump, tattoo, thrum. **2** *the rules were* ***drummed into*** *us at school* **instill,** drive, din, hammer, drill, implant, ingrain, inculcate. **3** *they* ***drummed up*** *support* **round up,** gather, collect, summon, attract, canvass, solicit, petition.

– ORIGIN Dutch or German *tromme*.

drum[2] ▶ **noun** any of several fish, many edible, that make a drumming sound by vibrating the swim bladder, found mainly in estuarine and shallow coastal waters.

drum and bass /bās/ ▶ **noun** a type of dance music consisting largely of electronic drums and bass.

drum·beat /ˈdrəmˌbēt/ ▶ **noun** a stroke or pattern of strokes on a drum.

drum·head /ˈdrəmˌhed/ ▶ **noun** the membrane or skin of a drum.

drum kit ▶ **noun** a set of drums, cymbals, and other percussion instruments.

drum·lin /ˈdrəmlin/ ▶ **noun** Geology a mound or small hill consisting of compacted boulder clay.

– ORIGIN probably from Scottish Gaelic and Irish *druim* 'ridge.'

drum ma·jor ▶ **noun 1** a noncommissioned officer commanding regimental drummers. **2** the male leader of a marching band, who twirls a baton.

drum ma·jor·ette ▶ **noun** the female leader of a marching band, who twirls a baton.

drum·mer /ˈdrəmər/ ▶ **noun** a person who plays a drum or drums.

drum roll ▶ **noun** a rapid succession of drumbeats.

drum·stick /ˈdrəmˌstik/ ▶ **noun 1** a stick used for beating a drum. **2** the lower cut of the leg of a cooked chicken or similar bird.

drunk /drəNGk/ past part. of **DRINK** ▶ **adjective** affected by alcohol to such an extent that one is not in control of oneself.

– SYNONYMS **intoxicated,** inebriated, drunken, tipsy, under the influence; informal loaded, bombed, tight, plastered, sloshed, pickled, tanked (up), three sheets to the wind.

– ANTONYMS sober.

▶ **noun** a person who is drunk or who often drinks too much.

– SYNONYMS **drunkard,** alcoholic, dipsomaniac, inebriate; informal boozer, wino, alky.

CHOOSE THE RIGHT WORD

drunk, blotto, drunken, inebriated, intoxicated, tight, tipsy

Anyone who is obviously or legally under the influence of alcohol is said to be **drunk**. **Drunken** means the same thing, but only *drunk* should be used predicatively, that is, after a linking verb (*she was drunk*) while *drunken* is more often used to modify a noun (*a drunken sailor*) and, in some cases, to imply habitual drinking to excess. *Drunken* is also used to modify nouns that do not refer to a person (*a drunken celebration*). To say **intoxicated** or **inebriated** is a more formal and less offensive way of calling someone *drunk*, with *intoxicated* implying that the individual is only slightly drunk, and *inebriated* implying drunkenness to the point of excitement or exhilaration (*the streets were filled with inebriated revelers*). **Tight** and **tipsy** are two of the more common slang expressions (there are literally hundreds more) meaning *drunk*. Like *intoxicated*, *tipsy* implies that someone is only slightly drunk, while *tight* implies obvious drunkenness but without any loss of muscular coordination. An elderly woman who has had one sherry too many might be described as *tipsy*, but someone who has been drinking all evening and is still able to stand up and give a speech might be described as *tight*. Either condition is preferable to being **blotto**, a word that means drunk to the point of incomprehensibility or unconsciousness.

drunk·ard /ˈdrəNGkərd/ ▶ **noun** a person who is often drunk.

– ORIGIN German.

drunk driv·ing ▶ **noun** the crime of driving a vehicle with too much alcohol in the blood.

drunk·en /ˈdrəNGkən/ ▶ **adjective 1** drunk. **2** caused by or showing the effects of drink: *a drunken stupor*.

– DERIVATIVES **drunk·en·ly** adverb **drunk·en·ness** noun.

– ORIGIN Old English.

CHOOSE THE RIGHT WORD

See **DRUNK**.

drupe /dro͞op/ ▶ **noun** Botany a fleshy fruit with thin skin and a central stone, e.g., a plum or olive.

– ORIGIN Latin *drupa* 'overripe olive.'

dry /drī/ ▶ **adjective** (**drier, driest**) **1** free from moisture or liquid. **2** not producing or yielding water, oil, or milk. **3** without grease or other lubrication. **4** serious and boring. **5** (of humor) subtle and expressed in a matter-of-fact way. **6** (of wine) not sweet. **7** not allowing the sale or drinking of alcohol.

– SYNONYMS **1 arid,** parched, waterless, dehydrated, desiccated, withered, shriveled, wizened. **2 dull,** uninteresting, boring, unexciting, tedious, dreary, monotonous, unimaginative, sterile; informal deadly. **3 wry,** subtle, laconic, ironic, sardonic, sarcastic, cynical.
– ANTONYMS wet, moist.

▶ **verb** (**dries, drying, dried**) **1** make or become dry. **2** preserve something by evaporating the moisture from it. **3** (**dry up**) (of a supply or flow) decrease and stop. **4** (**dry up**) informal stop talking. **5** (**dry out**) informal overcome one's addiction to alcohol.

– SYNONYMS **1 parch,** scorch, bake, sear, dehydrate, desiccate, wither, shrivel. **2 wipe,** towel, rub dry, drain.
– ANTONYMS wet, moisten.

– DERIVATIVES **dry·ness** noun.
– ORIGIN Old English.

CHOOSE THE RIGHT WORD

dry, arid, dehydrated, desiccated, parched, sere

Almost anything lacking in moisture (in relative terms)—whether it's a piece of bread, the basement of a house, or the state of Arizona—may be described as **dry**, a word that also connotes a lack of life or spirit (*a dry lecture on cell division*). **Arid**, on the other hand, applies to places or things that have been deprived of moisture and are therefore extremely or abnormally *dry* (*one side of the island was arid*); it is most commonly used to describe a desertlike region or climate that is lifeless or barren. **Desiccated** is used as a technical term for something from which moisture has been removed, and in general use it suggests lifelessness, although it is applied very often to people who have lost their vitality (*a desiccated old woman who never left her house*) or to animal and vegetable products that have been completely deprived of their vital juices (*desiccated oranges hanging limply from the tree*). **Dehydrated** is very close in meaning to *desiccated* and is often the preferred adjective when describing foods from which the moisture has been extracted (*they lived on dehydrated fruit*). *Dehydrated* may also refer to an unwanted loss of moisture (*the virus had left him seriously dehydrated*), as may the less formal term **parched**, which refers to an undesirable or uncomfortable lack of water in either a human being or a place (*parched with thirst; the parched landscape*). **Sere** is associated primarily with places and means *dry* or *arid* (*a harsh, sere land where few inhabitants could survive*).

dry·ad /ˈdrīˌad, -əd/ ▶ **noun** (in folklore and classical mythology) a nymph living in a tree or forest.
– ORIGIN from Greek *drus* 'tree.'

dry cell (also **dry battery**) ▶ **noun** an electric cell (or battery) in which the electrolyte is absorbed in a solid to form a paste.

dry-clean ▶ **verb** clean a garment with a chemical solvent rather than water.

dry dock ▶ **noun** a dock that can be drained of water to allow a ship's hull to be repaired.

dry·er /ˈdrīər/ (also **drier**) ▶ **noun** a machine or device for drying something, especially the hair or laundry.

dry fly ▶ **noun** an artificial fishing fly that floats lightly on the water.

dry goods ▶ **plural noun** fabric, thread, clothing, and related merchandise, especially as distinct from hardware and groceries.

dry ice ▶ **noun 1** solid carbon dioxide. **2** white mist produced with this as a theatrical effect.

dry·ly /ˈdrīlē/ ▶ **adverb** variant spelling of DRILY.

dry rot ▶ **noun** a fungus causing wood to decay in conditions where there is poor ventilation.

dry run ▶ **noun** a rehearsal of a performance or procedure.

dry·suit /ˈdrīˌso͞ot/ ▶ **noun** a waterproof rubber suit for water sports, under which warm clothes can be worn.

Ds ▶ **symbol** the chemical element darmstadtium.

DSc ▶ **abbreviation** Doctor of Science.

DSL ▶ **abbreviation** digital subscriber line, a method of routing digital data on copper telephone wires, allowing high-speed Internet access and simultaneous use of the line for voice transmission.

DSP ▶ **abbreviation** digital signal processor or processing.

DST ▶ **abbreviation** daylight saving time.

DTD ▶ **abbreviation** document type definition; a template that sets out the format and tag structure of an XML or SGML-compliant document.

DTP ▶ **abbreviation** desktop publishing.

DTs ▶ **plural noun** informal delirium tremens.

du·al /ˈd(y)o͞oəl/ ▶ **adjective** consisting of two parts, elements, or aspects.

– SYNONYMS **double,** twofold, duplex, binary, twin, matching, paired, coupled.
– ANTONYMS single.

– DERIVATIVES **du·al·i·ty** /d(y)o͞oˈalitē/ noun **du·al·ly** adverb.
– ORIGIN Latin *dualis*, from *duo* 'two.'

du·al·ism /ˈd(y)o͞oəˌlizəm/ ▶ **noun 1** division into two opposed or contrasted aspects, such as good and evil or mind and matter. **2** the quality or state of having two parts, elements, or aspects.
– DERIVATIVES **du·al·ist** noun & adjective **du·al·is·tic** /ˌd(y)o͞oəˈlistik/ adjective.

dub[1] /dəb/ ▶ **verb** (**dubs, dubbing, dubbed**) **1** give someone an unofficial name or nickname. **2** knight someone by touching their shoulder with a sword in a special ceremony.

– SYNONYMS **name,** call, nickname, label, christen, term, tag.

– ORIGIN Old French *adober* 'equip with armor.'

dub[2] ▶ **verb** (**dubs, dubbing, dubbed**) **1** provide a movie with a soundtrack in a different language from the original. **2** add sound effects or music to a movie or a recording. **3** make a copy of a recording. ▶ **noun 1** an act of dubbing sound effects or music. **2** a style of popular music originating from the remixing of recorded music (especially reggae).
– ORIGIN abbreviation of DOUBLE.

du·bi·ous /ˈd(y)o͞obēəs/ ▶ **adjective 1** hesitating or doubtful. **2** probably not honest; morally suspect: *dubious sales methods.* **3** of questionable value: *he has the dubious distinction of being Hollywood's top gossip columnist.*

– SYNONYMS **1 doubtful,** uncertain, unsure, hesitant, skeptical, suspicious; informal iffy. **2 suspicious,**

suspect, untrustworthy, unreliable, questionable; informal shady.
– ANTONYMS certain, trustworthy.

– DERIVATIVES **du·bi·ous·ly** adverb **du·bi·ous·ness** noun.
– ORIGIN from Latin *dubium* 'a doubt.'

dub·ni·um /'dəbnēəm/ ▶ **noun** a very unstable chemical element made by high-energy atomic collisions.
– ORIGIN from *Dubna* in Russia.

Du·bon·net /,d(y)o͞obə'nā/ ▶ **noun** trademark a sweet red vermouth made in France.
– ORIGIN from the name of a family of French wine merchants.

du·cal /'d(y)o͞okəl/ ▶ **adjective** relating to a duke or dukedom.

duc·at /'dəkət/ ▶ **noun** a former European gold coin.
– ORIGIN Italian *ducato*.

duch·ess /'dəCHis/ ▶ **noun 1** the wife or widow of a duke. **2** a woman holding a rank equivalent to duke.
– ORIGIN Old French.

duch·y /'dəCHē/ ▶ **noun** (pl. **duchies**) the territory of a duke or duchess.
– ORIGIN Old French *duche*.

duck[1] /dək/ ▶ **noun** (pl. same or **ducks**) **1** a waterbird with a broad blunt bill, short legs, and webbed feet. **2** a female duck. Contrasted with **DRAKE**.
– PHRASES **like water off a duck's back** (of a critical remark) having no effect.
– ORIGIN Old English.

duck[2] ▶ **verb 1** lower the head or body quickly to avoid being hit or seen. **2** push someone under water. **3** informal avoid an unwelcome duty.

– SYNONYMS **1 bend down,** stoop, crouch, squat, hunch down, hunker down. **2 shirk,** dodge, evade, avoid, elude, escape, sidestep.

▶ **noun** a quick lowering of the head.
– DERIVATIVES **duck·er** noun.
– ORIGIN Germanic.

duck[3] ▶ **noun** a strong untwilled linen or cotton fabric, used chiefly for casual or work clothes and sails.
– ORIGIN from Middle Dutch *doek* 'linen, linen cloth.'

duck-billed plat·y·pus ▶ **noun** see **PLATYPUS**.

duck·boards /'dək,bôrdz/ ▶ **plural noun** wooden slats joined together to form a path over muddy ground.

duck·ling /'dəkliNG/ ▶ **noun** a young duck.

duck·weed /'dək,wēd/ ▶ **noun** a tiny flowering plant that floats in large quantities on still water.

duck·y /'dəkē/ ▶ **adjective** informal excellent; delightful.
▶ **noun** Brit. informal a friendly form of address.

duct /dəkt/ ▶ **noun 1** a tube or passageway in a building or machine for air, cables, etc. **2** a tube in the body through which tears or other fluids pass.

– SYNONYMS **tube,** channel, canal, vessel, conduit, pipe, outlet, inlet, flue, shaft, vent.

▶ **verb** convey something through a duct.
– DERIVATIVES **duct·ing** noun.
– ORIGIN Latin *ductus* 'leading, aqueduct.'

duc·tile /'dəktl, -,tīl/ ▶ **adjective** (of a metal) able to be drawn out into a thin wire.
– DERIVATIVES **duc·til·i·ty** /dək'tilitē/ noun.

duct tape ▶ **noun** strong cloth-backed waterproof adhesive tape.

duct·work /'dəkt,wərk/ ▶ **noun** a system or network of ducts.

dud /dəd/ informal ▶ **noun 1** a thing that fails to work properly. **2** (**duds**) clothes. ▶ **adjective** failing to work or meet a standard.
– ORIGIN unknown.

dude /do͞od/ ▶ **noun** informal **1** a man. **2** a stylish man.
– ORIGIN probably from German dialect *Dude* 'fool.'

dude ranch ▶ **noun** (in the western US) a cattle ranch converted to a vacation center for tourists.

dudg·eon /'dəjən/ ▶ **noun** (in phrase **in high dudgeon**) feeling resentful or angry.
– ORIGIN unknown.

due /d(y)o͞o/ ▶ **adjective 1** expected at or planned for a certain time: *the baby's due in June*. **2** owed or deserving something: *he was due for a raise*. **3** needing to be paid; owing. **4** proper: *driving without due care and attention*. **5** required as a legal or moral duty.

– SYNONYMS **1** *their fees were due* **owing,** owed, payable, outstanding, overdue, unpaid, unsettled. **2** *the general's statement is due today* **expected,** anticipated, scheduled, awaited, required. **3 deserved,** merited, warranted, justified, owing, appropriate, fitting, right, rightful, proper. **4 proper,** correct, suitable, appropriate, adequate, sufficient.

▶ **noun 1** (**dues**) fees. **2** (**one's due/dues**) a person's right.

– SYNONYMS **fee,** subscription, charge, payment, contribution, levy.

▶ **adverb** (of a point of the compass) directly.

– SYNONYMS **directly,** straight, exactly, precisely, dead.

– PHRASES **due to 1** caused by. **2** because of. **give someone their due** be fair to someone. **in due course** at the appropriate time.
– ORIGIN Old French *deu* 'owed.'

USAGE

Some people think that you should not use **due to** to mean 'because of' for the reason that **due** is an adjective and should not be used as a preposition. However, this use is now common and acceptable in standard English.

du·el /'d(y)o͞oəl/ ▶ **noun 1** historical a prearranged contest with deadly weapons between two people to settle a point of honor. **2** a contest between two parties.

– SYNONYMS **1 single combat,** fight, confrontation, head-to-head; informal shoot-out. **2 contest,** match, game, meet, encounter, clash.

▶ **verb** (**duels, dueling, dueled**) fight a duel.
– DERIVATIVES **du·el·ist** noun.
– ORIGIN Latin *duellum*, literary form of *bellum* 'war.'

du·en·na /d(y)o͞o'enə/ ▶ **noun** an older woman acting as a governess and chaperone to girls in a Spanish family.
– ORIGIN Spanish.

due proc·ess ▶ **noun** fair treatment through the normal judicial system, especially as a citizen's entitlement.

du·et /d(y)o͞o'et/ ▶ **noun 1** a performance by two singers, instrumentalists, or dancers. **2** a musical composition for two performers. ▶ **verb** (**duets, duetting, duetted**) perform a duet.
– ORIGIN Italian *duetto*.

duff[1] /dəf/ ▶ **noun** decaying vegetable matter covering the ground under trees.
– ORIGIN uncertain.

duff[2] ▸ **noun** informal a person's buttocks: *I did not get where I am today by sitting on my duff.*
– ORIGIN uncertain.

duf·fel /ˈdəfəl/ (also **duffle**) ▸ **noun 1** a coarse woolen cloth with a thick nap. **2** a duffel bag.
– ORIGIN from *Duffel*, a town in Belgium.

duf·fel bag ▸ **noun** a cylindrical canvas bag closed by a drawstring.

duf·fer /ˈdəfər/ ▸ **noun** informal an incompetent or stupid person, especially an elderly one.
– ORIGIN from Scots *dowfart*.

dug[1] /dəg/ past and past participle of **DIG**.

dug[2] ▸ **noun** the udder, teat, or nipple of a female animal.
– ORIGIN perhaps Old Norse.

du·gong /ˈdo͞ogäNG, -gôNG/ ▸ **noun** (pl. same or **dugongs**) a sea cow (mammal) found in the Indian Ocean.
– ORIGIN Malay.

dug·out /ˈdəgˌout/ ▸ **noun 1** a trench that is roofed over as a shelter for troops. **2** a low shelter at the side of a sports field for a team's coaches and substitutes. **3** (also **dugout canoe**) a canoe made from a hollowed tree trunk.

duh /də, do͞o/ ▸ **exclamation** informal used to comment on an action perceived as foolish or stupid: *I left the keys in the ignition—duh!*

dui·ker /ˈdīkər/ ▸ **noun** (pl. same or **duikers**) a small African antelope.
– ORIGIN Dutch, 'diver.'

du jour /də ˈZHo͝or, ˌd(y)o͞o/ ▸ **adjective** informal enjoying great but probably short-lived popularity: *black comedy is the genre du jour.*
– ORIGIN French, 'of the day.'

duke /d(y)o͞ok/ ▸ **noun 1** a man holding the highest hereditary title in Britain and some other countries. **2** chiefly historical (in parts of Europe) a male ruler of a small independent state.
– DERIVATIVES **duke·dom** noun.
– ORIGIN Latin *dux* 'leader.'

dul·cet /ˈdəlsit/ ▸ **adjective** often ironic (of a sound) sweet and soothing.
– ORIGIN Latin *dulcis* 'sweet.'

dul·ci·mer /ˈdəlsəmər/ ▸ **noun** (also **hammered dulcimer**) a musical instrument with strings that are struck with hand-held hammers.
– ORIGIN Old French *doulcemer*.

dull /dəl/ ▸ **adjective 1** not interesting or exciting: *a very dull book*. **2** lacking brightness; not shiny. **3** (of the weather) overcast. **4** slow to understand; rather stupid. **5** not clearly felt or heard: *a dull pain in his jaw*.

> – SYNONYMS **1 uninteresting,** boring, tedious, monotonous, unimaginative, uneventful, featureless, colorless, lifeless, unexciting, uninspiring, flat, bland, stodgy, dreary; informal deadly, dullsville. **2 overcast,** cloudy, gloomy, dark, dismal, dreary, somber, gray, murky, sunless. **3 drab,** dreary, somber, dark, subdued, muted. **4 muffled,** muted, quiet, soft, faint, indistinct, stifled. **5 unintelligent,** stupid, slow, brainless, mindless, foolish, idiotic; informal dense, dim, halfwitted, thick.
> – ANTONYMS interesting, bright.

▸ **verb** make or become dull.

> – SYNONYMS **lessen,** decrease, diminish, reduce, dampen, blunt, deaden, allay, ease.
> – ANTONYMS intensify.

– DERIVATIVES **dull·ness** noun **dul·ly** adverb.
– ORIGIN Old English.

> **CHOOSE THE RIGHT WORD**
>
> See **STUPID**.

dull·ard /ˈdələrd/ ▸ **noun** a slow or stupid person.

dulse /dəls/ ▸ **noun** a dark red edible seaweed with flattened fronds.
– ORIGIN from Irish and Scottish Gaelic *duileasg*.

du·ly /ˈd(y)o͞olē/ ▸ **adverb** in accordance with what is required, appropriate, or expected.

> – SYNONYMS **1 properly,** correctly, appropriately, suitably, fittingly. **2 at the right time,** on time, punctually.

dumb /dəm/ ▸ **adjective 1** offensive unable to speak; lacking the power of speech. **2** temporarily unable or unwilling to speak. **3** informal stupid. **4** (of a computer terminal) having no independent processing capability.

> – SYNONYMS **1 mute,** speechless, tongue-tied, silent, at a loss for words. **2 stupid,** unintelligent, ignorant, dense, brainless, foolish, slow, dull, simple; informal thick, dim, daft.
> – ANTONYMS talkative, clever.

▸ **verb** (**dumb something down**) informal make something less intellectually challenging so as to appeal to a wider audience.
– DERIVATIVES **dumb·ly** adverb **dumb·ness** noun.
– ORIGIN Old English.

> **USAGE**
>
> Avoid **dumb** in the sense meaning 'not able to speak,' as it is likely to cause offense; use alternatives such as **speech-impaired**.

> **CHOOSE THE RIGHT WORD**
>
> See **STUPID**.

dumb·bell /ˈdəmˌbel/ ▸ **noun 1** a short bar with a weight at each end, used for exercise or muscle-building. **2** informal a stupid person.

dumb·found /ˈdəmˌfound/ (also **dumfound**) ▸ **verb** greatly astonish someone.

> – SYNONYMS *they were dumbfounded at his popularity* **astonish,** astound, amaze, stagger, startle, stun, confound, stupefy, daze, take aback; informal flabbergast.

– ORIGIN blend of **DUMB** and **CONFOUND**.

dum·bo /ˈdəmbō/ ▸ **noun** (pl. **dumbos**) informal a stupid person.

dumb·struck /ˈdəmˌstrək/ ▸ **adjective** so shocked or surprised as to be unable to speak.

dumb·wait·er /ˈdəmˌwātər/ ▸ **noun** a small elevator for carrying food and dishes between floors.

dum·dum /ˈdəmˌdəm/ (also **dumdum bullet**) ▸ **noun** a kind of soft-nosed bullet that expands on impact.
– ORIGIN from *Dum Dum*, a town and arsenal near Calcutta, India.

dum-dum ▸ **noun** informal a stupid person.

dum·my /ˈdəmē/ ▸ **noun** (pl. **dummies**) **1** a model of a human being. **2** an object designed to resemble and act as a substitute for the real one. **3** (in sports) a pretended pass or kick. **4** informal a stupid person.

– SYNONYMS **1 mannequin,** model, figure. **2** (as adj.) *a dummy attack on the airfield* **simulated,** practice, trial, mock, make-believe; informal pretend.

▸ **verb** (**dummies, dummying, dummied**) create a prototype of a book or page.
– ORIGIN first meaning 'a person who cannot speak': from **DUMB**.

dump /dəmp/ ▸ **noun 1** a site where garbage or waste is left. **2** a heap of garbage left at a dump. **3** informal an unpleasant or dreary place. **4** informal an act of defecation. **5** an act of dumping stored computer data.

– SYNONYMS **1 transfer station,** garbage dump, landfill site, rubbish heap, dumping ground. **2 hovel,** slum; informal hole, pigsty.

▸ **verb 1** get rid of garbage or something unwanted. **2** put something down heavily or carelessly. **3** informal abandon someone. **4** copy stored computer data to a different location. **5** send goods to a foreign market for sale at a low price.

– SYNONYMS **1 put down,** set down, deposit, place, shove, unload, drop, throw down; informal stick, park, plunk, plonk. **2 dispose of,** get rid of, throw away/out, discard, jettison; informal ditch, junk.

– PHRASES **dump on** informal abuse or criticize (someone).
– ORIGIN perhaps from Old Norse.

dump·ling /'dəmpliNG/ ▸ **noun 1** a small savory ball of dough boiled in water or in a stew. **2** a pastry consisting of fruit enclosed in a sweet dough and baked.
– ORIGIN probably from the former adjective *dump* 'of the consistency of dough.'

dumps /dəmps/ ▸ **plural noun** (in phrase **(down) in the dumps**) informal depressed or unhappy.
– ORIGIN probably from Dutch *domp* 'haze, mist.'

dump·ster /'dəmpstər/ (also **Dumpster** trademark) ▸ **noun** a large trash receptacle designed to be hoisted and emptied into a truck.

dump truck ▸ **noun** a truck with a body that tilts or opens at the back for unloading.

dump·y /'dəmpē/ ▸ **adjective** (**dumpier, dumpiest**) short and stout.

– SYNONYMS **short,** squat, stubby; **plump,** stout, chubby, chunky, portly, fat, bulky; informal tubby, roly-poly, pudgy, porky.
– ANTONYMS tall, slender.

dun[1] /dən/ ▸ **noun** a dull grayish-brown color.
– ORIGIN Old English.

dun[2] ▸ **verb** (**duns, dunning, dunned**) persistently demand that someone repays a debt.
– ORIGIN perhaps from former *Dunkirk privateer* (with connotations of a pirate making aggressive demands).

dunce /dəns/ ▸ **noun** a person who is slow at learning.
– ORIGIN first referring to a follower of the Scottish theologian John *Duns* Scotus, whose followers were ridiculed as enemies of learning.

dunce cap ▸ **noun** a paper cone formerly put on the head of a dunce at school as a mark of disgrace.

dun·der·head /'dəndər,hed/ ▸ **noun** informal a stupid person.
– DERIVATIVES **dun·der·head·ed** adjective.
– ORIGIN perhaps from former Scots *dunder, dunner* 'resounding noise.'

dune /d(y)o͞on/ ▸ **noun** a mound or ridge of sand formed by the wind, especially on the coast or in a desert.

– SYNONYMS **bank,** mound, hillock, hummock, knoll, ridge, heap, drift.

– ORIGIN Dutch.

dung /dəNG/ ▸ **noun** manure.
– ORIGIN Old English.

dun·ga·rees /,dəNGgə'rēz/ ▸ **plural noun** blue jeans or overalls.
– ORIGIN Hindi, 'coarse calico.'

dung bee·tle ▸ **noun** a beetle whose larvae feed on dung, especially a scarab.

dun·geon /'dənjən/ ▸ **noun** a strong underground prison cell, especially in a castle.
– ORIGIN Old French.

dung·hill /'dəNG,hil/ ▸ **noun** a heap of dung or refuse.

dunk /dəNGk/ ▸ **verb 1** dip food into a drink or soup before eating it. **2** immerse someone or something in water.
– ORIGIN German *tunken* 'dip or plunge.'

dun·lin /'dənlin/ ▸ **noun** (pl. same or **dunlins**) a sandpiper with a downcurved bill and reddish-brown upper parts.
– ORIGIN probably from **DUN**[1].

dun·no /də'nō/ ▸ **contraction** informal (I) do not know.

du·o /'d(y)o͞o-ō/ ▸ **noun** (pl. **duos**) **1** a pair of people or things, especially in music or entertainment. **2** Music a duet.
– ORIGIN Latin, 'two.'

du·o·dec·i·mal /,d(y)o͞oə'desəməl, ,d(y)o͞o-ō-/ ▸ **adjective** relating to a system of counting that has twelve as a base.
– ORIGIN Latin *duodecimus* 'twelfth.'

du·o·de·num /,d(y)o͞oə'dēnəm, d(y)o͞o'ädn-əm/ ▸ **noun** (pl. **duodenums**) the first part of the small intestine immediately beyond the stomach.
– DERIVATIVES **du·o·de·nal** /-'dēnl, -'ädnəl/ adjective.
– ORIGIN Latin.

du·o·logue /'d(y)o͞oə,läg, -,lôg/ ▸ **noun** a play or part of a play with speaking roles for only two actors.

du·op·o·ly /d(y)o͞o'äpəlē/ ▸ **noun** (pl. **duopolies**) a situation in which two suppliers dominate a market.

dupe /d(y)o͞op/ ▸ **verb** deceive or trick someone.

– SYNONYMS **deceive,** trick, hoodwink, hoax, swindle, defraud, cheat, double-cross; gull, mislead, take in, fool, inveigle; informal con, do, rip off, shaft, sucker, snooker, pull the wool over someone's eyes, pull a fast one on.

▸ **noun** a person who has been deceived or tricked.

– SYNONYMS **victim,** pawn, puppet, instrument, fool, innocent; informal sucker, pigeon, patsy, sap, stooge, fall guy.

– ORIGIN French dialect *dupe* 'hoopoe,' from the bird's supposedly stupid appearance.

du·ple /'d(y)o͞opəl/ ▸ **adjective** (of musical rhythm) based on two main beats to the measure.
– ORIGIN Latin *duplus*.

du·plex /'d(y)o͞opleks/ ▸ **noun 1** a residential building divided into two apartments. **2** an apartment on two floors. ▸ **adjective** having two parts.
– ORIGIN Latin.

du·pli·cate ▸ **adjective** /'d(y)o͞opləkit/ **1** exactly like something else. **2** having two corresponding parts.

– SYNONYMS **matching,** identical, twin, corresponding, equivalent.

▶ **noun** /ˈd(y)o͞opləkit/ one of two or more identical things.

– SYNONYMS **copy,** photocopy, facsimile, reprint, replica, reproduction, clone; trademark Xerox, photostat.

▶ **verb** /ˈd(y)o͞opləˌkāt/ **1** make or be an exact copy of something. **2** multiply something by two. **3** do something again unnecessarily.

– SYNONYMS **1 copy,** photocopy, photostat, xerox, reproduce, replicate, reprint, run off. **2 repeat,** do again, redo, replicate.

– DERIVATIVES **du·pli·ca·tion** /ˌd(y)o͞opləˈkāsʜən/ noun.
– ORIGIN Latin *duplicare*.

du·pli·ca·tor /ˈd(y)o͞opləˌkātər/ ▶ **noun** a machine for copying something.

du·plic·i·ty /d(y)o͞oˈplisitē/ ▶ **noun** dishonest behavior that is intended to deceive someone.

– SYNONYMS **deceitfulness,** deceit, deception, double-dealing, underhandedness, dishonesty, fraud, fraudulence, chicanery, trickery, subterfuge, skulduggery, treachery; informal crookedness, shadiness, dirty tricks, shenanigans, monkey business.
– ANTONYMS honesty.

– DERIVATIVES **du·plic·i·tous** adjective.

du·ra·ble /ˈd(y)o͝orəbəl/ ▶ **adjective 1** hard-wearing. **2** (of goods) not for immediate consumption and so able to be kept.

– SYNONYMS **1 hard-wearing,** wear-resistant, heavy-duty, tough, long-lasting, strong, sturdy, robust, utilitarian. **2 lasting,** long-lasting, long-term, enduring, persistent, abiding, permanent, undying, everlasting.
– ANTONYMS delicate, short-lived.

– DERIVATIVES **du·ra·bil·i·ty** /ˌd(y)o͝orəˈbilitē/ noun **du·ra·bly** adverb.
– ORIGIN Latin *durabilis*.

du·ra·ble goods ▶ **plural noun** goods not for immediate consumption and able to be kept for a period of time.

du·ra ma·ter /ˈd(y)o͝orə ˈmätər, ˈmā-/ ▶ **noun** the tough outermost membrane enveloping the brain and spinal cord.
– ORIGIN Latin, 'hard mother.'

du·ra·tion /d(y)o͝orˈāsʜən/ ▶ **noun** the time during which something continues: *a flight of over eight hours' duration*.

– SYNONYMS **length,** time, period, term, span, extent, stretch.

– PHRASES **for the duration 1** until the end of something. **2** informal for a very long time.
– ORIGIN Latin.

du·ress /d(y)o͝oˈres/ ▶ **noun** threats or violence used to force a person into doing something: *confessions extracted under duress*.

– SYNONYMS **coercion,** compulsion, force, pressure, intimidation, threats, constraint; informal arm-twisting.

– ORIGIN from Latin *durus* 'hard.'

du·ri·an /ˈdo͝orēən, -rēˌän/ ▶ **noun** a tropical Asian fruit with a fetid smell but pleasant taste.
– ORIGIN Malay.

dur·ing /ˈd(y)o͝oriɴɢ/ ▶ **preposition 1** throughout the course of a period of time. **2** at a particular point in the course of: *he met the prime minister during his first visit to the country*.

– ORIGIN from Latin *durare* 'to last.'

du·rum wheat /ˈd(y)o͝orəm/ ▶ **noun** a kind of hard wheat, yielding flour from which pasta is made.
– ORIGIN from Latin *durus* 'hard.'

dusk /dəsk/ ▶ **noun** the darker stage of twilight.

– SYNONYMS **twilight,** nightfall, sunset, sundown, evening, close of day, semidarkness; literary gloaming.
– ANTONYMS dawn.

– ORIGIN Old English, 'dark, swarthy.'

dusk·y /ˈdəskē/ ▶ **adjective** (**duskier, duskiest**) **1** dark or soft in color. **2** literary poorly lit; dim.
– DERIVATIVES **dusk·i·ly** adverb **dusk·i·ness** noun.

dust /dəst/ ▶ **noun 1** fine, dry powder consisting of tiny particles of earth or waste matter. **2** any material in the form of tiny particles: *coal dust*.

– SYNONYMS **dirt,** grime, grit, powder, particles.

▶ **verb 1** remove dust from the surface of something. **2** cover something lightly with a powdered substance. **3** (**dust something off**) bring something out for use again after a long period of neglect.

– SYNONYMS **1 wipe,** clean, brush, sweep. **2** *dust the cake with powdered sugar* **sprinkle,** scatter, powder, dredge, sift, cover.

– PHRASES **when the dust settles** when things quiet down.
– ORIGIN Old English.

dust bowl ▶ **noun** a dry area where vegetation has been lost and soil reduced to dust and eroded.

dust cov·er ▶ **noun** a dust jacket or drop cloth.

dust dev·il ▶ **noun** a small whirlwind or air vortex over land, visible as a column of dust and debris.

dust·er /ˈdəstər/ ▶ **noun** a cloth for dusting furniture.

dust jack·et ▶ **noun** a removable paper cover on a book.

dust·pan /ˈdəstˌpan/ ▶ **noun** a flat hand-held container into which dust and waste can be swept.

dust storm ▶ **noun** a strong wind carrying clouds of fine dust and sand.

dust-up ▶ **noun** informal a fight or quarrel.

dust·y /ˈdəstē/ ▶ **adjective** (**dustier, dustiest**) **1** covered with or resembling dust. **2** (of a color) dull or muted. **3** staid and uninteresting: *the society has banished its dusty, fusty, middle-aged-male image*.

– SYNONYMS **1 dirty,** grimy, grubby. **2 powdery,** crumbly, chalky, granular, soft, gritty.

– DERIVATIVES **dust·i·ly** adverb **dust·i·ness** noun.

Dutch /dəcʜ/ ▶ **adjective** relating to the Netherlands or its language. ▶ **noun** the language of the Netherlands.
– PHRASES **go Dutch** share the cost of a meal equally.
– ORIGIN Dutch *dutsch* 'Dutch, German.'

Dutch auc·tion ▶ **noun** a method of selling in which the price is reduced until a buyer is found.

Dutch cap ▶ **noun** a woman's lace cap with triangular flaps on each side, worn as part of Dutch traditional dress.

Dutch cour·age ▶ **noun** confidence gained from drinking alcohol.

Dutch elm dis·ease ▶ **noun** a disease of elm trees, caused by a fungus.

Dutch·man /ˈdəcʜmən/ (or **Dutchwoman** /ˈdəcʜˌwo͝omən/) ▶ **noun** (pl. **Dutchmen** or **Dutchwomen**) a person from the Netherlands, or a person of Dutch descent.

Dutch ov·en ▸ **noun** a covered earthenware or cast-iron pot used for slow cooking.

Dutch un·cle ▸ **noun** informal a person giving firm but benevolent advice.

du·ti·a·ble /ˈd(y)o͞otēəbəl/ ▸ **adjective** (of goods) on which customs or other duties have to be paid.

dut·i·ful /ˈd(y)o͞otəfəl/ ▸ **adjective** **1** doing one's duty in an obedient way. **2** done because of a feeling of obligation rather than enthusiasm: *dutiful applause greeted his speech.*

– SYNONYMS **conscientious,** responsible, dedicated, devoted, attentive, obedient, deferential.
– ANTONYMS remiss.

– DERIVATIVES **du·ti·ful·ly** adverb.

du·ty /ˈd(y)o͞otē/ ▸ **noun** (pl. **duties**) **1** something one has to do because it is morally right or legally necessary: *it's my duty to uphold the law.* **2** a task required as part of one's job. **3** a payment charged on the import, export, manufacture, or sale of goods.

– SYNONYMS **1** *a sense of duty* **responsibility,** obligation, commitment, allegiance, loyalty. **2** *it was his duty to attend the king* **job,** task, assignment, mission, function, role. **3 tax,** levy, tariff, excise, toll, rate.

– PHRASES **on** (or **off**) **duty** doing (or not doing) one's regular work.
– ORIGIN Old French *duete.*

du·ty-bound ▸ **adjective** morally or legally obliged to do something.

du·ty-free ▸ **adjective & adverb** (of goods) exempt from payment of duty.

du·vet /ˌd(y)o͞oˈvā/ ▸ **noun** a soft, thick quilt used instead of an upper sheet and blankets.
– ORIGIN French, 'down.'

DVD ▸ **abbreviation** a high-density videodisc.

DVD-R ▸ **abbreviation** DVD recordable, a DVD that can be recorded on once only.

DVD-ROM ▸ **abbreviation** DVD read-only memory, a DVD used in a computer for displaying data.

DVD-RW (also **DVD-RAM**) ▸ **abbreviation** DVD rewritable (or random-access memory), a DVD on which recordings can be made and erased a number of times.

DVM ▸ **abbreviation** Doctor of Veterinary Medicine.

dwarf /dwôrf/ ▸ **noun** (pl. **dwarfs** or **dwarves** /dwôrvz/) **1** a member of a mythical race of short, stocky humanlike creatures. **2** a person who is unusually small. **3** (also **dwarf star**) a star of relatively small size and low luminosity. ▸ **adjective** (of an animal or plant) much smaller than is usual for its type or species. ▸ **verb** cause to seem small in comparison: *the church is dwarfed by cranes.*

– SYNONYMS **1 dominate,** tower over, loom over, overshadow. **2 overshadow,** outshine, surpass, exceed, outclass, outstrip, outdo, top.

– DERIVATIVES **dwarf·ish** adjective.
– ORIGIN Old English.

USAGE

Although the use of **dwarf** to mean 'an unusually small person' is normally considered offensive, there is no term that has been established as an acceptable general alternative.

dwarf·ism /ˈd(w)ôrfizəm/ ▸ **noun** unusually low stature or small size.

dweeb /dwēb/ ▸ **noun** informal a boring, studious, or socially inept person.
– ORIGIN perhaps from **DWARF** and *feeb* 'a feeble-minded person.'

dwell /dwel/ ▸ **verb** (past and past part. **dwelt** or **dwelled**) **1** formal live in or at a place. **2** (**dwell on**) think, speak, or write at length about something.

– SYNONYMS **1 reside,** live, be housed, lodge, stay; informal put up; formal abide. **2** (**dwell on**) **linger over,** mull over, muse on, brood about/over, think about, be preoccupied by, obsess about, harp on about.

– DERIVATIVES **dwell·er** noun.
– ORIGIN Old English.

dwell·ing /ˈdweliNG/ (also **dwelling place**) ▸ **noun** formal a house or other place where someone lives.

dwin·dle /ˈdwindl/ ▸ **verb** gradually become smaller or weaker: *a weekly audience that's dwindled to less than nine million.*

– SYNONYMS **diminish,** decrease, reduce, lessen, shrink, wane.
– ANTONYMS increase.

– ORIGIN Old English, 'fade away.'

Dy ▸ **symbol** the chemical element dysprosium.

dy·ad /ˈdīad/ ▸ **noun** technical something consisting of two elements or parts.
– DERIVATIVES **dy·ad·ic** /dīˈadik/ adjective.
– ORIGIN from Latin *dyas.*

dye /dī/ ▸ **noun** a natural or synthetic substance used to color something.

– SYNONYMS **coloring,** dyestuff, pigment, tint, stain, wash.

▸ **verb** (**dyes, dyeing, dyed**) color something with dye.

– SYNONYMS **color,** tint, pigment, stain, wash.

– DERIVATIVES **dy·er** noun.
– ORIGIN Old English.

dyed-in-the-wool ▸ **adjective** having firm beliefs that will never change: *a dyed-in-the-wool socialist.*

– SYNONYMS **inveterate,** confirmed, entrenched, established, long-standing, deep-rooted, diehard; complete, absolute, thorough, thoroughgoing, out-and-out, full-bore, true blue, firm, unshakable, staunch, steadfast, committed, devoted, dedicated, loyal, unswerving; informal card-carrying.

dye·stuff /ˈdīˌstəf/ ▸ **noun** a substance that is used as a dye or that yields a dye.

dy·ing /ˈdī-iNG/ present participle of **DIE**[1].

dyke[1] /dīk/ (also **dike**) ▸ **noun** variant spelling of **DIKE**[1].
– ORIGIN Old Norse.

dyke[2] (also **dike**) ▸ **noun** informal a lesbian.
– DERIVATIVES **dyke·y** adjective.
– ORIGIN unknown.

dy·nam·ic /dīˈnamik/ ▸ **adjective** **1** (of a process or system) constantly changing or progressing: *the dynamic market in Latin America.* **2** full of energy and new ideas. **3** Physics relating to forces producing motion. Often contrasted with **STATIC**.

– SYNONYMS **energetic,** spirited, active, lively, vigorous, forceful, high-powered, aggressive, enterprising; informal go-getting, go-ahead.

▶ **noun** a force that stimulates change or progress: *evaluation is part of the basic dynamic of the project.*
– DERIVATIVES **dy·nam·i·cal** adjective **dy·nam·i·cal·ly** /-ik(ə)lē/ adverb.
– ORIGIN Greek *dunamikos.*

dy·nam·ic range ▶ **noun** the range of sound intensity that occurs in a piece of music or that can be handled by a piece of equipment.

dy·nam·ics /dīˈnamiks/ ▶ **plural noun 1** (treated as sing.) the branch of mechanics concerned with the motion of bodies under the action of forces. **2** the forces that stimulate change or progress within a system or process. **3** the varying levels of volume of sound in a musical performance.

dy·na·mism /ˈdīnəˌmizəm/ ▶ **noun** the quality of being full of energy, vigor, or enthusiasm: *the prosperity and dynamism of Barcelona.*

dy·na·mite /ˈdīnəˌmīt/ ▶ **noun 1** a high explosive made of nitroglycerine. **2** informal a very impressive or potentially dangerous person or thing: *that policy is political dynamite.* ▶ **verb** blow something up with dynamite.
– ORIGIN from Greek *dunamis* 'power.'

dy·na·mo /ˈdīnəˌmō/ ▶ **noun** (pl. **dynamos**) **1** a machine for converting mechanical energy into electrical energy. **2** informal an extremely energetic person.
– ORIGIN short for *dynamo-electric machine.*

dy·na·mom·e·ter /ˌdīnəˈmämitər/ ▶ **noun** an instrument that measures the power output of an engine.

dy·nast /ˈdīˌnast, -nəst/ ▶ **noun** a member of a dynasty, especially a hereditary ruler.

dy·nas·ty /ˈdīnəstē/ ▶ **noun** (pl. **dynasties**) **1** a series of rulers of a country who belong to the same family. **2** a succession of prominent people from the same family.

– SYNONYMS **family,** house, line, lineage, regime, empire.

– DERIVATIVES **dy·nas·tic** /dīˈnastik/ adjective **dy·nas·ti·cal·ly** /dīˈnastik(ə)lē/ adverb.
– ORIGIN Greek *dunasteia* 'lordship.'

dyne /dīn/ ▶ **noun** Physics force required to give a mass of one gram an acceleration of one centimeter per second every second.
– ORIGIN Greek *dunamis* 'force, power.'

dys- ▶ **combining form** bad; difficult (used especially in medical terms): *dyspepsia.*
– ORIGIN from Greek *dus-.*

dys·en·ter·y /ˈdisənˌterē/ ▶ **noun** a disease in which the intestines are infected, resulting in severe diarrhea.
– ORIGIN Greek *dusenteria.*

dys·func·tion·al /disˈfəNGkSHənl/ ▶ **adjective 1** not operating normally or properly. **2** unable to deal adequately with normal relationships between people.
– DERIVATIVES **dys·func·tion** noun **dys·func·tion·al·ly** adverb.

dys·lex·i·a /disˈleksēə/ ▶ **noun** a disorder involving difficulty in learning to read or interpret words, letters, and other symbols.
– DERIVATIVES **dys·lex·ic** /-ˈleksik/ adjective & noun.
– ORIGIN from DYS- and Greek *lexis* 'speech.'

dys·men·or·rhe·a /ˌdismenəˈrēə/ ▶ **noun** Medicine painful menstruation.

dys·mor·phi·a /disˈmôrfēə/ ▶ **noun** Medicine deformity or abnormality in the shape or size of a part of the body.
– DERIVATIVES **dys·mor·phic** /disˈmôrfik/ adjective.
– ORIGIN Greek *dusmorphia* 'misshapenness.'

dys·pep·sia /disˈpepsēə, -ˈpepSHə/ ▶ **noun** indigestion.
– ORIGIN Greek *duspepsia.*

dys·pep·tic /disˈpeptik/ ▶ **adjective 1** relating to or having dyspepsia (indigestion). **2** irritable; bad-tempered.

dys·pha·sia /disˈfāZHə/ ▶ **noun** a disorder marked by difficulty in using language coherently, due to brain disease or damage.
– DERIVATIVES **dys·pha·sic** /-ˈfāzik/ adjective.
– ORIGIN from Greek *phatos* 'spoken.'

dys·pho·ri·a /disˈfôrēə/ ▶ **noun** a state of unease or general dissatisfaction.
– DERIVATIVES **dys·phor·ic** /-ˈfôrik/ adjective.
– ORIGIN from Greek *dusphoros* 'hard to bear.'

dys·pla·sia /disˈplāZHə/ ▶ **noun** the enlargement of an organ or tissue by the proliferation of abnormal cells.
– DERIVATIVES **dys·plas·tic** /disˈplastik/ adjective.
– ORIGIN from Greek *plasis* 'formation.'

dys·prax·i·a /disˈpraksēə/ ▶ **noun** a disorder of the brain in childhood resulting in poor physical coordination.
– ORIGIN from Greek *dus-* 'bad or difficult' + *praxis* 'action.'

dys·pro·si·um /disˈprōzēəm/ ▶ **noun** a soft silvery-white metallic chemical element of the lanthanide series.
– ORIGIN from Greek *dusprositos* 'hard to get at.'

dys·to·pi·a /disˈtōpēə/ ▶ **noun** an imaginary place or society in which everything is bad.
– DERIVATIVES **dys·to·pi·an** adjective & noun.
– ORIGIN from DYS- + UTOPIA.

dys·tro·phy /ˈdistrəfē/ ▶ **noun** a disorder in which an organ or tissue of the body wastes away. See also MUSCULAR DYSTROPHY.
– DERIVATIVES **dys·troph·ic** /disˈträfik/ adjective.
– ORIGIN from DYS- + Greek *-trophia* 'nourishment.'

Ee

E[1] (also **e**) ▸ **noun** (pl. **Es** or **E's**) **1** the fifth letter of the alphabet. **2** referring to the fifth item in a set. **3** Music the third note of the scale of C major.

E[2] ▸ **abbreviation 1** East or Eastern. **2** informal the drug Ecstasy or a tablet of Ecstasy. **3** Physics energy.

e[1] ▸ **symbol 1** (€) euro or euros. **2** (*e*) Mathematics the transcendental number that is the base of natural logarithms, approximately equal to 2.71828.

e[2] /ē/ ▸ **noun** (pl. **e's**) an email system, message, or messages. ▸ **verb** (**e's e'ing e'd**) **1** send an email to someone: *e me to make an offer.* **2** send (a message) by email.

e- ▸ **prefix** referring to the use of electronic data transfer, especially through the Internet.
– ORIGIN from **ELECTRONIC**, on the pattern of *email*.

ea. ▸ **abbreviation** each.

each /ēch/ ▸ **determiner & pronoun** every one of two or more people or things, regarded separately. ▸ **adverb** to, for, or by every one of a group.

> – SYNONYMS **apiece,** per person, per head, per capita; informal a pop.

– ORIGIN Old English.

each oth·er ▸ **pronoun** the other one or ones.

ea·ger /ˈēgər/ ▸ **adjective 1** strongly wanting to do or have: *I was eager to help.* **2** keenly expectant or interested.

> – SYNONYMS **1 keen,** enthusiastic, avid, ardent, zealous, highly motivated, committed, earnest. **2** *we were eager for news* **anxious,** impatient, agog, longing, yearning, wishing, hoping; informal itching, dying, raring.
> – ANTONYMS apathetic.

– DERIVATIVES **ea·ger·ly** adverb **ea·ger·ness** noun.
– ORIGIN Old French *aigre* 'keen.'

ea·gle /ˈēgəl/ ▸ **noun** a large keen-sighted bird of prey with long broad wings and a large hooked bill.
– DERIVATIVES **ea·glet** noun.
– ORIGIN Latin *aquila*.

ea·gle-eyed ▸ **adjective** sharp-sighted and very observant.

ea·gle owl ▸ **noun** a very large owl with ear tufts and a deep hoot.

ear[1] /i(ə)r/ ▸ **noun 1** the organ of hearing and balance in humans and other vertebrates, especially the external part of this. **2** an ability to recognize and appreciate music or language. **3** willingness to listen: *she offers a sympathetic ear to worried pet owners.*

> – SYNONYMS *he has an ear for a good song* **appreciation,** feel, instinct, intuition, sense.

– DERIVATIVES **eared** adjective.
– PHRASES **be all ears** informal be listening eagerly. **one's ears are burning** one is subconsciously aware of being talked about. **have someone's ear** have access to and influence with someone. **have** (or **keep**) **an ear to the ground** be well informed about events and trends. **be out on one's ear** informal be abruptly dismissed from a job. **up to one's ears in** informal very busy with.
– ORIGIN Old English.

> **WORD LINKS**
> **aural** *relating to the ear*

ear[2] ▸ **noun** the seed-bearing head of a cereal plant.
– ORIGIN Old English.

ear·ache /ˈi(ə)rˌāk/ ▸ **noun** pain inside the ear.

ear·drum /ˈi(ə)rˌdrəm/ ▸ **noun** the membrane of the middle ear, which vibrates in response to sound waves.

ear·ful /ˈi(ə)rˌfo͝ol/ ▸ **noun** informal a prolonged amount of talking, typically an angry reprimand.

ear·hole /ˈi(ə)rˌhōl/ ▸ **noun** the external opening of the ear.

earl /ərl/ ▸ **noun** a British nobleman ranking above a viscount and below a marquess.
– DERIVATIVES **earl·dom** noun.
– ORIGIN Old English.

Earl Grey ▸ **noun** a kind of China tea flavored with bergamot.
– ORIGIN probably named after the 2nd *Earl Grey*, said to have been given the recipe by a Chinese mandarin.

ear·lobe /ˈi(ə)rˌlōb/ ▸ **noun** see **LOBE**.

ear·ly /ˈərlē/ ▸ **adjective** (**earlier, earliest**) **& adverb 1** before the usual or expected time. **2** belonging or happening at the beginning of a particular period or sequence: *he's in his early fifties.*

> – SYNONYMS **1** *early copies of the book* **advance,** initial, preliminary, first. **2** *an early death* **untimely,** premature, unseasonable, before time. **3** *early man* **primitive,** ancient, prehistoric, primeval. **4** *an early official statement* **prompt,** timely, quick, speedy, rapid, fast. **5** *expectant crowds arrived early* **in advance,** in good time, ahead of schedule, with time to spare, before the last moment. **6** *I was planning to finish work early today* **prematurely,** before the usual time, too soon, ahead of schedule.
> – ANTONYMS late, overdue.

– DERIVATIVES **ear·li·ness** noun.
– PHRASES **at the earliest** not before the time or date specified. **early bird** humorous a person who gets up or arrives early. **early** (or **earlier**) **on** at an early (or earlier) stage.
– ORIGIN Old English.

Ear·ly Eng·lish ▸ **adjective** referring to a style of English Gothic architecture typical of the late 12th and 13th centuries, marked by pointed arches and narrow pointed windows.

ear·ly mu·sic ▶ **noun** medieval, Renaissance, and early baroque music, especially as revived and played on period instruments.

ear·mark /ˈi(ə)rˌmärk/ ▶ **verb** set aside for a particular purpose: *the government has earmarked $15 million to fight hackers.*

– SYNONYMS **set aside,** keep (back), reserve, designate, assign, allocate.

▶ **noun 1** an identifying feature. **2** an identifying mark on the ear of a domesticated animal.

ear·muffs /ˈi(ə)rˌməfs/ ▶ **plural noun** a pair of soft fabric coverings, connected by a band, worn over the ears to protect them from cold or noise.

earn /ərn/ ▶ **verb 1** obtain money in return for work or services. **2** receive deservedly for one's behavior or achievements: *he earned a master's degree in English.* **3** (of capital invested) gain money as interest or profit.

– SYNONYMS **1 be paid,** take home, gross, receive, get, make, collect, bring in; informal pocket, bank. **2 deserve,** merit, warrant, justify, be worthy of, gain, win, secure, obtain.
– ANTONYMS lose.

– DERIVATIVES **earn·er** noun.
– ORIGIN Old English.

earned in·come /ərnd/ ▶ **noun** money derived from paid work as opposed to profit from investments.

ear·nest[1] /ˈərnist/ ▶ **adjective** very serious and sincere.

– SYNONYMS **1 serious,** solemn, grave, sober, humorless, staid, intense. **2 devout,** heartfelt, wholehearted, sincere, impassioned, fervent, intense.
– ANTONYMS frivolous, half-hearted.

– DERIVATIVES **ear·nest·ly** adverb **ear·nest·ness** noun.
– PHRASES **in earnest 1** with greater effort or intensity than before. **2** sincere and serious about one's intentions.
– ORIGIN Old English.

ear·nest[2] ▶ **noun** a sign or promise of what is to come.
– ORIGIN Old French *erres* 'a pledge.'

earn·ings /ˈərniNGz/ ▶ **plural noun** money or income earned.

– SYNONYMS **income,** pay, wages, salary, stipend, remuneration, fees, revenue, yield, profit, takings, proceeds.

ear·phone /ˈi(ə)rˌfōn/ ▶ **noun** an electrical device worn on the ear to listen to radio or recorded sound.

ear·piece /ˈi(ə)rˌpēs/ ▶ **noun** the part of a telephone, radio receiver, or other device that is applied to the ear during use.

ear-pierc·ing ▶ **adjective** loud and shrill. ▶ **noun** the piercing of the lobes or edges of the ears to allow earrings to be worn.

ear·plug /ˈi(ə)rˌpləg/ ▶ **noun** a piece of wax, absorbent cotton, or rubber placed in the ear as protection against noise or water.

ear·ring /ˈi(ə)rˌ(r)iNG/ ▶ **noun** a piece of jewelry worn on the lobe or edge of the ear.

ear·shot /ˈi(ə)rˌSHät/ ▶ **noun** the range or distance over which one can hear or be heard.

ear-split·ting ▶ **adjective** very loud.

earth /ərTH/ ▶ **noun 1** (also **Earth**) the planet on which we live. **2** the substance of the land surface; soil. **3** the underground lair of a badger or fox.

– SYNONYMS **1 world,** globe, planet. **2 land,** ground, terra firma, floor. **3 soil,** clay, dust, dirt, loam, ground, turf.

▶ **verb** Brit. connect an electrical device to earth.
– DERIVATIVES **earth·ward** /ˈərTHwərd/ adjective & adverb **earth·wards** adverb.
– PHRASES **come** (or **bring**) **back** (**down**) **to earth** return to reality. **on earth** used for emphasis: *what on earth are you doing?*
– ORIGIN Old English.

WORD LINKS

terrestrial *relating to the earth*
geography, **geology** *study of the earth*

earth·bound /ˈərTHˌbound/ ▶ **adjective 1** confined to the earth or to material things. **2** moving toward the earth.

earth·en /ˈərTHən/ ▶ **adjective 1** made of compressed earth. **2** (of a pot) made of baked or fired clay.

earth·en·ware /ˈərTHənˌwer/ ▶ **noun** pottery made of fired clay.

earth·ling /ˈərTHliNG/ ▶ **noun** (in science fiction) an inhabitant of the earth.

earth·ly /ˈərTHlē/ ▶ **adjective 1** relating to the earth or human life. **2** worldly rather than spiritual. **3** informal used for emphasis: *there was no earthly reason to rush.*

– SYNONYMS **worldly,** temporal, mortal, human, material, carnal, fleshly, bodily, physical, corporeal, sensual.
– ANTONYMS spiritual, heavenly.

– DERIVATIVES **earth·li·ness** noun.

earth·quake /ˈərTHˌkwāk/ ▶ **noun** a sudden violent shaking of the ground, caused by movements within the earth's crust.

– SYNONYMS **(earth) tremor,** shock, convulsion; informal quake.

WORD LINKS

seismic *relating to earthquakes*
seismology *study of earthquakes*

earth sci·en·ces ▶ **plural noun** the branches of science concerned with the physical composition of the earth and its atmosphere.

earth-shat·ter·ing ▶ **adjective** informal very important or shocking.

earth·work /ˈərTHˌwərk/ ▶ **noun** a large artificial bank of soil, especially one made as a defense in ancient times.

earth·worm /ˈərTHˌwərm/ ▶ **noun** a burrowing worm that lives in the soil.

earth·y /ˈərTHē/ ▶ **adjective** (**earthier**, **earthiest**) **1** resembling or suggestive of soil: *an earthy smell.* **2** direct and uninhibited about sex or bodily functions.

– SYNONYMS **1 down-to-earth,** unsophisticated, unrefined, simple, plain, unpretentious, natural. **2 bawdy,** ribald, racy, rude, crude, coarse, indelicate, indecent; informal raunchy.

– DERIVATIVES **earth·i·ly** adverb **earth·i·ness** noun.

ear trum·pet ▶ **noun** a trumpet-shaped device formerly used as a hearing aid.

ear·wax /ˈi(ə)rˌwaks/ ▶ **noun** the protective yellow waxy substance produced in the passage of the outer ear.

ear·wig /ˈi(ə)rˌwig/ ▶ **noun** a small insect with a pair of pincers at its rear end. ▶ **verb** (**earwigs, earwigging, earwigged**) Brit. informal eavesdrop on a conversation.
– ORIGIN Old English.

ease /ēz/ ▶ **noun 1** lack of difficulty or effort: *he beat his opponent with ease.* **2** freedom from worries or problems.

– SYNONYMS **1 effortlessness,** no trouble, simplicity. **2 naturalness,** casualness, informality, composure, nonchalance, insouciance. **3 affluence,** wealth, prosperity, luxury, plenty, comfort, enjoyment, well-being.
– ANTONYMS difficulty.

▶ **verb 1** make something less serious or severe. **2** (**ease off/up**) become less intense or unpleasant: *the gale eased off a bit.* **3** move carefully or gradually. **4** (of share prices, interest rates, etc.) decrease in value or amount.

– SYNONYMS **1 relieve,** alleviate, soothe, moderate, dull, deaden, numb. **2** *the rain **eased off*** **let up,** abate, subside, die down, slacken off, diminish, lessen. **3 calm,** quieten, pacify, soothe, comfort, console. **4 slide,** slip, squeeze, guide, maneuver, inch, edge.
– ANTONYMS aggravate, intensify.

– DERIVATIVES **ease·ful** adjective (literary).
– PHRASES **at ease** Military in a relaxed attitude with the feet apart and the hands behind the back.
– ORIGIN Old French *aise.*

ea·sel /ˈēzəl/ ▶ **noun** a wooden frame on legs for holding an artist's work in progress.
– ORIGIN Dutch *ezel* 'ass.'

ease·ment /ˈēzmənt/ ▶ **noun** Law a right to cross or otherwise use someone else's land for a specified purpose.

eas·i·ly /ˈēz(ə)lē/ ▶ **adverb 1** without difficulty or effort. **2** without doubt; definitely. **3** very probably.

– SYNONYMS **effortlessly,** comfortably, simply, without difficulty, readily, without a hitch.

east /ēst/ ▶ **noun** (**the east**) **1** the direction in which the sun rises at the equinoxes, on the right-hand side of a person facing north. **2** the eastern part of a place. **3** (**the East**) the regions or countries lying to the east of Europe, especially China, Japan, and India. **4** (**the East**) the former communist states of eastern Europe. ▶ **adjective 1** lying toward, near, or facing the east. **2** (of a wind) blowing from the east. ▶ **adverb** to or toward the east.
– DERIVATIVES **east·bound** /ˈēs(t)ˌbound/ adjective & adverb.
– ORIGIN Old English.

Eas·ter /ˈēstər/ (also **Easter Day** or **Easter Sunday**) ▶ **noun** the Christian festival celebrating the resurrection of Jesus.
– ORIGIN Old English.

Eas·ter egg ▶ **noun** a chocolate egg or decorated hard-boiled egg given as a gift at Easter.

east·er·ly /ˈēstərlē/ ▶ **adjective & adverb 1** facing or moving toward the east. **2** (of a wind) blowing from the east. ▶ **noun** (pl. **easterlies**) a wind blowing from the east.

east·ern /ˈēstərn/ ▶ **adjective 1** situated in, directed toward, or facing the east. **2** (**Eastern**) relating to or characteristic of the regions to the east of Europe.
– DERIVATIVES **east·ern·most** /ˈēstərnˌmōst/ adjective.

east·ern·er /ˈēstərnər/ ▶ **noun** a person from the east of a region or country.

East·ern time ▶ **noun** the standard time in a zone including the eastern states of the US and parts of Canada.

east-north·east ▶ **noun** the direction midway between east and northeast.

east-south·east ▶ **noun** the direction midway between east and southeast.

east·ward /ˈēs(t)wərd/ ▶ **adjective** in an easterly direction. ▶ **adverb** (also **eastwards**) toward the east.
– DERIVATIVES **east·ward·ly** adjective & adverb.

eas·y /ˈēzē/ ▶ **adjective** (**easier, easiest**) **1** achieved without great effort; not difficult. **2** free from worry or problems: *the easy life of the rich.* **3** not anxious or awkward. **4** informal, derogatory (of a woman) very willing to have sex.

– SYNONYMS **1 uncomplicated,** undemanding, effortless, painless, trouble-free, simple, straightforward, elementary, smooth sailing; informal a piece of cake, child's play, a cinch. **2 natural,** casual, informal, unceremonious, unreserved, unaffected, easygoing, amiable, affable, genial, good-humored, carefree, nonchalant, unconcerned; informal laid-back. **3 quiet,** tranquil, serene, peaceful, untroubled, contented, relaxed, comfortable, secure, safe. **4** *an easy pace* **leisurely,** unhurried, comfortable, undemanding, easygoing, gentle, sedate, moderate, steady.
– ANTONYMS difficult, demanding.

▶ **exclamation** be careful!
– DERIVATIVES **eas·i·ness** noun.
– PHRASES **easy on the eye** (or **ear**) informal pleasant to look at (or listen to). **go** (or **be**) **easy on** informal **1** do not be too harsh with someone. **2** do not use too much of something. **take it easy** do something in a leisurely way; relax.

eas·y chair ▶ **noun** a large, comfortable armchair.

eas·y·go·ing /ˈēzēˌgōiNG/ ▶ **adjective** relaxed and open-minded.

– SYNONYMS **relaxed,** even-tempered, placid, happy-go-lucky, carefree, imperturbable, undemanding, patient, tolerant, lenient, broad-minded, understanding; informal laid-back, unflappable.
– ANTONYMS intolerant.

eas·y lis·ten·ing ▶ **noun** popular music that is tuneful and undemanding.

eas·y street ▶ **noun** informal a state of financial security.

eat /ēt/ ▶ **verb** (past **ate** /āt/; past part. **eaten** /ˈētn/) **1** put food into the mouth and chew and swallow it. **2** (**eat out** or **in**) have a meal in a restaurant (or at home). **3** (**eat something away**) gradually erode or destroy something. **4** (**eat into**) use up a part of: *my loan payments are eating into my savings.* **5** (**eat something up**) use resources in very large quantities.

– SYNONYMS **1 consume,** devour, swallow, partake of, munch, chomp; informal tuck into, put away. **2 have a meal,** feed, snack, breakfast, lunch, dine; informal graze.

▶ **noun** (**eats**) informal light food or snacks.
– DERIVATIVES **eat·er** noun.
– PHRASES **eat one's heart out** long for something that cannot be achieved. **eat one's words** admit that one was wrong. **what's eating you** (or **him** etc.)? informal what is worrying or annoying you (or him etc.)?
– ORIGIN Old English.

eat·a·ble /ˈētəbəl/ ▶ **adjective** fit to be eaten as food. ▶ **noun** (**eatables**) items of food.

eat·er·y /ˈētərē/ ▶ **noun** (pl. **eateries**) informal a restaurant or cafe.

eat·ing ap·ple ▶ **noun** an apple suitable for eating raw.

eau de co·logne /ˌō də kəˈlōn/ ▶ **noun** (pl. **eaux de cologne** pronunc. same) a toilet water with a strong scent.
– ORIGIN French, 'water of Cologne.'

eau de toi·lette /ˌō də twäˈlet/ ▶ **noun** (pl. **eaux de toilette** pronunc. same) a dilute form of perfume; toilet water.
– ORIGIN French.

eau de vie /ˌō də ˈvē/ ▶ **noun** (pl. **eaux de vie** pronunc. same) brandy.
– ORIGIN French, 'water of life.'

eaves /ēvz/ ▶ **plural noun** the part of a roof that meets or overhangs the walls of a building.
– ORIGIN Old English.

eaves·drop /ˈēvzˌdräp/ ▶ **verb** (**eavesdrops, eavesdropping, eavesdropped**) secretly listen to a conversation.

– SYNONYMS **listen in,** spy, overhear.

– DERIVATIVES **eaves·drop·per** noun.
– ORIGIN from former *eavesdrop* 'the ground on to which water drips from the eaves.'

ebb /eb/ ▶ **noun** the movement of the tide out to sea.
▶ **verb 1** (of tidewater) move away from the land; recede. **2** gradually become less or weaker: *my confidence ebbed away.*

– SYNONYMS **1 recede,** go out, retreat. **2 diminish,** dwindle, wane, fade (away), peter out, decline, flag.
– ANTONYMS flow, increase.

– PHRASES **at a low ebb** in a weakened or depressed state.
– ORIGIN Old English.

Eb·o·la fe·ver /ēˈbōlə/ ▶ **noun** an infectious, generally fatal disease caused by a virus and marked by fever and severe internal bleeding.
– ORIGIN named after a river in the Democratic Republic of Congo.

E·bon·ics /ēˈbäniks/ ▶ **noun** (treated as sing.) American black English regarded as a language in its own right rather than as a dialect of standard English.

eb·on·ite /ˈebəˌnīt/ ▶ **noun** another term for **VULCANITE**.

eb·on·ized /ˈebəˌnīzd/ ▶ **adjective** (of furniture) made to look like ebony.

eb·on·y /ˈebənē/ ▶ **noun 1** heavy blackish or very dark brown wood from a tree of tropical and warm regions. **2** a very dark brown or black color.
– ORIGIN Greek *ebenos* 'ebony tree.'

e-book /ˈē ˌbo͝ok/ ▶ **noun** an electronic version of a printed book that can be read on a personal computer or special hand-held device.

e·bul·lient /iˈbo͝olyənt, iˈbəlyənt/ ▶ **adjective** cheerful and full of energy.

– SYNONYMS **exuberant,** buoyant, cheerful, cheery, merry, jolly, sunny, jaunty, animated, sparkling, vivacious, irrepressible; informal bubbly, bouncy, upbeat, chirpy, full of beans.
– ANTONYMS depressed.

– DERIVATIVES **e·bul·lience** noun **e·bul·lient·ly** adverb.
– ORIGIN from Latin *ebullire* 'boil up.'

e-busi·ness ▶ **noun 1** an online business. **2** another term for **E-COMMERCE**.

EC ▶ **abbreviation 1** European Commission. **2** European Community.

ec·cen·tric /ikˈsentrik/ ▶ **adjective 1** unconventional and slightly strange. **2** technical not placed centrally or not having its axis placed centrally.

– SYNONYMS **unconventional,** abnormal, anomalous, odd, strange, peculiar, weird, bizarre, outlandish, idiosyncratic, quirky; informal oddball, kooky, cranky.
– ANTONYMS conventional.

▶ **noun** a person who is unconventional and slightly strange.

– SYNONYMS **oddity,** free spirit, misfit; informal oddball, weirdo.

– DERIVATIVES **ec·cen·tri·cal·ly** adverb.
– ORIGIN Greek *ekkentros*.

WORD TOOLKIT

eccentric ...	quirky ...	bizarre ...
millionaire	comedy	twist
inventor	humor	coincidence
loner	mannerism	ritual
recluse	charm	antics
aristocrat	lyric	spectacle
genius	sensibility	juxtaposition
uncle	melody	incident
spinster	styling	behavior

ec·cen·tric·i·ty /ˌeksenˈtrisitē/ ▶ **noun** (pl. **eccentricities**) **1** the quality of being unconventional and slightly strange. **2** an eccentric act or habit.

ec·cle·si·al /iˈklēzēəl/ ▶ **adjective** formal relating to a Christian Church or denomination.
– ORIGIN from Greek *ekklēsia* 'assembly, church.'

ec·cle·si·as·tic /iˌklēzēˈastik/ formal ▶ **noun** a member of the Christian clergy. ▶ **adjective** ecclesiastical.

ec·cle·si·as·ti·cal /iˌklēzēˈastikəl/ ▶ **adjective** relating to the Christian Church or its clergy.
– DERIVATIVES **ec·cle·si·as·ti·cal·ly** adverb.
– ORIGIN Greek *ekklēsiastikos*.

ec·cle·si·ol·o·gy /iˌklēzēˈäləjē/ ▶ **noun 1** the study of churches, especially church architecture. **2** theology as applied to the nature and structure of the Christian Church.
– DERIVATIVES **ec·cle·si·o·log·i·cal** /iˌklēzēəˈläjikəl/ adjective **ec·cle·si·ol·o·gist** /-jist/ noun.

ECG ▶ **abbreviation** electrocardiogram or electrocardiograph.

ech·e·lon /ˈesнəˌlän/ ▶ **noun 1** a level or rank in an organization, profession, or society. **2** a formation of troops, ships, aircraft, or vehicles in parallel rows with the end of each row projecting further than the one in front.
– ORIGIN French *échelon*.

e·chid·na /əˈkidnə/ ▶ **noun** (pl. **echidnas**) a spiny egg-laying mammal native to Australia and New Guinea.
– ORIGIN Greek *ekhidna* 'viper.'

ech·i·na·cea /ˌekəˈnāsнə/ ▶ **noun** a North American plant used in herbal medicine.
– ORIGIN Greek *ekhinos* 'hedgehog' (from the appearance of the flowers).

echi·no·derm /iˈkīnəˌdərm, ˈekənəˌdərm/ ▶ **noun** a marine invertebrate (sea creature) of a large group that includes starfishes and sea urchins.
– ORIGIN from Greek *ekhinos* 'hedgehog, sea urchin' + *derma* 'skin.'

ech·o /ˈekō/ ▶ **noun** (pl. **echoes**) **1** a sound caused by the reflection of sound waves from a surface back to the listener. **2** a reflected radio or radar beam. **3** something suggestive of or similar to something else: *his early work shows echoes of Manet and Whistler.*

– SYNONYMS **reverberation,** reflection, ringing, repetition, repeat.

▶ **verb** (**echoes, echoing, echoed**) **1** (of a sound) reverberate or be repeated after the original sound has stopped. **2** be suggestive of or similar to: *his political opinions echoed his father's.* **3** repeat someone's words or opinions.

– SYNONYMS **1 reverberate,** resonate, resound, reflect, ring, vibrate. **2 repeat,** restate, reiterate, imitate, parrot, mimic, reproduce, recite.

– DERIVATIVES **ech·o·ey** adjective.
– ORIGIN Greek *ēkhō.*

ech·o·car·di·og·ra·phy /ˌekōˌkärdēˈägrəfē/ ▶ **noun** the use of ultrasound waves to investigate the action of the heart.
– DERIVATIVES **ech·o·car·di·o·gram** /ˌekōˈkärdēəˌgram/ noun **ech·o·car·di·o·graph** /ˌekōˈkärdēəˌgraf/ noun **ech·o·car·di·o·graph·ic** /-ˌkärdēəˈgrafik/ adjective.

ech·o cham·ber ▶ **noun** an enclosed space for producing echoes.

e·cho·ic /eˈkō-ik/ ▶ **adjective 1** relating to or like an echo. **2** representing a sound by imitation; onomatopoeic.

ech·o·lo·ca·tion /ˌekōlōˈkāsHən/ ▶ **noun** the location of objects by reflected sound, in particular as used by animals such as dolphins and bats.

ech·o sound·er ▶ **noun** a device for determining the depth of the seabed or detecting objects in water by measuring the time taken for echoes to return to the listener.

echt /ekt/ ▶ **adjective** authentic and typical.
– ORIGIN German.

e·clair /āˈkler, iˈkler/ (also **éclair**) ▶ **noun** a log-shaped pastry filled with cream and topped with chocolate icing.
– ORIGIN French *éclair* 'lightning.'

ec·lamp·si·a /iˈklam(p)sēə/ ▶ **noun** Medicine a condition in which a pregnant woman with high blood pressure experiences convulsions.
– DERIVATIVES **ec·lamp·tic** /iˈklam(p)tik/ adjective.
– ORIGIN Greek *eklampsis* 'sudden development.'

é·clat /āˈklä/ ▶ **noun** brilliant or successful effect: *a few of the men landed with the same éclat as their leader.*
– ORIGIN French.

ec·lec·tic /iˈklektik/ ▶ **adjective** using ideas from a wide variety of sources: *he thrived on an eclectic diet of classical and jazz.* ▶ **noun** a person whose ideas or tastes are derived from a wide variety of sources.
– DERIVATIVES **ec·lec·ti·cal·ly** adverb **ec·lec·ti·cism** /iˈklektiˌsizəm/ noun.
– ORIGIN Greek *eklektikos.*

e·clipse /iˈklips/ ▶ **noun 1** an occasion when one planet, the moon, etc., passes between another and the observer, or in front of a planet's source of light. **2** a sudden loss of significance or power. ▶ **verb 1** (of a planet, the moon, etc.) obscure the light coming from or shining on another. **2** make less significant or powerful: *he was one of the composers whose fame has been eclipsed by Mozart.*

– SYNONYMS **outshine,** overshadow, surpass, exceed, outclass, outstrip, outdo, transcend.

– ORIGIN Greek *ekleipsis.*

e·clip·tic /iˈkliptik/ ▶ **noun** Astronomy a great circle on the celestial sphere representing the sun's apparent circular path among the stars during the year.

eco- ▶ **combining form** representing ECOLOGY.

ec·o·friend·ly/ˈēkō-/ ▶ **adjective** not harmful to the environment.

ec·o·la·bel·ing /ˌekō ˈlābəliNG, ˈēkō-/ ▶ **noun** the use of labels to identify products that meet recognized environmental standards.
– DERIVATIVES **ec·o·la·bel** noun.

E. co·li /ē ˈkōlī/ ▶ **noun** the bacterium *Escherichia coli,* found in the intestines of humans and other animals, some strains of which can cause severe food poisoning.

e·co·log·i·cal foot·print ▶ **noun** the sum of an individual's or other entity's impact on the environment, based on consumption and pollution.

e·col·o·gy /iˈkäləjē/ ▶ **noun** the branch of biology concerned with the relations of organisms to one another and to their surroundings.
– DERIVATIVES **ec·o·log·i·cal** /ˌekəˈläjikəl, ˌēkə-/ adjective **ec·o·log·i·cal·ly** /ˌekəˈläjik(ə)lē, ˌēkə-/ adverb **e·col·o·gist** /-jist/ noun.
– ORIGIN from Greek *oikos* 'house.'

e·com·merce (also **e-business**) ▶ **noun** commercial transactions conducted on the Internet.

e·con·o·met·rics /iˌkänəˈmetriks/ ▶ **plural noun** (treated as sing.) the branch of economics concerned with the use of statistical methods in describing economic systems.
– DERIVATIVES **e·con·o·met·ric** adjective **e·con·o·me·tri·cian** /iˌkänəməˈtrisHən/ noun.

ec·o·nom·ic /ˌekəˈnämik, ˌēkə-/ ▶ **adjective 1** relating to economics or the economy of a country or region. **2** profitable, or concerned with profitability: *organizations must become larger if they are to remain economic.* **3** sparing in the use of resources or money.

– SYNONYMS **1 financial,** monetary, budgetary, commercial, fiscal. **2 profitable,** moneymaking, lucrative, remunerative, fruitful, productive.
– ANTONYMS unprofitable.

ec·o·nom·i·cal /ˌekəˈnämikəl, ˌēkə-/ ▶ **adjective 1** giving good value or return in relation to the resources used or money spent: *a small, economical car.* **2** careful not to waste resources or money.

– SYNONYMS **1 cheap,** inexpensive, low-cost, budget, economy, cut-price, bargain. **2 thrifty,** provident, prudent, sensible, frugal.
– ANTONYMS expensive, spendthrift.

– DERIVATIVES **ec·o·nom·i·cal·ly** /ˌekəˈnämik(ə)lē, ˌēkə-/ adverb.
– PHRASES **economical with the truth** euphemistic lying or deliberately withholding information.

CHOOSE THE RIGHT WORD

economical, frugal, miserly, parsimonious, provident, sparing, thrifty

If you don't like to spend money unnecessarily, you may simply be **economical**, which means that you manage your finances wisely and avoid any unnecessary expenses. If you're **thrifty**, you're both industrious and clever in managing your resources (*a thrifty shopper who never leaves home without her coupons*). **Frugal**, on the other hand, means that you tend to be sparing with money—sometimes getting a little carried away in your efforts—by avoiding any form of luxury or lavishness (*too frugal to take a taxi, even at night*). If you're **sparing**, you exercise such restraint in your spending that you sometimes deprive yourself (*sparing to the point where she allowed herself only one new item of clothing a season*). If you're **provident**, however, you're focused on providing for the future (*never one to be provident, she spent her allowance the day she received it*). **Miserly** and **parsimonious** are both used to describe frugality in its most extreme form. But while being *frugal* might be considered a virtue, being *parsimonious* is usually considered to be a fault or even a vice (*they could have been generous with their wealth, but they chose to lead a parsimonious life*). And no one wants to be called *miserly*, which implies being stingy out of greed rather than need (*so miserly that he reveled in his riches while those around him were starving*).

ec·o·nom·ic mi·grant ▶ **noun** a person who travels from one country to another to improve their standard of living.

ec·o·nom·ics /ˌekəˈnämiks, ˌēkə-/ ▶ **plural noun** (often treated as sing.) the branch of knowledge concerned with the production, consumption, and transfer of wealth.

e·con·o·mist /iˈkänəmist/ ▶ **noun** an expert in economics.

e·con·o·mize /iˈkänəˌmīz/ ▶ **verb** spend less; reduce one's expenses.

– SYNONYMS **save (money),** cut costs, cut back, make cutbacks, retrench, scrimp.

e·con·o·my /iˈkänəmē/ ▶ **noun** (pl. **economies**) **1** the state of a country or region in terms of the production and consumption of goods and services and the supply of money. **2** the careful use of resources so as to avoid waste: *the outboard engine increases fuel economy.* **3** a financial saving. **4** (also **economy class**) the cheapest class of air or rail travel.

– SYNONYMS **1 wealth,** financial resources, financial management. **2 thrift,** thriftiness, prudence, careful budgeting, economizing, saving, restraint, frugality.
– ANTONYMS extravagance.

▶ **adjective** offering good value for money: *an economy pack.*
– PHRASES **economy of scale** a proportionate saving in costs gained by an increased level of production.
– ORIGIN Greek *oikonomia* 'household management.'

ec·o·re·gion /ˈekōˌrējən, ˈēkō-/ ▶ **noun** a major ecosystem defined by distinctive geography and receiving uniform solar radiation and moisture.

ec·o·sphere /ˈekōˌsfi(ə)r, ˈēkō-/ ▶ **noun** a region in which life exists or could exist; the biosphere.

ec·o·sys·tem /ˈekōˌsistəm, ˈēkō-/ ▶ **noun** a biological community of interacting animals and plants and their environment.

ec·o·tour·ism /ˌekōˈto͝orizəm, ˌēkō-/ ▶ **noun** tourism directed toward unspoiled natural environments and intended to support conservation efforts.
– DERIVATIVES **ec·o·tour** noun **ec·o·tour·ist** noun.

ec·o·war·ri·or /ˈēkō-/ ▶ **noun** informal a person involved in protest activities aimed at protecting the environment.

ec·ru /ˈekro͞o/ ▶ **noun** a light cream or beige color.
– ORIGIN French, 'unbleached.'

ec·sta·sy /ˈekstəsē/ ▶ **noun** (pl. **ecstasies**) **1** an overwhelming feeling of happiness or joyful excitement. **2** (**Ecstasy**) an illegal amphetamine-based drug. **3** old use an emotional or religious frenzy or trance.

– SYNONYMS **rapture,** bliss, joy, elation, euphoria, rhapsodies.
– ANTONYMS misery.

– ORIGIN from Greek *ekstasis* 'standing outside oneself.'

CHOOSE THE RIGHT WORD

See **RAPTURE**.

ec·stat·ic /ekˈstatik/ ▶ **adjective** very happy or excited.

– SYNONYMS **enraptured,** elated, euphoric, rapturous, joyful, overjoyed, blissful; informal over the moon, on top of the world.

▶ **noun** a person who is subject to mystical experiences.
– DERIVATIVES **ec·stat·i·cal·ly** adverb.

ECT ▶ **abbreviation** electroconvulsive therapy.

ec·to·morph /ˈektəˌmôrf/ ▶ **noun** Physiology a person with a lean and delicate body build. Compare with **ENDOMORPH** and **MESOMORPH**.

ec·top·ic preg·nan·cy /ekˈtäpik/ ▶ **noun** a pregnancy in which the fetus develops outside the uterus, typically in a Fallopian tube.
– ORIGIN Greek *ektopos* 'out of place.'

ec·to·plasm /ˈektəˌplazəm/ ▶ **noun** a substance that supposedly comes out of the body of a medium during a trance.
– DERIVATIVES **ec·to·plas·mic** /ˌektəˈplazmik/ adjective.
– ORIGIN from Greek *ektos* 'outside' + *plasma* 'formation.'

Ec·ua·dor·e·an /ˌekwəˈdôrēən/ (also **Ecuadorian**) ▶ **noun** a person from Ecuador. ▶ **adjective** relating to Ecuador.

ec·u·men·i·cal /ˌekyəˈmenikəl/ ▶ **adjective 1** representing a number of different Christian Churches. **2** promoting unity among the world's Christian Churches.
– DERIVATIVES **ec·u·men·i·cal·ly** adverb.
– ORIGIN from Greek *oikoumenē* 'the inhabited earth.'

ec·u·me·nism /ˈekyəməˌnizəm, eˈkyo͞omə-/ ▶ **noun** the aim of promoting unity among the world's Christian Churches.

ec·ze·ma /ˈegzəmə, ˈeksə-, igˈzēmə/ ▶ **noun** a condition in which patches of skin become rough and inflamed, causing itching and bleeding.
– ORIGIN Greek *ekzema*.

ed. ▶ **abbreviation 1** edited by. **2** edition. **3** editor. **4** education.

E·dam /ˈēdəm/ ▶ **noun** a round yellow cheese with a red wax coating.
– ORIGIN from *Edam* in the Netherlands.

ed·a·ma·me /ˌedəˈmämā/ ▶ **noun** a dish of green soybeans boiled or steamed in their pods.
– ORIGIN Japanese, literally 'beans on a branch.'

ed·dy /ˈedē/ ▶ **noun** (pl. **eddies**) a circular movement of water causing a small whirlpool.

– SYNONYMS **swirl,** whirlpool, vortex.

▶ **verb** (**eddies, eddying, eddied**) (of water, air, smoke, etc.) move in a circular way.

– SYNONYMS **swirl,** whirl, spiral, wind, twist.

– ORIGIN probably related to an Old English word meaning 'again, back.'

e·del·weiss /ˈādlˌwīs, -ˌvīs/ ▶ **noun** a mountain plant with small flowers and gray-green leaves.
– ORIGIN from German *edel* 'noble' + *weiss* 'white.'

e·de·ma /iˈdēmə/ (Brit. **oedema**) ▶ **noun** an excess of watery fluid in the cavities or tissues of the body.
– ORIGIN Greek *oidēma*.

E·den /ˈēdn/ ▶ **noun 1** (also **Garden of Eden**) the place where Adam and Eve lived in the biblical story of

the Creation. **2** a place or state of great happiness or unspoiled beauty.
– DERIVATIVES **E·den·ic** /i'denik/ adjective.
– ORIGIN Hebrew.

e·den·tate /ē'den,tāt/ ▶ **noun** a mammal of a group that has no incisor or canine teeth, including the anteaters and sloths.
– ORIGIN from Latin *edentare* 'make toothless.'

edge /ej/ ▶ **noun 1** the outside limit of an object, area, or surface. **2** the sharpened side of a blade. **3** the line along which two surfaces of a solid meet. **4** a slight advantage over close rivals: *Europe is losing its competitive edge.* **5** an intense or striking quality: *the chef has a fiery edge to her cooking.*

– SYNONYMS **1 border,** boundary, extremity, fringe, margin, side, lip, rim, brim, brink, verge, perimeter. **2 sharpness,** severity, bite, sting, sarcasm, malice, spite, venom. **3 advantage,** lead, head start, the whip hand, the upper hand, dominance.
– ANTONYMS middle.

▶ **verb 1** provide something with an edge or border. **2** move carefully or furtively: *I tried to edge away from her.*

– SYNONYMS **1 border,** fringe, skirt, surround, enclose, encircle, bound. **2 trim,** decorate, finish, border, fringe. **3 creep,** inch, work one's way, ease oneself, sidle, steal.

– DERIVATIVES **edged** adjective **edg·er** noun.
– PHRASES **on edge** tense, nervous, or irritable. **set someone's teeth on edge** (especially of a sound) cause intense discomfort or irritation to someone.
– ORIGIN Old English.

CHOOSE THE RIGHT WORD

See **BORDER**.

edge·wise /'ej,wīz/ (also **edgeways** /-,wāz/) ▶ **adverb** with the edge uppermost or toward the viewer.
– PHRASES **get a word in edgewise** manage to break into a lively conversation or monologue.

edg·ing /'ejiNG/ ▶ **noun** something forming an edge or border.

edg·y /'ejē/ ▶ **adjective** (**edgier, edgiest**) **1** tense, nervous, or irritable. **2** informal avant-garde and unconventional.

– SYNONYMS **tense,** nervous, on edge, anxious, apprehensive, uneasy, unsettled, twitchy, jumpy, nervy, keyed up, restive; informal uptight, wired.
– ANTONYMS calm.

– DERIVATIVES **edg·i·ly** adverb **edg·i·ness** noun.

EDI ▶ **abbreviation** electronic data interchange.

ed·i·ble /'edəbəl/ ▶ **adjective** fit to be eaten. ▶ **noun** (**edibles**) items of food.
– DERIVATIVES **ed·i·bil·i·ty** /,edə'bilitē/ noun.
– ORIGIN Latin *edibilis*.

e·dict /'ēdikt/ ▶ **noun** an official order or proclamation.
– ORIGIN Latin *edictum* 'something proclaimed.'

ed·i·fice /'edəfis/ ▶ **noun** formal **1** a large, imposing building. **2** a complex system: *the edifice of economic reform degenerated into corruption.*
– ORIGIN Latin *aedificium*.

ed·i·fy /'edə,fī/ ▶ **verb** (**edifies, edifying, edified**) give educational or morally improving instruction to someone.

– SYNONYMS **educate,** instruct, teach, school, tutor, train, guide; enlighten, inform, cultivate, develop, improve, better.

– DERIVATIVES **ed·i·fi·ca·tion** /,edəfi'kāSHən/ noun **ed·i·fy·ing** /'edə,fī-iNG/ adjective.
– ORIGIN Latin *aedificare* 'build.'

ed·it /'edit/ ▶ **verb** (**edits, editing, edited**) **1** prepare written material for publication by correcting, shortening, or improving it. **2** prepare material for a movie or a radio or television program. **3** change online text on a computer or word processor. **4** be editor of a newspaper or magazine.

– SYNONYMS **correct,** check, copy-edit, improve, polish, modify, adapt, revise, rewrite, reword, shorten, condense, cut, abridge.

▶ **noun** a change made as a result of editing.
– DERIVATIVES **ed·it·a·ble** /'editəbəl/ adjective.
– ORIGIN from **EDITOR**.

e·di·tion /i'diSHən/ ▶ **noun 1** a particular form or version of a published written work. **2** the total number of copies of a book, newspaper, etc., issued at one time. **3** a particular instance of a regular radio or television program.

– SYNONYMS **issue,** number, volume, printing, impression, publication, program, version.

– ORIGIN Latin.

ed·i·tor /'editər/ ▶ **noun 1** a person who is in charge of a newspaper, magazine, or multiauthor book. **2** a person who commissions or prepares written or recorded material for publication or broadcasting.
– DERIVATIVES **ed·i·tor·ship** noun.
– ORIGIN Latin.

ed·i·to·ri·al /,edi'tôrēəl/ ▶ **adjective** relating to the commissioning or preparing of material for publication. ▶ **noun** a newspaper article giving an opinion on a topical issue.
– DERIVATIVES **ed·i·to·ri·al·ist** noun **ed·i·to·ri·al·ly** adverb.

ed·i·to·ri·al·ize /,edi'tôrēə,līz/ ▶ **verb** (of a newspaper or editor) express opinions rather than just report news.

EDP ▶ **abbreviation** electronic data processing.

EDT ▶ **abbreviation** Eastern Daylight Time.

ed·u·cate /'ejə,kāt/ ▶ **verb 1** give intellectual and moral instruction to someone. **2** give someone information on a particular subject: *a campaign to educate consumers about food safety.* **3** (as adj. **educated**) showing or having had a good education: *a polished, educated, girl.*

– SYNONYMS **1 teach,** school, tutor, instruct, coach, train, inform, enlighten. **2** (as adj. **educated**) **informed,** literate, schooled, tutored, well read, learned, knowledgeable, enlightened, intellectual, academic, erudite, scholarly, cultivated, cultured.

– DERIVATIVES **ed·u·ca·ble** /-kəbəl/ adjective **ed·u·ca·tive** /-,kātiv/ adjective **ed·u·ca·tor** /-,kātər/ noun.
– ORIGIN Latin *educare* 'lead out.'

ed·u·cat·ed guess ▶ **noun** a guess based on knowledge and experience.

ed·u·ca·tion /,ejə'kāSHən/ ▶ **noun 1** the process of teaching or learning. **2** the theory and practice of teaching. **3** information about or training in a particular subject: *health education.* **4** (**an education**) an enlightening experience: *traveling has been quite an education for this former teacher.*

– SYNONYMS **1 teaching,** schooling, tuition, tutoring, instruction, coaching, training, guidance, enlightenment. **2 learning,** knowledge, literacy, scholarship, enlightenment.

– DERIVATIVES **ed·u·ca·tion·ist** noun.

ed·u·ca·tion·al /ˌejəˈkāsʜənl/ ▶ **adjective 1** of or relating to the provision of education. **2** intended or serving to educate or enlighten.

– SYNONYMS **1** *an educational establishment* **academic,** scholastic, learning, teaching, pedagogic. **2** *an educational experience* **instructive,** instructional, educative, informative, illuminating, enlightening; formal **edifying.**

– DERIVATIVES **ed·u·ca·tion·al·ist** noun **ed·u·ca·tion·al·ly** adverb.

Ed·ward·i·an /edˈwôrdēən, -ˈwär-/ ▶ **adjective** relating to the reign of King Edward VII (1901–10). ▶ **noun** a person who lived during the Edwardian period.

EEC ▶ **abbreviation** European Economic Community.

EEG ▶ **abbreviation** electroencephalogram or electroencephalograph.

eel /ēl/ ▶ **noun** a snakelike fish with a very long, thin body and small fins.
– DERIVATIVES **eel-like** /-ˌlīk/ adjective **eel·y** adjective.
– ORIGIN Old English.

EEOC ▶ **abbreviation** Equal Employment Opportunity Commission.

e'er /e(ə)r/ ▶ **adverb** literary form of **EVER**.

ee·rie /ˈi(ə)rē/ ▶ **adjective** (**eerier, eeriest**) strange and frightening.

– SYNONYMS **uncanny,** sinister, ghostly, unnatural, unearthly, supernatural, other-worldly, strange, abnormal, weird, freakish; informal creepy, scary, spooky.

– DERIVATIVES **ee·ri·ly** adverb **ee·ri·ness** noun.
– ORIGIN probably from Old English, 'cowardly.'

ef·face /iˈfās/ ▶ **verb 1** cause to disappear: *nothing could efface the bitter memory.* **2** (**efface oneself**) make oneself appear unimportant. **3** erase a mark from a surface.
– DERIVATIVES **ef·face·ment** noun.
– ORIGIN French *effacer.*

ef·fect /iˈfekt/ ▶ **noun 1** a change that is a result of an action or other cause. **2** the state of being or becoming operative: *the agreement took effect in 2004.* **3** the extent to which something succeeds: *wind power can be used to great effect.* **4** (**effects**) personal belongings. **5** (**effects**) the lighting, sound, or scenery used in a play or movie. **6** Physics a physical phenomenon, typically named after its discoverer.

– SYNONYMS **1** *the effect of these changes* **result,** consequence, upshot, outcome, repercussions, end result, aftermath. **2** *the effect of the drug* **impact,** action, effectiveness, power, potency, strength, success. **3** *the dead man's effects* **belongings,** possessions, worldly goods, chattels, property; informal things, stuff.
– ANTONYMS cause.

▶ **verb** bring about: *the senator effected many policy changes.*

– SYNONYMS **achieve,** accomplish, carry out, manage, bring off, execute, conduct, engineer, perform, do, cause, bring about, produce.

– PHRASES **for effect** in order to impress people. **in effect** in practice, even if not formally acknowledged.
– ORIGIN Latin *effectus.*

USAGE

On the confusion of **effect** and **affect**, see the note at **AFFECT**[1].

ef·fec·tive /iˈfektiv/ ▶ **adjective 1** producing a desired or intended result. **2** (of a law or policy) operative. **3** existing in fact, though not formally acknowledged as such: *he remains in effective control of the military.*

– SYNONYMS **1 successful,** effectual, potent, powerful, helpful, beneficial, advantageous, valuable, useful. **2 convincing,** compelling, strong, forceful, persuasive, plausible, credible, logical, reasonable, cogent. **3 operative,** in force, in effect, valid, official, legal, binding. **4 virtual,** practical, essential, actual.
– ANTONYMS ineffective.

– DERIVATIVES **ef·fec·tive·ly** adverb **ef·fec·tive·ness** noun.

CHOOSE THE RIGHT WORD

effective, effectual, efficacious, efficient

All of these adjectives mean producing or capable of producing a result, but they are not interchangeable. Use **effective** when you want to describe something that produces a definite effect or result (*an effective speaker who was able to rally the crowd's support*) and **efficacious** when it produces the desired effect or result (*an efficacious remedy that cured her almost immediately*). If something produces the desired effect or result in a decisive manner, use **effectual** (*an effectual recommendation that got him the job*), an adjective that is often employed when looking back after an event is over (*an effectual strategy that finally turned the tide in their favor*). Reserve the use of **efficient** for when you want to imply skill and economy of energy in producing the desired result (*so efficient in her management of the company that layoffs were not necessary*). When applied to people, *efficient* means capable or competent (*an efficient homemaker*) and places less emphasis on the achievement of results and more on the skills involved.

ef·fec·tu·al /iˈfekcʜo͞oəl/ ▶ **adjective 1** producing an intended result; effective. **2** (of a legal document) valid or binding.
– DERIVATIVES **ef·fec·tu·al·ly** adverb.

CHOOSE THE RIGHT WORD

See **EFFECTIVE**.

ef·fem·i·nate /iˈfemənət/ ▶ **adjective** (of a man) having characteristics regarded as typical of a woman.

– SYNONYMS **womanish,** effete, foppish, unmanly, feminine; informal camp, campy, limp-wristed.
– ANTONYMS manly.

– DERIVATIVES **ef·fem·i·na·cy** /iˈfemənəsē/ noun **ef·fem·i·nate·ly** adverb.
– ORIGIN from Latin *effeminare* 'make feminine.'

ef·fen·di /iˈfendē/ ▶ **noun** (pl. **effendis**) a man of high education or social standing in an eastern Mediterranean or Arab country.
– ORIGIN Turkish *efendi.*

ef·fer·ves·cent /ˌefərˈvesənt/ ▶ **adjective 1** (of a liquid) giving off bubbles; fizzy. **2** lively and enthusiastic.

– SYNONYMS **fizzy,** sparkling, carbonated, aerated, gassy, bubbly.
– ANTONYMS still.

– DERIVATIVES **ef·fer·vesce** /ˌefərˈves/ verb **ef·fer·ves·cence** noun.
– ORIGIN from Latin *effervescere* 'boil up.'

ef·fete /iˈfēt/ ▶ **adjective 1** no longer effective; weak. **2** (of a man) affected or effeminate.
– DERIVATIVES **ef·fete·ly** adverb **ef·fete·ness** noun.

– ORIGIN Latin *effetus* 'worn out by bearing young.'

ef·fi·ca·cious /ˌefiˈkāsHəs/ ▶ **adjective** successful in producing an intended effect; effective.
– DERIVATIVES **ef·fi·ca·cious·ly** adverb.
– ORIGIN from Latin *efficere* 'accomplish.'

> **CHOOSE THE RIGHT WORD**
>
> See **EFFECTIVE**.

ef·fi·ca·cy /ˈefikəsē/ ▶ **noun** the ability to produce an intended result.

ef·fi·cien·cy /iˈfisHənsē/ ▶ **noun** (pl. **efficiencies**) **1** the quality of being efficient. **2** a means of using resources in a less wasteful way: *the company will seek to maximize cost efficiencies.*

> – SYNONYMS **1 economy,** productivity, cost-effectiveness, organization, order, orderliness, regulation. **2 competence,** capability, ability, proficiency, expertise, skill, effectiveness.
> – ANTONYMS inefficiency, incompetence.

ef·fi·cien·cy a·part·ment (also **efficiency**) ▶ **noun** an apartment in which one room typically contains the kitchen, living, and sleeping quarters, with a separate bathroom.

ef·fi·cient /iˈfisHənt/ ▶ **adjective** working well with minimum waste of money or effort.

> – SYNONYMS **1 economic,** productive, effective, cost-effective, streamlined, organized, methodical, systematic, orderly. **2 competent,** capable, able, proficient, skillful, skilled, effective, productive, organized, businesslike.
> – ANTONYMS inefficient, incompetent.

– DERIVATIVES **ef·fi·cient·ly** adverb.
– ORIGIN from Latin *efficere* 'accomplish.'

> **CHOOSE THE RIGHT WORD**
>
> See **EFFECTIVE**.

ef·fi·gy /ˈefijē/ ▶ **noun** (pl. **effigies**) a sculpture or model of a person.
– ORIGIN Latin *effigies*.

ef·flo·res·cence /ˌefləˈresəns/ ▶ **noun 1** literary a very high stage of development: *an efflorescence of art.* **2** the crystallization of salts on a surface such as brick.
– DERIVATIVES **ef·flo·res·cent** adjective.
– ORIGIN from Latin *florescere* 'begin to bloom.'

ef·flu·ent /ˈeflo͞oənt/ ▶ **noun** liquid waste or sewage discharged into a river or the sea.
– ORIGIN from Latin *effluere* 'flow out.'

ef·flu·vi·um /iˈflo͞ovēəm/ ▶ **noun** (pl. **effluvia** /-vēə/) an unpleasant or harmful smell or discharge.
– ORIGIN Latin.

ef·fort /ˈefərt/ ▶ **noun 1** a vigorous or determined attempt to do something. **2** physical or mental vigor: *he put considerable effort into achieving this goal.*

> – SYNONYMS **1 attempt,** try, endeavor; informal shot, stab, bash. **2 achievement,** accomplishment, feat, undertaking, enterprise, work, result, outcome. **3 exertion,** energy, work, application; informal elbow grease.

– DERIVATIVES **ef·fort·ful** adjective.
– ORIGIN Old French *esforcier*.

ef·fort·less /ˈefərtlis/ ▶ **adjective** done or achieved without effort; natural and easy.

> – SYNONYMS **easy,** undemanding, unchallenging, painless, simple, uncomplicated, straightforward, elementary; fluent, natural; informal as easy as pie, child's play, kids' stuff, a cinch, no sweat, a breeze, duck soup, a snap.
> – ANTONYMS difficult.

– DERIVATIVES **ef·fort·less·ly** adverb **ef·fort·less·ness** noun.

ef·fron·ter·y /iˈfrəntərē/ ▶ **noun** insolent or disrespectful behavior.

> – SYNONYMS **impudence,** impertinence, insolence, audacity, temerity, presumption, nerve, gall, cheek, shamelessness, impoliteness, disrespect, bad manners; informal brass, chutzpah.

– ORIGIN Latin *effrons* 'shameless, barefaced.'

ef·ful·gent /iˈfo͝oljənt, iˈfəl-/ ▶ **adjective** literary shining brightly.
– DERIVATIVES **ef·ful·gence** noun.
– ORIGIN from Latin *effulgere*.

ef·fu·sion /iˈfyo͞ozHən/ ▶ **noun 1** a discharge of something, especially a liquid. **2** an unrestrained expression of feelings in speech or writing: *effusions of patriotic bigotry.*
– ORIGIN from Latin *effundere* 'pour out.'

ef·fu·sive /iˈfyo͞osiv/ ▶ **adjective** expressing gratitude or approval in an unrestrained way.

> – SYNONYMS **gushing,** gushy, unrestrained, extravagant, fulsome, demonstrative, lavish, enthusiastic, lyrical; expansive, wordy, verbose.
> – ANTONYMS restrained.

– DERIVATIVES **ef·fu·sive·ly** adverb **ef·fu·sive·ness** noun.

e-fit /ˈē ˌfit/ ▶ **noun** an electronic picture of a person's face made from photographs of separate facial features, created by a computer program.

EFL ▶ **abbreviation** English as a foreign language.

e.g. ▶ **abbreviation** for example.
– ORIGIN from Latin *exempli gratia* 'for the sake of example.'

e·gal·i·tar·i·an /iˌgaləˈterēən/ ▶ **adjective** believing in or based on the principle that all people are equal and deserve equal rights and opportunities. ▶ **noun** a person who supports the principle of equality for all.
– DERIVATIVES **e·gal·i·tar·i·an·ism** noun.
– ORIGIN French *égalitaire*.

egg[1] /eg/ ▶ **noun 1** an oval or round object laid by a female bird, reptile, fish, or invertebrate and containing an ovum that can develop into a new organism. **2** an infertile egg of a chicken, used for food. **3** the cell in female humans and animals that is capable of producing young; an ovum. **4** informal, dated a person of a specified kind: *he's a good egg.*

> – SYNONYMS **ovum,** gamete; (**eggs**) roe, spawn.

– DERIVATIVES **egg·y** adjective.
– PHRASES **kill the goose that lays the golden eggs** destroy a reliable and valuable source of income. **with egg on one's face** informal appearing foolish or ridiculous.
– ORIGIN Old English.

> **WORD LINKS**
>
> **ovoid** *egg-shaped*

egg[2] ▶ **verb** (**egg someone on**) urge or encourage someone to do something foolish or risky: *Earl didn't really want to enter the talent contest, but his friends egged him on.*

– SYNONYMS **urge,** goad, incite, provoke, push, drive, spur on, prod.

– ORIGIN Old Norse, 'incite.'

egg·beat·er /'eg,bētər/ ▸ **noun 1** a kitchen utensil used for beating ingredients such as eggs or cream. **2** informal a helicopter.

egg·head /'eg,hed/ ▸ **noun** informal, derogatory a very intelligent or studious person.

egg·nog /'eg,näg, -,nôg/ ▸ **noun** a drink consisting of eggs, cream, and flavorings, often with alcohol.

egg·plant /'eg,plant/ ▸ **noun** the dark purple, egg-shaped fruit of a plant of the nightshade family.

egg·shell /'eg,sHel/ ▸ **noun** the thin, brittle outer layer of an egg. ▸ **adjective 1** (of china) very thin and delicate. **2** referring to a paint that dries with a slight sheen.

egg white ▸ **noun** the clear substance around the yolk of an egg that turns white when cooked or beaten.

e·go /'ēgō/ ▸ **noun** (pl. **egos**) **1** a person's sense of their own worth and importance: *staying fit is a great boost to the ego.* **2** the part of the mind that is responsible for the interpretation of reality and a sense of personal identity. Compare with **ID** and **SUPEREGO**.

– ORIGIN Latin, 'I.'

e·go·cen·tric /,ēgō'sentrik/ ▸ **adjective** thinking only of oneself; self-centered.

– DERIVATIVES **e·go·cen·tric·al·ly** /-(ə)lē/ adverb **e·go·cen·tric·i·ty** /,ēgōsen'trisitē/ noun **e·go·cen·trism** /,ēgō'sentrizəm/ noun.

e·go·ism /'ēgō,izəm/ ▸ **noun** another term for **EGOTISM**.

– DERIVATIVES **e·go·ist** noun **e·go·is·tic** /-'istik/ adjective.

e·go·ma·ni·a /,ēgō'mānēə/ ▸ **noun** obsessive self-centeredness.

– DERIVATIVES **e·go·ma·ni·ac** /-nē,ak/ noun **e·go·ma·ni·a·cal** /-mə'nīəkəl/ adjective.

e·go·tism /'ēgə,tizəm/ ▸ **noun** the quality of being excessively conceited or self-centered.

– SYNONYMS **self-centeredness,** egomania, egocentricity, self-interest, selfishness, self-seeking, self-serving, self-regard, self-obsession; narcissism, vanity, conceit, self-importance; boastfulness.

CHOOSE THE RIGHT WORD

See **PRIDE**.

e·go·tist /'ēgə,tist/ ▸ **noun** an excessively conceited or self-centered person.

– SYNONYMS **self-seeker,** egocentric, egomaniac, narcissist; boaster, braggart; informal swank, show-off, bighead, showboat.

– DERIVATIVES **e·go·tis·tic** /,ēgə'tistik/ adjective **e·go·tis·ti·cal** /,ēgə'tistikəl/ adjective.

e·go trip ▸ **noun** informal something that a person does to feel self-important.

e·gre·gious /i'grējəs/ ▸ **adjective** outstandingly bad; shocking.

– DERIVATIVES **e·gre·gious·ly** adverb **e·gre·gious·ness** noun.

– ORIGIN Latin *egregius* 'illustrious' (literally 'standing out from the flock').

e·gress /'ē,gres/ ▸ **noun** formal **1** the action of going out of or leaving a place. **2** a way out.

– ORIGIN from Latin *egressus* 'gone out.'

e·gret /'ēgrit, 'ē,gret, 'egrit/ ▸ **noun** a heron with mainly white plumage, having long plumes in the breeding season.

– ORIGIN Old French *aigrette*.

E·gyp·tian /i'jipsHən/ ▸ **noun 1** a person from Egypt. **2** the language used in ancient Egypt. ▸ **adjective** relating to Egypt.

E·gyp·tol·o·gy /,ējip'täləjē/ ▸ **noun** the study of the language, history, and culture of ancient Egypt.

– DERIVATIVES **E·gyp·to·log·i·cal** /i,jiptə'läjikəl/ adjective **E·gyp·tol·o·gist** noun.

eh /ā, e/ ▸ **exclamation** used to ask for something to be repeated or explained or to elicit agreement.

Eid /ēd/ (also **Id**) ▸ **noun 1** (in full **Eid ul-Fitr** /ēd o͝ol 'fētr/) the Muslim festival marking the end of the fast of Ramadan. **2** (in full **Eid ul-Adha** /ēd o͝ol 'ädə/) the festival marking the culmination of the annual pilgrimage to Mecca.

– ORIGIN Arabic, 'feast.'

ei·der /'īdər/ (also **eider duck**) ▸ **noun** (pl. same or **eiders**) a northern sea duck, the male of which has mainly black-and-white plumage.

– ORIGIN Old Norse.

ei·der·down /'īdər,doun/ ▸ **noun 1** the down from a female eider duck. **2** chiefly Brit. a quilt or comforter filled with down (originally from the female eider duck) or another soft material.

ei·det·ic /ī'detik/ ▸ **adjective** relating to mental images that are unusually vivid and detailed.

– ORIGIN Greek *eidētikos*.

eight /āt/ ▸ **cardinal number 1** one more than seven; 8. (Roman numeral: **viii** or **VIII**.) **2** an eight-oared rowing shell or its crew.

– PHRASES **pieces of eight** historical Spanish dollars, equivalent to eight reals.

– ORIGIN Old English.

eight·een /ā'tēn, 'ā,tēn/ ▸ **cardinal number** one more than seventeen; 18. (Roman numeral: **xviii** or **XVIII**.)

– DERIVATIVES **eight·eenth** /ā'tēnTH, 'ā,tēnTH/ ordinal number.

eight·een-wheel·er ▸ **noun** a large tractor-trailer with eighteen wheels.

eighth /'ā(t)TH/ ▸ **ordinal number 1** that is number eight in a sequence; 8th. **2** (**an eighth** or **one eighth**) each of eight equal parts into which something is divided.

eighth note ▸ **noun** a musical note having the value of half a quarter note, shown by a solid dot with a hooked stem.

eight·y /'ātē/ ▸ **cardinal number** (pl. **eighties**) ten less than ninety; 80. (Roman numeral: **lxxx** or **LXXX**.)

– DERIVATIVES **eight·i·eth** /'ātēiTH/ ordinal number.

eigh·ty-six /,ātē 'siks/ (also **86**) informal ▸ **noun** someone regarded as undesirable as a restaurant or bar patron. ▸ **verb 1** refuse to serve someone: *he got 86ed from a reservation casino*. **2** reject, discard, or cancel.

ein·stein·i·um /īn'stīnēəm/ ▸ **noun** an unstable radioactive chemical element made by high-energy atomic collisions.

– ORIGIN named after the German-born physicist Albert *Einstein*.

eis·tedd·fod /ī'steTH,väd/ ▸ **noun** (pl. **eisteddfods** or **eisteddfodau** /-'vädī/) a competitive festival of music and poetry in Wales.

– ORIGIN Welsh, 'session.'

ei·ther /ˈēT͟Hər, ˈīT͟Hər/ ▶ **conjunction & adverb** **1** used before the first of two alternatives specified (the other being introduced by 'or'). **2** (adv.) used to indicate a similarity or link with a statement just made: *You don't like him, do you? I don't either.* **3** for that matter; moreover. ▶ **determiner & pronoun** **1** one or the other of two people or things. **2** each of two.
– ORIGIN Old English.

USAGE

In good English, it is important that **either** and **or** are correctly placed so that the structures following each word balance each other. For example, it is better to say *I'm going to buy either a new camera or a new video* rather than *I'm either going to buy a new camera or a video.*

e·jac·u·late ▶ **verb** /iˈjakyəˌlāt/ **1** (of a man or male animal) eject semen from the penis at the moment of orgasm. **2** dated say something suddenly. ▶ **noun** /-ˌlit/ semen that has been ejaculated.
– DERIVATIVES **e·jac·u·la·tion** /iˌjakyəˈlāsHən/ noun **e·jac·u·la·tor** /iˈjakyəˌlātər/ noun **e·jac·u·la·to·ry** /-ləˌtôrē/ adjective.
– ORIGIN Latin *ejaculari* 'dart out.'

e·ject /iˈjekt/ ▶ **verb** **1** force or throw something out violently or suddenly. **2** make someone leave a place or post. **3** (of a pilot) escape from an aircraft by means of an ejection seat.

– SYNONYMS **1 emit,** spew out, discharge, disgorge, give off, send out, belch, vent. **2 expel,** throw out, remove, oust, evict, banish; informal kick out, boot out.

– DERIVATIVES **e·jec·tion** /iˈjeksHən/ noun **e·jec·tor** /iˈjektər/ noun.
– ORIGIN Latin *eicere* 'throw out.'

CHOOSE THE RIGHT WORD

eject, dismiss, evict, expel, oust

Want to get rid of someone? You can **eject** him or her, which means to throw or cast out (*he was ejected from the meeting room*). If you hope the person never comes back, use **expel**, a verb that suggests driving someone out of a country, an organization, etc., for all time (*to be expelled from school*); it can also imply the use of voluntary force (*to expel air from the lungs*). If you exercise force or the power of law to get rid of someone or something, **oust** is the correct verb (*ousted after less than two years in office*). If as a property owner you are turning someone out of a house or a place of business, you'll want to **evict** the person (*she was evicted for not paying the rent*). **Dismiss** is by far the mildest of these terms, suggesting that you are rejecting or refusing to consider someone or something (*to dismiss a legal case*). It is also commonly used of loss of employment (*dismissed from his job for excessive tardiness*).

e·jec·tion seat (also **ejector seat**) ▶ **noun** an aircraft seat that can throw its occupant from the craft in an emergency.

eke /ēk/ ▶ **verb** (**eke something out**) **1** make a living with difficulty. **2** make something last longer by using it sparingly: *retired folk hunting for bargains to eke out their social security money.*
– ORIGIN Old English, 'increase.'

EKG ▶ **abbreviation** **1** electrocardiogram. **2** electrocardiograph. **3** electrocardiography.

el /el/ ▶ **noun** **1** (**the El**) an elevated railroad or section of railroad, especially in Chicago. **2** a train running on such a railroad.

e·lab·o·rate ▶ **adjective** /iˈlab(ə)rit/ involving many carefully arranged parts; detailed and complicated.

– SYNONYMS **1 complicated,** complex, intricate, involved, detailed. **2 ornate,** decorated, embellished, adorned, ornamented, fancy, fussy, busy.
– ANTONYMS simple, plain.

▶ **verb** /iˈlabəˌrāt/ **1** develop or present a theory or policy in detail. **2** (**elaborate on**) add more detail to something already said.

– SYNONYMS *please **elaborate on** your explanation* **expand on,** enlarge on, add to, flesh out, develop, fill out, amplify.

– DERIVATIVES **e·lab·o·rate·ly** adverb **e·lab·o·ra·tion** /iˌlabəˈrāsHən/ noun **e·lab·o·ra·tive** /-ˌrātiv/ adjective.
– ORIGIN from Latin *elaborare* 'work out.'

é·lan /āˈlän, āˈlan/ (also **elan**) ▶ **noun** energy and stylishness: *he played the march with great élan.*
– ORIGIN French.

e·land /ˈēlənd/ ▶ **noun** a large African antelope with spiral horns.
– ORIGIN Dutch, 'elk.'

e·lapse /iˈlaps/ ▶ **verb** (of time) pass.
– ORIGIN Latin *elabi* 'slip away.'

e·las·tic /iˈlastik/ ▶ **adjective** **1** able to return to normal size or shape after being stretched or squeezed. **2** flexible and adaptable: *the definition of ethnicity is elastic.*

– SYNONYMS **1 stretchy,** elasticated, springy, flexible, pliable, supple. **2 adaptable,** flexible, adjustable, accommodating, variable, fluid, versatile.
– ANTONYMS rigid.

▶ **noun** cord, tape, or fabric that returns to its original length or shape after being stretched.
– DERIVATIVES **e·las·ti·cal·ly** /-(ə)lē/ adverb **e·las·tic·i·ty** /iˌlaˈstisitē, ēˌla-/ noun **e·las·ti·cize** /iˈlastəˌsīz/ verb.
– ORIGIN Greek *elastikos* 'propulsive.'

CHOOSE THE RIGHT WORD

See **FLEXIBLE**.

e·las·tic band ▶ **noun** a rubber band.

e·las·ti·cized /iˈlastəˌsīzd/ ▶ **adjective** (of a garment or material) made elastic with rubber thread or tape.

e·las·tin /iˈlastin/ ▶ **noun** an elastic, fibrous protein found in connective body tissue.

e·las·to·mer /iˈlastəmər/ ▶ **noun** a natural or synthetic polymer with elastic properties, e.g., rubber.
– DERIVATIVES **e·las·to·mer·ic** /iˌlastəˈmerik/ adjective.

e·lat·ed /iˈlātid/ ▶ **adjective** very happy and excited.

– SYNONYMS **thrilled,** delighted, overjoyed, ecstatic, euphoric, jubilant, rapturous, in raptures, walking on air, on cloud nine, in seventh heaven; informal on top of the world, over the moon, tickled pink.
– ANTONYMS miserable.

– ORIGIN Latin *elatus* 'raised.'

e·la·tion /iˈlāsHən/ ▶ **noun** great happiness and excitement.

el·bow /ˈelˌbō/ ▶ **noun** **1** the joint between the forearm and the upper arm. **2** a piece of piping or something similar bent through an angle. ▶ **verb** **1** hit or push someone with one's elbow. **2** (often **elbow one's way**) move by pushing past people with one's elbows.
– PHRASES **up to one's elbows in** deeply involved in something.
– ORIGIN Old English.

el·bow grease ▶ **noun** informal hard physical work, especially vigorous cleaning.

el·bow room ▶ **noun** informal adequate space to move or work in.

eld·er[1] /ˈeldər/ ▶ **adjective** (of one or more out of a group of people) of a greater age.

– SYNONYMS **older**, senior.

▶ **noun 1** (**one's elder**) a person older than oneself. **2** a leader or senior figure in a community. **3** an official or minister in certain Protestant Churches.

– SYNONYMS **leader**, patriarch, father.

– ORIGIN Old English.

eld·er[2] ▶ **noun** a small tree or shrub with white flowers and bluish-black or red berries.
– ORIGIN Old English.

el·der·ber·ry /ˈeldərˌberē/ ▶ **noun** (pl. **elderberries**) the berry of the elder, used for making jelly or wine.

el·der·flow·er /ˈeldərˌflou(-ə)r/ ▶ **noun** the flower of the elder, used to make wines and cordials.

eld·er·ly /ˈeldərlē/ ▶ **adjective** old or aging.

– SYNONYMS **aged**, old, aging, long in the tooth, gray-haired, in one's dotage; informal getting on, over the hill.
– ANTONYMS youthful.

eld·er states·man ▶ **noun** an experienced and respected politician or other public figure.

eld·est /ˈeldəst/ ▶ **adjective** (of one out of a group of people) oldest.

El Do·ra·do /ˌel dəˈrädō/ (also **eldorado**) ▶ **noun** (pl. **El Dorados**) a place of great abundance and wealth.
– ORIGIN Spanish, 'the gilded one,' a country or city formerly believed to exist in South America.

el·e·cam·pane /ˌelikamˈpān/ ▶ **noun** a plant with yellow daisylike flowers and bitter roots that are used in herbal medicine.
– ORIGIN from Latin *enula* 'helenium' (a plant of the daisy family) + *campana*, probably meaning 'of the fields.'

e·lect /iˈlekt/ ▶ **verb 1** choose someone to hold public office or another position by voting. **2** choose to do something: *the manager elected to leave him out of the project.*

– SYNONYMS **1 vote in**, vote for, return, cast one's vote for, choose, pick, select. **2 choose**, decide, opt, prefer, vote.

▶ **adjective 1** (of a person) chosen or singled out. **2** (**-elect**) elected to a position but not yet in office: *the president-elect.*
– DERIVATIVES **e·lect·a·bil·i·ty** /iˌlektəˈbilitē/ noun **e·lect·a·ble** adjective.
– ORIGIN Latin *eligere* 'pick out.'

e·lec·tion /iˈlekshən/ ▶ **noun 1** a formal process by which a person is elected, especially to a public office. **2** the action of electing someone.

– SYNONYMS **ballot**, vote, poll, primary.

WORD LINKS

psephology *study of elections*

e·lec·tion·eer·ing /iˌlekshəˈni(ə)riNG/ ▶ **noun** the action of campaigning to be elected to a political position.

e·lec·tive /iˈlektiv/ ▶ **adjective 1** relating to or appointed by election. **2** (of a course of study, medical treatment, etc.) chosen by the person concerned; not compulsory.

e·lec·tor /iˈlektər, -ˌtôr/ ▶ **noun 1** a person who has the right to vote in an election. **2** a member of the electoral college. **3** (**Elector**) historical a German prince entitled to take part in the election of the Holy Roman Emperor.

e·lec·tor·al /iˈlektərəl/ ▶ **adjective** relating to elections or electors.
– DERIVATIVES **e·lec·tor·al·ly** adverb.

e·lec·tor·al col·lege ▶ **noun** a group of people chosen to represent the members of a political party in the election of a leader.

e·lec·tor·ate /iˈlektərət/ ▶ **noun 1** the group of people in a country or area who are entitled to vote in an election. **2** historical the office or territories of a German elector.

e·lec·tric /iˈlektrik/ ▶ **adjective 1** relating to, worked by, or producing electricity. **2** very exciting or intense: *the atmosphere was electric.*

– SYNONYMS *the atmosphere was electric* **exciting**, charged, electrifying, thrilling, dramatic, dynamic, stimulating, galvanizing.

▶ **noun** (**electrics**) Brit. the system of electric wiring and parts in a house or vehicle.
– ORIGIN from Greek *ēlektron* 'amber' (because rubbing amber causes static electricity).

e·lec·tri·cal /iˈlektrikəl/ ▶ **adjective** relating to, operating by, or producing electricity.
– DERIVATIVES **e·lec·tri·cal·ly** adverb.

e·lec·tri·cal storm ▶ **noun** a thunderstorm or other violent disturbance of the electrical condition of the atmosphere.

e·lec·tric blan·ket ▶ **noun** an electrically wired blanket used for heating a bed.

e·lec·tric blue ▶ **noun** a steely or brilliant light blue.

e·lec·tric chair ▶ **noun** a chair in which convicted criminals are executed by electrocution.

e·lec·tric eel ▶ **noun** a large eel-like freshwater fish of South America, which uses pulses of electricity to kill its prey.

e·lec·tric fence ▶ **noun** a fence through which an electric current can be passed, giving an electric shock to any person or animal touching it.

e·lec·tric gui·tar ▶ **noun** a guitar with a built-in pickup that converts sound vibrations into electrical signals for amplification.

e·lec·tri·cian /ilekˈtrishən, ˌēlek-/ ▶ **noun** a person who installs and maintains electrical equipment.

e·lec·tric·i·ty /ilekˈtrisitē, ˌēlek-/ ▶ **noun 1** a form of energy resulting from the existence of charged particles (such as electrons), either statically as a buildup of charge or dynamically as a current. **2** the supply of electric current to a building. **3** great excitement or intense emotion: *the atmosphere was charged with sexual electricity.*

e·lec·tric shock ▶ **noun** a sudden discharge of electricity through a part of the body.

e·lec·tri·fy /iˈlektrəˌfī/ ▶ **verb** (**electrifies, electrifying, electrified**) **1** pass an electric current through something. **2** convert a machine or system to the use of electrical power. **3** (as adj. **electrifying**) very exciting or impressive: *an electrifying performance.*

– SYNONYMS **excite**, thrill, stimulate, arouse, rouse, inspire, stir (up), exhilarate, galvanize, fire (with enthusiasm), fire (up) someone's imagination, invigorate, animate, light a fire under.

– DERIVATIVES **e·lec·tri·fi·ca·tion** /iˌlektrəfiˈkāsʜən/ noun.

e·lec·tro /iˈlektrō/ ▶ **noun** a style of dance music with a fast beat and synthesized backing track.

e·lec·tro·car·di·og·ra·phy /iˌlektrōˌkärdēˈägrəfē/ ▶ **noun** the measurement and recording of activity in the heart using electrodes placed on the skin.
– DERIVATIVES **e·lec·tro·car·di·o·gram** /iˌlektrōˈkärdēəˌgram/ noun **e·lec·tro·car·di·o·graph** /iˌlektrōˈkärdiəˌgraf/ noun **e·lec·tro·car·di·o·graph·ic** /-ˌkärdiəˈgrafik/ adjective.

e·lec·tro·con·vul·sive /iˌlektrōkənˈvəlsiv/ ▶ **adjective** relating to the treatment of mental illness by applying electric shocks to the brain.

e·lec·tro·cute /iˈlektrəˌkyo͞ot/ ▶ **verb** injure or kill someone by electric shock.
– DERIVATIVES **e·lec·tro·cu·tion** /iˌlektrəˈkyo͞osʜən/ noun.

e·lec·trode /iˈlektrōd/ ▶ **noun** a conductor through which electricity enters or leaves something.
– ORIGIN from **ELECTRIC** + Greek *hodos* 'way.'

e·lec·tro·dy·nam·ics /iˌlektrōdīˈnamiks/ ▶ **plural noun** (usu. treated as sing.) the branch of mechanics concerned with the interaction of electric currents with magnetic or electric fields.
– DERIVATIVES **e·lec·tro·dy·nam·ic** adjective.

e·lec·tro·en·ceph·a·log·ra·phy /iˌlektrōənˌsefəˈlägrəfē/ ▶ **noun** the measurement and recording of electrical activity in the brain.
– DERIVATIVES **e·lec·tro·en·ceph·a·lo·gram** /iˌlektrōənˈsefələˌgram/ noun **e·lec·tro·en·ceph·a·lo·graph** /iˌlektrōənˈsefələˌgraf/ noun.

e·lec·trol·y·sis /ilekˈträlәsis, ˌēlek-/ ▶ **noun 1** chemical decomposition produced by passing an electric current through a conducting liquid. **2** the removal of hair roots or blemishes on the skin by means of an electric current.
– DERIVATIVES **e·lec·tro·lyt·ic** /iˌlektrəˈlitik/ adjective.

e·lec·tro·lyte /iˈlektrəˌlīt/ ▶ **noun 1** a liquid or gel that contains ions and can be decomposed by electrolysis, e.g., that present in a battery. **2** (usu. **electrolytes**) the ions, such as sodium and potassium, in cells, blood, or other organic matter.
– ORIGIN from Greek *lutos* 'released.'

e·lec·tro·mag·net /iˌlektrōˈmagnit/ ▶ **noun** a metal core made into a magnet by the passage of electric current through a surrounding coil.

e·lec·tro·mag·net·ic /iˌlektrōmagˈnetik/ ▶ **adjective** relating to the interrelation of electric currents or fields and magnetic fields.
– DERIVATIVES **e·lec·tro·mag·net·i·cal·ly** /-(ə)lē/ adverb **e·lec·tro·mag·net·ism** /iˌlektrōˈmagnəˌtizəm/ noun.

e·lec·tro·mag·net·ic ra·di·a·tion ▶ **noun** a kind of radiation including visible light, radio waves, gamma rays, and X-rays, in which electric and magnetic fields vary simultaneously.

e·lec·tro·me·chan·i·cal /iˌlektrōməˈkanikəl/ ▶ **adjective** referring to a mechanical device that is electrically operated.

e·lec·tro·mo·tive /iˌlektrəˈmōtiv/ ▶ **adjective** tending to produce an electric current.

e·lec·tro·mo·tive force ▶ **noun** a difference in potential that tends to give rise to an electric current.

e·lec·tron /iˈlekˌträn/ ▶ **noun** Physics a stable negatively charged subatomic particle found in all atoms and acting as the primary carrier of electricity in solids.

e·lec·tron·ic /ilekˈtränik, ˌēlek-/ ▶ **adjective 1** having components such as microchips and transistors that control and direct electric currents. **2** relating to electrons or electronics. **3** relating to or carried out by means of a computer or other electronic device: *electronic shopping*.
– DERIVATIVES **e·lec·tron·i·cal·ly** /-(ə)lē/ adverb.

e·lec·tron·ic·a /ilekˈtränikə, ˌēlek-/ ▶ **noun** a style of popular electronic music deriving from techno and rave.

e·lec·tron·ic pub·lish·ing ▶ **noun** the issuing of written material as electronic files rather than on paper.

e·lec·tron·ics /ilekˈträniks, ˌēlek-/ ▶ **plural noun 1** (usu. treated as sing.) the branch of physics and technology concerned with the design of circuits using transistors and microchips, and with the behavior and movement of electrons. **2** (treated as pl.) circuits or devices using transistors, microchips, etc.

e·lec·tron mi·cro·scope ▶ **noun** a microscope with high magnification and resolution, employing electron beams in place of light.

e·lec·tro·pho·re·sis /iˌlektrəfəˈrēsis/ ▶ **noun** the movement of charged particles in a fluid or gel under the influence of an electric field.
– DERIVATIVES **e·lec·tro·pho·ret·ic** /-ˈretik/ adjective.
– ORIGIN from Greek *phorēsis* 'being carried.'

e·lec·tro·plate /iˈlektrəˌplāt/ ▶ **verb** coat a metal object with another metal using electrolysis. ▶ **noun** electroplated articles.

e·lec·tro·scope /iˈlektrəˌskōp/ ▶ **noun** an instrument for detecting and measuring electric charge.

e·lec·tro·shock /iˈlektrəˌsʜäk/ ▶ **adjective** another term for **ELECTROCONVULSIVE**.

e·lec·tro·stat·ic /iˌlektrəˈstatik/ ▶ **adjective** relating to stationary electric charges or fields as opposed to electric currents.
– DERIVATIVES **e·lec·tro·stat·ic·al·ly** adverb **e·lec·tro·stat·ics** plural noun.

e·lec·tro·sur·ger·y /iˌlektrōˈsərjərē/ ▶ **noun** surgery using a high-frequency electric current to cut tissue.
– DERIVATIVES **e·lec·tro·sur·gi·cal** /-ˈsərjikəl/ adjective.

e·lec·tro·ther·a·py /iˌlektrōˈᴛʜerəpē/ ▶ **noun** the use of electric currents passed through the body to treat paralysis and other disorders.

e·lec·trum /iˈlektrəm/ ▶ **noun** an alloy of gold with at least 20 percent of silver, used for jewelry.
– ORIGIN Greek *ēlektron* 'amber, electrum.'

el·e·gant /ˈeləgənt/ ▶ **adjective 1** graceful and stylish. **2** pleasingly clever but simple: *an unbelievably elegant theory of everything*.

– SYNONYMS **1 stylish,** graceful, tasteful, sophisticated, classic, chic, smart, poised, cultivated, polished, cultured. **2** *an elegant solution* **neat,** simple, apt.
– ANTONYMS inelegant.

– DERIVATIVES **el·e·gance** noun **el·e·gant·ly** adverb.
– ORIGIN Latin *elegans* 'discriminating.'

WORD TOOLKIT

See **GRACIOUS**.

el·e·gi·ac /ˌeləˈjīək, eˈlējēˌak/ ▶ **adjective 1** relating to or characteristic of an elegy. **2** sad; mournful: *the elegiac,*

bittersweet tone of the narrator's voice.
– DERIVATIVES **el·e·gi·a·cal·ly** /ˌeləˈjīək(ə)lē/ adverb.

el·e·gy /ˈeləjē/ ▶ **noun** (pl. **elegies**) a mournful poem, typically a lament for someone who has died.
– ORIGIN Greek *elegos* 'mournful poem.'

el·e·ment /ˈeləmənt/ ▶ **noun 1** an essential or typical part: *there are four elements to the proposal.* **2** a small amount: *an element of danger.* **3** (**the elements**) rain and other bad weather. **4** (also **chemical element**) each of more than one hundred substances that cannot be chemically changed or broken down. **5** any of the four substances (earth, water, air, and fire) formerly believed to be the basic constituents of all matter. **6** a distinct group within a larger group: *right-wing elements in the army.* **7** a part in an electric device consisting of a wire through which an electric current is passed to provide heat.

– SYNONYMS **1 component,** constituent, part, section, portion, piece, segment, aspect, factor, feature, facet, ingredient, strand, detail, member. **2 trace,** touch, hint, smattering, soupçon. **3** (**the elements**) **weather,** climate; wind, rain, snow.

– PHRASES **in one's element** in a situation in which one feels happy or relaxed.
– ORIGIN Latin *elementum* 'principle, rudiment.'

el·e·men·tal /ˌeləˈmentl/ ▶ **adjective 1** forming an essential or typical feature; fundamental: *the sauces are made from a few elemental ingredients.* **2** relating to or resembling the powerful forces of nature: *elemental hatred.* **3** relating to a chemical element.

el·e·men·ta·ry /ˌeləˈment(ə)rē/ ▶ **adjective 1** relating to the most basic aspects of a subject. **2** straightforward and simple to understand: *elementary tasks.* **3** Chemistry not able to be decomposed into elements or other primary constituents.

– SYNONYMS **1** *an elementary astronomy course* **basic,** rudimentary, preparatory, introductory. **2** *a lot of the work is elementary* **easy,** simple, straightforward, uncomplicated, undemanding, painless, child's play, smooth sailing; informal a piece of cake.
– ANTONYMS advanced, difficult.

– DERIVATIVES **el·e·men·tar·i·ly** /-rəlē/ adverb.

el·e·men·ta·ry par·ti·cle ▶ **noun** any of various fundamental subatomic particles, including those that are the smallest and most basic constituents of matter (leptons and quarks) or are combinations of these, and those that transmit one of the four fundamental interactions in nature (gravitational, electromagnetic, strong, and weak).

el·e·men·ta·ry school ▶ **noun** a primary school for the first four to eight grades, and usually including kindergarten.

el·e·phant /ˈeləfənt/ ▶ **noun** (pl. same or **elephants**) a very large mammal with a trunk, curved tusks, and large ears, native to Africa and southern Asia.
– ORIGIN Greek *elephas* 'ivory, elephant.'

el·e·phan·ti·a·sis /ˌeləfənˈtīəsis/ ▶ **noun** a medical condition in which a limb becomes hugely enlarged, typically caused by a type of parasitic worm.

el·e·phan·tine /ˌeləˈfantēn, -ˌtīn, ˈeləfənˌtēn, -ˌtīn/ ▶ **adjective** typical of or like an elephant, especially in being large or clumsy.

el·e·vate /ˈeləˌvāt/ ▶ **verb 1** lift something to a higher position. **2** raise to a higher level or status: *the prize elevated her to the front rank of writers.*

– SYNONYMS **1 raise,** lift (up), raise up/aloft, hoist, hike up, haul up. **2 promote,** upgrade, move up, raise; informal kick upstairs.
– ANTONYMS lower, demote.

– ORIGIN Latin *elevare* 'to raise.'

el·e·vat·ed /ˈeləˌvātid/ ▶ **adjective** having a high intellectual or moral level.

– SYNONYMS **1 raised,** overhead, in the air, high up. **2 lofty,** grand, fine, sublime, inflated, pompous, bombastic. **3 high,** high-ranking, lofty, exalted, grand, noble.

el·e·va·tion /ˌeləˈvāsʜən/ ▶ **noun 1** the action of elevating someone or something: *his elevation to superstar status.* **2** the height of a place above sea level. **3** the angle of something with the horizontal. **4** a particular side of a building, or a scale drawing of this.
– DERIVATIVES **el·e·va·tion·al** adjective.

el·e·va·tor /ˈeləˌvātər/ ▶ **noun** a platform or compartment for raising and lowering people or things to different floors of a building.

e·lev·en /iˈlevən/ ▶ **cardinal number 1** one more than ten; 11. (Roman numeral: **xi** or **XI**.) **2** a sports team of eleven players.
– DERIVATIVES **e·lev·en·fold** /-ˌfōld/ adjective & adverb.
– ORIGIN Old English.

e·lev·enth /iˈlevənᴛʜ/ ▶ **ordinal number 1** that is number eleven in a sequence; 11th. **2** (**an eleventh/one eleventh**) each of eleven equal parts into which something is divided.
– PHRASES **the eleventh hour** the latest possible moment.

elf /elf/ ▶ **noun** (pl. **elves** /elvz/) a supernatural creature of folk tales, represented as a small human figure with pointed ears.

– SYNONYMS **pixie,** fairy, sprite, imp, brownie; gnome, goblin, hobgoblin; leprechaun, puck, troll.

– DERIVATIVES **elf·ish** adjective **elv·en** /ˈelvən/ adjective (literary) **elv·ish** /ˈelvisʜ/ adjective.
– ORIGIN Old English.

elf·in /ˈelfən/ ▶ **adjective** like an elf, especially in being small and delicate.

e·lic·it /iˈlisit/ ▶ **verb** (**elicits, eliciting, elicited**) draw out or produce a response or reaction: *my alternative parenting choices have often elicited criticism.*

– SYNONYMS **obtain,** draw out, extract, bring out, evoke, induce, prompt, generate, trigger, provoke.

– DERIVATIVES **e·lic·i·ta·tion** /iˌlisiˈtāsʜən/ noun **e·lic·i·tor** /-tər/ noun.
– ORIGIN Latin *elicere* 'draw out by trickery.'

e·lide /iˈlīd/ ▶ **verb 1** omit a sound or syllable when speaking. **2** join or merge things together.
– ORIGIN Latin *elidere* 'crush out.'

el·i·gi·ble /ˈeləjəbəl/ ▶ **adjective 1** meeting the conditions to do or receive something: *you may be eligible for a refund.* **2** desirable or suitable as a wife or husband.

– SYNONYMS **1 entitled,** permitted, allowed, qualified, able. **2 desirable,** suitable, available, single, unmarried, unattached.

– DERIVATIVES **el·i·gi·bil·i·ty** /ˌeləjəˈbilitē/ noun.
– ORIGIN Latin *eligibilis.*

e·lim·i·nate /iˈliməˌnāt/ ▶ **verb 1** completely remove or get rid of something. **2** exclude from consideration or further participation: *the team was eliminated from the competition.*

– SYNONYMS **1 remove,** get rid of, put an end to, do away with, end, stop, eradicate, destroy, stamp out. **2 knock out,** exclude, rule out, disqualify.

– DERIVATIVES **e·lim·i·na·tion** /iˌliməˈnāsʜən/ noun **e·lim·i·na·tor** /-ˌnātər/ noun.
– ORIGIN Latin *eliminare* 'turn out of doors.'

e·li·sion /iˈlizʜən/ ▸ **noun 1** the omission of a sound or syllable in speech. **2** the action of joining or merging things.
– ORIGIN Latin.

e·lite /əˈlēt, āˈlēt/ (also **élite**) ▸ **noun** a group of people regarded as the best in a particular society or organization: *China's educated elite.*

– SYNONYMS **best,** pick, cream, crème de la crème, flower, high society, beautiful people, aristocracy, ruling class.
– ANTONYMS dregs.

– ORIGIN French, 'selection, choice.'

e·lit·ism /əˈlēˌtizəm, āˈlē-/ ▸ **noun 1** the belief that a society or system should be run by a group of people regarded as superior to others. **2** the superior attitude or behavior associated with an elite: *the elitism that weakened our education system for a century.*
– DERIVATIVES **e·lit·ist** adjective & noun.

e·lix·ir /iˈliksər/ ▸ **noun** a magical potion, especially one supposedly able to make people live forever.
– ORIGIN Arabic.

E·liz·a·be·than /iˌlizəˈbētʜən/ ▸ **adjective** relating to or typical of the reign of Queen Elizabeth I (1558–1603). ▸ **noun** a person alive during the reign of Queen Elizabeth I.

elk /elk/ ▸ **noun 1** (pl. same or **elks**) a large North American red deer; a wapiti. **2** (pl. same or **elks**) British term for **MOOSE**. **3** (**Elk**) a member of the the Benevolent and Protective Order of Elks, a charitable fraternal organization.
– ORIGIN probably Old English.

el·lipse /iˈlips/ ▸ **noun** a regular oval shape resulting when a cone is cut by an oblique plane that does not intersect the base.

el·lip·sis /iˈlipsis/ ▸ **noun** (pl. **ellipses** /-sēz/) **1** the omission of words from speech or writing. **2** a set of dots indicating such an omission.
– ORIGIN Greek *elleipsis.*

el·lip·soid /iˈlipsoid/ ▸ **noun** a symmetrical three-dimensional figure with a circular cross-section when viewed along one axis and elliptical cross-sections when viewed along the other axes.
– DERIVATIVES **el·lip·soi·dal** /ilipˈsoidl, ˌelip-/ adjective.

el·lip·tic /iˈliptik/ ▸ **adjective** relating to or having the shape of an ellipse.
– DERIVATIVES **el·lip·tic·i·ty** /iˌlipˈtisitē, ˌelip-/ noun.

el·lip·ti·cal /iˈliptikəl/ ▸ **adjective 1** (of speech or writing) having a word or words deliberately omitted: *a superficial, elliptical narrative.* **2** another term for **ELLIPTIC**.
– DERIVATIVES **el·lip·ti·cal·ly** /-(ə)lē/ adverb.

elm /elm/ ▸ **noun** a tall deciduous tree with serrated leaves.
– ORIGIN Old English.

El Ni·ño /el ˈnēnyō/ ▸ **noun** (pl. **El Niños**) an irregular and complex cycle of climatic changes including unusually warm water off northern Peru and Ecuador.
– ORIGIN Spanish, 'the Christ child,' so called because the characteristic signs of an El Niño appear around Christmas time.

el·o·cu·tion /ˌeləˈkyo͞osʜən/ ▸ **noun** the skill of speaking clearly and pronouncing words distinctly.
– DERIVATIVES **el·o·cu·tion·ist** noun.
– ORIGIN from Latin *eloqui* 'speak out.'

e·lon·gate /iˈlôngˌgāt, iˈläng-/ ▸ **verb** (usu. as adj. **elongated**) make or become longer: *polar bears have elongated snouts.*
– DERIVATIVES **e·lon·ga·tion** /iˌlôngˈgāsʜən, ēˌlông-, iˌläng-, ēˌläng-/ noun.
– ORIGIN Latin *elongare* 'place at a distance.'

e·lope /iˈlōp/ ▸ **verb** run away secretly in order to get married.
– DERIVATIVES **e·lope·ment** noun.
– ORIGIN Old French *aloper.*

el·o·quence /ˈeləkwəns/ ▸ **noun** fluent or persuasive speaking or writing.
– ORIGIN Latin *eloquentia.*

el·o·quent /ˈeləkwənt/ ▸ **adjective 1** fluent or persuasive in speaking or writing. **2** clearly expressing something: *an art that is eloquent of America's cultural diversity.*

– SYNONYMS **articulate,** fluent, expressive, persuasive, well expressed, effective, lucid, vivid.
– ANTONYMS inarticulate.

– DERIVATIVES **el·o·quent·ly** adverb.

else /els/ ▸ **adverb 1** in addition; besides. **2** different; instead.
– PHRASES **or else 1** used to introduce the second of two alternatives. **2** used as a threat or warning: *she'd better shape up, or else.*
– ORIGIN Old English.

else·where /ˈelsˌ(h)wer/ ▸ **adverb** in, at, or to another place or other places. ▸ **pronoun** another place.

ELT ▸ **abbreviation** English language teaching.

e·lu·ci·date /iˈlo͞osiˌdāt/ ▸ **verb** make something easier to understand.
– DERIVATIVES **e·lu·ci·da·tion** /iˌlo͞osiˈdāsʜən/ noun.
– ORIGIN Latin *elucidare.*

CHOOSE THE RIGHT WORD

See **CLARIFY**.

e·lude /iˈlo͞od/ ▸ **verb 1** cleverly escape from or avoid someone or something. **2** fail to be understood or achieved by: *the logic of this eluded her.*

– SYNONYMS **evade,** avoid, get away from, dodge, escape from, lose, shake off, give the slip to, slip away from, throw off the scent.

– ORIGIN Latin *eludere.*

e·lu·sive /iˈlo͞osiv/ ▸ **adjective** difficult to find, catch, or achieve: *the elusive golden moon bear.*

– SYNONYMS **1 difficult to find,** evasive, slippery. **2 indefinable,** intangible, impalpable, fugitive, fleeting, transitory, ambiguous.

– DERIVATIVES **e·lu·sive·ly** adverb **e·lu·sive·ness** noun.
– ORIGIN from Latin *eludere* 'elude.'

el·ver /ˈelvər/ ▸ **noun** a young eel.
– ORIGIN from dialect *eel-fare* 'the passage of young eels up a river,' from **FARE** in its original sense 'a journey.'

elves /elvz/ plural of **ELF**.

E·ly·sian /iˈlizʜən, iˈlē-/ ▸ **adjective** relating to or like paradise.

– ORIGIN from *Elysium* or the *Elysian Fields* in Greek mythology, where heroes were taken when they died.

EM ▸ **abbreviation 1** electromagnetic. **2** emergency medicine.

em /em/ ▸ **noun** Printing **1** a unit for measuring the width of printed matter, equal to the height of the type size being used. **2** a unit of measurement equal to twelve points.

'em /əm/ ▸ **contraction** informal them: *let 'em know who's boss.*
– ORIGIN abbreviation of **THEM**.

e·ma·ci·at·ed /i'māsнē,ātid/ ▸ **adjective** abnormally thin and weak.

> – SYNONYMS **thin,** skeletal, bony, gaunt, wasted, thin as a rake, scrawny, skinny, scraggy, skin and bones, starved, cadaverous, shriveled, shrunken, withered.
> – ANTONYMS fat.

– DERIVATIVES **e·ma·ci·a·tion** /i,māsнē'āsнən/ noun.
– ORIGIN from Latin *emaciare* 'make thin.'

e·mail /'ē ,māl/ ▸ **noun 1** a message sent electronically from one computer user to another or others via a network. **2** the system of sending emails. ▸ **verb** mail someone or send a message using email.
– DERIVATIVES **e·mail·er** noun.

em·a·nate /'emə,nāt/ ▸ **verb 1** (**emanate from**) come or spread out from a source. **2** give out: *he emanated compassion.*
– ORIGIN Latin *emanare* 'flow out.'

em·a·na·tion /,emə'nāsнən/ ▸ **noun 1** something that emanates or comes from a source. **2** the action of coming from a source.

e·man·ci·pate /i'mansə,pāt/ ▸ **verb 1** set someone free, especially from legal, social, or political restrictions. **2** free someone from slavery.
– DERIVATIVES **e·man·ci·pa·tion** /i,mansə'pāsнən/ noun **e·man·ci·pa·to·ry** /-pə,tôrē/ adjective.
– ORIGIN Latin *emancipare* 'transfer as property.'

e·mas·cu·late /i'maskyə,lāt/ ▸ **verb 1** make weaker or less effective: *the world wars emasculated British power.* **2** deprive a man of his male role or identity.
– DERIVATIVES **e·mas·cu·la·tion** /i,maskyə'lāsнən/ noun.
– ORIGIN Latin *emasculare* 'castrate.'

em·balm /em'bä(l)m/ ▸ **verb** preserve a corpse from decay, usually by injection of a preservative.
– DERIVATIVES **em·balm·er** noun.
– ORIGIN Old French *embaumer*.

em·bank·ment /em'baNGkmənt/ ▸ **noun 1** a wall or bank built to prevent flooding by a river. **2** a bank of earth or stone built to carry a road or railroad over low ground.

em·bar·go /em'bärgō/ ▸ **noun** (pl. **embargoes**) an official ban, especially on trade or other commercial activity with a particular country.

> – SYNONYMS **ban,** bar, prohibition, stoppage, veto, moratorium, restriction, block, boycott.

▸ **verb** (**embargoes, embargoing, embargoed**) ban something officially.

> – SYNONYMS **ban,** bar, prohibit, stop, outlaw, blacklist, restrict, block, boycott.
> – ANTONYMS allow.

– ORIGIN Spanish.

em·bark /em'bärk/ ▸ **verb 1** go on board a ship or aircraft. **2** (**embark on**) begin a new project or course of action.

> – SYNONYMS **1 board (ship),** go on board, go aboard; informal hop on, jump on. **2** (**embark on**) **begin,** start, undertake, set out on, take up, turn one's hand to, get down to, enter into, venture into, launch into, plunge into, engage in.
> – ANTONYMS disembark.

– DERIVATIVES **em·bar·ka·tion** /,embär'kāsнən/ noun.
– ORIGIN French *embarquer*.

em·bar·ras de ri·chesses /äNbä'rä də rē'sнes/ ▸ **noun** more resources than one knows what to do with.
– ORIGIN French, 'embarrassment of riches.'

em·bar·rass /em'barəs/ ▸ **verb 1** make someone feel awkward, self-conscious, or ashamed. **2** (**be embarrassed**) be put in financial difficulties.

> – SYNONYMS **humiliate,** shame, put someone to shame, abash, mortify, fluster, discomfit; informal show up.

– ORIGIN French *embarrasser*.

em·bar·rassed /em'barəst/ ▸ **adjective** feeling or showing embarrassment.

> – SYNONYMS *the officer's flashlight caught a pair of embarrassed teens in the back seat* **humiliated,** mortified, red-faced, blushing, abashed, shamed, ashamed, shamefaced, self-conscious, uncomfortable, discomfited, disconcerted, flustered; informal with egg on one's face.

em·bar·rass·ing /em'barəsiNG/ ▸ **adjective** causing embarrassment.

> – SYNONYMS *many embarrassing moments have been preserved on videotape* **humiliating,** shameful, mortifying, ignominious, awkward, uncomfortable, compromising; informal cringeworthy, toe-curling.

em·bar·rass·ment /-mənt/ ▸ **noun 1** a feeling of self-consciousness, shame, or awkwardness. **2** a cause of self-consciousness, shame, or awkwardness: *her extreme views might be an embarrassment to the movement.*

> – SYNONYMS **1 humiliation,** mortification, shame, shamefacedness, awkwardness, self-consciousness, discomfort, discomfiture. **2 difficulty,** predicament, plight, problem, mess; informal bind, pickle, fix.

em·bas·sy /'embəsē/ ▸ **noun** (pl. **embassies**) **1** the official home or offices of an ambassador. **2** chiefly historical a deputation or mission sent by one country to another.
– ORIGIN Old French *ambasse*.

em·bat·tled /em'batld/ ▸ **adjective 1** troubled by many difficulties: *the embattled chancellor.* **2** prepared for war because surrounded by enemy forces. **3** (of a building) having battlements.

em·bed /em'bed/ (also **imbed**) ▸ **verb** (**embeds, embedding, embedded**) **1** fix something firmly and deeply in a surrounding mass. **2** cause an idea or feeling to be firmly lodged in a culture or someone's mind: *this myth is embedded in the national consciousness.* **3** attach a journalist to a military unit during a conflict.

em·bel·lish /em'belisн/ ▸ **verb 1** make something more attractive; decorate. **2** add extra, often exaggerated, details to a story to make it more interesting.

> – SYNONYMS **decorate,** adorn, ornament, beautify, enhance, trim, garnish, gild, deck, bedeck, festoon, emblazon.

– DERIVATIVES **em·bel·lish·ment** noun.
– ORIGIN Old French *embellir*.

em·ber /'embər/ ▶ **noun** a small piece of burning wood or coal in a dying fire.
– ORIGIN Old English.

em·bez·zle /em'bezəl/ ▶ **verb** steal money placed in one's trust or under one's control.

> – SYNONYMS **misappropriate,** steal, thieve, pilfer, purloin, appropriate, siphon off, pocket; informal filch, pinch.

– DERIVATIVES **em·bez·zle·ment** noun **em·bez·zler** noun.
– ORIGIN Old French *embesiler*.

em·bit·ter /em'bitər/ ▶ **verb** (usu. as adj. **embittered**) make someone bitter or resentful.

em·bla·zon /em'blāzn/ ▶ **verb 1** display a design on something in a noticeable way: *T-shirts emblazoned with the names of baseball teams.* **2** depict a heraldic device on something.

em·blem /'embləm/ ▶ **noun 1** a heraldic design or symbol as a distinctive badge of a nation, organization, or family. **2** a symbol representing a quality or idea: *the bards wore white, as an emblem of peace.*

> – SYNONYMS **symbol,** representation, token, image, figure, mark, sign, crest, badge, device, insignia, coat of arms, shield, logo, trademark.

– ORIGIN Greek *emblēma* 'insertion.'

> **CHOOSE THE RIGHT WORD**
>
> **emblem, attribute, image, sign, symbol, token, type**
>
> When it comes to representing or embodying the invisible or intangible, you can't beat a **symbol**. It applies to anything that serves as an outward sign of something immaterial or spiritual (*the cross as a symbol of salvation*; *the crown as a symbol of monarchy*), although the association between the symbol and what it represents does not have to be based on tradition or convention and may, in fact, be quite arbitrary (*the annual gathering at the cemetery became a symbol of the family's long and tragic history*). An **emblem** is a visual symbol or pictorial device that represents the character or history of a family, a nation, or an office (*the eagle is an emblem of the United States*). It is very close in meaning to **attribute**, which is an object that is conventionally associated with either an individual, a group, or an abstraction (*the spiked wheel as an attribute of St. Catherine*; *the scales as an attribute of justice*). An **image** is also a visual representation or embodiment, but in a much broader sense (*veins popping, he was the image of the angry father*). **Sign** is often used in place of *symbol* to refer to a simple representation of an agreed-upon meaning (*the upraised fist as a sign of victory; the white flag as a sign of surrender*), but a *symbol* usually embodies a wider range of meanings, while a *sign* can be any object, event, or gesture from which information can be deduced (*her faltering voice was a sign of her nervousness*). A **token**, on the other hand, is something offered as a symbol or reminder (*he gave her his class ring as a token of his devotion*) and a **type**, particularly in a religious context, is a symbol or representation of something not present (*Jerusalem as the type of heaven*; *the paschal lamb as the type of Christ*).

em·blem·at·ic /ˌembləˈmatik/ ▶ **adjective** representing a particular quality or idea: *Mill was an emblematic figure of his age.*

em·bod·i·ment/ em'bädēmənt, im-/ ▶ **noun 1** a physical or visible form of an idea or quality: *dance was the embodiment of cultural tradition.* **2** the representation of something in a physical or visible form.

em·bod·y /em'bädē/ ▶ **verb** (**embodies, embodying, embodied**) **1** give a physical or visible form to an idea or quality. **2** include or contain as a constituent part: *the changes in law embodied in the Civil Rights Act.*

> – SYNONYMS **1 personify,** manifest, symbolize, represent, express, epitomize, stand for, typify, exemplify. **2 incorporate,** include, contain.

em·bold·en /em'bōldən/ ▶ **verb** give courage or confidence to someone.

em·bo·lism /'embəˌlizəm/ ▶ **noun** obstruction of an artery, typically by a clot of blood or an air bubble.
– ORIGIN Greek *embolismos*.

em·bo·lus /'embələs/ ▶ **noun** (pl. **emboli** /-ˌlī, -ˌlē/) a blood clot, air bubble, fatty deposit, or other object obstructing a blood vessel.
– DERIVATIVES **em·bol·ic** /em'bälik/ adjective.
– ORIGIN Greek *embolos* 'peg, stopper.'

em·bon·point /ˌänbôn'pwan/ ▶ **noun** plumpness, especially of a woman's bosom.
– ORIGIN from French *en bon point* 'in good condition.'

em·boss /em'bôs, -'bäs/ ▶ **verb** carve or mold a raised design on a surface.
– DERIVATIVES **em·boss·er** noun.
– ORIGIN from former French *embosser*.

em·brace /em'brās/ ▶ **verb 1** hold someone closely in one's arms, especially to show affection. **2** include or contain something. **3** accept or support a belief or change willingly.

> – SYNONYMS **1 hug,** take/hold in one's arms, hold, cuddle, clasp/draw to one's bosom, squeeze, clutch, enfold. **2 welcome,** welcome with open arms, accept, take on board, take up, take to one's heart, adopt, espouse. **3 include,** take in, comprise, contain, incorporate, encompass, cover, subsume.

▶ **noun** an act of embracing someone.

> – SYNONYMS **hug,** cuddle, squeeze, clinch, caress.

– DERIVATIVES **em·brace·a·ble** adjective.
– ORIGIN Old French *embracer*.

em·bra·sure /em'brāzʜər/ ▶ **noun 1** an opening or recess around a window or door forming an enlargement of the area from the inside. **2** an opening in a wall or parapet, used for shooting through.
– ORIGIN from former French *embraser* 'widen an opening.'

em·bro·ca·tion /ˌembrə'kāsʜən/ ▶ **noun** a liquid medication rubbed on the body to relieve pain from strains.
– ORIGIN Latin.

em·broi·der /em'broidər/ ▶ **verb 1** sew decorative needlework patterns on something. **2** add false or exaggerated details to a story.
– DERIVATIVES **em·broi·der·er** noun.
– ORIGIN Old French *enbrouder*.

em·broi·der·y /em'broid(ə)rē/ ▶ **noun** (pl. **embroideries**) **1** the art or pastime of embroidering. **2** embroidered cloth.

em·broil /em'broil/ ▶ **verb** involve someone deeply in a conflict or difficult situation.
– ORIGIN French *embrouiller* 'to muddle.'

em·bry·o /'embrēˌō/ ▶ **noun** (pl. **embryos**) **1** an unborn animal in the process of development, especially an unborn human being in the first eight weeks from fertilization of the egg. Compare with **FETUS**. **2** the part of a seed that develops into a new plant. **3** something at an early stage of development.
– ORIGIN Greek *embruon* 'fetus.'

em·bry·ol·o·gy /ˌembrēˈäləjē/ ▶ **noun** the branch of biology and medicine concerned with the study of embryos.
– DERIVATIVES **em·bry·o·log·i·cal** /ˌembrēəˈläjikəl/ adjective **em·bry·ol·o·gist** /-jist/ noun.

em·bry·on·ic /ˌembrēˈänik/ ▶ **adjective** **1** relating to an embryo. **2** in an early stage of development: *the plan is still in its embryonic stages.*

em·cee /ˌemˈsē/ informal ▶ **noun** a master of ceremonies. ▶ **verb** (**emcees, emceeing, emceed**) act as a master of ceremonies at a public entertainment or large social occasion.

e·mend /iˈmend/ ▶ **verb** correct and revise written material.
– DERIVATIVES **e·men·da·tion** /ˌēmənˈdāshən, ˌemən-/ noun.
– ORIGIN Latin *emendare.*

em·er·ald /ˈem(ə)rəld/ ▶ **noun** **1** a bright green precious stone that is a variety of beryl. **2** a bright green color.
– ORIGIN Old French *esmeraud.*

e·merge /iˈmərj/ ▶ **verb** **1** become gradually visible. **2** begin to exist or become apparent: *the jogging boom emerged during the 1970s.* **3** (of facts) become known. **4** recover from or survive a difficult period.

> – SYNONYMS **1 appear,** come out, come into view, become visible, surface, materialize, issue, come forth. **2 become known,** become apparent, be revealed, come to light, come out, turn up, transpire, unfold, turn out, prove to be the case.

– ORIGIN Latin *emergere.*

e·mer·gence /iˈmərjəns/ ▶ **noun** the process of coming into being.

> – SYNONYMS *the emergence of the environmental movement* **appearance,** arrival, coming, materialization, advent, inception, dawn, birth, origination, start, development.

e·mer·gen·cy /iˈmərjənsē/ ▶ **noun** (pl. **emergencies**) **1** a serious, unexpected, and often dangerous situation requiring immediate action. **2** the emergency room in a hospital.

> – SYNONYMS **crisis,** disaster, catastrophe, calamity, plight.

▶ **adjective** arising from or used in an emergency: *an emergency exit.*

> – SYNONYMS **1 urgent,** crisis, extraordinary. **2 reserve,** standby, backup, fallback.

– ORIGIN Latin *emergentia.*

e·mer·gen·cy room ▶ **noun** the department of a hospital that provides immediate treatment for acute illnesses and trauma.

e·mer·gent /iˈmərjənt/ ▶ **adjective** in the process of coming into being: *a newly emergent middle class.*

e·mer·i·tus /iˈmerətəs/ ▶ **adjective** having retired but allowed to keep a title as an honor: *an emeritus professor.*
– ORIGIN Latin.

em·er·y /ˈem(ə)rē/ ▶ **noun** a grayish-black form of the mineral corundum used in powdered form for smoothing and polishing.
– ORIGIN Old French *esmeri.*

em·er·y board ▶ **noun** a strip of thin wood or cardboard coated with emery or another abrasive and used as a nail file.

e·met·ic /iˈmetik/ ▶ **adjective** (of a substance) causing vomiting. ▶ **noun** a substance that causes vomiting.
– ORIGIN Greek *emetikos.*

EMF ▶ **abbreviation** **1** electromagnetic field(s). **2** (**emf**) electromotive force.

em·i·grant /ˈemigrənt/ ▶ **noun** a person who emigrates to another country.

em·i·grate /ˈemiˌgrāt/ ▶ **verb** leave one's own country in order to settle permanently in another.

> – SYNONYMS **move abroad,** move overseas, leave one's country, migrate, relocate, resettle.
> – ANTONYMS immigrate.

– DERIVATIVES **em·i·gra·tion** /ˌemiˈgrāshən/ noun.
– ORIGIN Latin *emigrare.*

é·mi·gré /ˈeməˌgrā/ ▶ **noun** a person who has emigrated to another country, especially for political reasons.
– ORIGIN French.

em·i·nence /ˈemənəns/ ▶ **noun** **1** the quality of being highly accomplished and respected within a particular area of activity. **2** an important or distinguished person. **3** (**His/Your Eminence**) a title given to a Roman Catholic cardinal. **4** literary a piece of rising ground.
– ORIGIN Latin *eminentia.*

em·i·nent /ˈemənənt/ ▶ **adjective** **1** respected; distinguished. **2** outstanding or obvious: *the eminent reasonableness of their claim.*

> – SYNONYMS **illustrious,** distinguished, renowned, esteemed, preeminent, notable, noted, noteworthy, great, prestigious, important, outstanding, celebrated, prominent, well known, acclaimed, exalted.
> – ANTONYMS unknown.

– DERIVATIVES **em·i·nent·ly** adverb.

em·i·nent do·main ▶ **noun** Law the right of a government to take over private property for public use, with payment of compensation.

e·mir /əˈmi(ə)r/ (also **amir** pronunc. same) ▶ **noun** a title of various Muslim (mainly Arab) rulers.
– ORIGIN Arabic, 'commander.'

e·mir·ate /əˈmi(ə)rˌāt, əˈmi(ə)rit, ˈemərit/ ▶ **noun** the rank, lands, or reign of an emir.

em·is·sar·y /ˈeməˌserē/ ▶ **noun** (pl. **emissaries**) a person sent as a diplomatic representative on a special mission.
– ORIGIN Latin *emissarius* 'scout, spy.'

e·mis·sion /iˈmishən/ ▶ **noun** **1** the action of emitting something, especially heat, light, gas, or radiation. **2** a substance that is emitted.

> – SYNONYMS **discharge,** release, outpouring, outflow, outrush, leak.

e·mis·sions tra·ding ▶ **noun** a system by which countries and organizations receive permits to produce a specified amount of carbon dioxide and other greenhouse gases, which they may trade with others.

e·mit /iˈmit/ ▶ **verb** (**emits, emitting, emitted**) **1** discharge or give out gas, radiation, etc. **2** make a sound.

> – SYNONYMS **1 discharge,** release, give out/off, pour out, radiate, leak, ooze, disgorge, eject, belch, spew out, exude. **2 utter,** voice, let out, produce, give vent to, come out with.

– DERIVATIVES **e·mit·ter** noun.
– ORIGIN Latin *emittere.*

Em·men·tal /ˈemənˌtäl/ (also **Emmenthal** pronunc. same) ▶ **noun** a hard Swiss cheese with holes in it, similar to Gruyère.
– ORIGIN a valley in Switzerland where the cheese was first made.

Em·my /ˈemē/ ▶ **noun** (pl. **Emmys**) a statuette awarded annually to an outstanding television program or performer.
– ORIGIN said to be from *Immy*, short for *image orthicon tube* (a kind of television camera tube).

e·mo /ˈēmō/ ▶ **noun 1** a style of popular music derived from hardcore punk music and characterized by emotional, usually introspective lyrics. **2** the subculture or style associated with this music.

e·mol·lient /iˈmälyənt/ ▶ **adjective 1** softening or soothing the skin. **2** attempting to avoid conflict; calming. ▶ **noun** a substance that softens the skin.
– ORIGIN from Latin *emollire* 'make soft.'

e·mol·u·ment /iˈmälyəmənt/ ▶ **noun** formal a salary, fee, or benefit from employment.
– ORIGIN Latin *emolumentum*.

e·mote /iˈmōt/ ▶ **verb** show emotion in an exaggerated way: *he failed to cry, or at least emote, when his mother died.*
– ORIGIN from **EMOTION**.

e·mo·ti·con /iˈmōtəˌkän/ ▶ **noun** a representation of a facial expression such as a smile, formed with keyboard characters and used in email or texting to show the writer's feelings.
– ORIGIN blend of **EMOTION** and **ICON**.

e·mo·tion /iˈmōsHən/ ▶ **noun 1** a strong feeling, such as joy or anger. **2** instinctive feeling as distinguished from reasoning or knowledge.

> – SYNONYMS **1 feeling,** sentiment, reaction, response, instinct, intuition. **2 passion,** strength of feeling, heart.

– DERIVATIVES **e·mo·tion·less** adjective.
– ORIGIN from Latin *emovere* 'disturb.'

e·mo·tion·al /iˈmōsHənəl/ ▶ **adjective 1** relating to a person's emotions. **2** showing intense feeling: *an emotional speech*. **3** easily affected by or openly displaying emotion: *I'm emotional, sensitive, and shy.*

> – SYNONYMS **1 passionate,** hot-blooded, ardent, fervent, warm, responsive, excitable, temperamental, demonstrative, sensitive. **2 poignant,** moving, touching, affecting, powerful, stirring, emotive, impassioned, dramatic; informal tear-jerking.
> – ANTONYMS cold, clinical.

– DERIVATIVES **e·mo·tion·al·ism** /-ˌizəm/ noun **e·mo·tion·al·ize** /-ˌlīz/ verb **e·mo·tion·al·ly** adverb.

e·mo·tive /iˈmōtiv/ ▶ **adjective** arousing intense feeling.
– DERIVATIVES **e·mo·tive·ly** adverb.

> **USAGE**
>
> **Emotive** and **emotional** have similar meanings but they are not exactly the same. **Emotive** means 'arousing intense feeling' (*hunting is a highly emotive issue*), while **emotional** tends to mean 'showing intense feeling' (*an emotional speech*).

em·pa·na·da /empəˈnädə/ ▶ **noun** a Spanish or Latin American pastry turnover with a savory filling.
– ORIGIN Spanish.

em·pan·el /emˈpanl/ ▶ **verb** variant spelling of **IMPANEL**.

em·pa·thize /ˈempəˌTHīz/ ▶ **verb** understand and share the feelings of another.

> – SYNONYMS *I can **empathize with** her parents* **identify with,** sympathize with, understand, share the feelings of, be in tune with; relate to, feel for, have insight into; informal put oneself in the shoes of.

em·pa·thy /ˈempəTHē/ ▶ **noun** the ability to understand and share the feelings of another person.
– DERIVATIVES **em·pa·thet·ic** /ˌempəˈTHetik/ adjective **em·path·ic** /emˈpaTHik/ adjective.
– ORIGIN Greek *empatheia*.

> **USAGE**
>
> Do not confuse **empathy** and **sympathy**. **Empathy** means 'the ability to understand and share the feelings of another person' (*the artist developed a considerable empathy with his elderly subject*), whereas **sympathy** means 'the feeling of being sorry for someone who is unhappy or in difficulty' (*they had great sympathy for the flood victims*).

em·per·or /ˈemp(ə)rər/ ▶ **noun** the ruler of an empire.
– ORIGIN Latin *imperator* 'military commander.'

em·per·or pen·guin ▶ **noun** the largest kind of penguin, which breeds in the Antarctic and has a yellow patch on each side of the head.

em·pha·sis /ˈemfəsis/ ▶ **noun** (pl. **emphases** /-ˌsēz/) **1** special importance, value, or prominence given to something: *management is placing greater emphasis on improving productivity*. **2** stress given to a word or words in speaking.

> – SYNONYMS **1 prominence,** importance, significance, value, stress, weight, accent, attention, priority. **2** *the emphasis is on the word 'little'* **stress,** accent, weight, beat.

– ORIGIN Greek.

em·pha·size /ˈemfəˌsīz/ ▶ **verb** give special importance or prominence to something.

> – SYNONYMS **stress,** underline, highlight, focus attention on, point up, lay stress on, draw attention to, spotlight, foreground.
> – ANTONYMS understate.

em·phat·ic /emˈfatik/ ▶ **adjective 1** showing or giving emphasis. **2** definite and clear: *an emphatic win*.

> – SYNONYMS **forceful,** firm, vehement, wholehearted, energetic, vigorous, direct, insistent, certain, definite, out-and-out, decided, categorical, unqualified, unconditional, unequivocal, unambiguous, absolute, explicit, downright, outright, clear.

– DERIVATIVES **em·phat·i·cal·ly** /emˈfatik(ə)lē/ adverb.

em·phy·se·ma /ˌemfəˈsēmə, -ˈzēmə/ (also **pulmonary emphysema**) ▶ **noun** a condition in which the air sacs of the lungs are damaged and enlarged, causing breathlessness.
– DERIVATIVES **em·phy·sem·a·tous** /ˌemfəˈsemətəs, -ˈsēmə-, -ˈzemə-, -ˈzēmə-/ adjective.
– ORIGIN Greek *emphusēma*.

em·pire /ˈemˌpī(ə)r/ ▶ **noun 1** a large group of states ruled over by a single monarch or ruling authority. **2** a large commercial organization under the control of one person or group: *an entertainment empire*.

> – SYNONYMS **1 kingdom,** realm, domain, territory, commonwealth, power. **2 business,** firm, company, corporation, multinational, conglomerate, group, consortium, operation.

▶ **adjective** (usu. **Empire**) (of a dress) having a low neck and high waistline, a style popular during the First Empire (1804-15) in France.
– ORIGIN Latin *imperium*.

WORD LINKS

imperial *relating to an empire*

em·pir·i·cal /em'pirikəl/ (also **empiric** /em'pirik/) ▶ **adjective** based on observation or experience rather than theory or logic: *empirical studies of seed dispersal.*
– DERIVATIVES **em·pir·i·cal·ly** adverb.
– ORIGIN Greek *empeirikos.*

em·pir·i·cism /em'pirə,sizəm/ ▶ **noun** the theory that all knowledge is derived from experience and observation.
– DERIVATIVES **em·pir·i·cist** noun & adjective.

em·place·ment /em'plāsmənt/ ▶ **noun** a structure or platform on which a gun is placed for firing.

em·ploy /em'ploi/ ▶ **verb 1** give work to someone and pay them for it. **2** make use of. **3** keep someone occupied.

– SYNONYMS **1** *she employed a chauffeur* **hire,** engage, recruit, take on, sign up, appoint, retain. **2** (as adj. **employed**) *it is a myth that most employed people have adequate health insurance for their families* **working,** in work, in employment, holding down a job, earning, salaried, waged. **3** *the team employed subtle psychological tactics* **use,** utilize, make use of, apply, exercise, practice, put into practice, exert, bring into play, bring to bear, draw on, resort to, turn to, have recourse to. **4** *Julio was employed in carving a stone figure* **occupy,** engage, involve, keep busy, tie up.
– ANTONYMS dismiss.

– DERIVATIVES **em·ploy·a·bil·i·ty** /em,ploi-ə'bilitē/ noun **em·ploy·a·ble** adjective.
– PHRASES **in the employ of** employed by.
– ORIGIN Old French *employer.*

em·ploy·ee /em'ploi-ē, ,emploi'ē/ ▶ **noun** a person employed for wages or a salary.

– SYNONYMS **worker,** member of the staff, staff member, blue-collar worker, white-collar worker, workman, laborer, hand; (**employees**) personnel, staff, workforce.

em·ploy·er /em'ploi-ər/ ▶ **noun** a person or organization that employs people.

em·ploy·ment /em'ploimənt/ ▶ **noun 1** the action of employing someone or something. **2** the state of having paid work: *a fall in the numbers in full-time employment.* **3** a person's work or profession.

– SYNONYMS **work,** labor, service, job, post, position, situation, occupation, profession, trade, business, line of work.

em·po·ri·um /em'pôrēəm/ ▶ **noun** (pl. **emporia** /-'pôrēə/ or **emporiums**) a large store selling a wide variety of goods.
– ORIGIN Greek *emporion.*

em·pow·er /em'pou(-ə)r/ ▶ **verb 1** give authority or power to someone. **2** make someone stronger or more confident.

– SYNONYMS **1 authorize,** entitle, permit, allow, license, enable. **2 emancipate,** unshackle, set free, liberate, enfranchise.
– ANTONYMS forbid.

– DERIVATIVES **em·pow·er·ment** noun.

em·press /'empris/ ▶ **noun 1** a female emperor. **2** the wife or widow of an emperor.

emp·ty /'em(p)tē/ ▶ **adjective** (**emptier, emptiest**) **1** containing nothing; not filled or occupied. **2** not likely to be fulfilled: *an empty threat.* **3** having no meaning or purpose: *an empty life going nowhere.*

– SYNONYMS **1 vacant,** unoccupied, uninhabited, bare, clear, free. **2 meaningless,** hollow, idle, vain, futile, worthless, useless, ineffectual. **3 futile,** pointless, purposeless, worthless, meaningless, fruitless, valueless, of no value, senseless.
– ANTONYMS full, occupied.

▶ **verb** (**empties, emptying, emptied**) **1** remove the contents from a container. **2** (of a place, vehicle, or container) become empty: *the bus emptied in a flash.* **3** (of a river) flow into the sea or a lake.

– SYNONYMS **1 unload,** unpack, clear, evacuate, drain. **2 remove,** take out, extract, tip out, pour out.
– ANTONYMS fill, replace.

▶ **noun** (pl. **empties**) informal a bottle or glass left empty of its contents.
– DERIVATIVES **emp·ti·ly** adverb **emp·ti·ness** noun.
– ORIGIN Old English, 'at leisure, empty.'

emp·ty-hand·ed ▶ **adjective** having failed to obtain or achieve what one wanted.

emp·ty-head·ed ▶ **adjective** unintelligent and foolish.

emp·ty nest·er ▶ **noun** informal a parent whose children have grown up and left home.

em·py·re·an /em'pirēən, ,empə'rēən/ ▶ **noun** (**the empyrean**) literary heaven or the sky.
– ORIGIN Greek *empurios*, referring to the highest part of heaven.

EMS ▶ **abbreviation 1** emergency medical service. **2** European Monetary System.

EMT ▶ **abbreviation** emergency medical technician.

EMU ▶ **abbreviation** Economic and Monetary Union.

e·mu /'ēm(y)o͞o/ ▶ **noun** a large flightless fast-running Australian bird similar to an ostrich.
– ORIGIN Portuguese *ema.*

em·u·late /'emyə,lāt/ ▶ **verb 1** try to do as well as or better than a person or an achievement. **2** Computing reproduce the function or action of (a different computer or software system).

– SYNONYMS **imitate,** copy, mirror, echo, follow, model oneself on, take a page out of someone's book.

– DERIVATIVES **em·u·la·tion** /,emyə'lāsʜən/ noun **em·u·la·tor** /-,lātər/ noun.
– ORIGIN Latin *aemulari* 'to rival or equal.'

e·mul·si·fi·er /i'məlsə,fī(ə)r/ ▶ **noun** a substance that stabilizes an emulsion, especially an additive used to stabilize processed foods.

e·mul·si·fy /i'məlsə,fī/ ▶ **verb** (**emulsifies, emulsifying, emulsified**) make into or become an emulsion.
– DERIVATIVES **e·mul·si·fi·a·ble** /-,fīəbəl/ adjective **e·mul·si·fi·ca·tion** /i,məlsəfi'kāsʜən/ noun.

e·mul·sion /i'məlsʜən/ ▶ **noun 1** a liquid in which particles of one liquid are evenly dispersed in the other. **2** a type of matte paint for walls. **3** a light-sensitive coating for photographic films and plates, containing crystals of a silver compound dispersed in a medium such as gelatin.
– ORIGIN Latin.

en /en/ ▶ **noun** Printing a unit of measurement equal to half an em.
– ORIGIN the letter *N*, since it is approximately this width.

en·a·ble /en'ābəl/ ▶ **verb 1** provide someone with the ability or means to do something. **2** make something possible. **3** chiefly Computing make a device or system operational. **4** (as adj. **-enabled**) adapted for use with the specified application or system: *WAP-enabled cell phones.*

– SYNONYMS **allow,** permit, let, equip, empower, make able, fit, authorize, entitle, qualify.
– ANTONYMS prevent.

– DERIVATIVES **en·a·ble·ment** noun **en·a·bler** noun.

en·act /en'akt/ ▶ **verb 1** make a bill or other proposal law. **2** act out a role or play.

– SYNONYMS **1 make (into) law,** pass, approve, ratify, validate, sanction, authorize. **2 act out,** perform, appear in, stage, mount, put on, present.
– ANTONYMS repeal.

– DERIVATIVES **en·ac·tor** noun.

en·act·ment /en'aktmənt/ ▶ **noun 1** the process of enacting something. **2** a law that has been passed.

e·nam·el /i'naməl/ ▶ **noun 1** a colored shiny substance applied to metal, glass, or pottery for decoration or protection. **2** the hard glossy substance that covers the crown of a tooth. **3** a paint that dries to give a smooth, hard coat. ▶ **verb** (**enamels, enameling, enameled**) (usu. as adj. **enameled**) coat or decorate something with enamel.
– DERIVATIVES **e·nam·el·er** noun.
– ORIGIN Old French *amail* 'enamel.'

en·am·or /i'namər/ (chiefly Brit. **enamour**) ▶ **verb** (**be enamored of/with/by**) be filled with love or admiration for: *half the village are enamored of her.*
– ORIGIN Old French *enamourer.*

en bloc /äɴ 'bläk/ ▶ **adverb** all together or all at once.
– ORIGIN French.

en·camp /en'kamp/ ▶ **verb** settle in or establish a camp.

en·camp·ment /en'kampmənt/ ▶ **noun 1** a place where a camp is set up. **2** the process of setting up a camp.

en·cap·su·late /en'kaps(y)ə,lāt/ ▶ **verb 1** express clearly and in few words: *can you encapsulate the idea in two sentences?* **2** enclose something in or as if in a capsule.
– DERIVATIVES **en·cap·su·la·tion** /en,kaps(y)ə'lāsʜən/ noun.

en·case /en'kās/ ▶ **verb** enclose or cover something in a case or close-fitting surround.
– DERIVATIVES **en·case·ment** noun.

en·caus·tic /en'kôstik/ ▶ **adjective** (in painting and ceramics) decorated with colored clays or pigments mixed with hot wax, which are burned in as an inlay. ▶ **noun** the art or process of encaustic painting.
– ORIGIN Greek *enkaustikos.*

en·ceph·a·li·tis /en,sefə'lītis/ ▶ **noun** inflammation of the brain.
– DERIVATIVES **en·ceph·a·lit·ic** /-'litik/ adjective.
– ORIGIN from Greek *enkephalos* 'brain.'

en·ceph·a·log·ra·phy /en,sefə'lägrəfē/ ▶ **noun** any of various techniques for recording the structure or electrical activity of the brain.
– DERIVATIVES **en·ceph·a·lo·gram** /en'sefələ,gram/ noun.

en·ceph·a·lo·my·e·li·tis /en,sefələ,mīə'lītis/ ▶ **noun** inflammation of the brain and spinal cord, typically caused by acute infection with a virus.

en·ceph·a·lop·a·thy /en,sefə'läpəᴛʜē/ ▶ **noun** (pl. **encephalopathies**) a disease in which the functioning of the brain is affected, especially by viral infection or toxins in the blood.

en·chant /en'ᴄʜant/ ▶ **verb 1** fill someone with delight. **2** put someone under a spell.
– DERIVATIVES **en·chant·er** noun **en·chant·ment** noun **en·chant·ress** /en'ᴄʜantris/ noun.
– ORIGIN French *enchanter.*

en·chant·ing /en'ᴄʜantiɴɢ/ ▶ **adjective** delightfully charming or attractive.

– SYNONYMS **captivating,** charming, delightful, adorable, lovely, attractive, appealing, engaging, fetching, irresistible, fascinating.

– DERIVATIVES **en·chant·ing·ly** adverb.

WORD TOOLKIT

enchanting ...	irresistible ...	appealing ...
story	force	option
music	urge	idea
voice	temptation	prospect
place	charm	alternative
evening	impulse	quality
experience	attraction	design
performance	smile	candidate

en·chi·la·da /,enᴄʜə'lädə/ ▶ **noun** a tortilla filled with meat or cheese and served with chili sauce.
– PHRASES **the whole enchilada** informal the whole situation; everything.
– ORIGIN Latin American Spanish.

en·ci·pher /en'sīfər/ ▶ **verb** convert something into a coded form.
– DERIVATIVES **en·ci·pher·ment** noun.

en·cir·cle /en'sərkəl/ ▶ **verb** surround or form a circle around someone or something.
– DERIVATIVES **en·cir·cle·ment** noun.

encl. (also **enc.**) ▶ **abbreviation 1** enclosed. **2** enclosure.

en·clave /'en,klāv, 'äɴɢ-/ ▶ **noun 1** a small territory surrounded by a larger territory whose inhabitants are of a different nationality or culture. **2** a group that is different from those surrounding it: *the engineering department is a male enclave.*
– ORIGIN from Old French *enclaver* 'enclose.'

en·close /en'klōz/ ▶ **verb 1** surround or close off on all sides: *breakwaters enclosed the harbor.* **2** (**enclose something in/within**) place an object inside a container. **3** place another document or an object in an envelope together with a letter.

– SYNONYMS **1 surround,** circle, ring, encircle, bound, close in, wall in. **2 include,** insert, put in, send.

– ORIGIN Old French *enclore.*

WORD LINKS

claustrophobia *fear of enclosed spaces*

en·clo·sure /en'klōzʜər/ ▶ **noun 1** an area that is enclosed by a fence, wall, or other barrier. **2** a document or object placed in an envelope together with a letter.

– SYNONYMS **compound,** pen, corral, fold, stockade, ring, paddock, yard, run, coop.

en·code /en'kōd/ ▶ **verb** convert something into a coded form.
– DERIVATIVES **en·cod·er** noun.

en·co·mi·um /en'kōmēəm/ ▶ **noun** (pl. **encomiums** or **encomia** /-mēə/) formal a speech or piece of writing praising someone or something.
– ORIGIN Greek *enkōmion* 'eulogy.'

en·com·pass /en'kəmpəs/ ▸ **verb 1** include a wide range or number of things. **2** surround or cover: *the estate encompasses twelve acres.*

– SYNONYMS **include,** cover, embrace, incorporate, take in, contain, comprise, involve, deal with.

en·core /'än,kôr/ ▸ **noun** a repeated or additional performance of an item at the end of a concert, as called for by an audience. ▸ **exclamation** again! (as called by an audience at the end of a concert).
– ORIGIN French, 'still, again.'

en·coun·ter /en'koun(t)ər/ ▸ **verb 1** unexpectedly be faced with something difficult. **2** unexpectedly meet someone.

– SYNONYMS **1 experience,** run into, meet, come up against, face, be faced with, confront, suffer. **2 meet,** run into, come across/upon, stumble across/on, chance on, happen on; informal bump into.

▸ **noun 1** an unexpected or casual meeting. **2** a confrontation or difficult struggle: *his close encounter with death.*

– SYNONYMS **1 meeting,** chance meeting. **2 battle,** fight, skirmish, clash, scuffle, confrontation, struggle; informal run-in, set-to, scrap.

– ORIGIN Old French *encontrer.*

en·cour·age /en'kərij, -'kə-rij/ ▸ **verb 1** give support, confidence, or hope to someone. **2** help an activity, belief, etc., to develop.

– SYNONYMS **1 hearten,** cheer, buoy up, uplift, inspire, motivate, spur on, stir, fire up, stimulate, embolden; informal buck up. **2** (as adj. **encouraging**) *the results are very encouraging* **promising,** hopeful, auspicious, favorable, heartening, reassuring, cheering, comforting, welcome, pleasing, gratifying. **3** *she encouraged him to go* **persuade,** coax, urge, press, push, pressure, prod, egg on. **4** *the municipal government must encourage local businesses* **support,** back, promote, further, foster, nurture, cultivate, strengthen, stimulate.
– ANTONYMS discourage.

– DERIVATIVES **en·cour·ag·er** noun **en·cour·ag·ing** adjective.
– ORIGIN French *encourager.*

en·cour·age·ment /en'kərijmənt, -'kə-rijmənt/ ▸ **noun 1** the action of encouraging someone to do something. **2** something that encourages someone: *his success served as an encouragement to younger artists.*

– SYNONYMS **1 support,** cheering up, inspiration, motivation, stimulation, morale-boosting; informal a shot in the arm. **2 persuasion,** coaxing, urging, prodding, prompting, inducement, incentive, carrot. **3 backing,** sponsorship, support, promotion, furtherance, fostering, nurture, cultivation, stimulation.

en·croach /en'krōch/ ▸ **verb 1** (**encroach on**) gradually intrude on a person's territory, rights, etc. **2** advance gradually beyond expected or acceptable limits: *the sea has encroached all around the coast.*
– DERIVATIVES **en·croach·ment** noun.
– ORIGIN Old French *encrochier* 'seize.'

en croute /än 'kroot/ ▸ **adjective & adverb** in a pastry crust.
– ORIGIN French.

en·crust /en'krəst/ ▸ **verb** cover something with a hard surface layer.
– DERIVATIVES **en·crus·ta·tion** /,enkrəs'tāshən/ noun.

en·crypt /en'kript/ ▸ **verb** convert something into code.
– DERIVATIVES **en·cryp·tion** /-'kripshən/ noun.
– ORIGIN from Greek *kruptos* 'hidden.'

en·cum·ber /en'kəmbər/ ▸ **verb** prevent from moving or acting freely: *they were encumbered with cameras, tape recorders, and other gadgets.*
– ORIGIN Old French *encombrer* 'block up.'

en·cum·brance /en'kəmbrəns/ ▸ **noun 1** something that prevents freedom of action or movement. **2** Law a mortgage or other claim on property or assets.

en·cyc·li·cal /en'siklikəl/ ▸ **noun** a letter sent by the pope to all bishops of the Roman Catholic Church.
– ORIGIN from Greek *enkuklios* 'circular, general.'

en·cy·clo·pe·di·a /en,sīklə'pēdēə/ ▸ **noun** a book or set of books giving information on many subjects or on many aspects of one subject, typically arranged alphabetically.
– ORIGIN mock Greek *enkuklopaideia,* for *enkuklios paideia* 'all-round education.'

en·cy·clo·pe·dic /en,sīklə'pēdik/ ▸ **adjective 1** having detailed information on a wide variety of subjects: *an encyclopedic knowledge of food.* **2** relating to encyclopedias or information suitable for an encyclopedia.

en·cy·clo·pe·dist /en,sīklə'pēdist/ ▸ **noun** a person who writes, edits, or contributes to an encyclopedia.

end /end/ ▸ **noun 1** the final part of something. **2** the furthest part of something. **3** the stopping of a state or situation: *they called for an end to violence.* **4** a person's death or downfall. **5** a goal or desired result. **6** a part or share of an activity: *your end of the deal.* **7** a small piece that is left after use. **8** the part of an athletic field or court defended by one team or player.

– SYNONYMS **1 conclusion,** termination, ending, finish, close, resolution, climax, finale, culmination, denouement. **2 extremity,** limit, edge, border, boundary, periphery, point, tip, head, top, bottom. **3 aim,** goal, purpose, objective, object, target, intention, aspiration, wish, desire, ambition.
– ANTONYMS beginning, means.

▸ **verb 1** come or bring to an end; finish. **2** (**end in**) have something as its result: *the match ended in a draw.* **3** (**end up**) eventually reach or come to a particular state or place.

– SYNONYMS **1 finish,** conclude, terminate, close, stop, cease, culminate, climax. **2 break off,** call off, bring to an end, put an end to, stop, finish, terminate, discontinue, cancel.
– ANTONYMS begin.

– PHRASES **be the end** informal be the limit of what one can tolerate. **end it all** commit suicide. **the end of one's rope** having no patience or energy left. **in the end** eventually. **keep** (or **hold**) **one's end up** informal perform well in a demanding situation. **make** (**both**) **ends meet** earn just enough money to live on. **no end** informal very much. **no end of** informal a vast number or amount of. **on end 1** continuously. **2** upright.
– ORIGIN Old English.

en·dan·ger /en'dānjər/ ▸ **verb** put someone or something in danger.

– SYNONYMS **jeopardize,** risk, put at risk, put in danger, be a danger to, threaten, compromise, imperil.
– ANTONYMS safeguard.

– DERIVATIVES **en·dan·ger·ment** noun.

en·dan·gered /en'dānjərd/ ▸ **adjective** in danger of becoming extinct.

en·dear /en'di(ə)r/ ▸ **verb** make someone popular or well liked: *her personality endeared her to everyone.*

en·dear·ing /en'di(ə)rɪɴɢ/ ▸ **adjective** inspiring affection.

> – SYNONYMS **charming,** appealing, attractive, engaging, winning, captivating, enchanting, cute, sweet, delightful, lovely.

– DERIVATIVES **en·dear·ing·ly** adverb.

en·dear·ment /en'di(ə)rmənt/ ▸ **noun 1** a word or phrase expressing love or affection. **2** love or affection.

en·deav·or /en'devər/ ▸ **verb** try hard to do or achieve something.

> – SYNONYMS **try,** attempt, seek, strive, struggle, labor, toil, work.

▸ **noun 1** a serious attempt to achieve something. **2** serious and prolonged effort: *the museum's treasures spanned forty thousand years of human endeavor.*

> – SYNONYMS **1 attempt,** try, bid, effort. **2 undertaking,** enterprise, venture, exercise, activity, exploit, deed, act, action, move.

– ORIGIN from the former phrase *put oneself in devoir* 'do one's utmost.'

en·dem·ic /en'demik/ ▸ **adjective 1** (of a disease or condition) regularly found among particular people or in a certain area. **2** (of a plant or animal) native or restricted to a certain area.
– DERIVATIVES **en·de·mism** /'endəˌmizəm/ noun.
– ORIGIN Greek *endēmios* 'native.'

end·game /'en(d)ˌgām/ ▸ **noun** the final stage of a game such as chess or bridge, when few pieces or cards remain.

end·ing /'endiɴɢ/ ▸ **noun** an end or final part.

> – SYNONYMS **end,** finish, close, conclusion, resolution, summing-up, denouement, finale.
> – ANTONYMS beginning.

en·dive /'enˌdīv, 'änˌdēv/ ▸ **noun 1** a plant with bitter curly or smooth leaves, eaten in salads. **2** (also **Belgian endive**) a chicory crown.
– ORIGIN Old French.

end·less /'en(d)ləs/ ▸ **adjective 1** seeming to have no limits in size or amount: *the possibilities are endless.* **2** continuing indefinitely: *video screens showing endless catwalk shows.* **3** (of a belt, chain, or tape) having the ends joined to allow for continuous action.

> – SYNONYMS **1 unlimited,** limitless, infinite, inexhaustible, boundless, unbounded, ceaseless, unending, everlasting, constant, continuous, interminable, unfailing, perpetual, eternal, never-ending. **2 countless,** innumerable, numerous, a multitude of; informal umpteen, no end of; literary myriad.
> – ANTONYMS limited, few.

– DERIVATIVES **end·less·ly** adverb **end·less·ness** noun.

> **CHOOSE THE RIGHT WORD**
>
> See **ETERNAL**.

end·most /'en(d)ˌmōst/ ▸ **adjective** nearest to the end.

endo- ▸ **combining form** internal; within: *endoderm.*
– ORIGIN from Greek *endon* 'within.'

en·do·crine /'endəkrin/ ▸ **adjective** (of a gland) producing hormones or other products directly into the blood.
– ORIGIN from Greek *krinein* 'sift.'

en·do·cri·nol·o·gy /ˌendəkrə'näləjē/ ▸ **noun** the branch of physiology and medicine concerned with endocrine glands and hormones.
– DERIVATIVES **en·do·cri·nol·o·gist** noun.

en·dog·e·nous /en'däjənəs/ ▸ **adjective** technical relating to an internal cause or origin. Often contrasted with **EXOGENOUS**.
– DERIVATIVES **en·dog·e·nous·ly** adverb.

en·do·me·tri·o·sis /ˌendōˌmētrē'ōsis/ ▸ **noun** a condition in which tissue from the mucous membrane lining the uterus appears outside it, causing pelvic pain.

en·do·me·tri·um /ˌendō'mētrēəm/ ▸ **noun** the mucous membrane lining the uterus.
– DERIVATIVES **en·do·me·tri·al** adjective.
– ORIGIN from Greek *mētra* 'womb.'

en·do·morph /'endəˌmôrf/ ▸ **noun** Physiology a person with a soft round body build and a high proportion of fat tissue. Compare with **ECTOMORPH** and **MESOMORPH**.

en·dor·phin /en'dôrfin/ ▸ **noun** any of a group of chemical compounds produced in the body that have a painkilling effect.
– ORIGIN blend of **ENDOGENOUS** and **MORPHINE**.

en·dorse /en'dôrs/ ▸ **verb 1** declare one's public approval of someone or something. **2** sign a check on the back to specify another person as the payee or to accept responsibility for paying it.

> – SYNONYMS **support,** back, agree with, approve (of), favor, subscribe to, recommend, champion, uphold, sanction.
> – ANTONYMS oppose.

– DERIVATIVES **en·dors·a·ble** adjective **en·dors·er** noun.
– ORIGIN Latin *indorsare*.

en·dorse·ment /en'dôrsmənt/ ▸ **noun 1** a declaration of approval: *the president's endorsement of the plan.* **2** the action of endorsing a check or bill of exchange.

> – SYNONYMS **support,** backing, approval, seal of approval, agreement, recommendation, patronage, sanction.

en·do·scope /'endəˌskōp/ ▸ **noun** an instrument that can be introduced into the body to view its internal parts.
– DERIVATIVES **en·do·scop·ic** /ˌendə'skäpik/ adjective **en·do·scop·i·cal·ly** /ˌendə'skäpik(ə)lē/ adverb **en·dos·co·py** /en'däskəpē/ noun.

en·do·skel·e·ton /ˌendō'skelitn/ ▸ **noun** an internal skeleton, such as that of vertebrates.

en·do·sperm /'endəˌspərm/ ▸ **noun** the part of a seed that acts as a food store for the developing plant embryo.

en·do·ther·mic /ˌendə'ᴛʜərmik/ ▸ **adjective** (of a chemical reaction) accompanied by the absorption of heat.

en·dow /en'dou/ ▸ **verb 1** provide a person or institution with an income or property, especially by a bequest in a will. **2** provide with a quality, ability, or feature: *these singers are endowed with magnificent voices.* **3** establish a university post, annual prize, etc., by donating funds.

> – SYNONYMS **1 finance,** fund, pay for, subsidize, sponsor. **2** *he was endowed with great strength* **provide,** supply, furnish, equip, favor, bless, grace.

– ORIGIN Old French *endouer*.

en·dow·ment /en'doumənt/ ▸ **noun 1** money given to a college or other institution to provide it with an income. **2** a natural quality or ability.

– SYNONYMS **gift,** present, grant, funding, award, donation, contribution, subsidy, sponsorship, bequest, legacy.

▶ **adjective** referring to a form of life insurance involving payment of a fixed sum to the insured person on a specified date, or to their estate should they die before this date.

end·pa·per /'en(d),pāpər/ ▶ **noun** a leaf of paper at the beginning or end of a book, fixed to the inside of the cover.

end·point /'en(d),point/ (also **end point**) ▶ **noun** the final stage of a period or process.

en·due /en'd(y)o͞o/ ▶ **verb** (**endues, enduing, endued**) literary (usu. **be endued with**) provide someone or something with a quality or ability.
– ORIGIN Old French *enduire.*

en·dur·ance /en'd(y)o͝orəns/ ▶ **noun 1** the ability to endure something unpleasant and prolonged. **2** the capacity of something to withstand prolonged wear and tear.

– SYNONYMS **1 toleration,** tolerance, forbearance, patience, acceptance, resignation, stoicism. **2 resistance,** durability, permanence, longevity, strength, toughness, stamina, staying power, fortitude.

en·dure /en'd(y)o͝or/ ▶ **verb 1** suffer something unpleasant and prolonged patiently. **2** remain in existence.

– SYNONYMS **1 undergo,** go through, live through, experience, cope with, deal with, face, suffer, tolerate, put up with, brave, bear, withstand. **2 last,** live, live on, go on, survive, abide, continue, persist, remain.

– DERIVATIVES **en·dur·a·ble** adjective.
– ORIGIN Latin *indurare* 'harden.'

end-us·er ▶ **noun** the person who uses a particular product.

end·ways /'en(d),wāz/ (also **endwise**) ▶ **adverb** with the end facing upward, forward, or toward the viewer.

ENE ▶ **abbreviation** east-northeast.

en·e·ma /'enəmə/ ▶ **noun** a medical procedure in which fluid is injected into the rectum, especially to empty it.
– ORIGIN Greek.

en·e·my /'enəmē/ ▶ **noun** (pl. **enemies**) **1** a person who is actively opposed or hostile to someone or something. **2** (**the enemy**) (treated as sing. or pl.) a hostile nation or its armed forces in wartime. **3** a thing that damages or opposes something: *boredom is the great enemy of happiness.*

– SYNONYMS **opponent,** adversary, rival, antagonist, combatant, challenger, competitor, opposition, competition, the other side; literary foe.
– ANTONYMS friend, ally.

– ORIGIN Latin *inimicus.*

en·er·get·ic /,enər'jetik/ ▶ **adjective** showing or involving great energy or activity.

– SYNONYMS **1** *an energetic woman* **active,** lively, dynamic, spirited, animated, bouncy, bubbly, sprightly, tireless, indefatigable, enthusiastic; informal full of beans. **2** *energetic exercises* **vigorous,** strenuous, brisk, hard, arduous, demanding, taxing, tough, rigorous. **3** *an energetic advertising campaign* **forceful,** vigorous, aggressive, hard-hitting, high-powered, all-out, determined, bold, intensive; informal in-your-face.
– ANTONYMS lethargic.

– DERIVATIVES **en·er·get·i·cal·ly** adverb.
– ORIGIN from Greek *energein* 'operate, work in or upon.'

en·er·gy /'enərjē/ ▶ **noun** (pl. **energies**) **1** the strength and vitality required to keep active: *she had boundless energy and a zest for life.* **2** (**energies**) the physical and mental effort that is put into something. **3** power derived from physical or chemical resources to provide light and heat or to work machines. **4** Physics the capacity of matter and radiation to perform work.

– SYNONYMS **vitality,** vigor, strength, stamina, animation, spirit, verve, enthusiasm, zest, exuberance, dynamism, drive; informal punch, bounce, oomph, go, get-up-and-go.

– DERIVATIVES **en·er·gize** /'enər,jīz/ verb.
– ORIGIN Greek *energeia.*

en·er·vate /'enər,vāt/ ▶ **verb** make someone feel drained of energy.
– DERIVATIVES **en·er·va·tion** /,enər'vāshən/ noun.
– ORIGIN Latin *enervare* 'weaken (by extraction of the sinews).'

en·fant ter·ri·ble /äN,fäN te'rēbl(ə)/ ▶ **noun** (pl. **enfants terribles** pronunc. same) a person who behaves in an unconventional or controversial way.
– ORIGIN French, 'terrible child.'

en·fee·ble /en'fēbəl/ ▶ **verb** weaken someone or something.
– DERIVATIVES **en·fee·ble·ment** noun.

en·fi·lade /'enfə,lād, -,läd/ ▶ **noun** a volley of gunfire directed along a line of soldiers from end to end. ▶ **verb** direct a volley of gunfire along a line of soldiers.
– ORIGIN French.

en·fold /en'fōld/ ▶ **verb** surround or envelop someone or something.

en·force /en'fôrs/ ▶ **verb 1** make sure that a law, rule, or duty is obeyed or fulfilled. **2** (often as adj. **enforced**) force or require something to happen: *months of enforced idleness.*

– SYNONYMS **1 impose,** apply, administer, carry out, implement, bring to bear, put into effect. **2 force,** compel, coerce, exact.

– DERIVATIVES **en·force·a·ble** adjective **en·force·ment** noun **en·forc·er** noun.

en·fran·chise /en'fran,CHīz/ ▶ **verb 1** give the right to vote to someone. **2** historical free a slave.
– DERIVATIVES **en·fran·chise·ment** noun.

en·gage /en'gāj/ ▶ **verb 1** attract or involve someone's interest or attention. **2** (**engage in/with**) participate or become involved in: *he was engaged in a lively conversation with the barber.* **3** employ someone. **4** promise to do something. **5** enter into combat with an enemy force. **6** (of a part of a machine or engine) move into position so as to come into operation.

– SYNONYMS **1 capture,** catch, arrest, grab, draw, attract, gain, hold, grip, absorb, occupy. **2 employ,** hire, recruit, take on, enroll, appoint. **3** *the chance to engage in in a wide range of pursuits* **participate in,** join in, take part in, partake in/of, enter into, embark on. **4 attack,** fall on, take on, clash with, encounter, meet, fight, do battle with.
– ANTONYMS lose, dismiss.

– ORIGIN French *engager.*

en·gaged /en'gājd/ ▶ **adjective 1** busy; occupied. **2** having formally agreed to marry. **3** Brit. (of a telephone line) unavailable because already in use; busy.

CHOOSE THE RIGHT WORD

See **BUSY**.

en·gage·ment /en'gājmənt/ ▶ **noun 1** a formal agreement to get married. **2** an appointment. **3** the state of being involved in something. **4** a battle between armed forces.

– SYNONYMS **1 appointment,** meeting, arrangement, commitment, date, assignation, rendezvous. **2 participation,** involvement. **3 battle,** fight, clash, confrontation, encounter, conflict, skirmish, action, hostilities.

en·gag·ing /en'gājiNG/ ▶ **adjective** charming and attractive.

– SYNONYMS **charming,** attractive, appealing, pleasing, pleasant, agreeable, likable, lovable, sweet, winning, fetching; Scottish bonny.
– ANTONYMS unappealing.

– DERIVATIVES **en·gag·ing·ly** adverb.

en·gen·der /en'jendər/ ▶ **verb** give rise to a feeling, situation, or condition.

– SYNONYMS **cause,** give rise to, bring about, occasion, lead to, result in, produce, create, generate, arouse, rouse, inspire, provoke, kindle, trigger, spark, stir up, whip up.

– ORIGIN Old French *engendrer*.

en·gine /'enjən/ ▶ **noun 1** a machine with moving parts that converts power into motion. **2** a railroad locomotive. **3** historical a mechanical device, especially one used in warfare: *a siege engine*.

– SYNONYMS **motor,** generator, machine, turbine.

– DERIVATIVES **en·gine·less** adjective.
– ORIGIN Latin *ingenium* 'talent, device.'

en·gi·neer /,enjə'ni(ə)r/ ▶ **noun 1** a person who designs, builds, or maintains engines, machines, or structures. **2** a person who controls an engine, especially on an aircraft or ship. **3** a person who cleverly plans something.

– SYNONYMS **1** *a structural engineer* **designer,** planner, builder. **2** *a repair engineer* **mechanic,** repairer, technician, maintenance man, operator, driver.

▶ **verb 1** design and build a machine or structure. **2** cleverly plan something: *she engineered another meeting with him*.

– SYNONYMS **bring about,** arrange, pull off, bring off, contrive, maneuver, negotiate, organize, orchestrate, plan, mastermind.

en·gi·neer·ing /,enjə'ni(ə)riNG/ ▶ **noun 1** the branch of science and technology concerned with the design, building, and use of engines, machines, and structures. **2** an area of study or activity concerned with development in a particular area: *software engineering*.

Eng·lish /'iNG(g)lisH/ ▶ **noun** the language of England, now used in many varieties throughout the world. ▶ **adjective** relating to England.

– DERIVATIVES **Eng·lish·ness** noun.

Eng·lish break·fast ▶ **noun** a substantial cooked breakfast, typically including bacon and eggs.

Eng·lish·man /'iNG(g)lisH,mən/ (or **Englishwoman** /'iNG(g)lisH,wo͝omən/) ▶ **noun** (pl. **Englishmen** or **Englishwomen**) a person from England.

Eng·lish muf·fin ▶ **noun** a flat, circular, spongy bread roll made from yeast dough and eaten split, toasted, and buttered.

en·gorge /en'gôrj/ ▶ **verb** (often as adj. **engorged**) swell or cause to swell with blood, water, etc.

– DERIVATIVES **en·gorge·ment** noun.
– ORIGIN Old French *engorgier* 'feed to excess.'

en·grained /en'grānd/ ▶ **adjective** variant spelling of **INGRAINED**.

en·grave /en'grāv/ ▶ **verb 1** cut or carve words or a design on a hard surface. **2** cut a design as lines on a metal plate for printing. **3** (**be engraved on** or **in**) be permanently fixed in one's mind.

– DERIVATIVES **en·grav·er** noun.
– ORIGIN from **GRAVE**[3].

en·grav·ing /en'grāviNG/ ▶ **noun 1** a print made from an engraved plate, block, or other surface. **2** the process or art of cutting or carving a design on a hard surface.

– SYNONYMS **etching,** print, plate, picture, illustration, inscription.

en·gross /en'grōs/ ▶ **verb** involve or occupy someone completely: *the notes totally engrossed him*.

– SYNONYMS **absorb,** engage, involve, interest, occupy, preoccupy, rivet, grip, fascinate, captivate, enthrall.

– DERIVATIVES **en·gross·ing** adjective.
– ORIGIN from Latin *in grosso* 'wholesale.'

en·gulf /en'gəlf/ ▶ **verb 1** (of a natural force) sweep over something so as to completely surround or cover it. **2** (of a feeling) powerfully affect or overwhelm someone.

– SYNONYMS **swamp,** inundate, flood, deluge, immerse, swallow up, submerge, bury, envelop, overwhelm.

– DERIVATIVES **en·gulf·ment** noun.

en·hance /en'hans/ ▶ **verb** increase the quality, value, or extent of: *the system is intended to enhance the user's online shopping experience*.

– SYNONYMS **improve,** add to, strengthen, boost, increase, intensify, heighten, magnify, amplify, inflate, build up, supplement, augment.
– ANTONYMS diminish.

– DERIVATIVES **en·hance·ment** noun **en·hanc·er** noun.
– ORIGIN Old French *enhauncer*.

e·nig·ma /i'nigmə/ ▶ **noun** a person or thing that is mysterious or difficult to understand.

– SYNONYMS **mystery,** puzzle, riddle, conundrum, paradox.

– ORIGIN Greek *ainigma* 'riddle.'

CHOOSE THE RIGHT WORD

See **RIDDLE**[1].

en·ig·mat·ic /,enig'matik/ ▶ **adjective** difficult to understand; mysterious: *an enigmatic smile*.

– DERIVATIVES **en·ig·mat·i·cal** adjective **en·ig·mat·i·cal·ly** /-(ə)lē/ adverb.

en·join /en'join/ ▶ **verb 1** instruct or urge someone to do something. **2** (**enjoin someone from**) Law prohibit someone from performing an action by an injunction.

– ORIGIN Old French *enjoindre*.

CHOOSE THE RIGHT WORD

See **PROHIBIT**.

en·joy /en'joi/ ▸ verb **1** take pleasure in an activity or occasion. **2** (**enjoy oneself**) have a pleasant time. **3** possess and benefit from: *these professions enjoy high status.*

– SYNONYMS **1 like,** be fond of, take pleasure in, be keen on, delight in, relish, revel in, adore, lap up, savor, luxuriate in, bask in; informal get a thrill out of. **2** (**enjoy oneself**) **have fun,** have a good time, make merry, celebrate, revel; informal party, have a whale of a time, let one's hair down. **3 benefit from,** be blessed with, be favored with, be endowed with, possess, own, boast.
– ANTONYMS dislike, lack.

– ORIGIN Old French *enjoier* 'give joy to' or *enjoïr* 'enjoy.'

en·joy·a·ble /en'joi-əbəl/ ▸ adjective giving delight or pleasure.

– SYNONYMS **entertaining,** amusing, delightful, pleasant, congenial, convivial, agreeable, pleasurable, satisfying.
– ANTONYMS disagreeable.

– DERIVATIVES **en·joy·a·bil·i·ty** /en,joi-ə'bilitē/ noun **en·joy·a·bly** adverb.

en·joy·ment /en'joimənt/ ▸ noun **1** the state or process of taking pleasure in something: *the weather didn't mar our enjoyment of the trip.* **2** a thing that gives pleasure. **3** the fact of having and benefiting from something.

– SYNONYMS **pleasure,** fun, entertainment, amusement, recreation, relaxation, happiness, merriment, joy, satisfaction, liking.

en·large /en'lärj/ ▸ verb **1** make or become bigger. **2** (**enlarge on**) speak or write about something in greater detail.

– SYNONYMS **1 extend,** expand, grow, add to, amplify, augment, magnify, build up, stretch, widen, broaden, lengthen, elongate, deepen, thicken. **2 swell,** distend, bloat, bulge, dilate, blow up, puff up. **3** (**enlarge on**) **elaborate on,** expand on, add to, flesh out, add detail to, develop, fill out, embellish, embroider.
– ANTONYMS reduce, shrink.

– DERIVATIVES **en·larg·er** noun.

en·large·ment /en'lärjmənt/ ▸ noun **1** the action of enlarging something or the state of being enlarged. **2** a photograph that is larger than the original negative or than an earlier print.

en·light·en /en'lītn/ ▸ verb **1** give someone greater knowledge and understanding about something. **2** (as adj. **enlightened**) rational, tolerant, and well informed.

– SYNONYMS **1 inform,** tell, make aware, open someone's eyes, illuminate; informal put someone in the picture. **2** (as adj. **enlightened**) **informed,** aware, sophisticated, liberal, tolerant, open-minded, broad-minded, educated, knowledgeable, rational, civilized, refined, cultured.

en·light·en·ment /en'lītnmənt/ ▸ noun **1** the gaining of knowledge and understanding. **2** (**the Enlightenment**) a European intellectual movement of the late 17th and 18th centuries emphasizing reason and individualism rather than tradition.

– SYNONYMS **insight,** understanding, awareness, education, learning, knowledge, illumination, awakening, instruction, teaching, open-mindedness, broad-mindedness, culture, refinement, cultivation, civilization.

en·list /en'list/ ▸ verb **1** enroll or be enrolled in the armed services. **2** ask for someone's help in doing something.

– SYNONYMS **1 join up,** enroll, sign up, volunteer, register. **2 recruit,** call up, enroll, sign up, draft, conscript, mobilize. **3 obtain,** engage, secure, win, get.
– ANTONYMS discharge, demobilize.

– DERIVATIVES **en·list·ee** /,enlist'ē/ noun **en·list·ment** noun.

en·list·ed man ▸ noun a member of the armed forces below the rank of officer.

en·liv·en /en'līvən/ ▸ verb **1** make more interesting or appealing: *the vegetables are enlivened by a spicy coconut sauce.* **2** make someone more cheerful or lively.

– SYNONYMS **1** *a meeting enlivened by her wit* **liven up,** spice up; informal perk up, pep up. **2** *the visit had enlivened my mother* **cheer up,** brighten up, liven up, perk up, raise someone's spirits, uplift, gladden, buoy up, animate, vivify, vitalize, invigorate, restore, revive, refresh, stimulate, rouse, boost; informal buck up, pep up.

en masse /än 'mas/ ▸ adverb all together.
– ORIGIN French, 'in a mass.'

en·mesh /en'mesн/ ▸ verb (usu. **be enmeshed in**) entangle someone or something.

en·mi·ty /'enmitē/ ▸ noun (pl. **enmities**) the state of being an enemy; hostility.

– SYNONYMS **hostility,** animosity, antagonism, friction, antipathy, animus, acrimony, bitterness, rancor, resentment, ill feeling, bad feeling, ill will, bad blood, hatred, loathing, odium.
– ANTONYMS friendship.

– ORIGIN Old French *enemistie.*

en·no·ble /en'nōbəl/ ▸ verb **1** give someone a noble rank or title. **2** give greater dignity to: *ennoble the mind and uplift the spirit.*
– DERIVATIVES **en·no·ble·ment** noun.

en·nui /än'wē/ ▸ noun listlessness and dissatisfaction arising from boredom.
– ORIGIN French.

e·nol·o·gy /ē'näləjē/ ▸ noun the study of wines.
– DERIVATIVES **e·no·log·i·cal** /,ēnə'läjikəl/ adjective **e·nol·o·gist** /-jist/ noun.
– ORIGIN from Greek *oinos* 'wine.'

e·nor·mi·ty /i'nôrmitē/ ▸ noun (pl. **enormities**) **1** (**the enormity of**) the extreme seriousness or extent of something bad. **2** great size or scale: *he shook his head at the enormity of the task.* **3** a serious crime or sin.

– SYNONYMS **1 wickedness,** vileness, heinousness, baseness, depravity, outrageousness. **2 immensity,** hugeness, size, extent, magnitude.

– ORIGIN Latin *enormitas,* from *norma* 'pattern, standard.'

USAGE

The earliest meaning of **enormity** was 'a crime' and some people therefore object to its use in modern English as another way of saying **immensity** (as in *the enormity of the task*). However, this use is now broadly accepted in standard English.

e·nor·mous /i'nôrməs/ ▸ adjective very large; huge.

– SYNONYMS **huge,** vast, immense, gigantic, giant, massive, colossal, mammoth, tremendous, extensive, mighty, monumental, mountainous; informal mega, monster, whopping, ginormous.
– ANTONYMS tiny.

– DERIVATIVES **e·nor·mous·ly** adverb **e·nor·mous·ness** noun.

e·nough /i'nəf/ ▶ **determiner & pronoun** as much or as many as is necessary or desirable.

– SYNONYMS **1** *they had enough food* **sufficient,** adequate, ample, abundant, the necessary; informal plenty of. **2** *there's enough for everyone* **sufficient,** plenty, an adequate amount, as much as necessary, a sufficiency, an ample supply, one's fill.
– ANTONYMS insufficient.

▶ **adverb 1** to the required degree or extent. **2** to a moderate degree.
– PHRASES **enough is enough** no more will be tolerated.
– ORIGIN Old English.

en pas·sant /ˌän pä'sänt, äɴ pä'säɴ/ ▶ **adverb** by the way; in passing.
– ORIGIN French.

en·quire, etc. /en'kwīr/ ▶ **verb** chiefly British spelling of **INQUIRE**, etc.

en·rage /en'rāj/ ▶ **verb** make someone very angry.

– SYNONYMS **1** *the students were enraged at these new rules* **anger,** infuriate, incense, madden, inflame, antagonize, provoke; informal drive mad/crazy, make someone see red, make someone's blood boil. **2** (as adj. **enraged**) *an enraged mob* **furious,** infuriated, irate, incensed, raging, incandescent, fuming, seething, beside oneself; informal mad, livid, foaming at the mouth.
– ANTONYMS placate.

en·rap·ture /en'rapcHər/ ▶ **verb** give great pleasure to someone.
– DERIVATIVES **en·rapt** /en'rapt/ adjective.

en·rich/ en'ricH/ ▶ **verb 1** improve the quality or value of: *photography has enriched my life.* **2** make someone wealthy or wealthier.

– SYNONYMS **enhance,** improve, better, add to, augment, supplement, complement, refine.

– DERIVATIVES **en·rich·ment** noun.

en·riched u·ra·ni·um ▶ **noun** uranium containing an increased proportion of the fissile isotope U-235, making it more explosive.

en·roll /en'rōl/ (Brit. **enrol**) ▶ **verb** officially register or recruit someone as a member or student.

– SYNONYMS **1 register,** sign on/up, put one's name down, apply, volunteer, enter, join. **2 accept,** admit, take on, sign on/up, recruit, engage.

– ORIGIN Old French *enroller.*

en·roll·ment /en'rōlmənt/ (Brit. **enrolment**) ▶ **noun 1** the action of enrolling or being enrolled. **2** the number of people enrolled.

en route /än 'ro͞ot, en, äɴ/ ▶ **adverb** on the way.
– ORIGIN French.

en·sconce /en'skäns/ ▶ **verb** settle in a comfortable, safe, or secret place: *he was ensconced in a conference room.*
– ORIGIN from former *sconce*, referring to a small fort or earthwork.

en·sem·ble /än'sämbəl/ ▶ **noun 1** a group of musicians, actors, or dancers who perform together. **2** a group of items viewed as a whole, in particular a set of clothes worn together. **3** a musical passage for a whole choir or group of instruments.

– SYNONYMS **1 group,** band, company, troupe, cast, chorus, corps; informal combo. **2 whole,** unit, body, set, collection, combination, composite, package. **3 outfit,** costume, suit; informal getup.

– ORIGIN French.

en·shrine /en'sHrīn/ ▶ **verb 1** preserve a right, tradition, or idea in a form that ensures it will be respected: *the train operators claim that their subsidy is enshrined in European law.* **2** place a holy or precious object in an appropriate place or container.
– DERIVATIVES **en·shrine·ment** noun.

en·shroud /en'sHroud/ ▶ **verb** literary envelop something completely and hide it from view.

en·sign /'ensən, 'enˌsīn/ ▶ **noun 1** a flag, especially a military or naval one indicating nationality. **2** the lowest rank of commissioned officer in the US Navy and Coast Guard, above chief warrant officer and below lieutenant.
– ORIGIN Old French *enseigne.*

en·slave /en'slāv/ ▶ **verb 1** make someone a slave. **2** make someone completely dominated by something.
– DERIVATIVES **en·slave·ment** noun **en·slav·er** noun.

en·snare /en'sner/ ▶ **verb** put someone in a difficult situation or under the control of another.

– SYNONYMS *the larvae construct pits to ensnare their prey* **capture,** catch, trap, entrap, snare, net; entangle, embroil, enmesh.

en·sue /en'so͞o/ ▶ **verb** (**ensues, ensuing, ensued**) happen afterward or as a result: *once the auction starts, pandemonium ensues.*

– SYNONYMS **result,** follow, develop, succeed, emerge, arise, proceed, stem.

– ORIGIN Old French *ensivre.*

en·sure /en'sHo͝or/ ▶ **verb 1** make certain that something will occur or be so. **2** (**ensure against**) make sure that a problem does not occur.

– SYNONYMS **1 make sure,** make certain, see to it, check, confirm, establish, verify. **2 secure,** guarantee, assure, certify.

– ORIGIN Old French *enseurer.*

USAGE

On the difference between **ensure** and **insure**, see the note at **INSURE**.

ENT ▶ **abbreviation** ear, nose, and throat (as a department in a hospital).

en·tab·la·ture /en'tabləcHər, -ˌcHo͝or/ ▶ **noun** Architecture the upper part of a classical building supported by columns, comprising the architrave, frieze, and cornice.
– ORIGIN Italian *intavolatura* 'boarding.'

en·tail /en'tāl/ ▶ **verb 1** involve something as an unavoidable part or consequence: *any major surgery entails a certain degree of risk.* **2** Law limit the inheritance of property over a number of generations so that ownership remains within a family or group.

– SYNONYMS **involve,** necessitate, require, need, demand, call for, mean, imply, cause, give rise to, occasion.

– DERIVATIVES **en·tail·ment** noun.
– ORIGIN from Old French *taille* 'notch, tax.'

en·tan·gle /en'taNGgəl/ ▶ **verb** (usu. **be entangled in/with**) **1** make something tangled. **2** involve someone in a complicated situation.

– SYNONYMS **1** *their parachutes became entangled* **twist,** intertwine, entwine, tangle, snarl, knot, coil. **2** *he was entangled in a lawsuit* **involve,** embroil, mix up, catch up, bog down, mire.

en·tan·gle·ment /en'taNGgəlmənt/ ▶ **noun 1** a complicated or compromising relationship or situation. **2** a barrier, typically made of stakes and barbed wire, placed to impede enemy soldiers or vehicles.

en·tente /än'tänt/ (also **entente cordiale** /kôr'dyäl/) ▶ **noun** a friendly understanding or informal alliance between countries.
– ORIGIN from French *entente cordiale* 'friendly understanding.'

en·ter /'entər/ ▶ **verb 1** come or go into a place. **2** (often **enter into**) begin to be involved in or do something: *the firm entered into talks to join the consortium.* **3** join an institution or profession. **4** register as a participant in a competition, exam, etc. **5** (**enter into**) undertake to be bound by an agreement. **6** write or key information in a book, computer, etc.

– SYNONYMS **1 go into,** come into, get into, set foot in, gain access to. **2 penetrate,** pierce, puncture, perforate. **3 join,** enroll in, enlist in, volunteer for, sign up for. **4 go in for,** register for, enroll for, sign on/up for, compete in, take part in, participate in. **5 record,** write, put down, take down, note, jot down, register, log. **6 key (in),** type (in).
– ANTONYMS leave.

– ORIGIN Old French *entrer*.

en·ter·ic /en'terik/ ▶ **adjective** relating to or occurring in the intestines.
– ORIGIN Greek *enterikos*.

en·ter·i·tis /ˌentə'rītis/ ▶ **noun** inflammation of the small intestine, usually accompanied by diarrhea.

en·ter·o·vi·rus /ˌentərō'vīrəs/ ▶ **noun** any of a group of RNA viruses (including those causing polio and hepatitis A) that typically occur in the gastrointestinal tract, sometimes spreading to the central nervous system or other parts of the body.

en·ter·prise /'entərˌprīz/ ▶ **noun 1** a large project. **2** a business or company. **3** initiative and resourcefulness: *their success was thanks to a mixture of talent and enterprise.*

– SYNONYMS **1 undertaking,** endeavor, venture, exercise, activity, operation, task, business, project, scheme. **2 initiative,** resourcefulness, imagination, ingenuity, inventiveness, originality, creativity. **3 business,** company, firm, venture, organization, operation, concern, establishment; informal outfit.

– ORIGIN Old French, 'something undertaken.'

en·ter·pris·ing /'entərˌprīziNG/ ▶ **adjective** showing initiative and resourcefulness.

– SYNONYMS **resourceful,** entrepreneurial, imaginative, ingenious, inventive, creative, adventurous, bold; informal go-ahead.

– DERIVATIVES **en·ter·pris·ing·ly** adverb.

en·ter·tain /ˌentər'tān/ ▶ **verb 1** provide someone with amusement or enjoyment. **2** receive someone as a guest and give them food and drink. **3** give consideration to: *I entertained little hope of success.*

– SYNONYMS **1 amuse,** please, charm, cheer, interest, engage, occupy. **2 receive,** play host/hostess to, throw a party for, wine and dine, feed, fete. **3 consider,** contemplate, think of, countenance.
– ANTONYMS bore, reject.

– ORIGIN French *entretenir*.

en·ter·tain·er /ˌentər'tānər/ ▶ **noun** a person, such as a singer or comedian, whose job is to entertain others.

en·ter·tain·ing /ˌentər'tāniNG/ ▶ **adjective** providing amusement or enjoyment.
– DERIVATIVES **en·ter·tain·ing·ly** adverb.

en·ter·tain·ment /ˌentər'tānmənt/ ▶ **noun 1** the provision of amusement or enjoyment. **2** an event or performance designed to entertain people.

– SYNONYMS **amusement,** pleasure, leisure, recreation, relaxation, fun, enjoyment, diversion, interest.

en·thrall /en'THrôl/ ▶ **verb** fascinate someone and hold their attention.

– SYNONYMS *the exhibit enthralled me* **captivate,** charm, enchant, bewitch, fascinate, beguile, entrance, delight; win, ensnare, absorb, engross, rivet, grip, transfix, hypnotize, mesmerize, spellbind.

– DERIVATIVES **en·thrall·ment** noun.

en·throne /en'THrōn/ ▶ **verb** mark the new reign or period of office of a monarch or bishop by a ceremony in which they sit on a throne.
– DERIVATIVES **en·throne·ment** noun.

en·thuse /en'THo͞oz/ ▶ **verb 1** express great enthusiasm for something: *they enthused over my new look.* **2** make someone interested and enthusiastic.

en·thu·si·asm /en'THo͞ozēˌazəm/ ▶ **noun 1** great enjoyment, interest, or approval. **2** something that arouses enthusiasm.

– SYNONYMS **keenness,** eagerness, passion, fervor, zeal, zest, gusto, energy, vigor, fire, spirit, interest, commitment, devotion; informal get-up-and-go.
– ANTONYMS apathy.

– ORIGIN Greek *enthous* 'possessed by a god.'

en·thu·si·ast /en'THo͞ozēˌast/ ▶ **noun** a person who is full of enthusiasm for something.

– SYNONYMS **fan,** devotee, supporter, follower, aficionado, lover, admirer; informal buff.

en·thu·si·as·tic /enˌTHo͞ozē'astik/ ▶ **adjective** having or showing great enjoyment, interest, or approval.

– SYNONYMS **keen,** eager, avid, ardent, fervent, passionate, zealous, excited, wholehearted, committed, devoted, fanatical, earnest.
– ANTONYMS apathetic.

– DERIVATIVES **en·thu·si·as·ti·cal·ly** adverb.

en·tice /en'tīs/ ▶ **verb** persuade someone to do something by offering something pleasant or beneficial.

– SYNONYMS **tempt,** lure, attract, appeal to, invite, persuade, beguile, coax, woo, lead on, seduce; informal sweet-talk.

– DERIVATIVES **en·tice·ment** noun **en·tic·ing** adjective.
– ORIGIN Old French *enticier*.

CHOOSE THE RIGHT WORD

See **TEMPT**.

en·tire /en'tīr/ ▶ **adjective** including everything, everyone, or every part; whole.

– SYNONYMS **whole,** complete, total, full.

– ORIGIN Old French *entier*.

en·tire·ly /en'tīrlē/ ▸ **adverb** wholly; completely.

– SYNONYMS **1 absolutely,** completely, totally, wholly, utterly, quite, altogether, thoroughly. **2 solely,** only, exclusively, purely, merely, just, alone.

en·tire·ty /en'tī(ə)rtē, -'tīritē/ ▸ **noun** (**the entirety**) the whole of something: *the ambition to acquaint oneself with the entirety of science.*

– PHRASES **in its entirety** as a whole.

en·ti·tle /en'tītl/ ▸ **verb 1** give someone a right to do or receive: *employees are normally entitled to severance pay.* **2** give a title to a book, play, etc.

– SYNONYMS **1 qualify,** make eligible, authorize, allow, permit, enable, empower. **2 name,** title, call, label, designate, dub.

en·ti·tle·ment /en'tītlmənt/ ▸ **noun 1** the fact of having a right to something: *full entitlement to fees and maintenance should be offered.* **2** the amount to which a person has a right: *many have exhausted their welfare entitlements.*

en·ti·tle·ment pro·gram ▸ **noun** a government program that guarantees certain benefits to a particular group or segment of the population.

en·ti·ty /'entitē/ ▸ **noun** (pl. **entities**) a thing that has its own distinct and independent existence.

– SYNONYMS **being,** creature, individual, organism, life form, body, object, article, thing.

– ORIGIN French *entité*.

en·tomb /en'to͞om/ ▸ **verb 1** place a dead body in a tomb. **2** bury in or under something: *the miners were entombed in a tunnel all night.*

– DERIVATIVES **en·tomb·ment** noun.

en·to·mol·o·gy /ˌentə'mäləjē/ ▸ **noun** the branch of zoology concerned with the study of insects.

– DERIVATIVES **en·to·mo·log·i·cal** /-mə'läjikəl/ adjective **en·to·mol·o·gist** noun.

– ORIGIN from Greek *entomon* 'insect.'

en·tou·rage /ˌänto͞o'räzʜ/ ▸ **noun** a group of people who accompany an important person.

– ORIGIN French.

en·tr'acte /'änˌtrakt, än'trakt/ ▸ **noun 1** an interval between two acts of a play or opera. **2** a piece of music or a dance performed during such an interval.

– ORIGIN French.

en·trails /'entrālz, 'entrəlz/ ▸ **plural noun** a person's or animal's intestines or internal organs.

– ORIGIN Latin *intralia* 'internal things.'

en·train /en'trān/ ▸ **verb** formal board a train.

en·trance[1] /'entrəns/ ▸ **noun 1** an opening through which one may enter a place. **2** an act of entering. **3** the right, means, or opportunity to enter: *he studied at home to gain entrance to Stanford University.*

– SYNONYMS **1 entry,** entryway, way in, access, approach, door, portal, gate, opening, mouth, foyer, lobby, porch. **2 appearance,** arrival, entry, coming. **3 admission,** admittance, (right of) entry, entrée, access.
– ANTONYMS exit, departure.

en·trance[2] /en'trans/ ▸ **verb 1** fill someone with wonder and delight. **2** cast a spell on someone.

– SYNONYMS **enchant,** bewitch, beguile, captivate, mesmerize, hypnotize, spellbind, transfix, enthrall, engross, absorb, fascinate, stun, electrify, charm, delight; informal bowl over, knock out.

– DERIVATIVES **en·trance·ment** noun **en·tranc·ing** adjective.

en·trant /'entrənt/ ▸ **noun** a person who enters, joins, or takes part in something.

– SYNONYMS **competitor,** contestant, contender, participant, candidate, applicant.

en·trap /en'trap/ ▸ **verb** (**entraps, entrapping, entrapped**) **1** catch someone or something in a trap. **2** (of a police officer) trick someone into committing a crime in order to have them prosecuted.

– DERIVATIVES **en·trap·ment** noun.

en·treat /en'trēt/ ▸ **verb** ask someone to do something in an earnest or emotional way.

– SYNONYMS **implore,** beg, plead with, pray, ask, request, bid, enjoin, appeal to, call on; literary beseech.

– ORIGIN Old French *entraitier*.

en·treat·y /en'trētē/ ▸ **noun** (pl. **entreaties**) an earnest or emotional request.

en·tre·chat /ˌäntrə'sʜä/ ▸ **noun** Ballet a vertical jump during which the dancer repeatedly crosses the feet and beats them together.

– ORIGIN French.

en·tre·côte /'äntrəˌkōt/ ▸ **noun** a boned steak cut off the sirloin.

– ORIGIN French.

en·trée /'änˌtrā, ˌän'trā/ ▸ **noun 1** the main course of a meal. **2** the right to enter a place or social group: *their veneer of respectability gave them an entrée to the business community.*

– ORIGIN French.

en·trench /en'trencʜ/ ▸ **verb 1** establish something so firmly that change is difficult: *prejudice is entrenched in our society.* **2** establish a military force in trenches or other fortified positions.

– SYNONYMS (as adj. **entrenched**) *they tend to cling to entrenched attitudes* **ingrained,** established, fixed, firm, deep-seated, deep-rooted, unshakable, ineradicable.

– DERIVATIVES **en·trench·ment** noun.

en·tre·pôt /'äntrəˌpō/ ▸ **noun** a port or other place that acts as a center for import and export.

– ORIGIN French.

en·tre·pre·neur /ˌäntrəprə'no͝or, -'nər/ ▸ **noun** a person who sets up a business or businesses, taking financial risks in the hope of profit.

– SYNONYMS **businessman/businesswoman**; dealer, trader; promoter, impresario; informal wheeler-dealer, whiz kid, mover and shaker, go-getter.

– DERIVATIVES **en·tre·pre·neur·i·al** adjective **en·tre·pre·neur·i·al·ism** noun **en·tre·pre·neur·i·al·ly** adverb **en·tre·pre·neur·ism** noun.

– ORIGIN French.

en·tro·py /'entrəpē/ ▸ **noun** Physics a quantity expressing how much of a system's thermal energy is unavailable for conversion into mechanical work.

– DERIVATIVES **en·tro·pic** /en'träpik/ adjective.

– ORIGIN from Greek *tropē* 'transformation.'

en·trust /en'trəst/ ▸ **verb 1** (**entrust someone with**) give a responsibility to someone. **2** (**entrust something to**) put something into someone's care.

– SYNONYMS **1** *he was entrusted with the job* **charge,** invest, endow; burden, encumber, saddle. **2** *the authority* ***entrusted to*** *our committee* **assign to,** confer on, bestow on, vest in, consign to, delegate to, give to, grant to, vouchsafe to.

en·try /'entrē/ ▶ **noun** (pl. **entries**) **1** an act of entering. **2** an entrance, such as a door. **3** the right, means, or opportunity to enter: *she was refused entry to the meeting.* **4** an item recorded in a list, diary, ledger, or reference book. **5** a person who enters a competition.

– SYNONYMS **1 appearance,** arrival, entrance, coming. **2 entrance,** entryway, way in, access, approach, door, portal, gate, entrance hall, foyer, lobby. **3 admission,** admittance, entrance, access. **4 item,** record, note, memo, memorandum. **5 submission,** application, entry form.
– ANTONYMS departure, exit.

en·try-lev·el ▶ **adjective** suitable for a beginner or first-time user.

en·try·way /'entrē,wā/ ▶ **noun** a way in to somewhere or something; an entrance.

en·twine /en'twīn/ ▶ **verb** wind or twist things together.

– SYNONYMS **wind around,** twist around, coil around; weave, intertwine, interlace; entangle, tangle; twine.

e·nu·mer·ate /i'n(y)o͞omə,rāt/ ▶ **verb 1** mention a number of things one by one. **2** formal count people or things.

– SYNONYMS **list,** itemize, set out, give; cite, name, specify, identify, spell out, detail, particularize.

– DERIVATIVES **e·nu·mer·a·ble** /i'n(y)o͞omərəbəl/ adjective **e·nu·mer·a·tion** /i,n(y)o͞omə'rāsʜən/ noun.
– ORIGIN Latin *enumerare* 'count out.'

e·nu·mer·a·tor /i'n(y)o͞omə,rātər/ ▶ **noun** a person employed in taking a census of the population.

e·nun·ci·ate /i'nənsē,āt/ ▶ **verb 1** say or pronounce something clearly. **2** set out a policy or theory precisely.
– DERIVATIVES **e·nun·ci·a·tion** /i,nənsē'āsʜən/ noun.
– ORIGIN Latin *enuntiare* 'announce clearly.'

en·u·re·sis /,enyə'rēsis/ ▶ **noun** involuntary urination, especially by children at night.
– ORIGIN Latin.

en·vel·op /en'veləp/ ▶ **verb** (**envelops, enveloping, enveloped**) wrap up, cover, or surround completely: *we were enveloped in fog and rain.*

– SYNONYMS **surround,** cover, enfold, engulf, encircle, cocoon, sheathe, swathe, enclose, cloak, veil, shroud.

– DERIVATIVES **en·vel·op·ment** noun.
– ORIGIN Old French *envoluper.*

en·vel·ope /'envə,lōp, 'änvə-/ ▶ **noun 1** a flat paper container with a sealable flap, used to enclose a letter or document. **2** a structure or layer that covers or encloses something.
– PHRASES **push the envelope** informal approach or extend the limits of what is possible. [from aviation slang, relating to graphs of aerodynamic performance.]
– ORIGIN from French *envelopper* 'envelop.'

en·vi·a·ble /'envēəbəl/ ▶ **adjective** arousing or likely to arouse envy; desirable: *he has an enviable record of success.*
– DERIVATIVES **en·vi·a·bly** adverb.

en·vi·ous /'envēəs/ ▶ **adjective** feeling or showing envy.

– SYNONYMS **jealous,** covetous, desirous, grudging, begrudging, resentful; informal green with envy.

– DERIVATIVES **en·vi·ous·ly** adverb.

WORD TOOLKIT

envious ...	jealous ...	grudging ...
glance	rage	respect
eyes	boyfriend/girlfriend	admiration
friends	lover	acknowledgment
thoughts	type	praise
colleague	glare	recognition

en·vi·ron·ment /en'vīrənmənt, -'vī(ə)rn-/ ▶ **noun 1** the surroundings or conditions in which a person, animal, or plant lives or operates. **2** (**the environment**) the natural world, especially as affected by human activity. **3** the overall structure within which a computer, user, or program operates.

– SYNONYMS **1 situation,** setting, milieu, background, backdrop, context, conditions, ambience, atmosphere. **2 the natural world,** nature, the earth, the ecosystem, the biosphere, Mother Nature, wildlife, flora and fauna, the countryside.

– DERIVATIVES **en·vi·ron·men·tal** /en,vīrən'men(t)l, -,vī(ə)rn-/ adjective **en·vi·ron·men·tal·ly** adverb.

WORD LINKS

ecology *study of the environment*

en·vi·ron·men·tal·ist /en,vīrən'men(t)l-ist, -,vī(ə)rn-/ ▶ **noun** a person who is concerned about protecting the environment.

– SYNONYMS **conservationist,** ecologist, nature-lover, green; informal eco-warrior, tree-hugger.

– DERIVATIVES **en·vi·ron·men·tal·ism** noun.

en·vi·rons /en'vīrənz, -'vī(ə)rnz/ ▶ **plural noun** the area surrounding a place.

– SYNONYMS **surroundings,** surrounding area, vicinity, vicinage; locality, neighborhood, district, region; precincts.

– ORIGIN French.

en·vis·age /en'vizij/ ▶ **verb 1** think of something as a possible or desirable future event. **2** form a mental picture of something.

– SYNONYMS **1 foresee,** predict, forecast, anticipate, expect, think likely. **2 imagine,** contemplate, picture, conceive of, think of.

– ORIGIN French *envisager.*

en·vi·sion /en'vizʜən/ ▶ **verb** imagine something as a future possibility.

en·voy /'en,voi, 'än,voi/ ▶ **noun 1** a messenger or representative, especially one on a diplomatic mission. **2** (also **envoy extraordinary**) a diplomat ranking below ambassador and above chargé d'affaires.

– SYNONYMS **ambassador,** emissary, diplomat, representative, delegate, spokesperson, agent, intermediary, mediator; informal go-between.

– ORIGIN from French *envoyé* 'sent.'

en·vy /'envē/ ▶ **noun** (pl. **envies**) **1** discontented longing aroused by someone else's possessions, qualities, or luck. **2** (**the envy of**) a person or thing that arouses envy: *you can have a barbecue that will be the envy of your neighbors.*

– SYNONYMS **jealousy,** covetousness, resentment, bitterness.

▶ **verb** (**envies, envying, envied**) long to have something that belongs to someone else.

– SYNONYMS **1 be envious of,** be jealous of, be resentful of. **2 covet,** desire, aspire to, wish for, want, long for, yearn for, hanker after, crave.

– ORIGIN Old French *envie.*

en·wrap /en'rap/ ▶ **verb** (**enwraps, enwrapping, enwrapped**) cover or envelop someone or something.

en·zyme /'enzīm/ ▶ **noun** a substance produced by a living organism that acts as a catalyst to bring about a specific biochemical reaction.
– DERIVATIVES **en·zy·mat·ic** /ˌenzə'matik/ adjective **en·zy·mic** /en'zīmik, -'zimik/ adjective.
– ORIGIN from modern Greek *enzumos* 'leavened.'

E·o·cene /'ēəˌsēn/ ▶ **adjective** Geology relating to the second epoch of the Tertiary period (56.5 to 35.4 million years ago), when the first horses and whales appeared.
– ORIGIN from Greek *ēōs* 'dawn' + *kainos* 'new.'

e·on /'ēən, 'ēˌän/ (also chiefly Brit. **aeon**) ▶ **noun 1** an indefinite and very long period of time: *they'd left eons ago.* **2** a major division of geological time, subdivided into eras.
– ORIGIN Greek *aiōn* 'age.'

EP ▶ **abbreviation 1** (of a record or compact disc) extended-play. **2** European Parliament.

ep- ▶ **prefix** variant spelling of **EPI-** shortened before a vowel or *h.*

EPA ▶ **abbreviation** Environmental Protection Agency.

épa·ter /ā'pätā/ ▶ **verb** (in phrase **épater les bourgeois** /lā bo͝or'zHwä/) shock people regarded as conventional or complacent.
– ORIGIN French.

ep·au·let /'epəˌlet, ˌepə'let/ (also **epaulette**) ▶ **noun** an ornamental shoulder piece on a military uniform.
– ORIGIN French, 'little shoulder.'

é·pée /ˌe'pā/ ▶ **noun** a sharp-pointed dueling sword, used, with the end blunted, in fencing.
– ORIGIN French, 'sword.'

e·phed·rine /ə'fedrin, 'efəˌdrēn/ ▶ **noun** a drug that causes constriction of the blood vessels and widening of the bronchial passages, used to relieve asthma and hay fever.
– ORIGIN from *ephedra*, a plant which is the source of the drug.

e·phem·er·a /ə'fem(ə)rə/ ▶ **plural noun** items of short-lived interest or usefulness, especially those later valued by collectors.
– ORIGIN Greek, 'things lasting only a day.'

e·phem·er·al /ə'fem(ə)rəl/ ▶ **adjective** lasting or living for a very short time.

– SYNONYMS **transitory,** transient, fleeting, passing, short-lived, momentary, brief, short, temporary, impermanent, short-term.
– ANTONYMS permanent.

– DERIVATIVES **e·phem·er·al·i·ty** /əˌfemə'ralitē/ noun **e·phem·er·al·ly** adverb.

CHOOSE THE RIGHT WORD

See **TEMPORARY**.

epi- (also **ep-**) ▶ **prefix 1** upon: *epigraph.* **2** above: *epidermis.*
– ORIGIN from Greek *epi.*

ep·ic /'epik/ ▶ **noun 1** a long poem describing the adventures of heroic or legendary figures or the history of a nation. **2** a long movie or book portraying heroic adventures or covering a long period of time. ▶ **adjective 1** relating to an epic. **2** grand or heroic in scale: *an epic journey around the world.*

– SYNONYMS *their epic journey* **ambitious,** heroic, grand, great; monumental.

– DERIVATIVES **ep·i·cal** adjective **ep·i·cal·ly** /-(ə)lē/ adverb.
– ORIGIN from Greek *epos* 'word, song.'

ep·i·cene /'epiˌsēn/ ▶ **adjective 1** having characteristics of both sexes or no characteristics of either sex. **2** effeminate.
– ORIGIN Greek *epikoinos.*

ep·i·cen·ter /'epiˌsentər/ (Brit. **epicentre**) ▶ **noun** the point on the earth's surface directly above the origin of an earthquake. Compare with **FOCUS** (sense 5 of the noun).

ep·i·cure /'epiˌkyo͝or/ ▶ **noun** a person who takes particular pleasure in fine food and drink.
– ORIGIN from *Epicurus* (see **EPICUREAN**).

Ep·i·cu·re·an /ˌepikyə'rēən, ˌepi'kyo͝orēən/ ▶ **noun 1** a follower of the ancient Greek philosopher Epicurus, who taught that pleasure, particularly mental pleasure, was the highest good. **2** (**epicurean**) an epicure. ▶ **adjective 1** relating to Epicurus or his ideas. **2** (**epicurean**) relating to or suitable for an epicure.
– DERIVATIVES **Ep·i·cu·re·an·ism** /ˌepəkyə'rēəˌnizəm, -'kyo͝orēə-/ noun.

ep·i·cy·cle /'epiˌsīkəl/ ▶ **noun** Geometry a small circle whose center moves around the circumference of a larger one.
– DERIVATIVES **ep·i·cy·clic** /ˌepi'sīklik, 'epi-/ adjective.
– ORIGIN Old French.

ep·i·dem·ic /ˌepi'demik/ ▶ **noun 1** a widespread occurrence of an infectious disease in a community at a particular time. **2** a widespread outbreak of something undesirable: *an epidemic of violent crime.*

– SYNONYMS **1 outbreak,** plague, pandemic. **2 spate,** rash, wave, eruption, plague, outbreak, craze, upsurge.

▶ **adjective** relating to or like an epidemic.
– ORIGIN Greek *epidēmia.*

ep·i·de·mi·ol·o·gy /ˌepiˌdēmē'äləjē/ ▶ **noun** the study of the spread and control of diseases.
– DERIVATIVES **ep·i·de·mi·o·log·i·cal** /-ə'läjikəl/ adjective **ep·i·de·mi·ol·o·gist** noun.

ep·i·der·mis /ˌepi'dərmis/ ▶ **noun 1** the surface layer of an animal's skin, overlying the dermis. **2** the outer layer of tissue in a plant.
– DERIVATIVES **ep·i·der·mal** /-'dərməl/ adjective.
– ORIGIN Greek.

ep·i·did·y·mis /ˌepi'didəməs/ ▶ **noun** (pl. **epididymides** /-'didəmiˌdēz, -di'dimiˌdēz/) a highly convoluted duct behind the testis, along which sperm passes to the vas deferens.
– DERIVATIVES **ep·i·did·y·mal** /-məl/ adjective.
– ORIGIN from Greek *didumos* 'testicle.'

ep·i·du·ral /ˌepi'd(y)o͝orəl/ ▶ **noun** an anesthetic delivered into the space around the dura mater (outermost membrane) of the spinal cord, used especially in childbirth. ▶ **adjective** on or around the outermost membrane of the spinal cord.

ep·i·glot·tis /ˌepi'glätəs/ ▶ **noun** a flap of cartilage behind the root of the tongue, which descends during swallowing to cover the opening of the windpipe.
– ORIGIN Greek.

ep·i·gone /ˈepiˌgōn/ ▶ **noun** literary a follower or imitator of a distinguished artist, philosopher, musician, etc.
– ORIGIN Greek *epigonoi* 'those born afterwards.'

ep·i·gram /ˈepiˌgram/ ▶ **noun 1** a concise and witty saying or remark. **2** a short witty poem.
– DERIVATIVES **ep·i·gram·mat·ic** /ˌepigrəˈmatik/ adjective.
– ORIGIN Greek *epigramma.*

CHOOSE THE RIGHT WORD

See **SAYING**.

ep·i·graph /ˈepiˌgraf/ ▶ **noun 1** an inscription on a building, statue, or coin. **2** a short quotation introducing a book or chapter.
– ORIGIN Greek *epigraphein* 'write on.'

ep·i·la·tion /ˌepəˈlāsʜən/ ▶ **noun** the removal of hair by the roots.
– DERIVATIVES **ep·i·la·tor** /ˈepəˌlātər/ noun.
– ORIGIN French *épiler.*

ep·i·lep·sy /ˈepəˌlepsē/ ▶ **noun** a disorder of the nervous system causing periodic loss of consciousness or convulsions.
– DERIVATIVES **ep·i·lep·tic** /ˌepəˈleptik/ adjective & noun.
– ORIGIN Greek *epilēpsia*, from *epilambanein* 'seize, attack.'

ep·i·logue /ˈepəˌlôg, -ˌläg/ (also **epilog**) ▶ **noun** a section or speech at the end of a book or play that comments on or acts as a conclusion to what has happened.
– ORIGIN Greek *epilogos.*

ep·i·neph·rine /ˌepiˈnefrin/ ▶ **noun** another term for **ADRENALINE.**

e·piph·a·ny /iˈpifənē/ ▶ **noun** (pl. **epiphanies**) **1** (**Epiphany**) the occasion on which Jesus appeared to the Magi (Gospel of Matthew, chapter 2). **2** (**Epiphany**) the festival commemorating this, on January 6. **3** a moment of sudden and great revelation or understanding.
– DERIVATIVES **ep·i·phan·ic** /ˌepəˈfanik/ adjective.
– ORIGIN from Greek *epiphainein* 'reveal.'

ep·i·phyte /ˈepəˌfīt/ ▶ **noun** a plant that grows on a tree or other plant but is not a parasite.
– DERIVATIVES **ep·i·phyt·ic** /ˌepəˈfitik/ adjective.
– ORIGIN from Greek *epi* 'upon' + *phuton* 'plant.'

e·pis·co·pa·cy /iˈpiskəpəsē/ ▶ **noun** (pl. **episcopacies**) **1** the government of a Church by bishops. **2** (**the episcopacy**) the bishops of a region or Church as a group.

e·pis·co·pal /iˈpiskəpəl/ ▶ **adjective 1** relating to a bishop or bishops. **2** (of a Church) governed by or having bishops.
– DERIVATIVES **e·pis·co·pal·ly** adverb.
– ORIGIN Latin *episcopus* 'bishop.'

E·pis·co·pal Church ▶ **noun** the Anglican Church in Scotland and the US, with elected bishops.

e·pis·co·pa·lian /iˌpiskəˈpālēən/ ▶ **adjective 1** relating to the government of a Church by bishops. **2** of or belonging to an episcopal Church. ▶ **noun 1** a supporter of the government of a Church by bishops. **2** (**Episcopalian**) a member of the Episcopal Church.
– DERIVATIVES **e·pis·co·pa·lian·ism** noun.

e·pis·co·pate /iˈpiskəpət, -ˌpāt/ ▶ **noun 1** the position or period of office of a bishop. **2** (**the episcopate**) the bishops of a Church or region as a group.

e·pi·si·ot·o·my /iˌpēzēˈätəmē/ ▶ **noun** (pl. **episiotomies**) a surgical cut that may be made at the opening of the vagina during childbirth to make a difficult delivery easier.
– ORIGIN from Greek *epision* 'pubic region.'

ep·i·sode /ˈepiˌsōd/ ▶ **noun 1** an event or a sequence of events. **2** each of the separate installments into which a serialized story or program is divided.

– SYNONYMS **1 incident,** event, occurrence, chapter, experience, occasion, interlude, adventure, exploit. **2 installment,** chapter, passage, part, portion, section, program, show. **3 period,** spell, bout, attack, phase; informal dose.

– ORIGIN Greek *epeisodion.*

ep·i·sod·ic /ˌepəˈsädik/ ▶ **adjective 1** made up of a series of separate events. **2** occurring at irregular intervals.
– DERIVATIVES **ep·i·sod·i·cal·ly** /-(ə)lē/ adverb.

e·pis·te·mol·o·gy /iˌpistəˈmäləjē/ ▶ **noun** the branch of philosophy that deals with knowledge.
– DERIVATIVES **ep·i·ste·mic** /ˌepəˈstemik, -ˈstē-/ adjective **e·pis·te·mo·log·i·cal** /-məˈläjikəl/ adjective **e·pis·te·mol·o·gist** /-jist/ noun.
– ORIGIN Greek *epistēmē* 'knowledge.'

e·pis·tle /iˈpisəl/ ▶ **noun 1** formal or humorous a letter. **2** (**Epistle**) a book of the New Testament in the form of a letter from an Apostle.
– ORIGIN Greek *epistolē*, from *epistellein* 'send news.'

e·pis·to·lar·y /iˈpistəˌlerē/ ▶ **adjective 1** relating to the writing of letters. **2** (of a literary work) in the form of letters.

ep·i·taph /ˈepiˌtaf/ ▶ **noun 1** words written in memory of a person who has died, especially as an inscription on a tombstone. **2** something that is a reminder of a person, time, or event: *the story makes a sorry epitaph to a great career.*
– ORIGIN Greek *epitaphion* 'funeral oration.'

ep·i·the·li·um /ˌepəˈᴛʜēlēəm/ ▶ **noun** (pl. **epithelia** /-lēə/) the thin tissue forming the outer layer of the body's surface and lining the alimentary canal and other hollow structures.
– DERIVATIVES **ep·i·the·li·al** /-lēəl/ adjective.
– ORIGIN Latin.

ep·i·thet /ˈepəˌᴛʜet/ ▶ **noun 1** a word or phrase expressing a characteristic quality of the person or thing mentioned. **2** such a word or phrase used as an insult: *she constantly hurls racist epithets at him.*
– ORIGIN Greek *epitheton.*

e·pit·o·me /iˈpitəmē/ ▶ **noun** (**the epitome of**) a perfect example of a quality or type: *she was the epitome of a well-bred New Englander.*

– SYNONYMS **personification,** embodiment, incarnation, essence, quintessence, archetype, paradigm, exemplar, model.

– ORIGIN Greek.

e·pit·o·mize /iˈpitəˌmīz/ ▶ **verb** be a perfect example of: *the patriotic spirit was epitomized by the poetry of Rupert Brooke.*

ep·och /ˈepək/ ▶ **noun 1** a long period of time marked by particular events or characteristics: *the Victorian epoch.* **2** the beginning of a period of history. **3** Geology a division of time that is a subdivision of a period and is itself subdivided into ages.

– SYNONYMS **era,** age, period, time, eon.

– DERIVATIVES **ep·och·al** /ˈepəkəl/ adjective.
– ORIGIN Greek *epokhē* 'stoppage, fixed point of time.'

ep·och-mak·ing ▶ **adjective** very important and likely to have a great effect on a particular period of time.

ep·o·nym /ˈepəˌnim/ ▸ **noun 1** a word that comes from the name of a person. **2** a person after whom a discovery, invention, place, etc., is named.

e·pon·y·mous /əˈpänəməs/ ▸ **adjective 1** (of a person) giving their name to something. **2** (of a thing) named after a particular person or group.
– ORIGIN Greek *epōnumos*.

ep·ox·ide /eˈpäkˌsīd/ ▸ **noun** an organic compound whose molecule contains a three-membered ring involving an oxygen atom and two carbon atoms.
– ORIGIN from Greek *epi-* 'in addition' + OXIDE.

ep·ox·y /iˈpäksē/ (also **epoxy resin**) ▸ **noun** (pl. **epoxies**) an adhesive, plastic, paint, etc., made from synthetic polymers containing epoxide groups.

EPROM /ˈēˌpräm/ ▸ **noun** Computing a read-only memory whose contents can be erased and reprogrammed using special means.
– ORIGIN from *erasable programmable ROM*.

Ep·som salts /ˈepsəm/ ▸ **plural noun** crystals of magnesium sulfate, used as a laxative.
– ORIGIN named after the town of *Epsom* in Surrey, where the salts were first found occurring naturally.

EQ ▸ **abbreviation 1** educational quotient. **2** emotional quotient.
– ORIGIN after **IQ**.

eq·ua·ble /ˈekwəbəl/ ▸ **adjective 1** calm and even-tempered. **2** not varying greatly: *an equable climate*.

– SYNONYMS **1** *an equable man* **even-tempered,** calm, composed, collected, self-possessed, relaxed, easygoing; mellow, mild, tranquil, placid, stable, levelheaded; imperturbable, unexcitable, untroubled, well balanced; informal unflappable, together, laid-back. **2** *an equable climate* **stable,** constant, uniform, unvarying, consistent, unchanging, changeless; moderate, temperate.
– ANTONYMS temperamental, extreme.

– DERIVATIVES **eq·ua·bil·i·ty** /ˌekwəˈbilitē/ noun **eq·ua·bly** /-blē/ adverb.
– ORIGIN from Latin *aequare* 'make equal.'

e·qual /ˈēkwəl/ ▸ **adjective 1** being the same in quantity, size, degree, value, or status. **2** evenly or fairly balanced: *an equal contest*. **3** (**equal to**) having the ability or resources to meet a challenge.

– SYNONYMS **1 identical,** uniform, alike, like, the same, matching, equivalent, corresponding. **2 impartial,** nonpartisan, fair, just, equitable, unprejudiced, nondiscriminatory. **3 evenly matched,** even, balanced, level, nip and tuck, neck and neck.
– ANTONYMS different, unequal.

▸ **noun** a person or thing that is equal to another.

– SYNONYMS **equivalent,** peer, fellow, like, counterpart, match, parallel.

▸ **verb** (**equals, equaling, equaled**) **1** be equal or equivalent to something. **2** match or rival: *he equaled the championship record*.

– SYNONYMS **1 be equal to,** be equivalent to, be the same as, come to, amount to, make, total, add up to. **2 match,** reach, parallel, be level with.

– ORIGIN Latin *aequalis*, from *aequus* 'even, level, equal.'

e·qual·i·ty /iˈkwälitē/ ▸ **noun** the state of being equal.

– SYNONYMS **fairness,** equal rights, equal opportunities, impartiality, even-handedness, justice.

e·qual·ize /ˈēkwəˌlīz/ ▸ **verb** make or become equal.
– DERIVATIVES **e·qual·i·za·tion** /ˌēkwəliˈzāshən/ noun.

e·qual·iz·er /ˈēkwəˌlīzər/ ▸ **noun** a thing that has an equalizing effect.

e·qual·ly /ˈēkwəlē/ ▸ **adverb 1** in an equal way or to an equal extent: *all children should be treated equally*. **2** in amounts or parts that are equal.

USAGE

The expression **equally as**, as in *follow-up discussion is equally as important* should be avoided: just use **equally** or **as** on its own.

e·qual op·por·tu·ni·ty ▸ **noun** the policy of treating employees and others without discrimination, especially on the basis of their sex, race, or age: *an equal opportunity employer*.

e·quals sign (also **equal sign**) ▸ **noun** the symbol =.

e·qua·nim·i·ty /ˌēkwəˈnimitē, ˌekwə-/ ▸ **noun** calmness of temper; composure.

– SYNONYMS **composure,** calm, levelheadedness, self-possession, presence of mind, serenity, tranquility, imperturbability, equilibrium, poise, aplomb, sangfroid, nerve; informal cool.
– ANTONYMS anxiety.

– DERIVATIVES **e·quan·i·mous** /iˈkwänəməs/ adjective.
– ORIGIN Latin *aequanimitas*.

e·quate /iˈkwāt/ ▸ **verb 1** consider one thing as equal or equivalent to another: *customers equate their name with quality*. **2** make two or more things the same or equal to each other: *we must equate supply and demand*.

– SYNONYMS **1** *he equates criticism with treachery* **identify,** compare, bracket, class, associate, connect, link, relate. **2 equalize,** balance, even out/up, level, square, add up, tally, match.

e·qua·tion /iˈkwāzhən/ ▸ **noun 1** Mathematics a statement that the values of two mathematical expressions are equal (indicated by the sign =). **2** Chemistry a formula representing the changes that occur in a chemical reaction. **3** the process of equating one thing with another.

e·qua·tor /iˈkwātər/ ▸ **noun** an imaginary line around the earth at equal distances from the poles, dividing the earth into northern and southern hemispheres.
– ORIGIN Latin *aequator*, in the phrase *circulus aequator diei et noctis* 'circle equalizing day and night.'

e·qua·to·ri·al /ˌekwəˈtôrēəl/ ▸ **adjective** relating to, at, or near the equator.
– DERIVATIVES **e·qua·to·ri·al·ly** adverb.

eq·uer·ry /ˈekwərē, əˈkwerē/ ▸ **noun** (pl. **equerries**) **1** a male officer of the British royal household acting as an attendant to a member of the royal family. **2** historical an officer of a prince's or nobleman's household who was responsible for the stables.
– ORIGIN Old French *esquierie* 'company of squires, prince's stables.'

e·ques·tri·an /iˈkwestrēən/ ▸ **adjective 1** relating to horse riding. **2** depicting or representing a person on horseback: *an equestrian statue*. ▸ **noun** (fem. **equestrienne** /iˌkwestrēˈen/) a person who rides a horse.
– ORIGIN from Latin *equus* 'horse.'

e·ques·tri·an·ism /iˈkwestrēəˌnizəm/ ▸ **noun** the skill or sport of horse riding.

equi- ▶ **combining form** equal; equally: *equidistant.*
– ORIGIN Latin *aequus* 'equal.'

e·qui·dis·tant /ˌēkwiˈdistənt, ˌekwi-/ ▶ **adjective** at equal distances.
– DERIVATIVES **e·qui·dis·tance** noun.

e·qui·lat·er·al /ˌēkwəˈlatərəl, ˌekwə-/ ▶ **adjective** (of a triangle) having all sides the same length.

e·qui·lib·ri·um /ˌēkwəˈlibrēəm, ˌekwə-/ ▶ **noun** (pl. **equilibria** /-ˈlibrēə/) **1** a state in which opposing forces or influences are balanced. **2** the state of being physically balanced. **3** a calm state of mind.

– SYNONYMS **balance,** stability, poise, symmetry, harmony.
– ANTONYMS imbalance.

– ORIGIN Latin *aequilibrium*, from *libra* 'balance.'

e·quine /ˈekwīn, ˈēˌkwīn/ ▶ **adjective 1** relating to horses or other members of the horse family. **2** resembling a horse.
▶ **noun** a horse or other member of the horse family.
– ORIGIN from Latin *equus* 'horse.'

e·qui·noc·tial /ˌēkwəˈnäksʜəl, ˌekwə-/ ▶ **adjective 1** relating to or at the time of the equinox. **2** at or near the equator.

e·qui·nox /ˈekwəˌnäks, ˈēkwə-/ ▶ **noun** the time or date (twice each year, about September 22 and March 20) at which the sun crosses the celestial equator and when day and night are of equal length.
– ORIGIN Latin *aequinoctium*, from *aequus* 'equal' + *nox* 'night.'

e·quip /iˈkwip/ ▶ **verb** (**equips, equipping, equipped**) **1** supply with the items needed for a purpose: *all bedrooms are equipped with a color TV.* **2** prepare someone for a situation, activity, or task: *a course that equips students with the skills needed to enter the profession.*

– SYNONYMS **1** *the boat was equipped with a flare gun* **provide,** furnish, supply, issue, stock, provision, arm. **2** *the course will equip them for the workplace* **prepare,** qualify, ready, suit, train.

– ORIGIN French *équiper.*

eq·ui·page /ˈekwəpij/ ▶ **noun 1** old use equipment. **2** historical a carriage and horses with attendants.

e·quip·ment /iˈkwipmənt/ ▶ **noun 1** the items needed for a particular purpose. **2** the process of supplying these items.

– SYNONYMS **apparatus,** paraphernalia, tools, utensils, implements, hardware, gadgetry, things; informal stuff, gear.

e·qui·poise /ˈekwəˌpoiz/ ▶ **noun** a state of balance between different forces or interests.

eq·ui·ta·ble /ˈekwitəbəl/ ▶ **adjective** treating everyone fairly and equally.

WORD TOOLKIT

equitable ...	unbiased ...	neutral ...
distribution	opinion	position
share	reporting	zone
treatment	source	ground
solution	data	country
compensation	jury	territory
terms	expert	party

– SYNONYMS **fair,** just, impartial, even-handed, unbiased, unprejudiced, egalitarian; informal fair and square.
– ANTONYMS unfair.

– DERIVATIVES **eq·ui·ta·bly** /-əblē/ adverb.

eq·ui·ta·tion /ˌekwiˈtāsʜən/ ▶ **noun** formal the art and practice of horse riding.
– ORIGIN Latin.

eq·ui·ty /ˈekwitē/ ▶ **noun** (pl. **equities**) **1** the quality of being fair and impartial. **2** Law a branch of law that developed alongside common law and is concerned with fairness and justice. **3** the value of a mortgaged property after all the charges and debts secured against it have been paid. **4** the value of the shares issued by a company. **5** (**equities**) stocks and shares that do not pay a fixed amount of interest.
– ORIGIN Latin *aequitas*, from *aequus* 'equal.'

e·quiv·a·lent /iˈkwivələnt/ ▶ **adjective** (often **equivalent to**) **1** equal in value, amount, function, meaning, etc. **2** having the same or a similar effect.

– SYNONYMS **comparable,** corresponding, commensurate, similar, parallel, analogous.

▶ **noun** a person or thing that is equivalent to another.

– SYNONYMS **counterpart**, parallel, alternative, analog, twin.

– DERIVATIVES **e·quiv·a·lence** noun **e·quiv·a·len·cy** /iˈkwivələnsē/ noun **e·quiv·a·lent·ly** adverb.
– ORIGIN from Latin *aequivalere* 'be of equal worth.'

WORD TOOLKIT

See **IDENTICAL**.

e·quiv·o·cal /iˈkwivəkəl/ ▶ **adjective** unclear in meaning or intention; ambiguous.

– SYNONYMS **ambiguous,** indefinite, noncommittal, vague, imprecise, inexact, inexplicit, hazy, unclear, ambivalent, uncertain, unsure.
– ANTONYMS definite.

– DERIVATIVES **e·quiv·o·cal·ly** adverb.
– ORIGIN from Latin *aequus* 'equal' + *vocare* 'to call.'

e·quiv·o·cate /iˈkwivəˌkāt/ ▶ **verb** use ambiguous or evasive language.
– DERIVATIVES **e·quiv·o·ca·tion** /iˌkwivəˈkāsʜən/ noun.

ER ▶ **abbreviation 1** emergency room. **2** Queen Elizabeth.
– ORIGIN sense 2 from Latin *Elizabetha Regina.*

Er ▶ **symbol** the chemical element erbium.

er /ə, ər/ ▶ **exclamation** expressing hesitation: *Er, I'm not sure.*
– ORIGIN natural exclamation.

ERA ▶ **abbreviation 1** Baseball earned run average. **2** Equal Rights Amendment.

e·ra /ˈi(ə)rə, ˈerə/ ▶ **noun 1** a long and distinct period of history. **2** Geology a major division of time that is a subdivision of an eon and is itself subdivided into periods.

– SYNONYMS **age,** epoch, period, time, date, day, generation.

– ORIGIN Latin *aera*, plural of *aes* 'money, counter.'

e·rad·i·cate /iˈradiˌkāt/ ▶ **verb** remove or destroy something completely.

– SYNONYMS **eliminate,** get rid of, remove, obliterate, extinguish, exterminate, destroy, annihilate, kill, wipe out.

– DERIVATIVES **e·rad·i·ca·tion** /iˌradiˈkāsʜən/ noun **e·rad·i·ca·tor** noun.

– ORIGIN Latin *eradicare* 'tear up by the roots,' from *radix* 'root.'

CHOOSE THE RIGHT WORD

See **DESTROY**.

e·rase /i'rās/ ▶ **verb 1** rub something out. **2** remove all traces of something.

– SYNONYMS **delete,** rub out, wipe off, blank out, expunge, excise, remove, obliterate.

– DERIVATIVES **e·ras·a·ble** /-əbəl/ adjective **e·ra·sure** /i'rāsHər/ noun.
– ORIGIN Latin *eradere* 'scrape away.'

e·ras·er /i'rāsər/ ▶ **noun** a piece of rubber or plastic used to rub out something written.

er·bi·um /'ərbēəm/ ▶ **noun** a soft silvery-white metallic chemical element of the lanthanide series.
– ORIGIN named after *Ytterby* in Sweden (see **YTTERBIUM**).

ere /e(ə)r/ ▶ **preposition & conjunction** literary or old use before (in time).
– ORIGIN Old English.

e·rect /i'rekt/ ▶ **adjective 1** rigidly upright or straight. **2** (of a body part) enlarged and rigid, especially in sexual excitement.

– SYNONYMS **upright,** straight, vertical, perpendicular, standing (on end), bristling, stiff.

▶ **verb 1** construct a building, wall, etc. **2** create or establish: *the party that erected the welfare state.*

– SYNONYMS **build,** construct, put up, assemble, put together, fabricate, raise.
– ANTONYMS demolish, dismantle.

– DERIVATIVES **e·rect·ly** adverb **e·rect·ness** noun **e·rec·tor** noun.
– ORIGIN Latin *erigere* 'set up.'

e·rec·tile /i'rektl, -ˌtīl/ ▶ **adjective** able to become erect.

e·rec·tile dys·func·tion ▶ **noun** inability of a man to maintain an erection sufficient for satisfying sexual activity.

e·rec·tion /i'reksHən/ ▶ **noun 1** the action of erecting a structure or object. **2** a building or other upright structure. **3** an erect state of the penis.

er·e·mite /'erəˌmīt/ ▶ **noun** a Christian hermit.
– DERIVATIVES **er·e·mit·ic** /ˌerə'mitik/ adjective **er·e·mit·i·cal** /ˌerə'mitikəl/ adjective.
– ORIGIN Latin *eremita.*

erg /ərg/ ▶ **noun** Physics a unit of work or energy.
– ORIGIN from Greek *ergon* 'work.'

er·go /'ərgō, 'ergō/ ▶ **adverb** therefore.
– ORIGIN Latin.

er·go·nom·ic /ərgə'nämik/ ▶ **adjective 1** relating to ergonomics. **2** designed to improve people's efficiency in their working environment.
– DERIVATIVES **er·go·nom·ic·al·ly** adverb.

er·go·nom·ics /ˌərgə'nämiks/ ▶ **plural noun** (treated as sing.) the study of people's efficiency in their working environment.
– ORIGIN Greek *ergon* 'work.'

er·got /'ərgət, -ˌgät/ ▶ **noun** a disease of rye and other cereals, caused by a fungus.
– ORIGIN French.

er·i·ca /'erikə/ ▶ **noun** a plant of a large genus including the heaths.
– ORIGIN Greek *ereikē.*

er·i·ca·ceous /ˌeri'kāsHəs/ ▶ **adjective** relating to plants of the heather family.

Er·in /'erən/ ▶ **noun** old use or literary Ireland.
– ORIGIN Irish.

Er·i·tre·an /ˌerə'trēən, -'trāən/ ▶ **noun** a person from the nation of Eritrea in NE Africa. ▶ **adjective** relating to Eritrea.

ERM ▶ **abbreviation** Exchange Rate Mechanism.

er·mine /'ərmən/ ▶ **noun** (pl. same or **ermines**) **1** a stoat. **2** the white winter fur of the stoat, used for trimming the ceremonial robes of judges or members of the nobility.
– ORIGIN Old French *hermine*, probably from Latin *mus Armenius* 'Armenian mouse.'

e·rode /i'rōd/ ▶ **verb 1** gradually wear or be worn away. **2** gradually destroy or weaken: *the country's manufacturing base has been severely eroded.*

– SYNONYMS **wear away,** abrade, grind down, crumble, weather, undermine, weaken, deteriorate, destroy.

– ORIGIN Latin *erodere*, from *rodere* 'gnaw.'

e·rog·e·nous /i'räjənəs/ ▶ **adjective** (of a part of the body) sensitive to sexual stimulation.
– ORIGIN from Greek *erōs* 'sexual love.'

e·ro·sion /i'rōzHən/ ▶ **noun** the process of eroding something or the result of being eroded.

– SYNONYMS **wearing away,** abrasion, attrition, weathering, dissolution, deterioration, disintegration, destruction.

– DERIVATIVES **e·ro·sion·al** adjective **e·ro·sive** /i'rōsiv/ adjective.

e·rot·ic /i'rätik/ ▶ **adjective** relating to or arousing sexual desire or excitement.

– SYNONYMS **sexually arousing,** sexually stimulating, titillating, suggestive, pornographic, sexually explicit; informal steamy, blue, X-rated; euphemistic adult.

– DERIVATIVES **e·rot·i·cal·ly** adverb.
– ORIGIN Greek *erōtikos*, from *erōs* 'sexual love.'

e·rot·i·ca /i'rätikə/ ▶ **plural noun** (treated as sing. or pl.) erotic literature or art.

e·rot·i·cism /i'rätiˌsizəm/ ▶ **noun 1** the quality of being erotic. **2** sexual desire or excitement.

e·rot·i·cize /i'rätəˌsīz/ ▶ **verb** give something the quality of being able to arouse sexual desire or excitement.
– DERIVATIVES **e·rot·i·ci·za·tion** /iˌrätəsə'zāsHən/ noun.

e·ro·to·ma·ni·a /iˌrätə'mānēə, -ˌrōtə-/ ▶ **noun 1** excessive sexual desire. **2** a delusion in which a person believes that another person is in love with them.
– DERIVATIVES **e·ro·to·ma·ni·ac** /-'mānēˌak/ noun.

err /ər, er/ ▶ **verb 1** make a mistake. **2** (often as adj. **erring**) do wrong: *her erring husband.*
– PHRASES **err on the side of** display more rather than less of a particular quality in one's actions: *they erred on the side of caution.*
– ORIGIN Latin *errare* 'to stray.'

er·rand /'erənd/ ▶ **noun** a short journey made to deliver or collect something, especially on someone else's behalf.

– SYNONYMS **task,** job, chore, assignment, mission.

– ORIGIN Old English, 'message, mission.'

er·rant /ˈerənt/ ▶ **adjective 1** formal or humorous straying from the accepted course or standards. **2** old use or literary traveling in search of adventure.
– DERIVATIVES **er·rant·ry** noun.
– ORIGIN sense 1 from Latin *errare* 'err'; sense 2 from Old French *errant* 'traveling.'

er·rat·ic /iˈratik/ ▶ **adjective** not happening at regular times or following a regular pattern; unpredictable: *her behavior was becoming erratic.*

– SYNONYMS **unpredictable,** inconsistent, changeable, variable, inconstant, irregular, fitful, unstable, varying, fluctuating, unreliable.
– ANTONYMS consistent.

– DERIVATIVES **er·rat·i·cal·ly** adverb.

er·ra·tum /iˈrätəm, -ˈrā-, -ˈrat-/ ▶ **noun** (pl. **errata** /-tə/) an error in printing or writing, especially as noted in a list added to a book or published in a subsequent edition of a newspaper or journal.
– ORIGIN Latin, 'error.'

er·ro·ne·ous /iˈrōnēəs/ ▶ **adjective** wrong; incorrect.

– SYNONYMS **wrong,** incorrect, mistaken, in error, inaccurate, untrue, false, fallacious; unsound, specious, faulty, flawed; informal off the beam, way out.
– ANTONYMS correct.

– DERIVATIVES **er·ro·ne·ous·ly** adverb.
– ORIGIN Latin *erroneus*, from *errare* 'to stray, err.'

er·ror /ˈerər/ ▶ **noun 1** a mistake. **2** the state of being wrong in behavior or judgment: *the crash was caused by human error.* **3** technical the amount by which something is inaccurate in a calculation or measurement.

– SYNONYMS **mistake,** inaccuracy, miscalculation, blunder, slip, oversight, misconception, delusion, misprint; informal boo-boo, slip-up.

– ORIGIN Latin, from *errare* 'to stray, err.'

CHOOSE THE RIGHT WORD

See **MISTAKE**.

er·satz /ˈerˌsäts, -ˌzäts, erˈzäts/ ▶ **adjective 1** (of a product) made or used as a poor-quality substitute for something else. **2** not real or genuine: *ersatz emotion.*
– ORIGIN German, 'replacement.'

Erse /ərs/ ▶ **noun** the Scottish or Irish Gaelic language.
– ORIGIN early Scots form of **IRISH**.

erst·while /ˈərstˌ(h)wīl/ ▶ **adjective** former. ▶ **adverb** old use formerly.

e·ruc·ta·tion /iˌrəkˈtāsʜən/ ▶ **noun** formal a belch.
– ORIGIN Latin.

er·u·dite /ˈer(y)əˌdīt/ ▶ **adjective** having or showing knowledge or learning.
– DERIVATIVES **er·u·di·tion** /ˌer(y)o͝oˈdisʜən/ noun.
– ORIGIN Latin *eruditus*.

e·rupt /iˈrəpt/ ▶ **verb 1** (of a volcano) forcefully eject lava, rocks, ash, or gases. **2** break out suddenly: *fierce fighting erupted.* **3** give way to feelings in a sudden and noisy way: *the crowd erupted into applause.* **4** (of a spot, rash, etc.) suddenly appear on the skin.

– SYNONYMS *fighting erupted* **break out,** flare up, blow up, explode, burst out.

– DERIVATIVES **e·rup·tive** adjective.
– ORIGIN Latin *erumpere* 'break out.'

e·rup·tion /iˈrəpsʜən/ ▶ **noun** an act or instance of erupting.

– SYNONYMS **1 discharge,** explosion, lava flow, pyroclastic flow. **2 outbreak,** flare-up, upsurge, outburst, explosion, wave, spate.

er·y·sip·e·las /ˌerəˈsipələs/ ▶ **noun** a skin disease causing large raised red patches on the face and legs.
– ORIGIN Greek *erusipelas*.

er·y·the·ma /ˌerəˈᴛʜēmə/ ▶ **noun** reddening of the skin, usually in patches, as a result of injury or irritation causing dilatation of the blood capillaries.
– DERIVATIVES **er·y·the·mal** /-məl/ adjective **er·y·them·a·tous** /-ˈᴛʜemətəs, -ˈᴛʜēmətəs/ adjective.
– ORIGIN Greek *eruthēma*, from *eruthros* 'red.'

e·ryth·ro·cyte /iˈriᴛʜrəˌsīt/ ▶ **noun** a blood cell that contains hemoglobin and transports oxygen to the tissues; a red blood cell.

Es ▶ **symbol** the chemical element einsteinium.

es·ca·late /ˈeskəˌlāt/ ▶ **verb 1** increase rapidly: *costs started to escalate.* **2** become more intense or serious: *the crisis escalated.*

– SYNONYMS **1 increase rapidly,** soar, rocket, shoot up, spiral; informal go through the roof. **2 grow,** develop, mushroom, increase, heighten, intensify, accelerate.
– ANTONYMS plunge, subside.

– DERIVATIVES **es·ca·la·tion** /ˌeskəˈlāsʜən/ noun.
– ORIGIN first in the sense 'travel on an escalator': from **ESCALATOR**.

es·ca·la·tor /ˈeskəˌlātər/ ▶ **noun** a moving staircase consisting of a circulating belt of steps driven by a motor.
– ORIGIN French *escalade*, referring to a former method of military attack using ladders.

es·ca·lope /ˌeskəˈlōp, iˈskäləp, -ˈskal-/ ▶ **noun** a thin slice of meat, especially veal, coated in breadcrumbs and fried.
– ORIGIN Old French, 'shell.'

es·ca·pade /ˈeskəˌpād/ ▶ **noun** an incident involving daring and adventure.

– SYNONYMS **exploit,** stunt, caper, antic(s); adventure, venture; deed, feat, experience; incident, occurrence, event.

es·cape /iˈskāp/ ▶ **verb 1** break free from imprisonment or control. **2** elude or get free from someone. **3** succeed in avoiding something dangerous or undesirable: *she narrowly escaped death.* **4** fail to be noticed or remembered by: *his name escapes me.* **5** (of gas, liquid, or heat) leak from a container.

– SYNONYMS **1 run away,** run off, get away, break out, break free, bolt, make one's getaway, slip away, abscond; informal vamoose, skedaddle, fly the coop. **2** *he escaped his pursuers* **get away from,** elude, avoid, dodge, shake off; informal give someone the slip. **3** *they cannot escape their duties* **avoid,** evade, elude, cheat, sidestep, circumvent, steer clear of, shirk. **4 leak (out),** spill (out), seep (out), discharge, flow (out), pour (out).

▶ **noun 1** an act of escaping. **2** a means of escaping. **3** (also **escape key**) Computing a key that interrupts the current operation.

– SYNONYMS **1 getaway,** breakout, flight. **2 leak,** spill, seepage, discharge, outflow, outpouring.

– DERIVATIVES **es·cap·ee** /iˌskāˈpē, ˌeskāˈpē/ noun **es·cap·er** noun.
– ORIGIN Old French *eschaper*.

es·cape clause ▶ **noun** a clause in a contract that specifies the conditions under which a party can be freed from an obligation.

es·cape·ment /i'skāpmənt/ ▶ **noun 1** a mechanism that connects and regulates the moving parts in a clock or watch. **2** the part of the mechanism in a piano that enables the hammer to fall back as soon as it has struck the string. **3** a mechanism in a typewriter that shifts the carriage a small fixed amount to the left after a key is pressed and released.

es·cap·ism /i'skāp,izəm/ ▶ **noun** the habit of trying to distract oneself from unpleasant realities by engaging in fantasy or forms of entertainment.
– DERIVATIVES **es·cap·ist** noun & adjective.

es·cap·ol·o·gist /i,skā'päləjist, ,eskā-/ ▶ **noun** an entertainer who specializes in breaking free from ropes, handcuffs, and chains.
– DERIVATIVES **es·cap·ol·o·gy** noun.

es·car·got /,eskär'gō/ ▶ **noun** a snail, especially as an item on a menu.
– ORIGIN French.

es·carp·ment /i'skärpmənt/ ▶ **noun** a long, steep slope at the edge of a plateau or separating areas of land at different heights.
– ORIGIN French *escarpement.*

es·cha·tol·o·gy /,eskə'täləjē/ ▶ **noun** the part of theology concerned with death, judgment, and destiny.
– DERIVATIVES **es·cha·to·log·i·cal** /e,skatl'äjikəl, ,eskətl-/ adjective.
– ORIGIN Greek *eskhatos* 'last.'

es·cheat /es'CHēt/ ▶ **noun** chiefly historical the return of property to the government, or (in feudal law) to a lord, if the owner should die without legal heirs.
– ORIGIN Old French *eschete.*

es·chew /es'CHōō/ ▶ **verb** deliberately avoid doing or being involved in something.
– DERIVATIVES **es·chew·al** noun.
– ORIGIN Old French *eschiver.*

es·cort ▶ **noun** /'es,kôrt/ **1** a person, vehicle, or group accompanying another in order to protect or guard them or as a mark of rank. **2** a person who accompanies a member of the opposite sex to a social event. **3** euphemistic a prostitute.

– SYNONYMS **guard,** bodyguard, protector, minder, attendant, chaperone, entourage, retinue, protection, convoy.

▶ **verb** /i'skôrt/ accompany a person, vehicle, or group somewhere: *he escorted her back to her hotel.*

– SYNONYMS **1 conduct,** accompany, guide, usher, shepherd, take, lead. **2 partner,** accompany, chaperone.

– ORIGIN French *escorte.*

es·cri·toire /,eskri'twär/ ▶ **noun** a small writing desk with drawers and compartments.
– ORIGIN French.

es·crow /'eskrō/ ▶ **noun** Law a bond, deed, or other document kept by a third party and taking effect only when a specified condition has been fulfilled: *the board holds funds in escrow.*
– ORIGIN Old French *escroe* 'scrap, scroll.'

es·cutch·eon /i'skəCHən/ ▶ **noun 1** a shield or emblem bearing a coat of arms. **2** a flat piece of metal framing a keyhole, door handle, or light switch.
– PHRASES **a blot on one's escutcheon** something that damages one's reputation or character.
– ORIGIN Old French *escuchon,* from Latin *scutum* 'shield.'

ESE ▶ **abbreviation** east-southeast.

-ese ▶ **suffix** forming adjectives and nouns. **1** referring to an inhabitant or language of a country or city: *Chinese.* **2** often derogatory (especially with reference to language) referring to character or style: *journalese.*
– ORIGIN from Latin *-ensis.*

es·ker /'eskər/ ▶ **noun** Geology a long winding ridge of sediment deposited by meltwater from a retreating glacier or ice sheet.
– ORIGIN Irish *eiscir.*

Es·ki·mo /'eskə,mō/ ▶ **noun** (pl. same or **Eskimos**) **1** a member of a people inhabiting northern Canada, Alaska, Greenland, and eastern Siberia. **2** either of the two main languages of the Eskimo (Inuit and Yupik).
▶ **adjective** relating to the Eskimos or their languages.
– ORIGIN an Algonquian word, perhaps in the sense 'people speaking a different language.'

USAGE

The word **Eskimo** is now regarded by some people as offensive and the peoples inhabiting the regions of northern Canada and parts of Greenland and Alaska prefer to call themselves **Inuit**. The term **Eskimo**, however, is the only term that covers both the Inuit and the Yupik (peoples of Siberia, the Aleutian Islands, and Alaska), and is still widely used.

ESL ▶ **abbreviation** English as a second language.

ESN ▶ **abbreviation** electronic serial number.

ESOL /'ē,säl/ ▶ **abbreviation** English for speakers of other languages.

e·soph·a·gus /i'säfəgəs/ ▶ **noun** (pl. **esophagi** /-,gī, -,jī/) the muscular tube that connects the throat to the stomach.
– DERIVATIVES **e·soph·a·ge·al** /i,säfə'jēəl/ adjective.
– ORIGIN Greek *oisophagos.*

es·o·ter·ic /,esə'terik/ ▶ **adjective** intended for or understood by only a small number of people who have a specialized knowledge of something.

– SYNONYMS **abstruse,** obscure, arcane, rarefied, recondite, abstract, enigmatic, cryptic, complex, complicated, incomprehensible, impenetrable, mysterious.

– DERIVATIVES **es·o·ter·i·cal·ly** adverb.
– ORIGIN Greek *esōterikos.*

es·o·ter·i·ca /,esə'terikə/ ▶ **plural noun** subjects or publications understood by or intended for people with a specialized knowledge of something.

ESP ▶ **abbreviation** extrasensory perception.

es·pa·drille /'espə,dril/ ▶ **noun** a light canvas shoe with a sole made of rope or rubber molded to look like rope.
– ORIGIN French.

es·pal·ier /i'spalyər, -yā/ ▶ **noun** a fruit tree or ornamental shrub whose branches are trained to grow flat against a wall.
– ORIGIN French.

es·par·to /i'spärtō/ (also **esparto grass**) ▶ **noun** (pl. **espartos**) a coarse grass native to Spain and North Africa, used to make ropes, wickerwork, and paper.
– ORIGIN Spanish.

es·pe·cial /i'speSHəl/ ▶ **adjective 1** notable; special: *the interior carvings are of especial interest.* **2** for or

belonging chiefly to one person or thing.
– ORIGIN Latin *specialis*.

es·pe·cial·ly /i'speSHəlē/ ▶ **adverb 1** used to single out one person or thing over all others: *both of them were nervous, especially Geoffrey.* **2** to a great extent; very much: *he didn't especially like dancing.*

– SYNONYMS **1 mainly,** mostly, chiefly, particularly, principally, largely, primarily. **2** *a committee formed especially for the purpose* **expressly,** specially, specifically, exclusively, just, particularly, explicitly. **3** *he is especially talented* **exceptionally,** particularly, unusually, extraordinarily, uncommonly, uniquely, remarkably, outstandingly.

USAGE

Although similar in meaning, the words **especially** and **specially** are not interchangeable. In the broadest terms both can mean 'particularly' (*a song written especially for Jonathan* or *a song written specially for Jonathan*). However, in sentences such as *both of them were nervous, especially Geoffrey,* where **especially** means 'in particular, chiefly,' **specially** is informal and should not be used in written English.

Es·pe·ran·to /ˌespə'räntō/ ▶ **noun** an artificial language invented in 1887 as an international means of communication.
– DERIVATIVES **Es·pe·ran·tist** /-tist/ noun.
– ORIGIN from *Dr Esperanto*, a pen name of the inventor; the literal sense is 'one who hopes.'

es·pi·o·nage /'espēəˌnäzH, -ˌnäj/ ▶ **noun** the practice of spying or of using spies.
– ORIGIN French.

es·pla·nade /'espləˌnäd, -ˌnād/ ▶ **noun** a long, open, level area, typically beside the sea, along which people may walk for pleasure.
– ORIGIN French.

es·pous·al /i'spouzəl, -səl/ ▶ **noun** an act of adopting or supporting a cause, belief, or way of life: *his espousal of unorthodox religious views.*

es·pouse /i'spouz/ ▶ **verb** adopt or support a cause, belief, or way of life.
– ORIGIN Old French *espouser*.

es·pres·so /e'spresō/ (also **expresso** /ik'spresō/) ▶ **noun** (pl. **espressos**) strong black coffee made by forcing steam through ground coffee beans.
– ORIGIN from Italian *caffè espresso* 'pressed out coffee.'

es·prit/ e'sprē/ ▶ **noun** liveliness.
– ORIGIN French.

es·prit de corps /eˌsprē də 'kôr/ ▶ **noun** a feeling of pride and loyalty uniting the members of a group.
– ORIGIN French, 'spirit of the body.'

es·py /i'spī/ ▶ **verb** (**espies, espying, espied**) literary catch sight of someone or something.
– ORIGIN Old French *espier*.

Esq. ▶ **abbreviation** Esquire.

-esque ▶ **suffix** (forming adjectives) in the style of: *Kafkaesque.*
– ORIGIN French.

es·quire /'eskwīr, i'skwīr/ ▶ **noun 1** (**Esquire**) a title added to a lawyer's surname. **2** historical a young nobleman who acted as an attendant to a knight.
– ORIGIN Old French *esquier*, from Latin *scutarius* 'shield-bearer.'

-ess ▶ **suffix** forming nouns referring to females: *abbess.*
– ORIGIN French *-esse.*

USAGE

In modern English, many people regard feminine forms such as **poetess** or **authoress** as old-fashioned or sexist. It is therefore often better to use the gender-neutral base form instead (e.g. *she's a famous author*).

es·say ▶ **noun** /'esā/ **1** a piece of writing on a particular subject. **2** formal an attempt or effort.

– SYNONYMS **article,** composition, theme, paper, dissertation, thesis, discourse, study, assignment, treatise, piece, feature.

▶ **verb** /e'sā/ formal attempt: *Donald essayed a smile.*
– DERIVATIVES **es·say·ist** /'esā-ist/ noun.
– ORIGIN Old French *essai* 'trial'; the verb is an alteration of **ASSAY**.

es·sence /'esəns/ ▶ **noun 1** the basic or most important feature of something, which determines its character: *conflict is the essence of drama.* **2** an extract obtained from a plant or other substance and used for flavoring or perfume.

– SYNONYMS **1 nature,** heart, core, substance, basis, principle, quintessence, soul, spirit, reality; informal nitty-gritty. **2 extract,** concentrate, elixir, juice, oil.

– PHRASES **in essence** basically; fundamentally. **of the essence** very important.
– ORIGIN Latin *essentia*, from *esse* 'be.'

es·sen·tial /i'senCHəl/ ▶ **adjective 1** absolutely necessary. **2** central to the nature of something; fundamental: *the essential weakness of the plaintiff's case.*

– SYNONYMS **1 crucial,** key, vital, indispensable, all-important, critical, imperative. **2 basic,** inherent, fundamental, quintessential, intrinsic, underlying, characteristic, innate, primary.
– ANTONYMS unimportant, incidental.

▶ **noun 1** a thing that is absolutely necessary. **2** (**essentials**) the fundamental elements of something: *the essentials of democracy.*

– SYNONYMS **1 necessity,** prerequisite; informal must. **2** (**essentials**) **fundamentals,** basics, rudiments, first principles, foundations; essence, basis, core, kernal, crux; informal nitty-gritty, nuts and bolts.

– DERIVATIVES **es·sen·tial·ly** adverb.

es·sen·tial oil ▶ **noun** a natural oil extracted from a plant.

EST ▶ **abbreviation** Eastern Standard Time.

est. ▶ **abbreviation 1** established. **2** estimated.

es·tab·lish /i'stablisH/ ▶ **verb 1** set something up on a firm or permanent basis. **2** bring about contact or communication with a person, group, or country: *the two countries established diplomatic relations.* **3** make something accepted or recognized by other people: *he had established his reputation as a journalist.* **4** discover the facts of a situation or find something out for certain: *investigators are trying to establish the cause of the fire.*

– SYNONYMS **1 set up,** start, initiate, institute, found, create, inaugurate. **2 prove,** demonstrate, show, indicate, determine, confirm.

– ORIGIN Old French *establir*, from Latin *stabilire* 'make firm.'

es·tab·lished /i'stablisHt/ ▶ **adjective 1** having been in existence for a long time and therefore generally accepted. **2** recognized by the government as the national Church or religion.

– SYNONYMS *established practice* **accepted,** traditional, orthodox, set, fixed, official, usual, customary, common, normal, general, prevailing, accustomed, familiar, expected, conventional, standard.

es·tab·lish·ment /i'stabliSHmənt/ ▶ **noun 1** the action of establishing something or the state of being established. **2** a business organization, institution, or household. **3 (the Establishment)** a group in a society who have power and influence in matters of policy or opinion, and who are seen as being opposed to change.

– SYNONYMS **1 foundation,** institution, formation, inception, creation, installation, inauguration. **2 business,** firm, company, concern, enterprise, venture, organization, operation; informal outfit. **3 institution,** place, premises, institute. **4** *criticism of the Establishment* **the authorities,** the powers that be, the system, the ruling class.

es·tab·lish·men·tar·i·an /i,stabliSHmən'terēən/ ▶ **adjective** supporting the principle of an established Church. ▶ **noun** a person who supports the principle of an established Church.

es·tate /i'stāt/ ▶ **noun 1** a property consisting of a large house and extensive grounds. **2** a property where crops such as coffee or rubber are cultivated or where wine is produced. **3** all the money and property owned by a person at the time of their death. **4** old use or literary a particular state, period, or condition in life: *the holy estate of matrimony.*

– SYNONYMS **1 property,** grounds, garden(s), park, parkland, land(s), territory. **2** *an industrial estate* **area,** development, complex. **3 plantation,** farm, ranch, holding, forest, vineyard. **4 assets,** capital, wealth, riches, holdings, fortune, property, effects, possessions, belongings.

– ORIGIN Old French *estat*, from Latin *status* 'state, condition.'

es·teem /i'stēm/ ▶ **noun** respect and admiration.

– SYNONYMS **respect,** admiration, acclaim, appreciation, recognition, honor, reverence, estimation, regard.

▶ **verb 1** respect and admire: *he was esteemed as a philosopher.* **2** formal consider: *I should esteem it an honor if you would allow me to escort you.*

– SYNONYMS **respect,** admire, value, regard highly, appreciate, like, prize, treasure, revere.

– ORIGIN Latin *aestimare* 'to estimate.'

es·ter /'estər/ ▶ **noun** an organic chemical compound formed by a reaction between an acid and an alcohol.

es·thet·ic, etc. ▶ **adjective** variant spelling of **AESTHETIC,** etc.

es·ti·ma·ble /'estəməbəl/ ▶ **adjective** worthy of great respect.

– DERIVATIVES **es·ti·ma·bly** /-blē/ adverb.

es·ti·mate ▶ **verb** /'estə,māt/ roughly calculate the value, number, or amount of something: *the contract is estimated to be worth about $1 million.*

– SYNONYMS **1 calculate,** approximate, guess, evaluate, judge, assess, weigh up. **2 consider,** believe, reckon, deem, judge, rate.

▶ **noun** /'estəmit/ **1** an approximate calculation of the value, number, or amount of something. **2** a written statement indicating the likely price that will be charged for a particular piece of work. **3** a judgment or opinion.

– SYNONYMS **calculation,** approximation, estimation, guess, assessment, evaluation, quotation, valuation; informal guesstimate.

– DERIVATIVES **es·ti·ma·tion** /,estə'māSHən/ noun.

– ORIGIN Latin *aestimare* 'determine, appraise.'

es·ti·ma·tor /'estə,mātər/ ▶ **noun 1** a person who estimates the price, value, number, quantity, or extent of something. **2** Statistics a quantity used or evaluated as an estimate of the value of a parameter.

Es·to·ni·an /e'stōnēən/ ▶ **noun** a person from Estonia. ▶ **adjective** relating to Estonia.

es·top·pel /e'stäpəl/ ▶ **noun** Law the principle that precludes a person from asserting something contrary to what is implied by a previous action or statement of that person or by a previous pertinent judicial determination.

es·tra·di·ol /,estrə'dīôl, -,äl/ (Brit. **oestradiol**) ▶ **noun** a major estrogen produced in the ovaries.

es·tranged /i'strānjd/ ▶ **adjective 1** no longer on friendly terms with someone: *she was estranged from her daughter.* **2** (of a husband or wife) no longer living with their spouse.

– ORIGIN from Old French *estranger*, from Latin *extraneare* 'treat as a stranger.'

es·trange·ment /i'strānjmənt/ ▶ **noun** the state of being estranged.

– SYNONYMS *the estrangement between Vita and her family* **alienation,** disaffection, parting, separation, divorce, break-up, split, breach.

es·tro·gen /'estrəjən/ (Brit. **oestrogen**) ▶ **noun** any of a group of hormones that produce and maintain female physical and sexual characteristics.

– ORIGIN from **ESTRUS.**

es·trus /'estrəs/ (Brit. **oestrus**) ▶ **noun** a regularly occurring period of time during which many female mammals are fertile and sexually receptive to males.

– ORIGIN Greek *oistros* 'gadfly or frenzy.'

es·tu·ar·y /'esCHo͞o,erē/ ▶ **noun** (pl. **estuaries**) the mouth of a large river, where it enters the sea and becomes affected by the tides.

– DERIVATIVES **es·tu·a·rine** /'esCHo͞oə,rīn, -ə,rēn/ adjective.

– ORIGIN Latin *aestuarium* 'tidal part of a shore.'

ET ▶ **abbreviation 1** (in North America) Eastern time. **2** extraterrestrial.

ETA[1] ▶ **abbreviation** estimated time of arrival.

ETA[2] /'etə/ ▶ **abbreviation** a Basque separatist movement in Spain.

– ORIGIN Basque, from the initial letters of *Euzkadi ta Azkatasuna* 'Basque homeland and liberty.'

e-tail·er ▶ **noun** a retailer who sells goods via electronic transactions on the Internet.

et al. /,et 'al, ,et 'äl/ ▶ **abbreviation** and others.

– ORIGIN Latin *et alii.*

etc. ▶ **abbreviation** et cetera.

et cet·er·a /et 'setərə, 'setrə/ (also **etcetera**) ▶ **adverb** and other similar things; and so on.

– ORIGIN Latin, from *et* 'and' and *cetera* 'the rest.'

etch /eCH/ ▶ **verb 1** engrave metal, glass, or stone by drawing on a protective coating with a needle, and then covering it with acid to attack the exposed parts. **2** cut a text or design on a surface: *her initials were etched on the table.* **3 (be etched)** be clearly visible: *exhaustion* *was etched on his face.* **4** (**be etched on/in**) be fixed permanently in someone's mind: *the date would be etched on his memory for the rest of his life.*

– SYNONYMS **engrave,** carve, inscribe, incise, score, mark, scratch.

– DERIVATIVES **etch·er** noun.
– ORIGIN Dutch *etsen.*

etch·ing /ˈecHiNG/ ▸ **noun 1** the art or process of etching. **2** a print produced by etching.

– SYNONYMS **engraving,** print, plate.

ETD ▸ **abbreviation** estimated time of departure.

e·ter·nal /iˈtərnl/ ▸ **adjective 1** lasting or existing forever. **2** valid for all time: *eternal truths.*

– SYNONYMS **everlasting,** never-ending, endless, perpetual, undying, immortal, abiding, permanent, enduring, constant, continual, continuous, sustained, uninterrupted, unbroken, nonstop, around/round-the-clock.

– DERIVATIVES **e·ter·nal·ly** adverb.
– PHRASES **eternal triangle** a relationship between three people involving sexual rivalry.
– ORIGIN Latin *aeternalis.*

CHOOSE THE RIGHT WORD

eternal, endless, everlasting, interminable, never-ending, unending

There are some things in life that seem to exist beyond the boundaries of time. **Endless** is the most informal and has the broadest scope of all these adjectives. It can mean without end in time (*an endless argument*) or space (*the endless universe*), and it implies never stopping, or going on continuously as if in a circle (*to consult an endless succession of doctors*). **Unending** is a less formal word used to describe something that endures or has no end, and it can be used either in an approving sense (*unending devotion*) or a disapproving one (*unending conflict*). **Never-ending** is a more emphatic term than *unending*; it, too, can be used in either a positive or a negative sense (*a never-ending delight; a never-ending source of embarrassment*). In contrast, **interminable** is almost always used in a disapproving or negative sense for something that lasts a long time (*interminable delays in construction*). **Everlasting** refers to something that will continue to exist once it is created, while **eternal** implies that it has always existed and will continue to exist in the future. In Christian theology, for example, believers in the *eternal* God look forward to *everlasting* life.

e·ter·ni·ty /iˈtərnitē/ ▸ **noun** (pl. **eternities**) **1** unending time. **2** Theology endless life after death. **3** (**an eternity**) informal an undesirably long period of time.

– SYNONYMS **1 ever,** all time, perpetuity. **2 a long time,** an age, ages, a lifetime, hours, years, forever.

eth·ane /ˈeTHˌān/ ▸ **noun** a flammable hydrocarbon gas present in petroleum and natural gas.
– ORIGIN from **ETHER**.

eth·a·nol /ˈeTHəˌnôl, -ˌnäl/ ▸ **noun** chemical name for **ALCOHOL** (sense 1).

e·ther /ˈēTHər/ ▸ **noun 1** a highly flammable liquid used as an anesthetic and as a solvent. **2** (also **aether**) chiefly literary the sky or the upper regions of air.
– DERIVATIVES **e·ther·ic** /iˈTHerik, iˈTHi(ə)rik/ adjective.
– ORIGIN Greek *aithēr* 'upper air.'

e·the·re·al /iˈTHi(ə)rēəl/ ▸ **adjective 1** extremely delicate and light. **2** heavenly or spiritual.

– SYNONYMS **1** *her ethereal beauty* **delicate,** exquisite; fragile, airy, fine, subtle. **2** *ethereal beings* **celestial,** heavenly, spiritual, other-worldly.
– ANTONYMS substantial, earthly.

– DERIVATIVES **e·the·re·al·i·ty** /iˌTHi(ə)rēˈalitē/ noun **e·the·re·al·ly** adverb.

E·ther·net /ˈēTHərˌnet/ ▸ **noun** a system for connecting a number of computer systems to form a local area network.
– ORIGIN blend of **ETHER** and **NETWORK**.

eth·ic /ˈeTHik/ ▸ **noun** a set of moral principles or rules of behavior: *the Puritan work ethic.*
– ORIGIN Latin *ethice.*

eth·i·cal /ˈeTHikəl/ ▸ **adjective 1** relating to moral principles or the branch of knowledge concerned with these. **2** morally correct.

– SYNONYMS **moral,** morally correct, right-minded, principled, good, just, honorable, fair.

– DERIVATIVES **eth·i·cal·ly** adverb.

eth·ics /ˈeTHiks/ ▸ **plural noun 1** the moral principles that govern a person's behavior or the way in which an activity is conducted. **2** the branch of knowledge concerned with moral principles.

– SYNONYMS **morals,** morality, values, principles, ideals, standards (of behavior).

– DERIVATIVES **eth·i·cist** /ˈeTHisist/ noun.

E·thi·o·pi·an /ˌēTHēˈōpēən/ ▸ **noun** a person from Ethiopia. ▸ **adjective** relating to Ethiopia.

eth·nic /ˈeTHnik/ ▸ **adjective 1** relating to a group of people who have a common national or cultural tradition. **2** referring to origin by birth rather than by present nationality: *ethnic Albanians.* **3** belonging to or characteristic of a non-Western cultural tradition: *ethnic music.*

– SYNONYMS **racial,** race-related, national, cultural, folk, tribal, ethnological.

– DERIVATIVES **eth·ni·cal·ly** /-(ə)lē/ adverb **eth·nic·i·ty** /eTHˈnisitē/ noun.
– ORIGIN Greek *ethnikos* 'heathen,' from *ethnos* 'nation.'

eth·nic cleans·ing ▸ **noun** the mass expulsion or killing of members of an ethnic or religious group in an area by those of another group.

eth·no·cen·tric /ˌeTHnōˈsentrik/ ▸ **adjective** assessing other cultures according to the particular values or characteristics of one's own.
– DERIVATIVES **eth·no·cen·tri·cal·ly** /-(ə)lē/ adverb **eth·no·cen·tric·i·ty** /-ˌsenˈtrisitē/ noun **eth·no·cen·trism** /-ˌtrizəm/ noun.

eth·nog·ra·phy /eTHˈnägrəfē/ ▸ **noun** the scientific description of peoples and cultures.
– DERIVATIVES **eth·nog·ra·pher** noun **eth·no·graph·ic** /ˌeTHnəˈgrafik/ adjective.

eth·nol·o·gy /eTHˈnäləjē/ ▸ **noun** the study of the characteristics of different peoples and the differences and relationships between them.
– DERIVATIVES **eth·no·log·i·cal** /ˌeTHnəˈläjikəl/ adjective **eth·nol·o·gist** noun.

e·thol·o·gy /ēˈTHäləjē/ ▸ **noun 1** the science of animal behavior. **2** the study of human behavior from a biological perspective.
– DERIVATIVES **e·tho·log·i·cal** /ˌēTHəˈläjikəl/ adjective **e·thol·o·gist** noun.
– ORIGIN Greek *ēthologia.*

e·thos /'ēTHäs/ ▶ **noun** the characteristic spirit and attitudes of a culture, era, or community.
– ORIGIN Greek *ēthos* 'nature, disposition.'

eth·yl /'eTHəl/ ▶ **noun** the radical $-C_2H_5$, present in alcohol and ethane.
– ORIGIN German.

eth·yl al·co·hol ▶ **noun** another term for **ALCOHOL** (sense 1).

eth·yl·ene /'eTHə,lēn/ ▶ **noun** a flammable hydrocarbon gas present in natural gas and coal gas.

eth·yl·ene gly·col ▶ **noun** a colorless viscous alcohol used as an antifreeze and in the manufacture of polyesters.

e·ti·o·lat·ed /'ētēə,lātid/ ▶ **adjective** (of a plant) pale and weak due to a lack of light.
– ORIGIN French *étioler*.

e·ti·ol·o·gy /,ētē'äləjē/ ▶ **noun 1** Medicine the cause of a disease or condition. **2** the investigation of a cause or a reason.
– DERIVATIVES **e·ti·o·log·i·cal** /,ētēə'läjikəl/ adjective.
– ORIGIN from Greek *aitia* 'a cause.'

et·i·quette /'etikit, -,ket/ ▶ **noun** the customary rules of polite or correct behavior in a society or among members of a profession.

– SYNONYMS **protocol,** manners, accepted behavior, the rules, decorum, good form; courtesy, propriety, formalities, niceties; custom, convention; informal the done thing, the thing to do.

– ORIGIN French, 'list of ceremonial observances of a court.'

E·trus·can /i'trəskən/ ▶ **noun 1** a person from Etruria, an ancient nation state of west-central Italy that was at its height *c.*500 BC. **2** the language of Etruria. ▶ **adjective** relating to Etruria.
– ORIGIN Latin *Etruscus*.

et seq. /et sek/ ▶ **adverb** and what follows (used in page references).
– ORIGIN from Latin *et sequens*.

-ette ▶ **suffix** forming nouns referring to: **1** small size: *kitchenette*. **2** an imitation or substitute: *leatherette*. **3** female gender: *suffragette*.
– ORIGIN Old French.

é·tude /ā't(y)o͞od/ ▶ **noun** a short musical composition or exercise.
– ORIGIN French, 'study.'

et·y·mol·o·gy /,etə'mäləjē/ ▶ **noun** (pl. **etymologies**) an account of the origins and the developments in meaning of a word.
– DERIVATIVES **et·y·mo·log·i·cal** /-mə'läjikəl/ adjective **et·y·mo·log·i·cal·ly** /-mə'läjik(ə)lē/ adverb **et·y·mol·o·gist** noun.
– ORIGIN Greek *etumologia*.

EU ▶ **abbreviation** European Union.

Eu ▶ **symbol** the chemical element europium.

eu·ca·lyp·tus /,yo͞okə'liptəs/ (also **eucalypt** /'yo͞okə,lipt/) ▶ **noun** (pl. **eucalyptuses**) **1** an evergreen Australasian tree valued for its wood, oil, gum, and resin. **2** the oil from eucalyptus leaves, used for its medicinal properties.
– ORIGIN Latin, from Greek *eu* 'well' + *kaluptos* 'covered,' because the unopened flower is protected by a cap.

eu·car·y·ote ▶ **noun** variant spelling of **EUKARYOTE**.

Eu·cha·rist /'yo͞okərist/ ▶ **noun 1** the Christian ceremony commemorating the Last Supper, in which consecrated bread and wine are consumed. **2** the consecrated bread and wine used in this ceremony, especially the bread.
– DERIVATIVES **Eu·cha·ris·tic** /,yo͞okə'ristik/ adjective.
– ORIGIN Greek *eukharistia* 'thanksgiving.'

eu·chre /'yo͞okər/ ▶ **noun** a card game played with the thirty-two highest cards, the aim being to win at least three of the five tricks played.
– ORIGIN German dialect *Juckerspiel*.

Eu·clid·e·an /yo͞o'klidēən/ ▶ **adjective** (of systems of geometry) based on the principles of the Greek mathematician Euclid (*c.*300 BC).

eu·gen·ics /yo͞o'jeniks/ ▶ **plural noun** the science of improving a population by controlled breeding, in such a way as to increase the occurrence of desirable mental and physical characteristics.
– DERIVATIVES **eu·gen·ic** adjective **eu·gen·i·cist** /-'jenisist/ noun & adjective.
– ORIGIN from Greek *eu* 'well' + *genēs* 'born.'

eu·kar·y·ote /yo͞o'karē,ōt, -ēət/ (also **eucaryote**) ▶ **noun** Biology an organism whose genetic material is DNA in the form of chromosomes contained within a distinct nucleus (i.e., all living organisms other than bacteria). Compare with **PROKARYOTE**.
– ORIGIN from *eu-* 'easily (formed)' + *karyo-* 'kernel' + *-ote*.

eu·lo·gize /'yo͞olə,jīz/ ▶ **verb** praise someone or something highly.
– DERIVATIVES **eu·lo·gist** /-jist/ noun **eu·lo·gis·tic** /,yo͞olə'jistik/ adjective.

eu·lo·gy /'yo͞oləjē/ ▶ **noun** (pl. **eulogies**) a speech or piece of writing that praises someone or something highly, typically someone who has just died.
– ORIGIN Greek *eulogia* 'praise.'

eu·nuch /'yo͞onək/ ▶ **noun** a man who has been castrated.
– ORIGIN Greek *eunoukhos* 'bedroom guard' (eunuchs were formerly employed to guard the women's living areas at eastern courts).

eu·phe·mism /'yo͞ofə,mizəm/ ▶ **noun** (when referring to something unpleasant or embarrassing) a mild or less direct word used rather than one that is blunt or may be considered offensive.
– DERIVATIVES **eu·phe·mis·tic** /,yo͞ofə'mistik/ adjective **eu·phe·mis·ti·cal·ly** /-(ə)lē/ adverb.
– ORIGIN Greek *euphēmismos*, from *eu* 'well' + *phēmē* 'speaking.'

eu·pho·ni·ous /yo͞o'fōnēəs/ ▶ **adjective** sounding pleasant.
– DERIVATIVES **eu·pho·ni·ous·ly** adverb.

eu·pho·ni·um /yo͞o'fōnēəm/ ▶ **noun** a brass musical instrument resembling a small tuba.
– ORIGIN from Greek *euphōnos* 'having a pleasing sound.'

eu·pho·ny /'yo͞ofənē/ ▶ **noun** the quality of having a pleasant sound.

eu·phor·bi·a /yo͞o'fôrbēə/ ▶ **noun** a plant of a large genus that includes the spurges.
– ORIGIN named after *Euphorbus*, an ancient Greek physician.

eu·pho·ri·a /yo͞o'fôrēə/ ▶ **noun** a feeling of intense happiness.

– SYNONYMS **elation,** happiness, joy, delight, glee, excitement, exhilaration, jubilation, exultation, ecstasy, bliss, rapture.
– ANTONYMS misery.

– DERIVATIVES **eu·phor·ic** /yo͞oˈfôrik, -ˈfär-/ adjective **eu·phor·i·cal·ly** /yo͞oˈfôrik(ə)lē, -ˈfär-/ adverb.
– ORIGIN Greek, from *euphoros* 'borne well, healthy.'

> **CHOOSE THE RIGHT WORD**
>
> See **RAPTURE**.

Eur·a·sian /yo͝orˈāzʜən/ ▶ **adjective 1** of mixed European (or European-American) and Asian parentage. **2** relating to Eurasia (the landmass of Europe and Asia together). ▶ **noun** a person of Eurasian parentage.

eu·re·ka /yo͝oˈrēkə, yə-/ ▶ **exclamation** a cry of joy or satisfaction when one finds or discovers something.
– ORIGIN Greek *heurēka* 'I have found it,' said to have been uttered by Archimedes when he hit on a method of determining the purity of gold.

Eu·ro /ˈyərō, ˈyo͝orō/ ▶ **adjective** informal European, especially concerned with the European Union.

eu·ro /ˈyərō, ˈyo͝orō/ ▶ **noun** (pl. **euros**) a basic unit of money of twelve member countries of the European Union.

Eu·ro·cen·tric /ˌyərōˈsentrik, ˌyo͝orō-/ ▶ **adjective** regarding European culture as the most important; chiefly concerned with Europe.
– DERIVATIVES **Eu·ro·cen·trism** /-ˈsenˌtrizəm/ noun.

Eu·ro·crat /ˈyərəˌkrat, ˈyo͝orə-/ ▶ **noun** informal, chiefly derogatory a bureaucrat in the administration of the European Union.

Eu·ro·dol·lar /ˈyərōˌdälər, ˈyo͝orō-/ ▶ **noun** a US dollar held in Europe or elsewhere outside the US.

Eu·ro·land /ˈyərōˌland, ˈyo͝orō-/ (also **Eurozone** /ˈyərōˌzōn, ˈyo͝orō-/) ▶ **noun** the economic region formed by those member countries of the European Union that have adopted the euro.

Eu·ro·pe·an /ˌyərəˈpēən, ˌyo͝orə-/ ▶ **noun 1** a person from Europe. **2** a person of European parentage. ▶ **adjective** relating to Europe or the European Union.
– DERIVATIVES **Eu·ro·pe·an·ism** /-ˌnizəm/ noun **Eu·ro·pe·an·ize** /ˌyərəˈpēəˌnīz, ˌyo͝orə-/ verb.

Eu·ro·pe·an Un·ion ▶ **noun** an economic and political association of certain European countries, with free trade between member countries.

eu·ro·pi·um /yəˈrōpēəm/ ▶ **noun** a soft silvery-white metallic element of the lanthanide series.
– ORIGIN from *Europe*.

Eu·ro·pop /ˈyo͝orōˌpop/ ▶ **noun** pop music from continental Europe with simple tunes and words, often sung in English.

Eu·ro·trash /ˈyərōˌtrasʜ, ˈyo͝orō-/ ▶ **noun** informal rich European socialites, especially those living in the US.

Eu·sta·chian tube /yo͞oˈstāsʜ(ē)ən, -kēən/ ▶ **noun** a narrow passage leading from the pharynx to the cavity of the middle ear that equalizes the pressure on each side of the eardrum.
– ORIGIN named after the Italian anatomist Bartolomeo *Eustachio*.

eu·tha·na·sia /ˌyo͞otʜəˈnāzʜə/ ▶ **noun** the painless killing of a patient who has an incurable disease or who is in an irreversible coma.
– ORIGIN from Greek *eu* 'well' + *thanatos* 'death.'

eu·troph·ic /yo͞oˈträfik, -trō-/ ▶ **adjective** (of a lake or other body of water) rich in nutrients and so supporting a dense plant population, the decomposition of which kills animal life by depriving it of oxygen.
– ORIGIN from Greek *eu* 'well' + *trephein* 'nourish.'

EVA ▶ **abbreviation 1** ethyl vinyl acetate. **2** (in space) extravehicular activity.

e·vac·u·ate /iˈvakyəˌwāt/ ▶ **verb 1** remove someone from a place of danger to a safer place. **2** leave a dangerous place. **3** technical remove the contents from a container. **4** empty the bowels.

> – SYNONYMS **1 remove,** move out, take away. **2 leave,** vacate, abandon, move out of, withdraw from, retreat from, flee. **3** *police evacuated the area* **clear,** empty.

– DERIVATIVES **e·vac·u·a·tion** /iˌvakyo͞oˈāsʜən/ noun.
– ORIGIN Latin *evacuare*.

e·vac·u·ee /iˌvakyo͞oˈē/ ▶ **noun** a person evacuated from a place of danger.

e·vade /iˈvād/ ▶ **verb 1** escape or avoid someone or something, especially by cunning. **2** avoid dealing with or discussing: *don't try to evade the issue*. **3** avoid paying tax or duty, especially by illegitimate means.

> – SYNONYMS **1 elude,** avoid, dodge, escape (from), steer clear of, sidestep, lose, leave behind, shake off; informal give someone the slip. **2 avoid,** dodge, sidestep, bypass, skirt around, fudge; informal duck (out of), cop out of.
> – ANTONYMS confront.

– DERIVATIVES **e·vad·er** noun.
– ORIGIN Latin *evadere*.

e·val·u·ate /iˈvalyo͞oˌāt/ ▶ **verb 1** form an idea of the amount or value of something. **2** Mathematics find a numerical expression or equivalent for a formula, function, or equation.

> – SYNONYMS **assess,** judge, gauge, rate, estimate, appraise, weigh up; informal size up.

– DERIVATIVES **e·val·u·a·tion** /iˌvalyo͞oˈāsʜən/ noun **e·val·u·a·tive** /-yo͞oˌātiv, -ətiv/ adjective **e·val·u·a·tor** /-yo͞oˌātər/ noun.

ev·a·nes·cent /ˌevəˈnesənt/ ▶ **adjective** chiefly literary quickly fading from sight, memory, or existence.
– DERIVATIVES **ev·a·nesce** /ˌevəˈnes/ verb **ev·a·nes·cence** noun.
– ORIGIN from Latin *evanescere* 'disappear.'

> **CHOOSE THE RIGHT WORD**
>
> See **TEMPORARY**.

e·van·gel·i·cal /ˌivanˈjelikəl/ ▶ **adjective 1** relating to a tradition within Protestant Christianity emphasizing the authority of the Bible and salvation through personal faith in Jesus. **2** relating to the teaching of the gospel or Christianity. **3** passionate in supporting something. ▶ **noun** a member of the evangelical tradition in the Christian Church.
– DERIVATIVES **e·van·gel·i·cal·ism** /-izəm/ noun **e·van·gel·i·cal·ly** adverb.
– ORIGIN from Greek *euangelos* 'bringing good news.'

e·van·ge·list /iˈvanjəlist/ ▶ **noun 1** a person who tries to convert others to Christianity. **2** the writer of one of the four Gospels. **3** a passionate supporter of something.
– DERIVATIVES **e·van·ge·lism** /iˈvanjəˌlizəm/ noun **e·van·ge·lis·tic** /iˌvanjəˈlistik/ adjective.

e·van·ge·lize /iˈvanjəˌlīz/ ▶ **verb 1** convert or try to convert someone to Christianity. **2** preach the gospel.
– DERIVATIVES **e·van·ge·li·za·tion** /iˌvanjəliˈzāsʜən/ noun.

e·vap·o·rate /iˈvapəˌrāt/ ▶ **verb 1** turn from liquid into vapor. **2** cease to exist: *my patience evaporated*.

– SYNONYMS **1 vaporize,** dry up. **2 end,** pass (away), fizzle out, peter out, wear off, vanish, fade, disappear, melt away.
– ANTONYMS condense, materialize.

– DERIVATIVES **e·vap·o·ra·tion** /i,vapə'rāsHən/ noun **e·vap·o·ra·tive** /i'vapə,rātiv/ adjective **e·vap·o·ra·tor** /-,rātər/ noun.
– ORIGIN Latin *evaporare.*

e·vap·o·rat·ed milk ▶ **noun** thick milk that has had some of the liquid removed by evaporation.

e·va·sion /i'vāzHən/ ▶ **noun 1** the action of evading or avoiding something. **2** a statement that avoids dealing with something.

e·va·sive /i'vāsiv/ ▶ **adjective 1** avoiding a direct answer to a question. **2** intended to avoid or escape: *evasive action.*

– SYNONYMS **equivocal,** prevaricating, elusive, ambiguous, noncommittal, vague, unclear, oblique.

– DERIVATIVES **e·va·sive·ly** adverb **e·va·sive·ness** noun.

eve /ēv/ ▶ **noun 1** the day or period of time immediately before an event. **2** literary evening.
– ORIGIN short form of **EVEN**[2].

e·ven[1] /'ēvən/ ▶ **adjective 1** flat and smooth; level. **2** equal in number, amount, or value. **3** not varying much in speed, quality, etc.; regular: *just bike at an even pace.* **4** equally balanced: *the match was even.* **5** (of a person's temper) placid; calm. **6** (of a number) able to be divided by two without a remainder.

– SYNONYMS **1 flat,** smooth, uniform, level, plane. **2 uniform,** constant, steady, stable, consistent, unvarying, unchanging, regular. **3 tied,** drawn, all square, level, neck and neck, nip and tuck; informal even-steven(s).
– ANTONYMS bumpy, irregular, unequal.

▶ **verb** make or become even.
▶ **adverb** used for emphasis: *he knows even less than I do.*
– DERIVATIVES **e·ven·ly** adverb **e·ven·ness** noun.
– PHRASES **even as** at the very same time as. **even if** despite the possibility that. **even now** (or **then**) **1** in spite of what has (or had) happened. **2** at this (or that) very moment. **even so** nevertheless. **even though** despite the fact that.
– ORIGIN Old English.

e·ven[2] ▶ **noun** old use or literary evening.
– ORIGIN Old English.

e·ven-hand·ed /ēvən'handid/ ▶ **adjective** fair and impartial.
– DERIVATIVES **e·ven-hand·ed·ly** adverb **e·ven-hand·ed·ness** noun.

eve·ning /'ēvniNG/ ▶ **noun** the period of time at the end of the day.

– SYNONYMS **dusk,** twilight, nightfall, sunset, sundown, night.

– ORIGIN Old English.

eve·ning prim·rose ▶ **noun** a plant with pale yellow flowers that open in the evening, used for a medicinal oil.

eve·ning star ▶ **noun** (**the evening star**) the planet Venus, seen shining in the western sky after sunset.

e·ven mon·ey ▶ **noun** (in betting) odds offering an equal chance of winning or losing.

e·ven·song /'ēvən,sôNG, 'evən,säNG/ ▶ **noun** (especially in the Anglican Church) a service of evening prayers, psalms, and canticles.

e·vent /i'vent/ ▶ **noun 1** a thing that happens or takes place. **2** a public or social occasion. **3** each of several contests making up a sports competition.

– SYNONYMS **1 occurrence,** happening, incident, affair, occasion, phenomenon, function, gathering; informal do. **2 competition,** contest, tournament, match, fixture, race, game, sport, discipline.

– DERIVATIVES **e·vent·less** adjective.
– PHRASES **in any event** (or **at all events**) whatever happens or may have happened. **in the event of/that** if the specified thing happens.
– ORIGIN Latin *eventus.*

e·vent·ful /i'ventfəl/ ▶ **adjective** marked by interesting or exciting events.

– SYNONYMS **busy,** action-packed, full, lively, active, hectic.
– ANTONYMS dull.

e·vent ho·ri·zon ▶ **noun** Astronomy a hypothetical boundary around a black hole beyond which no light or other radiation can escape.

e·ven·tide /'ēvən,tīd/ ▶ **noun** old use or literary evening.

e·vent·ing /i'ventiNG/ ▶ **noun** a riding competition in which competitors must take part in each of several contests.
– DERIVATIVES **e·vent·er** noun.

e·ven·tu·al /i'venCHōōəl/ ▶ **adjective** occurring at the end of a process or period of time: *he was optimistic about the eventual outcome of the talks.*

– SYNONYMS **final,** ultimate, resulting, ensuing, consequent, subsequent.

e·ven·tu·al·i·ty /i,venCHōō'alitē/ ▶ **noun** (pl. **eventualities**) a possible event or outcome.

e·ven·tu·al·ly /i'venCHōōəlē/ ▶ **adverb** in the end, especially after a long delay: *eventually, after midnight, I arrived at the hotel.*

– SYNONYMS **in the end,** in due course, by and by, in time, after a time, finally, at last, ultimately, in the long run, at the end of the day, one day, some day, sometime, sooner or later.

e·ven·tu·ate /i'venCHōō,āt/ ▶ **verb** formal **1** occur as a result. **2** (**eventuate in**) lead to something as a result.

ev·er /'evər/ ▶ **adverb 1** at any time. **2** used in comparisons and questions for emphasis: *I felt better than ever.* **3** at all times; always. **4** increasingly: *having to borrow ever larger sums.*

– SYNONYMS **1 at any time,** at any point, on any occasion, under any circumstances, on any account, until now. **2 always,** forever, eternally, continually, constantly, endlessly, perpetually, incessantly.

– PHRASES **ever so** informal very.
– ORIGIN Old English.

ev·er·green /'evər,grēn/ ▶ **adjective 1** (of a plant) retaining green leaves throughout the year. Contrasted with **DECIDUOUS**. **2** having a lasting freshness or appeal: *the timeless quality of our evergreen brand.* ▶ **noun** an evergreen plant.

ev·er·last·ing /,evər'lastiNG/ ▶ **adjective** lasting forever or a very long time.

– SYNONYMS **eternal,** endless, never-ending, perpetual, undying, abiding, enduring, infinite.
– ANTONYMS transient, occasional.

– DERIVATIVES **ev·er·last·ing·ly** adverb.

CHOOSE THE RIGHT WORD

See **ETERNAL**.

ev·er·more /ˌevərˈmôr/ ▸ **adverb** literary always; forever.

eve·ry /ˈevrē/ ▸ **determiner 1** used to refer to all the members of a set without exception. **2** indicating how often something happens: *every thirty minutes.* **3** all possible: *every effort was made.*
– PHRASES **every bit as** (in comparisons) equally as. **every other** each alternate in a series.

eve·ry·bod·y /ˈevrēˌbädē, -ˌbədē/ ▸ **pronoun** every person.

– SYNONYMS **everyone,** every person, each person, all, one and all, all and sundry, the whole world, the public.
– ANTONYMS nobody.

eve·ry·day /ˈevrēˌdā/ ▸ **adjective 1** daily. **2** ordinary; commonplace.

– SYNONYMS **1 daily,** day-to-day, ongoing; formal quotidian. **2 commonplace,** ordinary, common, usual, regular, familiar, conventional, routine, run-of-the-mill, garden-variety, standard, stock, household, domestic.
– ANTONYMS unusual.

Eve·ry·man /ˈevrēˌman/ ▸ **noun** an ordinary or typical person.

eve·ry·one /ˈevrēˌwən/ ▸ **pronoun** every person.

– SYNONYMS see **EVERYBODY**.

eve·ry one ▸ **pronoun** each one.

eve·ry·thing /ˈevrēˌTHiNG/ ▸ **pronoun 1** all things, or all the things of a group or class. **2** the most important thing or aspect: *money isn't everything.*

eve·ry·where /ˈevrēˌ(h)wer/ ▸ **adverb 1** in or to all places. **2** in many places; very common: *sandwich bars are everywhere.*

– SYNONYMS **all over,** all around, in every nook and cranny, far and wide, near and far, high and low, [here, there, and everywhere], the world over, worldwide; informal all over the place, all over the map.
– ANTONYMS nowhere.

e·vict /iˈvikt/ ▸ **verb** legally force someone to leave a building or piece of land.

– SYNONYMS **expel,** eject, remove, dislodge, turn out, throw out, drive out, dispossess; informal chuck out, kick out, boot out, throw someone out on their ear.

– DERIVATIVES **e·vic·tion** /iˈvikSHən/ noun.
– ORIGIN from Latin *evincere* 'overcome, defeat.'

CHOOSE THE RIGHT WORD

See **EJECT**.

ev·i·dence /ˈevədəns/ ▸ **noun 1** information or signs indicating whether something is true or valid. **2** information used to establish facts in a legal investigation or acceptable as testimony in a court of law.

– SYNONYMS **1 proof,** confirmation, verification, substantiation, corroboration. **2 testimony,** witness statement, declaration, submission; Law deposition, affidavit. **3 signs,** indications, marks, traces, suggestions, hints.

▸ **verb** be or show evidence of: *the city's economic growth is evidenced by the creation of new jobs.*
– PHRASES **in evidence** noticeable; conspicuous.
– ORIGIN Latin *evidentia.*

ev·i·dent /ˈevədənt/ ▸ **adjective** clear or obvious.

– SYNONYMS **obvious,** apparent, noticeable, conspicuous, visible, discernible, clear, plain, manifest, patent; informal as clear as day.

ev·i·den·tial /ˌeviˈdenCHəl/ ▸ **adjective** formal relating to or providing evidence.

ev·i·den·tia·ry /ˌeviˈdenSHərē/ ▸ **adjective** chiefly Law another term for **EVIDENTIAL**.

ev·i·dent·ly /ˈevidəntlē, ˈeviˌdentlē, ˌevəˈdentlē/ ▸ **adverb 1** plainly or obviously. **2** it would seem that.

– SYNONYMS **1** *he was evidently dismayed* **obviously,** clearly, plainly, unmistakably, manifestly, patently. **2** *evidently, she believed herself superior* **seemingly,** apparently, as far as one can tell, from all appearances, on the face of it, it seems, it appears.

e·vil /ˈēvəl/ ▸ **adjective 1** very immoral, cruel, and wicked. **2** associated with the devil: *evil spirits.* **3** very unpleasant: *an evil smell.*

– SYNONYMS **1** *an evil deed* **wicked,** bad, wrong, immoral, sinful, vile, iniquitous, villainous, vicious, malicious, malevolent, demonic, diabolical, fiendish, dark, monstrous. **2** *an evil spirit* **harmful,** bad, malign. **3 unpleasant,** disagreeable, nasty, horrible, foul, filthy, vile.
– ANTONYMS good, virtuous.

▸ **noun 1** extreme wickedness. **2** something harmful or undesirable: *the evil of censorship.*

– SYNONYMS **1** *the evil in our midst* **wickedness,** badness, wrongdoing, sin, sinfulness, immorality, vice, iniquity, corruption, villainy. **2** *nothing but evil will result* **harm,** pain, misery, sorrow, suffering, trouble, disaster, misfortune, woe.
– ANTONYMS good.

– DERIVATIVES **e·vil·ly** adverb **e·vil·ness** noun.
– PHRASES **the evil eye** a gaze superstitiously believed to cause harm.
– ORIGIN Old English.

e·vil·do·er /ˈēvəlˌdo͞oər/ ▸ **noun** a person who does evil things.

e·vince /iˈvins/ ▸ **verb** formal reveal the presence of a quality or feeling.
– ORIGIN Latin *evincere* 'overcome, defeat.'

e·vis·cer·ate /iˈvisəˌrāt/ ▸ **verb** formal disembowel someone or something.
– DERIVATIVES **e·vis·cer·a·tion** /iˌvisəˈrāSHən/ noun.
– ORIGIN Latin *eviscerare.*

e·voc·a·tive /iˈväkətiv/ ▸ **adjective** bringing strong images, memories, or feelings to mind: *wonderfully evocative family snapshots.*

– SYNONYMS **reminiscent,** suggestive, redolent; expressive, vivid, powerful, haunting, moving, poignant.

e·voke /iˈvōk/ ▸ **verb 1** bring to the mind: *he said the race evoked memories of his own days as a top athlete.* **2** obtain a response.

– SYNONYMS **bring to mind,** put someone in mind of, conjure up, summon (up), invoke, elicit, induce, kindle, awaken, arouse.

– DERIVATIVES **ev·o·ca·tion** /ˌēvōˈkāSHən, ˌevə-/ noun.
– ORIGIN Latin *evocare* 'call on a spirit.'

ev·o·lu·tion /ˌevəˈlo͞oSHən/ ▸ **noun 1** the process by which different kinds of living organism are believed to have developed from earlier forms. **2** the gradual development of something.

– SYNONYMS **1 development,** progress, rise, expansion, growth. **2 natural selection,** Darwinism, adaptation, development.

– DERIVATIVES **ev·o·lu·tion·ar·i·ly** /ˌevəˌlo͞oSHəˈne(ə)rəlē/ adverb **ev·o·lu·tion·ar·y** /-ˌnerē/ adjective.
– ORIGIN Latin, 'unrolling.'

ev·o·lu·tion·ist /ˌevəˈlo͞oSHənist/ ▸ **noun** a person who believes in the theories of evolution and natural selection.
– DERIVATIVES **ev·o·lu·tion·ism** /-ˌnizəm/ noun.

e·volve /iˈvälv/ ▸ **verb 1** develop gradually: *over the years, the business evolved into the one he runs today.* **2** (of an organism) develop from earlier forms by evolution.

– SYNONYMS **develop,** progress, advance, grow, expand, spread.

– ORIGIN Latin *evolvere.*

ewe /yo͞o/ ▸ **noun** a female sheep.
– ORIGIN Old English.

ew·er /ˈyo͞oər/ ▸ **noun** a large jug with a wide mouth.
– ORIGIN Old French *aiguiere.*

ex[1] /eks/ ▸ **preposition** without; excluding.

ex[2] ▸ **noun** informal a former husband, wife, or other partner in a relationship.

ex- (also **e-**; **ef-** before *f*) ▸ **prefix 1** out: *exclude.* **2** upward: *extol.* **3** thoroughly: *excruciating.* **4** giving rise to: *exasperate.* **5** former: *ex-husband.*
– ORIGIN Latin or Greek *ex* 'out of.'

ex·ac·er·bate /igˈzasərˌbāt/ ▸ **verb** make something bad worse.

– SYNONYMS **aggravate,** worsen, inflame, compound, intensify, increase, heighten, magnify, add to.
– ANTONYMS reduce.

– DERIVATIVES **ex·ac·er·ba·tion** /igˌzasərˈbāSHən/ noun.
– ORIGIN Latin *exacerbare* 'make harsh.'

ex·act /igˈzakt/ ▸ **adjective 1** correct in every detail: *an exact replica.* **2** not approximate; precise: *the exact time of the solstice.* **3** accurate and careful about minor details.

– SYNONYMS **1** *an exact description* **precise,** accurate, correct, faithful, close, true, literal, strict, perfect. **2** *an exact record keeper* **careful,** meticulous, painstaking, punctilious, conscientious, scrupulous.
– ANTONYMS inaccurate, careless.

▸ **verb 1** demand and obtain something from someone. **2** take revenge on someone.

– SYNONYMS **1 demand,** require, impose, extract, compel, force, wring. **2 inflict,** impose, administer, mete out, wreak.

– DERIVATIVES **ex·act·ness** noun.
– ORIGIN from Latin *exigere* 'complete, ascertain, enforce.'

ex·act·ing /igˈzaktiNG/ ▸ **adjective** demanding a great deal of effort or skill.

– SYNONYMS **demanding,** stringent, testing, challenging, arduous, laborious, hard, taxing, grueling, punishing, tough.
– ANTONYMS easy, easygoing.

WORD TOOLKIT

See **FINICKY**.

ex·ac·tion /igˈzakSHən/ ▸ **noun** formal **1** the action of exacting or demanding a payment. **2** a sum of money demanded.

ex·ac·ti·tude /igˈzaktəˌt(y)o͞od/ ▸ **noun** the quality of being exact.

ex·act·ly /igˈzak(t)lē/ ▸ **adverb 1** used to emphasize the accuracy of something: *she stayed for exactly two weeks in each state.* **2** used to confirm or agree with what has just been said.

– SYNONYMS **1 precisely,** entirely, absolutely, completely, totally, just, quite, in every respect. **2 accurately,** precisely, unerringly, faultlessly, perfectly, faithfully.

ex·ag·ger·ate /igˈzajəˌrāt/ ▸ **verb 1** make something seem larger, better, or worse than it really is. **2** (as adj. **exaggerated**) enlarged or altered beyond normal proportions.

– SYNONYMS **overstate,** overemphasize, overestimate, inflate, embellish, embroider, elaborate, overplay, dramatize; informal blow all out of proportion.
– ANTONYMS understate.

– DERIVATIVES **ex·ag·ger·at·ed·ly** adverb **ex·ag·ger·a·tion** /igˌzajəˈrāSHən/ noun.
– ORIGIN Latin *exaggerare* 'heap up.'

ex·alt /igˈzôlt/ ▸ **verb 1** praise someone or something highly. **2** raise someone to a higher rank or position.
– ORIGIN Latin *exaltare.*

ex·al·ta·tion /ˌegzôlˈtāSHən, ˌeksôl-/ ▸ **noun 1** extreme happiness. **2** the action of praising or elevating someone or something.

ex·alt·ed /igˈzôltid, eg-/ ▸ **adjective 1** at a high level: *the exalted rank of inspector.* **2** (of an idea) noble; lofty.

ex·am /igˈzam/ ▸ **noun 1** short for **EXAMINATION** (sense 2). **2** a medical test: *an eye exam.*

ex·am·i·na·tion /igˌzaməˈnāSHən/ ▸ **noun 1** a detailed inspection or investigation. **2** a formal test of knowledge or ability in a subject or skill. **3** the action of examining someone or something.

– SYNONYMS **1** *items spread out for examination* **scrutiny,** inspection, perusal, study, investigation, consideration, analysis. **2** *a medical examination* **inspection,** checkup, assessment, appraisal, test, scan. **3** *a school examination* **test,** exam, quiz, assessment.

ex·am·ine /igˈzamən/ ▸ **verb 1** inspect someone or something closely to determine their nature or condition. **2** test someone's knowledge or ability. **3** Law formally question a defendant or witness in court.

– SYNONYMS **1 inspect,** scrutinize, investigate, look at, study, appraise, analyze, review, survey; informal check out. **2 test,** quiz, question, assess, appraise.

– DERIVATIVES **ex·am·i·nee** /igˌzaməˈnē/ noun **ex·am·in·er** noun.
– ORIGIN Latin *examinare* 'weigh, test.'

ex·am·ple /igˈzampəl/ ▸ **noun 1** a thing that is typical of its kind or that illustrates a general rule. **2** a person or thing regarded in terms of their suitability to be imitated.

– SYNONYMS **1 specimen,** sample, instance, case, illustration. **2 precedent,** lead, model, pattern, ideal, standard. **3 warning,** lesson, deterrent, disincentive.

– PHRASES **for example** used to introduce something chosen as a typical case. **make an example of** punish someone as a warning to others.
– ORIGIN Latin *exemplum.*

ex·as·per·ate /ig'zaspəˌrāt/ ▶ **verb** irritate someone intensely.

– SYNONYMS **infuriate,** anger, annoy, irritate, madden, provoke, irk, vex, gall, get on someone's nerves, rub the wrong way; informal aggravate, rile, bug, tee off, tick off.

– DERIVATIVES **ex·as·per·at·ed** adjective **ex·as·per·at·ing** adjective **ex·as·per·a·tion** /igˌzaspə'rāsHən/ noun.
– ORIGIN Latin *exasperare* 'irritate to anger.'

ex ca·the·dra /ˌeks kə'THēdrə/ ▶ **adverb & adjective** with the full authority of office (especially that of the pope).
– ORIGIN Latin, 'from the teacher's chair.'

ex·ca·vate /'ekskəˌvāt/ ▶ **verb 1** make a hole or channel by digging. **2** carefully remove earth from an area in order to find buried remains. **3** dig out objects or material from the ground.

– SYNONYMS **unearth,** dig up, uncover, reveal, disinter, exhume, dig out, quarry, mine.

– DERIVATIVES **ex·ca·va·tion** /ˌekskə'vāsHən/ noun **ex·ca·va·tor** /'ekskəˌvātər/ noun.
– ORIGIN Latin *excavare* 'hollow out.'

ex·ceed /ik'sēd/ ▶ **verb 1** be greater in number or size than: *our sales should exceed $2.1 billion*. **2** go beyond what is stipulated by a set limit. **3** be better than something; surpass.

– SYNONYMS **be more than,** be greater than, be over, go beyond, top, surpass.

– ORIGIN Latin *excedere*.

ex·ceed·ing·ly /ik'sēdiNGlē/ ▶ **adverb** extremely; very.

ex·cel /ik'sel/ ▶ **verb** (**excels, excelling, excelled**) be exceptionally good at an activity or subject.

– SYNONYMS **shine,** be excellent, be outstanding, be skillful, be talented, stand out, be second to none.

– ORIGIN Latin *excellere*.

ex·cel·lence /'eksələns/ ▶ **noun** the quality of being excellent.

– SYNONYMS **distinction,** quality, superiority, brilliance, greatness, caliber, eminence.

Ex·cel·len·cy /'eksələnsē/ ▶ **noun** (pl. **Excellencies**) (**His, Your,** etc. **Excellency**) a title or form of address for certain high officials of state, especially ambassadors, or of the Roman Catholic Church.

ex·cel·lent /'eksələnt/ ▶ **adjective** extremely good; outstanding.

– SYNONYMS **very good,** outstanding, superb, exceptional, marvelous, wonderful, splendid; informal terrific, fantastic.
– ANTONYMS inferior.

ex·cept /ik'sept/ ▶ **preposition** not including; other than.

– SYNONYMS **excluding,** not including, excepting, except for, omitting, not counting, but, besides, apart from, aside from, barring, bar, other than; informal outside of.

▶ **conjunction** used before a statement that is not included in one just made.
▶ **verb** exclude from a category or group: *present company excepted*.
– ORIGIN from Latin *excipere* 'take out.'

USAGE

On the confusion of **except** and **accept**, see the note at **ACCEPT**.

ex·cept·ing /ik'septiNG/ ▶ **preposition** except for; apart from.

ex·cep·tion /ik'sepsHən/ ▶ **noun** a person or thing that is not included in a general statement or that does not follow a rule.

– SYNONYMS **anomaly,** irregularity, deviation, special case, peculiarity, abnormality, oddity.

– PHRASES **take exception to** object strongly to something.

ex·cep·tion·a·ble /ik'sepsHənəbəl/ ▶ **adjective** formal open to objection; causing disapproval or offense.

ex·cep·tion·al /ik'sepsHənəl/ ▶ **adjective 1** unusually good. **2** unusual; not typical: *the drug could only be used in exceptional circumstances*.

– SYNONYMS **1** *the drought was exceptional* **unusual,** abnormal, atypical, out of the ordinary, rare, unprecedented, unexpected, surprising. **2** *her exceptional ability* **outstanding,** extraordinary, remarkable, special, phenomenal, prodigious.
– ANTONYMS normal, average.

– DERIVATIVES **ex·cep·tion·al·ly** adverb.

WORD TOOLKIT

exceptional ...	unique ...	remarkable ...
circumstances	opportunity	achievement
case	features	recovery
quality	combination	career
service	perspective	transformation
value	insight	similarity

ex·cerpt ▶ **noun** /'ekˌsərpt/ a short extract from a movie or piece of music or writing.

– SYNONYMS **extract,** part, section, piece, portion, snippet, clip, citation, quotation, quote, line, passage, fragment.

▶ **verb** /ik'sərpt/ take a short extract from a piece of writing.
– ORIGIN from Latin *excerpere* 'pluck out.'

ex·cess ▶ **noun** /ik'ses, 'ekses/ **1** an amount that is more than necessary, permitted, or desirable. **2** extreme behavior, especially in eating or drinking too much: *bouts of alcoholic excess*. **3** (**excesses**) unacceptable or illegal behavior.

– SYNONYMS **1 surplus,** surfeit, overabundance, superabundance, superfluity, glut. **2 remainder,** leftovers, extra, rest, residue. **3 overindulgence,** intemperance, immoderation, profligacy, extravagance, self-indulgence.
– ANTONYMS lack, restraint.

▶ **adjective** exceeding a permitted or desirable amount.

– SYNONYMS *excess oil* **surplus,** superfluous, redundant, unwanted, unneeded, excessive, extra.

– ORIGIN Latin *excessus*.

ex·cess bag·gage ▶ **noun** luggage weighing more than the limit allowed on an aircraft, liable to an extra charge.

ex·ces·sive /ik'sesiv/ ▶ **adjective** more than is necessary, normal, or desirable.

– SYNONYMS **1 immoderate,** intemperate, overindulgent, unrestrained, uncontrolled, extravagant. **2 exorbitant,** extortionate, unreasonable, outrageous, uncalled for, inordinate, unwarranted, disproportionate; informal over the top.

– DERIVATIVES **ex·ces·sive·ly** adverb **ex·ces·sive·ness** noun.

ex·change /iks'CHānj/ ▶ **noun 1** an act of giving something and receiving something else in return. **2** a short conversation or argument. **3** the changing of money to its equivalent in another currency. **4** a building or institution in which commodities are traded. **5** a set of equipment that connects telephone lines during a call.

– SYNONYMS **1 interchange,** trade, trading, swapping, traffic, trafficking. **2 conversation,** dialogue, chat, talk, discussion.

▶ **verb** give something and receive something else in return.

– SYNONYMS **trade,** swap, switch, change.

– DERIVATIVES **ex·change·a·ble** adjective **ex·chang·er** noun.
– ORIGIN Old French *eschangier.*

ex·change rate ▶ **noun** the value at which one currency may be exchanged for another.

ex·cheq·uer /eks'CHekər, iks-/ ▶ **noun 1** a royal or national treasury. **2** (**Exchequer**) (in the UK) the account at the Bank of England into which public money is paid.
– ORIGIN Old French *eschequier* 'chessboard' (accounts were kept on a checkered tablecloth by means of counters).

ex·cise[1] /'ek,sīz/ ▶ **noun** a tax charged on certain goods, such as alcohol, and licenses for certain activities.
– ORIGIN Dutch *excijs.*

ex·cise[2] /ik'sīz/ ▶ **verb 1** cut something out surgically. **2** remove a section from a piece of writing or music.
– DERIVATIVES **ex·ci·sion** /-'sizHən/ noun.
– ORIGIN Latin *excidere* 'cut out.'

ex·cit·a·ble /ik'sītəbəl/ ▶ **adjective** easily excited.

– SYNONYMS **temperamental,** volatile, mercurial, emotional, sensitive, highly strung, tempestuous, hotheaded, fiery.
– ANTONYMS placid.

– DERIVATIVES **ex·cit·a·bil·i·ty** /ik,sītə'bilitē/ noun **ex·cit·a·bly** /-əblē/ adverb.

ex·cite /ik'sīt/ ▶ **verb 1** make someone feel very enthusiastic and eager. **2** arouse someone sexually. **3** give rise to: *the new sauces are exciting particular interest.* **4** increase the energy or activity in a physical or biological system.

– SYNONYMS **1 thrill,** exhilarate, animate, enliven, rouse, stir, stimulate, galvanize. **2 provoke,** stir up, rouse, arouse, kindle, trigger, spark, incite, cause.
– ANTONYMS bore.

– DERIVATIVES **ex·ci·ta·tion** /ek,sī'tāsHən/ noun **ex·cit·a·to·ry** /ik'sītə,tôrē/ (chiefly Physiology) adjective **ex·cit·ed** adjective.
– ORIGIN Latin *excitare.*

ex·cite·ment /ik'sītmənt/ ▶ **noun 1** a feeling of great enthusiasm and eagerness. **2** something that arouses great enthusiasm and eagerness. **3** sexual arousal.

– SYNONYMS **1** *the excitement of seeing a leopard in the wild* **thrill,** pleasure, delight, joy; informal kick, buzz. **2** *the excitement in her eyes* **exhilaration,** elation, animation, enthusiasm, eagerness, anticipation.

ex·cit·ing /ik'sītiNG/ ▶ **adjective** causing great enthusiasm and eagerness.

– SYNONYMS **thrilling,** exhilarating, stirring, rousing, stimulating, intoxicating, electrifying, invigorating, gripping, compelling, powerful, dramatic.

– DERIVATIVES **ex·cit·ing·ly** adverb.

ex·claim /ik'sklām/ ▶ **verb** cry out suddenly, especially in surprise, anger, or pain.

– SYNONYMS **cry out,** declare, proclaim, blurt out, call out, shout, yell.

– ORIGIN Latin *exclamare.*

ex·cla·ma·tion /,eksklə'māsHən/ ▶ **noun** a sudden cry or remark.
– DERIVATIVES **ex·clam·a·to·ry** /ik'sklamə,tôrē/ adjective.

ex·cla·ma·tion point (also **exclamation mark**) ▶ **noun** a punctuation mark (!) indicating an exclamation.

ex·clude /ik'sklōōd/ ▶ **verb 1** prevent someone from entering or participating in something. **2** deliberately leave out when considering or doing something: *this information was excluded from the judicial investigation.*

– SYNONYMS **1 keep out,** deny access to, shut out, bar, ban, prohibit. **2 rule out,** preclude. **3 be exclusive of,** not include.
– ANTONYMS admit, include.

– DERIVATIVES **ex·clud·a·ble** adjective **ex·clud·er** noun.
– ORIGIN Latin *excludere.*

ex·clud·ing /ik'sklōōdiNG/ ▶ **preposition** not taking someone or something into account; except.

ex·clu·sion /ik'sklōōzHən/ ▶ **noun** the action of excluding someone or something from something.
– DERIVATIVES **ex·clu·sion·ar·y** /-,nerē/ adjective.

ex·clu·sive /ik'sklōōsiv/ ▶ **adjective 1** restricted to the person, group, or area concerned: *the problem isn't exclusive to Atlanta.* **2** high-class and expensive; select. **3** not including other things. **4** unable to exist or be true if something else exists or is true: *when it comes to hedges, fast growing and low maintenance are mutually exclusive.* **5** (of a story) not published or broadcast elsewhere.

– SYNONYMS **1 select,** chic, high-class, elite, fashionable, stylish, elegant, premier, upmarket, upscale; informal **posh,** classy, swish. **2 sole,** unshared, unique, individual, personal, private. **3** *prices exclusive of sales tax* **not including,** excluding, leaving out, omitting, excepting.
– ANTONYMS inclusive.

▶ **noun** a story published or broadcast by only one source.
– DERIVATIVES **ex·clu·sive·ly** adverb **ex·clu·sive·ness** noun **ex·clu·siv·i·ty** /,ekskloo'sivitē/ noun.
– ORIGIN Latin *exclusivus.*

ex·com·mu·ni·cate /,ekskə'myōōni,kāt/ ▶ **verb** officially ban someone from the sacraments and services of the Christian Church.
– DERIVATIVES **ex·com·mu·ni·ca·tion** /,ekskə,myōōni'kāsHən/ noun.
– ORIGIN Latin *excommunicare.*

ex-con ▶ **noun** informal an ex-convict; a former prisoner.
– ORIGIN abbreviation.

ex·co·ri·ate /ik'skôrē,āt/ ▶ **verb 1** formal criticize someone severely. **2** Medicine damage or remove part of the surface of the skin.
– DERIVATIVES **ex·co·ri·a·tion** /ik,skôrē'āsHən/ noun.
– ORIGIN Latin *excoriare* 'to skin.'

ex·cre·ment /'ekskrəmənt/ ▶ **noun** waste matter emptied from the bowels; feces.

– SYNONYMS **feces,** stools, droppings, excreta; ordure, dung, manure; dirt, muck, mess; informal poop, poo, turds, doo-doo.

– DERIVATIVES **ex·cre·men·tal** /,ekskrə'men(t)l/ adjective.
– ORIGIN Latin *excrementum.*

ex·cres·cence /ik'skresəns/ ▸ **noun 1** an abnormal growth protruding from a body or plant. **2** an unattractive object or feature.
– ORIGIN from Latin *excrescere* 'grow out.'

ex·cre·ta /ik'skrētə/ ▸ **noun** waste discharged from the body, especially feces and urine.
– ORIGIN Latin.

ex·crete /ik'skrēt/ ▸ **verb** discharge a waste substance from the body.
– DERIVATIVES **ex·cre·tion** /ik'skrēsʜən/ noun **ex·cre·to·ry** /'ekskri,tôrē/ adjective.
– ORIGIN Latin *excernere* 'sift out.'

ex·cru·ci·at·ing /ik'skro͞osʜē,ātiɴɢ/ ▸ **adjective 1** intensely painful. **2** very embarrassing, awkward, or tedious.

– SYNONYMS **agonizing,** severe, acute, intense, violent, racking, searing, piercing, stabbing, unbearable, unendurable; informal splitting, killing.

– DERIVATIVES **ex·cru·ci·at·ing·ly** adverb.
– ORIGIN from Latin *excruciare* 'torment.'

ex·cul·pate /'ekskəl,pāt/ ▸ **verb** formal show or declare that someone is not guilty of wrongdoing.
– DERIVATIVES **ex·cul·pa·tion** /,ekskəl'pāsʜən/ noun **ex·cul·pa·to·ry** /,eks'kəlpə,tôrē/ adjective.
– ORIGIN Latin *exculpare* 'free from blame.'

ex·cur·sion /ik'skərzʜən/ ▸ **noun** a short journey or trip, especially one taken for leisure.

– SYNONYMS **outing,** trip, jaunt, expedition, journey, tour, day out, drive, run; informal spin.

– DERIVATIVES **ex·cur·sion·ist** noun.
– ORIGIN from Latin *excurrere* 'run out.'

CHOOSE THE RIGHT WORD

See **JOURNEY**.

ex·cur·sus /ek'skərsəs/ ▸ **noun** (pl. same or **excursuses**) a detailed discussion of a particular point in a book.
– ORIGIN Latin, 'excursion.'

ex·cuse ▸ **verb** /ik'skyo͞oz/ **1** try to find reasons for a fault or offense; try to justify: *she did nothing to hide or excuse his cruelty*. **2** forgive a minor fault or a person committing one: *sit down—excuse the mess*. **3** release someone from a duty or requirement. **4** allow someone to leave a room or gathering. **5** (**excuse oneself**) say politely that one is leaving.

– SYNONYMS **1 forgive,** pardon. **2 justify,** defend, condone, forgive, overlook, disregard, ignore, tolerate, explain, mitigate. **3 let off,** release, relieve, exempt, absolve, free.
– ANTONYMS punish, condemn.

▸ **noun** /ik'skyo͞os/ **1** a reason given to justify a fault or offense. **2** something said to conceal the real reason for an action. **3** (**an excuse for**) informal a poor or inadequate example of: *you pathetic excuse for a human being!*

– SYNONYMS **1 justification,** defense, reason, explanation, mitigating circumstances, mitigation. **2 pretext,** pretense. informal story, alibi.

– DERIVATIVES **ex·cus·a·ble** /-zəbəl/ adjective **ex·cus·a·bly** /-zəblē/ adverb.
– PHRASES **excuse me 1** a polite apology. **2** used to ask someone to repeat what they have just said.
– ORIGIN Latin *excusare* 'to free from blame.'

ex·ec /eg'zek/ ▸ **noun** informal an executive (businessperson): *top execs*.
– ORIGIN abbreviation.

ex·e·cra·ble /'eksikrəbəl/ ▸ **adjective** extremely bad or unpleasant.
– DERIVATIVES **ex·e·cra·bly** /-blē/ adverb.
– ORIGIN Latin *execrabilis*.

ex·e·crate /'eksi,krāt/ ▸ **verb** feel or express great hatred for someone or something.
– DERIVATIVES **ex·e·cra·tion** /,eksi'krāsʜən/ noun.
– ORIGIN Latin *exsecrari* 'curse.'

ex·e·cut·a·ble /'eksi,kyo͞otəbəl/ Computing ▸ **adjective** (of a file or program) able to be run by a computer. ▸ **noun** an executable file or program.

ex·e·cute /'eksi,kyo͞ot/ ▸ **verb 1** put a plan, order, or course of action into effect: *the companies have executed a five-year agreement*. **2** perform a skillful action or maneuver. **3** carry out a sentence of death on a condemned person. **4** make a legal document valid by signing or sealing it. **5** carry out a judicial sentence, the terms of a will, or other order. **6** run a computer file or program.

– SYNONYMS **1 carry out,** accomplish, bring off/about, implement, achieve, complete, engineer; informal pull off. **2 put to death,** kill, hang, behead, electrocute, shoot.

– ORIGIN Latin *executare*.

ex·e·cu·tion /,eksi'kyo͞osʜən/ ▸ **noun 1** the carrying out of a plan, order, or course of action. **2** the killing of a condemned person. **3** the way in which something is produced or carried out.

– SYNONYMS **1 implementation,** carrying out, performance, accomplishment, bringing off/about, attainment, realization. **2 killing,** capital punishment, the death penalty.

ex·e·cu·tion·er /,eksi'kyo͞osʜ(ə)nər/ ▸ **noun** an official who executes condemned criminals.

ex·ec·u·tive /ig'zekyətiv, eg-/ ▸ **noun 1** a senior manager in a business. **2** a decision-making committee or other group in an organization. **3** (**the executive**) the branch of a government responsible for putting decisions or laws into effect.

– SYNONYMS **1 director,** manager, senior official, administrator; informal boss, exec, suit. **2 administration,** management, directorate, government, authority.

▸ **adjective** having the power to put plans, actions, or laws into effect.

– SYNONYMS **administrative,** managerial, decision-making, lawmaking, governing, controlling.

ex·ec·u·tor /ig'zekyətər/ ▸ **noun** a person appointed by someone to carry out the terms of their will.

ex·ec·u·trix /ig'zekyə,triks/ ▸ **noun** (pl. **executrices** /-,trisēz/ or **executrixes**) a female executor of a will.

ex·e·ge·sis /,eksi'jēsis/ ▸ **noun** (pl. **exegeses** /-sēz/) critical explanation of a written work, especially of the Bible.
– DERIVATIVES **ex·e·get·i·cal** /-'jetikəl/ adjective.
– ORIGIN Greek.

ex·e·gete /'eksə,jēt/ ▸ **noun** a person who interprets a written work, especially the Bible.

ex·em·plar /ig'zemplər, -,plär/ ▸ **noun** a person or thing serving as a typical example or appropriate model.
– ORIGIN Latin *exemplarium*.

ex·em·pla·ry /ig'zemplərē/ ▸ **adjective 1** providing a good example to others; very good. **2** (of a punishment) serving as a warning.

– SYNONYMS **perfect,** ideal, model, faultless, flawless, impeccable, irreproachable.
– ANTONYMS deplorable.

ex·em·pli·fy /igˈzempləˌfī/ ▶ **verb** (**exemplifies, exemplifying, exemplified**) be or give a typical example of: *the best dry sherry is exemplified by the fino of Jerez.*

– SYNONYMS **typify,** epitomize, be an example of, be representative of, symbolize, illustrate, demonstrate.

– DERIVATIVES **ex·em·pli·fi·ca·tion** /igˌzempləfiˈkāsʜən/ noun.

ex·empt /igˈzem(p)t/ ▶ **adjective** free from an obligation or requirement imposed on others: *since he is only 13, he is exempt from prosecution.*

– SYNONYMS **free,** not liable, not subject, immune, excepted, excused, absolved.

▶ **verb** make someone exempt from something.

– SYNONYMS **excuse,** free, release, exclude, grant immunity, spare, absolve; informal let off.

– ORIGIN Latin *exemptus* 'taken out, freed.'

CHOOSE THE RIGHT WORD

See **ABSOLVE**.

ex·emp·tion /igˈzem(p)sʜən/ ▶ **noun 1** the process of exempting or state of being exempt from something: *exemption from antitrust laws.* **2** (also **personal exemption**) an amount of money that can be earned or received free of tax.

– SYNONYMS **immunity,** exception, dispensation, indemnity, exclusion, freedom, release, relief, absolution.

ex·er·cise /ˈeksərˌsīz/ ▶ **noun 1** physical activity carried out for the sake of health and fitness. **2** an activity carried out for a specific purpose: *a public relations exercise.* **3** a task set to practice or test a skill. **4** (**exercises**) military drills or training maneuvers. **5** the application of a power, right, or process: *the exercise of authority.*

– SYNONYMS **1 physical activity,** a workout, working out, movement, training. **2 task,** piece of work, problem, assignment, practice. **3 maneuver,** operation, deployment.

▶ **verb 1** use or apply a power, right, or quality: *the industry has exercised restraint so far.* **2** do physical activity. **3** worry or perplex someone.

– SYNONYMS **1 use,** employ, make use of, utilize, practice, apply. **2 work out,** do exercises, train. **3 concern,** occupy, worry, trouble, bother, disturb, prey on someone's mind.

– DERIVATIVES **ex·er·cis·a·ble** /-əbəl/ adjective **ex·er·cis·er** noun.
– ORIGIN from Latin *exercere* 'keep busy, practice.'

ex·er·cise ball ▶ **noun** a lightweight, inflated plastic ball 18–36 inches (45–91 cm) across, used in exercises for fitness and physiotherapy.

ex·er·cise bike ▶ **noun** a stationary piece of exercise equipment resembling an ordinary bicycle.

ex·ert /igˈzərt/ ▶ **verb 1** apply or bring to bear a force, influence, or quality. **2** (**exert oneself**) make a physical or mental effort.

– SYNONYMS **1 bring to bear,** apply, use, utilize, deploy. **2** (**exert oneself**) **work hard,** labor, toil, make an effort, endeavor, push oneself.

– ORIGIN Latin *exserere* 'put forth.'

ex·er·tion /igˈzərsʜən/ ▶ **noun 1** physical or mental effort. **2** the application of a force, influence, or quality.

ex·e·unt /ˈeksēənt, ˈeksēˌo͝ont/ ▶ **verb** (as a stage direction) (actors) leave the stage.
– ORIGIN Latin, 'they go out.'

ex·fo·li·ate /eksˈfōlēˌāt/ ▶ **verb 1** (of a material) be shed from a surface in scales or layers. **2** wash or rub part of the body with a granular substance to remove dead skin cells.
– DERIVATIVES **ex·fo·li·ant** /eksˈfōlēənt/ noun **ex·fo·li·a·tion** /eksˌfōlēˈāsʜən/ noun **ex·fo·li·a·tor** /-ˌātər/ noun.
– ORIGIN Latin *exfoliare* 'strip of leaves.'

ex gra·ti·a /eks ˈgrāsʜēə/ ▶ **adverb & adjective** (of payment) given as a gift or favor rather than because of any legal requirement.
– ORIGIN Latin, 'from favor.'

ex·hale /eksˈhāl, ˈeksˌhāl/ ▶ **verb 1** breathe out. **2** give off vapor or fumes.
– DERIVATIVES **ex·ha·la·tion** /ˌeks(h)əˈlāsʜən/ noun.
– ORIGIN Latin *exhalare*.

ex·haust /igˈzôst/ ▶ **verb 1** tire someone out. **2** use up all of: *the company exhausted these funds in six months.* **3** explore a subject or possibilities so fully that there is nothing left to be said or discovered. **4** expel gas or steam from an engine or other machine.

– SYNONYMS **1 tire out,** wear out, overtire, fatigue, weary, drain; informal take it out of someone, poop (out), tucker out. **2** (as adj. **exhausting**) **tiring,** wearying, taxing, wearing, draining, arduous, strenuous, onerous, demanding, grueling; informal killing. **3 use up,** get through, consume, finish, deplete, spend, empty, drain; informal blow.
– ANTONYMS invigorate, replenish.

▶ **noun 1** waste gases or air expelled from an engine or other machine. **2** the system through which waste gases are expelled.
– DERIVATIVES **ex·haust·er** noun **ex·haust·i·ble** adjective.
– ORIGIN Latin *exhaurire* 'drain out.'

ex·haust·ed /igˈzôstid/ ▶ **adjective 1** very tired. **2** completely used up.

– SYNONYMS **1 tired out,** worn out, weary, dog-tired, ready to drop, drained, fatigued; informal done in, all in, bushed, knocked out, wiped out, pooped, tuckered out, fried, zonked. **2** *exhausted reserves* **used up,** consumed, finished, spent, depleted; empty, drained.

ex·haus·tion /igˈzôscʜən/ ▶ **noun 1** a state of extreme tiredness. **2** the action of using something up.

– SYNONYMS **tiredness,** fatigue, weariness, debility, enervation.

ex·haus·tive /igˈzôstiv/ ▶ **adjective** covering all aspects fully.

– SYNONYMS **comprehensive,** all-inclusive, complete, full, encyclopedic, thorough, in-depth; detailed, meticulous, painstaking.
– ANTONYMS perfunctory.

– DERIVATIVES **ex·haus·tive·ly** adverb **ex·haus·tive·ness** noun.

ex·hib·it /igˈzibit/ ▶ **verb 1** publicly display an item in an art gallery or museum. **2** show a quality: *he exhibited great humility.*

– SYNONYMS **1 put on display,** show, display, unveil, present. **2 show,** reveal, display, manifest, indicate, demonstrate, express, evince, evidence.

▶ **noun 1** an object or collection of objects on display in an art gallery or museum. **2** Law a document or other object produced in a court as evidence.

– SYNONYMS **item,** piece, artifact, display, collection.

– DERIVATIVES **ex·hib·i·tor** noun.
– ORIGIN Latin *exhibere* 'hold out.'

ex·hi·bi·tion /ˌeksəˈbisʜən/ ▶ **noun 1** a public display of items in an art gallery or museum. **2** a display or demonstration of a skill or quality.

– SYNONYMS **1 exposition,** display, show, showing, presentation. **2 display,** show, demonstration, manifestation, expression.

– PHRASES **make an exhibition of oneself** behave very foolishly in public.

ex·hi·bi·tion·ism /ˌeksəˈbisʜəˌnizəm/ ▶ **noun 1** behavior that is intended to attract attention to oneself. **2** a mental condition in which a person feels an urge to display their genitals in public.
– DERIVATIVES **ex·hi·bi·tion·ist** noun **ex·hi·bi·tion·is·tic** /-ˌbisʜəˈnistik/ adjective.

ex·hil·a·rate /igˈziləˌrāt/ ▶ **verb** make someone feel very happy or full of energy.

– SYNONYMS *the fireworks display exhilarated us* **thrill,** excite, intoxicate, elate, delight, invigorate, stimulate.

– DERIVATIVES **ex·hil·a·rat·ing** adjective **ex·hil·a·ra·tion** /igˌziləˈrāsʜən/ noun.
– ORIGIN Latin *exhilarare* 'make cheerful.'

ex·hort /igˈzôrt/ ▶ **verb** strongly urge someone to do something.

– SYNONYMS **urge,** encourage, call on, enjoin, charge, press, bid, appeal to, entreat, implore; literary beseech.

– DERIVATIVES **ex·hor·ta·tion** /ˌegzôrˈtāsʜən, ˌeksôr-/ noun.
– ORIGIN Latin *exhortari.*

ex·hume /igˈz(y)o͞om, eksˈ(y)o͞om/ ▶ **verb** dig out something buried, especially a corpse from the ground.

– SYNONYMS **disinter,** dig up, disentomb.
– ANTONYMS bury.

– DERIVATIVES **ex·hu·ma·tion** /ˌegz(y)o͞oˈmāsʜən, ˌeks(h)yo͞o-/ noun.
– ORIGIN Latin *exhumare.*

ex·i·gen·cy /ˈeksijənsē, igˈzijənsē/ ▶ **noun** (pl. **exigencies**) an urgent need or demand: *the exigencies of contemporary life.*
– ORIGIN Latin *exigentia.*

ex·i·gent /ˈeksijənt/ ▶ **adjective** pressing; demanding.

ex·ig·u·ous /igˈzigyo͞oəs, ikˈsig-/ ▶ **adjective** formal very small.
– ORIGIN Latin *exiguus* 'scanty.'

ex·ile /ˈegˌzīl, ˈekˌsīl/ ▶ **noun 1** the state of being barred from one's native country. **2** a person who lives in exile.

– SYNONYMS **1 banishment,** expulsion, deportation, eviction, isolation. **2 expatriate,** émigré, deportee, displaced person, refugee.

▶ **verb** expel and bar someone from their native country.
– ORIGIN Latin *exilium* 'banishment.'

ex·ist /igˈzist/ ▶ **verb 1** be real; be present in a place or situation: *his supporters say the deal never existed.* **2** be alive; live.

– SYNONYMS **1 live,** be alive, be, be present. **2 prevail,** occur, be found, be in existence, be the case; formal obtain. **3 survive,** subsist, live, support oneself, manage, make do, get by, scrape by, make ends meet, eke out a living.

– ORIGIN Latin *exsistere* 'come into being.'

ex·ist·ence /igˈzistəns/ ▶ **noun 1** the fact or state of existing. **2** a way of living: *a rural existence.*

– SYNONYMS **1 survival,** continuation. **2 way of life,** life, lifestyle, situation.

ex·ist·ent /igˈzistənt/ ▶ **adjective** existing.

ex·is·ten·tial /ˌegziˈstencʜəl/ ▶ **adjective 1** relating to existence. **2** concerned with existentialism.
– DERIVATIVES **ex·is·ten·tial·ly** adverb.

ex·is·ten·tial·ism /ˌegziˈstencʜəˌlizəm/ ▶ **noun** a philosophical theory that emphasizes that human beings are free agents, responsible for their own actions.
– DERIVATIVES **ex·is·ten·tial·ist** noun & adjective.

ex·it /ˈegzit, ˈeksit/ ▶ **noun 1** a way out of a building, room, or passenger vehicle. **2** an act of leaving. **3** a place for traffic to leave a major road or roundabout.

– SYNONYMS **1 way out,** door, escape route, egress. **2 turning,** turnoff, junction. **3 departure,** leaving, withdrawal, going, retreat, flight, exodus, escape.
– ANTONYMS entrance, arrival.

▶ **verb** (**exits, exiting, exited**) **1** go out of or leave a place. **2** terminate a computer process or program.

– SYNONYMS **leave,** go out, depart, withdraw, retreat.
– ANTONYMS enter.

– ORIGIN Latin, 'he or she goes out.'

ex·it poll ▶ **noun** a poll of people leaving a polling station, asking how they voted.

ex ni·hi·lo /ˈeks ˈnē(h)əlō, ˈnī(h)əlō/ ▶ **adverb** formal out of nothing: *he created a paradise ex nihilo.*
– ORIGIN Latin.

exo- ▶ **prefix** external; from outside: *exoskeleton.*
– ORIGIN Greek *exō* 'outside.'

ex·o·bi·ol·o·gy /ˌeksōbīˈäləjē/ ▶ **noun** the branch of science concerned with the possibility and likely nature of life on other planets or in space.
– DERIVATIVES **ex·o·bi·ol·o·gist** noun.

ex·o·crine /ˈeksəˌkrin, ˈeksəˌkrēn/ ▶ **adjective** (of a gland) producing hormones or other products through ducts rather than directly into the blood.
– ORIGIN from Greek *krinein* 'sift.'

ex·o·dus /ˈeksədəs/ ▶ **noun** a mass departure of people.
– ORIGIN Greek *exodos.*

ex of·fi·ci·o /ˈeks əˈfisʜēō/ ▶ **adverb & adjective** by virtue of one's position or status.
– ORIGIN from Latin *ex* 'out of, from' + *officium* 'duty.'

ex·og·e·nous /ekˈsäjənəs/ ▶ **adjective** technical relating to an external cause or origin. Often contrasted with **ENDOGENOUS**.
– DERIVATIVES **ex·og·e·nous·ly** adverb.

ex·on·er·ate /igˈzänəˌrāt/ ▶ **verb** officially state that someone has not done something wrong or illegal.

– SYNONYMS **absolve,** clear, acquit, find innocent, discharge; formal exculpate.
– ANTONYMS convict.

– DERIVATIVES **ex·on·er·a·tion** /igˌzänəˈrāsʜən/ noun.
– ORIGIN Latin *exonerare* 'free from a burden.'

CHOOSE THE RIGHT WORD

See **ABSOLVE**.

ex·o·plan·et /ˈeksōˌplanit/ ▸ **noun** a planet that orbits a star outside the solar system: *most of the 100 known exoplanets are comparable in mass to Jupiter.*

ex·or·bi·tant /igˈzôrbitənt/ ▸ **adjective** (of a price or amount charged) unreasonably high.

– SYNONYMS **extortionate,** excessive, prohibitive, outrageous, unreasonable, inflated. informal steep, stiff.
– ANTONYMS cheap.

– DERIVATIVES **ex·or·bi·tant·ly** adverb.
– ORIGIN from Latin *exorbitare* 'go off the track.'

ex·or·cise /ˈeksôrˌsīz, ˈeksər-/ (or **exorcize**) ▸ **verb** drive out a supposed evil spirit from a person or place.
– DERIVATIVES **ex·or·cism** /ˈeksôrˌsizəm, ˈeksər-/ noun **ex·or·cist** /ˈeksôrˌsist, ˈeksər-/ noun.
– ORIGIN Greek *exorkizein.*

ex·o·skel·e·ton /ˌeksōˈskelitn/ ▸ **noun** the rigid external covering of the body in insects and some other invertebrate animals.

ex·o·ther·mic /ˌeksəˈTHərmik/ ▸ **adjective** (of a chemical reaction) accompanied by the release of heat.

ex·ot·ic /igˈzätik/ ▸ **adjective 1** originating in or typical of a distant foreign country. **2** strikingly colorful or unusual: *youths with exotic haircuts.*

– SYNONYMS **1** *exotic birds* **foreign,** nonnative, alien, tropical. **2** *exotic places* **foreign,** faraway, far-off, far-flung, distant. **3 striking,** colorful, eye-catching, unusual, unconventional, extravagant, outlandish.

▸ **noun** an exotic plant or animal.
– DERIVATIVES **ex·ot·i·cal·ly** /-(ə)lē/ adverb **ex·ot·i·cism** /igˈzätəˌsizəm/ noun.
– ORIGIN Greek *exōtikos* 'foreign.'

WORD TOOLKIT

See **UNFAMILIAR**.

ex·ot·i·ca /igˈzätikə/ ▸ **plural noun** unusual and interesting objects: *Hawaiian exotica.*

ex·ot·ic danc·er ▸ **noun** a striptease dancer.

ex·pand /ikˈspand/ ▸ **verb 1** make or become larger or more extensive. **2** (**expand on**) give more details about something.

– SYNONYMS **1** *metals expand when heated* **enlarge,** increase in size, swell, lengthen, stretch, spread, thicken, fill out. **2** *the company is expanding* **grow,** enlarge, increase in size, extend, augment, broaden, widen, develop, diversify, build up, branch out, spread. **3** (**expand on**) **elaborate on,** enlarge on, go into detail about, flesh out, develop.
– ANTONYMS contract.

– DERIVATIVES **ex·pand·a·bil·i·ty** /ikˌspandəˈbilitē/ noun **ex·pand·a·ble** adjective **ex·pand·er** noun.
– ORIGIN Latin *expandere* 'spread out.'

ex·pand·ed /ikˈspandid/ ▸ **adjective 1** (of a material) having a light cellular structure. **2** relatively broad in shape.

ex·panse /ikˈspans/ ▸ **noun** a wide continuous area of something: *a vast expanse of sand dunes.*

– SYNONYMS **area,** stretch, sweep, tract, swathe, belt, region, sea, carpet, blanket, sheet.

ex·pan·sion /ikˈspanSHən/ ▸ **noun 1** the action of becoming larger or more extensive. **2** the political strategy of extending a state's territory by encroaching on that of other nations.

– SYNONYMS **1** *expansion and contraction* **enlargement,** swelling, lengthening, elongation, stretching, thickening. **2** *the expansion of the company* **growth,** increase in size, enlargement, extension, development, diversification, spread.
– ANTONYMS contraction.

– DERIVATIVES **ex·pan·sion·ar·y** /ikˈspanSHəˌnerē/ adjective.

ex·pan·sion card (also **expansion board**) ▸ **noun** a circuit board that can be inserted in a computer to give extra facilities or memory.

ex·pan·sion·ism /ikˈspanSHəˌnizəm/ ▸ **noun** the policy of extending a state's territory by encroaching on that of other nations.
– DERIVATIVES **ex·pan·sion·ist** noun & adjective.

ex·pan·sive /ikˈspansiv/ ▸ **adjective 1** covering a wide area; extensive. **2** relaxed, friendly, and communicative.

– SYNONYMS **1** *expansive farmland* **extensive,** sweeping, rolling. **2** *expansive coverage* **wide-ranging,** extensive, broad, wide, comprehensive, thorough. **3 communicative,** forthcoming, sociable, friendly, outgoing, affable, chatty, talkative.

– DERIVATIVES **ex·pan·sive·ly** adverb **ex·pan·sive·ness** noun.

ex par·te /eks ˈpärtē/ ▸ **adjective & adverb** Law with respect to or in the interests of one side only.
– ORIGIN Latin, 'from a side.'

ex·pat /eksˈpat/ ▸ **noun & adjective** informal short for **EXPATRIATE**.

ex·pa·ti·ate /ikˈspāSHēˌāt/ ▸ **verb** speak or write at length or in detail: *professors shuffling forth to expatiate on the American dream.*
– DERIVATIVES **ex·pa·ti·a·tion** /ikˌspāSHēˈāSHən/ noun.
– ORIGIN Latin *exspatiari* 'move beyond one's usual bounds.'

ex·pa·tri·ate /eksˈpātrēit/ ▸ **noun** a person who lives outside their native country. ▸ **adjective** living outside one's native country.
– DERIVATIVES **ex·pa·tri·a·tion** /eksˌpātrēˈāSHən/ noun.
– ORIGIN Latin *expatriare.*

ex·pect /ikˈspekt/ ▸ **verb 1** regard something as likely to happen. **2** regard someone as likely to do or be something. **3** believe that someone will arrive soon. **4** require or demand something because it is appropriate or a person's duty: *Picasso quickly mastered the style that was expected of a fashionable portrait painter.* **5** (**be expecting**) informal be pregnant.

– SYNONYMS **1 suppose,** presume, imagine, assume, surmise; informal guess, figure, reckon. **2 anticipate,** envisage, await, look for, hope for, look forward to, contemplate, bargain for/on, predict, forecast. **3 require,** ask for, call for, want, insist on, demand.

– DERIVATIVES **ex·pect·a·ble** adjective.
– ORIGIN Latin *exspectare* 'look out for.'

ex·pect·an·cy /ikˈspektənsē/ ▸ **noun** (pl. **expectancies**) **1** hope or anticipation that something will happen. **2** something expected: *a life expectancy of 22 to 25 years.*

ex·pect·ant /ikˈspektənt/ ▸ **adjective 1** hoping or anticipating that something is about to happen. **2** (of a woman) pregnant. **3** (of a man) about to become a father.
– DERIVATIVES **ex·pect·ant·ly** adverb.

ex·pec·ta·tion /ˌekspekˈtāSHən/ ▸ **noun 1** belief that something will happen or be the case. **2** a thing that is expected to happen.

– SYNONYMS **1 supposition,** assumption, presumption, conjecture, calculation, prediction, hope. **2 anticipation,** expectancy, eagerness, excitement, suspense.

ex·pec·to·rant /ik'spektərənt/ ▶ **noun** a medicine that helps to bring up phlegm from the air passages, used to treat coughs.

ex·pec·to·rate /ik'spektəˌrāt/ ▶ **verb** cough or spit out phlegm from the throat or lungs.
– DERIVATIVES **ex·pec·to·ra·tion** /ikˌspektə'rāsʜən/ noun.
– ORIGIN Latin *expectorare* 'expel from the chest.'

ex·pe·di·ent /ik'spēdēənt/ ▶ **adjective 1** convenient and practical although not always fair or right: *either side could break the agreement if it were expedient to do so.* **2** suitable or appropriate.

– SYNONYMS **convenient,** advantageous, useful, beneficial, helpful, practical, pragmatic, politic, prudent, judicious.

▶ **noun** a means of achieving an end.

– SYNONYMS **measure,** means, method, stratagem, scheme, plan, move, tactic, maneuver, device, contrivance, ploy, ruse.

– DERIVATIVES **ex·pe·di·ence** noun **ex·pe·di·en·cy** noun **ex·pe·di·ent·ly** adverb.
– ORIGIN from Latin *expedire* (see **EXPEDITE**).

ex·pe·dite /'ekspəˌdīt/ ▶ **verb** make an action or process happen sooner or be accomplished more quickly.
– DERIVATIVES **ex·pe·dit·er** (also **expeditor**) noun.
– ORIGIN Latin *expedire* 'extricate, put in order.'

ex·pe·di·tion /ˌekspə'disʜən/ ▶ **noun 1** a journey undertaken by a group of people with a particular purpose. **2** formal promptness or speed in doing something.

– SYNONYMS **journey,** voyage, tour, safari, trek, mission, quest, hike, trip.

– DERIVATIVES **ex·pe·di·tion·ar·y** /ˌekspə'disʜəˌnerē/ adjective.

CHOOSE THE RIGHT WORD

See **JOURNEY**.

ex·pe·di·tious /ˌekspə'disʜəs/ ▶ **adjective** quick and efficient.
– DERIVATIVES **ex·pe·di·tious·ly** adverb.

ex·pel /ik'spel/ ▶ **verb** (**expels, expelling, expelled**) **1** force someone to leave a school, organization, or place. **2** force something out, especially from the body.

– SYNONYMS **throw out,** bar, ban, debar, drum out, banish, exile, deport, evict; informal chuck out.
– ANTONYMS admit.

– DERIVATIVES **ex·pel·la·ble** adjective **ex·pel·lee** /ˌekspel'lē/ noun.
– ORIGIN Latin *expellere,* from *pellere* 'to drive.'

CHOOSE THE RIGHT WORD

See **EJECT**.

ex·pend /ik'spend/ ▶ **verb** spend or use up a resource.
– ORIGIN Latin *expendere.*

ex·pend·a·ble /ik'spendəbəl/ ▶ **adjective** able to be sacrificed or abandoned because of little significance when compared to an overall purpose.

– SYNONYMS **dispensable,** replaceable, nonessential, inessential, unnecessary, not required, superfluous.
– ANTONYMS indispensable.

– DERIVATIVES **ex·pend·a·bil·i·ty** /ikˌspendə'bilitē/ noun.

ex·pend·i·ture /ik'spendicʜər/ ▶ **noun 1** the action of spending funds. **2** the amount of money spent. **3** the use of energy or other resources.

ex·pense /ik'spens/ ▶ **noun 1** the cost of something. **2** (**expenses**) specific costs spent in carrying out a job or task. **3** something on which money must be spent: *tolls are a daily expense.*

– SYNONYMS **cost,** expenditure, spending, outlay, outgoings, payment, price, charge, fees, overhead, tariff, bill.
– ANTONYMS income, profit.

– PHRASES **at the expense of 1** paid for by someone. **2** so as to harm something.
– ORIGIN from Latin *expendere* 'weigh or pay out.'

ex·pense ac·count ▶ **noun** an arrangement under which money spent in the course of business is later repaid by one's employer.

ex·pen·sive /ik'spensiv/ ▶ **adjective** costing a lot of money.

– SYNONYMS **costly,** high-priced, dear, overpriced, exorbitant, extortionate; informal steep, stiff, pricey.
– ANTONYMS cheap.

– DERIVATIVES **ex·pen·sive·ly** adverb **ex·pen·sive·ness** noun.

ex·pe·ri·ence /ik'spi(ə)rēəns/ ▶ **noun 1** practical contact with and observation of facts or events. **2** knowledge or skill gained over time. **3** an event that leaves an impression on one: *a frightening experience.*

– SYNONYMS **1 skill,** practical knowledge, understanding, familiarity, involvement, participation, contact, acquaintance, exposure, background, track record, history; informal know-how. **2 incident,** occurrence, event, happening, episode, adventure.

▶ **verb 1** encounter or undergo an event or situation. **2** feel an emotion.

– SYNONYMS **undergo,** go through, encounter, face, meet, come across, come up against, come into contact with.

– ORIGIN Latin *experientia.*

ex·pe·ri·enced /ik'spi(ə)rēənst/ ▶ **adjective** having knowledge or skill in a particular field gained over time.

– SYNONYMS **knowledgeable,** skillful, skilled, expert, proficient, trained, competent, capable, seasoned, practiced, mature, veteran.

ex·pe·ri·en·tial /ekˌspi(ə)rē'encʜəl/ ▶ **adjective** involving or based on experience and observation.
– DERIVATIVES **ex·pe·ri·en·tial·ly** adverb.

ex·per·i·ment /ik'sperəmənt/ ▶ **noun 1** a scientific procedure undertaken to make a discovery, test a theory, or demonstrate a fact. **2** a new idea or method that is tried out without being sure of the outcome: *the previous experiment in democracy ended in disaster.*

– SYNONYMS **test,** investigation, trial, examination, observation, research, assessment, evaluation, appraisal, analysis, study.

▶ **verb 1** perform a scientific experiment. **2** try out new ideas or methods.

– SYNONYMS **carry out experiments,** test, trial, try out, assess, appraise, evaluate.

– DERIVATIVES **ex·per·i·men·ta·tion** /ikˌsperəmən'tāsʜən/ noun **ex·per·i·ment·er** noun.
– ORIGIN Latin *experimentum.*

ex·per·i·men·tal /ikˌsperəˈmen(t)l/ ▶ **adjective 1** based on new ideas and not yet fully tested or established: *an experimental drug.* **2** relating to scientific experiments. **3** (of art, music, etc.) departing from established conventions; innovative.

– SYNONYMS **1 exploratory,** investigational, trial, test, pilot, speculative, tentative, preliminary. **2 new,** innovative, creative, radical, avant-garde, alternative, unorthodox, unconventional, cutting-edge.

– DERIVATIVES **ex·per·i·men·tal·ism** /-izəm/ noun **ex·per·i·men·tal·ist** /-ist/ noun **ex·per·i·men·tal·ly** adverb.

ex·pert /ˈekˌspərt/ ▶ **noun** a person who has great knowledge or skill in a particular area.

– SYNONYMS **specialist,** authority, professional, pundit, maestro, virtuoso, master, wizard, connoisseur, aficionado; informal ace, pro, hotshot, maven.
– ANTONYMS amateur.

▶ **adjective** having or involving great knowledge or skill.

– SYNONYMS **skillful,** skilled, adept, accomplished, experienced, practiced, knowledgeable, talented, masterly, virtuoso; informal ace, crack, mean.
– ANTONYMS incompetent.

– DERIVATIVES **ex·pert·ly** adverb.
– ORIGIN Latin *expertus.*

ex·per·tise /ˌekspərˈtēz, -ˈtēs/ ▶ **noun** great skill or knowledge in a particular field.

– SYNONYMS **skill,** prowess, proficiency, competence, knowledge, ability, aptitude, capability; informal know-how.

ex·pi·ate /ˈekspēˌāt/ ▶ **verb** make amends for guilt or wrongdoing.
– DERIVATIVES **ex·pi·a·tion** /ˌekspēˈāsʜən/ noun **ex·pi·a·to·ry** /ˈekspēəˌtôrē/ adjective.
– ORIGIN Latin *expiare* 'appease by sacrifice.'

ex·pi·ra·tion /ˌekspəˈrāsʜən/ ▶ **noun** the ending of the fixed period for which a contract is valid: *the expiration of the lease.*

ex·pire /ikˈspīr/ ▶ **verb 1** (of a document or agreement) come to the end of its period of validity. **2** (of a period of time) come to an end. **3** (of a person) die. **4** technical breathe out air from the lungs.

– SYNONYMS **1 run out,** become invalid, become void, lapse, end, finish, stop, terminate. **2 die,** pass away, breathe one's last; informal kick the bucket, croak, buy the farm.

– DERIVATIVES **ex·pir·a·to·ry** /ikˈspīrəˌtôrē/ adjective.
– ORIGIN Latin *exspirare* 'breathe out.'

ex·plain /ikˈsplān/ ▶ **verb 1** make something clear by giving a detailed description. **2** give a reason or justification for: *Cassie found it necessary to explain her black eye.* **3** (**explain oneself**) justify one's motives or behavior. **4** (**explain something away**) make something seem less embarrassing by giving an excuse or reason for it.

– SYNONYMS **1 describe,** make clear, spell out, put into words, define, elucidate, expound, clarify, throw light on. **2 account for,** give a reason for, excuse.

– DERIVATIVES **ex·plain·a·ble** adjective **ex·plain·er** noun.
– ORIGIN Latin *explanare.*

CHOOSE THE RIGHT WORD

See **CLARIFY**.

ex·pla·na·tion /ˌekspləˈnāsʜən/ ▶ **noun 1** a statement or description that makes something clear. **2** a reason or justification for an action or belief.

– SYNONYMS **1 clarification,** description, statement, interpretation, definition, commentary. **2 account,** reason, justification, answer, excuse, defense, vindication.

ex·plan·a·to·ry /ikˈsplanəˌtôrē/ ▶ **adjective** intended to explain something.
– DERIVATIVES **ex·plan·a·to·ri·ly** /ikˌsplanəˈtôrəlē/ adverb.

ex·ple·tive /ˈeksplitiv/ ▶ **noun** an oath or swear word.

– SYNONYMS **swear word,** oath, curse, obscenity, profanity, four-letter word, dirty word; informal cuss word, cuss; formal imprecation; (**expletives**) bad language, foul language, strong language, swearing.

– ORIGIN from Latin *expletivus* 'acting to fill out.'

ex·pli·ca·ble /ekˈsplikəbəl, ˈeksplik-/ ▶ **adjective** able to be explained or understood.
– ORIGIN from Latin *explicare* 'unfold.'

ex·pli·cate /ˈeksplіˌkāt/ ▶ **verb** analyze and explain an idea or literary work in detail.
– DERIVATIVES **ex·pli·ca·tion** /ˌekspliˈkāsʜən/ noun **ex·pli·ca·tor** /-ˌkātər/ noun.
– ORIGIN Latin *explicare* 'unfold.'

CHOOSE THE RIGHT WORD

See **CLARIFY**.

ex·plic·it /ikˈsplisit/ ▶ **adjective 1** clear and detailed, with no room for confusion or doubt. **2** describing or showing sexual activity in a direct and detailed way.

– SYNONYMS **1 clear,** plain, straightforward, crystal clear, precise, exact, specific, unequivocal, unambiguous, detailed. **2 graphic,** candid, full-frontal, uncensored.
– ANTONYMS vague.

– DERIVATIVES **ex·plic·it·ly** adverb **ex·plic·it·ness** noun.
– ORIGIN from Latin *explicare* 'unfold.'

ex·plode /ikˈsplōd/ ▶ **verb 1** burst or shatter violently as a result of the release of internal energy. **2** suddenly express an emotion. **3** increase suddenly in number or extent: *the herbal medicine market has exploded.* **4** show a belief or theory to be false. **5** (as adj. **exploded**) (of a diagram) showing parts of something in the normal relative positions but slightly separated from each other.

– SYNONYMS **1 blow up,** detonate, go off, burst, erupt. **2 lose one's temper,** blow up; informal fly off the handle, hit the roof, blow one's top/lid/stack. **3 increase rapidly,** mushroom, snowball, escalate, burgeon, rocket. **4 disprove,** refute, rebut, repudiate, debunk; informal shoot full of holes, blow out of the water.

– DERIVATIVES **ex·plod·er** noun.
– ORIGIN Latin *explodere* 'drive out by clapping.'

ex·ploit ▶ **verb** /ikˈsploit/ **1** make use of a person or situation in an unfair way, so as to gain advantage for oneself: *people desperate to lose weight were being exploited by unscrupulous salesmen.* **2** make good use of a resource.

– SYNONYMS **1 take advantage of,** abuse, impose on, treat unfairly, misuse, ill-treat; informal walk (all) over. **2 utilize,** make use of, put/turn to good use, make the most of, capitalize on, benefit from; informal cash in on.

▶ **noun** /ˈekˌsploit/ a bold or daring act.

– SYNONYMS **feat,** deed, act, adventure, stunt, escapade, achievement.

– DERIVATIVES **ex·ploit·a·ble** adjective **ex·ploi·ta·tion** /ˌeksploiˈtāsHən/ noun **ex·ploit·er** /ikˈsploitər/ noun.
– ORIGIN Old French *esploit* 'success, progress.'

ex·ploit·a·tive /ikˈsploitətiv/ (also **exploitive** /ikˈsploitiv/) ▶ **adjective** treating someone unfairly so as to make money or gain an advantage.

ex·plo·ra·tion /ˌekspləˈrāsHən/ ▶ **noun 1** the action of traveling through an unfamiliar area in order to learn about it. **2** thorough analysis of a subject or theme.

– SYNONYMS **investigation,** study, survey, research, inspection, examination, scrutiny, observation.

ex·plore /ikˈsplôr/ ▶ **verb 1** travel through an unfamiliar area in order to learn about it. **2** inquire into or examine in detail: *she explored the possibility of going back to school.* **3** examine something by touch.

– SYNONYMS **1 travel through,** tour, survey, scout, reconnoiter. **2 investigate,** look into, consider, examine, research, survey, scrutinize, study, review; informal check out.

– DERIVATIVES **ex·plor·a·to·ry** /ikˈsplôrəˌtôrē/ adjective **ex·plor·er** noun.
– ORIGIN Latin *explorare* 'search out.'

ex·plo·sion /ikˈsplōzHən/ ▶ **noun 1** an act of exploding. **2** a sudden increase in amount or extent: *an explosion in information technology.*

– SYNONYMS **1 detonation,** eruption, bang, blast, boom. **2 outburst,** flare-up, outbreak, eruption, storm, rush, surge, fit, paroxysm. **3 sudden increase,** mushrooming, snowballing, escalation, multiplication, burgeoning, rocketing.

ex·plo·sive /ikˈsplōsiv/ ▶ **adjective 1** able or likely to explode. **2** likely to cause an outburst of anger or controversy. **3** (of an increase) sudden and dramatic.

– SYNONYMS **1 volatile,** inflammable, flammable, combustible, incendiary. **2 fiery,** stormy, violent, volatile, passionate, tempestuous, turbulent, touchy, irascible. **3 tense,** highly charged, overwrought, dangerous, perilous, hazardous, sensitive, delicate, unstable, volatile.

▶ **noun** a substance that can be made to explode.

– SYNONYMS **bomb,** charge, incendiary (device).

– DERIVATIVES **ex·plo·sive·ly** adverb **ex·plo·sive·ness** noun.

ex·po /ˈekspō/ ▶ **noun** (pl. **expos**) a large exhibition.
– ORIGIN abbreviation of **EXPOSITION**.

ex·po·nent /ikˈspōnənt, ˈekspōnənt/ ▶ **noun 1** a person who promotes an idea or theory. **2** a person who does a particular thing skillfully. **3** Mathematics a raised figure beside a number indicating how many times that number is to be multiplied by itself (e.g., 3 in $2^3 = 2 \times 2 \times 2$).
– ORIGIN from Latin *exponere* 'present, explain.'

ex·po·nen·tial /ˌekspəˈnencHəl/ ▶ **adjective 1** (of an increase) becoming more and more rapid. **2** relating to or expressed by a mathematical exponent.
– DERIVATIVES **ex·po·nen·tial·ly** adverb.

ex·port ▶ **verb** /ikˈspôrt, ˈekspôrt/ **1** send goods or services to another country for sale. **2** spread or introduce ideas or customs to another country. ▶ **noun** /ˈekˌspôrt/ **1** an article or service sold abroad. **2** the sale of goods or services to other countries.
– DERIVATIVES **ex·port·a·ble** /ikˈspôrtəbəl/ adjective **ex·por·ta·tion** /ˌekspôrˈtāsHən/ noun **ex·port·er** noun.
– ORIGIN Latin *exportare.*

ex·pose /ikˈspōz/ ▶ **verb 1** make something visible by uncovering it. **2** reveal the true nature of: *he has been exposed as a liar.* **3** (**expose someone to**) make someone vulnerable to possible harm or risk. **4** (as adj. **exposed**) unprotected from the weather. **5** (**expose oneself**) publicly and indecently display one's genitals. **6** subject photographic film to light.

– SYNONYMS **1** *at low tide the rocks are exposed* **reveal,** uncover, lay bare. **2** *he was exposed to radiation* **lay open,** subject, put at risk of, put in jeopardy of, leave unprotected from. **3** *they were exposed to new ideas* **introduce to,** bring into contact with, make aware of, familiarize with, acquaint with. **4 uncover,** reveal, unveil, unmask, detect, find out, denounce, condemn; informal blow the whistle on.
– ANTONYMS cover, protect.

– DERIVATIVES **ex·pos·er** noun.
– ORIGIN Latin *exponere* 'present, explain.'

ex·po·sé /ˌekspōˈzā/ ▶ **noun** a report in the media that reveals something shocking.

– SYNONYMS **revelation,** disclosure, exposure; report, feature, piece, column; informal scoop, tell-all.
– ANTONYMS cover-up.

– ORIGIN French, 'shown, set out.'

ex·po·si·tion /ˌekspəˈzisHən/ ▶ **noun 1** a detailed description and explanation of a theory. **2** a large public exhibition of art or trade goods. **3** Music the part of a movement in which the principal themes are first presented.
– DERIVATIVES **ex·po·si·tion·al** adjective.
– ORIGIN Latin.

ex·pos·i·tor /ikˈspäzitər/ ▶ **noun** a person who explains complicated ideas or theories.
– DERIVATIVES **ex·pos·i·to·ry** /ikˈspäziˌtôrē/ adjective.

ex post fac·to /ˌeks pōst ˈfaktō/ ▶ **adjective & adverb** formal with retrospective action or effect.
– ORIGIN from Latin *ex postfacto* 'in the light of subsequent events.'

ex·pos·tu·late /ikˈspäscHəˌlāt/ ▶ **verb** express strong disapproval or disagreement.
– DERIVATIVES **ex·pos·tu·la·tion** /ikˌspäscHəˈlāsHən/ noun.
– ORIGIN Latin *expostulare* 'demand.'

ex·po·sure /ikˈspōzHər/ ▶ **noun 1** the state of being exposed to something harmful: *a few simple practices can reduce exposure to bacteria.* **2** a physical condition resulting from being exposed to severe weather conditions. **3** the revelation of something secret. **4** the publicizing of information or an event. **5** the quantity of light reaching a photographic film, as determined by shutter speed and lens aperture.

– SYNONYMS **1 frostbite,** cold, hypothermia. **2 uncovering,** revelation, disclosure, unveiling, unmasking, discovery, detection. **3 publicity,** advertising, public attention, media interest; informal hype.

ex·pound /ikˈspound/ ▶ **verb** present and explain a theory or idea in detail.

– SYNONYMS **present,** put forward, set forth, propose, propound; explain, give an explanation of, detail, spell out, describe.

– DERIVATIVES **ex·pound·er** noun.
– ORIGIN Latin *exponere* 'present, explain.'

ex·press[1] /ik'spres/ ▸ **verb 1** convey a thought or feeling in words or by gestures and behavior. **2** squeeze out liquid or air. **3** Mathematics represent something by a figure, symbol, or formula.

– SYNONYMS **communicate,** convey, indicate, show, demonstrate, reveal, put across/over, get across/over, articulate, put into words, voice, give voice to, state, air, give vent to.

– DERIVATIVES **ex·press·i·ble** adjective.
– ORIGIN Old French *expresser.*

ex·press[2] ▸ **adjective 1** operating at high speed. **2** (of a delivery service) using a special messenger.

– SYNONYMS **rapid,** swift, fast, high-speed, nonstop, direct.

▸ **adverb** by express train or delivery service.
▸ **noun 1** (also **express train**) a train that stops at few stations and so travels quickly. **2** a special delivery service. ▸ **verb** send something by express messenger or delivery.
– ORIGIN from **EXPRESS**[3].

ex·press[3] ▸ **adjective 1** stated clearly and openly: *it was his express wish that the event should continue.* **2** specifically identified to the exclusion of anything else: *the league was formed with the express purpose of raising the level of soccer.*

– SYNONYMS **1 explicit,** clear, direct, plain, distinct, unambiguous, categorical. **2 sole,** specific, particular, special, specified.
– ANTONYMS vague.

– DERIVATIVES **ex·press·ly** adverb.
– ORIGIN Latin *expressus* 'distinctly presented.'

ex·pres·sion /ik'spreshən/ ▸ **noun 1** the action of expressing thoughts or feelings. **2** a look on someone's face that conveys a particular feeling: *a sad expression.* **3** a word or phrase expressing an idea. **4** Mathematics a collection of symbols expressing a quantity.

– SYNONYMS **1 utterance,** uttering, voicing, declaration, articulation. **2 indication,** demonstration, show, exhibition, token, illustration. **3 look,** appearance, air, manner, countenance, mien. **4 idiom,** phrase, turn of phrase, term, proverb, saying, adage, maxim. **5 emotion,** feeling, spirit, passion, intensity, style.

– DERIVATIVES **ex·pres·sion·less** adjective.

ex·pres·sion·ism /ik'spreshə,nizəm/ ▸ **noun** a style in art, music, or drama in which the artist or writer seeks to express the inner world of emotion rather than external reality.
– DERIVATIVES **ex·pres·sion·ist** noun & adjective **ex·pres·sion·is·tic** /ik,spreshə'nistik/ adjective.

ex·pres·sive /ik'spresiv/ ▸ **adjective 1** effectively conveying thought or feeling. **2** (**expressive of**) conveying a quality or idea.

– SYNONYMS **1 eloquent,** meaningful, demonstrative, suggestive. **2 emotional,** passionate, poignant, moving, stirring, emotionally charged, lyrical.
– ANTONYMS undemonstrative.

– DERIVATIVES **ex·pres·sive·ly** adverb **ex·pres·sive·ness** noun **ex·pres·siv·i·ty** /,ekspre'sivitē/ noun.

ex·press·way /ik'spres,wā/ ▸ **noun** a highway designed for fast traffic, with a dividing strip between the traffic in opposite directions and two or more lanes in each direction.

ex·pro·pri·ate /,eks'prōprē,āt/ ▸ **verb** (of the government) take property from its owner for public use or benefit.
– DERIVATIVES **ex·pro·pri·a·tion** /,eks,prōprē'āshən/ noun **ex·pro·pri·a·tor** noun.
– ORIGIN Latin *expropriare.*

ex·pul·sion /ik'spəlshən/ ▸ **noun** the action of expelling someone or something.

– SYNONYMS **1 removal,** debarment, dismissal, exclusion, ejection, banishment, eviction. **2 discharge,** ejection, excretion, voiding, evacuation, elimination, passing.
– ANTONYMS admission.

– DERIVATIVES **ex·pul·sive** /ik'spəlsiv/ adjective.
– ORIGIN Latin.

ex·punge /ik'spənj/ ▸ **verb** completely remove something undesirable or unpleasant.

– SYNONYMS **erase,** remove, delete, rub out, wipe out, efface; cross out, strike out, blot out, blank out; destroy, obliterate, eradicate, eliminate.

– ORIGIN Latin *expungere* 'mark for deletion by means of points.'

ex·pur·gate /'ekspər,gāt/ ▸ **verb** remove matter regarded as obscene or unsuitable from a piece of writing.

– SYNONYMS **censor,** bowdlerize, cut, edit; clean up, sanitize.

– DERIVATIVES **ex·pur·ga·tion** /,ekspər'gāshən/ noun **ex·pur·ga·tor** noun.
– ORIGIN Latin *expurgare* 'cleanse thoroughly.'

ex·quis·ite /ek'skwizit, 'ekskwizit/ ▸ **adjective 1** very beautiful and delicate. **2** highly refined: *exquisite taste.* **3** intensely felt: *the exquisite pain of love.*

– SYNONYMS **1 beautiful,** lovely, elegant, fine, delicate, fragile, dainty, subtle. **2** *exquisite taste* **discriminating,** discerning, sensitive, fastidious, refined.

– DERIVATIVES **ex·quis·ite·ly** adverb **ex·quis·ite·ness** noun.
– ORIGIN from Latin *exquirere* 'seek out.'

ex·tant /'ekstənt, ek'stant/ ▸ **adjective** still in existence.
– ORIGIN from Latin *exstare* 'be visible or prominent.'

ex·tem·po·ra·ne·ous /ik,stempə'rānēəs/ ▸ **adjective** another term for **EXTEMPORARY**.
– DERIVATIVES **ex·tem·po·ra·ne·ous·ly** adverb.

ex·tem·po·rar·y /ik'stempə,rerē/ ▸ **adjective** spoken or done without preparation.
– ORIGIN from **EXTEMPORE**.

ex·tem·po·re /ik'stempərē/ ▸ **adjective & adverb** spoken or done without preparation.
– ORIGIN from Latin *ex tempore* 'on the spur of the moment.'

ex·tem·po·rize /ik'stempə,rīz/ ▸ **verb** compose or perform something without preparation; improvise.
– DERIVATIVES **ex·tem·po·ri·za·tion** /ik,stempəri'zāshən/ noun.

ex·tend /ik'stend/ ▸ **verb 1** make something larger or longer in space or time. **2** occupy a specified area or continue for a specified distance. **3** offer or give: *he extended a warm welcome to new members.* **4** stretch out the body or a limb. **5** strain or exert someone to the utmost.

– SYNONYMS **1** *he attempted to extend his dominions* **expand,** enlarge, increase, lengthen, widen, broaden. **2** *we have extended our range of services* **widen,** expand, broaden, augment, supplement, increase, add to, enhance, develop. **3** *extending the life of the charter* **prolong,** lengthen, increase,

stretch out, protract, spin out, string out. **4** *the garden extends down to the road* **continue,** carry on, stretch, reach. **5** *he extended a hand in greeting* **hold out,** reach out, hold forth, stretch out, outstretch, offer, give, proffer.
– ANTONYMS reduce, shorten.

– DERIVATIVES **ex·tend·a·ble** /-əbəl/ adjective **ex·tend·er** noun **ex·tend·i·ble** /-əbəl/ adjective **ex·ten·si·bil·i·ty** /ik,stensə'bilitē/ noun **ex·ten·si·ble** /-'stensəbəl/ adjective.
– ORIGIN Latin *extendere.*

ex·tend·ed fam·i·ly ▶ **noun** a family that extends beyond the parents and children to include grandparents and other relatives.

ex·ten·sion /ik'stensHən/ ▶ **noun 1** the action of extending something. **2** a part added to a building to enlarge it. **3** an additional period of time allowed for something. **4** an extra telephone on the same line as the main one. **5** (**extensions**) lengths of long artificial hair woven into a person's own hair. **6** (also **extension cord**) an additional length of electric cable that can be plugged into a fixed socket and has another socket on the end.
– SYNONYMS **1 addition,** add-on, adjunct, annex, wing. **2 expansion,** increase, enlargement, widening, broadening, deepening, augmentation, enhancement, development, growth. **3 prolongation,** lengthening, increase.
– DERIVATIVES **ex·ten·sion·al** adjective.
– ORIGIN Latin.

ex·ten·sive /ik'stensiv/ ▶ **adjective 1** covering a large area. **2** large in amount or scale: *an extensive collection of antiques.* **3** (of agriculture) obtaining a relatively small crop from a large area with a minimum of capital and labor.
– SYNONYMS **1 large,** sizable, substantial, considerable, ample, great, vast. **2 comprehensive,** thorough, exhaustive, broad, wide, wide-ranging, catholic.
– DERIVATIVES **ex·ten·sive·ly** adverb **ex·ten·sive·ness** noun.

ex·ten·sor /ik'stensər, -sôr/ ▶ **noun** a muscle whose contraction extends a limb or other part of the body.

ex·tent /ik'stent/ ▶ **noun 1** the area covered by something. **2** the size or scale of something: *they have no idea of the extent of the problem.* **3** the degree to which something is the case: *all couples edit the truth to some extent.*
– SYNONYMS **1 area,** size, expanse, length, proportions, dimensions. **2 degree,** scale, level, magnitude, scope, size, reach, range.
– ORIGIN Old French *extente.*

ex·ten·u·at·ing /ik'stenyoo͞,ātiNG/ ▶ **adjective** showing reasons why an offense should be treated less seriously: *hunger and poverty are not treated by the courts as extenuating circumstances.*
– DERIVATIVES **ex·ten·u·a·tion** /ik,stenyoo͞'āsHən/ noun.
– ORIGIN from Latin *extenuare* 'make thin.'

ex·te·ri·or /ik'sti(ə)rēər/ ▶ **adjective** relating to, forming, or on the outside of something.
– SYNONYMS **outer,** outside, outermost, outward, external.
– ANTONYMS interior.
▶ **noun** the outer surface or structure of something.
– SYNONYMS **outside,** external surface, outward appearance, facade.
– ANTONYMS interior.
– DERIVATIVES **ex·te·ri·or·ly** adverb.
– ORIGIN Latin.

ex·ter·mi·nate /ik'stərmə,nāt/ ▶ **verb** destroy someone or something completely.
– SYNONYMS **kill,** destroy, wipe out, eliminate, eradicate, annihilate, extirpate.
– DERIVATIVES **ex·ter·mi·na·tion** /ik,stərmə'nāsHən/ noun **ex·ter·mi·na·tor** noun.
– ORIGIN Latin *exterminare* 'drive out.'

CHOOSE THE RIGHT WORD
See **DESTROY**.

ex·ter·nal /ik'stərnl/ ▶ **adjective 1** belonging to or forming the outside of something. **2** coming from a source outside the person or thing affected: *many external factors can influence the incidence of cancer.* **3** relating to another country or institution.
– SYNONYMS **outer,** outside, outermost, outward, exterior.
– ANTONYMS internal.
▶ **noun** (**externals**) the outward features of something.
– DERIVATIVES **ex·ter·nal·ly** adverb.
– ORIGIN Latin.

ex·ter·nal ear ▶ **noun** the parts of the ear outside the eardrum, especially the pinna.

ex·ter·nal·ize /ik'stərnə,līz/ ▶ **verb 1** express a thought or feeling in words or actions. **2** give external existence or physical form to something.
– DERIVATIVES **ex·ter·nal·i·za·tion** /ik,stərnəli'zāsHən/ noun.

ex·tinct /ik'stiNG(k)t/ ▶ **adjective 1** (of a species or other large group) having no living members. **2** no longer in existence. **3** (of a volcano) not having erupted in recorded history.
– SYNONYMS **1 vanished,** lost, gone, died out, wiped out, destroyed. **2 inactive.**
– ANTONYMS living, dormant.
– ORIGIN from Latin *exstinguere* 'extinguish.'

ex·tinc·tion /ik'stiNG(k)sHən/ ▶ **noun** the state of being or process of becoming extinct.
– SYNONYMS **dying out,** disappearance, vanishing, extermination, destruction, elimination, eradication, annihilation.

ex·tin·guish /ik'stiNGgwisH/ ▶ **verb 1** put out a fire or light. **2** put an end to: *no human life should be extinguished for the benefit of another.* **3** cancel a debt by full payment.
– SYNONYMS **douse,** quench, put out, stamp out, smother, snuff out.
– ANTONYMS light.
– DERIVATIVES **ex·tin·guish·er** noun.
– ORIGIN Latin *exstinguere.*

ex·tir·pate /'ekstər,pāt/ ▶ **verb** completely destroy something.
– SYNONYMS **weed out,** destroy, eradicate, stamp out, root out, wipe out, eliminate, suppress, crush, put down, put an end to, get rid of.
– DERIVATIVES **ex·tir·pa·tion** /,ekstər'pāsHən/ noun.
– ORIGIN Latin *exstirpare.*

CHOOSE THE RIGHT WORD
See **DESTROY**.

ex·tol /ik'stōl/ ▶ **verb** (**extols, extolling, extolled**) praise someone or something enthusiastically.

– SYNONYMS **praise,** wax lyrical about, sing the praises of, acclaim, applaud, celebrate, eulogize, rave about, enthuse over; formal **laud.**
– ANTONYMS criticize.

– ORIGIN Latin *extollere.*

ex·tort /ik'stôrt/ ▶ **verb** obtain something by force, threats, or other unfair means.

– SYNONYMS **extract,** exact, wring, wrest, screw, squeeze.

– DERIVATIVES **ex·tor·tion** /ik'stôrSHən/ noun **ex·tor·tion·ist** /ik'stôrSHənist/ noun.
– ORIGIN Latin *extorquere.*

ex·tor·tion·ate /ik'stôrSHənit/ ▶ **adjective** (of a price) much too high.

– SYNONYMS **exorbitant,** excessive, outrageous, unreasonable, inordinate, inflated.

– DERIVATIVES **ex·tor·tion·ate·ly** adverb.

ex·tra /'ekstrə/ ▶ **adjective** added to an existing or usual amount or number.

– SYNONYMS **additional,** more, added, supplementary, further, auxiliary, ancillary, subsidiary, secondary.

▶ **adverb 1** to a greater extent than usual. **2** in addition.

– SYNONYMS **exceptionally,** particularly, specially, especially, extremely.

▶ **noun 1** an item in addition to what is usual or necessary, for which an extra charge is made. **2** a person taking part in a crowd scene in a movie or play.

– SYNONYMS **addition,** supplement, bonus, adjunct, addendum, add-on.

– ORIGIN probably from **EXTRAORDINARY.**

extra- ▶ **prefix 1** outside; beyond: *extramarital.* **2** beyond the scope of: *extracurricular.*
– ORIGIN Latin *extra* 'outside.'

ex·tract ▶ **verb** /ik'strakt/ **1** remove something with care or effort. **2** obtain a substance or resource from something by a special method. **3** obtain something from someone unwilling to give it: *in the Middle Ages, they would torture people to extract a false confession.* **4** select a passage from a written work, movie, or piece of music for quotation, performance, or reproduction.

– SYNONYMS **1 take out,** draw out, pull out, remove, withdraw, release, extricate. **2 wrest,** exact, wring, screw, squeeze, obtain by force, extort. **3 squeeze out,** press out, obtain.
– ANTONYMS insert.

▶ **noun** /'ek,strakt/ **1** a short passage taken from a written work, movie, or piece of music. **2** the concentrated form of the active ingredient of a substance: *vanilla extract.*

– SYNONYMS **1 excerpt,** passage, citation, quotation. **2 distillation,** distillate, concentrate, essence, juice.

– DERIVATIVES **ex·tract·a·ble** adjective **ex·trac·tive** adjective.
– ORIGIN Latin *extrahere* 'draw out.'

ex·trac·tion /ik'strakSHən/ ▶ **noun 1** the action of extracting something. **2** the ethnic origin of someone's family: *a woman of Polish extraction.*

ex·trac·tor /ik'straktər/ ▶ **noun** a machine or device used to extract something. ▶ **adjective** referring to a fan used for removing unpleasant smells and stale air from a room.

ex·tra·cur·ric·u·lar /,ekstrəkə'rikyələr/ ▶ **adjective** (of an activity at a school or college) done in addition to the normal curriculum.

ex·tra·dite /'ekstrə,dīt/ ▶ **verb** hand over a person accused or convicted of a crime in another state or a foreign country to the legal authority of that state or country.
– DERIVATIVES **ex·tra·di·tion** /,ekstrə'diSHən/ noun.
– ORIGIN from French *extradition.*

ex·tra·mar·i·tal /,ekstrə'maritl/ ▶ **adjective** occurring outside marriage.

ex·tra·mu·ral /,ekstrə'myo͝orəl/ ▶ **adjective 1** outside the boundaries of a town or city. **2** Brit. (of a course of study) arranged for people who are not full-time members of a university or other educational establishment.
– DERIVATIVES **ex·tra·mu·ral·ly** adverb.
– ORIGIN from Latin *extra muros* 'outside the walls.'

ex·tra·ne·ous /ik'strānēəs/ ▶ **adjective 1** unrelated to the subject; irrelevant. **2** of external origin.

– SYNONYMS **irrelevant,** immaterial, beside the point, unrelated, unconnected, inapposite, inapplicable.

– DERIVATIVES **ex·tra·ne·ous·ly** adverb.
– ORIGIN Latin *extraneus.*

ex·tra·net /'ekstrə,net/ ▶ **noun** an intranet that can be partially accessed by authorized outside users, enabling organizations to exchange data in a secure way.

ex·tra·or·di·naire /,ekstrə,ôrdn'er/ ▶ **adjective** outstanding in a particular area: *a gardener extraordinaire.*
– ORIGIN French.

ex·traor·di·nar·y /ik'strôrdn,erē, ,ekstrə'ôrdn-/ ▶ **adjective 1** very unusual or remarkable. **2** (of a meeting) specially arranged rather than being one of a regular series. **3** (of an official) specially employed: *Ambassador Extraordinary.*

– SYNONYMS **1** *an extraordinary coincidence* **remarkable,** exceptional, amazing, astonishing, astounding, sensational, stunning, incredible, unbelievable, phenomenal; informal **fantastic.** **2** *extraordinary speed* **very great,** tremendous, enormous, immense, prodigious, stupendous, monumental.
– ANTONYMS unremarkable.

– DERIVATIVES **ex·traor·di·nar·i·ly** /-,erəlē/ adverb **ex·traor·di·nar·i·ness** noun.
– ORIGIN from Latin *extra ordinem* 'outside the normal course of events.'

ex·traor·di·nar·y ren·di·tion ▶ **noun** another term for **RENDITION** (sense 3).

ex·trap·o·late /ik'strapə,lāt/ ▶ **verb 1** use a fact or conclusion that is valid for one situation and apply it to a different or larger one. **2** extend a graph by inferring unknown values from trends in the known data.
– DERIVATIVES **ex·trap·o·la·tion** /ik,strapə'lāSHən/ noun **ex·trap·o·la·tive** /-,lātiv/ adjective.
– ORIGIN from **EXTRA-** + a shortened form of **INTERPOLATE.**

ex·tra·sen·so·ry per·cep·tion /,ekstrə'sensərē/ ▶ **noun** the supposed faculty of perceiving things by means other than the known senses, e.g., by telepathy, precognition, or clairvoyance.

ex·tra·ter·res·tri·al /,ekstrətə'restrēəl/ ▶ **adjective** relating to things beyond the earth or its atmosphere. ▶ **noun** a fictional being from outer space.

ex·trav·a·gant /ik'stravəgənt/ ▶ **adjective 1** lacking restraint in spending money or using resources. **2** costing a great deal. **3** exceeding what is reasonable or appropriate: *extravagant claims about the product.*

– SYNONYMS **1 spendthrift,** profligate, wasteful, prodigal, lavish. **2 excessive,** immoderate, exaggerated, gushing, unrestrained, effusive, fulsome. **3 ornate,** elaborate, fancy, overelaborate, ostentatious, exaggerated; informal flashy.
– ANTONYMS thrifty, moderate.

– DERIVATIVES **ex·trav·a·gance** noun **ex·trav·a·gant·ly** adverb.
– ORIGIN from Latin *extravagari* 'diverge greatly.'

ex·trav·a·gan·za /ikˌstravə'ganzə/ ▶ **noun** an elaborate and spectacular entertainment.

– SYNONYMS **spectacular,** display, spectacle, show, pageant.

– ORIGIN Italian *estravaganza* 'extravagance.'

ex·tra·ve·hic·u·lar /ˌekstrəvē'hikyələr/ ▶ **adjective** referring to activity performed in space outside a spacecraft.

ex·tra vir·gin ▶ **adjective** (of olive oil) of a particularly fine grade, made from the first pressing of the olives.

ex·treme /ik'strēm/ ▶ **adjective 1** to the highest degree; very great. **2** highly unusual; exceptional: *in extreme cases the soldier may be discharged.* **3** very severe or serious. **4** not moderate, especially politically. **5** furthest from the center or a given point: *the extreme north of Canada.* **6** (of a sport) performed in a dangerous environment.

– SYNONYMS **1** *extreme danger* **utmost,** (very) great, greatest (possible), maximum, great, acute, enormous, severe, serious. **2** *extreme measures* **drastic,** serious, desperate, dire, radical, far-reaching, draconian. **3 radical,** extremist, immoderate, fanatical, revolutionary, subversive, militant. **4 dangerous,** hazardous, risky, high-risk; informal white-knuckle. **5 furthest,** farthest, utmost, remotest, ultra-.
– ANTONYMS slight, moderate.

▶ **noun 1** either of two things that are as different from each other as possible. **2** the most extreme degree: *extremes of temperature.*

– SYNONYMS **extremity,** antithesis, opposite, (opposite) pole, limit, contrast.

– ORIGIN Latin *extremus* 'outermost, utmost.'

ex·treme·ly /ik'strēmlē/ ▶ **adverb** to a very high degree.

– SYNONYMS **very,** exceptionally, especially, extraordinarily, tremendously, immensely, hugely, supremely, highly, mightily; informal awfully, terribly, seriously, mighty.
– ANTONYMS slightly.

ex·treme unc·tion ▶ **noun** (in the Roman Catholic Church) a former name for the sacrament of anointing of the sick, especially when administered to the dying.

ex·trem·ist /ik'strēmist/ ▶ **noun** a person who holds extreme political or religious views.

– SYNONYMS **fanatic,** radical, zealot, fundamentalist, hardliner, militant, activist.
– ANTONYMS moderate.

– DERIVATIVES **ex·trem·ism** /-ˌmizəm/ noun.

ex·trem·i·ty /ik'stremitē/ ▶ **noun** (pl. **extremities**) **1** the furthest point or limit. **2** (**extremities**) the hands and feet. **3** severity or seriousness: *the extremity of the violence.* **4** extreme difficulty or hardship.

ex·tri·cate /'ekstriˌkāt/ ▶ **verb** free from a difficult or restrictive situation or place: *the company has to extricate itself from its current financial mess.*

– SYNONYMS **extract,** free, release, disentangle, get out, remove, withdraw, disengage; informal get someone/oneself off the hook.

– DERIVATIVES **ex·tri·ca·tion** /ˌekstri'kāsʜən/ noun.
– ORIGIN Latin *extricare* 'unravel.'

ex·trin·sic /ik'strinzik, -sik/ ▶ **adjective** coming or operating from outside; not part of the essential nature of something: *extrinsic environmental influences.*
– DERIVATIVES **ex·trin·si·cal·ly** adverb.
– ORIGIN Latin *extrinsecus* 'outward.'

ex·tro·vert /'ekstrəˌvərt/ ▶ **noun 1** an outgoing, socially confident person. **2** Psychology a person predominantly concerned with external things or objective considerations. ▶ **adjective** relating to or typical of an extrovert.

– SYNONYMS **outgoing,** extroverted, sociable, gregarious, lively, ebullient, exuberant, uninhibited, unreserved.
– ANTONYMS introverted.

– DERIVATIVES **ex·tro·ver·sion** /ˌekstrə'vərzʜən/ noun **ex·tro·vert·ed** adjective.
– ORIGIN from *extro-* (variant of **EXTRA-**) + Latin *vertere* 'to turn.'

ex·trude /ik'stro͞od/ ▶ **verb 1** thrust or force something out. **2** shape a material such as metal or plastic by forcing it through a die.

– SYNONYMS **force out,** thrust out, squeeze out, express, eject, expel, release, emit.

– DERIVATIVES **ex·tru·sion** /ik'stro͞ozʜən/ noun.
– ORIGIN Latin *extrudere.*

ex·tru·sive /ik'stro͞osiv/ ▶ **adjective** (of rock) that has been forced out at the earth's surface as lava or other volcanic deposits.

ex·u·ber·ant /ig'zo͞obərənt/ ▶ **adjective 1** lively and cheerful. **2** literary growing profusely.

– SYNONYMS **ebullient,** buoyant, cheerful, high-spirited, cheery, lively, vivacious, enthusiastic, irrepressible, energetic, animated, full of life, sparkling; informal bubbly, bouncy, full of beans.

– DERIVATIVES **ex·u·ber·ance** noun **ex·u·ber·ant·ly** adverb.
– ORIGIN from Latin *exuberare* 'be abundantly fruitful.'

ex·ude /ig'zo͞od/ ▶ **verb 1** (of liquid or a smell) discharge or be discharged slowly and steadily. **2** clearly display an emotion or quality: *silk skirts exuding elegance.*

– SYNONYMS **1** *milkweed exudes a milky sap* **give off/out,** discharge, release, emit, issue; ooze, secrete. **2** *he exuded self-confidence* **emanate,** radiate, ooze, emit; display, show, exhibit, manifest.

– DERIVATIVES **ex·u·da·tion** /ˌeksyo͞o'dāsʜən, ˌeksə-/ noun.
– ORIGIN Latin *exsudare,* from *sudare* 'to sweat.'

ex·ult /ig'zəlt/ ▶ **verb** show or feel triumphant elation.
– DERIVATIVES **ex·ul·ta·tion** /ˌeksəl'tāsʜən, ˌegzəl-/ noun.
– ORIGIN Latin *exsultare.*

ex·ult·ant /ig'zəltnt/ ▶ **adjective** triumphantly happy.

– SYNONYMS **jubilant,** thrilled, triumphant, delighted, exhilarated, happy, overjoyed, joyous, joyful, gleeful, excited, rejoicing, ecstatic, euphoric, elated, rapturous, in raptures, enraptured, on cloud nine, in seventh heaven; informal over the moon.

– DERIVATIVES **ex·ult·an·cy** noun **ex·ult·ant·ly** adverb.

ex·vo·to /eks 'vōtō/ ▶ **noun** (pl. **ex-votos**) an offering given in order to fulfill a vow.
– ORIGIN from Latin *ex voto* 'from a vow.'

eye /ī/ ▸ **noun 1** the organ of sight in humans and animals. **2** the small hole in a needle through which the thread is passed. **3** a small metal loop into which a hook is fitted as a fastener on a garment. **4** a person's opinion or feelings: *to European eyes, the city seems overcrowded.* **5** an eyelike marking on an animal or bird. **6** a round, dark spot on a potato from which a new shoot grows. **7** the calm region at the center of a storm. ▸ **verb** (**eyes, eyeing** or **eying, eyed**) look at someone or something closely or with interest.

– SYNONYMS **look at,** observe, view, gaze at, stare at, regard, contemplate, survey, scrutinize, consider, glance at, watch; informal check out, size up, eyeball.

– PHRASES **be all eyes** be watching eagerly and attentively. **an eye for an eye and a tooth for a tooth** doing the same thing in return is the appropriate way to deal with an offense or crime. [from the Book of Exodus, chapter 21.] **give someone the eye** informal look at someone with sexual interest. **have an eye for** be able to recognize and judge something wisely. **have one's eye on** aim to acquire something. **have** (or **keep**) **one's eye on** keep someone under careful observation. **have** (or **with**) **an eye to** have (or having) as one's objective. **have eyes in the back of one's head** know what is going on around one even when one cannot see it. **keep an eye out** (or **open**) look out for something. **make eyes at** look at someone with sexual interest. **one in the eye for** a disappointment or setback for someone. **open someone's eyes** cause someone to realize something. **see eye to eye** be in full agreement. **a twinkle** (or **gleam**) **in someone's eye** something that is as yet no more than an idea or dream. **up to one's eyes** informal very busy. **with one's eyes open** fully aware of possible difficulties.
– ORIGIN Old English.

WORD LINKS

ocular, **ophthalmic**, **optic** *relating to the eye*
ophthalmology *branch of medicine dealing with the eye*

eye·ball /'ī,bôl/ ▸ **noun** the round part of the eye of a vertebrate, within the eyelids and socket. ▸ **verb** informal stare at someone or something closely.
– PHRASES **eyeball to eyeball** face to face with someone, especially in an aggressive way.

eye·brow /'ī,brou/ ▸ **noun** the strip of hair growing on the ridge above a person's eye socket.
– PHRASES **raise one's eyebrows** (or **an eyebrow**) show surprise or mild disapproval.

eye-catch·ing ▸ **adjective** immediately appealing or noticeable.

eye con·tact ▸ **noun** the act of looking directly into one another's eyes: *make eye contact with your interviewers.*

eye·ful /'ī,fo͝ol/ ▸ **noun** informal **1** a long steady look. **2** an eye-catching person or thing.

eye·glass /'ī,glas/ ▸ **noun 1** a single lens for correcting or assisting poor eyesight, especially a monocle. **2** (**eyeglasses**) another term for **GLASSES**.

eye·hole /'ī,hōl/ ▸ **noun** a hole to look through, especially in a curtain or mask.

eye·lash /'ī,lasʜ/ ▸ **noun** each of the short hairs growing on the edges of the eyelids.

eye·let /'īlit/ ▸ **noun 1** a small round hole made in leather or cloth, used for threading a lace, string, or rope through. **2** a metal ring reinforcing an eyelet.
– ORIGIN Old French *oillet.*

eye·lid /'ī,lid/ ▸ **noun** each of the upper and lower folds of skin that cover the eye when closed.

eye·lin·er /'ī,līnər/ ▸ **noun** a cosmetic applied as a line around the eyes.

eye-o·pen·er ▸ **noun** informal an event or situation that proves to be unexpectedly revealing.

eye·patch /'ī,pacʜ/ ▸ **noun** a patch worn to protect an injured eye.

eye·piece /'ī,pēs/ ▸ **noun** the lens that is closest to the eye in a microscope or other optical instrument.

eye-pop·ping ▸ **adjective** informal astonishingly large or blatant.

eye·shade /'ī,sʜād/ ▸ **noun** a translucent visor used to protect the eyes from strong light.

eye·shad·ow /'ī,sʜadō/ ▸ **noun** a colored cosmetic applied to the eyelids or to the skin around the eyes.

eye·shot /'ī,sʜät/ ▸ **noun** the distance for which one can see: *he is within eyeshot.*

eye·sight /'ī,sīt/ ▸ **noun** a person's ability to see.

eye sock·et ▸ **noun** the cavity in the skull that encloses an eyeball with its surrounding muscles.

eye·sore /'ī,sôr/ ▸ **noun** a very ugly thing.

eye·tooth /'ī',to͞otʜ/ ▸ **noun** a canine tooth, especially one in the upper jaw.
– PHRASES **give one's eyeteeth for** (or **to be**) do anything in order to have or be something: *I'd give my eyeteeth for a new car.*

eye track·ing ▸ **noun** a technology that monitors eye movements as a means of detecting abnormalities or of studying how people interact with text or online documents.

eye·wash /'ī,wôsʜ, -,wäsʜ/ ▸ **noun 1** liquid for cleansing a person's eye. **2** informal nonsense.

eye·wear /ī,wer/ ▸ **noun** things worn on the eyes, such as spectacles and contact lenses.

eye·wit·ness /'ī'witnəs/ ▸ **noun** a person who has seen something happen and can give a first-han d description of it.

– SYNONYMS **observer,** onlooker, witness, bystander, passerby.

eyr·ie /'e(ə)rē, 'i(ə)rē/ ▸ **noun** variant spelling of **AERIE**.

F[1] (also **f**) ▶ **noun** (pl. **Fs** or **F's**) **1** the sixth letter of the alphabet. **2** Music the fourth note of the scale of C major.

F[2] ▶ **abbreviation 1** Fahrenheit. **2** farad(s). **3** female. **4** franc(s). ▶ **symbol 1** the chemical element fluorine. **2** Physics force.

f ▶ **abbreviation 1** Grammar feminine. **2** (in textual references) folio. **3** Music forte. **4** (in racing results) furlong(s). ▶ **symbol 1** focal length. **2** Electronics frequency.

fa /fä/ ▶ **noun** Music the fourth note of a major scale, coming after 'mi' and before 'sol'.
– ORIGIN the first syllable of *famuli*, taken from a Latin hymn.

FAA ▶ **abbreviation** Federal Aviation Administration.

fab /fab/ ▶ **adjective** informal fabulous; wonderful.

Fa·bi·an /'fābēən/ ▶ **noun** a member or supporter of the Fabian Society, an organization that aims to establish socialism in a gradual way that does not involve revolution. ▶ **adjective 1** relating to the Fabians. **2** using cautious delaying tactics to wear out an enemy.
– DERIVATIVES **Fa·bi·an·ism** /-ˌnizəm/ noun **Fa·bi·an·ist** /-ist/ noun.
– ORIGIN from the name of the Roman general Quintus *Fabius* Maximus Verrucosus (d.203 BC), known for his delaying tactics.

fa·ble /'fābəl/ ▶ **noun 1** a short story with a moral, typically featuring animals as characters. **2** a myth or legend. **3** a false statement; a nonfactual account.

> – SYNONYMS **parable,** allegory, myth, legend, story, tale.

– ORIGIN Old French, from Latin *fabula* 'story.'

> **CHOOSE THE RIGHT WORD**
>
> See **FICTION**.

fa·bled /'fābəld/ ▶ **adjective 1** famous: *a fabled guitarist.* **2** mythical or imaginary: *a fabled beast.*

fab·ric /'fabrik/ ▶ **noun 1** material produced by weaving or knitting textile fibers; cloth. **2** the walls, floor, and roof of a building. **3** the essential structure of a system or organization: *the fabric of society.*

> – SYNONYMS **1 cloth,** material, textile, stuff. **2 structure,** construction, makeup, organization, framework, essence.

– ORIGIN Latin *fabrica* 'something skillfully produced.'

fab·ri·cate /'fabrəˌkāt/ ▶ **verb 1** invent something, typically in order to deceive other people: *police officers had fabricated evidence to secure convictions.* **2** construct or manufacture an industrial product.

> – SYNONYMS **falsify,** fake, counterfeit, invent, make up.

– DERIVATIVES **fab·ri·ca·tion** /ˌfabrə'kāsʜən/ noun **fab·ri·ca·tor** /-ˌkātər/ noun.
– ORIGIN Latin *fabricare* 'manufacture.'

fab·ric soft·en·er ▶ **noun** liquid used to soften clothes when they are being washed.

fab·u·list /'fabyəlist/ ▶ **noun 1** a person who composes fables. **2** a liar.

fab·u·lous /'fabyələs/ ▶ **adjective 1** very great; extraordinary: *his fabulous wealth.* **2** informal wonderful. **3** mythical.

> – SYNONYMS **1 stupendous,** prodigious, phenomenal, exceptional, fantastic, breathtaking, staggering, unthinkable, unimaginable, incredible, undreamed of. **2** *a fabulous time* see **EXCELLENT**.

– DERIVATIVES **fab·u·lous·ly** adverb **fab·u·lous·ness** noun.
– ORIGIN Latin *fabulosus* 'celebrated in fable,' from *fabula* 'story.'

fa·cade /fə'säd/ (also **façade**) ▶ **noun 1** the face of a building, especially the front. **2** a deceptive outward appearance: *her facade of bravery crumbled and she burst into tears.*

> – SYNONYMS **1 front,** frontage, face, elevation, exterior, outside. **2 show,** front, appearance, pretense, simulation, affectation, act, charade, mask, veneer.

– ORIGIN French, from *face* 'face.'

face /fās/ ▶ **noun 1** the front part of a person's head from the forehead to the chin, or the corresponding part in an animal. **2** an expression on someone's face. **3** the front or main surface of something. **4** a vertical or sloping side of a mountain or cliff. **5** an aspect: *the unacceptable face of social drinking.*

> – SYNONYMS **1 countenance,** physiognomy, features, profile; literary visage, lineaments. **2 expression,** look, appearance, mien, air. **3** *he made a face* **grimace,** scowl, wince, frown, pout. **4 side,** aspect, surface, plane, facet, wall, elevation.

▶ **verb 1** be positioned with the face or front toward or in a particular direction: *the house faces due east.* **2** confront and deal with or accept: *I had to face the fact that I might never have a child.* **3** have a difficult event or situation ahead of one: *the president is facing a political crisis.* **4** (**face off**) get ready to argue or fight with someone. **5** cover the surface of something with a layer of a different material.

> – SYNONYMS **1 look out on,** front on to, look toward, look over/across, overlook, be opposite (to). **2 accept,** get used to, adjust to, learn to live with, cope with, deal with, come to terms with, become resigned to. **3 beset,** worry, trouble, confront, torment, plague, bedevil. **4 brave,** face up to, encounter, meet (head-on), confront. **5 cover,** clad, veneer, surface, dress, laminate, coat, line.

– DERIVATIVES **faced** adjective.
– PHRASES **face the music** be confronted with the unpleasant results of one's actions. **face to face** close together and looking directly at one another. **get out of someone's face** stop harassing or annoying someone. **in the face of** when confronted with something. **in**

one's face directly at or against one: *she slammed the door in my face.* **lose** (or **save**) **face** suffer (or avoid) humiliation. **make a face** produce an expression on one's face that shows dislike, disgust, or amusement. **on the face of it** apparently. **to someone's face** used to refer to remarks made openly and directly to someone.
– ORIGIN Old French, from Latin *facies* 'appearance, face.'

face card ▶ **noun** a playing card that is a king, queen, or jack of a suit.

face·cloth /ˈfās,klôTH/ ▶ **noun** a washcloth used specifically for one's face.

face·down /,fāsˈdoun/ ▶ **adverb & adjective** with the face, front, or upper part downward: *all of the papers were laid facedown on the table.*

face·less /ˈfāsləs/ ▶ **adjective 1** (of a person) remote and impersonal: *faceless bureaucrats.* **2** (of a place) having no distinguishing characteristics or identity.

face·lift /ˈfāslift/ ▶ **noun 1** a surgical operation to remove unwanted wrinkles by tightening the skin of the face. **2** a procedure carried out to improve the appearance of something.

> – SYNONYMS **renovation,** redecoration, refurbishment, revamp, makeover.

face mask ▶ **noun 1** a protective mask covering the face or part of the face. **2** (also **facial mask**) a cosmetic preparation spread over the face to improve the skin.

face-off ▶ **noun 1** a direct confrontation. **2** Ice Hockey the start of play.

face·plate /ˈfāsplāt/ ▶ **noun 1** a protective or decorative cover for a piece of equipment or an electrical fitting. **2** the transparent window of a diver's or astronaut's helmet.

face-sav·ing ▶ **adjective** preserving one's reputation or dignity.

fac·et /ˈfasət/ ▶ **noun 1** one of the sides of a cut gemstone. **2** an aspect: *every facet of our business.*

> – SYNONYMS **aspect,** feature, factor, side, dimension, strand, component, element.

– DERIVATIVES **fac·et·ed** adjective.
– ORIGIN French *facette* 'little face.'

face time ▶ **noun 1** time spent in face-to-face contact with someone: *we need to sit down for some face time, just you and me.* **2** time spent being filmed or photographed by the media: *the authors all wanted face time at our events.*

fa·ce·tious /fəˈsēSHəs/ ▶ **adjective** showing inappropriate humor or trying to be amusing at an inappropriate time.

> – SYNONYMS **flippant,** flip, glib, frivolous, tongue-in-cheek, joking, jokey, jocular, playful.
> – ANTONYMS serious.

– DERIVATIVES **fa·ce·tious·ly** adverb **fa·ce·tious·ness** noun.
– ORIGIN French *facétieux.*

face val·ue ▶ **noun** the value printed or depicted on a coin, postage stamp, etc.
– PHRASES **take something at face value** accept or believe that something is what it appears to be.

fa·cial /ˈfāSHəl/ ▶ **adjective** relating to or affecting the face. ▶ **noun** a beauty treatment for the face.
– DERIVATIVES **fa·cial·ly** adverb.

fa·cial mask ▶ **noun** another term for FACE MASK (sense 2).

fa·cial tis·sue ▶ **noun** a tissue that is used to blow one's nose, contain a sneeze, etc.

fa·ci·es /ˈfā,SHēz, ˈfāSHē,ēz/ ▶ **noun 1** Medicine the facial expression of a person that is typical of a particular disease or condition. **2** Geology the character of a rock expressed by its formation, composition, and fossil content.
– ORIGIN from Latin, 'form, appearance, face.'

fac·ile /ˈfasəl/ ▶ **adjective 1** (of an idea, remark, etc.) simplistic and lacking careful thought. **2** (of success) easily achieved.
– ORIGIN Latin *facilis* 'easy.'

fa·cil·i·tate /fəˈsili,tāt/ ▶ **verb** make something easy or easier.

> – SYNONYMS **make easier,** ease, make possible, smooth the way for, enable, assist, help (along), aid, promote, hasten, speed up.
> – ANTONYMS impede.

– DERIVATIVES **fa·cil·i·ta·tion** /fə,siliˈtāSHən/ noun **fa·cil·i·ta·tive** /-,tātiv/ adjective.
– ORIGIN from Latin *facilis* 'easy.'

fa·cil·i·ta·tor /fəˈsili,tātər/ ▶ **noun** someone or something that helps to produce a result, especially by directing or leading an activity: *a support group facilitator.*

fa·cil·i·ty /fəˈsilətē/ ▶ **noun** (pl. **facilities**) **1** a building, service, or piece of equipment provided for a particular purpose. **2** a natural ability to do something well and easily.

> – SYNONYMS **1** *a wealth of local facilities* **amenity,** resource, service, benefit, convenience, equipment. **2** *a medical facility* **establishment,** center, station, location, premises, site, post, base. **3 ease,** effortlessness, skill, adroitness, smoothness, fluency, slickness.

fac·ing /ˈfāsiNG/ ▶ **noun 1** a piece of material attached to the edge of a garment at the neck, armhole, etc., and turned inside, used to strengthen the edge. **2** an outer layer covering the surface of a wall. ▶ **adjective** positioned so as to face something.

fac·sim·i·le /fakˈsiməlē/ ▶ **noun** an exact copy, especially of written or printed material.
– ORIGIN from Latin *fac!* 'make!' and *simile,* from *similis* 'like.'

fact /fakt/ ▶ **noun 1** a thing that is definitely known to be true. **2** (**facts**) information used as evidence or as part of a report.

> – SYNONYMS **1** *a fact we cannot ignore* **reality,** actuality, certainty, truth, verity, gospel. **2** *every fact was double-checked* **detail,** particular, finding, point, factor, feature, characteristic, aspect; (**facts**) information, data.
> – ANTONYMS lie, fiction.

– PHRASES **before** (or **after**) **the fact** Law before (or after) the committing of a crime. **facts and figures** precise details. **a fact of life** something that must be accepted, even if unpleasant. **the facts of life** information about sex and reproduction. **the face of the matter** the truth. **in** (**point of**) **fact** in reality.
– ORIGIN Latin *factum* 'an act.'

fact-find·ing ▶ **adjective** having the purpose of discovering and establishing facts about something: *a fact-finding investigation.*

fac·tion[1] /ˈfakSHən/ ▶ **noun 1** a small group within a larger one whose members disagree with some of the beliefs of the larger group. **2** a state of conflict within an organization.

– SYNONYMS **1 clique,** coterie, caucus, bloc, camp, group, grouping, splinter group. **2 infighting,** dissent, dispute, discord, strife, conflict, friction, argument, disagreement, disunity, schism.

– DERIVATIVES **fac·tion·al** adjective **fac·tion·al·ism** /-l,izəm/ noun.
– ORIGIN Latin *facere* 'do, make.'

fac·tion² ▶ **noun** a type of literature or cinema in which real events are used as a basis for a fictional story or dramatization.
– ORIGIN blend of **FACT** and **FICTION**.

fac·tious /'faksʜəs/ ▶ **adjective** relating to or causing disagreement.
– ORIGIN Latin *factiosus.*

fac·ti·tious /fak'tisʜəs/ ▶ **adjective** not genuine; made up.
– ORIGIN Latin *facticius* 'made by art.'

fac·toid /'fak,toid/ ▶ **noun 1** a piece of unreliable information that is repeated so often that it becomes accepted as fact. **2** a brief or trivial piece of information.

fac·tor /'faktər/ ▶ **noun 1** a circumstance, fact, or influence that contributes to a result: *ill health was an important factor in his decision to retire early.* **2** Mathematics a number or quantity that when multiplied with another produces a given number or expression. **3** a level on a scale of measurement: *sunblock with a protection factor of 15.* **4** any of a number of substances in the blood that are involved in clotting. **5** a gene that determines a hereditary characteristic. **6** an agent who buys and sells goods on commission. **7** Finance a business that buys another firm's invoices at a discount and then collects the money due from them for itself.

– SYNONYMS **element,** part, component, ingredient, strand, constituent, feature, facet, aspect, characteristic, consideration, influence, circumstance.

▶ **verb** (**factor something in/out**) include (or exclude) something as relevant when making a decision.
– ORIGIN Latin *facere* 'do.'

fac·to·ri·al /fak'tôrēəl/ Mathematics ▶ **noun** the product of an integer and all the integers below it, e.g., 4 × 3 × 2 × 1 (*factorial* 4, denoted by *4!* and equal to 24). ▶ **adjective** relating to a factor or factorial.

fac·tor·ize /'faktə,rīz/ ▶ **verb** Mathematics break down or be able to be broken down into factors.
– DERIVATIVES **fac·tor·i·za·tion** /,faktərə'zāsʜən/ noun.

fac·tor VIII /,faktər 'āt/ (also **factor eight**) ▶ **noun** a blood protein involved in the clotting of blood, a lack of which causes one of the main forms of hemophilia.

fac·to·ry /'fakt(ə)rē/ ▶ **noun** (pl. **factories**) a building where goods are manufactured or assembled chiefly by machine.

– SYNONYMS **plant,** works, yard, mill, facility, workshop, shop.

– ORIGIN Latin *factorium* 'oil press.'

fac·to·ry farm·ing ▶ **noun** a system of rearing poultry, pigs, or cattle indoors under strictly controlled conditions.

fac·to·ry floor ▶ **noun** the workers in a company or industry, rather than the management.

fac·to·ry out·let ▶ **noun** a store in which goods, especially surplus stock, are sold directly by the manufacturers at a discount.

fac·to·ry ship ▶ **noun** a fishing vessel with facilities for immediate processing of the catch on board.

fac·to·tum /fak'tōtəm/ ▶ **noun** (pl. **factotums**) an employee who does all kinds of work.
– ORIGIN from Latin *fac!* 'do!' + *totum* 'the whole thing.'

fac·tu·al /'fakcʜo͞oəl/ ▶ **adjective** based on or concerned with fact or facts.

– SYNONYMS **truthful,** true, accurate, authentic, historical, genuine, true-to-life, correct, exact.
– ANTONYMS fictitious.

– DERIVATIVES **fac·tu·al·ly** adverb.

fac·ul·ta·tive /'fakəl,tātiv/ ▶ **adjective 1** Biology adopting a particular mode of life in response to conditions: *facultative biennials.* **2** occurring optionally in response to circumstances, rather than by nature: *evidence that mountain birds make facultative altitudinal movements.*

fac·ul·ty /'fakəltē/ ▶ **noun** (pl. **faculties**) **1** a basic mental or physical power: *the faculty of sight.* **2** an ability: *his faculty for taking the initiative.* **3** (treated as sing. or pl.) the teaching or research staff of a college or university. **4** a group of university departments concerned with a particular area of knowledge.

– SYNONYMS **1 power,** capability, capacity, facility; (**faculties**) senses, wits, reason, intelligence. **2 teaching staff,** teachers; department.

– ORIGIN Latin *facultas,* from *facilis* 'easy.'

fad /fad/ ▶ **noun** a temporary widespread enthusiasm for something; a craze.

– SYNONYMS **craze,** vogue, trend, fashion, mode, mania, rage.

– DERIVATIVES **fad·dish** adjective **fad·dism** /-,izəm/ noun **fad·dist** noun.
– ORIGIN uncertain.

fade /fād/ ▶ **verb 1** gradually grow faint and disappear. **2** lose or cause to lose color. **3** (of a movie or video image or recorded sound) become more or less clear or loud.

– SYNONYMS **1 grow pale,** become bleached, become washed out, lose color, discolor, blanch. **2 (grow) dim,** grow faint, fail, dwindle, die away, wane, disappear, vanish, decline, melt away. **3 decline,** die out, diminish, decay, crumble, collapse, fail.
– ANTONYMS brighten.

▶ **noun** an act of fading.
– ORIGIN Old French *fader.*

fade-in ▶ **noun** a gradual increase in sound volume or in the visibility of a filmed scene.

fade-out ▶ **noun** a gradual decrease, until disappearance, in sound volume or in the visibility of a filmed scene.

fad·er /'fādər/ ▶ **noun** a device for varying the volume of sound in a movie or video recording, or the intensity of light.

fa·do /'fäᴛʜo͞o/ ▶ **noun** (pl. **fados**) a type of popular Portuguese song, usually with a sad theme.
– ORIGIN Portuguese, 'fate.'

fae·ces, etc. ▶ **plural noun** British spelling of **FECES**, etc.

fa·er·ie /'ferē/ (also **faery**) ▶ **noun** old use or literary **1** a fairy. **2** fairyland.
– ORIGIN introduced as a variant of *fairy* by the English poet Edmund Spenser in *The Faerie Queene.*

Faer·o·ese /,fe(ə)rō'ēz/ (also chiefly Brit. **Faroese**) ▶ **noun** (pl. same) **1** a person from the Faeroe Islands. **2** the language of the Faeroe Islands.

fag¹ /fag/ ▶ **noun** informal, derogatory a male homosexual.
– DERIVATIVES **fag·gy** adjective.
– ORIGIN short for **FAGGOT** (sense 1).

fag² ▶ **noun** Brit. informal a cigarette.
– ORIGIN from *fag end* 'cigarette end,' originally meaning 'last and least important part.'

fag³ Brit. ▶ **noun 1** informal a tiring or unwelcome task. **2** an underclassman at a private school who does minor chores for an older student. ▶ **verb** (**fags**, **fagging**, **fagged**) **1** (of a private-school student) act as a fag. **2** (as adj. **fagged out**) informal exhausted. **3** informal work hard.
– ORIGIN unknown.

fag·got /'fagət/ ▶ **noun 1** informal, derogatory a male homosexual. **2** British spelling of FAGOT.
– DERIVATIVES **fag·got·y** adjective.

fag·ot /'fagət/ (Brit. **faggot**) ▶ **noun** a bundle of sticks bound together as fuel.
– ORIGIN Old French *fagot*, from Greek *phakelos* 'bundle.'

fag·ot·ing /'fagətiNG/ (Brit. **faggoting**) ▶ **noun** embroidery in which threads are fastened together in bundles.

Fahr. ▶ **abbreviation** Fahrenheit.

Fahr·en·heit /'farən,hīt/ ▶ **adjective** relating to a scale of temperature on which water freezes at 32° and boils at 212°.
– ORIGIN named after the German physicist Gabriel Daniel *Fahrenheit*.

fa·ience /fī'äns, fā-/ ▶ **noun** a type of glazed ceramic earthenware.
– ORIGIN from *Faenza*, a town in Italy.

fail /fāl/ ▶ **verb 1** be unsuccessful in achieving something. **2** be unable to meet the standards set by a test. **3** neglect to do something: *she failed to keep the appointment*. **4** not happen in the way expected: *chaos has failed to materialize*. **5** stop working properly. **6** become weaker or less good: *his sight was failing*. **7** let someone down: *her courage failed her*. **8** go out of business.

– SYNONYMS **1 be unsuccessful,** fall through, fall flat, collapse, founder, backfire, miscarry, come unstuck; informal flop, bomb. **2 be unsuccessful in,** not make the grade; informal flunk. **3 let down,** disappoint, desert, abandon, betray, be disloyal to. **4 break (down),** stop working, cut out, crash, malfunction, go wrong; informal conk out. **5 deteriorate,** degenerate, decline, fade. **6 collapse,** crash, go under, go bankrupt, cease trading; informal fold, go bust.
– ANTONYMS succeed, pass, improve.

▶ **noun** a mark that is not high enough to pass an exam or test.
– PHRASES **never fail to do something** used to indicate that something invariably happens: *such comments never fail to annoy him*. **without fail** whatever happens.
– ORIGIN from Latin *fallere* 'deceive.'

failed /fāld/ ▶ **adjective 1** not having achieved an intended goal or result: *failed negotiations*. **2** no longer operating or functional: *a failed backup system*.

fail·ing /'fāliNG/ ▶ **noun** a weakness in a person's character.

– SYNONYMS **fault,** shortcoming, weakness, imperfection, deficiency, defect, flaw, frailty.
– ANTONYMS strength.

▶ **preposition** if not.

fail·o·ver /'fāl,ōvər/ ▶ **noun** Computers the capability to switch automatically to a backup system in the event of a failure, or the process of doing this.

fail-safe ▶ **adjective 1** causing machinery to return to a safe condition if a breakdown occurs. **2** unlikely or unable to fail.

fail·ure /'fālyər/ ▶ **noun 1** lack of success. **2** an unsuccessful person or thing. **3** an instance of not doing something that is expected: *their failure to comply with the rules*. **4** an instance of something not functioning properly.

– SYNONYMS **1 lack of success,** defeat, collapse, foundering. **2 fiasco,** debacle, catastrophe, disaster; informal flop, washout, dead loss. **3 loser,** underachiever, ne'er-do-well, disappointment; informal no-hoper, dud. **4 negligence,** dereliction, omission, oversight. **5 breakdown,** malfunction, crash. **6 collapse,** crash, bankruptcy, insolvency, liquidation, closure.
– ANTONYMS success.

fain /fān/ old use ▶ **adverb** gladly. ▶ **adjective** willing or obliged to do something.
– ORIGIN Old English, 'happy.'

faint /fānt/ ▶ **adjective 1** not clearly seen, heard, or smelled. **2** (of a hope, chance, or idea) slight. **3** close to losing consciousness.

– SYNONYMS **1 indistinct,** vague, unclear, indefinite, ill-defined, imperceptible, pale, light, faded. **2 quiet,** muted, muffled, stifled, feeble, weak, low, soft, gentle. **3 slight,** slender, slim, small, tiny, remote, vague. **4 dizzy,** giddy, lightheaded, unsteady; informal woozy.
– ANTONYMS clear, loud, strong.

▶ **verb** briefly lose consciousness because of an inadequate supply of oxygen to the brain.

– SYNONYMS **pass out,** lose consciousness, black out, keel over, swoon.

▶ **noun** a sudden loss of consciousness.

– SYNONYMS **blackout,** fainting fit, loss of consciousness, coma, swoon.

– DERIVATIVES **faint·ness** noun.
– ORIGIN Old French *faindre* 'feign.'

USAGE

Do not confuse **faint** with **feint**. **Faint** means 'not clearly seen, heard, or smelled' (*the faint murmur of voices*) or 'lose consciousness,' whereas **feint** means 'a pretended attacking movement' or 'make a pretended attacking movement'.

faint-heart·ed ▶ **adjective** timid.

faint·ly /'fāntlē/ ▶ **adverb 1** feebly, indistinctly. **2** very slightly.

– SYNONYMS **1** *Maria called his name faintly* **indistinctly,** softly, gently, weakly, in a whisper. **2** *he looked faintly bewildered* **slightly,** vaguely, somewhat, quite, fairly, rather, a little, a bit, a touch, a shade.

fair¹ /fe(ə)r/ ▶ **adjective 1** treating people equally. **2** just or appropriate in the circumstances. **3** considerable in size or amount: *I do a fair bit of business traveling*. **4** moderately good. **5** (of hair or complexion) light; blond. **6** (of weather) fine and dry. **7** old use beautiful.

– SYNONYMS **1 just,** equitable, honest, impartial, unbiased, unprejudiced, neutral, even-handed. **2 fine,** dry, bright, clear, sunny, cloudless. **3 blond/blonde,** yellow, golden, flaxen, light. **4 pale,** light, pink, white, creamy. **5 reasonable,** passable, tolerable, satisfactory, acceptable, respectable, decent, all right, good enough, pretty good.
– ANTONYMS inclement, dark, poor.

▶ **adverb 1** in a fair way. **2** dialect very: *she'll be fair delighted to see you.*
– DERIVATIVES **fair·ness** noun.
– PHRASES **fair and square 1** with absolute accuracy. **2** honestly and straightforwardly. **fair enough** used to admit that something is reasonable or acceptable. **the fair sex** (also **the fairer sex**) dated or humorous women. **no fair** informal unfair: *ooh, he brought his posse ... no fair.*
– ORIGIN Old English.

fair² ▶ **noun 1** a gathering of sideshows, rides, and other amusements for public entertainment. **2** an event at which people, businesses, etc., display and sell goods. **3** an exhibition held to promote particular products.

– SYNONYMS **1 fete,** gala, festival, carnival. **2 market,** bazaar, exchange, sale. **3 exhibition,** display, show, exposition.

– ORIGIN Latin *feria*, from *feriae* 'holy days' (on which fairs were often held).

fair cop·y ▶ **noun** a copy of written or printed matter produced after final corrections have been made.

fair game ▶ **noun** a person or thing regarded as a reasonable target for criticism or exploitation.

fair·ground /'fe(ə)r,ground/ ▶ **noun** an outdoor area where a fair is held.

Fair Isle ▶ **noun** a traditional multicolored geometric design used in woolen knitwear.
– ORIGIN *Fair Isle* in the Shetland Islands, where the design was first devised.

fair·ly /'fe(ə)rlē/ ▶ **adverb 1** with justice. **2** moderately. **3** actually (used for emphasis): *he fairly snarled at her.*

– SYNONYMS **1 justly,** equitably, impartially, without bias, without prejudice, even-handedly, equally. **2 reasonably,** passably, tolerably, adequately, moderately, quite, relatively, comparatively; informal pretty. **3 positively,** really, simply, absolutely.

fair-mind·ed ▶ **adjective** judging things in a fair and impartial way.

fair play ▶ **noun** respect for the rules or equal treatment for all.

fair trade ▶ **noun** trade in which fair prices are paid to producers in developing countries.

fair use ▶ **noun** legally defined limits on the right to reproduce or cite copyrighted material without obtaining permission.

fair·way /'fe(ə)r,wā/ ▶ **noun 1** the part of a golf course between a tee and a green. **2** a channel in a river or harbor that can be used by shipping.

fair-weath·er friend ▶ **noun** a person whose friendship cannot be relied on in times of difficulty.

fair·y /'fe(ə)rē/ ▶ **noun** (pl. **fairies**) **1** a small imaginary being of human form that has magical powers. **2** informal, derogatory a male homosexual.

– SYNONYMS **sprite,** pixie, elf, imp, brownie, puck, leprechaun.

– ORIGIN Old French *faerie* 'fairyland,' from *fae* 'a fairy.'

fair·y god·moth·er ▶ **noun** a female character in fairy tales who brings unexpected good fortune to the hero or heroine.

fair·y·land /'fe(ə)rē,land/ ▶ **noun** the imaginary home of fairies.

fair·y ring ▶ **noun** a ring of dark grass caused by the growth of certain fungi, once believed to have been made by fairies dancing.

fair·y tale ▶ **noun 1** a children's story about magical and imaginary beings and lands. **2** an untrue account. ▶ **adjective** magical, idealized, or perfect: *a fairy-tale romance.*

fait ac·com·pli /'fet əkäm'plē, 'fāt/ ▶ **noun** a thing that has been done or decided and cannot now be altered.
– ORIGIN French, 'accomplished fact.'

faith /fāTH/ ▶ **noun 1** complete trust or confidence in someone or something. **2** strong belief in a religion. **3** a system of religious belief.

– SYNONYMS **1 trust,** belief, confidence, conviction, reliance. **2 religion,** belief, creed, church, persuasion, ideology, doctrine.
– ANTONYMS mistrust.

– ORIGIN from Latin *fides*.

faith-based ▶ **adjective** affiliated with or based on an organized religion: *faith-based nonprofit organizations.*

faith·ful /'fāTHfəl/ ▶ **adjective 1** remaining loyal. **2** remaining sexually loyal to a lover or to a husband or wife. **3** true to the facts or the original: *a faithful copy.*

– SYNONYMS **1 loyal,** constant, true, devoted, staunch, steadfast, dedicated, committed, trusty, dependable, reliable. **2 accurate,** precise, exact, true, strict, realistic, authentic.
– ANTONYMS disloyal, treacherous.

▶ **noun** (**the faithful**) those who are faithful to a particular religion or political party.
– DERIVATIVES **faith·ful·ly** adverb **faith·ful·ness** noun.

faith heal·ing ▶ **noun** a method of treating a sick person through the power of religious faith and prayer, rather than by medical means.

faith·less /'fāTHlis/ ▶ **adjective 1** disloyal, especially to a lover or spouse. **2** without religious faith.
– DERIVATIVES **faith·less·ness** noun.

fa·ji·tas /fə'hētəz/ ▶ **plural noun** a Mexican dish consisting of strips of spiced meat with vegetables and cheese, wrapped in a soft tortilla.
– ORIGIN Mexican Spanish, 'little strips.'

fake /fāk/ ▶ **adjective** not genuine.

– SYNONYMS **1 counterfeit,** forged, fraudulent, sham, pirated, false, bogus; informal phony, dud. **2 imitation,** artificial, synthetic, simulated, reproduction, replica, ersatz, man-made, dummy, false, mock; informal pretend. **3 feigned,** faked, put-on, assumed, invented, affected.
– ANTONYMS genuine, real, authentic.

▶ **noun** a person or thing that is not genuine.

– SYNONYMS **1 forgery,** counterfeit, copy, sham, fraud, hoax, imitation; informal phony, rip-off. **2 charlatan,** quack, sham, fraud, impostor; informal phony.

▶ **verb 1** make something that seems genuine in order to deceive other people: *she faked her spouse's signature.* **2** pretend to have a particular feeling or illness. **3** (**fake someone out**) deceive someone: *later we'll learn some moves to help you fake out your opponent.*

– SYNONYMS **1 forge,** counterfeit, falsify, copy, pirate. **2 feign,** pretend, simulate, put on, affect.

– DERIVATIVES **fak·er** noun **fak·er·y** noun.
– ORIGIN uncertain.

CHOOSE THE RIGHT WORD

See **QUACK²**.

fa·kir /fə'ki(ə)r, 'fākər/ ▶ **noun** a Muslim (or, loosely, a Hindu) holy man who lives on charitable donations.
– ORIGIN Arabic, 'needy man.'

fa·la·fel /fə'läfəl/ (also **felafel**) ▶ **noun** a Middle Eastern dish of spiced mashed chickpeas formed into balls and deep-fried.
– ORIGIN Arabic, 'pepper.'

fal·con /'falkən, 'fôl-/ ▶ **noun** a fast-flying bird of prey with long pointed wings.
– ORIGIN Old French *faucon*.

fal·con·er /'falkənər, 'fôl-/ ▶ **noun** someone who keeps, trains, or hunts with birds of prey.

fal·con·ry /'falkənrē, 'fôl-/ ▶ **noun** the skill of keeping birds of prey and training them to hunt.

fall /fôl/ ▶ **verb** (past **fell**; past part. **fallen**) **1** move downward quickly and without control. **2** collapse to the ground. **3** hang or slope down: *the land fell away in a steep bank*. **4** decrease. **5** occur: *her birthday fell on a Sunday*. **6** be captured or defeated in a battle or contest. **7** (of someone's face) show dismay or disappointment. **8** become: *she fell silent*. **9** (**fall off**) become detached and drop to the ground. **10** (**fall to**) become someone's duty.

– SYNONYMS **1 drop,** descend, plummet, plunge, sink, dive, tumble, cascade. **2 topple over,** tumble over, fall down/over, collapse. **3 subside,** recede, drop, retreat, go down, sink. **4** *the level of unemployment is falling* **decrease,** decline, diminish, fall off, drop off, lessen, dwindle, plummet, plunge, slump, sink. **5 occur,** take place, happen, come about. **6** *the town fell to the barbarians* **surrender,** yield, submit, give in, capitulate, succumb, be taken, be overwhelmed.
– ANTONYMS rise.

▶ **noun 1** an act of falling. **2** a decrease. **3** a defeat or downfall. **4** a thing that falls or has fallen. **5** a waterfall. **6** autumn.

– SYNONYMS **1** *an accidental fall* **tumble,** trip, spill, topple. **2** *a fall in sales* **decline,** fall-off, drop, decrease, cut, dip, reduction, slump; informal crash. **3** *the fall of the Roman Empire* **downfall,** collapse, failure, decline, destruction, overthrow, demise. **4** *the fall of the city* **surrender,** capitulation, yielding, submission, defeat.
– ANTONYMS rise.

– PHRASES **fall apart** (or **to pieces**) **1** break up, come apart, or disintegrate: *their marriage is likely to fall apart*. **2** (of a person) lose one's capacity to cope: *he fell apart when his mother died*. **fall back** retreat. **fall behind 1** fail to keep up with one's competitors. **2** fail to keep a commitment to repay: *borrowers falling behind with their mortgage payments*. **fall back on** turn to something when in difficulty. **fall for** informal **1** fall in love with. **2** be deceived by. **fall foul of** come into conflict with. **fall in** (or **into**) **line** do what one is told or what other people do. [with reference to military formation.] **fall into place** begin to make sense. **fall in with 1** meet someone by chance and become involved with them. **2** agree to something. **fall on 1** attack someone fiercely or unexpectedly. **2** be someone's duty. **fall out** have an argument. **fall short (of) 1** (of a missile) fail to reach its target. **2** fail to reach a required standard. **fall through** (of a plan, project, etc.) not happen or be completed.
– ORIGIN Old English.

fal·la·cious /fə'lāsʜəs/ ▶ **adjective** based on a mistaken belief; wrong: *a fallacious argument*.

fal·la·cy /'faləsē/ ▶ **noun** (pl. **fallacies**) **1** a mistaken belief. **2** a mistake in reasoning that makes an argument invalid.

– SYNONYMS **misconception,** misbelief, delusion, misapprehension, misinterpretation, misconstruction, error, mistake; untruth, inconsistency, myth.

– ORIGIN from Latin *fallere* 'deceive.'

fall·back /'fôl,bak/ ▶ **noun** an alternative plan for use in an emergency.

fall·en /'fôlən/ past participle of **FALL** ▶ **adjective 1** dated (of a woman) regarded as having lost her honor as a result of an extramarital sexual relationship. **2** killed in battle.

fall·en an·gel ▶ **noun** (in Christian, Jewish, and Muslim tradition) an angel who rebelled against God and was cast out of heaven.

fall guy ▶ **noun** informal a person who is blamed for something that is not their fault; a scapegoat.

fal·li·ble /'faləbəl/ ▶ **adjective** capable of making mistakes or being wrong.

– SYNONYMS **error-prone,** errant, liable to err, open to error; imperfect, flawed, weak.

– DERIVATIVES **fal·li·bil·i·ty** /,falə'bilətē/ noun.
– ORIGIN from Latin *fallere* 'deceive.'

fall·ing-out ▶ **noun** a quarrel.

fall·ing star ▶ **noun** a meteor or shooting star.

fall line ▶ **noun** the line of steepest descent down a slope, as for skiing or a watercourse.

fall·off /'fôl,ôf/ ▶ **noun** a decrease.

Fal·lo·pi·an tube /fə'lōpēən/ ▶ **noun** (in a female mammal) either of a pair of tubes along which eggs travel from the ovaries to the uterus.
– ORIGIN named after the Italian anatomist Gabriello *Fallopio*.

fall·out /'fôl,out/ ▶ **noun 1** radioactive particles spread over a wide area after a nuclear explosion. **2** the bad results of a situation or action: *the political fallout from his decision*.

fal·low[1] /'falō/ ▶ **adjective 1** (of farmland) plowed but left for a period of time without being planted with crops. **2** (of a period of time) when nothing is done or achieved.
– ORIGIN Old English.

fal·low[2] ▶ **noun** a pale brown or reddish yellow color.
– ORIGIN Old English.

fal·low deer ▶ **noun** a small Eurasian deer with a white-spotted reddish-brown coat in summer.
– ORIGIN Old English, 'pale brown.'

false /fôls/ ▶ **adjective 1** not correct or true; wrong. **2** invalid or illegal: *false imprisonment*. **3** not genuine; artificial: *false eyelashes*. **4** based on something that is not true or correct: *a false sense of security*. **5** literary (of a person) not faithful.

– SYNONYMS **1 incorrect,** untrue, wrong, inaccurate, untruthful, fictitious, fabricated, invented, made up, trumped up, counterfeit, forged, fraudulent. **2 disloyal,** faithless, unfaithful, untrue, inconstant, treacherous, double-crossing, deceitful, dishonest, duplicitous. **3 fake,** artificial, imitation, synthetic, simulated, reproduction, replica, ersatz, man-made, dummy, mock; informal pretend.
– ANTONYMS correct, faithful, genuine.

– DERIVATIVES **false·ly** adverb **false·ness** noun **fal·si·ty** /'fôlsətē/ noun.
– ORIGIN from Latin *falsum* 'fraud.'

false a·larm ▶ noun a warning given about something that does not happen.

false col·or ▶ noun representation in color other than the natural one in order to enhance visible information: *false-color infrared images*.

false dawn ▶ noun **1** a transient light that precedes the rising of the sun by about two or three hours. **2** a promising situation that comes to nothing.

false e·con·o·my ▶ noun an apparent financial saving that in fact leads to greater expenditure.

false front ▶ noun a facade or appearance that is intended to deceive: *I was ready to put on a false front and be civil to my parents*.

false·hood /'fôls,ho͝od/ ▶ noun **1** the state of being untrue. **2** a lie.

– SYNONYMS **1 lie,** untruth, fib, falsification, fabrication, invention, fiction. **2** *he accused me of falsehood* **lying,** untruthfulness, fabrication, invention, perjury, telling stories; deceit, deception, pretense, artifice, double-crossing, treachery.
– ANTONYMS truth, honesty.

CHOOSE THE RIGHT WORD

See **FICTION**.

false mem·o·ry ▶ noun an apparent memory of an event, especially one of childhood sexual abuse, that did not actually happen, sometimes arising from techniques used in psychoanalysis.

false move ▶ noun an unwise action that could have dangerous consequences.

false neg·a·tive ▶ noun an incorrect test result indicating the absence of a condition that is in fact present.

false pos·i·tive ▶ noun an incorrect test result indicating the presence of a condition that is in fact absent.

false pre·tens·es ▶ plural noun behavior intended to deceive other people.

false start ▶ noun **1** an occasion when a competitor in a race starts before the official signal has been given, so that the race has to be started again. **2** an unsuccessful attempt to begin something.

false step ▶ noun **1** a slip or stumble. **2** a mistake.

fal·set·to /fôl'setō/ ▶ noun (pl. **falsettos**) a high-pitched voice above a person's natural range, used by male singers.
– ORIGIN Italian, from *falso* 'false.'

fals·ies /'fôlsēz/ ▶ plural noun pads in women's clothing used to increase the apparent size of the breasts.

fal·si·fy /'fôlsə,fī/ ▶ verb (**falsifies, falsifying, falsified**) alter information or evidence so as to mislead others.

– SYNONYMS **forge,** fake, counterfeit, fabricate, alter, change, doctor, tamper with, manipulate, misrepresent, misreport, distort.

– DERIVATIVES **fal·si·fi·able** /,fôlsə'fīəbəl/ adjective **fal·si·fi·ca·tion** /,fôlsəfə'kāsнən/ noun.

fal·ter /'fôltər/ ▶ verb **1** lose strength or momentum. **2** move or speak hesitantly.

– SYNONYMS **hesitate,** delay, drag one's feet, stall, waver, vacillate, be indecisive, be irresolute; informal hem and haw, sit on the fence.

– DERIVATIVES **fal·ter·ing** adjective.
– ORIGIN perhaps from **FOLD**[1].

fame /fām/ ▶ noun the state of being famous.

– SYNONYMS **renown,** celebrity, stardom, popularity, prominence, distinction, esteem, eminence, repute.
– ANTONYMS obscurity.

famed /fāmd/ ▶ adjective famous; well known.

fa·mil·iar /fə'milyər/ ▶ adjective **1** well known as a result of long or close association: *a familiar figure*. **2** frequently encountered; common: *the situation was all too familiar*. **3** (**familiar with**) having a good knowledge of: *we're familiar with the terrain of northwest Minnesota*. **4** more friendly or informal than is appropriate. **5** friendly.

– SYNONYMS **1 well known,** recognized, accustomed, everyday, day-to-day, habitual, customary, routine. **2** (**familiar with**) **acquainted with,** conversant with, versed in, knowledgeable of, well informed in/of, au fait with; informal (well) up on. **3 overfamiliar,** presumptuous, disrespectful, forward, bold, impudent, impertinent.

▶ noun **1** (also **familiar spirit**) a spirit supposedly attending and obeying a witch. **2** a close friend or associate.
– DERIVATIVES **fa·mil·iar·ly** adverb.
– ORIGIN from Latin *familia* 'household servants, family.'

fa·mil·iar·i·ty /fə,milē'aritē, -,mil'yar-/ ▶ noun (pl. **familiarities**) **1** close acquaintance with or knowledge of something. **2** relaxed friendliness or intimacy between people. **3** inappropriate informality or intimacy.

– SYNONYMS **1** *a familiarity with politics* **acquaintance,** awareness, knowledge, experience, insight, understanding, comprehension. **2** *our familiarity allows us to give each other nicknames* **closeness,** intimacy, friendliness, friendship. **3** *the unnecessary familiarity made me dislike him at once* **overfamiliarity,** presumption, forwardness, boldness, cheek, impudence, impertinence, disrespect.

fa·mil·iar·ize /fə'milyə,rīz/ ▶ verb (**familiarize someone with**) give someone better knowledge or understanding of something.
– DERIVATIVES **fa·mil·iar·i·za·tion** /fə,milyərə'zāsнən/ noun.

fam·i·ly /'fam(ə)lē/ ▶ noun (pl. **families**) **1** a group consisting of parents and their children living together as a unit. **2** a group of people related by blood or marriage. **3** the children of a person or couple. **4** all the descendants of a common ancestor: *the house has been in the family for 300 years*. **5** a group of things that are alike in some way. **6** Biology a main category into which animals and plants are divided, ranking above genus and below order.

– SYNONYMS **1 relatives,** relations, (next of) kin, clan, tribe; informal folks. **2 children,** little ones, youngsters; informal kids. **3 species,** order, class, genus, phylum.

▶ adjective designed to be suitable for children as well as adults: *family entertainment*.
– DERIVATIVES **fa·mil·ial** /fə'milēəl, -'milyəl/ adjective.
– PHRASES **in the family way** informal pregnant.
– ORIGIN Latin *familia* 'household servants, family.'

fam·i·ly name ▶ noun a surname.

fam·i·ly plan·ning ▶ noun the control of the number of children in a family by means of contraception.

fam·i·ly prac·tice ▸ **noun** the branch of medicine designed to provide basic health care to all the members of a family.
– DERIVATIVES **fam·i·ly prac·ti·tion·er** noun.

fam·i·ly room ▸ **noun** a room in a house where family members relax and enjoy recreation.

fam·i·ly tree ▸ **noun** a diagram showing the relationship between people in several generations of a family.

fam·i·ly val·ues ▸ **plural noun** values supposedly characteristic of a traditional family unit, typically those of high moral standards and discipline.

fam·ine /ˈfamən/ ▸ **noun** a severe shortage of food.

> – SYNONYMS **1 food shortage,** hunger, starvation, malnutrition. **2 shortage,** scarcity, lack, dearth, deficiency, insufficiency, shortfall.
> – ANTONYMS plenty.

– ORIGIN from Latin *fames*.

fam·ished /ˈfamisнt/ ▸ **adjective** informal extremely hungry.

> – SYNONYMS **ravenous,** hungry, starving, starved, empty, unfed; informal peckish.
> – ANTONYMS replete.

– ORIGIN Latin *fames* 'hunger.'

fa·mous /ˈfāməs/ ▸ **adjective 1** known about by many people. **2** informal magnificent.

> – SYNONYMS **well known,** prominent, famed, popular, renowned, noted, eminent, distinguished, celebrated, illustrious, legendary.
> – ANTONYMS unknown.

– ORIGIN from Latin *fama* 'fame.'

fa·mous·ly /ˈfāməslē/ ▸ **adverb 1** as is widely known: *they have famously reclusive lifestyles.* **2** excellently: *we got along famously.*

fan[1] /fan/ ▸ **noun 1** a device with rotating blades that creates a current of air for cooling or ventilation. **2** a hand-held device that is waved so as to cool the user.
▸ **verb** (**fans, fanning, fanned**) **1** wave something so as to drive a current of air toward someone or something. **2** (of an air current) increase the strength of a fire. **3** make a belief or emotion stronger: *newspapers fanned national tensions.* **4** (**fan out**) spread out from a central point to cover a wide area.
– ORIGIN Latin *vannus*.

fan[2] ▸ **noun** a person who has a strong interest in or admiration for a particular sport, art form, famous person, etc.

> – SYNONYMS **enthusiast,** devotee, admirer, lover, aficionado, supporter, follower, disciple, adherent; informal buff.

– DERIVATIVES **fan·dom** noun.
– ORIGIN abbreviation of **FANATIC**.

fa·nat·ic /fəˈnatik/ ▸ **noun 1** a person who holds extreme or dangerous religious or political opinions. **2** informal a person with an obsessive enthusiasm for a pastime or hobby.

> – SYNONYMS **extremist,** militant, dogmatist, bigot, zealot, radical, diehard; informal maniac.

– DERIVATIVES **fa·nat·i·cism** /fəˈnatəˌsizəm/ noun.
– ORIGIN from Latin *fanaticus* 'of a temple, inspired by a god.'

fa·nat·i·cal /fəˈnatikəl/ ▸ **adjective 1** filled with excessive and single-minded zeal. **2** obsessively concerned with something.

> – SYNONYMS **1 zealous,** extremist, extreme, militant, gung-ho, dogmatic, radical, diehard, intolerant, single-minded, blinkered, inflexible, uncompromising. **2 enthusiastic,** eager, keen, fervent, passionate, obsessive, obsessed, fixated, compulsive; informal wild, nuts, crazy.

– DERIVATIVES **fa·nat·i·cal·ly** adverb.

fan belt ▸ **noun** a belt driving the fan that cools the radiator of a motor vehicle.

fan·boy /ˈfanˌboi/ (or **fangirl** /ˈfanˌgərl/) ▸ **noun** informal, derogatory an obsessive male (or female) fan, usually of movies, comic books, or science fiction.

fan·ci·er /ˈfansēər/ ▸ **noun** a person who has a special interest in or breeds a particular animal.

fan·ci·ful /ˈfansəfəl/ ▸ **adjective 1** overimaginative and unrealistic. **2** existing only in the imagination. **3** highly ornamental or imaginative in design.
– DERIVATIVES **fan·ci·ful·ly** /-f(ə)lē/ adverb **fan·ci·ful·ness** noun.

fan club ▸ **noun** an organized group of fans of a famous person or team.

fan·cy /ˈfansē/ ▸ **adjective** (**fancier, fanciest**) **1** elaborate or highly decorated. **2** sophisticated or expensive: *a fancy Italian restaurant.*

> – SYNONYMS **elaborate,** ornate, ornamental, decorative, embellished, intricate, ostentatious, showy, flamboyant, lavish, expensive; informal flashy, snazzy, posh, classy.
> – ANTONYMS plain.

▸ **verb** (**fancies, fancying, fancied**) **1** informal find someone sexually attractive: *I think Sid fancies your sister.* **2** informal want or want to do: *would you fancy some dessert?* **3** (**fancy oneself**) informal have an unduly high opinion of oneself, or of one's ability in a particular area: *she fancies herself a gourmet cook.* **4** used to express surprise: *fancy that!*

> – SYNONYMS **1 be attracted to,** find attractive, be infatuated with, be taken with; informal have a crush on, carry a torch for. **2 wish for,** want, desire, long for, yearn for, crave, thirst for, hanker after, dream of, covet. **3 imagine,** believe, think, be under the impression; informal reckon.

▸ **noun** (pl. **fancies**) **1** a superficial or brief feeling of attraction. **2** the power of imagining things. **3** something that is imagined.

> – SYNONYMS **1 whim,** foible, urge, whimsy, fascination, fad, craze, enthusiasm, passion, caprice. **2 fantasy,** dreaming, imagination, creativity.

– DERIVATIVES **fan·ci·ly** /ˈfansəlē/ adverb **fan·ci·ness** noun.
– PHRASES **take** (or **catch**) **someone's fancy** appeal to someone. **take a fancy to** become fond of someone or something.
– ORIGIN from **FANTASY**.

fan·cy-free ▸ **adjective** not emotionally involved with anyone.

fan·dan·go /fanˈdaNGgō/ ▸ **noun** (pl. **fandangoes** or **fandangos**) **1** a lively Spanish dance for two people. **2** a foolish or frivolous act or thing.
– ORIGIN Spanish.

fan·fare /ˈfanˌfer/ ▸ **noun 1** a short ceremonial tune or flourish played on brass instruments. **2** great media attention surrounding the introduction of something.
– ORIGIN French.

fan·fic /ˈfanˌfik/ ▸ **noun** short for **FAN FICTION**.

fan fic·tion ▶ **noun** a genre of amateur writing based on characters and events from mass entertainment or popular culture.

fang /faNG, fäNG/ ▶ **noun 1** a large sharp tooth, especially a canine tooth of a dog or wolf. **2** a tooth with which a snake injects poison. **3** the biting mouthpart of a spider.
– DERIVATIVES **fanged** adjective.
– ORIGIN from Old Norse, 'capture, grasp.'

fan·girl ▶ **noun** see **FANBOY**.

fan·light /ˈfanˌlīt/ ▶ **noun** a small semicircular window over a door or another window.

fan·ny /ˈfanē/ ▶ **noun** (pl. **fannies**) **1** informal a person's buttocks. **2** Brit. vulgar slang a woman's genitals.
– ORIGIN unknown.

fan·ny pack ▶ **noun** a small pouch worn around the waist and used for storing valuables and small items.

fan·tab·u·lous /fanˈtabyələs/ ▶ **adjective** informal excellent; wonderful.
– ORIGIN blend of **FANTASTIC** and **FABULOUS**.

fan·tail /ˈfanˌtāl/ ▶ **noun 1** a fan-shaped tail or end of something. **2** a domestic pigeon of a broad-tailed variety.
– DERIVATIVES **fan-tailed** adjective.

fan·ta·sia /fanˈtāZHə, fantəˈzēə/ ▶ **noun 1** a musical composition that does not follow a conventional form. **2** a musical composition based on several familiar tunes.
– ORIGIN Italian, 'fantasy.'

fan·ta·size /ˈfantəˌsīz/ ▶ **verb** daydream about desirable but unlikely situations or events: *she fantasized about living on a boat in the Caribbean*.
– DERIVATIVES **fan·ta·sist** noun.

fan·tas·tic /fanˈtastik/ ▶ **adjective 1** hard to believe or unlikely to happen: *fantastic schemes*. **2** informal very good, attractive, or large.

– SYNONYMS **1 fanciful,** extravagant, extraordinary, irrational, wild, absurd, far-fetched, unthinkable, implausible, improbable, unlikely; informal crazy. **2 strange,** weird, bizarre, outlandish, grotesque, surreal, exotic. **3 marvelous,** wonderful, sensational, outstanding, superb, excellent; informal terrific, fabulous; Brit. informal brilliant.
– ANTONYMS ordinary.

– DERIVATIVES **fan·tas·tic·al** adjective **fan·tas·tic·al·ly** /-(ə)lē/ adverb.

fan·ta·sy /ˈfantəsē/ ▶ **noun** (pl. **fantasies**) **1** the imagining of unlikely or impossible things. **2** a daydream about a situation or event that is desirable but unlikely to happen. **3** a type of imaginative fiction involving magic and adventure.

– SYNONYMS **1 imagination,** fancy, invention, make-believe, creativity, vision, daydreaming, reverie. **2 dream,** daydream, pipe dream, fanciful notion, wish, fond hope, delusion; informal pie in the sky.
– ANTONYMS realism.

– ORIGIN Greek *phantasia* 'imagination, appearance.'

fan·zine /ˈfanˌzēn, fanˈzēn/ ▶ **noun** a magazine for fans of a particular team, performer, activity, etc.
– ORIGIN blend of **FAN²** and **MAGAZINE**.

FAQ /fak/ ▶ **abbreviation** frequently asked questions.

far /fär/ ▶ **adverb** (**farther, farthest** or **further, furthest**) **1** at, to, or by a great distance. **2** over a long time. **3** by a great deal.

– SYNONYMS **1 a long way,** a great distance, a good way, afar. **2 much,** considerably, markedly, greatly, significantly, substantially, appreciably, by a long way, by a mile, easily.

▶ **adjective 1** situated at a great distance. **2** distant from the center. **3** more distant than another object of the same kind: *the far corner*.

– SYNONYMS **1 distant,** faraway, far-off, remote, out of the way, far-flung, outlying. **2 further,** opposite.
– ANTONYMS near.

– PHRASES **as far as 1** to the extent that. **2** for a great enough distance to reach: *I decided to walk as far as the reservoir*. **be a far cry from** be very different from. **by far** by a great amount. **far and away** by a very large amount. **far and wide** over a large area. **far gone 1** in a bad or worsening state. **2** advanced in time. **go far 1** achieve a great deal. **2** be worth or amount to much. **go too far** go beyond what is reasonable or acceptable. **(in) so far as** to the extent that.
– ORIGIN Old English.

far·ad /ˈfarəd, -ˌad/ ▶ **noun** the SI unit of electrical capacitance.
– ORIGIN from the name of the English physicist Michael *Faraday*.

far·a·day /ˈfarəˌdā/ ▶ **noun** a unit of electrical charge equal to 96,485 coulombs.
– ORIGIN named after Michael *Faraday*, English physicist.

far·a·way /ˈfärəˌwā/ ▶ **adjective 1** distant in space or time. **2** seeming remote from one's present situation; dreamy: *a faraway look*.

farce /färs/ ▶ **noun 1** a comic play involving ridiculously improbable situations and events. **2** this type of humor or performance. **3** an absurd or ridiculous event: *the debate turned into a drunken farce*.

– SYNONYMS **mockery,** travesty, parody, sham, pretense, charade, joke; informal shambles.
– ANTONYMS tragedy.

– ORIGIN French, 'stuffing' (from the former practice of 'stuffing' comic interludes into religious plays).

far·ci·cal /ˈfärsikəl/ ▶ **adjective** absurd or ridiculous.
– DERIVATIVES **far·ci·cal·ly** adverb.

fare /fer/ ▶ **noun 1** the money a passenger on public transportation has to pay. **2** a passenger in a taxi. **3** a range of food.

– SYNONYMS **1 price,** cost, charge, fee, toll, tariff. **2 food,** meals, cooking, cuisine.

▶ **verb** perform in a particular way: *the party fared badly in the spring elections*.

– SYNONYMS **get on,** get along, cope, manage, do, survive; informal make out.

– ORIGIN Old English.

Far East ▶ **noun** China, Japan, and other countries of east Asia.
– DERIVATIVES **Far East·ern** adjective.

fare·well /ferˈwel/ ▶ **exclamation** goodbye.

– SYNONYMS **goodbye,** so long, adieu, au revoir, ciao; informal bye, see you (later); Brit. informal ta-ta, cheerio, cheers.

▶ **noun** an act of parting or of marking someone's departure.

– SYNONYMS **goodbye,** adieu, leave-taking, parting, departure, send-off.

far-fetched ▶ **adjective** very difficult to believe.

far-flung ▶ **adjective** distant or remote.

far·i·na·ceous /ˌfarəˈnāsʜəs/ ▶ **adjective 1** made of flour or meal. **2** containing or resembling starch; starchy.
– ORIGIN Latin *farina* 'flour.'

farm /färmiɴɢ/ ▶ **noun 1** an area of land and its buildings used for growing crops and rearing animals. **2** a place for breeding or growing something: *a fish farm*.

> – SYNONYMS **ranch,** farmstead, plantation, estate, farmland, dairy farm. Austral./NZ **station.**

▶ **verb 1** make one's living by growing crops or keeping livestock. **2** (**farm something out**) send out or subcontract work to others.

> – SYNONYMS **1 breed,** rear, keep, raise, tend. **2** *we* ***farmed out*** *the warehouse construction to another firm* **contract out,** outsource, subcontract, delegate.

– ORIGIN Old French *ferme*, from Latin *firmare* 'fix, settle.'

farm·er /ˈfärmər/ ▶ **noun** a person who owns or manages a farm.

farm·hand /ˈfärmˌhand/ ▶ **noun** a worker on a farm.

farm·house /ˈfärmˌhous/ ▶ **noun** a house attached to a farm.

farm·ing /ˈfärmiɴɢ/ ▶ **noun** the activity or business of growing crops and raising livestock.

> – SYNONYMS **agriculture,** cultivation, ranching, farm management, husbandry, agronomy, agribusiness.

farm·land /ˈfärmˌland/ ▶ **noun** (also **farmlands**) land used for farming.

farm·stead /ˈfärmˌsted/ ▶ **noun** a farm and its buildings.

farm·yard /ˈfärmˌyärd/ ▶ **noun** a yard or small area of land surrounded by or next to farm buildings.

far·o /ˈferō/ ▶ **noun** a gambling card game in which players bet on the order in which the cards will appear.
– ORIGIN French *pharaon* 'pharaoh,' said to have been the name of the king of hearts.

Far·o·ese /ˌfe(ə)rōˈēz, -ˈēs/ ▶ **noun & adjective** chiefly British spelling of **FAEROESE**.

far-off ▶ **adjective** distant in time or space.

far out ▶ **adjective 1** unconventional. **2** informal excellent.

far·ra·go /fəˈrägō, -ˈrā-/ ▶ **noun** (pl. **farragoes**) a confused mixture.
– ORIGIN Latin, 'mixed fodder.'

far-reach·ing ▶ **adjective** having many important effects or implications.

far·ri·er /ˈfarēər/ ▶ **noun** a smith who shoes horses.
– DERIVATIVES **far·ri·er·y** noun.
– ORIGIN from Latin *ferrum* 'iron, horseshoe.'

far·row /ˈfarō/ ▶ **noun** a litter of pigs. ▶ **verb** (of a sow) give birth to piglets.
– ORIGIN Old English, 'young pig.'

far-see·ing ▶ **adjective** having foresight; farsighted.

Far·si /ˈfärsē/ ▶ **noun** the modern form of the Persian language, spoken in Iran.
– ORIGIN from the Persian word for 'Persia.'

far·sight·ed /ˈfärˌsītid, -ˈsītid/ ▶ **adjective 1** unable to see things clearly if they are relatively close to the eyes. **2** having or showing an awareness of what may happen in the future: *a farsighted exit strategy is very much a factor for both candidates*.

fart /färt/ informal ▶ **verb 1** emit wind from the anus. **2** (**fart around/about**) waste time on silly or unimportant things. ▶ **noun 1** an emission of wind from the anus. **2** a boring or unpleasant person.
– ORIGIN Old English.

far·ther /ˈfär<u>TH</u>ər/ ▶ **adverb & adjective** variant form of **FURTHER**.

> **USAGE**
>
> On the difference in use between **farther** and **further**, see the note at **FURTHER**.

farth·est /ˈfär<u>TH</u>ist/ ▶ **adjective & adverb** variant form of **FURTHEST**.

far·thing /ˈfär<u>TH</u>iɴɢ/ ▶ **noun 1** a former coin of the UK, equal to a quarter of an old penny. **2** chiefly Brit. the least possible amount: *she didn't care a farthing*.
– ORIGIN Old English, 'fourth.'

far·thin·gale /ˈfär<u>TH</u>iɴɢˌgāl/ ▶ **noun** historical a hooped petticoat or circular pad of fabric around the hips, formerly worn under women's skirts to extend and shape them.
– ORIGIN French *verdugale*.

Far West ▶ **noun** the region of North America west of the Rocky Mountains.

fas·ces /ˈfasˌēz/ ▶ **plural noun** historical a bundle of rods with a projecting ax blade, used as a symbol of a magistrate's power in ancient Rome.
– ORIGIN Latin, from *fascis* 'bundle.'

fas·ci·a /ˈfasʜ(ē)ə, ˈfā-/ (also chiefly Brit. **facia**) ▶ **noun 1** a board covering the ends of rafters or other fittings. **2** a detachable covering for the front of a cellular phone. **3** (in classical architecture) a long flat surface between moldings on an architrave. **4** Brit. the dashboard of a motor vehicle.
– ORIGIN Latin, 'band, door frame.'

fas·ci·cle /ˈfasikəl/ ▶ **noun 1** Anatomy & Biology a bundle of fibrous or stringy structures. **2** a separately published installment of a book or other printed work.
– ORIGIN Latin *fasciculus* 'little bundle.'

fas·ci·nate /ˈfasəˌnāt/ ▶ **verb** attract or interest someone very much.
– ORIGIN Latin *fascinare* 'bewitch.'

fas·ci·nat·ing /ˈfasəˌnātiɴɢ/ ▶ **adjective** extremely interesting.

> – SYNONYMS **interesting,** captivating, engrossing, absorbing, enchanting, enthralling, spellbinding, riveting, engaging, compelling, compulsive, gripping, charming, attractive, intriguing, diverting, entertaining.
> – ANTONYMS boring.

– DERIVATIVES **fas·ci·nat·ing·ly** adverb.

fas·ci·na·tion /ˌfasəˈnāsʜən/ ▶ **noun 1** the state of being very attracted to and interested in someone or something. **2** the power of something to attract or interest someone.

> – SYNONYMS **interest,** preoccupation, passion, obsession, compulsion, allure, lure, charm, attraction, appeal, pull, draw.

> **USAGE**
>
> Be careful to distinguish between the expressions **fascination with** and **fascination for**. A person has a **fascination with** something they are very interested in (*her fascination with the British royal family*), whereas something interesting holds a **fascination for** a person (*circuses have a fascination for children*).

fas·cism /ˈfasʜˌizəm/ ▶ **noun 1** a right-wing system of government characterized by extreme nationalistic beliefs and strict obedience to a leader or the state. **2** extreme right-wing or intolerant views or practices.
– DERIVATIVES **fas·cist** noun & adjective **fa·scis·tic** /faˈsʜistik/ adjective.
– ORIGIN Italian *fascismo*, from Latin *fascis* 'bundle.'

fash·ion /ˈfasʜən/ ▶ **noun 1** a style of clothing, hair, behavior, etc., that is currently popular. **2** the production and marketing of new styles of clothing and cosmetics. **3** a way of doing something: *they strolled across in a leisurely fashion*.

– SYNONYMS **1 vogue,** trend, craze, rage, mania, fad, style, look, convention, mode; informal thing. **2 clothes,** clothing design, couture; the garment industry; informal the rag trade. **3 manner,** way, method, style, approach, mode.

▶ **verb** form or make something: *a bench fashioned out of a fallen tree trunk*.

– SYNONYMS **construct,** build, make, manufacture, cast, shape, form, mold, sculpt, forge, hew, carve.

– PHRASES **after a fashion** to a certain extent but not perfectly. **in** (or **out of**) **fashion** fashionable (or unfashionable).
– ORIGIN Old French *façon*, from Latin *facere* 'do, make.'

fash·ion·a·ble /ˈfasʜ(ə)nəbəl/ ▶ **adjective** in or influenced by a style that is currently popular.

– SYNONYMS **in vogue,** in fashion, popular, up to date, up to the minute, modern, all the rage, trendsetting, stylish, chic, modish; informal trendy, classy, cool, tony.

– DERIVATIVES **fash·ion·a·bil·i·ty** /ˌfasʜ(ə)nəˈbilətē/ noun **fash·ion·a·bly** adverb.

fash·ion·is·ta /ˌfasʜəˈnēstə/ ▶ **noun** informal **1** a designer at a leading fashion house. **2** a devoted follower of fashion.

fast[1] /fast/ ▶ **adjective 1** moving or capable of moving at high speed. **2** taking place or acting rapidly. **3** (of a clock or watch) ahead of the correct time. **4** firmly fixed or attached. **5** (of a dye) not fading in light or when washed. **6** (of photographic film) needing only a short exposure. **7** involving or engaging in exciting or immoral activities.

– SYNONYMS **1 speedy,** quick, swift, rapid, high-speed, accelerated, express, blistering, breakneck, hasty, hurried; informal nippy, scorching, supersonic. **2 secure,** fastened, tight, firm, closed, shut, immovable. **3 loyal,** devoted, faithful, firm, steadfast, staunch, true, boon, bosom, inseparable.
– ANTONYMS slow, loose.

▶ **adverb 1** at high speed. **2** within a short time. **3** firmly or securely.

– SYNONYMS **1 quickly,** rapidly, swiftly, speedily, briskly, at full tilt, hastily, hurriedly, in a hurry. informal lickety-split. **2 securely,** firmly, tight. **3** *he's fast asleep* **deeply,** sound, completely.

– PHRASES **fast asleep** in a deep sleep. **pull a fast one** informal try to gain an unfair advantage.
– ORIGIN Old English.

fast[2] ▶ **verb** go without food or drink, especially for religious or medical reasons.

– SYNONYMS **eat nothing,** go without food, go hungry, starve oneself, go on a hunger strike.

▶ **noun** an act or period of fasting.
– ORIGIN Old English.

fast·back /ˈfas(t)ˌbak/ ▶ **noun** a car with a rear that slopes continuously from the roof to the bumper.

fast·ball /ˈfas(t)ˌbôl/ ▶ **noun** a baseball pitch thrown at or near a pitcher's top speed, usually faster than 90 mph.

fast breed·er ▶ **noun** a nuclear reactor using high-speed neutrons.

fas·ten /ˈfasən/ ▶ **verb 1** close or do up securely. **2** fix or hold something in place. **3** (**fasten on**) pick out and concentrate on something: *critics fastened on two sections of the report*.

– SYNONYMS **1 bolt,** lock, secure, make fast, chain, seal. **2 attach,** fix, affix, clip, pin, tack, stick, join. **3 tie (up),** tether, hitch, truss, fetter, lash, anchor, strap, rope.
– ANTONYMS unlock, untie.

– DERIVATIVES **fas·ten·er** noun **fas·ten·ing** noun.
– ORIGIN Old English, 'make sure, confirm.'

fast food ▶ **noun** easily prepared food sold in snack bars and restaurants as a quick meal.

fast for·ward ▶ **noun** on a player of recorded media, a control for moving the content forward rapidly. ▶ **verb** (**fast-forward**) move the content of recorded media forward with this control.

fas·tid·i·ous /fasˈtidēəs/ ▶ **adjective 1** very careful about accuracy and detail. **2** very concerned about cleanliness.
– DERIVATIVES **fas·tid·i·ous·ly** adverb **fas·tid·i·ous·ness** noun.
– ORIGIN Latin *fastidium* 'loathing.'

WORD TOOLKIT

See **FINICKY**.

fast lane ▶ **noun 1** a highway lane for fast-moving traffic. **2** a hectic or highly pressured lifestyle: *Hong Kong's high-rise corporate fast lane*.

fast·ness /ˈfas(t)nəs/ ▶ **noun 1** a secure place well protected by natural features. **2** the ability of a dye to maintain its color.

fast-talk ▶ **verb** informal pressure someone into doing something by using rapid or misleading speech.

fast track ▶ **noun** a rapid way of achieving something. ▶ **verb** (**fast-track**) speed up the development or progress of something.

fat /fat/ ▶ **noun 1** a natural oily substance found in animal bodies, deposited under the skin or around certain organs. **2** such a substance, or a similar one made from plants, used in cooking. **3** Chemistry any of a group of organic compounds of glycerol and acids that form the main constituents of animal and vegetable fat.

– SYNONYMS **1 blubber,** fatty tissue, adipose tissue, cellulite. **2 oil,** grease, lard, suet, butter, margarine.

▶ **adjective** (**fatter, fattest**) **1** (of a person or animal) having much excess fat. **2** (of food) containing much fat. **3** informal large or substantial: *fat profits*. **4** informal very little: *fat chance*.

– SYNONYMS **1 obese,** overweight, plump, stout, chubby, portly, flabby, paunchy, potbellied, corpulent; informal tubby. **2 fatty,** greasy, oily. **3 thick,** big, chunky, substantial, sizable.
– ANTONYMS thin, slim, lean.

– DERIVATIVES **fat·ness** noun **fat·tish** adjective.
– PHRASES **live off the fat of the land** have the best of everything.
– ORIGIN Old English.

fa·tal /ˈfātl/ ▶ **adjective 1** causing death. **2** leading to failure or disaster: *a fatal mistake*.

– SYNONYMS **1 deadly,** lethal, mortal, death-dealing, terminal, incurable, untreatable, inoperable. **2 disastrous,** devastating, ruinous, catastrophic, calamitous, dire.
– ANTONYMS harmless, beneficial.

– DERIVATIVES **fa·tal·ly** adverb.
– ORIGIN from Latin *fatum* (see **FATE**).

fa·tal·ism /ˈfātlˌizəm/ ▶ **noun 1** the belief that all events are decided in advance by a supernatural power and that humans have no control over them. **2** an attitude characterized by the belief that nothing can be done to prevent something from happening.
– DERIVATIVES **fa·tal·ist** noun **fa·tal·is·tic** /ˌfātlˈistik/ adjective.

fa·tal·i·ty /fāˈtalətē, fə-/ ▶ **noun** (pl. **fatalities**) an occurrence of death by accident, in war, or from disease.

fat burn·er ▶ **noun** an over-the-counter drug that claims to burn calories by increasing the body's metabolism.

fat cat ▶ **noun** derogatory a wealthy and powerful business executive or politician.

fate /fāt/ ▶ **noun 1** the development of events outside a person's control, regarded as decided in advance by a supernatural power. **2** the outcome of a situation for someone or something: *after his show was canceled, his wife's series suffered the same fate.* **3** (**the Fates**) Greek & Roman Mythology the three goddesses (Clotho, Lachesis, and Atropos) who controlled the lives of humans.

– SYNONYMS **1 destiny,** providence, the stars, chance, luck, serendipity, fortune, karma, kismet. **2 future,** destiny, outcome, end, lot. **3 death,** demise, end, sentence.

▶ **verb** (**be fated**) be destined to happen or act in a particular way: *it was as if they were fated to meet again.*

– SYNONYMS **predestine,** preordain, destine, mean, doom.

– ORIGIN Latin *fatum* 'that which has been spoken.'

fate·ful /ˈfātfəl/ ▶ **adjective** having far-reaching and usually disastrous consequences.
– DERIVATIVES **fate·ful·ly** adverb.

fat·head /ˈfatˌhed/ ▶ **noun** informal a stupid person.

fa·ther /ˈfäT͟Hər/ ▶ **noun 1** a male parent. **2** an important male figure in the origin and early history of something: *Jung was one of the fathers of modern psychoanalysis.* **3** literary a male ancestor. **4** (often as a title or form of address) a priest. **5** (**the Father**) (in Christian belief) God.

– SYNONYMS **1** informal **dad,** daddy, pop, pa, old man; informal, dated pater. **2 originator,** initiator, founder, inventor, creator, author, architect.

▶ **verb** be the father of someone.

– SYNONYMS **sire,** spawn, breed, give life to.

– DERIVATIVES **fa·ther·hood** noun **fa·ther·less** adjective.
– ORIGIN Old English.

WORD LINKS

paternal *relating to a father*
patricide *killing of one's father*

Fa·ther Christ·mas ▶ **noun** a British name for **SANTA CLAUS**.

fa·ther-in-law ▶ **noun** (pl. **fathers-in-law**) the father of one's husband or wife.

fa·ther·land /ˈfäT͟Hərˌland/ ▶ **noun** a person's native country.

fa·ther·ly /ˈfäT͟Hərlē/ ▶ **adjective** like a father, especially in being protective and affectionate.
– DERIVATIVES **fa·ther·li·ness** noun.

Fa·ther's Day ▶ **noun** a day of the year on which fathers are honored with gifts and greeting cards (usually the third Sunday in June).

fath·om /ˈfaT͟Həm/ ▶ **noun** a unit of length equal to six feet (1.8 meters), used in measuring the depth of water. ▶ **verb 1** understand or find an explanation for: *he couldn't fathom why she was so anxious.* **2** measure the depth of water.
– DERIVATIVES **fath·om·a·ble** adjective **fath·om·less** adjective.
– ORIGIN Old English, 'something that embraces' (the original measurement was based on the span of a person's outstretched arms).

fa·tigue /fəˈtēg/ ▶ **noun 1** extreme tiredness. **2** brittleness in metal or other materials caused by repeated stress. **3** (**fatigues**) loose-fitting clothing of a sort worn by soldiers. **4** (also **fatigue duty**) a menial nonmilitary task assigned to a soldier.

– SYNONYMS **tiredness,** weariness, exhaustion.
– ANTONYMS energy.

▶ **verb** (**fatigues, fatiguing, fatigued**) make someone extremely tired.

– SYNONYMS **tire out,** exhaust, wear out, drain, weary, overtire; informal knock out, take it out of.

– ORIGIN from Latin *fatigare* 'tire out.'

fat·so /ˈfatsō/ ▶ **noun** (pl. **fatsos**) informal, derogatory a fat person.

fat·ten /ˈfatn/ ▶ **verb** make or become fat or fatter.

fat·ty /ˈfatē/ ▶ **adjective** (**fattier, fattiest**) **1** containing a large amount of fat. **2** Medicine involving abnormal amounts of fat being deposited in a part of the body: *fatty degeneration of the arteries.*

– SYNONYMS **greasy,** fat, oily, creamy, rich.

▶ **noun** (pl. **fatties**) informal, derogatory a fat person.
– DERIVATIVES **fat·ti·ness** noun.

fat·ty ac·id ▶ **noun** an organic acid whose molecule contains a hydrocarbon chain.

fat·u·ous /ˈfacho͞oəs/ ▶ **adjective** silly and pointless.

– SYNONYMS **silly,** foolish, stupid, inane, idiotic, vacuous, asinine; pointless, senseless, ridiculous, ludicrous, absurd.
– ANTONYMS sensible.

– DERIVATIVES **fat·u·ous·ly** adverb **fat·u·ous·ness** noun.
– ORIGIN Latin *fatuus* 'foolish.'

fat·wa /ˈfätwä/ ▶ **noun** an authoritative ruling on a point of Islamic law.
– ORIGIN Arabic, 'decide a point of law.'

fau·cet /ˈfôsit, ˈfäs-/ ▶ **noun** a device for controlling a flow of liquid or gas from a pipe or container; a tap.
– ORIGIN Old French *fausset.*

fault /fôlt/ ▶ **noun 1** an unattractive or unsatisfactory feature; a defect or mistake. **2** responsibility for an accident or misfortune: *it's not my fault he's in this mess.* **3** (in tennis) a service that breaks the rules. **4** an extended break in the continuity of layers of rock formation, caused by movement of the earth's crust.

– SYNONYMS **1** *he has his faults* **defect,** failing, imperfection, blemish, flaw, shortcoming, weakness, weak point, vice. **2** *engineers have located the fault* **defect,** flaw, imperfection, bug, error, mistake, inaccuracy, oversight; informal glitch. **3 responsibility,** liability, culpability, guilt.
– ANTONYMS strength.

▶ **verb** criticize someone or something for being unsatisfactory: *her colleagues could not fault her dedication to the job.*

– SYNONYMS **find fault with,** criticize, attack, condemn; informal knock.

– PHRASES **at fault 1** responsible for an undesirable situation or event; in the wrong: *we recover compensation from the person at fault.* **2** mistaken or defective: *he suspected that his calculator was at fault.* **find fault** make a criticism or objection. —— **to a fault** to an excessive extent: *he was generous to a fault.*
– ORIGIN from Latin *fallere* 'deceive.'

CHOOSE THE RIGHT WORD

See **SIN[1]**.

fault·less /fôltləs/ ▶ **adjective** free from defect or error.

– SYNONYMS **perfect,** flawless, without fault, error-free, impeccable, accurate, precise, exact, correct, exemplary.
– ANTONYMS flawed.

– DERIVATIVES **fault·less·ly** adverb.

fault line /'fôlt ˌlīn/ ▶ **noun 1** the intersection of a geological fault with the earth's surface. **2** an undesirable or unbridgeable division: *the fault lines separating cultural politics and historical interpretation.*

fault·y /'fôltē/ ▶ **adjective (faultier, faultiest) 1** not working or made correctly. **2** (of thinking or reasoning) containing mistakes.

– SYNONYMS **1 malfunctioning,** broken, damaged, defective, not working, out of order; informal on the blink, acting up. **2 flawed,** unsound, defective, inaccurate, incorrect, erroneous, wrong.
– ANTONYMS working, sound.

faun /fôn/ ▶ **noun** Roman Mythology a lustful god of woods and fields, represented as a man with a goat's horns, ears, legs, and tail.
– ORIGIN from the name of the god *Faunus.*

fau·na /'fônə, 'fänə/ ▶ **noun** (pl. **faunas**) the animals of a particular region, habitat, or period of time. Compare with **FLORA**.
– DERIVATIVES **fau·nal** adjective.
– ORIGIN Latin, from *Fauna,* a goddess of woods and fields.

Faus·ti·an /foustēən/ ▶ **adjective** relating to the German astronomer Johann Faust, who was reputed to have sold his soul to the Devil.

Fauve /fōv/ ▶ **noun** a member of a group of early 20th-century French artists who painted in very bright colors.
– DERIVATIVES **Fauv·ism** noun **Fauv·ist** noun & adjective.
– ORIGIN French, 'wild beast,' with reference to a remark by the art critic Louis Vauxcelles.

faux /fō/ ▶ **adjective** made in imitation; artificial.
– ORIGIN French, 'false.'

faux pas /fō 'pä, 'fō ˌpä/ ▶ **noun** (pl. same) an embarrassing blunder in a social situation.
– ORIGIN French, 'false step.'

CHOOSE THE RIGHT WORD

See **MISTAKE**.

fa·va bean /'fävə ˌbēn/ ▶ **noun** another term for **BROAD BEAN**.
– ORIGIN from Latin *faba* 'bean.'

fave /fāv/ ▶ **noun & adjective** informal short for **FAVORITE**.

fa·vor /'fāvər/ (Brit. **favour**) ▶ **noun 1** approval or liking: *training is looked upon with favor by many employers.* **2** an act of kindness beyond what is due or usual: *I've come to ask you a favor.* **3** special treatment given to one person at the expense of another. **4** a small gift or souvenir: *they gave out personalized pens as party favors.* **5** old use a thing such as a badge that is worn as a mark of favor or support.

– SYNONYMS **1 approval,** approbation, goodwill, kindness, benevolence. **2 good turn,** service, good deed, act of kindness, courtesy.
– ANTONYMS disservice, disapproval.

▶ **verb 1** regard with approval or liking: *these politicians favor raising taxes.* **2** give unfairly preferential treatment to: *critics say the new regulations favor the worst polluters.* **3** work to someone's or something's advantage: *the soil and climate here don't favor tall trees.* **4** informal look like a parent or other relative. **5 (favor someone with)** give someone something they wish for.

– SYNONYMS **1 advocate,** recommend, approve of, be in favor of, support, back, champion, campaign for, press for, lobby for, promote; informal push for. **2 prefer,** go for, choose, opt for, select, pick, like better, be biased toward. **3 benefit,** be to the advantage of, help, assist, aid, advance, be of service to.
– ANTONYMS oppose.

– PHRASES **in favor** meeting with approval: *they were not in favor with the party.* **in someone's favor** to someone's advantage: *events were moving in his favor.* **in favor of** to be replaced by: *will today's teenage athletes drop soccer in favor of basketball, tennis, or golf?*
– ORIGIN Latin, from *favere* 'show kindness to.'

fa·vor·a·ble /'fāv(ə)rəbəl/ ▶ **adjective 1** expressing approval or agreement: *a favorable response.* **2** advantageous or helpful: *favorable economic conditions.* **3** suggesting a good outcome: *a favorable prognosis.*

– SYNONYMS **1 approving,** positive, complimentary, full of praise, flattering, glowing, enthusiastic, kind, good. **2 advantageous,** beneficial, in one's favor, good, right, suitable, appropriate, auspicious, promising, encouraging. **3 positive,** affirmative, assenting, approving, encouraging, reassuring.
– ANTONYMS critical, unfavorable.

– DERIVATIVES **fa·vor·a·bly** adverb.

fa·vor·ite /'fāv(ə)rət/ ▶ **adjective** preferred to all others of the same kind.

– SYNONYMS **favored,** preferred, chosen, choice, best-loved, dearest, pet.

▶ **noun 1** a favorite person or thing. **2** the competitor thought most likely to win.

– SYNONYMS **first choice,** pick, preference, pet, darling, the apple of one's eye; informal golden boy, teacher's pet. informal fair-haired boy/girl.

fa·vor·ite son ▶ **noun 1** a famous man who is particularly admired in his native area: *a brilliant idea from Toledo's favorite son.* **2** a person supported as a presidential candidate by delegates from the candidate's home state.

fa·vor·it·ism /'fāv(ə)rəˌtizəm/ ▶ **noun** the unfair favoring of one person or group at the expense of another.

favour, etc. ▶ **noun & verb** British spelling of **FAVOR**, etc.

fawn[1] /fôn, fän/ ▶ **noun 1** a young deer in its first year. **2** a light brown color.
– ORIGIN Old French *faon.*

fawn[2] ▸ **verb 1** try to please someone by flattering them or paying them too much attention. **2** (of a dog) show extreme devotion, especially by rubbing against someone.
– DERIVATIVES **fawn·ing** adjective.
– ORIGIN Old English, 'make or be glad.'

fax /faks/ ▸ **noun 1** an exact copy of a document made by electronic scanning and sent by telecommunications links. **2** the making or sending of documents in this way. **3** (also **fax machine**) a machine for sending and receiving such documents. ▸ **verb 1** send a document by fax. **2** contact someone by fax.
– ORIGIN abbreviation of FACSIMILE.

faze /fāz/ ▸ **verb** informal disconcert or unsettle someone.
– ORIGIN dialect *feeze* 'drive off,' from Old English.

FBI ▸ **abbreviation** Federal Bureau of Investigation.

FCC ▸ **abbreviation** Federal Communications Commission.

FDA ▸ **abbreviation** Food and Drug Administration.

FDIC ▸ **abbreviation** Federal Deposit Insurance Corporation, a body that underwrites most private bank deposits.

FDR ▸ **abbreviation** Franklin Delano Roosevelt.

Fe ▸ **symbol** the chemical element iron.
– ORIGIN from Latin *ferrum*.

fe·al·ty /'fēltē/ ▸ **noun** historical the loyalty sworn to a feudal lord by a tenant or vassal.
– ORIGIN Old French *feaulte*.

fear /fi(ə)r/ ▸ **noun 1** an unpleasant emotion caused by the threat of danger, pain, or harm. **2** the likelihood of something unwelcome happening: *she observed them without fear of attracting attention.*

> – SYNONYMS **1 terror,** fright, fearfulness, horror, alarm, panic, trepidation, dread, anxiety, angst, apprehension, nervousness. **2 phobia,** aversion, antipathy, dread, nightmare, horror, terror; informal hang-up.

▸ **verb 1** be afraid of someone or something. **2** (**fear for**) be anxious about: *she feared for her son's safety.*

> – SYNONYMS **1 be afraid of,** be fearful of, be scared of, be apprehensive of, dread, live in fear of, be terrified of. **2 suspect,** be afraid, have a sneaking suspicion, be inclined to think, have a hunch.

– ORIGIN Old English, 'danger.'

fear·ful /'fi(ə)rfəl/ ▸ **adjective 1** showing or causing fear. **2** informal very great.

> – SYNONYMS **1 afraid,** scared, frightened, scared stiff, scared to death, terrified, petrified, nervous, apprehensive, uneasy, anxious, timid; informal jittery. **2 terrible,** dreadful, awful, appalling, frightful, ghastly, horrific, horrible, shocking, gruesome.
> – ANTONYMS unafraid.

– DERIVATIVES **fear·ful·ly** adverb **fear·ful·ness** noun.

fear·less /'fi(ə)rlis/ ▸ **adjective** without fear; brave.

> – SYNONYMS **brave,** courageous, bold, audacious, intrepid, valiant, plucky, heroic, daring, unafraid; informal gutsy.
> – ANTONYMS timid, cowardly.

– DERIVATIVES **fear·less·ly** adverb **fear·less·ness** noun.

fear·some /'fi(ə)rsəm/ ▸ **adjective** frightening, especially in appearance.

> – SYNONYMS **frightening,** horrifying, terrifying, menacing, chilling, spine-chilling, alarming, unnerving, daunting, formidable, forbidding, dismaying, disquieting, disturbing; informal scary.

– DERIVATIVES **fear·some·ly** adverb.

> **WORD TOOLKIT**
>
> See **FORMIDABLE**.

fea·si·ble /'fēzəbəl/ ▸ **adjective 1** able to be done easily. **2** likely; probable.

> – SYNONYMS **practicable,** practical, workable, achievable, attainable, realizable, viable, realistic, possible; informal doable.
> – ANTONYMS impracticable.

– DERIVATIVES **fea·si·bil·i·ty** /ˌfēzə'bilətē/ noun **fea·si·bly** adverb.
– ORIGIN Old French *faisible*, from Latin *facere* 'do, make.'

> **USAGE**
>
> Some people object to the use of **feasible** to mean 'likely' or 'probable' (as in *the most feasible explanation*). This sense has been in the language for centuries, however, and is generally considered to be acceptable.

feast /fēst/ ▸ **noun 1** a large meal, especially one marking a special occasion. **2** an annual religious celebration. **3** a day dedicated to a particular saint.

> – SYNONYMS **banquet,** dinner, treat; informal spread.

▸ **verb 1** have a feast. **2** (**feast on**) eat large quantities of something.

> – SYNONYMS **1 gorge,** dine, binge. **2** (**feast on**) devour, consume, partake of, eat one's fill of; informal stuff one's face with, pig out on.

– PHRASES **feast one's eyes on** gaze at someone or something with pleasure. **feast or famine** either too much of something or too little.
– ORIGIN from Latin *festus* 'joyous.'

feast day ▸ **noun** a day on which an annual Christian celebration is held.

feat /fēt/ ▸ **noun** an achievement requiring great courage, skill, or strength.

> – SYNONYMS **achievement,** accomplishment, coup, triumph, undertaking, enterprise, venture, exploit, operation, exercise, endeavor, effort.

– ORIGIN Old French *fait*.

feath·er /'feT͟Hər/ ▸ **noun** any of the flat structures growing from a bird's skin, consisting of a partly hollow horny shaft fringed with fine strands.

> – SYNONYMS **plume,** quill; (**feathers**) plumage, down.

▸ **verb 1** turn an oar so that the blade passes through the air edgewise. **2** (as adj. **feathered**) covered or decorated with feathers.
– DERIVATIVES **feath·er·y** adjective.
– PHRASES **a feather in one's cap** an achievement to be proud of. **feather one's nest** make oneself richer, usually at someone else's expense.
– ORIGIN Old English.

feath·er·bed /'feT͟Hərˌbed/ ▸ **noun** a bed with a mattress stuffed with feathers. ▸ **verb** provide someone or something with very favorable economic or working conditions.

feath·er·brained /'feT͟Hərˌbrānd/ ▸ **adjective** silly or absentminded.

feath·er·ing /'feT͟HəriNG/ ▸ **noun 1** a bird's plumage. **2** the feathers of an arrow. **3** featherlike markings.

feath·er-light /ˈfeT͟Hərˌlīt/ ▶ **adjective** extremely light: *feather-light fabrics.*

feath·er·weight /ˈfeT͟Hərˌwāt/ ▶ **noun 1** a weight in boxing between bantamweight and lightweight. **2** a person or thing of little or no importance.

fea·ture /ˈfēCHər/ ▶ **noun 1** a distinctive element or aspect: *the town has many interesting features.* **2** a part of the face, such as the mouth or nose. **3** a newspaper or magazine article or a broadcast program devoted to a particular topic. **4** (also **feature film**) a full-length movie forming the main item in a movie theater program.

– SYNONYMS **1 characteristic,** attribute, quality, property, trait, hallmark, aspect, facet, factor, ingredient, component, element. **2** *her delicate features* **face,** countenance, physiognomy; informal mug. literary lineaments, visage. **3 centerpiece,** special attraction, highlight, focal point, focus, conversation piece. **4 article,** piece, item, report, story, column.

▶ **verb 1** have as a feature: *the hotel features a swimming pool and spacious gardens.* **2** have as an important actor or participant. **3** have an important or notable part in: *floral designs feature prominently in Persian rugs.*

– SYNONYMS **1 present,** promote, make a feature of, spotlight, highlight, showcase, foreground. **2 star,** appear, participate.

– DERIVATIVES **fea·tured** adjective.
– ORIGIN Old French *faiture* 'form.'

fea·ture-length /ˈfēCHərˌleNG(k)TH/ ▶ **adjective** about the same length as a typical movie: *a feature-length documentary.*

fea·ture·less /ˈfēCHərləs/ ▶ **adjective** lacking in distinguishable or interesting characteristics: *featureless suburban wasteland.*

Feb. ▶ **abbreviation** February.

fe·brile /ˈfebˌrīl, ˈfēˌbrīl/ ▶ **adjective 1** having or showing the symptoms of a fever. **2** overactive and excitable: *Poe's febrile imagination.*
– ORIGIN Latin *febrilis,* from *febris* 'fever.'

Feb·ru·ar·y /ˈfeb(y)o͞oˌerē, ˈfebro͞o-/ ▶ **noun** (pl. **Februaries**) the second month of the year.
– ORIGIN Latin *februarius,* from *februa,* the name of a purification feast held in this month.

fe·ces /ˈfēsēz/ (Brit. **faeces**) ▶ **plural noun** waste matter remaining after food has been digested, passed out of the body through the anus.
– DERIVATIVES **fe·cal** /fēkl/ adjective.
– ORIGIN Latin, plural of *faex* 'dregs.'

feck·less /ˈfekləs/ ▶ **adjective** irresponsible and lacking strength of character.
– DERIVATIVES **feck·less·ly** adverb **feck·less·ness** noun.
– ORIGIN from Scots and northern English dialect *effeck,* variant of **EFFECT**.

fe·cund /ˈfekənd, ˈfē-/ ▶ **adjective 1** very fertile: *a lush and fecund garden.* **2** producing many new and creative ideas: *these were her most fecund years.*
– DERIVATIVES **fe·cun·di·ty** /feˈkəndətē, fiˈkən-/ noun.
– ORIGIN Latin *fecundus.*

CHOOSE THE RIGHT WORD

See **FERTILE**.

Fed /fed/ ▶ **noun** informal a federal official, especially an FBI agent.

fed /fed/ past and past participle of **FEED**.

Fe·da·yeen /ˌfedāˈēn, -dīˈēn/ ▶ **plural noun** an Arab or Muslim commando force, especially one operating against Israel or against occupying forces in Iraq.
– ORIGIN from Arabic *fidā'ī* 'one who gives his life for another or for a cause.'

fed·er·al /ˈfed(ə)rəl/ ▶ **adjective 1** relating to a system of government in which several states unite under a central authority but remain independent in internal affairs. **2** relating to the central government of a federation: *federal laws.* **3** (**Federal**) US historical relating to the Northern States in the Civil War.
– DERIVATIVES **fed·er·al·ly** adverb.
– ORIGIN Latin *foedus* 'league, covenant.'

fed·er·al case ▶ **noun 1** a criminal case under the jurisdiction of a federal court. **2** a matter of great concern or with dire consequences: *I'm not trying to make a federal case out of this but you've got to do something.*

fed·er·al·ism /ˈfed(ə)rəˌlizəm/ ▶ **noun** the federal principle or system of government.
– DERIVATIVES **fed·er·al·ist** noun & adjective.

Fed·er·al Re·serve ▶ **noun** the banking authority that has the functions of a central bank.

fed·er·ate /ˈfedəˌrāt/ ▶ **verb** (of a number of states or organizations) unite on a federal basis.

fed·er·a·tion /ˌfedəˈrāSHən/ ▶ **noun 1** a group of states that have a central government but are independent in internal affairs. **2** an organization within which smaller divisions have some internal independence.

– SYNONYMS **confederation,** confederacy, association, league, alliance, coalition, union, syndicate, guild, consortium.

Fed·Ex /ˌfedeks/ (also **Fedex**) ▶ **verb** trademark send by courier, especially Federal Express: *the tape was FedExed to New York on Friday.*

fe·do·ra /fəˈdôrə/ ▶ **noun** a soft felt hat with a curled brim and the crown creased lengthways.
– ORIGIN from *Fédora,* a play written by the French dramatist Victorien Sardou.

fed up ▶ **adjective** informal annoyed or bored.

fee /fē/ ▶ **noun 1** a payment given for professional advice or services. **2** a sum of money paid in order to join an organization, gain admission to somewhere, etc.

– SYNONYMS **payment,** wage, salary, price, charge, bill, tariff, rate; (**fees**) remuneration, dues, earnings, pay; formal emolument.

– ORIGIN Old French *feu* 'an estate held on condition of feudal service.'

fee·ble /ˈfēbəl/ ▶ **adjective** (**feebler, feeblest**) **1** lacking physical or mental strength. **2** not convincing or impressive: *a feeble excuse.*

– SYNONYMS **1 weak,** weakened, debilitated, enfeebled, frail, decrepit, infirm, delicate, sickly, ailing, unwell, poorly. **2 ineffective,** unconvincing, implausible, unsatisfactory, poor, weak, flimsy, lame. **3 cowardly,** faint-hearted, spineless, timid, timorous, fearful, unassertive, weak, ineffectual; informal sissy, chicken. **4 faint,** dim, weak, pale, soft, subdued, muted.
– ANTONYMS strong.

– DERIVATIVES **fee·ble·ness** noun **fee·bly** adverb.
– ORIGIN from Latin *flebilis* 'lamentable.'

WORD TOOLKIT

See **WEAK**.

fee·ble-mind·ed ▶ **adjective** **1** foolish; stupid. **2** dated having less than average intelligence.

feed /fēd/ ▶ **verb** (past and past part. **fed** /fed/) **1** give food to a person or animal. **2** provide enough food for: *she needed money to feed and clothe her family.* **3** eat: *slugs and snails feed at night.* **4** supply with material, power, water, etc.: *a lake fed by waterfalls.* **5** pass something gradually through a confined space. **6** prompt an actor with a line.

– SYNONYMS **1 cater for/to,** provide for, cook for, dine, nourish. **2 eat,** graze, browse. **3 supply,** provide, give, deliver.

▶ **noun** **1** an act of feeding or of being fed. **2** food for domestic animals. **3** a device or pipe for supplying material to a machine. **4** the supply of raw material to a machine or device. **5** a broadcast distributed by a satellite or network from a central source to a large number of radio or television stations.

– SYNONYMS **fodder,** food, provender.

– ORIGIN Old English.

feed·back /ˈfēdˌbak/ ▶ **noun** **1** comments about a product or a person's performance, used as a basis for improvement. **2** the return of a fraction of the output of an amplifier, microphone, or other device to the input of the same device, causing distortion or a whistling sound.

feed·er /ˈfēdər/ ▶ **noun** **1** a person or animal that eats a particular food or in a particular way. **2** a thing that feeds or supplies something. **3** a road or rail route linking outlying districts with a main system.

feed·ing fren·zy ▶ **noun** **1** an aggressive group attack on prey by a number of sharks or piranhas. **2** an episode of frantic and unscrupulous competition for something, especially on the part of journalists covering a sensational story.

feed·lot /ˈfēdˌlät/ ▶ **noun** an enclosed area where livestock are fed and fattened for market.

feed·stock /ˈfēdˌstäk/ ▶ **noun** raw material used to supply a machine or industrial process.

fee-for-serv·ice ▶ **adjective** (of professional and especially medical services) charging a set fee for every service provided: *clinicians will be permitted to bill on a fee-for-service basis.*

feel /fēl/ ▶ **verb** (past and past part. **felt** /felt/) **1** notice, be aware of, or examine by touch or through physical sensation: *she felt her hand on his shoulder.* **2** give a sensation of a particular quality when touched: *his hair felt rough.* **3** experience an emotion or sensation: *I felt angry and upset.* **4** be affected by: *investors who have felt the effects of the recession.* **5** have a belief, attitude, or impression: *I felt that he hated me.* **6** (**feel up to**) have the strength or energy to do something.

– SYNONYMS **1 touch,** stroke, caress, fondle, finger, paw, handle. **2** *she felt a breeze on her back* **perceive,** sense, detect, discern, notice, be aware of, be conscious of. **3** *he will not feel any pain* **experience,** undergo, go through, bear, endure, suffer. **4 grope,** fumble, scrabble. **5 believe,** think, consider it right, be of the opinion, hold, maintain, judge; informal reckon, figure.

▶ **noun** **1** an act of feeling. **2** the sense of touch. **3** a sensation given by something when touched. **4** an impression given by something: *a cafe with a European feel.*

– SYNONYMS **1 texture,** finish, touch, consistency. **2 atmosphere,** ambience, aura, mood, feeling, air, impression, spirit; informal vibes. **3 aptitude,** knack, flair, bent, talent, gift, ability.

– PHRASES **feel free (to do something)** have no hesitation or shyness (often used as an invitation or for reassurance): *feel free to say what you like.* **feel like (doing) something** be inclined to have or do: *I feel like celebrating.* **get a feel for** become familiar with something. **have a feel for** have a sensitive appreciation or understanding of something.

– ORIGIN Old English.

feel·er /ˈfēlər/ ▶ **noun** **1** an animal organ such as an antenna that is used for testing things by touch. **2** a tentative proposal intended to find out someone's attitude or opinion.

feel-good ▶ **adjective** informal causing a feeling of happiness and well-being: *a feel-good movie.*

feel·ing /ˈfēliNG/ ▶ **noun** **1** an emotional state or reaction. **2** (**feelings**) the emotional side of a person's character: *I don't want to hurt her feelings.* **3** strong emotion. **4** a belief or opinion. **5** (**feeling for**) a sensitivity to or intuitive understanding of something. **6** the capacity to experience the sense of touch: *she lost all feeling in her leg.* **7** the sensation of touching or being touched: *the feeling of silk next to your skin.*

– SYNONYMS **1** *a rush of feeling* **compassion,** sympathy, empathy, fellow feeling, concern, pity, sorrow, commiseration. **2** *a feeling of nausea* **sensation,** sense, perception, awareness, consciousness. **3** (**feelings**) *he hurt her feelings* **sensibilities,** sensitivities, self-esteem, pride. **4** *the strength of her feeling* **love,** affection, fondness, tenderness, warmth, emotion, passion, desire. **5** *I had a feeling that I would win* **(sneaking) suspicion,** notion, inkling, hunch, impression, intuition, instinct, funny feeling, fancy, idea. **6** *my feeling is that it is true* **opinion,** belief, view, impression, intuition, instinct, hunch, estimation, guess. **7** (**feeling for**) *he had a feeling for poetry* **aptitude,** knack, flair, bent, talent, feel, gift, ability.

▶ **adjective** showing emotion or sensitivity.

– DERIVATIVES **feel·ing·ly** adverb.

fee sim·ple ▶ **noun** (pl. **fees simple**) Law a permanent and absolute tenure in land with freedom to dispose of it at will.

feet /fēt/ plural of **FOOT**.

feet first ▶ **adjective & adverb** **1** without hesitation or preparation: *the show requires the audience to jump in feet first.* **2** after death; as a corpse: *everyone told me they were going to carry me out feet first.*

feh /fe/ ▶ **exclamation** conveying disapproval, displeasure, or disgust: *the greatest writer in the English language? Feh!*

– ORIGIN Yiddish.

feign /fān/ ▶ **verb** pretend to feel or have: *he feigned surprise.*

– ORIGIN Old French *feindre.*

feint /fānt/ ▶ **noun** a deceptive or pretended attacking movement in boxing or fencing. ▶ **verb** make a feint.

– ORIGIN from French *feindre* 'feign.'

USAGE

On the confusion of **feint** and **faint**, see the note at **FAINT**.

feist·y /ˈfīstē/ ▶ **adjective** (**feistier, feistiest**) lively and spirited.

– DERIVATIVES **feist·i·ly** adverb **feist·i·ness** noun.
– ORIGIN from former *feist* 'small dog.'

fe·la·fel ▶ **noun** variant spelling of **FALAFEL**.

feld·spar /ˈfel(d),spär/ (also **felspar**) ▶ **noun** a mineral forming igneous rocks, consisting chiefly of aluminum silicates.
– ORIGIN German *Feldspat* 'field spar.'

fe·lic·i·ta·tions /fə,lisəˈtāsʜənz/ ▶ **plural noun** formal congratulations.

fe·lic·i·tous /fəˈlisətəs/ ▶ **adjective** well chosen or appropriate: *a felicitous phrase.*

– SYNONYMS **apt,** well chosen, fitting, suitable, appropriate, apposite, pertinent, germane, relevant.
– ANTONYMS inappropriate.

– DERIVATIVES **fe·lic·i·tous·ly** adverb.

fe·lic·i·ty /fəˈlisətē/ ▶ **noun** (pl. **felicities**) **1** great happiness. **2** the ability to express oneself in an appropriate way. **3** an appropriate or well-chosen feature of a work of literature: *his reviews shimmer with verbal felicities.*
– ORIGIN Latin *felicitas.*

fe·line /ˈfē,līn/ ▶ **adjective** relating to or resembling a cat or cats. ▶ **noun** a cat or other animal of the cat family.
– ORIGIN from Latin *feles* 'cat.'

fell¹ /fel/ past of **FALL**.

fell² ▶ **verb 1** cut down a tree. **2** knock someone down. **3** stitch down the edge of a seam to lie flat.

– SYNONYMS **1 cut down,** chop down, hack down, saw down, clear. **2 knock down,** knock to the ground, floor, strike down, knock out; informal deck, flatten, lay out.

– ORIGIN Old English.

fell³ ▶ **adjective** literary very evil or fierce.
– PHRASES **in one fell swoop** all in one go. [from Shakespeare's *Macbeth* (IV. iii. 219).]
– ORIGIN Old French *fel.*

fel·la·ti·o /fəˈlāsʜ(ē),ō/ ▶ **noun** stimulation of a man's penis with the mouth.
– DERIVATIVES **fel·late** verb.
– ORIGIN from Latin *fellare* 'to suck.'

fell·er¹ /ˈfelər/ ▶ **noun** nonstandard spelling of **FELLOW**.

fell·er² ▶ **noun** a person who cuts down trees.

fel·low /ˈfelō/ ▶ **noun 1** a man or boy. **2** a person in the same situation or associated with another: *they raised money for their fellows in need.* **3** a thing of the same kind as another. **4** a member of a learned society. **5** (also **research fellow**) a graduate receiving funds for a period of research. **6** Brit. a member of the governing body of certain colleges.

– SYNONYMS **1 man,** boy, person, individual, character; informal guy, dude, lad; Brit. informal chap, bloke. **2 companion,** friend, comrade, partner, associate, coworker, colleague; informal pal, buddy; Brit. informal mate.

▶ **adjective** sharing a particular activity, situation, or condition: *a fellow sufferer.*
– ORIGIN Old English, 'partner, colleague.'

fel·low feel·ing ▶ **noun** sympathy based on shared experiences.

fel·low·ship /ˈfelō,sʜip/ ▶ **noun 1** friendliness and companionship based on shared interests. **2** a group of people meeting to pursue a shared interest or aim. **3** the position of a fellow of a college or society.

– SYNONYMS **1 companionship,** comradeship, camaraderie, friendship, sociability, solidarity. **2 association,** organization, society, club, league, union, guild, alliance, fraternity, brotherhood.

fel·low trav·el·er ▶ **noun 1** a person who is sympathetic with a group's aims and policies without being a member of it: *journalists who are regarded as fellow travelers of the administration.* **2** chiefly historical a person who sympathizes with the Communist Party but is not a member of it.
– DERIVATIVES **fel·low trav·el·ing** adjective.

fel·on /ˈfelən/ ▶ **noun** a person who has committed a felony.
– ORIGIN Old French, 'wicked, a wicked person.'

fel·o·ny /ˈfelənē/ ▶ **noun** (pl. **felonies**) a crime regarded as more serious than a misdemeanor.
– DERIVATIVES **fe·lo·ni·ous** /fəˈlōnēəs/ adjective **fe·lo·ni·ous·ly** adverb.

felt¹ /felt/ ▶ **noun** cloth made by rolling and pressing wool, which causes the fibers to mat together. ▶ **verb 1** mat together or become matted. **2** (as adj. **felted**) covered with felt.
– ORIGIN Old English.

felt² past and past participle of **FEEL**.

felt-tip pen (also **felt-tipped pen**) ▶ **noun** a pen with a writing point made of felt or tightly packed fibers.

fe·luc·ca /fəˈlo͞okə, -ˈləkə/ ▶ **noun** a small boat propelled by oars or sails, used especially on the Nile.
– ORIGIN Arabic.

FEMA /ˈfēmə/ ▶ **abbreviation** Federal Emergency Management Agency.

fe·male /ˈfē,māl/ ▶ **adjective 1** referring to the sex that can bear offspring or produce eggs. **2** relating to or typical of women or female animals. **3** (of a plant or flower) having a pistil but no stamens. **4** (of a fitting) manufactured hollow so that a corresponding male part can be inserted. ▶ **noun** a female person, animal, or plant.
– DERIVATIVES **fe·male·ness** noun.
– ORIGIN from Latin *femina* 'woman.'

fem·i·nine /ˈfemənin/ ▶ **adjective 1** having qualities traditionally associated with women, especially delicacy and prettiness. **2** relating to women; female. **3** Grammar (of a gender of nouns and adjectives in certain languages) treated as female.

– SYNONYMS **womanly,** ladylike, soft, gentle, tender, delicate, pretty.
– ANTONYMS masculine.

– DERIVATIVES **fem·i·nine·ly** adverb **fem·i·nin·i·ty** /,feməˈninətē/ noun.
– ORIGIN from Latin *femina* 'woman.'

fem·i·nism /ˈfemə,nizəm/ ▶ **noun** a movement or theory supporting women's rights on the grounds of equality of the sexes.
– DERIVATIVES **fem·i·nist** noun & adjective.

fem·i·nize /ˈfemə,nīz/ ▶ **verb** make something more feminine or female.
– DERIVATIVES **fem·i·ni·za·tion** /,femənəˈzāsʜən/ noun.

femme fa·tale /,fem fəˈtal, fəˈtäl/ ▶ **noun** (pl. **femmes fatales** pronunc. same) an attractive and seductive woman.
– ORIGIN French, 'disastrous woman.'

femto- ▶ **combining form** referring to a factor of one quadrillionth (10^{-15}): *femtojoule.*
– ORIGIN from Danish or Norwegian *femten* 'fifteen.'

fe·mur /ˈfēmər/ ▶ **noun** (pl. **femurs** or **femora** /ˈfemərə/) the bone of the thigh.
– DERIVATIVES **fem·o·ral** /ˈfemərəl/ adjective.
– ORIGIN Latin, 'thigh.'

fen[1] /fen/ ▶ **noun** a low and marshy or frequently flooded area of land.
– DERIVATIVES **fen·ny** adjective.
– ORIGIN Old English.

fen[2] ▶ **noun** (pl. same) a unit of money of China, equal to one hundredth of a yuan.
– ORIGIN Chinese, 'a hundredth part.'

fence /fens/ ▶ **noun 1** a barrier enclosing an area, typically consisting of posts connected by wire, wood, etc. **2** a large upright obstacle in steeplechasing, show jumping, or cross-country races. **3** informal a dealer in stolen goods. **4** a guard or guide on a plane or other tool.

– SYNONYMS **barrier,** paling, railing, enclosure, barricade, stockade.

▶ **verb 1** surround or protect something with a fence. **2** (**fence something in/off**) enclose or separate with a fence for protection or to prevent escape: *everything is fenced in to keep out the wolves.* **3** informal deal in stolen goods. **4** practice the sport of fencing.

– SYNONYMS **1 enclose,** surround, encircle. **2 confine,** pen in, coop up, shut in/up, corral.

– DERIVATIVES **fenc·er** noun.
– PHRASES **side of the fence** either of the opposing positions involved in a conflict: *whatever side of the fence you are on, the issue is here to stay.* **sit on the fence** avoid making a decision.
– ORIGIN shortening of DEFENSE.

fenc·ing /ˈfensiNG/ ▶ **noun 1** the sport of fighting with blunted swords in order to score points. **2** a series of fences. **3** material for making fences.

fend /fend/ ▶ **verb 1** (**fend for oneself**) look after and provide for oneself. **2** (**fend someone/thing off**) defend oneself from an attack or attacker.

– SYNONYMS **1** (**fend for oneself**) **take care of oneself,** look after oneself, cope alone, stand on one's own two feet, get by. **2** (**fend someone/thing off**) **ward off,** head off, stave off, hold off, repel, repulse, resist, fight off.

– ORIGIN shortening of DEFEND.

fend·er /ˈfendər/ ▶ **noun 1** the mudguard or area around the wheel well of a vehicle. **2** a low frame around a fireplace to keep in falling coals. **3** a cushioning device hung over a ship's side to protect it against impact.

fen·es·tra·tion /ˌfenəˈstrāSHən/ ▶ **noun** Architecture the arrangement of windows in a building.
– ORIGIN from Latin *fenestra* 'window.'

feng shui /ˈfəNG ˈSHwē, -SHwā/ ▶ **noun** an ancient Chinese system of designing buildings and positioning objects inside buildings to ensure a favorable flow of energy.
– ORIGIN from the Chinese words for 'wind' and 'water.'

fen·nel /ˈfenl/ ▶ **noun** a plant whose leaves and seeds are used as an herb, and whose base is eaten as a vegetable.
– ORIGIN Latin *faeniculum.*

fen·ta·nyl /ˈfentənil, ˈfentn-il/ ▶ **noun** a fast-acting narcotic analgesic and sedative that is sometimes abused for its heroinlike effect.

fen·u·greek /ˈfenyəˌgrēk/ ▶ **noun** a white-flowered plant with seeds that are used as a spice.
– ORIGIN from Latin *faenum graecum* 'Greek hay' (the Romans used it as fodder).

fe·ral /ˈfi(ə)rəl, ˈferəl/ ▶ **adjective 1** (of an animal or plant) wild, especially after having been domesticated. **2** resembling a wild animal.
– ORIGIN from Latin *fera* 'wild animal.'

fer·ma·ta /ferˈmätə, fər-/ ▶ **noun** Music a pause of unspecified length on a note or rest, or the mark (𝄐) that designates this.

fer·ment ▶ **verb** /fərˈment/ **1** undergo or cause to undergo fermentation. **2** stir up disorder.
▶ **noun** /ˈfərment/ a state of unrest or excitement, especially among a large group of people: *the creative ferment of postwar Britain.*
– DERIVATIVES **fer·ment·a·ble** /fərˈmentəbəl/ adjective **fer·ment·er** /fərˈmentər/ noun.
– ORIGIN from Latin *fermentum* 'yeast.'

fer·men·ta·tion /ˌfərmənˈtāSHən/ ▶ **noun** the chemical breakdown of a substance by bacteria, yeasts, or other microorganisms, such as when sugar is converted into alcohol.
– DERIVATIVES **fer·ment·a·tive** /fərˈmen(t)ətiv/ adjective.

fer·mi·on /ˈfermēˌän, ˈfər-/ ▶ **noun** Physics a subatomic particle, such as a nucleon, that has a spin of a half integer.
– ORIGIN named after the Italian physicist Enrico *Fermi.*

fer·mi·um /ˈfermēəm, ˈfər-/ ▶ **noun** an unstable radioactive chemical element made by high-energy atomic collisions.

fern /fərn/ ▶ **noun** (pl. same or **ferns**) a flowerless plant that has feathery or leafy fronds and reproduces by spores.
– DERIVATIVES **fern·er·y** noun (pl. **ferneries**) **fern·y** adjective.
– ORIGIN Old English.

fe·ro·cious /fəˈrōSHəs/ ▶ **adjective 1** savagely fierce, cruel, or violent. **2** informal very great; extreme.

– SYNONYMS **1** *ferocious animals* **fierce,** savage, wild, predatory, ravening, aggressive, dangerous. **2** *a ferocious attack* **brutal,** vicious, violent, bloody, barbaric, savage, frenzied.
– ANTONYMS gentle, mild.

– DERIVATIVES **fe·ro·cious·ly** adverb **fe·roc·i·ty** /fəˈräsətē/ noun.
– ORIGIN from Latin *ferox* 'fierce.'

-ferous (usu. **-iferous**) ▶ **combining form** having or containing a specified thing: *Carboniferous.*
– ORIGIN from Latin *-fer* 'producing.'

fer·ret /ˈferət/ ▶ **noun 1** a domesticated albino or brown polecat, used, especially in Europe, for catching rabbits. **2** informal a search. ▶ **verb** (**ferrets, ferreting, ferreted**) **1** search for something in a place or container. **2** (**ferret something out**) discover something by determined searching. **3** (usu. as n. **ferreting**) hunt with ferrets.
– DERIVATIVES **fer·ret·er** noun **fer·ret·y** adjective.
– ORIGIN Old French *fuiret.*

fer·ric /ˈferik/ ▶ **adjective** Chemistry relating to iron with a valence of three.
– ORIGIN from Latin *ferrum* 'iron.'

Fer·ris wheel /ˈferis/ ▶ **noun** a fairground ride consisting of a giant vertical revolving wheel with passenger cars suspended on its outer edge.
– ORIGIN named after the American engineer George W. G. *Ferris.*

fer·ro·e·lec·tric /ˌferō-iˈlektrik/ ▶ **adjective** displaying permanent electric polarization that varies in strength with the applied electric field.
– DERIVATIVES **fer·ro·e·lec·tric·i·ty** /ˌferō-iˌlekˈtrisətē/ noun.

fer·ro·mag·net·ic /ˌferōˌmagˈnetik/ ▶ **adjective** Physics having the ability to become magnetic and to retain magnetic properties, as iron and some other metals do.
– DERIVATIVES **fer·ro·mag·ne·tism** /ˌferōˈmagnəˌtizəm/ noun.

fer·rous /ˈferəs/ ▶ **adjective 1** (of metals) containing iron. **2** Chemistry relating to iron with a valence of two.

fer·rule /ˈferəl/ ▶ **noun** a metal ring or cap used to strengthen the end of a handle, stick, or tube.
– ORIGIN Old French *virelle.*

fer·ry /ˈferē/ ▶ **noun** (pl. **ferries**) a boat or ship for carrying passengers and goods, especially as a regular service. ▶ **verb** (**ferries, ferrying, ferried**) carry someone or something by ferry or other transport.

– SYNONYMS **transport,** convey, carry, run, ship, shuttle.

– DERIVATIVES **fer·ry·man** noun (pl. **ferrymen**).
– ORIGIN Old Norse.

fer·tile /ˈfərtl/ ▶ **adjective 1** (of soil or land) producing or capable of producing abundant vegetation or crops. **2** (of a person, animal, or plant) able to conceive young or produce seed. **3** producing new and inventive ideas: *a fertile imagination.*

– SYNONYMS **1 productive,** fruitful, fecund, rich, lush. **2 creative,** inventive, innovative, visionary, original, ingenious, prolific.
– ANTONYMS barren.

– DERIVATIVES **fer·til·i·ty** /fərˈtilitē/ noun.
– ORIGIN Latin *fertilis.*

CHOOSE THE RIGHT WORD

fertile, fecund, fruitful, prolific

A **fertile** woman is one who has the power to produce offspring, just as *fertile* soil produces crops and a *fertile* imagination produces ideas. This adjective pertains to anything in which seeds (or thoughts) can take root and grow. A woman with ten children might be described as **fecund**, which means that she is not only capable of producing many offspring but has actually done it. A woman can be *fertile*, in other words, without necessarily being *fecund*. **Fruitful**, whose meaning is very close to that of *fecund* when used to describe plants and may replace *fertile* in reference to soil or land, pertains specifically to something that promotes fertility or fecundity (*a fruitful downpour*). It can also apply in a broader sense to anything that bears or promotes results (*a fruitful idea*; *a fruitful discussion*). While it's one thing to call a woman with a large family *fecund*, **prolific** is more usually applied to animals or plants in the literal sense of fertility, and suggests reproducing in great quantity or with rapidity. Figuratively, prolific is often used of highly productive creative efforts (*a prolific author with 40 titles published*).

fer·ti·lize /ˈfərtlˌīz/ ▶ **verb 1** introduce sperm or pollen into an egg, female animal, or plant to develop a new individual. **2** add fertilizer to soil or land.
– DERIVATIVES **fer·til·i·za·tion** /ˌfərtl-iˈzāshən/ noun.

fer·ti·liz·er /ˈfərtlˌīzər/ ▶ **noun** a chemical or natural substance added to soil to increase its fertility.

– SYNONYMS **plant food,** dressing, manure, muck, guano, compost.

fer·vent /ˈfərvənt/ ▶ **adjective** intensely passionate.

– SYNONYMS **impassioned,** passionate, intense, vehement, ardent, sincere, heartfelt, enthusiastic, zealous, fanatical, wholehearted, avid, eager, keen, committed, dedicated, devout.
– ANTONYMS apathetic.

– DERIVATIVES **fer·ven·cy** noun **fer·vent·ly** adverb.
– ORIGIN from Latin *fervere* 'boil.'

WORD TOOLKIT

See **ZEALOUS**.

fer·vid /ˈfərvid/ ▶ **adjective** intensely or excessively enthusiastic.
– DERIVATIVES **fer·vid·ly** adverb.
– ORIGIN Latin *fervidus.*

fer·vor /ˈfərvər/ (Brit. **fervour**) ▶ **noun** intense and passionate feeling: *the party swept to power on a tide of patriotic fervor.*

– SYNONYMS **passion,** ardor, intensity, zeal, vehemence, emotion, warmth, avidity, eagerness, keenness, enthusiasm, excitement, animation, vigor, energy, fire, spirit.
– ANTONYMS apathy.

fes·cue /ˈfeskyo͞o/ ▶ **noun** a narrow-leaved grass, some kinds of which are used for pasture and fodder.
– ORIGIN Old French *festu.*

fess /fes/ ▶ **verb** informal (**fess up**) confess; own up: *he fessed up about his relationship to Lawrence.*

-fest ▶ **combining form** informal in nouns referring to a festival or large gathering of a specified kind: *a media-fest.*
– ORIGIN from German *Fest* 'festival.'

fes·tal /ˈfestəl/ ▶ **adjective** relating to a festival; festive.
– ORIGIN from Latin *festa* 'feast.'

fes·ter /ˈfestər/ ▶ **verb 1** (of a wound or sore) become septic. **2** (of food or rubbish) become rotten. **3** (of a negative feeling or problem) become worse or more intense: *hate can breed and fester for centuries.*
– ORIGIN Old French *festrir.*

fes·ti·val /ˈfestəvəl/ ▶ **noun 1** a day or period of celebration, typically for religious reasons. **2** an organized series of concerts, movies, etc.

– SYNONYMS **celebration,** festivity, fete, fair, gala, carnival, fiesta, jamboree, feast day, holiday, holy day.

– ORIGIN Latin *festa* 'feast.'

fes·tive /ˈfestiv/ ▶ **adjective 1** relating to a festival. **2** typical of a festival or celebration; happy.

– SYNONYMS **jolly,** merry, joyous, joyful, happy, jovial, lighthearted, cheerful, jubilant, celebratory.

– DERIVATIVES **fes·tive·ly** adverb.

fes·tiv·i·ty /feˈstivətē/ ▶ **noun** (pl. **festivities**) **1** joyful celebration. **2** (**festivities**) activities or events celebrating a special occasion.

fes·toon /fesˈto͞on/ ▶ **verb** decorate something with chains of flowers, lights, etc.

– SYNONYMS **decorate,** adorn, ornament, trim, deck (out), hang, drape, swathe, garland, wreathe, bedeck; informal do up/out, get up.

▶ **noun** a decorative chain of flowers, leaves, or ribbons, hung in a curve.
– ORIGIN Italian *festone* 'festive ornament.'

fet·a /ˈfetə/ (also **feta cheese**) ▶ **noun** a salty Greek cheese made from the milk of sheep or goats.
– ORIGIN modern Greek *pheta.*

fe·tal /ˈfētl/ ▶ **adjective 1** relating to a fetus. **2** (of a posture) typical of a fetus, with the limbs folded in front of the body.

fetch /fecH/ ▶ **verb 1** go for and bring back someone or something. **2** sell for a particular price: *the old ax fetched $50 at auction.*

> – SYNONYMS **1 go and get,** go for, call for, summon, pick up, collect, bring, carry, convey, transport. **2 sell for,** bring in, raise, realize, yield, make, command; informal go for.

– DERIVATIVES **fetch·er** noun.
– ORIGIN Old English.

fetch·ing /ˈfecHiNG/ ▶ **adjective** attractive: *a fetching black miniskirt.*

> – SYNONYMS **attractive,** appealing, sweet, pretty, lovely, delightful, charming, captivating, enchanting; Scottish & N. English bonny.

– DERIVATIVES **fetch·ing·ly** adverb.

fete /fāt, fet/ (also **fête**) ▶ **noun** a celebration or festival. ▶ **verb** praise, welcome, or entertain publicly: *in New York, she was feted like royalty.*
– ORIGIN French.

fet·id /ˈfetid/ ▶ **adjective** smelling very unpleasant.
– ORIGIN Latin *fetidus.*

fet·ish /ˈfetisH/ ▶ **noun 1** an object worshiped for its supposed magical powers. **2** a form of sexual desire in which sexual pleasure is gained from an object, part of the body, or activity. **3** something that a person is obsessively devoted to: *a fetish for detail.*
– DERIVATIVES **fet·ish·ism** noun **fet·ish·ist** noun **fet·ish·is·tic** /ˌfetiˈsHistik/ adjective.
– ORIGIN French *fétiche.*

fet·ish·ize /ˈfetiˌsHīz/ ▶ **verb 1** make something the object of a sexual fetish. **2** have an excessive and irrational commitment to: *an author who fetishizes privacy.*
– DERIVATIVES **fet·ish·i·za·tion** /ˌfetisHiˈzāsHən/ noun.

fet·lock /ˈfetˌläk/ ▶ **noun** a joint of a horse's leg between the knee and the hoof.
– ORIGIN Germanic.

fe·tor /ˈfētər/ ▶ **noun** a strong, foul smell.
– ORIGIN Latin.

fet·ter /ˈfetər/ ▶ **verb 1** restrict the freedom of: *like most schools, it just rolls on, fettered by routine.* **2** restrain someone with chains or shackles. ▶ **noun 1** (**fetters**) restraints or controls. **2** a chain or shackle placed around a prisoner's ankles.
– ORIGIN Old English.

fet·tle /ˈfetl/ ▶ **noun** condition: *I was in fine fettle.*
– ORIGIN Old English, 'strip of material.'

fet·tuc·ci·ne /ˌfetəˈcHēnē/ ▶ **plural noun** pasta made in ribbons.
– ORIGIN Italian, 'little ribbons.'

fe·tus /ˈfētəs/ ▶ **noun** (pl. **fetuses**) an unborn mammal, in particular an unborn human more than eight weeks after conception.
– ORIGIN Latin, 'pregnancy, childbirth, offspring.'

feud /fyo͞od/ ▶ **noun 1** a prolonged and bitter dispute. **2** a state of prolonged hostility and violence between two groups.

> – SYNONYMS **vendetta,** conflict, quarrel, row, rivalry, hostility, strife.

▶ **verb** take part in a feud.

> – SYNONYMS **quarrel,** fight, clash, argue, squabble, dispute.

– ORIGIN Old French *feide* 'hostility.'

feu·dal /ˈfyo͞odl/ ▶ **adjective** relating to feudalism.
– ORIGIN from Latin *feodum* 'fee.'

feu·dal·ism /ˈfyo͞odlˌizəm/ ▶ **noun** the social system in medieval Europe, in which the nobility held lands in exchange for military service, and those at a lower level in society worked and fought for the nobles in exchange for land and protection.

fe·ver /ˈfēvər/ ▶ **noun 1** an abnormally high body temperature, usually accompanied by shivering, headache, and in severe instances, delirium. **2** great excitement or agitation: *election fever.*

> – SYNONYMS **1 feverishness,** high temperature; Medicine pyrexia; informal temperature. **2 excitement,** mania, frenzy, agitation, passion.

– ORIGIN Latin *febris.*

> **WORD LINKS**
>
> **febrile** *having a fever*

fe·vered /ˈfēvərd/ ▶ **adjective 1** having or showing the symptoms of fever. **2** nervously excited or agitated: *the fevered chants of the crowd.*

fe·ver·few /ˈfēvərˌfyo͞o/ ▶ **noun** an aromatic plant with feathery leaves and daisylike flowers, used as an herbal remedy for headaches.
– ORIGIN Latin *febrifuga,* from *febris* 'fever' + *fugare* 'drive away.'

fe·ver·ish /ˈfēv(ə)risH/ ▶ **adjective 1** having or showing the symptoms of a fever: *a feverish cold.* **2** displaying a frenetic excitement or energy: *the next couple of weeks were spent in a whirl of feverish activity.*

> – SYNONYMS **1 febrile,** fevered, hot, burning. **2 frenzied,** frenetic, hectic, agitated, excited, restless, nervous, worked up, overwrought, frantic, furious, hysterical, wild, uncontrolled, unrestrained.

– DERIVATIVES **fe·ver·ish·ly** adverb **fe·ver·ish·ness** noun.

fe·ver pitch ▶ **noun** a state of extreme excitement.

few /fyo͞o/ ▶ **determiner, pronoun, & adjective 1** (**a few**) a small number of. **2** not many.

> – SYNONYMS **not many,** hardly any, scarcely any, a small number of, a handful of, a couple of, one or two.
> – ANTONYMS many.

▶ **noun** (**the few**) a select minority of people.
– PHRASES **every few** once in every small group of (typically units of time): *she visits every few weeks.* **few and far between** scarce. **no fewer than** a surprisingly large number of. **quite a few** a fairly large number.
– ORIGIN Old English.

> **USAGE**
>
> Many people use the words **fewer** and **less** incorrectly. The rule is that **fewer** should be used with plural nouns, as in *eat fewer cookies* or *there are fewer people here today.* Use **less** with nouns referring to things that cannot be counted, as in *a job with less money.* It is wrong to use **less** with a plural noun (*less cookies, less people*).

fey /fā/ ▶ **adjective 1** unworldly and vague. **2** able to see into the future; clairvoyant.
– ORIGIN Old English, 'fated to die soon.'

fez /fez/ ▶ **noun** (pl. **fezzes**) a flat-topped conical red hat, worn by men in some Muslim countries.
– ORIGIN Turkish *fes,* named after the city of *Fez* in Morocco.

ff ▶ **abbreviation** Music fortissimo.

ff. ▶ **abbreviation** **1** folios. **2** following pages.

FHA ▶ **abbreviation** Federal Housing Administration.

fi·an·cé /ˌfēˌänˈsā, fēˈänsā/ ▶ **noun** (fem. **fiancée** pronunc. same) a person to whom another is engaged to be married.
– ORIGIN French.

fi·as·co /fēˈaskō/ ▶ **noun** (pl. **fiascos**) a ridiculous or humiliating failure.

– SYNONYMS **failure,** disaster, catastrophe, debacle, farce, mess; informal flop, washout, shambles.
– ANTONYMS success.

– ORIGIN from Italian *far fiasco* 'fail in a performance,' literally 'make a bottle.'

fi·at /ˈfēət, ˈfēˌät/ ▶ **noun** an official order or authorization.
– ORIGIN Latin, 'let it be done.'

fib /fib/ ▶ **noun** a trivial lie. ▶ **verb** (**fibs**, **fibbing**, **fibbed**) tell a fib.
– DERIVATIVES **fib·ber** noun.
– ORIGIN perhaps from former *fible-fable* 'nonsense,' from **FABLE**.

fi·ber /ˈfībər/ (Brit. **fibre**) ▶ **noun** **1** a thread or strand from which a plant or animal tissue, mineral substance, or textile is formed. **2** a substance formed of fibers. **3** substances in vegetables, fruit, and some other foods, that are difficult to digest and therefore help the passage of food through the body. **4** strength of character: *a lack of moral fiber*.

– SYNONYMS **thread,** strand, filament, wisp, yarn.

– ORIGIN Latin *fibra* 'fiber, entrails.'

fiber·board /ˈfībərˌbôrd/ ▶ **noun** a building material made of wood fibers compressed into boards.

fi·ber·glass /ˈfībərˌglas/ ▶ **noun** **1** a reinforced plastic material composed of glass fibers embedded in a resin matrix. **2** a textile fabric made from woven glass fibers.

fi·ber op·tics ▶ **plural noun** (treated as sing.) the use of thin flexible transparent fibers to transmit light signals, chiefly for telecommunications or for internal inspection of the body.
– DERIVATIVES **fi·ber-op·tic** adjective.

Fi·bo·nac·ci se·ries /ˌfēbəˈnächē ˈsi(ə)rēz/ ▶ **noun** Mathematics a series of numbers in which each number (**Fibonacci number**) is the sum of the two preceding numbers (e.g., the series 1, 1, 2, 3, 5, 8, etc.).
– ORIGIN named after the Italian mathematician Leonardo *Fibonacci*.

fibre, etc. ▶ **noun** British spelling of **FIBER**, etc.

fi·bril /ˈfībrəl, ˈfib-/ ▶ **noun** technical a small or slender fiber.
– ORIGIN Latin *fibrilla* 'little fiber.'

fi·bril·late /ˈfibrəˌlāt/ ▶ **verb** (of a muscle, especially in the heart) make a quivering movement due to uncoordinated contraction of the individual fibers.
– DERIVATIVES **fi·bril·la·tion** /ˌfibrəˈlāsʜən/ noun.

fi·brin /ˈfībrən/ ▶ **noun** an insoluble protein formed as a fibrous mesh during the clotting of blood.

fi·brin·o·gen /fīˈbrinəjən/ ▶ **noun** a soluble protein present in blood plasma, from which fibrin is produced.

fi·bro·blast /ˈfībrəˌblast, ˈfib-/ ▶ **noun** a cell in connective tissue that produces collagen and other fibers.

fi·broid /ˈfīˌbroid/ ▶ **adjective** relating to fibers or fibrous tissue. ▶ **noun** a noncancerous tumor of fibrous tissues, typically developing in the wall of the uterus.

fi·bro·my·al·gia /ˌfībrōmīˈalj(ē)ə/ ▶ **noun** a chronic disorder characterized by musculoskeletal pain, fatigue, and tenderness in localized areas.

fi·bro·sis /fīˈbrōsəs/ ▶ **noun** the thickening and scarring of connective tissue, usually as a result of injury.
– DERIVATIVES **fi·brot·ic** /fīˈbrätik/ adjective.

fi·brous /ˈfībrəs/ ▶ **adjective** consisting of or characterized by fibers.

fib·u·la /ˈfibyələ/ ▶ **noun** (pl. **fibulae** /ˈfibyəlē, -ˌlī/ or **fibulas**) the outer of the two bones between the knee and the ankle, parallel with the tibia.
– ORIGIN Latin, 'brooch.'

FICA /ˈfīkə/ ▶ **abbreviation** Federal Insurance Contributions Act, the law the governs deductions from salary and wages to fund Social Security.

fick·le /ˈfikəl/ ▶ **adjective** changeable, especially as regards one's loyalties.

– SYNONYMS **capricious,** flighty, giddy, changeable, volatile, mercurial, erratic, unpredictable, unreliable, unsteady.
– ANTONYMS constant.

– DERIVATIVES **fick·le·ness** noun.
– ORIGIN Old English, 'deceitful.'

fic·tion /ˈfiksʜən/ ▶ **noun** **1** literary works in prose describing imaginary events and people. **2** something that is invented or untrue: *keeping up the fiction that they were happily married*. **3** a false belief or statement, accepted as true for the sake of convenience.

– SYNONYMS **1 novels,** stories, literature, creative writing. **2 fabrication,** invention, lie, fib, tall tale, untruth, falsehood, fantasy, nonsense.
– ANTONYMS fact.

– DERIVATIVES **fic·tion·al** adjective **fic·tion·ally** adverb **fic·tion·ist** noun.
– ORIGIN Latin.

CHOOSE THE RIGHT WORD

fiction, deception, fable, fabrication, falsehood, figment

If a young child tells you there is a dinosaur under his bed, you might assume that his story is a **fiction**, but it is probably a **figment**. A *fiction* is a story that is invented either to entertain or to deceive (*her excuse was ingenious, but it was pure fiction*), while *figment* suggests the operation of fancy or imagination (*a figment of his imagination*). If a child hides his sandwich under the sofa cushions and tells you that a dinosaur ate it, this would be a **fabrication**, which is a story that is intended to deceive. Unlike a *figment*, which is mostly imagined, a *fabrication* is a false but thoughtfully constructed story in which some truth is often interwoven (*the city's safety record was a fabrication designed to lure tourists downtown*). A **falsehood** is basically a lie—a statement or story that one knows to be false but tells with intent to deceive (*a deliberate falsehood about where the money had come from*). A **deception**, on the other hand, is an act that deceives but not always intentionally (*a foolish deception designed to prevent her parents from worrying*). A **fable** is a fictitious story that deals with events or situations that are clearly fantastic, impossible, or incredible. It often gives animals or inanimate objects the power to speak and conveys a lesson of practical wisdom, as in *Aesop's Fables*.

fic·tion·al·ize /ˈfiksʜənəˌlīz/ ▶ **verb** make a true story into a fictional one.

fic·ti·tious /fik'tisHəs/ ▶ **adjective** **1** imaginary or invented; not real or true. **2** referring to the characters and events found in fiction.

– SYNONYMS **false,** fake, fabricated, bogus, spurious, assumed, affected, adopted, invented, made up; informal pretend, phony.
– ANTONYMS genuine.

fic·tive /'fiktiv/ ▶ **adjective** created by the imagination.
– DERIVATIVES **fic·tive·ness** noun.

fi·cus /'fīkəs/ ▶ **noun** (pl. same) a tree, shrub, or plant of the fig family, especially a potted one.

fid·dle /'fidl/ ▶ **noun** informal **1** a violin. **2** chiefly Brit. an act of fraud or cheating.

– SYNONYMS **fraud,** swindle, confidence trick; informal racket, scam.

▶ **verb** **1** touch or fidget with something restlessly or nervously. **2** informal falsify figures, data, or records. **3** informal play the violin.

– SYNONYMS **1 fidget,** play, toy, finger, handle. **2 adjust,** tinker, play (about/around), fool about/around, meddle, interfere, tamper; informal tweak, mess about/around. **3 falsify,** manipulate, massage, rig, distort, misrepresent, doctor, tamper with, interfere with; informal fix, cook (the books).

– DERIVATIVES **fid·dler** noun.
– PHRASES **fit as a fiddle** in very good health. **play second fiddle to** take a subordinate role to someone or something.
– ORIGIN from Old English *fithele* 'violin.'

fid·dle-fad·dle /'fidl ˌfadl/ ▶ **noun** trivial matters; nonsense.

fid·dler crab ▶ **noun** a small amphibious crab, the males of which have one greatly enlarged claw.

fid·dle·sticks /'fidlˌstiks/ ▶ **exclamation** informal, dated nonsense.

fi·del·i·ty /fə'delətē/ ▶ **noun** **1** continuing faithfulness to a person, cause, or belief. **2** the degree of exactness with which something is copied or reproduced.

– SYNONYMS **1 faithfulness,** loyalty, constancy, allegiance, commitment, devotion. **2 accuracy,** exactness, precision, correctness, strictness, closeness, authenticity.
– ANTONYMS disloyalty.

– ORIGIN from Latin *fidelis* 'faithful.'

fidg·et /'fijit/ ▶ **verb** (**fidgets, fidgeting, fidgeted**) make small movements through nervousness or impatience.

– SYNONYMS **1 wriggle,** squirm, twitch, jiggle, shuffle, be agitated; informal be jittery. **2 play,** fuss, toy, twiddle, fool about/around; informal fiddle, mess about/around.

▶ **noun** **1** a person who fidgets. **2** (**the fidgets**) mental or physical restlessness.
– ORIGIN from former *fidge* 'to twitch.'

fidg·et·y /'fijitē/ ▶ **adjective** inclined to fidget; uneasy or restless.

– SYNONYMS **restless,** restive, on edge, uneasy, nervous, nervy, keyed up, anxious, agitated; informal jittery, twitchy.

fi·du·ci·ar·y /fə'do͞osHēˌerē, -SHərē/ Law ▶ **adjective** involving trust, especially with regard to the relationship between a trustee and a beneficiary.
▶ **noun** (pl. **fiduciaries**) a trustee.

fie /fī/ ▶ **exclamation** old use used to express disgust or outrage.
– ORIGIN Latin *fi*, an exclamation of disgust at an unpleasant smell.

fief /fēf/ ▶ **noun** **1** historical an estate of land held on condition of feudal service. **2** a person's area of operation or control.
– DERIVATIVES **fief·dom** /'fēfdəm/ noun.
– ORIGIN Old French, variant of *feu* 'fee.'

field /fēld/ ▶ **noun** **1** an area of open land, especially one planted with crops, or a pasture. **2** a piece of land used for a sport or game. **3** a subject of study or area of activity: *experts in the field of design*. **4** a region or space with a particular property: *a magnetic field*. **5** a range within which objects are visible from a particular viewpoint or through a piece of equipment: *the webcam's field of view*. **6** (**the field**) all the participants in a contest or sport. **7** a scene of a battle or a military campaign.

– SYNONYMS **1 meadow,** pasture, paddock, grassland; literary lea, mead, greensward. **2 playing field,** ground, sports field; ballpark, soccer field; Brit. pitch. **3 area,** sphere, discipline, province, department, domain, territory, branch, subject. **4 scope,** range, sweep, reach, extent. **5 competitors,** entrants, competition, applicants, candidates, runners.

▶ **verb** **1** chiefly Baseball attempt to catch or stop the ball and return it after it has been hit. **2** select someone to play in a game or to run in an election. **3** deal with a difficult question, problem, etc.

– SYNONYMS **1 catch,** stop, retrieve, return, throw back. **2 deal with,** handle, cope with, answer, reply to, respond to.

▶ **adjective** **1** carried out or working in the natural environment, rather than in a laboratory or office: *a field operation*. **2** (of military equipment) light and mobile for use.
– DERIVATIVES **field·er** noun.
– PHRASES **in the field** **1** (of troops) engaged in combat or maneuvers. **2** engaged in practical work in the natural environment. **play the field** informal have a series of casual sexual relationships.
– ORIGIN Old English.

field corn ▶ **noun** corn that is grown as livestock feed or for processing as a market grain, in contrast to sweet corn.

field day ▶ **noun** an opportunity for action or success, especially at the expense of others: *he's having a field day bossing people around*.

field·er's choice ▶ **noun** Baseball a play in which the fielding team's decision to put out another player allows the batter to reach first base safely.

field e·vents ▶ **plural noun** track-and-field contests other than races, such as throwing and jumping events.

field glass·es ▶ **plural noun** binoculars for outdoor use.

field goal ▶ **noun** **1** Football a goal scored by a placekick, scoring three points. **2** Basketball a basket scored while the clock is running and the ball is in play.

field guide ▶ **noun** a book for the identification of birds, flowers, minerals, or other things in their natural environment.

field hock·ey ▶ **noun** hockey played on a field, as opposed to ice hockey.

field hos·pi·tal ▶ **noun** a temporary hospital set up near a battlefield.

field·ing /'fēldiNG/ ▶ **noun** **1** Baseball & Cricket the activity or skills involved in being a fielder. **2** Military the deployment of personnel or materiel: *the fielding of a software bridging capability.*

field mar·shal ▸ **noun** the highest rank of army officer in the UK and several other countries.

field mouse ▸ **noun** a common dark brown mouse with a long tail and large eyes.

field mush·room ▸ **noun** the common edible mushroom.

field of·fi·cer (also **field-grade officer**) ▸ **noun** a major, lieutenant colonel, or colonel.

field of vi·sion ▸ **noun** the entire area that a person or animal is able to see when their eyes are fixed in one position.

field test ▸ **noun** (also **field trial**) a test carried out in the environment in which a product is to be used. ▸ **verb** (**field-test**) test a product in the environment in which it is to be used.

field trip ▸ **noun** an expedition made by students or research workers to study something at first hand.

field·work /ˈfēldˌwərk/ ▸ **noun** practical work conducted by a researcher in the field rather than in a laboratory or office.

fiend /fēnd/ ▸ **noun 1** an evil spirit or demon. **2** a very wicked or cruel person. **3** informal a person who is very interested in something: *an exercise fiend.*
– ORIGIN Old English, 'an enemy, the devil.'

fiend·ish /ˈfēndisн/ ▸ **adjective 1** very cruel or unpleasant. **2** informal very complex.

– SYNONYMS **1 wicked,** cruel, vicious, evil, malevolent, villainous, brutal, savage, barbaric, barbarous, inhuman, murderous, ruthless, merciless. **2 cunning,** clever, ingenious, crafty, canny, wily, devious. **3 difficult,** complex, challenging, complicated, intricate.

– DERIVATIVES **fiend·ish·ly** adverb.

fierce /fi(ə)rs/ ▸ **adjective 1** violent or aggressive; ferocious. **2** intense or powerful: *her fierce determination never to lose the new order in her life.*

– SYNONYMS **1 ferocious,** savage, vicious, aggressive. **2 aggressive,** cutthroat, keen, intense, strong, relentless, dog-eat-dog. **3 intense,** powerful, vehement, passionate, impassioned, fervent, ardent. **4 powerful,** strong, violent, forceful, stormy, howling, raging, tempestuous.
– ANTONYMS gentle, mild.

– DERIVATIVES **fierce·ly** adverb **fierce·ness** noun.
– ORIGIN Latin *ferus* 'untamed.'

fier·y /ˈfī(ə)rē/ ▸ **adjective** (**fierier**, **fieriest**) **1** resembling or consisting of fire. **2** quick-tempered or passionate.

– SYNONYMS **1 burning,** blazing, on fire, flaming, ablaze. **2 bright,** brilliant, vivid, intense, rich. **3 passionate,** impassioned, excitable, spirited, quick-tempered, volatile, explosive, impetuous.

– DERIVATIVES **fier·i·ly** adverb **fier·i·ness** noun.

fi·es·ta /fēˈestə/ ▸ **noun 1** (in Spanish-speaking regions) a religious festival. **2** an event marked by festivities or celebration.
– ORIGIN Spanish.

FIFA /ˈfēfə/ ▸ **abbreviation** Fédération Internationale de Football Association, the international governing body of soccer.

fife /fīf/ ▸ **noun** a small shrill flute played in military bands.
– ORIGIN German *Pfeife* 'pipe.'

FIFO /ˈfīˌfō/ ▸ **abbreviation** first in first out (chiefly with reference to methods of stock valuation or data storage). Compare with **LIFO**.

fif·teen /fifˈtēn, ˈfifˌtēn/ ▸ **cardinal number 1** one more than fourteen; 15. (Roman numeral: **xv** or **XV**.) **2** a team of fifteen players, especially in rugby.
– DERIVATIVES **fif·teenth** ordinal number.
– ORIGIN Old English.

fifth /fi(f)тн/ ▸ **ordinal number 1** that is number five in a sequence; 5th. **2** (**a fifth/one fifth**) each of five equal parts into which something is divided. **3** a musical interval spanning five consecutive notes in a scale, in particular (also **perfect fifth**) an interval of three whole steps and a half step.
– DERIVATIVES **fifth·ly** adverb.
– PHRASES **take** (or **plead**) **the fifth** exercise the right guaranteed by the Fifth Amendment to the Constitution to refuse to answer questions in order to avoid incriminating oneself.

fifth col·umn ▸ **noun** a group within a country at war who are working for its enemies.
– DERIVATIVES **fifth col·umn·ist** noun.
– ORIGIN from the Spanish Civil War, when General Mola, leading four columns of troops toward Madrid, declared that he had a fifth column inside the city.

fifth wheel ▸ **noun 1** a superfluous person or thing: *she had said that he wouldn't be a fifth wheel on this trip.* **2** a coupling between a trailer and the vehicle that pulls it.

fif·ty /ˈfiftē/ ▸ **cardinal number** (pl. **fifties**) ten less than sixty; 50. (Roman numeral: **l** or **L**.)
– DERIVATIVES **fif·ti·eth** ordinal number.
– ORIGIN Old English.

fif·ty-fif·ty ▸ **adjective & adverb** with equal shares or chances.

fig /fig/ ▸ **noun** a soft pear-shaped fruit with sweet flesh and many small seeds.
– PHRASES **not give** (or **care**) **a fig** not care at all.
– ORIGIN Old French *figue.*

fig. ▸ **abbreviation** figure: *see fig. 7a.*

fight /fīt/ ▸ **verb** (past and past part. **fought** /fôt/) **1** take part in a violent struggle involving physical force or weapons. **2** take part in a war or contest. **3** (**fight back**) counterattack or retaliate in a fight, struggle, or contest. **4** (**fight someone/thing off**) defend oneself against an attack by someone or something. **5** quarrel or argue. **6** struggle to overcome, end, or prevent: *he came to power with a pledge to fight corruption.* **7** try very hard to obtain or do something: *doctors fought to save her life.*

– SYNONYMS **1 brawl,** exchange blows, scuffle, grapple, wrestle, tussle, spar; informal scrap, roughhouse. **2 do battle,** serve one's country, go to war, take up arms, engage, meet, clash, skirmish. **3 wage,** engage in, conduct, prosecute, undertake. **4 quarrel,** argue, bicker, squabble, fall out, feud, wrangle; Brit. row; informal scrap. **5 campaign,** strive, battle, struggle, crusade, agitate, lobby, push, press. **6 oppose,** contest, confront, challenge, appeal against, take a stand against, dispute, resist. **7 repress,** restrain, suppress, stifle, smother, hold back, fight back, keep in check, curb, choke back; informal keep the lid on.

▸ **noun 1** an act of fighting. **2** a vigorous struggle or campaign.

– SYNONYMS **1 brawl,** scuffle, disturbance, fisticuffs, fracas, melee, skirmish, clash, tussle; informal scrap, rough house, dust-up. dated affray. **2 boxing match,** bout, match, contest. **3 battle,** engagement, conflict, struggle, war, campaign, crusade, action, hostilities. **4 argument,** quarrel, squabble, wrangle, disagreement, falling-out, dispute, feud; Brit. row; informal tiff, spat, scrap. **5 struggle,** battle, campaign, push, effort. **6 will,** resistance, spirit, pluck, grit, strength, backbone, determination, resolution, resolve.

– PHRASES **fight fire with fire** use the weapons or tactics of one's opponent, even if one finds them distasteful. **fight it out** settle a dispute by fighting or competing aggressively: *they fought it out in court.* **fight one's way** move forward with difficulty.
– ORIGIN Old English.

fight·er /'fītər/ ▶ **noun 1** a person or animal that fights. **2** a fast military aircraft designed for attacking other aircraft.

– SYNONYMS **1 soldier,** fighting man/woman, warrior, combatant, serviceman, servicewoman; (**fighters**) troops, personnel, militia. **2 boxer,** pugilist, prizefighter, wrestler.

fight·ing chance ▶ **noun** a possibility of success if great effort is made.

fig leaf ▶ **noun** a leaf of a fig tree, used to conceal the genitals of naked people in paintings and sculpture.
– ORIGIN with reference to the story of Adam and Eve in the Bible, who made clothes out of fig leaves after becoming aware of their nakedness.

fig·ment /'figmənt/ ▶ **noun** a thing that exists only in a person's imagination.
– ORIGIN Latin *figmentum.*

CHOOSE THE RIGHT WORD

See **FICTION**.

fig·ur·al /'figyərəl/ ▶ **adjective** another term for **FIGURATIVE**.

fig·u·ra·tion /,figyə'rāsʜən/ ▶ **noun 1** decoration using designs. **2** the representation of people or things in art as they appear in real life. **3** Music use of elaborate counterpoint.

fig·ur·a·tive /'figyərətiv/ ▶ **adjective 1** not using words in their literal sense; metaphorical. **2** (of art) representing people or things as they appear in real life.

– SYNONYMS **metaphorical,** nonliteral, symbolic, allegorical, representative, emblematic.
– ANTONYMS literal.

– DERIVATIVES **fig·ur·a·tive·ly** adverb.

fig·ure /'figyər/ ▶ **noun 1** a number or numerical symbol. **2** an amount of money. **3** a person's bodily shape, especially that of a woman. **4** an important or distinctive person: *he became something of a cult figure.* **5** an artistic representation of a person or animal. **6** a geometrical shape defined by one or more lines. **7** a diagram or illustrative drawing. **8** a short succession of musical notes from which longer passages are developed.

– SYNONYMS **1 statistic,** number, quantity, amount, level, total, sum; (**figures**) data, statistics. **2 digit,** numeral, character, symbol. **3 price,** cost, amount, value, valuation. **4 shape,** outline, form, silhouette, proportions, physique, build, frame. **5 person,** personage, individual, character, personality, celebrity. **6 shape,** pattern, design, motif. **7 diagram,** illustration, drawing, picture, plate.

▶ **verb 1** play a significant part in something. **2** (**figure someone/thing out**) understand someone or something. **3** calculate an amount arithmetically. **4** informal think or consider: *I figured I was safe here.* **5** (**figure on**) informal expect something to happen or be the case.

– SYNONYMS **1** *he figures in many myths* **feature,** appear, be featured, be mentioned, be referred to. **2** (**figure someone/thing out**) **work out,** fathom, puzzle out, decipher, make sense of, think through, get to the bottom of, understand, comprehend, see, grasp, get the hang of; informal crack; Brit. informal suss out.

– ORIGIN Latin *figura* 'figure, form.'

fig·ure eight ▶ **noun** an object or movement having the shape of the number eight.

fig·ure·head /'figyər,hed/ ▶ **noun 1** a person who is leader in name only, lacking real power. **2** a carved bust or full-length figure set at the prow of an old-fashioned sailing ship.

fig·ure of speech ▶ **noun** a word or phrase used in a nonliteral sense to create a particular effect in speech or writing.

fig·ure skat·ing ▶ **noun** a type of ice skating in which the skater combines a number of movements including steps, jumps, and turns.

fig·ur·ine /,figyə'rēn/ ▶ **noun** a small statue of a person.
– ORIGIN Italian *figurina* 'small figure.'

Fi·ji·an /,fējēən, fi'jēən/ ▶ **noun** a person from Fiji. ▶ **adjective** relating to Fiji.

fil·a·ment /'filəmənt/ ▶ **noun 1** a slender threadlike object or fiber. **2** a metal wire in an electric light bulb, which glows white-hot when an electric current is passed through it. **3** Botany the slender part of a stamen that supports the anther.
– DERIVATIVES **fil·a·men·ta·ry** /,filə'mentərē/ adjective **fil·a·men·tous** /,filə,mentəs/ adjective.
– ORIGIN Latin *filamentum.*

fil·a·ri·a·sis /,filə'rīəsəs/ ▶ **noun** a disease caused by infestation with parasitic worms, transmitted by biting flies and mosquitoes in the tropics.
– ORIGIN from Latin *Filaria,* former name of a genus of nematode worms.

fil·bert /'filbərt/ ▶ **noun** a cultivated hazelnut.
– ORIGIN from French *noix de filbert* (so named because it ripens around August 20, the feast day of St. *Philibert*).

filch /filcʜ/ ▶ **verb** informal steal something small.
– ORIGIN unknown.

file[1] /fīl/ ▶ **noun 1** a folder or box for keeping loose papers together and in order. **2** Computing a collection of data or programs stored under a single identifying name. **3** a line of people or things one behind another. **4** Military a small detachment of troops.

– SYNONYMS **1 folder,** portfolio, binder. **2 dossier,** document, record, report, data, information, documentation, archives. **3 line,** column, row, queue, string, chain, procession.

▶ **verb 1** place a document in a file. **2** officially place a legal document, application, or charge on record. **3** walk one behind the other.

– SYNONYMS **1 categorize,** classify, organize, put in order, order, arrange, catalog, store, archive. **2 bring,** press, lodge. **3 walk in a line,** queue, march, parade, troop.

– ORIGIN Latin *filum* 'a thread.'

file[2] ▶ **noun** a tool with a roughened surface or surfaces, used for smoothing or shaping a hard material.
▶ **verb** smooth or shape something with a file.

– SYNONYMS **smooth,** buff, rub down, polish, shape, scrape, abrade, rasp, manicure.

– ORIGIN Old English.

fi·lé /fi'lā, 'fēlā/ ▶ **noun** powdered sassafras leaves used to flavor or thicken soup, especially gumbo.
– ORIGIN from French *filer* 'to twist.'

file·name /'fīl,nām/ ▶ **noun** an identifying name given to a computer file.

file-shar·ing ▶ **noun** the practice of or ability to transmit files from one computer to another over a network or the Internet: *file-sharing software*.

fi·let /fi'lā, 'filā/ ▶ **noun & verb** variant spelling of **FILLET** in all culinary senses.

fi·let mi·gnon /fi'lā mēn'yōN/ ▶ **noun** a small, tender cut of beef from the end of the tenderloin.
– ORIGIN French, literally 'dainty fillet.'

fil·i·al /'filēəl, 'filyəl/ ▶ **adjective** relating to or due from a son or daughter: *no one can accuse me of neglecting my filial duty*.
– ORIGIN from Latin *filius* 'son,' *filia* 'daughter.'

fil·i·bus·ter /'filə,bəstər/ ▶ **noun** prolonged speaking that obstructs progress in a lawmaking assembly.
▶ **verb** obstruct the progress of legislation by prolonged speaking.
– ORIGIN French *flibustier*, first applied to pirates in the West Indies.

fil·i·gree /'filə,grē/ (also **filagree**) ▶ **noun** delicate ornamental work of fine gold, silver, or copper wire.
– DERIVATIVES **fil·i·greed** adjective.
– ORIGIN from Latin *filum* 'thread' + *granum* 'seed.'

fil·ings /'filiNGz/ ▶ **plural noun** small particles rubbed off by a file.

Fil·i·pi·no /,filə'pēnō/ ▶ **noun** (pl. **Filipinos**; fem. **Filipina**, pl. **Filipinas**) **1** a person from the Philippines. **2** the national language of the Philippines. ▶ **adjective** relating to Filipinos or their language.

fill /fil/ ▶ **verb 1** make or become full: *his wardrobe is filled with designer clothes*. **2** block up a hole or gap. **3** be an overwhelming presence in: *the smell of garlic filled the air*. **4** cause someone to experience a feeling. **5** satisfy a need. **6** occupy a period of time. **7** hold and perform the duties of a position or role.

– SYNONYMS **1 fill up,** top up, charge. **2 crowd into,** throng, pack (into), occupy, squeeze into, cram (into). **3 stock,** pack, load, supply, replenish. **4 block up,** stop (up), plug, seal, caulk. **5 pervade,** permeate, suffuse, penetrate, infuse. **6 occupy,** hold, take up.
– ANTONYMS empty, clear, leave.

▶ **noun** (**one's fill**) as much as one wants or can bear.
– PHRASES **fill in** act as a substitute. **fill someone in** give someone information. **fill out** put on weight. **fill something out** (or **in**) complete a form by adding information. **fill someone's shoes** (or **boots**) informal take over someone's role and fulfill it satisfactorily.
– ORIGIN Old English.

fill·er[1] /'filər/ ▶ **noun 1** something used to fill a gap or cavity, or to increase bulk. **2** an item serving only to fill space or time in a broadcast, conversation, etc.

fill·er[2] ▶ **noun** (pl. same) a unit of money of Hungary, equal to one hundredth of a forint.
– ORIGIN Hungarian.

fil·let /'filit/ ▶ **noun 1** a boneless piece of meat from near the loins or ribs of an animal. **2** a boned side of a fish. **3** a band or ribbon binding the hair. **4** Architecture a narrow flat band separating two moldings. ▶ **verb** (**fillets, filleting, filleted**) **1** remove the bones from a fish. **2** cut meat or fish into boneless strips.
– ORIGIN Old French *filet* 'thread.'

fill·ing /'filiNG/ ▶ **noun 1** a quantity of material that fills or is used to fill something. **2** a piece of material used to fill a cavity in a tooth.

– SYNONYMS **stuffing,** padding, wadding, filler, contents.

▶ **adjective** (of food) leaving one feeling pleasantly full.

– SYNONYMS **substantial,** hearty, ample, satisfying, square, heavy, stodgy.

fill·ing sta·tion ▶ **noun** a gas station.

fil·lip /'filəp/ ▶ **noun** a stimulus or boost: *the latest initiative will bring a fillip to the area's economy*.
– ORIGIN in imitation of making a flick with the fingers.

fil·ly /'filē/ ▶ **noun** (pl. **fillies**) **1** a young female horse, especially one less than four years old. **2** humorous a lively girl or young woman.
– ORIGIN Old Norse.

film /film/ ▶ **noun 1** a thin, flexible strip of plastic or other material coated with a light-sensitive substance, used in a camera to produce photos or motion pictures. **2** a movie; a motion picture. **3** motion pictures considered as an art or industry. **4** material in the form of a very thin flexible sheet. **5** a thin layer covering a surface.

– SYNONYMS **1 layer,** coat, coating, covering, cover, skin, patina, tissue. **2 movie,** picture, feature film, motion picture, video, DVD. **3 movies,** cinema, pictures, films, the motion picture industry, the silver screen, the big screen.

▶ **verb 1** make a movie of a story, event, etc.; capture an event or performance on film. **2** become covered with a thin layer of something.

– SYNONYMS **1 photograph,** record on film, shoot, capture on film, videotape. **2 cloud,** mist, haze, blur.

– ORIGIN Old English, 'membrane.'

film·ic /'filmik/ ▶ **adjective** relating to movies or cinematography.

film·mak·er /'film,mākər/ ▶ **noun** a person who directs or produces movies.
– DERIVATIVES **film·mak·ing** noun.

film noir /,film 'nwär/ ▶ **noun** a style of movie marked by a mood of pessimism, fatalism, and menace.
– ORIGIN French, 'black film.'

film·og·ra·phy /fil'mägrəfē/ ▶ **noun** (pl. **filmographies**) a list of movies or television projects by one director or actor, or on one subject.

film stock ▶ **noun** photographic or cinematic film that has not been exposed or processed.

film·strip /'film,strip/ ▶ **noun** a series of transparencies in a strip for projection.

film·y /'filmē/ ▶ **adjective** (**filmier, filmiest**) **1** thin and translucent: *a flowing robe of filmy chiffon*. **2** covered with a thin film.

fi·lo /'fēlō/ (also **phyllo**) ▶ **noun** a kind of flaky pastry in the form of very thin sheets.
– ORIGIN modern Greek *phullo* 'leaf.'

fi·lo·vi·rus /'fēlō,vīrəs, 'fī-/ ▶ **noun** an RNA virus of a group that causes certain severe fevers characterized by hemorrhages.

fils /fēs/ ▸ **noun** used after a French surname to distinguish a son from a father of the same name.
– ORIGIN French, 'son.'

fil·ter /'filtər/ ▸ **noun 1** a device or substance that allows liquid or gas to pass through it, but holds back any solid particles. **2** a screen, plate, or layer that absorbs some of the light passing through it. **3** a piece of computer software that processes data before passing it to another application, for example to remove unwanted material.

> – SYNONYMS **strainer,** sifter, sieve, gauze, mesh, net.

▸ **verb 1** pass something through a filter. **2** move gradually in or out of somewhere: *the sun filtered through the window.* **3** (of information) gradually become known.

> – SYNONYMS **1 sieve,** strain, sift, clarify, purify, refine, treat. **2 seep,** percolate, leak, trickle, ooze, leach.

– DERIVATIVES **fil·ter·a·ble** adjective **fil·tra·tion** /fil'trāsHən/ noun.
– ORIGIN Latin *filtrum* 'felt used as a filter.'

fil·ter-feed·ing ▸ **adjective** (of an aquatic animal) feeding by filtering out plankton or nutrients suspended in the water.

fil·ter tip ▸ **noun** a filter attached to a cigarette for removing impurities from the inhaled smoke.

filth /filTH/ ▸ **noun 1** disgusting dirt. **2** obscene and offensive language or printed material.

> – SYNONYMS **dirt,** muck, grime, mud, sludge, slime, excrement, excreta, ordure, sewage, pollution.

– ORIGIN Old English.

filth·y /'filTHē/ ▸ **adjective** (**filthier, filthiest**) **1** disgustingly dirty. **2** obscene and offensive. **3** (of a mood) bad-tempered and aggressive.

> – SYNONYMS **1 dirty,** mucky, grimy, foul, squalid, sordid, soiled, stained, polluted, contaminated, unwashed. **2** *filthy jokes* **obscene,** rude, vulgar, dirty, smutty, improper, coarse, bawdy, lewd; informal blue. **3** *he was in a filthy mood* **bad,** foul, irritable, grumpy, grouchy, cross; informal cranky, ornery.
> – ANTONYMS clean, pleasant.

▸ **adverb** informal extremely: *she's filthy rich.*
– DERIVATIVES **filth·i·ly** adverb **filth·i·ness** noun.

WORD TOOLKIT

filthy ...	grubby ...	grimy ...
water	little hands	windows
habit	paws	floors
streets	mitts	mirror
animals	fingernails	pots and pans
conditions	children	dishes

fil·trate /'fil,trāt/ ▸ **noun** a liquid that has passed through a filter.

fin /fin/ ▸ **noun 1** a flattened part that projects from the body of a fish or other aquatic animal, used for propelling, steering, and balancing. **2** an underwater swimmer's flipper. **3** a projection on an aircraft, rocket, or car, for providing aerodynamic stability.
– DERIVATIVES **finned** adjective.
– ORIGIN Old English.

fin. ▸ **abbreviation 1** finance. **2** financial. **3** finish.

fi·na·gle /fə'nāgəl/ ▸ **verb** informal obtain something in a dishonest or devious way.
– DERIVATIVES **fi·na·gler** noun.
– ORIGIN from dialect *fainaigue* 'cheat.'

fi·nal /'fīnl/ ▸ **adjective 1** coming at the end; last. **2** allowing no further doubt or dispute: *the decision of the judges is final.*

> – SYNONYMS **1 last,** closing, concluding, finishing, end, ultimate, eventual. **2 irrevocable,** unalterable, absolute, conclusive, irrefutable, incontrovertible, indisputable, unchallengeable, binding.
> – ANTONYMS first, provisional.

▸ **noun 1** the last game in a tournament, which will decide the overall winner. **2** (**finals**) a series of games forming the final stage of a competition. **3** an exam at the end of a term, academic year, or particular class.
– ORIGIN from Latin *finis* 'end.'

WORD TOOLKIT

final ...	irrevocable ...	conclusive ...
decision	damage	evidence
score	undertaking	proof
analysis	divorce	results
word	loss	data
version	changes	argument
outcome	step	research

fi·nal cut ▸ **noun** the final edited version of a filmed production or sound recording.

fi·na·le /fə'nalē, -'nälē/ ▸ **noun** the last part of a piece of music, a performance, or a public event.

> – SYNONYMS **climax,** culmination, end, ending, finish, close, conclusion, termination, denouement.
> – ANTONYMS opening.

– ORIGIN Italian.

fi·nal·ist /'fīnl-ist/ ▸ **noun** a person or team competing in a final or finals.

fi·nal·i·ty /fī'nalətē, fi-/ ▸ **noun** (pl. **finalities**) the fact or quality of being final and unable to be changed.

fi·nal·ize /'fīnl,īz/ ▸ **verb** complete or decide on a final version of a plan or agreement.
– DERIVATIVES **fi·nal·i·za·tion** /,fīnl-ə'zāsHən/ noun.

fi·nal·ly /'fīn(ə)lē/ ▸ **adverb 1** after a long time and much difficulty or delay. **2** as a final point in a series.

> – SYNONYMS **1 eventually,** ultimately, in the end, after a long time, at (long) last, in the long run, in the fullness of time. **2 lastly,** last, in conclusion. **3 conclusively,** irrevocably, decisively, definitively, for ever, for good, once and for all.

fi·nal so·lu·tion ▸ **noun** the Nazi policy (1941–45) of exterminating Jews.

fi·nance /'fīnans, fə'nans/ ▸ **noun 1** the management of large amounts of money by governments or large organizations. **2** funds to support an enterprise. **3** (**finances**) the money available to a country, state, organization, or person.

> – SYNONYMS **1 financial affairs,** money matters, economics, commerce, business, investment. **2 funds,** money, capital, cash, resources, assets, reserves, funding.

▸ **verb** provide funding for a person or enterprise.

> – SYNONYMS **fund,** pay for, back, capitalize, endow, subsidize, invest in, sponsor; informal bankroll.

– ORIGIN Old French.

fi·nance com·pa·ny ▸ **noun** a company concerned primarily with providing money, as for short-term loans.

fi·nan·cial /fə'nancHəl, fī-/ ▸ **adjective** relating to finance.

– SYNONYMS **monetary,** money, economic, pecuniary, fiscal, banking, commercial, business, investment.

– DERIVATIVES **fi·nan·cial·ly** adverb.

fi·nan·cial plan·ner ▶ **noun** someone who is employed to manage savings and investments.

fi·nan·cial year ▶ **noun** British term for **FISCAL YEAR**.

fin·an·cier /ˌfinənˈsi(ə)r, fəˈnanˌsi(ə)r/ ▶ **noun** a person who manages the finances of governments or other large organizations.
– ORIGIN French.

finch /finCH/ ▶ **noun** a songbird of a large group including the canary and goldfinch, most of which have short stubby bills.
– ORIGIN Old English.

find /fīnd/ ▶ **verb** (past and past part. **found**) **1** discover someone or something by chance or by searching. **2** recognize or discover to be present or to be the case: *vitamin B12 is found in dairy products.* **3** confirm something by research or calculation. **4** reach or arrive at a state or point by a natural or normal process. **5** Law (of a court) officially declare to be the case: *he was found guilty of fraud.* **6** (**find against** or **for**) Law (of a court) make a decision against (or in favor of) someone.

– SYNONYMS **1** *I found the book I wanted* **locate,** spot, pinpoint, unearth, obtain, search out, track down, root out, come across/upon, run across/into, chance on, happen on, stumble on, encounter; informal bump into. **2** *they say they've found a cure for rabies* **discover,** invent, come up with, hit on. **3** *you'll find that it's a lively area* **realize,** become aware, discover, observe, notice, note, learn. **4** *I find their decision strange* **consider,** think, feel to be, look on as, view as, see as, judge, deem, regard as. **5** *he was found guilty* **judge,** deem, rule, declare, pronounce.
– ANTONYMS lose.

▶ **noun** a valuable or interesting discovery.

– SYNONYMS **1** *an archaeological find* **discovery,** acquisition. **2** *this table is a real find* **bargain,** godsend, boon, catch, asset; informal good buy.

– DERIVATIVES **find·a·ble** adjective.
– PHRASES **find favor** be liked or prove acceptable: *the ballet did not find favor with the public.* **find someone out** discover that someone has lied or been dishonest. **find something out** discover information or a fact.
– ORIGIN Old English.

find·er /ˈfīndər/ ▶ **noun 1** a person who finds someone or something. **2** a small telescope attached to a large one, used to locate an object for observation. **3** a viewfinder in a camera.

fin de siè·cle /ˌfan də sēˈəkl(ə)/ ▶ **adjective** relating to or typical of the end of a century, especially the 19th century.
– ORIGIN French, 'end of century.'

find·ing /ˈfīndiNG/ ▶ **noun** a conclusion reached as a result of an inquiry, investigation, or trial.

fine[1] /fīn/ ▶ **adjective 1** of very high quality. **2** satisfactory. **3** healthy and feeling well. **4** (of the weather) bright and clear. **5** very thin: *fine hair.* **6** of delicate or intricate workmanship. **7** difficult to distinguish because precise or subtle: *the ear makes fine distinctions between different noises.*

– SYNONYMS **1** *fine wines* **good,** choice, select, excellent, first-class, first-rate, great, exceptional, outstanding, splendid, magnificent, exquisite, superb, wonderful, superlative, prime, quality, special, superior, of distinction, premium, classic, vintage; informal A1, top-notch. **2** *a fine fellow* **worthy,** admirable, praiseworthy, laudable, upright, upstanding, respectable. **3 all right,** acceptable, suitable, good (enough), passable, satisfactory, adequate, reasonable, tolerable; informal OK, okay. **4 healthy,** well, good, all right, (fighting) fit, thriving, in good shape/condition; informal OK, okay, in fine fettle, in the pink. **5 fair,** dry, bright, clear, sunny, cloudless, balmy. **6 keen,** quick, alert, sharp, razor-sharp, acute, bright, brilliant, astute, clever, intelligent. **7 elegant,** stylish, expensive, smart, chic, fashionable, fancy, sumptuous, lavish, opulent; informal flashy. **8 flyaway,** wispy, delicate, thin, light. **9 sheer,** light, lightweight, thin, flimsy, diaphanous, filmy, see-through. **10 subtle,** ultra-fine, nice, hairsplitting.

▶ **adverb** informal in a satisfactory or pleasing way.
▶ **verb 1** (usu. **fine down**) make or become thinner. **2** clarify beer or wine by causing the precipitation of sediment.
– DERIVATIVES **fine·ly** adverb **fine·ness** noun.
– PHRASES **the finer points** the more complex or detailed aspects: *he went on to discuss the finer points of his work.*
– ORIGIN Old French *fin*.

fine[2] ▶ **noun** a sum of money imposed as a punishment by a court of law or other authority.

– SYNONYMS **penalty,** forfeit, damages, fee, excess charge.

▶ **verb** punish someone by a fine.
– ORIGIN Old French *fin* 'end, payment.'

fine art ▶ **noun** art intended to appeal mainly or solely to the sense of beauty, such as painting.
– PHRASES **have something down to a fine art** achieve a high level of skill in something through experience.

fine print ▶ **noun** another term for **SMALL PRINT**.

fin·er·y /ˈfīnərē/ ▶ **noun** showy clothes or decoration.

fines herbes /ˌfēnˈ(z)erb/ ▶ **plural noun** mixed herbs used in cooking.
– ORIGIN French, 'fine herbs.'

fi·nesse /fəˈnes/ ▶ **noun 1** impressive delicacy and skill: *his acting showed considerable dignity and finesse.* **2** subtle skill in handling people or situations. **3** (in bridge and whist) an attempt to win a trick with a card that is not a certain winner. ▶ **verb 1** do something with great subtlety and skill. **2** slyly attempt to avoid blame when dealing with a situation.
– ORIGIN French.

fine-tooth comb (also **fine-toothed comb**) ▶ **noun** (in phrase **with a fine-tooth comb**) with a very thorough search or analysis.

fine-tune ▶ **verb** make small adjustments to something in order to achieve the best performance.

fin·ger /ˈfiNGgər/ ▶ **noun 1** each of the four slender jointed parts attached to either hand (or five, if the thumb is included). **2** a measure of liquor in a glass, based on the breadth of a finger. **3** a long, narrow object.

– SYNONYMS **digit.**

▶ **verb 1** touch or feel someone or something with the fingers. **2** informal inform on someone. **3** Music play a passage with a particular sequence of positions of the fingers.

– SYNONYMS **touch,** feel, handle, stroke, rub, caress, fondle, toy with, play (about/around) with, fiddle with.

– DERIVATIVES **fin·gered** adjective **fin·ger·less** adjective.
– PHRASES **have a finger in every pie** be involved in a large number of activities. **have** (or **keep**) **one's finger on the pulse of something** be aware of the latest trends and developments of something: *she keeps her finger on the pulse of the fashion scene.* **lay a finger on** touch someone with the intention of harming them. **put one's finger on** identify something exactly.
– ORIGIN Old English.

fin·ger·board /ˈfiNGgər,bôrd/ ▸ **noun** a flat strip on the neck of a stringed instrument, against which the strings are pressed in order to vary the pitch.

fin·ger bowl ▸ **noun** a small bowl holding water for rinsing the fingers at a meal.

fin·ger food ▸ **noun** food that can conveniently be eaten with the fingers.

fin·ger·ing /ˈfiNGgəriNG/ ▸ **noun** a way or technique of using the fingers to play a musical instrument.

fin·ger·mark /ˈfiNGgər,märk/ ▸ **noun** a mark left on a surface by a dirty or greasy finger.

fin·ger·nail /ˈfiNGgər,nāl/ ▸ **noun** the nail on the upper surface of the tip of each finger.

fin·ger paint ▸ **noun** thick paint designed to be applied with the fingers, used by young children.

fin·ger·pick /ˈfiNGgər,pik/ ▸ **verb** play a guitar or similar instrument using the fingernails or plectrums worn on the fingertips.

fin·ger·print /ˈfiNGgər,print/ ▸ **noun** a mark made on a surface by a person's fingertip, useful for identification. ▸ **verb** record a person's fingerprints.

fin·ger·tip /ˈfiNGgər,tip/ ▸ **noun** the tip of a finger. ▸ **adjective** using or operated by the fingers: *fingertip controls.*
– PHRASES **at one's fingertips** (especially of information) readily available.

fin·i·al /ˈfinēəl/ ▸ **noun 1** a distinctive section or ornament at the highest point of a roof, pinnacle, or similar structure. **2** an ornament at the top, end, or corner of an object.
– ORIGIN from Latin *finis* 'end.'

fin·ick·y /ˈfinikē/ ▸ **adjective 1** fussy about one's requirements: *a finicky eater.* **2** excessively detailed or elaborate.
– DERIVATIVES **fin·ick·i·ness** noun.
– ORIGIN probably from FINE[1].

WORD TOOLKIT

finicky ...	fastidious ...	exacting ...
eater	attention	standards
customer	detail	task
appetite	art	specifications
tastes	care	schedule
child	grooming	process

fin·is /ˈfinis, fiˈnē/ ▸ **noun** the end (printed at the end of a book or shown at the end of a movie).
– ORIGIN Latin.

fin·ish /ˈfinisH/ ▸ **verb 1** bring or come to an end. **2** consume the whole or the remainder of food or drink. **3** reach the end of a race or other competition. **4** (**finish with**) have no more need or desire for someone or something. **5** complete the manufacture or decoration of something by giving it an attractive surface appearance.

– SYNONYMS **1 complete,** end, conclude, close, terminate, wind up, achieve, accomplish, fulfill; informal wrap up, sew up. **2 consume,** eat, devour, drink, finish off, polish off, use (up), exhaust, empty, drain, get through; informal down. **3 end,** come to an end, stop, conclude, come to a close, cease.
– ANTONYMS start.

▸ **noun 1** an end or final stage. **2** the place at which a race or competition ends. **3** the way in which a manufactured article is finished: *nylon with a shiny finish.*

– SYNONYMS **1 end,** ending, completion, conclusion, close, termination, finale, denouement. **2 surface,** texture, coating, covering, lacquer, glaze, veneer, gloss, patina, sheen, luster.
– ANTONYMS start.

– DERIVATIVES **fin·ish·er** noun.
– PHRASES **finish someone off** kill or comprehensively defeat someone. **finish up 1** complete an action or process: *the electrician should finish up by Friday.* **2** end by doing something or being in a particular position: *we finished up tired and humiliated.*
– ORIGIN Latin *finire.*

fin·ish·ing school ▸ **noun** a private school where girls are taught how to behave correctly in fashionable society.

fin·ish·ing touch ▸ **noun** a final detail that completes and improves a piece of work.

fi·nite /ˈfīnīt/ ▸ **adjective** limited in size or extent.

– SYNONYMS **limited,** restricted, determinate, fixed.
– ANTONYMS infinite.

– DERIVATIVES **fi·nite·ly** adverb **fi·nite·ness** noun.
– ORIGIN Latin *finitus* 'finished.'

fi·ni·to /fəˈnētō/ ▸ **adjective** informal finished: *his door closed, and that was it—the end, finito.*
– ORIGIN Italian.

fink /fiNGk/ informal ▸ **noun** an unpleasant or contemptible person, especially one who acts as an informant. ▸ **verb** (**fink on**) inform on to the authorities: *it turns out that Wally's been finking on us for years.*
– ORIGIN unknown.

Finn /fin/ ▸ **noun** a person from Finland.

Finn·ish /ˈfinisH/ ▸ **noun** the language of the Finns. ▸ **adjective** relating to the Finns or their language.

fiord ▸ **noun** variant spelling of FJORD.

fir /fər/ ▸ **noun** an evergreen coniferous tree with upright cones and flat needle-shaped leaves.
– ORIGIN probably Old Norse.

fire /fīr/ ▸ **noun 1** the state of burning, in which substances combine chemically with oxygen from the air and give out bright light, heat, and smoke. **2** an instance of burning in which something is destroyed. **3** wood or coal burned in a hearth or stove for heating or cooking. **4** passionate emotion or enthusiasm. **5** the firing of guns. **6** strong criticism: *we took a lot of fire for our initial tax proposal.*

– SYNONYMS **1 blaze,** conflagration, inferno, flames, burning, combustion. **2 dynamism,** energy, vigor, animation, vitality, exuberance, zest, elan, passion, zeal, spirit, verve, vivacity, enthusiasm; informal go, get-up-and-go, oomph. **3 gunfire,** firing, shooting, bombardment, shelling, volley, salvo, hail.

▸ **verb 1** shoot a bullet or projectile from a gun or other weapon. **2** informal dismiss someone from a job. **3** stimulate: *this personal testimony fired the girls' imagination.* **4** (**fire someone up**) fill someone with enthusiasm. **5** direct a rapid succession of questions or statements toward someone. **6** supply a furnace, power station, etc., with fuel. **7** bake or dry pottery or bricks in a kiln. **8** old use set fire to something.

– SYNONYMS **1** *someone fired a gun* **shoot,** discharge, let off, set off. **2 dismiss,** discharge, give someone their notice, lay off, let go; informal sack. **3 stimulate,** stir up, excite, awaken, rouse, inflame, animate, inspire, motivate.

– PHRASES **catch fire** begin to burn. **fire away** informal go ahead. **firing on all cylinders** functioning at a peak level. **light a fire under someone** stimulate someone to work or act more quickly or enthusiastically. **on fire 1** burning. **2** very excited. **set fire to** (or **set something on fire**) cause something to burn. **set the world on fire** do something remarkable or sensational. **under fire 1** being shot at. **2** being strongly criticized.

– ORIGIN Old English.

WORD LINKS

arson *crime of setting fire to property*
pyromania *obsessive desire to set fire to things*

fire a·larm ▸ **noun** a device making a loud noise that gives warning of a fire.

fire ant ▸ **noun** a tropical American ant that has a painful and sometimes dangerous sting.

fire·arm /ˈfī(ə)rˌärm/ ▸ **noun** a rifle, pistol, or other portable gun.

fire·ball /ˈfīrˌbôl/ ▸ **noun 1** a ball of flame or fire. **2** a large bright meteor. **3** an energetic or hot-tempered person.

fire·bomb /ˈfīrˌbäm/ ▸ **noun** a bomb designed to cause a fire. ▸ **verb** attack something with a firebomb.

fire·brand /ˈfīrˌbrand/ ▸ **noun** a passionate supporter of a particular cause.

fire·break /ˈfīrˌbrāk/ ▸ **noun** an obstacle that prevents fire from spreading, especially a strip of open space in a forest.

fire·brick /ˈfīrˌbrik/ ▸ **noun** a brick capable of withstanding intense heat, used especially to line furnaces and fireplaces.

fire com·pa·ny ▸ **noun** another term for **FIRE DEPARTMENT.**

fire·crack·er /ˈfīrˌkrakər/ ▸ **noun** a firework that explodes with a loud bang.

fire·damp /ˈfīrˌdamp/ ▸ **noun** a gas, chiefly methane, that forms an explosive mixture with air in coal mines.

fire de·part·ment ▸ **noun** the department of a local or municipal authority in charge of preventing and fighting fires.

fire door ▸ **noun 1** a fire-resistant door to prevent the spread of fire. **2** a door to the outside of a building, used as an emergency exit.

fire drill ▸ **noun** a practice of the emergency procedures to be used in case of fire.

fire-eat·er ▸ **noun** an entertainer who appears to eat fire.

fire en·gine ▸ **noun** a vehicle carrying firefighters and their equipment.

fire es·cape ▸ **noun** a staircase or ladder used for escaping from a burning building.

fire ex·tin·guish·er ▸ **noun** a portable device that discharges a jet of liquid, foam, or gas to extinguish a fire.

fire·fight /ˈfīrˌfīt/ ▸ **noun** Military a battle using guns rather than bombs or other weapons.

fire·fight·er /ˈfīrˌfītər/ ▸ **noun** a person whose job is to extinguish fires.

fire·fly /ˈfīrˌflī/ ▸ **noun** (pl. **fireflies**) a kind of beetle that glows in the dark.

fire·house /ˈfīrˌhous/ ▸ **noun** a fire station.

fire i·rons ▸ **plural noun** tools for tending a domestic fire, especially tongs, a poker, and a shovel.

fire·light /ˈfīrˌlīt/ ▸ **noun** light from a fire in a fireplace.

fire·man /ˈfīrmən/ ▸ **noun** (pl. **firemen**) a firefighter.

fire·place /ˈfīrˌplās/ ▸ **noun** a partially enclosed space at the base of a chimney for a domestic fire.

fire·pow·er /ˈfīrˌpou(-ə)r/ ▸ **noun** the destructive capacity of guns, missiles, or a military force.

fire·proof /ˈfīrˌpro͞of/ ▸ **adjective** able to withstand fire or great heat.

fire sale ▸ **noun 1** a sale of merchandise, sometimes damaged, from a business that has suffered a fire. **2** a sale of merchandise or assets from a seller facing bankruptcy.

fire·side /ˈfīrˌsīd/ ▸ **noun** the part of a room around a fireplace.

fire·side chat ▸ **noun** an informal and intimate conversation.

fire sta·tion ▸ **noun** a facility at which a fire department houses its fire engines and other equipment.

fire·storm /ˈfīrˌstôrm/ ▸ **noun** a very intense and destructive fire, fanned by strong currents of air drawn in from the surrounding area.

fire·trap /ˈfīrˌtrap/ ▸ **noun** a building without any or enough fire exits.

fire·wall /ˈfīrˌwôl/ ▸ **noun 1** a wall or partition designed to stop the spread of fire. **2** a part of a computer system or network that blocks unauthorized access to a network while allowing outward communication.

fire·wa·ter /ˈfīrˌwôtər, -ˌwätər/ ▸ **noun** humorous or dated strong alcohol.

Fire·Wire /ˈfī(ə)rˌwī(ə)r/ ▸ **noun** trademark a technology that allows high-speed data exchange between computers or between devices and computers.

fire·wood /ˈfīrˌwo͝od/ ▸ **noun** wood that is burned as fuel.

fire·work /ˈfīrˌwərk/ ▸ **noun 1** a device containing chemicals that burn or explode when it is ignited, producing spectacular colored lights and loud noises. **2** (**fireworks**) an outburst of anger or a display of great skill or energy.

fir·ing line ▸ **noun 1** the front line of troops in a battle. **2** a position where one is likely to be criticized or blamed: *the chief executive is in the firing line again.*

fir·ing squad ▸ **noun** a group of soldiers appointed to shoot a condemned person.

fir·kin /ˈfərkən/ ▸ **noun** chiefly historical a small cask used chiefly for liquids, butter, or fish.

– ORIGIN probably from Dutch *vierde* 'fourth' (a firkin originally contained a quarter of a barrel).

firm[1] /fərm/ ▸ **adjective 1** having a surface or structure that does not give way or sink under pressure. **2** solidly in place and stable. **3** having steady power or strength: *a firm grip.* **4** showing determination and strength of character. **5** fixed or definite: *she had no firm plans.*

– SYNONYMS **1 hard,** solid, unyielding, resistant, compacted, compressed, dense, stiff, rigid, set.

2 **secure,** stable, steady, strong, fixed, fast, tight, immovable, rooted, stationary, motionless. **3 resolute,** determined, decided, resolved, steadfast, adamant, emphatic, insistent, single-minded, wholehearted, unfaltering, unwavering, unflinching, unswerving, unbending, committed. **4 close,** good, boon, intimate, inseparable, dear, special, constant, devoted, loving, faithful, long-standing, steady, steadfast. **5 definite,** fixed, settled, decided, cut-and-dried, established, confirmed, agreed.
– ANTONYMS soft, unstable.

▶ **verb 1** make something firm. **2** (often **firm something up**) make an agreement or plan explicit and definite. ▶ **adverb** in a determined way: *he vowed to stand firm.*
– DERIVATIVES **firm·ly** adverb **firm·ness** noun.
– PHRASES **a firm hand** strict discipline or control.
– ORIGIN Latin *firmus.*

firm[2] ▶ **noun** a business organization.

– SYNONYMS **business,** company, concern, enterprise, organization, corporation, conglomerate, office, bureau, agency, consortium; informal outfit, operation.

– ORIGIN Latin *firmare* 'confirm by signature, settle.'

fir·ma·ment /ˈfərməmənt/ ▶ **noun** literary the heavens; the sky.
– ORIGIN Latin *firmamentum.*

firm·ware /ˈfərmˌwer/ ▶ **noun** Computing software permanently programmed into a read-only memory.

first /fərst/ ▶ **ordinal number 1** coming before all others in time or order; 1st. **2** before doing something else. **3** before all others in position, rank, or importance. **4** informal something never previously achieved or occurring.

– SYNONYMS **1 earliest,** initial, opening, introductory. **2 fundamental,** basic, rudimentary, primary, key, cardinal, central, chief, vital, essential. **3 foremost,** principal, highest, greatest, paramount, top, main, overriding, central, core; informal number-one. **4 top,** best, prime, premier, winning, champion.
– ANTONYMS last.

– PHRASES **at first** at the beginning. **of the first order** (or **magnitude**) of the highest quality or degree: *a soprano of the first order.*
– ORIGIN Old English.

first aid ▶ **noun** emergency medical help given to a sick or injured person until full treatment is available.
– DERIVATIVES **first-aid·er** noun.

first base ▶ **noun** Baseball the base that is the first destination of a runner.
– PHRASES **get to first base** informal succeed in the first step of an undertaking.

first·born /ˈfərstˌbôrn/ ▶ **noun** the first child to be born to someone.

first class ▶ **noun 1** a set of people or things grouped together as the best. **2** the best accommodations in an aircraft, train, or ship. ▶ **adjective & adverb 1** relating to the first class; of the best quality: *a first-class Thai restaurant.* **2** of or relating to a class of mail given priority: *send it out first class.*

first-de·gree ▶ **adjective 1** (of burns) affecting only the surface of the skin and causing reddening. **2** Law (of crime, especially murder) in the most serious category.

first·hand /ˈfərstˈhand/ ▶ **adjective & adverb** from the original source or personal experience; direct: *firsthand knowledge.*
– PHRASES **at first hand** directly or from personal experience.

first la·dy ▶ **noun** the wife of the president of the US or other head of state.

first-line ▶ **adjective** of first resort: *first-line drugs for HIV exposure.*

first·ly /ˈfərstlē/ ▶ **adverb** in the first place; first.

first mate ▶ **noun** the officer second in command to the master of a merchant ship.

first name ▶ **noun** a personal name given to someone at birth or baptism and used before a family name.
– PHRASES **be on a first-name basis** have a friendly and informal relationship.

First Na·tion ▶ **noun** (in Canada) any of several indigenous American Indian and Inuit communities that enjoy official status.

first of·fend·er ▶ **noun** a person who is convicted of a criminal offense for the first time.

first of·fi·cer ▶ **noun 1** the first mate on a merchant ship. **2** the second in command to the captain on an aircraft.

first per·son ▶ **noun** the form of a pronoun or verb used to refer to oneself, or to a group including oneself.

first prin·ci·ples ▶ **plural noun** the basic or fundamental concepts or assumptions on which a theory, system, or method is based.

first-rate ▶ **adjective** of the best class, quality, or condition; excellent.

first re·fus·al ▶ **noun** the privilege of deciding whether to accept or reject something before it is offered to others.

first re·spond·er ▶ **noun** someone designated or trained to respond to an emergency: *the department is extending its smallpox vaccination program to first responders.*

first run ▶ **noun** the period when a movie, play, or television program is first shown or performed: *this series was great during the first run and it is even better now.*
– DERIVATIVES **first-run** adjective.

first strike ▶ **noun** an opening attack with nuclear weapons.

first string ▶ **noun 1** the best players on a sports team, who normally play the most. **2** the outstanding people or things in a group: *these aren't the first string of gangster movies.*

First World ▶ **noun** the industrialized capitalist countries of western Europe, North America, Japan, Australia, and New Zealand.

firth /fərTH/ ▶ **noun** a narrow inlet of the sea.
– ORIGIN Old Norse.

fis·cal /ˈfiskəl/ ▶ **adjective 1** relating to financial matters. **2** relating to the income received by a government, especially as raised through taxes.
– DERIVATIVES **fis·cal·ly** adverb.
– ORIGIN Latin *fiscalis.*

fis·cal year ▶ **noun** a year as reckoned for taxing or accounting purposes.

fish[1] /fiSH/ ▶ **noun** (pl. same or **fishes**) **1** a cold-blooded animal with a backbone, gills, and fins, living in water. **2** the flesh of fish as food. **3** informal a person who is slightly strange: *he's an odd fish.* ▶ **verb 1** catch fish with a net or hook and line. **2** (**fish something out**) pull or take something out of water or a container. **3** grope or feel for something hidden. **4** (**fish for**) try to get a response or information by indirect means: *I wasn't fishing for compliments.*

– SYNONYMS **1 go fishing,** angle, trawl. **2** (**fish something out**) **pull out,** haul out, remove, extricate, extract, retrieve, rescue, save. **3 search,** delve, look, hunt, grope, fumble, ferret, rummage.

– DERIVATIVES **fish·a·ble** adjective **fish·ing** noun.
– PHRASES **a big fish** an important person. **a cold fish** a person who is unfriendly or shows little emotion. **a fish out of water** a person who feels out of place in their surroundings. **have other** (or **bigger**) **fish to fry** have more important matters to deal with.
– ORIGIN Old English.

USAGE

The normal plural of **fish** is **fish** (*he caught two huge fish*), but the older form **fishes** is still used when referring to different kinds of fish: *freshwater fishes of Pennsylvania.*

WORD LINKS

piscine *relating to fish*
ichthyology *study of fish*

fish² ▶ **noun 1** (also **fishplate**) a flat piece fixed across a joint to strengthen or connect it, e.g., in railroad track. **2** a long curved piece of wood lashed to a ship's damaged mast or spar as a temporary repair.
– ORIGIN probably from French *ficher* 'to fix.'

fish and chips ▶ **noun** batter-fried fish fillets served with french fries.

fish·bowl /ˈfisʜˌbōl/ ▶ **noun** a round glass bowl for keeping pet fish in.

fish·cake /ˈfisʜˌkāk/ ▶ **noun** a patty of shredded fish and mashed potato.

fish·er /ˈfisʜər/ ▶ **noun** old use a fisherman.

fish·er·man /ˈfisʜərmən/ ▶ **noun** (pl. **fishermen**) a person who catches fish for a living or for sport.

fish·er·y /ˈfisʜərē/ ▶ **noun** (pl. **fisheries**) **1** a place where fish are reared, or caught in large numbers. **2** the occupation or industry of catching or rearing fish.

fish·eye /ˈfisʜˌī/ ▶ **noun** a very wide-angle lens with a field of vision covering up to 180°, the scale being reduced toward the edges.

fish·hook /ˈfisʜˌho͝ok/ ▶ **noun** a hook, typically barbed and baited, for catching fish.

fish·ing line ▶ **noun** a long thread of silk or nylon attached to a baited hook and used for catching fish.

fish·ing rod ▶ **noun** a long, tapering rod to which a fishing line is attached.

fish·meal /ˈfisʜˌmēl/ ▶ **noun** ground dried fish used as fertilizer or animal feed.

fish·mon·ger /ˈfisʜˌməNGgər, -ˌmäNGgər/ ▶ **noun** a person or store that sells fish for food.

fish·net /ˈfisʜˌnet/ ▶ **noun** an open mesh fabric resembling a fishing net.

fish·plate /ˈfisʜˌplāt/ ▶ **noun** another term for FISH².

fish sauce ▶ **noun** a Thai and Vietnamese sauce used as a flavoring or condiment, prepared from fermented anchovies and salt.

fish·stick /ˈfisʜˌstik/ ▶ **noun** a small oblong piece of flaked or ground fish coated in batter or breadcrumbs.

fish story ▶ **noun** an incredible or far-fetched story.

fish·tail /ˈfisʜˌtāl/ ▶ **noun** a thing that is forked like a fish's tail. ▶ **verb** (of a vehicle) travel with its rear end sliding uncontrollably from side to side.

fish·wife /ˈfisʜˌwīf/ ▶ **noun** (pl. **fishwives** /-ˌwīvz/) a woman with a loud, harsh voice.

fish·y /ˈfisʜē/ ▶ **adjective** (**fishier, fishiest**) **1** referring to or resembling a fish or fish. **2** informal causing feelings of doubt or suspicion.

fis·sile /ˈfisəl, ˈfisˌīl/ ▶ **adjective 1** (of an atom or element) able to undergo nuclear fission. **2** (chiefly of rock) easily split.
– ORIGIN Latin *fissilis.*

fis·sion /ˈfisʜən, ˈfizʜən/ ▶ **noun 1** the action of splitting into two or more parts. **2** a reaction in which an atomic nucleus splits in two, releasing much energy. **3** Biology reproduction by means of a cell dividing into two or more new cells. ▶ **verb** (of atoms) undergo fission.
– DERIVATIVES **fis·sion·a·ble** adjective.

fis·sure /ˈfisʜər/ ▶ **noun** a long, narrow crack. ▶ **verb** split; crack.
– ORIGIN Latin *fissura.*

fist /fist/ ▶ **noun** a person's hand when the fingers are bent in toward the palm and held there tightly.
– DERIVATIVES **fist·ed** adjective **fist·ful** /ˈfistˌfo͝ol/ noun.
– ORIGIN Old English.

fist·fight /ˈfistˌfīt/ ▶ **noun** a fight with bare fists.

fist·i·cuffs /ˈfistiˌkəfs/ ▶ **plural noun** fighting with the fists.

fis·tu·la /ˈfiscʜələ/ ▶ **noun** (pl. **fistulas** or **fistulae** /ˈfiscʜəlē/) an abnormal or surgically made passage between a hollow or tubular organ and the body surface, or between two hollow or tubular organs.
– ORIGIN Latin, 'pipe, flute, fistula.'

fit¹ /fit/ ▶ **adjective** (**fitter, fittest**) **1** of a suitable quality, standard, or type: *food fit for human consumption.* **2** having the necessary qualities or skills to do something competently. **3** in good health, especially through regular physical exercise.

– SYNONYMS **1 suitable,** appropriate, suited, apposite, fitting, good enough, apt. **2 competent,** able, capable, ready, prepared, equipped. **3 healthy,** well, in good health, in (good) shape, in trim, in good condition, fighting fit, athletic, muscular, strapping, strong, robust, hale and hearty.
– ANTONYMS unsuitable, incapable.

▶ **verb** (**fits, fitting, fitted** or **fit**) **1** be of the right shape and size for someone or something. **2** be of the right size, shape, or number to occupy a position or place: *we can all fit in her car.* **3** fix something into place. **4** (often **be fitted with**) provide something with a component or article. **5** join together to form a whole. **6** be suitable for; match: *the punishment should fit the crime.* **7** make someone suitable for a role or task: *a business degree fits the student for a professional career.* **8** (usu. **be fitted for**) try clothing on someone in order to make or alter it to the correct size.

– SYNONYMS **1 lay,** install, put in, position, place, fix, arrange. **2 equip,** provide, supply, fit out, furnish. **3 join,** connect, piece together, attach, unite, link. **4 be appropriate to,** suit, match, correspond to, tally with, go with, accord with. **5 qualify,** prepare, make ready, train.

▸ **noun** the way in which something fits.
– DERIVATIVES **fit·ly** adverb.
– PHRASES **fit in** be compatible with other members of a group or in harmony with other elements of a situation. **fit someone/thing in** (or **into**) manage to find time to see someone or do something. **fit someone/thing out** (or **up**) provide someone or something with necessary items. **see fit** consider it correct or acceptable.
– ORIGIN unknown.

fit[2] ▸ **noun 1** a sudden attack of an illness, such as epilepsy, in which a person makes violent, uncontrolled movements and often loses consciousness. **2** a sudden short period of coughing, laughter, etc. **3** a sudden burst of intense feeling: *a fit of jealous rage*.

– SYNONYMS **1 convulsion,** spasm, paroxysm, seizure, attack. **2 outbreak,** outburst, attack, bout, spell. **3 tantrum,** frenzy.

– PHRASES **in** (or **by**) **fits and starts** with irregular bursts of activity.
– ORIGIN Old English, 'conflict.'

fit·ful /ˈfitfəl/ ▸ **adjective** not continuous, regular, or steady: *a few hours' fitful sleep*.
– DERIVATIVES **fit·ful·ly** adverb **fit·ful·ness** noun.

fit·ness /ˈfitnis/ ▸ **noun 1** the condition of being physically fit and healthy: *disease and lack of fitness are closely related*. **2** the quality of being suitable to fulfill a particular role or task: *he had a year in which to establish his fitness for the office*.

– SYNONYMS **1 good health,** strength, robustness, vigor, athleticism, toughness, stamina. **2 suitability,** capability, competence, ability, aptitude, readiness, preparedness.

fit·ted /ˈfitid/ ▸ **adjective 1** made to fill a space or to cover something closely. **2** chiefly Brit. (of a room) equipped with matching units of furniture.

fit·ter /ˈfitər/ ▸ **noun 1** a person who puts together or installs machinery, engine parts, or other equipment: *a pipe fitter*. **2** a person who supervises the cutting, fitting, or alteration of clothes or shoes.

fit·ting /ˈfitiNG/ ▸ **noun 1** a small part attached to a piece of furniture or equipment. **2** an occasion when one tries on a garment that is being made or altered.

– SYNONYMS **1 attachment,** part, piece, component, accessory, apparatus. **2 furnishings,** furniture, fixtures, fitments, equipment.

▸ **adjective** appropriate; right or proper.

– SYNONYMS **apt,** appropriate, suitable, apposite, fit, proper, right, seemly, correct.
– ANTONYMS unsuitable.

– DERIVATIVES **fit·ting·ly** adverb.

fit·ting room ▸ **noun** a room in a store where one can try on clothes before buying them.

five /fīv/ ▸ **cardinal number** one more than four; 5. (Roman numeral: **v** or **V**.)
– DERIVATIVES **five·fold** /ˈfīvˌfōld/ adjective & adverb.
– ORIGIN Old English.

five o'clock shad·ow ▸ **noun** a slight growth of beard visible on a man's chin several hours after he has shaved.

fiv·er /ˈfīvər/ informal ▸ **noun 1** a five-dollar bill. **2** Brit. a five-pound note.

five-spice ▸ **noun** a blend of five powdered spices, typically fennel seeds, cinnamon, cloves, star anise, and peppercorns, used in Chinese cooking.

five-star ▸ **adjective 1** (especially of a hotel or restaurant) denoting the highest class or quality: *a five-star luxury resort*. **2** (in the armed forces) referring to the highest military rank, awarded only in wartime: *a five-star general*.

fix /fiks/ ▸ **verb 1** attach or position something securely. **2** (**fix on**) direct or be directed unwaveringly toward: *her gaze fixed on Jess*. **3** decide or settle on: *no date has yet been fixed*. **4** make unchanging or permanent: *the rate of interest is fixed for two years*. **5** repair something. **6** make arrangements for something. **7** (**be fixing to do something**) informal be intending or planning to do something: *you're fixing to get into trouble*. **8** informal influence the outcome of something in an underhanded way. **9** informal provide someone with food or drink: *I'll fix you a sandwich*.

– SYNONYMS **1 fasten,** attach, affix, secure, connect, couple, link, install, stick, glue, pin, nail, screw, bolt, clamp, clip. **2 lodge,** stick, embed. **3 focus,** direct, level, point, train. **4 repair,** mend, put right, get working, restore. **5 arrange,** organize, contrive, manage, engineer; informal swing, wangle. **6 arrange,** put in order, adjust, style, groom, comb, brush; informal do. **7 prepare,** cook, make, get; informal rustle up. **8 decide on,** select, choose, settle, set, arrange, establish, allot, designate, name, appoint, specify. **9 rig,** tamper with, skew, influence; informal fiddle.

▸ **noun** informal **1** a difficult or awkward situation. **2** a dose of a narcotic drug to which one is addicted. **3** an act of fixing something.

– SYNONYMS **1 predicament,** plight, difficulty, awkward situation, corner, tight spot, mess; informal pickle, jam, hole, scrape, bind. **2 fraud,** swindle, trick, charade, sham; informal setup, fiddle.

– DERIVATIVES **fix·a·ble** adjective.
– PHRASES **fix someone up** informal **1** provide someone with something: *they'll fix him up with a room*. **2** arrange for someone to meet a possible romantic partner. **fix something up** arrange or organize something. **get a fix on** find out the position, nature, or facts of.
– ORIGIN Latin *fixus* 'fixed.'

fix·ate /ˈfikˌsāt/ ▸ **verb** (**fixate on** or **be fixated on**) be obsessively interested in someone or something.

fix·a·tion /fikˈsāSHən/ ▸ **noun 1** an obsessive interest in someone or something. **2** the process by which some plants and microorganisms combine chemically with nitrogen or carbon dioxide in the air to form solid compounds.

– SYNONYMS **obsession,** preoccupation, mania, addiction, compulsion; informal thing, bee in one's bonnet.

fix·a·tive /ˈfiksətiv/ ▸ **noun** a substance used to fix, protect, or stabilize something.

fixed /fikst/ ▸ **adjective 1** fastened securely in position. **2** not changing or able to be changed. **3** (of contests) with the outcome dishonestly arranged in advance: *charges of fixed games on the front pages*. **4** (**fixed for**) informal situated in terms of: *how are you fixed for cash?*

– SYNONYMS **predetermined,** set, established, arranged, specified, decided, agreed, determined, confirmed, prescribed, definite, defined, explicit, precise.

– DERIVATIVES **fix·ed·ly** /ˈfiksidlē/ adverb.

fixed as·sets ▸ **plural noun** assets that are bought for long-term use and are not likely to be converted quickly into cash, such as land, buildings, and equipment. Compare with **CURRENT ASSETS**.

fixed-in·come ▸ **adjective 1** Finance (of investments) paying a constant rate of return: *fixed-income mutual funds.* **2** having an income that does not increase: *fixed-income seniors.*

fixed-wing ▸ **adjective** (of aircraft) of the conventional type as opposed to those with rotating wings, such as helicopters.

fix·er /ˈfiksər/ ▸ **noun 1** a person who arranges or manipulates something, especially in an illicit or devious way: *alleged price fixers who avoided arrest.* **2** a substance used for fixing a photographic image.

fix·ings /ˈfiksiNGz/ ▸ **plural noun** the ingredients necessary to prepare a dish or meal.

fix·i·ty /ˈfiksitē/ ▸ **noun** the state of being unchanging or permanent.

fix·ture /ˈfiksCHər/ ▸ **noun 1** a piece of equipment or furniture that is fixed in position in a building or vehicle. **2** (**fixtures**) articles attached to a house or land and considered legally part of it so that they normally remain in place when an owner moves. **3** informal a person or thing that has become firmly established in a particular place.

fizz /fiz/ ▸ **verb 1** (of a liquid) produce bubbles of gas and make a hissing sound. **2** make a buzzing or crackling sound.

– SYNONYMS **bubble,** sparkle, effervesce, froth.

▸ **noun 1** the quality of being fizzy. **2** informal a fizzy drink, especially sparkling wine. **3** liveliness.

– SYNONYMS **1 bubbles,** sparkle, fizziness, effervescence, gassiness, froth. **2 crackle,** buzz, hiss, white noise.

– ORIGIN imitating the sound.

fiz·zle /ˈfizəl/ ▸ **verb 1** make a feeble hissing or spluttering sound. **2** (**fizzle out**) gradually become less successful; end in a disappointing way.
– ORIGIN probably imitating the sound.

fizz·y /ˈfizē/ ▸ **adjective** (**fizzier, fizziest**) (of a drink) containing bubbles of gas.

– SYNONYMS **sparkling,** effervescent, carbonated, gassy, bubbly, frothy.
– ANTONYMS still, flat.

– DERIVATIVES **fizz·i·ness** noun.

fjord /fēˈôrd, fyôrd/ (also **fiord**) ▸ **noun** a long, narrow, deep inlet of the sea between high cliffs, found especially in Norway.
– ORIGIN Norwegian.

FL ▸ **abbreviation** Florida.

fl. ▸ **abbreviation 1** floruit. **2** fluid.

Fla. ▸ **abbreviation** Florida.

flab /flab/ ▸ **noun** informal soft, loose excess flesh on a person's body.

flab·ber·gast /ˈflabərˌgast/ ▸ **verb** (usu. as adj. **flabbergasted**) informal surprise someone greatly.
– ORIGIN unknown.

flab·by /ˈflabē/ ▸ **adjective** (**flabbier, flabbiest**) **1** (of a part of a person's body) soft, loose, and fleshy. **2** lacking force, strength, or tight control; not impressive or effective: *a flabby script.*
– DERIVATIVES **flab·bi·ness** noun.
– ORIGIN alteration of earlier *flappy.*

flac·cid /ˈfla(k)səd/ ▸ **adjective** soft and limp.
– DERIVATIVES **flac·cid·i·ty** /fla(k)ˈsidətē/ noun.
– ORIGIN from Latin *flaccus* 'flabby.'

flack ▸ **noun** variant spelling of FLAK.

flag[1] /flag/ ▸ **noun 1** an oblong piece of cloth that, usually attached to a pole, is displayed as a symbol of a country or organization or as a signal. **2** a device or symbol resembling a flag, used as a marker.

– SYNONYMS **banner,** standard, ensign, pennant, streamer, colors.

▸ **verb** (**flags, flagging, flagged**) **1** mark something for attention. **2** (**flag someone down**) signal to a driver to stop. **3** direct or alert someone by waving a flag or using hand signals.

– SYNONYMS **1 indicate,** identify, point out, mark, label, tag, highlight. **2** (**flag someone down**) **hail,** wave down, stop, halt.

– PHRASES **fly the flag 1** (of a ship) be registered in a particular country and sail under its flag. **2** represent one's country or show that one is a member of a party or organization.
– ORIGIN unknown.

flag[2] ▸ **noun** a flagstone.
– DERIVATIVES **flagged** adjective.
– ORIGIN probably Scandinavian.

flag[3] ▸ **noun** a plant of the iris family, with long sword-shaped leaves.
– ORIGIN unknown.

flag[4] ▸ **verb** (**flags, flagging, flagged**) **1** become tired or less enthusiastic. **2** (as adj. **flagging**) becoming weaker or less dynamic: *the country's flagging economy.*

– SYNONYMS **1 tire,** grow tired, wilt, weaken, grow weak, droop. **2 fade,** decline, wane, ebb, diminish, decrease, lessen, dwindle.
– ANTONYMS revive.

– ORIGIN related to former *flag* 'drooping.'

Flag Day ▸ **noun** June 14, the anniversary of the adoption of the official US flag in 1777.

flag·el·late[1] /ˈflajəˌlāt/ ▸ **verb** whip someone, either as a form of religious punishment or for sexual pleasure.
– DERIVATIVES **flag·el·la·tion** /ˌflajəˈlāSHən/ noun.
– ORIGIN Latin *flagellare* 'whip.'

flag·el·late[2] /ˈflajələt, -ˌlāt/ ▸ **adjective** (of a single-celled organism) having one or more flagella used for swimming.

fla·gel·lum /fləˈjeləm/ ▸ **noun** (pl. **flagella** /-ˈjelə/) Biology a long, thin projection that enables many single-celled organisms to swim.
– ORIGIN Latin, 'little whip.'

flag foot·ball ▸ **noun** a form of football in which pulling a strip of plastic (a flag) from a ballcarrier's loosely attached belt is the equivalent of tackling.

flag·on /ˈflagən/ ▸ **noun** a large bottle or other container in which wine, cider, or beer is sold or served.
– ORIGIN from Latin *flasco.*

flag·pole /ˈflagˌpōl/ ▸ **noun** a pole used for flying a flag.

fla·grant /ˈflāgrənt/ ▸ **adjective** very obvious and unashamed: *a flagrant violation of the law.*

– SYNONYMS **blatant,** glaring, obvious, conspicuous, barefaced, shameless, brazen, undisguised.

– DERIVATIVES **fla·grant·ly** adverb.
– ORIGIN Latin *flagrare* 'blaze.'

flag·ship /ˈflagˌSHip/ ▸ **noun 1** the ship in a fleet that carries the commanding admiral. **2** the best or most important thing owned or produced by an organization.

flag·staff /ˈflag,staf/ ▶ **noun** a flagpole.

flag·stone /ˈflag,stōn/ ▶ **noun** a flat square or rectangular stone slab, used for paving.

flag stop ▶ **noun** a bus stop at which the bus halts only if requested by a passenger or if signaled.

flag-wav·ing ▶ **noun** a display of extreme patriotism.

flail /flāl/ ▶ **verb 1** swing or wave one's arms or legs wildly. **2** (usu. **flail around/about**) struggle to move while swinging one's arms and legs wildly. ▶ **noun** a tool or machine with a swinging action, used for threshing.
– ORIGIN Latin *flagellum* 'little whip.'

flair /fler/ ▶ **noun 1** a natural ability or talent. **2** stylishness.

– SYNONYMS **1 aptitude,** talent, gift, instinct, ability, facility, knack, skill. **2 style,** elegance, panache, dash, elan, poise, taste; informal class.

– ORIGIN French.

USAGE

On the confusion of **flair** with **flare**, see the note at **FLARE**.

flak /flak/ (also **flack**) ▶ **noun 1** antiaircraft fire. **2** strong criticism.
– ORIGIN abbreviation of German *Fliegerabwehrkanone* 'aviator-defense gun.'

flake[1] /flāk/ ▶ **noun** a small, flat, very thin piece of something.

– SYNONYMS **sliver,** wafer, shaving, paring, chip, fragment, scrap, shred.

▶ **verb 1** come away from a surface in flakes. **2** separate something into flakes.

– SYNONYMS **peel off,** chip, blister, come off.

– ORIGIN probably Germanic.

flake[2] ▶ **verb** (**flake out**) informal fall asleep or drop from exhaustion.
– ORIGIN from **FLAG[4]**.

flak jack·et ▶ **noun** a sleeveless jacket made of heavy fabric reinforced with metal, worn as protection against bullets and shrapnel.

flak·y /ˈflākē/ ▶ **adjective** (**flakier, flakiest**) **1** breaking or separating easily into flakes. **2** informal unconventional or eccentric.
– DERIVATIVES **flak·i·ness** noun.

flam·bé /flämˈbā/ ▶ **adjective** (after a noun) (of food) covered with liquor and set alight briefly: *steak flambé*. ▶ **verb** (**flambés, flambéing, flambéed** /-ˈbād/) cover food with liquor and set it alight briefly.
– ORIGIN French, 'singed.'

flam·beau /ˈflam,bō/ ▶ **noun** (pl. **flambeaus** or **flambeaux** /-,bōz/) **1** a flaming torch. **2** a branched candlestick.
– ORIGIN French, from *flambe* 'a flame.'

flam·boy·ant /flamˈboiənt/ ▶ **adjective 1** confident and lively in a way that attracts the attention of other people. **2** brightly colored or highly decorated.

– SYNONYMS **1 ostentatious,** exuberant, confident, lively, animated, vibrant, vivacious. **2 colorful,** bright, vibrant, vivid, dazzling, bold, showy, gaudy, garish, loud; informal jazzy, flashy.
– ANTONYMS restrained.

– DERIVATIVES **flam·boy·ance** noun **flam·boy·ant·ly** adverb.
– ORIGIN French, 'flaming, blazing.'

flame /flām/ ▶ **noun 1** a hot glowing body of ignited gas produced by something on fire. **2** a brilliant orange-red color.

– SYNONYMS **fire,** blaze, conflagration, inferno.

▶ **verb 1** give off flames. **2** set something alight. **3** (of a strong emotion) appear suddenly and fiercely. **4** (of a person's face) become red with embarrassment or anger. **5** informal send an abusive email message to someone.
– PHRASES **burst into flame** (or **flames**) suddenly begin to burn fiercely: *the grass looked ready to burst into flame.* **old flame** informal a former lover.
– ORIGIN Latin *flamma.*

fla·men·co /fləˈmeNGkō/ ▶ **noun** a style of Spanish guitar music accompanied by singing and dancing.
– ORIGIN Spanish, 'like a Gypsy' (literally 'Fleming,' i.e., 'a Flemish person').

flame·proof /ˈflām,pro͞of/ ▶ **adjective 1** (of fabric) treated so as to be nonflammable. **2** (of cookware) able to be used either in an oven or on a stovetop.

flame·throw·er /ˈflām,THrōər/ ▶ **noun** a weapon that sprays out burning fuel.

flam·ing /ˈflāmiNG/ ▶ **adjective 1** sending out flames. **2** very hot. **3** full of passion: *the ache of flaming desire.* **4** full of anger: *their flaming disputes.* **5** informal expressing annoyance: *that flaming dog!*

fla·min·go /fləˈmiNGgō/ ▶ **noun** (pl. **flamingos** or **flamingoes**) a wading bird with mainly pink or scarlet plumage and a long neck and legs.
– ORIGIN Spanish *flamengo.*

flam·ma·ble /ˈflaməbəl/ ▶ **adjective** easily set on fire.
– DERIVATIVES **flam·ma·bil·i·ty** /,flaməˈbilətē/ noun.

USAGE

For advice on the words **flammable** and **inflammable**, see the note at **INFLAMMABLE**.

flan /flan/ ▶ **noun 1** a custard with a caramel topping. **2** a baked dish consisting of an open-topped pastry case with a savory or sweet filling.
– ORIGIN Old French *flaon.*

flange /flanj/ ▶ **noun** a projecting flat rim on an object for strengthening it or attaching it to something.
– DERIVATIVES **flanged** adjective.
– ORIGIN perhaps from Old French *flanchir* 'to bend.'

flank /flaNGk/ ▶ **noun 1** the side of a person's or animal's body between the ribs and the hip. **2** the side of something such as a building or mountain. **3** the left or right side of a group of people.

– SYNONYMS **1 side,** haunch, quarter, thigh. **2 side,** wing, sector, face, aspect.

▶ **verb** be situated on each or on one side of: *the road is flanked by avenues of trees.*

– SYNONYMS **edge,** bound, line, border, fringe.

– ORIGIN Old French *flanc.*

flank·er /ˈflaNGkər/ ▶ **noun 1** Rugby a wing forward. **2** Military a fortification to the side of a force or position.

flan·nel /ˈflanl/ ▶ **noun 1** a kind of soft-woven woolen or cotton fabric. **2** (**flannels**) trousers made of woolen flannel. ▶ **verb** (**flannels, flannelling, flannelled**) Brit. informal use empty or insincere talk to avoid dealing with a difficult subject.
– ORIGIN probably from Welsh *gwlanen* 'woolen article.'

flap /flap/ ▶ **verb** (**flaps, flapping, flapped**) move or be moved up and down or from side to side.

– SYNONYMS **1** *ducks flapped their wings* **beat,** flutter, agitate, vibrate, wag, thrash, flail. **2** *the flag flapped in the breeze* **flutter,** wave, fly, blow, swing, ripple, stir.

▶ **noun 1** a piece of something attached on one side only, that covers an opening. **2** a hinged or sliding section of an aircraft wing, used to control upward movement. **3** a single flapping movement. **4** informal a state of worry or panic.

– SYNONYMS **1 beat,** stroke, flutter, movement. **2 panic,** fluster; informal state, stew, tizzy.

– DERIVATIVES **flap·py** adjective.
– ORIGIN uncertain.

flap·jack /ˈflapˌjak/ ▶ **noun** a pancake.
– ORIGIN from **FLAP** (in the dialect sense 'toss a pancake') + **JACK**[1].

flap·per /ˈflapər/ ▶ **noun** informal (in the 1920s) a fashionable and unconventional young woman.

flare /fle(ə)r/ ▶ **noun 1** a sudden brief burst of flame or light. **2** a device producing a very bright flame as a signal or marker. **3** a gradual widening toward the hem of a garment.

– SYNONYMS **1 blaze,** flame, flash, burst, flicker. **2 signal,** beacon, rocket, light, torch.

▶ **verb 1** burn or shine with a sudden intensity. **2** (usu. **flare up**) suddenly start or become stronger or more violent: *rioting flared up in other towns and cities.* **3** (**flare up**) suddenly become angry. **4** gradually become wider at one end.

– SYNONYMS **1 blaze,** flash, flare up, flame, burn, flicker. **2 spread,** splay, broaden, widen, dilate.

– ORIGIN unknown.

USAGE

Do not confuse **flare** with **flair**: **flare** means 'burn' or 'gradually become wider,' whereas **flair** means 'a natural ability or talent.' Trousers whose legs widen from the knees down are **flared**, not **flaired**.

flare-up ▶ **noun** a sudden outburst, especially of violence or an undesirable medical symptom: *a flare-up between the two countries.*

flash /flasʜ/ ▶ **verb 1** shine or cause to shine with a bright but brief or irregular light. **2** move or pass swiftly: *the scenery flashed by.* **3** display or be displayed briefly or repeatedly: *a message flashed up on the screen.* **4** informal display something in an obvious way so as to impress people: *they flash their money around.* **5** informal (of a man) show the genitals in public.

– SYNONYMS **1 shine,** flare, blaze, gleam, glint, sparkle, burn, blink, wink, flicker, shimmer, twinkle, glimmer, glisten. **2 zoom,** streak, tear, shoot, dash, dart, fly, whistle, hurtle, rush, bolt, race, speed, career; informal belt, barrel. **3 show off,** flaunt, flourish, display, parade.

▶ **noun 1** a sudden brief burst of bright light. **2** a camera attachment that produces a flash of light, for taking photographs in poor light. **3** a sudden or brief occurrence: *a flash of inspiration.* **4** a bright patch of color.

– SYNONYMS **flare,** blaze, burst, gleam, glint, sparkle, flicker, shimmer, twinkle, glimmer.

▶ **adjective** informal stylish or expensive in a way designed to attract attention and impress people; flashy.
– PHRASES **flash in the pan** a sudden but brief success. **in a flash** very quickly.
– ORIGIN uncertain.

flash·back /ˈflasʜˌbak/ ▶ **noun 1** a scene in a movie or novel set in a time earlier than the main story. **2** a sudden vivid memory of a past event.

flash·bulb /ˈflasʜˌbəlb/ ▶ **noun** a light bulb for one-time use that flashes in order to illuminate a photographic subject.

flash·card /ˈflasʜˌkärd/ ▶ **noun** a card containing a small amount of clearly displayed information, held up for students to see, as an aid to learning.

flash drive ▶ **noun** a removable data storage device containing flash memory that has no moving parts.

flash·er /ˈflasʜər/ ▶ **noun 1** a device or signal in which a light flashes on and off. **2** informal a person, especially a man, who exposes his genitals in public.

flash flood ▶ **noun** a sudden local flood resulting from extreme rainfall.

flash-for·ward ▶ **noun** a narrative device, used especially in movies, in which the action jumps to a future scene or development: *a flash-forward set in a mental clinic.* ▶ **verb** jump to future time in a narrative.

flash·ing /ˈflasʜiɴɢ/ ▶ **noun** a strip of metal used to seal the junction of a roof with another surface.

flash·light /ˈflasʜˌlīt/ ▶ **noun 1** a battery-operated portable light. **2** a light giving an intense flash, used for photographing at night or indoors.

flash mem·o·ry ▶ **noun** Computing memory that retains data in the absence of a power supply.

flash mob ▶ **noun** a public gathering of complete strangers, organized via the Internet or cell phone, who perform a pointless act and then disperse again.
– DERIVATIVES **flash mobber** noun **flash mobbing** noun.

flash·point /ˈflasʜˌpoint/ ▶ **noun 1** a point or place at which anger or violence flares up. **2** Chemistry the temperature at which a flammable compound gives off enough vapor to ignite in air.

flash·y /ˈflasʜē/ ▶ **adjective** (**flashier, flashiest**) stylish or expensive in a way designed to attract attention and impress other people.

– SYNONYMS **ostentatious,** flamboyant, showy, conspicuous, extravagant, expensive, vulgar, tasteless, brash, garish, loud, gaudy; informal snazzy, fancy, swanky, flash, glitzy.
– ANTONYMS understated.

– DERIVATIVES **flash·i·ly** adverb **flash·i·ness** noun.

flask /flask/ ▶ **noun 1** a conical or round bottle with a narrow neck. **2** chiefly Brit. a thermos. **3** a hip flask. **4** Brit. a lead-lined container for radioactive nuclear waste.
– ORIGIN Latin *flasca.*

flat[1] /flat/ ▶ **adjective** (**flatter, flattest**) **1** having a level and even surface. **2** not sloping; horizontal. **3** with a level surface and little height or depth: *a flat cap.* **4** (of shoes) without high heels. **5** flat-chested. **6** without liveliness or interest: *a flat voice.* **7** (of a carbonated drink) no longer fizzy. **8** (of something kept inflated) having lost some or all of its air. **9** (of a fee, charge, or price) unvarying; fixed. **10** (of a negative statement) definite and firm: *a flat denial.* **11** (of musical sound) below true or normal pitch. **12** (after a noun) (of a note or key) lower by a half step than a particular note or key: *E flat.*

– SYNONYMS **1 level,** horizontal, smooth, even, plane. **2 calm,** still, glassy, smooth, placid, like a millpond. **3 stretched out,** prone, spread-eagled,

prostrate, supine, recumbent. **4 monotonous,** toneless, lifeless, droning, boring, dull, tedious, uninteresting, unexciting. **5 inactive,** slow, sluggish, slack, quiet, depressed. **6 deflated,** punctured, burst, blown. **7 fixed,** set, invariable, regular, constant. **8 outright,** direct, absolute, definite, positive, straight, plain, explicit, categorical.
– ANTONYMS sloping, rough, uneven.

▶ **adverb 1** in or to a horizontal position. **2** so as to become level and even. **3** informal completely; absolutely: *she turned him down flat.* **4** emphasizing the speed of an action: *in ten minutes flat.*

– SYNONYMS **stretched out,** outstretched, spread-eagled, sprawling, prone, prostrate.

▶ **noun 1** the flat part of something. **2** (**flats**) an area of low level ground, especially near water. **3** informal a flat tire. **4** an upright section of stage scenery. **5** a musical note that is a semitone lower than the corresponding one of natural pitch, indicated by the sign ♭.
– DERIVATIVES **flat·ly** adverb **flat·ness** noun **flat·tish** adjective.
– PHRASES **fall flat** fail to produce the intended effect. **flat out** as fast or as hard as possible.
– ORIGIN Old Norse.

flat[2] ▶ **noun** chiefly Brit. an apartment.
– ORIGIN related to FLAT[1].

flat·bed /ˈflatˌbed/ ▶ **adjective** referring to a vehicle whose body consists of an open platform without raised sides or ends, used for carrying loads. ▶ **noun 1** a flatbed vehicle, or its open platform. **2** Computing a scanner or other device that keeps paper flat during use.

flat·bread /ˈflatˌbred/ ▶ **noun** an unleavened bread.

flat-chest·ed ▶ **adjective** (of a woman) having small breasts.

flat feet ▶ **plural noun** feet with arches that are lower than usual.

flat·fish /ˈflatˌfisн/ ▶ **noun** (pl. same or **flatfishes**) a sea fish, such as a flounder or sole, that swims on its side with both eyes on the upper side of its flattened body.

flat-foot·ed ▶ **adjective 1** having flat feet. **2** informal clumsy.

flat·i·ron /ˈflatˌīərn/ ▶ **noun** historical an iron heated on a hotplate or fire.

flat·line /ˈflatˌlīn/ ▶ **verb** informal die.
– DERIVATIVES **flat·lin·er** noun.
– ORIGIN with reference to the continuous straight line displayed on a heart monitor when a person dies.

flat·ten /ˈflatn/ ▶ **verb 1** make or become flat or flatter. **2** informal knock someone down.

– SYNONYMS **1 level,** even out, smooth out, make/become flat. **2 squash,** compress, press down, crush, compact, trample. **3 demolish,** raze (to the ground), tear down, knock down, destroy, wreck, devastate.
– ANTONYMS crumple.

– DERIVATIVES **flat·ten·er** noun.

flat·ter /ˈflatər/ ▶ **verb 1** praise or compliment someone excessively or insincerely. **2** (**be flattered**) feel honored and pleased. **3** (**flatter oneself**) believe something good about oneself, especially something that has no basis in reality. **4** (of clothing or a color) make someone appear attractive. **5** (often as adj. **flattering**) paint or draw someone so that they appear more attractive than in reality.

– SYNONYMS **1 compliment,** praise, express admiration for, fawn on, humor, wheedle; Brit. blarney; informal sweet-talk, soft-soap, butter up, play up to. **2 honor,** gratify, please, delight; informal tickle pink. **3 suit,** become, look good on, go well with; informal do something for.
– ANTONYMS insult, offend.

– DERIVATIVES **flat·ter·er** noun.
– ORIGIN Old French *flater.*

flat·ter·ing /ˈflatəriNG/ ▶ **adjective 1** full of praise and compliments. **2** pleasing or gratifying. **3** enhancing someone's appearance.

– SYNONYMS **1 complimentary,** praising, favorable, admiring, appreciative, fulsome, honeyed, obsequious, ingratiating, sycophantic. **2 pleasing,** gratifying, an honor. **3 becoming,** enhancing.
– ANTONYMS unflattering.

flat·ter·y /ˈflatərē/ ▶ **noun** (pl. **flatteries**) excessive or insincere praise.

– SYNONYMS **praise,** adulation, compliments, blandishments, honeyed words, fawning; Brit. blarney; informal sweet talk, soft soap, buttering up.

flat·top /ˈflatˌtäp/ ▶ **noun 1** a short haircut in which hair on top of the head is trimmed to a level plane. **2** informal an aircraft carrier.

flat·u·lent /ˈflacнələnt/ ▶ **adjective** suffering from a buildup of gas in the intestines or stomach.
– DERIVATIVES **flat·u·lence** noun.
– ORIGIN Latin *flatus* 'blowing.'

fla·tus /ˈflātəs/ ▶ **noun** Medicine gas from the stomach or intestines, especially when voided through the rectum.

flat·ware /ˈflatˌwe(ə)r/ ▶ **noun 1** eating utensils such as knives, forks, and spoons. **2** relatively flat dishes such as plates and saucers.

flat·worm /ˈflatˌwərm/ ▶ **noun** a type of worm, such as a tapeworm, with a flattened body that lacks blood vessels.

flaunt /flônt, flänt/ ▶ **verb** display something proudly or in a way intended to attract attention.

– SYNONYMS **show off,** display, make a great show of, put on show/display, parade, draw attention to, brag about, crow about, vaunt; informal flash.

– ORIGIN unknown.

USAGE

Be careful not to confuse **flaunt** with **flout**. **Flaunt** means 'display something in a way intended to attract attention' (*some students like to flaunt their wealth*), while **flout** means 'openly fail to follow a rule or convention' (*the tendency of some athletes to flout regulations*).

flau·tist /ˈflôtist, ˈflou-/ ▶ **noun** another term for FLUTIST.
– ORIGIN Italian *flautista.*

fla·vo·noid /ˈflāvəˌnoid/ ▶ **noun** any of a group of naturally occurring chemical compounds including several white or yellow plant pigments.
– ORIGIN from Latin *flavus* 'yellow.'

fla·vor /ˈflāvər/ (Brit. **flavour**) ▶ **noun 1** the distinctive taste of a food or drink. **2** a particular quality or atmosphere: *the resort has a distinctly Italian flavor.*

– SYNONYMS **1 taste,** savor, tang. **2 flavoring,** seasoning, taste, tang, relish, bite, piquancy, spice. **3 character,** quality, feel, feeling, ambience, atmosphere, air, mood, tone, spirit. **4 impression,** suggestion, hint, taste.

▶ **verb** alter or add to the taste of food or drink by adding a particular ingredient: *cottage cheese flavored with chives.*

– SYNONYMS **season,** spice (up), add piquancy to, ginger up, enrich, infuse.

– DERIVATIVES **fla·vor·ful** adjective **fla·vor·less** adjective **fla·vor·some** adjective.
– PHRASES **flavor of the month** a person or thing that is currently popular.
– ORIGIN Old French *flaor* 'a smell.'

fla·vor·ing /ˈflāvəriNG/ ▶ **noun** a substance used to add to or alter the flavor of a food or drink.

flavour, etc. ▶ **noun** British spelling of **FLAVOR**, etc.

flaw /flô/ ▶ **noun 1** a mark or flaw that spoils something. **2** a fundamental weakness or mistake.

– SYNONYMS **defect,** blemish, fault, imperfection, deficiency, weakness, weak spot/point, failing; Computing **bug**; informal **glitch**.
– ANTONYMS strength.

▶ **verb** (usu. as adj. **flawed**) spoil or weaken.

– SYNONYMS **1** (as adj. **flawed**) *flawed crystals* **faulty,** defective, unsound, imperfect, blemished, broken, cracked, scratched. **2** (as adj. **flawed**) *a flawed strategy* **unsound,** distorted, inaccurate, incorrect, erroneous, fallacious, wrong.
– ANTONYMS flawless.

– ORIGIN perhaps from an Old Norse word meaning 'stone slab.'

flaw·less /ˈflôləs/ ▶ **adjective** without any imperfections or defects.

– SYNONYMS **perfect,** unblemished, unmarked, unimpaired, whole, intact, sound, unbroken, undamaged, mint, pristine, impeccable, immaculate, accurate, correct, faultless, error-free, exemplary, model, ideal, copybook.
– ANTONYMS flawed.

– DERIVATIVES **flaw·less·ly** adverb.

flax /flaks/ ▶ **noun 1** a blue-flowered plant that is grown for its seed (flaxseed or linseed) and for thread made from its stalks. **2** thread made from flax, used to make linen.
– ORIGIN Old English.

flax·en /ˈflaksən/ ▶ **adjective** literary (of hair) pale yellow.

flax·seed /ˈflak(s)ˌsēd/ ▶ **noun** the seeds of the flax plant used as a nutritional supplement rich in omega-3 fatty acids, and (especially when called **LINSEED**) as the source of linseed oil.

flay /flā/ ▶ **verb 1** strip the skin from a body or carcass. **2** whip or beat someone so hard that some of their skin is removed. **3** criticize someone harshly.
– ORIGIN Old English.

flea /flē/ ▶ **noun** a small wingless jumping insect that feeds on the blood of mammals and birds.
– PHRASES **a flea in one's ear** a sharp reprimand.
– ORIGIN Old English.

flea-bit·ten ▶ **adjective 1** bitten by or infested with fleas. **2** shabby or run-down.

flea col·lar ▶ **noun** an insecticide-treated collar for a pet dog or cat.

flea mar·ket ▶ **noun** an indoor or outdoor market selling the secondhand goods of various vendors at low prices.

fleck /flek/ ▶ **noun 1** a very small patch of color or light. **2** a small particle: *flecks of dust.* ▶ **verb** mark or dot with small areas of a particular color or small pieces of something: *her brown hair was flecked with gray.*
– ORIGIN perhaps from Old Norse, or from German, Dutch *vlecke*.

fled /fled/ past and past participle of **FLEE**.

fledge /flej/ ▶ **verb 1** (of a young bird) develop wing feathers that are large enough for flight. **2** (as adj. **fledged**) having just taken on a particular role: *a newly fledged Detective Inspector.*
– ORIGIN from Old English, 'ready to fly.'

fledg·ling /ˈflejliNG/ (also **fledgeling**) ▶ **noun** a young bird that has just developed wing feathers that are large enough for flight. ▶ **adjective** new and inexperienced: *a fledgling democracy.*

flee /flē/ ▶ **verb** (**flees, fleeing**; past and past part. **fled** /fled/) run away.

– SYNONYMS **run away,** run off, run for it, make off, take off, take to one's heels, make a break for it, bolt, beat a (hasty) retreat, make a quick exit, escape; informal beat it, clear out/off, skedaddle, scram.

– ORIGIN Old English.

fleece /flēs/ ▶ **noun 1** the wool coat of a sheep. **2** a soft, warm fabric with a texture similar to sheep's wool, or a jacket made from this. ▶ **verb** informal swindle someone by charging them too much money.
– DERIVATIVES **fleec·y** adjective.
– ORIGIN Old English.

fleet[1] /flēt/ ▶ **noun 1** a group of ships sailing together. **2** (**the fleet**) a country's navy. **3** a number of vehicles or aircraft operating together.

– SYNONYMS **navy,** naval force, (naval) task force, armada, flotilla, squadron, convoy.

– ORIGIN Old English.

fleet[2] ▶ **adjective** fast and nimble.
– DERIVATIVES **fleet·ness** noun.
– PHRASES **fleet of foot** able to walk or move swiftly.
– ORIGIN probably from Old Norse.

fleet[3] ▶ **verb** literary move or pass quickly.
– ORIGIN Old English.

Fleet Ad·mi·ral ▶ **noun** an admiral of the highest rank in the US Navy.

fleet·ing /ˈflētiNG/ ▶ **adjective** lasting for a very short time.

– SYNONYMS **brief,** short-lived, quick, momentary, cursory, transient, ephemeral, passing, transitory.
– ANTONYMS lasting.

– DERIVATIVES **fleet·ing·ly** adverb.

CHOOSE THE RIGHT WORD

See **TEMPORARY**.

Flem·ing /ˈflemiNG/ ▶ **noun 1** a Flemish person. **2** a member of the Flemish-speaking people living in northern and western Belgium.
– ORIGIN Old English.

Flem·ish /ˈflemiSH/ ▶ **noun 1** (**the Flemish**) the people of Flanders, a region divided between Belgium, France, and the Netherlands. **2** the Dutch language as spoken in Flanders. ▶ **adjective** relating to the Flemish people or language.
– ORIGIN Dutch *Vlāmisch*.

flesh /flesH/ ▶ **noun 1** the soft substance in the body consisting of muscle tissue and fat. **2** the edible soft part of a fruit or vegetable. **3** (**the flesh**) the physical aspects and needs of the human body: *pleasures of the flesh.*

– SYNONYMS **1 tissue,** skin, muscle, fat, meat, body. **2 pulp,** marrow, meat. **3** *the pleasures of the flesh* **the body,** human nature, physicality, sensuality, sexuality.

▶ **verb** (**flesh something out**) give more information or details about something: *the governor fleshed out his economic philosophy.*

– PHRASES **flesh and blood 1** a close relative; one's family. **2** used to emphasize people's physical and emotional reality, often in contrast to something abstract, spiritual, or mechanical: *an embodiment of feminine ideals rather than a flesh and blood woman.* **in the flesh** in person or (of a thing) in its actual state. **make someone's flesh crawl** make someone feel fear, horror, or disgust.

– ORIGIN Old English.

flesh-col·ored ▶ **adjective** of the color of European people's skin: *wildly undulating flesh-colored clay tiles.*

flesh·ly /ˈfleshlē/ ▶ **adjective** (**fleshlier, fleshliest**) relating to the body and its needs.

flesh·pots /ˈflesh,päts/ ▶ **plural noun** places where people can satisfy their sexual desires.

– ORIGIN from the *fleshpots of Egypt* mentioned in the Bible (Book of Exodus).

flesh wound ▶ **noun** a wound that breaks the skin but does not damage bones or vital organs.

flesh·y /ˈfleshē/ ▶ **adjective** (**fleshier, fleshiest**) **1** having a lot of flesh; plump. **2** (of leaves or fruit) soft and thick. **3** resembling flesh.

– DERIVATIVES **flesh·i·ness** noun.

fleur-de-lis /,flər dlˈē, ,flo͝or-/ (also **fleur-de-lys**) ▶ **noun** (pl. **fleurs-de-lis** pronunc. same) a representation of a lily made up of three petals bound together near their bases.

– ORIGIN Old French *flour de lys* 'flower of the lily.'

flew /flo͞o/ past of FLY[1].

flex /fleks/ ▶ **verb 1** bend a limb or joint. **2** tighten a muscle. **3** warp or bend and then return to the proper shape.

– ORIGIN Latin *flectere.*

flex-fu·el ▶ **adjective** referring to a motor vehicle that will run on gasoline, ethanol, or these two in any combination: *flex-fuel subcompacts have captured 20% of Brazil's new car market.*

flex·i·bil·i·ty /,fleksəˈbilətē/ ▶ **noun** the quality of being flexible.

– SYNONYMS **1 pliability,** suppleness, elasticity, stretchiness, springiness, spring, resilience, bounce; informal give. **2 adaptability,** adjustability, versatility, open-endedness, freedom, latitude. **3 willingness to compromise,** give and take, amenability, cooperation, tolerance.
– ANTONYMS rigidity.

flex·i·ble /ˈfleksəbəl/ ▶ **adjective 1** capable of bending easily without breaking. **2** able to change or be changed in response to different circumstances.

– SYNONYMS **1 bendy,** pliable, supple, pliant, plastic, elastic, stretchy, springy, resilient, bouncy. **2 adaptable,** adjustable, variable, versatile, open-ended, open. **3 accommodating,** amenable, willing to compromise, cooperative, tolerant.
– ANTONYMS rigid, inflexible.

– DERIVATIVES **flex·i·bly** /-blē/ adverb.

CHOOSE THE RIGHT WORD

flexible, elastic, limber, pliable, pliant, resilient, supple

If you can bend over and touch your toes, you are **flexible**. But a dancer or gymnast is **limber**, an adjective that specifically applies to a body that has been brought into condition through training (*to stay limber, she did yoga every day*). *Flexible* applies to whatever can be bent without breaking, whether or not it returns to its original shape (*a flexible plastic hose; a flexible electrical conduit*); it does not necessarily refer, as *limber* does, to the human body. Unlike *flexible*, **resilient** implies the ability to spring back into shape after being bent or compressed, or to recover one's health or spirits quickly (*so young and resilient that she was back at work in a week*). **Elastic** is usually applied to substances or materials that are easy to stretch or expand and that quickly recover their shape or size (*pants with an elastic waist*), while **supple** is applied to whatever is easily bent, twisted, or folded without breaking or cracking (*a soft, supple leather*). When applied to the human body, *supple* suggests the ability to move effortlessly. **Pliant** and **pliable** may be used to describe either people or things that are easily bent or manipulated. *Pliant* suggests a tendency to bend without force or pressure from the outside, while *pliable* suggests the use of force or submission to another's will. A *pliant* person is merely adaptable, but a *pliable* person is easy to influence and eager to please.

flex·ion /ˈflekshən/ (also **flection**) ▶ **noun** the action of bending or the condition of being bent.

flex·or /ˈflek,sər, -,sôr/ ▶ **noun** a muscle whose contraction bends a limb or other part of the body.

flex·time /ˈfleks,tīm/ ▶ **noun** a system by which employees work an agreed total number of hours but have some flexibility as to when they start and finish work each day.

flick /flik/ ▶ **verb 1** make a sudden sharp movement. **2** hit or remove something with a flick of the fingers: *she flicked some ash off her sleeve.* **3** (**flick through**) look quickly through a book or a collection of papers.

– SYNONYMS **1** *he flicked the switch* **click,** snap, flip, jerk, throw. **2** *the horse flicked its tail* **swish,** twitch, wave, wag, waggle, shake. **3** (**flick through**) **thumb through,** leaf through, flip through, skim, scan, look through, browse through, dip into, glance at/through.

▶ **noun 1** a sudden sharp movement up and down or from side to side. **2** the sudden release of a finger or thumb held bent against another finger. **3** informal a movie.

– SYNONYMS **jerk,** snap, flip, whisk.

– ORIGIN representing sudden movement.

flick·er[1] /ˈflikər/ ▶ **verb 1** shine or burn unsteadily. **2** (of a feeling) be felt or shown briefly. **3** make small, quick movements.

– SYNONYMS **1 glimmer,** dance, twinkle, sparkle, wink, flash. **2 flutter,** quiver, tremble, shiver, shudder, jerk, twitch.

▶ **noun 1** a flickering movement or light. **2** a brief feeling or indication of emotion: *a flicker of alarm.*

– ORIGIN Old English, 'to flutter.'

flick·er[2] ▶ **noun** any of several colorful North American woodpeckers that are often ground feeders.

fli·er /ˈflīər/ ▶ **noun** variant spelling of FLYER.

flight /flīt/ ▶ **noun 1** the action or process of flying. **2** a journey made in an aircraft or in space. **3** the path of something through the air. **4** the action of running away: *the enemy were in flight.* **5** a very imaginative idea or story: *a flight of fancy.* **6** a flock of birds flying together. **7** a series of steps between floors or levels. **8** a unit of about six aircraft operating together. **9** the tail of an arrow or dart.

– SYNONYMS **1 aviation,** flying, air transport, aeronautics. **2 flock,** swarm, cloud, throng. **3 escape,** getaway, hasty departure, exit, exodus, breakout, bolt, disappearance.

– PHRASES **take flight 1** (of a bird) take off and fly. **2** run away.
– ORIGIN Old English; related to **FLY**[1].

flight at·tend·ant ▸ **noun** a steward or stewardess on an aircraft.

flight deck ▸ **noun 1** the cockpit of a large aircraft. **2** the deck of an aircraft carrier, used as a runway.

flight feath·er ▸ **noun** any of the large feathers in a bird's wing that support it during flight.

flight·less /ˈflītlis/ ▸ **adjective** (of a bird or insect) naturally unable to fly.

flight path ▸ **noun** the route taken by an aircraft or spacecraft.

flight re·cord·er ▸ **noun** an electronic device in an aircraft that records technical details during a flight, used in the event of an accident to discover its cause.

flight·y /ˈflītē/ ▸ **adjective** (**flightier, flightiest**) irresponsible and uninterested in serious things.
– DERIVATIVES **flight·i·ness** noun.

flim·flam /ˈflimˌflam/ ▸ **noun** informal **1** insincere and unconvincing talk. **2** a confidence trick.
– ORIGIN an invented word.

flim·sy /ˈflimzē/ ▸ **adjective** (**flimsier, flimsiest**) **1** weak and fragile. **2** (of clothing) light and thin. **3** unconvincing: *a flimsy excuse.*

– SYNONYMS **1 insubstantial,** fragile, frail, rickety, ramshackle, makeshift, jerry-built, shoddy. **2 thin,** light, fine, filmy, floaty, diaphanous, sheer, delicate, gossamer, gauzy. **3 weak,** feeble, poor, inadequate, insufficient, thin, unsubstantial, unconvincing, implausible.
– ANTONYMS sturdy.

– DERIVATIVES **flim·si·ly** adverb **flim·si·ness** noun.
– ORIGIN probably from **FLIMFLAM**.

flinch /flinCH/ ▸ **verb 1** make a quick, nervous movement as an instinctive reaction to fear or pain. **2** (**flinch from**) avoid something through fear or anxiety.

– SYNONYMS **1 wince,** start, shudder, quiver, jerk. **2** *he never flinched from his duty* **shrink from,** recoil from, shy away from, dodge, evade, avoid, duck, balk at.

– ORIGIN Old French *flenchir* 'turn aside.'

CHOOSE THE RIGHT WORD

See **WINCE**.

fling /fliNG/ ▸ **verb** (past and past part. **flung** /fləNG/) **1** throw something forcefully. **2** move or go suddenly and forcefully: *he flung out his arm.* **3** (**fling oneself into**) take part in an activity or enterprise with great enthusiasm. **4** (**fling something on/off**) put on or take off clothes carelessly and rapidly.

– SYNONYMS **throw,** hurl, toss, sling, launch, pitch, lob; informal chuck, heave.

▸ **noun 1** a short period of enjoyment or wild behavior. **2** a short sexual relationship. **3** a Highland fling.

– SYNONYMS **1 good time,** party, spree, fun and games; informal binge, bash, night on the town. **2 affair,** love affair, relationship, romance, liaison, entanglement, involvement.

– ORIGIN perhaps related to an Old Norse word meaning 'flog.'

flint /flint/ ▸ **noun 1** a hard gray rock consisting of nearly pure silica. **2** a piece of this rock. **3** a piece of flint or a metal alloy, used to produce a spark in a cigarette lighter.
– ORIGIN Old English.

flint·lock /ˈflintˌläk/ ▸ **noun** an old-fashioned type of gun fired by a spark from a flint.

flint·y /ˈflintē/ ▸ **adjective** (**flintier, flintiest**) **1** relating to, containing, or resembling flint. **2** stern and showing no emotion: *a flinty stare.*
– DERIVATIVES **flint·i·ly** adverb **flint·i·ness** noun.

flip /flip/ ▸ **verb** (**flips, flipping, flipped**) **1** turn over with a sudden, quick movement: *the plane flipped over.* **2** press a button or switch in order to turn a machine or device on or off. **3** move or toss something with a quick action. **4** (**flip through**) look through a book, magazine, etc. **5** (also **flip one's lid**) informal suddenly become very angry or lose one's self-control.

– SYNONYMS **1 overturn,** turn over, tip over, roll (over), upturn, capsize, upend, invert, knock over, keel over, topple over, turn turtle. **2 flick,** click, throw, push, pull. **3** (**flip through**) **thumb through,** leaf through, flick through, skim through, scan, look through, browse through, dip into, glance at/through, peruse, run one's eye over.

▸ **noun** a flipping action or movement.
▸ **adjective** not serious or respectful.
– ORIGIN probably a shortened form of **FILLIP**.

flip chart ▸ **noun** a very large pad of paper bound so that pages can be turned over at the top, used on a stand at presentations.

flip-flop ▸ **noun** a light sandal with a thong that passes between the big and second toes.

flip·pant /ˈflipənt/ ▸ **adjective** not treating something with the appropriate seriousness or respect.

– SYNONYMS **frivolous,** facetious, tongue-in-cheek, disrespectful, irreverent, cheeky; informal flip, saucy, sassy.
– ANTONYMS serious.

– DERIVATIVES **flip·pan·cy** /ˈflipənsē/ noun **flip·pant·ly** adverb.
– ORIGIN from **FLIP**.

flip·per /ˈflipər/ ▸ **noun 1** a broad, flat limb without fingers, used for swimming by sea animals such as seals and turtles. **2** each of a pair of flat rubber attachments worn on the feet for underwater swimming. **3** a pivoted arm in a pinball machine.

flip·ping /ˈflipiNG/ ▸ **adjective** Brit. informal used for emphasis or to express mild annoyance.

flip side ▸ **noun** informal **1** the reverse or less pleasant aspect of a situation. **2** dated the B-side of a pop single record.

flirt /flərt/ ▸ **verb 1** behave as if one finds another person sexually attractive but without intending to have a relationship with them. **2** (**flirt with**) show a casual interest in an idea or activity. **3** (**flirt with**) deliberately behave in such a way as to risk danger or death. ▸ **noun** a person who likes to flirt.

– SYNONYMS **1 tease,** coquette, heartbreaker. **2 (flirt with) tease,** lead on, toy with. **3 (flirt with) dabble in,** toy with, trifle with, play with, tinker with, dip into, scratch the surface of.

– DERIVATIVES **flir·ta·tion** /-'tāsHən/ noun **flirt·y** adjective **(flirtier, flirtiest).**
– ORIGIN uncertain.

flir·ta·tious /ˌflərt'tāsHəs/ ▸ **adjective** liking to flirt with people.
– DERIVATIVES **flir·ta·tious·ly** adverb.

flit /flit/ ▸ **verb (flits, flitting, flitted)** move swiftly and lightly.
– ORIGIN Old Norse.

flit·ter /'flitər/ ▸ **verb** move quickly here and there.
– ORIGIN from **FLIT.**

float /flōt/ ▸ **verb 1** rest on the surface of a liquid without sinking. **2** move slowly, hover, or be suspended in a liquid or the air: *clouds floated across the sky.* **3** put forward an idea as a suggestion or to test other people's reactions. **4** offer the shares of a company for sale on the stock market for the first time. **5** allow a currency to have a variable rate of exchange against other currencies. **6** provide funds to begin an enterprise with the expectation of being paid back with the enterprise's first proceeds: *would you float us the cash to stock our hotdog cart?*

– SYNONYMS **1 stay afloat,** stay on the surface, be buoyant, be buoyed up. **2 hover,** levitate, be suspended, hang, defy gravity. **3 drift,** glide, sail, slip, slide, waft. **4 launch,** offer, sell, introduce.
– ANTONYMS sink.

▸ **noun 1** a lightweight object or device designed to float on water. **2** a small floating object attached to a fishing line that moves when a fish bites. **3** a platform mounted on a truck and carrying a display in a procession. **4** a sum of money used for change at the beginning of a period of selling in a store, stall, etc. **5** a soft drink with a scoop of ice cream floating in it. **6** a hand tool with a rectangular blade used for smoothing plaster.
– DERIVATIVES **float·er** noun.
– ORIGIN Old English.

float·a·tion ▸ **noun** variant spelling of **FLOTATION.**

float·ing /'flōtiNG/ ▸ **adjective** not settled or living permanently in one place: *the region's floating population.*

– SYNONYMS **unsettled,** transient, temporary, migrant, wandering, nomadic, migratory, itinerant.

float·ing-point ▸ **adjective** Computing referring to a method of encoding numbers as two sequences of bits, one representing the number's significant digits and the other an exponent.

float·ing rib ▸ **noun** any of the lower ribs that are not attached directly to the breastbone.

float·plane /'flōtˌplān/ ▸ **noun** a seaplane.

float·y /'flōtē/ ▸ **adjective** giving the impression of floating, or of being able to float: *this floaty pale dress that swirls around her legs.*

floc·cu·lent /'fläkyələnt/ ▸ **adjective** having or resembling tufts of wool.
– ORIGIN Latin *flocculus* 'tuft of wool.'

flock[1] /fläk/ ▸ **noun 1** a number of birds moving or resting together. **2** a number of domestic animals, especially sheep, that are kept together. **3 (a flock/flocks)** a large number or crowd: *a flock of children.* **4** a Christian congregation under the charge of a particular minister.

– SYNONYMS **1 flight,** swarm, cloud, gaggle, skein. **2 herd,** drove.

▸ **verb** gather or move in a flock or crowd: *tourists flocked to the area.*

– SYNONYMS **1** *people flocked around her* **gather,** collect, congregate, assemble, converge, mass, crowd, throng, cluster, swarm. **2** *tourists flock to the place* **stream,** go in large numbers, swarm, crowd, troop.

– ORIGIN Old English.

flock[2] ▸ **noun** a soft material for stuffing cushions and quilts, made of wool refuse or torn-up cloth.
– ORIGIN Latin *floccus.*

floe /flō/ ▸ **noun** a sheet of floating ice.
– ORIGIN probably from Norwegian *flo* 'layer.'

flog /fläg/ ▸ **verb (flogs, flogging, flogged) 1** beat someone with a whip or stick as a punishment. **2** informal talk about or promote something repeatedly or at excessive length: *the issue has been flogged to death already.*

– SYNONYMS **whip,** thrash, lash, scourge, birch, cane, beat.

– DERIVATIVES **flog·ger** noun.
– ORIGIN perhaps from Latin *flagellare* 'to whip.'

flood /fləd/ ▸ **noun 1** an overflow of a large amount of water over dry land. **2 (the Flood)** the flood described in the Bible, brought by God because of the wickedness of the human race. **3** an overwhelming quantity of things or people appearing at once: *a flood of refugees.* **4** an outpouring of tears or emotion. **5** the rising of the tide.

– SYNONYMS **1 inundation,** deluge, torrent, overflow, flash flood; Brit. spate. **2 gush,** outpouring, torrent, rush, stream, surge, cascade. **3 succession,** series, string, barrage, volley, battery, avalanche, torrent, stream, storm.

▸ **verb 1** cover or become covered with water in a flood. **2** (of a river) become swollen and overflow its banks. **3** (usu. **be flooded out**) drive someone out of their home or business with a flood: *most of the families who have been flooded out will receive compensation.* **4** arrive in very large numbers: *letters of support and sympathy flooded in.* **5** fill completely: *she flooded the room with light.* **6** overfill the carburetor of an engine with fuel, causing the engine to fail to start.

– SYNONYMS **1** *the town was flooded* **inundate,** swamp, deluge, immerse, submerge, drown, engulf. **2** *the river could flood* **overflow,** burst its banks, brim over, run over. **3 glut,** swamp, saturate, oversupply. **4 pour,** stream, flow, surge, swarm, pile, crowd.

– ORIGIN Old English.

flood·gate /'flədˌgāt/ ▸ **noun 1** a gate that can be opened or closed to control a flow of water, especially the lower gate of a lock. **2 (the floodgates)** controls or restraints holding something back: *the case could open the floodgates for thousands of similar claims.*

flood·light /'flədˌlīt/ ▸ **noun** a large, powerful light used to illuminate a stage, sports field, etc. ▸ **verb** (past and past part. **floodlit** /'flədˌlit/) (usu. as adj. **floodlit**) light up a stage, sports field, etc., with floodlights.

flood·plain /'flədˌplān/ ▸ **noun** an area of low-lying ground next to a river that regularly becomes flooded.

flood tide ▸ **noun** an incoming tide.

floor /flôr/ ▶ **noun 1** the lower surface of a room. **2** a story of a building. **3** the bottom of the sea, a cave, etc. **4** a minimum level of prices or wages. **5** (**the floor**) the part of a lawmaking body in which members sit and from which they speak. **6** (**the floor**) the right to speak in a debate: *other speakers have the floor.*

– SYNONYMS **1 ground,** flooring. **2 story,** level, deck, tier, stage.

▶ **verb 1** provide a room with a floor. **2** informal knock someone to the ground. **3** informal completely baffle someone.

– SYNONYMS **1 knock down,** knock over, fell; informal deck, lay out. **2 baffle,** defeat, confound, perplex, puzzle, disconcert; informal throw, beat, stump.

– DERIVATIVES **floor·ing** noun.
– ORIGIN Old English.

floor·board /ˈflôrˌbôrd/ ▶ **noun** a long plank making up part of a wooden floor.

floor ex·er·cise ▶ **noun 1** a routine of gymnastic exercises performed without the use of any apparatus. **2** any fitness exercise performed on the floor, without special equipment.

floor lamp ▶ **noun** a tall lamp designed to stand on the floor.

floor man·ag·er ▶ **noun 1** an employee in a large store who supervises salespeople. **2** the stage manager of a television production.

floor plan ▶ **noun** a scale diagram of the arrangement of rooms in one story of a building.

floor sam·ple ▶ **noun** an article of merchandise that has been displayed in a store and is offered for sale at a reduced price.

floor show ▶ **noun** an entertainment presented on the floor of a nightclub or restaurant.

floo·zy /ˈflo͞ozē/ (also **floozie**) ▶ **noun** (pl. **floozies**) informal, chiefly humorous a girl or woman who has a reputation for promiscuity.
– ORIGIN uncertain.

flop /fläp/ ▶ **verb** (**flops, flopping, flopped**) **1** hang or swing loosely. **2** sit or lie down heavily and clumsily. **3** informal fail totally.

– SYNONYMS **1 hang,** dangle, droop, sag. **2 collapse,** slump, crumple, sink, drop. **3 be unsuccessful,** fail, fall flat, founder; informal bomb, tank.

▶ **noun 1** a heavy, clumsy fall. **2** informal a total failure.

– SYNONYMS **failure,** disaster, fiasco, debacle, catastrophe. informal washout, also-ran.
– ANTONYMS success.

– ORIGIN variant of **FLAP**.

-flop ▶ **combining form** Computing floating-point operations per second.

flop·house /ˈfläpˌhous/ ▶ **noun** informal a place providing cheap accommodations for homeless people.

flop·py /ˈfläpē/ ▶ **adjective** (**floppier, floppiest**) not firm or rigid; flopping or hanging loosely.

– SYNONYMS **limp,** flaccid, slack, flabby, relaxed, drooping, droopy, loose, flowing.
– ANTONYMS erect, stiff.

▶ **noun** (pl. **floppies**) (also **floppy disk**) Computing a flexible removable magnetic disk used for storing data.

flo·ra /ˈflôrə/ ▶ **noun** (pl. **floras**) **1** the plants of a particular region, habitat, or period of time. Compare with **FAUNA**. **2** the bacteria found naturally in the intestines.
– ORIGIN Latin *flos* 'flower.'

flo·ral /ˈflôrəl/ ▶ **adjective** relating to or decorated with flowers.
– DERIVATIVES **flo·ral·ly** adverb.

Flor·en·tine /ˈflôrənˌtēn, -tīn/ ▶ **adjective 1** relating to the city of Florence in Italy. **2** (**florentine**) (after a noun) (of food) served on top of or prepared with spinach: *chicken florentine.* ▶ **noun 1** a person from Florence. **2** a cookie consisting mainly of nuts and preserved fruit, coated on one side with chocolate.

flo·res·cence /flôrˈesəns, fləˈres-/ ▶ **noun** the process of flowering.

flo·ret /ˈflôrət/ ▶ **noun 1** one of the small flowers making up a composite flowerhead. **2** one of the flowering stems making up a head of cauliflower or broccoli.
– ORIGIN Latin *flos* 'flower.'

flo·ri·bun·da /ˌflôrəˈbəndə/ ▶ **noun** a plant, especially a rose, that bears dense clusters of flowers.
– ORIGIN Latin, from *floribundus* 'freely flowering.'

flo·ri·cul·ture /ˈflôriˌkəlCHər/ ▶ **noun** the growing of flowers.

flor·id /ˈflôrid, ˈflär-/ ▶ **adjective 1** having a red or flushed complexion. **2** too elaborate or ornate: *florid prose.*
– DERIVATIVES **flor·id·ly** adverb.
– ORIGIN Latin *floridus.*

flor·in /ˈflôrən, ˈflär-/ ▶ **noun 1** a former British coin worth two shillings. **2** an English gold coin of the 14th century. **3** a guilder, a former coin of the Netherlands.
– ORIGIN Italian *fiorino* 'little flower' (originally referring to a Florentine coin bearing a fleur-de-lis).

flo·rist /ˈflôrist/ ▶ **noun** a person who sells and arranges cut flowers.
– DERIVATIVES **flo·rist·ry** noun.

flo·ru·it /ˈflôr(y)o͞oit/ ▶ **verb** used to indicate when a historical figure lived, worked, or was most active.
– ORIGIN Latin, 'he or she flourished.'

floss /flôs, fläs/ ▶ **noun 1** (also **dental floss**) a soft thread used to clean between the teeth. **2** untwisted silk threads used in embroidery. **3** the rough silk enveloping a silkworm's cocoon. ▶ **verb** clean between one's teeth with dental floss.
– DERIVATIVES **floss·y** adjective.
– ORIGIN Old French *flosche* 'down, nap of velvet.'

flo·ta·tion /flōˈtāSHən/ (also **floatation**) ▶ **noun 1** the action of floating. **2** the process of offering a company's shares for sale on the stock market for the first time.

flo·til·la /flōˈtilə/ ▶ **noun** a small fleet of ships or boats.
– ORIGIN Spanish.

flot·sam /ˈflätsəm/ ▶ **noun** wreckage found floating on the sea.
– PHRASES **flotsam and jetsam** useless or discarded objects.
– ORIGIN Old French *floteson.*

flounce[1] /flouns/ ▶ **verb** move in a way that draws attention to oneself in order to emphasize one's impatience or annoyance. ▶ **noun** an exaggerated action expressing annoyance or impatience.
– ORIGIN perhaps related to Norwegian *flunsa* 'hurry.'

flounce[2] ▶ **noun** a wide ornamental strip of material gathered and sewn to a skirt or dress; a frill.
– DERIVATIVES **flounced** adjective **flounc·y** adjective.
– ORIGIN from an alteration of former *frounce* 'a fold or pleat,' from Old French *fronce.*

floun·der[1] /'floundər/ ▶ **verb 1** stagger clumsily in mud or water. **2** have trouble doing or understanding something.

– SYNONYMS **1** *floundering in the water* **struggle,** thrash, flail, twist and turn, splash, stagger, stumble, reel, lurch, blunder. **2** *she floundered, not knowing what to say* **struggle,** be out of one's depth, be confused; informal scratch one's head, be flummoxed, be fazed, be floored.

– ORIGIN perhaps a blend of **FOUNDER**[3] and **BLUNDER**.

USAGE

On the confusion of **flounder** and **founder**, see the note at **FOUNDER**[3].

floun·der[2] ▶ **noun** a small flatfish of shallow coastal waters.
– ORIGIN Old French *flondre*.

flour /'flou(ə)r/ ▶ **noun** a powder produced by grinding grain, used to make bread, cakes, and pastry.
▶ **verb** sprinkle something with flour.
– DERIVATIVES **flour·y** adjective.
– ORIGIN from **FLOWER** in the sense 'the best part,' first used to mean 'the finest quality of ground wheat.'

flour·ish /'flərisн/ ▶ **verb 1** grow or develop in a healthy or vigorous way. **2** be working or at the height of one's career during a particular period. **3** wave something around dramatically.

– SYNONYMS **1** *ferns flourish in the shade* **grow,** thrive, prosper, do well, burgeon, increase, multiply, proliferate, run riot. **2** *the arts flourished* **thrive,** prosper, bloom, be in good health, be vigorous, be in its heyday, make progress, advance, expand; informal go places. **3 brandish,** wave, shake, wield, swing, display, show off.
– ANTONYMS wither, decline.

▶ **noun 1** an exaggerated gesture or movement, made especially to attract attention. **2** an ornamental flowing curve in handwriting. **3** a fanfare played by brass instruments.
– ORIGIN Old French *florir*.

flout /flout/ ▶ **verb** openly fail to follow a rule, law, or convention.

– SYNONYMS **defy,** refuse to obey, disobey, break, violate, fail to comply with, fail to observe, contravene, infringe, breach, commit a breach of, transgress against, ignore, disregard.
– ANTONYMS observe.

– ORIGIN perhaps from Dutch *fluiten* 'play the flute, hiss scornfully.'

USAGE

On the confusion of **flout** and **flaunt**, see the note at **FLAUNT**.

flow /flō/ ▶ **verb 1** move steadily and continuously in a current or stream. **2** move steadily and freely: *people flowed into the courtyard*. **3** (of the sea or a tidal river) move toward the land; rise. **4** (**flow from**) result from; be caused by: *there are certain advantages that may flow from that decision*.

– SYNONYMS **1 pour,** run, course, circulate, stream, swirl, surge, sweep, gush, cascade, roll, rush, trickle, seep, ooze, dribble. **2 result,** proceed, arise, follow, ensue, stem, originate, emanate, spring.

▶ **noun 1** the action of flowing. **2** a steady, continuous stream: *the flow of traffic*. **3** the rise of a tide or a river.

– SYNONYMS **movement,** motion, current, circulation, stream, swirl, surge, gush, rush, spate, tide, trickle, ooze.

– PHRASES **go with the flow** informal be relaxed and accept a situation, rather than trying to alter or control it.
– ORIGIN Old English.

flow chart (also **flow diagram**) ▶ **noun** a diagram showing a sequence of operations or functions making up a complex process or computer program.

flow·er /'flou(-ə)r/ ▶ **noun 1** the part of a plant from which the seed or fruit develops, usually having brightly colored petals. **2** (often in phrase **in flower**) the state or period in which a plant's flowers have developed and opened. **3** (**the flower of**) the best of a group: *the flower of Ireland's youth*.

– SYNONYMS **bloom,** blossom.

▶ **verb 1** produce flowers. **2** develop richly and fully: *a musical form that flowered in the nineteenth century*.
– ORIGIN Old French *flour, flor*, from Latin *flos*.

WORD LINKS

floral *relating to flowers*
florist *person who sells flowers*

flow·ered /'flou(-ə)rd/ ▶ **adjective** decorated with patterns of flowers.

flow·er girl ▶ **noun 1** a young girl attending the bridge at a wedding. **2** historical a woman or girl who sells flowers, especially in the street.

flow·er head ▶ **noun** a compact mass of flowers at the top of a stem, especially a flat cluster of florets.

flow·er·pot /'flou(-ə)r,pät/ ▶ **noun** an earthenware or plastic container in which to grow a plant.

flow·er pow·er ▶ **noun** the promotion by hippies of peace and love as means of changing the world.

flow·er·y /'flou(-ə)rē/ ▶ **adjective 1** full of, decorated with, or resembling flowers. **2** (of speech or writing) elaborate.

flow·ing /'flōiNG/ ▶ **adjective 1** (especially of long hair or clothing) hanging or draping loosely and gracefully. **2** (of a line or contour) smoothly continuous: *the flowing curves of the lawn*. **3** (of language, movement, or style) graceful and fluent.
– DERIVATIVES **flow·ing·ly** adverb.

flown /flōn/ past participle of **FLY**[1].

fl. oz. ▶ **abbreviation** fluid ounce.

flu /flo͞o/ ▶ **noun** influenza.

flub /fləb/ informal ▶ **verb** (**flubs, flubbing, flubbed**) botch or bungle: *she flubbed her lines*. ▶ **noun** a thing badly or clumsily done; a blunder.

fluc·tu·ate /'fləkCHo͞o,āt/ ▶ **verb** rise and fall irregularly in number or amount: *her weight has fluctuated between 112 and 154 pounds*.

– SYNONYMS **vary,** change, shift, alter, waver, swing, oscillate, alternate, rise and fall.

– DERIVATIVES **fluc·tu·a·tion** /,fləkCHo͞o'āSHən/ noun.
– ORIGIN Latin *fluctuare* 'undulate.'

flue /flo͞o/ ▶ **noun 1** a duct in a chimney for smoke and waste gases. **2** a pipe or passage for conveying heat.
– ORIGIN unknown.

flu·ent /'flo͞oənt/ ▶ **adjective 1** speaking or writing in an articulate and natural way. **2** (of a language) used easily and accurately. **3** smoothly graceful and easy: *a runner in fluent motion.*

– SYNONYMS **articulate,** eloquent, silver-tongued, communicative, natural, effortless.
– ANTONYMS inarticulate.

– DERIVATIVES **flu·en·cy** noun **flu·ent·ly** adverb.
– ORIGIN from Latin *fluere* 'to flow.'

fluff /fləf/ ▶ **noun 1** soft fibers gathered in small light clumps. **2** the soft fur or feathers of a young mammal or bird. **3** informal a mistake. ▶ **verb 1** (usu. **fluff something up/out**) make something fuller and softer by shaking or patting. **2** informal fail to accomplish properly: *he fluffed his only line.*
– ORIGIN probably from Flemish *vluwe*.

fluff·y /'fləfē/ ▶ **adjective** (**fluffier, fluffiest**) **1** resembling or covered with fluff. **2** (of food) light in texture. **3** informal frivolous, silly, or vague: *fluffy game shows.*
– DERIVATIVES **fluff·i·ness** noun.

flu·gel·horn /'flo͞ogəlˌhôrn/ ▶ **noun** a brass musical instrument like a cornet but with a fuller tone.
– ORIGIN from German *Flügel* 'wing' + *Horn* 'horn.'

flu·id /'flo͞oid/ ▶ **noun** a substance, such as a liquid or gas, that has no fixed shape and yields easily to external pressure.

– SYNONYMS **liquid,** solution, liquor, gas, vapor.

▶ **adjective 1** able to flow easily. **2** not settled or stable: *today's fluid social environment.* **3** (of movement) smoothly elegant or graceful.

– SYNONYMS **1 free-flowing,** runny, liquid, liquefied, melted, molten, gaseous. **2 smooth,** fluent, flowing, effortless, easy, continuous, graceful, elegant.
– ANTONYMS solid.

– DERIVATIVES **flu·id·i·ty** /flo͞o'idətē/ noun **flu·id·ly** adverb.
– ORIGIN Latin *fluidus*.

flu·id ounce ▶ **noun 1** a unit of capacity equal to one sixteenth of a pint (approximately 0.03 liter). **2** Brit. a unit of capacity equal to one twentieth of a pint (approximately 0.028 liter).

fluke[1] /flo͞ok/ ▶ **noun** a lucky chance occurrence.
– DERIVATIVES **fluk·y** (also **flukey**) adjective (**flukier, flukiest**).
– ORIGIN perhaps a dialect word.

fluke[2] ▶ **noun** a parasitic flatworm that typically has suckers and hooks for attachment to the host.
– ORIGIN Old English.

fluke[3] ▶ **noun 1** a broad triangular plate on the arm of an anchor. **2** either of the lobes of a whale's tail.
– ORIGIN perhaps from **FLUKE**[2] (because of the shape).

flume /flo͞om/ ▶ **noun 1** an artificial channel for water. **2** a water slide at a swimming pool or amusement park.
– ORIGIN Latin *flumen* 'river.'

flum·mer·y /'fləmərē/ ▶ **noun** empty talk; nonsense.
– ORIGIN Welsh *llymru*.

flum·mox /'fləməks/ ▶ **verb** informal baffle or bewilder someone.
– ORIGIN probably dialect.

flung /fləNG/ past and past participle of **FLING**.

flunk /fləNGk/ ▶ **verb** informal **1** fail an exam. **2** (**flunk out**) (of a student) leave or be dismissed from school or college as a result of failing to reach the required standard.
– ORIGIN perhaps related to **FUNK**[1].

flun·ky /'fləNGkē/ (also **flunkey**) ▶ **noun** (pl. **flunkies** or **flunkeys**) **1** chiefly derogatory a person who performs menial tasks. **2** chiefly historical a uniformed manservant or footman.
– ORIGIN perhaps from **FLANK** in the sense 'a person who stands at one's flank.'

fluo·resce /flo͝o(ə)'res, flôr'es/ ▶ **verb** shine or glow brightly due to fluorescence.

fluo·res·cence /flo͝o(ə)'resəns, flôr'esəns/ ▶ **noun 1** light given out by a substance when it is exposed to radiation such as that of ultraviolet light or X-rays. **2** the property of giving out light in this way.
– ORIGIN from **FLUORSPAR** (which fluoresces).

fluo·res·cent /ˌflo͝o(ə)'resənt, flôr'esənt/ ▶ **adjective 1** having or showing fluorescence. **2** (of lighting) based on fluorescence from a substance illuminated by ultraviolet light. **3** vividly colorful.

fluor·i·date /'flo͝orəˌdāt, 'flôr-/ ▶ **verb** add traces of fluorides to something.
– DERIVATIVES **fluor·i·da·tion** /ˌflo͝orə'dāSHən, ˌflôr-/ noun.

fluor·ide /'flo͝orˌīd, 'flôr-/ ▶ **noun 1** a compound of fluorine with another element or group. **2** a fluorine-containing salt added to water supplies or toothpaste to reduce tooth decay.

fluor·i·nate /'flo͝orəˌnāt, 'flôr-/ ▶ **verb 1** introduce fluorine into a compound. **2** another term for **FLUORIDATE**.
– DERIVATIVES **fluor·i·na·tion** /ˌflo͝orə'nāSHən, ˌflôr-/ noun.

fluor·ine /'flo͝orˌēn, flôr-/ ▶ **noun** a poisonous, extremely reactive, pale yellow gaseous chemical element.
– ORIGIN from *fluor* (see **FLUORSPAR**).

fluo·rite /'flo͝orˌīt, flôr-/ ▶ **noun** a mineral form of calcium fluoride.

fluor·o·car·bon /ˌflo͝orō'kärbən, ˌflôrō-/ ▶ **noun** a compound formed by replacing one or more of the hydrogen atoms in a hydrocarbon with fluorine atoms. Fluorocarbons are widely used in lubricants, cleaners, and aerosols.

fluor·o·quin·o·lone /ˌflo͝orō'kwinˌōn, ˌflôrō-/ ▶ **noun** any of a class of therapeutic antibiotics that are active against a range of bacteria associated with human and animal diseases. Their use in livestock has sparked concerns about the spread of bacteria resistant to them in humans.

fluor·o·scope /'flo͝orəˌskōp, 'flôr-/ ▶ **noun** an instrument used for viewing X-ray images without taking and developing X-ray photographs.
– DERIVATIVES **fluor·o·scop·ic** /ˌflo͝orə'skäpik, ˌflôr-/ adjective **fluo·ros·co·py** /flo͝or'äskəpē, flôr-/ noun.

flu·or·spar /'flo͝orˌspär, 'flôr-/ ▶ **noun** another term for **FLUORITE**.
– ORIGIN from Latin *fluor* 'a flow' + **SPAR**[3].

flur·ried /'flərēd, 'flə-rēd/ ▶ **adjective** agitated, confused, or anxious.

flur·ry /'flərē, 'flə-rē/ ▶ **noun** (pl. **flurries**) **1** a small swirling mass of snow, leaves, etc., moved by a gust of wind. **2** a sudden short spell of activity or excitement. **3** a number of things arriving suddenly and at the same time: *a flurry of emails.*

– SYNONYMS **1 swirl,** whirl, eddy, shower, gust. **2 burst,** outbreak, spurt, fit, spell, bout, rash, eruption.

– ORIGIN from former *flurr* 'fly up, flutter,' probably influenced by **HURRY**.

flush[1] /fləsh/ ▶ **verb 1** (of a person's skin or face) become red and hot, typically through illness or emotion. **2** (**be flushed with**) be excited or very pleased by: *flushed with success, I was getting into my stride.* **3** clean something by passing large quantities of water through it. **4** remove or dispose of something by flushing with water. **5** force a person or animal out of hiding: *their task was to flush out the rebels.*

– SYNONYMS **1 blush,** redden, go pink, go red, go crimson, go scarlet, color (up). **2 rinse,** wash, sluice, swill, cleanse, clean. **3 chase,** force, drive, dislodge, expel.

▶ **noun 1** a reddening of the face or skin. **2** a sudden rush of intense emotion. **3** a period of freshness and vigor: *the first flush of youth.* **4** an act of flushing something with water.

– SYNONYMS **blush,** color, rosiness, pinkness, ruddiness, bloom.
– ANTONYMS pallor.

– DERIVATIVES **flush·er** noun.
– ORIGIN perhaps influenced by **FLASH** and **BLUSH**.

flush[2] ▶ **adjective** (usu. **flush with**) **1** completely level with another surface. **2** informal having plenty of something, especially money.
– ORIGIN probably related to **FLUSH**[1].

flush[3] ▶ **noun** (in poker) a hand of cards all of the same suit.
– ORIGIN Latin *fluxus* 'flux.'

flust·er /ˈfləstər/ ▶ **verb** (often as adj. **flustered**) make someone agitated or confused. ▶ **noun** a flustered state.
– ORIGIN perhaps Scandinavian.

flute /flo͞ot/ ▶ **noun 1** a high-pitched wind instrument consisting of a tube with holes along it. **2** a tall, narrow wine glass. **3** Architecture an ornamental vertical groove in a column. ▶ **verb** speak in a melodious way.
– ORIGIN Old French *flahute.*

flut·ed /flo͞otid/ ▶ **adjective** (of an object) having a series of decorative grooves.

flut·ing /ˈflo͞otiNG/ ▶ **noun 1** a sound reminiscent of that of a flute: *the silvery fluting of a blackbird.* **2** a groove or set of grooves forming a surface decoration.

flut·ist /ˈflo͞otist/ ▶ **noun** a flute player.

flut·ter /ˈflətər/ ▶ **verb 1** fly unsteadily by flapping the wings quickly and lightly. **2** move with a light irregular motion: *flags fluttered in the breeze.* **3** (of a pulse or heartbeat) beat irregularly.

– SYNONYMS **1** *butterflies fluttered around* **flit,** hover, dance. **2** *a robin fluttered its wings* **flap,** beat, quiver, agitate, vibrate, ruffle. **3** *she fluttered her eyelashes* **flicker,** bat. **4** *flags fluttered* **flap,** wave, ripple, undulate, quiver, fly.

▶ **noun 1** an act of fluttering. **2** a state of nervous excitement. **3** Electronics rapid variation in the pitch or amplitude of a signal, especially of recorded sound. Compare with **wow**[2].
– DERIVATIVES **flut·ter·y** adjective.
– ORIGIN Old English.

flut·y /ˈflo͞otē/ (also **flutey**) ▶ **adjective** (**flutier, flutiest**) reminiscent of the sound of a flute: *a high, fluty voice.*

flu·vi·al /ˈflo͞ovēəl/ ▶ **adjective** chiefly Geology relating to or found in a river.
– ORIGIN from Latin *fluvius* 'river.'

flux /fləks/ ▶ **noun 1** continuous change: *urban life is in a constant state of flux.* **2** technical the action of flowing. **3** Medicine an abnormal discharge from or within the body. **4** Physics the total amount of radiation, or of electric or magnetic field lines, passing through an area. **5** a substance mixed with a solid to lower the melting point, used in soldering or smelting.
– ORIGIN Latin *fluxus.*

fly[1] /flī/ ▶ **verb** (**flies, flying, flew** /flo͞o/; past part. **flown** /flōn/) **1** (of a winged creature or aircraft) move through the air. **2** control the flight of an aircraft. **3** carry or accomplish in an aircraft: *by June 22, the squadron had flown 207 sorties.* **4** go or move quickly: *his fingers flew across the keyboard.* **5** move or be thrown quickly through the air. **6** wave or flutter in the wind. **7** (of a flag) be displayed on a flagpole. **8** (**fly at**) attack someone verbally or physically. **9** old use run away; flee.

– SYNONYMS **1 wing,** glide, soar, wheel, take wing, take to the air, hover, swoop. **2 pilot,** operate, control, maneuver, steer. **3** *the ship flew a French flag* **display,** show, exhibit, hoist, raise, wave. **4 dash,** race, rush, bolt, zoom, dart, speed, hurry, career, hurtle; informal tear.

▶ **noun** (pl. **flies**) **1** an opening at the crotch of a pair of pants, closed with a zipper or buttons. **2** a flap of material covering the opening of a tent. **3** (**the flies**) the space over the stage in a theater.
– DERIVATIVES **fly·a·ble** adjective.
– PHRASES **fly in the face of** oppose or be the opposite of what is usual or expected. **fly off the handle** informal lose one's temper suddenly.
– ORIGIN Old English.

fly[2] ▶ **noun** (pl. **flies**) **1** a flying insect with a single pair of transparent wings and sucking or piercing mouthparts. **2** used in names of other flying insects, e.g., *dragonfly.* **3** a fishing bait consisting of a natural or artificial flying insect.
– PHRASES **a fly in the ointment** a minor irritation that spoils the enjoyment of something. **fly on the wall** an unnoticed observer.
– ORIGIN Old English.

fly·a·way /ˈflīə,wā/ ▶ **adjective** (of hair) fine and difficult to control.

fly·by /ˈflī,bī/ ▶ **noun** (pl. **flybys**) a flight past a point, especially the close approach of a spacecraft to a planet or moon for observation.

fly-by-night ▶ **adjective** unreliable or untrustworthy, especially in financial matters.

fly-by-wire ▶ **adjective** referring to a semiautomatic computer-regulated system for controlling an aircraft or spacecraft.

fly·catch·er /ˈflī,kaCHər, -,keCHər/ ▶ **noun** a perching bird that catches flying insects.

fly·er /ˈflīər/ (also **flier**) ▶ **noun 1** a person or thing that flies. **2** informal a fast-moving person or thing. **3** a small leaflet advertising an event or product. **4** a flying start.

fly-fish·ing ▶ **noun** the sport of fishing using a rod and an artificial fly as bait.

fly·ing /ˈflī-iNG/ ▶ **adjective 1** able to move through the air. **2** hasty; brief: *a flying visit.*
– PHRASES **with flying colors** very well; with particular merit.

fly·ing but·tress ▶ **noun** Architecture a buttress slanting from a separate column, typically forming an arch with the wall it supports.

fly·ing fish ▶ **noun** a fish of warm seas that leaps out of the water and uses its winglike pectoral fins to glide for some distance.

fly·ing sau·cer ▸ noun a disk-shaped flying craft supposedly piloted by aliens.

fly·ing squir·rel ▸ noun a small tree squirrel that has skin joining the fore and hind limbs for gliding from tree to tree.

fly·ing start ▸ noun **1** a start of a race in which the competitors are already moving at speed as they pass the starting point. **2** a good beginning giving an advantage over competitors.

fly·leaf /ˈflīˌlēf/ ▸ noun (pl. **flyleaves** /-ˌlēvz/) a blank page at the beginning or end of a book.

fly·o·ver /ˈflīˌōvər/ ▸ noun **1** a low flight by one or more aircraft over a specific location. **2** a ceremonial flight of aircraft past a person or place. **3** Brit. an overpass.

fly·pa·per /ˈflīˌpāpər/ ▸ noun sticky, poison-treated strips of paper that are hung indoors to catch and kill flies.

fly·sheet /ˈflīˌsʜēt/ ▸ noun a fabric cover pitched over a tent to give extra protection against bad weather.

fly swat·ter ▸ noun an implement used for swatting insects, typically a square of plastic mesh attached to a wire handle.

fly·way /ˈflīˌwā/ ▸ noun a route regularly used by large numbers of migrating birds.

fly·weight /ˈflīˌwāt/ ▸ noun a weight in boxing and other sports intermediate between light flyweight and bantamweight.

fly·wheel /ˈflīˌ(h)wēl/ ▸ noun a heavy wheel in a machine that is used to increase momentum and thereby provide greater stability or a reserve of available power.

FM ▸ abbreviation frequency modulation: *FM radio.*

Fm ▸ symbol the chemical element fermium.

fm ▸ abbreviation **1** fathom(s). **2** femtometer.

fmr. ▸ abbreviation former.

f-num·ber ▸ noun Photography the ratio of the focal length of a camera lens to the diameter of the aperture being used for a particular shot.

FOAF (also **FOF**) ▸ abbreviation friend of a friend.

foal /fōl/ ▸ noun a young horse or related animal. ▸ verb (of a mare) give birth to a foal.
– ORIGIN Old English.

foam /fōm/ ▸ noun **1** a mass of small bubbles formed on or in liquid. **2** a liquid substance containing many small bubbles: *shaving foam.* **3** (also **foam rubber**) a lightweight form of rubber or plastic made by solidifying foam.

> – SYNONYMS **froth,** spume, surf, spray, fizz, effervescence, bubbles, head, lather, suds.

▸ verb form or produce foam.

> – SYNONYMS **froth,** fizz, effervesce, bubble, lather, ferment, boil, seethe.

– DERIVATIVES **foam·y** adjective.
– PHRASES **foam at the mouth** informal be very angry.
– ORIGIN Old English.

FOB ▸ abbreviation **1** Military forward operating base. **2** Commerce (preceding a geographic location) free on board; indicating the point at which shipping charges are applicable.

fob[1] /fäb/ ▸ noun **1** a chain attached to a watch for carrying in a vest or waistband pocket. **2** (also **fob pocket**) a small pocket for carrying a watch. **3** a tab on a key ring.
– ORIGIN probably related to German dialect *Fuppe* 'pocket.'

fob[2] ▸ verb (**fobs, fobbing, fobbed**) **1** (**fob someone off**) try to deceive someone into accepting excuses or something inferior. **2** (**fob something off on**) give something inferior to someone.
– ORIGIN perhaps related to German *foppen* 'deceive, banter.'

fo·cac·cia /fōˈkäcʜ(ē)ə/ ▸ noun a type of flat Italian bread made with olive oil and flavored with herbs.
– ORIGIN Italian.

fo·cal /ˈfōkəl/ ▸ adjective relating to a focus, especially the focus of a lens.
– DERIVATIVES **fo·cal·ly** adverb.

fo·cal length ▸ noun the distance between the center of a lens or curved mirror and its focus.

fo·cal point ▸ noun **1** the point at which rays or waves from a lens or mirror meet, or the point from which rays or waves going in different directions appear to proceed. **2** the center of interest or activity: *a fireplace serves as the focal point of any room.*

fo'c'·sle /ˈfōksəl/ ▸ noun variant spelling of FORECASTLE.

fo·cus /ˈfōkəs/ ▸ noun (pl. **focuses** or **foci** /ˈfōˌsī, -ˌkī/) **1** the center of interest or activity. **2** the state or quality of having or producing a clear, well-defined image: *his face is out of focus.* **3** the point at which an object must be situated in order for a lens or mirror to produce a clear image of it. **4** a focal point. **5** the point of origin of an earthquake. Compare with EPICENTER. **6** Geometry a fixed point with reference to which an ellipse, parabola, or other curve is drawn.

> – SYNONYMS **1 center,** focal point, central point, center of attention, hub, pivot, nucleus, heart, cornerstone, linchpin. **2 subject,** theme, concern, subject matter, topic, point, essence, gist.

▸ verb (**focuses, focusing, focused** or **focusses, focussing, focussed**) **1** (of a person or their eyes) adapt to the prevailing level of light and become able to see clearly. **2** (**focus on**) pay particular attention to: *I was able to focus on a single project.* **3** adjust the focus of a telescope, camera, etc. **4** (of rays or waves) meet or cause to meet at a single point.

> – SYNONYMS **1 bring into focus,** aim, point, turn. **2** (**focus on**) **concentrate,** center, zero in, zoom in, address oneself to, pay attention to, pinpoint, revolve around.

– DERIVATIVES **fo·cus·er** noun.
– ORIGIN Latin, 'domestic hearth.'

fo·cus group ▸ noun a group of people assembled to assess a new product, political campaign, etc.

fod·der /ˈfädər/ ▸ noun **1** food for cattle and other livestock. **2** people or things regarded only as material to satisfy a need: *young people ending up as factory fodder.*
– ORIGIN Old English.

foe /fō/ ▸ noun formal or literary an enemy or opponent.
– ORIGIN from Old English, 'hostile.'

fog /fôg, fäg/ ▸ noun **1** a thick cloud of tiny water droplets suspended in the atmosphere at or near the earth's surface that restricts visibility. **2** a state or cause of confusion. **3** Photography cloudiness obscuring the image on a developed negative or print.

> – SYNONYMS **mist,** smog, murk, haze; Brit. informal pea-souper.

▸ verb (**fogs, fogging, fogged**) **1** cover or become covered with steam. **2** bewilder or confuse: *the sedative still*

fogged Jack's mind. **3** Photography make a film, negative, or print cloudy.
– ORIGIN perhaps from **FOGGY**.

fog bank ▶ **noun** a dense mass of fog, especially at sea.

fog·bound /ˈfôgˌbound, ˈfäg-/ ▶ **adjective** surrounded or hidden by fog.

fo·gey /ˈfōgē/ (also **fogy**) ▶ **noun** (pl. **fogeys** or **fogies**) a very old-fashioned or conservative person.
– DERIVATIVES **fo·gey·ish** adjective **fo·gey·ism** noun.
– ORIGIN unknown.

fog·gy /ˈfôgē, ˈfägē/ ▶ **adjective** (**foggier**, **foggiest**) **1** full of fog. **2** confused or unclear: *my memories of the event are foggy.*

– SYNONYMS **1 misty,** smoggy, hazy, murky. **2** *a foggy memory* **muddled,** confused, dim, hazy, shadowy, cloudy, blurred, obscure, vague, indistinct, unclear.
– ANTONYMS clear.

– PHRASES **not have the foggiest (idea)** informal have no idea at all.
– ORIGIN perhaps from Norwegian *fogg* 'grass that grows in a field after a crop of hay has been cut.'

fog·horn /ˈfôgˌhôrn, ˈfäg-/ ▶ **noun** a device making a loud, deep sound as a warning to ships in fog.

fo·gy /ˈfōgē/ ▶ **noun** variant spelling of **FOGEY**.

FOIA ▶ **abbreviation** Freedom of Information Act.

foi·ble /ˈfoibəl/ ▶ **noun** a minor weakness or eccentricity.
– ORIGIN from former French form of Old French *fieble* 'feeble.'

foie gras /fwä ˈgrä/ (also **pâté de foie gras** /ˈpatā də fwä ˌgrä/) ▶ **noun** a pâté made from the liver of a fattened goose.

foil[1] /foil/ ▶ **verb 1** prevent something wrong or undesirable from succeeding. **2** prevent someone from doing something.

– SYNONYMS **thwart,** frustrate, stop, defeat, block, prevent, obstruct, hinder, snooker, scotch. Brit. informal scupper.
– ANTONYMS assist.

– ORIGIN first meaning 'trample down': perhaps from Old French *fouler* 'to full cloth, trample.'

CHOOSE THE RIGHT WORD

See **THWART**.

foil[2] ▶ **noun 1** metal hammered or rolled into a thin, flexible sheet. **2** a person or thing that contrasts with and so emphasizes the qualities of another: *silver foliage provides the perfect foil for bright flower colors.*

– SYNONYMS **contrast,** complement, antithesis.

– ORIGIN Latin *folium* 'leaf.'

foil[3] ▶ **noun** a light, blunt-edged fencing sword with a button on its point.
– ORIGIN unknown.

foist /foist/ ▶ **verb** (**foist someone/thing on**) impose an unwelcome person or thing on: *electricity privatization was foisted on the public.*
– ORIGIN Dutch dialect *vuisten* 'take in the hand.'

fold[1] /fōld/ ▶ **verb 1** bend something over on itself so that one part of it covers another. **2** (often as adj. **folding**) be able to be folded into a flatter shape. **3** cover or wrap something in a flexible material. **4** affectionately hold someone in one's arms. **5** informal (of a company) go out of business. **6** (**fold something in/into**) mix an ingredient gently with another ingredient.

– SYNONYMS **1 double,** crease, turn, bend, tuck, pleat. **2 fail,** collapse, founder, go bankrupt, cease trading, be wound up, be shut (down); informal crash, go bust, go under, go to the wall, go belly up.

▶ **noun 1** a folded part or thing: *drooping folds of skin.* **2** a line or crease produced by folding. **3** chiefly Brit. a slight hill or hollow. **4** Geology a bend or curvature of strata.

– SYNONYMS **crease,** knife-edge, wrinkle, crinkle, pucker, furrow, pleat.

– DERIVATIVES **fold·a·ble** adjective.
– PHRASES **fold one's arms** cross one's arms over one's chest. **fold one's hands** bring or hold one's hands together.
– ORIGIN Old English.

fold[2] ▶ **noun 1** a pen or enclosure for sheep. **2** (**the fold**) a group with shared aims and values: *Welcome back to the fold, Brother Ben.*
– ORIGIN Old English.

-fold ▶ **suffix** forming adjectives and adverbs from cardinal numbers. **1** in an amount multiplied by: *threefold.* **2** consisting of a specified number of parts: *twofold.*
– ORIGIN Old English.

fold·a·way /ˈfōldəˌwā/ ▶ **adjective** designed to be folded up for easy storage or transport.

fold·er /ˈfōldər/ ▶ **noun 1** a folding cover or holder for storing loose papers. **2** Computing a directory containing related files.

fol·de·rol /ˈfäldəˌräl, ˈfôldəˌrôl/ ▶ **noun** trivial or nonsensical fuss.
– ORIGIN from a meaningless refrain in old songs.

fold·out /ˈfōlˌdout/ ▶ **noun** (of a page, a furniture part, or a bed) designed to be opened out for use and then folded away: *a foldout map.* ▶ **noun** a page or piece of furniture designed in such a way.

fo·li·age /ˈfōl(ē)ij/ ▶ **noun** the leaves of a plant.
– ORIGIN Old French *feuillage.*

fo·li·ar /ˈfōlēər/ ▶ **adjective** technical relating to leaves.

fo·li·ate /ˈfōlēət, -ˌāt/ ▶ **adjective** decorated with leaves or a leaflike pattern.

fo·lic ac·id /ˈfōlik, ˈfä-/ ▶ **noun** a vitamin of the B complex found especially in leafy green vegetables, liver, and kidneys.
– ORIGIN from Latin *folium* 'leaf.'

fo·lie à deux /fôˌlē ä ˈdœ/ ▶ **noun** (pl. **folies à deux**) delusion or mental illness shared by two people in a close relationship.
– ORIGIN French, 'shared madness.'

fo·li·o /ˈfōlēˌō/ ▶ **noun** (pl. **folios**) **1** a sheet of paper folded once to form two leaves (four pages) of a book. **2** a book made up of such sheets. **3** an individual leaf of paper numbered on the front side only. **4** the page number in a printed book.
– ORIGIN from Latin *folium* 'leaf.'

folk /fōk/ ▶ **plural noun 1** (also **folks**) informal people in general. **2** (**one's folks**) one's family, especially one's parents. **3** (also **folk music**) traditional music of unknown authorship, passed on by word of mouth.

– SYNONYMS **1 people,** individuals, 'men, women, and children', (living) souls, citizenry, inhabitants, residents, populace, population. **2 relatives,** relations, family, people; informal peeps.

▸ adjective originating from the beliefs, culture, and customs of ordinary people: *folk wisdom*.
– DERIVATIVES **folk·ish** adjective.
– PHRASES **just (plain) folks** ordinary, down-to-earth, unpretentious people.
– ORIGIN Old English.

folk art ▸ noun art created by people who have no academic training in art or who are not publicly identified as artists. Folk art typically reflects cultural traditions and values.

folk dance ▸ noun a traditional dance of a particular people or area.

folk et·y·mol·o·gy ▸ noun **1** a popular but mistaken account of the origin of a word or phrase. **2** the process by which the form of an unfamiliar or foreign word is adapted to a more familiar form through popular use.

folk·ie /ˈfōkē/ ▸ noun informal a singer, player, or fan of folk music.

folk·lore /ˈfōkˌlôr/ ▸ noun the traditional beliefs, stories, and customs of a community, passed on by word of mouth.
– DERIVATIVES **folk·lor·ic** /-ˌlôrik/ adjective **folk·lor·ist** noun.

folk med·i·cine ▸ noun treatment of disease or injury based on tradition rather than on modern scientific practice, and typically using simple, locally available remedies.

folk sing·er ▸ noun a singer of folk songs.

folk·son·o·my /ˌfōkˈsänəmē/ ▸ noun the activity of sorting information into categories derived from the consensus of the information users, or the result of this.

folk·sy /ˈfōksē/ ▸ adjective (**folksier, folksiest**) traditional and homey, especially in an artificial way: *his carefully cultivated, folksy image*.
– DERIVATIVES **folk·si·ness** noun.

folk tale ▸ noun a traditional story originally passed on by word of mouth.

fol·li·cle /ˈfälikəl/ ▸ noun a small cavity in the body, especially one in which the root of a hair develops.
– DERIVATIVES **fol·lic·u·lar** /fəˈlikyələr/ adjective.
– ORIGIN Latin *folliculus* 'little bag.'

fol·low /ˈfälō/ ▸ verb **1** move or travel behind someone or something. **2** go after someone so as to observe them. **3** go along a route or path. **4** come after in time or order: *the six years that followed his death*. **5** (also **follow on from**) happen as a result of something else. **6** be a logical consequence. **7** act according to an instruction or example. **8** accept someone as a guide, example, or leader of a movement. **9** take an interest in or pay close attention to: *supporters who have followed the team through thick and thin*. **10** understand someone or something. **11** practice or undertake a career or course of action. **12** (**follow something through**) continue an action or task to its conclusion. **13** (**follow something up**) pursue or investigate something further.

> – SYNONYMS **1 come behind,** come after, go behind, go after, walk behind. **2 accompany,** go along with, go around with, travel with, escort, attend; informal tag along with. **3 shadow,** trail, stalk, track; informal tail. **4 obey,** comply with, conform to, adhere to, stick to, keep to, act in accordance with, abide by, observe. **5 understand,** comprehend, take in, grasp, fathom, see; informal make heads or tails of, figure out. **6 be a fan of,** be a supporter of, support, watch, keep up with.
> – ANTONYMS lead, flout.

– PHRASES **follow one's nose 1** trust one's instincts. **2** go straight ahead. **follow suit 1** do the same as someone else. **2** (in card games) play a card of the suit led.
– ORIGIN Old English.

fol·low·er /ˈfälō-ər/ ▸ noun **1** a supporter, fan, or disciple. **2** a person who follows someone or something.

> – SYNONYMS **1 disciple,** apostle, defender, champion, believer, worshiper. **2 fan,** enthusiast, admirer, devotee, lover, supporter, adherent.
> – ANTONYMS leader, opponent.

– DERIVATIVES **fol·low·er·ship** noun.

fol·low·ing /ˈfälō-iNG/ ▸ preposition coming after or as a result of. ▸ noun a group of supporters or admirers.

> – SYNONYMS **admirers,** supporters, backers, fans, adherents, devotees, public, audience.
> – ANTONYMS opposition.

▸ adjective next in time or order.

> – SYNONYMS **next,** ensuing, succeeding, subsequent, successive.
> – ANTONYMS preceding.

fol·low-through ▸ noun the continuing of an action or task to its conclusion.

fol·low-up ▸ noun **1** an activity carried out to monitor or further develop earlier work. **2** a work that follows or builds on an earlier work.

fol·ly /ˈfälē/ ▸ noun (pl. **follies**) **1** lack of good sense; foolishness. **2** a foolish act or idea. **3** an ornamental building with no practical purpose, built in a park or large landscaped yard.

> – SYNONYMS **foolishness,** foolhardiness, stupidity, idiocy, lunacy, madness, rashness, recklessness, irresponsibility.
> – ANTONYMS wisdom.

– ORIGIN Old French *folie* 'madness.'

fo·ment /ˈfōˌment, fōˈment/ ▸ verb stir up trouble or violence.
– DERIVATIVES **fo·men·ta·tion** /ˌfōmenˈtāsHən, -mən-/ noun.
– ORIGIN Latin *fomentare* 'bathe part of the body with warm or medicated lotions.'

fond /fänd/ ▸ adjective **1** (**fond of**) feeling affection for someone or having a liking for something. **2** affectionate; loving: *fond memories of our childhood*. **3** (of a hope or belief) not likely to be fulfilled; foolishly optimistic.

> – SYNONYMS **1** *she was fond of dancing* **keen on,** partial to, enthusiastic about, attached to; informal into. **2 adoring,** devoted, doting, loving, caring, affectionate, indulgent. **3 unrealistic,** naive, foolish, overoptimistic, absurd, vain.
> – ANTONYMS indifferent, uncaring.

– DERIVATIVES **fond·ly** adverb **fond·ness** noun.
– ORIGIN unknown.

fon·dant /ˈfändənt/ ▸ noun **1** a thick paste made of sugar and water, used in making candy and cake icing. **2** a candy made of fondant.
– ORIGIN French, 'melting.'

fon·dle /ˈfändl/ ▸ verb stroke or caress someone lovingly or erotically.

> – SYNONYMS **caress,** stroke, pat, pet, finger, tickle, play with.

▸ noun an act of fondling.
– DERIVATIVES **fon·dler** noun.
– ORIGIN from **FOND**.

fon·due /fän'd(y)o͞o/ ▶ **noun** a dish in which small pieces of food are dipped into melted cheese, a hot sauce, or hot oil.
– ORIGIN French, 'melted.'

font[1] /fänt/ ▶ **noun** a large stone bowl in a church that holds the water used in baptism.
– ORIGIN Latin *fons* 'spring, fountain.'

font[2] (Brit. also **fount**) ▶ **noun** Printing a set of type of a particular face and size.
– ORIGIN French *fonte* 'casting.'

fon·ta·nel /ˌfäntn'el/ (Brit. **fontanelle**) ▶ **noun** a soft area between the bones of the skull in a baby or fetus, where the sutures are not yet fully formed.
– ORIGIN Old French, 'little fountain.'

fon·ti·na /fän'tēnə/ ▶ **noun** a pale yellow Italian cheese.
– ORIGIN Italian.

food /fo͞od/ ▶ **noun** any nutritious substance that people or animals eat or drink or that plants absorb to maintain life and growth.

– SYNONYMS **nourishment,** sustenance, nutriment, fare, cooking, cuisine, foodstuffs, refreshments, meals, provisions, rations; informal eats, grub, vittles, nosh; literary viands; dated victuals.

– PHRASES **food for thought** something that merits serious consideration.
– ORIGIN Old English.

WORD LINKS

alimentary *relating to food*

food chain ▶ **noun** a series of organisms each dependent on the next as a source of food.

food court ▶ **noun** an area, typically in a shopping mall, where fast food outlets and tables and chairs are located.

food·ie /'fo͞odē/ (also **foody**) ▶ **noun** (pl. **foodies**) informal a person with a strong interest in food; a gourmet.

food poi·son·ing ▶ **noun** illness caused by bacteria or other toxins in food, typically with vomiting and diarrhea.

food proc·es·sor ▶ **noun 1** an electric kitchen appliance used for chopping, mixing, or puréeing foods. **2** a company that converts agricultural products into processed foods.

food·stuff /'fo͞odˌstəf/ ▶ **noun** a substance suitable to be eaten as food.

food sup·ple·ment ▶ **noun** a substance ingested to remedy a real or perceived deficiency in a person's diet.

fool /fo͞ol/ ▶ **noun 1** a person who acts unwisely. **2** historical a jester or clown.

– SYNONYMS **1 idiot,** ass, halfwit, blockhead, dunce, simpleton; informal nincompoop, clod, dimwit, dummy, fathead, numbskull, nitwit, twit, dork, twerp, schmuck; Brit. informal berk. **2** *she made a fool of me* **laughingstock,** dupe, gull; informal stooge, sap, sucker, fall guy.
– ANTONYMS genius.

▶ **verb 1** trick or deceive someone. **2** (**fool around**) act in a joking or silly way. **3** (**fool around**) engage in casual or extramarital sex.

– SYNONYMS **1 deceive,** trick, hoax, dupe, take in, mislead, delude, hoodwink, bluff, gull; informal bamboozle, take for a ride, sucker. **2 pretend,** make believe, put on an act, act, sham, fake, joke, jest; informal kid; Brit. informal have on.

– DERIVATIVES **fool·er·y** noun.
– PHRASES **make a fool of 1** trick or deceive someone so that they look foolish. **2** (**make a fool of oneself**) behave in an incompetent or inappropriate way.
– ORIGIN Old French *fol* 'fool, foolish.'

fool·har·dy /'fo͞olˌhärdē/ ▶ **adjective** bold in a reckless way.
– DERIVATIVES **fool·har·di·ly** /-ˌhärdl-ē/ adverb **fool·har·di·ness** noun.
– ORIGIN from Old French *fol* 'foolish' + *hardi* 'emboldened.'

fool·ish /'fo͞olisн/ ▶ **adjective** lacking good sense or judgment; silly or unwise.

– SYNONYMS **stupid,** idiotic, senseless, mindless, unintelligent, thoughtless, imprudent, unwise, ill-advised, rash, reckless, foolhardy; informal **dumb,** dim, dim-witted, half-witted, moronic, thick, harebrained, daft.
– ANTONYMS sensible, wise.

– DERIVATIVES **fool·ish·ly** adverb **fool·ish·ness** noun.

WORD TOOLKIT

foolish ...	silly ...	vacuous ...
mistake	hat	rhetoric
child	superstition	expression
grin	joke	celebrity
decision	game	statement
idea	story	existence
behavior	song	TV show

fool·proof /'fo͞olˌpro͞of/ ▶ **adjective** incapable of going wrong or being misused.

– SYNONYMS **infallible,** dependable, reliable, trustworthy, certain, sure, guaranteed, safe, sound, tried and tested, watertight, airtight, flawless, perfect; informal sure-fire.

fool's gold ▶ **noun** a brassy yellow mineral that can be mistaken for gold, especially pyrite.

foot /fo͝ot/ ▶ **noun** (pl. **feet**) **1** the part of the leg below the ankle, on which a person walks. **2** the base or bottom of something vertical. **3** the end of a bed where the occupant's feet normally rest. **4** a unit of length equal to 12 inches (30.48 cm). **5** Poetry a group of syllables making up a basic unit of meter.

– SYNONYMS **1 paw,** hoof, pad. **2 bottom,** base, lowest part, end, foundation.

▶ **verb** informal **1** pay a bill. **2** (**foot it**) go somewhere on foot.
– DERIVATIVES **foot·less** adjective.
– PHRASES **feet of clay** a flaw or weakness in a person otherwise admired. **get** (or **start**) **off on the right** (or **wrong**) **foot** make a good (or bad) start. **have** (or **keep**) **one's feet on the ground** be (or remain) practical and sensible. **have** (or **get**) **a foot in the door** have (or gain) a first introduction to a profession or organization. **have one foot in the grave** humorous be very old or ill. **land** (or **fall**) **on one's feet** have good luck or success. **on** (or **by**) **foot** walking rather than using transport. **put one's best foot forward** begin with as much effort and determination as possible. **put one's foot down** informal be firm when faced with opposition or disobedience. **put one's foot in one's mouth** informal say or do something tactless or embarrassing. **under one's feet** in one's way. **under foot** on the ground.
– ORIGIN Old English.

WORD LINKS

podiatry *medical treatment of the feet*

foot·age /ˈfo͝otij/ ▶ **noun 1** a length of film made for movies or television. **2** size or length measured in feet.

foot-and-mouth dis·ease ▶ **noun** a disease caused by a virus in cattle and sheep, causing ulcers on the hoofs and around the mouth.

foot·ball /ˈfo͝otˌbôl/ ▶ **noun 1** a team game played in North America with an oval ball on a field marked out as a gridiron. **2** a large inflated oval ball used in football. **3** (in the UK) soccer. **4** (in the UK) a soccer ball.

foot·board /ˈfo͝otˌbôrd/ ▶ **noun 1** an upright panel forming the foot of a bed. **2** a board acting as a step up to a vehicle such as a train.

foot·bridge /ˈfo͝otˌbrij/ ▶ **noun** a bridge for pedestrians.

foot·er /ˈfo͝otər/ ▶ **noun 1** a person or thing of a specified number of feet in length or height: *a six-footer*. **2** a line of writing appearing at the foot of each page of a book or document.

foot·fall /ˈfo͝otˌfôl/ ▶ **noun** the sound of a footstep or footsteps.

foot·hill /ˈfo͝otˌhil/ ▶ **noun** a low hill at the base of a mountain or mountain range.

foot·hold /ˈfo͝otˌhōld/ ▶ **noun 1** a secure position from which further progress may be made: *the company has failed to gain a foothold in Japan*. **2** a place where one can place a foot to give secure support while climbing.

foot·ing /ˈfo͝otiNG/ ▶ **noun 1** (**one's footing**) a secure grip with one's feet. **2** the basis on which something is established or operates: *we are on equal footing with our competitors in the market*. **3** the foundations of a wall.

– SYNONYMS **1** *a solid financial footing* **basis,** base, foundation. **2** *on an equal footing* **standing,** status, position, condition, arrangement, basis, relationship, terms.

foot·lights /ˈfo͝otˌlīts/ ▶ **plural noun** a row of spotlights along the front of a stage at the level of the actors' feet.

foot·lock·er /ˈfo͝otˌläkər/ ▶ **noun** a small trunk or chest, typically the width of a single bed.

foot·loose /ˈfo͝otˌlo͞os/ ▶ **adjective** free to go where one likes and do as one pleases.

foot·man /ˈfo͝otmən/ ▶ **noun** (pl. **footmen**) a uniformed servant whose duties include admitting visitors.

foot·note /ˈfo͝otˌnōt/ ▶ **noun** an additional piece of information printed at the bottom of a page.

foot·path /ˈfo͝otˌpaTH/ ▶ **noun** a path for people to walk along.

foot·plate /ˈfo͝otˌplāt/ ▶ **noun** a platform for placing one or both feet on a piece of machinery or equipment.

foot·print /ˈfo͝otˌprint/ ▶ **noun** the mark left by a foot or shoe on a surface or the ground.

foot·rest /ˈfo͝otˌrest/ ▶ **noun** a support for the feet, used when sitting.

foot·sie /ˈfo͝otsē/ ▶ **noun** (in phrase **play footsie** (or **footsies**)) informal touch someone's feet lightly with one's own as a playful expression of romantic interest.

foot sol·dier ▶ **noun 1** a soldier who fights on foot. **2** a low-ranking person who nevertheless does valuable work.

foot·sore /ˈfo͝otˌsôr/ ▶ **adjective** having sore feet from much walking.

foot·step /ˈfo͝otˌstep/ ▶ **noun** a step taken in walking, especially as heard by another person.
– PHRASES **follow** (or **tread**) **in someone's footsteps** do as another person did before.

foot·stool /ˈfo͝otˌsto͞ol/ ▶ **noun** a low stool for resting the feet on when sitting.

foot-tap·ping ▶ **adjective** having a strong rhythmical musical beat.

foot·wear /ˈfo͝otˌwer/ ▶ **noun** shoes, boots, and other coverings for the feet.

foot·work /ˈfo͝otˌwərk/ ▶ **noun** the way in which one moves one's feet in dancing and sport.

fop /fäp/ ▶ **noun** a man who is excessively concerned with his clothes and appearance.
– DERIVATIVES **fop·per·y** noun **fop·pish** adjective.
– ORIGIN perhaps related to FOB[2].

for /fôr, fər/ ▶ **preposition 1** affecting or relating to. **2** in favor of. **3** on behalf of. **4** because of. **5** so as to get, have, or do. **6** in the direction of. **7** over a distance or during a period of time. **8** in exchange for or in place of. **9** in relation to the expected norm of: *she was tall for her age*. **10** indicating an occasion in a series. ▶ **conjunction** literary because; since.
– PHRASES **be in for it** informal be about to be punished or get into trouble.
– ORIGIN Old English.

fo·ra /ˈfôrə/ plural of FORUM (sense 2).

for·age /ˈfôrij, ˈfär-/ ▶ **verb 1** search for food. **2** search for something: *she foraged in her pocket for a tissue*. ▶ **noun** food for horses and cattle.
– DERIVATIVES **for·ag·er** noun.
– ORIGIN Old French *fourrager*.

fo·ra·men /fəˈrāmən/ ▶ **noun** (pl. **foramina** /-ˈramənə/) Anatomy an opening, hole, or passage, especially in a bone.
– ORIGIN Latin.

for·ay /ˈfôrˌā, ˈfärˌā/ ▶ **noun 1** a sudden attack or raid into enemy territory. **2** a spirited attempt to become involved in a new activity: *this is the firm's first foray into cookbook publishing*. ▶ **verb** attempt a new activity.
– DERIVATIVES **for·ay·er** noun.
– ORIGIN from Old French *forrier* 'forager.'

for·bade /fərˈbad, fôr-, -ˈbād/ (also **forbad** /fərˈbad, fôr-/) past of FORBID.

for·bear[1] /fərˈber, fôr-/ ▶ **verb** (past **forbore** /fərˈbôr, fôr-/; past part. **forborne** /fərˈbôrn, fôr-/) stop oneself from doing something.
– ORIGIN Old English.

USAGE

Do not confuse **forbear** with **forebear**. **Forbear** means 'stop oneself from doing something' (*he doesn't forbear to write about the bad times*), while **forebear** (which is also sometimes spelled **forbear**) means 'an ancestor' (*our Stone Age forebears*).

for·bear[2] ▶ **noun** variant spelling of FOREBEAR.

for·bear·ance /fôrˈberəns, fər-/ ▶ **noun** the quality of being patient and tolerant toward others.

CHOOSE THE RIGHT WORD

See ABSTINENCE.

for·bear·ing /fôr'beriNG, fər-/ ▸ **adjective** patient and restrained.

for·bid /fər'bid, fôr-/ ▸ **verb** (**forbids, forbidding, forbade** /-'bad, -'bād/ or **forbad** /-'bad/; past part. **forbidden**) **1** refuse to allow something. **2** order someone not to do something.

– SYNONYMS **prohibit,** ban, outlaw, make illegal, veto, proscribe, embargo, bar, debar, rule out.
– ANTONYMS permit.

– ORIGIN Old English.

CHOOSE THE RIGHT WORD

See **PROHIBIT**.

for·bid·den /fər'bidn, fôr-/ ▸ **adjective** not allowed; banned.

– SYNONYMS **prohibited,** banned, verboten, taboo, illegal, illicit, against the law.

– PHRASES **forbidden fruit** a thing that is desired all the more because it is not allowed. [with reference to the Book of Genesis.]

for·bid·ding /fər'bidiNG, fôr-/ ▸ **adjective** appearing unfriendly or threatening.

– SYNONYMS **threatening,** ominous, menacing, sinister, daunting, off-putting.

– DERIVATIVES **for·bid·ding·ly** adverb.

for·bore /fər'bôr, fôr-/ past of **FORBEAR**[1].

for·borne /fər'bôrn, fôr-/ past participle of **FORBEAR**[1].

force /fôrs/ ▸ **noun 1** physical strength or energy accompanying action or movement: *we had to lean against the force of the wind.* **2** strong pressure on someone to do something backed by the use or threat of violence. **3** influence or power: *the force of public opinion.* **4** a person or thing having power or influence. **5** an organized group of military personnel, police, or workers. **6** Physics an influence that changes the motion of a body or produces motion or stress in a stationary body.

– SYNONYMS **1 strength,** power, energy, might, effort. **2 coercion,** compulsion, constraint, duress, pressure, oppression, harassment, intimidation, violence; informal arm-twisting. **3 power,** potency, weight, effectiveness, persuasiveness, validity, strength, significance, influence, authority; informal punch. **4 body,** group, outfit, party, team, detachment, unit, squad.

▸ **verb 1** make someone do something against their will. **2** make a way through or into something by force. **3** push into a specified position using force: *thieves tried to force open the cash register.* **4** achieve something by effort. **5** (**force something on**) impose something on: *the new technology is being forced on retailers by the banks.* **6** make a plant develop or mature more quickly than normal.

– SYNONYMS **1 compel,** coerce, make, constrain, oblige, impel, drive, pressure, pressurize, press-gang, bully; informal lean on, twist someone's arm. **2** *water was forced through a hole* **propel,** push, thrust, shove, drive, press, pump. **3 break open,** knock/smash/break down, kick in.

– DERIVATIVES **forc·er** noun.
– PHRASES **force someone's hand** make someone do something. **in force 1** in great strength or numbers. **2** (**in/into force**) in or into effect.
– ORIGIN Old French.

forced /fôrst/ ▸ **adjective 1** obtained or imposed by coercion or physical power. **2** (of a gesture or expression) affected or unnatural.

– SYNONYMS **1** *forced labor* **enforced,** compulsory, obligatory, mandatory, involuntary, imposed, required. **2** *a forced smile* **strained,** unnatural, artificial, false, feigned, simulated, contrived, labored, affected, hollow; informal phony, pretend, put on.
– ANTONYMS voluntary, natural.

forced land·ing ▸ **noun** the abrupt landing of an aircraft in an emergency.

force-feed ▸ **verb** force someone to eat food.

force field ▸ **noun 1** another term for **FIELD** (sense 4 of the noun): *a classical molecular mechanical force field.* **2** (chiefly in science fiction and paranormal literature) an area of space in which a particular exotic force exerts its effects.

force·ful /'fôrsfəl/ ▸ **adjective** powerful, assertive, or vigorous.

– SYNONYMS **1 dynamic,** energetic, assertive, authoritative, vigorous, powerful, strong, pushy; informal in-your-face, go-ahead, feisty. **2 convincing,** cogent, compelling, strong, powerful, persuasive, coherent.
– ANTONYMS weak.

– DERIVATIVES **force·ful·ly** adverb **force·ful·ness** noun.

force ma·jeure /ˌfôrs mä'ZHər/ ▸ **noun 1** Law unforeseeable circumstances that prevent someone from fulfilling a contract. **2** superior strength.
– ORIGIN French.

force·meat /'fôrsˌmēt/ ▸ **noun** a mixture of chopped and seasoned meat or vegetables used as a stuffing or garnish.

for·ceps /'fôrsəps, -ˌseps/ ▸ **plural noun 1** a pair of pincers used in surgery or in a laboratory. **2** a large surgical instrument with broad blades, used to assist in the delivery of a baby.
– ORIGIN Latin, 'tongs, pincers.'

for·ci·ble /'fôrsəbəl/ ▸ **adjective** done by force.
– DERIVATIVES **for·ci·bly** adverb.

ford /fôrd/ ▸ **noun** a shallow place in a river or stream where it can be crossed. ▸ **verb** cross a river or stream at a ford.
– DERIVATIVES **ford·a·ble** adjective.
– ORIGIN Old English.

fore /fôr/ ▸ **adjective** situated or placed in front. ▸ **noun** the front part of something, especially a ship. ▸ **exclamation** called out as a warning to people in the path of a golf ball.
– PHRASES **to the fore** in or to a prominent or leading position.
– ORIGIN Old English.

fore- ▸ **combining form 1** before; in advance: *foreshorten.* **2** in or at the front of: *forecourt.*

fore and aft ▸ **adjective 1** backward and forward. **2** (of a ship's sail or rigging) set lengthwise, not on the yards.

fore·arm[1] /'fôrˌärm/ ▸ **noun** the part of a person's arm from the elbow to the wrist.

fore·arm[2] /fôr'ärm/ ▸ **verb** (**be forearmed**) be prepared in advance for danger or attack.

fore·bear /'fôrˌber/ (also **forbear**) ▸ **noun** an ancestor.
– ORIGIN from **FORE** + former *beer* 'someone who exists.'

USAGE

Forebear (meaning 'an ancestor') can also be spelled **forbear** and is often confused with the verb **forbear**. See the note at **FORBEAR**[1].

fore·bode /fôr'bōd/ ▶ **verb** old use act as an advance warning of something bad.

– SYNONYMS **presage,** augur, portend, herald, warn of, forewarn of, foreshadow, be an omen of, indicate, signify, signal, promise, threaten, spell, denote.

fore·bod·ing /fôr'bōdiNG/ ▶ **noun** a feeling that something bad is going to happen. ▶ **adjective** suggesting that something bad is going to happen.

fore·brain /'fôr,brān/ ▶ **noun** the front part of the brain.

fore·cast /'fôr,kast/ ▶ **verb** (past and past part. **forecast** or **forecasted**) predict or estimate a future event or trend.

– SYNONYMS **predict,** prophesy, prognosticate, foretell, foresee.

▶ **noun** a prediction or estimate, especially of the weather or a financial trend.

– SYNONYMS **prediction,** prophecy, prognostication, prognosis.

– DERIVATIVES **fore·cast·er** noun.

fore·cas·tle /'fōksəl, 'fôr,kasəl/ (also **fo'c's'le**) ▶ **noun** the front part of a ship below the deck.

fore·close /fôr'klōz/ ▶ **verb 1** take possession of a mortgaged property when a person fails to keep up with their mortgage payments. **2** rule out or prevent a course of action.

– DERIVATIVES **fore·clo·sure** /fôr'klōZHər/ noun.

– ORIGIN Old French *forclore* 'shut out.'

fore·court /'fôr,kôrt/ ▶ **noun 1** an open area in front of a large building. **2** the part of a tennis court between the service line and the net.

fore·doom /fôr'do͞om/ ▶ **verb** (**be foredoomed**) literary be condemned beforehand to certain failure.

fore·fa·ther /'fôr,fäT͟Hər/ (or **foremother** /'fôr,məT͟Hər/) ▶ **noun** an ancestor.

fore·fin·ger /'fôr,fiNGgər/ ▶ **noun** the finger next to the thumb.

fore·foot /'fôr,fo͝ot/ ▶ **noun** (pl. **forefeet**) each of the two front feet of a four-footed animal.

fore·front /'fôr,frənt/ ▶ **noun** the leading position or place: *he has always been at the forefront of research.*

fore·gath·er /fôr'gaT͟Hər/ (also **forgather**) ▶ **verb** formal assemble or gather together.

fore·go[1] ▶ **verb** variant spelling of **FORGO**.

fore·go[2] /fôr'gō/ ▶ **verb** (**foregoes, foregoing, forewent** /fôr'went/; past part. **foregone** /'fôr,gôn/) old use come before someone or something in place or time.

fore·go·ing /fôr'gōiNG/ ▶ **adjective** previously mentioned.

fore·gone /'fôr,gôn/ past participle of **FOREGO**[1], **FOREGO**[2].

– PHRASES **a foregone conclusion** an easily predictable result.

fore·ground /'fôr,ground/ ▶ **noun 1** the part of a view or picture nearest to the observer. **2** the most prominent or important position. ▶ **verb** make something the most important feature.

fore·hand /'fôr,hand/ ▶ **noun** (in tennis and other racket sports) a stroke played with the palm of the hand facing in the direction of the stroke.

fore·head /'fôrəd, 'fôr,hed/ ▶ **noun** the part of the face above the eyebrows.

for·eign /'fôrən, 'fär-/ ▶ **adjective 1** relating to or typical of a country or language other than one's own. **2** dealing with or involving other countries. **3** coming or introduced from outside: *the difficulty of introducing foreign genes into plants.* **4** (**foreign to**) not familiar to or typical of: *aisles of food and cosmetics entirely foreign to the average consumer.*

– SYNONYMS **alien,** overseas, nonnative, imported, distant, external, far-off, exotic, strange, unknown, unfamiliar.
– ANTONYMS domestic, native.

– DERIVATIVES **for·eign·ness** noun.
– ORIGIN Old French *forein, forain.*

for·eign bod·y ▶ **noun** an unwanted object that has entered the body from outside.

for·eign·er /'fôrənər, 'fär-/ ▶ **noun 1** a person from a foreign country. **2** informal a stranger or outsider.

– SYNONYMS **alien,** nonnative, stranger, outsider, immigrant, landed immigrant, settler, newcomer, incomer.
– ANTONYMS native, national.

WORD LINKS

xenophobia *irrational dislike or fear of foreigners*

for·eign ex·change ▶ **noun** the currency of other countries.

For·eign Le·gion ▶ **noun** a military formation of the French army composed chiefly of non-Frenchmen.

for·eign min·is·ter ▶ **noun** a government minister in charge of relations with foreign countries.

fore·knowl·edge /fôr'näləj/ ▶ **noun** awareness of something before it happens or exists.

fore·land /'fôrlənd/ ▶ **noun 1** an area of land in front of a particular feature. **2** a piece of land that juts out into the sea; a promontory.

fore·leg /'fôr,leg/ ▶ **noun** either of the front legs of a four-footed animal.

fore·limb /'fôr,lim/ ▶ **noun** either of the front limbs of an animal.

fore·lock /'fôr,läk/ ▶ **noun** a lock of hair growing just above the forehead.

fore·man /'fôrmən/ (or **forewoman** /'fôr,wo͝omən/) ▶ **noun** (pl. **foremen** or **forewomen**) **1** a worker who supervises other workers. **2** (in a court of law) a leader of a jury, who speaks on its behalf.

fore·mast /'fôr,mast, -məst/ ▶ **noun** the mast of a ship nearest the bow.

fore·most /'fôr,mōst/ ▶ **adjective** highest in rank, importance, or position: *one of the foremost art collectors of his day.*

– SYNONYMS **leading,** principal, premier, prime, top, greatest, best, supreme, preeminent, ranking, outstanding, most important, most notable; informal number-one.
– ANTONYMS minor.

▶ **adverb** in the first place.

fore·name /ˈfôrˌnām/ ▸ **noun** another term for **FIRST NAME**.

fore·noon /ˈfôrˌno͞on/ ▸ **noun** the morning.

fo·ren·sic /fəˈrenzik, -sik/ ▸ **adjective** **1** relating to the use of scientific methods to investigate crime. **2** relating to courts of law. ▸ **noun** (**forensics**) forensic tests or techniques.
– DERIVATIVES **fo·ren·si·cal·ly** adverb.
– ORIGIN Latin *forensis* 'in open court, public.'

fo·ren·sic med·i·cine ▸ **noun** the application of medical knowledge to the investigation of crime, particularly in establishing the causes of injury or death.

fore·or·dain /ˌfôrôrˈdān/ ▸ **verb** (of God or fate) appoint or determine something beforehand.

fore·paw /ˈfôrˌpô/ ▸ **noun** either of the front paws of a quadruped.

fore·play /ˈfôrˌplā/ ▸ **noun** sexual activity that precedes intercourse.

fore·run·ner /ˈfôrˌrənər/ ▸ **noun** a person or thing that comes before and influences someone or something else.

fore·sail /ˈfôrˌsāl, -səl/ ▸ **noun** the main sail on a foremast.

fore·see /fôrˈsē/ ▸ **verb** (**foresees, foreseeing, foresaw** /fôrˈsô/; past part. **foreseen**) be aware of something beforehand; predict.

– SYNONYMS **anticipate,** expect, envisage, predict, forecast, foretell, prophesy.

– DERIVATIVES **fore·see·a·ble** adjective **fore·see·a·bly** adverb.

fore·shad·ow /fôrˈshadō/ ▸ **verb** be a warning or indication of: *changes have begun that could foreshadow a new workplace structure*.

fore·shore /ˈfôrˌshôr/ ▸ **noun** the part of a shore between high- and low-water marks, or between the water and cultivated or developed land.

fore·short·en /fôrˈshôrtn/ ▸ **verb** **1** depict an object or view as being closer or shallower than in reality, so as to convey an effect of perspective. **2** reduce something in time or scale.

fore·sight /ˈfôrˌsīt/ ▸ **noun** **1** the ability to predict and prepare for future events and needs. **2** the front sight of a gun.

– SYNONYMS **forethought,** planning, farsightedness, vision, anticipation, prudence, care, caution.
– ANTONYMS hindsight.

– DERIVATIVES **fore·sight·ed** /ˈfôrˌsītid/ adjective.

fore·skin /ˈfôrˌskin/ ▸ **noun** the retractable roll of skin covering the end of the penis.

for·est /ˈfôrəst, ˈfär-/ ▸ **noun** **1** a large area covered with trees and undergrowth. **2** a mass of vertical or tangled objects: *a forest of pillars*. ▸ **verb** (usu. as adj. **forested**) plant land with trees.
– DERIVATIVES **for·est·a·tion** /ˌfôrəˈstāshən, ˌfär-/ noun.
– ORIGIN from Latin *forestis silva* 'outside wood.'

fore·stall /fôrˈstôl/ ▸ **verb** **1** prevent or delay something anticipated by taking action before it happens: *he forestalled the Board's plans by obtaining an injunction*. **2** prevent someone from doing something by anticipating what they are going to do.
– ORIGIN from Old English, 'an ambush.'

for·est·er /ˈfôrəstər/ ▸ **noun** a person in charge of a forest or skilled in forestry.

for·est·ry /ˈfôrəstrē, ˈfär-/ ▸ **noun** the science or practice of planting, managing, and caring for forests.

fore·taste /ˈfôrˌtāst/ ▸ **noun** a sample of something that is to come: *it had been an exceptionally warm day, a foretaste of heatwaves to come*.

fore·tell /fôrˈtel/ ▸ **verb** (past and past part. **foretold** /fôrˈtōld/) predict the future.

– SYNONYMS **predict,** forecast, prophesy, foresee, anticipate, envisage, warn of.

fore·thought /ˈfôrˌthôt/ ▸ **noun** careful consideration of what will be necessary or may happen in the future.

fore·to·ken /ˈfôrˌtōkən/ ▸ **verb** literary be a sign of a future event.

fore·told /fôrˈtōld/ past and past participle of **FORETELL**.

for·ev·er /fəˈrevər, fô-/ ▸ **adverb** **1** (also **for ever**) for all future time. **2** a very long time. **3** continually; all the time.

– SYNONYMS **1 for always,** evermore, for ever and ever, for good, for all time, until the end of time, eternally, forevermore; informal until the cows come home. **2 always,** continually, constantly, perpetually, incessantly, endlessly, persistently, repeatedly, regularly; informal 24-7.

fore·warn /fôrˈwôrn/ ▸ **verb** warn someone of a possible future danger or problem.

fore·went /fôrˈwent/ past of **FOREGO**[1], **FOREGO**[2].

fore·wing /ˈfôrˌwiNG/ ▸ **noun** either of the two front wings of a four-winged insect.

fore·word /ˈfôrˌwərd/ ▸ **noun** a short introduction to a book.

forex /ˈfôˌreks/ ▸ **abbreviation** foreign exchange.

for·feit /ˈfôrfit/ ▸ **verb** (**forfeits, forfeiting, forfeited**) **1** lose or be deprived of property or a right as a penalty for a fault or mistake. **2** lose or give up as a necessary result: *she had forfeited her studies after marriage*.

– SYNONYMS **lose,** be deprived of, surrender, relinquish, sacrifice, give up, renounce, forgo.

▸ **noun** **1** a penalty for a fault or mistake. **2** Law a right, privilege, or item of property lost as a result of wrongdoing.

– SYNONYMS **penalty,** sanction, punishment, penance, fine, confiscation, loss, forfeiture, surrender.

▸ **adjective** lost as a penalty for wrongdoing.
– DERIVATIVES **for·fei·ture** /ˈfôrfəCHər/ noun.
– ORIGIN Old French *forfaire* 'transgress.'

for·fend /fôrˈfend/ ▸ **verb** (in phrase **heaven forfend**) used to express dismay or horror at the thought of something happening: *Invite him back? Heaven forfend!*

for·gath·er /fôrˈgaTHər/ ▸ **verb** variant spelling of **FOREGATHER**.

for·gave /fərˈgāv/ past of **FORGIVE**.

forge[1] /fôrj/ ▸ **verb** **1** make or shape a metal object by heating and hammering the metal. **2** create something strong or successful: *the two women forged a close bond*. **3** produce a fraudulent copy or imitation of a banknote, work of art, signature, etc.

– SYNONYMS **1 hammer out,** beat out, fashion. **2 build,** construct, form, create, establish, set up. **3 fake,** falsify, counterfeit, copy, imitate, pirate.

▸ **noun** **1** a blacksmith's workshop. **2** a furnace or hearth for melting or refining metal.

– DERIVATIVES **forg·er** noun.
– ORIGIN Old French *forger*.

forge² ▶ **verb 1** move forward gradually or steadily. **2** (**forge ahead**) make progress.
– ORIGIN perhaps from a pronunciation of **FORCE**.

for·ger·y /ˈfôrjərē/ ▶ **noun** (pl. **forgeries**) **1** the action of forging a banknote, work of art, etc. **2** a forged or copied item.

– SYNONYMS **fake,** counterfeit, fraud, imitation, replica, copy, pirate copy; informal phony.

for·get /fərˈget/ ▶ **verb** (**forgets, forgetting, forgot** /fərˈgät/; past part. **forgotten** /fərˈgätn/ or **forgot**) **1** fail to remember something. **2** accidentally fail to do something. **3** deliberately cease to think of someone or something. **4** (**forget oneself**) fail to behave in an appropriate way.

– SYNONYMS **1 fail to remember,** be unable to remember. **2 leave behind,** fail to take/bring, leave home without. **3** *I forgot to close the door* **neglect,** fail, omit.
– ANTONYMS remember.

– DERIVATIVES **for·get·ta·ble** adjective.
– ORIGIN Old English.

for·get·ful /fərˈgetfəl/ ▶ **adjective** apt or likely not to remember.

– SYNONYMS **1 absentminded,** amnesiac, vague, scatterbrained, disorganized, dreamy, abstracted, with a mind/memory like a sieve. **2** *forgetful of the time* **heedless,** careless, inattentive to, negligent about, oblivious to, unconcerned about, indifferent to.

– DERIVATIVES **for·get·ful·ly** adverb **for·get·ful·ness** noun.

for·get-me-not ▶ **noun** a low-growing plant with bright blue flowers.
– ORIGIN translating Old French *ne m'oubliez mye*; said to ensure that the wearer of the flower would never be forgotten by a lover.

for·give /fərˈgiv/ ▶ **verb** (past **forgave** /fərˈgāv/; past part. **forgiven**) **1** stop feeling angry or resentful toward someone for an offense or mistake. **2** no longer feel angry about or wish to punish an offense, flaw, or mistake.

– SYNONYMS **1 pardon,** excuse, exonerate, absolve. **2 excuse,** overlook, disregard, ignore, make allowances for, turn a blind eye to, condone, indulge, tolerate.
– ANTONYMS blame, resent.

– DERIVATIVES **for·giv·a·ble** adjective.
– ORIGIN Old English.

CHOOSE THE RIGHT WORD

See **ABSOLVE**.

for·give·ness /fərˈgivnəs/ ▶ **noun** the action of forgiving or the state of being forgiven.

– SYNONYMS **pardon,** absolution, exoneration, indulgence, clemency, mercy, reprieve, amnesty.
– ANTONYMS punishment.

for·giv·ing /fərˈgiviNG/ ▶ **adjective 1** ready and willing to forgive: *Taylor was in a forgiving mood.* **2** tolerant: *these flooring planks are more forgiving of heavy traffic than real wood.*

– SYNONYMS **merciful,** lenient, compassionate, magnanimous, humane, softhearted, forbearing, tolerant, indulgent, understanding.
– ANTONYMS merciless, vindictive.

for·go /fôrˈgō/ (also **forego**) ▶ **verb** (**forgoes, forgoing, forwent** /fôrˈwent/; past part. **forgone** /ˈfôrˌgôn/) go without something desirable.

– SYNONYMS **do without,** go without, give up, waive, renounce, surrender, relinquish, part with, drop, sacrifice, abstain from, refrain from, eschew, cut out; informal swear off; formal forswear, abjure.

– ORIGIN Old English.

for·got /fərˈgät/ past and past participle of **FORGET**.

for·got·ten /fərˈgätn/ past participle of **FORGET**.

for·int /ˈfôrˌint/ ▶ **noun** the basic unit of money of Hungary.
– ORIGIN Hungarian.

fork /fôrk/ ▶ **noun 1** a small implement with two or more prongs used for lifting or holding food. **2** a farm or garden tool with prongs, used for digging or lifting. **3** each of a pair of supports in which a bicycle or motorcycle wheel revolves. **4** the point where a road, path, or river divides into two parts. **5** either of the parts where a road, path, or river divides. ▶ **verb 1** divide into two parts. **2** take one route or the other at a fork. **3** dig or lift something with a fork. **4** (**fork something out/over/up**) informal pay money for something, especially reluctantly.

– SYNONYMS **split,** branch, divide, separate, part, diverge, go in different directions, bifurcate.

– ORIGIN Latin *furca* 'pitchfork, forked stick.'

forked /fôrkt/ ▶ **adjective** having a divided or pronged end.

fork·lift /ˈfôrkˌlift/ ▶ **noun** (also **forklift truck**) a vehicle with a pronged device in front for lifting and carrying heavy loads.

for·lorn /fərˈlôrn, fôr-/ ▶ **adjective 1** pitifully sad and lonely. **2** unlikely to succeed or be fulfilled: *a forlorn attempt to escape.*

– SYNONYMS **1 unhappy,** sad, miserable, sorrowful, dejected, despondent, disconsolate, wretched, down, downcast, dispirited, downhearted, crestfallen, depressed, melancholy, gloomy, glum, mournful, despairing, doleful, woebegone; informal blue, down in the mouth, down in the dumps, fed up. **2 hopeless,** useless, futile, pointless, purposeless, vain, unavailing.
– ANTONYMS happy.

– DERIVATIVES **for·lorn·ly** adverb **for·lorn·ness** noun.
– PHRASES **forlorn hope** a persistent hope that is unlikely to be fulfilled. [from Dutch *verloren hoop* 'lost troop', originally referring to a band of soldiers picked to begin an attack, many of whom would not survive.]
– ORIGIN Old English, 'depraved, lost.'

WORD TOOLKIT

See **MELANCHOLY**.

form /fôrm/ ▶ **noun 1** the visible shape or arrangement of something. **2** a particular way in which a thing exists or appears: *a press release in the form of an eight-page booklet.* **3** a type of something. **4** a printed document with blank spaces for information to be inserted. **5** the state of an athlete with regard to their current standard of play: *illness has affected her form.* **6** details of previous performances by a racehorse or greyhound. **7** a person's mood and state of health: *she was in good form.* **8** the usual or correct method or procedure.

– SYNONYMS **1 shape,** configuration, formation, structure, construction, arrangement, appearance, exterior, outline, format, layout, design. **2 body,** shape, figure, frame, physique, anatomy; informal vital statistics. **3 manifestation,** appearance, embodiment, incarnation, semblance, shape, guise. **4 kind,** sort, type, class, category, variety, genre, brand, style. **5 questionnaire,** document, coupon, sheet, slip. **6 condition,** fitness, fettle, shape, health.

▶ **verb 1** bring together parts to create something. **2** go to make up: *the ideas that form the basis of the book.* **3** establish or develop something. **4** make or be made into a certain form: *form the dough into balls.*

– SYNONYMS **1 make,** construct, build, manufacture, fabricate, assemble, put together, create, fashion, shape. **2 formulate,** devise, conceive, work out, think up, lay, draw up, put together, produce, fashion, concoct, forge, hatch; informal dream up. **3 set up,** establish, found, launch, create, institute, start, inaugurate. **4 materialize,** come into being/existence, emerge, develop, take shape, gather, accumulate, collect, amass. **5 arrange,** draw up, line up, assemble, organize, sort, order. **6 comprise,** make, make up, constitute, compose, add up to.
– ANTONYMS dissolve, disappear.

– DERIVATIVES **form·a·ble** adjective **form·less** adjective.
– PHRASES **in form** playing or performing well. **off** (or **out of**) **form** not playing or performing well.
– ORIGIN Latin *forma* 'a mold or form.'

for·mal /'fôrməl/ ▶ **adjective 1** suitable for or referring to an official or important occasion: *formal evening wear.* **2** officially recognized: *a formal complaint.* **3** having a recognized form, structure, or set of rules: *he had little formal education.* **4** (of language) characterized by more elaborate grammatical structures and conservative vocabulary. **5** concerned with outward form rather than content.

– SYNONYMS **1 ceremonial,** ritualistic, ritual, official, conventional, traditional, stately, solemn, ceremonious. **2 aloof,** reserved, remote, detached, unapproachable, stiff, stuffy, correct, proper; informal standoffish. **3 official,** legal, authorized, approved, certified, endorsed, sanctioned, licensed, recognized.
– ANTONYMS informal, casual, unofficial.

– DERIVATIVES **for·mal·ly** adverb.

form·al·de·hyde /fôr'maldəˌhīd, fər-/ ▶ **noun** a colorless pungent gas, used in solution as a preservative for biological specimens.
– ORIGIN blend of **FORMIC ACID** and **ALDEHYDE**.

for·ma·lin /'fôrməlin/ ▶ **noun** a solution of formaldehyde in water.

for·mal·ism /'fôrməˌlizəm/ ▶ **noun** (in art, music, literature, etc.) concern or excessive concern with rules and outward form rather than the content of something.
– DERIVATIVES **for·mal·ist** noun.

for·mal·i·ty /fôr'malətē/ ▶ **noun** (pl. **formalities**) **1** a thing done to follow convention or rules: *a statutory declaration that all the formalities have been complied with.* **2** correct and formal behavior. **3** (**a formality**) a thing done or occurring as a matter of course.

– SYNONYMS **1 ceremony,** ritual, protocol, decorum, solemnity. **2 aloofness,** reserve, remoteness, detachment, unapproachability, stiffness, stuffiness, correctness; informal standoffishness.
– ANTONYMS informality.

for·mal·ize /'fôrməˌlīz/ ▶ **verb 1** give something legal or official status. **2** give something a definite form or shape.
– DERIVATIVES **for·mal·i·za·tion** /ˌfôrməli'zāsʜən/ noun.

for·mat /'fôrˌmat/ ▶ **noun 1** the way in which something is arranged or presented. **2** the shape, size, and presentation of a book, document, etc. **3** the medium in which a sound recording is made available: *LP and CD formats.* **4** Computing a defined structure for the processing, storage, or display of data.

– SYNONYMS **design,** style, appearance, look, form, shape, size, arrangement, plan, structure, scheme, composition, configuration.

▶ **verb** (**formats, formatting, formatted**) (especially in computing) arrange or put something into a particular format.
– ORIGIN from Latin *formatus liber* 'shaped book.'

for·ma·tion /fôr'māsʜən/ ▶ **noun 1** the action of forming or the process of being formed. **2** a structure or arrangement: *strange rock formations.* **3** a formal arrangement of aircraft in flight or troops.

– SYNONYMS **1** *the formation of the island* **emergence,** genesis, development, evolution, shaping, origin. **2** *the formation of a new government* **establishment,** setting up, institution, foundation, creation, inauguration. **3 configuration,** arrangement, grouping, pattern, array, alignment, order.
– ANTONYMS destruction, dissolution.

– DERIVATIVES **for·ma·tion·al** adjective.

for·ma·tive /'fôrmətiv/ ▶ **adjective** having an important influence on the development of someone or something: *his formative years in Victorian Scotland.*
– DERIVATIVES **for·ma·tive·ly** adverb.

form·er[1] /'fôrmər/ ▶ **adjective 1** having previously been: *her former husband.* **2** relating to or occurring in the past. **3** (**the former**) referring to the first of two things mentioned.

– SYNONYMS **1 one-time,** erstwhile, sometime, ex-, previous, preceding, earlier, prior, last; formal quondam. **2 earlier,** old, past, bygone, olden, long ago, gone by, long past, of old. **3 first-mentioned,** first.
– ANTONYMS future, current, latter.

– ORIGIN Old English.

form·er[2] ▶ **noun** a person or thing that forms something.

for·mer·ly /'fôrmərlē/ ▶ **adverb** in the past.

– SYNONYMS **previously,** earlier, before, until now/then, once, once upon a time, at one time, in the past.

For·mi·ca /fôr'mīkə, fər-/ ▶ **noun** trademark a hard plastic laminate used for countertops, cupboard doors, etc.
– ORIGIN unknown.

for·mic ac·id /'fôrmik/ ▶ **noun** an acid present in the fluid produced by some ants.
– ORIGIN from Latin *formica* 'ant.'

for·mi·da·ble /'fôrmədəbəl, fôr'midəbəl, fər'mid-/ ▶ **adjective** inspiring fear or respect through being impressively large, powerful, or capable.

– SYNONYMS **1 intimidating,** daunting, indomitable, forbidding, alarming, frightening, awesome, fearsome; humorous redoubtable. **2 accomplished,** masterly, virtuoso, expert, impressive, powerful, terrific, superb; informal tremendous, nifty, crack, ace, wizard, magic, mean, wicked, deadly.

– DERIVATIVES **for·mi·da·bly** adverb.
– ORIGIN Latin *formidabilis*.

WORD TOOLKIT

formidable ...	fearsome ...	daunting ...
opponent	creature	task
competitor	battle	challenge
barrier	beast	prospect
partnership	temper	odds
adversary	warrior	proposition
candidate	attack	mission
threat	claws	circumstances
intellect	predator	schedule
talent	teeth	responsibility

form let·ter ▶ **noun** a standardized letter to deal with frequently occurring matters.

for·mu·la /ˈfôrmyələ/ ▶ **noun** (pl. **formulae** /-ˌlē, -ˌlī/ (in senses 1 and 2) or **formulas**) **1** a mathematical relationship or rule expressed in symbols. **2** (also **chemical formula**) a set of chemical symbols showing the elements present in a compound and their relative proportions. **3** a method for achieving something: *at ZDC, we stick to our proven formula for success.* **4** a fixed form of words used in a particular situation. **5** a list of ingredients with which something is made. **6** a baby's liquid food preparation based on cow's milk or soy protein. **7** a classification of race car: *Formula One.*

– SYNONYMS **1 form of words,** set expression, rubric, phrase, saying. **2 recipe,** prescription, blueprint, plan, policy, method, procedure.

– ORIGIN Latin, 'small shape or mold.'

for·mu·la·ic /ˌfôrmyəˈlāik/ ▶ **adjective 1** made up of or containing a set form of words. **2** following a rule or style too closely: *the lyrics are dry and formulaic.*
– DERIVATIVES **for·mu·la·i·cal·ly** adverb.

for·mu·lar·y /ˈfôrmyəˌlerē/ ▶ **noun** (pl. **formularies**) **1** an official list giving details of prescribable medicines. **2** a collection of set forms for use in religious ceremonies.
– ORIGIN French *formulaire* 'book of formulae.'

for·mu·late /ˈfôrmyəˌlāt/ ▶ **verb 1** create or prepare something methodically. **2** express an idea in a concise or systematic way.

– SYNONYMS **1 devise,** conceive, work out, think up, lay, draw up, form, concoct, contrive, forge, hatch, prepare, develop. **2 express,** phrase, word, define, specify, put into words, frame, couch, put, articulate, say.

– DERIVATIVES **for·mu·la·tor** noun.

for·mu·la·tion /ˌfôrmyəˈlāsʜən/ ▶ **noun 1** the action of creating or preparing something. **2** a mixture prepared according to a formula.

for·ni·cate /ˈfôrniˌkāt/ ▶ **verb** formal or humorous have sexual intercourse with someone one is not married to.
– DERIVATIVES **for·ni·ca·tion** /ˌfôrniˈkāsʜən/ noun **for·ni·ca·tor** noun.
– ORIGIN from Latin *fornix* 'vaulted chamber,' later 'brothel.'

for·sake /fərˈsāk, fôr-/ ▶ **verb** (past **forsook** /-ˈso͝ok/; past part. **forsaken**) chiefly literary **1** abandon someone. **2** give up something valued or pleasant.
– ORIGIN Old English.

for·sooth /fərˈso͞otʜ/ ▶ **adverb** old use or humorous indeed.

for·swear /fôrˈswe(ə)r/ ▶ **verb** (past **forswore** /fôrˈswôr/; past part. **forsworn** /fôrˈswôrn/) formal agree to give up or do without something.

for·syth·i·a /fərˈsitʜēə/ ▶ **noun** a shrub whose bright yellow flowers appear in early spring before its leaves.
– ORIGIN named after the Scottish botanist William *Forsyth.*

fort /fôrt/ ▶ **noun** a building constructed to defend a place against attack.

– SYNONYMS **fortress,** castle, citadel, bunker, stronghold, fortification, bastion.

– PHRASES **hold (down) the fort** take responsibility for something while someone is away.
– ORIGIN from Latin *fortis* 'strong.'

for·te[1] /ˈfôrˌtā, fôrt/ ▶ **noun** a thing at which someone excels: *photo sessions are not his forte.*

– SYNONYMS **strength,** strong point, specialty, strong suit, talent, skill, gift; informal thing.

– ORIGIN French, 'strong.'

for·te[2] ▶ **adverb & adjective** Music loud or loudly.
– ORIGIN Italian, 'strong, loud.'

for·te·pi·an·o /ˌfôrtāpēˈanō, -pēˈänō/ ▶ **noun** (pl. **fortepianos**) a piano, especially one of the kind made in the 18th and early 19th centuries.
– ORIGIN from **FORTE**[2] + **PIANO**[2].

forth /fôrtʜ/ ▶ **adverb** formal or literary **1** out and away from a starting point. **2** so as to be revealed. **3** onward in time.
– PHRASES **and so forth** and so on.
– ORIGIN Old English.

forth·com·ing /fôrtʜˈkəmiɴɢ, ˈfôrtʜˌkəmiɴɢ/ ▶ **adjective 1** about to happen or appear. **2** ready or made available when required: *help was not forthcoming.* **3** willing to reveal information.

– SYNONYMS **1 coming,** upcoming, approaching, imminent, impending, future. **2 communicative,** talkative, chatty, informative, expansive, expressive, frank, open, candid.
– ANTONYMS past, current, reticent.

forth·right /ˈfôrtʜˌrīt/ ▶ **adjective** direct and outspoken.

– SYNONYMS **frank,** direct, straightforward, honest, candid, open, sincere, outspoken, straight, blunt, plain-spoken, no-nonsense, bluff, matter-of-fact, to the point; informal upfront.
– ANTONYMS secretive, evasive.

– DERIVATIVES **forth·right·ly** adverb **forth·right·ness** noun.
– ORIGIN Old English.

forth·with /fôrtʜˈwitʜ/ ▶ **adverb** without delay.

for·ti·fi·ca·tion /ˌfôrtəfəˈkāsʜən/ ▶ **noun 1** a defensive wall or other structure built to strengthen a place against attack. **2** the action of fortifying something.

for·ti·fy /ˈfôrtəˌfī/ ▶ **verb** (**fortifies, fortifying, fortified**) **1** provide a place with defensive structures as protection against attack. **2** encourage or strengthen someone. **3** add liquor to wine to make port, sherry, etc. **4** make food more nutritious by adding vitamins.

– SYNONYMS **1 strengthen,** secure, barricade, protect, buttress, shore up. **2 invigorate,** strengthen, energize, enliven, animate, vitalize, buoy up; informal pep up, buck up.
– ANTONYMS weaken.

– DERIVATIVES **for·ti·fi·er** noun.
– ORIGIN Latin *fortificare.*

for·tis·si·mo /fôrˈtisəˌmō/ ▶ **adverb & adjective** Music very loud or loudly.
– ORIGIN Italian.

for·ti·tude /ˈfôrtəˌto͞od/ ▶ **noun** courage and strength in bearing pain or trouble.

> – SYNONYMS **courage,** bravery, endurance, resilience, mettle, strength of character, backbone, grit; informal guts.

– ORIGIN Latin *fortitudo.*

fort·night /'fôrt,nīt/ ▶ **noun** chiefly Brit. a period of two weeks.
– DERIVATIVES **fort·night·ly** adjective & adverb.
– ORIGIN Old English, 'fourteen nights.'

For·tran /'fôr,tran/ ▶ **noun** a high-level computer programming language used especially for scientific applications.

for·tress /'fôrtrəs/ ▶ **noun** a fort or a strongly fortified town.

> – SYNONYMS **fort,** castle, citadel, bunker, stronghold, fortification.

– ORIGIN Old French *forteresse* 'strong place.'

for·tu·i·tous /fôr't(y)o͞oətəs/ ▶ **adjective 1** happening by chance rather than intention. **2** happening by a lucky chance; fortunate.
– DERIVATIVES **for·tu·i·tous·ly** adverb **for·tu·i·tous·ness** noun **for·tu·i·ty** noun (pl. **fortuities**).
– ORIGIN Latin *fortuitus.*

> **USAGE**
>
> The traditional, etymological meaning of *fortuitous* is 'happening by chance': a *fortuitous meeting* is a chance meeting, which might turn out to be either a good thing or a bad thing. In modern uses, however, *fortuitous* tends more often to be used to refer to fortunate outcomes, and the word has become more or less a synonym for 'lucky' or 'fortunate.' This use is frowned upon as being not etymologically correct and is best avoided except in informal contexts.

> **CHOOSE THE RIGHT WORD**
>
> See **ACCIDENTAL**.

for·tu·nate /'fôrCHənət/ ▶ **adjective 1** having or happening by good luck; lucky. **2** favorable; advantageous: *in the fortunate position of being headhunted to join a major firm.*

> – SYNONYMS **1 lucky,** favored, blessed, leading a charmed life, in luck; informal born with a silver spoon in one's mouth. **2 favorable,** advantageous, happy.
> – ANTONYMS unfavorable, unlucky.

for·tu·nate·ly /'fôrCHənətlē/ ▶ **adverb** it is fortunate that.

> – SYNONYMS **luckily,** as luck would have it, happily, mercifully, thankfully.

for·tune /'fôrCHən/ ▶ **noun 1** chance as a force affecting people's lives. **2** luck, especially good luck. **3** (**fortunes**) the success or failure of a person or enterprise. **4** a large amount of money or assets.

> – SYNONYMS **1 chance,** accident, coincidence, serendipity, destiny, providence, happenstance. **2 luck,** fate, destiny, predestination, the stars, karma, kismet, lot. **3** *an upswing in their fortunes* **circumstances,** state of affairs, condition, position, situation. **4 wealth,** money, riches, assets, resources, means, possessions, property, estate.

– PHRASES **a small fortune** informal a large amount of money. **tell someone's fortune** predict a person's future by palmistry or similar methods.
– ORIGIN Latin *Fortuna,* a goddess personifying luck or chance.

for·tune cook·ie ▶ **noun** a thin folded cookie containing a slip of paper with a prediction or aphorism written on it, served in Chinese restaurants.

for·tune-tell·er ▶ **noun** a person who predicts what will happen in people's lives.
– DERIVATIVES **for·tune-tell·ing** noun.

for·ty /'fôrtē/ ▶ **cardinal number** (pl. **forties**) ten less than fifty; 40. (Roman numeral: **xl** or **XL.**)
– DERIVATIVES **for·ti·eth** ordinal number.
– PHRASES **forty winks** informal a short daytime sleep.
– ORIGIN Old English.

for·ty-five ▶ **noun** a phonograph record played at 45 rpm.

fo·rum /'fôrəm/ ▶ **noun** (pl. **forums**) **1** a meeting or medium for an exchange of views. **2** (pl. **fora** /'fôrə/) (in ancient Roman cities) a public square or marketplace used for judicial and other business.

> – SYNONYMS **meeting,** assembly, gathering, rally, conference, seminar, convention, symposium.

– ORIGIN Latin, 'what is out of doors.'

for·ward /'fôrwərd/ ▶ **adverb** (also **forwards**) **1** in the direction that one is facing or traveling. **2** onward so as to make progress. **3** ahead in time. **4** in or near the front of a ship or aircraft.

> – SYNONYMS **1 ahead,** forwards, onward, onwards, on, further. **2 toward the front,** out, forth, into view, up.
> – ANTONYMS backward, back.

▶ **adjective 1** toward the direction that one is facing or traveling. **2** relating to the future. **3** bold or overfamiliar. **4** progressing toward a successful conclusion: *the decision is a forward step.* **5** situated in or near the front of a ship or aircraft.

> – SYNONYMS **1 onward,** advancing. **2 front,** advance, foremost, leading. **3 future,** forward-looking, for the future, anticipatory. **4 bold,** brazen, shameless, familiar, overfamiliar, presumptuous, cheeky; informal fresh.
> – ANTONYMS backward, rear.

▶ **noun** an attacking player in soccer, hockey, or other sports.
▶ **verb 1** send a letter or email on to a further address. **2** send a document or goods. **3** help something to develop or progress.

> – SYNONYMS **1 send on,** post on, redirect, readdress, pass on. **2 send,** dispatch, transmit, carry, convey, deliver, ship.

– DERIVATIVES **for·ward·er** noun **for·ward·ly** adverb **for·ward·ness** noun.
– ORIGIN Old English.

for·ward-look·ing (also **forward-thinking**) ▶ **adjective** favoring innovation; progressive.

for·went /fôr'went/ past of **FORGO**.

fos·sil /'fäsəl/ ▶ **noun 1** the remains or impression of a prehistoric plant or animal that have become hardened into rock. **2** humorous an old or outdated person or thing.
– ORIGIN from Latin *fossilis* 'dug up.'

fos·sil fu·el ▶ **noun** a natural fuel such as coal or gas, formed in the geological past from the remains of animals and plants.

fos·sil·ize /'fäsə,līz/ ▶ **verb** preserve an animal or plant so that it becomes a fossil.
– DERIVATIVES **fos·sil·i·za·tion** /,fäsəli'zāSHən/ noun.

fos·ter /'fôstər, 'fäs-/ ▶ **verb 1** promote the development of: *they hope the visit will foster improved relations* *between the two countries.* **2** bring up a child that is not one's own by birth.

– SYNONYMS **1 encourage,** promote, further, nurture, help, aid, assist, support, back. **2 bring up,** rear, raise, care for, take care of, look after, provide for.

– DERIVATIVES **fos·ter·age** noun **fos·ter·er** noun.
– ORIGIN Old English, 'feed, nourish.'

fought /fôt/ past and past participle of **FIGHT**.

foul /foul/ ▶ **adjective 1** having a very unpleasant smell or taste; disgusting. **2** very unpleasant: *he was in a foul mood.* **3** wicked or obscene. **4** not allowed by the rules of a sport. **5** polluted or contaminated.

– SYNONYMS **1 disgusting,** revolting, repulsive, repugnant, abhorrent, loathsome, offensive, sickening, nauseating; informal ghastly, gruesome, gross. **2 contaminated,** polluted, infected, tainted, impure, filthy, dirty, unclean. **3 vulgar,** crude, coarse, filthy, dirty, obscene, indecent, naughty, offensive; informal blue.
– ANTONYMS pleasant.

▶ **noun** (in sports) a piece of play that is not allowed by the rules.

▶ **verb 1** make something foul or polluted. **2** (of an animal) dirty something with excrement. **3** (in sports) commit a foul against an opponent. **4** (**foul out**) Basketball be put out of the game for exceeding the permitted number of fouls. **5** (**foul out**) Baseball (of a batter) be made out by hitting a foul ball that is caught by an opposing player. **6** (**foul something up**) make a mistake with or spoil something. **7** cause a cable or anchor to become entangled or jammed.

– SYNONYMS **1 dirty,** pollute, contaminate, poison, taint, sully. **2 tangle up,** entangle, snarl, catch, entwine.

– DERIVATIVES **foul·ly** adverb **foul·ness** noun.
– ORIGIN Old English.

WORD TOOLKIT

See **DIRTY**.

fou·lard /fo͞oˈlärd/ ▶ **noun** a thin, soft material of silk or silk and cotton.
– ORIGIN French.

foul ball ▶ **noun** Baseball a ball struck so that it falls or will fall outside the lines extending from home plate past first and third bases.

foul-mouthed ▶ **adjective** using bad language.

foul play ▶ **noun 1** unfair play in a game or sport. **2** criminal or violent activity, especially murder.

foul-up ▶ **noun** a problem caused by a stupid mistake.

found[1] /found/ past and past participle of **FIND**.

found[2] ▶ **verb 1** establish an institution or organization. **2** (**be founded on**) be based on a particular principle or idea.

– SYNONYMS **establish,** set up, start, begin, get going, institute, inaugurate, launch.

– ORIGIN Old French *fonder*.

found[3] ▶ **verb 1** melt and mold metal. **2** fuse materials to make glass. **3** make an object by melting and molding metal.
– ORIGIN Latin *fundere* 'melt, pour.'

foun·da·tion /founˈdāsнən/ ▶ **noun 1** the lowest load-bearing part of a building, typically below ground level. **2** a basis for something: *the Chinese laid the scientific foundation for many modern discoveries.* **3** justification or reason: *there was no foundation for the claim.* **4** an institution or organization. **5** the establishment of an institution or organization. **6** a cream or powder applied to the face as a base for other makeup.

– SYNONYMS **1 footing,** foot, base, substructure, underpinning. **2 justification,** grounds, evidence, basis. **3 institution,** establishment, charitable body, agency.

– DERIVATIVES **foun·da·tion·al** adjective.

foun·da·tion stone ▶ **noun** a stone laid at a ceremony to celebrate the laying of a building's foundation.

found·er[1] /ˈfoundər/ ▶ **noun** a person who founds an institution or settlement.

– SYNONYMS **originator,** creator, (founding) father, architect, developer, pioneer, author, inventor, mastermind.

found·er[2] ▶ **noun** the owner or operator of a foundry.

found·er[3] ▶ **verb 1** (of a plan or undertaking) fail; come to nothing. **2** (of a ship) fill with water and sink. **3** (of a horse) stumble or fall.

– SYNONYMS **1 fail,** be unsuccessful, fall flat, fall through, collapse, backfire, meet with disaster; informal flop, bomb. **2 sink,** go to the bottom, go down, be lost at sea.
– ANTONYMS succeed.

– ORIGIN Old French *fondrer* 'submerge, collapse.'

USAGE

The words **founder** and **flounder** are often confused. **Founder** chiefly means 'fail' (*a proposed merger between the two airlines foundered last year*), while **flounder** means 'have trouble doing or understanding something' (*the school was floundering in confusion about its role in the world*).

found·ing fa·ther ▶ **noun 1** a person who starts or helps start a movement or institution. **2** (**Founding Father**) a member of the convention that drew up the US Constitution in 1787.

found·ling /ˈfoundlіɴɢ/ ▶ **noun** a young child who has been abandoned by its parents and is found and cared for by others.

found ob·ject ▶ **noun** an object found or picked up at random and considered aesthetically pleasing.

found·ry /ˈfoundrē/ ▶ **noun** (pl. **foundries**) a workshop or factory for casting metal.

fount[1] /fänt, fount/ ▶ **noun 1** a source of a desirable quality: *he was a fount of wisdom.* **2** literary a spring or fountain.
– ORIGIN from **FOUNTAIN**.

fount[2] ▶ **noun** Brit. variant spelling of **FONT**[2].

foun·tain /ˈfountn/ ▶ **noun 1** an ornamental structure in a pool or lake from which a jet of water is pumped into the air. **2** a source of something desirable: *Susan is a fountain of knowledge about the area.* **3** literary a natural spring of water.

– SYNONYMS **1 jet,** spray, spout, spurt, cascade, water feature. **2 source,** fount, well, reservoir, fund, mine.

▶ **verb** spurt or cascade like a fountain.
– ORIGIN Old French *fontaine*.

foun·tain·head /ˈfountn,hed/ ▶ **noun** an original source of something.

foun·tain pen ▸ noun a pen with a container from which ink flows continuously to the nib.

four /fôr/ ▸ cardinal number one more than three; 4. (Roman numeral: **iv** or **IV**.)
– DERIVATIVES **four·fold** adjective & adverb.
– ORIGIN Old English.

four-by-four (also **4 × 4**) ▸ noun a vehicle with four-wheel drive.

four-di·men·sion·al ▸ adjective having the three dimensions of space (length, breadth, and depth) plus time.

4H (also **Four-H**) ▸ noun a government-sponsored organization with many local branches that teaches agricultural and practical skills to children in rural areas.

four-leaf clo·ver ▸ noun **1** a clover leaf with four leaflets instead of the usual three, thought to bring good luck. **2** a stylized representation of this.

four-let·ter word ▸ noun any of several short words referring to sex or excretion, regarded as rude or offensive.

four-post·er (also **four-poster bed**) ▸ noun a bed with a post at each corner, sometimes supporting a canopy.

four·score /'fôr'skôr/ ▸ cardinal number old use eighty.

four·some /'fôrsəm/ ▸ noun a group of four people.

four-square ▸ adjective **1** (of a building) having a square shape and solid appearance. **2** firm and resolute. ▸ adverb in a firm and resolute way: *the senator had come out four-square in favor of the line-item veto.*

four-stroke ▸ adjective (of an internal-combustion engine) having a cycle of four strokes (intake, compression, combustion, and exhaust).

four·teen /ˌfôr'tēn, 'fôrˌtēn/ ▸ cardinal number one more than thirteen; 14. (Roman numeral: **xiv** or **XIV**.)
– DERIVATIVES **four·teenth** ordinal number.

fourth /fôrTH/ ▸ ordinal number **1** that is number four in a sequence; 4th. **2** (**a fourth/one fourth**) a quarter: *a fourth of the pizza is gone.* **3** Music an interval spanning four consecutive notes in a diatonic scale.
– DERIVATIVES **fourth·ly** adverb.

fourth di·men·sion ▸ noun time regarded as a dimension comparable to the three linear dimensions.

fourth es·tate ▸ noun journalism; the press.

Fourth of Ju·ly ▸ noun another term for INDEPENDENCE DAY.

4WD ▸ abbreviation four-wheel drive.

four-wheel drive ▸ noun a transmission system that provides power directly to all four wheels of a vehicle.

fowl /foul/ ▸ noun (pl. same or **fowls**) **1** (also **domestic fowl**) a domesticated bird kept for its eggs or flesh; a cock or hen. **2** any domesticated bird, e.g., a turkey. **3** birds as a group, especially as the quarry of hunters.
– DERIVATIVES **fowl·er** noun **fowl·ing** noun.
– ORIGIN Old English.

fox /fäks/ ▸ noun **1** an animal of the dog family with a pointed muzzle and bushy tail. **2** informal a cunning or sly person. **3** informal a sexually attractive woman. ▸ verb informal baffle or deceive someone.
– ORIGIN Old English.

fox·glove /'fäks,gləv/ ▸ noun a tall plant with pinkish-purple or white bell-shaped flowers growing up the stem.

fox·hole /'fäks,hōl/ ▸ noun a hole in the ground used by troops as a shelter against enemy fire or as a firing point.

fox·hound /'fäks,hound/ ▸ noun a breed of dog with smooth hair and drooping ears, trained to hunt foxes in packs.

fox hunt·ing ▸ noun the sport of hunting a fox across country with a pack of hounds, carried out by people on foot and horseback.

fox·tail /'fäks,tāl/ ▸ noun a common meadow grass that has soft brushlike flowering spikes.

fox·trot /'fäks,trät/ ▸ noun a ballroom dance with alternation of slow and quick steps.

fox·y /'fäksē/ ▸ adjective (**foxier**, **foxiest**) **1** resembling a fox. **2** cunning or sly. **3** informal (of a woman) sexually attractive.
– DERIVATIVES **fox·i·ly** adverb **fox·i·ness** noun.

foy·er /'foiər, 'foiˌā/ ▸ noun a large entrance hall in a hotel or theater.

> – SYNONYMS **entrance hall**, hallway, entry, entryway, porch, reception area, atrium, concourse, lobby, anteroom.

– ORIGIN French, 'hearth, home.'

Fr. ▸ abbreviation Father (as a courtesy title of priests).
– ORIGIN from French *frère* 'brother.'

fr. ▸ abbreviation franc(s).

fra·cas /'frākəs, 'frak-/ ▸ noun (pl. **fracases**) a noisy disturbance or quarrel.

> – SYNONYMS **disturbance**, brawl, melee, rumpus, skirmish, struggle, scuffle, clash, fisticuffs, altercation; informal roughhouse, scrap, set-to, shindig, dust-up. Law, dated affray.

– ORIGIN French.

frac·tal /'fraktəl/ ▸ noun Mathematics a curve or geometrical figure, each part of which has the same statistical character as the whole.
– ORIGIN French.

frac·tion /'frakSHən/ ▸ noun **1** a numerical quantity that is not a whole number (e.g., ½, 0.5). **2** a very small part, amount, or proportion. **3** Chemistry each of the parts of a mixture, with different boiling points, which may be separated by distillation.

> – SYNONYMS **1** *a fraction of the population* **tiny part**, fragment, snippet, snatch. **2** *he moved a fraction closer* **bit**, little, touch, soupçon, trifle, mite, shade, jot; informal smidgen, tad.
> – ANTONYMS whole.

– ORIGIN Latin.

> **CHOOSE THE RIGHT WORD**
>
> See **FRAGMENT**.

frac·tion·al /'frakSHənl/ ▸ adjective **1** relating to or expressed as a fraction. **2** very small in amount.
– DERIVATIVES **frac·tion·al·ly** adverb.

frac·tious /'frakSHəs/ ▸ adjective **1** easily irritated. **2** difficult to control.

> – SYNONYMS **grumpy**, bad-tempered, irascible, irritable, crotchety, grouchy, cantankerous, tetchy, testy, ill-tempered, peevish, cross, pettish, waspish, crabby, crusty, cranky, ornery.

– DERIVATIVES **frac·tious·ly** adverb **frac·tious·ness** noun.
– ORIGIN from FRACTION, probably on the pattern of *faction, factious*.

frac·ture /ˈfrakCHər/ ▸ **noun 1** a crack or break, especially in a bone or layer of rock. **2** the cracking or breaking of a hard object or material.

– SYNONYMS **break,** crack, split, rupture, fissure.

▸ **verb 1** break or cause to break. **2** (of a group) split up or fragment.

– SYNONYMS **break,** crack, split, rupture, snap, shatter, fragment, splinter.

– ORIGIN Latin *fractura.*

frag·ile /ˈfrajəl, -ˌjīl/ ▸ **adjective 1** easily broken, damaged, or destroyed. **2** (of a person) not strong; delicate.

– SYNONYMS **1 breakable,** delicate, brittle, flimsy, dainty, fine. **2 tenuous,** shaky, insecure, vulnerable, flimsy. **3 weak,** delicate, frail, debilitated, ill, unwell, poorly, sickly.
– ANTONYMS sturdy, robust.

– DERIVATIVES **fra·gil·i·ty** /frəˈjilitē/ noun.
– ORIGIN Latin *fragilis.*

frag·ile X syn·drome ▸ **noun** an inherited condition characterized by an X chromosome that is abnormally susceptible to damage, especially by folic acid deficiency. Affected individuals tend to be mentally handicapped.

frag·ment ▸ **noun** /ˈfragmənt/ **1** a small part broken off or detached. **2** an isolated or incomplete part: *a fragment of conversation.*

– SYNONYMS **1 piece,** bit, particle, speck, chip, shard, sliver, splinter, flake. **2 snatch,** snippet, scrap, bit.

▸ **verb** /ˈfragˌment, ˌfragˈment/ break into fragments.

– SYNONYMS **break up,** crack open, shatter, splinter, fracture, disintegrate, fall to pieces, fall apart.

– ORIGIN Latin *fragmentum.*

CHOOSE THE RIGHT WORD

fragment, fraction, part, piece, portion, section, segment

The whole is equal to the sum of its **parts** — *part* being a general term for any of the components of a whole. But how did the whole come apart? **Fragment** suggests that breakage has occurred (*fragments of pottery*) and often refers to a brittle substance such as glass or pottery. **Segment** suggests that the whole has been separated along natural or pre-existing lines of division (*a segment of an orange*), and **section** suggests a substantial and clearly separate *part* that fits closely with other parts to form the whole (*a section of a bookcase*). **Fraction** usually suggests a less substantial but still clearly delineated *part* (*a fraction of her income*), and a **portion** is a *part* that has been allotted or assigned to someone (*her portion of the program*). Finally, the very frequently used **piece** is any *part* that is separate from the whole.

frag·men·tar·y /ˈfragmənˌterē/ ▸ **adjective** consisting of small disconnected or incomplete parts.
– DERIVATIVES **frag·men·tar·i·ly** /ˌfragmənˈterəlē/ adverb.

frag·men·ta·tion /ˌfragmənˈtāSHən/ ▸ **noun** the process of breaking or the state of being broken into fragments.

fra·grance /ˈfrāgrəns/ ▸ **noun 1** a pleasant, sweet smell. **2** a perfume or aftershave.

– SYNONYMS **1 sweet smell,** scent, perfume, bouquet, aroma, nose. **2 perfume,** scent, eau de toilette.

– DERIVATIVES **fra·granced** adjective.

fra·grant /ˈfrāgrənt/ ▸ **adjective** having a pleasant, sweet smell.

– SYNONYMS **sweet-scented,** sweet-smelling, scented, perfumed, aromatic.
– ANTONYMS smelly.

– DERIVATIVES **fra·grant·ly** adverb.
– ORIGIN from Latin *fragrare* 'smell sweet.'

frail /frāl/ ▸ **adjective 1** (of a person) weak and delicate. **2** easily damaged or broken.

– SYNONYMS **1** *a frail old lady* **weak,** delicate, feeble, infirm, ill, unwell, sickly, poorly. **2** *a frail structure* **fragile,** easily damaged, delicate, flimsy, insubstantial, unsteady, unstable, rickety.
– ANTONYMS strong, robust.

– DERIVATIVES **frail·ness** noun.
– ORIGIN Old French *fraile.*

WORD TOOLKIT

See **WEAK**.

frail·ty /ˈfrāltē/ ▸ **noun** (pl. **frailties**) **1** the condition of being frail or weak. **2** weakness in a person's character or morals.

frame /frām/ ▸ **noun 1** a rigid structure surrounding a picture, door, etc. **2** (**frames**) a metal or plastic structure holding the lenses of a pair of glasses. **3** the rigid supporting structure of a vehicle, building, or other object. **4** a person's body with reference to its size or build: *her slim frame.* **5** the underlying structure of a system, concept, or written work: *the novels rested on a frame of moral truth.* **6** a single complete picture in a series forming a movie, television, or video film. **7** another term for **RACK**[1] (sense 3 of the noun). **8** a round of play in bowling.

– SYNONYMS **1 framework,** structure, substructure, skeleton, casing, chassis, shell. **2 body,** figure, form, shape, physique, anatomy, build.

▸ **verb 1** place a picture in a frame. **2** formulate or develop a plan or system. **3** surround so as to create an attractive image: *short hair cut to frame the face.* **4** informal produce false evidence against an innocent person to make them appear guilty of a crime.

– SYNONYMS **1 mount,** set in a frame. **2 formulate,** draw up, draft, shape, compose, put together, form, devise.

– DERIVATIVES **framed** adjective **frame·less** adjective **fram·er** noun.
– PHRASES **frame of mind** a particular mood. **frame of reference** a set of values according to which judgments can be made.
– ORIGIN Old English, 'be useful,' later 'prepare timber for building.'

frame-up ▸ **noun** informal a conspiracy to incriminate someone falsely.

frame·work /ˈfrāmˌwərk/ ▸ **noun** a supporting or underlying structure.

– SYNONYMS **1 frame,** structure, skeleton, chassis, support, scaffolding. **2 structure,** shape, fabric, order, scheme, system, organization, anatomy; informal makeup.

franc /fraNGk/ ▸ **noun** the basic unit of money of France, Belgium, Switzerland, Luxembourg, and several other countries (replaced in France, Belgium, and Luxembourg by the euro in 2002).
– ORIGIN from Latin *Francorum Rex* 'king of the Franks,' the inscription on 14th-century gold coins.

fran·chise /ˈfranˌCHīz/ ▸ **noun 1** formal permission granted by a government or company to a person or

group enabling them to sell certain products or provide a service. **2** a business or service run under a franchise. **3** the right to vote in public elections. ▶ **verb 1** grant a franchise to someone. **2** grant a franchise for goods or a service.
– DERIVATIVES **fran·chi·see** /ˌfranˌCHīˈzē/ noun **fran·chis·er** (also **franchisor**) /ˌfranCHəˈzôr/ noun.
– ORIGIN Old French.

Fran·cis·can /franˈsiskən/ ▶ **noun** a monk or nun of a Christian religious order following the precepts of the Italian monk St. Francis of Assisi. ▶ **adjective** relating to St. Francis or the Franciscans.

fran·ci·um /ˈfransēəm/ ▶ **noun** an unstable radioactive chemical element of the alkali-metal group.
– ORIGIN from *France*.

Franco- (also **franco-**) ▶ **combining form 1** French; French and ...: *francophone* | *Franco-American*. **2** relating to France: *Francophile*.
– ORIGIN from Latin *Francus* 'Frank.'

Fran·co·phile /ˈfraNGkəˌfīl/ ▶ **noun** a person who is fond of or greatly admires France or the French.

fran·co·phone /ˈfraNGkəˌfōn/ ▶ **adjective** French-speaking. ▶ **noun** a French-speaking person.

fran·gi·ble /ˈfranjəbəl/ ▶ **adjective** literary or technical fragile; brittle.
– ORIGIN Latin *frangibilis*.

fran·gi·pan·i /ˌfranjəˈpanē, -ˈpänē/ ▶ **noun** (pl. **frangipanis**) **1** a tropical American tree or shrub with fragrant white, pink, or yellow flowers. **2** perfume obtained from the frangipani plant.
– ORIGIN named after the Marquis Muzio *Frangipani*, an Italian nobleman who invented a perfume for gloves.

Frank /fraNGk/ ▶ **noun** a member of a Germanic people that conquered Gaul in the 6th century.
– DERIVATIVES **Frank·ish** adjective & noun.
– ORIGIN from Old English *Franca*.

frank[1] /fraNGk/ ▶ **adjective 1** honest and direct, especially when dealing with unpleasant matters. **2** open or undisguised: *he looked at her with frank admiration*.

> – SYNONYMS **1 candid,** direct, forthright, plain, plain-spoken, straight, to the point, matter-of-fact, open, honest; informal upfront. **2 undisguised,** open, unconcealed, naked, unmistakable, clear, obvious, transparent, patent, evident.
> – ANTONYMS evasive.

– DERIVATIVES **frank·ness** noun.
– ORIGIN Latin *francus* 'free.'

frank[2] ▶ **verb** stamp an official mark on a letter or parcel to indicate that postage has been paid or does not need to be paid. ▶ **noun** a franking mark on a letter or parcel.
– ORIGIN from FRANK[1], in the former sense 'free of obligation.'

Frank·en·food /ˈfraNGkənˌfo͞od/ ▶ **noun** informal, derogatory a genetically modified food.
– ORIGIN from FRANKENSTEIN.

Frank·en·stein /ˈfraNGkənˌstīn/ (also **Frankenstein's monster**) ▶ **noun** a thing that becomes terrifying or destructive to its maker.
– ORIGIN from a character in a novel by Mary Shelley, Victor *Frankenstein*, who creates a manlike monster.

frank·furt·er /ˈfraNGkˌfərtər/ ▶ **noun** a seasoned smoked sausage made of beef and pork.
– ORIGIN from German *Frankfurter Wurst* 'Frankfurt sausage.'

frank·in·cense /ˈfraNGkənˌsens/ ▶ **noun** an aromatic resinous substance obtained from an African tree and burned as incense.
– ORIGIN from Old French *franc encens* 'high-quality incense.'

frank·ly /ˈfraNGklē/ ▶ **adverb 1** in an honest and direct way. **2** to be frank.

> – SYNONYMS **1 candidly,** directly, plainly, straightforwardly, forthrightly, openly, honestly, without beating about/around the bush, bluntly. **2 to be frank,** to be honest, to tell the truth, in all honesty.

fran·tic /ˈfrantik/ ▶ **adjective 1** distraught with fear, anxiety, or other emotion. **2** done in a hurried and chaotic way: *frantic efforts to put out the fires*.

> – SYNONYMS **panic-stricken,** panicky, beside oneself, at one's wits' end, distraught, overwrought, worked up, frenzied, frenetic, fraught, feverish, desperate; informal in a state, tearing one's hair out.
> – ANTONYMS calm.

– DERIVATIVES **fran·ti·cal·ly** adverb **fran·tic·ness** noun.
– ORIGIN Old French *frenetique* 'violently mad.'

frap·pé /fraˈpā/ ▶ **adjective** (of a drink) iced or chilled. ▶ **noun 1** a drink served with ice or frozen to a slushy consistency. **2** (**frappe** /frap/) a milkshake, especially one made with ice cream.
– ORIGIN French.

fra·ter·nal /frəˈtərnl/ ▶ **adjective 1** relating to or like a brother; brotherly. **2** relating to a fraternity. **3** (of twins) developed from separate ova (female reproductive cells) and therefore not identical.
– DERIVATIVES **fra·ter·nal·ly** adverb.
– ORIGIN Latin *frater* 'brother.'

fra·ter·ni·ty /frəˈtərnətē/ ▶ **noun** (pl. **fraternities**) **1** a male students' society in a college or university. **2** a group of people sharing the same profession or interests: *the medical fraternity*. **3** friendship and shared support within a group.

> – SYNONYMS **1 society,** club, association, group. **2 brotherhood,** fellowship, kinship, friendship, mutual support, solidarity, community. **3 profession,** community, trade, set, circle.

frat·er·nize /ˈfratərˌnīz/ ▶ **verb** (usu. **fraternize with**) be on friendly terms, especially with someone whom one is not supposed to be friendly with.
– DERIVATIVES **frat·er·ni·za·tion** /ˌfratərniˈzāSHən/ noun.

frat·ri·cide /ˈfratrəˌsīd/ ▶ **noun 1** the killing of one's brother or sister. **2** the accidental killing of one's own forces in war.
– DERIVATIVES **frat·ri·cid·al** /ˌfratrəˈsīdl/ adjective.
– ORIGIN from Latin *frater* 'brother' + **-CIDE**.

Frau /frou/ ▶ **noun** a title or form of address for a married or widowed German woman.
– ORIGIN German.

fraud /frôd/ ▶ **noun 1** the crime of deceiving someone to gain money or personal advantage. **2** a person who deceives others into believing that he or she has certain qualities or abilities.

> – SYNONYMS **1 deception,** cheating, swindling, trickery, embezzlement, deceit, double-dealing, chicanery. **2 swindle,** racket, deception, trick, cheat, hoax; informal scam, con, hustle, rip-off, sting, fiddle. **3 impostor,** fake, sham, charlatan, swindler, fraudster, confidence trickster; informal phony.

– ORIGIN Latin *fraus* 'deceit, injury.'

fraud·u·lent /'frôjələnt/ ▸ **adjective 1** done by or involving fraud. **2** intended to deceive.

– SYNONYMS **dishonest,** cheating, swindling, corrupt, criminal, deceitful, double-dealing, duplicitous; informal crooked, shady, dirty.
– ANTONYMS honest.

– DERIVATIVES **fraud·u·lence** noun **fraud·u·lent·ly** adverb.

WORD TOOLKIT

See **ILLEGAL**.

fraught /frôt/ ▸ **adjective 1** (**fraught with**) filled with something undesirable. **2** causing or feeling anxiety or stress.

– SYNONYMS **1** *a world fraught with danger* **full of,** filled with, rife with. **2 anxious,** worried, stressed, upset, distraught, overwrought, worked up, agitated, distressed, desperate, frantic, panic-stricken, panicky, beside oneself, at one's wits' end, at the end of one's tether.

– ORIGIN from Dutch *vracht* 'ship's cargo.'

Fräu·lein /'froi,līn/ ▸ **noun** a title or form of address for an unmarried German woman.
– ORIGIN German.

fray[1] /frā/ ▸ **verb 1** (of a fabric, rope, or cord) unravel or become worn at the edge. **2** (of a person's nerves or temper) show the effects of strain.

– SYNONYMS **1** (as adj. **frayed**) **worn,** threadbare, tattered, ragged, the worse for wear; informal raggedy, tatty. **2** (as adj. **frayed**) **strained,** fraught, tense, edgy, stressed.

– ORIGIN Old French *freiier*.

fray[2] ▸ **noun** (**the fray**) **1** a very competitive or demanding situation: *with new manufacturers entering the fray, the competition is certain to intensify.* **2** a battle or fight.
– ORIGIN from Old French *afrayer* 'disturb, startle.'

fraz·zle /'frazəl/ informal ▸ **verb 1** (as adj. **frazzled**) completely exhausted. **2** make something shrivel up with burning. ▸ **noun** (**a frazzle**) **1** an exhausted state. **2** a burned state.
– ORIGIN perhaps from **FRAY**[1] and former *fazle* 'ravel out.'

freak /frēk/ ▸ **noun 1** informal a person who is obsessed with a particular activity or interest: *a fitness freak.* **2** a very unusual and unexpected event. **3** (also **freak of nature**) a person, animal, or plant with a physical abnormality. **4** informal a person regarded as strange because of their unusual appearance or behavior.

– SYNONYMS **1 enthusiast,** fan, devotee, lover, aficionado; informal nut, fanatic, addict, maniac. **2 anomaly,** aberration, rarity, oddity, fluke, twist of fate. **3 aberration,** abnormality, oddity, monster, monstrosity, mutant, chimera. **4 eccentric,** misfit, oddity; informal oddball, weirdo, nut, wacko, kook.

▸ **adjective** very unusual and unexpected: *a freak accident.*

– SYNONYMS **unusual,** anomalous, aberrant, atypical, unrepresentative, irregular, exceptional, isolated.

▸ **verb** (usu. **freak out**) informal react or cause to react in a wild, shocked, or excited way.
– DERIVATIVES **freak·ish** adjective.
– ORIGIN probably from a dialect word.

freak show ▸ **noun 1** a sideshow at a fair, featuring abnormally developed people or animals. **2** an unusual or grotesque event viewed for pleasure, especially when it is in bad taste: *his latest film is a fabulous freak show.*

freak·y /'frēkē/ ▸ **adjective** (**freakier, freakiest**) informal very odd or strange.
– DERIVATIVES **freak·i·ly** adverb **freak·i·ness** noun.

freck·le /'frekəl/ ▸ **noun** a small light brown spot on the skin. ▸ **verb** cover or become covered with freckles.
– DERIVATIVES **freck·ly** /'frekl-ē, 'freklē/ adjective.
– ORIGIN Old Norse.

free /frē/ ▸ **adjective** (**freer, freest**) **1** able to do what one wants; not under the control of anyone else. **2** not confined, obstructed, or fixed: *they set the birds free.* **3** not having or not filled with things to do: *I spent my free time shopping.* **4** not occupied or in use. **5** (**free of/from**) not containing or affected by something undesirable. **6** available without charge. **7** (usu. **free with**) using or spending something without restraint. **8** behaving or speaking without restraint. **9** (of art, music, etc.) not following the normal conventions. **10** (of a translation) conveying the general meaning; not literal.

– SYNONYMS **1 free of charge,** without charge, for nothing, complimentary, gratis; informal for free, on the house. **2** *free of any pressures* **without,** unencumbered by, unaffected by, clear of, rid of, exempt from, not liable to, safe from, immune to, excused of. **3 unoccupied,** not busy, available, off duty, off work, on leave, at leisure, with time to spare. **4 vacant,** empty, available, unoccupied, not in use. **5 independent,** self-governing, self-determining, sovereign, autonomous, democratic. **6 on the loose,** at liberty, at large, loose, unrestrained. **7** *you are free to leave* **able,** in a position, allowed, permitted. **8 unobstructed,** unimpeded, unrestricted, unhampered, clear, open. **9** *she was free with her money* **generous,** liberal, open-handed, unstinting.
– ANTONYMS busy, occupied, confined.

▸ **adverb** without cost or payment.
▸ **verb** (**frees, freeing, freed**) **1** make someone or something free. **2** make something available for a purpose.

– SYNONYMS **1 release,** set free, let go, liberate, set loose, untie. **2 extricate,** release, get out, cut free, pull free, rescue.
– ANTONYMS confine, trap.

– DERIVATIVES **free·ness** noun.
– PHRASES **free and easy** informal and relaxed. **a free hand** freedom to act completely as one wishes. **a free ride** a situation in which someone benefits without making a fair contribution. **the free world** the noncommunist countries of the world, as formerly opposed to the Soviet bloc.
– ORIGIN Old English.

-free ▸ **combining form** free of or from: *tax-free.*

free a·gent ▸ **noun 1** a person who can act without restrictions imposed by others. **2** an athlete who is not bound by a contract and can join another team.

free-as·so·ci·ate ▸ **verb** allow the mind to supply whatever word, thought, or image is suggested by one previously mentioned or noted: *people then start to free-associate and shout out ideas.*
– DERIVATIVES **free as·so·ci·a·tion** noun.

free·base /'frē,bās/ ▸ **noun** cocaine that has been purified by heating with ether, taken by inhaling the fumes or smoking the residue. ▸ **verb** take cocaine in this way.

free·bie /'frēbē/ ▸ **noun** informal a thing given free of charge.

free·board /'frē,bôrd/ ▸ **noun** the height of a ship's side between the waterline and the deck.

free·boot·er /ˈfrēˌbo͞otər/ ▸ **noun** a person who behaves in an illegal way for their own advantage.
– DERIVATIVES **free·boot·ing** adjective.
– ORIGIN Dutch *vrijbuiter*.

free·born /ˈfrēˌbôrn/ ▸ **adjective** not born in slavery.

freed·man /ˈfrēdmən, -ˌman/ ▸ **noun** (pl. **freedmen**) historical an emancipated slave.

free·dom /ˈfrēdəm/ ▸ **noun 1** the power or right to act, speak, or think as one wants. **2** the state of being free: *clothing that allows maximum freedom of movement.* **3** (**freedom from**) the state of not being subject to or affected by something undesirable. **4** unrestricted use of something: *the dog had the freedom of the house.*

– SYNONYMS **1 liberty,** liberation, release, deliverance. **2 independence,** self-government, self-determination, self-rule, home rule, sovereignty, autonomy, democracy. **3** *freedom from political accountability* **exemption,** immunity, dispensation, impunity. **4 right,** entitlement, privilege, prerogative, discretion, latitude, elbow room, license, free rein, a free hand, carte blanche.
– ANTONYMS captivity, obligation.

CHOOSE THE RIGHT WORD

See **LIBERTY**.

free·dom fight·er ▸ **noun** a person who takes part in a struggle to achieve political freedom.

free en·ter·prise ▸ **noun** an economic system in which private businesses compete with each other with little state control.

free fall ▸ **noun 1** downward movement under the force of gravity. **2** a rapid decline that cannot be stopped: *the euro was in free fall.* ▸ **verb** (**free-fall**) fall rapidly.

free-for-all ▸ **noun** a disorganized or unrestricted situation or event in which everyone may take part.

free-form ▸ **adjective** not in a regular or formal structure.

free·hand /ˈfrēˌhand/ ▸ **adjective & adverb** done by hand without the aid of instruments such as rulers.

free·hold /ˈfrēˌhōld/ ▸ **noun** chiefly Brit. permanent and absolute ownership of land or property with the freedom to sell it when one wishes.
– DERIVATIVES **free·hold·er** noun.

free kick ▸ **noun** (in soccer and rugby) an unimpeded kick of the stationary ball awarded when the opposing team has broken the rules.

free·lance /ˈfrēˌlans/ ▸ **adjective** self-employed and hired to work for different companies on particular assignments. ▸ **adverb** earning one's living as a freelance. ▸ **noun** (also **freelancer**) a freelance worker. ▸ **verb** earn one's living as a freelance.
– ORIGIN first referring to a mercenary: from **FREE** + **LANCE**.

free·load·er /ˈfrēˌlōdər/ ▸ **noun** informal a person who takes advantage of others' generosity without giving anything in return.
– DERIVATIVES **free·load** /ˈfrēˌlōd/ verb.

free love ▸ **noun** dated the practice of having sexual relationships freely, without being faithful to one partner.

free·ly /ˈfrēlē/ ▸ **adverb 1** not under the control of someone else. **2** without restriction or restraint: *a world where people cannot speak freely.* **3** in abundant amounts. **4** willingly and readily.

– SYNONYMS **1 openly,** candidly, frankly, directly, without beating about/around the bush, without mincing one's words. **2 voluntarily,** willingly, readily, of one's own accord, of one's own free will, without being told to.

free·man /ˈfrēmən/ ▸ **noun** (pl. **freemen**) **1** a person who is entitled to full political and civil rights. **2** historical a person who is not a slave or serf.

free mar·ket ▸ **noun** an economic system in which prices are determined by supply and demand rather than controlled by a government.

Free·ma·son /ˈfrēˈmāsən/ ▸ **noun** a member of an international order whose members help each other and hold secret ceremonies.
– DERIVATIVES **Free·ma·son·ry** noun.

fre·er /ˈfrēər/ ▸ **adjective** comparative of **FREE**.

free rad·i·cal ▸ **noun** a highly reactive molecule with one odd electron not paired up in a chemical bond.

free-range ▸ **adjective** (of livestock or their produce) kept or produced in natural conditions, where the animals may move around freely.

free·sia /ˈfrēzʜə/ ▸ **noun** a small plant with fragrant, colorful, tubular flowers, native to southern Africa.
– ORIGIN named after the German physician Friedrich H. T. *Freese*.

free speech ▸ **noun** the right to express any opinions without censorship.

free spir·it ▸ **noun** an independent or uninhibited person: *they raised their children to be free spirits.*

fre·est /ˈfrēəst/ ▸ **adjective** superlative of **FREE**.

free·stand·ing /ˈfrēˈstandiɴɢ/ ▸ **adjective** not attached to or supported by another structure.

free·style /ˈfrēˌstīl/ ▸ **noun** (usu. before another noun) a contest, race, or type of sport in which there are few restrictions on the style or technique that competitors employ. ▸ **verb** perform or compete in an unrestricted or improvised fashion.
– DERIVATIVES **free·styl·er** noun.

free·think·er /ˈfrēˈᴛʜɪɴɢkər/ ▸ **noun** a person who questions or rejects accepted opinions, especially those concerning religious belief.

free throw ▸ **noun** Basketball an unimpeded attempt at a basket (worth one point) awarded to a player following a foul or other infringement.

free trade ▸ **noun** international trade left to its natural course without tariffs or other restrictions.

free verse ▸ **noun** poetry that does not rhyme or have a regular rhythm.

free·ware /ˈfrēˌwe(ə)r/ ▸ **noun** software that is available free of charge.

free·way /ˈfrēˌwā/ ▸ **noun** an express highway, especially one with controlled access.

free·wheel /ˈfrēˌ(h)wēl/ ▸ **verb 1** ride on a bicycle without using the pedals. **2** (as adj. **freewheeling**) not concerned with rules or the results of one's actions. ▸ **noun** a bicycle wheel that is able to revolve freely when no power is being applied to the pedals.
– DERIVATIVES **free·wheel·er** noun.

free will ▸ **noun** the power to act according to one's own wishes.

freeze /frēz/ ▶ **verb** (past **froze** /frōz/; past part. **frozen** /ˈfrōzən/) **1** (with reference to a liquid) turn or be turned into ice or another solid as a result of extreme cold. **2** block or become blocked or rigid with ice. **3** be or make very cold. **4** store something at a very low temperature in order to preserve it. **5** become suddenly motionless with fear or shock. **6** hold at a fixed level or in a fixed state: *the Act has given the police powers to freeze the assets of suspects.* **7** (of a computer screen) suddenly become locked. **8** (**freeze someone out**) informal make someone feel left out by being hostile or cold toward them.

– SYNONYMS **1 ice over,** ice up, solidify. **2 stand still,** stop dead in one's tracks, go rigid, become motionless, become paralyzed. **3 fix,** hold, set, limit, restrict, cap.
– ANTONYMS thaw.

▶ **noun 1** an act of holding something at a fixed level or in a fixed state. **2** a period of very cold weather.
– DERIVATIVES **freez·a·ble** adjective.
– ORIGIN Old English.

freeze-dry ▶ **verb** preserve something by rapidly freezing it and then removing the ice in a vacuum.

freeze-frame ▶ **noun 1** a single frame forming a motionless image from a film or videotape. **2** the facility or process of stopping a film or videotape to obtain a freeze-frame.

freez·er /ˈfrēzər/ ▶ **noun** a refrigerated cabinet or room for preserving food at very low temperatures.

freeze-up ▶ **noun 1** an instance of something freezing: *gas line freeze-up.* **2** a period when freezing temperatures prevail: *areas where they hunt seals after freeze-up.*

freez·ing /ˈfrēziNG/ ▶ **adjective 1** below 32°F (0°C). **2** very cold. **3** (of fog or rain) consisting of droplets that freeze rapidly on contact with a surface.

– SYNONYMS **1 icy,** bitter, chill, frosty, glacial, arctic, wintry, subzero, raw, biting. **2 frozen,** numb with cold, chilled to the bone/marrow.
– ANTONYMS balmy, hot.

▶ **noun** the freezing point of water (32°F/0°C).

freez·ing point ▶ **noun** the temperature at which a liquid turns into a solid when cooled.

freight /frāt/ ▶ **noun 1** transport of goods in bulk by truck, train, ship, or aircraft. **2** goods transported by freight.

– SYNONYMS **goods,** cargo, merchandise.

▶ **verb 1** transport goods by freight. **2** (**be freighted with**) be laden or burdened with: *each word was freighted with anger.*
– ORIGIN Dutch and German *vrecht.*

freight car ▶ **noun** a railroad car for carrying freight.

freight·er /ˈfrātər/ ▶ **noun** a large ship or aircraft designed to carry freight.

French /frenCH/ ▶ **adjective** relating to France or its people or language. ▶ **noun** the language of France, also used in parts of Belgium, Switzerland, Canada, and elsewhere.
– DERIVATIVES **French·ness** noun.
– PHRASES **excuse** (or **pardon**) **my French** informal used to apologize for swearing.

French bread ▶ **noun** white bread in a long, crisp loaf.

French Ca·na·di·an ▶ **noun** a Canadian whose native language is French. ▶ **adjective** relating to French Canadians.

French chalk ▶ **noun** a kind of steatite (talc) used for marking cloth and removing grease.

French dress·ing ▶ **noun** a salad dressing of vinegar, oil, and seasonings.

French fries ▶ **plural noun** potato cut into strips and deep-fried.

French horn ▶ **noun** a brass instrument with a coiled tube, valves, and a wide bell.

French·i·fy /ˈfrenCHi,fī/ ▶ **verb** (**Frenchifies, Frenchifying, Frenchified**) often derogatory make someone or something French in form or character.

French kiss ▶ **noun** a kiss with contact between tongues.
– DERIVATIVES **French kiss·ing** noun.

French·man /ˈfrenCHmən/ (or **Frenchwoman**) ▶ **noun** (pl. **Frenchmen** or **Frenchwomen**) a person who is French by birth or descent.

French toast ▶ **noun** bread coated in egg and milk and fried.

French win·dow ▶ **noun** each of a pair of casement windows extending to the floor in an outside wall, serving as a window and door.

French·wom·an /ˈfrenCH,wo͝omən/ ▶ **noun** (pl. **Frenchwomen**) a female who is French by birth or descent.

fre·net·ic /frəˈnetik/ ▶ **adjective** fast and energetic in a disorganized or uncontrolled way.
– DERIVATIVES **fre·net·i·cal·ly** adverb **fre·net·i·cism** /frəˈneti,sizəm/ noun.
– ORIGIN from Greek *phrenitis* 'delirium.'

fren·zied /ˈfrenzēd/ ▶ **adjective** wildly excited or uncontrolled.

– SYNONYMS **frantic,** wild, frenetic, hectic, feverish, fevered, mad, crazed, manic, furious, uncontrolled.
– ANTONYMS calm.

– DERIVATIVES **fren·zied·ly** adverb.

fren·zy /ˈfrenzē/ ▶ **noun** (pl. **frenzies**) a state or period of uncontrolled excitement or wild behavior.

– SYNONYMS **hysteria,** madness, mania, delirium, wild excitement, fever, lather, passion, panic, fury, rage.

– ORIGIN Latin *phrenesia.*

Fre·on /ˈfrē,än/ ▶ **noun** trademark an aerosol propellant, refrigerant, or organic solvent consisting of one or more of a group of chlorofluorocarbons and related compounds.

fre·quen·cy /ˈfrēkwənsē/ ▶ **noun** (pl. **frequencies**) **1** the rate at which something occurs in a given period or sample: *the lightning strikes seemed to increase in frequency.* **2** the fact or state of being frequent. **3** the number of cycles per second of a sound, light, or radio wave. **4** the particular waveband at which radio signals are broadcast or transmitted.

fre·quen·cy mod·u·la·tion ▶ **noun** the varying of the frequency of a wave, used as a means of broadcasting an audio signal by radio.

fre·quent ▶ **adjective** /ˈfrēkwənt/ **1** occurring or done many times at short intervals. **2** doing something often; regular: *he was a frequent visitor to Paris.*

– SYNONYMS **recurrent,** recurring, repeated, periodic, continual, habitual, regular, successive, numerous, several.
– ANTONYMS occasional.

▶ **verb** /frēˈkwent/ visit a place often or regularly.

– SYNONYMS **visit,** patronize, spend time in, visit regularly, haunt; informal hang out at.
– ANTONYMS avoid.

– DERIVATIVES **fre·quent·er** /frē'kwentər-/ noun.
– ORIGIN Latin *frequens* 'crowded, frequent.'

fre·quen·ta·tive /frē'kwentətiv/ ▶ **adjective** Grammar (of a verb or verbal form) expressing frequent repetition or intensity of action.

fre·quent·ly /'frēkwəntlē/ ▶ **adverb** at frequent intervals.

– SYNONYMS **often,** all the time, habitually, regularly, customarily, routinely, again and again, repeatedly, recurrently, continually; old use oftentimes.

fres·co /'freskō/ ▶ **noun** (pl. **frescoes** or **frescos**) a painting done on wet plaster on a wall or ceiling, in which the colors become fixed as the plaster dries.
– DERIVATIVES **fres·coed** adjective.
– ORIGIN Italian, 'cool, fresh.'

fresh /fresн/ ▶ **adjective 1** not previously known or used; new or different: *a fresh approach to treating problem skin.* **2** (of food) recently made or picked; not frozen or preserved. **3** recently created and so not impaired: *the memory was fresh in their minds.* **4** (**fresh from/out of**) (of a person) having just had a particular experience or come from a particular place: *we were fresh out of art school.* **5** pleasantly clean and cool: *fresh air.* **6** (of the wind) cool and fairly strong. **7** (of water) not salty. **8** full of energy. **9** informal too familiar toward someone, especially in a sexual way.

– SYNONYMS **1 new,** modern, original, novel, different, innovative. **2 recently made,** just picked, crisp, raw, natural, unprocessed. **3 refreshed,** rested, restored, energetic, vigorous, invigorated, lively, sprightly, bright, alert, bouncing, perky; informal full of beans, bright-eyed and bushy-tailed. **4 bracing,** brisk, strong, invigorating, chilly, cool; informal nippy. **5 cool,** crisp, refreshing, invigorating, pure, clean, clear. **6 impudent,** impertinent, insolent, presumptuous, forward, cheeky, disrespectful, rude; informal mouthy, saucy, lippy, sassy.
– ANTONYMS stale, old.

▶ **adverb** newly; recently.
– DERIVATIVES **fresh·ly** adverb **fresh·ness** noun.
– ORIGIN Old English, 'not salt, fit for drinking.'

fresh·en /'fresнən/ ▶ **verb 1** make or become fresh. **2** top off a drink. **3** (of wind) become stronger and colder.
– DERIVATIVES **fresh·en·er** noun.

fresh·et /'fresнət/ ▶ **noun 1** the flood of a river from heavy rain or melted snow. **2** a rush of fresh water flowing into the sea.
– ORIGIN probably from Old French *freschete.*

fresh·man /'fresнmən/ ▶ **noun** (pl. **freshmen**) a first-year student at a high school, college, or university.

fresh·wa·ter /'fresн'wôtər, -'wätər/ ▶ **adjective** relating to or found in fresh water; not of the sea.

fret[1] /fret/ ▶ **verb** (**frets, fretting, fretted**) **1** be constantly or visibly anxious. **2** gradually wear away something.

– SYNONYMS **worry,** be anxious, distress oneself, upset oneself, concern oneself, agonize, lose sleep.

▶ **noun** chiefly Brit. a state of anxiety.
– ORIGIN Old English, 'devour, consume.'

fret[2] ▶ **noun** each of a sequence of ridges on the fingerboard of some stringed instruments, used for fixing the positions of the fingers. ▶ **verb** (**frets, fretting, fretted**) provide a stringed instrument with frets.
– ORIGIN unknown.

fret[3] ▶ **noun** an ornamental design of vertical and horizontal lines. ▶ **verb** (**frets, fretting, fretted**) decorate something with fretwork.
– ORIGIN Old French *frete* 'trelliswork.'

fret·ful /'fretfəl/ ▶ **adjective** anxious or upset.
– DERIVATIVES **fret·ful·ly** adverb **fret·ful·ness** noun.

fret·saw /'fret,sô/ ▶ **noun** a saw with a narrow blade for cutting designs in thin wood or metal.

fret·work /'fret,wərk/ ▶ **noun** decorative patterns cut in wood with a fretsaw.

Freud·i·an /'froidēən/ ▶ **adjective 1** relating to or influenced by the Austrian psychotherapist Sigmund Freud and his methods of psychoanalysis. **2** able to be analyzed in terms of unconscious thoughts or desires: *a Freudian slip.* ▶ **noun** a follower of Freud or his methods.
– DERIVATIVES **Freud·i·an·ism** /-,nizəm/ noun.

Fri. ▶ **abbreviation** Friday.

fri·a·ble /'frīəbəl/ ▶ **adjective** easily crumbled.
– DERIVATIVES **fri·a·bil·i·ty** /,frīə'bilətē/ noun.
– ORIGIN from Latin *friare* 'to crumble.'

fri·ar /'frīər/ ▶ **noun** a member of certain religious orders of men.
– ORIGIN Old French *frere.*

fri·ar·y /'frīərē/ ▶ **noun** (pl. **friaries**) a building or community occupied by friars.

fric·as·see /'frikə,sē, ,frikə'sē/ ▶ **noun** a dish of stewed or fried pieces of meat served in a thick white sauce.
– DERIVATIVES **fric·as·seed** adjective.
– ORIGIN French.

fric·a·tive /'frikətiv/ ▶ **adjective** referring to a type of consonant (e.g., *f*) made by the friction of breath in a narrow opening.
– ORIGIN from Latin *fricare* 'to rub.'

fric·tion /'friksнən/ ▶ **noun 1** the resistance that one surface or object encounters when moving over another. **2** the action of one surface or object rubbing against another. **3** conflict or disagreement: *a number of issues are causing friction between the two countries.*

– SYNONYMS **1 rubbing,** chafing, grating, rasping, scraping, resistance, drag, abrasion. **2 discord,** disagreement, dissension, dispute, conflict, hostility, animosity, antipathy, antagonism, resentment, acrimony, bitterness, bad feeling.
– ANTONYMS harmony.

– DERIVATIVES **fric·tion·al** adjective **fric·tion·less** adjective.
– ORIGIN from Latin *fricare* 'to rub.'

Fri·day /'frīdā, -dē/ ▶ **noun** the day of the week before Saturday and following Thursday.
– ORIGIN Old English, named after the Germanic goddess *Frigga.*

fridge /frij/ ▶ **noun** a refrigerator.

fried /frīd/ past and past participle of **FRY**[1].

friend /frend/ ▶ **noun 1** a person that one likes and knows well. **2** a person who supports a particular cause or organization. **3** (**Friend**) a Quaker.

– SYNONYMS **companion,** comrade, confidant, confidante, familiar, intimate, soulmate, playmate, ally, associate; informal pal, buddy, bud, chum, amigo, compadre, homeboy; Brit. informal mate.
– ANTONYMS enemy.

– DERIVATIVES **friend·less** adjective.
– PHRASES **friend of the court** another term for **AMICUS**.
– ORIGIN Old English.

friend·ly /ˈfrendlē/ ▶ **adjective** (**friendlier, friendliest**) **1** kind and pleasant. **2** on good terms; not hostile. **3** (in combination) not harmful to a specified thing: *environment-friendly*. **4** Military relating to or allied with one's own forces: *two soldiers were killed by friendly fire*.

– SYNONYMS **1** *a friendly woman* **amiable,** companionable, sociable, gregarious, comradely, neighborly, hospitable, easy to get along with, affable, genial, cordial, warm, affectionate, convivial; informal chummy. **2** *friendly conversation* **amicable,** cordial, pleasant, easy, relaxed, casual, informal, close, intimate, familiar.
– ANTONYMS hostile.

▶ **noun** (pl. **friendlies**) Brit. a game or match not forming part of a serious competition.
– DERIVATIVES **friend·li·ly** adverb **friend·li·ness** noun.

friend·ly fire ▶ **noun** another term for **FRATRICIDE** (sense 2).

friend·ship /ˈfrend,sʜip/ ▶ **noun** **1** a relationship between friends. **2** the state of being friends.

– SYNONYMS **1** *lasting friendships* **relationship,** attachment, association, bond, tie, link, union. **2** *ties of friendship* **friendliness,** affection, camaraderie, comradeship, companionship, fellowship, closeness, affinity, unity, intimacy.
– ANTONYMS hostility.

frieze /frēz/ ▶ **noun** **1** a broad horizontal band of sculpted or painted decoration. **2** Architecture the part of an entablature between the architrave and the cornice.
– ORIGIN Latin *frisium*.

frig·ate /ˈfrigit/ ▶ **noun** a warship with a mixed armament, generally lighter than a destroyer.
– ORIGIN Italian *fregata*.

frig·ate bird ▶ **noun** a tropical seabird with a deeply forked tail and a long hooked bill.

fright /frīt/ ▶ **noun** **1** a sudden intense feeling of fear. **2** a shock.

– SYNONYMS **1 fear,** terror, horror, alarm, panic, dread, trepidation, dismay, nervousness. **2 scare,** shock, surprise, turn, jolt, start.

– PHRASES **look a fright** informal look ridiculous or very disheveled. **take fright** suddenly become frightened.
– ORIGIN Old English.

fright·en /ˈfrītn/ ▶ **verb** **1** make someone afraid. **2** (**frighten someone/thing off**) make someone or something too afraid to do something.

– SYNONYMS **scare,** startle, alarm, terrify, petrify, shock, chill, panic, unnerve, intimidate; informal spook.

– DERIVATIVES **fright·ened** adjective **fright·en·er** noun.

fright·en·ing /ˈfrītn-ɪɴɢ/ ▶ **adjective** causing fear or anxiety.

– SYNONYMS **terrifying,** horrifying, alarming, startling, chilling, spine-chilling, hair-raising, blood-curdling, disturbing, unnerving, intimidating, daunting, eerie, sinister, fearsome, nightmarish, menacing; informal scary, spooky, creepy.

– DERIVATIVES **fright·en·ing·ly** adverb.

fright·ful /ˈfrītfəl/ ▶ **adjective** **1** very unpleasant, serious, or shocking. **2** informal terrible; awful.

– SYNONYMS **horrible,** horrific, ghastly, horrendous, awful, dreadful, terrible, nasty; informal horrid.

– DERIVATIVES **fright·ful·ly** adverb **fright·ful·ness** noun.

fright wig ▶ **noun** a wig with the hair arranged sticking out, as worn by a clown.

frig·id /ˈfrijid/ ▶ **adjective** **1** very cold. **2** (especially of a woman) unable to be sexually aroused. **3** stiff or formal in style: *the house is no frigid art museum*.

– SYNONYMS **1 very cold,** bitterly cold, bitter, freezing, frozen, frosty, icy, chilly, chill, wintry, subzero, arctic, Siberian, polar, glacial; informal nippy. **2 stiff,** formal, stony, wooden, unemotional, passionless, unfeeling, distant, aloof, remote, reserved, unapproachable; frosty, cold, icy, cool, unsmiling, forbidding, unfriendly, unwelcoming; informal standoffish.
– ANTONYMS hot, friendly.

– DERIVATIVES **fri·gid·i·ty** /frəˈjidətē/ noun **frig·id·ly** adverb.
– ORIGIN Latin *frigidus*.

fri·jo·les /frēˈhōlēz/ ▶ **plural noun** (in Mexican cooking) beans.

frill /fril/ ▶ **noun** **1** a strip of gathered or pleated material used as a decorative edging. **2** a frill-like fringe of feathers, hair, skin, etc., on a bird or other animal. **3** (**frills**) unnecessary extra features: *a comfortable room with no frills*.
– DERIVATIVES **frilled** adjective **frill·y** adjective.
– ORIGIN Flemish *frul*.

fringe /frinj/ ▶ **noun** **1** a border of threads, tassels, or twists, used to edge clothing or material. **2** chiefly Brit. the front part of someone's hair, cut so as to hang over the forehead; bangs. **3** a natural border of hair or fibers in an animal or plant. **4** an outer part or edge of an area, group, or activity: *loners living on the fringes of society*.

– SYNONYMS **1 edge,** border, margin, extremity, perimeter, periphery, rim, limits, outskirts. **2 edging,** border, trimming, frill, flounce, ruffle.
– ANTONYMS middle.

▶ **adjective** not part of the mainstream; unconventional: *fringe theater*.

– SYNONYMS **alternative,** avant-garde, experimental, innovative, left-field, radical.
– ANTONYMS mainstream.

▶ **verb** provide with or form a fringe: *the sea is fringed by palm trees*.
– DERIVATIVES **fring·ing** noun **fring·y** adjective.
– ORIGIN Old French *frenge*.

fringe ben·e·fit ▶ **noun** an additional benefit, especially one given to an employee.

frip·per·y /ˈfripərē/ ▶ **noun** (pl. **fripperies**) **1** showy or unnecessary ornament. **2** a frivolous or trivial thing.
– ORIGIN Old French *freperie* 'secondhand clothes.'

Fris·bee /ˈfrizbē/ ▶ **noun** trademark a plastic disk designed for skimming through the air as an outdoor game.
– ORIGIN said to be named after the pie tins of the *Frisbie* bakery in Connecticut.

Fri·sian /ˈfrizʜən, ˈfrē-/ ▶ **noun** **1** a person from Frisia or Friesland in the Netherlands. **2** the Germanic language spoken in northern parts of the Netherlands and adjacent islands. ▶ **adjective** relating to Frisia or Friesland.

frisk /frisk/ ▶ **verb** **1** pass the hands over someone in a search for hidden weapons or drugs. **2** skip or move playfully; frolic.
– ORIGIN Old French *frisque* 'alert, lively.'

frisk·y /ˈfriskē/ ▶ **adjective** (**friskier, friskiest**) playful and full of energy.

– SYNONYMS **lively,** bouncy, bubbly, perky, active, energetic, animated, playful, coltish, skittish, spirited, high-spirited, in high spirits, exuberant; informal full of beans.

fris·son /frē'sôN/ ▶ **noun** a sudden strong feeling of excitement or fear; a thrill.
– ORIGIN French.

frit·il·lar·y /'fritl,erē/ ▶ **noun** (pl. **fritillaries**) **1** a plant with hanging bell-like flowers. **2** a butterfly with orange-brown wings checkered with black.
– ORIGIN Latin *fritillaria*.

frit·ta·ta /frē'tätə/ ▶ **noun** an Italian dish made with fried beaten eggs, resembling a Spanish omelet.
– ORIGIN Italian.

frit·ter[1] /'fritər/ ▶ **verb** (**fritter something away**) waste time, money, or energy on trivial matters.
– ORIGIN from former *fitter* 'break into fragments.'

frit·ter[2] ▶ **noun** a piece of fruit, vegetable, or meat that is coated in batter and deep-fried.
– ORIGIN Old French *friture*.

fritz /frits/ ▶ **noun** (in phrase **go** or **be on the fritz**) informal (of a machine) stop working properly.
– ORIGIN said to be a use of *Fritz*, with allusion to cheap German imports into the US before World War I.

friv·o·lous /'frivələs/ ▶ **adjective 1** not having any serious purpose or value. **2** (of a person) not serious or responsible.

– SYNONYMS **flippant,** glib, facetious, joking, jokey, lighthearted, fatuous, inane; informal flip.
– ANTONYMS serious.

– DERIVATIVES **fri·vol·i·ty** /fri'välətē/ noun **friv·o·lous·ly** adverb.
– ORIGIN Latin *frivolus* 'silly, trifling.'

frizz /friz/ ▶ **verb** (of hair) form into a mass of tight curls. ▶ **noun** a mass of tightly curled hair.
– ORIGIN French *friser*.

friz·zle[1] /'frizəl/ ▶ **verb** fry something until crisp or burned.
– ORIGIN from **FRY**[1], probably influenced by **SIZZLE**.

friz·zle[2] ▶ **verb** form hair into tight curls.
– ORIGIN from **FRIZZ**.

friz·zy /'frizē/ ▶ **adjective** (**frizzier, frizziest**) formed of a mass of small, tight curls.
– DERIVATIVES **friz·zi·ness** noun.

fro /frō/ ▶ **adverb** see **TO AND FRO** at **TO**.
– ORIGIN Old Norse.

frock /fräk/ ▶ **noun 1** chiefly Brit. a dress. **2** a loose outer garment, especially a long gown worn by monks or priests.
– ORIGIN Old French *froc*.

frock coat ▶ **noun** a man's double-breasted, long-skirted coat, now worn chiefly on formal occasions.

frog[1] /frôg, fräg/ ▶ **noun 1** a tailless amphibian with a short squat body and very long hind legs for leaping. **2** (**Frog**) informal, derogatory a French person.
– DERIVATIVES **frog·gy** adjective.
– PHRASES **have a frog in one's throat** informal find it hard to speak because of hoarseness.
– ORIGIN Old English: sense 2 is partly from the reputation of the French for eating frogs' legs.

frog[2] ▶ **noun 1** a thing used to hold or fasten something. **2** an ornamental coat fastener consisting of a spindle-shaped button and a loop.
– ORIGIN perhaps from **FROG**[1], influenced by Italian *forchetta* or French *fourchette* 'small fork.'

frog[3] ▶ **noun** an elastic horny pad in the sole of a horse's hoof.
– ORIGIN perhaps from **FROG**[1]; perhaps also influenced by Italian *forchetta* or French *fourchette* (see **FROG**[2]).

frog·man /'frôg,man, 'fräg-, -mən/ ▶ **noun** (pl. **frogmen**) a diver equipped with a rubber suit, flippers, and breathing equipment.

frog·march /'frôg,märcH, 'fräg-/ ▶ **verb** force someone to walk forward with their arms pinned from behind.

frol·ic /'frälik/ ▶ **verb** (**frolics, frolicking, frolicked**) play or move around in a cheerful and lively way. ▶ **noun** a lively or playful act or activity.
– DERIVATIVES **frol·ick·er** noun.
– ORIGIN from Dutch *vrolijk* 'merry, cheerful.'

frol·ic·some /'fräliksəm/ ▶ **adjective** lively and playful.

from /frəm/ ▶ **preposition 1** indicating the point at which a journey, process, or action starts. **2** indicating the source of something. **3** indicating the starting point of a range. **4** indicating separation, removal, or prevention. **5** indicating a cause. **6** indicating a difference.
– PHRASES **from time to time** occasionally.
– ORIGIN Old English.

frond /fränd/ ▶ **noun** the leaf or leaflike part of a palm, fern, or similar plant.
– ORIGIN Latin *frons* 'leaf.'

front /frənt/ ▶ **noun 1** the side or part of an object that presents itself to view or that is normally seen first. **2** the position directly ahead. **3** the forward-facing part of a person's body. **4** any face of a building, especially that of the main entrance: *the west front of the cathedral.* **5** the furthest position that an armed force has reached. **6** Meteorology the forward edge of an advancing mass of air. **7** a particular situation or area of activity: *good news on the job front.* **8** an organized political group. **9** a deceptive appearance or way of behaving: *I put on a brave front.* **10** a person or organization serving as a cover for secret or illegal activities. **11** boldness and confidence.

– SYNONYMS **1 fore,** foremost part, forepart, nose, head, bow, prow, foreground. **2 frontage,** face, facing, facade. **3 head,** beginning, start, top, lead. **4 appearance,** air, face, manner, exterior, veneer, (outward) show, act, pretense. **5 cover,** blind, disguise, facade, mask, cloak, screen, smokescreen, camouflage.
– ANTONYMS back.

▶ **adjective** of or at the front.

– SYNONYMS **leading,** lead, first, foremost.
– ANTONYMS back, last.

▶ **verb 1** have the front facing toward something. **2** place or be placed at the front of something. **3** provide something with a front or facing. **4** lead or be prominent in: *the group is fronted by two girl singers.* **5** present or host a television or radio program. **6** act as a front for secret or illegal activity.
– DERIVATIVES **front·ward** adjective & adverb **front·wards** adverb.
– PHRASES **in front of** in the presence of. **out front 1** at or to the front; in front: *two station wagons stopped out front.* **2** in the auditorium of a theater. **up front 1** at or near the front: *the floor plan has an open living area up front.* **2** in advance: *every fee must be paid up front.* **3** open and direct; frank: *I vowed to be up front with her.*
– ORIGIN Latin *frons* 'forehead, front.'

front·age /ˈfrəntij/ ▸ **noun 1** the facade of a building. **2** a piece of land adjoining a street or waterway.

front·age road ▸ **noun** a subsidiary road running parallel to a main road or highway and giving access to houses and businesses. Also called **SERVICE ROAD**.

fron·tal /ˈfrəntl/ ▸ **adjective 1** relating to or at the front. **2** relating to the forehead or front part of the skull.
– DERIVATIVES **fron·tal·ly** adverb.

fron·tal lobe ▸ **noun** each of the paired lobes of the brain lying immediately behind the forehead.

front and cen·ter ▸ **adverb** prominently; at the forefront: *trade negotiators put this issue front and center.*

front burn·er ▸ **noun** the focus of attention: *a revamp of the 1872 Mining Law is next up on the front burner.*

front court ▸ **noun 1** the part of a basketball court where each team tries to score against its opponent. **2** the players on a team who usually play closest to the other team's basket when trying to score.

front desk ▸ **noun** the main desk at a hotel or motel, for checking in or out and handling requests from guests.

front-end ▸ **adjective 1** informal (of money) paid or charged at the beginning of a transaction. **2** Computing (of a device or program) directly accessed by the user and allowing access to further devices or programs.

fron·tier /ˌfrənˈti(ə)r/ ▸ **noun 1** a border separating two countries. **2** the extreme limit of settled land beyond which lies wilderness. **3** the limit of knowledge or achievement in a particular area: *fundamental problems at the frontiers of cosmology.*

> – SYNONYMS **border,** boundary, borderline, dividing line, perimeter, limit, edge.

– ORIGIN Old French *frontiere*.

fron·tiers·man /ˌfrənˈti(ə)rzmən/ (or **frontierswoman** /ˌfrənˈti(ə)rzˌwo͝omən/) ▸ **noun** (pl. **frontiersmen** or **frontierswomen** /ˌfrənˈti(ə)rzˌwimin/) a man (or woman) living in the region of a frontier.

fron·tis·piece /ˈfrəntisˌpēs/ ▸ **noun** an illustration facing the title page of a book.
– ORIGIN Latin *frontispicium* 'facade.'

front line ▸ **noun 1** the part of an army that is closest to the enemy. **2** the most important position in an area of activity: *we're on the front line of world theater.*

front·man /ˈfrəntˌman, -mən/ ▸ **noun** (pl. **frontmen**) **1** the leader of a band. **2** a person who represents an illegal organization to give it an appearance of legitimacy.

front of·fice ▸ **noun** the management or administrative officers of a business or other organization.

front-page ▸ **adjective 1** appearing on the first page of a newspaper or similar publication and containing important or remarkable news: *they ran a front-page story headlined "White-Collar Chic."* **2** worthy of being printed on the first page of a newspaper, etc.: *dishonest research has become front-page news.*

front run·ner ▸ **noun** the leading contestant in a race or other competition.

front-wheel drive ▸ **noun** a transmission system that provides power to the front wheels of a motor vehicle.

frosh /fräsʜ/ ▸ **noun** informal freshman or freshmen: *I went to private school for my frosh and sophomore year.*

frost /frôst/ ▸ **noun 1** a deposit of white ice crystals formed on surfaces when the temperature falls below freezing. **2** a period of cold weather when frost forms. ▸ **verb 1** cover or be covered with frost. **2** decorate a cake, cupcake, etc., with icing. **3** tint hair strands to lighten the color of isolated strands.
– ORIGIN Old English.

frost·bite /ˈfrôs(t)ˌbīt/ ▸ **noun** injury to body tissues, especially the nose, fingers, or toes, caused by exposure to extreme cold.
– DERIVATIVES **frost·bit·ten** /ˈfrôs(t)ˌbitn/ adjective.

frost·ed /ˈfrôstid/ ▸ **adjective 1** covered with frost. **2** (of glass) having a textured surface so that it is difficult to see through. **3** (of food) decorated with icing. **4** (of hair) having isolated strands tinted a light color.

frost·ing /ˈfrôstiɴɢ/ ▸ **noun 1** icing. **2** a roughened matte finish on otherwise shiny material such as glass or steel.

frost·y /ˈfrôstē/ ▸ **adjective** (**frostier, frostiest**) **1** (of the weather) very cold with frost forming on surfaces. **2** cold and unfriendly.

> – SYNONYMS **1 cold,** freezing, frozen, icy, bitter, chill, wintry, arctic; informal nippy. **2 unfriendly,** cold, frigid, icy, glacial, inhospitable, unwelcoming, forbidding, hostile, stony.
> – ANTONYMS warm, friendly.

– DERIVATIVES **frost·i·ly** adverb **frost·i·ness** noun.

froth /frôᴛʜ/ ▸ **noun 1** a mass of small bubbles in liquid. **2** worthless or superficial talk, ideas, or activities: *the network has to explain the substance rather than the froth of politics.*

> – SYNONYMS **foam,** head, bubbles, frothiness, fizz, effervescence, lather, suds.

▸ **verb 1** form or produce froth. **2** be very angry or agitated.

> – SYNONYMS **bubble,** fizz, effervesce, foam, lather, churn, seethe.

– ORIGIN Old Norse.

froth·y /ˈfrôᴛʜē, -ᴛʜē/ ▸ **adjective** (**frothier, frothiest**) **1** full of or covered with a mass of small bubbles. **2** light and entertaining but of little substance: *lots of frothy interviews.*
– DERIVATIVES **froth·i·ly** adverb **froth·i·ness** noun.

frou-frou /ˈfro͞oˌfro͞o/ ▸ **noun** (usu. before another noun) frills or other ornamentation: *a little frou-frou skirt.*
– ORIGIN French.

frown /froun/ ▸ **verb 1** furrow one's brows to show disapproval, displeasure, or concentration. **2** (**frown on**) disapprove of: *casual sex is still frowned upon.*

> – SYNONYMS **1 scowl,** glower, glare, lower/lour, make a face, look daggers, give someone a black look, knit/furrow one's brows; informal give someone a dirty look. **2** (**frown on**) **disapprove of,** take a dim view of, take exception to, object to, look askance at, not take kindly to.
> – ANTONYMS smile.

▸ **noun** an act of frowning.
– ORIGIN Old French *froignier*.

frowz·y /ˈfrouzē/ (also **frowsy**) ▸ **adjective** scruffy, dingy, and neglected in appearance.
– ORIGIN unknown.

froze /frōz/ past of **FREEZE**.

fro·zen /ˈfrōzən/ past participle of **FREEZE**.

fruc·ti·fy /ˈfrəktəˌfī/ ▸ **verb** (**fructifies, fructifying, fructified**) formal **1** make or become fruitful. **2** bear fruit.
– ORIGIN Latin *fructificare*.

fruc·tose /'frək,tōs, 'fro͝ok-, -,tōz/ ▶ **noun** a simple sugar found chiefly in honey and fruit.
– ORIGIN from Latin *fructus* 'fruit.'

fru·gal /'fro͞ogəl/ ▶ **adjective 1** using only as much money or food as is necessary: *a frugal way of life.* **2** (of a meal) simple, plain, and costing little.

– SYNONYMS **1 thrifty,** economical, careful, cautious, prudent, provident, sparing, abstemious, austere, self-denying, ascetic, spartan. **2 meager,** scanty, scant, paltry, skimpy, plain, simple, spartan, inexpensive, cheap, economical.
– ANTONYMS extravagant, lavish.

– DERIVATIVES **fru·gal·i·ty** /fro͞o'galətē/ noun **fru·gal·ly** adverb.
– ORIGIN Latin *frugalis.*

CHOOSE THE RIGHT WORD

See **ECONOMICAL**.

fru·gi·vore /'fro͞oji,vôr/ ▶ **noun** an animal that feeds on fruit.
– DERIVATIVES **fru·giv·o·rous** /fro͞o'jivərəs/ adjective.
– ORIGIN from Latin *frux* 'fruit.'

fruit /fro͞ot/ ▶ **noun 1** the sweet and fleshy product of a tree or other plant that contains seed and can be eaten as food. **2** Botany the seed-bearing structure of a plant, e.g., an acorn. **3** the result or reward of work or activity: *the state is encouraging people to enjoy the fruits of their labor.* **4** informal, derogatory a male homosexual. ▶ **verb** (of a plant) produce fruit.
– ORIGIN Latin *fructus* 'enjoyment of produce, harvest.'

fruit·ar·i·an /fro͞o'te(ə)rēən/ ▶ **noun** a person who eats only fruit.
– DERIVATIVES **fruit·ar·i·an·ism** noun.

fruit bat ▶ **noun** a large bat that feeds chiefly on fruit or nectar.

fruit·cake /'fro͞ot,kāk/ ▶ **noun 1** a dense cake containing dried fruits and nuts. **2** informal an eccentric or mad person.

fruit cock·tail ▶ **noun** a chopped fruit salad, often sold in cans.

fruit fly ▶ **noun** a small fly that feeds on fruit in both its adult and larval stages.

fruit·ful /'fro͞otfəl/ ▶ **adjective 1** producing much fruit; fertile. **2** producing good results: *fruitful research.*

– SYNONYMS **productive,** constructive, useful, worthwhile, helpful, beneficial, valuable, rewarding, profitable, advantageous.
– ANTONYMS barren, futile.

– DERIVATIVES **fruit·ful·ly** adverb **fruit·ful·ness** noun.

CHOOSE THE RIGHT WORD

See **FERTILE**.

fruit·ing bod·y ▶ **noun** the spore-producing organ of a fungus, often seen as a toadstool.

fru·i·tion /fro͞o'isʜən/ ▶ **noun 1** the fulfillment of a plan or project. **2** literary the state or action of producing fruit.

– SYNONYMS **fulfillment,** realization, actualization, materialization, achievement, attainment, accomplishment, success, completion, consummation, conclusion, close, finish, perfection, maturity.

– ORIGIN from Latin *frui* 'enjoy.'

fruit·less /'fro͞otləs/ ▶ **adjective 1** failing to achieve the desired results; unproductive: *a fruitless search for contentment.* **2** not producing fruit.

– SYNONYMS **futile,** vain, in vain, to no avail, to no effect, idle, pointless, useless, worthless, hollow, ineffectual, ineffective, unproductive, unrewarding, profitless, unsuccessful, unavailing, abortive.
– ANTONYMS fruitful, productive.

– DERIVATIVES **fruit·less·ly** adverb **fruit·less·ness** noun.

fruit sal·ad ▶ **noun** a mixture of different types of chopped fruit.

fruit·y /'fro͞otē/ ▶ **adjective** (**fruitier, fruitiest**) **1** relating to, resembling, or containing fruit. **2** (of a voice) deep and rich. **3** informal, derogatory relating to or associated with homosexuals.
– DERIVATIVES **fruit·i·ness** noun.

frump /frəmp/ ▶ **noun** an unattractive woman who wears dowdy old-fashioned clothes.
– DERIVATIVES **frump·y** adjective.
– ORIGIN probably from Dutch *verrompelen* 'wrinkle.'

frus·trate /'frəs,trāt/ ▶ **verb 1** prevent a plan or action from progressing or succeeding. **2** prevent someone from doing or achieving something. **3** make someone annoyed or dissatisfied as a result of being unable to do something.

– SYNONYMS **1 thwart,** defeat, foil, block, stop, counter, spoil, check, forestall, scotch, derail, snooker; informal stymie; Brit. informal scupper. **2 exasperate,** infuriate, discourage, dishearten, disappoint.
– ANTONYMS further, satisfy.

– DERIVATIVES **frus·trat·ed** adjective **frus·trat·ing** adjective.
– ORIGIN Latin *frustrare* 'disappoint.'

frus·tra·tion /frə'strāsʜən/ ▶ **noun 1** the feeling of being upset or annoyed as a result of being unable to do something. **2** a cause of dissatisfaction or annoyance: *the frustrations of travel.* **3** the prevention of the progress, success, or fulfillment of something.

fry[1] /frī/ ▶ **verb** (**fries, frying, fried**) **1** cook or be cooked in hot fat or oil. **2** informal (of a person) burn or overheat. ▶ **noun** (pl. **fries**) **1** a fried dish or meal: *we'll have one burger and two fish fries.* **2** a gathering where fried food is served: *Friday night is the Rotary fish fry.* **3** (**fries**) French fries.
– ORIGIN Old French *frire.*

fry[2] ▶ **plural noun** young fish, especially when newly hatched.
– ORIGIN Old Norse.

fry·er /'frīər/ ▶ **noun 1** a large, deep container for frying food. **2** a small young chicken suitable for frying.

fry·ing pan (also **frypan** /'frī,pan/) ▶ **noun** a shallow pan with a long handle, used for frying food.
– PHRASES **out of the frying pan into the fire** from a bad situation to one that is worse.

FSBO /'fiz,bō/ ▶ **abbreviation** for sale by owner; relating to sales of private homes by their owners: *visit our home buying page to see FSBO homes for sale.*

FSH ▶ **abbreviation** follicle-stimulating hormone, a hormone that promotes the formation of ova or sperm.

f-stop ▶ **noun** a camera setting corresponding to a particular f-number.

FT ▶ **abbreviation 1** full-time. **2** Basketball free throw.

Ft. ▶ **abbreviation** Fort: *Ft. Lauderdale.*

ft. ▸ abbreviation foot or feet.

FTC ▸ abbreviation Federal Trade Commission.

FTP ▸ abbreviation Computing file transfer protocol, a standard for the exchange of program and data files across a network.

fu·bar /ˈfo͞oˌbär/ ▸ adjective out of working order; seriously, perhaps irreparably, damaged: *the clock in the hall is fubar.*
– ORIGIN acronym from *fucked up beyond all recognition* (or *repair*).

fuch·sia /ˈfyo͞oSHə/ ▸ noun **1** an ornamental shrub with drooping tubular flowers that are typically of two different colors. **2** a vivid purplish-red color.
– ORIGIN named after the German botanist Leonhard *Fuchs*.

fuck /fək/ vulgar slang ▸ verb **1** have sexual intercourse with someone. **2** damage or ruin something. ▸ noun an act of sexual intercourse. ▸ exclamation a strong expression of annoyance or contempt.
– PHRASES **fuck off** go away. **fuck someone/thing up** **1** damage someone emotionally. **2** do something badly.
– ORIGIN Germanic.

fuck-up ▸ noun vulgar slang **1** a mess or botched job: *near misses, complete misses, and total fuck-ups.* **2** someone who regularly botches things: *I was a C-student fuck-up.*

fud·dled /ˈfədld/ ▸ adjective confused or stupefied, especially with alcohol: *my head was aching and my brain seemed fuddled.*

fud·dy-dud·dy /ˈfədē ˌdədē/ ▸ noun (pl. **fuddy-duddies**) informal a person who is old-fashioned and who often disapproves of modern ideas, behavior, etc.
– ORIGIN unknown.

fudge /fəj/ ▸ noun **1** a soft candy made from sugar, butter, and milk or cream. **2** an attempt to fudge an issue. ▸ verb **1** present or deal with an issue in a vague way, especially to conceal the truth or mislead people. **2** manipulate facts or figures so as to present a more desirable picture.

– SYNONYMS **evade,** avoid, dodge, skirt, duck, gloss over, cloud, hedge, beat about the bush, equivocate.

– ORIGIN probably from former *fadge* 'to fit.'

fueh·rer ▸ noun variant spelling of **FÜHRER**.

fu·el /ˈfyo͞oəl/ ▸ noun **1** material such as coal, gas, or oil that is burned to produce heat or power. **2** food, drink, or drugs as a source of energy. **3** something that stirs up argument or strong emotion. ▸ verb (**fuels, fueling, fueled**) **1** supply something with fuel. **2** stir up or strengthen: *the slide in share prices fueled demands for government intervention.*

– SYNONYMS **1 power,** fire, drive, run. **2 fan,** feed, stoke up, inflame, intensify, stimulate, encourage, provoke, incite, sustain.

– ORIGIN Old French *fouaille*.

fu·el cell ▸ noun a cell producing an electric current directly from a chemical reaction.

fu·el in·jec·tion ▸ noun the direct introduction of fuel under pressure into the combustion units of an internal-combustion engine, as a way of improving a car's performance.

fuel rod ▸ noun a rod-shaped fuel element in a nuclear reactor.

fu·gal /ˈfyo͞ogəl/ ▸ adjective relating to a fugue.

fu·gi·tive /ˈfyo͞ojətiv/ ▸ noun a person who has escaped from captivity or is in hiding.

– SYNONYMS **escapee,** runaway, deserter, absconder, refugee.

▸ adjective quick to disappear; fleeting: *a fugitive glimpse.*
– ORIGIN from Latin *fugere* 'flee.'

fugue /fyo͞og/ ▸ noun **1** a musical composition in which a short melody or phrase is introduced by one part and successively taken up by others. **2** Psychiatry a period during which someone loses their memory or sense of identity and may leave their home or usual surroundings.
– ORIGIN Latin *fuga* 'flight.'

füh·rer /ˈfyo͞orər/ (also **fuehrer**) ▸ noun the title used by Hitler as leader of Germany.
– ORIGIN German, 'leader.'

ful·crum /ˈfo͝olkrəm, ˈfəl-/ ▸ noun (pl. **fulcra** /-krə/ or **fulcrums**) the point on which a lever turns or is supported.
– ORIGIN Latin, 'post of a couch.'

ful·fill /fo͝olˈfil/ (Brit. **fulfil**) ▸ verb **1** achieve or realize something desired, promised, or predicted: *I fulfilled a childhood dream when I became champion.* **2** satisfy or meet a requirement or condition. **3** (**fulfill oneself**) gain happiness or satisfaction by fully developing one's abilities.

– SYNONYMS **1 achieve,** attain, realize, make happen, succeed in, bring to completion, bring to fruition, satisfy. **2 carry out,** perform, accomplish, execute, do, discharge, conduct. **3 meet,** satisfy, comply with, conform to, fill, answer.

– DERIVATIVES **ful·fill·ing** adjective.
– ORIGIN Old English, 'fill up, make full.'

ful·filled /fo͝olˈfild/ ▸ adjective satisfied or happy.

– SYNONYMS **satisfied,** content, contented, happy, pleased, at peace.
– ANTONYMS discontented.

ful·fill·ment /fo͝olˈfilmənt/ (Brit. **fulfilment**) ▸ noun **1** a feeling of satisfaction or happiness as a result of fully developing one's abilities. **2** the action of fulfilling something.

full /fo͝ol/ ▸ adjective **1** containing or holding as much or as many as possible; having no empty space. **2** (**full of**) having a large number or quantity of something. **3** not lacking or omitting anything; complete: *I don't know the full story.* **4** (**full of**) unable to stop talking or thinking about: *they had their photographs taken and he was full of it.* **5** plump or rounded. **6** (of flavor, sound, or color) strong or rich.

– SYNONYMS **1 filled,** brimming, brimful, packed, loaded, crammed, crowded, bursting, overflowing, congested; informal jam-packed, wall-to-wall, chock-a-block, chock-full, awash. **2 replete,** full up, satisfied, sated, satiated; informal stuffed. **3 eventful,** interesting, exciting, lively, action-packed, busy, active. **4 comprehensive,** thorough, exhaustive, all-inclusive, all-encompassing, all-embracing, in-depth, complete, entire, whole, unabridged, uncut. **5 plump,** rounded, buxom, shapely, ample, curvaceous, voluptuous; informal busty, curvy, well endowed, zaftig. **6 loose-fitting,** loose, baggy, voluminous, roomy, capacious, billowing.
– ANTONYMS empty.

▸ adverb **1** straight; directly. **2** very.
– PHRASES **full of oneself** very self-satisfied and proud of oneself. **full on 1** running at or providing maximum

power or capacity. **2** so as to make a direct impact. **3** (**full-on**) informal unrestrained: *hours of full-on fun.* **full speed** (or **steam**) **ahead** proceeding with as much speed or energy as possible. **full up** filled to capacity. **in full** **1** with nothing omitted: *your life story in full.* **2** to the full amount due: *their relocation costs would be paid in full.* **3** to the utmost; completely: *the textbooks have failed to exploit in full the opportunities offered.*
– ORIGIN Old English.

full·back /ˈfo͝olˌbak/ ▶ **noun 1** Football an offensive player in the backfield. **2** a defender who plays at the side in a game such as soccer or field hockey.

full-blood·ed ▶ **adjective** wholehearted and enthusiastic.

full-blown ▶ **adjective** fully developed.

full-bod·ied ▶ **adjective** rich and satisfying in flavor or sound.

full bore ▶ **adverb** at full speed or maximum capacity. ▶ **adjective** referring to firearms with a relatively large caliber.

full-court press ▶ **noun 1** Basketball a defensive tactic in which members of a team cover their opponents throughout the court and not just near their own basket. **2** an instance of aggressive pressure: *if the president were to mount a full-court press for the space station.*

full·er·ene /ˌfo͝oləˈrēn/ ▶ **noun** Chemistry a form of carbon having a molecule consisting of atoms joined together in a hollow structure.
– ORIGIN shortening of *buckminsterfullerene* (the first known example, named after the American architect Richard Buckminster Fuller).

ful·ler's earth /ˈfo͝olərz/ ▶ **noun** a type of clay used to treat cloth during manufacture.

full-fledged ▶ **adjective 1** completely developed or established; of full status: *a full-fledged police detective.* **2** (of a bird) having fully developed wing feathers and able to fly.

full-fron·tal ▶ **adjective** fully exposing the front of the body, especially the genitals.

full-grown ▶ **adjective** having reached maturity: *full-grown wheat.*

full house ▶ **noun 1** a theater or meeting that is filled to capacity. **2** a poker hand with three of a kind and a pair. **3** a winning card at bingo in which all the numbers have been successfully marked off.

full-length ▶ **adjective 1** of the standard length: *a full-length Disney cartoon.* **2** (of a garment or curtain) extending to, or almost to, the ground. **3** (of a mirror or portrait) showing the whole human figure. ▶ **adverb** (usu. **full length**) (of a person) with the body lying stretched out and flat: *Lucy flung herself full length on the floor.*

full moon ▶ **noun** the phase of the moon in which its whole disk is illuminated.

full·ness /ˈfo͝olnəs/ ▶ **noun 1** the state of being full. **2** richness or abundance.
– PHRASES **in the fullness of time** after a due length of time has passed.

full-scale ▶ **adjective 1** (of a model or representation) of the same size as the thing represented. **2** as complete and thorough as possible: *a full-scale search of the area.*

full stop ▶ **noun** Brit. another term for **PERIOD** (sense 4 of the noun).

full-time ▶ **adjective** using the whole of a person's available working time. ▶ **adverb** on a full-time basis. ▶ **noun** (**full time**) Brit. the end of a sports match.
– DERIVATIVES **full-tim·er** noun.

ful·ly /ˈfo͝olē/ ▶ **adverb 1** completely or entirely. **2** no less or fewer than: *fully 65 percent.*

> – SYNONYMS **completely,** entirely, wholly, totally, perfectly, quite, altogether, thoroughly, in all respects, (up) to the hilt.
> – ANTONYMS partly.

ful·ly fledged ▶ **adjective** British term for **FULL-FLEDGED**.

ful·mar /ˈfo͝olmər, -ˌmär/ ▶ **noun** a large gray and white northern seabird.
– ORIGIN from Old Norse, 'stinking gull' (because of its habit of regurgitating its stomach contents when disturbed).

ful·mi·nate /ˈfo͝olməˌnāt, ˈfəl-/ ▶ **verb** protest strongly about something.
– DERIVATIVES **ful·mi·na·tion** /ˌfo͝olməˈnāshən, -fəl-/ noun.
– ORIGIN Latin *fulminare* 'strike with lightning.'

ful·some /ˈfo͝olsəm/ ▶ **adjective 1** excessively complimentary or flattering. **2** of large size or quantity; generous or plentiful: *fulsome details.*
– DERIVATIVES **ful·some·ly** adverb **ful·some·ness** noun.

> **USAGE**
>
> Although the earliest sense of **fulsome** was 'plentiful,' this meaning was replaced by the negative sense 'excessively flattering' and is now generally thought to be incorrect. The word is often heard in phrases such as **fulsome praise**, however, where the speaker just means that the praise is abundant rather than excessively flattering.

fu·ma·role /ˈfyo͞oməˌrōl/ ▶ **noun** an opening in or near a volcano, through which hot sulfurous gases emerge.
– ORIGIN Latin *fumariolum* 'vent, hole for smoke.'

fum·ble /ˈfəmbəl/ ▶ **verb 1** use the hands clumsily while doing or handling something. **2** (of the hands) do or handle something clumsily. **3** (**fumble around/about**) move around clumsily using the hands to find one's way. **4** express oneself or deal with something clumsily or nervously. **5** (in ball games) fail to catch or field the ball cleanly.

> – SYNONYMS **grope,** fish, scrabble, feel.

▶ **noun** an act of fumbling.
– DERIVATIVES **fum·bler** noun **fum·bling** adjective.
– ORIGIN German *fommeln* or Dutch *fommelen.*

fume /fyo͞om/ ▶ **noun** a gas or vapor that smells strongly or is dangerous to inhale.

> – SYNONYMS **smoke,** vapor, gas, exhaust, pollution.

▶ **verb 1** send out fumes. **2** feel extremely angry.

> – SYNONYMS **be furious,** seethe, be livid, be incensed, boil, be beside oneself, spit; informal foam at the mouth, see red.

– DERIVATIVES **fum·ing** adjective.
– ORIGIN Latin *fumus* 'smoke.'

fu·mi·gate /ˈfyo͞oməˌgāt/ ▶ **verb** use the fumes of certain chemicals to disinfect a contaminated area.

> – SYNONYMS **disinfect,** purify, sterilize, sanitize, decontaminate, cleanse, clean out.

– DERIVATIVES **fu·mi·gant** /-gənt/ noun **fu·mi·ga·tion** /ˌfyo͞oməˈgāshən/ noun **fu·mi·ga·tor** /-ˌgātər/ noun.
– ORIGIN Latin *fumigare.*

fun /fən/ ▶ **noun 1** lighthearted enjoyment. **2** a source of this: *exercise can be great fun.* **3** playfulness: *she's full of fun.*

– SYNONYMS **1 enjoyment,** entertainment, amusement, pleasure, jollification, merrymaking, recreation, leisure, relaxation, a good time; informal living it up, a ball. **2 merriment,** cheerfulness, jollity, joviality, high spirits, mirth, laughter, hilarity, lightheartedness, levity.
– ANTONYMS boredom.

▶ **adjective** informal enjoyable.

– SYNONYMS **enjoyable,** entertaining, amusing, pleasurable, pleasant, agreeable, convivial.

– PHRASES **make fun of** tease or laugh at in a mocking way.
– ORIGIN unknown.

func·tion /'fəNGKSHən/ ▶ **noun 1** an activity that is natural to or the purpose of a person or thing. **2** a large or formal social event or ceremony. **3** a computer operation corresponding to a single instruction from the user. **4** Mathematics a relation or expression involving one or more variables.

– SYNONYMS **1 purpose,** task, use, role. **2 responsibility,** duty, role, province, activity, assignment, task, job, mission. **3 social event,** party, social occasion, affair, gathering, reception, soirée. informal do, bash.

▶ **verb 1** work or operate in a proper or particular way. **2** (**function as**) fulfill the purpose or task of: *the building functions as a youth center.*

– SYNONYMS **1 work,** go, run, be in working/running order, operate. **2 act,** serve, operate, perform, do duty.

– ORIGIN French *fonction.*

func·tion·al /'fəNGKSHənl/ ▶ **adjective 1** relating to or having a function. **2** designed to be practical and useful, rather than attractive. **3** working or operating. **4** (of a disease) affecting the operation rather than the structure of an organ.

– SYNONYMS **1 practical,** useful, utilitarian, workaday, serviceable, no-frills. **2 working,** in working order, functioning, in service, in use, going, running, operative; informal up and running.

– DERIVATIVES **func·tion·al·ly** adverb.

func·tion·al·ism /'fəNGKSHənl,izəm/ ▶ **noun** the theory that the design of an object should be governed by its use rather than an attractive appearance.
– DERIVATIVES **func·tion·al·ist** noun & adjective.

func·tion·al·i·ty /,fəNGKSHə'nalətē/ ▶ **noun 1** the quality of being functional. **2** the range of operations that can be run on a computer or other electronic system.

func·tion·ar·y /'fəNGKSHə,nerē/ ▶ **noun** (pl. **functionaries**) an official.

func·tion key ▶ **noun** a key on a computer keyboard that can be assigned a particular function or operation.

fund /fənd/ ▶ **noun 1** a sum of money saved or made available for a purpose. **2** (**funds**) financial resources. **3** a large stock of something.

– SYNONYMS **1 collection,** kitty, reserve, pool, purse, savings, coffers. **2 money,** cash, wealth, means, assets, resources, savings, capital, reserves, the wherewithal.

▶ **verb** provide money for something: *a project funded by the Arts Council.*

– SYNONYMS **finance,** pay for, back, capitalize, subsidize, endow, invest in, sponsor; informal bankroll.

– DERIVATIVES **fund·er** noun **fund·ing** noun.
– ORIGIN Latin *fundus* 'bottom, piece of landed property.'

fun·da·ment /'fəndəmənt/ ▶ **noun 1** the foundation or basis of something. **2** humorous a person's buttocks.
– ORIGIN Latin *fundamentum,* from *fundare* 'to found.'

fun·da·men·tal /,fəndə'mentl/ ▶ **adjective** of central importance: *a fundamental difference of opinion.*

– SYNONYMS **basic,** underlying, core, rudimentary, root, primary, prime, cardinal, principal, chief, key, central, vital, essential.
– ANTONYMS secondary, incidental.

▶ **noun** a central or basic rule or principle.

fun·da·men·tal·ism /,fəndə'mentl,izəm/ ▶ **noun 1** a form of Protestant Christianity that promotes the belief that everything written in the Bible is literally true. **2** the strict following of the basic underlying doctrines of any religion or ideology.
– DERIVATIVES **fun·da·men·tal·ist** noun & adjective.

fun·da·men·tal·ly /,fəndə'mentl-ē/ ▶ **adverb** in central or primary respects.

– SYNONYMS **essentially,** in essence, basically, at heart, at bottom, deep down, profoundly, primarily, above all.

fund-rais·er ▶ **noun 1** a person who raises money for an organization or cause. **2** an event held to raise money for an organization or cause.
– DERIVATIVES **fund-rais·ing** noun.

fu·ner·al /'fyo͞on(ə)rəl/ ▶ **noun** a ceremony held shortly after a person's death, usually including the person's burial or cremation.

– SYNONYMS **burial,** interment, entombment, committal, laying to rest, cremation.

– PHRASES **it's your funeral** informal said to warn someone that the consequences of an unwise act are their own responsibility.
– ORIGIN Latin *funeralia.*

fu·ner·al di·rec·tor ▶ **noun** a person whose business is preparing dead bodies for burial or cremation and making arrangements for funerals.

fu·ner·al home (also **funeral parlor**) ▶ **noun** an establishment where people who have died are prepared for burial or cremation.

fu·ner·ar·y /'fyo͞onə,rerē/ ▶ **adjective** relating to a funeral or to other rites in which people who have died are commemorated.

fu·ne·re·al /fyə'ni(ə)rēəl, fyo͞o-/ ▶ **adjective** having the somber quality or atmosphere appropriate to a funeral.

fun·gi /'fən,jī, -,gī/ plural of **FUNGUS**.

fun·gi·cide /'fənjə,sīd, 'fəNGgə-/ ▶ **noun** a chemical that destroys fungus.
– DERIVATIVES **fun·gi·cid·al** /,fənjə'sīdl, ,fəNGgə-/ adjective.

fun·gus /'fəNGgəs/ ▶ **noun** (pl. **fungi** /-jī, -gī/) a spore-producing organism, such as a mushroom, that has no leaves or flowers and grows on other plants or on decaying matter.
– DERIVATIVES **fun·gal** /'fəNGgəl/ adjective **fun·goid** /'fəNG,goid/ adjective.
– ORIGIN Latin, perhaps from Greek *spongos* 'sponge.'

fu·nic·u·lar /fyo͞o'nikyələr/ ▶ **adjective** (of a railroad on a steep slope) operated by cables attached to cars that balance each other while one goes up and the other goes down. ▶ **noun** a funicular railroad.
– ORIGIN from Latin *funiculus* 'little rope.'

funk[1] /fo͝oNGk, fəNGk/ informal ▶ **noun** (also **blue funk**) **1** a state of depression: *falling into a deep funk*. **2** chiefly Brit. a state of panic or fear. ▶ **verb** chiefly Brit. avoid something out of fear.
– ORIGIN perhaps from **FUNK**[2] in the informal sense 'tobacco smoke.'

funk[2] ▶ **noun** a style of popular dance music of US black origin, having a strong rhythm.
– ORIGIN perhaps from French dialect *funkier* 'blow smoke on.'

funk·y /'fəNGkē/ ▶ **adjective** (**funkier, funkiest**) informal **1** (of music) having a strong dance rhythm. **2** unconventionally modern and stylish. **3** strongly musty: *a funky smell*.
– DERIVATIVES **funk·i·ly** adverb **funk·i·ness** noun.

fun·nel /'fənl/ ▶ **noun 1** a utensil that is wide at the top and narrow at the bottom, used for guiding liquid or powder into a small opening. **2** a metal chimney on a ship or steam engine. ▶ **verb** (**funnels, funneling, funneled**) guide or move through a funnel or narrow space: *the wind was funneling through the gorge*.
– ORIGIN Provençal *fonilh*.

fun·nel cloud ▶ **noun** a rotating, funnel-shaped cloud forming the core of a tornado or waterspout.

fun·ny /'fənē/ ▶ **adjective** (**funnier, funniest**) **1** causing laughter or amusement. **2** strange; peculiar. **3** suspicious: *there's something funny going on*. **4** informal slightly unwell.

> – SYNONYMS **1 amusing,** humorous, witty, comic, comical, hilarious, hysterical, riotous, uproarious, farcical; informal rib-tickling, priceless. **2 strange,** peculiar, odd, weird, bizarre, curious, freakish, quirky, unusual. **3 suspicious,** suspect, dubious, untrustworthy, questionable; informal fishy, dodgy.
> – ANTONYMS serious.

– DERIVATIVES **fun·ni·ly** adverb.

fun·ny bone ▶ **noun** informal the part of the elbow over which a sensitive nerve passes.

fun·ny busi·ness ▶ **noun** deceptive, disobedient, or lecherous behavior: *funny business in the fund industry*.

fun·ny farm ▶ **noun** informal, derogatory a psychiatric hospital.

fun run ▶ **noun** informal an uncompetitive run for sponsored runners, held in support of a charity.

fur /fər/ ▶ **noun 1** the short, soft hair of certain animals. **2** the skin of an animal with fur on it, used in making clothes. **3** a coat made from fur. **4** a coating formed on the tongue as a symptom of sickness. ▶ **verb** (**furs, furring, furred**) Brit. coat or clog something up.
– DERIVATIVES **furred** adjective.
– PHRASES **the fur will fly** informal there will be a dramatic argument.
– ORIGIN from Old French *forrer* 'to line, sheathe.'

fur·be·low /'fərbəˌlō/ ▶ **noun 1** a strip of gathered or pleated material attached to a skirt or petticoat. **2** (**furbelows**) showy ornaments or trimmings.
– ORIGIN French *falbala* 'trimming, flounce.'

fur·bish /'fərbisʜ/ ▶ **verb** (usu. as adj. **furbished**) give a fresh look to (something old or shabby); renovate: *the newly furbished church*.

fu·ri·ous /'fyo͝orēəs/ ▶ **adjective 1** extremely angry. **2** full of energy, intensity, or anger: *he strode off at a furious pace*.

> – SYNONYMS **1 very angry,** enraged, infuriated, irate, incensed, fuming, ranting, raving, seething, beside oneself, outraged; informal hopping mad, wild, livid. **2 fierce,** heated, passionate, fiery, tumultuous, turbulent, tempestuous, violent, stormy, acrimonious.
> – ANTONYMS pleased, calm.

– DERIVATIVES **fu·ri·ous·ly** adverb.
– ORIGIN Latin *furiosus*, from *furia* 'fury.'

furl /fərl/ ▶ **verb** roll or fold something up neatly and securely.
– DERIVATIVES **furled** adjective.
– ORIGIN French *ferler*.

fur·long /'fərˌlôNG, -ˌläNG/ ▶ **noun** an eighth of a mile, 220 yards.
– ORIGIN from the Old English words for 'furrow' + 'long' (originally referring to the length of a furrow in a field).

fur·lough /'fərlō/ ▶ **noun** leave of absence, especially from military duty.
– ORIGIN Dutch *verlof*.

fur·nace /'fərnəs/ ▶ **noun 1** an enclosed chamber in which material can be heated to very high temperatures. **2** a very hot place.
– ORIGIN from Latin *fornus* 'oven.'

fur·nish /'fərnisʜ/ ▶ **verb 1** provide a room or building with furniture and fittings. **2** (**furnish someone with**) supply someone with equipment or information: *she was able to furnish me with details of the incident*. **3** be a source of something.

> – SYNONYMS **1 fit out,** provide with furniture, appoint, equip, outfit. **2** *they furnished us with boots* **supply,** provide, equip, issue; informal fix up.

– DERIVATIVES **fur·nished** adjective **fur·nish·er** noun.
– ORIGIN Old French *furnir*.

fur·nish·ing /'fərnisʜiNG/ ▶ **noun 1** (**furnishings**) furniture and fittings in a room or building. **2** (as adj.) referring to fabrics used for curtains or upholstery: *furnishing fabrics*.

fur·ni·ture /'fərnicʜər/ ▶ **noun 1** the movable articles that are used to make a room or building suitable for living or working in, such as tables, chairs, or desks. **2** the small accessories or fittings that are required or desired for a particular task or function: *pendants, finials, and other decorative furniture*.
– ORIGIN French *fourniture*.

fu·ror /'fyo͝orˌôr, -ər/ (Brit. **furore** /ˌfyo͝o'rôrē/) ▶ **noun** an outbreak of public anger or excitement.

> – SYNONYMS **commotion,** uproar, outcry, fuss, upset, brouhaha, stir; informal to-do, hoo-ha, hullabaloo.

– ORIGIN Italian.

fur·ri·er /'fərēər/ ▶ **noun** a person who prepares or deals in furs.

fur·row /'fərō, 'fə-rō/ ▶ **noun 1** a long, narrow trench made in the ground by a plow. **2** a rut or groove. **3** a deep wrinkle on a person's face. ▶ **verb 1** make a furrow in the ground or the surface of something. **2** (of a person's forehead) become wrinkled: *his brow furrowed in concentration*.
– ORIGIN Old English.

fur·ry /'fərē/ ▶ **adjective** (**furrier, furriest**) covered with or like fur.
– DERIVATIVES **fur·ri·ness** noun.

fur seal ▶ **noun** a seal whose thick underside fur is used commercially as sealskin.

fur·ther /'fərTHər/ used as comparative of **FAR** ▶ **adverb** (also **farther** /'färTHər/) **1** at, to, or by a greater distance. **2** over a greater expanse of space or time. **3** beyond the point already reached. **4** at or to a more advanced or desirable stage. **5** in addition; also.

– SYNONYMS see **FURTHERMORE**.

▶ **adjective 1** (also **farther**) more distant in space. **2** additional.

– SYNONYMS **additional,** more, extra, supplementary, new, fresh.

▶ **verb** help the progress or development of something.

– SYNONYMS **promote,** advance, forward, develop, facilitate, aid, assist, help, boost, encourage.
– ANTONYMS impede.

– PHRASES **not go any further** (of a secret) not be told to anyone else. **until further notice** used to indicate that a situation will not change until another announcement is made: *the museum is closed to the public until further notice*.
– ORIGIN Old English, related to **FORTH**.

USAGE

Is there any difference between **further** and **farther**? When talking about distance, either form can be used: *she moved further down the train* and *she moved farther down the train* are both correct. However you should use **further** when you mean 'beyond or in addition to what has already been done' (*have you anything further to say?*) or 'additional' (*phone for further information*).

fur·ther·ance /ˈfərT͟Hərəns/ ▶ **noun** the action of helping a scheme or plan to progress.

fur·ther·more /ˈfərT͟Hərˌmôr/ ▶ **adverb** in addition; besides.

– SYNONYMS **moreover,** further, what's more, also, additionally, in addition, besides, as well, too, on top of that, into the bargain.

fur·ther·most /ˈfərT͟Hərˌmōst/ (also **farthermost** /ˈfärT͟Hərˌmōst/) ▶ **adjective** at the greatest distance from something.

fur·thest /ˈfərT͟Hist/ (also **farthest** /ˈfärT͟Hist/) used as superlative of **FAR** ▶ **adjective 1** situated at the greatest distance. **2** covering the greatest area or distance.

– SYNONYMS **most distant,** remotest, farthest, furthermost, farthermost, outer, outermost, extreme.
– ANTONYMS nearest.

▶ **adverb 1** at or by the greatest distance. **2** over the greatest distance or area. **3** to the most extreme or advanced point.

fur·tive /ˈfərtiv/ ▶ **adjective** done in a secretive or guilty way.

– SYNONYMS **surreptitious,** secretive, secret, clandestine, hidden, covert, conspiratorial, cloak-and-dagger, sneaky; informal shifty.
– ANTONYMS open.

– DERIVATIVES **fur·tive·ly** adverb **fur·tive·ness** noun.
– ORIGIN Latin *furtivus*, from *furtum* 'theft.'

fu·ry /ˈfyo͝orē/ ▶ **noun** (pl. **furies**) **1** extreme anger. **2** extreme strength or violence: *the fury of the storm*. **3** (**Furies**) Greek Mythology three goddesses who punished wrongdoers.

– SYNONYMS **1 rage,** anger, wrath, outrage; literary ire. **2 ferocity,** violence, turbulence, tempestuousness, savagery, severity, intensity, vehemence, force.

– ORIGIN from Latin *furere* 'be mad, rage.'

fuse[1] /fyo͞oz/ ▶ **verb 1** join or blend to form a single entity. **2** melt a material or object with intense heat, so as to join it with something else. **3** provide a circuit or electrical appliance with a fuse. ▶ **noun** a safety device consisting of a strip of wire that melts and breaks an electric circuit if the current exceeds a safe level.
– ORIGIN from Latin *fundere* 'pour, melt.'

fuse[2] (also **fuze**) ▶ **noun 1** a length of material along which a small flame moves to explode a bomb or firework. **2** a device in a bomb that controls the timing of the explosion. ▶ **verb** fit a fuse to a bomb.
– ORIGIN Latin *fusus* 'spindle.'

fuse box ▶ **noun** a box or board containing the fuses for electrical circuits in a building.

fu·se·lage /ˈfyo͞osəˌläzʜ, -zə-/ ▶ **noun** the main body of an aircraft.
– ORIGIN French, from *fuseler* 'shape into a spindle.'

fu·si·ble /ˈfyo͞ozəbəl/ ▶ **adjective** able to be fused or melted easily.

fu·sil·lade /ˈfyo͞osəˌläd, -ˌlād/ ▶ **noun** a series of shots fired at the same time or in rapid succession.
– ORIGIN French.

fu·sion /ˈfyo͞ozʜən/ ▶ **noun 1** the process or result of fusing things to form a single entity. **2** a reaction in which light atomic nuclei fuse to form a heavier nucleus, releasing much energy. **3** popular music that is a mixture of different styles, especially jazz and rock. ▶ **adjective** referring to food or cooking that combines elements of both eastern and western cuisine.
– ORIGIN Latin, from *fundere* 'pour, melt.'

fuss /fəs/ ▶ **noun 1** a display of unnecessary or excessive excitement or activity. **2** a protest or complaint.

– SYNONYMS **1 commotion,** excitement, stir, confusion, disturbance, brouhaha, uproar, furor, tempest in a teapot; informal hoo-ha, to-do, song and dance, dog and pony show. **2 protest,** complaint, objection, argument; Brit. row. **3 trouble,** bother, inconvenience, effort, exertion, labor; informal hassle.

▶ **verb 1** show unnecessary or excessive concern about something. **2** pay too much attention to someone: *his mother fussed over him all the time*.

– SYNONYMS **worry,** fret, be agitated, be worked up, make a big thing out of, make a mountain out of a molehill; informal be in a tizzy.

– ORIGIN perhaps Anglo-Irish.

fuss·pot /ˈfəsˌpät/ ▶ **noun** informal a fussy person.

fuss·y /ˈfəsē/ ▶ **adjective** (**fussier, fussiest**) **1** too concerned about one's requirements and therefore hard to please. **2** full of unnecessary detail or decoration.

– SYNONYMS **1 particular,** finicky, fastidious, hard to please; informal persnickety, choosy, picky. **2 over-elaborate,** ornate, fancy, busy, cluttered.

– DERIVATIVES **fuss·i·ly** adverb **fuss·i·ness** noun.

fus·tian /ˈfəsᴄʜən/ ▶ **noun** a thick, hard-wearing twilled cloth.
– ORIGIN from Latin *pannus fustaneus* 'cloth from *Fostat*,' a suburb of Cairo.

fus·ty /ˈfəstē/ ▶ **adjective** (**fustier, fustiest**) **1** smelling stale and damp or stuffy. **2** old-fashioned.
– DERIVATIVES **fus·ti·ness** noun.
– ORIGIN Old French *fuste* 'smelling of the cask.'

fu·tile /ˈfyo͞otl, -ˌtil/ ▶ **adjective** producing no useful results; pointless.

– SYNONYMS **fruitless,** vain, pointless, useless, ineffectual, forlorn, hopeless.
– ANTONYMS useful.

– DERIVATIVES **fu·tile·ly** adverb **fu·til·i·ty** /ˈfyo͞oˈtilətē/ noun.
– ORIGIN Latin *futilis*.

fu·ton /ˈfo͞oˌtän/ ▶ **noun 1** a Japanese padded mattress with no springs, able to be rolled up when not in use. **2** a type of low wooden sofa bed with such a mattress.
– ORIGIN Japanese.

fu·ture /ˈfyo͞ocHər/ ▶ **noun 1** (**the future**) time that is still to come. **2** events or conditions occurring or existing in time still to come. **3** a prospect of success or happiness: *I might have a future as an artist.* **4** Grammar a tense of verbs expressing events that have not yet happened. **5** (**futures**) contracts for assets bought at agreed prices but delivered and paid for later.

– SYNONYMS **1** *plans for the future* **time to come,** what lies ahead, the hereafter. **2** *her future lay in acting* **destiny,** fate, fortune, prospects, chances.
– ANTONYMS past.

▶ **adjective 1** existing or occurring in the future. **2** planned or destined to hold a particular position: *his future wife*. **3** Grammar (of a tense) expressing an event yet to happen.

– SYNONYMS **1 later,** to come, following, forthcoming, ensuing, succeeding, subsequent, coming, impending, approaching. **2** *her future husband* **to be,** destined, intended, planned, prospective.
– ANTONYMS previous, past.

– PHRASES **in the future** from now on.
– ORIGIN from Latin *futurus* 'going to be.'

fu·ture per·fect ▶ **noun** Grammar a tense of verbs expressing an action expected to be completed in the future, in English exemplified by *will have done*.

fu·ture shock ▶ **noun** a state of distress or disorientation caused by rapid social or technological change.

fu·tur·ism /ˈfyo͞ocHəˌrizəm/ ▶ **noun 1** concern with events and trends of the future or that anticipate the future. **2** (**Futurism**) an early 20th-century artistic movement that strongly rejected traditional forms and embraced modern technology.
– DERIVATIVES **fu·tur·ist, Fu·tur·ist** adjective & noun.

fu·tur·is·tic /ˌfyo͞ocHəˈristik/ ▶ **adjective 1** having or involving very modern technology or design. **2** (of a movie or book) set in the future.
– DERIVATIVES **fu·tur·is·ti·cal·ly** adverb.

fu·tu·ri·ty /fyo͞oˈto͝orətē, -ˈcHo͝orətē/ ▶ **noun** (pl. **futurities**) **1** the future time. **2** a future event.

fuze /fyo͞oz/ ▶ **noun** variant spelling of **FUSE**[2].

fuzz[1] /fəz/ ▶ **noun** a frizzy mass of hair or fiber. ▶ **verb** make or become fuzzy.
– ORIGIN probably German or Dutch.

fuzz[2] ▶ **noun** (**the fuzz**) informal the police.
– ORIGIN unknown.

fuzz·y /ˈfəzē/ ▶ **adjective** (**fuzzier, fuzziest**) **1** having a frizzy texture or appearance. **2** indistinct or vague: *a fuzzy picture*.

– SYNONYMS **1 frizzy,** fluffy, woolly, downy. **2 blurred,** indistinct, unclear, out of focus, misty. **3 unclear,** imprecise, unfocused, nebulous, vague, hazy, loose, woolly.
– ANTONYMS smooth, sharp, clear.

– DERIVATIVES **fuzz·i·ly** adverb **fuzz·i·ness** noun.

fuzz·y log·ic ▶ **noun** a form of logic in which predicates can have fractional values rather than simply being true or false.

F-word ▶ **noun** euphemistic the word 'fuck'.

FX ▶ **abbreviation** visual or sound effects.
– ORIGIN from the pronunciation of *effects*.

FYI ▶ **abbreviation** for your information.

Gg

G¹ (also **g**) ▶ **noun** (pl. **Gs** or **G's**) **1** the seventh letter of the alphabet. **2** referring to the next item after F in a set. **3** Music the fifth note in the scale of C major.

G² ▶ **abbreviation 1** giga- (10^9). **2** informal grand (a thousand dollars). **3** the force exerted by the earth's gravitational field. ▶ **symbol** referring to movies that are suitable for audiences of all ages.

g ▶ **abbreviation 1** Chemistry gas. **2** gram(s). ▶ **symbol** Physics the acceleration due to gravity (9.81 m/s^{-2}).

G8 ▶ **abbreviation** Group of Eight, a group of eight industrial nations whose heads of government meet regularly.

GA ▶ **abbreviation** Georgia.

Ga ▶ **symbol** the chemical element gallium.

gab /gab/ ▶ **verb** (**gabs, gabbing, gabbed**) informal talk at length.
– PHRASES **the gift of (the) gab** the ability to speak fluently and persuasively.
– ORIGIN from **GOB²**.

gab·ar·dine /ˈgabərˌdēn/ ▶ **noun** a smooth, hard-wearing worsted or cotton cloth, used especially for making raincoats.
– ORIGIN Old French *gauvardine*.

gab·ble /ˈgabəl/ ▶ **verb** talk rapidly and in a way that is hard to understand. ▶ **noun** rapid, unintelligible talk.
– DERIVATIVES **gab·bler** noun.
– ORIGIN Dutch *gabbelen*.

gab·by /ˈgabē/ ▶ **adjective** (**gabbier gabbiest**) informal excessively or annoyingly talkative.

gab·er·dine /ˈgabərˌdēn/ ▶ **noun** variant spelling of **GABARDINE**.

gab·fest /ˈgabˌfest/ ▶ **noun** informal **1** a conference or other gathering with prolonged talking: *these summits are merely empty gabfests*. **2** a lengthy conversation.

ga·ble /ˈgābəl/ ▶ **noun 1** the triangular upper part of a wall at the end of a ridged roof. **2** a gable-shaped canopy over a window or door.
– DERIVATIVES **ga·bled** adjective.
– ORIGIN Old Norse.

Gab·o·nese /ˌgabəˈnēz, -ˈnēs/ ▶ **noun** (pl. same) a person from Gabon, a country in West Africa. ▶ **adjective** relating to Gabon.

gad /gad/ ▶ **verb** (**gads, gadding, gadded**) (**gad about/ around**) informal enjoy oneself by visiting many different places or traveling from one place to another.
– ORIGIN from former *gadling* 'wanderer.'

gad·a·bout /ˈgadəˌbout/ ▶ **noun** informal a person who is always traveling from one place to another enjoying themselves.

gad·fly /ˈgadˌflī/ ▶ **noun** (pl. **gadflies**) **1** a large fly that bites livestock. **2** an annoying person.
– ORIGIN from **GAD**, or former *gad* 'goad, spike.'

gadg·et /ˈgajit/ ▶ **noun** a small mechanical device or tool.

> – SYNONYMS **device,** appliance, apparatus, instrument, implement, tool, utensil, contrivance, contraption, machine, mechanism, invention; informal gizmo.

– DERIVATIVES **gadg·et·ry** noun.
– ORIGIN probably from French *gâchette* 'lock mechanism.'

gad·o·lin·i·um /ˌgadlˈinēəm/ ▶ **noun** a soft silvery-white metallic chemical element of the lanthanide series.
– ORIGIN named after the Finnish mineralogist Johan *Gadolin*.

gad·wall /ˈgadˌwôl/ ▶ **noun** a brownish-gray freshwater duck that is found across Eurasia and North America.

gad·zooks /ˌgadˈzo͞oks/ ▶ **exclamation** old use expressing surprise or annoyance.
– ORIGIN alteration of *God's hooks*, i.e., the nails by which Christ was fastened to the cross.

Gael /gāl/ ▶ **noun** a Gaelic-speaking person.
– ORIGIN Scottish Gaelic *Gaidheal*.

Gael·ic /ˈgālik/ ▶ **noun 1** (also **Scottish Gaelic**) a Celtic language spoken in western Scotland, brought from Ireland in the 5th and 6th centuries AD. **2** (also **Irish Gaelic**) the Celtic language of Ireland; Irish. ▶ **adjective** relating to the Celtic languages and their speakers.

gaff /gaf/ ▶ **noun 1** a stick with a hook or barbed spear, for landing large fish. **2** Sailing a spar to which the head of a fore-and-aft sail is bent.
– ORIGIN Provençal *gaf* 'hook.'

gaffe /gaf/ ▶ **noun** an embarrassing blunder or mistake.

> – SYNONYMS **blunder,** mistake, error, slip, faux pas, indiscretion, solecism; informal slip-up, blooper, boo-boo, howler.

– ORIGIN French.

gaf·fer /ˈgafər/ ▶ **noun 1** the chief electrician in a movie or television production unit. **2** informal an old man.
– ORIGIN probably from **GODFATHER**.

gag¹ /gag/ ▶ **noun 1** a piece of cloth put in or over a person's mouth to prevent them from speaking. **2** a restriction on free speech. ▶ **verb** (**gags, gagging, gagged**) **1** put a gag on someone. **2** prevent someone from speaking freely. **3** choke or retch.

> – SYNONYMS **1 silence,** muzzle, suppress, stifle, censor, curb, restrain. **2 retch,** heave.

– ORIGIN perhaps imitating a person choking.

gag² ▶ **noun** a joke or funny story.

> – SYNONYMS **joke,** quip, jest, witticism; informal crack, wisecrack, one-liner.

– ORIGIN unknown.

ga·ga /ˈgäˌgä/ ▶ **adjective** informal rambling in speech or thought, especially as a result of old age.
– ORIGIN French.

gage¹ /gāj/ ▶ **noun** old use **1** a valued object given as a guarantee of someone's good faith. **2** a glove or other object thrown down as a challenge to fight.
– ORIGIN Old French.

gage² ▶ **noun & verb** variant spelling of **GAUGE**.

gag·gle /ˈgagəl/ ▶ **noun 1** a flock of geese. **2** informal a noisy group of people: *a gaggle of children*.
– ORIGIN imitating the noise that a goose makes.

gag or·der ▶ **noun** a judge's order that a case may not be discussed in public.

gag rule ▶ **noun** a regulation or directive that prohibits discussion of a particular matter: *York violated the gag rule at the expense of his own job*.

Gai·a /ˈgīə/ ▶ **noun** the earth viewed as a vast self-regulating organism.
– ORIGIN coined by the English scientist James Lovelock, from the name of the Greek goddess *Gaia*.

gai·e·ty /ˈgāitē/ ▶ **noun** (pl. **gaieties**) **1** the state or quality of being lighthearted and cheerful. **2** lively celebrations or festivities.
– ORIGIN French *gaieté*.

gail·lar·di·a /gəˈlärdēə/ ▶ **noun** a plant of the daisy family cultivated for its bright red and yellow flowers.

gai·ly /ˈgālē/ ▶ **adverb 1** in a lighthearted and cheerful way. **2** without thinking of the consequences of one's actions. **3** with a bright appearance.

gain /gān/ ▶ **verb 1** obtain or secure: *troops gained control of the town*. **2** reach or arrive at a place. **3** (**gain on**) come closer to a person or thing being chased. **4** increase the amount or rate of weight or speed. **5** increase in value. **6** (**gain in**) improve or progress in some way: *she has gained in confidence*. **7** benefit: *both of them stood to gain from the relationship*. **8** (of a clock or watch) become fast.

> – SYNONYMS **1 obtain,** get, secure, acquire, come by, procure, attain, achieve, earn, win, capture; informal land. **2** *they stood to gain from the deal* **profit,** make money, benefit, do well. **3** *she gained weight* **put on,** increase in, build up. **4** *they're **gaining on** us* **catch up to/with,** catch; reduce someone's lead, narrow the gap.
> – ANTONYMS lose.

▶ **noun 1** a thing that is gained. **2** an increase in wealth or resources.

> – SYNONYMS **1 profit,** earnings, income, yield, return, reward, advantage, benefit; informal take. **2 increase,** addition, rise, increment, advance.
> – ANTONYMS loss.

– DERIVATIVES **gain·er** noun.
– ORIGIN Old French *gaignier*.

> **CHOOSE THE RIGHT WORD**
>
> See **GET**.

gain·ful /ˈgānfəl/ ▶ **adjective** (of employment) useful and for which one is paid.

> – SYNONYMS **profitable,** paid, well paid, remunerative, lucrative, moneymaking, rewarding, fruitful, worthwhile, useful, productive, constructive, beneficial, advantageous, valuable.

– DERIVATIVES **gain·ful·ly** adverb.

gain·say /ˌgānˈsā, ˈgānˌsā/ ▶ **verb** (past and past part. **gainsaid**) formal deny or contradict a fact or statement.
– ORIGIN from former *gain-* 'against' + **SAY**.

gait /gāt/ ▶ **noun 1** a person's way of walking. **2** the pattern of steps of a horse or dog at a particular speed.

> – SYNONYMS **walk,** step, stride, pace, tread, way of walking, bearing, carriage, deportment.

– ORIGIN Old Norse, 'street.'

gait·er /ˈgātər/ ▶ **noun 1** a covering of cloth or leather for the ankle and lower leg. **2** a shoe or overshoe extending to the ankle or above.
– DERIVATIVES **gait·ered** adjective.
– ORIGIN French *guêtre*.

gal /gal/ ▶ **noun** informal a girl or young woman.

gal. ▶ **abbreviation** gallon(s).

ga·la /ˈgālə, ˈgalə/ ▶ **noun** a social occasion with special entertainments: (as adj.) *a gala affair*.

> – SYNONYMS **festival,** fair, fete, carnival, pageant, jubilee, jamboree, celebration.

– ORIGIN Old French *gale* 'rejoicing.'

ga·lac·tic /gəˈlaktik/ ▶ **adjective** relating to a galaxy or galaxies.
– DERIVATIVES **ga·lac·tic·al·ly** adverb.

ga·lan·gal /gəˈlaNGgəl/ (also **galingale** /ˈgalinˌgāl/) ▶ **noun** an Asian plant of the ginger family, used in cooking and herbal medicine.
– ORIGIN Old French *galingale*.

gal·ax·y /ˈgaləksē/ ▶ **noun** (pl. **galaxies**) **1** a system of millions or billions of stars held together by gravitational attraction. **2** (**the Galaxy**) the galaxy of which the solar system is a part; the Milky Way. **3** a large and impressive group of people or things: *a galaxy of celebrities*.
– ORIGIN from Greek *galaxias kuklos* 'milky vault' (referring to the Milky Way).

gale /gāl/ ▶ **noun 1** a very strong wind. **2** an outburst of laughter.

> – SYNONYMS **1 high wind,** blast, squall, storm, tempest, hurricane, tornado, cyclone, whirlwind, typhoon. **2 peal,** howl, hoot, shriek, roar, fit, paroxysm.

– ORIGIN perhaps related to an Old Norse word meaning 'mad, frantic.'

ga·le·na /gəˈlēnə/ ▶ **noun** a metallic gray or black mineral consisting of lead sulfide.
– ORIGIN Latin, 'lead ore.'

ga·lette /gəˈlet/ ▶ **noun 1** a round, flat, crusty cake. **2** a buckwheat pancake or crepe with a sweet or savory filling.
– ORIGIN French.

Gal·i·le·an¹ /ˌgaləˈlēən/ ▶ **adjective** relating to the Italian astronomer and physicist Galileo Galilei.

Gal·i·le·an² ▶ **noun** a person from Galilee, the region of ancient Palestine associated with the ministry of Jesus and now part of Israel. ▶ **adjective** relating to Galilee.

gall¹ /gôl/ ▶ **noun** bold and disrespectful behavior: *she had the gall to ask him for money*.
– ORIGIN Old English.

gall² ▶ **noun 1** annoyance or resentment. **2** a sore on the skin made by rubbing. ▶ **verb 1** make someone feel annoyed or resentful. **2** make the skin sore by rubbing.
– DERIVATIVES **gall·ing** adjective.
– ORIGIN Old English.

gall³ ▶ **noun** an abnormal growth on plants and trees, caused by the presence of insect larvae, mites, or fungi.
– ORIGIN Latin *galla*.

gall. ▸ abbreviation gallon(s).

gal·lant ▸ adjective 1 /ˈgalənt/brave or heroic. 2 /gəˈlant, -ˈlänt/(of a man) polite and charming to women.

– SYNONYMS 1 **brave,** courageous, valiant, bold, plucky, daring, fearless, intrepid, heroic, stouthearted; informal gutsy, spunky. 2 **chivalrous,** gentlemanly, courteous, polite, attentive, respectful, gracious, considerate, thoughtful.
– ANTONYMS cowardly, discourteous.

▸ noun /gəˈlant, -ˈlänt, ˈgalənt/ a man who is charmingly attentive to women.
– DERIVATIVES **gal·lant·ly** adverb.
– ORIGIN Old French *galant*.

gal·lant·ry /ˈgaləntrē/ ▸ noun (pl. **gallantries**) 1 courageous behavior. 2 polite attention paid by men to women.

gall·blad·der /ˈgôlˌbladər/ ▸ noun a small sac-shaped organ beneath the liver, in which bile is stored.

gal·le·on /ˈgalēən, ˈgalyən/ ▸ noun historical a large square-rigged sailing ship with three or more decks and masts.
– ORIGIN French *galion* or Spanish *galeón*.

gal·le·ri·a /ˌgaləˈrēə/ ▸ noun a long covered passageway, typically lined with stores and other businesses.
– ORIGIN Italian.

gal·ler·y /ˈgalərē/ ▸ noun (pl. **galleries**) 1 a room or building in which works of art are displayed. 2 a balcony or upper floor projecting from a back or side wall inside a hall or church. 3 the highest balcony in a theater, having the least expensive seats. 4 a long room or passage forming a portico or colonnade. 5 a horizontal underground passage in a mine.
– DERIVATIVES **gal·ler·ied** adjective.
– PHRASES **play to the gallery** do something intended to win approval or make oneself popular.
– ORIGIN Italian *galleria*.

gal·ley /ˈgalē/ ▸ noun (pl. **galleys**) 1 historical a low, flat ship with one or more sails and up to three banks of oars, often manned by slaves or criminals. 2 a narrow kitchen in a ship or aircraft. 3 (also **galley proof**) a printer's proof in the form of long single-column strips.
– ORIGIN Greek *galaia*; sense 3 is from French *galée* referring to an oblong tray for holding setup type.

gal·liard /ˈgalyərd/ ▸ noun historical a lively dance in triple time for two people.
– ORIGIN Old French *gaillard* 'valiant.'

Gal·lic /ˈgalik/ ▸ adjective 1 relating to or characteristic of France or the French. 2 relating to the Gauls.
– DERIVATIVES **Gal·li·cize** verb.
– ORIGIN Latin *Gallicus*, from *Gallus* 'a Gaul.'

gal·lic ac·id ▸ noun an organic acid extracted from tannins that has antioxidant properties.

Gal·li·cism /ˈgaliˌsizəm/ ▸ noun a French word or phrase adopted in another language.

gal·li·mau·fry /ˌgaləˈmôfrē/ ▸ noun a jumble or mixture.
– ORIGIN former French *galimafrée* 'unappetizing dish.'

gal·li·na·ceous /ˌgaləˈnāshəs/ ▸ adjective relating to the order of birds that includes domestic poultry and game birds such as grouse, partridges, and pheasants.

gal·li·um /ˈgalēəm/ ▸ noun a soft silvery-white metallic chemical element that melts just above normal room temperature.
– ORIGIN from Latin *Gallia* 'France' or *gallus* 'cock.'

gal·li·um ar·sen·ide ▸ noun a metallic compound that is used to make light-emitting diodes, integrated circuits, and some other computer components.

gal·li·vant /ˈgaləˌvant/ ▸ verb informal go from place to place enjoying oneself.
– ORIGIN perhaps from **GALLANT**.

gal·lon /ˈgalən/ ▸ noun 1 a unit of volume for measuring liquids, equal to four quarts (or eight pints): in the US, equivalent to 3.79 liters; in Britain (also **imperial gallon**), equivalent to 4.55 liters. 2 (**gallons**) informal large quantities of something.
– ORIGIN Old French *galon*.

gal·lop /ˈgaləp/ ▸ noun 1 the fastest pace of a horse, with all the feet off the ground together in each stride. 2 a ride on a horse at a gallop. ▸ verb (**gallops, galloping, galloped**) 1 go at the pace of a gallop. 2 move or progress very rapidly.
– ORIGIN Old French *galoper*.

gal·lows /ˈgalōz/ ▸ plural noun (usu. treated as sing.) 1 a structure consisting of two uprights and a crosspiece, used for hanging a person. 2 (**the gallows**) execution by hanging.
– ORIGIN Old English.

gal·lows hu·mor ▸ noun grim and ironical humor in a desperate or hopeless situation.

gall·stone /ˈgôlˌstōn/ ▸ noun a small hard mass formed abnormally in the gallbladder or bile ducts, causing pain and obstruction.

Gal·lup poll /ˈgaləp/ ▸ noun trademark an assessment of public opinion by questioning a representative sample of the population, used in forecasting voting results in an election.
– ORIGIN named after the American statistician George H. *Gallup*.

gall wasp ▸ noun a small winged antlike insect, the female of which lays eggs in plant tissue that cause a gall to form when the larvae hatch.

ga·loot /gəˈlo͞ot/ ▸ noun informal a clumsy or stupid person.
– ORIGIN unknown.

ga·lore /gəˈlôr/ ▸ adjective in large quantities: *there were prizes galore*.
– ORIGIN from Irish *go leor* 'to sufficiency.'

ga·losh /gəˈläsh/ ▸ noun (usu. **galoshes**) a waterproof rubber overshoe.
– ORIGIN from Latin *gallica solea* 'Gallic shoe.'

ga·lumph /gəˈləmf/ ▸ verb informal move in a clumsy, heavy, or noisy way.
– ORIGIN coined by Lewis Carroll in *Through the Looking-Glass*; perhaps a blend of **GALLOP** and **TRIUMPH**.

gal·van·ic /galˈvanik/ ▸ adjective 1 relating to or involving electric currents produced by chemical action. 2 sudden and dramatic.
– DERIVATIVES **gal·van·i·cal·ly** adverb.
– ORIGIN French *galvanique*, from the name of the Italian physiologist Luigi *Galvani*, known for his discovery of the twitching of frogs' legs in an electric field.

gal·va·nize /ˈgalvəˌnīz/ ▸ verb 1 make someone do something by shocking or exciting them: *a bang on the door galvanized her into action*. 2 (as adj. **galvanized**) (of iron or steel) coated with a protective layer of zinc.
– DERIVATIVES **gal·va·ni·za·tion** /ˌgalvəniˈzāshən/ noun.
– ORIGIN from the name of the Italian physiologist Luigi *Galvani*.

gal·va·nom·e·ter /ˌgalvəˈnämitər/ ▸ noun an instrument for detecting and measuring small electric currents.

Gam·bi·an /ˈgambēən/ ▶ **noun** a person from Gambia, a country in West Africa. ▶ **adjective** relating to Gambia.

gam·bit /ˈgambit/ ▶ **noun 1** an opening action or remark intended to gain someone an advantage. **2** (in chess) an opening move in which a player makes a sacrifice for the sake of some compensating advantage.
– ORIGIN Italian *gambetto* 'tripping up.'

gam·ble /ˈgambəl/ ▶ **verb 1** play games of chance for money. **2** bet a sum of money. **3** take risky action in the hope of a successful result: *they are gambling on a turnaround in the company's fortunes.*

> – SYNONYMS **1 bet,** place a bet, wager, hazard. **2 take a chance,** take a risk. informal stick one's neck out.

▶ **noun** a risky undertaking.

> – SYNONYMS *I took a gamble* **risk,** chance, shot/leap in the dark, speculation, lottery, potluck.

– DERIVATIVES **gam·bler** noun.
– ORIGIN from former *gamel* 'play games,' or from the verb **GAME**[1].

gam·bol /ˈgambəl/ ▶ **verb** (**gambols, gamboling, gamboled**) run or jump about playfully. ▶ **noun** an act of gamboling.
– ORIGIN Italian *gambata* 'trip up.'

game[1] /gām/ ▶ **noun 1** an activity taken part in for amusement. **2** a form of competitive activity or sport played according to rules. **3** a complete period of play, ending in a final result. **4** a single portion of play, forming a scoring unit within a game. **5** (**games**) a meeting for sporting contests. **6** the equipment used in playing a board game, computer game, etc. **7** informal a type of activity or business: *he was in the restaurant game.* **8** a secret plan or trick. **9** wild mammals or birds hunted for sport or food.

> – SYNONYMS **1 pastime,** diversion, entertainment, amusement, distraction, recreation, sport, activity. **2 match,** contest, fixture, meeting, tie, clash.

▶ **adjective** eager and willing to do something new or challenging: *they were game for anything.*

> – SYNONYMS **willing,** prepared, ready, disposed, interested, eager, keen, enthusiastic.

▶ **verb** play at games of chance for money.
– DERIVATIVES **game·ly** adverb **game·ness** noun **game·ster** noun.
– PHRASES **ahead of the game** ahead of one's competitors. **beat someone at their own game** use someone's own methods to outdo them. **the game is up** the deception or crime is revealed and so cannot succeed. **the only game in town** the best, the most important, or the only thing worth considering. **play the game** behave in a fair or honorable way. **play games** behave or conduct business in a way that lacks due seriousness or respect: *don't play games with me!*
– ORIGIN Old English, 'amusement, fun.'

game[2] ▶ **adjective** dated (of a person's leg) lame.
– ORIGIN unknown.

game bird ▶ **noun 1** a bird shot for sport or food. **2** a bird of a large group that includes pheasants, grouse, quails, guineafowl, etc.

game·cock /ˈgāmˌkäk/ ▶ **noun** a rooster bred and trained for cockfighting.

game fish ▶ **noun** (pl. same) a fish caught by anglers for sport, especially (in fresh water) salmon and trout and (in the sea) marlins, sharks, bass, and mackerel.

game·keep·er /ˈgāmˌkēpər/ ▶ **noun** a person employed to breed and protect game for a large estate.

gam·e·lan /ˈgaməˌlan/ ▶ **noun** a traditional instrumental group in Java and Bali, including many bronze percussion instruments.
– ORIGIN Javanese.

game plan ▶ **noun** a plan for success in sports, politics, or business: *he's revised his game plan to make sure he stays in charge.*

game point ▶ **noun** (in tennis and other sports) a point that if won by a player or side will also win them the game.

gam·er /ˈgāmər/ ▶ **noun 1** a participant in a computer or role-playing game. **2** (especially in sports) a person known for consistently making a strong effort regardless of challenging or adverse conditions.

game show ▶ **noun** a television program in which people compete to win prizes.

games·man·ship /ˈgāmzmənˌsʜip/ ▶ **noun** the art of winning games by using tactics to make one's opponent less confident.
– DERIVATIVES **games·man** noun.

gam·ete /ˈgamēt, gəˈmēt/ ▶ **noun** a cell that is able to unite with another of the opposite sex in sexual reproduction to form a zygote.
– ORIGIN Greek *gametē* 'wife,' *gametēs* 'husband,' from *gamos* 'marriage.'

game the·o·ry ▶ **noun** the mathematical study of strategies for dealing with competitive situations where the outcome of a participant's choice of action depends critically on the actions of other participants.

ga·me·to·cyte /gəˈmētəˌsīt/ ▶ **noun** Biology a cell that divides by meiosis to form a spermatozoon or an ovum.

gam·e·to·gen·e·sis /gəˌmētəˈjenəsis/ ▶ **noun** Biology the formation of gametes from gametocytes.

ga·me·to·phyte /gəˈmētəˌfīt/ ▶ **noun** Botany the sexual form of a plant in the alternation of generations.

game warden ▶ **noun** a person, often a government employee, who oversees hunting and wildlife in a particular area.

gam·ey ▶ **adjective** variant spelling of **GAMY**.

gam·ine /ˈgamēn/ ▶ **adjective** (of a girl) attractively boyish in appearance. ▶ **noun** a girl who is attractively boyish in appearance.
– ORIGIN French.

gam·ma /ˈgamə/ ▶ **noun** the third letter of the Greek alphabet (Γ, γ), represented as 'g'. ▶ **adjective** relating to gamma rays.

gam·ma glob·u·lin /ˈgläbyələn/ ▶ **noun** a mixture of blood proteins, mainly immunoglobulins, often given to boost immunity.

gam·ma rays (also **gamma radiation**) ▶ **plural noun** penetrating electromagnetic radiation of shorter wavelength than X-rays.

gam·ut /ˈgamət/ ▶ **noun 1** the complete range or scope of something: *the whole gamut of human emotion.* **2** a complete scale of musical notes; the range of a voice or instrument. **3** historical a musical scale consisting of seven overlapping scales, containing all the recognized notes used in medieval music.
– PHRASES **run the gamut** experience, display, or perform the complete range of something: *they ran the gamut of electronic dance music.*
– ORIGIN from Latin *gamma ut* the lowest musical note in the medieval scale.

CHOOSE THE RIGHT WORD

See **RANGE**.

gam·y /ˈgāmē/ (also **gamey**) ▶ **adjective** (**gamier, gamiest**) (of meat) having the strong flavor or smell of game when it is slightly decomposed and so ready to cook.
– DERIVATIVES **gam·i·ness** noun.

gan·der /ˈgandər/ ▶ **noun 1** a male goose. **2** informal a look or glance.
– ORIGIN Old English.

gang /gaNG/ ▶ **noun 1** an organized group of criminals or rowdy young people. **2** informal a group of people who regularly meet and do things together. **3** an organized group of people doing manual work. **4** a set of switches, sockets, or other devices grouped together.

– SYNONYMS **band,** group, crowd, pack, horde, throng, mob, herd, swarm, troop; informal bunch, gaggle, load.

▶ **verb 1** (**gang together**) form a group or gang. **2** (**gang up**) join together to oppose or intimidate someone: *the other children ganged up on him.*
– ORIGIN Old Norse, 'gait, course, going.'

gang·bang /ˈgaNG,baNG/ ▶ **noun** informal **1** a gang rape. **2** a sexual orgy. **3** an instance of violence involving members of a criminal gang.
– DERIVATIVES **gang·bang·er** noun.

gang·bust·ers /ˈgaNG,bəstər/ ▶ **plural noun** (in phrase **go** (or **like**) **gangbusters**) informal used to refer to great energy, speed, or success: *four-wheel-drive sales are going gangbusters.*

gang·land /ˈgaNG,land/ ▶ **noun** the world of criminal gangs.

gan·gli·on /ˈgaNGglēən/ ▶ **noun** (pl. **ganglia** /-glēə/ or **ganglions**) Anatomy & Medicine **1** a structure containing a number of nerve cells, often forming a swelling on a nerve fiber. **2** a mass of gray matter within the central nervous system. **3** an abnormal but harmless swelling on the sheath of a tendon.
– DERIVATIVES **gan·gli·on·ic** /,gaNGglēˈänik/ adjective.
– ORIGIN Greek.

gan·gly /ˈgaNGglē/ (also **gangling**) ▶ **adjective** (**ganglier, gangliest**) informal long or tall, thin, and awkward in movement: *a doe and a gangling half-grown fawn burst out of the trees.*

gang·plank /ˈgaNG,plaNGk/ ▶ **noun** a movable plank used to board or leave a ship or boat.

gang rape ▶ **noun** the rape of one person by a group of other people.

gan·grene /ˈgaNGgrēn, gaNGˈgrēn/ ▶ **noun** the death and decomposition of body tissue, caused by an obstructed blood supply or bacterial infection.
– DERIVATIVES **gan·gre·nous** /ˈgaNGgrənəs/ adjective.
– ORIGIN Greek *gangraina.*

gang·sta /ˈgaNGstə/ ▶ **noun 1** informal a member of a street gang. **2** (also **gangsta rap**) a type of rap music featuring aggressive lyrics, often with reference to gang violence.

gang·ster /ˈgaNGstər/ ▶ **noun** a member of an organized gang of violent criminals.

– SYNONYMS **hoodlum,** racketeer, thug, villain, criminal, Mafioso; informal mobster, crook, hood, tough.

– DERIVATIVES **gang·ster·ism** noun.

gang·way /ˈgaNG,wā/ ▶ **noun 1** a movable bridge linking a ship to the shore. **2** a raised platform or walkway providing a passage. **3** Brit. a passage between rows of seats in an auditorium, aircraft, etc.

gan·ja /ˈgänjə/ ▶ **noun** marijuana.
– ORIGIN Hindi.

gan·net /ˈganit/ ▶ **noun 1** a large seabird with mainly white plumage. **2** Brit. informal a greedy person.
– ORIGIN Old English.

gan·try /ˈgantrē/ ▶ **noun** (pl. **gantries**) a bridgelike overhead structure supporting equipment such as a crane or railroad signals.
– ORIGIN probably from **GALLON** + **TREE**.

gaol ▶ **noun** Brit. variant spelling of **JAIL**.

gap /gap/ ▶ **noun 1** a break or hole in an object or between two objects. **2** a space, interval, or break.

– SYNONYMS **1 opening,** aperture, space, breach, chink, slit, crack, crevice, cleft, cavity, hole, interstice. **2 pause,** intermission, interval, interlude, break, recess, breathing space, breather, respite, hiatus, lull. **3 omission,** blank, lacuna. **4** *the gap between rich and poor* **chasm,** gulf, separation, contrast, difference, disparity, divergence, imbalance.

– DERIVATIVES **gap·py** adjective.
– ORIGIN Old Norse, 'chasm.'

gape /gāp/ ▶ **verb 1** stare with one's mouth open wide in amazement or wonder. **2** (often as adj. **gaping**) be or become wide open: *a gaping wound.*

– SYNONYMS **1 stare,** goggle, gaze, ogle; informal rubberneck. **2** (as adj. **gaping**) **wide,** broad, vast, yawning, cavernous.

▶ **noun 1** an open-mouthed stare. **2** a wide opening.
– ORIGIN Old Norse.

ga·rage /gəˈräZH, -ˈräj/ ▶ **noun 1** a building in which a car or other motor vehicle is kept. **2** an establishment that provides services and repairs for motor vehicles. **3** (also **garage rock**) a form of unpolished pop music incorporating elements of rock, blues, and soul. ▶ **verb** put or keep a motor vehicle in a garage.
– ORIGIN French, from *garer* 'to shelter.'

ga·rage sale ▶ **noun** a sale of unwanted goods held in or outside of a garage; a yard sale.

ga·ram ma·sa·la /,gärəm məˈsälə/ ▶ **noun** a spice mixture used in Indian cooking.
– ORIGIN Urdu, 'pungent spice.'

garb /gärb/ ▶ **noun** clothing of a particular kind: *women in riding garb.* ▶ **verb** dress in distinctive clothes: *a motorcyclist garbed in black leather.*
– ORIGIN Italian *garbo* 'elegance.'

gar·bage /ˈgärbij/ ▶ **noun 1** domestic rubbish or waste. **2** something worthless or meaningless.

– SYNONYMS **1 trash,** refuse, waste, rubbish, detritus, litter, junk, scrap, scraps, leftovers, remains. **2 nonsense,** rubbish, balderdash, claptrap, twaddle, dross; informal hogwash, baloney, tripe, bilge, bull, bunk, poppycock, rot, piffle.

– ORIGIN Old French.

gar·bage can ▶ **noun** a container, typically plastic or metal, for household refuse.

gar·bage dis·pos·al ▶ **noun** an electric device fitted to the waste pipe of a kitchen sink for grinding up food waste.

gar·ban·zo /gärˈbänzō/ (also **garbanzo bean**) ▶ **noun** (pl. **garbanzos**) another term for **CHICKPEA**.
– ORIGIN Spanish.

gar·ble /ˈgärbəl/ ▶ **verb** reproduce a message or transmission in a confused and distorted way.

– SYNONYMS **mix up,** muddle, jumble, confuse, obscure, distort.

– DERIVATIVES **gar·bler** noun.
– ORIGIN Arabic, 'sift.'

gar·çon /gärˈsôn/ ▶ **noun** a waiter in a French restaurant.
– ORIGIN French, 'boy.'

gar·den /ˈgärdn/ ▶ **noun 1** a piece of cultivated land for growing flowers or vegetables. **2** (**gardens**) ornamental grounds laid out for public enjoyment.

– SYNONYMS plot, bed, patch, flower garden, vegetable garden, herb garden.

▶ **verb** cultivate or work in a garden.
– DERIVATIVES **gar·den·er** noun.
– ORIGIN Old French *jardin.*

WORD LINKS

horticultural *relating to gardens*

gar·den a·part·ment ▶ **noun** a ground-floor apartment with a door opening onto a yard or garden.

gar·den cen·ter ▶ **noun** a place where plants and gardening equipment are sold.

gar·de·nia /gärˈdēnyə/ ▶ **noun** a tree or shrub of warm climates, with large fragrant white or yellow flowers.
– ORIGIN named after the Scottish naturalist Dr. Alexander *Garden.*

gar·den par·ty ▶ **noun** a social event held on a lawn or in a garden.

gar·den-va·ri·e·ty ▶ **adjective** of the usual or ordinary type; commonplace.

gar·fish /ˈgärˌfisʜ/ ▶ **noun** any of a number of long, slender freshwater fish with beaklike jaws and sharply pointed teeth.

gar·gan·tu·an /gärˈgancʜo͞oən/ ▶ **adjective** very large; enormous.
– ORIGIN from *Gargantua,* a giant in a book by the French writer Rabelais.

gar·gle /ˈgärgəl/ ▶ **verb** wash one's mouth and throat with a liquid that is kept in motion by breathing through it. ▶ **noun 1** a liquid used for gargling. **2** an act of gargling.
– ORIGIN from Old French *gargouille* 'throat.'

gar·goyle /ˈgärˌgoil/ ▶ **noun** a spout in the form of a grotesque carved face or figure, set below the roof of a building to carry rainwater away.
– ORIGIN Old French *gargouille* 'throat,' also 'gargoyle.'

gar·ish /ˈgarisʜ/ ▶ **adjective** unpleasantly bright and showy; lurid.

– SYNONYMS **gaudy,** lurid, loud, harsh, showy, glittering, brash, tasteless, vulgar; informal flashy.
– ANTONYMS drab, tasteful.

– DERIVATIVES **gar·ish·ly** adverb **gar·ish·ness** noun.
– ORIGIN unknown.

gar·land /ˈgärlənd/ ▶ **noun** a wreath of flowers and leaves, worn on the head or hung as a decoration. ▶ **verb** decorate someone or something with a garland.
– ORIGIN Old French *garlande.*

gar·lic /ˈgärlik/ ▶ **noun** the bulb of a plant of the onion family, having a strong taste and smell and used as a flavoring in cooking.
– DERIVATIVES **gar·lick·y** adjective.
– ORIGIN Old English, from *gār* 'spear' + *lēac* 'leek.'

gar·lic mus·tard ▶ **noun** a European mustard plant that grows wild in the eastern US and that has both medicinal and culinary uses.

gar·ment /ˈgärmənt/ ▶ **noun** an item of clothing.

– SYNONYMS (**garments**) **clothes,** clothing, dress, garb, wardrobe, costume, attire; informal threads, gear, togs. formal apparel.

– ORIGIN Old French *garnement* 'equipment.'

gar·ner /ˈgärnər/ ▶ **verb** gather or collect: *the series has garnered more than thirty-five awards.*
– ORIGIN Old French *gernier.*

gar·net /ˈgärnit/ ▶ **noun** a deep red semiprecious stone.
– ORIGIN perhaps from Latin *granatum,* as in *pomum granatum* 'pomegranate,' because the garnet is similar in color to the fruit.

gar·nish /ˈgärnisʜ/ ▶ **verb 1** decorate food with a small amount of another food: *pheasant breast garnished with truffles.* **2** Law order that money or wages be seized to settle a debt.

– SYNONYMS **decorate,** adorn, ornament, trim, dress, embellish.

▶ **noun** a small amount of food used to decorate other food.

– SYNONYMS **decoration,** adornment, ornament, embellishment, enhancement, finishing touch.

– ORIGIN Old French *garnir* 'equip, arm.'

gar·nish·ee /ˌgärniˈsʜē/ ▶ **verb** variant of **GARNISH** (sense 2 of the verb). ▶ **noun** someone who is served with a garnishment.

gar·nish·ment /ˈgärnisʜmənt/ ▶ **noun** Law a court order directing that money or wages of a third party be seized to satisfy a debt.

gar·ret /ˈgarit/ ▶ **noun** a top-floor or attic room.
– ORIGIN Old French *garite* 'watchtower.'

gar·ri·son /ˈgarəsən/ ▶ **noun** a group of troops stationed in a fortress or town to defend it.

– SYNONYMS **1 troops,** forces, militia, soldiers, force, detachment, unit. **2 base,** camp, station, barracks, fort, command post.

▶ **verb** provide a place with a garrison.

– SYNONYMS **station,** post, deploy, base, site, place, billet.

– ORIGIN Old French *garison.*

gar·rote /gəˈrät, -ˈrōt/ (also **garotte**; **garrotte**) ▶ **verb** strangle someone with a wire or cord. ▶ **noun** a wire, cord, or other implement used to strangle someone.
– ORIGIN Spanish *garrote* 'cudgel, garrote.'

gar·ru·lous /ˈgar(y)ələs/ ▶ **adjective** excessively talkative.

– SYNONYMS **talkative,** loquacious, voluble, verbose, chatty, gossipy, effusive, expansive, forthcoming, conversational, communicative; informal mouthy, having the gift of the gab.
– ANTONYMS taciturn.

– DERIVATIVES **gar·ru·li·ty** /gəˈro͞olitē/ noun **gar·ru·lous·ly** adverb.
– ORIGIN Latin *garrulus.*

WORD TOOLKIT

See **TALKATIVE**.

gar·ter /'gärtər/ ▶ **noun 1** a band worn around the leg to keep up a stocking or sock. **2** a suspender for a sock or stocking.
– ORIGIN Old French *gartier*.

gar·ter snake ▶ **noun 1** a common harmless North American snake with longitudinal stripes. **2** a venomous burrowing African snake, typically dark with lighter bands.

gas /gas/ ▶ **noun** (pl. **gases** or **gasses**) **1** an airlike fluid substance that expands freely to fill any space available. **2** a flammable gas used as a fuel. **3** a gas used as an anesthetic. **4** gasoline. **5** (**a gas**) informal an entertaining or amusing person or thing. **6** Mining an explosive mixture of firedamp with air. ▶ **verb** (**gases, gassing, gassed**) **1** harm or kill someone or something with gas. **2** informal talk excessively about trivial things.
– DERIVATIVES **gas·ser** noun.
– ORIGIN invented by the Belgian chemist J. B. van Helmont; suggested by Greek *khaos* 'chaos.'

gas·bag /'gas,bag/ ▶ **noun** informal a person who talks excessively about trivial things.

gas cham·ber ▶ **noun** an airtight room that can be filled with poisonous gas to kill people or animals.

gas·e·ous /'gasēəs, 'gasHəs/ ▶ **adjective** relating to or having the characteristics of a gas.

gas guz·zler ▶ **noun** informal a car with high fuel consumption.

gash /gasH/ ▶ **noun** a long, deep cut or wound.

> – SYNONYMS **cut,** laceration, slash, slit, split, wound, injury.

▶ **verb** make a gash in something.

> – SYNONYMS **cut,** lacerate, slash, slit, split, wound, injure.

– ORIGIN from Old French *garcer* 'to chap, crack.'

gas·ket /'gaskit/ ▶ **noun** a sheet or ring of rubber or other material sealing the junction between two surfaces in an engine or other device.
– ORIGIN perhaps from French *garcette* 'thin rope.'

gas·light /'gas,līt/ ▶ **noun** light from a lamp that uses a jet of burning gas.
– DERIVATIVES **gas·lit** /-,lit/ adjective.

gas mask ▶ **noun** a protective mask used to cover the face as a defense against poison gas.

gas·o·hol /'gasə,hôl, -,häl/ ▶ **noun** a mixture of gasoline and ethanol used as fuel for internal-combustion engines.

gas·o·line /,gasə'lēn, 'gasəlēn/ ▶ **noun** a light fuel oil obtained by distilling petroleum and used in internal-combustion engines.

gas·om·e·ter /gas'ämitər/ ▶ **noun** a large tank in which gas is stored before being distributed to consumers.

gasp /gasp/ ▶ **verb 1** take a quick breath with the mouth open, from pain, breathlessness, or astonishment. **2** (**gasp for**) struggle for air by gasping.

> – SYNONYMS **1 catch one's breath,** gulp, draw in one's breath. **2 pant,** puff, huff and puff, wheeze, breathe hard/heavily, choke, fight for breath.

▶ **noun** a sudden quick breath.

> – SYNONYMS **gulp,** pant, puff.

– PHRASES **the last gasp** the point of exhaustion, death, or completion.
– ORIGIN Old Norse, 'to yawn.'

gas sta·tion ▶ **noun** a service station, especially one without repair facilities.

gas·sy /'gasē/ ▶ **adjective** (**gassier, gassiest**) resembling or full of gas.

gas·tric /'gastrik/ ▶ **adjective** relating to the stomach.
– ORIGIN from Greek *gastēr* 'stomach.'

gas·tric juice ▶ **noun** an acid fluid produced by the stomach glands, which helps digestion.

gas·tri·tis /ga'strītis/ ▶ **noun** inflammation of the lining of the stomach.

gas·tro·en·ter·i·tis /,gastrō,entə'rītis/ ▶ **noun** inflammation of the stomach and intestines, causing diarrhea and vomiting.

gas·tro·en·ter·ol·o·gy /,gastrō,entə'räləjē/ ▶ **noun** the branch of medicine that deals with disorders of the stomach and intestines.
– DERIVATIVES **gas·tro·en·te·rol·o·gist** noun.
– ORIGIN from Greek *gastēr* 'stomach' and *enteron* 'intestine.'

gas·tro·nome /'gastrə,nōm/ ▶ **noun** a gourmet.

gas·tron·o·my /ga'stränəmē/ ▶ **noun** the practice or art of choosing, preparing, and eating good food.
– DERIVATIVES **gas·tro·nom·ic** /,gastrə'nämik/ adjective.
– ORIGIN Greek *gastronomia*.

gas·tro·pod /'gastrə,päd/ ▶ **noun** Zoology any of a large class of mollusks including snails, slugs, and whelks.
– ORIGIN from Greek *gastēr* 'stomach' + *pous* 'foot.'

gas·works /'gas,wərks/ ▶ **plural noun** (treated as sing.) a place where gas is manufactured and processed.

gat /gat/ ▶ **noun** informal, dated a revolver or pistol.

gate /gāt/ ▶ **noun 1** a hinged barrier used to close an opening in a wall, fence, or hedge. **2** an exit from an airport building to an aircraft. **3** a hinged or sliding barrier for controlling the flow of water on a waterway. **4** the number of people who pay to attend a sports event. **5** an electric circuit with an output that depends on the combination of several inputs.

> – SYNONYMS **barrier,** turnstile, gateway, doorway, entrance, entryway, exit, door, portal.

▶ **verb** Brit. confine a student to school or college.
– DERIVATIVES **gat·ed** adjective.
– ORIGIN Old English.

-gate ▶ **combining form** in nouns referring to a scandal, especially one involving a cover-up: *Irangate*.
– ORIGIN suggested by the *Watergate* scandal in the US, 1972.

ga·teau /gä'tō, ga-/ ▶ **noun** (pl. **gateaus** or **gateaux** /-'tōz/) a rich cake with layers of cream or fruit.
– ORIGIN French.

gate-crash ▶ **verb** enter a party without an invitation or ticket.
– DERIVATIVES **gate-crash·er** noun.

gat·ed com·mu·ni·ty ▶ **noun** a residential area, typically fenced in, that has a guarded entrance for vehicular and pedestrian traffic.

gate·fold /'gāt,fōld/ ▶ **noun** an oversized folded page in a book or magazine, intended to be opened out for reading.

gate·house /'gāt,hous/ ▶ **noun 1** a house standing by the gateway to a country estate. **2** historical a room over a city or palace gate, often used as a prison.

gate·keep·er /'gāt,kēpər/ ▶ **noun** an attendant at a gate.

gate·keep·ing /ˈgātˌkēpiNG/ ▶ **noun 1** the activity of controlling, and usually limiting, general access to something: *her agent will be practicing a little more gatekeeping.* **2** Computing a service that controls access to files, computers, networks, etc.

gate·leg ta·ble /ˈgātˌleg/ ▶ **noun** a table with hinged legs that may be swung out from the center to support folding leaves.

gate·post /ˈgātˌpōst/ ▶ **noun** a post on which a gate is hinged or against which it shuts.

gate·way /ˈgātˌwā/ ▶ **noun 1** an opening in a wall or fence that can be closed by a gate. **2** (**gateway to**) a means of entering somewhere or achieving something: *college education is a gateway to the middle class.* **3** Computing a device used to connect two different computer networks, especially a connection to the Internet.

gate·way drug ▶ **noun** a habit-forming drug that may lead to the use of more seriously addictive drugs.

gath·er /ˈgaT͟Hər/ ▶ **verb 1** come or bring together; assemble or collect. **2** increase in speed, force, etc. **3** understand something to be the case as a result of information or evidence: *I gather he's resigned.* **4** collect plants or fruits for food. **5** harvest a crop. **6** draw together or toward oneself: *she gathered the child in her arms.* **7** pull fabric together in a series of folds by drawing thread through it.

> – SYNONYMS **1 congregate,** assemble, meet, collect, get together, convene, muster, rally, converge. **2 summon,** call together, bring together, assemble, convene, rally, round up, muster, marshal. **3 harvest,** reap, crop, pick, pluck, collect. **4 understand,** believe, be led to believe, conclude, infer, assume, take it, surmise, hear, learn, discover. **5 pleat,** pucker, tuck, fold, ruffle.
> – ANTONYMS disperse.

▶ **noun** (**gathers**) a part of a garment that is gathered.
– DERIVATIVES **gath·er·er** noun.
– ORIGIN Old English.

gath·er·ing /ˈgaT͟HəriNG/ ▶ **noun** a group of people assembled for a purpose.

> – SYNONYMS **assembly,** meeting, convention, rally, council, congress, congregation, audience, crowd, group, throng, mass; informal get-together.

Gat·ling gun /ˈgatliNG/ ▶ **noun** historical a rapid-fire, crank-driven machine gun with a cylindrical cluster of several barrels.
– ORIGIN named after the American inventor Richard J. *Gatling.*

ga·tor /ˈgātər/ ▶ **noun** informal an alligator.

GATT /gat/ ▶ **abbreviation** General Agreement on Tariffs and Trade.

gauche /gōsH/ ▶ **adjective** unsophisticated and awkward when dealing with others.

> – SYNONYMS **awkward,** gawky, inelegant, graceless, ungraceful, clumsy, ungainly, maladroit, inept, unsophisticated.
> – ANTONYMS elegant, sophisticated.

– DERIVATIVES **gauche·ly** adverb **gauche·ness** noun.
– ORIGIN French, 'left.'

gau·che·rie /ˌgōsHəˈrē/ ▶ **noun** awkward or unsophisticated ways.
– ORIGIN French.

gau·cho /ˈgoucHō/ ▶ **noun** (pl. **gauchos**) a cowboy from the South American plains.
– ORIGIN Latin American Spanish.

gaud·y /ˈgôdē/ ▶ **adjective** (**gaudier, gaudiest**) tastelessly bright or showy: *gaudy multicolored shorts.*

> – SYNONYMS **garish,** lurid, loud, glaring, harsh, showy, glittering, ostentatious, tasteless; informal flashy, tacky.
> – ANTONYMS drab, tasteful.

– DERIVATIVES **gaud·i·ly** adverb **gaud·i·ness** noun.
– ORIGIN probably from Old French *gaudir* 'rejoice.'

gauge /gāj/ (chiefly technical also **gage**) ▶ **noun 1** an instrument that measures and gives a visual display of the amount, level, or contents of something. **2** the thickness, size, or capacity of a wire, tube, bullet, etc., especially as a standard measure. **3** the distance between the rails of a railroad track.

> – SYNONYMS **meter,** measure, indicator, dial, scale, display.

▶ **verb 1** judge or assess a situation or mood: *it is difficult to gauge his true feelings.* **2** estimate or measure the amount or level of something. **3** measure the dimensions of an object with a gauge.

> – SYNONYMS **1 measure,** calculate, compute, work out, determine, ascertain, count, weigh, quantify, put a figure on. **2 assess,** evaluate, determine, estimate, form an opinion of, appraise, weigh up, judge, guess; informal size up.

– DERIVATIVES **gaug·er** noun.
– ORIGIN Old French.

Gaul /gôl/ ▶ **noun** a person from the ancient European region of Gaul.
– ORIGIN Latin *Gallus.*

Gaul·ish /ˈgôlisH/ ▶ **noun** the Celtic language of the ancient Gauls. ▶ **adjective** relating to the ancient Gauls.

Gaull·ist /ˈgôˌlist/ ▶ **noun** a supporter of the principles and policies of the French statesman Charles de Gaulle, characterized chiefly by conservatism and nationalism. ▶ **adjective** relating to Gaullists or Gaullism.
– DERIVATIVES **Gaull·ism** /ˈgôˌlizəm/ noun.

gaunt /gônt/ ▶ **adjective 1** lean and haggard, especially through suffering or age. **2** (of a place) grim or desolate.

> – SYNONYMS **haggard,** drawn, thin, lean, skinny, spindly, spare, bony, angular, rawboned, pinched, hollow-cheeked, scrawny, scraggy, as thin as a rail, cadaverous, skeletal, emaciated, skin and bone(s), wasted, withered; informal like a bag of bones.
> – ANTONYMS plump.

– DERIVATIVES **gaunt·ly** adverb **gaunt·ness** noun.
– ORIGIN unknown.

> **WORD TOOLKIT**
>
> See **THIN**.

gaunt·let[1] /ˈgôntlit, ˈgänt-/ ▶ **noun 1** a strong glove with a long, loose wrist. **2** a leather glove with steel plates, worn as part of medieval armor.
– PHRASES **take up** (or **throw down**) **the gauntlet** accept (or issue) a challenge. [from the medieval custom of issuing a challenge by throwing one's gauntlet to the ground; a person accepted the challenge by picking it up.]
– ORIGIN Old French *gantelet.*

gaunt·let[2] ▶ **noun** (in phrase **run the gauntlet**) **1** go through an intimidating crowd or experience in order to reach a goal. **2** historical undergo the military punishment of receiving blows while running between two rows of men with sticks.

– ORIGIN from Swedish *gata* 'lane' + *lopp* 'course,' influenced by **GAUNTLET**[1].

gauss /gous/ ▶ **noun** (pl. same or **gausses**) a unit of magnetic flux density, equal to one ten-thousandth of a tesla.
– ORIGIN named after the German mathematician Karl Friedrich *Gauss*.

Gauss·i·an dis·tri·bu·tion /ˈgousēən/ ▶ **noun** another term for **NORMAL DISTRIBUTION**.

gauze /gôz/ ▶ **noun 1** a thin transparent fabric. **2** thin, loosely woven cloth used for dressing wounds. **3** (also **wire gauze**) a fine wire mesh.
– DERIVATIVES **gauz·y** adjective.
– ORIGIN French *gaze*.

gave /gāv/ past of **GIVE**.

gav·el /ˈgavəl/ ▶ **noun** a small hammer with which an auctioneer, judge, or chair of a meeting hits a surface to call for attention or order.
– ORIGIN unknown.

gav·el-to-gav·el ▶ **adjective** (of media coverage of an event or trial) from beginning to end and all-inclusive: *C-SPAN plans gavel-to-gavel coverage from the convention floor.*

ga·votte /gəˈvät/ ▶ **noun** a medium-paced French dance, popular in the 18th century.
– ORIGIN Provençal *gavoto* 'dance of the mountain people.'

gawk /gôk/ ▶ **verb** stare in a stupid or rude way. ▶ **noun** an awkward or shy person.
– DERIVATIVES **gawk·er** noun.
– ORIGIN perhaps from Old Norse, 'to heed.'

gawk·y /ˈgôkē/ ▶ **adjective** nervously awkward and ungainly.
– DERIVATIVES **gawk·i·ly** adverb **gawk·i·ness** noun.

gawp /gôp/ ▶ **verb** informal stare in a stupid or rude way.
– DERIVATIVES **gawp·er** noun.
– ORIGIN perhaps from **GAPE**.

gay /gā/ ▶ **adjective** (**gayer, gayest**) **1** (especially of a man) homosexual. **2** relating to homosexuals. **3** dated lighthearted and carefree. **4** dated brightly colored; showy. ▶ **noun** a homosexual person, especially a man.
– DERIVATIVES **gay·ness** noun.
– ORIGIN Old French *gai*.

gay·dar /ˈgāˌdär/ ▶ **noun** informal the supposed ability of homosexuals to recognize one another by interpreting very slight indications.
– ORIGIN from **GAY** + **RADAR**.

ga·za·ni·a /gəˈzānēə/ ▶ **noun** a tropical herbaceous plant of the daisy family, with flowers that are typically orange or yellow.

gaze /gāz/ ▶ **verb** look steadily and intently.

– SYNONYMS **stare,** gape, look fixedly, eye, scrutinize, ogle; informal rubberneck, eyeball.

▶ **noun** a steady intent look.

– SYNONYMS **stare,** gape, fixed look, regard, scrutiny.

– DERIVATIVES **gaz·er** noun.
– ORIGIN perhaps related to **GAWK**.

ga·ze·bo /gəˈzēbō/ ▶ **noun** (pl. **gazebos**) a freestanding roofed structure with a wide view of the surrounding area, found typically in parks and backyards.
– ORIGIN perhaps from **GAZE**, in imitation of Latin future tenses ending in *-ebo*.

ga·zelle /gəˈzel/ ▶ **noun** a small antelope with curved horns and white underparts.
– ORIGIN French.

ga·zette /gəˈzet/ ▶ **noun** a journal or newspaper, especially the official journal of an organization.
– ORIGIN from Venetian *gazeta de la novità* 'a halfpennyworth of news.'

gaz·et·teer /ˌgaziˈti(ə)r/ ▶ **noun** a list of place names published as a book or part of a book.
– ORIGIN Italian *gazzetta* 'gazette.'

ga·zil·lion /gəˈzilyən/ ▶ **cardinal number** informal a very large number or quantity.
– ORIGIN humorous formation on the pattern of *billion*.

gaz·pa·cho /gäˈspäCHō/ ▶ **noun** (pl. **gazpachos**) a cold Spanish soup made chiefly from tomatoes and peppers.
– ORIGIN Spanish.

GB ▶ **abbreviation 1** Great Britain. **2** (also **Gb**) Computing gigabyte(s) or gigabit(s).

Gd ▶ **symbol** the chemical element gadolinium.

GDP ▶ **abbreviation** gross domestic product.

GDR ▶ **abbreviation** historical German Democratic Republic.

Ge ▶ **symbol** the chemical element germanium.

gear /gi(ə)r/ ▶ **noun 1** (**gears**) a set of toothed wheels that connect the engine to the wheels of a vehicle and work together to alter its speed. **2** a particular setting of gears in a vehicle: *I never left third gear.* **3** informal equipment, possessions, or clothing.

– SYNONYMS **1 equipment,** apparatus, paraphernalia, tools, utensils, implements, instruments, rig, tackle. **2 belongings,** possessions, effects, paraphernalia, bits and pieces; informal things, stuff. **3 clothes,** clothing, garments, outfits, attire, garb, wardrobe; informal togs, threads. formal apparel.

▶ **verb 1** design or adjust gears to give a particular speed or power output. **2** adapt something for a particular purpose or group: *an activity program geared to senior citizens.* **3** (**gear (someone/thing) up**) prepare to do something, or prepare someone to do something: *we're gearing up to expand out of California.*
– PHRASES **in** (or **out of**) **gear** with a gear (or no gear) engaged.
– ORIGIN Scandinavian.

gear·box /ˈgi(ə)rˌbäks/ ▶ **noun** a set of gears with its casing, especially in a motor vehicle; the transmission.

gear·ing /ˈgi(ə)riNG/ ▶ **noun 1** the set or arrangement of gears in a machine. **2** British term for **LEVERAGE** (sense 3).

gear·shift /ˈgi(ə)rˌSHift/ (also **shift lever**) ▶ **noun** a lever used to engage or change gears in a motor vehicle.

gear·wheel /ˈgi(ə)rˌ(h)wēl/ ▶ **noun 1** a toothed wheel in a set of gears. **2** (on a bicycle) a cogwheel driven directly by the chain.

geck·o /ˈgekō/ ▶ **noun** (pl. **geckos** or **geckoes**) a lizard of warm regions, with adhesive pads on the feet.
– ORIGIN Malay.

GED ▶ **abbreviation** general equivalency degree (or diploma).

gee[1] /jē/ (also **gee whiz** /ˈjē ˈ(h)wiz/) ▶ **exclamation** informal a mild expression of surprise, enthusiasm, or sympathy.
– ORIGIN perhaps an abbreviation of **JESUS**.

gee[2] ▶ **exclamation** (**gee up**) a command to a horse to go faster. ▶ **verb** (**gees, geeing, geed**) (**gee someone up**) encourage someone to put more effort into something.
– ORIGIN unknown.

gee·gaw /ˈgēgô/ ▶ **noun** a showy object, especially one that is useless or worthless: *overpriced geegaws to hang in their kitchen.*

geek /gēk/ ▶ **noun** informal **1** a person who is unfashionable or awkward in the company of other people. **2** an obsessive enthusiast: *a computer geek.*
– DERIVATIVES **geek·dom** noun **geek·y** adjective (**geekier, geekiest**).
– ORIGIN from English dialect *geck* 'fool.'

geese /gēs/ plural of GOOSE.

geez ▶ **exclamation** variant spelling of JEEZ.

gee·zer /ˈgēzər/ ▶ **noun** informal, derogatory an old man.
– ORIGIN from a dialect pronunciation of earlier *guiser* 'mummer.'

ge·fil·te fish /gəˈfiltə/ ▶ **noun** a dish of fishcakes boiled in broth and served chilled.
– ORIGIN Yiddish, 'stuffed fish.'

Gei·ger count·er /ˈgīgər/ ▶ **noun** a device for measuring radioactivity.
– ORIGIN named after the German physicist Hans *Geiger.*

gei·sha /ˈgāshə, ˈgē-/ ▶ **noun** (pl. same or **geishas**) a Japanese hostess trained to entertain men with conversation, dance, and song.
– ORIGIN Japanese, 'entertainer.'

gel[1] /jel/ ▶ **noun 1** a jellylike substance, especially one used in cosmetic or medicinal products. **2** Chemistry a semisolid suspension of a solid dispersed in a liquid.
▶ **verb** (**gels, gelling, gelled**) **1** Chemistry form into a gel. **2** smooth or style the hair with gel.
– ORIGIN from GELATIN.

gel[2] (also **jell**) ▶ **verb 1** (of jelly or a similar substance) set or become firmer. **2** take definite form or begin to work well: *we had new players and it took some time for the team to gel.*

gel·a·tin /ˈjelətn/ ▶ **noun** a clear water-soluble protein obtained from animal bones, used in food preparation, photographic processing, and glue.
– ORIGIN French *gélatine.*

ge·lat·i·nous /jəˈlatn-əs/ ▶ **adjective 1** having a jellylike consistency. **2** of or like the protein gelatin.

ge·la·to /jəˈlätō/ ▶ **noun** an Italian-style ice cream.

gel·cap /ˈjel,kap/ ▶ **noun** a gelatin capsule containing liquid medication or other substance to be taken orally.

geld /geld/ ▶ **verb** castrate a male animal.
– ORIGIN from an Old Norse word meaning 'barren.'

geld·ing /ˈgelding/ ▶ **noun** a castrated male horse.

gel·ig·nite /ˈjelig,nīt/ ▶ **noun** a high explosive made from nitroglycerine and nitrocellulose in a base of wood pulp and sodium.
– ORIGIN probably from GELATIN + Latin *lignis* 'wood.'

gel pen ▶ **noun** a pen that uses a gel-based ink, combining the permanence of oil-based ink and the smooth glide of water-based ink.

gem /jem/ ▶ **noun 1** a precious or semiprecious stone, especially one that has been cut and polished. **2** an outstanding person or thing: *a gem of a book.*

> – SYNONYMS **1 jewel,** precious stone, semiprecious stone; informal rock, sparkler. **2 masterpiece,** classic, treasure, prize, find; informal one in a million; old use the bee's knees.

– ORIGIN Latin *gemma* 'bud, jewel.'

gem·i·nate /ˈjemənit/ ▶ **adjective** Phonetics (of a consonant sound) doubled.

Gem·i·ni /ˈjemə,nī, -,nē/ ▶ **noun 1** a constellation and the third sign of the zodiac (the Twins), which the sun enters about May 21. **2** (**a Gemini**) a person born when the sun is in this sign.
– DERIVATIVES **Gem·i·ni·an** /-,nīən/ noun & adjective.
– ORIGIN Latin, 'twins.'

gems·bok /ˈgemz,bäk/ ▶ **noun** a large African antelope with black-and-white head markings and long straight horns.
– ORIGIN Dutch, 'chamois.'

gem·stone /ˈjem,stōn/ ▶ **noun** a gem used in a piece of jewelry.

-gen ▶ **combining form** referring to a substance that produces something: *allergen.*
– ORIGIN from Greek *genēs* '-born, of a specified kind.'

gen·darme /ˈzhändärm/ ▶ **noun** a paramilitary police officer in French-speaking countries.
– ORIGIN French, from *gens d'armes* 'men of arms.'

gen·dar·me·rie /zhänˈdärmərē/ ▶ **noun 1** the headquarters of a force of gendarmes. **2** a force of gendarmes.

gen·der /ˈjendər/ ▶ **noun 1** Grammar a class (usually masculine, feminine, common, or neuter) into which nouns and pronouns are placed in some languages. **2** the state of being male or female (with reference to social or cultural differences). **3** the members of one or the other sex.
– DERIVATIVES **gen·dered** adjective.
– ORIGIN Old French *gendre.*

> **USAGE**
>
> The words **gender** and **sex** both have the sense 'the state of being male or female,' but they are used in different ways: **sex** usually refers to biological differences, while **gender** tends to refer to cultural or social ones.

gen·der gap ▶ **noun** a discrepancy in opportunities, status, attitudes, etc., between men and women.

gen·der-neu·tral ▶ **adjective 1** involving, directed at, or designed for use by both sexes equally: *gender-neutral bathrooms.* **2** (of language) not specific to one sex; referring to a person of either sex: *the need for a gender-neutral pronoun.*

gene /jēn/ ▶ **noun** a distinct sequence of DNA forming part of a chromosome, by which offspring inherit characteristics from a parent.
– DERIVATIVES **gen·ic** /ˈjenik/ adjective.
– ORIGIN German *Gen.*

ge·ne·al·o·gy /,jēnēˈäləjē, -ˈal-/ ▶ **noun** (pl. **genealogies**) **1** a line of descent traced continuously from an ancestor. **2** the study of lines of descent.

> – SYNONYMS **lineage,** line (of descent), family tree, bloodline, pedigree, ancestry, heritage, parentage, family, stock, blood, roots.

– DERIVATIVES **ge·ne·a·log·i·cal** /,jēnēəˈläjikəl/ adjective **ge·ne·al·o·gist** noun.
– ORIGIN from Greek *genea* 'race, generation' + *logos* 'account.'

gene-al·tered ▶ **adjective** (especially in journalism) genetically modified: *the much ballyhooed, vine-ripened, gene-altered, rot-resistant tomato.*

gene pool ▶ **noun** the stock of different genes in a particular species of animal or plant.

gen·er·a /ˈjenərə/ plural of GENUS.

gen·er·al /ˈjenərəl/ ▸ adjective 1 affecting or concerning all or most people or things; not specialized or limited: *books of general interest*. 2 involving only the main features or elements; not detailed. 3 chief or principal: *the general manager*.

– SYNONYMS 1 *suitable for general use* **widespread,** common, extensive, universal, wide, popular, public, mainstream. 2 *a general pay increase* **comprehensive,** overall, across the board, blanket, global, universal, mass, wholesale. 3 **usual,** customary, habitual, traditional, normal, conventional, typical, standard, regular, accepted, prevailing, routine, established, everyday. 4 *a general description* **broad,** rough, loose, approximate, unspecific, vague, imprecise, inexact.
– ANTONYMS restricted, unusual, detailed.

▸ noun 1 a commander of an army, or an army officer ranking above lieutenant general. 2 short for BRIGADIER GENERAL, LIEUTENANT GENERAL, or MAJOR GENERAL.
– PHRASES **in general** 1 usually; mainly. 2 as a whole.
– ORIGIN Latin *generalis*.

gen·er·al an·es·the·tic ▸ noun an anesthetic that affects the whole body and causes a loss of consciousness.

gen·er·al de·liv·er·y ▸ noun mail delivery to a post office for collection by the addressee.

gen·er·al e·lec·tion ▸ noun 1 a regular election of candidates for office, as opposed to a primary election. 2 a regular election for state or national offices.

gen·er·al·is·si·mo /ˌjenərəˈlisəˌmō/ ▸ noun (pl. **generalissimos**) the commander of a combined military force consisting of army, navy, and air force units.
– ORIGIN from Italian, 'having greatest authority.'

gen·er·al·ist /ˈjenərəlist/ ▸ noun a person who is competent in several different fields or activities.

gen·er·al·i·ty /ˌjenəˈralitē/ ▸ noun (pl. **generalities**) 1 a statement or principle that is general rather than specific: *you're talking in generalities*. 2 the quality or state of being general. 3 (**the generality**) the majority.

gen·er·al·ize /ˈjenərəˌlīz/ ▸ verb 1 make a general or broad statement based on specific cases: *you cannot generalize about the actions of one set of employees*. 2 make something more common or more widely applicable. 3 (as adj. **generalized**) (of a disease) affecting much or all of the body; not localized.
– DERIVATIVES **gen·er·al·iz·a·ble** adjective **gen·er·al·i·za·tion** /ˌjenərəliˈzāSHən/ noun.

gen·er·al·ly /ˈjenərəlē/ ▸ adverb 1 in most cases. 2 without regard to details or exceptions. 3 by or to most people; widely.

– SYNONYMS 1 **normally,** in general, as a rule, by and large, mainly, mostly, for the most part, predominantly, on the whole, usually. 2 **widely,** commonly, extensively, universally, popularly.

gen·er·al prac·ti·tion·er ▸ noun a doctor who provides primary health care to patients of any age.
– DERIVATIVES **gen·er·al prac·tice** noun.

gen·er·al-pur·pose ▸ adjective having a range of potential uses or functions.

gen·er·al·ship /ˈjenərəlˌSHip/ ▸ noun the skill and practice of exercising military command.

gen·er·al staff ▸ noun the staff assisting a military commander.

gen·er·al store ▸ noun a store, typically in a rural area, that carries a wide variety of merchandise such as food, housewares, hardware, and dry goods, without being divided into departments.

gen·er·al strike ▸ noun a strike of workers in all or most industries.

gen·er·ate /ˈjenəˌrāt/ ▸ verb create or produce: *the article generated much reader interest*.

– SYNONYMS **create,** make, produce, engender, spawn, precipitate, prompt, provoke, trigger, spark, stir up, induce.

– ORIGIN Latin *generare*.

gen·er·a·tion /ˌjenəˈrāSHən/ ▸ noun 1 all of the people born and living at about the same time: *he was one of the cleverest entrepreneurs of his generation*. 2 the average period (about thirty years) in which children grow up and have children of their own. 3 a set of members of a family regarded as a single stage in descent. 4 a group of people of similar age involved in an activity: *a new generation of actors*. 5 a stage in the development of a product: *the next generation of cell phones*. 6 the production or creation of something.

– SYNONYMS 1 **age,** age group, peer group. 2 **crop,** batch, wave, range.

– DERIVATIVES **gen·er·a·tion·al** adjective.

gen·er·a·tion gap ▸ noun a difference in attitudes between people of different generations, leading to lack of understanding.

Gen·er·a·tion X ▸ noun the generation born between the mid 1960s and the mid 1970s, typically seen as lacking a sense of direction and feeling that they have no role in society.
– DERIVATIVES **Gen·er·a·tion X·er** noun.

gen·er·a·tive /ˈjenərətiv, -ˌrātiv/ ▸ adjective capable of production or reproduction.

gen·er·a·tor /ˈjenəˌrātər/ ▸ noun 1 a person or thing that generates something. 2 a dynamo or similar machine for converting mechanical energy into electricity.

ge·ner·ic /jəˈnerik/ ▸ adjective 1 referring to a class, group, or genus; not specific: *Indians are fond of saag (a generic term for leafy greens)*. 2 (of goods) having no brand name.
– DERIVATIVES **ge·ner·i·cal·ly** adverb.
– ORIGIN from Latin *genus* 'stock, race.'

gen·er·os·i·ty /ˌjenəˈräsitē/ ▸ noun 1 the quality of being kind and generous. 2 the fact of being plentiful or large: *diners cannot complain about the generosity of portions*.

– SYNONYMS **liberality,** lavishness, magnanimity, bounty, munificence, open-handedness, largesse, unselfishness, altruism, charity.
– ANTONYMS meanness, selfishness.

gen·er·ous /ˈjenərəs/ ▸ adjective 1 freely giving more than is necessary or expected. 2 kind toward others. 3 larger or more plentiful than is usual: *a generous helping of rice*.

– SYNONYMS 1 **liberal,** lavish, magnanimous, giving, open-handed, bountiful, unselfish, ungrudging, free, unstinting, munificent; literary bounteous. 2 **plentiful,** copious, ample, liberal, large, abundant, rich.
– ANTONYMS mean, selfish, meager.

– DERIVATIVES **gen·er·ous·ly** adverb.
– ORIGIN Latin *generosus* 'noble, magnanimous.'

WORD TOOLKIT

generous ...	unselfish ...	benevolent ...
support	player	dictator
offer	service	creator
donation	devotion	fund
gift	commitment	society
terms	love	force
portion	efforts	patriarch
benefactor	courage	organization

gen·e·sis /'jenəsis/ ▶ **noun 1** the origin of something. **2** (**Genesis**) the first book of the Bible, which includes the story of the creation of the world.

– SYNONYMS **origin,** source, root, beginning, start.

– ORIGIN Greek, 'generation, creation.'

gene ther·a·py ▶ **noun** the introduction of normal genes into cells in place of missing or defective ones in order to correct genetic disorders.

ge·net·ic /jə'netik/ ▶ **adjective 1** relating to genes or heredity. **2** relating to genetics. **3** relating to the origin of something.

– DERIVATIVES **ge·net·i·cal** adjective **ge·net·i·cal·ly** adverb.

– ORIGIN from GENESIS.

ge·net·i·cal·ly mod·i·fied /jə'netik(ə)lē 'mädə,fīd/ ▶ **adjective** (of a plant or animal) containing genetic material that has been artificially altered so as to produce a desired characteristic.

ge·net·ic blue·print ▶ **noun** (not in technical use) a genomic map: *determining the genetic blueprints for all malaria parasites.*

ge·net·ic code ▶ **noun** the means by which DNA and RNA molecules carry genetic information.

ge·net·ic en·gi·neer·ing ▶ **noun** the deliberate modification of a plant or animal by altering its genetic material.

ge·net·ic fin·ger·print·ing ▶ **noun** the analysis of DNA from samples of body tissues or fluids in order to identify individuals.

ge·net·ics /jə'netiks/ ▶ **plural noun** (treated as sing.) the study of the way in which inherited characteristics are passed from one generation to another.

– DERIVATIVES **ge·net·i·cist** noun.

ge·net·ic screen·ing ▶ **noun** the screening, especially by DNA analysis, of a population or individual for genetic susceptibility to particular disorders and diseases.

ge·net·ic test·ing ▶ **noun** the sequencing of human DNA to discover genetic differences, anomalies, or mutations that may prove pathological: *genetic testing for Huntington's disease.*

ge·ni·al /'jēnyəl, -nēəl/ ▶ **adjective** friendly and cheerful.

– SYNONYMS **friendly,** affable, cordial, amiable, warm, easygoing, approachable, sympathetic, good-natured, good-humored, cheerful, hospitable, companionable, sociable, convivial, outgoing, gregarious; informal chummy.
– ANTONYMS unfriendly.

– DERIVATIVES **ge·ni·al·i·ty** /,jēnē'alitē/ noun **gen·ial·ly** adverb.

– ORIGIN Latin *genialis* 'nuptial, productive.'

-genic ▶ **combining form 1** producing or produced by: *carcinogenic.* **2** well suited to: *photogenic.*

ge·nie /'jēnē/ ▶ **noun** (pl. **genii** /-nē,ī/ or **genies**) (in Arabian folklore) a spirit, especially one capable of granting wishes when summoned.

– ORIGIN Latin *genius* (see GENIUS).

ge·ni·i /'jēnē,ī/ plural of GENIE.

gen·i·tal /'jenitl/ ▶ **adjective** referring to the human or animal reproductive organs. ▶ **noun** (**genitals**) a person or animal's external reproductive organs.

– DERIVATIVES **gen·i·tal·ly** adverb.

– ORIGIN Latin *genitalis.*

gen·i·ta·li·a /,jeni'tālēə, -'tālyə/ ▶ **plural noun** formal or technical a person or animal's genitals.

– ORIGIN Latin.

gen·i·tive /'jenitiv/ ▶ **noun** the grammatical case of a word that is used to show possession or close association.

– ORIGIN from Latin *genitivus casus* 'case of production or origin.'

ge·ni·to·u·ri·nar·y /,jenitō'yŏŏrə,nerē/ ▶ **adjective** relating to the genital and urinary organs.

gen·ius /'jēnyəs/ ▶ **noun** (pl. **geniuses**) **1** exceptional intellectual power or other natural ability: *a painter of genius.* **2** an exceptionally intelligent or able person. **3** the prevalent character of a nation, period, etc.

– SYNONYMS **1 brilliance,** intelligence, intellect, ability, cleverness, brains. **2 talent,** gift, flair, aptitude, facility, knack, ability, expertise, capacity, faculty. **3 brilliant person,** mastermind, Einstein, intellectual, brain, prodigy; informal egghead, brainiac, whiz kid.

– ORIGIN Latin, also in the sense 'spirit present at one's birth.'

gen·o·cide /'jenə,sīd/ ▶ **noun** the deliberate killing of a very large number of people from a particular ethnic group or nation.

– DERIVATIVES **gen·o·cid·al** /,jenə'sīdl/ adjective.

– ORIGIN from Greek *genos* 'race' + -CIDE.

ge·nome /'jē,nōm/ ▶ **noun 1** the full set of the chromosomes of an animal, plant, or other life form. **2** the complete set of genetic material present in an animal, plant, or other life form.

– ORIGIN blend of GENE and CHROMOSOME.

ge·no·mics /jē'nōmiks, -'näm-/ ▶ **plural noun** the branch of biology concerned with the structure, function, evolution, and mapping of genomes.

– DERIVATIVES **ge·no·mic** adjective.

gen·o·type /'jenə,tīp, 'jē-/ ▶ **noun** the genetic makeup of an individual animal, plant, or other life form.

– DERIVATIVES **gen·o·typ·ic** adjective.

gen·re /'zhänrə/ ▶ **noun** a style or category of art or literature.

– SYNONYMS **category,** class, classification, group, set, type, sort, kind, variety.

▶ **adjective** referring to a style of painting showing scenes from ordinary life.

– ORIGIN French, 'a kind.'

gent /jent/ ▶ **noun** informal **1** a gentleman. **2** (**the Gents**) Brit. a men's restroom.

gen·teel /jen'tēl/ ▶ **adjective** polite and refined in an affected or exaggerated way.

– SYNONYMS **refined,** respectable, well mannered, courteous, polite, proper, correct, seemly, well bred, ladylike, gentlemanly, dignified, gracious.
– ANTONYMS uncouth.

– DERIVATIVES **gen·teel·ly** adverb.

– ORIGIN French *gentil* 'well born.'

> CHOOSE THE RIGHT WORD
>
> See **URBANE**.

gen·tian /'jencHən/ ▸ **noun** a plant of temperate and mountainous regions with violet or blue trumpet-shaped flowers.
– ORIGIN Latin *gentiana*.

Gen·tile /'jentīl/ ▸ **adjective** not Jewish. ▸ **noun** a person who is not Jewish.
– ORIGIN Latin *gentilis* 'relating to a family or nation.'

gen·til·i·ty /jen'tilitē/ ▸ **noun** polite and refined behavior, especially as typical of a high social class: *the ideal of Victorian gentility was to distance oneself from the taint of commerce.*
– ORIGIN from Old French *gentil* 'high-born, noble.'

gen·tle /'jentl/ ▸ **adjective** (**gentler**, **gentlest**) **1** mild or kind; not rough or violent: *a gentle and loving mother.* **2** not harsh or severe. **3** old use noble or courteous.

> – SYNONYMS **1 kind,** tender, sympathetic, considerate, understanding, compassionate, humane, mild, placid, serene. **2 light,** soft, quiet, low. **3 gradual,** slight, easy, slow, imperceptible.
> – ANTONYMS brutal, strong, loud, steep.

– DERIVATIVES **gen·tle·ness** noun **gen·tly** adverb.
– ORIGIN Old French *gentil* 'high-born, noble.'

gent·le·folk /'jentl,fōk/ ▸ **plural noun** old use people of noble birth or good social position.

gent·le·man /'jentlmən/ ▸ **noun** (pl. **gentlemen**) **1** a courteous or honorable man. **2** a man of good social position. **3** (in polite or formal use) a man.
– DERIVATIVES **gen·tle·man·ly** adjective.

gen·tle·man's a·gree·ment ▸ **noun** an arrangement based on trust rather than on a legal contract.

gen·tle·wom·an /'jentl,wo͝omən/ ▸ **noun** (pl. **gentlewomen**) old use a woman of noble birth or good social position.

gen·tri·fy /'jentrə,fī/ ▸ **verb** (**gentrifies**, **gentrifying**, **gentrified**) renovate or improve a house or district so that it is in keeping with middle-class taste.
– DERIVATIVES **gen·tri·fi·ca·tion** /,jentrəfi'kāsHən/ noun **gen·tri·fi·er** noun.

gen·try /'jentrē/ ▸ **noun** (**the gentry**) people of good social position.
– ORIGIN Old French *genterie*.

gen·u·flect /'jenyə,flekt/ ▸ **verb** lower the body briefly by bending one knee to the ground in worship or as a sign of respect.
– DERIVATIVES **gen·u·flec·tion** /,jenyə'fleksHən/ noun.
– ORIGIN Latin *genuflectere*.

gen·u·ine /'jenyo͞oin/ ▸ **adjective 1** truly what it is said to be; authentic: *a genuine leather handbag.* **2** able to be trusted; sincere.

> – SYNONYMS **1 authentic,** real, actual, original, bona fide, true; informal the real McCoy, the real thing, kosher. **2 sincere,** honest, truthful, straightforward, direct, frank, candid, open, natural; informal straight, upfront.
> – ANTONYMS bogus, insincere.

– DERIVATIVES **gen·u·ine·ly** adverb **gen·u·ine·ness** noun.
– ORIGIN Latin *genuinus*.

ge·nus /'jēnəs/ ▸ **noun** (pl. **genera** /'jenərə/) **1** a category in the classification of animals and plants that ranks above species and below family, shown by a capitalized Latin name, e.g., *Leo.* **2** a class of things that have common characteristics.
– ORIGIN Latin, 'birth, race, stock.'

Gen-X /'jen 'eks/ ▸ **noun** short for **GENERATION X**.
– DERIVATIVES **Gen-X·er** /'jen 'eksər/ noun.

geo- ▸ **combining form** relating to the earth: *geology.*
– ORIGIN from Greek *gē* 'earth.'

ge·o·cen·tric /,jēō'sentrik/ ▸ **adjective 1** having the earth as the center, as in former astronomical systems. Compare with **HELIOCENTRIC**. **2** Astronomy measured from or considered in relation to the center of the earth.

ge·o·chem·is·try /,jēō'keməstrē/ ▸ **noun** the study of the chemical composition of the earth and its constituent materials.

ge·ode /'jēōd/ ▸ **noun 1** a small cavity in rock lined with crystals or other mineral matter. **2** a rock containing such a cavity.
– ORIGIN from Greek *geōdēs* 'earthy.'

ge·o·des·ic /,jēə'desik, -'dē-/ ▸ **adjective 1** referring to the shortest possible line between two points on a sphere or other curved surface. **2** (of a dome) constructed from struts that follow geodesic lines and form an open framework of triangles and polygons.

ge·od·e·sy /jē'ädəsē/ ▸ **noun** the branch of mathematics concerned with the shape and area of the earth.
– DERIVATIVES **ge·od·e·sist** noun.
– ORIGIN Greek *geōdaisia*.

ge·o·det·ic /,jēə'detik/ ▸ **adjective** relating to geodesy, especially as applied to land surveying.

ge·og·ra·phy /jē'ägrəfē/ ▸ **noun 1** the study of the physical features of the earth and of human activity as it relates to these. **2** the way in which the physical features of a place are arranged: *the rugged geography of British Columbia.*
– DERIVATIVES **ge·og·ra·pher** noun **ge·o·graph·ic** /,jēə'grafik/ adjective **ge·o·graph·i·cal** /,jēə'grafikəl/ adjective **ge·o·graph·i·cal·ly** /,jēə'grafik(ə)lē/ adverb.

ge·ol·o·gy /jē'äləjē/ ▸ **noun 1** the science that deals with the physical structure and substance of the earth. **2** the geological features of a district.
– DERIVATIVES **ge·o·log·ic** /,jēə'läjik/ adjective **ge·o·log·i·cal** /,jēə'läjikəl/ adjective **ge·o·log·i·cal·ly** /,jēə'läjik(ə)lē/ adverb **ge·ol·o·gist** noun.

ge·o·man·cy /'jēə,mansē/ ▸ **noun** the art of siting buildings so as to encourage good fortune.
– DERIVATIVES **ge·o·man·cer** noun **ge·o·man·tic** /,jēə'mantik/ adjective.

ge·o·met·ric /,jēə'metrik/ ▸ **adjective 1** relating to geometry. **2** (of a design) consisting of regular lines and shapes.
– DERIVATIVES **ge·o·met·ri·cal** adjective **ge·o·met·ri·cal·ly** adverb.

ge·o·met·ric mean ▸ **noun** the central number in a geometric progression (e.g., 9 in 3, 9, 27).

ge·o·met·ric pro·gres·sion (also **geometric series**) ▸ **noun** a sequence of numbers with a constant ratio between each number and the one before (e.g., 1, 3, 9, 27, 81, in which each number in the sequence is multiplied by 3 to create the next number).

ge·om·e·try /jē'ämətrē/ ▸ **noun 1** (pl. **geometries**) the branch of mathematics concerned with the properties and relations of points, lines, surfaces, and solids. **2** the shape and relative arrangement of the parts of something.

– DERIVATIVES **ge·om·e·tri·cian** /ˌjēəməˈtrisHən/ noun.
– ORIGIN Greek *geometria.*

ge·o·mor·phol·o·gy /ˌjēōˌmôrˈfäləjē/ ▶ **noun** the study of the physical features of the surface of the earth and their relation to its geological structures.
– DERIVATIVES **ge·o·mor·pho·log·i·cal** /-ˌmôrfəˈläjikəl/ adjective **ge·o·mor·phol·o·gist** noun.

ge·o·phys·ics /ˌjēōˈfiziks/ ▶ **plural noun** (treated as sing.) the physics of the earth.
– DERIVATIVES **ge·o·phys·i·cal** adjective **ge·o·phys·i·cist** noun.

ge·o·po·lit·i·cal /ˌjēōpəˈlitikəl/ ▶ **adjective** relating to politics, especially international relations, as influenced by geographical factors.
– DERIVATIVES **ge·o·pol·i·tics** /ˌjēōˈpäləˌtiks/ noun.

geor·gette /jôrˈjet/ ▶ **noun** a thin silk or crêpe dress material.
– ORIGIN named after the French dressmaker *Georgette* de la Plante.

Geor·gian[1] /ˈjôrjən/ ▶ **adjective 1** relating to or characteristic of the reigns of the British Kings George I–IV (1714–1830). **2** relating to British neoclassical architecture of this period.

Geor·gian[2] ▶ **noun 1** a person from the country of Georgia. **2** the official language of Georgia. ▶ **adjective** relating to Georgians or Georgian.

Geor·gian[3] ▶ **adjective** relating to the US state of Georgia. ▶ **noun** a person from Georgia.

ge·o·sta·tion·ar·y /ˌjēōˈstāsHəˌnerē/ ▶ **adjective** (of an artificial satellite) orbiting in such a way that it appears to be stationary above a fixed point on the earth's surface.

ge·o·stra·te·gic /ˌjēōstrəˈtējik/ ▶ **adjective** relating to the strategy required in dealing with international political problems.

ge·o·ther·mal /ˌjēōˈTHərməl/ ▶ **adjective** relating to or produced by the internal heat of the earth.

ge·ra·ni·um /jəˈrānēəm/ ▶ **noun 1** a garden plant with red, pink, or white flowers; a pelargonium. **2** a plant or small shrub of a genus that comprises the cranesbills.
– ORIGIN Greek *geranion.*

ger·ber·a /ˈgərbərə/ ▶ **noun** a tropical plant of the daisy family, with large brightly colored flowers.
– ORIGIN named after the German naturalist Traugott *Gerber.*

ger·bil /ˈjərbəl/ ▶ **noun** a mouselike desert rodent, often kept as a pet.
– ORIGIN Latin *gerbillus* 'little jerboa.'

ger·i·at·ric /ˌjerēˈatrik/ ▶ **adjective 1** relating to old people. **2** informal very old or out of date; decrepit. ▶ **noun** an old person, especially one receiving special care.
– ORIGIN from Greek *gēras* 'old age' + *iatros* 'doctor.'

> **USAGE**
>
> **Geriatric** is the normal term used to refer to the health care of old people (*a geriatric ward*). When used outside such situations, it carries overtones of being decrepit and can be offensive if used with reference to people.

ger·i·at·rics /ˌjerēˈatriks/ ▶ **plural noun** (treated as sing. or pl.) the branch of medicine or social science concerned with the health and care of old people.
– DERIVATIVES **ger·i·a·tri·cian** /ˌjerēəˈtrisHən/ noun.

germ /jərm/ ▶ **noun 1** a microorganism, especially one that causes disease. **2** a portion of an organism capable of developing into a new one or part of one. **3** an initial stage from which something may develop: *the germ of an idea.*

> – SYNONYMS **1 microbe,** microorganism, bacillus, bacterium, virus; informal bug. **2** *the germ of an idea* **start,** beginnings, seed, embryo, bud, root, origin, source.

– ORIGIN Latin *germen* 'seed, sprout.'

Ger·man /ˈjərmən/ ▶ **noun 1** a person from Germany. **2** the language of Germany, Austria, and parts of Switzerland. ▶ **adjective** relating to Germany or German.
– DERIVATIVES **Ger·man·ize** verb.

ger·mane /jərˈmān/ ▶ **adjective** relevant to a subject under consideration: *considerations germane to a foreign policy decision.*
– ORIGIN Latin *germanus* 'genuine, of the same parents.'

Ger·man·ic /jərˈmanik/ ▶ **adjective 1** referring to the language family that includes English, German, Dutch, Frisian, and the Scandinavian languages. **2** referring to the peoples of ancient northern and western Europe speaking such languages. **3** characteristic of Germans or Germany. ▶ **noun 1** the Germanic languages. **2** the ancient language from which the Germanic languages developed.

ger·ma·ni·um /jərˈmānēəm/ ▶ **noun** a shiny gray chemical element with semiconducting properties.
– ORIGIN from Latin *Germanus* 'German.'

Ger·man mea·sles ▶ **plural noun** (usu. treated as sing.) another term for **RUBELLA**.

Ger·man shep·herd ▶ **noun** a large breed of dog often used as guard dogs or for police work; an Alsatian.

germ cell ▶ **noun** Biology a cell that is able to unite with another of the opposite sex in sexual reproduction; a gamete.

ger·mi·cide /ˈjərməˌsīd/ ▶ **noun** a substance that destroys harmful microorganisms.
– DERIVATIVES **ger·mi·cid·al** /ˌjərməˈsīdl/ adjective.

ger·mi·nal /ˈjərmənl/ ▶ **adjective 1** relating to a germ cell or embryo. **2** in the earliest stage of development: *a germinal idea.* **3** providing material for future development.
– ORIGIN from Latin *germen* 'sprout, seed.'

ger·mi·nate /ˈjərməˌnāt/ ▶ **verb** (of a seed or spore) begin to grow and put out shoots after a period of being dormant.
– DERIVATIVES **ger·mi·na·tion** /ˌjərməˈnāsHən/ noun.
– ORIGIN Latin *germinare* 'sprout forth, bud.'

germ war·fare ▶ **noun** the use of disease-spreading microorganisms as a military weapon.

ger·on·tol·o·gy /ˌjerənˈtäləjē/ ▶ **noun** the scientific study of old age and old people.
– DERIVATIVES **ge·ron·to·log·i·cal** /jəˌräntlˈäjikəl/ adjective **ger·on·tol·o·gist** noun.

ger·ry·man·der /ˈjerēˌmandər/ ▶ **verb** alter the boundaries of a constituency so as to favor one political party in an election.
– ORIGIN from Governor Elbridge *Gerry* of Massachusetts + **SALAMANDER**, from the similarity between a salamander and the shape of a voting district created when he was in office.

ger·und /ˈjerənd/ ▶ **noun** Grammar a verb form that functions as a noun, in English ending in *-ing* (e.g., *asking* in *do you mind my asking you?*).
– ORIGIN Latin *gerundum.*

ges·so /ˈjesō/ ▸ **noun** a hard compound of plaster of Paris or whiting in glue, used in sculpture.
– ORIGIN Italian.

ge·stalt /gəˈSHtält, -ˈSHtôlt/ ▸ **noun** Psychology an organized whole that is perceived as more than the sum of its parts.
– ORIGIN German, 'form, shape.'

Ge·sta·po /gəˈstäpō/ ▸ **noun** the German secret police under Nazi rule.
– ORIGIN German, from *Geheime Staatspolizei* 'secret state police.'

ges·ta·tion /jeˈstāSHən/ ▸ **noun 1** the process of developing in the uterus between conception and birth. **2** the development of something over a period of time: *the gestation of a musical can take months.*
– DERIVATIVES **ges·tate** /ˈjeˌstāt/ verb **ges·ta·tion·al** /-SHənl/ adjective.
– ORIGIN from Latin *gestare* 'carry, carry in the womb.'

ges·tic·u·late /jeˈstikyəˌlāt/ ▸ **verb** gesture dramatically instead of speaking or to emphasize one's words.
– DERIVATIVES **ges·tic·u·la·tion** /jeˌstikyəˈlāSHən/ noun.
– ORIGIN Latin *gesticulari.*

ges·ture /ˈjesCHər/ ▸ **noun 1** a movement of part of the body to express an idea or meaning. **2** an action performed to convey one's feelings or intentions: *the prisoners were released as a gesture of goodwill.* **3** an action performed for show in the knowledge that it will have no effect.

– SYNONYMS **1 signal,** sign, motion, indication, gesticulation. **2 action,** act, deed, move.

▸ **verb** make a gesture.

– SYNONYMS **signal,** motion, gesticulate, wave, indicate, give a sign.

– DERIVATIVES **ges·tur·al** adjective.
– ORIGIN Latin *gestura.*

ge·sund·heit /gəˈzo͝ontīt/ ▸ **exclamation** used to wish good health to someone who has just sneezed.
– ORIGIN from German *Gesundheit* 'health.'

get /get/ ▸ **verb** (**gets, getting, got**/gät/; past part. **got, gotten** /ˈgätn/) **1** come to have or hold something. **2** experience or suffer something. **3** pick up, fetch, or deal with something. **4** reach a particular state or condition. **5** succeed in obtaining, achieving, or experiencing something. **6** catch or thwart someone. **7** move to or from a specified position or place. **8** persuade someone to do something. **9** begin to be or do something, especially gradually or by chance: *we got talking.* **10** travel by or catch a form of transport. **11** informal punish, injure, or kill someone. **12** used with past participle to form the passive: *the field got flooded.*

– SYNONYMS **1** *where did you get that hat?* **obtain,** acquire, come by, receive, gain, earn, win, be given; informal get (a) hold of, score. **2** *she got the flu* **contract,** develop, go down with, catch, fall ill with. **3** *get the children from school* **fetch,** collect, go/come for, call for, pick up, bring, deliver, convey. **4** *I'll get dinner* **prepare,** get ready, cook, make; informal fix, rustle up. **5** *your coffee is getting cold* **become,** grow, turn, go. **6** *I didn't get what he said* **hear,** catch, make out, follow, take in. **7** *I don't get the joke* **understand,** comprehend, grasp, see, fathom, follow. **8** *have the police got their man?* **capture,** catch, arrest, apprehend, seize; informal collar, grab, pick up. **9** *we got there early* **arrive,** reach, make it, turn up, appear, present oneself, come along; informal show up. **10** *we got her to go* **persuade,** induce, prevail on, influence, talk into.
– ANTONYMS give.

– DERIVATIVES **get·ta·ble** adjective **get·ter** noun.
– PHRASES **be out to get someone** be determined to punish or harm someone: *they think we are the bad guys and out to get them.* **get something across** manage to communicate an idea clearly. **get along** have a harmonious or friendly relationship: *they seem to get along pretty well.* **get around 1** persuade someone to do or allow something. **2** deal successfully with a problem. **get around to** find the time to deal with a task. **get at 1** reach or gain access to somewhere. **2** informal imply something: *what are you getting at?* **3** informal discover or determine something: *Purcell's statement gets at the heart of the issue.* **get away** escape or leave. **get away with** escape blame or punishment for something. **get back at** take revenge on someone. **get by** manage with difficulty to live. **get down to** begin to do or give serious attention to something. **get in on** become involved in (a profitable or exciting activity). **get it on** informal have sexual intercourse. **get off** informal **1** escape a punishment. **2** vulgar slang have an orgasm. **get off on** informal be excited or aroused by (something): *some guys get off on that kind of attention.* **get on 1** make progress with a task. **2** (**be getting on**) informal be old or comparatively old. **get over** recover from an illness or an unpleasant experience. **get something over** manage to communicate something. **get something over with** deal with an unpleasant but necessary task promptly. **get through 1** pass or endure a difficult experience or period. **2** use up a large amount or number of something. **3** make contact by telephone. **4** succeed in communicating with someone. **get to** informal annoy or upset someone. **get together** gather socially or to cooperate. **get up** rise from bed after sleeping. **get up to** be involved in something.
– ORIGIN Old Norse, 'obtain, beget, guess.'

CHOOSE THE RIGHT WORD

get, acquire, attain, gain, obtain, procure, secure

Get is a very broad term meaning to come into possession of. You can *get* something by fetching it (*get some groceries*), by receiving it (*get a birthday gift*), by earning it (*get interest on a bank loan*), or by any of a dozen other familiar means. It is such a common, over-used word that many writers try to substitute **obtain** for it whenever possible, perhaps because it sounds less colloquial. But it can also sound pretentious (*all employees were required to obtain an annual physical exam*) and should be reserved for contexts where the emphasis is on seeking something out (*to obtain blood samples*). **Acquire** often suggests a continued, sustained, or cumulative acquisition (*to acquire poise as one matures*), but it can also hint at deviousness (*to acquire the keys to the safe*). Use **procure** if you want to emphasize the effort involved in bringing something to pass (*procure a mediated divorce settlement*) or if you want to imply maneuvering to possess something (*procure a reserved parking space*). But beware: *Procure* is so often used to describe the act of obtaining partners to gratify the lust of others (*to procure a prostitute*) that it has acquired somewhat unsavory overtones. **Gain** also implies effort, usually in *getting* something advantageous or profitable (*gain entry, gain victory*). In a similar vein, **secure** underscores the difficulty involved in bringing something to pass and the desire to place it beyond danger (*secure a permanent peace; secure a lifeline*). **Attain** should be reserved for achieving a high goal or desirable result (*If she attains the summit of Mt. Everest, she will secure for herself a place in mountaineering history*).

get·a·way /'getə͵wā/ ▶ **noun 1** an escape, especially after committing a crime. **2** a short vacation.

get-go ▶ **noun** informal the very beginning: *it was a terrific marriage right from the get-go*.

get-to·geth·er ▶ **noun** an informal social gathering.

get·up /'getəp/ ▶ **noun** informal an outfit, especially an unusual one: *our Halloween getups were really scary*.

gey·ser /'gīzər/ ▶ **noun** a hot spring in which water intermittently boils, sending a tall column of water and steam into the air.
– ORIGIN named after a spring in Iceland.

Gha·na·ian /gə'nāən, gə'nīən/ ▶ **noun** a person from Ghana. ▶ **adjective** relating to Ghana.

ghast·ly /'gastlē/ ▶ **adjective (ghastlier, ghastliest) 1** causing great horror or fear. **2** informal very unpleasant. **3** very white.

> – SYNONYMS **1 terrible,** frightful, horrible, grim, awful, horrifying, shocking, appalling, gruesome, horrendous, monstrous. **2 unpleasant,** objectionable, disagreeable, distasteful, awful, terrible, dreadful, frightful, detestable, vile; informal horrible, horrid.
> – ANTONYMS pleasant.

– DERIVATIVES **ghast·li·ness** noun.
– ORIGIN Old English, 'terrify.'

ghat /gôt, gät/ ▶ **noun 1** (in the Indian subcontinent) a flight of steps leading down to a river. **2** (in the Indian subcontinent) a mountain pass.
– ORIGIN Hindi.

GHB ▶ **abbreviation** (sodium) gamma-hydroxybutyrate, a designer drug with anesthetic properties.

ghee /gē/ ▶ **noun** clarified butter used in Indian cooking.
– ORIGIN from Sanskrit, 'sprinkled.'

gher·kin /'gərkin/ ▶ **noun** a small pickled cucumber.
– ORIGIN Greek *angourion* 'cucumber.'

ghet·to /'getō/ ▶ **noun** (pl. **ghettos** or **ghettoes**) **1** a part of a city occupied by people of a particular race, nationality, or ethnic group. **2** historical the Jewish quarter in a city.
– ORIGIN perhaps from Italian *getto* 'foundry' (because the first ghetto was established on the site of a foundry in Venice), or from Italian *borghetto* 'small borough.'

ghet·to blast·er ▶ **noun** informal a large portable radio and cassette or CD player.

ghet·to·ize /'getō͵īz/ ▶ **verb** put in an isolated or segregated place, group, or situation: *they were black and quickly ghettoized in northern cities*.
– DERIVATIVES **ghet·to·i·za·tion** /͵getō-i'zāsнən/ noun.

ghost /gōst/ ▶ **noun 1** an apparition of a dead person that is believed to appear to the living. **2** a faint trace: *the ghost of a smile*.

> – SYNONYMS **specter,** phantom, wraith, spirit, presence, apparition; informal spook.

▶ **verb** act as ghostwriter of a book.
– PHRASES **give up the ghost** die or stop functioning.
– ORIGIN Old English, 'spirit, soul.'

> **WORD LINKS**
> **spectral** *relating to a ghost*

ghost·ing /'gōstiNG/ ▶ **noun** the appearance of a secondary image on a television or other display screen.

ghost·ly /'gōstlē/ ▶ **adjective (ghostlier, ghostliest)** relating to or like a ghost; eerie.

> – SYNONYMS **supernatural,** unearthly, spectral, phantom, unnatural, eerie, weird, uncanny; informal spooky.

ghost town ▶ **noun** a town with few or no remaining inhabitants.

ghost·writ·er /'gōst͵rītər/ ▶ **noun** a person employed to write material for another person who is the named author.
– DERIVATIVES **ghost·write** verb.

ghoul /go͞ol/ ▶ **noun 1** an evil spirit, especially one supposed to rob graves and feed on dead bodies. **2** a person with an unhealthy interest in death or disaster.
– DERIVATIVES **ghoul·ish** adjective **ghoul·ish·ly** adverb **ghoul·ish·ness** noun.
– ORIGIN Arabic.

GHQ ▶ **abbreviation** General Headquarters.

GHz (also **gHz**) ▶ **abbreviation** gigahertz.

GI[1] ▶ **noun** (pl. **GIs**) a private in the Army.
– ORIGIN abbreviation of *government* (or *general*) *issue* (referring to military equipment).

GI[2] ▶ **abbreviation** glycemic index.

gi·ant /'jīənt/ ▶ **noun 1** an imaginary or mythical being of human form but superhuman size. **2** an unusually tall or large person or thing. **3** a star of relatively great size and luminosity.

> – SYNONYMS **colossus,** mammoth, monster, leviathan, ogre.
> – ANTONYMS dwarf.

▶ **adjective** very large; gigantic.

> – SYNONYMS **huge,** colossal, massive, enormous, gigantic, mammoth, vast, immense, monumental, mountainous, titanic, towering, gargantuan; informal mega, monster, whopping, ginormous.
> – ANTONYMS miniature.

– DERIVATIVES **gi·ant·ess** noun.
– ORIGIN Greek *gigas*.

> **WORD TOOLKIT**
> See **COLOSSAL**.

gi·ant-kill·er ▶ **noun** a person or team that defeats a much more powerful opponent.
– DERIVATIVES **gi·ant-kill·ing** noun.

gib·ber /'jibər/ ▶ **verb** speak rapidly and in a way that is difficult to understand.
– ORIGIN imitating the sound.

gib·ber·ish /'jibərisн/ ▶ **noun** speech or writing that is meaningless or difficult to understand.

gib·bet /'jibit/ ▶ **noun** historical **1** a gallows. **2** an upright post with an arm on which the bodies of executed criminals were left hanging.
– ORIGIN Old French *gibet* 'little staff, cudgel, gallows.'

gib·bon /'gibən/ ▶ **noun** a small ape with long, powerful arms, native to the forests of SE Asia.
– ORIGIN from an Indian dialect word.

gib·bous /'gibəs/ ▶ **adjective** (of the moon) having the illuminated part greater than a semicircle and less than a circle.
– ORIGIN Latin *gibbosus*.

gibe /jīb/ (also **jibe**) ▶ **noun** an insulting or mocking remark.

– SYNONYMS **taunt,** sneer, jeer, insult, barb; informal dig, put-down.

▶ **verb** make insulting or mocking remarks.
– ORIGIN perhaps from Old French *giber* 'handle roughly.'

gib·lets /ˈjiblits/ ▶ **plural noun** the liver, heart, gizzard, and neck of a chicken or other fowl.
– ORIGIN Old French *gibelet* 'game bird stew.'

gid·dy /ˈgidē/ ▶ **adjective** (**giddier, giddiest**) **1** having or causing a sensation of spinning and losing one's balance; dizzy. **2** excitable and not interested in serious things.

– SYNONYMS **1 dizzy,** lightheaded, faint, unsteady, wobbly, reeling; informal woozy. **2 flighty,** silly, frivolous, skittish, irresponsible; informal dizzy.

– DERIVATIVES **gid·di·ly** adverb **gid·di·ness** noun.
– ORIGIN Old English, 'insane.'

gid·dy-up /ˌgidē ˈəp/ ▶ **exclamation** said to make a horse start moving or go faster.
– ORIGIN from a pronunciation of *get up*.

GIF /jif/ ▶ **noun** Computing **1** a format for image files. **2** a file in this format.
– ORIGIN from the initial letters of *graphic interchange format*.

gift /gift/ ▶ **noun 1** a thing given willingly to someone without payment; a present. **2** a natural ability or talent: *she has a gift for math.* **3** informal a very easy task.

– SYNONYMS **1 present,** handout, donation, offering, bonus, award, endowment. **2 talent,** flair, aptitude, facility, knack, bent, ability, skill, capacity, faculty.

▶ **verb 1** give something as a gift. **2** (**gift someone with**) provide someone with an ability or talent. **3** (as adj. **gifted**) having exceptional talent or ability.

– SYNONYMS (as adj. **gifted**) *a gifted young percussionist* **talented,** skilled, accomplished, expert, able, proficient, intelligent, clever, bright, brilliant, precocious; informal crack, ace.
– ANTONYMS inept.

– DERIVATIVES **gift·ed·ness** noun.
– PHRASES **look a gift horse in the mouth** find fault with something that has been received as a gift or favor.
– ORIGIN Old Norse.

CHOOSE THE RIGHT WORD

See **PRESENT**[3].

gift cer·tif·i·cate ▶ **noun** a voucher that can be exchanged for merchandise in a store, given as a present.

gift wrap ▶ **noun** decorative paper for wrapping gifts. ▶ **verb** (**gift-wrap**) wrap a gift in decorative paper.

gig[1] /gig/ informal ▶ **noun 1** a live performance by a musician or other performer. **2** a task or assignment: *spotting whales seemed like a great gig.* ▶ **verb** (**gigs, gigging, gigged**) perform a gig or gigs.
– ORIGIN unknown.

gig[2] ▶ **noun** chiefly historical a light two-wheeled carriage pulled by one horse.
– ORIGIN probably from former *gig* 'a flighty girl.'

gig[3] ▶ **noun** informal short for **GIGABYTE**.

giga- ▶ **combining form 1** referring to a factor of one billion (10^9): *gigawatt.* **2** Computing referring to a factor of 2^{30}.
– ORIGIN from Greek *gigas* 'giant.'

gig·a·bit /ˈgigəˌbit, ˈjig-/ ▶ **noun** a unit of information stored in a computer equal to one billion (10^9) or (strictly) 2^{30} bits.

gig·a·byte /ˈgigəˌbīt, ˈjig-/ ▶ **noun** a unit of information stored in a computer equal to one billion (10^9) or (strictly) 2^{30} bytes.

gig·a·flop /ˈgigəˌfläp/ ▶ **noun** Computing a unit of computing speed equal to one billion floating-point operations per second.

gig·a·hertz /ˈgigəˌhərts, ˈjig-/ ▶ **noun** a unit of frequency equivalent to one billion hertz.

gi·gan·tic /jīˈgantik/ ▶ **adjective** very great in size or extent.

– SYNONYMS **huge,** enormous, vast, giant, massive, colossal, mammoth, immense, monumental, mountainous, gargantuan; informal mega, monster, whopping, humongous, ginormous.
– ANTONYMS tiny.

– DERIVATIVES **gi·gan·ti·cal·ly** adverb.
– ORIGIN from Latin *gigas* 'giant.'

gi·gan·tism /jīˈgantizəm/ ▶ **noun** chiefly Biology unusual or abnormal largeness.

gig·a·watt /ˈgigəˌwät, ˈjig-/ ▶ **noun** a unit of power equal to one billion watts.

gig·gle /ˈgigəl/ ▶ **verb** laugh lightly in a nervous or silly way.

– SYNONYMS **titter,** snigger, snicker, tee-hee, chuckle, chortle, laugh.

▶ **noun** a nervous or silly laugh.

– SYNONYMS **titter,** snigger, snicker, tee-hee, chuckle, chortle, laugh.

– DERIVATIVES **gig·gler** noun **gig·gly** adjective.
– ORIGIN imitating the sound.

gig·o·lo /ˈjigəˌlō/ ▶ **noun** (pl. **gigolos**) a young man paid by an older woman to be her escort or lover.
– ORIGIN French, 'male dancing partner.'

gigue /zhēg/ ▶ **noun** Music a lively piece of music in the style of a dance, typically of the Renaissance or baroque period.
– ORIGIN French, literally 'jig.'

Gi·la mon·ster /ˈhēlə/ ▶ **noun** a venomous lizard native to the Southwest and Mexico.

gild /gild/ ▶ **verb 1** cover something thinly with gold. **2** (as adj. **gilded**) wealthy and privileged: *gilded youth.*
– DERIVATIVES **gild·er** noun **gild·ing** noun.
– PHRASES **gild the lily** try to improve what is already beautiful or excellent. [misquotation of a line from Shakespeare's *King John* IV. ii.]
– ORIGIN Old English.

gill[1] /gil/ ▶ **noun 1** the breathing organ of fish and some amphibians. **2** the vertical plates on the underside of mushrooms and many toadstools. ▶ **verb** gut or clean a fish.
– DERIVATIVES **gilled** adjective.
– PHRASES **to the gills** until completely full.
– ORIGIN Old Norse.

gill[2] /jil/ ▶ **noun** a unit of measure for liquids, equal to a quarter of a pint.
– ORIGIN Old French *gille* 'measure or container for wine.'

gilt /gilt/ ▶ **adjective** covered thinly with gold leaf or gold paint. ▶ **noun** gold leaf or gold paint applied in a thin layer to a surface.
– ORIGIN from **GILD**.

gim·bal /ˈgimbəl, ˈjim-/ (also **gimbals**) ▶ **noun** a device for keeping an instrument such as a compass horizontal in a moving vessel or aircraft.
– ORIGIN Old French *gemel* 'twin.'

gim·crack /ˈjimˌkrak/ ▶ **adjective** showy but flimsy or poorly made. ▶ **noun** a cheap and showy ornament.
– DERIVATIVES **gim·crack·er·y** /-ˌkrakərē/ noun.
– ORIGIN unknown.

gim·let /ˈgimlit/ ▶ **noun** a small T-shaped tool with a screw-tip for boring holes.
– ORIGIN Old French *guimbelet* 'little drill.'

gim·mick /ˈgimik/ ▶ **noun** something intended to attract attention rather than fulfill a useful purpose.
– DERIVATIVES **gim·mick·ry** noun **gim·mick·y** adjective.
– ORIGIN unknown.

gimp /gimp/ ▶ **noun** informal, often offensive **1** a physically handicapped person. **2** a limp. **3** a feeble or contemptible person.
– DERIVATIVES **gimp·y** adjective.

gin[1] /jin/ ▶ **noun 1** a clear alcoholic spirit distilled from grain or malt and flavored with juniper berries. **2** (also **gin rummy**) a form of the card game rummy.
– ORIGIN abbreviation of *genever*, a kind of Dutch gin.

gin[2] ▶ **noun 1** a machine for separating cotton from its seeds. **2** a trap for catching small game.
– ORIGIN Old French *engin* 'engine.'

gin and ton·ic ▶ **noun** a cocktail made with gin and tonic water, and usually a slice of lime.

gin·ger /ˈjinjər/ ▶ **noun 1** a hot spice made from the rhizome of a SE Asian plant. **2** a light reddish-yellow color. ▶ **verb 1** (**ginger someone/thing up**) make someone or something more lively or exciting. **2** flavor something with ginger.
– DERIVATIVES **gin·ger·y** adjective.
– ORIGIN Latin *gingiber*.

gin·ger ale ▶ **noun** a carbonated soft drink flavored with ginger.

gin·ger·bread /ˈjinjərˌbred/ ▶ **noun 1** cake made with molasses and flavored with ginger. **2** fancy decoration, especially on the facade of a building.

gin·ger·ly /ˈjinjərlē/ ▶ **adverb** in a careful or cautious way.
– ORIGIN perhaps from Old French *gensor* 'delicate.'

gin·ger snap ▶ **noun** a hard, ginger-flavored cookie.

ging·ham /ˈgiNGəm/ ▶ **noun** lightweight cotton cloth with a check pattern.
– ORIGIN from a Malay word meaning 'striped.'

gin·gi·vi·tis /ˌjinjəˈvītis/ ▶ **noun** inflammation of the gums.
– ORIGIN from Latin *gingiva* 'gum.'

gink·go /ˈgiNGkō/ (also **gingko**) ▶ **noun** (pl. **ginkgos** or **ginkgoes**) a Chinese tree with fan-shaped leaves and yellow flowers.
– ORIGIN Chinese.

gi·nor·mous /jīˈnôrməs, jī-/ ▶ **adjective** informal very large.
– ORIGIN blend of **GIANT** and **ENORMOUS**.

gin·seng /ˈjinseNG/ ▶ **noun** the tuber of an east Asian and North American plant, believed to have medicinal properties.
– ORIGIN from Chinese 'man' + the name of a kind of herb.

gip·sy ▶ **noun** variant spelling of **GYPSY**.

gi·raffe /jəˈraf/ ▶ **noun** (pl. same or **giraffes**) a large African mammal with a very long neck and legs, the tallest living animal.
– ORIGIN French *girafe*, from Arabic.

gird /gərd/ ▶ **verb** (past and past part. **girded** or **girt** /gərt/) literary encircle or secure something with a belt or band.
– PHRASES **gird (up) one's loins** prepare and strengthen oneself for something difficult.
– ORIGIN Old English.

gird·er /ˈgərdər/ ▶ **noun** a large metal beam used in building bridges and large buildings.
– ORIGIN from **GIRD**.

gir·dle /ˈgərdl/ ▶ **noun 1** a belt or cord worn around the waist. **2** a woman's elasticized corset extending from waist to thigh. ▶ **verb** encircle something with a girdle or belt.
– ORIGIN Old English, related to **GIRD** and **GIRTH**.

girl /gərl/ ▶ **noun 1** a female child. **2** a young woman. **3** a person's girlfriend.

– SYNONYMS **young woman,** young lady, miss; Scottish lass, lassie. informal gal, chick, broad, dame, babe. Austral. informal sheila.

– DERIVATIVES **girl·hood** noun **girl·ish** adjective **girl·ish·ly** adverb.
– ORIGIN perhaps related to German *gör* 'child.'

girl·friend /ˈgərlˌfrend/ ▶ **noun 1** a person's regular female companion in a romantic or sexual relationship. **2** a woman's female friend.

– SYNONYMS **sweetheart,** lover, partner, significant other, girl, woman; informal steady, (main) squeeze.

girl·ie /ˈgərlē/ (also **girly**) ▶ **adjective 1** often derogatory typical of or resembling a girl. **2** depicting nude or partially nude young women in erotic poses: *girlie magazines*. ▶ **noun** (pl. **girlies**) informal a girl or young woman.

Girl Scout ▶ **noun** a member of the Girl Scouts of America.

girt /gərt/ past participle of **GIRD**.

girth /gərTH/ ▶ **noun 1** the measurement around the middle of something. **2** a band attached to a saddle and fastened around a horse's belly.
– ORIGIN Old Norse.

GIS ▶ **abbreviation** geographic information system, a software application for storing and manipulating geographic information.

gist /jist/ ▶ **noun** the main or general meaning of a speech or piece of writing.
– ORIGIN from Old French *cest action gist* 'this action lies,' meaning that there were sufficient grounds to proceed in a legal case.

Git·mo /ˈgitˌmō/ ▶ **noun** informal the US naval base or detention facility at Guantánamo Bay, Cuba.
– ORIGIN representing a pronunciation of *GTMO,* an abbreviation of *Guantánamo*.

give /giv/ ▶ **verb** (**gives, giving, gave** /gāv/; past part. **given**) **1** cause someone to receive or have something. **2** carry out an action or make a sound. **3** cause to experience or suffer: *he gives me the creeps*. **4** present an appearance or impression. **5** state or put forward information. **6** alter in shape under pressure rather than resist or break. **7** concede that someone deserves something.

– SYNONYMS **1** *she gave them $2000* **donate,** contribute, present, award, grant, bestow, hand (over), bequeath, leave. **2** *can I give him a message?* **convey,** pass on, impart, communicate, transmit,

send, deliver, relay. **3** *she gave her life for them* **sacrifice,** give up, relinquish, devote, dedicate. **4** *she gave a party* **organize,** arrange, lay on, throw, host, hold, have. **5** *Dominic gave a bow* **perform,** execute, make, do. **6** *she gave a shout* **utter,** let out, emit, produce, make.
– ANTONYMS receive, take.

▶ **noun** the capacity of something to bend under pressure.
– DERIVATIVES **giv·er** noun.
– PHRASES **give and take** willingness on both sides of a relationship to make concessions. **give something away** reveal something secret. **give the game away** accidentally reveal something secret. **give in** stop fighting or arguing. **give or take** informal to within a specified amount. **give out** stop operating. **give something off/out** produce and send out a smell, heat, etc. **give rise to** cause something to happen. **give up** stop making an effort and accept that one has failed. **give someone up** hand over a wanted person. **give something up** stop doing, eating, or drinking something regularly.
– ORIGIN Old English.

CHOOSE THE RIGHT WORD

give, afford, award, bestow, confer, donate, grant

You **give** a birthday present, **grant** a favor, **bestow** charity, and **confer** an honor. While all of these verbs mean to convey something or transfer it from one's own possession to that of another, the circumstances surrounding that transfer dictate which word is the best one. *Give* is the most general, meaning to pass over, deliver, or transmit something (*give him encouragement*). *Grant* implies that a request or desire has been expressed, and that the receiver is dependent on the giver's discretion (*grant permission for the trip*). **Award** suggests that the giver is in some sense a judge, and that the thing given is deserved (*award a scholarship*), while *bestow* implies that something is given as a gift and may imply condescension on the part of the giver (*bestow a large sum of money on a needy charity*). To *confer* is to give an honor, a privilege, or a favor; it implies that the giver is a superior (*confer a knighthood; confer a college degree*). **Donate** implies that the giving is to a public cause or charity (*donate a painting to the local art museum*), and to **afford** is to give or bestow as a natural consequence (*the window afforded a fine view of the mountains*).

give·a·way /ˈgivəˌwā/ ▶ **noun** informal **1** something that reveals the truth about something: *the shape of the parcel was a dead giveaway.* **2** something given free, especially for promotional purposes.

giv·en /ˈgivən/ past participle of GIVE ▶ **adjective** **1** specified or stated. **2** (**given to**) inclined to. ▶ **preposition** taking into account. ▶ **noun** an established fact or situation.

giv·en name ▶ **noun** another term for FIRST NAME.

giz·mo /ˈgizmō/ ▶ **noun** (pl. **gizmos**) informal a clever device; a gadget.
– ORIGIN unknown.

giz·zard /ˈgizərd/ ▶ **noun** a muscular, thick-walled part of a bird's stomach for grinding food.
– ORIGIN Old French.

gla·brous /ˈglābrəs/ ▶ **adjective** technical free from hair or down; smooth.
– ORIGIN from Latin *glaber* 'hairless, smooth.'

gla·cé /glaˈsā/ ▶ **adjective** (of fruit) preserved in sugar.
– ORIGIN French, 'iced.'

gla·cial /ˈglāsHəl/ ▶ **adjective** **1** relating to ice, especially in the form of glaciers. **2** very cold or unfriendly.
– DERIVATIVES **gla·cial·ly** adverb.
– ORIGIN Latin *glacialis* 'icy.'

gla·cial pe·ri·od ▶ **noun** an ice age.

gla·ci·at·ed /ˈglāsHēˌātid/ ▶ **adjective** covered or having been covered by glaciers or ice sheets.

gla·ci·a·tion /ˌglāsHēˈāsHən/ ▶ **noun** **1** the state or result of being covered by glaciers or ice sheets. **2** an ice age.

gla·cier /ˈglāsHər/ ▶ **noun** a slowly moving mass of ice formed by the accumulation of snow on mountains or near the poles.
– ORIGIN French, from *glace* 'ice.'

glad /glad/ ▶ **adjective** (**gladder, gladdest**) **1** feeling pleasure or happiness. **2** grateful: *I'm glad for the second chance.* **3** causing happiness.

– SYNONYMS **1 pleased,** happy, gratified, delighted, thrilled, overjoyed; informal over the moon. **2** *I'd be glad to help* **willing,** eager, happy, pleased, delighted, ready, prepared.
– ANTONYMS dismayed, reluctant.

– DERIVATIVES **glad·ness** noun.
– ORIGIN Old English, 'bright, shining.'

glad·den /ˈgladn/ ▶ **verb** make someone glad.

glade /glād/ ▶ **noun** an open space in a forest or other wooded area.
– ORIGIN unknown.

glad-hand ▶ **verb** (especially of a politician) greet or welcome someone warmly.
– DERIVATIVES **glad-hand·er** noun.

glad·i·a·tor /ˈgladēˌātər/ ▶ **noun** (in ancient Rome) a man trained to fight with weapons against other men or wild animals in an arena.
– DERIVATIVES **glad·i·a·to·ri·al** /ˌgladēəˈtôrēəl/ adjective.
– ORIGIN Latin.

glad·i·o·lus /ˌgladēˈōləs/ ▶ **noun** (pl. **gladioli** /-lī/) a plant with sword-shaped leaves and tall stems of brightly colored flowers.
– ORIGIN Latin.

glad·ly /ˈgladlē/ ▶ **adverb** with pleasure: *we gladly accepted the senator's invitation.*

– SYNONYMS **with pleasure,** happily, cheerfully, willingly, readily, eagerly, freely, ungrudgingly.

glad rags ▶ **plural noun** informal clothes for a party or special occasion.

Glad·stone bag /ˈgladˌstōn/ ▶ **noun** a bag having two equal compartments joined by a hinge.
– ORIGIN named after the British Liberal statesman W. E. *Gladstone.*

glam /glam/ informal ▶ **adjective** glamorous. ▶ **verb** (**glams, glamming, glammed**) (**glam someone up**) make someone look glamorous.

glam·or·ize /ˈglaməˌrīz/ ▶ **verb** make something, especially something bad, seem attractive or desirable.
– DERIVATIVES **glam·or·i·za·tion** /ˌglaməriˈzāsHən/ noun.

glam·or·ous /ˈglamərəs/ ▶ **adjective** excitingly attractive and appealing.

– SYNONYMS **1 beautiful,** elegant, chic, stylish, fashionable. **2 exciting,** glittering, glossy, colorful, exotic; informal glitzy, jet-setting.
– ANTONYMS dowdy, dull.

– DERIVATIVES **glam·or·ous·ly** adverb.

glam·our /ˈglamər/ (also **glamor**) ▶ **noun** an attractive and exciting quality.

– SYNONYMS **1** *she had undeniable glamour* **beauty,** allure, elegance, chic, style, charisma, charm, magnetism. **2** *the glamour of TV* **allure,** attraction, fascination, charm, magic, romance, excitement, thrill; informal glitz, glam.

▶ **adjective** referring to photography or publications that feature a culture of beauty and excitement: *a glamour model.*
– ORIGIN first meaning 'magic': from **GRAMMAR**, with reference to the occult practices associated with learning in medieval times.

glance /glans/ ▶ **verb 1** take a brief or hurried look. **2** hit something and bounce off at an angle.

– SYNONYMS **1 look briefly,** look quickly, peek, peep, glimpse, catch a glimpse. **2** *I glanced through the report* **read quickly (through),** scan (through), skim (through), leaf through, flick through, flip through, thumb through, browse (through).

▶ **noun** a brief or hurried look.
– DERIVATIVES **glanc·ing** adjective.
– ORIGIN Old French *glacier* 'to slip.'

gland /gland/ ▶ **noun 1** an organ of the body that produces particular chemical substances. **2** a lymph node.
– ORIGIN from Latin *glandulae* 'throat glands.'

glan·du·lar /ˈglanjələr/ ▶ **adjective** relating to or affecting a gland or glands.

glans /glanz/ ▶ **noun** (pl. **glandes** /ˈglandēz/) the rounded part forming the end of the penis or clitoris.
– ORIGIN Latin, 'acorn.'

glare /gle(ə)r/ ▶ **verb 1** stare in an angry way. **2** shine with a dazzling light. **3** (as adj. **glaring**) highly obvious: *a glaring error.*

– SYNONYMS **1 scowl,** glower, look daggers, frown, lower/lour; informal give someone a dirty look. **2** *the sun glared out of the sky* **blaze,** beam, shine brightly, be dazzling, be blinding. **3** (as adj. **glaring**) **obvious,** conspicuous, unmistakable, inescapable, unmissable, striking, flagrant, blatant.

▶ **noun 1** an angry stare. **2** dazzling light. **3** overwhelming public attention: *his visit will be conducted in the full glare of publicity.*

– SYNONYMS **1 scowl,** glower, angry stare, frown, black look; informal dirty look. **2 blaze,** dazzle, shine, beam, brilliance.

– DERIVATIVES **glar·ing·ly** adverb **glar·y** adjective.
– ORIGIN from Dutch and German *glaren* 'to gleam or glare.'

glas·nost /ˈglazˌnōst, ˈglas-, ˈgläz-, ˈgläs-/ ▶ **noun** (in the former Soviet Union) the policy or practice of more open government.
– ORIGIN Russian *glasnost'* 'the fact of being public, openness.'

glass /glas/ ▶ **noun 1** a hard, brittle, transparent substance made by fusing sand with soda and lime. **2** a drinking container made of glass. **3** chiefly Brit. a mirror. **4** a lens or optical instrument, in particular a monocle or a magnifying lens. ▶ **verb** cover or enclose something with glass.
– DERIVATIVES **glass·ful** noun **glass·ware** noun.
– ORIGIN Old English.

glass block (also **glass brick**) ▶ **noun** a block of tempered glass used as a construction material, or these collectively: *a wide swath of glass block from the tub platform to the ceiling.*

glass·blow·ing /ˈglasˌblō-ɪɴɢ/ ▶ **noun** the craft of making glassware by blowing semimolten glass through a long tube.
– DERIVATIVES **glass·blow·er** noun.

glass ceil·ing ▶ **noun** a situation in which certain groups, especially women and minorities, find that progress in a profession is blocked although there are no official barriers to advancement.

glass·es /ˈglasiz/ ▶ **plural noun** a pair of lenses set in a frame that rests on the nose and ears, used to correct defective eyesight.

glass·y /ˈglasē/ ▶ **adjective** (**glassier, glassiest**) **1** resembling glass. **2** (of a person's eyes or expression) showing no interest or liveliness.
– DERIVATIVES **glass·i·ly** adverb.

Glas·we·gian /glazˈwējən, -jēən, glas-/ ▶ **noun** a person from Glasgow, Scotland. ▶ **adjective** relating to Glasgow, Scotland.

glau·co·ma /glôˈkōmə/ ▶ **noun** a condition of increased pressure within the eyeball, causing gradual loss of sight.
– ORIGIN Greek *glaukōma.*

glau·cous /ˈglôkəs/ ▶ **adjective** technical or literary **1** dull grayish-green or blue in color. **2** covered with a powdery bloom like that on grapes.
– ORIGIN Greek *glaukos.*

glaze /glāz/ ▶ **verb 1** fit panes of glass into a window frame or similar structure. **2** enclose or cover something with glass. **3** cover something with a glaze. **4** lose brightness and liveliness: *transactions complex enough to make an accountant's eyes glaze over.*

– SYNONYMS **cover,** coat, varnish, lacquer, polish; ice, frost.

▶ **noun 1** a glasslike substance fused onto the surface of pottery to form an impervious decorative coating. **2** a liquid such as milk or beaten egg, used to form a shiny coating on food. **3** Art a thin topcoat of transparent paint used to modify the tone of an underlying color.

– SYNONYMS **coating,** topping, varnish, lacquer, polish; icing, frosting.

– DERIVATIVES **glaz·ing** noun.
– ORIGIN from **GLASS**.

gla·zier /ˈglāzʜər/ ▶ **noun** a person whose profession is fitting glass into windows and doors.

GLBT ▶ **abbreviation** gay, lesbian, bisexual, and transgendered: *a planned GLBT cable channel.*

gleam /glēm/ ▶ **verb** shine brightly, especially with reflected light.

– SYNONYMS **shine,** glint, glitter, shimmer, glimmer, sparkle, twinkle, flicker, wink, glisten, flash.

▶ **noun 1** a faint or brief light. **2** a brief or faint sign of a quality or emotion: *there was a gleam of mischief in her eyes.*

– SYNONYMS **flash,** glimmer, glint, shimmer, twinkle, sparkle, flicker, beam, ray, shaft.

– DERIVATIVES **gleam·ing** adjective.
– PHRASES **a gleam in someone's eye** see **EYE**.
– ORIGIN Old English.

glean /glēn/ ▶ **verb 1** collect information or objects gradually from various sources. **2** historical gather leftover grain after a harvest.

– DERIVATIVES **glean·er** noun.
– ORIGIN Latin *glennare*.

glean·ings /ˈglēniNGz/ ▶ **plural noun** things gathered from various sources.

glee /glē/ ▶ **noun 1** great delight. **2** a song for men's voices in three or more parts.
– ORIGIN Old English, 'entertainment, music, fun.'

glee club ▶ **noun** an amateur choir or chorus.

glee·ful /ˈglēfəl/ ▶ **adjective** very happy, especially in a gloating way.
– DERIVATIVES **glee·ful·ly** adverb.

glen /glen/ ▶ **noun** a narrow valley.
– ORIGIN Scottish Gaelic and Irish *gleann*.

glib /glib/ ▶ **adjective** (**glibber**, **glibbest**) using words easily, but without much thought or sincerity.

– SYNONYMS **slick,** smooth-talking, fast-talking, silver-tongued, smooth; disingenuous, insincere, facile, shallow, superficial, flippant; informal flip, sweet-talking.
– ANTONYMS sincere.

– DERIVATIVES **glib·ly** adverb **glib·ness** noun.
– ORIGIN Germanic.

glide /glīd/ ▶ **verb 1** move with a smooth, quiet, continuous motion. **2** fly without power or in a glider.

– SYNONYMS **1** *a gondola glided past* **slide,** slip, sail, float, drift, flow. **2** *seagulls gliding over the waves* **soar,** wheel, plane, fly.

▶ **noun** an instance of gliding.
– DERIVATIVES **glid·ing** noun.
– ORIGIN Old English.

glid·er /ˈglīdər/ ▶ **noun** a light aircraft designed to fly without using an engine.

glim·mer /ˈglimər/ ▶ **verb** shine faintly with a wavering light. ▶ **noun 1** a faint or wavering light. **2** a faint sign of a feeling or quality: *a glimmer of hope*.
– DERIVATIVES **glim·mer·ing** adjective & noun.
– ORIGIN probably Scandinavian.

glimpse /glimps/ ▶ **noun** a brief or partial view.

– SYNONYMS **glance,** brief/quick look, sight, sighting, peek, peep.

▶ **verb** see someone or something briefly or partially.

– SYNONYMS **catch sight of,** sight, spot, notice, discern, spy, pick out, make out; formal espy.

– ORIGIN probably Germanic.

glint /glint/ ▶ **verb** give out or reflect small flashes of light. ▶ **noun 1** a small flash of reflected light. **2** an expression of an emotion in a person's eyes: *the unmistakable glint of interest in her eye*.
– ORIGIN probably Scandinavian.

glis·san·do /gliˈsändō/ ▶ **noun** (pl. **glissandi** /-dē/ or **glissandos**) Music a continuous slide upward or downward between two notes.
– ORIGIN Italian.

glis·ten /ˈglisən/ ▶ **verb** (of something wet or oily) shine or sparkle. ▶ **noun** a sparkling light reflected from something wet or oily.
– ORIGIN Old English.

glis·ter /ˈglistər/ literary ▶ **verb** sparkle; glitter. ▶ **noun** a sparkle.
– ORIGIN probably from German *glistern* or Dutch *glisteren*.

glitch /gliCH/ ▶ **noun** informal **1** a sudden fault or failure of equipment. **2** an unexpected setback in a plan.
– ORIGIN unknown.

glit·ter /ˈglitər/ ▶ **verb 1** shine with a bright, shimmering reflected light. **2** (as adj. **glittering**) impressively successful or glamorous: *a glittering career*.

– SYNONYMS **sparkle,** twinkle, glint, shimmer, glimmer, wink, flash, shine.

▶ **noun 1** bright, shimmering reflected light. **2** tiny pieces of sparkling material used for decoration. **3** an attractive but superficial quality: *a stylist's life is not all glitter and glamour*.

– SYNONYMS **sparkle,** twinkle, glint, shimmer, glimmer, flicker, flash.

– DERIVATIVES **glit·ter·y** adjective.
– ORIGIN Old Norse.

glit·te·ra·ti /ˌglitəˈrätē/ ▶ **plural noun** informal fashionable people involved in show business or other glamorous activity.
– ORIGIN blend of **GLITTER** and **LITERATI**.

glitz /glits/ ▶ **noun** informal showy but superficial display.
– DERIVATIVES **glitz·y** adjective.
– ORIGIN from **GLITTER**, suggested by **RITZY**.

glitz·y /ˈglitsē/ ▶ **adjective** (**glitzier**, **glitziest**) informal ostentatiously attractive (often used to suggest superficial glamor): *I wanted something glitzy to wear to the launch party*.
– DERIVATIVES **glitz·i·ly** /-səlē/ adverb **glitz·i·ness** noun.

gloam·ing /ˈglōmiNG/ ▶ **noun** (**the gloaming**) literary twilight; dusk.
– ORIGIN Old English.

gloat /glōt/ ▶ **verb** be smug or pleased about one's own success or another person's misfortune.
– DERIVATIVES **gloat·er** noun **gloat·ing** adjective & noun.
– ORIGIN uncertain.

glob /gläb/ ▶ **noun** informal a lump of a semiliquid substance.
– ORIGIN perhaps a blend of **BLOB** and **GOB**[1].

glob·al /ˈglōbəl/ ▶ **adjective 1** relating to the whole world; worldwide. **2** relating to or including the whole of something, or of a group of things. **3** Computing operating or applying through the whole of a file or program.

– SYNONYMS **1 worldwide,** international, world, intercontinental, universal. **2 comprehensive,** overall, general, all-inclusive, all-encompassing, universal, broad.

– DERIVATIVES **glob·al·ly** adverb.

glob·al·ism /ˈglōbəˌlizəm/ ▶ **noun** the operation or planning of economic and foreign policy on a global basis.
– DERIVATIVES **glob·al·ist** /ˈglōbəlist/ noun & adjective.

glob·al·i·za·tion /ˌglōbəliˈzāSHən/ ▶ **noun** the process by which businesses start operating on a global scale.
– DERIVATIVES **glob·al·ize** /ˈglōbəˌlīz/ verb.

glob·al vil·lage ▶ **noun** the world considered as a single community linked by telecommunications.

glob·al warm·ing ▶ **noun** the gradual increase in the overall temperature of the earth's atmosphere due to the greenhouse effect caused by increased levels of pollutants.

globe /glōb/ ▶ **noun 1** a spherical or rounded object. **2** (**the globe**) the earth. **3** a spherical representation of the earth.
– DERIVATIVES **glo·bose** /ˈglōbōs/ adjective.
– ORIGIN Latin *globus*.

globe·trot·ter /ˈglōbˌträtər/ ▶ **noun** informal a person who travels widely.
– DERIVATIVES **globe·trot·ting** /ˈglōbˌträtiNG/ noun & adjective.

glob·u·lar /ˈgläbyələr/ ▶ **adjective 1** globe-shaped; spherical. **2** composed of globules.

glob·ule /ˈgläbyo͞ol/ ▶ **noun** a small round particle of a substance; a drop.
– ORIGIN Latin *globulus* 'little globe.'

glob·u·lin /ˈgläbyəlin/ ▶ **noun** any of a group of simple proteins found in blood serum.

glock·en·spiel /ˈgläkənˌspēl, -ˌSHpēl/ ▶ **noun** a musical percussion instrument containing tuned metal pieces that are struck with small hammers.
– ORIGIN German, 'bell play.'

glom /gläm/ ▶ **verb** (**gloms, glomming, glommed**) informal **1** become stuck or joined: *muddy leaves will glom onto your tires.* **2** steal: *he was about to glom my wallet.*

gloom /glo͞om/ ▶ **noun 1** partial or total darkness. **2** a state of depression or despondency.

– SYNONYMS **1 darkness,** dark, murk, shadows, shade. **2 despondency,** depression, dejection, melancholy, unhappiness, sadness, misery, woe, despair.
– ANTONYMS light, happiness.

– PHRASES **gloom and doom** see **DOOM**.
– ORIGIN unknown.

gloom·y /ˈglo͞omē/ ▶ **adjective** (**gloomier, gloomiest**) **1** dark or poorly lit. **2** causing or feeling depression or despondency: *despite the gloomy forecasts, a political crisis looks unlikely.*

– SYNONYMS **1 dark,** shadowy, murky, sunless, dim, dingy. **2 despondent,** depressed, downcast, downhearted, dejected, dispirited, disheartened, demoralized, crestfallen, glum, melancholy; informal down in the mouth, down in the dumps. **3 pessimistic,** depressing, downbeat, disheartening, disappointing, unfavorable, bleak, black.
– ANTONYMS bright, cheerful.

– DERIVATIVES **gloom·i·ly** adverb **gloom·i·ness** noun.

glop /gläp/ ▶ **noun** informal sloppy or sticky semifluid matter.
– DERIVATIVES **glop·py** adjective.
– ORIGIN uncertain.

glo·ri·fy /ˈglôrəˌfī/ ▶ **verb** (**glorifies, glorifying, glorified**) **1** represent something as admirable, especially undeservedly. **2** (as adj. **glorified**) made to appear more important or special than is the case: *he was nothing more than a glorified janitor.* **3** praise and worship God.
– DERIVATIVES **glo·ri·fi·ca·tion** /ˌglôrəfiˈkāSHən/ noun.

glo·ri·ous /ˈglôrēəs/ ▶ **adjective 1** having or bringing glory: *his glorious career with the quartet is coming to an end.* **2** very beautiful or impressive. **3** very enjoyable.

– SYNONYMS **wonderful,** marvelous, magnificent, superb, sublime, spectacular, lovely, fine, delightful; informal stunning, fantastic, terrific, tremendous, sensational, heavenly, divine, gorgeous, fabulous, awesome.
– ANTONYMS undistinguished.

– DERIVATIVES **glo·ri·ous·ly** adverb **glo·ri·ous·ness** noun.

glo·ry /ˈglôrē/ ▶ **noun** (pl. **glories**) **1** great fame or honor won by notable achievements: *he began his pursuit of Olympic glory with the 100 meters.* **2** magnificence; great beauty. **3** a very beautiful or impressive thing. **4** worship and thanksgiving offered to God.

– SYNONYMS **1 honor,** distinction, prestige, fame, renown, kudos, eminence, acclaim, celebrity, praise, recognition. **2 magnificence,** splendor, grandeur, majesty, greatness, nobility, opulence, beauty, elegance.
– ANTONYMS shame.

▶ **verb** (**glory in**) take great pride or pleasure in: *he gloried in the power of public office.*

– SYNONYMS *we **gloried in** our independence* **delight in,** take pleasure in, revel in, rejoice in, exult in, relish, savor, be proud of; informal get a kick out of, get a thrill out of.

– PHRASES **in (all) one's glory** in a state of great happiness or radiance.
– ORIGIN Latin *gloria.*

glo·ry hole ▶ **noun 1** a funnel-shaped surface excavation from which ore is mined. **2** informal a hole in a wall through which fellatio or male masturbation is conducted secretly. **3** dated, informal an untidy room or cupboard used for storage.

gloss[1] /gläs, glôs/ ▶ **noun 1** the shine on a smooth surface. **2** (also **gloss paint**) a type of paint that dries to a shiny surface. **3** an attractive appearance that conceals something ordinary or unpleasant: *the gloss of suburban life.*

– SYNONYMS **shine,** sheen, luster, gleam, patina, polish, brilliance, shimmer.

▶ **verb 1** apply a glossy substance to something. **2** (**gloss over**) try to conceal or pass over something by mentioning it briefly or misleadingly.

– SYNONYMS *he tried to **gloss over** his problems* **conceal,** cover up, hide, disguise, mask, veil, play down, minimize, understate.

– ORIGIN unknown.

CHOOSE THE RIGHT WORD

See **POLISH**.

gloss[2] ▶ **noun** a translation or explanation of a word, phrase, or passage. ▶ **verb** provide a translation or explanation of a word, phrase, or passage.
– ORIGIN Old French *glose.*

glos·sa·ry /ˈgläsərē, ˈglô-/ ▶ **noun** (pl. **glossaries**) an alphabetical list of words relating to a specific subject, dialect, or written work, with explanations.
– ORIGIN Latin *glossarium.*

gloss·y /ˈgläsē, ˈglô-/ ▶ **adjective** (**glossier, glossiest**) **1** shiny and smooth. **2** superficially attractive and stylish.

– SYNONYMS **shiny,** gleaming, lustrous, brilliant, glistening, glassy, polished, lacquered, glazed.
– ANTONYMS dull.

▶ **noun** (pl. **glossies**) informal a magazine printed on glossy paper with many color photographs.
– DERIVATIVES **gloss·i·ly** adverb **gloss·i·ness** noun.

WORD TOOLKIT

glossy ...	lustrous ...	satiny ...
paper	hair	dress
brochure	gold	fabric
photos	metal	finish
lips	fur	sheets
leaves	wool	skin

glot·tal /ˈglätl/ ▸ **adjective** relating to the glottis (part of the larynx).

glot·tal stop ▸ **noun** a speech sound made by opening and closing the glottis, sometimes used instead of a properly sounded *t*.

glot·tis /ˈglätis/ ▸ **noun** the part of the larynx consisting of the vocal cords and the slitlike opening between them.
– ORIGIN Greek.

glove /gləv/ ▸ **noun 1** a covering for the hand with separate parts for each finger and the thumb. **2** a padded protective covering for the hand used in boxing and other sports.
– DERIVATIVES **gloved** adjective.
– PHRASES **fit like a glove** (of clothes) fit exactly. **the gloves are** (or **come**) **off** used to indicate that something will be done in an uncompromising and perhaps brutal way: *they had begun a civil campaign, but now the gloves are off.*
– ORIGIN Old English.

glove com·part·ment (also **glovebox**) ▸ **noun** a small storage compartment in the dashboard of a motor vehicle.

glow /glō/ ▸ **verb 1** give out a steady light without flame. **2** especially of one's complexion, look or feel warm or healthy: *she was glowing with excitement.* **3** look very pleased or happy.

– SYNONYMS **1 shine,** gleam, glimmer, flicker, flare. **2 smolder,** burn.

▸ **noun 1** a steady light. **2** a feeling or appearance of warmth or health. **3** a strong feeling of pleasure or well-being: *a glow of pride.*

– SYNONYMS **radiance,** light, gleam, glimmer.

– ORIGIN Old English.

glow·er /ˈglouər/ ▸ **verb** have an angry or sullen expression. ▸ **noun** an angry or sullen look.
– ORIGIN perhaps from Scandinavian.

glow·ing /ˈglōiNG/ ▸ **adjective** expressing great praise: *a glowing report.*

– SYNONYMS **1 bright,** radiant, incandescent, luminous, smoldering; literary lambent. **2 rosy,** pink, red, ruddy, flushed, blushing, burning. **3 vivid,** vibrant, bright, brilliant, rich, intense, radiant. **4 complimentary,** favorable, enthusiastic, admiring, rapturous, fulsome.

– DERIVATIVES **glow·ing·ly** adverb.

glow-worm ▸ **noun** a type of beetle, the wingless female of which glows to attract males.

glox·in·i·a /gläkˈsinēə/ ▸ **noun** a tropical American plant with large, velvety, bell-shaped flowers.
– ORIGIN named after the German botanist Benjamin P. *Gloxin.*

glu·cose /ˈglo͞okōs/ ▸ **noun** a simple sugar that is an important energy source in living organisms.
– ORIGIN Greek *gleukos* 'sweet wine.'

glue /glo͞o/ ▸ **noun** an adhesive substance used for sticking objects or materials together.

– SYNONYMS **adhesive,** gum, paste, (rubber) cement, mucilage; informal stickum.

▸ **verb** (**glues, gluing** or **glueing, glued**) **1** fasten or join things with glue. **2** (**be glued to**) informal be paying very close attention to something.

– SYNONYMS **stick,** paste, fix, seal, cement.

– DERIVATIVES **glue·y** adjective.
– ORIGIN Latin *gluten.*

glue-sniff·ing ▸ **noun** the practice of inhaling intoxicating fumes from certain types of glue.

glug /gləg/ informal ▸ **verb** (**glugs, glugging, glugged**) pour or drink liquid with a hollow gurgling sound. ▸ **noun** a hollow gurgling sound.
– DERIVATIVES **glug·ga·ble** adjective.
– ORIGIN imitating the sound.

glum /gləm/ ▸ **adjective** (**glummer, glummest**) sad or dejected.

– SYNONYMS **gloomy,** downcast, dejected, despondent, crestfallen, disheartened, depressed, doleful, miserable, woebegone; informal fed up, down in the dumps, down in the mouth.
– ANTONYMS cheerful.

– DERIVATIVES **glum·ly** adverb.
– ORIGIN variant of **GLOOM**.

glut /glət/ ▸ **noun** an excessively abundant supply. ▸ **verb** (**gluts, glutting, glutted**) supply or fill something to excess.
– ORIGIN probably from Latin *gluttire* 'to swallow.'

glu·ten /ˈglo͞otn/ ▸ **noun** a substance containing a number of proteins that is found in wheat and other cereal grains.
– ORIGIN Latin, 'glue.'

glu·te·us /ˈglo͞otēəs/ ▸ **noun** (pl. **glutei** /-tēˌī/) any of three muscles in each buttock that move the thigh.
– DERIVATIVES **glu·te·al** /-tēəl/ adjective.
– ORIGIN Greek *gloutos* 'buttock.'

glu·ti·nous /ˈglo͞otn-əs/ ▸ **adjective 1** like glue in texture; sticky. **2** excessively sentimental; sickly: *glutinous ballads.*
– ORIGIN Latin *glutinosus.*

glut·ton /ˈglətn/ ▸ **noun 1** an excessively greedy eater. **2** a person who is very eager for something difficult or challenging: *I was a glutton for punishment.*
– DERIVATIVES **glut·ton·ous** adjective.
– ORIGIN Latin *glutto.*

glut·ton·y /ˈglətn-ē/ ▸ **noun** the habit or fact of eating excessively.

gly·ce·mic in·dex /glīˈsēmik/ ▸ **noun** a scale that ranks foods from 1 to 100 based on their effect on blood-sugar levels.

glyc·er·in /ˈglisərin/ (Brit. **glycerine** /-rin, -ˌrēn, ˌglisəˈrēn/) ▸ **noun** another term for **GLYCEROL**.
– ORIGIN French *glycerin.*

glyc·er·ol /ˈglisəˌrôl, -ˌräl/ ▸ **noun** a colorless, sweet liquid formed as a byproduct in soap manufacture, used in making cosmetics, explosives, and antifreeze.

gly·cine /ˈglīsēn/ ▸ **noun** Biochemistry the simplest naturally occurring amino acid. It is a constituent of most proteins.

gly·co·gen /ˈglīkəjən/ ▸ **noun** a substance deposited in bodily tissues as a store of glucose.

gly·col /ˈglīkôl, -kōl/ ▸ **noun** short for **ETHYLENE GLYCOL**.

gly·col·y·sis /glīˈkäləsis/ ▸ **noun** the breakdown of glucose by enzymes, releasing energy.

gly·co·side /ˈglīkəˌsīd/ ▸ **noun** a compound formed from a simple sugar and another compound by replacement of a hydroxyl group in the sugar molecule.

glyph /glif/ ▸ **noun 1** a hieroglyphic character. **2** Architecture

an ornamental carved groove, as on a Greek frieze. **3** Computing a small graphic symbol.
– ORIGIN Greek *gluphē* 'carving.'

GM ▶ **abbreviation** **1** general manager. **2** genetically modified.

gm ▶ **abbreviation** gram(s).

G-man ▶ **noun** informal an FBI agent.
– ORIGIN probably an abbreviation of *Government man*.

GMO ▶ **abbreviation** genetically modified organism.

GMT ▶ **abbreviation** Greenwich Mean Time.

gnarled /närld/ ▶ **adjective** knobbly, rough, and twisted, especially with age.
– ORIGIN from former *knarre* 'rugged rock or stone.'

gnarl·y /'närlē/ ▶ **adjective** (**gnarlier, gnarliest**) **1** gnarled. **2** informal dangerous, challenging, or unpleasant. **3** informal extremely amazing or excellent.

gnash /nash/ ▶ **verb** grind one's teeth together, especially as a sign of anger.
– ORIGIN perhaps from Old Norse.

gnat /nat/ ▶ **noun** a small two-winged fly resembling a mosquito.
– ORIGIN Old English.

gnaw /nô/ ▶ **verb** **1** bite at or nibble something persistently. **2** cause persistent anxiety or pain: *his conscience gnawed at him.*
– ORIGIN Old English.

gneiss /nīs/ ▶ **noun** a metamorphic rock with a banded or layered structure, typically consisting of feldspar, quartz, and mica.
– ORIGIN German.

gnoc·chi /'näkē/ ▶ **plural noun** (in Italian cooking) small dumplings made from potato, semolina, or flour.
– ORIGIN Italian.

gnome /nōm/ ▶ **noun** **1** an imaginary creature like a tiny man, supposed to guard the earth's treasures underground. **2** a small garden ornament in the form of a bearded man with a pointed hat.
– DERIVATIVES **gnom·ish** adjective.
– ORIGIN Latin *gnomus*.

gno·mic /'nōmik/ ▶ **adjective** clever but often difficult to understand: *I had to have the gnomic response interpreted for me.*
– DERIVATIVES **gno·mi·cal·ly** adverb.
– ORIGIN from Greek *gnōmē* 'thought, opinion.'

gno·sis /'nōsis/ ▶ **noun** knowledge of spiritual mysteries.
– ORIGIN Greek, 'knowledge.'

Gnos·ti·cism /'nästəˌsizəm/ ▶ **noun** a heretical movement of the 2nd-century Christian Church, teaching that mystical knowledge (gnosis) of the supreme divine being enables the human spirit to be redeemed.
– DERIVATIVES **Gnos·tic** /'nästik/ adjective & noun.

GNP ▶ **abbreviation** gross national product.

gnu /n(y)o͞o/ ▶ **noun** a large African antelope with a long head and a beard and mane.
– ORIGIN from Khoikhoi and San.

go[1] ▶ **verb** (**goes, going, went** /went/; past part. **gone** /gôn, gän/) **1** move to or from a place. **2** pass into or be in a specified state: *my mind went blank.* **3** (often **go into**) start an activity or course of action: *I'll go skiing | she went into business.* **4** engage in an activity on a regular basis. **5** lie or extend in a certain direction. **6** come to an end; cease to exist. **7** disappear or be used up. **8** (of time) pass. **9** pass time in a particular way: *they went for months without talking.* **10** have a particular outcome. **11** (**be going to be/do**) used to express a future tense. **12** function or operate. **13** be matching. **14** be acceptable or permitted: *anything goes.* **15** fit into or be regularly kept in a particular place. **16** make a specified sound. **17** informal say. **18** (**go by/under**) be known or called by a specified name.

– SYNONYMS **1** *he's gone into town* **travel,** move, proceed, make your way, journey, advance, progress, pass. **2** *the road goes to Amherst* **lead,** stretch, reach, extend. **3** **leave,** depart, go away, withdraw, absent oneself, exit, set off, start out, get under way, take oneself off, be on one's way. informal make tracks. **4** **be used up,** be spent, be exhausted, be consumed. **5** **become,** get, turn, grow. **6** **turn out,** work out, develop, progress, result, end (up); informal pan out. **7** **match,** harmonize, blend, be complementary, coordinate, be compatible. **8** **function,** work, run, operate. **9** *interest rates are **going down*** **decrease,** fall, drop, decline, plummet, plunge, slump. **10** *you should have **gone into** the subject more thoroughly* **investigate,** examine, inquire into, look into, research, probe, explore, delve into, consider, review, analyze. **11** *the lecture went on for hours* **last,** continue, carry on, run on, proceed, endure, persist, take. **12** *I'm not sure what went on* **happen,** take place, occur, transpire; informal go down. **13** *he's **going out with** Kate* **see,** take out, be someone's boyfriend/girlfriend, be in a relationship with; informal date, go with. **14** *the terrible things she has **gone through*** **undergo,** experience, face, suffer, live through, endure. **15** *she **went through** Sue's bag* **search,** look through, hunt through, rummage in/through, rifle through. **16** *I have to **go through** the report* **examine,** study, scrutinize, inspect, look over, scan, check.

▶ **noun** (pl. **goes**) informal **1** an attempt: *give it a go.* **2** a single item, action, or spell of activity: *the remedies cost up to five bucks a go.* **3** spirit or energy.

– SYNONYMS *here, have a go* **try,** attempt, effort, bid; informal shot, stab, crack.

– PHRASES **go about** begin or carry on with an activity. **go along with** agree to something. **go around** **1** be sufficient to supply everybody present. **2** circulate or be communicated within a group: *there's a rumor going around.* **go at** energetically attack or tackle something. **go back** (of two people) have known each other for a specified, usually long period of time: *Victor and I go back longer than I care to admit.* **go back on** fail to keep a promise. **go down** **1** be defeated in a contest. **2** obtain a specified reaction: *the show went down well.* **go for** **1** decide on something. **2** attempt to gain something. **3** attack someone. **go in for** like or regularly take part in something. **going!, gone!** an auctioneer's announcement that bidding is closing or closed. **go into** **1** investigate or inquire into something. **2** (of a whole number) be capable of dividing another, typically without a remainder. **go off** **1** (of a bomb or gun) explode or fire. **2** informal begin to dislike someone or something. **go on** **1** continue or persevere. **2** take place. **go out** **1** stop shining or burning. **2** (of the tide) ebb. **3** carry on a regular romantic relationship with someone. **go over** examine or check the details of something. **go through** **1** undergo a difficult experience. **2** examine something carefully. **3** informal use up or spend something. **go under** become bankrupt. **go with** **1** give one's consent or agreement to (a person or their views). **2** have a romantic relationship with (someone). **go without** suffer lack or hardship. **have——going for**

one informal—is in one's favor. **make a go of** informal be successful in something. **on the go** informal very active or busy. **to go** (of food or drink from a restaurant or cafe) to be eaten or drunk off the premises.
– ORIGIN Old English.

USAGE

For information on the use of **go** followed by **and** (as in *I must go and change*), see the note at **AND**.

go² ▶ **noun** a Japanese board game of territorial possession and capture.

goad /gōd/ ▶ **verb 1** keep annoying or criticizing someone until they react. **2** urge cattle on with a goad.
– SYNONYMS **provoke,** spur, prod, egg on, hound, badger, rouse, stir, move, stimulate, motivate, prompt, induce, encourage, urge, inspire; impel, pressure.
▶ **noun 1** a thing that stimulates someone into action. **2** a spiked stick used for driving cattle.
– ORIGIN Old English.

go-a·head informal ▶ **noun** (**the go-ahead**) permission to proceed. ▶ **adjective** enterprising and ambitious.

goal /gōl/ ▶ **noun 1** (in soccer, football, etc.) a pair of posts linked by a crossbar and forming a space into or over which the ball has to be sent to score. **2** an instance of sending the ball into or over a goal. **3** an aim or desired result: *my goal is to make movies.*
– SYNONYMS **objective,** aim, end, target, intention, plan, purpose, ambition, aspiration.
– DERIVATIVES **goal·less** adjective.
– ORIGIN unknown.

goal·ie /ˈgōlē/ ▶ **noun** informal a goalkeeper.

goal·keep·er /ˈgōlˌkēpər/ ▶ **noun** a player in soccer or field hockey whose role is to stop the ball from entering the goal.

goal kick ▶ **noun** Soccer a free kick taken by the defending side after attackers send the ball over the end line outside the goal.

goal line ▶ **noun** in field sports, a line on which the goal is placed or which acts as the boundary beyond which a try or touchdown is scored.

goal·post /ˈgōlˌpōst/ ▶ **noun** either of the two upright posts of a goal.
– PHRASES **move the goalposts** unfairly alter the conditions or rules of something while it is still happening.

goal·scor·er /ˈgōlˌskôrər/ ▶ **noun** a player who scores a goal.
– DERIVATIVES **goal·scor·ing** adjective.

goal·tend·er /ˈgōlˌtendər/ ▶ **noun** a goalkeeper, especially in hockey.

go-a·round ▶ **noun 1** an instance of an activity or pattern that occurs repeatedly: *this is the third go-around for clearance talks.* **2** Aviation a circular flight pattern following an abandoned landing attempt.

goat /gōt/ ▶ **noun 1** a hardy domesticated mammal that has backward-curving horns and (in the male) a beard. **2** a wild mammal related to the goat, such as the ibex. **3** informal a lecherous man.
– DERIVATIVES **goat·ish** adjective **goat·y** adjective.
– PHRASES **get someone's goat** informal irritate someone.
– ORIGIN Old English.

goat-an·te·lope ▶ **noun** a mammal of a group including the chamois, with characteristics of both goats and antelopes.

goat·ee /gōˈtē/ ▶ **noun** a small pointed beard like that of a goat.
– DERIVATIVES **goat·eed** adjective.

goat·herd /ˈgōtˌhərd/ ▶ **noun** a person who looks after goats.

goat·skin /ˈgōtˌskin/ ▶ **noun** leather made from the skin of a goat.

gob¹ /gäb/ informal ▶ **noun 1** a lump of a slimy or thick semiliquid substance. **2** (**gobs of**) a lot of: *he wants to make gobs of money selling DVDs.* ▶ **verb** (**gobs, gobbing, gobbed**) Brit. spit.
– ORIGIN Old French *gobe* 'mouthful, lump.'

gob² ▶ **noun** Brit. informal a person's mouth.
– ORIGIN perhaps from Scottish Gaelic.

gob·ble¹ /ˈgäbəl/ ▶ **verb 1** eat hurriedly and noisily. **2** use a large amount of something very quickly: *impractical ventures gobbled up the rock star's cash.*
– SYNONYMS **guzzle,** bolt, gulp, devour, wolf down; informal put away, scarf (down/up), tuck into, demolish.
– DERIVATIVES **gob·bler** noun.
– ORIGIN probably from **GOB¹**.

gob·ble² ▶ **verb** (of a male turkey) make a swallowing sound in the throat.
– DERIVATIVES **gob·bler** noun.
– ORIGIN imitating the sound.

gob·ble·dy·gook /ˈgäbəldēˌgo͝ok, -ˌgo͞ok/ (also **gobbledegook**) ▶ **noun** informal language that is difficult to understand because of excessive use of technical terms.
– ORIGIN probably imitating a turkey's gobble.

go-be·tween ▶ **noun** an intermediary or negotiator.

gob·let /ˈgäblit/ ▶ **noun** a drinking glass with a foot and a stem.
– ORIGIN Old French *gobelet* 'little cup.'

gob·lin /ˈgäblin/ ▶ **noun** (in folklore and fairy tales) a small, ugly, mischievous creature.
– ORIGIN Old French *gobelin.*

go·by /ˈgōbē/ ▶ **noun** (pl. **gobies**) a small sea fish, typically with a sucker on the underside.
– ORIGIN Greek *kōbios.*

go-cart ▶ **noun** variant spelling of **GO-KART**.

God /gäd/ ▶ **noun 1** (in Christianity and other religions that believe in only one God) the creator and supreme ruler of the universe. **2** (**god**) a superhuman being or spirit worshiped as having power over nature and human life. **3** (**god**) a greatly admired or influential person. **4** (**the gods**) informal the gallery in a theater.
– SYNONYMS **1** *a gift from God* **the Lord,** the Almighty, the Creator, the Maker, the Godhead; Allah, Jehovah, Yahweh; (God) the Father, (God) the Son, the Holy Ghost/Spirit, the Holy Trinity; the Great Spirit, Gitchi Manitou; humorous the Man Upstairs. **2** (**god**) *sacrifices to appease the gods* **deity,** goddess, divine being, divinity, immortal.
▶ **exclamation** used to express surprise, anger, etc., or for emphasis.
– DERIVATIVES **god·hood** noun **god·like** adjective.
– PHRASES **God the Father, (the) Son, and (the) Holy Ghost** (in Christian doctrine) the persons of the Trinity. **God's gift** chiefly ironic the best possible person for

someone: *he thought he was God's gift to women.*
– ORIGIN Old English.

god·child /ˈgäd,CHīld/ ▸ noun (pl. **godchildren** /-,CHildrən/) a person in relation to a godparent.

god·damn /ˈgädˈdam/ (also **goddam** or **goddamned**) ▸ adjective, adverb, & noun informal used for emphasis, especially to express anger or frustration: (as adj.) *this goddamn weather* | (as n.) *I don't give a goddamn what you do!*

god·daugh·ter /ˈgäd,dôtər/ ▸ noun a female godchild.

god·dess /ˈgädis/ ▸ noun **1** a female god. **2** a woman who is greatly admired, especially for her beauty.

go·de·tia /gəˈdēSHə/ ▸ noun a North American plant with showy lilac to red flowers.
– ORIGIN named after the Swiss botanist Charles H. *Godet.*

god·fa·ther /ˈgäd,fäT͟Hər/ ▸ noun **1** a male godparent. **2** a male leader of a Mafia family.

God·fear·ing ▸ adjective earnestly religious.

god·for·sak·en /ˈgädfər,sākən/ ▸ adjective (of a place) unattractive, remote, or depressing.

God·giv·en ▸ adjective **1** received from God: *the God-given power to work miracles.* **2** possessed without question, as if by divine authority: *the union man's God-given right to strike.*

god·head /ˈgäd,hed/ ▸ noun **1** (**the Godhead**) God. **2** divine nature.

god·less /ˈgädlis/ ▸ adjective **1** not believing in a god or God. **2** wicked; very bad.

god·ly /ˈgädlē/ ▸ adjective (**godlier**, **godliest**) devoutly religious; pious.
– DERIVATIVES **god·li·ness** noun.

god·moth·er /ˈgäd,məT͟Hər/ ▸ noun a female godparent.

god·par·ent /ˈgäd,pe(ə)rənt, -,par-/ ▸ noun a person who presents a child at baptism and promises to take responsibility for their religious education.

god·send /ˈgäd,send/ ▸ noun something very helpful or welcome at a particular time.

god·son /ˈgäd,sən/ ▸ noun a male godchild.

God·speed /ˈgädˈspēd/ ▸ exclamation dated an expression of good wishes to a person starting a journey.

god·wit /ˈgädwit/ ▸ noun a large long-legged wading bird with a long bill.
– ORIGIN unknown.

go·er /ˈgōər/ ▸ noun (often in combination) a person who regularly attends a specified place or event: *a theatergoer.*

goes /gōōz/ third person singular present of **GO**[1].

go·fer /ˈgōfər/ (also **gopher**) ▸ noun informal a person who runs errands.
– ORIGIN from *go for* (i.e., go and fetch).

go-get·ter ▸ noun informal an energetic and very enterprising person.
– DERIVATIVES **go-get·ting** adjective.

gog·gle /ˈgägəl/ ▸ verb **1** look with wide open eyes. **2** (of the eyes) protrude or open wide. ▸ noun (**goggles**) close-fitting protective glasses with side shields.
– ORIGIN probably representing oscillating movement.

gog·gle-eyed ▸ adjective having wide-open eyes, especially through astonishment.

go-go ▸ adjective referring to an unrestrained and erotic style of dancing to pop music.

go·ing /ˈgōiNG/ ▸ noun **1** the condition of the ground as regards its suitability for horse racing or walking. **2** conditions for, or progress in, an activity or enterprise: *the company sold its advertising airtime for $500 million, good going in a recession.* ▸ adjective (of a price) usual or current.

go·ing con·cern ▸ noun a thriving business.

go·ing-o·ver ▸ noun informal **1** a thorough cleaning or inspection. **2** an attack or heavy defeat.

go·ings-on ▸ plural noun informal suspect or unusual activities.

goi·ter /ˈgoitər/ (Brit. **goitre**) ▸ noun a swelling of the neck resulting from enlargement of the thyroid gland.
– DERIVATIVES **goi·trous** /ˈgoitrəs/ adjective.
– ORIGIN French, or from Old French *goitron* 'gullet.'

go-kart (also **go-cart**) ▸ noun a small race car with a lightweight body.

gold /gōld/ ▸ noun **1** a yellow precious metal, used in jewelry and decoration and to guarantee the value of currencies. **2** a deep yellow or yellow-brown color. **3** coins or articles made of gold.
– ORIGIN Old English.

gold card ▸ noun a credit card that provides benefits not available on a standard card.

gold-dig·ger ▸ noun informal a woman who forms relationships with men purely for financial gain.

gold disc ▸ noun a framed golden replica of a compact disc awarded to a recording artist or group for sales exceeding a specified figure.

gold dust ▸ noun fine particles of gold.

gold·en /ˈgōldən/ ▸ adjective **1** made of or resembling gold. **2** (of a period) very happy and prosperous. **3** excellent: *a golden opportunity.* **4** (of celebrations) marking the fiftieth anniversary: *their golden wedding anniversary.*

> – SYNONYMS **blond/blonde,** yellow, fair, flaxen.
> – ANTONYMS dark.

– DERIVATIVES **gold·en·ly** adverb.

gold·en age ▸ noun the period when something is most successful: *the golden age of musical theater.*

gold·en boy (or **golden girl**) ▸ noun informal a very popular or successful young person.

Gold·en De·li·cious ▸ noun a variety of eating apple with a greenish-yellow skin.

gold·en ea·gle ▸ noun a large eagle with yellow-tipped head feathers.

Gold·en Fleece ▸ noun **1** Mythology the fleece of a golden ram, guarded by an unsleeping dragon. **2** a goal that is highly desirable but difficult to achieve.

gold·en goose ▸ noun a continuing source of wealth or profit that may be exhausted if it is misused.

gold·en hand·cuffs ▸ plural noun informal benefits provided by an employer to discourage an employee from working elsewhere.

gold·en hand·shake ▸ noun informal a payment given to someone who is laid off or retires early.

gold·en old·ie ▸ noun informal an old song or movie that is still well known and popular.

gold·en re·triev·er ▸ noun a breed of retriever with a thick golden-colored coat.

gold·en·rod /ˈgōldən,räd/ ▸ **noun** a plant with tall spikes of small bright yellow flowers.

gold·en rule ▸ **noun** a basic principle that should always be followed.

gold·en·seal /ˈgōldən,sēl/ ▸ **noun** a woodland plant of the buttercup family whose bright yellow root has medicinal and antibacterial properties.

gold·field /ˈgōld,fēld/ ▸ **noun** a district in which gold is found as a mineral.

gold·finch /ˈgōld,fincH/ ▸ **noun** a gregarious finch with bright yellow plumage.

gold·fish /ˈgōld,fisH/ ▸ **noun** (pl. same or **goldfishes**) a small reddish-golden carp popular in ponds and aquariums.

gold·fish bowl ▸ **noun 1** a spherical glass container for goldfish. **2** a place or situation lacking privacy.

gold leaf ▸ **noun** gold beaten into a very thin sheet, used in gilding.

gold med·al ▸ **noun** a medal made of or colored gold, awarded for first place in a competition.

gold mine ▸ **noun 1** a place where gold is mined. **2** a source of wealth or resources.

gold plate ▸ **noun 1** a thin layer of gold applied as a coating to another metal. **2** dishes, flatware, etc., made of or plated with gold.

gold rush ▸ **noun** a rapid movement of people to a newly discovered goldfield.

gold·smith /ˈgōld,smitH/ ▸ **noun** a person who makes gold articles.

gold stand·ard ▸ **noun** historical the system by which the value of a currency was defined in terms of gold.

go·lem /ˈgōləm/ ▸ **noun** (in Jewish legend) a clay figure brought to life by magic.
– ORIGIN Hebrew, 'shapeless mass.'

golf /gälf, gôlf/ ▸ **noun** a game played on an outdoor course, the aim of which is to strike a small hard ball with a club into a series of small holes with the fewest possible strokes. ▸ **verb** (usu. as n. **golfing**) play golf.
– DERIVATIVES **golf·er** noun.
– ORIGIN perhaps related to Dutch *kolf* 'club.'

golf club ▸ **noun 1** a club used to hit the ball in golf, with a heavy wooden or metal head and a slender shaft. **2** a membership organization for golf players, or its premises.

golf course ▸ **noun** a course on which golf is played, typically consisting of 18 holes.

Go·li·ath /gəˈlīəTH/ ▸ **noun** a person or thing of enormous size or strength.
– ORIGIN from the name of a giant in the Bible, killed by David.

gol·li·wog /ˈgälē,wäg/ ▸ **noun** dated a soft doll with a black face and fuzzy hair.
– ORIGIN from *Golliwogg*, a doll character in books by the US writer Bertha Upton.

gol·ly /ˈgälē/ ▸ **exclamation** informal used to express surprise or delight.
– ORIGIN euphemism for **God**.

go·nad /ˈgōnad/ ▸ **noun** a bodily organ that produces gametes; a testis or ovary.
– DERIVATIVES **go·nad·al** /gōˈnadl/ adjective.
– ORIGIN Latin *gonades*, plural of *gonas*.

gon·do·la /ˈgändələ, gänˈdōlə/ ▸ **noun 1** a flat-bottomed boat used on Venetian canals, having a high point at each end and worked by one oar at the stern. **2** a cabin on a ski lift, or suspended from an airship or balloon.
– ORIGIN Venetian Italian.

gon·do·lier /,gändlˈi(ə)r/ ▸ **noun** a person who propels and steers a gondola.

gone /gôn/ past participle of **GO**[1] ▸ **adjective 1** no longer present, available, or in existence. **2** informal having reached a specified time in a pregnancy: *she's four months gone*.

> – SYNONYMS **1 away,** absent, off, out, missing. **2 past,** over (and done with), no more, done, finished, ended, forgotten. **3 used up,** consumed, finished, spent, depleted.

▸ **preposition** Brit. **1** (of time) past. **2** (of age) older than.

gon·er /ˈgônər/ ▸ **noun** informal a person or thing that is doomed or cannot be saved.

gong /gäNG, gôNG/ ▸ **noun** a metal disk with a turned rim, giving a resonant note when struck.
– ORIGIN Malay.

gon·na /ˈgônə, ˈgənə/ ▸ **contraction** informal going to: *we're gonna win this game*.

gon·or·rhe·a /,gänəˈrēə/ (Brit. **gonorrhoea**) ▸ **noun** a sexually transmitted disease causing discharge from the urethra or vagina.
– ORIGIN from Greek *gonos* 'semen' + *rhoia* 'flux.'

goo /go͞o/ ▸ **noun** informal a sticky or slimy substance.
– ORIGIN perhaps from *burgoo*, a nautical slang term for porridge.

goo·ber /ˈgo͞obər/ ▸ **noun** informal **1** a dimwitted person; a yokel. **2** (also **goober pea**) a peanut.

good /go͝od/ ▸ **adjective** (**better** /ˈbetər/, **best** /best/) **1** having the required qualities; of a high standard. **2** morally right, polite, or obedient. **3** enjoyable, pleasant, or satisfying. **4** appropriate or suitable. **5** (**good for**) beneficial to. **6** thorough: *have a good look around*. **7** at least: *a good 20 years ago*.

> – SYNONYMS **1 fine,** superior, excellent, superb, outstanding, magnificent, exceptional, marvelous, wonderful, first-rate, first-class, quality; informal great, ace, terrific, fantastic, fabulous, class, awesome, wicked; Brit. informal brilliant. **2** *a good person* **virtuous,** righteous, upright, upstanding, moral, ethical, principled, law-abiding, blameless, honorable, decent, respectable, trustworthy; informal squeaky clean. **3** *the children are good at school* **well behaved,** obedient, dutiful, polite, courteous, respectful. **4** *a good driver* **capable,** able, proficient, adept, adroit, accomplished, skillful, talented, masterly, expert; informal mean, wicked, nifty, crackerjack. **5** *a good friend* **close,** intimate, dear, bosom, special, best, loyal. **6** *a good time was had by all* **enjoyable,** pleasant, agreeable, pleasurable, delightful, lovely, amusing. **7** *it was good of you to come* **kind,** generous, charitable, gracious, noble, altruistic, unselfish. **8** *a good time to call* **convenient,** suitable, appropriate, fitting, fit, opportune, timely, favorable. **9** *bananas are good for you* **wholesome,** healthy, nourishing, nutritious, beneficial. **10** *good food* **tasty,** appetizing, flavorsome, palatable, succulent; informal scrumptious, yummy. **11** *a good reason* **valid,** genuine, authentic, legitimate, sound, bona fide, convincing, compelling. **12** *good weather* **fine,** fair, dry, bright, clear, sunny, cloudless, calm, warm, mild.
> – ANTONYMS bad, wicked, naughty.

▶ **noun 1** behavior that is right or acceptable. **2** something beneficial: *he resigned for the good of the country.* **3** (**goods**) products or possessions.

– SYNONYMS **1 virtue,** righteousness, goodness, morality, integrity, honesty, truth, honor. **2** *it's for your own good* **benefit,** advantage, profit, gain, interest, welfare, well-being. **3** (**goods**) **merchandise,** wares, stock, commodities, produce, products, articles.
– ANTONYMS wickedness, disadvantage.

– PHRASES **as good as** very nearly. **be —— to the good** have a specified net profit or advantage. **come up with** (or **deliver**) **the goods** informal do what is expected or required. **do someone good** be beneficial to someone. **for good** forever. **good and ——** informal used as an intensifier before an adjective or adverb: *it'll be good and dark by then.* **the Good Book** the Bible. **good for you!** well done! **a good word** words recommending or defending a person. **in good time 1** with no risk of being late. **2** (also **all in good time**) in due course but without haste. **make something good** (or **make good on something**) **1** compensate for loss, damage, or expense. **2** fulfill a promise or claim.
– ORIGIN Old English.

good·bye /ˌgo͝odˈbī/ (also **goodby**) ▶ **exclamation** used to express good wishes when parting or ending a conversation.

– SYNONYMS **farewell,** adieu, au revoir, ciao, adios; informal bye, bye-bye, so long, see you (later); Brit. informal cheerio, cheers, ta-ta.

▶ **noun** (pl. **goodbyes**; also **goodbys**) an instance of saying 'goodbye'; a parting.
– ORIGIN contraction of *God be with you!*

good faith ▶ **noun** honesty or sincerity of intention.

good-for-noth·ing ▶ **adjective** worthless and lazy. ▶ **noun** a worthless and lazy person.

Good Fri·day ▶ **noun** the Friday before Easter Sunday, on which the Crucifixion of Jesus is commemorated in the Christian Church.

good-heart·ed ▶ **adjective** kind and well meaning.

good-hu·mored ▶ **adjective** friendly or cheerful.

good·ie ▶ **noun** variant spelling of **GOODY**.

good-look·ing ▶ **adjective** physically attractive.

– SYNONYMS **attractive,** beautiful, pretty, handsome, lovely, stunning, striking, arresting, gorgeous, prepossessing, fetching; Scottish bonny; informal easy on the eye, cute, foxy. old use comely.
– ANTONYMS ugly.

good·ly /ˈgo͝odlē/ ▶ **adjective** (**goodlier**, **goodliest**) considerable in size or quantity.

good-na·tured ▶ **adjective** kind and unselfish.

good·ness /ˈgo͝odnis/ ▶ **noun 1** the quality of being good. **2** the nutritious element of food.

– SYNONYMS **1 virtue,** good, righteousness, morality, integrity, rectitude, honesty, honor, decency, respectability, nobility, worth, merit. **2 kindness,** humanity, benevolence, tenderness, warmth, affection, love, goodwill, sympathy, compassion, care, concern, understanding, generosity, charity.

▶ **exclamation** expressing surprise, anger, etc.

good night ▶ **exclamation** expressing good wishes on parting at night or before going to bed.

good old boy ▶ **noun** informal, often derogatory **1** a member of a network of men that has controlling influence in some sphere. **2** a Southern white male regarded as typical in being somewhat unsophisticated.

goods and chat·tels ▶ **plural noun** all kinds of personal possessions.

good-sized ▶ **adjective** adequately or generously large: *the text is supplied in good-sized clear print.*

good-tem·pered ▶ **adjective** not easily angered.

good-time ▶ **adjective** interested in pleasure more than anything else.

good·will /ˌgo͝odˈwil/ ▶ **noun 1** friendly or helpful feelings or attitude. **2** the established reputation of a business regarded as an asset and calculated as part of its value when it is sold.

– SYNONYMS **kindness,** compassion, goodness, benevolence, consideration, charity, decency, neighborliness.
– ANTONYMS hostility.

good·y /ˈgo͝odē/ ▶ **noun** (also **goodie**) (pl. **goodies**) informal something attractive or desirable, especially something tasty to eat. ▶ **exclamation** expressing childish delight.

good·y bag ▶ **noun** a bag containing a selection of desirable items, especially one given to party guests as they leave or to customers as a promotional offer.

good·y-good·y informal ▶ **noun** a person who behaves well so as to impress other people. ▶ **adjective** virtuous in a smug or showy way.

good·y two-shoes ▶ **noun** another term for **GOODY-GOODY**.

goo·ey /ˈgo͞oē/ ▶ **adjective** (**gooier, gooiest**) informal **1** soft and sticky. **2** excessively sentimental: *gooey nostalgia.*
– DERIVATIVES **goo·ey·ness** noun.

goof /go͞of/ informal ▶ **noun 1** a mistake. **2** a foolish or stupid person. ▶ **verb 1** fool around. **2** make a mistake. **3** (**goof off**) evade a duty.
– ORIGIN unknown.

CHOOSE THE RIGHT WORD

See **MISTAKE**.

goof·ball /ˈgo͞ofˌbôl/ ▶ **noun** informal **1** a naive, silly, or stupid person. **2** a narcotic pill, especially a barbiturate.

goof·y /ˈgo͞ofē/ ▶ **adjective** (**goofier, goofiest**) informal **1** foolish; harmlessly eccentric. **2** (in surfing, snowboarding, etc.) having the right leg in front of the left on the board.
– DERIVATIVES **goof·i·ly** adverb **goof·i·ness** noun.

goo·gle /ˈgo͞ogəl/ ▶ **verb 1** use an Internet search engine, especially Google: *she spent the afternoon googling aimlessly.* **2** search for the name of someone or something on the Internet in order to find information about them.

gook[1] /go͝ok/ ▶ **noun** informal, offensive a person of SE Asian descent.
– ORIGIN unknown.

gook[2] /go͝ok, gək/ ▶ **noun** informal a sloppy wet or viscous substance: *all that gook she kept putting on her hair.*

goon /go͞on/ ▶ **noun** informal **1** a foolish or eccentric person. **2** a thug.
– ORIGIN perhaps from dialect *gooney* 'stupid person.'

goose /go͞os/ ▶ **noun** (pl. **geese**) **1** a large waterbird with a long neck and webbed feet. **2** a female goose. **3** informal a

foolish person. ▶ **verb** informal poke someone between the buttocks.
– ORIGIN Old English.

goose·ber·ry /'go͞os,berē/ ▶ **noun** (pl. **gooseberries**) a round edible yellowish-green berry with a hairy skin.
– ORIGIN the first element perhaps from **GOOSE**, or perhaps from Old French *groseille*.

goose·bumps /'go͞os,bəmps/ ▶ **plural noun** a state of the skin in which small bumps appear and hairs are erect, resulting from cold, emotion, or fear.

goose·flesh /'go͞os,flesʜ/ ▶ **noun** another term for **GOOSEBUMPS**.

goose step ▶ **noun** a military marching step in which the legs are not bent at the knee. ▶ **verb** (**goose-step**) march with the legs kept straight.

GOP ▶ **abbreviation** Grand Old Party (the Republican Party).

go·pher /'gōfər/ ▶ **noun 1** (also **pocket gopher**) a burrowing American rodent with pouches on its cheeks. **2** variant spelling of **GOFER**.
– ORIGIN perhaps from Canadian French *gaufre* 'honeycomb' (because the gopher 'honeycombs' the ground with its burrows).

Gor·di·an knot /'gôrdēən/ ▶ **noun** (in phrase **cut the Gordian knot**) solve a difficult problem in a direct or forceful way.
– ORIGIN from the legendary knot tied by King *Gordius* and cut through by Alexander the Great in response to the prophecy that whoever untied it would rule Asia.

gore[1] /gôr/ ▶ **noun** blood that has been shed, especially as a result of violence.
– ORIGIN Old English, 'dung, dirt.'

gore[2] ▶ **verb** (of an animal such as a bull) pierce or stab someone with a horn or tusk.
– ORIGIN unknown.

gore[3] ▶ **noun** a triangular or tapering piece of material used in making a garment, sail, or umbrella.
– DERIVATIVES **gored** adjective.
– ORIGIN Old English, 'triangular piece of land.'

gorge /gôrj/ ▶ **noun** a steep, narrow valley or ravine.

> – SYNONYMS **ravine,** canyon, gully, defile, chasm, gulch, coulee, gulf.

▶ **verb** eat a large amount greedily.

> – SYNONYMS *they gorged themselves on cake* **stuff,** cram, fill, overindulge; informal pig out.

– DERIVATIVES **gorg·er** noun.
– PHRASES **one's gorge rises** one is sickened or disgusted.
– ORIGIN Old French, 'throat.'

gor·geous /'gôrjəs/ ▶ **adjective 1** beautiful; very attractive. **2** informal very pleasant.

> – SYNONYMS **1 good-looking,** attractive, beautiful, pretty, handsome, lovely, stunning; Scottish bonny; informal cute, foxy, fanciable, hot. old use comely. **2 spectacular,** splendid, superb, wonderful, grand, impressive, awe-inspiring, awesome, stunning, breathtaking; informal sensational, fabulous, fantastic. **3 resplendent,** magnificent, sumptuous, luxurious, elegant, dazzling, brilliant.
> – ANTONYMS ugly, drab.

– DERIVATIVES **gor·geous·ly** adverb **gor·geous·ness** noun.
– ORIGIN Old French *gorgias* 'fine, elegant.'

gor·get /'gôrjit/ ▶ **noun 1** historical an article of clothing or piece of armor covering the throat. **2** a patch of color on the throat of a bird.
– ORIGIN Old French *gorgete*.

Gor·gon /'gôrgən/ (also **gorgon**) ▶ **noun 1** Greek Mythology each of three sisters with snakes for hair, who had the power to turn anyone who looked at them to stone. **2** a fierce or repulsive woman.
– ORIGIN Greek *gorgos* 'terrible.'

Gor·gon·zo·la /,gôrgən'zōlə/ ▶ **noun** a rich, strong-flavored Italian cheese with bluish-green veins.
– ORIGIN named after the Italian village of *Gorgonzola*.

go·ril·la /gə'rilə/ ▶ **noun 1** a powerfully built great ape of central Africa, the largest living primate. **2** informal a heavily built aggressive-looking man.
– ORIGIN Greek.

gorse /gôrs/ ▶ **noun** a yellow-flowered shrub with thin prickly leaves.
– ORIGIN Old English.

gor·y /'gôrē/ ▶ **adjective** (**gorier, goriest**) **1** involving violence and bloodshed. **2** covered in blood.

> – SYNONYMS **grisly,** gruesome, violent, bloody, brutal, savage; ghastly, frightful, horrid, fearful, hideous, macabre, horrible, horrific.

– DERIVATIVES **gor·i·ness** noun.
– PHRASES **the gory details** humorous explicit details.

gosh /gäsʜ/ ▶ **exclamation** informal used to express surprise or for emphasis.
– ORIGIN euphemism for **GOD**.

gos·hawk /'gäs,hôk/ ▶ **noun** a short-winged hawk resembling a large sparrowhawk.
– ORIGIN Old English, 'goose-hawk.'

gos·ling /'gäzlɪɴɢ/ ▶ **noun** a young goose.
– ORIGIN Old Norse.

gos·pel /'gäspəl/ ▶ **noun 1** the teachings of Jesus. **2** (**Gospel**) the record of Jesus's life and teaching in the first four books of the New Testament. **3** (**Gospel**) each of the first four books of the New Testament. **4** (also **gospel truth**) something absolutely true. **5** (also **gospel music**) a style of black American evangelical religious singing.
– ORIGIN Old English, 'good news.'

gos·sa·mer /'gäsəmər/ ▶ **noun** a fine, filmy substance consisting of cobwebs spun by small spiders. ▶ **adjective** very fine and insubstantial.
– ORIGIN probably from **GOOSE** + **SUMMER**, perhaps from the time around St. Martin's day (November 11) when geese were eaten and gossamer is seen.

gos·sip /'gäsəp/ ▶ **noun 1** casual conversation or unproven reports about other people. **2** chiefly derogatory a person who likes talking about other people's private lives.

> – SYNONYMS **1 news,** rumors, scandal, hearsay, tittle-tattle; informal dirt, buzz, scuttlebutt. **2 chat,** talk, conversation, chatter, heart-to-heart, tête-à-tête; informal gabfest, jaw, gas, chinwag. **3 gossipmonger,** busybody, scandalmonger, rumor-monger, muckraker.

▶ **verb** (**gossips, gossiping, gossiped**) engage in gossip.

> – SYNONYMS **1 talk,** whisper, tell tales, spread rumors; informal dish, dish the dirt. **2** *people sat around gossiping* **chat,** talk, converse; informal shoot the breeze, gas, chew the fat, jaw, chinwag.

– DERIVATIVES **gos·sip·er** noun **gos·sip·y** adjective.
– ORIGIN Old English, 'godfather or godmother,' later 'a close friend.'

gos·sip col·umn ▶ **noun** a section of a newspaper devoted to gossip about well-known people.

got /gät/ past and past participle of **GET**.

Goth /gäTH/ ▶ **noun 1** a member of a Germanic people that invaded the Roman Empire between the 3rd and 5th centuries. **2** (also **goth**) a young person of a group favoring black clothing and a style of rock music having apocalyptic or mystical lyrics.
– ORIGIN Greek *Gothoi*.

Goth·ic /ˈgäTHik/ ▶ **adjective 1** relating to the style of architecture prevalent in western Europe in the 12th–16th centuries, characterized by pointed arches and elaborate tracery. **2** very gloomy or horrifying. **3** (of lettering) derived from the angular style of handwriting with broad vertical downstrokes used in medieval western Europe. **4** relating to the ancient Goths. ▶ **noun 1** Gothic architecture. **2** the extinct language of the Goths.

goth·ic nov·el ▶ **noun** an English type of fiction popular in the 18th to early 19th centuries, characterized by an atmosphere of mystery and horror.

go-to ▶ **adjective** informal (usually of people representing some resource) of first resort: *he's Hollywood's go-to guy when a trained bear is needed.*

got·ta /ˈgätə/ ▶ **contraction** informal have got to: *you gotta be careful.*

got·ten /ˈgätn/ past participle of **GET**.

gouache /gwäsH, go͞oˈäsH/ ▶ **noun 1** a method of painting using watercolors thickened with a type of glue. **2** watercolors thickened with a type of glue.
– ORIGIN French.

Gou·da /ˈgo͞odə/ ▶ **noun** a flat round Dutch cheese with a yellow rind.
– ORIGIN made in *Gouda* in the Netherlands.

gouge /gouj/ ▶ **verb 1** make a rough hole or groove in a surface. **2** (**gouge something out**) cut or force something out roughly or brutally. ▶ **noun 1** a chisel with a concave blade. **2** a hole or groove made by gouging.
– DERIVATIVES **goug·er** noun.
– ORIGIN Old French.

gou·lash /ˈgo͞oˌläsH/ ▶ **noun** a Hungarian stew of meat and vegetables, flavored with paprika.
– ORIGIN from Hungarian *gulyás* 'herdsman' + *hús* 'meat.'

gou·ra·mi /go͞oˈrämē/ ▶ **noun** (pl. same or **gouramis**) an Asian fish of a large group including many kinds popular in aquariums.
– ORIGIN Malay.

gourd /gôrd, go͝ord/ ▶ **noun 1** the large hard-skinned fleshy fruit of a climbing or trailing plant. **2** a container made from the hollowed and dried skin of a gourd.
– ORIGIN Old French *gourde*.

gour·mand /go͝orˈmänd/ ▶ **noun 1** a person who enjoys eating, sometimes to excess. **2** a person who is knowledgeable about good food; a gourmet.
– ORIGIN Old French.

gour·man·dize /ˈgo͝ormənˌdīz/ ▶ **verb** eat good food, especially to excess.

gour·met /ˌgôrˈmā, ˌgo͝or-/ ▶ **noun** a person who is knowledgeable about good food.

> – SYNONYMS **gastronome,** epicure, epicurean, connoisseur; informal foodie.

▶ **adjective** (of food or a meal) high quality.
– ORIGIN French.

gout /gout/ ▶ **noun 1** a disease that causes the joints to swell and become painful. **2** literary a drop or spot.
– DERIVATIVES **gout·y** adjective.
– ORIGIN Latin *gutta* 'drop.'

gov. ▶ **abbreviation 1** government. **2** governor.

gov·ern /ˈgəvərn/ ▶ **verb 1** conduct the policy and affairs of a country, state, organization, or people. **2** control or influence: *the wines are governed by strict regulations.* **3** Grammar (of a word) require that another word or group of words be in a particular case.

> – SYNONYMS **1 rule,** preside over, control, be in charge of, command, run, head, manage, oversee, supervise. **2 determine,** decide, control, constrain, regulate, direct, rule, dictate, shape, affect.

– DERIVATIVES **gov·ern·a·bil·i·ty** /ˌgəvərnəˈbilitē/ noun **gov·ern·a·ble** adjective.
– ORIGIN Greek *kubernan* 'to steer.'

gov·ern·ance /ˈgəvərnəns/ ▶ **noun** the action or style of governing something.

gov·ern·ess /ˈgəvərnis/ ▶ **noun** a woman employed to teach children in a private household.

gov·ern·ing bod·y ▶ **noun** a group of people who govern an institution such as a school in partnership with the managers.

gov·ern·ment /ˈgəvər(n)mənt/ ▶ **noun 1** (treated as sing. or pl.) the group of people who govern a nation or state. **2** the system by which a nation, state, or community is governed. **3** the action or way of governing a nation, state, or organization: *he believed in strong government.*

> – SYNONYMS **administration,** executive, regime, authority, council, powers that be, cabinet, ministry.

– DERIVATIVES **gov·ern·men·tal** /ˌgəvər(n)ˈmentl/ adjective.

gov·er·nor /ˈgəvə(r)nər/ ▶ **noun 1** the elected executive head of a US state. **2** an official appointed to govern a town or region. **3** the representative of the British Crown in a colony or in a Commonwealth country that regards the British monarch as head of state. **4** a member of a governing body. **5** Brit. informal a person's employer or manager.

> – SYNONYMS **leader,** ruler, chief, head, administrator, principal, director, chairman, chairwoman, chair, superintendent, commissioner, controller; informal boss.

– DERIVATIVES **gov·er·nor·ship** /-ˌsHip/ noun.

Gov·er·nor Gen·er·al ▶ **noun** (pl. **Governors General**) the chief representative of the British Crown in a Commonwealth country of which the British monarch is head of state.

govt. ▶ **abbreviation** government.

gown /goun/ ▶ **noun 1** a long dress worn on formal occasions. **2** a protective garment worn in a hospital by surgical staff or patients. **3** a loose cloak indicating a person's profession or status, worn by a judge, academic, or university student. **4** the members of a university as distinct from the residents of a town.

> – SYNONYMS **dress,** evening gown, prom dress/gown, wedding gown; robe, dressing gown.

▶ **verb** (**be gowned**) be dressed in a gown.
– ORIGIN Latin *gunna* 'fur garment.'

goy /goi/ ▶ **noun** (pl. **goyim** /ˈgoi-im/ or **goys**) informal, derogatory a Jewish word for a non-Jew.
– DERIVATIVES **goy·ish** adjective.
– ORIGIN Hebrew, 'people, nation.'

GP ▶ **abbreviation 1** general practitioner. **2** Grand Prix.

GPA ▶ **abbreviation** grade point average.

GPO ▶ **abbreviation** **1** government printing office. **2** general post office. **3** group purchasing organization.

GPRS ▶ **abbreviation** general packet radio services, a technology for radio transmission of small packets of data, especially between cell phones and the Internet.

GPS ▶ **abbreviation** Global Positioning System (a satellite navigational system).

gr. ▶ **abbreviation** **1** grain(s). **2** gram(s). **3** gross.

grab /grab/ ▶ **verb** (**grabs, grabbing, grabbed**) **1** seize someone or something suddenly and roughly. **2** informal obtain quickly or when an opportunity arises: *get into town early to grab a parking space*. **3** informal impress: *how does that grab you?*

– SYNONYMS **seize,** grasp, snatch, take hold of, grip, clasp, clutch, catch.

▶ **noun** **1** a quick sudden attempt to seize something. **2** a mechanical device for moving loads.
– DERIVATIVES **grab·ber** noun.
– PHRASES **up for grabs** informal available.
– ORIGIN German and Dutch *grabben*.

grab bag ▶ **noun** **1** an eclectic or miscellaneous assortment: *financing a grab bag of more than 20 right-wing front groups*. **2** a container from which a person takes a wrapped item at random, not knowing the contents.

grab·by /'grabē/ ▶ **adjective** informal **1** having or showing a selfish desire for something; greedy. **2** attracting attention; arousing people's interest: *a grabby angle on a news story*.

grace /grās/ ▶ **noun** **1** elegance of movement. **2** polite good will: *she had the grace to look sheepish*. **3** (**graces**) attractive qualities or behavior. **4** (in Christian belief) the free and unearned favor of God. **5** a person's favor. **6** a period officially allowed for an obligation to be met: *the sport has three years' grace before the ban comes into force*. **7** a short prayer of thanks said before or after a meal. **8** (**His**, **Her**, or **Your Grace**) used as forms of description or address for a duke, duchess, or archbishop.

– SYNONYMS **1 elegance,** poise, finesse, polish, fluency, smoothness, suppleness. **2** *he had the grace to apologize* **courtesy,** decency, (good) manners, politeness, respect. **3** *he fell from grace* **favor,** approval, approbation, acceptance, esteem, regard, respect.
– ANTONYMS awkwardness.

▶ **verb** **1** bring honor to something by one's presence. **2** make more attractive: *a fresh wreath graced an upstairs window*.

– SYNONYMS **adorn,** embellish, decorate, ornament, enhance.

– PHRASES **the** (**Three**) **Graces** Greek Mythology three beautiful goddesses believed to personify charm, grace, and beauty. **with good** (or **bad**) **grace** in a willing (or reluctant) way.
– ORIGIN Latin *gratia*.

grace·ful /'grāsfəl/ ▶ **adjective** having or showing grace or elegance.

– SYNONYMS **elegant,** fluid, fluent, easy, polished, supple.

– DERIVATIVES **grace·ful·ly** adverb **grace·ful·ness** noun.

grace·less /'grāslis/ ▶ **adjective** lacking grace, elegance, or charm.
– DERIVATIVES **grace·less·ly** adverb **grace·less·ness** noun.

grace note ▶ **noun** Music an extra note added to ornament a melody.

gra·cious /'grāsнəs/ ▶ **adjective** **1** polite, kind, and pleasant. **2** elegant in a way associated with upper-class status or wealth: *magazines devoted to gracious living*. **3** (in Christian belief) showing God's grace.

– SYNONYMS **courteous,** polite, civil, well mannered, tactful, diplomatic, kind, considerate, thoughtful, obliging, accommodating, hospitable.

▶ **exclamation** expressing polite surprise.
– DERIVATIVES **gra·cious·ly** adverb **gra·cious·ness** noun.

WORD TOOLKIT

gracious ...	elegant ...	stylish ...
host/hostess	style	clothes
smile	simplicity	shoes
hospitality	design	production
manners	dining	leather
gesture	dress	apartment
winner	room	decor
concession	home	sunglasses
reception	hotel	furniture

grack·le /'grakəl/ ▶ **noun** a songbird of the American blackbird family with glossy black plumage.

grad /grad/ ▶ **noun** informal term for **GRADUATE**.

gra·da·tion /grā'dāsнən/ ▶ **noun** **1** a scale of successive changes, stages, or degrees. **2** a stage in a such a scale.
– DERIVATIVES **gra·da·tion·al** adjective.

grade /grād/ ▶ **noun** **1** a specified level of rank, quality, proficiency, or value: *the worst grade of coffee*. **2** a mark indicating the quality of a student's work. **3** a class in a school comprising children grouped according to age or ability. **4** the steepness of a road or hill; gradient.

– SYNONYMS **1** *hotels within the same grade* **category,** class, classification, ranking, quality, grouping, group, bracket. **2** *his job is of the lowest grade* **rank,** level, standing, position, class, status, order, echelon. **3 mark,** score, assessment, evaluation, appraisal. **4 year,** class.

▶ **verb** **1** arrange people or things in groups according to quality, size, ability, etc.: *caviar is graded according to the size of its grains*. **2** pass gradually from one level to another. **3** reduce a road to an easier gradient.

– SYNONYMS **classify,** class, categorize, bracket, sort, group, arrange, pigeonhole, rank, evaluate, rate, value.

– PHRASES **make the grade** informal succeed.
– ORIGIN Latin *gradus* 'step.'

grade cross·ing ▶ **noun** a place where a railroad and a road cross at the same level.

grade point av·er·age ▶ **noun** (abbr.: **GPA**) an indication of a student's academic achievement arrived at by averaging grades where A=4, B=3, C=2, and D=1.

grad·er /'grādər/ ▶ **noun** **1** a person or thing that grades: *a certified beef grader*. **2** a wheeled machine for leveling the ground or making roads. **3** (in combination) a student in a specified grade in school: *a fifth grader*.

grade school ▶ **noun** elementary school.

gra·di·ent /'grādēənt/ ▶ **noun** **1** a sloping part of a road or railroad. **2** the degree to which the ground slopes. **3** a change in the magnitude of a property (e.g., temperature) observed in passing from one point or moment to another.

– SYNONYMS **slope,** incline, grade, hill, rise, ramp, bank.

– ORIGIN from **GRADE**.

grad·u·al /'grajōōəl/ ▶ **adjective 1** taking place in stages over an extended period. **2** (of a slope) not steep.

– SYNONYMS **1 slow,** steady, measured, unhurried, cautious, piecemeal, step-by-step, bit-by-bit, progressive, continuous. **2 gentle,** moderate, slight, easy.
– ANTONYMS abrupt, steep.

– DERIVATIVES **grad·u·al·ness** noun.
– ORIGIN Latin *gradualis*.

grad·u·al·ism /'grajōōə,lizəm/ ▶ **noun** a policy or theory of gradual rather than sudden change.
– DERIVATIVES **grad·u·al·ist** noun.

grad·u·al·ly /'grajōōəlē/ ▶ **adverb** in a gradual manner: *the icicles gradually got longer throughout the day | gradually add the flour mixture.*

– SYNONYMS **slowly,** steadily, slowly but surely, cautiously, gently, gingerly, piecemeal, bit by bit, by degrees, progressively, systematically.

grad·u·ate ▶ **noun** /'grajōōit/ a person who has been awarded a high-school diploma, a college degree, or a certificate of training. ▶ **verb** /'grajōō,āt/ **1** successfully complete high school, a college degree program, or a course of training. **2** (**graduate to**) move up to something more advanced. **3** arrange or mark out something in a scale in gradations. **4** change gradually.
– ORIGIN from Latin *graduare* 'take a degree.'

grad·u·ate school ▶ **noun** a division of a university offering advanced programs beyond the bachelor's degree.

grad·u·a·tion /,grajōō'āsʜən/ ▶ **noun 1** the receiving or conferring of an academic degree or diploma. **2** the ceremony at which degrees are conferred. **3** the action of dividing into degrees or other proportionate divisions on a graduated scale. **4** a mark on a container or instrument indicating a degree of quantity.

graf·fi·ti /grə'fētē/ ▶ **plural noun** (treated as sing. or pl.) writing or drawings on a surface in a public place. ▶ **verb** write or draw graffiti on a surface.
– DERIVATIVES **graf·fi·tist** noun.
– ORIGIN Italian.

graft[1] /graft/ ▶ **noun 1** a shoot or twig inserted into a slit on the trunk or stem of a living plant, from which it receives sap. **2** a piece of living body tissue that is transplanted surgically to replace diseased or damaged tissue. **3** an operation in which tissue is transplanted.

– SYNONYMS *a skin graft* **transplant,** implant.

▶ **verb 1** insert or transplant something as a graft. **2** add or attach to something else, especially inappropriately: *plate glass windows had been grafted onto an eighteenth-century building.*

– SYNONYMS **1 transplant,** implant. **2 splice,** join, insert, fix.

– ORIGIN Greek *graphion* 'writing implement.'

graft[2] informal ▶ **noun** bribery and other corrupt measures adopted to gain power or money in politics or business.
– DERIVATIVES **graft·er** noun.
– ORIGIN unknown.

Grail /grāl/ (also **Holy Grail**) ▶ **noun** (in medieval legend) the cup or platter used by Jesus at the Last Supper, especially as the object of quests by knights.
– ORIGIN Old French *graal*.

grain /grān/ ▶ **noun 1** wheat or other cultivated cereal used as food. **2** a single seed or fruit of a cereal. **3** a small hard particle of a substance such as sand. **4** the smallest unit of weight in the troy and avoirdupois systems. **5** the smallest possible amount: *there wasn't a grain of truth in the rumors.* **6** the lengthwise arrangement of fibers, particles, or layers in wood, paper, rock, etc.

– SYNONYMS **1 kernel,** seed. **2 granule,** particle, speck, bit, scrap, crumb, fragment, morsel. **3 trace,** hint, tinge, suggestion, shadow, soupçon, ounce, iota, jot, scrap, shred; informal smidgen. **4 texture,** weave, pattern, nap.

– DERIVATIVES **grained** adjective.
– PHRASES **against the grain** contrary to one's nature or instinct.
– ORIGIN Latin *granum*.

grain·y /'grānē/ ▶ **adjective** (**grainier, grainiest**) **1** consisting of grains; granular. **2** (of a photograph) showing visible grains of emulsion.
– DERIVATIVES **grain·i·ness** noun.

gram[1] /gram/ (Brit. also **gramme**) ▶ **noun** a metric unit of mass equal to one thousandth of a kilogram.
– ORIGIN Greek *gramma* 'small weight.'

gram[2] ▶ **noun** informal grandmother.

gram·mar /'gramər/ ▶ **noun 1** the whole structure of a language, including the rules for the way words are formed and their relationship to each other in a sentence. **2** knowledge and use of the rules or principles of grammar: *bad grammar.* **3** a book on grammar.
– ORIGIN from Greek *grammatikē tekhnē* 'art of letters.'

gram·mar·i·an /grə'me(ə)rēən/ ▶ **noun** a person who studies and writes about grammar.

gram·mar school ▶ **noun 1** another term for **ELEMENTARY SCHOOL**. **2** (in the UK, especially formerly) a state secondary school that admits students on the basis of their ability.

gram·mat·i·cal /grə'matikəl/ ▶ **adjective** relating to or following the rules of grammar.
– DERIVATIVES **gram·mat·i·cal·i·ty** /-,mati'kalitē/ noun **gram·mat·i·cal·ly** adverb.

Gram·my /'gramē/ ▶ **noun** (pl. **Grammys** or **Grammies**) an annual award given by the American National Academy of Recording Arts and Sciences for achievement in the music industry.
– ORIGIN blend of **GRAMOPHONE** and **EMMY**.

gram·o·phone /'gramə,fōn/ ▶ **noun** dated, chiefly Brit. a record player.
– ORIGIN formed by reversing the elements of *phonogram* 'sound recording.'

gram·pus /'grampəs/ ▶ **noun** (pl. **grampuses**) a killer whale or other dolphinlike sea animal.
– ORIGIN Old French *grapois* (influenced by **GRAND**).

gra·na·ry /'grānərē, 'gran-/ ▶ **noun** (pl. **granaries**) **1** a storehouse for threshed grain. **2** a region growing large quantities of cereal.
– ORIGIN Latin *granarium*.

grand /grand/ ▶ **adjective 1** magnificent and impressive. **2** large or ambitious in scope or scale: *a grand plan for converting dying neighborhoods into thriving communities.* **3** of the highest importance or rank. **4** dignified, noble, or proud. **5** informal excellent. **6** (in combination) (in names of family relationships) referring to one generation removed in ascent or descent: *a grand-niece.*

– SYNONYMS **1 magnificent,** imposing, impressive, awe-inspiring, splendid, resplendent, majestic, monumental, palatial, stately, upscale, upmarket; informal fancy, posh, swish. **2 ambitious,** bold, epic, big, extravagant. **3 august,** distinguished, illustrious, eminent, venerable, dignified, proud. **4 excellent,** marvelous, splendid, first-class, first-rate, wonderful, outstanding; informal superb, terrific, great, super; Brit. informal **brilliant.**
– ANTONYMS humble, poor.

▶ **noun 1** (pl. same) informal a thousand dollars or pounds. **2** a grand piano.
– DERIVATIVES **grand·ly** adverb **grand·ness** noun.
– ORIGIN Latin *grandis* 'full-grown, great.'

grand·child /ˈgran(d)ˌCHīld/ ▶ **noun** (pl. **grandchildren** /ˈgran(d)ˌCHildrən/) a child of one's son or daughter.

grand·dad /ˈgranˌdad/ (also **grandad, grandaddy**) ▶ **noun** informal one's grandfather. ▶ **adjective** (of a shirt) having a collar in the form of a narrow upright band.

grand·daugh·ter /ˈgranˌdôtər/ ▶ **noun** a daughter of one's son or daughter.

grand duke ▶ **noun 1** (in Europe, especially formerly) a prince or nobleman ruling over a small independent country. **2** historical a son (or grandson) of a Russian tsar.

grande dame /ˈgran ˈdam, ˈgrän ˈdäm/ ▶ **noun** a woman who is influential within a particular area of activity.
– ORIGIN French, 'grand lady.'

gran·dee /granˈdē/ ▶ **noun 1** a Spanish or Portuguese nobleman of the highest rank. **2** a high-ranking or eminent man.
– ORIGIN from Spanish and Portuguese *grande* 'grand.'

gran·deur /ˈgranjər, ˈgranˌdyo͝or/ ▶ **noun 1** the quality of being grand and impressive: *the wild grandeur of the mountains.* **2** high rank or social importance.

– SYNONYMS **splendor,** magnificence, glory, resplendence, majesty, greatness, stateliness, pomp, ceremony.

grand·fa·ther /ˈgran(d)ˌfäT͟Hər/ ▶ **noun 1** the father of one's father or mother. **2** a founder or originator of something. ▶ **verb** exempt from a new law or regulation: *smokers who worked here before the ban have been grandfathered.*

grand·fa·ther clause ▶ **noun** a clause exempting certain classes of people or things from the requirements of a new piece of legislation.

grand·fa·ther clock ▶ **noun** a clock in a tall freestanding wooden case, driven by weights.

Grand Gui·gnol /grän gēnˈyôl/ ▶ **noun** dramatic entertainment of a sensational or horrific nature.
– ORIGIN *Guignol* was the bloodthirsty chief character in a French puppet show; the entertainment originated at the *Grand Guignol* theater in Paris.

gran·di·flo·ra /ˌgrandəˈflôrə/ ▶ **adjective** (of a cultivated plant) bearing large flowers.
– ORIGIN from Latin *grandis* 'great' + *flos* 'flower.'

gran·dil·o·quent /granˈdiləkwənt/ ▶ **adjective** using long or difficult words in order to impress.
– DERIVATIVES **gran·dil·o·quence** noun **gran·dil·o·quent·ly** adverb.
– ORIGIN Latin *grandiloquus* 'grand-speaking.'

gran·di·ose /ˈgrandēˌōs, ˌgrandēˈōs/ ▶ **adjective** very large or ambitious, especially in a way that is intended to impress: *the city was built on a vast and grandiose scale.*
– DERIVATIVES **gran·di·ose·ly** adverb **gran·di·os·i·ty** /ˌgrandēˈäsitē/ noun.
– ORIGIN Italian *grandioso.*

grand ju·ry ▶ **noun** Law a jury selected to examine the validity of an accusation prior to trial.

grand lar·ce·ny ▶ **noun** Law theft of personal property having a value above a legally specified amount.

grand·ma /ˈgran(d)ˌmä, ˈgram-/ ▶ **noun** informal one's grandmother.

grand mal /ˌgran(d) ˈmäl, ˈmal/ ▶ **noun** a serious form of epilepsy with muscle spasms and prolonged loss of consciousness. Compare with **PETIT MAL.**
– ORIGIN French, 'great sickness.'

grand mas·ter ▶ **noun 1** (also **grandmaster**) a chess player of the highest class. **2** (**Grand Master**) the head of an order of chivalry or of Freemasons.

grand·moth·er /ˈgran(d)ˌməT͟Hər/ ▶ **noun** the mother of one's father or mother.

grand op·er·a ▶ **noun** an opera on a serious theme in which the entire libretto (including dialogue) is sung.

grand·pa /ˈgran(d)ˌpä, ˈgram-/ ▶ **noun** informal one's grandfather.

grand·par·ent /ˈgran(d)ˌpe(ə)rənt, -ˌpar-/ ▶ **noun** a grandmother or grandfather.

grand pi·an·o ▶ **noun** a large full-toned piano that has the body, strings, and soundboard arranged horizontally and is supported by three legs.

Grand Prix /ˌgräN ˈprē, ˌgran/ ▶ **noun** (pl. **Grands Prix** pronunc. same) a race forming part of an auto-racing or motorcycling world championship.
– ORIGIN French, 'great or chief prize.'

grand slam ▶ **noun 1** the winning of each of a group of major championships or matches in a particular sport in the same year. **2** Bridge the bidding and winning of all thirteen tricks.

grand·son /ˈgran(d)ˌsən/ ▶ **noun** the son of one's son or daughter.

grand·stand /ˈgran(d)ˌstand/ ▶ **noun** the main spectator area at a racetrack or sports arena. ▶ **verb** (usu. as n. **grandstanding**) derogatory seek to attract applause or favorable attention from spectators or the media.

grand to·tal ▶ **noun** the final amount after everything is added up.

grand tour ▶ **noun 1** historical a cultural tour of Europe formerly undertaken by upper-class young men. **2** a guided tour of a building, exhibit, or institution.

grange /grānj/ ▶ **noun 1** (**the Grange**) in the US, a farmers' association that sponsors community activities and political lobbying. **2** Brit. a country house with farm buildings attached. **3** old use a barn.
– ORIGIN Old French.

gran·ite /ˈgranit/ ▶ **noun** a very hard rock consisting mainly of quartz, mica, and feldspar.
– DERIVATIVES **gra·nit·ic** /grəˈnitik/ adjective.
– ORIGIN from Italian *granito* 'grained.'

gran·ny /ˈgranē/ (also **grannie**) ▶ **noun** (pl. **grannies**) informal one's grandmother.

gran·ny knot ▶ **noun** a square knot with the ends crossed the wrong way and therefore liable to slip.

Gran·ny Smith ▶ **noun** a bright green variety of apple with crisp, tart flesh.
– ORIGIN named after Maria Ann (*Granny*) *Smith*, who first produced such apples.

gra·no·la /grə'nōlə/ ▶ **noun** a kind of breakfast cereal or snack food consisting typically of rolled oats, honey, nuts, and dried fruits.

grant /grant/ ▶ **verb 1** agree to give something to someone or allow them to do something. **2** give something formally or legally to: *someone with a fear of torture would be granted asylum*. **3** admit to someone that something is true.

– SYNONYMS **1** *he granted them leave of absence* **allow,** permit, agree to, accord, afford, vouchsafe. **2** *he granted them $20,000* **give,** award, bestow on, confer on, present with, endow with. **3 admit,** accept, concede, allow, appreciate, recognize, acknowledge, confess.
– ANTONYMS refuse, deny.

▶ **noun 1** a sum of money given by a government or public body for a particular purpose. **2** the action of granting something.

– SYNONYMS **award,** bursary, endowment, scholarship, allowance, subsidy, contribution, handout, donation, gift.

– DERIVATIVES **gran·tee** /gran'tē/ noun **gran·tor** /gran'tôr, 'grantər/ (also **granter**) noun.
– PHRASES **take someone/thing for granted 1** fail to appreciate someone or something as a result of overfamiliarity. **2** assume that something is true.
– ORIGIN Old French *granter* 'consent to support.'

CHOOSE THE RIGHT WORD

See **GIVE**.

grant·ed /'grantid/ ▶ **adverb** admittedly; it is true. ▶ **conjunction** (**granted that**) even assuming that.

gran·u·lar /'granyələr/ ▶ **adjective 1** resembling or consisting of granules. **2** having a roughened surface.
– DERIVATIVES **gran·u·lar·i·ty** /,granyə'laritē/ noun.

gran·u·lat·ed /'granyə,lātid/ ▶ **adjective 1** in the form of granules. **2** technical having a roughened surface.
– DERIVATIVES **gran·u·la·tion** /,granyə'lāsʜən/ noun.

gran·ule /'granyo͞ol/ ▶ **noun** a small hard particle of a substance.
– ORIGIN Latin *granulum* 'little grain.'

grape /grāp/ ▶ **noun** a green, purple, or black berry growing in clusters on a vine, eaten as fruit and used in making wine.
– DERIVATIVES **grap·ey** adjective.
– ORIGIN Old French, 'bunch of grapes.'

grape·fruit /'grāp,fro͞ot/ ▶ **noun** (pl. same) a large round yellow citrus fruit with a slightly bitter taste.

grape hy·a·cinth ▶ **noun** a small plant with clusters of small globular blue flowers.

grape·shot /'grāp,sʜät/ ▶ **noun** historical ammunition consisting of a number of small iron balls fired together from a cannon.

grape·vine /'grāp,vīn/ ▶ **noun 1** a vine bearing grapes. **2** (**the grapevine**) informal the spreading of information through rumor and informal conversation: *I heard on the grapevine that he'd been very impressive*.

graph /graf/ ▶ **noun** a diagram showing the relation between two or more sets of numbers or quantities, typically plotted along a pair of lines at right angles.
– ORIGIN abbreviation of *graphic formula*.

-graph ▶ **combining form 1** referring to something written or drawn in a specified way: *autograph*. **2** referring to an instrument that records something: *seismograph*.
– ORIGIN from Greek *graphos* 'written, writing.'

graph·ic /'grafik/ ▶ **adjective 1** relating to visual art, especially involving drawing, engraving, or lettering. **2** giving vividly explicit detail: *graphic descriptions of sexual practices*. **3** in the form of a graph.

– SYNONYMS **1 visual,** pictorial, illustrative, diagrammatic. **2 vivid,** explicit, detailed, realistic, descriptive, powerful, colorful, lurid, shocking.
– ANTONYMS vague.

▶ **noun** a visual image displayed on a computer screen or stored as data.
– ORIGIN Greek *graphē* 'writing, drawing.'

WORD TOOLKIT

graphic ...	picturesque ...	vivid ...
image	village	memory
detail	town	color
violence	setting	description
depiction	view	account
representation	landscape	imagination
scene	spot	dream
portrayal	location	reminder
footage	harbor	example

graph·i·cal /'grafikəl/ ▶ **adjective 1** relating to or in the form of a graph. **2** relating to visual art or computer graphics.
– DERIVATIVES **graph·i·cal·ly** adverb.

graph·ic arts ▶ **plural noun** visual arts based on the use of line and tone rather than three-dimensional work or the use of color.

graph·ic de·sign ▶ **noun** the art of combining words and pictures in advertisements, magazines, or books.

graph·ic nov·el ▶ **noun** a novel in comic-strip format.

graph·ics /'grafiks/ ▶ **plural noun** (usu. treated as sing.) the use of drawings, designs, or pictures to illustrate books, magazines, etc.

graph·ite /'gra,fīt/ ▶ **noun** a gray form of carbon used as pencil lead and as a solid lubricant in machinery.
– DERIVATIVES **gra·phit·ic** /grə'fitik/ adjective.
– ORIGIN from Greek *graphein* 'write.'

graph·ol·o·gy /gra'fäləjē/ ▶ **noun** the study of handwriting, especially as used to analyze a person's character.
– DERIVATIVES **graph·o·log·i·cal** /,grafə'läjikəl/ adjective **graph·ol·o·gist** noun.
– ORIGIN from Greek *graphē* 'writing.'

graph pa·per ▶ **noun** paper printed with a network of small squares, used for drawing graphs or other diagrams.

-graphy ▶ **combining form** forming nouns referring to. **1** a descriptive science: *geography*. **2** a technique of producing images: *radiography*. **3** a style of writing or drawing: *calligraphy*. **4** writing about a specified subject: *hagiography*. **5** a written or printed list: *filmography*.
– DERIVATIVES **-graphic** combining form.
– ORIGIN Greek *-graphia* 'writing.'

grap·nel /'grapnəl/ ▶ **noun** a device with iron claws, attached to a rope and used for dragging or grasping.
– ORIGIN Old French *grapon*.

grap·ple /'grapəl/ ▶ **verb 1** take a firm hold of someone and struggle to overcome them. **2** (**grapple with**) struggle to deal with or understand: *Europe is grappling with a fuel crisis*.

– SYNONYMS **1 wrestle,** struggle, tussle, scuffle, battle. **2 deal,** cope, get to grips, tackle, confront, face.

– DERIVATIVES **grap·pler** noun.
– ORIGIN from Old French *grapil* 'small hook.'

grasp /grasp/ ▸ **verb 1** seize and hold someone or something firmly. **2** take an opportunity eagerly. **3** understand something fully.

– SYNONYMS **1 grip,** clutch, clasp, clench, squeeze, catch, seize, grab, snatch. **2 understand,** comprehend, take in, see, apprehend, assimilate, absorb; informal get.

▸ **noun 1** a firm grip. **2** a person's capacity to achieve or understand something: *the top job was within her grasp.*

– SYNONYMS **1 grip,** hold, squeeze. **2 reach,** scope, power, range, sights. **3 understanding,** comprehension, awareness, grip, knowledge, mastery, command.

– DERIVATIVES **grasp·a·ble** adjective **grasp·er** noun.
– ORIGIN perhaps related to **GROPE**.

grasp·ing /'graspiNG/ ▸ **adjective** greedy for wealth.

– SYNONYMS **greedy,** acquisitive, avaricious, rapacious, mercenary, materialistic; informal tightfisted, tight, money-grubbing.

grass /gräs/ ▸ **noun 1** vegetation consisting of short plants with long, narrow leaves. **2** ground covered with grass. **3** informal marijuana. **4** Brit. informal a police informer. ▸ **verb 1** cover an area with grass. **2** (often **grass on**) Brit. informal inform the police of someone's criminal activity.
– PHRASES **not let the grass grow under one's feet** not delay in taking action. **put someone/thing out to grass 1** put an animal out to graze. **2** informal force someone to retire.
– ORIGIN Old English; sense 4 is perhaps related to rhyming slang *grasshopper* 'copper.'

grass·hop·per /'gras,häpər/ ▸ **noun** an insect with long hind legs that are used for jumping and for producing a chirping sound.

grass·land /'gras,land/ ▸ **noun** (also **grasslands**) a large area of grass-covered land, especially one used for grazing.

grass roots ▸ **plural noun** the most basic level of an activity or organization.

grass wid·ow ▸ **noun** a woman whose husband is away often or for a long time.
– ORIGIN first referring to an unmarried woman with a child: perhaps from the idea of a couple having lain on the grass instead of in bed.

grass·y /'grasē/ ▸ **adjective** (**grassier, grassiest**) covered with or resembling grass.

grate[1] /grāt/ ▸ **verb 1** shred food by rubbing it on a grater. **2** make an unpleasant scraping sound. **3** have an irritating effect: *the fly's buzzing grated on my nerves.*

– SYNONYMS **1 shred,** pulverize, mince, grind, crush, crumble. **2 grind,** rub, rasp, scrape, jar, creak.

– ORIGIN Old French *grater.*

grate[2] ▸ **noun 1** a metal frame for holding fuel in a fireplace. **2** the recess of a fireplace.
– ORIGIN Old French.

grate·ful /'grātfəl/ ▸ **adjective** feeling or showing one's appreciation of something that has been done for one.

– SYNONYMS **thankful,** appreciative, indebted, obliged, in someone's debt, beholden.

– DERIVATIVES **grate·ful·ly** adverb.
– ORIGIN Latin *gratus* 'pleasing, thankful.'

grat·er /'grātər/ ▸ **noun** a device having a surface covered with sharp-edged holes, used for grating food.

grat·i·fi·ca·tion /,gratəfi'kāsHən/ ▸ **noun 1** pleasure, especially when gained from the satisfaction of a desire: *a thirst for sexual gratification.* **2** a source of pleasure.

grat·i·fy /'gratə,fī/ ▸ **verb** (**gratifies, gratifying, gratified**) **1** give pleasure or satisfaction to: *he was gratified that they liked the book.* **2** indulge or satisfy a desire.
– ORIGIN Latin *gratificari* 'give or do as a favor.'

grat·in /'grätn, 'gratn/ ▸ **noun** a casserole with a light browned crust of breadcrumbs or melted cheese.
– ORIGIN French.

grat·ing[1] /'grātiNG/ ▸ **adjective 1** sounding harsh and unpleasant. **2** irritating: *his grating confrontational personality.*
– DERIVATIVES **grat·ing·ly** adverb.

grat·ing[2] ▸ **noun** a framework of parallel or crossed bars that covers an opening.

grat·is /'gratis/ ▸ **adverb & adjective** free of charge.
– ORIGIN Latin.

grat·i·tude /'gratə,t(y)o͞od/ ▸ **noun** the quality of being grateful; appreciation of kindness.

– SYNONYMS **thanks,** gratefulness, thankfulness, appreciation, indebtedness, recognition, acknowledgment.

– ORIGIN Latin *gratitudo.*

gra·tu·i·tous /grə't(y)o͞oitəs/ ▸ **adjective 1** having no justifiable reason or purpose: *studios were under pressure to tone down gratuitous violence.* **2** free of charge.

– SYNONYMS **unjustified,** uncalled for, unwarranted, unprovoked, undue; indefensible, unjustifiable; needless, unnecessary, inessential, unmerited, groundless, senseless, wanton, indiscriminate; excessive, immoderate, inordinate, inappropriate.
– ANTONYMS necessary, paid.

– DERIVATIVES **gra·tu·i·tous·ly** adverb.
– ORIGIN Latin *gratuitus* 'given freely, spontaneous.'

gra·tu·i·ty /grə't(y)o͞oitē/ ▸ **noun** (pl. **gratuities**) formal a sum of money given to someone who has provided a service; a tip.
– ORIGIN Latin *gratuitas* 'gift.'

CHOOSE THE RIGHT WORD

See **PRESENT**[3].

gra·ve[1] /grāv/ ▸ **noun 1** a hole dug in the ground for a coffin or a corpse. **2** (**the grave**) death.

– SYNONYMS **tomb,** burial place, last resting place, vault, mausoleum, sepulcher.

– PHRASES **dig one's own grave** do something foolish that causes one's downfall. **turn in one's grave** (of a dead person) be likely to have been angry or distressed about something had they been alive.
– ORIGIN Old English.

grave[2] ▸ **adjective 1** giving cause for alarm or concern: *he was in grave danger.* **2** solemn or serious: *her face was grave.*

– SYNONYMS **1 serious,** important, weighty, profound, significant, momentous, critical, urgent, pressing, dire, terrible, dreadful. **2 solemn,** serious, sober, unsmiling, grim, somber, dour.
– ANTONYMS trivial, lighthearted.

– DERIVATIVES **grave·ly** adverb.
– ORIGIN Latin *gravis* 'heavy, serious.'

grave[3] ▶ **verb** (past part. **graven** or **graved**) **1** literary fix something firmly in the mind. **2** old use engrave something on a surface.
– ORIGIN Old English, 'dig.'

grave ac·cent /gräv, grāv/ ▶ **noun** a mark (`) placed over a vowel in some languages to indicate a change in its sound quality.
– ORIGIN French *grave* 'heavy, serious.'

grave·dig·ger /ˈgrāvˌdigər/ ▶ **noun** a person who digs graves.

grav·el /ˈgravəl/ ▶ **noun** a loose mixture of small stones and coarse sand, used for paths and roads. ▶ **verb** (**gravels, graveling, graveled**) cover something with gravel.
– ORIGIN Old French.

gra·vel·ly /ˈgravəlē/ ▶ **adjective 1** resembling, containing, or consisting of gravel. **2** (of a voice) deep and rough-sounding.

grav·en im·age ▶ **noun** a carved figure of a god used as an idol.
– ORIGIN with reference to the Book of Exodus, chapter 20.

grav·er /ˈgrāvər/ ▶ **noun** an engraving tool.

Graves' dis·ease ▶ **noun** a swelling of the neck and protrusion of the eyes resulting from hyperthyroidism.

grave·stone /ˈgrāvˌstōn/ ▶ **noun** an inscribed headstone marking a grave.

grave·yard /ˈgrāvˌyärd/ ▶ **noun** a burial ground, especially one beside a church.

– SYNONYMS **cemetery,** churchyard, burial ground, necropolis, memorial park; informal boneyard; historical potter's field; archaic God's acre.

grave·yard shift ▶ **noun** a work shift that runs from midnight to 8 a.m.

gra·vim·e·ter /grəˈvimitər/ ▶ **noun** an instrument for measuring the force of gravity at different places.

grav·i·met·ric /ˌgravəˈmetrik/ ▶ **adjective 1** relating to the measurement of weight. **2** relating to the measurement of gravity.

grav·i·tas /ˈgraviˌtäs/ ▶ **noun** a dignified and serious manner.
– ORIGIN Latin.

grav·i·tate /ˈgraviˌtāt/ ▶ **verb 1** be drawn toward a place, person, or thing: *his children gravitated toward careers in music.* **2** Physics move, or tend to move, toward a center of gravity.

grav·i·ta·tion /ˌgraviˈtāsʜən/ ▶ **noun 1** movement, or a tendency to move, toward a center of gravity. **2** Physics gravity.
– DERIVATIVES **grav·i·ta·tion·al** adjective **grav·i·ta·tion·al·ly** adverb.

grav·i·ty /ˈgravitē/ ▶ **noun 1** the force that attracts a body toward the center of the earth, or toward any other physical body having mass. **2** extreme importance or seriousness: *the gravity of environmental crimes.* **3** a solemn or serious manner.

– SYNONYMS **1 seriousness,** importance, significance, weight, consequence, magnitude, acuteness, urgency, dreadfulness. **2 solemnity,** seriousness, sobriety, severity, grimness, somberness, dourness.

– ORIGIN Latin *gravitas* 'weight, seriousness.'

grav·lax /ˈgrävˌläks/ ▶ **noun** a Scandinavian dish of dry-cured salmon marinated in herbs.
– ORIGIN Swedish.

gra·vure /grəˈvyo͝or/ ▶ **noun** short for **PHOTOGRAVURE**.

gra·vy /ˈgrāvē/ ▶ **noun** (pl. **gravies**) a sauce made by adding stock, flour, and seasoning to the fat and juices that come out of meat during cooking.
– ORIGIN perhaps from Old French *grané*.

gra·vy boat ▶ **noun** a long, narrow vessel used for serving gravy.

gra·vy train ▶ **noun** informal a situation in which someone can easily make a lot of money.

gray /grā/ (also chiefly Brit. **grey**) ▶ **adjective 1** of a color between black and white, as of ashes or lead. **2** (of hair) turning gray or white with age. **3** (of the weather) cloudy and dull; without sun. **4** dull and nondescript: *gray, faceless men.* **5** not accounted for in official statistics: *the gray economy.*

– SYNONYMS **1** silvery, gunmetal, slate, charcoal, smoky. **2 cloudy,** overcast, dull, dark, sunless, murky, gloomy, cheerless. **3 pale,** wan, ashen, pasty, pallid, colorless, waxen. **4 characterless,** colorless, nondescript, flat, bland, dull, boring, tedious, monotonous. **5** *a gray area* **ambiguous,** doubtful, unclear, uncertain, indefinite, debatable.

▶ **noun** gray color.
▶ **verb** (especially of hair) become gray.
– DERIVATIVES **gray·ish** adjective **gray·ness** noun.
– ORIGIN Old English.

gray a·re·a ▶ **noun** an area of activity that does not easily fit into an existing category and is difficult to deal with.

gray·beard /ˈgrāˌbi(ə)rd/ ▶ **noun** humorous an old man.

gray·ling /ˈgrālɪɴɢ/ ▶ **noun** an edible silvery-gray freshwater fish with horizontal violet stripes.

gray mat·ter ▶ **noun 1** the darker tissue of the brain and spinal cord. **2** informal intelligence.

gray seal ▶ **noun** a large North Atlantic seal with a spotted grayish coat.

gray squir·rel ▶ **noun** a tree squirrel with mainly gray fur, native to eastern North America and introduced elsewhere.

gray wa·ter ▶ **noun** Ecology the relatively clean wastewater from baths, sinks, washing machines, and kitchen appliances.

graze[1] /grāz/ ▶ **verb 1** (of cattle, sheep, etc.) eat grass in a field. **2** informal eat frequent snacks at irregular intervals.

– SYNONYMS **feed,** eat, crop, nibble, browse.

– DERIVATIVES **graz·er** noun.
– ORIGIN Old English.

graze[2] ▶ **verb 1** scrape and break the skin on part of the body. **2** touch something lightly in passing.

– SYNONYMS **1 scrape,** skin, scratch, chafe, scuff, rasp. **2 touch,** brush, shave, skim, kiss, scrape, clip, glance off.

▶ **noun** a slight injury caused by grazing the skin.

– SYNONYMS **scratch,** scrape, abrasion.

– ORIGIN perhaps from **GRAZE**[1].

graz·ing /ˈgrāzɪɴɢ/ ▶ **noun** grassland suitable for use as pasture.

GRE ▶ **abbreviation** Graduate Record Examination, a set of tests usually required of applicants to US graduate schools in fields other than business, law, and medicine.

grease /grēs/ ▶ **noun 1** a thick oily substance, especially one used to lubricate machinery. **2** animal fat used or produced in cooking.

– SYNONYMS **oil,** fat, lubricant.

▶ **verb** smear or lubricate something with grease.
– PHRASES **grease the palm of** informal bribe someone. **like greased lightning** informal very rapidly.
– ORIGIN Old French *graisse*.

grease gun ▶ **noun** a device for pumping grease under pressure to a particular point.

grease mon·key ▶ **noun** derogatory or humorous an auto mechanic.

grease·paint /ˈgrēsˌpānt/ ▶ **noun** a waxy substance used as makeup by actors.

greas·er /ˈgrēsər, -zər/ ▶ **noun 1** informal a rough young man, especially one who greases back his hair and who consorts with a tough group. **2** an auto mechanic or an unskilled engineer on a ship.

greas·y /ˈgrēsē, -zē/ ▶ **adjective** (**greasier, greasiest**) **1** covered with or resembling grease. **2** polite or friendly in a way that seems excessive and insincere.

– SYNONYMS **oily,** fatty, buttery, oleaginous, slippery, slick, slimy, slithery; informal slippy.

– DERIVATIVES **greas·i·ly** adverb **greas·i·ness** noun.

greas·y spoon ▶ **noun** informal a shabby cafe serving inexpensive fried meals.

great /grāt/ ▶ **adjective 1** much higher than average in amount, extent, or intensity. **2** much higher than average in ability, quality, or importance: *a great Italian composer*. **3** informal excellent. **4** used to emphasize a description: *I was a great fan of Hank's*. **5** (**Greater**) referring to an area that includes the center of a city and a large urban area around it: *Greater Los Angeles*. **6** (in combination) (in names of family relationships) referring to one degree further removed upward or downward: *a great-aunt*.

– SYNONYMS **1 considerable,** substantial, significant, serious, exceptional, extraordinary. **2 large,** big, extensive, expansive, broad, wide, vast, immense, huge, enormous, massive; informal humongous, whopping, ginormous. **3 prominent,** eminent, distinguished, illustrious, celebrated, acclaimed, admired, esteemed, renowned, notable, famous, well known, leading, top, major. **4 magnificent,** imposing, impressive, awe-inspiring, grand, splendid, majestic. **5 expert,** skillful, skilled, adept, accomplished, talented, fine, masterly, master, brilliant, virtuoso, marvelous, outstanding, first-class, superb; informal crack, class. **6 keen,** eager, enthusiastic, devoted, ardent, fanatical, passionate, dedicated, committed. **7 enjoyable,** delightful, lovely, excellent, marvelous, wonderful, fine, splendid; informal terrific, fantastic, fabulous, super, cool; Brit. informal brilliant.
– ANTONYMS little, small, minor, modest.

▶ **noun** a famous and successful person.
▶ **adverb** informal very well.
– ORIGIN Old English.

great ape ▶ **noun** a large ape of a family closely related to humans, including the gorilla and chimpanzees.

great-aunt ▶ **noun** an aunt of one's father or mother.

Great Dane ▶ **noun** a very large and powerful dog with short hair.

great di·vide ▶ **noun 1** a distinction regarded as significant that is difficult to ignore or overcome: *the great divide between workers and management*. **2** an event, date, or place regarded as a point of significant and irrevocable change or difference: *to our parents the war was the great divide*.

great horned owl ▶ **noun** a large owl found throughout North and South America, with hornlike ear tufts.

great·ly /ˈgrātlē/ ▶ **adverb** very much.

– SYNONYMS **very much,** extremely, considerably, substantially, significantly, markedly, seriously, materially, enormously, vastly, immensely, tremendously, mightily.

great-neph·ew ▶ **noun** a son of one's nephew or niece.

great·ness /ˈgrātnəs/ ▶ **noun** the quality of being great, distinguished, or eminent.

– SYNONYMS **1** *a child destined for greatness* **eminence,** distinction, celebrity, fame, prominence, renown, importance. **2** *her greatness as a writer* **brilliance,** genius, prowess, talent, expertise, mastery, artistry, skill, proficiency, flair.

great-niece ▶ **noun** a daughter of one's nephew or niece.

great room ▶ **noun** a large room in a modern house that combines features of a living room with those of a dining room or family room.

great-un·cle ▶ **noun** an uncle of one's mother or father.

Great War ▶ **noun** World War I.

greave /grēv/ ▶ **noun** historical a piece of armor for the shin.
– ORIGIN Old French *greve* 'shin, greave.'

grebe /grēb/ ▶ **noun** a diving waterbird with a long neck and a very short tail.
– ORIGIN French.

Gre·cian /ˈgrēsʜən/ ▶ **adjective** relating to ancient Greece, especially its architecture.

Greco- (also **Graeco-**) ▶ **combining form** Greek; Greek and ...: *Greco-Roman*.
– ORIGIN Latin *Graecus* 'Greek.'

greed /grēd/ ▶ **noun 1** a strong and selfish desire for possessions, wealth, or power. **2** a desire to eat more food than is necessary.

– SYNONYMS **1 avarice,** acquisitiveness, covetousness, materialism, mercenariness; informal money-grubbing. **2 gluttony,** hunger, voracity, self-indulgence; informal piggishness. **3 desire,** appetite, hunger, thirst, craving, longing, yearning, hankering; informal itch.
– ANTONYMS generosity, temperance, indifference.

greed·y /ˈgrēdē/ ▶ **adjective** (**greedier, greediest**) **1** having an excessive desire for food. **2** having or showing a strong and selfish desire for wealth or power: *people driven from their land by greedy developers*.

– SYNONYMS **1 gluttonous,** ravenous, voracious; informal piggish, piggy. **2 avaricious,** acquisitive, covetous, grasping, materialistic, mercenary; informal money-grubbing.

– DERIVATIVES **greed·i·ly** adverb **greed·i·ness** noun.
– ORIGIN Old English.

CHOOSE THE RIGHT WORD

greedy, acquisitive, covetous, avaricious, rapacious, gluttonous

The desire for money and the things it can buy is often associated with Americans. But not all Americans are

greedy, which implies an insatiable desire to possess or acquire something, beyond what one needs or deserves (*greedy for profits*). Someone who is *greedy* for food might be called **gluttonous**, which emphasizes consumption as well as desire (*a gluttonous appetite for sweets*), but *greedy* is a derogatory term only when the object of longing is itself evil or when it cannot be possessed without harm to oneself or others (*a reporter greedy for information*). A *greedy* child may grow up to be an **avaricious** adult, which implies a fanatical greediness for money or other valuables. **Rapacious** is an even stronger term, with an emphasis on taking things by force (*so rapacious in his desire for land that he forced dozens of families from their homes*). **Acquisitive**, on the other hand, is a more neutral word suggesting a willingness to exert effort in acquiring things (*an acquisitive woman who filled her house with antiques and artwork*), and not necessarily material things (*a probing, acquisitive mind*). **Covetous**, in contrast to *acquisitive*, implies an intense desire for something as opposed to the act of acquiring or possessing it. It is often associated with the Ten Commandments (*Thou shalt not covet thy neighbor's wife*) and suggests a longing for something that rightfully belongs to another.

Greek /grēk/ ▶ **noun** **1** a person from Greece. **2** the ancient or modern language of Greece. ▶ **adjective** relating to Greece.
– PHRASES **it's all Greek to me** informal I can't understand it at all.

green /grēn/ ▶ **adjective** **1** of the color between blue and yellow in the spectrum; colored like grass. **2** covered with grass or other vegetation. **3** (**Green**) concerned with or supporting protection of the environment. **4** (of a plant or fruit) young or unripe. **5** inexperienced or naive. **6** in an untreated or original state; not cured, seasoned, etc.

– SYNONYMS **1** olive green, pea green, emerald green, lime green, avocado, pistachio, jade. **2** **verdant,** grassy, leafy. **3** **environmental,** ecological, conservationist, eco-, eco-friendly. **4** **inexperienced,** callow, raw, unseasoned, untried, naive, innocent, unworldly; informal wet behind the ears.

▶ **noun** **1** green color or material. **2** a piece of common grassy land, especially in the center of a town or village. **3** an area of smooth, very short grass immediately surrounding a hole on a golf course. **4** (**greens**) green vegetables. **5** (**Green**) a member or supporter of an environmentalist group or party.
▶ **verb** **1** make or become green. **2** make something less harmful to the environment.
– DERIVATIVES **green·ish** adjective **green·ness** noun.
– PHRASES **the green-eyed monster** jealousy personified. [from Shakespeare's *Othello*.]
– ORIGIN Old English.

green au·dit ▶ **noun** an assessment of a business as regards its observance of practices that seek to minimize harm to the environment.

green·back /ˈgrēnˌbak/ ▶ **noun** informal a dollar.

green bean ▶ **noun** the immature pod of any of various bean plants, eaten as a vegetable.

green belt ▶ **noun** an area of open land around a city, on which building is restricted.

Green Be·ret ▶ **noun** informal a member of the US Army Special Forces, or a British commando.

green card ▶ **noun** a permit that allows a foreign national to live and work permanently in the US.

green·er·y /ˈgrēnərē/ ▶ **noun** green foliage or vegetation.

green·field /ˈgrēnˌfēld/ ▶ **adjective** (of a site) previously undeveloped or built on.

green·fly /ˈgrēnˌflī/ ▶ **noun** (pl. **greenflies**) a green aphid.

green·gage /ˈgrēnˌgāj/ ▶ **noun** a small greenish plum.
– ORIGIN named after the English botanist Sir William *Gage*.

green·gro·cer /ˈgrēnˌgrōsər/ ▶ **noun** chiefly Brit. a person who sells fruit and vegetables.
– DERIVATIVES **green·gro·cer·y** noun.

green·horn /ˈgrēnˌhôrn/ ▶ **noun** informal an inexperienced or naive person.

green·house /ˈgrēnˌhous/ ▶ **noun** a glass building in which plants that need protection from cold weather are grown.

green·house ef·fect ▶ **noun** the trapping of the sun's warmth in a planet's lower atmosphere, because visible radiation from the sun passes through the atmosphere more readily than infrared radiation coming from the planet's surface.

green·house gas ▶ **noun** a gas, such as carbon dioxide, that contributes to the greenhouse effect by absorbing infrared radiation.

Green·land·er /ˈgrēnˌləndər/ ▶ **noun** a person from Greenland.

green light ▶ **noun** **1** a green traffic light giving permission to proceed. **2** permission to go ahead with a project.

green on·ion ▶ **noun** a small immature onion with a long green stem, eaten chiefly in salads; a scallion.

green pep·per ▶ **noun** an unripe sweet pepper, green in color and eaten as a vegetable.

green rev·o·lu·tion ▶ **noun** a large increase in crop production in developing countries achieved by the use of artificial fertilizers, pesticides, and high-yield crop varieties.

green room ▶ **noun** a room in a theater or studio in which performers can relax when they are not performing.

greens·keep·er /ˈgrēnzˌkēpər/ ▶ **noun** a person employed to look after a golf course.

green·stone /ˈgrēnˌstōn/ ▶ **noun** **1** a greenish igneous rock containing feldspar and hornblende. **2** chiefly NZ a variety of jade.

green stuff ▶ **noun** informal money: *the company's green stuff piled up to some $60 billion.*

green tea ▶ **noun** tea made from unfermented leaves, produced mainly in China and Japan.

green thumb ▶ **noun** a natural talent for growing plants.

Green·wich Mean Time ▶ **noun** the time measured at the Greenwich meridian, used as the standard time in a zone that includes the British Isles.
– ORIGIN from *Greenwich* in London, former site of the Royal Observatory.

Green·wich me·rid·i·an ▶ **noun** the meridian of zero longitude, passing through Greenwich, England.

green·wood /ˈgrēnˌwo͝od/ ▶ **noun** old use woods or forest in leaf, especially as a refuge for medieval outlaws.

greet /grēt/ ▶ **verb** **1** give a word or sign of welcome when meeting someone. **2** react to or acknowledge in a particular way. **3** (of a sight or sound) become apparent to a person arriving somewhere.

– SYNONYMS **1 say hello to,** address, salute, hail, welcome, meet, receive. **2** *the decision was greeted with outrage* **receive,** respond to, react to, take.

– DERIVATIVES **greet·er** noun.
– ORIGIN Old English.

greet·ing /ˈgrētiNG/ ▶ **noun 1** a word or sign of welcome when meeting someone. **2** (usu. **greetings**) a formal expression of good wishes.

– SYNONYMS **1 hello,** salutation, welcome, reception. **2 best wishes,** good wishes, congratulations, compliments, regards, respects.
– ANTONYMS farewell.

greet·ing card ▶ **noun** a decorative card sent to express good wishes on a particular occasion.

gre·gar·i·ous /griˈge(ə)rēəs/ ▶ **adjective 1** fond of company; sociable. **2** (of animals) living in flocks, herds, or colonies.

– SYNONYMS **sociable,** convivial, companionable, outgoing.
– ANTONYMS unsociable.

– DERIVATIVES **gre·gar·i·ous·ly** adverb **gre·gar·i·ous·ness** noun.
– ORIGIN Latin *gregarius*, from *grex* 'a flock.'

Gre·go·ri·an cal·en·dar /grəˈgôrēən/ ▶ **noun** the modified form of the Julian calendar introduced in 1582 by Pope Gregory XIII, and still used today.

Gre·go·ri·an chant /grəˈgôrēən/ ▶ **noun** medieval church plainsong.
– ORIGIN named after St. *Gregory* the Great.

grem·lin /ˈgremlin/ ▶ **noun** a mischievous creature regarded as responsible for unexplained mechanical or electrical faults.
– ORIGIN a World War II term: perhaps suggested by **GOBLIN**.

gre·nade /grəˈnād/ ▶ **noun** a small bomb thrown by hand or launched mechanically.
– ORIGIN from Old French *pome grenate* 'pomegranate'; the bomb was regarded as resembling a pomegranate.

Gre·na·di·an /grəˈnādēən/ ▶ **noun** a person from the Caribbean country of Grenada. ▶ **adjective** relating to Grenada.

gren·a·dier /ˌgrenəˈdi(ə)r/ ▶ **noun 1** historical a soldier armed with grenades. **2** (**Grenadiers** or **Grenadier Guards**) (in the UK) the first regiment of the royal household infantry.

gren·a·dine /ˈgrenəˌdēn, ˌgrenəˈdēn/ ▶ **noun** a sweet syrup made in France from pomegranates.
– ORIGIN French.

grew /groo/ past of **GROW**.

grey, etc. ▶ **adjective** chiefly British spelling of **GRAY**, etc.

grey·hound /ˈgrāˌhound/ ▶ **noun** a swift, slender breed of dog used in racing.
– ORIGIN Old English.

grid /grid/ ▶ **noun 1** a framework of bars that are parallel to or cross each other. **2** a network of lines that cross each other to form a series of squares or rectangles. **3** a network of cables or pipes for distributing power, especially high-voltage electricity. **4** a pattern of lines marking the starting places on an auto-racing track.
– ORIGIN from **GRIDIRON**.

grid·dle /ˈgridl/ ▶ **noun** a heavy, flat iron plate that is heated and used for cooking food. ▶ **verb** cook food on a griddle.
– ORIGIN Old French *gredil*.

grid·i·ron /ˈgridˌīərn/ ▶ **noun 1** a frame of parallel metal bars used for grilling meat or fish over an open fire. **2** a grid pattern, especially of streets. **3** a football field, marked with regularly spaced parallel lines.
– ORIGIN alteration of former *gredile* 'griddle.'

grid·lock /ˈgridˌläk/ ▶ **noun** a traffic jam affecting a whole network of intersecting streets.
– DERIVATIVES **grid·locked** adjective.

grief /grēf/ ▶ **noun 1** intense sorrow, especially caused by someone's death. **2** informal trouble or annoyance.

– SYNONYMS **sorrow,** misery, sadness, anguish, pain, distress, heartache, heartbreak, agony, woe, desolation.
– ANTONYMS joy.

– PHRASES **come to grief** have an accident; meet with disaster.
– ORIGIN Old French.

griev·ance /ˈgrēvəns/ ▶ **noun** a real or imagined cause for complaint.

– SYNONYMS **complaint,** objection, grumble, grouse, ill feeling, bad feeling, resentment; informal gripe.

grieve /grēv/ ▶ **verb 1** feel intense sorrow, especially as a result of someone's death. **2** cause great distress to someone.

– SYNONYMS **1 mourn,** sorrow, cry, sob, weep. **2 sadden,** upset, distress, pain, hurt, wound, break someone's heart.
– ANTONYMS rejoice.

– DERIVATIVES **griev·er** noun.
– ORIGIN Old French *grever* 'burden, encumber.'

CHOOSE THE RIGHT WORD

See **MOURN**.

griev·ous /ˈgrēvəs/ ▶ **adjective** formal (of something bad) very severe or serious: *the loss of his father was a grievous blow*.
– DERIVATIVES **griev·ous·ly** adverb.

grif·fin /ˈgrifin/ (also **gryphon** /ˈgrifən/ or **griffon** /ˈgrifən/) ▶ **noun** a mythical creature with the head and wings of an eagle and the body of a lion.
– ORIGIN Old French *grifoun*.

grif·fon /ˈgrifən/ ▶ **noun 1** a dog of a small terrierlike breed. **2** a large vulture with pale brown plumage.
– ORIGIN variant of **GRIFFIN**.

grift /grift/ ▶ **verb** engage in petty swindling. ▶ **noun** a petty swindle.
– DERIVATIVES **grift·er** noun.

grill /gril/ ▶ **noun 1** a metal framework used for cooking food on an open fire; gridiron. **2** a restaurant serving grilled food: *the bar and grill on Polk Street*. **3** a dish of food cooked using a grill. **4** variant form of **GRILLE**. **5** Brit. the broiling unit of an oven; broiler. ▶ **verb 1** cook food using a grill. **2** informal question someone in a relentless or aggressive way.
– ORIGIN Old French *graille* 'grille.'

grille /gril/ (also **grill**) ▶ **noun** a grating or screen of metal bars or wires.
– ORIGIN French.

grim /grim/ ▶ **adjective** (**grimmer, grimmest**) **1** very serious or gloomy; forbidding. **2** horrifying, depressing, or worrying: *the grim realities of warfare.*

– SYNONYMS **1 stern,** forbidding, uninviting, unsmiling, dour, formidable. **2 dreadful,** ghastly, horrible, terrible, awful, appalling, frightful, shocking, grisly, gruesome, depressing, distressing, upsetting. **3 bleak,** dismal, dingy, wretched, miserable, depressing, cheerless, joyless, gloomy, uninviting.
– ANTONYMS amiable, pleasant.

– DERIVATIVES **grim·ly** adverb **grim·ness** noun.
– ORIGIN Old English.

grim·ace /ˈgriməs, griˈmās/ ▶ **noun** a twisted expression on a person's face, expressing disgust, pain, or wry amusement. ▶ **verb** make a grimace.
– ORIGIN French.

grime /grīm/ ▶ **noun** dirt ingrained on a surface. ▶ **verb** make something black or dirty with grime.
– DERIVATIVES **grim·y** adjective (**grimier, grimiest**).
– ORIGIN German and Dutch.

Grim Reap·er ▶ **noun** a personification of death in the form of a cloaked skeleton wielding a large scythe.

grin /grin/ ▶ **verb** (**grins, grinning, grinned**) smile broadly.

– SYNONYMS *Liam grinned at us* **smile,** beam, smirk.

▶ **noun** a broad smile.

– SYNONYMS *a silly grin* **smile,** beam, smirk.

– PHRASES **grin and bear it** suffer pain or misfortune without complaining.
– ORIGIN Old English.

CHOOSE THE RIGHT WORD

See **SMILE**.

Grinch /grinCH/ ▶ **noun** informal a spoilsport or killjoy.
– ORIGIN the name of a character in the children's story *How the Grinch Stole Christmas* by Dr. Seuss.

grind /grīnd/ ▶ **verb** (past and past part. **ground**) **1** reduce something to small particles or powder by crushing it. **2** make something sharp or smooth by rubbing it against a hard or abrasive surface or tool. **3** rub together or move gratingly. **4** (**grind someone down**) weaken someone by treating them harshly over a long period of time. **5** (**grind something out**) produce something slowly and laboriously. **6** (as adj. **grinding**) (of a difficult situation) oppressive and seemingly endless: *grinding poverty.* **7** informal (of a dancer) rotate the hips.

– SYNONYMS **1 crush,** pound, pulverize, mill, crumble. **2 rub,** grate, scrape. **3 sharpen,** whet, hone, put an edge on, mill, machine, polish, smooth.

▶ **noun** hard, dull work: *the daily grind.*

– SYNONYMS **drudgery,** toil, labor, exertion, chores.

– DERIVATIVES **grind·ing·ly** adverb.
– PHRASES **grind to a halt** (or **come to a grinding halt**) slow down gradually and then stop completely.
– ORIGIN Old English.

CHOOSE THE RIGHT WORD

See **LABOR**.

grind·er /ˈgrīndər/ ▶ **noun 1** a machine or tool that grinds: *a meat grinder.* **2** a person employed to grind something. **3** a tooth, especially a molar. **4** a submarine sandwich.

grind·stone /ˈgrīndˌstōn/ ▶ **noun 1** a thick revolving disk of abrasive material used for sharpening or polishing metal objects. **2** a millstone.
– PHRASES **keep one's nose to the grindstone** work hard and continuously.

grin·go /ˈgriNGgō/ ▶ **noun** (pl. **gringos**) informal, derogatory (in Latin America) a white English-speaking person.
– ORIGIN Spanish, 'foreign, foreigner.'

grip /grip/ ▶ **verb** (**grips, gripping, gripped**) **1** take and keep a firm hold of something. **2** affect deeply: *she was gripped by a feeling of panic.* **3** (often as adj. **gripping**) hold someone's attention or interest: *a gripping drama.*

– SYNONYMS **1 grasp,** clutch, clasp, take hold of, clench, cling to, grab, seize, squeeze. **2 afflict,** affect, take over, beset. **3** (as adj. **gripping**) **engrossing,** enthralling, absorbing, riveting, captivating, spellbinding, fascinating, compelling, thrilling, exciting, action-packed, dramatic.

▶ **noun 1** a firm hold. **2** an understanding of something. **3** a part or attachment by which something is held in the hand. **4** old use a traveling bag. **5** a member of a camera crew responsible for moving and setting up equipment.

– SYNONYMS **1 grasp,** hold. **2 traction,** purchase, friction, adhesion. **3 control,** power, hold, stranglehold, clutches, influence.

– DERIVATIVES **grip·per** noun.
– PHRASES **come** (or **get**) **to grips with** begin to deal with or understand. **in the grip of** dominated or affected by something undesirable or adverse: *people caught in the grip of a drug problem.* **lose one's grip** become unable to understand or control one's situation.
– ORIGIN Old English.

gripe /grīp/ ▶ **verb 1** informal complain or grumble. **2** (as adj. **griping**) (of pain in the stomach or intestines) sudden and acute. ▶ **noun 1** informal a minor complaint. **2** pain in the stomach or intestines; colic.
– ORIGIN Old English, 'grasp, clutch.'

gris·ly /ˈgrizlē/ ▶ **adjective** (**grislier, grisliest**) causing horror or disgust.
– DERIVATIVES **gris·li·ness** noun.
– ORIGIN Old English.

USAGE

Grisly and **grizzly** are often confused. **Grisly** means 'causing horror or disgust,' as in *a grisly murder*, whereas a **grizzly** is a kind of large North American bear.

grist /grist/ ▶ **noun 1** grain that is ground to make flour. **2** malt crushed to make mash for brewing.
– PHRASES **grist for the mill** useful experience or knowledge.
– ORIGIN Old English, 'grinding.'

gris·tle /ˈgrisəl/ ▶ **noun** tough inedible cartilage in meat.
– DERIVATIVES **gris·tly** adjective.
– ORIGIN Old English.

grit /grit/ ▶ **noun 1** small loose particles of stone or sand. **2** (also **gritstone** /ˈgritˌstōn/) a coarse sandstone. **3** courage and determination. ▶ **verb** (**grits, gritting, gritted**) spread grit on an icy road.
– DERIVATIVES **grit·ter** noun.
– PHRASES **grit one's teeth 1** clench one's teeth. **2** be determined to do or continue to do something difficult or unpleasant.
– ORIGIN Old English.

grits /grits/ ▶ **plural noun** a dish of coarsely ground corn kernels boiled with water or milk.
– ORIGIN Old English, 'bran, mill dust.'

grit·ty /ˈgritē/ ▶ **adjective** (**grittier, grittiest**) **1** containing or covered with grit. **2** showing courage and

determination. **3** showing something unpleasant as it really is; uncompromising: *a gritty prison drama*.
– DERIVATIVES **grit·ti·ly** adverb **grit·ti·ness** noun.

griz·zled /ˈgrizəld/ ▶ **adjective** having gray or gray-streaked hair.
– ORIGIN Old French *gris* 'gray.'

griz·zly /ˈgrizlē/ (also **grizzly bear**) ▶ **noun** (pl. **grizzlies**) a large variety of brown bear often having white-tipped fur, native to western North America.
– ORIGIN from GRIZZLED.

USAGE

On the confusion of **grizzly** and **grisly**, see the note at GRISLY.

groan /grōn/ ▶ **verb 1** make a deep sound of pain or despair. **2** make a low creaking sound when pressure or weight is applied. **3** (**groan under**) be weighed down by: *a table groaning under an assortment of richly spiced dishes*.

– SYNONYMS **1 moan,** cry. **2 complain,** grumble, moan, mutter; informal grouse, bellyache, bitch, whinge. **3 creak,** grate, rasp.

▶ **noun** a groaning sound.

– SYNONYMS **1 moan,** cry. **2 complaint,** grumble, grievance, moan, muttering; informal grouse, gripe. **3 creaking,** creak, grating, grinding.

– DERIVATIVES **groan·er** noun.
– ORIGIN Old English.

gro·cer /ˈgrōsər/ ▶ **noun** a person who sells food and small household items.
– ORIGIN Old French *grossier*.

gro·cer·y /ˈgrōs(ə)rē/ ▶ **noun** (pl. **groceries**) **1** a grocer's store or business. **2** (**groceries**) items of food sold in a grocer's store or supermarket.

grog /gräg/ ▶ **noun 1** liquor (originally rum) mixed with water. **2** informal alcoholic drink.
– ORIGIN said to be from the nickname of Edward Vernon, an English admiral who ordered diluted rum to be served out to sailors.

grog·gy /ˈgrägē/ ▶ **adjective** (**groggier, groggiest**) feeling dazed, weak, or unsteady.
– DERIVATIVES **grog·gi·ly** adverb **grog·gi·ness** noun.

groin[1] /groin/ ▶ **noun 1** the area between the abdomen and the thigh on either side of the body. **2** the region of the genitals. **3** Architecture a curved edge formed by two intersecting roof arches.
– ORIGIN perhaps from an Old English word meaning 'depression, abyss.'

groin[2] ▶ **noun** a low wall or barrier built out into the sea from a beach to prevent the beach from shifting or being eroded.

grom·met /ˈgrämit/ ▶ **noun** a protective eyelet in a hole that a rope or cable passes through.
– ORIGIN from former French *gourmer* 'to curb.'

groom /gro͞om, gro͝om/ ▶ **verb 1** brush and clean a horse's or dog's coat. **2** (often as adj. **groomed**) keep oneself neat and tidy in appearance: *a beautifully groomed woman*. **3** prepare or train someone for a particular purpose or activity: *she had been groomed to take over her father's business*. **4** (of a pedophile) prepare a child for a meeting, especially via an Internet chat room.

– SYNONYMS **1 curry,** brush, clean, rub down. **2 brush,** comb, arrange, do; informal fix. **3 prepare,** prime, condition, coach, train, drill, teach, school.

▶ **noun 1** a person employed to take care of horses. **2** a bridegroom.
– ORIGIN unknown.

groove /gro͞ov/ ▶ **noun 1** a long, narrow cut in a hard material. **2** a spiral track cut in a phonograph record, into which the stylus fits. **3** an established routine or habit. **4** informal a rhythmic pattern in popular or jazz music.

– SYNONYMS **furrow,** channel, trench, trough, rut, gutter, canal, hollow, indentation.

▶ **verb 1** make a groove or grooves in something. **2** informal dance to or play pop or jazz music.
– DERIVATIVES **grooved** adjective **groov·er** noun.
– PHRASES **in** (or **into**) **the groove 1** informal performing consistently well or confidently: *it might take me a couple of races to get back into the groove*. **2** indulging in relaxed and spontaneous enjoyment: *the music swings and gets people in the groove*.
– ORIGIN Dutch *groeve* 'furrow, pit.'

groov·y /ˈgro͞ovē/ ▶ **adjective** (**groovier, grooviest**) informal, dated or humorous fashionable and exciting.
– DERIVATIVES **groov·i·ly** adverb **groov·i·ness** noun.

grope /grōp/ ▶ **verb 1** feel about uncertainly with one's hands. **2** informal fondle someone for sexual pleasure, especially against their will.

– SYNONYMS **fumble,** scrabble, fish, ferret, rummage, feel, search, hunt.

▶ **noun** informal an act of groping someone.
– DERIVATIVES **grop·er** noun.
– ORIGIN Old English.

gros·beak /ˈgrōsˌbēk/ ▶ **noun** a songbird with a stout conical bill and brightly colored plumage.
– ORIGIN from French *gros* 'big, fat' + *bec* 'beak.'

gros·grain /ˈgrōˌgrān/ ▶ **noun** a heavy ribbed fabric, typically of silk or rayon.
– ORIGIN French, 'coarse grain.'

gros point /ˈgrō ˌpoint/ ▶ **noun** a type of needlepoint embroidery consisting of stitches crossing two or more threads of the canvas in each direction.
– ORIGIN French, 'large stitch.'

gross /grōs/ ▶ **adjective 1** unattractively large. **2** informal very unpleasant; repulsive. **3** very obvious and unacceptable: *gross misconduct*. **4** rude or vulgar. **5** (of income, profit, or interest) without deduction of tax or other contributions. Often contrasted with NET[2]. **6** (of weight) including contents or other variable items.

– SYNONYMS **1** *the place smelled gross* **disgusting,** repulsive, revolting, foul, nasty, obnoxious, sickening, nauseating, stomach-churning. **2** *a gross distortion of the truth* blatant, obvious, barefaced, shameless, brazen, out and out, utter, complete. **3** *their gross income* **total,** full, overall, combined, before deductions, before tax.
– ANTONYMS pleasant, net.

▶ **adverb** without tax or other contributions having been deducted.

▶ **verb 1** produce or earn an amount of money as gross profit or income. **2** (**gross someone out**) informal disgust someone.

– SYNONYMS **earn,** make, bring in, take, get, receive; informal rake in.

▶ **noun 1** (pl. same) an amount equal to twelve dozen; 144. **2** (pl. **grosses**) a gross profit or income.
– DERIVATIVES **gross·ly** adverb **gross·ness** noun.
– ORIGIN Old French *gros* 'large'; sense 1 of the noun is from French *grosse douzaine* 'large dozen.'

gross do·mes·tic prod·uct ▸ **noun** the total value of goods produced and services provided within a country during one year.

gross na·tion·al prod·uct ▸ **noun** the total value of goods produced and services provided by a country during one year, equal to the gross domestic product plus the net income from foreign investments.

gro·tesque /grō'tesk/ ▸ **adjective 1** comically or repulsively ugly or distorted. **2** shocking or offensive: *a grotesque waste of money.*

> – SYNONYMS **1 misshapen,** deformed, distorted, twisted, monstrous, hideous, freakish, unnatural, abnormal, strange; informal weird. **2 outrageous,** monstrous, shocking, appalling, preposterous, ridiculous, ludicrous, unbelievable, incredible.

▸ **noun 1** a grotesque figure or image. **2** a style of decorative painting or sculpture in which human and animal forms are interwoven with flowers and foliage.
– DERIVATIVES **gro·tesque·ly** adverb **gro·tesque·ness** noun.
– ORIGIN from Italian *opera* or *pittura grottesca* 'work or painting like that found in a grotto.'

gro·tes·quer·ie /grō'teskərē/ ▸ **noun** (pl. **grotesqueries**) the quality of being grotesque, or things that are grotesque.

grot·to /'grätō/ ▸ **noun** (pl. **grottoes** or **grottos**) a small picturesque cave, especially an artificial one in a park or garden.
– ORIGIN Italian *grotta.*

grot·ty /'grätē/ ▸ **adjective** (**grottier, grottiest**) Brit. informal **1** unpleasant and of poor quality. **2** unwell.
– DERIVATIVES **grot·ti·ness** noun.
– ORIGIN from GROTESQUE.

grouch /groucн/ informal ▸ **noun 1** a person who is often grumpy. **2** a complaint or grumble. ▸ **verb** complain; grumble.
– ORIGIN from Old French *grouchier* 'to grumble, murmur.'

grouch·y /'groucнē/ ▸ **adjective** (**grouchier, grouchiest**) irritable and bad-tempered; grumpy.
– DERIVATIVES **grouch·i·ly** adverb.

ground[1] /ground/ ▸ **noun 1** the solid surface of the earth. **2** land or soil of a particular kind: *marshy ground.* **3** an area of land or sea with a particular use: *fishing grounds.* **4** (**grounds**) an area of enclosed land surrounding a large house. **5** (**grounds**) reasons for doing or believing something. **6** a prepared surface to which paint or other decoration is applied. **7** (**grounds**) small pieces of solid matter in a liquid, especially coffee, that settle at the bottom.

> – SYNONYMS **1 floor,** earth, terra firma. **2 earth,** soil, turf, land, terrain. **3 stadium,** field, arena, park, track. **4** *the mansion's grounds* **estate,** gardens, park, land, property, surroundings, territory. **5** *grounds for dismissal* **reason,** cause, basis, foundation, justification, rationale, argument, occasion, excuse, pretext.

▸ **verb 1** ban or prevent a pilot or aircraft from flying. **2** run a ship aground. **3** (**be grounded in/on**) have as a firm theoretical or practical basis: *an area of research grounded in classical physics.* **4** informal (of a parent) refuse to allow a child to go out socially, as a punishment.

> – SYNONYMS **1 base,** found, establish, root, build, form. **2** *she was well grounded in the classics* **teach,** instruct, coach, tutor, educate, school, train, drill.

– PHRASES **be thick** (or **thin**) **on the ground** exist in large (or small) numbers or amounts. **break new ground** achieve or create something new. **gain ground** become more popular or accepted. **get off the ground** start happening or functioning successfully. **give** (or **lose**) **ground** retreat or lose one's advantage. **go to ground** (of a fox or other animal) enter its burrow. **hold** (or **stand**) **one's ground** not retreat or lose one's advantage. **on the ground** in a place where real, practical work is done.
– ORIGIN Old English.

ground[2] past and past participle of GRIND.

ground ball (also **grounder**) ▸ **noun** Baseball a hit ball that travels along the ground.

ground·break·ing /'ground,brākiNG/ ▸ **adjective** involving completely new methods or discoveries.

WORD TOOLKIT

groundbreaking ...	newsworthy ...	noteworthy ...
work	event	feature
research	story	achievement
study	item	contribution
technology	information	performance
exhibition	topic	accomplishment

ground con·trol ▸ **noun** (treated as sing. or pl.) the personnel and equipment that monitor and direct the flight and landing of aircraft or spacecraft.

ground cov·er ▸ **noun** low-growing, spreading plants that help to prevent weeds or stabilize soil.

ground floor ▸ **noun** the floor of a building at ground level.

ground glass ▸ **noun 1** glass with a smooth ground surface that makes it nontransparent. **2** glass ground into an abrasive powder.

ground·hog /'ground,häg, -,hôg/ ▸ **noun** another term for WOODCHUCK.

ground·ing /'groundiNG/ ▸ **noun** basic training or instruction in a subject.

ground·less /'ground-lis/ ▸ **adjective** not based on any good reason.

ground rules ▸ **plural noun** basic principles controlling the way in which something is done.

ground·sel /'groun(d)səl/ ▸ **noun** a plant of the daisy family with small yellow flowers.
– ORIGIN Old English.

grounds·keep·er /'groun(d)z,kēpər/ (Brit. **groundsman**) ▸ **noun** a person who maintains a sports field, a park, or the grounds of a school or other institution.

ground speed ▸ **noun** an aircraft's speed relative to the ground.

ground squir·rel ▸ **noun** a burrowing squirrel of a large group including the chipmunks.

ground·swell /'groun(d),swel/ ▸ **noun** a buildup of opinion in a large section of the population.

ground·wa·ter /'ground,wôtər, -,wätər/ ▸ **noun** water held underground in the soil or in rock.

ground·work /'ground,wərk/ ▸ **noun** preliminary or basic work.

ground ze·ro ▸ **noun 1** the point on the earth's surface directly below an exploding nuclear bomb. **2** informal a starting point or base for an activity: *his favorite phase was ground zero, when ideas would fly around.* **3** (**Ground Zero**) the site of the former World Trade Center in New York City, since the terrorist attacks of September 11, 2001.

group /groōp/ ▶ **noun** (treated as sing. or pl.) **1** a number of people or things located, gathered, or classed together. **2** a number of musicians who play popular music together. **3** a division of an air force. **4** Chemistry a set of elements occupying a column in the periodic table and having broadly similar properties. **5** Chemistry a combination of atoms having a recognizable identity in a number of compounds.

> – SYNONYMS **1 category,** class, classification, grouping, cluster, set, batch, type, sort, kind, variety, family. **2 crowd,** party, body, band, company, gathering, congregation, assembly, collection, cluster, clump, knot, flock, pack, troop, gang; informal bunch. **3 band,** ensemble, act; informal lineup, combo, outfit.

▶ **verb** place in or form a group or groups: *sofas and chairs were grouped around a low table.*

> – SYNONYMS **1 categorize,** classify, class, catalog, sort, bracket, pigeonhole. **2 assemble,** collect, organize, place, arrange, range, line up, lay out.

– ORIGIN Italian *gruppo.*

group dy·nam·ic ▶ **plural noun** (also treated as sing.) Psychology the processes involved when people in a group interact with each other, or the study of these.

group·er /ˈgroōpər/ ▶ **noun** a large heavy-bodied fish found in warm seas.
– ORIGIN Portuguese *garoupa.*

group home ▶ **noun** a home where a small number of unrelated people requiring support or supervision, such as the mentally ill, can live together.

group·ie /ˈgroōpē/ ▶ **noun** informal a person who follows a pop group or celebrity, often in the hope of a sexual relationship with them.

group·ing /ˈgroōpiNG/ ▶ **noun** a group of people with a shared interest or aim, especially within a larger organization.

group ther·a·py ▶ **noun** a form of psychiatric therapy in which patients meet to discuss their problems.

grouse[1] /grous/ ▶ **noun** (pl. same) a medium-sized game bird with a plump body and feathered legs.
– ORIGIN perhaps related to Latin *gruta* or to Old French *grue* 'crane.'

grouse[2] ▶ **verb** complain or grumble. ▶ **noun** a grumble or complaint.
– ORIGIN unknown.

grout /grout/ ▶ **noun** a mortar or paste for filling crevices, especially the gaps between wall or floor tiles. ▶ **verb** fill in crevices with grout.
– ORIGIN perhaps related to French dialect *grouter* 'grout a wall.'

grove /grōv/ ▶ **noun** a small wood, orchard, or group of trees.
– ORIGIN Old English.

grov·el /ˈgrävəl, ˈgrə-/ ▶ **verb** (**grovels, groveling, groveled**) **1** crouch or crawl on the ground. **2** act in a very humble way in an attempt to gain forgiveness or favorable treatment.

> – SYNONYMS **1 prostrate oneself,** lie, kneel, cringe. **2 be obsequious,** fawn on, kowtow, bow and scrape, toady, dance attendance on, ingratiate oneself with; informal crawl, creep, suck up to, lick someone's boots.

– DERIVATIVES **grov·el·er** noun.
– ORIGIN from an Old Norse word meaning 'face downward.'

grow /grō/ ▶ **verb** (past **grew**; past part. **grown**) **1** (of a living thing) undergo natural development by increasing in size and changing physically. **2** (of a plant) germinate and develop. **3** become larger or greater over a period of time; increase. **4** become gradually or increasingly: *we grew braver.* **5** (**grow up**) become an adult. **6** (**grow on**) become gradually more appealing to: *the tune grows on you.* **7** (**grow out of**) become too large to wear a garment. **8** (**grow out of**) become too mature to continue to do something: *she had long since grown out of her disco phase.*

> – SYNONYMS **1 enlarge,** get bigger, get larger, get taller, expand, increase in size, extend, spread, swell, multiply, snowball, mushroom, balloon, build up, mount up, pile up. **2 sprout,** germinate, spring up, develop, bud, bloom, flourish, thrive, run riot. **3 cultivate,** produce, propagate, raise, rear, farm. **4 become,** get, turn, begin to be.
> – ANTONYMS shrink, decline.

– ORIGIN Old English.

grow·er /ˈgrōər/ ▶ **noun 1** someone who grows a particular type of crop: *tomato growers.* **2** a plant that grows in a specified way.

grow·ing pains ▶ **plural noun 1** pains that can occur in the limbs of young children. **2** difficulties experienced in the early stages of an enterprise.

growl /groul/ ▶ **verb 1** (especially of a dog) make a low sound of hostility in the throat. **2** say something in a low, angry voice. **3** make a low rumbling sound.

> – SYNONYMS **snarl,** bark, yap, bay.

▶ **noun** a growling sound.
– ORIGIN probably imitating the sound.

growl·er /ˈgroulər/ ▶ **noun 1** a person or thing that growls. **2** a small iceberg.

grown /grōn/ past participle of **GROW**.

grown-up ▶ **adjective** adult.

> – SYNONYMS **adult,** mature, of age, fully grown, independent.

▶ **noun** informal an adult.

> – SYNONYMS **adult,** woman, man, grown man/woman.
> – ANTONYMS child.

growth /grōTH/ ▶ **noun 1** the process of growing. **2** something that has grown or is growing. **3** a tumor or other abnormal formation.

> – SYNONYMS **1 enlargement,** increase in size, expansion, extension, swelling, multiplication, mushrooming, snowballing, rise, escalation, buildup, development. **2 tumor,** malignancy, cancer, lump, swelling.

growth hor·mone ▶ **noun** a hormone that stimulates growth in animal or plant cells.

growth in·dus·try ▶ **noun** an industry that is developing particularly rapidly.

growth ring ▶ **noun** a concentric layer of wood, shell, or bone developed during a regular period of growth.

growth stock ▶ **noun** a company stock that tends to increase in capital value rather than yield high income.

grub /grəb/ ▶ **noun 1** the larva of an insect, especially a beetle. **2** informal food. ▶ **verb** (**grubs, grubbing, grubbed**) **1** dig shallowly in soil. **2** (**grub something up**) dig something up. **3** search clumsily and unmethodically: *I began grubbing around in the wastebasket.*

– DERIVATIVES **grub·ber** noun.
– ORIGIN perhaps related to Dutch *grobbelen*, also to **GRAVE**[1].

grub·by /ˈgrəbē/ ▶ **adjective** (**grubbier, grubbiest**) **1** dirty; grimy. **2** involving activities that are dishonest or immoral: *a grubby affair*.

> – SYNONYMS **dirty,** grimy, filthy, mucky, unwashed, stained, soiled; informal cruddy, grungy, yucky.
> – ANTONYMS clean.

– DERIVATIVES **grub·bi·ness** noun.

> **WORD TOOLKIT**
> See **FILTHY**.

grudge /grəj/ ▶ **noun** a long-lasting feeling of resentment or dislike: *he held a grudge against his former boss*.

> – SYNONYMS **grievance,** resentment, bitterness, rancor, ill will, animosity, antipathy, antagonism; informal a chip on one's shoulder.

▶ **verb 1** be resentfully unwilling to give or allow something: *he grudged the money spent on her*. **2** feel resentful that someone has achieved something: *I don't grudge him his moment of triumph*.
– ORIGIN related to **GROUCH**.

grudg·ing /ˈgrəjiNG/ ▶ **adjective** given or allowed only reluctantly or resentfully: *a grudging apology*.

> **WORD TOOLKIT**
> See **ENVIOUS**.

gru·el /ˈgro͞oəl/ ▶ **noun** a thin liquid food of oatmeal boiled in milk or water.
– ORIGIN Old French.

gruel·ing /ˈgro͞oəliNG/ ▶ **adjective** extremely tiring and demanding.

> – SYNONYMS **exhausting,** tiring, taxing, draining, demanding, exacting, difficult, arduous, strenuous, back-breaking, punishing, crippling; informal murderous.

– DERIVATIVES **gruel·ing·ly** adverb.
– ORIGIN from former *gruel* 'exhaust, punish.'

grue·some /ˈgro͞osəm/ ▶ **adjective** causing disgust or horror.

> – SYNONYMS **grisly,** ghastly, frightful, horrid, horrifying, hideous, horrible, grim, awful, dreadful, terrible, horrific; informal sick, gross.
> – ANTONYMS pleasant.

– DERIVATIVES **grue·some·ly** adverb **grue·some·ness** noun.
– ORIGIN from Scots *grue* 'feel horror, shudder.'

gruff /grəf/ ▶ **adjective 1** (of a person's voice) rough and low in pitch. **2** abrupt or unfriendly in manner.

> – SYNONYMS **1** *a gruff reply* **abrupt,** brusque, curt, short, blunt; taciturn; surly, grumpy, crusty, ungracious; informal grouchy. **2** *a gruff voice* **rough,** guttural, throaty, gravelly, husky, croaking, rasping, hoarse, harsh; low.
> – ANTONYMS friendly, soft.

– DERIVATIVES **gruff·ly** adverb **gruff·ness** noun.
– ORIGIN from Flemish and Dutch *grof* 'coarse, rude.'

> **CHOOSE THE RIGHT WORD**
> See **BRUSQUE**.

grum·ble /ˈgrəmbəl/ ▶ **verb 1** complain in a bad-tempered but muted way. **2** make a low rumbling sound.

> – SYNONYMS **complain,** grouse, whine, mutter, carp, make a fuss; informal moan, bellyache, bitch, whinge.

▶ **noun** a complaint.

> – SYNONYMS **complaint,** grouse, grievance, protest; informal grouch, moan, beef, gripe.

– DERIVATIVES **grum·bler** noun.
– ORIGIN probably Germanic.

grump /grəmp/ ▶ **noun** informal **1** a grumpy person. **2** a period of sulking.

grump·y /ˈgrəmpē/ ▶ **adjective** (**grumpier, grumpiest**) bad-tempered and sulky.

> – SYNONYMS **bad-tempered,** crabby, tetchy, touchy, irascible, cantankerous, curmudgeonly, surly, fractious; informal grouchy, cranky, ornery.
> – ANTONYMS good-humored.

– DERIVATIVES **grump·i·ly** adverb **grump·i·ness** noun.
– ORIGIN imitating sounds expressing displeasure.

grunge /grənj/ ▶ **noun 1** a style of rock music with a loud, harsh guitar sound. **2** a casual, deliberately untidy style of fashion including loose, layered clothing and ripped jeans. **3** informal grime; dirt.
– DERIVATIVES **grun·gy** adjective.
– ORIGIN perhaps from by **GRUBBY** and **DINGY**.

grunt /grənt/ ▶ **verb 1** (of an animal, especially a pig) make a low, short guttural sound. **2** make a low sound as a result of physical effort or to show agreement. ▶ **noun** a grunting sound.
– DERIVATIVES **grunt·er** noun.
– ORIGIN Old English.

Gru·yère /gro͞oˈyer, grē-/ ▶ **noun** a Swiss cheese with a firm texture.
– ORIGIN named after *Gruyère*, a district in Switzerland.

gryph·on ▶ **noun** variant spelling of **GRIFFIN**.

GSA ▶ **abbreviation 1** General Services Administration, a federal department that manages supplies, properties, and services for all other departments. **2** Girl Scouts of America.

GSM ▶ **abbreviation** Global System (or Standard) for Mobile.

G-spot ▶ **noun** an area of the wall of the vagina believed to be very sensitive to sexual stimulation.
– ORIGIN first as *Gräfenberg spot*, from *Gräfenberg* and Dickinson, the American gynecologists who first described it.

GST ▶ **abbreviation** generation-skipping tax.

G-string ▶ **noun** a skimpy undergarment covering the genitals, consisting of a narrow strip of cloth attached to a waistband.

G-suit ▶ **noun** a garment lined with pressurized air pouches, worn by fighter pilots and astronauts to enable them to withstand high gravitational forces.
– ORIGIN abbreviation of *gravity-suit*.

GT ▶ **noun** a high-performance car.
– ORIGIN short for Italian *gran turismo* 'great touring.'

GTi ▶ **noun** a GT car with a fuel-injection engine.

gua·ca·mo·le /ˌgwäkəˈmōlē/ ▶ **noun** a dish of mashed avocado mixed with chili peppers, tomatoes, and other ingredients.
– ORIGIN Nahuatl, 'avocado sauce.'

guai·a·cum /ˈgwīəkəm/ ▶ **noun** an evergreen tree of the Caribbean and tropical America, formerly important for its hard, heavy, oily wood.
– ORIGIN Latin.

gua·nine /ˈgwänēn/ ▸ **noun** Biochemistry a purine derivative that is one of the four constituent bases of nucleic acids.

gua·no /ˈgwänō/ ▸ **noun** the excrement of seabirds, used as a fertilizer.
– ORIGIN Quechua.

gua·ra·na /gwəˈränə/ ▸ **noun** a substance prepared from the seeds of a Brazilian shrub, believed to have medicinal properties.
– ORIGIN Tupi.

Gua·ra·ni /gwärəˈnē/ ▸ **noun** (pl. same) **1** a member of an American Indian people of Paraguay and adjacent regions. **2** the language of the Guarani. **3** (**guarani**) the basic unit of money of Paraguay.
– ORIGIN Spanish.

guar·an·tee /ˌgarənˈtē/ ▸ **noun 1** an assurance that certain conditions will be fulfilled or that certain things will be done. **2** an assurance that a product will remain in working order for a particular length of time. **3** something that makes an outcome certain: *a degree is no guarantee of a fast-track career.* **4** money or a valuable item given or promised as an assurance that something will be done. **5** variant spelling of **GUARANTY**.

– SYNONYMS **1 warranty. 2 promise,** assurance, word (of honor), pledge, vow, oath, commitment. **3 collateral,** security, surety, bond.

▸ **verb** (**guarantees, guaranteeing, guaranteed**) **1** provide a guarantee for something: *the company guarantees to refund your money.* **2** promise with certainty: *no one can guarantee a profit on stocks and shares.* **3** provide financial security for something.

– SYNONYMS **1 promise,** swear, pledge, vow, give one's word, give an assurance, give an undertaking. **2 underwrite,** put up collateral for.

– ORIGIN perhaps from Spanish *garante*.

guar·an·tor /ˌgarənˈtôr, ˈgarəntər/ ▸ **noun** a person or organization that gives or acts as a guarantee.

guar·an·ty /ˈgarənˌtē/ (also **guarantee**) ▸ **noun** (pl. **guaranties**) **1** a formal pledge to pay another person's debt or to perform another person's obligation in the case of default. **2** a thing serving as security for a pledge.

guard /gärd/ ▸ **verb 1** watch over someone or something in order to protect or control them. **2** protect against damage or harm: *the company fiercely guarded its independence.* **3** (**guard against**) take precautions against: *farmers must guard against sudden changes in the market.*

– SYNONYMS **protect,** defend, shield, secure, cover, mind, stand guard over, watch, keep an eye on.

▸ **noun 1** a person, especially a soldier, assigned to protect a person or to control access to somewhere. **2** (treated as sing. or pl.) a body of soldiers guarding a place or person. **3** a prison employee who guards the inmates. **4** a defensive posture taken up in a fight. **5** a state of looking out for possible dangers or difficulties: *he let his guard slip.* **6** a device worn or fitted on something to prevent injury or damage: *a retractable blade guard.*

– SYNONYMS **1 sentry,** sentinel, watchman, nightwatchman, protector, defender, guardian, lookout, watch. **2 warden,** warder, keeper, jailer; informal screw. **3 cover,** shield, screen, fender, bumper, buffer.

– PHRASES **on** (or **off**) **guard** prepared (or unprepared) for a surprise or difficulty. **under guard** being guarded.
– ORIGIN Old French *garder*.

guard·ed /ˈgärdid/ ▸ **adjective** cautious and having possible reservations: *the proposals were given a guarded welcome.*

– SYNONYMS **cautious,** careful, circumspect, wary, chary, reluctant, noncommittal; informal cagey.

– DERIVATIVES **guard·ed·ly** adverb.

guard·house /ˈgärdˌhous/ (also **guardroom** /ˈgärdˌro͞om, -ˌro͞om/) ▸ **noun** a building for soldiers guarding the entrance to a military camp or for the detention of military prisoners.

guard·i·an /ˈgärdēən/ ▸ **noun 1** a person who defends or protects something. **2** a person legally responsible for someone unable to manage their own affairs, especially a child whose parents have died.

– SYNONYMS **protector,** defender, preserver, custodian, warden, guard, keeper, curator, caretaker, steward, trustee.

– DERIVATIVES **guard·i·an·ship** noun.
– ORIGIN Old French *garden*.

WORD LINKS

tutelary *relating to a guardian*

guard·i·an an·gel ▸ **noun** a spirit believed to watch over and protect a person or place.

guard of hon·or ▸ **noun** another term for **HONOR GUARD**.

guard·rail /ˈgärdˌrāl/ ▸ **noun 1** a rail that prevents people from falling off or being hit by something. **2** a strong fence at the side of a road or traffic lane to prevent vehicles from leaving it.

guards·man /ˈgärdzmən/ ▸ **noun** (pl. **guardsmen**) a member of the US National Guard.

guar gum /gwär/ ▸ **noun** a gum used in the food and paper industries, obtained from the seeds of an African and Asian bean plant.
– ORIGIN Hindi.

Gua·te·ma·lan /ˌgwätəˈmälən/ ▸ **noun** a person from Guatemala in Central America. ▸ **adjective** relating to Guatemala.

gua·va /ˈgwävə/ ▸ **noun** a tropical American fruit with pink juicy flesh.
– ORIGIN probably from Taino (an extinct Caribbean language).

gu·ber·na·to·ri·al /ˌgo͞obərnəˈtôrēəl/ ▸ **adjective** relating to a governor, particularly of a US state.
– ORIGIN Latin *gubernator* 'governor.'

gudg·eon[1] /ˈgəjən/ ▸ **noun** a small freshwater fish often used as bait by anglers.
– ORIGIN Old French *goujon*.

gudg·eon[2] ▸ **noun 1** a pivot or spindle on which something swings or rotates. **2** the tubular part of a hinge into which the pin fits. **3** a socket at the stern of a boat, into which the rudder is fitted. **4** a pin holding two blocks of stone together.
– ORIGIN from Old French *gouge* 'chisel.'

guel·der rose /ˈgeldər/ ▸ **noun** a shrub with heads of fragrant creamy-white flowers followed by translucent red berries.
– ORIGIN from Dutch *geldersche roos* 'rose of *Gelderland*' (a province of the Netherlands).

Guern·sey /ˈgərnzē/ ▸ **noun** (pl. **Guernseys**) **1** a breed of dairy cattle from Guernsey in the Channel Islands, noted for producing rich, creamy milk. **2** (**guernsey**) a thick sweater made from oiled wool.

guer·ril·la /gəˈrilə/ (also **guerilla**) ▶ **noun** a member of a small independent group fighting against the government or regular forces.

– SYNONYMS **rebel,** irregular, freedom fighter, radical, revolutionary, terrorist, member of the resistance.

– ORIGIN Spanish, 'little war.'

guess /ges/ ▶ **verb 1** estimate or suppose something without having enough information to be sure of being right. **2** correctly estimate: *she's guessed where we're going.* **3** (**I guess**) informal I suppose: *I guess I'd better tell you.*

– SYNONYMS **1 estimate,** reckon, judge, speculate, conjecture, hypothesize, surmise. **2 suppose,** think, imagine, expect, suspect, dare say; informal reckon.

▶ **noun** an estimate or conclusion formed by guessing.

– SYNONYMS **hypothesis,** theory, conjecture, surmise, estimate, belief, opinion, supposition, speculation, suspicion, impression, feeling.

– DERIVATIVES **guess·er** noun.
– ORIGIN perhaps from Dutch *gissen.*

guess·ti·mate (also **guestimate**) informal ▶ **noun** /ˈgestəmit/ an estimate based on a mixture of guesswork and calculation. ▶ **verb** /ˈgestəˌmāt/ estimate something by using a mixture of guesswork and calculation.

guess·work /ˈgesˌwərk/ ▶ **noun** the process or results of guessing.

guest /gest/ ▶ **noun 1** a person invited to visit someone's home or to a social occasion. **2** a person invited to take part in a broadcast or entertainment. **3** a person staying at a hotel or guest house.

– SYNONYMS **1 visitor,** caller, company. **2 client,** customer, resident, boarder, lodger, patron, diner, vacationer, tourist.
– ANTONYMS host.

▶ **verb** appear as a guest in a broadcast or entertainment.
– PHRASES **guest of honor** the most important guest at an occasion.
– ORIGIN Old Norse.

guest·book /ˈgestˌbo͝ok/ ▶ **noun 1** a book in which visitors to a public building or private home write their names and addresses, and sometimes remarks. **2** a Web page where visitors to a site may leave their names and comments.

guest house ▶ **noun 1** a small, separate house on the grounds of a larger house, used for accommodating overnight guests. **2** a private house offering accommodations to paying guests.

guest room ▶ **noun 1** a room in a private home for accommodating guests. **2** a hotel room.

guest work·er ▶ **noun** a person with temporary permission to work in another country.

guff /gəf/ ▶ **noun** informal ridiculous talk or ideas; nonsense.
– ORIGIN first meaning 'whiff of a bad smell.'

guf·faw /gəˈfô/ ▶ **noun** a loud, deep laugh. ▶ **verb** give a loud, deep laugh.
– ORIGIN imitating the sound.

guid·ance /ˈgīdns/ ▶ **noun 1** advice or information aimed at solving a problem or difficulty. **2** the directing of the movement or position of something.

– SYNONYMS **1 advice,** counsel, instruction, suggestions, tips, hints, pointers, guidelines. **2 direction,** control, leadership, management, supervision.

guide /gīd/ ▶ **noun 1** a person who advises or shows the way to other people. **2** something that helps a person make a decision or form an opinion: *your resting pulse rate is a rough guide to your physical condition.* **3** a book providing information on a subject. **4** a structure or marking that directs the movement or positioning of something.

– SYNONYMS **1 escort,** attendant, courier, leader, usher. **2 outline,** template, example, exemplar, model, pattern, guideline, yardstick, precedent. **3 guidebook,** travel guide, vade mecum, companion, handbook, manual, directory, A to Z, instructions, directions; informal bible.

▶ **verb 1** show someone the way to a place. **2** direct the positioning or movement of something. **3** (as adj. **guided**) directed by remote control or internal equipment: *a guided missile.* **4** direct or influence the behavior or development of: *his entire life was guided by his religious beliefs.*

– SYNONYMS **1 lead,** conduct, show, usher, shepherd, direct, steer, pilot, escort. **2 direct,** steer, manage, conduct, run, be in charge of, govern, preside over, supervise, oversee. **3 advise,** counsel, direct.

– ORIGIN Old French.

guide·book /ˈgīdˌbo͝ok/ ▶ **noun** a book containing information about a place for visitors or tourists.

guide dog ▶ **noun** a dog that has been trained to lead a blind person.

guide·line /ˈgīdˌlīn/ ▶ **noun** a general rule, principle, or piece of advice.

guild /gild/ ▶ **noun 1** a medieval association of craftsmen or merchants. **2** an association of people who do the same work or have the same interests or aims.

– SYNONYMS **association,** society, union, league, organization, company, fellowship, club, order, lodge.

– ORIGIN Old English.

guild·er /ˈgildər/ ▶ **noun** (pl. same or **guilders**) **1** (until the introduction of the euro in 2002) the basic unit of money of the Netherlands. **2** historical a gold or silver coin formerly used in the Netherlands, Germany, and Austria.
– ORIGIN Dutch.

guild·hall /ˈgildˌhôl/ ▶ **noun 1** the meeting place of a guild or corporation. **2** Brit. a town hall.

guile /gīl/ ▶ **noun** clever but dishonest or devious behavior.

– SYNONYMS **cunning,** craftiness, craft, artfulness, artifice, wiliness, slyness, deviousness; deception, deceit, duplicity, underhandedness, double-dealing, trickery.
– ANTONYMS honesty.

– DERIVATIVES **guile·ful** adjective.
– ORIGIN Old French.

guile·less /ˈgīllis/ ▶ **adjective** innocent, honest, and sincere.
– DERIVATIVES **guile·less·ly** adverb.

guil·le·mot /ˈgiləˌmät/ ▶ **noun** an auk with a narrow pointed bill, nesting on cliff ledges.
– ORIGIN French.

guil·lo·tine /ˈgiləˌtēn, ˈgēə-/ ▶ **noun 1** a machine with a heavy blade that slides down a frame, used for

beheading people. **2** a device with a descending or sliding blade used for cutting paper or sheet metal. ▶ **verb** execute someone with a guillotine.
– ORIGIN named after the French physician Joseph-Ignace *Guillotin*, who recommended its use for executions.

guilt /gilt/ ▶ **noun 1** the fact of having committed an offense or crime. **2** a feeling of having done something wrong.

– SYNONYMS **1 culpability,** blameworthiness, responsibility. **2 remorse,** shame, regret, contrition, self-reproach, a guilty conscience.
– ANTONYMS innocence.

– ORIGIN Old English.

guilt·less /ˈgiltlis/ ▶ **adjective** having no guilt; innocent.
– DERIVATIVES **guilt·less·ly** adverb.

guilt trip ▶ **noun** informal a feeling of guilt about something, especially when this feeling is self-indulgent or deliberately provoked by another person.

guilt·y /ˈgiltē/ ▶ **adjective** (**guiltier, guiltiest**) **1** responsible for a particular wrongdoing, fault, or mistake: *he was found guilty of manslaughter.* **2** having or showing a feeling of guilt: *a guilty conscience.*

– SYNONYMS **1 culpable,** to blame, at fault, in the wrong, responsible. **2 ashamed,** guilt-ridden, conscience-stricken, remorseful, sorry, contrite, repentant, penitent, regretful, rueful, shamefaced.
– ANTONYMS innocent.

– DERIVATIVES **guilt·i·ly** adverb **guilt·i·ness** noun.

guin·ea /ˈginē/ ▶ **noun** a former British gold coin with a value of 21 shillings (now £1.05).
– ORIGIN named after *Guinea* in West Africa (the source of the gold from which the first guineas were minted).

guin·ea fowl ▶ **noun** (pl. same) a large African game bird with slate-colored, white-spotted plumage.

guin·ea pig ▶ **noun 1** a tailless South American rodent, often kept as a pet. **2** a person or thing used in an experiment.

guise /gīz/ ▶ **noun** an outward form, appearance, or way of presenting someone or something: *the country has carried on whaling under the guise of scientific research.*

– SYNONYMS **1** *in the guise of a swan* **likeness,** appearance, semblance, form, shape, image; disguise. **2** *payments made under the guise of consultancy fees* **pretense,** disguise, front, facade, cover, blind, screen, smokescreen.

– ORIGIN Old French.

gui·tar /giˈtär/ ▶ **noun** a stringed musical instrument with six (or occasionally twelve) strings, played by plucking or strumming with the fingers or a plectrum.
– DERIVATIVES **gui·tar·ist** noun.
– ORIGIN Spanish *guitarra.*

Gu·ja·ra·ti /ˌgo͝ojəˈrätē/ (also **Gujerati**) ▶ **noun** (pl. **Gujaratis**) **1** a person from the Indian state of Gujarat. **2** the language of the Gujaratis. ▶ **adjective** relating to the Gujaratis or their language.

Gu·lag /ˈgo͞oläg/ ▶ **noun** (**the Gulag**) a system of harsh labor camps maintained in the Soviet Union 1930–1955.
– ORIGIN Russian.

gulch /gəlCH/ ▶ **noun** a narrow, steep-sided ravine.
– ORIGIN perhaps from dialect *gulch* 'to swallow.'

gulf /gəlf/ ▶ **noun 1** a deep inlet of the sea almost surrounded by land, with a narrow mouth. **2** a deep ravine. **3** a substantial difference between two people, ideas, or situations: *the gulf between rich and poor.*

– SYNONYMS **1 bay,** inlet, cove, bight, fjord, estuary, sound; Scottish firth. **2 gap,** divide, separation, difference, contrast.

– ORIGIN Italian *golfo.*

Gulf War syn·drome ▶ **noun** an unexplained medical condition affecting some veterans of the 1991 Gulf War, characterized by fatigue, chronic headaches, and skin and breathing disorders.

gull[1] /gəl/ ▶ **noun** a long-winged seabird having white plumage with a gray or black back.
– ORIGIN Celtic.

gull[2] ▶ **verb** fool or deceive someone. ▶ **noun** a person who is fooled or deceived.
– ORIGIN unknown.

Gul·lah /ˈgələ/ ▶ **noun** (pl. same or **Gullahs**) **1** a member of a black people living on the coast of South Carolina and nearby islands. **2** the Creole language of the Gullah, having an English base with West African elements.
– ORIGIN perhaps a shortening of *Angola.*

gul·let /ˈgəlit/ ▶ **noun** the passage by which food passes from the mouth to the stomach; the esophagus.
– ORIGIN Old French *goulet* 'little throat.'

gul·li·ble /ˈgələbəl/ ▶ **adjective** easily persuaded to believe something.

– SYNONYMS **credulous,** naive, easily deceived, impressionable, unsuspecting, ingenuous, innocent, inexperienced, green; informal wet behind the ears.
– ANTONYMS suspicious.

– DERIVATIVES **gul·li·bil·i·ty** /ˌgələˈbilitē/ noun.
– ORIGIN from GULL[2].

CHOOSE THE RIGHT WORD

gullible, callow, credulous, ingenuous, naive, trusting, unsophisticated

Some people will believe anything. Those who are truly **gullible** are the easiest to deceive, which is why they so often make fools of themselves. Those who are merely **credulous** might be a little too quick to believe something, but they usually aren't stupid enough to act on it. **Trusting** suggests the same willingness to believe (*a trusting child*), but it isn't necessarily a bad way to be (*a person so trusting he completely disarmed his enemies*). No one likes to be called **naive** because it implies a lack of street smarts (*she's so naive she'd accept a ride from a stranger*), but when applied to things other than people, it can describe a simplicity and absence of artificiality that is quite charming (*the naive style in which nineteenth-century American portraits were often painted*). Most people would rather be thought of as **ingenuous**, meaning straightforward and sincere (*an ingenuous confession of the truth*), because it implies the simplicity of a child without the negative overtones. **Callow**, however, comes down a little more heavily on the side of immaturity and almost always goes hand-in-hand with youth. Whether young or old, someone who is **unsophisticated** suffers from a lack of experience.

gull-wing ▶ **adjective** (of a door on a car or aircraft) opening upward.

gul·ly /ˈgəlē/ (also **gulley**) ▶ **noun** (pl. **gullies, gulleys**) **1** a ravine or deep channel caused by the action of running water. **2** a gutter or drain.
– ORIGIN French *goulet* (see GULLET).

gulp /gəlp/ ▶ **verb 1** swallow drink or food quickly or in large mouthfuls. **2** swallow with difficulty as a result of strong emotion: *she gulped, trying hard to stop crying.*

– SYNONYMS **1 swallow,** quaff, swill down; informal swig, down, knock back. **2 gobble,** guzzle, devour, bolt, wolf down. **3** *she gulped back her tears* **choke back,** fight/hold back, suppress, stifle, smother.

▶ **noun 1** an act of gulping. **2** a large mouthful of liquid drunk quickly.

– SYNONYMS **mouthful,** swallow, draft; informal swig.

– ORIGIN probably from Dutch *gulpen*.

gum[1] /gəm/ ▶ **noun 1** a thick sticky substance produced by some trees and shrubs. **2** glue used for sticking paper or other light materials together. **3** chewing gum or bubble gum. ▶ **verb** (**gums, gumming, gummed**) **1** cover or fasten something with gum or glue. **2** (**gum something up**) clog up a mechanism and prevent it from working properly.
– ORIGIN Old French *gomme*.

gum[2] ▶ **noun** the firm area of flesh around the roots of the teeth in the upper or lower jaw.
– ORIGIN Old English.

gum ar·a·bic ▶ **noun** a gum produced by some kinds of acacia tree, and used as glue and in incense.

gum·bo /ˈgəmbō/ ▶ **noun** (pl. **gumbos**) (in Cajun cooking) a spicy chicken or seafood soup thickened with okra, filé, or roux.
– ORIGIN Angolan.

gum·drop /ˈgəmˌdräp/ ▶ **noun** a firm, jellylike candy.

gum·my[1] /ˈgəmē/ ▶ **adjective** (**gummier, gummiest**) sticky.

gum·my[2] ▶ **adjective** (**gummier, gummiest**) toothless: *a gummy grin*.

gum·my[3] ▶ **noun** (pl. **gummies**) a candy made to imitate a gummy bear but in another shape, such as a shark or a heart.

gum·my bear ▶ **noun** a small chewy translucent candy made in the shape of a bear.

gump·tion /ˈgəmpsHən/ ▶ **noun** informal initiative and resourcefulness.
– ORIGIN unknown.

gum·shoe /ˈgəmˌsHo͞o/ ▶ **noun** informal, dated a detective.
– ORIGIN from *gumshoes* in the sense 'sneakers,' suggesting stealth.

gum tree ▶ **noun** a tree that produces gum, especially a eucalyptus.

gun /gən/ ▶ **noun 1** a weapon incorporating a metal tube from which bullets or shells are propelled by explosive force. **2** a device using pressure to send out a substance or object: *a grease gun*. **3** a gunman: *a hired gun*.

– SYNONYMS **firearm,** sidearm, handgun, weapon; informal piece, rod, gat, heater.

▶ **verb** (**guns, gunning, gunned**) **1** (**gun someone down**) shoot someone with a gun. **2** (**be gunning for**) be actively looking for an opportunity to blame or attack someone. **3** make a vehicle's engine operate at excessive speed.
– PHRASES **go great guns** informal proceed forcefully or successfully. **jump the gun** informal act before the proper or appropriate time. **stick to one's guns** informal refuse to compromise or change. **under the gun** informal under great pressure: *manufacturers are under the gun to offer green alternatives*.
– ORIGIN perhaps from a familiar form of the Scandinavian name *Gunnhildr*, from *gunnr* + *hildr*, both meaning 'war.'

gun·boat /ˈgənˌbōt/ ▶ **noun** a small ship armed with guns.

gun·boat di·plo·ma·cy ▶ **noun** foreign policy supported by the use or threat of military force.

gun·cot·ton /ˈgənˌkätn/ ▶ **noun** an explosive made by steeping cotton or wood pulp in a mixture of nitric and sulfuric acids.

gun dog ▶ **noun** a dog trained to retrieve game that has been shot.

gun·fight /ˈgənˌfīt/ ▶ **noun** a fight involving an exchange of gunfire.
– DERIVATIVES **gun·fight·er** noun.

gun·fire /ˈgənˌfī(ə)r/ ▶ **noun** the repeated firing of a gun or guns.

gung-ho /ˈgəNG ˈhō/ ▶ **adjective** too eager to take part in fighting or warfare.
– ORIGIN from a Chinese word taken to mean 'work together' and adopted as a slogan by US Marines.

gunk /gəNGk/ ▶ **noun** informal an unpleasantly sticky or messy substance.
– ORIGIN the trademark of a US detergent.

gun·man /ˈgənmən/ ▶ **noun** (pl. **gunmen**) a man who uses a gun to commit a crime or terrorist act.

– SYNONYMS **armed criminal,** assassin, sniper, terrorist, gunfighter; informal hit man, gunslinger, shootist.

gun·met·al /ˈgənˌmetl/ ▶ **noun 1** a gray corrosion-resistant form of bronze containing zinc. **2** a dull bluish-gray color.

gun·nel /ˈgənl/ ▶ **noun** variant spelling of **GUNWALE**.

gun·ner /ˈgənər/ ▶ **noun** a person, especially in military service, who operates a gun.

gun·ner·y /ˈgənərē/ ▶ **noun** the design, manufacture, or firing of heavy guns.

gun·ner·y ser·geant ▶ **noun** a noncommissioned officer in the US Marine Corps ranking above staff sergeant and below master sergeant.

gun·ny /ˈgənē/ ▶ **noun** coarse fabric, typically made from jute fiber and used for making sacks.

gun·play /ˈgənˌplā/ ▶ **noun** the use of guns.

gun·point /ˈgənˌpoint/ ▶ **noun** (in phrase **at gunpoint**) while threatening someone or being threatened with a gun.

gun·pow·der /ˈgənˌpoudər/ ▶ **noun** an explosive consisting of a powdered mixture of saltpeter, sulfur, and charcoal.

gun·run·ner /ˈgənˌrənər/ ▶ **noun** a person involved in the illegal sale or importing of firearms.
– DERIVATIVES **gun·run·ning** noun.

gun·ship /ˈgənˌsHip/ ▶ **noun** a heavily armed helicopter.

gun·shot /ˈgənˌsHät/ ▶ **noun** a shot fired from a gun.

gun-shy ▶ **adjective** (especially of a hunting dog) alarmed at the sound of a gun.

gun·sight /ˈgənˌsīt/ ▶ **noun** a device on a gun enabling it to be aimed accurately.

gun·sling·er /ˈgənˌsliNGər/ ▶ **noun** informal a person who carries a gun.

gun·smith /ˈgənˌsmiTH/ ▶ **noun** a person who makes and sells small firearms.

gun·wale /ˈgənl/ (also **gunnel**) ▶ **noun** the upper edge or planking of the side of a boat.

– PHRASES **to the gunwales** informal so as to be almost overflowing.
– ORIGIN from **GUN** + **WALE** (because it was formerly used to support guns).

gup·py /ˈgəpē/ ▶ **noun** (pl. **guppies**) a small freshwater fish native to tropical America, popular in aquariums.
– ORIGIN named after the Trinidadian clergyman R. J. Lechmere *Guppy*, who sent the first specimen to the British Museum.

gur·gle /ˈgərgəl/ ▶ **verb** make a hollow bubbling sound.
▶ **noun** a gurgling sound.
– ORIGIN perhaps from Latin *gurgulio* 'gullet.'

Gur·kha /ˈgo͝orkə/ ▶ **noun 1** a member of any of several Nepalese peoples noted for their ability as soldiers. **2** a member of a regiment in the British army established for Nepalese recruits.
– ORIGIN a Nepalese place name.

gur·ney /ˈgərnē/ ▶ **noun** (pl. **gurneys**) a stretcher on wheels for transporting hospital patients.
– ORIGIN apparently named after J. T. *Gurney* of Boston, Massachusetts.

gu·ru /ˈgo͞oro͞o, go͞oˈro͞o/ ▶ **noun 1** a Hindu spiritual teacher. **2** each of the ten first leaders of the Sikh religion. **3** an influential teacher or expert on a particular subject: *a management guru.*

> – SYNONYMS **1 spiritual teacher,** tutor, sage, mentor, spiritual leader, master. **2 expert,** authority, pundit, leading light, master, specialist.
> – ANTONYMS disciple.

– ORIGIN Sanskrit, 'weighty, grave.'

gush /gəsʜ/ ▶ **verb 1** flow in a strong, fast stream.
2 express approval in a very enthusiastic way.

> – SYNONYMS **1 surge,** stream, spout, spurt, jet, rush, pour, spill, cascade, flood. **2** *everyone gushed about the script* **enthuse,** rave, be enthusiastic, be effusive, rhapsodize, go into raptures, wax lyrical; informal go mad, go wild, go crazy.

▶ **noun** a strong, fast stream.

> – SYNONYMS **surge,** stream, spout, spurt, jet, rush, outpouring, spill, outflow, cascade, flood, torrent.

– DERIVATIVES **gush·ing** adjective.
– ORIGIN probably imitating the sound.

gush·er /ˈgəsʜər/ ▶ **noun** an oil well from which oil gushes without being pumped.

gush·y /ˈgəsʜē/ ▶ **adjective** (**gushier, gushiest**) expressing approval in a very enthusiastic way.

gus·set /ˈgəsit/ ▶ **noun 1** a piece of material sewn into a garment to strengthen or enlarge a part of it. **2** a bracket strengthening an angle of a structure.
– ORIGIN Old French *gousset* 'small pod or shell.'

gust /gəst/ ▶ **noun 1** a brief, strong rush of wind. **2** a sudden burst of rain, sound, etc.

> – SYNONYMS **flurry,** blast, puff, blow, rush, squall.

▶ **verb** blow in gusts.
– ORIGIN Old Norse.

gus·to /ˈgəstō/ ▶ **noun** enthusiasm and energy.
– ORIGIN Italian.

gust·y /ˈgəstē/ ▶ **adjective** (**gustier, gustiest**)
1 characterized by or blowing in gusts: *a gusty morning.*
2 having or showing gusto: *gusty female vocals.*
– DERIVATIVES **gust·i·ly** /ˈgəstəlē/ adverb **gust·i·ness** noun.

gut /gət/ ▶ **noun 1** the stomach or intestine. **2** (**guts**) internal organs that have been removed or exposed. **3** (**guts**) the internal parts or essence of something. **4** (**guts**) informal courage and determination. **5** fiber from the intestines of animals, used for violin or racket strings.

> – SYNONYMS **1 stomach,** belly, abdomen, paunch, intestines, viscera; informal tummy, insides, innards. **2** *he has a lot of guts* **courage,** bravery, backbone, nerve, pluck, spirit, daring, grit, fearlessness, determination. informal moxie.

▶ **verb** (**guts, gutting, gutted**) **1** take out the internal organs of a fish or other animal before cooking it. **2** remove or destroy the internal parts of: *the building was gutted by fire.*

> – SYNONYMS **1 clean (out),** disembowel, draw; formal eviscerate. **2 strip,** empty, devastate, lay waste, ravage, ruin, wreck.

▶ **adjective** informal instinctive: *a gut feeling.*

> – SYNONYMS **instinctive,** intuitive, deep-seated, involuntary, spontaneous, unthinking, knee-jerk.

– PHRASES **bust a gut** informal **1** make a strenuous effort: *a problem that nobody's going to bust a gut trying to solve.* **2** laugh uncontrollably.
– ORIGIN Old English.

> **WORD LINKS**
>
> **visceral** *relating to the gut*

gut·less /ˈgətləs/ ▶ **adjective** informal lacking courage or determination.
– DERIVATIVES **gut·less·ness** noun.

guts·y /ˈgətsē/ ▶ **adjective** (**gutsier, gutsiest**) informal **1** showing courage and determination. **2** (of food or drink) having a strong flavor.
– DERIVATIVES **guts·i·ness** noun.

gut·ta-per·cha /ˌgətə ˈpərcʜə/ ▶ **noun** a hard, tough substance resembling rubber, obtained from certain Malaysian trees.
– ORIGIN Malay.

gut·ter /ˈgətər/ ▶ **noun 1** a shallow trough beneath the edge of a roof, or a channel at the side of a street, for carrying off rainwater. **2** (**the gutter**) a very poor or squalid environment.

> – SYNONYMS **drain,** trough, trench, ditch, sluice, sewer, channel, conduit, pipe.

▶ **verb** (of a flame) flicker and burn unsteadily.
– ORIGIN Old French *gotiere.*

gut·ter·snipe /ˈgətərˌsnīp/ ▶ **noun** a scruffy, badly behaved child who spends most of their time on the street.

gut·tur·al /ˈgətərəl/ ▶ **adjective 1** (of a speech sound) produced in the throat and harsh-sounding. **2** (of a way of speaking) characterized by guttural sounds.
– DERIVATIVES **gut·tur·al·ly** adverb.
– ORIGIN from Latin *guttur* 'throat.'

gut-wrench·ing ▶ **adjective** informal extremely upsetting or unpleasant: *gut-wrenching violence.*

guy[1] /gī/ ▶ **noun 1** informal a man. **2** (**guys**) informal people of either sex.

> – SYNONYMS **man,** fellow; informal lad, fella, gent, chap, dude, joe, hombre.

▶ **verb** make fun of someone.

guy[2] ▶ **noun** a rope or line fixed to the ground to secure a tent.
– ORIGIN probably German.

Guy·a·nese /ˌgīəˈnēz, -ˈnēs/ ▶ **noun** (pl. same) a person from Guyana, a country on the NE coast of South America. ▶ **adjective** relating to Guyana.

guz·zle /ˈgəzəl/ ▶ **verb** eat or drink something greedily.

– SYNONYMS **1 gobble,** bolt, wolf, devour; informal scarf down, tuck into. **2 gulp down,** quaff, swill; informal knock back, swig, slug.

– DERIVATIVES **guz·zler** noun.
– ORIGIN perhaps from Old French *gosillier* 'chatter, vomit.'

gybe ▶ **verb & noun** British spelling of **JIBE**[2].

gym /jim/ ▶ **noun 1** a gymnasium. **2** a private club with facilities for improving or maintaining physical fitness. **3** gymnastics.

gym bag ▶ **noun** a bag for holding sports equipment and clothing.

gym·kha·na /jimˈkänə/ ▶ **noun** an event consisting of a series of competitions on horseback, typically for children.
– ORIGIN Urdu, 'racket court.'

gym·na·si·um /jimˈnāzēəm/ ▶ **noun** (pl. **gymnasiums** or **gymnasia** /-zēə/) a hall or building equipped for gymnastics, games, and other physical exercise.
– ORIGIN from Greek *gumnazein* 'exercise naked.'

gym·nast /ˈjimnist/ ▶ **noun** a person trained in gymnastics.

gym·nas·tics /jimˈnastiks/ ▶ **plural noun** (also treated as sing.) exercises involving physical agility, flexibility, and coordination.
– DERIVATIVES **gym·nas·tic** adjective.

gym·no·sperm /ˈjimnəˌspərm/ ▶ **noun** a plant of a large group that have seeds that are not protected by an ovary or fruit, such as conifers.
– ORIGIN from Greek *gumnos* 'naked.'

gy·ne·col·o·gy /ˌgīnəˈkäləjē, ˌjinə-/ (Brit. **gynaecology**) ▶ **noun** the branch of medicine concerned with conditions and diseases specific to women and girls, especially those affecting the reproductive system.
– DERIVATIVES **gyn·e·co·log·i·cal** /-kəˈläjikəl/ adjective **gyn·e·co·log·i·cal·ly** /-kəˈläjik(ə)lē/ adverb **gy·ne·col·o·gist** noun.
– ORIGIN Greek *gunē* 'woman, female.'

gyn·e·co·mas·ti·a /ˌgīnəkōˈmastēə/ ▶ **noun** Medicine enlargement of a man's breasts, usually due to hormone imbalance or hormone therapy.

gyp /jip/ ▶ **verb** (**gyps, gypping, gypped**) informal cheat or swindle someone.
– ORIGIN unknown.

gyp·sum /ˈjipsəm/ ▶ **noun** a soft white or gray mineral used to make plaster of Paris and in the building industry.
– ORIGIN Latin.

gyp·sy /ˈjipsē/ (also **gipsy**) ▶ **noun** (pl. **gypsies**) **1** a member of a traveling people with dark skin and hair who speak a langauge (Romany) related to Hindi. **2** someone with an unconventional or transient lifestyle. ▶ **adjective** (of a business or merchant) nonunion or unlicensed: *gypsy trucking firms.*
– DERIVATIVES **gyp·sy·ish** adjective.
– ORIGIN from *gipcyan*, short for **EGYPTIAN** (because Gypsies were believed to have come from Egypt).

gyp·sy moth ▶ **noun** a European moth, introduced to the US in the 19th century, whose caterpillar feeds on tree foliage and can be a serious pest.

gy·rate /ˈjīrāt/ ▶ **verb 1** move in a circle or spiral. **2** dance by rotating the hips in a suggestive way.

– SYNONYMS **rotate,** revolve, wheel, turn, whirl, circle, pirouette, twirl, swirl, spin, swivel.

– DERIVATIVES **gy·ra·tion** noun **gy·ra·tor** noun **gy·ra·to·ry** adjective.
– ORIGIN Latin *gyrare* 'revolve.'

gyre /jīr/ ▶ **verb** literary whirl. ▶ **noun** a spiral or vortex.
– ORIGIN Latin *gyrare.*

gyr·fal·con /ˈjərˌfalkən, -ˌfôl-/ ▶ **noun** a large arctic falcon, with mainly gray or white plumage.
– ORIGIN probably related to German *gēr* 'spear.'

gy·ro[1] /ˈjīrō/ ▶ **noun** (pl. **gyros**) a gyroscope or gyrocompass.

gy·ro[2] /ˈyērō, ˈzhirō/ ▶ **noun** (pl. **gyros**) a sandwich made with slices of spiced meat cooked on a spit, served with salad in pita bread.

gy·ro·com·pass /ˈjīrōˌkəmpəs/ ▶ **noun** a compass in which the direction of true north is maintained by a gyroscope rather than magnetism.
– ORIGIN from Greek *guros* 'a ring.'

gy·ro·scope /ˈjīrəˌskōp/ ▶ **noun** a device used to provide stability or maintain a fixed direction, consisting of a wheel or disk spinning rapidly about an axis that is itself free to alter in direction.
– DERIVATIVES **gy·ro·scop·ic** adjective.

H¹ /ācʜ/ (also **h**) ▶ **noun** (pl. **Hs** or **H's**) the eighth letter of the alphabet.

H² ▶ **abbreviation** **1** (of a pencil lead) hard. **2** height. **3** Physics henry(s). ▶ **symbol** the chemical element hydrogen.

h ▶ **abbreviation** **1** (in measuring the height of horses) hand(s). **2** hour(s).

ha¹ ▶ **abbreviation** hectare(s).

ha² /hä/ (also **hah**) ▶ **exclamation** used to express surprise, suspicion, triumph, or some other emotion.

ha·be·as cor·pus /ˈhābēəs ˈkôrpəs/ ▶ **noun** Law a writ requiring that a person who has been arrested be brought before a judge or into court, to decide whether their detention is lawful.
– ORIGIN Latin, 'you shall have the body (in court).'

hab·er·dash·er /ˈhabərˌdasʜər/ ▶ **noun** a person who sells men's clothing.
– DERIVATIVES **hab·er·dash·er·y** noun.
– ORIGIN probably from Old French *hapertas*, perhaps the name of a fabric.

hab·it /ˈhabit/ ▶ **noun** **1** something that a person does regularly. **2** informal an addiction to a drug. **3** a long, loose garment worn by a monk or nun.

> – SYNONYMS **1 custom,** practice, routine, way; formal wont. **2 addiction,** dependence, craving, fixation.

– ORIGIN Latin *habitus* 'condition, appearance.'

hab·it·a·ble /ˈhabitəbəl/ ▶ **adjective** of a good enough condition to live in.
– DERIVATIVES **hab·it·a·bil·i·ty** noun.
– ORIGIN Latin *habitabilis*.

hab·i·tat /ˈhabiˌtat/ ▶ **noun** the natural home or environment of an animal or plant.
– ORIGIN Latin, 'it inhabits.'

hab·i·ta·tion /ˌhabiˈtāsʜən/ ▶ **noun** **1** the fact of living somewhere. **2** formal a house or home.

hab·it-form·ing ▶ **adjective** (of a drug) addictive.

ha·bit·u·al /həˈbicʜo͞oəl/ ▶ **adjective** **1** done regularly and in a way that is difficult to stop: *her father's habitual complaints*. **2** regular; usual: *his habitual dress*.

> – SYNONYMS **1 constant,** persistent, continual, continuous, perpetual, nonstop, endless, never-ending; informal eternal. **2 inveterate,** confirmed, compulsive, incorrigible, hardened, ingrained, chronic, regular. **3 customary,** accustomed, regular, usual, normal, characteristic; literary wonted.
> – ANTONYMS occasional.

– DERIVATIVES **ha·bit·u·al·ly** adverb.

> **WORD TOOLKIT**
>
> See **INCORRIGIBLE**.

ha·bit·u·ate /həˈbicʜo͞oˌāt/ ▶ **verb** make or become used to something.
– DERIVATIVES **ha·bit·u·a·tion** noun.

ha·bit·u·é /həˈbicʜo͞oˌā/ ▶ **noun** a person who regularly goes to a particular place.
– ORIGIN French, 'accustomed.'

ha·ček /ˈhaˌcʜek/ ▶ **noun** a mark (ˇ) placed over a letter to alter the sound in Slavic and other languages.
– ORIGIN Czech, 'little hook.'

ha·ci·en·da /ˌhäsēˈendə/ ▶ **noun** (in Spanish-speaking countries) a large estate with a house.
– ORIGIN Spanish.

hack¹ /hak/ ▶ **verb** **1** cut something with rough or heavy blows. **2** kick something wildly or roughly. **3** use a computer to gain unauthorized access to data in another system. **4** (**hack it**) informal manage; cope.

> – SYNONYMS **cut,** chop, hew, lop, slash.

▶ **noun** a rough cut or blow.
– DERIVATIVES **hack·a·ble** adjective **hack·er** noun.
– ORIGIN Old English.

hack² ▶ **noun** **1** a writer, especially a journalist, who produces mediocre or unoriginal work. **2** a horse for ordinary riding, or one that can be hired. **3** a ride on a horse. **4** a taxicab. ▶ **verb** ride a horse.
– DERIVATIVES **hack·er·y** noun.
– ORIGIN abbreviation of **HACKNEY**.

hack·ing cough ▶ **noun** a dry, frequent cough.

hack·le /ˈhakəl/ ▶ **noun** **1** (**hackles**) hairs along an animal's back that rise when it is angry or alarmed. **2** a long, narrow feather on the neck or lower back of a domestic rooster or other bird.
– PHRASES **make someone's hackles rise** make someone angry or indignant.
– ORIGIN Germanic.

hack·ney /ˈhaknē/ ▶ **noun** (pl. **hackneys**) chiefly historical **1** a horse with a high-stepping trot, used in harness. **2** a horse-drawn vehicle kept for hire.
– ORIGIN probably from *Hackney* in East London, where horses were formerly kept.

hack·neyed /ˈhaknēd/ ▶ **adjective** (of a phrase or idea) unoriginal and used too often.

> – SYNONYMS **overused,** overdone, overworked, worn out, timeworn, stale, tired, threadbare, trite, banal, clichéd.
> – ANTONYMS original.

– ORIGIN from the former verb *hackney* 'use a horse for general purposes.'

hack·saw /ˈhakˌsô/ ▶ **noun** a saw with a narrow blade set in a frame, used for cutting metal.

had /had/ past and past participle of **HAVE**.

had·dock /ˈhadək/ ▶ **noun** (pl. same) a silvery-gray edible fish of North Atlantic coastal waters.
– ORIGIN Old French *hadoc*.

Ha·des /ˈhādēz/ ▶ **noun** **1** Greek Mythology the underworld;

the home of the spirits of the dead. **2** informal hell.
– ORIGIN Greek *Haidēs*, a name of Pluto, the god of the dead.

Ha·dith /hə'dēᴛʜ/ ▶ **noun** (pl. same or **Hadiths**) a collection of Islamic traditions containing sayings of the prophet Muhammad.
– ORIGIN Arabic, 'tradition.'

had·n't /'hadnt/ ▶ **contraction** had not.

had·ron /'had,rän/ ▶ **noun** Physics a subatomic particle of a type that is held in atomic nuclei, such as a baryon or meson.
– ORIGIN from Greek *hadros* 'bulky.'

hadst /hadst/ old-fashioned second person singular past of **HAVE**.

haf·ni·um /'hafnēəm/ ▶ **noun** a hard silver-gray metal resembling zirconium.
– ORIGIN from *Hafnia*, the Latin form of *Havn*, a former name of Copenhagen.

haft /haft/ ▶ **noun** the handle of a knife, ax, or spear.
– ORIGIN Old English.

hag /hag/ ▶ **noun 1** an ugly old woman. **2** a witch.
– ORIGIN perhaps from Old English.

hag·fish /'hag,fisʜ/ ▶ **noun** (pl. same or **hagfishes**) a primitive jawless sea fish with a slimy eel-like body and a rasping tongue used for feeding on dead or dying fish.

hag·gard /'hagərd/ ▶ **adjective** looking exhausted and ill.

> – SYNONYMS **drawn,** tired, exhausted, drained, careworn, gaunt, pinched, hollow-cheeked, hollow-eyed.

– ORIGIN French *hagard*.

hag·gis /'hagis/ ▶ **noun** (pl. same) a Scottish dish consisting of seasoned sheep's or calf's offal mixed with suet and oatmeal, boiled in a bag traditionally made from the animal's stomach.
– ORIGIN probably from earlier *hag* 'hack, hew,' from Old Norse.

hag·gle /'hagəl/ ▶ **verb** argue or negotiate with someone about the price of something.

> – SYNONYMS **barter,** bargain, negotiate, wrangle.

– DERIVATIVES **hag·gler** noun.
– ORIGIN Old Norse.

hag·i·og·ra·phy /,hagē'ägrəfē, ,hāgē-/ ▶ **noun 1** literature concerned with the lives of saints. **2** a biography that idealizes its subject.
– DERIVATIVES **hag·i·og·ra·pher** noun **hag·i·o·graph·ic** /,hagēə'grafik, ,hāgēə-/ adjective **hag·i·o·graph·i·cal** /,hagēə'grafəkəl, ,hāgēə-/ adjective.

hah ▶ **exclamation** another spelling of **HA²**.

ha-ha /'hä ,hä, ,hä 'hä/ ▶ **noun** a ditch with a wall on its inner side below ground level, forming a boundary to a park or garden without interrupting the view.
– ORIGIN said to be from the cry of surprise uttered on coming across such an obstacle.

hai·ku /'hī,ko͞o, ,hī'ko͞o/ ▶ **noun** (pl. same or **haikus**) a Japanese poem of seventeen syllables, in three lines of five, seven, and five.
– ORIGIN Japanese.

hail¹ /hāl/ ▶ **noun 1** pellets of frozen rain falling in showers. **2** a large number of things hurled forcefully through the air.

> – SYNONYMS *a hail of missiles* **barrage,** volley, shower, stream, salvo.

▶ **verb** (**it hails, it is hailing, it hailed**) hail falls.
– ORIGIN Old English.

hail² ▶ **verb 1** call out to someone to attract attention. **2** describe enthusiastically: *he was hailed as a literary genius.* **3** (**hail from**) have one's home or origins in.

> – SYNONYMS **1 call out to,** shout to, address, greet, salute, say hello to. **2** *he hailed a cab* **flag down,** wave down. **3 acclaim,** praise, applaud. **4** *he hails from Australia* **come from,** be from, be a native of.

▶ **exclamation** old use expressing greeting or praise.
– ORIGIN from former *hail* 'healthy.'

Hail Mar·y ▶ **noun** (pl. **Hail Marys**) a prayer to the Virgin Mary used chiefly by Roman Catholics.

hail·stone /'hāl,stōn/ ▶ **noun** a pellet of hail.

hail·storm /'hāl,stôrm/ ▶ **noun** a storm of heavy hail.

hair /he(ə)r/ ▶ **noun 1** any of the fine threadlike strands growing from the skin of mammals and other animals, or from the outer layer of a plant. **2** strands of hair collectively, especially on a person's head.

> – SYNONYMS **1 head of hair,** shock of hair, mane, mop, locks, tresses, curls. **2 hairstyle,** haircut; informal hairdo. **3 fur,** wool, coat, fleece, pelt, mane.

– DERIVATIVES **hair·less** adjective.
– PHRASES **hair of the dog** informal an alcoholic drink taken to cure a hangover. [from *hair of the dog that bit you*, formerly recommended as a remedy for the bite of a mad dog.] **a hair's breadth** a very small margin. **let one's hair down** informal enjoy oneself in an uninhibited way. **make someone's hair stand on end** alarm someone. **split hairs** make small and unnecessary distinctions.
– ORIGIN Old English.

hair·ball /'he(ə)r,bôl/ ▶ **noun** a ball of hair that collects in the stomach of an animal as a result of the animal licking its coat.

hair·band /'he(ə)r,band/ ▶ **noun** a band worn over the top of the head and behind the ears to keep the hair off the face.

hair·brush /'he(ə)r,brəsʜ/ ▶ **noun** a brush for smoothing one's hair.

hair·cut /'heər,kət/ ▶ **noun 1** the style in which someone's hair is cut. **2** an act of cutting someone's hair.

hair·do /'he(ə)r,do͞o/ ▶ **noun** (pl. **hairdos**) informal the style of a person's hair.

hair·dress·er /'he(ə)r,dresər/ ▶ **noun** a person who cuts and styles hair.

> – SYNONYMS **hairstylist,** stylist, coiffeur, coiffeuse, barber.

– DERIVATIVES **hair·dress·ing** noun.

hair·dry·er /'he(ə)r,drīər/ (also **hairdrier**) ▶ **noun** an electrical device for drying the hair with warm air.

hair·line /'he(ə)r,līn/ ▶ **noun** the edge of a person's hair. ▶ **adjective** very thin or fine: *a hairline fracture.*

hair·net /'he(ə)r,net/ ▶ **noun** a small piece of fine net used to hold the hair in place.

hair·piece /'he(ə)r,pēs/ ▶ **noun** a patch or bunch of false hair used to add to a person's natural hair.

hair·pin /'he(ə)r,pin/ ▶ **noun** a U-shaped pin for fastening the hair.

hair·pin turn ▶ **noun** a sharp U-shaped bend in a road.

hair-rais·ing ▶ **adjective** extremely alarming or frightening.

hair shirt ▸ noun a shirt made of stiff cloth woven from horsehair, formerly worn as a penance for having done wrong.

hair-split·ting ▸ noun the making of small and unnecessary distinctions.

hair·spray /ˈhe(ə)rˌsprā/ ▸ noun a solution sprayed on hair to keep it in place.

hair·spring /ˈhe(ə)rˌspriNG/ ▸ noun a flat coiled spring that regulates the timekeeping in some clocks and watches.

hair·style /ˈhe(ə)rˌstīl/ ▸ noun a way in which someone's hair is cut or arranged.
– DERIVATIVES **hair·styl·ing** noun **hair·styl·ist** noun.

hair trig·ger ▸ noun a firearm trigger set for release at the slightest pressure. ▸ adjective (**hair-trigger**) liable to change suddenly and violently.

hair·y /ˈhe(ə)rē/ ▸ adjective (**hairier, hairiest**) **1** covered with or resembling hair. **2** informal dangerous or frightening: *a hairy mountain road*.

– SYNONYMS **1 shaggy,** bushy, long-haired, woolly, furry, fleecy. **2 bearded,** unshaven, stubbly, bristly; formal hirsute. **3 risky,** dangerous, perilous, hazardous, tricky; informal dicey.

– DERIVATIVES **hair·i·ness** noun.

Hai·tian /ˈhāSHən/ ▸ noun a person from Haiti. ▸ adjective relating to Haiti.

haj·i /ˈhajē/ (also **hajji**) ▸ noun (pl. **hajis**) a Muslim who has been to Mecca as a pilgrim.
– ORIGIN Arabic.

hajj /haj/ (also **haj**) ▸ noun the pilgrimage to Mecca that all Muslims are expected to make at least once if they can afford to do so.
– ORIGIN Arabic, 'pilgrimage.'

hake /hāk/ ▸ noun (pl. same or **hakes**) a long-bodied edible fish with strong teeth.
– ORIGIN perhaps from Old English, 'hook.'

ha·lal /həˈläl, həˈlal/ ▸ adjective (of meat) prepared as prescribed by Muslim law.
– ORIGIN Arabic, 'according to religious law.'

hal·berd /ˈhalbərd, ˈhôl-/ (also **halbert**) ▸ noun historical a combined spear and battle-ax.
– ORIGIN German *helmbarde*.

hal·cy·on /ˈhalsēən/ ▸ adjective (of a past time) idyllically happy and peaceful: *halcyon days*.
– ORIGIN first referring to a mythical bird (usually identified with a species of kingfisher) said to breed in a nest floating at sea and to calm the wind and waves: from Greek *alkuōn* 'kingfisher.'

hale[1] /hāl/ ▸ adjective (of an old person) strong and healthy.
– ORIGIN Old English, 'whole.'

hale[2] ▸ verb old use haul.
– ORIGIN Old French *haler*.

half /haf/ ▸ noun (pl. **halves** /havz/) **1** either of two equal or matching parts into which something is or can be divided. **2** either of two equal periods into which a sports game or performance is divided. **3** a halfback. ▸ predeterminer & pronoun an amount equal to a half. ▸ adjective forming a half. ▸ adverb **1** to the extent of half. **2** partly: *half-cooked*.
– PHRASES **go halves** share the cost of something equally. **half a chance** informal the slightest opportunity. **half past one** (**two**, etc.) thirty minutes after one (two, etc.) o'clock. **not half 1** not nearly. **2** informal not at all. **too —— by half** excessively ——: *he's too charming by half*.
– ORIGIN Old English.

half-and-half ▸ adverb & adjective in equal parts. ▸ noun a mixture of milk and cream.

half-assed ▸ adjective vulgar slang done without much skill or effort.

half·back /ˈhafˌbak/ ▸ noun **1** Football an offensive back usually positioned behind the quarterback and to the side of the fullback. **2** a usually defensive player in a ball game such as soccer or field hockey whose position is between the forwards and the fullbacks.

half-baked ▸ adjective informal not well planned or considered.

half blood ▸ noun **1** offensive another term for **HALF-BREED**. **2** dated the relationship between people having one parent in common. **3** dated a person related to another in this way.

half-breed ▸ noun offensive a person whose parents are of different races, especially an American Indian and a person of white European ancestry.

half-broth·er (or **half-sister**) ▸ noun a brother (or sister) with whom one has only one parent in common.

half-caste ▸ noun offensive a person whose parents are of different races.

half-cock ▸ noun the partly raised position of the cock of a gun.
– DERIVATIVES **half-cocked** adjective.
– PHRASES **at half-cock** when only partly ready.

half dol·lar ▸ noun a US or Canadian coin worth fifty cents.

half-doz·en (also **half a dozen**) ▸ noun a group of six.

half-har·dy ▸ adjective (of a plant) able to grow outdoors except in severe frost.

half-heart·ed ▸ adjective without enthusiasm or energy.

– SYNONYMS **unenthusiastic,** cool, lukewarm, tepid, apathetic.
– ANTONYMS enthusiastic.

– DERIVATIVES **half-heart·ed·ly** adverb **half-heart·ed·ness** noun.

half hitch ▸ noun a knot formed by making a loop in a rope and passing one end through it.

half hour ▸ noun **1** (also **half an hour**) a period of thirty minutes. **2** a point in time thirty minutes after the beginning of an hour of the clock.
– DERIVATIVES **half-hour·ly** adjective & adverb.

half-life ▸ noun the time taken for the radioactivity of a substance to fall to half its original value.

half-light ▸ noun dim light, such as that at dusk.

half-mast ▸ noun the position of a flag that is being flown some way below the top of its staff as a mark of respect for a recent death.

half meas·ures ▸ plural noun actions or policies that are not forceful or decisive enough.

half-moon ▸ noun **1** the moon when only half its surface is visible from the earth. **2** a semicircular or crescent-shaped object.

half nel·son ▸ noun see **NELSON**.

half note ▶ **noun** a musical note having the time value of two quarter notes or half a whole note, represented by a ring with a stem.

half step ▶ **noun** the smallest interval used in classical Western music, equal to a twelfth of an octave or half a tone; a semitone.

half-tim·bered ▶ **adjective** having walls with a timber frame and a brick or plaster filling.

half·time /ˈhafˌtīm/ ▶ **noun** a short interval between two halves of a game or contest.

half·tone /ˈhafˌtōn/ ▶ **noun** a reproduction of a photographic image in which the different shades are produced by dots of varying sizes.

half-track ▶ **noun** a vehicle with wheels at the front and caterpillar tracks at the rear.

half-truth ▶ **noun** a statement that is only partly true.

half-vol·ley ▶ **noun** (in tennis and soccer) a strike or kick of the ball immediately after it bounces.

half·way /ˈhafˈwā/ ▶ **adverb & adjective 1** at or to a point equal in distance between two others. **2** (as adv.) to some extent: *halfway decent.*

– SYNONYMS **1** *he started running down the passage and then stopped halfway* **midway,** in the middle, in the center; partway, part of the way. **2** *the halfway point* **midway,** middle, mid, central, center, intermediate. **3** *she seemed halfway friendly* **to some extent/degree,** in some measure, relatively, comparatively, moderately, somewhat, (up) to a point; just about, almost, nearly.

– PHRASES **meet someone halfway** compromise; concede some points in order to gain others.

half·way house ▶ **noun 1** the halfway point in a process. **2** a place where drug addicts, discharged prisoners, or psychiatric patients can stay for a short time to prepare themselves for a return to normal life.

half·wit /ˈhafˌwit/ ▶ **noun** informal a stupid person.
– DERIVATIVES **half-wit·ted** adjective.

hal·i·but /ˈhaləbət/ ▶ **noun** (pl. same) a large edible marine flatfish.
– ORIGIN from former *haly* 'holy' + *butt* 'flatfish' (because it was often eaten on holy days).

hal·ide /ˈhaˌlīd, ˈhā-/ ▶ **noun** a chemical compound formed from a halogen and another element or group: *silver halide.*

hal·i·to·sis /ˌhaliˈtōsəs/ ▶ **noun** unpleasant-smelling breath.
– ORIGIN Latin *halitus* 'breath.'

hall /hôl/ ▶ **noun 1** an area in a building into which rooms open; a corridor. **2** the room or space just inside the front entrance of a house. **3** a large room for meetings, concerts, etc. **4** (also **residence hall**) a college or university building in which students live. **5** Brit. a large country house. **6** the main living room of a medieval house.

– SYNONYMS **1 entrance hall,** hallway, entry, entrance, lobby, foyer, vestibule, atrium. **2 assembly room,** meeting room, chamber, auditorium, theater, house.

– ORIGIN Old English.

hal·le·lu·jah /ˌhaləˈlo͞oyə/ (also **alleluia** /ˌaləˈlo͞oyə/) ▶ **exclamation** God be praised.
– ORIGIN Hebrew, 'praise ye the Lord.'

hall·mark /ˈhôlˌmärk/ ▶ **noun 1** an official mark stamped on articles made of gold, silver, or platinum as a guarantee of their purity. **2** a distinctive feature of something: *tiny bubbles are the hallmark of fine champagne.* ▶ **verb** stamp an object with a hallmark.
– ORIGIN from *Goldsmiths' Hall* in London, where articles were tested and stamped.

hal·lo /həˈlō/ ▶ **exclamation** variant spelling of **HELLO**.

Hall of Fame ▶ **noun** an establishment commemorating the achievements of a group of people, especially athletes.

hal·loo /həˈlo͞o/ ▶ **exclamation 1** used to attract someone's attention. **2** used to encourage dogs during a hunt.
– ORIGIN probably from Old French *haloer* 'pursue or urge on with shouts.'

hal·lowed /ˈhalōd/ ▶ **adjective 1** made holy: *a hallowed shrine.* **2** greatly honored and respected: *the hallowed ground of Fenway Park.*
– ORIGIN Old English, related to **HOLY**.

WORD TOOLKIT

See **HOLY**.

Hal·low·een /ˌhaləˈwēn, ˌhälə-, -ōˈēn/ (also **Hallowe'en**) ▶ **noun** the night of October 31, the eve of All Saints' Day.
– ORIGIN shortened form of *All Hallow Even*, from *hallow* 'saint, holy person' + **EVEN**[2].

hal·lu·ci·nate /həˈlo͞osənˌāt/ ▶ **verb** experience a seemingly real perception of something not actually present.
– ORIGIN Latin *hallucinari* 'go astray in thought.'

hal·lu·ci·na·tion /həˌlo͞osənˈāsʜən/ ▶ **noun** an experience involving a seemingly real perception of something not actually present.

– SYNONYMS *he continued to suffer from horrific hallucinations* **delusion,** illusion, figment of the imagination, mirage, chimera, fantasy.

hal·lu·ci·na·to·ry /həˈlo͞osənəˌtôrē/ ▶ **adjective** resembling or causing hallucinations: *hallucinatory drugs.*

hal·lu·ci·no·gen /həˈlo͞osənəjən/ ▶ **noun** a drug causing hallucinations.
– DERIVATIVES **hal·lu·ci·no·gen·ic** adjective.

hall·way /ˈhôlˌwā/ ▶ **noun** another term for **HALL** (sense 2).

ha·lo /ˈhālō/ ▶ **noun** (pl. **haloes** or **halos**) **1** (in a painting) a circle of light surrounding the head of a holy person. **2** a circle of light around the sun or moon, refracted through ice crystals in the atmosphere. ▶ **verb** (**haloes, haloing, haloed**) surround someone or something with a halo, or with something resembling a halo.
– ORIGIN Greek *halōs* 'disc of the sun or moon.'

hal·o·gen /ˈhaləjən/ ▶ **noun** any of the nonmetallic chemical elements fluorine, chlorine, bromine, iodine, and astatine. ▶ **adjective** using a filament surrounded by iodine vapor or that of another halogen: *a halogen bulb.*
– ORIGIN from Greek *hals* 'salt.'

hal·on /ˈhāˌlän/ ▶ **noun** any of a number of gaseous compounds of carbon with halogens, used in fire extinguishers.
– ORIGIN from **HALOGEN**.

halt[1] /hôlt/ ▶ **verb** bring or come to an abrupt stop.

– SYNONYMS **1** *halt at the barrier* **stop,** come to a halt, come to a stop, come to a standstill, pull up. **2** *a strike halted production* **stop,** bring to a stop, put a stop to, suspend, arrest, check, curb, stem, staunch, block, stall.

▶ **noun** a stopping of movement or activity.

– SYNONYMS **1 stop,** standstill. **2 stoppage,** break, pause, interval, interruption.
– ANTONYMS start.

– PHRASES **call a halt** stop something: *he decided to call a halt to all further discussions.*
– ORIGIN German *halten* 'to hold.'

halt² ▶ **adjective** old use lame or limping.
– ORIGIN Old English.

halt·er /ˈhôltər/ ▶ **noun 1** a rope or strap placed around the head of an animal and used to lead or tether it. **2** old use a noose for hanging a person. **3** a strap by which the bodice of a sleeveless dress or top is fastened or held behind the neck, leaving the shoulders and back bare. **4** a top with such a neck. ▶ **verb** put a halter on an animal.
– ORIGIN Old English.

hal·ter neck ▶ **noun** (also **halter top**) a style of woman's top that is fastened behind the neck, leaving the shoulders, upper back, and arms bare.

halt·ing /ˈhôltiNG/ ▶ **adjective** slow and hesitant.

– SYNONYMS **hesitant,** faltering, hesitating, stumbling, stammering, stuttering, broken, imperfect.
– ANTONYMS fluent.

– DERIVATIVES **halt·ing·ly** adverb.

hal·vah /ˈhälvä/ (also **halva**) ▶ **noun** a Middle Eastern confection made of sesame flour and honey.
– ORIGIN Arabic and Persian, 'sweetmeat.'

halve /hav, häv/ ▶ **verb 1** divide something into two parts of equal size. **2** reduce or be reduced by half: *pre-tax profits halved to $5 million.*

halves /havz, hävz/ plural of **HALF**.

hal·yard /ˈhalyərd/ ▶ **noun** a rope used for raising and lowering a sail, yard, or flag on a ship.
– ORIGIN from **HALE²**.

ham¹ /ham/ ▶ **noun 1** meat from the upper part of a pig's leg that has been salted and dried or smoked. **2** (**hams**) the back of the thigh or the thighs and buttocks.
– ORIGIN from a Germanic word meaning 'be crooked.'

ham² ▶ **noun 1** a bad actor, especially one who overacts. **2** (also **radio ham**) informal an amateur radio operator. ▶ **verb** (**hams, hamming, hammed**) informal overact.
– ORIGIN perhaps from the first syllable of **AMATEUR**.

ham·a·dry·ad /ˌhaməˈdrīəd/ ▶ **noun** (in classical mythology) a nymph who lives in a tree and dies when the tree dies.
– ORIGIN from Greek *hama* 'together' + *drus* 'tree.'

ham·burg·er /ˈhamˌbərgər/ ▶ **noun** a small patty of ground beef, fried, broiled, or grilled and typically served on a bun or roll.
– ORIGIN German, from the city of *Hamburg* in Germany.

ham-fist·ed /ˈham ˌfistid/ (also **ham-handed**) ▶ **adjective** informal clumsy; awkward.

ham·let /ˈhamlit/ ▶ **noun** a small village or settlement.
– ORIGIN Old French *hamelet.*

ham·mam /haˈmäm, həˈmäm/ ▶ **noun** a Turkish bath.
– ORIGIN from Turkish or Arabic, 'bath.'

ham·mer /ˈhamər/ ▶ **noun 1** a tool consisting of a heavy metal head mounted at the end of a handle, used for breaking things and driving in nails. **2** an auctioneer's mallet, tapped to indicate a sale. **3** a part of a mechanism that hits another, e.g., one exploding the charge in a gun. **4** a heavy metal ball attached to a wire for throwing in an athletic contest. ▶ **verb 1** hit something repeatedly. **2** (**hammer away**) work hard and persistently. **3** (**hammer something in/into**) make something stick in someone's mind by constant repetition: *a story that has been hammered into her since childhood.* **4** (**hammer something out**) laboriously work out the details of a plan or agreement. **5** informal utterly defeat a person or team in a contest.

– SYNONYMS **beat,** batter, bang, pummel, pound, knock, thump.

– PHRASES **come** (or **go**) **under the hammer** be sold at an auction. **hammer and tongs** informal with great energy or enthusiasm.
– ORIGIN Old English.

ham·mer and sick·le ▶ **noun** the symbols of the industrial worker and the peasant used as the emblem of the former Soviet Union and of international communism.

ham·mer drill ▶ **noun** a power drill that delivers a rapid succession of blows.

ham·mer·head /ˈhamərˌhed/ ▶ **noun** a shark with flattened extensions on either side of the head.

ham·mer·lock /ˈhamərˌläk/ ▶ **noun** an armlock in which a person's arm is bent up behind their back.

ham·mer·toe /ˈhamərˌtō/ ▶ **noun** a toe that is bent permanently downward, typically as a result of pressure from footwear.

ham·mock /ˈhamək/ ▶ **noun** a wide strip of canvas or rope mesh suspended at both ends, used as a bed.
– ORIGIN from Taino (an extinct Caribbean language).

Ham·mond or·gan /ˈhamənd/ ▶ **noun** trademark a type of electronic organ.
– ORIGIN named after the American mechanical engineer Laurens *Hammond.*

ham·my /ˈhamē/ ▶ **adjective** (**hammier, hammiest**) informal (of acting) exaggerated or overly theatrical.

ham·per¹ /ˈhampər/ ▶ **noun 1** a large basket with a lid, used for laundry. **2** a basket with a handle and a hinged lid, used for food, cutlery, etc., on a picnic.
– ORIGIN Old French *hanaper* 'case for a goblet.'

hamper² ▶ **verb** slow down or prevent the movement or progress of: *their work is hampered by lack of funds.*

– SYNONYMS **hinder,** obstruct, impede, inhibit, delay, slow down, hold up, interfere with, handicap, hamstring.
– ANTONYMS help.

– ORIGIN perhaps related to German *hemmen* 'restrain.'

ham·ster /ˈhamstər/ ▶ **noun** a burrowing rodent with a short tail and large cheek pouches, native to Europe and North Asia, often kept as a pet.
– ORIGIN German *hamustro* 'corn-weevil.'

ham·string /ˈhamˌstriNG/ ▶ **noun 1** any of five tendons at the back of a person's knee. **2** the large tendon at the back of the hind leg of a horse or other four-legged animal. ▶ **verb** (past and past part. **hamstrung**) **1** cripple a person or animal by cutting their hamstrings. **2** prevent someone or something from taking action or making progress.
– ORIGIN from **HAM¹** + **STRING**.

Han /han/ ▸ **noun 1** the Chinese dynasty that ruled almost continuously from 206 BC until AD 220. **2** the dominant ethnic group in China.

hand /hand/ ▸ **noun 1** the end part of the arm beyond the wrist. **2** a pointer on a clock or watch indicating the passing of units of time. **3** (**hands**) a person's power or control: *taking the law into their own hands.* **4** an active role: *he had a big hand in organizing the event.* **5** help in doing something: *do you need a hand?* **6** a person who does physical work, especially in a factory, on a farm, or on board a ship. **7** informal a round of applause. **8** the set of cards dealt to a player in a card game. **9** a person's handwriting or workmanship. **10** a unit of measurement of a horse's height, equal to 4 inches (10.16 cm). **11** dated a promise of marriage made by or on behalf of a woman.

– SYNONYMS **1 fist,** palm; informal paw, mitt. **2 handwriting,** writing, script. **3 worker,** employee, workman, laborer, hired hand, operative, craftsman.

▸ **verb 1** give something to someone. **2** (**hand something down**) pass something to a successor or descendant. **3** (**hand something in**) give something to a person in authority for their attention. **4** (**hand something out**) distribute something among a group.

– SYNONYMS **pass,** give, present, let someone have.

▸ **adjective 1** operated by or held in the hand: *hand luggage.* **2** done or made manually: *hand signals.*

– PHRASES **at hand** easy to reach; near. **by hand** by a person and not a machine. **get** (or **keep**) **one's hand in** become (or remain) practiced in something. **hand in glove** in close association. **hand in hand** closely associated or connected. (**from**) **hand to mouth** satisfying only one's immediate needs; with no money in reserve. **hands down** easily and decisively. **in hand 1** in progress or receiving attention. **2** ready for use if required. **in safe hands** protected by someone trustworthy. **make** (or **lose** or **spend**) **money hand over fist** informal make (or lose or spend) money very rapidly. **on hand** present and available. **on someone's hands 1** as someone's responsibility. **2** at someone's disposal: *he has time on his hands.* **on the one** (or **the other**) **hand** used to present factors for (and against) something. **out of hand 1** not under control. **2** without taking time to think: *the proposal was rejected out of hand.* **to hand** within easy reach. **turn one's hand to** do something that is different from one's usual occupation.

– ORIGIN Old English.

WORD LINKS

manual *relating to the hands*

hand·bag /ˈhan(d)ˌbag/ ▸ **noun** a woman's purse.

hand·ball /ˈhan(d)ˌbôl/ ▸ **noun 1** a game similar to squash, in which the ball is hit with the hand in a walled court. **2** Soccer unlawful touching of the ball with the hand or arm.

hand·bell /ˈhan(d)ˌbel/ ▸ **noun** a small bell, especially one of a set tuned to a range of notes and played by a group of people.

hand·bill /ˈhan(d)ˌbil/ ▸ **noun** a small printed advertisement or other notice distributed by hand.

hand·book /ˈhan(d)ˌbo͝ok/ ▸ **noun** a book giving basic information or instructions.

– SYNONYMS **manual,** instructions, ABC, A to Z, companion, guide, guidebook, vade mecum.

hand·brake /ˈhan(d)ˌbrāk/ ▸ **noun 1** the emergency or parking brake on a motor vehicle. **2** a brake operated by hand, as on a bicycle.

hand·cart /ˈhan(d)ˌkärt/ ▸ **noun** a small cart pushed or drawn by hand.

hand·clap /ˈhan(d)ˌklap/ ▸ **noun** a clapping of the hands.

hand·craft·ed /ˈhan(d)ˌkraftid/ ▸ **adjective** made skillfully by hand.

hand·cuff /ˈhan(d)ˌkəf/ ▸ **noun** (**handcuffs**) a pair of lockable linked metal rings for securing a prisoner's wrists.

– SYNONYMS **manacles,** shackles, irons; informal cuffs, bracelet.

▸ **verb** put handcuffs on someone.

– SYNONYMS **manacle,** shackle, clap/put someone in irons; informal cuff.

hand·ful /ˈhan(d)ˌfo͝ol/ ▸ **noun** (pl. **handfuls**) **1** a quantity that fills the hand. **2** a small number or amount. **3** informal a person who is difficult to deal with or control.

– SYNONYMS **few,** small number, small amount, small quantity, sprinkling, smattering, one or two, some, not many.
– ANTONYMS lot.

hand gre·nade ▸ **noun** a hand-thrown grenade.

hand·grip /ˈhan(d)ˌgrip/ ▸ **noun 1** a handle for holding onto something. **2** a grasp with the hand, especially considered in terms of its strength, as in a handshake.

hand·gun /ˈhan(d)ˌgən/ ▸ **noun** a gun designed for use with one hand.

hand·held /ˈhandˌheld/ ▸ **adjective** designed to be held in the hand: *a handheld metal detector.*

hand·hold /ˈhandˌhōld/ ▸ **noun** something for a hand to grip on.

hand·i·cap /ˈhandēˌkap/ ▸ **noun 1** a condition that restricts a person's ability to function physically, mentally, or socially. **2** something that makes progress or success difficult: *not being able to drive was something of a handicap.* **3** a disadvantage placed on a superior competitor in a sport in order to make the chances more equal, such as the extra weight given to a racehorse on the basis of its previous performance. **4** the number of strokes by which a golfer normally exceeds par for a course.

– SYNONYMS **1 disability,** infirmity, defect, impairment, affliction. **2 impediment,** hindrance, obstacle, barrier, constraint, disadvantage, stumbling block.
– ANTONYMS benefit, advantage.

▸ **verb** (**handicaps, handicapping, handicapped**) make it difficult for someone or something to progress or succeed: *the industry was handicapped by an acute manpower shortage.*

– SYNONYMS **hamper,** impede, hinder, impair, hamstring, restrict, constrain.
– ANTONYMS help.

– ORIGIN from the phrase *hand in cap,* an old gambling game which involved players putting their hands into a cap in which money had been deposited.

hand·i·capped /ˈhandēˌkapt/ ▸ **adjective** (of a person) having a condition that restricts their ability to function physically, mentally, or socially.

USAGE

Until quite recently the word **handicapped** was the standard term used to refer to people with physical and mental disabilities. For a brief period in the second half of the 20th century, it looked as if **handicapped** would be replaced by **disabled**, but both words are now acceptable and interchangeable in standard American English, and neither word has been overtaken by newer coinages such as **differently abled** or **physically** (or **mentally**) **challenged**.

hand·i·craft /ˈhandēˌkraft/ ▶ **noun 1** an activity involving the making of decorative objects by hand. **2** decorative objects made by hand.

hand·i·work /ˈhandēˌwərk/ ▶ **noun 1** (**one's handiwork**) something that one has made or done. **2** the making of things by hand.

hand·ker·chief /ˈhaNGkərCHif, -CHēf/ ▶ **noun** (pl. **handkerchiefs** or **handkerchieves** /ˈhaNGkərCHivz, -CHēvz/) a square of cotton or other material for wiping one's nose.

han·dle /ˈhandl/ ▶ **verb 1** feel or manipulate something with the hands. **2** deal or cope with a situation, person, or problem: *he handled the interview confidently*. **3** control or manage something commercially. **4** (**handle oneself**) behave oneself in a particular way. **5** (of a vehicle) respond in a particular way when being driven: *the new model does not handle well*.

– SYNONYMS **1 hold,** pick up, grasp, grip, lift, finger. **2 control,** drive, steer, operate, maneuver. **3 deal with,** manage, tackle, take care of, look after, take charge of, attend to, see to, sort out. **4 trade in,** deal in, buy, sell, supply, peddle, traffic in.

▶ **noun 1** the part by which a thing is held, carried, or controlled. **2** a way of understanding, controlling, or approaching a person or situation: *they seem unable to get a handle on the problem*. **3** informal the name of a person or place.

– SYNONYMS **grip,** haft, hilt, stock, shaft.

– DERIVATIVES **han·dled** adjective **hand·ling** noun.
– ORIGIN Old English.

han·dle·bar /ˈhandlˌbär/ (also **handlebars**) ▶ **noun** the steering bar of a bicycle or motorcycle.

han·dle·bar mus·tache ▶ **noun** a wide, thick mustache with the ends curving slightly upward.

han·dler /ˈhandlər/ ▶ **noun 1** a person who handles a particular type of article: *baggage handlers*. **2** a person who trains or has charge of an animal. **3** a person who trains or manages another person.

hand·made /ˈhan(d)ˈmād/ ▶ **adjective** made by hand rather than machine.

hand·maid·en /ˈhan(d)ˌmādn/ ▶ **noun 1** old use a female servant. **2** a subservient partner or element: *shipping is the handmaiden of commerce and industry*.

hand-me-down ▶ **noun** a garment or other item that has been passed on from another person.

hand·off /ˈhandˌôf, -ˌäf/ ▶ **noun 1** a transfer of power, control, or responsibility. **2** Football an exchange made by handing the ball to a teammate.

hand·out /ˈhandˌout/ ▶ **noun 1** an amount of money or other aid given to a person or organization. **2** a piece of printed information provided free of charge, especially to accompany a lecture.

hand·o·ver /ˈhandˌōvər/ ▶ **noun** an act of handing something over.

hand-pick ▶ **verb** select someone or something carefully.

hand·print /ˈhandˌprint/ ▶ **noun** the mark left by the impression of a hand.

hand·rail /ˈhan(d)ˌrāl/ ▶ **noun** a rail fixed to posts or a wall for people to hold onto for support.

hand·saw /ˈhan(d)ˌsô/ ▶ **noun** a wood saw worked by one hand.

hand·set /ˈhan(d)ˌset/ ▶ **noun 1** the part of a telephone that is held up to speak into and listen to. **2** a hand-held control device for a piece of electronic equipment.

hands-free ▶ **adjective** (especially of a telephone) designed to be operated without using the hands.

hand·shake /ˈhan(d)ˌSHāk/ ▶ **noun** an act of shaking a person's hand.
– DERIVATIVES **hand·shak·ing** noun.

hands-off ▶ **adjective** not involving or requiring direct control or intervention: *her hands-off management style*.

hand·some /ˈhansəm/ ▶ **adjective** (**handsomer, handsomest**) **1** (of a man) good-looking. **2** (of a woman) striking and strong-featured rather than conventionally pretty. **3** (of a thing) well made and of obvious quality. **4** (of an amount) large: *a handsome profit*.

– SYNONYMS **1 good-looking,** attractive, striking; informal hunky, cute. **2 substantial,** considerable, sizable, princely, generous, lavish, ample, bumper; informal tidy.
– ANTONYMS ugly.

– DERIVATIVES **hand·some·ly** adverb **hand·some·ness** noun.
– ORIGIN from **HAND**, first meaning 'easy to handle or use.'

hands-on ▶ **adjective** involving or offering active participation.

hand·spring /ˈhandˌspriNG/ ▶ **noun** a jump through the air onto one's hands followed by another onto one's feet.

hand·stand /ˈhandˌstand/ ▶ **noun** an act of balancing upside down on one's hands.

hand-to-hand ▶ **adjective** (of fighting) at close quarters and involving physical contact between the opponents.

hand·work /ˈhandˌwərk/ ▶ **noun** work done with the hands: *the transition from handwork to machine production*.
– DERIVATIVES **hand·worked** adjective.

hand·wo·ven /ˈhandˈwōvən/ ▶ **adjective** made on a hand-operated loom.

hand·writ·ing /ˈhan(d)ˌrītiNG/ ▶ **noun 1** writing with a pen or pencil rather than by typing or printing. **2** a person's particular style of writing.
– PHRASES **the handwriting** (or **writing**) **is on the wall** there are clear signs that something unpleasant or unwelcome is going to happen. [with reference to Belshazzar's feast in the Bible (Book of Daniel, chapter 5), at which mysterious writing appeared on the wall foretelling Belshazzar's overthrow.]

hand·writ·ten /ˈhan(d)ˌritn/ ▶ **adjective** written with a pen or pencil.

hand·y /ˈhandē/ ▶ **adjective** (**handier, handiest**) **1** convenient to handle or use; useful. **2** in a convenient place or position. **3** skillful with one's hands.

– SYNONYMS **1 useful,** convenient, practical, neat, easy to use, user-friendly, helpful, functional. **2 ready,** to hand, within reach, accessible, readily available, nearby, at the ready. **3 skillful,** skilled, dexterous, deft, adept, proficient.

– DERIVATIVES **hand·i·ly** adverb **hand·i·ness** noun.

hand·y·man /ˈhandēˌman/ ▶ **noun** (pl. **handymen**) a person employed to do renovations or domestic repairs.

hang /haNG/ ▶ **verb** (past and past part. **hung** except in sense 2) **1** suspend or be suspended from above with the lower part not attached. **2** (past and past part. **hanged**) kill someone by suspending them from a rope tied around the neck (used as a form of capital punishment). **3** attach something so as to allow free movement about the point of attachment (such as a hinge): *hanging a door.* **4** (of fabric or a garment) fall or drape in a particular way. **5** attach meat or game to a hook and leave it until it is ready to cook. **6** paste wallpaper to a wall. **7** remain static in the air: *a cloud of smoke hung over the city.* **8** (of something bad or unwelcome) be oppressively present or imminent: *a sense of dread hung over him.*

– SYNONYMS **1** *lights hung from the trees* **be suspended,** dangle, swing, sway, hover, float. **2** *hang the picture at eye level* **suspend,** put up, pin up, display. **3 decorate,** adorn, drape, festoon, deck out. **4 send to the gallows,** execute, lynch; informal string up.

▶ **noun** the way in which something hangs or is hung.
▶ **exclamation** dated used in expressions as a mild oath.
– PHRASES **get the hang of** informal learn how to operate or do something. **hang around 1** wait around; loiter. **2** (**hang around with**) associate with someone. **hang back** remain behind. **hang fire** delay taking action. **hang on 1** hold tightly. **2** informal wait for a short time. **3** be dependent on: *so much hangs on exam results.* **4** listen closely to something. **hang out** informal spend time relaxing or enjoying oneself. **hang tough** informal be or remain inflexible or firmly resolved. **hang up** end a telephone conversation by cutting the connection.
– ORIGIN Old English.

USAGE

Hang has two past tense and past participle forms: **hanged** and **hung**. Use **hung** in general situations (*they hung out the washing*), but use **hanged** to refer to execution of someone by hanging (*the prisoner was hanged*).

hang·ar /ˈhaNGər/ ▶ **noun** a large building in which aircraft are kept.
– ORIGIN French.

hang·dog /ˈhaNGˌdôg, -ˌdäg/ ▶ **adjective** having a dejected or guilty appearance; shamefaced.

hang·er /ˈhaNGər/ ▶ **noun 1** a person who hangs something. **2** (also **coat hanger**) a curved frame of wood, plastic, or metal with a hook at the top, for hanging clothes from a rail.

hang·er-on ▶ **noun** (pl. **hangers-on**) someone who tries to associate with a rich or powerful person in order to benefit from the relationship.

hang glid·er ▶ **noun** an unpowered flying device for a single person, consisting of a frame with fabric stretched over it from which the operator is suspended.
– DERIVATIVES **hang-glide** verb **hang-glid·ing** noun.

hang·ing /ˈhaNGiNG/ ▶ **noun 1** the practice of hanging condemned criminals as a form of capital punishment. **2** a decorative piece of fabric hung on the wall of a room or around a bed. ▶ **adjective** suspended in the air.

hang·man /ˈhaNGmən, -ˌman/ ▶ **noun** (pl. **hangmen**) an executioner who hangs condemned people.

hang·nail /ˈhaNGˌnāl/ ▶ **noun** a piece of torn skin at the root of a fingernail.
– ORIGIN Old English.

hang·out /ˈhaNGˌout/ ▶ **noun** informal a place where someone spends a great deal of time.

hang·o·ver /ˈhaNGˌōvər/ ▶ **noun 1** a severe headache or other aftereffects caused by drinking too much alcohol. **2** a custom, feeling, etc., that has survived from the past: *this feeling of insecurity was a hangover from her schooldays.*

hang-up ▶ **noun** informal an emotional problem or inhibition.

– SYNONYMS **neurosis,** phobia, preoccupation, fixation, obsession, inhibition, mental block; informal complex, thing, issue, bee in one's bonnet.

hank /haNGk/ ▶ **noun** a coil or length of wool, hair, or other material.
– ORIGIN Old Norse.

hank·er /ˈhaNGkər/ ▶ **verb** (**hanker after/for/to do**) feel a desire for or to do: *she hankered after a traditional white wedding.*

– SYNONYMS **yearn,** long, wish, hunger, thirst, lust, ache; informal itch.

– ORIGIN probably related to **HANG**.

han·ky /ˈhaNGkē/ (also **hankie**) ▶ **noun** (pl. **hankies**) informal a handkerchief.

han·ky-pan·ky /ˈpaNGkē/ ▶ **noun** informal behavior considered to be slightly improper.
– ORIGIN uncertain.

Han·o·ve·ri·an /ˌhanəˈve(ə)rēən/ ▶ **adjective** relating to the royal house of Hanover, who ruled as monarchs in Britain from 1714 to 1901.

Han·sard /ˈhansərd/ ▶ **noun** the official word-for-word record of debates in the British, Canadian, Australian, New Zealand, or South African parliament.
– ORIGIN named after the English printer Thomas C. *Hansard.*

Han·sen's dis·ease /ˈhansənz/ ▶ **noun** another term for **LEPROSY**.
– ORIGIN named after the Norwegian physician Gerhard H. A. *Hansen.*

han·som /ˈhansəm/ (also **hansom cab**) ▶ **noun** historical a two-wheeled horse-drawn cab for two passengers, with the driver seated behind.
– ORIGIN named after the English architect Joseph A. *Hansom.*

han·ta·vi·rus /ˈhantəˌvīrəs/ ▶ **noun** one of several viruses, carried by rodents, that can cause disease in humans.
– ORIGIN from *Hantaan* (a river in Korea where the virus was first isolated).

Ha·nuk·kah /ˈKHänəkə, ˈhänəkə/ (also **Chanukkah**) ▶ **noun** an eight-day Jewish festival of lights held in December, commemorating the rededication of the Jewish Temple in Jerusalem.
– ORIGIN Hebrew, 'consecration.'

hap·haz·ard /ˌhapˈhazərd/ ▶ **adjective** having no particular order or plan; disorganized.

– SYNONYMS **random,** disorderly, indiscriminate, chaotic, hit-and-miss, aimless, chance; informal higgledy-piggledy.
– ANTONYMS methodical.

– DERIVATIVES **hap·haz·ard·ly** adverb.

hap·less /'haplis/ ▶ **adjective** unlucky; unfortunate.

– SYNONYMS **unfortunate,** unlucky, unhappy, wretched, miserable.
– ANTONYMS lucky.

– DERIVATIVES **hap·less·ly** adverb.

hap·loid /'hap,loid/ ▶ **adjective** (of a cell or nucleus) containing a single set of unpaired chromosomes. Compare with **DIPLOID**.

hap·pen /'hapən/ ▶ **verb 1** take place; occur. **2** come about by chance: *it just so happened that she turned up that afternoon.* **3** (**happen on**) come across something by chance: *I happened on a street with a few restaurants.* **4** chance to do something or come about. **5** (**happen to**) be experienced by: *the same thing happened to me.* **6** (**happen to**) become of: *I don't care what happens to the money.*

– SYNONYMS **1 occur,** take place, come about, arise, develop, result, transpire; informal go down; literary come to pass. **2** *I happened to be in Yuma* **chance,** have the good/bad luck.

– PHRASES **as it happens** actually; as a matter of fact.

CHOOSE THE RIGHT WORD

happen, befall, occur, transpire

When things **happen**, they come to pass either for a reason or by chance (*it happened the day after school started; she happened upon the scene of the accident*), but the verb is more frequently associated with chance (*it happened to be raining when we got there*). **Occur** can also refer either to something that comes to pass either accidentally or as planned, but it should only be used interchangeably with *happen* when the subject is a definite or actual event (*the tragedy occurred last winter*). Unlike *happen, occur* also carries the implication of something that presents itself to sight or mind (*it never occurred to me that he was lying*). **Transpire** is a more formal (and some would say undesirable) word meaning to *happen* or *occur,* and it conveys the sense that something has leaked out or become known (*he told her exactly what had transpired while she was away*). While things that *happen, occur,* or *transpire* can be either positive or negative, when something **befalls** it is usually unpleasant (*he had no inkling of the disaster that would befall him when he got home*).

hap·pen·ing /'hap(ə)niNG/ ▶ **noun** an event or occurrence.

– SYNONYMS **occurrence,** event, incident, episode, affair.

▶ **adjective** informal fashionable.

hap·pen·stance /'hapən,stans/ ▶ **noun** coincidence.
– ORIGIN blend of **HAPPEN** and **CIRCUMSTANCE**.

hap·pi·ly /'hapəlē/ ▶ **adverb 1** in a happy way. **2** it is fortunate that.

– SYNONYMS **1** *he smiled happily* **cheerfully,** contentedly, cheerily, merrily, joyfully. **2** *I will happily do as you ask* **gladly,** willingly, readily, freely. **3** *happily, we are living in enlightened times* **fortunately,** luckily, thankfully, mercifully, as luck would have it.

hap·pi·ness /'hapēnis/ ▶ **noun** the condition of being happy.

– SYNONYMS *trying to rediscover the happiness we once knew* **pleasure,** contentment, well-being, satisfaction, cheerfulness, good spirits, merriment, joy, joyfulness, delight, elation, jubilation.
– ANTONYMS sadness.

hap·py /'hapē/ ▶ **adjective** (**happier, happiest**) **1** feeling or showing pleasure or contentment. **2** willing to do something. **3** fortunate and convenient: *a happy coincidence.* **4** (in combination) informal inclined to use a particular thing too readily or at random: *trigger-happy.*

– SYNONYMS **1 cheerful,** cheery, merry, joyful, jovial, jolly, carefree, in good spirits, in a good mood, pleased, contented, content, satisfied, gratified, delighted, sunny, radiant, elated, jubilant; literary blithe. **2 glad,** pleased, delighted, more than willing. **3 fortunate,** lucky, timely, convenient.
– ANTONYMS sad, unhappy, unfortunate.

hap·py-go-luck·y ▶ **adjective** cheerfully unconcerned about the future.

hap·py hour ▶ **noun** a period of the day when drinks are sold at reduced prices in a bar or restaurant.

hap·py hunt·ing ground ▶ **noun** a place where success or enjoyment can be found.
– ORIGIN referring to the optimistic hope of American Indians for good hunting grounds in the afterlife.

hap·py me·di·um ▶ **noun** a satisfactory compromise.

hap·tic /'haptik/ ▶ **adjective** technical relating to the sense of touch.
– ORIGIN Greek *haptikos* 'able to touch or grasp.'

ha·ra-ki·ri /,härə 'ki(ə)rē, ,harə-, ,harē 'karē/ ▶ **noun** a method of ritual suicide involving cutting open the stomach with a sword, formerly practiced in Japan by samurai.
– ORIGIN from the Japanese words for 'belly' + 'cutting.'

ha·ram /'he(ə)rəm, 'harəm/ ▶ **adjective** forbidden by Islamic law.
– ORIGIN Arabic.

ha·rangue /hə'raNG/ ▶ **verb** address a person or group in a loud and aggressive or critical way. ▶ **noun** a forceful and aggressive or critical speech.
– ORIGIN Latin *harenga.*

ha·rass /hə'ras, 'harəs/ ▶ **verb 1** torment someone by putting constant pressure on them or by saying or doing unpleasant things to them: *he had been harassed by the police.* **2** (as adj. **harassed**) feeling tired or tense as a result of too many demands made on one: *harassed parents.* **3** make repeated small-scale attacks on an enemy in order to wear down their resistance.

– SYNONYMS **1 persecute,** intimidate, hound, pester, bother; informal hassle, bug, ride. **2** (as adj. **harassed**) **stressed,** hard-pressed, careworn, worried, troubled; informal hassled.

– DERIVATIVES **ha·rass·er** noun **ha·rass·ment** noun.
– ORIGIN French *harasser,* from *harer* 'set a dog on.'

har·bin·ger /'härbənjər/ ▶ **noun** a person or thing that announces or signals the approach of something: *this plant is the first harbinger of spring.*
– ORIGIN Old French *herbergier* 'provide lodging for.'

har·bor /'härbər/ (Brit. **harbour**) ▶ **noun** a place on the coast where ships may moor in shelter.

– SYNONYMS **port,** dock, haven, marina, mooring, wharf, anchorage, waterfront.

▶ **verb 1** keep a thought or feeling secretly in one's mind. **2** give a refuge or shelter to someone or something. **3** carry the germs of a disease.

– SYNONYMS **1 shelter,** conceal, hide, shield, protect, give asylum to. **2 bear,** hold, nurse, foster.

– ORIGIN Old English, 'shelter.'

hard /härd/ ▸ **adjective 1** solid, firm, and rigid; not easily broken, bent, or pierced. **2** requiring or showing a great deal of endurance or effort; difficult. **3** (of a person) not showing any signs of weakness; tough. **4** done with a great deal of force or strength: *a hard whack*. **5** harsh or unpleasant to the senses: *the hard light of morning*. **6** (of information or a subject of study) concerned with precise facts that can be proved. **7** (of drink) strongly alcoholic. **8** (of a drug) very addictive. **9** (of pornography) very obscene and explicit. **10** referring to an extreme faction within a political party: *the hard left*. **11** (of water) containing mineral salts.

– SYNONYMS **1 firm,** solid, rigid, stiff, unbreakable, unyielding, compacted, compressed, tough, strong. **2 arduous,** strenuous, tiring, exhausting, back-breaking, grueling, heavy, laborious, demanding, uphill. **3 industrious,** diligent, assiduous, conscientious, energetic, keen, enthusiastic, indefatigable. **4 difficult,** puzzling, complicated, complex, intricate, knotty, thorny, problematic. **5 harsh,** unpleasant, grim, austere, difficult, bad, bleak, tough. **6 forceful,** heavy, strong, sharp, violent, powerful.
– ANTONYMS soft, easy, gentle.

▸ **adverb 1** with a great deal of effort or force. **2** so as to be solid or firm. **3** to the fullest extent possible.

– SYNONYMS **1 forcefully,** roughly, heavily, sharply, violently. **2 diligently,** industriously, assiduously, conscientiously, energetically, doggedly; informal like mad, like crazy. **3 closely,** intently, critically, carefully, searchingly.

– DERIVATIVES **hard·ish** adjective **hard·ness** noun.
– PHRASES **be hard put** find it very difficult. **hard and fast** (of a rule or distinction) fixed and definitive. **hard at it** informal busily working. **hard feelings** feelings of resentment. **hard luck** used to express sympathy or commiserations. **hard of hearing** not able to hear well. **hard on** following soon after. **hard up** informal short of money. **the hard way** through suffering or learning from the unpleasant consequences of mistakes: *his reputation was earned the hard way*. **play hard to get** informal deliberately adopt an uninterested attitude.
– ORIGIN Old English.

hard·back /ˈhärd,bak/ ▸ **noun** a book bound in stiff covers.

hard·ball /ˈhärd,bôl/ ▸ **noun 1** baseball, especially as contrasted with softball. **2** informal uncompromising and ruthless methods or dealings, especially in politics: *the leadership played hardball to win the vote*.

hard-bit·ten ▸ **adjective** tough and cynical.

hard·board /ˈhärd,bôrd/ ▸ **noun** stiff board made of compressed and treated wood pulp.

hard-boiled ▸ **adjective 1** (of an egg) boiled until solid. **2** (of a person) tough and cynical.

hard cash ▸ **noun** coins and bills as opposed to other forms of payment.

hard cop·y ▸ **noun** a printed version on paper of data held in a computer.

hard core ▸ **noun 1** the most committed or uncompromising members of a group. **2** very explicit pornography. **3** (usu. **hardcore**) a type of rock or dance music that is experimental, loud, and played aggressively.

hard·cov·er /ˈhärd,kəvər/ ▸ **noun** another term for **HARDBACK.**

hard disk (also **hard drive**) ▸ **noun** Computing a rigid nonremovable magnetic disk with a large data storage capacity.

hard drive ▸ **noun** Computing a self-contained storage device containing a read-write mechanism plus one or more hard disks, inside a sealed unit.

hard·en /ˈhärdn/ ▸ **verb 1** make or become hard or harder. **2** (as adj. **hardened**) fixed in a bad habit or way of life: *hardened criminals*.

– SYNONYMS **1** *this glue will harden in four hours* **solidify,** set, stiffen, thicken, cake, congeal. **2** *their suffering had hardened them* **toughen,** desensitize, inure, numb. **3** (as adj. **hardened**) **inveterate,** seasoned, habitual, chronic, compulsive, confirmed, incorrigible.
– ANTONYMS soften.

– DERIVATIVES **hard·en·er** noun.

hard hat ▸ **noun 1** a rigid protective helmet, as worn at construction sites. **2** informal a worker who wears a hard hat.

hard·head·ed /ˈhärd,hedid/ ▸ **adjective** tough and realistic.

hard-heart·ed ▸ **adjective** unsympathetic or uncaring.

hard-hit·ting ▸ **adjective** uncompromisingly direct and honest.

har·di·hood /ˈhärdē,ho͝od/ ▸ **noun** dated boldness; daring.

hard la·bor ▸ **noun** a type of punishment that takes the form of heavy physical work.

hard line ▸ **noun** a strict and uncompromising policy or attitude: *he takes a hard line on most moral issues*. ▸ **adjective** uncompromising; strict.
– DERIVATIVES **hard·lin·er** noun.

hard·ly /ˈhärdlē/ ▸ **adverb 1** almost no; almost not; almost none: *there was hardly any wind*. **2** no or not. **3** only with great difficulty. **4** only a very short time before: *the party had hardly started when the police arrived*.

– SYNONYMS **scarcely,** barely, only just, just.

hard-nosed ▸ **adjective** informal realistic and tough-minded.

hard-on ▸ **noun** vulgar slang an erection of the penis.

hard pal·ate ▸ **noun** the bony front part of the roof of the mouth.

hard·pan /ˈhärd,pan/ ▸ **noun** a hardened layer, occurring in or below the soil, that resists penetration by water and plant roots.

hard-pressed ▸ **adjective** in difficulties or under pressure: *she'd be hard-pressed to find anyone else who'd put up with her*.

hard rock ▸ **noun** very loud rock music with a heavy beat.

hard·scape /ˈhärd,skāp/ ▸ **noun** the nonliving or constructed fixtures of a planned outdoor area.

hard·scrab·ble /ˈhärd,skrabəl/ ▸ **adjective 1** returning little in exchange for great effort: *her uncle's hardscrabble peanut farm*. **2** characterized by chronic poverty and hardship: *a hardscrabble coal town in the mountains*.

hard sell ▸ **noun** a policy or technique of aggressive selling or advertising.

hard·ship /ˈhärd,sʜip/ ▸ **noun** severe suffering or difficulty.

– SYNONYMS **difficulty,** privation, destitution, poverty, austerity, need, distress, suffering, adversity.
– ANTONYMS prosperity, ease.

hard·tack /ˈhärd,tak/ ▶ **noun** old use hard dry bread or biscuit, especially as rations for sailors or soldiers.

hard·top /ˈhärd,täp/ ▶ **noun** a motor vehicle with a rigid roof that in some cases is detachable.

hard·ware /ˈhärd,we(ə)r/ ▶ **noun 1** tools and other items used in the home and in activities such as gardening. **2** the machines, wiring, and other physical components of a computer. **3** heavy military equipment such as tanks and missiles.

– SYNONYMS **equipment,** apparatus, gear, paraphernalia, tackle, machinery.

hard-wear·ing ▶ **adjective** able to stand much wear.

hard-wired ▶ **adjective** Electronics involving permanently connected circuits rather than software.

hard·wood /ˈhärd,wo͝od/ ▶ **noun** the wood from broad-leaved trees as opposed to that of conifers.

har·dy /ˈhärdē/ ▶ **adjective** (**hardier, hardiest**) **1** capable of enduring difficult conditions; robust. **2** (of a plant) able to survive outside during winter.

– SYNONYMS **robust,** healthy, fit, strong, sturdy, tough, rugged.
– ANTONYMS delicate.

– DERIVATIVES **har·di·ness** noun.
– ORIGIN Old French *hardi.*

hare /he(ə)r/ ▶ **noun** a fast-running, long-eared mammal resembling a large rabbit, with very long hind legs. ▶ **verb** run very fast.
– ORIGIN Old English.

hare·bell /ˈhe(ə)r,bel/ ▶ **noun** a plant with pale blue bell-shaped flowers.

hare·brained /ˈhe(ə)r,brānd/ ▶ **adjective** foolish and unlikely to succeed: *steer clear of harebrained schemes.*

Ha·re Krish·na /,härē ˈkrisнnə, ,harē/ ▶ **noun** a member of a religious sect based on the worship of the Hindu god Krishna.
– ORIGIN Sanskrit, 'O Vishnu Krishna,' a devotional chant.

hare·lip /ˈhe(ə)r,lip/ ▶ **noun** offensive term for CLEFT LIP.

USAGE

The word **harelip** can cause offense and should be avoided; use **cleft lip** instead.

har·em /ˈhe(ə)rəm, ˈhar-/ ▶ **noun 1** the separate part of a Muslim household reserved for women. **2** the wives and concubines of a polygamous Muslim man.
– ORIGIN Arabic, 'prohibited place.'

har·i·cot /ˈhari,kō/ ▶ **noun** a round white variety of French bean.
– ORIGIN French.

ha·ris·sa /həˈrēsə/ ▶ **noun** a hot sauce or paste used in North African cuisine, made from chili peppers, paprika, and olive oil.
– ORIGIN Arabic.

hark /härk/ ▶ **verb 1** literary listen. **2** (**hark back to**) recall or remind one of something in the past.
– ORIGIN Germanic.

hark·en ▶ **verb** variant spelling of HEARKEN.

har·le·quin /ˈhärlik(w)ən/ ▶ **noun** (**Harlequin**) a character in traditional pantomime, wearing a mask and a diamond-patterned costume. ▶ **adjective** in varied colors; variegated.
– ORIGIN former French *Herlequin*, the leader of a legendary troop of demon horsemen.

har·lot /ˈhärlət/ ▶ **noun** old use a prostitute or promiscuous woman.
– DERIVATIVES **har·lot·ry** noun.
– ORIGIN Old French, 'young man, knave.'

harm /härm/ ▶ **noun 1** physical injury to a person. **2** damage done to something. **3** an adverse effect: *there was no harm in looking, was there?*

– SYNONYMS **injury,** damage, mischief, detriment, disservice.
– ANTONYMS good.

▶ **verb 1** physically injure someone. **2** damage or have an adverse effect on: *when we use products that waste energy, we harm the environment.*

– SYNONYMS **1 hurt,** injure, wound, lay a finger on, mistreat, ill-treat, maltreat. **2 damage,** spoil, affect, undermine, ruin.
– ANTONYMS heal, help.

– ORIGIN Old English.

harm·ful /ˈhärmfəl/ ▶ **adjective** causing or likely to cause harm.

– SYNONYMS **damaging,** injurious, detrimental, dangerous, unhealthy, unwholesome, hurtful, destructive, hazardous.
– ANTONYMS beneficial.

– DERIVATIVES **harm·ful·ly** adverb **harm·ful·ness** noun.

harm·less /ˈhärmlis/ ▶ **adjective** not able or likely to cause harm.

– SYNONYMS **1 safe,** innocuous, gentle, mild, nontoxic. **2 inoffensive,** innocuous, innocent, blameless, gentle.
– ANTONYMS harmful, objectionable.

– DERIVATIVES **harm·less·ly** adverb **harm·less·ness** noun.

WORD TOOLKIT

harmless ...	benign ...	nontoxic ...
fun	neglect	paint
drug	lesion	cleaning products
bacteria	tumor	compound
flirting	disease	ingredients
creature	growth	concentration
prank	dictatorship	chemicals

har·mon·ic /härˈmänik/ ▶ **adjective 1** relating to or characterized by harmony. **2** Music relating to a harmonic. ▶ **noun** Music a tone produced by vibration of a string in any of certain fractions (half, third, etc.) of its length.
– DERIVATIVES **har·mon·i·cal·ly** adverb.

har·mon·i·ca /härˈmänikə/ ▶ **noun** a small rectangular wind instrument with a row of metal reeds that produce different notes.

har·mo·ni·ous /härˈmōnēəs/ ▶ **adjective 1** tuneful; not discordant. **2** arranged in a pleasing way so that each part goes well with the others: *dishes providing a harmonious blend of color, flavor, and aroma.* **3** free from disagreement or conflict.

– SYNONYMS **1 melodious,** tuneful, musical, sweet-sounding, mellifluous, dulcet, euphonious. **2 friendly,** amicable, cordial, amiable, congenial,

peaceful, in harmony, in tune. **3 balanced,** coordinated, pleasing, tasteful.
– ANTONYMS discordant, hostile.

– DERIVATIVES **har·mo·ni·ous·ly** adverb **har·mo·ni·ous·ness** noun.

har·mo·ni·um /här'mōnēəm/ ▶ **noun** a keyboard instrument in which the notes are produced by air driven through metal reeds by foot-operated bellows.
– ORIGIN from Greek *harmonios* 'harmonious.'

har·mo·nize /'härməˌnīz/ ▶ **verb 1** add notes to a melody to produce harmony. **2** sing or play in harmony. **3** make or be harmonious or in agreement: *unsweetened coconut harmonizes well with many Indian dishes.* **4** make things consistent with each other.

– SYNONYMS **1 coordinate,** go together, match, blend, mix, balance, tone in, be compatible, be harmonious, suit each other, set each other off. **2 standardize,** coordinate, integrate, synchronize, make consistent, bring into line, systematize.
– ANTONYMS clash.

– DERIVATIVES **har·mo·ni·za·tion** /ˌhärmənə'zāsʜən/ noun **har·mo·niz·er** noun.

har·mo·ny /'härmənē/ ▶ **noun** (pl. **harmonies**) **1** the combination of musical notes sounded at the same time to produce a pleasing effect. **2** a pleasing quality when things are arranged together well. **3** a state of agreement and peaceful existence: *images of racial harmony.*

– SYNONYMS **1 tunefulness,** euphony, unison, melodiousness. **2 accord,** agreement, peace, friendship, fellowship, cooperation, understanding, rapport, unity.
– ANTONYMS dissonance, disagreement.

– ORIGIN Latin *harmonia* 'joining, concord.'

har·ness /'härnis/ ▶ **noun 1** a set of straps and fittings by which a horse or other animal is fastened to a cart, plow, etc., and is controlled by its driver. **2** an arrangement of straps for fastening something such as a parachute to a person's body or for restraining a young child. ▶ **verb 1** fit a horse or other animal with a harness. **2** control and use so as to achieve or produce something: *we will harness new technology to keep the police ahead of the criminals.*
– PHRASES **in harness** in the routine of daily work.
– ORIGIN Old French *harneis* 'military equipment.'

harp /härp/ ▶ **noun** a musical instrument consisting of a frame supporting a series of parallel strings of different lengths, played by plucking with the fingers. ▶ **verb** (**harp on**) keep talking or writing about something in a boring way.
– DERIVATIVES **harp·ist** noun.
– ORIGIN Old English.

har·poon /ˌhär'po͞on/ ▶ **noun** a barbed spearlike missile attached to a long rope and thrown by hand or fired from a gun, used for catching whales and other large sea creatures. ▶ **verb** spear something with a harpoon.
– DERIVATIVES **har·poon·er** noun.
– ORIGIN Greek *harpē* 'sickle.'

harp seal ▶ **noun** a slender North Atlantic seal that typically has a dark harp-shaped mark on its gray back.

harp·si·chord /'härpsiˌkôrd/ ▶ **noun** a keyboard instrument similar in shape to a grand piano, with horizontal strings plucked by points of quill, leather, or plastic operated by pressing the keys.
– DERIVATIVES **harp·si·chord·ist** noun.
– ORIGIN from Latin *harpa* 'harp' + *chorda* 'string.'

har·py /'härpē/ ▶ **noun** (pl. **harpies**) **1** Greek & Roman Mythology a monster with a woman's head and body and a bird's wings and claws. **2** an unpleasant woman.
– ORIGIN Greek *harpuiai* 'snatchers.'

har·que·bus /'(h)ärk(w)əbəs/ (also **arquebus**) ▶ **noun** a former type of portable gun supported on a tripod or a forked rest.
– ORIGIN French *harquebuse.*

har·ri·dan /'haridn/ ▶ **noun** a bossy or aggressive old woman.
– ORIGIN perhaps from French *haridelle* 'old horse.'

har·ri·er¹ /'harēər/ ▶ **noun** a long-winged, slender bird of prey.
– ORIGIN from **HARRY**.

har·ri·er² ▶ **noun** a hound of a breed used for hunting hares.
– ORIGIN from **HARE**.

har·row /'harō/ ▶ **noun** an implement consisting of a heavy frame set with teeth that is dragged over plowed land to break up or spread the soil. ▶ **verb 1** use a harrow to break up soil. **2** (as adj. **harrowing**) very distressing.

– SYNONYMS (as adj. **harrowing**) **distressing,** traumatic, upsetting, shocking, disturbing, painful, agonizing.

– ORIGIN Old Norse.

har·rumph /hə'rəmf/ ▶ **verb 1** clear the throat noisily. **2** grumpily express disapproval.
– ORIGIN imitating the sound.

har·ry /'harē/ ▶ **verb** (**harries, harrying, harried**) **1** carry out repeated attacks on an enemy. **2** harass someone continuously.

– SYNONYMS **harass,** hound, torment, pester, worry, badger, nag, plague; informal hassle, bug.

– ORIGIN Old English.

harsh /härsʜ/ ▶ **adjective 1** unpleasantly rough or intense to the senses: *a harsh white light.* **2** cruel or severe. **3** (of climate or conditions) difficult to survive in; hostile.

– SYNONYMS **1 grating,** rasping, strident, raucous, discordant, jarring, dissonant. **2 garish,** loud, glaring, gaudy, lurid. **3 cruel,** savage, barbarous, merciless, inhumane, ruthless, brutal, hard-hearted, unfeeling, unrelenting. **4 severe,** stringent, firm, stiff, stern, rigorous, uncompromising, draconian. **5 rude,** discourteous, unfriendly, sharp, bitter, unkind, critical, disparaging. **6 austere,** grim, spartan, hard, inhospitable. **7 cold,** freezing, icy, bitter, hard, severe, bleak.
– ANTONYMS kind, mild, gentle.

– DERIVATIVES **harsh·en** verb **harsh·ly** adverb **harsh·ness** noun.
– ORIGIN German *harsch* 'rough.'

hart /härt/ ▶ **noun** an adult male deer, especially a red deer over five years old.
– ORIGIN Old English.

har·te·beest /'härt(ə)ˌbēst/ ▶ **noun** a large African antelope with a long head and sloping back.
– ORIGIN from Dutch *hert* 'hart' + *beest* 'beast.'

har·um-scar·um /'he(ə)rəm 'ske(ə)rəm/ ▶ **adjective** reckless or impetuous.
– ORIGIN from **HARE** and **SCARE**.

har·vest /'härvist/ ▶ **noun 1** the process or period of gathering in crops. **2** the season's yield or crop.

– SYNONYMS **crop,** yield, vintage, produce.

▶ **verb** gather a crop as a harvest.

– SYNONYMS **gather,** bring in, reap, pick, collect.

– DERIVATIVES **har·vest·a·ble** adjective **har·vest·er** noun.
– ORIGIN Old English, 'autumn.'

har·vest·man /'härvəstmən/ ▶ **noun** (pl. **harvestmen**) another term for **DADDY LONGLEGS**.

har·vest moon ▶ **noun** the full moon that is seen closest to the time of the autumnal equinox.

har·vest mouse ▶ **noun** a small mouse that nests among the stalks of growing grains.

has /haz/ third person singular present of **HAVE**.

has-been ▶ **noun** informal a person or thing that is outdated or no longer significant.

hash[1] /hasн/ ▶ **noun** a dish of diced cooked meat reheated with potatoes. ▶ **verb 1** make (meat or other food) into a hash. **2** (**hash something out**) come to agreement on something after much discussion.
– PHRASES **make a hash of** informal make a mess of something. **settle someone's hash** informal deal with someone in a forceful and decisive way.
– ORIGIN French *hache* 'ax.'

hash[2] ▶ **noun** informal hashish.

hash[3] (also **hash mark, hash sign**) ▶ **noun** the symbol #.

hash browns ▶ **plural noun** a dish of chopped and fried cooked potatoes.

hash·ish /'ha,sнēsн/ ▶ **noun** an extract of the cannabis plant.
– ORIGIN Arabic, 'dry herb, powdered hemp leaves.'

Ha·sid /кнä'sēd, 'кнäsid, 'häsid/ (also **Chasid**, **Chassid**, or **Hassid**) ▶ **noun** (pl. **Hasidim** /,кнäsē'dēm, hä'sēdim/) a follower of Hasidism, a mystical Jewish movement founded in the eighteenth century and represented today by fundamentalist communities in Israel and New York.
– DERIVATIVES **Ha·sid·ic** /кнä'sedik, hä'sēdik/ adjective **Has·i·dism** /'hasi,dizəm/ noun.
– ORIGIN from Hebrew, 'pious.'

has·n't /'haznt/ ▶ **contraction** has not.

hasp /hasp/ ▶ **noun** a hinged metal plate that forms part of a fastening for a door or lid and is fitted over a metal loop and secured by a pin or padlock.
– ORIGIN Old English.

Has·sid ▶ **noun** variant spelling of **HASID**.

has·si·um /'hasēəm/ ▶ **noun** a very unstable chemical element made by high-energy atomic collisions.
– ORIGIN from *Hassias*, the Latin name for the German state of *Hesse*.

has·sle /'hasəl/ informal ▶ **noun 1** annoying inconvenience. **2** a situation of conflict or disagreement: *she didn't want to get into a hassle with her dad over money.*

– SYNONYMS **inconvenience,** bother, nuisance, trouble, annoyance, irritation, fuss; informal aggravation, headache, pain in the neck.

▶ **verb** harass or pester someone.

– SYNONYMS **harass,** pester, be on at, badger, hound, bother, nag, torment; informal bug.

– ORIGIN unknown.

has·sock /'hasək/ ▶ **noun 1** a thick, firmly padded cushion, in particular a footstool. **2** a firm clump of grass or matted vegetation in marshy ground.
– ORIGIN Old English, in sense 2.

hast /hast/ old-fashioned second person singular present of **HAVE**.

haste /hāst/ ▶ **noun** speed or urgency in doing something.

– SYNONYMS **1** *working with feverish haste* **speed,** hurriedness, swiftness, rapidity, quickness, briskness, alacrity; old use celerity. **2** *the note was clearly written* ***in haste*** **quickly,** rapidly, fast, speedily, in a rush, in a hurry.
– ANTONYMS delay.

– ORIGIN Old French.

has·ten /'hāsən/ ▶ **verb 1** be quick to do something; move quickly. **2** make something happen sooner than expected.

– SYNONYMS **1 hurry,** rush, dash, race, fly, speed; informal zip, scoot, hotfoot it, hightail it. **2 speed up,** bring on, precipitate, advance.
– ANTONYMS dawdle, delay.

hast·y /'hāstē/ ▶ **adjective** (**hastier, hastiest**) **1** done with speed or urgency. **2** acting too quickly and without much thought: *the medics were a little hasty in predicting an early death for him.*

– SYNONYMS **hurried,** rash, impetuous, impulsive, reckless, precipitate, spur-of-the-moment.
– ANTONYMS considered.

– DERIVATIVES **hast·i·ly** adverb **hast·i·ness** noun.

hat /hat/ ▶ **noun** a shaped covering for the head, typically with a brim and a crown.
– DERIVATIVES **hat·ful** noun **hat·less** adjective **hat·ted** adjective.
– PHRASES **keep something under one's hat** keep something a secret. **pass the hat** collect contributions of money. **take one's hat off to someone** used to express admiration or praise for someone. **talk through one's hat** informal talk foolishly or ignorantly. **throw one's hat in the ring** express willingness to take up a challenge, especially to enter a political race.
– ORIGIN Old English.

hat·band /'hat,band/ ▶ **noun** a decorative ribbon around a hat, just above the brim.

hatch[1] /hacн/ ▶ **noun 1** a small opening in a floor, wall, or roof allowing access from one area to another. **2** a door in an aircraft, spacecraft, or submarine. **3** an opening in the deck of a boat or ship.
– ORIGIN Old English, referring to the lower half of a divided door.

hatch[2] ▶ **verb 1** (of a young bird, fish, or reptile) emerge or cause to emerge from its egg. **2** (of an egg) open and produce a young animal. **3** think up a plot or plan. ▶ **noun** a newly hatched brood.
– ORIGIN unknown.

hatch·back /'hacн,bak/ ▶ **noun** a car with a door across the full width at the back end that opens upward.

hatch·er·y /'hacнərē/ ▶ **noun** (pl. **hatcheries**) an establishment where fish or poultry eggs are hatched.

hatch·et /'hacнit/ ▶ **noun** a small ax with a short handle.
– PHRASES **bury the hatchet** end a quarrel or conflict. [referring to an American Indian custom.]
– ORIGIN Old French *hachette* 'little ax.'

hatch·et job ▶ **noun** informal a fierce spoken or written attack.

hatch·et man ▶ **noun** informal a person employed to carry out unpleasant tasks on behalf of someone else.

hatch·ling /'hacнling/ ▶ **noun** a newly hatched young animal.

hatch·way /ˈhaCH,wā/ ▶ **noun** an opening or hatch, especially in a ship's deck.

hate /hāt/ ▶ **verb** feel intense dislike for someone or something.

– SYNONYMS **1 loathe,** detest, despise, dislike, abhor, shrink from, be unable to bear/stand; formal abominate. **2 be sorry,** be reluctant, be loath.

▶ **noun** intense dislike.

– SYNONYMS **hatred,** loathing, abhorrence, abomination, aversion, disgust.
– ANTONYMS love.

▶ **adjective** (of a hostile act) motivated by intense dislike or prejudice: *a hate crime*.
– DERIVATIVES **hat·er** noun.
– ORIGIN Old English.

hate·ful /ˈhātfəl/ ▶ **adjective** arousing or deserving hate; very unpleasant.
– DERIVATIVES **hate·ful·ly** adverb **hate·ful·ness** noun.

hath /haTH/ old-fashioned third person singular present of **HAVE**.

hath·a yo·ga /ˈhäTHə/ ▶ **noun** a system of physical exercises and breathing control used in yoga.
– ORIGIN *hatha* from Sanskrit, 'force.'

ha·tred /ˈhātrid/ ▶ **noun** intense dislike or ill will.

– SYNONYMS see **HATE**.

hat·ter /ˈhatər/ ▶ **noun** a person who makes and sells hats.
– PHRASES **(as) mad as a hatter** informal completely insane.

hat trick ▶ **noun** three successes of the same kind, especially (in ice hockey or soccer) three goals scored by the same player in a game.
– ORIGIN (in cricket) referring to the presentation of a new hat to a bowler taking a hat trick.

haugh·ty /ˈhôtē/ ▶ **adjective (haughtier, haughtiest)** behaving in an arrogant and superior way toward others.
– DERIVATIVES **haugh·ti·ly** adverb **haugh·ti·ness** noun.
– ORIGIN Old French *hault* 'high.'

haul /hôl/ ▶ **verb 1** pull or drag something with effort. **2** transport something in a truck or cart.

– SYNONYMS **drag,** pull, heave, lug, hump; informal schlep.

▶ **noun 1** a quantity of something obtained, especially illegally: *they escaped with a haul of antiques*. **2** a number of fish caught at one time. **3** a distance to be traveled: *the thirty-mile haul to Boston*.

– SYNONYMS **booty,** loot, plunder, spoils, stolen goods; informal swag.

– DERIVATIVES **haul·er** noun.
– ORIGIN variant of **HALE**[2].

haul·age /ˈhôlij/ ▶ **noun** the commercial transport of goods.

haunch /hônCH, hänCH/ ▶ **noun 1** the buttock and thigh of a human or animal. **2** the leg and loin of an animal, as food.
– ORIGIN Old French *hanche*.

haunt /hônt, hänt/ ▶ **verb 1** (of a ghost) appear regularly in a place. **2** (of a person) visit a place often. **3** be persistently and disturbingly present in the mind: *both men are haunted by memories of death*.

– SYNONYMS **torment,** disturb, trouble, worry, plague, prey on.

▶ **noun** a place frequented by a specified person: *the bar was a favorite haunt of artists*.

– SYNONYMS **meeting place,** stomping ground, stamping ground, spot, venue; informal hangout.

– DERIVATIVES **haunt·er** noun.
– ORIGIN Old French *hanter*.

haunt·ed /ˈhôntid, ˈhän-/ ▶ **adjective 1** (of a place) frequented by a ghost. **2** having or showing signs of great distress.

– SYNONYMS **1 possessed,** cursed, jinxed, eerie. **2 tormented,** anguished, tortured, obsessed, troubled, worried.

haunt·ing /ˈhôntiNG, ˈhän-/ ▶ **adjective** beautiful or sad in a way that is hard to forget: *the haunting sound of the flutes*.

– SYNONYMS **evocative,** affecting, stirring, powerful, poignant, memorable.

– DERIVATIVES **haunt·ing·ly** adverb.

haute cou·ture /ˌōt ˌkoo͞ˈto͝or/ ▶ **noun** the designing and making of high-quality clothes by leading fashion houses.
– ORIGIN French, 'high dressmaking.'

haute cui·sine /ˌōt ˌkwəˈzēn/ ▶ **noun** high-quality cooking in the traditional French style.
– ORIGIN French, 'high cookery.'

hau·teur /hōˈtər/ ▶ **noun** proud haughtiness of manner.
– ORIGIN French.

Ha·va·na /həˈvanə/ ▶ **noun** a cigar made in Cuba or from Cuban tobacco.
– ORIGIN named after *Havana*, the capital of Cuba.

have /hav/ ▶ **verb (has, having, had) 1** possess, own, or hold something. **2** experience: *I had difficulty keeping awake*. **3** be able to make use of something. **4 (have to)** be obliged to; must. **5** perform a particular action: *he had a look around*. **6** show a personal quality or characteristic. **7** suffer from an illness or disability. **8** cause to be or be done: *she had dinner ready*. **9** place, hold, or keep something in a particular position. **10** receive something from someone. **11** take or invite someone into one's home. **12** eat or drink something. **13 (not have)** refuse to allow or accept something. **14 (be had)** informal be cheated or deceived.

– SYNONYMS **1** *he had a new car* **own,** be in possession of, be blessed with, boast, enjoy. **2** *the apartment has five rooms* **comprise,** consist of, contain, include, incorporate, be composed of, be made up of. **3** *we've decided to have a party* **organize,** hold, give, throw, put on, lay on. **4** *I have to get up at six* **must,** be obliged to, be required to, be compelled to, be forced to, be bound to. **5** *she* **had** *a blue dress* **on be wearing,** be dressed in, be clothed in, be decked out in, sport.

▶ **auxiliary verb** used with a past participle to form the perfect, pluperfect, and future perfect tenses, and the conditional mood.
– PHRASES **have had it** informal be beyond repair or revival. **have (got) it in for someone** informal behave in a hostile way toward someone. **have (got) nothing on** informal **1** be not nearly as good as (someone or something), especially in a particular respect: *bright though his three sons were, they had nothing on Sally*. **2 have nothing (or something) on someone** know nothing (or something) discreditable or incriminating about someone: *I am not worried—they've got nothing on me*. **have it out** informal attempt to settle a dispute by confrontation. **the haves and the have-nots** informal people with plenty of money and those who are poor.
– ORIGIN Old English.

USAGE

Be careful not to write **of** when you mean **have** or **'ve**: *I could've told you that*, not *I could of told you that*. The mistake occurs because the pronunciation of **have** can sound the same as that of **of**, so that the words are confused when they are written down.

ha·ven /ˈhāvən/ ▸ **noun 1** a place of safety. **2** a harbor or small port.

– SYNONYMS **refuge,** retreat, shelter, sanctuary, oasis.

– ORIGIN Old English.

have·n't /ˈhavənt/ ▸ **contraction** have not.

hav·er·sack /ˈhavərˌsak/ ▸ **noun** a small, sturdy bag carried on the back or over the shoulder, especially by soldiers and hikers.
– ORIGIN from former German *Habersack* 'bag used to carry oats.'

hav·oc /ˈhavək/ ▸ **noun 1** widespread destruction. **2** great confusion or disorder.

– SYNONYMS **chaos,** mayhem, bedlam, pandemonium, a shambles.

– PHRASES **play havoc with** completely disrupt something.
– ORIGIN Old French *havot*.

haw[1] /hô/ ▸ **noun** the red fruit of the hawthorn.
– ORIGIN Old English.

haw[2] ▸ **verb** see **HEM AND HAW** at **HEM**[2].

Ha·wai·ian /həˈwīən, -ˈwoi-ən/ ▸ **noun 1** a person from Hawaii. **2** the language of Hawaii. ▸ **adjective** relating to Hawaii.

Ha·wai·ian shirt ▸ **noun** a brightly colored and gaily patterned shirt.

hawk[1] /hôk/ ▸ **noun 1** a fast-flying bird of prey with broad rounded wings and a long tail. **2** any bird of prey used in falconry. **3** a person who advocates aggressive policies in foreign affairs. ▸ **verb** hunt game with a trained hawk.
– DERIVATIVES **hawk·ish** adjective.
– ORIGIN Old English.

hawk[2] ▸ **verb** offer goods for sale in the street.
– ORIGIN probably from **HAWKER**.

hawk[3] ▸ **verb 1** clear the throat noisily. **2** (**hawk something up**) bring phlegm up from the throat.
– ORIGIN probably imitating the sound.

hawk·er /ˈhôkər/ ▸ **noun** a person who travels around selling goods.
– ORIGIN probably from German or Dutch.

haw·ser /ˈhôzər/ ▸ **noun** a thick rope or cable for mooring or towing a ship.
– ORIGIN from Old French *haucier* 'to hoist.'

haw·thorn /ˈhôˌTHôrn/ ▸ **noun** a thorny shrub or tree with white, pink, or red blossoms and small dark red fruits (haws).
– ORIGIN Old English.

hay /hā/ ▸ **noun** grass that has been mown and dried for use as fodder.
– DERIVATIVES **hay·ing** noun.
– PHRASES **hit the hay** informal go to bed. **make hay (while the sun shines)** make good use of an opportunity while it lasts.
– ORIGIN Old English.

hay fe·ver ▸ **noun** an allergy to pollen or dust, causing sneezing and watery eyes.

hay·loft /ˈhāˌlôft/ ▸ **noun** a loft over a stable or in a barn used for storing hay or straw.

hay·mak·er /ˈhāˌmākər/ ▸ **noun 1** a person involved in making hay. **2** informal a forceful blow.
– DERIVATIVES **hay·mak·ing** noun.

hay·seed /ˈhāˌsēd/ ▸ **noun** informal, derogatory a simple, unsophisticated country person.

hay·stack /ˈhāˌstak/ ▸ **noun** a large packed pile of hay.

hay·wire /ˈhāˌwīr/ ▸ **adjective** informal out of control: *everybody's weather is going haywire*.
– ORIGIN from the use of hay-baling wire in makeshift repairs.

haz·ard /ˈhazərd/ ▸ **noun 1** a danger or risk of danger: *many people view fast food as a health hazard*. **2** an obstacle, such as a bunker, on a golf course. **3** literary chance; probability.

– SYNONYMS **danger,** risk, peril, menace, jeopardy, threat.

▸ **verb 1** say something in a tentative way. **2** put something at risk of being lost.
– ORIGIN Persian or Turkish, 'dice.'

haz·ard lights ▸ **plural noun** flashing indicator lights on a vehicle, used to warn that the vehicle is stationary or unexpectedly slow.

haz·ard·ous /ˈhazərdəs/ ▸ **adjective** risky; dangerous: *a hazardous construction site*.

– SYNONYMS **risky,** dangerous, unsafe, perilous, precarious, fraught with danger, high-risk; informal dicey.
– ANTONYMS safe.

– DERIVATIVES **haz·ard·ous·ly** adverb.

haz·ard pay ▸ **noun** extra payment for working under dangerous conditions.

haze[1] /hāz/ ▸ **noun 1** a thin mist typically caused by fine particles of dust, pollutants, or water vapor. **2** a state of mental confusion: *I went to bed in an alcoholic haze*.

– SYNONYMS **mist,** fog, cloud, vapor, smoke, steam.

▸ **verb 1** cover or conceal with a haze.
– ORIGIN probably from **HAZY**.

haze[2] ▸ **verb** force a new or potential recruit to the military, a college fraternity, etc., to perform strenuous, humiliating, or dangerous tasks: *rookies were mercilessly hazed*.
– ORIGIN originally Scots and dialect in the sense 'frighten, scold, or beat.'

ha·zel /ˈhāzəl/ ▸ **noun 1** a shrub or small tree bearing catkins in spring and edible nuts in autumn. **2** a reddish-brown or greenish-brown color, especially of someone's eyes.
– ORIGIN Old English.

ha·zel·nut /ˈhāzəlˌnət/ ▸ **noun** the round brown edible nut of the hazel.

haz·mat /ˈhazmat/ ▸ **noun** (often as modifier) dangerous substances; hazardous material: *hazmat shipments*.

ha·zy /ˈhāzē/ ▸ **adjective** (**hazier, haziest**) **1** covered by a haze. **2** vague, unclear, or confused: *those days are a hazy memory*.

– SYNONYMS **1 misty,** foggy, smoggy, murky. **2 vague,** dim, nebulous, blurred, fuzzy.

– DERIVATIVES **ha·zi·ly** adverb **ha·zi·ness** noun.
– ORIGIN unknown.

H-bomb ▶ **noun** short for **HYDROGEN BOMB**.

HDL ▶ **abbreviation** high-density lipoprotein.

HD radio ▶ **noun 1** trademark a technology for broadcasting terrestrial radio signals digitally that permits multicasting in traditional radio bandwidths. **2** a radio capable of receiving these signals.

HDTV ▶ **abbreviation** high-definition television.

He ▶ **symbol** the chemical element helium.

he /hē/ ▶ **pronoun** (third person sing.) **1** used to refer to a man, boy, or male animal previously mentioned or easily identified. **2** used to refer to a person or animal of unspecified sex. ▶ **noun** a male; a man.
– ORIGIN Old English.

USAGE

Until recently, **he** was used to refer to both males and females when a person's sex was not specified; this is now regarded as outdated and sexist. One solution is to use **he or she**, but this can be awkward if used repeatedly. An alternative is to use **they**, especially where it occurs after an indefinite pronoun such as **everyone** or **someone** (as in *everyone needs to feel that they matter*): this is becoming more and more accepted both in speech and in writing.

head /hed/ ▶ **noun 1** the upper part of the body, containing the brain, mouth, and sense organs. **2** a person in charge of something. **3** the front, forward, or upper part or end of something. **4** a person considered as a unit: *they paid fifty dollars a head*. **5** (treated as pl.) a specified number of animals: *seventy head of cattle*. **6** a compact mass of leaves or flowers at the top of a stem. **7** the cutting or operational end of a tool or mechanism. **8** a part of a computer or a tape or video recorder that transfers information to and from a tape or disk. **9** the source of a river or stream. **10** the foam on top of a glass of beer. **11** (**heads**) the side of a coin bearing the image of a head. **12** pressure of water or steam in an engine or other confined space: *a good head of steam*. **13** informal a toilet, especially on a boat or ship.

– SYNONYMS **1 skull,** cranium; informal nut. **2 brain(s),** brainpower, intellect, intelligence, gray matter. informal smarts. **3** *a head for business* **aptitude,** talent, gift, capacity. **4 leader,** chief, controller, governor, superintendent, commander, captain, director, manager, principal, president; informal boss. **5 front,** beginning, start, top.

▶ **adjective** chief; principal.

– SYNONYMS **chief,** principal, leading, main, first, top, highest.

▶ **verb 1** be or act as the head of: *the foreign policy team is headed by an academic*. **2** (**head someone/thing off**) intercept someone or something and force them to turn aside. **3** (**head someone/thing off**) forestall. **4** (also **be headed**) move in a specified direction: *I headed for the exit*. **5** give a title or heading to something. **6** Soccer shoot or pass the ball with the head.

– SYNONYMS **1 command,** control, lead, manage, direct, supervise, superintend, oversee, preside over. **2** (**head someone/thing off**) *he went to head off the cars* **intercept**, divert, redirect, reroute, turn away. **3** (**head someone/thing off**) *they headed off a confrontation* **forestall,** avert, stave off, nip in the bud, prevent, avoid, stop.

– DERIVATIVES **head·ed** adjective **head·less** adjective.
– PHRASES **come to a head** reach a crisis. **go to someone's head 1** (of alcohol) make someone slightly drunk. **2** (of success) make someone conceited. **head first 1** with the head in front of the rest of the body. **2** without thinking beforehand. **a head for** a talent for or an ability to cope with something: *a head for heights*. —— **one's head off** informal talk, laugh, shout, etc., unrestrainedly. **head over heels 1** turning over completely in forward motion. **2** madly in love. **a head start** an advantage granted or gained at the beginning. **keep** (or **lose**) **one's head** remain (or fail to remain) calm. **keep one's head above water** avoid falling into debt or difficulty. **make heads or tails of** understand something at all. **off the top of one's head** without careful thought. **out of one's head** crazy. **over someone's head 1** (also **above someone's head**) beyond someone's ability to understand. **2** without consulting someone. **turn someone's head** make someone conceited.
– ORIGIN Old English.

head·ache /'hed,āk/ ▶ **noun 1** a continuous pain in the head. **2** informal a cause of worry or trouble.

– SYNONYMS **1 sore head,** migraine. **2 problem,** worry, hassle, pain in the neck, bind.

– DERIVATIVES **head·ach·y** adjective.

head·band /'hed,band/ ▶ **noun** a band of fabric worn around the head as a decoration or to keep the hair off the face.

head·bang·er /'hed,baNGər/ ▶ **noun** informal a fan or performer of heavy metal music.

head·board /'hed,bôrd/ ▶ **noun** an upright panel at the head of a bed.

head·butt /'hed,bət/ ▶ **verb** attack someone by hitting them hard with the head. ▶ **noun** an act of headbutting.

head·case /'hed,kās/ ▶ **noun** informal a mentally ill or unstable person.

head count ▶ **noun** a count of the number of people present or available.

head·dress /'hed,dres/ ▶ **noun** an ornamental covering for the head.

head·er /'hedər/ ▶ **noun 1** Soccer a shot or pass made with the head. **2** informal a headlong fall or dive. **3** a line of writing at the top of each page of a book or document. **4** (also **header tank**) a raised tank of water maintaining pressure in a plumbing system. **5** a brick or stone laid at right angles to the face of a wall.

head·gear /'hed,gi(ə)r/ ▶ **noun 1** hats and other items worn on the head. **2** orthodontic equipment worn on the head and attached to braces on the teeth.

head·hunt /'hed,hənt/ ▶ **verb 1** approach someone already employed elsewhere to fill a vacant position. **2** (as n. **headhunting**) the practice among some societies of collecting the heads of dead enemies as trophies.
– DERIVATIVES **head·hunt·er** noun.

head·ing /'hediNG/ ▶ **noun 1** a title at the top of a page or section of a book. **2** a direction or bearing. **3** the top of a curtain extending above the hooks or wire by which it is suspended.

– SYNONYMS **title,** caption, legend, rubric, headline.

head·land /'hedlənd, 'hed,land/ ▶ **noun** a narrow piece of land projecting into the sea.

head·light /'hed,līt/ (also **headlamp** /'hed,lamp/) ▶ **noun** a powerful light at the front of a motor vehicle or railroad engine.

head·line /ˈhed,līn/ ▸ **noun** **1** a heading at the top of an article or page in a newspaper or magazine. **2** (**the headlines**) a summary of the most important items of news. ▸ **verb** **1** provide an article with a headline. **2** appear as the star performer at a concert.

head·lin·er /ˈhed,līnər/ ▸ **noun** a performer or act that is promoted as the star attraction on a program or advertisement.

head·lock /ˈhed,läk/ ▸ **noun** a method of restraining someone by holding an arm firmly around their head.

head·long /ˈhed,lôNG, -,läNG/ ▸ **adverb & adjective** **1** with the head first. **2** in a rush.

– SYNONYMS **1** *he fell headlong into the tent* **head first,** on one's head. **2** *she rushed headlong to join the craze* **without thinking,** precipitously, impetuously, rashly, recklessly, hastily. **3** *a headlong dash* **breakneck,** whirlwind; reckless, precipitate, precipitous, hasty, careless, headless.
– ANTONYMS cautiously, cautious.

head·man /ˈhedmən/ ▸ **noun** (pl. **headmen**) the leader of a tribe.

head·mas·ter /ˈhed,mastər/ (or **headmistress**) ▸ **noun** the man (or woman) in change of a school, especially a private school; the principal.

head of state ▸ **noun** a president, monarch, or other official leader of a country, who may also be the head of government.

head-on ▸ **adjective & adverb** **1** with or involving the front of a vehicle. **2** with or involving direct confrontation.

head·phones /ˈhed,fōnz/ ▸ **plural noun** a pair of earphones joined by a band placed over the head.

head·piece /ˈhed,pēs/ ▸ **noun** a device worn on the head.

head·quar·ter /ˈhed,kwôrtər/ ▸ **verb** (**be headquartered**) have headquarters at a specified place.

head·quar·ters /ˈhed,kwôrtərz/ ▸ **noun** (treated as sing. or pl.) **1** the managerial and administrative center of an organization. **2** the premises occupied by a military commander and the commander's staff.

– SYNONYMS **head office,** HQ, base, nerve center, mission control.

head·rest /ˈhed,rest/ ▸ **noun** a padded support for the head on the back of a seat.

head·room /ˈhed,ro͞om, -,ro͝om/ ▸ **noun** the space between the top of a vehicle or a person's head and the ceiling or other structure above.

head·scarf /ˈhed,skärf/ ▸ **noun** (pl. **headscarves** /-,skärvz/) a square of fabric worn as a covering for the head.

head·set /ˈhed,set/ ▸ **noun** a set of headphones with a microphone attached.

head·ship /ˈhed,SHip/ ▸ **noun** the position of leader: *the rising rate of female headship.*

head·shrink·er /ˈhed,SHriNGkər/ ▸ **noun** informal a psychiatrist, psychologist, or psychotherapist.

head·stone /ˈhed,stōn/ ▸ **noun** an inscribed stone slab set up at the head of a grave.

head·strong /ˈhed,strôNG/ ▸ **adjective** determined to do things in one's own way, regardless of advice to the contrary.

– SYNONYMS **willful,** strong-willed, stubborn, obstinate, obdurate; contrary, perverse, wayward.

heads-up ▸ **noun** informal an advance warning of something: *I had a heads-up on what would happen.*

head-to-head ▸ **adjective & adverb** involving two parties confronting each other in a dispute or contest.

head-turn·ing ▸ **adjective** very noticeable or attractive.

head·wa·ters /ˈhed,wôtərz, -,wätərz/ ▸ **plural noun** the tributary streams of a river close to or forming its source.

head·way /ˈhed,wā/ ▸ **noun** (in phrase **make headway**) make progress.

head·wind /ˈhed,wind/ ▸ **noun** a wind blowing from directly in front.

head·word /ˈhed,wərd/ ▸ **noun** a word that begins a separate entry in a reference book such as a dictionary.

head·y /ˈhedē/ ▸ **adjective** (**headier, headiest**) **1** exciting or exhilarating: *the heady days following the election.* **2** (of alcohol) intoxicating.

– SYNONYMS **1** **exhilarating,** exciting, stimulating, thrilling, intoxicating. **2** **potent,** intoxicating, strong.

– DERIVATIVES **head·i·ly** adverb.

heal /hēl/ ▸ **verb** **1** make or become sound or healthy again. **2** put right an undesirable situation.

– SYNONYMS **1** **cure,** make better, restore to health, treat. **2** **get better,** be cured, recover, recuperate, mend, be on the mend. **3** **put right,** repair, resolve, reconcile, settle; informal **patch up.**

– DERIVATIVES **heal·er** noun.
– ORIGIN Old English.

health /helTH/ ▸ **noun** **1** the state of being free from illness or injury. **2** a person's mental or physical condition.

– SYNONYMS **1** **well-being,** fitness, good condition, strength, robustness, vigor. **2** *her poor health forced her to retire* **condition,** state of health, physical shape, constitution.
– ANTONYMS illness.

– ORIGIN Old English.

WORD LINKS

salubrious *good for the health*

health·care /ˈhelTH,ke(ə)r/ ▸ **noun** the maintenance and improvement of physical and mental health through the provision of medical services.

health cen·ter ▸ **noun** an establishment housing local medical services.

health club ▸ **noun** a private club with exercise facilities and health and beauty treatments.

health food ▸ **noun** food that is thought to be good for one's health.

health·ful /ˈhelTHfəl/ ▸ **adjective** good for one's health.
– DERIVATIVES **health·ful·ly** adverb **health·ful·ness** noun.

CHOOSE THE RIGHT WORD

See **SANITARY**.

health tour·ism ▸ **noun** the practice of traveling abroad in order to receive medical treatment.

health·y /ˈhelTHē/ ▸ **adjective** (**healthier, healthiest**) **1** having or promoting good health. **2** normal, sensible, or desirable. **3** of a very satisfactory size or amount: *a healthy profit.*

– SYNONYMS **1 well,** fit, in good shape, in fine fettle, in tip-top condition, strong, fighting fit; informal in the pink. **2 wholesome,** good for you, health-giving, nutritious, nourishing, invigorating, sanitary, hygienic.

– DERIVATIVES **health·i·ly** adverb **health·i·ness** noun.

heap /hēp/ ▸ **noun 1** a pile of a substance or of a number of objects. **2** informal a large amount or number: *we have heaps of room.* **3** informal an old vehicle in bad condition.

– SYNONYMS **pile,** stack, mound, mountain.

▸ **verb 1** put in or form a heap. **2** (**heap something with**) load something with a large amount of something. **3** (**heap something on**) give much praise, abuse, etc., to: *the press heaped abuse on him.*

– SYNONYMS **pile (up),** stack (up), make a mound of.

– ORIGIN Old English.

hear /hi(ə)r/ ▸ **verb** (past and past part. **heard** /hərd/) **1** perceive a sound with the ear. **2** be told about something. **3** (**have heard of**) be aware of the existence of: *nobody had heard of my college.* **4** (**hear from**) receive a letter or phone call from someone. **5** listen to someone or something. **6** listen to and judge a case or person bringing a case in a court of law.

– SYNONYMS **1 make out,** catch, get, perceive, overhear. **2 learn,** find out, discover, gather, glean. **3 try,** judge, adjudicate on.

– DERIVATIVES **hear·a·ble** adjective **hear·er** noun.

– PHRASES **hear! hear!** used to express full agreement with something in a speech. **will** (or **would**) **not hear of** will (or would) not allow or agree to.

– ORIGIN Old English.

hear·ing /ˈhi(ə)riNG/ ▸ **noun 1** the faculty of perceiving sounds. **2** the range within which sounds may be heard; earshot. **3** an opportunity to state one's case: *a fair hearing.* **4** an act of listening to evidence before an official or in a court of law.

– SYNONYMS **1 earshot,** hearing distance. **2 trial,** court case, inquiry, inquest, tribunal.

WORD LINKS

auditory, **aural** *relating to hearing*

hear·ing aid ▸ **noun** a small amplifying device worn in or on the ear by a partially deaf person.

heark·en /ˈhärkən/ (also **harken**) ▸ **verb** (usu. **hearken to**) old use listen.

– ORIGIN Old English.

hear·say /ˈhi(ə)rˌsā/ ▸ **noun** information received from others that cannot be proved.

hearse /hərs/ ▸ **noun** a vehicle for carrying the coffin at a funeral.

– ORIGIN Old French *herce* 'harrow, frame.'

heart /härt/ ▸ **noun 1** the hollow muscular organ in the chest that pumps the blood around the body. **2** the central, innermost, or vital part: *the heart of the city.* **3** a person's capacity for feeling love or compassion. **4** mood or feeling: *a change of heart.* **5** courage or enthusiasm. **6** a shape representing a heart with two equal curves meeting at a point at the bottom and a cusp at the top. **7** (**hearts**) one of the four suits in a deck of playing cards.

– SYNONYMS **1 center,** middle, hub, core. **2 essence,** crux, core, nub, root, meat, substance, kernel; informal nitty-gritty. **3 compassion,** sympathy, humanity, fellow feeling(s), empathy, understanding, soul, goodwill. **4 emotions,** feelings, sentiments, soul, mind. **5 enthusiasm,** spirit, determination, resolve, nerve.

– PHRASES **after one's own heart** sharing one's tastes. **at heart** in one's real nature, in contrast to how one may appear. **break someone's heart** overwhelm someone with sadness. **by heart** from memory. **close** (or **dear**) **to one's heart** very important to one. **from the** (or **the bottom of one's**) **heart** in a very sincere way. **have a heart of gold** have a very kind nature. **have the heart to do something** be insensitive enough to do something. **have one's heart in one's mouth** be very alarmed or apprehensive. **in one's heart of hearts** in one's innermost feelings. **tug** (or **pull**) **at one's heartstrings** arouse strong feelings of love or pity. **take something to heart** be very upset by criticism. **wear one's heart on one's sleeve** show one's feelings openly.

– ORIGIN Old English.

WORD LINKS

cardiac *relating to the heart*
coronary *relating to the heart's arteries*
cardiology *branch of medicine concerning the heart*

heart·ache /ˈhärtˌāk/ ▸ **noun** distress or grief.

– SYNONYMS **anguish,** suffering, distress, unhappiness, grief, misery, sorrow, sadness, heartbreak, pain, hurt, woe.
– ANTONYMS happiness.

heart at·tack ▸ **noun** a sudden occurrence of coronary thrombosis.

heart·beat /ˈhärtˌbēt/ ▸ **noun** a pulsation of the heart.

– PHRASES **a heartbeat away** very close.

heart·break /ˈhärtˌbrāk/ ▸ **noun** overwhelming distress.

heart·break·er /ˈhärtˌbrākər/ ▸ **noun 1** a person who is very attractive but who is irresponsible in emotional relationships. **2** a story or event that causes overwhelming distress.

heart·break·ing /ˈhärtˌbrākiNG/ ▸ **adjective** causing overwhelming distress.

– SYNONYMS **distressing,** upsetting, disturbing, heart-rending, tragic, painful, sad, agonizing, harrowing.
– ANTONYMS comforting.

heart·bro·ken /ˈhärtˌbrōkən/ ▸ **adjective** suffering from overwhelming distress.

– SYNONYMS **anguished,** devastated, broken-hearted, heavy-hearted, grieving, grief-stricken, inconsolable, crushed, shattered, desolate, despairing; miserable, sorrowful, sad, despondent.

heart·burn /ˈhärtˌbərn/ ▸ **noun** a form of indigestion felt as a burning sensation in the chest, caused by acid regurgitation into the esophagus.

heart·en /ˈhärtn/ ▸ **verb** make more cheerful or confident: *he was heartened by the increase in party membership.*

– DERIVATIVES **heart·en·ing** adjective.

heart fail·ure ▸ **noun** severe failure of the heart to function properly, especially as a cause of death.

heart·felt /ˈhärtˌfelt/ ▸ **adjective** deeply and strongly felt.

– SYNONYMS **sincere,** genuine, from the heart, earnest, profound, deep, wholehearted, honest.
– ANTONYMS insincere.

hearth /härTH/ ▶ **noun** the floor or area in front of a fireplace.
– ORIGIN Old English.

hearth·rug /ˈhärTHˌrəg/ ▶ **noun** a rug laid in front of a fireplace.

heart·i·ly /ˈhärtl-ē/ ▶ **adverb 1** in a hearty way. **2** very: *I'm heartily sick of them.*

> – SYNONYMS **1 wholeheartedly,** warmly, profoundly, eagerly, enthusiastically. **2 thoroughly,** completely, absolutely, exceedingly, downright, quite; informal seriously, real, mighty.

heart·land /ˈhärtˌland/ ▶ **noun 1** the central or most important part of a country or area. **2** the central part of the US; the Midwest.

heart·less /ˈhärtlis/ ▶ **adjective** lacking any pity for others; very unkind or unfeeling.

> – SYNONYMS **unfeeling,** unsympathetic, unkind, uncaring, hard-hearted, cold, callous, cruel, merciless, pitiless, inhuman.
> – ANTONYMS compassionate.

– DERIVATIVES **heart·less·ly** adverb **heart·less·ness** noun.

heart-rend·ing ▶ **adjective** very sad or distressing.

heart·sick /ˈhärtˌsik/ (also **heartsore** /ˈhärtˌsôr/) ▶ **adjective** literary despondent from grief or loss of love.

heart-stop·ping ▶ **adjective** very exciting.

heart·throb /ˈhärtˌTHräb/ ▶ **noun** informal a man, typically a celebrity, whose good looks excite romantic feelings.

heart-to-heart ▶ **adjective** (of a conversation) intimate and personal.

heart·warm·ing /ˈhärtˌwôrmiNG/ ▶ **adjective** emotionally rewarding or uplifting.

> – SYNONYMS **touching,** heartening, stirring, uplifting, cheering, gratifying.
> – ANTONYMS distressing.

heart·wood /ˈhärtˌwo͝od/ ▶ **noun** the dense inner part of a tree trunk, yielding the hardest timber.

heart·y /ˈhärtē/ ▶ **adjective** (**heartier, heartiest**) **1** enthusiastic and friendly. **2** cheerful and full of energy: *a big bluff hearty man.* **3** (of a feeling or opinion) deeply felt. **4** (of a meal) wholesome and filling.

> – SYNONYMS **1 exuberant,** jovial, ebullient, cheerful, lively, loud, animated, vivacious, energetic, spirited. **2 wholehearted,** heartfelt, sincere, genuine, real. **3 robust,** healthy, hardy, fit, vigorous, sturdy, strong. **4 substantial,** large, ample, satisfying, filling, generous.

– DERIVATIVES **heart·i·ness** noun.

heat /hēt/ ▶ **noun 1** the quality of being hot; high temperature. **2** heat as a form of energy arising from the random movement of molecules. **3** a source or level of heat for cooking. **4** intensity of feeling: *an attempt to take some heat out of the debate.* **5** (**the heat**) informal great pressure to do or achieve something: *the heat is on.* **6** a preliminary round in a race or contest.

> – SYNONYMS **1 warmth,** hotness, high temperature. **2 passion,** intensity, vehemence, fervor, excitement, agitation, anger.
> – ANTONYMS cold, apathy.

▶ **verb 1** make or become hot or warm. **2** (**heat up**) become more intense and exciting. **3** (as adj. **heated**) passionate.

> – SYNONYMS **1** *the food was heated* **warm (up),** reheat, cook, keep warm, microwave. **2** *the pipes expand as they heat up* **get hot,** get warm, warm up. **3** (as adj. **heated**) *a heated argument* **vehement,** passionate, impassioned, animated, lively, acrimonious, angry, bitter, furious, fierce. **4** (as adj. **heated**) *Robert grew heated as he spoke of the risks* **excited,** animated, worked up, wound up, keyed up; informal het up.
> – ANTONYMS cool.

– DERIVATIVES **heat·ed·ly** adverb.
– PHRASES **in the heat of the moment** while temporarily angry or excited and without stopping to think. **in heat** (of a female mammal) in a sexual state of readiness for mating.
– ORIGIN Old English.

> **WORD LINKS**
> **thermal** *relating to heat*

heat·er /ˈhētər/ ▶ **noun** a device for warming something.

heat ex·haus·tion ▶ **noun** a condition caused by prolonged exposure to heat during activity and characterized by weakness, profuse sweating, dizziness, and nausea.

heath /hēTH/ ▶ **noun 1** an area of open uncultivated land, especially in Britain, covered with heather, gorse, and coarse grasses. **2** a dwarf shrub with small pink or purple bell-shaped flowers, found on heaths and moors.
– ORIGIN Old English.

heath·en /ˈhēT͟Hən/ ▶ **noun** derogatory a person who does not belong to a widely held religion (especially Christianity, Judaism, or Islam) as regarded by people who do. ▶ **adjective** relating to heathens.
– DERIVATIVES **heath·en·ish** adjective **heath·en·ism** noun.
– ORIGIN Old English.

heath·er /ˈheT͟Hər/ ▶ **noun** a dwarf shrub with purple flowers, found on moors and heaths.
– DERIVATIVES **heath·er·y** adjective.
– ORIGIN Old English.

heath·land /ˈhēTHˌland/ ▶ **noun** an extensive area of heath.

heat·ing /ˈhētiNG/ ▶ **noun** equipment or devices used to provide heat, especially to a building.

heat·proof /ˈhētˌpro͞of/ ▶ **adjective** able to resist great heat.

heat-seek·ing ▶ **adjective** (of a missile) able to detect and home in on heat produced by a target.

heat·stroke /ˈhētˌstrōk/ ▶ **noun** a feverish condition caused by failure of the body's temperature-regulating mechanism when exposed to very high temperatures.

heat wave ▶ **noun** a prolonged period of unusually hot weather.

heave /hēv/ ▶ **verb** (past and past part. **heaved** or Nautical **hove** /hōv/) **1** lift, haul, or throw something heavy with great effort. **2** rise and fall rhythmically or spasmodically: *his shoulders heaved as he wept.* **3** produce a sigh noisily. **4** try to vomit. **5** (**heave to**) (of a ship) come to a stop.

> – SYNONYMS **1 haul,** pull, drag, tug; informal yank. **2 throw,** fling, cast, hurl, lob, pitch; informal chuck, sling. **3 let out,** breathe, give, emit, utter. **4 rise and fall,** roll, swell, surge, churn, seethe. **5 retch,** vomit, cough up, be/get sick; informal throw up, puke, barf, upchuck, hurl, spew.

▸ noun an act of heaving something.
– DERIVATIVES **heav·er** noun.
– PHRASES **heave in sight** (or **into view**) (especially of a ship) come into view.
– ORIGIN Old English.

heave-ho ▸ noun (**the heave-ho**) informal dismissal from a job or contest.

heav·en /ˈhevən/ ▸ noun **1** (in various religions) the place where God or the gods live and where good people go after death. **2** (**the heavens**) literary the sky. **3** a place or state of great happiness. **4** (also **heavens**) used in exclamations as a substitute for 'God'.

> – SYNONYMS **1 paradise,** the hereafter, the next world, the afterworld, nirvana, Zion, Elysium. **2 bliss,** ecstasy, rapture, contentment, happiness, delight, joy, paradise.
> – ANTONYMS hell.

– DERIVATIVES **heav·en·ward** adjective & adverb **heav·en·wards** adverb.
– PHRASES **the heavens open** it suddenly starts to rain very heavily. **in seventh heaven** very happy; ecstatic.
– ORIGIN Old English.

> **WORD LINKS**
>
> **celestial** *relating to heaven*

heav·en·ly /ˈhevənlē/ ▸ adjective **1** relating to heaven; divine. **2** relating to the sky. **3** informal very pleasant; wonderful.

> – SYNONYMS **1 divine,** angelic, holy, celestial. **2 celestial,** cosmic, stellar, sidereal. **3 delightful,** wonderful, glorious, sublime, exquisite, beautiful, lovely, gorgeous, enchanting; informal divine, super, fantastic, fabulous.

WORD TOOLKIT

heavenly ...	divine ...	angelic ...
host	intervention	face
kingdom	right	voice
reward	inspiration	smile
light	law	wings
experience	retribution	child
gates	guidance	souls

heav·en·ly bod·y ▸ noun a planet, star, or other object in space.

heav·en-sent ▸ adjective happening unexpectedly and at a very favorable time.

heav·i·ly /ˈhevəlē/ ▸ adverb **1** slowly and laboriously. **2** decisively. **3** to excess. **4** to a considerable degree. **5** densely.

> – SYNONYMS **1** *Dad walked heavily* **laboriously,** slowly, ponderously, awkwardly, clumsily. **2** *we were heavily defeated* **decisively,** conclusively, roundly, soundly, utterly, completely, thoroughly. **3** *he drank heavily* **excessively,** immoderately, copiously, intemperately. **4** *I became heavily involved in politics* **deeply,** extremely, greatly, exceedingly, tremendously, profoundly. **5** *the area is heavily planted with trees* **densely,** closely, thickly.

heav·y /ˈhevē/ ▸ adjective (**heavier**, **heaviest**) **1** weighing a great deal. **2** very dense, thick, or substantial: *heavy gray clouds*. **3** of more than the usual size, amount, or force: *heavy traffic*. **4** striking or falling with force: *he felt a heavy blow on his shoulder*. **5** needing much physical effort. **6** not delicate or graceful. **7** serious or difficult to understand: *a heavy discussion*. **8** informal full of anger or other strong emotion and difficult to deal with: *things were getting heavy*. **9** (of music, especially rock) having a strong bass component and a forceful rhythm. **10** (of ground) muddy or full of clay.

> – SYNONYMS **1 weighty,** hefty, substantial, ponderous, solid, dense, cumbersome, unwieldy. **2 forceful,** hard, strong, violent, powerful, mighty, sharp, severe. **3 strenuous,** hard, physical, difficult, arduous, demanding, back-breaking, grueling. **4 intense,** fierce, relentless, severe, serious. **5 substantial,** filling, stodgy, rich, big.
> – ANTONYMS light.

▸ noun (pl. **heavies**) informal a large, strong man, especially one hired for protection.
– DERIVATIVES **heav·i·ness** noun.
– ORIGIN Old English.

heav·y-du·ty ▸ adjective designed to withstand a great deal of use or wear.

heav·y go·ing ▸ noun a person or situation that is difficult or boring.

heav·y-hand·ed ▸ adjective clumsy, insensitive, or overly forceful.

> – SYNONYMS **1 clumsy,** awkward, maladroit; informal ham-fisted, all thumbs. **2 insensitive,** oppressive, overbearing, harsh, severe, tactless, undiplomatic, inept.
> – ANTONYMS dexterous, sensitive.

heav·y-heart·ed ▸ adjective depressed or melancholy.

heav·y hit·ter (also **big hitter**) ▸ noun informal an important or powerful person.

heav·y hy·dro·gen ▸ noun another term for **DEUTERIUM**.

heav·y in·dus·try ▸ noun the manufacture of large, heavy articles and materials in bulk.

heav·y met·al ▸ noun **1** a type of very loud harsh-sounding rock music with a strong beat. **2** a metal of relatively high density, or of high relative atomic weight.

heav·y pet·ting ▸ noun sexual activity between two people that stops short of intercourse.

heav·y·set /ˈhevēˌset/ ▸ adjective (of a person) broad and strongly built.

heav·y wa·ter ▸ noun water in which the hydrogen in the molecules is partly or wholly replaced by the isotope deuterium, used especially in nuclear reactors.

heav·y·weight /ˈhevēˌwāt/ ▸ noun **1** a weight in boxing and other sports, typically the heaviest category. **2** informal an influential person. ▸ adjective **1** of above-average weight. **2** informal serious or influential: *heavyweight news coverage*.

He·bra·ic /hēˈbrāik/ ▸ adjective relating to Hebrew or the Hebrew people.

He·brew /ˈhēbro͞o/ ▸ noun **1** a member of an ancient people living in what is now Israel and Palestine, whose scriptures and traditions form the basis of the Jewish religion. **2** the language of the Hebrews, in its ancient or modern form.
– ORIGIN from a Hebrew word understood to mean 'one from the other side (of the river).'

heck /hek/ ▸ exclamation used for emphasis, or to express surprise, annoyance, etc.
– ORIGIN euphemistic alteration of **HELL**.

heck·le /ˈhekəl/ ▶ **verb** interrupt a public speaker with derisive comments or abuse.
– DERIVATIVES **heck·ler** noun.
– ORIGIN from a dialect form of **HACKLE**.

hec·tare /ˈhekˌte(ə)r/ ▶ **noun** a metric unit of square measure, equal to 10,000 square meters (2.471 acres).
– ORIGIN from Greek *hekaton* 'hundred.'

hec·tic /ˈhektik/ ▶ **adjective** full of frantic activity.

– SYNONYMS **frantic,** frenetic, frenzied, feverish, manic, busy, active, fast and furious.
– ANTONYMS leisurely.

– DERIVATIVES **hec·ti·cal·ly** adverb.
– ORIGIN Greek *hektikos* 'habitual.'

hec·tor /ˈhektər/ ▶ **verb** talk to someone in a bullying way.
– DERIVATIVES **hec·tor·ing** adjective.
– ORIGIN from the Trojan warrior *Hector* in Homer's *Iliad*.

he'd /hēd/ ▶ **contraction 1** he had. **2** he would.

hedge /hej/ ▶ **noun 1** a fence or boundary formed by closely growing bushes. **2** a way of protecting oneself against financial loss or another adverse situation: *a hedge against inflation*. ▶ **verb 1** surround something with a hedge. **2** avoid making a definite statement or commitment. **3** protect an investor or investment against loss by making compensating contracts or transactions.
– DERIVATIVES **hedg·er** noun.
– PHRASES **hedge one's bets** avoid committing oneself when faced with a difficult choice.
– ORIGIN Old English.

hedge fund ▶ **noun** a limited partnership of investors that uses high-risk methods in hopes of realizing large capital gains.

hedge·hog /ˈhejˌhôg, -ˌhäg/ ▶ **noun** a small mammal with a spiny coat, able to roll itself into a ball for defense.

hedge·row /ˈhejˌrō/ ▶ **noun** a hedge of wild bushes and occasional trees bordering a road or field.

he·don·ism /ˈhēdnˌizəm/ ▶ **noun** behavior based on the belief that pleasure is the most important thing in life.
– DERIVATIVES **he·don·ist** noun **he·don·is·tic** /ˌhēdnˈistik/ adjective.
– ORIGIN from Greek *hēdonē* 'pleasure.'

hee·bie-jee·bies /ˈhēbē ˈjēbēz/ ▶ **plural noun** (**the heebie-jeebies**) informal a state of nervous fear or anxiety.
– ORIGIN unknown.

heed /hēd/ ▶ **verb** pay attention to someone or something.

– SYNONYMS **pay attention to,** take notice of, take note of, listen to, consider, take to heart, take into account, obey, adhere to, abide by, observe.
– ANTONYMS disregard.

▶ **noun** careful attention.

– SYNONYMS *he* ***paid*** *no* ***heed*** **attention,** notice, note, regard, thought.

– DERIVATIVES **heed·ful** adjective.
– ORIGIN Old English.

heed·less /ˈhēdlis/ ▶ **adjective** showing a reckless lack of care or attention.
– DERIVATIVES **heed·less·ly** adverb **heed·less·ness** noun.

hee-haw /ˈhē ˌhô/ ▶ **noun** the loud, harsh cry of a donkey or mule. ▶ **verb** make the loud, harsh cry of a donkey or mule.

heel[1] /hēl/ ▶ **noun 1** the back part of the foot below the ankle. **2** the part of a shoe or boot supporting the heel. **3** the part of the palm of the hand next to the wrist. **4** informal, dated an inconsiderate or untrustworthy man. ▶ **exclamation** a command to a dog to walk close behind its owner. ▶ **verb** fit a new heel on a shoe or boot.
– DERIVATIVES **heeled** adjective.
– PHRASES **at** (or **on**) **the heels of** following closely after someone or something. **bring someone to heel** bring someone under control. **cool one's heels** be kept waiting. **take to one's heels** run away. **kick up one's heels** have a lively, enjoyable time.
– ORIGIN Old English.

heel[2] ▶ **verb** (of a ship) lean over owing to the pressure of wind or an uneven load.
– ORIGIN Germanic.

heel·ball /ˈhēlˌbôl/ ▶ **noun** a mixture of hard wax and lampblack used by shoemakers for polishing or in brass rubbing.

heft /heft/ ▶ **verb 1** lift or carry something heavy. **2** lift or hold something to test its weight. ▶ **noun 1** the weight of someone or something. **2** ability or influence.
– ORIGIN probably from **HEAVE**.

heft·y /ˈheftē/ ▶ **adjective** (**heftier**, **heftiest**) **1** large and heavy. **2** (of a number or amount) considerable: *she could face a hefty fine*.

– SYNONYMS **1 burly,** sturdy, strapping, bulky, strong, muscular, big, solid, well built; informal hulking, beefy. **2 powerful,** violent, hard, forceful, mighty. **3 substantial,** sizable, considerable, stiff, large, heavy; informal whopping.
– ANTONYMS light.

– DERIVATIVES **heft·i·ly** adverb.

He·ge·li·an /həˈgālēən/ ▶ **adjective** relating to the German philosopher Georg Hegel or his philosophy. ▶ **noun** a follower of Hegel.
– DERIVATIVES **He·ge·li·an·ism** /həˈgālēəˌnizəm/ noun.

he·gem·o·ny /həˈjemənē, ˈhejəˌmōnē/ ▶ **noun** dominance of one social group or country over others.
– DERIVATIVES **heg·e·mon·ic** /ˌhegəˈmänik/ adjective.
– ORIGIN from Greek *hēgemōn* 'leader.'

He·gi·ra /hiˈjīrə, ˈhejərə/ (also **Hejira** or **Hijra**) ▶ **noun 1** Muhammad's departure from Mecca to Medina in AD 622, marking the consolidation of the first Muslim community. **2** the Muslim era reckoned from this date.
– ORIGIN Arabic, 'departure.'

heif·er /ˈhefər/ ▶ **noun** a young female cow that has not had a calf.
– ORIGIN Old English.

height /hīt/ ▶ **noun 1** the measurement of someone or something from head to foot or from base to top. **2** the distance of something above ground or sea level. **3** the quality of being tall or high. **4** a high place. **5** the most intense part or period: *the height of the attack*. **6** an extreme example: *it would be the height of bad manners not to attend the wedding*.

– SYNONYMS **1 tallness,** stature, elevation, altitude. **2** *mountain heights* **summit,** top, peak, crest, crown, tip, cap, pinnacle. **3** *the height of their fame* **highest point,** peak, zenith, pinnacle, climax.
– ANTONYMS width, nadir.

– ORIGIN Old English.

WORD LINKS

acrophobia *fear of heights*

height·en /ˈhītn/ ▶ **verb 1** make or become more intense. **2** make something higher.

– SYNONYMS **intensify,** increase, enhance, add to, augment, boost, strengthen, deepen, magnify, reinforce.
– ANTONYMS reduce.

Heim·lich ma·neu·ver /ˈhīmlik, ˈhīmlikH/ ▶ **noun** a first-aid procedure for dislodging an obstruction from a person's windpipe, in which a sudden strong pressure is applied on the abdomen between the navel and the rib cage.
– ORIGIN named after the American physician Henry J. *Heimlich.*

hei·nous /ˈhānəs/ ▶ **adjective** very wicked: *a heinous crime*.

– SYNONYMS **odious,** wicked, evil, atrocious, monstrous, abominable, detestable, despicable, horrific, terrible, awful, abhorrent, loathsome, hideous, unspeakable, execrable.
– ANTONYMS admirable.

– DERIVATIVES **hei·nous·ly** adverb **hei·nous·ness** noun.
– ORIGIN Old French *haineus.*

heir /e(ə)r/ ▶ **noun 1** a person who is legally entitled to the property or rank of another on that person's death. **2** a person who continues the work of a predecessor.

– SYNONYMS **successor,** next in line, inheritor, beneficiary, legatee.

– DERIVATIVES **heir·less** adjective **heir·ship** noun.
– ORIGIN Old French.

heir ap·par·ent ▶ **noun** (pl. **heirs apparent**) **1** an heir whose rights cannot be taken away by the birth of another heir. **2** a person who is most likely to take on the job or role of another.

heir·ess /ˈe(ə)ris/ ▶ **noun** a female heir, especially to vast wealth.

– SYNONYMS **successor,** next in line, inheritor, beneficiary, legatee.

heir·loom /ˈe(ə)rˌlo͞om/ ▶ **noun** a valuable object that has belonged to a family for several generations.
– ORIGIN from **HEIR** + **LOOM**[1] (in the former senses 'tool, heirloom').

heir pre·sump·tive ▶ **noun** (pl. **heirs presumptive**) an heir whose rights may be taken away by the birth of another heir.

heist /hīst/ informal ▶ **noun** a robbery. ▶ **verb** steal something.
– ORIGIN from a pronunciation of **HOIST**.

He·ji·ra ▶ **noun** variant spelling of **HEGIRA**.

held /held/ past and past participle of **HOLD**[1].

hel·i·cal /ˈhelikəl, ˈhē-/ ▶ **adjective** having the shape or form of a helix; spiral.
– DERIVATIVES **hel·i·cal·ly** adverb.

hel·i·ces /ˈhēləˌsēz/ plural of **HELIX**.

hel·i·cop·ter /ˈheliˌkäptər/ ▶ **noun** a type of aircraft powered by one or two sets of horizontally revolving rotors.
– ORIGIN from Greek *helix* 'spiral' + *pteron* 'wing.'

he·li·o·cen·tric /ˌhēlēəˈsentrik/ ▶ **adjective 1** having the sun as the center, as in the accepted astronomical model of the solar system. Compare with **GEOCENTRIC**. **2** Astronomy measured from or considered in relation to the center of the sun.
– ORIGIN from Greek *hēlios* 'sun.'

he·li·o·graph /ˈhēlēəˌgraf/ ▶ **noun 1** a device that reflects sunlight in flashes from a movable mirror, used to send signals. **2** a message sent using a heliograph.
– DERIVATIVES **he·li·o·graph·ic** /ˌhēlēəˈgrafik/ adjective.
– ORIGIN from Greek *hēlios* 'sun.'

he·li·o·sphere /ˈhēlēəˌsfi(ə)r/ ▶ **noun** the region of space, including the solar system, in which the solar wind has a significant influence.
– DERIVATIVES **he·li·o·spher·ic** /ˌhēlēəˈsferik, -ˈsfi(ə)rik/ adjective.
– ORIGIN from Greek *hēlios* 'sun.'

he·li·o·trope /ˈhēlēəˌtrōp/ ▶ **noun** a plant of the borage family with fragrant purple or blue flowers.
– ORIGIN from Greek *hēlios* 'sun' + *trepein* 'to turn.'

hel·i·pad /ˈheləˌpad/ ▶ **noun** a landing and takeoff area for helicopters.

hel·i·port /ˈheləˌpôrt/ ▶ **noun** an airport or landing place for helicopters.

hel·i-ski·ing /ˈheliˌskē-iNG/ ▶ **noun** skiing in which the skier is taken up the mountain by helicopter.

he·li·um /ˈhēlēəm/ ▶ **noun** a light colorless gas that does not burn.
– ORIGIN from Greek *hēlios* 'sun.'

he·lix /ˈhēliks/ ▶ **noun** (pl. **helices** /-ləˌsēz/) an object with a three-dimensional spiral shape like that of a wire wound in a single layer around a cylinder or cone.
– ORIGIN Greek.

hell /hel/ ▶ **noun 1** (in various religions) a place of evil and everlasting suffering to which the wicked are sent after death. **2** a state or place of great suffering.

– SYNONYMS **1 the underworld,** the netherworld, eternal damnation, perdition, hellfire, fire and brimstone, the Inferno, Hades. **2 misery,** torture, agony, purgatory, torment, a nightmare.
– ANTONYMS heaven, bliss.

▶ **exclamation** used to express annoyance or surprise or for emphasis.
– DERIVATIVES **hell·ward** adverb & adjective.
– PHRASES **all hell breaks loose** informal suddenly there is chaos. **come hell or high water** whatever difficulties may occur. **for the hell of it** informal just for fun. **give someone hell** informal reprimand someone severely. **hell for leather** as fast as possible. **like hell** informal very fast, much, hard, etc. **not a hope in hell** informal no chance at all. **until hell freezes over** forever.
– ORIGIN Old English.

WORD LINKS

infernal *relating to hell*

he'll /hēl/ ▶ **contraction** he will or he shall.

hell-bent ▶ **adjective** determined to achieve something at all costs.

hell·cat /ˈhelˌkat/ ▶ **noun** a spiteful, violent woman.

hel·le·bore /ˈheləˌbôr/ ▶ **noun** a poisonous winter-flowering plant with large white, green, or purplish flowers.
– ORIGIN Greek *helleboros.*

Hel·lene /ˈhelēn/ ▶ **noun** a Greek.
– ORIGIN named after *Hellen,* who was held in Greek mythology to be the ancestor of all the Greeks.

Hel·len·ic /heˈlenik/ ▶ **adjective 1** Greek. **2** relating to ancient Greek culture between *c.*1050 BC and *c.*300 BC. ▶ **noun** the Greek language.

Hel·len·ism /ˈhelə,nizəm/ ▸ **noun 1** the national character or culture of Greece, especially ancient Greece. **2** the study or imitation of ancient Greek culture.
– DERIVATIVES **Hel·len·ist** noun **Hel·len·ize** verb.

Hel·len·is·tic /,heləˈnistik/ ▸ **adjective** relating to ancient Greek culture from the death of Alexander the Great (323 BC) to the defeat of Cleopatra and Mark Antony by Octavian in 31 BC.

hell·fire /ˈhel,fīr/ ▸ **noun** the fire said to exist in hell.

hell·hole /ˈhel,hōl/ ▸ **noun** a very unpleasant place.

hell·hound /ˈhel,hound/ ▸ **noun** a demon in the form of a dog.

hell·ish /ˈhelisH/ ▸ **adjective 1** relating to or like hell. **2** informal extremely difficult or unpleasant.
– DERIVATIVES **hell·ish·ly** adverb **hell·ish·ness** noun.

hel·lo /həˈlō, heˈlō, ˈhelō/ (also **hallo** or **hullo**) ▸ **exclamation 1** used as a greeting or to attract someone's attention. **2** (often pronounced with a prolonged final vowel) expressing sarcasm or anger: *hello! were you even listening?*
– ORIGIN from French *ho* 'ho!' + *là* 'there.'

hell·rais·er /ˈhel,rāzər/ ▸ **noun** a person who causes trouble by violent, drunken, or outrageous behavior.

Hell's An·gel ▸ **noun** a member of a gang of male motorcycle enthusiasts, originally known for their lawless behavior.

helm /helm/ ▸ **noun 1** a tiller or wheel for steering a ship or boat. **2** (**the helm**) a position of leadership. ▸ **verb 1** steer a boat or ship. **2** manage the running of something.
– ORIGIN Old English.

hel·met /ˈhelmit/ ▸ **noun** a hard or padded protective hat.
– DERIVATIVES **hel·met·ed** adjective.
– ORIGIN Old French, 'little helmet.'

helms·man /ˈhelmzmən/ ▸ **noun** (pl. **helmsmen**) a person who steers a ship or boat.

hel·ot /ˈhelət/ ▸ **noun 1** (in part of ancient Greece) a member of a class of people having a status in between slaves and citizens. **2** a serf or slave.
– ORIGIN Greek *Heilōtes*.

help /help/ ▸ **verb 1** make it easier for someone to do something. **2** improve a situation or problem. **3** (**help someone to**) serve someone with food or drink. **4** (**help oneself**) take something without asking permission. **5** (**can/could not help**) cannot or could not stop oneself doing: *he couldn't help laughing.*

> – SYNONYMS **1 assist,** aid, abet, lend a hand, give assistance, come to the aid of, be of service, do someone a favor, do someone a service, do someone a good turn, rally around, pitch in. **2 support,** contribute to, give money to, donate to, promote, boost, back. **3 relieve,** soothe, ease, alleviate, improve, lessen. **4** *he could not help laughing* **resist,** avoid, refrain from, keep from, stop.
> – ANTONYMS hinder, impede.

▸ **noun 1** the action of helping someone. **2** a person or thing that helps someone. **3** a person employed to do household tasks.

> – SYNONYMS **1 assistance,** aid, support, succor, benefit, use, advantage, service. **2 relief,** alleviation, improvement, healing.
> – ANTONYMS hindrance.

– ORIGIN Old English.

help·er /ˈhelpər/ ▸ **noun** a person who helps.

> – SYNONYMS **assistant,** aide, deputy, auxiliary, supporter, second, mate, right-hand man/woman, man/girl Friday, attendant; informal gal Friday.

help·er cell ▸ **noun** a T cell that influences or controls the differentiation or activity of other cells of the immune system.

help·ful /ˈhelpfəl/ ▸ **adjective 1** giving or ready to give help. **2** useful.

> – SYNONYMS **1 obliging,** of assistance, supportive, accommodating, cooperative, neighborly, eager to please. **2 useful,** beneficial, valuable, constructive, informative, instructive. **3 handy,** useful, convenient, practical, easy-to-use, serviceable; informal neat, nifty.
> – ANTONYMS useless.

– DERIVATIVES **help·ful·ly** adverb **help·ful·ness** noun.

help·ing /ˈhelpiNG/ ▸ **noun** a portion of food served to one person at one time.

> – SYNONYMS **portion,** serving, piece, slice, share, plateful; informal dollop.

help·less /ˈhelplis/ ▸ **adjective 1** unable to defend oneself or to act without help. **2** uncontrollable: *helpless laughter.*

> – SYNONYMS **dependent,** incapable, powerless, paralyzed, defenseless, vulnerable, exposed, unprotected.
> – ANTONYMS independent.

– DERIVATIVES **help·less·ly** adverb **help·less·ness** noun.

help·line /ˈhelp,līn/ ▸ **noun** a telephone service providing help with problems.

help·mate /ˈhelp,māt/ (also **helpmeet** /-,mēt/) ▸ **noun** a helpful companion or partner.

hel·ter-skel·ter /ˈheltər ˈskeltər/ ▸ **adjective & adverb** in a hasty and confused or disorganized way. ▸ **noun** Brit. a tall spiral slide winding around a tower at a fair. ▸ **noun** disorder; confusion.
– ORIGIN perhaps symbolic of running feet or from former *skelte* 'hasten.'

hem[1] /hem/ ▸ **noun** the edge of a piece of cloth or item of clothing that has been turned under and stitched down. ▸ **verb** (**hems, hemming, hemmed**) **1** make a hem on a piece of cloth or item of clothing. **2** (**hem someone/thing in**) surround someone or something and restrict their space or movement.
– ORIGIN Old English.

hem[2] ▸ **exclamation** expressing the sound made when coughing or clearing the throat to attract attention or show hesitation.
– PHRASES **hem and haw** hesitate; be indecisive.

he-man ▸ **noun** informal a very well-built, masculine man.

he·ma·tite /ˈhēmə,tīt/ ▸ **noun** a reddish-black mineral consisting of iron oxide.
– ORIGIN from Greek *haimatitēs lithos* 'blood-like stone.'

he·ma·tol·o·gy /,hēməˈtäləjē/ ▸ **noun** the branch of medicine concerned with the study and treatment of the blood.
– DERIVATIVES **he·ma·to·log·i·cal** /-təˈläjikəl/ adjective **he·ma·tol·o·gist** noun.
– ORIGIN from Greek *haima* 'blood.'

he·ma·to·ma /,hēməˈtōmə/ ▸ **noun** a solid swelling of clotted blood within the tissues.
– ORIGIN from Greek *haima* 'blood.'

hemi- ▶ **prefix** half: *hemisphere.*
– ORIGIN Greek *hēmi-*.

hem·i·ple·gi·a /ˌheməˈplēj(ē)ə/ ▶ **noun** paralysis of one side of the body.
– DERIVATIVES **hem·i·ple·gic** noun & adjective.

hem·i·sphere /ˈheməˌsfi(ə)r/ ▶ **noun** **1** a half of a sphere. **2** a half of the earth, usually as divided into northern and southern halves by the equator, or into western and eastern halves by an imaginary line passing through the North and South Poles. **3** (also **cerebral hemisphere**) each of the two parts of the cerebrum (the main part of the brain) of a vertebrate.
– DERIVATIVES **hem·i·spher·ic** /ˌheməˈsfi(ə)rik, -ˈsferik/ adjective **hem·i·spher·i·cal** /ˌheməˈsfi(ə)rikəl, -ˈsferikəl/ adjective.

hem·line /ˈhemˌlīn/ ▶ **noun** the level of the lower edge of a garment such as a skirt or coat.

hem·lock /ˈhemˌläk/ ▶ **noun** **1** a very poisonous plant of the parsley family, with fernlike leaves and small white flowers. **2** a poison obtained from this plant.
– ORIGIN Old English.

he·mo·glo·bin /ˈhēməˌglōbin/ ▶ **noun** a red protein containing iron, responsible for transporting oxygen in the blood.
– ORIGIN a shortened form of *hematoglobulin*, in the same sense, from Greek *haima* 'blood' + **GLOBULE**.

he·mo·lyt·ic /ˌhēməˈlitik/ ▶ **adjective** relating to or involving the rupture or destruction of red blood cells: *hemolytic anemia.*

he·mo·phil·i·a /ˌhēməˈfilēə/ ▶ **noun** a medical condition in which the ability of the blood to clot is greatly reduced, causing severe bleeding from even a slight injury.
– ORIGIN from Greek *haima* 'blood' + **-PHILIA**.

he·mo·phil·i·ac /ˌhēməˈfilēˌak/ ▶ **noun** a person with hemophilia.

hem·or·rhage /ˈhem(ə)rij/ ▶ **noun** **1** a severe loss of blood from a ruptured blood vessel. **2** a damaging loss of valuable people or resources: *the continuing hemorrhage of doctors.* ▶ **verb** **1** bleed heavily from a ruptured blood vessel. **2** use or spend something valuable in large amounts: *the business was hemorrhaging cash.*
– ORIGIN from Greek *haima* 'blood' + *rhēgnunai* 'burst.'

hem·or·rhoid /ˈhem(ə)ˌroid/ ▶ **noun** a swollen vein or group of veins (piles) in the region of the anus.
– ORIGIN from Greek *haimorrhoides phlebes* 'bleeding veins.'

he·mo·sta·sis /ˌhēməˈstāsəs, heme-/ ▶ **noun** the stopping of a flow of blood.
– DERIVATIVES **he·mo·stat·ic** /-ˈstatik/ adjective.

hemp /hemp/ ▶ **noun** **1** the cannabis plant. **2** the fiber of the cannabis plant, extracted from the stem and used to make rope, strong fabrics, paper, etc. **3** marijuana.
– ORIGIN Old English.

hen /hen/ ▶ **noun** **1** a female bird, especially of a domestic fowl. **2** (**hens**) domestic fowls of either sex.
– ORIGIN Old English.

hen·bane /ˈhenˌbān/ ▶ **noun** a poisonous plant of the nightshade family, with sticky hairy leaves and an unpleasant smell.

hence /hens/ ▶ **adverb** **1** as a consequence; for this reason. **2** from now; in the future: *two years hence.* **3** (also **from hence**) old use from here.

– SYNONYMS **consequently,** as a consequence, for this reason, therefore, so, accordingly, as a result, that being so.

– ORIGIN Old English.

hence·forth /ˈhensˌfôrTH/ (also **henceforward**) ▶ **adverb** from this or that time on.

hench·man /ˈhenCHmən/ ▶ **noun** (pl. **henchmen**) **1** chiefly derogatory a faithful supporter or assistant, especially one prepared to engage in criminal or dishonest activities. **2** historical a squire or page attending a prince or nobleman.
– ORIGIN from Old English *hengest* 'male horse' + **MAN**, the first sense being probably 'a groom.'

henge /henj/ ▶ **noun** a prehistoric monument consisting of a circle of stone or wooden uprights.
– ORIGIN from *Stonehenge*, a monument of this type in Wiltshire, from two Old English words meaning 'stone' + 'to hang.'

hen·na /ˈhenə/ ▶ **noun** a reddish-brown dye made from the powdered leaves of a tropical shrub, used especially to color the hair and decorate the body. ▶ **verb** (**hennas, hennaing, hennaed**) dye the hair with henna.
– ORIGIN Arabic.

hen par·ty ▶ **noun** informal a social gathering for women only.

hen·peck /ˈhenˌpek/ ▶ **verb** (usu. as adj. **henpecked**) (of a woman) continually criticize and nag (her husband or other male partner).

hen·ry /ˈhenrē/ ▶ **noun** (pl. **henries** or **henrys**) Physics the SI unit of inductance.
– ORIGIN named after the American physicist Joseph *Henry*.

hep[1] /hep/ ▶ **adjective** old-fashioned term for **HIP[3]**.

hep[2] ▶ **noun** informal short for **HEPATITIS**: *hep C.*

hep·a·rin /ˈhepərin/ ▶ **noun** a compound found in the liver and other tissues that prevents blood clotting or coagulating, used in the treatment of thrombosis.
– ORIGIN from Greek *hēpar* 'liver.'

he·pat·ic /həˈpatik/ ▶ **adjective** relating to the liver.
– ORIGIN from Greek *hēpar* 'liver.'

hep·a·ti·tis /ˌhepəˈtitis/ ▶ **noun** a disease in which the liver becomes inflamed, causing jaundice and other symptoms, mainly spread by a series of viruses (**hepatitis A, B,** and **C**) transmitted in blood or food.

hep·cat /ˈhepˌkat/ ▶ **noun** informal, dated a stylish or fashionable person.
– ORIGIN from *hep* (variant of **HIP[3]** + *cat* (an informal term for a man, especially among jazz enthusiasts).

hepta- ▶ **combining form** seven; having seven: *heptathlon.*
– ORIGIN Greek *hepta* 'seven.'

hep·ta·gon /ˈheptəˌgän/ ▶ **noun** a plane figure with seven straight sides and angles.

hep·tath·lon /hepˈtaTHˌlän/ ▶ **noun** an athletic contest for women that consists of seven separate events.
– DERIVATIVES **hep·tath·lete** noun.
– ORIGIN from **HEPTA-** + Greek *athlon* 'contest.'

her /hər/ ▶ **pronoun** (third person sing.) **1** used as the object of a verb or preposition to refer to a female person or animal previously mentioned. **2** referring to a ship, country, or other thing regarded as female. ▶ **possessive determiner** **1** belonging to or associated with a female person or animal previously mentioned. **2** (**Her**) used in titles: *Her Royal Highness.*
– ORIGIN Old English.

her·ald /ˈherəld/ ▶ **noun 1** an official employed to oversee matters concerning state ceremonies and the use of coats of arms. **2** historical a person who carried official messages, made proclamations, and oversaw tournaments. **3** a person or thing viewed as a sign that something is about to happen: *daffodils are the herald of spring.*

– SYNONYMS **1** *a herald announced the armistice* **messenger,** courier. **2 harbinger,** sign, indicator, signal, portent, omen; literary foretoken.

▶ **verb 1** be a sign that something is about to happen: *the speech heralded a change in policy.* **2** describe in enthusiastic terms: *he was heralded as the next Sinatra.*

– SYNONYMS **1** *shouts heralded their approach* **proclaim,** announce, broadcast, publicize, declare, advertise. **2** *the speech heralded a policy change* **signal,** indicate, announce, usher in, pave the way for, be a harbinger of; literary foretoken, betoken.

– ORIGIN Old French *herault.*

he·ral·dic /həˈraldik/ ▶ **adjective** relating to heraldry.
– DERIVATIVES **he·ral·di·cal·ly** adverb.

her·ald·ry /ˈherəldrē/ ▶ **noun** the system by which coats of arms are drawn up, described, and regulated.

herb /(h)ərb/ ▶ **noun 1** any plant whose leaves, seeds, or flowers are used for flavoring food or in medicine. **2** Botany any seed-bearing plant that does not have a woody stem and dies down to the ground after flowering.
– DERIVATIVES **herb·y** adjective.
– ORIGIN Latin *herba* 'grass, green crops.'

her·ba·ceous /(h)ərˈbāsʜəs/ ▶ **adjective** relating to herbs (in the botanical sense).

her·ba·ceous bor·der ▶ **noun** a garden border consisting mainly of flowering plants that live for several years.

herb·age /ˈ(h)ərbij/ ▶ **noun** herbaceous plants, especially grass used for grazing.

herb·al /ˈ(h)ərbəl/ ▶ **adjective** relating to or made from herbs. ▶ **noun** a book that describes herbs and their culinary and medicinal properties.

her·bal·ism /ˈ(h)ərbəˌlizəm/ ▶ **noun** the study or practice of using herbs for medicinal or therapeutic purposes.

herb·al·ist /ˈ(h)ərbəlist/ ▶ **noun** a person who practices herbalism, or one who grows or sells herbs for medicinal purposes.

her·bar·i·um /(h)ərˈbe(ə)rēəm/ ▶ **noun** (pl. **herbaria** /-ˈbe(ə)rēə/) a collection of dried plants organized in a systematic way.

herbed /(h)ərbd/ ▶ **adjective** cooked or flavored with herbs.

herb·i·cide /ˈ(h)ərbəˌsīd/ ▶ **noun** a poisonous substance used to destroy unwanted plants.

her·biv·ore /ˈ(h)ərbəˌvôr/ ▶ **noun** an animal that feeds on plants.
– DERIVATIVES **her·biv·o·rous** /(h)ərˈbiv(ə)rəs/ adjective.

Her·cu·le·an /ˌhərkyəˈlēən, hərˈkyo͞olēən/ ▶ **adjective** requiring great strength or effort: *a Herculean task.*
– ORIGIN named after *Hercules,* a hero of Roman and Greek mythology famed for his strength.

herd /hərd/ ▶ **noun 1** a large group of animals, especially hoofed mammals, that live or are kept together. **2** derogatory a large group of people: *herds of tourists.*

– SYNONYMS **drove,** flock, pack, fold, swarm, mass, crowd, horde.

▶ **verb 1** move in a particular direction. **2** keep or look after livestock.
– DERIVATIVES **herd·er** noun.
– ORIGIN Old English.

herd in·stinct ▶ **noun** an inclination or natural tendency to behave or think like the majority of a group.

herds·man /ˈhərdzmən/ ▶ **noun** (pl. **herdsmen**) the owner or keeper of a herd of domesticated animals.

here /hi(ə)r/ ▶ **adverb 1** in, at, or to this place or position. **2** (usu. **here is/are**) used when introducing or handing over something or someone. **3** used when indicating a time, point, or situation that has arrived or is happening. ▶ **exclamation** used to attract someone's attention.
– PHRASES **here and now** at the present time. **here and there** in various places. **here's to** used to wish someone health or success before drinking. **neither here nor there** of no importance or relevance.
– ORIGIN Old English.

here·a·bouts /ˈhirəˌbouts/ (also **hereabout**) ▶ **adverb** near this place.

here·af·ter /hi(ə)rˈaftər/ ▶ **adverb** formal **1** from now on or at some time in the future. **2** after death. ▶ **noun** (**the hereafter**) life after death.

here·by /ˌhi(ə)rˈbī, ˈhi(ə)rˌbī/ ▶ **adverb** formal as a result of this.

he·red·i·tar·y /həˈrediˌterē/ ▶ **adjective 1** passed on by or relating to inheritance. **2** (of a characteristic or disease) able to be passed on genetically from parents to their offspring.

– SYNONYMS **1 inherited,** bequeathed, handed down, passed down, family, ancestral. **2 genetic,** inborn, inherited, inbred, innate, in the family, in the blood, in the genes.

– DERIVATIVES **he·red·i·tar·i·ly** /həˌrediˈte(ə)rəlē/ adverb.

he·red·i·ty /həˈreditē/ ▶ **noun 1** the passing on of physical or mental characteristics genetically from one generation to another. **2** the inheriting of a title, office, or right.
– ORIGIN Latin *hereditas* 'heirship.'

Her·e·ford /ˈhərfərd, ˈherə-/ ▶ **noun** an animal of a breed of red and white beef cattle.
– ORIGIN from *Hereford* in west central England.

here·in /ˌhi(ə)rˈin/ ▶ **adverb** formal in this document, book, or matter.

here·in·af·ter /ˌhi(ə)rinˈaftər/ ▶ **adverb** formal further on in this document.

here·of /ˌhi(ə)rˈəv/ ▶ **adverb** formal of this document.

her·e·sy /ˈherəsē/ ▶ **noun** (pl. **heresies**) **1** belief or opinion that goes against traditional religious doctrine. **2** opinion that differs greatly from what is generally accepted.
– ORIGIN Greek *hairesis* 'choice, sect.'

her·e·tic /ˈherətik/ ▶ **noun 1** a person who holds beliefs or opinions that go against traditional religious doctrine. **2** a person whose opinion differs greatly from that which is generally accepted.
– DERIVATIVES **he·ret·i·cal** /həˈretikəl/ adjective **he·ret·i·cal·ly** adverb.

here·to /ˌhi(ə)rˈto͞o/ ▶ **adverb** formal to this matter or document.

here·to·fore /ˈhi(ə)rtəˌfôr/ ▶ **adverb** formal before now.

here·un·der /ˌhi(ə)rˈəndər/ ▶ **adverb** formal **1** as provided for under the terms of this document. **2** further on in this document.

here·up·on /ˌhi(ə)rəˈpän/ ▸ **adverb** old use after or as a result of this.

here·with /ˌhirˈwɪᴛʜ, -ˈwiᴛʜ/ ▸ **adverb** formal with this letter or document.

her·it·a·ble /ˈheritəbəl/ ▸ **adjective** able to be inherited.
– DERIVATIVES **her·it·a·bil·i·ty** /ˌheritəˈbilitē/ noun **her·it·a·bly** adverb.

her·it·age /ˈheritij/ ▸ **noun 1** property that is or may be inherited; an inheritance. **2** valued things such as historic buildings that have been passed down from previous generations.

> – SYNONYMS **1 tradition,** history, past, background, culture, customs. **2 ancestry,** lineage, descent, extraction, parentage, roots, heredity, birth.

▸ **adjective** (of a plant variety) not hybridized with another; old-fashioned: *heritage roses.*
– ORIGIN Old French, from *heriter* 'inherit.'

her·maph·ro·dite /hərˈmafrədīt/ ▸ **noun 1** a person or animal with both male and female sex organs or characteristics. **2** Botany a plant having stamens and pistils in the same flower.
– DERIVATIVES **her·maph·ro·dit·ic** /-ˌmafrəˈditik/ adjective **her·maph·ro·dit·ism** /-diˌtizəm/ noun.
– ORIGIN Greek *hermaphroditos,* first the name of the son of Hermes and Aphrodite who became joined in one body with the nymph Salmacis.

her·me·neu·tic /ˌhərməˈn(y)o͞otik/ ▸ **adjective** relating to interpretation, especially of the Bible or literary texts.
– DERIVATIVES **her·me·neu·ti·cal** adjective.
– ORIGIN Greek *hermēneutikos.*

her·me·neu·tics /ˌhərməˈn(y)o͞otiks/ ▸ **plural noun** (usu. treated as sing.) the branch of knowledge that deals with interpretation, especially of the Bible or literary texts.

her·met·ic /hərˈmetik/ ▸ **adjective 1** (of a seal or closure) complete and airtight. **2** insulated or protected from outside influences: *a hermetic society.*
– DERIVATIVES **her·met·i·cal·ly** adverb.
– ORIGIN from Latin *Hermes Trismegistus* 'thrice-greatest Hermes,' the legendary founder of alchemy and astrology identified with the Greek god Hermes.

her·mit /ˈhərmit/ ▸ **noun 1** a person living in solitude for religious reasons. **2** a person who prefers to live alone.

> – SYNONYMS **recluse,** loner, ascetic; historical anchorite, anchoress; old use eremite.

– DERIVATIVES **her·mit·ic** /hərˈmitik/ adjective.
– ORIGIN from Greek *erēmos* 'solitary.'

her·mit·age /ˈhərmitij/ ▸ **noun** the home of a hermit, especially when small and remote.

her·mit crab ▸ **noun** a crab with a soft abdomen that lives in shells cast off by other shellfish.

her·ni·a /ˈhərnēə/ ▸ **noun** (pl. **hernias**) a condition in which part of an organ (typically the intestine) protrudes through the wall of the cavity containing it.
– DERIVATIVES **her·ni·a·ted** /ˈhərnēˌātid/ adjective **her·ni·a·tion** /hərnēˈāsʜən/ noun.
– ORIGIN Latin.

he·ro /ˈhi(ə)rō/ ▸ **noun** (pl. **heroes**) **1** a person who is admired for their courage or outstanding achievements. **2** the chief male character in a book, play, or movie. **3** (in mythology and folklore) a person of superhuman qualities. **4** a submarine sandwich.

> – SYNONYMS **1 star,** superstar, megastar, idol, celebrity, favorite, darling; informal celeb. **2 main character,** starring role, male protagonist, (male) lead, leading man; informal good guy.
> – ANTONYMS villain.

– ORIGIN Greek *hērōs.*

he·ro·ic /həˈrōik/ ▸ **adjective 1** relating to or like a hero or heroine; very brave. **2** grand or ambitious in size or intention: *this is filmmaking on a heroic scale.*

> – SYNONYMS **brave,** courageous, valiant, intrepid, bold, fearless, daring; informal gutsy, spunky.
> – ANTONYMS cowardly.

▸ **noun** (**heroics**) brave or dramatic behavior or talk.
– DERIVATIVES **he·ro·i·cal·ly** adverb.

her·o·in /ˈherō-in/ ▸ **noun** a highly addictive painkilling drug obtained from morphine.
– ORIGIN German, from Latin *heros* 'hero' (because of its effects on the user's self-esteem).

her·o·ine /ˈherō-in/ ▸ **noun 1** a woman admired for her courage or outstanding achievements. **2** the chief female character in a book, play, or movie.

> – SYNONYMS **1 star,** superstar, megastar, idol, celebrity, favorite, darling; informal celeb. **2 main character,** female protagonist, lead, leading lady, prima donna, diva.

her·o·ism /ˈherōˌizəm/ ▸ **noun** great bravery.

> – SYNONYMS **bravery,** courage, valor, daring, fearlessness, pluck; informal guts, spunk, moxie.
> – ANTONYMS cowardice.

her·on /ˈherən/ ▸ **noun** a large fish-eating wading bird with long legs, a long neck, and a long pointed bill.
– ORIGIN Old French.

her·on·ry /ˈherənrē/ ▸ **noun** (pl. **heronries**) a breeding colony of herons, typically in a group of trees.

hero wor·ship ▸ **noun** extreme admiration for someone.
▸ **verb** (**hero-worship**) admire someone very much.

her·pes /ˈhərpēz/ ▸ **noun** a disease caused by a virus, affecting the skin (often with blisters) or the nervous system.
– DERIVATIVES **her·pet·ic** /hərˈpetik/ adjective.
– ORIGIN Greek *herpēs* 'shingles.'

her·pes sim·plex ▸ **noun** a form of herpes that may produce cold sores, genital inflammation, or conjunctivitis.

her·pes·vi·rus /ˈhərpēzˌvīrəs/ ▸ **noun** any of a group of viruses causing herpes and other diseases.

her·pes zos·ter /ˈzästər/ ▸ **noun 1** medical name for **SHINGLES**. **2** a herpesvirus that causes shingles and chicken pox.
– ORIGIN Greek *herpēs* 'shingles' and *zōstēr* 'girdle, belt.'

her·pe·tol·o·gy /ˌhərpəˈtäləjē/ ▸ **noun** the branch of zoology concerned with reptiles and amphibians.
– DERIVATIVES **her·pe·to·log·i·cal** /-təˈläjəkəl/ adjective **her·pe·tol·o·gist** noun.
– ORIGIN Greek *herpeton* 'creeping thing.'

Herr /he(ə)r/ ▸ **noun** a title or form of address for a German-speaking man, corresponding to *Mr.*
– ORIGIN from German *hērro* 'more exalted.'

her·ring /ˈherɪɴɢ/ ▸ **noun** an edible silvery fish that is found in shoals in coastal waters.
– ORIGIN Old English.

her·ring·bone /ˈherɪɴɢˌbōn/ ▸ **noun** a zigzag pattern consisting of columns of short parallel lines, with all the lines in one column sloping one way and all the lines in the next column sloping the other way.

her·ring gull ▸ noun a common northern gull with gray black-tipped wings.

hers /hərz/ ▸ possessive pronoun used to refer to a thing or things belonging to or associated with a female person or animal previously mentioned.

USAGE

There is no apostrophe: the spelling should be **hers** not *her's*.

her·self /hər'self/ ▸ pronoun (third person sing.) **1** (reflexive) used as the object of a verb or preposition to refer to a female person or animal previously mentioned as the subject of the clause. **2** (emphatic) she or her personally.

hertz /hərts/ ▸ noun (pl. same) the SI unit of frequency, equal to one cycle per second.
– ORIGIN named after the German physicist H. R. *Hertz*.

he's /hēz/ ▸ contraction **1** he is. **2** he has.

hes·i·tant /'hezitənt/ ▸ adjective slow to act or speak as a result of indecision or reluctance.

– SYNONYMS **1 uncertain,** undecided, unsure, doubtful, dubious, ambivalent, of two minds, wavering, vacillating, irresolute, indecisive, hemming and hawing. informal iffy. **2 timid,** diffident, shy, bashful, insecure, nervous.
– ANTONYMS certain, decisive, confident.

– DERIVATIVES **hes·i·tance** noun **hes·i·tan·cy** noun **hes·i·tant·ly** adverb.

WORD TOOLKIT

See **UNWILLING**.

hes·i·tate /'hezi,tāt/ ▸ verb **1** pause indecisively. **2** be reluctant to do something: *please do not hesitate to contact me*.

– SYNONYMS **1 pause,** delay, wait, stall, be uncertain, be unsure, be doubtful, be indecisive, vacillate, waver, hem and haw. informal dilly-dally. **2** ***don't hesitate to*** *to ask* **be reluctant to,** be unwilling to, be disinclined to, scruple to, have misgivings about, have qualms about, think twice about.

– DERIVATIVES **hes·i·ta·tion** /,hezi'tāsʜən/ noun.
– ORIGIN Latin *haesitare* 'stick fast.'

het·er·o /'hetərō/ ▸ noun & adjective informal short for **HETEROSEXUAL**.

hetero- ▸ combining form other; different: *heterosexual*.
– ORIGIN Greek *heteros* 'other.'

het·er·o·cy·clic /,hetərō'sīklik, -'siklik/ ▸ adjective referring to a chemical compound whose molecule contains a ring of atoms of at least two elements (one of which is generally carbon).

het·er·o·dox /'hetərə,däks/ ▸ adjective not following the usual or accepted standards or beliefs.
– DERIVATIVES **het·er·o·dox·y** noun.
– ORIGIN from Greek *heteros* 'other' + *doxa* 'opinion.'

het·er·o·ge·ne·ous /,hetərə'jēnēəs/ ▸ adjective consisting of many different kinds of people or things; varied: *a heterogeneous collection*.
– DERIVATIVES **het·er·o·ge·ne·i·ty** /-jə'nēətē/ noun **het·er·o·ge·ne·ous·ly** adverb.
– ORIGIN from Greek *heteros* 'other' + *genos* 'a kind.'

het·er·ol·o·gous /,hetə'räləgəs/ ▸ adjective chiefly Biology not homologous.
– DERIVATIVES **het·er·ol·o·gy** /-'räləjē/ noun.

het·er·o·mor·phic /,hetərə'môrfik/ ▸ adjective Biology occurring in two or more different forms, especially at different stages in the life cycle.
– DERIVATIVES **het·er·o·morph** /'hetərə,môrf/ noun.

het·er·o·sex·ism /,hetərō'sek,sizəm/ ▸ noun discrimination or prejudice against homosexuals on the assumption that heterosexuality is the norm.
– DERIVATIVES **het·er·o·sex·ist** adjective.

het·er·o·sex·u·al /,hetərō'seksʜōōəl/ ▸ adjective **1** sexually attracted to the opposite sex. **2** (of a sexual relationship) between a man and a woman. ▸ noun a heterosexual person.
– DERIVATIVES **het·er·o·sex·u·al·i·ty** /-,seksʜōō'alitē/ noun **het·er·o·sex·u·al·ly** adverb.
– ORIGIN from Greek *heteros* 'other.'

het up /,het 'əp/ ▸ adjective informal angry and agitated.
– ORIGIN from dialect *het* 'heated, hot.'

heu·ris·tic /hyōō'ristik/ ▸ adjective **1** allowing a person to discover or learn something for themselves. **2** Computing proceeding to a solution by trial and error or by rules that are only loosely defined. ▸ noun **1** (**heuristics**) (usu. treated as sing.) the study and use of heuristic techniques. **2** a heuristic process or method.
– DERIVATIVES **heu·ris·ti·cal·ly** adverb.
– ORIGIN Greek *heuriskein* 'to find.'

hew /hyōō/ ▸ verb (past part. **hewn** /hyōōn/ or **hewed**) **1** chop or cut wood, coal, etc., with an ax, pick, or other tool. **2** (**be hewn**) be cut or formed from a hard material: *a seat hewn out of a fallen tree trunk*. **3** (**hew to**) conform or adhere to.
– ORIGIN Old English.

hex[1] /heks/ ▸ verb cast a spell on someone. ▸ noun **1** a magic spell. **2** a witch.
– ORIGIN German *hexen*.

hex[2] ▸ adjective short for **HEXADECIMAL**.

hexa- (also **hex-** before a vowel) ▸ combining form six; having six: *hexagon*.
– ORIGIN Greek *hex* 'six.'

hex·a·dec·i·mal /,heksə'des(ə)məl/ ▸ adjective Computing relating to or using a system of numerical notation that has 16 rather than 10 as its base.

hex·a·gon /'heksə,gän/ ▸ noun a plane figure with six straight sides and angles.
– DERIVATIVES **hex·ag·o·nal** /hek'sagənl/ adjective.

hex·a·gram /'heksə,gram/ ▸ noun a six-pointed star formed by two intersecting equilateral triangles.

hex·a·he·dron /,heksə'hēdrən/ ▸ noun (pl. **hexahedra** or **hexahedrons**) a solid figure with six plane faces.
– DERIVATIVES **hex·a·he·dral** adjective.

hex·am·e·ter /hek'samitər/ ▸ noun a line of verse consisting of six metrical feet.

hex·ane /'hek,sān/ ▸ noun a colorless liquid hydrocarbon of the alkane series, commonly used as a solvent.

hex·a·va·lent /,heksə'vālənt/ ▸ adjective Chemistry having a valence of six.

hey /hā/ ▸ exclamation used to attract attention or to express surprise, interest, annoyance, etc.

hey·day /'hā,dā/ ▸ noun (**one's heyday**) the period of someone's or something's greatest success, popularity, activity, etc.: *the paper has lost millions of readers since its heyday in 1964*.
– ORIGIN first used as an exclamation of joy or surprise.

HF ▸ abbreviation Physics high frequency.

Hf ▸ symbol the chemical element hafnium.

Hg ▸ symbol the chemical element mercury.
– ORIGIN abbreviation of Latin *hydrargyrum*.

HHS ▸ abbreviation (Department of) Health and Human Services.

HI ▸ abbreviation Hawaii.

hi /hī/ ▸ exclamation informal used as a friendly greeting.

hi·a·tal her·ni·a /hī'ātəl/ (also **hiatus hernia**) ▸ noun a condition in which an organ (usually the stomach) protrudes through the diaphragm at the opening for the esophagus.

hi·a·tus /hī'ātəs/ ▸ noun (pl. **hiatuses**) a pause or gap in a series, sequence, or process: *there was a brief hiatus in the war.*

– SYNONYMS **pause,** break, gap, lacuna, interval, intermission, interlude, interruption.

– ORIGIN Latin, 'gaping.'

Hib /hib/ ▸ noun a bacterium that causes meningitis in very young children or babies.
– ORIGIN from the initial letters of *Haemophilus influenzae type B*.

hi·ba·chi /hə'bäCHē/ ▸ noun (pl. **hibachis**) a portable apparatus for grilling foods over charcoal.
– ORIGIN Japanese *hibachi, hi-hachi*, from *hi* 'fire' + *hachi* 'bowl, pot.'

hi·ber·nate /'hībər,nāt/ ▸ verb (of an animal) spend the winter in a state like deep sleep.
– DERIVATIVES **hi·ber·na·tion** /,hībər'nāSHən/ noun **hi·ber·na·tor** noun.
– ORIGIN Latin *hibernare*.

Hi·ber·ni·an /hī'bərnēən/ ▸ adjective Irish (now chiefly used in names). ▸ noun an Irish person (now chiefly used in names).
– ORIGIN Latin *Hibernia*, from Celtic.

hi·bis·cus /hī'biskəs/ ▸ noun a plant of the mallow family with large brightly colored flowers.
– ORIGIN Greek *hibiskos* 'marsh mallow.'

hic·cup /'hikəp/ (also **hiccough** pronunc. same) ▸ noun **1** a gulping sound in the throat caused by an involuntary spasm of the diaphragm and respiratory organs. **2** a minor difficulty or setback. ▸ verb (**hiccups, hiccuping, hiccuped**) make the sound of a hiccup or series of hiccups.
– DERIVATIVES **hic·cup·y** adjective.
– ORIGIN imitating the sound.

hick /hik/ ▸ noun informal an unsophisticated person from the country.

hick·ey /'hikē/ ▸ noun (pl. **hickeys**) informal a temporary red mark on the skin caused by biting or sucking during sexual play.
– ORIGIN unknown.

hick·o·ry /'hik(ə)rē/ ▸ noun **1** a tree found in chiefly in North America with tough, heavy wood and edible nuts. **2** a stick made of hickory wood.
– ORIGIN from *pohickery*, the local Virginian name, from Algonquian.

hid /hid/ past of HIDE[1].

hid·den /'hidn/ past participle of HIDE[1]. ▸ adjective

– SYNONYMS **1 concealed,** secret, invisible, unseen, camouflaged. **2 obscure,** unclear, concealed, cryptic, arcane, mysterious, secret, covert, abstruse, deep.
– ANTONYMS visible, obvious.

– DERIVATIVES **hid·den·ness** noun.

hid·den a·gen·da ▸ noun a secret motive or plan.

hide[1] /hīd/ ▸ verb (past **hid** /hid/; past part. **hidden** /'hidn/) **1** put or keep out of sight: *I hid the key under a flowerpot.* **2** conceal oneself. **3** keep something secret.

– SYNONYMS **1 conceal,** secrete, put out of sight, cache; informal stash. **2** (as adj. **hidden**) *a hidden camera* **concealed,** secret, invisible, unseen, camouflaged. **3 conceal oneself,** secrete oneself, take cover, lie low, go to ground; informal hole up. **4 obscure,** block out, blot out, obstruct, cloud, shroud, veil, eclipse, camouflage. **5 keep secret,** conceal, cover up, keep quiet about, hush up, suppress, disguise, mask; informal keep a/the lid on. **6** (as adj. **hidden**) *a hidden meaning* **obscure,** unclear, concealed, cryptic, arcane, mysterious, secret, covert, abstruse, deep.
– ANTONYMS reveal.

▸ noun Brit. a camouflaged shelter used to watch wild animals or birds at close quarters.
– PHRASES **hide one's light under a bushel** keep quiet about one's talents or accomplishments. [with biblical reference to the Gospel of Matthew, chapter 15.]
– ORIGIN Old English.

hide[2] ▸ noun the skin of an animal, especially when made into leather.
– PHRASES **neither hide nor hair of** not the slightest trace of.
– ORIGIN Old English.

hide-and-seek ▸ noun a children's game in which one player tries to find other players who have hidden themselves.

hide·a·way /'hīdə,wā/ ▸ noun a place where one can hide or be alone.

– SYNONYMS **retreat,** refuge, hiding place, hideout, safe house, den.

▸ adjective designed to be concealed when not in use: *a hideaway bed.*

hide·bound /'hīd,bound/ ▸ adjective unwilling or unable to abandon old-fashioned ideas or customs in favor of new ways of thinking.

hid·e·ous /'hidēəs/ ▸ adjective **1** extremely ugly. **2** extremely unpleasant.

– SYNONYMS **1 ugly,** repulsive, repellent, unsightly, revolting, grotesque. **2 horrific,** terrible, appalling, awful, dreadful, frightful, horrible, horrendous, horrifying, shocking, sickening, gruesome, ghastly.
– ANTONYMS beautiful, pleasant.

– DERIVATIVES **hid·e·ous·ly** adverb **hid·e·ous·ness** noun.
– ORIGIN Old French *hidos, hideus*.

hide·out /'hīd,out/ ▸ noun a hiding place, especially one used by someone who has broken the law.

hid·ey-hole /'hīdē,hōl/ (also **hidy-hole**) ▸ noun informal a hiding place.

hid·ing[1] /'hīding/ ▸ noun **1** a physical beating. **2** informal a severe defeat.

– SYNONYMS **beating,** thrashing, whipping, drubbing; informal licking, belting, pasting, walloping.

– ORIGIN from HIDE[2].

hid·ing[2] ▸ noun the action of hiding or the state of being hidden: *he had gone into hiding.*

hie /hī/ ▸ verb (**hies, hieing** or **hying, hied**) old use go quickly.
– ORIGIN Old English, 'strive, pant.'

hi·er·ar·chi·cal /ˌhī(ə)'rärkikəl/ ▶ **adjective** arranged in order of rank or status.
– DERIVATIVES **hi·er·ar·chi·cal·ly** adverb.

hi·er·ar·chy /'hī(ə)ˌrärkē/ ▶ **noun** (pl. **hierarchies**) **1** a system in which people are ranked one above the other according to their status or authority. **2** a classification of things according to their relative importance.

– SYNONYMS **ranking,** order, pecking order, grading, ladder, scale.

– ORIGIN from Greek *hierarkhēs* 'sacred ruler.'

hi·er·at·ic /ˌhī(ə)'ratik/ ▶ **adjective** relating to priests.
– ORIGIN Greek *hieratikos*.

hi·er·o·glyph /'hī(ə)rəˌglif/ ▶ **noun** a picture of an object representing a word, syllable, or sound, especially as found in the ancient Egyptian writing system.

hi·er·o·glyph·ic /ˌhī(ə)rə'glifik/ ▶ **noun** (**hieroglyphics**) writing consisting of hieroglyphs. ▶ **adjective** relating to or written in hieroglyphs.
– ORIGIN from Greek *hieros* 'sacred' + *gluphē* 'carving.'

hi·er·o·phant /'hī(ə)rəˌfant/ ▶ **noun** a person, especially a priest, who interprets sacred mysteries or other things that are very difficult to understand.
– DERIVATIVES **hi·er·o·phan·tic** adjective.
– ORIGIN from Greek *hieros* 'sacred' + *phainein* 'show.'

hi-fi /'hī 'fī/ informal ▶ **adjective** relating to the reproduction of high-fidelity sound. ▶ **noun** (pl. **hi-fis**) a set of equipment for reproducing high-fidelity sound.

hig·gle·dy-pig·gle·dy /'higəldē 'pigəldē/ ▶ **adverb & adjective** in confusion or disorder.
– ORIGIN probably with reference to the irregular herding together of pigs.

high /hī/ ▶ **adjective 1** extending far upward. **2** of a specified height. **3** far above ground or sea level. **4** great or greater than normal in amount, value, size, or intensity: *high blood pressure*. **5** (of a period or movement) at its peak: *high summer*. **6** great in rank or status; important. **7** culturally or morally superior: *a man with high ideals*. **8** (of a sound or note) at or near the top of a musical scale; not deep or low. **9** informal under the influence of drugs or alcohol. **10** (of food) strong-smelling because beginning to go bad. **11** (of game) slightly decomposed and so ready to cook.

– SYNONYMS **1 tall,** lofty, towering, giant, big, multistory, high-rise, elevated. **2 high-ranking,** ranking, leading, top, prominent, senior, influential, powerful, important, exalted. **3 inflated,** excessive, unreasonable, expensive, exorbitant, extortionate; informal steep, stiff. **4 high-pitched,** shrill, piercing, squeaky, penetrating, soprano, treble, falsetto. **5 intoxicated,** hallucinating; informal stoned, wrecked, off your head.
– ANTONYMS low, deep.

▶ **noun 1** a high point, level, or figure. **2** an area of high atmospheric pressure. **3** informal a state of intense happiness.
▶ **adverb 1** at or to a considerable or specified height. **2** at a high price. **3** (of a sound) at or to a high pitch.

– SYNONYMS **at a great height,** high up, way up, in the sky, aloft, overhead, to a great height.
– ANTONYMS low.

– PHRASES **from on high 1** from a very high place. **2** from remote high authority or heaven. **high and dry 1** stranded by the sea as it retreats. **2** in a very difficult position. **high and low** in many different places. **high and mighty** informal arrogant. **the high ground** a position of superiority. **it is high time that ——** it is past the time when something should have happened or been done. **on one's high horse** informal behaving arrogantly or pompously. **run high 1** (of a river) be full and close to overflowing, with a strong current. **2** (of feelings) be intense.
– ORIGIN Old English.

high altar ▶ **noun** the chief altar of a church.

high·ball /'hīˌbôl/ ▶ **noun** a drink consisting of whiskey and a mixer such as soda or ginger ale, served in a tall glass with ice.

high beam ▶ **noun 1** the brightest setting of a vehicle's headlights. **2** (**high beams**) the headlights of a vehicle when set on high beam: *the glare from his high beams*.

high-born ▶ **adjective** having noble parents.

high·brow /'hīˌbrou/ ▶ **adjective** often derogatory concerned with serious artistic or cultural ideas; intellectual or refined.

– SYNONYMS **intellectual,** scholarly, bookish, academic, educated, donnish, bluestocking; erudite, learned; informal brainy.
– ANTONYMS lowbrow.

▶ **noun** a person of this type.

high chair ▶ **noun** a small chair with long legs for a baby or small child, fitted with a tray and used at mealtimes.

High Church ▶ **noun** a tradition within the Anglican Church that emphasizes the importance of ritual and the authority of bishops and priests.

high-class ▶ **adjective** of a high standard, quality, or social class.

– SYNONYMS **superior,** first-rate; excellent, select, choice, premier, top, top-flight, deluxe, top-quality, upmarket, upscale; informal top-notch, top-drawer, A1, classy, posh.

high com·mand ▶ **noun** the commander-in-chief and associated senior staff of an army, navy, or air force.

high com·mis·sion ▶ **noun** an embassy of one Commonwealth country in another.
– DERIVATIVES **high com·mis·sion·er** noun.

high court ▶ **noun 1** a supreme court of justice. **2** the US Supreme Court.

high-end ▶ **adjective** referring to the most expensive of a range of products.

high·er ed·u·ca·tion ▶ **noun** education beyond high school, especially at a college or university.

high ex·plo·sive ▶ **noun** a powerful chemical explosive of the kind used in shells and bombs.

high·fa·lu·tin /ˌhīfə'lo͞otn/ ▶ **adjective** informal grand or self-important in a pompous or pretentious way.
– ORIGIN perhaps from HIGH + *fluting*.

high fash·ion ▶ **noun** another term for HAUTE COUTURE.

high fi·del·i·ty ▶ **noun** the reproduction of sound with little distortion.

high fi·nance ▶ **noun** financial transactions involving large sums of money.

high five ▶ **noun** informal a gesture of celebration or greeting in which two people slap each other's palms with their arms raised.

high·fli·er /'hīflīər/ ▶ **noun 1** someone who is very successful, especially academically or in business.

2 a stock that trades at a high price or that has risen sharply.

high-flown ▸ **adjective** (especially of language) extravagant or intended to impress.

high fre·quen·cy ▸ **noun** (in radio) a frequency of 3–30 megahertz.

high gear ▸ **noun** a gear that makes a wheeled vehicle move fast.

High Ger·man ▸ **noun** the standard literary and spoken form of German, originally used in the highlands in the south of Germany.

high-grade ▸ **adjective 1** of very good quality. **2** (of a medical condition) of a more serious kind; major: *a high-grade tumor.*

high-hand·ed ▸ **adjective** using one's authority forcefully and without considering the feelings of other people.

high-hat ▸ **noun 1** a snobbish or supercilious person. **2** variant spelling of **HI-HAT**. ▸ **adjective** snobbish or supercilious.

high-im·pact ▸ **adjective** (of physical exercises, especially aerobics) placing a great deal of stress on the body.

high jinks /jiNGks/ ▸ **plural noun** high-spirited fun.

high jump ▸ **noun** (**the high jump**) an athletic event in which competitors jump as high as possible over a bar that is raised after each round.
– DERIVATIVES **high jump·er** noun.

high·land /ˈhīlənd/ ▸ **noun** (also **highlands**) **1** an area of high or mountainous land. **2** (**the Highlands**) the mountainous northern part of Scotland.
– DERIVATIVES **high·land·er** noun.

High·land fling ▸ **noun** an energetic solo Scottish dance consisting of a series of complex steps.

high-lev·el ▸ **adjective 1** involving senior people; of relatively high importance: *high-level negotiations.* **2** (of a computer programming language) having instructions resembling an existing language such as English, making it relatively easy to use.

high life ▸ **noun** an extravagant social life as enjoyed by wealthy people.

high·light /ˈhīˌlīt/ ▸ **noun 1** an outstanding part of an event or period of time: *that season was the highlight of his career.* **2** a bright or reflective area in a painting, picture, or design. **3** (**highlights**) bright tints in the hair, produced by bleaching or dyeing.

– SYNONYMS **high point,** climax, peak, pinnacle, height, zenith, summit, focus, feature.

▸ **verb 1** draw attention to: *the issues highlighted by the report.* **2** mark something with a highlighter. **3** create highlights in hair.

– SYNONYMS **spotlight,** call attention to, focus on, underline, show up, bring out, accentuate, accent, stress, emphasize.
– ANTONYMS play down.

high·light·er /ˈhīˌlītər/ ▸ **noun 1** a broad felt-tipped pen used to overlay transparent fluorescent color on a part of a text or illustration. **2** a cosmetic used to emphasize the cheekbones or other facial features.

high·ly /ˈhīlē/ ▸ **adverb 1** to a high degree or level. **2** favorably.

high-main·te·nance ▸ **adjective 1** needing a lot of work to keep in good condition: *high-maintenance bricks and mortar.* **2** informal (of a person or relationship) demanding a lot of attention.

High Mass ▸ **noun** a Roman Catholic mass with full ritual procedure, including music and incense.

high-mind·ed ▸ **adjective** having strong moral principles.

high·ness /ˈhīnis/ ▸ **noun 1** (**His, Her, Your Highness**) a title given to a person of royal rank, or used in addressing them. **2** the quality of being high: *the highness of her cheekbones.*

high-oc·tane ▸ **adjective 1** (of gasoline) having a high octane number and therefore allowing an engine to run smoothly. **2** powerful or dynamic: *a high-octane career.*

high-pitched ▸ **adjective** (of a sound) high in pitch.

high-pow·ered ▸ **adjective** informal (of a person) dynamic and forceful.

high-pres·sure ▸ **adjective 1** involving a high degree of activity and exertion; stressful: *a high-pressure career.* **2** (of a salesperson or sales pitch) employing a high degree of coercion; insistent. **3** involving or using much physical force: *high-pressure jets of water.* **4** referring to a condition of the atmosphere with the pressure above average.

high priest ▸ **noun 1** a chief priest of a non-Christian religion. **2** (also **high priestess**) the leader of a cult or movement.

high-pro·file ▸ **adjective** attracting much attention or publicity: *a high-profile court case.*

high re·lief ▸ **noun** see **RELIEF** (sense 8).

high-rise ▸ **adjective** (of a building) having many stories. ▸ **noun** a building with many stories.

high road ▸ **noun** a morally superior approach toward something: *she took the high road and refused to engage in negative campaigning.*

high roll·er ▸ **noun** informal a person who gambles or spends large sums of money.

high school ▸ **noun** a secondary school that typically comprises grades 9 through 12.

high seas ▸ **plural noun** (**the high seas**) the open ocean, especially the areas that are not under the control of any one country.

high sea·son ▸ **noun** the most popular time of year for a vacation, when prices are highest.

high sher·iff ▸ **noun** see **SHERIFF**.

high so·ci·e·ty ▸ **noun** see **SOCIETY** (sense 3).

high spir·its ▸ **plural noun** lively and cheerful behavior or mood.
– DERIVATIVES **high-spir·it·ed** adjective.

high spot ▸ **noun** the most enjoyable part of an experience or period of time.

high street Brit. ▸ **noun** the main street of a town. ▸ **adjective** (**high-street**) catering to the needs of the ordinary public: *high-street fashion.*

high-strung ▸ **adjective** very nervous and easily upset.

high·tail /ˈhīˌtāl/ ▸ **verb** informal move or travel fast.

high tea ▸ **noun** Brit. a meal eaten in the late afternoon or early evening, typically consisting of a cooked dish and tea.

high-tech /ˈhī ˈtek/ (also **hi-tech**) ▸ **adjective 1** using, needing, or involved in high technology. **2** (of architecture and interior design) functional in style and using materials such as steel, plastic, and glass.

high tech·nol·o·gy ▸ **noun** advanced technological development, especially in electronics.

high-ten·sile ▸ **adjective** (of metal) very strong under tension.

high tide (also **high water**) ▸ **noun 1** the state of the tide when at its highest level. **2** the highest point of something: *the high tide of nationalism.*

high-top ▸ **adjective** referring to a sneaker with a laced upper that extends above the ankle. ▸ **noun** (**high-tops**) a pair of such shoes.

high trea·son ▸ **noun** see **TREASON**.

high-wa·ter mark ▸ **noun** the level reached by the sea at high tide, or by a lake or river during a flood.

high·way /ˈhīˌwā/ ▸ **noun 1** a main road, especially one connecting major towns or cities. **2** (chiefly in official use) a public road.

high·way·man /ˈhīˌwāmən/ ▸ **noun** (pl. **highwaymen**) historical a man, typically on horseback, who held up and robbed travelers.

high wire ▸ **noun** a high tightrope. ▸ **adjective** requiring great skill or judgment.

hi-hat (also **high-hat**) ▸ **noun** a pair of foot-operated cymbals forming part of a drum kit.

hi·jab /hiˈjäb/ ▸ **noun** a head covering worn in public by some Muslim women.
– ORIGIN from an Arabic word meaning 'to veil.'

hi·jack /ˈhīˌjak/ ▸ **verb 1** illegally seize control of an aircraft, ship, vehicle, etc., while it is traveling somewhere. **2** take over something and use it for a new purpose: *the organization had been hijacked by extremists.*

– SYNONYMS **commandeer,** seize, take over, appropriate, expropriate.

▸ **noun** an instance of hijacking an aircraft, ship, etc.
– DERIVATIVES **hi·jack·er** noun.
– ORIGIN unknown.

Hij·ra /ˈhijrə/ ▸ **noun** variant spelling of **HEGIRA**.

hike /hīk/ ▸ **noun 1** a long walk, especially in the country or wilderness. **2** a sharp increase, especially in price. **3** informal a long distance.

– SYNONYMS **1 walk,** trek, tramp, trudge, slog, march, ramble. **2 increase,** rise.

▸ **verb 1** go on a hike. **2** pull or lift up clothing. **3** increase a price sharply.

– SYNONYMS **1 walk,** trek, tramp, trudge, slog, march, ramble, backpack. **2 increase,** raise, up, put up, push up; informal jack up, bump up.

– DERIVATIVES **hik·er** noun.
– ORIGIN unknown.

hi·lar·i·ous /həˈle(ə)rēəs/ ▸ **adjective** extremely funny.

– SYNONYMS **very funny,** hysterical, uproarious, rib-tickling; informal side-splitting, priceless, a scream, a hoot.

– DERIVATIVES **hi·lar·i·ous·ly** adverb.
– ORIGIN Greek *hilaros* 'cheerful.'

hi·lar·i·ty /həˈle(ə)ritē/ ▸ **noun** a state of great amusement causing loud laughter.

hill /hil/ ▸ **noun** a naturally raised area of land, not as high or craggy as a mountain.

– SYNONYMS **high ground,** hillock, hillside, rise, mound, knoll, hummock, fell, mountain.

– PHRASES **over the hill** informal old and past one's prime.
– ORIGIN Old English.

hill·bil·ly /ˈhilˌbilē/ ▸ **noun** (pl. **hillbillies**) informal, chiefly derogatory an unsophisticated country person.
– ORIGIN from **HILL** + *Billy* (informal form of the man's name *William*).

hill·ock /ˈhilək/ ▸ **noun** a small hill or mound.
– DERIVATIVES **hill·ock·y** adjective.

hill·side /ˈhilˌsīd/ ▸ **noun** the sloping side of a hill.

hill sta·tion ▸ **noun** a town in the low mountains of the Indian subcontinent, popular as a vacation-resort during the hot season.

hill·top /ˈhilˌtäp/ ▸ **noun** the summit of a hill.

hill·y /ˈhilē/ ▸ **adjective** (**hillier, hilliest**) having many hills.
– DERIVATIVES **hill·i·ness** noun.

hilt /hilt/ ▸ **noun** the handle of a sword, dagger, or knife.
– PHRASES **to the hilt** completely.
– ORIGIN Old English.

him /him/ ▸ **pronoun** (third person sing.) used as the object of a verb or preposition to refer to a male person or animal previously mentioned.
– ORIGIN Old English.

USAGE

Why is it often said that you should say *I could never be as good as he* rather than *I could never be as good as him*? For a discussion of this issue, see the note at **PERSONAL PRONOUN**.

Him·a·la·yan /ˌhiməˈlāən/ ▸ **adjective** relating to the Himalayas, a mountain system in southern Asia.

him·self /himˈself/ ▸ **pronoun** (third person sing.) **1** (reflexive) used as the object of a verb or preposition to refer to a male person or animal previously mentioned as the subject of the clause. **2** (emphatic) he or him personally.

hind[1] /hīnd/ ▸ **adjective** situated at the back.
– ORIGIN perhaps from Old English, 'behind.'

hind[2] ▸ **noun** a female deer.
– ORIGIN Old English.

hind·er[1] /ˈhindər/ ▸ **verb** delay or impede someone or something.

– SYNONYMS **hamper,** impede, inhibit, thwart, foil, delay, interfere with, slow down, hold back, hold up, restrict, handicap, hamstring.
– ANTONYMS facilitate.

– ORIGIN Old English, 'damage.'

CHOOSE THE RIGHT WORD

See **PROHIBIT**.

hind·er[2] /ˈhīndər/ ▸ **adjective** situated at or toward the back.
– ORIGIN perhaps from Old English, 'backward.'

Hin·di /ˈhindē/ ▸ **noun** a language of northern India derived from Sanskrit. ▸ **adjective** relating to Hindi.
– ORIGIN Urdu.

hind·limb /ˈhīn(d)ˌlim/ ▸ **noun** either of the two back limbs of an animal.

hind·most /ˈhīn(d)ˌmōst/ ▸ **adjective** farthest back.

hind·quar·ters /'hīn(d),kwôrtərz/ ▶ **plural noun** the hind legs and adjoining parts of a four-legged animal.

hin·drance /'hindrəns/ ▶ **noun** a thing that delays or impedes someone or something.

– SYNONYMS **impediment,** obstacle, barrier, obstruction, handicap, hurdle, restraint, restriction, encumbrance, complication, delay, drawback, setback, difficulty, inconvenience, hitch, stumbling block, fly in the ointment, hiccup.
– ANTONYMS aid, help.

hind·sight /'hīn(d),sīt/ ▶ **noun** understanding of a situation or event after it has happened.

Hin·du /'hindo͞o/ ▶ **noun** (pl. **Hindus**) a follower of Hinduism. ▶ **adjective** relating to Hinduism.
– ORIGIN Urdu.

Hin·du·ism /'hindo͞o,izəm/ ▶ **noun** a major religious and cultural tradition of the Indian subcontinent, including belief in reincarnation and the worship of a large number of gods and goddesses.
– DERIVATIVES **Hin·du·ize** verb.

Hin·du·sta·ni /,hindo͞o'stänē/ ▶ **noun** a group of languages and dialects spoken in NW India that includes Hindi and Urdu.

hind·wing /'hīn(d),wiNG/ ▶ **noun** either of the two back wings of a four-winged insect.

hinge /hinj/ ▶ **noun** a movable joint or mechanism by which a door, gate, or lid opens and closes or that connects linked objects. ▶ **verb** (**hinges, hinging, hinged**) **1** attach or join something with a hinge. **2** (**hinge on**) depend entirely on: *the city's future is likely to hinge on the election.*
– ORIGIN related to **HANG**.

hin·ny /'hinē/ ▶ **noun** (pl. **hinnies**) the offspring of a female donkey and a male horse.
– ORIGIN Greek *hinnos.*

hint /hint/ ▶ **noun 1** a slight or indirect indication. **2** a very small trace of something. **3** a small item of practical information.

– SYNONYMS **1 clue,** inkling, suggestion, indication, sign, signal, intimation. **2 tip,** suggestion, pointer, guideline, recommendation. **3 trace,** touch, suspicion, suggestion, dash, soupçon; informal smidgen, tad.

▶ **verb 1** indicate something indirectly. **2** (**hint at**) be a slight indication of: *a sound that hinted at deep power.*

– SYNONYMS **imply,** insinuate, intimate, suggest, refer to, drive at, mean; informal get at.

– ORIGIN probably from an Old English word meaning 'grasp.'

hin·ter·land /'hintər,land/ (also **hinterlands**) ▶ **noun 1** the remote areas of a country, away from the coast and major rivers. **2** the area around or beyond a major town or port.
– ORIGIN German.

hip[1] /hip/ ▶ **noun** a projection of the pelvis and upper thigh bone on each side of the body.
– DERIVATIVES **hipped** adjective.
– PHRASES **be joined at the hip** informal (of two people) be inseparable.
– ORIGIN Old English.

hip[2] ▶ **noun** the fruit of a rose.
– ORIGIN Old English.

hip[3] ▶ **adjective** (**hipper, hippest**) informal **1** very fashionable. **2** (**hip to**) aware of or informed about something.
– DERIVATIVES **hip·ness** noun.
– ORIGIN unknown.

hip[4] ▶ **exclamation** introducing a communal cheer: *hip, hip, hooray!*
– ORIGIN unknown.

hip·bone /'hip,bōn/ ▶ **noun** a large bone forming the main part of the pelvis on each side of the body.

hip flask ▶ **noun** a small flask for liquor, carried in a hip pocket.

hip-hop ▶ **noun** a style of pop music of US black and Hispanic origin, featuring rap with an electronic backing.
– DERIVATIVES **hip-hop·per** noun.
– ORIGIN probably from **HIP**[3].

hip·pie /'hipē/ ▶ **noun** variant spelling of **HIPPY**.

hip·po /'hipō/ ▶ **noun** (pl. same or **hippos**) informal a hippopotamus.

Hip·po·crat·ic oath /'hipə'kratik/ ▶ **noun** an oath formerly taken by medical doctors to observe a code of professional behavior (parts of which are still used in some medical schools).
– ORIGIN from the name of the ancient Greek physician *Hippocrates.*

hip·po·drome /'hipə,drōm/ ▶ **noun 1** an arena for equestrian or other sporting events. **2** (in ancient Greece or Rome) a course for chariot or horse races.
– ORIGIN from Greek *hippos* 'horse' + *dromos* 'race, course.'

hip·po·pot·a·mus /,hipə'pätəməs/ ▶ **noun** (pl. **hippopotamuses** or **hippopotami** /-,mī, -,mē/) a large African mammal with a thick skin and massive jaws, living partly on land and partly in water.
– ORIGIN from Greek *hippos ho potamios* 'river horse.'

hip·py /'hipē/ (also **hippie**) ▶ **noun** (pl. **hippies**) (especially in the 1960s) a young person, typically having long hair, who advocates peace and free love and dresses unconventionally.
– DERIVATIVES **hip·pie·dom** noun **hip·py·ish** adjective.
– ORIGIN from **HIP**[3].

hip·ster /'hipstər/ ▶ **noun** informal a person who follows the latest trends and fashions.
– ORIGIN from **HIP**[3].

hip·sters /'hipstərz/ ▶ **plural noun** pants with a waistline at the hips; hip-huggers.
– ORIGIN from **HIP**[1].

hire /hīr/ ▶ **verb 1** appoint someone as an employee. **2** employ someone for a short time to do a particular job. **3** (**hire oneself out**) make oneself available for temporary employment.

– SYNONYMS **1 rent,** lease, charter. **2 employ,** engage, recruit, appoint, take on, sign up.
– ANTONYMS dismiss.

▶ **noun 1** the action of hiring someone or something. **2** a recently recruited employee.
– DERIVATIVES **hire·a·ble** adjective **hir·er** noun.
– PHRASES **for hire** available to be hired.
– ORIGIN Old English.

hire·ling /'hīrliNG/ ▶ **noun** chiefly derogatory a person who is willing to undertake any kind of work provided that they are paid.

hir·sute /'hər,so͞ot, hər'so͞ot, 'hi(ə)r,so͞ot/ ▶ **adjective** having a great deal of hair on the face or body; hairy.
– DERIVATIVES **hir·sute·ness** noun.
– ORIGIN Latin *hirsutus.*

his /hiz/ ▶ **possessive determiner 1** belonging to or associated with a male person or animal previously mentioned. **2** (**His**) used in titles: *His Honor*. ▶ **possessive pronoun** used to refer to a thing belonging to or associated with a male person or animal previously mentioned.
– ORIGIN Old English.

His·pan·ic /hiˈspanik/ ▶ **adjective** relating to Spain or to Spanish-speaking countries, especially those of Latin America. ▶ **noun** a Spanish-speaking person, especially one of Latin American descent, living in the US.
– DERIVATIVES **His·pan·i·cize** /hiˈspaniˌsīz/ verb.
– ORIGIN from Latin *Hispania* 'Spain.'

> **USAGE**
>
> In the US, **Hispanic** is the standard accepted term when referring to Spanish-speaking people living in the US. Other, more specific terms such as **Latino** and **Chicano** are also used where occasion demands.

hiss /his/ ▶ **verb 1** make a sharp sound like that made when pronouncing the letter *s*, often as a sign of disapproval or mockery. **2** whisper something in an urgent or angry way.

> – SYNONYMS **1 fizz,** whistle, wheeze. **2 jeer,** catcall, whistle, hoot.
> – ANTONYMS cheer.

▶ **noun 1** a hissing sound. **2** electrical interference at audio frequencies.

> – SYNONYMS **1 fizz,** whistle, wheeze. **2 jeer,** catcall, whistle, abuse, derision.
> – ANTONYMS cheer.

– ORIGIN imitating the sound.

his·ta·mine /ˈhistəˌmēn, -ˌmin/ ▶ **noun** a compound that is released by cells in response to injury and in allergic reactions.
– ORIGIN from Greek *histos* 'web, tissue' and **AMINE**.

his·to·gram /ˈhistəˌgram/ ▶ **noun** Statistics a diagram consisting of rectangles whose height is proportional to the frequency of a variable and whose width is equal to the class interval.

his·tol·o·gy /hiˈstäləjē/ ▶ **noun** the branch of biology concerned with the microscopic structure of tissues.
– DERIVATIVES **his·to·log·i·cal** /ˌhistəˈläjikəl/ adjective **his·tol·o·gist** noun.
– ORIGIN from Greek *histos* 'web, tissue.'

his·to·pa·thol·o·gy /ˌhistōpəˈᴛʜäləjē/ ▶ **noun** the branch of medicine concerned with the changes in tissues caused by disease.
– DERIVATIVES **his·to·path·o·log·i·cal** /ˌhistōˌpaᴛʜəˈläjikəl/ adjective **his·to·pa·thol·o·gist** noun.
– ORIGIN from Greek *histos* 'web, tissue.'

his·to·ri·an /hiˈstôrēən/ ▶ **noun** an expert in history.

his·tor·ic /hiˈstôrik, -ˈstär-/ ▶ **adjective 1** famous or important in history, or likely to be so in the future: *a historic occasion*. **2** Grammar (of a tense) used in describing past events.

> – SYNONYMS **significant,** notable, important, momentous, memorable, groundbreaking; informal earth-shattering.

> **USAGE**
>
> **Historic** and **historical** do not have the same meaning. **Historic** means 'famous or important in history' (*a historic occasion*), whereas **historical** chiefly means 'relating to history' (*historical evidence*).

his·tor·i·cal /hiˈstôrikəl, -ˈstär-/ ▶ **adjective 1** relating to history: *historical evidence*. **2** belonging to or set in the past. **3** (of the study of a subject) based on an analysis of its development over a period.

> – SYNONYMS **1 documented,** recorded, chronicled, authentic, factual, actual. **2 past,** bygone, ancient, old, former.

– DERIVATIVES **his·tor·i·cal·ly** adverb.

his·tor·i·cism /hiˈstôrəˌsizəm, -ˈstär-/ ▶ **noun 1** the theory that social and cultural developments are determined by history. **2** excessive regard for past styles of art and architecture.
– DERIVATIVES **his·tor·i·cist** noun **his·tor·i·cize** verb.

his·to·ric·i·ty /ˌhistəˈrisitē/ ▶ **noun** historical authenticity.

his·tor·ic pres·ent /ˈprezənt/ ▶ **noun** Grammar the present tense used instead of the past in vivid narrative or informal speech.

his·to·ri·og·ra·phy /hiˌstôrēˈägrəfē, -ˌstär-/ ▶ **noun 1** the study of the writing of history and of written histories. **2** the writing of history.
– DERIVATIVES **his·to·ri·og·ra·pher** noun **his·to·ri·o·graph·ic** /-əˈgrafik/ adjective **his·to·ri·o·graph·i·cal** /-əˈgrafikəl/ adjective.

his·to·ry /ˈhist(ə)rē/ ▶ **noun** (pl. **histories**) **1** the study of past events. **2** the past considered as a whole. **3** the past events connected with someone or something: *a patient with a complicated medical history*. **4** a continuous record of past events or trends.

> – SYNONYMS **1 the past,** former times, the olden days, yesterday, antiquity. **2 chronicle,** archive, record, report, narrative, account, study. **3 background,** past, life story, experiences, record.

– PHRASES **be history** informal be dismissed or dead; be finished.
– ORIGIN Greek *historia* 'narrative, history.'

his·tri·on·ic /ˌhistrēˈänik/ ▶ **adjective 1** excessively theatrical or dramatic. **2** formal relating to actors or acting. ▶ **noun** (**histrionics**) exaggerated behavior designed to attract attention.

> – SYNONYMS **dramatics,** theatrics, tantrums; affectation.

– DERIVATIVES **his·tri·on·i·cal·ly** adverb.
– ORIGIN from Latin *histrio* 'actor.'

hit /hit/ ▶ **verb** (**hits, hitting, hit**) **1** strike someone or something with the hand or a tool, bat, weapon, etc. **2** come into contact with someone or something quickly and forcefully. **3** strike a target. **4** cause harm or distress to: *the area was badly hit by layoffs*. **5** be suddenly realized by: *it hit me that I was successful*. **6** (**hit on**) informal suddenly discover or think of something. **7** (**hit on**) informal make sexual advances toward. **8** (**hit out**) make a strongly worded criticism or attack. **9** informal reach or arrive at a place, level, or figure.

> – SYNONYMS **1 strike,** smack, slap, beat, punch, thump, thrash, batter, club, pummel, cuff, swat; informal whack, wallop, bash, clout, belt, slug, clobber. **2 crash into,** run into, smash into, knock into, bump into, plow into, collide with, meet head-on. **3 devastate,** affect badly, upset, shatter, crush, traumatize; informal knock sideways. **4 occur to,** strike, dawn on, come to; enter one's head, cross one's mind, come to mind, spring to one's mind. **5** (**hit on**) *she hit on a novel idea for fund-raising* **discover,** come up with, think of, conceive of, dream up, invent, devise.

▶ **noun** **1** an instance of hitting or being hit. **2** a successful movie, pop record, etc. **3** Computing an instance of identifying an item of data that matches the requirements of a search. **4** an instance of a particular website being accessed by a user. **5** informal a murder carried out by a criminal organization. **6** informal a dose of an addictive drug.

– SYNONYMS **1 blow,** slap, smack, thump, punch, knock, bang; informal whack, wallop, bash, clout, slug, belt. **2 success,** sellout, winner, triumph, sensation, bestseller; informal smash hit, chart-topper, crowd-puller.
– ANTONYMS failure.

– DERIVATIVES **hit·ter** noun.
– PHRASES **hit-and-miss** done or occurring at random. **hit-and-run** (of a road accident) from which the driver responsible leaves rapidly without helping the other people involved. **hit someone below the belt 1** Boxing give one's opponent an illegal low blow. **2** behave unfairly toward someone. **hit the ground running** informal start something new with energy and enthusiasm. **hit it off** informal be naturally well suited. **hit the nail on the head** find exactly the right answer. **hit the road** (or **trail**) informal set out on a journey.
– ORIGIN Old Norse, 'come upon, meet with.'

hitch /hicн/ ▶ **verb** **1** move something into a different position with a jerk: *she hitched up her skirt and ran.* **2** fasten or tether an animal with a rope. **3** informal travel or obtain a lift by hitch-hiking.

– SYNONYMS **1 pull,** lift, raise; informal yank. **2 harness,** yoke, couple, fasten, connect, attach.

▶ **noun** **1** a temporary difficulty. **2** a temporary knot used to fasten one thing to another.

– SYNONYMS **problem,** difficulty, snag, setback, obstacle, complication; informal glitch, hiccup.

– PHRASES **get hitched** informal get married.
– ORIGIN unknown.

hitch·er /'hicнər/ ▶ **noun** a hitch-hiker.

hitch·hike /'hicн,hīk/ ▶ **verb** travel by getting free rides in passing vehicles: *he dropped out in 1976 and hitchhiked west.*
– DERIVATIVES **hitch·hik·er** noun.

hi-tech ▶ **adjective** variant spelling of **HIGH-TECH**.

hith·er /'hiтнər/ ▶ **adverb** old use to or toward this place.
– PHRASES **hith·er and thith·er** (also **hither and yon**) to and fro.
– ORIGIN Old English.

hith·er·to /'hiтнər,to͞o, ,hiтнər'to͞o/ ▶ **adverb** until the point in time under discussion.

Hit·ler·i·an /hit'le(ə)rēən/ ▶ **adjective** relating to or characteristic of the Austrian-born Nazi leader and Chancellor of Germany, Adolf Hitler.

hit list ▶ **noun** a list of people to be killed for criminal or political reasons.

hit man ▶ **noun** informal a hired assassin.

hit-or-miss /',hid ôr 'mis/ ▶ **adjective** as likely to be unsuccessful as successful: *her work can be hit-or-miss.*

– SYNONYMS **erratic,** haphazard, disorganized, sloppy, unmethodical, uneven, inconsistent, random; informal slaphappy.
– ANTONYMS meticulous.

hit pa·rade ▶ **noun** dated a list of popular things, especially of best-selling songs.
– ORIGIN from the 20th-century weekly listing of the current best-selling pop records.

Hit·tite /'hitīt/ ▶ **noun** **1** a member of an ancient people who established an empire in the western peninsula of Asia and Syria *c.*1700–1200 BC. **2** the language of the Hittites. ▶ **adjective** relating to the Hittites.

HIV ▶ **abbreviation** human immunodeficiency virus (the virus that causes AIDS).

hive /hīv/ ▶ **noun** **1** a beehive. **2** a place full of people working hard. ▶ **verb** place bees in a hive.
– ORIGIN Old English.

hives /hīvz/ ▶ **plural noun** (treated as sing. or pl.) a very itchy rash of round, red weals on the skin, caused by an allergic reaction.
– ORIGIN unknown.

HIV-pos·i·tive ▶ **adjective** having had a positive result in a blood test for HIV.

HK ▶ **abbreviation** Hong Kong.

hl ▶ **abbreviation** hectoliter(s).

HMO ▶ **abbreviation** health maintenance organization; an organization to which subscribers pay a predetermined fee in return for a range of medical services.

HMS ▶ **abbreviation** Her or His Majesty's Ship.

Ho ▶ **symbol** the chemical element holmium.

ho¹ /hō/ ▶ **noun** (pl. **hos** or **hoes**) informal **1** a prostitute. **2** derogatory a woman.
– ORIGIN representing a dialect pronunciation of **WHORE**.

ho² /hō/ ▶ **exclamation** **1** an expression of surprise, admiration, triumph, or derision. **2** used as the second element of various exclamations: *heave ho!* **3** used to call for attention: *ho there!*

hoa·gie /'hōgē/ ▶ **noun** another term for **SUBMARINE SANDWICH**.

hoard /hôrd/ ▶ **noun** **1** a secret store of money or valuables. **2** a store of useful information.

– SYNONYMS **cache,** stockpile, store, collection, supply, reserve; informal stash.

▶ **verb** gradually collect something and store it away.

– SYNONYMS **stockpile,** store up, put aside, put by, lay by, set aside, cache, save, squirrel away; informal salt away.
– ANTONYMS squander.

– DERIVATIVES **hoard·er** noun.
– ORIGIN Old English.

USAGE

Hoard and **horde** are sometimes confused. A **hoard** is 'a secret store' (*a hoard of treasure*), while **horde** is a word showing disapproval when talking about 'a large group of people' (*hordes of greedy shareholders*).

hoar·frost /'hôr,frôst, -,fräst/ ▶ **noun** a grayish-white, feathery deposit of frost.

hoarse /hôrs/ ▶ **adjective** (of a voice) rough and harsh.

– SYNONYMS **rough,** harsh, croaky, throaty, gruff, husky, grating, rasping.

– DERIVATIVES **hoarse·ly** adverb **hoars·en** verb **hoarse·ness** noun.
– ORIGIN Old English.

hoar·y /'hôrē/ ▶ **adjective** (**hoarier, hoariest**) **1** old and having gray or white hair. **2** old and unoriginal: *a hoary old adage.*
– DERIVATIVES **hoar·i·ly** adverb **hoar·i·ness** noun.

hoax /hōks/ ▶ **noun** a humorous or cruel trick.

> – SYNONYMS **practical joke,** prank, trick, deception, fraud; informal con, spoof, scam.

▶ **verb** deceive someone with a hoax.
– DERIVATIVES **hoax·er** noun.
– ORIGIN probably from **HOCUS-POCUS**.

hob·bit /ˈhäbit/ ▶ **noun** a member of an imaginary race similar to humans, of small size and with hairy feet.
– ORIGIN invented by the British writer J. R. R. Tolkien, and said by him to mean 'hole-dweller.'

hob·ble /ˈhäbəl/ ▶ **verb 1** walk awkwardly, typically because of pain. **2** strap together the legs of a horse or other animal to prevent it from straying.

> – SYNONYMS **limp,** shamble, totter, dodder, stagger, stumble.

▶ **noun** an awkward way of walking.
– DERIVATIVES **hob·bler** noun.
– ORIGIN probably related to Dutch *hobbelen* 'rock from side to side.'

hob·by /ˈhäbē/ ▶ **noun** (pl. **hobbies**) a leisure activity that a person does regularly for pleasure.

> – SYNONYMS **pastime,** leisure activity, sideline, diversion, relaxation, recreation, amusement.

– ORIGIN from a familiar form of the man's name *Robin*.

hob·by·horse /ˈhäbēˌhôrs/ ▶ **noun 1** a child's toy consisting of a stick with a model of a horse's head at one end. **2** a rocking horse. **3** a person's favorite topic of conversation.

hob·by·ist /ˈhäbēist/ ▶ **noun** a person with a particular hobby.

hob·gob·lin /ˈhäbˌgäblən/ ▶ **noun** a mischievous imp.
– ORIGIN from *hob*, familiar form of the names *Robin* and *Robert*, used in the sense 'country fellow.'

hob·nail /ˈhäbˌnāl/ ▶ **noun** a short heavy-headed nail used to reinforce the soles of boots.
– DERIVATIVES **hob·nailed** adjective.

hob·nob /ˈhäbˌnäb/ ▶ **verb** (**hobnobs, hobnobbing, hobnobbed**) informal spend time socially with rich or important people.

> – SYNONYMS **associate,** mix, fraternize, socialize, spend time, go around, mingle, consort, rub elbows; informal hang around/out.

– ORIGIN from former *hob or nob*, or *hob and nob*, probably meaning 'give and take.'

ho·bo /ˈhōˌbō/ ▶ **noun** (pl. **hoboes** or **hobos**) a homeless person; a tramp.
– ORIGIN unknown.

Hob·son's choice /ˈhäbsənz/ ▶ **noun** a choice of taking what is offered or nothing at all.
– ORIGIN named after Thomas *Hobson*, who hired out horses, making the customer take the one nearest the door or none at all.

hock[1] /häk/ ▶ **noun 1** the joint in the hind leg of a four-legged animal, between the knee and the fetlock. **2** a knuckle of pork or ham.
– ORIGIN from an Old English word meaning 'heel.'

hock[2] ▶ **verb** informal pawn an object.
– PHRASES **in hock 1** having been pawned. **2** in debt.
– ORIGIN from Dutch *hok* 'hutch, prison, debt.'

hock·ey /ˈhäkē/ ▶ **noun 1** short for **ICE HOCKEY**. **2** short for **FIELD HOCKEY**.
– ORIGIN unknown.

ho·cus-po·cus /ˌhōkəsˈpōkəs/ ▶ **noun 1** meaningless talk used to deceive someone. **2** a form of words used by a conjuror.
– ORIGIN from *hax pax max Deus adimax*, a mock Latin phrase used by conjurors.

hod /häd/ ▶ **noun 1** a builder's V-shaped open trough attached to a short pole, used for carrying bricks. **2** a coal scuttle.
– ORIGIN Old French *hotte* 'pannier.'

hodge·podge /ˈhäjˌpäj/ ▶ **noun** a confused mixture.

> – SYNONYMS **mixture,** mixed bag, assortment, jumble, ragbag, miscellany, medley, potpourri, melange, mishmash.

Hodg·kin's dis·ease /ˈhäjkinz/ ▶ **noun** a cancerous disease causing enlargement of the lymph nodes, liver, and spleen.
– ORIGIN named after the English physician Thomas *Hodgkin*.

hoe /hō/ ▶ **noun** a long-handled gardening tool with a thin metal blade, used mainly for weeding. ▶ **verb** (**hoes, hoeing, hoed**) use a hoe to turn earth or cut through weeds.
– DERIVATIVES **ho·er** noun.
– ORIGIN Old French *houe*.

hoe·down /ˈhōˌdoun/ ▶ **noun** a gathering for lively folk dancing.

hog /hôg, häg/ ▶ **noun 1** a castrated male pig reared for slaughter. **2** informal a greedy person. ▶ **verb** (**hogs, hogging, hogged**) informal take or use most or all of something selfishly.

> – SYNONYMS **monopolize,** dominate, corner, control, take over.

– DERIVATIVES **hog·ger** noun **hog·gish** adjective.
– PHRASES **go (the) whole hog** informal do something completely or thoroughly.
– ORIGIN Old English.

ho·gan /ˈhōˌgän, -gən/ ▶ **noun** a traditional Navajo hut of logs and earth.

hog·back /ˈhôgˌbak, ˈhäg-/ (also **hog's back**) ▶ **noun** a long steep hill or mountain ridge.

hogs·head /ˈhôgzˌhed, ˈhägz-/ ▶ **noun 1** a large cask. **2** a measure of liquid volume for wine or beer.

hog-tie ▶ **verb 1** secure by fastening together the hands and feet of a person, or all four feet of an animal. **2** impede or hinder greatly.

hog·wash /ˈhôgˌwôsʜ, ˈhägˌwäsʜ/ ▶ **noun** informal nonsense.
– ORIGIN first meaning 'kitchen swill for pigs.'

hog·weed /ˈhôgˌwēd, ˈhäg-/ ▶ **noun** a large white-flowered weed of the parsley family.

ho-hum /ˈhō ˈhəm/ ▶ **exclamation** used to express boredom or resignation. ▶ **adjective** boring: *a ho-hum script*.
– ORIGIN imitative of a yawn.

hoi pol·loi /ˈhoi pəˌloi/ ▶ **plural noun** derogatory the ordinary people.
– ORIGIN Greek, 'the many.'

hoi·sin sauce /ˈhoisin, hoiˈsin/ ▶ **noun** a sweet, spicy, dark red sauce made from soybeans, used in Chinese cooking.
– ORIGIN from two Cantonese words meaning 'sea' + 'fresh.'

hoist /hoist/ ▶ **verb 1** raise something by means of ropes and pulleys. **2** haul or lift something up.

– SYNONYMS **raise,** lift, haul up, heave up, winch up, pull up, elevate.

▶ **noun 1** an act of hoisting something. **2** a device for hoisting something.

– SYNONYMS **crane,** winch, pulley, windlass.

– DERIVATIVES **hoist·er** noun.
– ORIGIN probably from Dutch *hijsen* or German *hiesen.*

hoi·ty-toi·ty /'hoitē 'toitē/ ▶ **adjective** snobbish or haughty.
– ORIGIN from former *hoit* 'romp.'

hok·ey /'hōkē/ ▶ **adjective** (**hokier, hokiest**) informal excessively sentimental or artificial.
– ORIGIN from **HOKUM**.

ho·kum /'hōkəm/ ▶ **noun** informal **1** nonsense; rubbish. **2** unoriginal or sentimental material in a movie, book, etc.
– ORIGIN unknown.

hold[1] /hōld/ ▶ **verb** (past and past part. **held** /held/) **1** grasp, carry, or support someone or something. **2** contain or be able to contain: *the tank held twenty-four gallons.* **3** have, own, or occupy something. **4** keep or detain someone. **5** stay or keep at a certain value or level: *MCI shares held at 99 cents.* **6** have a belief or opinion. **7** (**hold someone/thing in**) regard someone or something in a particular way: *the speed limit is held in contempt by many drivers.* **8** (**hold someone to**) make someone keep a promise. **9** continue to follow a course. **10** arrange and take part in a meeting or conversation. **11** informal refrain from adding or using something: *a strawberry margarita, but hold the tequila.*

– SYNONYMS **1 clasp,** clutch, grasp, grip, clench, cling to, hold on to, embrace, hug, squeeze. **2** *the police were holding him* **detain,** imprison, lock up, keep behind bars, confine, intern, incarcerate. **3 take,** contain, accommodate, fit, have room for. **4** *the court held that there was no evidence* **maintain,** consider, take the view, believe, think, feel, deem, be of the opinion, rule, decide; informal reckon. **5** *they held a meeting* **convene,** call, summon, conduct, organize, run.
– ANTONYMS release.

▶ **noun 1** an act or way of grasping someone or something. **2** a handhold. **3** a degree of power or control: *Tom had some kind of hold over his father.*

– SYNONYMS **1 grip,** grasp, clasp, clutch. **2 influence,** power, control, grip, dominance, authority, sway.

– PHRASES **get hold of 1** grasp something. **2** informal find or contact someone. **hold something against someone** continue to feel resentful for something that someone has done. **hold back** hesitate. **hold something down** informal succeed in keeping a job. **hold fast 1** remain tightly secured. **2** continue to believe in a principle. **hold forth** talk at length. **hold good** (or **true**) remain true or valid. **hold it** informal wait or stop doing something. **hold off** (of bad weather) fail to occur. **hold someone/thing off 1** resist an attacker or challenge. **2** postpone an action or decision. **hold on 1** wait; stop. **2** keep going in difficult circumstances. **hold out 1** resist difficult circumstances. **2** continue to be enough. **hold out for** continue to demand something. **hold something over 1** postpone something. **2** use a piece of information to intimidate (someone). **hold up** remain strong. **hold someone/thing up 1** delay someone or something. **2** rob someone using the threat of violence. **3** present someone or something as an example. **no holds barred** without rules or restrictions. **on hold** waiting to be dealt with or connected by telephone. **take hold** start to have an effect.
– ORIGIN Old English.

hold[2] ▶ **noun** a storage space in the lower part of a ship or aircraft.
– ORIGIN from **HOLE**.

hold·er /'hōldər/ ▶ **noun 1** a device or implement for holding something: *a cigarette holder.* **2** a person who holds something: *holders of two American hostages | a US passport holder.* **3** the possessor of a trophy, championship, or record: *the record holder in the 100-yard dash.*

– SYNONYMS **1 bearer,** owner, possessor, keeper. **2 container,** receptacle, case, cover, housing, sheath.

hold·ing /'hōldiNG/ ▶ **noun 1** an area of land held by lease. **2** (**holdings**) stocks and other financial assets owned by a person or organization.

hold·ing com·pa·ny ▶ **noun** a company created to buy shares in other companies, which it then controls.

hold·ing pat·tern ▶ **noun 1** the flight path maintained by an aircraft awaiting permission to land. **2** a state or period of no progress or change.

hold·o·ver /'hōld,ōvər/ ▶ **noun** a person or thing surviving from an earlier time, especially someone surviving in office or remaining on a sports team.

hold·up /'hōld,əp/ ▶ **noun 1** a cause of delay. **2** a robbery carried out with the threat of violence.

– SYNONYMS **1 delay,** setback, hitch, snag, difficulty, problem, glitch, hiccup, traffic jam, tailback. **2 robbery,** raid, armed robbery, mugging; informal stickup, heist.

hole /hōl/ ▶ **noun 1** a hollow space in a solid object or surface. **2** an opening or gap in or passing through something. **3** (in golf) a hollow in the ground into which the ball must be hit. **4** informal an awkward or unpleasant place or situation.

– SYNONYMS **1 opening,** aperture, orifice, gap, space, interstice, fissure, vent, chink, breach, crack, rupture, puncture. **2 pit,** crater, depression, hollow, cavern, cave, chamber. **3 burrow,** lair, den, earth, sett/set.

▶ **verb 1** make a hole or holes in something. **2** Golf hit the ball into a hole. **3** (**hole up**) informal hide oneself.
– DERIVATIVES **hol·ey** adjective.
– PHRASES **hole in one** (pl. **holes in one**) Golf a shot that enters the hole from the tee. **in the hole** informal in debt: *$50,000 in the hole.* **make a hole in** use a large amount of something.
– ORIGIN Old English.

hole in the heart ▶ **noun** an abnormal opening present from birth in the wall between the chambers of the heart, resulting in inadequate circulation of oxygenated blood.

hole-in-the-wall ▶ **noun** informal a small dingy place, especially a bar or restaurant.

Ho·li /'hōlē/ ▶ **noun** a Hindu spring festival celebrated in honor of Krishna.
– ORIGIN Sanskrit.

hol·i·day /'hälə,dā/ ▶ **noun 1** a day of national or religious celebration when no work is done. **2** chiefly Brit. a vacation.

– SYNONYMS **day of observance,** festival, feast day, fiesta, celebration, anniversary, jubilee, saint's day, feast day.

▸ **verb** spend a holiday in a particular place.
– ORIGIN Old English, 'holy day.'

ho·li·er-than-thou ▸ **adjective** offensively certain that one is morally superior to others.

ho·li·ness /'hōlēnis/ ▸ **noun 1** the state of being holy. **2** (**His/Your Holiness**) the title of the Pope, Orthodox patriarchs, and the Dalai Lama.

ho·lism /'hōl,izəm/ ▸ **noun** Medicine the treating of the whole person, taking into account mental and social factors, rather than just the symptoms of a disease.
– DERIVATIVES **ho·lis·tic** /hō'listik/ adjective.
– ORIGIN from Greek *holos* 'whole.'

hol·lan·daise sauce /'hälən,dāz/ ▸ **noun** a creamy sauce made of butter, egg yolks, and vinegar.
– ORIGIN French *hollandais* 'Dutch.'

hol·ler /'hälər/ informal ▸ **verb** give a loud shout. ▸ **noun** a loud shout.
– ORIGIN related to **HALLOO**.

hol·low /'hälō/ ▸ **adjective 1** having a hole or empty space inside. **2** curving inward; concave: *hollow cheeks.* **3** (of a sound) echoing. **4** worthless or insincere: *hollow election promises.*

> – SYNONYMS **1 empty,** hollowed out, void. **2 sunken,** deep-set, concave, depressed, recessed. **3 worthless,** meaningless, empty, profitless, fruitless, pointless, pyrrhic. **4 insincere,** false, deceitful, hypocritical, sham, untrue.
> – ANTONYMS solid, convex.

▸ **noun 1** a hole or depression. **2** a small valley.

> – SYNONYMS **1 hole,** pit, cavity, crater, trough, depression, indentation, dip. **2 valley,** vale, dale, dell.

▸ **verb 1** form by making a hole: *the pond was hollowed out by hand.* **2** make a depression in.

> – SYNONYMS **gouge,** scoop, dig, cut, excavate, channel.

– DERIVATIVES **hol·low·ly** adverb **hol·low·ness** noun.
– ORIGIN Old English, 'cave.'

hol·ly /'hälē/ ▸ **noun** an evergreen shrub with prickly dark green leaves and red berries.
– ORIGIN Old English.

hol·ly·hock /'hälē,häk/ ▸ **noun** a tall plant of the mallow family, with large showy flowers.
– ORIGIN from **HOLY** + former *hock* 'mallow.'

hol·mi·um /'hōlmēəm/ ▸ **noun** a soft silvery-white metallic element.
– ORIGIN from *Holmia*, Latinized form of *Stockholm*, the capital of Sweden.

hol·o·caust /'hälə,kôst, 'hōlə-/ ▸ **noun 1** destruction or killing on a mass scale. **2** (**the Holocaust**) the mass murder of Jews under the German Nazi regime in World War II.
– ORIGIN from Greek *holos* 'whole' + *kaustos* 'burnt.'

Hol·o·cene /'hälə,sēn, 'hōlə-/ ▸ **adjective** Geology relating to the present epoch (from about 10,000 years ago, following the Pleistocene).
– ORIGIN from Greek *kainos* 'new.'

hol·o·gram /'hälə,gram, 'hōlə-/ ▸ **noun** a photographic image formed in such a way that it looks three-dimensional when it is lit up.
– DERIVATIVES **hol·o·graph·ic** adjective **hol·og·ra·phy** noun.
– ORIGIN from Greek *holos* 'whole.'

hol·o·graph /'hälə,graf, 'hōlə-/ ▸ **noun** a manuscript handwritten by its author.

hol·ster /'hōlstər/ ▸ **noun** a holder for carrying a handgun, worn on a belt or under the arm. ▸ **verb** put a gun into its holster.
– ORIGIN unknown.

ho·ly /'hōlē/ ▸ **adjective** (**holier, holiest**) **1** dedicated to God or a religious purpose. **2** morally and spiritually excellent.

> – SYNONYMS **1 saintly,** godly, pious, religious, devout, God-fearing, spiritual. **2 sacred,** consecrated, hallowed, sanctified, venerated, revered.
> – ANTONYMS sinful, irreligious.

– ORIGIN Old English.

WORD TOOLKIT

holy ...	hallowed ...	venerated ...
city	halls	figures
grail	ground	relic
water	turf	saint
book	portals	masters
scriptures	corridors	icon
shrine	institution	tradition

ho·ly day ▸ **noun** a religious festival.

Ho·ly Fa·ther ▸ **noun** the Pope.

ho·ly or·ders ▸ **plural noun** see **ORDER** (sense 10 of the noun).

Ho·ly Roll·er (also **holy roller**) ▸ **noun** informal, derogatory a member of an evangelical Christian group that expresses religious fervor by frenzied excitement or trances.

Ho·ly Ro·man Em·pire ▸ **noun** the western part of the Roman Empire, as revived by Charlemagne in 800.

Ho·ly See ▸ **noun** the office of Pope, or people associated with the Pope in governing the Roman Catholic Church.

Ho·ly Spir·it (or **Holy Ghost**) ▸ **noun** (in Christianity) the third person of the Trinity; God as spiritually active in the world.

ho·ly war ▸ **noun** a war waged in support of a religious cause.

ho·ly wa·ter ▸ **noun** water blessed by a priest and used in religious ceremonies and rituals.

Ho·ly Week ▸ **noun** the week before Easter.

Ho·ly Writ ▸ **noun** sacred writings as a whole, especially the Bible.

hom·age /'(h)ämij/ ▸ **noun** honor or respect shown publicly to someone: *they paid homage to the local boy who became president.*

> – SYNONYMS **respect,** honor, reverence, worship, admiration, esteem, adulation, tribute.
> – ANTONYMS contempt.

– ORIGIN Old French.

CHOOSE THE RIGHT WORD

See **HONOR**.

hom·bre /'ämbrā, -brē/ ▸ **noun** informal a man, especially one of a particular type: *their quarterback is one tough hombre.*

hom·burg /'hämbərg/ ▸ **noun** a man's felt hat having a narrow curled brim and a lengthwise indentation in the crown.
– ORIGIN named after the German town of *Homburg*.

home /hōm/ ▶ noun **1** the place where someone lives. **2** an institution for people needing professional care. **3** a place where something flourishes or from which it originated: *Barcelona became the home of Modernism*. **4** the finishing point in a race. **5** (in games) the place where a player is free from attack.

– SYNONYMS **1 residence,** house, accommodations, property, quarters, lodgings, address, place; informal pad; formal abode, dwelling. **2 homeland,** native land, hometown, birthplace, roots, fatherland, mother country, motherland. **3 institution,** hospice, shelter, refuge, retreat, asylum, hostel.

▶ adjective **1** relating to the home. **2** made, done, or intended for use in the home. **3** relating to someone's own country. **4** (in team sports) referring to a team's own ground.

– SYNONYMS **domestic,** internal, local, national.
– ANTONYMS foreign, international.

▶ adverb **1** to or at someone's home. **2** to the end of something: *a couple more questions and you're home*. **3** to the intended or correct position: *he slid the bolt home noisily*.

▶ verb **1** (of an animal) return by instinct to its territory. **2** (**home in on**) move or be aimed toward a target or destination.

– PHRASES **at home 1** comfortable and at ease. **2** ready to receive visitors. **bring something home to** make someone realize the significance of something. **close to home** (of a remark) uncomfortably accurate. **home free** having successfully achieved or being within sight of achieving one's objective: *at 7-0 they should have been home free*.

– ORIGIN Old English.

home·bod·y /ˈhōmˌbädē/ ▶ noun (pl. **homebodies**) informal a person who likes to stay at home, especially one who is perceived as unadventurous.

home·boy /ˈhōmˌboi/ (or **homegirl** /ˈhōmˌgərl/) ▶ noun informal **1** a person from one's own town or neighborhood. **2** (especially among urban black people) a member of a peer group or gang.

home brew ▶ noun beer or other alcoholic drink brewed at home.

home·buy·er /ˈhōmˌbīər/ ▶ noun a person who buys a house or condominium.

home·com·ing /ˈhōmˌkəmiNG/ ▶ noun an instance of returning home.

home ec /ˈhōm ˈek/ ▶ noun informal short for **HOME ECONOMICS**.

home ec·o·nom·ics ▶ plural noun (often treated as sing.) the study of cookery and household management.

home front ▶ noun the civilian population and activities of a nation whose armed forces are engaged in a foreign war.

home fur·nish·ings ▶ plural noun curtains, chair coverings, and other cloth items used to decorate a room.

home·grown /ˈhōmˈgrōn/ ▶ adjective grown or produced in one's own garden or country.

home·land /ˈhōmˌland/ ▶ noun **1** a person's native land. **2** a self-governing state occupied by a particular people: *they are fighting for a Kurd homeland*. **3** historical any of ten partially self-governing areas in South Africa assigned to particular African peoples.

home·less /ˈhōmlis/ ▶ adjective not having anywhere to live.

– SYNONYMS **of no fixed abode,** without a roof over one's head, on the streets, vagrant, destitute.

– DERIVATIVES **home·less·ness** noun.

home·ly /ˈhōmlē/ ▶ adjective (**homelier, homeliest**) (of a person) unattractive.

– SYNONYMS **unattractive,** plain, unprepossessing, ugly.

– DERIVATIVES **home·li·ness** noun.

home·made /ˈhō(m)ˈmād/ ▶ adjective made at home.

home·mak·er /ˈhōmˌmākər/ ▶ noun a person who manages a home.

home mov·ie ▶ noun a movie made at home or without professional equipment or expertise, especially one featuring one's own activities.

Home Of·fice ▶ noun the British government department dealing with law and order, immigration, etc., in England and Wales.

ho·me·o·path /ˈhōmēəˌpaTH/ ▶ noun a person who practices homeopathy.

ho·me·op·a·thy /ˌhōmēˈäpəTHē/ ▶ noun a system of complementary medicine in which disease is treated by minute doses of natural substances that would normally produce symptoms of the disease.

– DERIVATIVES **ho·me·o·path·ic** adjective /ˈhōmēəˌpaTHik/.

– ORIGIN from Greek *homoios* 'like' + *patheia* 'suffering, feeling.'

ho·me·o·sta·sis /ˌhōmēəˈstāsis/ ▶ noun the tendency of the body to keep its own temperature, blood pressure, etc., at a constant level.

– DERIVATIVES **ho·me·o·stat·ic** /-ˈstatik/ adjective.

– ORIGIN from Greek *homoios* 'like' + *stasis* 'stoppage, standing.'

home·own·er /ˈhōmˌōnər/ ▶ noun a person who owns their own home.

home page ▶ noun a person's or organization's introductory document on the Internet.

home plate Baseball ▶ noun a five-sided rubber mat next to which a baseball batter stands and over which the pitcher must throw the ball for a strike.

ho·mer /ˈhōmər/ Baseball, informal ▶ noun a home run. ▶ verb hit a home run.

Ho·mer·ic /hōˈmerik/ ▶ adjective relating to the ancient Greek poet Homer or to the epic poems that he is thought to have written.

home·room /ˈhōmˌro͞om, -ˌro͝om/ ▶ noun a classroom in which fixed groups of students gather, usually daily, for school administrative purposes.

home rule ▶ noun the government of a place by its own citizens.

home run ▶ noun Baseball a hit that allows the batter to make a complete circuit of the bases.

home·school·er /ˈhōmˈsko͞olər/ ▶ plural noun **1** a child who is educated at home by their parents. **2** a parent who educates their child or children at home.

home·school·ing /ˈhōmˈsko͞oliNG/ ▶ noun the education of children at home by their parents.

– DERIVATIVES **home·school** verb.

Home Sec·re·tar·y ▶ noun (in the UK) the foreign minister; the counterpart of the US secretary of state.

home·sick /ˈhōmˌsik/ ▶ adjective missing one's home during a time away from it.

home·spun /ˈhōmˌspən/ ▶ **adjective 1** simple and unsophisticated. **2** (of cloth or yarn) made or spun at home. ▶ **noun** homespun cloth.

home·stead /ˈhōmˌsted/ ▶ **noun** a farmhouse with surrounding land and outbuildings.
– DERIVATIVES **home·stead·er** noun **home·stead·ing** noun.

home stretch ▶ **noun** the final stretch of a racetrack, or the final stage of a process: *when vacation shopping reaches its home stretch.*

home truth ▶ **noun** an unpleasant fact about oneself, pointed out by someone else.

home·ward /ˈhōmwərd/ ▶ **adverb** (also **homewards**) toward home. ▶ **adjective** going or leading toward home.

home·work /ˈhōmˌwərk/ ▶ **noun 1** school work that a student is required to do at home. **2** preparation for an event or situation. **3** paid work done in one's own home.
– DERIVATIVES **home·work·er** noun.

home·wreck·er /ˈhōmˌrekər/ ▶ **noun** informal someone who is blamed for the breakup of a marriage or family, such as an adulterous partner.

hom·ey /ˈhōmē/ (also **homy**) ▶ **adjective** (**homier, homiest**) **1** comfortable and cozy. **2** unsophisticated. ▶ **noun** variant of **HOMIE**.

hom·i·cide /ˈhäməˌsīd, ˈhōmə-/ ▶ **noun** the killing of another person.

– SYNONYMS **murder,** manslaughter, killing, slaughter, butchery, assassination.

– DERIVATIVES **hom·i·cid·al** /ˌhäməˈsīdl, ˌhōmə-/ adjective.
– ORIGIN from Latin *homo* 'man' + **-CIDE**.

hom·ie /ˈhōmē/ (also **homey**) ▶ **noun** (pl. **homies** or **homeys**) informal a homeboy or homegirl.

hom·i·let·ic /ˌhäməˈletik/ ▶ **adjective** relating to or like a homily; morally uplifting.

hom·i·ly /ˈhäməlē/ ▶ **noun** (pl. **homilies**) **1** a talk on a religious subject that is intended to be spiritually uplifting. **2** a tedious talk on a moral issue.
– DERIVATIVES **hom·i·list** noun.
– ORIGIN Greek *homilia* 'discourse.'

hom·ing /ˈhōmiNG/ ▶ **adjective 1** (of a pigeon or other animal) able to return home from a great distance. **2** (of a weapon) able to find and hit a target electronically.

hom·i·nid /ˈhäməˌnid/ ▶ **noun** a member of a family of primates that includes humans and their fossil ancestors.
– ORIGIN from Latin *homo* 'man.'

hom·i·noid /ˈhäməˌnoid/ ▶ **noun** Zoology a primate of a group that includes humans, their fossil ancestors, and the great apes.

hom·i·ny /ˈhämənē/ ▶ **noun** coarsely ground corn used to make grits.
– ORIGIN Algonquian.

ho·mo /ˈhōmō/ informal, chiefly derogatory ▶ **noun** (pl. **homos**) a homosexual man. ▶ **adjective** homosexual.

homo- ▶ **combining form 1** same: *homogeneous.* **2** relating to homosexual love: *homoerotic.*
– ORIGIN from Greek *homos* 'same.'

ho·mo·e·rot·ic /ˌhōmō-iˈrätik/ ▶ **adjective** concerning or arousing sexual desire centered on a person of the same sex.
– DERIVATIVES **ho·mo·e·rot·i·cism** /-ˌsizəm/ noun.

ho·mo·ge·ne·ous /ˌhōməˈjēnēəs/ ▶ **adjective 1** of the same kind; alike. **2** consisting of parts all of the same kind: *a homogeneous society.*
– DERIVATIVES **ho·mo·ge·ne·i·ty** /ˌhōməjəˈnēitē, ˌhämə-/ noun **ho·mo·ge·ne·ous·ly** adverb **ho·mo·ge·ne·ous·ness** noun.
– ORIGIN from Greek *homos* 'same' + *genos* 'race, kind.'

ho·mog·e·nize /həˈmäjəˌnīz/ ▶ **verb 1** treat milk so that the particles of fat are broken down and the cream does not separate. **2** make different things more similar or uniform.
– DERIVATIVES **ho·mog·e·ni·za·tion** /həˌmäjənīˈzāsHən/ noun **ho·mog·e·niz·er** noun.

hom·o·graph /ˈhäməˌgraf, ˈhōmə-/ ▶ **noun** each of two or more words having the same spelling but different meanings and origins (e.g. **BOW**[1] and **BOW**[2] in this dictionary).

ho·mol·o·gous /hōˈmäləgəs, hə-/ ▶ **adjective 1** having a similar relative position or structure; corresponding. **2** Biology (of organs) similar in position, structure, and evolutionary origin.
– DERIVATIVES **ho·mol·o·gize** /hōˈmäləˌjīz, hə-/ verb **ho·mol·o·gy** /hōˈmäləjē, hə-/ noun.
– ORIGIN Greek *homologos* 'agreeing, consistent.'

ho·mo·logue /ˈhōməˌlôg, -ˌläg/ (also **homolog**) ▶ **noun** technical a thing that has the same relative position or structure as another.

hom·o·nym /ˈhäməˌnim, ˈhōmə-/ ▶ **noun** each of two or more words having the same spelling or pronunciation but different meanings and origins (e.g. **CAN**[1] and **CAN**[2] in this dictionary).
– DERIVATIVES **ho·mon·y·mous** /hōˈmänəməs/ adjective.
– ORIGIN Greek *homōnumos* 'having the same name.'

ho·mo·pho·bi·a /ˌhōməˈfōbēə/ ▶ **noun** an extreme and irrational hatred or fear of homosexuality and homosexuals.
– DERIVATIVES **ho·mo·phobe** /ˈhōməˌfōb/ noun **ho·mo·pho·bic** /-ˈfōbik/ adjective.

ho·mo·phone /ˈhäməˌfōn, ˈhōmə-/ ▶ **noun** each of two or more words having the same pronunciation but different meanings, origins, or spelling (e.g., *new* and *knew*).
– ORIGIN from Greek *phōnē* 'sound, voice.'

ho·mop·ter·an /hōˈmäptərən/ ▶ **noun** any of a group of insects, including aphids and cicadas, in which the forewings are uniform in texture.

Ho·mo sa·pi·ens /ˈhōmō ˈsāpēənz/ ▶ **noun** the primate species to which modern humans belong.
– ORIGIN Latin, 'wise man.'

ho·mo·sex·u·al /ˌhōməˈseksHo͞oəl/ ▶ **adjective** feeling or involving sexual attraction to people of one's own sex. ▶ **noun** a homosexual person.
– DERIVATIVES **ho·mo·sex·u·al·i·ty** /-ˌseksHo͞oˈalitē/ noun **ho·mo·sex·u·al·ly** adverb.

ho·mun·cu·lus /həˈməNGkyələs, hō-/ ▶ **noun** (pl. **homunculi** /-ˌlī/) a very small human or humanlike creature.
– ORIGIN Latin, 'little man.'

hom·y ▶ **adjective** variant spelling of **HOMEY**.

hon /hən/ ▶ **noun** informal short for **HONEY** (sense 2).

Hon. ▶ **abbreviation 1** (in official job titles) Honorary. **2** (in titles of judges and, in the UK, nobility and members of parliament) Honorable.

hon·cho /ˈhänCHō/ ▶ **noun** (pl. **honchos**) informal a leader.
– ORIGIN Japanese, 'group leader.'

Hon·du·ran /hänˈd(y)o͝orən/ ▶ **noun** a person from Honduras, a country in Central America. ▶ **adjective** relating to Honduras.

hone /hōn/ ▸ **verb 1** make better or more efficient: *she honed her singing skills.* **2** sharpen a tool with a whetstone.
– ORIGIN Old English, 'stone.'

hon·est /'änist/ ▸ **adjective 1** truthful and sincere. **2** fairly earned through hard work: *an honest living.* **3** simple and unpretentious.

> – SYNONYMS **1** *an honest man* **upright,** honorable, principled, virtuous, good, decent, law-abiding, trustworthy, scrupulous, ethical, upstanding, right-minded. **2** *I haven't been honest with you* **truthful,** sincere, candid, frank, open, forthright, straight; informal upfront.
> – ANTONYMS dishonest.

▸ **adverb** informal genuinely; really.
– ORIGIN Latin *honestus.*

hon·est·ly /'änistlē/ ▸ **adverb 1** in an honest way. **2** really (used for emphasis).

> – SYNONYMS **1 fairly,** lawfully, legally, legitimately, honorably, decently, ethically; informal on the level. **2 sincerely,** genuinely, truthfully, truly, wholeheartedly, to be honest, to be frank, in all honesty, in all sincerity.

hon·est-to-God ▸ **adjective** informal genuine; real.

hon·est-to-good·ness ▸ **adjective** genuine and straightforward.

hon·es·ty /'änistē/ ▸ **noun 1** the quality of being honest and sincere: *they spoke with honesty about their fears.* **2** a plant of the mustard family with round, flat translucent seed pods.

> – SYNONYMS **1 integrity,** uprightness, honor, righteousness, virtue, goodness, probity, trustworthiness. **2 sincerity,** candor, frankness, directness, truthfulness, truth, openness, straightforwardness.
> – ANTONYMS dishonesty, insincerity.

hon·ey /'hənē/ ▸ **noun** (pl. **honeys**) **1** a sweet, sticky yellowish-brown fluid made by bees from flower nectar. **2** darling; sweetheart. **3** informal an excellent example of something: *it's a honey of a car.* **4** informal an attractive girl.
– ORIGIN Old English.

hon·ey·bee /'hənē,bē/ ▸ **noun** the common bee.

hon·ey·comb /'hənē,kōm/ ▸ **noun 1** a structure of six-sided cells of wax, made by bees to store honey and eggs. **2** a structure resembling a bee's honeycomb. ▸ **verb** fill an area with cavities or tunnels.

hon·ey·dew /'hənē,d(y)o͞o/ ▸ **noun** a sweet, sticky substance produced by aphids (small insects) feeding on the sap of plants.

hon·ey·dew mel·on ▸ **noun** a variety of melon with pale skin and sweet green flesh.

hon·eyed /'hənēd/ ▸ **adjective 1** containing or coated with honey. **2** soothing and soft: *honeyed words.* **3** having a warm yellow color.

hon·ey·moon /'hənē,mo͞on/ ▸ **noun 1** a vacation taken by a newly married couple. **2** an initial period of enthusiasm or goodwill. ▸ **verb** go on a honeymoon.
– DERIVATIVES **hon·ey·moon·er** noun.
– ORIGIN first referring to affection waning like the moon, then to the first month after marriage.

hon·ey·pot /'hənē,pät/ ▸ **noun** a place to which many people are attracted.

hon·ey·suck·le /'hənē,səkəl/ ▸ **noun** a climbing shrub with fragrant yellow and pink flowers.

hon·ey·trap /'hənē,trap/ ▸ **noun** a plan in which an attractive person entices another person into revealing information or doing something unwise.

honk /hängk, hôngk/ ▸ **noun 1** the cry of a goose. **2** the sound of a car horn. ▸ **verb** make a honk.
– ORIGIN imitating the sound.

hon·ky /'hängkē, 'hông-/ ▸ **noun** (pl. **honkies**) informal, derogatory (among black people) a white person.
– ORIGIN unknown.

hon·ky-tonk /'hängkē ,tängk, 'hôngkē ,tôngk/ ▸ **noun** informal **1** a cheap or disreputable bar or club. **2** ragtime piano music.
– ORIGIN unknown.

hon·or /'änər/ (Brit. **honour**) ▸ **noun 1** great respect. **2** a clear sense of what is morally right. **3** something that is a privilege and a pleasure: *he had the honor of introducing the president.* **4** a person or thing that brings credit to something. **5** an award or title given as a reward for achievement. **6** (**honors**) a course of degree studies more specialized than for an ordinary program. **7** (**honors**) a special distinction for academic achievement. **8** (**His, Your,** etc. **Honor**) a title of respect for a judge or mayor. **9** dated a woman's chastity. **10** Bridge an ace, king, queen, or jack.

> – SYNONYMS **1 integrity,** honesty, uprightness, morality, probity, principles, high-mindedness, decency, scrupulousness, fairness, justness. **2 distinction,** privilege, glory, kudos, cachet, prestige. **3 reputation,** good name, character, repute, image, standing, status. **4 privilege,** pleasure, compliment.
> – ANTONYMS shame.

▸ **verb 1** regard someone or something with great respect. **2** pay public respect to: *talented writers were honored at a special ceremony.* **3** fulfill a duty or keep an agreement.

> – SYNONYMS **1 respect,** esteem, admire, look up to, value, cherish, revere, venerate. **2 applaud,** acclaim, praise, salute, recognize, celebrate, pay tribute to. **3 fulfill,** observe, keep, obey, heed, follow, carry out, keep to, abide by, adhere to, comply with, conform to, be true to.
> – ANTONYMS disobey, break.

CHOOSE THE RIGHT WORD

honor, deference, homage, obeisance, reverence

The Ten Commandments instruct us to "**Honor** thy father and mother." But what does *honor* entail? While all of these nouns describe the respect or esteem that one shows to another, *honor* implies acknowledgment of a person's right to such respect (*honor one's ancestors; honor the dead*). **Homage** is honor with praise or tributes added, and it connotes a more worshipful attitude (*pay homage to the king*). **Reverence** combines profound respect with love or devotion (*he treated his wife with reverence*), while **deference** suggests courteous regard for a superior, often by yielding to the person's status or wishes (*show deference to one's elders*). **Obeisance** is a show of honor or reverence by an act or gesture of submission or humility, such as a bow or a curtsy (*the schoolchildren were instructed to pay obeisance when the Queen arrived*).

hon·or·a·ble /'änərəbəl/ ▸ **adjective 1** bringing or worthy of honor. **2** (**Honorable**) a title indicating eminence or distinction, given especially to judges and certain high officials.

– SYNONYMS **1 honest,** moral, principled, righteous, decent, respectable, virtuous, good, upstanding, upright, noble, fair, trustworthy, law-abiding. **2 illustrious,** distinguished, eminent, great, glorious, prestigious.
– ANTONYMS dishonorable.

– DERIVATIVES **hon·or·a·bly** adverb.

hon·or·a·ble men·tion ▶ **noun** a commendation for a candidate in an exam or competition who is not awarded a prize.

hon·o·rar·i·um /ˌänəˈre(ə)rēəm/ ▶ **noun** (pl. **honorariums** or **honoraria** /-ˈre(ə)rēə/) a voluntary payment for professional services that are offered without charge.
– ORIGIN Latin, referring to a gift made to someone entering public office.

hon·or·ar·y /ˈänəˌrerē/ ▶ **adjective 1** (of a title or position) given as an honor. **2** (of a person) holding such a title or position: *an honorary member of the club.*

– SYNONYMS **titular,** nominal, in name only, unofficial, token.

hon·or guard ▶ **noun** a group of soldiers ceremonially welcoming an important visitor or escorting a casket in a funeral.

hon·or·if·ic /ˌänəˈrifik/ ▶ **adjective** given as a mark of respect.

hon·or roll ▶ **noun** a list of people who have attained an honor, especially a list of students who have earned excellent grades.

hon·or sys·tem ▶ **noun** a system of payment or examination that relies solely on the honesty of the people concerned.

hon·our, etc. ▶ **noun & verb** British spelling of **HONOR**, etc.

hooch /ho͞oCH/ (also **hootch**) ▶ **noun** informal strong alcoholic drink, especially inferior or illicit whiskey.
– ORIGIN abbreviation of *Hoochinoo*, an Alaskan Indian people who made alcoholic liquor.

hood[1] /ho͝od/ ▶ **noun 1** a covering for the head and neck with an opening for the face. **2** the metal part covering the engine of a vehicle. **3** a protective canopy. ▶ **verb** put a hood on or over someone.
– DERIVATIVES **hood·ed** adjective.
– ORIGIN Old English.

hood[2] ▶ **noun** informal a gangster or violent criminal.
– ORIGIN abbreviation of **HOODLUM**.

hood[3] ▶ **noun** informal a neighborhood.

-hood ▶ **suffix** forming nouns referring to. **1** a condition or quality: *womanhood.* **2** a collection or group: *brotherhood.*
– ORIGIN Old English.

hood·ie /ˈho͝odē/ (also **hoody**) ▶ **noun** (pl. **hoodies**) a hooded garment, especially a sweatshirt.

hood·lum /ˈho͞odləm, ˈho͝od-/ ▶ **noun** a gangster or other violent criminal.

– SYNONYMS **gangster,** mobster, heavy, hit man, thug, criminal; informal hood.

– ORIGIN unknown.

hoo·doo /ˈho͞oˌdo͞o/ ▶ **noun 1** a run or cause of bad luck. **2** voodoo. ▶ **verb** (**hoodoos**, **hoodooing**, **hoodooed**) bring bad luck to someone or something.
– ORIGIN alteration of **VOODOO**.

hood·wink /ˈho͝odˌwiNGk/ ▶ **verb** deceive or trick someone.
– ORIGIN from **HOOD**[1] + **WINK** in the former sense 'close the eyes.'

hood·y ▶ **noun** variant spelling of **HOODIE**.

hoo·ey /ˈho͞oē/ ▶ **noun** informal nonsense.
– ORIGIN unknown.

hoof /ho͝of, ho͞of/ ▶ **noun** (pl. **hoofs** or **hooves** /ho͝ovz, ho͞ovz/) the horny part of the foot of a horse, cow, etc.
– DERIVATIVES **hoofed** adjective.
– PHRASES **hoof it** informal **1** go on foot. **2** dance. **on the hoof** informal **1** without great thought or preparation. **2** (of livestock) not yet slaughtered.
– ORIGIN Old English.

hoof·er /ˈho͞ofər, ˈho͝ofər/ ▶ **noun** informal a professional dancer.

hoo-ha /ˈho͞o ˌhä/ ▶ **noun** informal a commotion or fuss.
– ORIGIN unknown.

hook /ho͝ok/ ▶ **noun 1** a piece of curved metal or other material for catching hold of things or hanging things on. **2** a short swinging punch made with the elbow bent and rigid. **3** a thing designed to catch people's attention. **4** a catchy passage in a song.

– SYNONYMS **1 peg,** nail. **2 fastener,** clasp, hasp, clip.

▶ **verb 1** attach or fasten something with a hook. **2** bend into a curved shape: *he hooked his thumbs in his belt.* **3** catch a fish with a hook. **4** (**be hooked**) informal be very interested or addicted. **5** (in golf) hit the ball in a curving path.

– SYNONYMS **1 attach,** hitch, fasten, fix, secure, hang, clasp. **2 catch,** land, net, take, bag.

– PHRASES **by hook or by crook** by any possible means. **hook, line, and sinker** completely. **hook up 1** link to electronic equipment. **2** meet or join another person or people. **off the hook 1** informal no longer in trouble. **2** (of a telephone receiver) not on its rest.
– ORIGIN Old English.

hook·ah /ˈho͝okə, ˈho͞okə/ ▶ **noun** an oriental tobacco pipe with a long, flexible tube that draws the smoke through water in a bowl.
– ORIGIN Urdu.

hook and eye ▶ **noun** a small metal hook and loop used to fasten a garment.

hooked /ho͝okt/ ▶ **adjective 1** having or resembling a hook or hooks. **2** informal captivated or addicted.

– SYNONYMS **1 curved,** hook-shaped, aquiline, angular, bent. **2** *she got* **hooked on** *cocaine | he was* **hooked on** *reality TV* **addicted to,** dependent on; obsessed with, fanatical about, enthusiastic about; informal mad about.

hook·er /ˈho͝okər/ ▶ **noun** informal a prostitute.

hook·up /ˈho͝okˌəp/ ▶ **noun 1** a connection to electricity, a utility, a communications system, etc. **2** informal a relationship initiated for a purpose, especially sex: *a date tomorrow night with my hookup from last week.*

hook·worm /ˈho͝okˌwərm/ ▶ **noun** a parasitic worm with hooklike mouthparts that can infest the intestines.

hook·y /ˈho͝okē/ (also **hookey**) ▶ **noun** (in phrase **play hooky**) informal stay away from school or work without permission or explanation.

hoo·li·gan /ˈho͞oləgin/ ▶ **noun** a violent young troublemaker.

– SYNONYMS **lout,** thug, vandal, delinquent, ruffian, troublemaker. informal tough, bruiser.

– DERIVATIVES **hoo·li·gan·ism** noun.
– ORIGIN perhaps from *Hooligan*, the surname of a fictional rowdy Irish family in a music-hall song.

hoop /hōōp/ ▶ **noun 1** a circular band of a rigid material. **2** a large ring used as a toy or for circus performers to jump through. **3** the round metal rim from which a basketball net is suspended. **4** (**hoops**) informal the game of basketball: *the UNC quarterback might not return to hoops.*

– SYNONYMS **ring,** band, circle, wheel, circlet, loop.

▶ **verb** bind or surround with hoops.
– DERIVATIVES **hooped** adjective.
– ORIGIN Old English.

hoop·la /ˈhōōˌplä, ˈhŏŏpˌlä/ ▶ **noun** informal excitement surrounding an event or situation.

hoo·poe /ˈhōōˌpō, -ˌpōō/ ▶ **noun** a salmon-pink bird with a long bill, a large crest, and black-and-white wings and tail.
– ORIGIN Latin *upupa*, imitating the bird's call.

hoop·ster /ˈhōōpstər/ ▶ **noun** informal a basketball player.

hoo·ray /həˈrā, hōō-/ ▶ **exclamation** hurrah.

hoot /hōōt/ ▶ **noun 1** a low sound made by owls or a similar sound made by a horn, siren, etc. **2** a shout of scorn or disapproval. **3** an outburst of laughter. **4** (**a hoot**) informal a very amusing person or thing. ▶ **verb** make or cause to make a hoot.
– PHRASES **not care** (or **give**) **a hoot** (or **two hoots**) informal not care at all.
– ORIGIN perhaps imitating the sound.

hootch /hōōCH/ ▶ **noun** variant spelling of **HOOCH**.

hoot·en·an·ny /ˈhōōtnˌanē/ ▶ **noun** (pl. **hootenannies**) informal an informal gathering with country or folk music and sometimes dancing.
– ORIGIN (originally US, referring to a gadget or 'thingamajig'): of unknown origin.

hoot·er /ˈhōōtər/ ▶ **noun** informal **1** a person's nose. **2** (**hooters**) a woman's breasts.

hooves /hŏŏvz, hōōvz/ plural of **HOOF**.

hop[1] /häp/ ▶ **verb** (**hops, hopping, hopped**) **1** jump along on one foot. **2** (of a bird or animal) jump along with two or all feet at once. **3** jump over or off something. **4** informal move or go somewhere quickly: *hop in then and we'll be off.*

– SYNONYMS *he hopped over the fence* **jump,** bound, spring, bounce, leap, vault.

▶ **noun 1** a hopping movement. **2** a short journey or distance. **3** an informal dance.

– SYNONYMS *the rabbit had a hop around* **jump,** bound, bounce, leap, spring.

– PHRASES **hopping mad** informal very angry.
– ORIGIN Old English.

hop[2] ▶ **noun** a climbing plant whose dried flowers (**hops**) are used in brewing to give beer a bitter flavor.
– DERIVATIVES **hop·py** adjective.
– ORIGIN from German or Dutch.

hope /hōp/ ▶ **noun 1** a feeling of expectation and desire for something to happen. **2** a cause or source of hope: *her only hope is surgery.*

– SYNONYMS **1 aspiration,** desire, wish, expectation, ambition, aim, plan, dream. **2 optimism,** expectation, confidence, faith, belief.
– ANTONYMS pessimism.

▶ **verb 1** expect and want something to happen. **2** intend if possible to do something.

– SYNONYMS **1 expect,** anticipate, look for, be hopeful of, dream of. **2** *we hope to move in on Monday* **aim,** intend, be looking, have the intention, have in mind, plan.

– DERIVATIVES **hop·er** noun.
– ORIGIN Old English.

hope chest ▶ **noun** a chest containing household linen and clothing stored by a woman in preparation for her marriage.

hope·ful /ˈhōpfəl/ ▶ **adjective** feeling or inspiring hope.

– SYNONYMS **1 optimistic,** full of hope, confident, sanguine, positive, buoyant, bullish, upbeat. **2 promising,** encouraging, heartening, reassuring, favorable, optimistic.
– ANTONYMS pessimistic, discouraging.

▶ **noun** a person likely or hoping to succeed.
– DERIVATIVES **hope·ful·ness** noun.

hope·ful·ly /ˈhōpfəlē/ ▶ **adverb 1** in a hopeful way. **2** it is to be hoped that.

– SYNONYMS **1 optimistically,** full of hope, confidently, buoyantly, expectantly. **2 all being well,** if all goes well, God willing, with luck, knock (on) wood, fingers crossed.

USAGE

The traditional sense of **hopefully** is 'in a hopeful way.' The newer use, meaning 'it is to be hoped that' (as in *hopefully, it should be finished next year*) is now the most common, although some people still think that it is incorrect.

hope·less /ˈhōplis/ ▶ **adjective 1** feeling or causing despair. **2** very bad or incompetent.

– SYNONYMS **1 forlorn,** beyond hope, lost, irreparable, irreversible, incurable, impossible, futile. **2 bad,** poor, awful, terrible, dreadful, appalling, atrocious, incompetent; informal pathetic, useless, lousy, rotten, rubbish.
– ANTONYMS competent.

– DERIVATIVES **hope·less·ly** adverb **hope·less·ness** noun.

Ho·pi /ˈhōpē/ ▶ **noun** (pl. same or **Hopis**) **1** a member of an American Indian people living chiefly in NE Arizona. **2** the language of the Hopi.
– ORIGIN Hopi.

hop·per /ˈhäpər/ ▶ **noun 1** a container that tapers downward and discharges its contents at the bottom. **2** a person or thing that hops.

hop·scotch /ˈhäpˌskäCH/ ▶ **noun** a children's game of hopping into and over squares marked on the ground to retrieve a marker.
– ORIGIN from **HOP[1]** + **SCOTCH** in the sense 'put and end to, stop.'

horde /hôrd/ ▶ **noun 1** chiefly derogatory a large group of people. **2** an army or tribe of nomadic warriors.

– SYNONYMS **crowd,** mob, pack, gang, troop, army, swarm, mass, throng.

– ORIGIN Turkish *ordu* 'royal camp.'

USAGE

On the confusion of **horde** and **hoard**, see the note at **HOARD**.

hore·hound /ˈhôrˌhound/ ▶ **noun** a plant of the mint

family, traditionally used as a medicinal herb.
– ORIGIN Old English.

ho·ri·zon /hə'rīzən/ ▶ **noun 1** the line at which the earth's surface and the sky appear to meet. **2** the limit of a person's knowledge, experience, or interest: *she wanted to leave home and broaden her horizons.*
– PHRASES **on the horizon** about to happen; imminent.
– ORIGIN from Greek *horizōn* 'limiting.'

hor·i·zon·tal /ˌhôrə'zän(t)l/ ▶ **adjective** parallel to the plane of the horizon; at right angles to the vertical.

– SYNONYMS **level,** flat, parallel.
– ANTONYMS vertical.

▶ **noun** a horizontal line, plane, or structure.
– DERIVATIVES **hor·i·zon·tal·i·ty** /-ˌzän'talitē/ noun **hor·i·zon·tal·ly** adverb.

hor·i·zon·tal sta·bi·liz·er ▶ **noun** a horizontal airfoil at the tail of an aircraft.

hor·mone /'hôrˌmōn/ ▶ **noun** a substance produced by a living thing and carried by blood or sap to regulate the action of specific cells or tissues.
– DERIVATIVES **hor·mo·nal** /hôr'mōnl/ adjective.
– ORIGIN Greek *hormōn* 'setting in motion.'

hor·mone re·place·ment ther·a·py ▶ **noun** treatment with certain hormones to make symptoms of menopause or osteoporosis less severe.

horn /hôrn/ ▶ **noun 1** a hard bony outgrowth, often curved and pointed, found in pairs on the heads of cattle, sheep, and other animals. **2** the substance of which horns are composed. **3** a brass wind instrument, conical in shape or wound into a spiral. **4** an instrument sounding a signal. **5** a pointed projection or object.
– DERIVATIVES **horned** adjective.
– PHRASES **blow one's own horn** talk boastfully about one's achievements. **draw** (or **pull**) **in one's horns** become less assertive or ambitious. **horn in** informal interfere or intrude. **on the horns of a dilemma** faced with a decision involving equally unfavorable alternatives.
– ORIGIN Old English.

horn·beam /'hôrnˌbēm/ ▶ **noun** a deciduous tree with hard pale wood.

horn·bill /'hôrnˌbil/ ▶ **noun** a tropical bird with a hornlike structure on its large curved bill.

horn·blende /'hôrnˌblend/ ▶ **noun** a dark brown, black, or green mineral present in many rocks.
– ORIGIN German.

hor·net /'hôrnit/ ▶ **noun** a kind of large wasp, typically red and yellow or red and black.
– PHRASES **stir up a hornets' nest** cause a situation full of difficulties or angry feelings.
– ORIGIN Old English.

horn of plen·ty ▶ **noun** a cornucopia.

horn·pipe /'hôrnˌpīp/ ▶ **noun 1** a lively solo dance traditionally performed by sailors. **2** a piece of music for such a dance.

horn-rimmed ▶ **adjective** (of glasses) having rims made of horn or a similar substance.

horn·y /'hôrnē/ ▶ **adjective** (**hornier, horniest**) **1** made of or resembling horn. **2** hard and rough. **3** informal sexually aroused or arousing.
– DERIVATIVES **horn·i·ness** noun.

ho·rol·o·gy /hə'räləjē/ ▶ **noun 1** the study and measurement of time. **2** the art of making clocks and watches.
– DERIVATIVES **hor·o·log·i·cal** /ˌhôrə'läjikəl/ adjective **ho·rol·o·gist** noun.
– ORIGIN from Greek *hōra* 'time.'

hor·o·scope /'hôrəˌskōp, 'härə-/ ▶ **noun** a forecast of a person's future based on the relative positions of the stars and planets at the time of that person's birth.
– ORIGIN from Greek *hōra* 'time' + *skopos* 'observer.'

hor·ren·dous /hə'rendəs, hô-/ ▶ **adjective** highly unpleasant or horrifying.
– DERIVATIVES **hor·ren·dous·ly** adverb.
– ORIGIN Latin *horrendus*.

hor·ri·ble /'hôrəbəl, 'här-/ ▶ **adjective 1** causing or likely to cause horror. **2** very unpleasant.

– SYNONYMS **1 dreadful,** awful, terrible, shocking, appalling, horrifying, horrific, horrendous, grisly, ghastly, gruesome, harrowing, unspeakable, abhorrent. **2 nasty,** horrid, disagreeable, obnoxious, disgusting, hateful, odious, objectionable, insufferable.
– ANTONYMS pleasant.

– DERIVATIVES **hor·ri·bly** adverb.

hor·rid /'hôrid, 'här-/ ▶ **adjective 1** causing horror. **2** very unpleasant.
– DERIVATIVES **hor·rid·ly** adverb **hor·rid·ness** noun.

hor·ri·fic /hô'rifik, hə-/ ▶ **adjective** causing horror.

– SYNONYMS **dreadful,** horrendous, horrible, terrible, atrocious, horrifying, shocking, appalling, harrowing, hideous, grisly, ghastly, sickening.

– DERIVATIVES **hor·rif·i·cal·ly** adverb.

hor·ri·fy /'hôrəˌfī, 'här-/ ▶ **verb** (**horrifies, horrifying, horrified**) fill someone with horror.

– SYNONYMS **shock,** appall, outrage, scandalize, offend, disgust, revolt, nauseate, sicken.

– DERIVATIVES **hor·ri·fied** adjective **hor·ri·fy·ing** adjective.
– ORIGIN Latin *horrificare*.

hor·ror /'hôrər, 'här-/ ▶ **noun 1** an intense feeling of fear, shock, or disgust. **2** a cause of horror. **3** intense dislike: *he had a horror of modernity.* **4** informal a badly behaved or mischievous child.

– SYNONYMS **1 terror,** fear, fright, alarm, panic. **2 dismay,** consternation, alarm, distress, disgust, shock.
– ANTONYMS delight, satisfaction.

– ORIGIN from Latin *horrere* 'shudder, (of hair) stand on end.'

hors de com·bat /ˌôr də käm'bä/ ▶ **adjective** out of action due to injury or damage.
– ORIGIN French, 'out of the fight.'

hors d'oeuvre /ôr 'dərv, 'dœvrə/ ▶ **noun** (pl. same or **hors d'oeuvres** pronunc. same or /'dərvz/) a savory appetizer.
– ORIGIN French, 'outside the work.'

horse /hôrs/ ▶ **noun 1** a large four-legged mammal with a flowing mane and tail, used for riding and for pulling heavy loads. **2** an adult male horse, as opposed to a mare or colt. **3** (treated as sing. or pl.) cavalry. **4** a structure on which something is mounted or supported: *a clothes horse.*

– SYNONYMS **mount,** charger, nag, colt, stallion, mare, filly, bronco.

▶ **verb** (**horse around**) informal fool around.
– PHRASES **from the horse's mouth** from the person directly concerned in the matter. **hold one's horses** informal wait a moment.
– ORIGIN Old English.

WORD LINKS

equine *relating to horses*
equestrian *relating to horse riding*

horse·back /'hôrs,bak/ ▶ **adjective** mounted on a horse.
– PHRASES **on horseback** mounted on a horse.

horse chest·nut ▶ **noun 1** a large deciduous tree producing nuts enclosed in a spiny case. **2** the fruit or seed of this tree.
– ORIGIN horse chestnuts are said to have been an Eastern remedy for chest diseases in horses.

horse·flesh /'hôrs,flesн/ ▶ **noun** horses considered as a group.

horse·fly /'hôrs,flī/ ▶ **noun** (pl. **horseflies**) a large fly that bites horses and other large mammals.

horse·hair /'hôrs,he(ə)r/ ▶ **noun** hair from the mane or tail of a horse, used in furniture for padding.

horse lat·i·tudes ▶ **plural noun** a belt of calm air and sea occurring in both the northern and southern hemispheres between the trade winds and the westerlies.
– ORIGIN uncertain.

horse laugh ▶ **noun** a loud, coarse laugh.

horse·man /'hôrsmən/ (or **horsewoman** /'hôrs,wo͝omən/) ▶ **noun** (pl. **horsemen** or **horsewomen** /'hôrs,wimin/) a rider on horseback, especially a skilled one.
– DERIVATIVES **horse·man·ship** noun.

horse·play /'hôrs,plā/ ▶ **noun** rough, boisterous play.

horse·pow·er /'hôrs,pou(-ə)r/ ▶ **noun** (pl. same) an imperial unit of power equal to 550 foot-pounds per second (about 750 watts), especially as a measurement of engine power.

horse race ▶ **noun 1** a race between two or more horses ridden by jockeys. **2** a very close contest: *the election was still a horse race.*
– DERIVATIVES **horse rac·ing** noun.

horse·rad·ish /'hôrs,radisн/ ▶ **noun** a plant of the mustard family grown for its strong-tasting root, which is often made into a sauce.

horse sense ▶ **noun** informal common sense.

horse·shoe /'hôr(s),sнo͞o/ ▶ **noun 1** a U-shaped iron band attached to the base of a horse's hoof. **2** (**horseshoes**) (treated as sing.) a game in which horseshoes are thrown at a stake in the ground.

horse·tail /'hôrs,tāl/ ▶ **noun** a flowerless plant with a jointed stem and narrow leaves.

horse-trad·ing ▶ **noun** informal hard and shrewd bargaining.

horse·whip /'hôrs,(h)wip/ ▶ **noun** a long whip used for driving and controlling horses. ▶ **verb** (**horsewhips, horsewhipping, horsewhipped**) beat someone or something with a horsewhip.

hors·ey /'hôrsē/ (also **horsy**) ▶ **adjective** (**horsier, horsiest**) **1** relating to or resembling a horse. **2** very interested in horses or horse racing.

horst /hôrst/ ▶ **noun** Geology a raised elongated block of the earth's crust lying between two faults.
– ORIGIN German, 'heap.'

hor·ta·to·ry /'hôrtə,tôrē/ ▶ **adjective** formal strongly urging someone to do something.
– ORIGIN from Latin *hortari* 'exhort.'

hor·ti·cul·ture /'hôrti,kəlcнər/ ▶ **noun** the art or practice of garden cultivation and management.
– DERIVATIVES **hor·ti·cul·tur·al** /,hôrti'kəlcнərəl/ adjective **hor·ti·cul·tur·ist** (also **horticulturalist**) noun.
– ORIGIN from Latin *hortus* 'garden.'

ho·san·na /hō'zanə, -'zä-/ (also **hosannah**) ▶ **noun & exclamation** a biblical cry of praise or joy.
– ORIGIN from a Hebrew phrase meaning 'save, we pray.'

hose /hōz/ ▶ **noun 1** a flexible tube conveying water. **2** (treated as pl.) stockings, socks, and tights.

– SYNONYMS **pipe,** tube, duct, outlet, pipeline, siphon.

▶ **verb** water or spray something with a hose.
– ORIGIN Old English.

ho·sier·y /'hōzнərē/ ▶ **noun** stockings, socks, and tights.

hos·pice /'häspis/ ▶ **noun 1** a home providing care for people who are sick or terminally ill. **2** old use a lodging for travelers, especially one run by a religious order.
– ORIGIN Latin *hospitium.*

hos·pi·ta·ble /hä'spitəbəl, 'häspitəbəl/ ▶ **adjective** **1** friendly and welcoming to guests or strangers. **2** (of an environment) pleasant and favorable for living in.

– SYNONYMS **welcoming,** friendly, sociable, cordial, gracious, accommodating, warm.

– DERIVATIVES **hos·pi·ta·bly** adverb.

hos·pi·tal /'hä,spitl/ ▶ **noun** an institution providing medical and surgical treatment and nursing care for sick or injured people.

– SYNONYMS **infirmary,** clinic, sanatorium, hospice; Military field hospital.

– ORIGIN Latin *hospitale.*

hos·pi·tal·i·ty /,häspi'talitē/ ▶ **noun** the friendly and generous treatment of guests or strangers.

– SYNONYMS **friendliness,** neighborliness, sociability, welcome, warmth, kindness, cordiality, generosity.

hos·pi·tal·ize /'häspitl,īz/ ▶ **verb** admit someone to a hospital for treatment.
– DERIVATIVES **hos·pi·tal·i·za·tion** /,häspitl-li'zāsнən/ noun.

Host /hōst/ ▶ **noun** (**the Host**) the bread consecrated in the Christian Eucharist (Holy Communion).
– ORIGIN Latin *hostia* 'victim.'

host[1] /hōst/ ▶ **noun 1** a person who receives or entertains guests. **2** the presenter of a television or radio program. **3** a place or organization that holds and organizes an event to which others are invited. **4** Computing a computer that mediates multiple access to databases or provides other services to a network. **5** an animal or plant on or in which a parasite lives.

– SYNONYMS **1 party-giver,** hostess, entertainer. **2 presenter,** compère, anchor, anchorman, anchorwoman, announcer.
– ANTONYMS guest.

▶ **verb** act as host at an event or for a television or radio program.

– SYNONYMS **present,** introduce, compère, front, anchor.

– ORIGIN Latin *hospes* 'host, guest.'

host[2] ▶ **noun** (**a host/hosts of**) a large number of people or things.
– ORIGIN Latin *hostis* 'stranger, enemy,' later 'army.'

hos·ta /ˈhōstə, ˈhästə/ ▸ **noun** a shade-tolerant plant with ornamental foliage.
– ORIGIN named after the Austrian physician Nicolaus T. *Host.*

hos·tage /ˈhästij/ ▸ **noun** a person held prisoner in an attempt to make others give in to a demand.

– SYNONYMS **captive,** prisoner, detainee, internee.

– PHRASES **a hostage to fortune** an act or remark regarded as unwise because it invites trouble in the future.
– ORIGIN Latin *obsidatus* 'the state of being a hostage.'

hos·tel /ˈhästl/ ▸ **noun** an establishment that provides cheap food and lodging for a particular group of people.
– ORIGIN Old French.

host·ess /ˈhōstis/ ▸ **noun 1** a female host. **2** a woman employed at a restaurant to welcome and seat customers.

hos·tile /ˈhästl, ˈhäˌstīl/ ▸ **adjective 1** showing or feeling dislike or opposition. **2** relating to a military enemy. **3** (of a takeover bid) opposed by the company to be bought.

– SYNONYMS **1 unfriendly,** unkind, unsympathetic, antagonistic, aggressive, confrontational, belligerent. **2 unfavorable,** adverse, bad, harsh, grim, inhospitable, forbidding. **3** *they are hostile to the idea* **opposed,** averse, antagonistic, ill-disposed, unsympathetic, antipathetic, against; informal **anti.**
– ANTONYMS friendly, favorable.

– DERIVATIVES **hos·tile·ly** adverb.
– ORIGIN from Latin *hostis* 'stranger, enemy.'

CHOOSE THE RIGHT WORD

hostile, adverse, bellicose, belligerent, inimical

Few people have trouble recognizing hostility when confronted with it. Someone who is **hostile** displays an attitude of intense ill will and acts like an enemy (*the audience grew hostile after waiting an hour for the show to start*). Both **bellicose** and **belligerent** imply a readiness or eagerness to fight, but the former is used to describe a state of mind or temper (*after drinking all night, he was in a bellicose mood*), while the latter is normally used to describe someone who is actively engaged in hostilities (*the belligerent brothers were at it again*). While *hostile* and *belligerent* usually apply to people, **adverse** and **inimical** are used describe tendencies or influences. *Inimical* means having an antagonistic tendency (*remarks that were inimical to everything she believed in*), and *adverse* means turned toward something in opposition (*an adverse wind; under adverse circumstances*). Unlike *hostile*, *adverse* and *inimical* need not connote the involvement of human feeling.

hos·til·i·ty /häˈstilitē/ ▸ **noun** (pl. **hostilities**) **1** hostile behavior. **2** (**hostilities**) acts of warfare: *a cessation of hostilities.*

– SYNONYMS **1 antagonism,** unfriendliness, malevolence, venom, hatred, aggression, belligerence. **2 opposition,** antagonism, animosity, antipathy. **3** *a cessation of hostilities* **fighting,** armed conflict, combat, warfare, war, bloodshed, violence.

hot /hät/ ▸ **adjective** (**hotter, hottest**) **1** having a high temperature. **2** feeling or producing an uncomfortable sensation of heat. **3** feeling or showing anger, lust, or other strong emotion. **4** informal currently popular, fashionable, or interesting: *they know the hottest dance moves.* **5** informal very knowledgeable or skillful. **6** (**hot on**) informal strict about something. **7** informal (of goods) stolen.

– SYNONYMS **1** *hot food* **heated,** sizzling, roasting, boiling, scorching, scalding, red-hot. **2** *a hot day* **very warm,** balmy, summery, tropical, scorching, searing, blistering, sweltering, torrid, sultry; informal boiling, baking, roasting. **3 spicy,** peppery, fiery, strong, piquant, powerful. **4 fierce,** intense, keen, competitive, cutthroat, ruthless, aggressive, violent. **5** *she's hot on local history* **knowledgeable,** well informed, au fait, well up, well versed; informal clued up.
– ANTONYMS cold, mild.

▸ **verb** (**hots, hotting, hotted**) (**hot up** or **hot something up**) Brit. informal become or make more intense or exciting.
– DERIVATIVES **hot·ness** noun.
– PHRASES **have the hots for** informal be sexually attracted to someone. **hot under the collar** informal angry or resentful. **in hot water** informal in trouble. **make it** (or **things**) **hot for** informal stir up trouble for someone.
– ORIGIN Old English.

hot air ▸ **noun** informal empty or boastful talk.

hot-air bal·loon ▸ **noun** another term for **BALLOON** (sense 2 of the noun).

hot·bed /ˈhätˌbed/ ▸ **noun 1** an environment where a particular activity happens or flourishes: *the country was a hotbed of revolt.* **2** a bed of earth heated by fermenting manure, for raising or forcing plants.

hot-blood·ed ▸ **adjective** lustful; passionate.

hot but·ton ▸ **adjective** informal arousing passionate emotions or debate: *a hot-button issue.*

hot·cake /ˈhätˌkāk/ ▸ **noun** a pancake.
– PHRASES **like hotcakes** quickly and in great quantity, especially because of popularity: *his latest CD is selling like hotcakes.*

hot dog ▸ **noun 1** a hot sausage served in a long, soft roll. **2** a person who shows off, especially a skier or surfer. ▸ **verb** (**hotdog**) (**hotdogs, hotdogging, hotdogged**) informal perform stunts.

ho·tel /hōˈtel/ ▸ **noun** an establishment providing accommodations and meals for travelers and tourists.
– ORIGIN French *hôtel.*

ho·te·lier /ˌôtelˈyā, hōtlˈi(ə)r/ ▸ **noun** a person who owns or manages a hotel.

hot flash ▸ **noun** a sudden feeling of heat in the skin or face, often as a symptom of menopause.

hot·foot /ˈhätˌfo͝ot/ ▸ **adverb** in eager haste. ▸ **verb** (**hotfoot it**) hurry eagerly.

hot·head /ˈhätˌhed/ ▸ **noun** a rash or quick-tempered person.
– DERIVATIVES **hot-head·ed** adjective.

hot·house /ˈhätˌhous/ ▸ **noun 1** a heated greenhouse. **2** an environment that encourages rapid growth or development. ▸ **verb** educate a child to a higher level than is usual for their age.

hot key ▸ **noun** Computing a key or combination of keys providing quick access to a function within a program.

hot·line /ˈhätˌlīn/ ▸ **noun** a direct telephone line set up for a specific purpose.

hot·ly /ˈhätlē/ ▸ **adverb** in a passionate, excited, or angry way: *the rumors were hotly denied.*

– SYNONYMS **vehemently,** vigorously, strenuously, fiercely, heatedly.

hot mon·ey ▶ **noun** capital that is frequently transferred between financial institutions in an attempt to maximize interest or profit.

hot pants ▶ **plural noun** women's tight, brief shorts.

hot plate ▶ **noun** a flat heated metal or ceramic surface used for cooking food or keeping it hot.

hot po·ta·to ▶ **noun** informal a controversial issue that is difficult to deal with.

hot rod ▶ **noun** a motor vehicle that has been specially modified to give it extra power and speed. ▶ **verb** (**hot-rod**) **1** modify a vehicle or other device to make it faster or more powerful. **2** drive a hot rod.
– DERIVATIVES **hot-rod·der** noun.

hot seat ▶ **noun** (**the hot seat**) informal **1** the position of a person who carries full responsibility for something. **2** the electric chair.

hot·shot /ˈhät,sʜät/ ▶ **noun** informal an important or exceptionally able person.

hot spot ▶ **noun 1** a place of significant activity or danger. **2** a small area with a high temperature in comparison to its surroundings. **3** (also **wireless hot spot**) a place in a public building with a signal that allows wireless connection to the Internet.

hot spring ▶ **noun** a spring of naturally hot water, typically heated by subterranean volcanic activity.

hot stuff ▶ **noun** informal **1** a person or thing of outstanding talent or interest. **2** a sexually exciting person, book, etc.

hot-tem·pered ▶ **adjective** easily angered.

Hot·ten·tot /ˈhätn,tät/ ▶ **noun & adjective** offensive formerly used to refer to the Khoikhoi peoples of South Africa and Namibia.
– ORIGIN Dutch.

hot tick·et ▶ **noun** informal a person or thing that is in great demand.

hot·tie /ˈhätē/ (also **hotty**) ▶ **noun** informal a sexually attractive person.

hot tub ▶ **noun** a large tub filled with hot bubbling water, used for recreation or therapy.

hot-wa·ter bot·tle (also **hot-water bag**) ▶ **noun** a rubber container that is filled with hot water and used for warming a bed or part of the body.

hot-wire ▶ **verb** informal start the engine of a vehicle by bypassing the ignition switch.

Hou·di·ni /ho͞oˈdēnē/ ▶ **noun** a person skilled at escaping from difficult situations.
– ORIGIN named after the American magician and escape artist Harry *Houdini* (Erik Weisz).

hound /hound/ ▶ **noun** a dog of a breed used for hunting. ▶ **verb** harass or pursue relentlessly: *she was hounded by the media.*

– SYNONYMS **pursue,** chase, stalk, harry, harass, pester, badger, torment.

– ORIGIN Old English.

hounds·tooth /ˈhoun(d)z,to͞oᴛʜ/ ▶ **noun** a large checked pattern with notched corners.

hour /ou(ə)r/ ▶ **noun 1** a period of 60 minutes, one of the twenty-four equal parts that a day is divided into. **2** a time of day specified as an exact number of hours from midnight or midday. **3** a period set aside for a particular purpose or activity: *leisure hours.* **4** a point in time: *the store is half-full even at this hour.*
– PHRASES **on the hour** at an exact hour, or on each hour, of the day or night.
– ORIGIN Greek *hōra* 'season, hour.'

hour·glass /ˈou(ə)r,glas/ ▶ **noun** a device with two connected glass bulbs containing sand that takes an hour to fall from the upper to the lower bulb. ▶ **adjective** shaped like an hourglass: *her hourglass figure.*

hou·ri /ˈho͝orē/ ▶ **noun** (pl. **houris**) a beautiful young woman, especially one of the virgin companions of the faithful in the Muslim Paradise.
– ORIGIN from an Arabic word meaning 'having eyes with a marked contrast of black and white.'

hour·ly /ˈou(ə)rlē/ ▶ **adjective 1** done or occurring every hour. **2** calculated hour by hour. ▶ **adverb 1** every hour. **2** by the hour.

house ▶ **noun** /hous/ **1** a building for people to live in. **2** a building devoted to a particular activity or purpose: *a house of prayer.* **3** a firm or institution: *a fashion house.* **4** a religious community that occupies a particular building. **5** a residential hall at a school or college. **6** a lawmaking assembly. **7** a dynasty: *the House of Stewart.* **8** (also **house music**) a style of fast electronic dance music. **9** Astrology one of twelve divisions of the celestial sphere.

– SYNONYMS **1 residence,** home; informal pad. formal dwelling, abode, habitation, domicile. **2 family,** clan, tribe, dynasty, line, bloodline, lineage. **3 firm,** business, company, corporation, enterprise, establishment, institution, concern, organization, operation; informal outfit. **4 assembly,** legislative body, congress, senate, chamber, council, parliament.

▶ **adjective** /hous/ **1** (of an animal or plant) kept in or infesting buildings. **2** relating to resident medical staff at a hospital. **3** relating to a firm, institution, or society: *a house journal.*
▶ **verb** /houz/ **1** provide someone with shelter or accommodations. **2** provide space for: *the museum houses a collection of Roman sculpture.* **3** enclose or encase something.

– SYNONYMS **1 accommodate,** give someone a roof over their head, lodge, quarter, board, billet, take in, put up. **2 contain,** hold, store, cover, protect, enclose.

– DERIVATIVES **house·ful** /ˈhous,fo͝ol/ noun.
– PHRASES **like a house on fire** (or **afire**) informal vigorously, excellently. **keep house** run a household. **on the house** at the management's expense. **put one's house in order** make necessary reforms.
– ORIGIN Old English.

house ar·rest ▶ **noun** the state of being kept as a prisoner in one's own house.

house·boat /ˈhous,bōt/ ▶ **noun** a boat that is equipped for use as a home.

house·bound /ˈhous,bound/ ▶ **adjective** unable to leave one's house, often due to illness or old age.

house·boy /ˈhous,boi/ ▶ **noun** a boy or man employed to undertake domestic duties.

house·break /ˈhous,brāk/ ▶ **verb** (past. **housebroke** /ˈhous,brōk/; past participle **housebroken** /ˈhous,brōkən/) **1** train a pet to urinate and defecate outside the house or only in a special place. **2** informal or humorous teach someone good manners or neatness.

house·break·ing /ˈhous,brākiNG/ ▶ **noun** the action of breaking into a building to commit a crime.
– DERIVATIVES **house·break·er** noun.

house·coat /ˈhous,kōt/ ▶ **noun** a woman's long, loose robe for casual wear around the house.

house·dress /ˈhous,dres/ ▶ **noun** a simple, usually washable, dress suitable for wearing while doing housework.

house·fly /ˈhous,flī/ ▶ **noun** (pl. **houseflies**) a common small fly often found in and around houses.

house·hold /ˈhous,(h)ōld/ ▶ **noun** a house and its occupants regarded as a unit.

– SYNONYMS **1 family,** house, occupants, clan, tribe; informal brood. **2** *household goods* **domestic,** family, everyday, ordinary, common, commonplace, regular, practical, workaday.

– DERIVATIVES **house·hold·er** noun.

house·hold name (also **household word**) ▶ **noun** a famous person or thing.

house-hunt·ing ▶ **noun** the process of seeking a house to buy or rent.
– DERIVATIVES **house-hunt·er** noun.

house hus·band ▶ **noun** a man who lives with a partner and carries out the household duties traditionally done by a housewife.

house·keep·er /ˈhous,kēpər/ ▶ **noun** a person, typically a woman, employed to manage a household.

house·keep·ing /ˈhous,kēpiNG/ ▶ **noun 1** the management of a household. **2** the department in a hotel, etc. that oversees its cleaning, linen, and glassware. **3** operations such as record-keeping and maintenance in an organization or a computer that support its real work.

house lights ▶ **plural noun** the lights in the area of a theater where the audience sits.

house·maid /ˈhous,mād/ ▶ **noun** a female employee who cleans rooms.

house mar·tin ▶ **noun** a black-and-white bird of the swallow family, nesting on buildings.

house·mas·ter /ˈhous,mastər/ (or **housemistress**) ▶ **noun** chiefly Brit. a teacher in charge of a house at a boarding school.

house·mate /ˈhous,māt/ ▶ **noun** a person with whom one shares a house.

house mouse ▶ **noun** a grayish-brown mouse found abundantly as a scavenger in houses.

House of Com·mons ▶ **noun** the part of Parliament in the UK whose members are elected by voters.

House of Lords ▶ **noun 1** the part of Parliament in the UK whose members are peers and bishops and are not elected by voters. **2** a committee of specially qualified members of the House of Lords, appointed as the ultimate judicial appeal court of England and Wales.

House of Rep·re·sent·a·tives ▶ **noun** the lower house of the US Congress.

house·plant /ˈhous,plant/ ▶ **noun** a plant grown indoors.

house-proud ▶ **adjective** very concerned with the cleanliness and appearance of one's home.

house-sit ▶ **verb** live in and look after a house while its owner is away.
– DERIVATIVES **house-sit·ter** noun.

house spar·row ▶ **noun** a common brown and gray sparrow that nests in the eaves and roofs of houses.

house style ▶ **noun** a company's preferred manner of presentation and layout of written material.

house-to-house ▶ **adjective & adverb** performed at or taken to each house in turn.

house-train ▶ **verb** train a pet to urinate and defecate outside the house.

house·wares /ˈhous,we(ə)rz/ ▶ **noun** kitchen utensils and similar household items.

house·warm·ing /ˈhous,wôrmiNG/ ▶ **noun** a party celebrating a move to a new home.

house·wife /ˈhous,wīf/ ▶ **noun** (pl. **housewives** /-,wīvz/) a married woman whose main occupation is caring for her family and running the household.
– DERIVATIVES **house·wife·ly** adjective **house·wif·er·y** /-,wīfərē/ noun.

house·work /ˈhous,wərk/ ▶ **noun** cleaning and other work done in running a home.

hous·ing /ˈhouziNG/ ▶ **noun 1** houses and apartments as a whole. **2** the provision of accommodations. **3** a rigid casing for a piece of equipment.

– SYNONYMS **1 accommodations,** houses, homes, living quarters; formal dwellings. **2 casing,** covering, case, cover, holder, sleeve.

HOV ▶ **abbreviation** high-occupancy vehicle.

hove /hōv/ Nautical past tense of **HEAVE**.

hov·el /ˈhəvəl, ˈhävəl/ ▶ **noun** a small squalid or run-down dwelling.

– SYNONYMS **shack,** shanty, hut, slum; informal dump, hole.

– ORIGIN unknown.

hov·er /ˈhəvər/ ▶ **verb 1** remain in one place in the air. **2** linger close at hand in an uncertain way. **3** remain near a particular level or between two states: *the temperature hovered around ten degrees.*

– SYNONYMS **1 hang,** be poised, be suspended, float, fly, drift. **2 wait,** linger, loiter.

▶ **noun** an act of hovering.
– DERIVATIVES **hov·er·er** noun.
– ORIGIN unknown.

hov·er·craft /ˈhəvər,kraft/ ▶ **noun** (pl. same) a vehicle or craft that travels over land or water on a cushion of air.

how /hou/ ▶ **adverb 1** in what way or by what means. **2** in what condition or health. **3** to what extent or degree. **4** the way in which.
– PHRASES **how about?** would you like? **how do you do?** said when meeting a person for the first time in a formal situation. **how many** what number. **how much** what amount or price. **how's that for——?** isn't that a remarkable instance of——?
– ORIGIN Old English.

how·dah /ˈhoudə/ ▶ **noun** a seat for riding on the back of an elephant or camel, usually having a canopy.
– ORIGIN Urdu.

how·dy /ˈhoudē/ ▶ **exclamation** an informal friendly greeting.
– ORIGIN alternative of *how d'ye.*

how·ev·er /houˈevər/ ▶ **adverb 1** used to introduce a statement that contrasts with a previous one. **2** in whatever way or to whatever extent.

– SYNONYMS **nevertheless,** nonetheless, even so, but, for all that, despite that, in spite of that.

how·itz·er /ˈhouətsər/ ▶ **noun** a short gun for firing shells at a steep angle.
– ORIGIN Dutch *houwitser*.

howl /houl/ ▶ **noun 1** a long wailing cry made by an animal. **2** a loud cry of pain, amusement, etc.

– SYNONYMS **1 baying,** cry, bark, yelp, yowl. **2 wail,** cry, yell, yelp, bellow, roar, shout, shriek, scream, screech.

▶ **verb** make a howling sound.

– SYNONYMS **1 bay,** cry, bark, yelp, yowl. **2 wail,** cry, yell, bawl, bellow, shriek, scream, screech, caterwaul, ululate; informal holler.

– ORIGIN probably imitating the sound.

howl·er /ˈhoulər/ ▶ **noun** informal a stupid mistake.

howl·ing /ˈhouliNG/ ▶ **adjective** informal great: *the meal was a howling success.*

how·so·ev·er /ˌhousōˈevər/ formal or old use ▶ **adverb** to whatever extent. ▶ **conjunction** in whatever way.

h.p. (also **HP**) ▶ **abbreviation 1** high pressure. **2** horsepower.

HQ ▶ **abbreviation** headquarters.

HR ▶ **abbreviation 1** House of Representatives. **2** human resources.

hr. ▶ **abbreviation** hour(s).

HRH ▶ **abbreviation** Brit. Her (or His) Royal Highness.

HRT ▶ **abbreviation** hormone replacement therapy.

Hs ▶ **symbol** the chemical element hassium.

HTML ▶ **abbreviation** Computing Hypertext Markup Language.

HTTP ▶ **abbreviation** Computing Hypertext Transfer (or Transport) Protocol.

hub /həb/ ▶ **noun 1** the central part of a wheel, rotating on or with the axle. **2** the center of an activity, region, or network.

– SYNONYMS **center,** core, heart, focus, focal point, nucleus, kernel, nerve center.
– ANTONYMS periphery.

hub·bub /ˈhəbəb/ ▶ **noun 1** a loud, confused noise caused by a crowd. **2** a busy, noisy situation.

– SYNONYMS **1 noise,** din, racket, commotion, clamor, cacophony, babel, rumpus; Brit. informal row. **2 confusion,** chaos, commotion, pandemonium, bedlam, mayhem, tumult, fracas, hurly-burly; informal hullabaloo.

– ORIGIN perhaps Irish.

hub·by /ˈhəbē/ ▶ **noun** (pl. **hubbies**) informal a husband.

hub·cap /ˈhəbˌkap/ ▶ **noun** a cover for the hub of a motor vehicle's wheel.

hu·bris /ˈ(h)yo͞obris/ ▶ **noun** excessive pride or self-confidence.
– DERIVATIVES **hu·bris·tic** adjective.
– ORIGIN Greek.

huck·ster /ˈhəkstər/ ▶ **noun 1** a person who sells small items, either door-to-door or from a stall. **2** a person who uses aggressive selling techniques.
– DERIVATIVES **huck·ster·ism** noun.
– ORIGIN probably German.

HUD /həd/ ▶ **abbreviation** (Department of) Housing and Urban Development.

hud·dle /ˈhədl/ ▶ **verb 1** crowd together. **2** curl one's body into a small space.

– SYNONYMS **1 crowd,** cluster, gather, bunch, throng, flock, collect, group, congregate. **2 curl up,** snuggle, nestle, hunch up.
– ANTONYMS disperse.

▶ **noun** a number of people or things grouped closely together.

– SYNONYMS **group,** cluster, bunch, collection; informal gaggle.

– ORIGIN perhaps German.

hue /(h)yo͞o/ ▶ **noun 1** a color or shade. **2** technical the quality of a color, dependent on its dominant wavelength, by virtue of which it is discernible as red, green, etc. **3** an aspect: *men of all political hues.*

– SYNONYMS **color,** shade, tone, tint, tinge.

– ORIGIN Old English.

hue and cry ▶ **noun** clamor or public outcry.
– ORIGIN from Old French *hu e cri* 'outcry and cry.'

huff /həf/ ▶ **verb** (often in phrase **huff and puff**) **1** breathe out noisily. **2** show one's annoyance in an obvious way. ▶ **noun** a fit of petty annoyance.
– ORIGIN imitating the sound.

huff·y /ˈhəfē/ ▶ **adjective** (**huffier, huffiest**) easily offended.
– DERIVATIVES **huff·i·ly** adverb **huff·i·ness** noun.

hug /həg/ ▶ **verb** (**hugs, hugging, hugged**) **1** hold someone or something tightly in one's arms or against one's body. **2** keep close to: *a few craft hugged the shore.*

– SYNONYMS **embrace,** cuddle, squeeze, clasp, clutch, hold tight.

▶ **noun** an act of hugging.

– SYNONYMS **embrace,** cuddle, squeeze, bear hug.

– DERIVATIVES **hug·ga·ble** adjective **hug·ger** noun.
– ORIGIN probably Scandinavian.

huge /(h)yo͞oj/ ▶ **adjective** very large; enormous.

– SYNONYMS **enormous,** vast, immense, massive, colossal, prodigious, gigantic, gargantuan, mammoth, monumental, giant, towering, mountainous; informal mega, monster, astronomical, ginormous.
– ANTONYMS tiny.

– DERIVATIVES **huge·ly** adverb **huge·ness** noun.
– ORIGIN Old French *ahuge*.

Hu·gue·not /ˈhyo͞ogəˌnät/ ▶ **noun** a French Protestant of the 16th–17th centuries.
– ORIGIN French.

huh /hə/ ▶ **exclamation** used to express scorn or surprise, or in questions to invite agreement.

hu·la /ˈho͞olə/ (also **hula-hula**) ▶ **noun** a dance performed by Hawaiian women, in which the dancers sway their hips.
– ORIGIN Hawaiian.

hu·la hoop (also trademark **Hula-Hoop**) ▶ **noun** a large hoop spun around the body by gyrating the hips.

hulk /həlk/ ▶ **noun 1** an old ship stripped of fittings and permanently moored. **2** a large or clumsy person or thing.
– ORIGIN Old English, 'fast ship.'

hulk·ing /ˈhəlkiNG/ ▶ **adjective** informal very large or clumsy.

hull[1] /həl/ ▸ **noun** the main body of a ship or other vessel.

– SYNONYMS **framework,** body, shell, frame, skeleton, structure.

– ORIGIN perhaps the same word as **HULL**[2], or related to **HOLD**[2].

hull[2] ▸ **noun 1** the outer covering of a fruit or seed. **2** the cluster of leaves and stalk on a strawberry or raspberry. ▸ **verb** remove the hulls from (fruit, seeds, or grain).
– ORIGIN Old English.

hul·la·ba·loo /'hələbəˌlo͞o, ˌhələbə'lo͞o/ ▸ **noun** informal a commotion or uproar.
– ORIGIN from *hallo, hullo,* etc.

hul·lo /hə'lō/ ▸ **exclamation** variant spelling of **HELLO**.

hum /həm/ ▸ **verb** (**hums, humming, hummed**) **1** make a low continuous sound like that of a bee. **2** sing with closed lips. **3** informal be in a very busy state.

– SYNONYMS **1 purr,** drone, murmur, buzz, whirr, throb. **2 be busy,** be active, be lively, buzz, bustle, be a hive of activity, throb.

▸ **noun** a low continuous sound.

– SYNONYMS **murmur,** drone, purr, buzz.

– DERIVATIVES **hum·ma·ble** adjective **hum·mer** noun.
– ORIGIN imitating the sound.

hu·man /'(h)yo͞omən/ ▸ **adjective 1** relating to or characteristic of human beings. **2** showing the better qualities of human beings, such as kindness.

– SYNONYMS **1 mortal,** flesh and blood, fallible, weak, frail, imperfect, vulnerable, physical, bodily, fleshly. **2 compassionate,** humane, kind, considerate, understanding, sympathetic.

▸ **noun** (also **human being**) a person.

– SYNONYMS **person,** human being, Homo sapiens, man, woman, individual, mortal, (living) soul, earthling; (**humans**) the human race, humanity, humankind, mankind, people.

– DERIVATIVES **hu·man·ly** adverb **hu·man·ness** noun.
– ORIGIN from Latin *homo* 'man, human being.'

WORD LINKS

anthropology *study of humankind*

hu·mane /(h)yo͞o'mān/ ▸ **adjective 1** kind or considerate toward people or animals. **2** formal (of a branch of learning) intended to civilize people.

– SYNONYMS **compassionate,** kind, considerate, understanding, sympathetic, tolerant, forbearing, forgiving, merciful, humanitarian, charitable.
– ANTONYMS cruel.

– DERIVATIVES **hu·mane·ly** adverb **hu·mane·ness** noun.

WORD TOOLKIT

humane ...	**lenient ...**	**solicitous ...**
treatment	punishment	hospitality
prison	scoring	husband/wife
trap	laws	suitor
death	judge	service

Hu·mane So·ci·e·ty ▸ **noun** trademark a nonprofit organization that attempts to prevent cruelty to animals and often operates animal shelters.

hu·man in·ter·est ▸ **noun** the aspect of a news story that interests people because it describes other people's experiences or emotions.

hu·man·ism /'(h)yo͞oməˌnizəm/ ▸ **noun 1** a system of thought that regards people as capable of using their intelligence to live their lives, rather than relying on religious belief. **2** a Renaissance cultural movement that revived interest in ancient Greek and Roman thought.
– DERIVATIVES **hu·man·ist** noun & adjective **hu·man·is·tic** /ˌ(h)yo͞omə'nistik/ adjective.

hu·man·i·tar·i·an /(h)yo͞oˌmani'te(ə)rēən/ ▸ **adjective** concerned with or seeking to improve human welfare: *humanitarian aid.*

– SYNONYMS **1 compassionate,** humane, unselfish, altruistic, generous. **2 charitable,** philanthropic, public-spirited, socially concerned.

▸ **noun** a humanitarian person.

– SYNONYMS **philanthropist,** altruist, benefactor, social reformer, good Samaritan, do-gooder.

– DERIVATIVES **hu·man·i·tar·i·an·ism** noun.

USAGE

Sentences such as *this is the worst humanitarian disaster this country has seen* show a loose use of **humanitarian** to mean 'human.' This use is especially common in journalism but is best avoided in careful writing.

hu·man·i·ty /(h)yo͞o'manitē/ ▸ **noun** (pl. **humanities**) **1** human beings as a whole. **2** the condition of being human. **3** sympathy and kindness toward other people. **4** (**humanities**) studies concerned with human culture, such as literature, art, or history.

– SYNONYMS **1 humankind,** mankind, man, people, the human race, Homo sapiens. **2 compassion,** brotherly love, fellow feeling, humaneness, kindness, consideration, understanding, sympathy, tolerance.

hu·man·ize /'(h)yo͞oməˌnīz/ ▸ **verb 1** make something more pleasant or suitable for people. **2** give a human character to something.
– DERIVATIVES **hu·man·i·za·tion** /ˌhyo͞oməni'zāsʜən/ noun.

hu·man·kind /'(h)yo͞omənˌkīnd/ ▸ **noun** human beings as a whole.

hu·man na·ture ▸ **noun** the general characteristics and feelings shared by all people.

hu·man·oid /'(h)yo͞oməˌnoid/ ▸ **adjective** resembling a human in appearance or character. ▸ **noun** a being resembling a human.

hu·man re·sourc·es ▸ **plural noun 1** the collective personnel of a business or organization. **2** the department of a business or organization that deals with the administration, management, and training of personnel.

hu·man rights ▸ **plural noun** basic rights to which every person is entitled, such as freedom.

hum·ble /'həmbəl/ ▸ **adjective** (**humbler, humblest**) **1** having or showing a modest or low estimate of one's own importance. **2** of low rank. **3** not large or special: *a small, humble chalet.*

– SYNONYMS **1 meek,** deferential, respectful, submissive, self-effacing, unassertive, modest, unassuming, self-deprecating. **2 lowly,** poor, undistinguished, mean, common, ordinary, simple, modest.
– ANTONYMS proud, arrogant.

▸ **verb** make someone feel less important or proud.

– SYNONYMS **humiliate,** demean, lower, degrade, debase, mortify, shame.

– DERIVATIVES **hum·bly** adverb.
– PHRASES **eat humble pie** make a humble apology and accept humiliation. [from former *umbles* meaning 'offal,' considered inferior food.]
– ORIGIN Latin *humilis* 'low, lowly.'

WORD TOOLKIT

humble ...	meek ...	deferential ...
opinion	voice	tone
servant	acceptance	treatment
apologies	husband/wife	standard
request	little mouse	society
heart	whimper	habits

hum·bug /ˈhəmˌbəg/ ▶ **noun 1** false or misleading talk or behavior. **2** a person who is not sincere or honest.
– DERIVATIVES **hum·bug·ger·y** noun.
– ORIGIN unknown.

hum·ding·er /ˈhəmˈdiNGər/ ▶ **noun** informal a remarkable or outstanding person or thing.
– ORIGIN unknown.

hum·drum /ˈhəmˌdrəm/ ▶ **adjective** lacking excitement or variety; dull.

– SYNONYMS **mundane,** dull, dreary, boring, tedious, monotonous, prosaic, routine, ordinary, everyday, run-of-the-mill, workaday, pedestrian.

– ORIGIN probably from **HUM**.

hu·mec·tant /(h)yo͞oˈmektənt/ ▶ **adjective** retaining or preserving moisture. ▶ **noun** a substance used to reduce the loss of moisture.
– ORIGIN from Latin *humectare* 'moisten.'

hu·mer·us /ˈ(h)yo͞omərəs/ ▶ **noun** (pl. **humeri** /-məˌrī/) the bone of the upper arm, between the shoulder and the elbow.
– DERIVATIVES **hu·mer·al** adjective.
– ORIGIN Latin, 'shoulder.'

hu·mid /ˈ(h)yo͞omid/ ▶ **adjective** (of the air or weather) damp and warm.

– SYNONYMS **muggy,** close, sultry, sticky, steamy, clammy, heavy.
– ANTONYMS dry, fresh.

– DERIVATIVES **hu·mid·ly** adverb.
– ORIGIN Latin *humidus*.

hu·mid·i·fi·er /(h)yo͞oˈmidəˌfī(ə)r/ ▶ **noun** a device that increases indoor atmospheric moisture.

hu·mid·i·fy /(h)yo͞oˈmidəˌfī/ ▶ **verb** (**humidifies, humidifying, humidified**) (often as adj. **humidified**) increase the level of moisture in air.
– DERIVATIVES **hu·mid·i·fi·ca·tion** /-ˌmidəfiˈkāSHən/ noun.

hu·mid·i·ty /(h)yo͞oˈmiditē/ ▶ **noun 1** the state or quality of being humid. **2** a measure of the amount of water vapor in the atmosphere or a gas.

hu·mi·dor /ˈ(h)yo͞omiˌdôr/ ▶ **noun** an airtight container for keeping cigars or tobacco moist.

hu·mil·i·ate /(h)yo͞oˈmilēˌāt/ ▶ **verb** make someone feel ashamed or foolish in front of another.

– SYNONYMS **embarrass,** mortify, humble, shame, disgrace, chasten, deflate, crush, squash, demean, take down a peg or two; informal show up, put down, cut down to size, make someone eat crow.
– ANTONYMS dignify.

– DERIVATIVES **hu·mil·i·a·ting** adjective **hu·mil·i·a·tor** noun.
– ORIGIN Latin *humiliare* 'make humble.'

hu·mil·i·a·tion /(h)yo͞oˌmilēˈāSHən/ ▶ **noun** the state of being humiliated: *the humiliation of having been left at the altar.*

– SYNONYMS **embarrassment,** mortification, shame, indignity, ignominy, disgrace, dishonor, degradation, discredit, loss of face, blow to one's pride.

hu·mil·i·ty /(h)yo͞oˈmilitē/ ▶ **noun** the quality of having a modest view of one's importance.

– SYNONYMS **modesty,** humbleness, meekness, respect, deference, diffidence.
– ANTONYMS pride.

hum·ming·bird /ˈhəmiNGˌbərd/ ▶ **noun** a small long-billed tropical American bird able to hover by beating its wings extremely fast.

hum·mock /ˈhəmək/ ▶ **noun** a small hill or mound.
– DERIVATIVES **hum·mock·y** adjective.
– ORIGIN unknown.

hum·mus /ˈho͝oməs, ˈhəm-/ ▶ **noun** a thick Middle Eastern dip made from chickpeas puréed with olive oil and garlic.
– ORIGIN Arabic.

hu·mon·gous /(h)yo͞oˈmäNGgəs, -ˈməNG-/ (also **humungous**) ▶ **adjective** informal very large; enormous.
– ORIGIN perhaps from **HUGE** and **MONSTROUS**.

hu·mor /ˈ(h)yo͞omər/ (Brit. **humour**) ▶ **noun 1** the quality of being amusing. **2** a state of mind: *her good humor vanished.* **3** (also **cardinal humor**) each of four fluids of the body that were formerly believed to determine a person's physical and mental qualities.

– SYNONYMS **1 comedy,** funny side, hilarity, absurdity, ludicrousness, satire, irony. **2 jokes,** jests, quips, witticisms, funny remarks, wit, comedy; informal gags, wisecracks. **3 mood,** temper, disposition, spirits.
– ANTONYMS seriousness.

▶ **verb** agree with someone's wishes so as to keep the person in a good mood.

– SYNONYMS **indulge,** accommodate, pander to, cater to, give in to, go along with, flatter, mollify, placate.

– DERIVATIVES **hu·mor·less** adjective.
– PHRASES **out of humor** in a bad mood.
– ORIGIN Latin 'moisture.'

hu·mor·ist /ˈ(h)yo͞omərist/ ▶ **noun** a writer or speaker who is known for being amusing.

hu·mor·ous /ˈ(h)yo͞omərəs/ ▶ **adjective 1** causing amusement. **2** having or showing a sense of humor.

– SYNONYMS **amusing,** funny, comic, comical, entertaining, diverting, witty, jocular, lighthearted, hilarious.
– ANTONYMS serious.

– DERIVATIVES **hu·mor·ous·ly** adverb **hu·mor·ous·ness** noun.

humour, etc. ▶ **noun** British spelling of **HUMOR**, etc.

hump /həmp/ ▶ **noun 1** a rounded raised mass of earth or land. **2** a rounded part projecting from the back of a camel or other animal or as an abnormality on a person's back.

– SYNONYMS **protuberance,** prominence, lump, bump, knob, protrusion, projection, bulge, swelling, growth, outgrowth.

▶ **verb 1** informal lift or carry something heavy with difficulty. **2** (as adj. **humped**) having a hump. **3** vulgar slang have sex with someone.

– SYNONYMS *he humped boxes up the stairs* **heave,** carry, lug, lift, hoist, heft; informal schlep, tote.

– DERIVATIVES **hump·less** adjective **hump·y** adjective.
– PHRASES **over the hump** informal past the most difficult part of something.
– ORIGIN probably related to German *humpe* 'hump.'

hump·back /'həmp,bak/ ▶ **noun 1** (also **humpback whale**) a baleen whale that has a hump and long white flippers. **2** another term for **HUNCHBACK**.
– DERIVATIVES **hump·backed** adjective.

hu·mun·gous ▶ **adjective** variant spelling of **HUMONGOUS**.

hu·mus /'(h)yo͞oməs/ ▶ **noun** the organic component of soil, formed from dead and dying leaves and other plant material.
– ORIGIN Latin, 'soil.'

Hum·vee /'həm'vē/ ▶ **noun** trademark a modern, multipurpose military vehicle.
– ORIGIN alteration, from the initials of *high-mobility multipurpose vehicle*.

Hun /hən/ ▶ **noun 1** a member of an Asiatic people who invaded Europe in the 4th–5th centuries. **2** informal, derogatory a German (especially during World Wars I and II).
– ORIGIN Greek *Hounnoi*.

hunch /hənch/ ▶ **verb** raise one's shoulders and bend the top of one's body forward. ▶ **noun** a belief that something is true, based on a feeling rather than evidence.

– SYNONYMS **feeling,** guess, suspicion, impression, inkling, idea, notion, fancy, intuition; informal gut feeling.

– ORIGIN unknown.

hunch·back /'hənch,bak/ ▶ **noun** offensive a person with a hump on his or her back.
– DERIVATIVES **hunch·backed** adjective.

hun·dred /'həndrid/ ▶ **cardinal number 1** ten more than ninety; 100. (Roman numeral: **c** or **C**.) **2** (**hundreds**) informal an unspecified large number. **3** (**the —— hundreds**) the years of a specified century: *the early nineteen hundreds*. **4** used to express whole hours in the twenty-four-hour system.
– DERIVATIVES **hun·dred·fold** adjective & adverb **hun·dredth** ordinal number.
– PHRASES **a** (or **one**) **hundred percent 1** entirely. **2** informal completely fit and healthy. **3** informal maximum effort and commitment.
– ORIGIN Old English.

hun·dred·weight /'həndrid,wāt/ ▶ **noun** (pl. same or **hundredweights**) **1** (also **short hundredweight**) a unit of weight equal to 100 lb (about 45.4 kg). **2** (also **metric hundredweight**) a unit of weight equal to 50 kg. **3** (also **long hundredweight**) Brit. a unit of weight equal to 112 lb (about 50.8 kg).

hung /həng/ past and past participle of **HANG** ▶ **adjective 1** (of a jury) unable to agree on a verdict. **2** (of an elected body in the UK and Canada) having no political party with an overall majority. **3** (**hung up about/on**) informal have an obsession or problem about.

Hun·gar·i·an /həng'ge(ə)rēən/ ▶ **noun 1** a person from Hungary. **2** the official language of Hungary. ▶ **adjective** relating to Hungary.

hun·ger /'hənggər/ ▶ **noun 1** a feeling of discomfort and a need to eat, caused by a lack of food. **2** a strong desire: *his hunger for money*.

– SYNONYMS **1 lack of food,** starvation, malnutrition, undernourishment. **2 desire,** craving, longing, yearning, hankering, appetite, thirst; informal itch.

▶ **verb** (**hunger after/for**) have a strong desire for someone or something.

– SYNONYMS *all actors hunger after such a role* **desire,** crave, long for, yearn for, pine for, ache for, hanker after, thirst for, lust for; informal itch for, be dying for.

– ORIGIN Old English.

hun·ger strike ▶ **noun** a prolonged refusal to eat, carried out as a protest.

hung·o·ver /'həng'ōvər/ (also **hung over**) ▶ **adjective** suffering from a hangover.

hun·gry /'hənggrē/ ▶ **adjective** (**hungrier, hungriest**) **1** feeling or showing hunger. **2** having a strong desire: *a party hungry for power*.

– SYNONYMS **1 ravenous,** famished, starving, starved, malnourished, undernourished, underfed; informal peckish. **2** *they are hungry for success* **eager,** keen, avid, longing, yearning, aching, greedy, craving, desirous of, hankering after; informal itching, dying.
– ANTONYMS full.

– DERIVATIVES **hun·gri·ly** adverb **hun·gri·ness** noun.

hunk /həngk/ ▶ **noun 1** a large piece cut or broken from something larger. **2** informal a strong, sexually attractive man.

– SYNONYMS **chunk,** wedge, block, slab, lump, square, gobbet.

– DERIVATIVES **hunk·y** (**hunkier, hunkiest**) adjective.
– ORIGIN probably Dutch or German.

hunk·er /'həngkər/ ▶ **verb 1** squat or crouch down low. **2** (**hunker down**) approach a task seriously.
– ORIGIN probably related to German *hocken*.

hun·kers /'həngkərz/ ▶ **plural noun** informal a person's haunches.
– ORIGIN from **HUNKER**.

hunk·y-do·ry /'həngkē 'dôrē/ ▶ **adjective** informal fine; going well.
– ORIGIN *hunky* from Dutch *honk* 'home'; the origin of *dory* is unknown.

hunt /hənt/ ▶ **verb 1** chase and kill a wild animal for sport or food. **2** try to find by thorough searching: *he desperately hunted for a new job*. **3** (**hunt someone down**) chase and capture someone. **4** (as adj. **hunted**) appearing alarmed or harassed.

– SYNONYMS **1 chase,** stalk, pursue, course, track, trail. **2 search,** seek, look high and low, scour the area.

▶ **noun 1** an act of hunting. **2** a group of people who meet regularly to hunt animals as a sport.

– SYNONYMS **1 chase,** pursuit. **2 search,** quest.

– DERIVATIVES **hunt·ing** noun.
– ORIGIN Old English.

hunt·er /'hən(t)ər/ ▶ **noun 1** a person or animal that hunts. **2** a breed of horse developed for stamina in fox hunting.
– DERIVATIVES **hunt·ress** /'həntris/ noun.

hunt·er-gath·er·er ▶ **noun** a member of a nomadic people who live chiefly by hunting, fishing, and harvesting wild food.

hunt·ing ground ▶ **noun** a place where people are likely to find what they are looking for.

Hun·ting·ton's dis·ease ▸ **noun** a hereditary disease marked by degeneration of brain cells, causing chorea (disorder of the nervous system) and progressive dementia.
– ORIGIN named after the American neurologist George *Huntington.*

hunts·man /'həntsmən/ ▸ **noun** (pl. **huntsmen**) **1** a person who hunts. **2** an official in charge of hounds during a fox hunt.

hur·dle /'hərdl/ ▸ **noun 1** one of a series of upright frames that athletes in a race must jump over. **2** (**hurdles**) a hurdle race. **3** a problem or difficulty that must be overcome: *the project must still clear several hurdles before work can start.*

– SYNONYMS **obstacle,** difficulty, problem, barrier, bar, snag, stumbling block, impediment, obstruction, complication, hindrance.

▸ **verb 1** run in a hurdle race. **2** jump over a hurdle or other obstacle while running.
– DERIVATIVES **hur·dler** noun.
– ORIGIN Old English.

hur·dy-gur·dy /'hərdē ˌgərdē/ ▸ **noun** (pl. **hurdy-gurdies**) **1** a musical instrument with a droning sound played by turning a handle, with keys worked by the other hand. **2** informal a barrel organ.
– ORIGIN probably imitating the instrument's sound.

hurl /hərl/ ▸ **verb 1** throw someone or something with great force. **2** shout abuse or insults.

– SYNONYMS **throw,** toss, fling, launch, pitch, cast, lob; informal chuck, sling.

– ORIGIN probably influenced by German *hurreln.*

hurl·ing /'hərliNG/ ▸ **noun** an Irish game resembling hockey, played with a shorter stick.

hurl·y-burl·y /'hərlē 'bərlē/ ▸ **noun** busy and noisy activity.
– ORIGIN from **HURL**.

hur·rah /ho͝o'rä, hə-/ (also **hooray, hurray**) ▸ **exclamation** used to express joy or approval.
– ORIGIN alteration of **HUZZAH**.

hur·ri·cane /'həriˌkān, 'hə-ri-/ ▸ **noun** a severe storm with a violent wind, in particular a tropical cyclone in the Caribbean.

– SYNONYMS **typhoon,** storm, windstorm, whirlwind, gale, tempest.

– ORIGIN Spanish *huracán.*

hur·ri·cane lamp ▸ **noun** an oil lamp in which the flame is protected from the wind by a glass chimney.

hur·ry /'hərē, 'hə-rē/ ▸ **verb** (**hurries, hurrying, hurried**) **1** move or act quickly. **2** do quickly or too quickly: *guided tours tend to be hurried.*

– SYNONYMS **1 be quick,** hurry up, hasten, speed up, run, dash, rush, race, scurry, scramble, scuttle, sprint; informal get a move on, step on it, hightail it, hotfoot it. **2 hustle,** hasten, push, urge. **3** (as adj. **hurried**) *a hurried greeting* **quick,** fast, swift, rapid, speedy, brisk, cursory, perfunctory, brief, short, fleeting. **4** (as adj. **hurried**) *a hurried decision* **hasty,** rushed, precipitate, spur-of-the-moment.
– ANTONYMS dawdle, delay.

▸ **noun 1** great speed or urgency in doing something. **2** a need for speed or haste; urgency: *relax, what's the hurry?*

– SYNONYMS **rush,** haste, speed, urgency, hustle and bustle.

– DERIVATIVES **hur·ried·ly** adverb.
– PHRASES **in a hurry** informal easily; readily: *you won't forget that in a hurry.*
– ORIGIN imitating the movement.

hurt /hərt/ ▸ **verb** (past and past part. **hurt**) **1** cause pain or injury to someone. **2** feel pain. **3** upset or distress someone.

– SYNONYMS **1 be painful,** ache, be sore, be tender, smart, sting, burn, throb; informal be agony. **2 injure,** wound, damage, disable, bruise, cut, gash, graze, scrape, scratch. **3 distress,** pain, wound, sting, upset, sadden, devastate, grieve, mortify.

▸ **noun 1** injury or pain. **2** unhappiness or distress.

– SYNONYMS **distress,** pain, suffering, grief, misery, anguish, upset, sadness, sorrow.

▸ **adjective 1** injured. **2** feeling distress.

– SYNONYMS **1** *my hurt hand* **injured,** wounded, bruised, grazed, cut, gashed, sore, painful, aching. **2** *Anne's hurt expression* **pained,** aggrieved, offended, distressed, upset, sad, mortified; informal miffed.

– ORIGIN Old French *hurter* 'to strike.'

hurt·ful /'hərtfəl/ ▸ **adjective** causing mental pain or distress.

– SYNONYMS **upsetting,** distressing, wounding, unkind, cruel, nasty, mean, malicious, spiteful.

– DERIVATIVES **hurt·ful·ly** adverb.

hur·tle /'hərtl/ ▸ **verb** move at great speed, especially in an uncontrolled way.

– SYNONYMS **speed,** rush, run, race, career, whiz, zoom, charge, shoot, streak, gallop, fly, go like the wind; informal belt, pelt, tear, barrel, go like a bat out of hell.

– ORIGIN from **HURT**.

hus·band /'həzbənd/ ▸ **noun** a married man considered in relation to his wife. ▸ **verb** use resources economically.
– ORIGIN Old Norse, 'master of a house.'

hus·band·man /'həzbəndmən/ ▸ **noun** (pl. **husbandmen**) old use a farmer.

hus·band·ry /'həzbəndrē/ ▸ **noun 1** the care, cultivation, and breeding of crops and animals; farming. **2** management and careful use of resources.

hush /həSH/ ▸ **verb 1** make or become quiet. **2** (**hush something up**) prevent something from becoming public.

– SYNONYMS **1 silence,** quiet (down), shush, gag, muzzle; informal shut up. **2** (**hush something up**) *management took steps to hush up the dangers* **keep secret,** conceal, hide, suppress, cover up, keep quiet about, sweep under the carpet.

▸ **noun** a silence.

– SYNONYMS **silence,** quiet, stillness, peace, calm, tranquility.
– ANTONYMS noise.

– ORIGIN from former *husht* 'silent,' 'be quiet!'

hush-hush ▸ **adjective** informal highly secret or confidential.

hush mon·ey ▸ **noun** informal money paid to someone to prevent them from revealing information.

hush pup·py ▸ **noun** a small deep-fried ball of cornmeal batter.

husk /həsk/ ▸ **noun** the dry outer covering of some fruits or seeds.

– SYNONYMS **shell,** hull, pod, case, covering, integument; Botany pericarp.

▶ **verb** remove the husk or husks from fruit or seeds.

– ORIGIN probably from German *hūske* 'sheath.'

husk·y[1] /ˈhəskē/ ▶ **adjective** (**huskier, huskiest**) **1** sounding low-pitched and slightly hoarse: *her deliciously husky voice.* **2** big and strong.

– SYNONYMS *a husky voice* **throaty,** gruff, gravelly, hoarse, croaky, rough, guttural, harsh, rasping, raspy.
– ANTONYMS shrill, soft.

– DERIVATIVES **husk·i·ly** adverb **husk·i·ness** noun.

husky[2] ▶ **noun** (pl. **huskies**) a powerful dog of a breed with a thick double coat, used in the Arctic for pulling sleds.
– ORIGIN from a North American dialect word meaning 'Eskimo.'

hus·sar /həˈzär/ ▶ **noun** a soldier in a light cavalry regiment that adopted a dress uniform modeled on that of the Hungarian light horsemen of the 15th century.
– ORIGIN Hungarian *huszár.*

hus·sy /ˈhəsē, ˈhəzē/ ▶ **noun** (pl. **hussies**) an immoral or impudent girl or woman.
– ORIGIN from **HOUSEWIFE**.

hust·ings /ˈhəstiNGz/ ▶ **noun** (treated as pl. or sing.) (**the hustings**) the political meetings and other campaigning that take place before an election.
– ORIGIN Old Norse, 'household assembly held by a leader.'

hus·tle /ˈhəsəl/ ▶ **verb** **1** push roughly; jostle. **2** (**hustle someone into**) pressure someone into doing something without time for consideration. **3** informal obtain something dishonestly or by aggressive methods. **4** informal work as a prostitute.

– SYNONYMS **1 push,** shove, thrust, manhandle, frogmarch. **2** *I was hustled into joining their church* **coerce,** force, compel, pressure, badger, hound, harass, nag, urge, goad, browbeat. **3** *we got hustled by a guy selling expired tickets* **swindle,** cheat, trick, bamboozle, hoodwink; informal con, fleece, rip off.

▶ **noun** busy movement and activity: *the hustle and bustle of the big city.*

– SYNONYMS **confusion,** bustle, tumult, hubbub, activity, action, liveliness, excitement, whirl; informal comings and goings, ballyhoo, hoo-ha, hullabaloo.

– ORIGIN Dutch *hutselen* 'shake, toss.'

hus·tler /ˈhəslər/ ▶ **noun** informal **1** an aggressively enterprising person; a go-getter. **2** an enterprising and often dishonest person, especially one trying to sell something. **3** an expert player, especially at pool or billiards, who pretends to be less skillful than they are and lures or challenges less skilled, especially amateur, players into games in order to win money from them. **4** a female prostitute. **5** a male prostitute, especially for homosexual clients.

hut /hət/ ▶ **noun** a small simple house or shelter.

– SYNONYMS **shack,** shanty, cabin, cabana, shelter, shed, lean-to, hovel.

– ORIGIN German *hütte.*

hutch /həCH/ ▶ **noun** **1** a box with a wire mesh front, used for keeping rabbits or other small domesticated animals. **2** a cupboard or dresser typically with open shelves above.
– ORIGIN Latin *hutica* 'storage chest.'

Hu·tu /ˈhōōtōō/ ▶ **noun** (pl. same or **Hutus** or **Bahutu** /baˈhōōtōō/) a member of a people forming the majority population in Rwanda and Burundi.

huz·zah /həˈzä/ ▶ **exclamation** old use or ironic used to express approval or delight.
– ORIGIN perhaps first used as a sailor's cry.

HVAC ▶ **abbreviation** heating, ventilation, and air conditioning.

hwy ▶ **abbreviation** highway.

hy·a·cinth /ˈhīəˌsinTH/ ▶ **noun** a plant with fragrant bell-shaped flowers.
– ORIGIN named after *Hyacinthus,* a youth loved by the god Apollo in Greek mythology.

hy·a·line /ˈhīəlin, -ˌlīn/ ▶ **adjective** Anatomy & Zoology having a glassy, translucent appearance: *hyaline cartilage.*

hy·brid /ˈhīˌbrid/ ▶ **noun** **1** the offspring of two plants or animals of different species or varieties, such as a mule. **2** a thing made by combining two different elements: *tae-bo, a hybrid of aerobics and Thai kick-boxing.*

– SYNONYMS **1 cross,** crossbreed, mixture, blend, combination, composite, fusion, amalgam. **2** (as adj.) *a hybrid organization* **composite,** crossbred, interbred, mixed, blended, compound.

– DERIVATIVES **hy·brid·i·ty** /hīˈbriditē/ noun.
– ORIGIN Latin *hybrida* 'offspring of a tame sow and wild boar, child of a freeman and slave, etc.'

hy·brid car ▶ **noun** a car with a gasoline engine and an electric motor, each of which can propel it.

hy·brid·ize /ˈhībriˌdīz/ ▶ **verb** breed individuals of two different species or varieties to produce hybrids.
– DERIVATIVES **hy·brid·i·za·tion** /ˌhībrədiˈzāSHən/ noun.

hy·dra /ˈhīdrə/ ▶ **noun** a minute freshwater invertebrate animal with a tubular body and a ring of tentacles around the mouth.
– ORIGIN named after the *Hydra* of Greek mythology, a snake with many heads that grew again if they were cut off.

hy·dran·gea /hīˈdrānjə/ ▶ **noun** a shrub with large white, blue, or pink clusters of flowers.
– ORIGIN from Greek *hudro-* 'water' + *angeion* 'container.'

hy·drant /ˈhīdrənt/ ▶ **noun** an upright water pipe with a nozzle to which a fire hose can be attached.

hy·drate ▶ **noun** /ˈhīˌdrāt/ a compound in which water molecules are chemically bound to another compound or an element. ▶ **verb** /ˌhīˈdrāt/ cause something to absorb or combine with water.
– DERIVATIVES **hy·dra·tion** /hīˈdrāSHən/ noun.

hy·drau·lic /hīˈdrôlik/ ▶ **adjective** relating to or operated by a liquid moving in a confined space under pressure.
– DERIVATIVES **hy·drau·li·cal·ly** adverb.
– ORIGIN from Greek *hudro-* 'water' + *aulos* 'pipe.'

hy·drau·lics /hīˈdrôliks/ ▶ **plural noun** (usu. treated as sing.) the branch of science concerned with the use of liquids moving under pressure to provide mechanical force.

hy·dra·zine /ˈhīdrəˌzēn/ ▶ **noun** Chemistry a colorless volatile alkaline liquid with powerful reducing properties, used in chemical synthesis and rocket fuels.

hy·dride /ˈhīˌdrīd/ ▶ **noun** Chemistry a compound of hydrogen with a metal.

hy·dro /ˈhīdrō/ ▶ **noun** (pl. **hydros**) **1** a hydroelectric power plant. **2** hydroelectricity.

hydro- (also **hydr-**) ▸ **combining form 1** relating to water or fluid: *hydraulic*. **2** combined with hydrogen: *hydrocarbon*.
– ORIGIN from Greek *hudōr* 'water.'

hy·dro·car·bon /ˈhīdrəˌkärbən/ ▸ **noun** a compound of hydrogen and carbon, such as those that are the chief components of petroleum and natural gas.

hy·dro·ceph·a·lus /ˌhīdrōˈsefələs/ ▸ **noun** a condition in which fluid accumulates in the brain.
– DERIVATIVES **hy·dro·ce·phal·ic** /ˌhīdrōsəˈfalik/ adjective **hy·dro·ceph·a·ly** noun.
– ORIGIN from Greek *hudro-* 'water' + *kephalē* 'head.'

hy·dro·chlo·ric ac·id /ˌhīdrəˈklôrik/ ▸ **noun** a corrosive acid containing hydrogen and chlorine.

hy·dro·chlo·ride /ˌhīdrəˈklôˌrīd/ ▸ **noun** a compound of an organic base with hydrochloric acid.

hy·dro·cor·ti·sone /ˌhīdrəˈkôrtiˌzōn/ ▸ **noun** a steroid hormone used to treat inflammation and rheumatism.

hy·dro·cy·an·ic ac·id /ˌhīdrōsīˈanik/ ▸ **noun** a highly poisonous acidic solution of hydrogen cyanide.

hy·dro·dy·nam·ics /ˌhīdrōdīˈnamiks/ ▸ **plural noun** (treated as sing.) the branch of science concerned with the forces acting on or exerted by fluids (especially liquids).
– DERIVATIVES **hy·dro·dy·nam·ic** adjective **hy·dro·dy·nam·ic·al·ly** adverb.

hy·dro·e·lec·tric /ˌhīdrōəˈlektrik/ ▸ **adjective** relating to the generation of electricity using flowing water to drive a turbine that powers a generator.
– DERIVATIVES **hy·dro·e·lec·tric·i·ty** /-əlekˈtrisitē/ noun.

hy·dro·foil /ˈhīdrəˌfoil/ ▸ **noun 1** a boat fitted with structures (known as foils) that lift the hull clear of the water to increase speed. **2** each of the foils of a hydrofoil.

hy·dro·gel /ˈhīdrəˌjel/ ▸ **noun** a gel in which the liquid component is water.

hy·dro·gen /ˈhīdrəjən/ ▸ **noun** a colorless, odorless, highly flammable gas that is the lightest of the chemical elements.

hy·dro·gen·ate /ˈhīdrəjəˌnāt, hīˈdräjənāt/ ▸ **verb** combine a substance with hydrogen.
– DERIVATIVES **hy·dro·gen·a·tion** /ˌhīdrəjəˈnāshən, hīˌdräjə-/ noun.

hy·dro·gen bomb ▸ **noun** a nuclear bomb whose destructive power comes from the fusion of isotopes of hydrogen (deuterium and tritium).

hy·dro·gen per·ox·ide ▸ **noun** a colorless liquid used in some disinfectants and bleaches.

hy·dro·gen sul·fide ▸ **noun** a colorless poisonous gas with a smell of rotten eggs, made by the action of acids on sulfides.

hy·drog·ra·phy /hīˈdrägrəfē/ ▸ **noun** the science of surveying and charting seas, lakes, and rivers.
– DERIVATIVES **hy·drog·ra·pher** noun **hy·dro·graph·ic** /ˌhīdrəˈgrafik/ adjective.

hy·drol·o·gy /hīˈdräləjē/ ▸ **noun** the branch of science concerned with the properties and distribution of water on the earth's surface.
– DERIVATIVES **hy·dro·log·ic** /ˌhīdrəˈläjik/ adjective **hy·dro·log·i·cal** /ˌhīdrəˈläjikəl/ adjective **hy·drol·o·gist** noun.

hy·drol·y·sis /hīˈdräləsis/ ▸ **noun** Chemistry the chemical breakdown of a compound due to reaction with water.
– DERIVATIVES **hy·dro·lyt·ic** /ˌhīdrəˈlitik/ adjective.

hy·dro·lyze /ˈhīdrəˌlīz/ (Brit **hydrolyse**) ▸ **verb** break down a compound by chemical reaction with water.

hy·drom·e·ter /hīˈdrämitər/ ▸ **noun** an instrument for measuring the density of liquids.

hy·drop·a·thy /hīˈdräpəTHē/ ▸ **noun** the treatment of illness through the use of water, either internally or by external means such as steam baths.
– DERIVATIVES **hy·dro·path·ic** /ˌhīdrəˈpaTHik/ adjective.

hy·dro·phil·ic /ˌhīdrəˈfilik/ ▸ **adjective** having a tendency to mix with or dissolve in water.

hy·dro·pho·bi·a /ˌhīdrəˈfōbēə/ ▸ **noun 1** extreme fear of water, especially as a symptom of rabies. **2** rabies.

hy·dro·pho·bic /ˌhīdrəˈfōbik/ ▸ **adjective 1** tending to repel or fail to mix with water. **2** relating to or suffering from hydrophobia.

hy·dro·phone /ˈhīdrəˌfōn/ ▸ **noun** a microphone that detects sound waves under water.

hy·dro·plane /ˈhīdrəˌplān/ ▸ **noun 1** a light, fast motorboat designed to skim over the surface of water. **2** a finlike attachment that enables a moving submarine to rise or fall in the water. **3** a seaplane. ▸ **verb** another term for **AQUAPLANE**.

hy·dro·pon·ics /ˌhīdrəˈpäniks/ ▸ **plural noun** (treated as sing.) the growing of plants in sand, gravel, or liquid, with added nutrients but without soil.
– DERIVATIVES **hy·dro·pon·ic** adjective **hy·dro·pon·i·cal·ly** adverb.
– ORIGIN from Greek *hudōr* 'water' + *ponos* 'labor.'

hy·dro·sphere /ˈhīdrəˌsfir/ ▸ **noun** the seas, lakes, and other waters of the earth's surface, considered as a group.

hy·dro·stat·ic /ˌhīdrəˈstatik/ ▸ **adjective** relating to the pressure and other characteristics of liquid that is not in motion.
– DERIVATIVES **hy·dro·stat·ics** plural noun.

hy·dro·ther·a·py /ˌhīdrəˈTHerəpē/ ▸ **noun 1** the use of exercises in a pool to treat conditions such as arthritis. **2** another term for **HYDROPATHY**.

hy·dro·ther·mal /ˌhīdrəˈTHərməl/ ▸ **adjective** relating to the action of heated water in the earth's crust.
– DERIVATIVES **hy·dro·ther·mal·ly** adverb.

hy·dro·ther·mal vent ▸ **noun** an opening in the sea floor out of which heated mineral-rich water flows.

hy·drous /ˈhīdrəs/ ▸ **adjective** containing water.

hy·drox·ide /hīˈdräkˌsīd/ ▸ **noun** a compound containing OH negative ions together with a metallic element.

hy·drox·yl /hīˈdräksəl/ ▸ **noun** Chemistry the radical –OH, present in alcohols and many other organic compounds.

hy·dro·zo·an /ˌhīdrəˈzōən/ ▸ **noun** a small marine or freshwater animal related to jellyfish and corals and belonging to a group that includes hydras and the Portuguese man-of-war. ▸ **adjective** relating to the hydrozoans.

hy·e·na /hīˈēnə/ ▸ **noun** a doglike carnivorous African mammal with an erect mane.
– ORIGIN Greek *huaina* 'female pig.'

hy·giene /ˈhīˌjēn/ ▸ **noun** conditions or practices that help to prevent illness or disease, especially the keeping of oneself and one's surroundings clean.

– SYNONYMS **cleanliness,** sanitation, sterility, purity, disinfection.

– ORIGIN from Greek *hugieinē tekhnē* 'art of health.'

hy·gi·en·ic /hī'jenik, -'jē-/ ▶ **adjective** clean and free of the organisms that spread disease.

– SYNONYMS **sanitary,** clean, germ-free, disinfected, sterilized, sterile, antiseptic, aseptic.
– ANTONYMS insanitary.

– DERIVATIVES **hy·gi·en·i·cal·ly** adverb.

CHOOSE THE RIGHT WORD

See **SANITARY**.

hy·gien·ist /hī'jenəst, -jē-/ ▶ **noun** a person working with a dentist who specializes in scaling and polishing teeth and giving advice on oral hygiene.

hy·grom·e·ter /hī'grämitər/ ▶ **noun** an instrument for measuring humidity.
– ORIGIN Greek *hugros* 'wet.'

hy·gro·scop·ic /ˌhīgrə'skäpik/ ▶ **adjective** tending to absorb moisture from the air.

hy·ing /'hī-iNG/ present participle of **HIE**.

hy·men /'hīmən/ ▶ **noun** a membrane that partially closes the opening of the vagina and is usually broken on the first occasion a woman or girl has sex.
– ORIGIN Greek *humēn* 'membrane.'

hy·me·nop·ter·an /ˌhīmə'näptərən/ ▶ **noun** an insect having four transparent wings, belonging to a large group that includes the bees, wasps, and ants.
– DERIVATIVES **hy·me·nop·ter·ous** /-tərəs/ adjective.
– ORIGIN Greek *humenopteros* 'membrane-winged.'

hymn /him/ ▶ **noun** a religious song of praise, especially a Christian song in praise of God. ▶ **verb** praise or celebrate something.
– ORIGIN Greek *humnos* 'ode or song in praise.'

hym·nal /'himnəl/ ▶ **noun** a book of hymns.

hym·no·dy /'himnədē/ ▶ **noun** the singing or composing of hymns.
– ORIGIN Greek *humnōidia*.

hy·oid /'hīˌoid/ ▶ **noun** a U-shaped bone in the neck that supports the tongue. ▶ **adjective** relating to this bone.
– ORIGIN from Greek *huoeidēs* 'shaped like the letter upsilon (ʊ).'

hype[1] /hīp/ informal ▶ **noun** extravagant or excessive publicity or sales promotion. ▶ **verb** publicize something in an excessive or extravagant way.
– ORIGIN unknown.

hype[2] ▶ **verb** (**be hyped up**) informal be stimulated or very excited.
– ORIGIN abbreviation of **HYPODERMIC**.

hy·per /'hīpər/ ▶ **adjective** informal full of nervous energy; hyperactive.

hyper- ▶ **prefix 1** over; beyond; above: *hypersonic*. **2** excessively; above normal: *hyperactive*.
– ORIGIN Greek *huper* 'over, beyond.'

hy·per·ac·tive /ˌhīpər'aktiv/ ▶ **adjective** abnormally or extremely active.
– DERIVATIVES **hy·per·ac·tiv·i·ty** /-ˌak'tivitē/ noun.

hy·per·bar·ic /ˌhīpər'barik/ ▶ **adjective** relating to or involving a gas at a pressure greater than normal.
– ORIGIN from Greek *barus* 'heavy.'

hy·per·bo·la /hī'pərbələ/ ▶ **noun** (pl. **hyperbolas** or **hyperbolae** /-lē/) a symmetrical curve formed when a cone is cut by a plane nearly parallel to the cone's axis.
– ORIGIN from Greek *huperbolē* 'excess.'

hy·per·bo·le /hī'pərbəlē/ ▶ **noun** a way of speaking or writing that deliberately exaggerates things for effect.

– SYNONYMS **exaggeration,** overstatement, magnification, embroidery, embellishment, excess, overkill.
– ANTONYMS understatement.

– ORIGIN Greek *huperbolē* 'excess.'

hy·per·bol·ic /ˌhīpər'bälik/ ▶ **adjective 1** (of language) deliberately exaggerated. **2** relating to a hyperbola.
– DERIVATIVES **hy·per·bol·i·cal·ly** adverb.

hy·per·crit·i·cal /ˌhīpər'kritikəl/ ▶ **adjective** excessively and unreasonably critical.

hy·per·drive /'hīpərˌdrīv/ ▶ **noun** (in science fiction) a supposed propulsion system for travel in hyperspace.

hy·per·e·mi·a /ˌhīpə'rēmēə/ ▶ **noun** an excess of blood in the vessels supplying an organ or other part of the body.
– DERIVATIVES **hy·per·e·mic** /-'rēmik/ adjective.

hy·per·gly·ce·mi·a /ˌhīpərglī'sēmēə/ (Brit. **hyperglycaemia**) ▶ **noun** an excess of glucose in the bloodstream, often associated with the common form of diabetes.
– DERIVATIVES **hy·per·gly·ce·mic** adjective.

hy·per·i·cin /hī'perəsin/ ▶ **noun** a substance found in the leaves and flowers of St. John's wort, believed to have properties similar to those of antidepressant drugs.
– ORIGIN from **HYPERICUM**.

hy·per·i·cum /hī'perikəm/ ▶ **noun** a yellow-flowered plant of a family that includes St. John's wort.
– ORIGIN Greek *hupereikon*.

hy·per·in·fla·tion /hīpərin'flāsHən/ ▶ **noun** inflation of prices or wages occurring at a very high rate.

hy·per·ki·net·ic /ˌhīpərkə'netik/ ▶ **adjective 1** frenetic; hyperactive. **2** relating to mental disorders marked by hyperactivity and inability to concentrate.

hy·per·link /'hīpərˌliNGk/ ▶ **noun** Computing a link from a hypertext document to another location, activated by clicking on a highlighted word or image.

hy·per·mar·ket /'hīpərˌmärkit/ ▶ **noun** Brit. a very large supermarket.

hy·per·me·di·a /ˌhīpər'mēdēə/ ▶ **noun** Computing an extension to hypertext providing multimedia facilities, such as sound and video.

hy·per·re·al /ˌhīpə(r)'rēəl/ ▶ **adjective 1** exaggerated in comparison to reality. **2** (of art) extremely realistic.

hy·per·sen·si·tive /ˌhīpər'sensitiv/ ▶ **adjective** abnormally or excessively sensitive.

hy·per·son·ic /ˌhīpər'sänik/ ▶ **adjective 1** relating to speeds of more than five times the speed of sound (Mach 5). **2** relating to sound frequencies above about a billion hertz.

hy·per·space /'hīpərˌspās/ ▶ **noun 1** space of more than three dimensions. **2** (in science fiction) a notional space–time continuum in which it is possible to travel faster than light.

hy·per·ten·sion /ˌhīpər'tensHən/ ▶ **noun** abnormally high blood pressure.
– DERIVATIVES **hy·per·ten·sive** /-'tensiv/ adjective.

hy·per·text /'hīpərˌtekst/ ▶ **noun** Computing a software system allowing users to move quickly between related documents or sections of text.

hy·per·ther·mi·a /ˌhīpər'THərmēə/ ▶ **noun** the condition of having an abnormally high body temperature.

hy·per·thy·roid·ism /ˌhīpərˈTHīroiˌdizəm/ ▶ **noun** overactivity of the thyroid gland, resulting in an increased rate of metabolism.
– DERIVATIVES **hy·per·thy·roid** adjective.

hy·per·ton·ic /ˌhīpərˈtänik/ ▶ **adjective** **1** having a higher osmotic pressure than a particular fluid, typically a body fluid or intracellular fluid. **2** having abnormally high muscle tone.

hy·per·tro·phy /hīˈpərtrəfē/ ▶ **noun** abnormal enlargement of an organ or tissue resulting from an increase in size of its cells.
– DERIVATIVES **hy·per·troph·ic** /ˌhīpərˈträfik, -ˈtrō-/ adjective **hy·per·troph·ied** /-trəfēd/ adjective.
– ORIGIN from Greek *-trophia* 'nourishment.'

hy·per·ven·ti·late /ˌhīpərˈventlˌāt/ ▶ **verb** **1** breathe at an abnormally rapid rate. **2** be or become overexcited.
– DERIVATIVES **hy·per·ven·ti·la·tion** /-ˌventlˈāSHən/ noun.

hy·pha /ˈhīfə/ ▶ **noun** (pl. **hyphae** /-fē/) Botany each of the filaments that make up the mycelium of a fungus.
– ORIGIN Greek *huphē* 'web.'

hy·phen /ˈhīfən/ ▶ **noun** the sign (-) used to join words to show that they have a combined meaning or that they are grammatically linked, or to divide a word into parts between one part and the next.
– ORIGIN from Greek *huphen* 'together.'

USAGE

When phrasal verbs such as **build up** and **catch up** are made into nouns, they are written either as one word (*a buildup of pressure*) or with a hyphen (*we're always playing catch-up*). However, a normal phrasal verb should not have a hyphen: *continue to build up your pension*.

hy·phen·ate /ˈhīfəˌnāt/ ▶ **verb** write words with a hyphen.
– DERIVATIVES **hy·phen·a·tion** /ˌhīfəˈnāSHən/ noun.

hyp·na·gog·ic /ˌhipnəˈgäjik, -ˈgō-/ (also **hypnogogic**) ▶ **adjective** relating to the state immediately before sleep.
– DERIVATIVES **hyp·na·gog·i·a** noun.

hyp·no·sis /hipˈnōsis/ ▶ **noun** the practice of causing a person to enter a state of consciousness in which they lose the power of voluntary action and respond readily to suggestions or commands.
– ORIGIN Greek *hupnos* 'sleep.'

hyp·no·ther·a·py /ˌhipnōˈTHerəpē/ ▶ **noun** the use of hypnosis to treat physical or mental problems.
– DERIVATIVES **hyp·no·ther·a·pist** noun.

hyp·not·ic /hipˈnätik/ ▶ **adjective** **1** producing or relating to hypnosis. **2** causing one to feel very relaxed or drowsy. **3** (of a drug) causing sleep.
– DERIVATIVES **hyp·not·i·cal·ly** adverb.

hyp·no·tism /ˈhipnəˌtizəm/ ▶ **noun** the study or practice of hypnosis.
– DERIVATIVES **hyp·no·tist** noun.

hyp·no·tize /ˈhipnəˌtīz/ ▶ **verb** put someone into a state of hypnosis.

– SYNONYMS **entrance,** spellbind, enthrall, transfix, captivate, bewitch, enrapture, grip, rivet, absorb.

hy·po /ˈhīpō/ ▶ **noun** **1** the chemical sodium thiosulfate used as a photographic fixer. **2** (pl. **hypos**) informal a hypodermic needle or syringe.

hypo- (also **hyp-**) ▶ **prefix** **1** under: *hypodermic*. **2** below normal: *hypoglycemia*.
– ORIGIN from Greek *hupo* 'under.'

hy·po·al·ler·gen·ic /ˌhīpōˌalərˈjenik/ ▶ **adjective** unlikely to cause an allergic reaction.

hy·po·chlo·rous ac·id /ˌhīpəˈklôrəs/ ▶ **noun** a weak acid with oxidizing properties formed when chlorine dissolves in cold water, used in bleaching and water treatment.
– DERIVATIVES **hy·po·chlo·rite** /-ˌrīt/ noun.

hy·po·chon·dri·a /ˌhīpəˈkändrēə/ ▶ **noun** excessive anxiety about one's health.
– ORIGIN Greek *hupokhondria*, referring to the soft body area below the ribs, once thought to be the seat of melancholy.

hy·po·chon·dri·ac /ˌhīpəˈkändrēˌak/ ▶ **noun** a person who is excessively worried about their health.

hy·poc·ri·sy /hiˈpäkrisē/ ▶ **noun** (pl. **hypocrisies**) the practice of claiming to have higher moral standards than is the case.
– ORIGIN Greek *hupokrisis* 'acting of a theatrical part.'

hyp·o·crite /ˈhipəˌkrit/ ▶ **noun** a person who claims to have higher moral standards than is the case.
– DERIVATIVES **hyp·o·crit·i·cal** adjective **hyp·o·crit·i·cal·ly** adverb.

hy·po·der·mic /ˌhīpəˈdərmik/ ▶ **adjective** **1** (of a needle or syringe) used to inject a drug or other substance beneath the skin. **2** relating to the region immediately beneath the skin. ▶ **noun** a hypodermic syringe or injection.
– DERIVATIVES **hy·po·der·mi·cal·ly** adverb.
– ORIGIN from Greek *derma* 'skin.'

hy·po·gly·ce·mi·a /ˌhīpōglīˈsēmēə/ (Brit. **hypoglycaemia**) ▶ **noun** lack of glucose in the bloodstream.
– DERIVATIVES **hy·po·gly·ce·mic** adjective.

hy·po·ma·ni·a /ˌhīpəˈmānēə/ ▶ **noun** a mild form of mania, marked by elation and hyperactivity.
– DERIVATIVES **hy·po·man·ic** /-ˈmanik/ adjective.

hy·po·ten·sion /ˌhīpəˈtenSHən/ ▶ **noun** abnormally low blood pressure.
– DERIVATIVES **hy·po·ten·sive** adjective.

hy·pot·e·nuse /hīˈpätnˌ(y)o͞os/ ▶ **noun** the longest side of a right triangle, opposite the right angle.
– ORIGIN from Greek *hupoteinousa grammē* 'subtending line.'

hy·po·thal·a·mus /ˌhīpəˈTHaləməs/ ▶ **noun** (pl. **hypothalami** /-ˌmī/) a region of the front part of the brain below the thalamus, controlling body temperature, thirst, and hunger, and involved in sleep and emotional activity.
– DERIVATIVES **hy·po·tha·lam·ic** /ˌhīpōˌTHəˈlamik/ adjective.

hy·po·ther·mi·a /ˌhīpəˈTHərmēə/ ▶ **noun** the condition of having an abnormally low body temperature.
– ORIGIN from Greek *thermē* 'heat.'

hy·poth·e·sis /hīˈpäTHəsis/ ▶ **noun** (pl. **hypotheses** /-ˌsēz/) a proposed explanation of something made on the basis of limited evidence, used as a starting point for further investigation.
– ORIGIN Greek *hupothesis* 'foundation.'

hy·poth·e·size /hīˈpäTHəˌsīz/ ▶ **verb** put forward an explanation as a hypothesis.

hy·po·thet·i·cal /ˌhīpəˈTHetikəl/ ▶ **adjective** based on an assumption or imagined situation rather than fact.

– SYNONYMS **theoretical,** speculative, conjectured, notional, supposed, assumed; academic, imaginary.
– ANTONYMS actual.

– DERIVATIVES **hy·po·thet·i·cal·ly** adverb.

hy·po·thy·roid·ism /ˌhīpōˈᴛʜīroiˌdizəm/ ▶ **noun** abnormally low activity of the thyroid gland, resulting in retarded growth and mental development.
– DERIVATIVES **hy·po·thy·roid** adjective.

hy·pox·i·a /hīˈpäksēə/ ▶ **noun** a situation in which not enough oxygen reaches the body tissues.
– DERIVATIVES **hy·pox·ic** adjective.

hy·rax /ˈhīˌraks/ ▶ **noun** a small mammal with a short tail, found in Africa and Arabia.
– ORIGIN Greek *hurax* 'shrew-mouse.'

hys·sop /ˈhisəp/ ▶ **noun** a small bushy plant whose bitter minty leaves are used in cooking and herbal medicine.
– ORIGIN Greek *hyssōpos*.

hys·ter·ec·to·my /ˌhistəˈrektəmē/ ▶ **noun** (pl. **hysterectomies**) a surgical operation to remove all or part of the uterus.
– ORIGIN from Greek *hustera* 'womb.'

hys·te·ri·a /hiˈsterēə, -ˈsti(ə)rēə/ ▶ **noun 1** extreme or uncontrollable emotion or excitement: *a note of hysteria crept into his voice.* **2** dated a psychological disorder involving a change in self-awareness or the conversion of psychological stress into physical symptoms.

– SYNONYMS **frenzy,** feverishness, hysterics, agitation, mania, panic, alarm, distress.
– ANTONYMS calm.

– ORIGIN Greek *hustera* 'womb' (hysteria once being thought to be caused by a disorder of the womb).

hys·ter·ic /hiˈsterik/ ▶ **noun 1** (**hysterics**) wildly emotional behavior. **2** (**hysterics**) informal uncontrollable laughter. **3** a person suffering from hysteria.

hys·ter·i·cal /hiˈsterikəl/ ▶ **adjective 1** in a state of uncontrolled excitement or other strong emotion. **2** informal very funny.

– SYNONYMS **1 overwrought,** overemotional, out of control, frenzied, frantic, wild, beside oneself, manic, delirious; informal in a state. **2 very funny,** hilarious, uproarious, rib-tickling; informal side-splitting, priceless, a scream, a hoot.
– ANTONYMS calm.

– DERIVATIVES **hys·ter·i·cal·ly** adverb.

Hz ▶ **abbreviation** hertz.

I[1] (also i) ▶ **noun** (pl. **Is** or **I's**) **1** the ninth letter of the alphabet. **2** the Roman numeral for one.

I[2] /ī/ ▶ **pronoun** (first person sing.) used by a speaker to refer to himself or herself.
– ORIGIN Old English.

I[3] ▶ **abbreviation 1** (preceding a highway number) Interstate. **2** (**I.**) Island(s) or Isle(s). ▶ **symbol** the chemical element iodine.

IA ▶ **abbreviation** Iowa.

IAEA ▶ **abbreviation** International Atomic Energy Agency.

i·amb /ˈīamb/ ▶ **noun** Poetry a metrical foot consisting of one short (or unstressed) syllable followed by one long (or stressed) syllable.
– ORIGIN Greek *iambos*.

i·am·bic /īˈambik/ Poetry ▶ **adjective** (of poetry or poetic meter) using iambs. ▶ **noun** (**iambics**) verse using iambs.

IAQ ▶ **abbreviation** indoor air quality.

i·at·ro·gen·ic /īˌatrəˈjenik/ ▶ **adjective** (of illness) caused by medical treatment.
– ORIGIN Greek *iatros* 'physician.'

I-beam ▶ **noun** a girder that has the shape of a capital I when viewed in section.

I·be·ri·an /īˈbi(ə)rēən/ ▶ **adjective** relating to Iberia (the peninsula that consists of modern Spain and Portugal). ▶ **noun** a person from Iberia.

i·bex /ˈīˌbeks/ ▶ **noun** (pl. **ibexes**) a wild mountain goat with long curved horns.
– ORIGIN Latin.

IBF ▶ **abbreviation** International Boxing Federation.

ib·id. /ˈibid/ ▶ **adverb** in the same source (referring to the work cited in the previous note).
– ORIGIN abbreviation of Latin *ibidem* 'in the same place.'

i·bis /ˈībis/ ▶ **noun** (pl. same or **ibises**) a large wading bird with a long downcurved bill, a long neck, and long legs.
– ORIGIN Greek.

IBS ▶ **abbreviation** irritable bowel syndrome.

i·bu·pro·fen /ˌībyo͞oˈprōfən/ ▶ **noun** a synthetic compound used as a painkiller and to reduce inflammation.
– ORIGIN from the chemical name.

IC ▶ **abbreviation** integrated circuit.

ICBM ▶ **abbreviation** intercontinental ballistic missile.

ICC ▶ **abbreviation 1** Interstate Commerce Commission. **2** International Criminal Court.

ICE ▶ **abbreviation 1** Immigration and Customs Enforcement. **2** in case of emergency; referring to a program in which cell phone users store their emergency contact information in their phone's address book.

ice /īs/ ▶ **noun 1** frozen water, a brittle transparent crystalline solid. **2** a frozen mixture of fruit juice or flavored water and sugar.

> – SYNONYMS **1** icicles, black ice, frost, permafrost, hoar (frost); literary rime. **2 sorbet,** water ice, sherbet, gelato, ice cream. **3 coldness,** coolness, frostiness, iciness, hostility, unfriendliness.

▶ **verb 1** decorate something with icing. **2** (usu. **ice up/over**) become covered or blocked with ice.
– DERIVATIVES **iced** adjective.
– PHRASES **break the ice** start the conversation at the beginning of a social gathering so as to make people feel more relaxed. **on ice 1** (of wine, food, or biological material) kept chilled by being surrounded by ice. **2** (especially of a plan or proposal) held in reserve for future consideration: *the recommendation was put on ice*. **3** (of an entertainment) performed by skaters: *Cinderella on Ice*. **on thin ice** in a precarious or risky situation.
– ORIGIN Old English.

> **WORD LINKS**
>
> **glacial** *relating to ice*

ice age ▶ **noun** a period when ice covered much of the earth's surface, in particular during the Pleistocene period.

ice·berg /ˈīsˌbərg/ ▶ **noun** a large mass of ice floating in the sea.
– PHRASES **the tip of the iceberg** the small noticeable part of a much larger situation or problem.
– ORIGIN Dutch *ijsberg*.

ice·berg let·tuce ▶ **noun** a kind of lettuce having a closely packed round head of crisp pale leaves.

ice·box /ˈīsˌbäks/ ▶ **noun 1** a chilled container for keeping food cold. **2** dated a refrigerator.

ice·break·er /ˈīsˌbrākər/ ▶ **noun** a ship designed for breaking a channel through ice.

ice cap ▶ **noun** a permanent covering of ice over a large area, especially at the North and South Poles.

ice cream ▶ **noun** a semi-soft frozen dessert made with sweetened and flavored milk fat.

ice cream cone ▶ **noun 1** a cone-shaped wafer for holding ice cream. **2** ice cream served in such a cone.

ice danc·ing ▶ **noun** a form of ice skating involving choreographed dance moves performed by skaters in pairs.

iced tea ▶ **noun** a chilled drink of black tea served in a glass.

ice field ▶ **noun** a large flat expanse of floating ice, especially in Polar regions.

ice fish·ing ▶ **noun** fishing through holes drilled in the ice on a lake or reservoir.
– DERIVATIVES **ice-fish** verb.

ice floe ▶ **noun** see **FLOE**.

ice hock·ey ▶ **noun** a form of hockey played on an ice rink between two teams of six skaters.

Ice·land·er /ˈīsləndər/ ▶ **noun** a person from Iceland.

Ice·lan·dic /īsˈlandik/ ▶ **noun** the language of Iceland. ▶ **adjective** relating to Iceland or its language.

ice pack ▶ **noun** a bag filled with ice and held against part of the body to reduce swelling or lower temperature.

ice pick ▶ **noun** a small pick used by climbers or for breaking ice.

ice skate ▶ **noun** a boot with a blade attached to the sole, used for skating on ice. ▶ **verb** skate on ice as a sport or pastime.
– DERIVATIVES **ice skat·er** noun **ice skat·ing** noun.

I Ching /ˈē ˈCHiNG, ˈjiNG/ ▶ **noun** an ancient Chinese manual for foretelling the future.
– ORIGIN Chinese, 'book of changes.'

ich·thy·ol·o·gy /ˌikTHēˈäləjē/ ▶ **noun** the branch of zoology concerned with fish.
– DERIVATIVES **ich·thy·o·log·i·cal** /-əˈläjikəl/ adjective **ich·thy·ol·o·gist** noun.
– ORIGIN from Greek *ikhthus* 'fish.'

ich·thy·o·saur /ˈikTHēəˌsôr/ (also **ichthyosaurus** /ˌikTHēəˈsôrəs/) ▶ **noun** a fossil marine reptile with a long pointed head, four flippers, and a vertical tail.

i·ci·cle /ˈīsikəl/ ▶ **noun** a hanging, tapering piece of ice formed when dripping water freezes.
– ORIGIN from Old English.

ic·ing /ˈīsiNG/ ▶ **noun** a mixture of sugar with liquid or butter and often flavoring, used as a coating for cakes or cookies.
– PHRASES **the icing on the cake** an additional thing that makes something already good even better.

ick·y /ˈikē/ ▶ **adjective** (**ickier, ickiest**) informal **1** unpleasantly sticky. **2** distastefully sentimental. **3** nasty or repulsive.
– ORIGIN perhaps related to **SICK**[1] or to the child's word *ickle* 'little.'

i·con /ˈīˌkän/ ▶ **noun 1** (also **ikon**) (in the Orthodox Church) a painting of Jesus or another holy figure, typically on wood, that is itself treated as holy and used as an aid to prayer. **2** a person or thing admired as a symbol of a particular idea, quality, time, etc.: *an iron-jawed icon of American manhood.* **3** a small symbol on a computer screen that represents a program, option, or window.
– ORIGIN Greek *eikōn* 'image.'

i·con·ic /īˈkänik/ ▶ **adjective** referring to someone or something regarded as a symbol of a particular idea, quality, period, etc.: *he became an iconic figure for directors around the world.*
– DERIVATIVES **i·con·i·cal·ly** adverb.

i·con·o·clast /īˈkänəˌklast/ ▶ **noun 1** a person who attacks cherished beliefs or established values and practices. **2** (in the past) a person who destroyed images used in religious worship.
– DERIVATIVES **i·con·o·clasm** noun **i·con·o·clas·tic** /īˌkänəˈklastik/ adjective.
– ORIGIN from Greek *eikōn* 'image' + *klan* 'to break.'

i·co·nog·ra·phy /ˌīkəˈnägrəfē/ ▶ **noun** (pl. **iconographies**) **1** the use or study of images or symbols in visual arts. **2** the images or symbols associated with a person or movement. **3** the illustration of a subject by drawings or figures.
– DERIVATIVES **i·co·nog·ra·pher** noun **i·con·o·graph·ic** /īˌkänəˈgrafik/ adjective.

i·co·nol·o·gy /ˌīkəˈnäləjē/ ▶ **noun 1** the study of visual imagery and its symbolism and interpretation, especially in social or political terms. **2** symbolism: *the iconology of a work of art.*
– DERIVATIVES **i·con·o·log·i·cal** /īˌkänəˈläjikəl/ adjective.

i·co·nos·ta·sis /ˌīkəˈnästəsis/ ▶ **noun** (pl. **iconostases** /-ˌsēz/) a screen bearing icons, separating the sanctuary of many Eastern churches from the nave.
– ORIGIN from Greek *eikōn* 'image' + *stasis* 'standing.'

i·co·sa·he·dron /īˌkōsəˈhēdrən, īˌkäsə-/ ▶ **noun** (pl. **icosahedra** /-drə/ or **icosahedrons**) a three-dimensional shape with twenty plane faces.
– DERIVATIVES **i·co·sa·he·dral** /-drəl/ adjective.
– ORIGIN from Greek *eikosaedros* 'twenty-faced.'

ICT ▶ **abbreviation** information and computing technology.

ICU ▶ **abbreviation** intensive care unit.

i·cy /ˈīsē/ ▶ **adjective** (**icier, iciest**) **1** covered with or consisting of ice. **2** very cold: *an icy wind.* **3** very unfriendly or hostile: *her voice was icy.*

> – SYNONYMS **1 iced (over),** frozen, frosty, slippery, treacherous; literary rimy. **2 freezing,** chill, biting, bitter, raw, arctic. **3 unfriendly,** hostile, forbidding, cold, chilly, frosty, stern.

– DERIVATIVES **i·ci·ly** adverb **i·ci·ness** noun.

ID ▶ **abbreviation 1** identification or identity. **2** Idaho.

id /id/ ▶ **noun** Psychoanalysis the part of the unconscious mind consisting of a person's basic inherited instincts, needs, and feelings. Compare with **EGO** and **SUPEREGO**.
– ORIGIN Latin, 'that.'

id. ▶ **abbreviation** idem.

I'd /īd/ ▶ **contraction 1** I had. **2** I should or I would.

IDE ▶ **abbreviation** Computing Integrated Drive Electronics, a standard for interfacing computers and their peripherals.

i·de·a /īˈdēə/ ▶ **noun 1** a thought or suggestion about a possible course of action. **2** a mental impression: *shop around to get an idea of what things cost.* **3** a belief: *nineteenth-century ideas about drinking.* **4** (**the idea**) the aim or purpose: *the idea was to bring people into bookstores.*

> – SYNONYMS **1 concept,** notion, conception, thought. **2 plan,** scheme, design, proposal, proposition, suggestion, aim, intention, objective, goal. **3 thought,** theory, view, opinion, feeling, belief. **4 sense,** feeling, suspicion, fancy, inkling, hunch, notion. **5 estimate,** approximation, guess, conjecture; informal guesstimate.

– ORIGIN Greek, 'form, pattern.'

i·de·al /īˈdē(ə)l/ ▶ **adjective 1** most suitable; perfect: *an ideal opportunity to brush up on her French.* **2** desirable or perfect but existing only in the imagination: *in an ideal world, we might have made a different decision.*

> – SYNONYMS **perfect,** faultless, exemplary, classic, archetypal, quintessential, model, ultimate, utopian, fairy-tale.

▶ **noun 1** a person or thing regarded as perfect. **2** a principle or standard that is worth trying to achieve: *tolerance and freedom, the liberal ideals.*

> – SYNONYMS **1** *an ideal to aim at* **model,** pattern, archetype, exemplar, example, perfection, epitome, last word. **2** *liberal ideals* **principle,** standard, value, belief, conviction, ethos.

– DERIVATIVES **i·de·al·ly** adverb.

i·de·al gas ▸ **noun** Chemistry a hypothetical gas whose molecules occupy negligible space and have no interactions, and that consequently obeys the gas laws exactly.

i·de·al·ism /ī'dē(ə),lizəm/ ▸ **noun 1** the belief that ideals can be achieved, even when this is unrealistic. **2** (in art or literature) the representation of things as perfect or better than in reality.
– DERIVATIVES **i·de·al·ist** noun.

i·de·al·is·tic /ī,dē(ə)'listik/ ▸ **adjective** believing that ideals can be achieved, even when this is unrealistic: *some say I'm drawing a wildly idealistic portrait of what the Church can become.*

> – SYNONYMS **Utopian,** visionary, romantic, quixotic, unrealistic, impractical.

– DERIVATIVES **i·de·al·is·ti·cal·ly** /ī,dē(ə)'listik(ə)lē/ adverb.

i·de·al·ize /ī'dē(ə),līz/ ▸ **verb** (often as adj. **idealized**) regard or represent as perfect or better than in reality: *her idealized account of their life together.*
– DERIVATIVES **i·de·al·i·za·tion** /ī,dē(ə)li'zāsHən/ noun.

i·de·a·tion /,īdē'āsHən/ ▸ **noun** Psychology the formation of ideas or concepts: *paranoid ideation.*
– DERIVATIVES **i·de·a·tion·al** /-sHənl/ adjective **i·de·a·tion·al·ly** adverb.

i·dée fixe /ē,dā 'fēks/ ▸ **noun** (pl. **idées fixes** pronunc. same) an idea that dominates someone's mind; an obsession.
– ORIGIN French, 'fixed idea.'

i·dem /'ī,dem, 'idem/ ▸ **adverb** used in quotations to indicate an author or word that has just been mentioned.
– ORIGIN Latin, 'the same.'

i·den·ti·cal /ī'dentikəl/ ▸ **adjective 1** exactly alike or the same: *four girls in identical green outfits.* **2** (of twins) developed from a single fertilized ovum, and therefore of the same sex and very similar in appearance.

> – SYNONYMS **(exactly) the same,** indistinguishable, twin, duplicate, interchangeable, alike, matching.
> – ANTONYMS different.

– DERIVATIVES **i·den·ti·cal·ly** adverb.
– ORIGIN Latin *identicus.*

WORD TOOLKIT

identical ...	same ...	equivalent ...
twins	time	amounts
results	place	levels
sequences	page	units
copies	sex	value
circumstances	day	doses
DNA	team	rates

i·den·ti·fi·ca·tion /ī,dentəfi'kāsHən/ ▸ **noun 1** the action of identifying someone or something or the fact of being identified. **2** an official document or other proof of one's identity.

> – SYNONYMS **1 recognition,** singling out, pinpointing, naming. **2 determination,** establishing, ascertainment, discovery, diagnosis. **3 ID,** papers, documents, credentials, card, pass, badge.

i·den·ti·fy /ī'dentə,fī/ ▸ **verb** (**identifies, identifying, identified**) **1** prove or recognize who or what a person or thing is: *he couldn't identify his attackers.* **2** recognize something as being worthy of attention: *a system that ensures that the student's needs are identified.* **3** (**identify with**) feel that one understands or shares the feelings of another person. **4** (**identify with**) associate someone or something closely with: *the policy was closely identified with the prime minister.*

> – SYNONYMS **1 recognize,** pick out, spot, point out, pinpoint, put one's finger on, name. **2 determine,** establish, ascertain, make out, discern, distinguish. **3** *we identify sport with glamour* **associate,** link, connect, relate. **4** *he **identified with** the team captain* **empathize with,** sympathize with, understand, relate to, feel for.

– DERIVATIVES **i·den·ti·fi·a·ble** adjective **i·den·ti·fi·a·bly** adverb **i·den·ti·fi·er** noun.

i·den·ti·ty /ī'dentitē/ ▸ **noun** (pl. **identities**) **1** the fact of being who or what a person or thing is: *he knows the identity of the bombers.* **2** the characteristics determining who or what a person or thing is and distinguishing them from others: *a sense of national identity.* **3** a close similarity or feeling of understanding.

> – SYNONYMS **individuality,** self, personality, character, originality, distinctiveness, uniqueness.

– ORIGIN Latin *identitas,* from *idem* 'same.'

i·den·ti·ty cri·sis ▸ **noun** Psychiatry a period of uncertainty and confusion in which a person's sense of identity becomes insecure, typically due to a change in their expected aims or role in society.

i·den·ti·ty theft ▸ **noun** the fraudulent use of another person's name and other personal information in order to obtain money or goods.

id·e·o·gram /'idēə,gram, 'īdēə-/ (also **ideograph** /'idēə,graf, 'īdēə-/) ▸ **noun** a character used in a writing system to symbolize the idea of a thing rather than the sounds used to say it (e.g., a numeral).

i·de·o·logue /'īdēə,lôg, -,läg, 'idēə-/ ▸ **noun** a person who follows a system of ideas and principles in a strict and inflexible way.

i·de·ol·o·gy /,īdē'äləjē, ,idē-/ ▸ **noun** (pl. **ideologies**) **1** a system of ideas and principles forming the basis of an economic or political theory. **2** the set of beliefs held by a particular social group: *bourgeois ideology.*

> – SYNONYMS **belief**; doctrine, creed, theory.

– DERIVATIVES **i·de·o·log·i·cal** /-ə'läjikəl/ adjective **i·de·o·log·i·cal·ly** /-ə'läjik(ə)lē/ adverb **i·de·ol·o·gist** noun.
– ORIGIN from Greek *idea* 'form.'

ides /īdz/ ▸ **plural noun** (in the ancient Roman calendar) a day falling roughly in the middle of each month, from which other dates were calculated.
– ORIGIN Latin *idus* (plural).

id·i·o·cy /'idēəsē/ ▸ **noun** (pl. **idiocies**) extremely stupid behavior.

id·i·o·lect /'idēə,lekt/ ▸ **noun** the way that a particular person uses language.
– ORIGIN from Greek *idios* 'own, distinct.'

id·i·om /'idēəm/ ▸ **noun 1** a group of words whose meaning is different from the meanings of the individual words (e.g., *rain cats and dogs*). **2** a form of language and grammar used by particular people at a particular time or place. **3** a style of expression in music or art that is characteristic of a particular group or place: *a restrained classical idiom.*
– ORIGIN Greek *idiōma* 'private property.'

id·i·o·mat·ic /,idēə'matik/ ▸ **adjective** using or relating to expressions that are natural to a native speaker: *he spoke fluent, idiomatic English.*

> – SYNONYMS **colloquial,** everyday, conversational, vernacular, natural.

– DERIVATIVES **id·i·o·mat·i·cal·ly** adverb.

id·i·o·path·ic /ˌidēəˈpaᴛʜik/ ▶ **adjective** relating to any disease or condition that arises spontaneously or for which the cause is unknown.

id·i·o·syn·cra·sy /ˌidēəˈsiɴɢkrəsē/ ▶ **noun** (pl. **idiosyncrasies**) **1** a distinctive or unusual way of behaving or thinking peculiar to a particular person. **2** a distinctive characteristic of something: *the idiosyncrasies of the prison system.*

– SYNONYMS **peculiarity,** oddity, eccentricity, mannerism, quirk, characteristic.

– ORIGIN Greek *idiosunkrasia.*

id·i·o·syn·crat·ic /ˌidēəsiɴɢˈkratik, ˌidē-ō-/ ▶ **adjective** peculiar or distinctively individual: *her idiosyncratic diet.*
– DERIVATIVES **id·i·o·syn·crat·i·cal·ly** adverb.

id·i·ot /ˈidēət/ ▶ **noun 1** informal a stupid person. **2** old use a mentally disabled person.

– SYNONYMS **fool,** ass, halfwit, blockhead, dunce, simpleton; informal nincompoop, clod, dimwit, dummy, fathead, numbskull; informal nitwit, twit, dork, twerp, moron, schmuck.
– ANTONYMS genius.

– ORIGIN Greek *idiōtēs* 'layman, ignorant person.'

id·i·ot·ic /ˌidēˈätik/ ▶ **adjective** very stupid or foolish.
– DERIVATIVES **id·i·ot·i·cal·ly** adverb.

id·i·ot sa·vant ▶ **noun** (pl. **idiot savants** or **idiots savants** pronunc. same) a person who has a mental disability or learning difficulties but is gifted in a particular way, such as the ability to perform feats of memory.
– ORIGIN French, 'knowledgeable idiot.'

i·dle /ˈīdl/ ▶ **adjective 1** tending to avoid work; lazy. **2** not working or not in use. **3** having no purpose or effect: *she did not make idle threats.*

– SYNONYMS **1 lazy,** indolent, slothful, shiftless, work-shy. **2 unemployed,** jobless, out of work, unoccupied; informal on the dole. **3 unoccupied,** spare, empty, unfilled. **4 frivolous,** trivial, trifling, minor, insignificant, unimportant, empty, meaningless, vain.
– ANTONYMS industrious, busy.

▶ **verb 1** spend time doing nothing. **2** (of an engine) run slowly while out of gear.
– DERIVATIVES **i·dle·ness** noun **i·dler** noun **i·dly** adverb.
– ORIGIN Old English, 'empty, useless.'

CHOOSE THE RIGHT WORD

See **LOITER**.

i·dol /ˈīdl/ ▶ **noun 1** a statue or picture of a god that is itself worshiped. **2** a person who is greatly admired: *a soccer idol.*

– SYNONYMS **1 icon,** effigy, statue, figurine, totem. **2 hero,** heroine, star, superstar, icon, celebrity, darling; informal pinup, heartthrob.

– ORIGIN Greek *eidōlon.*

i·dol·a·try /īˈdälətrē/ ▶ **noun 1** the practice of worshiping statues or pictures of a god or gods. **2** extreme admiration or devotion.
– DERIVATIVES **i·dol·a·ter** noun **i·dol·a·trous** adjective.
– ORIGIN from Greek *eidōlon* 'idol' + *-latreia* 'worship.'

i·dol·ize /ˈīdlˌīz/ ▶ **verb** admire or love someone greatly or excessively.

– SYNONYMS **hero-worship,** worship, revere, venerate, look up to, exalt; informal put on a pedestal.

– DERIVATIVES **i·dol·i·za·tion** /ˌīdl-iˈzāsʜən/ noun.

CHOOSE THE RIGHT WORD

See **REVERE**.

i·dyll /ˈīdl/ ▶ **noun 1** a very happy or peaceful period or situation. **2** a short poem or piece of writing describing a picturesque country scene or incident.
– ORIGIN Greek *eidullion* 'little form.'

i·dyl·lic /īˈdilik/ ▶ **adjective** extremely happy, peaceful, or picturesque.

– SYNONYMS **perfect,** wonderful, blissful, halcyon, happy; literary Arcadian.

– DERIVATIVES **i·dyl·li·cal·ly** adverb.

i.e. ▶ **abbreviation** that is to say.
– ORIGIN from Latin *id est* 'that is.'

IEEE /ˌaɪ ˌtrɪpəl ˈi/ ▶ **abbreviation** Institute of Electrical and Electronics Engineers.

if /if/ ▶ **conjunction 1** on the condition or in the event that. **2** despite the possibility or fact that. **3** whether. **4** every time that; whenever. **5** expressing a polite request or tentative opinion. **6** expressing surprise or regret.

– SYNONYMS **provided,** providing, on condition that, presuming, supposing, assuming, as long as, in the event that.

▶ **noun** a situation that is not certain: *there are so many ifs and buts in the policy.*
– PHRASES **if anything** used to suggest tentatively that something may be the case (often the opposite of something previously implied): *I haven't made much of this—if anything, I've played it down.* **if so** if that is the case.
– ORIGIN Old English.

USAGE

If and **whether** are more or less interchangeable in sentences like *I'll see if he left an address* and *I'll see whether he left an address,* although **whether** is more formal and more suitable for written use.

if·fy /ˈifē/ ▶ **adjective** (**iffier, iffiest**) informal **1** uncertain. **2** seeming bad or wrong in some way.

ig·loo /ˈiglo͞o/ ▶ **noun** a dome-shaped Eskimo house, typically built from blocks of solid snow.
– ORIGIN Inuit, 'house.'

ig·ne·ous /ˈignēəs/ ▶ **adjective** Geology (of rock) formed when molten rock cools and solidifies.
– ORIGIN Latin *ignis* 'fire.'

ig·nite /igˈnīt/ ▶ **verb 1** catch fire or set on fire. **2** provoke or stir up: *the words ignited new fury in him.*

– SYNONYMS **1 catch fire,** burst into flames, explode. **2 light,** set fire to, set alight, kindle.
– ANTONYMS extinguish.

– DERIVATIVES **ig·ni·ter** noun.
– ORIGIN Latin *ignis* 'fire.'

ig·ni·tion /igˈnisʜən/ ▶ **noun 1** the action of catching fire or setting something on fire. **2** the process of starting the combustion of fuel in the cylinders of an internal-combustion engine. **3** the mechanism for bringing this about.

ig·no·ble /igˈnōbəl/ ▶ **adjective** (**ignobler, ignoblest**) **1** not good or honest; dishonorable. **2** of humble origin or social status.
– DERIVATIVES **ig·no·bly** adverb.
– ORIGIN Latin *ignobilis.*

ig·no·min·i·ous /ˌignəˈminēəs/ ▸ **adjective** deserving or causing public disgrace or shame: *an ignominious defeat.*
– DERIVATIVES **ig·no·min·i·ous·ly** adverb.
– ORIGIN Latin *ignominiosus.*

ig·no·min·y /ˈignəˌminē, igˈnäminē/ ▸ **noun** public shame or disgrace.

ig·no·ra·mus /ˌignəˈrāməs, -ˈraməs/ ▸ **noun** (pl. **ignoramuses**) an ignorant or stupid person.
– ORIGIN Latin, 'we do not know.'

ig·no·rance /ˈignərəns/ ▸ **noun** lack of knowledge or information.

> – SYNONYMS **1 lack of knowledge,** lack of education, unenlightenment. **2 unfamiliarity,** incomprehension, inexperience, innocence.
> – ANTONYMS education, knowledge.

ig·no·rant /ˈignərənt/ ▸ **adjective 1** lacking knowledge or education. **2** (often **ignorant of**) not informed about or aware of a particular subject or fact: *I was ignorant of the effects of radiotherapy.* **3** informal not polite; rude.

> – SYNONYMS **1 uneducated,** unschooled, illiterate, uninformed, unenlightened, inexperienced, unsophisticated. **2 unaware,** unconscious, unfamiliar, unacquainted, uninformed; informal in the dark.
> – ANTONYMS educated, knowledgeable.

– DERIVATIVES **ig·no·rant·ly** adverb.
– ORIGIN from Latin *ignorare* 'not know.'

WORD TOOLKIT

ignorant ...	illiterate ...	uninformed ...
masses	peasants	readers
fool	adults	investors
comments	villagers	voters
bigot	parents	decision
bliss	children	consumers

ig·nore /igˈnôr/ ▸ **verb 1** deliberately take no notice of: *I shouted to her but she ignored me.* **2** fail to consider something important.

> – SYNONYMS **1 snub,** look right through, cold-shoulder, take no notice of, pay no attention to; informal blank. **2 disregard,** take no account of, fail to observe, disobey, defy, overlook, brush aside, turn a blind eye to.
> – ANTONYMS acknowledge, obey.

– ORIGIN Latin *ignorare* 'not know.'

CHOOSE THE RIGHT WORD

See **NEGLECT**.

i·gua·na /iˈgwänə/ ▸ **noun** a large tropical American lizard with a spiny crest along the back.
– ORIGIN Arawak.

i·ke·ba·na /ˌikəˈbänə, ˌēke-/ ▸ **noun** the art of Japanese flower arrangement.
– ORIGIN Japanese, 'living flowers.'

i·kon ▸ **noun** variant spelling of **ICON** (sense 1).

IL ▸ **abbreviation** Illinois.

il·e·um /ˈilēəm/ ▸ **noun** (pl. **ilea** /ˈilēə/) the third and lowest part of the small intestine, between the jejunum and the cecum.
– DERIVATIVES **il·e·al** /-əl/ adjective.
– ORIGIN Latin, variant of **ILIUM**.

il·i·ac /ˈilēˌak/ ▸ **adjective** relating to the ilium or the nearby regions of the lower body.

il·i·um /ˈilēəm/ ▸ **noun** (pl. **ilia** /ˈilēə/) the large broad bone forming the upper part of each half of the pelvis.
– ORIGIN Latin.

ilk /ilk/ ▸ **noun** a type: *fascists, racists, and others of that ilk.*
– ORIGIN Old English, related to **ALIKE**.

ill /il/ ▸ **adjective 1** not in good health; unwell. **2** bad, harmful, or unfavorable: *she suffered no ill effects.*

> – SYNONYMS **1 unwell,** sick, poorly, peaked, indisposed, nauseous, queasy; informal under the weather. **2** *ill effects* **harmful,** damaging, detrimental, deleterious, adverse, injurious, destructive, dangerous.
> – ANTONYMS well, beneficial.

▸ **adverb 1** badly, wrongly, or imperfectly: *ill-chosen.* **2** only with difficulty: *she could ill afford the cost.*

> – SYNONYMS **1 barely,** scarcely, hardly, only just. **2 inadequately,** insufficiently, poorly, badly.

▸ **noun 1** a problem or misfortune: *the ills of society.* **2** evil or harm.

> – SYNONYMS **problem,** trouble, difficulty, misfortune, trial, tribulation; informal headache, hassle.

– PHRASES **ill at ease** uncomfortable or embarrassed. **speak** (or **think**) **ill of** say (or think) something critical about.
– ORIGIN Old Norse, 'evil, difficult.'

Ill. ▸ **abbreviation** Illinois.

I'll /īl/ ▸ **contraction** I will; I shall.

ill-ad·vised ▸ **adjective** unwise or badly thought out.

ill-bred ▸ **adjective** badly brought up or rude.

ill-con·ceived ▸ **adjective** not carefully planned or considered.

il·le·gal /i(l)ˈlēgəl/ ▸ **adjective** against the law.

> – SYNONYMS **unlawful,** illicit, illegitimate, criminal, fraudulent, corrupt, dishonest, outlawed, banned, forbidden, prohibited, proscribed, unlicensed, unauthorized; informal crooked, shady.
> – ANTONYMS legal.

– DERIVATIVES **il·le·gal·i·ty** noun (pl. **illegalities**) **il·le·gal·ly** adverb.

USAGE

Illegal and **unlawful** have slightly different meanings. An illegal act is against the law, but an **unlawful** one only goes against the rules that apply in a particular situation. For example, handball in soccer is **unlawful**, but not **illegal**.

WORD TOOLKIT

illegal ...	fraudulent ...	corrupt ...
drugs	claims	officials
dumping	transaction	government
weapons	documents	politician
substances	accounting	system
gambling	conveyance	regime
entry	election	society
parking	charges	judge

il·leg·i·ble /i(l)ˈlejəbəl/ ▸ **adjective** not clear enough to be read.

> – SYNONYMS **unreadable,** indecipherable, unintelligible.

– DERIVATIVES **il·leg·i·bil·i·ty** noun **il·leg·i·bly** adverb.

il·le·git·i·mate /ˌi(l)ləˈjitəmit/ ▶ **adjective** **1** not allowed by law or a particular set of rules: *the strike was condemned as illegitimate.* **2** (of a child) having parents who are not married to each other.

– SYNONYMS **illegal,** unlawful, illicit, criminal, felonious, fraudulent, corrupt, dishonest; informal crooked, shady.
– ANTONYMS legal, legitimate.

– DERIVATIVES **il·le·git·i·ma·cy** noun **il·le·git·i·mate·ly** adverb.

ill-equipped ▶ **adjective** not having the necessary equipment or resources.

ill-fat·ed ▶ **adjective** destined to fail or have bad luck.

ill-found·ed ▶ **adjective** not based on fact or reliable evidence.

ill-got·ten ▶ **adjective** acquired by illegal or unfair means.

il·lib·er·al /i(l)ˈlib(ə)rəl/ ▶ **adjective** restricting freedom of thought or behavior.

il·lic·it /i(l)ˈlisit/ ▶ **adjective** forbidden by law, rules, or accepted standards: *an illicit relationship.*

– SYNONYMS **illegal,** unlawful, criminal, outlawed, banned, forbidden, prohibited, proscribed, unlicensed, unauthorized, improper, disapproved of.
– ANTONYMS legal.

– DERIVATIVES **il·lic·it·ly** adverb.
– ORIGIN Latin *illicitus.*

il·lim·it·a·ble /i(l)ˈlimitəbəl/ ▶ **adjective** having no limits or end.
– DERIVATIVES **il·lim·it·a·bly** adverb.

il·lit·er·ate /i(l)ˈlitərit/ ▶ **adjective** **1** unable to read or write. **2** having no knowledge of a particular subject or activity: *voters who are politically illiterate.*
– DERIVATIVES **il·lit·er·a·cy** /-əsē/ noun.
– PHRASES **functionally illiterate** lacking the literacy necessary for coping with most jobs and many everyday situations.

WORD TOOLKIT

See **IGNORANT**.

ill-judged ▶ **adjective** lacking careful thought; unwise.

ill-man·nered ▶ **adjective** having bad manners; rude.

ill-na·tured ▶ **adjective** bad-tempered and sullen.

ill·ness /ˈilnis/ ▶ **noun** a disease or period of sickness.

– SYNONYMS **sickness,** poor health, disease, ailment, disorder, complaint, indisposition, malady, affliction, infection; informal bug, virus.
– ANTONYMS health.

il·log·i·cal /i(l)ˈläjikəl/ ▶ **adjective** not sensible or based on sound reasoning.

– SYNONYMS **irrational,** unreasonable, erroneous, invalid, spurious, fallacious, specious.

– DERIVATIVES **il·log·i·cal·i·ty** noun (pl. **illogicalities**) **il·log·i·cal·ly** adverb.

ill-starred ▶ **adjective** unlucky.

ill-tem·pered ▶ **adjective** irritable or surly.

ill-treat ▶ **verb** treat someone or something cruelly.
– DERIVATIVES **ill-treat·ment** noun.

il·lu·mi·nate /iˈlo͞oməˌnāt/ ▶ **verb** **1** light something up. **2** (usu. as adj. **illuminating**) help to clarify or explain something: *a most illuminating discussion.* **3** decorate a page or initial letter in a manuscript with gold, silver, or colored designs.

– SYNONYMS (as adj. **illuminating**) **informative,** enlightening, revealing, explanatory, instructive, helpful, educational.
– ANTONYMS confusing.

– DERIVATIVES **il·lu·mi·na·tor** noun.
– ORIGIN Latin *illuminare* 'illuminate,' from *lumen* 'light.'

il·lu·mi·na·ti /iˌlo͞oməˈnätē/ ▶ **plural noun** people claiming to possess special knowledge or understanding.
– ORIGIN plural of Italian *illuminato* or Latin *illuminatus* 'enlightened.'

il·lu·mi·na·tion /iˌlo͞oməˈnāsʜən/ ▶ **noun** **1** lighting or light. **2** (**illuminations**) a display of lights on a building or other structure. **3** understanding or enlightenment: *he had moments of intense spiritual illumination.*

– SYNONYMS **light,** lighting, radiance, gleam, glow, glare.

il·lu·mine /iˈlo͞omən/ ▶ **verb** literary light something up.

ill-use /ˈil ˈyo͞oz/ ▶ **verb** treat someone badly.

il·lu·sion /iˈlo͞ozʜən/ ▶ **noun** **1** a false or unreal idea or belief: *he had no illusions about her.* **2** something that seems to exist but does not, or that seems to be something it is not: *he uses color to give an illusion of space.*

– SYNONYMS **1 delusion,** misapprehension, misconception, false impression, mistaken impression, fantasy, dream, fancy. **2 appearance,** impression, semblance. **3 mirage,** hallucination, apparition, figment of the imagination, trick of the light.

– ORIGIN Latin, from *illudere* 'to mock.'

il·lu·sion·ist /iˈlo͞ozʜənist/ ▶ **noun** a magician or conjuror.

il·lu·sive /iˈlo͞osiv/ ▶ **adjective** chiefly literary deceptive; illusory.

il·lu·so·ry /iˈlo͞osərē, -zərē/ ▶ **adjective** apparently real but not actually so.

– SYNONYMS **false,** imagined, imaginary, fanciful, unreal, sham, fallacious.
– ANTONYMS genuine.

– DERIVATIVES **il·lu·so·ri·ly** adverb.

il·lus·trate /ˈiləˌstrāt/ ▶ **verb** **1** provide a book, magazine, etc., with pictures. **2** make something clear by using examples, charts, or pictures. **3** act as an example of: *the World Cup illustrated what high standards our players must achieve.*

– SYNONYMS **1 decorate,** ornament, accompany, support. **2 explain,** elucidate, clarify, demonstrate, show, point up; informal get across/over.

– DERIVATIVES **il·lus·tra·tor** noun.
– ORIGIN Latin *illustrare* 'light up.'

il·lus·tra·tion /ˌiləˈstrāsʜən/ ▶ **noun** **1** a picture illustrating a book, magazine, etc. **2** the action of illustrating something. **3** an example that proves something or helps to explain it: *the case provides a good illustration of the legal problems.*

– SYNONYMS **1 picture,** drawing, sketch, figure, plate, image, print. **2 example,** sample, case, instance, exemplification, demonstration.

il·lus·tra·tive /iˈləstrətiv, ˈiləˌstrātiv/ ▶ **adjective** **1** serving as an example or explanation. **2** relating to

pictorial illustration.
– DERIVATIVES **il·lus·tra·tive·ly** adverb.

il·lus·tri·ous /i'ləstrēəs/ ▶ **adjective** famous and admired for past achievements.
– ORIGIN Latin *illustris* 'clear, bright.'

ill will ▶ **noun** hostility or animosity toward someone.

IM ▶ **abbreviation** Computing **1** instant message. **2** instant messaging.

im- ▶ **prefix** variant spelling of **IN-**[1], **IN-**[2] before *b*, *m*, *p* (as in *imbibe*, *immodest*, *impart*).

I'm /īm/ ▶ **contraction** I am.

im·age /'imij/ ▶ **noun 1** a likeness of a person or thing in the form of a picture or statue. **2** a picture of someone or something seen on a television or computer screen, through a lens, or as a reflection. **3** the impression that a person, organization, or product presents to the public: *the band's squeaky-clean image*. **4** a picture in the mind. **5** a person or thing that closely resembles another: *he's the image of his father*. **6** a simile or metaphor.

– SYNONYMS **1 likeness,** depiction, portrayal, representation, painting, picture, portrait, drawing, photograph. **2 conception,** impression, perception, notion, idea. **3 persona,** profile, face.

▶ **verb** make or form an image of someone or something.
– DERIVATIVES **im·age·less** adjective.
– ORIGIN Latin *imago*.

WORD LINKS

iconography *study of images*

CHOOSE THE RIGHT WORD

See **EMBLEM**.

im·ag·er /'imijər/ ▶ **noun** an electronic or other device that records images.

im·age·ry /'imij(ə)rē/ ▶ **noun 1** language using similes and metaphors that produces images in the mind. **2** visual symbolism. **3** visual images as a whole.

im·ag·i·na·ble /i'maj(ə)nəbəl/ ▶ **adjective** possible to be thought of or believed.
– DERIVATIVES **i·mag·i·na·bly** adverb.

im·ag·i·nar·y /i'majə͵nerē/ ▶ **adjective 1** existing only in the imagination. **2** Mathematics expressed in terms of the square root of −1 (represented by *i* or *j*): *imaginary numbers*.

– SYNONYMS **unreal,** nonexistent, fictional, pretend, make-believe, invented, made-up, illusory.
– ANTONYMS real.

– DERIVATIVES **im·ag·i·nar·i·ly** adverb.

im·ag·i·na·tion /i͵majə'nāsHən/ ▶ **noun 1** the faculty or action of forming ideas or images in the mind: *her story captured the public's imagination*. **2** the ability of the mind to be creative or resourceful.

– SYNONYMS **1 mind's eye,** fancy. **2 creativity,** vision, inventiveness, resourcefulness, ingenuity, originality.

im·ag·i·na·tive /i'maj(ə)nətiv/ ▶ **adjective** having or showing creativity or inventiveness.

– SYNONYMS **creative,** visionary, inventive, resourceful, ingenious, original, innovative.

– DERIVATIVES **i·mag·i·na·tive·ly** adverb **i·mag·i·na·tive·ness** noun.

CHOOSE THE RIGHT WORD

See **CREATIVE**.

im·ag·ine /i'majən/ ▶ **verb 1** form a mental image of someone or something. **2** believe that something unreal exists. **3** suppose or assume: *we imagined that Mabel would move away after Ned died*.

– SYNONYMS **1 visualize,** envisage, picture, see in one's mind's eye, dream up, think up/of, conceive. **2 assume,** presume, expect, take it (as read), suppose.

– DERIVATIVES **i·mag·in·er** noun.
– ORIGIN from Latin *imaginare* 'form an image of' and *imaginari* 'picture to oneself.'

im·ag·ing /'imijiNG/ ▶ **noun** the process or activity of creating images of physical objects using digitizing equipment: *diagnostic imaging of the brain*.

im·ag·in·ings /i'majəniNGz/ ▶ **plural noun** thoughts or fantasies.

im·ag·ism /'imə͵jizəm/ ▶ **noun** a movement in early 20th-century English and American poetry that aimed to achieve clarity of expression through the use of precise images.
– DERIVATIVES **im·ag·ist** noun.

i·ma·go /i'māgō, i'mä-/ ▶ **noun** (pl. **imagos** or **imagines** /i'māgə͵nēz/) the final and fully developed adult stage of an insect.
– ORIGIN Latin, 'image.'

i·mam /i'mäm/ ▶ **noun 1** the person who leads prayers in a mosque. **2 (Imam)** a title of various Muslim leaders.
– DERIVATIVES **i·mam·ate** /-͵māt/ noun.
– ORIGIN Arabic, 'leader.'

IMAX /'ī͵maks/ ▶ **noun** trademark a technique of wide-screen cinematography that produces an image approximately ten times larger than that from standard 35 mm film.

im·bal·ance /im'baləns/ ▶ **noun** a lack of proportion or balance.

im·be·cile /'imbəsəl, -͵sil/ ▶ **noun** informal a stupid person. ▶ **adjective** stupid; idiotic.
– DERIVATIVES **im·be·cil·ic** /͵imbə'silik/ adjective **im·be·cil·i·ty** /͵imbə'silitē/ (pl. **imbecilities**) noun.
– ORIGIN from Latin *imbecillus* 'weak, without a supporting staff.'

im·bed ▶ **verb** variant spelling of **EMBED**.

im·bibe /im'bīb/ ▶ **verb 1** formal or humorous drink alcohol. **2** literary absorb ideas or knowledge.
– DERIVATIVES **im·bib·er** noun.
– ORIGIN Latin *imbibere*.

im·bro·glio /im'brōlyō/ ▶ **noun** (pl. **imbroglios**) a very confused or complicated situation.
– ORIGIN Italian.

im·bue /im'byo͞o/ ▶ **verb** (**imbues, imbuing, imbued**) fill with a feeling or quality: *we were imbued with a sense of purpose*.

– SYNONYMS **permeate,** saturate, suffuse, inject, inculcate, fill.

– ORIGIN Latin *imbuere* 'moisten.'

IMF ▶ **abbreviation** International Monetary Fund.

im·i·tate /'imi͵tāt/ ▶ **verb 1** follow someone or something as a model. **2** copy a person's speech or behavior, especially to amuse people. **3** make a copy of or simulate something.

– SYNONYMS **1 copy,** emulate, follow, echo, ape, parrot; informal rip off. **2 mimic,** do an impression of, impersonate, parody, caricature; informal take off, send up.

– DERIVATIVES **im·i·ta·ble** /ˈimitəbəl/ adjective **im·i·ta·tor** noun.
– ORIGIN Latin *imitari.*

CHOOSE THE RIGHT WORD

imitate, ape, copy, impersonate, mimic, mock

A young girl might **imitate** her mother by answering the phone in exactly the same tone of voice, while a teenager who deliberately *imitates* the way her mother talks for the purpose of irritating her would more accurately be said to **mimic** her. *Imitate* implies following something as an example or model (*he imitated the playing style of his music teacher*), while *mimic* suggests imitating someone's mannerisms for fun or ridicule (*they liked to mimic the teacher's southern drawl*). To **copy** is to imitate or reproduce something as closely as possible (*he copied the style of dress and speech used by the other gang members*). When someone assumes another person's appearance or mannerisms, sometimes for the purpose of perpetrating a fraud, he or she is said to **impersonate** (*arrested for impersonating a police officer; a comedian well known for impersonating political figures*). **Ape** and **mock** both imply an unflattering imitation. Someone who mimics in a contemptuous way is said to *ape* (*he entertained everyone in the office by aping the boss's phone conversations with his wife*), while someone who imitates with the intention of belittling or irritating is said to *mock* (*the students openly mocked their teacher's attempt to have a serious discussion about sex*).

im·i·ta·tion /ˌimiˈtāSHən/ ▶ **noun 1** a copy. **2** the action of imitating someone or something.

– SYNONYMS **1** *an imitation of a sailor's hat* **copy,** simulation, reproduction, replica, forgery. **2** (as adj.) *imitation ivory* **artificial,** synthetic, mock, fake, simulated, man-made, manufactured, substitute, ersatz. **3** *learning by imitation* **emulation,** copying. **4** *a perfect imitation of Elvis* **impersonation,** impression, parody, caricature; informal takeoff, sendup, spoof.

im·i·ta·tive /ˈimiˌtātiv/ ▶ **adjective 1** following a model or example. **2** (of a word) reproducing a natural sound (e.g., *fizz*); onomatopoeic.
– DERIVATIVES **im·i·ta·tive·ly** adverb.

im·mac·u·late /iˈmakyəlit/ ▶ **adjective 1** completely clean, neat, or tidy. **2** free from flaws or mistakes: *an immaculate safety record.*

– SYNONYMS **1 clean,** spotless, shining, shiny, gleaming, perfect, pristine, mint, flawless, faultless, unblemished; informal tip-top, A1. **2** *his immaculate record* **impeccable,** unsullied, spotless, unblemished, untarnished; informal squeaky clean.
– ANTONYMS dirty, damaged.

– DERIVATIVES **im·mac·u·la·cy** noun **im·mac·u·late·ly** adverb.
– ORIGIN Latin *immaculatus.*

Im·mac·u·late Con·cep·tion ▶ **noun** (in the Roman Catholic Church) the doctrine that the Virgin Mary was free of the sin common to all human beings from the moment she was conceived.

im·ma·nent /ˈimənənt/ ▶ **adjective 1** present as a natural part of something; inherent: *love is a force immanent in the world.* **2** (of God) permanently present throughout the universe.
– DERIVATIVES **im·ma·nence** noun.
– ORIGIN from Latin *immanere* 'remain within.'

im·ma·te·ri·al /ˌi(m)məˈti(ə)rēəl/ ▶ **adjective 1** unimportant under the circumstances; irrelevant. **2** spiritual rather than physical.
– DERIVATIVES **im·ma·te·ri·al·i·ty** /-ˌti(ə)rēˈalitē/ noun.

im·ma·ture /ˌiməˈCHo͝or, -ˈt(y)o͝or/ ▶ **adjective 1** not fully developed. **2** lacking the emotional or intellectual development of an adult or mature person; childish.

– SYNONYMS **childish,** babyish, infantile, juvenile, puerile, callow.

– DERIVATIVES **im·ma·ture·ly** adverb **im·ma·tu·ri·ty** noun.

WORD TOOLKIT

See **YOUTHFUL**.

im·meas·ur·a·ble /iˈmezHərəbəl/ ▶ **adjective** too large or extreme to measure.
– DERIVATIVES **im·meas·ur·a·bly** adverb.

im·me·di·a·cy /iˈmēdēəsē/ ▶ **noun 1** the quality of providing direct and instant involvement with something: *the immediacy of television images.* **2** lack of delay; speed.

im·me·di·ate /iˈmēdē-it/ ▶ **adjective 1** occurring or done at once. **2** most urgent: *the immediate concern was how to avoid taxes.* **3** nearest in time, space, or relationship. **4** direct: *a coronary was the immediate cause of death.*

– SYNONYMS **1 instant,** instantaneous, prompt, swift, speedy, rapid, quick. **2 current,** present, urgent, pressing. **3 nearest,** close, next-door, adjacent, adjoining.
– ANTONYMS delayed.

– ORIGIN Latin *immediatus.*

im·me·di·ate·ly /iˈmēdē-itlē/ ▶ **adverb 1** at once. **2** very close in time, space, or relationship.

– SYNONYMS **1 straightaway,** at once, right away, instantly, (right) now, directly, forthwith, here and now, there and then; informal pronto. **2 directly,** right, exactly, precisely, squarely, just, dead; informal smack dab.
– ANTONYMS later.

▶ **conjunction** chiefly Brit. as soon as.

im·me·mo·ri·al /ˌi(m)məˈmôrēəl/ ▶ **adjective** existing from before what can be remembered or found in records: *they had lived there from time immemorial.*
– DERIVATIVES **im·me·mo·ri·al·ly** adverb.

im·mense /iˈmens/ ▶ **adjective** very large or great.

– SYNONYMS **huge,** massive, vast, enormous, gigantic, colossal, monumental, towering, giant, mammoth; informal monster, whopping, ginormous.
– ANTONYMS tiny.

– DERIVATIVES **im·men·si·ty** noun.
– ORIGIN Latin *immensus* 'immeasurable.'

WORD TOOLKIT

See **COLOSSAL**.

im·mense·ly /iˈmenslē/ ▶ **adverb** to a great extent; extremely.

im·merse /iˈmərs/ ▶ **verb 1** dip or submerge someone or something in a liquid. **2** (**immerse oneself** or **be immersed**) involve oneself deeply in an activity or interest.

– SYNONYMS **1 dip,** submerge, dunk, duck, sink. **2 absorb,** engross, occupy, engage, involve, bury, preoccupy; informal lose.

– ORIGIN Latin *immergere* 'dip into.'

im·mer·sion /i'mərzhən, -shən/ ▶ **noun 1** the action of immersing someone or something in a liquid. **2** deep involvement in an interest or activity.

im·mer·sive /i'mərsiv/ ▶ **adjective** (of a computer display) generating a three-dimensional image that appears to surround the user.

im·mi·grant /'imigrənt/ ▶ **noun** a person who comes to live permanently in a foreign country.

– SYNONYMS **newcomer,** settler, incomer, migrant, non-native, foreigner, alien, expatriate.
– ANTONYMS native.

im·mi·grate /'imi,grāt/ ▶ **verb** come to live permanently in a foreign country: *the Mennonites immigrated to western Canada in the 1870s.*

– DERIVATIVES **im·mi·gra·tion** /,imi'grāshən/ noun.
– ORIGIN Latin *immigrare.*

im·mi·nent /'imənənt/ ▶ **adjective** about to happen.

– SYNONYMS **near,** close (at hand), impending, approaching, coming, forthcoming, on the way, expected, looming.
– ANTONYMS distant.

– DERIVATIVES **im·mi·nence** noun **im·mi·nent·ly** adverb.
– ORIGIN from Latin *imminere* 'overhang, impend.'

im·mis·ci·ble /i(m)'misəbəl/ ▶ **adjective** (of liquids) not forming a homogeneous mixture when mixed.

im·mo·bile /i(m)'mōbəl, -bēl, -bīl/ ▶ **adjective 1** not moving; motionless. **2** unable to move or be moved.

– SYNONYMS **motionless,** still, stock-still, static, stationary, rooted to the spot, rigid, frozen, transfixed.

– DERIVATIVES **im·mo·bil·i·ty** /,i(m)mō'bilitē/ noun.

im·mo·bi·lize /i(m)'mōbə,līz/ ▶ **verb** prevent someone or something from moving or operating as normal.

– DERIVATIVES **im·mo·bi·li·za·tion** /-,mōbəli'zāshən/ noun **im·mo·bi·li·zer** noun.

im·mod·er·ate /i(m)'mädərit/ ▶ **adjective** not sensible or restrained; excessive.

– DERIVATIVES **im·mod·er·ate·ly** adverb.

im·mod·est /i(m)'mädist/ ▶ **adjective 1** tending to be boastful. **2** tending to show off one's body.

– SYNONYMS **indecorous,** improper, indecent, indelicate, immoral, forward, bold, brazen, shameless.

– DERIVATIVES **im·mod·est·ly** adverb **im·mod·es·ty** noun.

im·mo·late /'imə,lāt/ ▶ **verb** kill or offer something as a sacrifice, especially by burning.

– DERIVATIVES **im·mo·la·tion** /,imə'lāshən/ noun.
– ORIGIN Latin *immolare* 'sprinkle with sacrificial meal.'

im·mor·al /i(m)'môrəl, -'märəl/ ▶ **adjective** not following accepted standards of morality.

– SYNONYMS **wicked,** bad, wrong, unethical, unprincipled, unscrupulous, dishonest, corrupt, sinful, impure.
– ANTONYMS moral, ethical.

– DERIVATIVES **im·mor·al·i·ty** /,imə'ralitē, ,imô-/ noun (pl. **immoralities**) **im·mor·al·ly** adverb.

USAGE

On the difference between **immoral** and **amoral**, see the note at **AMORAL**.

im·mor·tal /i(m)'môrtl/ ▶ **adjective 1** living forever. **2** deserving to be remembered forever: *an immortal children's book.*

– SYNONYMS **1 undying,** deathless, eternal, everlasting, imperishable, indestructible. **2 timeless,** perennial, classic, time-honored, enduring, evergreen.
– ANTONYMS mortal, ephemeral.

▶ **noun 1** an immortal being, especially a Greek or Roman god. **2** a person who will remain famous for a long time.

– DERIVATIVES **im·mor·tal·i·ty** /,i(m),môr'talitē/ noun.

im·mor·tal·ize /i(m)'môrtl,īz/ ▶ **verb** cause someone or something to be remembered for a very long time.

im·mov·a·ble /i(m)'mo͞ovəbəl/ ▶ **adjective 1** not able to be moved. **2** not able to be changed or persuaded: *an immovable truth.* **3** Law (of property) consisting of land, buildings, or other permanent items.

– SYNONYMS **1 fixed,** secure, set firm, set fast, stuck, jammed, stiff. **2 motionless,** unmoving, stationary, still, stock-still, rooted to the spot, transfixed, paralyzed, frozen.
– ANTONYMS mobile.

– DERIVATIVES **im·mov·a·bly** adverb.

im·mune /i'myo͞on/ ▶ **adjective 1** having a natural resistance to a particular infection. **2** relating to such resistance: *the immune system.* **3** not affected or influenced by something: *no one is immune to her charm.* **4** protected or exempt from a duty or penalty.

– SYNONYMS **resistant,** not subject, not liable, not vulnerable, protected from, safe from, secure against.
– ANTONYMS susceptible, liable.

– ORIGIN Latin *immunis* 'exempt from public service or charge.'

im·mune re·sponse ▶ **noun** the reaction of the cells and fluids of the body to the presence of an antigen (harmful substance).

im·mune sys·tem ▶ **noun** the organs and processes of the body that provide resistance to infection and toxins.

im·mu·ni·ty /i'myo͞onitē/ ▶ **noun** (pl. **immunities**) **1** the ability of an organism to resist a particular infection: *immunity to rubella.* **2** exemption from a duty or penalty: *the rebels were given immunity from prosecution.*

– SYNONYMS **1 resistance,** protection, defense. **2 exemption,** exception, freedom, indemnity, privilege, prerogative, license, impunity, protection.
– ANTONYMS susceptibility, liability.

im·mu·nize /'imyə,nīz/ ▶ **verb** make a person or animal immune to infection, typically by inoculation.

– SYNONYMS **vaccinate,** inoculate, inject.

– DERIVATIVES **im·mu·ni·za·tion** /,imyəni'zāshən/ noun.

im·mu·no·de·fi·cien·cy /,imyənōdə'fishənsē, i,myo͞o-/ ▶ **noun** failure of the immune system to protect the body from infection.

im·mu·no·glob·u·lin /,imyənō'gläbyələn, i,myo͞o-/ ▶ **noun** a protein produced in the blood that functions as an antibody.

im·mu·nol·o·gy /,imyə'näləjē/ ▶ **noun** the branch of medicine and biology concerned with immunity to infection.

– DERIVATIVES **im·mu·no·log·ic** /ˌimyənəˈläjik, iˌmyo͞o-/ adjective **im·mu·no·log·i·cal** /ˌimyənəˈläjikəl, iˌmyo͞o-/ adjective **im·mu·nol·o·gist** noun.

im·mu·no·sup·pres·sion /ˌimyənōsəˈpresʜən, iˌmyo͞o-/ ▶ **noun** prevention of a person's natural response to infection, especially as induced to help the survival of an organ after a transplant operation.
– DERIVATIVES **im·mu·no·sup·pres·sant** noun **im·mu·no·sup·pressed** adjective.

im·mu·no·ther·a·py /ˌimyənōˈᴛʜerəpē, iˌmyo͞o-/ ▶ **noun** the prevention or treatment of disease with substances that stimulate the body's resistance to infection.

im·mure /iˈmyo͝or/ ▶ **verb** confine or imprison someone.
– ORIGIN Latin *immurare*.

im·mu·ta·ble /iˈmyo͞otəbəl/ ▶ **adjective** not changing or able to be changed.
– DERIVATIVES **im·mu·ta·bil·i·ty** /iˌmyo͞otəˈbilitē/ noun **im·mu·ta·bly** adverb.

i-Mode /ˈī ˌmōd/ ▶ **noun** a technology that allows data to be transferred to and from Internet sites via cell phones.

imp /imp/ ▶ **noun 1** a small, mischievous devil. **2** a mischievous child.
– ORIGIN from an Old English word meaning 'a young shoot.'

im·pact ▶ **noun** /ˈimˌpakt/ **1** an act of one object hitting another. **2** a marked effect or influence: *man's impact on the environment*.

> – SYNONYMS **1 collision,** crash, smash, bump, knock. **2 effect,** influence, consequences, repercussions, ramifications.

▶ **verb** /imˈpakt/ **1** hit another object. **2** have a strong effect: *high interest rates have impacted on retail spending*. **3** press something firmly into something else.

> – SYNONYMS **1 crash into,** smash into, collide with, hit, strike, smack into, bang into. **2** *interest rates impacted on spending* **affect,** influence, hit, have an effect, make an impression.

– DERIVATIVES **im·pact·ful** /imˈpaktfəl/ adjective **im·pac·tor** /imˈpaktər/ noun.
– ORIGIN from Latin *impingere* 'drive in.'

im·pact·ed /imˈpaktid/ ▶ **adjective** (of a tooth) wedged between another tooth and the jaw.
– DERIVATIVES **im·pac·tion** noun.

im·pair /imˈpe(ə)r/ ▶ **verb 1** weaken or damage something. **2** (as adj. **impaired**) having a disability of a specified kind: *hearing-impaired*.

> – SYNONYMS **weaken,** damage, harm, undermine, diminish, reduce, lessen, decrease.
> – ANTONYMS improve, enhance.

– DERIVATIVES **im·pair·ment** noun.
– ORIGIN Old French *empeirier*.

im·pal·a /imˈpalə, -ˈpälə/ ▶ **noun** (pl. same) an antelope of southern and East Africa, with lyre-shaped horns.
– ORIGIN Zulu.

im·pale /imˈpāl/ ▶ **verb** pierce someone or something with a sharp object.
– DERIVATIVES **im·pale·ment** noun **im·pal·er** noun.
– ORIGIN Latin *impalare*.

im·pal·pa·ble /imˈpalpəbəl/ ▶ **adjective 1** unable to be felt by touch. **2** not easily understood.
– DERIVATIVES **im·pal·pa·bly** adverb.

im·pan·el /imˈpanl/ (also **empanel**) ▶ **verb** (**impanels, impaneling, impaneled**) enroll a jury or enroll someone onto a jury.
– DERIVATIVES **im·pan·el·ment** noun.
– ORIGIN Old French *empaneller*.

im·part /imˈpärt/ ▶ **verb 1** communicate information. **2** give a quality: *the mushrooms impart a woody flavor to the salad*.

> – SYNONYMS **communicate,** pass on, convey, transmit, relay, relate, tell, make known, report, announce.

– ORIGIN Latin *impartire* 'give a share of.'

im·par·tial /imˈpärsʜəl/ ▶ **adjective** treating everyone equally; not biased.

> – SYNONYMS **unbiased,** unprejudiced, neutral, nonpartisan, disinterested, detached, dispassionate, objective.
> – ANTONYMS biased, partisan.

– DERIVATIVES **im·par·ti·al·i·ty** /-ˌpärsʜēˈalitē/ noun **im·par·tial·ly** adverb.

im·pass·a·ble /imˈpasəbəl/ ▶ **adjective** impossible to travel along or over.
– DERIVATIVES **im·pass·a·bil·i·ty** /-ˌpasəˈbilitē/ noun.

im·passe /ˈimˌpas, imˈpas/ ▶ **noun** a situation in which progress is impossible; a deadlock.

> – SYNONYMS **deadlock,** dead end, stalemate, standoff, standstill.

– ORIGIN French.

im·pas·sioned /imˈpasʜənd/ ▶ **adjective** filled with or showing great emotion.

im·pas·sive /imˈpasiv/ ▶ **adjective** not feeling or showing emotion.
– DERIVATIVES **im·pas·sive·ly** adverb **im·pas·siv·i·ty** /ˌimpəˈsivitē/ noun.

im·pas·to /imˈpastō, -ˈpästō/ ▶ **noun** the process or technique of laying on paint thickly so that it stands out from a surface.
– ORIGIN Italian.

im·pa·tiens /imˈpāsʜənz/ ▶ **noun** a plant of the balsam family with abundant red, pink, or white flowers.

im·pa·tient /imˈpāsʜənt/ ▶ **adjective 1** lacking patience or tolerance. **2** restlessly eager: *they were impatient for change*.

> – SYNONYMS **1 restless,** agitated, nervous, anxious. **2 anxious,** eager, keen; informal itching, dying. **3 irritated,** annoyed, angry, tetchy, snappy, cross, curt, brusque.
> – ANTONYMS patient.

– DERIVATIVES **im·pa·tience** noun **im·pa·tient·ly** adverb.

im·peach /imˈpēcʜ/ ▶ **verb 1** charge the holder of a public office with misconduct. **2** question the validity or worth of something.
– DERIVATIVES **im·peach·a·ble** adjective **im·peach·ment** noun.
– ORIGIN Old French *empecher* 'impede.'

im·pec·ca·ble /imˈpekəbəl/ ▶ **adjective** without any faults or mistakes; perfect.

WORD TOOLKIT

impeccable ...	flawless ...	pristine ...
timing	skin	wilderness
taste	execution	beaches
credentials	technique	environment
manners	game	nature
character	beauty	forest
integrity	diamond	lakes
style	craftsmanship	landscape

– SYNONYMS **flawless,** faultless, unblemished, spotless, stainless, perfect, exemplary, irreproachable; informal squeaky clean.
– ANTONYMS imperfect.

– DERIVATIVES **im·pec·ca·bil·i·ty** /-ˌpekəˈbilitē/ noun **im·pec·ca·bly** adverb.
– ORIGIN Latin *impeccabilis* 'not liable to sin.'

im·pe·cu·ni·ous /ˌimpəˈkyōōnēəs/ ▶ **adjective** having little or no money.
– DERIVATIVES **im·pe·cu·ni·os·i·ty** /-ˌkyōōnēˈäsitē/ noun.
– ORIGIN from **IN-**[1] + Latin *pecuniosus* 'wealthy.'

im·ped·ance /imˈpēdns/ ▶ **noun** the total resistance of an electric circuit to the flow of alternating current.

im·pede /imˈpēd/ ▶ **verb** delay or block the progress or action of: *matters that would impede progress.*

– SYNONYMS **hinder,** obstruct, hamper, hold back/up, delay, interfere with, disrupt, retard, slow (down).
– ANTONYMS facilitate.

– ORIGIN Latin *impedire* 'shackle the feet of.'

im·ped·i·ment /imˈpedəmənt/ ▶ **noun 1** a hindrance or obstruction. **2** (also **speech impediment**) a defect in a person's speech, such as a lisp or stammer.

– SYNONYMS **1 hindrance,** obstruction, obstacle, barrier, bar, block, check, curb, restriction. **2 defect,** impairment, stammer, stutter, lisp.

im·pel /imˈpel/ ▶ **verb** (**impels, impelling, impelled**) **1** drive or urge someone to do something. **2** drive someone or something forward.
– DERIVATIVES **im·pel·ler** noun.
– ORIGIN Latin *impellere.*

im·pend·ing /imˈpendiNG/ ▶ **adjective** (especially of something bad or important) be about to happen: *a sense of impending danger.*

– SYNONYMS **imminent,** close (at hand), near, approaching, coming, brewing, looming, threatening.

– ORIGIN from Latin *impendere* 'overhang.'

im·pen·e·tra·ble /imˈpenətrəbəl/ ▶ **adjective** **1** impossible to get through or into. **2** impossible to understand.

– SYNONYMS **1 unbreakable,** indestructible, solid, thick, unyielding. **2 impassable,** dense, thick, overgrown. **3 incomprehensible,** unfathomable, unintelligible, baffling, bewildering, confusing, opaque.

– DERIVATIVES **im·pen·e·tra·bil·i·ty** /-ˌpenətrəˈbilitē/ noun **im·pen·e·tra·bly** adverb.

im·pen·i·tent /imˈpenitnt/ ▶ **adjective** not feeling shame or regret.
– DERIVATIVES **im·pen·i·tence** noun **im·pen·i·tent·ly** adverb.

im·per·a·tive /imˈperətiv/ ▶ **adjective 1** vitally important; essential. **2** giving an authoritative command. **3** Grammar (of a mood of a verb) expressing a command, as in *Come here!*

– SYNONYMS **vital,** crucial, critical, essential, pressing, urgent.

▶ **noun** an essential or urgent thing.
– DERIVATIVES **im·per·a·tive·ly** adverb.
– ORIGIN Latin *imperativus* 'specially ordered.'

im·per·cep·ti·ble /ˌimpərˈseptəbəl/ ▶ **adjective** too slight or gradual to be seen, heard, or felt.

– SYNONYMS **unnoticeable,** undetectable, indiscernible, invisible, inaudible, impalpable, slight, small, subtle, faint.

– DERIVATIVES **im·per·cep·ti·bly** adverb.

im·per·fect /imˈpərfikt/ ▶ **adjective 1** faulty or incomplete. **2** Grammar (of a tense) referring to a past action in progress but not completed at the time in question.

– SYNONYMS **faulty,** flawed, defective, inferior, second-rate, shoddy, substandard, damaged, blemished, torn, broken, cracked, scratched.

– DERIVATIVES **im·per·fect·ly** adverb.

im·per·fec·tion /ˌimpərˈfekSHən/ ▶ **noun 1** a fault, blemish, or undesirable feature. **2** the state of being faulty or incomplete.

im·pe·ri·al /imˈpi(ə)rēəl/ ▶ **adjective 1** relating to an empire or an emperor. **2** typical of an emperor; majestic. **3** (of weights and measures) based on a nonmetric system formerly used for all measures in the UK, and still used for some.
– DERIVATIVES **im·pe·ri·al·ly** adverb.
– ORIGIN Latin *imperialis.*

im·pe·ri·al·ism /imˈpi(ə)rēəˌlizəm/ ▶ **noun** a policy of extending a country's power and influence through establishing colonies or by military force.
– DERIVATIVES **im·pe·ri·al·ist** /imˈpi(ə)rēəlist/ noun & adjective **im·pe·ri·al·is·tic** /imˌpi(ə)rēəˈlistik/ adjective.

im·per·il /imˈperəl/ ▶ **verb** (**imperils, imperiled, imperiling**) put someone or something in danger.
– DERIVATIVES **im·per·il·ment** noun.

im·pe·ri·ous /imˈpi(ə)rēəs/ ▶ **adjective** expecting to be obeyed without question; arrogant and domineering.

– SYNONYMS **peremptory,** high-handed, overbearing, domineering, authoritarian, dictatorial, authoritative, bossy, arrogant; informal pushy, high and mighty.

– DERIVATIVES **im·pe·ri·ous·ly** adverb **im·pe·ri·ous·ness** noun.
– ORIGIN Latin *imperiosus.*

im·per·ish·a·ble /imˈperiSHəbəl/ ▶ **adjective** lasting forever.
– DERIVATIVES **im·per·ish·a·bly** adverb.

im·per·ma·nent /imˈpərmənənt/ ▶ **adjective** not lasting or unchanging.
– DERIVATIVES **im·per·ma·nence** noun **im·per·ma·nent·ly** adverb.

im·per·me·a·ble /imˈpərmēəbəl/ ▶ **adjective** not allowing fluid to pass through.
– DERIVATIVES **im·per·me·a·bil·i·ty** /-ˌpərmēəˈbilitē/ noun.

im·per·mis·si·ble /ˌimpərˈmisəbəl/ ▶ **adjective** not permitted or allowed.

im·per·son·al /imˈpərsənl/ ▶ **adjective 1** not influenced by or involving personal feelings. **2** lacking human qualities; cold or anonymous: *an impersonal high-rise.* **3** Grammar (of a verb) used only with *it* as a subject (as in *it is snowing*).

– SYNONYMS **aloof,** distant, remote, detached, unemotional, unsentimental, cold, cool, indifferent, unconcerned, formal, stiff, businesslike, matter-of-fact; informal standoffish.

– DERIVATIVES **im·per·son·al·i·ty** /-ˌpərsəˈnalitē/ noun **im·per·son·al·ly** adverb.

im·per·son·ate /imˈpərsəˌnāt/ ▶ **verb** pretend to be another person to entertain or deceive people.

– SYNONYMS **imitate,** mimic, do an impression of, ape, parody, caricature, satirize, lampoon, masquerade as, pose as, pass oneself off as; informal take off on.

– DERIVATIVES **im·per·son·a·tion** /-ˌpərsəˈnāSHən/ noun **im·per·son·a·tor** noun.
– ORIGIN from IN-² + Latin *persona* 'person.'

CHOOSE THE RIGHT WORD

See IMITATE.

im·per·ti·nent /imˈpərtn-ənt/ ▶ **adjective 1** not showing proper respect. **2** formal not relevant or pertinent.

– SYNONYMS **rude,** insolent, impolite, ill-mannered, disrespectful, impudent, cheeky, presumptuous, forward.
– ANTONYMS polite, respectful.

– DERIVATIVES **im·per·ti·nence** noun **im·per·ti·nent·ly** adverb.

im·per·turb·a·ble /ˌimpərˈtərbəbəl/ ▶ **adjective** not easily upset or excited.
– DERIVATIVES **im·per·turb·a·bil·i·ty** /-tərbəˈbilitē/ noun **im·per·turb·a·bly** adverb.

im·per·vi·ous /imˈpərvēəs/ ▶ **adjective 1** not allowing fluid to pass through. **2** (**impervious to**) unable to be affected by: *he worked, apparently impervious to the heat.*
– DERIVATIVES **im·per·vi·ous·ly** adverb **im·per·vi·ous·ness** noun.

im·pet·u·ous /imˈpeCHo͞oəs/ ▶ **adjective** acting or done quickly and without thought or care.

– SYNONYMS **impulsive,** rash, hasty, reckless, foolhardy, imprudent, ill-considered, spontaneous, impromptu, spur-of-the-moment.

– DERIVATIVES **im·pet·u·os·i·ty** /-ˌpeCHo͞oˈäsitē/ noun **im·pet·u·ous·ly** adverb **im·pet·u·ous·ness** noun.
– ORIGIN Latin *impetuosus.*

im·pe·tus /ˈimpitəs/ ▶ **noun 1** the force or energy with which a body moves. **2** something that makes a process happen or happen more quickly: *the main impetus for change has been the enforcement of legislation.*

– SYNONYMS **1 momentum,** drive, thrust, energy, force, power, push. **2 motivation,** stimulus, incentive, inspiration, driving force.

– ORIGIN Latin, 'assault, force.'

im·pi·e·ty /imˈpī-itē/ ▶ **noun** lack of religious respect or reverence.

im·pinge /imˈpinj/ ▶ **verb** (**impinges, impinging, impinged**) **1** have an effect: *these laws clearly impinge on freedom of speech.* **2** advance over an area belonging to another; encroach.
– DERIVATIVES **im·pinge·ment** noun.
– ORIGIN Latin *impingere* 'drive something in or at.'

im·pi·ous /ˈimpēəs, imˈpī-/ ▶ **adjective** not showing respect or reverence.
– DERIVATIVES **im·pi·ous·ly** adverb.

imp·ish /ˈimpiSH/ ▶ **adjective** inclined to do naughty things for fun; mischievous.
– DERIVATIVES **imp·ish·ly** adverb **imp·ish·ness** noun.

im·plac·a·ble /imˈplakəbəl/ ▶ **adjective 1** unwilling to stop opposing someone or something: *an implacable enemy of the arts.* **2** unable to be stopped; relentless.
– DERIVATIVES **im·plac·a·bil·i·ty** /-ˌplakəˈbilitē/ noun **im·plac·a·bly** adverb.
– ORIGIN from IN-¹ + Latin *placabilis* 'easily calmed.'

im·plant ▶ **verb** /imˈplant/ **1** insert tissue or an artificial object into the body for medical purposes. **2** establish an idea in the mind. **3** (of a fertilized egg) become attached to the wall of the uterus.

– SYNONYMS **1 insert,** embed, bury, inject, transplant, graft. **2 instill,** inculcate, introduce, plant, sow.

▶ **noun** /ˈimˌplant/ a thing that has been implanted.
– DERIVATIVES **im·plan·ta·tion** /ˌimplanˈtāSHən/ noun.
– ORIGIN Latin *implantare* 'engraft.'

im·plant·able /imˈplantəbəl/ ▶ **adjective** capable of or designed for being implanted in living tissue: *an implantable defibrillator.*

im·plau·si·ble /imˈplôzəbəl/ ▶ **adjective** not seeming reasonable or probable.

– SYNONYMS **unlikely,** improbable, questionable, doubtful, debatable, unconvincing, far-fetched.
– ANTONYMS convincing.

– DERIVATIVES **im·plau·si·bil·i·ty** /-ˌplôzəˈbilitē/ noun **im·plau·si·bly** adverb.

WORD TOOLKIT

See IMPOSSIBLE.

im·ple·ment ▶ **noun** /ˈimpləmənt/ a tool, utensil, or other piece of equipment that is used for a particular purpose.

– SYNONYMS **tool,** utensil, instrument, device, apparatus, gadget, contraption, appliance; informal gizmo.

▶ **verb** /-ˌment/ put a decision, plan, or agreement into effect.

– SYNONYMS **execute,** apply, put into effect, put into practice, carry out/through, perform, enact, fulfill.
– ANTONYMS abolish, cancel.

– DERIVATIVES **im·ple·men·ta·tion** /ˌimpləmənˈtāSHən/ noun **im·ple·ment·er** /-ˌmentər/ noun.
– ORIGIN from Latin *implere* 'fill up, employ.'

CHOOSE THE RIGHT WORD

See TOOL.

im·pli·cate /ˈimpliˌkāt/ ▶ **verb 1** show someone to be involved in a crime. **2** (**be implicated in**) bear some of the responsibility for: *he was implicated in the bombing of the hotel.* **3** convey a meaning indirectly; imply something.

– SYNONYMS **incriminate,** involve, connect, embroil, enmesh.

– DERIVATIVES **im·pli·ca·tive** /ˈimpliˌkātiv, imˈplikətiv/ adjective.
– ORIGIN Latin *implicare* 'fold in, involve, imply.'

im·pli·ca·tion /ˌimpliˈkāSHən/ ▶ **noun 1** the conclusion that can be drawn from something although it is not stated directly. **2** a likely consequence of something. **3** the state of being involved in something.

– SYNONYMS **1 suggestion,** inference, insinuation, innuendo, intimation, imputation. **2 consequence,** result, ramification, repercussion, reverberation, effect. **3 incrimination,** involvement, connection, entanglement, association.

– DERIVATIVES **im·pli·ca·tion·al** adjective.

im·plic·it /imˈplisit/ ▶ **adjective 1** suggested though not directly stated. **2** (**implicit in**) always to be found in: *the problems implicit in all social theory.* **3** with no qualification or question: *an implicit faith.*

– SYNONYMS **1 implied,** inferred, understood, hinted at, suggested, unspoken, unstated, tacit, taken for granted. **2 inherent,** latent, underlying,

inbuilt, incorporated. **3 absolute,** complete, total, wholehearted, utter, unqualified, unconditional, unshakable, unquestioning, firm.
– ANTONYMS explicit.

– DERIVATIVES **im·plic·it·ly** adverb **im·plic·it·ness** noun.
– ORIGIN Latin *implicitus.*

im·plode /im'plōd/ ▶ **verb** collapse violently inward.
– DERIVATIVES **im·plo·sion** noun **im·plo·sive** adjective.
– ORIGIN from **IN-²** + Latin *plodere, plaudere* 'to clap.'

im·plore /im'plôr/ ▶ **verb** beg someone earnestly or desperately to do something.

– SYNONYMS **plead with,** beg, entreat, appeal to, ask, request, call on, exhort, urge.

– DERIVATIVES **im·plor·ing·ly** adverb.
– ORIGIN Latin *implorare* 'invoke with tears.'

im·ply /im'plī/ ▶ **verb** (**implies, implying, implied**) **1** suggest something rather than state it directly. **2** suggest something as a likely consequence: *the forecast traffic increase implied more pollution.*

– SYNONYMS **1 insinuate,** suggest, infer, hint, intimate, give someone to understand, make out. **2 involve,** entail, mean, point to, signify, indicate, presuppose.

– ORIGIN Latin *implicare* 'fold in, involve.'

USAGE

The words **imply** and **infer** can describe the same situation, but from different points of view. If a person **implies** something, as in *he implied that the General was a traitor,* it means that they are suggesting something but not saying it directly. If you **infer** something from what has been said, as in *we inferred from his words that the General was a traitor,* this means that you come to the conclusion that this is what they really mean.

im·po·lite /ˌimpə'līt/ ▶ **adjective** not having or showing good manners.

– SYNONYMS **rude,** bad-mannered, ill-mannered, discourteous, uncivil, disrespectful, insolent, impudent, impertinent, cheeky; informal lippy.

– DERIVATIVES **im·po·lite·ly** adverb **im·po·lite·ness** noun.

im·pol·i·tic /im'päliˌtik/ ▶ **adjective** not wise or prudent.

im·pon·der·a·ble /im'pändərəbəl/ ▶ **adjective** difficult or impossible to assess. ▶ **noun** a factor that is difficult or impossible to assess.

im·port /im'pôrt/ ▶ **verb 1** bring goods or services into a country from abroad. **2** transfer data into a computer file or document.

– SYNONYMS **bring in,** buy in, ship in.
– ANTONYMS export.

▶ **noun 1** an article or service imported from abroad. **2** the action of importing goods or services. **3** the implied meaning of something. **4** importance.

– SYNONYMS **1 meaning,** sense, essence, gist, drift, message, thrust, substance, implication. **2 importance,** significance, consequence, momentousness, magnitude, substance, weight, note, gravity, seriousness.
– ANTONYMS insignificance.

– DERIVATIVES **im·port·a·ble** adjective **im·por·ta·tion** /ˌimpôr'tāsʜən/ noun **im·port·er** noun.
– ORIGIN Latin *importare* 'bring in.'

im·por·tance /im'pôrtns/ ▶ **noun** the state or fact of being important.

– SYNONYMS **1** *the signing of the treaty was an event of immense importance* **significance,** momentousness, moment, import, consequence, note, weight, seriousness, gravity. **2** *she had a fine sense of her own importance* **status,** eminence, prestige, worth, influence, power, authority.
– ANTONYMS insignificance.

im·por·tant /im'pôrtnt/ ▶ **adjective 1** of great significance or value. **2** having great authority or influence: *important modern writers.*

– SYNONYMS **1 significant,** consequential, momentous, of great import, major, valuable, necessary, crucial, vital, essential, pivotal, decisive, far-reaching, historic. **2 powerful,** influential, well connected, high-ranking, prominent, eminent, notable, distinguished, esteemed, respected, great, prestigious.
– ANTONYMS insignificant.

– DERIVATIVES **im·por·tant·ly** adverb.

im·por·tu·nate /im'pôrcʜənit/ ▶ **adjective** very persistent.
– DERIVATIVES **im·por·tu·nate·ly** adverb **im·por·tu·ni·ty** /ˌimpôr't(y)o͞onitē/ noun (pl. **importunities**).
– ORIGIN Latin *importunus* 'inconvenient.'

im·por·tune /ˌimpôr't(y)o͞on, im'pôrcʜən/ ▶ **verb** harass someone with persistent requests.
– ORIGIN Latin *importunus* (see **IMPORTUNATE**).

im·pose /im'pōz/ ▶ **verb 1** introduce something that must be obeyed or done. **2** force something to be accepted. **3** take unreasonable advantage of someone. **4** (**impose oneself**) exert firm control over something: *the director was unable to impose himself on the production.*

– SYNONYMS **1** *they plan to impose a tax on fuel* **levy,** charge, apply, enforce, set, establish, institute, introduce, bring into effect. **2** *he imposed his ideas on everyone* **foist,** force, inflict, press. **3** *she had imposed on Mark's kindness* **take advantage of,** exploit, take liberties with, bother, trouble, disturb, inconvenience, put out, put to trouble.
– ANTONYMS abolish.

– ORIGIN Latin *imponere* 'inflict, deceive.'

im·pos·ing /im'pōzɪɴɢ/ ▶ **adjective** grand and impressive.

– SYNONYMS **impressive,** spectacular, striking, dramatic, commanding, arresting, awesome, formidable, splendid, grand, majestic.
– ANTONYMS modest.

– DERIVATIVES **im·pos·ing·ly** adverb.

im·po·si·tion /ˌimpə'zisʜən/ ▶ **noun 1** the action of introducing something that must be obeyed or done. **2** something that has been imposed; an unwelcome demand or burden.

– SYNONYMS **1 imposing,** foisting, forcing, inflicting. **2 levying,** charging, application, enforcement, enforcing, setting, establishment, introduction. **3 burden,** encumbrance, liberty, bother, worry; informal hassle.

im·pos·si·ble /im'päsəbəl/ ▶ **adjective 1** not able to occur, exist, or be done. **2** very difficult to deal with: *I was in an impossible situation.*

– SYNONYMS **1** *gale-force winds made fishing impossible* **out of the question,** impracticable, nonviable, unworkable. **2** *an impossible dream* **unattainable,** unachievable, unobtainable, hopeless, impracticable, unworkable. **3** *an impossible customer* **unreasonable,** difficult, awkward, intolerable,

unbearable, exasperating, maddening, infuriating.
– ANTONYMS possible.

– DERIVATIVES **im·pos·si·bil·i·ty** /im,päsə'bilitē/ noun (pl. **impossibilities**) **im·pos·si·bly** adverb.

WORD TOOLKIT

impossible ...	unattainable ...	implausible ...
task	goal	scenario
odds	dream	claim
feat	standard	explanation
mission	beauty	story
demands	perfection	ending
question	woman	theory
choice	level	excuses

im·pos·tor /im'pästər/ (also **imposter**) ▶ **noun** a person who pretends to be someone else in order to deceive or defraud others.

– SYNONYMS **impersonator,** deceiver, hoaxer, fraudster, fake, fraud; informal phony.

– ORIGIN Latin.

CHOOSE THE RIGHT WORD

See **QUACK**[2].

im·pos·ture /im'päschər/ ▶ **noun** an act of pretending to be someone else in order to deceive others.

im·po·tent /'impətnt/ ▶ **adjective 1** unable to take effective action; powerless. **2** (of a man) unable to achieve an erection or orgasm.

– SYNONYMS **powerless,** ineffective, ineffectual, useless, feeble, paralyzed, incapacitated.
– ANTONYMS powerful, effective.

– DERIVATIVES **im·po·tence** noun **im·po·ten·cy** noun **im·po·tent·ly** adverb.

im·pound /im'pound/ ▶ **verb 1** seize and take legal possession of something. **2** shut up domestic animals in an enclosure. **3** (of a dam) hold back water.

– SYNONYMS **confiscate,** appropriate, take possession of, seize, commandeer, expropriate, requisition, take over.

– DERIVATIVES **im·pound·ment** noun.

im·pov·er·ish /im'päv(ə)rish/ ▶ **verb** (often as adj. **impoverished**) **1** make a person or area poor. **2** make worse in quality: *impoverished soil.*
– DERIVATIVES **im·pov·er·ish·ment** noun.
– ORIGIN Old French *empoverir.*

im·prac·ti·ca·ble /im'praktikəbəl/ ▶ **adjective** impossible to be done in practice: *it was impracticable to widen the road here.*

– SYNONYMS **unworkable,** unfeasible, nonviable, unachievable, unattainable, impractical.
– ANTONYMS practicable.

– DERIVATIVES **im·prac·ti·ca·bil·i·ty** /-,praktikə'bilitē/ noun **im·prac·ti·ca·bly** adverb.

im·prac·ti·cal /im'praktikəl/ ▶ **adjective** not adapted for use or action; not sensible: *impractical high heels.*

– SYNONYMS **1 unrealistic,** unworkable, unfeasible, nonviable, ill-thought-out, absurd, idealistic, fanciful, romantic, starry-eyed, pie-in-the-sky; informal cockeyed, crackpot, crazy. **2 unsuitable,** not sensible, inappropriate, unserviceable.
– ANTONYMS realistic, practical.

– DERIVATIVES **im·prac·ti·cal·i·ty** /-,prakti'kalitē/ noun **im·prac·ti·cal·ly** adverb.

im·pre·ca·tion /,impri'kāshən/ ▶ **noun** formal a spoken curse.
– ORIGIN from Latin *imprecari* 'invoke evil.'

im·pre·cise /,impri'sīs/ ▶ **adjective** not exact or detailed.

– SYNONYMS **1 vague,** loose, indistinct, inaccurate, nonspecific, sweeping, broad, general, hazy, fuzzy, woolly, nebulous, ambiguous, equivocal, uncertain. **2 inexact,** approximate, rough; informal ballpark.
– ANTONYMS exact.

– DERIVATIVES **im·pre·cise·ly** adverb **im·pre·ci·sion** /-'sizhən/ noun.

im·preg·na·ble /im'preg-nəbəl/ ▶ **adjective 1** unable to be captured or broken into. **2** unable to be overcome: *Dallas forged an impregnable lead.*
– DERIVATIVES **im·preg·na·bil·i·ty** /-,pregnə'bilitē/ noun **im·preg·na·bly** adverb.
– ORIGIN Old French *imprenable.*

WORD TOOLKIT

See **INDOMITABLE**.

im·preg·nate /im'preg,nāt/ ▶ **verb 1** soak or saturate something with a substance. **2** fill with a feeling or quality: *an atmosphere impregnated with tension.* **3** make someone pregnant.
– DERIVATIVES **im·preg·na·tion** /,impreg'nāshən/ noun.
– ORIGIN Latin *impregnare.*

im·pre·sa·ri·o /,imprə'särē,ō, -'se(ə)r-/ ▶ **noun** (pl. **impresarios**) a person who organizes and often finances theatrical or musical productions.
– ORIGIN Italian.

impress ▶ **verb** /im'pres/ **1** make someone feel admiration and respect. **2** (**impress something on**) emphasize the importance of something to someone. **3** make a mark or design on something using a stamp or seal.

– SYNONYMS **1 make an impression on,** have an impact on, influence, affect, move, stir, rouse, excite, inspire, dazzle, awe. **2** (**impress something on**) **emphasize to,** stress to, bring home to, instill in, inculcate into, drum into.
– ANTONYMS disappoint.

▶ **noun** /'im,pres/ **1** an act of impressing a mark. **2** a mark made by pressure. **3** a person's characteristic quality: *his desire to put his own impress on the films he made.*
– ORIGIN Old French *empresser* 'press in.'

im·pres·sion /im'preshən/ ▶ **noun 1** an idea, feeling, or opinion. **2** an effect produced on someone: *his quick wit made a good impression.* **3** an imitation of a person or thing, done to entertain. **4** a mark impressed on a surface. **5** the printing of a number of copies of a publication for issue at one time. **6** a particular printed version of a book, especially one reprinted with no or only minor alteration.

– SYNONYMS **1 feeling,** sense, fancy, (sneaking) suspicion, inkling, intuition, hunch, notion, idea. **2 opinion,** view, image, picture, perception, reaction, judgment, verdict, estimation. **3 impact,** effect, influence. **4 indentation,** dent, mark, outline, imprint. **5 impersonation,** imitation, caricature; informal takeoff.

im·pres·sion·a·ble /im'presh(ə)nəbəl/ ▶ **adjective** easily influenced.

– SYNONYMS **easily influenced,** suggestible, susceptible, persuadable, pliable, malleable, pliant, ingenuous, trusting, naive, gullible.

– DERIVATIVES **im·pres·sion·a·bil·i·ty** /-prəsʜ(ə)nə'bilitē/ noun.

im·pres·sion·ism /im'presʜə,nizəm/ ▶ **noun** a style or movement in painting concerned with showing the visual impression of a particular moment, especially the shifting effects of light.
– DERIVATIVES **Im·pres·sion·ist** /im'presʜənist/ noun & adjective.
– ORIGIN from French *impressionniste*.

im·pres·sion·ist /im'presʜənist/ ▶ **noun** an entertainer who impersonates famous people.

im·pres·sion·is·tic /im,presʜə'nistik/ ▶ **adjective** **1** based on personal impressions or reactions. **2** (**Impressionistic**) in the style of Impressionism.
– DERIVATIVES **im·pres·sion·is·ti·cal·ly** adverb.

im·pres·sive /im'presiv/ ▶ **adjective** arousing admiration through size, quality, or skill.

> – SYNONYMS **magnificent,** majestic, imposing, splendid, spectacular, grand, awe-inspiring, stunning, breathtaking.

– DERIVATIVES **im·pres·sive·ly** adverb **im·pres·sive·ness** noun.

im·pri·ma·tur /,imprə'mätər, -'mātər/ ▶ **noun** **1** a person's authoritative approval. **2** an official license issued by the Roman Catholic Church to print a religious book.
– ORIGIN Latin, 'let it be printed.'

im·print ▶ **verb** /im'print/ **1** make a mark on an object by pressure. **2** make an impression or effect on: *he'd always have this ghastly image imprinted on his mind.*

> – SYNONYMS **stamp,** print, impress, mark, emboss.

▶ **noun** /'imprint/ **1** a mark made by pressure. **2** a printer's or publisher's name and other details in a publication. **3** a brand name under which books are published.

> – SYNONYMS **impression,** print, mark, stamp, indentation.

– ORIGIN Latin *imprimere* 'impress, imprint.'

im·pris·on /im'prizən/ ▶ **verb** put or keep someone in prison.

> – SYNONYMS **incarcerate,** send to prison, jail, lock up, put away, intern, detain, hold prisoner, hold captive; informal send up/down, send up the river.

– DERIVATIVES **im·pris·on·ment** noun.

im·prob·a·ble /im'präbəbəl/ ▶ **adjective** not likely to be true or to happen.

> – SYNONYMS **1 unlikely,** doubtful, dubious, debatable, questionable, uncertain. **2 unconvincing,** unbelievable, implausible, unlikely.

– DERIVATIVES **im·prob·a·bil·i·ty** /-,präbə'bilitē/ noun (pl. **improbabilities**) **im·prob·a·bly** adverb.

im·promp·tu /im'präm(p),t(y)o͞o/ ▶ **adjective & adverb** done without being planned or rehearsed.

> – SYNONYMS **unrehearsed,** unprepared, unscripted, extempore, extemporized, improvised, spontaneous, unplanned; informal off-the-cuff.

▶ **noun** (pl. **impromptus**) a short piece of instrumental music, especially a solo, similar to an improvisation.
– ORIGIN from Latin *in promptu* 'in readiness.'

im·prop·er /im'präpər/ ▶ **adjective** **1** not following accepted standards of behavior. **2** not modest or decent.

> – SYNONYMS **1 unacceptable,** unprofessional, irregular, unethical, dishonest. **2 unseemly,** unfitting, unbecoming, unladylike, ungentlemanly, inappropriate, indelicate, indecent, immodest, indecorous, immoral. **3 indecent,** risqué, suggestive, naughty, dirty, filthy, vulgar, crude, rude, obscene, lewd; informal blue, raunchy, steamy.
> – ANTONYMS proper, seemly.

– DERIVATIVES **im·prop·er·ly** adverb.

im·prop·er frac·tion ▶ **noun** a fraction in which the numerator is greater than the denominator, such as ⁵⁄₄.

im·pro·pri·e·ty /,imprə'prī-itē/ ▶ **noun** (pl. **improprieties**) behavior that fails to conform to standards of morality or honesty.

im·prove /im'pro͞ov/ ▶ **verb** **1** make or become better: (as adj. **improved**) *improved road and rail links.* **2** (**improve on**) achieve or produce something better than something else. **3** (as adj. **improving**) giving moral or intellectual benefit.

> – SYNONYMS **1 make better,** ameliorate, upgrade, refine, enhance, boost, build on, raise. **2 get better,** advance, progress, develop, make headway, make progress, pick up, look up, move forward. **3 recover,** get better, recuperate, rally, revive, be on the mend.
> – ANTONYMS worsen, deteriorate.

– DERIVATIVES **im·prov·a·bil·i·ty** /im,pro͞ovə'bilitē/ noun **im·prov·a·ble** adjective **im·prov·er** noun.
– ORIGIN Old French *emprower*.

im·prove·ment /im'pro͞ovmənt/ ▶ **noun** **1** the action of making or becoming better. **2** a thing that improves something or is better than something else: *home improvements*.

> – SYNONYMS **advance,** development, upgrade, refinement, enhancement, betterment, amelioration, boost, augmentation, rally, recovery, upswing.

im·prov·i·dent /im'prävidənt/ ▶ **adjective** not providing for future needs.
– DERIVATIVES **im·prov·i·dence** noun **im·prov·i·dent·ly** adverb.

im·prov·i·sa·tion /im,prävi'zāsʜən/ ▶ **noun** **1** the action of improvising something. **2** a piece of music, drama, or verse created without preparation.
– DERIVATIVES **im·prov·i·sa·tion·al** adjective.

im·pro·vise /'imprə,vīz/ ▶ **verb** **1** create and perform music, drama, or verse without preparation. **2** make something from whatever is available.

> – SYNONYMS **1 extemporize,** ad-lib; informal speak off the cuff, play (it) by ear, wing it. **2 contrive,** devise, throw together, cobble together, rig up; informal whip up, rustle up.

– DERIVATIVES **im·pro·vi·sa·to·ry** /im'prävizə,tôrē/ adjective **im·pro·vis·er** noun.
– ORIGIN from Latin *improvisus* 'unforeseen.'

im·pru·dent /im'pro͞odnt/ ▶ **adjective** not thinking about the results of an action; rash.
– DERIVATIVES **im·pru·dence** noun **im·pru·dent·ly** adverb.

im·pu·dent /'impyəd(ə)nt/ ▶ **adjective** not showing proper respect to someone; impertinent.

> – SYNONYMS **impertinent,** insolent, cheeky, cocky, brazen; presumptuous, forward, disrespectful, insubordinate; rude, impolite, ill-mannered, discourteous; informal saucy, sassy, lippy.
> – ANTONYMS polite.

– DERIVATIVES **im·pu·dence** noun **im·pu·dent·ly** adverb.
– ORIGIN Latin *impudens* 'shameless.'

im·pugn /im'pyo͞on/ ▸ **verb** express doubts about the honesty or validity of a fact or statement.
– ORIGIN Latin *impugnare* 'assail.'

im·pulse /'im,pəls/ ▸ **noun 1** a sudden strong urge to act, without thinking about the results. **2** something that causes something to happen; an impetus: *the impulse for the book came from personal experience.* **3** a pulse of electrical energy. **4** Physics a force acting briefly on a body and producing a change of momentum.

– SYNONYMS **1 urge,** instinct, drive, compulsion, itch, whim, desire, fancy, notion. **2 spontaneity,** impetuosity, recklessness, rashness.

– ORIGIN Latin *impulsus* 'a push.'

im·pul·sion /im'pəlsʜən/ ▸ **noun 1** a strong urge to do something. **2** the influence behind an action or process.

im·pul·sive /im'pəlsiv/ ▸ **adjective** acting or done without thinking ahead.

– SYNONYMS **1 hasty,** sudden, quick, precipitate, impetuous, impromptu, spontaneous, snap, unplanned, unpremeditated, thoughtless, rash, reckless. **2 impetuous,** instinctive, passionate, intuitive, emotional, devil-may-care.
– ANTONYMS cautious, premeditated.

– DERIVATIVES **im·pul·sive·ly** adverb **im·pul·sive·ness** noun **im·pul·siv·i·ty** /,im,pəl'sivitē/ noun.

im·pu·ni·ty /im'pyo͞onitē/ ▸ **noun** freedom from punishment or from the harmful results of an action: *rebels crossed the border with impunity.*
– ORIGIN Latin *impunitas.*

im·pure /im'pyo͝or/ ▸ **adjective 1** mixed with unwanted substances. **2** morally wrong, especially in sexual matters.

im·pu·ri·ty /im'pyo͝oritē/ ▸ **noun** (pl. **impurities**) **1** the quality or state of being impure. **2** a substance that spoils the purity of something.

– SYNONYMS **1** *the impurity of the air* **contamination,** pollution; dirtiness, filthiness, foulness, unwholesomeness. **2** *the impurities in beer* **contaminant,** pollutant, foreign body; dross, dirt, filth. **3** *sin and impurity* **immorality,** sin, sinfulness, wickedness; lustfulness, lechery, lewdness, lasciviousness, obscenity, crudeness, indecency, impropriety, vulgarity, coarseness.

im·pute /im'pyo͞ot/ ▸ **verb** believe that something undesirable has been done or caused by someone or something: *the crimes imputed to the prince.*
– DERIVATIVES **im·put·a·ble** adjective **im·pu·ta·tion** /,impyə'tāsʜən/ noun.
– ORIGIN Latin *imputare* 'enter in the account.'

IN ▸ **abbreviation** Indiana.

In ▸ **symbol** the chemical element indium.

in /in/ ▸ **preposition 1** so as to be enclosed, surrounded, or inside. **2** expressing a period of time during which an event takes place. **3** expressing the length of time before an event is expected to happen. **4** expressing a state, condition, or quality. **5** expressing inclusion or involvement. **6** indicating the means of expression used: *put it in writing.* **7** indicating a person's occupation or profession. **8** expressing a value as a proportion of a whole: *ten cents in the dollar.* ▸ **adverb 1** expressing movement that results in being inside or surrounded. **2** expressing the state of being enclosed or surrounded. **3** present at one's home or office. **4** expressing arrival at a destination. **5** (of the tide) rising or at its highest level. ▸ **adjective** informal fashionable.
– PHRASES **be in for** be going to experience something, especially something unpleasant. **in on** knowing a secret. **in that** for the reason that. **in with** informal enjoying friendly relations with. **the ins and outs** informal all the details.
– ORIGIN Old English.

in. ▸ **abbreviation** inch(es).

in-[1] ▸ **prefix 1** (added to adjectives) not: *infertile.* **2** (added to nouns) without; a lack of: *inaction.*
– ORIGIN Latin.

in-[2] ▸ **prefix** in; into; toward; within: *influx.*
– ORIGIN from **IN** or Latin *in.*

in·a·bil·i·ty /,inə'bilitē/ ▸ **noun** the state of being unable to do something.

in ab·sen·tia /,in əb'sensʜ(ē)ə/ ▸ **adverb** while not present.
– ORIGIN Latin, 'in absence.'

in·ac·ces·si·ble /,inak'sesəbəl/ ▸ **adjective 1** unable to be reached or used. **2** difficult to understand or appreciate. **3** (of a person) not open to advances; unapproachable.
– DERIVATIVES **in·ac·ces·si·bil·i·ty** /,inaksesə'bilətē/ noun **in·ac·ces·si·bly** adverb.

in·ac·cu·rate /,in'akyərit/ ▸ **adjective** not accurate or correct.

– SYNONYMS **inexact,** imprecise, incorrect, wrong, erroneous, faulty, imperfect, defective, unreliable, false, mistaken, untrue.

– DERIVATIVES **in·ac·cu·ra·cy** noun (pl. **inaccuracies**) **in·ac·cu·rate·ly** adverb.

in·ac·tion /in'aksʜən/ ▸ **noun** lack of action where some is expected or appropriate.

in·ac·ti·vate /in'aktə,vāt/ ▸ **verb** make something inactive or inoperative.
– DERIVATIVES **in·ac·ti·va·tion** /-,aktə'vāsʜən/ noun.

in·ac·tive /in'aktiv/ ▸ **adjective** not active or working.

– SYNONYMS **1** *I was terribly inactive over the holidays* **idle,** indolent, lazy, lifeless, slothful, lethargic, inert, sluggish, unenergetic, listless, torpid, sedentary. **2** *the computer is currently inactive* **inoperative,** nonfunctioning, idle; not working, out of service, unused, not in use; dormant.

– DERIVATIVES **in·ac·tiv·i·ty** /,inak'tivitē/ noun.

WORD TOOLKIT

See **INERT**.

in·ad·e·quate /,in'adikwit/ ▸ **adjective 1** not enough or not good enough: *inadequate funding.* **2** unable to deal with a situation or with life.

– SYNONYMS **1 insufficient,** deficient, poor, scant, scarce, sparse, in short supply, paltry, meager. **2 incapable,** incompetent, ineffective, inefficient, inept, unfit; informal not up to snuff/scratch.

– DERIVATIVES **in·ad·e·qua·cy** /-kwəsē/ noun (pl. **inadequacies**) **in·ad·e·quate·ly** adverb.

in·ad·mis·si·ble /,inəd'misəbəl/ ▸ **adjective 1** (especially of evidence in court) not accepted as valid. **2** not to be allowed.
– DERIVATIVES **in·ad·mis·si·bil·i·ty** /,inəd,misə'bilitē/ noun.

in·ad·vert·ent /,inəd'vərtnt/ ▸ **adjective** not deliberate or intentional.
– DERIVATIVES **in·ad·vert·ence** noun.
– ORIGIN from **IN-**[1] + Latin *advertere* 'turn the mind to.'

in·ad·vert·ent·ly /ˌinəd'vərtntlē/ ▶ **adverb** unintentionally: *his name had been inadvertently omitted from the list.*

– SYNONYMS **accidentally,** by accident, unintentionally, by mistake, mistakenly, unwittingly.
– ANTONYMS intentionally.

in·ad·vis·a·ble /ˌinəd'vīzəbəl/ ▶ **adjective** likely to have undesirable results; unwise.
– DERIVATIVES **in·ad·vis·a·bil·i·ty** /ˌinədˌvīzə'bilitē/ noun.

in·al·ien·a·ble /in'ālēənəbəl/ ▶ **adjective** unable to be taken away from or given away by the possessor: *inalienable rights.*
– DERIVATIVES **in·al·ien·a·bly** adverb.

in·ane /i'nān/ ▶ **adjective** lacking sense or meaning; silly.
– DERIVATIVES **in·ane·ly** adverb **in·an·i·ty** /i'nanitē/ noun (pl. **inanities**).
– ORIGIN Latin *inanis* 'empty, vain.'

in·an·i·mate /in'anəmit/ ▶ **adjective** not alive: *inanimate objects like stones.*

in·ap·pli·ca·ble /in'aplikəbəl, ˌinə'plik-/ ▶ **adjective** not relevant or appropriate.
– DERIVATIVES **in·ap·pli·ca·bil·i·ty** /-ˌaplikə'bilitē/ noun.

in·ap·pro·pri·ate /ˌinə'prōprē-it/ ▶ **adjective** not suitable or appropriate.

– SYNONYMS **unsuitable,** unfitting, unseemly, unbecoming, improper, out of place/keeping, inapposite; informal out of order.

– DERIVATIVES **in·ap·pro·pri·ate·ly** adverb **in·ap·pro·pri·ate·ness** noun.

in·apt /in'apt/ ▶ **adjective** not suitable or appropriate.
– DERIVATIVES **in·apt·ly** adverb.

in·ar·gu·a·ble /ˌin'ärgyo͞oəbəl/ ▶ **adjective** not subject to debate or argument: *an inarguable fact.*
– DERIVATIVES **in·ar·gu·a·bly** adverb.

in·ar·tic·u·late /ˌinär'tikyəlit/ ▶ **adjective 1** unable to express one's ideas or feelings clearly or easily. **2** not expressed in words.
– DERIVATIVES **in·ar·tic·u·la·cy** noun **in·ar·tic·u·late·ly** adverb **in·ar·tic·u·late·ness** noun.

in·as·much /ˌinəz'məCH/ ▶ **adverb (inasmuch as) 1** to the extent that. **2** considering that; since.

in·at·ten·tive /ˌinə'tentiv/ ▶ **adjective** not paying attention.
– DERIVATIVES **in·at·ten·tion** /ˌinə'tenSHən/ noun **in·at·ten·tive·ly** adverb **in·at·ten·tive·ness** noun.

in·au·di·ble /ˌin'ôdəbəl/ ▶ **adjective** unable to be heard.

– SYNONYMS **unclear,** indistinct, faint, muted, soft, low, muffled, whispered, muttered, murmured, mumbled.

– DERIVATIVES **in·au·di·bil·i·ty** /ˌinôdə'bilitē/ noun **in·au·di·bly** adverb.

in·au·gu·ral /in'ôg(y)ərəl/ ▶ **adjective** marking the beginning of an organization or period of office.

in·au·gu·rate /in'ôg(y)əˌrāt/ ▶ **verb 1** introduce a new system, project, or period. **2** admit someone formally to a position or office. **3** mark the opening of an organization or the first public use of a service with a special ceremony.

– SYNONYMS **1 initiate,** begin, start, institute, launch, get going, get under way, establish, bring in, usher in; informal kick off. **2 install,** instate, swear in, invest, ordain, crown.

– DERIVATIVES **in·au·gu·ra·tion** /-ôg(y)ə'rāSHən/ noun **in·au·gu·ra·tor** noun.
– ORIGIN from Latin *inauguratus* 'consecrated after interpreting omens.'

in·aus·pi·cious /ˌinô'spiSHəs/ ▶ **adjective** not likely to lead to success; unpromising.
– DERIVATIVES **in·aus·pi·cious·ly** adverb **in·aus·pi·cious·ness** noun.

in·au·then·tic /ˌinô'THentik/ ▶ **adjective** not authentic, genuine, or sincere.
– DERIVATIVES **in·au·then·tic·i·ty** /-ôTHən'tisitē/ noun.

in-be·tween ▶ **adjective** informal situated somewhere between two extremes or recognized categories; intermediate: *I am not unconscious, but in some in-between state.* ▶ **noun** an intermediate thing: *successes, failures, and in-betweens.*

in·board /'inˌbôrd/ ▶ **adverb & adjective** within or toward the center of a ship, aircraft, or vehicle.

in·born /'in'bôrn/ ▶ **adjective** existing from birth.

in·bound /'inˌbound/ ▶ **adjective & adverb** traveling back toward an original point of departure.

in-box ▶ **noun** the window on a computer screen in which received emails are displayed.

in·bred /'inˌbred/ ▶ **adjective 1** produced by breeding from closely related people or animals. **2** existing from birth; inborn.

in·breed /'inˌbrēd/ ▶ **verb** (past and past part. **inbred** /'inˌbred/) (often as n. **inbreeding**) breed from closely related people or animals.

in·built /'inˌbilt/ ▶ **adjective** present as an original or essential part: *his inbuilt sense of direction.*

Inc. /iNGk/ ▶ **abbreviation** Incorporated.

In·ca /'iNGkə/ ▶ **noun 1** a member of a South American Indian people living in the central Andes before the Spanish conquest in the early 1530s. **2** the supreme ruler of the Incas.
– DERIVATIVES **In·can** adjective.
– ORIGIN Quechua, 'lord, royal person.'

in·cal·cu·la·ble /in'kalkyələbəl, iNG-/ ▶ **adjective 1** too great to be calculated or estimated. **2** not able to be calculated or estimated.
– DERIVATIVES **in·cal·cu·la·bil·i·ty** /-ˌkalkyələ'bilitē/ noun **in·cal·cu·la·bly** adverb.

in cam·er·a ▶ **adverb** see **CAMERA**.

in·can·des·cent /ˌinkən'desənt/ ▶ **adjective 1** glowing as a result of being heated. **2** (of an electric light) containing a filament that glows white-hot when heated by a current passed through it. **3** informal very angry.
– DERIVATIVES **in·can·des·cence** noun **in·can·des·cent·ly** adverb.
– ORIGIN from Latin *incandescere* 'glow.'

in·can·ta·tion /ˌinkan'tāSHən/ ▶ **noun** words said as a magic spell or charm.
– DERIVATIVES **in·can·ta·to·ry** /in'kantəˌtôrē/ adjective.
– ORIGIN from Latin *incantare* 'chant, bewitch.'

in·ca·pa·ble /ˌin'kāpəbəl/ ▶ **adjective 1 (incapable of)** lacking the ability or required quality to do something. **2** unable to behave rationally or take care of oneself.

– SYNONYMS **incompetent,** inept, inadequate, ineffective, ineffectual, unfit, unqualified; informal not up to it.
– ANTONYMS competent.

– DERIVATIVES **in·ca·pa·bil·i·ty** /ˌinˌkāpə'bilitē/ noun.

in·ca·pac·i·tate /ˌinkəˈpasiˌtāt/ ▸ **verb** prevent someone from functioning in a normal way.
– DERIVATIVES **in·ca·pac·i·tant** noun **in·ca·pac·i·ta·tion** /-ˌpasiˈtāsʜən/ noun.
– ORIGIN from **INCAPACITY**.

in·ca·pac·i·ty /ˌinkəˈpasitē/ ▸ **noun** (pl. **incapacities**) **1** inability to do something or to function normally. **2** legal disqualification.

in·car·cer·ate /inˈkärsəˌrāt/ ▸ **verb** imprison or confine someone.
– DERIVATIVES **in·car·cer·a·tion** /-ˌkärsəˈrāsʜən/ noun.
– ORIGIN Latin *incarcerare*.

in·car·nate ▸ **adjective** /inˈkärnit, -ˌnāt/ **1** (of a god or spirit) in human form. **2** represented in physical form: *she was beauty incarnate.* ▸ **verb** /ˈinkärˌnāt/ **1** be the living embodiment of a quality. **2** embody or represent a god or spirit in human form.
– ORIGIN from Latin *incarnare* 'make flesh.'

in·car·na·tion /ˌinkärˈnāsʜən/ ▸ **noun 1** a physical embodiment of a god, spirit, or quality: *they regarded the dictator as the incarnation of evil.* **2** (**the Incarnation**) (in Christian belief) the embodiment of God the Son in human flesh as Jesus. **3** (with reference to reincarnation) each of a series of earthly lifetimes or forms.

in·cau·tious /inˈkôsʜəs/ ▸ **adjective** not concerned about potential problems or risks.
– DERIVATIVES **in·cau·tion** noun **in·cau·tious·ly** adverb.

in·cen·di·ar·y /inˈsendēˌerē/ ▸ **adjective 1** (of a bomb) designed to cause fires. **2** tending to stir up conflict. ▸ **noun** (pl. **incendiaries**) a bomb designed to cause fires.
– DERIVATIVES **in·cen·di·a·rism** /-dēəˌrizəm/ noun.
– ORIGIN Latin *incendiarius*.

in·cense[1] /ˈinˌsens/ ▸ **noun** a gum, spice, or other substance that is burned for the sweet smell it produces. ▸ **verb** perfume with incense.
– ORIGIN Latin *incensum* 'something burnt, incense.'

in·cense[2] /inˈsens/ ▸ **verb** make someone very angry.

> – SYNONYMS **enrage,** infuriate, anger, madden, outrage, exasperate, antagonize, provoke; informal make someone see red.
> – ANTONYMS placate.

– ORIGIN Latin *incendere* 'set fire to.'

in·cen·tive /inˈsentiv/ ▸ **noun** a thing that motivates or encourages someone to do something.

> – SYNONYMS **inducement,** motivation, motive, reason, stimulus, spur, impetus, encouragement, carrot; informal sweetener.
> – ANTONYMS deterrent.

– ORIGIN Latin *incentivum* 'something that incites.'

in·cen·tiv·ize /inˈsentəˌvīz/ ▸ **verb** provide with an incentive for doing something: *this is likely to incentivize management to find savings.*

in·cep·tion /inˈsepsʜən/ ▸ **noun** the establishment or starting point of an institution or activity.
– ORIGIN from Latin *incipere* 'begin.'

in·cer·ti·tude /inˈsərtiˌt(y)o͞od/ ▸ **noun** a state of uncertainty.

in·ces·sant /inˈsesənt/ ▸ **adjective** continuing without stopping.
– DERIVATIVES **in·ces·sant·ly** adverb.
– ORIGIN from Latin *in-* 'not' + *cessare* 'cease.'

in·cest /ˈinˌsest/ ▸ **noun** sexual intercourse between people classed as being too closely related to marry each other.
– ORIGIN from Latin *in-* 'not' + *castus* 'chaste.'

in·ces·tu·ous /inˈsesʜo͞oəs/ ▸ **adjective 1** involving sex between people who are too closely related to marry each other. **2** excessively close and resistant to outside influence: *a small, incestuous legal community.*
– DERIVATIVES **in·ces·tu·ous·ly** adverb.

inch /inʜ/ ▸ **noun 1** a unit of length equal to one twelfth of a foot (2.54 cm). **2** a quantity of rainfall that would cover a horizontal surface to a depth of one inch. **3** a very small amount or distance: *don't yield an inch.* ▸ **verb** move along slowly and carefully.
– PHRASES **every inch 1** the whole area or distance. **2** entirely; very much so. (**to**) **within an inch of** almost to the point of; very close to.
– ORIGIN Latin *uncia* 'twelfth part.'

in·cho·ate /inˈkō-it, -āt/ ▸ **adjective** just begun and so not fully formed or developed.
– DERIVATIVES **in·cho·ate·ly** adverb.
– ORIGIN from Latin *incohare* 'begin.'

inch·worm /ˈinʜˌwərm/ ▸ **noun** a caterpillar that moves forward by arching and straightening its body.

in·ci·dence /ˈinsidəns/ ▸ **noun 1** the occurrence, rate, or frequency of something undesirable: *an increased incidence of cancer.* **2** Physics the intersection of a line or ray with a surface.

in·ci·dent /ˈinsidənt/ ▸ **noun 1** an instance of something happening; an event. **2** a violent event, such as an attack. **3** the occurrence of dangerous or exciting events: *the plane landed without incident.*

> – SYNONYMS **1 event,** occurrence, episode, happening, affair, business, adventure, exploit, escapade. **2 disturbance,** commotion, clash, confrontation, scene, accident, fracas, contretemps. **3** *the journey was not without incident* **excitement,** adventure, drama, crisis, danger.

▸ **adjective 1** (**incident to**) resulting from. **2** (of light or other radiation) falling on a surface. **3** Physics relating to the intersection of a line or ray with a surface.
– ORIGIN from Latin *incidere* 'fall upon, happen to.'

in·ci·den·tal /ˌinsiˈdentl/ ▸ **adjective 1** occurring in connection with or as a result of something else: *the risks incidental to a firefighter's job.* **2** occurring as a minor accompaniment to something else: *incidental expenses.*

> – SYNONYMS **1 secondary,** subsidiary, minor, peripheral, background, by-the-by, unimportant, insignificant, tangential. **2 chance,** accidental, random, fluky, fortuitous, serendipitous, coincidental, unlooked-for.
> – ANTONYMS essential.

▸ **noun** an incidental detail or expense.

> **CHOOSE THE RIGHT WORD**
>
> See **ACCIDENTAL**.

in·ci·den·tal·ly /ˌinsiˈdent(ə)lē/ ▸ **adverb 1** by the way. **2** in an incidental way.

> – SYNONYMS **1 by the way,** by the by, in passing, speaking of which; informal as it happens. **2 by chance,** by accident, accidentally, fortuitously, by a fluke, by happenstance.

in·ci·den·tal mu·sic ▸ **noun** music used in a movie or play as a background.

in·cin·er·ate /inˈsinəˌrāt/ ▸ **verb** destroy something by burning.

– DERIVATIVES **in·cin·er·a·tion** /-ˌsinəˈrāsʜən/ noun.
– ORIGIN Latin *incinerare* 'burn to ashes.'

in·cin·er·a·tor /inˈsinəˌrātər/ ▶ **noun** a device for burning waste material.

in·cip·i·ent /inˈsipēənt/ ▶ **adjective** beginning to happen or develop.
– DERIVATIVES **in·cip·i·ent·ly** adverb.
– ORIGIN from Latin *incipere* 'undertake, begin.'

in·cise /inˈsīz/ ▶ **verb** **1** make a cut or cuts in a surface. **2** cut a mark or decoration into a surface.
– ORIGIN Latin *incidere* 'cut into.'

in·ci·sion /inˈsizʜən/ ▶ **noun** **1** a cut made as part of a surgical operation. **2** the action of cutting into something.

in·ci·sive /inˈsīsiv/ ▶ **adjective** **1** showing or having clear thought and sharp insight: *incisive questions*. **2** (of an action) quick and direct.

– SYNONYMS **penetrating,** acute, sharp, razor-sharp, keen, astute, trenchant, shrewd, piercing, perceptive, insightful, perspicacious; concise, succinct, pithy, to the point, crisp, clear.
– ANTONYMS rambling, vague.

– DERIVATIVES **in·ci·sive·ly** adverb **in·ci·sive·ness** noun.

in·ci·sor /inˈsīzər/ ▶ **noun** a narrow-edged tooth at the front of the mouth, adapted for cutting.

in·cite /inˈsīt/ ▶ **verb** **1** encourage or stir up violent or unlawful behavior. **2** urge someone to act in a violent or unlawful way.

– SYNONYMS **1 stir up,** whip up, encourage, stoke up, fuel, kindle, inflame, instigate, provoke, excite, trigger, spark off. **2 provoke,** encourage, urge, goad, spur on, egg on, drive, prod, prompt; informal put up to.
– ANTONYMS discourage, deter.

– DERIVATIVES **in·cite·ment** noun **in·cit·er** noun.
– ORIGIN Latin *incitare*.

in·ci·vil·i·ty /ˌinsəˈvilətē/ ▶ **noun** (pl. **incivilities**) rude or offensive speech or behavior.

in·clem·ent /inˈklemənt/ ▶ **adjective** (of the weather) unpleasantly cold or wet.
– DERIVATIVES **in·clem·en·cy** noun (pl. **inclemencies**).

in·cli·na·tion /ˌinkləˈnāsʜən, ˌiɴɢklə-/ ▶ **noun** **1** a person's natural tendency to act or feel in a particular way: *Jack was a scientist by inclination*. **2** (**inclination for/to/toward**) an interest in or liking for something. **3** a slope or slant. **4** the angle at which a straight line or plane slopes away from another.

– SYNONYMS **tendency,** propensity, leaning, predisposition, predilection, impulse, bent, liking, taste, penchant, preference.
– ANTONYMS aversion.

in·cline ▶ **verb** /inˈklīn/ **1** tend or be willing to think or do: *I was inclined to accept her offer*. **2** (**be inclined**) have a specified tendency or talent: *Sam was mathematically inclined*. **3** lean or turn away from the vertical or horizontal. **4** bend the head forward and downward.

– SYNONYMS **1 predispose,** lead, make, dispose, prejudice, prompt, induce. **2** *I incline to the opposite view* **tend to/toward,** lean to/toward, swing to/toward, veer to/toward, gravitate to/toward, be drawn to/toward, prefer, favor, go for. **3 bend,** bow, nod, bob, lower, dip.

▶ **noun** /ˈinˌklīn/ an inclined surface or plane; a slope.

– SYNONYMS **slope,** gradient, grade, pitch, ramp, bank, ascent, rise, hill, dip, descent.

– ORIGIN Latin *inclinare* 'to bend toward.'

in·clined plane ▶ **noun** a plane inclined at an angle to the horizontal, used to make it easier to raise a load.

in·clude /inˈklo͞od/ ▶ **verb** **1** have or contain something as part of a whole: *the price includes bed and breakfast*. **2** make or treat someone or something as part of a whole or group.

– SYNONYMS **1 incorporate,** comprise, encompass, cover, embrace, take in, number, contain. **2 allow for,** count, take into account, take into consideration. **3 add,** insert, put in, append, enter.
– ANTONYMS exclude, leave out.

– ORIGIN Latin *includere* 'shut in.'

in·clud·ing /inˈklo͞odiɴɢ/ ▶ **preposition** containing someone or something as part of a whole or group.

in·clu·sion /inˈklo͞ozʜən/ ▶ **noun** **1** the action of including or the state of being included. **2** a person or thing that is included.

in·clu·sion·a·ry /inˈklo͞ozʜəˌnerē/ ▶ **adjective** designed for or accommodating people who differ in age, income, race, or some other quality: *inclusionary membership policies*.

in·clu·sive /inˈklo͞osiv/ ▶ **adjective** **1** including all the expected or required services or items. **2** (**inclusive of**) containing a specified element as part of a whole. **3** (after a noun) including the limits stated: *the ages of 55 to 59 inclusive*. **4** not excluding any section of society or any party: *an inclusive peace process*.

– SYNONYMS **all-in,** comprehensive, overall, full, all-around, umbrella, catch-all, all-encompassing.
– ANTONYMS exclusive, limited.

– DERIVATIVES **in·clu·sive·ly** adverb **in·clu·sive·ness** noun.

in·cog·ni·to /ˌinkägˈnētō, inˈkägniˌtō/ ▶ **adjective & adverb** having one's true identity concealed. ▶ **noun** (pl. **incognitos**) a false identity.
– ORIGIN Italian, 'unknown.'

in·co·her·ent /ˌinkōˈhi(ə)rənt, ˌiɴɢ-, -ˈher-/ ▶ **adjective** **1** (of language or a speaker) difficult to understand. **2** not logical or well organized.
– DERIVATIVES **in·co·her·ence** noun **in·co·her·en·cy** noun (pl. **incoherencies**) **in·co·her·ent·ly** adverb.

in·come /ˈinˌkəm, ˈiɴɢ-/ ▶ **noun** money received during a particular period for work or from investments.

– SYNONYMS **earnings,** salary, wages, pay, remuneration, revenue, receipts, take, profits, proceeds, yield, dividend.
– ANTONYMS expenditure, outgoings.

in·come tax ▶ **noun** tax levied directly on personal income.

in·com·ing /ˈinˌkəmiɴɢ/ ▶ **adjective** **1** coming in. **2** (of an official or administration) having just been elected or appointed to succeed another.

– SYNONYMS **1 arriving,** approaching, inbound, inward, returning, homeward. **2 new,** next, future, elect, designate.
– ANTONYMS outward, outgoing.

▶ **noun** (**incomings**) revenue; income.

in·com·men·su·ra·ble /ˌinkəˈmensərəbəl, -sʜər-/ ▶ **adjective** **1** not able to be judged or measured by the same standards. **2** Mathematics (of numbers) in a ratio that cannot be expressed by means of integers.

in·com·men·su·rate /ˌinkəˈmensərit, -sʜə-/ ▶ **adjective** **1** (**incommensurate with**) not in keeping or in proportion with something. **2** another term for INCOMMENSURABLE (sense 1).

in·com·mode /ˌinkəˈmōd/ ▶ **verb** formal cause inconvenience to someone.
– ORIGIN Latin *incommodare*.

in·com·mo·di·ous /ˌinkəˈmōdēəs/ ▶ **adjective** formal or dated causing inconvenience or discomfort.

in·com·mu·ni·ca·ble /ˌinkəˈmyo͞onikəbəl/ ▶ **adjective** not able to be communicated to others.

in·com·mu·ni·ca·do /ˌinkəˌmyo͞oniˈkädō/ ▶ **adjective & adverb** not able to communicate with other people.
– ORIGIN Spanish *incomunicado*.

in·com·pa·ra·ble /inˈkämp(ə)rəbəl/ ▶ **adjective** so good or impressive that nothing can be compared to it: *the furnishings are of incomparable beauty.*
– DERIVATIVES **in·com·pa·ra·bly** adverb.

in·com·pat·i·ble /ˌinkəmˈpatəbəl, ˌiNG-/ ▶ **adjective** **1** (of two things) not able to exist or be used together. **2** (of two people) not able to live or work together without disagreeing.

– SYNONYMS **mismatched,** unsuited, poles apart, irreconcilable, inconsistent, conflicting, opposed, opposite, contradictory, at odds, at variance.
– ANTONYMS harmonious, consistent.

– DERIVATIVES **in·com·pat·i·bil·i·ty** /-ˌpatəˈbilitē/ noun (pl. **incompatibilities**).

in·com·pe·tent /inˈkämpətənt, iNG-/ ▶ **adjective** **1** not sufficiently skillful to do something successfully. **2** Law not qualified to act in a particular capacity.

– SYNONYMS **inept,** unskilled, inexpert, amateurish, unprofessional, bungling, blundering, clumsy; informal useless, not up to it.

▶ **noun** an incompetent person.
– DERIVATIVES **in·com·pe·tence** noun **in·com·pe·ten·cy** noun **in·com·pe·tent·ly** adverb.

in·com·plete /ˌinkəmˈplēt, ˌiNG-/ ▶ **adjective** not finished or having all the necessary parts.

– SYNONYMS **1 unfinished,** uncompleted, partial, half-finished. **2 deficient,** insufficient, partial, sketchy, fragmentary.
– ANTONYMS completed, full.

– DERIVATIVES **in·com·plete·ly** adverb **in·com·plete·ness** noun **in·com·ple·tion** noun.

WORD TOOLKIT

incomplete ...	cursory ...	vague ...
information	glance	notion
picture	examination	memory
knowledge	reading	promises
work	inspection	reference
sentence	investigation	answers

in·com·pre·hen·si·ble /ˌinkämprəˈhensəbəl, inˌkäm-/ ▶ **adjective** not able to be understood.

– SYNONYMS **unintelligible,** impenetrable, unclear, indecipherable, unfathomable, abstruse, difficult, involved.
– ANTONYMS intelligible, clear.

– DERIVATIVES **in·com·pre·hen·si·bil·i·ty** /inˌkämprəhensəˈbilitē/ noun **in·com·pre·hen·si·bly** adverb **in·com·pre·hen·sion** /ˌinkämprəˈhenSHən, inˌkäm-/ noun.

in·con·ceiv·a·ble /ˌinkənˈsēvəbəl/ ▶ **adjective** not able to be imagined or grasped mentally.
– DERIVATIVES **in·con·ceiv·a·bly** adverb.

in·con·clu·sive /ˌinkənˈklo͞osiv, ˌiNG-/ ▶ **adjective** not leading to a firm conclusion or result.
– DERIVATIVES **in·con·clu·sive·ly** adverb **in·con·clu·sive·ness** noun.

in·con·gru·ent /inˈkäNGgro͞oənt, ˌinkənˈgro͞o-/ ▶ **adjective** out of place; incongruous.
– DERIVATIVES **in·con·gru·ent·ly** adverb.

in·con·gru·ous /inˈkäNGgro͞oəs/ ▶ **adjective** out of place or not appropriate in a particular situation.
– DERIVATIVES **in·con·gru·i·ty** /ˌinkənˈgro͞o-itē, ˌiNG-, -käNG-/ noun (pl. **incongruities**) **in·con·gru·ous·ly** adverb.

in·con·se·quen·tial /ˌinkänsəˈkwenCHəl/ ▶ **adjective** not important or significant.
– DERIVATIVES **in·con·se·quen·ti·al·i·ty** /-ˌkwenCHēˈalitē/ noun **in·con·se·quen·tial·ly** adverb.

WORD TOOLKIT

inconsequential ...	petty ...	paltry ...
matter	crime	sum
details	jealousy	salary
piece	rules	attendance
role	insult	meal
event	complaint	gain

in·con·sid·er·a·ble /ˌinkənˈsidərəbəl/ ▶ **adjective** small in size, amount, extent, etc.: *a not inconsiderable number.*

in·con·sid·er·ate /ˌinkənˈsidərit/ ▶ **adjective** thoughtlessly causing hurt or inconvenience to others.

– SYNONYMS **thoughtless,** unthinking, insensitive, selfish, self-centered, impolite, discourteous, rude; tactless, undiplomatic; informal ignorant.
– ANTONYMS thoughtful.

– DERIVATIVES **in·con·sid·er·ate·ly** adverb **in·con·sid·er·ate·ness** noun.

in·con·sist·ent /ˌinkənˈsistənt/ ▶ **adjective** **1** having parts or elements that differ from or contradict each other. **2** (**inconsistent with**) not in keeping with.

– SYNONYMS **1 erratic,** changeable, unpredictable, variable, unstable, fickle, unreliable, volatile; informal up and down. **2 incompatible,** conflicting, at odds, at variance, irreconcilable, out of keeping, contrary.

– DERIVATIVES **in·con·sist·en·cy** noun (pl. **inconsistencies**) **in·con·sist·ent·ly** adverb.

in·con·sol·a·ble /ˌinkənˈsōləbəl/ ▶ **adjective** not able to be comforted or consoled.
– DERIVATIVES **in·con·sol·a·bly** adverb.

in·con·spic·u·ous /ˌinkənˈspikyo͞oəs/ ▶ **adjective** not clearly visible or noticeable.
– DERIVATIVES **in·con·spic·u·ous·ly** adverb **in·con·spic·u·ous·ness** noun.

in·con·stant /inˈkänstənt/ ▶ **adjective** frequently changing; variable or irregular.
– DERIVATIVES **in·con·stan·cy** noun.

in·con·test·a·ble /ˌinkənˈtestəbəl/ ▶ **adjective** not able to be disputed.
– DERIVATIVES **in·con·test·a·bly** adverb.

in·con·ti·nent /inˈkäntənənt, -ˈkäntn-ənt/ ▶ **adjective** **1** unable to control when one urinates or defecates. **2** lacking self-control.
– DERIVATIVES **in·con·ti·nence** noun **in·con·ti·nent·ly** adverb.

in·con·tro·vert·i·ble /inˌkäntrəˈvərtəbəl/ ▶ **adjective** not able to be denied or disputed.
– DERIVATIVES **in·con·tro·vert·i·bly** adverb.

in·con·ven·ience /ˌinkənˈvēn-yəns/ ▶ **noun** the state of being slightly troublesome or difficult.

– SYNONYMS **trouble,** nuisance, bother, problem, disruption, difficulty, disturbance; informal aggravation, hassle, headache, pain, pain in the neck.

▶ **verb** cause someone slight trouble or difficulty.

– SYNONYMS **trouble,** bother, put out, put to any trouble, disturb, impose on.

in·con·ven·ient /ˌinkənˈvēn-yənt/ ▶ **adjective** causing trouble, difficulties, or discomfort.

– SYNONYMS **awkward,** difficult, inopportune, badly timed, unsuitable, inappropriate, unfortunate.

– DERIVATIVES **in·con·ven·ient·ly** adverb.

in·cor·po·rate /inˈkôrpəˌrāt/ ▶ **verb 1** take in or contain as part of a whole: *some schemes incorporated all these variations.* **2** combine ingredients into one substance. **3** (often as adj. **incorporated**) form a company or other organization as a legal corporation.

– SYNONYMS **1 absorb,** include, subsume, assimilate, integrate, swallow up. **2 include,** contain, embrace, build in, offer, boast. **3 blend,** mix, combine, fold in, stir in.

– DERIVATIVES **in·cor·po·ra·tion** /-ˌkôrpəˈrāsʜən/ noun **in·cor·po·ra·tive** /inˈkôrpəˌrātiv/ adjective **in·cor·po·ra·tor** noun.

– ORIGIN Latin *incorporare* 'embody.'

in·cor·po·re·al /ˌinkôrˈpôrēəl/ ▶ **adjective** not having a physical body or form.

in·cor·rect /ˌinkəˈrekt/ ▶ **adjective 1** not true or factually accurate; wrong: *the doctor gave you incorrect advice.* **2** not following accepted standards or rules.

– SYNONYMS **1 wrong,** erroneous, mistaken, untrue, false, fallacious, flawed; informal wide of the mark. **2 inappropriate,** unsuitable, unacceptable, improper, unseemly; informal out of order.

– DERIVATIVES **in·cor·rect·ly** adverb **in·cor·rect·ness** noun.

in·cor·ri·gi·ble /inˈkôrijəbəl, -ˈkär-/ ▶ **adjective** not able to be changed or reformed: *he's an incorrigible liar.*

– DERIVATIVES **in·cor·ri·gi·bil·i·ty** /-ˌkôrijəˈbilitē, -ˌkär-/ noun **in·cor·ri·gi·bly** adverb.

– ORIGIN Latin *incorrigibilis.*

WORD TOOLKIT

incorrigible ...	hardened ...	habitual ...
optimist	criminal	offender
flirt	cynic	drunkenness
womanizer	soldier	smoker
spendthrift	warrior	liar
gossip	terrorist	snoring

in·cor·rupt·i·ble /ˌinkəˈrəptəbəl/ ▶ **adjective 1** not able to be corrupted, especially by taking bribes. **2** not subject to death or decay; everlasting.

– DERIVATIVES **in·cor·rupt·i·bil·i·ty** /-ˌrəptəˈbilitē/ noun.

in·crease ▶ **verb** /inˈkrēs/ become or make greater in size, amount, or intensity: *car use is increasing at an alarming rate.*

– SYNONYMS **1 grow,** get bigger, get larger, enlarge, expand, swell, rise, climb, mount, intensify, strengthen, extend, spread, widen. **2 add to,** make larger, make bigger, augment, supplement, top up, build up, extend, raise, swell, inflate, intensify, heighten; informal up, bump up.

▶ **noun** /ˈinˌkrēs/ an instance of growing or making greater.

– SYNONYMS **growth,** rise, enlargement, expansion, extension, increment, gain, addition, augmentation, surge; informal hike.
– ANTONYMS decrease.

– DERIVATIVES **in·creas·ing** adjective **in·creas·ing·ly** adverb.

– PHRASES **on the increase** becoming greater, more common, or more frequent.

– ORIGIN Latin *increscere.*

in·cred·i·ble /inˈkredəbəl/ ▶ **adjective 1** impossible or hard to believe. **2** informal very good.

– SYNONYMS **1 unbelievable,** unconvincing, far-fetched, implausible, improbable, inconceivable, unimaginable. **2 wonderful,** marvelous, spectacular, remarkable, phenomenal, prodigious, breathtaking; informal fantastic, terrific.

– DERIVATIVES **in·cred·i·bil·i·ty** /-ˌkredəˈbilitē/ noun **in·cred·i·bly** adverb.

in·cred·u·lous /inˈkrejələs/ ▶ **adjective** unwilling or unable to believe something.

– DERIVATIVES **in·cre·du·li·ty** /ˌinkrəˈd(y)o͞olitē/ noun **in·cred·u·lous·ly** adverb.

in·cre·ment /ˈiɴɢkrəmənt, ˈin-/ ▶ **noun** an increase or addition, especially one of a series on a fixed scale.

– DERIVATIVES **in·cre·men·tal** adjective **in·cre·men·tal·ly** adverb.

– ORIGIN Latin *incrementum.*

in·crim·i·nate /inˈkriməˌnāt/ ▶ **verb** make someone appear guilty of a crime or wrongdoing: (as adj. **incriminating**) *incriminating evidence.*

– DERIVATIVES **in·crim·i·na·tion** /-ˌkriməˈnāsʜən/ noun **in·crim·i·na·to·ry** /-nəˌtôrē/ adjective.

– ORIGIN Latin *incriminare* 'accuse.'

in-crowd ▶ **noun** (**the in-crowd**) informal a small group of people perceived by others to be particularly fashionable or popular.

in·cu·bate /ˈinkyəˌbāt, ˈiɴɢ-/ ▶ **verb 1** (of a bird) sit on eggs to keep them warm and hatch them. **2** keep bacteria, cells, etc., at a suitable temperature so that they develop. **3** (of an infectious disease) develop slowly without noticeable signs.

– DERIVATIVES **in·cu·ba·tion** /ˌinkyəˈbāsʜən, ˌiɴɢ-/ noun.

– ORIGIN Latin *incubare* 'lie on.'

in·cu·ba·tor /ˈinkyəˌbātər, ˈiɴɢ-/ ▶ **noun 1** a machine used to hatch eggs or grow microorganisms under controlled conditions. **2** an enclosed machine providing a controlled and protective environment for the care of premature babies.

in·cu·bus /ˈiɴɢkyəbəs, ˈin-/ ▶ **noun** (pl. **incubi** /-ˌbī/) **1** a male demon believed to have sex with sleeping women. **2** literary a cause of difficulty or anxiety.

– ORIGIN Latin *incubo* 'nightmare.'

in·cul·cate /inˈkəlˌkāt, ˈinkəl-/ ▶ **verb** fix an idea in someone's mind by constantly repeating it.

– DERIVATIVES **in·cul·ca·tion** /ˌinkəlˈkāsʜən/ noun.

– ORIGIN Latin *inculcare* 'press in.'

in·cum·ben·cy /inˈkəmbənsē/ ▶ **noun** (pl. **incumbencies**) the period during which an office is held.

in·cum·bent /inˈkəmbənt/ ▶ **adjective 1** (**incumbent on**) necessary for someone as a duty. **2** currently holding an office or post. ▶ **noun 1** the holder of an office or post. **2** (in the Christian Church) the holder of a benefice.

– ORIGIN from Latin *incumbere* 'lie or lean on.'

in·cur /in'kər, ING-/ ▶ **verb** (**incurs, incurring, incurred**) do something that results in one experiencing something unpleasant or unwelcome: *he incurred the crowd's anger.*

– SYNONYMS **bring on oneself,** expose oneself to, lay oneself open to, run up, earn, sustain, experience.

– ORIGIN Latin *incurrere* 'run into or toward.'

in·cur·a·ble /ˌin'kyo͝orəbəl/ ▶ **adjective 1** not able to be cured. **2** not able to be changed: *he's an incurable romantic.*

– SYNONYMS **1 untreatable,** inoperable, irremediable; terminal, fatal; chronic. **2 inveterate,** dyed-in-the-wool, confirmed, established, absolute, complete, utter, thoroughgoing, out-and-out; incorrigible, hopeless.

▶ **noun** an incurable person.

– DERIVATIVES **in·cur·a·bly** adverb.

in·cu·ri·ous /in'kyo͝orēəs/ ▶ **adjective** not eager to know something; lacking curiosity.

– DERIVATIVES **in·cu·ri·os·i·ty** /-ˌkyo͝orē'äsitē/ noun **in·cu·ri·ous·ly** adverb.

in·cur·sion /in'kərZHən/ ▶ **noun** a sudden or brief invasion or attack.

– ORIGIN from Latin *incurrere* 'run into or toward.'

Ind. ▶ **abbreviation 1** (often of politicians) Independent. **2** Indian. **3** Indiana.

in·debt·ed /in'detid/ ▶ **adjective 1** owing gratitude to someone: *Alex obviously feels indebted to his rescuer.* **2** owing money.

– DERIVATIVES **in·debt·ed·ness** noun.

– ORIGIN from Old French *endetter* 'involve in debt.'

in·de·cent /in'dēsənt/ ▶ **adjective 1** not following accepted standards of behavior in relation to sexual matters. **2** not appropriate in the circumstances: *he was buried with indecent haste.*

– SYNONYMS **1 obscene,** dirty, filthy, rude, naughty, vulgar, smutty, pornographic; informal **blue;** euphemistic adult. **2 unseemly,** improper, unbecoming, inappropriate.

– DERIVATIVES **in·de·cen·cy** noun (pl. **indecencies**) **in·de·cent·ly** adverb.

in·de·cent as·sault ▶ **noun** sexual assault that does not involve rape.

in·de·cent ex·po·sure ▶ **noun** the crime of intentionally showing one's genitals in public.

in·de·ci·pher·a·ble /ˌindi'sīfərəbəl/ ▶ **adjective** not able to be read or understood.

in·de·ci·sive /ˌindi'sīsiv/ ▶ **adjective 1** not able to make decisions quickly. **2** not settling an issue: *an indecisive battle.*

– SYNONYMS **1** *an indecisive leader* **irresolute,** hesitant, tentative, weak; vacillating, dithering, wavering; blowing hot and cold, unsure, uncertain; undecided. **2** *an indecisive result* **inconclusive,** proving nothing, open, indeterminate, unclear, ambiguous.

– DERIVATIVES **in·de·ci·sion** /ˌindi'siZHən/ noun **in·de·ci·sive·ly** adverb **in·de·ci·sive·ness** noun.

in·dec·o·rous /ˌin'dekərəs, ˌindi'kôrəs/ ▶ **adjective** not in keeping with good taste and propriety; improper.

in·deed /in'dēd/ ▶ **adverb 1** used to emphasize a statement or answer. **2** used to introduce a further and stronger or more surprising point.

– ORIGIN from *in deed.*

in·de·fat·i·ga·ble /ˌində'fatigəbəl/ ▶ **adjective** never tiring or stopping.

– DERIVATIVES **in·de·fat·i·ga·bly** adverb.

– ORIGIN Latin *indefatigabilis,* from *fatigare* 'wear out.'

in·de·fen·si·ble /ˌində'fensəbəl/ ▶ **adjective** not able to be justified or defended.

– DERIVATIVES **in·de·fen·si·bly** adverb.

in·de·fin·a·ble /ˌində'fīnəbəl/ ▶ **adjective** not able to be defined or described exactly.

– DERIVATIVES **in·de·fin·a·bly** /-blē/ adverb.

in·def·i·nite /in'defənit/ ▶ **adjective 1** not clearly expressed or defined; vague. **2** lasting for an unknown or unstated length of time.

– DERIVATIVES **in·def·i·nite·ly** adverb **in·def·i·nite·ness** noun.

in·def·i·nite ar·ti·cle ▶ **noun** Grammar the words *a* or *an.*

in·def·i·nite pro·noun ▶ **noun** Grammar a pronoun that does not refer to any person or thing in particular, e.g., *anything, everyone.*

in·del·i·ble /in'deləbəl/ ▶ **adjective 1** unable to be forgotten: *the beauty of the valley made an indelible impression on him.* **2** (of ink or a mark) unable to be removed.

– DERIVATIVES **in·del·i·bly** adverb.

– ORIGIN Latin *indelebilis.*

in·del·i·cate /in'delikit/ ▶ **adjective 1** lacking sensitive understanding or tact. **2** slightly indecent.

– DERIVATIVES **in·del·i·ca·cy** noun **in·del·i·cate·ly** adverb.

in·dem·ni·fy /in'demnəˌfī/ ▶ **verb** (**indemnifies, indemnifying, indemnified**) **1** compensate someone for harm or loss. **2** protect or insure someone against legal responsibility for their actions.

– DERIVATIVES **in·dem·ni·fi·ca·tion** /-ˌdemnəfi'kāSHən/ noun **in·dem·ni·fi·er** noun.

in·dem·ni·ty /in'demnitē/ ▶ **noun** (pl. **indemnities**) **1** security or protection against a loss. **2** security against or exemption from legal responsibility for one's actions. **3** a sum of money paid to compensate for damage or loss, especially by a country defeated in war.

– ORIGIN from Latin *indemnis* 'unhurt, free from loss.'

in·dent ▶ **verb** /in'dent/ **1** form hollows, dents, or notches in something. **2** begin a line of writing further from the margin than the other lines. ▶ **noun** /in'dent, 'inˌdent/ a space left by indenting writing.

– DERIVATIVES **in·dent·er** (also **indentor**) noun.

– ORIGIN Latin *indentare.*

in·den·ta·tion /ˌinden'tāSHən/ ▶ **noun 1** a deep recess or notch on an edge or surface. **2** the action of indenting something, especially a line of writing.

in·den·ture /in'denCHər/ ▶ **noun 1** a formal agreement or contract, such as one formerly binding an apprentice to work for an employer. **2** historical a contract by which a person agreed to work for a set period for a landowner in a British colony in exchange for passage to the colony. ▶ **verb** chiefly historical bind someone by an indenture as an apprentice or laborer.

– DERIVATIVES **in·den·ture·ship** noun.

in·de·pend·ence /ˌində'pendəns/ ▶ **noun** the fact or state of being independent.

– SYNONYMS **1 self-government,** self-rule, home rule, self-determination, sovereignty, autonomy. **2 impartiality,** neutrality, disinterestedness, detachment, objectivity.

CHOOSE THE RIGHT WORD

See **LIBERTY**.

In·de·pend·ence Day ▸ **noun** a national holiday on July 4 celebrating the anniversary of the adoption of the Declaration of Independence in 1776.

in·de·pend·ent /ˌindəˈpendənt/ ▸ **adjective 1** free from outside control or influence: *you should take independent advice*. **2** (of a country) self-governing. **3** having or earning enough money to support oneself. **4** not connected with another person or thing; separate. **5** (of broadcasting, a school, etc.) not supported by public funds.

– SYNONYMS **1 self-governing,** self-ruling, self-determining, sovereign, autonomous, nonaligned, free. **2 separate,** different, unconnected, unrelated, discrete. **3 private,** private-sector, fee-paying, privatized, deregulated, denationalized. **4 impartial,** unbiased, unprejudiced, neutral, disinterested, uninvolved, detached, dispassionate, objective, nonpartisan.
– ANTONYMS related, biased.

▸ **noun** an independent person or organization.
– DERIVATIVES **in·de·pend·en·cy** noun.

in·de·pend·ent·ly /ˌindəˈpendəntlē/ ▸ **adverb** on one's own: *I prefer to work independently*.

– SYNONYMS **alone,** on one's own, separately, individually, unaccompanied, solo, unaided, unassisted, without help, by one's own efforts, under one's own steam, single-handedly.

in-depth ▸ **adjective** comprehensive and thorough.

in·de·scrib·a·ble /ˌindiˈskrībəbəl/ ▸ **adjective** too unusual, extreme, or vague to be adequately described.
– DERIVATIVES **in·de·scrib·a·bly** adverb.

in·de·struct·i·ble /ˌindiˈstrəktəbəl/ ▸ **adjective** not able to be destroyed.

– SYNONYMS **unbreakable,** shatterproof, vandal-proof, durable; lasting, enduring, everlasting, undying, immortal, imperishable; literary adamantine.
– ANTONYMS fragile.

– DERIVATIVES **in·de·struct·i·bil·i·ty** /-ˌstrəktəˈbilitē/ noun **in·de·struct·i·bly** adverb.

in·de·ter·mi·na·ble /ˌindiˈtərmənəbəl/ ▸ **adjective** not able to be determined.

in·de·ter·mi·nate /ˌindiˈtərmənit/ ▸ **adjective 1** not exactly known, established, or defined: *a woman of indeterminate age*. **2** Mathematics (of a quantity) having no definite or definable value.
– DERIVATIVES **in·de·ter·mi·na·cy** noun **in·de·ter·mi·nate·ly** adverb.

in·dex /ˈinˌdeks/ ▸ **noun** (pl. **indexes** or especially in technical use **indices** /-dəˌsēz/) **1** an alphabetical list of names or subjects with references to the places in a book where they occur. **2** an alphabetical list or catalog of books or documents. **3** a sign or measure of something: *dress was an index of social class*. **4** a number representing the relative value or magnitude of something in terms of a standard: *a price index*. **5** Mathematics an exponent or other superscript or subscript number appended to a quantity.

– SYNONYMS **list,** listing, inventory, catalog, register, directory, database.

▸ **verb 1** record items in or provide something with an index. **2** link the value of prices, wages, etc., automatically to the value of a price index.
– DERIVATIVES **in·dex·a·ble** adjective **in·dex·a·tion** /ˌindekˈsāsʜən/ noun **in·dex·er** noun.
– ORIGIN Latin, 'forefinger, informer, sign.'

in·dex fin·ger ▸ **noun** the forefinger.

In·di·a ink ▸ **noun** deep black ink used especially in drawing and technical graphics.
– ORIGIN first used of Chinese and Japanese pigments imported to Europe via India.

In·di·an /ˈindēən/ ▸ **noun 1** a person from India. **2** dated an American Indian. ▸ **adjective 1** relating to India. **2** dated relating to American Indians.
– DERIVATIVES **In·di·an·ize** verb **In·di·an·ness** noun.

USAGE

Do not use the outdated terms **Indian** or **Red Indian** to refer to American native peoples; use **American Indian** or **Native American** instead.

In·di·an sum·mer ▸ **noun** a period of dry, warm weather occurring in late autumn.

in·di·cate /ˈindiˌkāt/ ▸ **verb 1** point out or show something. **2** be a sign of: *sales indicate a growing market for such art*. **3** mention something briefly or indirectly. **4** (**be indicated**) be necessary or recommended: *treatment for shock may be indicated*. **5** Brit. (of a driver) use a turn signal.

– SYNONYMS **1 point to,** be a sign of, be evidence of, demonstrate, show, testify to, be symptomatic of, denote, mark, signal, reflect, signify, suggest, imply. **2 state,** declare, make known, communicate, announce, put on record. **3 specify,** designate, stipulate, show.

– ORIGIN Latin *indicare*.

in·di·ca·tion /ˌindiˈkāsʜən/ ▸ **noun 1** a sign or piece of information that indicates something: *early indications of success*. **2** a reading given by a gauge or meter. **3** a symptom that suggests certain medical treatment is necessary: *heavy bleeding is a common indication for hysterectomy*.

– SYNONYMS **sign,** signal, indicator, symptom, mark, demonstration, pointer, guide, hint, clue, omen, warning.

CHOOSE THE RIGHT WORD

See **SIGN**.

in·dic·a·tive /inˈdikətiv/ ▸ **adjective 1** acting as a sign: *having recurrent dreams is not necessarily indicative of any psychological problem*. **2** Grammar (of a form of a verb) expressing a simple statement of fact (e.g., *she left*). ▸ **noun** Grammar an indicative verb.

in·di·ca·tor /ˈindiˌkātər/ ▸ **noun 1** a thing that shows a state or level: *car ownership as an indicator of affluence*. **2** a gauge or meter that gives particular information: *a speed indicator*. **3** a chemical compound that changes color at a specific pH value or in the presence of a particular substance, and can be used to monitor a chemical change.

– SYNONYMS **measure,** gauge, meter, barometer, guide, index, mark, sign, signal.

in·di·ces /ˈindiˌsēz/ plural of **INDEX**.

in·dict /inˈdīt/ ▸ **verb** formally accuse someone of or charge them with a crime.
– ORIGIN Latin *indicere* 'proclaim, appoint.'

in·dict·a·ble /inˈdītəbəl/ ▸ **adjective** (of an offense) making the person who commits it liable to be charged with a crime that warrants a trial by jury.

in·dict·ment /in'dītmənt/ ▶ **noun 1** Law a formal charge or accusation of a crime. **2** an indication that a system or situation is bad and deserves to be condemned: *these escalating crime figures are an indictment of our society.*

– SYNONYMS **charge,** accusation, impeachment, arraignment, prosecution, citation, summons.

in·die /'indē/ ▶ **adjective** informal (of a pop group or record label) not belonging or linked to a major record company.

in·dif·fer·ence /in'dif(ə)rəns/ ▶ **noun** lack of interest, concern, or sympathy: *his apparent indifference infuriated her.*

– SYNONYMS **detachment,** lack of concern, disinterest, lack of interest, nonchalance, boredom, unresponsiveness, impassivity, coolness.
– ANTONYMS concern.

in·dif·fer·ent /in'dif(ə)rənt/ ▶ **adjective 1** having no particular interest in or feelings about something. **2** not particularly good; mediocre.

– SYNONYMS **1 detached,** unconcerned, uninterested, uncaring, casual, nonchalant, offhand, unenthusiastic, unimpressed, unmoved, impassive, cool. **2 mediocre,** ordinary, average, middle-of-the-road, uninspired, undistinguished, unexceptional, pedestrian, forgettable, amateurish; informal no great shakes, nothing to write home about.
– ANTONYMS enthusiastic, brilliant.

– DERIVATIVES **in·dif·fer·ent·ly** adverb.
– ORIGIN Latin, 'making no difference.'

in·dig·e·nize/in'dijə,nīz/ ▶ **verb** bring something under the control or influence of native people.
– DERIVATIVES **in·dig·e·ni·za·tion** /-,dijəni'zāsHən/ noun.

in·dig·e·nous /in'dijənəs/ ▶ **adjective** originating or occurring naturally in a particular place; native.
– ORIGIN Latin *indigena* 'a native.'

WORD TOOLKIT

See **ORIGINAL**.

in·di·gent /'indijənt/ ▶ **adjective** very poor. ▶ **noun** a person who is very poor.
– DERIVATIVES **in·di·gence** noun.
– ORIGIN Latin, from *indigere* 'to lack.'

in·di·gest·i·ble /,indi'jestəbəl/ ▶ **adjective 1** difficult or impossible to digest. **2** difficult to read or understand.
– DERIVATIVES **in·di·gest·i·bil·i·ty** /-,jestə'bilitē/ noun **in·di·gest·i·bly** adverb.

in·di·ges·tion /,indi'jescHən, -dī-/ ▶ **noun** pain or discomfort in the stomach caused by difficulty in digesting food.

in·dig·nant /in'dignənt/ ▶ **adjective** feeling or showing offense and annoyance.

– SYNONYMS **aggrieved,** affronted, displeased, resentful, angry, annoyed, offended, exasperated; informal peeved, irked, sore, put out.

– DERIVATIVES **in·dig·nant·ly** adverb.
– ORIGIN Latin, from *indignari* 'regard as unworthy.'

in·dig·na·tion /,indig'nāsHən/ ▶ **noun** annoyance caused by what is seen as unfair treatment.

in·dig·ni·ty /in'dignitē/ ▶ **noun** (pl. **indignities**) treatment or circumstances that cause one to feel ashamed or embarrassed.

in·di·go /'indi,gō/ ▶ **noun** (pl. **indigos**) **1** a dark blue dye obtained from a tropical plant. **2** a dark blue color.
– ORIGIN Portuguese, from Greek *indikos* 'Indian (dye).'

in·di·rect /,ində'rekt/ ▶ **adjective 1** not direct: *an indirect route.* **2** (of taxation) charged on goods and services rather than income or profits. **3** (of costs) arising from the regular expenses involved in running a business or from subsidiary work.

– SYNONYMS **1 incidental,** secondary, subordinate, ancillary, collateral, concomitant, contingent. **2 roundabout,** circuitous, meandering, winding, tortuous. **3 oblique,** implicit, implied.

– DERIVATIVES **in·di·rec·tion** noun **in·di·rect·ly** adverb **in·di·rect·ness** noun.

in·di·rect ob·ject ▶ **noun** Grammar a person or thing that is affected by the action of a transitive verb but is not the main object (e.g., *him* in *give him the book*).

in·di·rect speech ▶ **noun** another term for **REPORTED SPEECH**.

in·dis·cern·i·ble /,indi'sərnəbəl/ ▶ **adjective** impossible to see or distinguish clearly.

in·dis·ci·pline /in'disəplin/ ▶ **noun** disorderly or uncontrolled behavior.

in·dis·creet /,indi'skrēt/ ▶ **adjective** too ready to reveal things that should remain secret or private.

– SYNONYMS **imprudent,** unwise, impolitic, injudicious, incautious, irresponsible, ill-judged, careless, rash; undiplomatic, indelicate, tactless.

– DERIVATIVES **in·dis·creet·ly** adverb.

in·dis·cre·tion /,indi'skresHən/ ▶ **noun** behavior or an act or remark that is indiscreet or shows a lack of good judgment.

CHOOSE THE RIGHT WORD

See **SIN**[1].

in·dis·crim·i·nate /,indi'skrimənit/ ▶ **adjective** done or acting at random or without careful judgment.
– DERIVATIVES **in·dis·crim·i·nate·ly** adverb.

in·dis·pen·sa·ble /,indi'spensəbəl/ ▶ **adjective** absolutely necessary.
– DERIVATIVES **in·dis·pen·sa·bil·i·ty** /-,spensə'bilitē/ noun.

in·dis·posed /,indi'spōzd/ ▶ **adjective 1** slightly unwell. **2** unwilling to do something.

in·dis·po·si·tion /,indispə'zisHən/ ▶ **noun** a slight illness.

in·dis·put·a·ble /,indis'pyo͞otəbəl/ ▶ **adjective** unable to be challenged or denied.
– DERIVATIVES **in·dis·put·a·bil·i·ty** /,indispyo͞otə'bilitē/ noun **in·dis·put·a·bly** adverb.

in·dis·sol·u·ble /,indi'sälyəbəl/ ▶ **adjective** unable to be destroyed; lasting.

in·dis·tinct /,indis'tiNGkt/ ▶ **adjective** not clear or sharply defined.
– DERIVATIVES **in·dis·tinct·ly** adverb **in·dis·tinct·ness** noun.

in·dis·tin·guish·a·ble /indis'tiNGgwisHəbəl/ ▶ **adjective** not able to be identified as different or distinct.
– DERIVATIVES **in·dis·tin·guish·a·bly** /-blē/ adverb.

in·di·um /'indēəm/ ▶ **noun** a soft silvery-white metallic chemical element resembling zinc, used in some alloys and semiconductor devices.
– ORIGIN from **INDIGO**.

in·di·vid·u·al /,ində'vijəwəl/ ▶ **adjective 1** single; separate. **2** relating to or for one particular person: *the individual needs of the children.* **3** striking or unusual; original: *a highly individual musical style.*

– SYNONYMS **1 single,** separate, discrete, independent, lone. **2 unique,** characteristic, distinctive, distinct, particular, idiosyncratic, peculiar, personal, special. **3 original,** exclusive, different, unusual, novel, unorthodox, out of the ordinary.
– ANTONYMS multiple, shared, ordinary.

▶ **noun 1** a single person or item as distinct from a group. **2** a person of a particular kind: *a selfish individual*. **3** a person who is unusual or different from other people.

– SYNONYMS **person,** human being, soul, creature, character; informal type, sort, customer.

– ORIGIN from Latin *in-* 'not' + *dividere* 'to divide.'

in·di·vid·u·al·ism /ˌində'vijo͞oəˌlizəm/ ▶ **noun 1** independence and self-reliance. **2** a social theory that favors the idea that individual people should have freedom of action rather than be controlled by society or the government.
– DERIVATIVES **in·di·vid·u·al·ist** noun & adjective **in·di·vid·u·al·is·tic** /-ˌvijo͞oə'listik/ adjective.

in·di·vid·u·al·i·ty /ˌindəˌvijə'walitē/ ▶ **noun** the quality or character of a person or thing that makes them different from others.

in·di·vid·u·al·ize /ˌində'vijo͞oəˌlīz/ ▶ **verb** make or alter something in such a way as to suit the needs or wishes of a particular person.

in·di·vid·u·al·ly /ˌində'vijəwəlē/ ▶ **adverb 1** one by one; singly; separately: *individually wrapped cheese slices*. **2** in a distinctive manner: *each sign is individually designed and crafted*. **3** personally; in an individual capacity: *partnerships and individually owned companies*.

– SYNONYMS **separately,** singly, one by one, one at a time, independently.

in·di·vid·u·ate /ˌində'vijo͞oˌāt/ ▶ **verb** distinguish someone or something from other people or things of the same kind.
– DERIVATIVES **in·di·vid·u·a·tion** /-ˌvijo͞o'āsHən/ noun.

in·di·vis·i·ble /ˌindi'vizəbəl/ ▶ **adjective 1** unable to be divided or separated. **2** (of a number) unable to be divided by another number exactly without leaving a remainder.
– DERIVATIVES **in·di·vis·i·bil·i·ty** /ˌindivizə'bilitē/ noun **in·di·vis·i·bly** adverb.

in·doc·tri·nate /in'däktrəˌnāt/ ▶ **verb** make someone accept a set of beliefs, without allowing them to consider any alternatives.
– DERIVATIVES **in·doc·tri·na·tion** /-ˌdäktrə'nāsHən/ noun.
– ORIGIN from DOCTRINE.

In·do-Eu·ro·pe·an /ˌindō-/ ▶ **noun 1** the family of languages spoken over the greater part of Europe and Asia as far as northern India. **2** a person who speaks an Indo-European language. ▶ **adjective** relating to Indo-European languages.

in·do·lent /'indələnt/ ▶ **adjective** wanting to avoid activity or exertion; lazy.
– DERIVATIVES **in·do·lence** noun **in·do·lent·ly** adverb.
– ORIGIN Latin, 'not giving pain.'

in·dom·i·ta·ble /in'dämitəbəl/ ▶ **adjective** impossible to subdue or defeat.
– DERIVATIVES **in·dom·i·ta·bil·i·ty** /-ˌdämitə'bilitē/ noun **in·dom·i·ta·bly** adverb.
– ORIGIN Latin *indomitabilis* 'unable to be tamed.'

In·do·ne·sian /ˌində'nēzHən/ ▶ **noun 1** a person from Indonesia. **2** the group of languages spoken in Indonesia. ▶ **adjective** relating to Indonesia.

WORD TOOLKIT

indomitable ...	unassailable ...	impregnable ...
spirit	lead	fortress
courage	position	barrier
enemy	truth	wall
strength	record	defense
presence	authority	vault
determination	logic	stronghold
faith	reputation	castle

in·door /'inˌdôr/ ▶ **adjective** situated, done, or used inside a building or under cover.

in·doors /in'dôrz/ ▶ **adverb** into or within a building. ▶ **noun** the area or space inside a building.

in·drawn /'inˌdrôn/ ▶ **adjective 1** (of breath) taken in. **2** (of a person) shy and introspective.

in·du·bi·ta·ble /in'd(y)o͞obitəbəl/ ▶ **adjective** formal impossible to doubt; unquestionable.
– DERIVATIVES **in·du·bi·ta·bly** adverb.
– ORIGIN Latin *indubitabilis*.

in·duce /in'd(y)o͞os/ ▶ **verb 1** persuade or influence someone to do something. **2** bring about or cause: *herbs to induce sleep*. **3** cause a pregnant woman to go into labor by the use of drugs or other artificial means. **4** produce an electric charge or current or a magnetic state by induction.

– SYNONYMS **1 persuade,** convince, prevail on, get, make, prompt, encourage, cajole into, talk into. **2 bring about,** cause, produce, create, give rise to, generate, engender.
– ANTONYMS dissuade.

– DERIVATIVES **in·duc·er** noun **in·duc·i·ble** adjective.
– ORIGIN Latin *inducere* 'lead in.'

in·duce·ment /in'd(y)o͞osmənt/ ▶ **noun 1** a thing that persuades or influences someone to do something. **2** a bribe.

in·duct /in'dəkt/ ▶ **verb 1** formally admit someone to an organization or establish them in a position. **2** enlist someone for military service.
– DERIVATIVES **in·duc·tee** noun /ˌindək'tē/.
– ORIGIN Latin *inducere* 'lead in.'

in·duc·tance /in'dəktəns/ ▶ **noun** Physics the property of an electric conductor or circuit that causes an electromotive force to be generated by a change in the current flowing.

in·duc·tion /in'dəksHən/ ▶ **noun 1** the action or process of introducing someone to an organization or establishing them in a position. **2** the action or process of inducing something. **3** a method of reasoning in which a general rule or conclusion is drawn from particular facts or examples. **4** the production of an electric or magnetic state in an object by bringing an electrified or magnetized object close to it (without touching it). **5** the drawing of the fuel mixture into the cylinders of an internal-combustion engine.

in·duc·tive /in'dəktiv/ ▶ **adjective 1** using a method of reasoning that draws general conclusions from particular facts or examples. **2** relating to electric or magnetic induction. **3** Physics possessing inductance.
– DERIVATIVES **in·duc·tive·ly** adverb.

in·dulge /in'dəlj/ ▶ **verb 1** (**indulge in**) allow oneself to enjoy the pleasure of something: *we indulged in an ice cream sundae*. **2** satisfy a desire or interest: *she was able to indulge a growing passion for literature*. **3** allow someone to do or have whatever they wish.

– SYNONYMS **1 satisfy,** gratify, fulfill, feed, yield to, give in to, go along with. **2 pamper,** spoil, overindulge, coddle, mollycoddle, cosset, pander to, wait on hand and foot.

– ORIGIN Latin *indulgere* 'give free rein to.'

in·dul·gence /in'dəljəns/ ▸ **noun 1** the action of allowing oneself to do something pleasurable. **2** a thing that is indulged in; a luxury. **3** a willingness to tolerate someone's faults. **4** an extension of the time in which a bill or debt has to be paid. **5** chiefly historical (in the Roman Catholic Church) the setting aside or cancellation by the Pope of the punishment still due for sins after absolution.

– SYNONYMS **1 satisfaction,** gratification, fulfillment. **2 self-gratification,** self-indulgence, overindulgence, intemperance, excess, extravagance, hedonism. **3 extravagance,** luxury, treat, nonessential, extra, frill. **4 pampering,** coddling, mollycoddling, cosseting. **5 tolerance,** forbearance, understanding, compassion, sympathy, leniency.
– ANTONYMS asceticism, intolerance.

in·dul·gent /in'dəljənt/ ▸ **adjective 1** readily indulging someone or overlooking their faults. **2** self-indulgent.

– SYNONYMS **generous,** permissive, easygoing, liberal, tolerant, forgiving, forbearing, lenient, kind, kindly, softhearted.
– ANTONYMS strict.

– DERIVATIVES **in·dul·gent·ly** adverb.

in·dus·tri·al /in'dəstrēəl/ ▸ **adjective** relating to or used in industry, or having many industries. ▸ **noun** (**industrials**) industrial companies or traded investments in them.
– DERIVATIVES **in·dus·tri·al·ly** adverb.

in·dus·tri·al·ism /in'dəstrēə,lizəm/ ▸ **noun** a social or economic system based on manufacturing industries.

in·dus·tri·al·ist /in'dəstrēəlist/ ▸ **noun** a person who owns or controls a manufacturing business.

– SYNONYMS **manufacturer,** factory owner, captain of industry, magnate, tycoon.

in·dus·tri·al·ize /in'dəstrēə,līz/ ▸ **verb** (often as adj. **industrialized**) develop industries in a country or region on a wide scale.
– DERIVATIVES **in·dus·tri·al·i·za·tion** /in,dəstrēəli'zāsʜən/ noun.

in·dus·tri·al park ▸ **noun** an area of land developed as a site for factories and other industrial use.

in·dus·tri·al re·la·tions ▸ **plural noun** the relations between management and workers in industry.

in·dus·tri·al-strength ▸ **adjective** very strong or powerful.

in·dus·tri·ous /in'dəstrēəs/ ▸ **adjective** hard-working.

– SYNONYMS **hard-working,** diligent, assiduous, dedicated, conscientious, studious; busy, active, bustling, energetic, productive; with one's shoulder to the wheel, with one's nose to the grindstone.
– ANTONYMS indolent.

– DERIVATIVES **in·dus·tri·ous·ly** adverb **in·dus·tri·ous·ness** noun.

CHOOSE THE RIGHT WORD

See **BUSY**.

in·dus·try /'indəstrē/ ▸ **noun** (pl. **industries**) **1** economic activity concerned with the processing of raw materials and manufacture of goods in factories. **2** a particular branch of economic or commercial activity: *the tourist industry.* **3** hard work.

– SYNONYMS **1 manufacturing,** production, construction, trade, commerce. **2 business,** trade, field, line of business, profession. **3 activity,** energy, effort, endeavor, hard work, industriousness, diligence, application.

– ORIGIN Latin *industria* 'diligence.'

In·dy /'indē/ ▸ **noun** a form of auto racing in which specially constructed cars are driven around a banked, regular, typically oval circuit, which allows for exceptionally high speeds.
– ORIGIN named after *Indianapolis,* where the principal Indy race is held.

in·e·bri·ate ▸ **verb** /i'nēbrē,āt/ (usu. as adj. **inebriated**) make someone drunk. ▸ **adjective** /-brē-it/ drunk.
– DERIVATIVES **in·e·bri·a·tion** /i,nēbrē'āsʜən/ noun.
– ORIGIN Latin *inebriare.*

in·ed·i·ble /,in'edəbəl/ ▸ **adjective** not fit for eating.

in·ef·fa·ble /in'efəbəl/ ▸ **adjective 1** too great or extreme to be expressed in words: *the ineffable beauty of the Everglades.* **2** too sacred to be spoken.
– DERIVATIVES **in·ef·fa·bil·i·ty** /-efə'bilitē/ noun **in·ef·fa·bly** adverb.
– ORIGIN Latin *ineffabilis.*

in·ef·fec·tive /,ini'fektiv/ ▸ **adjective** not producing any or the desired effect.

– SYNONYMS **1 unsuccessful,** unproductive, unprofitable, ineffectual, unavailing, to no avail, fruitless, futile. **2 ineffectual,** inefficient, inadequate, incompetent, incapable, unfit, inept; informal useless, hopeless.
– ANTONYMS effective.

– DERIVATIVES **in·ef·fec·tive·ly** adverb **in·ef·fec·tive·ness** noun.

in·ef·fec·tu·al /,ini'fekcʜōōəl/ ▸ **adjective 1** not producing any or the desired effect. **2** lacking the necessary forcefulness in a role or situation.
– DERIVATIVES **in·ef·fec·tu·al·ly** adverb.

in·ef·fi·cient /,ini'fisʜənt/ ▸ **adjective** failing to make the best use of time or resources.

– SYNONYMS **1 ineffective,** ineffectual, incompetent, inept, disorganized. **2 uneconomical,** wasteful, unproductive, time-wasting, slow, unsystematic.

– DERIVATIVES **in·ef·fi·cien·cy** noun **in·ef·fi·cient·ly** adverb.

in·e·las·tic /ini'lastik/ ▸ **adjective** (of a material) not elastic.
– DERIVATIVES **in·e·las·tic·al·ly** adverb **in·e·las·tic·i·ty** /ini,la'stisitē, inē,la-/ noun.

in·el·e·gant /in'eligənt/ ▸ **adjective** not elegant or graceful.
– DERIVATIVES **in·el·e·gance** noun **in·el·e·gant·ly** adverb.

in·el·i·gi·ble /,in'eləjəbəl/ ▸ **adjective** not eligible.
– DERIVATIVES **in·el·i·gi·bil·i·ty** /,in'eləjə'bilitē/ noun.

in·e·luc·ta·ble /,ini'ləktəbəl/ ▸ **adjective** unable to be resisted or avoided; inescapable.
– DERIVATIVES **in·e·luc·ta·bly** adverb.
– ORIGIN Latin *ineluctabilis.*

in·ept /i'nept/ ▸ **adjective** awkward or clumsy; incompetent.

– SYNONYMS **incompetent,** unskillful, unskilled, inexpert, amateurish; clumsy, awkward, maladroit,

bungling, blundering.
– ANTONYMS competent.

– DERIVATIVES **in·ept·i·tude** /-ti,t(y)o͞od/ noun **in·ept·ly** adverb **in·ept·ness** noun.
– ORIGIN Latin *ineptus* 'not suitable.'

in·e·qual·i·ty /,ini'kwälitē/ ▶ **noun** (pl. **inequalities**) lack of equality.

– SYNONYMS **imbalance,** inequity, inconsistency, disparity, discrepancy, dissimilarity, difference, bias, prejudice, discrimination, unfairness.

in·eq·ui·ta·ble /in'ekwitəbəl/ ▶ **adjective** unfair; unjust.
– DERIVATIVES **in·eq·ui·ta·bly** adverb.

in·eq·ui·ty /in'ekwitē/ ▶ **noun** (pl. **inequities**) lack of fairness or justice.

in·e·rad·i·ca·ble /,inə'radikəbəl/ ▶ **adjective** unable to be destroyed or removed.
– DERIVATIVES **in·e·rad·i·ca·bly** adverb.

in·ert /i'nərt/ ▶ **adjective 1** lacking the ability or strength to move. **2** without active chemical properties.
– DERIVATIVES **in·ert·ly** adverb **in·ert·ness** noun.
– ORIGIN Latin *iners*, 'unskilled, inactive.'

WORD TOOLKIT

inert ...	motionless ...	inactive ...
gas	body	duty
element	form	lifestyle
particle	water	members
placebo	traffic	children

in·ert gas ▶ **noun** another term for **NOBLE GAS**.

in·er·tia /i'nərsнə/ ▶ **noun 1** lack of desire or ability to move or change. **2** Physics a property of matter by which it continues in its existing state of rest or continues moving in a straight line, unless changed by an external force.
– DERIVATIVES **in·er·tial** adjective.

in·es·cap·a·ble /,ini'skāpəbəl/ ▶ **adjective** unable to be avoided or denied.
– DERIVATIVES **in·es·cap·a·bil·i·ty** /-,skāpə'bilitē/ noun **in·es·cap·a·bly** adverb.

in·es·sen·tial /,ini'sencнəl/ ▶ **adjective** not absolutely necessary. ▶ **noun** an inessential thing.

in·es·ti·ma·ble /in'estəməbəl/ ▶ **adjective** too great to be measured.
– DERIVATIVES **in·es·ti·ma·bly** adverb.

in·ev·i·ta·ble /in'evitəbəl/ ▶ **adjective** certain to happen; unavoidable.

– SYNONYMS **unavoidable,** inescapable, inexorable, assured, certain, sure.
– ANTONYMS avoidable.

▶ **noun** (**the inevitable**) a situation that is unavoidable.
– DERIVATIVES **in·ev·i·ta·bil·i·ty** /-,evitə'bilitē/ noun.
– ORIGIN Latin *inevitabilis*.

in·ev·i·ta·bly /in'evitəblē/ ▶ **adverb** unavoidably.

– SYNONYMS **unavoidably,** necessarily, automatically, naturally, as a matter of course, of necessity, inescapably, certainly, surely; informal like it or not.

in·ex·act /,inig'zakt/ ▶ **adjective** not quite accurate.
– DERIVATIVES **in·ex·ac·ti·tude** /,inig'zaktə,t(y)o͞od/ noun **in·ex·act·ly** adverb **in·ex·act·ness** noun.

in·ex·cus·a·ble /,inik'skyo͞ozəbəl/ ▶ **adjective** too bad to be justified or tolerated.
– DERIVATIVES **in·ex·cus·a·bly** adverb.

in·ex·haust·i·ble /,inig'zôstəbəl/ ▶ **adjective** (of an amount or supply of something) available in unlimited quantities.
– DERIVATIVES **in·ex·haust·i·bly** adverb.

in·ex·o·ra·ble /in'eksərəbəl/ ▶ **adjective 1** impossible to stop or prevent: *the inexorable march of new technology*. **2** (of a person) impossible to persuade; unrelenting.
– DERIVATIVES **in·ex·o·ra·bil·i·ty** /-,eksərə'bilitē/ noun **in·ex·o·ra·bly** adverb.
– ORIGIN Latin *inexorabilis*.

in·ex·pen·sive /,inik'spensiv/ ▶ **adjective** not costing a great deal; cheap.

– SYNONYMS **cheap,** affordable, low-cost, economical, competitive, reasonable, budget, economy, bargain, cut-rate, reduced.

– DERIVATIVES **in·ex·pen·sive·ly** adverb **in·ex·pen·sive·ness** noun.

in·ex·pe·ri·ence /,inik'spi(ə)rēəns/ ▶ **noun** lack of experience.

in·ex·pe·ri·enced /,inik'spi(ə)rēənst/ ▶ **adjective** lacking experience: *she's inexperienced, but we expect her to become an excellent teacher*.

– SYNONYMS **inexpert,** untrained, unqualified, unskilled, unseasoned, naive, new, callow, immature; informal wet behind the ears, wide-eyed.

in·ex·pert /in'ekspərt/ ▶ **adjective** lacking skill or knowledge in a particular field.
– DERIVATIVES **in·ex·pert·ly** adverb.

in·ex·pli·ca·ble /,inek'splikəbəl, in'eksplikəbəl/ ▶ **adjective** unable to be explained or accounted for.
– DERIVATIVES **in·ex·pli·ca·bil·i·ty** /'inek,splikə'bilitē/ noun **in·ex·pli·ca·bly** adverb.

in·ex·press·i·ble /,inik'spresəbəl/ ▶ **adjective** (of a feeling) too strong to be described or expressed in words.
– DERIVATIVES **in·ex·press·i·bly** adverb.

in·ex·pres·sive /,inik'spresiv/ ▶ **adjective** showing no expression.
– DERIVATIVES **in·ex·pres·sive·ly** adverb **in·ex·pres·sive·ness** noun.

in·ex·tin·guish·a·ble /,inik'stiNGgwisнəbəl/ ▶ **adjective** unable to be extinguished.

in ex·tre·mis /,in ek'strāmēs, ik'strēmis/ ▶ **adverb 1** in an extremely difficult situation. **2** at the point of death.
– ORIGIN Latin.

in·ex·tri·ca·ble /,inik'strikəbəl, in'ekstri-/ ▶ **adjective** impossible to disentangle or separate: *the past and the present are inextricable*.
– DERIVATIVES **in·ex·tri·ca·bly** adverb.

in·fal·li·bil·i·ty /in,falə'bilitē/ ▶ **noun 1** the quality of being infallible; the inability to be wrong. **2** (also **papal infallibility**) (in the Roman Catholic Church) the doctrine that in specified circumstances the pope is incapable of error in pronouncing dogma.

in·fal·li·ble /in'faləbəl/ ▶ **adjective 1** incapable of making mistakes or being wrong. **2** never failing; always effective.
– DERIVATIVES **in·fal·li·bly** adverb.

in·fa·mous /'infəməs/ ▶ **adjective 1** well known for some bad quality or deed. **2** morally bad; wicked.

– SYNONYMS **notorious,** disreputable, scandalous.
– ANTONYMS reputable.

– DERIVATIVES **in·fa·mous·ly** adverb.

in·fa·my /ˈinfəmē/ ▶ **noun** (pl. **infamies**) **1** the state of being known for something bad. **2** a wicked act.

in·fan·cy /ˈinfənsē/ ▶ **noun 1** the state or period of being a baby or very young child. **2** the early stage in the development or growth of something: *opinion polls were in their infancy.*

– SYNONYMS **beginnings,** early days, early stages, emergence, dawn, outset, birth, inception.
– ANTONYMS end.

in·fant /ˈinfənt/ ▶ **noun** a baby or very young child.

– SYNONYMS **baby,** newborn, young child, tiny tot, little one; Medicine neonate; Scottish bairn.

– ORIGIN from Latin *infans* 'unable to speak.'

in·fan·ta /inˈfantə/ ▶ **noun** historical a daughter of the king or queen of Spain or Portugal.
– ORIGIN Spanish and Portuguese.

in·fan·ti·cide /inˈfantiˌsīd/ ▶ **noun** the killing of a baby or very young child.

in·fan·tile /ˈinfənˌtīl, ˈinfənt-il/ ▶ **adjective 1** relating to or affecting babies and very young children. **2** derogatory childish.

in·fan·til·ism /ˈinfəntlˌizəm, inˈfan-/ ▶ **noun 1** childish behavior. **2** Psychology a condition in which characteristics or behavior of babies or very young children persist into adult life.

in·fan·try /ˈinfəntrē/ ▶ **noun** soldiers who fight on foot.
– DERIVATIVES **in·fan·try·man** noun (pl. **infantrymen**).
– ORIGIN Italian *infanteria,* from *infante* 'youth, infantryman.'

in·farct /ˈinˌfärkt/ ▶ **noun** Medicine a small area of dead tissue resulting from a failure of the blood supply.
– DERIVATIVES **in·farc·tion** /inˈfärkshən/ noun.
– ORIGIN Latin *infarctus.*

in·fat·u·ate /inˈfachōōˌāt/ ▶ **verb** (**be infatuated with**) have an intense but usually short-lived passion for someone.
– DERIVATIVES **in·fat·u·a·tion** /-ˌfachōōˈāshən/ noun.
– ORIGIN Latin *infatuare* 'make foolish.'

in·fect /inˈfekt/ ▶ **verb 1** affect a person, part of the body, etc., with an organism that causes disease. **2** contaminate something.

– SYNONYMS **contaminate,** pollute, taint, foul, poison, blight.

– ORIGIN Latin *inficere* 'to taint.'

in·fec·tion /inˈfekshən/ ▶ **noun 1** the process of infecting someone or something or the state of being infected. **2** an infectious disease.

– SYNONYMS **1 disease,** virus, illness, ailment, disorder, sickness; informal bug. **2 contamination,** poison, bacteria, germs; Medicine sepsis.

in·fec·tious /inˈfekshəs/ ▶ **adjective 1** (of a disease or disease-causing organism) liable to be transmitted through the environment. **2** (of a person or animal) likely to spread infection. **3** likely to spread to or influence other people: *her enthusiasm is infectious.*

– SYNONYMS **communicable,** contagious, transmittable, transmissible, transferable; informal catching.

– DERIVATIVES **in·fec·tious·ly** adverb **in·fec·tious·ness** noun.

in·fec·tious mon·o·nu·cle·o·sis ▶ **noun** an infectious disease caused by a virus, resulting in swollen lymph glands and long-term lack of energy.

in·fec·tive /inˈfektiv/ ▶ **adjective** capable of causing infection.

in·fe·lic·i·tous /ˌinfəˈlisitəs/ ▶ **adjective** unfortunate; inappropriate.
– DERIVATIVES **in·fe·lic·i·tous·ly** adverb.

in·fe·lic·i·ty /ˌinfəˈlisitē/ ▶ **noun** (pl. **infelicities**) **1** an inappropriate remark or action. **2** old use unhappiness or misfortune.

in·fer /inˈfər/ ▶ **verb** (**infers, inferring, inferred**) work something out from evidence and reasoning rather than from direct statements.

– SYNONYMS **deduce,** conclude, surmise, reason; gather, understand, presume, assume, figure, take it, read between the lines.

– DERIVATIVES **in·fer·a·ble** (also **inferrable**) adjective.
– ORIGIN Latin *inferre* 'bring in, bring about.'

USAGE

On the use of **imply** and **infer**, see the note at **IMPLY**.

in·fer·ence /ˈinf(ə)rəns/ ▶ **noun 1** a conclusion reached on the basis of evidence and reasoning. **2** the process of reaching a conclusion in this way.
– DERIVATIVES **in·fer·en·tial** /ˌinfəˈrenchəl/ adjective.

in·fe·ri·or /inˈfi(ə)rēər/ ▶ **adjective 1** lower in rank, status, or quality. **2** of low standard or quality. **3** chiefly Anatomy low or lower in position. **4** (of a letter or symbol) written or printed below the line.

– SYNONYMS **1 second-class,** lower-ranking, subordinate, junior, minor, lowly, humble, menial, beneath someone. **2 second-rate,** mediocre, substandard, low-grade, unsatisfactory, shoddy, poor; informal crummy, lousy.
– ANTONYMS superior.

▶ **noun** a person lower than another in rank, status, or ability.

– SYNONYMS **subordinate,** junior, underling, minion.

– DERIVATIVES **in·fe·ri·or·i·ty** /inˌfi(ə)rēˈôritē, -ˈäritē/ noun.
– ORIGIN Latin, from *inferus* 'low.'

in·fe·ri·or·i·ty com·plex ▶ **noun** a feeling that one is of lower status or has less ability than other people, resulting in aggressive or withdrawn behavior.

in·fer·nal /inˈfərnl/ ▶ **adjective 1** relating to hell or the underworld. **2** informal very annoying: *an infernal nuisance.*
– DERIVATIVES **in·fer·nal·ly** adverb.
– ORIGIN Latin *infernus* 'underground.'

in·fer·no /inˈfərnō/ ▶ **noun** (pl. **infernos**) **1** a large uncontrollable fire. **2** (**Inferno**) hell.
– ORIGIN Italian, from Latin *infernus* 'underground.'

in·fer·tile /inˈfərtl/ ▶ **adjective 1** unable to have children or (of an animal) bear young. **2** (of land) unable to produce crops or vegetation.

– SYNONYMS **1** *she was infertile* **sterile,** barren; childless, unable to procreate/reproduce, impotent; Medicine infecund. **2** *infertile soil* **barren,** unfruitful, unproductive; sterile, impoverished, arid.

– DERIVATIVES **in·fer·til·i·ty** /ˌinfərˈtilitē/ noun.

in·fest /inˈfest/ ▶ **verb** (of insects or organisms) be present in large numbers, typically so as to cause damage or disease.

– SYNONYMS (as adj. **infested**) *the bedding was infested with fleas* **overrun,** swarming, teeming, crawling, alive, plagued.

– DERIVATIVES **in·fes·ta·tion** /ˌinfeˈstāsʜən/ noun.
– ORIGIN Latin *infestare* 'assail.'

in·fi·del /ˈinfədl, -ˌdel/ ▶ **noun** chiefly old use a person who has no religion or whose religion is not that of the majority.
– ORIGIN Latin *infidelis.*

in·fi·del·i·ty /ˌinfiˈdelitē/ ▶ **noun** (pl. **infidelities**) **1** the action or state of being sexually unfaithful. **2** lack of religious faith.

in·fight·ing /ˈinˌfītiɴɢ/ ▶ **noun** conflict within a group or organization.

in·fill /ˈinˌfil/ ▶ **noun** (also **infilling**) material or buildings used to fill a space or hole. ▶ **verb** fill or block up a space or hole.

in·fil·trate /ˈinfilˌtrāt, inˈfil-/ ▶ **verb 1** enter or gain access to an organization or place in a gradual and surreptitious way. **2** pass slowly into or through something.

– SYNONYMS **penetrate,** insinuate oneself into, worm one's way into, sneak into, slip into, creep into, invade.

– DERIVATIVES **in·fil·tra·tion** /ˌinfilˈtrāsʜən/ noun **in·fil·tra·tor** noun.

in·fi·nite /ˈinfənit/ ▶ **adjective 1** without limits and impossible to measure or calculate: *the infinite number of stars in the universe.* **2** very great in amount or degree: *he bathed the wound with infinite care.*

– SYNONYMS **boundless,** unbounded, unlimited, limitless, never-ending, incalculable, untold, countless, uncountable, innumerable, numberless, immeasurable.
– ANTONYMS limited.

– DERIVATIVES **in·fi·nite·ly** adverb **in·fin·i·tude** /inˈfiniˌt(y)o͞od/ noun.
– ORIGIN Latin *infinitus.*

in·fin·i·tes·i·mal /ˌinfiniˈtes(ə)məl/ ▶ **adjective** extremely small.
– DERIVATIVES **in·fin·i·tes·i·mal·ly** adverb.
– ORIGIN Latin *infinitesimus.*

in·fin·i·tive /inˈfinitiv/ ▶ **noun** the basic form of a verb, often occurring in English with the word *to,* as in *to see, to ask.*
– DERIVATIVES **in·fin·i·ti·val** /-finiˈtīvəl/ adjective.
– ORIGIN from Latin *infinitus.*

in·fin·i·ty /inˈfinitē/ ▶ **noun** (pl. **infinities**) **1** the state or quality of having no limit and being impossible to measure or calculate. **2** a very great number or amount. **3** Mathematics a number greater than any assignable quantity or countable number (symbol ∞).

in·firm /inˈfərm/ ▶ **adjective** physically weak.
– ORIGIN Latin *infirmus.*

in·fir·ma·ry /inˈfərm(ə)rē/ ▶ **noun** (pl. **infirmaries**) a hospital or place set aside for the care of sick or injured people.

in·fir·mi·ty /inˈfərmitē/ ▶ **noun** (pl. **infirmities**) physical or mental weakness.

in fla·gran·te de·lic·to /ˌin fləˈgräntā dəˈliktō, fləˈgrantē/ ▶ **adverb** in the very act of doing something wrong, especially having illicit sex.
– ORIGIN Latin, 'in the heat of the crime.'

in·flame /inˈflām/ ▶ **verb 1** make something stronger or worse: *comments that inflamed what was already a sensitive situation.* **2** arouse strong feelings in someone. **3** cause inflammation in a part of the body.

– SYNONYMS **1 enrage,** incense, anger, madden, infuriate, exasperate, provoke, antagonize; informal make someone see red. **2 aggravate,** exacerbate, intensify, worsen, compound. **3** (as adj. **inflamed**) *the cut became inflamed* **swollen,** red, hot, burning, itchy, sore, painful, tender, infected.
– ANTONYMS placate.

in·flam·ma·ble /inˈflaməbəl/ ▶ **adjective** easily set on fire.
– DERIVATIVES **in·flam·ma·bil·i·ty** /-ˌflaməˈbilitē/ noun.

USAGE

The words **inflammable** and **flammable** both mean 'easily set on fire.' It is, however, safer to use **flammable** to avoid ambiguity, as the *in-* part of **inflammable** can give the impression that the word means 'nonflammable'.

in·flam·ma·tion /ˌinfləˈmāsʜən/ ▶ **noun** a condition in which an area of the skin or body becomes reddened, swollen, hot, and often painful, especially as a reaction to injury or infection.

in·flam·ma·to·ry /inˈflaməˌtôrē/ ▶ **adjective 1** relating to or causing inflammation. **2** arousing or intended to arouse angry or violent feelings.

in·flat·a·ble /inˈflātəbəl/ ▶ **adjective** capable of being inflated. ▶ **noun** a plastic or rubber object that is inflated before use.

in·flate /inˈflāt/ ▶ **verb 1** expand something by filling it with air or gas. **2** increase something by a large or excessive amount. **3** (as adj. **inflated**) exaggerated: *an inflated view of her own importance.* **4** bring about inflation of a currency or in an economy.

– SYNONYMS **1 blow up,** pump up, fill, puff up/out, dilate, distend, swell, bloat. **2 increase,** raise, boost, escalate, put up; informal hike up, jack up. **3** (as adj. **inflated**) *inflated prices* **high,** sky-high, excessive, unreasonable, outrageous, exorbitant, extortionate; informal steep. **4** (as adj. **inflated**) *an inflated opinion of himself* **exaggerated,** immoderate, aggrandized, overblown, overstated.
– ANTONYMS deflate, lower.

– ORIGIN Latin *inflare* 'blow into.'

in·fla·tion /inˈflāsʜən/ ▶ **noun 1** the action of inflating something. **2** a general increase in prices and fall in the value of money.
– DERIVATIVES **in·fla·tion·ar·y** adjective **in·fla·tion·ist** /-nist/ noun & adjective.

in·flect /inˈflekt/ ▶ **verb 1** Grammar (of a word) change by inflection. **2** vary the intonation or pitch of the voice.
– ORIGIN Latin *inflectere.*

in·flec·tion /inˈfleksʜən/ ▶ **noun 1** Grammar a change in the form of a word (typically the ending) to show a grammatical function or quality such as tense, mood, person, number, case, and gender. **2** a variation in intonation or pitch of the voice. **3** chiefly Mathematics a change of curvature from convex to concave.
– DERIVATIVES **in·flec·tion·al** adjective.

in·flex·i·ble /inˈfleksəbəl/ ▶ **adjective 1** not able to be altered or adapted. **2** unwilling to change or compromise. **3** not able to be bent; stiff.
– DERIVATIVES **in·flex·i·bil·i·ty** /-ˌfleksəˈbilitē/ noun **in·flex·i·bly** adverb.

in·flict /inˈflikt/ ▶ **verb** (**inflict something on**) **1** cause someone to suffer something unpleasant: *they inflicted serious injuries on the other men.* **2** impose something unwelcome on someone: *she is wrong to inflict her beliefs on everyone else.*

– SYNONYMS **1 give,** administer, deal out, mete out, exact, wreak. **2 impose,** force, thrust, foist.

– DERIVATIVES **in·flic·tion** noun.
– ORIGIN Latin *infligere* 'strike against.'

in·flight /ˈinˌflīt/ ▶ **adjective** occurring or provided during an aircraft flight: *inflight entertainment*.

in·flo·res·cence /ˌinflôˈresəns, -flə-/ ▶ **noun 1** the complete flowerhead of a plant, including stems, stalks, bracts, and flowers. **2** the process of flowering.
– ORIGIN Latin *inflorescere* 'come into flower.'

in·flow /ˈinˌflō/ ▶ **noun 1** the movement of liquid or air into a place. **2** the movement of a lot of money, people, or things into a place.

in·flu·ence /ˈinflo͞oəns/ ▶ **noun 1** the power or ability to have an effect on someone's beliefs or actions. **2** a person or thing with the power or ability to do this. **3** the power arising out of one's status, contacts, or wealth.

– SYNONYMS **1 effect,** impact, control, spell, hold. **2** *a good* ***influence on*** *her* **example to,** role model for, inspiration to. **3 power,** authority, sway, leverage, weight, pull; informal clout.

▶ **verb** have an effect on: *feminist ideas have influenced the lawmakers.*

– SYNONYMS **1 affect,** have an impact on, determine, guide, control, shape, govern, decide, change, alter. **2 sway,** bias, prejudice, manipulate, persuade, induce.

– DERIVATIVES **in·flu·enc·er** noun.
– PHRASES **under the influence** informal affected by alcohol or drugs.
– ORIGIN Latin *influere* 'flow in.'

in·flu·en·tial /ˌinflo͞oˈenCHəl/ ▶ **adjective** having great influence.

– SYNONYMS **powerful,** controlling, important, authoritative, leading, significant, instrumental, guiding.

– DERIVATIVES **in·flu·en·tial·ly** adverb.

in·flu·en·za /ˌinflo͞oˈenzə/ ▶ **noun** a highly contagious infection of the nose, throat, and lungs, spread by a virus and causing fever, severe aching, and catarrh.
– ORIGIN Italian, 'influence.'

in·flux /ˈinˌfləks/ ▶ **noun 1** the arrival or entry of large numbers of people or things. **2** an inflow of water into a river, lake, or the sea.
– ORIGIN Latin *influxus*.

in·fo /ˈinfō/ ▶ **noun** informal information.

in·fo·mer·cial /ˈinfōˌmərSHəl/ ▶ **noun** a long television advertisement that gives a great deal of information about a product in a supposedly objective way.
– ORIGIN blend of **INFORMATION** and **COMMERCIAL**.

in·form /inˈfôrm/ ▶ **verb 1** give facts or information to someone. **2 (inform on)** give information about someone's involvement in a crime to the police. **3** have an important influence on; determine the nature of: *religion informs every aspect of their lives.*

– SYNONYMS **1 tell,** notify, apprise, advise, impart to, communicate to, let someone know, brief, enlighten, send word to. **2** *he* ***informed on*** *two colleagues* **betray,** give away, denounce, incriminate, report on; informal rat on/out, squeal on, snitch on, tell on, blow the whistle on, finger.

– ORIGIN Latin *informare* 'shape, describe.'

in·for·mal /inˈfôrməl/ ▶ **adjective 1** relaxed, friendly, or unofficial. **2** (of clothes) suitable for everyday wear; casual. **3** referring to the language of everyday speech and writing, rather than that used in official and formal situations.

– SYNONYMS **1 unofficial,** casual, relaxed, easygoing, low-key. **2 colloquial,** vernacular, idiomatic, popular, familiar, everyday; informal slangy, chatty. **3 casual,** relaxed, comfortable, everyday; informal comfy.
– ANTONYMS formal.

– DERIVATIVES **in·for·mal·i·ty** /ˌinfôrˈmalitē/ noun **in·for·mal·ly** adverb.

in·form·ant /inˈfôrmənt/ ▶ **noun 1** a person who gives information to someone else. **2** an informer.

in·for·mat·ics /ˌinfərˈmatiks/ ▶ **plural noun** (treated as sing.) Computing the science of processing data for storage and retrieval.

in·for·ma·tion /ˌinfərˈmāSHən/ ▶ **noun 1** facts or knowledge provided or learned. **2** what is conveyed or represented by a particular arrangement or sequence of things: *genetically transmitted information.*

– SYNONYMS **facts,** particulars, details, figures, statistics, data, knowledge, intelligence; informal info, the 411.

– DERIVATIVES **in·for·ma·tion·al** adjective **in·for·ma·tion·al·ly** adverb.

CHOOSE THE RIGHT WORD

See **KNOWLEDGE**.

in·for·ma·tion sci·ence ▶ **noun** Computing the study of processes for storing and retrieving information.

in·for·ma·tion su·per·high·way ▶ **noun** an extensive electronic network such as the Internet, used for the rapid transfer of information in digital form.

in·for·ma·tion tech·nol·o·gy ▶ **noun** the study or use of systems such as computers and telecommunications for storing, retrieving, and sending information.

in·for·ma·tive /inˈfôrmətiv/ ▶ **adjective** providing useful information.

– SYNONYMS **instructive,** illuminating, enlightening, revealing, explanatory, factual, educational, edifying.

– DERIVATIVES **in·for·ma·tive·ly** adverb.

in·formed /inˈfôrmd/ ▶ **adjective 1** having or showing knowledge: *an informed readership*. **2** (of a decision or judgment) based on an understanding of the facts.

– SYNONYMS **knowledgeable,** enlightened, educated, briefed, up to date, up to speed, in the picture, in the know, au fait; informal clued in.
– ANTONYMS ignorant.

in·form·er /inˈfôrmər/ ▶ **noun** a person who informs on another person to the police or other authority.

– SYNONYMS **informant,** betrayer, traitor, Judas, collaborator, stool pigeon, fifth columnist, spy, Benedict Arnold, double agent, infiltrator, plant, tattletale; informal rat, squealer, whistle-blower, snitch, fink, stoolie.

in·fo·tain·ment /ˌinfōˈtānmənt/ ▶ **noun** broadcast programs that present news and serious subjects in an entertaining way.
– ORIGIN blend of **INFORMATION** and **ENTERTAINMENT**.

infra- ▶ **prefix** below: *infrasonic*.
– ORIGIN Latin *infra* 'below.'

in·frac·tion /inˈfrakSHən/ ▶ **noun** a breaking of a law, agreement, or set of rules.
– ORIGIN Latin, from *infringere* 'infringe.'

in·fra dig /ˌinfrə ˈdig/ ▶ **adjective** informal beneath one's dignity.
– ORIGIN from Latin *infra dignitatem.*

in·fra·or·der /ˈinfrəˌôrdər/ ▶ **noun** Biology a taxonomic category that ranks below a suborder.

in·fra·red /ˌinfrəˈred/ ▶ **noun** electromagnetic radiation having a wavelength just greater than that of red light but less than that of microwaves, emitted particularly by heated objects. ▶ **adjective** relating to such radiation.

in·fra·son·ic /ˌinfrəˈsänik/ ▶ **adjective** relating or referring to sound waves with a frequency below the range that can be heard by the human ear.

in·fra·sound /ˈinfrəˌsound/ ▶ **noun** infrasonic sound waves.

in·fra·struc·ture /ˈinfrəˌstrəkCHər/ ▶ **noun** the basic physical and organizational structures (e.g., buildings, roads, and power supplies) needed for a society or enterprise to function.
– DERIVATIVES **in·fra·struc·tur·al** /ˌinfrəˈstrəkCHərəl/ adjective.

in·fre·quent /inˈfrēkwənt/ ▶ **adjective** not occurring often; rare.
– DERIVATIVES **in·fre·quen·cy** noun **in·fre·quent·ly** adverb.

in·fringe /inˈfrinj/ ▶ **verb 1** break the terms of a law, agreement, etc. **2** limit or restrict someone's rights: *such widespread surveillance could infringe on personal liberties.*
– DERIVATIVES **in·fringe·ment** noun **in·fring·er** noun.
– ORIGIN Latin *infringere.*

in·fu·ri·ate /inˈfyo͞orēˌāt/ ▶ **verb** make someone very irritated or angry.

> – SYNONYMS **enrage,** incense, provoke, anger, madden, exasperate; informal make someone see red.
> – ANTONYMS please.

– DERIVATIVES **in·fu·ri·at·ing** adjective.
– ORIGIN Latin *infuriare.*

in·fuse /inˈfyo͞oz/ ▶ **verb 1** fill something with a quality: *a play infused with humor.* **2** soak tea, herbs, etc., to extract the flavor or healing properties. **3** Medicine allow a liquid to flow into a vein or tissue.
– DERIVATIVES **in·fus·er** noun.
– ORIGIN Latin *infundere* 'pour in.'

in·fu·sion /inˈfyo͞ozHən/ ▶ **noun 1** a drink or remedy prepared by soaking tea or herbs. **2** a new or additional element introduced into something: *the company needs a serious infusion of cash.* **3** the action of infusing something.

in·gen·ious /inˈjēnyəs/ ▶ **adjective** clever, original, and inventive.

> – SYNONYMS **inventive,** creative, imaginative, original, innovative, pioneering, resourceful, enterprising, inspired, clever.
> – ANTONYMS unimaginative.

– DERIVATIVES **in·gen·ious·ly** adverb.
– ORIGIN Latin *ingeniosus.*

> **CHOOSE THE RIGHT WORD**
>
> See **CREATIVE**.

in·gé·nue /ˈanjəˌno͞o, ˈänzH-/ ▶ **noun** an innocent or unsophisticated young woman.
– ORIGIN French.

in·ge·nu·i·ty /ˌinjəˈn(y)o͞oitē/ ▶ **noun** the quality of being clever, original, and inventive.
– ORIGIN Latin *ingenuitas* 'ingenuousness.'

in·gen·u·ous /inˈjenyo͞oəs/ ▶ **adjective** innocent and unsuspecting.

> – SYNONYMS **naive,** innocent, simple, childlike, trusting, trustful, wide-eyed, inexperienced, artless, guileless.
> – ANTONYMS artful.

– DERIVATIVES **in·gen·u·ous·ly** adverb **in·gen·u·ous·ness** noun.
– ORIGIN Latin *ingenuus* 'native, inborn.'

> **CHOOSE THE RIGHT WORD**
>
> See **GULLIBLE**.

in·gest /inˈjest/ ▶ **verb** take food or drink into the body by swallowing or absorbing it.
– DERIVATIVES **in·ges·tion** noun.
– ORIGIN Latin *ingerere* 'bring in.'

in·glo·ri·ous /inˈglôrēəs/ ▶ **adjective** causing shame; dishonorable.

in·go·ing /ˈinˌgōiNG/ ▶ **adjective** going toward or into.

in·got /ˈiNGgət/ ▶ **noun** a rectangular block of steel, gold, or other metal.
– ORIGIN perhaps from an Old English word meaning 'pour, cast.'

in·grain /inˈgrān/ ▶ **verb** firmly fix or establish (a habit, belief, or attitude) in a person. ▶ **adjective** /ˈinˌgrān/ (of a textile) composed of fibers that have been dyed different colors before being woven.

in·grained /inˈgrānd/ (also **engrained**) ▶ **adjective 1** (of a habit or attitude) firmly established and hard to change. **2** (of dirt) deeply embedded.
– ORIGIN from the old use of *grain* to mean 'kermes, cochineal' (the first meaning was 'dyed with cochineal').

in·grate /ˈinˌgrāt/ formal or literary ▶ **noun** an ungrateful person. ▶ **adjective** ungrateful.
– ORIGIN Latin *ingratus.*

in·gra·ti·ate /inˈgrāsHēˌāt/ ▶ **verb** (**ingratiate oneself**) try to gain favor with someone by flattering or trying to please them.
– DERIVATIVES **in·gra·ti·at·ing** adjective **in·gra·ti·a·tion** /-ˌgrāsHēˈāsHən/ noun.
– ORIGIN from Latin *in gratiam* 'into favor.'

in·grat·i·tude /inˈgratiˌt(y)o͞od/ ▶ **noun** a lack of gratitude for something that has been done for one.

in·gre·di·ent /inˈgrēdēənt, iNG-/ ▶ **noun 1** any of the substances that are combined to make a particular dish. **2** one of the parts or elements of something: *their romance had all the ingredients of a fairy tale.*

> – SYNONYMS **constituent,** component, element, item, part, strand, unit, feature, aspect, attribute.

– ORIGIN Latin *ingredi* 'enter.'

in·gress /ˈinˌgres/ ▶ **noun 1** the action of entering or coming in. **2** a place or means of access.
– ORIGIN Latin *ingressus.*

in-group ▶ **noun** an exclusive, typically small, group of people with a shared interest or identity: *an in-group of scholars involved in sociological debates.*

in·grown /ˈinˌgrōn/ (also **ingrowng** /ˈinˌgrōiNG/) ▶ **adjective** (of a toenail) growing inward into the flesh of the toe.

in·gui·nal /ˈiNGgwənəl/ ▶ **adjective** relating to the groin.
– ORIGIN Latin *inguinalis.*

in·hab·it /in'habit/ ▶ **verb** (**inhabits, inhabiting, inhabited**) live in or occupy a place.

– SYNONYMS **live in,** occupy, settle, people, populate, colonize.

– DERIVATIVES **in·hab·it·a·ble** adjective.
– ORIGIN Latin *inhabitare.*

in·hab·it·ant /in'habitnt/ ▶ **noun** a person or animal that lives in or occupies a place.

– SYNONYMS **resident,** occupant, occupier, settler, local, native; (**inhabitants**) population, populace, people, public, community, citizenry, townsfolk, townspeople.

in·hal·ant /in'hālənt/ ▶ **noun** a medicine that is inhaled.

in·hale /in'hāl/ ▶ **verb** breathe in air, gas, smoke, etc.

– SYNONYMS **breathe in,** draw in, suck in, sniff (in), drink in, gasp.
– ANTONYMS exhale.

– DERIVATIVES **in·ha·la·tion** /ˌinhə'lāsʜən/ noun.
– ORIGIN Latin *inhalare.*

in·hal·er /in'hālər/ ▶ **noun** a portable device used for inhaling a medicine.

in·here /in'hi(ə)r/ ▶ **verb** (**inhere in/within**) formal be an essential or permanent part of something.
– ORIGIN Latin *inhaerere* 'stick to.'

in·her·ent /in'hi(ə)rənt, -'her-/ ▶ **adjective** existing in someone or something as a permanent or essential part or quality: *the risks inherent in our business.*
– DERIVATIVES **in·her·ent·ly** adverb.

in·her·it /in'herit/ ▶ **verb** (**inherits, inheriting, inherited**) **1** receive money, property, or a title as an heir at the death of the previous holder. **2** have a quality or characteristic that one's parents or ancestors also possessed: *she inherited her mother's strong-willed nature.* **3** receive or be left with a situation, object, etc., from a predecessor or former owner.

– SYNONYMS **be bequeathed,** be left, be willed, come into, succeed to, assume, take over.

– DERIVATIVES **in·her·it·a·ble** adjective **in·her·i·tor** noun.
– ORIGIN Latin *inhereditare* 'appoint as heir.'

in·her·it·ance /in'heritəns/ ▶ **noun 1** money, property, or a title received on the death of the previous owner. **2** the action of inheriting something.

– SYNONYMS **legacy,** bequest, endowment, birthright, heritage, patrimony.

WORD LINKS

hereditary *relating to inheritance*

in·her·it·ance tax ▶ **noun** tax levied on property and money acquired by inheritance.

in·hib·it /in'hibit/ ▶ **verb** (**inhibits, inhibiting, inhibited**) **1** hinder or restrict an action or process: *cold inhibits plant growth.* **2** make someone unable to act in a relaxed and natural way.

– SYNONYMS **impede,** hinder, hamper, hold back, discourage, interfere with, obstruct, slow down, retard.
– ANTONYMS assist, allow.

– ORIGIN Latin *inhibere.*

CHOOSE THE RIGHT WORD

See **THWART**.

in·hib·it·ed /in'hibitid/ ▶ **adjective** unable to act in a relaxed and natural way: *she was so inhibited that most people thought she was cold and unfeeling.*

– SYNONYMS **reserved,** reticent, guarded, self-conscious, insecure, withdrawn, repressed, undemonstrative, shy, diffident, bashful; informal uptight.

in·hi·bi·tion /ˌin(h)i'bisʜən/ ▶ **noun 1** a feeling that makes someone unable to act in a relaxed and natural way. **2** the action of inhibiting something.

in·hib·i·tor /in'hibitər/ ▶ **noun** a substance that slows down or prevents a particular chemical reaction or other process.
– DERIVATIVES **in·hib·i·to·ry** adjective.

in·hos·pi·ta·ble /ˌinhä'spitəbəl, in'häs-/ ▶ **adjective** **1** (of an environment) harsh and difficult to live in. **2** unwelcoming.

in-house ▶ **adjective & adverb** within an organization.

in·hu·man /in'(h)yo͞omən/ ▶ **adjective 1** lacking good human qualities; cruel or brutal. **2** not human in nature or character.

– SYNONYMS **1** *inhuman treatment* **cruel,** harsh, inhumane, brutal, callous, sadistic, savage, vicious, barbaric. **2** *inhuman shapes* **monstrous,** devilish, ghostly, demonic, animal, bestial; unearthly.
– ANTONYMS humane.

– DERIVATIVES **in·hu·man·ly** adverb.

in·hu·mane /ˌin(h)yo͞o'mān/ ▶ **adjective** showing no compassion for the misery or suffering of other people; cruel.
– DERIVATIVES **in·hu·mane·ly** adverb.

in·hu·man·i·ty /ˌin(h)yo͞o'manitē/ ▶ **noun** (pl. **inhumanities**) cruel or brutal behavior.

in·im·i·cal /i'nimikəl/ ▶ **adjective** harmful or unfavorable: *the policy was inimical to America's real interests.*
– DERIVATIVES **in·im·i·cal·ly** adverb.
– ORIGIN from Latin *inimicus* 'enemy.'

CHOOSE THE RIGHT WORD

See **HOSTILE**.

in·im·i·ta·ble /i'nimitəbəl/ ▶ **adjective** impossible to imitate; unique.
– DERIVATIVES **in·im·i·ta·bly** adverb.

in·iq·ui·ty /i'nikwitē/ ▶ **noun** (pl. **iniquities**) highly unfair or immoral behavior.
– DERIVATIVES **in·iq·ui·tous** adjective.
– ORIGIN Latin *iniquitas.*

in·i·tial /i'nisʜəl/ ▶ **adjective** existing or occurring at the beginning: *our initial impression was favorable.*

– SYNONYMS **beginning,** opening, commencing, starting, first, earliest, primary, preliminary, preparatory, introductory, inaugural.
– ANTONYMS final.

▶ **noun** the first letter of a name or word.
▶ **verb** (**initials, initialing, initialed**) mark a document with one's initials as a sign of approval or authorization.
– ORIGIN from Latin *initium* 'beginning.'

in·i·tial·ism /i'nisʜəˌlizəm/ ▶ **noun** an abbreviation consisting of initial letters pronounced separately (e.g., *CPU*).

in·i·tial·ize /i'nisʜəˌlīz/ ▶ **verb** Computing **1** (often **be initialized to**) set to the value or put in the condition appropriate to the start of an operation: *the counter is*

initialized to one. **2** format (a computer disk).
– DERIVATIVES **in·i·tial·i·za·tion** /iˌnisHəli'zāsHən/ noun.

in·i·tial·ly /i'nisHəlē/ ▶ **adverb** at first: *initially, we thought it might be pilot error.*

– SYNONYMS **at first,** at the start, at the outset, in/at the beginning, to begin with, to start with, originally.

in·i·ti·ate ▶ **verb** /i'nisHēˌāt/ **1** cause a process or action to begin. **2** admit someone into a society or group with a formal ceremony or ritual. **3 (initiate someone into)** introduce someone to a new activity or skill: *they were initiated into the mysteries of mathematics.*

– SYNONYMS **1 begin,** start (off), commence, institute, inaugurate, launch, instigate, establish, set up. **2** *initiated into the club* **introduce,** admit, induct, install, swear in, ordain, invest.
– ANTONYMS end, expel.

▶ **noun** /i'nisHēit/ a person who has been initiated into a society, group, or new activity.
– DERIVATIVES **in·i·ti·a·tion** /iˌnisHē'āsHən/ noun **in·i·ti·a·tor** /i'nisHēˌātər/ noun **in·i·ti·a·to·ry** /-əˌtôrē/ adjective.
– ORIGIN Latin *initiare* 'begin.'

in·i·ti·a·tive /i'nisH(ē)ətiv/ ▶ **noun 1** the ability to act independently and with a fresh approach. **2** the power or opportunity to act before others do: *we have lost the initiative.* **3** a new development or fresh approach to a problem: *a new initiative against car theft.*

– SYNONYMS **1 enterprise,** resourcefulness, inventiveness, imagination, ingenuity, originality, creativity. **2 advantage,** upper hand, edge, lead, start. **3 scheme,** plan, strategy, measure, proposal, step, action.

– PHRASES **on one's own initiative** without being prompted by other people. **take** (or **seize**) **the initiative** be the first to take action in a particular situation: *antiglobalization groups have seized the initiative in the dispute.*

in·ject /in'jekt/ ▶ **verb 1** introduce a drug or other substance into the body with a syringe: *the doctor injected a painkilling drug.* **2** administer a drug or medicine to a person or animal with a syringe: *he injected himself with adrenaline.* **3** introduce something under pressure into a passage, cavity, or solid material. **4** introduce a new or different element into something: *she tried to inject scorn into her tone.*

– SYNONYMS **1 administer,** take; informal shoot (up), mainline, fix. **2 inoculate,** vaccinate. **3 insert,** introduce, feed, push, force, shoot. **4 introduce,** instill, infuse, imbue, breathe.

– DERIVATIVES **in·ject·a·ble** adjective & noun **in·jec·tor** noun.
– ORIGIN Latin *inicere* 'throw in.'

in·jec·tion /in'jeksHən/ ▶ **noun 1** an act of giving a person or animal a drug using a syringe. **2** a substance that is injected. **3** a large sum of additional money used to help a situation, business, etc.

– SYNONYMS **1 inoculation,** vaccination, immunization, booster; informal jab, shot. **2 addition,** introduction, investment, dose, infusion, insertion.

in-joke ▶ **noun** a joke that is shared exclusively by a small group.

in·ju·di·cious /ˌinjoo'disHəs/ ▶ **adjective** showing poor judgment; unwise.
– DERIVATIVES **in·ju·di·cious·ly** adverb.

in·junc·tion /in'jəNG(k)sHən/ ▶ **noun 1** an order made by a court of law stating that a person must or must not do something. **2** an authoritative warning.

– SYNONYMS **order,** ruling, direction, directive, command, instruction, mandate.

– DERIVATIVES **in·junc·tive** /-'jəNG(k)tiv/ adjective.
– ORIGIN Latin.

in·jure /'injər/ ▶ **verb 1** do physical harm to someone or something. **2** harm or damage: *a company's reputation could be injured by a libel suit.*

– SYNONYMS **1 hurt,** wound, damage, harm, disable, break; Medicine traumatize. **2 damage,** mar, spoil, weaken, ruin, blight, blemish, tarnish, blacken.

in·jured /'injərd/ ▶ **adjective 1** physically harmed. **2** offended or upset: *his injured pride.*

– SYNONYMS **1 hurt,** wounded, damaged, sore, bruised, broken, fractured; Medicine traumatized. **2 upset,** hurt, wounded, offended, reproachful, pained, aggrieved.
– ANTONYMS healthy.

in·ju·ri·ous /in'jo͝orēəs/ ▶ **adjective 1** causing or likely to cause harm or damage. **2** (of language) libelous.

in·ju·ry /'injərē/ ▶ **noun** (pl. **injuries**) **1** an instance of being physically harmed. **2** the fact of being injured; harm or damage.

– SYNONYMS **1 wound,** bruise, cut, gash, scratch, graze; Medicine trauma, lesion. **2 harm,** hurt, damage, pain, suffering. **3 offense,** abuse, injustice, disservice, affront, insult.

– ORIGIN Latin *injuria* 'a wrong.'

in·jus·tice /in'jəstis/ ▶ **noun 1** lack of justice or fairness. **2** an unjust act or occurrence.

– SYNONYMS **1 unfairness,** one-sidedness, inequity, bias, prejudice, discrimination, intolerance, exploitation, corruption. **2 wrong,** offense, crime, sin, outrage, scandal, disgrace, affront.

ink /iNGk/ ▶ **noun 1** a colored fluid used for writing, drawing, or printing. **2** a black liquid squirted by a cuttlefish, octopus, or squid to confuse a predator.
▶ **verb 1** write or mark words or a design with ink. **2** cover metal type or a stamp with ink before printing.
– ORIGIN Old French *enque.*

ink·jet print·er /'iNGkˌjet/ ▶ **noun** a printer in which the characters are formed by minute jets of ink.

ink·ling /'iNGkliNG/ ▶ **noun** a slight suspicion; a hint.
– ORIGIN from former *inkle* 'say in an undertone.'

ink·well /'iNGkˌwel/ ▶ **noun** historical a container for ink, usually fitted into a hole in a desk.

ink·y /'iNGkē/ ▶ **adjective** (**inkier, inkiest**) **1** as dark as ink. **2** stained with ink.

in·laid /'inˌlād/ past and past participle of **INLAY**.

in·land /'inˌland, -lənd/ ▶ **adjective & adverb 1** in or into the interior of a country. **2** (as adj.) chiefly Brit. carried on within a country; domestic: *inland trade.*

– SYNONYMS **interior,** inshore, internal, upcountry.
– ANTONYMS coastal.

▶ **noun** the interior of a country or region.
– DERIVATIVES **in·land·er** noun.

in-law ▶ **noun** a relative by marriage. ▶ **combining form** related by marriage: *father-in-law.*

in·lay /ˌin'lā/ ▶ **verb** (past and past part. **inlaid**) decorate an object by embedding pieces of a different material in its surface. ▶ **noun** /'inˌlā/ **1** inlaid decoration. **2** a material or substance used for inlaying. **3** a filling shaped to fit a cavity in a tooth.

in·let /ˈinˌlet, -lit/ ▶ **noun 1** a small arm of the sea, a lake, or a river. **2** a place or means of entry: *an air inlet.* **3** (in tailoring and dressmaking) an inserted piece of material.

– SYNONYMS **1 cove,** bay, bight, creek, estuary, fjord, sound; Scottish firth. **2 vent,** flue, shaft, duct, channel, pipe.

inline (also **in-line**) ▶ **adjective 1** having parts arranged in a line. **2** forming an integral part of a continuous sequence of operations or machines.

inline skate (also **in-line skate**) ▶ **noun** a roller skate in which the wheels are fixed in a single line along the sole of the boot.
– DERIVATIVES **in·line skat·er** noun **in·line skat·ing** noun.

in lo·co pa·ren·tis /in ˌlōkō pəˈrentis/ ▶ **adverb & adjective** (of a teacher or other adult) in the place of a parent; as a guardian.
– ORIGIN Latin.

in·mate /ˈinˌmāt/ ▶ **noun** a person living in an institution such as a prison or hospital.

– SYNONYMS **1 prisoner,** convict, captive, detainee, internee. **2 patient,** mental patient, resident.

– ORIGIN probably from **INN** + **MATE**[1].

in me·mo·ri·am /ˌin məˈmôrēəm/ ▶ **preposition** in memory of a dead person.
– ORIGIN Latin.

in·most /ˈinˌmōst/ ▶ **adjective** closest to the center; innermost.

inn /in/ ▶ **noun** an establishment that provides food, drink, and accommodations, especially for travelers.
– ORIGIN Old English.

in·nards /ˈinərdz/ ▶ **plural noun** informal **1** internal organs; entrails. **2** the internal workings of a device or machine.

in·nate /iˈnāt/ ▶ **adjective** inborn; natural.
– DERIVATIVES **in·nate·ly** adverb **in·nate·ness** noun.
– ORIGIN Latin *innatus*.

in·ner /ˈinər/ ▶ **adjective 1** situated inside; close to the center. **2** mental or spiritual: *inner strength.* **3** private; not expressed.

– SYNONYMS **1 central,** innermost. **2 internal,** interior, inside, innermost. **3 hidden,** secret, deep, underlying, veiled.
– ANTONYMS outer.

▶ **noun** an inner part.

in·ner cit·y ▶ **noun** an area in or near the center of a city, especially when associated with social and economic problems.

in·ner ear ▶ **noun** the part of the ear embedded in the temporal bone, consisting of the semicircular canals and the cochlea.

in·ner·most /ˈinərˌmōst/ ▶ **adjective 1** furthest in; closest to the center. **2** (of thoughts) most private and deeply felt.

in·ner tube ▶ **noun** a separate inflatable tube inside a tire.

in·ning /ˈiniNG/ ▶ **noun** Baseball each division of a game during which both sides have a turn at batting.
– ORIGIN Old English, 'a putting or getting in.'

in·nings /ˈiniNGz/ ▶ **noun** (pl. same) (treated as sing.) Cricket each of the divisions of a game during which one side has a turn at batting.

inn·keep·er /ˈinˌkēpər/ ▶ **noun** chiefly old use a person who runs an inn.

in·no·cence /ˈinəsəns/ ▶ **noun** the state, quality, or fact of being innocent.

– SYNONYMS **1** *he protested his innocence* **guiltlessness,** blamelessness. **2** *she took advantage of his innocence* **naivety,** credulity, inexperience, gullibility, ingenuousness.

in·no·cent /ˈinəsənt/ ▶ **adjective 1** not guilty of a crime or offense. **2** having had little experience of life, especially of sexual matters. **3** not directly involved in an event yet suffering its consequences: *an innocent bystander.* **4** not intended to cause offense: *an innocent remark.* **5** (**innocent of**) without experience or knowledge of something: *a man innocent of war's cruelties.*

– SYNONYMS **1 guiltless,** blameless, clean, irreproachable, above reproach, honest, upright, law-abiding. **2 harmless,** innocuous, safe, inoffensive, unobjectionable. **3 naive,** ingenuous, trusting, credulous, impressionable, easily led, inexperienced, unsophisticated, artless.
– ANTONYMS guilty.

▶ **noun** an innocent person.
– DERIVATIVES **in·no·cent·ly** adverb.
– ORIGIN Latin, 'not harming.'

in·noc·u·ous /iˈnäkyo͞oəs/ ▶ **adjective** not harmful or offensive.

– SYNONYMS **1 harmless,** safe, nontoxic, edible. **2** *an innocuous comment* **inoffensive,** unobjectionable, unexceptionable, harmless, anodyne.
– ANTONYMS harmful, offensive.

– DERIVATIVES **in·noc·u·ous·ly** adverb.
– ORIGIN Latin *innocuus*.

in·no·vate /ˈinəˌvāt/ ▶ **verb** introduce new methods, ideas, or products.
– DERIVATIVES **in·no·va·tor** noun **in·no·va·to·ry** /-vəˌtôrē/ adjective.
– ORIGIN Latin *innovare* 'renew, alter.'

in·no·va·tion /ˌinəˈvāSHən/ ▶ **noun 1** the action of introducing new methods, ideas, or products. **2** a new method, idea, or product.

– SYNONYMS **change,** alteration, upheaval, reorganization, restructuring, novelty, departure.

in·no·va·tive /ˈinəˌvātiv/ ▶ **adjective 1** featuring new ideas or methods; advanced and original: *innovative designs.* **2** (of a person) original and creative in their thinking.

– SYNONYMS **original,** new, novel, fresh, unusual, experimental, inventive, ingenious, pioneering, groundbreaking, revolutionary, radical.

in·nu·en·do /ˌinyo͞oˈendō/ ▶ **noun** (pl. **innuendoes** or **innuendos**) a remark that makes an indirect reference to something, typically something rude or unpleasant.

– SYNONYMS **insinuation,** suggestion, intimation, implication; aspersion, slur.

– ORIGIN Latin, 'by nodding at, by pointing to.'

in·nu·mer·a·ble /iˈn(y)o͞omərəbəl/ ▶ **adjective** too many to be counted.

in·nu·mer·ate /iˈn(y)o͞omərit/ ▶ **adjective** without a basic knowledge of mathematics and arithmetic.
– DERIVATIVES **in·nu·mer·a·cy** /-rəsē/ noun.

in·oc·u·late /iˈnäkyəˌlāt/ ▶ **verb 1** another term for **VACCINATE**. **2** introduce cells or microorganisms into a

substance in which they can be grown.
– DERIVATIVES **in·oc·u·la·tion** /iˌnäkyəˈlāsʜən/ noun **in·oc·u·la·tor** noun.
– ORIGIN Latin *inoculare*.

in·of·fen·sive /ˌinəˈfensiv/ ▶ **adjective** not objectionable or harmful.
– DERIVATIVES **in·of·fen·sive·ly** adverb **in·of·fen·sive·ness** noun.

in·op·er·a·ble /inˈäp(ə)rəbəl/ ▶ **adjective 1** not able to be safely treated or removed by a surgical operation: *an inoperable brain tumor*. **2** not able to be used. **3** impractical; unworkable.

in·op·er·a·tive /inˈäp(ə)rətiv/ ▶ **adjective** not working or taking effect.

in·op·por·tune /ˌinˌäpərˈt(y)o͞on/ ▶ **adjective** happening at an inconvenient time.

in·or·di·nate /iˈnôrdn-it/ ▶ **adjective** unusually large; excessive.
– DERIVATIVES **in·or·di·nate·ly** adverb.
– ORIGIN Latin *inordinatus*.

in·or·gan·ic /ˌinôrˈganik/ ▶ **adjective 1** not consisting of or coming from living matter. **2** Chemistry relating or referring to compounds that do not contain carbon.
– DERIVATIVES **in·or·gan·i·cal·ly** adverb.

in·pa·tient /ˈinˌpāsʜənt/ ▶ **noun** a patient who stays in a hospital while receiving treatment.

in·put /ˈinˌpo͝ot/ ▶ **noun 1** what is put or taken in or operated on by any process or system. **2** a person's contribution: *I'd value your input*. **3** energy supplied to a device or system; an electrical signal. **4** a place or device from which electricity, data, etc., enters a system. ▶ **verb** (**inputs, inputting**; past and past part. **input** or **inputted**) put data into a computer.
– DERIVATIVES **in·put·ter** noun.

in·quest /ˈinˌkwest, ˈɪɴɢ-/ ▶ **noun 1** a judicial inquiry to find out the facts relating to a particular incident. **2** an inquiry by a coroner's court into the cause of a death.

– SYNONYMS **inquiry,** investigation, probe, examination, review, hearing.

– ORIGIN Old French *enqueste*.

in·quire /inˈkwīr/ (also chiefly Brit. **enquire**) ▶ **verb 1** ask someone for information. **2** (**inquire after**) ask about someone's health or situation. **3** (**inquire into**) investigate something.

– SYNONYMS **1 ask,** query, question. **2** *we are* ***inquiring into*** *the incident* **investigate,** probe, look into, make inquiries of/about, research, examine, explore, delve into; informal check out.

– DERIVATIVES **in·quir·er** noun.
– ORIGIN Latin *inquirere*.

in·quir·ing /inˈkwīrɪɴɢ/ ▶ **adjective 1** interested in learning new things: *an open, inquiring mind*. **2** (of a look) expressing a wish for information.
– DERIVATIVES **in·quir·ing·ly** adverb.

in·quir·y /inˈkwī(ə)rē, ˈinˌkwī(ə)rē, ˈinkwərē/ ▶ **noun** (pl. **inquiries**) **1** an act of asking for information. **2** an official investigation.

– SYNONYMS **1 question,** query. **2 investigation,** probe, examination, exploration, inquest, hearing.

in·qui·si·tion /ˌinkwiˈzisʜən, ˌɪɴɢ-/ ▶ **noun 1** a period of long and intensive questioning or investigation. **2** the verdict of an official inquiry.
– ORIGIN Latin, 'examination.'

in·quis·i·tive /inˈkwizitiv, ɪɴɢ-/ ▶ **adjective 1** eager to learn things. **2** too curious about other people's affairs; prying.
– DERIVATIVES **in·quis·i·tive·ly** adverb **in·quis·i·tive·ness** noun.

in·quis·i·tor /inˈkwizitər/ ▶ **noun** a person conducting a long, intensive, or relentless period of questioning or investigation.
– DERIVATIVES **in·quis·i·to·ri·al** /inˌkwiziˈtôrēəl/ adjective.

in re ▶ **preposition** in the legal case of; with regard to: *in re Mancet's Estate*.

in·road /ˈinˌrōd/ ▶ **noun** (usu. in phrase **make inroads in/into**) a gradual entry into or effect on a place or situation: *the firm is beginning to make inroads into the US market*.

in·rush /ˈinˌrəsʜ/ ▶ **noun** a sudden inward rush or flow.
– DERIVATIVES **in·rush·ing** adjective & noun.

INS ▶ **abbreviation** Immigration and Naturalization Service, a former federal agency that was absorbed into Immigration and Customs Enforcement.

in·sa·lu·bri·ous /ˌinsəˈlo͞obrēəs/ ▶ **adjective** not clean or well kept; seedy or squalid.

in·sane /inˈsān/ ▶ **adjective 1** seriously mentally ill. **2** extremely foolish; irrational.

– SYNONYMS **1 mad,** of unsound mind, certifiable, psychotic, schizophrenic, unhinged; informal crazy, nuts, raving mad, bonkers, loony. **2 stupid,** idiotic, nonsensical, absurd, ridiculous, ludicrous, preposterous; informal crazy, mad, daft.
– ANTONYMS sane.

– DERIVATIVES **in·sane·ly** adverb **in·san·i·ty** /inˈsanitē/ noun (pl. **insanities**).
– ORIGIN Latin *insanus*.

in·sa·tia·ble /inˈsāsʜəbəl/ ▶ **adjective** impossible to satisfy.
– DERIVATIVES **in·sa·tia·bil·i·ty** /-ˌsāsʜəˈbilitē/ noun **in·sa·tia·bly** adverb.

in·scribe /inˈskrīb/ ▶ **verb 1** write or carve words or symbols on a surface. **2** write a dedication to someone in a book. **3** Geometry draw a figure within another so that their boundaries touch but do not intersect.
– ORIGIN Latin *inscribere*.

in·scrip·tion /inˈskripsʜən/ ▶ **noun 1** words or symbols inscribed on a monument, in a book, etc. **2** the action of inscribing something.
– DERIVATIVES **in·scrip·tion·al** adjective.

in·scru·ta·ble /inˈskro͞otəbəl/ ▶ **adjective** impossible to understand or interpret.
– DERIVATIVES **in·scru·ta·bil·i·ty** /-ˌskro͞otəˈbilitē/ noun **in·scru·ta·bly** adverb.
– ORIGIN Latin *inscrutabilis*.

in·seam /ˈinˌsēm/ ▶ **noun** the seam in a pair of pants from the crotch to the bottom of the leg, or the length of this.

in·sect /ˈinˌsekt/ ▶ **noun** a small invertebrate animal with a body divided into three segments (head, thorax, and abdomen), six legs, two antennae, and usually one or two pairs of wings.

– SYNONYMS **bug**; informal creepy-crawly.

– ORIGIN from Latin *animal insectum* 'segmented animal.'

WORD LINKS

entomology *study of insects*

in·sec·ti·cide /in'sekti,sīd/ ▸ **noun** a substance used for killing insects.
– DERIVATIVES **in·sec·ti·cid·al** /-,sekti'sīdl/ adjective.

in·sec·tile /in'sektl, -,tīl/ ▸ **adjective** resembling an insect.

in·sec·ti·vore /in'sektə,vôr/ ▸ **noun** **1** an animal that feeds on insects and other invertebrates. **2** Zoology a mammal of an order that includes the shrews, moles, and hedgehogs.
– DERIVATIVES **in·sec·tiv·o·rous** /,in,sek'tivərəs/ adjective.

in·se·cure /,insi'kyo͝or/ ▸ **adjective** **1** not confident or self-assured. **2** not firm or firmly fixed. **3** (of a place) easily broken into; not protected.

– SYNONYMS **1 unconfident,** uncertain, unsure, doubtful, diffident, hesitant, self-conscious, anxious, fearful. **2 unprotected,** unguarded, vulnerable, unsecured. **3 unstable,** rickety, wobbly, shaky, unsteady, precarious.
– ANTONYMS confident, stable.

– DERIVATIVES **in·se·cure·ly** adverb **in·se·cu·ri·ty** noun (pl. **insecurities**).

in·sem·i·nate /in'semə,nāt/ ▸ **verb** introduce semen into the vagina of a woman or a female animal.
– DERIVATIVES **in·sem·i·na·tion** /-,semə'nāsʜən/ noun **in·sem·i·na·tor** noun.
– ORIGIN Latin *inseminare* 'sow.'

in·sen·sate /in'sen,sāt, -sit/ ▸ **adjective** **1** lacking physical sensation. **2** lacking sympathy for other people; unfeeling. **3** completely lacking sense or reason.

in·sen·si·ble /in'sensəbəl/ ▸ **adjective** **1** unconscious. **2** numb; without feeling. **3** (**insensible of/to**) unaware of or indifferent to something. **4** too small or gradual to be noticed.
– DERIVATIVES **in·sen·si·bly** adverb **in·sen·si·bil·i·ty** /in,sensə'bilitē/ noun.

in·sen·si·tive /in'sensitiv/ ▸ **adjective** **1** showing or having no concern for the feelings of other people. **2** not able to feel something physically: *she was remarkably insensitive to pain.* **3** not aware of or able to respond to something: *politicians had been insensitive to local issues.*

– SYNONYMS **1 heartless,** unfeeling, inconsiderate, thoughtless, thick-skinned; hard-hearted, uncaring, unsympathetic, unkind. **2** *he was* ***insensitive to*** *her feelings* **impervious to,** oblivious to, unaware of, unresponsive to, indifferent to.
– ANTONYMS compassionate.

– DERIVATIVES **in·sen·si·tive·ly** adverb **in·sen·si·tiv·i·ty** /-,sensi'tivitē/ noun.

in·sen·ti·ent /in'sensʜ(ē)ənt/ ▸ **adjective** incapable of feeling; inanimate.
– DERIVATIVES **in·sen·ti·ence** noun.

in·sep·a·ra·ble /in'sep(ə)rəbəl/ ▸ **adjective** **1** unable to be separated or treated separately. **2** very friendly and close.
– DERIVATIVES **in·sep·a·ra·bil·i·ty** /-,sep(ə)rə'bilitē/ noun **in·sep·a·ra·bly** adverb.

in·sert ▸ **verb** /in'sərt/ **1** place or fit something into something else: *she inserted her key into the lock.* **2** include text in a piece of writing.

– SYNONYMS **put,** place, push, thrust, slide, slip, load, fit, slot, install; informal pop, stick.
– ANTONYMS extract, remove.

▸ **noun** /'in,sərt/ **1** a loose page or section in a magazine. **2** an ornamental section of cloth inserted into a garment. **3** a shot inserted in a film or video.
– DERIVATIVES **in·sert·a·ble** adjective **in·sert·er** noun.
– ORIGIN Latin *inserere* 'put in.'

in·ser·tion /in'sərsʜən/ ▸ **noun** **1** the action of inserting something. **2** a change or new item inserted in a piece of writing. **3** each appearance of an advertisement in a newspaper or magazine.

in·serv·ice ▸ **adjective** (of training) intended to take place during the course of employment.

in·set ▸ **noun** /'in,set/ **1** a thing inserted; an insert. **2** a small picture or map inserted within the border of a larger one. ▸ **verb** /in'set/ (**insets, insetting**; past and past part. **inset** or **insetted**) **1** put something in as an inset. **2** decorate something with an inset: *tables inset with ceramic tiles.*

in·shore /'in'sʜôr/ ▸ **adjective** **1** at sea but close to the shore. **2** operating at sea but near the coast. ▸ **adverb** toward or closer to the shore.

in·side ▸ **noun** /'in'sīd/ **1** the inner side, surface, or part of something. **2** (**insides**) informal the stomach and bowels. **3** the part of a road furthest from the center. **4** the side of a curve where the edge is shorter.

– SYNONYMS **1 interior,** center, core, middle, heart. **2** (**insides**) **stomach,** gut, bowels, intestines; informal tummy, belly, guts.

▸ **adjective** /,in'sīd, 'in,sīd/ **1** situated on or in, or coming from, the inside. **2** known or done by someone within an organization: *inside information.* **3** (in some sports) referring to positions nearer to the center of the field.

– SYNONYMS **1 inner,** interior, internal, innermost. **2 confidential,** classified, restricted, privileged, private, secret, exclusive; informal hush-hush.
– ANTONYMS outside.

▸ **preposition & adverb** /,in'sīd/ **1** situated or moving within. **2** within a person's body or mind. **3** indoors. **4** informal in prison. **5** (in some sports) closer to the center of the field than. **6** in less than the period of time specified.
– PHRASES **inside of** informal **1** within: *something inside of me wanted to believe him.* **2** in less than (the period of time specified): *rerigging a ship for a voyage inside of a week.* **on the inside** informal in a position in which one can get private information.

in·side job ▸ **noun** informal a crime committed by or with the help of a person associated with the place where it occurred.

in·side out ▸ **adverb** with the inner surface turned outward.
– PHRASES **know something inside out** know something very thoroughly. **turn something inside out** **1** turn the inner surface of something outward. **2** change something utterly: *it is not so easy to turn your whole life inside out.*

in·sid·er /in'sīdər/ ▸ **noun** a person within an organization, especially someone who has information unavailable to people outside it.

in·sid·er trad·ing ▸ **noun** the illegal practice of trading on the stock exchange with the benefit of confidential information.

in·side track ▸ **noun** **1** the inner, shorter track of a racetrack. **2** a position of advantage: *he always had the inside track for the starring role.*

in·sid·i·ous /in'sidēəs/ ▸ **adjective** proceeding or spreading gradually or without being noticed, but causing serious harm.
– DERIVATIVES **in·sid·i·ous·ly** adverb **in·sid·i·ous·ness** noun.
– ORIGIN Latin *insidiosus* 'cunning.'

in·sight /ˈinˌsīt/ ▶ **noun 1** the ability to see and understand the truth about someone or something. **2** an understanding of the nature of someone or something: *a fascinating insight into the town's industrial heritage.*

– SYNONYMS **intuition,** perception, understanding, comprehension, appreciation, judgment, discernment, vision, imagination, wisdom.

– DERIVATIVES **in·sight·ful** /inˈsītfəl/ adjective **in·sight·ful·ly** adverb /inˈsītfəlē/.

in·sig·ni·a /inˈsignēə/ ▶ **noun** (pl. same or **insignias**) a badge or emblem of someone's rank, position, or membership in a group or organization.
– ORIGIN Latin, 'signs, badges.'

in·sig·nif·i·cant /ˌinsigˈnifikənt/ ▶ **adjective** having little or no importance or value.

– SYNONYMS **unimportant,** trivial, trifling, negligible, inconsequential, of no account, paltry, petty, insubstantial; informal piddling.

– DERIVATIVES **in·sig·nif·i·cance** noun **in·sig·nif·i·cant·ly** adverb.

in·sin·cere /ˌinsinˈsi(ə)r/ ▶ **adjective** not expressing one's true feelings.

– SYNONYMS **false,** fake, hollow, artificial, feigned, pretended, put-on, disingenuous, hypocritical, cynical; informal phony, pretend.

– DERIVATIVES **in·sin·cere·ly** adverb **in·sin·cer·i·ty** /-ˈseritē/ noun (pl. **insincerities**).

in·sin·u·ate /inˈsinyəˌwāt/ ▶ **verb 1** suggest or hint at something bad in an indirect and unpleasant way. **2** (**insinuate oneself into**) maneuver oneself gradually into a favorable position: *he insinuated himself into the president's confidence.*
– DERIVATIVES **in·sin·u·at·ing** adjective.
– ORIGIN Latin *insinuare*, from *sinuare* 'to curve.'

in·sin·u·a·tion /inˌsinyo͞oˈāsʜən/ ▶ **noun** an unpleasant hint or suggestion.

in·sip·id /inˈsipid/ ▶ **adjective 1** lacking flavor. **2** not interesting or exciting.
– DERIVATIVES **in·si·pid·i·ty** /ˌinsəˈpiditē/ noun **in·sip·id·ly** adverb.
– ORIGIN Latin *insipidus*.

WORD TOOLKIT

insipid ...	tedious ...	uneventful ...
performance	process	day
lyrics	work	life
display	task	vacation
dialogue	exercise	childhood
music	reading	summer
commentary	negotiations	conclusion

in·sist /inˈsist/ ▶ **verb 1** demand or state something forcefully, without accepting refusal. **2** (**insist on**) persist in doing something.

– SYNONYMS **1 stand firm,** stand one's ground, be resolute, be determined, hold out, persist, be emphatic, lay down the law, not take no for an answer; informal stick to one's guns, put one's foot down. **2 demand,** command, order, require. **3 maintain,** assert, protest, swear, declare, repeat.

– ORIGIN Latin *insistere* 'persist.'

in·sist·ent /inˈsistənt/ ▶ **adjective 1** demanding something and not allowing refusal: *she was very insistent that I call her.* **2** repeated and demanding attention.

– SYNONYMS **persistent,** determined, tenacious, unyielding, dogged, unrelenting, importunate, relentless, inexorable.

– DERIVATIVES **in·sist·ence** noun **in·sis·tent·ly** adverb.

in si·tu /ˌin ˈsīto͞o, ˈsē-/ ▶ **adverb & adjective** in the original or appropriate position.
– ORIGIN Latin.

in·so·bri·e·ty /ˌinsəˈbrī-itē/ ▶ **noun** drunkenness.

in·so·far /ˌinsōˈfär/ ▶ **adverb** (**insofar as**) to the extent that: *his philosophy spoke of personal problems only insofar as they illustrated general ones.*

in·sole /ˈinˌsōl/ ▶ **noun 1** a removable sole worn inside a shoe for warmth or to improve the fit. **2** the fixed inner sole of a boot or shoe.

in·so·lent /ˈinsələnt/ ▶ **adjective** rude and disrespectful.

– SYNONYMS **impertinent,** impudent, cheeky, ill-mannered, bad mannered, rude, impolite, discourteous, disrespectful, insubordinate; cocky; informal fresh, lippy, sassy, saucy.
– ANTONYMS polite.

– DERIVATIVES **in·so·lence** noun **in·so·lent·ly** adverb.
– ORIGIN Latin, 'immoderate, arrogant.'

in·sol·u·ble /inˈsälyəbəl/ ▶ **adjective 1** impossible to solve. **2** (of a substance) unable to be dissolved.
– DERIVATIVES **in·sol·u·bil·i·ty** /-ˌsälyəˈbilitē/ noun.

in·sol·vent /inˈsälvənt/ ▶ **adjective** not having enough money to pay debts owed.
– DERIVATIVES **in·sol·ven·cy** noun.

in·som·ni·a /inˈsämnēə/ ▶ **noun** the condition of being unable to sleep.
– DERIVATIVES **in·som·ni·ac** /-nēˌak/ noun & adjective.
– ORIGIN Latin.

in·so·much /ˌinsōˈməcʜ/ ▶ **adverb** (**insomuch that/as**) to the extent that.

in·sou·ci·ant /inˈso͞osēənt, ˌaɴso͞oˈsyäɴ/ ▶ **adjective** casually unconcerned.
– DERIVATIVES **in·sou·ci·ance** noun **in·sou·ci·ant·ly** /inˈso͞osēəntlē/ adverb.
– ORIGIN French.

in·spect /inˈspekt/ ▶ **verb 1** look at someone or something closely. **2** examine someone or something to ensure that they reach an official standard.

– SYNONYMS **examine,** check, scrutinize, investigate, vet, test, monitor, survey, study, look over; informal check out, give something a/the once-over.

– ORIGIN Latin *inspicere* 'look into, examine.'

in·spec·tion /inˈspeksʜən/ ▶ **noun** an examination or investigation: *on further inspection, we detected a slight crack in the pipe.*

– SYNONYMS **examination,** checkup, survey, scrutiny, exploration, investigation; informal once-over, going-over.

in·spec·tor /inˈspektər/ ▶ **noun 1** an official who ensures that regulations are obeyed. **2** a police officer ranking below a superintendent or police chief.

– SYNONYMS **examiner,** scrutineer, investigator, surveyor, assessor, supervisor, monitor, watchdog, ombudsman, auditor.

– DERIVATIVES **in·spec·tor·ate** noun **in·spec·to·ri·al** /ˌinspekˈtôrēəl/ adjective **in·spec·tor·ship** noun.

in·spi·ra·tion /ˌinspəˈrāsʜən/ ▸ **noun 1** the process of being filled with a feeling or with the urge to do something: *the Rocky Mountains have provided inspiration for many artists.* **2** a person or thing that inspires other people. **3** a sudden clever idea. **4** the process of breathing in.

– SYNONYMS **1 stimulus,** motivation, encouragement, influence, spur, fillip; informal shot in the arm. **2 creativity,** invention, innovation, ingenuity, imagination, originality, insight, vision. **3 bright idea,** revelation; informal brainstorm, brainwave.

– DERIVATIVES **in·spi·ra·tion·al** adjective.

in·spire /inˈspīr/ ▸ **verb 1** give someone the desire, enthusiasm, or confidence to do something. **2** create a feeling in a person. **3** give rise to: *the film was successful enough to inspire a sequel.* **4** breathe in air; inhale.

– SYNONYMS **1 stimulate,** motivate, encourage, influence, move, spur, energize, galvanize. **2** (as adj. **inspiring**) *inspiring essays* **inspirational,** encouraging, heartening, uplifting, stirring, rousing, electrifying, moving. **3 give rise to,** lead to, bring about, prompt, spawn, engender. **4 arouse,** awaken, prompt, induce, ignite, trigger, kindle, produce, bring out.

– DERIVATIVES **in·spir·a·to·ry** /inˈspīrəˌtôrē/ adjective **in·spir·er** noun.
– ORIGIN Latin *inspirare* 'breathe or blow into.'

in·spired /inˈspīrd/ ▸ **adjective 1** displaying creativity or excellence. **2** (of air or another substance) that has been breathed in.

– SYNONYMS **outstanding,** wonderful, marvelous, excellent, magnificent, exceptional, first-class, virtuoso, superlative; informal tremendous, superb, awesome, out of this world; Brit. informal brilliant.

inst. ▸ **abbreviation** institution; institute.

in·sta·bil·i·ty /ˌinstəˈbilitē/ ▸ **noun** (pl. **instabilities**) lack of stability.

– SYNONYMS **unreliability,** uncertainty, unpredictability, insecurity, volatility, capriciousness, changeability, variability, inconsistency, mutability.
– ANTONYMS stability.

in·stall /inˈstôl/ ▸ **verb 1** place or fix equipment in position ready for use. **2** establish someone in a new place or role.

– SYNONYMS **1 put,** place, station, site, insert. **2 swear in,** induct, inaugurate, invest, appoint, ordain, consecrate, anoint, enthrone, crown. **3 ensconce,** position, settle, seat, plant, sit (down); informal plonk, park.
– ANTONYMS remove.

– DERIVATIVES **in·stall·er** noun.
– ORIGIN Latin *installare.*

in·stal·la·tion /ˌinstəˈlāsʜən/ ▸ **noun 1** the action of installing or establishing someone or something. **2** a large piece of equipment installed for use. **3** a military or industrial establishment. **4** an art exhibit constructed within a gallery.

in·stall·ment /inˈstôlmənt/ (Brit **instalment**) ▸ **noun 1** a sum of money due as one of several payments made over a period of time. **2** one of several parts of something published or broadcast at intervals.

– SYNONYMS **1 payment,** repayment, tranche, portion. **2 part,** episode, chapter, issue, program, section, segment, volume.

– ORIGIN Old French *estalement.*

in·stance /ˈinstəns/ ▸ **noun 1** an example or single occurrence of something. **2** a particular case: *she hired a writer, in this instance a novelist.*

– SYNONYMS **example,** occasion, occurrence, case, illustration, sample.

▸ **verb** give something as an example.
– PHRASES **for instance** as an example. **in the first instance** in the first stage of a series of actions.
– ORIGIN Latin *instantia* 'presence, urgency.'

in·stant /ˈinstənt/ ▸ **adjective 1** happening immediately. **2** (of food) processed to allow quick preparation. **3** dated urgent; pressing.

– SYNONYMS **1 immediate,** instantaneous, on-the-spot, prompt, swift, speedy, rapid, **quick;** informal snappy. **2 prepared,** precooked, microwaveable.
– ANTONYMS delayed.

▸ **noun 1** a precise moment of time. **2** a very short time.

– SYNONYMS **moment,** minute, second, split second, trice, twinkling of an eye, flash; informal jiffy.

– ORIGIN Latin.

in·stan·ta·ne·ous /ˌinstənˈtānēəs/ ▸ **adjective** occurring or done immediately.
– DERIVATIVES **in·stan·ta·ne·i·ty** /inˌstantnˈē-itē/ noun **in·stan·ta·ne·ous·ly** adverb.

in·stan·ti·ate /inˈstancʜēˌāt/ ▸ **verb** represent something by a particular instance or example.
– DERIVATIVES **in·stan·ti·a·tion** /-ˌstancʜēˈāsʜən/ noun.

in·stant·ly /ˈinstəntlē/ ▸ **adverb** at once; immediately: *she fell asleep almost instantly.*

– SYNONYMS **immediately,** at once, straightaway, right away, instantaneously, forthwith, there and then, here and now, this/that minute, this/that second.

in·stant mes·sag·ing ▸ **noun** the exchange of typed messages between computer users in real time via the Internet.
– DERIVATIVES **in·stant mes·sage** noun.

in·stant re·play ▸ **noun** an immediate playback of part of a television broadcast, typically one in slow motion showing an incident in a sports event.

in·stead /inˈsted/ ▸ **adverb 1** as an alternative or substitute. **2** (**instead of**) in place of.

– SYNONYMS **as an alternative,** in lieu, alternatively, alternately, rather, on second thoughts.

in·step /ˈinˌstep/ ▸ **noun** the part of a person's foot between the ball and the ankle.
– ORIGIN unknown.

in·sti·gate /ˈinstiˌgāt/ ▸ **verb 1** cause something to happen or begin: *they instigated legal proceedings.* **2** (**instigate someone to/to do**) encourage someone to do something, especially something bad.
– DERIVATIVES **in·sti·ga·tion** /ˌinstiˈgāsʜən/ noun **in·sti·ga·tor** noun.
– ORIGIN Latin *instigare* 'urge, incite.'

in·still /inˈstil/ ▸ **verb 1** gradually establish an idea or attitude in someone's mind: *her mother instilled in Harriet a love for cooking.* **2** put a liquid into something in drops.
– DERIVATIVES **in·stil·la·tion** /ˌinstəˈlāsʜən/ noun.
– ORIGIN Latin *instillare.*

in·stinct /'inˌstiNGkt/ ▶ **noun 1** an inborn tendency to behave in a certain way. **2** a natural ability or skill. **3** a feeling based on intuition rather than facts or reasoning.

– SYNONYMS **1 inclination,** urge, drive, compulsion, intuition, feeling, sixth sense, nose. **2 talent,** gift, ability, aptitude, skill, flair, feel, knack.

– DERIVATIVES **in·stinc·tu·al** /ins'tiNGkCHo͞oəl/ adjective.
– ORIGIN Latin *instinctus* 'impulse.'

in·stinc·tive /in'stiNG(k)tiv/ ▶ **adjective** based on instinct rather than conscious thought or training.

– SYNONYMS **intuitive,** natural, instinctual, innate, inborn, inherent, unconscious, subconscious, automatic, reflex, knee-jerk; informal gut.

– DERIVATIVES **in·stinc·tive·ly** adverb.

in·sti·tute /'instiˌt(y)o͞ot/ ▶ **noun** an organization for the promotion of science, education, culture, or a particular profession.

– SYNONYMS **organization,** establishment, institution, foundation, center, academy, school, college, university, society, association, federation, body.

▶ **verb 1** begin or establish a scheme, policy, legal action, etc. **2** appoint someone to a position, especially as a cleric.

– SYNONYMS **set up,** inaugurate, found, establish, organize, initiate, set in motion, get under way, get off the ground, start, launch.
– ANTONYMS abolish, end.

– ORIGIN from Latin *instituere* 'establish.'

in·sti·tu·tion /ˌinsti't(y)o͞oSHən/ ▶ **noun 1** an important organization such as a university, bank, hospital, or church. **2** an organization providing residential care for people with special needs. **3** an established law or custom. **4** informal a well-established and familiar person or thing. **5** the establishment or introduction of something.

– SYNONYMS **1 establishment,** organization, institute, foundation, center, academy, school, college, university, society, association, body. **2 (residential) home,** hospital, asylum, prison. **3** *the institution of marriage* **practice,** custom, convention, tradition.

in·sti·tu·tion·al /ˌinsti't(y)o͞oSHənl/ ▶ **adjective 1** relating to an institution. **2** typical of an institution, especially in being impersonal or unimaginative.

– SYNONYMS **organized,** established, bureaucratic, conventional, procedural, formal, formalized, systematic, systematized, structured, regulated.

– DERIVATIVES **in·sti·tu·tion·al·ism** /-ˌizəm/ noun **in·sti·tu·tion·al·ly** adverb.

in·sti·tu·tion·al·ize /ˌinsti't(y)o͞oSHənlˌīz/ ▶ **verb 1** establish as an accepted part of an organization or culture: *claims that racism is institutionalized in education*. **2** place someone in a residential institution. **3** (**be/become institutionalized**) be or become apathetic and dependent after a long period in a residential institution.

– DERIVATIVES **in·sti·tu·tion·al·i·za·tion** /ˌinstiˌt(y)o͞oSHənl-i'zāSHən/ noun.

in·struct /in'strəkt/ ▶ **verb 1** tell or order someone to do something. **2** teach someone a subject or skill. **3** inform someone of a fact or situation.

– SYNONYMS **1 order,** direct, command, tell, mandate; old use bid. **2 teach,** coach, train, educate, tutor, guide, school, show.

– ORIGIN Latin *instruere* 'construct, equip, teach.'

in·struc·tion /in'strəkSHən/ ▶ **noun 1** an act of telling someone to do something; an order. **2** (**instructions**) detailed information about how something should be done. **3** teaching or education. **4** a code in a computer program that defines and carries out an operation.

– SYNONYMS **1 order,** command, directive, direction, decree, injunction, mandate, commandment; old use bidding. **2 (instructions) directions,** handbook, manual, guide, advice, guidance. **3 teaching,** coaching, schooling, lessons, classes, lectures, training, drill, guidance.

– DERIVATIVES **in·struc·tion·al** adjective.

in·struc·tive /in'strəktiv/ ▶ **adjective** useful and informative.
– DERIVATIVES **in·struc·tive·ly** adverb.

in·struc·tor /in'strəktər/ ▶ **noun 1** a teacher. **2** a college or university teacher ranking below assistant professor.

– SYNONYMS **trainer,** coach, teacher, tutor, adviser, counselor, guide.

in·stru·ment /'instrəmənt/ ▶ **noun 1** a tool or implement, especially for precision work. **2** a measuring device, especially in a vehicle or aircraft. **3** (also **musical instrument**) a device for producing musical sounds. **4** a means of pursuing an aim: *her car is the instrument of her freedom*. **5** a person who is exploited by another. **6** a formal or legal document.

– SYNONYMS **1 implement,** tool, utensil, device, apparatus, gadget. **2 gauge,** meter, indicator, dial, display. **3 agent,** cause, agency, channel, medium, means, vehicle.

– ORIGIN Latin *instrumentum*.

CHOOSE THE RIGHT WORD

See **TOOL**.

in·stru·men·tal /ˌinstrə'mentl/ ▶ **adjective 1** serving as a means of achieving something. **2** (of music) performed on instruments. **3** relating to an implement or measuring device.

– SYNONYMS *the space program has always been instrumental in our efforts to make medical advances* **involved,** active, influential, contributory; helpful, useful, of service; significant, important, crucial, critical, essential, pivotal, key; (**be instrumental in**) play a part in, contribute to, be a factor in, have a hand in; add to, help, promote, advance, further; be conducive to, lead to, cause.

▶ **noun** a piece of music performed by instruments, with no vocals.

– DERIVATIVES **in·stru·men·tal·i·ty** /ˌinstrəmən'talitē, -men-/ noun **in·stru·men·tal·ly** adverb.

in·stru·men·tal·ist /ˌinstrə'mentl-ist/ ▶ **noun** a player of a musical instrument.

in·stru·men·ta·tion /ˌinstrəmən'tāSHən, -men-/ ▶ **noun 1** the instruments used in a piece of music. **2** the arrangement of a piece of music for particular instruments. **3** measuring instruments as a group.

in·stru·ment pan·el ▶ **noun** a surface in front of a driver's or pilot's seat where the vehicle's or aircraft's instruments are situated.

in·sub·or·di·nate /ˌinsə'bôrdn-it/ ▶ **adjective** disobedient to orders or authority.
– DERIVATIVES **in·sub·or·di·na·tion** /-ˌbôrdn'āSHən/ noun.

in·sub·stan·tial /ˌinsəb'stanCHəl/ ▶ **adjective** lacking strength and solidity.

– DERIVATIVES **in·sub·stan·ti·al·i·ty** /-ˌstanchēˈalitē/ noun **in·sub·stan·tial·ly** adverb.

in·suf·fer·a·ble /inˈsəf(ə)rəbəl/ ▶ **adjective 1** too extreme to bear; intolerable. **2** unbearably arrogant or conceited.
– DERIVATIVES **in·suf·fer·a·bly** adverb.
– ORIGIN from Latin *sufferre* 'suffer.'

in·suf·fi·cient /ˌinsəˈfishənt/ ▶ **adjective** not enough for a purpose.

– SYNONYMS **inadequate,** deficient, poor, scant, scanty, not enough, too little, too few.

– DERIVATIVES **in·suf·fi·cien·cy** /ˌinsəˈfishənsē/ noun **in·suf·fi·cient·ly** adverb.

in·su·lar /ˈins(y)ələr/ ▶ **adjective 1** ignorant of or uninterested in cultures, ideas, or peoples outside one's own experience. **2** relating to an island.
– DERIVATIVES **in·su·lar·i·ty** /ˌins(y)əˈlaritē/ noun.
– ORIGIN from Latin *insula* 'island.'

in·su·late /ˈins(y)əˌlāt/ ▶ **verb 1** place material between one thing and another to prevent loss of heat or intrusion of sound. **2** cover something with nonconducting material to prevent the passage of electricity. **3** protect someone from something unpleasant.

– SYNONYMS **1 wrap,** sheathe, cover, encase, enclose, lag, soundproof. **2 protect,** save, shield, shelter, screen, cushion, cocoon.

– DERIVATIVES **in·su·la·tor** noun.
– ORIGIN from Latin *insula* 'island.'

in·su·la·tion /ˌins(y)əˈlāshən/ ▶ **noun 1** material used to insulate something. **2** the action of insulating or state of being insulated: *his comparative insulation from the world.*

in·su·lin /ˈinsələn/ ▶ **noun** a hormone produced in the pancreas that regulates glucose levels in the blood, and the lack of which causes diabetes.
– ORIGIN from Latin *insula* 'island' (with reference to the islets of Langerhans in the pancreas).

in·sult ▶ **verb** /inˈsəlt/ speak to or treat someone with disrespect or abuse.

– SYNONYMS **1 abuse,** be rude to, call someone names, slight, disparage, discredit, malign, defame, denigrate, offend, hurt, humiliate; informal bad-mouth. **2** (as adj. **insulting**) *once you send that insulting message, there's no taking it back* **abusive,** rude, offensive, disparaging, belittling, derogatory, deprecating, disrespectful, uncomplimentary; informal bitchy, catty.
– ANTONYMS compliment.

▶ **noun** /ˈinˌsəlt/ **1** a disrespectful or abusive remark or action. **2** a thing so worthless as to be offensive: *the pay offer is an absolute insult.*

– SYNONYMS **jibe,** affront, slight, slur, barb, indignity, abuse, aspersions; informal dig, put-down.

– DERIVATIVES **in·sult·ing·ly** adverb.
– ORIGIN Latin *insultare* 'jump or trample on.'

in·su·per·a·ble /inˈso͞op(ə)rəbəl/ ▶ **adjective** impossible to overcome.
– DERIVATIVES **in·su·per·a·bly** adverb.
– ORIGIN Latin *insuperabilis.*

in·sup·port·a·ble /ˌinsəˈpôrtəbəl/ ▶ **adjective 1** unable to be supported or justified. **2** unable to be endured; intolerable.
– DERIVATIVES **in·sup·port·a·bly** adverb.

in·sur·ance /inˈsho͝orəns/ ▶ **noun 1** an arrangement by which a company or the government guarantees to provide compensation for loss, damage, illness, or death in return for payment of a specified premium. **2** money paid as compensation under an insurance policy. **3** a thing providing protection against a possible event: *jackets hung on their chairs, insurance against the air conditioning.*

– SYNONYMS **indemnity,** assurance, protection, security, cover, safeguard, warranty.

in·sur·ance pol·i·cy ▶ **noun** a contract of insurance.

in·sure /inˈsho͝or/ ▶ **verb 1** arrange for compensation in the event of damage to or loss of property, or a death, in exchange for regular payments to a company. **2** (**insure someone against**) protect someone against a possible event. **3** another term for **ENSURE**.

– SYNONYMS **provide insurance for,** indemnify, cover, assure, protect, underwrite, warrant.

– DERIVATIVES **in·sur·a·ble** adjective.
– ORIGIN alteration of **ENSURE**.

USAGE

There is considerable overlap between the meaning and use of **insure** and **ensure**. In both US and British English the main meaning of **insure** is 'arrange for compensation in the event of damage or loss'; **ensure** is not used at all in this sense. For the general senses, **insure** and **ensure** are often interchangeable, but **insure** tends to be more common in US English.

in·sured /inˈsho͝ord/ ▶ **adjective** covered by insurance: *an insured risk.* ▶ **noun** (**the insured**) (pl. same) a person or organization covered by insurance.

in·sur·er /inˈsho͝orər/ ▶ **noun** a company that provides insurance.

in·sur·gent /inˈsərjənt/ ▶ **noun** a rebel or revolutionary. ▶ **adjective** relating to rebels.
– DERIVATIVES **in·sur·gence** noun **in·sur·gen·cy** noun (pl. **insurgencies**).
– ORIGIN from Latin *insurgere* 'rise up.'

in·sur·mount·a·ble /ˌinsərˈmountəbəl/ ▶ **adjective** too great to be overcome.
– DERIVATIVES **in·sur·mount·a·bly** adverb.

in·sur·rec·tion /ˌinsəˈrekshən/ ▶ **noun** a violent uprising against authority.
– DERIVATIVES **in·sur·rec·tion·ar·y** adjective **in·sur·rec·tion·ist** noun & adjective.
– ORIGIN Latin, from *insurgere* 'rise up.'

in·sus·cep·ti·ble /ˌinsəˈseptəbəl/ ▶ **adjective** not likely to be affected by something.
– DERIVATIVES **in·sus·cep·ti·bil·i·ty** /ˌinsəˌseptəˈbilitē/ noun.

in·tact /inˈtakt/ ▶ **adjective** not damaged in any way.

– SYNONYMS **whole,** entire, complete, unbroken, undamaged, unscathed, unblemished, unmarked, in one piece.
– ANTONYMS damaged.

– DERIVATIVES **in·tact·ness** noun.
– ORIGIN Latin *intactus* 'untouched.'

in·tact fam·i·ly ▶ **noun** a nuclear family in which membership has remained constant, without divorce or other divisive factors.

in·ta·glio /inˈtalyō, -ˈtäl-/ ▶ **noun** (pl. **intaglios**) **1** an incised or engraved design. **2** a gem with an incised design.
– ORIGIN Italian.

in·take /ˈinˌtāk/ ▶ **noun 1** an amount or quantity taken in. **2** an act of taking something in. **3** a place or structure through which something is taken in.

in·tan·gi·ble /inˈtanjəbəl/ ▶ **adjective** **1** unable to be touched; not physical: *the intangible gift of joy.* **2** vague and abstract. ▶ **noun** an abstract or intangible thing.
– DERIVATIVES **in·tan·gi·bil·i·ty** /-ˌtanjəˈbilitē/ noun **in·tan·gi·bly** adverb.

in·te·ger /ˈintijər/ ▶ **noun** a whole number.
– ORIGIN from Latin, 'intact, whole.'

in·te·gral ▶ **adjective** /ˈintigrəl, inˈteg-/ **1** necessary to make a whole complete; fundamental: *games are an integral part of the curriculum.* **2** included as part of a whole. **3** forming a whole; complete. **4** Mathematics relating to an integer or integers.

– SYNONYMS **1 essential,** fundamental, component, basic, intrinsic, inherent, vital, necessary. **2 built-in,** inbuilt, integrated, inboard, fitted. **3 unified,** integrated, comprehensive, holistic, all-embracing.
– ANTONYMS peripheral, supplementary.

▶ **noun** /ˈintigrəl/ Mathematics a function of which a given function is the derivative, and which may express the area under the curve of a graph of the function.
– DERIVATIVES **in·te·gral·ly** adverb.

in·te·gral cal·cu·lus ▶ **noun** Mathematics the part of calculus concerned with the integrals of functions.

in·te·grate ▶ **verb** /ˈintiˌgrāt/ **1** combine or be combined to form a whole: *transport planning should be integrated with energy policy.* **2** make or become accepted as a member of a social group. **3** Mathematics find the integral of a function.

– SYNONYMS **combine,** amalgamate, merge, unite, fuse, blend, consolidate, meld, mix, incorporate, assimilate, homogenize, desegregate.
– ANTONYMS separate.

– DERIVATIVES **in·te·gra·ble** /-grəbəl/ adjective **in·te·gra·tive** /-ˌgrātiv/ adjective **in·te·gra·tor** noun.
– ORIGIN Latin *integrare* 'make whole.'

in·te·grat·ed cir·cuit ▶ **noun** an electronic circuit on a small piece of semiconducting material, performing the same function as a larger circuit of separate components.

in·te·gra·tion /ˌintiˈgrāsHən/ ▶ **noun** **1** the action of combining things to form a whole. **2** the mixing of peoples or groups who were previously segregated.
– DERIVATIVES **in·te·gra·tion·ist** noun.

in·teg·ri·ty /inˈtegritē/ ▶ **noun** **1** the quality of being honest and having strong moral principles. **2** the state of being whole or unified. **3** the quality of being sound in construction.

– SYNONYMS **1 honesty,** probity, rectitude, uprightness, fairness, honor, sincerity, truthfulness, trustworthiness. **2 unity,** coherence, cohesion, solidity. **3 soundness,** strength, sturdiness, solidity, durability, stability, rigidity.
– ANTONYMS dishonesty.

– ORIGIN Latin *integritas.*

in·teg·u·ment /inˈtegyəmənt/ ▶ **noun** a tough outer protective layer, especially of an animal or plant.
– DERIVATIVES **in·teg·u·men·ta·ry** /-ˌtegyəˈmentərē/ adjective.
– ORIGIN Latin *integumentum.*

in·tel·lect /ˈintlˌekt/ ▶ **noun** **1** the faculty of using the mind to think logically and understand things. **2** an intelligent person.

– SYNONYMS **mind,** brain(s), intelligence, reason, judgment, gray matter, brain cells.

– ORIGIN Latin *intellectus* 'understanding.'

in·tel·lec·tu·al /ˌintlˈekcHo͞oəl/ ▶ **adjective** **1** having a highly developed ability to think logically and understand things. **2** relating or appealing to the intellect.

– SYNONYMS **1 learned,** academic, erudite, bookish, highbrow, scholarly, donnish. **2 mental,** cerebral, rational, conceptual, theoretical, analytical, logical, cognitive.

▶ **noun** a person with a highly developed intellect.
– DERIVATIVES **in·tel·lec·tu·al·ly** adverb.

in·tel·lec·tu·al·ism /ˌintlˈekcHo͞oəˌlizəm/ ▶ **noun** the use of the intellect at the expense of the emotions.
– DERIVATIVES **in·tel·lec·tu·al·ist** noun.

in·tel·lec·tu·al·ize /ˌintlˈekcHo͞oəˌlīz/ ▶ **verb** **1** make something seem rational or logical. **2** talk or write in a logical or intellectual way.

in·tel·lec·tu·al prop·er·ty ▶ **noun** Law intangible property that is the result of creativity, e.g., patents or copyrights.

in·tel·li·gence /inˈtelijəns/ ▶ **noun** **1** the ability to gain and apply knowledge and skills. **2** the collection of secret information of military or political value. **3** secret information collected about an enemy or competitor.

– SYNONYMS **1 intellect,** cleverness, brainpower, judgment, reasoning, acumen, wit, insight, perception. **2 information,** facts, details, particulars, data, knowledge.

– ORIGIN Latin *intelligentia.*

in·tel·li·gence quo·tient ▶ **noun** a number representing a person's reasoning ability, compared to the statistical norm, 100 being average.

in·tel·li·gent /inˈtelijənt/ ▶ **adjective** **1** having intelligence, especially of a high level. **2** (of a device) able to vary its state or action in response to varying situations and past experience. **3** (of a computer terminal) having its own processing capability.

– SYNONYMS **clever,** bright, quick-witted, smart, astute, sharp, insightful, perceptive, penetrating, educated, knowledgeable, enlightened; informal brainy.

– DERIVATIVES **in·tel·li·gent·ly** adverb.

in·tel·li·gent de·sign ▶ **noun** a theory that life, or the universe, cannot have arisen by chance and was designed and created by some intelligent entity.

in·tel·li·gent·si·a /inˌteliˈjentsēə/ ▶ **noun** (treated as sing. or pl.) intellectuals or highly educated people as a class.

in·tel·li·gi·ble /inˈtelijəbəl/ ▶ **adjective** able to be understood.

– SYNONYMS **comprehensible,** understandable, accessible, digestible, user-friendly, clear, coherent, plain, unambiguous.

– DERIVATIVES **in·tel·li·gi·bil·i·ty** /-ˌtelijəˈbilitē/ noun **in·tel·li·gi·bly** adverb.
– ORIGIN Latin *intelligibilis.*

in·tem·per·ate /inˈtemp(ə)rit/ ▶ **adjective** **1** lacking self-control. **2** characterized by excessive drinking of alcohol.
– DERIVATIVES **in·tem·per·ance** noun **in·tem·per·ate·ly** adverb.

in·tend /inˈtend/ ▶ **verb** **1** have a course of action as one's aim or plan. **2** plan that something should be, do, or mean something: *the book was intended as a satire.* **3** (**intend for/to do**) design or plan something for a particular purpose. **4** (**be intended for**) be meant for the use of someone.

– SYNONYMS **plan,** mean, have in mind, aim, propose, hope, expect, envisage.

– DERIVATIVES **in·tend·er** noun.
– ORIGIN Latin *intendere* 'intend, extend, direct.'

CHOOSE THE RIGHT WORD

intend, aim, design, mean, plan, propose, purpose

If you **intend** to do something, you may or may not be serious about getting it done (*I intend to clean out the garage some day*) but at least you have a goal in mind. Although **mean** can also imply either a firm resolve (*I mean to go, with or without her permission*) or a vague intention (*I've been meaning to write her for weeks*), it is a less formal word that usually connotes a certain lack of determination or a weak resolve. **Plan**, like *mean* and *intend*, may imply a vague goal (*I plan to tour China some day*), but it is often used to suggest that you're taking active steps (*I plan to leave as soon as I finish packing*). **Aim** indicates that you have an actual goal or purpose in mind and that you're putting some effort behind it (*she had aimed to become a psychiatrist*), without the hint of failure conveyed by *mean*. If you **propose** to do something, you declare your intention ahead of time (*I propose that we set up a meeting next week*), and if you **purpose** to do it, you are even more determined to achieve your goal (*I purpose to write a three-volume history of baseball in America*). **Design** suggests forethought in devising a plan (*design a strategy that will keep everyone happy*).

in·tend·ed /inˈtendid/ ▶ **adjective** planned or meant. ▶ **noun** (**one's intended**) informal one's fiancé(e).

in·tense /inˈtens/ ▶ **adjective 1** very great in force, degree, or strength: *the job demands intense concentration.* **2** very earnest or serious.

– SYNONYMS **1 extreme,** great, acute, fierce, severe, high, exceptional, extraordinary, harsh, strong, powerful, violent; informal serious. **2 passionate,** impassioned, zealous, vehement, fervent, earnest, eager, committed.
– ANTONYMS mild, apathetic.

– DERIVATIVES **in·tense·ly** adverb **in·tense·ness** noun.
– ORIGIN Latin *intensus* 'stretched tightly, strained.'

in·ten·si·fi·er /inˈtensəˌfīər/ ▶ **noun 1** a thing that makes something more intense. **2** Grammar an adverb used to give force or emphasis (e.g., *really* in *my feet are really cold*).

in·ten·si·fy /inˈtensəˌfī/ ▶ **verb** (**intensifies, intensifying, intensified**) increase in degree, force, or strength: *the war has intensified.*

– SYNONYMS **escalate,** increase, step up, raise, strengthen, reinforce, pick up, build up, heighten, deepen, extend, expand, amplify, magnify, aggravate, exacerbate, worsen, inflame, compound.
– ANTONYMS abate.

– DERIVATIVES **in·ten·si·fi·ca·tion** /-ˌtensəfiˈkāshən/ noun.

in·ten·si·ty /inˈtensitē/ ▶ **noun** (pl. **intensities**) **1** the quality of being great in force, degree, or strength: *the pain grew in intensity.* **2** chiefly Physics the measurable amount of a property, such as force or brightness.

– SYNONYMS **1 strength,** power, force, severity, ferocity, fierceness, harshness, violence. **2 passion,** ardor, fervor, vehemence, fire, emotion, eagerness.

in·ten·sive /inˈtensiv/ ▶ **adjective 1** concentrated on a single subject or into a short time: *an intensive course in Arabic.* **2** (of agriculture) aiming to achieve maximum production within a limited area. **3** (in combination) concentrating on or making much use of something: *labor-intensive methods.*

– SYNONYMS **thorough,** thoroughgoing, in-depth, rigorous, exhaustive, vigorous, detailed, minute, meticulous, painstaking, methodical, extensive.
– ANTONYMS cursory.

– DERIVATIVES **in·ten·sive·ly** adverb **in·ten·sive·ness** noun.

in·ten·sive care ▶ **noun** special medical treatment given to a dangerously ill patient.

in·tent /inˈtent/ ▶ **noun** something intended; a plan or intention.

– SYNONYMS **aim,** intention, purpose, objective, goal.

▶ **adjective 1** (**intent on**) determined to do something. **2** (**intent on**) concentrating hard on something. **3** showing earnest and eager attention.

– SYNONYMS **1** *he was* ***intent on*** *proving his point* **bent on,** set on, determined to (be), insistent on, resolved to (be), hell-bent on, keen on, committed to, determined to (be). **2 attentive,** absorbed, engrossed, fascinated, enthralled, rapt, focused, concentrating, preoccupied.
– ANTONYMS distracted.

– DERIVATIVES **in·tent·ly** adverb **in·tent·ness** noun.
– PHRASES **to** (or **for**) **all intents and purposes** in all important respects. **with intent** Law with the intention of committing a crime.
– ORIGIN Latin *intendere* 'intend.'

in·ten·tion /inˈtenchən/ ▶ **noun 1** an aim or plan. **2** (**one's intentions**) a man's plans in respect to marriage.

– SYNONYMS **aim,** purpose, intent, objective, goal.

– DERIVATIVES **in·ten·tioned** adjective.

in·ten·tion·al /inˈtenchənl/ ▶ **adjective** done on purpose; deliberate.

– SYNONYMS **deliberate,** done on purpose, willful, calculated, conscious, intended, planned, meant, knowing.

– DERIVATIVES **in·ten·tion·al·i·ty** /inˌtenchəˈnalitē/ noun **in·ten·tion·al·ly** adverb.

in·ter /inˈtər/ ▶ **verb** (**inters, interring, interred**) place a corpse in a grave or tomb.

– SYNONYMS **bury,** lay to rest, consign to the grave, entomb.
– ANTONYMS exhume.

– ORIGIN Old French *enterrer*.

inter- ▶ **prefix 1** between; among: *interbreed.* **2** so as to affect both; mutually: *interaction.*
– ORIGIN Latin *inter.*

in·ter·act /ˌintərˈakt/ ▶ **verb** (of two people or things) act so as to affect each other.
– DERIVATIVES **in·ter·ac·tion** noun.

in·ter·ac·tive /ˌintərˈaktiv/ ▶ **adjective 1** influencing each other. **2** (of a computer or other electronic device) allowing a two-way flow of information between it and a user.
– DERIVATIVES **in·ter·ac·tive·ly** adverb **in·ter·ac·tiv·i·ty** /-akˈtivitē/ noun.

in·ter a·li·a /ˈintər ˈālēə, ˈälēə/ ▶ **adverb** among other things.
– ORIGIN Latin.

in·ter·breed /ˌintərˈbrēd/ ▶ **verb** (past and past part. **interbred**) breed or cause to breed with an animal of a different race or species.

in·ter·ca·lar·y /inˈtərkəˌlerē, ˌintərˈkalərē/ ▶ **adjective** **1** (of a day or a month) inserted in the calendar to harmonize it with the solar year, e.g., February 29 in leap years. **2** inserted between or among other things: *elaborate intercalary notes and footnotes.*
– ORIGIN from Latin *intercalare.*

in·ter·cede /ˌintərˈsēd/ ▶ **verb** intervene on behalf of someone.
– ORIGIN Latin *intercedere.*

in·ter·cel·lu·lar /ˌintərˈselyələr/ ▶ **adjective** located or occurring between cells.

in·ter·cept ▶ **verb** /ˌintərˈsept/ stop a person, vehicle, or communication so as to prevent them from continuing to a destination.

– SYNONYMS **stop,** head off, cut off, catch, seize, block, interrupt.

▶ **noun** /ˈintərˌsept/ **1** an act of intercepting someone or something. **2** Mathematics the point at which a line cuts the axis of a graph.
– DERIVATIVES **in·ter·cep·tion** /ˌintərˈsepsʜən/ noun **in·ter·cep·tor** /ˌintərˈseptər/ noun.
– ORIGIN Latin *intercipere* 'catch between.'

in·ter·ces·sion /ˌintərˈsesʜən/ ▶ **noun** **1** the action of intervening on behalf of someone. **2** the saying of a prayer on behalf of another person.
– DERIVATIVES **in·ter·ces·sor** noun **in·ter·ces·so·ry** adjective.
– ORIGIN Latin.

in·ter·change ▶ **verb** /ˌintərˈcʜānj/ **1** exchange things with each other. **2** put each of two things in the other's place. ▶ **noun** /ˈintərˌcʜānj/ **1** the action of exchanging people or things. **2** an exchange of words. **3** a road junction on several levels so that traffic streams do not intersect.

in·ter·change·a·ble /ˌintərˈcʜānjəbəl/ ▶ **adjective** **1** (of things) able to be interchanged. **2** very similar: *interchangeable disco divas.*
– DERIVATIVES **in·ter·change·a·bil·i·ty** /ˌintərˌcʜānjəˈbilitē/ noun **in·ter·change·a·bly** adverb.

in·ter·cit·y /ˈintərˌsitē/ ▶ **adjective** existing or traveling between cities.

in·ter·com /ˈintərˌkäm/ ▶ **noun** an electrical device allowing one-way or two-way communication.
– ORIGIN short for *intercommunication.*

in·ter·com·mu·ni·cat·ing /ˌintərkəˈmyo͞oniˌkātiɴɢ/ ▶ **adjective** (of two rooms) having a shared connecting door.

in·ter·com·mu·ni·ca·tion /ˌintərkəˌmyo͞oniˈkāsʜən/ ▶ **noun** the process of communicating between people or groups.

in·ter·con·nect /ˌintərkəˈnekt/ ▶ **verb** connect with each other.
– DERIVATIVES **in·ter·con·nec·tion** noun.

in·ter·con·ti·nen·tal /ˌintərˌkäntnˈentl/ ▶ **adjective** relating to or traveling between continents.

in·ter·cool·er /ˌintərˈko͞olər/ ▶ **noun** a device for cooling gas between successive compressions, especially in a supercharged engine.
– DERIVATIVES **in·ter·cool** verb.

in·ter·course /ˈintərˌkôrs/ ▶ **noun** **1** communication or dealings between people. **2** sexual intercourse.

– SYNONYMS **1 dealings,** relations, relationships, contact, interchange, communication, networking. **2 sexual intercourse,** sex, sexual relations, mating, copulation, fornication; technical coitus.

– ORIGIN Latin *intercursus.*

in·ter·crop /ˌintərˈkräp/ ▶ **verb** (**intercrops, intercropping, intercropped**) (often as n. **intercropping** /ˈintərˌkräpiɴɢ/) grow a crop among plants of a different kind.

in·ter·cut /ˌintərˈkət/ ▶ **verb** (**intercuts, intercutting, intercut**) alternate scenes with contrasting scenes in a movie.

in·ter·de·nom·i·na·tion·al /ˌintərdiˌnäməˈnāsʜənl/ ▶ **adjective** relating to more than one religious denomination.

in·ter·de·part·men·tal /ˌintərdiˌpärtˈmentl, -ˌdēpärt-/ ▶ **adjective** relating to more than one department.

in·ter·de·pend·ent /ˌintərdiˈpendənt/ ▶ **adjective** dependent on each other.
– DERIVATIVES **in·ter·de·pend·ence** noun **in·ter·de·pend·en·cy** noun.

in·ter·dict ▶ **noun** /ˈintərˌdikt/ **1** an authoritative order forbidding something. **2** (in the Roman Catholic Church) a sentence barring a person or place from ecclesiastical functions and privileges.

– SYNONYMS **prohibition,** ban, bar, veto, embargo, moratorium, injunction.

▶ **verb** /ˌintərˈdikt/ prohibit or forbid something.
– DERIVATIVES **in·ter·dic·tion** /ˌintərˈdiksʜən/ noun.
– ORIGIN from Latin *interdicere* 'interpose, forbid by decree.'

CHOOSE THE RIGHT WORD

See **PROHIBIT**.

in·ter·dis·ci·pli·nar·y /ˌintərˈdisəpliˌnerē/ ▶ **adjective** relating to more than one branch of knowledge.

in·ter·est /ˈint(ə)rist/ ▶ **noun** **1** the state of wanting to know about something or someone. **2** the quality of arousing curiosity or holding the attention: *a tale full of interest.* **3** a subject that one enjoys doing or studying. **4** a share, right, or stake in property or a financial undertaking. **5** money paid for the use of money that is lent. **6** a person's advantage or benefit. **7** a group in politics or business having a common concern.

– SYNONYMS **1 attentiveness,** attention, regard, notice, curiosity, enjoyment, delight. **2** *this will be of interest* **concern,** consequence, importance, import, significance, note, relevance, value. **3 hobby,** pastime, leisure pursuit, amusement, recreation, diversion, passion. **4 stake,** share, claim, investment, involvement, concern.
– ANTONYMS boredom.

▶ **verb** **1** arouse someone's curiosity or attention. **2** (**interest someone in**) persuade someone to do or obtain something. **3** (as adj. **interested**) involved in something and so not impartial.

– SYNONYMS **1 appeal to,** be of interest to, attract, intrigue, amuse, divert, entertain, arouse someone's curiosity, whet someone's appetite; informal tickle someone's fancy. **2** (as adj. **interested**) *an interested crowd* **attentive,** fascinated, riveted, gripped, captivated, agog, intrigued, curious, keen, eager. **3** (as adj. **interested**) *interested parties* **partisan,** partial, biased, prejudiced, preferential; concerned, involved, affected.

– DERIVATIVES **in·ter·est·ed·ly** adverb.
– PHRASES **in the interests** (or **interest**) **of something** for the benefit of: *in the interests of security we are keeping the information confidential.* **of interest** interesting:

much of it is of interest to historians.
– ORIGIN Latin *interesse* 'differ, be important.'

in·ter·est·ing /ˈint(ə)ristiNG, ˈintəˌrestiNG/ ▶ **adjective** arousing curiosity or interest.

– SYNONYMS **absorbing,** engrossing, fascinating, riveting, gripping, compelling, captivating, engaging, enthralling, appealing, entertaining, stimulating, diverting, intriguing.

– DERIVATIVES **in·ter·est·ing·ly** adverb.

in·ter·face /ˈintərˌfās/ ▶ **noun 1** a point where two things meet and interact. **2** a device or program enabling a user to communicate with a computer, or for connecting two items of hardware or software. **3** chiefly Physics a surface forming a boundary between two portions of matter or space. ▶ **verb** (**interface with**) **1** interact with another person, system, etc. **2** Computing connect with something by an interface.

in·ter·fac·ing /ˈintərˌfāsiNG/ ▶ **noun** an extra layer of material or an adhesive stiffener, applied to the facing of a garment to add support.

in·ter·faith /ˈintərˈfāTH/ ▶ **adjective** relating to or between different religions.

in·ter·fere /ˌintərˈfi(ə)r/ ▶ **verb 1** become involved in something without being asked or required to do so: *she tried not to interfere in her children's lives.* **2** (**interfere with**) prevent something from continuing or being carried out properly. **3** (**interfere with**) handle or adjust something without permission. **4** Physics (of waves of the same wavelength) interact to produce interference.

– SYNONYMS **1 butt in,** barge in, intrude, meddle, tamper, encroach; informal poke one's nose in, stick one's oar in. **2** (**interfere with**) **impede,** obstruct, stand in the way of, hinder, inhibit, restrict, constrain, hamper, handicap, disturb, disrupt, influence, affect, confuse.

– DERIVATIVES **in·ter·fer·er** noun **in·ter·fer·ing** adjective.
– ORIGIN Old French *s'entreferir* 'strike each other.'

in·ter·fer·ence /ˌintərˈfi(ə)rəns/ ▶ **noun 1** the action of interfering with someone or something. **2** disturbance to radio signals caused by unwanted signals from other sources. **3** Physics the combination of waves of the same wavelength from two or more sources, producing a new wave pattern.

– SYNONYMS **1 intrusion,** intervention, involvement, meddling, prying. **2 disruption,** disturbance, static, noise.

– DERIVATIVES **in·ter·fe·ren·tial** /-fəˈrenCHəl/ adjective.

in·ter·fer·on /ˌintərˈfi(ə)rˌän/ ▶ **noun** a protein released by animal cells that prevents a virus from reproducing.

in·ter·fuse /ˌintərˈfyo͞oz/ ▶ **verb** literary join or mix things together.
– DERIVATIVES **in·ter·fu·sion** noun.

in·ter·ga·lac·tic /ˌintərgəˈlaktik/ ▶ **adjective** relating to or situated between galaxies.

in·ter·gla·cial /ˌintərˈglāSHəl/ ▶ **adjective** Geology relating to a period of milder climate between two glacial periods.

in·ter·gov·ern·men·tal /ˌintərˌgəvər(n)ˈmentl/ ▶ **adjective** relating to or conducted between governments.

in·ter·im /ˈintərəm/ ▶ **noun** (**the interim**) the time between two events. ▶ **adjective** in or for the time between two events; provisional.
– ORIGIN from Latin, 'meanwhile.'

in·te·ri·or /inˈti(ə)rēər/ ▶ **adjective 1** situated within or inside something; inner. **2** remote from the coast or frontier; inland. **3** relating to a country's internal affairs. **4** within the mind or soul: *an interior monologue.*

– SYNONYMS **1 inside,** inner, internal, inland, upcountry, central. **2 internal,** home, domestic, national, state, civil, local. **3 inner,** mental, spiritual, psychological, private, personal, secret.

▶ **noun 1** the interior part of a building, country, etc. **2** the internal affairs of a country.

– SYNONYMS **1 inside,** depths, recesses, bowels, belly, heart. **2 center,** heartland.
– ANTONYMS exterior.

– DERIVATIVES **in·te·ri·or·ize** verb **in·te·ri·or·ly** adverb.
– ORIGIN Latin, 'inner.'

in·te·ri·or dec·o·ra·tion ▶ **noun** the decoration of the interior of a building or room, with regard for color combination and artistic effect.

in·te·ri·or de·sign ▶ **noun** the design, decoration, and furnishings of the interior of a room or building.

in·te·ri·or·i·ty /inˌti(ə)rēˈôritē, -ˈär-/ ▶ **noun** the quality of being interior or inward.

in·ter·ject /ˌintərˈjekt/ ▶ **verb** say something suddenly as an interruption.
– ORIGIN Latin *interjicere* 'interpose.'

in·ter·jec·tion /ˌintərˈjekSHən/ ▶ **noun** an exclamation or interruption.

in·ter·lace /ˌintərˈlās/ ▶ **verb 1** cross or be crossed together; interweave. **2** (**interlace something with**) mingle or intersperse something with: *discussion interlaced with mathematics.*

in·ter·lard /ˌintərˈlärd/ ▶ **verb** (**interlard something with**) intersperse speech or writing with contrasting words and phrases.

in·ter·leave /ˌintərˈlēv/ ▶ **verb 1** place something between the layers of something else. **2** insert blank leaves between the pages of a book.

in·ter·li·brar·y loan /ˌintərˈlībrerē/ ▶ **noun** a system in which one library borrows a book from another library for the use of an individual.

in·ter·line /ˌintərˈlīn/ ▶ **verb** put an extra lining in a garment or curtain.

in·ter·lin·e·ar /ˌintərˈlinēər/ ▶ **adjective** written between the lines of another piece of writing.

in·ter·link /ˌintərˈliNGk/ ▶ **verb** join or connect things together.
– DERIVATIVES **in·ter·link·age** noun.

in·ter·lock /ˌintərˈläk/ ▶ **verb** (of two or more things) engage with each other by overlapping or fitting together. ▶ **noun 1** a device for connecting or coordinating the function of components. **2** (also **interlock fabric**) a fabric with closely interlocking stitches allowing it to stretch.

in·ter·loc·u·tor /ˌintərˈläkyətər/ ▶ **noun** formal a person who takes part in a conversation.
– DERIVATIVES **in·ter·lo·cu·tion** /-ləˈkyo͞oSHən/ noun.
– ORIGIN from Latin *interloqui* 'interrupt (with speech).'

in·ter·loc·u·to·ry /ˌintərˈläkyəˌtôrē/ ▶ **adjective** Law (of a decree or judgment) given provisionally during the course of a legal action.

in·ter·lop·er /ˈintərˌlōpər, ˌintərˈlōpər/ ▶ **noun** a person who is present in a place or situation where they are not wanted or do not belong.

– ORIGIN from INTER- + *-loper*, from Dutch *landlooper* 'vagabond.'

in·ter·lude /ˈintər,lo͞od/ ▸ **noun 1** a period of time or activity that contrasts with what goes before or after it: *a romantic interlude*. **2** a pause between the acts of a play. **3** a piece of music played between other pieces or between the verses of a hymn.
– ORIGIN Latin *interludium*.

in·ter·mar·ry /,intərˈmarē/ ▸ **verb** (**intermarries, intermarrying, intermarried**) (of people of different races, castes, or religions) marry each other.
– DERIVATIVES **in·ter·mar·riage** noun.

in·ter·me·di·ar·y /,intərˈmēdē,erē/ ▸ **noun** (pl. **intermediaries**) a person who acts as a link between people in order to try to bring about an agreement.

– SYNONYMS **mediator,** go-between, negotiator, arbitrator, peacemaker, middleman, broker.

▸ **adjective** intermediate.

in·ter·me·di·ate /,intərˈmēdē-it/ ▸ **adjective 1** coming between two things in time, place, or character: *an intermediate stage of development*. **2** having a level of knowledge or skill between basic and advanced.

– SYNONYMS **halfway,** in-between, middle, mid, midway, intervening, transitional.

▸ **noun** a thing coming between other things in time, place, or character.
– DERIVATIVES **in·ter·me·di·a·cy** noun **in·ter·me·di·a·tion** /-,mēdēˈāsʜən/ noun.
– ORIGIN from Latin *inter-* 'between' + *medius* 'middle.'

in·ter·ment /inˈtərmənt/ ▸ **noun** the burial of a corpse in a grave or tomb.

in·ter·mez·zo /,intərˈmetsō/ ▸ **noun** (pl. **intermezzi** /-ˈmetsē/ or **intermezzos**) **1** a short connecting instrumental movement in an opera or other musical work. **2** a short piece for a solo instrument. **3** a light dramatic or other performance between the acts of a play.
– ORIGIN Italian.

in·ter·mi·na·ble /inˈtərmənəbəl/ ▸ **adjective** endless or seemingly endless.
– DERIVATIVES **in·ter·mi·na·bly** adverb.
– ORIGIN Latin *interminabilis*.

CHOOSE THE RIGHT WORD

See **ETERNAL**.

in·ter·min·gle /,intərˈmiɴɢgəl/ ▸ **verb** mix or mingle together.

in·ter·mis·sion /,intərˈmisʜən/ ▸ **noun 1** a pause or break. **2** an interval between parts of a play or movie.
– ORIGIN Latin.

in·ter·mit·tent /,intərˈmitnt/ ▸ **adjective** occurring at irregular intervals: *intermittent rain*.

– SYNONYMS **sporadic,** irregular, fitful, spasmodic, discontinuous, isolated, random, patchy, scattered, occasional, periodic.
– ANTONYMS continuous.

– DERIVATIVES **in·ter·mit·ten·cy** noun **in·ter·mit·tent·ly** adverb.
– ORIGIN Latin, 'ceasing.'

in·ter·mix /,intərˈmiks/ ▸ **verb** mix together.
– DERIVATIVES **in·ter·mix·a·ble** adjective **in·ter·mix·ture** noun.

in·ter·mod·al /,intərˈmodl/ ▸ **adjective** involving two or more different modes of transport.

in·ter·mo·lec·u·lar /,intərməˈlekyələr/ ▸ **adjective** existing or occurring between molecules.

in·tern ▸ **verb** /inˈtərn/ confine someone as a prisoner.
▸ **noun** /ˈin,tərn/ **1** a recent medical graduate receiving supervised training in a hospital and acting as an assistant physician or surgeon. **2** a student or trainee who does a job to gain work experience.
– DERIVATIVES **in·tern·ment** /inˈtərnmənt/ noun **in·tern·ship** /-,sʜip/ noun.
– ORIGIN from Latin *internus* 'inward, internal.'

in·ter·nal /inˈtərnl/ ▸ **adjective 1** relating to or situated on the inside. **2** inside the body. **3** relating to affairs and activities within a country. **4** existing or used within an organization. **5** in one's mind or soul.

– SYNONYMS **1 inner,** interior, inside, central. **2 domestic,** home, interior, civil, local, national, state.
– ANTONYMS external, foreign.

▸ **noun** (**internals**) inner parts or features.
– DERIVATIVES **in·ter·nal·i·ty** /,intərˈnalitē/ noun **in·ter·nal·ly** adverb.
– ORIGIN Latin *internalis*.

in·ter·nal com·bus·tion en·gine ▸ **noun** an engine in which power is generated by the expansion of hot gases from the burning of fuel with air inside the engine.

in·ter·nal ex·ile ▸ **noun** banishment from a part of one's own country as a punishment.

in·ter·nal·ize /inˈtərnl,īz/ ▸ **verb** unconsciously make an attitude or belief part of one's behavior.
– DERIVATIVES **in·ter·nal·i·za·tion** /in,tərnl-iˈzāsʜən/ noun.

in·ter·nal mar·ket ▸ **noun 1** another term for **SINGLE MARKET**. **2** a system within an organization whereby departments buy each other's services.

in·ter·nal med·i·cine ▸ **noun** a branch of medicine specializing in the diagnosis and nonsurgical treatment of diseases.

in·ter·na·tion·al /,intərˈnasʜənl/ ▸ **adjective 1** existing or occurring between nations. **2** agreed on or used by all or many nations.

– SYNONYMS **global,** worldwide, world, intercontinental, universal, cosmopolitan, multiracial, multinational.
– ANTONYMS national, local.

▸ **noun** (**International**) any of four associations founded (1864–1936) to promote socialism or communism.
– DERIVATIVES **in·ter·na·tion·al·i·ty** /-,nasʜəˈnalitē/ noun **in·ter·na·tion·al·ly** adverb.

In·ter·na·tion·al Date Line ▸ **noun** an imaginary North–South line through the Pacific Ocean, chiefly along the meridian furthest from Greenwich, to the east of which the date is a day earlier than it is to the west.

in·ter·na·tion·al·ism /,intərˈnasʜənl,izəm/ ▸ **noun** the belief in or promotion of cooperation and understanding between nations.
– DERIVATIVES **in·ter·na·tion·al·ist** noun.

in·ter·na·tion·al·ize /,intərˈnasʜənl,īz/ ▸ **verb** make something international in scope or nature.
– DERIVATIVES **in·ter·na·tion·al·i·za·tion** /-,nasʜənl-iˈzāsʜən/ noun.

in·ter·na·tion·al law ▸ **noun** a set of rules established by custom or treaty and recognized by nations as binding in their relations with one another.

international style ▸ **noun** a style of 20th-century architecture characterized by the use of steel and reinforced concrete, simple lines, and strict geometric forms.

in·ter·ne·cine /ˌintərˈnesēn, -ˈnēsēn, -sin/ ▶ **adjective** **1** destructive to both sides in a conflict. **2** relating to conflict within a group: *internecine rivalries*.
– ORIGIN Latin *internecinus*.

in·tern·ee /ˌintərˈnē/ ▶ **noun** a prisoner.

In·ter·net /ˈintərˌnet/ ▶ **noun** a global computer network providing a variety of information and communication facilities.

in·ter·op·er·a·ble /ˌintərˈäp(ə)rəbəl/ ▶ **adjective** (of computer systems or software) able to exchange and make use of information.
– DERIVATIVES **in·ter·op·er·a·bil·i·ty** /-ˌäp(ə)rəˈbilitē/ noun.

in·ter·pen·e·trate /ˌintərˈpeniˌtrāt/ ▶ **verb** (of different things) mix or merge together.
– DERIVATIVES **in·ter·pen·e·tra·tion** /-ˌpeniˈtrāsʜən/ noun.

in·ter·per·son·al /ˌintərˈpərsənəl/ ▶ **adjective** relating to relationships between people.
– DERIVATIVES **in·ter·per·son·al·ly** adverb.

in·ter·phase /ˈintərˌfāz/ ▶ **noun** Biology the resting phase between successive mitotic divisions of a cell, or between the first and second divisions of meiosis.

in·ter·plan·e·tar·y /ˌintərˈplaniˌterē/ ▶ **adjective** situated or traveling between planets.

in·ter·play /ˈintərˌplā/ ▶ **noun** the way in which things interact: *the painting has a dramatic interplay of light and shade*.

In·ter·pol /ˈintərˌpōl/ ▶ **noun** an international organization that coordinates investigations made by the police forces of member countries into international crimes.
– ORIGIN from *Inter(national) pol(ice)*.

in·ter·po·late /inˈtərpəˌlāt/ ▶ **verb** **1** insert something different or additional into something else. **2** add a remark to a conversation. **3** Mathematics insert an intermediate term into a series by estimating it from surrounding known values.
– DERIVATIVES **in·ter·po·la·tion** /-ˌtərpəˈlāsʜən/ noun **in·ter·po·la·tor** noun.
– ORIGIN Latin *interpolare* 'refurbish, alter.'

in·ter·pose /ˌintərˈpōz/ ▶ **verb** **1** insert between one thing and another: *she interposed herself between the newcomers*. **2** intervene between parties. **3** say something as an interruption.
– DERIVATIVES **in·ter·po·si·tion** /ˌintərpəˈzisʜən/ noun.
– ORIGIN Latin *interponere* 'put in.'

in·ter·pret /inˈtərprit/ ▶ **verb** (**interprets, interpreting, interpreted**) **1** explain the meaning of something. **2** translate aloud the words of a person speaking a different language. **3** understand as having a particular meaning: *he interpreted her silence as indifference*. **4** perform a creative work in a way that conveys one's understanding of the creator's ideas.

> – SYNONYMS **1 explain,** elucidate, expound, clarify. **2 understand,** construe, take (to mean), see, regard. **3 decipher,** decode, translate, understand.

– DERIVATIVES **in·ter·pret·a·ble** adjective **in·ter·pre·ta·tive** (also **interpretive**) adjective.
– ORIGIN Latin *interpretari* 'explain, translate.'

> **CHOOSE THE RIGHT WORD**
>
> See **CLARIFY**.

in·ter·pre·ta·tion /inˌtərpriˈtāsʜən/ ▶ **noun** **1** the action of explaining the meaning of something. **2** an explanation. **3** the way in which a performer expresses a creative work.

> – SYNONYMS **1 explanation,** elucidation, exposition, clarification, analysis. **2 meaning,** understanding, explanation, inference. **3 rendition,** execution, presentation, performance, reading, playing, singing.

– DERIVATIVES **in·ter·pre·ta·tion·al** adjective.

in·ter·pret·er /inˈtərpritər/ ▶ **noun** a person who interprets foreign speech aloud as it is spoken.

in·ter·ra·cial /ˌintərˈrāsʜəl/ ▶ **adjective** existing between or involving different races.
– DERIVATIVES **in·ter·ra·cial·ly** adverb.

in·ter·reg·num /ˌintərˈregnəm/ ▶ **noun** (pl. **interregnums**) a period between reigns or political regimes when normal government is suspended.
– ORIGIN Latin.

in·ter·re·late /ˌintərəˈlāt/ ▶ **verb** relate or connect to one other.
– DERIVATIVES **in·ter·re·lat·ed·ness** noun **in·ter·re·la·tion** noun **in·ter·re·la·tion·ship** noun.

in·ter·ro·gate /inˈterəˌgāt/ ▶ **verb** ask someone questions in a detailed or aggressive way.
– DERIVATIVES **in·ter·ro·ga·tion** /inˌterəˈgāsʜən/ noun **in·ter·ro·ga·tor** noun.
– ORIGIN Latin *interrogare* 'question.'

in·ter·rog·a·tive /ˌintəˈrägətiv/ ▶ **adjective** **1** expressing a question: *a hard, interrogative stare*. **2** Grammar used in questions. ▶ **noun** a word used in questions, e.g., *how* or *what*.
– DERIVATIVES **in·ter·rog·a·tive·ly** adverb.

in·ter·rog·a·to·ry /ˌintəˈrägəˌtôrē/ ▶ **adjective** expressing a question; questioning.

in·ter·rupt /ˌintəˈrəpt/ ▶ **verb** **1** stop the continuous progress of something. **2** stop a person who is speaking by saying or doing something. **3** break the continuity of a line, surface, or view.

> – SYNONYMS **1 suspend,** discontinue, adjourn, break off, stop, halt; informal put on ice. **2 cut in (on),** break in (on), barge in (on), intrude, intervene; informal butt in (on), chime in (on).

– DERIVATIVES **in·ter·rupt·er** (also **interruptor**) noun **in·ter·rupt·i·ble** adjective **in·ter·rup·tive** adjective.
– ORIGIN Latin *interrumpere* 'break, interrupt.'

in·ter·rup·tion /ˌintəˈrəpsʜən/ ▶ **noun** **1** an act, remark, or period that stops the progress of something. **2** the action of interrupting someone or something.

> – SYNONYMS **1 cutting in,** barging in, interference, intervention, intrusion, disturbance; informal butting in. **2 suspension,** breaking off, discontinuance, stopping.

in·ter·sect /ˌintərˈsekt/ ▶ **verb** **1** divide something by passing or lying across it. **2** (of lines, roads, etc.) cross or cut each other.
– ORIGIN Latin *intersecare* 'cut, intersect.'

in·ter·sec·tion /ˌintərˈseksʜən/ ▶ **noun** **1** a point at which roads intersect or cross each other. **2** a point or line common to lines or surfaces that intersect.
– DERIVATIVES **in·ter·sec·tion·al** adjective.

in·ter·sex /ˈintərˌseks/ ▶ **noun** the condition of having both male and female sex organs or characteristics; hermaphroditism.

in·ter·sex·u·al /ˌintərˈseksʜo͞oəl/ ▶ **adjective** **1** existing or occurring between the sexes. **2** relating to the

condition of having both male and female sex organs or characteristics; hermaphroditic.
– DERIVATIVES **in·ter·sex·u·al·i·ty** /-ˌsekshōōˈalitē/ noun.

in·ter·space /ˈintərˌspās/ ▶ **noun** a space between objects. ▶ **verb** /ˌintərˈspās/ (usu. **be interspaced**) put or occupy a space between: *five pearls interspaced with diamonds*.

in·ter·sperse /ˌintərˈspərs/ ▶ **verb** scatter or place things among or between other things.
– DERIVATIVES **in·ter·sper·sion** noun.
– ORIGIN Latin *interspergere* 'scatter between.'

in·ter·state /ˈintərˌstāt/ ▶ **adjective** existing or carried on between states. ▶ **noun** one of a system of highways extending across the US.

in·ter·stel·lar /ˌintərˈstelər/ ▶ **adjective** occurring or situated between stars.

in·ter·stice /inˈtərstis/ ▶ **noun** (pl. **interstices** /-stiˌsēz/) a small space between things.
– ORIGIN Latin *interstitium*.

in·ter·sti·tial /ˌintərˈstishəl/ ▶ **adjective** relating to or found in small spaces between things.
– DERIVATIVES **in·ter·sti·tial·ly** adverb.

in·ter·tex·tu·al·i·ty /ˌintərˌtekschōōˈalitē/ ▶ **noun** the relationship between pieces of writing.
– DERIVATIVES **in·ter·tex·tu·al** /-ˈtekschōōəl/ adjective.

in·ter·trib·al /ˌintərˈtrībəl/ ▶ **adjective** existing or occurring between different tribes.

in·ter·twine /ˌintərˈtwīn/ ▶ **verb** twist or twine together.

in·ter·val /ˈintərvəl/ ▶ **noun 1** a period of time between two events. **2** a pause in activity, especially (Brit.) a pause between parts of a performance or a sports match. **3** a space or gap between things: *the path is marked with rocks at intervals.* **4** the difference in pitch between two sounds.

– SYNONYMS **intermission,** interlude, break, recess, time out.

– ORIGIN Latin *intervallum* 'space between ramparts, interval.'

in·ter·vene /ˌintərˈvēn/ ▶ **verb 1** come between people or things so as to prevent or alter a situation: *he intervened in the dispute.* **2** (usu. as adj. **intervening**) occur or be between events or things.

– SYNONYMS **intercede,** involve oneself, get involved, step in, interfere, intrude.

– DERIVATIVES **in·ter·ven·er** (also **intervenor**) noun.
– ORIGIN Latin *intervenire* 'come between.'

in·ter·ven·tion /ˌintərˈvenshən/ ▶ **noun 1** the action of intervening between people or things to influence or control a situation. **2** action taken to improve a medical disorder.
– DERIVATIVES **in·ter·ven·tion·al** adjective.

in·ter·ven·tion·ist /ˌintərˈvenshənist/ ▶ **adjective** favoring intervention to influence or control a situation. ▶ **noun** a person who favors intervening to influence or control a situation.
– DERIVATIVES **in·ter·ven·tion·ism** noun.

in·ter·view /ˈintərˌvyōō/ ▶ **noun 1** an occasion on which a journalist or broadcaster puts questions to a person. **2** a formal meeting at which a person is asked questions to assess their suitability for a job or college admission. **3** a session of formal questioning of a person by the police.

– SYNONYMS **meeting,** discussion, interrogation, cross-examination, debriefing, audience, talk, chat; informal grilling.

▶ **verb** hold an interview with someone.

– SYNONYMS **talk to,** question, quiz, interrogate, cross-examine, debrief, poll, canvass, sound out; informal grill, pump.

– DERIVATIVES **in·ter·view·ee** /ˌintərˌvyōōˈē/ noun.
– ORIGIN French *entrevue*.

in·ter·view·er /ˈintərˌvyōōər/ ▶ **noun** a person who conducts an interview.

– SYNONYMS **questioner,** interrogator, examiner, assessor, journalist, reporter, inquisitor.

in·ter·war /ˌintərˈwôr/ ▶ **adjective** existing in the period between two wars, especially the two world wars.

in·ter·weave /ˌintərˈwēv/ ▶ **verb** (past **interwove** /ˌintərˈwōv/; past part. **interwoven** /ˌintərˈwōvən/) weave or become woven together.

in·tes·tate /inˈtestāt, -tit/ ▶ **adjective** not having made a will before dying.
– DERIVATIVES **in·tes·ta·cy** /-təsē/ noun.

in·tes·tine /inˈtestən/ (also **intestines**) ▶ **noun** the long tubular organ leading from the end of the stomach to the anus.
– DERIVATIVES **in·tes·ti·nal** /inˈtestənəl/ adjective.
– ORIGIN Latin *intestinum*.

in·ti·fa·da /ˌintəˈfädə/ ▶ **noun** the Palestinian uprising against Israeli occupation of the West Bank and Gaza Strip, beginning in 1987.
– ORIGIN Arabic.

in·ti·ma·cy /ˈintəməsē/ ▶ **noun** (pl. **intimacies**) **1** close familiarity or friendship. **2** a familiar or private act or remark.

– SYNONYMS **closeness,** togetherness, rapport, attachment, familiarity, friendliness, affection, warmth.
– ANTONYMS formality.

in·ti·mate[1] /ˈintəmit/ ▶ **adjective 1** close and friendly: *they're on intimate terms.* **2** private and personal. **3** euphemistic having a sexual relationship. **4** involving very close connection: *her intimate involvement with the community.* **5** (of knowledge) detailed. **6** having a relaxed and cozy atmosphere.

– SYNONYMS **1 close,** bosom, dear, cherished, fast, firm. **2 friendly,** warm, welcoming, hospitable, relaxed, informal, cozy, comfortable. **3 personal,** private, confidential, secret, inward. **4 detailed,** thorough, exhaustive, deep, in-depth, profound.
– ANTONYMS distant, formal, cold.

▶ **noun** a very close friend.
– DERIVATIVES **in·ti·mate·ly** adverb.
– ORIGIN from Latin *intimare* 'impress, make familiar.'

in·ti·mate[2] /ˈintəˌmāt/ ▶ **verb** state something, especially in an indirect way.

– SYNONYMS **1 announce,** state, make known, disclose, reveal, divulge, let it be known. **2 imply,** suggest, hint at, indicate, insinuate.

– DERIVATIVES **in·ti·ma·tion** /ˌintəˈmāshən/ noun.
– ORIGIN Latin *intimare* (see **INTIMATE**[1]).

in·tim·i·date /inˈtimiˌdāt/ ▶ **verb** frighten someone, especially so as to force them into doing something.

– SYNONYMS **frighten,** menace, scare, terrorize, threaten, browbeat, bully, harass, hound; informal lean on.

– DERIVATIVES **in·tim·i·da·tion** /-ˌtimiˈdāshən/ noun **in·tim·i·da·tor** /-ˈtimiˌdātər/ noun **in·tim·i·da·to·ry**

/-ˌtimidəˌtôrē/ adjective.
– ORIGIN Latin *intimidare* 'make timid.'

in·to /ˈintōō/ ▶ **preposition 1** expressing movement or direction to a point on or within. **2** expressing a change of state or the result of an action. **3** so as to turn toward. **4** about or concerning. **5** expressing division. **6** informal very interested in.

in·tol·er·a·ble /inˈtälərəbəl/ ▶ **adjective** unable to be endured.

> – SYNONYMS **unbearable,** insufferable, insupportable, unendurable, more than flesh and blood can stand, too much to bear.
> – ANTONYMS bearable.

– DERIVATIVES **in·tol·er·a·bly** adverb.

in·tol·er·ant /inˈtälərənt/ ▶ **adjective** not tolerant of views or behavior that differ from one's own.

> – SYNONYMS **1 bigoted,** narrow-minded, prejudiced, illiberal. **2 allergic,** sensitive, hypersensitive.

– DERIVATIVES **in·tol·er·ance** noun **in·tol·er·ant·ly** adverb.

in·to·na·tion /ˌintəˈnāshən, -tō-/ ▶ **noun 1** the rise and fall of the voice in speaking. **2** the action of saying something with little rise and fall of the voice. **3** accuracy of musical pitch.
– DERIVATIVES **in·to·na·tion·al** adjective.

in·tone /inˈtōn/ ▶ **verb** say or recite something with little rise and fall of the pitch of the voice.
– ORIGIN Latin *intonare*.

in to·to /ˌin ˈtōtō/ ▶ **adverb** as a whole.
– ORIGIN Latin.

in·tox·i·cant /inˈtäksikənt/ ▶ **noun** a substance that causes someone to lose their self-control.

in·tox·i·cate /inˈtäksikāt/ ▶ **verb 1** (of alcoholic drink or a drug) cause someone to lose their self-control. **2** excite or exhilarate someone.
– DERIVATIVES **in·tox·i·ca·tion** /-ˌtäksiˈkāshən/ noun.
– ORIGIN Latin *intoxicare*.

in·tox·i·cat·ing /inˈtäksikāting/ ▶ **adjective 1** (of alcoholic drink or a drug) liable to cause intoxication. **2** exhilarating or exciting.

> – SYNONYMS **1** *intoxicating drink* **alcoholic,** strong, hard. **2** *an intoxicating sense of freedom* **heady,** exhilarating, thrilling, stirring, stimulating, invigorating, powerful, potent, electrifying; informal mind-blowing.
> – ANTONYMS nonalcoholic.

intra- ▶ **prefix** (added to adjectives) on the inside; within: *intramural*.
– ORIGIN Latin, 'inside.'

in·trac·ta·ble /inˈtraktəbəl/ ▶ **adjective 1** hard to solve or deal with. **2** (of a person) stubborn.
– DERIVATIVES **in·trac·ta·bil·i·ty** /-ˌtraktəˈbilitē/ noun **in·trac·ta·bly** adverb.

> **CHOOSE THE RIGHT WORD**
>
> See **STUBBORN**.

in·tra·mu·ral /ˌintrəˈmyōōrəl/ ▶ **adjective 1** situated or done within a building. **2** taking place within a single educational institution.
– ORIGIN from **INTRA-** + Latin *murus* 'wall.'

in·tra·net /ˈintrəˌnet/ ▶ **noun** a private communications network created with Internet software.

in·tran·si·gent /inˈtransijənt, -zi-/ ▶ **adjective** refusing to change one's views.

> – SYNONYMS **uncompromising,** inflexible, unbending, unyielding, unwavering, stubborn, obstinate, pigheaded.
> – ANTONYMS compliant.

▶ **noun** a person who refuses to change their views.
– DERIVATIVES **in·tran·si·gence** noun **in·tran·si·gen·cy** noun **in·tran·si·gent·ly** adverb.
– ORIGIN from Spanish *los intransigentes* (a name adopted by extreme republicans).

in·tran·si·tive /inˈtransitiv, -zi-/ ▶ **adjective** Grammar (of a verb) not taking a direct object, e.g., *die* in *he died suddenly*. The opposite of **TRANSITIVE**.
– DERIVATIVES **in·tran·si·tive·ly** adverb **in·tran·si·tiv·i·ty** /-ˌtransiˈtivitē, -zi-/ noun.

in·tra·u·ter·ine /ˌintrəˈyōōtərin, -rīn/ ▶ **adjective** within the uterus.

in·tra·u·ter·ine de·vice ▶ **noun** a contraceptive device fitted inside the uterus, which prevents the implantation of fertilized eggs.

in·tra·ve·nous /ˌintrəˈvēnəs/ ▶ **adjective** within or into a vein or veins.
– DERIVATIVES **in·tra·ve·nous·ly** adverb.

in·trep·id /inˈtrepid/ ▶ **adjective** not afraid of danger or difficulty; brave or bold.

> – SYNONYMS **fearless,** unflinching, bold, daring, heroic, dynamic, brave, valiant, doughty, indomitable.
> – ANTONYMS fearful.

– DERIVATIVES **in·tre·pid·i·ty** /ˌintrəˈpiditē/ noun **in·trep·id·ly** adverb.
– ORIGIN Latin *intrepidus* 'not alarmed.'

> **CHOOSE THE RIGHT WORD**
>
> See **BOLD**.

in·tri·ca·cy /ˈintrikəsē/ ▶ **noun** (pl. **intricacies**) **1** the quality of being complicated or detailed. **2** (**intricacies**) complicated details.

in·tri·cate /ˈintrikit/ ▶ **adjective** very complicated or detailed.

> – SYNONYMS **complex,** complicated, convoluted, tangled, elaborate, ornate, detailed.
> – ANTONYMS simple.

– DERIVATIVES **in·tri·cate·ly** adverb.
– ORIGIN from Latin *intricare* 'entangle.'

WORD TOOLKIT

intricate ...	complex ...	convoluted ...
design	system	logic
pattern	issue	argument
detail	structure	story
web	interaction	explanation
network	relationship	plot
carving	trait	reasoning
embroidery	mixture	scheme
melody	organism	thinking

in·trigue ▶ **verb** /inˈtrēg/ (**intrigues, intriguing, intrigued**) **1** arouse someone's curiosity or interest. **2** plot something illegal or harmful.

> – SYNONYMS **interest,** fascinate, arouse someone's curiosity, attract, engage.

▶ **noun** /ˈinˌtrēg/ **1** the plotting of something illegal or harmful. **2** a secret love affair.

– SYNONYMS **plotting,** conniving, scheming, machination, double-dealing, subterfuge.

– DERIVATIVES **in·tri·guer** noun **in·tri·guing** adjective **in·tri·guing·ly** adverb.
– ORIGIN French *intriguer* 'tangle, plot.'

CHOOSE THE RIGHT WORD

See **PLOT**.

in·trin·sic /in'trinzik, -sik/ ▶ **adjective** belonging to the basic nature of someone or something; essential: *the club was an intrinsic part of New York nightlife.*

– SYNONYMS **inherent,** innate, inborn, inbred, congenital, natural; integral, basic, fundamental, essential.

– DERIVATIVES **in·trin·si·cal·ly** adverb.
– ORIGIN Latin *intrinsecus* 'inwardly, inwards.'

in·tro /'intrō/ ▶ **noun** (pl. **intros**) informal an introduction.

intro- ▶ **prefix** into; inward: *introvert.*
– ORIGIN Latin *intro* 'to the inside.'

in·tro·duce /ˌintrə'd(y)o͞os/ ▶ **verb 1** bring something into use or operation for the first time. **2** present someone by name to another. **3** (**introduce something to**) cause someone to learn about a subject or experience an activity for the first time. **4** insert something. **5** occur at the start of: *a horn solo introduces the symphony.* **6** provide an opening announcement for a television or radio program. **7** present new legislation for debate in a lawmaking assembly.

– SYNONYMS **1 institute,** initiate, launch, inaugurate, establish, found, bring in, set in motion, start, begin, get going. **2 present,** make known, acquaint with. **3 insert,** inject, put, force, shoot, feed. **4 instill,** infuse, inject, add.
– ANTONYMS end, remove.

– DERIVATIVES **in·tro·duc·er** noun.
– ORIGIN Latin *introducere.*

in·tro·duc·tion /ˌintrə'dəksʜən/ ▶ **noun 1** the action of introducing someone or something. **2** a thing newly brought in. **3** an act of introducing one person to another. **4** a thing that introduces another, such as a section at the beginning of a book. **5** a book or course of study intended for people who are beginning to study a subject. **6** a person's first experience of a subject or activity.

– SYNONYMS **1 institution,** establishment, initiation, launch, inauguration, foundation. **2 presentation,** meeting, audience. **3 foreword,** preface, preamble, prologue, prelude; informal intro.
– ANTONYMS ending, epilogue.

in·tro·duc·to·ry /ˌintrə'dəktərē/ ▶ **adjective** serving as an introduction; basic or preliminary.

– SYNONYMS **1 opening,** initial, starting, initiatory, first, preliminary. **2 elementary,** basic, rudimentary, entry-level.
– ANTONYMS final, advanced.

in·tro·it /'inˌtrō-it, -ˌtroit/ ▶ **noun** (in the Christian Church) a psalm or antiphon sung or said while the priest approaches the altar for Holy Communion.
– ORIGIN Latin *introitus.*

in·tro·spec·tion /ˌintrə'spekshən/ ▶ **noun** the examination of one's own thoughts or feelings.
– ORIGIN from Latin *introspicere* 'look into' or from *introspectare* 'keep looking into.'

in·tro·spec·tive /ˌintrə'spektiv/ ▶ **adjective** given to examining one's own thoughts or feelings: *an introspective poet.*

– SYNONYMS **inward-looking,** self-analyzing, introverted, introvert, contemplative, thoughtful, reflective; informal **navel-gazing.**

– DERIVATIVES **in·tro·spec·tive·ly** adverb.

in·tro·vert /'intrəˌvərt/ ▶ **noun** a shy, quiet person who is mainly concerned with their own thoughts and feelings. ▶ **adjective** another term for **INTROVERTED**.
– DERIVATIVES **in·tro·ver·sion** noun.
– ORIGIN from Latin *intro-* 'to the inside' + *vertere* 'to turn.'

in·tro·vert·ed /'intrəˌvərtid/ ▶ **adjective 1** relating to an introvert. **2** (of a community, company, or other group) concerned principally with its own affairs.

– SYNONYMS **shy,** reserved, withdrawn, reticent, diffident, retiring, quiet; introspective, introvert, inward-looking; pensive.
– ANTONYMS extroverted.

in·trude /in'tro͞od/ ▶ **verb 1** enter a place or situation where one is unwelcome or uninvited. **2** interrupt and disturb: *the noise began to intrude into her thoughts.*

– SYNONYMS **encroach,** impinge, trespass, infringe, invade, violate, disturb, disrupt.

– ORIGIN Latin *intrudere.*

in·trud·er /in'tro͞odər/ ▶ **noun** a person who intrudes, especially one who enters a building with criminal intent.

– SYNONYMS **trespasser,** interloper, invader, infiltrator, burglar, housebreaker; informal gatecrasher.

in·tru·sion /in'tro͞ozʜən/ ▶ **noun 1** the action of entering a place or situation where one is unwelcome or uninvited. **2** a thing that intrudes.

in·tru·sive /in'tro͞osiv/ ▶ **adjective 1** unwelcome or uninvited and causing disturbance or annoyance. **2** (of igneous rock) that has been forced when molten into cracks in neighboring rocks.

– SYNONYMS **1** *intrusive neighbors* **intruding,** invasive, inquisitive, prying; informal nosy. **2** *intrusive questions* **personal,** prying, impertinent.

– DERIVATIVES **in·tru·sive·ly** adverb **in·tru·sive·ness** noun.

in·tu·it /in't(y)o͞o-it/ ▶ **verb** (past and past part. **intuited**) understand or work something out by intuition.
– ORIGIN Latin *intueri* 'contemplate.'

in·tu·i·tion /ˌint(y)o͞o'isʜən/ ▶ **noun** the ability to understand or know something immediately, without conscious reasoning.

– SYNONYMS **1 instinct,** feeling, insight, sixth sense. **2 hunch,** feeling in one's bones, inkling, sneaking suspicion, premonition; informal gut feeling.

in·tu·i·tive /in't(y)o͞oitiv/ ▶ **adjective 1** based on what one feels to be true; instinctive. **2** (chiefly of computer software) easy to use and understand.

– SYNONYMS **instinctive,** innate, inborn, inherent, natural, unconscious, subconscious; informal gut.

– DERIVATIVES **in·tu·i·tive·ly** adverb **in·tu·i·tive·ness** noun.

In·u·it /'in(y)o͞o-it/ ▶ **noun 1** (pl. same or **Inuits**) a member of a people of northern Canada and parts of Greenland and Alaska. **2** the language of the Inuit.
– ORIGIN Inuit, 'people.'

USAGE

For an explanation of the terms **Inuit** and **Eskimo**, see the note at **ESKIMO**.

I·nuk·ti·tut /i'n(y)o͝okti,to͞ot/ ▶ **noun** the Inuit language.
– ORIGIN Inuit, 'the Inuit way.'

in·un·date /'inən,dāt/ ▶ **verb 1** overwhelm with things to be dealt with: *we've been inundated with complaints.* **2** flood something.
– DERIVATIVES **in·un·da·tion** /,inən'dāsнən/ noun.
– ORIGIN Latin *inundare* 'flood.'

in·ure /i'n(y)o͝or/ ▶ **verb** (**be inured to**) become used to something, especially something unpleasant.
– ORIGIN from an Old French phrase meaning 'in use or practice.'

in u·ter·o /in 'yo͞otərō/ ▶ **adverb & adjective** in a woman's uterus; before birth.
– ORIGIN Latin.

in·vade /in'vād/ ▶ **verb 1** (of an armed force) enter a country so as to conquer or occupy it. **2** enter somewhere in large numbers. **3** intrude on: *his privacy was being invaded.* **4** (of a parasite or disease) spread into the body.

– SYNONYMS **1 occupy,** conquer, capture, seize, take (over), annex, overrun, storm. **2 intrude on,** violate, encroach on, infringe on, trespass on, disturb, disrupt.
– ANTONYMS leave, liberate.

– DERIVATIVES **in·vad·er** noun.
– ORIGIN Latin *invadere.*

in·va·lid¹ /'invəlid/ ▶ **noun** a person made weak or disabled by illness or injury. ▶ **verb** (**be invalided**) be removed from active service in the armed forces because of injury or illness.

– SYNONYMS **disable,** incapacitate, hospitalize, put out of action, lay up.

– DERIVATIVES **in·va·lid·ism** /-,izəm/ noun.
– ORIGIN from **INVALID²**.

in·va·lid² /in'valid/ ▶ **adjective 1** not valid or officially recognized. **2** not true because based on incorrect information or faulty reasoning.

– SYNONYMS **1 void,** null and void, not binding, illegitimate, inapplicable. **2 false,** fallacious, spurious, unsound, wrong, untenable.

– DERIVATIVES **in·val·id·ly** adverb.
– ORIGIN Latin *invalidus* 'not strong.'

in·val·i·date /in'vali,dāt/ ▶ **verb 1** make or prove an argument or theory to be incorrect or faulty. **2** make an official document or procedure no longer legally valid.
– DERIVATIVES **in·val·i·da·tion** /-,vali'dāsнən/ noun.

in·va·lid·i·ty /,invə'liditē/ ▶ **noun** the fact of being invalid.

in·val·u·a·ble /in'valyo͞oəbəl/ ▶ **adjective** very useful.

– SYNONYMS **indispensable,** irreplaceable, all-important, crucial, vital, worth its weight in gold.
– ANTONYMS dispensable.

– DERIVATIVES **in·val·u·a·bly** adverb.

in·var·i·a·ble /in've(ə)rēəbəl/ ▶ **adjective 1** never changing. **2** Mathematics (of a quantity) constant.
– DERIVATIVES **in·var·i·a·bil·i·ty** /-,ve(ə)rēə'bilitē/ noun.

in·var·i·a·bly /in've(ə)rēəblē/ ▶ **adverb** in every case or on every occasion; always.

– SYNONYMS **always,** at all times, without fail, without exception, consistently, habitually, unfailingly.

in·va·sion /in'vāzнən/ ▶ **noun 1** an instance of invading a country. **2** the arrival of a large number of people or things. **3** an intrusion: *random drug testing is an invasion of privacy.*

– SYNONYMS **1 occupation,** conquering, capture, seizure, annexation, takeover. **2 violation,** infringement, interruption, encroachment, disturbance, disruption, breach.
– ANTONYMS withdrawal.

in·va·sive /in'vāsiv/ ▶ **adjective 1** tending to invade or intrude: *invasive grasses.* **2** (of medical procedures) involving the introduction of instruments or other objects into the body.

in·vec·tive /in'vektiv/ ▶ **noun** strongly abusive or critical language.
– ORIGIN Latin *invectivus* 'attacking.'

in·veigh /in'vā/ ▶ **verb** (**inveigh against**) speak or write about someone with great hostility.
– ORIGIN Latin *invehi* 'be carried into, attack.'

in·vei·gle /in'vāgəl/ ▶ **verb** persuade someone to do something by deception or flattery: *he can inveigle any woman into bed in minutes.*
– ORIGIN Old French *aveugler* 'to blind.'

CHOOSE THE RIGHT WORD

See **TEMPT**.

in·vent /in'vent/ ▶ **verb 1** create or design a new device or process. **2** make up a false story, name, etc.

– SYNONYMS **1 originate,** create, design, devise, develop. **2 make up,** fabricate, concoct, hatch, contrive, dream up; informal cook up.

– ORIGIN Latin *invenire* 'contrive, discover.'

in·ven·tion /in'vensнən/ ▶ **noun 1** the action of inventing something. **2** a newly created device or process. **3** a false story. **4** a person's creative ability.

– SYNONYMS **1 origination,** creation, development, design, discovery. **2 innovation,** contraption, contrivance, device, gadget. **3 fabrication,** concoction, (piece of) fiction, story, tale, lie, untruth, falsehood, fib.

in·ven·tive /in'ventiv/ ▶ **adjective** having or showing creativity or original thought.

– SYNONYMS **creative,** original, innovative, imaginative, resourceful, unusual, fresh, novel, new, groundbreaking, unorthodox, unconventional.
– ANTONYMS unimaginative.

– DERIVATIVES **in·ven·tive·ly** adverb **in·ven·tive·ness** noun.

CHOOSE THE RIGHT WORD

See **CREATIVE**.

in·ven·tor /in'ventər/ ▶ **noun** a person who creates or designs a new device or process.

– SYNONYMS **originator,** creator, designer, deviser, developer, author, architect, father.

in·ven·to·ry /'invən,tôrē/ ▶ **noun** (pl. **inventories**) **1** a complete list of items such as goods in stock or the contents of a building. **2** a quantity of goods in stock.

– SYNONYMS **list,** listing, catalog, record, register, checklist, log, archive.

▶ **verb** (**inventories, inventorying, inventoried**) make an inventory of items.
– ORIGIN Latin *inventarium* 'a list of what is found.'

in·verse /'invərs, in'vərs/ ▶ **adjective** opposite in position, direction, order, or effect. ▶ **noun 1** a thing that is the opposite or reverse of another. **2** Mathematics a reciprocal quantity.
– DERIVATIVES **in·verse·ly** adverb.
– ORIGIN Latin *inversus*.

in·verse pro·por·tion (also **inverse ratio**) ▶ **noun** a relation between two quantities such that one increases in proportion as the other decreases.

in·ver·sion /in'vərZHən/ ▶ **noun 1** the action of inverting something or the state of being inverted. **2** (also **temperature** or **thermal inversion**) a reversal of the normal decrease of air temperature with altitude, or of water temperature with depth.
– DERIVATIVES **in·ver·sive** /-'vərsiv/ adjective.

in·vert /in'vərt/ ▶ **verb** put something upside down or in the opposite position, order, or arrangement.
– DERIVATIVES **in·vert·er** noun **in·vert·i·ble** adjective.
– ORIGIN Latin *invertere* 'turn inside out.'

in·ver·te·brate /in'vərtəbrit, -ˌbrāt/ ▶ **noun** an animal having no backbone, such as a mollusk. ▶ **adjective** relating to invertebrates.

in·vest /in'vest/ ▶ **verb 1** put money into financial schemes, shares, or property with the expectation of making a profit. **2** devote time or energy to an undertaking with the expectation of a worthwhile result. **3** (**invest in**) informal buy something whose usefulness will repay the cost. **4** (**invest someone/thing with**) provide someone or something with a quality: *these weapons are invested with an almost mystical value by collectors.* **5** formally appoint someone to a rank or office.

– SYNONYMS **1 put in,** put up, advance, expend, spend; informal lay out. **2** (**invest in**) **put money into,** sink money into, fund, back, finance, underwrite.

– DERIVATIVES **in·vest·a·ble** adjective **in·ves·tor** noun.
– ORIGIN Latin *investire* 'clothe'; sense 1 is influenced by Italian *investire*.

in·ves·ti·gate /in'vestiˌgāt/ ▶ **verb 1** carry out a systematic or formal inquiry into an incident or allegation so as to establish the truth. **2** carry out research into a subject. **3** make a search or systematic inquiry.

– SYNONYMS **inquire into,** look into, go into, probe, explore, scrutinize, analyze, study, examine; informal check out.

– ORIGIN Latin *investigare* 'trace out.'

in·ves·ti·ga·tion /inˌvesti'gāSHən/ ▶ **noun 1** the action of investigating something or someone. **2** a formal inquiry or systematic study.

– SYNONYMS **examination,** inquiry, study, inspection, exploration, analysis, research, scrutiny, probe, review.

in·ves·ti·ga·tive /in'vestiˌgātiv/ ▶ **adjective 1** relating to investigation or research. **2** (of journalism or a journalist) investigating and seeking to expose dishonesty or injustice.

in·ves·ti·ga·tor /in'vestiˌgātər/ ▶ **noun** a person who investigates.

– SYNONYMS **researcher,** examiner, analyst, inspector, scrutineer, detective.

– DERIVATIVES **in·ves·ti·ga·to·ry** /-gəˌtôrē/ adjective.

in·ves·ti·ture /in'vestiCHər, -ˌCHo͝or/ ▶ **noun 1** the action of formally investing a person with honors or rank. **2** a ceremony at which this takes place.

in·vest·ment /in'ves(t)mənt/ ▶ **noun 1** the action of investing money in something for profit. **2** a thing worth buying because it may be profitable or useful in the future.

– SYNONYMS **1 investing,** speculation, outlay, funding, backing, financing, underwriting. **2 stake,** payment, outlay, venture, proposition.

in·vest·ment bank ▶ **noun** a bank that deals in securities and provides services for large investors.
– DERIVATIVES **in·vest·ment bank·er** noun **in·vest·ment bank·ing** noun.

in·vet·er·ate /in'vetərit/ ▶ **adjective 1** having a long-standing and firmly established habit or interest: *an inveterate gambler*. **2** (of a feeling or habit) firmly established.

– SYNONYMS **1** *an inveterate gambler* **confirmed,** hardened, incorrigible, addicted, compulsive, obsessive; informal pathological, chronic. **2** *an inveterate Democrat* **staunch,** steadfast, committed, devoted, dedicated, dyed-in-the-wool, diehard.

– DERIVATIVES **in·vet·er·a·cy** noun **in·vet·er·ate·ly** adverb.
– ORIGIN Latin *inveteratus* 'made old.'

in·vid·i·ous /in'vidēəs/ ▶ **adjective** unacceptable, unfair, and likely to arouse resentment or anger in others.

– SYNONYMS **1 unpleasant,** awkward, difficult, undesirable, unenviable. **2 unfair,** unjust, unwarranted.

– DERIVATIVES **in·vid·i·ous·ly** adverb **in·vid·i·ous·ness** noun.
– ORIGIN Latin *invidiosus*, from *invidia* 'hostility.'

in·vig·or·ate /in'vigəˌrāt/ ▶ **verb** give strength or energy to someone or something.

– SYNONYMS **revitalize,** energize, refresh, revive, enliven, liven up, perk up, wake up, animate, galvanize, fortify, rouse, exhilarate; informal buck up, pep up.
– ANTONYMS tire.

– DERIVATIVES **in·vig·or·at·ing** adjective **in·vig·or·a·tion** /inˌvigə'rāSHən/ noun.
– ORIGIN Latin *invigorare* 'make strong.'

in·vin·ci·ble /in'vinsəbəl/ ▶ **adjective** too powerful to be defeated or overcome.

– SYNONYMS **invulnerable,** indestructible, unconquerable, unbeatable, indomitable, unassailable, impregnable.
– ANTONYMS vulnerable.

– DERIVATIVES **in·vin·ci·bil·i·ty** /-ˌvinsə'bilitē/ noun **in·vin·ci·bly** adverb.
– ORIGIN from Latin *in-* 'not' + *vincibilis* 'able to be overcome.'

in·vi·o·la·ble /in'vīələbəl/ ▶ **adjective** never to be broken, infringed or violated: *inviolable rules*.
– DERIVATIVES **in·vi·o·la·bil·i·ty** /inˌvīələ'bilitē/ noun **in·vi·o·la·bly** adverb.

in·vi·o·late /in'vīəlit/ ▶ **adjective** that is or should be free from injury or attack.
– ORIGIN from Latin *in-* 'not' + *violare* 'violate.'

in·vis·i·ble /in'vizəbəl/ ▶ **adjective 1** unable to be seen, either by nature or because hidden. **2** relating to earnings that a country makes from the sale of services rather than tangible commodities.

– SYNONYMS **unseen,** imperceptible, undetectable, inconspicuous, unnoticed, unobserved, hidden, out of sight.
– ANTONYMS visible.

– DERIVATIVES **in·vis·i·bil·i·ty** /-ˌvizə'bilitē/ noun **in·vis·i·bly** adverb.

WORD TOOLKIT

invisible ...	undetectable ...	veiled ...
force	levels	threat
man	steroid	reference
barrier	drug	warning
line	changes	criticism
enemy	virus	insult
ink	substances	suggestion
God	concentrations	anger

in·vi·ta·tion /ˌinvi'tāsHən/ ▶ **noun 1** a written or spoken request inviting someone to go somewhere or to do something. **2** the action of inviting someone to go somewhere or to do something. **3** a situation or action that is likely to result in a particular outcome: *his tactics were an invitation to disaster*.

– SYNONYMS **request,** call, summons; informal invite.

in·vite ▶ **verb** /in'vīt/ **1** ask someone in a friendly or formal way to go somewhere or to do something. **2** request something formally or politely. **3** tend to result in a particular outcome.

– SYNONYMS **1 ask,** summon. **2 ask for,** request, call for, appeal for, solicit, seek. **3 cause,** induce, provoke, ask for, encourage, lead to, bring on oneself, arouse.

▶ **noun** /'inˌvīt/ informal an invitation.
– DERIVATIVES **in·vi·tee** /ˌinvī'tē/ noun **in·vit·er** noun.
– ORIGIN Latin *invitare*.

in·vit·ing /in'vītiNG/ ▶ **adjective** tempting or attractive.

– SYNONYMS **tempting,** enticing, alluring, attractive, appealing, appetizing, mouthwatering, intriguing, seductive.
– ANTONYMS repellent.

– DERIVATIVES **in·vit·ing·ly** adverb.

in vi·tro /in 'vēˌtrō/ ▶ **adjective & adverb** (of biological processes) taking place in a test tube or elsewhere outside a living organism.
– ORIGIN Latin, 'in glass.'

in vi·vo /in 'vēvō/ ▶ **adverb & adjective** (of biological processes) taking place in a living organism.
– ORIGIN Latin, 'in a living thing.'

in·vo·ca·tion /ˌinvə'kāsHən/ ▶ **noun 1** the action of appealing to someone or something as an authority or in support of an argument. **2** an appeal to a god or spirit.

in·voice /'inˌvois/ ▶ **noun** a list of goods or services provided, with a statement of the sum due. ▶ **verb** send an invoice to someone for goods or services.
– ORIGIN from French *envoyer* 'send.'

in·voke /in'vōk/ ▶ **verb 1** appeal to someone or something as an authority or in support of an argument. **2** call on a god or spirit in prayer or as a witness. **3** call earnestly for something. **4** give rise to: *how could she explain the accident without invoking his wrath?*

– SYNONYMS **1 cite,** refer to, resort to, have recourse to, turn to. **2 pray to,** call on, appeal to. **3 bring forth,** bring out, elicit, conjure up, generate.

– ORIGIN Latin *invocare*.

in·vol·un·tar·y /in'välənˌterē/ ▶ **adjective 1** done without conscious control. **2** (especially of muscles or nerves) involved in processes that are not consciously controlled. **3** done against someone's will.

– SYNONYMS **1 reflex,** automatic, instinctive, unintentional, uncontrollable. **2 compulsory,** obligatory, mandatory, forced, prescribed.
– ANTONYMS deliberate, optional.

– DERIVATIVES **in·vol·un·tar·i·ly** /inˌvälən'te(ə)rəlē, -'välənˌter-/ adverb.

WORD TOOLKIT

See **SPONTANEOUS**.

in·vo·lut·ed /'invəˌlōōtid/ ▶ **adjective** formal complicated or intricate.
– ORIGIN Latin *involutus* 'wrapped up.'

in·volve /in'välv/ ▶ **verb 1** (of a situation or event) include something as a necessary part or result. **2** cause to experience or participate in an activity or situation: *his car was stolen and involved in a crash*. **3** (**be/get involved**) be or become occupied or engrossed in something. **4** (**be involved**) be in a romantic relationship with someone.

– SYNONYMS **1 entail,** require, necessitate, demand, call for. **2 include,** take in, incorporate, encompass, comprise, cover. **3** *social workers involved in the case* **associated with,** connected with/to, concerned with. **4** *he had been involved in burglaries* **implicated,** caught up, mixed up. **5 engrossed,** absorbed, immersed, caught up, preoccupied, intent.
– ANTONYMS preclude, exclude.

– ORIGIN Latin *involvere* 'entangle, enfold.'

in·volved /in'välvd/ ▶ **adjective** difficult to understand; complicated.

– SYNONYMS **complicated,** intricate, complex, elaborate, convoluted, confusing.

in·volve·ment /in'välvmənt/ ▶ **noun 1** the fact or condition of being involved with or participating in something. **2** emotional or personal association with someone.

– SYNONYMS **1** *his involvement in a plot to overthrow the government* **participation,** collaboration, collusion, complicity, association, connection, entanglement. **2** *emotional involvement* **attachment,** friendship, intimacy, commitment.

in·vul·ner·a·ble /in'vəlnərəbəl/ ▶ **adjective** impossible to harm or damage.

– SYNONYMS **impervious,** immune; indestructible, impregnable, unassailable, invincible, secure.

– DERIVATIVES **in·vul·ner·a·bil·i·ty** /-ˌvəlnərə'bilitē/ noun **in·vul·ner·a·bly** adverb.

-in-wait·ing ▶ **combining form 1** referring to a position as attendant to a royal person: *lady-in-waiting*. **2** awaiting a turn or about to happen: *a political administration-in-waiting*.

in·ward /'inwərd/ ▶ **adjective 1** directed or proceeding toward the inside. **2** mental or spiritual. ▶ **adverb** (also **inwards**) **1** toward the inside. **2** into or toward the mind or spirit.

– SYNONYMS **inside,** toward the inside, into the interior, within, inwards.

– DERIVATIVES **in·ward·ly** adverb **in·ward·ness** noun.

in-your-face ▶ **adjective** informal blatantly aggressive or provocative.
– ORIGIN from *in your face,* used as an insult.

I/O ▶ **abbreviation** Electronics input-output.

IOC ▶ **abbreviation** International Olympic Committee.

i·o·dide /ˈīəˌdīd/ ▶ **noun** a compound of iodine with another element or group.

i·o·dine /ˈīəˌdīn/ ▶ **noun 1** a black crystalline nonmetallic chemical element of the halogen group. **2** an antiseptic solution of iodine in alcohol.
– ORIGIN from Greek *iōdēs* 'violet-colored.'

i·o·dized /ˈīəˌdīzd/ ▶ **adjective** impregnated with iodine: *iodized salt.*

i·on /ˈīən, ˈīˌän/ ▶ **noun** an atom or molecule with a net electric charge through loss or gain of electrons, either positive (a **cation**) or negative (an **anion**).
– ORIGIN Greek, 'going.'

i·on ex·change ▶ **noun** the exchange of ions of the same charge between an insoluble solid and a solution in contact with it, used in water-softening and other purification processes.

I·o·ni·an /īˈōnēən/ ▶ **noun** a person from the Ionian Islands, a chain of islands off the western coast of mainland Greece. ▶ **adjective** relating to the Ionians or the Ionian Islands.

I·on·ic /īˈänik/ ▶ **adjective** relating to a classical order of architecture characterized by a column with scroll shapes on the top.
– ORIGIN Greek *Iōnikos.*

i·on·ic /īˈänik/ ▶ **adjective 1** relating to ions. **2** (of a chemical bond) formed by the attraction of ions with opposite charges. Often contrasted with **COVALENT**.
– DERIVATIVES **i·on·i·cal·ly** adverb.

i·on·ize /ˈīəˌnīz/ ▶ **verb** convert an atom, molecule, or substance into an ion or ions, typically by removing one or more electrons.
– DERIVATIVES **i·on·iz·a·ble** adjective **i·on·i·za·tion** /ˌīəniˈzāsʜən/ noun.

i·on·iz·er /ˈīəˌnīzər/ ▶ **noun** a device that produces ions, especially one used to improve the quality of the air in a room.

i·on·o·sphere /īˈänəˌsfi(ə)r/ ▶ **noun** the layer of the atmosphere above the mesosphere that contains a high concentration of ions and electrons and is able to reflect radio waves.
– DERIVATIVES **i·on·o·spher·ic** /īˌänəˈsfi(ə)rik, -ˈsfer-/ adjective.

i·o·ta /īˈōtə/ ▶ **noun 1** the ninth letter of the Greek alphabet (Ι, ι), represented as 'i'. **2** an extremely small amount: *it won't make an iota of difference.*

– SYNONYMS **(little) bit,** mite, speck, scrap, shred, ounce, jot.

– ORIGIN Greek.

IOU ▶ **noun** a signed document acknowledging a debt.
– ORIGIN representing the pronunciation of *I owe you.*

IP ▶ **abbreviation** Computing Internet Protocol.

IPA ▶ **abbreviation** International Phonetic Alphabet.

ip·e·cac /ˈipikak/ ▶ **noun** the dried rhizome of a South American shrub, or a drug prepared from this, used as an emetic and expectorant.
– ORIGIN Portuguese.

IPO ▶ **abbreviation** initial public offering, the first issue of a company's shares to the public, used as a means of raising startup or expansion capital.

iPod /ˈīˌpäd/ ▶ **noun** trademark a type of personal digital audio player.

ip·so fac·to /ˈipsō ˈfaktō/ ▶ **adverb** by that very fact or act.
– ORIGIN Latin.

IQ ▶ **abbreviation** intelligence quotient.

IR ▶ **abbreviation** infrared.

Ir ▶ **symbol** the chemical element iridium.

IRA /ˈīrə/ ▶ **abbreviation** individual retirement account.

I·ra·ni·an /iˈrānēən, iˈrä-/ ▶ **noun** a person from Iran. ▶ **adjective** relating to Iran.

I·ra·qi /iˈräkē, iˈrakē/ ▶ **noun** (pl. **Iraqis**) **1** a person from Iraq. **2** the form of Arabic spoken in Iraq. ▶ **adjective** relating to Iraq.

i·ras·ci·ble /iˈrasəbəl/ ▶ **adjective** hot-tempered; irritable.
– DERIVATIVES **i·ras·ci·bil·i·ty** /iˌrasəˈbilitē/ noun **i·ras·ci·bly** adverb.
– ORIGIN Latin *irascibilis,* from *ira* 'anger.'

i·rate /īˈrāt/ ▶ **adjective** very angry.
– DERIVATIVES **i·rate·ly** adverb.
– ORIGIN Latin *iratus.*

IRC ▶ **abbreviation** Computing Internet Relay Chat.

ire /ī(ə)r/ ▶ **noun** chiefly literary anger.
– ORIGIN Latin *ira.*

i·ren·ic /īˈrenik, īˈrē-/ ▶ **adjective** formal intended or intending to maintain or bring about peace.
– ORIGIN from Greek *eirēnē* 'peace.'

ir·i·des·cent /ˌiriˈdesənt/ ▶ **adjective** showing bright colors that seem to change when seen from different angles.
– DERIVATIVES **ir·i·des·cence** noun **ir·i·des·cent·ly** adverb.
– ORIGIN from Latin *iris* 'rainbow.'

i·rid·i·um /iˈridēəm/ ▶ **noun** a hard, dense silvery-white metallic element.
– ORIGIN from Latin *iris* 'rainbow' (so named because it forms compounds of various colors).

ir·i·dol·o·gy /ˌiriˈdäləjē/ ▶ **noun** (in alternative medicine) a method of diagnosing illnesses or conditions by examining the iris of the eye.
– DERIVATIVES **ir·i·dol·o·gist** noun.

i·ris /ˈīris/ ▶ **noun 1** a colored ring-shaped membrane behind the cornea of the eye, with the pupil in the center. **2** a plant with sword-shaped leaves and purple or yellow flowers.
– ORIGIN Greek, 'rainbow, iris.'

I·rish /ˈīrisʜ/ ▶ **noun** (also **Irish Gaelic**) the Celtic language of Ireland. ▶ **adjective** relating to Ireland or Irish.
– DERIVATIVES **I·rish·man** noun (pl. **Irishmen**) **I·rish·ness** noun **I·rish·wom·an** noun (pl. **Irishwomen**).
– ORIGIN Old English.

I·rish cof·fee ▶ **noun** coffee mixed with a dash of Irish whiskey and served with cream on top.

I·rish set·ter ▶ **noun** a breed of setter (dog) with a long, silky dark red coat and a long feathered tail.

I·rish wolf·hound ▶ **noun** a large grayish hound with a rough coat.

irk /ərk/ ▶ **verb** irritate or annoy someone.
– ORIGIN perhaps from Old Norse, 'to work.'

irk·some /'ərksəm/ ▶ **adjective** irritating or annoying.
– DERIVATIVES **irk·some·ly** adverb.

i·ron /'īərn/ ▶ **noun 1** a strong, hard magnetic silvery-gray metal, used in construction and manufacturing. **2** a tool made of iron. **3** a hand-held implement with a flat heated steel base, used to smooth clothes. **4** a golf club used for hitting the ball at a high angle. **5** (**irons**) handcuffs or chains used as a restraint.

– SYNONYMS (as adj.) *an iron will* **uncompromising,** unrelenting, unyielding, unbending, rigid, steely.
– ANTONYMS flexible.

▶ **verb 1** smooth clothes with an iron. **2** (**iron something out**) settle a difficulty or problem.
– PHRASES **have many** (or **other**) **irons in the fire** have a range of options or be involved in several activities.
– ORIGIN Old English.

I·ron Age ▶ **noun** the period that followed the Bronze Age, when weapons and tools came to be made of iron.

i·ron·clad /'īərn,klad/ ▶ **adjective 1** covered or protected with iron. **2** impossible to weaken or change: *an ironclad guarantee.*

Iron Cur·tain ▶ **noun** (**the Iron Curtain**) a barrier regarded as separating the former Soviet bloc and the West before the decline of communism in eastern Europe.

iron fist ▶ **noun** (also **iron hand**) harsh and strictly enforced control: *touting the need for Uncle Sam's iron fist.*

i·ron·ic /ī'ränik/ ▶ **adjective 1** expressing an idea with words that usually mean the opposite in order to be humorous or emphasize a point. **2** happening in the opposite way to what is expected.

– SYNONYMS **1 sarcastic,** sardonic, satirical, dry, wry, double-edged, mocking, derisive, scornful. **2 paradoxical,** funny, strange.

– DERIVATIVES **i·ron·i·cal** adjective **i·ron·i·cal·ly** adverb.

i·ron·ing /'īərniNG/ ▶ **noun** clothes that need to be or have just been ironed.

i·ron·ing board ▶ **noun** a long, narrow board with folding legs, on which clothes are ironed.

i·ro·nist /'īrənist, 'īərnist/ ▶ **noun** a person who uses irony.
– DERIVATIVES **i·ro·nize** verb.

i·ron lung ▶ **noun** a rigid case fitted over a patient's body, used to provide artificial respiration by means of mechanical pumps.

i·ron maid·en ▶ **noun** a former instrument of torture consisting of a coffin-shaped box lined with iron spikes.

i·ron man ▶ **noun 1** an exceptionally strong man. **2** a sporting contest involving several events and requiring a great deal of stamina.

i·ron·stone /'īərn,stōn/ ▶ **noun 1** sedimentary rock containing iron compounds. **2** a kind of dense opaque stoneware.

i·ron·wood /'īərn,wo͝od/ ▶ **noun** any of a number of trees that produce very hard timber, including the hornbeam.

i·ron·work /'īərn,wərk/ ▶ **noun** things made of iron.

i·ron·works /'īərn,wərks/ ▶ **noun** a place where iron is smelted or iron goods are made.

i·ro·ny /'īrənē, 'iərnē/ ▶ **noun** (pl. **ironies**) **1** the expression of meaning through the use of words that normally mean the opposite, typically in order to be humorous or emphasize a point. **2** a situation that is the opposite to what is expected.

– SYNONYMS **1 sarcasm,** mockery, ridicule, derision, scorn. **2 paradox.**

– ORIGIN Greek *eirōneia* 'pretended ignorance.'

Ir·o·quois /'irə,kwoi/ ▶ **noun** (pl. same) a member of a former group of six American Indian peoples who lived mainly in southern Ontario and Quebec and northern New York State.
– ORIGIN French, from an Algonquian language.

ir·ra·di·ate /i'rādē,āt/ ▶ **verb 1** expose someone or something to radiation. **2** shine light on something, or appear to do so: *happiness filled her, irradiating her whole face.*
– DERIVATIVES **ir·ra·di·a·tion** /i,rādē'āsHən/ noun.
– ORIGIN Latin *irradiare.*

ir·ra·tion·al /i'rasHənl/ ▶ **adjective** not logical or reasonable.

– SYNONYMS **unreasonable,** illogical, groundless, baseless, unfounded, unjustifiable.
– ANTONYMS rational, logical.

– DERIVATIVES **ir·ra·tion·al·i·ty** /i,rasHə'nalitē/ noun **ir·ra·tion·al·ly** adverb.

ir·rec·on·cil·a·ble /i,rekən'sīləbəl, i'rekən,sī-/ ▶ **adjective 1** incompatible: *the two points of view were irreconcilable.* **2** not able to be resolved: *irreconcilable differences.*
– DERIVATIVES **ir·rec·on·cil·a·bly** adverb.

ir·re·cov·er·a·ble /,iri'kəvərəbəl/ ▶ **adjective** not able to be recovered or remedied.
– DERIVATIVES **ir·re·cov·er·a·bly** adverb.

ir·re·deem·a·ble /,iri'dēməbəl/ ▶ **adjective** not able to be saved, improved, or corrected.
– DERIVATIVES **ir·re·deem·a·bly** adverb.

ir·re·den·tist /,iri'dentist/ ▶ **noun** a person believing that territory formerly belonging to their own country should be restored to it.
– DERIVATIVES **ir·re·den·tism** /-,tizəm/ noun.
– ORIGIN Italian *irredentista.*

ir·re·duc·i·ble /,iri'd(y)o͞osəbəl/ ▶ **adjective** not able to be reduced or simplified.
– DERIVATIVES **ir·re·duc·i·bly** adverb.

ir·ref·u·ta·ble /,irə'fyo͞otəbəl, i'refyə-/ ▶ **adjective** impossible to deny or disprove.

– SYNONYMS **indisputable,** undeniable, unquestionable, incontrovertible, incontestable, beyond question, beyond doubt, conclusive, definite, definitive, decisive.

– DERIVATIVES **ir·ref·u·ta·bly** adverb.

ir·re·gard·less /,iri'gärdlis/ ▶ **adjective & adverb** informal regardless.
– ORIGIN probably a blend of **IRRESPECTIVE** and **REGARDLESS.**

ir·reg·u·lar /i'regyələr/ ▶ **adjective 1** not even or regular in shape, arrangement, or occurrence: *an irregular heartbeat.* **2** contrary to the rules or to that which is normal or established: *irregular financial dealings.* **3** (of troops) not belonging to regular army units. **4** Grammar (of a word) having inflections that do not conform to the usual rules.

– SYNONYMS **1 uneven,** crooked, misshapen, lopsided, asymmetrical, twisted. **2 rough,** bumpy, uneven, pitted, rutted, lumpy, knobbly, gnarled.

3 inconsistent, unsteady, uneven, fitful, patchy, variable, varying, changeable, inconstant, erratic, unstable, spasmodic, intermittent. **4 improper,** illegitimate, unethical, unprofessional; informal shady, dodgy. **5 guerrilla,** underground, paramilitary, partisan, mercenary, terrorist.

▶ **noun** a member of an irregular military force.

– SYNONYMS **guerrilla,** paramilitary, resistance fighter, partisan, mercenary, terrorist.

– DERIVATIVES **ir·reg·u·lar·i·ty** /iˌregyəˈlaritē/ noun (pl. **irregularities**) **ir·reg·u·lar·ly** adverb.

ir·rel·e·vant /iˈreləvənt/ ▶ **adjective** not relevant to the subject or matter in question.

– SYNONYMS **beside the point,** immaterial, unconnected, unrelated, peripheral, extraneous.

– DERIVATIVES **ir·rel·e·vance** noun **ir·rel·e·van·cy** noun (pl. **irrelevancies**) **ir·rel·e·vant·ly** adverb.

ir·re·li·gious /ˌiriˈlijəs/ ▶ **adjective** without religious belief, or showing no respect for religion.

– DERIVATIVES **ir·re·li·gion** noun.

ir·re·me·di·a·ble /ˌiriˈmēdēəbəl/ ▶ **adjective** impossible to remedy.

– DERIVATIVES **ir·re·me·di·a·bly** adverb.

ir·re·mov·a·ble /ˌiriˈmo͞ovəbəl/ ▶ **adjective** not able to be removed.

ir·rep·a·ra·ble /iˈrep(ə)rəbəl/ ▶ **adjective** impossible to repair or put right: *irreparable brain damage.*

– SYNONYMS **irreversible,** irrevocable, irrecoverable, unrepairable, beyond repair.

– DERIVATIVES **ir·rep·a·ra·bly** adverb.

ir·re·place·a·ble /iriˈplāsəbəl/ ▶ **adjective** impossible to replace if lost or damaged.

ir·re·press·i·ble /ˌiriˈpresəbəl/ ▶ **adjective** not able to be controlled or restrained.

– SYNONYMS **ebullient,** exuberant, buoyant, breezy, jaunty, high-spirited, vivacious, animated, full of life, lively; informal bubbly, bouncy, peppy, chipper, chirpy, full of beans.

– DERIVATIVES **ir·re·press·i·bly** adverb.

ir·re·proach·a·ble /ˌiriˈprōCHəbəl/ ▶ **adjective** not able to be criticized; faultless.

– DERIVATIVES **ir·re·proach·a·bly** adverb.

ir·re·sist·i·ble /ˌiriˈzistəbəl/ ▶ **adjective** too tempting or powerful to be resisted.

– SYNONYMS **1 captivating,** enticing, alluring, enchanting, fascinating, seductive.
2 uncontrollable, overwhelming, overpowering, ungovernable, compelling.

– DERIVATIVES **ir·re·sist·i·bly** adverb.

WORD TOOLKIT

See **ENCHANTING**.

ir·res·o·lute /i(r)ˈrezəˌlo͞ot/ ▶ **adjective** uncertain.

– DERIVATIVES **ir·res·o·lute·ly** adverb **ir·res·o·lu·tion** /-ˌrezəˈlo͞osHən/ noun.

ir·re·solv·a·ble /ˌiriˈzälvəbəl/ ▶ **adjective** impossible to solve.

ir·re·spec·tive /ˌiriˈspektiv/ ▶ **adjective** (**irrespective of**) regardless of.

ir·re·spon·si·ble /ˌiriˈspänsəbəl/ ▶ **adjective** not showing a proper sense of responsibility.

– SYNONYMS **reckless,** rash, careless, unwise, imprudent, ill-advised, injudicious, hasty, impetuous, foolhardy, foolish, unreliable, undependable, untrustworthy.

– DERIVATIVES **ir·re·spon·si·bil·i·ty** /-ˌspänsəˈbilitē/ noun **ir·re·spon·si·bly** adverb.

ir·re·triev·a·ble /ˌiriˈtrēvəbəl/ ▶ **adjective** not able to be improved or put right.

– DERIVATIVES **ir·re·triev·a·bly** adverb.

ir·rev·er·ent /iˈrev(ə)rənt/ ▶ **adjective** disrespectful.

– SYNONYMS **disrespectful,** impertinent, cheeky, flippant, rude, discourteous.
– ANTONYMS respectful.

– DERIVATIVES **ir·rev·er·ence** noun **ir·rev·er·ent·ly** adverb.

ir·re·vers·i·ble /ˌiriˈvərsəbəl/ ▶ **adjective** impossible to be reversed or altered.

– DERIVATIVES **ir·re·vers·i·bil·i·ty** /-ˌvərsəˈbilitē/ noun **ir·re·vers·i·bly** adverb.

ir·rev·o·ca·ble /ˌiˈrevəkəbəl/ ▶ **adjective** not able to be changed, reversed, or recovered: *an irrevocable decision.*

– SYNONYMS **irreversible,** unalterable, unchangeable, immutable, final, binding, permanent, set in stone.

– DERIVATIVES **ir·rev·o·ca·bil·i·ty** /iˌrevəkəˈbilitē/ noun **ir·rev·o·ca·bly** adverb.

– ORIGIN Latin *irrevocabilis.*

WORD TOOLKIT

See **FINAL**.

ir·ri·gate /ˈirigāt/ ▶ **verb 1** supply water to land or crops by means of channels. **2** Medicine apply a flow of water or medication to an organ or wound.

– DERIVATIVES **ir·ri·ga·ble** /-gəbəl/ adjective **ir·ri·ga·tion** /ˌiriˈgāsHən/ noun **ir·ri·ga·tor** /-ˌgātər/ noun.

– ORIGIN Latin *irrigare* 'moisten.'

ir·ri·ta·ble /ˈiritəbəl/ ▶ **adjective 1** easily annoyed or angered. **2** Medicine abnormally sensitive.

– SYNONYMS **bad-tempered,** short-tempered, irascible, tetchy, testy, grumpy, grouchy, crotchety, cantankerous, fractious, curmudgeonly.
– ANTONYMS good-humored.

– DERIVATIVES **ir·ri·ta·bil·i·ty** /ˌiritəˈbilitē/ noun **ir·ri·ta·bly** adverb.

ir·ri·ta·ble bow·el syn·drome ▶ **noun** a condition involving recurrent abdominal pain and diarrhea or constipation.

ir·ri·tant /ˈiritənt/ ▶ **noun 1** a substance that irritates part of the body. **2** a source of continual annoyance.

– SYNONYMS **annoyance,** (source of) irritation, thorn in someone's side/flesh, nuisance; informal pain (in the neck), headache, burr in/under someone's saddle.

▶ **adjective** causing irritation to the body.

ir·ri·tate /ˈiriˌtāt/ ▶ **verb 1** make someone annoyed or angry. **2** cause inflammation in a part of the body.

– SYNONYMS **1 annoy,** bother, vex, make cross, exasperate, infuriate, anger, madden, rub the wrong way; informal aggravate, peeve, rile, needle, get (to), bug, tee off, tick off. **2 inflame,** hurt, chafe, scratch, scrape, rub.
– ANTONYMS delight, soothe.

– DERIVATIVES **ir·ri·tat·ing** adjective **ir·ri·tat·ing·ly** adverb.

– ORIGIN Latin *irritare.*

ir·ri·ta·tion /ˌiriˈtāsʜən/ ▶ **noun** the state of feeling annoyed or angry.

– SYNONYMS **annoyance,** exasperation, vexation, indignation, anger, displeasure, chagrin.
– ANTONYMS delight.

ir·rup·tion /iˈrəpsʜən/ ▶ **noun** a sudden forcible entry.
– DERIVATIVES **ir·rupt** /iˈrəpt/ verb **ir·rup·tive** /iˈrəptiv/ adjective.
– ORIGIN Latin *irrumpere* 'break into.'

IRS ▶ **abbreviation** Internal Revenue Service.

is /iz/ third person singular present of **BE**.

ISA ▶ **abbreviation** Computing industry standard architecture.

ISBN ▶ **abbreviation** international standard book number.

is·che·mi·a /isˈkēmēə/ ▶ **noun** an inadequate blood supply to a part of the body, especially the heart muscles.
– DERIVATIVES **is·che·mic** adjective.
– ORIGIN Greek *iskhaimos* 'stopping blood.'

ISDN ▶ **abbreviation** integrated services digital network, a telecommunications network through which sound, images, and data can be transmitted as digitized signals.

-ise ▶ **suffix** chiefly Brit. variant spelling of **-IZE**.

USAGE

For advice on the use of **-ise** or **-ize**, see the note at **-IZE**.

i·sin·glass /ˈīzənˌglas, ˈīzinɢ-/ ▶ **noun** a kind of gelatin obtained from fish.
– ORIGIN from Dutch *huysenblas* 'sturgeon's bladder.'

Is·lam /isˈläm, iz-/ ▶ **noun 1** the religion of the Muslims, based on belief in one God and regarded by them to have been revealed through Muhammad as the Prophet of Allah. **2** the Muslim world.
– DERIVATIVES **Is·lam·i·za·tion** /isˌlämiˈzāsʜən, iz-/ noun **Is·lam·ize** /ˈisləˌmīz, ˈiz-/ verb.
– ORIGIN Arabic, 'submission.'

Is·lam·ic /isˈlämik/ ▶ **adjective** relating to Islam.
– DERIVATIVES **Is·lam·i·cize** /isˈlämiˌsīz, iz-/ verb.

Is·lam·ism /ˈisləˌmizəm, ˈiz-/ ▶ **noun** Islamic extremism or fundamentalism.
– DERIVATIVES **Is·lam·ist** /ˈisləˌmist, ˈiz-/ (also **Islamicist** /isˈlämiˌsist, iz-/) noun & adjective.

Is·lam·o·pho·bi·a /isˌläməˈfōbēə, iz-/ ▶ **noun** a hatred or fear of Islam or Muslims.

is·land /ˈīlənd/ ▶ **noun 1** a piece of land surrounded by water. **2** a thing that is isolated, detached, or surrounded: *the last island of democracy in this country.*

– SYNONYMS **isle,** islet, atoll; (**islands**) archipelago.

– DERIVATIVES **is·land·er** noun.
– ORIGIN Old English.

WORD LINKS

insular *relating to an island*

isle /īl/ ▶ **noun** literary (except in place names) an island.
– ORIGIN Old French *ile*.

is·let /ˈīlət/ ▶ **noun** a small island.

is·lets of Lang·er·hans /ˈlanɢərˌhanz, ˈlänɢərˌhäns/ ▶ **plural noun** groups of cells in the pancreas that produce insulin.
– ORIGIN named after the German anatomist Paul *Langerhans*.

ism /ˈizəm/ ▶ **noun** informal, chiefly derogatory a distinctive system, philosophy, or ideology.

is·n't /ˈizənt/ ▶ **contraction** is not.

ISO ▶ **abbreviation 1** International Organization for Standardization. **2** (in personal ads) in search of.

i·so·bar /ˈīsəˌbär/ ▶ **noun** a line on a map connecting points having the same atmospheric pressure.
– DERIVATIVES **i·so·bar·ic** /ˌīsəˈbarik, -ˈbär-/ adjective.
– ORIGIN Greek *isobaros* 'of equal weight.'

i·so·late /ˈīsəˌlāt/ ▶ **verb 1** place someone or something apart or alone. **2** Chemistry & Biology obtain or extract a compound, microorganism, etc., in a pure form. **3** cut off the electrical or other connection to something.

– SYNONYMS **separate,** segregate, detach, cut off, shut away, alienate, distance, cloister, seclude, cordon off, seal off, close off, fence off.
– ANTONYMS integrate.

▶ **noun** /ˈīsəˌlit/ an isolated person or thing.
– DERIVATIVES **i·so·la·tor** noun.
– ORIGIN from **ISOLATED**.

i·so·lat·ed /ˈīsəˌlātid/ ▶ **adjective 1** remote; lonely: *isolated villages.* **2** single; exceptional: *isolated incidents of unrest.*

– SYNONYMS **1 remote,** out of the way, outlying, off the beaten track, in the back of beyond, godforsaken, inaccessible, cut-off; informal in the middle of nowhere, in the sticks, jerkwater. **2 solitary,** lonely, secluded, lonesome, reclusive, hermitlike. **3 unique,** lone, solitary, unusual, exceptional, untypical, freak.
– ANTONYMS accessible.

– ORIGIN French *isolé*, from Latin *insulatus* 'made into an island.'

i·so·la·tion /ˌīsəˈlāsʜən/ ▶ **noun** the process of isolating someone or something or the fact of being isolated.

– SYNONYMS **1 solitariness,** loneliness, friendlessness. **2 remoteness,** inaccessibility.
– ANTONYMS contact.

– PHRASES **in isolation** without relation to others; separately.

i·so·la·tion·ism /ˌīsəˈlāsʜəˌnizəm/ ▶ **noun** a policy of remaining apart from the political affairs of other countries.
– DERIVATIVES **i·so·la·tion·ist** noun.

i·so·mer /ˈīsəmər/ ▶ **noun 1** Chemistry each of two or more compounds with the same formula but a different arrangement of atoms and different properties. **2** Physics each of two or more atomic nuclei with the same atomic number and mass number but different energy states.
– DERIVATIVES **i·so·mer·ic** /ˌīsəˈmerik/ adjective **i·som·er·ism** /īˈsäməˌrizəm/ noun **i·som·er·ize** /īˈsäməˌrīz/ verb.
– ORIGIN Greek *isomerēs* 'sharing equally.'

i·so·met·ric /ˌīsəˈmetrik/ ▶ **adjective 1** having equal dimensions. **2** Physiology involving an increase in muscle tension but no contraction of the muscle. **3** (of perspective drawing) having the three main dimensions represented by axes 120° apart.
– DERIVATIVES **i·so·met·ri·cal·ly** adverb **i·som·e·try** /īˈsämitrē/ noun.
– ORIGIN Greek *isometria* 'equality of measure.'

i·so·met·rics /ˌīsəˈmetriks/ ▶ **plural noun** a system of physical exercises in which muscles are made to act against each other or against a fixed object.

i·so·mor·phic /ˌīsəˈmôrfik/ ▶ **adjective** having a similar form and relationship.

– DERIVATIVES **i·so·mor·phism** noun **i·so·morph·ous** adjective.

i·sos·ce·les /ī'säsə,lēz/ ▶ **adjective** (of a triangle) having two sides of equal length.
– ORIGIN Greek *isoskelēs*.

i·so·therm /'īsə,THərm/ ▶ **noun** a line on a map or diagram connecting points having the same temperature.
– DERIVATIVES **i·so·ther·mal** /,īsə'THərməl/ adjective & noun.
– ORIGIN from Greek *isos* 'equal' + *thermē* 'heat.'

i·so·ton·ic /,īsə'tänik/ ▶ **adjective 1** Physiology (of a muscle action) taking place with normal contraction. **2** (of a drink) containing essential salts and minerals in the same concentration as normally found in the body.
– ORIGIN Greek *isotonos*.

i·so·tope /'īsə,tōp/ ▶ **noun** Chemistry each of two or more forms of the same element that contain equal numbers of protons but different numbers of neutrons in their nuclei.
– DERIVATIVES **i·so·top·ic** /,īsə'täpik/ adjective.
– ORIGIN from Greek *isos* 'equal' + *topos* 'place,' because the isotopes occupy the same place in the periodic table.

i·so·trop·ic /,īsə'träpik, -'trōpik/ ▶ **adjective** Physics having the same size or properties when measured in different directions.
– ORIGIN from Greek *isos* 'equal' + *tropos* 'a turn.'

ISP ▶ **abbreviation** Internet service provider.

Is·rae·li /iz'rālē/ ▶ **noun** (pl. **Israelis**) a person from Israel. ▶ **adjective** relating to the modern country of Israel.

Is·ra·el·ite /'izrēə,līt/ ▶ **noun** a member of the ancient Hebrew nation.

is·sei /'ē(s),sā/ ▶ **noun** (pl. same) a Japanese immigrant to North America. Compare with **NISEI** and **SANSEI**.

is·sue /'isHōō/ ▶ **noun 1** an important topic or problem to be discussed or resolved: *environmental issues*. **2** the action of supplying or distributing something. **3** each of a regular series of publications. **4** (**issues**) personal problems or difficulties. **5** formal or Law children of one's own.

> – SYNONYMS **1 matter,** question, point at issue, affair, case, subject, topic, problem, situation. **2 edition,** number, installment, copy, impression. **3 issuing,** release, publication, distribution.

▶ **verb** (**issues, issuing, issued**) **1** supply or distribute something. **2** formally send out or make known: *the minister issued a statement*. **3** (**issue from**) come, go, or flow out from: *exotic smells issued from a nearby building*.

> – SYNONYMS **1 release,** put out, deliver, publish, broadcast, circulate, distribute. **2 supply,** provide, furnish, arm, equip, fit out, rig out; informal fix up.

– DERIVATIVES **is·su·ance** /-əns/ noun **is·su·er** noun.
– PHRASES **at issue** under discussion. **make an issue of** treat something too seriously or as a problem. **take issue with** disagree with or challenge.
– ORIGIN Old French.

isth·mus /'isməs/ ▶ **noun** (pl. **isthmuses**) a narrow strip of land with sea on either side, linking two larger areas of land.
– ORIGIN Greek *isthmos*.

IT ▶ **abbreviation** information technology.

it /it/ ▶ **pronoun** (third person sing.) **1** used to refer to a thing previously mentioned or easily identified. **2** referring to an animal or child of unspecified sex. **3** used to identify a person: *it's me*. **4** used as a subject in statements about time, distance, or weather: *it is raining*. **5** used to refer to something specified later in the sentence: *it is impossible to get there today*. **6** used to refer to the situation or circumstances: *if it's convenient*. **7** exactly what is needed or desired.
– ORIGIN Old English, neuter of **HE**.

It. ▶ **abbreviation 1** Italian. **2** Italy.

I·tal·ian /i'talyən/ ▶ **noun 1** a person from Italy. **2** the language of Italy, descended from Latin. ▶ **adjective** relating to Italy or Italian.
– DERIVATIVES **I·tal·ian·ize** /i'talyə,nīz/ verb.

I·tal·ian·ate /i'talyə,nāt/ ▶ **adjective** Italian in character or appearance.

Italian ice ▶ **noun** a frozen dessert consisting of fruit juice or purée in a sugar syrup.

i·tal·ic /i'talik, ī'tal-/ ▶ **adjective** referring to the sloping typeface used especially for emphasis and in foreign words. ▶ **noun** (also **italics**) an italic typeface or letter.
– ORIGIN Greek *Italikos* 'Italian.'

i·tal·i·cize /i'tali,sīz, ī'tal-/ ▶ **verb** print or format text in italics.

itch /icH/ ▶ **noun 1** an uncomfortable sensation that causes a desire to scratch the skin. **2** informal an impatient desire.

> – SYNONYMS **1 tingling,** irritation, itchiness, prickle. **2 longing,** yearning, craving, ache, hunger, thirst, urge, hankering; informal yen.

▶ **verb 1** have an itch. **2** informal feel an impatient desire to do something: *he was itching to get outside*.

> – SYNONYMS **1 tingle,** be irritated, be itchy, sting, hurt, be sore. **2 long,** yearn, ache, burn, crave, hanker for/after, hunger, thirst, be eager, be desperate; informal be dying.

– ORIGIN Old English.

itch·y /'icHē/ ▶ **adjective** (**itchier, itchiest**) having or causing an itch.
– DERIVATIVES **itch·i·ness** noun.
– PHRASES **have itchy feet** informal have a strong urge to travel.

it'd /'itid/ ▶ **contraction 1** it had. **2** it would.

i·tem /'ītəm/ ▶ **noun** an individual article or unit: *an item of clothing*.

> – SYNONYMS **1 thing,** article, object, piece, element, constituent, component, ingredient. **2 issue,** matter, affair, case, subject, topic, question, point. **3 report,** story, article, piece, write-up, bulletin, feature, review.

– PHRASES **be an item** informal (of a couple) be in a romantic or sexual relationship.
– ORIGIN Latin, 'in like manner, also.'

i·tem·ize /'ītə,mīz/ ▶ **verb 1** present something as a list of individual items or parts. **2** identify various deductions on one's tax return in order to get credit for them: *you can take the deduction even if you don't itemize*.

it·er·ate /'itə,rāt/ ▶ **verb 1** do or say something repeatedly. **2** make repeated use of a mathematical or computational procedure, applying it each time to the result of the previous application.
– DERIVATIVES **it·er·a·tion** /,itə'rāsHən/ noun **it·er·a·tive** /'itə,rātiv, -rətiv/ adjective.
– ORIGIN Latin *iterare*.

i·tin·er·ant /ī'tinərənt, i'tin-/ ▶ **adjective** traveling from place to place. ▶ **noun** an itinerant person.
– ORIGIN Latin *itinerari* 'travel.'

i·tin·er·ar·y /ī'tinə,rerē, i'tin-/ ▶ **noun** (pl. **itineraries**) a planned route or journey.

– SYNONYMS **route,** plan, schedule, timetable, program.

-itis ▶ **suffix** forming names of diseases that cause inflammation: *cystitis.*
– ORIGIN Greek *-itēs.*

it'll /'itl/ ▶ **contraction 1** it will. **2** it shall.

its /its/ ▶ **possessive determiner 1** belonging to or associated with a thing previously mentioned or easily identified. **2** belonging to or associated with a child or animal of unspecified sex.

USAGE

A common error in writing is to confuse the possessive **its** (as in *turn the camera on its side*) with the form **it's** (short for either **it is** or **it has**, as in *it's my fault; it's been a hot day*).

it's /its/ ▶ **contraction 1** it is. **2** it has.

it·self /it'self/ ▶ **pronoun** (third person sing.) **1** (reflexive) used to refer to something previously mentioned as the subject of the clause: *his horse hurt itself.* **2** (emphatic) used to emphasize a particular thing or animal mentioned: *she wanted him more than life itself.*
– PHRASES **in itself** viewed in its essential qualities.

it·ty-bit·ty /'itē 'bitē/ (also **itsy-bitsy** /'itsē 'bitsē/) ▶ **adjective** informal very small; tiny.

IUD ▶ **abbreviation** intrauterine device.

IV ▶ **abbreviation** intravenous or intravenously.

I've /īv/ ▶ **contraction** I have.

IVF ▶ **abbreviation** in vitro fertilization.

i·vied /'īvēd/ ▶ **adjective** covered in ivy.

I·vies /'īvēz/ ▶ **plural noun** the Ivy League schools collectively, or other schools perceived as being of equal stature.

I·vo·ri·an /ī'vôrēən/ ▶ **noun** a person from the Ivory Coast, a country in West Africa. ▶ **adjective** relating to the Ivory Coast.

i·vo·ry /'īvərē/ ▶ **noun** (pl. **ivories**) **1** a hard creamy-white substance that forms the main part of the tusks of an elephant or walrus. **2** the creamy-white color of ivory. **3** (**the ivories**) informal the keys of a piano.
– ORIGIN Old French *ivurie.*

i·vo·ry tow·er ▶ **noun** a privileged or secluded existence in which someone does not have to face the normal difficulties of life.

i·vy /'īvē/ ▶ **noun** (pl. **ivies**) a woody evergreen climbing plant, typically with shiny five-pointed leaves.
– ORIGIN Old English.

I·vy League ▶ **noun** a group of long-established and prestigious universities in the eastern US.
– ORIGIN with reference to the ivy traditionally growing over their walls.

I·yen·gar /ē'yeNGgär/ ▶ **noun** a type of yoga focusing on the correct alignment of the body, making use of straps, wooden blocks, and other objects to help achieve the correct postures.
– ORIGIN named after the Indian yoga teacher B. K. S. *Iyengar.*

-ize ▶ **suffix** forming verbs meaning: **1** make or become: *privatize.* **2** cause to resemble: *Americanize.* **3** treat in a specified way: *pasteurize.* **4** treat or cause to combine with a specified substance: *carbonize.* **5** perform or subject someone to a specified practice: *hospitalize.*
– ORIGIN Greek *-izein.*

USAGE

Many verbs that end in **-ize** can also end in **-ise**, especially in British English. However, there are a small number of verbs that must always be spelled with **-ise** at the end. This is either because **-ise** forms part of a larger word element, such as *-mise* in **compromise**, or because the verb corresponds to a noun that has **-s-** in the stem, such as **televise** (from *television*).

Jj

J[1] (also **j**) ▶ **noun** (pl. **Js** or **J's**) the tenth letter of the alphabet.

J[2] ▶ **abbreviation 1** (in card games) jack. **2** Physics joule(s).

jab /jab/ ▶ **verb** (**jabs, jabbing, jabbed**) poke someone or something roughly or quickly with a sharp or pointed object.

– SYNONYMS *he jabbed the officer with his finger* **poke**, prod, dig, nudge, thrust, stab, push.

▶ **noun 1** a quick, sharp poke or blow. **2** informal an injection, especially a vaccination.

– SYNONYMS *a jab in the ribs* **poke**, prod, dig, nudge, thrust, stab, push.

– ORIGIN apparently symbolic of the action.

jab·ber /ˈjabər/ ▶ **verb** talk rapidly and excitedly. ▶ **noun** rapid, excited talk.
– ORIGIN imitating the sound.

ja·bot /zʜaˈbō, ja-/ ▶ **noun** an ornamental ruffle on the front of a shirt or blouse.
– ORIGIN French.

jac·a·ran·da /ˌjakəˈrandə/ ▶ **noun** a tropical American tree with blue trumpet-shaped flowers and sweet-smelling wood.
– ORIGIN Tupi-Guarani.

jack[1] /jak/ ▶ **noun 1** a device for lifting heavy objects, especially one for raising the axle of a motor vehicle off the ground. **2** a playing card with a picture of a soldier, page, or knave on it, normally ranking next below a queen. **3** a phone jack. **4** the small white ball at which players aim in lawn bowling. **5** a small metal piece used in games of tossing and catching. **6** (**jacks**) a game played by tossing and catching jacks. **7** a small national flag flown at the bow of a vessel in harbor. **8** the male of various animals, e.g., the donkey. **9** used in names of animals and plants that are smaller than similar kinds, e.g., **jack pine**. ▶ **verb 1** (**jack something up**) raise something with a jack. **2** (**jack something up**) informal increase something by a considerable amount: *the hotels have jacked up their prices.* **3** (**jack off**) vulgar slang masturbate.
– PHRASES **jack of all trades (and master of none)** a person who can do many different types of work (but has special skill in none). **not know jack** informal be ignorant: *you don't have to know jack about music to be a producer.*
– ORIGIN from *Jack*, familiar form of the man's name *John*.

jack[2] ▶ **verb** informal steal something.

jack·al /ˈjakəl/ ▶ **noun** a wild dog that feeds on the decaying flesh of dead animals, found in Africa and southern Asia.
– ORIGIN Turkish *çakal*.

jack·ass /ˈjakˌas/ ▶ **noun 1** a stupid person. **2** a male ass or donkey.

jack·boot /ˈjakˌbo͞ot/ ▶ **noun** a large leather military boot reaching to the knee.
– DERIVATIVES **jack·boot·ed** adjective.

jack·daw /ˈjakˌdô/ ▶ **noun** a small gray-headed Eurasian crow, noted for its inquisitiveness.

jack·et /ˈjakit/ ▶ **noun 1** an outer garment extending to the waist or hips, with sleeves. **2** an outer covering placed around something for protection or insulation. **3** the skin of a potato. ▶ **verb** (**jackets, jacketing, jacketed**) cover something with a jacket.
– ORIGIN Old French *jaquet*.

Jack Frost ▶ **noun** frost represented as a human being.

jack·fruit /ˈjakˌfro͞ot/ ▶ **noun** the very large edible fruit of an Asian tree.
– ORIGIN from Portuguese *jaca* + **FRUIT**.

jack·ham·mer /ˈjakˌhamər/ ▶ **noun** a portable pneumatic hammer or drill. ▶ **verb** beat or hammer something heavily or loudly and repeatedly.

jack-in-the-box ▶ **noun** a toy consisting of a box containing a figure on a spring that pops up when the lid is opened.

jack-in-the-pul·pit ▶ **noun** a woodland plant having a purple or green spadix that is followed by bright red berries.
– ORIGIN so named because the erect spadix overarched by the spathe resembles a person in a pulpit.

jack·knife /ˈjakˌnīf/ ▶ **noun** (pl. **jackknives**) **1** a large knife with a folding blade. **2** a dive in which the body is bent at the waist and then straightened. ▶ **verb** (**jackknifes, jackknifing, jackknifed**) **1** move one's body into a bent or doubled-up position. **2** (of a tractor-trailer or other articulated vehicle) bend into a V-shape in an uncontrolled skidding movement. **3** (of a diver) perform a jackknife.

jack-o'-lan·tern /ˈjak ə ˌlantərn/ ▶ **noun** a lantern made from a hollowed-out pumpkin in which holes are cut to represent facial features, made especially for Halloween.

jack pine ▶ **noun** a small, hardy North American pine with short needles.

jack·pot /ˈjakˌpät/ ▶ **noun** a large cash prize in a game or lottery.
– PHRASES **hit the jackpot** informal have great or unexpected success.
– ORIGIN first used in a form of poker, where the pot, or bets made, accumulated until a player could open the bidding with two jacks or better.

jack·rab·bit /ˈjakˌrabət/ ▶ **noun** a hare found in open country in western North America.
– ORIGIN abbreviation of *jackass-rabbit*, because of its long ears.

Jack Rus·sell /ˈrəsəl/ (also **Jack Russell terrier**) ▶ **noun** a small breed of terrier with short legs.

– ORIGIN named after the English clergyman Rev. John *(Jack) Russell*.

Jac·o·be·an /ˌjakəˈbēən/ ▶ **adjective** relating to or characteristic of the reign of James I of England (1603–1625). ▶ **noun** a person who lived in the Jacobean period.
– ORIGIN from Latin *Jacobus* 'James.'

Jac·o·bite /ˈjakəˌbīt/ ▶ **noun** a supporter of the deposed James II and his descendants in their claim to the British throne after the Revolution of 1688.
– DERIVATIVES **Jac·o·bit·ism** /-bītˌizəm/ noun.

Ja·cob's lad·der ▶ **noun** a plant with blue or white flowers and slender pointed leaves formed in ladderlike rows.
– ORIGIN with biblical reference to Jacob's dream of a ladder reaching to heaven (Book of Genesis).

jac·quard /ˈjaˌkärd, jəˈkärd/ ▶ **noun 1** a piece of equipment consisting of perforated cards, fitted to a loom for weaving patterned and brocaded fabrics. **2** a fabric made on a jacquard loom.
– ORIGIN named after the French weaver Joseph M. *Jacquard*.

ja·cuz·zi /jəˈko͞ozē/ ▶ **noun** (pl. **jacuzzis**) trademark a large bath with jets of water that massage the body.
– ORIGIN named after the Italian-born American inventor Candido *Jacuzzi*.

jade[1] /jād/ ▶ **noun 1** a hard bluish-green stone used for ornaments and jewelry. **2** a light, bluish-green color.
– ORIGIN French, from Spanish *piedra de ijada* 'stone for colic,' which it was believed to cure.

jade[2] ▶ **noun** old use **1** a bad-tempered or disreputable woman. **2** an old or worn-out horse.
– ORIGIN unknown.

jad·ed /ˈjādid/ ▶ **adjective** tired or lacking enthusiasm after having had too much of something.
– ORIGIN from JADE[2].

jade·ite /ˈjādˌīt/ ▶ **noun** a green, blue, or white form of jade.

JAG ▶ **abbreviation** judge advocate general.

jag[1] /jag/ ▶ **verb** (**jags, jagging, jagged**) stab, pierce, or prick something. ▶ **noun** a sharp projection.
– DERIVATIVES **jag·gy** adjective.
– ORIGIN perhaps representing sudden movement or unevenness.

jag[2] ▶ **noun** informal a period of unrestrained activity or emotion: *a crying jag*.
– ORIGIN unknown.

jag·ged /ˈjagid/ ▶ **adjective** with rough, sharp points sticking out.

> – SYNONYMS **spiky,** barbed, ragged, rough, uneven, irregular, serrated.
> – ANTONYMS smooth.

– DERIVATIVES **jag·ged·ly** adverb **jag·ged·ness** noun.

> **WORD TOOLKIT**
>
> See SPIKY.

jag·uar /ˈjagˌwär/ ▶ **noun** a large, heavily built cat that has a yellowish-brown coat with black spots, found mainly in Central and South America.
– ORIGIN Tupi-Guarani.

Jah /jä, yä/ ▶ **noun** the Rastafarian name for God.
– ORIGIN representing a Hebrew abbreviation of YAHWEH.

jai a·lai /ˈhī (ə)ˌlī/ ▶ **noun** a game in which a ball is thrown using a long, curved wicker basket.
– ORIGIN Spanish.

jail /jāl/ (Brit. also **gaol**) ▶ **noun** a place for holding people accused or convicted of a crime.

> – SYNONYMS **prison,** lockup, jailhouse, detention center, penitentiary; informal clink, cooler, slammer, inside, can, pen, pokey, big house.

▶ **verb** put someone in jail.

> – SYNONYMS **imprison,** incarcerate, lock up, put away, detain; informal send down/up, send up the river, put behind bars, put inside.
> – ANTONYMS acquit, release.

– ORIGIN Old French *jaiole* and *gayole*.

jail·bait /ˈjālˌbāt/ ▶ **noun** informal a young woman, or young women as a group, regarded as sexually attractive but under the legal age of consent.

jail·bird /ˈjālˌbərd/ ▶ **noun** informal a person who is or has repeatedly been in prison.

jail·break /ˈjālˌbrāk/ ▶ **noun** an escape from jail.

jail·er /ˈjālər/ ▶ **noun 1** a person in charge of a jail or its prisoners. **2** someone who forcibly confines someone else.

jail·house /ˈjālˌhous/ ▶ **noun** a prison.

Jain /jān/ ▶ **noun** a follower of Jainism. ▶ **adjective** relating to Jainism.
– ORIGIN Sanskrit.

Jain·ism /ˈjāˌnizəm/ ▶ **noun** an Indian religion characterized by nonviolence and strict self-discipline.

jake /jāk/ ▶ **adjective** informal all right; satisfactory.
– ORIGIN unknown.

ja·la·pe·ño /ˌhäləˈpānyō, -ˈpē-/ ▶ **noun** (pl. **jalapeños**) a very hot green chili pepper.
– ORIGIN Mexican Spanish, from the Mexican city of *Jalapa*.

ja·lop·y /jəˈläpē/ ▶ **noun** (pl. **jalopies**) informal a dilapidated old car.
– ORIGIN unknown.

jal·ou·sie /ˈjaləˌsē/ ▶ **noun** a blind or shutter made of a row of angled slats.
– ORIGIN French, 'jealousy.'

jam[1] /jam/ ▶ **verb** (**jams, jamming, jammed**) **1** squeeze or pack tightly into a space: *four of us were jammed in one compartment*. **2** push something roughly and forcibly into position: *he jammed his hat on*. **3** crowd onto a road or area so as to block it. **4** become or make unable to function due to a part becoming stuck: *the photocopier jammed*. **5** (**jam something on**) apply something forcibly: *he jammed on the brakes*. **6** make a radio transmission unintelligible by causing interference. **7** informal improvise with other musicians.

> – SYNONYMS **1 stuff,** shove, force, ram, thrust, press, push, wedge, stick, cram. **2 crowd,** pack, pile, press, squeeze, sandwich, cram, throng, mob, fill, block, clog, congest. **3 stick,** become stuck, catch, seize (up).

▶ **noun 1** an instance of something jamming or becoming stuck. **2** informal an awkward situation. **3** short for TRAFFIC JAM. **4** informal an improvised performance by a group of musicians.

> – SYNONYMS *we are in a real jam* **predicament,** plight, tricky situation, problem, dilemma, muddle, mess; informal fix, tight spot.

– DERIVATIVES **jam·mer** noun.
– ORIGIN probably symbolic of the action.

jam² ▶ noun a thick spread made from sweetened fruit.
– ORIGIN perhaps from JAM¹.

Ja·mai·can /jəˈmākən/ ▶ noun a person from Jamaica. ▶ adjective relating to Jamaica.

jamb /jam/ ▶ noun a side post of a doorway, window, or fireplace.
– ORIGIN French *jambe* 'leg, vertical support.'

jam·ba·lay·a /ˌjəmbəˈlīə/ ▶ noun a Cajun dish of rice with shrimp, chicken, and vegetables.
– ORIGIN Provençal *jambalaia*.

jam·bo·ree /ˌjambəˈrē/ ▶ noun **1** a lavish or noisy celebration or party. **2** a large rally of Boy Scouts or Girl Scouts.
– ORIGIN unknown.

jam-packed ▶ adjective informal extremely crowded or full to capacity.

Jan. ▶ abbreviation January.

Jane Doe /ˈjān ˈdō/ ▶ noun an anonymous female party in a legal action or an unidentified woman.

jan·gle /ˈjaNGgəl/ ▶ verb **1** make or cause to make a ringing metallic sound. **2** (of a person's nerves) be set on edge. ▶ noun a ringing metallic sound.
– DERIVATIVES **jan·gly** adjective.
– ORIGIN Old French *jangler*.

jan·is·sar·y /ˈjaniˌserē/ ▶ noun (pl. **janissaries**) historical a Turkish infantryman in the Sultan's guard.
– ORIGIN French *janissaire*.

jan·i·tor /ˈjanitər/ ▶ noun a caretaker of a building; a custodian.
– DERIVATIVES **jan·i·to·ri·al** /ˌjaniˈtôrēəl/ adjective.
– ORIGIN Latin, from *janua* 'door.'

Jan·u·ar·y /ˈjanyo͞oˌerē/ ▶ noun (pl. **Januaries**) the first month of the year.
– ORIGIN from Latin *Januarius mensis* 'month of *Janus*' (the Roman god of beginnings).

Jap /jap/ ▶ noun & adjective informal, offensive short for JAPANESE.

ja·pan /jəˈpan/ ▶ noun a black glossy varnish originating in Japan. ▶ verb (**japans, japanning, japanned**) varnish something with japan.

Jap·a·nese /ˌjapəˈnēz, -ˈnēs/ ▶ noun (pl. same) **1** a person from Japan. **2** the language of Japan. ▶ adjective relating to Japan.

Jap·a·nese bee·tle ▶ noun a metallic green and copper beetle that is a garden pest in both its adult and larval stages.

jape /jāp/ ▶ noun dated a practical joke.
– ORIGIN probably from Old French *japer* 'to yelp, yap' and *gaber* 'to mock.'

ja·pon·i·ca /jəˈpänikə/ ▶ noun an Asian shrub of the rose family, with bright red flowers.
– ORIGIN Latin, 'Japanese.'

jar¹ /jär/ ▶ noun a wide-mouthed cylindrical container made of glass or pottery.

– SYNONYMS **pot,** container, crock.

– ORIGIN French *jarre*.

jar² ▶ verb (**jars, jarring, jarred**) **1** send a painful or uncomfortable shock through a part of the body. **2** strike against something with an unpleasant vibration or jolt. **3** have an unpleasant or annoying effect: *a laugh that jarred on the ears.* **4** conflict or clash with something: *the play's symbolism jarred with the realism of its setting.*

– SYNONYMS **1 jolt,** jerk, shake, vibrate. **2 grate,** set someone's teeth on edge, irritate, annoy, get on someone's nerves. **3 clash,** conflict, contrast, be incompatible, be at variance, be at odds.

▶ noun an instance of jarring.
– DERIVATIVES **jar·ring** adjective.
– ORIGIN probably imitating the sensation.

jar·di·nière /ˌjärdnˈi(ə)r, ˌZHärdnˈye(ə)r/ ▶ noun **1** an ornamental pot or stand for displaying plants. **2** a garnish of mixed vegetables.
– ORIGIN French, 'female gardener.'

jar·gon /ˈjärgən/ ▶ noun words or expressions used by a particular group that are difficult for other people to understand.

– SYNONYMS **slang,** idiom, cant, argot, gobbledygook; informal lingo, -speak, -ese.

– DERIVATIVES **jar·gon·is·tic** /ˌjärgəˈnistik/ adjective **jar·gon·ize** verb.
– ORIGIN Old French *jargoun*.

jas·mine /ˈjazmən/ ▶ noun a shrub or climbing plant with sweet-smelling white, pink, or yellow flowers.
– ORIGIN French *jasmin*, from Persian.

jas·per /ˈjaspər/ ▶ noun an opaque reddish-brown variety of quartz.
– ORIGIN Old French *jasp(r)e*.

jaun·dice /ˈjôndis/ ▶ noun **1** yellowing of the skin or whites of the eyes, caused especially by a liver disorder. **2** bitterness or resentment.
– DERIVATIVES **jaun·diced** adjective.
– ORIGIN Old French *jaunice* 'yellowness.'

jaunt /jônt/ ▶ noun a short trip for pleasure.

– SYNONYMS **trip,** outing, excursion, tour, drive, ride, run; informal spin, junket.

– ORIGIN unknown.

CHOOSE THE RIGHT WORD

See JOURNEY.

jaun·ty /ˈjôntē/ ▶ adjective (**jauntier, jauntiest**) having a lively and self-confident manner.
– DERIVATIVES **jaun·ti·ly** adverb **jaun·ti·ness** noun.
– ORIGIN French *gentil* 'well-born.'

Ja·va /ˈjävə, ˈjavə/ ▶ noun trademark a computer programming language designed to work across different computer systems.

Ja·van /ˈjävən, ˈjavən/ ▶ noun a person from the Indonesian island of Java. ▶ adjective relating to Java.

Jav·a·nese /ˌjävəˈnēz, -ˈnēs/ ▶ noun (pl. same) **1** a person from Java. **2** the language of central Java. ▶ adjective relating to Java.

jave·lin /ˈjav(ə)lən/ ▶ noun a long, light spear thrown in a competitive sport or as a weapon.
– ORIGIN Old French *javeline*.

jaw /jô/ ▶ noun **1** each of the upper and lower bony structures in vertebrates forming the framework of the mouth and containing the teeth. **2** (**jaws**) the grasping, biting, or crushing mouthparts of an invertebrate. **3** (**jaws**) the gripping parts of a tool such as a wrench or vice.

– SYNONYMS (**jaws**) **mouth,** maw, muzzle, mandibles; informal chops.

▶ **verb** informal talk or gossip at length.
– ORIGIN Old French *joe* 'cheek, jaw.'

jaw·bone /ˈjôˌbōn/ ▶ **noun** a bone of the jaw, especially that of the lower jaw.

jaw-drop·ping ▶ **adjective** informal amazing.

jaw·line /ˈjôˌlīn/ ▶ **noun** the contour of the lower edge of a person's jaw.

jay /jā/ ▶ **noun** a noisy bird of the crow family with boldly patterned plumage.
– ORIGIN Latin *gaius, gaia*.

jay·walk /ˈjāˌwôk/ ▶ **verb** walk across a street in violation of pedestrian laws, especially where there is no crosswalk or at an intersection when the traffic has the right of way.
– DERIVATIVES **jay·walk·er** noun.
– ORIGIN from **JAY** in the former sense 'silly person.'

jazz /jaz/ ▶ **noun** a type of music of black American origin, typically instrumental and characterized by improvisation. ▶ **verb** (**jazz something up**) make something more lively or attractive.
– PHRASES **and all that jazz** informal and other similar things.
– ORIGIN unknown.

jazz·y /ˈjazē/ ▶ **adjective** (**jazzier, jazziest**) **1** relating to or like jazz. **2** bright, colorful, and showy.

jct. ▶ **abbreviation** junction.

jeal·ous /ˈjeləs/ ▶ **adjective 1** envious of someone else's achievements or advantages. **2** having a resentful suspicion that one's partner is sexually attracted to or involved with someone else: *a jealous husband*. **3** very protective of one's rights or possessions: *they kept a jealous eye over their interests*.

– SYNONYMS **1 envious,** covetous, resentful, grudging, green with envy. **2 suspicious,** distrustful, possessive, proprietorial, overprotective. **3 protective,** vigilant, watchful, mindful, careful.
– ANTONYMS trusting.

– DERIVATIVES **jeal·ous·ly** adverb.
– ORIGIN Old French *gelos*.

WORD TOOLKIT

See **ENVIOUS**.

jeal·ous·y /ˈjeləsē/ ▶ **noun** (pl. **jealousies**) the state or feeling of being jealous.

– SYNONYMS **envy,** resentment, bitterness; humorous the green-eyed monster.

jeans /jēnz/ ▶ **plural noun** casual pants made of denim.
– ORIGIN from Latin *Janua* 'Genoa,' where *jean*, a type of hard-wearing cotton cloth, was originally made.

jeep /jēp/ ▶ **noun** trademark a sturdy motor vehicle with four-wheel drive.
– ORIGIN probably from the World War II vehicle's model code *GP* (*general purpose*), influenced by 'Eugene the Jeep,' a creature in the *Popeye* comic strip.

jee·pers /ˈjēpərz/ ▶ **exclamation** used to express surprise or alarm.
– ORIGIN alteration of *Jesus*.

jeer /ji(ə)r/ ▶ **verb** make rude and mocking remarks to someone.

– SYNONYMS **taunt,** mock, ridicule, deride, insult, abuse, heckle, catcall (at), boo (at), whistle at, scoff at, sneer at.
– ANTONYMS applaud, cheer.

▶ **noun** a rude and mocking remark.

– SYNONYMS **taunt,** sneer, insult, shout, jibe, boo, catcall; derision, teasing, scoffing, abuse, scorn, heckling, catcalling.
– ANTONYMS applause, cheer.

– ORIGIN unknown.

jeez /jēz/ ▶ **exclamation** a mild expression used to show surprise or annoyance.

je·had ▶ **noun** variant spelling of **JIHAD**.

Je·ho·vah /jəˈhōvə/ ▶ **noun** a form of the Hebrew name of God.
– ORIGIN Hebrew.

Je·ho·vah's Wit·ness ▶ **noun** a member of a Christian sect that denies many traditional Christian doctrines and preaches that Jesus will return to earth at the Last Judgment.

je·june /jiˈjo͞on/ ▶ **adjective 1** naive and simplistic. **2** (of ideas or writings) dull.
– ORIGIN Latin *jejunus* 'fasting, barren.'

je·ju·num /jiˈjo͞onəm/ ▶ **noun** the part of the small intestine between the duodenum and ileum.
– ORIGIN Latin, 'fasting' (because it is usually found to be empty after death).

Jek·yll /ˈjekəl/ ▶ **noun** (in phrase **a Jekyll and Hyde**) a person who displays alternately good and evil personalities.
– ORIGIN after the central character in Robert Louis Stevenson's story *The Strange Case of Dr. Jekyll and Mr. Hyde*.

jell /jel/ ▶ **verb** variant spelling of **GEL²**.

jel·la·ba /jəˈläbə/ ▶ **noun** variant spelling of **DJELLABA**.

jel·lied /ˈjelēd/ ▶ **adjective** (of food) set in a jelly.

jell·o /ˈjelō/ (also trademark **Jell-O**) ▶ **noun** a fruit-flavored gelatin dessert made up from a powder.

Jell·o shot ▶ **noun** an alcoholic beverage consisting of liquor incorporated into sweetened gelatin dessert and chilled in a small container.
– ORIGIN from Jell-O, the proprietary name of a gelatin dessert.

jel·ly /ˈjelē/ ▶ **noun** (pl. **jellies**) **1** a sweet semisolid spread made from fruit juice and sugar boiled to a thick consistency. **2** a substance with a similar semisolid consistency: *the eggs are encased in an amber-colored jelly*. **3** a gumdrop or other candy made with gelatin.
– ORIGIN Old French *gelee* 'frost, jelly.'

jel·ly bean ▶ **noun** a bean-shaped candy with a jellylike center and a firm sugar coating.

jel·ly·fish /ˈjelēˌfisн/ ▶ **noun** (pl. same or **jellyfishes**) a sea animal with a soft bell- or saucer-shaped body that has stinging tentacles around the edge.

jel·ly roll ▶ **noun** a cylindrical cake made from a flat sponge cake spread with a filling such as jam and rolled up.

jen·ny /ˈjenē/ ▶ **noun** (pl. **jennies**) a female donkey or ass.
– ORIGIN familiar form of the woman's name *Janet*.

jeop·ard·ize /ˈjepərˌdīz/ ▶ **verb** put someone or something into a situation where there is a risk of loss, harm, or failure.

– SYNONYMS **threaten,** endanger, imperil, risk, compromise, prejudice.
– ANTONYMS safeguard.

jeop·ard·y /ˈjepərdē/ ▶ **noun** danger of loss, harm, or failure.

– SYNONYMS **danger,** peril, risk.

– ORIGIN from Old French *ieu parti* '(evenly) divided game.'

jer·bo·a /jərˈbōə/ ▶ **noun** a rodent with very long hind legs found in deserts from North Africa to central Asia.
– ORIGIN Arabic.

jer·e·mi·ad /ˌjerəˈmīəd, -ˌad/ ▶ **noun** a long, mournful complaint.
ORIGIN French *jérémiade*, with reference to the Lamentations of Jeremiah in the Old Testament.

jerk[1] /jərk/ ▶ **noun 1** a quick, sharp, sudden movement. **2** informal a stupid person.

– SYNONYMS **1** *she gave the reins a jerk* **yank,** tug, pull, wrench. **2** *the elevator stopped with a jerk* **jolt,** lurch, bump, jump, bounce, jounce, shake.

▶ **verb 1** move or raise something with a jerk. **2 (jerk someone around)** informal deal with someone dishonestly or unfairly.

– SYNONYMS **1** *she jerked her arm free* **yank,** tug, pull, wrench, wrest, drag, snatch. **2** *the car jerked along* **jolt,** lurch, bump, bounce, jounce.

– DERIVATIVES **jerk·er** noun.
– ORIGIN uncertain.

jerk[2] ▶ **verb** prepare pork or chicken by marinating it in spices and barbecuing it over a wood fire. ▶ **noun** meat that has been marinated and barbecued over a wood fire.
– ORIGIN Spanish *charquear*.

jer·kin /ˈjərkin/ ▶ **noun** a sleeveless jacket.
– ORIGIN unknown.

jerk·y[1] /ˈjərkē/ ▶ **adjective (jerkier, jerkiest)** moving in abrupt stops and starts.

– SYNONYMS **convulsive,** spasmodic, fitful, twitchy, shaky.
– ANTONYMS smooth.

– DERIVATIVES **jerk·i·ly** adverb **jerk·i·ness** noun.

jerk·y[2] ▶ **noun** meat that has been cured by being cut into long, thin strips and dried.
– ORIGIN from American Spanish *charqui*.

jer·o·bo·am /ˌjerəˈbōəm/ ▶ **noun** a wine bottle with a capacity four times larger than that of an ordinary bottle.
– ORIGIN named after *Jeroboam*, a king of Israel (Book of Kings 1).

Jer·ry /ˈjerē/ ▶ **noun** (pl. **Jerries)** informal, derogatory a German.
– ORIGIN probably from **GERMAN**.

jer·ry-built ▶ **adjective** badly or hastily built.
– DERIVATIVES **jer·ry-build·er** noun.
– ORIGIN uncertain: perhaps from the name of a firm of builders in Liverpool.

jer·sey /ˈjərzē/ ▶ **noun** (pl. **jerseys) 1** a knitted garment with long sleeves. **2** a distinctive shirt worn by a player in certain sports. **3** a soft knitted fabric. **4 (Jersey)** an animal of a breed of light brown dairy cattle.
– ORIGIN first referring to fabric made in the Channel Island of *Jersey*.

Je·ru·sa·lem ar·ti·choke /jəˈro͞os(ə)ləm, -ˈro͞oz-/ ▶ **noun** a knobbly root vegetable with white flesh.
– ORIGIN from Italian *girasole* 'sunflower.'

jest /jest/ ▶ **noun** a joke. ▶ **verb** speak or act in a joking way.
– ORIGIN Latin *gesta* 'actions, exploits.'

jest·er /ˈjestər/ ▶ **noun** historical a professional joker or "fool" at a medieval court.

Jes·u·it /ˈjezHo͞oit, ˈjez(y)o͞o-/ ▶ **noun** a member of the Society of Jesus, a Roman Catholic order of priests founded by St. Ignatius Loyola.

Jes·u·it·i·cal /ˌjezHo͞oˈitikəl, ˌjez(y)o͞o-/ ▶ **adjective 1** relating to the Jesuits. **2** using evasive language, in a way once associated with Jesuits.

Je·sus /ˈjēzəs/ (also **Jesus Christ**) ▶ **noun** the central figure of the Christian religion, believed by Christians to be the Messiah and the Son of God. ▶ **exclamation** informal expressing irritation, dismay, or surprise.

jet[1] /jet/ ▶ **noun 1** a rapid stream of liquid or gas forced out of a small opening. **2** an aircraft powered by jet engines.

– SYNONYMS **stream,** spurt, spray, fountain, rush, spout, gush, surge, burst.

▶ **verb (jets, jetting, jetted) 1** spurt out in a jet. **2** travel by jet aircraft.
– ORIGIN from French *jeter* 'to throw.'

jet[2] ▶ **noun 1** a hard black semiprecious mineral. **2** (also **jet black**) a glossy black color.
– ORIGIN Old French *jaiet*.

je·té /zHəˈtā/ ▶ **noun** Ballet a spring from one foot to the other, with the following leg extended backward while in the air.
– ORIGIN French.

jet en·gine ▶ **noun** an aircraft engine that provides force for forward movement by ejecting a high-speed jet of gas obtained by burning fuel in air.

jet·foil /ˈjetˌfoil/ ▶ **noun** a type of passenger-carrying hydrofoil.
– ORIGIN from **JET[1]** and **HYDROFOIL**.

jet lag ▶ **noun** extreme tiredness and other effects felt by a person after a long flight across different time zones.
– DERIVATIVES **jet-lagged** adjective.

jet·lin·er /ˈjetˌlīnər/ ▶ **noun** a large jet aircraft that carries passengers.

jet pro·pul·sion ▶ **noun** propulsion by the backward ejection of a high-speed jet of gas or liquid.

jet·sam /ˈjetsəm/ ▶ **noun** unwanted material or goods that have been thrown overboard from a ship and washed ashore.
– ORIGIN from **JETTISON**.

jet set ▶ **noun (the jet set)** informal fashionable and wealthy people who frequently travel abroad for pleasure.
– DERIVATIVES **jet-set·ter** noun **jet-set·ting** adjective.

jet ski ▶ **noun** trademark a small jet-propelled vehicle that skims across the surface of water and is ridden in a similar way to a motorcycle.
– DERIVATIVES **jet-ski·er** noun **jet-ski·ing** noun.

jet stream ▶ **noun** any of several narrow bands of very strong predominantly westerly air currents encircling the globe several miles above the earth.

jet·ti·son /ˈjetisən, -zən/ ▶ **verb 1** throw or drop something from an aircraft or ship. **2** abandon or discard an unwanted person or thing.

– SYNONYMS **dump,** drop, ditch, throw out, get rid of, discard, dispose of, scrap.

– ORIGIN Old French *getaison.*

jet·ty /ˈjetē/ ▶ **noun** (pl. **jetties**) **1** a landing stage or small pier for boats. **2** a construction built out into the water to protect a harbor, riverbank, or coastline.

– SYNONYMS **pier,** landing (stage), quay, wharf, dock, levee, breakwater, mole.

– ORIGIN Old French *jetee.*

jeu·nesse do·rée /zʜəˌnes dôˈrā/ ▶ **noun** fashionable, wealthy, and stylish young people.
– ORIGIN French, 'gilded youth.'

Jew /jo͞o/ ▶ **noun** a member of the people whose traditional religion is Judaism and who trace their origins to the ancient Hebrew people of Israel.
– ORIGIN Hebrew, 'Judah.'

jew·el /ˈjo͞oəl/ ▶ **noun 1** a precious stone. **2** (**jewels**) pieces of jewelry. **3** a hard precious stone used as a bearing in a watch or other device. **4** a highly valued person or thing: *she was a jewel of a nurse.*

– SYNONYMS **1 gem,** gemstone, (precious) stone; informal sparkler, rock. **2 showpiece,** pride (and joy), cream, crème de la crème, jewel in the crown, prize, pick.

– DERIVATIVES **jew·eled** adjective.
– PHRASES **the jewel in the crown** the most valuable or successful part of something.
– ORIGIN Old French *joel.*

jew·el box ▶ **noun** a storage box for a compact disc.

jew·el·er /ˈjo͞o(ə)lər/ (Brit. **jeweller**) ▶ **noun** a person who makes or sells jewelry.

jew·el·ry /ˈjo͞o(ə)lrē/ (Brit. **jewellery**) ▶ **noun** personal ornaments such as necklaces, rings, or bracelets.

Jew·ess /ˈjo͞o-is/ ▶ **noun** usu. offensive a Jewish woman or girl.

Jew·ish /ˈjo͞o-isʜ/ ▶ **adjective** relating to Jews or Judaism.
– DERIVATIVES **Jew·ish·ness** noun.

Jew·ish New Year ▶ **noun** another term for **ROSH HASHANAH**.

Jew·ry /ˈjo͞orē/ ▶ **noun** Jews as a group.

Jew's harp ▶ **noun** a small musical instrument like a U-shaped harp, held between the teeth and struck with a finger.

Je·ze·bel /ˈjezəˌbel, -bəl/ ▶ **noun** a shameless or immoral woman.
– ORIGIN the name of the wife of King Ahab in the Bible.

jiao /jyou/ ▶ **noun** (pl. same) a unit of money of China, equal to one tenth of a yuan.
– ORIGIN Chinese.

jib /jib/ ▶ **noun 1** Sailing a triangular sail set in front of the mast. **2** the projecting arm of a crane.
– ORIGIN unknown.

jibe[1] /jīb/ ▶ **noun & verb** variant spelling of **GIBE**.

jibe[2] (Brit. **gybe**) Sailing ▶ **verb 1** change course by swinging the sail across a following wind. **2** (of a sail or boom) swing across the wind. ▶ **noun** an act of jibing.
– ORIGIN from former Dutch *gijben.*

jibe[3] ▶ **verb** (usu. **jibe with**) informal be in accordance or agree with something.
– ORIGIN unknown.

jif·fy /ˈjifē/ (also **jiff**) ▶ **noun** informal a moment.
– ORIGIN unknown.

jig /jig/ ▶ **noun 1** a lively dance with leaping movements. **2** a device that holds a piece of work and guides the tool operating on it. ▶ **verb** (**jigs, jigging, jigged**) **1** move up and down jerkily. **2** dance a jig.
– ORIGIN unknown.

jig·ger[1] /ˈjigər/ ▶ **noun 1** a machine or vehicle with a part that rocks or moves to and fro. **2** a measure of liquor or wine. ▶ **verb** informal rearrange or tamper with something.

jig·ger[2] ▶ **noun** variant spelling of **CHIGGER**.

jig·gle /ˈjigəl/ ▶ **verb** move lightly and quickly from side to side or up and down. ▶ **noun** an instance of jiggling.
– DERIVATIVES **jig·gly** adjective.
– ORIGIN from **JOGGLE** and **JIG**.

jig·gy /ˈjigē/ ▶ **adjective** informal **1** uninhibited, especially in a sexual way. **2** trembling or nervous, especially as the result of drug withdrawal.

jig·saw /ˈjigˌsô/ ▶ **noun 1** a puzzle consisting of a picture printed on cardboard or wood and cut into many interlocking shapes that have to be fitted together. **2** a machine saw with a fine blade enabling it to cut curved lines.

ji·had /jiˈhäd/ (also **jehad**) ▶ **noun** (in Islam) a war or struggle against unbelievers.
– DERIVATIVES **ji·had·ist** noun.
– ORIGIN Arabic, 'effort.'

ji·had·i /jiˈhädē/ (also **jehadi**) ▶ **noun** (pl. **jihadis**) a person involved in a jihad.

jilt /jilt/ ▶ **verb** abruptly break off a relationship with a lover.

– SYNONYMS **leave,** walk out on, throw over, finish with, break up with, stand up, leave at the altar; informal ditch, dump, drop, run out on, give someone the brush off.

– ORIGIN unknown.

Jim Crow /ˈjim ˈkrō/ ▶ **noun 1** the former practice of segregating black people in the US. **2** offensive a black person.
– DERIVATIVES **Jim Crow·ism** noun.
– ORIGIN a black character in a plantation song.

jim·my /ˈjimē/ (also Brit. **jemmy** /ˈjemē/) ▶ **noun** (pl. **jimmies**) a short crowbar, used especially by burglars. ▶ **verb** (**jimmies, jimmying, jimmied**) informal force open a window or door with a jimmy.
– ORIGIN familiar form of the man's name *James.*

jim·son weed /ˈjimsən/ ▶ **noun** a strong-smelling poisonous plant with large, trumpet-shaped white flowers and toothed leaves.
– ORIGIN (originally as *Jamestown weed*): named after *Jamestown* in Virginia.

jin·gle /ˈjiɴɢgəl/ ▶ **noun 1** a light ringing sound such as that made by metal objects being shaken together. **2** a short, easily remembered slogan, verse, or tune.

– SYNONYMS *the jingle of money* **clink,** chink, tinkle, jangle.

▶ **verb** make a light ringing sound.

– SYNONYMS *the keys jingled* **clink,** chink, tinkle, jangle.

– DERIVATIVES **jin·gler** noun **jin·gly** adjective.
– ORIGIN imitating the sound.

jin·go·ism /ˈjiɴɢgōˌizəm/ ▶ **noun** chiefly derogatory extreme patriotism in the form of aggressive foreign policy.

– DERIVATIVES **jin·go·ist** noun **jin·go·is·tic** /ˌjiNGgō'istik/ adjective.
– ORIGIN from *by jingo!* in a song adopted by those who supported the sending of a British fleet into Turkish waters to resist Russia in 1878.

jink /jiNGk/ ▶ **verb** change direction suddenly and nimbly. ▶ **noun** a sudden quick change of direction.
– ORIGIN from Scots *high jinks*, referring to antics at drinking parties.

jinn /jin/ (also **djinn**) ▶ **noun** (pl. same or **jinns**) (in Arabian and Muslim mythology) an intelligent spirit able to appear in human or animal form.

jinx /jiNGks/ ▶ **noun** a person or thing that brings bad luck.
– SYNONYMS **curse,** spell, the evil eye, hex, black magic, voodoo, bad luck.
▶ **verb** bring bad luck to someone or something.
– SYNONYMS **curse,** cast a spell on, hex.
– ORIGIN probably from Latin *jynx* 'wryneck.'

jir·ga /'jərgə/ ▶ **noun** (in Afghanistan) a tribal council.
– ORIGIN Pashto,'council, assembly.'

jit·ter /'jitər/ informal ▶ **noun 1** (**the jitters**) a feeling of extreme nervousness. **2** slight irregular variation in an electrical signal. ▶ **verb** act nervously.
– DERIVATIVES **jit·ter·i·ness** noun **jit·ter·y** adjective.
– ORIGIN unknown.

jit·ter·bug /'jitərˌbəg/ ▶ **noun** a fast dance performed to swing music, popular in the 1940s. ▶ **verb** (**jitterbugs, jitterbugging, jitterbugged**) dance the jitterbug.

jiu·jit·su ▶ **noun** variant spelling of **JUJITSU**.

jive /jīv/ ▶ **noun** a style of lively dance popular in the 1940s and 1950s, performed to swing music or rock and roll. ▶ **verb** dance the jive.
– DERIVATIVES **jiv·er** noun.
– ORIGIN unknown.

job /jōb/ ▶ **noun 1** a paid position of regular employment. **2** a task or piece of work. **3** informal a crime, especially a robbery. **4** informal a procedure to improve the appearance of something: *a nose job.*
– SYNONYMS **1 position,** post, situation, appointment, occupation, profession, trade, career, work, vocation, calling, métier. **2 task,** piece of work, assignment, mission, project, undertaking, operation, duty, chore, errand, responsibility, charge, role, function; informal department.
▶ **verb** (**jobs, jobbing, jobbed**) (usu. as adj. **jobbing**) do casual or occasional work.
– PHRASES **do the job** informal achieve the required result: *a piece of board will do the job.* **do a job on someone** informal do something that harms or defeats an opponent.
– ORIGIN unknown.

job·ber /'jäbər/ ▶ **noun 1** a person who does casual or occasional work. **2** informal a professional wrestler who frequently loses a match.

job·less /'jäbləs/ ▶ **adjective** without a paid job.
– SYNONYMS **unemployed,** out of work, without work, laid off.
– ANTONYMS employed.
– DERIVATIVES **job·less·ness** noun.

job lot ▶ **noun** a batch of articles sold or bought at one time, especially at a discount.

job-share ▶ **verb** (of two part-time employees) share a single full-time job. ▶ **noun** an arrangement in which two part-time employees share a full-time job.
– DERIVATIVES **job-shar·er** noun.

jock /jäk/ ▶ **noun** informal **1** an enthusiast or participant in a particular sport or other activity. **2** a disk jockey. **3** a young man who is socially adept and physically fit but not very intelligent. **4** a pilot.

jock·ey /'jäkē/ ▶ **noun** (pl. **jockeys**) a professional rider in horse races. ▶ **verb** (**jockeys, jockeying, jockeyed**) struggle to gain or achieve something: *drivers are constantly jockeying for position.*

jock·strap /'jäkˌstrap/ ▶ **noun** a support or pouch worn to protect a man's genitals, especially in sports.
– ORIGIN from slang *jock* 'genitals.'

jo·cose /jō'kōs/ ▶ **adjective** formal playful or humorous.
– DERIVATIVES **jo·cose·ly** adverb **jo·cos·i·ty** /-'käsitē/ noun (pl. **jocosities**).
– ORIGIN from Latin *jocus* 'jest, joke.'

joc·u·lar /'jäkyələr/ ▶ **adjective** humorous or amusing.
– DERIVATIVES **joc·u·lar·i·ty** /ˌjäkyə'laritē/ noun **joc·u·lar·ly** adverb.
– ORIGIN Latin *jocularis*.

joc·und /'jäkənd, 'jō-/ ▶ **adjective** formal cheerful and lighthearted.
– ORIGIN Latin *jucundus* 'pleasant, agreeable.'

jodh·purs /'jädpərz/ ▶ **plural noun** trousers worn for horse riding that are close-fitting below the knee.
– ORIGIN named after the Indian city of *Jodhpur*.

Joe Blow ▶ **noun** informal a name for a hypothetical average man.

jog /jäg/ ▶ **verb** (**jogs, jogging, jogged**) **1** run at a steady, gentle pace, especially for exercise. **2** (**jog along/on**) continue in a steady, uneventful way. **3** knock something slightly.
– SYNONYMS **1 run,** trot, lope. **2 nudge,** prod, poke, push, bump, jar.
▶ **noun 1** a spell of jogging. **2** a gentle running pace. **3** a slight push or knock.
– DERIVATIVES **jog·ger** noun.
– PHRASES **jog someone's memory** make someone remember something.
– ORIGIN from **JAG**[1].

jog·gle /'jägəl/ ▶ **verb** move with repeated small jerks.
– ORIGIN from **JOG**.

john /jän/ ▶ **noun** informal **1** a toilet. **2** a prostitute's client.
– ORIGIN from the man's name *John*.

John Bull ▶ **noun** a character representing England or the typical Englishman.
– ORIGIN from a character in John Arbuthnot's satire *Law is a Bottomless Pit; or, the History of John Bull.*

John Doe ▶ **noun** an anonymous male party in a legal action or an unidentified man.
– ORIGIN originally in legal use as a name of a fictitious plaintiff, corresponding to *Richard Roe*, used to represent the defendant.

John Do·ry /'dôrē/ ▶ **noun** (pl. **John Dories**) an edible dory (fish) of the eastern Atlantic and Mediterranean, with a black oval mark on each side.

John Han·cock ▶ **noun** informal a person's signature: *put your John Hancock right here.*
– ORIGIN from the fact that John Hancock's signature was written large and legibly on the Declaration of Independence.

john·ny-come-late·ly ▶ **noun** informal a newcomer to or late starter at a place or area of activity.

joie de vi·vre /ˌzHwä də ˈvēvrə/ ▸ **noun** lively enjoyment of life.
– ORIGIN French.

join /join/ ▸ **verb 1** link or become linked to. **2** unite to form a whole: *they joined up with local environmentalists.* **3** become a member or employee of an organization. **4** (also **join in**) take part in an activity. **5** meet or go somewhere with someone. **6** (**join up**) become a member of the armed forces.

– SYNONYMS **1** *the two parts are joined with clay* **connect,** unite, couple, fix, affix, attach, fasten, stick, glue, fuse, weld, amalgamate, bond, link, yoke, merge, secure, make fast, tie, bind. **2** *the path joins a major road* **meet,** touch, reach. **3 help in,** participate in, get involved in, contribute to, enlist in, join up, sign up, band together, get together, team up.
– ANTONYMS separate, leave.

▸ **noun** a place where things are connected or fastened together.
– DERIVATIVES **join·a·ble** adjective.
– PHRASES **join forces** combine efforts.
– ORIGIN Old French *joindre.*

CHOOSE THE RIGHT WORD

join, combine, conjoin, connect, consolidate, unite

It is possible for an individual to **join** an investment club, to **consolidate** his or her financial resources, and to **combine** a background in economics with a strong interest in retirement planning. All of these words mean to bring together or to attach two or more things. *Join* is the general term for bringing into contact or conjunction two discrete things (*join two pieces of wood; join one's friends in celebration*), while **conjoin** emphasizes both the separateness of the things that are joined and the unity that results (*her innate brilliance, conjoined with a genuine eagerness to learn, made her the ideal candidate for the job*). In contrast, to *combine* is to mix or mingle things together, often to the point where they merge with one another (*combine the ingredients for a cake*). *Consolidate* also implies a merger of distinct and separate elements, but the emphasis here is on achieving greater compactness, strength, or efficiency (*consolidate their furnishings and buy a new house together*). **Connect** implies a loose or obvious attachment of things to each other, but with each thing's identity or physical separateness preserved (*the two families were connected by blood; she connected the computer to the printer*). In a physical context, it differs from *join* in that it implies an intervening element that permits movement; in other words, the bones are *connected* by ligaments, but bricks are *joined* by mortar. When things are joined or combined so closely that they form a single thing, they are said to **unite** (*the parties were united in their support of the new law*).

join·er /ˈjoinər/ ▸ **noun 1** informal a person who readily joins groups or campaigns. **2** dated a person who constructs the wooden parts of a building.

joint /joint/ ▸ **noun 1** a point at which parts are joined. **2** a structure in the body by which two bones are fitted together. **3** the part of a plant stem from which a leaf or branch grows. **4** Brit. a large piece of meat; a roast. **5** informal a place for eating, drinking, or entertainment: *a burger joint.* **6** informal a marijuana cigarette.

– SYNONYMS **join,** junction, intersection, link, connection, weld, seam, coupling.

▸ **adjective 1** shared, held, or made by two or more people: *a joint account.* **2** sharing in an achievement or activity.

– SYNONYMS **common,** shared, communal, collective, mutual, cooperative, collaborative, concerted, combined, united, allied.
– ANTONYMS separate.

▸ **verb 1** (usu. as adj. **jointed**) provide or fasten something with joints. **2** cut beef, fowl, etc., at the joint, creating separate pieces for roasting, frying, etc.
– PHRASES **out of joint 1** (of a joint of the body) dislocated. **2** in a state of disorder.
– ORIGIN from Old French *joindre* 'to join.'

Joint Chiefs of Staff ▸ **noun** the chiefs of the Army and Air Force, the commandant of the Marine Corps, and the chief of Naval Operations.

joint·er /ˈjointər/ ▸ **noun** a plane for preparing a wooden edge for joining to another.

joint·ly /ˈjointlē/ ▸ **adverb** together; in collaboration: *the two companies will jointly develop business software.*

– SYNONYMS **together,** in partnership, in cooperation, in collaboration, cooperatively, in conjunction, in combination, mutually, in league.

joint-stock ▸ **adjective** relating to joint ownership by shareholders.

joist /joist/ ▸ **noun** a length of lumber or steel supporting the floor or ceiling of a building.
– ORIGIN from Old French *giste* 'beam supporting a bridge.'

jo·jo·ba /hōˈhōbə/ ▸ **noun** an oil extracted from the seeds of a North American shrub, used in cosmetics.
– ORIGIN Mexican Spanish.

joke /jōk/ ▸ **noun 1** a thing that someone says to cause amusement or laughter. **2** a trick played for fun. **3** informal a ridiculously inadequate person or thing: *public transportation is a joke.*

– SYNONYMS **1 witticism,** jest, quip, pun; informal gag, wisecrack, crack, funny, one-liner. **2 trick,** prank, stunt, hoax, jape; informal leg-pulling, spoof. **3 laughingstock,** object of ridicule, butt, stooge. **4 farce,** travesty, waste of time.

▸ **verb** make jokes.

– SYNONYMS **tell jokes,** jest, banter, quip; informal wisecrack, josh.

– DERIVATIVES **jok·ey** (also **joky**) adjective **jok·ing·ly** adverb.
– PHRASES **the joke is on someone** informal someone looks foolish, especially after trying to make someone else look so.
– ORIGIN perhaps from Latin *jocus.*

jok·er /ˈjōkər/ ▸ **noun 1** a person who is fond of joking. **2** informal a foolish or ridiculous person. **3** a playing card with the figure of a jester, used as a wild card.

– SYNONYMS **comedian,** comedienne, comic, humorist, wit, jester, prankster, practical joker, clown.

– PHRASES **the joker in the deck** a person or factor likely to have an unpredictable effect.

jol·li·fi·ca·tion /ˌjäləfiˈkāsHən/ ▸ **noun** lively celebration with others; merrymaking.

jol·li·ty /ˈjälitē/ ▸ **noun** (pl. **jollities**) **1** lively and cheerful activity. **2** the quality of being cheerful.

jol·ly[1] /ˈjälē/ ▸ **adjective** (**jollier, jolliest**) **1** happy and cheerful. **2** lively and entertaining.

– SYNONYMS **cheerful,** happy, cheery, good-humored, jovial, merry, sunny, joyful, lighthearted,

in high spirits, buoyant, bubbly, genial; informal chipper, chirpy, perky; literary blithe.
– ANTONYMS miserable.

▶ **verb** (**jollies, jollying, jollied**) informal encourage in a friendly way: *he jollied her along.*
▶ **adverb** Brit. informal very.
▶ **noun** (pl. **jollies**) Brit. informal a party or celebration.
– DERIVATIVES **jol·li·ly** adverb **jol·li·ness** noun.
– PHRASES **get one's jollies** informal have fun or find pleasure.
– ORIGIN Old French *jolif* 'pretty.'

jol·ly[2] (also **jolly boat**) ▶ **noun** (pl. **jollies**) a ship's boat that is smaller than a cutter.
– ORIGIN perhaps related to **YAWL**.

Jol·ly Rog·er /'jälē 'räjər/ ▶ **noun** a pirate's flag with a white skull and crossbones on a black background.
– ORIGIN unknown.

jolt /jōlt/ ▶ **verb 1** push or shake someone or something abruptly and roughly. **2** shock someone into taking action.

– SYNONYMS **1 push,** jar, bump, knock, bang, shake, jog. **2 bump,** bounce, jerk, rattle, lurch, shudder, jounce. **3 startle,** surprise, shock, stun, shake; informal rock, knock sideways.

▶ **noun 1** a sudden or violent movement. **2** a surprise or shock.

– SYNONYMS **bump,** bounce, shake, jerk, lurch, jounce.

– ORIGIN unknown.

jon·quil /'jänkwəl/ ▶ **noun** a narcissus with small sweet-smelling yellow flowers.
– ORIGIN Spanish *junquillo.*

Jor·da·ni·an /jôr'dānēən/ ▶ **noun** a person from Jordan.
▶ **adjective** relating to Jordan.

josh /jäsh/ ▶ **verb** informal tease someone playfully.
– DERIVATIVES **josh·er** noun.
– ORIGIN unknown.

Josh·u·a tree /'jäshōōə/ ▶ **noun** a tall branching yucca of SW North America, with clusters of spiky leaves.
– ORIGIN probably from *Joshua* in the Bible, the plant being likened to a man with a spear.

jos·tle /'jäsəl/ ▶ **verb 1** push or bump against someone roughly. **2** (**jostle for**) struggle or compete forcefully for: *they jostled for control of the company.*

– SYNONYMS **1 push,** shove, elbow, barge into, bang into, bump against, knock against. **2** *photographers jostled for position* **struggle,** vie, jockey, scramble, fight.

– ORIGIN from **JOUST**.

jot /jät/ ▶ **verb** (**jots, jotting, jotted**) write something quickly. ▶ **noun** a very small amount: *his rich voice has not lost a jot of its power.*
– ORIGIN from Greek *iōta*, the smallest letter of the Greek alphabet (see **IOTA**).

jot·tings /'jätingz/ ▶ **plural noun** brief, sketchy, or incomplete notes or drawings.

joule /jōōl/ ▶ **noun** the unit of work or energy in the SI system.
– ORIGIN named after the English physicist James P. *Joule.*

jounce /jouns/ ▶ **verb** jolt or bounce.
– ORIGIN uncertain.

jour·nal /'jərnl/ ▶ **noun 1** a newspaper or magazine dealing with a particular subject. **2** a diary or daily record.

– SYNONYMS **1 periodical,** magazine, gazette, review, newsletter, news-sheet, bulletin, newspaper, paper, daily, weekly, monthly, quarterly. **2 diary,** log, logbook, daybook, weblog, blog, chronicle, history, yearbook.

▶ **verb** (**journals, journaling, journaled**) write in a journal or diary.
– ORIGIN Old French *jurnal.*

jour·nal·ese /,jərnl'ēz/ ▶ **noun** informal an unoriginal and poor writing style supposedly typical of journalists.

jour·nal·ism /'jərnl,izəm/ ▶ **noun** the activity or profession of being a journalist.

jour·nal·ist /'jərnl-ist/ ▶ **noun** a person who writes for newspapers or magazines or prepares news or features to be broadcast on radio or television.

– SYNONYMS **reporter,** correspondent, columnist, newsman, newswoman; informal news hound, hack, stringer.

– DERIVATIVES **jour·nal·is·tic** /,jərnl'istik/ adjective.

jour·ney /'jərnē/ ▶ **noun** (pl. **journeys**) an act of traveling from one place to another.

– SYNONYMS **trip,** expedition, tour, trek, travels, voyage, cruise, ride, drive, crossing, passage, flight, odyssey, pilgrimage, safari, globetrotting; old use peregrinations.

▶ **verb** (**journeys, journeying, journeyed**) travel somewhere.

– SYNONYMS **travel,** go, voyage, sail, cruise, fly, hike, trek, ride, drive, make one's way.

– DERIVATIVES **jour·ney·er** noun.
– ORIGIN Old French *jornee* 'day, a day's travel, a day's work.'

CHOOSE THE RIGHT WORD

journey, excursion, expedition, jaunt, pilgrimage, trip, voyage

While all of these nouns refer to a course of travel to a particular place, usually for a specific purpose, there is a big difference between a **jaunt** to the nearest beach and an **expedition** to the rainforest. While a **trip** may be either long or short, for business or pleasure, and taken at either a rushed or a leisurely pace (*a ski trip; a trip to Europe*), a **journey** suggests that a considerable amount of time and distance will be covered and that the travel will take place over land (*a journey into the Australian outback*). A long trip by water or through air or space is a **voyage** (*a voyage to the Galapagos Islands; a voyage to Mars*), while a short, casual trip for pleasure or recreation is a *jaunt* (*a jaunt to the local shopping mall*). **Excursion** also applies to a brief pleasure trip, usually no more than a day in length, that returns to the place where it began (*an afternoon excursion to the zoo*). Unlike the rest of these nouns, *expedition* and **pilgrimage** apply to *journeys* that are undertaken for a specific purpose. An *expedition* is usually made by an organized group or company (*a scientific expedition; an expedition to locate new sources of oil*), while a *pilgrimage* is a journey to a place that has religious or emotional significance (*the Muslims' annual pilgrimage to Mecca; a pilgrimage to the place where her father died*).

jour·ney·man /'jərnēmən/ ▶ **noun** (pl. **journeymen**) **1** a skilled worker who is employed by another. **2** a worker or athlete who is reliable but not outstanding.
– ORIGIN from **JOURNEY** in the former sense 'day's work.'

joust /joust/ ▸ **verb 1** (of a medieval knight) fight an opponent on horseback with lances. **2** (usu. as n. **jousting**) compete for superiority with someone: *he ignored Sam's verbal jousting.* ▸ **noun** a medieval contest in which knights on horseback fought with lances.
– DERIVATIVES **joust·er** noun.
– ORIGIN Old French *jouster* 'bring together.'

Jove /jōv/ ▸ **noun** (in phrase **by Jove**) dated used for emphasis or to indicate surprise.
– ORIGIN another name for the Roman god Jupiter.

jo·vi·al /'jōvēəl/ ▸ **adjective** cheerful and friendly.

– SYNONYMS **cheerful,** jolly, happy, cheery, jocular, good-humored, convivial, genial, good-natured, affable, outgoing, smiling, merry, sunny; literary blithe.
– ANTONYMS miserable.

– DERIVATIVES **jo·vi·al·i·ty** /ˌjōvē'alitē/ noun **jo·vi·al·ly** adverb.
– ORIGIN Latin *jovialis* 'of Jupiter' (referring to the influence of the planet Jupiter).

Jo·vi·an /'jōvēən/ ▸ **adjective 1** relating to the planet Jupiter or the class of giant planets to which Jupiter belongs. **2** (in Roman mythology) relating to the god Jove (or Jupiter). ▸ **noun** a hypothetical or fictional inhabitant of the planet Jupiter.

jowl /joul/ ▸ **noun 1** the lower part of a person's cheek, especially when fleshy. **2** the cheek of a pig used as meat: *hog jowls and collard greens.* **3** the loose skin at the throat of cattle.
– DERIVATIVES **jowl·y** adjective.
– ORIGIN Old English.

joy /joi/ ▸ **noun 1** great pleasure and happiness. **2** a cause of great pleasure and happiness.

– SYNONYMS **delight,** pleasure, jubilation, triumph, exultation, rejoicing, happiness, elation, euphoria, bliss, ecstasy, rapture.
– ANTONYMS misery.

– ORIGIN Old French *joie.*

joy·ful /'joifəl/ ▸ **adjective** feeling or causing great pleasure or happiness.

– SYNONYMS **1 cheerful,** happy, jolly, merry, sunny, joyous, cheery, smiling, jovial, mirthful, gleeful, pleased, delighted, thrilled, jubilant, elated, ecstatic; informal over the moon, on cloud nine. **2** *joyful news* **pleasing,** happy, good, cheering, gladdening, welcome, gratifying, heartwarming.
– ANTONYMS sad.

– DERIVATIVES **joy·ful·ly** adverb **joy·ful·ness** noun.

joy·less /'joiləs/ ▸ **adjective** not giving or feeling any pleasure or satisfaction; grim or dismal.

joy·ous /'joiəs/ ▸ **adjective** chiefly literary full of happiness and joy.
– DERIVATIVES **joy·ous·ly** adverb **joy·ous·ness** noun.

joy·ride /'joiˌrīd/ ▸ **noun** informal **1** a fast ride in a stolen vehicle. **2** a ride for enjoyment.
– DERIVATIVES **joy·rid·er** noun **joy·rid·ing** noun.

joy·stick /'joiˌstik/ ▸ **noun** informal **1** the control column of an aircraft. **2** a lever for controlling the movement of an image on a computer screen.

JP ▸ **abbreviation** Justice of the Peace.

JPEG /'jāˌpeg/ ▸ **noun** Computing a format for compressing images.
– ORIGIN abbreviation of *Joint Photographic Experts Group.*

Jr. ▸ **abbreviation** junior (in names): *George Smith, Jr.*

ju·bi·lant /'jo͞obələnt/ ▸ **adjective** happy and triumphant.

– SYNONYMS **overjoyed,** exultant, triumphant, joyful, elated, thrilled, gleeful, euphoric, ecstatic; informal over the moon, on cloud nine.
– ANTONYMS despondent.

– DERIVATIVES **ju·bi·lant·ly** adverb.

ju·bi·la·tion /ˌjo͞obə'lāsʜən/ ▸ **noun** a feeling of great happiness and triumph.
– ORIGIN from Latin *jubilare* 'shout for joy.'

ju·bi·lee /'jo͞obəˌlē, ˌjo͞obə'lē/ ▸ **noun** a special anniversary, especially one celebrating twenty-five or fifty years of something.

– SYNONYMS **anniversary,** commemoration, celebration, festival.

– ORIGIN from a Hebrew word meaning 'ram's-horn trumpet,' with which a year of emancipation and restoration, kept every fifty years, was proclaimed.

Judaeo- ▸ **combining form** chiefly British spelling of **Judeo-**.

Ju·da·ic /jo͞o'dāik/ ▸ **adjective** relating to Judaism or the ancient Jews.

Ju·da·ism /'jo͞odēˌizəm, -dā-/ ▸ **noun** the religion of the Jews, based on the Old Testament and the Talmud.
– DERIVATIVES **Ju·da·ist** noun.
– ORIGIN Greek *Ioudaïsmos.*

Ju·da·ize /'jo͞odēˌīz, -dā-/ ▸ **verb** make someone or something Jewish.
– DERIVATIVES **Ju·da·i·za·tion** noun.

Ju·das /'jo͞odəs/ ▸ **noun** a person who betrays a friend.
– ORIGIN from *Judas* Iscariot, the disciple who betrayed Christ.

jud·der /'jədər/ ▸ **verb** chiefly Brit. shake rapidly and forcefully.
– DERIVATIVES **jud·der·y** adjective.
– ORIGIN imitating the sound.

Judeo- (also Brit. **Judaeo-**) ▸ **combining form** Jewish; Jewish and ...: *Judeo-Christian.*
– ORIGIN from Latin *Judaeus* 'Jewish.'

judge /jəj/ ▸ **noun 1** a public officer appointed or elected to decide cases in a court of law. **2** a person who decides the results of a competition. **3** a person with the necessary knowledge or skill to give an opinion.

– SYNONYMS **1 justice,** jurist, justice of the peace, magistrate, sheriff. **2 adjudicator,** referee, umpire, arbiter, assessor, examiner, moderator, scrutineer; informal ref, ump.

▸ **verb 1** form an opinion about: *a work should be judged on its own merits.* **2** give a verdict on a case or person in a court of law. **3** decide the results of a competition.

– SYNONYMS **1 conclude,** decide, consider, believe, think, deduce, infer, gauge, estimate, guess, surmise, conjecture, regard as, rate as; informal reckon, figure. **2** *she was judged innocent* **pronounce,** decree, rule, find. **3 adjudicate,** arbitrate, moderate, referee, umpire. **4 assess,** evaluate, appraise, examine, review.

– ORIGIN Latin *judex.*
– DERIVATIVES **judge·ship** /-ˌsʜip/ noun.

judg·ment /'jəjmənt/ (also chiefly Brit. **judgement**) ▸ **noun 1** the ability to make considered decisions or form sensible opinions: *an error of judgment.* **2** an opinion or conclusion. **3** a decision of a court of law or judge.

– SYNONYMS **1 sense,** discernment, perception, discrimination, understanding, powers of reasoning, reason, logic. **2 opinion,** view, estimate, appraisal, conclusion, diagnosis, assessment, impression, conviction, perception, thinking. **3** *a court judgment* **verdict,** decision, adjudication, ruling, pronouncement, decree, finding, sentence.

– PHRASES **against one's better judgment** opposite to what one feels to be wise. **sit in judgment** assume the right to judge or criticize someone.

judg·men·tal /jəj'mentl/ (also chiefly Brit. **judgemental**) ▶ **adjective 1** relating to the use of judgment. **2** excessively critical.

– SYNONYMS **critical,** censorious, disapproving, disparaging, deprecating, negative, overcritical.

– DERIVATIVES **judg·men·tal·ly** adverb.

judg·ment call ▶ **noun 1** a ruling by a sports official that is based on observation and may be appealed. **2** any subjective observation or judgment.

Judg·ment Day ▶ **noun** the time of the Last Judgment; the end of the world.

ju·di·ca·ture /'jo͞odikə,cho͝or, -,kācHər/ ▶ **noun 1** the administration of a national or state justice system. **2 (the judicature)** judges as a group.
– ORIGIN from Latin *judicare* 'to judge.'

ju·di·cial /jo͞o'disHəl/ ▶ **adjective** relating to a court of law or judge.
– DERIVATIVES **ju·di·cial·ly** adverb.
– ORIGIN from Latin *judicium* 'judgment.'

USAGE

On the difference between **judicial** and **judicious**, see the note at **JUDICIOUS**.

ju·di·ci·ar·y /jo͞o'disHē,erē, -'disHərē/ ▶ **noun** (pl. **judiciaries**) (usu. **the judiciary**) the system of judges of a country or state.

ju·di·cious /jo͞o'disHəs/ ▶ **adjective** having or done with good judgment; sensible.

– SYNONYMS **wise,** sensible, prudent, shrewd, astute, canny, discerning, sagacious, strategic, politic, expedient.
– ANTONYMS ill-advised.

– DERIVATIVES **ju·di·cious·ly** adverb **ju·di·cious·ness** noun.

USAGE

Judicious and **judicial** do not mean the same thing. **Judicious** means 'having or done with good judgment, sensible' (*the judicious use of public investment*), whereas **judicial** means 'relating to a court of law or judge' (*the judicial system*).

ju·do /'jo͞odō/ ▶ **noun** a sport of unarmed combat using holds and leverage to unbalance the opponent.
– ORIGIN Japanese, 'gentle way.'

jug /jəg/ ▶ **noun 1** a large container for liquids, with a handle and a narrow mouth. **2 (jugs)** vulgar slang a woman's breasts. **3 (the jug)** informal prison.
– ORIGIN perhaps from *Jug*, familiar form of the woman's names *Joan*, *Joanna*, and *Jenny*.

jug band ▶ **noun** a group of jazz, blues, or folk musicians using simple or improvised instruments such as jugs and washboards.

jug·ger·naut /'jəgər,nôt/ ▶ **noun** a huge, powerful, and overwhelming force or institution: *you can't fight the juggernaut of bureaucracy.*
– ORIGIN Sanskrit, 'Lord of the world,' referring to an image of the Hindu god Krishna carried on a heavy chariot.

jug·gle /'jəgəl/ ▶ **verb 1** continuously throw up and catch a number of objects so as to keep at least one in the air at any time. **2** manage to deal with several activities at the same time. **3** organize or manipulate facts so as to present them in the most effective or favorable way.
– DERIVATIVES **jug·gler** noun.
– ORIGIN Old French *jogler*.

jug·u·lar /'jəgyələr/ ▶ **adjective** relating to the neck or throat. ▶ **noun** (also **jugular vein**) any of several large veins in the neck, carrying blood from the head.
– PHRASES **go for the jugular** attack an opponent's weakest point in an aggressive way.
– ORIGIN from Latin *jugulum* 'collarbone, throat.'

juice /jo͞os/ ▶ **noun 1** the liquid present in fruit or vegetables, often made into a drink. **2 (juices)** fluid produced by the stomach. **3 (juices)** liquid coming from meat or other food in cooking. **4** informal fuel or electrical energy. **5 (juices)** informal a person's creative abilities.

– SYNONYMS **liquid,** fluid, sap, extract, concentrate, essence.

▶ **verb 1** extract the juice from fruit or vegetables. **2 (juice something up)** informal liven something up: *juice up the plot with some love interest.*
– ORIGIN Latin *jus* 'broth, vegetable juice.'

juic·er /'jo͞osər/ ▶ **noun** a device for extracting juice from fruit and vegetables.

juic·y /'jo͞osē/ ▶ **adjective (juicier, juiciest) 1** full of juice. **2** informal interestingly scandalous: *a juicy bit of gossip.* **3** informal likely to be rewarding or profitable: *juicy projects.*

– SYNONYMS **1 succulent,** tender, moist, ripe. **2 sensational,** fascinating, intriguing, exciting, graphic, lurid.
– ANTONYMS dry.

– DERIVATIVES **juic·i·ly** adverb **juic·i·ness** noun.

ju·jit·su /,jo͞o'jitso͞o/ (also **jiujitsu**) ▶ **noun** a Japanese system of unarmed combat and physical training.
– ORIGIN Japanese, 'gentle skill.'

ju·ju /'jo͞o,jo͞o/ ▶ **noun 1** a charm or fetish, especially as used by some West African peoples. **2** supernatural power believed to be possessed by a charm or fetish.
– ORIGIN West African.

ju·jube /'jo͞o,jo͞ob/ ▶ **noun 1** an edible berrylike fruit of a shrub, formerly eaten as a cough cure. **2** a jujube-flavored lozenge or candy.
– ORIGIN Latin *jujuba*.

juke·box /'jo͞ok,bäks/ ▶ **noun** a machine that plays a selected musical recording when a coin is inserted.
– ORIGIN *juke* is from a word in a Creole language meaning 'disorderly.'

Jul. ▶ **abbreviation** July.

ju·lep /'jo͞oləp/ ▶ **noun 1** a sweet drink made from sugar syrup. **2** short for **MINT JULEP**.
– ORIGIN Latin *julapium*.

Jul·ian cal·en·dar /'jo͞olyən, -lēən/ ▶ **noun** a calendar introduced by the Roman general Julius Caesar, in which the year consisted of 365 days, every fourth year having 366 (replaced by the Gregorian calendar).

ju·li·enne /jo͞olē'en/ ▶ **noun** a portion of food cut into short, thin strips. ▶ **verb** cut food into short, thin strips.
– ORIGIN French.

Ju·ly /jo͝o'lī/ ▶ **noun** (pl. **Julys**) the seventh month of the year.
– ORIGIN from Latin *Julius mensis* 'month of July,' named after the Roman general Julius Caesar.

jum·ble /'jəmbəl/ ▶ **noun** an untidy collection of things.

– SYNONYMS **heap,** muddle, mess, tangle, confusion, disarray, chaos, hodgepodge; informal shambles.

▶ **verb** mix things up in a confused way.

– SYNONYMS **mix up,** muddle (up), disorganize, disorder, tangle, confuse.

– ORIGIN uncertain.

jum·bo /'jəmbō/ informal ▶ **noun** (pl. **jumbos**) **1** a very large person or thing. **2** (also **jumbo jet**) a very large airliner. ▶ **adjective** very large.
– ORIGIN probably from **MUMBO-JUMBO**.

jump /jəmp/ ▶ **verb 1** push oneself off the ground using the muscles in one's legs and feet. **2** move over, onto, or down from somewhere by jumping. **3** move suddenly and quickly: *I jumped to my feet.* **4** make an uncontrolled movement in surprise. **5** (**jump at/on**) accept an opportunity or offer eagerly. **6** (**jump on**) informal attack or criticize someone suddenly. **7** pass abruptly from one subject or state to another. **8** rise suddenly and by a large amount: *prices jumped two percent in two weeks.* **9** (**be jumping**) informal (of a place) be very lively.

– SYNONYMS **1 leap,** spring, bound, vault, hop, skip, caper, dance, prance. **2** *pretax profits jumped* **rise,** go up, shoot up, soar, surge, climb, increase; informal skyrocket. **3** *the noise made her jump* **start,** jolt, flinch, recoil, shudder.

▶ **noun 1** an act of jumping. **2** a large or sudden change or increase. **3** an obstacle to be jumped by a horse.

– SYNONYMS **1 leap,** spring, bound, hop, skip. **2 rise,** leap, increase, upsurge, upswing; informal hike. **3 start,** jerk, spasm, shudder.

– PHRASES **get** (or **have**) **the jump on someone** informal get (or have) an advantage over someone as a result of one's prompt action. **jump down someone's throat** informal respond to someone in a sudden and angry way. **jump out** have a strong visual or mental impact; be very striking: *advertising posters that really jump out at you.* **jump ship** (of a sailor) leave a ship without permission. **jump through hoops** go through a complicated procedure in order to achieve something. **one jump ahead** one stage ahead of a rival.
– ORIGIN probably imitating the sound of feet landing on the ground.

jump cut ▶ **noun** (in movies or television) an abrupt transition from one scene to another.

jumped-up ▶ **adjective** informal considering oneself to be more important than one really is.

jump·er[1] /'jəmpər/ ▶ **noun 1** a collarless sleeveless dress, usually worn over a blouse. **2** Brit. a sweater.
– ORIGIN perhaps from Old French *jupe* 'loose jacket or tunic.'

jump·er[2] ▶ **noun** a person or animal that jumps.

jump·er ca·ble ▶ **noun** each of a pair of cables fitted with clips at either end, used for recharging a battery in a motor vehicle by connecting it to the battery in another.

jump jet ▶ **noun** a jet aircraft that can take off and land vertically.

jump-off ▶ **noun** a deciding round in a show-jumping competition.

jump rope ▶ **noun** a length of rope used for jumping by swinging it over the head and under the feet.

jump-start ▶ **verb 1** start a car with a dead battery by using jumper cables or by a sudden release of the clutch while it is being pushed. **2** give impetus to something that is progressing slowly or has stopped. ▶ **noun** an act of jump-starting something.

jump·suit /'jəm(p),so͞ot/ ▶ **noun** a one-piece garment incorporating a pair of pants and a sleeved top.
– ORIGIN first referring to a garment worn when parachuting.

jump·y /'jəmpē/ ▶ **adjective** (**jumpier, jumpiest**) informal **1** anxious and uneasy. **2** stopping and starting abruptly.

– SYNONYMS **nervous,** on edge, edgy, tense, anxious, restless, fidgety, keyed up, overwrought; informal jittery, uptight, het up, antsy.
– ANTONYMS calm.

– DERIVATIVES **jump·i·ly** adverb **jump·i·ness** noun.

Jun. ▶ **abbreviation** June.

jun·co /'jəNGkō/ ▶ **noun** (pl. **juncos**) a small North American songbird related to the buntings, with mainly gray and brown plumage.
– ORIGIN from Latin *juncus* 'rush, reed.'

junc·tion /'jəNGkSHən/ ▶ **noun 1** a point where two or more things meet or are joined. **2** a place where roads or railroad lines meet. **3** the action of joining things or the state of being joined.

– SYNONYMS **crossroads,** intersection, interchange, turn, turnoff, cloverleaf, exit.

– ORIGIN from Latin *jungere* 'to join.'

junc·tion box ▶ **noun** a box containing a junction of electric wires or cables.

junc·ture /'jəNGkCHər/ ▶ **noun 1** a particular point in time. **2** a place where things join.
– ORIGIN Latin *junctura* 'joint.'

June /jo͞on/ ▶ **noun** the sixth month of the year.
– ORIGIN from Latin *Junius mensis* 'month of June,' from *Junonius* 'sacred to the goddess Juno.'

June bug ▶ **noun** a large brown scarab beetle that appears in late spring and early summer.

June·teenth /,jo͞on'tēnTH/ ▶ **noun** a festival held annually on June 19 by some African Americans to commemorate emancipation from slavery in Texas on that day in 1865.
– ORIGIN blend of *June* and *(nine)teenth.*

Jung·i·an /'yo͝oNGgēən/ ▶ **adjective** relating to the Swiss psychologist Carl Jung or his work. ▶ **noun** a follower of Jung or his work.

jun·gle /'jəNGgəl/ ▶ **noun 1** an area of land with dense forest and tangled vegetation, typically in the tropics. **2** a very complex or competitive situation: *a jungle of competing technologies.* **3** a style of dance music with very fast electronic drum tracks and slower synthesized bass lines.
– DERIVATIVES **jun·gly** adjective.
– PHRASES **the law of the jungle** the principle that people who are strongest and most selfish will be most successful.
– ORIGIN Sanskrit, 'rough and arid terrain.'

jun·gle gym ▶ **noun** a structure of connected bars or rope for children to climb on.

jun·glist /ˈjəNGglist/ ▶ **noun** a performer or fan of jungle music. ▶ **adjective** of or relating to jungle music.

jun·ior /ˈjo͞onyər/ ▶ **adjective** **1** relating to young or younger people. **2** relating to students in the third year of a four-year course at college or high school. **3** (after a name) referring to the younger of two people with the same name in a family. **4** low or lower in rank or status: *a junior officer*.

– SYNONYMS **younger,** minor, subordinate, lower, lesser, low-ranking, inferior, secondary.
– ANTONYMS senior, older.

▶ **noun** **1** a person who is a specified number of years younger than someone else: *he's five years her junior*. **2** a student in the third year at college or high school. **3** (in sports) a young competitor, typically under the age of 16 or 18. **4** a person with low rank or status.
– ORIGIN Latin.

jun·ior col·lege ▶ **noun** a two-year college offering complete courses of training or preparation for completion at a four-year college.

jun·ior high school ▶ **noun** a school intermediate between an elementary school and a high school.

ju·ni·per /ˈjo͞onəpər/ ▶ **noun** an evergreen shrub or small tree with berries that are used to flavor gin.
– ORIGIN Latin *juniperus*.

junk[1] /jəNGk/ ▶ **noun** informal **1** useless or worthless articles or material; rubbish. **2** heroin.

– SYNONYMS **rubbish,** clutter, odds and ends, bric-a-brac, refuse, trash, litter, scrap, waste, debris.

▶ **verb** informal get rid of something regarded as worthless or useless.
– ORIGIN unknown.

junk[2] ▶ **noun** a flat-bottomed sailboat used in China and the East Indies.
– ORIGIN Malay.

junk bond ▶ **noun** a high-yielding high-risk security, typically issued to finance a takeover.

junk DNA ▶ **noun** genomic DNA that does not encode proteins and whose function is not well understood.

jun·ket /ˈjəNGkit/ ▶ **noun** **1** a dish of sweetened curds of milk. **2** informal an extravagant trip enjoyed by officials at public expense. ▶ **verb** (**junkets, junketing, junketed**) informal take part in an extravagant trip at public expense.
– ORIGIN first referring to a cream cheese made in a rush basket: from Old French *jonquette* 'rush basket.'

junk food ▶ **noun** preprepared food with little nutritional value.

junk·ie /ˈjəNGkē/ (also **junky**) ▶ **noun** informal **1** a drug addict. **2** a person with an obsessive interest in or enthusiasm for something: *a media junkie*.
– ORIGIN from JUNK[1].

junk mail ▶ **noun** informal unsolicited advertising or promotional material received through the mail or email.

junk·y /ˈjəNGkē/ ▶ **adjective** useless or of little value: *her junky blue car*. ▶ **noun** (pl. **junkies**) variant spelling of JUNKIE.

junk·yard /ˈjəNGk,yärd/ ▶ **noun** a place where scrap is collected before being discarded, reused, or recycled.

Ju·no·esque /,jo͞onōˈesk/ ▶ **adjective** (of a woman) tall and shapely.
– ORIGIN named after the Roman goddess *Juno*.

jun·ta /ˈho͞ontə, ˈjəntə/ ▶ **noun** a military or political group that rules a country after taking power by force.
– ORIGIN Spanish and Portuguese, 'deliberative or administrative council.'

Ju·pi·ter /ˈjo͞opitər/ ▶ **noun** the largest planet in the solar system, fifth in order from the sun.

Ju·ras·sic /jəˈrasik/ ▶ **adjective** Geology relating to the second period of the Mesozoic era (about 208 to 146 million years ago), when large reptiles were dominant and the first birds appeared.
– ORIGIN French *jurassique*, from the *Jura* Mountains between France and Switzerland.

ju·rid·i·cal /jo͝oˈridikəl/ ▶ **adjective** Law relating to judicial action and the law.
– DERIVATIVES **ju·rid·i·cal·ly** adverb.
– ORIGIN Latin *juridicus*.

ju·ris·dic·tion /,jo͝orisˈdiksHən/ ▶ **noun** **1** the official power to make legal decisions and judgments: *the Arizona court had no jurisdiction over the defendants*. **2** the area or sphere of activity over which the legal authority of a court or other institution extends. **3** a system of courts of law.
– DERIVATIVES **ju·ris·dic·tion·al** adjective.
– ORIGIN Latin.

CHOOSE THE RIGHT WORD

jurisdiction, authority, command, dominion, power, sovereignty, sway

The **authority** of our elected officials refers to their *power* (often conferred by rank or office) to give orders, require obedience, or make decisions. Their authority is normally limited by their **jurisdiction**, which is a legally predetermined division of a larger whole, within which someone has a right to rule or decide (*the matter was beyond his jurisdiction*). The president of the United States has more **power** than any other American official, which means that he has the ability to exert force or control over something. He does not, however, have the *authority* to make laws on his own. As commander in chief, he does have **command** over the nation's armed forces, implying that he has the kind of authority that can enforce obedience. Back in the days when Great Britain had **dominion**, or supreme authority, over the American colonies, it was the king of England who held **sway** over this country's economic and political life—an old-fashioned word that stresses the sweeping scope of one's power. But his **sovereignty**, which emphasizes absolute or autonomous rule over something considered as a whole, was eventually challenged. The rest, as they say, is history.

ju·ris·pru·dence /,jo͝orisˈpro͞odns/ ▶ **noun** **1** the theory or philosophy of law. **2** a legal system.
– DERIVATIVES **ju·ris·pru·den·tial** /-pro͞oˈdencHəl/ adjective.
– ORIGIN Latin *jurisprudentia*.

ju·rist /ˈjo͝orist/ ▶ **noun** **1** a lawyer or a judge. **2** an expert in law.
– DERIVATIVES **ju·ris·tic** /jo͝oˈristik/ adjective.
– ORIGIN Latin *jurista*.

ju·ror /ˈjo͝orər, -ôr/ ▶ **noun** a member of a jury.

ju·ry /ˈjo͝orē/ ▶ **noun** (pl. **juries**) **1** a group of people (typically twelve) sworn to give a verdict in a legal case on the basis of evidence given in court. **2** a group of people judging a competition.
– PHRASES **the jury is out** a decision has not yet been reached.
– ORIGIN Old French *juree* 'oath, inquiry.'

ju·ry-rigged ▸ **adjective 1** (of a ship) having makeshift rigging. **2** makeshift; improvised.
– DERIVATIVES **ju·ry-rig** verb.
– ORIGIN *jury* perhaps from Old French *ajurie* 'aid.'

jus /zHo͞o(s), jo͞os/ ▸ **noun** (especially in French cuisine) a thin gravy or sauce made from meat juices.
– ORIGIN French, 'juice.'

just /jəst/ ▸ **adjective 1** morally right and fair. **2** appropriate or deserved: *we got our just deserts.* **3** (of an opinion) well founded; justifiable.

> – SYNONYMS **1** *a just society* **fair,** fair-minded, equitable, even-handed, impartial, unbiased, objective, neutral, disinterested, unprejudiced, honorable, upright, decent, principled. **2** *a just reward* **deserved,** well deserved, well earned, merited, rightful, due, proper, fitting, appropriate, defensible, justified, justifiable.
> – ANTONYMS unfair.

▸ **adverb 1** exactly. **2** exactly or nearly at this or that moment. **3** very recently. **4** by a small amount. **5** simply; only.

> – SYNONYMS **1 exactly,** precisely, absolutely, completely, totally, entirely, perfectly, utterly, thoroughly; informal dead. **2 narrowly,** only just, by a hair's breadth, by the skin of one's teeth, barely, scarcely, hardly; informal by a whisker.

– DERIVATIVES **just·ly** adverb **just·ness** noun.
– PHRASES **just in case** as a precaution. **just so 1** arranged or done very carefully. **2** formal expressing agreement.
– ORIGIN Latin *justus*.

jus·tice /'jəstis/ ▸ **noun 1** behavior or treatment that is morally right and fair. **2** the quality of being right and fair: *the justice of his case.* **3** the administration of law in a way that is fair and morally right. **4** a judge or magistrate.

> – SYNONYMS **1 fairness,** justness, fair play, fair-mindedness, equity, right, rightness, even-handedness, honesty, morality. **2 validity,** justification, soundness, well-foundedness, legitimacy. **3 judge,** jurist, magistrate, justice of the peace, sheriff.

– PHRASES **bring someone to justice** arrest and try someone in court for a crime. **do oneself justice** perform as well as one is able. **do someone/thing justice** treat someone or something with due fairness.
– ORIGIN Old French *justise* 'administration of the law.'

> **WORD LINKS**
>
> **judicial** *relating to a system of justice*

jus·tice of the peace ▸ **noun** a magistrate appointed to hear minor cases, perform marriages, grant licenses, etc., in a town, county, or other local district.

jus·ti·ci·a·ble /jə'stisH(ē)əbəl/ ▸ **adjective** Law subject to trial in a court of law.

jus·ti·fi·a·ble /'jəstə,fīəbəl, ,jəstə'fī-/ ▸ **adjective** able to be shown to be right or reasonable: *the paper takes justifiable pride in its political coverage.*

> – SYNONYMS **valid,** legitimate, warranted, well founded, justified, just, reasonable, tenable, defensible, sound, warrantable.
> – ANTONYMS unjustifiable, unwarranted.

– DERIVATIVES **jus·ti·fi·a·bil·i·ty** /,jəstə,fīə'bilitē/ noun **jus·ti·fi·a·bly** adverb.

jus·ti·fi·ca·tion /,jəstəfi'kāsHən/ ▸ **noun 1** the action of justifying something. **2** good reason for something that exists or has been done: *there's no justification for the job losses.*

> – SYNONYMS **grounds,** reason, basis, rationale, premise, vindication, explanation, defense, argument, case.

jus·ti·fy /'jəstə,fī/ ▸ **verb (justifies, justifying, justified) 1** prove something to be right or reasonable. **2** be a good reason for: *the situation was grave enough to justify further investigation.* **3** adjust written words so that the lines of type form straight edges at both sides.

> – SYNONYMS **1 give grounds for,** give reasons for, explain, account for, defend, vindicate, excuse, exonerate. **2 warrant,** be good reason for.

– DERIVATIVES **jus·tif·i·ca·to·ry** /jə'stifəkə,tôrē, ,jəstəfi'kātôrē/ adjective **jus·ti·fi·er** noun.
– ORIGIN Latin *justificare* 'do justice to.'

jut /jət/ ▸ **verb (juts, jutting, jutted)** extend out, over, or beyond the main body or line of something.

> – SYNONYMS **stick out,** project, protrude, bulge out, overhang, beetle.

– ORIGIN from **JET**[1].

Jute /jo͞ot/ ▸ **noun** a member of a Germanic people that settled in southern Britain in the 5th century.
– DERIVATIVES **Jut·ish** adjective.
– ORIGIN Old English.

jute /jo͞ot/ ▸ **noun** rough fiber made from the stems of a tropical plant, used for making rope or sacking.
– ORIGIN Bengali.

ju·ve·nile /'jo͞ovə,nīl, -vənl/ ▸ **adjective 1** relating to young people or animals. **2** childish; immature.

> – SYNONYMS **1 young,** teenage, adolescent, junior. **2 childish,** immature, puerile, infantile, babyish.
> – ANTONYMS adult, mature.

▸ **noun 1** a young person or animal. **2** Law a person below the age at which ordinary criminal prosecution is possible (18 in most countries).

> – SYNONYMS **child,** youngster, teenager, adolescent, minor, junior; informal kid.
> – ANTONYMS adult.

– DERIVATIVES **ju·ve·nil·i·ty** /jo͞ovə'nilitē/ noun.
– ORIGIN Latin *juvenilis*.

> **WORD TOOLKIT**
>
> See **YOUTHFUL**.

ju·ve·nile de·lin·quen·cy ▸ **noun** the regular committing of criminal acts by a young person.
– DERIVATIVES **ju·ve·nile de·lin·quent** noun.

ju·ve·nil·i·a /,jo͞ovə'nilēə/ ▸ **plural noun** works produced by an author or artist when young.
– ORIGIN Latin.

jux·ta·pose /'jəkstə,pōz, ,jəkstə'pōz/ ▸ **verb** place things close together, especially so as to show a contrast: *a world of obscene extravagance juxtaposed with abject poverty.*
– DERIVATIVES **jux·ta·po·si·tion** /,jəkstəpə'zisHən/ noun.
– ORIGIN French *juxtaposer*.

Language Guide

1. Grammar

Grammar is the system and structure of a language. It embodies all the principles by which the language works. All good writing begins with an understanding of the fundamentals of grammar: parts of speech and how they combine into phrases, clauses, sentences, and paragraphs.

■ PARTS OF SPEECH

Noun

A noun is a word that identifies or names a person, place, thing, action, or quality. There are two types of nouns: proper and common.

PROPER NOUNS

A noun that names a particular person, place, or thing is a **proper noun**. It always begins with a capital letter:

Benito Mussolini	Cairo	the Chrysler Building
Jell-O	Mount Everest	

COMMON NOUNS

A noun that names a type of person, place, or thing is a **common noun**. There are three kinds of common nouns: concrete, abstract, and collective.

A **concrete noun** names someone or something that you can see or touch:

arm	giraffe	hamburger
lake	stapler	

An **abstract noun** names something intangible (that is, something that can neither be seen nor touched):

assistance	bravery	disappointment
flavor	wit	

A **collective noun** names a group of persons or things:

audience	colony	herd
platoon	set	

SINGULAR AND PLURAL NOUNS

A noun that names one person, place, or thing is **singular**. A noun that names more than one person, place, or thing is **plural**. The spelling of a singular noun almost always changes when it becomes a plural. Most plurals can be formed by adding *s* or *es*, but many nouns do not follow this format.

bean/beans; fort/forts
beach/beaches; toothbrush/toothbrushes
leaf/leaves; party/parties; woman/women

If the spelling of a plural noun is in doubt, it is always advisable to consult a dictionary.

APPOSITIVES

An **appositive** is a noun (or a unit of words that acts as a noun) whose meaning is a direct copy or extension of the meaning of the preceding noun in the sentence. In other words, the appositive and the preceding noun refer to the same person, place, or thing. The appositive helps to characterize or elaborate on the preceding noun in a specific way.

The wedding cake, a chocolate <u>masterpiece</u>, was the hit of the reception.
[The noun *cake* and the appositive *masterpiece* are the same thing.]

His primary objective, <u>to write the great American novel</u>, was never realized.
[The noun *objective* and the appositive *to write the great American novel* are the same thing.]

Eleanor's math teacher, <u>Mrs. Kennedy</u>, is retiring next year.
[The noun *teacher* and the appositive *Mrs. Kennedy* are the same person.]

POSSESSIVES

A **possessive** is a noun whose form has changed in order to show possession. Certain rules can be followed to determine how the form should change for any given noun.

In the case of a singular noun, add an apostrophe and an *s*:

<u>Lincoln's</u> inaugural address
<u>the baby's</u> favorite blanket

EXCEPTION: Most singular nouns that end in *s* follow the preceding rule with no difficulty (e.g., *Chris's*, *Dickens's*), but some singular nouns that end in *s* may be exempted from the rule because the pronunciation of the plural is less awkward with just an apostrophe and no final *s*:

<u>Ramses'</u> dynasty
<u>Aristophanes'</u> great comedic works

In the case of a plural noun that ends in *s*, add just an apostrophe:

the <u>Lincolns'</u> summer home
our <u>babies'</u> double stroller

In the case of a plural noun that does not end in *s*, add an apostrophe and an *s*:

<u>men's</u> footwear
the <u>fungi's</u> rapid reproduction

In the case of a compound noun (a noun made of more than one word), only the last word takes the possessive form:

my <u>sister-in-law's</u> house
the <u>commander in chief's</u> personal staff

In the case of joint possession (that is, where two or more nouns possess the same thing together), only the last of the possessing nouns takes the possessive form:

<u>Ryan and Saul's</u> nickel collection
[There is only one nickel collection, and *both* Ryan and Saul own it *together*.]

<u>Gramma and Grampa's</u> photo albums
[However many photo albums there may be, they all belong to *both* Gramma and Grampa *together*.]

In the case of individual possession by two or more nouns (that is, two or more nouns possess the same type of thing, but separately and distinctly), each of the possessing nouns takes the possessive form:

<u>Lenny's and Suzanne's</u> footprints on the beach
[Lenny and Suzanne *each* left *their own distinct* footprints on the beach.]

<u>Strauss's and Khachaturian's</u> waltzes
[Strauss and Khachaturian *each* composed *their own distinct* waltzes.]

Pronoun

A **pronoun** is a word that represents a person or thing without giving the specific name of the person or thing. There are five classes of pronouns: personal, relative, demonstrative, indefinite, and interrogative.

A **personal pronoun** is used to refer to the person speaking (first person), the person spoken to (second person), or the person or thing spoken about (third person) and is always either singular (refering to one person or thing) or plural (refering to more than one person or thing). Here are the various forms of personal pronoun, which are explained further down:

Number	Person	Nominative	Objective	Possessive	Possessive used as an adjective	Reflexive
Singular	1st person	I	me	mine	my	myself
	2nd person	you	you	yours	your	yourself
	3rd person masculine	he	him	his	his	himself
	3rd person feminine	she	her	hers	her	herself
	3rd person neuter	it	it	its	its	itself
Plural	1st person	we	us	ours	our	ourselves
	2nd person	you	you	yours	your	yourselves
	3rd person	they	them	theirs	their	themselves

Reflexive personal pronouns are so called because they reflect the action of the verb back to the subject. It is incorrect to use a reflexive pronoun as the subject of a verb.

incorrect:	Denise and myself will fix the car. [The reflexive pronoun *myself* has no subject to refer to; the wording should be "Denise and I."]
correct:	I just hurt myself. [The reflexive pronoun *myself* refers to the subject *I*.]

A reflexive pronoun that adds force or emphasis to a noun or another pronoun is called "intensive":

You yourself must return the ladder.
Terri and Phil want to wallpaper the kitchen themselves.

A **relative pronoun** introduces a descriptive clause. The relative pronouns are *which, that, who, whoever, whose, whom,* and *whomever.*

Wendy was the pianist who won the scholarship.
Is Mr. Leonard the teacher whose book was just published?
Whoever wrote the speech is a genius.
I attended the morning meeting, which lasted for three hours.

A **demonstrative pronoun** is specific. It is used to point out particular persons, places, or things. The demonstrative pronouns are *this, that, these,* and *those.*

These are the finest fabrics available.
I'll look at those first.
What is this?

An **indefinite pronoun** is nonspecific. It is used to refer to persons, places, or things without particular identification. There are numerous indefinite pronouns, including the following:

all	everyone	none
any	everything	no one
anybody	few	other
anyone	little	others
anything	many	several
both	most	some
each	much	somebody
either	neither	someone
everybody	nobody	something

George brought two desserts, but I didn't try either.
Many are called, but few are chosen.
Can somebody please answer the phone?

An **interrogative pronoun** is used to ask a question. The interrogative pronouns are *who, which,* and *what.*

Who wants to buy a raffle ticket?
Which of the two applicants has more practical experience?
What is the purpose of another debate?

PRONOUN CASES

The case of a pronoun is what determines its relation to the other words in the sentence. There are three pronoun cases: nominative, objective, and possessive.

Nominative case

The nominative pronouns are *I*, *you*, *he*, *she*, *it*, *we*, *they*, *who*, and *whoever*.

A pronoun that is the subject (or part of the subject) of a sentence is in the nominative case:

They loved the movie.
Mark and I are going to the Bahamas

A pronoun that is a predicate is in the nominative case:

It was she who wrote the poem.
The winner will probably be you.

However, the nominative can sometimes sound dated:

Who is there? It is I.
["It is me" would be more colloquial.]

Objective case

The objective pronouns are *me*, *you*, *him*, *her*, *it*, *us*, *them*, *whom*, and *whomever*.

A pronoun that is the direct object of a verb is in the objective case:

Stephen already invited them.
Should we keep it?

A pronoun that is the indirect object of a verb is in the objective case:

Captain Mackenzie told us many seafaring tales.
I'll give you the recipe tomorrow.

A pronoun that is the object of a preposition is in the objective case:

Does she think this job is beneath her?
To whom was it addressed?

Possessive case

A possessive pronoun shows ownership.

The possessive pronouns used as predicate nominatives are *mine*, *yours*, *his*, *hers*, *its*, *ours*, *theirs*, and *whose*.

The blue station wagon is mine.
None of the cash was theirs.

The possessive pronouns used as adjectives are *my*, *your*, *his*, *her*, *its*, *our*, *their*, and *whose*.

Whose test scores were the highest?
I believe this is your package.

TIP

A possessive pronoun never has an apostrophe. Remember, the word *it's* is the contraction of *it is* or *it has*—not the possessive form of *it*, whereas *its* is like *yours*, *ours*, etc.

- possessive: Life has its ups and downs.
- contraction: It's good to see you.

SINGULAR AND PLURAL AGREEMENT

It is important to identify a pronoun as singular or plural and to make certain that the associated verb form is in agreement. The pronouns that tend to cause the most problems for writers and speakers are the indefinite pronouns.

Some indefinite pronouns are always singular and therefore always require a singular verb. These include *everybody*, *everyone*, *somebody*, *someone*, *nobody*, *one*, *either*, and *neither*.

Nobody wants to leave.
Don't get up unless someone knocks on the door.
Either of these two colors is fine.

Other indefinite pronouns may be singular or plural, depending on the particular reference. These include *any*, *all*, *some*, *most*, and *none*.

If any of these marbles are yours, let me know.
[The noun *marbles* is plural.]

If any of this cake is yours, let me know.
[The noun *cake* is singular.]

Most of the potatoes are already gone.
[The noun *potatoes* is plural.]

Most of the evening is already gone.
[The noun *evening* is singular.]

Verb

A **verb** is a word that expresses an action or a state of being.

An **action verb** expresses a physical or mental action:

break	eat	intercept
operate	unveil	wish

A **state of being verb** expresses a condition or state of being:

be	become	is
lack	seem	smell

TRANSITIVE VERBS

A **transitive verb** expresses an action that is performed on someone or something. The someone or something is the **direct object**. Notice in each of the following examples that the direct object receives the action of the verb.

Ingrid restores antique furniture.
[transitive verb: *restores*; direct object: *furniture*]

Hernandez pitched the ball.
[transitive verb: *pitched*; direct object: *ball*]

Did you feed the children?
[transitive verb: *feed*; direct object: *children*]

Sometimes a transitive verb has both a direct object and an indirect object. An **indirect object** is the person or thing to whom or for whom the verb's action is being performed. Notice in each of the following examples that the direct object receives the action of the verb, while the indirect object identifies who or what the action affected.

The captain handed us our orders.
[transitive verb: *handed*; direct object: *orders*; indirect object: *us*]

Did you give the plants some water?
[transitive verb: *give*; direct object: *water*; indirect object: *plants*]

I tossed a pen to Herman.
[transitive verb: *tossed*; direct object: *pen*; indirect object: *Herman*]

TIP

Remember: A direct object answers *what or whom?* An indirect object answers *to what or whom?* or *for what or whom?* These questions demonstrate how to find the direct and indirect objects in the six example sentences above:

direct objects:	*What* does Ingrid restore?	furniture
	What did Hernandez pitch?	ball
	Whom did you feed?	children
	What did the captain hand?	orders
	Did you give *what*?	water
	What did I toss?	pen
indirect objects:	*To whom* did the captain hand orders?	us
	Did you give water *to what*?	plants
	To whom did I toss a pen?	Herman

INTRANSITIVE VERBS

An **intransitive verb** does not have an object. Notice in each of the following examples that the verb expresses an action that occurs without needing to be received.

We marched in the parade.
The tea kettle whistled.
Heidi sleeps on the third floor.

TIP

Remember: Because an intransitive verb does not have an object, the question *what or whom?* will be unanswerable in respect of the three example sentences above.

What did we march?

Whom did the kettle whistle?

What does Heidi sleep?

These questions simply cannot be answered; therefore the verbs are intransitive.

LINKING VERBS

A **linking verb** joins a word (or unit of words) that names a person or thing to another word (or unit of words) that renames or describes the person or thing. It is always intransitive and always expresses a state of being. The most common linking verbs are *to be* and all its forms, which include *am*, *is*, *was*, *are*, and *were*.

Other common linking verbs include the following:

act	appear	become
feel	grow	look
remain	seem	smell
sound	taste	turn

The air seemed humid yesterday.
What smells so good?
The days grow shorter.
I am a registered voter.
Kim remains a devout Catholic.
Butch and Sundance were the title characters.

Predicate adjectives and nominatives

The word (or unit of words) that a linking verb joins to the subject can be either an adjective or a noun, but its function is always the same: to tell something about the subject. An adjective that follows a linking verb is a **predicate adjective**. A noun that follows a linking verb is a **predicate nominative.**

predicate adjective: The air seemed humid yesterday.
What smells so good?
The days grow shorter.

predicate nominative: I am a registered voter.
Kim remains a devout Catholic.
Butch and Sundance were the title characters.

VOICE

The subject of a transitive verb either performs or receives the action. A verb whose subject performs is said to be in the **active voice.** A verb whose subject receives is said to be in the **passive voice.**

active voice: Brainerd & Sons built the storage shed.
[The subject *Brainerd & Sons* performed the action of building.]

Lucy will clean the kitchen.
[The subject *Lucy* will perform the action of cleaning.]

passive voice: The storage shed was built by Brainerd & Sons.
[The subject *shed* received the action of building.]

The kitchen will be cleaned by Lucy.
[The subject *kitchen* will receive the action of cleaning.]

MOOD

Verbs have a quality that shows the attitude or purpose of the speaker. This quality is called the **mood**. There are three verb moods: indicative, imperative, and subjunctive.

The **indicative mood** shows a statement or question of fact:

Does Paula know the combination to the safe?
Dr. Sliva is my dentist.

The **imperative mood** shows a command or request:

Make the most of your situation.
Proceed to the third traffic light.

The **subjunctive mood** shows a condition of doubtfulness, possibility, desirability, improbability, or unreality:

Should you decide to return the blouse, you will need the receipt.
If I were rich, I'd quit my job.

PERSON AND NUMBER

The **person** (first, second, or third) of a verb depends on to whom or to what the verb refers: the person speaking (first person), the person spoken to (second person), or the person or thing spoken about (third person).

The **number** (singular or plural) of a verb depends on whether the verb refers to a singular subject or a plural subject.

For nearly all verbs, the form of the verb changes only in the third person singular.

Person	Singular	Plural
first person	I *know*	we *know*
second person	you *know*	you *know*
third person	he *knows* she *knows* it *knows* Chris *knows* the teacher *knows*	they *know* Chris and Pat *know* the teachers *know*

TENSE

The **tense** of a verb shows the time of the verb's action. There are six verb tenses: present, present perfect, past, past perfect, future, and future perfect.

The **present tense** shows action occurring in the present:

I smell fresh coffee.

The present tense can also show the following:

action that is typical or habitual:	I design greenhouses. Stuart daydreams during math class.
action that will occur:	Lynne retires in six months. Our plane lands at midnight.
facts and beliefs:	March follows February. Greed destroys the spirit.

TIP

Yet another function of the present tense is what is called the historical present. This usage allows the writer or speaker to relate past actions in a present tone, which may enhance the descriptive flow of the text:

> The United States acquires the Oklahoma Territory from France in 1803 as part of the Louisiana Purchase. Following the War of 1812, the U.S. government begins a relocation program, forcing Indian tribes from the eastern United States to move into certain unsettled western areas, including Oklahoma. Because of their opposition to the U.S. government, most of these native people lend their support to the Confederate South during the American Civil War. In 1865, the war ends in utter defeat for the Confederacy, and all of the Oklahoma Territory soon falls under U.S. military rule.

When using the historical present, writers and speakers must be careful not to lapse into the past tense. For example, it would be an incorrect mix of tenses to say, "In 1865, the war ended in utter defeat for the Confederacy, and all of the Oklahoma Territory soon falls under U.S. military rule."

The **present perfect tense** is formed with the word *has* or *have*. It shows action begun in the past and completed by the time of the present:

James has checked the air in the tires at least three times.
I have read the book you're talking about.

The **past tense** shows action that occurred in the past:

Greg memorized his speech.
The mouse scurried across the room.

The **past perfect tense** is formed with the word *had*. It shows action that occurred in the past, prior to another past action:

Eugene had finished his story by the time we got to the airport.
The parrot had flown into another room long before we noticed an empty cage.

The **future tense** is formed with the word *will*. It shows action that is expected to occur in the future:

The president will address the nation this evening.
Tempers will flare when the truth comes out.

The **future perfect tense** is formed with the words *will have*. It shows action that is expected to occur in the future, prior to another future or expected action:

Noreen will have finished painting by the time we're ready to lay the carpet.
The candidates will have traveled thousands of miles before this campaign is over.

VERBALS

A verb form that acts as a part of speech other than a verb is a **verbal**. There are three types of verbals: infinitives, participles, and gerunds.

An **infinitive** is a verb form that can act as a noun, an adjective, or an adverb. It is preceded by the preposition *to*.

noun:	To steal is a crime. [The infinitive *to steal* is the subject.]
	Our original plan, to elope, was never discovered. [The infinitive *to elope* is an appositive.]
adjective:	Those are words to remember. [The infinitive *to remember* modifies the noun *words*.]
adverb:	The hill was too icy to climb. [The infinitive *to climb* modifies the predicate adjective *icy*.]
	He lived to golf. [The infinitive *to golf* modifies the verb *lived*.]

A **participle** is a verb form that has one of two uses: to make a verb phrase ("they were trying"; "the car has died") or to act as an adjective. A participle is a verbal only when it acts as an adjective.

A **present participle** always ends in *-ing*:

catching
laughing
winding

A **past participle** usually ends in *-ed*, *-en*, or *-t*:

given
lost
toasted

In the following examples, each participle acts as an adjective and is therefore a verbal:

Does the zoo have a laughing hyena?
We live on a winding road.
It was a lost opportunity.
Add a cup of toasted coconut.

A **gerund** is a verb form that acts as a noun. It always ends in *-ing*:

Reading is my favorite pastime.
The next step, varnishing, should be done in a well-ventilated area.
The doctor suggested guidelines for sensible dieting.

TIP

Remember: Both gerunds and present participles always end in *-ing*, but their functions are quite distinct. Also remember that a present participle is only a verbal when it acts as an adjective, *not* when it acts as a verb phrase.

verbal:	Her singing has improved this year. [Used as a noun, *singing* is a gerund, which is always a verbal.]
	Peterson hired the singing cowboys. [Used as an adjective, *singing* is a present participle that is also a verbal.]
not a verbal:	The birds are singing. [Used to form a verb phrase, *singing* is a present participle, but not a verbal]

Adjective

An **adjective** is a word that modifies a noun. There are two basic types of adjectives: descriptive and limiting.

DESCRIPTIVE ADJECTIVES

A **descriptive adjective** describes a noun. That is, it shows a quality or condition of a noun:

She is an upstanding citizen.
Josh has invited his zany friends.
That was a mighty clap of thunder.
I prefer the white shirt with the long sleeves.

Comparison of adjectives

Descriptive adjectives are able to indicate qualities and conditions by three degrees of comparison: positive, comparative, and superlative. Adjectives may be compared in downward or upward order.

For **downward comparisons**, all adjectives use the words *less* (comparative) and *least* (superlative).

DOWNWARD COMPARISONS

Positive	Comparative	Superlative
(the quality or condition)	(a degree lower than the positive)	(the lowest degree of the positive)
intelligent	less intelligent	least intelligent
kind	less kind	least kind
salty	less salty	least salty

For **upward comparisons**, there are three different formats:

UPWARD COMPARISONS

Positive	Comparative	Superlative
(the quality or condition)	(a degree higher than the positive)	(the highest degree of the positive)

1. Almost all one-syllable adjectives use the endings *-er* (comparative) and *-est* (superlative). Some adjectives with two or more syllables follow this format as well.

kind	kinder	kindest
straight	straighter	straightest
salty	saltier	saltiest

2. Most adjectives with two or more syllables use the words *more* (comparative) and *most* (superlative). Most one-syllable adjectives may use this format as an optional alternative to using *-er* and *-est*.

harmonious	more harmonious	most harmonious
impatient	more impatient	most impatient
talkative	more talkative	most talkative
kind	more kind	most kind

3. Some adjectives have irregular forms.

bad/ill	worse	worst
good/well	better	best
far	farther/further	farthest/furthest
little	less	least
many	more	most

TIP

Never "double compare" an adjective. Remember:

- Sometimes a descriptive adjective may use either *-er* or *more*, but it never uses both.

  correct: The red grapes are sweeter than the green ones.
  The red grapes are more sweet than the green ones.

  incorrect: The red grapes are more sweeter than the green ones.

- Sometimes a descriptive adjective may use either *-est* or *most*, but it never uses both.

  correct: Samson is the friendliest dog in the building.
  Samson is the most friendly dog in the building.

  incorrect: Samson is the most friendliest dog in the building.

LIMITING ADJECTIVES

A **limiting adjective** shows the limits of a noun. That is, it indicates the number or quantity of a noun, or it points out a certain specificity of a noun. There are three types of limiting adjectives: numerical adjectives, pronominal adjectives, and articles.

A **numerical adjective** is a number. It may be cardinal ("how many") or ordinal ("in what order"):

cardinal: We have served one million customers.
There are three prizes.
After Arizona was admitted, there were forty-eight states.

ordinal: You are the one millionth customer.
We won third prize.
Arizona was the forty-eighth state to be admitted.

A **pronominal adjective** is a pronoun that acts as an adjective. A pronominal adjective may be personal (*my*, *your*, *his*, *her*, *its*, *our*, *their*), demonstrative (*this*, *that*, *these*, *those*), indefinite (*all*, *any*, *few*, *other*, *several*, *some*), or interrogative (*which*, *what*).

personal: We loved her goulash.
The squirrel returned to its nest.

demonstrative: Those directions are too complicated.
This window is broken.

indefinite: Pick any card from the deck.
All luggage will be inspected.

interrogative: Which radios are on sale?
What color is the upholstery?

There are three **articles** in English: *a*, *an*, and *the*. Articles are classified as either indefinite (*a*, *an*) or definite (*the*).

indefinite: At dawn, a helicopter broke the silence.
An usher seated us.

definite: The paintings lacked imagination.

Adverb

An **adverb** is a word that modifies a verb, an adjective, or another adverb.

ADVERB MEANINGS

An adverb usually describes how, where, when, or to what extent something happens.

An **adverb of manner** describes *how*:

They argued loudly.

An **adverb of place** describes *where*:

Please stay nearby.

An **adverb of time** describes *when*:

I'll call you later.

An **adverb of degree** describes *to what extent*:

The laundry is somewhat damp.

ADVERB FUNCTIONS

A **relative adverb** introduces a subordinate clause:

I'll be out on the veranda when the clock strikes twelve.

A **conjunctive adverb** (also called a **transitional adverb**) joins two independent clauses:

Dinner is ready; however, you may have to heat it up.

An **interrogative adverb** introduces a question:

Where did Lisa go?

TIP

A great number of adverbs are created by adding the suffix *-ly* to an adjective:

hesitant + *-ly* = hesitantly
strong + *-ly* = strongly

This does not mean, however, that all adverbs end in *-ly*.

adverbs: fast, seldom, now

Nor does it mean that all words ending in *-ly* are adverbs.

adjectives: friendly, homely, dastardly

The way to determine if a word is an adverb or an adjective is to see how it is used in the sentence:

- If it modifies a noun, it is an adjective.
- If it modifies a verb, an adjective, or another adverb, it is an adverb.

An **independent adverb** functions independently from the rest of the sentence. That is, the meaning and grammatical correctness of the sentence would not change if the independent adverb were removed:

Besides, I never liked living in the city.

COMPARISON OF ADVERBS

Like adjectives, adverbs of manner may be compared in three degrees: positive, comparative, and superlative.

Most adverbs, especially those that end in *-ly*, take on the upward comparing words *more* and *most*:

Positive	Comparative	Superlative
nicely	more nicely	most nicely
diligently	more diligently	most diligently

Some adverbs take on the upward comparing suffixes *-er* and *-est*:

Positive	Comparative	Superlative
early	earlier	earliest
soon	sooner	soonest
close	closer	closest

Some adverbs have irregular upward comparisons:

Positive	Comparative	Superlative
much	more	most
little	less	least
badly	worse	worst
well	better	best
far	farther/further	farthest/furthest

Almost all adverbs take on the downward comparing words *less* and *least*:

Positive	Comparative	Superlative
nicely	less nicely	least nicely
diligently	less diligently	least diligently
early	less early	least early
soon	less soon	least soon
close	less close	least close

Preposition

A **preposition** is a word or group of words that governs a noun or pronoun by expressing its relationship to another word in the clause.

The suspects landed <u>in</u> jail.
[The relationship between the noun *jail* and the verb *landed* is shown by the preposition *in*.]

Please hide the packages <u>under</u> the bed.
[The relationship between the noun *bed* and the noun *packages* is shown by the preposition *under*.]

The guitarist playing <u>with</u> our band is Samantha's uncle.
[The relationship between the noun *band* and the participle *playing* is shown by the preposition *with*.]

I already knew <u>about</u> it.
[The relationship between the pronoun *it* and the verb *knew* is shown by the preposition *about*.]

TIP

Many words used as prepositions may be used as other parts of speech as well:

The closest village is <u>over</u> that hill.	[preposition]
He leaned <u>over</u> and whispered in my ear.	[adverb]
I told no one <u>but</u> Corinne.	[preposition]
We played our best, <u>but</u> the other team won.	[conjunction]
She is <u>but</u> a shadow of her former self.	[adverb]

COMMON PREPOSITIONS

aboard	around	beneath	contrary to
about	as	beside	despite
above	as far as	besides	down
according to	as for	between	during
across	as to	beyond	except
after	aside from	but	for
against	at	but for	from
ahead	because of	by	in
along	before	by means of	in addition to
along with	behind	by way of	in back of
amid	below	concerning	in case of

in front of
in lieu of
in place of
in regard to
in spite of
inside
instead of
into
like
near
next to
of
off
on
on account of
on behalf of
onto
opposite
out
out of
outside
over
past
per
prior to
regarding
round
since
thanks to
through
throughout
till
to
toward
under
underneath
unlike
until
up
upon
up to
with
within
without

Conjunction

A **conjunction** is a word (or unit of words) that connects words, phrases, clauses, or sentences. There are three kinds of conjunctions: coordinating, subordinating, and correlative.

COORDINATING CONJUNCTIONS

A **coordinating conjunction** connects elements that have the same grammatical rank—that is, it connects words to words (nouns to nouns, verbs to verbs, etc.), phrases to phrases, clauses to clauses, sentences to sentences. A coordinating conjunction is almost always one of these seven words: *and*, *but*, *for*, *nor*, *or*, *so*, *yet*.

Would you prefer rice or potatoes?
[The coordinating conjunction *or* connects the two nouns *rice* and *potatoes*.]

I have seen and heard enough.
[The coordinating conjunction *and* connects the two verbs *seen* and *heard*.]

Vinnie's cat lay on the chair purring softly yet twitching its tail.
[The coordinating conjunction *yet* connects the two participial phrases *purring softly* and *twitching its tail*.]

O'Donnell is the reporter whose name is on the story but who denies having written it.
[The coordinating conjunction *but* connects the two subordinate clauses *whose name is on the story* and *who denies having written it*.]

We wanted to see batting practice, so we got to the stadium early.
[The coordinating conjunction *so* connects the two sentences *We wanted to see batting practice* and *We got to the stadium early*, creating one sentence. Notice that a comma precedes the conjunction when two sentences are joined.]

SUBORDINATING CONJUNCTIONS

A **subordinating conjunction** belongs to a subordinate clause. It connects the subordinate clause to a main clause.

I could get there on time if only the ferry were still running.
[The subordinating conjunction *if only* connects the subordinate clause *if only the ferry were still running* to the main clause *I could get there on time*.]

Common subordinating conjunctions

after	but	since	until
although	even if	so	when
as	even though	so that	whenever
as if	how	than	where
as long as	if	that	whereas
as though	if only	though	wherever
because	in order that	till	while
before	rather than	unless	why

CORRELATIVE CONJUNCTIONS

Two coordinating conjunctions that function together are called a pair of correlative conjunctions. These are the most common pairs of correlative conjunctions:

both . . . and	either . . . or	neither . . . nor
not only . . . but	not only . . . but also	whether . . . or

The site in Denver offers the potential for both security and expansion.
[The pair of correlative conjunctions *both . . . and* connects the two nouns *security* and *expansion*.]

I'm running in tomorrow's race whether it is sunny or rainy.
[The pair of correlative conjunctions *whether . . . or* connects the two adjectives *sunny* and *rainy*.]

TIP

It would be incorrect to say:

Their dog is neither quiet nor obeys simple commands.

Why? Because the pair of correlative conjunctions *neither . . . nor* is being used to connect the adjective *quiet* to the verb phrase *obeys simple commands*. This is not a grammatically valid connection.

Remember: A pair of correlative conjunctions is comprised of two coordinating conjunctions, and a coordinating conjunction must connect elements that have the same grammatical rank—that is, it must connect words to words (nouns to nouns, verbs to verbs, etc.), phrases to phrases, clauses to clauses, sentences to sentences.

Therefore, the sentence must be reworded to make the grammatical ranks match. Here are two such corrected versions:

Their dog is neither quiet nor obedient.
[The adjective *quiet* is connected to the adjective *obedient*.]

Their dog neither stays quiet nor obeys simple commands.
[The verb phrase *stays quiet* is connected to the verb phrase *obeys simple commands*.]

Interjection

An interjection is a word or phrase that expresses emotion, typically in an abrupt or emphatic way. It is not connected grammatically to the rest of the sentence. When the emotion expressed is very strong, the interjection is followed by an exclamation point. Otherwise it is followed by a comma:

Stop! I can't let you in here.
Yeah! Dempsey has won another fight.
Ah, that was a wonderful meal.
No, I don't think that's true.

TIP

Interjections occur more often in speech than in writing. It is not wrong to use interjections in writing, but writers should do so sparingly. Remember, an interjection is essentially an interruption, and too many may disrupt the flow of the text.

■ WORD GROUPS

Phrase

A **phrase** is a unit of words that acts as a single part of speech.

NOUN PHRASES

A phrase made up of a noun and its modifiers is a **noun phrase**:

The biggest pumpkin won a blue ribbon.
A magnificent whooping crane flew overhead.

Most noun phrases can be replaced with a pronoun:

Give the tickets to the tall, dark-haired gentleman.
Give the tickets to him.

VERB PHRASES

A phrase made up of a main verb and its auxiliaries is a **verb phrase** (also called a **complete verb**):

We have been waiting for three hours.
What type of music do you prefer?

ADJECTIVE PHRASES

A phrase made up of a participle and its related words is an **adjective phrase** (also called an **adjectival phrase** or a **participial phrase**). Acting as a single adjective, it modifies a noun or pronoun:

Awakened by the siren, we escaped to safety.
[The adjective phrase *Awakened by the siren* modifies the pronoun *we*.]

Following his grandmother's directions, Harry baked a beautiful apple pie.
[The adjective phrase *Following his grandmother's directions* modifies the noun *Harry*.]

PREPOSITIONAL PHRASES

A phrase that begins with a preposition is a **prepositional phrase**. It can act as an adjective or an adverb:

adjective: The car with the sunroof is mine.
[The noun *car* is modified by the prepositional phrase *with the sunroof*.]

adverb: After the storm, we gathered the fallen branches.
[The verb *gathered* is modified by the prepositional phrase *After the storm*.]

Clause

A clause is a unit of words that contains a subject and a predicate.

INDEPENDENT CLAUSES

A clause that can stand by itself as a complete thought is an **independent clause**. Any independent clause can stand alone as a complete sentence:

The Milwaukee Brewers joined the National League in November 1997.
It is snowing.
Vitus is the patron saint of actors.
Bob called.
The Celts were highly ritualistic.

SUBORDINATE CLAUSES

A clause that cannot stand by itself as a complete thought is a **subordinate clause** (also called a **dependent clause**). It cannot be a part of a sentence unless it is related by meaning to the independent clause. Essentially, it exists to build upon the information conveyed by the independent clause. A subordinate clause can relate to the independent clause as an adjective, an adverb, or a noun:

adjective: The Milwaukee Brewers, who play at Miller Park, joined the National League in November 1997.

adverb: Bob called when you were at the store.

noun: Read what child development experts have to say about the virtues and drawbacks of homeschooling.

ELLIPTICAL CLAUSES

An **elliptical clause** deviates from the rule that states "a clause contains a subject and a predicate." What an elliptical clause does is *imply* both a subject and a predicate, even though both elements do not in fact appear in the clause:

While vacationing in Spain, Jo received word of her promotion.
[The elliptical clause implies the subject "she" and the predicate "was vacationing"—that is, it implies "While she was vacationing in Spain."]

Myers arrived on Saturday the 12th; Anderson, the following Monday.
[The elliptical clause implies the predicate "arrived the following Monday"—that is, it implies "Anderson arrived the following Monday."]

Elliptical clauses are valuable devices, as they allow the writer to avoid excessive wordiness, preserve a sense of variety, and enhance the rhythm of the text.

RESTRICTIVE CLAUSES

A clause that is essential to the meaning of the sentence—that is, it *restricts* the meaning of the sentence—is a **restrictive clause**. The content of a restrictive clause identifies a particular person, place, or thing. If the restrictive clause were to be removed, the meaning of the sentence would change. A restrictive clause begins with the relative pronoun *that*, *who*, or *whom*. It should never be set off with commas.

I'm returning the coat <u>that I bought last week</u>.
[The identification of the coat is important. It's not just any coat. It's specifically the one and only coat "that I bought last week." Without the restrictive clause, the identification would be lost.]

The president <u>who authorized the Louisiana Purchase</u> was Thomas Jefferson.
[The point of this sentence is to identify specifically the one and only president responsible for the Louisiana Purchase. Without the restrictive clause, the point of the sentence would be lost.]

NONRESTRICTIVE CLAUSES

A clause that is not essential to the meaning of the sentence—that is, it does *not restrict* the meaning of the sentence—is a **nonrestrictive clause**. The content of a nonrestrictive clause adds information to what has already been identified. If the nonrestrictive clause were to be removed, the meaning of the sentence would not change. A nonrestrictive clause begins with the relative pronoun *which*, *who*, or *whom*. It should always be set off with commas.

I'm returning my new coat, <u>which doesn't fit</u>.
President Jefferson, <u>who authorized the Louisiana Purchase</u>, was the third U.S. president.
[The clauses *which doesn't fit* and *who authorized the Louisiana Purchase* are informative but not necessary. Without them, the meaning of each sentence is still clear.]

Sentence

Properly constructed sentences are integral to good communication. By definition, a sentence is "a set of words that is complete in itself, typically containing a subject and predicate, conveying a statement, question, exclamation, or command, and consisting of a main clause and sometimes one or more subordinate clauses." Simply put, a sentence is a group of words that expresses a complete thought.

SUBJECT AND PREDICATE

The primary building blocks of a sentence are the subject and the predicate.

The **subject** (usually a noun or pronoun) is the part that the sentence is telling about. A **simple subject** is simply the person, place, or thing being discussed. A **complete subject** is the simple subject along with all the words directly associated with it:

<u>The large tropical plant in my office</u> has bloomed every summer.
[Here, the simple subject is *plant*. The complete subject is *The large tropical plant in my office*.]

Two or more subjects that belong to the same verb comprise what is called a **compound subject**:

Stan Garrison and the rest of the department are relocating next week.
[Here, the compound subject consists of *Stan Garrison* and *the rest of the department*. They share the verb phrase *are relocating*.]

The **predicate** (a verb) is the "action" or "being" part of the sentence—the part that tells something about the subject. A **simple predicate** is simply the main verb and its auxiliaries. A **complete predicate** is the simple predicate along with all the words directly associated with it:

The setting sun has cast a scarlet glow across the skyline.
[Here, the simple predicate is *has cast*. The complete predicate is *has cast a scarlet glow across the skyline*.]

Two or more predicates that have the same subject comprise what is called a **compound predicate**:

I wanted to buy some art but left empty-handed.
[Here, the compound predicate consists of *wanted to buy some art* and *left empty-handed*. They share the subject *I*.]

FOUR SENTENCE STRUCTURES

A **simple sentence** contains one independent clause. Its subject and/or predicate may or may not be compound, but its one and only clause is always independent:

Paula rode her bicycle.
[subject + predicate]

Honus Wagner and Nap Lajoie are enshrined in the Baseball Hall of Fame.
[compound subject + predicate]

The correspondents traveled across the desert and slept in makeshift shelters.
[subject + compound predicate]

Lunch and dinner are discounted on Sunday but are full price on Monday.
[compound subject + compound predicate]

A **compound sentence** contains two or more independent clauses. The following examples show the various ways that coordinating conjunctions (e. g., *and*, *but*, *yet*), conjunctive adverbs (e. g., *however*, *therefore*), and punctuation may be used to join the clauses in a compound sentence:

Ken made the phone calls and Maria addressed the envelopes.

The war lasted for two years, but the effects of its devastation will last for decades.

Judges and other officials should sign in by noon; exhibitors will start arriving at 2:00.

I have decided to remain on the East Coast; however, I am willing to attend the monthly meetings in Dallas.

FDR initiated the New Deal, JFK embraced the New Frontier, and LBJ envisioned the Great Society.

A **complex sentence** contains one independent clause and one or more subordinate clauses. Here the independent clause in each example is double-underlined, and the subordinate clauses are single-underlined:

Even though I majored in English, I was hired to teach applied physics.

We can have the party indoors if it gets too windy.

Before I agree, I have to read the final report that you drafted.

A **compound-complex sentence** contains two or more independent clauses and one or more subordinate clauses. Here the independent clauses are double-underlined, and the subordinate clauses are single-underlined:

Because the candidates have been so argumentative, some voters are confused and many have become disinterested.

We will begin painting tomorrow if the weather's nice, but if it rains, we will start on Thursday.

FOUR SENTENCE FUNCTIONS

A **declarative sentence** states a fact, an assertion, an impression, or a feeling. It ends with a period:

Florence is a beautiful city.

Lewis Carroll died in 1898.

I'm sorry I missed the end of your speech.

An **interrogative sentence** asks a question. It ends with a question mark:

Did you read the article about migrating geese patterns?

How do you spell your last name?

Mr. Young owns a kennel?

An **imperative sentence** makes a request or gives an order. It typically ends with a period but may end with an exclamation point:

Please lock the doors.

Do not throw trash in the recycling bins.

Think before you speak!

An **exclamatory sentence** expresses surprise, shock, or some other strong feeling. It ends with an exclamation point:

Look at this mess!

I can't believe how great this is!

I lost my purse!

Paragraph

A paragraph is a series of sentences that conveys a single theme. Paragraphs help writers organize thoughts, actions, and descriptions into readable units of information. The paragraph, as a unit of text, may have one of several functions. It may be descriptive, giving certain details or impressions about a person, thing, or event. It may be instructive, explaining a method or procedure. It may be conceptual, stating thoughts, feelings, or opinions.

Every paragraph should contain a sentence that states the main idea of the paragraph. This is called the **topic sentence**. The other sentences in the paragraph are the **supporting sentences**, and their function is just that—to support or elaborate on the idea set forth in the topic sentence. Most paragraphs begin with the topic sentence, as in the following example:

> Each Thanksgiving we make place cards decorated with pressed autumn leaves. After gathering the smallest and most colorful leaves from the maples and oaks in our backyard, we place the leaves between sheets of blotter paper, which we then cover with a large, heavy book. In just a day or two, the leaves are ready to be mounted on cards. We use plain index cards, folded in half. Using clear adhesive paper, we put one leaf on each card, leaving room for the guest's name.

Try reading the preceding paragraph without the topic sentence (the first sentence). The supporting information becomes less unified because it has no main idea to support. Now imagine adding to the paragraph the following sentence:

> Last year, three of our guests were snowed in at the airport.

This would be a misplaced addition to the paragraph, as it is unrelated to the topic sentence (that is, it has nothing to do with making Thanksgiving place cards). Because it introduces a new and distinct idea, it should become the topic sentence for a new and distinct paragraph.

■ SENTENCE STYLE

Sentence Types

Getting one's ideas across in words is the core of communication. Sentences provide the means to arrange ideas in a coherent way. Certainly, the rules of grammar should be observed when constructing a sentence, but the general rhythm of the sentence is also important. Sentences may be categorized into three general types: loose, periodic, and balanced. Good writers typically use a combination of these styles in order to create a flow of ideas that will hold the reader's interest.

A **loose sentence** gets to the main point quickly. It begins with a basic and complete statement, which is followed by additional information:

> The power went out, plunging us into darkness, silencing the drone of the television and leaving our dinner half-cooked.
> [The basic statement is *The power went out*. Everything that follows is additional information.]

A **periodic sentence** ends with the main point. It begins with additional information, thus imposing a delay before the basic statement is given:

> With no warning, like a herd of stampeding bison, a mob of fans crashed through the gate.

[The basic statement is *a mob of fans crashed through the gate*. Everything that precedes is additional information.]

A **balanced sentence** is comprised of grammatically equal or similar structures. The ideas in the sentence are linked by comparison or contrast:

To visit their island villa is to sample nirvana.

As writers become more comfortable with the basic rules of grammar and the general patterns of sentence structure, they are able to remain compliant with the rules while getting more creative with the patterns. Many well-constructed sentences will not agree precisely with any of the three preceding examples, but they should always evoke an answer of "yes" to two fundamental questions:

- Is the sentence grammatically correct?
- Will the meaning of the sentence be clear to the reader?

Flawed Sentences

Three types of "flawed sentences" are sentence fragments, run-on sentences, and sentences with improperly positioned modifiers.

SENTENCE FRAGMENTS

A **sentence fragment** is simply an incomplete sentence. Fundamental to every sentence is a complete thought that is able to stand on its own. Because a phrase or subordinate clause is not an independent thought, it cannot stand on its own as a sentence. To be a part of a sentence, it must either be connected to an independent clause or be reworded to become an independent clause. Consider this sentence fragment:

My English guest who stayed on for Christmas.

Here are three possible ways to create a proper sentence from that fragment:

Everyone left on Tuesday except Dan, my English guest who stayed on for Christmas.
[The fragment is added to the independent clause *Everyone left on Tuesday except Dan*.]

My English guest stayed on for Christmas.
[The fragment becomes an independent clause by removing the word *who*.]

Dan was my English guest who stayed on for Christmas.
[The fragment becomes an independent clause by adding the words *Dan was*.]

RUN-ON SENTENCES

A **run-on sentence** results when two or more sentences are improperly united into one sentence.

Characteristic of a run-on sentence is the absence of punctuation between the independent clauses or the use of incorrect punctuation (typically a comma) between the independent clauses:

Our flight was canceled we had to spend the night in Boston.

Our flight was canceled, we had to spend the night in Boston.

Here are three possible ways to correct the preceding run-on sentences:

Our flight was canceled; we had to spend the night in Boston.
[A semicolon provides a properly punctuated separation of the two independent clauses.]

Our flight was canceled, so we had to spend the night in Boston.
[A comma followed by a conjunction (*so*) provides a properly worded and punctuated separation of the two independent clauses.]

Our flight was canceled. We had to spend the night in Boston.
[The creation of two distinct sentences provides an absolute separation of the two independent clauses.]

MODIFIER PROBLEMS

The improper placement of modifying words, phrases, and clauses is a common mistake. The result is a sentence in which the modifier unintentionally refers to the wrong person or thing. The three principal culprits are dangling modifiers, misplaced modifiers, and squinting modifiers. Writers must be careful to avoid these troublesome errors in sentence construction. Review the following examples to see how an improperly placed modifier can be confusing to the reader. It is important to recognize the subtle differences between the incorrect sentences and their corrected versions.

A **dangling modifier** is an adjectival phrase or clause that lacks a proper connection because the word it is supposed to modify is missing.

dangling: While waiting for my son, a cat jumped onto the hood of my car.
[This wrongly implies that "a cat was waiting for my son."]

correct: While I was waiting for my son, a cat jumped onto the hood of my car.
While waiting for my son, I saw a cat jump onto the hood of my car.
A cat jumped onto the hood of my car while I was waiting for my son.
[The crucial word that was missing is "I."]

dangling: At age seven, her grandfather died of diphtheria.
[This wrongly implies that "her grandfather died when he was seven."]

correct: When she was seven, her grandfather died of diphtheria.
Her grandfather died of diphtheria when she was seven.
At age seven, she lost her grandfather when he died of diphtheria.
[The crucial word that was missing is "she."]

A **misplaced modifier** is a phrase or clause that is not positioned close enough to the word it is supposed to modify. It will seem to the reader that a different word is being modified.

misplaced: There was an outbreak in our school of chicken pox.
[This wrongly implies that there is "a school of chicken pox."]

correct: There was an outbreak of chicken pox in our school.
In our school there was an outbreak of chicken pox.
Our school experienced an outbreak of chicken pox.

misplaced: I was stopped by a policeman without a driver's license.
[This wrongly implies that there was "a policeman without a driver's license."]

correct: Driving without a license, I was stopped by a policeman.
I was stopped by a policeman, and I did not have a driver's license.

A **squinting modifier** is an adverb placed between two verbs. For the reader, it is often difficult to determine which verb the adverb is supposed to modify.

squinting: The stack of chairs she had arranged carefully collapsed in the wind.
[Was the stack of chairs "arranged carefully" or did it "carefully collapse"?]

correct: The stack of chairs she had carefully arranged collapsed in the wind.
[Of the two possible meanings, this is only one that makes sense.]

squinting: The stack of chairs she had arranged quickly collapsed in the wind.
[Was the stack of chairs "arranged quickly" or did it "quickly collapse"?]

correct: The stack of chairs she had quickly arranged collapsed in the wind.
The stack of chairs she had arranged collapsed quickly in the wind.
[Either meaning could make sense, so only the writer would know which version is correct.]

2. Spelling

Compounds

A compound adjective or noun is a single term formed from two or more distinct words. There are three spelling formats for compounds: open, hyphenated, and closed.

In an **open compound**, the component words are separate, with no hyphen (*well fed; wagon train*).

In a **hyphenated compound**, the component words are joined by a hyphen (*half-baked; city-state).*

In a **closed compound**, the component words are joined into a single word (*hardheaded; campfire).*

COMPOUND ADJECTIVES

For most cases of open compound adjectives, there is a general rule of thumb: the compound is left open when it is not followed by the modified noun; the compound is hyphenated when it is followed by the modified noun:

She was <u>well known</u> in the South for her poetry.
[The compound *well known* is open because it is not followed by the modified noun *She*.]

In the South, she was a <u>well-known poet</u>.
[The compound *well-known* is hyphenated because it is followed by the modified noun *poet*.]

A notable exception occurs when the first part of the compound adjective is an adverb that ends in *-ly*. In this case, the compound remains open, even when it is followed by the noun:

The woman who met us in the lobby was <u>beautifully dressed</u>.

A <u>beautifully dressed woman</u> met us in the lobby.

COMPOUND NOUNS

For spellers, the least troublesome compound nouns are familiar closed compounds:

cupcake downstairs fireplace

Other compound nouns can be troublesome. Although certain ones, such as *mother-in-law*, are always hyphenated, many compound nouns commonly occur in more than one acceptable format, such as *ice cap* or *icecap* and *vice president* or *vice-president*. For most spelling questions, the best resource is a dictionary; for questions pertaining specifically to compounds, an unabridged edition is recommended.

COMPOUND VERBS

When an open compound noun is used as a verb, a hyphen is added:

> Last summer, we conducted a field test of various compost tumblers. [noun]
>
> University veterinarians were able to field-test the procedure extensively. [verb]

TIP

Different dictionaries often disagree on the preferred spelling formats for a number of compounds, so writers are well advised to consult just one dictionary when establishing a spelling style.

Prefixes

A prefix is a group of letters added to the beginning of a word to adjust its meaning. In most cases, prefixes are affixed to the root word without hyphenation:

> antibacterial postwar semicircle

Often, however, a hyphen is customary, necessary, or preferable.

Certain prefixes almost always take a hyphen: *all-*, *ex-*, *full-*, *quasi-*, *self-*:

> all-encompassing ex-partner full-bodied
> quasi-liberal self-confidence

When the root word begins with a capital letter, the prefix takes a hyphen:

> anti-American pre-Conquest

Sometimes, without a hyphen, a word could be easily confused with another:

> We recovered our furniture.

Does this mean we *found* our *missing* furniture? Or did we *put new coverings on* our furniture? If the latter is meant, a hyphen would have avoided confusion:

> We re-covered our furniture.

Sometimes, a hyphen is not necessary but preferable. Without it, the word may look awkward. One such circumstance is when the last letter of the prefix and the first letter of the root word are both vowels, or when an awkward double consonant is created. For each of the following pairs of words, either spelling is acceptable:

> antiknock/anti-knock semiindependent/semi-independent
> preadapt/pre-adapt nonnegative/non-negative

TIP

Regarding the use of optional hyphens, the writer should establish a preferred style. Keeping a running list of hyphenated terms can help writers keep track of which spellings they have already used in their text, thus making the style consistent.

Suffixes

A suffix is a group of letters added to the end of a word to create a derivative or inflection of the word. There are exceptions to the following guidelines on how to spell with suffixes, but in most cases these rules apply:

A root word that ends in *e* drops the *e* when the suffix begins with a vowel:

rehearse/rehearsing

However, most words that end in *ce* or *ge* keep the *e* when the suffix begins with *a* or *o*:

service/serviceable
advantage/advantageous

A root word that ends in *e* keeps the *e* when the suffix begins with a consonant:

wise/wisely

A root word that ends in a *y* preceded by a consonant changes the *y* to *i* when the suffix begins with any letter other than *i*:

satisfy/satisfies/satisfying

A root word that ends in *ie* changes the *ie* to *y* when the suffix is *-ing*:

lie/lying

A root word that ends in *oe* keeps the *e* when the suffix begins with a vowel, unless the vowel is *e*:

toe/toeing/toed

A one-syllable root word that ends in a single consonant preceded by a single vowel doubles the consonant when the suffix is *-ed*, *-er*, or *-ing*. This rule also applies to root words with two or more syllables if the accent is on the last syllable.

stir/stirred
refer/referring

Numbers

Numbers are an important part of everyday communication, yet they often cause a writer to stumble, particularly over questions of spelling and style. The guidelines on *how* to spell out a number are fairly straightforward. The guidelines on *when* to spell out a number are not so precise.

HOW TO SPELL OUT NUMBERS

Cardinal Numbers

The most common problem associated with the spelling of whole cardinal numbers is punctuation. The rules are actually quite simple: Numeric amounts that fall between twenty and one hundred are always hyphenated. No other punctuation should appear in a spelled-out whole number, regardless of its size.

26	twenty-six
411	four hundred eleven
758	seven hundred fifty-eight
6,500	six thousand five hundred
33,003	thirty-three thousand three
972,923	nine hundred seventy-two thousand nine hundred twenty-three

Note: The word *and* does not belong in the spelling of a number. For example, "758" should not be spelled "seven hundred and fifty-eight."

Ordinal Numbers

The punctuation of spelled-out ordinal numbers typically follows the rules for cardinal numbers.

What should we do for their fifty-fifth anniversary?

He graduated two hundred twenty-ninth out of a class of two hundred thirty.

When ordinal numbers appear as numerals, they are affixed with *-th*, with the exception of those ending with the ordinal *first*, *second*, or *third*.

1st	2nd	3rd
4th	581st	32nd
73rd	907th	

Note: Sometimes 2nd is written as 2d, and 3rd as 3d.

Fractions

A fraction can appear in a number of formats, as shown here:

$\frac{3}{8}$	case fraction (or split fraction)
⅜	fraction with solidus
0.375	decimal fraction
three-eighths	spelled-out fraction

When acting as an adjective, a spelled-out fraction should always be hyphenated.

The Serbian democrats have won a two-thirds majority.

When acting as a noun, a spelled-out fraction may or may not be hyphenated, according to the writer's or publisher's preferred style.

At least four-fifths of the supply has been used up.
or
At least four fifths of the supply has been used up.

WHEN TO SPELL OUT NUMBERS

When to spell out a number, whole or fractional, is as much a matter of sense as of style. Text that is heavy with numbers, such as scientific or statistical material, could become virtually unreadable if the numbers were all spelled out. Conversely, conventional prose that occasionally makes mention of a quantity may look unbalanced with an occasional numeral here and there.

Often, the decision to spell or not to spell comes down to simple clarity:

Our standard paper size is $8\frac{1}{2}$by 11.
Our standard paper size is 8½ by 11.
Our standard paper size is eight and a half by eleven.
Our standard paper size is eight and one-half by eleven.

The preceding four sentences say exactly the same thing, but the best choice for readability is the first.

TIP

Numerals and other symbols should never begin a sentence. If the symbol should not or cannot be spelled out, the sentence needs to be reworded.

19 students have become mentors.
should be:
Nineteen students have become mentors.

1904 was the year that the hamburger became popular.
should be:
It was in 1904 that the hamburger became popular.

$10 was found on the stairs.
should be:
Ten dollars was found on the stairs.

6:00 is the earliest I can leave.
should be:
Six o'clock is the earliest I can leave.
or:
The earliest I can leave is 6:00.

$y = 2x + 1$ is a line with a slope of 2.
should be:
The line $y = 2x + 1$ has a slope of 2.

3. Punctuation

Punctuation is an essential element of good writing because it makes the author's meaning clear to the reader. Although precise punctuation styles may vary somewhat among published sources, there are a number of fundamental principles worthy of consideration. Discussed below are these punctuation marks used in English:

comma
semicolon
colon
period
question mark
exclamation point
apostrophe
quotation marks
parentheses
dash
hyphen

Comma

The comma is the most used punctuation mark in the English language. It signals to the reader a pause, which generally clarifies the author's meaning and establishes a sensible order to the elements of written language. Among the most typical functions of the comma are the following:

1. It can separate the clauses of a compound sentence when there are two independent clauses joined by a conjunction, especially when the clauses are not very short:
   It never occurred to me to look in the attic, and I'm sure it didn't occur to Rachel either.
   The Nelsons wanted to see the Grand Canyon at sunrise, but they overslept that morning.
2. It can separate the clauses of a compound sentence when there is a series of independent clauses, the last two of which are joined by a conjunction:
   The bus ride to the campsite was very uncomfortable, the cabins were not ready for us when we got there, the cook had forgotten to start dinner, and the rain was torrential.
3. It is used to precede or set off, and therefore indicate, a nonrestrictive dependent clause (a clause that could be omitted without changing the meaning of the main clause):

I read her autobiography, which was published last July.

They showed up at midnight, after most of the guests had gone home.

The coffee, which is freshly brewed, is in the kitchen.

4. It can follow an introductory phrase:

   Having enjoyed the movie so much, he agreed to see it again.

   Born and raised in Paris, she had never lost her French accent.

   In the beginning, they had very little money to invest.

5. It can set off words used in direct address:

   Listen, people, you have no choice in the matter.

   Yes, Mrs. Greene, I will be happy to feed your cat.

6. It can separate two or more coordinate adjectives (adjectives that could otherwise be joined with *and*) that modify one noun:

   The cruise turned out to be the most entertaining, fun, and relaxing vacation I've ever had.

   The horse was tall, lean, and sleek.

   Note that cumulative adjectives (those not able to be joined with *and*) are not separated by a comma:

   She wore bright yellow rubber boots.

7. It is used to separate three or more items in a series or list:

   Charlie, Melissa, Stan, and Mark will be this year's soloists in the spring concert.

   We need furniture, toys, clothes, books, tools, housewares, and other useful merchandise for the benefit auction.

   Note that the comma between the last two items in a series is sometimes omitted in less precise style:

   The most popular foods served in the cafeteria are pizza, hamburgers and nachos.

8. It is used to separate and set off the elements in an address or other geographical designation:

   My new house is at 1657 Nighthawk Circle, South Kingsbury, Michigan.

   We arrived in Pamplona, Spain, on Thursday.

9. It is used to set off direct quotations (note the placement or absence of commas with other punctuation):

   "Kim forgot her gloves," he said, "but we have a pair she can borrow."

   There was a long silence before Jack blurted out, "This must be the world's ugliest painting."

   "What are you talking about?" she asked in a puzzled manner.

   "Happy New Year!" everyone shouted.

10. It is used to set off titles after a person's name:

    Katherine Bentley, M.D.

    Martin Luther King, Jr., delivered the sermon.

Semicolon

The semicolon has two basic functions:

1. It can separate two main clauses, particularly when these clauses are of equal importance:

   The crowds gathered outside the museum hours before the doors were opened; this was one exhibit no one wanted to miss.

   She always complained when her relatives stayed for the weekend; even so, she usually was a little sad when they left.

2. It can be used as a comma is used to separate such elements as clauses or items in a series or list, particularly when one or more of the elements already includes a comma:

   The path took us through the deep, dark woods; across a small meadow into a cold, wet cave; and up a hillside overlooking the lake.

   Listed for sale in the ad were two bicycles; a battery-powered, leaf-mulching lawn mower; and a maple bookcase.

Colon

The colon has five basic functions:

1. It can introduce something, especially a list of items:

   In the basket were three pieces of mail: a postcard, a catalog, and a wedding invitation.

   Students should have the following items: backpack, loose-leaf notebook, pens and pencils, pencil sharpener, and ruler.

2. It can separate two clauses in a sentence when the second clause is being used to explain or illustrate the first clause:

   We finally understood why she would never go sailing with us: she had a deep fear of the water.

   Most of the dogs in our neighborhood are quite large: two of them are St. Bernards.

3. It can introduce a statement or a quotation:

   His parents say the most important rule is this: Always tell the truth.

   We repeated the final words of his poem: "And such is the plight of fools like me."

4. It can be used to follow the greeting in a formal or business letter:

   Dear Ms. Daniels:

   Dear Sir or Madam:

   Gentlemen:

5. It is used in the United States to separate minutes from hours, and seconds from minutes, in showing time of day and measured length of time:

   Please be at the restaurant before 6:45.

   Her best running time so far has been 00:12:35.

Period

The period has two basic functions:

1. It is used to mark the end of a sentence:

   It was reported that there is a shortage of nurses at the hospital. Several of the patients have expressed concern about this problem.

2. It is often used at the end of an abbreviation:

   On Fri., Sept. 12, Dr. Brophy noted that the patient's weight was 168 lb. and that his height was 6 ft. 2 in.

   (Note that another period is not added to the end of the sentence when the last word is an abbreviation.)

Question Mark and Exclamation Point

The only sentences that do not end in a period are those that end in either a question mark or an exclamation point.

Question marks are used to mark the end of a sentence that asks a direct question (generally, a question that expects an answer):

Is there any reason for us to bring more than a few dollars?
Who is your science teacher?

Exclamation points are used to mark the end of a sentence that expresses a strong feeling, typically surprise, joy, or anger:

I want you to leave and never come back!
What a beautiful view this is!

Apostrophe

The apostrophe has two basic functions:

1. It is used to show where a letter or letters are missing in a contraction.

   The directions are cont'd [continued] *on the next page.*

   We've [we have] *decided that if she can't* [cannot] *go, then we aren't* [are not] *going either.*

2. It can be used to show possession:

   The possessive of a singular noun or an irregular plural noun is created by adding an apostrophe and an *s*:

   the pilot's uniform

   Mrs. Mendoza's house

   a tomato's bright red color

   the oxen's yoke

   The possessive of a regular plural noun is created by adding just an apostrophe:

   the pilots' uniforms [referring to more than one pilot]

the Mendozas' house [referring to the Mendoza family]

the tomatoes' bright red color [referring to more than one tomato]

Quotation Marks

Quotation marks have two basic functions:

1. They are used to set off direct quotations (an exact rendering of someone's spoken or written words):

   "I think the new library is wonderful," she remarked to David.

   We were somewhat lost, so we asked, "Are we anywhere near the gallery?"

   In his letter he had written, "The nights here are quiet and starry. It seems like a hundred years since I've been wakened by the noise of city traffic and squabbling neighbors."

   Note that indirect quotes (which often are preceded by that, if, or whether) are not set off by quotation marks:

   He told me that he went to school in Boston.

   We asked if we could still get tickets to the game.

2. They can be used to set off words or phrases that have specific technical usage, or to set off meanings of words, or to indicate words that are being used in a special way in a sentence:

   The part of the flower that bears the pollen is the "stamen."

   When I said "plain," I meant "flat land," not "ordinary."

   Oddly enough, in the theater, the statement "break a leg" is meant as an expression of good luck.

   What you call "hoagies," we call "grinders" or "submarine sandwiches."

   He will never be a responsible adult until he outgrows his "Peter Pan" behavior.

   Note that sometimes single quotation marks, rather than double quotation marks, may be used to set off words or phrases:

   The part of the flower that bears the pollen is the 'stamen.'

   What is most important is to be consistent in such usage. Single quotation marks are also used to set off words or phrases within material already in double quotation marks, as:

   "I want the sign to say 'Ellen's Bed and Breakfast' in large gold letters," she explained.

Parentheses

Parentheses are used, in pairs, to enclose information that gives extra detail or explanation to the regular text.

Parentheses are used in two basic ways:

1. They can separate a word or words in a sentence from the rest of the sentence:

   On our way to school, we walk past the Turner Farm (the oldest dairy farm in town) and watch the cows being fed.

   The stores were filled with holiday shoppers (even more so than last year).

Note that the period goes outside the parentheses, because the words in the parentheses are only part of the sentence.

2. They can form a separate complete sentence:

   Please bring a dessert to the dinner party. (It can be something very simple.) I look forward to seeing you there.

   Note that the period goes inside the parentheses, because the words in the parentheses are a complete and independent sentence.

Dash

A dash is used most commonly to replace the usage of parentheses within sentences. If the information being set off is in the middle of the sentence, a pair of long (or "em") dashes is used; if it is at the end of the sentence, just one long dash is used:

On our way to school, we walk past the Turner Farm—the oldest dairy farm in town—and watch the cows being fed.

The stores were filled with holiday shoppers—even more so than last year.

Hyphen

A hyphen has three basic functions:

1. It can join two or more words to make a compound, especially when doing so makes the meaning more clear to the reader:

   We met to discuss long-range planning.

   There were six four-month-old piglets at the fair.

   That old stove was quite a coal-burner.

2. It can replace the word "to" when a span or range of data is given. This kind of hyphen is sometimes keyed as a short (or "en") dash:

   John Adams was president of the United States 1797–1801.

   Today we will look for proper nouns in the L–N section of the dictionary.

   The ideal weight for that breed of dog would be 75–85 pounds.

3. It can be used to break a word at the end of a line.

Wordfinder Index

Thematic Lists

Animals

Amphibians

axolotl
barking frog
bell toad
blind salamander
bullfrog
caecilian/coecilian
cane toad
cave salamander
chorus frog
congo eel/snake
cricket frog
dusky salamander
eft
flying frog
four-toed salamander
frog
giant salamander
giant toad
gopher frog
green frog
green salamander
hellbender
horned toad
hyla
Jefferson salamander
leopard frog
long-tailed salamander
marbled salamander
marine toad
midwife toad
mudpuppy
mud siren
narrow-mouthed frog
natterjack (toad)
newt
Olympic salamander
painted salamander
peeper/spring peeper
pickerel frog
purple salamander
red-backed salamander
red-legged frog
red salamander
robber frog
salamander
siren
slimy salamander
spadefoot toad
spotted frog
spotted salamander
tadpole
tailed toad
Texas salamander
tiger salamander
toad
tree frog
tree salamander
tree toad
two-lined salamander
waterdog
whistling frog
white-lipped frog
wood frog
worm salamander

Birds

blackbird
bluebird
blue jay
bobolink
bunting
cardinal
catbird
chat
chickadee
chuck-will's-widow
cowbird
creeper
crossbill
crow
cuckoo
dickcissel
dove
finch
flicker
flycatcher
gnatcatcher
goldfinch
grackle
grosbeak
hummingbird
junco
kingbird
kingfisher
kinglet
lark
longspur
magpie
martin
meadowlark
mockingbird
nighthawk
nightingale
nightjar
nuthatch
oriole
ovenbird
phoebe
pigeon
pipit
raven
redpoll
redstart
robin
sapsucker
shrike
siskin
skylark
sparrow
starling
swallow
swift
tanager
thrasher
thrush
titmouse
towhee
veery
vireo
warbler
waterthrush
waxwing
wheatear
whippoorwill
woodpecker
wood thrush
wren
yellowthroat

Birds of Prey

accipiter
American eagle
bald eagle
barn owl
barred owl
boreal owl
brown owl
burrowing owl
buteo
buzzard
caracara
chicken hawk
condor
eagle owl
eagle
falcon
falconet
fish eagle
fish hawk
golden eagle
goshawk
great gray owl
great horned owl
gyrfalcon
harpy eagle
harrier
hawk owl
horned owl
kestrel
kite
lammergeier
lanner
marsh harrier
marsh hawk
merlin
northern harrier
osprey
owl
peregrine falcon
pigeon hawk
red-tailed hawk
ringtail
rough-legged hawk
saker
saw-whet owl
screech owl
sea eagle
sharp-shinned hawk
short-eared owl
snowy owl
sparrow hawk
spotted owl
tawny eagle
tawny owl
tiercel

Chickens and Other Ground Birds

Ancona
bantam (chicken)
black grouse
blue grouse
bobwhite
brahma (chicken)
capercaillie
chukar
Cornish (chicken)
fool hen
francolin
grouse
guinea fowl
hazel grouse
Hungarian partridge
leghorn
partridge
peafowl/peacock/peahen
pheasant
Plymouth Rock
prairie chicken
ptarmigan
quail
Rhode Island Red
ringneck
ring-necked pheasant
Rock Cornish (game hen)
rock ptarmigan
ruffed grouse
sage grouse
sharp-tailed grouse
snow partridge
spruce grouse
Sussex
tragopan
turkey
White Rock
willow grouse
willow ptarmigan
Wyandot

Seabirds

See also **Penguins**

ancient murrelet
Arctic tern
Atlantic puffin
auk
auklet
baccalieu bird
bawk
black guillemot
black skimmer
black tern
black-footed albatross
Bonaparte's gull
booby
brown noddy
brown pelican
bull bird
cahow
Cassin's auklet
common murre
cormorant
duck
double-crested cormorant
dovekie
Franklin's gull
frigate bird
fulmar
gannet
glaucous gull
greater shearwater
guillemot
gull
gun-billed tern
herring gull
Iceland gull
jaeger
kittiwake
laughing gull
little auk
little gull
little tern
Manx shearwater
marbled murrelet
mew gull
Mother Carey's chicken
murre
murrelet
noddy
northern fulmar
northern gannet
parasitic jaeger
pelagic cormorant
pelican
petrel
pigeon guillemot
pomarine jaeger
prion
puffin
razorbill
ring-billed gull
roseate tern
Ross's gull
Sabine's gull
sea pigeon
sea swallow
seagull
shag
shearwater
skimmer
skua
sooty shearwater
sooty tern
storm petrel
tern
ticklace
tropicbird
turr
white pelican

Penguins

Adélie penguin
African jackass penguin
blue penguin
chinstrap penguin
emperor penguin
erect-crested penguin
fairy penguin
Fiordland crested penguin
Galapagos penguin
gentoo (penguin)
Humboldt penguin
king penguin
little penguin
macaroni penguin
Magellanic penguin

Peruvian penguin
rockhopper (penguin)
royal penguin
Snares Island penguin
yellow-eyed penguin

Shorebirds

adjutant stork
American egret
avocet
Baird's sandpiper
beach bird
bittern
brolga
cattle egret
coot
crane
curlew
dotterel
dowitcher
dunlin
egret
flamingo
gallinule
godwit
golden plover
great blue heron
great white egret
heron
ibis
jabiru
jacana
killdeer
lapwing
least bittern
limpkin
marabou
moorhen
oystercatcher
pectoral sandpiper
pewit
piping plover
plover
rail
red knot sandpiper
ringed plover
ruff/reeve
sanderling
sandhill crane
sandpiper
snipe
snowy egret
sora
spoonbill
stilt
stint
stork
tattler
turnstone
waterhen
whimbrel
whooping crane
willet
yellowlegs

Waterfowl

Arctic loon
barnacle goose
black duck
black swan
blue goose
brant
bufflehead
Canada goose
canvasback
eared grebe
eider
fulvous whistling duck
gadwall
garganey
goldeneye
gray goose
graylag
harlequin duck
helldiver
hooded merganser
horned grebe
king eider
long-tailed duck
loon
mallard
mandarin duck
merganser
mottled duck
Muscovy duck
mute swan
oldsquaw
Pacific loon
pied-billed grebe
pintail
red-breasted goose
redhead
red-necked grebe
red-throated loon
ring-necked duck
Ross's goose
ruddy duck
sawbill
scaup
scoter
shoveler
smew
snow goose
surf scoter
teal
trumpeter swan
tundra swan
baldpate
Western grebe
whistling swan
white-fronted goose
white-winged scoter
whooper
wigeon
wood duck
yellow-billed loon

Fish

albacore (tuna)
amberjack
anchovy
angelfish
anglerfish
bacalao
barbel
barracuda
bass
blackfish
blenny
blowfish
bluefish
bonito
bream
brill
brisling
buffalo fish
burbot
butterfish
carp
catfish
char
cod/codfish
conger eel
crappie
cusk
dogfish
dolphinfish
dorado
dory
Dover sole
eel
finnan (haddie)
flounder
fluke
flying fish
fugu
goby
grouper
grunion
grunt
haddock
hake
halibut
herring
John Dory
kingfish
kipper
lamprey
lemon sole
limpet
lox
lutefisk
mackerel
mahimahi
monkfish
moray eel
orange roughy
parrotfish
perch
pilchard
pollack
pompano
rainbow trout
ray
red mullet
red snapper
rockfish
rouget
sablefish
salmon
sand dab
sardine
scrod
sea bass
sea bream
sea trout
shad
shark
skate
smelt
snapper
sole
sprat
striped bass
sturgeon
sunfish
swordfish
tarpon
tilapia
tilefish
torsk
trout
tuna
turbot
wahoo
whitefish
wrasse
yellowtail

Sharks

angel shark
basking shark
blue shark
dogfish
great white shark
hammerhead
mackerel shark
mako
monkfish
nurse shark
porbeagle
requiem shark
shovelhead
thresher shark
tope
whale shark

Insects

ant
alderfly
amberwing
ant lion
aphid
army ant
assassin bug
backswimmer
bee
bedbug
beetle
blackfly
blowfly
bluebottle
boatman
boll weevil
booklouse
borer
botfly
bristletail
bumblebee
butterfly
caddisfly
carpenter ant
carpenter bee
carpet beetle
carrion beetle
chafer
chinch bug
cicada
click beetle
cluster fly
coccid
cockroach
Colorado beetle
corn borer
crane fly
cricket
cuckoo bee
cucumber beetle
damselfly
darner
deathwatch beetle
deerfly
diving beetle
dobsonfly
doodlebug
dragonfly
dung beetle
earwig
elater
emmet
engraver beetle
fire ant
firefly
flea
froghopper
fruit fly
furniture beetle
gall wasp
glowworm
gnat
Goliath beetle
grasshopper
greenbottle
harvester ant
Hercules beetle
honeybee
hornet
horsefly
housefly
ichneumon
Japanese beetle
June bug
katydid
ladybug
leafcutter
leafhopper
lightning bug
locust
louse
mayfly
mealy bug
Mexican bean beetle
mosquito
moth
mud dauber
no-see-um
paper wasp
pismire
potato beetle
praying mantis
rhinoceros beetle
roach
robber fly
rose chafer
rove beetle
sandfly
sawfly
sawyer
scarab beetle
scorpion fly
shadfly
snout beetle
snowflea
spittlebug
springtail
squash bug
stag beetle
stink bug
stonefly
termite
tiger beetle
tsetse fly
walking stick
water beetle
wasp
weevil
white ant
whitefly
yellow jacket

Butterflies

admiral
aguna
alpine
American lady
arctic
azure
banner
beauty
blue
bolla
brushfoot
buckeye
cabbage white
checkered skipper
checkerspot
clearwing
cloudywing
comma
copper
cracker
crescent
daggerwing
Diana
dogface
dotted blue
duskywing
elfin
emperor
flasher
fritillary
giant skipper
glassywing
greenstreak
groundstreak
hairstreak
harvester
heliconian
Julia
lady butterfly
leaf butterfly
leafwing
long dash
longtail
marble

metalmark
Mexican bluewing
milkweed butterfly
mimic
ministreak
monarch
mourning cloak
mulberry wing
orange
orangetip
orion
owl butterfly
painted lady
patch
peacock
pearly eye
pixie
powdered skipper
purple
purplewing
queen
question mark
red admiral
ringlet
roadside skipper
satyr
scallopwing
scrub hairstreak
shoemaker
silverdrop
silverspot
skipper
skipperling
soldier
sootywing
sulfur/sulphur
swallowtail
tortoiseshell
viceroy
white
white admiral
wood nymph
yellow
zebra

Moths

acrea moth
armyworm moth
bagworm moth
black witch
buck moth
bumblebee moth
burnet
carpenter moth
carpet moth
cecropia
clearwing
clothes moth
codling moth
cotton leafworm moth
ctenuchid
cutworm moth
Cynthia
dagger moth
day moth
diamondback moth
dried leaf moth
emperor moth
flannel moth
forester
geometer
grain moth
green cloverworm moth
gypsy moth
handmaid
hawk moth
honey-locust moth
hummingbird moth
imperial moth
Indian meal moth
lo moth
Isabella moth
leopard moth
luna moth
lunate moth
meal moth
Mediterranean flour moth
noctuid
oakworm moth
Pandora moth
pantry moth
pitch twigmoth
plume moth
polyphemus moth
Promethea moth
prominent
regal/royal moth
rosy maple moth
salt marsh moth
satin moth
saturnid
silkworm/silk moth
snout moth
sphinx
tentmaker
three-spotted fillip
tiger moth
tortrix
tussock
underwing
wax moth
yucca moth
Zimmerman pine moth

Mammals

Bears

Alaskan brown bear
American black bear
Asian black bear
black bear
blue bear
brown bear
cave bear (extinct)
cinnamon bear
giant panda
glacier bear
grizzly (bear)
Kodiak bear
Malayan sun bear
panda
polar bear
Siberian brown bear
silvertip grizzly (bear)
sloth bear
sun bear
white bear
yellow bear

Cats

DOMESTIC CATS

Abyssinian
American bobtail
American curl
American shorthair
American wirehair
angora
Balinese
Birman
bobtail
Bombay
British shorthair
Burmese
calico
chartreux
chinchilla (cat)
colorpoint shorthair
Cornish Rex
curl
Devon Rex
Egyptian mau
exotic
ginger
Havana brown
Himalayan
Javanese
Japanese bobtail
Korat
LaPerm
longhair
Maine coon
Manx
marmalade
Norwegian forest cat
ocicat
Oriental
Persian
ragdoll
Rex
Russian Blue
Scottish fold
Selkirk Rex
shorthair
Siamese
Siberian
Singapura
Somali
Sphynx
tabby
Tonkinese
tortoiseshell
Turkish angora
Turkish Van
wirehair

WILD CATS

Bengal tiger
bobcat
Canada lynx
caracal
catamount
cheetah
clouded leopard
cougar
eyra
cat
jaguar
jaguarundi
kodkod
leopard
leopard cat
lion
lynx
margay
mountain lion
ocelot
oncilla
panther
puma
serval
Siberian tiger
snow leopard
tiger
tiger cat
wildcat

Cattle

Aberdeen
Angus
African buffalo
Alderney
Ayrshire
banteng
beefalo
bison
Black Angus
Brahman
Brown Swiss
buffalo
Charolais
Chianina
fighting bull
Galloway
gaur
gayal
Guernsey
Hereford
Highland cattle
Holstein
Jersey
kouprey
Limousin
longhorn
musk ox
ox
plains bison
Red Angus
Red Poll
shorthorn
Simmental
Texas longhorn
water buffalo
wood bison
yak
zebu

Deer

axis
barren ground caribou
blacktail
brocket
caribou
chital
elk
fallow deer
moose
mule deer
muley
muntjac
musk deer
Père David's deer
Peary caribou
red deer
reindeer
roe
sika
wapiti
whitetail
woodland caribou

Dogs

DOMESTIC DOGS

affenpinscher
Afghan hound
Airedale (terrier)
Akita
Alaskan malamute
American Eskimo dog
American water spaniel
American pit bull (terrier)
Anatolian shepherd
Australian shepherd
Australian terrier
basenji
basset hound
beagle
bearded collie
Bedlington terrier
Belgian Malinois
Belgian sheepdog
Belgian Tervuren
Bernese mountain dog
Bichon Frisé
black and tan coonhound
Black Russian terrier
bloodhound
bluetick (coonhound)
border collie
border terrier
borzoi
Boston terrier
Bouvier des Flandres
boxer
Briard
Brittany (spaniel)
Brussels griffon
bull terrier
bulldog
bullmastiff
cairn terrier
Canaan dog
Cardigan Welsh corgi
Cavalier King Charles spaniel
Chesapeake Bay retriever
chihuahua
Chinese crested
chow chow
Clumber spaniel
cockapoo
cocker spaniel
collie
coonhound
curly-coated retriever
dachshund
Dalmatian
Dandie Dinmont (terrier)
Doberman (pinscher)
Australian cattle dog
English setter
English springer spaniel
English toy spaniel
field spaniel
Finnish spitz
flat-coated retriever
foxhound
French bulldog
German shepherd dog
German shorthaired pointer
German wirehaired pointer
giant schnauzer
Glen of Imaal terrier
golden retriever
Gordon setter
Great Dane
Great Pyrenees
greater Swiss mountain dog
greyhound
harrier
Havana silk dog/ Havanese
Ibizan (hound)
Irish setter
Irish terrier
Irish water spaniel
Irish wolfhound
Italian greyhound
Jack Russell terrier
Japanese chin
keeshond
kelpie
Kerry blue (terrier)
Komondor
kuvasz
labradoodle
Labrador retriever
Lakeland terrier
Lhasa apso
Löwchen
Maltese (terrier)
Manchester terrier
mastiff
miniature bull terrier
miniature pinscher
miniature poodle
miniature schnauzer
Neapolitan mastiff
Newfoundland
Norfolk terrier

Norwegian elkhound
Norwich terrier
Old English sheepdog
otterhound
papillon
Pekingese/Pekinese
Pembroke Welsh corgi
petit basset griffon Vendéen
pharaoh hound
pit bull (terrier)
Plott hound
pointer
Polish lowland sheepdog
Pomeranian
Portuguese water dog
pug
puli
redbone (coonhound)
Rhodesian ridgeback
Rottweiler
rough collie
Saluki
Samoyed
schipperke
Scottish deerhound
Scottish terrier
Sealyham terrier
Shar-Pei
Shetland sheepdog
Shiba Inu
Shih Tzu
Siberian husky
silky terrier
Skye terrier
smooth fox terrier
soft-coated wheaten terrier
Spinone (Italiano)
St. Bernard
Staffordshire bull terrier
Staffordshire terrier
staghound
standard poodle
standard schnauzer
Sussex spaniel
teacup poodle
Tibetan spaniel
Tibetan terrier
toy Manchester terrier
toy poodle
vizsla
Weimaraner
Welsh springer spaniel
Welsh terrier
West Highland (white) terrier
whippet
wire fox terrier
wirehaired pointing griffon
Yorkshire terrier

WILD DOGS

African wild/ hunting dog
Arctic fox
Arctic wolf
brush wolf
bush dog
coyote
cross fox
dhole
dingo
fox
gray wolf
jackal
prairie wolf
red fox
silver fox
swift fox
timber wolf
tundra wolf
wolf

Horses

American saddle horse
Andalusian
Appaloosa
Arabian
Belgian
Canadian
cayuse
Chincoteague pony
Clydesdale
Dartmoor pony
Falabella
Hanoverian
Lipizzaner
Morgan
mustang
Newfoundland pony
palomino
Percheron
polo pony
Quarter Horse
racehorse
Shetland pony
shire horse
Standardbred
Tennessee Walking Horse
thoroughbred
Waler

Marsupials

antechinus
bandicoot
cuscus
dasyure
flying phalanger
honey possum
kangaroo
koala
numbat
opossum/possum
pademelon
phalanger
pygmy possum
quoll
rat kangaroo
ringtail
Tasmanian devil
wallaby
wombat

Primates

ape
aye-aye
baboon
Barbary ape
bonobo
bush baby
capuchin
chimpanzee
colobus
douroucouli
drill
gelada
gibbon
gorilla
guenon
hamadryas
hanuman (langur)
howler
indri
langur
lemur
loris
macaque
mandrill
mangabey
marmoset
monkey
orangutan
proboscis monkey
rhesus monkey
silverback
spider monkey
squirrel monkey
tamarin
tarsier
titi
vervet
wanderoo

Rodents

agouti
Arctic ground squirrel
bandicoot rat
beaver
black squirrel
brown rat
bushy-tailed wood rat
capybara
cavy
chinchilla
chipmunk
collared lemming
coypu
deer mouse
dormouse
field mouse
flying squirrel
gerbil
golden hamster
gopher
gray squirrel
groundhog
ground squirrel
guinea pig
hamster
hoary marmot
house mouse
jerboa
jumping mouse
kangaroo mouse
kangaroo rat
lemming
marmot
mole rat
mouse
muskrat
Norway rat
paca
pack rat
pocket gopher
porcupine
prairie dog
rat
red squirrel
squirrel
suslik
viscacha
vole
water rat
water vole
woodchuck
woodmouse
wood rat

Seals

bearded seal
bedlamer
blueback
California sea lion
common seal
eared seal
earless seal
elephant seal
fur seal
gray seal
harp seal
hooded seal
leopard seal
monk seal
northern sea lion
ringed seal
sea dog
sea elephant
sea lion
spotted seal
square-flipper seal
walrus
whitecoat

Whales, Dolphins, and Porpoises

beaked whale
beluga
black dolphin
blue whale
bottlenose dolphin
bottlenose whale
bowhead
Burmeister's porpoise
cochito
common dolphin
Dall's porpoise
dusky dolphin
finback (whale)
finless porpoise
grampus
gray whale
harbor porpoise
hourglass dolphin
humpback (whale)
humpbacked dolphin
Irrawaddy dolphin
killer whale
minke (whale)
narwhal
orca
pilot whale
pothead
right whale
right whale dolphin
rorqual
rough-toothed dolphin
sei whale
spectacled porpoise
sperm whale
spinner dolphin
spotted dolphin
strap-toothed whale
striped dolphin
tucuxi
white whale
white-beaked dolphin
white-sided dolphin

Spiders and Other Arachnids

American dog tick
American house spider
ant mimic
argiope
banana spider
barn spider
basilica spider
bird spider
black widow
blue bug
bolas spider
bowl and doily spider
brown dog tick
brown recluse
brown spider
brown widow
castor bean tick
cattle tick
cave spider
cellar spider
chigger
cobweb weaver
combfooted spider
crab spider
cross spider
daddy longlegs
deer tick
dust mite
dwarf spider
false black widow
featherlegged spider
filmy dome spider
fishing spider
folding-door spider
funnel weaver
furrow spider
gall mite
garden spider
giant crab spider
giant hairy hadrurus
golden silk spider
grass spider
hairy mygalomorph
hammock spider
harvest mite
harvestman
hobo spider
huntsman spider
itch mite
jumping spider
lattice spider
lone star tick
lynx spider
marbled spider
micrathena
mite
northern widow
nursery web spider
ogre-faced spider
orb weaver
orchard spider
paralysis tick
pirate spider
platform spider
pseudoscorpion
purseweb spider
rabbit tick
ray spider
red widow
sac spider
scabies mite
schizomid
scorpion
shamrock spider
sheetweb spider
six-eyed crab spider
spider mite
spitting spider
star-bellied spider
sun spider/scorpion
tangleweb spider
tarantula
thick-jawed spider
three-footed mite
tick
trapdoor spider
triangle spider
velvet mite
vinegarone/ vinegaroon
wandering spider
water mite
whip scorpion
wind scorpion
wolf spider
wood spider
wood tick
yellow vejovis

Mollusks and Crustaceans

Bivalves

bar clam
bay scallop
cherrystone (clam)
clam
cockle
gaper
geoduck
littleneck
mussel
oyster
pearl oyster
pecten
piddock
quahog
razor clam
scallop
sea scallop
steamer
teredo
zebra mussel

Gastropods

abalone
conch
cowrie
haliotis
limpet
murex
nudibranch
periwinkle
sea slug
sea snail
slug
snail
volute
whelk
winkle

Cephalopods

bobtail squid
chambered nautilus
cuttlefish
nautilus
octopus
squid

Crustaceans

barnacle
black tiger shrimp
blue crab
brine shrimp
copepod
crab
crawdad
crawfish
crayfish
daphnia
doodlebug
Dungeness crab
fiddler crab
ghost shrimp
hermit crab
king crab
krill
land crab
langouste
langoustine
lobster
Norway lobster
pillbug
prawn
roly-poly
shrimp
snow crab
soft-shell crab
spider crab
spiny lobster
squill
stone crab
tiger shrimp
trilobite
wood louse

Reptiles

alligator
alligator snapping turtle
basilisk
blindworm
box turtle
caiman
chameleon
chuckwalla
crocodile
diamondback
flying dragon
flying lizard
frill lizard
galliwasp
gecko
gharial
Gila monster
glass lizard
goanna
green turtle
hawksbill
horned toad
iguana
Komodo dragon
leatherback turtle
lizard
loggerhead turtle
monitor lizard
mugger
painted turtle
skink
slow-worm
snapping turtle
terrapin
tortoise
tuatara
turtle

Snakes

adder
anaconda
asp
boa
boa constrictor
bull snake
cobra
constrictor
copperhead
coral snake
cottonmouth
death adder
diamondback
fer-de-lance
garter snake
grass snake
hamadryad
hognose snake
horned viper
king cobra
krait
mamba
massasauga
milk snake
pit viper
puff adder
python
rattlesnake
rock python
sidewinder
spitting cobra
taipan
viper
water moccasin
water snake
whip snake

Dinosaurs

Acanthopholis
Albertosaurus
Allosaurus
Amargasaurus
Ankylosaurus
Apatosaurus
Baryonyx
Brachiosaurus
Brontosaurus
Camarasaurus
Camptosaurus
Carnotaurus
Ceratosaurus
Corythosaurus
Deinonychus
Dilophosaurus
Diplodocus
Dryosaurus
Edmontosaurus
Euoplocephalus
Gallimimus
Gigantosaurus
Homalocephale
Hylaeosaurus
Hypacrosaurus
Iguanodon
Janenschia
Kentrosaurus
Lambeosaurus
Lesothosaurus
Maiasaura
Majungatholis
Mamenchisaurus
Megalosaurus
Megaraptor
Notoceratops
Ornithomimus
Ouranosaurus
Pachycephalo-saurus
Parasaurolophus
Plateosaurus
Protarchaeopteryx
Psittacosaurus
Pteranodon
Quaesitosaurus
Riojasaurus
Saichania
Saltopus
Sauropelta
Scelidosaurus
Scipionyx
Sinornithosaurus
Spinosaurus
Stegoceras
Stegosaurus
Styracosaurus
Triceratops
Tröodon
Tyrannosaurus (rex)/T. rex
Ultrasauros
Utahraptor
Velociraptor
Vulcanodon
Wannanosaurus
Xiaosaurus
Yangchuanosuarus
Zigongosaurus

Art

Art Schools, Styles, and Movements

abstract expressionism
Aesthetic Movement
Art Deco
Art Nouveau
Arts and Crafts
Ashcan
avant-garde
Barbizon
baroque
Bauhaus
Beaux Arts
Blaue Reiter
Bloomsbury Group
classicism
conceptual art
constructivism
cubism
Dada
deconstructivism
De Stijl
expressionism
fauvism
Florentine school
folk art
futurism
Grand Manner
Group of Seven
Impressionism
Jugendstil
magic realism
Mannerism
minimalism
modernism
naive art
naturalism
Nazarenes
neoclassicism
neo-Impressionism
neoplasticism
neo-realism
Neue Sachlichkeit
op art
performance art
photorealism
plein-air painting
pop art
post-Impressionism
postmodernism
Pre-Raphaelitism
primitive art
Purism
realism
Renaissance art
rococo
romanticism
socialist realism
social realism
Sturm und Drang
suprematism
surrealism
symbolism
tenebrism
ukiyo-e

Art Techniques and Media

acrylic painting
action painting
airbrushing
aquatint
batik
brass rubbing
calligraphy
cartooning
ceramics
charcoal
cire perdue
clay
cloisonné
collage
conté
distemper
decoupage
drawing
dry point
enameling
encaustic
engraving
etching
fresco
gouache
grisaille
illumination
impasto
intaglio
intarsia
linocut
lithography
lost wax
marbling
marquetry
mezzotint
montage
mosaic
mural painting
oil painting
painting
pastel
pen and ink
photography
photogravure
photomontage
pointillism
screen printing
sculpture
scumbling
sgraffito
silk-screen printing
sketching
stained glass
stonecutting
tachism
tempera
trompe l'oeil
watercolor
wood carving
woodcutting
wood engraving

Painting Techniques and Methods

acrylic painting
action painting
aquarelle
chiaroscuro
color-field painting
color wash
divisionism
encaustic
faux painting/ finishing
finger painting
genre painting
gouache
grisaille
grotesque
impasto
marbleizing/ marbling
miniature painting
mural painting
oil painting
pointillism
polychromy
rag painting
sand painting
scumbling
secco
silk painting
spray-can painting
sumi-e
tempera
tenebrism
watercolor
Yamato-e

Types and Forms of Painting

altarpiece
annunciation
capriccio
cave painting
cityscape
cloudscape
conversation piece
crucifixion
diorama
diptych
Ecce Homo
écorché
fête galante
fresco
half-length
icon
kakemono
landscape
miniature
mural
nativity
nocturne
noli me tangere
nude
old master
panorama
paysage
pietà
polyptych
portrait
predella
retable
riverscape
seascape
skyscape
still life
tondo
townscape
triptych
trompe l'œil
vanitas
wall painting

Geography

Layers of the Earth's Atmosphere

exosphere
ionosphere
mesosphere
ozone layer
stratosphere
thermosphere
troposphere

Cloud Types and Formations

altocumulus
altostratus
anabatic
anvil
arch/arcus
back-sheared
banner
billow
bow
calvus
cap cloud
capillatus
castellanus/ castellatus
chinook
cirrocumulus
cirrostratus
cirrus
cloudlet
congestus
contrail
cumuliform
cumulonimbus
cumulus
duplicatus
fall streaks
fibratus
flanking line
floccus
Foehn wall
fog
fractus
fumulus
funnel cloud
humilis
incus
intortus
iridescent
lacunosus
lenticularis
luminous
mackerel sky
mamma/ mammatus
mare's tails
mediocris
mesoscale
mother-of-pearl
mushroom
nacreous
nebulosus
nimbostratus
nimbus
noctilucent
opacus
orographic
pannus
perlucidus
pileus
praecipitatio
pyrocumulus
radiatus
rain cloud
scud cloud
spissatus
storm cloud
stratiformus
stratocumulus
stratus
streamer
thundercloud
thunderhead
translucidas
tuba
uncinus
undulatus
veil cloud
velum
vertebratus
virga
wall cloud
wave cloud

Constellations

Andromeda
Antlia: the Air Pump
Apus: Bird of Paradise
Aquarius: the Water Bearer/ Carrier
Aquila: the Eagle
Ara: the Altar
Aries: the Ram
Auriga: the Charioteer
Boötes: the Herdsman
Caelum: the Chisel
Camelopardalis: the Giraffe
Cancer: the Crab
Canes Venatici: the Hunting Dogs
Canis Major: the Big Dog
Canis Minor: the Little Dog
Capricornus: the Goat
Carina: the Ship's Keel
Cassiopeia
Centaurus: the Centaur
Cepheus: Cepheus
Cetus: the Whale
Chamaeleon: the Chameleon
Circinus: the Compass
Columba: the Dove
Coma Berenices: Berenice's Hair
Corona Australis: the Southern Crown
Coronas Borealis: the Northern Crown
Corvus: the Crow/Raven
Crater: the Cup
Crux: the Cross
Cygnus: the Swan
Delphinus: the Dolphin
Dorado: the Goldfish/ Swordfish
Draco: the Dragon
Equuleus: the Little Horse
Eridanus: the River
Eridanus Fornax: the Furnace
Gemini: the Twins
Grus: the Crane
Hercules
Horologium: the Clock
Hydra: the Sea Monster
Hydrus: the Sea Serpent
Indus: the Indian
Lacerta: the Lizard
Leo: the Lion
Leo Minor: the Little Lion
Lepus: the Hare
Libra: the Scales/Balance
Lupus: the Wolf
Lynx: the Lynx
Lyra: the Harp/Lyre
Mensa: the Table
Microscopium: the Microscope
Monoceros: the Unicorn
Musca: the Fly
Norma: the Rule
Octans: the Octant
Ophiuchus: the Serpent Bearer
Orion: the Hunter
Pavo: the Peacock
Pegasus: the Flying Horse
Perseus
Phoenix: the Firebird
Pictor: the Easel
Pisces: the Fishes
Piscis Austrinus: the Southern Fish
Puppis: the Ship's Stern or Poop Deck
Pyxis: the Ship's Compass
Reticulum: the Net
Sagitta: the Arrow
Sagittarius: the Archer
Scorpius: the Scorpion
Sculptor: the Sculptor
Scutum: the Shield
Serpens Caput: the Serpent
Sextans: the Sextant
Taurus: the Bull
Telescopium: the Telescope
Triangulum: the Triangle
Triangulum Australe: the Southern Triangle
Tucana: the Toucan
Ursa Major: the Great Bear
Ursa Minor: the Little Bear
Vela: the Sails
Virgo: the Virgin
Volans: the Flying Fish
Vulpecula: the Little Fox

Meteor Showers (and approx. peak date)

Quadrantids (January 4)
April Lyrids (April 22)
Eta Aquarids (May 5)
June Lyrids (June 16)
June Boötids (June 27)
South Delta Aquarids (July 27)
Perseids (August 12)
Draconids (October 8)
Orionids (October 22)
Taurids (November 4)
Leonids (November 17)
Geminids (December 14)
Ursids (December 23)

Rocks

Metamorphic

amphibolite
blueschist
eclogite
epidiorite
epidosite
gneiss
granulite
hornfels
lazurite
marble
mica schist
mylonite
phyllite
psammite
pyroxenite
quartzite
schist
serpentinite
slate
verdite

Sedimentary

arenite
argillite
breccia
chalk
chert
claystone
coal
conglomerate
diatomite
dolomite
flint
ironstone
limestone
marl
mudstone
oil shale
oolite
pholphorite
pisolite
radiolarite
rag
rudite
sandstone
shale
siltstone
tillite

Igneous

andesite
anorthosite
aplite
basalt
diorite
dolerite
dunite
elvan
felsite
gabbro
granite
greenstone
kimberlite
lamprophyre
lava
monzonite
obsidian
ophiolite
pegmatite
peridotite
phonolite
picrite
porphyry
pumice
rhyolite
syenite
tephrite
tonalite
trachyte
trap rock
tuff
variolite
vitrophyre

Star Types

astrometric binary
binary star
brown dwarf
cepheid
collapsar
dark star
double star
dwarf star
eclipsing binary
flare star
giant
lodestar
magnetar
neutron star
nova
polar
polar star
pulsar
quasar
red dwarf
red giant
supergiant
supernova
variable star
visual binary
white dwarf

Winds

Alaskan wind
amihan
anabatic wind
barrier wind
bayamo
Bellot wind
bergwind
bise
blue norther
bora
Boulder wind
buran
chinook
chocolatta north
collada
cow-killer
Diablo wind
drainage wind
dust devil
easterly/easterlies
etesian/Etesian
first gust
foehn/föhn
gale
geostrophic wind
glacier wind
gradient wind
haboob
harmattan
katabatic wind
khamsin
kona
land breeze
levanter
libeccio
maestro
meltemi
mistral
monsoon
mountain breeze
Newhall wind
nor'wester
palouser/Palouser
pampero
prevailing wind
Santa Ana (wind)
sea breeze
shamal
simoom/simoon
sirocco
snow devil
snow eater
solano
sou'wester
storm wind
straight-line wind
sundowner
Texas norther
trade winds
tramontana
valley breeze
Wasatch wind
westerly/westerlies
whirlwind
williwaw
zonda

Science

Branches of Science

acoustics
aerodynamics
agricultural science
agrophysics
anatomy
anthropology
astrobiology
astrodynamics
astrometry
astronomy
astrophysics
atomic physics
bacteriology
behavioral science
biochemistry
biogeography
biology
biophysics
biotechnology
botany
cartography
chemistry
climatology
computer science
conchology
cosmology
cryogenics
crystallography
cybernetics
cytology
dendrology
dynamics
earth science
ecology
economics
electrical engineering
electrodynamics
electronics
embryology
endocrinology
engineering
entomology
environmental science
epidemiology
ethnology
ethology
evolutionary biology
evolutionary psychology
exobiology
fluid mechanics
forensics
genetic engineering
genetics
geochemistry
geochronology
geodesy
geography
geology
geomorphology
geophysics
geostatics
glaciology
hematology
herpetology
histology
holography
hydrodynamics
hydrology
hydrostatics
ichthyology
immunology
information technology
kinesiology
limnology
linguistics
marine biology
mathematics
mechanics
medical physics
medicine
metallurgy
meteorology
microbiology
mineralogy
molecular biology
morphology
mycology
natural history
nephology
neurochemistry
neurology
neuroscience
nuclear chemistry
nuclear physics
oceanography
oncology
ontogeny
ophthalmology
optics
ornithology
paleobotany
paleoclimatology
paleogeography
paleontology
palynology
parasitology
particle physics
pathology
pedology
petrology
pharmacology
photochemistry
phycology
phylogeny
physics
physiography
physiology
phytology
phytopathology
psychiatry
psychology
quantum mechanics
radiochemistry
radiology
robotics
seismology
sociobiology
sociology
soil science
spectroscopy
statistics
stratigraphy

taxonomy
tectonics
thermodynamics
topography
toxicology
veterinary medicine
virology
volcanology/
vulcanology
zoogeography
zoology
zymurgy

Chemical Elements and Their Symbols

M = metal R = radioactive

Element	Symbol		
actinium	Ac		R
aluminum	Al	M	
americium	Am	M	R
antimony	Sb	M	
argon	Ar		
arsenic	As		
astatine	At		R
barium	Ba	M	
berkelium	Bk	M	R
beryllium	Be	M	
bismuth	Bi	M	
bohrium	Bh		R
boron	B		
bromine	Br		
cadmium	Cd	M	
calcium	Ca	M	
californium	Cf	M	R
carbon	C		
cerium	Ce	M	
cesium	Cs	M	
chlorine	Cl		
chromium	Cr	M	
cobalt	Co	M	
copper	Cu	M	
curium	Cm	M	R
darmstadtium	Ds		R
dubnium	Db		R
dysprosium	Dy	M	
einsteinium	Es		R
erbium	Er	M	
europium	Eu	M	
fermium	Fm	M	R
fluorine	F		
francium	Fr	M	R
gadolinium	Gd	M	
gallium	Ga	M	
germanium	Ge		
gold	Au	M	
hafnium	Hf	M	
hassium	Hs		R
helium	He		
holmium	Ho	M	
hydrogen	H		
indium	In	M	
iodine	I		
iridium	Ir	M	
iron	Fe	M	
krypton	Kr		
lanthanum	La	M	
lawrencium	Lr	M	R
lead	Pb	M	
lithium	Li	M	
lutetium	Lu		
magnesium	Mg	M	
manganese	Mn	M	
meitnerium	Mt	M	R
mendelevium	Md	M	R
mercury	Hg	M	
molybdenum	Mo	M	
neodymium	Nd	M	
neon	Ne		
neptunium	Np	M	R
nickel	Ni	M	
niobium	Nb	M	
nitrogen	N		
nobelium	Nb	M	R
osmium	Os	M	
oxygen	O		
palladium	Pd	M	
phosphorus	P		
platinum	Pt	M	
plutonium	Pu		R
polonium	Po	M	R
potassium	K	M	
praseodymium	Pr	M	
promethium	Pm	M	R
protactinium	Pa	M	R
radium	Ra	M	R
radon	Rn		R
rhenium	Re	M	
rhodium	Rh	M	
rubidium	Rb	M	
ruthenium	Ru	M	
rutherfordium	Rf		R
samarium	Sm	M	
scandium	Sc	M	
seaborgium	Sg		R
selenium	Se		
silicon	Si		
silver	Ag	M	
sodium	Na	M	
strontium	Sr	M	
sulfur	S		
tantalum	Ta	M	
technetium	Tc	M	R
tellurium	Te		
terbium	Tb	M	
thallium	Tl	M	
thorium	Th	M	R
thulium	Tm	M	
tin	Sn	M	
titanium	Ti	M	
tungsten	W	M	
uranium	U	M	R
vanadium	V	M	
xenon	Xe		
ytterbium	Yb	M	
yttrium	Y	M	
zinc	Zn	M	
zirconium	Zr	M	

Types of Chemical Compound

acetate
acid
alcohol
aldehyde
alkaloid
alkane
alkene
alkyne
amine
base
bromide
carbide
carbohydrate
carbonate
chloride
chlorofluorocarbon (CFC)
cyanide
epoxide
ester
fluoride
hydrocarbon
hydroxide
iodide
ketone
nitrate
nitride
nitro compound
oxide
paraffin (hydrocarbon)
phosphate
salt
silicate
silicone
sulfate
sulfide

Types of Radiation

alpha radiation
background radiation
backscatter
beta radiation
bremsstrahlung
Cerenkov/Cherenkov radiation
coherent radiation
cosmic rays
cyclotron radiation
electromagnetic radiation
gamma radiation
gravitational radiation
Hawking radiation
heat radiation
infrared (IR) radiation
insolation
ionizing radiation
light
microwaves
neutron radiation
particle radiation
radar (waves)
radio waves
solar radiation
submillimeter radiation
synchrotron radiation
thermal radiation
ultraviolet (UV) radiation
visible light
X-rays

Subatomic Particles

antielectron
antineutron
antiparticle
antiproton
antiquark
axion
baryon
boson
electron
fermion
gluon
hadron
Higgs (boson/particle)
hyperon
kaon
lambda particle
lepton
meson
muon
neutrino
neutron
nucleon
photon
pion
positron
proton
psi particle
quark
strange particle
tau particle
WIMP

Sports

acrobatics
aerobatics
aerobics
angling
aquaplaning
archery
badminton
ballooning
base-jumping
BMX
bocce
boxing
bullfighting
bungee jumping
caber tossing
canoeing
canyoning
caving
clay-pigeon shooting
climbing
crew
cross-country running
cycle racing
cycling
darts
deep-sea fishing
dinghy racing
diving
eventing
falconry
fencing
fishing
fly-fishing
fowling
freestyling
game fishing
gliding
greyhound racing
gymkhana
gymnastics
hang-gliding
harness racing
hiking
hockey
horse racing
hot-air ballooning
jet-skiing
kayaking
kiteboarding
kitesurfing
motocross
mountain biking
mountaineering
MX
orienteering
parachuting
paragliding
parapenting
parasailing
parascending
pigeon racing
pistol shooting
powerboat racing
quoits
rafting
riverboarding
rock climbing
rollerskating
rollerblading
rowing
sailing
scuba-diving
sculling
shooting
showjumping
skateboarding
skeet (shooting)
skin-diving
skydiving
snorkeling
spelunking
sprinting
steeplechasing
surfing
swimming
synchronized swimming
track and field
trapshooting
trotting
wakeboarding
walking
waterskiing
weightlifting
whitewater rafting
windsurfing
wrestling
yachting

Ball Games

Association football
Australian Rules football
bandy
baseball
basketball
beach volleyball
billiards
bocce
boule/boules
bowling
bowls
Canadian football
carpetball
court tennis
cricket
croquet
dodgeball
duckpin bowling
field hockey
flag football
foosball™
football
four square
Gaelic football
golf
handball
hockey
hurling
jai alai
kickball
lacrosse
lawn bowling
lawn tennis
miniature golf
netball
ninepins
paddleball
pelota
pétanque
Ping-Pong™
polo
pool
rackets
racquetball
rounders
rugby
rugby league
rugby union
sandlot ball/baseball
Skee-Ball™
shinty
skittles
snooker
soccer
softball
SPUD
squash
table tennis
tenpin bowling
volleyball
water polo

Gymnastic Events

asymmetric bars
balance beam
balls
clubs
floor exercise
high bar
hoops
horizontal bar
parallel bars
pommel horse
power tumbling
rhythmic (gymnastics)
ribbons
rings
ropes
sports aerobics
teamgym
trampoline
tumbling
uneven bars
vault

Swimming Strokes and Kicks

Australian crawl
backstroke
breaststroke
butterfly (stroke)
crawl
dog paddle
dolphin crawl
elementary backstroke
freestyle
front crawl
flutter kick
frog kick
overarm
scissor kick
sidestroke
trudgen
whip kick

Tennis Terms

ace
advantage
alley
backcourt
backhand
ball boy
ball girl
baseline
break
break point
chop
clay court
court
cross-court
deuce
double fault
doubles
drop shot
fault
foot-fault
forecourt
forehand
game
game point
grand slam
grass court
groundstroke
half court
half-volley
let
match point
mixed doubles
net
overhand
passing shot
rally
serve
service break
set
set point
slice
smash
topspin
volley

Track and Field Events

biathlon
cross-country run
decathlon
discus throw
hammer throw
heptathlon
high jump
hurdles
javelin throw
long jump
long distance
marathon
middle distance
modern pentathlon
pole vault
race walk
relay
road run
shot put
sprint
steeplechase
triathlon
triple jump
walk

Winter Sports

alpine skiing
biathlon
bobsled
cross-country skiing
curling
dogsled racing
downhill skiing
figure skating
free skating
freestyle skiing
giant slalom
heli-skiing
hockey
ice dancing
ice hockey
ice skating
luge
moguls
Nordic combined
skating
skeleton
skiing
skijoring
ski jumping
slalom
snowboarding
speed skating
super-G
tobogganing

Archaic Words

These words are no longer in everyday use but are sometimes used to impart an old-fashioned flavor to historical novels, for example, or in standard conversation or writing just for a humorous effect. Some, such as *bedlam*, reveal the origin of their current meaning, while others reveal the origin of a different modern word, as with *gentle*, the sense of which is preserved in *gentleman*. Some, such as *learn* and *let*, now mean the opposite of their former use.

abroad out of doors
accouchement birthing
advertisement a notice to readers in a book
afeard/afeared frightened
affright frighten (someone)
ague malaria or a similar illness
aliment food; nourishment
ambuscade an ambush
animalcule a microscopic animal
apothecary a person who prepared and sold medicine
appetency a longing or desire
assay attempt
asunder apart
audition the power of hearing
aught anything at all
avaunt go away
bane poison
baseborn of low birth or social standing
bedlam an asylum
behold see or observe
behoof benefit or advantage
beldam an old woman
bethink oneself of remember; recollect
betimes in good time; early
bibliopole a dealer in books
bijoux jewelry; trinkets
billow a large sea wave
blackguard a scoundrel
blow produce flowers or be in flower
bodkin a dagger
bootless (of a task) ineffectual; useless
breech a person's buttocks
bridewell a prison or reform school for petty offenders
brimstone sulfur
bruit a report or rumor
buck a fashionable and daring young man
bumper a generous glass of an alcoholic drink
burgess a full citizen of a town or borough
buss a kiss
caboose a kitchen on a ship's deck
cadet a younger son or daughter
caducity the infirmity of old age; senility
camelopard a giraffe
cannonade bombard
carl a man of low birth
ceil line or plaster the roof of (a building)
champaign open level countryside
chapman a peddler
chicane deceive; hoodwink
circumjacent surrounding
cicisbeo a married woman's male companion or lover
cispontine on the north side of the Thames in London
cleanse restore to health
clerk a literate or scholarly person
clew a ball of thread
clout a piece of cloth or clothing
collogue talk confidentially
commend entrust someone or something to
commons provisions shared in common; rations
communicant a person who imparts information
compass encircle or surround
compeer a companion or close associate
con study attentively or learn by heart (a piece of writing)
condition social position
conjure implore (someone) to do something
contemn treat or regard with contempt
contumely insolent or insulting language or treatment
cordwainer a shoemaker
corrupt rotten or putrid
corse a corpse
cottier a rural laborer living in a cottage
coxcomb a vain and conceited man; a dandy
coz cousin
crinkum-crankum elaborate decoration or detail
crookback a person with a hunchback
crumpet a person's head
cruse an earthenware pot or jar
cully a friendly form of address for a man
cutpurse a pickpocket
dame an elderly or mature woman
damsel a young unmarried woman
dandiprat a young or insignificant person
darbies handcuffs
dark ignorant
degrade reduce to a lower rank, especially as a punishment
degree social or official rank
delate report (an offense)
demesne a region or domain
demit resign from (an office or position)
demoralize corrupt the morals of
dight clothed or equipped
discover divulge (a secret)
disport frolic
dispraise censure or criticize
divers of varying types; several
doit a very small amount of money
dot a dowry from which only the interest or annual income was available to the husband
doxy a lover or mistress
drab a slovenly woman
drought thirst
egad exclamation of surprise, anger, or affirmation
embarrass hamper or impede
embouchure the mouth of a river
equipage gear; equipment
ere before (in time)
espousal a marriage or engagement
estate a particular state, period, or condition in life
esurient hungry
expectations one's prospects of inheritance
expiry death
fain pleased or willing under the circumstances
fainéant an idle or ineffective person
fair beautiful
fandangle a useless or purely ornamental thing
fane a shrine or temple
fare travel
fell an animal skin; a pelt
feminal feminine; womanly
fervent hot or glowing
fie exclamation used to express disgust or outrage
filibeg a kilt
fishwife a woman who sells fish

fizgig	a silly or flirtatious young woman
flux	diarrhea or dysentery
forfend	avert or prevent (something evil or unpleasant)
forsooth	indeed
fourscore	eighty
freak	a whim
frore	frozen or frosty
froward	(of a person) difficult to deal with; contrary
fruit	offspring
fudge	nonsense
furbish	polish (a weapon)
gadzooks	an expression of surprise or annoyance
gage	a valued object deposited as a guarantee
gallant	a dashing gentleman
gammer	an old woman
garland	a literary anthology
garth	a yard or garden
gaud	a trinket
gentle	noble or courteous
glabriety	baldness
glaciate	freeze over
glebe	a meadow
glim	a candle
go-cart	a baby walker
God's acre	a churchyard
goodly	attractive, excellent, or virtuous
goody	(with a name) an elderly woman of humble position
grateful	received with gratitude
greenwood	a forest
grimalkin	a cat
gudgeon	a credulous person
guerdon	a reward
gyve	a fetter or shackle
habiliment	clothing
halt	lame
handmaid	a female servant
hearken	listen
hence	from here
herbary	a herb garden
hereat	as a result of this
hereunto	to this document
hereupon	after or as a result of this
hie	go quickly
hight	named
hither	to or toward this place
hoar	frost
horse-coper	a person who deals in horses
horseless carriage	a car
host	an army
howbeit	nevertheless
husbandman	a farmer
immedicable	untreatable
imminent	overhanging
indite	write; compose
inscribe	enter the name of (someone) on a list
in sooth	actually
intelligence	news
intelligencer	a person who gathers intelligence
invest	surround (a place) in order to besiege or blockade it
iron horse	a steam locomotive
izzard	the letter Z
jade	a bad-tempered or disreputable woman
jakes	an outdoor toilet
job	turn a public office or a position of trust to private advantage
kickshaw	a fancy but insubstantial cooked dish
kine	cows collectively
kirtle	a woman's gown or a man's tunic
knave	a dishonest or unscrupulous man
larcener	thief
latchet	a narrow thong or lace for fastening a shoe or sandal
laud	praise
laver	a basin or similar container used for washing oneself
learn	teach
leech	a doctor or healer
leman	a lover or sweetheart
let	hinder
levant	abscond leaving unpaid debts
Levant	the eastern part of the Mediterranean
levy	a body of enlisted troops
lief	as happily; as gladly
like enough	probably
loathly	repulsive
lordling	a minor lord
love apple	a tomato
Lucifer	a match
lurdan	an idle or incompetent person
lying-in	seclusion before and after childbirth
magdalen	a reformed prostitute
mage	a magician or learned person
magnify	glorify; extol
maid	a girl or young woman
malapert	presumptuous and impudent
malison	a curse
man-at-arms	a soldier
marry	an expression of surprise, indignation, or emphatic assertion
mayhap	perhaps; possibly
mazed	bewildered
measure	a dance
meat	food of any kind
mechanical	a manual worker
meet	suitable or proper
melodist	a singer
methinks	it seems to me
moil	drudgery
mooncalf	a foolish person
morrow, the	the following day
mummer	an actor in the theater
natheless	nevertheless
natural	a person born with impaired intelligence
naught	nothing
nay	no
neat	a bovine animal or animals
nice	fastidious
nigh	near
nithing	a contemptible or despicable person
noise (something) about	talk about or make known publicly
nubbing-cheat	a gallows
numbles	a deer's entrails as food
orison	a prayer
orts	scraps; remains
otherwhere	elsewhere
otiose	lazy; slothful
overbrim	spill; overflow
overleap	jump over or across
overset	capsize; flip over
pale	an area within determined bounds or subject to a particular jurisdiction
palfrey	a docile riding horse
pate	a person's head
paynim	a pagan
peccant	sinful; offending
peeler	a police officer
pelf	money, especially when gained dishonestly
peradventure	perhaps
perchance	by some chance
peregrinate	travel or wander from place to place
periapt	a charm or amulet
pest	bubonic plague
pestilence	a fatal epidemic disease, especially bubonic plague
peterman	a thief or safecracker
physic	medicinal drugs or medical treatment
picaroon	a scoundrel
piepowder	a traveler or an itinerant merchant or trader
pismire	an ant
pistoleer	a soldier armed with a pistol
plain over	lament; cry over
plight	solemnly pledge or promise (faith or loyalty)
pollard	an animal that has lost its horns or cast its antlers
poltroon	an utter coward
popinjay	a parrot
pore on	think about
portage	the action of carrying or transporting
portion	a dowry
portion	a person's destiny or lot
posy	a short motto or line of verse inscribed inside a ring
potation	a beverage
pouncet-box	a small box with a perforated lid used for holding a substance impregnated with perfume
prithee	please
profess	teach (a subject) as a professor
purblind	nearsighted
purfle	an ornamental or embroidered edge of a garment
pythoness	a woman believed to be possessed by a spirit and to be able to foresee the future
quaggy	marshy or boggy
quality	high social standing

quean an impudent girl or woman
quick, the the living
quidnunc an inquisitive, gossipy person
quiz look intently at (someone)
quoth said (in *I/he/she quoth*)
rack (of a cloud) be driven by the wind
raiment clothing
rapscallion a mischievous person
rathe-ripe (of fruit) ripening early in the year; (of a person) precocious
reave carry out a plundering raid
receipt a recipe
recipe a medical prescription
recompense punish or reward appropriately
recreant cowardly
rede advice or counsel
reduce besiege and capture (a town or fortress)
relieve make (something) stand out
remit diminish
repair an abode or haunt
repulsive lacking friendliness or sympathy
riband a ribbon
rover a pirate
rude ignorant and uneducated
ruth a feeling of pity, distress, or grief
sables black mourning clothes
sacring the consecration of a bishop, a sovereign, or the Eucharistic elements
saddle-bow the pommel of a saddle
salamander a red-hot iron or poker
sanative healing
sanguinary involving or causing much bloodshed
sap make (a building, etc.) insecure by removing its foundations
saturnism lead poisoning
scantling a specimen, sample, or small amount
scapegrace a mischievous person; a rascal
scaramouch a boastful but cowardly person
schoolman a teacher
science knowledge
sciolist a person who pretends to be knowledgeable
scold a woman who nags or grumbles constantly
scot a taxlike payment
scrag a neck
scruple a very small amount of something, especially a quality
scullion a menial servant
scurvy worthless or contemptible
sea coal mineral coal
sea smoke fog
seizing a length of cord or rope on board a ship
sennight a week
sepulture burial
shambles a slaughterhouse
shrift forgiveness
shrive (of a priest) absolve (a person making a confession)
silly helpless; defenseless
sippet a small piece of bread or toast for dipping into soup or sauce
skirt an edge, border, or extreme part
slay kill in a violent way
slipshod (of shoes) worn down at the heel
slugabed a lazy person who stays in bed late
small beer weak beer
smite defeat or conquer
soak drink heavily
soft tack bread, especially as rations for sailors or soldiers
soil a stain
sooth truth
sore extremely; severely
speed success; prosperity
spence a pantry or larder
statuary a sculptor
steed a horse
stoup a container for drinking beer, etc.; a flagon
stripe a blow with a lash
strumpet a female prostitute or a promiscuous woman
success a good or bad outcome
suffer endure; tolerate
surety, of/for a for certain
swain a country youth
swash flamboyantly swagger about or wield a sword
sweeting darling
sweetmeat an item of confectionery or sweet food
taiga a forest
tantivy a rapid gallop or ride
tapster a person who serves at a bar
tenter a person in charge of something, especially factory machinery
thenceforth from that time, place, or point onward
thereunto to that
therewith with or in the thing mentioned
thither to or toward that place
thrice three times
tilt with engage in a contest with
timbrel a tambourine or similar instrument
'tis it is
tithe a tenth
tocsin an alarm bell or signal
tope drink to excess
trespass a sin or offense
trig neat and smart
trigon a triangle
troth faith or loyalty when pledged in a solemn undertaking
truck an exchange or transaction
turnkey a jailer
'tween between
tweeny a maid who assisted both the cook and the housemaid
twelvemonth a year
uncle a pawnbroker
uncommon remarkably
unhand release from one's grasp
up to snuff up to the required standard
usher an assistant teacher
vale a farewell; a send-off
varlet an unprincipled rogue
venery hunting
verily truly; certainly
verse a line of poetry
very real; genuine
virtue virginity
visionary existing only in the imagination
wain a wagon or cart
wait on/upon pay a respectful visit to
waits street singers of Christmas carols
ware of aware of
wassail revelry
wast second person singular past of *be*
watch remain awake as religious observance
watchful wakeful
watchword a military password
weasand the esophagus or gullet
ween think or suppose; be of the opinion
wench a girl or young woman
whence from what place or source
whereat at which
wherefore for what reason
wherewith with or by which
whilom formerly
white goods domestic linen
whither to what place or state
wife a woman, especially an old or uneducated one
wight a person of a specified kind
wise manner, way, or extent
withal in addition
without outside
wondrous wonderfully
wont accustomed
wonted usual
wool-stapler a dealer in wool
wright a maker or builder
yclept by the name of
ye you
yea yes
yoke the amount of land that one pair of oxen could plow in a day
yonder over there
zounds an expression of surprise or indignation

Literary Words

These words are used mainly, or with a special meaning, in poetry and other writing in an elevated, 'literary' style.

abode	a home
access	an outburst of an emotion
accursed	damned
achromatic	colorless
adamantine	unbreakable; impenetrable
adieu	goodbye
afar	at a distance
affianced	engaged to marry
afire	on fire
amarantine	everlasting
anathema	a curse; a hex
anon	soon
apace	quickly
Arcadian	idyllic; countrified
argent	silvery
argosy	a large merchant ship
arrant	utter
asunder	into pieces
atrabilious	melancholy or bad-tempered
aurora	the dawn
bacchanal	a drinking session; binge
bard	a poet
barque	a boat
beauteous	beautiful
bedew	sprinkle with water
bedizen	dress gaudily
befall	happen
befoul	pollute
beget	produce (a child)
begetter	an originator or creator
behest	a directive or command
behold	see
benison	a blessing
beseech	ask urgently and fervently
besmirch	make dirty or discolored
besprinkle	sprinkle with small drops or bits (of something)
bestrew	scatter
betake oneself	go to
betimes	early; ahead of schedule
betide	happen
betoken	be a warning of
blithe	happy
bosky	covered by trees or bushes
bourn	a boundary
bower	a bedroom
brand	a sword
brume	mist or fog
celerity	swiftness
cerulean	sky blue
choler	anger
cincture	a belt or girdle
circumvallate	surround with a rampart or wall
clarion	loud and clear
cleave to	stick fast to
clime	climate
cockcrow	dawn
connubial	relating to marriage; conjugal
contemn	despise; disdain
coronal	a crown
coruscate	flash or sparkle
cozen	swindle
crapulent	relating to the drinking of alcohol
crescent	growing
darkling	relating to growing darkness
dayspring	dawn; daybreak
deathly	fatal
deep, the	the sea
dell	a small valley
deracinate	pull up by the roots
dingle	a deep wooded valley
direful	dreadful
disenthrall	set free
divers	of varying types
Dives	a rich man
doff	remove; take off
dolor	great sorrow
dome	a stately building
drear	dreary
dulcify	sweeten
effulgent	shining brightly
eld	old age
embosom	embrace
eminence	a piece of rising ground
empyrean	the sky
enfetter	shackle
engirdle	surround
enkindle	arouse
ensorcelled	enchanted
ere	before
erne	a sea eagle
espy	catch sight of
ether	the clear sky
evanesce	disappear; vanish
evanescent	quickly fading
eventide	evening
faerie	a fairy
farewell	goodbye
fay	a fairy
fell	cruel
fervid	hot or glowing
fidus Achates	a faithful friend
finny	relating to fish
firmament	the sky
flaxen	pale yellow
fleer	jeer or laugh disrespectfully
flexuous	full of bends and curves
forebode	predict; warn of
foreknow	foresee
foretoken	an omen
forsake	abandon; renounce
fount	a spring or fountain
fulgent	shining brightly
fulguration	a flash like lightning
fuliginous	sooty; dusky
fulminate	explode violently
furbelow	adorn with trimmings
georgic	rustic; agricultural
gird	secure with a belt
glaive	a sword
glaucous	grayish-green; grayish-blue
glister	sparkle
gloaming	dusk
greensward	grassy ground
gyre	whirl or gyrate
hark	listen
hebetude	sluggishness
hither	to or toward this place
horripilation	goosebumps; hair standing on end
hymeneal	relating to marriage
hyperborean	arctic; polar
ichor	blood, or a fluid likened to it
illude	trick someone
illume/illumine	illuminate
imbrue	stain one's hand or sword with blood
impuissant	powerless
incarnadine	color (something) crimson; the color crimson
ingrate	ungrateful
inhume	bury
inly	inwardly
insatiate	never satisfied
ire	anger
isle	an island
knell	the sound of a bell
lachrymal	connected with weeping or tears
lachrymose	tearful; quick to cry
lacustrine	associated with lakes
lambent	softly glowing or flickering
lave	wash or wash over
lay	a song
lea	an area of grassy land
lenity	kindness or gentleness
limn	represent in painting or words
Lethe, the waters of	oblivion
lineaments	facial features
lightsome	lithe
lucent	shining
madding	acting madly; frenzied
mage	a magician or learned person
main, the	the open ocean
malefic	causing harm
manifold	many and various
mantled	covered
marge	a margin
mead	a meadow
mephitic	foul-smelling
mere	a lake or pond
miasma	a stench
moon	a month
morrow, the	the following day
muliebrity	womanliness
mutable	fickle
nescient	lacking knowledge; ignorant

nigh	near
niveous	snowy
nocuous	noxious, harmful, or poisonous
noisome	foul-smelling
noontide	noon
nymph	a beautiful young woman
oft/ofttimes	often
omphalos	a center or hub
orb	an eye
orgulous	proud or haughty
outspread	spread out
pellucid	translucent
perchance	by some chance
perfervid	intense and impassioned
perfidious	deceitful and untrustworthy
perfidy	a betrayal
phantasm	a ghost
philippic	a bitter verbal attack
pinion	a bird's wing
plaint	a lament or dirge
plangent	loud and mournful
plash	a splashing sound
plenteous	plentiful
plumbless	extremely deep
poesy	poetry
Pooterish	arrogant; snooty
pother	a commotion or fuss
previse	foresee
profound, the	the ocean depths
prothalamium	a song or poem celebrating a wedding
puissant	powerful or influential
pulchritude	beauty
pule	cry
purl	flow with a babbling sound
quidnunc	an inquisitive and gossipy person
realm	a kingdom
redolent	fragrant
refection	refreshment; a light meal
refulgent	shining brightly
rend	tear to pieces
repine	be discontented
revenant	a ghost
Rhadamanthine	stern and incorruptible in judgment
rime	frost
rimy	frost-covered
rive	split
roundelay	a short, simple song with a refrain
rubescent	reddening
rutilant	glowing or glittering with red or golden light
sans	without
scribe	write
sea-girt	surrounded by sea
sempiternal	everlasting
serpent	a snake
shade	a ghost
ship of the desert	a camel
shore	country by the sea
sigil	a sign or symbol
slay	kill
slumber	sleep
spume	froth; foam
star-crossed	ill-fated
steed	a horse
stilly	still and quiet
storied	celebrated in stories
strand	a shore
Stygian	very dark
sublunary	terrestrial; earthbound
summers	years of a person's age
sunder	split (something) apart
supernal	relating to the sky or the heavens
susurration/ susurrus	a whispering or rustling sound
swain	a young lover or suitor
sward	a field or meadow
swinge	strike hard; beat
sword, the	military power; violence
sylvan	wooded
tarry	delay leaving
temerarious	rash or reckless
tenebrous	dark; shadowy
thew	muscle
thewy	athletic; muscular
threescore	sixty
thrice	three times
tidings	news; information
toilsome	involving hard work
tope	drink alcohol to excess
trammel	a restriction or obstruction
transpierce	penetrate
travail	painful or laborious effort
trenchant	sharp-edged
troublous	full of troubles
tryst	a rendezvous between lovers
uncloak	uncover; reveal
unman	deprive of manly qualities
upheave	lift up; heave
Uranian	homosexual
vainglorious	conceited
verdurous	fresh and green
vermeil	brilliant red
vestal	chaste; pure
vesture	clothing
viands	food
virescent	greenish
viridescent	greenish or becoming green
visage	a person's face
visitant	a ghost
want	lack or be short of
wastrel	an idler or good-for-nothing
wax	become larger or stronger
wayfarer	a person who travels on foot
wed	marry
welkin, the	the sky or heaven
wellspring	a bountiful source
wind	blow (a bugle)
without	outside
wondrous	inspiring wonder
wont	accustomed
wonted	usual
wrathful	extremely angry
wreathe	twist or entwine
yesteryear	the (recent) past
yon	yonder; that
yore	of former ties or long ago
youngling	a young person or animal
zephyr	a soft, gentle breeze

US Presidents

Name	Life dates	Party	Term in office
1. George Washington	1732–1799	Federalist	1789–1797
2. John Adams	1735–1826	Federalist	1797–1801
3. Thomas Jefferson	1743–1826	Democratic-Republican	1801–1809
4. James Madison	1751–1836	Democratic-Republican	1809–1817
5. James Monroe	1758–1831	Democratic-Republican	1817–1825
6. John Quincy Adams	1767–1848	Democratic-Republican	1825–1829
7. Andrew Jackson	1767–1845	Democrat	1829–1837
8. Martin Van Buren	1782–1862	Democrat	1837–1841
9. William Henry Harrison	1773–1841	Whig	1841
10. John Tyler	1790–1862	Whig	1841–1845
11. James Knox Polk	1795–1849	Democrat	1845–1849
12. Zachary Taylor	1784–1850	Whig	1849–1850
13. Millard Fillmore	1800–1874	Whig	1850–1853
14. Franklin Pierce	1804–1869	Democrat	1853–1857
15. James Buchanan	1791–1868	Democrat	1857–1861
16. Abraham Lincoln	1809–1865	Republican	1861–1865
17. Andrew Johnson	1808–1875	Democrat	1865–1869
18. Ulysses Simpson Grant	1822–1885	Republican	1869–1877
19. Rutherford Birchard Hayes	1822–1893	Republican	1877–1881
20. James Abram Garfield	1831–1881	Republican	1881
21. Chester Alan Arthur	1830–1886	Republican	1881–1885
22. (Stephen) Grover Cleveland	1837–1908	Democrat	1885–1889
23. Benjamin Harrison	1833–1901	Republican	1889–1893
24. (Stephen) Grover Cleveland	1837–1908	Democrat	1893–1897
25. William McKinley	1843–1901	Republican	1897–1901
26. Theodore Roosevelt	1858–1919	Republican	1901–1909
27. William Howard Taft	1857–1930	Republican	1909–1913
28. (Thomas) Woodrow Wilson	1856–1924	Democrat	1913–1921
29. Warren Gamaliel Harding	1865–1923	Republican	1921–1923
30. (John) Calvin Coolidge	1872–1933	Republican	1923–1929
31. Herbert Clark Hoover	1874–1964	Republican	1929–1933
32. Franklin Delano Roosevelt	1882–1945	Democrat	1933–1945
33. Harry S Truman	1884–1972	Democrat	1945–1953
34. Dwight David Eisenhower	1890–1969	Republican	1953–1961
35. John Fitzgerald Kennedy	1917–1963	Democrat	1961–1963
36. Lyndon Baines Johnson	1908–1973	Democrat	1963–1969
37. Richard Milhous Nixon	1913–1994	Republican	1969–1974
38. Gerald Rudolph Ford	1913–2006	Republican	1974–1977
39. James Earl Carter, Jr.	1924–	Democrat	1977–1981
40. Ronald Wilson Reagan	1911–2004	Republican	1981–1989
41. George Herbert Walker Bush	1924–	Republican	1989–1993
42. William Jefferson Clinton	1946–	Democrat	1993–2001
43. George Walker Bush	1946–	Republican	2001–2009
44. Barack Hussein Obama	1961–	Democrat	2009–

US States

State	Abbreviations traditional	postal	Capital
Alabama	Ala.	AL	Montgomery
Alaska	Alas.	AK	Juneau
Arizona	Ariz.	AZ	Phoenix
Arkansas	Ark.	AR	Little Rock
California	Calif.	CA	Sacramento
Colorado	Colo.	CO	Denver
Connecticut	Conn.	CT	Hartford
Delaware	Del.	DE	Dover
Florida	Fla.	FL	Tallahassee
Georgia	Ga.	GA	Atlanta
Hawaii	—	HI	Honolulu
Idaho	Ida.	ID	Boise
Illinois	Ill.	IL	Springfield
Indiana	Ind.	IN	Indianapolis
Iowa	Ia.	IA	Des Moines
Kansas	Kan.	KS	Topeka
Kentucky	Ky.	KY	Frankfort
Louisiana	La.	LA	Baton Rouge
Maine	Me.	ME	Augusta
Maryland	Md.	MD	Annapolis
Massachusetts	Mass.	MA	Boston
Michigan	Mich.	MI	Lansing
Minnesota	Minn.	MN	St. Paul
Mississippi	Miss.	MS	Jackson
Missouri	Mo.	MO	Jefferson City

State	Abbreviations traditional	postal	Capital
Montana	Mont.	MT	Helena
Nebraska	Nebr.	NE	Lincoln
Nevada	Nev.	NV	Carson City
New Hampshire	N.H.	NH	Concord
New Jersey	N.J.	NJ	Trenton
New Mexico	N. Mex.	NM	Santa Fe
New York	N.Y.	NY	Albany
North Carolina	N.C.	NC	Raleigh
North Dakota	N. Dak.	ND	Bismarck
Ohio	—	OH	Columbus
Oklahoma	Okla.	OK	Oklahoma City
Oregon	Ore.	OR	Salem
Pennsylvania	Pa.	PA	Harrisburg
Rhode Island	R.I.	RI	Providence
South Carolina	S.C.	SC	Columbia
South Dakota	S. Dak.	SD	Pierre
Tennessee	Tenn.	TN	Nashville
Texas	Tex.	TX	Austin
Utah	—	UT	Salt Lake City
Vermont	Vt.	VT	Montpelier
Virginia	Va.	VA	Richmond
Washington	Wash.	WA	Olympia
West Virginia	W. Va.	WV	Charleston
Wisconsin	Wis.	WI	Madison
Wyoming	Wyo.	WY	Cheyenne

Countries of the World

Country	Capital	Continent/Area	Nationality
Afghanistan	Kabul	Asia	Afghan
Albania	Tirana	Europe	Albanian
Algeria	Algiers	Africa	Algerian
Andorra	Andorra la Vella	Europe	Andorran
Angola	Luanda	Africa	Angolan
Antigua and Barbuda	St. John's	North America	Antiguan, Barbudan
Argentina	Buenos Aires	South America	Argentinian, Argentine
Armenia	Yerevan	Europe	Armenian
Australia	Canberra	Australia	Australian
Austria	Vienna	Europe	Austrian
Azerbaijan	Baku	Europe	Azerbaijani
Bahamas,The	Nassau	North America	Bahamian
Bahrain	Manama	Asia	Bahraini
Bangladesh	Dhaka	Asia	Bangladeshi
Barbados	Bridgetown	North America	Barbadian
Belarus	Minsk	Europe	Belorussian, Belarussian, *or* Belarusian
Belgium	Brussels	Europe	Belgian
Belize	Belmopan	North America	Belizean
Benin	Porto Novo	Africa	Beninese
Bhutan	Thimphu	Asia	Bhutanese
Bolivia	La Paz; Sucre	South America	Bolivian
Bosnia and Herzegovina	Sarajevo	Europe	Bosnian, Herzegovinian
Botswana	Gaborone	Africa	Motswana, *sing.*, Batswana, *pl.*
Brazil	Brasilia	South America	Brazilian
Brunei	Bandar Seri Begawan	Asia	Bruneian
Bulgaria	Sofia	Europe	Bulgarian
Burkina Faso	Ouagadougou	Africa	Burkinese
Burma (Myanmar)	Rangoon (Yangon); Nay Pyi Taw	Asia	Burmese
Burundi	Bujumbura	Africa	Burundian, *n.*; Burundi, *adj.*
Cambodia	Phnom Penh	Asia	Cambodian
Cameroon	Yaoundé	Africa	Cameroonian
Canada	Ottawa	North America	Canadian
Cape Verde	Praia	Africa	Cape Verdean
Central African Republic	Bangui	Africa	Central African
Chad	N'Djamena	Africa	Chadian
Chile	Santiago	South America	Chilean
China	Beijing	Asia	Chinese
Colombia	Bogotá	South America	Colombian
Comoros	Moroni	Africa	Comoran
Congo, Democratic Republic of the (*formerly* Zaire)	Kinshasa	Africa	Congolese
Congo, Republic of the	Brazzaville	Africa	Congolese, *n.*; Congolese *or* Congo, *adj.*
Costa Rica	San José	North America	Costa Rican
Côte d'Ivoire	Yamoussoukro	Africa	Ivorian
Croatia	Zagreb	Europe	Croat, *n.*; Croatian, *adj.*
Cuba	Havana	North America	Cuban
Cyprus	Nicosia	Europe	Cypriot
Czech Republic	Prague	Europe	Czech
Denmark	Copenhagen	Europe	Dane, *n.*; Danish, *adj.*
Djibouti	Djibouti	Africa	Djiboutian

Country	Capital	Continent/Area	Nationality
Dominica	Roseau	North America	Dominican
Dominican Republic	Santo Domingo	North America	Dominican
Ecuador	Quito	South America	Ecuadorean
Egypt	Cairo	Africa	Egyptian
El Salvador	San Salvador	North America	Salvadoran
Equatorial Guinea	Malabo	Africa	Equatorial Guinean *or* Equatoguinean
Eritrea	Asmara	Africa	Eritrean
Estonia	Tallinn	Europe	Estonian
Ethiopia	Addis Ababa	Africa	Ethiopian
Fiji	Suva	Oceania	Fijian
Finland	Helsinki	Europe	Finn, *n.*; Finnish, *adj.*
France	Paris	Europe	French
Gabon	Libreville	Africa	Gabonese
Gambia	Banjul	Africa	Gambian
Georgia	Tbilisi	Europe	Georgian
Germany	Berlin	Europe	German
Ghana	Accra	Africa	Ghanaian
Greece	Athens	Europe	Greek
Grenada	St. George's	North America	Grenadian
Guatemala	Guatemala City	North America	Guatemalan
Guinea	Conakry	Africa	Guinean
Guinea-Bissau	Bissau	Africa	Guinea-Bissauan
Guyana	Georgetown	South America	Guyanese
Haiti	Port-au-Prince	North America	Haitian
Holy *See*	Vatican City	Europe	
Honduras	Tegucigalpa	North America	Honduran
Hungary	Budapest	Europe	Hungarian
Iceland	Reykjavik	Europe	Icelander, *n.*; Icelandic, *adj.*
India	New Delhi	Asia	Indian
Indonesia	Djakarta	Asia	Indonesian
Iran	Tehran	Asia	Iranian
Iraq	Baghdad	Asia	Iraqi
Ireland, Republic of	Dublin	Europe	Irish
Israel	Jerusalem	Asia	Israeli
Italy	Rome	Europe	Italian
Jamaica	Kingston	North America	Jamaican
Japan	Tokyo	Asia	Japanese
Jordan	Amman	Asia	Jordanian
Kazakhstan	Astana	Asia	Kazakhstani
Kenya	Nairobi	Africa	Kenyan
Kiribati	Tarawa	Oceania	I-Kiribati
Korea, North (*see* North Korea)			
Korea, South (*see* South Korea)			
Kuwait	Kuwait City	Asia	Kuwaiti
Kyrgyzstan	Bishkek	Asia	Kyrgyz
Laos	Vientiane	Asia	Lao *or* Laotian
Latvia	Riga	Europe	Latvian
Lebanon	Beirut	Asia	Lebanese
Lesotho	Maseru	Africa	Mosotho, *sing.*; Basotho, *pl.*; Basotho, *adj.*
Liberia	Monrovia	Africa	Liberian
Libya	Tripoli	Africa	Libyan
Liechtenstein	Vaduz	Europe	Liechtensteiner, *n.*; Liechtenstein, *adj.*
Lithuania	Vilnius	Europe	Lithuanian
Luxembourg	Luxembourg	Europe	Luxembourger, *n.*; Luxembourg, *adj.*
Macedonia	Skopje	Europe	Macedonian
Madagascar	Antananarivo	Africa	Malagasy
Malawi	Lilongwe	Africa	Malawian
Malaysia	Kuala Lumpur	Asia	Malaysian

Country	Capital	Continent/Area	Nationality
Maldives	Male	Asia	Maldivian
Mali	Bamako	Africa	Malian
Malta	Valletta	Europe	Maltese
Marshall Islands	Majuro	Oceania	Marshallese
Mauritania	Nouakchott	Africa	Mauritanian
Mauritius	Port Louis	Africa	Mauritian
Mexico	Mexico City	North America	Mexican
Micronesia	Kolonia	Oceania	Micronesian
Moldova	Chişinău	Europe	Moldovan
Monaco	Monaco	Europe	Monacan *or* Monegasque
Mongolia	Ulaanbaatar	Asia	Mongolian
Montenegro	Podgorica	Europe	Montenegrin
Morocco	Rabat	Africa	Moroccan
Mozambique	Maputo	Africa	Mozambican
Myanmar (*see* Burma)			
Namibia	Windhoek	Africa	Namibian
Nauru	Yaren District	Oceania	Nauruan
Nepal	Kathmandu	Asia	Nepalese
Netherlands	Amsterdam;	Europe	Dutchman *or* Dutchwoman, *n.*; Dutch, *adj.*
New Zealand	Wellington	Oceania	New Zealander, *n.*; New Zealand, *adj.*
Nicaragua	Managua	North America	Nicaraguan
Niger	Niamey	Africa	Nigerien
Nigeria	Abuja	Africa	Nigerian
North Korea	Pyongyang	Asia	North Korean
Norway	Oslo	Europe	Norwegian
Oman	Muscat	Asia	Omani
Pakistan	Islamabad	Asia	Pakistani
Palau	Koror	Oceania	Palauan
Panama	Panama City	North America	Panamanian
Papua New Guinea	Port Moresby	Oceania	Papua New Guinean
Paraguay	Asunción	South America	Paraguayan
Peru	Lima	South America	Peruvian
Philippines	Manila	Asia	Filipino, *n.*; Philippine, *adj.*
Poland	Warsaw	Europe	Pole, *n.*; Polish, *adj.*
Portugal	Lisbon	Europe	Portuguese
Qatar	Doha	Asia	Qatari
Romania	Bucharest	Europe	Romanian
Russia	Moscow	Europe & Asia	Russian
Rwanda	Kigali	Africa	Rwandan, Rwandese
Saint Kitts and Nevis	Basseterre	North America	Kittsian; Nevisian
Saint Lucia	Castries	North America	St. Lucian
Saint Vincent and the Grenadines	Kingstown	North America	St. Vincentian *or* Vincentian
Samoa (*formerly* Western Samoa)	Apia	Oceania	Samoan
San Marino	San Marino	Europe	Sammarinese
São Tomé and Príncipe	São Tomé	Africa	Sao Tomean
Saudi Arabia	Riyadh	Asia	Saudi *or* Saudi Arabian
Senegal	Dakar	Africa	Senegalese
Serbia	Belgrade	Europe	Serbian
Seychelles	Victoria	Indian Ocean	Seychellois, *n.*; Seychelles, *adj.*
Sierra Leone	Freetown	Africa	Sierra Leonean
Singapore	Singapore	Asia	Singaporean, *n.*; Singapore, *adj.*
Slovakia	Bratislava	Europe	Slovak
Slovenia	Ljubljana	Europe	Slovene, *n.*; Slovenian, *adj.*
Solomon Islands	Honiara	Oceania	Solomon Islander
Somalia	Mogadishu	Africa	Somali
South Africa	Pretoria; Cape Town	Africa	South African

Country	Capital	Continent/Area	Nationality
South Korea	Seoul	Asia	South Korean
Spain	Madrid	Europe	Spanish
Sri Lanka	Colombo	Asia	Sri Lankan
Sudan	Khartoum	Africa	Sudanese
Suriname	Paramaribo	South America	Surinamer, *n.*; Surinamese, *adj.*
Swaziland	Mbabane	Africa	Swazi
Sweden	Stockholm	Europe	Swede, *n.*; Swedish, *adj.*
Switzerland	Berne	Europe	Swiss
Syria	Damascus	Asia	Syrian
Taiwan	Taipei	Asia	Taiwanese
Tajikistan	Dushanbe	Asia	Tajik
Tanzania	Dodoma	Africa	Tanzanian
Thailand	Bangkok	Asia	Thai
Timor-Leste	Dili	Asia	Timor-Lestean
Togo	Lomé	Africa	Togolese
Tonga	Nuku'alofa	Oceania	Tongan
Trinidad and Tobago	Port-of-Spain	South America	Trinidadian; Tobagonian
Tunisia	Tunis	Africa	Tunisian
Turkey	Ankara	Asia & Europe	Turk, *n.*; Turkish, *adj.*
Turkmenistan	Ashgabat	Asia	Turkmen
Tuvalu	Funafuti	Oceania	Tuvaluan
Uganda	Kampala	Africa	Ugandan
Ukraine	Kiev	Europe	Ukrainian
United Arab Emirates	Abu Dhabi	Africa	Emirati *or* Emirian
United Kingdom	London	Europe	Briton, *n.*; British, *collective pl. & adj.*
United States of America	Washington, DC	North America	American
Uruguay	Montevideo	South America	Uruguayan
Uzbekistan	Tashkent	Asia	Uzbek
Vanuatu	Vila	Oceania	Ni-Vanuatu
Venezuela	Caracas	South America	Venezuelan
Vietnam	Hanoi	Asia	Vietnamese
Western Samoa (*see* Samoa)			
Yemen	Sana'a	Asia	Yemeni
Zaire (*see* Congo)			
Zambia	Lusaka	Africa	Zambian
Zimbabwe	Harare	Africa	Zimbabwean

K[1] (also **k**) ▶ **noun** (pl. **Ks** or **K's**) the eleventh letter of the alphabet.

K[2] ▶ **abbreviation 1** kelvin(s). **2** Computing kilobyte(s). **3** kilometer(s). **4** (in card games and chess) king. **5** Köchel (catalog of Mozart's works). **6** informal thousand. ▶ **symbol** the chemical element potassium.

k ▶ **abbreviation** kilo-.

Kab·ba·lah /'kabələ, kə'bä-/ (also **Kabbala, Cabbala, Cabala**, or **Qabalah**) ▶ **noun** the ancient Jewish tradition of mystical interpretation of the Bible.
– DERIVATIVES **Kab·ba·lism** /'kabə,lizəm/ noun **Kab·ba·list** /-list/ noun **Kab·ba·lis·tic** /,kabə'listik/ adjective.
– ORIGIN Hebrew, 'tradition.'

ka·bob ▶ **noun** variant spelling of **KEBAB**.

ka·bu·ki /kə'bo͞okē/ ▶ **noun** a form of traditional Japanese drama performed by men, with stylized song, mime, and dance.
– ORIGIN Japanese.

ka-ching /kə'CHING/ ▶ **noun** used to represent the sound of a cash register, especially with reference to making money.

Kad·dish /'kädiSH/ ▶ **noun 1** an ancient Jewish prayer sequence recited in the synagogue service. **2** a form of the Kaddish recited for the dead.
– ORIGIN from Aramaic, 'holy.'

Kaf·fir /'kafər/ ▶ **noun** offensive, chiefly S. African a black African.
– ORIGIN Arabic, 'infidel.'

USAGE

The word **Kaffir** is a racially abusive and offensive term, and in South Africa its use is actionable.

kaf·fi·yeh /kə'fē(y)ə/ ▶ **noun** variant spelling of **KEFFIYEH**.

Kaf·ka·esque /,käfkə'esk/ ▶ **adjective** relating to the Czech novelist Franz Kafka or his nightmarish fictional world.

kaf·tan /'kaftən, -,tan/ (also **caftan**) ▶ **noun 1** a woman's long, loose dress. **2** a man's long belted tunic, worn in the Near East.
– ORIGIN Persian.

ka·hu·na /kə'ho͞onə/ ▶ **noun** informal an important person.
– ORIGIN Hawaiian, 'wise man, shaman.'

kai·se·ki /kī'sekē/ ▶ **noun** a style of traditional Japanese cuisine in which a series of very small, intricate dishes are prepared; a meal served in this style.

kai·ser /'kīzər/ ▶ **noun** historical the German Emperor, the Emperor of Austria, or the head of the Holy Roman Empire.

kal·an·cho·e /,kalən'kō-ē, kə'laNGkō-ē/ ▶ **noun** a tropical succulent plant with clusters of tubular flowers.
– ORIGIN Chinese.

Ka·lash·ni·kov /kə'läSHnə,kôf, -,kôv/ ▶ **noun** a type of rifle or submachine gun made in Russia.
– ORIGIN named after the Russian designer Mikhail T. *Kalashnikov*.

kale /kāl/ (also **kail**) ▶ **noun** a variety of cabbage with large dark-green leaves and a loosely packed head.
– ORIGIN Latin *caulis* 'stem, cabbage.'

ka·lei·do·scope /kə'līdə,skōp/ ▶ **noun 1** a toy consisting of a tube containing mirrors and pieces of colored glass or paper, whose reflections produce changing patterns when the tube is rotated. **2** a constantly changing pattern: *the dancers moved in a kaleidoscope of color.*
– DERIVATIVES **ka·lei·do·scop·ic** /-,līdə'skäpik/ adjective.
– ORIGIN from Greek *kalos* 'beautiful' + *eidos* 'form' + **-SCOPE**.

kal·ends ▶ **plural noun** variant spelling of **CALENDS**.

Ka·ma Su·tra /'kämə 'so͞otrə/ ▶ **noun** an ancient Sanskrit work on the art of love and sexual technique.
– ORIGIN Sanskrit, 'love thread.'

ka·mi·ka·ze /,kämi'käzē/ ▶ **noun** (in World War II) a Japanese aircraft loaded with explosives and making a deliberate suicidal crash on an enemy target. ▶ **adjective** reckless or potentially self-destructive.
– ORIGIN from the Japanese words for 'divinity' and 'wind.'

kan·ga·roo /,kaNGgə'ro͞o/ ▶ **noun** a large Australian marsupial with a long, powerful tail and strong hind legs that enable it to travel by leaping.
– ORIGIN from an Aboriginal language.

kan·ga·roo court ▶ **noun** an unofficial court formed by a group of people to try someone regarded as guilty of an offense.

kan·ga·roo rat ▶ **noun** a seed-eating, hopping rodent with large cheek pouches and long hind legs, found from Canada to Mexico.

Kant·i·an /'käntēən/ ▶ **adjective** relating to the German philosopher Immanuel Kant or his philosophy. ▶ **noun** a follower of Kant's philosophy.
– DERIVATIVES **Kant·i·an·ism** noun.

ka·o·lin /'kāəlin/ ▶ **noun** a fine soft white clay, used for making china and in medicine.
– ORIGIN from a Chinese word meaning 'high hill.'

ka·pok /'kā,päk/ ▶ **noun** a cottonlike substance that grows around the seeds of a tropical tree, used as stuffing for cushions, soft toys, etc.
– ORIGIN Malay.

Ka·po·si's sar·co·ma /kə'pōsēz sär'kōmə, 'kapə,sēz, 'käpō,SHēz/ ▶ **noun** a form of cancer involving multiple tumors of the lymph nodes or skin, occurring chiefly in people with depressed immune systems, for example, as a result of AIDS.
– ORIGIN named after Moritz K. *Kaposi* (1837–1902), Hungarian dermatologist.

ka·put /kəˈpo͝ot, kä-/ ▸ **adjective** informal broken and useless.
– ORIGIN German *kaputt*.

kar·a·bi·ner /ˌkarəˈbēnər/ (also **carabiner**) ▸ **noun** a coupling link with a safety closure, used by rock climbers.
– ORIGIN from German *Karabiner-haken* 'spring hook.'

kar·a·kul /ˈkarəkəl/ (also **caracul**) ▸ **noun 1** a breed of Asian sheep with a dark curled fleece when young. **2** cloth or fur made from or resembling the fleece of the karakul.
– ORIGIN Russian.

kar·a·o·ke /ˌkarēˈōkē/ ▸ **noun** a form of entertainment in which people sing popular songs over prerecorded backing tracks.
– ORIGIN Japanese, 'empty orchestra.'

kar·at /ˈkarət/ (chiefly Brit. also **carat**) ▸ **noun** a measure of the purity of gold, pure gold being 24 karats.

ka·ra·te /kəˈrätē/ ▸ **noun** an oriental system of unarmed combat using the hands and feet to deliver and block blows.
– ORIGIN Japanese, 'empty hand.'

kar·ma /ˈkärmə/ ▸ **noun 1** (in Hinduism and Buddhism) the sum of a person's actions in this and previous lives, viewed as affecting their fate in this or future existences. **2** informal good or bad luck, viewed as resulting from one's actions.
– DERIVATIVES **kar·mic** adjective.
– ORIGIN Sanskrit, 'action, effect, fate.'

karst /kärst/ ▸ **noun** Geology a limestone region with underground streams and many cavities in the rock.
– DERIVATIVES **kars·tic** adjective.
– ORIGIN from German *der Karst*, a limestone region in Slovenia.

kart /kärt/ ▸ **noun** a small race car with a tubular frame, no suspension, and a rear-mounted engine.
– DERIVATIVES **kart·ing** noun.
– ORIGIN shortening of **GO-KART**.

kas·bah /ˈkäzbä/ (also **casbah**) ▸ **noun** a fortress in the old part of a North African city, and the narrow streets that surround it.
– ORIGIN Arabic.

Kash·mir·i /ˌkashˈmi(ə)rē, ˌkazh-/ ▸ **noun** (pl. **Kashmiris**) **1** a person from Kashmir. **2** the language of Kashmir. ▸ **adjective** relating to Kashmir.

ka·ta /ˈkätə/ ▸ **noun 1** a system of individual training exercises for practitioners of karate and other martial arts. **2** (pl. same or **katas**) an individual exercise of this kind.
– ORIGIN Japanese.

ka·ta·na /kəˈtänə/ ▸ **noun** a long, single-edged sword used by samurai.
– ORIGIN Japanese.

ka·ty·did /ˈkātēˌdid/ ▸ **noun** a large North American insect related to the grasshoppers, the male of which makes a sound that resembles its name.

ka·va /ˈkävə/ ▸ **noun** a Polynesian drink that causes drowsiness, made from the crushed roots of a plant of the pepper family.
– ORIGIN Tongan.

kay·ak /ˈkīˌak/ ▸ **noun** a canoe made of a light frame with a watertight covering. ▸ **verb** (**kayaks, kayaking, kayaked**) travel in a kayak.
– DERIVATIVES **kay·ak·er** noun.
– ORIGIN Inuit.

ka·zoo /kəˈzo͞o/ ▸ **noun** a musical instrument consisting of a pipe with a hole in it, over which is a membrane that produces a buzzing sound when the player hums into it.
– ORIGIN probably imitating the sound produced.

KB (also **Kb**) ▸ **abbreviation** kilobyte(s).

KC ▸ **abbreviation 1** Kansas City. **2** Kennel Club. **3** Knights of Columbus.

kcal ▸ **abbreviation** kilocalorie(s).

ke·a /ˈkēə/ ▸ **noun** a New Zealand parrot with a long, narrow bill and mainly olive-green plumage.
– ORIGIN Maori.

ke·bab /kəˈbäb/ (also **kabob**) ▸ **noun** a dish of pieces of meat, fish, or vegetables roasted or grilled on a skewer or spit.
– ORIGIN Arabic.

kedge /kej/ ▸ **verb** move a boat by hauling in a hawser attached at a distance to an anchor. ▸ **noun** a small anchor used for kedging a boat.
– ORIGIN perhaps from dialect *cadge* 'bind, tie.'

keel /kēl/ ▸ **noun** a lengthwise structure along the base of a ship, often extended downward to increase stability. ▸ **verb** (**keel over**) **1** fall over; collapse. **2** (of a boat or ship) turn over on its side; capsize.

– SYNONYMS **1 collapse,** faint, pass out, black out, swoon. **2 capsize,** turn turtle, turn upside down, founder, overturn, turn over, tip over.

– ORIGIN Old Norse.

keel·boat /ˈkēlˌbōt/ ▸ **noun 1** a yacht built with a permanent keel rather than a centerboard. **2** a large, flat freight boat used on rivers.

keel·haul /ˈkēlˌhôl/ ▸ **verb 1** humorous punish or reprimand someone severely. **2** historical punish someone by dragging them through the water under the keel of a ship.

keel·son /ˈkēlsən/ (also **kelson**) ▸ **noun** a structure running the length of a ship, that fastens the timbers or plates of the floor to the keel.
– ORIGIN from German *kiel* 'keel' + *swīn* 'swine' (used as the name of a timber).

keen[1] /kēn/ ▸ **adjective 1** eager and enthusiastic. **2** (**keen on**) interested in: *the school was very keen on sports.* **3** (of a blade) sharp. **4** (of a sense) highly developed. **5** quick to understand things: *her keen intellect.* **6** (of the air or wind) extremely cold.

– SYNONYMS **1** *I'm keen to help* **eager,** anxious, intent, impatient, determined; informal raring, itching, dying. **2** *a keen birdwatcher* **enthusiastic,** avid, ardent, fervent, conscientious, committed, dedicated. **3** *a girl he was keen on* **attracted to,** interested in, fond of, infatuated with, taken with, smitten with, enamored of; informal stuck on. **4** *a keen cutting edge* **sharp,** sharpened, honed, razor-sharp. **5** *a keen sense of duty* **intense,** acute, fierce, passionate, burning, fervent, strong, powerful. **6** *a keen mind* **acute,** penetrating, astute, incisive, sharp, perceptive, piercing, razor-sharp, shrewd, discerning, clever, intelligent, brilliant, bright, smart, wise, insightful.
– ANTONYMS reluctant, unenthusiastic.

– DERIVATIVES **keen·ly** adverb **keen·ness** noun.
– ORIGIN Old English, 'clever, brave.'

CHOOSE THE RIGHT WORD

keen, acute, astute, penetrating, perspicacious, sharp, shrewd

A knife can be **sharp**, even **keen**, but it can't be **astute**. While *keen* and *sharp* mean having a fine point or edge, they also pertain to mental agility and perceptiveness. You might describe someone as having a *keen* mind, which suggests the ability to grapple with complex problems, or to observe details and see them as part of a larger pattern (*a keen appreciation of what victory would mean for the Democratic party*) or a *keen* wit, which suggests an incisive or stimulating sense of humor. Someone who is *sharp* has an alert and rational mind, but is not necessarily well grounded in a particular field and may in some cases be cunning or devious (*sharp enough to see how the situation might be turned to her advantage*). An **astute** mind, in contrast, is one that has a thorough and profound understanding of a given subject or field (*an astute understanding of the legal principles involved*). Like *sharp*, **shrewd** implies both practicality and cleverness, but with an undercurrent of self-interest (*a shrewd salesperson*). **Acute** is close in meaning to *keen*, but with more emphasis on sensitivity and the ability to make subtle distinctions (*an acute sense of smell*). While a keen mind might see only superficial details, a **penetrating** mind would focus on underlying causes (*a penetrating analysis of the plan's feasibility*). **Perspicacious** is the most formal of these terms, meaning both perceptive and discerning (*a perspicacious remark; perspicacious judgment*).

keen² ▶ **verb 1** wail in grief for a dead person. **2** make an eerie wailing sound. ▶ **noun** an Irish funeral song accompanied with wailing as a lament for the dead.
– ORIGIN from Irish *caoinim* 'I wail.'

keep /kēp/ ▶ **verb** (past and past part. **kept** /kept/) **1** continue to have something. **2** continue in a specified condition, position, or activity: *I should have kept quiet, but I blundered on.* **3** save or retain something for use in the future. **4** store something in a regular place. **5** do something promised, agreed, or necessary: *I have to go and keep another appointment soon.* **6** (of food) remain in good condition. **7** make a note about something. **8** write in a diary. **9** make someone late. **10** provide accommodations and food for someone. **11** own and look after an animal. **12** (as adj. **kept**) (of a woman) supported financially in return for sex.

– SYNONYMS **1** *I kept the forms* **retain,** hold on to, save, store, put aside, set aside; informal hang on to. **2** *keep calm* **remain,** stay. **3** *he keeps going on about it* **persist in,** keep on, carry on, continue, insist on. **4** *keep the rules* **comply with,** obey, observe, conform to, abide by, adhere to, stick to, heed, follow, carry out, act on, make good (on), honor, keep to, stand by. **5** *keeping the old traditions* **preserve,** keep alive/up, carry on, perpetuate, maintain, uphold. **6** *he stole to keep his family* **provide for,** support, feed, maintain, sustain, take care of, look after. **7** *she keeps rabbits* **breed,** rear, raise, tend, farm, own.

▶ **noun 1** food, clothes, and other essentials for living. **2** the strongest or central tower of a castle.

– SYNONYMS **maintenance,** upkeep, sustenance, board, room and board, food, livelihood.

– PHRASES **for keeps** informal permanently. **keep from** avoid doing something. **keep someone from** prevent someone from doing something. **keep something from** cause something to remain a secret from someone. **keep on** continue to do something. **keep someone/thing on** continue to use or employ someone or something. **keep to 1** avoid leaving a path, road, or place. **2** stay on schedule or to the point being discussed. **3** fulfill a promise. **keep up** move at the same rate as someone or something else. **keep something up** continue a course of action. **keep up with 1** be aware of current events. **2** continue to be in contact with someone. **keep up with the Joneses** try hard not to be outdone by one's neighbors or friends.
– ORIGIN Old English.

keep·er /ˈkēpər/ ▶ **noun 1** a person who manages or looks after something or someone. **2** a goalkeeper. **3** an object that protects or secures another. **4** informal a thing worth keeping.

– SYNONYMS **curator,** custodian, guardian, conservator, administrator, overseer, steward, caretaker, attendant, concierge.

keep·ing /ˈkēpiNG/ ▶ **noun** (in phrase **in** or **out of keeping with**) harmonious or suitable (or inharmonious or unsuitable) in a particular situation: *the cuisine is in keeping with the hotel's Edwardian character.*

– SYNONYMS **consistent with,** in harmony with, in accord with, in agreement with, in line with, in character with, compatible with, appropriate to, befitting, suitable for.

keep·sake /ˈkēpˌsāk/ ▶ **noun** a small item kept in memory of the person who gave it or originally owned it.

kef·fi·yeh /kəˈfē(y)ə/ (also **kaffiyeh**) ▶ **noun** a headdress worn by Arab men, consisting of a square of fabric fastened by a band around the head.
– ORIGIN Arabic.

keg /keg/ ▶ **noun** a small barrel. ▶ **adjective** (of beer) supplied in a keg, to which carbon dioxide has been added.
– ORIGIN Old Norse.

keis·ter /ˈkēstər/ (also **keester**) ▶ **noun 1** informal a person's buttocks. **2** dated a suitcase, bag, or box for carrying belongings or goods.
– ORIGIN unknown.

ke·loid /ˈkēˌloid/ ▶ **noun** an area of fibrous tissue formed at the site of a scar or injury.
– ORIGIN from Greek *khēlē* 'crab's claw.'

kelp /kelp/ ▶ **noun** a very large brown seaweed with broad fronds divided into strips.
– ORIGIN unknown.

kel·pie /ˈkelpē/ ▶ **noun** a water spirit of Scottish folklore, typically taking the form of a horse.
– ORIGIN perhaps from Scottish Gaelic *cailpeach, colpach* 'bullock, colt.'

kel·vin /ˈkelvən/ ▶ **noun** the SI base unit of thermodynamic temperature, equal to one degree Celsius.
– ORIGIN named after the British physicist William T. *Kelvin.*

Kel·vin scale ▶ **noun** the scale of temperature with absolute zero as zero and the freezing point of water as 273.15 kelvins.

ken /ken/ ▶ **noun** (**one's ken**) one's range of knowledge or understanding. ▶ **verb** (**kens, kenning**; past and past part. **kenned** or **kent** /kent/) Scottish & N. English **1** know someone or something. **2** recognize someone or something.
– ORIGIN from Old English, 'tell, make known.'

ken·do /ˈkenˌdō/ ▶ **noun** a Japanese form of fencing with two-handed bamboo swords.
– ORIGIN Japanese, 'sword way.'

ken·nel /ˈkenl/ ▸ **noun 1** a small shelter for a dog. **2** (**kennels**) (treated as sing. or pl.) a boarding or breeding establishment for dogs. ▸ **verb** (**kennels, kenneling, kenneled**) put or keep a dog in a kennel or kennels.
– ORIGIN Old French *chenil.*

kent /kent/ past and past participle of **KEN**.

Ken·yan /ˈkenyən, ˈkēnyən/ ▸ **noun** a person from Kenya. ▸ **adjective** relating to Kenya.

kep·i /ˈkāpē, ˈkepē/ ▸ **noun** (pl. **kepis**) a French military cap with a horizontal peak.
– ORIGIN French *képi.*

kept /kept/ past and past participle of **KEEP**.

ker·a·tin /ˈkerətin/ ▸ **noun** a fibrous protein forming the main constituent of hair, feathers, hoofs, claws, and horns.
– ORIGIN from Greek *keras* 'horn.'

kerb, etc. /kərb/ ▸ **noun** British spelling of **CURB** (sense 1 of the noun), etc.

ker·chief /ˈkərCHəf, -ˌCHēf/ ▸ **noun 1** a piece of fabric used to cover the head. **2** dated a handkerchief.
– ORIGIN Old French *cuevrechief.*

kerf /kərf/ ▸ **noun 1** a slit made by cutting with a saw. **2** the cut end of a felled tree.
– ORIGIN Old English.

ker·nel /ˈkərnl/ ▸ **noun 1** the softer part of a nut, seed, or fruit stone contained within its hard shell. **2** the seed and hard husk of a cereal, especially wheat. **3** the central or most important part of something: *there is a kernel of truth in what he asserted.*
– ORIGIN Old English, 'small corn.'

ker·o·sene /ˈkerəˌsēn, ˈkar-, ˌkerəˈsēn, ˌkar-/ ▸ **noun** a light fuel oil, used in jet engines and domestic heaters and lamps.
– ORIGIN from Greek *kēros* 'wax.'

kes·trel /ˈkestrəl/ ▸ **noun** a small falcon that hovers with rapidly beating wings while searching for prey.
– ORIGIN perhaps from Old French *crecerelle.*

ke·ta·mine /ˈketəˌmēn, -min/ ▸ **noun** a medical drug used as an anesthetic and painkiller and also illegally as a hallucinogen.
– ORIGIN blend of **KETONE** and **AMINE**.

ketch /keCH/ ▸ **noun** a type of two-masted sailboat.
– ORIGIN probably from **CATCH**.

ketch·up /ˈkeCHəp/ (also **catsup**) ▸ **noun** a spicy sauce made chiefly from tomatoes and vinegar.
– ORIGIN perhaps from Chinese, 'tomato juice.'

ke·tone /ˈkēˌtōn/ ▸ **noun** any of a class of organic chemical compounds including acetone.
– ORIGIN from German *Aketon* 'acetone.'

ke·to·sis /kēˈtōsis/ ▸ **noun** the condition of having raised levels of ketones in the body, associated with abnormal fat metabolism and diabetes mellitus.
– DERIVATIVES **ke·tot·ic** /-ˈtätik/ adjective.

ket·tle /ˈketl/ ▸ **noun** a metal or plastic container with a lid, spout, and handle, used for boiling water.
– PHRASES **a different kettle of fish** informal something completely different from the one just mentioned. **the pot calling the kettle black** used to say that a person is criticizing someone for faults that they have themselves. **a fine** (or **pretty**) **kettle of fish** informal an awkward situation.
– ORIGIN Latin *catillus* 'little pot.'

ket·tle·drum /ˈketlˌdrəm/ ▸ **noun** a large drum shaped like a bowl, with adjustable pitch.

keV ▸ **abbreviation** kiloelectronvolt(s).

Kev·lar /ˈkevlär/ ▸ **noun** trademark a very strong synthetic fiber used to reinforce tires, helmets, and bulletproof vests.

key[1] /kē/ ▸ **noun** (pl. **keys**) **1** a small piece of shaped metal that is inserted into a lock and turned to open or close it. **2** an instrument for grasping and turning a screw, peg, or nut. **3** a lever pressed down by the finger in playing an instrument such as the organ, piano, or flute. **4** each of several buttons on a panel for operating a typewriter or computer terminal. **5** a means of achieving or understanding something: *discipline seems to be the key to her success.* **6** an explanatory list of symbols used in a map or table. **7** a word or system for solving a code. **8** a group of musical notes based on a particular note and comprising a scale.

> – SYNONYMS **1** *the key to the mystery* **answer,** clue, solution, explanation, basis, foundation. **2** *the key to success* **means,** way, route, path, passport, secret, formula.

▸ **adjective** vitally important: *he was a key figure in the civil war.*

> – SYNONYMS **crucial,** central, essential, indispensable, pivotal, critical, vital, principal, prime, major, leading, main, important.

▸ **verb** (**keys, keying, keyed**) **1** enter or operate on data by means of a computer keyboard. **2** (**be keyed up**) be nervous, tense, or excited. **3** (**key something to**) make something suitable for or in harmony with: *courses keyed to the needs of health professionals.*
– ORIGIN Old English.

key[2] /kē/ ▸ **noun** a low-lying island or reef in the Caribbean or off the coast of Florida.
– ORIGIN Spanish *cayo* 'reef.'

key·board /ˈkēˌbôrd/ ▸ **noun 1** a panel of keys for use with a computer or typewriter. **2** a set of keys on a piano or similar musical instrument. **3** an electronic musical instrument with keys arranged as on a piano. ▸ **verb** enter data by means of a keyboard.
– DERIVATIVES **key·board·er** noun.

key card (also **card key**) ▸ **noun** a small plastic card that can be used instead of a door key, containing magnetically encoded data.

key grip ▸ **noun** the person in a film crew who is in charge of the camera equipment.

key·hole /ˈkēˌhōl/ ▸ **noun** a hole in a lock into which the key is inserted.

Keynes·i·an /ˈkānzēən/ ▸ **adjective** relating to the theories of the English economist John Maynard Keynes, who believed that government spending on public works is necessary to stimulate the economy and provide employment.
– DERIVATIVES **Keynes·i·an·ism** noun.

key·note /ˈkēˌnōt/ ▸ **noun 1** a central theme: *individuality was the keynote of the Nineties.* **2** the note on which a musical key is based. ▸ **adjective** (of a speech) setting out the central theme of a conference.

key·pad /ˈkēˌpad/ ▸ **noun** a small keyboard or set of buttons for operating a portable electronic device or telephone.

key·punch /ˈkēˌpənch/ ▸ **noun** a device for transferring data by means of punched holes or notches on a series of cards or paper tape.

key ring ▸ **noun** a metal ring for holding keys together in a bunch.

key sig·na·ture ▸ **noun** Music a combination of sharps or flats after the clef at the beginning of each stave, indicating the key of a composition.

key·stone /ˈkēˌstōn/ ▸ **noun** **1** the central part of a policy or system: *he has made tax cuts the keystone of his domestic policy.* **2** a central stone at the summit of an arch, locking the whole together.

key·stroke /ˈkēˌstrōk/ ▸ **noun** a single pressing of a key on a keyboard.

key·word /ˈkēˌwərd/ ▸ **noun** **1** a word or idea of great significance: *homes and jobs are the keywords in the campaign.* **2** a word used in a computer system to indicate the content of a document. **3** a significant word mentioned in an index.

kg ▸ **abbreviation** kilogram(s).

khak·i /ˈkakē/ ▸ **noun** (pl. **khakis**) **1** a cotton or wool fabric of a dull brownish-yellow color, used especially in military clothing. **2** a dull greenish- or yellowish-brown color. **3** (**khakis**) clothing, especially pants, of this fabric and color.
– ORIGIN from Urdu, 'dust-colored.'

Khal·sa /ˈkälsə/ ▸ **noun** the company of fully initiated Sikhs to which devout orthodox Sikhs are ritually admitted at puberty.
– ORIGIN from Arabic, 'pure, belonging to.'

khan /kän/ ▸ **noun** a title given to rulers and officials in central Asia, Afghanistan, and some other Muslim countries.
– DERIVATIVES **khan·ate** noun.
– ORIGIN Turkic, 'lord, prince.'

khat /kät/ ▸ **noun** the leaves of an Arabian shrub, which are chewed (or drunk as an infusion) as a stimulant.
– ORIGIN Arabic.

kheer /ki(ə)r/ ▸ **noun** an Indian dessert consisting of rice and sugar boiled in milk or coconut milk, often flavored with cardamom and ground nuts.

Khmer /kəˈme(ə)r, kme(ə)r/ ▸ **noun** (pl. same or **Khmers**) **1** a person from Cambodia. **2** the official language of Cambodia.

Khoi·khoi /ˈkoiˌkoi/ (also **Khoi**) ▸ **noun** (pl. same) a member of a group of peoples of South Africa and Namibia.
– ORIGIN Nama (a Khoikhoi language), 'men of men.'

kHz ▸ **abbreviation** kilohertz.

kib·ble /ˈkibəl/ ▸ **verb** (usu. as adj. **kibbled**) grind or chop beans, grain, etc., coarsely. ▸ **noun** ground meal shaped into pellets, especially for pet food.
– ORIGIN unknown.

kib·butz /kiˈbo͝ots/ ▸ **noun** (pl. **kibbutzim** /kiˌbo͝otˈsēm/) a farming settlement in Israel in which work is shared by the whole community.
– ORIGIN modern Hebrew, 'gathering.'

kib·butz·nik /kiˈbo͝otsnik/ ▸ **noun** a member of a kibbutz.

kib·itz /ˈkibits/ ▸ **verb** informal **1** look on and offer unwelcome advice, especially at a card game. **2** speak informally; chat.
– DERIVATIVES **kib·itz·er** noun.
– ORIGIN Yiddish.

ki·bosh /kəˈbäsh, ˈkīˌbäsh/ (also **kybosh**) ▸ **noun** (in phrase **put the kibosh on**) informal put a decisive end to: *he put the kibosh on the deal.*
– ORIGIN unknown.

kick /kik/ ▸ **verb** **1** hit or propel someone or something forcibly with the foot. **2** strike out with the foot or feet. **3** informal succeed in giving up a habit or addiction. **4** (of a gun) recoil when fired.

> – SYNONYMS **1 boot,** punt; informal hoof. **2** informal *he was struggling to kick his drug habit* **give up,** break, abandon, end, stop, cease, desist from, renounce; informal shake, pack in, leave off, quit.

▸ **noun** **1** an instance of kicking. **2** informal a thrill of pleasurable excitement: *rich kids turning to crime just for kicks.* **3** informal the strong stimulating effect of alcohol or a drug.

> – SYNONYMS *I get a kick out of driving* **thrill,** excitement, stimulation, tingle, frisson; informal charge, buzz, high.

– PHRASES **kick against** resist or disagree with something. **kick around** (or **about**) lie unwanted or unused. **kick someone around** treat someone roughly or without respect. **kick something around** discuss an idea informally. **kick the bucket** informal die. **kick in** come into effect or operation. **a kick in the teeth** informal a serious setback. **kick off 1** (of a football or soccer game) be started or resumed by a player kicking the ball from the center spot. **2** (also **kick something off**) begin or cause something to begin. **kick oneself** be annoyed with oneself. **kick someone out** informal expel or dismiss someone.
– ORIGIN unknown.

kick-ass ▸ **adjective** informal forceful, vigorous, and aggressive: *he's a kick-ass guy who takes no prisoners.*

kick·back /ˈkikˌbak/ ▸ **noun** **1** a sudden forceful recoil. **2** informal an underhanded payment made to someone in return for help in arranging a business or political deal.

kick-box·ing ▸ **noun** a form of martial art that combines boxing with elements of karate, in particular kicking with bare feet.

kick·er /ˈkikər/ ▸ **noun** **1** the player in a team who scores by kicking or who kicks to gain positional advantage. **2** informal an unexpected and often unpleasant discovery or turn of events. **3** an extra clause in a contract.

kick·ing /ˈkiking/ ▸ **adjective** informal (especially of music) lively and exciting.

kick·off /ˈkikˌôf/ ▸ **noun** **1** the start or resumption of a soccer match, with a kick from the center spot. **2** informal the start of an event or activity.

kick-pleat ▸ **noun** an inverted pleat in a narrow skirt to allow freedom of movement.

kick·stand /ˈkikˌstand/ ▸ **noun** a rod attached to a bicycle or motorcycle that may be kicked into a vertical position to support the vehicle when it is stationary.

kick-start ▸ **verb** **1** start a motorcycle engine with a downward thrust of a pedal. **2** provide an impetus to start or boost a process: *the government could kick-start the economy by cutting interest rates.* ▸ **noun** **1** an act of kick-starting something. **2** a device to kick-start an engine.

kid[1] /kid/ ▸ **noun** **1** informal a child or young person. **2** a young goat.

– SYNONYMS **child,** youngster, baby, toddler, tot, infant, boy, girl, minor, juvenile, adolescent, teenager, youth, stripling. informal kiddie, rug rat, (little) nipper. derogatory brat.

– PHRASES **handle** (or **treat**) **someone/thing with kid gloves** deal with someone or something very carefully. **kids' stuff** informal something that is easy or simple to do.
– ORIGIN Old Norse.

kid² ▶ **verb** (**kids, kidding, kidded**) informal **1** fool someone into believing something. **2** (**kid around**) behave in a silly way.
– ORIGIN perhaps from KID[1], expressing the idea 'make a child or goat of.'

kid broth·er (or **kid sister**) ▶ **noun** informal a younger brother (or sister).

kid·die /'kidē/ (also **kiddy**) ▶ **noun** (pl. **kiddies**) informal a young child.

kid·do /'kidō/ ▶ **noun** (pl. **kiddos** or **kiddoes**) informal used as a friendly or slightly condescending form of address.

kid·dush /'kidəsн, kē'do͞osн/ ▶ **noun** a Jewish ceremony of prayer and blessing over wine, performed at a meal preceding the Sabbath or a holy day.
– ORIGIN Hebrew, 'sanctification.'

kid·nap /'kid,nap/ ▶ **verb** (**kidnaps, kidnapping, kidnapped;** also **kidnaps, kidnaping, kidnaped**) take someone by force and keep them captive, typically to obtain a ransom for their release.

– SYNONYMS **abduct,** carry off, capture, seize, snatch, take hostage.

▶ **noun** an instance of kidnapping someone.
– DERIVATIVES **kid·nap·per** noun.
– ORIGIN from KID[1] + slang *nap* 'seize.'

kid·ney /'kidnē/ ▶ **noun** (pl. **kidneys**) **1** each of a pair of organs in the abdominal cavity that remove waste products from the blood and excrete urine. **2** the kidney of a sheep, ox, or pig as food.
– ORIGIN unknown.

kid·ney bean ▶ **noun** a dark red kidney-shaped bean, eaten as a vegetable.

kid·ney ma·chine ▶ **noun** a machine that performs the functions of a person's kidney when one or both organs are damaged.

kid·ney stone ▶ **noun** a hard mass formed in the kidneys, typically consisting of insoluble calcium compounds.

kiel·ba·sa /kil'bäsə, kēl-/ ▶ **noun** a highly seasoned Polish sausage, typically containing garlic.
– ORIGIN Polish, literally 'sausage.'

kif /kif/ (also **kef** /kef/) ▶ **noun** a substance, especially powdered resin from the cannabis plant, smoked to produce a drowsy state.
– ORIGIN Arabic, 'enjoyment, well-being.'

ki·lim /kē'lēm, 'kiləm/ (also **kelim**) ▶ **noun** a carpet or rug woven without a pile, made in Turkey, Kurdistan, and neighboring areas.
– ORIGIN Persian.

kill /kil/ ▶ **verb** **1** cause the death of someone or something. **2** put an end to or defeat something. **3** informal overwhelm someone with an emotion: *the suspense is killing me.* **4** informal cause pain or distress to someone. **5** pass time, typically while waiting for an event.

– SYNONYMS **murder,** assassinate, eliminate, terminate, dispatch, execute, slaughter, exterminate, butcher, massacre; informal bump off, do away with, do in, take out, blow away, rub out, whack, waste; literary slay.

▶ **noun** **1** an act of killing, especially of one animal by another. **2** an animal or animals killed by a hunter or another animal.
– PHRASES **be in at the kill** be present at or benefit from the successful completion of an enterprise.
– ORIGIN probably Germanic.

kill·deer /'kil,di(ə)r/ (also **killdeer plover**) ▶ **noun** a widespread American plover with a plaintive call that resembles its name.

kill·er /'kilər/ ▶ **noun** **1** a person or thing that kills. **2** informal a very impressive or difficult thing. **3** informal a hilarious joke.

– SYNONYMS **murderer,** assassin, butcher, gunman, terminator, executioner; informal hit man.

kill·er whale ▶ **noun** a large toothed whale with black-and-white markings and a prominent fin on its back.

kil·li·fish /'kilē,fisн/ ▶ **noun** (pl. same or **killifishes**) a small, brightly colored fish of fresh or brackish water.
– ORIGIN probably from KILL and FISH[1].

kill·ing /'kiliɴɢ/ ▶ **noun** an act of causing death.

– SYNONYMS **murder,** assassination, homicide, manslaughter, execution, slaughter, massacre, butchery, bloodshed, carnage, extermination, genocide.

▶ **adjective** informal exhausting or unbearable.
– PHRASES **make a killing** make a great deal of money out of something.

kill·ing field ▶ **noun** a place where many people have been killed, especially during a war.

kill·joy /'kil,joi/ ▶ **noun** a person who spoils the enjoyment of others by behaving very seriously or disapprovingly.

kiln /kiln, kil/ ▶ **noun** a furnace or oven for burning, baking, or drying pottery, bricks, or lime.
– ORIGIN Latin *culina* 'kitchen, cooking stove.'

ki·lo /'kēlō/ ▶ **noun** (pl. **kilos**) a kilogram.

kilo- ▶ **combining form** referring to a factor of one thousand (10^3): *kilometer.*
– ORIGIN from Greek *khilioi* 'thousand.'

kil·o·byte /'kilə,bīt/ ▶ **noun** a unit of information stored in a computer equal to 1,024 bytes.

kil·o·cal·o·rie /'kilə,kalərē/ ▶ **noun** a unit of energy of one thousand calories (equal to one large calorie).

kil·o·gram /'kilə,gram/ ▶ **noun** the SI unit of mass, equal to 1,000 grams (approximately 2.205 lb).

kil·o·hertz /'kilə,hərts/ ▶ **noun** a measure of frequency equivalent to 1,000 cycles per second.

kil·o·joule /'kilə,jo͞ol, 'kilə,joul/ ▶ **noun** 1,000 joules, especially as a measure of the energy value of foods.

kil·o·li·ter /'kilə,lētər/ ▶ **noun** 1,000 liters (equivalent to 220 imperial gallons).

kil·o·me·ter /ki'lämitər, 'kilə,mētər/ (Brit. **kilometre**) ▶ **noun** a metric unit of measurement equal to 1,000 meters (approximately 0.62 miles).
– DERIVATIVES **kil·o·met·ric** /,kilə'metrik/ adjective.

kil·o·ton /'kilə,tən/ ▶ **noun** a unit of explosive power equivalent to 1,000 tons of TNT.

kil·o·volt /ˈkiləˌvōlt/ ▸ **noun** 1,000 volts.

kil·o·watt /ˈkiləˌwät/ ▸ **noun** 1,000 watts.

kil·o·watt-hour ▸ **noun** a measure of electrical energy equivalent to a power consumption of one thousand watts for one hour.

kilt /kilt/ ▸ **noun** a knee-length skirt of pleated tartan cloth, traditionally worn by men as part of Scottish Highland dress. ▸ **verb** (usu. as adj. **kilted**) arrange a garment or material in pleats.
– DERIVATIVES **kilt·ed** adjective.
– ORIGIN Scandinavian.

kil·ter /ˈkiltər/ ▸ **noun** (in phrase **out of kilter**) out of harmony or balance.
– ORIGIN unknown.

kim·chi /ˈkimCHē/ ▸ **noun** a Korean dish of spicy pickled cabbage.
– ORIGIN Korean.

ki·mo·no /kəˈmōnō, -nə/ ▸ **noun** (pl. **kimonos**) a long, loose Japanese robe having wide sleeves and tied with a sash.
– ORIGIN Japanese, 'wearing thing.'

kin /kin/ ▸ **noun** (treated as pl.) one's family and relations.

> – SYNONYMS **relatives,** relations, family, kith and kin, kindred, kinsfolk, kinsmen, kinswomen, people; informal folks.

▸ **adjective** (of a person) related.
– ORIGIN Old English.

kind[1] /kīnd/ ▸ **noun 1** a group or type of people or things with similar characteristics: *all kinds of music.* **2** character; nature: *language makes humans different in kind from other animals.* **3** (in the Christian Church) each of the elements (bread and wine) consumed during Holy Communion.

> – SYNONYMS **sort,** type, variety, style, form, class, category, genre, genus, species.

– PHRASES **in kind 1** in the same way. **2** (of payment) in goods or services as opposed to money. **kind of** informal rather. **of a kind** only partly deserving the name. **one of a kind** unique. **two** (or **three, four,** etc.) **of a kind** the same or very similar.
– ORIGIN Old English.

> **USAGE**
>
> When using **kind** to refer to a plural noun, it is incorrect to say *these kind of questions are not relevant* (that is, to have *kind* in the singular): you should use *kinds* instead (*these kinds of questions are not relevant*).

kind[2] ▸ **adjective** caring, friendly, and generous.

> – SYNONYMS **kindly,** good-natured, kind-hearted, warmhearted, caring, affectionate, loving, warm, considerate, obliging, compassionate, sympathetic, understanding, benevolent, benign, altruistic, unselfish, generous, charitable, philanthropic, helpful, thoughtful, humane; informal decent.
> – ANTONYMS unkind.

– ORIGIN Old English, 'natural, native.'

kind·a /ˈkīndə/ informal ▸ **contraction** kind of: *I think it's kinda funny.*

kin·der·gar·ten /ˈkindərˌgärtn, -ˌgärdn/ ▸ **noun** a school that prepares children for first grade.
– DERIVATIVES **kin·der·gar·ten·er** /-ˌgärtnər, -ˌgärd-/ (also **kindergartner**) noun.
– ORIGIN German, 'children's garden.'

kind-heart·ed ▸ **adjective** having a kind and sympathetic nature.
– DERIVATIVES **kind-heart·ed·ly** adverb **kind-heart·ed·ness** noun.

kin·dle /ˈkindl/ ▸ **verb 1** light a flame or set something on fire. **2** arouse an emotion or reaction: *his enthusiasm for politics was kindled by his wife.*

> – SYNONYMS **1 light,** ignite, set light to, set fire to; informal torch. **2 rouse,** arouse, wake, awaken, stimulate, inspire, stir (up), excite, fire, trigger, activate, spark.
> – ANTONYMS extinguish.

– ORIGIN from Old Norse, 'candle, torch.'

kin·dling /ˈkindliNG/ ▸ **noun** small sticks or twigs used for lighting fires.

kind·ly /ˈkīn(d)lē/ ▸ **adverb 1** in a kind way. **2** please (used in a polite request). ▸ **adjective** (**kindlier, kindliest**) kind; warm-hearted.

> – SYNONYMS **benevolent,** kind, kind-hearted, warmhearted, generous, good-natured, gentle, warm, compassionate, caring, loving, benign, well meaning, considerate.
> – ANTONYMS unkind, cruel.

– DERIVATIVES **kind·li·ness** noun.
– PHRASES **not take kindly to** not welcome or be pleased by something.

kind·ness /ˈkīn(d)nis/ ▸ **noun 1** the quality of being caring, friendly, and generous. **2** a kind act.

> – SYNONYMS **kindliness,** affection, warmth, gentleness, concern, care, consideration, altruism, unselfishness, compassion, sympathy, benevolence, generosity.
> – ANTONYMS unkindness.

kin·dred /ˈkindrid/ ▸ **noun 1** (treated as pl.) one's family and relations. **2** relationship by blood. ▸ **adjective** having similar qualities: *books on kindred subjects.*
– ORIGIN Old English.

kin·dred spir·it ▸ **noun** a person whose interests or attitudes are similar to one's own.

kine /kīn/ ▸ **plural noun** old use cows as a group; cattle.

kin·e·mat·ics /ˌkinəˈmatiks/ ▸ **plural noun** (treated as sing.) the branch of mechanics concerned with the motion of objects without reference to the forces that cause the motion.
– DERIVATIVES **kin·e·mat·ic** adjective.
– ORIGIN from Greek *kinēma* 'motion.'

ki·ne·si·ol·o·gy /kəˌnēsēˈäləjē, -zē-/ ▸ **noun** the study of the mechanics of body movements.

ki·ne·sis /kəˈnēsis/ ▸ **noun** technical movement; motion.
– ORIGIN Greek.

ki·net·ic /kəˈnetik/ ▸ **adjective 1** relating to or resulting from motion. **2** (of a work of art) depending on movement for its effect.
– DERIVATIVES **ki·net·i·cal·ly** adverb.
– ORIGIN Greek *kinētikos.*

ki·net·ic en·er·gy ▸ **noun** Physics energy that a body possesses as a result of being in motion. Compare with **POTENTIAL ENERGY.**

ki·net·ics /kəˈnetiks/ ▸ **plural noun** (treated as sing.) **1** the branch of chemistry concerned with the rates of chemical reactions. **2** Physics another term for **DYNAMICS** (sense 1).

ki·ne·to·scope /kəˈnetəˌskōp, -ˈnē-/ ▸ **noun** an early motion-picture device in which the images were viewed through a peephole.

kin·folk /ˈkinˌfōk/ (also **kinsfolk**) ▸ **plural noun** a person's family and other blood relations.

king /kiNG/ ▸ **noun 1** the male ruler of an independent country, especially one who inherits the position by birth. **2** the best or most important person or thing in an area of activity or group: *India's king of fruits, the mango.* **3** a playing card bearing a picture of a king, ranking next below an ace. **4** the most important chess piece, which the opponent has to checkmate in order to win. **5** a piece in checkers with extra capacity for moving, made by crowning an ordinary piece that has reached the opponent's baseline.

– SYNONYMS **ruler,** sovereign, monarch, Crown, His Majesty, emperor, prince, potentate.

– DERIVATIVES **king·ly** adjective **king·ship** noun.
– ORIGIN Old English.

king·bird /ˈkiNGˌbərd/ ▸ **noun** a large American tyrant flycatcher, typically with a gray head and back and yellowish or white underparts.

King Charles span·iel ▸ **noun** a small breed of spaniel with a white, black, and tan coat.
– ORIGIN named after King Charles II of England, Scotland, and Ireland.

king co·bra ▸ **noun** a brownish cobra native to the Indian subcontinent, the largest of all venomous snakes.

king·dom /ˈkiNGdəm/ ▸ **noun 1** a country, state, or territory ruled by a king or queen. **2** an area associated with or dominated by a particular person or thing: *the world they came upon was far from being a kingdom of brotherly love.* **3** the spiritual reign or authority of God. **4** each of the three divisions (animal, vegetable, and mineral) in which natural objects are classified.

– SYNONYMS **realm,** domain, dominion, country, empire, land, territory, nation, (sovereign) state, province.

– PHRASES **to kingdom come** informal into the next world.

king·fish·er /ˈkiNGˌfisHər/ ▸ **noun** a colorful bird with a long sharp beak that dives to catch fish in rivers and ponds.

King James Bi·ble (also **King James Version**) ▸ **noun** another name for **AUTHORIZED VERSION**.

king·let /ˈkiNGlit/ ▸ **noun** a very small greenish bird with a bright orange or yellow crown.

king·mak·er /ˈkiNGˌmākər/ ▸ **noun** a person who uses their political influence to bring a leader to power.
– ORIGIN first used with reference to the Earl of Warwick (1428–71).

king of beasts ▸ **noun** the lion.

King of Kings ▸ **noun** (in the Christian Church) God.

king·pin /ˈkiNGˌpin/ ▸ **noun 1** a main or large bolt in a central position. **2** a vertical bolt used as a pivot. **3** a person or thing that is essential to the success of an organization or operation.

king post ▸ **noun** an upright post in the center of a roof truss, extending from the tie beam to the apex of the truss.

king-sized (also **king-size**) ▸ **adjective** of a larger size than normal; very large.

kink /kiNGk/ ▸ **noun 1** a sharp twist or curve in something that is otherwise straight. **2** a flaw or obstacle in a plan or operation. **3** a quirk in a person's character. ▸ **verb** form a kink in something.
– ORIGIN German *kinke*.

kin·ka·jou /ˈkiNGkəˌjo͞o/ ▸ **noun** a mammal with a tail that can grasp things, found in the tropical forests of Central and South America.
– ORIGIN Algonquian.

kink·y /ˈkiNGkē/ ▸ **adjective (kinkier, kinkiest) 1** informal relating to or liking unusual sexual activities. **2** having kinks or twists.
– DERIVATIVES **kink·i·ly** adverb **kink·i·ness** noun.

kins·folk /ˈkinzˌfōk/ ▸ **plural noun** also **KINFOLK**.

kin·ship /ˈkinˌsHip/ ▸ **noun 1** family or blood relationship. **2** a sharing of characteristics or origins: *they felt a kinship with architects.*

kins·man /ˈkinzmən/ (or **kinswoman**) ▸ **noun** (pl. **kinsmen** or **kinswomen**) one of a person's blood relations.

ki·osk /ˈkēˌäsk/ ▸ **noun** a small open-fronted cubicle from which newspapers, refreshments, or tickets are sold.
– ORIGIN Turkish *köşk* 'pavilion.'

kip·per /ˈkipər/ ▸ **noun** a herring that has been split open, salted, and dried or smoked. ▸ **verb** cure a herring by splitting it open and salting and drying or smoking it.
– ORIGIN Old English, referring to a male salmon in the spawning season.

kirk /kərk/ ▸ **noun** Scottish & N. English **1** a church. **2** (**the Kirk** or **the Kirk of Scotland**) the Church of Scotland.
– ORIGIN from the same Old English root as **CHURCH**.

kirsch /ki(ə)rsH/ ▸ **noun** brandy distilled from the fermented juice of cherries.
– ORIGIN German.

kir·tle /ˈkərtl/ ▸ **noun** old use **1** a woman's gown or outer petticoat. **2** a man's tunic or coat.
– ORIGIN Old English.

kis·met /ˈkizmit, -ˌmet/ ▸ **noun** destiny or fate.
– ORIGIN Arabic, 'division, portion, lot.'

kiss /kis/ ▸ **verb 1** touch or caress someone with the lips as a sign of love, affection, or greeting. **2** Billiards (of a ball) lightly touch another ball.

– SYNONYMS informal peck, smooch, canoodle, neck, buss, make out, lock lips. formal osculate.

▸ **noun** a touch or caress with the lips.

– SYNONYMS French kiss; informal peck, smooch, smack, buss, X.

– DERIVATIVES **kiss·a·ble** adjective.
– PHRASES **kiss of death** an action that ensures that an enterprise will fail. **kiss of life 1** mouth-to-mouth resuscitation. **2** something that revives a failing enterprise. **kiss of peace** a ceremonial kiss given as a sign of unity, especially during the Christian Eucharist (Holy Communion).
– ORIGIN Old English.

kiss·er /ˈkisər/ ▸ **noun 1** a person who kisses someone. **2** informal a person's mouth.

kiss·ing cous·in ▸ **noun** a relative known well enough to greet with a kiss.

kiss·o·gram /ˈkisəˌgram/ ▸ **noun** a novelty greeting delivered by a person who accompanies it with a kiss.

kiss·y /ˈkisē/ ▸ **adjective** informal involving or fond of kissing; amorous.

Ki·swa·hi·li /ˌkiswäˈhēlē/ ▶ **noun** another term for **Swahili**.

kit[1] /kit/ ▶ **noun 1** a set of articles or equipment for a specific purpose. **2** a set of all the parts needed to assemble something.

– SYNONYMS **1 equipment,** tools, implements, instruments, gadgets, utensils, appliances, gear, tackle, hardware, paraphernalia; informal things, stuff; Military accoutrements. **2** *a model airplane kit* **set,** pack, do-it-yourself kit.

▶ **verb** (**kit someone/thing out**) provide someone or something with appropriate clothing or equipment.

– SYNONYMS **equip,** fit (out/up), furnish, supply, provide, issue, dress, clothe, attire, rig out, deck out; informal fix up.

– ORIGIN Dutch *kitte* 'wooden container.'

kit[2] ▶ **noun** the young of certain animals, e.g., the beaver, ferret, and mink.

kit bag ▶ **noun** a long cylindrical canvas bag for carrying a soldier's possessions.

kitch·en /ˈkicнən/ ▶ **noun 1** a room where food is prepared and cooked. **2** a set of cabinets and appliances installed in a kitchen.
– ORIGIN Old English.

kitch·en cab·i·net ▶ **noun** informal a group of unofficial political advisers considered to be too influential.

kitch·en·ette /ˌkicнəˈnet/ ▶ **noun** a small kitchen or part of a room equipped as a kitchen.

kitch·en gar·den ▶ **noun** a garden where vegetables and fruit are grown for household use.

kitch·en-sink ▶ **adjective** (of drama) dealing with working-class life in a very realistic way.

kitch·en·ware /ˈkicнənˌwe(ə)r/ ▶ **noun** kitchen utensils.

kite /kīt/ ▶ **noun 1** a toy consisting of a light frame with thin material stretched over it, flown in the wind at the end of a long string. **2** a long-winged bird of prey with a forked tail and a soaring flight. **3** Geometry a quadrilateral figure having two pairs of equal sides next to each other. ▶ **verb 1** (usu. as n. **kiting**) fly a kite. **2** informal write or use a check fraudulently.
– ORIGIN Old English.

kite·surf·ing /ˈkītˌsərfiNG/ (also **kiteboarding**) ▶ **noun** the sport of riding on a surfboard while harnessed or holding onto a specially designed kite, using the wind for propulsion.

kith /kiтн/ ▶ **noun** (in phrase **kith and kin**) one's family and other relations.
– ORIGIN Old English.

kitsch /kicн/ ▶ **noun** art, objects, or design considered to be tastelessly showy or sentimental.
– DERIVATIVES **kitsch·i·ness** noun **kitsch·y** adjective.
– ORIGIN German.

kit·ten /ˈkitn/ ▶ **noun 1** a young cat. **2** the young of certain other animals, such as the rabbit and beaver. ▶ **verb** give birth to kittens.
– PHRASES **have kittens** informal be very nervous or upset.
– ORIGIN Old French *chitoun*.

kit·ten heel ▶ **noun** a type of low stiletto heel.

kit·ten·ish /ˈkitn-isн/ ▶ **adjective** playful, lively, or flirtatious.
– DERIVATIVES **kit·ten·ish·ly** adverb.

kit·ti·wake /ˈkitēˌwāk/ ▶ **noun** a small gull that nests in colonies on sea cliffs and has a loud call that resembles its name.

kit·ty[1] /ˈkitē/ ▶ **noun** (pl. **kitties**) **1** a fund of money for use by a group of people. **2** a pool of money in some card games.
– ORIGIN unknown.

kit·ty[2] ▶ **noun** (pl. **kitties**) a pet name for a cat.

kit·ty-cor·ner ▶ **adjective & adverb** another term for **CATER-CORNERED**.

ki·wi /ˈkēwē/ ▶ **noun** (pl. **kiwis**) **1** a flightless, tailless New Zealand bird with hairlike feathers and a long downcurved bill. **2** (**Kiwi**) informal a New Zealander.
– ORIGIN Maori.

ki·wi fruit ▶ **noun** (pl. same) the fruit of an Asian climbing plant, with a thin hairy skin, green flesh, and black seeds.

kJ ▶ **abbreviation** kilojoule(s).

KKK ▶ **abbreviation** Ku Klux Klan.

Klans·man /ˈklanzmən/ (or **Klanswoman** /ˈklanzˈwo͝omən/) ▶ **noun** (pl. **Klansmen** or **Klanswomen**) a member of the Ku Klux Klan, an extremist right-wing secret society in the US.

klax·on /ˈklaksən/ ▶ **noun** trademark an electric horn or similar loud warning device.
– ORIGIN the name of the manufacturers.

klep·to·ma·ni·a /ˌkleptəˈmānēə, -ˈmānyə/ ▶ **noun** a recurrent urge to steal things.
– DERIVATIVES **klep·to·ma·ni·ac** noun & adjective.
– ORIGIN from Greek *kleptēs* 'thief.'

klieg light /klēg/ ▶ **noun** a powerful electric lamp used in filming.
– ORIGIN named after the American brothers, Anton T. and John H. *Kliegl*, who invented it.

klip·spring·er /ˈklipˌspriNGər/ ▶ **noun** a small antelope native to rocky regions of southern Africa.
– ORIGIN Dutch, 'rock jumper.'

kludge /klo͞oj/ ▶ **noun** informal something hastily or badly put together.
– ORIGIN invented word.

klutz /kləts/ ▶ **noun** informal a clumsy, awkward, or foolish person.
– DERIVATIVES **klutz·y** adjective.
– ORIGIN Yiddish, 'wooden block.'

km ▶ **abbreviation** kilometer(s).

knack /nak/ ▶ **noun 1** a skill at performing a task. **2** a tendency to do something: *he had the knack of falling asleep anywhere*.

– SYNONYMS **1 gift,** talent, flair, instinct, genius, ability, capability, capacity, aptitude, bent, facility, trick; informal the hang of something. **2 tendency,** habit, liability, propensity.

– ORIGIN probably from former *knack* 'sharp blow or sound.'

knap·sack /ˈnapˌsak/ ▶ **noun** a small rucksack used by soldiers and hikers.
– ORIGIN Dutch *knapzack*.

knap·weed /ˈnapˌwēd/ ▶ **noun** a plant with purple thistlelike flowerheads.
– ORIGIN from *knop* 'knob' (because of its rounded flower heads).

knave /nāv/ ▶ **noun 1** old use a dishonest or unscrupulous man. **2** (in cards) a jack.
– DERIVATIVES **knav·er·y** noun **knav·ish** adjective.
– ORIGIN Old English, 'boy, servant.'

knead /nēd/ ▶ **verb 1** work dough or clay with the hands. **2** massage a part of the body by squeezing and pressing it.
– ORIGIN Old English.

knee /nē/ ▶ **noun 1** the joint between the thigh and the lower leg. **2** the upper surface of a person's thigh when in a sitting position. ▶ **verb** (**knees, kneeing, kneed**) hit someone with the knee.
– PHRASES **bring someone to their knees** defeat someone or force them to submit.
– ORIGIN Old English.

knee·cap /ˈnēˌkap/ ▶ **noun** the convex bone in front of the knee joint. ▶ **verb** (**kneecaps, kneecapping, kneecapped**) shoot someone in the knee or leg as a punishment.

knee-high ▶ **noun** (usu. **knee-highs**) a sock or nylon stocking with an elasticized top that reaches the knee.

knee-jerk ▶ **noun** an involuntary kick caused by a blow on the tendon just below the knee. ▶ **adjective** automatic and unthinking: *a knee-jerk reaction*.

kneel /nēl/ ▶ **verb** (past and past part. **knelt** /nelt/ or also **kneeled**) fall or rest on a knee or the knees.
– ORIGIN Old English.

kneel·er /ˈnēlər/ ▶ **noun** a cushion or bench for kneeling on.

knell /nel/ literary ▶ **noun** the sound of a bell, especially when rung solemnly for a death or funeral. ▶ **verb** (of a bell) ring solemnly.
– ORIGIN Old English.

knelt /nelt/ past and past participle of **KNEEL**.

knew /n(y)o͞o/ past of **KNOW**.

knick·er·bock·ers /ˈnikərˌbäkərz/ ▶ **plural noun** short loose-fitting trousers gathered in at or just below the knee.
– ORIGIN from Diedrich *Knickerbocker*, the pretended author of Washington Irving's *History of New York*, the Dutch settlers in the book wearing short trousers that fastened at the knee.

knick·ers /ˈnikərz/ ▶ **plural noun 1** knickerbockers. **2** Brit. a woman's or girl's underpants.
– ORIGIN abbreviation of *knickerbockers*.

knick-knack /ˈnikˌnak/ ▶ **noun** a small ornament, usually one of little value.
– ORIGIN from **KNACK**.

knife /nīf/ ▶ **noun** (pl. **knives** /nīvz/) **1** a cutting instrument consisting of a blade fixed into a handle. **2** a cutting blade on a machine. ▶ **verb** stab someone with a knife.

– SYNONYMS **stab,** hack, gash, slash, lacerate, cut, bayonet, wound.

– PHRASES **at knifepoint** /ˈnīfˌpoint/ under threat of injury from a knife.
– ORIGIN Old Norse.

knife-edge ▶ **noun** the cutting edge of a knife.
– PHRASES **on a knife-edge** in a very tense or dangerous situation: *investors could be living on a knife-edge for the next twelve months.*

knife pleat ▶ **noun** a sharp, narrow pleat on a skirt.

knight /nīt/ ▶ **noun 1** (in the Middle Ages) a man raised to military rank after serving his sovereign or lord as a page and squire. **2** (in the UK) a man awarded a nonhereditary title by the sovereign and entitled to use 'Sir' in front of his name. **3** a chess piece, typically shaped like a horse's head, that moves by jumping to the opposite corner of a rectangle two squares by three. ▶ **verb** give a man the title of knight.
– DERIVATIVES **knight·ly** adjective.
– PHRASES **knight in shining armor** a gallant man who helps a woman in a difficult situation.
– ORIGIN Old English, 'boy, youth, servant.'

knight er·rant ▶ **noun** a medieval knight who wandered in search of opportunities to perform acts of chivalry and courage.

knight·hood /ˈnītˌho͝od/ ▶ **noun** the title, rank, or status of a knight.

knit /nit/ ▶ **verb** (**knits, knitting**; past and past part. **knitted** or (especially in sense 3) **knit**) **1** make a garment by interlocking loops of yarn with knitting needles or on a machine. **2** make a plain stitch in knitting. **3** unite or join together: *their two clans are knit together by common traditions.* **4** tighten one's eyebrows in a frown.

– SYNONYMS **unite,** unify, bond, fuse, coalesce, merge, meld, blend, join, link.

▶ **noun** (**knits**) knitted garments.
– DERIVATIVES **knit·ter** noun **knit·ting** noun.
– ORIGIN Old English.

knit·ting nee·dle ▶ **noun** a long, thin, pointed rod used as part of a pair for hand knitting.

knit·wear /ˈnitˌwe(ə)r/ ▶ **noun** knitted garments.

knives /nīvz/ plural of **KNIFE**.

knob /näb/ ▶ **noun 1** a rounded lump or ball at the end or on the surface of something. **2** a ball-shaped handle on a door or drawer. **3** a round control switch on a machine. **4** a small lump of something: *a knob of butter.* **5** vulgar slang a man's penis.

– SYNONYMS **lump,** bump, protrusion, protuberance, bulge, swelling, knot, nodule, boss.

– DERIVATIVES **knobbed** adjective **knob·by** adjective.
– ORIGIN German *knobbe* 'knot, knob.'

knock /näk/ ▶ **verb 1** strike a surface noisily to attract attention. **2** collide forcefully with someone or something. **3** strike someone or something so that they move or fall. **4** make a hole, dent, etc., in something by striking it. **5** informal criticize someone or something. **6** (of an engine) make a thumping or rattling noise.

– SYNONYMS **1 bang,** tap, rap, thump, pound, hammer, beat, strike, hit; informal bash. **2 collide with,** bump into, run into, crash into, smash into, plow into, impact. **3** *he deliberately knocked down the display of toilet paper in aisle 3* **fell,** floor, flatten, knock over, run over/down; demolish, pull down, tear down, destroy, raze, level, flatten, bulldoze.

▶ **noun 1** a sudden short sound caused by a blow. **2** a blow or collision. **3** a setback.

– SYNONYMS **tap,** rap, rat-a-tat, knocking, bang, banging, pounding, hammering, thump, thud.

– PHRASES **knock around** (or **about**) informal **1** travel or spend time without a specific purpose. **2** happen to be present. **knock something back** informal consume a drink quickly. **knock something down** informal **1** reduce the price of an article. **2** (at an auction) confirm a sale to a bidder by a knock with a hammer. **knock it off** informal stop doing something. **knock off** informal stop work.

knock something off informal produce a piece of work quickly and easily. **knock someone out 1** make someone unconscious. **2** informal astonish or greatly impress someone. **3** eliminate a competitor in a knockout competition. **knock someone up** vulgar slang make a woman pregnant. **the school of hard knocks** painful or difficult but useful life experiences.
– ORIGIN Old English.

knock·a·bout /'näkə͵bout/ ▶ **adjective** (of comedy) rough and slapstick.

knock·down /'näk͵doun/ ▶ **adjective 1** informal (of a price) very low. **2** (of furniture) easily dismantled.

knock·er /'näkər/ ▶ **noun 1** a hinged object fixed to a door and rapped by visitors to attract attention. **2** informal a person who continually finds fault. **3** (**knockers**) informal a woman's breasts.

knock-kneed ▶ **adjective** having legs that curve inward at the knee.

knock·off /'näk͵ôf/ ▶ **noun** informal a copy or imitation of a product.

knock·out /'näk͵out/ ▶ **noun 1** an act of making someone unconscious. **2** informal an extremely attractive or impressive person or thing.

knoll /nōl/ ▶ **noun** a small hill or mound.
– ORIGIN Old English.

knot /nät/ ▶ **noun 1** a fastening made by looping a piece of string, rope, etc., on itself and tightening it. **2** a tangled mass in hair, wool, or other fibers. **3** a hard mass in wood at the point where the trunk and a branch join. **4** a hard lump of tissue in the body. **5** a small group of people: *a knot of spectators*. **6** a unit of speed equivalent to one nautical mile per hour, used of ships, aircraft, or winds.

– SYNONYMS *a knot of people* **cluster,** group, band, huddle, bunch, circle, ring.

▶ **verb** (**knots, knotting, knotted**) **1** fasten something with a knot: *scarves were knotted loosely around their throats*. **2** make something tangled. **3** cause a muscle to become tense and hard. **4** (of the stomach) tighten as a result of tension.

– SYNONYMS **tie,** fasten, secure, bind, do up.

– PHRASES **tie someone (up) in knots** informal completely confuse someone. **tie the knot** informal get married.
– ORIGIN Old English; sense 6 comes from the former practice of measuring a ship's speed by using a float attached to a long knotted line.

knot gar·den ▶ **noun** a formal garden laid out in a complex design.

knot·grass /'nät͵gras/ ▶ **noun** a common plant with jointed creeping stems and small pink flowers.

knot·hole /'nät͵hōl/ ▶ **noun** a hole in a piece of wood where a knot has fallen out.

knot·ty /'nätē/ ▶ **adjective** (**knottier, knottiest**) **1** full of knots. **2** extremely difficult or complex: *a knotty problem*.

knot·weed /'nät͵wēd/ ▶ **noun** knotgrass or a related plant.

know /nō/ ▶ **verb** (past **knew** /n(y)o͞o/; past part. **known** /nōn/) **1** be aware of something through observation, inquiry, or information. **2** be absolutely sure of something. **3** be familiar or friendly with someone. **4** have a good command of a subject or language. **5** have personal experience of: *a man who had known better times*. **6** (usu. **be known as**) think of as having a particular characteristic, or give a particular name or title to: *the boss was universally known as 'Sir'* **7** old use have sex with someone.

– SYNONYMS **1** *she doesn't know I'm here* **be aware,** realize, be conscious, be cognizant. **2** *I know the rules* **be familiar with,** be conversant with, be acquainted with, be versed in, have a grasp of, understand, comprehend; informal be clued in on. **3** *do you know her?* **be acquainted with,** have met, be familiar with.

– DERIVATIVES **know·a·ble** adjective.
– PHRASES **be in the know** informal be aware of something known only to a few people. **know no bounds** have no limits. **know one's own mind** be decisive and certain. **know the ropes** have experience of the correct way of doing something. **know what's what** informal be experienced and competent in a particular area.
– ORIGIN Old English, 'recognize, identify.'

know-how ▶ **noun** practical knowledge or skill.

– SYNONYMS **expertise,** skill, proficiency, knowledge, understanding, mastery, technique; informal savvy.

know·ing /'nōiNG/ ▶ **adjective 1** suggesting that one has secret knowledge: *a knowing smile*. **2** chiefly derogatory experienced or shrewd.

– SYNONYMS **significant,** meaningful, expressive, suggestive, eloquent, superior.

– DERIVATIVES **know·ing·ly** adverb **know·ing·ness** noun.
– PHRASES **there is no knowing** no one can tell whether something is the case.

knowl·edge /'nälij/ ▶ **noun 1** information and skills gained through experience or education. **2** the total of what is known. **3** awareness of or familiarity with a fact or situation: *he denied all knowledge of the incident*.

– SYNONYMS **1 understanding,** comprehension, grasp, command, mastery, familiarity, acquaintance; informal know-how. **2 learning,** erudition, education, scholarship, schooling, wisdom. **3 awareness,** consciousness, realization, cognition, apprehension, perception, appreciation, cognizance.
– ANTONYMS ignorance.

– PHRASES **to (the best of) my knowledge 1** so far as I know. **2** as I know for certain.

WORD LINKS

gnostic *relating to knowledge*

CHOOSE THE RIGHT WORD

knowledge, erudition, information, learning, pedantry, scholarship, wisdom

How much do you know? **Knowledge** applies to any body of facts gathered by study, observation, or experience, and to the ideas inferred from these facts (*an in-depth knowledge of particle physics; firsthand knowledge about the company*). **Information** may be no more than a collection of data or facts (*information about vacation resorts*) gathered through observation, reading, or hearsay, with no guarantee of their validity (*false information that led to the arrest*). **Scholarship** emphasizes academic knowledge or accomplishment (*a special award for scholarship*), while **learning** is knowledge gained not only by study in schools and universities but by individual research and investigation (*a man of education and learning*), which puts it on a somewhat higher plane. **Erudition** is on a higher plane still, implying bookish knowledge that is beyond the average person's comprehension (*exhibit extraordinary *erudition in a doctoral dissertation*). **Pedantry**, on the other hand, is a negative term for a slavish attention to obscure facts or details or an undue display of learning (*the pedantry of modern literary criticism*). You can have extensive *knowledge* of a subject and even exhibit *erudition*, however, without attaining **wisdom**, the superior judgment and understanding that is based on both knowledge and experience.

knowl·edge·a·ble /ˈnälijəbəl/ (also **knowledgable**) ▶ **adjective** intelligent and well informed.

– SYNONYMS **1 well informed,** learned, well read, (well) educated, erudite, scholarly, cultured, cultivated, enlightened. **2** *he's knowledgeable about art* **conversant with,** familiar with, well acquainted with, au fait with, up on, up to date with, abreast of; informal clued in on.
– ANTONYMS ignorant.

– DERIVATIVES **know·ledge·a·bly** adverb.

knowl·edge base ▶ **noun 1** a store of information or data that is available to draw on. **2** the underlying set of facts and rules that a computer system has available to solve a problem.

knowl·edge work·er ▶ **noun** a person whose job involves handling or using information.

known /nōn/ past participle of KNOW ▶ **adjective 1** recognized, familiar, or within the scope of knowledge: *a subject little known to English readers.* **2** publicly acknowledged to be: *a known criminal.* **3** Mathematics (of a quantity or variable) having a value that can be stated.

– SYNONYMS **recognized,** well known, widely known, noted, celebrated, notable, notorious, acknowledged.

know-noth·ing ▶ **noun** an ignorant person.

knuck·le /ˈnəkəl/ ▶ **noun 1** each of the joints of a finger. **2** a knee-joint of a four-legged animal, or the part joining the leg to the foot. **3** a cut of meat consisting of the knuckle of a four-legged animal. ▶ **verb** rub or press something with the knuckles.
– PHRASES **knuckle down 1** apply oneself seriously to a task. **2** (also **knuckle under**) submit to someone's authority. **rap someone on the knuckles** rebuke or criticize someone.
– ORIGIN German or Dutch *knökel* 'little bone.'

knuck·le·ball /ˈnəkəlˌbôl/ (also **knuckler**) ▶ **noun** Baseball a slow pitch that has virtually no spin and moves erratically, typically made using the knuckles of the first joints of the index and middle fingers.

knuck·le·dust·er /ˈnəkəlˌdəstər/ ▶ **noun** a metal fitting worn over the knuckles in fighting to increase the effect of blows.

knuck·le·head /ˈnəkəlˌhed/ ▶ **noun** informal a stupid person.

knuck·le sand·wich ▶ **noun** informal a punch in the mouth.

knurl /nərl/ ▶ **noun** a small projecting knob or ridge.
– DERIVATIVES **knurled** adjective.
– ORIGIN apparently from German *knorre* 'knob.'

KO /ˌkāˈō/ ▶ **noun** a knockout in a boxing match. ▶ **verb** (**KO's**, **KO'ing**, **KO'd**) knock someone out in a boxing match.

ko·a·la /kōˈälə/ ▶ **noun** a bearlike tree-dwelling Australian marsupial that has thick gray fur and feeds on eucalyptus leaves.
– ORIGIN Dharuk (an Aboriginal language).

ko·an /ˈkōˌän/ ▶ **noun** (in Zen Buddhism) a paradox or puzzle that cannot be understood or answered in conventional terms, requiring a learner to abandon ordinary ways of understanding in order to move toward enlightenment.
– ORIGIN Japanese, 'matter for public thought.'

kof·ta /ˈkôftə/ ▶ **noun** (pl. same or **koftas**) (in Middle Eastern and Indian cooking) a spiced meatball.
– ORIGIN Urdu and Persian, 'pounded meat.'

kohl /kōl/ ▶ **noun** a black powder used as eye makeup.
– ORIGIN Arabic.

kohl·ra·bi /kōlˈräbē/ ▶ **noun** (pl. **kohlrabies**) a variety of cabbage with an edible turniplike stem.
– ORIGIN German.

koi /koi/ ▶ **noun** (pl. same) a large common Japanese carp.
– ORIGIN Japanese.

ko·la /ˈkōlə/ ▶ **noun** variant spelling of COLA (sense 2).

kol·khoz /kəlˈkôz, -ˈkʜôz/ ▶ **noun** (pl. same or **kolkhozes**) a collective farm in the former Soviet Union.
– ORIGIN Russian.

Ko·mo·do drag·on /kəˈmōdō/ ▶ **noun** a very large lizard native to Komodo and neighboring Indonesian islands.

kook /ko͝ok/ ▶ **noun** informal a mad or eccentric person.
– DERIVATIVES **kook·y** adjective (**kookier**, **kookiest**).
– ORIGIN probably from CUCKOO.

kook·a·bur·ra /ˈko͝okəˌbərə/ ▶ **noun** a very large, noisy Australasian kingfisher that feeds on reptiles and birds.
– ORIGIN Wiradhuri (an Aboriginal language).

ko·pek /ˈkōpek/ (also **copeck** or **kopeck**) ▶ **noun** a unit of money of Russia and some other countries of the former Soviet Union, equal to one hundredth of a ruble.
– ORIGIN Russian *kopeĭka* 'small lance.'

ko·ra /ˈkôrə/ ▶ **noun** a West African musical instrument shaped like a lute and played like a harp.
– ORIGIN a local word.

Ko·ran /kəˈrän, kô-, ˈkôrän/ (also **Quran** or **Qur'an**) ▶ **noun** the sacred book of Islam, believed to be the word of God as dictated to Muhammad and written down in Arabic.
– DERIVATIVES **Ko·ran·ic** /-ˈränik/ adjective.
– ORIGIN Arabic, 'recitation.'

Ko·re·an /kəˈrēən, kô-/ ▶ **noun 1** a person from Korea. **2** the language of Korea. ▶ **adjective** relating to Korea.

kor·ma /ˈkôrmə/ ▶ **noun** a mild Indian curry of meat or fish marinaded in yogurt or curds.
– ORIGIN Urdu, from Turkish *kavurma*.

ko·sher /ˈkōsʜər/ ▶ **adjective 1** (of food) prepared according to the requirements of Jewish law. **2** informal genuine and legitimate.
– ORIGIN Hebrew, 'proper.'

Ko·so·var /ˈkôsəˌvär, ˈkäs-/ ▶ **noun** a person from Kosovo.
– DERIVATIVES **Ko·so·van** /ˈkôsəˌvən, ˈkäs-/ noun & adjective.

kow·tow /ˈkouˈtou/ ▶ **verb 1** be excessively meek and obedient in one's behavior toward someone: *she didn't have to kowtow to a boss.* **2** historical kneel and touch the ground with the forehead as a gesture of deference or submission, as part of Chinese custom.
– ORIGIN Chinese.

KP ▶ **abbreviation** kitchen police, designating the US military personnel assigned to kitchen duties, or the assignment itself.

kph ▶ **abbreviation** kilometers per hour.

Kr ▶ **symbol** the chemical element krypton.

kraal /kräl/ S. African ▶ **noun 1** a traditional African village of huts. **2** an enclosure for sheep and cattle.
– ORIGIN Dutch.

kraft /kraft/ (also **kraft paper**) ▶ **noun** a kind of strong, smooth brown wrapping paper.
– ORIGIN Swedish, 'strength.'

kra·ken /'kräkən/ ▶ **noun** a mythical sea monster said to appear off the coast of Norway.
– ORIGIN Norwegian.

Kraut /krout/ ▶ **noun** informal, offensive a German.
– ORIGIN shortening of **SAUERKRAUT**.

krem·lin /'kremlin/ ▶ **noun 1** a citadel within a Russian town. **2** (**the Kremlin**) the citadel in Moscow, housing the Russian government.
– ORIGIN Russian *kreml'*.

krill /kril/ ▶ **plural noun** small shrimplike crustaceans that are the main food of baleen whales.
– ORIGIN Norwegian *kril* 'small fish fry.'

kris /krēs/ ▶ **noun** a Malay or Indonesian dagger with a wavy-edged blade.
– ORIGIN Malay.

kro·na /'krōnə/ ▶ **noun 1** (pl. **kronor** pronunc. same) the basic unit of money of Sweden. **2** (pl. **kronur** pronunc. same) the basic unit of money of Iceland.
– ORIGIN Swedish and Icelandic, 'crown.'

kro·ne /'krōnə/ ▶ **noun** (pl. **kroner** pronunc. same) the basic unit of money of Denmark and Norway.
– ORIGIN Danish and Norwegian, 'crown.'

kru·ger·rand /'kroōgə,rand/ (also **Kruger** /'kroōgər, 'kryər/) ▶ **noun** a South African gold coin bearing a portrait of President Kruger.

kryp·ton /'krip,tän/ ▶ **noun** an inert gaseous chemical element, present in trace amounts in the air.
– ORIGIN Greek *krupton* 'hidden.'

KS ▶ **abbreviation** Kansas.

Kshat·ri·ya /k(ə)'sHätrēə/ ▶ **noun** a member of the second-highest Hindu caste, that of the military.
– ORIGIN Sanskrit, 'rule, authority.'

kt ▶ **abbreviation** knot(s).

ku·dos /'k(y)oō,dōs, -,dōz, -,däs/ ▶ **noun** praise, admiration, and respect.

– SYNONYMS **prestige**, cachet, glory, honor, status, standing, distinction, admiration, respect, esteem.

– ORIGIN Greek.

USAGE

Despite appearances, **kudos** is not a plural word. The use of it as if it were a plural, as in *he received many kudos for his work*, is wrong (the correct use is *he received much kudos for his work*).

ku·du /'ko͝odo͞o/ ▶ **noun** (pl. same or **kudus**) a striped African antelope, the male of which has long spirally curved horns.
– ORIGIN Afrikaans.

Ku Klux Klan /'koō ,kləks 'klan/ ▶ **noun** an extremist right-wing secret society in the US whose members believe in the supremacy of white people.
– ORIGIN perhaps from Greek *kuklos* 'circle' and **CLAN**.

kuk·ri /'ko͝okrē/ ▶ **noun** (pl. **kukris**) a curved knife that broadens toward the point, used by Gurkhas.
– ORIGIN Nepalese.

ku·lak /koō'lak, -'läk/ ▶ **noun** historical a peasant in Russia wealthy enough to own a farm and hire workers.
– ORIGIN Russian, 'fist, tight-fisted person.'

küm·mel /'kiməl/ ▶ **noun** a sweet liqueur flavored with caraway and cumin seeds.
– ORIGIN German.

kum·quat /'kəm,kwät/ (also **cumquat**) ▶ **noun** an East Asian fruit like a small orange, with an edible sweet rind and acid pulp.
– ORIGIN Chinese, 'little orange.'

kun·da·li·ni /,ko͝ondl'ēnē/ ▶ **noun** (in yoga) latent female energy believed to lie coiled at the base of the spine.
– ORIGIN Sanskrit, 'snake.'

kung fu /'kəNG 'foō, 'ko͝oNG/ ▶ **noun** a Chinese martial art resembling karate.
– ORIGIN Chinese, from words meaning 'merit' and 'master.'

Kurd /kərd/ ▶ **noun** a member of a mainly Islamic people living in Kurdistan, an area composed of parts of Turkey, Iraq, Iran, Syria, Armenia, and Azerbaijan.
– ORIGIN the name in Kurdish.

Kurd·ish /'kərdisH/ ▶ **noun** the Iranian language of the Kurds. ▶ **adjective** relating to the Kurds.

kur·ta /'kərtə/ ▶ **noun** a loose collarless shirt worn by people from the Indian subcontinent.
– ORIGIN Urdu and Persian.

Ku·wai·ti /kə'wātē/ ▶ **noun** (pl. **Kuwaitis**) a person from Kuwait. ▶ **adjective** relating to Kuwait.

kV ▶ **abbreviation** kilovolt(s).

kvetch /k(ə)vecH, kfecH/ informal ▶ **noun 1** a person who complains a great deal. **2** a complaint. ▶ **verb** complain.
– ORIGIN Yiddish.

kW ▶ **abbreviation** kilowatt(s).

Kwan·zaa /'kwänzə/ ▶ **noun** a secular festival observed by many African Americans from December 26 to January 1 as a celebration of their cultural heritage and traditional values.
– ORIGIN Kiswahili.

kwash·i·or·kor /,kwäsHē'ôrkôr, -kər/ ▶ **noun** a form of malnutrition caused by a lack of protein in the diet, typically affecting young children in certain parts of Africa.
– ORIGIN a local word in Ghana.

kWh ▶ **abbreviation** kilowatt-hour(s).

KY ▶ **abbreviation** Kentucky.

Kyr·i·e /'ki(ə)rē,ā/ (also **Kyrie eleison** /i'lā-i,sän, -sən/) ▶ **noun** (in the Christian Church) a short repeated appeal to God used in many set forms of public worship.
– ORIGIN Greek *Kuriē eleēson* 'Lord, have mercy.'

L¹ (also l) ▸ **noun** (pl. **Ls** or **L's**) **1** the twelfth letter of the alphabet. **2** the Roman numeral for 50.

L² ▸ **abbreviation 1** (**L.**) Lake, Loch, or Lough. **2** large (as a clothes size). **3** (in tables of sports results) lost.

l ▸ **abbreviation 1** left. **2** (in horse racing) length(s). **3** (**l.**) line. **4** liter(s). ▸ **symbol** (in mathematical formulas) length.

£ /pound(z)/ ▸ **symbol** pound(s).
– ORIGIN the initial letter of Latin *libra* 'pound, balance.'

LA ▸ **abbreviation 1** Los Angeles. **2** Louisiana.

La ▸ **symbol** the chemical element lanthanum.

la /lä/ ▸ **noun** Music the sixth note of a major scale, coming after 'sol' and before 'ti'.
– ORIGIN the first syllable of *labii*, a word taken from a Latin hymn.

Lab /lab/ ▸ **abbreviation** a Labrador retriever.

lab /lab/ ▸ **noun** informal a laboratory.

la·bel /ˈlābəl/ ▸ **noun 1** a small piece of paper, fabric, etc., attached to an object and giving information about it. **2** the name or trademark of a fashion company. **3** a company that produces recorded music. **4** a classifying name given to a person or thing: *young women who dislike the feminist label.*

– SYNONYMS **1 tag,** ticket, tab, sticker, marker, docket. **2 description,** designation, name, epithet, nickname, sobriquet, title.

▸ **verb** (**labels, labeling, labeled**) **1** attach a label to something. **2** place someone or something in a category: *he was labeled as an anarchist.*

– SYNONYMS **1 tag,** ticket, mark, stamp. **2 categorize,** classify, class, describe, designate, identify, mark, stamp, brand, call, name, term, dub.

– ORIGIN Old French, 'ribbon.'

la·bi·a /ˈlābēə/ ▸ **plural noun** (sing. **labium** /ˈlābēəm/) the inner and outer folds of the vulva (the female external genitals).
– ORIGIN Latin, 'lips.'

la·bi·al /ˈlābēəl/ ▸ **adjective 1** chiefly Anatomy & Biology relating to the labia or lips. **2** Phonetics (of a consonant) produced with the lips partially or completely closed (e.g., *p* or *w*), or (of a vowel) produced with rounded lips (e.g., *oo*).

la·bile /ˈlāˌbīl, -bəl/ ▸ **adjective 1** technical liable to change; easily altered. **2** Chemistry easily broken down or displaced.
– ORIGIN Latin *labilis*.

la·bi·um /ˈlābēəm/ ▸ **noun** singular of LABIA.

la·bor /ˈlābər/ (Brit. **labour**) ▸ **noun 1** work, especially hard physical work. **2** workers as a group. **3** the process of childbirth.

– SYNONYMS **1 work,** toil, exertion, effort, industry, drudgery; informal slog, grind; old use travail. **2 workers,** employees, laborers, workforce, staff. **3 childbirth,** birth, delivery; technical parturition.

▸ **verb 1** work hard. **2** work at an unskilled manual job. **3** try hard to do something in the face of difficulty: *biologists have labored for years to develop hardier crops.* **4** move with difficulty. **5** (**labor under**) believe something that is not true: *you've been laboring under a misapprehension.*

– SYNONYMS **work (hard),** toil, slave (away), struggle, strive, exert oneself, endeavor, try hard; informal slog away, plug away.

– PHRASES **a labor of love** a task done for pleasure, not reward. **labor the point** repeat or emphasize something that has already been said and understood.
– ORIGIN Latin 'toil, trouble.'

CHOOSE THE RIGHT WORD

labor, drudgery, grind, toil, travail, work

Most people have to **work** for a living, meaning that they have to exert themselves mentally or physically in return for a paycheck. But *work* is not always performed by humans (*a machine that works like a charm*). **Labor** is not only human but usually physical work (*the labor required to build a stone wall*), although it can also apply to intellectual work of unusual difficulty (*the labor involved in writing a symphony*). Anyone who has been forced to perform **drudgery** knows that it is the most unpleasant, uninspiring, and monotonous kind of labor (*a forklift that eliminates the drudgery of stacking boxes; the drudgery of compiling a phone book*). A **grind** is even more intense and unrelenting than drudgery, emphasizing work that is performed under pressure in a dehumanizing way (*the daily grind of classroom teaching*). **Toil** suggests labor that is prolonged and very tiring (*farmers who toil endlessly in the fields*), but not necessarily physical (*mothers who toil to teach their children manners*). Those who **travail** endure pain, anguish, or suffering (*his hours of travail ended in heartbreak*).

lab·o·ra·to·ry /ˈlabrəˌtôrē/ ▸ **noun** (pl. **laboratories**) a room or building for scientific experiments, research, or teaching, or for the manufacture of drugs or chemicals.
– ORIGIN Latin *laboratorium*.

la·bor camp ▸ **noun** a prison camp in which punishment takes the form of heavy manual work.

La·bor Day ▸ **noun** a public holiday held in honor of working people in some countries on May 1, or (in the US and Canada) on the first Monday in September.

la·bored /ˈlābərd/ ▸ **adjective 1** done with great difficulty: *labored breathing.* **2** not natural or spontaneous: *a rather labored joke.*

– SYNONYMS **1** *labored breathing* **strained,** difficult, forced, laborious. **2** *a labored metaphor* **contrived,** forced, unconvincing, unnatural, artificial, overdone.
– ANTONYMS natural, easy.

la·bor·er /ˈlāb(ə)rər/ ▸ **noun** a person doing unskilled manual work.

– SYNONYMS **workman,** worker, manual worker, blue-collar worker, (hired) hand, roustabout, drudge, menial.

la·bor force ▸ **noun** the members of a population who are able to work.

la·bor-in·ten·sive ▸ **adjective** needing a large workforce or a large amount of work in relation to what is produced.

la·bo·ri·ous /lə'bôrēəs/ ▸ **adjective 1** requiring considerable time and effort. **2** showing obvious signs of effort: *a slow, laborious speech*.

– SYNONYMS **1 arduous,** hard, heavy, difficult, strenuous, grueling, punishing, exacting, tough, onerous, challenging, painstaking, time-consuming. **2 labored,** strained, forced, stiff, stilted, unnatural, artificial, ponderous.
– ANTONYMS easy, effortless.

– DERIVATIVES **la·bo·ri·ous·ly** adverb.

la·bor-sav·ing ▸ **adjective** designed to reduce the amount of work needed to carry out a task.

la·bor un·ion ▸ **noun** an organized association of workers formed to protect and further their rights and interests.

la·bour, etc. ▸ **noun** British spelling of LABOR, etc.

La·bour Par·ty ▸ **noun** a British political party formed to represent the interests of ordinary working people.

Lab·ra·dor /'labrə,dôr/ (also **Labrador retriever**) ▸ **noun** a breed of retriever with a black or yellow coat, used also as a guide dog.
– ORIGIN named after the *Labrador* Peninsula of eastern Canada.

la·bur·num /lə'bərnəm/ ▸ **noun** a small hardwood tree with hanging clusters of yellow flowers followed by pods of poisonous seeds.
– ORIGIN Latin.

lab·y·rinth /'lab(ə),rinTH/ ▸ **noun 1** a complicated irregular network of passages or paths. **2** an intricate and confusing arrangement: *the labyrinth of immigration laws*. **3** a complex bony structure in the inner ear that contains the organs of hearing and balance.
– ORIGIN Greek *laburinthos*, referring to the maze built to house the Minotaur in Greek mythology.

lab·y·rin·thine /,labə'rin,THēn, -'rinTHin, -'rin,THīn/ ▸ **adjective 1** resembling a labyrinth. **2** complicated and confusing.

– SYNONYMS **1** *labyrinthine corridors* **mazelike,** winding, twisting, serpentine, meandering. **2** *a labyrinthine system* **complicated,** intricate, complex, involved, tortuous, convoluted, elaborate, confusing, puzzling, mystifying, bewildering, baffling.

lac /lak/ ▸ **noun** a resinous substance produced by an Asian insect (the **lac insect**), used to make varnish, shellac, etc.
– ORIGIN Hindi or Persian.

lace /lās/ ▸ **noun 1** a delicate open fabric of cotton or silk made by looping, twisting, or knitting thread in patterns. **2** a cord or leather strip used to fasten a shoe or garment. ▸ **verb 1** fasten a shoe or garment with a lace or laces. **2** twist or tangle things together. **3** add an ingredient, especially alcohol, to a drink or dish to improve the flavor or to make it stronger: *coffee laced with brandy*.

– SYNONYMS **1 fasten,** do up, tie up, secure, knot. **2 flavor,** mix, blend, fortify, strengthen, season, spice (up), liven up, doctor, adulterate; informal spike.

– ORIGIN Old French *laz*.

lac·er·ate /'lasə,rāt/ ▸ **verb** tear or cut the flesh or skin.
– ORIGIN Latin *lacerare*.

lac·er·a·tion /,lasə'rāSHən/ ▸ **noun** a cut or wound.

– SYNONYMS **gash,** cut, wound, injury, tear, slash, scratch, scrape, abrasion, graze.

lace·wing /'lās,wiNG/ ▸ **noun** a delicate insect with large, clear membranous wings.

lach·ry·mal /'lakrəməl/ (also **lacrimal** or **lacrymal**) ▸ **adjective 1** formal or literary connected with weeping or tears. **2** Physiology & Anatomy concerned with the production of tears.
– ORIGIN from Latin *lacrima* 'tear.'

lach·ry·mose /'lakrə,mōs, -,mōz/ ▸ **adjective** formal or literary **1** tending to cry easily; tearful. **2** causing tears; sad.

lac·ing /'lāsiNG/ ▸ **noun 1** a laced fastening of a shoe or garment. **2** a dash of liquor added to a drink.

lack /lak/ ▸ **noun** the state of being without or not having enough of something: *the lack of funds available for research*.

– SYNONYMS **absence,** want, need, deficiency, dearth, shortage, shortfall, scarcity, paucity.
– ANTONYMS abundance.

▸ **verb** (also **lack for**) be without or without enough of: *he lacked imagination*.

– SYNONYMS **be without,** be in need of, be short of, be deficient in, be low on, be pressed for, need; informal be strapped for.

– ORIGIN perhaps partly from German *lak*, Dutch *laken*.

lack·a·dai·si·cal /,lakə'dāzikəl/ ▸ **adjective** lacking enthusiasm and thoroughness.
– DERIVATIVES **lack·a·dai·si·cal·ly** adverb.
– ORIGIN from the former exclamation *lackaday*, expressing surprise or grief.

lack·ey /'lakē/ ▸ **noun** (pl. **lackeys**) **1** a servant. **2** a person who is too willing to serve or obey others.
– ORIGIN French *laquais*.

lack·ing /'lakiNG/ ▸ **adjective** missing or not having enough of something: *she was shy and lacking in confidence*.

lack·lus·ter /'lak,ləstər/ ▸ **adjective 1** lacking energy or inspiration: *a lackluster performance*. **2** (of the hair or eyes) not shining.

– SYNONYMS **uninspired,** uninspiring, unimaginative, dull, humdrum, colorless, bland, insipid, flat, dry, lifeless, tame, prosaic, dreary, tedious.
– ANTONYMS inspired.

la·con·ic /lə'känik/ ▸ **adjective** using very few words: *his laconic reply suggested a lack of interest in the subject*.
– DERIVATIVES **la·con·i·cal·ly** /-(ə)lē/ adverb.
– ORIGIN Greek *Lakōnikos* 'Spartan,' the inhabitants of Sparta being known for their terse speech.

lac·quer /'lakər/ ▸ **noun 1** a varnish made of shellac or of synthetic substances. **2** the sap of an East Asian tree (the **lacquer tree**) used as a varnish. **3** a chemical substance sprayed on hair to keep it in place. ▸ **verb** (often as adj. **lacquered**) coat with lacquer.

– DERIVATIVES **lac·quered** adjective.
– ORIGIN from Hindi or Persian (see **LAC**).

lac·ri·mal ▸ **adjective** variant spelling of **LACHRYMAL**.

la·crosse /lə'krôs, -'kräs/ ▸ **noun** a team game, originally played by North American Indians, in which a ball is thrown, carried, and caught with a long-handled stick that has a net at one end.
– ORIGIN from French (*le jeu de*) *la crosse* '(the game of) the hooked stick.'

lac·ry·mal ▸ **adjective** variant spelling of **LACHRYMAL**.

lac·tate[1] /ˌlak'tāt/ ▸ **verb** (of a female mammal) produce milk.
– ORIGIN Latin *lactare* 'suckle.'

lac·tate[2] /'lakˌtāt/ ▸ **noun** Chemistry a salt or ester of lactic acid.

lac·ta·tion /lak'tāsʜən/ ▸ **noun** **1** the producing of milk by the mammary glands. **2** the process of suckling a baby or young animal.

lac·tic /'laktik/ ▸ **adjective** relating to or obtained from milk.
– ORIGIN Latin *lac* 'milk.'

lac·tic ac·id ▸ **noun** an organic acid present in sour milk and produced in the muscles during strenuous exercise.

lac·tose /'lakˌtōs, -ˌtōz/ ▸ **noun** Chemistry a compound sugar present in milk.

lac·to-veg·e·tar·i·an /'laktō-/ ▸ **noun** a person who eats only dairy products and vegetables.

la·cu·na /lə'k(y)o͞onə/ ▸ **noun** (pl. **lacunae** /-nī, -nē/ or **lacunas**) a gap or missing portion: *there are a few lacunae in the historical record.*
– ORIGIN Latin, 'pool.'

la·cus·trine /lə'kəstrin/ ▸ **adjective** technical or literary relating to lakes.
– ORIGIN from Latin *lacus* 'lake.'

lac·y /'lāsē/ ▸ **adjective** (**lacier, laciest**) made of, resembling, or trimmed with lace.

lad /lad/ ▸ **noun** a boy or young man.

– SYNONYMS **boy,** schoolboy, youth, youngster, juvenile, stripling; informal **kid.** derogatory **brat.**

– ORIGIN unknown.

lad·der /'ladər/ ▸ **noun** **1** a structure consisting of a series of bars or steps between two uprights, used for climbing up or down. **2** a series of stages by which progress can be made: *the career ladder.* **3** Brit. a run in a pair of tights or stockings. ▸ **verb** Brit. develop or cause to develop a run in tights or stockings.
– ORIGIN Old English.

lad·der-back ▸ **noun** an upright chair with a back resembling a ladder.

lad·die /'ladē/ ▸ **noun** informal, chiefly Scottish a boy or young man.

lad·en /'lādn/ ▸ **adjective** loaded or weighed down.

– SYNONYMS **loaded,** burdened, weighed down, overloaded, piled high, full, packed, stuffed, crammed; informal chock-full, chock-a-block.

la-di-da /ˌlä dē 'dä/ (also **lah-di-dah**) ▸ **adjective** informal pretentious or snobbish.
– ORIGIN imitating an affected way of speaking.

la·dies /'lādēz/ plural of **LADY**.

la·dies' man (also **lady's man**) ▸ **noun** informal a man who enjoys spending time and flirting with women.

la·dies' room ▸ **noun** a women's restroom in a public building.

La·di·no /lə'dēnō/ ▸ **noun** (pl. **Ladinos**) **1** the language of some Sephardic Jews, based on medieval Spanish. **2** (in Latin America) a person of mixed race or a Spanish-speaking white person.
– ORIGIN Spanish.

la·dle /'lādl/ ▸ **noun** a large long-handled spoon with a cup-shaped bowl, for serving soup, stew, or sauce. ▸ **verb** **1** serve or transfer soup or sauce with a ladle. **2** (**ladle something out**) distribute something in large amounts.
– DERIVATIVES **la·dle·ful** /-ˌfo͝ol/ noun.
– ORIGIN Old English.

la·dy /'lādē/ ▸ **noun** (pl. **ladies**) **1** (in polite or formal use) a woman. **2** a woman of high social position. **3** (**Lady**) (in the UK) a title used by peeresses, female relatives of peers, the wives and widows of knights, etc. **4** a polite and well-educated woman. **5** (**the Ladies**) a women's public toilet.

– SYNONYMS **1 woman,** female, girl; Scottish lass, lassie; informal **dame, broad;** Austral. informal **sheila.**
2 noblewoman, aristocrat, duchess, countess, peeress, viscountess, baroness.

– PHRASES **My Lady** a polite form of address to certain noblewomen.
– ORIGIN Old English, from words meaning 'loaf' and 'knead'; compare with **LORD**.

la·dy·bug /'lādēˌbəg/ (also **ladybird** /'lādēˌbərd/) ▸ **noun** a small beetle having a red or yellow back with black spots.

La·dy chap·el ▸ **noun** a chapel dedicated to the Virgin Mary in a church or cathedral.

La·dy Day ▸ **noun** the Christian feast of the Annunciation, March 25.

la·dy·fin·ger /'lādēˌfiɴɢgər/ ▸ **noun** a small finger-shaped sponge cake.

la·dy-in-wait·ing ▸ **noun** (pl. **ladies-in-waiting**) a woman who attends a queen or princess.

la·dy·kill·er /'lādēˌkilər/ ▸ **noun** informal a charming man who habitually seduces women.

la·dy·like /'lādēˌlīk/ ▸ **adjective** appropriate for or typical of a well-mannered woman or girl.

– SYNONYMS **genteel,** polite, refined, well bred, cultivated, polished, decorous, proper, respectable, well mannered, cultured, sophisticated, elegant.

la·dy of the night ▸ **noun** euphemistic a prostitute.

La·dy·ship /'lādēˌsʜip/ ▸ **noun** (**Her/Your Ladyship**) a respectful way of referring to or addressing a woman who has a title.

la·dy's maid ▸ **noun** chiefly historical a maid who attended to the personal needs of her mistress.

la·dy's man ▸ **noun** variant spelling of **LADIES' MAN**.

la·dy's man·tle ▸ **noun** a plant with greenish flowers, formerly used in herbal medicine.

la·dy's slip·per ▸ **noun** an orchid whose flower has a pouch- or slipper-shaped lip.

lag[1] /lag/ ▸ **verb** (**lags, lagging, lagged**) move or develop more slowly than another or others: *the country was lagging behind its European competitors.*

– SYNONYMS **fall behind,** trail, bring up the rear, dawdle, hang back, delay, loiter, linger, dally, straggle.

▶ **noun** (also **time lag**) a period of time between two events; a delay.
– ORIGIN perhaps Scandinavian.

CHOOSE THE RIGHT WORD

See **LOITER**.

lag² ▶ **verb** (**lags, lagging, lagged**) cover a water tank, pipes, etc., with material designed to prevent heat loss.
– ORIGIN from earlier *lag* 'piece of insulating cover.'

la·ger /ˈlägər/ ▶ **noun** a light effervescent beer.
– ORIGIN from German *Lagerbier* 'beer brewed for keeping.'

lag·gard /ˈlagərd/ ▶ **noun** a person who falls behind others. ▶ **adjective** slower than desired or expected.
– ORIGIN from **LAG¹**.

lag·ging /ˈlagiNG/ ▶ **noun** material providing heat insulation for a water tank, pipes, etc.

la·goon /ləˈgo͞on/ ▶ **noun 1** a stretch of salt water separated from the sea by a low sandbank or coral reef. **2** a small freshwater lake near a larger lake or river.
– ORIGIN Italian and Spanish *laguna*.

lah ▶ **noun** Music variant spelling of **LA**.

lah-di-dah ▶ **noun** variant spelling of **LA-DI-DA**.

la·i·cize /ˈlāəˌsīz/ ▶ **verb** formal withdraw clerical or ecclesiastical character or status from someone or something.
– DERIVATIVES **la·i·cism** /-ˌsizəm/ noun **la·i·ci·za·tion** /ˌlāəsəˈzāSHən/ noun.
– ORIGIN Latin *laicus*.

laid /lād/ past and past participle of **LAY¹**.

laid-back ▶ **adjective** informal relaxed and easygoing.

– SYNONYMS **relaxed,** easygoing, free and easy, casual, nonchalant, blasé, cool, calm, unconcerned, leisurely, unhurried; informal unflappable.
– ANTONYMS uptight.

lain /lān/ past participle of **LIE¹**.

lair /le(ə)r/ ▶ **noun 1** a wild animal's resting place. **2** a person's hiding place or den.
– ORIGIN Old English.

laird /le(ə)rd/ ▶ **noun** (in Scotland) a person who owns a large estate.
– ORIGIN Scots form of **LORD**.

lais·sez-faire /ˌlesā ˈfe(ə)r, ˌlezā/ ▶ **noun** a policy of allowing things to take their course without interfering, especially nonintervention by governments in the workings of the free market.
– ORIGIN French, 'allow to do.'

la·i·ty /ˈlāətē/ ▶ **noun** (**the laity**) people who are not members of the clergy.
– ORIGIN from **LAY²**.

lake¹ /lāk/ ▶ **noun 1** a large area of water surrounded by land. **2** a pool of liquid.

– SYNONYMS **pool,** pond, tarn, reservoir, lagoon, waterhole, watering hole, bayou (lake); Scottish loch.

– DERIVATIVES **lake·side** /ˈlākˌsīd/ noun.
– ORIGIN Latin *lacus* 'pool, lake.'

lake² ▶ **noun** a purplish-red pigment, originally made with lac.
– ORIGIN variant of **LAC**.

lakh /läk, lak/ ▶ **noun** Indian a hundred thousand.
– ORIGIN Sanskrit.

lam¹ /lam/ ▶ **verb** (**lams, lamming, lammed**) (often **lam into**) informal hit someone or something hard or repeatedly.
– ORIGIN perhaps Scandinavian.

lam² ▶ **noun** (in phrase **on the lam**) informal in the process of running away or escaping.
– ORIGIN from **LAM¹**.

la·ma /ˈlämə/ ▶ **noun 1** a title given to a spiritual leader in Tibetan Buddhism as a mark of respect. **2** a Tibetan or Mongolian Buddhist monk.
– ORIGIN Tibetan, 'superior one.'

La·marck·ism /ləˈmärˌkizəm/ ▶ **noun** the theory of evolution devised by the French naturalist Jean Baptiste de Lamarck (1744–1829), based on the proposition that characteristics acquired by an animal or plant in order to survive can be passed on to its offspring.
– DERIVATIVES **La·marck·i·an** /ləˈmärkēən/ noun & adjective.

la·ma·ser·y /ˈläməˌserē/ ▶ **noun** (pl. **lamaseries**) a monastery of lamas.

lamb /lam/ ▶ **noun 1** a young sheep. **2** a mild-mannered, gentle, or innocent person. ▶ **verb 1** (of a ewe) give birth to lambs. **2** tend ewes during the period when lambs are born.
– DERIVATIVES **lamb·ing** noun.
– PHRASES **the Lamb of God** a title of Jesus.
– ORIGIN Old English.

lam·ba·da /lamˈbädə/ ▶ **noun** a fast Brazilian dance that couples perform in close physical contact.
– ORIGIN Portuguese, 'a beating.'

lam·baste /lamˈbāst, -ˈbast/ (also **lambast** /-ˈbast/) ▶ **verb** criticize someone or something harshly.
– ORIGIN from **LAM¹** + dated *baste*, also meaning 'beat.'

lam·bent /ˈlambənt/ ▶ **adjective** literary glowing or flickering with a soft radiance.
– ORIGIN Latin *lambere* 'to lick.'

Lam·bru·sco /lamˈbro͞oskō, -ˈbro͝os-/ ▶ **noun** a sparkling red or white wine made from grapes grown in the Emilia-Romagna region of northern Italy.
– ORIGIN Italian, 'grape of the wild vine.'

lambs·wool /ˈlamzˌwo͝ol/ ▶ **noun** soft, fine wool from lambs, used to make knitted garments.

lame /lām/ ▶ **adjective 1** walking with difficulty as the result of an injury or illness affecting the leg or foot. **2** (of an explanation or excuse) unconvincingly feeble. **3** dull and uninspiring: *a lame, predictable storyline*.

– SYNONYMS **1 limping,** hobbling, crippled, disabled, incapacitated; old use game. **2 feeble,** weak, thin, flimsy, poor, unconvincing, implausible, unlikely.

▶ **verb** make a person or animal lame.
– DERIVATIVES **lame·ly** adverb **lame·ness** noun.
– ORIGIN Old English.

la·mé /laˈmā, lä-/ ▶ **noun** fabric with interwoven gold or silver threads.
– ORIGIN French.

lame·brain /ˈlāmˌbrān/ ▶ **adjective** informal a stupid person.

lame duck ▶ **noun 1** an ineffectual or unsuccessful person or thing. **2** a president or administration in the final period of office, after a successor has been elected.

la·mel·la /ləˈmelə/ ▶ **noun** (pl. **lamellae** /-ˈmelē, -ˈmelī/) technical a thin layer, membrane, or plate of tissue, especially in bone.
– DERIVATIVES **la·mel·lar** /-ˈmelər/ adjective **la·mel·late** /ˈlaməlit, ləˈmelit, ˈlaməˌlāt/ adjective.
– ORIGIN Latin, 'small, thin plate.'

la·ment /lə'ment/ ▶ noun **1** a passionate expression of grief. **2** a song, piece of music, or poem expressing grief or regret. ▶ verb **1** mourn a person's death. **2** (as adj. **the lamented** or **the late lamented**) a conventional way of referring to a dead person. **3** express regret or disappointment about something: *he lamented the modernization of the old buildings.*

– SYNONYMS **1 mourn,** grieve, sorrow, weep, cry, wail, keen. **2 complain about,** bewail, bemoan, deplore.
– ANTONYMS celebrate, welcome.

– DERIVATIVES **lam·en·ta·tion** /ˌlamən'tāsʜən/ noun.
– ORIGIN from Latin *lamenta* 'weeping.'

CHOOSE THE RIGHT WORD

See **MOURN**.

lam·en·ta·ble /'laməntəbəl, lə'mentəbəl/ ▶ adjective **1** (of circumstances or conditions) very bad: *the industry is in a lamentable state.* **2** (of an event or attitude) regrettable: *her prejudice showed lamentable immaturity.*

– SYNONYMS **deplorable,** regrettable, terrible, awful, wretched, woeful, dire, disastrous, desperate, grave, appalling, dreadful, pitiful, shameful, unfortunate; formal egregious.
– ANTONYMS wonderful.

– DERIVATIVES **la·men·ta·bly** /-əblē/ adverb.

lam·i·na /'lamənə/ ▶ noun (pl. **laminae** /-ˌnē, -ˌnī/) technical a thin layer, plate, or scale of sedimentary rock, organic tissue, or other material.
– DERIVATIVES **lam·i·nar** /'lamənər/ adjective.
– ORIGIN Latin.

lam·i·nate ▶ verb /'laməˌnāt/ **1** cover a flat surface with a layer of protective material. **2** manufacture something by sticking layers of material together. **3** split into layers or leaves. **4** beat or roll metal into thin plates. ▶ noun /-nit, -ˌnāt/ a laminated structure or material. ▶ adjective /-nit, -ˌnāt/ consisting or made of many layers of material stuck together.
– DERIVATIVES **lam·i·na·tion** /ˌlamə'nāsʜən/ noun.

Lam·mas /'laməs/ (also **Lammas Day**) ▶ noun the first day of August, formerly observed as a harvest festival.
– ORIGIN Old English, 'loaf mass.'

lam·mer·gei·er /'lamərˌgīər/ (also **lammergeyer**) ▶ noun a long-winged, long-tailed vulture, noted for dropping bones to break them and get at the marrow.
– ORIGIN German, from *Lämmer* 'lambs' + *Geier* 'vulture.'

lamp /lamp/ ▶ noun **1** an electric, oil, or gas device for giving light. **2** an electrical device producing ultraviolet or other radiation, especially for therapeutic purposes.
– ORIGIN Greek *lampas* 'torch.'

lamp·black /'lampˌblak/ ▶ noun a black pigment made from soot.

lamp·light /'lampˌlīt/ ▶ noun the light cast by a lamp.
– DERIVATIVES **lamp·lit** /-ˌlit/ adjective.

lam·poon /lam'po͞on/ ▶ verb publicly ridicule or mock someone or something. ▶ noun a speech or piece of writing that ridicules or mocks someone or something.
– ORIGIN French *lampon.*

CHOOSE THE RIGHT WORD

See **CARICATURE**.

lamp·post /'lam(p)ˌpōst/ ▶ noun a tall pole with a light at the top, used to light a street.

lam·prey /'lamprē/ ▶ noun (pl. **lampreys**) an eel-like jawless fish that has a sucker mouth with horny teeth and a rasping tongue.
– ORIGIN Latin *lampreda.*

lamp·shade /'lampˌsʜād/ ▶ noun a cover for a lamp, used to soften or direct its light.

LAN /lan/ ▶ abbreviation Computing local area network.

lance /lans/ ▶ noun **1** a long weapon with a wooden shaft and a pointed steel head, formerly used by a horseman in charging. **2** a metal pipe supplying a jet of oxygen to a furnace or to make a very hot flame for cutting. ▶ verb **1** prick or cut open an abscess or boil with a lancet or other sharp instrument. **2** pierce something.
– ORIGIN Latin *lancea.*

lance·let /'lanslit/ ▶ noun a small invertebrate marine animal.

lan·ce·o·late /'lansēəlit, -ˌlāt/ ▶ adjective technical having a narrow oval shape tapering to a point at each end.
– ORIGIN from Latin *lanceola* 'a small lance.'

lanc·er /'lansər/ ▶ noun a soldier of a cavalry regiment armed or formerly armed with lances.

lan·cet /'lansit/ ▶ noun a small, broad, two-edged surgical knife with a sharp point.
– ORIGIN Old French *lancette* 'small lance.'

lan·cet win·dow ▶ noun a slender window with a pointed arch, especially in a medieval church.

land /land/ ▶ noun **1** the part of the earth's surface that is not covered by water. **2** an area of ground in terms of its ownership or use: *the land north of town.* **3** (**the land**) ground or soil as a basis for agriculture. **4** a country or state.

– SYNONYMS **1 dry land,** terra firma, coast, coastline, shore. **2 grounds,** fields, property, acres, acreage, estate, real estate. **3 country,** nation, state, realm, kingdom, province, region, territory, area, domain.

▶ verb **1** go ashore. **2** put someone or something on land from a boat. **3** come down to the ground, or bring an aircraft or spacecraft to the ground. **4** bring a fish to land with a net or rod. **5** informal succeed in obtaining or achieving something desirable: *she landed a contract with a major film studio.* **6** (**land up**) reach a place or destination. **7** (**land up with**) end up with an unwelcome situation. **8** (**land someone in**) informal put someone in a difficult situation: *his exploits landed him in trouble.* **9** (**land someone with**) inflict something unwelcome on someone: *the mistake landed the company with a massive bill.* **10** informal inflict a blow on someone.

– SYNONYMS **1 disembark,** go ashore, debark, alight, light, get off, berth, dock, moor, (drop) anchor, tie up, put in, touch down, come to rest. **2 get,** obtain, acquire, secure, gain, net, win, achieve, attain, bag, carry off.
– ANTONYMS embark, take off.

– DERIVATIVES **land·less** adjective.
– PHRASES **how the land lies** what the situation is. **the land of Nod** humorous a state of sleep. [with reference to the biblical place name *Nod,* mentioned in the Book of Genesis, chapter 4.]
– ORIGIN Old English.

WORD LINKS

terrestrial *relating to land*

lan·dau /'lanˌdou/ ▶ noun historical a four-wheeled enclosed horse-drawn carriage.

– ORIGIN named after *Landau* in Germany, where it was first made.

land bridge ▶ noun an area of land formerly connecting two landmasses that are now separate.

land·ed /'landid/ ▶ adjective **1** owning much land, especially through inheritance. **2** consisting of or relating to land owned through inheritance.

land·er /'landər/ ▶ noun a spacecraft designed to land on the surface of a planet or moon.

land·fall /'lan(d),fôl/ ▶ noun **1** an arrival at land on a sea or air journey. **2** a collapse of a mass of land. **3** the contact of a hurricane with a landmass.

land·fill /'lan(d),fil/ ▶ noun **1** the disposal of waste material by burying it. **2** waste material that has been buried. **3** an area filled in by this process.

land·form /'lan(d),fôrm/ ▶ noun a natural feature of the earth's surface.

land·hold·er /'land,hōldər/ ▶ noun a landowner.

land·ing /'landiNG/ ▶ noun **1** a level area at the top of a staircase or between flights of stairs. **2** the action of coming to land or bringing something to land. **3** a place where people and goods can be landed from a boat.

land·ing craft ▶ noun a boat specially designed for putting troops and military equipment ashore on a beach.

land·ing gear ▶ noun the undercarriage of an aircraft.

land·ing stage ▶ noun a platform onto which passengers or cargo can be landed from a boat.

land·la·dy /'lan(d),lādē/ ▶ noun (pl. **landladies**) **1** a woman who rents out land or property. **2** a woman who owns or runs an inn, boardinghouse, or similar establishment.

– SYNONYMS **1 (property) owner,** proprietor, lessor, householder, landowner; slumlord. **2 licensee,** innkeeper, hotelier; Brit. publican; humorous mine host.
– ANTONYMS tenant.

land·line /'lan(d),līn/ ▶ noun a conventional telecommunications connection by cable laid across land.

land·locked /'lan(d),läkt/ ▶ adjective almost or entirely surrounded by land: *a landlocked country.*

land·lord /'lan(d),lôrd/ ▶ noun **1** a man (in legal use also a woman) who rents out land or property. **2** a man who owns or runs an inn, boardinghouse, or similar establishment.

– SYNONYMS **1 (property) owner,** proprietor, lessor, householder, landowner; slumlord. **2 licensee,** innkeeper, hotelier; Brit. publican; humorous mine host.
– ANTONYMS tenant.

land·lord·ism /'lan(d)lôr,dizəm/ ▶ noun the system whereby land or property is owned by landlords to whom tenants pay a fixed rent.

land·lub·ber /'lan(d),ləbər/ ▶ noun informal a person who is not used to the sea or sailing.

land·mark /'lan(d),märk/ ▶ noun **1** an object or feature of a landscape or town that is easily seen and recognized from a distance. **2** an event, discovery, or change marking an important stage or turning point: *a landmark in civil aviation technology.*

– SYNONYMS **1 feature,** sight, monument, building. **2** *a landmark in Indian history* **turning point,** milestone, watershed.

land·mass /'lan(d),mas/ ▶ noun a continent or other large body of land.

land·mine /'lan(d),mīn/ ▶ noun an explosive mine laid on or just under the surface of the ground.

land·own·er /'lan,dōnər/ ▶ noun a person who owns land.

– DERIVATIVES **land·own·er·ship** /'landōnər,SHip/ noun **land·own·ing** adjective & noun.

land·scape /'lan(d),skāp/ ▶ noun **1** all the visible features of an area of land. **2** a picture of an area of countryside. **3** the distinctive features of an area of intellectual activity: *the political landscape.*

– SYNONYMS **scenery,** country, countryside, topography, terrain, view, panorama.

▶ verb improve the appearance of a piece of land by changing its contours, planting trees and shrubs, etc.
▶ adjective referring to a format for printed material that is wider than it is high. Compare with **PORTRAIT**.

– DERIVATIVES **land·scap·er** noun **land·scap·ist** /-,skāpist/ noun.

– ORIGIN Dutch *lantscap.*

land·scape ar·chi·tec·ture ▶ noun the art and practice of designing the outdoor environment, especially so as to make parks or gardens harmonize with buildings or roads.

land·scape gar·den·ing ▶ noun the art and practice of laying out grounds in a way that is ornamental or that imitates natural scenery.

land·side /'lan(d),sīd/ ▶ noun the area of an airport terminal to which the general public has unrestricted access.

land·slide /'lan(d),slīd/ ▶ noun **1** the sliding down of a mass of earth or rock from a mountain or cliff. **2** an overwhelming majority of votes for one party in an election.

– SYNONYMS **1 avalanche,** rockfall, mudslide, rockslide. **2 decisive victory,** runaway victory, overwhelming majority; informal whitewash.

lands·man /'lan(d)zmən/ ▶ noun (pl. **landsmen**) a person unfamiliar with the sea or sailing.

land·ward /'lan(d)wərd/ ▶ adverb (also **landwards**) toward land. ▶ adjective facing toward land as opposed to sea.

lane /lān/ ▶ noun **1** a narrow road, especially in a rural area. **2** a division of a road intended to separate single lines of traffic according to speed or direction. **3** each of a number of parallel strips of track or water for competitors in a race. **4** a route or course regularly followed by ships or aircraft.

– SYNONYMS **road,** street, track, trail, alley, alleyway, passage, path.

– ORIGIN Old English.

lan·gous·tine /'laNGgə,stēn/ ▶ noun a small European lobster.

– ORIGIN French.

lan·guage /'laNGgwij/ ▶ noun **1** the method of human communication, either spoken or written, consisting of the use of words in a structured and conventional way. **2** the system of communication used by a particular community or country. **3** a particular style of speaking or writing: *legal language.* **4** the manner or style of a piece of writing or speech. **5** a system of symbols and rules for writing computer programs.

– SYNONYMS **1 speech,** speaking, talk, discourse, communication, words, vocabulary. **2 tongue,** mother tongue, native tongue, dialect, patois; informal lingo. **3 wording,** phrasing, phraseology, style, vocabulary, terminology, expressions, turn of phrase, parlance.

– ORIGIN Old French *langage*, from Latin *lingua* 'tongue.'

WORD LINKS

linguistic *relating to language*

lan·guid /ˈlaNGgwid/ ▶ **adjective 1** relaxed and not inclined to exert oneself physically. **2** weak or faint from illness or tiredness.

– SYNONYMS **1 relaxed,** unhurried, languorous, slow; listless, lethargic, sluggish, lazy, apathetic; informal laid-back. **2 sickly,** weak, faint, feeble, frail, delicate; tired, weary, fatigued.
– ANTONYMS energetic.

– DERIVATIVES **lan·guid·ly** adverb.

lan·guish /ˈlaNGgwisH/ ▶ **verb 1** grow weak or feeble. **2** be kept in an unpleasant place or situation: *he was languishing in jail.*

– SYNONYMS **1 deteriorate,** decline, go downhill, wither, droop, wilt, fade. **2 waste away,** rot, be abandoned, be neglected, be forgotten, suffer.
– ANTONYMS thrive.

– ORIGIN Old French *languir.*

lan·guor /ˈlaNG(g)ər/ ▶ **noun** tiredness or inactivity, especially when pleasurable.

– SYNONYMS **lassitude,** lethargy, listlessness, torpor, fatigue, weariness, sleepiness, drowsiness; laziness, idleness, indolence, inertia, sluggishness, apathy.
– ANTONYMS vigor.

– DERIVATIVES **lan·guor·ous** /-g(ə)rəs, ˈlaNGərəs/ adjective **lan·guor·ous·ly** /-g(ə)rəslē, ˈlaNGərəslē/ adverb.

La Ni·ña /lä ˈnēnyə/ ▶ **noun** an occasional cooling of the water in the equatorial Pacific, which is associated with widespread weather changes complementary to those of El Niño.
– ORIGIN Spanish, literally 'the girl child,' after *El Niño.*

lank /laNGk/ ▶ **adjective 1** (of hair) long, limp, and straight. **2** lanky.
– ORIGIN Old English, 'thin.'

lank·y /ˈlaNGkē/ ▶ **adjective** (**lankier, lankiest**) awkwardly thin and tall.

– SYNONYMS **tall, thin,** slender, slim, lean, lank, skinny, spindly, spare, gangling, gangly, gawky, rangy.
– ANTONYMS stocky.

– DERIVATIVES **lank·i·ness** noun.

lan·o·lin /ˈlanl-in/ ▶ **noun** a fatty substance found naturally on sheep's wool and used as a base for ointments.
– ORIGIN from Latin *lana* 'wool' + *oleum* 'oil.'

lan·tern /ˈlantərn/ ▶ **noun 1** a lamp enclosed in a metal frame with glass panels. **2** the light chamber at the top of a lighthouse. **3** a square, curved, or polygonal structure on the top of a dome or a room, with glass or open sides.
– ORIGIN Latin *lanterna.*

lan·tern-jawed ▶ **adjective** having long, thin jaws.

lan·tern slide ▶ **noun** historical a photographic slide for use in a magic lantern.

lan·tha·nide /ˈlanTHəˌnīd/ ▶ **noun** any of the series of fifteen rare-earth elements from lanthanum to lutetium in the periodic table.

lan·tha·num /ˈlanTHənəm/ ▶ **noun** a silvery-white rare-earth metallic chemical element.
– ORIGIN from Greek *lanthanein* 'escape notice' (because the element was not at first detected in cerium oxide).

lan·yard /ˈlanyərd/ (also **laniard**) ▶ **noun 1** a rope used to adjust the tension in a ship's rigging. **2** a cord passed around the neck, shoulder, or wrist for holding a whistle or similar object.
– ORIGIN Old French *laniere.*

La·o·tian /lāˈōsHən/ ▶ **noun** a person from the country of Laos in SE Asia. ▶ **adjective** relating to Laos.

lap[1] /lap/ ▶ **noun** the flat area between the waist and knees of a seated person.
– PHRASES **in someone's lap** as someone's responsibility. **in the lap of luxury** in conditions of great comfort and wealth.
– ORIGIN Old English, 'fold, flap.'

lap[2] ▶ **noun 1** one circuit of a track or racetrack. **2** a part of a journey or other undertaking: *the last lap of their four-day tour.* **3** an overlapping or projecting part. **4** a single turn of rope, thread, or cable around a drum or reel.

– SYNONYMS **circuit,** leg, circle, round, stretch.

▶ **verb** (**laps, lapping, lapped**) **1** overtake a competitor in a race to become one or more laps ahead. **2** (**lap someone/thing in**) literary enfold someone or something protectively in something soft: *he was lapped in blankets.*
– ORIGIN from LAP[1].

lap[3] ▶ **verb** (**laps, lapping, lapped**) **1** (of an animal) take up liquid with the tongue. **2** (**lap something up**) accept something with obvious pleasure: *she's lapping up all the attention.* **3** (of water) wash against something with a gentle rippling sound: *a sun-kissed island lapped by an azure sea.*

– SYNONYMS **1 drink,** lick up, sup, swallow, slurp, gulp. **2** (**lap something up**) **relish,** revel in, savor, delight in, wallow in, glory in, enjoy. **3 splash,** wash, swish, slosh, break, plash; literary purl.

▶ **noun** the action of water lapping.
– ORIGIN Old English.

lap·a·ros·co·py /ˌlapəˈräskəpē/ ▶ **noun** (pl. **laparoscopies**) a surgical procedure in which a fiber-optic instrument is inserted through the wall of the abdomen to enable the internal organs to be viewed.
– DERIVATIVES **lap·a·ro·scope** /ˈlap(ə)rəˌskōp/ noun **lap·a·ro·scop·ic** /ˌlap(ə)rəˈskäpik/ adjective.
– ORIGIN from Greek *lapara* 'flank.'

lap·a·rot·o·my /ˌlapəˈrätəmē/ ▶ **noun** (pl. **laparotomies**) a surgical incision into the abdomen, to make a diagnosis or in preparation for major surgery.

lap danc·ing ▶ **noun** erotic dancing in which the dancer performs a striptease near to or on the lap of a paying customer.
– DERIVATIVES **lap dance** noun **lap danc·er** noun.

lap·dog /ˈlapˌdôg, -ˌdäg/ ▶ **noun 1** a small pampered pet dog. **2** a person who is completely under the influence of another.

la·pel /ləˈpel/ ▶ **noun** the part on each side of a coat or jacket immediately below the collar that is folded back against the front opening.
– ORIGIN from LAP[1].

lap·i·dar·y /ˈlapəˌderē/ ▶ **adjective 1** relating to the engraving, cutting, or polishing of stones and gems. **2** (of language) elegant and concise. ▶ **noun** (pl. **lapidaries**) a person who cuts, polishes, or engraves stones and gems.
– ORIGIN from Latin *lapis* 'stone.'

lap·is laz·u·li /ˈlapis ˈlazyəˌlī, ˈlazʜəˌlī, ˈlazyəlē/ (also **lapis**) ▶ **noun 1** a bright blue rock used in jewelry. **2** the pigment ultramarine, originally made by crushing lapis lazuli.
– ORIGIN Latin, 'stone of lapis lazuli.'

lap joint ▶ **noun** a joint between shafts, rails, etc., made by halving the thickness of each part at the joint and fitting them together.

Lap·land·er /ˈlapˌlandər, -ləndər/ ▶ **noun** a person from Lapland, a region in northern Europe.

Lapp /lap/ ▶ **noun 1** a member of a people of the extreme north of Scandinavia. **2** the language of the Lapps.
– ORIGIN Swedish.

USAGE

Although the term **Lapp** is still widely used and is the most familiar term to many people, the people themselves prefer to be called **Sami**.

lap·pet /ˈlapit/ ▶ **noun 1** a fold or hanging piece of flesh in some animals. **2** a loose or overlapping part of a garment.
– ORIGIN from LAP[1].

lapse /laps/ ▶ **noun 1** a brief failure of concentration, memory, or judgment. **2** a decline from previously high standards: *his lapse into petty crime*. **3** a period of time between two events. **4** Law the termination of a right or privilege through disuse or failure to follow the appropriate procedures.

– SYNONYMS **1 failure,** slip, error, mistake, blunder, fault, omission; informal slip-up. **2 decline,** fall, deterioration, degeneration, backsliding, regression. **3 interval,** gap, pause, interlude, lull, hiatus, break.

▶ **verb 1** (of a right, privilege, or agreement) become invalid because it is not used, claimed, or renewed. **2** (usu. as adj. **lapsed**) stop following the rules and practices of a religion or doctrine: *a lapsed Catholic*. **3** (**lapse into**) pass gradually into a different, often worse state or condition: *the country lapsed into chaos*.

– SYNONYMS **1 expire,** run out, (come to an) end, cease, stop, terminate. **2 revert,** relapse, drift, slide, slip, sink.

– ORIGIN Latin *lapsus*.

lap·top /ˈlapˌtäp/ ▶ **noun** a portable microcomputer suitable for use while traveling.

lap·wing /ˈlapˌwiɴɢ/ ▶ **noun** a large crested plover (bird) with a dark green back, black-and-white head, and a loud call.
– ORIGIN Old English, from words meaning 'to leap' and 'move from side to side.'

lar·board /ˈlärˌbôrd, -bərd/ ▶ **noun** Nautical old-fashioned term for PORT[3].

lar·ce·ny /ˈlärs(ə)nē/ ▶ **noun** (pl. **larcenies**) theft of personal property.
– DERIVATIVES **lar·ce·nous** /-nəs/ adjective.
– ORIGIN Old French *larcin*.

larch /lärcʜ/ ▶ **noun** a northern coniferous tree with bunches of deciduous bright green needles and tough wood.
– ORIGIN German *larche*.

lard /lärd/ ▶ **noun** fat from the abdomen of a pig, prepared for use in cooking. ▶ **verb 1** insert strips of fat or bacon in meat before cooking. **2** add many obscure or technical expressions to talk or writing: *his conversation is larded with references to Coleridge*.
– ORIGIN Latin *lardum*.

lard·er /ˈlärdər/ ▶ **noun** a room or large cupboard for storing food.
– ORIGIN Latin *lardarium*.

lar·don /ˈlärdn/ ▶ **noun** (also **lardoon**) a chunk or strip of bacon inserted in meat before it is cooked.
– ORIGIN French.

lard·y /ˈlärdē/ ▶ **adjective** informal (of a person) fat.

large /lärj/ ▶ **adjective 1** of great or relatively great size, extent, or capacity. **2** of wide range or scope: *we can afford to take a larger view of the situation*.

– SYNONYMS **big,** great, sizable, substantial, considerable, huge, extensive, voluminous, vast, prodigious, massive, immense, enormous, colossal, king-size(d), heavy, mammoth, gigantic, giant, fat, stout, strapping, bulky, burly; informal jumbo, mega, whopping.
– ANTONYMS small.

▶ **verb** (**large it**) Brit. informal go out and have a good time.
– DERIVATIVES **large·ness** noun **larg·ish** adjective.
– PHRASES **at large 1** escaped or not yet captured. **2** as a whole: *society at large*.
– ORIGIN Latin *larga* 'copious.'

large in·tes·tine ▶ **noun** the part of the alimentary canal that consists of the cecum, colon, and rectum collectively.

large·ly /ˈlärjlē/ ▶ **adverb** on the whole; mostly.

– SYNONYMS **mostly,** mainly, to a large/great extent, chiefly, predominantly, primarily, principally, for the most part, in the main, on the whole.

large-scale ▶ **adjective** involving large numbers or a large area; extensive.

lar·gesse /lärˈzʜes, -ˈjes/ (also **largess**) ▶ **noun 1** generosity. **2** money or gifts given generously.

– SYNONYMS **generosity,** liberality, munificence, bountifulness, beneficence, charity, philanthropy, magnanimity, benevolence, charitableness.
– ANTONYMS meanness.

– ORIGIN Old French.

CHOOSE THE RIGHT WORD

See PRESENT[3].

lar·go /ˈlärˌgō/ ▶ **adverb & adjective** Music in a slow tempo and dignified style.
– ORIGIN Italian.

lar·i·at /ˈlarēət/ ▶ **noun** a rope used as a lasso or for tethering animals.
– ORIGIN from Spanish *la reata*.

lark[1] /lärk/ ▶ **noun** a brown songbird that sings while in flight.
– ORIGIN Old English.

lark[2] informal ▶ **noun** an amusing adventure or escapade. ▶ **verb** enjoy oneself by behaving in a playful and mischievous way.
– ORIGIN perhaps from dialect *lake* 'play.'

lark·spur /ˈlärkˌspər/ ▶ **noun** a Mediterranean plant resembling a delphinium.

lar·va /ˈlärvə/ ▸ **noun** (pl. **larvae** /-vē, -ˌvī/) the immature form of an insect or other animal that undergoes metamorphosis, e.g., a caterpillar or tadpole.
– DERIVATIVES **lar·val** /-vəl/ adjective.
– ORIGIN Latin, 'ghost, mask.'

la·ryn·ge·al /ləˈrinj(ē)əl, ˌlarənˈjēəl/ ▸ **adjective** relating to the larynx.

lar·yn·gi·tis /ˌlarənˈjītis/ ▸ **noun** inflammation of the larynx.

lar·ynx /ˈlariNGks, ˈler-/ ▸ **noun** (pl. **larynxes** or **larynges** /ləˈrinˌjēz/) the hollow muscular organ forming an air passage to the lungs and containing the vocal cords.
– ORIGIN Greek *larunx*.

la·sa·gna /ləˈzänyə/ (also **lasagne**) ▸ **noun 1** pasta in the form of sheets or wide strips. **2** an Italian dish consisting of lasagna baked with meat or vegetables and a cheese sauce.
– ORIGIN Italian.

las·civ·i·ous /ləˈsivēəs/ ▸ **adjective** feeling or showing obvious sexual desire.

– SYNONYMS **lecherous,** lewd, lustful, licentious, libidinous, salacious, lubricious, prurient, dirty, smutty, naughty, suggestive, indecent; Brit. informal randy; formal concupiscent.

– DERIVATIVES **las·civ·i·ous·ly** adverb **las·civ·i·ous·ness** noun.
– ORIGIN Latin *lascivia* 'lustfulness.'

la·ser /ˈlāzər/ ▸ **noun** a device that produces a beam of light of a type used for surgery, compact discs, and holograms.
– ORIGIN from the initial letters of *light amplification by stimulated emission of radiation*.

la·ser·disc /ˈlāzərˌdisk/ ▸ **noun** a disc resembling a large compact disc, used for high-quality video and for interactive multimedia.

la·ser print·er ▸ **noun** a computer printer in which a laser is used to form a pattern of electrically charged dots on a light-sensitive drum, which attracts toner.

lash /lasH/ ▸ **verb 1** beat a person or animal with a whip or stick. **2** beat forcefully against: *waves lashed the coast*. **3** (**lash out**) attack someone or something verbally or physically. **4** fasten something securely with a cord or rope. **5** (of an animal) move its tail quickly and violently.

– SYNONYMS **1 strike,** hit, take a swing at, set on, turn on, attack; informal lay into. **2 beat against,** dash against, pound, batter, hammer against, strike, hit, drum. **3** (**lash out**) *the president lashed out at the opposition* **criticize,** attack, condemn, censure; informal lay into, dis; Brit. informal have a go at. **4 fasten,** bind, tie (up), tether, hitch, knot, rope.

▸ **noun 1** a sharp blow or stroke with a whip or stick. **2** the flexible leather part of a whip. **3** an eyelash.
– ORIGIN probably imitating the sound.

lash·ing /ˈlasHiNG/ ▸ **noun 1** a whipping or beating. **2** a cord used to fasten something securely.

LASIK /ˈlāzik/ ▸ **noun** eye surgery to correct vision in which a laser reshapes the inner cornea.
– ORIGIN from the initial letters of *laser-assisted in situ keratomileusis*.

lass /las/ (also **lassie**) ▸ **noun** chiefly Scottish & N. English a girl or young woman.
– ORIGIN Old Norse, 'unmarried.'

las·si /ˈlasē/ ▸ **noun** a sweet or savory Indian drink made from a yogurt or buttermilk base with water.
– ORIGIN Hindi.

las·si·tude /ˈlasəˌt(y)o͞od/ ▸ **noun** physical or mental weariness; lack of energy.
– ORIGIN Latin *lassitudo*.

las·so /ˈlasō, ˈlaso͞o, laˈso͞o/ ▸ **noun** (pl. **lassos** or **lassoes**) a rope with a noose at one end, used especially in North America for catching cattle or horses. ▸ **verb** (**lassoes, lassoing, lassoed**) catch an animal with a lasso.
– ORIGIN Spanish *lazo*.

last¹ /last/ ▸ **adjective 1** coming after all others in time or order. **2** most recent in time: *last year*. **3** immediately preceding something in order: *their last album*. **4** lowest in importance or rank. **5** (**the last**) the least likely or suitable. **6** only remaining: *it's our last hope*.

– SYNONYMS **1 final,** closing, concluding, end, ultimate, terminal, later, latter. **2 rearmost,** hindmost, endmost, furthest (back). **3 previous,** preceding, prior, former, latest, most recent.
– ANTONYMS first, next.

▸ **adverb 1** on the last occasion before the present: *she was last seen on Friday evening*. **2** (in combination) after all others in order: *the last-named film*. **3** (in stating numbered points) lastly.
▸ **noun** (pl. same) **1** the last person or thing. **2** (**the last of**) the only remaining part of.
– PHRASES **at last** (or **at long last**) in the end; after much delay. **the last minute** the latest possible time before an event. **the last word 1** a final statement on a subject. **2** the most modern or advanced example of something: *the hotel is the last word in luxury*. **to the last** up to the last moment of a person's life.
– ORIGIN Old English.

last² ▸ **verb 1** continue for a specified period of time. **2** remain operating or usable for a considerable or specified length of time: *the car is built to last*. **3** (of provisions or resources) be enough for someone for a specified period of time: *there was only enough food to last them three months*. **4** (often **last something out**) manage to survive or endure something.

– SYNONYMS **1** *the hearing lasted for six days* **continue,** go on, carry on, keep on/going, take. **2** *he won't last long as manager* **survive,** endure, hold on/out, keep going, persevere, persist, stay, remain; informal stick it out, hang on, go the distance.
– ANTONYMS end.

– ORIGIN Old English.

last³ ▸ **noun** a shaped stand used by a shoemaker for shaping or repairing a shoe or boot.
– ORIGIN Old English.

last-ditch ▸ **adjective** referring to a final desperate attempt to achieve something.

last-gasp ▸ **adjective** done or happening at the last possible moment.

last·ing /ˈlastiNG/ ▸ **adjective** enduring or able to endure for a long time: *a lasting impression*.

– SYNONYMS **enduring,** long-lasting, long-lived, abiding, continuing, long-term, permanent, durable, stable, secure, long-standing, eternal, undying, everlasting, unending, never-ending.
– ANTONYMS passing, ephemeral.

Last Judg·ment ▸ **noun** the judgment of humankind expected in some religions to take place at the end of the world.

last·ly /ˈlastlē/ ▸ **adverb** as a final point; last.

last name ▸ **noun** a person's surname.

last rites ▸ **plural noun** (in the Christian Church) a religious ceremony performed for and in the presence of a person who is about to die.

Last Sup·per ▸ **noun** the meal eaten by Jesus and his disciples on the night before the Crucifixion.

last trump ▸ **noun** the trumpet blast that in some religions is thought will wake the dead on Judgment Day.

lat. ▸ **abbreviation** latitude.

latch /laCH/ ▸ **noun 1** a bar with a catch and lever used for fastening a door or gate. **2** a spring lock for an outer door that catches when the door is closed and can only be opened from the outside with a key. ▸ **verb** fasten a door or gate with a latch.
– PHRASES **latch onto** informal **1** join someone and remain with them as a constant and usually unwelcome companion. **2** take up an idea or trend enthusiastically: *Californians had a reputation for latching onto fads.* **3** understand the meaning of something.
– ORIGIN Old English, 'take hold of, grasp.'

latch·key /ˈlaCH,kē/ ▸ **noun** (pl. **latchkeys**) a key of a house's outer door.

latch·key child ▸ **noun** a child who is alone at home after school until a parent returns from work.

late /lāt/ ▸ **adjective 1** acting, arriving, or happening after the proper or usual time. **2** belonging or taking place far on in a particular time or period: *a woman in her late fifties.* **3** (**latest**) of most recent date or origin. **4** (**the/one's late**) (of a person) no longer alive: *his late wife.* **5** far on in the day or night.

> – SYNONYMS **1 behind schedule,** tardy, overdue, delayed, belated, behindhand. **2** (**later**) *a later chapter* **subsequent,** following, succeeding, future, upcoming, to come, ensuing, next. **3** (**latest**) **most recent,** newest, up to the minute, current, state-of-the-art, cutting-edge; informal in, with it, trendy, hip, hot, happening, cool. **4 dead,** departed, lamented, passed on/away; formal deceased.
> – ANTONYMS punctual, early.

▸ **adverb 1** after the proper or usual time. **2** (**later**) at a time in the near future; afterward. **3** toward the end of a period. **4** far on in the day or night. **5** (**late of**) formerly but not now living or working in a place.

> – SYNONYMS **1** *she had arrived late* **behind schedule,** behind time, behindhand, belatedly, tardily, at the last minute. **2** (**later**) *later, the film rights were sold* **subsequently,** eventually, then, next, later on, afterward, at a later date, in the future, in due course, by and by, in a while, in time; formal thereafter.

▸ **noun** (**the latest**) the most recent news or fashion.
– DERIVATIVES **late·ness** noun **lat·ish** (also **lateish**) adjective & adverb.
– PHRASES **at the latest** no later than the time specified. **of late** recently.
– ORIGIN Old English.

late·com·er /ˈlāt,kəmər/ ▸ **noun** a person who arrives late.

la·teen /ləˈtēn, la-/ ▸ **noun 1** (also **lateen sail**) a triangular sail on a long yard at an angle of 45° to the mast. **2** a ship rigged with such a sail.
– ORIGIN from French *voile Latine* 'Latin sail.'

late·ly /ˈlātlē/ ▸ **adverb** recently; not long ago.

> – SYNONYMS **recently,** not long ago, of late, latterly, in recent times.

la·tent /ˈlātnt/ ▸ **adjective** existing but not yet developed, apparent, or active: *her latent talent.*

> – SYNONYMS **dormant,** untapped, undiscovered, hidden, concealed, undeveloped, unrealized, unfulfilled, potential.

– DERIVATIVES **la·ten·cy** noun **la·tent·ly** adverb.
– ORIGIN Latin *latere* 'be hidden.'

WORD TOOLKIT

latent ...	potential ...	dormant ...
tuberculosis	problems	volcano
infection	benefits	plants
defect	buyers	seeds
factors	investors	account
homosexuality	risk	cells

la·tent heat ▸ **noun** Physics the heat required to convert a solid into a liquid or vapor, or a liquid into a vapor, without change of temperature.

la·tent im·age ▸ **noun** an image on exposed photographic film that has not yet been made visible by developing.

lat·er·al /ˈlatərəl, ˈlatrəl/ ▸ **adjective** relating to, toward, or from the side or sides. ▸ **noun** a lateral part, especially a shoot or branch growing out from the side of a stem.
– DERIVATIVES **lat·er·al·ly** adverb.
– ORIGIN Latin *lateralis.*

lat·er·ite /ˈlatə,rīt/ ▸ **noun** a reddish clayey topsoil found in tropical regions, sometimes used to make roads.
– ORIGIN from Latin *later* 'brick.'

la·tex /ˈlā,teks/ ▸ **noun 1** a milky fluid found in many plants, notably the rubber tree, that coagulates on exposure to the air. **2** a synthetic product resembling latex, used to make paints, coatings, etc.
– ORIGIN Latin, 'liquid, fluid.'

lath /laTH/ ▸ **noun** (pl. **laths**) a thin, flat strip of wood, especially one of a series forming a foundation for the plaster of a wall.
– ORIGIN Old English.

lathe /lāT͟H/ ▸ **noun** a machine for shaping wood or metal by means of a rotating drive that turns the piece being worked on against changeable cutting tools.
– ORIGIN probably from Danish *lad* 'structure, frame.'

lath·er /ˈlaT͟Hər/ ▸ **noun 1** a frothy white mass of bubbles produced by soap when mixed with water. **2** heavy sweat visible on a horse's coat as a white foam. **3** (**a lather**) informal a state of agitation or nervous excitement. ▸ **verb 1** form a lather. **2** rub something with soap until a lather is produced. **3** spread a substance thickly or liberally: *we lathered butter on our toast.*
– ORIGIN Old English.

la·thi /ˈlätē/ ▸ **noun** (pl. **lathis**) (in the Indian subcontinent) a long metal-bound bamboo stick used as a weapon, especially by police.
– ORIGIN Hindi.

Lat·in /ˈlatn/ ▸ **noun 1** the language of ancient Rome and its empire. **2** a person from a country whose language developed from Latin. ▸ **adjective 1** relating to the Latin language. **2** relating to countries using languages that developed from Latin, especially Latin America. **3** relating to the Western or Roman Catholic Church.
– DERIVATIVES **Lat·in·ism** /-,izəm/ noun **Lat·in·ist** /-ist/ noun **La·tin·i·ty** /ləˈtinətə, la-/ noun.
– ORIGIN Latin *Latinus* 'of Latium' (an ancient region in central Italy).

La·ti·na /lə'tēnə, la-/ ▶ **noun** fem. of **LATINO**.

Lat·in A·mer·i·can ▶ **adjective** relating to the parts of the American continent where Spanish or Portuguese is the main national language. ▶ **noun** a person from Latin America.

Lat·in·ate /'latn,āt/ ▶ **adjective** (of language) having the character of Latin.

Lat·in·ize /'latn,īz/ ▶ **verb** give a Latin or Latinate form to a word.
– DERIVATIVES **Lat·in·i·za·tion** noun.

La·ti·no /lə'tēnō, la-/ ▶ **noun** (pl. **Latinos**; fem. **Latina**, pl. **Latinas**) a Latin American inhabitant of the US. ▶ **adjective** relating to Latinos or Latinas.
– ORIGIN Latin American Spanish.

lat·i·tude /'latə,t(y)o͞od/ ▶ **noun 1** the angular distance of a place north or south of the equator. **2** (**latitudes**) regions with reference to their temperature and distance from the equator: *northern latitudes.* **3** scope for freedom of action or thought: *journalists have considerable latitude in criticizing public figures.*

> – SYNONYMS **freedom,** scope, leeway, (breathing) space, flexibility, liberty, independence, free rein, license.
> – ANTONYMS restriction.

– DERIVATIVES **lat·i·tu·di·nal** /,latə't(y)o͞odn-əl/ adjective **lat·i·tu·di·nal·ly** /,latə't(y)o͞odn-əlē/ adverb.
– ORIGIN Latin *latitudo* 'breadth.'

> **CHOOSE THE RIGHT WORD**
>
> See **RANGE**.

lat·i·tu·di·nar·i·an /,latə,t(y)o͞odn'erēən/ ▶ **adjective** liberal in religious views. ▶ **noun** a person with a liberal religious outlook.
– DERIVATIVES **lat·i·tu·di·nar·i·an·ism** /-,nizəm/ noun.

la·trine /lə'trēn/ ▶ **noun** a communal toilet in a camp or barracks.
– ORIGIN Latin *latrina*.

lat·te /'lä,tā/ (also **caffè latte** /ka'fā, kə-/) ▶ **noun** a drink of frothy steamed milk with a shot of espresso coffee.
– ORIGIN from Italian *caffè latte* 'milk coffee.'

lat·ter /'latər/ ▶ **adjective 1** nearer to the end than to the beginning. **2** recent: *in latter years.* **3** (**the latter**) referring to the second or second-mentioned of two people or things.

> – SYNONYMS **1 later,** closing, end, concluding, final. **2 last-mentioned,** second, last, final.
> – ANTONYMS earlier, former.

– ORIGIN Old English, 'slower.'

lat·ter-day ▶ **adjective** modern or contemporary, especially when resembling a person or thing of the past: *a latter-day Noah.*

Lat·ter-Day Saints ▶ **plural noun** the Mormons' name for themselves.

lat·ter·ly /'latərlē/ ▶ **adverb 1** recently. **2** in the later stages of a period of time.

lat·tice /'latis/ ▶ **noun 1** a structure or pattern consisting of strips crossing each other with square or diamond-shaped spaces left between. **2** a regular repeated three-dimensional arrangement of atoms, ions, or molecules in a metal or other crystalline solid.
– DERIVATIVES **lat·ticed** adjective **lat·tice·work** /'latis,wərk/ noun.
– ORIGIN Old French *lattis*.

Lat·vi·an /'latvēən/ ▶ **noun 1** a person from Latvia. **2** the language of Latvia. ▶ **adjective** relating to Latvia.

laud /'lôd/ ▶ **verb** formal praise someone or something highly.
– DERIVATIVES **lau·da·tion** /lô'dāsʜən/ noun.
– ORIGIN Latin *laudare*.

laud·a·ble /'lôdəbəl/ ▶ **adjective** deserving praise.

> – SYNONYMS **praiseworthy,** commendable, admirable, worthy, deserving, creditable, estimable, exemplary.
> – ANTONYMS shameful.

– DERIVATIVES **laud·a·bly** /-blē/ adverb.

lau·da·num /'lôdn-əm, 'lôdnəm/ ▶ **noun** a solution prepared from opium and formerly used as a painkiller.
– ORIGIN Latin.

laud·a·to·ry /'lôdə,tôrē/ ▶ **adjective** expressing praise.

laugh /laf/ ▶ **verb 1** make the sounds that express lively amusement. **2** (**laugh at**) make fun of. **3** (**laugh something off**) dismiss something by treating it lightheartedly. **4** (**be laughing**) informal be in a fortunate or successful position.

> – SYNONYMS **1 chuckle,** chortle, guffaw, giggle, titter, snigger, roar, split one's sides; informal be in stitches, be rolling in the aisles, crack up. **2** *people laughed at his theories* **ridicule,** mock, deride, scoff at, jeer at, sneer at, jibe at, make fun of, poke fun at, taunt, tease. **3** *you have to just **laugh off** their stupid remarks* **dismiss,** make a joke of, make light of, shrug off, brush aside; informal pooh-pooh.

▶ **noun 1** an act of laughing. **2** (**a laugh**) informal a cause of laughter.

> – SYNONYMS **1 chuckle,** chortle, guffaw, giggle, titter, snigger, roar, shriek. **2 joke,** prank, jest; informal lark, hoot, scream.

– DERIVATIVES **laugh·er** noun.
– PHRASES **have the last laugh** be eventually proved right or at an advantage. **laugh someone/thing out of court** dismiss someone or something as being obviously ridiculous. **laugh up one's sleeve** be secretly amused.
– ORIGIN Old English.

laugh·a·ble /'lafəbəl/ ▶ **adjective** so ridiculous as to be amusing.
– DERIVATIVES **laugh·a·bly** /-blē/ adverb.

laugh·ing gas ▶ **noun** nontechnical term for **NITROUS OXIDE**.

laugh·ing·stock /'lafiɴɢ,stäk/ ▶ **noun** a person who is ridiculed by everyone.

laugh·ter /'laftər/ ▶ **noun** the action or sound of laughing.

> – SYNONYMS **1 laughing,** chuckling, chortling, guffawing, giggling, tittering, sniggering. **2 amusement,** entertainment, humor, mirth, merriment, gaiety, hilarity, jollity, fun.

laugh track ▶ **noun** recorded laughter added to a comedy show, especially a television situation comedy.

launch[1] /lôncʜ, läncʜ/ ▶ **verb 1** move a boat or ship from land into the water. **2** send a rocket or missile on its course. **3** hurl or move forcefully: *I launched myself out of bed.* **4** begin an enterprise or introduce a new product. **5** (**launch into**) begin something energetically and enthusiastically.

> – SYNONYMS **1 propel,** fire, shoot, throw, hurl, fling, pitch, lob, let fly; informal chuck, heave, sling. **2 start,**

begin, initiate, put in place, set up, inaugurate, introduce; informal kick off.

▶ **noun 1** an act of launching something. **2** an occasion at which a new product or publication is introduced to the public.
– ORIGIN Old French *lancier* 'to lance.'

launch² ▶ **noun** a large motorboat, used especially for short trips.
– ORIGIN Spanish *lancha* 'pinnace.'

launch·er /ˈlônCHər, ˈlän-/ ▶ **noun** a structure that holds a rocket or missile during launching.

launch pad (also **launching pad**) ▶ **noun** the area on which a rocket stands for launching, typically a platform with a supporting structure.

laun·der /ˈlôndər, ˈlän-/ ▶ **verb 1** wash and iron clothes or linen. **2** informal pass illegally obtained money through legitimate businesses or foreign banks to conceal its origins.
– DERIVATIVES **laun·der·er** noun.
– ORIGIN from Latin *lavanda* 'things to be washed.'

laun·dress /ˈlôndrəs, ˈlän-/ ▶ **noun** dated a woman employed to launder clothes and linen.

laun·dro·mat /ˈlôndrəˌmat, ˈlän-/ ▶ **noun** trademark an establishment with coin-operated washing machines and dryers for public use.

laun·dry /ˌlôndrē, ˈlän-/ ▶ **noun** (pl. **laundries**) **1** clothes and linen that need to be washed or that have been newly washed. **2** a room or building where clothes and linen are washed and ironed.

laun·dry bas·ket ▶ **noun** a basket for dirty clothing.

laun·dry list ▶ **noun** a long or exhaustive list.

lau·re·ate /ˈlôrē-it, ˈlär-/ ▶ **noun 1** a person given an award for outstanding creative or intellectual achievement. **2** a Poet Laureate.
– DERIVATIVES **lau·re·ate·ship** /-ˌSHip/ noun.
– ORIGIN from Latin *laurea* 'laurel wreath.'

lau·rel /ˈlôrəl, ˈlär-/ ▶ **noun 1** an evergreen shrub or small tree with dark green glossy leaves. **2** (**laurels**) a crown woven from bay leaves and awarded as a sign of victory or mark of honor in classical times. **3** (**laurels**) honor or praise for an achievement.
– PHRASES **rest on one's laurels** be so satisfied with what one has already achieved that one makes no further effort.
– ORIGIN Latin *laurus*.

la·va /ˈlävə, ˈlavə/ ▶ **noun** hot molten or semifluid rock that erupts from a volcano or fissure, or solid rock formed when this cools.
– ORIGIN Italian.

la·vage /ləˈväZH, ˈlavij/ ▶ **noun** the process of washing out a body cavity, such as the colon or stomach.
– ORIGIN French *laver* 'to wash.'

la·va lamp ▶ **noun** a transparent electric lamp containing a viscous liquid in which a suspended waxy substance rises and falls in constantly changing shapes.

lav·a·to·ry /ˈlavəˌtôrē/ ▶ **noun** (pl. **lavatories**) a bathroom.

– SYNONYMS see **BATHROOM**.

– ORIGIN Latin *lavatorium* 'place for washing.'

lave /lāv/ ▶ **verb** literary wash something.
– ORIGIN Latin *lavare* 'to wash.'

lav·en·der /ˈlavəndər/ ▶ **noun 1** a small evergreen shrub with narrow strong-smelling leaves and bluish-purple flowers. **2** a pale bluish-purple color.
– ORIGIN Latin *lavandula*.

lav·en·der wa·ter ▶ **noun** a perfume made from distilled lavender.

la·ver /ˈlāvər/ (also **purple laver**) ▶ **noun** an edible seaweed with thin reddish-purple and green fronds.
– ORIGIN Latin.

lav·ish /ˈlaviSH/ ▶ **adjective 1** very rich, elaborate, or luxurious. **2** giving or given in large amounts: *lavish funding from abroad.*

– SYNONYMS **1 sumptuous,** luxurious, gorgeous, costly, expensive, opulent, grand, splendid, rich, fancy; informal posh, bling-bling. **2 generous,** liberal, bountiful, unstinting, unsparing, free, munificent, extravagant, abundant, copious, plentiful, prolific, excessive, wasteful, prodigal; literary plenteous.
– ANTONYMS meager, frugal.

▶ **verb** give in abundant or extravagant quantities: *he lavished money and attention on the family.*

– SYNONYMS **shower,** heap, pour, deluge, throw at, squander, dissipate.
– ANTONYMS begrudge, stint.

– DERIVATIVES **lav·ish·ly** adverb **lav·ish·ness** noun.
– ORIGIN from Old French *lavasse* 'deluge of rain.'

law /lô/ ▶ **noun 1** a rule or system of rules recognized by a country or community as regulating the actions of its members and enforced by the imposition of penalties. **2** such rules as a subject of study or as the basis of the legal profession. **3** statute law and the common law as distinct from equity. **4** a rule that controls correct behavior in a sport. **5** a statement of the fact that a particular natural or scientific phenomenon always occurs if certain conditions are present. **6** something that has binding force or effect: *his word was law.* **7** (**the law**) informal the police.

– SYNONYMS **1 regulation,** statute, ordinance, act, bill, decree, edict, rule, ruling, dictum, command, order, directive, dictate, diktat, fiat, bylaw; (**laws**) legislation, constitution, code. **2 principle,** rule, precept, commandment, belief, creed, credo, maxim, tenet, doctrine, canon.

– PHRASES **be a law unto oneself** behave in an unconventional or unpredictable way. **lay down the law** issue instructions in a domineering way. **take the law into one's own hands** illegally punish someone according to one's own ideas of justice.
– ORIGIN Old Norse, 'something laid down or fixed.'

WORD LINKS

legal, legislative *relating to laws*

law-a·bid·ing ▶ **adjective** obedient to the laws of society.

law·break·er /ˈlôˌbrākər/ ▶ **noun** a person who breaks the law.

law court ▶ **noun** a court of law.

law·ful /ˈlôfəl/ ▶ **adjective** following, permitted by, or recognized by the law or a set of rules.

– SYNONYMS **legitimate,** legal, licit, permissible, permitted, allowable, allowed, rightful, sanctioned, authorized, warranted; informal legit.
– ANTONYMS illegal.

– DERIVATIVES **law·ful·ly** adverb **law·ful·ness** noun.

law·giv·er /ˈlôˌgivər/ ▶ **noun** a person who draws up and enacts laws.

law·less /ˈlôləs/ ▶ **adjective** not governed by or obedient to laws.
– DERIVATIVES **law·less·ly** adverb **law·less·ness** noun.

law·mak·er /ˈlôˌmākər/ ▶ **noun** a member of a government who draws up laws.
– DERIVATIVES **law·mak·ing** /-ˌmākiNG/ adjective & noun.

law·man /ˈlôˌmən, -man/ ▶ **noun** (pl. **lawmen**) a law-enforcement officer, especially a sheriff.

lawn[1] /lôn/ ▶ **noun** an area of mown grass in a yard, garden, or park.
– ORIGIN Old French *launde* 'wooded district, heath.'

lawn[2] ▶ **noun** a fine linen or cotton fabric.
– ORIGIN probably from *Laon*, a French city important for linen manufacture.

lawn bowl·ing (Brit. **bowls**) ▶ **noun** a game played with wooden bowls, the object of which is to roll one's bowl as close as possible to a small white ball (the jack).

lawn·mow·er /ˈlônˌmōər/ ▶ **noun** a machine for cutting the grass on a lawn.

lawn ten·nis ▶ **noun** dated or formal tennis.

law of av·er·ag·es ▶ **noun** the supposed principle that future events are likely to turn out so that they balance any past events.

law of na·ture ▶ **noun** another term for **NATURAL LAW**.

law·ren·ci·um /lôˈrensēəm/ ▶ **noun** a very unstable chemical element made by high-energy collisions.
– ORIGIN named after the American physicist Ernest O. *Lawrence*.

law·suit /ˈlôˌso͞ot/ ▶ **noun** a claim or dispute brought to a court of law to be decided.

law·yer /ˈloi-ər, ˈlôyər/ ▶ **noun** a person who practices or studies law; an attorney or a counselor.

> – SYNONYMS **attorney,** attorney-at-law, counsel, counselor, legal practitioner, member of the bar, litigator, advocate; Brit. solicitor, barrister; informal mouthpiece, legal eagle; informal, derogatory ambulance chaser, shyster.

– DERIVATIVES **law·yer·ing** noun **law·yer·ly** adjective.

lax /laks/ ▶ **adjective 1** not strict, severe, or careful enough: *lax security arrangements.* **2** (of limbs or muscles) relaxed.

> – SYNONYMS **slack,** slipshod, negligent, remiss, careless, sloppy, slapdash, offhand, casual.
> – ANTONYMS strict.

– DERIVATIVES **lax·i·ty** noun **lax·ly** adverb **lax·ness** noun.
– ORIGIN Latin *laxus* 'loose, lax.'

lax·a·tive /ˈlaksətiv/ ▶ **noun** a medicine that causes a person to empty their bowels. ▶ **adjective** causing the bowels to empty.
– ORIGIN from Latin *laxare* 'loosen.'

lay[1] /lā/ ▶ **verb** (past and past part. **laid** /lād/) **1** put something down. **2** assign or place. **3** stake an amount of money in a bet. **4** put something down and set it in position for use. **5** (**lay something before**) present material for consideration and action to someone. **6** (of a female bird, reptile, etc.) produce an egg from inside the body. **7** cause a ghost to stop appearing. **8** vulgar slang (**get laid**) have sex.

> – SYNONYMS **1 put (down),** place, set (down), deposit, rest, position, shove; informal stick, dump, park, plonk. **2** *they tried to lay the blame on others* **assign to,** attribute to, ascribe to, allot to, attach to; hold someone accountable, hold someone responsible, find guilty. **3** *I'd lay money on it* **bet,** wager, gamble, stake.

▶ **noun 1** the general appearance of an area of land. **2** the position or direction in which something lies. **3** vulgar slang a sexual partner or act of sex.
– PHRASES **lay claim to** claim that one has a right to something or possesses a skill or quality. **lay something down 1** formulate and enforce a rule or principle. **2** build up a deposit of a substance. **3** store wine in a cellar. **4** pay or bet money. **lay something in/up** build up a stock in case of need. **lay into** informal attack someone violently. **the lay of the land 1** the features of an area. **2** the current situation. **lay off** informal give something up. **lay someone off** discharge a worker because of a shortage of work. **lay something on thick** (or **with a trowel**) informal greatly exaggerate or overemphasize something. **lay someone open to** expose someone to the risk of something. **lay someone out** prepare someone for burial after death. **lay something out 1** construct or arrange buildings or gardens according to a plan. **2** arrange and present material for printing and publication. **3** informal spend a sum of money. **lay something to rest 1** bury a body in a grave. **2** put an end to fear, anxiety, etc. **lay someone up** put someone out of action through illness or injury.
– ORIGIN Old English.

> **USAGE**
>
> The words **lay** and **lie** are often used incorrectly. **Lay** generally means 'put something down' (*they are going to lay the carpet*), whereas **lie** means 'be in a horizontal position to rest' (*why don't you lie down?*). The past tense and past participle of **lay** is **laid** (*they laid the carpet*); the past tense of **lie** is **lay** (*he lay on the floor*) and the past participle is **lain** (*she had lain awake for hours*).

lay[2] ▶ **adjective 1** not belonging to the clergy. **2** not having professional qualifications or expert knowledge in a particular subject.

> – SYNONYMS **1** *a lay preacher* **nonordained,** nonclerical, secular. **2** *science books for a lay audience* **nonexpert,** nonprofessional, nonspecialist, nontechnical, amateur, unqualified, untrained.

– ORIGIN Latin *laicus*.

lay[3] ▶ **noun 1** a short lyric or narrative poem intended to be sung. **2** literary a song.
– ORIGIN Old French *lai*.

lay[4] past of **LIE**[1].

lay·a·bout /ˈlāəˌbout/ ▶ **noun** derogatory a person who does little or no work.

lay·a·way /ˈlāəˌwā/ ▶ **noun** (also **layaway plan**) a system of paying a deposit to secure an item for later purchase: *she picked up a coat she had on layaway.*

lay broth·er (or **lay sister**) ▶ **noun** a person who has taken the vows of a religious order but is not ordained and is employed in ancillary or manual work.

lay·er /ˈlāər/ ▶ **noun 1** a sheet or thickness of material, typically one of several, covering a surface. **2** (in combination) a person or thing that lays something: *a cable-layer.* **3** a shoot fastened down to take root while attached to the parent plant.

> – SYNONYMS **sheet,** stratum, level, tier, seam, coat, coating, film, covering, blanket, skin.

▶ **verb** (often as adj. **layered**) arrange or cut something in a layer or layers.
– ORIGIN from **LAY**[1].

lay·ette /lā'et/ ▶ **noun** a set of clothing and bedclothes for a newborn child.
– ORIGIN French.

lay·man /'lāmən/ (or **laywoman** /'lā,wo͝omən/ or **layperson** /'lā,pərsən/) ▶ **noun** (pl. **laymen, laywomen, laypersons,** or **laypeople** /'lā,pēpəl/) **1** a member of a Church who is not a priest or minister. **2** a person without professional or specialized knowledge in a particular subject.

lay·off /'lā,ôf, -,äf/ ▶ **noun 1** an instance of discharging a worker or workers because of a shortage of work. **2** a temporary break from an activity.

lay·out /'lā,out/ ▶ **noun 1** the way in which something, especially a page, is laid out. **2** a thing set out in a particular way.

– SYNONYMS **arrangement,** design, plan, formation, format, configuration, composition, organization, geography, structure.

lay·o·ver /'lā,ōvər/ ▶ **noun** a rest or wait before a further stage in a journey.

lay read·er ▶ **noun** (in the Anglican Church) a layperson authorized to preach and to conduct some services but not to celebrate the Holy Communion.

lay·up /'lāəp/ ▶ **noun** Basketball a one-handed shot made from near the basket, especially one that rebounds off the backboard.

lay·wom·an /'lā,wo͝omən/ ▶ **noun** see **LAYMAN**.

laze /lāz/ ▶ **verb** spend time relaxing or doing very little.

– SYNONYMS **relax,** unwind, lounge about/around, loaf (about/around), loll about/around, lie around/about, take it easy, idle; informal hang around, chill (out), veg (out).

▶ **noun** a spell of lazing.

la·zy /'lāzē/ ▶ **adjective** (**lazier, laziest**) **1** unwilling to work or use energy. **2** showing a lack of effort or care: *a lazy investigation*.

– SYNONYMS **1 idle,** indolent, slothful, bone idle, work-shy, shiftless. **2 slow,** slow-moving, languid, leisurely, lethargic, sluggish, torpid.
– ANTONYMS industrious.

– DERIVATIVES **la·zi·ly** adverb **la·zi·ness** noun.
– ORIGIN perhaps related to German *lasich* 'languid, idle.'

la·zy·bones /'lāzē,bōnz/ ▶ **noun** (pl. same) informal a lazy person.

la·zy eye ▶ **noun** an eye with poor vision due to underuse, especially the unused eye in a squint.

lb. ▶ **abbreviation** pound(s) (in weight).
– ORIGIN from Latin *libra*.

l.c. ▶ **abbreviation 1** in the passage cited. **2** lower case.
– ORIGIN sense 1 from Latin *loco citato*.

LCD ▶ **abbreviation 1** Electronics & Computing liquid crystal display. **2** Mathematics lowest (or least) common denominator.

LCM ▶ **abbreviation** Mathematics lowest (or least) common multiple.

ld. ▶ **abbreviation 1** lead. **2** load.

LDS ▶ **abbreviation** Latter-Day Saints.

lea /lē/ ▶ **noun** literary an open area of grassy land.
– ORIGIN Old English.

leach /lēch/ ▶ **verb** (of a soluble substance) drain away from soil or other material by the action of water passing through it.
– ORIGIN Old English, 'to water.'

lead¹ /lēd/ ▶ **verb** (past and past part. **led** /led/) **1** draw, guide, or take a person or animal with one. **2** be a route or means of access: *the street led into the square*. **3** (**lead (up) to**) result in. **4** influence to do or believe something: *that may lead them to reconsider*. **5** be in charge of other people. **6** be in first place in a competition or contest. **7** have a particular way of life. **8** be best in an area of activity: *these companies lead the way in new technological developments*. **9** (often **lead (off) with**) begin with a particular action or item. **10** (**lead up to**) come before: *the weeks leading up to the election*. **11** (**lead someone on**) deceive someone into believing that one is attracted to them. **12** (in card games) play the first card in a trick or round of play.

– SYNONYMS **1** *Michelle led them into the house* **guide,** conduct, show (the way), usher, escort, steer, shepherd, accompany, see, take. **2** *this might lead to job losses* **result in,** cause, bring on/about, give rise to, create, produce, occasion, effect, generate, contribute to, promote, provoke, stir up, spark (off). **3** *what led you to believe him?* **cause,** induce, prompt, move, persuade, drive, make. **4** *she led a coalition of radicals* **control,** preside over, head, command, govern, run, manage, rule, be in charge of; informal head up. **5** *we were leading at halftime* **be ahead,** be winning, be in front, be in the lead, be first, outrun, outstrip, outpace, leave behind, outdo, outclass, beat. **6** *I want to lead a normal life* **live,** have, spend, follow, pass, enjoy.
– ANTONYMS follow.

▶ **noun 1** an example for others to follow: *others followed our lead*. **2** (**the lead**) first place in a competition or contest. **3** an amount by which a competitor is ahead of the others. **4** the chief part in a play or movie. **5** a strap or cord for restraining and guiding a dog. **6** a clue to be followed in solving a problem. **7** a wire conveying electric current from a source to an appliance, or connecting two points of a circuit together.

– SYNONYMS **1 example,** model, pattern, standard, guidance, direction, role model. **2 first place,** winning position, vanguard. **3** *a one-goal lead* **margin,** advantage, gap, edge. **4 leading role,** starring role, title role, principal role. **5 leash,** tether, rope, chain. **6 clue,** pointer, hint, tip, tip-off, suggestion, indication.

▶ **adjective 1** referring to the main item in a newspaper, magazine, or broadcast: *the lead article*. **2** playing the chief part in a musical group: *the lead singer*.

– SYNONYMS **leading,** first, top, foremost, front, pole, head, chief, principal, premier.

– PHRASES **lead someone down the garden path** informal give someone misleading clues or signals.
– ORIGIN Old English.

lead² /led/ ▶ **noun 1** a heavy bluish-gray soft metallic element. **2** graphite used as the part of a pencil that makes a mark. **3** (**leads**) lead frames holding the glass of a lattice or stained-glass window. **4** Nautical a lump of lead suspended on a line to determine the depth of water. **5** Printing a blank space between lines of print.
– ORIGIN Old English.

lead crys·tal /led/ (also **lead glass**) ▶ **noun** glass containing a substantial proportion of lead oxide, making it more refractive.

lead·ed /'ledid/ ▶ **adjective 1** framed, covered, or weighted with lead. **2** (of gasoline) containing lead.

lead·en /'ledn/ ▸ **adjective 1** dull, heavy, or slow: *he hoped sleep would loosen his leaden legs.* **2** dull gray in color.
– DERIVATIVES **lead·en·ly** adverb.

lead·er /'lēdər/ ▸ **noun 1** a person or thing that leads. **2** a person or thing that is the most successful or advanced in a particular area. **3** the principal player in a music group. **4** a short strip of nonfunctioning material at each end of a reel of film or recording tape for connection to the spool.

– SYNONYMS **chief,** head, principal, commander, captain, controller, superior, chairman, chair, director, manager, superintendent, supervisor, overseer, master, mistress, prime minister, president, premier, governor, ruler, monarch, sovereign; informal boss, skipper, numero uno, (head) honcho, boss man/lady.
– ANTONYMS follower, supporter.

– DERIVATIVES **lead·er·less** adjective.

lead·er board ▸ **noun** a scoreboard showing the names and current scores of the leading competitors, especially in a golf match.

lead·er·ship /'lēdər,sнip/ ▸ **noun 1** the state or position of being a leader. **2** the action of leading a group of people or an organization.

– SYNONYMS **1** *the leadership of the party* **control,** rule, command, dominion, headship, directorship, premiership, chairmanship, governorship, captaincy. **2** *firm leadership* **guidance,** direction, authority, management, supervision, government.

lead-in /'lēd ˌin/ ▸ **noun** an introduction to something.

lead·ing /'lēdiNG/ ▸ **adjective** most important or in first place.

– SYNONYMS **main,** chief, top, front, major, prime, principal, foremost, key, central, dominant, greatest, preeminent, star.
– ANTONYMS subordinate, minor.

lead·ing edge ▸ **noun** the forefront of technological development.

lead·ing light ▸ **noun** a person who is prominent or influential in a particular field or organization.

lead·ing ques·tion ▸ **noun** a question that prompts the desired answer.

lead-off /'lēd/ ▸ **adjective 1** (of an action) beginning a series or a process: *the album's lead-off track.* **2** (**leadoff**) Baseball referring to the first batter in a lineup or of an inning.

lead time /lēd/ ▸ **noun** the time between the beginning and completion of a production process.

lead-up /lēd/ ▸ **noun** an event or sequence that leads up to something else.

leaf /lēf/ ▸ **noun** (pl. **leaves**) **1** a flat, typically green structure that grows from the stem of a plant. **2** the state of having leaves: *the trees were in leaf.* **3** a single sheet of paper, especially in a book; a page. **4** gold, silver, or other metal in the form of very thin foil. **5** a hinged or detachable part, especially of a table.

– SYNONYMS **1** (**leaves**) **foliage,** greenery. **2 page,** sheet, folio.

▸ **verb 1** (**leaf through**) turn over pages or papers, reading them quickly or casually. **2** (of a plant) put out new leaves.

– SYNONYMS (**leaf through**) *I leafed through a magazine* **flip through,** flick through, thumb through, skim through/over, browse through, glance through/over, riffle through, scan, run one's eye over, peruse.

– DERIVATIVES **leaf·age** noun **leaf·less** adjective.
– PHRASES **turn over a new leaf** start to act or behave in a better way.
– ORIGIN Old English.

leaf·let /'lēflit/ ▸ **noun 1** a printed sheet of paper containing information or advertising and usually distributed free. **2** a small leaf, especially a component of a compound leaf.

– SYNONYMS **pamphlet,** booklet, brochure, handbill, circular, flyer, handout.

▸ **verb** (**leaflets, leafleting, leafleted**) distribute leaflets to people or an area.

leaf lit·ter ▸ **noun** another term for **LITTER** (sense 6 of the noun).

leaf mold ▸ **noun** soil consisting chiefly of decayed leaves.

leaf·y /'lēfē/ ▸ **adjective** (**leafier, leafiest**) **1** having many leaves. **2** full of trees and shrubs: *a leafy avenue.*
– DERIVATIVES **leaf·i·ness** noun.

league[1] /lēg/ ▸ **noun 1** a collection of people, countries, or groups that combine to help each other or promote something. **2** a class of quality or excellence: *the two men were not in the same league.* **3** a group of sports clubs that play each other over a period for a championship.

– SYNONYMS **1 alliance,** confederation, confederacy, federation, union, association, coalition, consortium, affiliation, cooperative, partnership, fellowship, syndicate. **2 class,** group, category, level, standard.

▸ **verb** (**leagues, leaguing, leagued**) join in a league or alliance.
– PHRASES **in league** (of people) conspiring with each other.
– ORIGIN Italian *lega.*

league[2] ▸ **noun** a former measure of distance, usually about three miles.
– ORIGIN Latin *leuga, leuca.*

leak /lēk/ ▸ **verb 1** (of a container or covering) accidentally allow contents to escape or enter through a hole or crack. **2** (of liquid, gas, etc.) escape or enter accidentally through a hole or crack. **3** deliberately disclose secret information.

– SYNONYMS **1 seep,** escape, ooze, drip, dribble, drain, run. **2 disclose,** divulge, reveal, make public, tell, expose, release, let slip.

▸ **noun 1** a hole or crack through which contents leak. **2** an instance of leaking.

– SYNONYMS **1 hole,** opening, puncture, perforation, gash, slit, break, crack, chink, fissure, rupture, tear. **2 escape,** leakage, discharge, seepage. **3 disclosure,** revelation, exposé.

– DERIVATIVES **leak·age** noun **leak·er** noun **leak·y** adjective.
– PHRASES **have** (or **take**) **a leak** informal urinate.
– ORIGIN probably from German or Dutch.

lean[1] /lēn/ ▸ **verb** (past and past part. **leaned** /lēnd/ or chiefly Brit. **leant** /lent/) **1** (**lean against/on**) slope and rest against. **2** be in or move into a sloping position. **3** (**lean on**) rely on someone for support. **4** (**lean to/toward**) favor a point of view. **5** (**lean on**) informal intimidate someone into doing something.

– SYNONYMS **1** **(lean against/on)** *Polly leaned against the door* **rest on/against,** recline on/against, be supported by. **2** *trees leaning in the wind* **slant,** incline, bend, tilt, slope, tip, list. **3** **(lean on)** **depend on,** rely on, count on, bank on, trust in, have faith in. **4** **(lean to/toward)** **tend toward,** incline toward, gravitate toward, favor, prefer, have a preference for, have an affinity with.

▶ **noun** an instance of leaning or sloping.
– ORIGIN Old English.

lean² ▶ **adjective** **1** (of a person) having no unwanted fat; thin. **2** (of meat) containing little fat. **3** (of a period of time) difficult because money or food is scarce: *the lean years of the Depression*. **4** (of an industry or organization) efficient and with no waste. **5** (of a vaporized fuel mixture) having a high proportion of air.

– SYNONYMS **1** **thin,** slim, slender, skinny, spare, angular, spindly, wiry, lanky. **2** **meager,** sparse, poor, mean, inadequate, insufficient, paltry.
– ANTONYMS fat, abundant.

▶ **noun** the lean part of meat.
– DERIVATIVES **lean·ness** noun.
– ORIGIN Old English.

WORD TOOLKIT

See **THIN**.

lean·ing /ˈlēniNG/ ▶ **noun** a tendency or preference: *communist leanings*.

– SYNONYMS **inclination,** tendency, bent, propensity, penchant, preference, predisposition, predilection, proclivity.

lean-to ▶ **noun** (pl. **lean-tos**) a building sharing a wall with a larger building and having a roof that leans against that wall.

leap /lēp/ ▶ **verb** (past or past part. **leaped** /lēpt/ or **leapt** /lept/) **1** jump high, far, or across something. **2** move quickly and suddenly: *Ann leapt to her feet*. **3** **(leap at)** accept something eagerly. **4** (especially of a price or amount) increase dramatically. **5** **(leap out)** be immediately noticeable.

– SYNONYMS **1** **jump,** vault, spring, bound, hop, clear. **2** **rise,** soar, rocket, skyrocket, shoot up, escalate.

▶ **noun** **1** an instance of leaping. **2** a sudden change or increase.

– SYNONYMS **rise,** surge, upsurge, escalation, upswing, upturn.

– DERIVATIVES **leap·er** noun.
– PHRASES **a leap in the dark** a daring step or enterprise with an unpredictable outcome. **by (**or **in) leaps and bounds** with very rapid progress.
– ORIGIN Old English.

leap·frog /ˈlēpˌfrôg, -ˌfräg/ ▶ **noun** a game in which players in turn vault with parted legs over others who are bending down. ▶ **verb** **(leapfrogs, leapfrogging, leapfrogged)** **1** vault over someone in the game of leapfrog. **2** reach a leading position by overtaking others or omitting a stage in a process: *the firm has leapfrogged over all its rivals*.

leap year ▶ **noun** a year, occurring once every four years, that has 366 days (February 29 being the additional day).

learn /lərn/ ▶ **verb** (past and past part. **learned** /lərnd/ or chiefly Brit. **learnt** /lərnt/) **1** gain knowledge of or skill in something through study or experience or by being taught. **2** become aware of something by information or from observation. **3** memorize something. **4** old use or informal teach someone.

– SYNONYMS **1** **master,** grasp, take in, absorb, assimilate, digest, familiarize oneself with; informal get the hang of. **2** **memorize,** learn by heart, learn by rote, get down pat. **3** **discover,** find out, become aware, be informed, hear, understand, gather; informal get wind of.

– DERIVATIVES **learn·a·ble** adjective.
– ORIGIN Old English.

learn·ed /ˈlərnid/ ▶ **adjective** having or showing much knowledge gained by studying.

– SYNONYMS **scholarly,** erudite, knowledgeable, widely read, cultured, intellectual, academic, literary, bookish, highbrow; informal **brainy.**
– ANTONYMS ignorant.

learn·er /ˈlərnər/ ▶ **noun** a person who is learning a subject or skill.

– SYNONYMS **beginner,** novice, starter, trainee, apprentice, student, pupil, fledgling, neophyte, tyro; informal **rookie, greenhorn.**
– ANTONYMS expert, veteran.

learn·ing /ˈlərniNG/ ▶ **noun** knowledge or skills gained through study or by being taught.

– SYNONYMS **study,** knowledge, education, schooling, tuition, teaching, scholarship, erudition, understanding, wisdom.
– ANTONYMS ignorance.

CHOOSE THE RIGHT WORD

See **KNOWLEDGE**.

learn·ing curve ▶ **noun** the rate of a person's progress in gaining experience or new skills.

learn·ing dis·a·bil·i·ty ▶ **noun** difficulty in gaining knowledge and skills to the level expected of one's age.
– DERIVATIVES **learn·ing-dis·a·bled** adjective.

USAGE

The term **learning disability** covers general conditions such as Down syndrome as well as more specific conditions such as dyslexia. It is considered less discriminatory and more positive than terms such as **mental handicap**, especially in official situations.

lease /lēs/ ▶ **noun** a contract by which one party conveys land, property, services, etc., to another for a specified time, in return for payment. ▶ **verb** rent something on lease.

– SYNONYMS **rent (out),** hire (out), charter, let (out), sublet.

– PHRASES **a new lease on life** a substantially improved chance to lead a happy or successful life.
– ORIGIN from Old French *lesser, laissier* 'let, leave.'

lease·hold /ˈlēsˌhōld/ ▶ **noun** **1** the holding of property by a lease. **2** a piece of land or property held by a lease.
– DERIVATIVES **lease·hold·er** noun.

leash /lēsH/ ▶ **noun** a strap or cord for restraining and guiding a dog. ▶ **verb** put a leash on a dog.
– ORIGIN from Old French *laissier* in the sense 'let an animal run on a slack lead.'

least /lēst/ ▶ **determiner & pronoun** (usu. **the least**) smallest in amount, extent, or significance. ▶ **adverb** to the

smallest extent or degree.
– PHRASES **at least 1** not less than. **2** if nothing else. **3** anyway. **at the least** (or **very least**) **1** not less than. **2** taking the most pessimistic view. **not in the least** not at all. **not least** in particular.
– ORIGIN Old English.

least·ways /ˈlēstˌwāz/ (also **leastwise**) ▶ **adverb** dialect or informal at least.

leath·er /ˈleT͟Hər/ ▶ **noun 1** a material made from the skin of an animal by tanning or a similar process. **2** a piece of leather as a polishing cloth. **3** (**leathers**) leather clothes worn by a motorcyclist. ▶ **adjective** referring to people, especially homosexuals, who wear leather clothing and accessories as a sign of rough masculinity: *leather bar*. ▶ **verb 1** (as adj. **leathered**) covered with leather. **2** informal beat with a leather strap.
– ORIGIN Old English.

leath·er·back /ˈleT͟Hərˌbak/ (also **leatherback turtle**) ▶ **noun** a very large black turtle with a thick leathery shell, living chiefly in tropical seas.

leath·er·ette /ˌleT͟Həˈret/ ▶ **noun** imitation leather.

leath·ern /ˈleT͟Hərn/ ▶ **adjective** old use made of leather.

leath·er·y /ˈleT͟H(ə)rē/ ▶ **adjective** having a tough, hard texture like leather.
– DERIVATIVES **leath·er·i·ness** noun.

leave[1] /lēv/ ▶ **verb** (past and past part. **left** /left/) **1** go away from someone or something. **2** stop living at, attending, or working for. **3** allow something to remain; go away without taking something. **4** (**leave something to**) let someone deal with or be responsible for something. **5** give something to someone in a will. **6** (**be left**) remain to be used or dealt with: *drink left from the wedding*. **7** cause to be in a particular state or position: *leave the door open*. **8** let someone do something without help or interference. **9** deposit something to be collected or dealt with. **10** have someone as a surviving relative after one's death: *he leaves a wife and three children*.

> – SYNONYMS **1** *I left the hotel* **go away,** depart, withdraw, retire, take one's leave, pull out, quit, decamp, flee, escape, abandon, desert, vacate; informal vamoose, push off, shove off, clear out/off, split, make tracks. **2** *the next morning we left for Taipei* **set off,** set sail, get going. **3** *he left his job in November* **resign,** retire, step down, give up, drop out; informal quit. **4** *he's left his wife* **abandon,** desert, jilt, leave in the lurch, leave high and dry, throw over; informal dump, ditch, walk/run out on. **5** *she left her purse on a bus* **leave behind,** forget, lose, mislay. **6** *I thought I'd leave it to the experts* **entrust,** hand over, pass on, refer, delegate. **7** *he left her $100,000* **bequeath,** will, endow, hand down.
> – ANTONYMS arrive.

– DERIVATIVES **leav·er** noun.
– PHRASES **leave someone/thing be** informal avoid disturbing or interfering with someone or something. **leave off** stop doing something. **leave someone/thing out** fail to include someone or something.
– ORIGIN Old English.

leave[2] ▶ **noun 1** (also **leave of absence**) time when one has permission to be absent from work or duty. **2** formal permission: *seeking leave to appeal*.

> – SYNONYMS **1 vacation,** break, furlough, sabbatical, leave of absence, holiday. **2 permission,** consent, authorization, sanction, dispensation, approval, clearance, blessing, agreement, assent; informal the go-ahead, the green light.

– PHRASES **take one's leave** formal say goodbye.
– ORIGIN Old English.

leav·en /ˈlevən/ ▶ **noun 1** a substance, typically yeast, added to dough to make it ferment and rise. **2** an influence or quality that modifies or improves something: *John's humor was the leaven of his charm*. ▶ **verb 1** (usu. as adj. **leavened**) make dough or bread ferment and rise by adding yeast or another leaven. **2** make an addition to improve something: *the debate was leavened by humor*.
– ORIGIN Latin *levamen* 'relief.'

leaves /lēvz/ plural of LEAF.

leave-tak·ing ▶ **noun** an act of saying goodbye.

leav·ings /ˈlēviNGz/ ▶ **plural noun** things that have been left as worthless.

Leb·a·nese /ˌlebəˈnēz, -ˈnēs/ ▶ **noun** (pl. same) a person from Lebanon. ▶ **adjective** relating to Lebanon.

Le·bens·raum /ˈlābənsˌroum, -bənz-/ ▶ **noun** territory that a state or nation believes is needed for its natural development.
– ORIGIN German, 'living space.'

lech·er /ˈleCHər/ ▶ **noun** a lecherous man.

> – SYNONYMS **womanizer,** libertine, debauchee, rake, roué; Don Juan, Casanova, Lothario, Romeo; informal lech, dirty old man; formal fornicator.

– DERIVATIVES **lech·er·y** noun.

lech·er·ous /ˈleCH(ə)rəs/ ▶ **adjective** having or showing excessive or offensive sexual desire.

> – SYNONYMS **lustful,** licentious, lascivious, libidinous, lewd, salacious, prurient; Brit. informal randy; formal concupiscent.

– DERIVATIVES **lech·er·ous·ly** adverb **lech·er·ous·ness** noun.
– ORIGIN from Old French *lechier* 'live in debauchery or gluttony.'

lec·i·thin /ˈlesəTHin/ ▶ **noun** a substance found in egg yolk and other animal and plant tissues, often used as an emulsifier in food processing.
– ORIGIN from Greek *lekithos* 'egg yolk.'

lec·tern /ˈlektərn/ ▶ **noun** a tall stand with a sloping top used to support a book or papers from which a speaker can read while standing up.
– ORIGIN Latin *lectrum*, from *legere* 'to read.'

lec·tion·ar·y /ˈlekSHəˌnerē/ ▶ **noun** (pl. **lectionaries**) a list or book of portions of the Bible to be read at church services.
– ORIGIN Latin.

lec·ture /ˈlekCHər/ ▶ **noun 1** an educational talk to an audience, especially one of students in a university. **2** a lengthy reprimand or warning.

> – SYNONYMS **1 speech,** talk, address, discourse, presentation, oration. **2 reprimand,** scolding, rebuke, reproach; informal dressing-down, telling-off, talking-to, tongue-lashing.

▶ **verb 1** give an educational talk or talks. **2** criticize or reprimand someone.

> – SYNONYMS **1 talk,** speak, discourse, hold forth, teach; informal spout, sound off. **2 reprimand,** scold, rebuke, reproach, take to task, berate, upbraid, remonstrate with, castigate; informal tell off, bawl out.

– ORIGIN Latin *lectura*.

lec·tur·er /ˈlekCHərər/ ▶ **noun** a person who gives lectures, such as a teacher at a college or university.

lec·ture·ship /ˈlekCHər,SHip/ ▸ **noun** a post as a lecturer.

LED ▸ **abbreviation** light-emitting diode, a semiconductor diode that glows when a voltage is applied.

led /led/ past and past participle of **LEAD**[1].

le·der·ho·sen /ˈlādər,hōzən/ ▸ **plural noun** leather shorts with suspenders, traditionally worn by men in the Alps.
– ORIGIN German.

ledge /lej/ ▸ **noun 1** a narrow horizontal surface projecting from a wall, cliff, or other vertical surface. **2** an underwater ridge, especially one of rocks near the seashore.
– ORIGIN perhaps from **LAY**[1].

ledg·er /ˈlejər/ ▸ **noun** a book in which financial accounts are kept.
– ORIGIN probably from variants of **LAY**[1] and **LIE**[1], influenced by Dutch *legger* and *ligger*.

ledg·er line (also **leger line**) ▸ **noun** Music a short line added for notes above or below the range of a staff.

lee /lē/ ▸ **noun 1** (also **lee side**) the side of something sheltered from the wind. Contrasted with **WEATHER**. **2** shelter from wind or weather given by an object.
– ORIGIN Old English, 'shelter.'

leech[1] /lēCH/ ▸ **noun 1** a worm that sucks the blood of animals or people, used in medicine for bloodletting. **2** a person who lives off others.
– ORIGIN Old English.

leech[2] ▸ **noun** old use a doctor or healer.
– ORIGIN Old English.

leek /lēk/ ▸ **noun** a vegetable related to the onion, with flat overlapping leaves forming an elongated cylindrical bulb.
– ORIGIN Old English.

leer /li(ə)r/ ▸ **verb** look or gaze in a lustful or unpleasant way. ▸ **noun** a lustful or unpleasant look.
– ORIGIN perhaps from an Old English word meaning 'cheek.'

leer·y /ˈli(ə)rē/ ▸ **adjective** (**leerier, leeriest**) informal cautious or wary: *a city leery of gang violence.*

> – SYNONYMS **wary,** cautious, careful, guarded, chary, suspicious, distrustful; worried, anxious, apprehensive.

– DERIVATIVES **leer·i·ness** noun.
– ORIGIN from **LEER**.

lees /lēz/ ▸ **plural noun** the sediment of wine in the bottom of the barrel.
– ORIGIN Latin *liae.*

lee shore ▸ **noun** a shore lying on the side of a ship that is sheltered from the wind (and onto which the ship could be blown).

lee·ward /ˈlēwərd, ˈlo͞oərd/ ▸ **adjective & adverb** on or toward the side sheltered from the wind or toward which the wind is blowing. Contrasted with **WINDWARD**. ▸ **noun** the leeward side.

lee·way /ˈlē,wā/ ▸ **noun 1** the amount of freedom to move or act that is available: *we have a lot of leeway in how we do our jobs.* **2** the sideways drift of a ship to leeward of the desired course.

> – SYNONYMS **freedom,** scope, latitude, space, room, liberty, flexibility, license, free hand, free rein.

left[1] /left/ ▸ **adjective 1** on, toward, or relating to the side of a person or thing that is to the west when the person or thing is facing north. **2** relating to a left-wing person or group.

> – SYNONYMS **left-hand,** sinistral; Nautical port; Heraldry sinister.
> – ANTONYMS right.

▸ **adverb** on or to the left side.
▸ **noun 1** (**the left**) the left-hand part, side, or direction. **2** a left turn. **3** a person's left fist, or a blow given with it. **4** (often **the Left**) (treated as sing. or pl.) a group or party with radical, reforming, or socialist views.
– DERIVATIVES **left·ish** adjective **left·most** /ˈlef(t),mōst/ adjective **left·ward** /ˈleftwərd/ adjective & adverb **left·wards** adverb.
– PHRASES **have two left feet** be clumsy or awkward.
– ORIGIN Old English, 'weak.'

left[2] past and past participle of **LEAVE**[1].

left field ▸ **noun 1** Baseball the part of the outfield to the left of center field from the perspective of home plate. **2** Baseball the position of the defensive player stationed in left field. **3** informal a surprising or unconventional position or direction. **4** a position of ignorance or confusion: *he's so far out in left field he doesn't know what's going on.*

left hand ▸ **noun** the region or direction on the left side of someone or something. ▸ **adjective 1** on or toward the left side. **2** done with or using the left hand.

left-hand·ed ▸ **adjective 1** (of a person) using the left hand more naturally than the right. **2** done with the left hand. **3** turning to the left; toward the left. **4** (of a screw) advanced by turning counterclockwise.

left-hand·er ▸ **noun 1** a left-handed person. **2** a blow struck with a person's left hand.

left·ie ▸ **noun** variant spelling of **LEFTY**.

left·ism /lef,tizəm/ ▸ **noun** the political views or policies of the Left.
– DERIVATIVES **left·ist** /ˈleftist/ noun & adjective.

left·o·ver /ˈleft,ōvər/ ▸ **noun** (**leftovers**) something, especially food, remaining after the rest has been used. ▸ **adjective** remaining; surplus.

left wing ▸ **noun 1** the radical, liberal, or socialist section of a political party or system. **2** the left side of a sports team on the field or of an army.
– DERIVATIVES **left-wing·er** noun.
– ORIGIN sense 1 is with reference to the National Assembly in France (1789–91), where the nobles sat to the president's right and the commoners to the left.

left·y /ˈleftē/ (also **leftie**) ▸ **noun** (pl. **lefties**) informal **1** a left-wing person. **2** a left-handed person.

leg /leg/ ▸ **noun 1** each of the limbs on which a person or animal moves and stands. **2** a long, thin support or prop, especially of a chair or table. **3** a section of a journey, process, or race. **4** (in sports) each of two games constituting a round of a competition. **5** (**legs**) informal sustained popularity or success: *some books have legs, others don't.*

> – SYNONYMS **1 limb,** member, shank; informal pin, peg. **2 part,** stage, section, phase, stretch, lap.

– DERIVATIVES **leg·ged** adjective.
– PHRASES **not have a leg to stand on** be unable to justify one's arguments or actions. **on one's** (or **its**) **last legs** near the end of life, usefulness, or existence.
– ORIGIN Old Norse.

leg·a·cy /ˈlegəsē/ ▸ **noun** (pl. **legacies**) **1** an amount of money or property left to someone in a will. **2** a situation that exists because of a past event or action: *all the ills in the country are the legacy of military rule.*

– SYNONYMS **bequest,** inheritance, endowment, gift, birthright, estate, heirloom.

▶ **adjective** (of computer hardware or software) that has been superseded but is difficult to replace because of its wide use.

– ORIGIN Old French *legacie*.

le·gal /'lēgəl/ ▶ **adjective 1** relating to or required by the law. **2** permitted by law.

– SYNONYMS **1 lawful,** legitimate, legalized, valid, permissible, permitted, sanctioned, authorized, licensed, allowed, allowable, aboveboard, acceptable, constitutional; informal legit. **2** *the legal system* **judicial,** juridical, forensic.
– ANTONYMS illegal.

– DERIVATIVES **le·gal·ly** adverb.
– ORIGIN Latin *legalis*.

le·gal age ▶ **noun** the age at which a person takes on the rights and responsibilities of an adult.

le·gal aid ▶ **noun** payment from public funds given to people who cannot afford to pay for legal advice or action.

le·gal·ese /ˌlēgə'lēz, -'lēs/ ▶ **noun** informal the formal and technical language of legal documents.

le·gal·ism /'lēgəˌlizəm/ ▶ **noun** the practice of keeping strictly to the law.
– DERIVATIVES **le·gal·ist** noun & adjective **le·gal·is·tic** /ˌlēgə'listik/ adjective.

le·gal·i·ty /lə'galətē/ ▶ **noun** (pl. **legalities**) **1** the quality or state of being legal. **2** (**legalities**) rules and duties imposed by law.

le·gal·ize /'lēgəˌlīz/ ▶ **verb** make something that was illegal allowed by the law.
– DERIVATIVES **le·gal·i·za·tion** /ˌlēgələ'zāshən, -ˌlī'zā-/ noun.

le·gal sep·a·ra·tion ▶ **noun** an arrangement by which a husband or wife remain married but live apart, following a court order.

le·gal ten·der ▶ **noun** coins or banknotes that must be accepted if offered in payment of a debt.

leg·ate /'legit/ ▶ **noun** a member of the clergy who represents the Pope.
– ORIGIN Latin *legatus*.

leg·a·tee /ˌlegə'tē/ ▶ **noun** a person who receives a legacy.
– ORIGIN from Latin *legare* 'delegate, bequeath.'

le·ga·tion /li'gāshən/ ▶ **noun 1** a diplomatic minister and their staff. **2** the official residence of a diplomat.

le·ga·to /li'gäto/ ▶ **adverb & adjective** Music in a smooth, flowing way.
– ORIGIN Italian, 'bound.'

leg·end /'lejənd/ ▶ **noun 1** a traditional story about the past that may or may not have a factual basis. **2** a very famous person: *a screen legend*. **3** an inscription or explanatory wording.

– SYNONYMS **1 myth,** saga, epic, folk tale, folk story, fable; (**legends**) lore, folklore, mythology. **2 celebrity,** star, superstar, icon, phenomenon, luminary, giant, hero; informal celeb, megastar. **3 caption,** inscription, dedication, slogan, heading, title.

▶ **adjective** very well known: *his speed and ferocity in attack were legend*.
– ORIGIN from Latin *legenda* 'things to be read.'

leg·end·ar·y /'lejənˌderē/ ▶ **adjective 1** relating to or based on traditional stories about the past. **2** remarkable enough to be famous: *France's legendary chefs*.

– SYNONYMS **1 fabled,** mythical, traditional, fairy-tale, storybook, mythological, fictional, fictitious. **2 famous,** celebrated, famed, renowned, acclaimed, illustrious, esteemed, honored, exalted, venerable, eminent, distinguished, great.

– DERIVATIVES **leg·end·ar·i·ly** /-ˌderəlē, ˌlejən'de(ə)r-/ adverb.

leg·er·de·main /ˌlejərdə'mān, 'lejərdəˌmān/ ▶ **noun 1** skillful use of the hands when performing conjuring tricks. **2** deception; trickery.
– ORIGIN from French *léger de main* 'dexterous' (literally 'light of hand').

le·ger line ▶ **noun** variant spelling of LEDGER LINE.

leg·gings /'legiNGz/ ▶ **plural noun 1** tight-fitting stretch pants worn by women and children. **2** protective coverings for the legs.

leg·gy /'legē/ ▶ **adjective** (**leggier, leggiest**) **1** long-legged. **2** (of a plant) having a long and straggly stem or stems.

leg·i·ble /'lejəbəl/ ▶ **adjective** (of handwriting or print) clear enough to read.
– DERIVATIVES **leg·i·bil·i·ty** /ˌlejə'bilətē/ noun **leg·i·bly** adverb.
– ORIGIN Latin *legibilis*.

le·gion /'lējən/ ▶ **noun 1** a division of 3,000–6,000 men in the ancient Roman army. **2** (**a legion/legions of**) a vast number of people or things.

– SYNONYMS **horde,** throng, multitude, crowd, mass, mob, gang, swarm, flock, herd, army.

▶ **adjective** great in number: *her fans are legion*.
– ORIGIN Latin.

le·gion·ar·y /'lējəˌnerē/ ▶ **noun** (pl. **legionaries**) a soldier in an ancient Roman legion.

le·gion·naire /ˌlējə'ner/ ▶ **noun 1** a member of the Foreign Legion. **2** a member of a national association for former servicemen and servicewomen.

le·gion·naires' dis·ease ▶ **noun** a form of pneumonia spread chiefly in water droplets through air conditioning systems.
– ORIGIN because identified after an outbreak at an American Legion meeting.

leg i·ron ▶ **noun** a metal band or chain placed around a prisoner's ankle as a restraint.

leg·is·late /'lejəˌslāt/ ▶ **verb** make laws.

leg·is·la·tion /ˌlejə'slāshən/ ▶ **noun** laws as a whole.

– SYNONYMS **law,** rules, rulings, regulations, acts, bills, statutes, ordinances.

– ORIGIN Latin, 'proposing of a law.'

leg·is·la·tive /'lejəˌslātiv/ ▶ **adjective 1** having the power to make laws. **2** relating to laws or a lawmaking body.
– DERIVATIVES **leg·is·la·tive·ly** adverb.

leg·is·la·tor /'lejəˌslātər/ ▶ **noun** a person who makes laws; a member of a legislature.

leg·is·la·ture /'lejəˌslāchər/ ▶ **noun** the lawmaking body of a country or state.

– SYNONYMS **parliament,** senate, congress, council, chamber, house.

le·git·i·mate ▶ **adjective** /li'jitəmit/ **1** in accordance with the law or rules. **2** (of a child) born of parents lawfully married to each other. **3** able to be defended or justified: *a legitimate excuse for being late*. **4** (of a sovereign) having a title based on strict hereditary right.

– SYNONYMS **1** *the legitimate use of such weapons* **legal,** lawful, authorized, permitted, sanctioned, approved, licensed; informal legit. **2** *the legitimate heir* **rightful,** lawful, genuine, authentic, real, true, proper; informal kosher. **3** *a legitimate excuse* **valid,** sound, admissible, acceptable, well founded, justifiable, reasonable, sensible, just, fair, bona fide.
– ANTONYMS illegal, invalid.

▸ **verb** /-ˌmāt/ make something lawful.
– DERIVATIVES **le·git·i·ma·cy** /-məsē/ noun **le·git·i·mate·ly** /-mitlē/ adverb **le·git·i·ma·tion** /liˌjitəˈmāsнən/ noun.
– ORIGIN from Latin *legitimare* 'make legal.'

le·git·i·mize /liˈjitəˌmīz/ ▸ **verb** make something lawful or legitimate.
– DERIVATIVES **le·git·i·mi·za·tion** /liˌjitəməˈzāsнən/ noun.

Le·go /ˈlegō/ ▸ **noun** trademark a toy consisting of interlocking plastic building blocks.
– ORIGIN from Danish *leg godt* 'play well.'

leg·room /ˈlegˌro͞om, -ˌro͝om/ ▸ **noun** space in which a seated person can put their legs.

leg·ume /ˈlegˌyo͞om, ləˈgyo͞om/ ▸ **noun 1** a plant of the pea family grown as a crop. **2** a seed, pod, or other edible part of a plant of the pea family.
– ORIGIN Latin *legumen.*

le·gu·mi·nous /liˈgyo͞omənəs/ ▸ **adjective** relating to plants of the pea family, typically having seeds in pods and root nodules containing nitrogen-fixing bacteria.

leg-up ▸ **noun 1** an act of helping someone to mount a horse or high object. **2** a boost to improve one's position.

leg warm·ers ▸ **plural noun** a pair of knitted garments covering the legs from ankle to knee or thigh.

leg·work /ˈlegˌwərk/ ▸ **noun** work that involves tiring or boring travel from place to place.

lei /lā/ ▸ **noun** a Polynesian garland of flowers.
– ORIGIN Hawaiian.

leish·man·i·a·sis /ˌlēsнməˈnīəsəs/ ▸ **noun** a tropical and subtropical disease transmitted by the bite of sandflies.
– ORIGIN named after the British pathologist William B. *Leishman.*

lei·sure /ˈlēzнər, ˈlezнər/ ▸ **noun** time spent in or free for relaxation or enjoyment.

– SYNONYMS **free time,** spare time, time off, rest, recreation, relaxation, R & R.
– ANTONYMS work.

– DERIVATIVES **lei·sured** adjective.
– PHRASES **at leisure 1** not occupied; free. **2** in an unhurried way. **at one's leisure** when convenient.
– ORIGIN Old French *leisir.*

lei·sure·ly /ˈlēzнərlē, ˈlezнər-/ ▸ **adjective** relaxed and unhurried.

– SYNONYMS **unhurried,** relaxed, easy, gentle, sedate, comfortable, restful, undemanding, slow.
– ANTONYMS hurried.

▸ **adverb** without hurry.
– DERIVATIVES **lei·sure·li·ness** noun.

lei·sure·wear /ˈlēzнərˌwe(ə)r, ˈlezнər-/ ▸ **noun** casual clothes worn for leisure activities.

leit·mo·tif /ˈlītmōˌtēf/ (also **leitmotiv** pronunc. same) ▸ **noun** a recurring theme in a musical or literary work.
– ORIGIN German *Leitmotiv.*

lem·ming /ˈleminɢ/ ▸ **noun 1** a short-tailed Arctic rodent that periodically migrates in large numbers. **2** a person who unthinkingly joins a mass movement, especially a rush to destruction.
– ORIGIN Norwegian and Danish.

lem·on /ˈlemən/ ▸ **noun 1** a pale yellow oval citrus fruit with thick skin and acidic juice. **2** a drink made from or flavored with lemon juice. **3** a pale yellow color. **4** informal an unsatisfactory or disappointing person or thing, especially an automobile.
– DERIVATIVES **lem·on·y** adjective.
– ORIGIN Old French *limon.*

lem·on·ade /ˌleməˈnād, ˈleməˌnād/ ▸ **noun** a sweetened drink made from lemon juice or lemon flavoring and sweetened water.

lem·on balm ▸ **noun** a bushy lemon-scented herb of the mint family.

lem·on grass ▸ **noun** a tropical grass that yields an oil that smells of lemon, used in Asian cooking.

le·mur /ˈlēmər/ ▸ **noun** a primate with a pointed snout and a long tail that lives in trees in Madagascar.
– ORIGIN from Latin *lemures* 'spirits of the dead' (from the animal's face).

lend /lend/ ▸ **verb** (past and past part. **lent** /lent/) **1** allow someone to use something on the understanding that it will be returned. **2** allow someone to use a sum of money under an agreement to pay it back later, typically with interest. **3** contribute or add a quality to: *the smile lent his face a boyish charm.* **4** (**lend itself to**) (of a thing) be suitable for something.

– SYNONYMS **1 loan,** advance. **2 add,** impart, give, bestow, confer, provide, supply, furnish, contribute.
– ANTONYMS borrow.

– DERIVATIVES **lend·er** noun.
– PHRASES **lend an ear** listen sympathetically or attentively.
– ORIGIN Old English.

lend·ing li·brar·y ▸ **noun** a public library from which books may be borrowed for a limited time.

length /lenɢ(k)тн, lenth/ ▸ **noun 1** the measurement or extent of something from end to end. **2** the amount of time occupied by something: *schools have reduced the length of summer vacation.* **3** a stretch or piece of something. **4** the quality of being long. **5** the full distance that a thing extends for. **6** the extent of a garment downward when worn. **7** the length of a horse or boat as a measure of the lead in a race. **8** a degree to which a course of action is taken: *they go to great lengths to avoid the press.*

– SYNONYMS **1 extent,** distance, span, reach, area, expanse, range. **2 period,** duration, stretch, span, term. **3** *a length of silk* **piece,** strip, section, swatch.

– PHRASES **at length 1** in detail; fully. **2** after a long time.
– ORIGIN Old English.

length·en /ˈlenɢ(k)тнən, ˈlenтнən/ ▸ **verb** make or become longer.

– SYNONYMS **extend,** elongate, increase, prolong, draw out, protract, spin out.
– ANTONYMS shorten.

length·ways /ˈlenɢ(k)тнˌwāz, ˈlenтн-/ ▸ **adverb** lengthwise.

length·wise /ˈlenɢ(k)тнˌwīz, ˈlenтн-/ ▸ **adverb** in a direction parallel with the length of something.
▸ **adjective** lying or moving lengthwise.

length·y /ˈlenɢ(k)тнē, ˈlenтнē/ ▸ **adjective** (**lengthier, lengthiest**) very or excessively long in time or extent.

– SYNONYMS **(very) long,** long-lasting, protracted, extended, long-drawn-out, prolonged, interminable, time-consuming, long-winded.
– ANTONYMS short.

– DERIVATIVES **length·i·ly** adverb.

le·ni·ent /'lēnēənt, 'lēnyənt/ ▸ **adjective** not as strict or severe as expected: *a lenient one-year sentence.*

– SYNONYMS **merciful,** forgiving, forbearing, tolerant, charitable, humane, indulgent, magnanimous, clement.
– ANTONYMS severe.

– DERIVATIVES **le·ni·ence** noun **le·ni·en·cy** noun **le·ni·ent·ly** adverb.
– ORIGIN from Latin *lenire* 'soothe.'

WORD TOOLKIT

See **HUMANE**.

Le·nin·ism /'lenə,nizəm/ ▸ **noun** Marxism as interpreted and applied by the Soviet premier Vladimir Ilich Lenin.
– DERIVATIVES **Le·nin·ist** noun & adjective.

lens /lenz/ ▸ **noun 1** a piece of glass or other transparent material with one or both sides curved for concentrating or dispersing light rays. **2** the light-gathering device of a camera, containing a group of compound lenses. **3** the transparent structure behind the iris in the eye, by which light is focused onto the retina.
– ORIGIN Latin, 'lentil.'

lens·man /'lenzmən, -,man/ ▸ **noun** (pl. **lensmen**) a professional photographer or cameraman.

Lent /lent/ ▸ **noun** (in the Christian Church) the period preceding Easter, during which some people give up food or other things that they enjoy.
– ORIGIN abbreviation of **LENTEN**.

lent /lent/ past and past participle of **LEND**.

Lent·en /'lent(ə)n/ ▸ **adjective** relating to Lent.
– ORIGIN Old English, 'spring, Lent.'

len·tic·u·lar /len'tikyələr/ ▸ **adjective 1** shaped like a lentil, especially by having two curved surfaces. **2** relating to the lens of the eye.

len·ti·go /len'tīgō, -'tē-/ ▸ **noun** (pl. **lentigines** /-'tijə,nēz/) a small brown patch on the skin, typically found in elderly people.
– ORIGIN Latin *lens* 'lentil.'

len·til /'lent(ə)l/ ▸ **noun** a pulse (edible seed) that is dried and then soaked and cooked before eating.
– ORIGIN Latin *lens* 'lentil.'

len·to /'lentō/ ▸ **adverb & adjective** Music slow or slowly.
– ORIGIN Italian.

Le·o /'lēō/ ▸ **noun 1** a constellation and the fifth sign of the zodiac (the Lion), which the sun enters about July 23. **2** (**a Leo**) a person born when the sun is in this sign.
– ORIGIN Latin.

le·o·nine /'lēə,nīn/ ▸ **adjective** relating to or resembling a lion or lions.
– ORIGIN from Latin *leo* 'lion.'

leop·ard /'lepərd/ ▸ **noun** (fem. **leopardess**) a large solitary cat with a black-spotted fawn or brown coat, found in the forests of Africa and southern Asia.
– ORIGIN Greek *leopardos*.

le·o·tard /'lēə,tärd/ ▸ **noun** a close-fitting, stretchy one-piece garment covering the body to the top of the thighs, worn for dance, gymnastics, and exercise.
– ORIGIN named after the French trapeze artist Jules *Léotard*.

lep·er /'lepər/ ▸ **noun 1** a person with leprosy. **2** a person who is rejected or avoided by others: *the story suggested she was a social leper.*
– ORIGIN from Greek *lepros* 'scaly.'

Lep·i·dop·ter·a /,lepə'däptərə/ ▸ **plural noun** an order of insects comprising the butterflies and moths.
– DERIVATIVES **lep·i·dop·ter·an** adjective & noun **lep·i·dop·ter·ist** /,lepə'däptərist/ noun **lep·i·dop·ter·ous** /-tərəs/ adjective.
– ORIGIN from Greek *lepis* 'scale' + *pteron* 'wing.'

lep·re·chaun /'leprə,kän, -,kôn/ ▸ **noun** (in Irish folklore) a small, mischievous sprite.
– ORIGIN Old Irish *luchorpán*.

lep·ro·sy /'leprəsē/ ▸ **noun** a contagious disease that causes discoloration and lumps on the skin and, in severe cases, disfigurement and deformities.

lep·rous /'leprəs/ ▸ **adjective** referring to or suffering from leprosy.

lep·ton /'leptän/ ▸ **noun** Physics a subatomic particle of a type that is not held in atomic nuclei, such as an electron or neutrino.
– ORIGIN from Greek *leptos* 'small.'

les·bi·an /'lezbēən/ ▸ **noun** a woman who is sexually attracted to other women. ▸ **adjective** referring to lesbians or homosexuality in women.
– DERIVATIVES **les·bi·an·ism** /-,nizəm/ noun.
– ORIGIN from *Lesbos*, Greek island and home of Sappho, who expressed affection for women in her poetry.

lese-maj·es·ty /,lez 'majəstē, ,lēz/ (also **lèse-majesté** /,lez ,mäjə'stā/) ▸ **noun 1** the insulting of a monarch; treason. **2** arrogant or disrespectful behavior.
– ORIGIN from Latin *laesa majestas* 'injured sovereignty.'

le·sion /'lēzʜən/ ▸ **noun** an area in an organ or tissue that has been damaged through injury or disease; a wound.
– ORIGIN from Latin *laedere* 'injure.'

less /les/ ▸ **determiner & pronoun 1** a smaller amount of; not as much. **2** fewer in number. ▸ **adverb** to a smaller extent; not so much. ▸ **preposition** minus.
– PHRASES **less is more** used to express the view that a minimalist approach is more effective.
– ORIGIN Old English.

USAGE

On the difference in use between **less** and **fewer**, see the note at **FEW**.

les·see /le'sē/ ▸ **noun** a person who holds the lease of a property.
– ORIGIN Old French *lesse*.

less·en /'lesən/ ▸ **verb** make or become less; diminish.

– SYNONYMS **1 reduce,** decrease, minimize, moderate, diminish, allay, assuage, alleviate, dull, deaden, take the edge off. **2 decrease,** decline, subside, slacken, abate, fade, die down, let up, ease off, tail off, drop (off/away), dwindle, ebb, wane, recede.
– ANTONYMS increase.

less·er /'lesər/ ▸ **adjective** not so great, large, or important as the other or the rest.

– SYNONYMS **1 less important,** minor, secondary, subsidiary, peripheral. **2 subordinate,** inferior, second-class, subservient, lowly, humble.
– ANTONYMS greater, superior.

less·er-known ▶ adjective not as well or widely known as others of the same kind.

les·son /ˈlesən/ ▶ noun **1** a period of learning or teaching. **2** a thing learned by teaching or experience. **3** a thing that acts as a warning or encouragement. **4** a passage from the Bible read aloud during a church service.

– SYNONYMS **1 class,** session, seminar, tutorial, lecture, period. **2 warning,** deterrent, caution, example, message, moral.

– ORIGIN Old French *leçon.*

les·sor /ˈlesˌôr, leˈsôr/ ▶ noun a person who leases a property to another.
– ORIGIN Old French.

lest /lest/ ▶ conjunction formal **1** to avoid the risk of. **2** because of the possibility of.
– ORIGIN Old English, 'whereby less that.'

USAGE

The word **lest** takes the *subjunctive* mood of a verb, meaning that the correct use is *she was worrying lest he be attacked* (not … *lest he was attacked*). See **SUBJUNCTIVE**.

let[1] /let/ ▶ verb (**lets, letting, let**) **1** allow someone to do something or something to happen. **2** used to express an intention, proposal, or instruction: *let's have a drink.* **3** chiefly Brit. rent out a room or other property. **4** used to express an assumption on which a theory or calculation is to be based: *let x = 10.*

– SYNONYMS *let him sleep for now* **allow,** permit, give permission to, give leave to, authorize, license, empower, enable, entitle; informal give the go-ahead to, OK.
– ANTONYMS prevent, prohibit.

▶ noun Brit. a period during which a room or property is rented.
– DERIVATIVES **let·ting** noun.
– PHRASES **let alone** not to mention. **let someone down** fail to support or help someone. **let fly** attack someone. **let someone/thing go 1** allow a person or animal to go free. **2** release one's grip on someone or something. **let oneself go 1** act in an uninhibited way. **2** become careless in one's habits or appearance. **let someone off 1** refrain from punishing someone. **2** excuse someone from a task or duty. **let something off** cause a gun, firework, or bomb to fire or explode. **let on** informal reveal information. **let something out 1** make a sound or cry. **2** make a piece of clothing looser or larger. **let up** informal become less intense.
– ORIGIN Old English, 'leave behind, leave out.'

let[2] ▶ noun (in racket sports) a situation in which a point is not counted and is played for again.
– PHRASES **without let or hindrance** formal without obstruction; freely.
– ORIGIN Old English, 'hinder.'

let·down /ˈletˌdoun/ ▶ noun a disappointment.

– SYNONYMS **disappointment,** anticlimax, comedown, nonevent, fiasco; informal washout.

le·thal /ˈlēTHəl/ ▶ adjective **1** able or enough to cause death. **2** very harmful or destructive.

– SYNONYMS **fatal,** deadly, mortal, terminal, life-threatening, murderous, poisonous, toxic, noxious, venomous, dangerous.
– ANTONYMS harmless, safe.

– DERIVATIVES **le·thal·i·ty** /lēˈTHalətē/ noun **le·thal·ly** adverb.
– ORIGIN Latin *lethalis.*

le·thar·gic /ləˈTHärjik/ ▶ adjective lacking energy and enthusiasm: *feeling depressed and lethargic.*

– SYNONYMS **sluggish,** inert, inactive, slow, lifeless, languid, listless, apathetic, weary, tired, fatigued, enervated.
– ANTONYMS energetic.

– DERIVATIVES **le·thar·gi·cal·ly** /ləˈTHärjik(ə)lē/ adverb.

leth·ar·gy /ˈleTHərjē/ ▶ noun a lack of energy and enthusiasm.
– ORIGIN from Greek *lēthargos* 'forgetful.'

let's /lets/ ▶ contraction let us.

let·ter /ˈletər/ ▶ noun **1** a symbol representing one or more of the sounds used in speech; any of the symbols of an alphabet. **2** a written, typed, or printed communication, sent by mail or messenger. **3** the precise terms of a statement or requirement: *adherence to the letter of the law.* **4** (**letters**) literature.

– SYNONYMS **1 character,** sign, symbol, figure. **2 message,** note, line, missive, dispatch, communication; formal epistle; (**letters**) correspondence, mail, post.

▶ verb carve or write letters on something.
– DERIVATIVES **let·ter·ing** noun.
– PHRASES **to the letter** precisely or exactly.
– ORIGIN Latin *litera* 'letter of the alphabet,' (plural) 'epistle, literature, culture.'

WORD LINKS

epistolary *relating to letter-writing*

let·ter bomb ▶ noun an explosive device hidden in a small package, which explodes when the package is opened.

let·ter car·ri·er ▶ noun a mail carrier.

let·ter·head /ˈletərˌhed/ ▶ noun a printed heading on stationery, stating the sender's name and address.

let·ter of cred·it ▶ noun a letter issued by one bank to another to serve as a guarantee for payments made to a specified person.

let·ter o·pen·er ▶ noun a blunt knife or other device used for opening envelopes.

let·ter·press /ˈletərˌpres/ ▶ noun printing from a hard, raised image under pressure, using viscous ink.

let·tuce /ˈletis/ ▶ noun a cultivated plant with edible leaves that are eaten in salads.
– ORIGIN Old French *letues.*

let·up ▶ noun informal a brief time when something becomes less intense, difficult, or tiring.

leu·cine /ˈlo͞oˌsēn, -sin/ ▶ noun a hydrophobic amino acid that is a constituent of most proteins and an essential nutrient in the diet of vertebrates.
– ORIGIN from Greek *leukos* 'white.'

leu·ke·mi·a /lo͞oˈkēmēə/ (Brit. **leukaemia**) ▶ noun a serious disease in which increased numbers of immature or abnormal white cells are produced, stopping the production of normal blood cells.
– DERIVATIVES **leu·ke·mic** /-ˈkēmik/ adjective.
– ORIGIN from Greek *leukos* 'white' + *haima* 'blood.'

leu·ko·cyte /ˈlo͞okəˌsīt/ (also Brit. **leucocyte**) ▶ noun a colorless cell that circulates in the blood and body fluids and acts against foreign substances and disease; a white blood cell.
– ORIGIN from Greek *leukos* 'white' + *kutos* 'vessel.'

Le·vant /lə'vant, lə'vänt/ ▶ **noun** (**the Levant**) historical the eastern part of the Mediterranean.
– DERIVATIVES **Le·van·tine** /'levənˌtīn, -ˌtēn, lə'vantin/ noun & adjective.
– ORIGIN from French, 'rising' (used to mean 'point of sunrise, east').

lev·ee[1] /'levē/ ▶ **noun 1** an embankment built to prevent a river from overflowing. **2** a ridge of sediment deposited naturally alongside a river. **3** a landing place; a quay.
– ORIGIN French, 'rising, lifting.'

lev·ee[2] ▶ **noun** old use a formal reception of visitors or guests.
– ORIGIN French, 'rising' (first referring to a reception held by a monarch after rising from bed).

lev·el /'levəl/ ▶ **noun 1** a position or stage on a scale of quantity, extent, rank, or quality. **2** a horizontal line or surface. **3** a height or distance from the ground or another base point: *storms caused river levels to rise*. **4** a floor of a multistory building. **5** a flat area of land. **6** (also **spirit level**) a device consisting of a sealed glass tube partially filled with a liquid, containing an air bubble whose position reveals whether a surface is perfectly level or plumb. **7** an instrument giving a line parallel to the plane of the horizon for testing whether things are horizontal.

– SYNONYMS **1 rank,** position, degree, grade, stage, standard, class, group, set, classification. **2** *a high level of employment* **quantity,** amount, extent, measure, degree, volume.

▶ **adjective 1** having a flat, horizontal surface. **2** having the same height, position, or value as someone or something else: *her face was level with his own*. **3** calm and steady.

– SYNONYMS **1** *a level surface* **flat,** smooth, even, uniform, plane, flush, horizontal. **2** *the scores were level* **equal,** even, drawn, tied, all square, neck and neck, on a par, evenly matched; informal even-steven, nip and tuck. **3** *a level voice* **steady,** even, uniform, regular, constant, unchanging.
– ANTONYMS uneven, unequal.

▶ **verb** (**levels, leveling, leveled**) **1** make or become level or flat. **2** make or become equal or similar. **3** aim or direct a weapon, criticism, or accusation. **4** (**level with**) informal be frank or honest with someone.

– SYNONYMS **1 even off,** even out, flatten, smooth (out). **2 equalize,** equal, even (up), make level. **3 aim,** point, direct, train, focus, turn.

– DERIVATIVES **lev·el·ly** adverb **lev·el·ness** noun.
– PHRASES **a level playing field** a situation in which everyone has an equal chance of succeeding. **on the level** informal honest; truthful.
– ORIGIN Old French *livel*.

lev·el·er /'lev(ə)lər/ ▶ **noun 1** a person or thing that levels something. **2** a situation or activity in which distinctions of class, age, or ability do not matter: *he valued the sport because it was a great leveler*.

lev·el·head·ed /'levəl'hedid/ ▶ **adjective** calm and sensible.

– SYNONYMS **sensible,** practical, realistic, prudent, pragmatic, reasonable, rational, mature, sound, sober, businesslike, no-nonsense, having your feet on the ground; informal unflappable, together.
– ANTONYMS excitable.

– DERIVATIVES **lev·el·head·ed·ly** adverb **lev·el·head·ed·ness** noun.

lev·er /'levər, 'lēvər/ ▶ **noun 1** a rigid bar resting on a pivot, used to move a load with one end when pressure is applied to the other. **2** an arm or handle that is moved to operate a mechanism.

– SYNONYMS **handle,** arm, switch, crowbar, bar, jimmy.

▶ **verb 1** lift or move something with a lever. **2** move with effort: *she levered herself up*.

– SYNONYMS **pry,** prize, force, wrench; informal jimmy.

– ORIGIN from Old French *lever* 'to lift.'

lev·er·age /'lev(ə)rij, 'lēv(ə)rij/ ▶ **noun 1** the exertion of force by means of a lever. **2** the power to influence: *states trying to regain their former leverage*. **3** the ratio of a company's loan capital (debt) to the value of its common stock (equity).

– SYNONYMS **1 force,** purchase, grip, hold, anchorage. **2** *more leverage in negotiations* **influence,** power, authority, weight, sway, pull, control, say, advantage, pressure; informal clout, muscle, teeth.

lev·er·aged buy·out ▶ **noun** the purchase of a controlling share in a company by its management, using capital borrowed from outside the company.

lev·er·et /'lev(ə)rit/ ▶ **noun** a young hare in its first year.
– ORIGIN Old French.

le·vi·a·than /lə'vīəᴛʜən/ ▶ **noun 1** a very large or powerful thing. **2** (in biblical use) a sea monster.
– ORIGIN Hebrew.

lev·i·tate /'levəˌtāt/ ▶ **verb** rise or cause to rise and hover in the air.
– DERIVATIVES **lev·i·ta·tion** /ˌlevə'tāsʜən/ noun.
– ORIGIN from Latin *levis* 'light.'

lev·i·ty /'levətē/ ▶ **noun** the treatment of a serious matter with humor or lack of respect.

– SYNONYMS **lightheartedness,** high spirits, cheerfulness, humor, gaiety, hilarity, frivolity, amusement, mirth, laughter, merriment, glee, jollity.
– ANTONYMS seriousness.

– ORIGIN Latin *levitas*.

le·vy /'levē/ ▶ **verb** (**levies, levying, levied**) **1** impose a tax, fee, or fine. **2** old use enlist someone for military service.

– SYNONYMS **impose,** charge, exact, raise, collect.

▶ **noun** (pl. **levies**) **1** an act of imposing a tax, fee, or fine: *a levy on energy-intensive industries*. **2** a sum of money raised by a tax, fee, or fine. **3** old use a body of enlisted troops.

– SYNONYMS **tax,** tariff, toll, excise, duty.

– ORIGIN Old French *lever* 'raise.'

lewd /lo͞od/ ▶ **adjective** crude and offensive in a sexual way.
– DERIVATIVES **lewd·ly** adverb **lewd·ness** noun.
– ORIGIN Old English.

lex·i·cal /'leksikəl/ ▶ **adjective 1** relating to the words of a language. **2** relating to a lexicon or dictionary.
– DERIVATIVES **lex·i·cal·ly** adverb.
– ORIGIN from Greek *lexikos* 'of words.'

lex·i·cog·ra·phy /ˌleksə'kägrəfē/ ▶ **noun** the practice of compiling dictionaries.
– DERIVATIVES **lex·i·cog·ra·pher** noun **lex·i·co·graph·ic** /-kə'grafik/ adjective.

lex·i·con /'leksiˌkän, -kən/ ▶ **noun 1** the vocabulary of a person, language, or subject area. **2** a dictionary.
– ORIGIN from Greek *lexikon biblion* 'book of words.'

ley /lā/ (also **ley line**) ▶ **noun** a supposed straight line connecting ancient sites, believed by some people to be associated with lines of energy and other paranormal phenomena.
– ORIGIN variant of **LEA**.

LF ▶ **abbreviation** low frequency.

LI ▶ **abbreviation** Long Island.

Li ▶ **symbol** the chemical element lithium.

li·a·bil·i·ty /ˌlīəˈbilətē/ ▶ **noun** (pl. **liabilities**) **1** the state of being legally responsible for something. **2** a thing for which someone is legally responsible, especially a debt. **3** a person or thing likely to cause embarrassment or difficulty.

– SYNONYMS **1 responsibility,** accountability. **2** *they have big liabilities* **obligations,** debts, arrears, dues, commitments. **3** *she was proving to be a liability* **hindrance,** handicap, nuisance, inconvenience, embarrassment, impediment, disadvantage, millstone, encumbrance, burden.
– ANTONYMS asset.

li·a·ble /ˈlī(ə)bəl/ ▶ **adjective 1** responsible by law. **2** (**liable to**) legally required to do something. **3** (**liable to do**) likely to do, be, or experience: *areas liable to flooding.*

– SYNONYMS **1 responsible,** accountable, answerable, blameworthy, at fault. **2 likely,** inclined, tending, apt, prone, given, subject, susceptible, vulnerable, exposed, in danger of, at risk of.

– ORIGIN perhaps from French *lier* 'to bind.'

li·aise /lēˈāz/ ▶ **verb 1** cooperate on a matter of shared concern. **2** (**liaise between**) act as a link to assist communication between people.

– SYNONYMS **cooperate,** collaborate, communicate, network, interface, link up; informal hook up.

– ORIGIN from **LIAISON**.

li·ai·son /ˈlēəˌzän, lēˈā-/ ▶ **noun 1** communication or cooperation between people or organizations. **2** a sexual relationship, especially a secret one.

– SYNONYMS **1 cooperation,** contact, association, connection, collaboration, communication, alliance, partnership. **2 love affair,** relationship, romance, attachment, fling.

– ORIGIN from French *lier* 'to bind.'

li·ai·son of·fi·cer ▶ **noun** a person who is employed to form a working relationship between two organizations to their mutual benefit.

li·a·na /lēˈänə, -ˈanə/ (also **liane** /-ˈän, -ˈan/) ▶ **noun** a woody climbing plant that hangs from trees, especially in tropical rainforests.
– ORIGIN French *liane* 'clematis, liana.'

li·ar /ˈlīər/ ▶ **noun** a person who tells lies.

– SYNONYMS **fibber,** deceiver, perjurer, dissembler, faker, hoaxer, impostor.

lib /lib/ ▶ **noun** informal (in the names of political movements) the liberation of a specified group: *women's lib.*
– DERIVATIVES **lib·ber** noun.

li·ba·tion /līˈbāsʜən/ ▶ **noun 1** a drink poured out as an offering to a god. **2** humorous an alcoholic drink.
– ORIGIN from Latin *libare* 'pour as an offering.'

li·bel /ˈlībəl/ ▶ **noun 1** the crime of publishing a false statement that is damaging to a person's reputation. Compare with **SLANDER**. **2** a published false statement that damages a person's reputation.

– SYNONYMS **defamation (of character),** character assassination, calumny, misrepresentation, scandalmongering, slur, smear; informal mud-slinging.

▶ **verb** (**libels, libeling, libeled**) publish a false and damaging statement about someone.

– SYNONYMS **defame,** malign, blacken someone's name, sully someone's reputation, smear, cast aspersions on, drag someone's name through the mud/mire, denigrate, traduce, slur.

– ORIGIN Latin *libellus* 'little book.'

li·bel·ous /ˈlībələs/ ▶ **adjective** containing or constituting a libel: *a libelous newspaper story.*

– SYNONYMS **defamatory,** denigratory, disparaging, derogatory, false, untrue, insulting, scurrilous.

lib·er·al /ˈlib(ə)rəl/ ▶ **adjective 1** willing to respect and accept behavior or opinions different from one's own. **2** (of a society, law, etc.) favorable to individual rights and freedoms. **3** (in politics favoring individual liberty, free trade, and moderate reform. **4** (**Liberal**) relating to Liberals or a Liberal Party. **5** (of an interpretation) broadly understood; not strictly literal. **6** given, used, or giving in generous amounts: *liberal amounts of wine were consumed.* **7** (of education) concerned with broadening general knowledge and experience.

– SYNONYMS **1 tolerant,** unprejudiced, broad-minded, open-minded, enlightened, permissive, free (and easy), easygoing, libertarian, indulgent, lenient. **2** *a liberal social agenda* **progressive,** advanced, modern, forward-looking, forward-thinking, enlightened, reformist, radical; informal go-ahead. **3** *a liberal interpretation of the law* **flexible,** broad, loose, rough, free, nonliteral. **4 abundant,** copious, ample, plentiful, lavish, generous, open-handed, unsparing, unstinting, free, munificent.
– ANTONYMS reactionary, strict.

▶ **noun 1** a person of liberal views. **2** (**Liberal**) a supporter or member of a Liberal Party.
– DERIVATIVES **lib·er·al·ism** /-ˌlizəm/ noun **lib·er·al·i·ty** /ˌlibəˈralətē/ noun **lib·er·al·ly** adverb.
– ORIGIN Latin *liberalis.*

lib·er·al arts ▶ **plural noun** academic subjects such as literature, philosophy, mathematics, and social and physical sciences as distinct from professional and technical subjects.

lib·er·al·ize /ˈlib(ə)rəˌlīz/ ▶ **verb** remove or loosen restrictions on something, typically an economic or political system.
– DERIVATIVES **lib·er·al·i·za·tion** /ˌlib(ə)rələˈzāsʜən, -ˌlīˈzā-/ noun.

lib·er·ate /ˈlibəˌrāt/ ▶ **verb 1** set someone free, especially from imprisonment or oppression. **2** (as adj. **liberated**) free from social conventions, especially with regard to sexual roles.

– SYNONYMS **(set) free,** release, let out, let go, set loose, save, rescue, emancipate; historical enfranchise.
– ANTONYMS imprison, enslave.

– DERIVATIVES **lib·er·a·tion** /ˌlibəˈrāsʜən/ noun **lib·er·a·tion·ist** /ˌlibəˈrāsʜənist/ noun **lib·er·a·tor** /-ˌrātər/ noun **lib·er·a·tor·y** /ˈlibərəˌtôrē/ adjective.
– ORIGIN Latin *liberare.*

lib·er·a·tion the·ol·o·gy ▶ **noun** a movement in Christian belief that attempts to address the problems of poverty and social injustice.

Li·be·ri·an /lī'bi(ə)rēən/ ▶ **noun** a person from Liberia, a country in in West Africa. ▶ **adjective** relating to Liberia.

lib·er·tar·i·an /ˌlibər'te(ə)rēən/ ▶ **noun** a person who believes that the government should intervene only minimally in the lives of its citizens.
– DERIVATIVES **lib·er·tar·i·an·ism** /ˌlibər'te(ə)rēəˌnizəm/ noun.

lib·er·tine /'libərˌtēn/ ▶ **noun** a man who behaves without moral principles, especially in sexual matters.
– DERIVATIVES **lib·er·tin·ism** /-ˌnizəm/ noun.
– ORIGIN Latin *libertinus* 'freed slave.'

lib·er·ty /'libərtē/ ▶ **noun** (pl. **liberties**) **1** the state of being free; freedom. **2** the power or scope to act as one pleases. **3** a right or privilege. **4** informal a disrespectful remark or action.

> – SYNONYMS **1 freedom,** independence, immunity, self-determination, autonomy, emancipation, sovereignty, self-government, self-rule, self-determination, civil liberties, human rights. **2** *he's not at liberty to discuss his real work* **able,** free, entitled, permitted.
> – ANTONYMS slavery.

– PHRASES **take liberties with 1** behave in an excessively familiar way toward someone. **2** treat something without strict faithfulness to the facts or to an original. **take the liberty** do something without first asking permission.
– ORIGIN Latin *libertas*.

> **CHOOSE THE RIGHT WORD**
>
> **liberty, freedom, independence, license, permission**
>
> The Fourth of July is the day on which Americans commemorate their nation's **independence**, a word that implies the ability to stand alone, without being sustained by anything else. While *independence* is usually associated with countries or nations, **freedom** and **liberty** more often apply to individuals. But unlike *freedom*, which implies an absence of restraint or compulsion (*the freedom to speak openly*), *liberty* implies the power to choose among alternatives rather than merely being unrestrained (*the liberty to select their own form of government*). *Freedom* can also apply to many different types of oppressive influences (*freedom from interruption; freedom to leave the room at any time*), while *liberty* often connotes deliverance or release (*he gave the slaves their liberty*). **License** may imply the *liberty* to disobey rules or regulations imposed on others, especially when there is an advantage to be gained in doing so (*poetic license*). But more often it refers to an abuse of *liberty* or the power to do whatever one pleases (*a license to sell drugs*). **Permission** is an even broader term than *license*, suggesting the capacity to act without interference or censure, usually with some degree of approval or authority (*permission to be absent from his post*).

li·bid·i·nous /lə'bidn-əs/ ▶ **adjective** having or showing a strong sex drive.
– ORIGIN from Latin *libido* 'desire, lust.'

li·bi·do /lə'bēdō/ ▶ **noun** (pl. **libidos**) sexual desire.
– DERIVATIVES **li·bid·i·nal** /-'bidn-əl/ adjective.
– ORIGIN Latin, 'desire, lust.'

Li·bra /'lēbrə, 'lī-/ ▶ **noun 1** a constellation and the seventh sign of the zodiac (the Scales), which the sun enters about September 23. **2** (**a Libra**) a person born when the sun is in this sign.
– DERIVATIVES **Li·bran** noun & adjective.
– ORIGIN Latin.

li·brar·i·an /lī'bre(ə)rēən/ ▶ **noun** a person in charge of or assisting in a library.
– DERIVATIVES **li·brar·i·an·ship** /-ˌship/ noun.

li·brar·y /'līˌbrerē, -brərē/ ▶ **noun** (pl. **libraries**) **1** a building or room containing a collection of books and periodicals for use by the public or the members of an institution. **2** a private collection of books. **3** an organized collection of movies, recorded music, etc., kept for research or borrowing. **4** (also **software library**) a collection of computer programs and software packages made generally available.
– ORIGIN Latin *libraria* 'bookshop.'

li·bret·to /lə'bretō/ ▶ **noun** (pl. **libretti** /-'bretē/ or **librettos**) the text of an opera or other long vocal work.
– DERIVATIVES **li·bret·tist** noun.
– ORIGIN Italian, 'small book.'

Lib·y·an /'libēən/ ▶ **noun** a person from Libya. ▶ **adjective** relating to Libya.

lice /līs/ plural of LOUSE.

li·cense /'līsəns/ ▶ **noun** (Brit. **licence**) **1** a permit from an authority to own, use, or do something. **2** freedom to behave without restraint: *the government has given the army too much license*. **3** the freedom of writer or artist to deviate from facts or accepted rules.

> – SYNONYMS **1 permit,** certificate, document, documentation, authorization, warrant, credentials, pass, papers. **2 franchise,** consent, sanction, warrant, charter, concession. **3 freedom,** liberty, free rein, latitude, independence, scope, carte blanche; informal a blank check.

▶ **verb** (Brit. also **licence**) **1** grant a license to someone. **2** authorize or permit something.

> – SYNONYMS **permit,** allow, authorize, give authority to, give permission to, certify, accredit, empower, entitle, enable, sanction.
> – ANTONYMS ban.

– DERIVATIVES **li·cens·a·ble** adjective **li·cens·er** (also **licensor**) noun.
– ORIGIN Latin *licentia* 'freedom, licentiousness.'

> **CHOOSE THE RIGHT WORD**
>
> See LIBERTY.

li·cen·see /ˌlīsən'sē/ ▶ **noun** the holder of a license, especially to sell alcoholic drinks.

li·cense plate ▶ **noun** a sign showing a unique series of letters or numbers, fixed to a vehicle to indicate that it has been registered with the government.

li·cen·sure /'līsənshər, -ˌshoor/ ▶ **noun** the granting or regulation of licenses, as for professionals.

li·cen·ti·ate /lī'sensh(ē)it/ ▶ **noun 1** the holder of a certificate of competence to practice a particular profession. **2** (in certain colleges and universities) a degree between that of bachelor and master or doctor.
– DERIVATIVES **li·cen·ti·ate·ship** /-ˌship/ noun.
– ORIGIN from Latin *licentiatus* 'having freedom.'

li·cen·tious /lī'senshəs/ ▶ **adjective** promiscuous and unprincipled in sexual matters.
– DERIVATIVES **li·cen·tious·ly** adverb **li·cen·tious·ness** noun.
– ORIGIN Latin *licentiosus*.

li·chen /'līkən/ ▶ **noun** a simple plant consisting of a fungus living in close association with an alga, typically growing on rocks, walls, and trees.
– DERIVATIVES **li·chened** adjective.
– ORIGIN Greek *leikhēn*.

lic·it /'lisit/ ▸ **adjective** formal not forbidden; lawful.
– ORIGIN Latin *licitus* 'allowed.'

lick /lik/ ▸ **verb 1** pass the tongue over something in order to taste, moisten, or clean it. **2** move lightly and quickly: *the flames licked around the wood.* **3** informal overcome someone decisively. ▸ **noun 1** an act of licking. **2** informal a small amount or quick application of something: *a lick of paint.* **3** informal a short phrase or solo in jazz or popular music.
– PHRASES **at a lick** informal at a fast pace. **a lick and a promise** informal a hasty performance of a task, especially of cleaning something. **lick someone's boots** (or vulgar slang **ass**) be excessively flattering or servile toward someone.
– ORIGIN Old English.

lick·ing /'likiNG/ ▸ **noun** informal a severe defeat or beating.

lic·o·rice /'lik(ə)risH, -ris/ ▸ **noun** a chewy black substance made from the juice of a root and used in making candies and medicine.
– ORIGIN Old French *licoresse*.

lid /lid/ ▸ **noun 1** a removable or hinged cover for the top of a container. **2** an eyelid.

– SYNONYMS **cover,** top, cap, covering, stopper.

– DERIVATIVES **lid·ded** adjective **lid·less** adjective.
– ORIGIN Old English.

li·do /'lēdō/ (also **lido deck**) ▸ **noun** (pl. **lidos**) a deck on a cruise ship where swimming pools are located.
– ORIGIN Italian, 'shore.'

lie[1] /lī/ ▸ **verb** (**lies, lying** /'lī-iNG/, **lay** /lā/; past part. **lain** /lān/) **1** be in or take up a horizontal or resting position on a supporting surface. **2** be or remain in a particular state: *many buildings were lying empty.* **3** be situated in a specified position or direction. **4** be found: *the solution lies in a return to traditional values.*

– SYNONYMS **1** *he was lying on the bed* **recline,** lie down, be recumbent, be prostrate, be supine, be prone, be stretched out, sprawl, rest, repose, lounge, loll. **2** *her bag lay on the chair* **be,** be situated, be positioned, be located, be placed, be found, be sited, be arranged, rest.
– ANTONYMS stand.

▸ **noun** the way, direction, or position in which something lies or comes to rest.
– PHRASES **let something lie** take no action on a problematic matter. **lie in state** (of the corpse of a person of national importance) be laid in a public place of honor before burial. **lie low** keep out of sight; avoid attention. **lie with** old use have sex with. **take something lying down** accept an insult or reprimand without protest.
– ORIGIN Old English.

USAGE

For the correct use of **lay** and **lie**, see the note at **LAY**[1].

lie[2] ▸ **noun 1** a deliberately false statement. **2** a situation involving deception or based on a mistaken impression.

– SYNONYMS **untruth,** falsehood, fib, fabrication, deception, invention, (piece of) fiction, falsification, white lie; informal tall story, whopper.
– ANTONYMS truth.

▸ **verb** (**lies, lying** /'lī-iNG/, **lied**) **1** tell a lie or lies. **2** present a false impression: *the camera cannot lie.*

– SYNONYMS **1 tell a lie,** fib, dissemble, perjure oneself. **2** (as n. **lying**) *she was no good at lying* **dishonesty,** fabrication, fibbing, perjury, untruthfulness, mendacity, misrepresentation, deceit, duplicity. **3** (as adj. **lying**) *he was a lying womanizer* **dishonest,** untruthful, false, mendacious, deceitful, duplicitous, double-dealing, two-faced.

– PHRASES **give the lie to** show that something assumed to be true is not true.
– ORIGIN Old English.

WORD LINKS

mendacious *telling lies*

Lieb·frau·milch /'lēbˌfrouˌmilcH, 'lēp-, -ˌmilk, -ˌmilKH/ ▸ **noun** a light white wine from the Rhine region.
– ORIGIN from German *lieb* 'dear' + *Frau* 'lady' (referring to the Virgin Mary) + *Milch* 'milk.'

lied /lēd, lēt/ ▸ **noun** (pl. **lieder** /'lēdər/) a type of German song, typically for solo voice with piano accompaniment.
– ORIGIN German.

lie de·tec·tor ▸ **noun** a device for determining whether a person is telling the truth.

lie-down ▸ **noun** chiefly Brit. a short rest on a bed or sofa.

lief /lēf/ ▸ **adverb** (**as lief**) old use as happily.
– ORIGIN Old English, 'dear, pleasant.'

liege /lēj, lēzH/ ▸ **noun** historical **1** (also **liege lord**) a lord or sovereign under the feudal system. **2** a person who served a lord in the feudal system.
– ORIGIN Old French.

lien /'lē(ə)n/ ▸ **noun** Law a right to keep the property of another person until a debt owed by that person is paid.
– ORIGIN Old French *loien*.

lieu /lo͞o/ ▸ **noun** (in phrase **in lieu**) instead: *rum was used by local merchants in lieu of cash.*
– ORIGIN French.

Lieut. ▸ **abbreviation** lieutenant.

lieu·ten·ant /lo͞o'tenənt/ ▸ **noun 1** a person who acts as a deputy or substitute for a superior. **2** a rank of officer in the Navy or Coast Guard.
– DERIVATIVES **lieu·ten·an·cy** /-'tenənsē/ noun (pl. **lieutenancies**).
– ORIGIN Old French, 'place-holding.'

lieu·ten·ant colo·nel ▸ **noun** a rank of officer in the Army, Air Force, or Marine Corps above major and below colonel.

lieu·ten·ant com·man·der ▸ **noun** a rank of officer in the Navy or Coast Guard, above lieutenant and below commander.

lieu·ten·ant gen·er·al ▸ **noun** a high rank of officer in the Army, Air Force, or Marine Corps above major general and below general.

lieu·ten·ant gov·er·nor ▸ **noun** a deputy state governor.

life /līf/ ▸ **noun** (pl. **lives** /līvz/) **1** the condition that distinguishes animals and plants from inorganic matter, including the ability to grow, breathe, and reproduce. **2** the existence of an individual human being or animal. **3** a particular type or aspect of people's existence: *school life.* **4** living things and their activity. **5** the period during which something continues to exist, function, or be valid. **6** vitality or energy. **7** informal a sentence of imprisonment for life. **8** a biography.

– SYNONYMS **1 existence,** being, living, animation, sentience, creation, viability. **2 living creatures,** fauna, flora, the ecosystem, the biosphere, the

ecosphere. **3 way of life,** lifestyle, situation, fate, lot. **4 lifetime,** lifespan, days, time (on earth), existence. **5 vitality,** animation, liveliness, vivacity, verve, high spirits, exuberance, zest, enthusiasm, energy, vigor, dynamism, elan, gusto, bounce, spirit, fire. **6 biography,** autobiography, history, chronicle, account, memoirs, diary.
– ANTONYMS death.

▸ **adjective** (in art) based on a living rather than an imagined form: *a life drawing.*
– PHRASES **as large as** (or **larger than**) **life** informal noticeably present. **not on your life** informal definitely not. **take one's life in one's hands** risk being killed.
– ORIGIN Old English.

WORD LINKS
animate, vital *having life*

life·belt /ˈlīfˌbelt/ ▸ **noun** a life preserver in the shape of a belt.

life·blood /ˈlīfˌbləd/ ▸ **noun** a vital factor or force: *intelligence is the lifeblood of antiterrorist operations.*

life·boat /ˈlīfˌbōt/ ▸ **noun 1** a type of boat launched from land to rescue people at sea. **2** a small boat kept on a ship for use in an emergency.

life·bu·oy /ˈlīfˌbo͞o-ē, -ˌboi/ ▸ **noun** a life preserver, especially one in the shape of a ring.

life cy·cle ▸ **noun** the series of changes in the life of an organism.

life ex·pec·tan·cy ▸ **noun** the period that a person may expect to live.

life force ▸ **noun** the force that gives something its vitality or strength.

life form ▸ **noun** any living thing.

life·guard /ˈlīfˌgärd/ ▸ **noun** a person employed to rescue swimmers who get into difficulty at a beach or swimming pool.

life in·sur·ance ▸ **noun** insurance that pays out a sum of money either on the death of the insured person or after a set period.

life jack·et ▸ **noun** a sleeveless inflatable jacket for keeping a person afloat in water.

life·less /ˈlīflis/ ▸ **adjective 1** dead or apparently dead. **2** not containing living things. **3** lacking vitality or excitement.

– SYNONYMS **1 dead,** stiff, cold, inert, inanimate; formal deceased. **2 barren,** sterile, bare, desolate, stark, bleak, arid, infertile, uninhabited. **3 lackluster,** apathetic, lethargic, uninspired, dull, colorless, characterless, wooden.
– ANTONYMS alive, lively.

– DERIVATIVES **life·less·ly** adverb **life·less·ness** noun.

life·like /ˈlīfˌlīk/ ▸ **adjective** very similar to the person or thing represented.

– SYNONYMS **realistic,** true to life, faithful, detailed, vivid, graphic, natural, naturalistic, representational.

life·line /ˈlīfˌlīn/ ▸ **noun 1** a thing on which someone or something depends or that provides a means of escape: *visitors are a lifeline for lonely elderly people.* **2** a rope thrown to rescue someone in water or used by sailors to secure themselves to a boat. **3** (in palmistry) a line on the palm of a person's hand, regarded as indicating how long they will live.

life·long /ˈlīfˌlôNG, -ˌläNG/ ▸ **adjective** lasting in a particular state throughout a person's life.

life part·ner ▸ **noun** a romantic partner to whom one has made a lifetime commitment.

life pre·serv·er ▸ **noun** a device made of buoyant or inflatable material, such as a life jacket or lifebelt, to keep someone afloat in water.

lif·er /ˈlīfər/ ▸ **noun** informal a person serving a life sentence in prison.

life raft ▸ **noun** an inflatable raft for use in an emergency at sea.

life·sav·er /ˈlīfˌsāvər/ ▸ **noun 1** informal a thing that saves someone from serious difficulty. **2** a ring-shaped life preserver.

life sci·enc·es ▸ **plural noun** the sciences concerned with the study of living organisms, including biology, botany, and zoology.

life sen·tence ▸ **noun** a punishment of life imprisonment.

life-size (also **life-sized**) ▸ **adjective** of the same size as the person or thing represented.

life-skill ▸ **noun** (often plural) a skill required for everyday life.

life·span /ˈlīfˌspan/ ▸ **noun** the length of time for which a person or animal lives or a thing functions.

life·style /ˈlīfˌstīl/ ▸ **noun** the way in which someone lives.

– SYNONYMS **way of life,** life, situation, conduct, behavior, ways, habits, mores.

life sup·port ▸ **noun** the maintenance of a patient's vital functions following an injury or serious illness.

life-threa·ten·ing ▸ **adjective** potentially fatal.

life·time /ˈlīfˌtīm/ ▸ **noun 1** the length of time that a person lives or a thing lasts. **2** informal a very long time.

– SYNONYMS **lifespan,** life, days, time (on earth), existence, career.

life·work /ˈlīfˈwərk/ ▸ **noun** the entire or principal work, labor, or task of a person's lifetime.

LIFO /ˈlīfō/ ▸ **abbreviation** last in first out (chiefly with reference to methods of stock valuation or data storage). Compare with **FIFO**.

lift /lift/ ▸ **verb 1** raise or be raised to a higher position or level. **2** pick someone or something up and move them to a different position. **3** formally remove or end a legal restriction, decision, or ban. **4** (**lift off**) (of an aircraft, spacecraft, or rocket) take off, especially vertically. **5** informal steal something.

– SYNONYMS **1 raise,** hoist, heave, haul up, heft, elevate, hold high, pick up, grab, take up, winch up, jack up. **2** *the fog had lifted* **clear,** rise, disperse, dissipate, disappear, vanish, dissolve. **3** *the ban has been lifted* **cancel,** remove, withdraw, revoke, rescind, end, stop, terminate. **4 (lift off) take off,** become airborne, be launched, take to the air, blast off.

▸ **noun 1** an act of lifting. **2** a free ride in another person's vehicle. **3** a device for carrying people up or down a mountain. **4** a feeling of increased cheerfulness: *winning the match has given everyone a lift.* **5** upward force exerted by the air on an airfoil. **6** Brit. an elevator.

– SYNONYMS *the goal will give his confidence a lift* **boost,** fillip, impetus, encouragement, spur, push; informal shot in the arm.

– DERIVATIVES **lift·a·ble** adjective **lift·er** noun.
– PHRASES **not lift a finger** refuse to make the slightest effort.
– ORIGIN Old Norse.

lift·off /ˈliftˌôf, -ˌäf/ ▶ **noun** the vertical takeoff of a spacecraft, rocket, or aircraft.

lig·a·ment /ˈligəmənt/ ▶ **noun 1** a short band of tough, flexible fibrous tissue that connects two bones or cartilages or holds together a joint. **2** a fold of membrane that supports a body organ and keeps it in position.
– DERIVATIVES **lig·a·men·tous** /ˌligəˈmentəs/ adjective.
– ORIGIN Latin *ligamentum* 'bond.'

li·ga·ture /ˈligəCHər, -ˌCHo͝or/ ▶ **noun 1** a thing used for tying something tightly, especially a cord used in surgery to tie up a bleeding artery. **2** Music a slur or tie. **3** Printing a character consisting of two or more joined letters, e.g., *æ*. ▶ **verb** bind or connect something with a ligature.
– ORIGIN Latin *ligatura*.

light[1] /līt/ ▶ **noun 1** the natural form of energy that makes things visible; electromagnetic radiation from about 390 to 740 nm in wavelength. **2** a source of illumination such as a lamp. **3** (**lights**) traffic lights. **4** a device producing a flame or spark. **5** an expression in someone's eyes. **6** understanding: *light dawned in her eyes.* **7** an area that is brighter or paler than its surroundings. **8** a window or section of a window.

– SYNONYMS **1 illumination,** brightness, shining, gleam, brilliance, radiance, luminosity, luminescence, incandescence, blaze, glare, glow, luster; literary refulgence, effulgence. **2 lamp,** lantern, flashlight, bulb, beacon, candle, torch. **3 daylight,** daytime, day, sunlight.
– ANTONYMS darkness.

▶ **verb** (past **lit**; past part. **lit** or **lighted**) **1** provide something with light. **2** ignite or be ignited.

– SYNONYMS **1 illuminate,** irradiate, floodlight; literary illumine. **2 set fire to,** ignite, kindle.

▶ **adjective 1** having a considerable amount of natural light. **2** (of a color) pale.

– SYNONYMS **1 bright,** well lit, sunny. **2 pale,** pastel, delicate, subtle, faded, bleached.
– ANTONYMS dark.

– DERIVATIVES **light·less** adjective **light·ness** noun.
– PHRASES **bring** (or **come**) **to light** make (or become) widely known or evident. **in a —— light** in the way specified. **in (the) light of** taking something into consideration. **light at the end of the tunnel** an indication that a period of difficulty is ending. **the light of day** general public attention. **light up 1** become illuminated. **2** become lively or happy. **light something up** ignite a cigarette, pipe, or cigar before smoking it. **see the light** understand or realize something. **throw** (or **cast** or **shed**) **light on** help to explain something by providing further information.
– ORIGIN Old English.

WORD LINKS

optics *study of the behavior of light*

light[2] ▶ **adjective 1** not heavy or heavy enough. **2** not strongly or heavily built or made. **3** relatively low in density, amount, or intensity: *traffic was light.* **4** carrying or suitable for small loads. **5** gentle or delicate. **6** not serious or challenging: *light entertainment.* **7** (of sleep or a sleeper) easily disturbed. **8** easily done. **9** cheerful or carefree.

– SYNONYMS **1 lightweight,** portable, underweight. **2 flimsy,** thin, lightweight, floaty, gauzy, diaphanous, filmy. **3** *a light dinner* **small,** modest, simple, insubstantial, frugal. **4** *light duties* **easy,** simple, undemanding, untaxing; informal cushy. **5** *a light touch* **gentle,** delicate, dainty, soft, faint, careful, sensitive, subtle. **6** *light entertainment* **undemanding,** middle-of-the-road, mainstream, lightweight, lowbrow, mass-market, superficial, frivolous, trivial.
– ANTONYMS heavy.

– DERIVATIVES **light·ish** adjective **light·ness** noun.
– PHRASES **make light of** treat something as unimportant. **make light work of** accomplish something quickly and easily.
– ORIGIN Old English.

light[3] ▶ **verb** (past and past part. **lit** /lit/ or **lighted**) (**light on**) come upon or discover someone or something by chance.
– ORIGIN Old English, 'descend, alight.'

light bulb ▶ **noun** a glass bulb containing inert gas, inserted into a lamp or ceiling socket, that provides light when an electric current is passed through it.

light cream ▶ **noun** thin cream with a relatively low fat content.

light·en[1] /ˈlītn/ ▶ **verb 1** make or become lighter in weight. **2** make or become less serious.

– SYNONYMS **1 reduce,** lessen, decrease, diminish, ease, alleviate, relieve. **2 cheer (up),** brighten, gladden, lift, boost, buoy (up), revive, restore, revitalize.
– ANTONYMS increase.

light·en[2] ▶ **verb** make or become brighter.

– SYNONYMS **1 brighten,** light up, illuminate, irradiate; literary illumine. **2 bleach,** whiten, blanch.
– ANTONYMS darken.

light·er[1] /ˈlītər/ ▶ **noun** a device producing a small flame, used to light cigarettes.

light·er[2] ▶ **noun** a flat-bottomed barge used to transfer goods to and from ships in harbor.
– ORIGIN from LIGHT[2] (in the sense 'unload'), or from German *luchter*.

light-fin·gered ▶ **adjective** informal prone to steal.

light-foot·ed ▶ **adjective** fast and nimble on one's feet.

light-head·ed /ˈlītˌhedid/ ▶ **adjective** dizzy and slightly faint.

– SYNONYMS **dizzy,** giddy, faint; informal woozy.

light·heart·ed /ˈlītˌhärtid/ ▶ **adjective 1** amusing and entertaining. **2** cheerful or carefree.

– SYNONYMS **carefree,** cheerful, cheery, happy, merry, glad, playful, blithe, bright, entertaining, amusing, diverting; informal upbeat; dated gay.
– ANTONYMS miserable.

– DERIVATIVES **light·heart·ed·ly** adverb.

light·house /ˈlītˌhous/ ▶ **noun** a tower or other structure containing a light to warn ships at sea.

light in·dus·try ▶ **noun** the manufacture of small or light articles.

light·ing /ˈlītiNG/ ▶ **noun 1** equipment for producing light. **2** the arrangement or effect of lights.

light·ly /ˈlītlē/ ▶ **adverb 1** with little force; gently. **2** to a slight extent or amount. **3** without sufficient care or thought.

– SYNONYMS **1** *Hermione kissed him lightly on the cheek* **softly,** gently, faintly, delicately. **2** *season very lightly with paprika* **sparingly,** sparsely, moderately, slightly, subtly. **3** *her views are not to be dismissed lightly* **carelessly,** airily, readily, heedlessly, uncaringly, unthinkingly, thoughtlessly, flippantly.

light me·ter ▶ **noun** an instrument measuring the intensity of light, used when taking photographs.

light·ning /ˈlītniNG/ ▶ **noun** a high-voltage electrical discharge between a cloud and the ground or within a cloud, accompanied by a bright flash. ▶ **adjective** very quick: *lightning speed.*
– ORIGIN from LIGHTEN[2].

USAGE

Do not confuse **lightning** with **lightening**. **Lightning** means 'a high-voltage electrical discharge and bright flash in the sky' (*thunder and lightning*) or *very quick,* whereas **lightening** is part of the verb **lighten** and means 'getting lighter' (*the sea was lightening from black to gray*).

light·ning bug ▶ **noun** another term for FIREFLY.

light·ning rod ▶ **noun** a metal rod or wire fixed in a high and exposed place to divert lightning into the ground.

light pen ▶ **noun 1** a hand-held penlike photosensitive device used for passing information to a computer. **2** a hand-held device for reading bar codes.

light pol·lu·tion ▶ **noun** excessive brightening of the night sky by street lights and other artificial sources.

light·ship /ˈlīt,SHip/ ▶ **noun** an anchored boat with a light to warn ships at sea.

light·weight /ˈlīt,wāt/ ▶ **noun 1** a weight in boxing and other sports between featherweight and welterweight. **2** informal a person of little importance. ▶ **adjective 1** of thin material or build. **2** lacking seriousness or importance: *lightweight magazine essays.*

– SYNONYMS **1 thin,** light, filmy, flimsy, insubstantial, summery. **2 trivial,** insubstantial, superficial, shallow, undemanding, frivolous.
– ANTONYMS heavy, serious.

light year ▶ **noun** Astronomy a unit of distance equivalent to the distance that light travels in one year, 9.4607×10^{12} km (nearly 6 trillion miles).

lig·ne·ous /ˈlignēəs/ ▶ **adjective** consisting of or resembling wood.
– ORIGIN Latin *ligneus* 'relating to wood.'

lig·nin /ˈlignin/ ▶ **noun** a complex organic substance found in the cell walls of many plants, making them rigid and woody.
– ORIGIN from Latin *lignum* 'wood.'

lig·nite /ˈlig,nīt/ ▶ **noun** a type of soft brownish coal.
– ORIGIN from Latin *lignum* 'wood.'

lik·a·ble /ˈlīkəbəl/ (also **likeable**) ▶ **adjective** pleasant; easy to like.

– SYNONYMS **pleasant,** friendly, agreeable, affable, amiable, genial, personable, nice, good-natured, engaging, appealing, endearing, convivial, congenial.
– ANTONYMS unpleasant.

– DERIVATIVES **lik·a·bly** /-blē/ adverb.

like[1] /līk/ ▶ **preposition 1** similar to. **2** in the same way as. **3** in a way appropriate to. **4** in this way. **5** such as. **6** used to ask about the nature of someone or something.

– SYNONYMS **1 similar to,** the same as, identical to, akin to, resembling. **2 in the manner of,** in the same way/manner as, in a similar way to. **3 such as,** for example, for instance, namely, in particular, viz. **4 characteristic of,** typical of, in character with.
– ANTONYMS unlike.

▶ **conjunction** informal **1** in the same way that. **2** as if.
▶ **noun 1** a similar person or thing. **2** (**the like**) things of the same kind.
▶ **adjective** having similar characteristics.
– PHRASES **like so** informal in this way.
– ORIGIN Old Norse.

USAGE

When writing formal English, do not use **like** to mean 'as if,' as in *he's behaving like he owns the place*; use **as if** or **as though** instead.

like[2] ▶ **verb 1** find someone or something pleasant or satisfactory. **2** wish for or want something.

– SYNONYMS **1 be fond of,** have a soft spot for, care about, think well/highly of, admire, respect; be attracted to, fancy, be keen on, be taken with; informal rate. **2 enjoy,** have a taste for, care for, be partial to, take pleasure in, be keen on, appreciate, love, adore, relish; informal have a thing about, be into, be mad about, be hooked on. **3** *feel free to say what you like* **choose,** please, wish, want, see/think fit, care to, will.
– ANTONYMS hate.

▶ **noun** (**likes**) the things one likes.
– ORIGIN Old English, 'be pleasing.'

like·li·hood /ˈlīklē,ho͝od/ ▶ **noun** the state or fact of being likely or probable.

– SYNONYMS **probability,** chance, prospect, possibility, odds, risk, threat, danger, hope, promise.

like·ly /ˈlīklē/ ▶ **adjective** (**likelier, likeliest**) **1** such as well might be the case; probable. **2** apparently suitable; promising.

– SYNONYMS **1 probable,** possible, odds-on, expected, anticipated; informal in the cards. **2 plausible,** reasonable, feasible, acceptable, believable, credible, tenable. **3 suitable,** promising, appropriate.
– ANTONYMS unlikely, implausible.

▶ **adverb** probably.
– PHRASES **a likely story!** used to express disbelief. **not likely!** informal certainly not.

like-mind·ed ▶ **adjective** having similar tastes or opinions.

lik·en /ˈlīkən/ ▶ **verb** (**liken someone/thing to**) point out that someone or something is similar to; compare: *he likened the election to a job interview.*

– SYNONYMS **compare,** equate, set beside.
– ANTONYMS contrast.

like·ness /ˈlīknis/ ▶ **noun 1** the fact of being alike; resemblance. **2** outward appearance: *humans are made in God's likeness.* **3** a portrait or other representation of a person.

– SYNONYMS **1 resemblance,** similarity, similitude, correspondence. **2 representation,** image, depiction, portrayal, picture, drawing, sketch, painting, portrait, photograph, study.
– ANTONYMS dissimilarity.

CHOOSE THE RIGHT WORD

likeness, affinity, analogy, resemblance, similarity, similitude
Two sisters who are only a year apart in age and who are very similar to each other in terms of appearance and personality would be said to bear a **likeness** to one another. **Similarity** applies to people or things that are merely somewhat alike (*there was a similarity between the two women, both of whom were raised in the Midwest*), while **resemblance** suggests a similarity only in appearance or in superficial or external ways (*with their short hair and blue eyes, they bore a strong resemblance to each other*). **Affinity** adds to *resemblance* a natural kinship, temperamental sympathy, common experience, or some other relationship (*she has an affinity for young children*). **Similitude** is a more literary word meaning *likeness* or *similarity* in reference to abstract things (*a similitude of the truth*). An **analogy** is a comparison of things that are basically unlike but share certain attributes or circumstances (*he drew an analogy between the human heart and a bicycle pump*).

like·wise /ˈlīkˌwīz/ ▶ **adverb 1** also; moreover. **2** in a similar way.
– SYNONYMS **1 also,** equally, in addition, too, as well, to boot, besides, moreover, furthermore. **2 the same,** similarly, correspondingly.

lik·ing /ˈlīkiNG/ ▶ **noun 1** a regard or fondness for someone or something. **2** a person's taste: *the coffee was just to his liking.*
– SYNONYMS **fondness,** love, affection, penchant, soft spot, attachment, taste, passion, preference, partiality, predilection, weakness.
– ANTONYMS dislike.

li·lac /ˈlīˌläk, -ˌlak, -lək/ ▶ **noun 1** a shrub or small tree with fragrant violet, pink, or white blossoms. **2** a pale pinkish-violet color.
– ORIGIN from Persian, 'bluish.'

Lil·li·pu·tian /ˌliləˈpyo͞oSHən/ ▶ **adjective** very small or unimportant. ▶ **noun** a very small or unimportant person or thing.
– ORIGIN from *Lilliput* in Jonathan Swift's *Gulliver's Travels*, a country inhabited by 6-inch-high people.

lilt /lilt/ ▶ **noun 1** a characteristic rising and falling of the voice when speaking. **2** a gentle rhythm in a tune. ▶ **verb** speak, sing, or sound with a lilt.
– ORIGIN unknown.

lil·y /ˈlilē/ ▶ **noun** (pl. **lilies**) a plant with large trumpet-shaped flowers on a tall, slender stem.
– ORIGIN Greek *leirion.*

lil·y-liv·ered ▶ **adjective** weak and cowardly.

lil·y of the val·ley ▶ **noun** a plant of the lily family, with broad leaves and small white bell-shaped flowers.

lil·y pad ▶ **noun** a leaf of a water lily.

lil·y-white ▶ **adjective 1** pure white. **2** totally innocent or pure.

li·ma bean /ˈlīmə/ ▶ **noun** an edible flat whitish bean.
– ORIGIN from *Lima*, the capital of Peru.

limb[1] /lim/ ▶ **noun 1** an arm, leg, or wing. **2** a large branch of a tree. **3** a projecting part of a structure, object, or natural feature.
– SYNONYMS **1 arm, leg,** wing, appendage; old use member. **2 branch,** bough.
– DERIVATIVES **limb·less** adjective.
– PHRASES **out on a limb** in a position where one is not supported by anyone else.
– ORIGIN Old English.

limb[2] ▶ **noun** Astronomy a specified edge of the disk of the sun, moon, or other celestial object.
– ORIGIN Latin *limbus* 'hem, border.'

lim·ber[1] /ˈlimbər/ ▶ **verb** (**limber up**) warm up in preparation for exercise or activity. ▶ **adjective** supple; flexible.
– ORIGIN perhaps from LIMBER[2] in the dialect sense 'cart shaft.'

CHOOSE THE RIGHT WORD

See FLEXIBLE.

lim·ber[2] ▶ **noun** the detachable front part of a gun carriage.
– ORIGIN probably related to Latin *limonarius.*

lim·bic sys·tem /ˈlimbik/ ▶ **noun** a complex system of nerves and networks in the brain, controlling the basic emotions and drives such as fear and hunger.
– ORIGIN from Latin *limbus* 'edge, border.'

lim·bo[1] /ˈlimbō/ ▶ **noun 1** (in some Christian beliefs) the place between heaven and hell where the souls of people who have not been baptized go when they die. **2** (pl. **limbos**) an uncertain period of waiting for a decision.
– ORIGIN from Latin *limbus* 'hem, border, limbo.'

lim·bo[2] ▶ **noun** (pl. **limbos**) a West Indian dance in which the dancer bends backward to pass under a horizontal bar that is progressively lowered toward the ground. ▶ **verb** (**limbos, limboing, limboed**) dance the limbo.
– ORIGIN from LIMBER[1].

lime[1] /līm/ ▶ **noun 1** a product obtained from burning chalk or limestone, used in agriculture to improve certain soils or in traditional building to make mortar and plaster. **2** any salt or alkali containing calcium. ▶ **verb** treat soil or water with lime.
– DERIVATIVES **lim·y** adjective.
– ORIGIN Old English.

lime[2] ▶ **noun 1** a rounded green citrus fruit similar to a lemon. **2** a bright light green color. **3** a drink made from lime juice.
– ORIGIN French.

lime[3] (also **lime tree**) ▶ **noun** a deciduous tree with heart-shaped leaves and yellowish blossoms.
– ORIGIN Old English.

lime·ade /ˌlīmˈād, ˈlīmˌād/ ▶ **noun** a drink made from lime juice sweetened with sugar.

lime·kiln /ˈlīmˌkil(n)/ ▶ **noun** a kiln for burning limestone to produce quicklime.

lime·light /ˈlīmˌlīt/ ▶ **noun 1** (**the limelight**) the focus of public attention. **2** an intense white light produced by heating lime, formerly used in theaters.
– SYNONYMS **attention,** interest, scrutiny, the public eye, publicity, prominence, the spotlight, fame, celebrity.
– ANTONYMS obscurity.

lim·er·ick /ˈlim(ə)rik/ ▶ **noun** a humorous five-line poem with a rhyme scheme *aabba*.
– ORIGIN said to be from the chorus 'will you come up to Limerick?', sung between improvised verses at a party.

lime·stone /ˈlīmˌstōn/ ▶ **noun** a hard sedimentary rock composed mainly of calcium carbonate.

Lim·ey /ˈlīmē/ ▶ **noun** (pl. **Limeys**) informal, often derogatory a British person.
– ORIGIN from the former practice of giving lime juice to sailors in the British navy.

lim·i·nal /ˈlimənl/ ▶ **adjective** technical **1** relating to a transitional or initial stage. **2** at or on a boundary or threshold.
– DERIVATIVES **lim·i·nal·i·ty** /ˌliməˈnalətē/ noun.
– ORIGIN from Latin *limen* 'threshold.'

lim·it /ˈlimit/ ▶ **noun 1** a point beyond which something does not or may not pass. **2** a restriction on the size or amount of something that is allowed or possible: *an age limit*. **3** the furthest extent of one's endurance.

– SYNONYMS **1 boundary (line),** border, frontier, bound, edge, perimeter, margin. **2 maximum,** ceiling, cap, cutoff point.

▶ **verb** (**limits**, **limiting**, **limited**) set a limit on; restrict: *try to limit the amount you drink*.

– SYNONYMS **restrict,** curb, cap, (hold in) check, restrain, circumscribe, regulate, control, govern, ration.

– DERIVATIVES **lim·it·er** noun.
– PHRASES **be the limit** informal be very annoying. **off limits** out of bounds. **within limits** up to a point.
– ORIGIN Latin *limes* 'boundary, frontier.'

lim·i·ta·tion /ˌliməˈtāshən/ ▶ **noun 1** a rule or condition that limits someone or something; a restriction. **2** a fault or failing. **3** the act of limiting something.

– SYNONYMS **1 restriction,** curb, restraint, control, check. **2 imperfection,** flaw, defect, failing, shortcoming, weak point, deficiency, frailty, weakness.
– ANTONYMS strength.

lim·it·ed /ˈlimitid/ ▶ **adjective 1** restricted in size, amount, extent, or ability. **2** (of a monarchy or government) operating under limitations of power set down in a constitution.

– SYNONYMS **restricted,** circumscribed, finite, small, tight, slight, in short supply, short, meager, scanty, sparse, inadequate, insufficient, paltry, poor, minimal.
– ANTONYMS limitless, ample.

lim·it·ed li·a·bi·li·ty ▶ **noun** the condition of being legally responsible for the debts of a company only to the extent of the value of one's shares when they were issued.

lim·it·less /ˈlimitlis/ ▶ **adjective** without a limit; very large or extensive: *limitless possibilities*.
– DERIVATIVES **lim·it·less·ly** adverb **lim·it·less·ness** noun.

limn /lim/ ▶ **verb** literary depict or describe someone or something in painting or words.
– DERIVATIVES **lim·ner** /ˈlim(n)ər/ noun.
– ORIGIN Latin *luminare* 'make light.'

lim·o /ˈlimō/ ▶ **noun** (pl. **limos**) informal a limousine.

lim·ou·sine /ˈliməˌzēn, ˌliməˈzēn/ ▶ **noun** a large, luxurious car.
– ORIGIN French, first referring to a caped cloak worn in the region of *Limousin*; the car originally had an outside driving compartment, covered with a canopy.

limp¹ /limp/ ▶ **verb 1** walk with difficulty because of an injured leg or foot. **2** (of a damaged ship or aircraft) move with difficulty.

– SYNONYMS **hobble,** hop, lurch, stagger, shuffle, totter, shamble.

▶ **noun** a walk hampered by an injury.
– ORIGIN related to former *limphalt* 'lame.'

limp² ▶ **adjective 1** not stiff or firm. **2** lacking energy or vigor.

– SYNONYMS **soft,** flaccid, loose, slack, lax, floppy, drooping, droopy, sagging.
– ANTONYMS firm.

– DERIVATIVES **limp·ly** adverb **limp·ness** noun.
– ORIGIN perhaps related to **LIMP¹**.

lim·pet /ˈlimpit/ ▶ **noun** a marine shellfish with a conical shell and a muscular foot for clinging tightly to rocks.
– ORIGIN Latin *lampreda* 'limpet, lamprey.'

lim·pet mine ▶ **noun** a mine that attaches magnetically to a ship's hull and explodes after a certain time.

lim·pid /ˈlimpid/ ▶ **adjective 1** (of a liquid or the eyes) clear. **2** (especially of writing or music) clear or melodious.

– SYNONYMS **1** *a limpid pool* **clear,** transparent, glassy, crystal clear, translucent, unclouded. **2** *his limpid prose style* **lucid,** clear, transparent, plain, unambiguous, simple; accessible.
– ANTONYMS opaque.

– DERIVATIVES **lim·pid·i·ty** /limˈpidətē/ noun **lim·pid·ly** adverb.
– ORIGIN Latin *limpidus*.

limp-wrist·ed ▶ **adjective** informal weak, feeble, or effeminate.

linch·pin /ˈlinchˌpin/ (also **lynchpin**) ▶ **noun 1** a vital or essential person or thing. **2** a pin through the end of an axle to keep a wheel in position.
– ORIGIN Old English.

lin·dane /ˈlinˌdān/ ▶ **noun** a synthetic insecticide, now restricted in use due to its persistence in the environment.
– ORIGIN named after the Dutch chemist Teunis van der *Linden*.

lin·den /ˈlindən/ ▶ **noun** a basswood or lime tree.
– ORIGIN Old English.

line¹ /līn/ ▶ **noun 1** a long, narrow mark or band. **2** a row or series of people or things. **3** a row of written or printed words. **4** a wrinkle in the skin. **5** a direction, course, or channel. **6** a limit or boundary: *the issue cut across class lines*. **7** a shape or outline. **8** a length of cord, wire, etc. **9** a telephone connection. **10** a railroad track or route. **11** a range of products. **12** an area of activity: *the stresses unique to their line of work*. **13** a connected series of military defenses facing an enemy force. **14** (also **line of battle**) an arrangement of troops for action in battle. **15** informal a remark intended to achieve a purpose: *he saved his best lines for single women*. **16** (**lines**) the words of an actor's part.

– SYNONYMS **1** *he drew a line through the name* **stroke,** dash, score, underline, underscore, slash, stripe, strip, band, belt. **2** *they waited in a line* **file,** rank, column, string, train, procession, row, queue. **3** *the opening line of the poem* **sentence,** phrase, clause, utterance; passage, extract, quotation, quote, citation. **4** *there were lines around her eyes* wrinkle, furrow, crease, crinkle, crow's foot. **5** *a line of flight* **course,** route, track, path. **6** *the county line* **boundary,** limit, border, frontier, touchline, margin, perimeter. **7** *the classic lines of the sports car* **contour,** outline, configuration, shape, design, profile, silhouette. **8** **cord,** rope, cable, wire, thread, string. **9** *a new line of cologne* **brand,** kind, sort, type, variety, make. **10** *my line is engineering* **line of work,** business, field, specialty, forte, province, department, sphere, area, area of expertise.

▶ **verb 1** stand or be positioned at intervals along a route. **2** (**line someone/thing up**) arrange people or things in a row. **3** (**line someone/thing up**) have someone or something prepared. **4** (as adj. **lined**) marked or covered with lines.

– SYNONYMS **1** *the driveway was lined by poplars* **border,** edge, fringe, bound. **2** (**line someone/thing up**) *we've **lined up** an all-star cast* **assemble,** get together, organize, prepare, arrange, fix up, book, schedule. **3** (as adj. **lined**) *lined paper* **ruled,** feint, striped, banded. **4** (as adj. **lined**) *a thin woman with a lined face* **wrinkled,** wrinkly, furrowed, wizened.

– PHRASES **come** (or **bring**) **into line** conform (or cause to conform) with something. **in line** under control. **in line for** likely to receive something. **in** (or **out of**) **line with** in (or not in) alignment or accordance with something. **lay it on the line** speak frankly. **line of fire** the expected path of gunfire or a missile. **on the line** at serious risk. **out of line** informal behaving inappropriately or badly.

– ORIGIN Old English; later influenced by Old French *ligne*.

line² ▶ **verb** cover the inner surface of something with a layer of different material.

– PHRASES **line one's pocket** make money, especially by dishonest means.

– ORIGIN from former *line* 'flax,' with reference to the use of linen for linings.

lin·e·age /ˈlinē-ij/ ▶ **noun** a person's ancestry or pedigree.

– SYNONYMS **ancestry,** family, parentage, birth, descent, extraction, genealogy, roots, origins.

lin·e·al /ˈlinēəl/ ▶ **adjective 1** in a direct line of descent or ancestry. **2** consisting of lines; linear.

– DERIVATIVES **lin·e·al·ly** adverb.

lin·e·a·ment /ˈlin(ē)əmənt/ ▶ **noun** (usu. **lineaments**) literary a distinctive feature of the face.

– ORIGIN Latin *lineamentum*.

lin·e·ar /ˈlinēər/ ▶ **adjective 1** arranged in or extending along a straight line. **2** consisting of lines. **3** progressing in a series of stages: *a linear narrative*. **4** involving one dimension only. **5** Mathematics able to be represented by a straight line on a graph.

– DERIVATIVES **lin·e·ar·i·ty** /ˌlinēˈaritē/ noun **lin·e·ar·ly** adverb.

lin·e·ar e·qua·tion ▶ **noun** an equation between two variables that gives a straight line when plotted on a graph.

lin·e·a·tion /ˌlinēˈāsʜən/ ▶ **noun 1** a line or linear marking. **2** the action of drawing lines or marking with lines.

line·back·er /ˈlīnˌbakər/ ▶ **noun** Football a defensive player normally positioned behind the line of scrimmage, but in front of the safeties.

line danc·ing ▶ **noun** a type of country and western dancing in which a line of dancers follow a choreographed pattern of steps.

– DERIVATIVES **line dance** noun **line danc·er** noun.

line draw·ing ▶ **noun** a drawing based on the use of line rather than shading.

line drive ▶ **noun** Baseball a powerfully hit ball that travels in the air and relatively close to and parallel with the ground.

line·man /ˈlīnmən/ ▶ **noun** (pl. **linemen**) **1** a person employed to lay and maintain railroad tracks. **2** a person employed to repair and maintain telephone or power lines. **3** Football a player normally positioned on the line of scrimmage.

line man·ag·er ▶ **noun** chiefly Brit. a manager to whom an employee is directly responsible.

– DERIVATIVES **line man·age·ment** noun.

lin·en /ˈlinin/ ▶ **noun 1** cloth woven from flax. **2** articles such as sheets or clothes that were traditionally made of linen.

– ORIGIN Old English.

line-out ▶ **noun** an electrical connection that carries output from a video or audio device.

lin·er¹ /ˈlīnər/ ▶ **noun 1** a large passenger ship. **2** a cosmetic for outlining or accentuating the eyes or lips.

– ORIGIN sense 1 is so named because such a ship traveled on a regular line or route.

lin·er² ▶ **noun** a lining of a garment, container, etc.

lin·er note ▶ **noun** (usu. **liner notes**) the printed text supplied with a compact disc or on the sleeve of a phonograph record.

lines·man /ˈlīnzmən/ ▶ **noun** (pl. **linesmen**) (in sports) an official who assists the referee or umpire in deciding whether the ball is out of play.

line·up /ˈlīnˌəp/ ▶ **noun 1** a group of people or things assembled for a purpose. **2** the schedule of television programs for a particular period. **3** a group of people assembled so that an eyewitness may identify a suspect for a crime from among them.

– SYNONYMS **1** **roster,** team, squad, side, configuration. **2** **cast,** bill, program.

lin·gam /ˈlinɢgəm/ ▶ **noun** Hinduism a phallus or phallic object as a symbol of Shiva, the god of reproduction.

– ORIGIN Sanskrit, 'mark, sexual characteristic.'

lin·ger /ˈlinɢgər/ ▶ **verb 1** be slow or reluctant to leave. **2** (**linger over**) spend a long time over something. **3** be slow to fade, disappear, or die: *the tradition seems to linger on*.

– SYNONYMS **1** **wait (around),** stand (around), remain, loiter; informal stick around, hang around. **2** **persist,** continue, remain, stay, endure, carry on, last.

– DERIVATIVES **lin·ger·er** noun.

– ORIGIN Germanic.

lin·ge·rie /ˌlänzʜəˈrā, -jə-/ ▶ **noun** women's underwear and nightclothes.

– ORIGIN French.

lin·go /ˈlinɢgō/ ▶ **noun** (pl. **lingos** or **lingoes**) informal **1** a foreign language. **2** the jargon of a particular subject or group.

– ORIGIN probably from Latin *lingua* 'tongue.'

lin·gua fran·ca /ˈlinɢgwə ˈfranɢkə/ ▶ **noun** (pl. **lingua francas**) a language used as a common language between speakers whose native languages are different.

– ORIGIN Italian, 'Frankish tongue.'

lin·gual /ˈlinɢgwəl/ ▶ **adjective** technical **1** relating to the tongue. **2** relating to speech or language.

– DERIVATIVES **lin·gual·ly** adverb.
– ORIGIN Latin *lingualis*.

lin·gui·ne /liNG'gwēnē/ ▶ **plural noun** small ribbons of pasta.
– ORIGIN Italian, 'little tongues.'

lin·guist /'liNGgwist/ ▶ **noun 1** a person skilled in foreign languages. **2** a person who studies linguistics.
– ORIGIN from Latin *lingua* 'language.'

lin·guis·tic /liNG'gwistik/ ▶ **adjective** relating to language or linguistics.
– DERIVATIVES **lin·guis·ti·cal·ly** / -tik(ə)lē/ adverb.

lin·guis·tics /liNG'gwistiks/ ▶ **plural noun** (treated as sing.) the scientific study of language and its structure.

lin·i·ment /'linəmənt/ ▶ **noun** an ointment rubbed on the body to relieve pain or bruising.
– ORIGIN Latin *linimentum*.

lin·ing /'līniNG/ ▶ **noun** a layer of different material covering or attached to the inside of something.

– SYNONYMS **backing,** facing, padding, insulation.

link /liNGk/ ▶ **noun 1** a relationship or connection between people or things. **2** something that enables people to communicate with each other. **3** a means of contact or transport between two places. **4** a code or instruction connecting one part of a computer program, website, etc., to another. **5** a loop in a chain.

– SYNONYMS **connection,** relationship, association, linkage, tie-up, tie, bond, attachment, affiliation.

▶ **verb** make, form, or suggest a link with or between: *a network of routes linking towns and villages.*

– SYNONYMS **1 join,** connect, fasten, attach, bind, secure, fix, tie, couple, yoke. **2** *the evidence linking him with the body* **associate,** connect, relate, bracket.
– ANTONYMS separate.

– DERIVATIVES **link·er** noun.
– ORIGIN Old Norse.

link·age /'liNGkij/ ▶ **noun 1** the action of linking people or things. **2** a system of links.

links /liNGks/ (also **golf links**) ▶ **plural noun** (treated as sing. or pl.) a golf course.
– ORIGIN Old English, 'rising ground.'

link·up /'liNGk,əp/ ▶ **noun 1** an instance of people or things linking. **2** a connection enabling people or machines to communicate with each other.

Lin·nae·an /li'nēən, -'nāən/ (also **Linnean**) ▶ **adjective** relating to the Swedish botanist Linnaeus (Latinized name of Carl von Linné) or his classification of animals and plants.

lin·net /'linit/ ▶ **noun** a mainly brown and gray finch with a reddish breast and forehead.
– ORIGIN from Old French *lin* 'flax' (because the bird feeds on flaxseeds).

li·no·cut /'līnō,kət/ ▶ **noun** a design carved in relief on a block of linoleum, used for printing.

lin·o·le·ic ac·id /,linə'lēik, -'lā-, lə'nōlēik/ ▶ **noun** a polyunsaturated fatty acid present in linseed oil and other oils and essential in the diet.
– ORIGIN from Latin *linum* 'flax.'

li·no·le·um /lə'nōlēəm/ ▶ **noun** a floor covering consisting of a canvas backing thickly coated with a preparation of linseed oil and powdered cork.
– ORIGIN from Latin *linum* 'flax' + *oleum* 'oil.'

lin·seed /'lin,sēd/ ▶ **noun** the seeds of the flax plant.
– ORIGIN Old English.

lin·seed oil ▶ **noun** oil extracted from linseed, used especially in paint and varnish.

lint /lint/ ▶ **noun 1** short, fine fibers that separate from cloth or yarn during processing. **2** a fabric with a raised nap on one side, used for dressing wounds.
– DERIVATIVES **lint·y** adjective.
– ORIGIN perhaps from Old French *linette* 'linseed.'

lin·tel /'lintl/ ▶ **noun** a horizontal support across the top of a door or window.
– DERIVATIVES **lin·teled** adjective.
– ORIGIN Old French.

Lin·ux /'linəks/ ▶ **noun** trademark an open-source version of the UNIX computer operating system.

li·on /'līən/ ▶ **noun** (fem. **lioness**) **1** a large tawny cat of Africa and NW India, the male of which has a shaggy mane. **2** a brave, strong, or fierce person. **3** (also **literary lion**) a famous author.
– PHRASES **the lion's share** the largest part of something.
– ORIGIN Greek *leōn*.

WORD LINKS

leonine *relating to lions*

li·on·heart·ed /'līən,härtid/ ▶ **adjective** brave and determined.

li·on·ize /'līə,nīz/ ▶ **verb** treat someone as a celebrity.
– DERIVATIVES **li·on·i·za·tion** /,līənə'zāSHən/ noun.

lip /lip/ ▶ **noun 1** either of the two fleshy parts forming the edges of the mouth opening. **2** the edge of a hollow container or an opening. **3** informal disrespectful talk.

– SYNONYMS **edge,** rim, brim, border, verge, brink.

– DERIVATIVES **lip·less** adjective **lipped** adjective.
– PHRASES **bite one's lip** stop oneself from saying something or laughing. **pass one's lips** be eaten, drunk, or spoken. **pay lip service to** express superficial respect or support for something.
– ORIGIN Old English.

li·pase /'lip,ās, 'lī,pās/ ▶ **noun** an enzyme produced by the pancreas that promotes the breakdown of fats.
– ORIGIN from Greek *lipos* 'fat.'

lip balm ▶ **noun** a preparation to prevent or relieve sore or chapped lips.

lip·gloss /'lip,gläs, -,glôs/ (also **lip gloss**) ▶ **noun** a glossy cosmetic applied to the lips.

lip·id /'lipid/ ▶ **noun** any of a class of fats that are insoluble in water and include many natural oils, waxes, and steroids.
– ORIGIN from Greek *lipos* 'fat.'

lip·o·pro·tein /,lipə'prō,tēn, ,lī-/ ▶ **noun** a soluble protein that transports lipids (a type of fat) in the blood.

lip·o·some /'lipə,sōm, 'lī-/ ▶ **noun** a tiny artificial container of insoluble fat enclosing a water droplet, used to carry drugs into body tissues.
– ORIGIN from Greek *lipos* 'fat' + *sōma* 'body.'

lip·o·suc·tion /'lipō,səkSHən, 'lī-/ ▶ **noun** a technique in cosmetic surgery for removing excess fat from under the skin by suction.

lip·py /'lipē/ informal ▶ **adjective** (**lippier, lippiest**) disrespectful; impertinent.

lip-read /,rēd/ ▶ **verb** understand speech from watching a speaker's lip movements.
– DERIVATIVES **lip-read·er** noun.

lip·stick /ˈlipˌstik/ ▶ **noun** colored cosmetic applied to the lips from a small solid stick.

lip-sync /ˌsiNGk/ (also **lip-synch**) ▶ **verb** (of an actor or singer) move the lips silently in time to prerecorded music or speech.

liq·ue·fy /ˈlikwəˌfī/ ▶ **verb** (**liquefies, liquefying, liquefied**) make or become liquid.
– DERIVATIVES **liq·ue·fac·tion** /ˌlikwəˈfaksHən/ noun.
– ORIGIN Latin *liquefacere*.

li·queur /liˈkər, -ˈk(y)o͝or/ ▶ **noun** a strong, sweet flavored alcoholic liquor.
– ORIGIN French.

liq·uid /ˈlikwid/ ▶ **noun** a substance that flows freely but remains at constant volume, such as water or oil.

– SYNONYMS **fluid,** moisture, solution, liquor, juice, sap.

▶ **adjective 1** relating to or in the form of a liquid. **2** clear, like water: *liquid dark eyes*. **3** (of a sound) pure and flowing. **4** (of assets) held in or easily converted into cash.

– SYNONYMS **fluid,** liquefied, melted, molten, thawed, dissolved, runny.
– ANTONYMS solid.

– DERIVATIVES **liq·uid·ly** adverb **liq·uid·ness** noun.
– ORIGIN Latin *liquidus*.

liq·ui·date /ˈlikwəˌdāt/ ▶ **verb 1** close a business and sell what it owns in order to pay its debts. **2** sell something in order to get money. **3** pay off a debt. **4** informal kill someone.
– DERIVATIVES **liq·ui·da·tion** /ˌlikwəˈdāsHən/ noun **liq·ui·da·tor** noun.
– ORIGIN Latin *liquidare* 'make clear.'

liq·uid crys·tal dis·play ▶ **noun** an electronic visual display in which the application of an electric current to a liquid crystal layer makes it opaque.

liq·uid·i·ty /liˈkwidətē/ ▶ **noun** the availability of liquid assets to a market or company.

liq·ui·fy /ˈlikwəˌfī/ ▶ **verb** variant spelling of LIQUEFY.

liq·uor /ˈlikər/ ▶ **noun 1** alcoholic drink, especially distilled spirits. **2** liquid that has been produced in or used for cooking.

– SYNONYMS **1 alcohol,** spirits, drink; informal booze, the hard stuff, hooch, moonshine. **2 stock,** broth, bouillon, juice, liquid.

– ORIGIN Latin.

li·ra /ˈli(ə)rə/ ▶ **noun 1** (pl. **lire** /ˈli(ə)rā, -rə/) (until the introduction of the euro in 2002) the basic monetary unit of Italy. **2** (pl. **lira**) the basic unit of money of Turkey.
– ORIGIN Italian.

-lish ▶ **suffix** forming nouns referring to a blend of a language with English, as used by native speakers of the first language: *Spanglish*.

lisle /līl/ ▶ **noun** a fine, smooth cotton thread formerly used for stockings.
– ORIGIN from *Lisle*, former spelling of the French city *Lille*.

lisp /lisp/ ▶ **noun** a speech defect in which *s* is pronounced like *th* in *thick* and *z* is pronounced like *th* in *this*. ▶ **verb** speak with a lisp.
– DERIVATIVES **lisp·er** noun.
– ORIGIN Old English.

lis·some /ˈlisəm/ (also **lissom**) ▶ **adjective** slim, supple, and graceful.
– DERIVATIVES **lis·some·ness** noun.
– ORIGIN from LITHE + *-some* 'characterized by being.'

list[1] /list/ ▶ **noun 1** a number of connected items or names written one below or one after the other. **2** a selvage of a piece of fabric. **3** (**lists**) historical a fence of stakes enclosing an area for a tournament.

– SYNONYMS **catalog,** inventory, record, register, roll, file, index, directory, checklist.

▶ **verb 1** make a list of people or things. **2** include someone or something in a list.

– SYNONYMS **record,** register, enter, itemize, enumerate, catalog, file, log, minute, categorize, inventory, classify, group, sort, rank, index.

– PHRASES **enter the lists** issue or accept a challenge.
– ORIGIN sense 1 of the noun from French *liste*; sense 2 from Old English; sense 3 from Old French *lisse*.

list[2] ▶ **verb** (of a ship) lean over to one side.

– SYNONYMS **lean (over),** tilt, tip, heel (over), pitch, incline, slant, slope, bank, careen, cant.

▶ **noun** an instance of leaning to one side.
– ORIGIN unknown.

lis·ten /ˈlisən/ ▶ **verb 1** give one's attention to a sound. **2** (**listen for** or **listen out for**) make an effort to hear something. **3** (**listen in**) listen to a private conversation. **4** respond to advice or a request: *politicians should listen to popular opinion*.

– SYNONYMS **1 pay attention,** be attentive, attend, concentrate, keep one's ears open, prick up one's ears; informal be all ears. **2 heed,** take heed of, take notice/note of, bear in mind, take into consideration/account.

▶ **noun** an act of listening.
– DERIVATIVES **lis·ten·er** noun.
– ORIGIN Old English, 'pay attention to.'

lis·ten·a·ble /ˈlisənəbəl/ ▶ **adjective** easy or pleasant to listen to.
– DERIVATIVES **lis·ten·a·bil·i·ty** /ˌlis(ə)nəˈbilitē/ noun.

lis·ten·ing post ▶ **noun** a station for intercepting electronic communications.

lis·te·ri·a /liˈstirēə/ ▶ **noun** a type of bacterium that infects humans and other animals through contaminated food.
– ORIGIN named after the English surgeon Joseph *Lister*.

lis·te·ri·o·sis /liˌsti(ə)rēˈōsis/ ▶ **noun** disease caused by infection with listeria, which can resemble influenza or meningitis and may cause miscarriage.

list·ing /ˈlistiNG/ ▶ **noun 1** a list or catalog. **2** an entry in a list.

list·less /ˈlis(t)lis/ ▶ **adjective** lacking energy or enthusiasm.

– SYNONYMS **lethargic,** lifeless, enervated, languid, inactive, inert, sluggish, apathetic, passive, supine, indifferent, uninterested, impassive.
– ANTONYMS energetic.

– DERIVATIVES **list·less·ly** adverb **list·less·ness** noun.

list price ▶ **noun** the price of an article as listed by the manufacturer.

lit[1] /lit/ past and past participle of LIGHT[1], LIGHT[3].

lit[2] ▶ **noun** short for LITERATURE: *chick lit*.

lit·a·ny /ˈlitn-ē/ ▶ **noun** (pl. **litanies**) **1** a series of prayers in church services, usually recited by the clergy and responded to by the people. **2** a long and boring list of

complaints, reasons, etc.
– ORIGIN Greek *litaneia* 'prayer.'

li·tchi /ˈlēCHē/ ▶ **noun** variant spelling of LYCHEE.

lite /līt/ ▶ **adjective 1** relating to low-fat or low-sugar versions of food or drink products. **2** (often in combination) informal referring to a simplified or less challenging version of something: *schmaltzy reggae-lite*.
– ORIGIN respelling of LIGHT².

li·ter /ˈlētər/ (Brit. **litre**) ▶ **noun** a metric unit of capacity equal to 1,000 cubic centimeters (about 2.1 pints).
– ORIGIN from French *litre*, from Greek *litra*, a Sicilian unit of money.

lit·er·a·cy /ˈlit(ə)rəsē/ ▶ **noun 1** the ability to read and write. **2** ability or knowledge in a particular area: *computer literacy*.

lit·er·al /ˈlit(ə)rəl/ ▶ **adjective 1** using or interpreting words in their usual or most basic sense. **2** (of a translation) representing the exact words of the original text. **3** informal absolute (used for emphasis): *fifteen years of literal hell*.

> – SYNONYMS **1 strict,** technical, original, true. **2 word for word,** verbatim, exact, accurate, faithful.
> – ANTONYMS figurative.

▶ **noun** Brit. a misprint of a letter.
– DERIVATIVES **lit·er·al·ness** noun.
– ORIGIN Latin *litera* 'letter of the alphabet.'

lit·er·al·ism /ˈlit(ə)rəˌlizəm/ ▶ **noun** the interpretation of words in their usual or most basic sense.
– DERIVATIVES **lit·er·al·ist** noun **lit·er·al·is·tic** /ˌlit(ə)rəˈlistik/ adjective.

lit·er·al·ly /ˈlit(ə)rəlē/ ▶ **adverb 1** in a literal way or sense. **2** informal used for emphasis rather than being actually true: *we were literally killing ourselves laughing*.

lit·er·ar·y /ˈlitəˌrerē/ ▶ **adjective 1** concerning the writing, study, or content of literature. **2** (of language) typical of or suitable for works of literature or formal writing.

> – SYNONYMS **1 artistic,** poetic, dramatic. **2 scholarly,** intellectual, academic, bookish, erudite, well read, cultured.

– DERIVATIVES **lit·er·ar·i·ness** noun.
– ORIGIN Latin *litera* 'letter of the alphabet.'

lit·er·ar·y crit·i·cism ▶ **noun** the art or practice of judging the qualities and character of works of literature.

lit·er·ate /ˈlitərit/ ▶ **adjective 1** able to read and write. **2** knowledgeable in a particular field: *computer literate*.

> – SYNONYMS **(well) educated,** well read, widely read, scholarly, learned, knowledgeable, cultured, cultivated.
> – ANTONYMS ignorant.

lit·er·a·ti /ˌlitəˈrätē/ ▶ **plural noun** educated people who are interested in literature.
– ORIGIN Latin.

lit·er·a·ture /ˈlit(ə)rəCHər, -ˌCHo͝or, -ˌt(y)o͝or/ ▶ **noun 1** written works such as novels, plays, and poems that are regarded as having artistic merit. **2** books and writings on a particular subject. **3** leaflets and other material giving information or advice.

> – SYNONYMS **1 writing,** poetry, drama, plays, prose. **2 publications,** reports, studies, material, documentation, leaflets, pamphlets, brochures, handouts, publicity, advertising.

lithe /līTH/ ▶ **adjective** slim, supple, and graceful.

> – SYNONYMS **agile,** graceful, supple, flexible, lissome, loose-limbed, nimble.
> – ANTONYMS clumsy.

– DERIVATIVES **lithe·ly** adverb **lithe·ness** noun.
– ORIGIN Old English, 'gentle, meek, mellow.'

lith·i·um /ˈliTHēəm/ ▶ **noun 1** a light, soft, silver-white metallic chemical element. **2** a lithium salt used as a drug in the treatment of bipolar disorder or depression.
– ORIGIN from Greek *lithos* 'stone.'

lith·o /ˈliTHō/ informal ▶ **noun** (pl. **lithos**) short for LITHOGRAPHY or LITHOGRAPH. ▶ **adjective** short for LITHOGRAPHIC. ▶ **verb** (**lithoes, lithoing, lithoed**) short for LITHOGRAPH.

lith·o·graph /ˈliTHəˌgraf/ ▶ **noun** a print made by lithography. ▶ **verb** print text or pictures by lithography.
– DERIVATIVES **lith·o·graph·ic** /ˌliTHəˈgrafik/ adjective.

li·thog·ra·phy /liˈTHägrəfē/ ▶ **noun** the process of printing from a flat metal (formerly stone) surface treated so as to repel the ink except where it is required for printing.
– DERIVATIVES **li·thog·ra·pher** noun.
– ORIGIN Greek *lithos* 'stone.'

li·thol·o·gy /liˈTHäləjē/ ▶ **noun** the study of the physical characteristics of rocks.
– DERIVATIVES **lith·o·log·i·cal** /ˌliTHəˈläjikəl/ adjective.

lith·o·sphere /ˈliTHəˌsfi(ə)r/ ▶ **noun** the rigid outer part of the earth, consisting of the crust and upper mantle.
– DERIVATIVES **lith·o·spher·ic** /ˌliTHəˈsferik, -ˈsfi(ə)r-/ adjective.

Lith·u·a·ni·an /ˌliTHəˈwānēən/ ▶ **noun 1** a person from Lithuania. **2** the language of Lithuania. ▶ **adjective** relating to Lithuania.

lit·i·gant /ˈlitəgənt/ ▶ **noun** a person involved in a dispute or claim being heard in a court of law.

lit·i·gate /ˈlitəˌgāt/ ▶ **verb** take a dispute or claim to a court of law.
– DERIVATIVES **lit·i·ga·tor** noun.
– ORIGIN Latin *litigare*.

lit·i·ga·tion /ˌlitəˈgāSHən/ ▶ **noun** the action or process of taking a dispute or claim to a court of law.

> – SYNONYMS **legal proceedings,** legal action, case, lawsuit, suit, prosecution, indictment.

li·ti·gious /ləˈtijəs/ ▶ **adjective** having a tendency to take legal action to settle disputes.
– DERIVATIVES **li·ti·gious·ness** noun.

lit·mus /ˈlitməs/ ▶ **noun** a dye obtained from certain lichens that is red under acid conditions and blue under alkaline conditions.
– ORIGIN from Old Norse words meaning 'dye' and 'moss.'

lit·mus pa·per ▶ **noun** paper stained with litmus, used as a test for acids or alkalis.

lit·mus test ▶ **noun** a reliable test of the truth or value of something.

li·to·tes /ˈlītəˌtēz, ˈlit-, līˈtōtēz/ ▶ **noun** ironical understatement in which something is expressed by the negative of its opposite (e.g., *I'm not unhappy about that* for *I'm happy about that*).
– ORIGIN Greek.

li·tre ▶ **noun** British spelling of LITER.

LittD ▶ **abbreviation** Doctor of Letters.
– ORIGIN from Latin *Litterarum Doctor*.

lit·ter /ˈlitər/ ▶ **noun 1** small items of trash left lying in a public place. **2** an untidy collection of things. **3** a number of young born to an animal at one time. **4** (also **cat litter**) absorbent material lining a tray where a cat can urinate and defecate indoors. **5** straw or other plant matter used as animal bedding. **6** (also **leaf litter**) decomposing leaves and other matter forming a layer on top of soil. **7** historical a vehicle containing a bed or seat enclosed by curtains and carried by men or animals. **8** a stretcher for carrying a sick or wounded person.

– SYNONYMS **trash,** rubbish, garbage, refuse, junk, waste, debris, detritus.

▶ **verb** make a place or area untidy with scattered articles: *clothes and newspapers littered the floor.*

– SYNONYMS **clutter up,** mess up, be scattered about/around, be strewn about/around.

– ORIGIN Old French *litiere,* from Latin *lectus* 'bed.'

lit·ter·bug /ˈlitərˌbəg/ ▶ **noun** informal a person who carelessly drops litter in public places.

lit·tle /ˈlitl/ ▶ **adjective 1** small in size, amount, or degree. **2** (of a person) young or younger. **3** short in time or distance. **4** relatively unimportant.

– SYNONYMS **1** *a little writing desk* **small,** compact, miniature, tiny, minute, minuscule, toy, baby, undersized, dwarf, midget; Scottish wee; informal teeny-weeny, teensy-weensy, vest-pocket. **2** *a little man* **short,** small, slight, petite, diminutive, tiny, elfin; Scottish wee; informal pint-sized. **3** *my little brother* **young,** younger, baby. **4** *I was a bodyguard for a little while* **brief,** short, quick, hasty, cursory. **5** *a few little problems* **minor,** unimportant, insignificant, trivial, trifling, petty, paltry, inconsequential, negligible.
– ANTONYMS big, large, elder, major.

▶ **determiner & pronoun 1** (**a little**) a small amount of something. **2** (**a little**) a short time or distance. **3** not much.

– SYNONYMS **1** (**a little**) *add a little vinegar* **some,** a bit of, a touch of, a dash of, a taste of, a spot of, a hint of, a dribble of, a splash of, a pinch of, a sprinkling of, a speck of; informal a smidgen of, a tad of. **2** (**a little**) *after a little, Oliver came in* **a short time,** a while, a bit, an interval, a short period, a minute, a moment, a second, an instant; informal a sec, a jiffy.

▶ **adverb** (**less, least**) **1** (**a little**) to a small extent. **2** hardly or not at all.

– SYNONYMS **1** (**a little**) *he reminded me a little of my father* **slightly,** somewhat, a little bit, quite, to some degree. **2** *he is little known as a singer* **hardly,** barely, scarcely, not much, only slightly. **3** *his art has been little seen in Canada* **rarely,** seldom, infrequently, hardly (ever), scarcely ever, not much.
– ANTONYMS well, often.

– DERIVATIVES **lit·tle·ness** noun.
– PHRASES **little by little** gradually.
– ORIGIN Old English.

CHOOSE THE RIGHT WORD

See **SMALL**.

lit·tle fin·ger ▶ **noun** the smallest finger, at the outer side of the hand.
– PHRASES **twist** (or **wind** or **wrap**) **someone around one's little finger** be able to make someone do whatever one wants.

Lit·tle League ▶ **noun** youth baseball or softball for children up to age 12.
– DERIVATIVES **Lit·tle Lea·guer** noun.

lit·tle peo·ple ▶ **plural noun 1** people of very small stature. **2** the ordinary people of a country or organization. **3** fairies or leprechauns.

lit·to·ral /ˈlitərəl/ ▶ **adjective** relating to the shore of the sea or a lake. ▶ **noun** a region lying along a shore.
– ORIGIN Latin *littoralis.*

li·tur·gi·cal /liˈtərjikəl/ ▶ **adjective** relating to liturgy or public worship.
– DERIVATIVES **li·tur·gi·cal·ly** adverb **lit·ur·gist** /ˈlitərjist/ noun.

lit·ur·gy /ˈlitərjē/ ▶ **noun** (pl. **liturgies**) a set form of public worship used in the Christian Church.
– ORIGIN Greek *leitourgia* 'public service, worship of the gods.'

liv·a·ble /ˈlivəbəl/ ▶ **adjective 1** worth living. **2** fit to live in. **3** (**livable with**) informal easy to live with.
– DERIVATIVES **liv·a·bil·i·ty** /ˌlivəˈbilətē/ noun.

live[1] /liv/ ▶ **verb 1** remain alive. **2** be alive at a particular time. **3** spend one's life in a particular way or under particular circumstances: *they are living in fear.* **4** make one's home in a particular place or with a particular person. **5** (**live in/out**) have one's home at (or away from) the place where one works or studies. **6** supply oneself with the means of staying alive: *they live by hunting and fishing.* **7** (**live for**) regard something as the most important aspect of one's life: *he lived for his painting.* **8** survive in someone's mind: *her name lived on.*

– SYNONYMS **1 exist,** be alive, be, have life, breathe, draw breath, walk the earth. **2 reside,** have one's home, lodge, inhabit, occupy. formal dwell; old use abide, bide. **3** *she had lived a difficult life* **experience,** spend, pass, lead, have, go through, undergo. **4** *he lived by scavenging* **survive,** make a living, eke out a living, subsist, support oneself, sustain oneself, make ends meet, keep body and soul together.
– ANTONYMS die.

– PHRASES **live something down** succeed in making other people forget something embarrassing or regrettable. **live it up** informal lead a very enjoyable life, usually by being extravagant and having an exciting social life. **live off** (or **on**) **1** depend on someone or something as a source of income or support. **2** eat as a major part of one's diet. **live rough** live outdoors as a result of being homeless. **live together** (of a couple not married to each other) share a home and have a sexual relationship. **live up to** fulfill expectations, a commitment, etc.: *the president lived up to his promise.* **live with 1** share a home and have a sexual relationship with a person to whom one is not married. **2** accept or tolerate something unpleasant.
– ORIGIN Old English.

live[2] /līv/ ▶ **adjective 1** living. **2** (of a musical performance) played in front of an audience. **3** (of a broadcast) transmitted at the time it occurs; not recorded. **4** of current or continuing interest and importance: *a live issue.* **5** (of a wire or device) connected to a source of electric current. **6** containing or using explosive that has not been detonated: *live ammunition.* **7** (of coals) burning. **8** (of yogurt) containing the living microorganisms by which it is formed.

– SYNONYMS **1 living,** alive, conscious, animate, vital. **2** *a live rail* **electrified,** charged, powered up, active, switched on. **3** *a live grenade* **unexploded,** explosive, active, primed. **4** *a live issue* **topical,** current, controversial, hot, burning, pressing, important, relevant.
– ANTONYMS dead, inanimate.

▶ **adverb** at the time of something's occurrence or performance: *the match will be televised live.*
– ORIGIN shortening of **ALIVE**.

live·able ▶ **adjective** variant spelling of **LIVABLE**.

live·bear·ing /ˈlīvˌbe(ə)riNG/ ▶ **adjective** bearing live young rather than laying eggs.
– DERIVATIVES **live·bear·er** /ˈlīvˌbe(ə)rər/ noun.

lived-in /ˈlivd ˌin/ ▶ **adjective** (of a room or building) showing comforting signs of wear and habitation.

live-in /ˈliv ˌin/ ▶ **adjective 1** (of a domestic employee) living in an employer's house. **2** living with someone as their sexual partner: *his live-in girlfriend.* **3** (of a course of study, treatment, etc.) residential.

live·li·hood /ˈlīvlēˌho͝od/ ▶ **noun** a means of earning money in order to live.

– SYNONYMS **(source of) income,** living, subsistence, bread and butter, job, work, employment, occupation.

– ORIGIN Old English, 'way of life.'

live·long /ˈlivˌlôNG, -ˌläNG/ ▶ **adjective** literary (of a period of time) entire: *all this livelong day.*

live·ly /ˈlīvlē/ ▶ **adjective** (**livelier, liveliest**) **1** full of life and energy. **2** (of a place) full of activity. **3** intellectually stimulating: *a lively debate.* **4** mentally quick and active: *her lively mind.*

– SYNONYMS **1 energetic,** active, animated, dynamic, full of life, outgoing, spirited, sprightly, high-spirited, vivacious, enthusiastic, vibrant, buoyant, exuberant, boisterous, effervescent, cheerful; informal chipper, chirpy, full of beans. **2 busy,** crowded, bustling, hectic, buzzing, vibrant, colorful. **3** *a lively debate* **stimulating,** interesting, vigorous, animated, spirited, heated.
– ANTONYMS quiet, dull.

– DERIVATIVES **live·li·ness** noun.
– PHRASES **look lively** informal move more quickly and energetically.

WORD TOOLKIT

See **ROWDY**.

liv·en /ˈlīvən/ ▶ **verb** (**liven someone/thing up** or **liven up**) make or become more lively or interesting.

liv·er¹ /ˈlivər/ ▶ **noun 1** a large organ in the abdomen that produces bile and neutralizes toxins. **2** the flesh of an animal's liver as food.
– ORIGIN Old English.

liv·er² ▶ **noun** a person who lives in a particular way: *a clean liver.*

liv·er spot ▶ **noun** a small brown spot on the skin.

liv·er·wort /ˈlivərˌwərt, -ˌwôrt/ ▶ **noun** a small flowerless green plant that grows in moist habitats.

liv·er·y /ˈliv(ə)rē/ ▶ **noun** (pl. **liveries**) **1** a special uniform worn by an official or a servant such as a footman. **2** a distinctive design and color scheme used on the vehicles or products of a company.
– DERIVATIVES **liv·er·ied** adjective.
– PHRASES **at livery** (of a horse) kept for the owner and fed and cared for at a fixed charge.
– ORIGIN first meaning 'the giving of food, provisions, or clothing to servants': from Old French *livree* 'delivered.'

liv·er·y sta·ble ▶ **noun** a stable where horses are kept at livery or may be hired out.

lives /līvz/ plural of **LIFE**.

live·stock /ˈlīvˌstäk/ ▶ **noun** farm animals.

live wire /līv/ ▶ **noun** informal an energetic and lively person.

liv·id /ˈlivid/ ▶ **adjective 1** informal furiously angry. **2** dark bluish-gray in color.

– SYNONYMS **furious,** enraged, very angry, infuriated, irate, incensed, fuming, ranting, raving, seething, beside oneself, outraged; informal hopping mad, wild.

– DERIVATIVES **li·vid·i·ty** /ləˈvidətē/ noun.
– ORIGIN Latin *lividus*.

liv·ing /ˈliviNG/ ▶ **noun 1** a way or style of life: *the benefits of country living.* **2** an income that is enough to live on, or the means of earning it.

– SYNONYMS **1 way of life,** lifestyle, life, conduct, behavior, activities, habits. **2 livelihood,** (source of) income, subsistence, keep, daily bread, bread and butter, job, work, employment, occupation.

▶ **adjective 1** alive. **2** (of a place) for living rather than working in: *living quarters.* **3** (of a language) still spoken and used.

– SYNONYMS **1 alive,** live, animate, sentient, breathing, existing. **2** *a living language* **current,** contemporary.
– ANTONYMS dead, extinct.

– PHRASES **in** (or **within**) **living memory** within or during a time that is remembered by people still alive. **the living image of** an exact copy or likeness of someone.

WORD TOOLKIT

See **ORGANIC**.

liv·ing room ▶ **noun** a room in a house for general everyday use.

liv·ing wage ▶ **noun** a wage that is high enough to enable someone to maintain a normal standard of living.

liv·ing will ▶ **noun** a written statement giving details of a person's wishes regarding their future medical treatment should they become unable to give informed consent.

liz·ard /ˈlizərd/ ▶ **noun** a four-legged reptile with a long body and tail and a rough, scaly, or spiny skin.
– ORIGIN Old French *lesard*.

ll. ▶ **abbreviation** (in textual references) lines.

'll ▶ **contraction** shall; will.

lla·ma /ˈlämə/ ▶ **noun** a domesticated animal of the camel family found in the Andes, used for carrying loads and valued for its soft woolly fleece.
– ORIGIN Spanish.

lm ▶ **abbreviation** lumen(s).

ln ▶ **abbreviation** Mathematics natural logarithm.
– ORIGIN from Latin *logarithmus naturalis*.

LNB ▶ **abbreviation** low noise blocker, a circuit on a satellite dish that selects the required signal from the transmission.

LNG ▶ **abbreviation** liquefied natural gas.

lo /lō/ ▶ **exclamation** old use used to draw attention to an interesting event.
– PHRASES **lo and behold** used to present a new scene or situation.
– ORIGIN first recorded in Old English.

loach /lōCH/ ▶ **noun** a small freshwater fish with several long, thin growths (barbels) near the mouth.
– ORIGIN Old French *loche*.

load /lōd/ ▶ **noun 1** a heavy or bulky thing being or about to be carried. **2** the total number or amount carried in a vehicle or container. **3** a weight or source of pressure. **4** (**a load/loads of**) informal a large quantity or amount of something. **5** the amount of work to be done by a person or machine. **6** the amount of power supplied by a source. **7** a burden of responsibility, worry, or grief: *their offer took a load off my mind.*

– SYNONYMS **1 cargo,** freight, consignment, delivery, shipment, goods, pack, bundle, parcel. **2** *a heavy teaching load* **commitment,** responsibility, duty, obligation, burden, onus.

▶ **verb 1** put a load or large quantity of something on or in a vehicle or container. **2** insert something into a device so that it will operate. **3** put ammunition into a firearm. **4** transfer data or a program into a computer's memory. **5** bias something so that a particular outcome is likely: *the odds were loaded against them before the match.*

– SYNONYMS **1 fill (up),** pack, stock, stack, stow, store, bundle, place, put, deposit, pile, stuff, cram; old use lade. **2 burden,** weigh down, saddle, oppress, charge, overburden, overwhelm, encumber, tax, strain, trouble, worry. **3** *he loaded the gun* **prime,** charge, set up, prepare. **4** *load the cassette into the camcorder* **insert,** put, place, slot, slide.

– DERIVATIVES **load·er** noun.
– PHRASES **get a load of** informal take a look at (used to draw attention to someone or something). **load the dice against** (or **in favor of**) put someone or something at a disadvantage (or an advantage).
– ORIGIN Old English, 'journey, conveyance.'

load·ed /'lōdid/ ▶ **adjective 1** carrying a load. **2** (of dice) weighted so that they will always fall in the same way when thrown. **3** having an underlying meaning or implication: *a loaded question.* **4** informal wealthy. **5** informal drunk.

– SYNONYMS **1 full,** filled, laden, packed, stuffed, crammed, brimming, stacked; informal chock-full, chock-a-block. **2** *a politically loaded word* **charged,** emotive, sensitive, delicate.

load fac·tor ▶ **noun** the ratio of the average or actual amount of some quantity and the maximum possible or permissible.

load·ing /'lōdiNG/ ▶ **noun 1** the application of a load to something. **2** the amount of load applied. **3** an increase in an insurance premium due to a factor that increases the risk involved.

load·mas·ter /'lōd,mastər/ ▶ **noun** the member of an aircraft's crew responsible for the cargo.

load·stone ▶ **noun** variant spelling of **LODESTONE**.

loaf[1] /lōf/ ▶ **noun** (pl. **loaves** /lōvz/) a quantity of bread that is shaped and baked in one piece.
– ORIGIN Old English.

loaf[2] ▶ **verb** spend time in an idle or aimless way.

– SYNONYMS **laze,** lounge, loll, idle; informal hang around, bum around.

– ORIGIN probably from **LOAFER**.

loaf·er /'lōfər/ ▶ **noun 1** a person who spends their time in an idle or aimless way. **2** trademark a casual leather shoe with a flat heel.
– ORIGIN perhaps from German *Landläufer* 'tramp.'

loam /lōm/ ▶ **noun 1** a fertile soil of clay and sand containing humus. **2** a paste of clay and water with sand and chopped straw, used in making bricks and plastering walls.
– DERIVATIVES **loam·y** adjective.
– ORIGIN Old English, 'clay.'

loan /lōn/ ▶ **noun 1** a thing that is borrowed, especially a sum of money that is expected to be paid back with interest. **2** the action of lending something.

– SYNONYMS **credit,** advance, mortgage, overdraft.

▶ **verb** give something as a loan.

– SYNONYMS **lend,** advance.

– PHRASES **on loan** being borrowed.
– ORIGIN Old Norse.

loan shark ▶ **noun** informal a moneylender who charges extremely high rates of interest.

loath /lōTH, lōTH/ (also **loth**) ▶ **adjective** reluctant; unwilling.

– SYNONYMS **reluctant,** unwilling, disinclined, averse, opposed, resistant.
– ANTONYMS eager, willing.

– ORIGIN Old English, 'hostile.'

USAGE

Do not confuse **loath** and **loathe**. **Loath** is an adjective meaning 'reluctant or unwilling' (*I was loath to leave*), whereas **loathe** is a verb meaning 'feel hatred or disgust for' (*she loathed him on sight*).

loathe /lōTH/ ▶ **verb** feel hatred or disgust for someone or something.

– SYNONYMS **hate,** detest, abhor, despise, abominate, not be able to bear/stand, execrate.
– ANTONYMS love.

– ORIGIN Old English, related to **LOATH**.

CHOOSE THE RIGHT WORD

See **DESPISE**.

loath·ing /'lōTHiNG/ ▶ **noun** hatred or disgust.

– SYNONYMS **hatred,** hate, detestation, abhorrence, abomination, antipathy, aversion, dislike, disgust, repugnance.

loath·some /'lōTHsəm, 'lōTH-/ ▶ **adjective** causing hatred or disgust.

– SYNONYMS **hateful,** detestable, abhorrent, repulsive, odious, repugnant, repellent, disgusting, revolting, sickening, nauseating, abominable, despicable, contemptible, reprehensible, vile, horrible, nasty, obnoxious, gross, foul, execrable; informal horrid; literary noisome.

loaves /lōvz/ plural of **LOAF**[1].

lob /läb/ ▶ **verb** (**lobs**, **lobbing**, **lobbed**) throw or hit something in a high arc. ▶ **noun** (in tennis) a ball lobbed over an opponent or a stroke producing this result.
– ORIGIN probably from German or Dutch.

lo·bar /'lō,bär, -bər/ ▶ **adjective** relating to or affecting a lobe, especially a lobe of a lung.

lo·bate /'lō,bāt/ ▶ **adjective** having a lobe or lobes.

lob·by /'läbē/ ▶ **noun** (pl. **lobbies**) **1** a room out of which one or more other rooms or corridors lead, typically one near the entrance of a public building. **2** a group of people trying to influence politicians on a particular issue: *members of the anti-abortion lobby.* **3** an organized attempt by members of the public to influence politicians.

– SYNONYMS **1 entrance (hall),** hallway, hall, vestibule, foyer, reception. **2** *the anti-hunt lobby* **pressure group,** interest group, movement, campaign, crusade, faction, camp.

▶ **verb** (**lobbies, lobbying, lobbied**) try to influence a politician on an issue.

– SYNONYMS **1 approach,** contact, petition, appeal to, pressurize, importune. **2 campaign,** crusade, press, push, ask, call, demand, promote, advocate, champion.

– DERIVATIVES **lob·by·ist** noun.
– ORIGIN Latin *lobia* 'covered walk.'

lobe /lōb/ ▶ **noun 1** a roundish projection or division of something. **2** (also **ear lobe**) the rounded fleshy part at the lower edge of the outer ear. **3** a major division of an organ such as the brain.
– DERIVATIVES **lobed** adjective.
– ORIGIN Greek *lobos.*

lo·bel·ia /lō'bēlēə, -'bēlyə/ ▶ **noun** a garden plant with blue or scarlet flowers.
– ORIGIN named after the Flemish botanist Matthias de *Lobel.*

lo·bot·o·mize /lə'bätə͵mīz/ ▶ **verb** perform a lobotomy on someone.

lo·bot·o·my /lə'bätəmē/ ▶ **noun** (pl. **lobotomies**) a surgical operation involving cutting into part of the brain, formerly used to treat mental illness.

lob·ster /'läbstər/ ▶ **noun 1** a large edible shellfish with large pincers. **2** the flesh of this animal as food.
– ORIGIN Old English.

lob·ster pot ▶ **noun** a basketlike trap in which lobsters are caught.

lob·ster ther·mi·dor /'THərmə͵dôr/ ▶ **noun** a dish of lobster cooked in a cream sauce, returned to its shell, sprinkled with cheese, and browned under the broiler.
– ORIGIN *thermidor* from *Thermidor,* the eleventh month of the French Republican calendar.

lo·cal /'lōkəl/ ▶ **adjective 1** relating to a particular area or to the area in which a person lives: *the local post office.* **2** (in technical use) relating to a particular region or part: *a local infection.* **3** Computing referring to a device that can be accessed without the use of a network.

– SYNONYMS **1** *the local council* **district,** regional, town, municipal, provincial, parish. **2** *a local restaurant* **neighborhood,** nearby, near, at hand, close by, handy, convenient. **3** *a local infection* **confined,** restricted, contained, localized.
– ANTONYMS national, widespread.

▶ **noun** a person who lives in a particular area.

– SYNONYMS **resident,** native, inhabitant, parishioner.
– ANTONYMS outsider.

– DERIVATIVES **lo·cal·ly** adverb.
– ORIGIN Latin *localis,* from *locus* 'place.'

lo·cal an·es·the·tic ▶ **noun** an anesthetic that affects only a part of the body.

lo·cal ar·e·a net·work ▶ **noun** a computer network that links devices within a building or group of adjacent buildings.

lo·cale /lō'kal/ ▶ **noun** a place where something happens or is set.
– ORIGIN French *local* 'locality.'

lo·cal gov·ern·ment ▶ **noun** the administration of a particular town, county, or district, with representatives elected by people who live there.

lo·cal·i·ty /lō'kalətē/ ▶ **noun** (pl. **localities**) **1** an area or neighborhood. **2** the position or site of something.

lo·cal·ize /'lōkə͵līz/ ▶ **verb 1** (often as adj. **localized**) restrict or assign something to a particular place: *a localized infection.* **2** make something local in character: *a more localized news service.*
– DERIVATIVES **lo·cal·iz·a·ble** adjective **lo·cal·i·za·tion** /͵lōkələ'zāSHən/ noun **lo·cal·iz·er** noun.

lo·cal time ▶ **noun** time as reckoned in a particular region or time zone.

lo·cate /'lō͵kāt, lō'kāt/ ▶ **verb 1** discover the exact place or position of: *engineers were working to locate the fault.* **2** (**be located**) be situated in a particular place.

– SYNONYMS **1 find,** pinpoint, track down, unearth, sniff out, smoke out, search out, uncover, run to earth. **2 situate,** site, position, place, base, put, build, establish, station.

– DERIVATIVES **lo·cat·a·ble** adjective **lo·ca·tor** noun.
– ORIGIN Latin *locare* 'to place.'

lo·ca·tion /lō'kāSHən/ ▶ **noun 1** a particular place or position. **2** the action of locating someone or something. **3** an actual place in which a movie or television broadcast is made, outside a studio.

– SYNONYMS **position,** place, situation, site, locality, locale, spot, whereabouts, scene, setting, area, environment, venue, address; technical locus.

– DERIVATIVES **lo·ca·tion·al** adjective.

loc. cit. /'läk 'sit/ ▶ **abbreviation** in the passage already quoted.
– ORIGIN Latin *loco citato.*

loch /läk, läKH/ ▶ **noun** Scottish **1** a lake. **2** a narrow strip of sea, almost surrounded by land.
– ORIGIN Scottish Gaelic.

lo·ci /'lō͵sī, -͵sē, -͵kē, -͵kī/ plural of LOCUS.

lo·ci clas·si·ci /'lō͵sī 'klasə͵sī, 'lō͵sē 'klasə͵sē, 'lō͵kē 'klasi͵kē, 'lō͵kī 'klasi͵kī/ plural of LOCUS CLASSICUS.

lock[1] /läk/ ▶ **noun 1** a mechanism for keeping a door or container fastened, operated by a key. **2** a similar device used to prevent the operation of a vehicle or other machine. **3** a short section of a canal or river with gates and sluices at each end that can be opened or closed to change the water level, used for raising and lowering boats. **4** informal a person or thing that is certain to succeed; a certainty. **5** (in wrestling and martial arts) a hold that prevents an opponent from moving a limb. **6** old use a mechanism for exploding the charge of a gun.

– SYNONYMS **bolt,** catch, fastener, clasp, hasp, latch, padlock.

▶ **verb 1** fasten or secure something with a lock. **2** (**lock something up**) shut and secure a building by fastening its doors with locks. **3** enclose or shut in by locking a door, fastening a lid, etc.: *the prisoners are locked in overnight.* **4** (**lock someone up/away**) imprison someone. **5** make or become fixed in one position or unable to to move: *the brakes locked.* **6** (**lock someone/thing in**) involve in (an embrace or struggle): *they were locked in a legal battle.* **7** (**lock on to**) locate and then track a target by radar or similar means.

– SYNONYMS **1 bolt,** fasten, secure, padlock, latch, chain. **2 (lock someone up/away) imprison,** jail, incarcerate, intern, send to prison, put behind bars, put under lock and key, cage, pen, coop up; informal send up/ down, put away, put inside. **3 become stuck,** stick, jam, seize. **4 (lock someone/thing in)** *he locked her in an embrace* **clasp,** clench, grasp, embrace, hug, squeeze.
– ANTONYMS unlock, open.

– DERIVATIVES **lock·a·ble** adjective.
– PHRASES **lock horns** become involved in a conflict or dispute. **lock, stock, and barrel** including everything. [referring to the complete mechanism of a firearm.]
– ORIGIN Old English.

lock² ▶ **noun 1** a section of a person's hair that coils or hangs in a piece. **2 (locks)** literary a person's hair.

– SYNONYMS **strand,** tress, curl, ringlet, hank, tuft, wisp, coil, tendril.

– ORIGIN Old English.

lock·down /ˈläkˌdoun/ ▶ **noun** the confining of prisoners to their cells.

lock·er /ˈläkər/ ▶ **noun** a small lockable cupboard or compartment in which belongings may be left temporarily.

lock·er room ▶ **noun** a changing room containing rows of lockers, especially in schools or gymnasiums.

lock·et /ˈläkit/ ▶ **noun** a small ornamental case worn on a chain around a person's neck, used to hold an item of sentimental value such as a tiny photograph or a lock of hair.
– ORIGIN Old French *locquet* 'small latch or lock.'

lock-in ▶ **noun** an arrangement that obliges a person or company to negotiate or trade only with a specific company.

lock·jaw /ˈläkˌjô/ ▶ **noun** spasm of the jaw muscles, causing the mouth to remain tightly closed, typically as a symptom of tetanus.

lock·nut /ˈläkˌnət/ ▶ **noun 1** a nut screwed down on another to keep it tight. **2** a nut designed so that, once tightened, it cannot be accidentally loosened.

lock·out /ˈläkˌout/ ▶ **noun** a situation in which an employer refuses to allow employees to enter their place of work until certain terms are agreed to.

lock·smith /ˈläkˌsmiTH/ ▶ **noun** a person who makes and repairs locks.

lock·step /ˈläkˌstep/ ▶ **noun 1** a way for a body of people to march with each as close as possible to the one in front. **2** close imitation of another's actions: *they raised prices in lockstep with those of foreign competitors.*

lock·up /ˈläkˌəp/ ▶ **noun 1** a makeshift jail. **2** the action of becoming fixed or immovable.

lo·co /ˌlōkō/ ▶ **adjective** informal crazy.
– ORIGIN Spanish, 'insane.'

lo·co·mo·tion /ˌlōkəˈmōSHən/ ▶ **noun** movement or the ability to move from one place to another.
– ORIGIN from Latin *loco* 'from a place' + *motio* 'motion.'

lo·co·mo·tive /ˌlōkəˈmōtiv/ ▶ **noun** a powered rail vehicle used for pulling trains. ▶ **adjective** relating to locomotion.

lo·co·mo·tor /ˌlōkəˈmōtər/ (also **locomotory**) ▶ **adjective** chiefly Biology relating to locomotion.

lo·co·weed /ˈlōkōˌwēd/ ▶ **noun 1** a plant of the pea family that, if eaten by livestock, can cause a brain disorder marked by unpredictable behavior and loss of coordination. **2** informal cannabis.

lo·cus /ˈlōkəs/ ▶ **noun** (pl. **loci** /ˈlōˌsī, -ˌsē, -ˌkē, -ˌkī/) **1** technical a particular position, point, or place. **2** Mathematics a curve or other figure formed by all the points satisfying a particular condition.
– ORIGIN Latin, 'place.'

lo·cus clas·si·cus /ˈlōkəs ˈklasikəs/ ▶ **noun** (pl. **loci classici** /ˈlōˌsī ˈklasəˌsī, ˈlōˌsē ˈklasəˌsē, ˈlōˌkē ˈklasiˌkē, ˈlōˌkī ˈklasiˌkī/) the best known or most authoritative passage on a particular subject.
– ORIGIN Latin, 'classical place.'

lo·cust /ˈlōkəst/ ▶ **noun** a large tropical grasshopper that migrates in vast swarms and is very destructive to vegetation.
– ORIGIN Latin *locusta.*

lo·cu·tion /lōˈkyo͞oSHən/ ▶ **noun 1** a word or phrase. **2** a person's particular style of speech.
– ORIGIN from Latin *loqui* 'speak.'

lode /lōd/ ▶ **noun** a vein of metal ore in the earth.
– ORIGIN Old English, 'way, course.'

lo·den /ˈlōdn/ ▶ **noun 1** a thick waterproof woolen cloth. **2** the dark green color in which such cloth is often made.
– ORIGIN German.

lode·star /ˈlōdˌstär/ ▶ **noun** a star that is used to guide the course of a ship, especially the Pole Star.

lode·stone /ˈlōdˌstōn/ (also **loadstone**) ▶ **noun 1** a piece of magnetite or other naturally magnetic mineral, able to be used as a magnet. **2** a person or thing that is a focus of attention or attraction.

lodge /läj/ ▶ **noun 1** a small house at the gates of a large house with grounds, occupied by a gatekeeper or other employee. **2** a small country house occupied by people engaged in hunting and shooting. **3** a branch or meeting place of an organization such as the Freemasons. **4** a beaver's den. **5** an American Indian tent or other dwelling.

– SYNONYMS **1** *a hunting lodge* **house,** chalet, cottage, cabin. **2** *a Masonic lodge* **section,** branch, chapter, wing, group.

▶ **verb 1** formally present a complaint, appeal, etc., to the proper authorities. **2** make or become firmly fixed or embedded in a place: *he had a bullet lodged in his skull.* **3** rent accommodations in another person's house. **4** provide someone with rented accommodations. **5 (lodge something in/with)** leave money or a valuable item in a place or with a person for safekeeping.

– SYNONYMS **1 submit,** register, enter, put forward, advance, lay, present, tender, proffer, put on record, record, table, file. **2** *the bullet lodged in his back* **become embedded,** get stuck, stick, catch, get caught, wedge. **3 reside,** board, stay, room, live; literary sojourn. **4 deposit,** put, bank, stash, store, stow, put away.

– ORIGIN Old French *loge* 'arbour, hut.'

lodge·ment /ˈläjmənt/ ▶ **noun 1** chiefly literary a place in which a person or thing is lodged. **2** the depositing of money in a particular bank or account.

lodge·pole pine /ˈläjpōl/ ▶ **noun** a straight-trunked pine tree traditionally used by some American Indians to construct lodges.

lodg·er /ˈläjər/ ▶ **noun** a person who pays rent to live in a property with the owner.

lodg·ing /ˈläjiNG/ ▶ **noun** **1** temporary accommodations. **2** (**lodgings**) a rented room or rooms, usually in the same house as the owner.

– SYNONYMS **accommodations,** rooms, chambers, living quarters, a roof over one's head, housing, shelter; informal digs, crib; formal residence, dwelling, abode.

lo·ess /les, ləs, ˈlōˌes/ ▶ **noun** a loosely compacted fine soil originally deposited by the wind.
– ORIGIN Swiss German *lösch* 'loose.'

lo-fi /ˈlō ˈfī/ (also **low-fi**) ▶ **adjective** relating to or using sound reproduction of a lower quality than hi-fi.
– ORIGIN from LOW[1] + *-fi* on the pattern of *hi-fi*.

loft /lôft, läft/ ▶ **noun** **1** a room or storage space directly under the roof of a house or other building. **2** a large, open living area in a converted warehouse or other large building. **3** a gallery in a church or hall. **4** a shelter with nest holes for pigeons. **5** Golf upward movement given to the ball in a stroke. **6** the thickness of an insulating material such as that in a sleeping bag. ▶ **verb** kick, hit, or throw a ball or missile high into the air.
– ORIGIN Old Norse, 'air, upper room.'

loft·y /ˈlôftē, ˈläf-/ ▶ **adjective** (**loftier**, **loftiest**) **1** tall and impressive. **2** morally good or admirable; noble: *lofty ideals*. **3** haughty and aloof.

– SYNONYMS **1 tall,** high, towering. **2** *lofty ideals* **noble,** exalted, high, high-minded, worthy, grand, fine, elevated. **3** *lofty disdain* **haughty,** arrogant, disdainful, supercilious, condescending, patronizing, scornful, contemptuous, self-important, conceited, snobbish; informal stuck-up, snooty.
– ANTONYMS low, short.

– DERIVATIVES **loft·i·ly** adverb **loft·i·ness** noun.

log[1] /lôg, läg/ ▶ **noun** **1** a part of the trunk or a large branch of a tree that has fallen or been cut off. **2** (also **logbook**) an official record of events during the voyage of a ship or aircraft. **3** a piece of equipment for measuring the speed of a ship, originally one consisting of a float attached to a knotted line.

– SYNONYMS **1** *a fallen log* **branch,** trunk, piece of wood; (**logs**) timber, firewood. **2 record,** register, logbook, journal, diary, minutes, ledger, account, tally.

▶ **verb** (**logs**, **logging**, **logged**) **1** enter information in an official record: *customs officials logged the contents of every ship*. **2** achieve a certain distance, speed, or time. **3** (**log in**/**on** or **out**/**off**) go through the procedures to begin (or finish) using a computer. **4** cut down an area of forest to use the wood commercially.

– SYNONYMS **1 register,** record, note, write down, put in writing, enter, file. **2** *the pilot had logged 95 hours* **attain,** achieve, chalk up, make, do, go, cover, clock.

– DERIVATIVES **log·ger** noun **log·ging** noun.
– ORIGIN unknown.

log[2] ▶ **noun** short for LOGARITHM.

lo·gan·ber·ry /ˈlōgənˌberē/ ▶ **noun** (pl. **loganberries**) an edible soft red fruit, similar to a raspberry.
– ORIGIN from the name of the American horticulturalist John H. *Logan*.

log·a·rithm /ˈlôgəˌriTHəm, ˈlägə-/ ▶ **noun** one of a series of numbers, representing the power to which a fixed number (the base) must be raised to produce a given number, used to simplify calculations.
– DERIVATIVES **log·a·rith·mic** /ˌlôgəˈriTHmik, ˌlägə-/ adjective.
– ORIGIN from Greek *logos* 'reckoning, ratio' + *arithmos* 'number.'

log·book /ˈlôgˌbo͝ok, ˈläg-/ ▶ **noun** a log of a ship or aircraft.

loge /lōZH/ ▶ **noun** a private box or enclosure in a theater. a mid-priced seating section in a stadium, often the back portion of a lower tier.
– ORIGIN from French.

log·ger·head /ˈlôgərˌhed, ˈlägər-/ ▶ **noun** (also **loggerhead turtle**) a large-headed reddish-brown turtle of warm seas.
– PHRASES **at loggerheads** engaged in strong dispute or disagreement. [perhaps from a use of *loggerhead* in a former sense 'long-handled iron instrument for heating liquids' (when used as a weapon).]
– ORIGIN from dialect *logger* 'block of wood for hobbling a horse' + HEAD.

log·gia /ˈlōj(ē)ə, ˈlô-/ ▶ **noun** a gallery or room with one or more open sides, especially with one side open to a garden.
– ORIGIN Italian, 'lodge.'

log·ic /ˈläjik/ ▶ **noun** **1** the science of reasoning. **2** good or valid reasoning: *the logic of the argument is faulty*. **3** an underlying system or set of principles used in preparing a computer or electronic device to perform a particular task.

– SYNONYMS **1 reason,** judgment, rationality, wisdom, sense, good sense, common sense, sanity. **2** *the logic of their argument* **reasoning,** rationale, argument.

– DERIVATIVES **lo·gi·cian** /ləˈjisHən, lō-/ noun.
– ORIGIN from Greek *logikē tekhnē* 'art of reason.'

log·i·cal /ˈläjikəl/ ▶ **adjective** **1** relating to or following the rules of logic. **2** capable of or showing rational thought. **3** expected or sensible under the circumstances: *the polar expedition is a logical extension of his Arctic travels*.

– SYNONYMS **1 reasoned,** rational, sound, cogent, valid, coherent, clear, systematic, orderly, methodical, analytical, consistent. **2** *the logical outcome* **natural,** reasonable, sensible, understandable, predictable, unsurprising, likely.
– ANTONYMS illogical.

– DERIVATIVES **log·i·cal·ly** adverb.

log·ic bomb ▶ **noun** Computing a set of instructions secretly incorporated into a program so that if a particular condition is satisfied they will be carried out, usually with harmful effects.

log·in /ˈlôgˌin, ˈläg-/ (also **logon**) ▶ **noun** an act of logging in to a computer, or the password needed to do so.

lo·gis·tics /ləˈjistiks, lō-/ ▶ **plural noun** (treated as sing. or pl.) **1** the detailed coordination of a large and complex project or event. **2** the commercial activity of transporting goods to customers.
– DERIVATIVES **lo·gis·tic** adjective **lo·gis·ti·cal** adjective **logistically** adverb.
– ORIGIN French *logistique* 'movement and supply of troops and equipment.'

log·jam /ˈlôgˌjam, ˈläg-/ ▶ **noun** **1** a situation that seems unable to be settled; deadlock. **2** a backlog.

lo·go /ˈlōˌgō/ ▶ **noun** (pl. **logos**) a design or symbol adopted by an organization to identify its products.

– SYNONYMS **design,** symbol, emblem, trademark, motif, monogram.

– ORIGIN Greek *logos* 'word.'

log·roll·ing /ˈlôgˌrōliNG, ˈläg-/ ▶ **noun 1** informal the practice of exchanging favors, especially in politics. **2** a sport in which two contestants stand on a floating log and try to knock each other off by spinning it with their feet.
– DERIVATIVES **log·roll·er** noun.

loin /loin/ ▶ **noun 1** the part of the body on both sides of the spine between the lowest ribs and the hipbones. **2** a cut of meat from the back or sides of an animal, near the tail. **3** (**loins**) literary a person's sexual organs.
– ORIGIN Old French *loigne*.

loin·cloth /ˈloinˌklôTH, -ˌkläTH/ ▶ **noun** a piece of cloth wrapped around the hips, worn by men in some hot countries as their only garment.

loi·ter /ˈloitər/ ▶ **verb** stand around without any obvious purpose.

> – SYNONYMS **linger,** wait, skulk, loaf, lounge, idle; informal hang about/around.

– DERIVATIVES **loi·ter·er** noun.
– ORIGIN perhaps from Dutch *loteren* 'wag about.'

> **CHOOSE THE RIGHT WORD**
>
> **loiter, dally, dawdle, idle, lag**
> Someone who hangs around downtown after the stores are closed and appears to be deliberately wasting time is said to **loiter**, a verb that connotes improper or sinister motives (*the police warned the boys not to loiter*). To **dawdle** is to pass time leisurely or to pursue something halfheartedly (*dawdle in a stationery shop; dawdle over a sinkful of dishes*). Someone who **dallies** dawdles in a particularly pleasurable and relaxed way, with connotations of amorous activity (*he dallied with his girlfriend when he should have been delivering papers*). **Idle** suggests that the person makes a habit of avoiding work or activity (*idle away the hours of a hot summer day*), while **lag** suggests falling behind or failing to maintain a desirable rate of progress (*she lagged several yards behind her classmates as they walked to the museum*).

Lo·li·ta /lōˈlētə/ ▶ **noun** (**a Lolita**) a sexually precocious young girl.
– ORIGIN a character in the novel *Lolita* by Vladimir Nabokov.

loll /läl/ ▶ **verb 1** sit, lie, or stand in a lazy, relaxed way. **2** hang loosely: *he let his head loll back*.
– ORIGIN probably symbolic of dangling.

lol·la·pa·loo·za /ˌläləpəˈlo͞ozə/ ▶ **noun** informal a very impressive or attractive person or thing.
– ORIGIN an invented word.

lol·li·pop /ˈlälēˌpäp/ ▶ **noun** a flat, rounded candy on the end of a stick.
– ORIGIN perhaps from dialect *lolly* 'tongue' + **POP**[1].

lol·ly·gag /ˈlälēˌgag/ ▶ **verb** (**lollygags, lollygagging, lollygagged**) informal spend time in an aimless way.
– ORIGIN unknown.

Lom·bard /ˈlämˌbärd, -bərd/ ▶ **noun 1** a member of a Germanic people who invaded Italy in the 6th century. **2** a person from Lombardy in northern Italy.
– DERIVATIVES **Lom·bar·dic** /lämˈbärdik/ adjective.
– ORIGIN Italian *lombardo*.

lone /lōn/ ▶ **adjective 1** having no companions; solitary. **2** lacking the support of other people: *I am by no means a lone voice*. **3** literary (of a place) remote and rarely visited.

> – SYNONYMS **1 solitary,** single, solo, unaccompanied, sole, isolated. **2** *a lone parent* **single,** unmarried, separated, divorced, widowed.

– ORIGIN shortening of **ALONE**.

lone·ly /ˈlōnlē/ ▶ **adjective** (**lonelier, loneliest**) **1** sad because one has no friends or company. **2** spent without company: *long, lonely hours*. **3** (of a place) remote and rarely visited.

> – SYNONYMS **1 isolated,** alone, friendless, lonesome, with no one to turn to, abandoned, rejected, unloved, unwanted. **2 deserted,** uninhabited, desolate, solitary, isolated, remote, out of the way, off the beaten track, secluded, in the back of beyond, godforsaken; informal in the middle of nowhere.

– DERIVATIVES **lone·li·ness** noun.

lone·ly hearts ▶ **plural noun** people looking for a lover or friend through the personal columns of a newspaper.

lon·er /ˈlōnər/ ▶ **noun** a person who prefers to be alone.

> – SYNONYMS **recluse,** introvert, lone wolf, hermit, misanthrope, outsider; historical anchorite.

lone·some /ˈlōnsəm/ ▶ **adjective** lonely.

long[1] /lôNG, läNG/ ▶ **adjective** (**longer** /ˈlôNGgər, ˈläNG-/, **longest** /ˈlôNGgist, ˈläNG-/) **1** of a great distance or duration. **2** having a particular length, distance, or duration: *the ship will be 150 yards long*. **3** relatively great in extent: *a long list*. **4** (of a ball in sports) traveling a great distance, or further than expected. **5** Phonetics (of a vowel) pronounced in a way that takes longer than a short vowel in the same position (e.g., in standard American English the vowel /o͞o/ in *food*). **6** (of odds in betting) reflecting a low level of probability. **7** (**long on**) informal well supplied with something: *an industry that's long on ideas but short on cash*.

> – SYNONYMS **lengthy,** extended, prolonged, protracted, long-lasting, drawn-out, endless, lingering, interminable.
> – ANTONYMS short, brief.

▶ **noun** a long time.
▶ **adverb** (**longer, longest**) **1** for a long time. **2** at a distant time: *long ago*. **3** throughout a particular period of time: *all day long*. **4** (with reference to the ball in sports) at, to, or over a great distance.
– DERIVATIVES **long·ish** /ˈlôNGgiSH, ˈläNG-/ adjective.
– PHRASES **as** (or **so**) **long as 1** during the whole time that. **2** provided that. **in the long run** (or **term**) eventually. **the long and the short of it** all that can or need be said. **long in the tooth** rather old. [originally said of horses, from the receding of the gums with age.]
– ORIGIN Old English.

long[2] ▶ **verb** (**long for/to do**) have a strong wish for or to do something.

> – SYNONYMS *I **longed for** the holidays* **yearn for,** pine for, ache for, hanker for/after, hunger for, thirst for, itch for, be eager for, be desperate for, crave, dream of, set one's heart on; informal be dying for.

– ORIGIN Old English, 'grow long,' also 'yearn.'

long. ▶ **abbreviation** longitude.

long·board /ˈlôNGˌbôrd, ˈläNG-/ ▶ **noun** a type of long surfboard.

long·boat /ˈlôNGˌbōt, ˈläNG-/ ▶ **noun 1** historical a large boat that could be launched from a sailing ship. **2** another term for **LONGSHIP**.

long·bow /ˈlôNGˌbō, ˈläNG-/ ▶ **noun** historical a large bow drawn by hand and shooting a long feathered arrow.

long-dis·tance ▶ **adjective 1** traveling or operating between distant places. **2** Athletics referring to a race distance of 6 miles or 10,000 meters (6 miles 376 yds), or longer. ▶ **adverb** between distant places.

long di·vi·sion ▶ **noun** the process of dividing one number by another with the calculations written down.

long-drawn (also **long-drawn-out**) ▶ **adjective** lasting a very long time, or too long.

longe /lənj/ ▶ **noun** variant of LUNGE[2].

lon·gev·i·ty /lôn'jevətē, län-/ ▶ **noun** long life.
– ORIGIN from Latin *longus* 'long' + *aevum* 'age.'

long face ▶ **noun** an unhappy or disappointed expression.

long·hand /'lôNG,hand, 'läNG-/ ▶ **noun** ordinary handwriting (as opposed to shorthand, typing, or printing).

long haul ▶ **noun 1** a relatively long distance in terms of travel or the transport of goods. **2** a lengthy and difficult task.

long·horn /'lôNG,hôrn, 'läNG-/ ▶ **noun** a breed of cattle with long horns.

long·house /'lôNG,hous, 'läNG-/ ▶ **noun** a large communal house in parts of Malaysia and Indonesia or among some North American Indians.

long·ing /'lôNGiNG/ ▶ **noun** a strong wish to do or have something.

– SYNONYMS **yearning,** craving, ache, burning, hunger, thirst, hankering, desire, wish, hope, aspiration; informal yen, itch.

▶ **adjective** having or showing a strong wish to do or have something: *a longing look*.
– DERIVATIVES **long·ing·ly** adverb.

lon·gi·tude /'länji,t(y)o͞od, 'lôn-/ ▶ **noun** the distance of a place east or west of the Greenwich meridian, measured in degrees.
– ORIGIN Latin *longitudo*.

lon·gi·tu·di·nal /,länjə't(y)o͞odn-əl, ,lôn-/ ▶ **adjective 1** running lengthwise. **2** relating to the distance of a place east or west of the Greenwich meridian.
– DERIVATIVES **lon·gi·tu·di·nal·ly** adverb.

long johns /jänz/ ▶ **plural noun** informal underwear with closely fitted legs reaching to the ankles.

long jump ▶ **noun** (**the long jump**) an athletic event in which competitors jump as far as possible along the ground in one leap.
– DERIVATIVES **long jump·er** noun.

long·leaf pine /'lôNG,lēf, 'läNG-/ ▶ **noun** a large pine tree with very long needles and cones, formerly an important source of turpentine.

long-life ▶ **adjective** (of perishable goods) treated so as to stay fresh for longer than usual.

long·line /'lôNG,līn, 'läNG-/ ▶ **noun** a deep-sea fishing line with a large number of hooks attached to it.

long-lived /livd/ ▶ **adjective** living or lasting a long time.

long-play·ing ▶ **adjective** (of a record) 12 inches (about 30 cm) in diameter and designed to rotate at 33⅓ revolutions per minute.

long-range ▶ **adjective 1** able to be used or be effective over long distances. **2** relating to a period of time far into the future.

long·ship /'lôNG,SHip, 'läNG-/ ▶ **noun** a long, narrow warship with oars and a sail, used by the Vikings.

long·shore /'lôNG,SHôr, 'läNG-/ ▶ **adjective** relating to or moving along the seashore.
– ORIGIN from *along shore*.

long·shore·man /,lôNG'SHôrmən, ,läNG-/ ▶ **noun** (pl. **longshoremen**) a person employed to load and unload ships.

long shot ▶ **noun** an attempt or guess that has only the slightest chance of succeeding or being accurate.
– PHRASES **not by a long shot** informal not at all.

long-stand·ing ▶ **adjective** having existed for a long time.

– SYNONYMS **well established,** time-honored, traditional, abiding, enduring.
– ANTONYMS new, recent.

long-suf·fer·ing ▶ **adjective** bearing problems or annoying behavior patiently.

– SYNONYMS **patient,** forbearing, tolerant, uncomplaining, philosophical, stoical, forgiving.

long suit ▶ **noun 1** (in bridge or whist) a situation in which a player holds several cards of one suit in a hand. **2** an outstanding personal quality or achievement: *tact was not his long suit*.

long-term ▶ **adjective** occurring over or relating to a long period of time: *the long-term effects of smoking*.

lon·gueur /lôNG'gər, läNG-/ ▶ **noun** a tedious period of time or passage in a book or piece of music.
– ORIGIN French, 'length.'

long un·der·wear ▶ **noun** a warm, close-fitting undergarment with ankle-length legs and often long sleeves.

long wave ▶ **noun 1** a radio wave of a wavelength above one kilometer (and a frequency below 300 kilohertz). **2** broadcasting using radio waves of 1 to 10 kilometers wavelength.

long·ways /'lôNG,wāz, 'läNG-/ ▶ **adverb** lengthwise.

long-wind·ed /'windid/ ▶ **adjective** lengthy and boring.

– SYNONYMS **verbose,** wordy, lengthy, long, prolix, interminable, rambling, tortuous, meandering, repetitious, repetitive.
– ANTONYMS concise, succinct.

loo /lo͞o/ ▶ **noun** Brit. informal a toilet.
– ORIGIN uncertain: one theory suggests the source is *Waterloo*, a trade name for iron cisterns in the early 20th century.

loo·fah /'lo͞ofə/ ▶ **noun** a long, rough, fibrous object used like a bath sponge, consisting of the dried inner parts of a tropical fruit.
– ORIGIN Egyptian Arabic.

look /lo͝ok/ ▶ **verb 1** direct one's gaze in a particular direction. **2** have the appearance or give the impression of being: *he looked unhappy*. **3** face in a particular direction: *the rooms look out over the harbor*.

– SYNONYMS **1 glance,** gaze, stare, gape, peer, peep, peek, watch, observe, view, regard, examine, inspect, eye, scan, scrutinize, survey, study, contemplate, take in, ogle, leer at; informal take a gander, rubberneck, get a load of, eyeball. **2 seem (to be),** appear (to be), come across/over as. **3 command a view of,** face, overlook, front.

▶ **noun 1** an act of looking at someone or something.

2 an expression of a feeling or thought by looking at someone: *he gave me a funny look.* **3** the appearance of someone or something: *the contemporary look of the city skyline.* **4** (**looks**) a person's facial appearance. **5** a style or fashion: *Italian designers unveiled their latest looks.*

– SYNONYMS **1 glance,** examination, study, inspection, scrutiny, peep, peek, glimpse; informal eyeful, once-over, squint. **2 expression,** mien, countenance. **3 appearance,** air, style, effect, ambience, impression, aspect, manner, demeanor.

▶ **exclamation** (also **look here!**) used to call attention to what one is going to say.

– PHRASES **look after** take care of. **look at 1** think of something in a particular way. **2** examine a matter and consider what action to take. **look down on** (also **look down one's nose at**) regard someone or something with a feeling of superiority. **look for** attempt to find. **look in** make a short visit. **look into** investigate. **look lively** (or **sharp**) informal be quick; get moving. **look on** watch without getting involved. **look out** be alert for possible trouble or danger. **look to 1** rely on someone to do something. **2** hope or expect to do something. **look up** improve. **look something up** search for and find a piece of information in a reference work. **look someone up** informal visit or contact someone. **look up to** have a great deal of respect for.

– ORIGIN Old English.

look·a·like /ˈlo͝okəˌlīk/ ▶ **noun** a person or thing that looks very similar to another.

– SYNONYMS **double,** twin, clone, living image, doppelgänger, replica; informal spitting image, dead ringer.

look·er /ˈlo͝okər/ ▶ **noun 1** a person with a particular appearance: *she's not a bad looker.* **2** informal a very attractive person.

look·ing glass ▶ **noun** a mirror.

look·out /ˈlo͝okˌout/ ▶ **noun 1** a place from which to keep watch. **2** a person stationed to keep watch for danger or trouble. **3** (**one's lookout**) informal one's own responsibility or problem.

– SYNONYMS **1 watchman,** watch, guard, sentry, sentinel, observer. **2** *that's your lookout* **problem,** concern, business, affair, responsibility, worry; informal pigeon.

– PHRASES **be on the lookout** (or **keep a lookout**) **for 1** be alert to possible danger or trouble. **2** keep searching for something.

look-see ▶ **noun** informal a brief look or inspection.

look·up /ˈlo͝okˌəp/ ▶ **noun** systematic retrieval of electronic information.

loom[1] /lo͞om/ ▶ **noun** a piece of equipment for weaving fabric.

– ORIGIN Old English, 'tool.'

loom[2] ▶ **verb 1** appear as a vague shape, especially one that is large or threatening: *vehicles loomed out of the darkness.* **2** (of an unwelcome event) seem about to happen: *there is a crisis looming.*

– SYNONYMS **1 emerge,** appear, materialize, take shape. **2 be imminent,** be on the horizon, impend, threaten, brew, be just around the corner.

– ORIGIN probably from German or Dutch.

loon[1] /lo͞on/ ▶ **noun** informal a silly or foolish person.

– ORIGIN from **LOON**[2] (referring to the bird's actions when escaping from danger), perhaps influenced by **LOONY**.

loon[2] ▶ **noun** another term for **DIVER** (sense 2).

– ORIGIN probably from Shetland dialect *loom.*

loon·y /ˈlo͞onē/ informal ▶ **noun** (pl. **loonies**) a crazy or silly person. ▶ **adjective** (**loonier, looniest**) crazy or silly.

– DERIVATIVES **loon·i·ness** noun.

– ORIGIN from **LUNATIC**.

loon·y bin ▶ **noun** informal, derogatory an institution for people with mental illnesses.

loop /lo͞op/ ▶ **noun 1** a shape produced by a curve that bends around and crosses itself. **2** an endless strip of tape or film allowing sounds or images to be continuously repeated. **3** a complete circuit for an electric current. **4** Computing a programmed sequence of instructions that is repeated until or while a particular condition is satisfied.

– SYNONYMS **coil,** ring, circle, noose, spiral, curl, bend, curve, arc, twirl, whorl, twist, helix.

▶ **verb 1** form into a loop or loops: *she looped her arms around his neck.* **2** follow a course that forms a loop or loops.

– SYNONYMS **1 coil,** wind, twist, snake, spiral, curve, bend, turn. **2 fasten,** tie, join, connect, knot, bind.

– PHRASES **in** (or **out of**) **the loop** informal aware (or unaware) of information known to only a privileged few. **loop the loop** (of an aircraft) fly in a vertical circle.

– ORIGIN unknown.

loop·er /ˈlo͞opər/ ▶ **noun 1** another term for **INCHWORM**. **2** Baseball a fly ball that becomes a hit by dropping out of the reach of the infielders.

loop·hole /ˈlo͞opˌ(h)ōl/ ▶ **noun** an inexact wording or omission in a law or contract that enables someone to avoid doing something.

– SYNONYMS **ambiguity,** means of evasion, discrepancy, inconsistency, omission, excuse, escape clause.

– ORIGIN from former *loop* 'opening in a wall' + **HOLE**.

loop·y /ˈlo͞opē/ ▶ **adjective** (**loopier, loopiest**) informal crazy or silly.

– DERIVATIVES **loop·i·ness** noun.

loose /lo͞os/ ▶ **adjective 1** not firmly or tightly fixed in place. **2** not held, tied, or packaged together. **3** not tied up or shut in: *the bull was loose in the field.* **4** (of a garment) not fitting tightly or closely. **5** not dense or compact in structure. **6** relaxed: *her loose, easy stride.* **7** not strict; inexact: *a loose interpretation.* **8** careless and indiscreet: *loose talk.* **9** dated promiscuous or immoral. **10** (of the ball in a game) in play but not in any player's possession.

– SYNONYMS **1 not secure,** unsecured, unattached, untied, detached, wobbly, unsteady, dangling, free. **2 free,** at large, at liberty, on the loose. **3 baggy,** roomy, oversized, voluminous, shapeless, sloppy. **4** *a loose interpretation* **vague,** imprecise, approximate, broad, general, rough, liberal.
– ANTONYMS secure, tight.

▶ **verb 1** release someone or something. **2** relax one's grip. **3** (usu. **loose something off**) fire a shot, bullet, etc.

– SYNONYMS **1 free,** let loose, release, untie, unchain, unfasten, unleash, relax. **2 relax,** slacken, loosen.
– ANTONYMS confine, tighten.

– DERIVATIVES **loose·ly** adverb **loose·ness** noun.

– PHRASES **on the loose** having escaped from prison or confinement.

– ORIGIN Old Norse.

USAGE

Do not confuse **loose** and **lose**; **loose** means 'not fixed in place or tied up' (*a loose tooth*), while **lose** means 'have something taken away' (*she might lose her job*) or 'become unable to find someone or something.'

loose can·non ▶ **noun** an unpredictable person who may cause unintentional harm or damage.

loose end ▶ **noun** a detail that is not yet settled or explained.
– PHRASES **be at loose ends** have nothing specific to do.

loose-leaf ▶ **adjective** (of a folder) having pages that can be taken out and put in separately.

loos·en /'lo͞osən/ ▶ **verb 1** make or become loose. **2** (**loosen up**) warm up in preparation for an activity.

– SYNONYMS **1 undo,** slacken, unfasten, detach, release, disconnect. **2 weaken,** relax, slacken, loose, let go.
– ANTONYMS tighten.

– DERIVATIVES **loos·en·er** noun.
– PHRASES **loosen someone's tongue** make someone talk freely.

loose·strife /'lo͞o(s),strīf/ ▶ **noun** a waterside plant with a tall upright spike of purple or yellow flowers.
– ORIGIN Greek *lusimakheion.*

loos·ey-goos·ey /'lo͞osē 'go͞osē/ ▶ **adjective** informal **1** not tense; relaxed and comfortable. **2** lacking in definition, care, or precision.
– ORIGIN from the expression *loose as a goose.*

loot /lo͞ot/ ▶ **noun 1** goods stolen from empty buildings during a war or riot. **2** goods stolen by a thief. **3** informal money.

– SYNONYMS **booty,** spoils, plunder, haul; informal swag, boodle.

▶ **verb** steal goods from empty buildings during a war or riot.

– SYNONYMS **plunder,** pillage, ransack, sack, rifle, rob, strip, gut.

– DERIVATIVES **loot·er** noun.
– ORIGIN Sanskrit, 'rob.'

lop /läp/ ▶ **verb** (**lops, lopping, lopped**) **1** cut off a branch or limb from a tree or body. **2** informal make something smaller or less by a particular amount: *the new highway lops an hour off commuting time.*
– DERIVATIVES **lop·per** noun.
– ORIGIN unknown.

lope /lōp/ ▶ **verb** run with a long bounding stride. ▶ **noun** a long bounding stride.
– ORIGIN Old Norse, 'leap.'

lop-eared ▶ **adjective** (of an animal) having drooping ears.
– DERIVATIVES **lop ears** plural noun.
– ORIGIN from former *lop* 'hang loosely or limply.'

lop·sid·ed /'läp,sīdid/ ▶ **adjective** with one side lower or smaller than the other.

– SYNONYMS **crooked,** askew, awry, off-center, uneven, out of true, asymmetrical, tilted, at an angle, slanting. informal cockeyed; Brit. informal wonky.
– ANTONYMS even, level.

– DERIVATIVES **lop·sid·ed·ly** adverb **lop·sid·ed·ness** noun.

lo·qua·cious /lō'kwāsнəs/ ▶ **adjective** talkative.

– SYNONYMS **talkative,** voluble, garrulous, chatty, gossipy; informal gabby, gassy.
– ANTONYMS reticent, taciturn.

– DERIVATIVES **lo·quac·i·ty** /lō'kwasətē/ noun.
– ORIGIN from Latin *loqui* 'to talk.'

lo·quat /'lō,kwät/ ▶ **noun** a small egg-shaped yellow fruit from an East Asian tree.
– ORIGIN Chinese dialect, 'rush orange.'

lord /lôrd/ ▶ **noun 1** (in the UK) a man of noble rank. **2** (**Lord**) (in the UK) a title given formally to a baron, less formally to a marquess, earl, or viscount, and as a courtesy title to a younger son of a duke or marquess. **3** (**the Lords**) (in the UK) the House of Lords, or its members. **4** a master or ruler. **5** (**Lord**) a name for God or Jesus.

– SYNONYMS **1 noble,** nobleman, peer, aristocrat. **2 master,** ruler, leader, chief, superior, monarch, sovereign, king, emperor, prince, governor, commander.

▶ **exclamation** (**Lord**) used in exclamations expressing surprise or worry, or for emphasis.
▶ **verb** (**lord it over**) act in an arrogant and bullying way toward someone.
– PHRASES **the Lord's Day** Sunday. **the Lord's Prayer** the prayer taught by Jesus to his disciples, beginning 'Our Father'.
– ORIGIN Old English, 'bread-keeper'; compare with **LADY**.

lord·ly /'lôrdlē/ ▶ **adjective** (**lordlier, lordliest**) characteristic of or suitable for a lord.
– DERIVATIVES **lord·li·ness** noun.

lord·ship /'lôrd,sнip/ ▶ **noun 1** (**His/Your Lordship**) (in the UK) a form of address to a judge, bishop, or nobleman. **2** supreme power or rule.

lore /lôr/ ▶ **noun** a body of traditions and knowledge relating to a particular subject: *farming lore.*
– ORIGIN Old English, 'instruction.'

lor·gnette /lôrn'yet/ (also **lorgnettes**) ▶ **noun** a pair of glasses or opera glasses held by a long handle at one side.
– ORIGIN French, from *lorgner* 'to squint.'

lor·i·keet /'lôrə,kēt, 'lär-/ ▶ **noun** a small bird of the lory family, found chiefly in New Guinea.
– ORIGIN from **LORY**.

lo·ris /'lôris/ ▶ **noun** (pl. **lorises**) a small, slow-moving primate that lives in thick vegetation in South Asia.
– ORIGIN French.

lor·ry /'lôrē, 'lärē/ ▶ **noun** (pl. **lorries**) Brit. a large, heavy motor vehicle for transporting goods or troops; a truck.
– ORIGIN uncertain.

lo·ry /'lôrē/ ▶ **noun** (pl. **lories**) a small Australasian or SE Asian parrot.
– ORIGIN Malay.

lose /lo͞oz/ ▶ **verb** (past and past part. **lost** /lôst, läst/) **1** no longer have or keep: *I've lost my appetite.* **2** have something taken away: *she was upset about losing her job.* **3** become unable to find something or someone. **4** fail to win a game or contest. **5** earn less money than one is spending. **6** waste or fail to take advantage of: *he may have lost his chance.* **7** (**be lost**) be destroyed or killed. **8** escape from a pursuer. **9** (**lose oneself in/be lost in**) be or become deeply absorbed in: *he had been lost in thought.* **10** (of a watch or clock) become slow by a particular amount of time.

– SYNONYMS **1 mislay,** misplace, be unable to find, lose track of. **2 escape from,** evade, elude, dodge, avoid, give someone the slip, shake off, throw off, leave behind, outdistance, outrun. **3 waste,** squander, let pass, miss; informal pass up, blow. **4 be defeated,** be beaten; informal come a cropper, go down.
– ANTONYMS find, seize, win.

– PHRASES **lose face** become less well respected. **lose heart** become discouraged. **lose it** informal lose control of one's temper or emotions. **lose out** not get a full chance or opportunity. **lose one's** (or **the**) **way** become lost.
– ORIGIN Old English, 'perish, destroy,' also 'become unable to find.'

USAGE

On the confusion of **lose** and **loose**, see the note at LOOSE.

los·er /ˈlo͞ozər/ ▶ **noun 1** a person or thing that loses or has lost a game or contest. **2** informal a person who is generally unsuccessful in life.

– SYNONYMS **failure,** underachiever, dead loss, write-off, has-been; informal also-ran.

los·ing bat·tle ▶ **noun** a struggle in which failure seems certain.

loss /lôs, läs/ ▶ **noun 1** the fact or process of losing something or someone. **2** a person, thing, or amount lost. **3** the feeling of grief after losing a valued person or thing. **4** a person or thing that is badly missed when lost.

– SYNONYMS **1** *the loss of the documents* **mislaying,** misplacement, forgetting. **2** *the loss of her husband* **death,** demise, passing away, bereavement. **3** *a loss of $15,000* **deficit,** debit, debt. **4** *Canadian losses in the war* **casualties,** fatalities, victims; dead.
– ANTONYMS recovery, profit.

– PHRASES **at a loss 1** uncertain or puzzled. **2** making less money than is spent in operating or producing something.
– ORIGIN Old English, 'destruction.'

loss lead·er ▶ **noun** a product sold at a loss to attract customers.

lost /lôst, läst/ past and past participle of LOSE ▶ **adjective** unable to find one's way; not knowing where one is.

– SYNONYMS **1 missing,** mislaid, misplaced, gone astray. **2 stray,** off course, going around in circles, adrift, at sea. **3** *a lost opportunity* **missed,** wasted, squandered, gone by the board(s); informal down the drain. **4** *lost traditions* **bygone,** past, former, old, vanished, forgotten, dead. **5** *lost species and habitats* **extinct,** died out, defunct, vanished, gone, destroyed, wiped out, exterminated. **6** *lost in thought* **engrossed,** absorbed, rapt, immersed, deep, intent, engaged, wrapped up.

– PHRASES **be lost for words** be so surprised or upset that one cannot think what to say. **be lost on** fail to be noticed or understood by: *the irony is lost on him*.

lost cause ▶ **noun** a person or thing that can no longer hope to succeed or be improved.

lost gen·er·a·tion ▶ **noun** the generation reaching maturity during and just after World War I, many of whose men were killed during those years.

lot /lät/ ▶ **pronoun** informal **1** (**a lot** or **lots**) a large number or amount of something. **2** (**the lot**) the whole number or amount.

– SYNONYMS **a large amount,** a fair amount, a good/great deal, an abundance, a wealth, a profusion, plenty; a large number, a considerable number; informal loads, masses, heaps, piles, stacks, oodles, tons.

▶ **adverb** (**a lot** or **lots**) informal a great deal.

– SYNONYMS *I work in pastels* ***a lot*** **a great deal,** a good deal, much; often, frequently, regularly.

▶ **noun 1** (treated as sing. or pl.) informal a particular group or set of people or things: *you lot think you're so clever*. **2** an item or set of items for sale at an auction. **3** a method of deciding something by choosing an item at random, especially one piece of paper from a number of pieces. **4** a person's destiny, luck, or situation in life: *many housewives are not happy with their lot*. **5** an area of land: *a parking lot*.

– SYNONYMS **1 group,** crowd, circle, crew; informal bunch, gang, mob. **2** *an auction lot* **item,** article, batch, group, bundle, parcel. **3** *his lot in life* **fate,** destiny, fortune, situation, circumstances, plight, predicament.

– PHRASES **draw** (or **cast**) **lots** decide something by choosing one piece of paper from a number of other pieces. **fall to someone's lot** become someone's task or responsibility. **throw in one's lot with** decide to join a person or group and share their fate.

USAGE

Although **a lot of** and **lots of** are very common in speech, they still have an informal feel and it is better to avoid them in formal English; use alternatives such as **many** or **a large number** instead.

The correct spelling is **a lot**; do not spell it as one word (*alot*).

– ORIGIN Old English.

lo-tech ▶ **adjective** variant spelling of LOW-TECH.

loth ▶ **adjective** variant spelling of LOATH.

Lo·thar·i·o /lōˈᴛʜe(ə)rēˌō, -ˈᴛʜär-/ ▶ **noun** (pl. **Lotharios**) a man who has many casual sexual relationships with women; a womanizer.
– ORIGIN from a character in Nicholas Rowe's tragedy *The Fair Penitent*.

lo·tion /ˈlōsʜən/ ▶ **noun** a thick creamy liquid applied to the skin as a medicine or cosmetic.

– SYNONYMS **ointment,** cream, balm, rub, moisturizer, lubricant, embrocation, liniment, salve, unguent.

– ORIGIN Latin.

lot·ter·y /ˈlätərē/ ▶ **noun** (pl. **lotteries**) **1** a means of raising money by selling numbered tickets and giving prizes to the holders of numbers drawn at random. **2** something whose success is governed by chance: *the Grand Prix was made a lottery by heavy rain*.

– SYNONYMS **raffle,** drawing, sweepstakes, lotto, pool.

– ORIGIN probably from Dutch *loterij*.

lot·to /ˈlätō/ ▶ **noun** (pl. **lottos**) **1** a children's game similar to bingo, using illustrated counters or cards. **2** a lottery.
– ORIGIN Italian.

lo·tus /ˈlōtəs/ ▶ **noun 1** a kind of large water lily. **2** (in Greek mythology) a legendary fruit that causes dreamy forgetfulness and an unwillingness to leave.
– ORIGIN Greek *lōtos*.

lo·tus-eat·er ▶ **noun** a person who indulges in pleasure and luxury rather than dealing with practical concerns.

lo·tus po·si·tion ▶ **noun** a cross-legged position for meditation, with the feet resting on the thighs.

louche /lo͞osн/ ▶ **adjective** having a bad reputation but still attractive: *a louche rock star.*
– ORIGIN French, 'squinting.'

loud /loud/ ▶ **adjective 1** producing or capable of producing much noise. **2** expressed forcefully: *the bold decision to introduce change despite loud protests from all.* **3** very bright and tasteless: *a loud checked suit.*

> – SYNONYMS **1 noisy,** blaring, booming, roaring, thunderous, resounding, sonorous, powerful, stentorian, deafening, ear-splitting, piercing, shrill, raucous; Music forte, fortissimo. **2 vociferous,** clamorous, insistent, vehement, emphatic. **3 garish,** gaudy, lurid, showy, flamboyant, ostentatious, vulgar, tasteless; informal flashy.
> – ANTONYMS quiet.

▶ **adverb** with much noise.
– DERIVATIVES **loud·en** verb **loud·ly** adverb **loud·ness** noun.
– PHRASES **out loud** so as to be heard; aloud.
– ORIGIN Old English.

loud·mouth /ˈloud,mouтн/ ▶ **noun** informal a person who talks too much or makes tactless remarks.

loud·speak·er /ˈloud,spēkər/ ▶ **noun** a device that converts electrical impulses into sound.

lough /läk, läкн/ ▶ **noun** (in Ireland) a loch.

lounge /lounj/ ▶ **verb** lie, sit, or stand in a relaxed or lazy way.

> – SYNONYMS **laze,** lie, loll, recline, relax, rest, take it easy, sprawl, slump, slouch, loaf, idle.

▶ **noun 1** a room in a hotel, theater, or airport in which to relax or wait. **2** a couch or sofa, especially a backless one having a headrest at one end.

> – SYNONYMS **1 waiting room,** waiting area, reception area, parlor. **2 bar,** tavern, pub, taproom, club, barroom.

– ORIGIN unknown.

lounge liz·ard ▶ **noun** informal an idle man who spends his time among rich and fashionable people.

loung·er /ˈlounjər/ ▶ **noun** a person who spends their time in a lazy or relaxed way.

loupe /lo͞op/ ▶ **noun** a small magnifying glass used by jewelers and watchmakers.
– ORIGIN from French.

lour ▶ **verb** variant spelling of LOWER[3].

louse /lous/ ▶ **noun 1** (pl. **lice** /līs/) a small wingless insect that lives as a parasite on humans, animals, and plants. **2** (pl. **louses**) informal an unpleasant person. ▶ **verb** (**louse something up**) informal spoil something.
– ORIGIN Old English.

lous·y /ˈlouzē/ ▶ **adjective** (**lousier, lousiest**) **1** informal very poor or bad. **2** infested with lice. **3** (**lousy with**) informal full of or teeming with something undesirable.
– DERIVATIVES **lous·i·ly** /-zəlē/ adverb **lous·i·ness** noun.

lout /lout/ ▶ **noun** a rough or aggressive man or boy.

> – SYNONYMS **hooligan,** ruffian, thug, boor, oaf, rowdy; informal tough, bruiser.

– DERIVATIVES **lout·ish** adjective.
– ORIGIN perhaps from an Old English word meaning 'bow down.'

lou·ver /ˈlo͞ovər/ (also **louvre**) ▶ **noun** each of a set of slanting slats fixed at intervals in a door, shutter, or cover to allow air or light through.
– DERIVATIVES **lou·vered** adjective.
– ORIGIN Old French *lover, lovier* 'skylight.'

lov·a·ble /ˈləvəbəl/ (also **loveable**) ▶ **adjective** inspiring love or affection.

> – SYNONYMS **adorable,** dear, sweet, cute, charming, lovely, likable, engaging, endearing, winning, winsome.
> – ANTONYMS hateful, loathsome.

– DERIVATIVES **lov·a·ble·ness** noun **lov·a·bly** /-blē/ adverb.

lov·age /ˈləvij/ ▶ **noun** a large white-flowered plant used as an herb in cooking.
– ORIGIN Old French *luvesche.*

love /ləv/ ▶ **noun 1** a strong feeling of affection. **2** strong affection linked with sexual attraction. **3** a great interest and pleasure in something. **4** a person or thing that one loves: *she was the love of his life.* **5** (in tennis, squash, etc.) a score of zero.

> – SYNONYMS **1 adoration,** devotion, affection, fondness, tenderness, attachment, warmth, passion, desire, lust, yearning, infatuation, besottedness. **2 liking,** taste, zeal, zest, enthusiasm, keenness, fondness, weakness, partiality, predilection, penchant. **3 compassion,** care, regard, concern, altruism, unselfishness, philanthropy, benevolence, humanity. **4 beloved,** loved one, dearest, darling, sweetheart, sweet, angel, honey.
> – ANTONYMS hatred.

▶ **verb 1** feel love for someone. **2** like or enjoy something very much. **3** (as adj. **loving**) showing love or great care.

> – SYNONYMS **1 be in love with,** adore, be devoted to, be infatuated with, be smitten with, be besotted with, idolize, worship, think the world of, dote on, care for, hold dear, cherish; informal be mad/crazy about, carry a torch for. **2 like,** delight in, relish, enjoy, have a soft spot for, have a weakness for, be addicted to, be taken with; informal have a thing about, be hooked on, get a kick out of. **3** (as adj. **loving**) **affectionate,** fond, devoted, adoring, doting, caring, tender, warm, close, amorous, passionate.
> – ANTONYMS hate.

– DERIVATIVES **love·less** adjective **lov·ing·ly** adverb.
– PHRASES **make love 1** have sex. **2** (**make love to**) dated pay romantic attention to someone. **there's no love lost between** the people mentioned dislike each other.
– ORIGIN Old English.

> **WORD LINKS**
>
> **amatory** *relating to love*

love·a·ble /ˈləvəbəl/ ▶ **adjective** variant spelling of LOVABLE.

love af·fair ▶ **noun 1** a romantic or sexual relationship between two people who are not married to each other. **2** an intense enthusiasm for something.

> – SYNONYMS **relationship,** affair, affaire, romance, liaison, fling, amour, entanglement, involvement, intrigue.

love·bird /ˈləv,bərd/ ▶ **noun 1** a very small African or Madagascan parrot that shows affection for its mate. **2** (**lovebirds**) informal an openly affectionate couple.

love bite ▶ **noun** a hickey.

love child ▶ **noun** a child born to parents who are not married to each other.

love han·dles ▸ plural noun informal excess fat at a person's waistline.

love-in ▸ noun informal (especially among hippies in the 1960s) a gathering at which people are encouraged to express friendship and physical attraction.

love-in-a-mist ▸ noun a plant whose blue flowers are surrounded by threadlike green bracts (modified leaves).

love life ▸ noun the part of a person's life concerning their relationships with lovers.

love·lorn /ˈləvˌlôrn/ ▸ adjective unhappy because one loves someone who does not feel the same in return.
– ORIGIN from LOVE + a former word meaning 'lost.'

love·ly /ˈləvlē/ ▸ adjective (**lovelier**, **loveliest**) **1** very beautiful. **2** very pleasant.

– SYNONYMS **1 beautiful,** pretty, attractive, good-looking, handsome, adorable, charming, engaging, enchanting, gorgeous, alluring, ravishing, glamorous; Scottish bonny; informal cute, foxy, drop-dead gorgeous. old use comely. **2 delightful,** marvelous, magnificent, stunning, splendid, wonderful, superb, pleasant, enjoyable; informal terrific, fabulous, heavenly, divine, amazing, glorious.
– ANTONYMS ugly, horrible.

▸ noun (pl. **lovelies**) informal a beautiful woman or girl.
– DERIVATIVES **love·li·ness** noun.

love·mak·ing /ˈləvˌmākiNG/ ▸ noun sexual intercourse and other sexual activity.

love nest ▸ noun informal a private place where two lovers spend time together.

lov·er /ˈləvər/ ▸ noun **1** a person in a sexual or romantic relationship with someone. **2** a person who enjoys a specified thing: *a music lover.*

– SYNONYMS **1 boyfriend, girlfriend,** beloved, sweetheart, inamorato/inamorata, mistress, partner, gigolo. dated beau; literary swain; old use paramour. **2 devotee,** admirer, fan, enthusiast, aficionado; informal buff, nut.

love seat ▸ noun a small sofa for two people.

love·sick /ˈləvˌsik/ ▸ adjective in love, or missing the person one loves, so much that one is unable to act normally.
– DERIVATIVES **love·sick·ness** noun.

love·y-dove·y /ˈləvē ˈdəvē/ ▸ adjective informal very affectionate or romantic.

lov·ing cup ▸ noun a two-handled cup passed around at banquets.

low[1] /lō/ ▸ adjective **1** not high or tall; of less than average height. **2** not far above the ground, horizon, or sea level. **3** below average in amount, extent, or intensity. **4** ranking below others in importance: *training was given low priority.* **5** lacking quality; inferior. **6** (of a sound) deep or quiet. **7** unfavorable: *she had a low opinion of herself.* **8** depressed or lacking energy. **9** lacking moral principles; unscrupulous or dishonest.

– SYNONYMS **1 short,** small, little, squat, stubby, stunted. **2 cheap,** economical, moderate, reasonable, affordable, modest, bargain, bargain-basement, rock-bottom. **3 scarce,** scant, meager, sparse, few, little, reduced, depleted, diminished. **4 inferior,** substandard, poor, low-grade, unsatisfactory, inadequate, second-rate. **5 quiet,** soft, faint, gentle, muted, subdued, muffled, hushed. **6 bass,** low-pitched, deep, rumbling, booming, sonorous. **7 depressed,** dejected, despondent, downhearted, downcast, down, miserable, dispirited, gloomy, glum, flat; informal fed up, down in the dumps, blue.
– ANTONYMS high, expensive, loud.

▸ noun **1** a low point, level, or figure. **2** an area of low atmospheric pressure.
▸ adverb **1** in or into a low position or state. **2** quietly or at a low pitch.
– DERIVATIVES **low·ish** adjective **low·ness** noun.
– ORIGIN Old Norse.

low[2] ▸ verb (of a cow) moo. ▸ noun a moo.
– ORIGIN Old English.

low·ball /ˈlōˌbôl/ informal ▸ adjective (of an estimate, bid, etc.) deceptively or unrealistically low. ▸ verb offer a deceptively or unrealistically low estimate or bid to.

low beam ▸ noun a vehicle headlight providing short-range illumination.

low·brow /ˈlōˌbrou/ ▸ adjective chiefly derogatory not intellectual or interested in culture.

Low Church ▸ noun a tradition within the Anglican Church that places relatively little emphasis on ritual and the authority of bishops and priests.

low com·e·dy ▸ noun comedy bordering on farce.

low·down /ˈlōˌdoun/ informal ▸ adjective unfair or dishonest. ▸ noun (**the lowdown**) the true or most important facts about something.

low-end ▸ adjective referring to the less expensive products in a range.

low·er[1] /ˈlōər/ ▸ adjective comparative of LOW[1]. **1** less high in position, importance, or amount. **2** (of a geological period or formation) older (and hence forming more deeply buried strata): *the Lower Cretaceous.* **3** (in place names) situated to the south.

– SYNONYMS **1 subordinate,** inferior, lesser, junior, minor, secondary, subsidiary, subservient. **2** *her lower lip* **bottom,** nether, bottommost, under.
– ANTONYMS upper.

– DERIVATIVES **low·er·most** /-ˌmōst/ adjective.

low·er[2] ▸ verb **1** move someone or something downward. **2** make or become less in amount, intensity, or value: *I lowered my voice to a whisper.* **3** (**lower oneself**) behave in a way that is humiliating.

– SYNONYMS **1 let down,** take down, drop, let fall. **2 soften,** modulate, quieten, hush, tone down, muffle, turn down, mute. **3 reduce,** decrease, lessen, bring down, cut, slash.
– ANTONYMS raise, increase.

low·er[3] /ˈlou(ə)r/ (also **lour**) ▸ verb **1** (of the sky) look dark and threatening. **2** look angry or sullen; scowl.

low·er·case /ˈlōərˌkās/ ▸ noun small letters as opposed to capitals.

low·er class /ˈlōər/ (also **lower classes**) ▸ noun the working class.

low·er court /ˈlōər/ ▸ noun Law a court whose decisions may be overruled by another on appeal.

low·er house /ˈlōər/ (also **lower chamber**) ▸ noun **1** one of two houses (often the larger) in a bicameral legislature or parliament and typically having the primary responsibility for legislation. **2** (often **the House**) the House of Representatives (of the US or of a US state). **3** (**the Lower House**) (in the UK) the House of Commons.

low·est com·mon de·nom·i·na·tor /lōist/ ▶ **noun 1** Mathematics the lowest common multiple of the denominators of several fractions. **2** derogatory the level of the least discriminating audience or other group.

low·est com·mon mul·ti·ple /lōist/ ▶ **noun** Mathematics the lowest quantity that is a multiple of two or more given quantities.

low-fi ▶ **adjective** variant spelling of LO-FI.

low fre·quen·cy ▶ **noun** (in radio) a frequency of 30–300 kilohertz.

low gear ▶ **noun** a gear that causes a vehicle to move slowly.

Low Ger·man ▶ **noun** a German dialect spoken in much of northern Germany.

low-grade ▶ **adjective 1** of low quality or strength. **2** (of a medical condition) of a less serious kind; minor: *a low-grade fever.*

low-hang·ing fruit ▶ **noun** informal a thing that can be won or obtained with little effort.

low-im·pact /ˈim,pakt/ ▶ **adjective 1** (of physical exercises) putting little stress on the body. **2** having relatively little effect on the environment.

low-key (also **low-keyed**) ▶ **adjective** not elaborate, showy, or intensive; restrained.

– SYNONYMS **restrained,** modest, understated, muted, subtle, quiet, low-profile, inconspicuous, unobtrusive, discreet.
– ANTONYMS ostentatious, obtrusive.

low·land /ˈlōlənd, -ˌland/ ▶ **noun 1** (also **lowlands**) low-lying country. **2** (**the Lowlands**) the part of Scotland lying south and east of the Highlands.
– DERIVATIVES **low·land·er** noun.

low-lev·el ▶ **adjective 1** of relatively little importance. **2** (of a computer programming language) similar to machine code in form.

low·life /ˈlō,līf/ ▶ **noun** (pl. **lowlifes**) **1** dishonest or immoral people or activities. **2** informal a dishonest or immoral person.

low·light /ˈlō,līt/ ▶ **noun 1** (**lowlights**) darker dyed streaks in the hair. **2** informal a disappointing or dull event or feature.

low·ly /ˈlōlē/ ▶ **adjective** (**lowlier, lowliest**) low in status or importance.

– SYNONYMS **humble,** low, low-ranking, common, ordinary, plain, modest, simple, obscure.
– ANTONYMS aristocratic, exalted.

▶ **adverb** to a low degree: *lowly paid workers.*
– DERIVATIVES **low·li·ness** noun.

low-ly·ing ▶ **adjective** (of land) not far above sea level.

low-pro·file ▶ **adjective** avoiding attention or publicity: *a low-profile campaign.*

low re·lief ▶ **noun** see RELIEF (sense 8).

low-rise ▶ **adjective 1** (of a building) having few stories. **2** (of trousers) cut so as to fit low on the hips rather than on the waist.

low sea·son ▶ **noun** the least popular time of year for a vacation, when prices are lowest.

low-slung ▶ **adjective 1** lower in height or closer to the ground than usual. **2** (of clothes) cut to fit low on the hips rather than the waist.

low spir·its ▶ **plural noun** a feeling of sadness and gloom.

low-tech /ˈlō ˈtek/ (also **lo-tech**) ▶ **adjective** using or needing only low technology: *low-tech solar heating systems.*

low tech·nol·o·gy ▶ **noun** less advanced technological development or equipment.

low tide (also **low water**) ▶ **noun** the state of the tide when at its lowest level.

low-wa·ter mark ▶ **noun** the level reached by the sea at low tide.

lox /läks/ ▶ **noun** smoked salmon.
– ORIGIN Yiddish.

loy·al /ˈloiəl/ ▶ **adjective** showing firm and constant support for a person, an organization, or one's country.

– SYNONYMS **faithful,** true, true-blue, devoted, constant, steadfast, staunch, dependable, reliable, trustworthy, trusty, patriotic, unswerving.
– ANTONYMS disloyal, treacherous.

– DERIVATIVES **loy·al·ly** adverb.
– ORIGIN French.

loy·al·ist /ˈloiəlist/ ▶ **noun 1** a person who remains loyal to the established ruler or government. **2** (**Loyalist**) a colonist of the American Revolutionary period who supported the British.
– DERIVATIVES **loy·al·ism** /-ˌlizəm/ noun.

loy·al·ty /ˈloiəltē/ ▶ **noun** (pl. **loyalties**) **1** the state of being loyal or faithful to a person, an organization, or one's country. **2** a strong feeling of support or commitment: *arguments with in-laws can cause divided loyalties.*

– SYNONYMS **allegiance,** faithfulness, fidelity, obedience, adherence, devotion, steadfastness, staunchness, dedication, commitment, patriotism; old use fealty.
– ANTONYMS disloyalty, treachery.

loz·enge /ˈläzənj/ ▶ **noun 1** a small tablet of medicine that is sucked to soothe a sore throat. **2** a diamond shape; a rhombus.
– ORIGIN Old French *losenge.*

LP ▶ **abbreviation** long-playing (phonograph record).

LPG ▶ **abbreviation** liquefied petroleum gas.

LPN ▶ **abbreviation** Licensed Practical Nurse.

Lr ▶ **symbol** the chemical element lawrencium.

LSAT /ˈel,sat/ ▶ **abbreviation** Law School Admission Test.

LSD ▶ **noun** lysergic acid diethylamide, a powerful drug that causes hallucinations.

Lt ▶ **abbreviation** Lieutenant.

Ltd ▶ **abbreviation** Brit. (after a company name) Limited.

Lu ▶ **symbol** the chemical element lutetium.

lub·ber /ˈləbər/ ▶ **noun** old use or dialect a big, clumsy person.
– DERIVATIVES **lub·ber·ly** adjective & adverb.
– ORIGIN perhaps from Old French *lobeor* 'swindler, parasite.'

lube /lo͞ob/ informal ▶ **noun** a lubricant. ▶ **verb** lubricate something.

lu·bri·cant /ˈlo͞obrəkənt/ ▶ **noun** a substance for lubricating machinery or part of the body.

lu·bri·cate /ˈlo͞obrə,kāt/ ▶ **verb** apply a substance such as oil or grease to machinery or part of the body to allow smooth movement.

– DERIVATIVES **lu·bri·ca·tion** /ˌlo͞obrəˈkāSHən/ noun **lu·bri·ca·tor** noun.
– ORIGIN Latin *lubricare* 'make slippery.'

lu·bri·cious /lo͞oˈbriSHəs/ ▶ **adjective** referring to sexual matters in a crude or offensive way.
– DERIVATIVES **lu·bri·cious·ly** adverb **lu·bric·i·ty** /-ˈbrisitē/ noun.
– ORIGIN Latin *lubricus* 'slippery.'

lu·cent /ˈlo͞osənt/ ▶ **adjective** literary glowing with or giving off light; shining.
– DERIVATIVES **lu·cen·cy** noun.
– ORIGIN from Latin *lucere* 'shine.'

lu·cid /ˈlo͞osid/ ▶ **adjective 1** easy to understand; clear: *a lucid account.* **2** showing an ability to think clearly. **3** literary bright or luminous.

– SYNONYMS **1 clear,** crystal-clear, intelligible, comprehensible, cogent, coherent, articulate. **2 rational,** sane, in possession of one's faculties, compos mentis, clear-headed, sober; informal all there.
– ANTONYMS confused.

– DERIVATIVES **lu·cid·i·ty** /lo͞oˈsidətē/ noun **lu·cid·ly** adverb.
– ORIGIN Latin *lucidus.*

Lu·ci·fer /ˈlo͞osəfər/ ▶ **noun 1** the Devil. **2 (lucifer)** old use a match.
– ORIGIN Latin, 'light-bringing, morning star.'

luck /lək/ ▶ **noun 1** good things that happen by chance: *it was just luck that the first goal went in.* **2** chance considered as a force that causes success or failure: *we both had bad luck and lost five thousand dollars.*

– SYNONYMS **1 good fortune,** good luck, stroke of luck, fluke; informal lucky break. **2 fortune,** fate, serendipity, chance, accident, a twist of fate.
– ANTONYMS bad luck, misfortune.

▶ **verb** informal **(luck into/onto)** find or obtain something by good luck.
– PHRASES **no such luck** informal unfortunately not. **try one's luck** attempt something risky.
– ORIGIN German *lucke.*

luck·i·ly /ˈləkəlē/ ▶ **adverb** it is fortunate that.

– SYNONYMS **fortunately,** happily, providentially, by good fortune, as luck would have it, mercifully, thankfully.

luck·less /ˈlækləs/ ▶ **adjective** having bad luck; unfortunate.

luck·y /ˈləkē/ ▶ **adjective (luckier, luckiest)** having, bringing, or resulting from good luck: *seven's my lucky number.*

– SYNONYMS **1 fortunate,** in luck, favored, charmed, successful. **2 providential,** fortunate, timely, opportune, serendipitous, chance, fortuitous, accidental.
– ANTONYMS unlucky.

lu·cra·tive /ˈlo͞okrətiv/ ▶ **adjective** producing a great deal of profit; profitable.

– SYNONYMS **profitable,** gainful, remunerative, moneymaking, well paid, rewarding, worthwhile.
– ANTONYMS unprofitable.

– DERIVATIVES **lu·cra·tive·ly** adverb.
– ORIGIN Latin *lucrativus.*

lu·cre /ˈlo͞okər/ ▶ **noun** literary money, especially when gained in an underhanded or dishonorable way.
– ORIGIN Latin *lucrum.*

lu·cu·bra·tion /ˌlo͞ok(y)əˈbrāSHən/ ▶ **noun** literary a scholarly or pedantic piece of writing.
– ORIGIN from Latin *lucubrare* 'work by lamplight.'

Lud·dite /ˈlədˌīt/ ▶ **noun 1** often derogatory a person opposed to industrialization or new technology. **2** a member of any of the bands of English workers who opposed mechanization and destroyed machinery in the early 19th century.
– DERIVATIVES **Lud·dism** /-ˌizəm/ noun **Lud·dit·ism** /-ˌītˌizəm/ noun.
– ORIGIN perhaps named after Ned *Lud,* a worker who destroyed machinery.

lu·dic /ˈlo͞odik/ ▶ **adjective** formal spontaneous; playful.
– ORIGIN French *ludique.*

lu·di·crous /ˈlo͞odəkrəs/ ▶ **adjective** absurd; ridiculous.

– SYNONYMS **absurd,** ridiculous, farcical, laughable, risible, preposterous, mad, insane, idiotic, stupid, asinine, nonsensical; informal crazy.
– ANTONYMS sensible.

– DERIVATIVES **lu·di·crous·ly** adverb **lu·di·crous·ness** noun.
– ORIGIN Latin *ludicrus.*

luff /ləf/ ▶ **verb** steer a sailing ship nearer the wind.
– ORIGIN Old French *lof.*

Luft·waf·fe /ˈlo͝oftˌwäfə, -ˌväfə/ ▶ **noun** the German air force until the end of World War II.
– ORIGIN from German *Luft* 'air' + *Waffe* 'weapon.'

lug[1] /ləg/ ▶ **verb (lugs, lugging, lugged)** carry or drag a heavy object with great effort.
– ORIGIN probably Scandinavian.

lug[2] ▶ **noun 1** a projection on an object by which it may be carried or fixed in place. **2** an uncouth, aggressive man.
– ORIGIN probably Scandinavian.

luge /lo͞oZH/ ▶ **noun** a light toboggan ridden in a sitting or lying position.
– ORIGIN Swiss French.

Lu·ger /ˈlo͞ogər/ ▶ **noun** trademark a type of German automatic pistol.
– ORIGIN named after the German firearms expert George *Luger.*

lug·gage /ˈləgij/ ▶ **noun** suitcases or other bags for a traveler's belongings.

– SYNONYMS **baggage,** bags, suitcases, cases.

– ORIGIN from LUG[1].

lug·ger /ˈləgər/ ▶ **noun** a small ship with two or three masts and a four-sided sail on each.

lug nut ▶ **noun** a large rounded nut used especially to attach a vehicle wheel to its axle.

lu·gu·bri·ous /ləˈg(y)o͞obrēəs/ ▶ **adjective** sad and dismal; mournful.

– SYNONYMS **mournful,** gloomy, sad, unhappy, melancholy, doleful, woeful, miserable, forlorn, somber, solemn, sorrowful, morose, dour, cheerless, joyless, dismal; funereal; literary dolorous.
– ANTONYMS cheerful.

– DERIVATIVES **lu·gu·bri·ous·ly** adverb **lu·gu·bri·ous·ness** noun.
– ORIGIN Latin *lugubris.*

lug·worm /ˈləgˌwərm/ ▶ **noun** a worm that lives in muddy sand, used as fishing bait.
– ORIGIN unknown.

luke·warm /ˈlo͞okˈwôrm/ ▶ **adjective 1** only slightly warm. **2** not enthusiastic or interested: *a lukewarm response.*

– SYNONYMS *a lukewarm response* **indifferent,** cool, half-hearted, apathetic, tepid, unenthusiastic, uninterested, noncommittal.
– ANTONYMS warm.

– ORIGIN from dialect *luke* 'tepid.'

lull /ləl/ ▶ **verb 1** calm someone or send them to sleep with soothing sounds or movements. **2** make someone feel secure or confident, even if they are at risk. **3** (of noise or a storm) become quiet or calm.

– SYNONYMS **soothe,** calm, quiet, still, assuage, allay, ease, quell.

▶ **noun** a temporary period of quiet or inactivity.

– SYNONYMS **1 pause,** respite, interval, break, suspension, breathing space, hiatus; informal letup, breather. **2** *the lull before the storm* **calm,** stillness, quiet, tranquility, peace, silence, hush.

– ORIGIN imitating sounds used to quieten a child.

lull·a·by /ˈləlәˌbī/ ▶ **noun** (pl. **lullabies**) a soothing song sung to send a child to sleep.
– ORIGIN from **LULL** + *bye-bye*.

lum·ba·go /ˌləmˈbāgō/ ▶ **noun** pain in the lower back.
– ORIGIN Latin.

lum·bar /ˈləmbər, -ˌbär/ ▶ **adjective** relating to the lower back.
– ORIGIN Latin *lumbaris*.

lum·bar punc·ture ▶ **noun** Medicine the taking of spinal fluid from the lower back through a hollow needle, usually for diagnosis.

lum·ber[1] /ˈləmbər/ ▶ **verb** move in a slow, heavy, awkward way.

– SYNONYMS **trundle,** stump, clump, plod, stumble, shamble, shuffle, trudge.

– ORIGIN uncertain.

lum·ber[2] ▶ **noun** partly prepared timber. ▶ **verb** cut and prepare forest timber for transport and sale.
– ORIGIN perhaps from **LUMBER**[1]; later associated with former *lumber* 'pawnbroker's shop.'

lum·ber·ing /ˈləmbəriNG/ ▶ **adjective** slow and clumsy: *he was a lumbering bear of a man.*

– SYNONYMS **clumsy,** awkward, slow, blundering, bumbling, ponderous, ungainly; informal clodhopping.
– ANTONYMS nimble, agile.

lum·ber·jack /ˈləmbərˌjak/ (also **lumberman** /ˈləmbərˌmən/) ▶ **noun** a person who fells trees, cuts them into logs, or transports them.

lum·ber·jack shirt ▶ **noun** a shirt of brushed cotton or flannel, typically with a check pattern.

lum·ber·yard /ˈləmbərˌyärd/ ▶ **noun** a place that sells lumber and other building materials.

lu·men /ˈlo͞omən/ ▶ **noun** Physics the SI unit of flux of light.
– ORIGIN Latin, 'light.'

lu·mi·naire /ˌlo͞oməˈner/ ▶ **noun** a complete electric light unit.
– ORIGIN French.

lu·mi·nance /ˈlo͞omənəns/ ▶ **noun 1** the component of a television signal that carries information on the brightness of the image. **2** Physics the intensity of light emitted from a surface per unit area in a given direction.

lu·mi·nar·y /ˈlo͞oməˌnerē/ ▶ **noun** (pl. **luminaries**) **1** a person who is influential or famous within an area of activity: *culinary luminaries.* **2** old use the sun or moon.

lu·mi·nesce /ˌlo͞oməˈnes/ ▶ **verb** produce light by luminescence.

lu·mi·nes·cence /ˌlo͞oməˈnesəns/ ▶ **noun** the production of light by a substance that has not been heated, as in fluorescence.
– DERIVATIVES **lu·mi·nes·cent** adjective.

lu·mi·nos·i·ty /ˌlo͞oməˈnäsətē/ ▶ **noun** (pl. **luminosities**) the quality of being bright or shining.

lu·mi·nous /ˈlo͞omənəs/ ▶ **adjective 1** bright or shining, especially in the dark. **2** Physics relating to visible light.

– SYNONYMS **shining,** bright, brilliant, radiant, dazzling, glowing, luminescent, phosphorescent, fluorescent, incandescent.
– ANTONYMS dark.

– DERIVATIVES **lu·mi·nous·ly** adverb.
– ORIGIN Latin *luminosus*.

CHOOSE THE RIGHT WORD

See **BRIGHT**.

lum·mox /ˈləməks/ ▶ **noun** informal a clumsy, stupid person.
– ORIGIN unknown.

lump[1] /ləmp/ ▶ **noun 1** an irregular mass or piece of something hard or solid. **2** a swelling under the skin. **3** informal a heavy, clumsy, or slow-witted person.

– SYNONYMS **1 chunk,** hunk, piece, block, wedge, slab, ball, knob, pat, clod, clump, nugget, gobbet. **2 swelling,** bump, bulge, protuberance, protrusion, growth, nodule, tumor.

▶ **verb** treat as alike, regardless of details: *Hong Kong and Bangkok tend to be lumped together in vacation brochures.*

– SYNONYMS **combine,** put, group, bunch, throw.

– PHRASES **a lump in the throat** a feeling of tightness in the throat caused by strong emotion.
– ORIGIN perhaps Germanic.

lump[2] ▶ **verb** (**lump it**) informal accept or put up with something whether one likes it or not.
– ORIGIN uncertain.

lump·ec·to·my /ˌləmˈpektəmē/ ▶ **noun** (pl. **lumpectomies**) a surgical operation in which a lump, typically a tumor, is removed from the breast.

lum·pen /ˈləmpən, ˈlo͝om-/ ▶ **adjective 1** lumpy and misshapen. **2** uncultured and stupid.
– ORIGIN abbreviation of **LUMPENPROLETARIAT**.

lum·pen·pro·le·tar·i·at /ˈləmpənˌprōləˈte(ə)rēət, ˈlo͝om-/ ▶ **noun** (in Marxism) the lower orders of society who are not interested in politics or revolutionary advancement.
– ORIGIN from German *Lumpen* 'rag, rogue' + **PROLETARIAT**.

lump·fish /ˈləmpˌfisH/ ▶ **noun** (pl. same or **lumpfishes**) a North Atlantic fish with edible roe.
– ORIGIN from German *lumpen*, Dutch *lompe*.

lump·ish /ˈləmpisH/ ▶ **adjective 1** stupid or slow-witted. **2** roughly or clumsily formed.
– DERIVATIVES **lump·ish·ly** adverb **lump·ish·ness** noun.

lump sum ▶ **noun** a single payment made at one time, as opposed to several installments.

lump·y /ˈləmpē/ ▶ **adjective** (**lumpier, lumpiest**) full of or covered with lumps.
– DERIVATIVES **lump·i·ly** adverb **lump·i·ness** noun.

lu·na·cy /ˈlo͞onəsē/ ▸ **noun** (pl. **lunacies**) **1** insanity (not in technical use). **2** great foolishness.
– ORIGIN from LUNATIC.

lu·nar /ˈlo͞onər/ ▸ **adjective** relating to, determined by, or resembling the moon.
– ORIGIN from Latin *luna* 'moon.'

lu·nar e·clipse ▸ **noun** an eclipse in which the moon passes into the earth's shadow.

lu·nar month ▸ **noun 1** a month measured between successive new moons (roughly 29½ days). **2** (in general use) four weeks.

lu·na·tic /ˈlo͞onəˌtik/ ▸ **noun 1** a person who is mentally ill (not in technical use). **2** a very foolish person.

> – SYNONYMS **maniac,** psychopath, madman, madwoman, idiot; informal loony, screwball, nutcase, headcase, psycho.

▸ **adjective 1** mentally ill (not in technical use). **2** very foolish.

> – SYNONYMS *a lunatic idea* **stupid,** foolish, idiotic, insane, absurd, ridiculous, ludicrous, preposterous, asinine; informal crazy, mad, daft.

– ORIGIN from Latin *luna* 'moon' (from the former belief that changes of the moon caused insanity).

lu·na·tic a·sy·lum ▸ **noun** dated a psychiatric hospital.

lu·na·tic fringe ▸ **noun** a small section within a group with extreme or eccentric views.

lunch /lənCH/ ▸ **noun** a meal eaten in the middle of the day. ▸ **verb** eat lunch.
– DERIVATIVES **lunch·er** noun.
– PHRASES **out to lunch** informal unbalanced or crazy.
– ORIGIN abbreviation of LUNCHEON.

lunch·eon /ˈlənCHən/ ▸ **noun** formal lunch.
– ORIGIN perhaps from Spanish *lonja* 'slice.'

lunch·meat /ˈlənCHˌmēt/ ▸ **noun** meat sold in slices for sandwiches; cold cuts.

lunch·time /ˈlənCHˌtīm/ ▸ **noun** the time when lunch is eaten.

lu·nette /lo͞oˈnet/ ▸ **noun 1** an arched window or other aperture in a domed ceiling. **2** a crescent-shaped or semicircular alcove containing a painting or statue.
– ORIGIN French, 'little moon.'

lung /ləNG/ ▸ **noun** each of the pair of organs within the ribcage of humans and most vertebrates, into which air is drawn in breathing.
– DERIVATIVES **lunged** adjective **lung·ful** /-ˌfo͝ol/ noun.
– ORIGIN Old English.

> **WORD LINKS**
>
> **pulmonary** *relating to the lungs*

lunge[1] /lənj/ ▸ **noun 1** a sudden forward movement of the body. **2** a thrust in fencing, in which the leading leg is bent while the back leg remains straightened.

> – SYNONYMS *Darren made a lunge at his attacker* **thrust,** dive, rush, charge, grab.

▸ **verb** (**lunges, lunging** or **lungeing, lunged**) make a sudden forward movement or thrust.

> – SYNONYMS *he lunged at her with a knife* **thrust,** dive, spring, launch oneself, rush.

– ORIGIN from French *allonger* 'lengthen.'

lunge[2] /lənj/ (also **longe** pronunc. same) ▸ **noun** a long rein on which a horse is made to move in a circle around its trainer.
– ORIGIN French *longe.*

lung·fish /ˈləNGˌfiSH/ ▸ **noun** (pl. same or **lungfishes**) a freshwater fish with one or two sacs that function as lungs, enabling it to breathe air and live dormant in mud to survive drought.

lun·gi /ˈlo͝oNGgē/ ▸ **noun** (pl. **lungis**) an item of clothing like a sarong, wrapped around the waist and extending to the ankles, worn in India and Burma (Myanmar).
– ORIGIN Urdu.

lunk /ləNGk/ (also **lunkhead**) ▸ **noun** informal a slow-witted person.
– ORIGIN probably from LUMP[1].

lu·pine[1] /ˈlo͞opin/ ▸ **noun** a plant with a tall stem bearing many small colorful flowers.
– ORIGIN Latin *lupinus.*

lu·pine[2] /ˈlo͞oˌpīn/ ▸ **adjective** relating to or like a wolf or wolves.
– ORIGIN from Latin *lupus* 'wolf.'

lu·pus /ˈlo͞opəs/ ▸ **noun** an ulcerous skin disease, especially **lupus vulgaris** (/ˌvəlˈge(ə)ris/) that is due to direct infection with tuberculosis.
– ORIGIN Latin, 'wolf.'

lu·pus er·y·the·ma·to·sus /ˌerəˌTHēməˈtōsəs/ ▸ **noun** an inflammatory disease causing scaly red patches on the skin.
– ORIGIN from LUPUS + Greek *eruthēma* 'reddening.'

lurch[1] /lərCH/ ▸ **verb** make a sudden unsteady movement; stagger.

> – SYNONYMS **1 stagger,** stumble, sway, reel, roll, totter, weave. **2 swing,** list, roll, pitch, veer, swerve.

▸ **noun** a sudden unsteady movement.
– ORIGIN unknown.

lurch[2] ▸ **noun** (in phrase **leave someone in the lurch**) leave someone in a difficult situation without assistance or support.
– ORIGIN from French *demeurer lourche* 'be discomfited' (*lourche* referring to a game resembling backgammon).

lure /lo͝or/ ▸ **verb** tempt someone to do something or to go somewhere.

> – SYNONYMS **tempt,** entice, attract, induce, coax, persuade, inveigle, seduce, beguile, draw.
> – ANTONYMS deter, put off.

▸ **noun 1** the attractive or tempting qualities of a person or thing: *the lure of the city.* **2** a type of bait used in fishing or hunting. **3** a bunch of feathers with a piece of meat attached to a long string, which a falconer swings around their head to recall a hawk.

> – SYNONYMS *the lure of the stage* **temptation,** attraction, pull, draw, appeal, inducement, allure, fascination, interest, glamour.

– ORIGIN Old French *luere.*

> **CHOOSE THE RIGHT WORD**
>
> See TEMPT.

lur·ex /ˈlo͝orˌeks/ ▸ **noun** trademark yarn or fabric incorporating a glittering metallic thread.
– ORIGIN unknown.

lu·rid /ˈlo͝orid/ ▸ **adjective 1** unpleasantly vivid in color. **2** deliberately shocking or sensational: *lurid accounts of murders.*

> – SYNONYMS **1 bright,** vivid, glaring, fluorescent, gaudy, loud. **2** *lurid details* **sensational,** colorful,

salacious, graphic, explicit, prurient, shocking, gruesome, gory, grisly; informal juicy.

– DERIVATIVES **lu·rid·ly** adverb **lu·rid·ness** noun.
– ORIGIN Latin *luridus* 'yellow, sallow.'

lurk /lərk/ ▶ **verb 1** wait in hiding so as to attack someone or something. **2** be present in an underlying or hidden way: *danger lurks beneath the surface.*

– SYNONYMS **skulk,** loiter, lie in wait, hide.

– ORIGIN perhaps from **LOWER**[3].

lurk·er /'lərkər/ ▶ **noun** a person who visits an Internet bulletin board or chat room but does not participate.

lus·cious /'ləsʜəs/ ▶ **adjective 1** having a pleasingly rich, sweet taste. **2** very pleasing to the senses: *luscious harmonies.* **3** (of a woman) sexually attractive.

– SYNONYMS **1** *luscious fruit* **delicious,** succulent, juicy, mouthwatering, sweet, tasty, appetizing; informal scrumptious, yummy. **2** *a luscious woman* **gorgeous,** nubile, ravishing, alluring, sultry, beautiful, stunning; informal foxy, cute.
– ANTONYMS unappetizing, plain, scrawny.

– DERIVATIVES **lus·cious·ly** adverb **lus·cious·ness** noun.
– ORIGIN perhaps from **DELICIOUS**.

lush[1] /ləsʜ/ ▶ **adjective 1** (of vegetation) growing thickly. **2** rich and pleasing to the senses: *the album's lush production.* **3** informal sexually attractive.

– SYNONYMS **1 profuse,** abundant, luxuriant, flourishing, rich, riotous, vigorous, dense, thick, rampant. **2 luxurious,** sumptuous, palatial, opulent, lavish, elaborate, extravagant, fancy; informal **plush,** posh, swanky, swank, swish, bling-bling.
– ANTONYMS sparse, austere.

– DERIVATIVES **lush·ly** adverb **lush·ness** noun.
– ORIGIN perhaps from Old French *lasche* 'lax.'

lush[2] ▶ **noun** informal a drunkard.
– ORIGIN perhaps from **LUSH**[1].

lust /ləst/ ▶ **noun 1** strong sexual desire. **2** a passionate desire for something: *a lust for power.*

– SYNONYMS **1 desire,** longing, passion, libido, sex drive, sexuality, lecherousness, lasciviousness. **2 greed,** desire, craving, eagerness, longing, yearning, hunger, thirst, appetite, hankering.

▶ **verb** (usu. **lust for/after**) feel strong desire for someone or something.
– ORIGIN Old English.

lus·ter /'ləstər/ (Brit. **lustre**) ▶ **noun 1** a soft sheen or glow. **2** prestige or distinction: *a celebrity player will add luster to the lineup.* **3** a thin metallic coating used to give an iridescent glaze to ceramics.
– DERIVATIVES **lus·tered** adjective **lus·ter·less** adjective.
– ORIGIN Latin *lustrare* 'illuminate.'

CHOOSE THE RIGHT WORD

See **POLISH**.

lust·ful /'ləs(t)fəl/ ▶ **adjective** filled with strong sexual desire.
– DERIVATIVES **lust·ful·ly** adverb **lust·ful·ness** noun.

lus·trous /'ləstrəs/ ▶ **adjective** having a soft glow or sheen.

– SYNONYMS **shiny,** shining, satiny, silky, glossy, gleaming, burnished, polished; bright, brilliant, luminous.
– ANTONYMS dull, dark.

– DERIVATIVES **lus·trous·ly** adverb **lus·trous·ness** noun.

WORD TOOLKIT

See **GLOSSY**.

CHOOSE THE RIGHT WORD

See **BRIGHT**.

lust·y /'ləstē/ ▶ **adjective** (**lustier, lustiest**) healthy and strong; vigorous.
– DERIVATIVES **lust·i·ly** adverb **lust·i·ness** noun.

lute /lo͞ot/ ▶ **noun** a stringed instrument with a long neck and a rounded body with a flat front, played by plucking.
– ORIGIN Old French *lut, leut.*

lu·te·nist /'lo͞otn-ist, 'lo͞otnist/ (also **lutanist**) ▶ **noun** a lute player.

lu·te·ti·um /lo͞o'tēsʜ(ē)əm/ ▶ **noun** a rare silvery-white metallic chemical element of the lanthanide series.
– ORIGIN from Latin *Lutetia,* the ancient name of Paris, where its discoverer lived.

Lu·ther·an /'lo͞otʜ(ə)rən/ ▶ **noun** a member of the Lutheran Church, a Protestant Church based on the beliefs and teachings of the German theologian Martin Luther. ▶ **adjective** relating to the teachings of Martin Luther or to the Lutheran Church.
– DERIVATIVES **Lu·ther·an·ism** /-ˌnizəm/ noun.

lu·thi·er /'lo͞otēər/ ▶ **noun** a maker of stringed instruments.
– ORIGIN from French *luth* 'lute.'

lux /ləks/ ▶ **noun** (pl. same) the SI unit of illumination.
– ORIGIN Latin, 'light.'

luxe /ləks, lo͝oks/ ▶ **noun** luxury.
– ORIGIN French.

lux·u·ri·ant /ˌləg'zʜo͝orēənt, ˌlək'sʜo͝or-/ ▶ **adjective 1** (of vegetation or hair) growing thickly and strongly. **2** rich and pleasing to the senses: *the novel's luxuriant prose.*
– DERIVATIVES **lux·u·ri·ance** noun **lux·u·ri·ant·ly** adverb.
– ORIGIN from Latin *luxuriare* 'grow rankly.'

lux·u·ri·ate /ˌləg'zʜo͝orēˌāt, ˌlək'sʜo͝or-/ ▶ **verb** (**luxuriate in**) take pleasure in something enjoyable.

lux·u·ri·ous /ˌləg'zʜo͝orēəs, ˌlək'sʜo͝or-/ ▶ **adjective 1** very elegant, comfortable, and expensive. **2** giving sensual pleasure: *long, luxurious baths.*

– SYNONYMS **opulent,** sumptuous, grand, palatial, magnificent, extravagant, fancy, deluxe, expensive, uptown, upmarket, upscale; informal plush, posh, classy, swanky, swank, swish, bling-bling.
– ANTONYMS plain, basic.

– DERIVATIVES **lux·u·ri·ous·ly** adverb **lux·u·ri·ous·ness** noun.

lux·u·ry /'ləksʜ(ə)rē, 'ləgzʜ(ə)-/ ▶ **noun** (pl. **luxuries**) **1** a state of great comfort and elegance, especially when involving great expense. **2** an item that is expensive and enjoyable but not essential.

– SYNONYMS **1 opulence,** sumptuousness, grandeur, magnificence, splendor, luxuriousness, affluence. **2 indulgence,** extravagance, treat, extra, frill.
– ANTONYMS simplicity, necessity.

▶ **adjective** expensive and elegant; luxurious: *a luxury yacht.*
– ORIGIN Latin *luxuria* 'lechery.'

LW ▶ **abbreviation** long wave.

lx ▶ **abbreviation** Physics lux.

ly·can·thrope /ˈlīkənˌᴛʜrōp/ ▶ **noun** a werewolf.

ly·can·thro·py /līˈkanᴛʜrəpē/ ▶ **noun** the mythical transformation of a person into a wolf.
– DERIVATIVES **ly·can·throp·ic** /ˌlīkənˈᴛʜräpik/ adjective.
– ORIGIN from Greek *lukos* 'wolf' + *anthrōpos* 'man.'

ly·chee /ˈlēᴄʜē/ (also **litchi**) ▶ **noun** a small round fruit with sweet white flesh, a large stone, and thin rough skin.
– ORIGIN Chinese.

lych·gate /ˈliᴄʜˌgāt/ ▶ **noun** a roofed gateway to a churchyard.
– ORIGIN from Old English *līc* 'body' (from the former practice of using such a gateway to shelter a coffin before burial).

ly·co·pene /ˈlīkəˌpēn/ ▶ **noun** a red pigment related to carotene and present in tomatoes and many berries and fruits.
– ORIGIN from Latin *Lycopersicon* a genus name including the tomato.

Ly·cra /ˈlīkrə/ ▶ **noun** trademark a synthetic elastic fiber or fabric used for close-fitting clothing.
– ORIGIN unknown.

lye /lī/ ▶ **noun** a strongly alkaline solution, especially of potassium hydroxide, used for washing or cleaning.
– ORIGIN Old English.

ly·ing[1] /ˈlī-iɴɢ/ present participle of **LIE**[1].

ly·ing[2] present participle of **LIE**[2].

Lyme dis·ease /līm/ ▶ **noun** a form of arthritis caused by bacteria that are transmitted by ticks.
– ORIGIN named after *Lyme, CT,* where an outbreak occurred.

lymph /limf/ ▶ **noun** a colorless fluid containing white blood cells that bathes the tissues of the body.
– ORIGIN Latin *lympha, limpa* 'water.'

lym·phat·ic /limˈfatik/ ▶ **adjective** relating to lymph or its production. ▶ **noun** a structure like a vein that conveys lymph in the body.
– ORIGIN Greek *numpholēptos* 'seized by nymphs'; now associated with **LYMPH**.

lym·phat·ic sys·tem ▶ **noun** the network of vessels through which lymph drains from the body tissues into the blood.

lymph node (also **lymph gland**) ▶ **noun** each of a number of small swellings in the body's lymphatic system where lymph is filtered and lymphocytes are formed.

lym·pho·cyte /ˈlimfəˌsīt/ ▶ **noun** a form of small leukocyte (white blood cell) with a single round nucleus, occurring especially in the lymphatic system.

lym·pho·ma /limˈfōmə/ ▶ **noun** (pl. **lymphomas**) cancer of the lymph nodes.

lynch /linᴄʜ/ ▶ **verb** (of a group) kill someone for an alleged crime without a legal trial, especially by hanging.
– DERIVATIVES **lynch·er** noun.
– ORIGIN named after Captain William *Lynch* of Virginia, head of an unofficial court of justice.

lynch·pin /ˈlinᴄʜˌpin/ ▶ **noun** variant spelling of **LINCHPIN**.

lynx /liɴɢks/ ▶ **noun** a wild cat with a short tail and tufted ears.
– ORIGIN Greek *lunx*.

lynx-eyed ▶ **adjective** keen-sighted.

ly·on·naise /ˌlīəˈnāz/ ▶ **adjective** (especially of sliced potatoes) cooked with onions or with a white wine and onion sauce.
– ORIGIN French, 'characteristic of the city of Lyons.'

lyre /līr/ ▶ **noun** a stringed instrument like a small U-shaped harp with strings fixed to a crossbar, used especially in ancient Greece.
– ORIGIN Greek *lura*.

lyre·bird /ˈlīrˌbərd/ ▶ **noun** a large Australian songbird, the male of which has a long lyre-shaped tail.

lyr·ic /ˈlirik/ ▶ **noun 1** (also **lyrics**) the words of a song. **2** a fairly short poem expressing the writer's emotions or mood. ▶ **adjective 1** (of poetry) expressing the writer's emotions or mood, usually briefly. **2** (of a singing voice) light.
– ORIGIN from Greek *lura* 'lyre.'

lyr·i·cal /ˈlirikəl/ ▶ **adjective 1** (of literature, art, or music) expressing the writer's emotions in an imaginative and pleasing way. **2** (of poetry) expressing the writer's emotions or mood; lyric. **3** relating to the words of a popular song.

> – SYNONYMS **1 expressive**, emotional, deeply felt, personal. **2 enthusiastic**, effusive, rapturous, ecstatic, euphoric, passionate, impassioned.
> – ANTONYMS unenthusiastic.

– DERIVATIVES **lyr·i·cal·ly** adverb.
– PHRASES **wax lyrical** talk in a very enthusiastic and unrestrained way.

lyr·i·cism /ˈlirəˌsizəm/ ▶ **noun** the expression of emotion in literature or music in an imaginative and pleasing way.

lyr·i·cist /ˈlirəsist/ ▶ **noun** a person who writes the words to popular songs.

ly·ser·gic ac·id /līˈsərjik, li-/ ▶ **noun** a substance prepared from natural ergot alkaloids or synthetically, from which the drug LSD can be made.
– ORIGIN from (*hydro*)*lys*(*is*) + *erg*(*ot*).

Mm

M[1] (also **m**) ▸ **noun** (pl. **Ms** or **M's**) **1** the thirteenth letter of the alphabet. **2** the Roman numeral for 1,000.

M[2] ▸ **abbreviation 1** male. **2** medium. **3** mega-. **4** Monsieur. **5** motorway.

m ▸ **abbreviation 1** married. **2** masculine. **3** Physics mass. **4** Chemistry meta-. **5** meter(s). **6** mile(s). **7** milli-. **8** million(s). **9** minute(s).

MA ▸ **abbreviation 1** Massachusetts. **2** Master of Arts.

ma /mä/ ▸ **noun** informal a person's mother.

ma'am /mam/ ▸ **noun** a term of respectful or polite address used for a woman; madam.

ma·ca·bre /mə'käbrə, -'käb/ ▸ **adjective** disturbing and horrifying because concerned with death or injury.
– ORIGIN French.

mac·ad·am /mə'kadəm/ ▸ **noun** broken stone used with tar or bitumen for surfacing roads and paths.
– ORIGIN named after the British surveyor John L. *McAdam*.

mac·a·da·mi·a /ˌmakə'dāmēə/ ▸ **noun** the round edible nut of an Australian tree.
– ORIGIN named after the Australian chemist John *Macadam*.

ma·caque /mə'käk, -'kak/ ▸ **noun** a medium-sized monkey with a long face and cheek pouches for holding food.
– ORIGIN from Bantu *makaku* 'some monkeys.'

mac·a·ro·ni /ˌmakə'rōnē/ ▸ **noun 1** pasta in the form of narrow curved tubes. **2** (pl. **macaronies**) an 18th-century British dandy who imitated continental fashions.
– ORIGIN Italian *maccaroni*.

mac·a·roon /ˌmakə'ro͞on/ ▸ **noun** a light cookie made with egg white and ground almonds or coconut.
– ORIGIN French *macaron*.

ma·caw /mə'kô/ ▸ **noun** a large brightly colored parrot with a long tail, native to Central and South America.
– ORIGIN Portuguese *macau*.

mac·chi·a·to /ˌmäkē'ätō/ ▸ **noun** espresso coffee with a dash of frothy steamed milk.
– ORIGIN Italian, 'stained, marked.'

Mace /mās/ ▸ **noun** trademark an irritant chemical used in an aerosol to disable attackers.

mace[1] /mās/ ▸ **noun 1** a ceremonial staff carried as a symbol of authority by certain officials. **2** historical a heavy club with a spiked metal head.
– ORIGIN Old French *masse* 'large hammer.'

mace[2] ▸ **noun** a spice consisting of the dried outer covering of the nutmeg.
– ORIGIN Latin *macir*.

Mac·e·do·ni·an /ˌmasə'dōnēən/ ▸ **noun** a person from the republic of Macedonia (formerly part of Yugoslavia), ancient Macedonia, or the modern Greek region of Macedonia. ▸ **adjective** relating to Macedonia.

mac·er·ate /'masəˌrāt/ ▸ **verb** soften or break up food by soaking in a liquid.
– DERIVATIVES **mac·er·a·tion** /ˌmasə'rāsHən/ noun.
– ORIGIN Latin *macerare*.

Mach /mäk, mäkH/ ▸ **noun** used with a numeral (as **Mach 1**, **Mach 2**, etc.) to indicate the speed of sound, twice the speed of sound, etc.
– ORIGIN named after the Austrian physicist Ernst *Mach*.

ma·chet·e /mə'sHetē/ ▸ **noun** a broad, heavy knife used as an implement or weapon.
– ORIGIN Spanish.

Mach·i·a·vel·li·an /ˌmakēə'velēən, ˌmäk-/ ▸ **adjective** cunning, scheming, and unscrupulous.
– ORIGIN from the Italian statesman and philosopher Niccolò *Machiavelli*.

ma·chic·o·la·tion /məˌcHikə'lāsHən/ ▸ **noun** (in medieval fortifications) an opening between the supports of a projecting structure, through which stones or burning objects could be dropped on attackers.
– DERIVATIVES **ma·chic·o·lat·ed** /mə'cHikəˌlātid/ adjective.
– ORIGIN from Provençal *macar* 'to crush' + *col* 'neck.'

ma·chin·a·ble /mə'sHēnəbəl/ ▸ **adjective** (of a material) able to be worked by a machine tool.
– DERIVATIVES **ma·chin·a·bil·i·ty** /məˌsHēnə'bilətē/ noun.

mach·i·na·tions /ˌmakə'nāsHənz, ˌmasHə-/ ▸ **plural noun** secret plots; scheming.
– ORIGIN from Latin *machinari* 'contrive.'

CHOOSE THE RIGHT WORD

See **PLOT**.

ma·chine /mə'sHēn/ ▸ **noun 1** a device using mechanical power and having several parts, for performing a particular task. **2** a well-organized group of influential people.

– SYNONYMS **1 device,** appliance, apparatus, engine, gadget, mechanism, tool, instrument, contraption. **2** *an efficient publicity machine* **organization,** system, structure, machinery; informal setup.

▸ **verb** make or operate on something with a machine.
– ORIGIN Greek *mēkhos* 'contrivance.'

ma·chine code (also **machine language**) ▸ **noun** a computer programming language consisting of instructions that a computer can respond to directly.

ma·chine gun ▸ **noun** an automatic gun that fires bullets in rapid succession for as long as the trigger is pressed. ▸ **verb** (**machine-gun**) shoot someone with a machine gun.

ma·chine-read·a·ble ▸ **adjective** in a form that a computer can process.

ma·chin·er·y /mə'sHēn(ə)rē/ ▸ **noun 1** machines as a whole, or the components of a machine. **2** an organized system or structure: *the machinery of the state*.

– SYNONYMS **1 equipment,** apparatus, plant, hardware, gear, gadgetry, technology. **2** *the machinery of local government* **workings,** organization, system, structure; informal setup.

ma·chine tool ▶ **noun** a fixed power tool for cutting or shaping metal, wood, etc.

ma·chine trans·la·tion ▶ **noun** translation carried out by a computer.

ma·chin·ist /məˈsʜēnist/ ▶ **noun** a person who operates a machine or who makes machinery.

ma·chis·mo /məˈcʜēzmō, -ˈkēz-/ ▶ **noun** strong or aggressive masculine pride.
– ORIGIN Mexican Spanish.

ma·cho /ˈmäcʜō, ˈmacʜō/ ▶ **adjective** showing aggressive pride in one's masculinity.

– SYNONYMS **manly,** male, masculine, virile, red-blooded; informal **butch.**

– ORIGIN Mexican Spanish.

mack·er·el /ˈmak(ə)rəl/ ▶ **noun** an edible sea fish with a greenish-blue back.
– ORIGIN Old French *maquerel.*

mack·in·tosh /ˈmakən,täsʜ/ (also **macintosh**) ▶ **noun** Brit. a full-length waterproof coat.
– ORIGIN named after the Scottish inventor Charles *Macintosh.*

mac·ra·mé /ˈmakrə,mā/ ▶ **noun** the craft of knotting cord or string in patterns to make decorative articles.
– ORIGIN French.

mac·ro /ˈmakrō/ ▶ **noun** (pl. **macros**) Computing a single instruction that expands automatically into a set of instructions to perform a particular task.

macro- ▶ **combining form** large; large-scale: *macroeconomics.*
– ORIGIN from Greek *makros* 'long, large.'

mac·ro·bi·ot·ic /,makrōbīˈätik/ ▶ **adjective** (of diet) consisting of unprocessed organic foods, based on Buddhist principles of the balance of yin and yang.
– ORIGIN from Greek *makros* 'long' + *bios* 'life.'

mac·ro·car·pa /ˈmakrə,kärpə/ ▶ **noun** a Californian cypress tree with a large spreading crown of horizontal branches.
– ORIGIN from Greek *makros* 'long' + *karpos* 'fruit.'

mac·ro·cosm /ˈmakrə,käzəm/ ▶ **noun** the whole of a complex structure (such as the world) contrasted with a small or representative part of it (a microcosm).
– DERIVATIVES **mac·ro·cos·mic** /,makrəˈkäzmik/ adjective.
– ORIGIN from Greek *makros kosmos* 'big world.'

mac·ro·ec·o·nom·ics /ˈmakrō,ekəˈnämiks, -,ēkə-/ ▶ **plural noun** (treated as sing.) the branch of economics concerned with large-scale economic factors, such as interest rates.

mac·ro lens ▶ **noun** a camera lens suitable for taking photographs unusually close to the subject.

mac·ro·mol·e·cule /,makrōˈmälə,kyo͞ol/ ▶ **noun** a molecule containing a very large number of atoms, such as a protein.
– DERIVATIVES **mac·ro·mo·lec·u·lar** /-məˈlekyələr/ adjective.

ma·cron /ˈmā,krän, ˈmak-, ˈmākrən/ ▶ **noun** a written or printed mark (¯) used to indicate a long vowel in some languages, or a stressed vowel in verse.

mac·ro·phage /ˈmakrə,fāj/ ▶ **noun** a large phagocytic cell found in stationary form in the tissues or as a mobile white blood cell, especially at sites of infection.

mac·ro·scop·ic /,makrəˈskäpik/ ▶ **adjective 1** visible to the naked eye; not microscopic. **2** relating to large-scale or general analysis.

mac·u·la /ˈmakyələ/ (also **macule** /ˈmak,yo͞ol/) ▶ **noun** (pl. **maculae** /-,lē, -,lī/) Medicine an area of skin discoloration.
– ORIGIN Latin.

ma·cum·ba /məˈko͝ombə/ ▶ **noun** a religion of African origin practiced among black people in Brazil, using sorcery, ritual dance, and fetishes.
– ORIGIN Portuguese.

mad /mad/ ▶ **adjective** (**madder**, **maddest**) **1** mentally ill. **2** very foolish; not sensible. **3** informal very angry. **4** informal very enthusiastic about something. **5** impulsive, confused, or frenzied. **6** (of a dog) having rabies.

– SYNONYMS **1 insane,** crazy, out of one's mind, deranged, demented, crazed, lunatic, unbalanced, unhinged, psychotic, non compos mentis; informal mental, nuts, nutty, off one's rocker, bonkers, loony, loopy, batty, cuckoo. **2** *a mad scheme* **foolish,** insane, stupid, lunatic, idiotic, foolhardy, absurd, ludicrous, silly, asinine, wild, crackbrained, senseless, preposterous; informal crazy, crackpot, daft. **3 angry,** furious, infuriated, enraged, fuming, incensed, beside oneself; informal livid, sore. **4** *he's mad about her* **passionate about,** fanatical about, ardent about, fervent about, devoted to, infatuated with; informal crazy about, gaga over/about, nuts about, wild about, hooked on. **5** *a mad dash to get ready* **frenzied,** frantic, frenetic, feverish, hysterical, wild, hectic, manic.
– ANTONYMS sane, sensible.

– DERIVATIVES **mad·ly** adverb.
– ORIGIN Old English.

Mad·a·gas·can /,madəˈgaskən/ ▶ **noun** a person from Madagascar. ▶ **adjective** relating to Madagascar.

mad·am /ˈmadəm/ ▶ **noun 1** a polite form of address for a woman. **2** a woman who runs a brothel.
– ORIGIN from French *ma dame* 'my lady.'

Mad·ame /məˈdäm, -ˈdam/ ▶ **noun** (pl. **Mesdames** /māˈdäm, -ˈdam/) a title or form of address for a French-speaking woman.

mad·cap /ˈmad,kap/ ▶ **adjective** foolish or reckless.

– SYNONYMS **1** *a madcap scheme* **reckless,** rash, foolhardy, foolish, harebrained, wild; informal crazy, crackpot. **2** *a madcap comedy* **zany,** eccentric; informal wacky.

mad cow dis·ease ▶ **noun** informal term for **BSE**.

MADD ▶ **abbreviation** Mothers Against Drunk Driving.

mad·den /ˈmadn/ ▶ **verb 1** drive someone insane. **2** make someone very annoyed.

– SYNONYMS **infuriate,** exasperate, irritate, incense, anger, enrage, provoke, make someone see red, inflame; informal aggravate, tee off, tick off, make someone's blood boil.
– ANTONYMS calm.

mad·der /ˈmadər/ ▶ **noun** a red dye or pigment obtained from the roots of a plant.
– ORIGIN Old English.

mad·ding /ˈmadiɴɢ/ ▶ **adjective** literary acting madly; frenzied: *far from the madding crowd.*

made /mād/ past and past participle of **MAKE**.

Ma·dei·ra /məˈdi(ə)rə, məˈde(ə)rə/ ▶ **noun** a strong sweet white wine from the island of Madeira in the Atlantic Ocean.

mad·e·leine /ˈmadl-ən, ˌmadl-ˈān/ ▶ **noun** a small rich sponge cake decorated with coconut and jam.
– ORIGIN probably named after *Madeleine* Paulmier, a French pastry cook.

Mad·e·moi·selle /ˌmad(ə)m(w)əˈzel, mamˈzel/ ▶ **noun** (pl. **Mesdemoiselles** /ˌmād(ə)m(w)əˈzel(z)/) a title or form of address for an unmarried French-speaking woman.
– ORIGIN from French *ma demoiselle* 'my damsel.'

made to meas·ure ▶ **adjective** specially made to fit a particular person or thing: *made-to-measure curtains.*

made-up ▶ **adjective 1** wearing makeup. **2** invented; untrue.

mad·house /ˈmadˌhous/ ▶ **noun 1** informal a scene of great confusion or uproar. **2** historical an institution for the mentally ill.

mad·man /ˈmadˌman, -mən/ (or **madwoman**) ▶ **noun** (pl. **madmen** or **madwomen**) **1** a person who is mentally ill. **2** a foolish or reckless person.

– SYNONYMS **lunatic,** maniac, psychotic, psychopath; informal loony, nut, nutcase, headcase, screwball, psycho.

mad·ness /ˈmadnəs/ ▶ **noun 1** the state of being mentally ill. **2** extremely foolish behavior. **3** frenzied or chaotic activity.

– SYNONYMS **1 insanity,** mental illness, dementia, derangement, lunacy, mania, psychosis. **2** *it is madness to allow children to roam around after dark* **folly,** foolishness, idiocy, stupidity, foolhardiness. **3** *it's absolute madness in here* **bedlam,** mayhem, chaos, pandemonium, uproar, turmoil.
– ANTONYMS sanity.

Ma·don·na /məˈdänə/ ▶ **noun** (**the Madonna**) the Virgin Mary.
– ORIGIN from Italian *ma donna* 'my lady.'

mad·ras /ˈmadrəs, məˈdras, məˈdräs/ ▶ **noun 1** a colorful striped or checked cotton fabric. **2** a hot spiced curry dish.
– ORIGIN named after the Indian city of *Madras*.

mad·ri·gal /ˈmadrigəl/ ▶ **noun** a 16th- or 17th-century song for several voices without instrumental accompaniment.
– ORIGIN Italian *madrigale*.

mael·strom /ˈmālˌsträm, -strəm/ ▶ **noun 1** a powerful whirlpool. **2** a state or situation of confused movement or turmoil: *they were caught up in a maelstrom of change.*
– ORIGIN Dutch.

mae·nad /ˈmēˌnad/ ▶ **noun** (in ancient Greece) a female follower of the god Bacchus, associated with frenzied rites.
– ORIGIN Greek *Mainas*.

maes·tro /ˈmīstrō/ ▶ **noun** (pl. **maestri** /ˈmīstrē/ or **maestros**) **1** a distinguished male conductor or performer of classical music. **2** a distinguished man in any area of activity.
– ORIGIN Italian, 'master.'

Ma·fi·a /ˈmäfēə/ ▶ **noun 1** (**the Mafia**) an international criminal organization originating in Sicily. **2** (**mafia**) a powerful group who secretly influence matters: *the top tennis mafia.*
– ORIGIN Italian.

Ma·fi·o·so /ˌmäfēˈōsō, -zō/ ▶ **noun** (pl. **Mafiosi** /-sē, -zē/) a member of the Mafia.

mag /mag/ ▶ **noun** informal a magazine (periodical).

mag·a·zine /ˌmagəˈzēn, ˈmagəˌzēn/ ▶ **noun 1** a periodical publication containing articles and illustrations. **2** a regular television or radio program dealing with a variety of items. **3** a chamber holding cartridges to be fed automatically to the breech of a gun. **4** a store for arms, ammunition, and explosives.

– SYNONYMS **journal,** periodical, supplement, fanzine; informal glossy, mag.

– ORIGIN Arabic, 'storehouse.'

mage /māj/ ▶ **noun** old use or literary a magician or learned person.
– ORIGIN anglicized form of Latin *magus*.

ma·gen·ta /məˈjentə/ ▶ **noun** a light reddish-purple color.
– ORIGIN named after *Magenta* in Italy.

mag·got /ˈmagət/ ▶ **noun** a soft-bodied legless larva of a fly or other insect, found in decaying matter.
– ORIGIN perhaps from Old Norse.

ma·gi /ˈmāˌjī/ plural of **MAGUS**.

mag·ic /ˈmajik/ ▶ **noun 1** the power of apparently using mysterious or supernatural forces to make things happen. **2** conjuring tricks performed to entertain. **3** a mysterious and fascinating quality: *the magic of the theater.* **4** informal exceptional skill or talent.

– SYNONYMS **1 sorcery,** witchcraft, wizardry, necromancy, enchantment, the supernatural, occultism, the occult, black magic, the black arts, voodoo, hoodoo. **2 illusion,** conjuring (tricks), sleight of hand, legerdemain; formal prestidigitation. **3 allure,** excitement, fascination, charm, glamour. **4** *the old Liverpool magic* **brilliance,** skill, accomplishment, expertise, art, finesse, talent.

▶ **adjective** apparently having supernatural powers.
▶ **verb** (**magics, magicking, magicked**) do or create by or as if by magic: *they magicked their island out of sight.*
– ORIGIN from Greek *magikē tekhnē* 'art of a magus.'

mag·i·cal /ˈmajikəl/ ▶ **adjective 1** relating to or using magic. **2** very pleasant or enjoyable.

– SYNONYMS **1 supernatural,** magic, mystical, other-worldly. **2 enchanting,** entrancing, spellbinding, bewitching, fascinating, captivating, alluring, enthralling, charming, lovely, delightful, beautiful, amazing; informal heavenly, gorgeous. **3 extraordinary,** remarkable, incredible, astonishing, astounding, staggering, miraculous.

– DERIVATIVES **mag·i·cal·ly** adverb.

mag·ic car·pet ▶ **noun** (especially in Arabian stories) a carpet that is able to transport people through the air.

ma·gi·cian /məˈjisʜən/ ▶ **noun 1** a person with magic powers. **2** a conjuror.

– SYNONYMS **1 sorcerer,** sorceress, witch, wizard, warlock, enchanter, enchantress, necromancer; formal thaumaturge. **2 illusionist,** conjuror; formal prestidigitator.

mag·ic lan·tern ▶ **noun** an early form of projector for showing photographic slides.

mag·ic mush·room ▶ **noun** informal a toadstool that causes hallucinations if eaten.

mag·ic re·al·ism (also **magical realism**) ▶ **noun** a type of literature in which realistic narrative is combined with surreal elements of dream or fantasy.

mag·is·te·ri·al /ˌmajəˈsti(ə)rēəl/ ▶ **adjective 1** having or showing great authority: *a magisterial volume.* **2** relating

to a magistrate.
– DERIVATIVES **mag·is·te·ri·al·ly** adverb.
– ORIGIN from Latin *magister* 'master.'

mag·is·tra·cy /ˈmajəstrəsē/ ▶ **noun** (pl. **magistracies**)
1 the position or authority of a magistrate.
2 magistrates as a group.

mag·is·trate /ˈmajəˌstrāt/ ▶ **noun** an official who administers the law, especially one with authority to judge minor cases and hold preliminary hearings.
– ORIGIN Latin *magistratus* 'administrator.'

mag·lev /ˈmagˌlev/ ▶ **noun** a transport system in which trains glide above a track, supported by magnetic repulsion.
– ORIGIN short for *magnetic levitation*.

mag·ma /ˈmagmə/ ▶ **noun** very hot fluid or semifluid material within the earth's crust from which lava and other igneous rock is formed by cooling.
– ORIGIN Greek.

Mag·na Car·ta /ˌmagnə ˈkärtə/ ▶ **noun** a charter of liberty and political rights signed by King John of England in 1215.
– ORIGIN Latin, 'great charter.'

mag·nan·i·mous /magˈnanəməs/ ▶ **adjective** generous or forgiving, especially toward a rival or less powerful person.

> – SYNONYMS **generous,** charitable, benevolent, beneficent, big-hearted, open-handed, munificent, philanthropic, noble, unselfish, altruistic.
> – ANTONYMS mean.

– DERIVATIVES **mag·na·nim·i·ty** /ˌmagnəˈnimətē/ noun **mag·nan·i·mous·ly** adverb.
– ORIGIN from Latin *magnus* 'great' + *animus* 'soul.'

mag·nate /ˈmagˌnāt, ˈmagnət/ ▶ **noun** a wealthy and influential businessman or businesswoman.
– ORIGIN Latin *magnas* 'great man.'

mag·ne·sia /magˈnēzнə, -ˈnēsнə/ ▶ **noun** a compound of magnesium used to reduce stomach acid and as a laxative.
– ORIGIN Greek, referring to a mineral from Magnesia in Asia Minor.

mag·ne·si·um /magˈnēzēəm, -zнəm/ ▶ **noun** a silvery-white metallic element that burns with a brilliant white flame.

mag·net /ˈmagnət/ ▶ **noun 1** a piece of iron or other material that can attract iron-containing objects and that points north and south when suspended. **2** a person or thing that has a powerful attraction: *the beach is a magnet for sun-worshipers.*
– ORIGIN from Greek *magnēs lithos* 'lodestone.'

mag·net·ic /magˈnetik/ ▶ **adjective 1** having the property of magnetism. **2** very attractive.

> – SYNONYMS **attractive,** irresistible, seductive, charismatic, hypnotic, alluring, fascinating, captivating.

– DERIVATIVES **mag·net·i·cal·ly** adverb.

mag·net·ic field ▶ **noun** a region around a magnet within which the force of magnetism acts.

mag·net·ic mine ▶ **noun** a mine that detonates when it comes near a magnetized body such as a ship or tank.

mag·net·ic north ▶ **noun** the direction in which the north end of a compass needle will point in response to the earth's magnetic field.

mag·net·ic pole ▶ **noun** each of the points near the geographical North and South Poles, indicated by the needle of a magnetic compass.

mag·net·ic res·o·nance im·ag·ing ▶ **noun** a technique for producing images of bodily organs by measuring the response of the atomic nuclei of body tissues to high-frequency radio waves when placed in a strong magnetic field.

mag·net·ic storm ▶ **noun** a disturbance of the magnetic field of the earth.

mag·net·ic tape ▶ **noun** tape used in recording sound, pictures, or computer data.

mag·net·ism /ˈmagnəˌtizəm/ ▶ **noun 1** the property displayed by magnets and produced by the motion of electric charges, which results in objects being attracted or pushed away. **2** the ability to attract and charm people.

mag·net·ite /ˈmagnəˌtīt/ ▶ **noun** a gray-black magnetic mineral that is an important form of iron ore.

mag·net·ize /ˈmagnəˌtīz/ ▶ **verb** give magnetic properties to something.

mag·ne·to /magˈnētō/ ▶ **noun** (pl. **magnetos**) a small electric generator containing a permanent magnet and used to provided high-voltage pulses, especially (formerly) in the ignition systems of internal-combustion engines.

mag·ne·tom·e·ter /ˌmagnəˈtämətər/ ▶ **noun** an instrument used for measuring magnetic forces, especially the earth's magnetism.

mag·ne·tron /ˈmagnəˌträn/ ▶ **noun** an electron tube for amplifying or generating microwaves, with the flow of electrons controlled by an external magnetic field.

mag·net school ▶ **noun** a public school offering special instruction and programs not available elsewhere.

Mag·nif·i·cat /magˈnifiˌkät, mänˈyifi-/ ▶ **noun** the hymn of the Virgin Mary (Gospel of Luke, chapter 1), sung as a regular part of a Christian service.
– ORIGIN Latin, 'magnifies,' from the opening words, which translate as 'my soul magnifies the Lord.'

mag·ni·fi·ca·tion /ˌmagnəfiˈkāsнən/ ▶ **noun 1** the action of magnifying something with a lens or microscope.
2 the degree to which something can be made to appear larger by means of a lens or microscope.

mag·nif·i·cence /magˈnifəsəns/ ▶ **noun** the quality of being very impressive or attractive: *the magnificence of nature.*

mag·nif·i·cent /magˈnifəsənt/ ▶ **adjective 1** very beautiful, impressive, or elaborate. **2** very good; excellent.

> – SYNONYMS **1 splendid,** spectacular, impressive, striking, glorious, superb, majestic, awe-inspiring, breathtaking, sublime, resplendent, sumptuous, grand, imposing, monumental, palatial, opulent, luxurious, lavish, rich, dazzling, beautiful.
> **2 excellent,** outstanding, marvelous, brilliant, wonderful, virtuoso, fine, superb.
> – ANTONYMS uninspiring, ordinary.

– DERIVATIVES **mag·nif·i·cent·ly** adverb.
– ORIGIN Latin *magnificus*.

mag·nif·i·co /magˈnifiˌkō/ ▶ **noun** (pl. **magnificoes**) informal an important or powerful person.
– ORIGIN from Italian, 'high-minded, excellent.'

mag·ni·fy /ˈmagnəˌfī/ ▶ **verb** (**magnifies, magnifying, magnified**) **1** make something appear larger than it is, especially with a lens or microscope. **2** intensify or increase: *that way we can magnify our efforts.* **3** old use praise someone or something highly.

– SYNONYMS **enlarge,** increase, augment, extend, expand, boost, enhance, maximize, amplify, intensify; informal blow up.
– ANTONYMS reduce, minimize.

– DERIVATIVES **mag·ni·fi·er** noun.
– ORIGIN Latin *magnificare.*

mag·ni·fy·ing glass ▶ **noun** a lens that produces an enlarged image, used to examine small or finely detailed things.

mag·nil·o·quent /mag'niləkwənt/ ▶ **adjective** formal using language that is excessively elaborate or pompous.

mag·ni·tude /'magnə,to͞od/ ▶ **noun 1** great size, extent, or importance: *events of tragic magnitude.* **2** the size of something. **3** the degree of brightness of a star.

– SYNONYMS **1 size,** extent, immensity, vastness, hugeness, enormity. **2 importance,** import, significance, consequence.

– ORIGIN Latin *magnitudo.*

mag·no·lia /mag'nōlyə/ ▶ **noun** a tree or shrub with large creamy-pink or -white waxy flowers.
– ORIGIN named after the French botanist Pierre *Magnol.*

mag·nox /'mag,näks/ ▶ **noun** a magnesium-based alloy used to enclose uranium fuel elements in some nuclear reactors.

mag·num /'magnəm/ ▶ **noun** (pl. **magnums**) **1** a wine bottle of twice the standard size, normally 1½ liters. **2** trademark a gun designed to fire cartridges that are more powerful than its caliber would suggest.
– ORIGIN Latin, 'great thing.'

mag·num o·pus /'magnəm 'ōpəs/ ▶ **noun** a work of art, music, or literature that is the most important that a person has produced.
– ORIGIN Latin, 'great work.'

mag·pie /'mag,pī/ ▶ **noun 1** a black and white bird with a long tail and a noisy cry. **2** a person who obsessively collects unimportant things.
– ORIGIN probably from dialect *maggot the pie, maggoty-pie,* from *Magot,* a former form of the woman's name *Marguerite,* + Latin *pica* 'magpie.'

ma·gus /'māgəs/ ▶ **noun** (pl. **magi** /'mā,jī/) **1** a priest of ancient Persia. **2** a sorcerer. **3** (**the Magi**) the three wise men from the East who brought gifts to the infant Jesus.
– ORIGIN Latin.

Mag·yar /'mag,yär/ ▶ **noun 1** a member of the predominant people in Hungary. **2** the Hungarian language.
– ORIGIN Hungarian.

ma·ha·ra·ja /,mähə'räjə, -'räzнə/ (also **maharajah**) ▶ **noun** historical an Indian prince.
– ORIGIN Hindi.

ma·ha·ra·ni /,mähə'ränē/ ▶ **noun** historical a maharaja's wife or widow.
– ORIGIN Hindi.

Ma·ha·ri·shi /,mähə'rēsнē, mə'härəsнē/ ▶ **noun** a great Hindu wise man or spiritual leader.
– ORIGIN Sanskrit.

ma·hat·ma /mə'hätmə, -'hatmə/ ▶ **noun** (in the Indian subcontinent) a holy or wise person regarded with love and respect.
– ORIGIN Sanskrit, 'great soul.'

Ma·ha·ya·na /,mähə'yänə/ ▶ **noun** one of the two major traditions of Buddhism (the other being Theravada), practiced especially in China, Tibet, Japan, and Korea.
– ORIGIN Sanskrit, 'great vehicle.'

Ma·hi·can /mə'hēkən/ (also **Mohican** /mō'hēkən/) ▶ **noun 1** a member of an American Indian people formerly inhabiting the Upper Hudson Valley in New York. **2** the Algonquian language of this people. ▶ **adjective** relating to the Mahicans.
– ORIGIN the name in the extinct Mahican language.

ma·hi·ma·hi /,mähē'mähē/ ▶ **noun** an edible marine fish of warm seas, with silver and bright blue or green coloration.
– ORIGIN from Hawaiian.

mah-jongg /mä 'zнäng, -zнông/ (also **mah-jong**) ▶ **noun** a Chinese game played with 136 or 144 small rectangular tiles.
– ORIGIN Chinese dialect, 'sparrows.'

ma·hog·a·ny /mə'hägənē/ ▶ **noun 1** hard reddish-brown wood from a tropical tree, used for furniture. **2** a rich reddish-brown color.
– ORIGIN unknown.

ma·hout /mə'hout/ ▶ **noun** (in the Indian subcontinent and SE Asia) a person who works with and rides an elephant.
– ORIGIN Hindi.

maid /mād/ ▶ **noun 1** a female domestic servant. **2** old use a girl or young woman.

maid·en /'mādn/ ▶ **noun** old use an unmarried girl or young woman, especially a virgin. ▶ **adjective 1** (of an older woman) unmarried. **2** first of its kind: *a maiden voyage.*
– ORIGIN Old English.

maid·en·hair fern /'mādn,he(ə)r/ ▶ **noun** a fern with fine stems and delicate fronds.

maid·en·head /'mādn,hed/ ▶ **noun** old use **1** a girl's or woman's virginity. **2** the hymen.

maid·en name ▶ **noun** the surname of a married woman before her marriage.

maid of hon·or ▶ **noun 1** a principal bridesmaid. **2** an unmarried noblewoman attending a queen or princess.

maid·serv·ant /'mād,sərvənt/ ▶ **noun** dated a female servant.

mail[1] /māl/ ▶ **noun 1** letters and packages sent by the postal system. **2** the postal system. **3** email.

– SYNONYMS *the mail arrived | we sent it by mail* **letters,** correspondence; post, postal system, postal service, post office; informal snail mail.

▶ **verb 1** send a letter or package using the postal system. **2** send email to someone.

– SYNONYMS **send,** post, dispatch, forward, ship.

– ORIGIN Old French *male* 'wallet.'

mail[2] ▶ **noun** historical flexible armor made of metal rings or plates.
– ORIGIN Old French *maille.*

mail·bag /'māl,bag/ ▶ **noun** a large sack or bag for carrying mail.

mail·box /'māl,bäks/ ▶ **noun 1** a box for mail at the entrance to a person's house. **2** a public box into which mail is placed for collection. **3** a computer file in which emails are stored.

mail car·ri·er ▶ **noun** a person who is employed to deliver and collect letters and parcels.

mail·er /ˈmālər/ ▸ **noun 1** the sender of a letter or package by mail. **2** a container for conveying items by mail, typically a padded envelope or protective tube. **3** a computer program that sends email.

mail·ing /ˈmāliNG/ ▸ **noun** an item of advertising mailed to a large number of people.

mail·ing list ▸ **noun** a list of the names and addresses of people to whom advertising matter or information may be mailed regularly.

mail·man /ˈmālˌman/ ▸ **noun** (pl. **mailmen**) a person who is employed to deliver and collect letters and packages.

mail or·der ▸ **noun** the selling of goods by mail.

maim /mām/ ▸ **verb** injure someone so that part of the body is permanently damaged.

– SYNONYMS **injure,** wound, cripple, disable, incapacitate, mutilate, disfigure, mangle.

– ORIGIN Old French *mahaignier*.

main /mān/ ▸ **adjective** chief in size or importance.

– SYNONYMS **principal,** chief, head, leading, foremost, most important, major, dominant, central, focal, key, prime, primary, first, fundamental, predominant, preeminent, paramount.
– ANTONYMS subsidiary, minor.

▸ **noun 1** a principal water or gas pipe or electricity cable. **2** (**the main**) old use or literary the open ocean.
– PHRASES **in the main** on the whole.
– ORIGIN from Old English, 'physical force.'

main·board /ˈmānˌbôrd/ ▸ **noun** another term for **MOTHERBOARD**.

main brace ▸ **noun** the rope attached to the main yard (spar) of a sailing ship.

main clause ▸ **noun** Grammar a clause that can form a complete sentence standing alone, having a subject and a verb.

main course ▸ **noun** the most substantial course of a meal.

main drag ▸ **noun** informal the main street of a town.

main·frame /ˈmānˌfrām/ ▸ **noun** a large high-speed computer, especially one supporting numerous workstations.

main·land /ˈmānlənd, -ˌland/ ▸ **noun** the main area of land of a country, not including islands and separate territories.

main line ▸ **noun 1** a chief railroad line. **2** informal a principal vein as a site for a drug injection. ▸ **verb** (**mainline**) informal inject a drug into a vein.

main·ly /ˈmānlē/ ▸ **adverb** for the most part; chiefly.

– SYNONYMS **mostly,** for the most part, in the main, on the whole, largely, by and large, to a large extent, predominantly, chiefly, principally, primarily.

main man ▸ **noun** informal a close and trusted friend.

main·mast /ˈmānˌmast/ ▸ **noun** the principal mast of a ship.

main·sail /ˈmānsəl, -ˌsāl/ ▸ **noun** the chief sail of a ship, especially the lowest sail on the mainmast of a square-rigged ship.

main·spring /ˈmānˌspriNG/ ▸ **noun 1** the most influential or important part: *faith was the mainspring of her life*. **2** the chief spring in a watch, clock, etc.

main·stay /ˈmānˌstā/ ▸ **noun 1** a thing on which something else is based or depends: *cotton is the mainstay of the economy*. **2** a rope or wire that extends from the top of the mainmast of a sailing ship to the foot of the mast nearest the front.

main·stream /ˈmānˌstrēm/ ▸ **noun** the ideas, attitudes, or activities that are shared by most people. ▸ **adjective** belonging to or typical of the mainstream. ▸ **verb** bring into the mainstream: *vegetarianism has been mainstreamed*.

main street ▸ **noun 1** the principal street of a town. **2** (**Main Street**) used in reference to the materialism, mediocrity, or parochialism regarded as typical of small-town life.
– ORIGIN sense 2 from the title of a novel (1920) by Sinclair Lewis.

main·tain /mānˈtān/ ▸ **verb 1** cause to continue in the same state or at the same level: *she maintained close links with India*. **2** keep a building, machine, or road in good condition by checking or repairing it regularly. **3** provide enough money to support someone. **4** strongly state that something is the case: *he has always maintained his innocence*.

– SYNONYMS **1 preserve,** conserve, keep, retain, keep going, prolong, perpetuate, sustain, carry on, continue. **2 look after,** service, care for, take care of, support, provide for, keep. **3 insist,** declare, assert, protest, affirm, profess, avow, claim, contend, argue; formal aver.
– ANTONYMS discontinue.

– DERIVATIVES **main·tain·a·bil·i·ty** /ˌmānˌtānəˈbilətē/ noun **main·tain·a·ble** adjective **main·tain·er** noun.
– ORIGIN Old French *maintenir*.

main·te·nance /ˈmānt(ə)nəns, ˈmāntn-əns/ ▸ **noun 1** the process of keeping something in the same state or in good condition. **2** Brit. the provision of financial support for a former husband or wife after divorce.

– SYNONYMS **1 preservation,** conservation, prolongation, continuation. **2 servicing,** service, repair, running repairs, care. **3 support,** upkeep, alimony, allowance.

ma·iol·i·ca /mīˈäləkə/ ▸ **noun** fine Italian earthenware with colored decoration on an opaque white glaze.
– ORIGIN from Italian *Maiolica* 'Majorca.'

maî·tre d'hô·tel /ˌmātrə dōˈtel, ˌmetrə/ (also **maître d'** /ˌmātrə ˈdē, ˌmātər/) ▸ **noun** (pl. **maîtres d'hôtel** (pronunc. same) or **maître d's**) the head waiter of a restaurant.
– ORIGIN French, 'master of the house.'

maize /māz/ ▸ **noun** technical or chiefly British term for **CORN**[1] (sense 1).
– ORIGIN Spanish *maíz*.

ma·jes·tic /məˈjestik/ ▸ **adjective** impressively grand or beautiful.

– SYNONYMS **stately,** dignified, distinguished, magnificent, grand, splendid, glorious, impressive, regal, noble, awe-inspiring, monumental, palatial, imposing.
– ANTONYMS modest.

– DERIVATIVES **ma·jes·ti·cal·ly** adverb.

maj·es·ty /ˈmajəstē/ ▸ **noun** (pl. **majesties**) **1** impressive grandeur or beauty. **2** royal power. **3** (**His, Your,** etc. **Majesty**) a title given to a sovereign or their wife or widow.

– SYNONYMS **stateliness,** dignity, magnificence, pomp, grandeur, splendor, glory, impressiveness, nobility.

– ORIGIN Latin *majestas*.

ma·jol·i·ca /mə'jälikə/ ▶ **noun** a kind of earthenware imitating Italian maiolica.

ma·jor /'mājər/ ▶ **adjective** **1** important, serious, or significant. **2** greater or more important; main: *he got the major share of the profit.* **3** (of a musical scale) having intervals of a half step between the third and fourth, and seventh and eighth notes. Contrasted with MINOR.

– SYNONYMS **1 greatest,** best, finest, most important, chief, main, prime, principal, leading, foremost, outstanding, preeminent. **2 crucial,** vital, important, big, significant, considerable, weighty, serious, key, utmost, great, paramount, prime.
– ANTONYMS minor, trivial.

▶ **noun** **1** a rank of officer in the US Army, Marine Corps, and Air Force, above captain and below lieutenant colonel. **2** Music a major key, interval, or scale. **3** a student's main subject or course. **4** a student specializing in a specified subject.
▶ **verb** (**major in**) specialize in a particular subject at a college or university.
– ORIGIN Latin, 'greater.'

Ma·jor·can /mə'jôrkən, mä'yôrkən/ ▶ **noun** a person from Majorca. ▶ **adjective** relating to Majorca.

ma·jor-do·mo /ˌmājər 'dōmō/ ▶ **noun** (pl. **major-domos**) the chief steward of a large household.
– ORIGIN Latin *major domus* 'highest official of the household.'

ma·jor gen·er·al ▶ **noun** a rank of officer in the US Army, Air Force, and Marine Corps, above brigadier general and below lieutenant general.

ma·jor·i·tar·i·an /mə,jôri'te(ə)rēən, -jär-/ ▶ **adjective** governed by or believing in decision by a majority.

ma·jor·i·ty /mə'jôrətē, -'jär-/ ▶ **noun** (pl. **majorities**) **1** the greater number. **2** the number by which votes for one candidate in an election are more than those for all other candidates combined. **3** the age when a person is legally a full adult, usually 18 or 21.

– SYNONYMS **1 most,** bulk, mass, best part, lion's share, (main) body, preponderance, predominance. **2 coming of age,** age of consent, adulthood, seniority.
– ANTONYMS minority.

USAGE

The main meaning of **majority** is 'the greater number' and it should be used with plural nouns: *the majority of cases.* It is not good English to use **majority** with nouns that do not take a plural to mean 'the greatest part,' as in *she ate the majority of the meal.*

ma·jor·i·ty rule ▶ **noun** the principle that the greater number of people should exercise greater power.

ma·jor league ▶ **noun** **1** the highest-level professional league or leagues in a sport, such as the American and National Leagues of baseball. **2** the highest attainable level in any endeavor or activity: *major-league corporations.*

ma·jus·cule /'majəsˌkyo͞ol/ ▶ **noun** a capital letter.
– ORIGIN from Latin *majuscula littera* 'somewhat greater letter.'

make /māk/ ▶ **verb** (past and past part. **made** /mād/) **1** form something by putting parts together or combining substances. **2** cause or bring about something. **3** force someone to do something. **4** (**make something into**) alter something so that it forms something else. **5** add up to: *one and one makes two.* **6** estimate, decide, or calculate something. **7** gain or earn money or profit. **8** be suitable for: *this fern makes a good house plant.* **9** manage to arrive at or achieve something. **10** prepare to go in a particular direction or do a particular thing: *I made toward the car.* **11** (**make it**) become successful. **12** arrange bedclothes tidily on a bed ready for use.

– SYNONYMS **1** *he makes models* **construct,** build, erect, assemble, put together, manufacture, produce, fabricate, create, form, forge, fashion, model, improvise. **2** *don't make such a noise* **cause,** create, bring about, produce, generate, give rise to, effect. **3** *I didn't want to go but she made me* **force,** compel, coerce, press, drive, dragoon, pressurize, oblige, require; informal railroad, steamroller. **4** *they made him chairman* **appoint,** designate, name, nominate, select, elect, vote in. **5** *he's made a lot of money* **acquire,** obtain, gain, get, secure, win, earn. **6** *he made dinner* **prepare,** concoct, cook, whip up, brew; informal fix.
– ANTONYMS destroy.

▶ **noun** the manufacturer or trade name of a product.

– SYNONYMS **brand,** marque, label, type, sort, kind, variety.

– PHRASES **have (got) it made** informal be in a position where success is certain. **make away with** steal something. **make do** manage with the limited means available. **make for 1** move toward. **2** tend to result in. **3** (**be made for**) be very suitable for. **make it up to** compensate someone for unfair treatment. **make something of 1** give attention or importance to. **2** understand the meaning of. **make off** leave hurriedly. **make off with** steal something. **make or break** be the factor that decides whether something will succeed or fail. **make someone/thing out 1** manage with difficulty to see, hear, or understand someone or something. **2** pretend to be or do something. **3** draw up a list or document. **make out** informal **1** make progress; get on. **2** engage in sexual activity. **make someone over** give someone a new image with cosmetics, hairstyling, and clothes. **make something over 1** transfer the possession of something. **2** redesign or refit something: *Anna helped to make over our website.* **make sail** spread a sail or sails, especially to begin a voyage. **make time** find the time to do something. **make up** become friendly again after a quarrel. **make someone up** apply cosmetics to someone. **make something up 1** put something together from parts or ingredients. **2** invent a story. **3** (also **make up for**) compensate for something. **make up one's mind** make a decision. **make way** allow room for someone or something else. **on the make** informal **1** trying to make money or gain an advantage. **2** looking for a sexual partner.
– ORIGIN Old English.

make-be·lieve ▶ **noun** a state of fantasy or pretense.

– SYNONYMS **fantasy,** pretense, daydreaming, invention, fabrication, charade, play-acting, masquerade.

▶ **adjective** imitating something real; pretend.

– SYNONYMS **imaginary,** imagined, made-up, fanciful, fictitious; informal pretend.
– ANTONYMS real, actual.

make-do ▶ **adjective** makeshift or temporary.

make·o·ver /'mākˌōvər/ ▶ **noun** a complete transformation of the appearance of someone or something.

mak·er /ˈmākər/ ▶ **noun** **1** a person or thing that makes something. **2** (**our, the**, etc. **Maker**) God.

– SYNONYMS **creator,** manufacturer, constructor, builder, producer.

– PHRASES **meet one's Maker** chiefly humorous die.

make·shift /ˈmākˌsʜift/ ▶ **adjective** acting as a temporary substitute or measure.

– SYNONYMS **temporary,** provisional, stopgap, standby, rough and ready, improvised, ad hoc.

make·up /ˈmākˌəp/ ▶ **noun** **1** cosmetics applied to the face. **2** the way in which something is formed or put together: *the makeup of the rock.* **3** the arrangement of written matter, illustrations, etc., on a printed page.

– SYNONYMS **1 cosmetics,** greasepaint; informal warpaint. **2 composition,** constitution, structure, configuration, arrangement. **3 character,** nature, temperament, personality, mentality, persona.

make·weight /ˈmākˌwāt/ ▶ **noun** **1** an unimportant person or thing that is only included to complete something. **2** something added to make up a required weight.

mak·ing /ˈmākiɴɢ/ ▶ **noun** **1** (**makings**) the necessary qualities. **2** (in phrase **be the making of**) bring about the success of.

– SYNONYMS (**makings**) *she had the makings of a great teacher* **qualities,** characteristics, ingredients, potential, capacity, capability, stuff.

ma·ko /ˈmākō, ˈmäkō/ ▶ **noun** (pl. **makos**) a large shark with a deep blue back and white underparts.
– ORIGIN Maori.

mal- ▶ **combining form** **1** bad; badly: *malodorous.* **2** wrong or incorrectly: *malfunction.* **3** not: *maladroit.*
– ORIGIN from Latin *male* 'badly.'

mal·a·chite /ˈmaləˌkīt/ ▶ **noun** a bright green mineral that contains copper.
– ORIGIN Greek *malakhē* 'mallow.'

mal·ad·just·ed /ˌmaləˈjəstid/ ▶ **adjective** failing to cope with normal social situations.

– SYNONYMS **disturbed,** unstable, neurotic, dysfunctional; informal mixed up, screwed up.

mal·ad·min·is·tra·tion /ˌmalədˈminəˈstrāsʜən/ ▶ **noun** formal dishonest or inefficient management or administration.
– DERIVATIVES **mal·ad·min·is·ter** /ˌmalədˈministər/ verb.

mal·a·droit /ˌmaləˈdroit/ ▶ **adjective** inefficient or clumsy.

mal·a·dy /ˈmalədē/ ▶ **noun** (pl. **maladies**) literary a disease or illness.

– SYNONYMS **illness,** sickness, disease, infection, ailment, disorder, complaint, affliction, infirmity; informal bug, virus.

– ORIGIN from Old French *malade* 'ill.'

Mal·a·gas·y /ˌmaləˈgasē/ ▶ **noun** (pl. same or **Malagasies**) **1** a person from Madagascar. **2** the language of Madagascar.

ma·laise /məˈlāz, -ˈlez/ ▶ **noun** a general feeling of unease, bad health, or low spirits.
– ORIGIN French.

mal·a·mute /ˈmaləˌmyo͞ot/ ▶ **noun** a powerful dog of a breed with a thick, gray coat, bred by the Inuit and used to pull sleds.
– ORIGIN from Inuit *malimiut*, the name of a people of Kotzebue Sound, Alaska, who developed the breed.

mal·a·prop·ism /ˈmaləˌpräpizəm/ (also **malaprop** /ˈmaləˌpräp/) ▶ **noun** the mistaken use of a word in place of a similar-sounding one (e.g., 'dance a *flamingo*' instead of *flamenco*).
– ORIGIN named after Mrs *Malaprop* in Richard Sheridan's play *The Rivals*.

ma·lar·i·a /məˈle(ə)rēə/ ▶ **noun** a disease that causes recurrent attacks of fever, caused by a parasite that is transmitted by mosquitoes.
– DERIVATIVES **ma·lar·i·al** adjective.
– ORIGIN from Italian *mala aria* 'bad air' (the disease was formerly thought to be caused by vapors given off by marshes).

ma·lar·key /məˈlärkē/ ▶ **noun** informal nonsense.
– ORIGIN unknown.

mal·a·thi·on /ˌmaləˈᴛʜīˌän/ ▶ **noun** a synthetic insecticide containing phosphorus.
– ORIGIN from its chemical name.

Ma·la·wi·an /məˈläwēən/ ▶ **noun** a person from Malawi in south central Africa. ▶ **adjective** relating to Malawi.

Ma·lay /məˈlā, ˈmāˌlā/ ▶ **noun** **1** a member of a people inhabiting Malaysia and Indonesia. **2** the language of the Malays. ▶ **adjective** relating to the Malays or their language.

Ma·lay·an /məˈlāən/ ▶ **noun** another term for **MALAY**. ▶ **adjective** relating to Malays or Malaya (now part of Malaysia).

Ma·lay·sian /məˈlāzʜən/ ▶ **noun** a person from Malaysia. ▶ **adjective** relating to Malaysia.

mal·con·tent /ˌmalkənˈtent, ˈmalkənˌtent/ ▶ **noun** a person who is dissatisfied and rebellious.

Mal·div·i·an /môlˈdivēən, mäl-/ ▶ **noun** a person from the Maldives, a country consisting of a chain of islands in the Indian Ocean. ▶ **adjective** relating to the Maldives.

male /māl/ ▶ **adjective** **1** relating to the sex that can fertilize or inseminate the female to give rise to offspring. **2** relating to or typical of men: *a deep male voice.* **3** (of a plant or flower) having stamens but lacking functional pistils. **4** (of a fitting) manufactured to fit inside a corresponding female part.

– SYNONYMS **masculine,** manly, virile, macho.
– ANTONYMS female.

▶ **noun** a male person, animal, or plant.
– DERIVATIVES **male·ness** noun.
– ORIGIN Old French *masle*.

WORD TOOLKIT

male ...	manly ...	mannish ...
colleague	men	haircut
hybrid	virtues	woman
lion	art	trousers
model	physique	boy

mal·e·dic·tion /ˌmaləˈdiksʜən/ ▶ **noun** a curse.
– ORIGIN from Latin *maledicere* 'speak evil of.'

mal·e·fac·tor /ˈmaləˌfaktər/ ▶ **noun** formal a criminal or other wrongdoer.
– ORIGIN from Latin *malefacere* 'do wrong.'

ma·lef·ic /məˈlefik/ ▶ **adjective** literary causing harm or destruction.
– DERIVATIVES **ma·lef·i·cent** /-ˈlefəsənt/ adjective.
– ORIGIN from Latin *male* 'ill' + *-ficus* 'doing.'

ma·lev·o·lent /mə'levələnt/ ▶ **adjective** wishing evil to others.
– DERIVATIVES **ma·lev·o·lence** noun **ma·lev·o·lent·ly** adverb.
– ORIGIN from Latin *male* 'ill' + *velle* 'to wish.'

mal·fea·sance /mal'fēzəns/ ▶ **noun** Law wrongdoing, especially by a public official.
– ORIGIN Old French *malfaisance*.

mal·for·ma·tion /ˌmalfôr'māshən, -fər-/ ▶ **noun 1** a part of the body that is not formed correctly. **2** the state of being abnormally shaped or formed.
– DERIVATIVES **mal·formed** /mal'fôrmd/ adjective.

mal·func·tion /mal'fəngkshən/ ▶ **verb** (of equipment or machinery) fail to function normally.

– SYNONYMS **break down,** fail, stop working, crash, go down; informal conk out, go kaput.

▶ **noun** a failure to function normally.

Ma·li·an /'mälēən/ ▶ **noun** a person from Mali, a country in West Africa. ▶ **adjective** relating to Mali.

mal·ice /'maləs/ ▶ **noun** the desire to harm someone.

– SYNONYMS **spite,** malevolence, ill will, vindictiveness, vengefulness, malignity, animus, enmity, rancor.
– ANTONYMS benevolence.

– ORIGIN Old French.

mal·ice a·fore·thought ▶ **noun** Law the intention to kill or harm, which distinguishes murder from unlawful killing.

ma·li·cious /mə'lishəs/ ▶ **adjective** intending or intended to do harm: *his talent for malicious gossip.*

– SYNONYMS **spiteful,** malevolent, vindictive, vengeful, resentful, malign, nasty, hurtful, cruel, catty, venomous, poisonous, barbed; informal bitchy.
– ANTONYMS benevolent.

– DERIVATIVES **ma·li·cious·ly** adverb **ma·li·cious·ness** noun.

ma·lign /mə'līn/ ▶ **adjective** harmful or evil.

– SYNONYMS *a malign influence* **harmful,** evil, bad, baleful, destructive, malignant, injurious.
– ANTONYMS beneficial.

▶ **verb** criticize someone in a spiteful way.

– SYNONYMS **defame,** slander, libel, blacken someone's name/character, smear, vilify, cast aspersions on, run down, denigrate, disparage, slur, abuse; informal bad-mouth, knock.
– ANTONYMS praise.

– DERIVATIVES **ma·lig·ni·ty** /-'lignətē/ noun **ma·lign·ly** adverb.
– ORIGIN Latin *malignus* 'tending to evil.'

ma·lig·nan·cy /mə'lignənsē/ ▶ **noun** (pl. **malignancies**) **1** the presence of a malignant tumor; cancer. **2** a cancerous growth. **3** the quality of being harmful or evil.

ma·lig·nant /mə'lignənt/ ▶ **adjective 1** harmful or evil. **2** (of a tumor) tending to grow uncontrollably or to recur after removal; cancerous.
– ORIGIN from Latin *malignare* 'plan maliciously.'

ma·lin·ger /mə'linggər/ ▶ **verb** pretend to be ill in order to avoid duty or work.
– DERIVATIVES **ma·lin·ger·er** noun.
– ORIGIN from French *malingre* 'weak, sickly.'

mall /môl/ ▶ **noun 1** a large enclosed pedestrian shopping area. **2** a sheltered walk or promenade.
– ORIGIN probably from *The Mall*, a walk in St. James's Park, London.

mal·lard /'malərd/ ▶ **noun** a wild duck, the male of which has a dark green head and white collar.
– ORIGIN Old French, 'wild drake.'

mal·le·a·ble /'malyəbəl, 'malēə-/ ▶ **adjective 1** able to be hammered or pressed into shape without breaking or cracking. **2** easily influenced: *a malleable youth.*
– DERIVATIVES **mal·le·a·bil·i·ty** /ˌmalyə'bilitē, ˌmalēə-/ noun.
– ORIGIN from Latin *malleus* 'a hammer.'

mal·let /'malət/ ▶ **noun 1** a hammer with a large wooden head. **2** a long-handled wooden stick with a head like a hammer, for hitting a croquet or polo ball.
– ORIGIN Latin *malleus*.

mal·low /'malō/ ▶ **noun** a plant with pink or purple flowers.
– ORIGIN Latin *malva*.

malm·sey /'mä(l)mzē/ ▶ **noun** a very sweet Madeira wine.
– ORIGIN from *Monemvasia*, a port in Greece.

mal·nour·ished /mal'nərisht, -'nə-risht/ ▶ **adjective** suffering from lack of food or of the right foods.
– DERIVATIVES **mal·nourish·ment** /-'nərishmənt/ noun.

mal·nu·tri·tion /ˌmalnoo'trishən/ ▶ **noun** the state of not having enough food or not eating enough of the right foods.

mal·oc·clu·sion /ˌmalə'kloozhən/ ▶ **noun** imperfect positioning of the teeth when the jaws are closed.

mal·o·dor·ous /mal'ōdərəs/ ▶ **adjective** smelling very unpleasant.

mal·prac·tice /mal'praktəs/ ▶ **noun** illegal, corrupt, or negligent professional behavior.

malt /môlt/ ▶ **noun** barley or other grain that has been soaked in water, allowed to sprout, and dried, used for brewing or distilling. ▶ **verb 1** convert grain into malt. **2** (as adj. **malted**) mixed with malt or a malt extract.
– ORIGIN Old English.

Mal·tese /môl'tēz/ ▶ **noun** (pl. same) a person from Malta. ▶ **adjective** relating to Malta.

Mal·tese cross ▶ **noun** a cross with arms of equal length that broaden from the center and have their ends indented in a shallow V-shape.
– ORIGIN so named because the cross was formerly worn by the Knights Hospitallers, a religious order based in Malta.

Mal·thu·sian /mal'th(y)oozhən, môl-/ ▶ **adjective** relating to the theory of the English economist Thomas Malthus that, if unchecked, the population tends to increase at a greater rate than its food supplies. ▶ **noun** a person who supports this theory.

malt liq·uor ▶ **noun** alcoholic liquor made from malt by fermentation rather than distillation; beer with a relatively high alcohol content.

malt·ose /'môlˌtōs, -ˌtōz/ ▶ **noun** a sugar produced by the breakdown of starch, e.g., by enzymes found in malt and saliva.

mal·treat /mal'trēt/ ▶ **verb** treat a person or animal badly or cruelly.

– SYNONYMS **ill-treat,** mistreat, abuse, ill-use, mishandle, misuse, persecute, harm, hurt, injure.

– DERIVATIVES **mal·treat·ment** noun.

malt whis·key ▶ **noun** whiskey made only from malted barley.

mal·ver·sa·tion /ˌmalvərˈsāsʜən/ ▶ **noun** formal corrupt behavior by a person in public office.
– ORIGIN from Latin *male* 'badly' + *versari* 'behave.'

mal·ware /ˈmalˌwe(ə)r/ ▶ **noun** software that is intended to damage or disable computers and computer systems.

mam /mäm/ ▶ **noun** informal a term of respectful or polite address used for a woman; ma'am.
– ORIGIN contraction of *madam*.

ma·ma /ˈmämə/ (also **mamma**) ▶ **noun 1** one's mother. **2** informal a mature woman: *she is one hot mama*.
– ORIGIN imitating a child's first syllables *ma, ma*.

mam·ba /ˈmämbə/ ▶ **noun** a large, highly venomous African snake.
– ORIGIN Zulu.

mam·bo /ˈmämbō/ ▶ **noun** (pl. **mambos**) a Latin American dance similar to the rumba.
– ORIGIN American Spanish.

mam·mal /ˈmaməl/ ▶ **noun** a warm-blooded vertebrate animal that has hair or fur, produces milk, and (typically) bears live young.
– DERIVATIVES **mam·ma·li·an** /məˈmālēən/ adjective.
– ORIGIN from Latin *mamma* 'breast.'

mam·ma·ry /ˈmamərē/ ▶ **adjective** relating to the breasts or other milk-producing organs of mammals: *a mammary gland*. ▶ **noun** (pl. **mammaries**) informal a breast.
– ORIGIN from Latin *mamma* 'breast.'

mam·mo·gram /ˈmaməˌgram/ ▶ **noun** an image obtained by mammography.

mam·mog·ra·phy /maˈmägrəfē/ ▶ **noun** a technique using X-rays to diagnose and locate tumors of the breasts.

Mam·mon /ˈmamən/ ▶ **noun** wealth regarded as an evil influence or false object of worship.
– ORIGIN from an Aramaic word meaning 'riches'; see Gospel of Matthew, chapter 6, and Gospel of Luke, chapter 16.

mam·moth /ˈmaməᴛʜ/ ▶ **noun** a large extinct form of elephant with a hairy coat and long curved tusks. ▶ **adjective** huge; enormous.
– ORIGIN Russian.

mam·my /ˈmamē/ ▶ **noun** (pl. **mammies**) informal **1** a child's name for their mother. **2** offensive (formerly in the South) a black nursemaid or nanny in charge of white children.

man /man/ ▶ **noun** (pl. **men**) **1** an adult human male. **2** a male member of a workforce, team, etc. **3** a husband or lover. **4** a person. **5** human beings in general: *places untouched by man*. **6** a piece or token used in a board game.

> – SYNONYMS **1 male,** gentleman, fellow, youth; informal guy, dude, hombre, gent, geezer. **2 human being,** human, person, mortal, individual, soul. **3 the human race,** Homo sapiens, humankind, humanity, human beings, humans, people, mankind.

▶ **verb** (**mans, manning, manned**) provide a place or machine with the personnel to run, operate, or defend it.

> – SYNONYMS **1 staff,** crew, occupy. **2 operate,** work, use.

▶ **exclamation** informal used for emphasis or to express surprise, admiration, or delight.
– PHRASES **man about town** a fashionable and sociable man. **the man in the street** the average man. **man of the cloth** a clergyman. **man of letters** a male scholar or author. **man to man** in a direct and frank way between two men. **to a man** with no exceptions.
– ORIGIN Old English.

> **USAGE**
>
> Many people now think that the use of **man** to refer to 'human beings in general' is old-fashioned or sexist. Alternative terms such as **the human race** or **humankind** may be used in some situations, but elsewhere there are no established alternatives, for example for the term **manpower**.

> **WORD LINKS**
>
> **male, masculine, virile** *relating to men*

-man ▶ **combining form** forming nouns referring to: **1** a man of a specified nationality or origin: *Frenchman*. **2** a person belonging to a specified group or having a specified occupation or role: *chairman*. **3** a ship of a specified kind: *merchantman*.

> **USAGE**
>
> The use of the form **-man** to create words referring to an occupation or role, as in **fireman** and **policeman**, is now often regarded as outdated and sexist. As a result, there has been a move away from **-man** compound words except where it is known that a man rather than a woman is being referred to. Alternative nonspecific terms that can be used instead include **firefighter** and **police officer**.

man·a·cle /ˈmanikəl/ ▶ **noun** a metal band or chain fastened around a person's hands or ankles to restrict their movement. ▶ **verb** restrict someone with a manacle or manacles.
– ORIGIN Old French *manicle* 'handcuff.'

man·age /ˈmanij/ ▶ **verb 1** be in charge of people or an organization. **2** control the use of money, time, or other resources. **3** succeed in doing or dealing with: *she eventually managed to buy a house*. **4** succeed or cope despite difficulties. **5** be free to attend an appointment.

> – SYNONYMS **1 be in charge of,** run, head, direct, control, preside over, lead, govern, rule, command, supervise, oversee, administer; informal head up. **2 accomplish,** achieve, carry out, perform, undertake, deal with, cope with. **3 cope,** get along/on, make do, survive, get by, muddle through/along, make ends meet; informal make out, hack it.

– DERIVATIVES **man·ag·ing** adjective.
– ORIGIN Italian *maneggiare* 'train a horse.'

man·age·a·ble /ˈmanijəbəl/ ▶ **adjective** able to be dealt with or controlled without difficulty.

> – SYNONYMS **1 achievable,** doable, practicable, feasible, reasonable, attainable, viable. **2 compliant,** tractable, pliant, biddable, docile, amenable, accommodating, acquiescent.

man·aged care ▶ **noun** a system of health care in which patients visit only certain doctors and hospitals, and in which the cost of treatment is monitored by a managing company.

man·age·ment /ˈmanijmənt/ ▶ **noun 1** the process of managing people or things. **2** the managers of an organization.

> – SYNONYMS **1 administration,** running, managing, organization, direction, leadership, control, governance, rule, command, supervision, guidance, operation. **2 managers,** employers, directors, board, directorate, executive, administration; informal bosses,

top brass.
– ANTONYMS employees.

man·age·ment ac·count·ing ▸ **noun** the provision of financial data and advice to a company for use in the organization and development of its business.
– DERIVATIVES **man·age·ment ac·count·ant** noun.

man·ag·er /'manijər/ ▸ **noun 1** a person who manages an organization, a group of staff, or a sports team. **2** a person in charge of the business affairs of an athlete, actor, or performer.

– SYNONYMS **executive,** head, supervisor, principal, director, superintendent, foreman, forewoman, overseer, organizer, administrator; informal boss, chief.

– DERIVATIVES **man·a·ge·ri·al** /ˌmanə'ji(ə)rēəl/ adjective **man·ag·er·ship** /-ˌsHip/ noun.

man-at-arms ▸ **noun** old use a soldier.

man·a·tee /'manəˌtē/ ▸ **noun** a large mammal that lives in the sea near tropical Atlantic coasts.
– ORIGIN Carib.

Man·che·go /man'CHāgō/ ▸ **noun** a Spanish cheese traditionally made with sheep's milk.
– ORIGIN Spanish.

Man·chu /'manˌCHo͞o, man'CHo͞o/ ▸ **noun** a member of a people originally living in Manchuria in NE China, who formed the last imperial dynasty of China (1644–1912).
– ORIGIN Manchu, 'pure.'

man·da·la /'mandələ, 'mən-/ ▸ **noun** an intricate circular design symbolizing the universe in Hinduism and Buddhism.
– ORIGIN Sanskrit, 'disc, circle.'

man·da·mus /man'dāməs/ ▸ **noun** a writ issued as a command to an inferior court or ordering a person to perform a public or statutory duty.
– ORIGIN from Latin, literally 'we command.'

man·da·rin /'mandərən/ ▸ **noun 1** (**Mandarin**) the official form of the Chinese language. **2** a high-ranking official in the former imperial Chinese civil service. **3** a powerful official or senior bureaucrat. **4** a small citrus fruit with a loose yellow-orange skin.
– ORIGIN Hindi *mantrī* 'counselor.'

man·da·rin col·lar ▸ **noun** a close-fitting upright collar.

man·da·rin duck ▸ **noun** a small East Asian duck, the male of which has an orange ruff and sail-like feathers on each side of the body.

man·date ▸ **noun** /'manˌdāt/ **1** an official order or authorization. **2** the authority to carry out a policy, regarded as given by voters to the winner of an election: *a government with a popular mandate*. **3** historical a commission from the League of Nations (the forerunner of the UN) to a member nation to administer a territory.

– SYNONYMS **1 authority,** approval, ratification, endorsement, sanction, authorization. **2 instruction,** directive, decree, command, order, injunction.

▸ **verb** /ˌman'dāt/ authorize someone to do something.
– ORIGIN Latin *mandatum* 'something commanded.'

man·da·to·ry /'mandəˌtôrē/ ▸ **adjective** required by law or mandate; compulsory.

– SYNONYMS **obligatory,** compulsory, binding, required, requisite, necessary.
– ANTONYMS optional.

– DERIVATIVES **man·da·to·ri·ly** /-ˌtôrəlē/ adverb.

man·di·ble /'mandəbəl/ ▸ **noun 1** the lower jawbone in a mammal or fish. **2** either of the upper and lower parts of a bird's beak. **3** either half of the crushing organ in an insect's mouthparts.
– ORIGIN from Latin *mandere* 'to chew.'

man·do·lin /ˌmandə'lin, 'mandələn/ ▸ **noun 1** a musical instrument resembling a lute, having paired metal strings plucked with a plectrum. **2** (also **mandoline** pronunc. same) a kitchen implement consisting of a frame with adjustable blades, for slicing vegetables.
– DERIVATIVES **man·do·lin·ist** /-'linist/ noun.
– ORIGIN Italian *mandolino* 'little mandola' (a *mandola* being an early form of mandolin).

man·drake /'manˌdrāk/ ▸ **noun** a plant with a forked fleshy root supposedly resembling the human form, used in herbal medicine and magic.
– ORIGIN Latin *mandragora.*

man·drel /'mandrəl/ ▸ **noun 1** a shaft or spindle in a lathe to which work is fixed while being turned. **2** a cylindrical rod around which metal or other material is forged or shaped.
– ORIGIN unknown.

man·drill /'mandrəl/ ▸ **noun** a large West African baboon with a red and blue face, the male having a blue rump.
– ORIGIN probably from **MAN** + a local word.

mane /mān/ ▸ **noun 1** a growth of long hair on the neck of a horse, lion, or other mammal. **2** a person's long flowing hair.
– ORIGIN Old English.

man-eat·er ▸ **noun 1** an animal that can kill and eat people. **2** informal a dominant woman who has many sexual partners.
– DERIVATIVES **man-eat·ing** adjective.

ma·nège /ma'nezH, mə-, -'nāzH/ ▸ **noun 1** a riding school. **2** the movements in which a horse is trained in a riding school.
– ORIGIN French.

ma·neu·ver /mə'n(y)o͞ovər/ (Brit. **manoeuvre**) ▸ **noun 1** a movement or series of moves requiring skill and care. **2** a carefully planned scheme or action. **3** (**maneuvers**) a large-scale military exercise.

– SYNONYMS **1 operation,** exercise, move, movement, action. **2 stratagem,** tactic, gambit, ploy, trick, dodge, ruse, scheme, device, plot, machination, artifice, subterfuge, intrigue.

▸ **verb 1** move skillfully or carefully. **2** carefully manipulate someone or something in order to achieve an aim.

– SYNONYMS **1 steer,** guide, drive, negotiate, jockey, navigate, pilot, direct, move, work. **2 manipulate,** contrive, manage, engineer, fix, organize, arrange, orchestrate, choreograph, stage-manage; informal wangle, pull strings.

– ORIGIN French *manœuvrer*, from Latin *manus* 'hand' + *operari* 'to work.'

ma·neu·ver·a·ble /mə'n(y)o͞ovərəbəl/ ▸ **adjective** (of a boat or aircraft) able to be maneuvered easily.
– DERIVATIVES **ma·neu·ver·a·bil·i·ty** /məˌno͞ovərə'bilətē/ noun.

man·ful /'manfəl/ ▸ **adjective** brave and determined.
– DERIVATIVES **man·ful·ly** adverb.

man·ga /'maNGˌga, 'mänˌga/ ▸ **noun** Japanese cartoons, comic books, and animated films with a science-fiction or fantasy theme.
– ORIGIN Japanese.

man·ga·bey /ˈmaNGgəˌbā/ ▶ **noun** a long-tailed monkey from West and central Africa.
– ORIGIN by wrong association with *Mangabey*, a region of Madagascar.

man·ga·nese /ˈmaNGgəˌnēz, -ˌnēs/ ▶ **noun** a hard gray metallic element used in special steels and magnetic alloys.
– ORIGIN Italian, alteration of *magnesia*.

ma·nge /mānj/ ▶ **noun** a skin disease in some animals that is caused by mites and results in severe itching and hair loss.
– ORIGIN from Old French *mangier* 'eat.'

man·gel-wur·zel /ˈmaNGgəl ˈwərzəl/ ▶ **noun** another term for **MANGOLD**.

man·ger /ˈmānjər/ ▶ **noun** a long trough from which horses or cattle feed.
– ORIGIN Old French *mangeure*, from Latin *manducare* 'to chew.'

man·gle[1] /ˈmaNGgəl/ ▶ **verb 1** destroy or severely damage something by tearing or crushing. **2** spoil or do something badly: *he was mangling Bach on the piano*.
– ORIGIN Old French *mahaignier* 'maim.'

man·gle[2] ▶ **noun** a large machine for ironing sheets, usually when they are damp, using heated rollers.
– ORIGIN from Greek *manganon* 'axis, engine.'

man·go /ˈmaNGgō/ ▶ **noun** (pl. **mangoes** or **mangos**) an oval tropical fruit with yellow flesh.
– ORIGIN Portuguese *manga*.

man·gold /ˈmaNGgōld/ ▶ **noun** a variety of beet with a large root, grown as feed for farm animals.
– ORIGIN German *Mangoldwurzel*.

man·go·steen /ˈmaNGgəˌstēn/ ▶ **noun** a tropical fruit with juicy white flesh inside a thick reddish-brown rind.
– ORIGIN Malay.

man·grove /ˈmanˌgrōv, ˈmaNG-/ ▶ **noun** a tree or shrub found in tropical coastal swamps, with tangled roots that grow above ground.
– ORIGIN probably from Taino (an extinct Caribbean language).

man·gy /ˈmānjē/ ▶ **adjective** (**mangier, mangiest**) **1** having mange. **2** in poor condition; shabby.

man·han·dle /ˈmanˌhandl/ ▶ **verb 1** move a heavy object with effort. **2** drag or push someone roughly.

man·hat·tan /manˈhatn, mən-/ ▶ **noun** a cocktail made of vermouth and whiskey.
– ORIGIN named after the New York island and borough of *Manhattan*.

man·hole /ˈmanˌhōl/ ▶ **noun** a covered opening allowing access to a sewer or other underground structure.

man·hood /ˈmanˌho͝od/ ▶ **noun 1** the state or period of being a man. **2** the men of a country or society. **3** the qualities traditionally associated with men, such as strength and sexual potency.

man-hour ▶ **noun** an hour regarded in terms of the amount of work that can be done by one person within this period.

man·hunt /ˈmanˌhənt/ ▶ **noun** an organized search for a suspect, criminal, or escaped prisoner.

ma·ni·a /ˈmānēə/ ▶ **noun 1** mental illness characterized by an overactive imagination and excited activity. **2** an excessive enthusiasm; an obsession.

> – SYNONYMS **obsession,** compulsion, fixation, fetish, fascination, preoccupation, passion, enthusiasm, desire, urge, craving, craze, fad, rage; informal thing.

– ORIGIN Greek, 'madness.'

-mania ▶ **combining form 1** referring to a specified type of mental abnormality or obsession: *kleptomania*. **2** referring to extreme enthusiasm: *Beatlemania*.
– DERIVATIVES **-maniac** combining form.

ma·ni·ac /ˈmānēˌak/ ▶ **noun 1** a person who behaves in an extremely wild or violent way. **2** informal a person with an extreme enthusiasm for something.

> – SYNONYMS **lunatic,** madman, madwoman, psychopath; informal loony, nutcase, nut, headcase, screwball, psycho, sicko.

– DERIVATIVES **ma·ni·a·cal** /məˈnīəkəl/ adjective **ma·ni·a·cal·ly** /məˈnīək(ə)lē/ adverb.

man·ic /ˈmanik/ ▶ **adjective 1** relating to a mental illness characterized by an overactive imagination and excited activity. **2** showing wild excitement and energy: *a manic grin*.

> – SYNONYMS **1 mad,** insane, deranged, demented, maniacal, wild, crazed, demonic, hysterical, raving, unhinged; informal crazy. **2** *manic activity* **frenzied,** feverish, frenetic, hectic, intense.
> – ANTONYMS sane, calm.

– DERIVATIVES **man·i·cal·ly** /-(ə)lē/ adverb.

man·ic de·pres·sion ▶ **noun** another term, especially formerly, for **BIPOLAR DISORDER**.
– DERIVATIVES **man·ic-de·pres·sive** adjective & noun.

Man·i·chae·an /ˌmanəˈkēən/ (also **Manichean**) ▶ **adjective 1** chiefly historical relating to Manichaeism. **2** relating to a contrast or conflict between opposites.
– DERIVATIVES **Man·i·chae·an·ism** /-ˈkēəˌnizəm/ noun.

Man·i·chae·ism /ˈmanəˌkēizəm/ (also **Manicheism**) ▶ **noun** a religious system with Christian, Gnostic, and pagan elements, founded in Persia in the 3rd century by Manes and based on a belief in an ancient conflict between light and darkness.
– ORIGIN from Latin *Manichaeus* 'of Manes.'

man·i·cure /ˈmaniˌkyo͝or/ ▶ **noun** a cosmetic treatment of the hands and nails. ▶ **verb 1** give a manicure to a person or the hands. **2** (as adj. **manicured**) (of a lawn or garden) neatly trimmed and maintained.
– DERIVATIVES **man·i·cur·ist** /ˈmaniˌkyo͝orist/ noun.
– ORIGIN from Latin *manus* 'hand' + *cura* 'care.'

man·i·fest[1] /ˈmanəˌfest/ ▶ **adjective** clear and obvious.

> – SYNONYMS **obvious,** clear, plain, apparent, evident, patent, distinct, definite, blatant, overt, glaring, transparent, conspicuous, undisguised.

▶ **verb 1** show or display: *she manifested signs of severe depression*. **2** (of an illness or disorder) become apparent. **3** (of a ghost) appear.

> – SYNONYMS **display,** show, exhibit, demonstrate, betray, present, reveal; formal evince.
> – ANTONYMS hide.

– DERIVATIVES **man·i·fest·ly** adverb.
– ORIGIN Latin *manifestus* 'caught in the act, flagrant.'

man·i·fest[2] ▶ **noun 1** a document listing a ship's contents, cargo, crew, and passengers. **2** a list of passengers or cargo in an aircraft.
– ORIGIN Italian *manifesto* 'manifesto.'

man·i·fes·ta·tion /ˌmanəfəˈstāSHən, -ˌfesˈtāSHən/ ▶ **noun 1** a sign that something exists or is happening: *graffiti* *was a manifestation of bored youth.* **2** an appearance of a god or spirit in physical form.

– SYNONYMS **1 display,** demonstration, show, exhibition, presentation. **2 sign,** indication, evidence, symptom, testimony, proof, mark, reflection, example, instance.

CHOOSE THE RIGHT WORD

See **SIGN**.

Man·i·fest Des·ti·ny ▶ **noun** the 19th-century doctrine or belief that US expansion throughout the American continents was both justified and inevitable.

man·i·fes·to /ˌmanəˈfestō/ ▶ **noun** (pl. **manifestos**) a public declaration of the policy and aims of a political party or other group.
– ORIGIN Italian.

man·i·fold /ˈmanəˌfōld/ ▶ **adjective 1** many and various. **2** having many different forms or aspects. ▶ **noun** a pipe with several openings that connect to other parts, especially one in an internal combustion engine conveying air and fuel from the carburetor to the cylinders or leading from the cylinders to the exhaust pipe.
– ORIGIN Old English.

WORD TOOLKIT

See **DIVERSE**.

man·i·kin /ˈmanikən/ (also **mannikin**) ▶ **noun 1** a very small person. **2** a jointed model of the human body.
– ORIGIN Dutch *manneken* 'little man.'

Ma·nil·a /məˈnilə/ (also **Manilla**) ▶ **noun 1** strong brown paper, originally made from a Philippine plant. **2** a cigar or cheroot made in Manila.
– ORIGIN from *Manila,* the capital of the Philippines.

man·i·oc /ˈmanēˌäk/ ▶ **noun** another term for **CASSAVA**.
– ORIGIN Tupi.

ma·nip·u·late /məˈnipyəˌlāt/ ▶ **verb 1** handle or control a tool, device, etc., in a skillful way. **2** control or influence someone in a clever or underhanded way. **3** alter or present information so as to mislead someone. **4** examine or treat part of the body by feeling or moving it with the hand.

– SYNONYMS **1 operate,** work, handle, turn, pull, push, twist, slide. **2 control,** influence, use to one's advantage, exploit, twist.

– DERIVATIVES **ma·nip·u·la·ble** /-ləbəl/ adjective **ma·nip·u·la·tion** /məˌnipyəˈlāsHən/ noun **ma·nip·u·la·tor** /-ˌlātər/ noun.
– ORIGIN from Latin *manipulus* 'handful.'

ma·nip·u·la·tive /məˈnipyələtiv, -ˌlātiv/ ▶ **adjective 1** controlling a person or situation in a clever or underhanded way. **2** relating to manipulation of an object or part of the body.

man·kind /ˌmanˈkīnd, ˈmanˌkīnd/ ▶ **noun** human beings as a whole; the human race.

– SYNONYMS **the human race,** humankind, humanity, human beings, humans, Homo sapiens, people, man, men and women.

man·ly /ˈmanlē/ ▶ **adjective** (**manlier, manliest**) **1** having qualities traditionally associated with men, such as courage and strength. **2** suitable for a man: *manly sports.*

– SYNONYMS **virile,** masculine, strong, all-male, red-blooded, muscular, muscly, strapping, well built, rugged, tough, powerful, brawny; informal hunky.
– ANTONYMS effeminate.

– DERIVATIVES **man·li·ness** noun.

WORD TOOLKIT

See **MALE**.

man-made ▶ **adjective** made or caused by human beings.

– SYNONYMS **artificial,** synthetic, manufactured, imitation, ersatz, simulated, mock, fake, faux.
– ANTONYMS natural, real.

WORD TOOLKIT

See **ARTIFICIAL**.

man·na /ˈmanə/ ▶ **noun 1** (in the Bible) the substance miraculously supplied as food to the Israelites in the wilderness (Book of Exodus, chapter 16). **2** something unexpected and very welcome or beneficial.
– ORIGIN Hebrew and Arabic.

manned /mand/ ▶ **adjective** having a human crew.

man·ne·quin /ˈmanikən/ ▶ **noun 1** a dummy used to display clothes in a store window. **2** dated a fashion model.
– ORIGIN French, from Dutch *manneken* 'little man.'

man·ner /ˈmanər/ ▶ **noun 1** a way in which something is done or happens. **2** a person's outward behavior or attitude toward other people. **3** (**manners**) polite social behavior. **4** a style in literature or art. **5** literary a kind or sort.

– SYNONYMS **1 way,** fashion, mode, means, method, methodology, system, style, approach, technique, procedure, process. **2** *her unfriendly manner* **behavior,** attitude, demeanor, air, aspect, mien, bearing, conduct. **3** (**manners**) **social graces,** politeness, Ps and Qs, etiquette, protocol, decorum, propriety, civility.

– PHRASES **all manner of** many different kinds of. **in a manner of speaking** in some sense. **to the manner born** naturally at ease in a particular job or situation.
– ORIGIN from Latin *manuarius* 'of the hand,' from *manus* 'hand.'

man·nered /ˈmanərd/ ▶ **adjective 1** behaving in a specified way: *well-mannered.* **2** (of behavior, art, literary style, etc.) marked by distinctive or exaggerated features intended to be impressive.

man·ner·ism /ˈmanəˌrizəm/ ▶ **noun 1** a habitual gesture or way of speaking or behaving. **2** the use of a very distinctive style in art, literature, or music. **3** (**Mannerism**) a style of 16th-century Italian art characterized by distortions in scale and perspective.

– SYNONYMS **idiosyncrasy,** quirk, oddity, foible, trait, peculiarity, habit, characteristic.

– DERIVATIVES **man·ner·ist** noun & adjective.

man·ner·ly /ˈmanərlē/ ▶ **adjective** well-mannered; polite.

man·ni·kin /ˈmanikən/ ▶ **noun** variant spelling of **MANIKIN**.

man·nish /ˈmanisH/ ▶ **adjective** (of a woman) looking or behaving like a man.

WORD TOOLKIT

See **MALE**.

ma·noeu·vre ▶ **noun & verb** British spelling of **MANEUVER**.

man-of-war (also **man-o'-war** /ˌmanə'wôr/) ▸ **noun** historical an armed sailing ship.

ma·nom·e·ter /mə'nämətər/ ▸ **noun** an instrument for measuring the pressure of fluids.
– ORIGIN from Greek *manos* 'thin, rarefied.'

man·or /'manər/ ▸ **noun 1** a large country house with lands. **2** (in medieval times) an area of land controlled by a lord.
– DERIVATIVES **ma·no·ri·al** /mə'nôrēəl/ adjective.
– ORIGIN Old French *maner* 'dwelling.'

man·pow·er /'manˌpouər/ ▸ **noun** the number of people working or available for work or service.

man·qué /mänɢ'kā/ ▸ **adjective** having never become what one might have been; unfulfilled: *an actor manqué*.
– ORIGIN French, from *manquer* 'to lack.'

man·sard /'manˌsärd, -sərd/ ▸ **noun** a roof with four sides, in each of which the lower part of the slope is steeper than the upper part.
– ORIGIN named after the French architect François *Mansart*.

manse /mans/ ▸ **noun 1** a house provided for a minister of certain Christian churches, especially the Scottish Presbyterian Church. **2** a large, stately house; a mansion.
– ORIGIN Latin *mansus* 'house.'

man·serv·ant /'manˌsərvənt/ ▸ **noun** (pl. **menservants**) a male servant.

man·sion /'mansʜən/ ▸ **noun** a large, impressive house.

> – SYNONYMS **estate,** stately home, hall, manor (house).
> – ANTONYMS hovel.

– ORIGIN Latin, 'place where someone stays.'

man-sized ▸ **adjective 1** of the size of a human being. **2** large enough to occupy, suit, or satisfy a man: *a man-sized breakfast*. **3** formidable: *a man-sized job*.

man·slaugh·ter /'manˌslôtər/ ▸ **noun** the crime of killing a person without intending to do so.

man·ta /'mantə/ ▸ **noun** (also **manta ray**) a very large ray (fish) of tropical seas.
– ORIGIN Latin American Spanish, 'large blanket.'

man·tel /'mantl/ (also **mantle**) ▸ **noun** a mantelpiece or mantelshelf.
– ORIGIN from **MANTLE**.

man·tel·piece /'mantlˌpēs/ ▸ **noun 1** a structure surrounding a fireplace. **2** a mantelshelf.

man·tel·shelf /'mantlˌsʜelf/ ▸ **noun** a shelf forming the top of a mantelpiece.

man·til·la /man'tē(y)ə, -'tilə/ ▸ **noun** (in Spain) a lace or silk scarf traditionally worn by women over the hair and shoulders.
– ORIGIN Spanish, 'little mantle or shawl.'

man·tis /'mantis/ (also **praying mantis**) ▸ **noun** (pl. same or **mantises**) a slender insect with a triangular head, typically waiting motionless for prey with its forelegs folded like hands in prayer.
– ORIGIN Greek, 'prophet.'

man·tle /'mantl/ ▸ **noun 1** a woman's loose sleeveless cloak or shawl. **2** a covering layer of something: *a mantle of snow*. **3** (also **gas mantle**) a mesh cover fixed around a gas jet to give a glowing light when heated. **4** an important role or responsibility that passes from one person to another. **5** the region of the earth's interior between the crust and the core, consisting of hot, dense silicate rock. ▸ **verb** literary cover or envelop something.
– ORIGIN Latin *mantellum* 'cloak.'

man·tra /'mantrə, 'män-/ ▸ **noun 1** (originally in Hinduism and Buddhism) a word or sound repeated to help concentration while meditating. **2** a Vedic hymn. **3** a frequently repeated statement or slogan.
– ORIGIN Sanskrit, 'instrument of thought.'

man·trap /'manˌtrap/ ▸ **noun** a trap for catching people.

man·u·al /'manyə(wə)l/ ▸ **adjective 1** relating to or operated with the hands: *a manual typewriter*. **2** using or working with the hands: *a manual worker*.

> – SYNONYMS **physical,** laboring, blue-collar, hand.

▸ **noun 1** a book giving instructions or information. **2** an organ keyboard played with the hands, not the feet.

> – SYNONYMS **handbook,** instructions, guide, companion, ABC, guidebook, vade mecum; informal bible.

– DERIVATIVES **man·u·al·ly** adverb.
– ORIGIN from Latin *manus* 'hand.'

man·u·fac·to·ry /ˌmanyə'fakt(ə)rē/ ▸ **noun** (pl. **manufactories**) old use a factory.

man·u·fac·ture /ˌmanyə'fakcʜər/ ▸ **verb 1** make something on a large scale using machinery. **2** make up evidence or a story.

> – SYNONYMS **1 make,** produce, mass-produce, build, construct, assemble, put together, turn out, process. **2 make up,** invent, fabricate, concoct, hatch, dream up, think up, contrive; informal cook up.

▸ **noun** the process of making goods on a large scale using machinery.

> – SYNONYMS **production,** making, manufacturing, mass production, construction, building, assembly.

– ORIGIN French, from Italian *manifattura*, influenced by Latin *manu factum* 'made by hand.'

man·u·fac·tur·er /ˌmanyə'fakcʜərər/ ▸ **noun** a person or organization that manufactures something: *local manufacturers are important sources of tax revenue*.

> – SYNONYMS **maker,** producer, builder, constructor, industrialist.

man·u·mit /ˌmanyə'mit/ ▸ **verb** (**manumits, manumitting, manumitted**) historical free someone from slavery.
– DERIVATIVES **man·u·mis·sion** /-'misʜən/ noun.
– ORIGIN Latin *manumittere* 'send forth from the hand.'

ma·nure /mə'n(y)o͝or/ ▸ **noun** animal dung used for fertilizing land. ▸ **verb** spread manure on land.
– ORIGIN Old French.

man·u·script /'manyəˌskript/ ▸ **noun 1** a handwritten book, document, or piece of music. **2** an author's handwritten or typed work, submitted for printing and publication.
– ORIGIN from Latin *manu* 'by hand' + *scriptus* 'written.'

Manx /manɢks/ ▸ **noun** the Celtic language formerly spoken on the Isle of Man, still used for some ceremonial purposes. ▸ **adjective** relating to the Isle of Man.
– ORIGIN from Old Irish *Manu* 'Isle of Man.'

Manx cat ▸ **noun** a breed of cat without a tail.

man·y /'menē/ ▸ **determiner, pronoun, & adjective** (**more, most**) a large number of people or things.

> – SYNONYMS **numerous,** a lot of, plenty of, countless, innumerable, scores of, untold, copious, abundant; informal lots of, umpteen, loads of, masses of, stacks

of, heaps of, oodles of, a slew of; literary myriad.
– ANTONYMS few.

▶ noun (**the many**) the majority of people.
– ORIGIN Old English.

man·za·nil·la /ˌmanzəˈnē(y)ə, -ˈnɪlə/ ▶ noun a pale, very dry Spanish sherry.
– ORIGIN Spanish, 'chamomile' (because the flavor is considered similar to that of chamomile).

ma·ña·na /mənˈyänə/ ▶ adverb tomorrow, or at some time in the future.
– ORIGIN Spanish.

Mao·ism /ˈmouˌizəm/ ▶ noun the communist policies and theories of the former Chinese head of state Mao Zedong.
– DERIVATIVES **Mao·ist** noun & adjective.

Ma·o·ri /ˈmourē/ ▶ noun (pl. same or **Maoris**) **1** a member of the aboriginal people of New Zealand. **2** the Polynesian language of the Maori.

map /map/ ▶ noun **1** a flat diagram of an area of land or sea showing physical features, cities, roads, etc. **2** a diagram or collection of data showing the arrangement, distribution, or sequence of something.

– SYNONYMS **plan**, chart, A to Z, atlas.

▶ verb (**maps, mapping, mapped**) **1** represent or record something on a map. **2** (**map something out**) plan something in detail.

– SYNONYMS **chart**, plot, draw, record.

– PHRASES **off the map** very distant or remote. **put someone/thing on the map** make someone or something famous.
– ORIGIN Latin *mappa* 'sheet, napkin.'

WORD LINKS

cartography *making of maps*

ma·ple /ˈmāpəl/ ▶ noun a tree or shrub with five-pointed leaves, winged fruits, and syrupy sap.
– ORIGIN Old English.

ma·ple leaf ▶ noun the leaf of the maple, used as the Canadian national emblem.

ma·ple syr·up ▶ noun sugary syrup produced from the sap of a maple tree.

ma·quette /maˈket/ ▶ noun a small model or sketch made by a sculptor as a basis for a larger work.
– ORIGIN French.

ma·quis /mäˈkē/ ▶ noun (pl. same) **1** (**the Maquis**) the French resistance movement during the German occupation of France in World War II. **2** dense evergreen vegetation characteristic of coastal regions in the Mediterranean.
– ORIGIN French, 'brushwood.'

mar /mär/ ▶ verb (**mars, marring, marred**) damage or spoil: *violence marred a number of New Year celebrations.*

– SYNONYMS **spoil,** impair, detract from, disfigure, blemish, scar, deface, ruin, damage, wreck, taint, tarnish.
– ANTONYMS enhance.

– ORIGIN Old English.

Mar. ▶ abbreviation March.

mar·a·bou /ˈmarəˌbo͞o/ ▶ noun **1** an African stork with a massive bill and large neck pouch. **2** down feathers from the marabou used as trimming for hats or clothing.
– ORIGIN French, from Arabic, 'holy man.'

ma·rac·a /məˈräkə/ ▶ noun a hollow gourd or gourd-shaped container filled with small beans, stones, etc., shaken as a musical instrument.
– ORIGIN Portuguese, from Tupi.

mar·a·schi·no /ˌmarəˈsʜēˌnō, -ˈskē-/ ▶ noun (pl. **maraschinos**) a strong, sweet liqueur made from a kind of cherry.
– ORIGIN Italian, from *marasca* (the name of the cherry).

mar·a·schi·no cher·ry ▶ noun a cherry preserved in maraschino.

mar·a·thon /ˈmarəˌᴛʜän/ ▶ noun **1** a long-distance running race, strictly one of 26 miles 385 yards (42.195 km). **2** a long and very difficult task.
– ORIGIN from *Marathōn* in Greece, the scene of a victory over the Persians in 490 BC; the modern race is based on the tradition that a messenger ran from Marathon to Athens (22 miles) with the news.

ma·raud /məˈrôd/ ▶ verb go about in search of goods to steal or people to attack.
– DERIVATIVES **ma·raud·er** noun.
– ORIGIN from French *maraud* 'rogue.'

mar·ble /ˈmärbəl/ ▶ noun **1** a hard form of limestone, typically with streaks of color running through it, that may be polished and used in sculpture and building. **2** a small ball of colored glass used as a toy. **3** (**marbles**) (treated as sing.) a game in which marbles are rolled along the ground. **4** (**one's marbles**) informal one's mental faculties. ▶ verb stain or streak something so that it looks like marble.
– DERIVATIVES **mar·bled** adjective.
– ORIGIN Greek *marmaros* 'shining stone.'

mar·bling /ˈmärbəlɪɴɢ/ ▶ noun **1** coloring or marking that resembles marble. **2** streaks of fat in lean meat.

marc /märk/ ▶ noun **1** the skins and other remains from grapes that have been pressed for winemaking. **2** an alcoholic spirit distilled from this.
– ORIGIN French, from *marcher* in the early sense 'to tread or trample.'

mar·ca·site /ˈmärkəˌsīt/ ▶ noun **1** a semiprecious stone consisting of iron pyrites. **2** a piece of polished metal cut as a gem.
– ORIGIN Latin *marcasita*.

March /märᴄʜ/ ▶ noun the third month of the year.
– ORIGIN from Latin *Martius mensis* 'month of Mars.'

march /märᴄʜ/ ▶ verb **1** walk in time with other people and with regular paces, like a soldier. **2** proceed quickly and with determination. **3** force someone to walk somewhere quickly. **4** take part in an organized procession to make a protest.

– SYNONYMS **1 stride,** walk, troop, step, pace, tread, slog, tramp, hike, trudge, parade, file. **2 strut,** flounce, storm, stomp, sweep.

▶ noun **1** an act of marching. **2** a procession organized as a protest. **3** a piece of music written to accompany marching.

– SYNONYMS **1 walk,** trek, hike. **2 parade,** procession, cortège, demonstration; informal demo. **3** *the march of technology* **progress,** advance, development, evolution, passage.

– DERIVATIVES **march·er** noun.
– PHRASES **on the march 1** engaged in marching. **2** making progress.
– ORIGIN French *marcher* 'to walk.'

March·es /ˈmärᴄʜiz/ ▶ plural noun an area of land on the border between two countries or territories.
– ORIGIN Old French *marche*, related to **MARK**[1].

March hare ▶ **noun** informal a brown hare in the breeding season, noted for its wild behavior.

march·ing or·ders ▶ **noun 1** instructions for troops to depart. **2** informal a dismissal from a place, job, etc.

mar·chion·ess /'märsʜ(ə)nəs/ ▶ **noun 1** the wife or widow of a marquess. **2** a woman holding the rank of marquess in her own right.
– ORIGIN Latin *marchionissa*, 'female ruler of a border territory.'

Mar·di Gras /'märdē ˌgrä/ ▶ **noun** a carnival held in some countries on Shrove Tuesday.
– ORIGIN French, 'fat Tuesday,' referring to the last day of feasting before the fast and penitence of Lent.

mare[1] /me(ə)r/ ▶ **noun** the female of a horse or related animal.
– ORIGIN Old English.

ma·re[2] /'märā/ ▶ **noun** (pl. **maria** /'märēə/) a large plain of volcanic rock on the surface of the moon.
– ORIGIN Latin *mare* 'sea'; these areas were once thought to be seas, as they appear dark by contrast with surrounding highland areas.

mare's nest ▶ **noun 1** a complicated situation. **2** a discovery that turns out to be illusory or worthless.

mare's tail ▶ **noun 1** a water plant with whorls of narrow leaves around a tall thick stem. **2** (**mare's tails**) long straight streaks of cirrus cloud.

mar·ga·rine /'märjərən/ ▶ **noun** a butter substitute made from vegetable oils or animal fats.
– ORIGIN French, from Greek *margaron* 'pearl' (because the crystals of the compounds from which it was first made had a pearly luster).

mar·ga·ri·ta /ˌmärgə'rētə/ ▶ **noun** a cocktail made with tequila and lemon or lime juice.
– ORIGIN Spanish equivalent of the woman's name *Margaret*.

mar·gin /'märjən/ ▶ **noun 1** an edge or border. **2** the blank border on each side of the print on a page. **3** an amount by which something is won. **4** an amount included or allowed for so as to ensure success or safety: *there was no margin for error*. **5** the furthest reach or limit: *the margins of acceptability*.

– SYNONYMS **1 edge,** side, verge, border, perimeter, brink, brim, rim, fringe, boundary, periphery, extremity. **2 leeway,** latitude, scope, room, space, allowance. **3** *they won by a narrow margin* **gap,** majority, amount.

– ORIGIN Latin *margo* 'edge.'

CHOOSE THE RIGHT WORD

See **BORDER**.

mar·gin·al /'märjənl/ ▶ **adjective 1** relating to or situated on an edge or border. **2** of minor importance. **3** (of a decision or distinction) very narrow.

– SYNONYMS *a very marginal case* **borderline,** disputable, questionable, doubtful.
– ANTONYMS considerable.

▶ **noun** Brit. a marginal parliamentary seat.
– DERIVATIVES **mar·gin·al·i·ty** /ˌmärjə'nalətē/ noun.

mar·gi·na·li·a /ˌmärjə'nālēə/ ▶ **plural noun** notes written or printed in the margin of a book or manuscript.

mar·gin·al·ize /'märjənəˌlīz/ ▶ **verb** treat a person, group, or idea as unimportant.
– DERIVATIVES **mar·gin·al·i·za·tion** /ˌmärjənələ'zāsʜən/ noun.

mar·gin·al·ly /'märjənəlē/ ▶ **adverb** to only a limited extent.

mar·grave /'märˌgrāv/ ▶ **noun** historical the hereditary title of some princes of the Holy Roman Empire.
– ORIGIN Dutch, from *marke* 'boundary' + *grave* 'count.'

mar·gue·rite /ˌmärg(y)ə'rēt/ ▶ **noun** another term for **OXEYE DAISY**.
– ORIGIN French form of the woman's name *Margaret*.

ma·ri·a /'märēə/ plural of **MARE**[2].

ma·ri·a·chi /ˌmärē'äcʜē/ ▶ **noun** (pl. **mariachis**) a musician performing traditional Mexican folk music.
– ORIGIN Mexican Spanish, 'street singer.'

mar·i·gold /'mariˌgōld/ ▶ **noun** a plant of the daisy family with yellow or orange flowers.
– ORIGIN from the woman's name *Mary* + dialect *gold* 'marigold.'

ma·ri·jua·na /ˌmarə'(h)wänə/ ▶ **noun** cannabis.
– ORIGIN Latin American Spanish.

ma·rim·ba /mə'rimbə/ ▶ **noun** a deep-toned xylophone of African origin.
– ORIGIN from Kimbundu (a Bantu language of western Angola).

ma·ri·na /mə'rēnə/ ▶ **noun** a purpose-built harbor with moorings for yachts and small boats.
– ORIGIN Italian or Spanish, from Latin *mare* 'sea.'

mar·i·nade ▶ **noun** /ˌmarə'nād/ a mixture of oil, vinegar, and spices, in which meat, fish, or other food is soaked before cooking in order to flavor or soften it. ▶ **verb** also /'marəˌnād/ another term for **MARINATE**.
– ORIGIN French, from Spanish *marinar* 'pickle in brine.'

ma·ri·na·ra /ˌmarə'narə, ˌmärə'närə/ ▶ **noun** (in Italian cooking) a sauce made from tomatoes, onions, and herbs.
– ORIGIN from Italian *alla marinara* 'sailor-style.'

mar·i·nate /'marəˌnāt/ ▶ **verb** soak meat, fish, or other food in a marinade.
– DERIVATIVES **mar·i·na·tion** /ˌmarə'nāsʜən/ noun.

ma·rine /mə'rēn/ ▶ **adjective 1** relating to the sea. **2** relating to shipping or a navy.

– SYNONYMS **1 seawater,** sea, saltwater, aquatic. **2 maritime,** nautical, naval, seafaring, seagoing, ocean-going.

▶ **noun** a member of a body of troops trained to serve on land or sea, in particular a member of the US Marine Corps.
– ORIGIN Latin *marinus*, from *mare* 'sea.'

mar·i·ner /'marənər/ ▶ **noun** formal or literary a sailor.

– SYNONYMS **sailor,** seaman, seafarer; informal sea dog, old salt; dated tar.

mar·i·on·ette /ˌmarēə'net/ ▶ **noun** a puppet worked by strings.
– ORIGIN French, from the woman's name *Marion*.

mar·i·tal /'maritl/ ▶ **adjective** relating to marriage or the relations between husband and wife.

– SYNONYMS **matrimonial,** conjugal, married, wedded, nuptial.

– DERIVATIVES **mar·i·tal·ly** adverb.
– ORIGIN Latin *maritus* 'husband.'

mar·i·time /'mariˌtīm/ ▶ **adjective 1** relating to shipping or other activity taking place at sea. **2** living or found in or near the sea. **3** (of a climate) moist and mild owing to the influence of the sea.

– SYNONYMS **naval,** marine, nautical, seafaring, seagoing, sea, ocean-going, oceanic, coastal.

– ORIGIN Latin *maritimus,* from *mare* 'sea.'

mar·jo·ram /ˈmärjərəm/ ▶ **noun** a plant of the mint family whose sweet-scented leaves are used as an herb in cooking.
– ORIGIN Latin *majorana.*

mark[1] /märk/ ▶ **noun 1** a small area on a surface having a different color from its surroundings. **2** something that indicates position or acts as a pointer. **3** a line, figure, or symbol made to identify or record something. **4** a sign or indication of a quality or feeling: *a mark of respect.* **5** a characteristic feature of something: *it is the mark of a civilized society to treat its elderly members well.* **6** a level or stage. **7** a grade awarded for a piece of work. **8** a particular model or type of a vehicle or machine.

– SYNONYMS **1 blemish,** streak, spot, fleck, blot, stain, smear, speck, smudge, blotch, bruise, scratch, scar, dent, chip, nick. **2** *books bearing the mark of a well-known bookseller* **logo,** seal, stamp, symbol, emblem, device, insignia, badge, brand, trademark, monogram, hallmark. **3** *a mark of respect* **sign,** token, symbol, emblem, badge, indication; evidence, proof. **4** *the mark of a civilized society* **characteristic,** feature, trait, attribute, quality, hallmark, stamp, indicator. **5** *unemployment had passed the two million mark* **point,** level, stage, degree. **6** *he got good marks for math* **grade,** grading, rating, score, percentage.

▶ **verb 1** make a mark on something. **2** write a word or symbol on an object to identify it. **3** indicate the position of something. **4** (**mark someone/thing out**) distinguish someone or something from other people or things. **5** indicate or acknowledge a significant event. **6** (**mark something up** or **down**) increase or reduce the price of an item. **7** assess a written work and give it a mark. **8** notice or pay careful attention to something.

– SYNONYMS **1 discolor,** stain, smear, smudge, streak, dirty, scratch, scar, dent. **2** *her possessions were clearly marked* **label,** identify, flag, tag, initial, highlight, name, brand. **3** *a ceremony was held to mark the occasion* **celebrate,** observe, recognize, acknowledge, keep, honor, commemorate, remember, solemnize. **4** *the incidents marked a new phase in their campaign* **represent,** signify, indicate, herald. **5** *his sword marked him out as an officer* **characterize,** distinguish, identify, typify. **6** *I have a pile of essays to mark* **assess,** evaluate, appraise, grade, correct.

– PHRASES **be quick off the mark** be fast in responding. **make its** (or **one's** or **a**) **mark** have a lasting or significant effect. **mark time 1** (of troops) march on the spot without moving forward. **2** pass one's time in routine activities while waiting for something to happen. **near** (or **close**) **to the mark** almost accurate. **off** (or **wide of**) **the mark** wrong or inaccurate. **on your mark(s)** be ready to start (used to instruct competitors in a race). **up to the mark** up to the required standard.
– ORIGIN Old English.

mark[2] ▶ **noun** (until the introduction of the euro in 2002) the basic unit of money of Germany.
– ORIGIN Old Norse.

mark·down /ˈmärkˌdoun/ ▶ **noun** a reduction in price.

marked /märkt/ ▶ **adjective 1** having a visible mark or other identifying feature. **2** clearly noticeable: *a marked increase in sales.* **3** singled out as a target for attack: *a marked man.*

– SYNONYMS **noticeable,** pronounced, decided, distinct, striking, clear, unmistakable, obvious, conspicuous, notable.
– ANTONYMS imperceptible.

– DERIVATIVES **mark·ed·ly** /ˈmärkədlē/ adverb.

mark·er /ˈmärkər/ ▶ **noun 1** an object used to indicate a position, place, or route. **2** a pen with a broad felt tip. **3** (in soccer) a player who guards an opponent. **4** a person who marks a test or exam.

mar·ket /ˈmärkit/ ▶ **noun 1** a regular gathering for the buying and selling of food, livestock, or other goods. **2** an outdoor space or hall where people offer goods for sale. **3** a particular area of commercial or competitive activity: *the export market.* **4** demand for a particular product or service: *the rapidly growing market for Internet software.*

– SYNONYMS **grocery store,** supermarket, store, convenience store, mart.

▶ **verb** (**markets, marketing, marketed**) advertise or promote something.

– SYNONYMS **sell,** retail, merchandise, trade, advertise, promote.

– DERIVATIVES **mar·ket·a·ble** /ˈmärkitəbəl/ adjective **mar·ket·er** noun.
– PHRASES **on the market** available for sale.
– ORIGIN Latin *mercatus.*

mar·ket·eer /ˌmärkəˈti(ə)r/ ▶ **noun 1** a person who sells products or services in a market. **2** a person who is in favor of a particular system of trade: *a free marketeer.*

mar·ket·ing /ˈmärkitiNG/ ▶ **noun** the promotion and selling of products or services.

mar·ket-mak·er ▶ **noun** Stock Exchange a dealer in securities or other assets who undertakes to buy or sell at specified prices at all times.

mar·ket·place /ˈmärkətˌplās/ ▶ **noun 1** an open space where a market is held. **2** a competitive or commercial area of activity: *the global marketplace.*

mar·ket re·search ▶ **noun** the activity of gathering information about consumers' needs and preferences.

mar·ket town ▶ **noun** a town of moderate size where a regular market is held.

mar·ket val·ue ▶ **noun** the amount for which something can be sold in an open market.

mark·ing /ˈmärkiNG/ ▶ **noun 1** an identifying mark. **2** (also **markings**) a pattern of marks on an animal's fur, feathers, or skin.

marks·man /ˈmärksmən/ ▶ **noun** (pl. **marksmen**) a person skilled in shooting.
– DERIVATIVES **marks·man·ship** /-ˌSHip/ noun.

mark·up /ˈmärˌkəp/ ▶ **noun 1** the amount added to the price of goods to cover overhead and profit. **2** a set of codes given to different elements of a body of computer data to indicate their relationship to the rest of the data.

marl[1] /märl/ ▶ **noun** rock or soil consisting of clay and lime, formerly used as fertilizer.
– ORIGIN Old French *marle.*

marl[2] ▶ **noun** a yarn or fabric with differently colored threads.
– ORIGIN shortening of *marbled.*

mar·lin /ˈmärlən/ ▸ **noun** a large edible fish of warm seas, with a pointed snout.
– ORIGIN from **MARLINSPIKE** (with reference to its pointed snout).

mar·lin·spike /ˈmärlənˌspīk/ (also **marlinespike**) ▸ **noun** a pointed metal tool used by sailors to separate strands of rope or wire.
– ORIGIN from Dutch *marlen* 'keep binding.'

mar·ma·lade /ˈmärməˌlād/ ▸ **noun** a preserve made from citrus fruit, especially bitter oranges.
– ORIGIN Portuguese *marmelada* 'quince jam,' from *marmelo* 'quince.'

mar·mo·re·al /märˈmôrēəl/ ▸ **adjective** literary made of or resembling marble.
– ORIGIN from Latin *marmor* 'marble.'

mar·mo·set /ˈmärməˌset, -ˌzet/ ▸ **noun** a small tropical American monkey with a silky coat and a long tail.
– ORIGIN Old French *marmouset* 'grotesque image.'

mar·mot /ˈmärmət/ ▸ **noun** a heavily built burrowing rodent.
– ORIGIN French *marmotte*.

Mar·o·nite /ˈme(ə)rəˌnīt/ ▸ **noun** a member of a Christian sect living chiefly in Lebanon.
– ORIGIN from the name of John *Maro*, a 5th-century Syrian religious leader.

ma·roon¹ /məˈro͞on/ ▸ **noun** a dark brownish-red color.
– ORIGIN from French *marron* 'chestnut'.

ma·roon² ▸ **verb** leave someone alone in a remote or inaccessible place.

> – SYNONYMS *schoolboys marooned on a desert island* **strand,** cast away, cast ashore, abandon, desert, leave behind, leave.

– ORIGIN from *Maroon*, a member of a group of black people descended from runaway slaves and living in parts of Suriname and the West Indies, from Spanish *cimarrón* 'runaway slave.'

marque /märk/ ▸ **noun** a make of car, as distinct from a specific model.
– ORIGIN French.

mar·quee /märˈkē/ ▸ **noun** a rooflike projection over the entrance to a theater, hotel, or other building.
– ORIGIN from **MARQUISE** (formerly a synonym for *marquee*).

mar·quess /ˈmärkwəs/ ▸ **noun** a British nobleman ranking above an earl and below a duke.
– ORIGIN variant of **MARQUIS**.

mar·que·try /ˈmärkətrē/ ▸ **noun** inlaid work made from small pieces of colored wood, used to decorate furniture.
– ORIGIN French *marqueter* 'become variegated.'

mar·quis /märˈkē, ˈmärkwəs/ ▸ **noun 1** (in some European countries) a nobleman ranking above a count and below a duke. **2** variant spelling of **MARQUESS**.
– ORIGIN Old French *marchis*.

mar·quise /märˈkēz/ ▸ **noun 1** the wife or widow of a marquis, or a woman holding the rank of marquis in her own right. **2** a ring set with a pointed oval gem or cluster of gems.
– ORIGIN French, feminine of **MARQUIS**.

mar·riage /ˈmarij/ ▸ **noun 1** the formal union of a man and a woman, by which they become husband and wife. **2** a combination of two or more elements.

> – SYNONYMS **1 matrimony,** wedlock, wedding, wedding ceremony, nuptials, union, match. **2** *a marriage of jazz, pop, and gospel* **union,** fusion, mixture, mix, blend, alliance, amalgamation, combination, hybrid.
> – ANTONYMS divorce, separation.

– ORIGIN Old French *mariage*.

> **WORD LINKS**
>
> **marital, matrimonial, nuptial, conjugal** *relating to marriage*

mar·riage·a·ble /ˈmarijəbəl/ ▸ **adjective** suitable for marriage, especially in terms of age.

mar·ried /ˈmarēd/ ▸ **adjective** united by marriage. ▸ **noun** (**marrieds**) married people.

mar·row /ˈmarō/ ▸ **noun** (also **bone marrow**) a soft fatty substance in the cavities of bones, in which blood cells are produced.
– PHRASES **to the marrow** to one's innermost being.
– ORIGIN Old English.

mar·row·bone /ˈmarōˌbōn/ ▸ **noun** a bone containing edible marrow.

mar·ry /ˈmarē/ ▸ **verb** (**marries, marrying, married**) **1** take someone as one's wife or husband in marriage. **2** join two people in marriage. **3** (**marry into**) become a member of a family by marriage. **4** join two things together in a harmonious way: *the show marries poetry with art.*

> – SYNONYMS **1 get married,** wed, become husband and wife; informal tie the knot, walk down the aisle, get hitched. **2** *the show marries poetry with art* **join,** unite, combine, fuse, mix, blend, merge, amalgamate.
> – ANTONYMS divorce, separate.

– ORIGIN Old French *marier*.

Mars /märz/ ▸ **noun** a small planet of the solar system, fourth in order from the sun and the nearest to the earth.

Mar·sa·la /märˈsälə/ ▸ **noun** a dark, sweet fortified dessert wine made in Sicily.
– ORIGIN named after *Marsala*, a town in Sicily.

marsh /märsн/ ▸ **noun** an area of low-lying land that is flooded in wet seasons or at high tide and typically remains waterlogged.

> – SYNONYMS **swamp,** marshland, bog, morass, mire, quagmire, slough, fen.

– DERIVATIVES **marsh·y** adjective.
– ORIGIN Old English.

mar·shal /ˈmärsнəl/ ▸ **noun 1** an officer of the highest rank in the armed forces of some countries. **2** a federal or municipal law-enforcement officer. **3** an official responsible for supervising public events. ▸ **verb** (**marshals, marshaling, marshaled**) **1** assemble a group of people, especially soldiers, in an orderly way. **2** bring facts, information, etc., together in an organized way. **3** direct the movement of an aircraft on the ground at an airport.

> – SYNONYMS **assemble,** gather (together), collect, muster, call together, draw up, line up, array, organize, group, arrange, deploy, position, summon, round up.

– ORIGIN Old French *mareschal* 'farrier, commander.'

Marsh Ar·ab ▸ **noun** a member of a semi-nomadic Arab people living in marshland in southern Iraq.

marsh gas ▶ noun gas, mainly methane, produced by decaying matter in marshes.

marsh·land /ˈmärsʜˌland/ ▶ noun (also **marshlands**) land consisting of marshes.

marsh·mal·low /ˈmärsʜˌmelō, -ˌmalō/ ▶ noun a spongy confection made from a mixture of sugar, egg white, and gelatin.

marsh mal·low ▶ noun a tall pink-flowered plant growing in marshes, whose roots were formerly used to make marshmallow.

marsh mar·i·gold ▶ noun a plant with large yellow flowers that grows in damp ground and shallow water.

mar·su·pi·al /märˈso͞opēəl/ ▶ noun a mammal, such as a kangaroo, whose young are born before they are fully developed and are carried and suckled in a pouch on the mother's belly.
– ORIGIN Greek *marsupion* 'little purse.'

mart /märt/ ▶ noun **1** a store. **2** a market.
– ORIGIN Dutch, variant of *marct* 'market.'

mar·ten /ˈmärtn/ ▶ noun a weasel-like forest mammal that is hunted for fur in some countries.
– ORIGIN from Old French *peau martrine* 'marten fur.'

mar·tial /ˈmärsʜəl/ ▶ adjective relating to or appropriate to war; warlike.

– SYNONYMS **military,** soldierly, warlike, fighting, militaristic; informal gung-ho.

– DERIVATIVES **mar·tial·ly** adverb.
– ORIGIN Latin *martialis*, from *Mars*, the name of the Roman god of war.

mar·tial arts ▶ plural noun various sports or skills that originated mainly in Japan, Korea, and China as forms of self-defense or attack, such as judo, karate, and kung fu.

mar·tial law ▶ noun government by the military forces of a country, during which ordinary laws are suspended.

Mar·tian /ˈmärsʜən/ ▶ noun a supposed inhabitant of the planet Mars. ▶ adjective relating to Mars.

mar·tin /ˈmärtn/ ▶ noun used in names of small short-tailed swallows, e.g., **house martin**.
– ORIGIN probably from the name of St. *Martin* of Tours.

mar·ti·net /ˌmärtnˈet/ ▶ noun a person who enforces strict discipline.
– ORIGIN named after Jean *Martinet*, a French soldier.

mar·tin·gale /ˈmärtnˌgāl/ ▶ noun a strap or set of straps running from the noseband or reins to the girth of a horse, used to prevent the horse from raising its head too high.
– ORIGIN French.

mar·ti·ni /märˈtēnē/ ▶ noun a cocktail made from gin and dry vermouth.
– ORIGIN named after *Martini* and Rossi, a maker of vermouth.

Mar·ti·niq·uan /ˌmärtnˈēkən/ (also **Martinican**) ▶ noun a person from Martinique, a French island in the Lesser Antilles. ▶ adjective relating to Martinique.

mar·tyr /ˈmärtər/ ▶ noun **1** a person who is killed because of their religious or political beliefs. **2** a person who exaggerates their difficulties in order to obtain sympathy. ▶ verb make someone a martyr.
– DERIVATIVES **mar·tyr·dom** /ˈmärtərdəm/ noun.
– ORIGIN Greek *martur* 'witness.'

mar·tyr·ol·o·gy /ˌmärtəˈräləjē/ ▶ noun (pl. **martyrologies**) **1** the study of martyrs. **2** a list of martyrs.

mar·vel /ˈmärvəl/ ▶ verb (**marvels, marveling, marveled**) be filled with wonder: *she marveled at the beauty of the scenery.*

– SYNONYMS **be amazed,** be astonished, be in awe, wonder.

▶ noun a person or thing that causes a feeling of wonder.

– SYNONYMS **wonder,** miracle, sensation, spectacle, phenomenon, prodigy.

– ORIGIN Old French *merveille*.

mar·vel·ous /ˈmärv(ə)ləs/ (Brit. **marvellous**) ▶ adjective **1** causing great wonder; extraordinary. **2** extremely good or pleasing.

– SYNONYMS **excellent,** splendid, wonderful, magnificent, superb, sensational, glorious, sublime, lovely, delightful; informal super, great, amazing, fantastic, terrific, tremendous, fabulous, cracking, awesome, divine, ace, wicked; Brit. informal smashing, brilliant.
– ANTONYMS commonplace, awful.

– DERIVATIVES **mar·vel·ous·ly** adverb.

Marx·ism /ˈmärkˌsizəm/ ▶ noun the political and economic theories of Karl Marx and Friedrich Engels, later developed by their followers as the basis for communism.
– DERIVATIVES **Marx·i·an** /-sēən/ noun & adjective **Marx·ist** noun & adjective.

mar·zi·pan /ˈmärzəˌpan, ˈmärtsə-/ ▶ noun a sweet paste of ground almonds, sugar, and egg whites, used to coat cakes or to make confectionery.
– ORIGIN Italian *marzapane*.

Ma·sai /ˈmäˌsī, mäˈsī/ (also **Maasai**) ▶ noun (pl. same or **Masais**) a member of a pastoral people living in Tanzania and Kenya.
– ORIGIN the Masai's name for themselves.

ma·sa·la /məˈsälə/ ▶ noun a mixture of spices ground into a paste or powder and used in Indian cooking.
– ORIGIN Urdu.

mas·car·a /maˈskarə/ ▶ noun a cosmetic for darkening and thickening the eyelashes.
– ORIGIN Italian, 'mask.'

mas·car·po·ne /ˌmäskärˈpōn(e)/ ▶ noun a soft, mild Italian cream cheese.
– ORIGIN Italian.

mas·cot /ˈmasˌkät, -kət/ ▶ noun a person, animal, or object that is identified with a person, group, team, etc., and supposed to bring good luck.
– ORIGIN French *mascotte*.

mas·cu·line /ˈmaskyələn/ ▶ adjective **1** having the qualities or appearance traditionally associated with men. **2** relating to men; male. **3** Grammar (of a gender of nouns and adjectives in certain languages) treated as male.

– SYNONYMS **1 virile,** macho, manly, male, muscular, muscly, strong, strapping, well built, rugged, robust, brawny, powerful, red-blooded, vigorous; informal hunky, laddish. **2 mannish,** unfeminine, unladylike; informal butch. **3** *a masculine trait* **male,** man's, men's, male-oriented.
– ANTONYMS feminine, effeminate.

– DERIVATIVES **mas·cu·lin·i·ty** /ˌmaskyəˈlinitē/ noun.
– ORIGIN from Latin *masculus* 'male.'

ma·ser /ˈmāzər/ ▶ noun a form of laser generating a beam of microwaves.
– ORIGIN from the initial letters of *microwave*

amplification (by the) stimulated emission (of) radiation.

MASH /mash/ ▶ **abbreviation** mobile army surgical hospital.

mash /mash/ ▶ **verb 1** crush or beat something to a soft mass. **2** (in brewing) mix powdered malt with hot water to form wort.

– SYNONYMS **pulp,** crush, purée, cream, pound, beat.

▶ **noun 1** a soft mass made by crushing a substance into a pulp. **2** bran mixed with hot water, given as a food to horses. **3** (in brewing) a mixture of powdered malt and hot water that is left standing until the sugars dissolve to form the wort. **4** Brit. informal mashed potatoes.
– ORIGIN Old English.

mashed potatoes ▶ **plural noun** a dish of potatoes that have been boiled until soft, then mashed, usually with butter and milk.

mash-up ▶ **noun 1** a recording created by digitally combining and synchronizing instrumental tracks with vocal tracks from two or more different songs: *a mash-up of Madonna's "Ray of Light" and the Sex Pistols.* **2** a video or Web-based product made by combining content or functionality from more than one source.

mask /mask/ ▶ **noun 1** a covering for all or part of the face, worn as a disguise, for protection or hygiene, or for theatrical effect. **2** a device used to filter inhaled air or to supply gas for breathing. **3** a likeness of a person's face molded or sculpted in clay or wax. **4** a face pack.

– SYNONYMS **pretense,** semblance, veil, screen, front, facade, veneer, disguise, cover, cloak, camouflage.

▶ **verb 1** cover someone's face or part of their face with a mask. **2** conceal or disguise: *brandy did not mask the bitter taste.* **3** cover an object or surface so as to protect it during painting or similar work.

– SYNONYMS **hide,** conceal, disguise, cover up, obscure, screen, cloak, camouflage.

– DERIVATIVES **masked** adjective.
– ORIGIN French *masque*, from Italian *maschera* or *mascara*.

masked ball ▶ **noun** a ball at which participants wear masks to conceal their faces.

mask·ing tape ▶ **noun** adhesive tape used in painting to cover areas on which paint is not wanted.

mas·och·ism /ˈmasəˌkizəm, ˈmaz-/ ▶ **noun** the tendency to enjoy one's own pain or humiliation.
– DERIVATIVES **mas·och·ist** noun **mas·och·is·tic** /ˌmasəˈkistik, ˌmaz-/ adjective.
– ORIGIN named after the Austrian novelist Leopold von Sacher-*Masoch*.

ma·son /ˈmāsən/ ▶ **noun 1** a builder and worker in stone. **2** (**Mason**) a Freemason.
– ORIGIN Old French *masson*.

Ma·son–Dix·on line /ˈdiksən/ (also **Mason and Dixon line**) ▶ **noun** the boundary between Maryland and Pennsylvania, taken as the northern limit of the slave-owning states before the abolition of slavery.
– ORIGIN named after Charles *Mason* (1728–1786) and Jeremiah *Dixon* (1733–1779), the 18th-cent. English astronomers who surveyed it in 1763–67.

Ma·son·ic /məˈsänik/ ▶ **adjective** relating to Freemasons.

ma·son jar ▶ **noun** a wide-mouthed glass jar with an airtight screw top, used for preserving fruit and vegetables.

ma·son·ry /ˈmāsənrē/ ▶ **noun 1** stonework. **2** (**Masonry**) Freemasonry.

masque /mask/ ▶ **noun** a form of dramatic entertainment popular in the 16th and 17th centuries, consisting of dancing and acting performed by players wearing masks.
– ORIGIN probably from *masker* 'person wearing a mask.'

mas·quer·ade /ˌmaskəˈrād/ ▶ **noun 1** an attempt to hide the truth or one's real feelings. **2** a masked ball. ▶ **verb 1** pretend to be someone that one is not. **2** be disguised or passed off as something else: *the idle gossip that masquerades as news.*
– ORIGIN French *mascarade*.

Mass /mas/ ▶ **noun 1** the Christian service of the Eucharist or Holy Communion, especially in the Roman Catholic Church. **2** a musical setting of parts of the liturgy used in the Mass.
– ORIGIN Latin *missa*, from *mittere* 'dismiss,' perhaps from the last words of the service, *Ite, missa est* 'Go, it is the dismissal.'

mass /mas/ ▶ **noun 1** a body of matter with no definite shape. **2** a large number of people or objects gathered together. **3** (**the masses**) the ordinary people. **4** (**the mass of**) the majority of. **5** (**a mass of**) a large amount of. **6** Physics the quantity of matter that a body contains, as measured by its acceleration under a given force or by the force exerted on it by a gravitational field.

– SYNONYMS **1** *a mass of fallen leaves* **pile,** heap, accumulation, aggregation, mat, tangle. **2** *a mass of cyclists* **crowd,** horde, throng, host, troop, army, herd, flock, swarm, mob, pack, flood, multitude. **3** *the mass of the population* **majority,** most, preponderance, greater part, best/better part, bulk, body.

▶ **adjective** done by or affecting large numbers of people or things: *a mass exodus.*

– SYNONYMS **widespread,** general, extensive, large-scale, wholesale, universal, indiscriminate.

▶ **verb** gather together into a single body or mass: *both countries began massing troops in the region.*

– SYNONYMS **assemble,** gather together, collect, rally.

– ORIGIN Latin *massa*.

mas·sa·cre /ˈmasikər/ ▶ **noun 1** a brutal slaughter of a large number of people. **2** informal a very heavy defeat.

– SYNONYMS **slaughter,** mass murder, mass execution, ethnic cleansing, genocide, holocaust, annihilation, liquidation, extermination, carnage, butchery, bloodbath, bloodletting.

▶ **verb 1** brutally kill a large number of people. **2** informal inflict a heavy defeat on an opponent.

– SYNONYMS **slaughter,** butcher, murder, kill, annihilate, exterminate, execute, liquidate, eliminate, mow down.

– ORIGIN French.

mas·sage /məˈsäzʜ, -ˈsäj/ ▶ **noun** the rubbing and kneading of parts of the body with the hands to relieve tension or pain.

– SYNONYMS **rub,** rubdown, kneading.

▶ **verb 1** give someone a massage. **2** manipulate figures to give a more acceptable result.

– SYNONYMS **1 rub,** knead, manipulate, pummel, work. **2 alter,** tamper with, manipulate, doctor, falsify, juggle, fiddle with, tinker with, distort, rig; informal cook, fiddle.

– ORIGIN French.

mas·sage par·lor ▶ **noun 1** a place where one can pay to have a massage. **2** euphemistic a brothel.

mas·seur /ma'sər, mə-/ ▶ **noun** (fem. **masseuse** /ma'so͞os, mə-, ma'sœz/) a person who provides massage professionally.
– ORIGIN French.

mas·sif /ma'sēf/ ▶ **noun** a compact group of mountains.
– ORIGIN French, 'massive.'

mas·sive /'masiv/ ▶ **adjective 1** large and heavy or solid. **2** exceptionally large, intense, or severe: *a massive heart attack*. **3** forming a solid or continuous mass.

– SYNONYMS **huge,** enormous, vast, immense, mighty, great, colossal, tremendous, gigantic, mammoth, monumental, giant, mountainous; informal monster, whopping, astronomical, ginormous, mega.
– ANTONYMS tiny.

– DERIVATIVES **mas·sive·ly** adverb **mas·sive·ness** noun.
– ORIGIN French *massif*.

mass-mar·ket ▶ **adjective** (of goods) produced in large quantities for many people.

mass me·di·a ▶ **noun** television, radio, and newspapers considered as a group; the media.

mass noun ▶ **noun** Grammar a noun referring to something that cannot be counted, in English usually a noun that has no plural form and is not used with *a* or *an*, e.g., *luggage, happiness*. Contrasted with **COUNT NOUN**.

mass num·ber ▶ **noun** Physics the total number of protons and neutrons in a nucleus.

mass-pro·duce /prə'do͞os/ ▶ **verb** produce goods in large quantities, using machinery.
– DERIVATIVES **mass pro·duc·tion** noun.

mast[1] /mast/ ▶ **noun 1** a tall upright post or spar on a boat, generally carrying a sail or sails. **2** any tall upright post, especially a flagpole or a television or radio transmitter.
– ORIGIN Old English.

mast[2] ▶ **noun** the fruit of beech and other forest trees, especially as food for pigs.
– ORIGIN Old English.

mas·tec·to·my /ma'stektəmē/ ▶ **noun** (pl. **mastectomies**) a surgical operation to remove all or part of a breast.
– ORIGIN from Greek *mastos* 'breast.'

mas·ter /'mastər/ ▶ **noun 1** a man in a position of authority, control, or ownership. **2** a person who is skilled in a particular art or activity: *a master of disguise*. **3** chiefly Brit. the head of a college or school. **4** a person who holds a second or further degree from a university. **5** an original movie, recording, or document from which copies can be made. **6** (**Master**) a title placed before a boy's name.

– SYNONYMS **1 lord,** overlord, lord and master, liege, ruler, sovereign, monarch. **2 expert,** genius, maestro, virtuoso, authority; informal ace, wizard, whiz, hotshot, pro, maven, crackerjack. **3 teacher,** schoolteacher, schoolmaster, tutor, instructor.
– ANTONYMS servant, student.

▶ **adjective 1** (of an artist) having great skill or expertise: *a master painter*. **2** skilled in a particular profession and able to teach others: *a master builder*. **3** main; principal: *the master bedroom*.

– SYNONYMS **expert,** adept, proficient, skilled, skillful, deft, dexterous, adroit, practiced, experienced, masterly, accomplished; informal crack, ace, crackerjack.
– ANTONYMS amateur.

▶ **verb 1** gain complete knowledge of or skill in a subject, technique, etc. **2** gain control of: *I managed to master my fears*. **3** make a master copy of a movie or record.

– SYNONYMS **1** *he'd mastered the technique* **learn,** become proficient in, pick up, grasp, understand; informal get the hang of. **2 overcome,** conquer, beat, quell, suppress, control, triumph over, subdue, vanquish, subjugate, curb, check, defeat, get the better of; informal lick.

– ORIGIN Latin *magister*.

mas·ter-at-arms ▶ **noun** a warrant officer responsible for police duties on board a ship.

mas·ter·class /'mastər,klas/ ▶ **noun** a class, especially in music, given to students by an expert in the field.

mas·ter·ful /'mastərfəl/ ▶ **adjective 1** powerful and able to control others. **2** performed or performing very skillfully.

– SYNONYMS **commanding,** powerful, imposing, magisterial, authoritative.
– ANTONYMS weak.

– DERIVATIVES **mas·ter·ful·ly** adverb.

mas·ter key ▶ **noun** a key that opens several locks, each of which also has its own key.

mas·ter·ly /'mastərlē/ ▶ **adjective** performed or performing very skillfully.

– SYNONYMS **expert,** adept, skillful, skilled, adroit, proficient, deft, dexterous, accomplished, polished, consummate.
– ANTONYMS inept.

mas·ter·mind /'mastər,mīnd/ ▶ **noun 1** a person who is extremely intelligent. **2** a person who plans and directs a complex scheme or enterprise.

– SYNONYMS **genius,** intellect; informal brain(s).

▶ **verb** plan and direct a complex scheme or enterprise.

– SYNONYMS **plan,** control, direct, be in charge of, run, conduct, organize, arrange, preside over, orchestrate, stage-manage, engineer, manage, coordinate.

mas·ter of cer·e·mo·nies ▶ **noun** a person in charge of procedure at a state occasion, formal event, or entertainment, who introduces the speakers or performers.

mas·ter·piece /'mastər,pēs/ ▶ **noun** a work of outstanding skill.

– SYNONYMS **magnum opus,** chef-d'œuvre, masterwork, pièce de résistance, tour de force, classic.

mas·ter ser·geant ▶ **noun** a high-ranking noncommissioned officer in the US armed forces.

mas·ter stroke /'mastər ,strōk/ ▶ **noun** an outstandingly skillful or clever move.

mas·ter·work /'mastər,wərk/ ▶ **noun** a masterpiece.

mas·ter·y /'mast(ə)rē/ ▶ **noun 1** complete knowledge or command of a subject or skill. **2** control or superiority: *man's mastery over nature*.

– SYNONYMS **1 proficiency,** ability, capability, knowledge, understanding, comprehension, command, grasp. **2 control,** domination, command, supremacy, superiority, power, authority, jurisdiction, dominion, sovereignty.

mast·head /'mast,hed/ ▶ **noun 1** the highest part of a ship's mast. **2** the name of a newspaper or magazine printed at the top of the first page. **3** a list of staff, owner, advertising rates, etc., in a newspaper or magazine.

mas·tic /ˈmastik/ ▶ **noun** **1** an aromatic gum from the bark of a Mediterranean tree, used in making varnish and chewing gum and as a flavoring. **2** a puttylike waterproof substance used as a filler and sealant in building.
– ORIGIN Greek *mastikhē*.

mas·ti·cate /ˈmastiˌkāt/ ▶ **verb** chew food.
– DERIVATIVES **mas·ti·ca·tion** /ˌmastiˈkāsʜən/ noun.
– ORIGIN Latin *masticare*.

mas·tiff /ˈmastif/ ▶ **noun** a dog of a large, strong breed with drooping ears and lips.
– ORIGIN Old French *mastin*.

mas·ti·tis /maˈstītis/ ▶ **noun** inflammation of the mammary gland in the breast or udder.
– ORIGIN from Greek *mastos* 'breast.'

mas·to·don /ˈmastəˌdän/ ▶ **noun** a large extinct elephantlike mammal.
– ORIGIN from Greek *mastos* 'breast' + *odous* 'tooth' (with reference to nipple-shaped projections on the crowns of its molar teeth).

mas·toid /ˈmasˌtoid/ (also **mastoid process**) ▶ **noun** a conical projection of the temporal bone behind the ear, to which neck muscles are attached, and that has air spaces linked to the middle ear.

mas·tur·bate /ˈmastərˌbāt/ ▶ **verb** stimulate one's genitals with one's hand for sexual pleasure.
– DERIVATIVES **mas·tur·ba·tion** /ˌmastərˈbāsʜən/ noun **mas·tur·ba·tor** noun **mas·tur·ba·to·ry** /-bəˌtôrē/ adjective.
– ORIGIN Latin *masturbari*.

mat /mat/ ▶ **noun** **1** a thick piece of material placed on the floor to protect it from dirt or as a decoration. **2** a piece of thick material for landing on in gymnastics or similar sports. **3** a small piece of material placed on a surface to protect it from the heat or moisture of an object placed on it. **4** a thick, untidy layer of hairy or woolly material.

– SYNONYMS *a thick mat of hair* **mass,** tangle, mop, thatch, shock, mane.

– ORIGIN Old English.

mat·a·dor /ˈmatəˌdôr/ ▶ **noun** a bullfighter whose task is to kill the bull.
– ORIGIN Spanish, 'killer.'

match[1] /macʜ/ ▶ **noun** **1** a contest in which people or teams compete against each other. **2** an exact equivalent. **3** a pair of things that are very similar or combine together well. **4** a person or thing that can compete with another as an equal in quality or strength. **5** a potential husband or wife. **6** a marriage.

– SYNONYMS **1 contest,** competition, game, tournament, meet, derby, bout, fight. **2** *an exact match* **lookalike,** double, twin, duplicate, mate, companion, counterpart, pair, replica, copy, doppelgänger; informal spitting image, dead ringer.

▶ **verb** **1** correspond in appearance; combine together well. **2** be equal to someone or something in quality or strength. **3** place one person or group in competition with another.

– SYNONYMS **1** *the jacket and pants do not match* **go with,** coordinate with, complement, suit, set off. **2** (as adj. **matching**) *red suede boots with a matching handbag | pick the two matching blocks from the pile* **corresponding,** equivalent, parallel, analogous, complementary, paired, twin, identical, alike. **3** *did their statements match?* **correspond,** tally, agree, coincide, square. **4** *no one can match him at chess* **equal,** compare with, be in the same league as, touch, rival, compete with; informal hold a candle to.

– ORIGIN Old English, 'mate, companion.'

match[2] ▶ **noun** **1** a short, thin stick tipped with a mixture that ignites when rubbed against a rough surface. **2** historical a piece of wick or cord used for lighting gunpowder.
– ORIGIN Old French *meche*.

match·book /ˈmacʜˌbo͝ok/ ▶ **noun** a small cardboard folder of matches with a striking surface on one side.

match·box /ˈmacʜˌbäks/ ▶ **noun** a small box in which matches are sold.

match·less /ˈmacʜləs/ ▶ **adjective** so good that no one or nothing is an equal.

match·lock /ˈmacʜˌläk/ ▶ **noun** historical a type of gun with a lock in which a piece of wick or cord was placed for igniting the powder.

match·mak·er /ˈmacʜˌmākər/ ▶ **noun** a person who tries to bring about marriages or relationships between other people.

match play ▶ **noun** Golf a play in which the score is reckoned by the number of holes won. Compare with STROKE PLAY.

match point ▶ **noun** (in tennis and some other sports) a point that, if won by one of the players will also win them the match.

match·stick /ˈmacʜˌstik/ ▶ **noun** the stem of a match. ▶ **adjective** Brit. drawn using thin straight lines: *matchstick men*.

match·up /ˈmacʜəp/ ▶ **noun** **1** a contest between athletes or sports teams. **2** a pairing or combining of people or things for some purpose.

mate[1] /māt/ ▶ **noun** **1** the sexual partner of an animal. **2** informal a person's spouse or other sexual partner. **3** one of a matched pair: *I've got one glove without a mate*. **4** (in combination) a fellow member or occupant: *his teammates*. **5** an officer on a merchant ship below the master. **6** Brit. informal a friend or companion. **7** chiefly Brit. an assistant to a skilled worker.

– SYNONYMS **1 partner,** husband, wife, spouse, consort, lover; informal better half, other half. **2 friend,** companion, schoolmate, classmate, workmate; informal pal, chum, buddy, amigo, compadre.

▶ **verb** **1** (of animals or birds) come together for breeding. **2** join or connect two things.

– SYNONYMS **breed,** couple, copulate, pair.

– ORIGIN German, 'comrade.'

mate[2] ▶ **noun & verb** Chess short for CHECKMATE.

ma·té /ˈmäˌtā/ (also **yerba maté** /ˈyerbə, ˈyər-/) ▶ **noun** an infusion of the bitter, caffeine-rich leaves of a South American shrub.
– ORIGIN from Spanish *mate*.

ma·ter /ˈmātər/ ▶ **noun** Brit. informal, dated mother.
– ORIGIN Latin.

ma·ter·fa·mil·i·as /ˌmātərfəˈmilēəs, ˌmätər-/ ▶ **noun** (pl. **matresfamilias** /ˌmäˌtrās-, ˌmātərz-/) the female head of a family or household.
– ORIGIN Latin.

ma·te·ri·al /mə'ti(ə)rēəl/ ▸ **noun 1** the substance from which something is or can be made. **2** items needed for doing or creating something. **3** cloth or fabric.

– SYNONYMS **1 matter,** substance, stuff, constituents. **2 fabric,** cloth, textiles. **3 information,** data, facts, facts and figures, statistics, evidence, details, particulars, background; informal info. **4** *cleaning materials* **things,** items, articles, stuff, supplies; Brit. informal gubbins. **5** *the materials for a new building* **constituent,** raw material, component, supplies.

▸ **adjective 1** consisting of or referring to physical objects rather than the mind or spirit: *the material world*. **2** essential or relevant: *evidence material to the case*.

– SYNONYMS **1 physical,** corporeal, fleshly, bodily, tangible, mundane, worldly, earthly, secular, temporal, concrete, real. **2** *information material to the inquiry* **relevant,** pertinent, applicable, germane, vital, essential, key.
– ANTONYMS spiritual.

– DERIVATIVES **ma·te·ri·al·i·ty** /mə,ti(ə)rē'alitē/ noun **ma·te·ri·al·ly** adverb.
– ORIGIN Latin *materia* 'matter.'

ma·te·ri·al·ism /mə'ti(ə)rēə,lizəm/ ▸ **noun 1** a tendency to consider material possessions and physical comfort as more important than spiritual values. **2** Philosophy the doctrine that nothing exists except matter.
– DERIVATIVES **ma·te·ri·al·ist** noun & adjective **ma·te·ri·al·is·tic** /mə,ti(ə)rēə'listik/ adjective.

ma·te·ri·al·ize /mə'ti(ə)rēə,līz/ ▸ **verb 1** become fact; happen: *the hoped-for investment boom did not materialize*. **2** appear.

– SYNONYMS **1 happen,** occur, come about, take place, transpire; informal come off; literary come to pass. **2 appear,** turn up, arrive, emerge, surface, pop up; informal show up.

– DERIVATIVES **ma·te·ri·al·i·za·tion** /mə,ti(ə)rēələ'zāsʜən/ noun.

ma·te·ri·el /mə,ti(ə)rē'el/ ▸ **noun** military materials and equipment.
– ORIGIN French *matériel*.

ma·ter·nal /mə'tərnl/ ▸ **adjective 1** relating to or characteristic of a mother. **2** related through the mother's side of the family.

– SYNONYMS **motherly,** protective, caring, nurturing, maternalistic.

– DERIVATIVES **ma·ter·nal·ly** adverb.
– ORIGIN French *maternel*, from Latin *mater* 'mother.'

ma·ter·ni·ty /mə'tərnətē/ ▸ **noun** motherhood. ▸ **adjective** relating to the period during pregnancy and shortly after childbirth: *maternity clothes*.

math /maᴛʜ/ ▸ **noun** mathematics.

math·e·mat·ics /maᴛʜ(ə)'matiks/ ▸ **plural noun** (usu. treated as sing.) the branch of science concerned with number, quantity, and space, either as abstract ideas (**pure mathematics**) or as applied to physics, engineering, and other subjects (**applied mathematics**).
– DERIVATIVES **math·e·mat·i·cal** /,maᴛʜ(ə)'matikəl/ adjective **math·e·mat·i·cal·ly** /-ik(ə)lē/ adverb **math·e·ma·ti·cian** /,maᴛʜ(ə)mə'tisʜən/ noun.
– ORIGIN from Greek *mathēma* 'science.'

mat·i·nee /,matn'ā/ ▸ **noun** an afternoon performance in a theater or movie theater.
– ORIGIN from French *matin* 'morning.'

mat·i·nee i·dol ▸ **noun** informal, dated a handsome actor admired chiefly by women.

mat·ins /'matnz/ ▸ **noun** a service of morning prayer, especially in the Anglican Church.
– ORIGIN Old French *matines* 'mornings.'

ma·tri·arch /'mātrē,ärk/ ▸ **noun 1** a woman who is the head of a family or tribe. **2** a powerful older woman.
– DERIVATIVES **ma·tri·ar·chal** /,mātrē'ärkəl/ adjective.
– ORIGIN from Latin *mater* 'mother.'

ma·tri·ar·chy /'mātrē,ärkē/ ▸ **noun 1** a form of social organization in which the mother or eldest female is the head of the family. **2** a society in which women hold most or all of the power.

ma·tri·ces plural of **MATRIX**.

mat·ri·cide /'matrə,sīd, 'mā-/ ▸ **noun 1** the killing of one's mother. **2** a person who kills their mother.
– DERIVATIVES **mat·ri·cid·al** /,matrə'sīdl, ,mā-/ adjective.
– ORIGIN from Latin *mater* 'mother' + *-cidium* 'killing.'

ma·tric·u·late /mə'trikyə,lāt/ ▸ **verb** enroll or be enrolled at a college or university.
– DERIVATIVES **ma·tric·u·la·tion** /mə,trikyə'lāsʜən/ noun.
– ORIGIN Latin *matriculare*.

mat·ri·lin·e·al /,matrə'linēəl, ,mā-/ ▸ **adjective** based on relationship with the mother or the female line of descent.
– DERIVATIVES **mat·ri·lin·e·al·ly** adverb.

mat·ri·mo·ni·al /,matrə'mōnēəl/ ▸ **adjective** of or relating to marriage or married people.

– SYNONYMS **marital,** conjugal, married, wedded, nuptial; literary connubial.

mat·ri·mo·ny /'matrə,mōnē/ ▸ **noun** the state of being married, or the ceremony of marriage.
– ORIGIN Latin *matrimonium*.

ma·trix /'mātriks/ ▸ **noun** (pl. **matrices** /'mātrisēz/ or **matrixes**) **1** an environment or material in which something develops. **2** a mold in which something is cast or shaped. **3** Mathematics a rectangular arrangement of quantities in rows and columns that is manipulated according to particular rules. **4** a gridlike array of elements; a lattice. **5** a mass of rock in which gems, crystals, or fossils are embedded.
– ORIGIN Latin, 'womb.'

ma·tron /'mātrən/ ▸ **noun 1** a dignified or sedate married woman. **2** a female prison officer.
– DERIVATIVES **ma·tron·ly** adjective.
– ORIGIN Latin *matrona*, from *mater* 'mother.'

ma·tron of hon·or ▸ **noun** a married woman attending the bride at a wedding.

matte /mat/ (also **matt**) ▸ **adjective** (of a surface, paint, etc.) not shiny: *matte white paint*. ▸ **noun 1** a matte color, paint, or finish. **2** a sheet of cardboard placed on the back of a picture, as a mount or to form a border.
– ORIGIN French *mat*.

mat·ted /'matid/ ▸ **adjective** (of hair or fur) tangled into a thick mass.

– SYNONYMS **tangled,** knotted, tousled, disheveled, uncombed, unkempt, ratty.

mat·ter /'matər/ ▸ **noun 1** physical substance or material in general, as distinct from mind and spirit; (in physics) that which occupies space and possesses mass. **2** a subject or situation under consideration: *complicated financial matters*. **3** (**the matter**) the reason for a problem: *what's the matter?* **4** written or printed material. **5** Law something to be tried or proved in court; a case.

> – SYNONYMS **1 material,** stuff, substance. **2 affair,** business, situation, concern, incident, episode, subject, topic, issue, question, point at issue, case.

▶ **verb** be important or significant: *it doesn't matter what she thinks.*

> – SYNONYMS **be important,** make any difference, be of consequence, be relevant, count, signify.

– PHRASES **as a matter of fact** in reality; in fact. **in the matter of** regarding. **a matter of 1** no more than a particular period of time: *they were shown the door in a matter of minutes.* **2** a question of. **a matter of course** the natural or expected thing. **no matter 1** regardless of. **2** it is of no importance.
– ORIGIN Latin *materia.*

mat·ter-of-fact ▶ **adjective** unemotional and practical.

> – SYNONYMS **unemotional,** practical, down-to-earth, sensible, realistic, unsentimental, pragmatic, businesslike, commonsensical, levelheaded, hardheaded, no-nonsense, straightforward.

mat·ting /'matiNG/ ▶ **noun** material used for mats, especially coarse fabric woven from a natural fiber.

mat·tock /'matək/ ▶ **noun** an agricultural tool similar to a pickax, but with one arm of the head curved like an adze and the other like a chisel edge.
– ORIGIN Old English.

mat·tress /'matrəs/ ▶ **noun** a fabric case filled with soft, firm, or springy material used for sleeping on.
– ORIGIN Arabic, 'carpet or cushion.'

mat·u·ra·tion /ˌmaCHə'rāSHən/ ▶ **noun 1** the action or process of maturing. **2** the formation of pus in a boil, abscess, etc.

ma·ture /mə'CHo͝or, -'t(y)o͝or/ ▶ **adjective 1** fully grown or physically developed; adult. **2** like an adult in mental or emotional development. **3** (of thought or planning) careful and thorough. **4** (of certain foods or drinks) ready for consumption. **5** due for payment.

> – SYNONYMS **1 adult,** of age, fully grown, in one's prime. **2 grown-up,** sensible, responsible, adult. **3 ripe,** ripened, mellow, seasoned, ready.
> – ANTONYMS immature.

▶ **verb 1** become mature. **2** (of an insurance policy) reach the end of its term and so become payable.

> – SYNONYMS **1 grow up,** come of age, reach adulthood. **2 ripen,** mellow, age. **3 develop,** grow, bloom, blossom, evolve.

– DERIVATIVES **ma·ture·ly** adverb.
– ORIGIN Latin *maturus* 'timely, ripe.'

> **CHOOSE THE RIGHT WORD**
>
> **mature, age, develop, mellow, ripen**
>
> Most of us would prefer to **mature** rather than simply **age**. *Mature* implies gaining wisdom, experience, or sophistication as well as adulthood; when applied to other living things, it indicates fullness of growth and readiness for normal functioning (*a mature crop of strawberries*). To *age*, on the other hand, is to undergo the changes that result from the passage of time, often with an emphasis on the negative or destructive changes that accompany growing old (*the tragedy aged him five years*). **Develop** is like *mature* in that it means to undergo a series of positive changes to attain perfection or effectiveness, but it can refer to a part as well as a whole organism (*the kitten's eyesight had begun to develop at three weeks*). **Ripen** is a less formal word meaning to *mature*, but it usually applies to fruit (*the apples ripened in the sun*). **Mellow** suggests the tempering or moderation of harshness that comes with time or experience. With its connotations of warmth, mildness, and sweetness, it is a more positive word than *mature* or *age* (*to mellow as one gets older*).

ma·tu·ri·ty /mə'CHo͝oritē, mə't(y)o͝or-/ ▶ **noun 1** the state, fact, or period of being mature. **2** the time when an insurance policy reaches the end of its term and so becomes payable.

> – SYNONYMS **1 adulthood,** coming of age, manhood, womanhood. **2 responsibility,** sense, wisdom.

ma·tu·ti·nal /mə't(y)o͞otn-əl, ˌmaCHə'tīnl/ ▶ **adjective** formal relating to or happening in the morning.
– ORIGIN Latin *matutinus* 'early.'

mat·zo /'mätsə/ (also **matzoh**) ▶ **noun** (pl. **matzos**) a cracker of unleavened bread, traditionally eaten by Jews during Passover.
– ORIGIN Yiddish, from Hebrew.

maud·lin /'môdlin/ ▶ **adjective** sentimental in a tearful or self-pitying way.
– ORIGIN from the name of Mary *Magdalen* in the Bible, typically represented weeping.

maul /môl/ ▶ **verb 1** (of an animal) wound a person or other animal by scratching and tearing. **2** handle or treat someone or something savagely or roughly.

> – SYNONYMS **savage,** attack, claw, scratch, lacerate, mangle, tear.

▶ **noun** a tool with a heavy head and a handle, used for crushing, ramming, and driving wedges; a beetle.
– ORIGIN from Latin *malleus* 'hammer.'

maun·der /'môndər/ ▶ **verb** talk or act in a rambling or aimless way.
– ORIGIN perhaps from former *maunder* 'to beg.'

Maun·dy Thurs·day /'môndē/ ▶ **noun** the Thursday before Easter, observed in the Christian Church as a commemoration of the Last Supper.
– ORIGIN Old French *mande,* from Latin *mandatum novum* 'new commandment' (referring to Christ's words in the Gospel of John, chapter 13).

Mau·ri·ta·ni·an /ˌmôri'tānēən, -'tānyən/ ▶ **noun** a person from Mauritania, a country in West Africa. ▶ **adjective** relating to Mauritania.

Mau·ri·tian /mô'risHən/ ▶ **noun** a person from the island of Mauritius in the Indian Ocean. ▶ **adjective** relating to Mauritius.

mau·so·le·um /ˌmôzə'lēəm, ˌmôsə-/ ▶ **noun** (pl. **mausolea** /-'lēə/ or **mausoleums**) a building containing a tomb or tombs.
– ORIGIN Greek *Mausōleion,* from *Mausōlos,* the name of a king to whose tomb the name was originally applied.

mauve /mōv, môv/ ▶ **noun** a pale purple color.
– ORIGIN French, 'mallow.'

ma·ven /'māvən/ ▶ **noun** informal an expert or connoisseur.
– ORIGIN Yiddish.

mav·er·ick /'mav(ə)rik/ ▶ **noun 1** an unconventional or independent-minded person. **2** an unbranded calf or yearling.

> – SYNONYMS **individualist,** nonconformist, free spirit, original, eccentric, rebel, dissenter, dissident.
> – ANTONYMS conformist.

– ORIGIN from Samuel A. *Maverick,* a Texas rancher who did not brand his cattle.

maw /mô/ ▶ noun the jaws or throat, especially of a voracious animal.
– ORIGIN Old English.

mawk·ish /ˈmôkisн/ ▶ adjective expressing emotion in an exaggerated or embarrassing way: *a mawkish ode to parenthood*.
– ORIGIN from former *mawk* 'maggot.'

max /maks/ ▶ noun & adjective short for MAXIMUM.

max·i /ˈmaksē/ ▶ noun (pl. **maxis**) a skirt or coat reaching to the ankle.

max·il·la /makˈsilə/ ▶ noun (pl. **maxillae** /makˈsilē, -ˈsilˌī/) **1** the bone of the upper jaw. **2** (in an insect or other arthropod) each of a pair of chewing mouthparts.
– DERIVATIVES **max·il·lar·y** /ˈmaksəˌlerē/ adjective.
– ORIGIN Latin, 'jaw.'

max·im /ˈmaksim/ ▶ noun a short statement expressing a general truth or rule of behavior.

– SYNONYMS **saying,** adage, aphorism, proverb, motto, saw, axiom, dictum, precept, epigram.

– ORIGIN from Latin *propositio maxima* 'most important proposition.'

CHOOSE THE RIGHT WORD

See SAYING.

max·i·mize /ˈmaksəˌmīz/ ▶ verb **1** make as great or large as possible: *the company is aiming to maximize profits*. **2** make the best use of something.
– DERIVATIVES **max·i·mi·za·tion** /ˌmaksəməˈzāsнən/ noun **max·i·miz·er** noun.

max·i·mum /ˈmaksəməm/ ▶ noun (pl. **maxima** or **maximums**) the greatest amount, size, or intensity possible or achieved.

– SYNONYMS **upper limit,** limit, utmost, greatest, most, peak, pinnacle, height, ceiling, top.
– ANTONYMS minimum.

▶ adjective greatest in amount, size, or intensity.

– SYNONYMS **greatest,** highest, biggest, largest, top, most, utmost, supreme.

– DERIVATIVES **max·i·mal** adjective.
– ORIGIN Latin, 'greatest thing.'

max·well /ˈmaksˌwel, -wəl/ ▶ noun a unit used in measuring the strength of a magnetic field.
– ORIGIN named after the Scottish physicist J. C. *Maxwell*.

May /mā/ ▶ noun **1** the fifth month of the year. **2** (**may**) the hawthorn or its blossom.
– ORIGIN from Latin *Maius mensis* 'month of the goddess *Maia*.'

may /mā/ ▶ modal verb (3rd sing. present **may**; past **might**) **1** expressing possibility. **2** expressing permission. **3** expressing a wish or hope.
– PHRASES **be that as it may** nevertheless.
– ORIGIN Old English.

USAGE

For an explanation of the difference in use between **may** and **can**, see the note at CAN[1].

Ma·ya /ˈmīə/ ▶ noun (pl. same or **Mayas**) a member of a Central American people whose civilization died out *c.*900 AD.
– DERIVATIVES **Ma·yan** adjective & noun.
– ORIGIN the Maya's name for themselves.

ma·ya /ˈmīə, ˈmäyə/ ▶ noun **1** (in Hinduism) the supernatural power wielded by gods and demons to produce illusions, or the power by which the universe becomes manifest. **2** (in Hinduism and Buddhism) the illusion or appearance of the phenomenal world.
– ORIGIN from Sanskrit *mā* 'create.'

may·ap·ple /ˈmāˌapəl/ ▶ noun an herbaceous plant of the barberry family with large, deeply divided leaves. The plant, which bears a yellow, egg-shaped edible fruit in May, has long been used medicinally.

may·be /ˈmābē/ ▶ adverb perhaps; possibly.

– SYNONYMS **perhaps,** possibly, for all you know; literary perchance.

May·day /ˈmāˌdā/ ▶ noun an international radio distress signal used by ships and aircraft.
– ORIGIN from the pronunciation of French *m'aider* from *venez m'aider* 'come and help me.'

May Day ▶ noun May 1, celebrated as a springtime festival or as a holiday in honor of workers.

may·fly /ˈmāˌflī/ ▶ noun (pl. **mayflies**) an insect with transparent wings that lives as an adult for only a very short time.

may·hap /ˈmāˌhap/ ▶ adverb old use perhaps; possibly.

may·hem /ˈmāˌhem/ ▶ noun violent disorder; chaos.

– SYNONYMS **chaos,** havoc, bedlam, pandemonium, uproar, turmoil, a riot, anarchy; informal a madhouse.

– ORIGIN first meaning 'the crime of maliciously injuring someone': from Old French.

may·n't /ˈmā(ə)nt/ ▶ contraction may not.

may·on·naise /ˈmāəˌnāz, ˌmāəˈnāz/ ▶ noun a thick creamy dressing made from egg yolks, oil, and vinegar.
– ORIGIN French.

may·or /ˈmāər/ ▶ noun the elected head of a city, town, or other municipality.
– DERIVATIVES **may·or·al** /māˈôrəl, ˈmāərəl/ adjective **may·or·ship** /-ˌsнip/ noun.
– ORIGIN from Latin *major* 'greater.'

may·or·al·ty /ˈmāərəltē/ ▶ noun (pl. **mayoralties**) the position or term of office of a mayor.

may·or·ess /ˈmāərəs/ ▶ noun **1** the wife of a mayor. **2** a woman elected as mayor.

may·pole /ˈmāˌpōl/ ▶ noun a decorated pole with long ribbons attached to the top, traditionally used for dancing around on May Day.

maze /māz/ ▶ noun **1** a network of paths and walls or hedges, designed as a puzzle, through which one has to find a way. **2** a confusing mass of information.

– SYNONYMS **labyrinth,** network, warren, web, tangle, confusion, jungle.

– ORIGIN related to AMAZE.

ma·zur·ka /məˈzərkə, -ˈzo͝or-/ ▶ noun a lively Polish dance in triple time.
– ORIGIN Polish, 'folk dance from Mazovia' (a region of Poland).

MB ▶ abbreviation **1** Bachelor of Medicine. **2** Manitoba. **3** (also **Mb**) Computing megabyte(s).
– ORIGIN sense 1 from Latin *Medicinae Baccalaureus*.

MBA ▶ abbreviation Master of Business Administration.

MBO ▶ abbreviation management buyout.

MC ▶ abbreviation **1** Master of Ceremonies. **2** (in the US) Member of Congress. **3** Military Cross. ▶ noun a person who provides entertainment at a club or party by instructing the DJ and performing rap music. ▶ **verb** (**MC's, MC'ing, MC'd**) perform as an MC.

MCC ▶ **abbreviation** Metropolitan Community Church.

Mc·Car·thy·ism /mə'kärTHēˌizəm/ ▶ **noun** a campaign against alleged communists in the US government and other organizations carried out under Senator Joseph McCarthy from 1950–54.
– DERIVATIVES **Mc·Car·thy·ite** /-THēˌīt/ adjective & noun.

Mc·Coy /mə'koi/ ▶ **noun** (in phrase **the real McCoy**) informal the real thing.
– ORIGIN uncertain.

Mc·Guf·fin /mə'gəfin/ ▶ **noun** an object or device in a movie or a book that serves merely as a trigger for the plot.
– ORIGIN a Scottish surname, said to have been borrowed by the English film director Alfred Hitchcock from a story involving such a factor.

m-com·merce ▶ **noun** commercial dealings carried out electronically by cell phone.

MD ▶ **abbreviation 1** Doctor of Medicine. **2** Maryland.
– ORIGIN sense 1 from Latin *Medicinae Doctor*.

Md ▶ **symbol** the chemical element mendelevium.

MDMA ▶ **abbreviation** methylenedioxymethamphetamine, the drug Ecstasy.

MDT ▶ **abbreviation** Mountain Daylight Time.

me /mē/ ▶ **pronoun** (first person sing.) used as the object of a verb or preposition or after 'than,' 'as,' or the verb 'to be,' to refer to the speaker himself or herself.
– ORIGIN Old English.

USAGE

The pronoun **me** should be used as the object of a verb or preposition, as in *John hates me*. It is wrong to use **me** as the subject of a verb, as in *John and me went to the store*; in this case **I** should be used instead. See **PERSONAL PRONOUN**.

me·a cul·pa /ˌmāə 'ko͝olˌpə, -ˌpä/ ▶ **exclamation** an acknowledgment that one is wrong or at fault.
– ORIGIN Latin, 'by my fault.'

mead¹ /mēd/ ▶ **noun** an alcoholic drink of fermented honey and water.
– ORIGIN Old English.

mead² ▶ **noun** literary a meadow.

mead·ow /'medō/ ▶ **noun 1** an area of grassland, especially one used for hay. **2** a piece of low ground near a river.
– SYNONYMS **field,** paddock, pasture; literary lea, mead.
– ORIGIN Old English.

mead·ow·sweet /'medōˌswēt, 'medə-/ ▶ **noun** a tall meadow plant with heads of creamy white fragrant flowers.

mea·ger /'mēgər/ ▶ **adjective** lacking in quantity or quality: *a meager diet of bread and beans*.
– SYNONYMS **inadequate,** scant, paltry, limited, restricted, sparse, negligible, skimpy, slender, pitiful, miserly, niggardly; informal measly, stingy.
– ANTONYMS abundant.
– DERIVATIVES **mea·ger·ness** noun.
– ORIGIN Latin *macer*.

meal¹ /mēl/ ▶ **noun 1** any of the regular daily occasions when food is eaten. **2** the food eaten during a meal.
– SYNONYMS dinner, lunch, breakfast, brunch, snack, feast, banquet; informal spread; formal repast.
– ORIGIN Old English.

WORD LINKS

prandial *relating to meals*

meal² ▶ **noun** the edible part of any grain or seed ground to a powder, used to make flour or to feed animals.
– ORIGIN Old English.

meal tick·et ▶ **noun** a person or thing that is exploited as a source of money.

meal·time /'mēlˌtīm/ ▶ **noun** the time at which a meal is eaten.

meal·y /'mēlē/ ▶ **adjective** (**mealier, mealiest**) **1** relating to or containing ground grain or seeds. **2** pale in color.

meal·y·bug /'mēlēˌbəg/ ▶ **noun** a sap-sucking scale insect that is coated with a white powdery wax and that can be a serious pest.

meal·y-mouthed /'mēlē 'mouT͟Hd, -ˌmouTHt/ ▶ **adjective** reluctant to speak frankly.
– ORIGIN perhaps from German *Mehl im Maule behalten* 'carry meal in the mouth' (i.e. be indirect in speech).

mean¹ /mēn/ ▶ **verb** (past and past part. **meant** /ment/) **1** intend to express or refer to something. **2** (of a word) have something as its explanation in the same language or its equivalent in another language. **3** intend to do or be the case: *they mean no harm*. **4** have something as a result. **5** intend or design for a particular purpose: *the coat was meant for a much larger person*. **6** be of specified importance to someone.
– SYNONYMS **1 signify,** denote, indicate, convey, designate, show, express, spell out, stand for, represent, symbolize, imply, suggest, intimate, portend. **2 intend,** aim, plan, have in mind, set out, want. **3** *this will mean war* **entail,** involve, necessitate, lead to, result in, give rise to, bring about, cause, engender, produce.
– PHRASES **mean business** be in earnest. **mean well** have good intentions, but not always carry them out.
– ORIGIN Old English.

CHOOSE THE RIGHT WORD

See **INTEND**.

mean² ▶ **adjective 1** unwilling to give or share things; not generous. **2** unkind or unfair. **3** vicious or aggressive. **4** poor in quality and appearance: *her home was mean and small*. **5** dated coming from a low social class. **6** informal excellent.
– SYNONYMS **1 miserly,** niggardly, parsimonious, penny-pinching, cheese-paring; informal tightfisted, stingy, tight, cheap. **2 unkind,** nasty, unpleasant, spiteful, malicious, unfair, shabby, horrible, despicable, contemptible, obnoxious, vile, loathsome, base, low; informal rotten.
– ANTONYMS generous, kind.
– DERIVATIVES **mean·ly** adverb **mean·ness** noun.
– ORIGIN first meaning 'common to two or more people': from Old English.

mean³ ▶ **noun 1** the average value of a set of quantities. **2** something in the middle of two extremes. ▶ **adjective**

1 calculated as a mean; average. **2** equally far from two extremes.
– ORIGIN Latin *medianus* 'middle.'

me·an·der /mēˈandər/ ▸ **verb 1** (of a river or road) follow a winding course. **2** wander or progress in a leisurely or aimless way. ▸ **noun** a bend of a river that curves back on itself.
– ORIGIN from the river *Maeander* in Turkey.

mean·ie /ˈmēnē/ (also **meany**) ▸ **noun** informal a mean or small-minded person.

mean·ing /ˈmēniNG/ ▸ **noun 1** what is meant by a word, idea, or action. **2** a sense of purpose.

> – SYNONYMS **1 significance,** sense, signification, import, gist, thrust, drift, implication, message. **2 definition,** sense, explanation, interpretation, connotation.

> **WORD LINKS**
> **semantic** *relating to meaning*

mean·ing·ful /ˈmēniNGfəl/ ▸ **adjective 1** having meaning. **2** important or worthwhile. **3** expressing something without words: *they exchanged meaningful glances.*

> – SYNONYMS **1 significant,** relevant, important, telling, expressive, eloquent, pointed, pregnant, revealing, suggestive. **2 sincere,** deep, serious, earnest, significant, important.

– DERIVATIVES **mean·ing·ful·ly** adverb **mean·ing·ful·ness** noun.

mean·ing·less /ˈmēniNGlis/ ▸ **adjective** having no meaning or significance.

> – SYNONYMS **unintelligible,** incomprehensible, incoherent, senseless, pointless.

– DERIVATIVES **mean·ing·less·ly** adverb **mean·ing·less·ness** noun.

means /mēnz/ ▸ **plural noun** (also treated as sing.) **1** an action or method for achieving a result: *language is a means of communication.* **2** a person's financial resources; income.

> – SYNONYMS **1 method,** way, manner, course, agency, channel, avenue, procedure, process, methodology, expedient. **2 money,** resources, capital, income, finance, funds, cash, the wherewithal, assets, wealth, riches, affluence, fortune.

– PHRASES **by all means** of course. **by means of** by using. **by no means** certainly not. **a man** (or **woman**) **of means** a rich man (or woman). **a means to an end** a thing that is not valued in itself but is useful in achieving an aim.
– ORIGIN plural of **MEAN**[3].

means test ▸ **noun** an official investigation into a person's finances to determine whether they qualify for a welfare payment or other public funds. ▸ **verb** (**means-test**) base (a welfare payment, etc.) on a means test.

meant /ment/ past and past participle of **MEAN**[1].

mean·time /ˈmēnˌtīm/ ▸ **adverb** (also **in the meantime**) in the period of time between two events; meanwhile.

> – SYNONYMS **1 for now,** for the moment, for the present, for the time being, in the meanwhile, in the meantime, in the interim. **2 at the same time,** simultaneously, concurrently.

mean·while /ˈmēnˌ(h)wīl/ ▸ **adverb 1** (also **in the meanwhile**) in the period of time between two events. **2** at the same time.

> – SYNONYMS **1 for now,** for the moment, for the present, for the time being, in the meanwhile, in the meantime, in the interim. **2 at the same time,** simultaneously, concurrently.

mea·sles /ˈmēzəlz/ ▸ **plural noun** (treated as sing.) an infectious disease spread by a virus, causing fever and a red rash.
– ORIGIN probably from Dutch *masel* 'spot.'

mea·sly /ˈmēzlē/ ▸ **adjective** (**measlier, measliest**) informal ridiculously small or few.

meas·ure /ˈmeZHər/ ▸ **verb 1** determine the size, amount, or degree of something by comparing it with a standard unit. **2** be of a specified size. **3** (**measure something out**) take an exact quantity of something. **4** assess the importance or value of: *it is hard to measure teaching ability.* **5** (**measure up**) reach the required standard.

> – SYNONYMS **quantify,** gauge, size, count, weigh, evaluate, assess, determine, calculate, compute.

▸ **noun 1** a means of achieving a purpose: *cost-cutting measures.* **2** a standard unit used to express size, amount, or degree. **3** a measuring device marked with standard units of size, amount, or degree. **4** (**a measure of**) a certain amount or degree of. **5** (**a measure of**) an indication of the extent or quality of. **6** a proposal for a law. **7** (**measures**) a group of rock strata: *coal measures.* **8** any of the sections, typically of equal time value, into which a musical composition is divided.

> – SYNONYMS **1 action,** act, course of action, deed, procedure, step, expedient, initiative, program. **2 statute,** act, bill, law. **3 ruler,** tape measure, gauge, meter, scale. **4** *sales are a measure of their success* **yardstick,** test, standard, barometer, touchstone, benchmark.

– DERIVATIVES **meas·ur·a·ble** /ˈmeZH(ə)rəbəl/ adjective **meas·ur·a·bly** adverb **meas·ur·er** noun.
– PHRASES **for good measure** as an amount or item that is additional to what is strictly required. **take** (or **get** or **have**) **the measure of** understand the character or abilities of.
– ORIGIN Latin *mensura*, from *metiri* 'to measure.'

meas·ured /ˈmeZHərd/ ▸ **adjective 1** slow and regular in rhythm. **2** (of language) carefully considered.

> – SYNONYMS **1 regular,** steady, even, rhythmic, unfaltering, slow, dignified, stately, sedate, leisurely, unhurried. **2 careful,** thoughtful, considered, reasoned, calculated.

meas·ure·less /ˈmeZHərlis/ ▸ **adjective** literary having no limits.

meas·ure·ment /ˈmeZHərmənt/ ▸ **noun 1** the action of measuring. **2** an amount, size, or extent found by measuring. **3** a standard unit used in measuring.

> – SYNONYMS **1 quantification,** evaluation, assessment, calculation, computation, mensuration. **2 size,** dimension, proportions, value, amount, quantity.

meas·ur·ing cup /ˈmeZH(ə)riNG/ ▸ **noun** a cup marked in graded amounts, used for measuring ingredients in cooking.

meat /mēt/ ▸ **noun 1** the flesh of an animal as food. **2** the chief part: *let's get to the meat of the matter.*

> – SYNONYMS **flesh.**

– ORIGIN Old English, 'food,' 'article of food.'

meat·ball /ˈmētˌbôl/ ▸ **noun** a ball of ground or chopped meat.

meat loaf ▶ **noun** ground or chopped meat baked in the shape of a loaf.

meat·pack·ing /ˈmēt,pakiNG/ ▶ **noun** the business of slaughtering animals and processing the meat for sale as food.

meat·y /ˈmētē/ ▶ **adjective** (**meatier, meatiest**) **1** resembling or full of meat. **2** fleshy or muscular. **3** full of substance or interest: *a meaty, scholarly book*.
– DERIVATIVES **meat·i·ness** noun.

Mec·ca /ˈmekə/ ▶ **noun** a place that attracts many people: *the area is a Mecca for skiers*.
– ORIGIN from the city of *Mecca* in Saudi Arabia, the holiest city for Muslims.

me·chan·ic /məˈkanik/ ▶ **noun** a skilled worker who repairs and maintains machinery.
– ORIGIN from Greek *mēkhanē* 'machine.'

me·chan·i·cal /məˈkanikəl/ ▶ **adjective** **1** relating to or operated by a machine or machinery. **2** done without thought; automatic. **3** relating to physical forces or motion.

> – SYNONYMS **1 mechanized,** machine-driven, automated, automatic. **2 automatic,** knee-jerk, unthinking, instinctive, habitual, routine, unemotional, unfeeling.
> – ANTONYMS manual.

– DERIVATIVES **me·chan·i·cal·ly** adverb.

me·chan·i·cal draw·ing ▶ **noun** a scale drawing done with precision instruments.

me·chan·i·cal en·gi·neer·ing ▶ **noun** the branch of engineering concerned with the design, construction, and use of machines.

me·chan·ics /məˈkaniks/ ▶ **plural noun** **1** (treated as sing.) the branch of study concerned with motion and forces producing motion. **2** machinery or working parts. **3** the practical aspects of something: *the mechanics of cello-playing*.

mech·an·ism /ˈmekə,nizəm/ ▶ **noun** **1** a piece of machinery. **2** the way in which something works or is brought about.

> – SYNONYMS **1 apparatus,** machine, machinery, appliance, device, instrument, tool, contraption, gadget; informal gizmo. **2** *a complaints mechanism* **procedure,** process, system, method, means, medium, channel.

mech·a·nis·tic /,mekəˈnistik/ ▶ **adjective** relating to the theory that all natural processes can be explained in purely physical terms.

mech·a·nize /ˈmekə,nīz/ ▶ **verb** equip a process or place with machines or automatic devices.
– DERIVATIVES **mech·a·ni·za·tion** /,mekənəˈzāSHən/ noun.

me·co·ni·um /miˈkōnēəm/ ▶ **noun** the dark green substance forming the first feces of a newborn infant.
– ORIGIN Latin, 'poppy juice.'

MEd /,em ˈed/ ▶ **abbreviation** Master of Education.

med. ▶ **abbreviation** **1** medium. **2** (**med**) informal medical: *med school*.

me·da·ka /məˈdäkə/ ▶ **noun** a small Japanese freshwater fish of variable color that is bred for aquariums and scientific studies.

med·al /ˈmedl/ ▶ **noun** a metal disk with an inscription or design, awarded for achievement or to mark an event.

> – SYNONYMS **decoration,** ribbon, star, badge, award, commendation, honor.

– ORIGIN Latin *medalia* 'half a denarius.'

med·al·ist /ˈmedl-ist/ (Brit. **medallist**) ▶ **noun** a person awarded a medal.

me·dal·lion /məˈdalyən/ ▶ **noun** **1** a piece of jewelry in the shape of a medal, worn as a pendant. **2** a decorative oval or circular painting, panel, or design. **3** a small flat round or oval cut of meat or fish.

Med·al of Hon·or (also **Congressional Medal of Honor**) ▶ **noun** the highest US military decoration, awarded by Congress to a member of the armed forces for gallantry and bravery in combat at the risk of life above and beyond the call of duty.

med·dle /ˈmedl/ ▶ **verb** interfere in something that is not one's concern.

> – SYNONYMS **1 interfere,** intrude, intervene, pry; informal poke one's nose in. **2 fiddle,** interfere, tamper, mess (around).

– DERIVATIVES **med·dler** noun **med·dle·some** /ˈmedlsəm/ adjective.
– ORIGIN Old French.

me·di·a /ˈmēdēə/ ▶ **noun** **1** television, radio, and newspapers as the means of mass communication. **2** plural of **MEDIUM**.

> **USAGE**
>
> The word **media** comes from the Latin plural of **medium**. In the normal sense 'television, radio, and newspapers,' it often behaves as a collective noun (one referring to a group of people or things, such as **staff**), and can correctly be used with either a singular or a plural verb: *the media was informed* or *the media were informed*.

me·di·ae·val ▶ **adjective** variant spelling of **MEDIEVAL**.

me·di·al /ˈmēdēəl/ ▶ **adjective** situated in the middle.
– DERIVATIVES **me·di·al·ly** adverb.
– ORIGIN Latin *medialis*.

me·di·an /ˈmēdēən/ ▶ **adjective** **1** technical situated in the middle. **2** having a value in the middle of a series of values arranged in order of magnitude. ▶ **noun** **1** a median value. **2** Geometry a straight line drawn from one of the angles of a triangle to the middle of the opposite side. **3** (also **median strip**) a strip of land between the lanes of opposing traffic on a divided highway.
– ORIGIN Latin *medianus*.

me·di·ate /ˈmēdē,āt/ ▶ **verb** **1** try to settle a dispute between other people or groups. **2** formal be a means of conveying or influencing: *the meaning of poems is mediated by the language employed*.

> – SYNONYMS **arbitrate,** conciliate, moderate, make peace, intervene, intercede, act as (an) intermediary, negotiate, liaise, referee.

– ORIGIN Latin *mediare* 'to place in the middle.'

me·di·a·tion /,mēdēˈāSHən/ ▶ **noun** the action of trying to settle a dispute.

> – SYNONYMS **arbitration,** conciliation, reconciliation, intervention, intercession, negotiation, shuttle diplomacy.

me·di·a·tor /ˈmēdē,ātər/ ▶ **noun** a person who tries to settle a dispute.

> – SYNONYMS **arbitrator,** arbiter, negotiator, conciliator, peacemaker, go-between, middleman,

intermediary, moderator, honest broker, liaison officer, umpire, referee, adjudicator, judge.

med·ic /ˈmedik/ ▶ **noun** a military medical corpsman who dispenses first aid at combat sites.

Med·i·caid /ˈmediˌkād/ ▶ **noun** a federal system of health insurance for people requiring financial assistance.

med·i·cal /ˈmedikəl/ ▶ **adjective** relating to the science or practice of medicine. ▶ **noun** an examination to assess a person's physical health.
– DERIVATIVES **med·i·cal·ly** adverb.
– ORIGIN from Latin *medicus* 'physician.'

med·i·cal cer·ti·fi·cate ▶ **noun** a doctor's certificate confirming that a person is either unfit or fit to work.

med·i·cal ex·am·in·er ▶ **noun** a physician employed by a local authority to conduct autopsies and determine causes of death.

med·i·cal of·fi·cer ▶ **noun** a doctor serving in the armed forces, in a prison, or in a public health service.

me·dic·a·ment /məˈdikəmənt, ˈmedikəˌment/ ▶ **noun** a medicine.

Med·i·care /ˈmediˌke(ə)r/ ▶ **noun** a federal system of health insurance for people over 65 years of age and for certain younger people with disabilities.

med·i·cate /ˈmediˌkāt/ ▶ **verb 1** give medicine or a drug to someone. **2** (as adj. **medicated**) containing a medicinal substance.
– ORIGIN Latin *medicari* 'give remedies to.'

med·i·ca·tion /ˌmedəˈkāsʜən/ ▶ **noun 1** a medicine or drug. **2** treatment with medicines.

me·dic·i·nal /məˈdisənl/ ▶ **adjective 1** having healing properties. **2** relating to medicines.

– SYNONYMS **curative,** healing, remedial, therapeutic, restorative, health-giving.

– DERIVATIVES **me·dic·i·nal·ly** adverb.

med·i·cine /ˈmedisən/ ▶ **noun 1** the science or practice of the treatment and prevention of disease. **2** a drug or other substance taken by mouth in order to treat or prevent disease.

– SYNONYMS **medication,** drug, prescription, treatment, remedy, cure, nostrum, panacea, cure-all.

– ORIGIN from Latin *medicus* 'physician.'

WORD LINKS

pharmaceutical *relating to medicines*

med·i·cine ball ▶ **noun** a large, heavy solid ball thrown and caught for exercise.

med·i·cine man ▶ **noun** (especially among North American Indians) a person believed to have magical powers of healing.

med·i·co /ˈmediˌkō/ ▶ **noun** (pl. **medicos**) informal a doctor or medical student.

me·di·e·val /ˌmed(ē)ˈēvəl, ˌmēd-, ˌmid-/ (also **mediaeval**) ▶ **adjective 1** relating to the Middle Ages. **2** informal outdated, primitive, or unsophisticated: *a country that is medieval in outlook.*
– DERIVATIVES **me·di·e·val·ize** verb **me·di·e·val·ly** adverb.
– ORIGIN from Latin *medium aevum* 'middle age.'

me·di·e·val·ist /ˌmed(ē)ˈēvəlist, ˌmēd-/ (also **mediaevalist**) ▶ **noun** a scholar of medieval history or literature.

me·di·na /məˈdēnə/ ▶ **noun** the old quarter of a North African town.
– ORIGIN Arabic, 'town.'

me·di·o·cre /ˌmēdēˈōkər/ ▶ **adjective** of only average quality; not very good.

– SYNONYMS **average,** ordinary, undistinguished, uninspired, indifferent, unexceptional, unexciting, unremarkable, run-of-the-mill, pedestrian, prosaic, lackluster, forgettable, amateurish; informal so-so.
– ANTONYMS excellent.

– ORIGIN Latin *mediocris* 'of middle height or degree.'

me·di·oc·ri·ty /ˌmēdēˈäkrətē/ ▶ **noun** (pl. **mediocrities**) **1** the state of being average in quality. **2** a person of average ability and lacking originality.

med·i·tate /ˈmedəˌtāt/ ▶ **verb 1** focus one's mind for a time for spiritual purposes or for relaxation. **2** (**meditate on/about**) think carefully about.

– SYNONYMS **contemplate,** think, consider, ponder, muse, reflect, deliberate, ruminate, brood, mull over.

– ORIGIN Latin *meditari* 'contemplate.'

med·i·ta·tion /ˌmedəˈtāsʜən/ ▶ **noun 1** the action or practice of meditating. **2** a speech or piece of writing expressing considered thoughts on a subject.

med·i·ta·tive /ˈmedəˌtātiv/ ▶ **adjective** involving or absorbed in focused thought or deep reflection.
– DERIVATIVES **med·i·ta·tive·ly** adverb.

Med·i·ter·ra·ne·an /ˌmedətəˈrānēən/ ▶ **adjective** relating to the Mediterranean Sea or the countries around it.
– ORIGIN Latin *mediterraneus* 'inland.'

Med·i·ter·ra·ne·an cli·mate ▶ **noun** a climate that has warm, wet winters and calm, hot, dry summers, characteristic of the Mediterranean region and parts of California, South Africa, and SW Australia.

me·di·um /ˈmēdēəm/ ▶ **noun** (pl. **media** or **mediums**) **1** a means by which something is expressed, communicated, or achieved: *using the latest technology as a medium for job creation.* **2** a substance through which a force or other influence is transmitted. **3** a form of storage for computer software, such as magnetic tape or disks. **4** a liquid with which pigments are mixed to make paint. **5** (pl. **mediums**) a person claiming to be able to communicate between the dead and the living. **6** the middle state between two extremes. **7** the substance in which an organism lives or is grown for scientific study.

– SYNONYMS *a medium of expression* **means,** method, avenue, channel, vehicle, organ, instrument, mechanism.

▶ **adjective** between two extremes; average.

– SYNONYMS **average,** middling, medium-sized, middle-sized, moderate, normal, standard.

– ORIGIN Latin, 'middle.'

med·lar /ˈmedlər/ ▶ **noun** a small brown applelike fruit.
– ORIGIN Old French *medler.*

med·ley /ˈmedlē/ ▶ **noun** (pl. **medleys**) **1** a varied mixture. **2** a collection of musical items performed as a continuous piece.
– ORIGIN Old French *medlee* 'melee.'

Mé·doc /māˈdôk, -ˈdäk/ ▶ **noun** (pl. same or **Médocs**) a red wine produced in the Médoc area of SW France.

me·dul·la /məˈdələ/ ▶ **noun 1** a distinct inner region of a body organ or tissue. **2** the soft internal tissue of a plant.
– ORIGIN Latin, 'pith or marrow.'

me·dul·la ob·lon·ga·ta/ äˌblôNGˈgätə/ ▶ **noun** the part of the spinal cord extending into the brain.

me·du·sa /məˈd(y)o͞osə, -zə/ ▶ **noun** (pl. **medusae** /-sē, -sī, -zē, -zī/ or **medusas**) the free-swimming stage in the life cycle of a jellyfish or related organism.
– ORIGIN from *Medusa*, a gorgon in Greek mythology with snakes in her hair.

meek /mēk/ ▶ **adjective** quiet, gentle, and submissive.

– SYNONYMS **submissive,** obedient, compliant, tame, biddable, acquiescent, timid, quiet, mild, gentle, docile, shy, diffident, unassuming, self-effacing.
– ANTONYMS assertive.

– DERIVATIVES **meek·ly** adverb **meek·ness** noun.
– ORIGIN Old Norse, 'soft, gentle.'

WORD TOOLKIT

See **HUMBLE**.

meer·kat /ˈmi(ə)rˌkat/ ▶ **noun** a small southern African mongoose.
– ORIGIN Dutch, 'sea cat.'

meer·schaum /ˈmi(ə)rˌSHôm, -SHəm/ ▶ **noun 1** a soft white claylike material. **2** a tobacco pipe with a bowl made from meerschaum.
– ORIGIN German, 'sea foam.'

meet[1] /mēt/ ▶ **verb** (past and past part. **met** /met/) **1** come together with someone at the same place and time. **2** see or be introduced to someone for the first time. **3** touch or join: *the wall curved to meet the ceiling.* **4** experience a situation. **5** (**meet with**) receive a reaction. **6** fulfill or satisfy a need or requirement.

– SYNONYMS **1 encounter,** come face to face with, run into, run across, come across/upon, chance on, happen on, stumble across; informal bump into. **2 get to know,** be introduced to, make the acquaintance of. **3 assemble,** gather, congregate, convene; formal foregather. **4 converge,** connect, touch, link up, intersect, cross, join.

▶ **noun** an organized event at which a number of races or other sporting contests are held.
– ORIGIN Old English.

meet[2] ▶ **adjective** old use suitable or proper.
– ORIGIN related to **METE**.

meet·ing /ˈmētiNG/ ▶ **noun 1** an organized gathering of people for a discussion or other purpose. **2** a situation in which people meet by chance or arrangement.

– SYNONYMS **1 gathering,** assembly, conference, congregation, convention, forum, summit, rally, consultation, audience, interview, conclave; informal get-together. **2 encounter,** contact, appointment, assignation, rendezvous; literary tryst. **3** *the meeting of land and sea* **convergence,** confluence, conjunction, union, intersection, crossing. **4** *an athletics meeting* **event,** tournament, meet, rally, competition, match, game, contest.

meet·ing·house /ˈmētiNGˌhous/ ▶ **noun 1** a Quaker place of worship. **2** historical a Protestant place of worship.

meg·a /ˈmegə/ ▶ **adjective** informal **1** very large. **2** of great significance or importance.

mega- ▶ **combining form 1** large: *megalith.* **2** referring to a factor of one million (10^6): *megabyte.*
– ORIGIN Greek *megas* 'great.'

meg·a·bucks /ˈmegəˌbəks/ ▶ **plural noun** informal a huge sum of money.

meg·a·byte /ˈmegəˌbīt/ ▶ **noun** a unit of information stored in a computer equal to one million or (strictly) 1,048,576 bytes.

meg·a·flop /ˈmegəˌfläp/ ▶ **noun** Computing a unit of computing speed equal to one million or (strictly) 1,048,576 floating-point operations per second.

meg·a·hertz /ˈmegəˌhərts/ ▶ **noun** (pl. same) a unit of frequency equal to one million hertz.

meg·a·lith /ˈmegəˌliTH/ ▶ **noun** a large stone that forms a prehistoric monument or part of one.
– DERIVATIVES **meg·a·lith·ic** /ˌmegəˈliTHik/ adjective.

meg·a·lo·ma·ni·a /ˌmegəlōˈmānēə/ ▶ **noun 1** the false belief that one is very powerful or important. **2** a strong desire for power.
– DERIVATIVES **meg·a·lo·ma·ni·ac** /ˌmegəlōˈmānēˌak/ noun & adjective.

meg·a·lop·o·lis /ˌmegəˈläpələs/ ▶ **noun** a very large, densely populated city.
– ORIGIN from Greek *polis* 'city.'

meg·a·phone /ˈmegəˌfōn/ ▶ **noun** a large cone-shaped device for amplifying the voice.

meg·a·pix·el /ˈmegəˌpiksəl/ ▶ **noun** Computing a unit of graphic resolution equivalent to 2^{20} or (strictly) 1,048,576 pixels.

meg·a·pode /ˈmegəˌpōd/ ▶ **noun** a large Australasian or SE Asian bird that lives on the ground and builds a mound of plant debris to incubate its eggs.
– ORIGIN from Greek *pous* 'foot.'

meg·a·star /ˈmegəˌstär/ ▶ **noun** informal a very famous entertainer or athlete.

meg·a·ton /ˈmegəˌtən/ ▶ **noun** a unit of explosive power equivalent to one million tons of TNT.

meg·a·volt /ˈmegəˌvōlt/ ▶ **noun** one million volts.

meg·a·watt /ˈmegəˌwät/ ▶ **noun** a unit of power equal to one million watts.

mei·o·sis /mīˈōsəs/ ▶ **noun** (pl. **meioses** /-sēz/) Biology the division of a cell that results in four cells, each with half the number of chromosomes of the original cell. Compare with **MITOSIS**.
– DERIVATIVES **mei·ot·ic** /mīˈätik/ adjective.
– ORIGIN Greek *meiōsis* 'lessening.'

Meis·sen /ˈmīsən/ ▶ **noun** fine porcelain produced at Meissen in Germany since 1710.

-meister ▶ **combining form** referring to a person who is skilled or prominent in a particular area of activity: *a media-meister.*
– ORIGIN from German *Meister* 'master.'

meit·ner·i·um /mītˈni(ə)rēəm/ ▶ **noun** a very unstable chemical element made by high-energy atomic collisions.
– ORIGIN named after the Swedish physicist Lise *Meitner*.

mel·a·mine /ˈmeləˌmēn/ ▶ **noun** a hard, heat-resistant plastic used to coat surfaces.
– ORIGIN German *Melamin*, from **AMINE**.

mel·an·cho·li·a /ˌmelənˈkōlēə/ ▶ **noun** dated severe depression.

mel·an·chol·y /ˈmelənˌkälē/ ▶ **noun** deep and long-lasting sadness.

– SYNONYMS **sadness,** sorrow, unhappiness, depression, despondency, dejection, gloom, misery; informal the blues.
– ANTONYMS happiness.

▶ **adjective** feeling or causing sadness.

– SYNONYMS **sad,** sorrowful, unhappy, gloomy, despondent, dejected, disconsolate, downcast, downhearted, woebegone, glum, miserable, morose, depressed, dispirited, mournful, doleful, lugubrious; informal down in the dumps, blue.
– ANTONYMS cheerful.

– DERIVATIVES **mel·an·chol·ic** /ˌmelən'kälik/ adjective.
– ORIGIN Greek *melankholia.*

WORD TOOLKIT

melancholy ...	forlorn ...	miserable ...
music	hope	life
thoughts	attempt	failure
eyes	cry	existence
lament	lover	experience
tale	victim	conditions

Mel·a·ne·sian /ˌmelə'nēzʜən/ ▶ **adjective** relating to the islands that make up Melanesia in the western Pacific. ▶ **noun** a person from Melanesia.

me·lange /mā'länj/ ▶ **noun** a varied mixture.
– ORIGIN French *mélange.*

mel·a·nin /'melənin/ ▶ **noun** a dark pigment in the hair and skin, responsible for tanning of skin exposed to sunlight.
– ORIGIN from Greek *melas* 'black.'

mel·a·no·ma /ˌmelə'nōmə/ ▶ **noun** a form of skin cancer that develops in melanin-forming cells.

mel·a·to·nin /ˌmelə'tōnin/ ▶ **noun** a hormone secreted by the pineal gland that inhibits melanin formation and is involved in regulating various physiological cycles.

Mel·ba toast /'melbə/ ▶ **noun** very thin crisp toast.
– ORIGIN named after the Australian opera singer Dame Nellie *Melba.*

meld /meld/ ▶ **verb** combine something with something else.
– ORIGIN perhaps a blend of **MELT** and **WELD.**

me·lee /'mā,lā, mā'lā/ ▶ **noun 1** a confused fight. **2** a confused crowd of people.
– ORIGIN French *mêlée.*

mel·lif·lu·ous /mə'liflōōəs/ ▶ **adjective** pleasingly smooth and musical to hear.
– DERIVATIVES **mel·lif·lu·ous·ly** adverb **mel·lif·lu·ous·ness** noun.
– ORIGIN from Latin *mel* 'honey' + *fluere* 'to flow.'

mel·lo·tron /'melə,trän/ ▶ **noun** an electronic keyboard instrument in which each key controls the playback of a single prerecorded musical sound.
– ORIGIN from **MELLOW** + *-tron,* from **ELECTRONIC.**

mel·low /'melō/ ▶ **adjective 1** pleasantly smooth or soft in sound, taste, or color. **2** relaxed and good-humored.

– SYNONYMS **1 sweet-sounding,** dulcet, melodious, mellifluous, soft, smooth, rich. **2 genial,** affable, amiable, good-humored, good-natured, pleasant, relaxed, easygoing.
– ANTONYMS harsh, rough.

▶ **verb** make or become mellow.
– ORIGIN perhaps related to **MEAL**[2].

CHOOSE THE RIGHT WORD

See **MATURE.**

me·lo·de·on /mə'lōdēən/ ▶ **noun 1** a small accordion. **2** a small organ similar to the harmonium.

me·lod·ic /mə'lädik/ ▶ **adjective 1** relating to melody. **2** pleasant-sounding.
– DERIVATIVES **me·lod·i·cal·ly** /-(ə)lē/ adverb.

me·lo·di·ous /mə'lōdēəs/ ▶ **adjective** pleasant-sounding; tuneful.

– SYNONYMS **tuneful,** melodic, musical, mellifluous, dulcet, sweet-sounding, harmonious, euphonious, lyrical.
– ANTONYMS discordant.

mel·o·dra·ma /'melə,drämə/ ▶ **noun 1** a play full of exciting events and with exaggerated characters and emotions. **2** exaggerated or extreme behavior or events.
– ORIGIN first referring to a play interspersed with songs and music: from Greek *melos* 'music' + French *drame* 'drama.'

mel·o·dra·mat·ic /ˌmelədrə'matik/ ▶ **adjective** overdramatic or exaggerated: *he flung the door open with a melodramatic flourish.*

– SYNONYMS **exaggerated,** histrionic, extravagant, overdramatic, overdone, sensationalized, overemotional, theatrical, stagy; informal hammy.

– DERIVATIVES **mel·o·dra·mat·i·cal·ly** /-ik(ə)lē/ adverb.

mel·o·dy /'melədē/ ▶ **noun** (pl. **melodies**) **1** a sequence of notes that is musically satisfying; a tune. **2** the arrangement of musical notes to form a tune. **3** the main part in harmonized music.

– SYNONYMS **tune,** air, strain, theme, song, refrain.

– ORIGIN from Greek *melos* 'song.'

mel·on /'melən/ ▶ **noun** a large round fruit with sweet pulpy flesh and many seeds.
– ORIGIN Greek *mēlopepōn.*

melt /melt/ ▶ **verb 1** make or become liquid by heating. **2** gradually disappear or disperse: *most of the crowd had melted away.* **3** become or make more tender or loving.

– SYNONYMS **1 liquefy,** thaw, defrost, soften, dissolve; technical deliquesce. **2 vanish,** disappear, fade, evaporate.
– ANTONYMS freeze, solidify.

– ORIGIN Old English.

melt·down /'melt,doun/ ▶ **noun 1** a disastrous collapse: *the coming economic meltdown.* **2** an accident in a nuclear reactor in which the fuel overheats and melts the reactor core.

melt·ing point ▶ **noun** the temperature at which a solid will melt.

melt·ing pot ▶ **noun** a place where different peoples, ideas, or styles are mixed together.

melt·wa·ter /'melt,wôtər, -,wätər/ (also **meltwaters**) ▶ **noun** water formed by the melting of snow and ice.

mem·ber /'membər/ ▶ **noun 1** a person or organization belonging to a group or society. **2** a part of a complex structure. **3** old use a part of the body, especially a limb. **4** the penis.

– SYNONYMS **subscriber,** associate, fellow, representative.

– ORIGIN Latin *membrum* 'limb.'

mem·ber·ship /'membər,ʜip/ ▶ **noun 1** the fact of being a member of a group. **2** the members or the number of members in a group.

mem·brane /'mem,brān/ ▶ **noun 1** a skinlike structure that lines, connects, or covers a cell or part of the body.

2 a thin pliable sheet of material forming a barrier or lining.
– DERIVATIVES **mem·bra·ne·ous** /mem'brānēəs/ adjective **mem·bra·nous** /'membrənəs, mem'brānəs/ adjective.
– ORIGIN Latin *membrum* 'limb.'

me·men·to /mə'men,tō/ ▶ **noun** (pl. **mementos** or **mementoes**) an object kept as a reminder of a person or event.

– SYNONYMS **souvenir,** keepsake, reminder, remembrance, token, memorial.

– ORIGIN Latin, 'remember!'

me·men·to mo·ri /mə'men,tō 'môrē/ ▶ **noun** (pl. same) an object kept as a reminder that death is inevitable.
– ORIGIN Latin, 'remember (that you have) to die.'

mem·o /'memō/ ▶ **noun** (pl. **memos**) a memorandum.

mem·oir /'mem,wär, -,wôr/ ▶ **noun 1** a historical account or biography written from personal knowledge. **2** (**memoirs**) an account written by a public figure of their life and experiences.

– SYNONYMS **1 account,** history, record, chronicle, narrative, story, portrayal, depiction, portrait, profile. **2** (**memoirs**) **autobiography,** life story, journal, diary.

– ORIGIN French *mémoire* 'memory.'

mem·o·ra·bil·i·a /,mem(ə)rə'bilēə/ ▶ **plural noun** objects kept or collected because of their associations with memorable people or events.

mem·o·ra·ble /'mem(ə)rəbəl/ ▶ **adjective** worth remembering or easily remembered.

– SYNONYMS **unforgettable,** momentous, significant, historic, remarkable, notable, noteworthy, important, outstanding, arresting, indelible, catchy, haunting.

– DERIVATIVES **mem·o·ra·bly** adverb.

mem·o·ran·dum /,memə'randəm/ ▶ **noun** (pl. **memoranda** /-də/ or **memorandums**) **1** a note sent from one person to another in an organization. **2** a formal record or report.
– ORIGIN Latin, 'something to be brought to mind.'

me·mo·ri·al /mə'môrēəl/ ▶ **noun** an object or structure established in memory of a person or event.

– SYNONYMS **1 monument,** cenotaph, mausoleum, statue, plaque, cairn, shrine, tombstone. **2 tribute,** testimonial, remembrance, memento.

▶ **adjective** in memory of someone.
– DERIVATIVES **me·mo·ri·al·ist** /mə'môrēəlist/ noun **me·mo·ri·al·ize** /mə'môrēə,līz/ verb.

Me·mo·ri·al Day ▶ **noun** a day on which people who died in active military service are remembered, officially observed in the US on the last Monday in May.

mem·o·rize /'memə,rīz/ ▶ **verb** learn something by heart.

– SYNONYMS **commit to memory,** remember, learn (by heart), become word-perfect in, get down pat.

mem·o·ry /'mem(ə)rē/ ▶ **noun** (pl. **memories**) **1** the faculty by which the mind stores and remembers information. **2** a person or thing remembered. **3** the length of time over which people's memory extends. **4** a computer's equipment or capacity for storing information.

– SYNONYMS **1 recollection,** remembrance, reminiscence, recall. **2 commemoration,** remembrance, honor, tribute, recognition, respect.

– PHRASES **in memory of** so as to honor and remind people of a dead person.
– ORIGIN Latin *memoria.*

WORD LINKS

mnemonic *helping the memory*

Mem·o·ry Stick ▶ **noun** trademark a small electronic device for storing data or transferring it to or from a computer, digital camera, etc.

mem·sa·hib /'mem,sä(h)ib, -,säb/ ▶ **noun** dated (in the Indian subcontinent) a respectful form of address for a married white woman.
– ORIGIN from an Indian pronunciation of *ma'am* + **SAHIB**.

men /men/ plural of **MAN**.

men·ace /'menəs/ ▶ **noun 1** a dangerous or harmful person or thing. **2** a threatening quality.

– SYNONYMS **1 threat,** intimidation, malevolence, oppression. **2 danger,** peril, risk, hazard, threat. **3 nuisance,** pest, troublemaker, mischief-maker.

▶ **verb** put someone or something at risk; threaten.

– SYNONYMS **1 threaten,** endanger, put at risk, jeopardize, imperil. **2 intimidate,** threaten, terrorize, frighten, scare, terrify. **3** (as adj. **menacing**) *a menacing tone of voice* **threatening,** ominous, intimidating, frightening, forbidding, hostile, sinister, baleful.

– ORIGIN from Latin *minax* 'threatening.'

mé·nage à trois /mā'näzʜ ä 't(r)wä, mə-/ ▶ **noun** an arrangement in which a married couple and the lover of one of them live together.
– ORIGIN French, 'household of three.'

me·nag·er·ie /mə'najərē, -'nazʜ-/ ▶ **noun** a collection of wild animals kept in captivity for showing to the public.
– ORIGIN French.

men·a·qui·none /,menə'kwin,ōn, -'kwī,nōn/ ▶ **noun** a member of the vitamin K group, a compound produced by bacteria in the intestines, essential for blood clotting.
– ORIGIN from its chemical name.

mend /mend/ ▶ **verb 1** restore something to its correct or working condition. **2** improve an unpleasant situation.

– SYNONYMS **repair,** fix, restore, sew (up), stitch, darn, patch, renew, renovate; informal patch up.
– ANTONYMS break.

▶ **noun** a repair in a material.
– DERIVATIVES **mend·a·ble** adjective **mend·er** noun.
– PHRASES **mend fences** resolve a disagreement with someone. **on the mend** improving in health or condition.
– ORIGIN shortening of **AMEND**.

men·da·cious /men'dāsʜəs/ ▶ **adjective** lying; untruthful.
– DERIVATIVES **men·da·cious·ly** adverb **men·dac·i·ty** /men'dasitē/ noun.
– ORIGIN Latin *mendax* 'lying.'

men·de·le·vi·um /,mendə'lēvēəm, -'lā-/ ▶ **noun** a very unstable chemical element made by high-energy collisions.
– ORIGIN named after the Russian chemist Dimitri *Mendeleev.*

Men·de·li·an /men'dēlēən/ ▶ **adjective** relating to the theory of heredity based on characteristics transmitted as genes, as developed by the Austrian botanist G. J. Mendel.
– DERIVATIVES **Men·del·ism** /'mendl,izəm/ noun.

men·di·cant /ˈmendikənt/ ▸ **adjective** **1** living by begging. **2** (of a religious order) originally dependent on charitable donations. ▸ **noun** **1** a beggar. **2** a member of a mendicant religious order.
– ORIGIN from Latin *mendicus* 'beggar.'

men·folk /ˈmen͵fōk/ ▸ **plural noun** the men of a family or community.

men·ha·den /menˈhādn, mən-/ ▸ **noun** a large deep-bodied fish of the herring family found along the east coast of North America and used to make fish meal and fertilizer.
– ORIGIN from Algonquian.

men·hir /ˈmen͵hi(ə)r/ ▸ **noun** a tall upright stone erected as a monument in prehistoric times.
– ORIGIN from Breton *men* 'stone' + *hir* 'long.'

me·ni·al /ˈmēnēəl/ ▸ **adjective** (of work) of low status and requiring little skill.

– SYNONYMS **unskilled,** lowly, humble, low-grade, low-status, humdrum, routine, boring, dull.

▸ **noun** a person with a menial job.
– ORIGIN Old French.

me·nin·ges /məˈninjēz/ ▸ **plural noun** (sing. **meninx** /ˈmēniNGks, ˈmen-/) the three membranes that enclose the brain and spinal cord.
– ORIGIN from Greek *mēninx* 'membrane.'

men·in·gi·tis /͵menənˈjītis/ ▸ **noun** a serious disease in which the meninges around the brain and spinal cord become inflamed owing to infection with a bacterium or virus.

me·nis·cus /məˈniskəs/ ▸ **noun** (pl. **menisci** /-kē, -kī/) **1** Physics the curved upper surface of a liquid in a tube. **2** a thin lens that curves outward on one side and inward on the other.
– ORIGIN Greek *mēniskos* 'crescent.'

Men·non·ite /ˈmenə͵nīt/ ▸ **noun** a member of a Protestant sect that emphasizes adult baptism and rejects church organization, military service, and public office.
– ORIGIN from the name of its founder, *Menno* Simons (1496–1561).

men·o·pause /ˈmenə͵pôz/ ▸ **noun** the ending of menstruation or the stage in a woman's life (typically between 45 and 50) when this occurs.
– DERIVATIVES **men·o·pau·sal** /͵menəˈpôzəl/ adjective.
– ORIGIN from Greek *mēn* 'month' + **PAUSE**.

me·nor·ah /məˈnôrə/ ▸ **noun** a candelabrum used in Jewish worship, typically with eight branches.
– ORIGIN Hebrew.

men·ses /ˈmen͵sēz/ ▸ **plural noun** blood discharged from the uterus at menstruation.
– ORIGIN Latin, plural of *mensis* 'month.'

men·stru·al /ˈmenstr(o͞o)əl/ ▸ **adjective** relating to menstruation.
– ORIGIN Latin *menstrualis*.

men·stru·ate /ˈmenstrə͵wāt, ˈmen͵strāt/ ▸ **verb** (of a woman) discharge blood from the lining of the uterus each month.

men·stru·a·tion /͵menstro͞oˈāSHən, menˈstrā-/ ▸ **noun** the process in a woman of discharging blood from the lining of the uterus each month from puberty until menopause, except during pregnancy.

men·su·ra·tion /͵mensHəˈrāSHən, ͵mensə-/ ▸ **noun** **1** the measurement of something. **2** the part of geometry concerned with measuring lengths, areas, and volumes.
– ORIGIN from Latin *mensurare* 'to measure.'

mens·wear /ˈmenz͵we(ə)r/ ▸ **noun** clothes for men.

men·tal /ˈmentl/ ▸ **adjective** **1** relating to or done by the mind. **2** relating to disorders or illnesses of the mind. **3** informal insane.

– SYNONYMS **1 intellectual,** cerebral, cognitive, rational. **2 psychiatric,** psychological, behavioral.
– ANTONYMS physical.

– ORIGIN from Latin *mens* 'mind.'

USAGE

The use of **mental** in sense 2 (as in **mental problems**) is now regarded as old-fashioned, even offensive, and has been largely replaced by **psychiatric**.

men·tal age ▸ **noun** a person's mental ability expressed as the age at which an average person reaches the same ability.

men·tal block ▸ **noun** an inability to remember something or perform a mental action.

men·tal·i·ty /menˈtalitē/ ▸ **noun** (pl. **mentalities**) a typical way of thinking of a person or group.

– SYNONYMS **way of thinking,** mindset, mind, psychology, attitude, outlook, makeup, disposition, character.

men·tal·ly /ˈmen(t)lē/ ▸ **adverb** in one's mind: *mentally, I was prepared to deal with the situation.*

– SYNONYMS **psychologically,** intellectually, in one's mind, in one's head, inwardly, internally.

men·tal·ly hand·i·capped ▸ **adjective** having underdeveloped intellectual ability that prevents one from functioning normally in society.

men·thol /ˈmen͵THôl, -͵THäl/ ▸ **noun** a minty substance found chiefly in peppermint oil, used as a flavoring and in decongestants.
– DERIVATIVES **men·tho·lat·ed** /ˈmenTHə͵lātid/ adjective.
– ORIGIN Latin *mentha* 'mint.'

men·tion /ˈmenCHən/ ▸ **verb** **1** refer to something briefly. **2** refer to someone as being noteworthy: *he is regularly mentioned as a possible Cabinet member.*

– SYNONYMS **1 allude to,** refer to, touch on, bring up, raise, broach. **2 state,** say, observe, remark, indicate, disclose, divulge, reveal.

▸ **noun** **1** a reference to someone or something. **2** a formal acknowledgment of something noteworthy.

– SYNONYMS **reference,** allusion, comment, citation; informal namecheck, name-drop, plug.

– ORIGIN Latin.

men·tor /ˈmen͵tôr, -tər/ ▸ **noun** **1** an experienced and trusted adviser. **2** an experienced person in an organization or educational institution who trains and advises new employees or students.

– SYNONYMS **adviser,** counselor, guide, guru, consultant, confidant(e), trainer, teacher, tutor, instructor.

▸ **verb** to advise or train someone, especially a younger colleague.
– ORIGIN from *Mentor*, the adviser of Telemachus in Homer's *Odyssey*.

men·u /ˈmenyo͞o/ ▸ **noun** **1** a list of dishes available in a restaurant. **2** the food to be served at a meal. **3** a list of commands or options displayed on a computer screen.

– SYNONYMS **bill of fare,** carte du jour, table d'hôte, wine list.

– ORIGIN French, 'detailed list.'

me·ow /mē'ou/ ▶ **noun** the characteristic cry of a cat.
▶ **verb** make a meow.
– ORIGIN imitating the sound.

Meph·is·to·phe·li·an /məˌfistə'fēlēən, ˌmefəstə-/ (also **Mephistophelean**) ▶ **adjective** literary wicked or evil.
– ORIGIN from *Mephistopheles*, an evil spirit to whom Faust, in the German legend, sold his soul.

me·phit·ic /mə'fitik/ ▶ **adjective** literary smelling very unpleasant.
– ORIGIN from Latin *mephitis* 'foul vapor.'

mer·can·tile /'mərkənˌtēl, -ˌtīl/ ▶ **adjective** relating to trade or commerce.
– ORIGIN from Italian *mercante* 'merchant.'

mer·can·til·ism /'mərkəntiˌlizəm, -ˌtē-, -ˌtī-/ ▶ **noun** belief in the benefits of profitable trading; commercialism.

Mer·ca·tor pro·jec·tion /mər'kātər/ ▶ **noun** a world map projection made onto a cylinder in such a way that all parallels of latitude have the same length as the equator.
– ORIGIN from *Mercator*, Latinized name of the Flemish geographer G. Kremer.

mer·ce·nar·y /'mərsəˌnerē/ ▶ **adjective** motivated chiefly by the desire to make money.

– SYNONYMS **grasping,** greedy, acquisitive, avaricious, materialistic, venal; informal money-grubbing.

▶ **noun** (pl. **mercenaries**) a professional soldier hired to serve in a foreign army.
– ORIGIN from Latin *mercenarius* 'hireling.'

mer·cer·ized /'mərsəˌrīzd/ ▶ **adjective** (of cotton) chemically treated to make it strong and shiny.
– ORIGIN named after J. *Mercer*, said to have invented the process.

mer·chan·dise ▶ **noun** /'mərCHənˌdīz, -ˌdīs/ goods for sale.

– SYNONYMS **goods,** wares, stock, commodities, produce, products.

▶ **verb** /'mərCHənˌdīz/ (or **merchandize**) promote the sale of goods.
– DERIVATIVES **mer·chan·dis·er** /-ˌdīzər/ noun.
– ORIGIN from Old French *marchand* 'merchant.'

mer·chan·dis·ing /'mərCHənˌdīziNG/ ▶ **noun 1** products used to promote a particular movie, pop music group, etc. **2** the promotion of goods in stores and other retail outlets.

mer·chant /'mərCHənt/ ▶ **noun 1** a wholesale trader. **2** a retail trader. **3** informal, derogatory a person fond of a particular activity: *a speed merchant.*

– SYNONYMS **trader,** tradesman, dealer, wholesaler, broker, agent, seller, retailer, supplier, buyer, vendor, distributor.

▶ **adjective** (of sailors or shipping) involved with commerce.
– ORIGIN Old French *marchant.*

mer·chant·a·ble /'mərCHəntəbəl/ ▶ **adjective** suitable for sale.

mer·chant·man /'mərCHəntmən/ ▶ **noun** (pl. **merchantmen**) a ship carrying merchandise.

mer·chant ma·rine ▶ **noun** a country's commercial shipping.

mer·ci·ful /'mərsifəl/ ▶ **adjective 1** showing compassion and forgiveness. **2** giving relief from suffering: *her death was a merciful release.*

– SYNONYMS **forgiving,** compassionate, pitying, forbearing, lenient, humane, mild, kind, softhearted, tenderhearted, sympathetic, humanitarian, liberal, generous, magnanimous.
– ANTONYMS cruel.

mer·ci·ful·ly /'mərsif(ə)lē/ ▶ **adverb 1** in a merciful way. **2** to one's great relief; fortunately.

mer·ci·less /'mərsiləs/ ▶ **adjective** showing no mercy.

– SYNONYMS **ruthless,** remorseless, pitiless, unforgiving, implacable, inexorable, relentless, inhumane, inhuman, unfeeling, severe, cold-blooded, hard-hearted, stony-hearted, heartless, harsh, callous, cruel, brutal.
– ANTONYMS compassionate.

– DERIVATIVES **mer·ci·less·ly** adverb **mer·ci·less·ness** noun.

mer·cu·ri·al /mərˌkyo͝orēəl/ ▶ **adjective 1** tending to change mood suddenly. **2** relating to the element mercury.

– SYNONYMS **volatile,** capricious, temperamental, excitable, fickle, changeable, unpredictable, variable, mutable, erratic, inconstant, inconsistent, unstable, unsteady, fluctuating, ever-changing, moody, flighty, wayward, impulsive; technical labile.
– ANTONYMS stable.

– ORIGIN Latin *mercurialis* 'relating to the god Mercury.'

WORD TOOLKIT

See **VARIABLE**.

Mer·cu·ry /'mərkyərē/ ▶ **noun** a small planet that is the closest to the sun in the solar system.
– DERIVATIVES **Mer·cu·ri·an** /mər'kyo͝orēən/ adjective.

mer·cu·ry /'mərkyərē/ ▶ **noun** a heavy silvery-white liquid metallic element used in some thermometers and barometers.
– DERIVATIVES **mer·cu·ric** /mərˌkyo͝orik/ adjective **mer·cu·rous** /'mərkyərəs/ adjective.
– ORIGIN from *Mercury*, the Roman messenger of the gods.

mer·cy /'mərsē/ ▶ **noun** (pl. **mercies**) **1** compassion or forgiveness shown toward someone in one's power to punish or harm. **2** something to be grateful for.

– SYNONYMS **pity,** compassion, leniency, clemency, charity, forgiveness, forbearance, kindness, sympathy, indulgence, tolerance, generosity, magnanimity.
– ANTONYMS ruthlessness, cruelty.

▶ **adjective** done from a desire to relieve suffering: *a mercy killing.*
▶ **exclamation** old use used to express surprise or fear.
– PHRASES **at the mercy of** completely in the power of.
– ORIGIN Latin *merces* 'reward, pity.'

mere[1] /mi(ə)r/ ▶ **adjective 1** that is nothing more than what is specified: *questions that cannot be answered by mere mortals.* **2** (**the merest**) the smallest or slightest.
– ORIGIN Latin *merus* 'pure, undiluted.'

mere[2] ▶ **noun** literary (except in place names) a lake or pond.
– ORIGIN Old English.

mere·ly /'mi(ə)rlē/ ▶ **adverb** just; only.

– SYNONYMS **only,** purely, solely, simply, just, but.

me·ren·gue /mə'reNGgā/ ▶ **noun** **1** a Caribbean style of dance music typically in duple and triple time. **2** a dance style associated with merengue, with alternating long and short stiff-legged steps.
– ORIGIN probably American Spanish.

mer·e·tri·cious /merə'trisHəs/ ▶ **adjective** appearing attractive but having no real value.
– ORIGIN from Latin *meretrix* 'prostitute.'

mer·gan·ser /mər'gansər/ ▶ **noun** a fish-eating diving duck with a long, thin, jagged, and hooked bill.
– ORIGIN from Latin *mergus* 'diver' + *anser* 'goose.'

merge /mərj/ ▶ **verb** **1** combine or be combined into a whole: *the two banks merged.* **2** blend gradually into something else.

– SYNONYMS **1 join (together),** join forces, unite, affiliate, team up. **2 amalgamate,** bring together, join, consolidate, conflate, unite, unify, combine, incorporate, integrate. **3 mingle,** blend, fuse, mix, intermix, intermingle, coalesce.
– ANTONYMS separate.

– ORIGIN Latin *mergere* 'to dip, plunge.'

merg·er /'mərjər/ ▶ **noun** a merging of two things, especially companies, into one.

– SYNONYMS **amalgamation,** combination, union, fusion, coalition, affiliation, unification, incorporation, consolidation, linkup, alliance.
– ANTONYMS split.

mer·guez /mər'gez/ ▶ **noun** (pl. same) a spicy beef and lamb sausage colored with red peppers, originally made in North Africa.
– ORIGIN French, from Arabic.

me·rid·i·an /mə'ridēən/ ▶ **noun** **1** a circle of constant longitude passing through a given place on the earth's surface and the poles. **2** any of twelve pathways in the body, believed by practitioners of Chinese medicine to be a channel for vital energy.
– ORIGIN from Latin *meridianum* 'noon' (because the sun crosses a meridian at noon).

me·rid·i·o·nal /mə'ridēənəl/ ▶ **adjective** **1** relating to the south, especially southern Europe. **2** relating to a meridian.

me·ringue /mə'raNG/ ▶ **noun** **1** beaten egg whites and sugar baked until crisp. **2** a small cake made of meringue.
– ORIGIN French.

me·ri·no /mə'rēnō/ ▶ **noun** (pl. **merinos**) **1** a breed of sheep with long, fine wool. **2** a soft woolen or wool-and-cotton material.
– ORIGIN Spanish.

mer·i·stem /'merə,stem/ ▶ **noun** a region of plant tissue consisting of actively dividing cells.
– ORIGIN from Greek *meristos* 'divisible.'

mer·it /'merit/ ▶ **noun** **1** the quality of being particularly good; excellence. **2** a good point or quality.

– SYNONYMS **1 excellence,** quality, caliber, worth, value, distinction, eminence. **2 good point,** strong point, advantage, benefit, value, asset, plus.
– ANTONYMS fault, disadvantage.

▶ **verb** (**merits, meriting, merited**) deserve or be worthy of: *offenses regarded as serious enough to merit dismissal.*

– SYNONYMS **deserve,** warrant, justify, earn, rate, be worthy of, be entitled to, have a right to, have a claim to.

– ORIGIN Latin *meritum* 'due reward.'

mer·i·toc·ra·cy /,meri'täkrəsē/ ▶ **noun** (pl. **meritocracies**) a society in which power is held by the people with the greatest ability.
– DERIVATIVES **mer·i·to·crat** /'meritə,krat/ noun **mer·i·to·crat·ic** /,meritə'kratik/ adjective.

mer·i·to·ri·ous /'meri,tôrēəs/ ▶ **adjective** deserving reward or praise.

mer·lin /'mərlən/ ▶ **noun** a small dark falcon.
– ORIGIN Old French *merilun.*

Mer·lot /mər'lō/ ▶ **noun** a red wine made from a variety of grape originally from the Bordeaux region of France.
– ORIGIN French.

mer·maid /'mər,mād/ ▶ **noun** a mythical sea creature with a woman's head and trunk and a fish's tail.
– ORIGIN from **MERE**[2] (in the former sense 'sea') + **MAID.**

mer·man /'mərmən/ ▶ **noun** (pl. **mermen**) a mythical sea creature with the head and torso of a man and a fish's tail.

mer·ri·ment /'merēmənt/ ▶ **noun** cheerfulness and fun.

mer·ry /'merē/ ▶ **adjective** (**merrier, merriest**) cheerful and lively.

– SYNONYMS **cheerful,** cheery, in high spirits, sunny, smiling, lighthearted, lively, carefree, joyful, joyous, jolly, convivial, festive, gleeful, happy, laughing; informal chirpy.
– ANTONYMS miserable.

– DERIVATIVES **mer·ri·ly** adverb **mer·ri·ness** noun.
– PHRASES **make merry** enjoy oneself with other people by dancing and drinking.
– ORIGIN Old English, 'pleasing, delightful.'

mer·ry-go-round ▶ **noun** **1** a revolving machine with model horses or cars on which people ride for amusement. **2** a continuous cycle of activities or events.

mer·ry·mak·ing /'merē,mākiNG/ ▶ **noun** cheerful celebration and fun.

me·sa /'māsə/ ▶ **noun** an isolated flat-topped hill with steep sides.
– ORIGIN Spanish, 'table.'

mé·sal·li·ance /,māzə'līəns, ,mā,zal'yäNs/ ▶ **noun** a marriage to a person of a lower social class.
– ORIGIN French, 'misalliance.'

mes·cal /me'skal, mə-/ ▶ **noun** **1** an intoxicating liquor distilled from a type of agave (plant). **2** a peyote cactus.
– ORIGIN Nahuatl.

mes·ca·line /'meskəlin, -,lēn/ (also **mescalin** /'meskəlin/) ▶ **noun** a drug that causes hallucinations, made from the peyote cactus.

Mes·dames /mā'däm/ plural of **MADAME.**

Mes·de·moi·selles /'mādəm(w)ə,zel, 'mād,mwä,zel/ plural of **MADEMOISELLE.**

mesh /mesH/ ▶ **noun** **1** material made of a network of wire or thread. **2** the spacing of the strands of a net. **3** a complex or constricting situation: *people caught in the mesh of history.*

– SYNONYMS **netting,** net, grille, screen, lattice, gauze.

▶ **verb** **1** become entangled or entwined. **2** (**mesh with**) be in harmony with. **3** (of a gearwheel) lock together with another.

– SYNONYMS **1 engage,** connect, lock, interlock. **2 harmonize,** fit together, match, dovetail, connect, interconnect.

– ORIGIN probably from Old English.

mes·mer·ic /mez'merik/ ▶ **adjective** completely capturing a person's attention so that they become unaware of their surroundings; hypnotic.
– DERIVATIVES **mes·mer·i·cal·ly** adverb.

mes·mer·ism /'mezmə,rizəm/ ▶ **noun** historical a therapeutic technique involving hypnotism.
– DERIVATIVES **mes·mer·ist** noun.
– ORIGIN named after the Austrian physician Franz A. *Mesmer*.

mes·mer·ize /'mezmə,rīz/ ▶ **verb** capture a person's attention completely.

Mes·o·lith·ic /,mezə'liTHik, ,mē-/ ▶ **adjective** Geology relating to the middle part of the Stone Age, between the end of the glacial period and the beginnings of agriculture.
– ORIGIN from Greek *mesos* 'middle' + *lithos* 'stone.'

mes·o·morph /'mezə,môrf, 'mē-/ ▶ **noun** Physiology a person with a compact and muscular body build. Compare with **ECTOMORPH** and **ENDOMORPH**.

me·son /'mez,än, 'mā,zän, 'mē,zän/ ▶ **noun** Physics a subatomic particle that is intermediate in mass between an electron and a proton.
– ORIGIN from Greek *mesos* 'middle.'

Mes·o·po·ta·mi·an /,mesəpə'tāmēən/ ▶ **adjective** relating to Mesopotamia, an ancient region of what is now Iraq. ▶ **noun** a person from Mesopotamia.

mes·o·sphere /'mezə,sfi(ə)r, 'mē-/ ▶ **noun** the region of the earth's atmosphere above the stratosphere and below the thermosphere.
– ORIGIN from Greek *mesos* 'middle.'

mes·o·the·li·o·ma /'mezə,THēlē'ōmə, ,mē-/ ▶ **noun** a cancer affecting the lining of the chest or abdomen, associated mainly with exposure to asbestos.

Mes·o·zo·ic /,mezə'zōik, ,mē-/ ▶ **adjective** Geology relating to the era between the Paleozoic and Cenozoic eras, about 245 to 65 million years ago, with evidence of the first mammals, birds, and flowering plants.
– ORIGIN from Greek *mesos* 'middle' + *zōion* 'animal.'

mes·quite /mə'skēt/ ▶ **noun** a spiny tree of the southwestern US and Mexico, yielding wood, medicinal products, and edible pods.
– ORIGIN Mexican Spanish *mezquite*.

mess /mes/ ▶ **noun 1** a dirty or untidy state. **2** a state of confusion or difficulty. **3** euphemistic a dog's or cat's excrement. **4** a place providing meals and recreational facilities for members of the armed forces. **5** a portion of semisolid food.

> – SYNONYMS **1 untidiness,** disorder, disarray, clutter, muddle, jumble, chaos; informal shambles. **2 plight,** predicament, tight spot, tight corner, difficulty, trouble, quandary, dilemma, problem, muddle, mix-up; informal jam, fix, pickle, hole.

▶ **verb 1** make something untidy or dirty. **2** (**mess about/around**) behave in a silly or playful way. **3** (**mess something up**) informal handle something badly. **4** (**mess someone up**) informal cause someone problems. **5** (**mess with**) informal meddle with. **6** eat in an armed forces' mess.

> – SYNONYMS **1 dirty,** clutter up, jumble, dishevel, rumple, muss up. **2** (**mess around/about**) **fool around,** fiddle around/about, play around, fidget, toy, trifle, tamper, tinker, interfere, meddle, monkey around/about. **3** (**mess something up**) **bungle,** spoil, make a mess of, ruin; informal botch, make a hash of, foul up, screw up, muff.

– ORIGIN Old French *mes* 'portion of food.'

mes·sage /'mesij/ ▶ **noun 1** a spoken, written, or electronic communication. **2** a significant point or central theme of a novel, speech, etc.

> – SYNONYMS **1 communication,** news, note, memo, email, letter, missive, report, bulletin, communiqué, dispatch. **2** *the message of his teaching* **meaning,** sense, import, idea, point, thrust, moral, gist, essence, implication.

▶ **verb** send a message to someone, especially by email.
– PHRASES **get the message** informal understand what is meant. **on** (or **off**) **message** (of a politician) following (or not following) the official party line.
– ORIGIN Old French.

mes·sage board ▶ **noun** a website where people can post and read messages, usually on a specific topic or area of interest.

Mes·sei·gneurs /,māsān'yər(z)/ plural of **MONSEIGNEUR**.

mes·sen·ger /'mesənjər/ ▶ **noun** a person who carries a message.

> – SYNONYMS **courier,** postman, runner, dispatch rider, envoy, emissary, agent, go-between.

mes·sen·ger RNA ▶ **noun** the form of RNA in which genetic information transcribed from DNA is transferred to a ribosome.

mess hall ▶ **noun** a room or building where groups of people, especially soldiers, eat together.

mes·si·ah /mə'sīə/ ▶ **noun 1** (**the Messiah**) the person sent by God to save the Jewish people, as prophesied in the Hebrew Bible (the Old Testament). **2** (**the Messiah**) Jesus regarded by Christians as the Messiah of the Hebrew prophecies. **3** a leader regarded as a savior of a country, group, etc.
– ORIGIN Hebrew, 'anointed.'

mes·si·an·ic /,mesē'anik/ ▶ **adjective 1** relating to the Messiah. **2** passionate or fervent: *messianic zeal*.
– DERIVATIVES **mes·si·a·nism** /'mesēə,nizəm, mə'sīə-/ noun.

Mes·sieurs /məs'yœ(r)(z), mās-, mə'si(ə)r(z)/ plural of **MONSIEUR**.

Mes·srs. /'mesərz/ plural of **MR.**
– ORIGIN abbreviation of **MESSIEURS**.

mess·y /'mesē/ ▶ **adjective** (**messier, messiest**) **1** untidy or dirty. **2** confused and difficult to deal with.

> – SYNONYMS **1 dirty,** filthy, grubby, soiled, grimy, mucky, muddy, stained, smeared, smudged, disheveled, scruffy, unkempt, rumpled, matted, tousled. **2 untidy,** disordered, in a muddle, chaotic, confused, disorganized, in disarray, cluttered; informal like a bomb's hit it. **3** *a messy legal battle* **complex,** tangled, confused, convoluted, unpleasant, nasty, bitter, acrimonious.
> – ANTONYMS clean, tidy.

– DERIVATIVES **mess·i·ly** adverb **mess·i·ness** noun.

WORD TOOLKIT

messy ...	disorderly ...	chaotic ...
hair	manner	scene
divorce	fashion	traffic
bedroom	movements	life
handwriting	crowd	event
eater	behavior	lifestyle
house	conduct	atmosphere

mes·ti·zo /me'stēzō/ ▶ noun (pl. **mestizos**; fem. **mestiza** /mə'stēzə/, pl. **mestizas**) a Latin American of mixed race, especially one of Spanish and American Indian parentage.
– ORIGIN Spanish, 'mixed.'

met /met/ past and past participle of **MEET**[1].

met. ▶ abbreviation **1** meteorology. **2** metropolitan.

meta- (also **met-** before a vowel or h) ▶ combining form **1** referring to a change of position or condition: *metamorphosis*. **2** referring to position behind, after, or beyond: *metacarpus*. **3** referring to something of a higher or second-order kind: *metalanguage*.
– ORIGIN from Greek *meta* 'with, across, after.'

me·tab·o·lism /mə'tabə,lizəm/ ▶ noun the chemical processes in a living organism by which food is used for tissue growth or energy production.
– DERIVATIVES **met·a·bol·ic** /'metə'bälik/ adjective.
– ORIGIN from Greek *metabolē* 'change.'

me·tab·o·lite /mə'tabə,līt/ ▶ noun a substance formed in or necessary for metabolism.

me·tab·o·lize /mə'tabə,līz/ ▶ verb (of the body or an organ) process a substance by metabolism.

met·a·car·pus /'metə,kärpəs/ ▶ noun (pl. **metacarpi** /-pē, -,pī/) the group of five bones of the hand between the wrist and the fingers.
– DERIVATIVES **met·a·car·pal** adjective & noun.
– ORIGIN Greek *metakarpion*.

met·al /'metl/ ▶ noun **1** a solid material that is typically hard, shiny, and able to be shaped and that can conduct electricity and heat, e.g., iron, copper, and gold. **2** heavy metal or similar rock music.
– ORIGIN Greek *metallon* 'mine, metal.'

met·a·lan·guage /'metə,laNG(g)wij/ ▶ noun a form of language used to describe or analyze another language.

met·al de·tec·tor ▶ noun an electronic device that gives a signal when it is close to metal.

met·al·ize /'metl,īz/ ▶ verb **1** coat something with a layer of metal. **2** make something metallic.

me·tal·lic /mə'talik/ ▶ adjective **1** relating to or resembling metal. **2** (of sound) sharp and ringing.
– DERIVATIVES **me·tal·li·cal·ly** /-ik(ə)lē/ adverb.

met·al·log·ra·phy /,metl'ägrəfē/ ▶ noun the descriptive science of the structure and properties of metals.
– DERIVATIVES **me·tal·lo·graph·ic** /'metl-ə'grafik/ adjective.

met·al·lur·gy /'metl,ərjē/ ▶ noun the scientific study of the properties, production, and purification of metals.
– DERIVATIVES **met·al·lur·gi·cal** adjective **met·al·lur·gist** noun.

met·al·work /'metl,wərk/ ▶ noun **1** the art of making things from metal. **2** objects made from metal.

met·a·mor·phic /'metə'môrfik/ ▶ adjective (of rock) having been changed by heat, pressure, or other natural agencies.
– DERIVATIVES **met·a·mor·phism** /'metə'môr,fizəm/ noun.

met·a·mor·phose /,metə'môr,fōz, -,fōs/ ▶ verb **1** (of an insect or amphibian) undergo metamorphosis. **2** change completely in form or nature.

met·a·mor·pho·sis /,metə'môrfəsəs/ ▶ noun (pl. **metamorphoses** /-fə,sēz/) **1** the transformation of an insect or amphibian from an immature form or larva to an adult form in distinct stages. **2** a change in form or nature.
– ORIGIN Greek, from *metamorphoun* 'transform, change shape.'

met·a·phor /'metə,fôr, -fər/ ▶ noun **1** a figure of speech in which a word or phrase is used of something to which it does not literally apply (e.g., *the long arm of the law*). **2** a thing seen as symbolic of something else.

– SYNONYMS **figure of speech**, image, trope, analogy, comparison, symbol.

– ORIGIN from Greek *metapherein* 'to transfer.'

met·a·phor·i·cal /,metə'fôrikəl/ (also **metaphoric** /,metə'fôrik/) ▶ adjective relating to or making use of metaphors.
– DERIVATIVES **met·a·phor·i·cal·ly** /,metə'fôrik(ə)lē/ adverb.

met·a·phys·ic /,metə'fizik/ ▶ noun a system of metaphysics.

met·a·phys·i·cal /,metə'fizikəl/ ▶ adjective **1** relating to metaphysics. **2** beyond physical matter: *the metaphysical battle between Good and Evil*. **3** referring to a group of 17th-century English poets (in particular John Donne, George Herbert, Andrew Marvell, and Henry Vaughan) known for their complex imagery.
– DERIVATIVES **met·a·phys·i·cal·ly** adverb.

met·a·phys·ics /,metə'fiziks/ ▶ plural noun (usu. treated as sing.) **1** philosophy concerned with abstract ideas such as the nature of existence or of truth and knowledge. **2** abstract theory with no basis in reality.
– DERIVATIVES **met·a·phy·si·cian** /-fə'zisHən/ noun.
– ORIGIN from Greek *ta meta ta phusika* 'the things after the Physics,' referring to the sequence of subjects treated in the works of Aristotle.

me·tas·ta·sis /mə'tastəsəs/ ▶ noun (pl. **metastases** /-,sēz/) the development of secondary tumors elsewhere in the body from the primary site of cancer.
– ORIGIN Greek, 'removal or change.'

met·a·tar·sal /,metə'tärsəl/ ▶ noun any of the bones of the foot.

met·a·tar·sus /,metə'tärsəs/ ▶ noun (pl. **metatarsi** /-tärsē/ /-tärsī/) the group of bones in the foot, between the ankle and the toes.

met·a·zo·an /,metə'zōən/ ▶ noun an animal other than a protozoan or sponge.
– ORIGIN from **META-** + Greek *zōion* 'animal.'

mete /mēt/ ▶ verb (**mete something out**) deal out justice, punishment, etc., to someone.
– ORIGIN Old English, 'measure.'

me·te·or /'mētēər, -ē,ôr/ ▶ noun a small body of matter from outer space that glows as a result of friction with the earth's atmosphere and appears as a shooting star.
– ORIGIN from Greek *meteōros* 'lofty.'

me·te·or·ic /,mētē'ôrik/ ▶ adjective **1** relating to meteors or meteorites. **2** (of change or development) very rapid: *her meteoric rise to the top of her profession*.

me·te·or·ite /'mētēə,rīt/ ▶ noun a piece of rock or metal that has fallen to the earth from space.

me·te·or·oid /'mētēə,roid/ ▶ noun a small body that would become a meteor if it entered the earth's atmosphere.

me·te·or·ol·o·gy /,mētēə'räləjē/ ▶ noun the study of atmospheric processes and conditions, especially for weather forecasting.
– DERIVATIVES **me·te·or·o·log·i·cal** /-rə'läjikəl/ adjective **me·te·or·ol·o·gist** noun.

me·ter[1] /'mētər/ ▶ noun a device that measures and records the quantity, degree, or rate of something. ▶ verb measure the quantity, degree, or rate of something with a meter.
– ORIGIN from **METE**.

me·ter² /ˈmētər/ (Brit. **metre**) ▸ **noun** the basic unit of length in the metric system, equal to 100 centimeters (approx. 39.37 inches).
– ORIGIN from Greek *metron* 'measure.'

me·ter³ (Brit. **metre**) ▸ **noun 1** the rhythm of a piece of poetry, determined by the number and length of feet in a line. **2** the basic pulse and rhythm of a piece of music.

-meter ▸ **combining form 1** in names of measuring instruments: *thermometer*. **2** in nouns referring to lines of poetry with a specified number of metrical feet: *hexameter*.
– ORIGIN from Greek *metron* 'measure.'

meth /meTH/ ▸ **noun** informal **1** short for **CRYSTAL METH**. **2** short for **METHADONE**.

meth·a·done /ˈmeTHəˌdōn/ ▸ **noun** a powerful painkiller, used as a substitute for morphine and heroin in the treatment of addiction.
– ORIGIN from its chemical name.

meth·am·phet·a·mine /ˌmeTHəmˈfetəˌmēn, -min/ ▸ **noun** a drug related to amphetamine, used illegally as a stimulant.

meth·ane /ˈmeTHˌān/ ▸ **noun** a colorless, odorless flammable gas that is the main constituent of natural gas.
– ORIGIN from **METHYL**.

meth·a·nol /ˈmeTHəˌnôl, -ˌnōl/ ▸ **noun** a poisonous flammable alcohol, used to make methylated spirit.

meth·e·drine /ˈmeTHəˌdrēn, -drin/ ▸ **noun** trademark another term for **METHAMPHETAMINE**.

me·thinks /miˈTHiNGks/ ▸ **verb** (past **methought**) old use or humorous it seems to me.
– ORIGIN Old English.

meth·od /ˈmeTHəd/ ▸ **noun 1** a way of doing something. **2** the quality of being well organized and systematic in one's thinking and behavior.

> – SYNONYMS **1 procedure,** technique, system, practice, routine, modus operandi, process, strategy, tactic, approach, way, manner, mode. **2** *there's no method in his approach* **order,** organization, structure, form, system, logic, planning, design, consistency.
> – ANTONYMS disorder.

– ORIGIN Greek *methodos* 'pursuit of knowledge.'

meth·od act·ing ▸ **noun** an acting technique in which an actor tries to identify completely with a character's emotions.

me·thod·i·cal /məˈTHädikəl/ (also **methodic**) ▸ **adjective** well organized and systematic.

> – SYNONYMS **orderly,** well ordered, well organized, well planned, efficient, businesslike, systematic, structured, logical, disciplined, consistent, scientific.

– DERIVATIVES **me·thod·i·cal·ly** /-ik(ə)lē/ adverb.

Meth·od·ist /ˈmeTHədəst/ ▸ **noun** a member of a Christian Protestant denomination originating in the 18th century and based on the ideas of Charles and John Wesley. ▸ **adjective** relating to Methodists or their beliefs.
– DERIVATIVES **Meth·od·ism** /-ˌdizəm/ noun.
– ORIGIN probably from the idea of following a specified 'method' of Bible study.

meth·od·ol·o·gy /ˌmeTHəˈdäləjē/ ▸ **noun** (pl. **methodologies**) a system of methods used in a particular activity or area of study.
– DERIVATIVES **meth·od·o·log·i·cal** /-dəˈläjikəl/ adjective.

me·thought /miˈTHôt/ past of **METHINKS**.

Me·thu·se·lah /məˈTH(y)o͞oz(ə)lə/ ▸ **noun 1** humorous a very old person. **2** (**methuselah**) a wine bottle of eight times the standard size.
– ORIGIN named after the biblical patriarch *Methuselah*, said to have lived for 969 years (Book of Genesis, chapter 5).

meth·yl /ˈmeTHəl/ ▸ **noun** Chemistry the radical $-CH_3$, derived from methane.
– ORIGIN from Greek *methu* 'wine' + *hulē* 'wood.'

meth·yl al·co·hol ▸ **noun** methanol.

meth·yl·ate /ˈmeTHəˌlāt/ ▸ **verb 1** mix or impregnate something with methanol or methylated spirit. **2** Chemistry introduce a methyl group into a molecule or compound.
– DERIVATIVES **meth·yl·a·tion** /ˌmeTHəˈlāSHən/ noun.

me·tic·u·lous /məˈtikyələs/ ▸ **adjective** very careful and precise.

> – SYNONYMS **careful,** conscientious, diligent, scrupulous, punctilious, painstaking, thorough, studious, rigorous, detailed, perfectionist, fastidious.
> – ANTONYMS careless.

– DERIVATIVES **me·tic·u·lous·ly** adverb **me·tic·u·lous·ness** noun.
– ORIGIN Latin *meticulosus* 'fearful.'

mé·tier /meˈtyā, ˈmeˌtyā/ ▸ **noun 1** a profession or occupation. **2** an occupation or activity that someone is good at.
– ORIGIN French.

met·o·nym /ˈmetəˌnim/ ▸ **noun** a word or phrase used as a substitute for something with which it is closely associated, e.g., *Washington* for the US government.
– DERIVATIVES **met·o·nym·ic** /ˌmetəˈnimik/ adjective **me·ton·y·my** /məˈtänəmē/ noun.
– ORIGIN Greek *metōnumia* 'change of name.'

me-too ▸ **adjective** informal **1** (of a product) designed to imitate or compete with another that has already been successful: *me-too drugs*. **2** (of a person or course of action) adopting the views or policies of another person, especially a competitor.

me·tre /ˈmētər/ ▸ **noun** British spelling of **METER²**, **METER³**.

met·ric /ˈmetrik/ ▸ **adjective** relating to or using the metric system.

met·ri·cal /ˈmetrikəl/ ▸ **adjective 1** relating to or composed in poetic meter. **2** relating to or involving measurement.
– DERIVATIVES **met·ri·cal·ly** /-ik(ə)lē/ adverb.

met·ric sys·tem ▸ **noun** the decimal measuring system based on the meter, liter, and gram as units of length, capacity, and weight or mass.

met·ric ton (also **tonne**) ▸ **noun** a unit of weight equal to 1,000 kilograms (2,205 lb).

met·ro /ˈmetrō/ ▸ **noun** (pl. **metros**) an underground railroad system in a city, especially Paris.
– ORIGIN French, from *Chemin de Fer Métropolitain* 'Metropolitan Railway.'

met·ro·nome /ˈmetrəˌnōm/ ▸ **noun** a musicians' device that marks time at a selected rate by giving a regular tick.
– DERIVATIVES **met·ro·nom·ic** /ˌmetrəˈnämik/ adjective.
– ORIGIN from Greek *metron* 'measure' + *nomos* 'law.'

me·trop·o·lis /mə'träp(ə)ləs/ ▶ **noun** the main city of a country or region.
– ORIGIN Greek, from *mētēr* 'mother' + *polis* 'city.'

met·ro·pol·i·tan /ˌmetrə'pälitn/ ▶ **adjective 1** relating to a large or capital city. **2** relating to the parent country of a colony. **3** Christian Church relating to a metropolitan. ▶ **noun 1** a person living in a large or capital city. **2** Christian Church a bishop having authority over the bishops of a province.

met·ro·sex·ual /ˌmetrō'sekSHōōəl/ ▶ **noun** informal a heterosexual urban man who enjoys shopping, fashion, and similar interests usually associated with women or homosexual men.
– ORIGIN from **METROPOLITAN** and **HETEROSEXUAL**.

met·tle /'metl/ ▶ **noun** spirit and strength in the face of difficulty.
– PHRASES **be on one's mettle** be ready to show one's ability or courage.
– ORIGIN variant spelling of **METAL**.

meu·nière /mœn'yer/ ▶ **adjective** (after a noun) cooked or served in lightly browned butter with lemon juice and parsley: *sole meunière.*
– ORIGIN from French *à la meunière* 'in the manner of a miller's wife.'

mew /myōō/ ▶ **verb** (of a cat or gull) make a characteristic high-pitched crying noise. ▶ **noun** a high-pitched crying noise.
– ORIGIN imitating the sound.

mewl /myōōl/ ▶ **verb 1** cry feebly. **2** make a high-pitched crying noise.
– ORIGIN imitating the sound.

mews /myōōz/ ▶ **noun** (pl. same) Brit. a row of houses or apartments converted from stables in a small street or square.

Mex·i·can /'meksəkən/ ▶ **noun** a person from Mexico. ▶ **adjective** relating to Mexico.

me·ze /me'ze/ (also **mezze**) ▶ **noun** (pl. same or **mezes**) (in Turkish, Greek, and Middle Eastern cooking) a selection of hot and cold hors d'oeuvres.
– ORIGIN Turkish, 'appetizer.'

me·zu·zah /mə'zōōzə/ ▶ **noun** a parchment inscribed with religious texts and attached in a case to the doorpost of a Jewish house as a sign of faith.
– ORIGIN from Hebrew *mĕzūzāh* 'doorpost.'

mez·za·nine /'mezəˌnēn, ˌmezə'nēn/ ▶ **noun 1** a low story between two others, typically between the ground and second floors of a building. **2** the lowest balcony of a theater or the front rows of the balcony.
– ORIGIN from Italian *mezzano* 'middle.'

mez·zo /'metsō, 'medzō/ (also **mezzo-soprano**) ▶ **noun** (pl. **mezzos**) a female singer with a voice pitched between soprano and contralto.
– ORIGIN Italian, 'half, middle.'

mez·zo·tint /'metsōˌtint, 'medzō-/ ▶ **noun** a print made from an engraved metal plate, the surface of which has been scraped and polished to give areas of shade and light respectively.
– ORIGIN from Italian *mezzo* 'half' + *tinto* 'tint.'

MF ▶ **abbreviation** medium frequency.

mfg. ▶ **abbreviation** manufacturing.

mfr. ▶ **abbreviation** manufacturer.

Mg ▶ **symbol** the chemical element magnesium.

mg ▶ **abbreviation** milligram(s).

Mgr. ▶ **abbreviation 1** (**mgr.**) manager. **2** Monseigneur. **3** Monsignor.

MHR ▶ **abbreviation** (in the US and Australia) Member of the House of Representatives.

MHz ▶ **abbreviation** megahertz.

MI ▶ **abbreviation** Michigan.

mi /mē/ ▶ **noun** Music the third note of a major scale, coming after 're' and before 'fa'.
– ORIGIN the first syllable of *mira*, in a Latin hymn.

mi. ▶ **abbreviation** mile(s).

MIA ▶ **abbreviation** missing in action.

mi·as·ma /mī'azmə, mē-/ ▶ **noun** literary **1** an unpleasant or unhealthy smell or vapor. **2** an oppressive or unpleasant atmosphere: *a miasma of despair.*
– ORIGIN Greek, 'defilement.'

mic /mīk/ ▶ **noun** informal a microphone.

mi·ca /'mīkə/ ▶ **noun** a mineral found as minute shiny scales in granite and other rocks.
– ORIGIN Latin, 'crumb.'

mice /mīs/ plural of **MOUSE**.

Mich·ael·mas /'mikəlməs/ ▶ **noun** the day of the Christian festival of St. Michael, September 29.
– ORIGIN Old English, 'Saint Michael's Mass.'

mick·ey /'mikē/ ▶ **noun** informal a Mickey Finn, or the drug used to make a Mickey Finn: *did you slip him a mickey?*

Mick·ey Finn /'mikē 'fin/ ▶ **noun** informal a drink to which a drug has been secretly added.
– ORIGIN probably the name of a notorious Chicago bar owner.

Mick·ey Mouse /ˌmikē 'mous/ ▶ **adjective** informal trivial or not of high quality.
– ORIGIN from the name of the character created by the cartoonist Walt Disney.

Mic·mac /'mikˌmak/ ▶ **noun** (pl. same or **Micmacs**) a member of an American Indian people living in the Maritime Provinces of Canada.
– ORIGIN the Micmacs' name for themselves.

mi·cro /'mīkrō/ ▶ **noun** (pl. **micros**) a microcomputer or microprocessor. ▶ **adjective** extremely small or small-scale.

micro- ▶ **combining form 1** very small or of reduced size: *microchip.* **2** referring to a factor of one millionth (10^{-6}): *microfarad.*
– ORIGIN Greek *mikros* 'small.'

mi·cro·a·nal·y·sis /ˌmīkrōə'naləsəs/ ▶ **noun** the analysis of chemical compounds using a sample of a few milligrams.

mi·crobe /'mīˌkrōb/ ▶ **noun** a microorganism, especially a bacterium causing disease.
– DERIVATIVES **mi·cro·bi·al** /mī'krōbēəl/ adjective.
– ORIGIN from Greek *mikros* 'small' + *bios* 'life.'

mi·cro·bi·ol·o·gy /ˌmīkrōˌbī'äləjē/ ▶ **noun** the scientific study of microorganisms.

mi·cro·brew·er·y /ˌmīkrō'brōōərē/ ▶ **noun** (pl. **microbreweries**) a brewery producing limited quantities of beer.
– DERIVATIVES **mi·cro·brew·er** noun.

mi·cro·burst /'mīkrōˌbərst/ ▶ **noun** a sudden, powerful, localized downdraft.

mi·cro·chip /ˈmīkrōˌchip/ ▶ **noun** a tiny wafer of silicon or similar material used to make an integrated circuit. ▶ **verb** (**microchips, microchipping, microchipped**) implant a microchip under the skin of a cat or dog so that they can be identified.

mi·cro·cir·cuit /ˈmīkrōˌsərkət/ ▶ **noun** a minute electric circuit, especially an integrated circuit.

mi·cro·cli·mate /ˈmīkrōˌklīmət/ ▶ **noun** the climate of a very small or restricted area.

mi·cro·code /ˈmīkrəˌkōd/ ▶ **noun** a very low-level set of instructions controlling the operation of a computer.

mi·cro·com·pu·ter /ˈmīkrōkəmˌpyo͞otər/ ▶ **noun** a small computer with a microprocessor as its central processor.

mi·cro·cosm /ˈmīkrəˌkäzəm/ ▶ **noun** a thing seen as a miniature representation of something much larger: *the city's population is a microcosm of modern Malaysia*.
– DERIVATIVES **mi·cro·cos·mic** /ˌmīkrəˈkäzmik/ adjective.
– ORIGIN from Greek *mikros kosmos* 'little world.'

mi·cro·derm·a·bra·sion /ˌmīkrōˌdərməˈbrāzhən/ ▶ **noun** a cosmetic treatment in which the face is sprayed with granular crystals to remove dead skin cells.

mi·cro·dot /ˈmīkrəˌdät/ ▶ **noun** **1** a photograph, especially of a printed document, reduced to a very small size. **2** informal a tiny tablet of LSD.

mi·cro·ec·o·nom·ics /ˌmīkrōˌekəˈnämiks, -ˌēkə-/ ▶ **plural noun** (treated as sing.) the part of economics concerned with single factors and the effects of individual decisions.

mi·cro·e·lec·tron·ics /ˌmīkrōiˌlekˈträniks/ ▶ **plural noun** (usu. treated as sing.) the design, manufacture, and use of microchips and microcircuits.

mi·cro·fi·ber /ˈmīkrōˌfībər/ ▶ **noun** a very fine synthetic yarn.

mi·cro·fiche /ˈmīkrəˌfēsh/ ▶ **noun** a flat piece of film containing greatly reduced photographs of the pages of a newspaper, catalog, or other document.
– ORIGIN from **MICRO-** + French *fiche* 'slip of paper.'

mi·cro·film /ˈmīkrəˌfilm/ ▶ **noun** a length of film containing greatly reduced photographs of a newspaper, catalog, or other document.

mi·cro·gram /ˈmīkrəˌgram/ ▶ **noun** one millionth of a gram.

mi·cro·graph /ˈmīkrəˌgraf/ ▶ **noun** a photograph taken using a microscope.

mi·cro·grav·i·ty /ˌmīkrōˈgravətē/ ▶ **noun** very weak gravity, as in an orbiting spacecraft.

mi·cro·li·ter /ˌmīkrōˈlētər/ ▶ **noun** one millionth of a liter.

mi·cro·man·age /ˌmīkrōˈmanij/ ▶ **verb** control every part, however small, of an enterprise or activity.
– DERIVATIVES **mi·cro·man·age·ment** noun.

mi·crom·e·ter /mīˈkrämətər/ ▶ **noun** **1** a gauge that measures small distances or thicknesses. **2** one millionth of a meter.

mi·cron /ˈmīˌkrän/ ▶ **noun** one millionth of a meter.

Mi·cro·ne·sian /ˌmīkrəˈnēzhən/ ▶ **noun** a person from Micronesia, an island group in the western Pacific. ▶ **adjective** relating to Micronesia.

mi·cro·nu·tri·ent /ˌmīkrōˈn(y)o͞otrēənt/ ▶ **noun** a chemical element or substance required in trace amounts by living things.

mi·cro·or·gan·ism /ˌmīkrōˈôrgəˌnizəm/ ▶ **noun** a microscopic organism, especially a bacterium or virus.

mi·cro·pay·ment /ˈmīkrōˌpāmənt/ ▶ **noun** a very small payment made each time a user accesses an Internet page or service.

mi·cro·phone /ˈmīkrəˌfōn/ ▶ **noun** a device for converting sound waves into electrical energy, which can then be amplified, transmitted, or recorded.

mi·cro·proc·es·sor /ˌmīkrōˈpräsesər, -ˈprōˌsesər/ ▶ **noun** an integrated circuit that can perform the role of a central processing unit of a computer.

mi·cro·scope /ˈmīkrəˌskōp/ ▶ **noun** an instrument used in scientific study for magnifying very small objects.
– ORIGIN from **MICRO-** + *skopein* 'look at.'

mi·cro·scop·ic /ˌmīkrəˈskäpik/ ▶ **adjective** **1** so small as to be visible only with a microscope. **2** very small. **3** relating to a microscope.
– DERIVATIVES **mi·cro·scop·i·cal·ly** /-ik(ə)lē/ adverb.

mi·cros·co·py /mīˈkräskəpē/ ▶ **noun** the use of a microscope.

mi·cro·sec·ond /ˈmīkrōˌsekənd/ ▶ **noun** one millionth of a second.

mi·cro·struc·ture /ˌmīkrōˈstrəkchər/ ▶ **noun** the fine structure in a material that can be made visible and examined with a microscope.

mi·cro·sur·ger·y /ˌmīkrōˈsərjərē/ ▶ **noun** intricate surgery performed using very small instruments and a microscope.

mi·cro·wave /ˈmīkrəˌwāv/ ▶ **noun** **1** an electromagnetic wave with a wavelength in the range 0.001–0.3 m, shorter than that of a normal radio wave but longer than those of infrared radiation. **2** (also **microwave oven**) an oven that uses microwaves to cook or heat food. ▶ **verb** cook food in a microwave oven.

mic·tu·rate /ˈmikchəˌrāt/ ▶ **verb** formal urinate.
– DERIVATIVES **mic·tu·ri·tion** /ˌmikchəˈrishən/ noun.
– ORIGIN Latin *micturire*.

mid /mid/ ▶ **adjective** relating to or in the middle part of a range. ▶ **preposition** literary in the middle of; amid.

mid- ▶ **combining form** **1** referring to the middle of: *midsection*. **2** in the middle; medium; half: *midway*.
– ORIGIN Old English.

mid·air /ˈmidˈe(ə)r/ ▶ **noun** a part of the air above ground level: *he caught Murray's keys in midair*.

Mi·das touch /ˈmīdəs/ ▶ **noun** the ability to make money out of anything one does.
– ORIGIN from *Midas*, king of Phrygia, who in Greek mythology was given the power to turn everything he touched into gold.

mid·brain /ˈmidˌbrān/ ▶ **noun** a small central part of the brainstem, developing from the middle of the embryonic brain.

mid·day /ˈmidˈdā/ ▶ **noun** the middle of the day; noon.

– SYNONYMS **noon**, twelve noon, high noon, noonday.
– ANTONYMS midnight.

mid·den /ˈmidn/ ▶ **noun** a dunghill or refuse heap.
– ORIGIN Scandinavian.

mid·dle /ˈmidl/ ▶ **adjective** **1** at an equal distance from the edges or ends of something; central. **2** intermediate in rank, quality, or ability.

– SYNONYMS **central,** mid, mean, medium, median, midway, halfway, equidistant.

▶ **noun 1** a middle point or position. **2** informal a person's waist and stomach.

– SYNONYMS **1 center,** midpoint, halfway point, dead center, hub, eye, heart, core, kernel. **2 midriff,** waist, belly, stomach; informal tummy.
– ANTONYMS edge.

– ORIGIN Old English.

mid·dle age ▶ **noun** the period after early adulthood and before old age, about 45 to 60.
– DERIVATIVES **mid·dle-aged** adjective.

Mid·dle Ag·es ▶ **plural noun** the period of European history from the fall of the Roman Empire in the West (5th century) to the fall of Constantinople (1453), or, more narrowly, from *c.*1000 to 1453.

Mid·dle A·mer·i·ca ▶ **noun** the conservative middle classes of the US, characterized as living in the Midwest.

mid·dle·brow /ˈmidlˈbrou/ ▶ **adjective** informal needing or involving only a moderate level of intellectual effort.

mid·dle C ▶ **noun** the C near the middle of the piano keyboard, written on the first ledger line below the treble staff or the first ledger line above the bass staff.

mid·dle class ▶ **noun** the social group made up of business and professional people, between the upper and working classes.

mid·dle dis·tance ▶ **noun 1** the part of a real or painted landscape between the foreground and the background. **2** Athletics a race distance between 800 and 5,000 meters.

mid·dle ear ▶ **noun** the air-filled central cavity of the ear, behind the eardrum.

Mid·dle East ▶ **noun** an area of SW Asia and northern Africa, stretching from the Mediterranean to Pakistan, in particular Iran, Iraq, Israel, Jordan, Lebanon, and Syria.
– DERIVATIVES **Mid·dle East·ern** adjective.

Mid·dle Eng·lish ▶ **noun** the English language from *c.*1150 to *c.*1470.

mid·dle ground ▶ **noun** an area of compromise or possible agreement between two opposing positions or groups.

mid·dle·man /ˈmidlˌman/ ▶ **noun** (pl. **middlemen**) **1** a person who buys goods from producers and sells them to retailers or consumers. **2** a person who arranges business or political deals between other people.

mid·dle name ▶ **noun** a person's name placed after the first name and before the surname.

mid·dle-of-the-road ▶ **adjective 1** (of views) not extreme; moderate. **2** (of music) popular with a wide range of people but rather bland or unadventurous.

mid·dle school ▶ **noun** a school for children in the sixth, seventh, and eighth grades.

mid·dle·weight /ˈmidlˌwāt/ ▶ **noun** a weight in boxing and other sports intermediate between welterweight and light heavyweight.

mid·dling /ˈmidliNG, ˈmidlin/ ▶ **adjective** moderate or average. ▶ **adverb** informal fairly or moderately.

mid·field /ˈmidˌfēld, midˈfēld/ ▶ **noun 1** (chiefly in soccer) the central part of the field. **2** the players who play in a central position between attack and defense.
– DERIVATIVES **mid·field·er** noun.

midge /mij/ ▶ **noun** a small two-winged fly that forms swarms near water, of which many kinds feed on blood.
– ORIGIN Old English.

mid·get /ˈmijit/ ▶ **noun** a very small person or thing. ▶ **adjective** very small: *a midget submarine.*

MIDI /ˈmidē/ ▶ **noun** a standard for interconnecting electronic musical instruments and computers.
– ORIGIN from the initial letters of *musical instrument digital interface.*

mid·i /ˈmidē/ ▶ **noun** (pl. **midis**) a woman's calf-length skirt, dress, or coat.

midi- ▶ **combining form** of medium size or length.

mid·land /ˈmidlənd/ ▶ **noun 1** the middle part of a country. **2** (**the Midlands**) the inland counties of central England. ▶ **adjective** (also **midlands**) relating to or in the middle part of a country or the Midlands.
– DERIVATIVES **mid·land·er** noun.

mid·life /midˈlīf/ ▶ **noun** the central period of a person's life, between around 45 and 60 years old.

mid·life cri·sis ▶ **noun** an emotional crisis of identity and self-confidence that can occur in early middle age.

mid·line /ˈmidˌlīn/ ▶ **noun** a median line or plane of bilateral symmetry, especially in an organism. ▶ **adjective** in the middle range of a product line, in terms of expense or features.

mid·night /ˈmidˌnīt/ ▶ **noun** twelve o'clock at night; the middle of the night.

mid·night blue ▶ **noun** a very dark blue.

mid·night sun ▶ **noun** the sun when seen at midnight during the summer within either the Arctic or Antarctic Circle.

mid·point /ˈmidˌpoint/ ▶ **noun 1** a point halfway through a period or process. **2** the exact middle point of something.

mid·rib /ˈmidˌrib/ ▶ **noun** a large strengthened vein running down the center of a leaf.

mid·riff /ˈmidˌrif/ ▶ **noun** the front of the body between the chest and the waist.
– ORIGIN Old English.

mid·sec·tion /ˈmidˌsekSHən/ ▶ **noun** the middle part of something.

mid·ship /ˈmidˌSHip/ ▶ **noun** the middle part of a ship or boat.

mid·ship·man /ˈmidˌSHipmən, midˈSHip-/ ▶ **noun** (pl. **midshipmen**) **1** a cadet in the US Navy. **2** a rank of officer in the British Royal Navy, above cadet and below sub lieutenant.

mid·ships /ˈmidˌSHips/ ▶ **adverb & adjective** another term for **AMIDSHIPS**.

midst /midst, mitst/ old use or literary ▶ **preposition** in the middle of. ▶ **noun** the middle point or part.
– PHRASES **in our** (or **your** or **their**) **midst** among us (or you or them).

mid·stream /ˈmidˈstrēm/ ▶ **noun** the middle of a stream or river.
– PHRASES **in midstream** in the middle of doing something.

mid·sum·mer /ˈmidˈsəmər/ ▶ **noun 1** the middle part of summer. **2** the summer solstice.

mid·term /ˈmidˌtərm/ ▶ **noun** the middle of a period of office, an academic term, or a pregnancy.

mid·town /ˈmid,toun/ ▶ **noun** the central part of a city between the downtown and uptown areas.

mid·way /ˈmid,wā, -ˈwā/ ▶ **adverb & adjective** in or toward the middle.

mid·week /ˈmid,wēk/ ▶ **noun** the middle of the week. ▶ **adjective & adverb** in the middle of the week.

Mid·west /ˈmidˈwest/ ▶ **noun** the region of northern states of the US from Ohio west to the Rocky Mountains.
– DERIVATIVES **Mid·west·ern** adjective **Mid·west·ern·er** noun.

mid·wife /ˈmid,wīf/ ▶ **noun** (pl. **midwives** /ˈmid,wīvz/) a person who is trained to help women in childbirth.
– DERIVATIVES **mid·wife·ry** /midˈwīf(ə)rē/ noun.
– ORIGIN probably from former *mid* 'with' + **WIFE** (in the sense 'woman').

mid·win·ter /ˈmidˈwintər/ ▶ **noun 1** the middle part of winter. **2** the winter solstice.

mien /mēn/ ▶ **noun** a person's look or manner.
– ORIGIN probably from French *mine* 'expression.'

mi·fep·ri·stone /,mifəˈpris,tōn/ ▶ **noun** a synthetic steroid that inhibits the action of progesterone, given orally in early pregnancy to induce abortion.

miffed /mifd/ ▶ **adjective** informal offended or irritated.
– ORIGIN uncertain.

might[1] /mīt/ ▶ **modal verb** (3rd sing. present **might**) past of **MAY**. **1** used to express possibility or make a suggestion. **2** used politely or tentatively in questions and requests.

might[2] ▶ **noun** great power or strength.

> – SYNONYMS **strength,** force, forcefulness, power, vigor, energy, brawn.

– PHRASES **with all one's might** using all one's power or strength.
– ORIGIN Old English.

might·n't /ˈmītnt/ ▶ **contraction** might not.

might·y /ˈmītē/ ▶ **adjective** (**mightier, mightiest**) **1** very powerful or strong. **2** informal very large.

> – SYNONYMS **powerful,** forceful, strong, hard, heavy, violent, vigorous, hefty.
> – ANTONYMS feeble.

▶ **adverb** informal extremely.
– DERIVATIVES **might·i·ly** adverb **might·i·ness** noun.

mi·gnon·ette /,minyəˈnet/ ▶ **noun** a plant with spikes of small fragrant greenish flowers.
– ORIGIN French.

mi·graine /ˈmī,grān/ ▶ **noun** a throbbing headache, typically affecting one side of the head and often accompanied by nausea and disturbed vision.
– ORIGIN French, from Greek *hēmi-* 'half' + *kranion* 'skull.'

mi·grant /ˈmīgrənt/ ▶ **noun 1** a person who moves from one place to another to find work. **2** an animal that migrates.

> – SYNONYMS **immigrant, emigrant,** nomad, itinerant, traveler, transient, wanderer, drifter.

▶ **adjective** tending to migrate or having migrated: *migrant workers.*

> – SYNONYMS **traveling,** wandering, drifting, nomadic, itinerant, transient.

mi·grate /ˈmī,grāt/ ▶ **verb 1** (of an animal) move from one habitat to another according to the seasons. **2** move to settle in a new area in order to find work. **3** Computing change or transfer from one system to another.
– DERIVATIVES **mi·gra·tion** /mīˈgrāsʜən/ noun **mi·gra·to·ry** /ˈmīgrə,tôrē/ adjective.
– ORIGIN Latin *migrare* 'to move, shift.'

mih·rab /ˈmi(ə)rəb/ ▶ **noun** a niche in the wall of a mosque at the point nearest to Mecca, toward which the congregation faces to pray.
– ORIGIN Arabic, 'place for prayer.'

mi·ka·do /miˈkädō/ ▶ **noun** historical a title given to the emperor of Japan.
– ORIGIN Japanese.

mike /mīk/ ▶ **noun** informal a microphone.

mil /mil/ ▶ **abbreviation** informal millions.

mi·la·dy /məˈlādē, mī-/ ▶ **noun** historical or humorous used to address or refer to an English noblewoman.

mil·age ▶ **noun** variant spelling of **MILEAGE**.

milch /milk, milcʜ/ ▶ **adjective** (of a domestic mammal) giving or kept for milk.
– ORIGIN from Old English *-milce* in *thrimilce* 'May' (when cows could be milked three times a day).

milch cow ▶ **noun** a source of easy profit.

mild /mīld/ ▶ **adjective 1** not severe, harsh, or extreme: *mild criticism.* **2** (of weather) fairly warm. **3** not sharp or strong in flavor. **4** gentle and calm: *his mild manner.*

> – SYNONYMS **1 gentle,** tender, soft, sympathetic, peaceable, good-natured, quiet, placid, docile, meek. **2** *a mild punishment* **lenient,** light. **3 warm,** balmy, temperate, clement. **4 bland,** tasteless, insipid.
> – ANTONYMS harsh, strong, severe.

▶ **noun** Brit. a kind of dark beer not strongly flavored with hops.
– DERIVATIVES **mild·ly** adverb **mild·ness** noun.
– ORIGIN Old English.

mil·dew /ˈmil,d(y)o͞o/ ▶ **noun** a coating of minute fungi that grows on plants or on materials such as paper or leather when they are damp.
– DERIVATIVES **mil·dewed** adjective.
– ORIGIN Old English.

mild steel ▶ **noun** strong, tough steel containing a small percentage of carbon.

mile /mīl/ ▶ **noun 1** (also **statute mile**) a unit of length equal to 5,280 feet (approximately 1.609 kilometers). **2** (**miles**) informal a very long way. ▶ **adverb** (**miles**) informal by a great amount or a long way: *the second tape is miles better.*
– PHRASES **be miles away** informal be lost in thought. **go the extra mile** try particularly hard to achieve something. **stand** (or **stick**) **out a mile** informal be very obvious or noticeable.
– ORIGIN Latin *milia*, plural of *mille* 'thousand'; a Roman 'mile' consisted of 1,000 paces (approximately 1,620 yards).

mile·age /ˈmīlij/ (also **milage**) ▶ **noun 1** a number of miles traveled or covered. **2** informal actual or potential benefit or advantage: *she got plenty of mileage out of the rumor.*

mile·post /ˈmīl,pōst/ ▶ **noun 1** a milestone. **2** a post one mile from the finishing post of a race.

mil·er /ˈmīlər/ ▶ **noun** informal a person or horse trained to run races of a mile.

mile·stone /ˈmīl,stōn/ ▶ **noun 1** a stone set up beside a road to mark the distance in miles to a particular place. **2** an event marking a significant new development or stage.

mil·foil /'mil,foil/ ▶ **noun** **1** another term for **YARROW**. **2** a water plant with whorls of submerged leaves.
– ORIGIN from Latin *mille* 'thousand' + *folium* 'leaf.'

mi·lieu /mil'yo͞o, -'yə(r)/ ▶ **noun** (pl. **milieux** pronunc. same, or **milieus** /mil'yo͞oz, -'yə(r)z/) a person's social environment: *his working-class milieu*.
– ORIGIN French, from *mi* 'mid' + *lieu* 'place.'

mil·i·tant /'milətənt/ ▶ **adjective** prepared to take aggressive action in support of a political or social cause.

– SYNONYMS **hard-line,** extreme, extremist, committed, zealous, fanatical, radical.

▶ **noun** a militant person.

– SYNONYMS **activist,** extremist, partisan, radical, zealot.

– DERIVATIVES **mil·i·tan·cy** noun **mil·i·tant·ly** adverb.

mil·i·tar·i·a /,mili'te(ə)rēə/ ▶ **plural noun** military articles of historical interest.

mil·i·ta·rism /'milətə,rizəm/ ▶ **noun** the belief that a country should maintain and readily use strong armed forces.
– DERIVATIVES **mil·i·ta·rist** noun & adjective **mil·i·ta·ris·tic** /,milətə'ristik/ adjective.

mil·i·ta·rize /'milətə,rīz/ ▶ **verb** (often as adj. **militarized**) **1** supply a place with soldiers and other military resources. **2** make something military in nature or similar to an army: *militarized police forces*.
– DERIVATIVES **mil·i·ta·ri·za·tion** /,milətərə'zāsʜən/ noun.

mil·i·tar·y /'milə,terē/ ▶ **adjective** relating to or characteristic of soldiers or armed forces.

– SYNONYMS **fighting,** service, army, armed, defense, martial.
– ANTONYMS civilian.

▶ **noun** (**the military**) the armed forces of a country.

– SYNONYMS **(armed) forces,** services, militia, army, navy, air force, marines.

– DERIVATIVES **mil·i·tar·i·ly** /,milə'te(ə)rəlē/ adverb.
– ORIGIN Latin *militaris*, from *miles* 'soldier.'

mil·i·tar·y hon·ors ▶ **plural noun** ceremonies performed by troops as a mark of respect at the burial of a member of the armed forces.

mil·i·tar·y-in·dus·tri·al com·plex ▶ **noun** a country's military establishment and arms industries, regarded as a strong influence on government.

mil·i·tar·y po·lice ▶ **noun** a military body responsible for policing and disciplinary duties in the armed forces.

mil·i·tate /'milə,tāt/ ▶ **verb** (**militate against**) be a powerful or decisive factor in preventing something: *these differences will militate against the two communities coming together*.

– SYNONYMS **work against,** hinder, discourage, be prejudicial to, be detrimental to.

– ORIGIN Latin *militare* 'wage war.'

USAGE

On the confusion between **militate** and **mitigate**, see the note at **MITIGATE**.

mi·li·tia /mə'lisʜə/ ▶ **noun** **1** a military force made up of civilians, used to supplement a regular army in an emergency. **2** a rebel force opposing a regular army.
– DERIVATIVES **mi·li·tia·man** /mə'lisʜəmən/ noun (pl. **militiamen**).
– ORIGIN Latin, 'military service.'

milk /milk/ ▶ **noun** **1** an opaque white fluid produced by female mammals to feed their young. **2** the milk of cows as a food and drink for humans. **3** the milklike juice of certain plants, such as the coconut. ▶ **verb** **1** draw milk from a cow or other animal. **2** exploit or defraud by taking small amounts of money over a period of time: *he had milked his grandmother of all her money*. **3** take full advantage of a situation.

– SYNONYMS **exploit,** take advantage of; informal bleed (dry), squeeze, fleece.

– ORIGIN Old English.

WORD LINKS

lactic *relating to milk*

milk choc·o·late ▶ **noun** solid chocolate that has been made with milk.

milk fe·ver ▶ **noun** an acute illness in cows or other female animals that have just produced young.

milk·maid /'milk,mād/ ▶ **noun** (in the past) a girl or woman who worked in a dairy.

milk·man /'milkmən, -,man/ ▶ **noun** (pl. **milkmen**) a man who delivers milk to houses.

milk run ▶ **noun** a routine, uneventful journey, especially by aircraft.
– ORIGIN RAF slang in World War II for a sortie that was as simple as a milkman's round.

milk·shake /'milk,sʜāk/ ▶ **noun** a cold drink made from milk blended with ice cream and a flavoring such as syrup or fruit.

milk·sop /'milk,säp/ ▶ **noun** a timid and indecisive person.

milk this·tle ▶ **noun** a thistle with a solitary purple flower and glossy leaves, used in herbal medicine.

milk tooth ▶ **noun** a temporary tooth in a child or young mammal.

milk·weed /'milk,wēd/ ▶ **noun** an herbaceous American plant that attracts butterflies and produces a milky sap.

milk·y /'milkē/ ▶ **adjective** (**milkier, milkiest**) **1** containing milk. **2** having a soft white color or clouded appearance.
– DERIVATIVES **milk·i·ly** adverb **milk·i·ness** noun.

Milk·y Way ▶ **noun** the galaxy of which our solar system is a part, visible at night as a faint band of light crossing the sky.

mill[1] /mil/ ▶ **noun** **1** a building equipped with machinery for grinding grain into flour. **2** a device or piece of machinery for grinding solid substances, such as peppercorns. **3** a building fitted with machinery for a manufacturing process: *a steel mill*.

– SYNONYMS **factory,** plant, works, workshop, shop, foundry.

▶ **verb** **1** grind something in a mill. **2** (**mill around/about**) move around in a confused mass. **3** cut or shape metal with a rotating tool. **4** (usu. as adj. **milled**) produce regular ribbed markings on the edge of a coin.

– SYNONYMS **1 grind,** pulverize, powder, granulate, pound, crush, press. **2** (**mill around/about**) **wander,** drift, swarm, crowd, fill, pack, throng.

– PHRASES **go** (or **put someone**) **through the mill** undergo (or make someone undergo) an unpleasant experience.
– ORIGIN Latin *mola* 'grindstone, mill.'

mill² ▸ **noun** a monetary unit used only in calculations, worth one thousandth of a dollar.
– ORIGIN from Latin *millesimum* 'thousandth part.'

mille·feuille /ˌmēl'fœy(ə), -fə'wē/ ▸ **noun** a cake consisting of thin layers of puff pastry and such fillings as whipped cream, custard, or fruit.
– ORIGIN French, 'thousand-leaf.'

mil·le·nar·i·an /ˌmilə'ne(ə)rēən/ ▸ **adjective** relating to or believing in Christian millenarianism. ▸ **noun** a person who believes in millenarianism.
– ORIGIN Latin *millenarius* 'having a thousand.'

mil·le·nar·i·an·ism /ˌmilə'ne(ə)rēəˌnizəm/ ▸ **noun** the belief in a future thousand-year age of blessedness, beginning with or culminating in the Second Coming of Jesus.
– DERIVATIVES **mil·le·nar·i·an·ist** noun & adjective.

mil·le·nar·y /'miləˌnerē/ ▸ **noun** (pl. **millenaries**) **1** a period of a thousand years. **2** a thousandth anniversary. ▸ **adjective** consisting of a thousand.

mil·len·ni·al /mi'lenēəl/ ▸ **adjective** relating to a millennium.

mil·len·ni·al·ism /mə'lenēəˌlizəm/ ▸ **noun** another term for **MILLENARIANISM**.
– DERIVATIVES **mil·len·ni·al·ist** noun & adjective.

mil·len·ni·um /mə'lenēəm/ ▸ **noun** (pl. **millennia** or **millenniums**) **1** a period of a thousand years, especially when calculated from the traditional date of the birth of Jesus. **2** (**the millennium**) the point at which one period of a thousand years ends and another begins. **3** (**the millennium**) Christian Theology the prophesied forthcoming thousand-year reign of Jesus. **4** an anniversary of a thousand years.
– ORIGIN from Latin *mille* 'thousand' + *annus* 'year.'

USAGE

The correct spelling is **millennium**, with a double **l** and a double **n**. The spelling with one **n** is a common mistake, arising from confusion with other similar words such as **millenarian**, correctly spelled with only one **n**.

mil·len·ni·um bug ▸ **noun** an inability in older computing software to deal correctly with dates of January 1, 2000 or later.

mill·er /'milər/ ▸ **noun** a person who owns or works in a grain mill.

mil·let /'milit/ ▸ **noun** a cereal that bears a large crop of small seeds, used to make flour or alcoholic drinks.
– ORIGIN French.

milli- ▸ **combining form** a thousand, especially a factor of one thousandth (10^{-3}): *milligram*.
– ORIGIN from Latin *mille* 'thousand.'

mil·liard /'milˌyärd, -yərd/ ▸ **noun** Brit., dated one thousand million; a billion.

mil·li·bar /'miləˌbär/ ▸ **noun** one thousandth of a bar, a unit of atmospheric pressure equivalent to 100 pascals.

mil·li·gram /'miləˌgram/ ▸ **noun** one thousandth of a gram.

mil·li·li·ter /'miləˌlētər/ ▸ **noun** one thousandth of a liter.

mil·li·me·ter /'miləˌmētər/ ▸ **noun** one thousandth of a meter.

mil·li·ner /'milənər/ ▸ **noun** a person who makes or sells women's hats.
– DERIVATIVES **mil·li·ner·y** /'miləˌnerē/ noun.
– ORIGIN from the name of the Italian city *Milan*, first meaning 'a native of Milan,' later 'a seller of fancy goods from Milan.'

mil·lion /'milyən/ ▸ **cardinal number** (pl. **millions** or (with numeral or quantifying word) same) **1** the number equivalent to a thousand multiplied by a thousand; 1,000,000 or 10^6. **2** (also **millions**) informal a very large number or amount.
– DERIVATIVES **mil·lionth** /-yənTH/ ordinal number.

mil·lion·aire /ˌmilyə'ne(ə)r, 'milyəˌne(ə)r/ ▸ **noun** (fem. **millionairess** /ˌmilyə'ne(ə)rəs/) a person whose money and property are worth one million dollars or more.

mil·li·pede /'miləˌpēd/ ▸ **noun** a small invertebrate animal with a long body composed of many segments, most of which have two pairs of legs.
– ORIGIN from Latin *mille* 'thousand' + *pes* 'foot.'

mil·li·sec·ond /'miləˌsekənd/ ▸ **noun** one thousandth of a second.

mill·pond /'milˌpänd/ ▸ **noun** an artificial pool providing a head of water to power a watermill.

mill·stone /'milˌstōn/ ▸ **noun 1** each of a pair of circular stones used for grinding grain. **2** a heavy and inescapable responsibility.

mill wheel ▸ **noun** a wheel used to drive a watermill.

mi·lo /'mīlō/ ▸ **noun** a drought-resistant variety of sorghum, an important cereal in the central US.
– ORIGIN Sesotho (an African language).

mi·lord /mə'lôrd, mī-/ ▸ **noun** historical or humorous used to address or refer to an English nobleman.

milque·toast /'milkˌtōst/ ▸ **noun** a timid or submissive person.
– ORIGIN from the name of an American cartoon character, Caspar *Milquetoast*, created by H. T. Webster.

milt /milt/ ▸ **noun 1** the semen of a male fish. **2** the reproductive gland of a male fish.
– ORIGIN Old English.

MIME /mīm, 'em 'ī 'em 'ē/ ▸ **noun** Computing a standard for formatting files such as text, graphics, and audio, so they can be sent over the Internet and seen or played by a Web browser or email application.
– ORIGIN an acronym for *multipurpose Internet mail extensions*.

mime /mīm/ ▸ **noun 1** the use of silent gestures and facial expressions to tell a story or convey a feeling, especially as a form of theatrical performance. **2** a performer of mime. ▸ **verb** use mime to act out a story or convey a feeling.
– ORIGIN Greek *mimos*.

mim·e·o·graph /'mimēəˌgraf/ ▸ **noun** a duplicating machine that produces copies from a stencil, now superseded by the photocopier.
– ORIGIN from Greek *mimeomai* 'I imitate.'

mi·me·sis /mə'mēsis, mī-/ ▸ **noun 1** imitation of reality in art and literature. **2** the quality of resembling another animal or plant.
– ORIGIN Greek.

mi·met·ic /mi'metik/ ▸ **adjective 1** imitating reality in art or literature. **2** resembling another animal or plant.

mim·ic /'mimik/ ▸ **verb** (**mimics, mimicking, mimicked**) **1** imitate someone in order to make fun of them or to entertain others. **2** (of an animal or plant) take on the appearance of another for protection. **3** imitate or copy something.

– SYNONYMS **imitate,** copy, impersonate, do an impression of, ape, caricature, parody.

▸ **noun** a person skilled in mimicking others.

– SYNONYMS **impersonator,** impressionist; informal copycat.

CHOOSE THE RIGHT WORD

See **IMITATE**.

mim·ic·ry /ˈmiməkrē/ ▸ **noun 1** imitation of someone or something. **2** the close external resemblance of an animal or plant to another.

CHOOSE THE RIGHT WORD

See **CARICATURE**.

mi·mo·sa /miˈmōsə, mī-, -zə/ ▸ **noun 1** an acacia tree with delicate fernlike leaves and yellow flowers. **2** a plant of a genus that includes the **SENSITIVE PLANT**. **3** a drink of champagne and orange juice.
– ORIGIN probably from Latin *mimus* 'mime' (because the plant mimics an animal's sensitivity to touch).

min. ▸ **abbreviation 1** minimum. **2** minute(s).

min·a·ret /ˌminəˈret/ ▸ **noun** a slender tower of a mosque, with a balcony from which Muslims are called to prayer.
– ORIGIN Arabic.

min·a·to·ry /ˈminəˌtôrē, ˈmī-/ ▸ **adjective** formal threatening.
– ORIGIN from Latin *minari* 'threaten.'

mince /mins/ ▸ **verb 1** cut up meat into very small pieces. **2** walk in an affected way with short, quick steps and swinging hips.

– SYNONYMS **grind,** chop up, cut up, dice, crumble, hash.

▸ **noun** something minced, especially mincemeat.
– DERIVATIVES **minc·er** noun.
– PHRASES **not mince (one's) words** speak in a direct way.
– ORIGIN Old French *mincier*.

mince·meat /ˈminsˌmēt/ ▸ **noun** a mixture of currants, raisins, apples, candied citrus peel, sugar, spices, and suet.
– PHRASES **make mincemeat of** informal defeat someone decisively.

mind /mīnd/ ▸ **noun 1** a person's faculty of consciousness and thought. **2** a person's ability to reason or remember things. **3** a person's attention or will. **4** an intelligent person.

– SYNONYMS **1 brain,** intelligence, intellect, brains, brainpower, wits, understanding, reasoning, judgment, sense, head; informal gray matter, smarts. **2 attention,** thoughts, concentration. **3 sanity,** mental faculties, senses, wits, reason, reasoning, judgment. **4 intellect,** thinker, brain, scholar, genius.

▸ **verb 1** be distressed or annoyed by someone or something. **2** feel concern about something. **3** take care with or watch out for: *mind your head on that cupboard!* **4** take care of someone or something temporarily.

– SYNONYMS **1 object,** care, be bothered, be annoyed, be upset, take offense, disapprove, look askance; informal give/care a damn. **2 be careful of,** watch out for, look out for, beware of. **3 look after,** take care of, keep an eye on, watch, attend to, care for.

– PHRASES **be of two minds** be unable to decide between alternatives. **give someone a piece of one's mind** informal rebuke someone. **have a** (or **a good**) **mind to do** be inclined to do. **in one's mind's eye** in one's imagination. **mind one's Ps & Qs** be careful to be polite and avoid giving offense. **never mind 1** do not be concerned or distressed. **2** let alone. **out of one's mind** not thinking sensibly; crazy. **put one in mind of** remind one of. **to my mind** in my opinion.
– ORIGIN Old English.

WORD LINKS

mental *relating to the mind*

mind-bend·ing ▸ **adjective** informal altering one's state of mind.

mind-blow·ing ▸ **adjective** informal overwhelmingly impressive.

mind-bog·gling ▸ **adjective** informal overwhelming; startling.

mind·ed /ˈmīndid/ ▸ **adjective** (often in combination) inclined to think in a particular way: *liberal-minded*.

mind·er /ˈmīndər/ ▸ **noun** a person employed to look after someone or something.

mind·ful /ˈmīndfəl/ ▸ **adjective** (**mindful of/that**) aware of or recognizing that.

mind game ▸ **noun** a series of actions intended to unsettle someone or to gain an advantage over them.

mind·less /ˈmīn(d)lis/ ▸ **adjective 1** acting or done without justification and with no concern for the consequences. **2** (**mindless of**) not thinking of or concerned about. **3** (of an activity) simple and repetitive.

– SYNONYMS **1 stupid,** idiotic, brainless, asinine, witless, empty-headed; informal dumb, dopey, dim, halfwitted, fatheaded, boneheaded. **2 unthinking,** thoughtless, senseless, gratuitous, wanton, indiscriminate. **3 mechanical,** routine, tedious, boring, monotonous, mind-numbing.

– DERIVATIVES **mind·less·ly** adverb **mind·less·ness** noun.

mind read·er ▸ **noun** a person who can supposedly discern what another person is thinking.

mind·set /ˈmīndˌset/ ▸ **noun** a person's established set of attitudes.

mine[1] /mīn/ ▸ **possessive pronoun** referring to a thing or things belonging to or associated with the speaker.
– ORIGIN Old English.

mine[2] ▸ **noun 1** a hole or passage dug in the earth for extracting coal or other minerals. **2** an abundant source: *the book is a mine of information.* **3** a type of bomb placed on or in the ground or water that detonates on contact.

– SYNONYMS **1 pit,** colliery, excavation, quarry. **2** *a mine of information* **store,** storehouse, reservoir, repository, gold mine, treasure house, treasury.

▸ **verb 1** extract coal and other minerals from a mine. **2** lay explosive mines on or in the ground or water. **3** exploit a source of information or skill: *his body of work should be mined for its fresh ideas.*

– SYNONYMS **quarry,** excavate, dig, extract.

– ORIGIN Old French.

mine·field /ˈmīnˌfēld/ ▸ **noun 1** an area planted with explosive mines. **2** a subject or situation presenting hidden risks.

min·er /ˈmīnər/ ▶ **noun** a person who works in a mine.

min·er·al /ˈmin(ə)rəl/ ▶ **noun 1** a solid inorganic substance that occurs naturally, such as copper. **2** an inorganic substance needed by the human body for good health, such as calcium. **3** a substance obtained by mining.
– ORIGIN Latin *minera* 'ore.'

min·er·al·o·gy /ˌminəˈräləjē, -ˈral-/ ▶ **noun** the scientific study of minerals.
– DERIVATIVES **min·er·al·og·i·cal** /ˌmin(ə)rəˈläjikəl/ adjective **min·er·al·o·gist** noun.

min·er·al oil ▶ **noun** a product produced by distilling petroleum, used as a lubricant or laxative.

min·er·al wa·ter ▶ **noun** water that naturally contains some dissolved salts.

mine·shaft /ˈmīnˌsHaft/ ▶ **noun** a deep, narrow shaft that gives access to a mine.

min·e·stro·ne /ˌminəˈstrōnē/ ▶ **noun** an Italian soup containing vegetables and pasta.
– ORIGIN from Italian *minestrare* 'serve at table.'

mine·sweep·er /ˈmīnˌswēpər/ ▶ **noun** a warship equipped for detecting and removing tethered explosive mines.

Ming /miNG/ ▶ **adjective** (of Chinese porcelain) made during the Ming dynasty (1368–1644), having vivid colors and elaborate designs.
– ORIGIN Chinese, 'clear or bright.'

min·gle /ˈmiNGgəl/ ▶ **verb 1** mix together. **2** move around and chat at a social function.

> – SYNONYMS **1 mix,** blend, intermingle, intermix, interweave, interlace, combine, merge, fuse, unite, join, amalgamate. **2 socialize,** circulate, associate, fraternize, get together; informal hobnob.
> – ANTONYMS separate.

– ORIGIN from former *meng* 'mix or blend.'

min·i /ˈminē/ ▶ **adjective** referring to a very small version of something. ▶ **noun** (pl. **minis**) a very short skirt or dress.

mini- ▶ **combining form** very small of its kind; miniature: *minibus.*

min·i·a·ture /ˈmin(ē)əCHər, -ˌCHo͝or/ ▶ **adjective** much smaller than normal in size.

> – SYNONYMS **small,** mini, little, small-scale, baby, toy, pocket, diminutive, vest-pocket; informal pint-sized; Scottish wee.
> – ANTONYMS giant.

▶ **noun 1** a thing that is much smaller than normal. **2** a very small and highly detailed portrait.
– DERIVATIVES **min·i·a·tur·ize** /ˈmin(ē)əCHəˌrīz/ verb.
– ORIGIN from Latin *minium* 'red lead' (formerly used to mark words in manuscripts).

> **CHOOSE THE RIGHT WORD**
>
> See **SMALL**.

min·i·a·tur·ist /ˈmin(ē)əˌCHo͝orist, -CHərist/ ▶ **noun** an artist who paints miniatures.

min·i·bar /ˈminēˌbär/ ▶ **noun** a refrigerator in a hotel room containing a selection of drinks.

min·i·bus /ˈminēˌbəs/ ▶ **noun** a small bus for about ten to fifteen passengers.

min·i·cam /ˈminēˌkam/ ▶ **noun** a hand-held video camera.

min·i·com·pu·ter /ˈminēkəmˌpyo͞otər/ ▶ **noun** a computer of medium power, more than a microcomputer but less than a mainframe.

min·i·disc /ˈminēˌdisk/ ▶ **noun** a disc similar to a small CD but able to record sound or data as well as play it back.

min·i·dress /ˈminēˌdres/ ▶ **noun** a very short dress.

min·im /ˈminim/ ▶ **noun** one sixtieth of a fluid dram, about one drop of liquid.
– ORIGIN from Latin *minimus* 'smallest.'

min·i·ma /ˈminəmə/ plural of **MINIMUM**.

min·i·mal /ˈminəməl/ ▶ **adjective 1** of a minimum amount, quantity, or degree. **2** (of art) using simple forms or structures. **3** (of music) characterized by the repetition and gradual alteration of short phrases.

> – SYNONYMS **very little,** very small, minimum, the least (possible), nominal, token, negligible.
> – ANTONYMS maximum.

– DERIVATIVES **min·i·mal·ly** adverb.

min·i·mal·ist /ˈminəməlist/ ▶ **adjective 1** relating to minimal art or music. **2** deliberately simple or basic in design. ▶ **noun** a person who creates minimal art or music.
– DERIVATIVES **min·i·mal·ism** /ˈminəməˌlizəm/ noun.

min·i·me ▶ **noun** informal a person who closely resembles a smaller or younger version of another.
– ORIGIN the name of a cloned character in the film *Austin Powers: The Spy Who Shagged Me.*

min·i·mize /ˈminəˌmīz/ ▶ **verb 1** reduce something to the smallest possible amount or degree. **2** represent something as less important than it really is.

> – SYNONYMS **1 keep down,** keep to a minimum, reduce, decrease, cut (down), lessen, curtail, prune; informal slash. **2 belittle,** make light of, play down, underrate, downplay, undervalue.
> – ANTONYMS maximize, exaggerate.

– DERIVATIVES **min·i·mi·za·tion** /ˌminəməˈzāsHən/ noun **min·i·miz·er** noun.

min·i·mum /ˈminəməm/ ▶ **noun** (pl. **minima** or **minimums**) the least or smallest amount, extent, or intensity possible or recorded: *they checked passports with the minimum of fuss.*

> – SYNONYMS **lowest level,** lower limit, rock bottom, least, lowest.

▶ **adjective** smallest or lowest in amount, extent, or intensity.

> – SYNONYMS **minimal,** least, smallest, least possible, slightest, lowest.
> – ANTONYMS maximum.

– ORIGIN Latin.

min·i·mum wage ▶ **noun** the lowest wage permitted by law or by agreement.

min·ion /ˈminyən/ ▶ **noun** a lowly employee or assistant of a powerful person.
– ORIGIN from French *mignon* 'pretty, dainty.'

min·i·pill ▶ **noun** a contraceptive pill containing progestin and not estrogen.

min·i·se·ries /ˈminēˌsi(ə)rēz/ ▶ **noun** a television drama shown in a small number of episodes.

min·i·skirt /ˈminēˌskərt/ ▶ **noun** a very short skirt.
– DERIVATIVES **min·i·skirt·ed** adjective.

min·is·ter /ˈminəstər/ ▶ **noun 1** a head of a government department. **2** a member of the clergy, especially in

Protestant Churches. **3** a diplomat, usually ranking below an ambassador, representing a country or sovereign in a foreign country.

> – SYNONYMS **1 member of the government,** member of the cabinet, secretary. **2 clergyman,** clergywoman, cleric, pastor, rector, priest, parson, vicar, curate; informal reverend, padre.

▶ **verb 1** (**minister to**) attend to the needs of. **2** act as a minister of religion.

> – SYNONYMS *doctors ministered to the injured* **tend to,** care for, take care of, look after, nurse, treat, attend to, see to, help.

– ORIGIN Latin, 'servant.'

min·is·te·ri·al /ˌminəˈsti(ə)rēəl/ ▶ **adjective** relating to a minister or ministers.
– DERIVATIVES **min·is·te·ri·al·ly** adverb.

min·is·tra·tions /ˌminəˈstrāsʜənz/ ▶ **plural noun 1** formal or humorous the provision of help or care. **2** the services of a minister of religion.
– DERIVATIVES **min·is·trant** /ˈminəstrənt/ noun.

min·is·try /ˈminəstrē/ ▶ **noun** (pl. **ministries**) **1** a government department headed by a minister. **2** a period of government under one minister. **3** the work or office of a minister of religion.

> – SYNONYMS **1 department,** bureau, agency, office. **2 the priesthood,** holy orders, the church.

min·i·van /ˈminēˌvan/ (also trademark **Mini Van**) ▶ **noun** a small van fitted with seats for passengers.

mink /miɴɢk/ ▶ **noun** a small stoatlike mammal farmed for its fur.
– ORIGIN Swedish.

min·ke /ˈmiɴɢkē/ ▶ **noun** a small rorqual whale with a dark gray back and white underparts.
– ORIGIN probably named after *Meincke*, a Norwegian whaler.

min·now /ˈminō/ ▶ **noun 1** a small freshwater fish of the carp family. **2** a minor or unimportant person.
– ORIGIN probably from Old English.

Mi·no·an /məˈnōən, mī-/ ▶ **adjective** relating to a Bronze Age civilization centered on Crete (*c.*3000–1050 BC).
– ORIGIN named after the legendary Cretan king *Minos*.

mi·nor /ˈmīnər/ ▶ **adjective 1** lesser in importance, seriousness, or significance: *minor alterations.* **2** (of a musical scale) having intervals of a half step between the second and third, and (usually) the fifth and sixth, and the seventh and eighth notes. Contrasted with **MAJOR**.

> – SYNONYMS **1 slight,** small, unimportant, insignificant, inconsequential, negligible, trivial, trifling, paltry, petty, nickel-and-dime; informal piffling. **2** *a minor poet* **little known,** unknown, lesser, unimportant, obscure, minor-league; informal small-time, two-bit.
> – ANTONYMS major, important.

WORD TOOLKIT

minor ...	slight ...	unimportant ...
injury	breeze	backwater
leagues	movement	town
offense	advantage	poet
miracle	exaggeration	literature
surgery	angle	colony
setback	possibility	paperwork

▶ **noun 1** a person under the age of full legal responsibility. **2** Music a minor key, interval, or scale. **3** a student's subsidiary subject or area of concentration.

> – SYNONYMS **child,** infant, youth, adolescent, teenager, boy, girl; informal kid.
> – ANTONYMS adult.

▶ **verb** (**minor in**) study a subsidiary subject in college.
– ORIGIN Latin, 'smaller, less.'

Mi·nor·can /məˈnôrkən/ ▶ **noun** a person from Minorca. ▶ **adjective** relating to Minorca.

mi·nor·i·ty /məˈnôrətē/ ▶ **noun** (pl. **minorities**) **1** the smaller number or part. **2** a relatively small group of people differing from the majority in race, religion, etc. **3** the state of being under the age of full legal responsibility.

mi·nor·i·ty lead·er ▶ **noun** the head of the minority party in a legislative body, especially the US Senate or House of Representatives.

mi·nor league ▶ **noun 1** a league below the level of the major league in a particular professional sport, especially baseball. **2** (as adj.) of lesser power or significance: *a minor-league villain.*
– DERIVATIVES **mi·nor lea·guer** noun.

Min·o·taur /ˈminəˌtôr, ˈmī-/ ▶ **noun** Greek Mythology a creature who was half-man and half-bull, kept in a labyrinth on Crete by King Minos.
– ORIGIN Greek *Minōtauros* 'bull of Minos.'

min·ox·i·dil /məˈnäksəˌdil/ ▶ **noun** a synthetic drug used in the treatment of hypertension and in lotions to promote hair growth.

min·strel /ˈminstrəl/ ▶ **noun** a medieval singer or musician.
– ORIGIN Old French *menestral* 'entertainer, servant.'

min·strel·sy /ˈminstrəlsē/ ▶ **noun** the activity of performing as a minstrel.

mint[1] /mint/ ▶ **noun 1** a plant used as an herb in cooking. **2** the flavor of mint, especially peppermint or spearmint. **3** a peppermint or spearmint candy or breath freshener.
– DERIVATIVES **mint·y** adjective.
– ORIGIN Greek *minthē*.

mint[2] ▶ **noun 1** a place where coins are made. **2** (**a mint**) informal a large sum of money. ▶ **adjective** as new; in perfect condition. ▶ **verb 1** make a coin by stamping metal. **2** produce something for the first time.

> – SYNONYMS **coin,** stamp, strike, cast, make, manufacture.

– ORIGIN from Latin *moneta* 'money.'

mint ju·lep ▶ **noun** a cocktail made with bourbon, crushed ice, sugar, and fresh mint.

min·u·et /ˌminyo͞oˈet/ ▶ **noun** a slow ballroom dance in triple time, popular in the 18th century.
– ORIGIN from French *menuet* 'fine, delicate.'

mi·nus /ˈmīnəs/ ▶ **preposition 1** with the subtraction of. **2** (of temperature) falling below zero by: *minus 32° Fahrenheit.* **3** informal lacking: *he was minus a finger.* ▶ **adjective 1** (before a number) below zero; negative. **2** (after a grade) slightly below: *C-minus.* **3** having a negative electric charge. ▶ **noun 1** (also **minus sign**) the symbol –, indicating subtraction or a negative value. **2** informal a disadvantage.
– ORIGIN Latin, neuter of *minor* 'less.'

mi·nus·cule /ˈminəˌskyo͞ol, minˈəsˌkyo͞ol/ ▶ **adjective** very small. ▶ **noun** a lowercase letter.

– ORIGIN from Latin *minuscula littera* 'somewhat smaller letter.'

USAGE

The correct spelling is **minuscule**, not *miniscule*, although the latter form is extremely common.

mi·nute[1] /'minit/ ▶ **noun 1** a period of time equal to sixty seconds or a sixtieth of an hour. **2** (**a minute**) informal a very short time. **3** (also **arc minute** or **minute of arc**) a measurement of an angle equal to one sixtieth of a degree.

– SYNONYMS **moment,** short time, little while, second, instant; informal sec, jiffy.

– PHRASES **up to the minute** up to date.
– ORIGIN from Latin *pars minuta prima* 'first very small part.'

mi·nute[2] /mī'n(y)o͞ot, mə-/ ▶ **adjective** (**minutest**) **1** very small. **2** very detailed or thorough: *he made a minute examination of the area.*

– SYNONYMS **1 tiny,** minuscule, microscopic, miniature; Scottish wee; informal teeny, teensy, teeny-weeny, teensy-weensy. **2** *minute detail* **exhaustive,** painstaking, meticulous, rigorous, thorough.
– ANTONYMS huge.

– DERIVATIVES **mi·nute·ly** adverb **mi·nute·ness** noun.
– ORIGIN Latin *minutus* 'lessened, made small.'

CHOOSE THE RIGHT WORD

See **SMALL**.

mi·nute[3] /'minit/ ▶ **noun 1** (**minutes**) a written summary of the points discussed at a meeting. **2** an official written message.

– SYNONYMS (**minutes**) **record(s),** proceedings, log, notes, transcript, summary.

▶ **verb** record the points discussed at a meeting.
– ORIGIN French *minute*, from the idea of a rough copy in 'small writing.'

min·ute·man /'minət,man/ ▶ **noun** (pl. **minutemen**) historical (during the American Revolution) an American militiaman who volunteered to be ready for service at a minute's notice.

min·ute steak /'minit/ ▶ **noun** a thin slice of steak cooked very quickly.

mi·nu·ti·ae /mə'n(y)o͞oshē,ē, -shē,ī/ ▶ **plural noun** small or precise details.
– ORIGIN Latin.

minx /mingks/ ▶ **noun** chiefly humorous an impudent, cunning, or flirtatious girl or young woman.
– DERIVATIVES **minx·y** adjective.
– ORIGIN unknown.

Mi·o·cene /'mīə,sēn/ ▶ **adjective** Geology relating to the fourth epoch of the Tertiary period (23.3 to 5.2 million years ago), when the first apes appeared.
– ORIGIN from Greek *meiōn* 'less' + *kainos* 'new.'

mi·ra·bi·le dic·tu /mə'räbə,lā 'diktoo͞, mə'rabəlē/ ▶ **adverb** wonderful to relate.
– ORIGIN Latin.

mir·a·cle /'mirikəl/ ▶ **noun 1** an extraordinary and welcome event believed to be the work of God or a saint. **2** a remarkable and welcome event: *it was a miracle that more people hadn't been killed.* **3** an outstanding example or achievement.

– SYNONYMS **wonder,** marvel, sensation, phenomenon.

– ORIGIN Latin *miraculum* 'object of wonder.'

mir·a·cle play ▶ **noun** a mystery play.

mi·rac·u·lous /mə'rakyələs/ ▶ **adjective** like a miracle; very surprising and welcome.

– SYNONYMS **amazing,** astounding, remarkable, extraordinary, incredible, unbelievable, sensational, phenomenal, inexplicable.

– DERIVATIVES **mi·rac·u·lous·ly** adverb.

mi·rage /mə'räzh/ ▶ **noun 1** an optical illusion caused by the refraction of light by heated air, in which a sheet of water seems to appear in a desert or on a hot road. **2** something that seems real or possible but is not in fact so: *such promised happiness is only a mirage.*
– ORIGIN French.

mire /mīr/ ▶ **noun 1** a stretch of swampy or boggy ground. **2** a difficult situation from which it is hard to escape. ▶ **verb** (**be mired**) **1** become stuck in mud. **2** become involved in a difficult situation.
– ORIGIN Old Norse.

mire·poix /mi(ə)r'pwä/ ▶ **noun** a mixture of chopped sautéed vegetables used in various sauces.
– ORIGIN named after the French general Duc de *Mirepoix*.

mir·ror /'mirər/ ▶ **noun 1** a piece of glass coated with metal that reflects a clear image. **2** something that accurately represents something else.

– SYNONYMS **looking glass;** Brit. glass.

▶ **verb 1** reflect someone or something. **2** correspond to: *the expansion in the Far East has been mirrored in the loss of investment to Eastern Europe.*

– SYNONYMS **reflect,** match, reproduce, imitate, copy, mimic, echo, parallel.

– ORIGIN Old French *mirour*.

mir·ror·ball /'mirər,bôl/ ▶ **noun** a revolving ball covered with small mirrored facets, used to provide lighting effects at discos.

mir·ror im·age ▶ **noun** an image that is identical in form to another but has the structure reversed, as if seen in a mirror.

mir·ror site ▶ **noun** an Internet site that stores contents copied from another site.

mirth /mərth/ ▶ **noun** amusement, especially as expressed in laughter.
– DERIVATIVES **mirth·ful** adjective.
– ORIGIN Old English.

mirth·less /'mərthləs/ ▶ **adjective** (of a smile or laugh) lacking real amusement.
– DERIVATIVES **mirth·less·ly** adverb.

MIRV /mərv/ ▶ **abbreviation** multiple independently targeted re-entry vehicle, an intercontinental nuclear missile with several independent warheads.

mir·y /'mīrē/ ▶ **adjective** very muddy or boggy.

MIS ▶ **abbreviation** Computing management information system; a computerized information-processing system designed to support the activities of company or organizational management.

mis- ▶ **prefix 1** (added to verbs and their derivatives) wrongly, badly, or unsuitably: *mismanage.* **2** (added to some nouns) expressing a negative sense: *misadventure.*
– ORIGIN Old English.

mis·ad·ven·ture /ˌmisədˈvenCHər/ ▶ **noun** an unfortunate incident; a mishap.

mis·a·ligned /ˌmisəˈlīnd/ ▶ **adjective** incorrectly aligned.
– DERIVATIVES **mis·a·lign·ment** /ˌmisəˈlīnmənt/ noun.

mis·al·li·ance /ˌmisəˈlīəns/ ▶ **noun** an unsuitable or unhappy alliance or marriage.

mis·an·thrope /ˈmisənˌTHrōp, ˈmiz-/ ▶ **noun** a person who dislikes and avoids other people.
– DERIVATIVES **mis·an·throp·ic** /ˌmisənˈTHräpik/ adjective **mis·an·thro·py** /misˈsanTHrəpē/ noun.
– ORIGIN from Greek *misein* 'to hate' + *anthrōpos* 'man.'

mis·ap·ply /ˌmisəˈplī/ ▶ **verb** (**misapplies, misapplying, misapplied**) use something for the wrong purpose or in the wrong way.
– DERIVATIVES **mis·ap·pli·ca·tion** /-ˌapləˈkāSHən/ noun.

mis·ap·pre·hen·sion /ˌmisˌapriˈhenSHən/ ▶ **noun** a mistaken belief.

mis·ap·pro·pri·ate /ˌmisəˈprōprēˌāt/ ▶ **verb** dishonestly take something for one's own use.

– SYNONYMS **embezzle,** expropriate, steal, thieve, pilfer, pocket, help oneself to; informal swipe, rip off.

– DERIVATIVES **mis·ap·pro·pri·a·tion** /-ˌprōprēˈāSHən/ noun.

mis·be·got·ten /ˌmisbəˈgätn/ ▶ **adjective** **1** badly designed or planned. **2** old use (of a child) illegitimate.

mis·be·have /ˌmisbiˈhāv/ ▶ **verb** behave badly.

– SYNONYMS **behave badly,** be naughty, be disobedient, get up to mischief, get up to no good, be rude; informal carry on, act up.

– DERIVATIVES **mis·be·hav·ior** /-ˈhāvyər/ noun.

misc. ▶ **abbreviation** miscellaneous.

mis·cal·cu·late /misˈkalkyəˌlāt/ ▶ **verb** calculate or assess something wrongly.
– DERIVATIVES **mis·cal·cu·la·tion** /ˌmisˌkalkyəˈlāSHən/ noun.

mis·call /misˈkôl/ ▶ **verb** call something by a wrong or inappropriate name.

mis·car·riage /misˈkarij, ˈmisˌkarij/ ▶ **noun** **1** the early and unplanned expulsion of a fetus from the womb, before it is able to survive independently. **2** an unsuccessful outcome; a failure.

mis·car·riage of jus·tice ▶ **noun** a failure of a court or judicial system to achieve justice.

mis·car·ry /misˈkarē, ˈmisˌkarē/ ▶ **verb** (**miscarries, miscarrying, miscarried**) **1** (of a pregnant woman) have a miscarriage. **2** (of a plan) fail to achieve an intended result.

mis·cast /misˈkast/ ▶ **verb** (**be miscast**) (of an actor) be given an unsuitable role.

mis·ceg·e·na·tion /miˌsejəˈnāSHən, ˌmisəjə-/ ▶ **noun** the interbreeding of people of different races.
– ORIGIN from Latin *miscere* 'to mix' + *genus* 'race.'

mis·cel·la·ne·a /ˌmisəˈlānēə/ ▶ **plural noun** different items collected together.

mis·cel·la·ne·ous /ˌmisəˈlānēəs/ ▶ **adjective** **1** (of a number of things or people) of various types. **2** composed of things of different kinds: *a miscellaneous collection of problems.*

– SYNONYMS **various,** varied, different, assorted, mixed, sundry, diverse, disparate, heterogeneous.

– DERIVATIVES **mis·cel·la·ne·ous·ly** adverb.
– ORIGIN Latin *miscellus* 'mixed.'

mis·cel·la·ny /ˈmisəˌlānē/ ▶ **noun** (pl. **miscellanies**) a collection of different things.

mis·chance /misˈCHans/ ▶ **noun** bad luck.

mis·chief /ˈmisCHif/ ▶ **noun** **1** playful misbehavior. **2** harm or trouble caused by someone or something.

– SYNONYMS **naughtiness,** bad behavior, misbehavior, misconduct, disobedience, wrongdoing; informal monkey business, shenanigans.

– ORIGIN Old French *meschief.*

mis·chie·vous /ˈmisCHivəs/ ▶ **adjective** **1** misbehaving or fond of misbehaving in a playful way. **2** intended to cause trouble.

– SYNONYMS **1 naughty,** bad, badly behaved, troublesome, disobedient, rascally. **2 playful,** wicked, impish, roguish.
– ANTONYMS well behaved.

– DERIVATIVES **mis·chie·vous·ly** adverb **mis·chie·vous·ness** noun.

mis·ci·ble /ˈmisəbəl/ ▶ **adjective** (of liquids) capable of being mixed together.
– ORIGIN from Latin *miscere* 'to mix.'

mis·com·mu·ni·ca·tion /ˌmiskəˌmyo͞onəˈkāSHən/ ▶ **noun** failure to communicate properly.

mis·con·ceive /ˌmiskənˈsēv/ ▶ **verb** **1** fail to understand something correctly. **2** (**be misconceived**) be badly judged or planned.

mis·con·cep·tion /ˌmiskənˈsepSHən/ ▶ **noun** a false or mistaken idea or belief.

– SYNONYMS **misapprehension,** misunderstanding, mistake, error, misinterpretation, misconstruction, misreading, misjudgment, misbelief, miscalculation, false impression, illusion, fallacy, delusion.

mis·con·duct /misˈkänˌdəkt/ ▶ **noun** unacceptable or improper behavior, especially by a professional person.

– SYNONYMS **1 wrongdoing,** criminality, unprofessionalism, malpractice, negligence, impropriety; formal maladministration. **2 misbehavior,** bad behavior, mischief, misdeeds, naughtiness.

mis·con·struc·tion /ˌmiskənˈstrəkSHən/ ▶ **noun** the action of misinterpreting something.

mis·con·strue /ˌmiskənˈstro͞o/ ▶ **verb** (**misconstrues, misconstruing, misconstrued**) interpret something wrongly.

mis·count /misˈkount/ ▶ **verb** count something incorrectly.

mis·cre·ant /ˈmiskrēənt/ ▶ **noun** a person who has done something wrong or unlawful.
– ORIGIN Old French *mescreant* 'disbelieving.'

mis·cue /misˈkyo͞o/ ▶ **verb** (**miscues, miscueing** or **miscuing, miscued**) (in billiards) fail to cue the ball properly. ▶ **noun** an act of miscueing the ball.

mis·deed /misˈdēd/ ▶ **noun** a wrong or unlawful act.

mis·de·mean·or /ˈmisdiˌmēnər/ (Brit. **misdemeanour**) ▶ **noun** **1** a minor wrongdoing. **2** Law (in the US and formerly in the UK) an offense regarded as less serious than a felony.

– SYNONYMS **wrongdoing,** crime, felony; misdeed, misconduct, offense, error, peccadillo, transgression, sin; old use trespass.

mis·di·ag·nose /misˈdī-igˌnōs, -ˌnōz/ ▶ **verb** make an incorrect diagnosis of an illness.
– DERIVATIVES **mis·di·ag·no·sis** /ˌmisˌdī-igˈnōsəs/ noun.

mis·di·al /ˌmisˈdī(ə)l/ ▶ **verb** (**misdials, misdialing, misdialed**) dial a telephone number incorrectly.

mis·di·rect /ˌmisdəˈrekt, -dī-/ ▶ **verb** direct or instruct someone wrongly.
– DERIVATIVES **mis·di·rec·tion** /-ˈreksHən/ noun.

mise en scène /ˌmēz ˌäN ˈsen/ ▶ **noun** **1** the arrangement of scenery and stage props in a play. **2** the setting of an event.
– ORIGIN French, 'putting on stage.'

mi·ser /ˈmīzər/ ▶ **noun** a person who hoards wealth and spends as little as possible.

– SYNONYMS **penny-pincher,** Scrooge; informal skinflint, cheapskate, tightwad.
– ANTONYMS spendthrift.

– ORIGIN from Latin, 'wretched.'

mis·er·a·ble /ˈmiz(ə)rəbəl/ ▶ **adjective** **1** deeply unhappy or depressed. **2** causing unhappiness or discomfort. **3** gloomy and humorless. **4** too small; inadequate: *all they pay me is a miserable $10,000 a year.*

– SYNONYMS **1 unhappy,** sad, sorrowful, melancholy, dejected, depressed, downhearted, downcast, despondent, disconsolate, wretched, glum, gloomy, forlorn, woebegone, mournful; informal blue, down in the dumps. **2** *their miserable surroundings* **dreary,** dismal, gloomy, drab, wretched, depressing, grim, cheerless, bleak, desolate.
– ANTONYMS cheerful, lovely.

– DERIVATIVES **mis·er·a·ble·ness** noun **mis·er·a·bly** adverb.

WORD TOOLKIT

See **MELANCHOLY**.

mis·er·i·cord /məˈzeriˌkôrd/ ▶ **noun** a ledge projecting from the underside of a hinged seat in a choir stall in a church, giving support to someone standing when the seat is folded up.
– ORIGIN from Latin *misericors* 'compassionate.'

mi·ser·ly /ˈmīzərlē/ ▶ **adjective** **1** unwilling to spend money; stingy. **2** (of a quantity) too small; inadequate.

– SYNONYMS **mean,** parsimonious, close-fisted, penny-pinching, grasping, niggardly, cheese-paring; informal stingy, tight, tightfisted, cheap.
– ANTONYMS generous.

– DERIVATIVES **mi·ser·li·ness** noun.

CHOOSE THE RIGHT WORD

See **ECONOMICAL**.

mis·er·y /ˈmiz(ə)rē/ ▶ **noun** (pl. **miseries**) **1** great unhappiness or distress. **2** a cause of misery.

– SYNONYMS **unhappiness,** distress, wretchedness, suffering, angst, anguish, anxiety, torment, pain, grief, heartache, heartbreak, despair, despondency, dejection, depression, gloom, sorrow; informal the blues.
– ANTONYMS contentment, pleasure.

mis·fire /misˈfīr/ ▶ **verb** **1** (of a gun) fail to fire properly. **2** (of an internal combustion engine) fail to ignite the fuel correctly. **3** fail to produce the intended result: *he didn't know that his plan had misfired.*

mis·fit /ˈmisˌfit/ ▶ **noun** a person whose behavior or attitude sets them apart from others.

mis·for·tune /misˈfôrcHən/ ▶ **noun** **1** bad luck. **2** an unfortunate event.

– SYNONYMS **problem,** difficulty, setback, trouble, adversity, (stroke of) bad luck, misadventure, mishap, blow, failure, accident, disaster, trial, tribulation.

mis·giv·ings /misˈgiviNGz/ ▶ **plural noun** feelings of doubt or anxiety about what might happen.

– SYNONYMS **qualms,** doubts, reservations; suspicions, second thoughts; trepidation, skepticism, unease, anxiety, apprehension, disquiet.

mis·gov·ern /misˈgəvərn/ ▶ **verb** govern a country unfairly or poorly.

mis·guid·ed /misˈgīdid/ ▶ **adjective** showing poor judgment or reasoning.

– SYNONYMS **unwise,** foolish, ill-advised, ill-judged, ill-considered, injudicious, imprudent, unsound, mistaken, misplaced.
– ANTONYMS wise.

mis·han·dle /misˈhandəl/ ▶ **verb** handle or deal with something unwisely or wrongly.

mis·hap /ˈmisˌhap/ ▶ **noun** an unlucky accident.

– SYNONYMS **accident,** trouble, problem, difficulty, setback, adversity, misfortune, blow, disaster, tragedy, catastrophe, calamity.

mis·hear /misˈhi(ə)r/ ▶ **verb** (past and past part. **misheard**) fail to hear (a person or their words) correctly.

mis·hit /ˌmisˈhit/ ▶ **verb** (**mishits, mishitting, mishit**) hit or kick a ball badly.

mish·mash /ˈmisHˌmasH, -ˌmäsH/ ▶ **noun** a confused mixture.
– ORIGIN from **MASH**.

mis·i·den·ti·fy /ˌmisīˈdentəˌfī/ ▶ **verb** (**misidentifies, misidentifying, misidentified**) identify someone or something incorrectly.
– DERIVATIVES **mis·i·den·ti·fi·ca·tion** /-īˌdentəfəˈkāsHən/ noun.

mis·in·form /ˌmisinˈfôrm/ ▶ **verb** give someone false or inaccurate information.
– DERIVATIVES **mis·in·for·ma·tion** /ˌmisinfərˈmāsHən/ noun.

mis·in·ter·pret /ˌmisinˈtərprət/ ▶ **verb** (**misinterprets, misinterpreting, misinterpreted**) interpret something wrongly.
– DERIVATIVES **mis·in·ter·pre·ta·tion** /-inˌtərprəˈtāsHən/ noun.

mis·judge /ˌmisˈjəj/ ▶ **verb** **1** form an incorrect opinion of someone or something. **2** estimate wrongly: *the horse misjudged the fence and Joe was thrown off.*
– DERIVATIVES **mis·judg·ment** (also **misjudgement**) noun.

mis·lay /misˈlā/ ▶ **verb** (past and past part. **mislaid**) lose an object by temporarily forgetting where one has left it.

– SYNONYMS **lose,** misplace, be unable to find.
– ANTONYMS find.

mis·lead /misˈlēd/ ▶ **verb** (past and past part. **misled** /misˈled/) give someone inaccurate or false information.

– SYNONYMS **deceive,** delude, take in, lie to, fool, hoodwink, misinform; informal lead up the garden path, take for a ride, give someone a bum steer.

mis·lead·ing /mis'lēdiNG/ ▶ **adjective** giving the wrong idea or impression.

– SYNONYMS **deceptive,** confusing, deceiving, equivocal, false.
– ANTONYMS clear, straightforward.

mis·man·age /mis'manij/ ▶ **verb** manage something badly or wrongly.
– DERIVATIVES **mis·man·age·ment** noun.

mis·match /'mis,maCH/ ▶ **noun** a failure to correspond or match: *a huge mismatch between supply and demand.* ▶ **verb** match people or things unsuitably or incorrectly.

mis·name /mis'nām/ ▶ **verb** give a wrong or inappropriate name to someone or something.

mis·no·mer /mis'nōmər/ ▶ **noun 1** an inaccurate or misleading name. **2** the wrong use of a name or term.
– ORIGIN from Old French *mesnommer* 'misname.'

mi·so /'mēsō/ ▶ **noun** a paste made from fermented soy beans and barley or rice malt, used in Japanese cooking.
– ORIGIN Japanese.

mi·sog·y·nist /mə'säjənist/ ▶ **noun** a man who hates women.
– DERIVATIVES **mi·sog·y·nis·tic** /mə,säjə'nistik/ adjective.

mi·sog·y·ny /mə'säjənē/ ▶ **noun** hatred of women.
– ORIGIN from Greek *misos* 'hatred' + *gunē* 'woman.'

mis·place /mis'plās/ ▶ **verb** put something in the wrong place.

mis·placed /mis'plāst/ ▶ **adjective 1** not appropriate in the circumstances. **2** (of a feeling) directed to an inappropriate person or thing: *a misplaced faith in the ability of scientists.*

mis·play ▶ **verb** /mis'plā/ **1** play a ball or card wrongly or badly. **2** err by misjudgment. ▶ **noun** an instance of playing a ball or card badly.

mis·print /mis,print/ ▶ **noun** an error in a printed work. ▶ **verb** print something incorrectly.

mis·pro·nounce /,misprə'nouns/ ▶ **verb** pronounce something wrongly.
– DERIVATIVES **mis·pro·nun·ci·a·tion** /-prə,nənsē'āSHən/ noun.

mis·quote /mis'kwōt/ ▶ **verb** quote someone or something inaccurately.
– DERIVATIVES **mis·quo·ta·tion** /,miskwō'tāSHən/ noun.

mis·read /mis'rēd/ ▶ **verb** (past and past part. **misread** /mis'red/) read or interpret something wrongly.

mis·rep·re·sent /,mis,repri'zent/ ▶ **verb** give a false or misleading account of someone or something.
– DERIVATIVES **mis·rep·re·sen·ta·tion** /mis,reprəzən'tāSHən/ noun.

mis·rule /mis'ro͞ol/ ▶ **noun 1** unfair or inefficient government of a country. **2** disruption of peace; disorder. ▶ **verb** govern a country badly.

miss[1] /mis/ ▶ **verb 1** fail to hit, reach, or come into contact with something aimed at. **2** fail to attend or take advantage of something. **3** avoid someone or something. **4** notice or feel the loss or absence of. **5** fail to notice, hear, or understand: *she had shrewd eyes that missed nothing.* **6** be too late for a passenger vehicle, etc.

– SYNONYMS **1 go wide of,** fall short of, pass, overshoot. **2** *she never missed a class* **fail to attend,** be absent from, cut, skip, omit. **3** *I left early to miss rush hour* **avoid,** beat, evade, escape, dodge, sidestep, elude, circumvent, bypass. **4** *he missed all his old friends* **pine for,** yearn for, ache for, long for.
– ANTONYMS hit, catch.

▶ **noun 1** a failure to hit, catch, or reach something. **2** an unsuccessful movie or recording.
– PHRASES **give something a miss** Brit. informal decide not to do or have something. **miss the boat** informal be too slow to take advantage of something.
– ORIGIN Old English.

miss[2] ▶ **noun 1** (**Miss**) a title used before the name of an unmarried woman or girl. **2** a girl or young woman.

– SYNONYMS **young woman,** young lady, girl, schoolgirl, missy; Scottish lass, lassie. literary maiden, maid, damsel.

– ORIGIN abbreviation of *mistress.*

mis·sal /'misəl/ ▶ **noun** a book that contains the set forms of worship used in the Catholic Mass.
– ORIGIN from Latin *missa* 'Mass.'

mis·shap·en /mis'SHāpən/ ▶ **adjective** not having the normal or natural shape.

mis·sile /'misəl/ ▶ **noun 1** an object that is forcibly propelled at a target. **2** an explosive weapon that is self-propelled or directed by remote control.
– ORIGIN Latin, from *mittere* 'send.'

miss·ing /'misiNG/ ▶ **adjective 1** absent and unable to be found. **2** not present when expected or supposed to be.

– SYNONYMS **1 lost,** mislaid, misplaced, absent, gone (astray), unaccounted for. **2 absent,** lacking, wanting.
– ANTONYMS present.

miss·ing link ▶ **noun** a supposed fossil form believed to be a link between humans and apes.

mis·sion /'misHən/ ▶ **noun 1** an important assignment, typically involving travel abroad. **2** an organization involved in a long-term assignment abroad. **3** a military or scientific operation or expedition. **4** the work carried out by a religious organization to spread its faith. **5** an aim or task that a person feels to be their duty: *he made it his mission to foster talent.*

– SYNONYMS **1 assignment,** commission, expedition, journey, trip, undertaking, operation, project. **2** *her mission in life* **vocation,** calling, goal, aim, quest, purpose, function, task, job, labor, work, duty.

– ORIGIN Latin.

mis·sion·ar·y /'misHə,nerē/ ▶ **noun** (pl. **missionaries**) a person sent on a religious mission.

– SYNONYMS **evangelist,** apostle, proselytizer, preacher.

▶ **adjective** relating to a missionary or religious mission.

mis·sion creep ▶ **noun** a gradual shift in objectives during a military campaign, often resulting in a longer involvement than was planned.

mis·sion state·ment ▶ **noun** a formal summary of the aims and values of an organization.

mis·sis ▶ **noun** variant spelling of **MISSUS**.

mis·sive /'misiv/ ▶ **noun** formal a letter.
– ORIGIN Latin *missivus.*

mis·spell /mis'spel/ ▶ **verb** (past and past part. **misspelt** or **misspelled**) spell a word wrongly.

mis·spend /mis'spend/ ▶ **verb** (past and past part. **misspent**) spend time or money foolishly or wastefully.

mis·state /mis'stāt/ ▶ **verb** state something wrongly or inaccurately.
– DERIVATIVES **mis·state·ment** noun.

mis·step /mis'step, 'mis,step/ ▶ **noun** a badly judged step.

mis·sus /'misəz, -əs/ (also **missis**) ▶ **noun** (**the missus**) informal or humorous a person's wife.

miss·y /'misē/ ▶ **noun** (pl. **missies**) an affectionate or scornful form of address to a young girl.

mist /mist/ ▶ **noun 1** a cloud of tiny water droplets in the atmosphere that limits visibility to a lesser extent than fog. **2** a condensed vapor settling on a surface.

– SYNONYMS **haze,** fog, smog, murk, cloud, vapor, steam, spray, condensation.

▶ **verb** cover or become covered with mist.
– ORIGIN Old English.

mis·take /mə'stāk/ ▶ **noun 1** a thing that is incorrect. **2** an error of judgment.

– SYNONYMS **error,** fault, inaccuracy, omission, slip, blunder, miscalculation, misunderstanding, oversight, misinterpretation, gaffe, faux pas, solecism; informal slip-up, boo-boo, goof, boner.

▶ **verb** (past **mistook** /mə'stŏŏk/; past part. **mistaken**) **1** (**mistake someone/thing for**) confuse someone or something with. **2** be wrong about: *I mistook the nature of our relationship.*

– SYNONYMS (**mistake someone/thing for**) **confuse with,** mix up with, take for.

– ORIGIN Old Norse, 'take in error.'

CHOOSE THE RIGHT WORD

mistake, blooper, blunder, error, faux pas, goof, slip

It would be a **mistake** to argue with your boss the day before he or she evaluates your performance, but to forget an important step in an assigned task would be an **error**. Although these nouns are used interchangeably in many contexts, a *mistake* is usually caused by poor judgment or a disregard of rules or principles (*it was a mistake not to tell the truth at the outset*), while an *error* implies an unintentional deviation from standards of accuracy or right conduct (*a mathematical error*). A **blunder** is a careless, stupid, or blatant mistake involving behavior or judgment; it suggests awkwardness or ignorance on the part of the person who makes it (*his blunder that ruined the evening*). A **slip** is a minor and usually accidental mistake that is the result of haste or carelessness (*her slip of the tongue spoiled the surprise*), while a **faux pas** (which means "false step" in French) is an embarrassing breach of etiquette (*it was a faux pas to have meat at the table when so many of the guests were vegetarians*). **Goofs** and **bloopers** are humorous mistakes. A *blooper* is usually a mix-up in speech, while to *goof* is to make a careless error that is honestly admitted (*she shrugged her shoulders and said, "I goofed!"*).

mis·tak·en /mə'stākən/ ▶ **adjective 1** wrong in one's opinion or judgment. **2** based on a misunderstanding or faulty judgment.

– SYNONYMS **1 inaccurate,** wrong, erroneous, incorrect, off the beam, false, fallacious, unfounded, misguided. **2 misinformed,** wrong, in error, under a misapprehension, barking up the wrong tree.
– ANTONYMS correct.

– DERIVATIVES **mis·tak·en·ly** adverb.

mis·ter /'mistər/ ▶ **noun 1** variant form of **Mr. 2** informal a form of address to a man.

mis·time /mis'tīm/ ▶ **verb** choose an inappropriate moment to do or say something.

mis·tle·toe /'misəl,tō/ ▶ **noun** a plant that grows as a parasite on trees and bears white berries in winter.
– ORIGIN Old English.

mis·took /mə'stŏŏk/ past of **MISTAKE**.

mis·tral /'mistrəl, mi'sträl/ ▶ **noun** a strong, cold northwesterly wind that blows through the Rhône valley and southern France.
– ORIGIN French.

mis·trans·late /,mis,tranz'lāt, -,trans'lāt/ ▶ **verb** translate something incorrectly.
– DERIVATIVES **mis·trans·la·tion** /-'lāshən/ noun.

mis·treat /mis'trēt/ ▶ **verb** treat a person or animal badly or unfairly.

– SYNONYMS **ill-treat,** maltreat, abuse, knock about/around, hit, beat, molest, injure, harm, hurt, misuse.

– DERIVATIVES **mis·treat·ment** noun.

mis·tress /'mistris/ ▶ **noun 1** a woman who controls or owns something. **2** a woman skilled in a particular subject or activity: *she's a mistress of the sound bite.* **3** a woman in a sexual relationship with a man who is married to someone else. **4** (**Mistress**) old use Mrs.
– ORIGIN Old French *maistresse*.

mis·tri·al /'mis,trī(ə)l/ ▶ **noun** a trial that is made invalid through an error in the proceedings.

mis·trust /mis'trəst/ ▶ **verb** have no trust in someone or something.

– SYNONYMS **be suspicious of,** be skeptical of, be wary of, be chary of, distrust, have doubts about, have misgivings about, have reservations about, suspect.

▶ **noun** lack of trust.
– DERIVATIVES **mis·trust·ful** /,mis'trəstfəl/ adjective.

mist·y /'mistē/ ▶ **adjective** (**mistier, mistiest**) **1** full of or covered with mist. **2** not clear or distinct: *a few misty memories.*

– SYNONYMS **hazy,** foggy, cloudy, blurred, vague, indistinct.
– ANTONYMS clear.

– DERIVATIVES **mist·i·ly** adverb **mist·i·ness** noun.

mis·un·der·stand /,mis,əndər'stand/ ▶ **verb** (past and past part. **misunderstood** /-,əndər'stŏŏd/) fail to understand someone or something correctly.

– SYNONYMS **misapprehend,** misinterpret, misconstrue, misconceive, mistake, misread, be mistaken, get the wrong idea.

mis·un·der·stand·ing /,mis,əndər'standiNG/ ▶ **noun** **1** a failure to understand something correctly. **2** a disagreement with someone.

– SYNONYMS **1 misinterpretation,** misreading, misapprehension, misconception, false impression. **2 disagreement,** difference (of opinion), dispute, falling-out, quarrel, argument, clash.

mis·use ▶ **verb** /mis'yōōz, 'mis,yōōz/ **1** use something wrongly. **2** treat someone badly or unfairly.

– SYNONYMS **put to wrong use,** misapply, misemploy, abuse, squander, waste, dissipate, misappropriate, embezzle.

▶ **noun** /,mis'yōōs, 'mis,yōōs/ the action of misusing something.

mite[1] /mīt/ ▶ **noun** a very tiny creature like a spider, several kinds of which live as parasites on animals or plants.
– ORIGIN Old English.

mite[2] ▸ **noun 1** a small child or animal. **2** a very small amount. ▸ **adverb** (**a mite**) informal slightly.
– ORIGIN Dutch (first referring to a Flemish copper coin of low value).

mi·ter /ˈmītər/ (Brit **mitre**) ▸ **noun 1** a tall headdress that tapers to a point at front and back, worn by bishops and senior abbots. **2** a joint made between two pieces of wood cut at an angle so as to form a corner of 90°. ▸ **verb** join pieces of wood by means of a miter.
– ORIGIN Greek *mitra* 'belt or turban.'

mit·i·gate /ˈmitəˌgāt/ ▸ **verb 1** make something bad less severe or serious. **2** (as adj. **mitigating**) (of a fact or circumstance) lessening the seriousness of or blame attached to an action.
– DERIVATIVES **mit·i·ga·tion** /ˌmitəˈgāsʜən/ noun.
– ORIGIN Latin *mitigare* 'soften, alleviate.'

> **USAGE**
>
> Do not confuse **mitigate** and **militate**. **Mitigate** means 'make something bad less severe' (*drainage schemes helped to mitigate the problem*), while **militate** is used with **against** to mean 'be a powerful factor in preventing' (*laws that militate against personal freedom*).

> **CHOOSE THE RIGHT WORD**
>
> See **ALLEVIATE**.

mi·to·chon·dri·on /ˌmītəˈkändrēən/ ▸ **noun** (pl. **mitochondria** /-drēə/) Biology a structure found in large numbers in most cells, in which respiration and energy production occur.
– DERIVATIVES **mi·to·chon·dri·al** /-drēəl/ adjective.
– ORIGIN from Greek *mitos* 'thread' + *khondrion* 'small granule.'

mi·to·sis /mīˈtōsəs/ ▸ **noun** (pl. **mitoses** /-sēz/) Biology the division of a cell that results in two daughter cells, each with the same number and kind of chromosomes as the original cell. Compare with **MEIOSIS**.
– ORIGIN from Greek *mitos* 'thread.'

mi·tre /ˈmītər/ ▸ **noun & verb** British spelling of **MITER**.

mitt /mit/ ▸ **noun 1** a mitten. **2** Baseball a glove worn by the catcher and first baseman. **3** a fingerless glove. **4** informal a person's hand.

mit·ten /ˈmitn/ ▸ **noun** a glove having a single section for all four fingers, with a separate section for the thumb.
– ORIGIN Old French *mitaine*.

mitz·vah /ˈmitsvə/ ▸ **noun** (pl. **mitzvoth** /ˈmitsˌvōt, -ˌvōs/) Judaism **1** a precept or commandment. **2** a good deed done from religious duty.
– ORIGIN from Hebrew *miṣwāh* 'commandment.'

mix /miks/ ▸ **verb 1** combine or be combined to form a whole. **2** make something by combining ingredients. **3** (**mix something up**) spoil the order or arrangement of a group of things. **4** (**mix someone/thing up**) confuse a person or thing with another. **5** combine signals or soundtracks into one to produce a recording. **6** enjoy meeting other people socially.

> – SYNONYMS **1 blend,** mingle, combine, jumble, fuse, unite, join, amalgamate, incorporate, meld, homogenize; technical admix; literary commingle. **2 associate,** socialize, keep company, consort, mingle, circulate, rub elbows; informal hang out/around, hobnob.
> – ANTONYMS separate.

▸ **noun 1** a mixture. **2** the proportion of different people or things making up a mixture. **3** a version of a sound recording mixed in a different way from the original.

> – SYNONYMS **mixture,** blend, combination, compound, fusion, union, amalgamation, medley, selection, assortment, variety.

– PHRASES **be mixed up in** (or **with**) be involved in dishonest or underhanded activity.
– ORIGIN from **MIXED**.

mixed /mikst/ ▸ **adjective 1** consisting of different kinds, qualities, or elements. **2** relating to or intended for both men and women.

> – SYNONYMS **1 assorted,** varied, variegated, miscellaneous, disparate, diverse, diversified, motley, sundry, jumbled, heterogeneous. **2** *mixed reactions* **ambivalent,** equivocal, contradictory, conflicting, confused, muddled.
> – ANTONYMS homogeneous.

– ORIGIN from Latin *miscere* 'to mix.'

mixed bag ▸ **noun** a varied assortment of things or people.

mixed bless·ing ▸ **noun** a thing that has both advantages and disadvantages.

mixed e·con·o·my ▸ **noun** an economic system combining private and public enterprise.

mixed farming ▸ **noun** farming of both crops and livestock.

mixed grill ▸ **noun** a dish of various grilled meats, mushrooms, and tomatoes.

mixed mar·riage ▸ **noun** a marriage between people of different races or religions.

mixed met·a·phor ▸ **noun** a combination of metaphors that produces a ridiculous effect (e.g., *this tower of strength will forge ahead*).

mixed-up ▸ **adjective** informal suffering from psychological or emotional problems.

mix·er /ˈmiksər/ ▸ **noun 1** a device for mixing things. **2** a person considered in terms of their ability to mix socially. **3** a social gathering. **4** a soft drink that can be mixed with alcohol.

mix·ol·o·gist /mikˈsäləjist/ ▸ **noun** informal a person who is skilled at mixing cocktails and other drinks.
– DERIVATIVES **mix·ol·o·gy** noun.

mix·ture /ˈmiksᴄʜər/ ▸ **noun 1** a substance made by mixing other substances together. **2** (**a mixture of**) a combination of different things in which each part is distinct: *the area is a bizarre mixture of ancient and modern*. **3** a combination of two or more substances that mix together without any chemical reaction occurring.

> – SYNONYMS **1 blend,** mix, brew, combination, concoction, composition, compound, alloy, amalgam. **2 assortment,** miscellany, medley, blend, variety, mixed bag, mix, diversity, collection, selection, hodgepodge, ragbag.

mix-up ▸ **noun** informal a confusion or misunderstanding.

> – SYNONYMS **confusion,** muddle, misunderstanding, mistake, error.

mi·zu·na /məˈzo͞onə/ ▸ **noun** a Japanese plant of the rape family, with leaves that are eaten in salads.
– ORIGIN from Japanese.

miz·zen /ˈmizən/ (also **mizzenmast** /ˈmizənˌmast/) ▸ **noun** the mast behind a ship's mainmast.
– ORIGIN from Italian *mezzano* 'middle.'

ml ▶ **abbreviation 1** mile or miles. **2** milliliter or milliliters.

MLA ▶ **abbreviation** Modern Language Association.

Mlle ▶ **abbreviation** (pl. **Mlles**) Mademoiselle.

MLS ▶ **abbreviation 1** Master of Library Science. **2** Multiple Listing Service, an organization that holds computerized listings of US real estate offered for sale. **3** Major League Soccer.

mm ▶ **abbreviation** millimeter or millimeters.

Mme ▶ **abbreviation** (pl. **Mmes**) Madame.

MMR ▶ **abbreviation** measles, mumps, and rubella (a vaccination given to children).

MMS ▶ **abbreviation** Multimedia Messaging Service, a system that enables cell phones to send and receive color pictures and sound clips as well as text messages.

MN ▶ **abbreviation** Minnesota.

Mn ▶ **symbol** the chemical element manganese.

mne·mon·ic /nə'mänik/ ▶ **noun** a pattern of letters or words that helps one to remember something. ▶ **adjective** helping or designed to help the memory.
– ORIGIN from Greek *mnēmōn* 'mindful.'

MO ▶ **abbreviation 1** Medical Officer. **2** Missouri. **3** modus operandi. **4** money order.

Mo ▶ **symbol** the chemical element molybdenum.

mo·a /'mōə/ ▶ **noun** a large extinct flightless bird resembling the emu, formerly found in New Zealand.
– ORIGIN Maori.

moan /mōn/ ▶ **noun 1** a low mournful sound, usually expressing suffering. **2** informal a minor complaint. ▶ **verb 1** make a moan. **2** complain or grumble.

> – SYNONYMS **1 groan,** wail, whimper, sob, cry. **2 complain,** grouse, grumble, whine, carp; informal gripe, grouch, bellyache, bitch, beef.

– DERIVATIVES **moan·er** noun.
– ORIGIN unknown.

moat /mōt/ ▶ **noun** a deep, wide ditch filled with water, surrounding and protecting a castle.
– DERIVATIVES **moat·ed** adjective.
– ORIGIN Old French *mote* 'mound.'

mob /mäb/ ▶ **noun 1** a disorderly crowd of people. **2** (**the Mob**) the Mafia. **3** (**the mob**) derogatory the ordinary people.

> – SYNONYMS **crowd,** horde, multitude, rabble, mass, throng, gathering, assembly.

▶ **verb** (**mobs, mobbing, mobbed**) crowd around someone or into somewhere in an unruly way.

> – SYNONYMS **surround,** crowd round, besiege, jostle.

– ORIGIN from Latin *mobile vulgus* 'excitable crowd.'

mo·bile /'mōbəl, 'mō,bēl, 'mō,bīl/ ▶ **adjective 1** able to move or be moved freely or easily. **2** (of a store or other service) set up in a vehicle so as to travel around. **3** able or willing to move between occupations, homes, or social classes. **4** (of the features of the face) readily changing expression.

> – SYNONYMS **1 able to move,** able to walk, walking; informal up and about. **2** *a mobile library* **traveling,** transportable, portable, movable, itinerant, peripatetic.
> – ANTONYMS immobile.

▶ **noun 1** /'mō,bēl/ a decorative structure hung so as to turn freely in the air. **2** /'mō,bīl/ chiefly Brit. a cell phone.
– PHRASES **upwardly** (or **downwardly**) **mobile** moving to a higher (or lower) social class.
– ORIGIN Latin *mobilis*.

mo·bile home ▶ **noun** a large camper used as permanent living accommodations.

mo·bile phone ▶ **noun** a cell phone.

mo·bil·i·ty /mō'bilətē/ ▶ **noun** the ability to move or be moved freely and easily.

mo·bi·lize /'mōbə,līz/ ▶ **verb 1** prepare and organize troops for active service. **2** organize people or resources for a particular task.

> – SYNONYMS **1** *mobilize the troops* **marshal,** deploy, muster, rally, call up, assemble, mass, organize, prepare. **2** *mobilizing support for the party* **generate,** arouse, awaken, excite, stimulate, stir up, encourage, inspire, whip up.

– DERIVATIVES **mo·bi·li·za·tion** /,mōbələ'zāsʜən/ noun.

Mö·bi·us strip /'mōbēəs/ ▶ **noun** a surface with one continuous side formed by joining the ends of a rectangular strip after twisting one end through 180°.
– ORIGIN named after the German mathematician August F. *Möbius*.

mo·blog /'mō,bläg/ ▶ **noun** a weblog whose content originates from cell phones and other portable wireless devices.

mob·ster /'mäbstər/ ▶ **noun** informal a gangster.

moc·ca·sin /'mäkəsən/ ▶ **noun** a soft leather shoe with the sole turned up and sewn to the upper, originally worn by North American Indians.
– ORIGIN Virginia Algonquian.

mo·cha /'mōkə/ ▶ **noun 1** a fine-quality coffee. **2** a drink or flavoring made with mocha and chocolate.
– ORIGIN named after *Mocha*, a port in Yemen on the Red Sea.

mo·chac·ci·no /,mōkə'cʜēnō/ ▶ **noun** (pl. **mochaccinos**) a cappuccino containing chocolate syrup or flavoring.
– ORIGIN blend of **MOCHA** and **CAPPUCCINO**.

mock /mäk/ ▶ **verb 1** tease or laugh at someone scornfully. **2** imitate someone in an unkind way. **3** (**mock something up**) make a replica or imitation of something.

> – SYNONYMS **ridicule,** jeer at, sneer at, deride, make fun of, laugh at, scoff at, tease, taunt. informal goof on, rag on.

▶ **adjective 1** not authentic or real: *a mock-Georgian house*. **2** (of an exam, battle, etc.) arranged for training or practice.

> – SYNONYMS **imitation,** artificial, man-made, simulated, synthetic, ersatz, fake, reproduction, pseudo, false, spurious; informal pretend.
> – ANTONYMS genuine.

▶ **noun** (**mocks**) Brit. informal exams taken in school as training for public exams.
– DERIVATIVES **mock·er** noun **mock·ing·ly** adverb.
– ORIGIN Old French *mocquer* 'deride.'

> **CHOOSE THE RIGHT WORD**
>
> See **IMITATE**.

mock·er·y /'mäk(ə)rē/ ▶ **noun** (pl. **mockeries**) **1** scornful teasing; ridicule. **2** an absurd or worthless version of something: *the contents of the bowl were a mockery of food*.
– PHRASES **make a mockery of** make something seem foolish or absurd.

mock-he·ro·ic ▶ **adjective** imitating the grandiose style of heroic literature in order to mock an ordinary subject.

mock·ing·bird /'mäkiNG,bərd/ ▶ **noun** a long-tailed American songbird, noted for its mimicry of the calls of other birds.

mock or·ange ▶ **noun** a bushy shrub with white flowers whose perfume resembles that of orange blossom.

mock-up ▶ **noun** a model of a machine or structure that is used for teaching or testing.

mod /mäd/ ▶ **noun** Brit. (especially in the 1960s) a young person of a group who wore stylish clothes and rode motor scooters. ▶ **adjective** informal modern.

mod·al /'mōdl/ ▶ **adjective** **1** relating to the way in which something is done. **2** Grammar relating to the mood of a verb. **3** (of music) using melodies or harmonies based on modes other than the ordinary major and minor scales.
– DERIVATIVES **mo·dal·i·ty** /mō'dalitē/ noun (pl. **modalities**) **mod·al·ly** adverb.

mod·al verb ▶ **noun** Grammar an auxiliary verb that expresses necessity or possibility, e.g., *must*, *shall*, *will*.

mod·ding /'mädiNG/ ▶ **noun** informal the activity of modifying hardware or software to perform in a way desired by the user but not envisioned or permitted by the manufacturer.
– DERIVATIVES **mod·der** noun.
– ORIGIN back formation from *modify*.

mode /mōd/ ▶ **noun** **1** a way in which something occurs or is done: *his preferred mode of travel was a kayak*. **2** a style or fashion in clothes, art, etc. **3** a set of musical notes forming a scale and from which melodies and harmonies are constructed. **4** Statistics the value that occurs most frequently in a given set of data.

– SYNONYMS **1 manner,** way, means, method, system, style, approach. **2** *the camera is in manual mode* **function,** position, operation, setting, option.

– ORIGIN Latin *modus* 'measure, manner.'

mod·el /'mädl/ ▶ **noun** **1** a three-dimensional copy of a person or thing, typically on a smaller scale. **2** something used as an example. **3** an excellent example of a quality: *she was a model of self-control*. **4** a person employed to display clothes by wearing them. **5** a person employed to pose for an artist or photographer. **6** a particular design or version of a product. **7** a simplified mathematical description of a system or process, used to assist calculations and predictions.

– SYNONYMS **1 replica,** copy, representation, mock-up, dummy, imitation, duplicate, reproduction, facsimile. **2** (as adj.) *model trains* **replica,** toy, miniature, dummy, imitation, duplicate, reproduction, facsimile. **3 prototype,** archetype, type, paradigm, version, mold, template, framework, pattern, design, blueprint. **4** *she was a model of patience* **ideal,** paragon, perfect example/specimen; perfection, acme, epitome, nonpareil, crème de la crème. **5** (as adj.) *a model teacher* **ideal,** perfect, exemplary, classic, flawless, faultless, nonpareil. **6 fashion model,** supermodel, mannequin; informal clothes horse.

▶ **verb** (**models, modeling, modeled**) **1** make or shape a figure in clay, wax, etc. **2** (**model something on**) use something as an example to follow. **3** display clothes by wearing them. **4** work as an artist's or photographer's model. **5** make a mathematical model of something. **6** (in drawing or painting) make something appear three-dimensional.
– DERIVATIVES **mod·el·er** noun.

mod·el house (also **model home**) ▶ **noun** a new house, especially a prefabricated one or one on the site of a new development, that is furnished and decorated to be shown to possible buyers.

mo·dem /'mōdəm, 'mō,dem/ ▶ **noun** a device for converting digital and analog signals, especially to enable a computer to be connected to a telephone line.
– ORIGIN blend of *modulator* and *demodulator*.

mod·er·ate ▶ **adjective** /'mäd(ə)rət/ **1** average in amount, intensity, or degree: *we walked at a moderate pace*. **2** (of a political position) not radical or extreme.

– SYNONYMS **1 average,** modest, medium, middling, tolerable, passable, adequate, fair; informal OK, so-so, bog-standard, fair-to-middling. **2** *moderate prices* **reasonable,** within reason, acceptable, affordable, inexpensive, fair, modest, low. **3** *moderate views* **middle-of-the-road,** nonextremist, liberal, pragmatic, centrist.
– ANTONYMS immoderate, extreme.

▶ **noun** /'mäd(ə)rət/ a person with moderate political views.

▶ **verb** /'mädə,rāt/ **1** make or become less extreme or intense. **2** be in charge of a decision-making body or a debate. **3** monitor an Internet bulletin board or chat room for inappropriate or offensive content.

– SYNONYMS **1 die down,** abate, let up, calm down, lessen, decrease, diminish, recede, weaken, subside. **2 curb,** control, check, temper, restrain, subdue, tame, lessen, decrease, lower, reduce, diminish, alleviate, allay, appease, ease, soothe, calm, tone down.
– ANTONYMS increase.

– ORIGIN from Latin *moderare* 'reduce, control.'

mod·er·ate·ly /'mäd(ə)rətlē/ ▶ **adverb** to a certain extent.

– SYNONYMS **somewhat,** quite, fairly, reasonably, comparatively, relatively, to some extent, tolerably, adequately; informal pretty.

mod·er·a·tion /,mädə'rāsHən/ ▶ **noun** **1** the avoidance of extremes in one's actions or opinions. **2** the action of making something less intense or extreme.

CHOOSE THE RIGHT WORD

See **ABSTINENCE**.

mod·e·ra·to /,mädə'rätō/ ▶ **adverb & adjective** Music at a moderate pace.
– ORIGIN Italian, 'moderate.'

mod·er·a·tor /'mädə,rātər/ ▶ **noun** **1** a person who helps people to settle a dispute. **2** a person who presides over a debate.

mod·ern /'mädərn/ ▶ **adjective** **1** relating to the present or to recent times. **2** having or using the most up-to-date techniques or equipment. **3** (in the arts) marked by a significant departure from traditional styles and values.

– SYNONYMS **1** *modern times* **present-day,** contemporary, present, current, twenty-first-century, latter-day, recent. **2** *her clothes are very modern* **fashionable,** up to date, trendsetting, stylish, chic, à la mode, the latest, new, newest, newfangled, advanced; informal trendy, cool, in, funky.
– ANTONYMS past, old-fashioned.

▶ **noun** a person who believes in a departure from traditional styles or values.
– DERIVATIVES **mo·der·ni·ty** /mä'dərnitē, mə-, -'der-/ noun **mod·ern·ly** adverb **mod·ern·ness** noun.
– ORIGIN Latin *modernus*.

mod·ern·ism /'mädər,nizəm/ ▶ **noun** **1** modern ideas, methods, or styles. **2** a movement in the arts that aims to depart significantly from traditional styles or ideas.
– DERIVATIVES **mod·ern·ist** /'mädərnist/ noun & adjective **mod·ern·is·tic** /,mädər'nistik/ adjective.

mod·ern·ize /'mädər,nīz/ ▶ **verb** bring something up to date with modern equipment, techniques, or ideas.
– SYNONYMS **update,** bring up to date, streamline, rationalize, overhaul, renovate, remodel, refashion, revamp.
– DERIVATIVES **mod·ern·i·za·tion** /,mädərnə'zāsʜən/ noun **mod·ern·iz·er** noun.

mod·est /'mädəst/ ▶ **adjective** **1** viewing one's abilities or achievements in a humble way. **2** relatively moderate, limited, or small: *drink modest amounts of alcohol*. **3** not showing off the body.
– SYNONYMS **1 humble,** self-deprecating, self-effacing, unassuming, shy, diffident, reserved, bashful. **2** *modest success* **moderate,** fair, limited, tolerable, passable, adequate, satisfactory, acceptable, unexceptional. **3** *a modest house* **small,** ordinary, simple, plain, humble, inexpensive, unostentatious, unpretentious. **4** *her modest dress* **demure,** decent, seemly, decorous, proper.
– ANTONYMS conceited, grand, indecent.
– DERIVATIVES **mod·est·ly** adverb.
– ORIGIN Latin *modestus* 'keeping due measure.'

mod·es·ty /'mädəstē/ ▶ **noun** the quality or state of being humble, decent, or moderate.
– SYNONYMS **humility,** self-effacement, shyness, bashfulness, self-consciousness, reserve.

mod·i·cum /'mädikəm, 'mōd-/ ▶ **noun** a small quantity of something.
– ORIGIN from Latin *modicus* 'moderate.'

mod·i·fi·ca·tion /,mädəfə'kāsʜən/ ▶ **noun** **1** the action of modifying something. **2** a change made.
– SYNONYMS **change,** adjustment, alteration, adaptation, refinement, revision, amendment; informal tweak.

mod·i·fi·er /'mädə,fīər/ ▶ **noun** **1** a person or thing that modifies something. **2** Grammar a word that qualifies the sense of a noun (e.g., *good* and *family* in *a good family house*).

mod·i·fy /'mädə,fī/ ▶ **verb** (**modifies, modifying, modified**) make partial or minor changes to something.
– SYNONYMS **1 change,** alter, adjust, adapt, amend, revise, refine; informal tweak. **2 moderate,** temper, soften, tone down, qualify.
– ORIGIN Latin *modificare*.

mod·ish /'mōdisʜ/ ▶ **adjective** currently fashionable.
– DERIVATIVES **mod·ish·ly** adverb **mod·ish·ness** noun.

mo·diste /mō'dēst/ ▶ **noun** dated a fashionable milliner or dressmaker.
– ORIGIN French.

mod·u·lar /'mäjələr/ ▶ **adjective** **1** made up of separate units. **2** Mathematics relating to a modulus.
– DERIVATIVES **mod·u·lar·i·ty** /,mäjə'le(ə)ritē/ noun.

mod·u·late /'mäjə,lāt/ ▶ **verb** **1** control or regulate something. **2** vary the strength, tone, or pitch of the voice. **3** adjust the amplitude or frequency of an oscillation or signal. **4** Music change from one key to another.
– DERIVATIVES **mod·u·la·tion** /,mäjə'lāsʜən/ noun **mod·u·la·tor** noun.
– ORIGIN Latin *modulari* 'to measure.'

mod·ule /'mäjo͞ol/ ▶ **noun** **1** each of a set of parts or units that can be used to make a more complex structure. **2** each of a set of independent units of study forming part of a course. **3** an independent self-contained unit of a spacecraft.
– ORIGIN Latin *modulus*.

mod·u·lus /'mäjələs/ ▶ **noun** (pl. **moduli** /-,lī, -,lē/) **1** Mathematics the magnitude of a number irrespective of whether it is positive or negative. **2** Physics a constant factor relating a physical effect to the force producing it.

mo·dus op·e·ran·di /'mōdəs ,äpə'randē, -,dī/ ▶ **noun** (pl. **modi operandi** /'mōdē, 'mōdī/) a way of operating or doing something.
– ORIGIN Latin.

mo·dus vi·ven·di /'mōdəs vi'vendē, -,dī/ ▶ **noun** (pl. **modi vivendi** /'mōdē, 'mōdī/) an arrangement allowing differing or conflicting groups to exist together peacefully.
– ORIGIN Latin.

Mo·gul /'mōgəl/ (also **Moghul** or **Mughal** pronunc. same) ▶ **noun** **1** a member of the Muslim dynasty of Mongol origin that ruled much of India in the 16th–19th centuries. **2** (**mogul**) an important or powerful person.
– SYNONYMS **magnate,** tycoon, VIP, notable, personage, baron, captain, king, lord; informal bigwig, big shot, big noise, top dog, top banana, big enchilada.
– ORIGIN Persian, 'Mongol.'

mo·gul /'mōgəl/ ▶ **noun** a bump on a ski slope formed by the repeated turns of skiers over the same path.
– ORIGIN probably from southern German dialect *Mugel, Mugl*.

mo·hair /'mō,he(ə)r/ ▶ **noun** a yarn or fabric made from the hair of the angora goat.
– ORIGIN Arabic, 'cloth made of goat's hair.'

Mo·ham·me·dan /mo͝o'hamid(ə)n, mō-/ ▶ **noun & adjective** variant spelling of **MUHAMMADAN**.

Mo·hawk /'mō,hôk/ ▶ **noun** (pl. same or **Mohawks**) **1** a member of an American Indian people originally inhabiting parts of what is now upper New York State. **2** the Iroquoian language of this people. **3** a hairstyle with the head shaved except for a strip of hair, typically standing erect, from the middle of the forehead to the back of the neck. ▶ **adjective** relating to the Mohawks or their language.
– ORIGIN from an American Indian language meaning 'maneaters.'

Mo·he·gan /mō'hēgən/ ▶ **noun** **1** a member of an American Indian people formerly inhabiting western parts of Connecticut and Massachusetts. **2** the Algonquian language of this people. ▶ **adjective** relating to the Mohegans or their language.
– ORIGIN Mohegan, 'people of the tidal waters.'

Mo·hi·can /mō'hēkən/ ▶ **adjective & noun** old-fashioned variant of **MAHICAN** or **MOHEGAN**.

moi /mwä/ ▶ **pronoun** humorous me.
– ORIGIN French.

moi·e·ty /ˈmoiətē/ ▶ **noun** (pl. **moieties**) formal or technical each of two parts into which a thing is or can be divided.
– ORIGIN from Old French *moite.*

moi·re /môˈrā, mwä-, mwär/ (also **moiré** /mwäˈrā, mô-/) ▶ **noun** silk fabric treated to give it an appearance like that of rippled water.
– ORIGIN French *moiré* 'mohair' (the treatment first being used on mohair).

moist /moist/ ▶ **adjective** slightly wet; damp.

> – SYNONYMS **1 damp,** steamy, humid, muggy, clammy, dank, wet, soggy, sweaty, sticky. **2 succulent,** juicy, soft, tender.
> – ANTONYMS dry.

– DERIVATIVES **moist·ly** adverb **moist·ness** noun.
– ORIGIN Old French *moiste.*

> **WORD TOOLKIT**
>
> See **RIPE**, **WET**.

mois·ten /ˈmoisən/ ▶ **verb** make or become slightly wet.

> – SYNONYMS **dampen,** wet, damp, water, humidify.

mois·ture /ˈmoisCHər/ ▶ **noun** tiny drops of water or other liquid in the air, in a substance, or condensed on a surface.

> – SYNONYMS **wetness,** wet, water, liquid, condensation, steam, vapor, dampness, damp, humidity.

mois·tur·ize /ˈmoisCHəˌrīz/ ▶ **verb** make something, especially the skin, less dry.
– DERIVATIVES **mois·tur·iz·er** noun.

mo·ji·to /mōˈhētō/ ▶ **noun** a cocktail originating in Cuba and consisting of white rum, lime or lemon juice, sugar, fresh mint, ice, and club soda.

mo·jo /ˈmōˌjō/ ▶ **noun** (pl. **mojos**) **1** a magic charm or spell. **2** power or influence.
– ORIGIN probably African.

mol /mōl/ ▶ **noun** Chemistry short for **MOLE**[4].

mo·lar[1] /ˈmōlər/ ▶ **noun** a grinding tooth at the back of a mammal's mouth.
– ORIGIN from Latin *mola* 'millstone.'

mo·lar[2] ▶ **adjective** Chemistry **1** relating to one mole of a substance. **2** (of a solution) containing one mole of solute per liter of solvent.

mo·las·ses /məˈlasəz/ ▶ **noun 1** a thick dark brown liquid obtained from raw sugar. **2** a paler, sweeter version of this used as a table syrup and in baking.
– ORIGIN from Latin *mellacium* 'must.'

mold[1] /mōld/ (Brit. **mould**) ▶ **noun 1** a hollow container used to give shape to molten or hot liquid material when it cools and hardens. **2** a distinctive type, style, or character: *he's a leader in the mold of Winston Churchill.* **3** a gelatin dessert or mousse.

> – SYNONYMS **1 cast,** die, matrix, form, shape, template, pattern, frame. **2** *an actress in the Hollywood mold* **pattern,** form, type, style, tradition, school.

▶ **verb 1** form an object out of a soft substance. **2** influence the development of something.

> – SYNONYMS **1 shape,** form, fashion, model, work, construct, make, create, sculpt, cast. **2 determine,** direct, control, guide, influence, shape, form, fashion, make.

– PHRASES **break the mold** end a restrictive pattern of events or behavior by doing things differently.
– ORIGIN probably from Old French *modle.*

mold[2] (Brit. **mould**) ▶ **noun** a furry growth of minute fungi occurring in moist warm conditions on organic matter.
– ORIGIN probably from former *moul* 'grow moldy.'

mold[3] (Brit. **mould**) ▶ **noun** soft loose earth, especially when rich in organic matter.
– ORIGIN Old English.

Mol·da·vi·an /mälˈdāvēən, mô-/ ▶ **noun** a person from Moldavia, a former principality of SE Europe. ▶ **adjective** relating to Moldavia.

mold·board /ˈmōldˌbôrd/ ▶ **noun** the blade or plate in a plow that turns the earth over.

mold·er /ˈmōldər/ (Brit. **moulder**) ▶ **verb** slowly decay.
– ORIGIN perhaps from **MOLD**[3].

mold·ing /ˈmōldiNG/ (Brit. **moulding**) ▶ **noun** a shaped strip of wood, stone, or plaster as a decorative architectural feature.

Mol·do·van /məlˈdōvən, mäl-, môl-/ ▶ **noun** a person from Moldova, a country in SE Europe. ▶ **adjective** relating to Moldova.

mold·y /ˈmōldē/ ▶ **adjective** (**moldier, moldiest**) **1** covered with or smelling of mold. **2** informal old-fashioned.
– DERIVATIVES **mold·i·ness** noun.

mo·le[1] /mōl/ ▶ **noun 1** a small burrowing mammal with dark velvety fur, a long muzzle, and very small eyes. **2** a spy who manages to gain an important position within the security defenses of a country. **3** someone within an organization who secretly passes on confidential information to another organization or country.
– ORIGIN Germanic.

mole[2] ▶ **noun** a small dark brown mark on the skin where there is a high concentration of melanin.
– ORIGIN Old English.

mole[3] ▶ **noun 1** a large solid structure acting as a pier, breakwater, or causeway. **2** a harbor formed by a mole.
– ORIGIN Latin *moles* 'mass.'

mole[4] ▶ **noun** Chemistry the SI unit of amount of substance.
– ORIGIN from German *Molekul* 'molecule.'

mo·le[5] /ˈmōlā/ ▶ **noun** a highly spiced Mexican sauce made chiefly from chili peppers and chocolate, served with meat.
– ORIGIN Mexican Spanish.

mo·lec·u·lar /məˈlekyələr/ ▶ **adjective** relating to or consisting of molecules.

mo·lec·u·lar bi·ol·o·gy ▶ **noun** the branch of biology concerned with the macromolecules (e.g., proteins and DNA) essential to life.

mo·lec·u·lar weight ▶ **noun** another term for **RELATIVE MOLECULAR MASS.**

mol·e·cule /ˈmäləˌkyo͞ol/ ▶ **noun** a group of atoms chemically bonded together, representing the smallest fundamental unit of a compound that can take part in a chemical reaction.
– ORIGIN French, from Latin *molecula* 'small mass.'

mole·hill /ˈmōlˌhil/ ▶ **noun** a small mound of earth thrown up by a burrowing mole.
– PHRASES **make a mountain out of a molehill** exaggerate the importance of a small problem.

mole·skin /ˈmōlˌskin/ ▶ **noun 1** the skin of a mole used as fur. **2** a thick cotton fabric with a soft pile surface.

mo·lest /məˈlest/ ▶ **verb 1** assault or abuse someone sexually. **2** dated pester or harass someone in a hostile way.

– SYNONYMS **1 harass,** harry, pester, persecute, torment. **2 (sexually) abuse,** (sexually) assault, interfere with, rape, violate; informal grope, paw; literary ravish.

– DERIVATIVES **mo·les·ta·tion** /ˌmōˌle-, ˌmōlə'stāsHən/ noun **mo·lest·er** noun.
– ORIGIN Latin *molestare* 'annoy.'

CHOOSE THE RIGHT WORD

See **ATTACK**.

moll /mäl/ ▸ **noun** informal **1** a gangster's girlfriend. **2** dated a prostitute.
– ORIGIN familiar form of the woman's name *Mary*.

mol·li·fy /'mäləˌfī/ ▸ **verb** (**mollifies, mollifying, mollified**) make someone feel less angry or anxious.
– DERIVATIVES **mol·li·fi·ca·tion** /ˌmäləfə'kāsHən/ noun.
– ORIGIN Latin *mollis* 'soft.'

CHOOSE THE RIGHT WORD

See **PACIFY**.

mol·lusk /'mäləsk/ (Brit. **mollusc**) ▸ **noun** an invertebrate animal of a large group including snails, slugs, and mussels, with a soft unsegmented body and often an external shell.
– DERIVATIVES **mol·lus·kan** /mə'ləsˌkən/ adjective.
– ORIGIN from Latin *mollis* 'soft.'

mol·ly /'mälē/ (also **mollie**) ▸ **noun** (pl. **mollies**) a small fish that is bred for aquariums in many colors, especially black.
– ORIGIN from the name of Count *Mollien*, a French statesman.

mol·ly·cod·dle /'mälēˌkädl/ ▸ **verb** treat someone in an indulgent or overprotective way.
– ORIGIN from *molly* 'girl' + **CODDLE**.

Mo·lo·tov cock·tail /'mäləˌtôf, -ˌtôv, 'mōlə-/ ▸ **noun** a simple incendiary device thrown by hand, consisting of a bottle of flammable liquid ignited by means of a wick.
– ORIGIN named after the Soviet statesman Vyacheslav *Molotov*, who led the Soviet campaign against Finland in World War II, when such weapons were used by the Finns.

molt /mōlt/ (Brit. **moult**) ▸ **verb** shed old feathers, hair, or skin, to make way for a new growth. ▸ **noun** a period of molting.
– ORIGIN from Latin *mutare* 'to change.'

mol·ten /'mōltn/ ▸ **adjective** (especially of metal, rock, or glass) liquefied by heat.
– ORIGIN old-fashioned past participle of **MELT**.

WORD TOOLKIT

See **RUNNY**.

mol·to /'mōlˌtō, 'môl-/ ▸ **adverb** Music very.
– ORIGIN Italian.

mo·lyb·de·num /mə'libdənəm/ ▸ **noun** a brittle silver-gray metallic element used in some steels and other alloys.
– ORIGIN Greek *molubdos* 'lead.'

mom /mäm/ ▸ **noun** informal one's mother.

mom-and-pop ▸ **adjective** informal referring to a small store or business of a type often run by a married couple: *a little mom-and-pop diner.*

mo·ment /'mōmənt/ ▸ **noun 1** a brief period of time. **2** an exact point in time. **3** formal importance: *the issues were of little moment.* **4** Physics a turning effect produced by a force on an object, expressed as the product of the force and the distance from its line of action to a given point.

– SYNONYMS **1 little while,** short time, bit, minute, instant, (split) second; informal sec, jiffy. **2 point (in time),** stage, juncture, instant, time, hour, second, minute, day.

– PHRASES **have one's** (or **its**) **moments** be very good at times. **moment of truth** a time when a person or thing is tested or a crisis has to be faced. **of the moment** currently popular, famous, or important.
– ORIGIN Latin *momentum* (see **MOMENTUM**).

mo·men·tar·i·ly /ˌmōmən'te(ə)rəlē/ ▸ **adverb 1** for a very short time. **2** very soon.

– SYNONYMS **1** *he paused momentarily* **briefly,** fleetingly, for a moment, for a second, for an instant. **2** *my husband will be here momentarily* **in a moment,** very soon, in a minute, in a second, shortly.

mo·men·tar·y /'mōmənˌterē/ ▸ **adjective** very brief or short-lived.

– SYNONYMS **brief,** short, short-lived, fleeting, passing, transitory, transient, ephemeral.
– ANTONYMS lengthy.

mo·men·tous /mō'men(t)əs, mə'-/ ▸ **adjective** very important or significant: *a momentous decision.*

– SYNONYMS **important,** significant, historic, critical, crucial, decisive, pivotal, consequential, far-reaching; informal earth-shattering.
– ANTONYMS insignificant.

– DERIVATIVES **mo·men·tous·ly** adverb **mo·men·tous·ness** noun.

mo·men·tum /mō'mentəm, mə-/ ▸ **noun** (pl. **momenta** /mō'mentə, mə-/) **1** the force gained by a moving object. **2** the driving force caused by the development of something: *the investigation gathered momentum.* **3** Physics the quantity of motion of a moving body, equal to the product of its mass and velocity.

– SYNONYMS **impetus,** energy, force, driving force, power, strength, thrust, speed, velocity.

– ORIGIN Latin *movimentum*, from *movere* 'to move.'

mom·ma ▸ **noun** variant spelling of **MAMA**.

mom·my /'mämē/ ▸ **noun** (pl. **mommies**) informal one's mother.

Mon. ▸ **abbreviation** Monday.

mon·ad /'mōˌnad/ ▸ **noun** technical a single unit; the number one.
– ORIGIN Greek *monas* 'unit.'

mon·arch /'mänərk, 'mänˌärk/ ▸ **noun 1** a king, queen, or emperor who rules a country or empire. **2** a large orange and black butterfly.

– SYNONYMS **sovereign,** ruler, Crown, crowned head, potentate, king, queen, emperor, empress, prince, princess.

– DERIVATIVES **mo·nar·chi·cal** /mə'närkikəl/ adjective.
– ORIGIN from Greek *monos* 'alone' + *arkhein* 'to rule.'

mon·ar·chism /'mänərˌkizəm, 'mänˌär-/ ▸ **noun** support for the principle that a monarch should rule a country.
– DERIVATIVES **mon·ar·chist** noun & adjective.

mon·ar·chy /'mänərkē, 'mänˌär-/ ▸ **noun** (pl. **monarchies**) **1** rule by a monarch. **2** a country ruled by a monarch.

mon·as·ter·y /'mänəˌsterē/ ▸ **noun** (pl. **monasteries**) a community of monks living under religious vows.

– SYNONYMS friary, abbey, priory, cloister.

– ORIGIN Greek *monastērion*, from *monazein* 'live alone.'

mo·nas·tic /mə'nastik/ ▶ **adjective 1** relating to monks or nuns or their communities. **2** resembling monks or their way of life, especially in being simple, plain, or solitary.
– DERIVATIVES **mo·nas·ti·cal·ly** /-ik(ə)lē/ adverb **mo·nas·ti·cism** /-tə,sizəm/ noun.

Mon·day /'məndā, -dē/ ▶ **noun** the day of the week before Tuesday and following Sunday.
– ORIGIN Old English, 'day of the moon.'

Mon·é·gasque /,mänə'gäsk, -'gask/ ▶ **noun** a person from Monaco. ▶ **adjective** relating to Monaco.
– ORIGIN French.

mon·e·ta·rism /'mänitə,rizəm, 'mən-/ ▶ **noun** the theory that inflation is best controlled by limiting the supply of money circulating in an economy.
– DERIVATIVES **mon·e·ta·rist** noun & adjective.

mon·e·tar·y /'mänə,terē, 'mən-/ ▶ **adjective** relating to money or currency.

– SYNONYMS **financial,** fiscal, pecuniary, money, cash, capital, economic, budgetary.

– DERIVATIVES **mon·e·tar·i·ly** /-,te(ə)rəlē/ adverb.

mon·e·tize /'mänə,tīz/ ▶ **verb 1** convert something into currency. **2** (as adj. **monetized**) (of a society) adapted to the use of money.
– DERIVATIVES **mon·e·ti·za·tion** /,mänətə'zāsнən, ,mänə,tī'zāsнən/ noun.

mon·ey /'mənē/ ▶ **noun 1** a means of payment in the form of coins and bills. **2** the assets, property, etc., owned by someone or something: *the college is very short of money*. **3** payment or profit: *he's making a lot of money*. **4** (**moneys** or **monies**) formal sums of money.

– SYNONYMS **cash,** hard cash, means, wherewithal, funds, capital, finances, notes, coins, change, currency, specie; informal dough, bread, loot, dinero.

– PHRASES **for my money** informal in my opinion. **put one's money where one's mouth is** informal take action to support one's statements.
– ORIGIN Latin *moneta* 'mint, money,' originally a title of the goddess Juno, in whose temple in ancient Rome money was minted.

mon·ey·bags /'mənē,bagz/ ▶ **noun** informal a wealthy person.

mon·eyed /'mənēd/ (also **monied**) ▶ **adjective** having much money; wealthy.

mon·ey-grub·bing ▶ **adjective** informal greedily concerned with making money.

mon·ey·lend·er /'mənē,lendər/ ▶ **noun** a person whose business is lending money, usually at a high rate of interest.

mon·ey·mak·er /'mənē,mākər/ ▶ **noun** a person or thing that earns a lot of money.
– DERIVATIVES **mon·ey·mak·ing** noun & adjective.

mon·ey mar·ket ▶ **noun** the trade in short-term loans between banks and other financial institutions.

mon·ey or·der ▶ **noun** a printed order for payment of a specified sum, issued by a bank or post office.

mon·ey sup·ply ▶ **noun** the total amount of money in circulation or in existence in a country.

-monger ▶ **combining form 1** referring to someone who trades in a particular thing: *fishmonger*. **2** chiefly derogatory referring to a person engaging in a particular activity: *rumor-monger*.
– ORIGIN Latin *mango* 'dealer.'

Mon·gol /'mänɢgəl/ ▶ **noun** a person from Mongolia.

USAGE

The use of the term **mongol** or **mongoloid** to refer to a person with Down syndrome is now unacceptable and considered offensive.

Mon·go·li·an /män'gōlēən, mänɢ-/ ▶ **noun 1** a person from Mongolia. **2** the language of Mongolia. ▶ **adjective** relating to Mongolia.

Mon·gol·oid /'mänɢgə,loid/ ▶ **adjective 1** relating to the division of humankind that includes the peoples native to east Asia, SE Asia, and Arctic North America. **2** (**mongoloid**) offensive affected with Down syndrome.

USAGE

The term **Mongoloid** is associated with outdated ideas about racial types; it is potentially offensive and best avoided.

mon·goose /'män,gōōs, 'mänɢ-/ ▶ **noun** (pl. **mongooses**) a small carnivorous mammal with a long body and tail, native to Africa and Asia.
– ORIGIN Marathi (a central Indian language).

mon·grel /'mänɢgrəl, 'mənɢ-/ ▶ **noun** a dog of a mixed breed.
– ORIGIN apparently related to **MINGLE** and **AMONG**.

mon·ied ▶ **adjective** variant spelling of **MONEYED**.

mon·ies /'mənēz/ plural of **MONEY**, used in financial contexts.

mon·i·ker /'mänikər/ (also **monicker**) ▶ **noun** informal a name.
– DERIVATIVES **mon·i·kered** adjective.
– ORIGIN unknown.

mon·ism /'män,izəm, 'mō,nizəm/ ▶ **noun** Philosophy a theory or doctrine that denies the existence of a distinction between things such as matter and mind.
– DERIVATIVES **mon·ist** noun & adjective.
– ORIGIN from Greek *monos* 'single.'

mon·i·tor /'mänətər/ ▶ **noun 1** a person or device that monitors something. **2** a display screen used to view a picture from a particular camera or an image generated by a computer. **3** a loudspeaker used by performers to hear what is being played or recorded. **4** a student with disciplinary or other special duties during school hours. **5** (also **monitor lizard**) a large tropical lizard.

– SYNONYMS **1 detector,** scanner, recorder, sensor, security camera, CCTV. **2** *UN monitors* **observer,** watchdog, overseer, supervisor, scrutineer. **3** *a computer monitor* **screen,** display, VDU.

▶ **verb** keep someone or something under observation, especially so as to regulate or record their activity or progress.

– SYNONYMS **observe,** watch, track, keep an eye on, keep under surveillance, record, note, oversee; informal keep tabs on.

– ORIGIN from Latin *monere* 'warn.'

monk /mənɢk/ ▶ **noun** a man belonging to a religious community, typically one living under vows of poverty, chastity, and obedience.
– DERIVATIVES **monk·ish** adjective.
– ORIGIN from Greek *monakhos* 'solitary.'

mon·key /ˈməNGkē/ ▶ **noun** (pl. **monkeys**) **1** a primate that typically has a long tail and lives in trees in tropical countries. **2** a mischievous child.

– SYNONYMS **simian**, primate, ape.

▶ **verb** (**monkeys, monkeying, monkeyed**) **1** (**monkey with**) tamper with something. **2** (**monkey around/about**) behave in a silly or playful way.

– SYNONYMS (**monkey with**) **tamper with,** fiddle with, interfere with, meddle with, tinker with, play with; informal mess with.

– PHRASES **make a monkey of** (or **out of**) make a fool of.
– ORIGIN unknown.

mon·key busi·ness ▶ **noun** informal mischievous or underhanded behavior.

mon·key puz·zle ▶ **noun** a coniferous tree with branches covered in spirals of tough spiny leaves.

mon·key suit ▶ **noun** informal a man's evening dress or formal suit.

mon·key wrench ▶ **noun** an adjustable wrench with large jaws.

monk·fish /ˈməNGkˌfisH/ ▶ **noun** (pl. same or **monkfishes**) an anglerfish, especially when used as food.

monks·hood /ˈməNGksˌho͝od/ ▶ **noun** a poisonous plant with blue or purple flowers.

mon·o[1] /ˈmänō/ ▶ **adjective 1** (of sound reproduction) using only one transmission channel. **2** monochrome. ▶ **noun 1** sound reproduction that uses only one transmission channel. **2** monochrome color reproduction.

mon·o[2] ▶ **noun** short for **INFECTIOUS MONONUCLEOSIS**.

mono- (also mon- before a vowel) ▶ **combining form 1** one; single: *monochromatic*. **2** (forming names of chemical compounds) containing one atom or group of a specified kind.
– ORIGIN Greek *monos* 'alone.'

mon·o·bas·ic /ˌmänōˈbāsik/ ▶ **adjective** Chemistry (of an acid) having one replaceable hydrogen atom.

mon·o·chro·mat·ic /ˌmänəkrōˈmatik/ ▶ **adjective 1** containing only one color. **2** (of light or other radiation) of a single wavelength or frequency.

mon·o·chrome /ˈmänəˌkrōm/ ▶ **noun** representation or reproduction of images in black and white or in varying tones of one color. ▶ **adjective** consisting of or displaying images in black and white or in varying tones of one color.
– ORIGIN Greek *monokhrōmatos* 'of a single color.'

mon·o·cle /ˈmänikəl/ ▶ **noun** a single lens worn to improve sight in one eye.
– ORIGIN Latin *monoculus* 'one-eyed.'

mon·o·clo·nal /ˌmänəˈklōnl/ ▶ **adjective** Biology relating to a clone or line of clones produced from a single individual or cell.

mon·o·coque /ˈmänəˌkōk, -ˌkäk/ ▶ **noun** an aircraft or vehicle structure in which the chassis and the body are built as a single piece.
– ORIGIN French, from *mono-* 'single' + *coque* 'shell.'

mon·o·cot·y·le·don /ˌmänəˌkätlˈēdn/ ▶ **noun** a flowering plant whose seeds have a single cotyledon (seed leaf).

mo·noc·u·lar /məˈnäkyələr, mä-/ ▶ **adjective** with, for, or using one eye.
– ORIGIN Latin *monoculus* 'having one eye.'

mon·o·cul·ture /ˈmänəˌkəlcHər/ ▶ **noun** the cultivation of a single crop in a particular area.

mon·o·dy /ˈmänədē/ ▶ **noun** (pl. **monodies**) **1** an ode sung by a single actor in a Greek tragedy. **2** music with only one melodic line.
– ORIGIN Greek *monōdos* 'singing alone.'

mo·noe·cious /məˈnēsHəs/ ▶ **adjective** (of a plant or invertebrate animal) having both the male and female reproductive organs in the same individual. Compare with **DIOECIOUS**.
– ORIGIN from Greek *monos* 'single' + *oikos* 'house.'

mon·o·fil·a·ment /ˌmänəˈfiləmənt/ ▶ **noun** a single strand of a synthetic fiber such as nylon.

mo·nog·a·my /məˈnägəmē/ ▶ **noun** the state of having only one husband, wife, or sexual partner at any one time.
– DERIVATIVES **mo·nog·a·mist** noun **mo·nog·a·mous** adjective.
– ORIGIN from Greek *monos* 'single' + *gamos* 'marriage.'

mon·o·glot /ˈmänəˌglät/ ▶ **adjective** using or speaking only one language.
– ORIGIN from Greek *monos* 'single' + *glōtta* 'tongue.'

mon·o·gram /ˈmänəˌgram/ ▶ **noun** a motif of two or more interwoven letters, typically a person's initials.
– DERIVATIVES **mon·o·grammed** adjective.

mon·o·graph /ˈmänəˌgraf/ ▶ **noun** a scholarly written study of a single subject.
– DERIVATIVES **mon·o·graph·ic** /ˌmänəˈgrafik/ adjective.

mon·o·hull /ˈmänōˌhəl/ ▶ **noun** a boat with only one hull, as opposed to a catamaran or multihull.

mon·o·lin·gual /ˌmänəˈliNGg(yə)wəl/ ▶ **adjective** speaking or expressed in only one language.

mon·o·lith /ˈmänəˌliTH/ ▶ **noun 1** a large single upright block of stone, especially a pillar or monument. **2** a very large organization or institution that is seen as impersonal and slow to change.
– ORIGIN from Greek *monos* 'single' + *lithos* 'stone.'

mon·o·lith·ic /ˌmänəˈliTHik/ ▶ **adjective 1** formed of a single large block of stone. **2** (of an organization or institution) large, impersonal, and slow to change.

mon·o·logue /ˈmänəˌlôg, -ˌläg/ ▶ **noun 1** a long speech by one actor in a play or movie. **2** a long, boring speech by one person during a conversation.
– ORIGIN Greek *monologos* 'speaking alone.'

mon·o·ma·ni·a /ˌmänəˈmānēə/ ▶ **noun** an obsessive preoccupation with one thing.
– DERIVATIVES **mon·o·ma·ni·ac** /-ˈmānēˌak/ noun.

mon·o·mer /ˈmänəmər/ ▶ **noun** a molecule that can be linked to other identical molecules to form a polymer.

mon·o·nu·cle·o·sis /ˌmänōˌn(y)o͞oklēˈōsəs/ ▶ **noun** short for **INFECTIOUS MONONUCLEOSIS**.

mon·o·phon·ic /ˌmänəˈfänik/ ▶ **adjective** full form of **MONO**[1] (sense 1 of the adjective).

mon·o·plane /ˈmänəˌplān/ ▶ **noun** an aircraft with one pair of wings.

mo·nop·o·list /məˈnäpəlist/ ▶ **noun** a person or organization that has exclusive control of the supply of a particular product or service.
– DERIVATIVES **mo·nop·o·lis·tic** /məˌnäpəˈlistik/ adjective.

mo·nop·o·lize /məˈnäpəˌlīz/ ▶ **verb** dominate or take control of: *bigger teams monopolize the most profitable TV deals.*
– DERIVATIVES **mo·nop·o·li·za·tion** /məˌnäpələˈzāsHən/ noun.

mo·nop·o·ly /mə'näpəlē/ ▶ noun (pl. **monopolies**) **1** the exclusive possession or control of the supply of a product or service. **2** an organization having a monopoly, or a product or service controlled by one. **3** exclusive possession or control of something: *men don't have a monopoly on unrequited love*.
– ORIGIN from Greek *monos* 'single' + *pōlein* 'sell.'

mon·o·rail /'mänə,rāl/ ▶ noun a railroad in which the track consists of a single rail.

mon·o·sac·cha·ride /,mänə'sakə,rīd/ ▶ noun a sugar (e.g., glucose) that cannot be broken down to give a simpler sugar.

mon·o·so·di·um glu·ta·mate /,mänə,sōdēəm 'glo͞otə,māt/ ▶ noun a compound used to add flavor to food.

mon·o·syl·lab·ic /,mänəsə'labik/ ▶ adjective **1** consisting of one syllable. **2** saying only brief words, or saying very little.

mon·o·syl·la·ble /,mänə'siləbəl, 'mänə,sil-/ ▶ noun a word of one syllable.

mon·o·the·ism /'mänə,THē,izəm/ ▶ noun the belief that there is a single god.
– DERIVATIVES **mon·o·the·ist** noun & adjective **mon·o·the·is·tic** /,mänəTHē'istik/ adjective.

mon·o·tone /'mänə,tōn/ ▶ noun a continuing sound, especially of someone's voice, that is unchanging in pitch.

mo·not·o·nous /mə'nätn-əs/ ▶ adjective **1** boring because of lack of change or variety: *a monotonous job*. **2** (of a sound) lacking variation of tone or pitch.

> – SYNONYMS **tedious,** boring, uninteresting, unexciting, dull, repetitive, repetitious, unvarying, unchanging, mechanical, mind-numbing, soul-destroying; informal deadly.
> – ANTONYMS interesting.

– DERIVATIVES **mo·not·o·nous·ly** adverb **mo·not·o·ny** /mə'nätn-ē/ noun.

mon·o·treme /'mänə,trēm/ ▶ noun a mammal that possesses a cloaca and lays eggs, i.e., a platypus or echidna.
– ORIGIN from Greek *monos* 'single' + *trēma* 'hole.'

mon·o·un·sat·u·rat·ed /,mänō,ən'sacHə,rātid/ ▶ adjective referring to fats whose molecules are saturated except for one multiple bond, believed to be healthier in the diet than polyunsaturated fats.

mon·ox·ide /mə'näk,sīd/ ▶ noun an oxide containing one atom of oxygen.

Mon·roe Doc·trine /mən'rō/ ▶ noun a principle of US policy, originated by President James Monroe in 1823, that any intervention by external powers in the politics of the Americas is a potentially hostile act against the US.

Mon·sei·gneur /,mōNsān'yər/ ▶ noun (pl. **Messeigneurs** /,māsān'yər(z)/) a title or form of address for a French-speaking prince, cardinal, archbishop, or bishop.
– ORIGIN French, 'my lord.'

Mon·sieur /mə'syœ(r), mə'syər/ ▶ noun (pl. **Messieurs** /mə'syœ(r)(z), mā-, mə'syər(z)/) a title or form of address for a French-speaking man, corresponding to *Mr.* or *sir*.
– ORIGIN French, 'my lord.'

Mon·si·gnor /män'sēnyər, mən-/ ▶ noun (pl. **Monsignori** /,mänsēn'yôrē/) the title of various senior Roman Catholic priests and officials.
– ORIGIN Italian.

mon·soon /män'so͞on, 'män,so͞on/ ▶ noun **1** a seasonal wind in the region of the Indian subcontinent and SE Asia, bringing rain when blowing from the southwest. **2** the rainy season (typically May to September) accompanying the monsoon.
– DERIVATIVES **mon·soon·al** adjective.
– ORIGIN Arabic, 'season.'

mons pu·bis /'mänz 'pyo͞obis/ ▶ noun the rounded mass of fatty tissue lying over the joint of the pubic bones.
– ORIGIN Latin, 'mount of the pubes.'

mon·ster /'mänstər/ ▶ noun **1** a large, ugly, and frightening imaginary creature. **2** a very cruel or wicked person.

> – SYNONYMS **1 giant,** mammoth, demon, dragon, colossus, leviathan. **2 fiend,** animal, beast, devil, demon, barbarian, savage, brute; informal swine.

▶ adjective informal extraordinarily large: *a monster 36-lb. carp*.
– ORIGIN Latin *monstrum*.

mon·strance /'mänstrəns/ ▶ noun (in the Roman Catholic Church) a container in which the consecrated Host is displayed for veneration.
– ORIGIN from Latin *monstrare* 'to show.'

mon·stros·i·ty /män'sträsətē/ ▶ noun (pl. **monstrosities**) **1** a very large and ugly building or other object. **2** a thing that is evil.

mon·strous /'mänstrəs/ ▶ adjective **1** very large and ugly or frightening. **2** very evil or wrong: *a monstrous crime*. **3** extraordinarily large: *a monstrous tidal wave*.

> – SYNONYMS **1 grotesque,** hideous, ugly, ghastly, gruesome, horrible, horrific, horrifying, grisly, disgusting, repulsive, dreadful, frightening, terrible, terrifying. **2 appalling,** wicked, abominable, terrible, horrible, dreadful, vile, outrageous, unspeakable, despicable, vicious, savage, barbaric, inhuman.
> – ANTONYMS beautiful, humane.

– DERIVATIVES **mon·strous·ly** adverb.

mons Ve·ne·ris /'mänz 'venərəs/ ▶ noun (in women) the mons pubis.
– ORIGIN Latin, 'mount of Venus.'

mon·tage /män'täzH, mōn-, mōN-/ ▶ noun **1** the technique of putting together separate photos or sections of filmed or videotaped images to form a composite whole. **2** a composite picture, video, etc., resulting from this.
– ORIGIN French.

mon·tane /män'tān, 'män,tān/ ▶ adjective relating to or inhabiting mountainous country.
– ORIGIN Latin, from *mons* 'mountain.'

Mon·te·ne·grin /,mäntə'negrən/ ▶ noun a person from Montenegro, a republic in the Balkans. ▶ adjective relating to Montenegro.

Mon·tes·so·ri /,mäntə'sôrē/ ▶ noun a system of education that aims to develop a child's natural interests and activities rather than use formal teaching methods.
– ORIGIN named after the Italian educationist Maria *Montessori*.

month /mənTH/ ▶ noun **1** each of the twelve named periods into which a year is divided. **2** a period of time between the same dates in successive calendar months. **3** a period of 28 days or four weeks.
– ORIGIN Old English, related to MOON (since in many early civilizations the calendar month was calculated as beginning with the new moon).

month·ly /ˈmənTHlē/ ▶ **adjective** done, produced, or happening once a month. ▶ **adverb** once a month. ▶ **noun** (pl. **monthlies**) a magazine published once a month.

mon·ty /ˈmäntē/ ▶ **noun** (**the full monty**) Brit. informal the full amount expected, desired, or possible.
– ORIGIN unknown; perhaps from *the full Montague Burton*, apparently meaning 'Sunday-best three-piece suit' (from the name of a tailor), or in reference to 'the full cooked English breakfast' insisted on by Field Marshal *Montgomery*.

mon·u·ment /ˈmänyəmənt/ ▶ **noun** **1** a statue or structure built to commemorate a person or event. **2** a structure or site of historical importance. **3** a lasting and memorable example of something: *the house is a monument to timeless elegance*.

> – SYNONYMS **memorial,** statue, pillar, cairn, column, obelisk, cross, cenotaph, tomb, mausoleum, shrine.

– ORIGIN Latin *monumentum*.

mon·u·men·tal /ˌmänyəˈmentl/ ▶ **adjective** **1** very large or impressive: *a monumental achievement*. **2** acting as a monument.

> – SYNONYMS **1 huge,** enormous, gigantic, massive, colossal, mammoth, immense, tremendous, mighty, stupendous. **2 significant,** important, majestic, memorable, remarkable, noteworthy, momentous, grand, awe-inspiring, heroic, epic.
> – ANTONYMS tiny.

– DERIVATIVES **mon·u·men·tal·i·ty** /ˌmänyəˌmenˈtalətē/ noun **mon·u·men·tal·ly** adverb.

moo /mo͞o/ ▶ **verb** (**moos, mooing, mooed**) (of a cow) make a long, deep sound. ▶ **noun** (pl. **moos**) the long, deep sound made by a cow.
– ORIGIN imitating the sound.

mooch /mo͞oCH/ ▶ **verb** **1** ask for or obtain something without paying for it. **2** informal (**mooch around/about**) stand or walk around in a bored or listless way.
– ORIGIN probably from Old French *muscher* 'hide, skulk.'

mood /mo͞od/ ▶ **noun** **1** a temporary state of mind. **2** an angry, irritable, or sulky state of mind: *she's in a mood*. **3** the atmosphere or overall tone of something: *the mood of modern times*. **4** Grammar a form or category of a verb expressing a fact, command, question, wish, or condition.

> – SYNONYMS **1 frame of mind,** state of mind, humor, temper. **2 bad mood,** temper, bad temper, sulk, low spirits, the doldrums, the blues. **3 atmosphere,** feeling, spirit, ambience, aura, character, flavor, feel, tone.

– ORIGIN Old English.

mood sta·bil·iz·er ▶ **noun** a drug used in the treatment of mental disorders that are characterized by unstable mood shifts.

mood swing ▶ **noun** an abrupt and apparently unaccountable change of mood.

mood·y /ˈmo͞odē/ ▶ **adjective** (**moodier, moodiest**) **1** tending to become bad-tempered or sulky. **2** giving a sad or mysterious impression.

> – SYNONYMS **temperamental,** emotional, volatile, capricious, erratic, bad-tempered, petulant, sulky, sullen, morose.
> – ANTONYMS cheerful.

– DERIVATIVES **mood·i·ly** adverb **mood·i·ness** noun.

moo·lah /ˈmo͞oˌlä/ ▶ **noun** informal money.
– ORIGIN unknown.

moo·li /ˈmo͞oˌlē/ ▶ **noun** a variety of large white slender radish.
– ORIGIN from Sanskrit, 'root.'

moon /mo͞on/ ▶ **noun** **1** (also **Moon**) the natural satellite of the earth, orbiting it every 28 days and shining by reflected light from the sun. **2** a natural satellite of any planet. **3** literary or humorous a month. ▶ **verb** **1** (usu. **moon around/about**) behave in a listless or dreamy way. **2** informal expose one's buttocks to someone as an insult or joke.

> – SYNONYMS **daydream,** loaf, idle, brood, mope, pine.

– PHRASES **over the moon** informal delighted.
– ORIGIN Old English, related to **MONTH**.

> **WORD LINKS**
>
> **lunar** *relating to the moon*

moon·beam /ˈmo͞onˌbēm/ ▶ **noun** a ray of moonlight.

moon boot ▶ **noun** a thickly padded boot with a fabric or plastic outer surface.

moon-faced ▶ **adjective** having a round face.

Moon·ie /ˈmo͞onē/ ▶ **noun** informal, often derogatory a member of the Unification Church.
– ORIGIN named after its founder, the Korean religious leader Sun Myung *Moon*.

moon·light /ˈmo͞onˌlīt/ ▶ **noun** the light of the moon. ▶ **verb** (past and past part. **moonlighted**) informal have a second job, especially at night, in addition to one's regular employment.
– DERIVATIVES **moon·light·er** noun **moon·lit** adjective.

moon·scape /ˈmo͞onˌskāp/ ▶ **noun** a rocky and barren landscape resembling the moon's surface.

moon·shine /ˈmo͞onˌSHīn/ ▶ **noun** informal **1** foolish talk or ideas. **2** liquor that has been made illicitly or smuggled.

> – SYNONYMS **alcohol,** corn liquor, corn mash, bootleg liquor/whiskey; informal white lightning, hooch, booze, homebrew, mountain dew, firewater, rotgut.

moon·stone /ˈmo͞onˌstōn/ ▶ **noun** a pearly white semiprecious form of the mineral feldspar.

moon·struck /ˈmo͞onˌstrək/ ▶ **adjective** unable to think or act normally, especially as a result of being in love.

moon·walk /ˈmo͞onˌwôk/ ▶ **verb** **1** walk on the moon. **2** move or dance in a way reminiscent of the weightless movement of walking on the moon.

moon·y /ˈmo͞onē/ ▶ **adjective** (**moonier, mooniest**) dreamy, especially as a result of being in love.

Moor /mo͝or/ ▶ **noun** a member of a Muslim people of NW Africa.
– DERIVATIVES **Moor·ish** adjective.
– ORIGIN Greek *Mauros* 'inhabitant of Mauretania' (an ancient region of N. Africa).

moor[1] /mo͝or/ ▶ **noun** chiefly Brit. a stretch of open uncultivated upland.
– ORIGIN Old English.

moor[2] ▶ **verb** secure a boat by attaching it by cable or rope to the shore or to an anchor.

> – SYNONYMS **tie (up),** secure, make fast, berth, dock.

– ORIGIN probably from Germanic.

moor·hen /ˈmo͝orˌhen/ ▶ **noun** a water bird with blackish plumage and a red and yellow bill.

moor·ing /ˈmo͝oriNG/ (also **moorings**) ▶ **noun** **1** a place where a boat is moored. **2** the ropes, chains, or anchors by which a boat is moored.

moor·land /ˈmo͝o(ə)rlənd, -ˌland/ ▶ **noun** (also **moorlands**) chiefly Brit. an extensive area of moor.

moose /mo͞os/ ▶ **noun** (pl. same) a large northern deer with broad antlers and a growth of skin hanging from the neck.
– ORIGIN from Abnaki (an American Indian language).

moot /mo͞ot/ ▶ **adjective** debatable or uncertain: *a moot point*. ▶ **verb** raise a question or topic for discussion: *the scheme was first mooted last October*. ▶ **noun** a mock trial examining a hypothetical case.
– ORIGIN Old English, 'assembly or meeting.'

mop /mäp/ ▶ **noun** **1** a bundle of thick loose strings or a sponge attached to a handle, used for wiping floors. **2** a thick mass of untidy hair.

> – SYNONYMS *a tousled mop of hair* **shock,** mane, tangle, mass.

▶ **verb** (**mops, mopping, mopped**) **1** clean or soak up liquid from something by wiping: *she mopped the floor*. **2** (**mop something up**) complete or put an end to something by dealing with the remaining parts: *troops mopped up the last pockets of resistance*.
– ORIGIN perhaps related to Latin *mappa* 'napkin.'

mope /mōp/ ▶ **verb** be listless and gloomy.

> – SYNONYMS **1 brood,** sulk, be miserable, be despondent, pine, eat one's heart out, fret, grieve; informal be down in the dumps. **2** *she was moping about the house* **languish,** moon, loaf; Brit. informal mooch; N. Amer. informal lollygag.

– ORIGIN perhaps Scandinavian.

mo·ped /ˈmōˌped/ ▶ **noun** a light motorcycle with an engine capacity below 50 cc.
– ORIGIN from Swedish *trampcykel med motor och pedaler* 'pedal cycle with motor and pedals.'

mop·pet /ˈmäpət/ ▶ **noun** informal an endearing small child.
– ORIGIN from former *moppe* 'baby or rag doll.'

mop·top /ˈmäpˌtäp/ ▶ **noun** a man's hairstyle in the form of a long shaggy bob.

MOR ▶ **abbreviation** (of music) middle-of-the-road.

mo·raine /məˈrān/ ▶ **noun** a mass of rocks and sediment carried down and deposited by a glacier.
– ORIGIN from French dialect *morre* 'snout.'

mor·al /ˈmôrəl, ˈmär-/ ▶ **adjective** **1** concerned with the principles of right and wrong behavior. **2** psychological rather than physical or practical: *moral support*. **3** based on or following the code of behavior that is considered socially right or acceptable: *they have a moral obligation to pay the money back*.

> – SYNONYMS **1 ethical,** good, virtuous, righteous, upright, upstanding, high-minded, principled, honorable, honest, just, noble. **2** *moral support* **psychological,** emotional, mental.
> – ANTONYMS immoral, unethical.

▶ **noun** **1** a lesson about right or wrong that can be learned from a story or experience. **2** (**morals**) standards of behavior, or principles of right and wrong.

> – SYNONYMS **1 lesson,** message, meaning, significance, import, point, teaching. **2** (**morals**) **moral code,** code of ethics, values, principles, standards, (sense of) morality, scruples.

– DERIVATIVES **mor·al·ly** adverb.
– ORIGIN Latin *moralis*.

mo·rale /məˈral/ ▶ **noun** the level of a person's or group's confidence or enthusiasm at a particular time: *the extra pay is aimed at boosting morale*.

> – SYNONYMS **confidence,** self-confidence, self-esteem, spirit(s), team spirit, esprit de corps, motivation.

– ORIGIN French *moral*.

mor·al·ism /ˈmôrəˌlizəm, ˈmär-/ ▶ **noun** the practice of moralizing, especially showing a tendency to make judgments about others' morality.

mor·al·ist /ˈmôrəlist/ ▶ **noun** **1** a teacher or student of morality. **2** a person with a tendency to moralize.
– DERIVATIVES **mor·al·is·tic** /ˌmôrəˈlistik/ adjective.

mo·ral·i·ty /məˈralətē, mô-/ ▶ **noun** (pl. **moralities**) **1** principles concerning the distinction between right and wrong or good and bad behavior. **2** a particular system of values and moral principles. **3** the extent to which an action is right or wrong.

> – SYNONYMS **1 ethics,** rights and wrongs, whys and wherefores. **2 virtue,** good behavior, righteousness, uprightness, morals, standards, principles, honesty, integrity, propriety, honor, decency.

mo·ral·i·ty play ▶ **noun** a kind of play, popular in the 15th and 16th centuries, that presents a lesson about right and wrong behavior, in which characters represent qualities such as good or evil.

mor·al·ize /ˈmôrəˌlīz, ˈmär-/ ▶ **verb** comment on issues of right or wrong behavior, especially in a disapproving way.
– DERIVATIVES **mor·al·iz·er** noun.

mor·al ma·jor·i·ty ▶ **noun** **1** the part of society in favor of strict moral standards. **2** (**Moral Majority**) a right-wing Christian movement in the US.

mor·al phi·los·o·phy ▶ **noun** the branch of philosophy concerned with ethics.

mor·al vic·to·ry ▶ **noun** a situation in which one's ideas or principles are shown to be fair or justified, even if one has not achieved one's aim.

mo·rass /məˈras, mô-/ ▶ **noun** **1** an area of muddy or boggy ground. **2** a complicated or confused situation: *a morass of lies*.
– ORIGIN Dutch *moeras*.

mor·a·to·ri·um /ˌmôrəˈtôrēəm, ˌmär-/ ▶ **noun** (pl. **moratoriums** or **moratoria** /-ˈtôrēə/) **1** a temporary ban on an activity. **2** a legal authorization to debtors to postpone payment.
– ORIGIN Latin.

Mo·ra·vi·an /məˈrāvēən/ ▶ **noun** **1** a person from Moravia in the Czech Republic. **2** a member of a Protestant Church founded by emigrants from Moravia. ▶ **adjective** relating to Moravia or the Moravian Church.

mo·ray /ˈmôrˌā, məˈrā/ (also **moray eel**) ▶ **noun** an eellike predatory fish of warm seas.
– ORIGIN Portuguese *moréia*.

mor·bid /ˈmôrbəd/ ▶ **adjective** **1** having or showing an unhealthy interest in unpleasant subjects, especially death and disease. **2** Medicine relating to or indicating disease.

> – SYNONYMS **ghoulish,** macabre, unhealthy, gruesome, unwholesome; informal sick.
> – ANTONYMS wholesome.

– DERIVATIVES **mor·bid·i·ty** /môrˈbidətē/ noun **mor·bid·ly** adverb.
– ORIGIN Latin *morbus* 'disease.'

mor·dant /ˈmôrdnt/ ▶ **adjective** (especially of humor) sharply sarcastic. ▶ **noun 1** a substance that combines with a dye, used to fix it in a material. **2** a corrosive liquid used to etch the lines on a printing plate.
– ORIGIN Latin *mordere* 'to bite.'

more /môr/ ▶ **determiner & pronoun** a greater or additional amount or degree.

– SYNONYMS **extra,** further, added, additional, supplementary, increased, new.
– ANTONYMS less, fewer.

▶ **adverb 1** forming the comparative of adjectives and adverbs. **2** to a greater extent. **3** again. **4** (**more than**) extremely: *I'm more than happy to oblige.*
– PHRASES **more or less 1** to a certain extent. **2** approximately. **no more 1** nothing or no further. **2** (**be no more**) no longer exist.
– ORIGIN Old English.

USAGE

Do not use **more** with an adjective that is already in a comparative (**-er**) form (as in *more better, more hungrier*); the correct use is *better* or *hungrier* (or *more hungry*).

mo·rel /məˈrel, mô-/ ▶ **noun** an edible fungus having a brown oval or pointed cap with an irregular honeycombed surface.
– ORIGIN French *morille.*

mo·rel·lo /məˈrelō/ ▶ **noun** (pl. **morellos**) a kind of sour dark cherry used in cooking.
– ORIGIN Italian, 'blackish.'

more·o·ver /môrˈōvər/ ▶ **adverb** in addition to what has been said; besides.

– SYNONYMS **besides,** furthermore, what's more, in addition, also, as well, too, to boot, additionally, on top of that, into the bargain.

mo·res /ˈmôrˌāz/ ▶ **plural noun** the customs and conventions of a community.
– ORIGIN Latin, plural of *mos* 'custom.'

mor·ga·nat·ic /ˌmôrgəˈnatik/ ▶ **adjective** (of a marriage) between a man of high rank and a woman of low rank who keeps her former status, their children having no claim to the father's possessions or title.
– ORIGIN from Latin *matrimonium ad morganaticam* 'marriage with a morning gift' (because a gift given by a husband on the morning after the marriage was the wife's only entitlement).

morgue /môrg/ ▶ **noun 1** a mortuary. **2** informal a newspaper's archive, or a collection of cuttings, photographs, or other reference material.
– ORIGIN French, originally the name of a building in Paris where bodies were kept until identified.

mor·i·bund /ˈmôrəˌbənd, ˈmär-/ ▶ **adjective 1** at the point of death. **2** in decline or lacking vitality or effectiveness: *the country's moribund economy.*
– ORIGIN from Latin *mori* 'to die.'

Mor·mon /ˈmôrmən/ ▶ **noun** a member of the Church of Jesus Christ of Latter-Day Saints, a religion founded in the US in 1830 by Joseph Smith Jr.
– DERIVATIVES **Mor·mon·ism** /-ˌnizəm/ noun.
– ORIGIN the name of a prophet to whom Smith attributed *The Book of Mormon*, a collection of supposed revelations.

morn /môrn/ ▶ **noun** literary morning.
– ORIGIN Old English.

mor·nay /môrˈnā/ ▶ **adjective** referring to or served in a cheese-flavored white sauce: *cauliflower mornay.*
– ORIGIN perhaps named after *Mornay*, the eldest son of the French cook Joseph Voiron, the inventor of the sauce.

morn·ing /ˈmôrniNG/ ▶ **noun 1** the period of time between midnight and noon, especially from sunrise to noon. **2** sunrise.

– SYNONYMS **1 before lunch,** a.m., forenoon; literary morn. **2 dawn,** daybreak, sunrise, sunup, first light.

▶ **adverb** (**mornings**) informal every morning.
– ORIGIN from **MORN**, on the pattern of *evening*.

morn·ing-af·ter pill ▶ **noun** a contraceptive pill that is effective up to about seventy-two hours after having sex.

morn·ing glo·ry ▶ **noun** a climbing plant of the convolvulus family with trumpet-shaped flowers.

morn·ing sick·ness ▶ **noun** nausea occurring during early pregnancy.

morn·ing star ▶ **noun** the planet Venus when visible in the east before sunrise.

Mo·roc·can /məˈräkən/ ▶ **noun** a person from Morocco in North Africa. ▶ **adjective** relating to Morocco.

mo·roc·co /məˈräkō/ ▶ **noun** fine flexible leather made (originally in Morocco) from goatskins.

mo·ron /ˈmôrˌän/ ▶ **noun** informal a stupid person.
– DERIVATIVES **mo·ron·ic** /məˈränik, mô-/ adjective.
– ORIGIN Greek *mōros* 'foolish.'

mo·rose /məˈrōs, mô-/ ▶ **adjective** sullen and bad-tempered.
– DERIVATIVES **mo·rose·ly** adverb **mo·rose·ness** noun.
– ORIGIN Latin *morosus* 'peevish.'

morph /môrf/ ▶ **verb** (in computer animation) change smoothly and gradually from one image to another.
– ORIGIN from **METAMORPHOSIS**.

mor·pheme /ˈmôrˌfēm/ ▶ **noun** Linguistics the smallest unit of meaning into which a word can be divided (e.g., *in, come, -ing*, forming *incoming*).

mor·phine /ˈmôrˌfēn/ ▶ **noun** a drug obtained from opium and used medicinally to relieve pain.
– ORIGIN named after the Roman god of sleep, *Morpheus*.

mor·phol·o·gy /môrˈfäləjē/ ▶ **noun** (pl. **morphologies**) **1** the branch of biology concerned with the forms and structures of living organisms. **2** the study of the forms of words. **3** the form, shape, or structure of something.
– DERIVATIVES **mor·pho·log·i·cal** /ˌmôrfəˈläjikəl/ adjective **mor·phol·o·gist** noun.

mor·ris danc·ing /môris, ˈmär-/ ▶ **noun** traditional English folk dancing performed outdoors by groups of dancers wearing costumes with small bells attached and carrying handkerchiefs or sticks.
– ORIGIN from *Moorish* (see **MOOR**).

mor·row /ˈmôrō, ˈmärō/ ▶ **noun** (**the morrow**) old use or literary the following day.
– ORIGIN Old English.

Morse code /môrs/ ▶ **noun** an alphabet or code in which letters are represented by combinations of long and short signals of light or sound.
– ORIGIN named after Samuel F. B. *Morse* (1791–1872), US inventor.

mor·sel /ˈmôrsəl/ ▶ **noun** a small piece of food.
– ORIGIN Old French, 'little bite.'

mor·ta·del·la /ˌmôrtəˈdelə/ ▶ **noun** a type of smooth-textured Italian sausage containing pieces of fat.

– ORIGIN from Latin *murtatum* 'sausage seasoned with myrtle berries.'

mor·tal /'môrtl/ ▶ **adjective 1** having to die at some time. **2** causing death: *a mortal wound.* **3** (of fear, pain, etc.) intense. **4** (of conflict or an enemy) lasting until death; never to be reconciled. **5** informal conceivable or imaginable: *every mortal thing.* **6** Christian Theology (of a sin) that deprives the soul of God's grace. Often contrasted with **VENIAL**.

– SYNONYMS **1** *all men are mortal* **perishable,** physical, bodily, corporeal, human, fleshly, earthly, impermanent, transient, ephemeral. **2** *a mortal blow* **fatal,** lethal, deadly, death-dealing, murderous, terminal. **3** *mortal enemies* **deadly,** sworn, irreconcilable, bitter, implacable, unrelenting, remorseless.
– ANTONYMS eternal.

▶ **noun** a human being.

– SYNONYMS **human (being),** person, man, woman, earthling.

– DERIVATIVES **mor·tal·ly** adverb.
– ORIGIN from Latin *mors* 'death.'

mor·tal·i·ty /môr'talətē/ ▶ **noun 1** the state of having to die at some time. **2** death, especially on a large scale. **3** (also **mortality rate**) the number of deaths in a particular area or period, or from a particular cause.

mor·tar /'môrtər/ ▶ **noun 1** a mixture of lime with cement, sand, and water, used to hold bricks or stones together. **2** a cup-shaped container in which substances are crushed or ground with a pestle. **3** a short cannon for firing shells at high angles. ▶ **verb 1** join bricks or stones together with mortar. **2** attack someone or something with shells fired from a mortar.
– ORIGIN Latin *mortarium* 'container in which substances are crushed or ground'; sense 1 is probably a transferred use of sense 2, the mortar being mixed in a trough or other container.

mor·tar·board /'môrtər,bôrd/ ▶ **noun 1** a hat with a stiff, flat square top and a tassel, worn as part of formal academic dress. **2** a small square board held horizontally by a handle on the underside, used for holding mortar.

mort·gage /'môrgij/ ▶ **noun 1** a legal agreement by which a person takes out a loan using property as security (usually a house that is being purchased). **2** an amount of money borrowed in a mortgage. ▶ **verb** give a bank the right to hold a person's house as security for the loan borrowed from them.
– ORIGIN Old French, 'dead pledge.'

mort·ga·gee /,môrgə'jē/ ▶ **noun** the lender in a mortgage.

mort·ga·gor /,môrgi'jôr, 'môrgijər/ ▶ **noun** the borrower in a mortgage.

mor·ti·cian /môr'tisʜən/ ▶ **noun** an undertaker.

mor·ti·fy /'môrtə,fī/ ▶ **verb** (**mortifies, mortifying, mortified**) **1** make someone feel embarrassed or humiliated. **2** use self-discipline to control one's physical desires. **3** (of flesh) become gangrenous.
– DERIVATIVES **mor·ti·fi·ca·tion** /,môrtəfə'kāsʜən/ noun **mor·ti·fy·ing** adjective.
– ORIGIN Old French *mortifier.*

mor·tise /'môrtis/ (also **mortice**) ▶ **noun** a hole or recess designed to receive a corresponding projection (a tenon) so that the two are held together. ▶ **verb 1** join two things together using a mortise and tenon. **2** cut a mortise in something.
– ORIGIN Old French *mortaise.*

mor·tise lock ▶ **noun** a lock set into the framework of a door in a recess or mortise.

mor·tu·ar·y /'môrcʜoo͞,erē/ ▶ **noun** (pl. **mortuaries**) a room or building in which dead bodies are kept until burial or cremation.

– SYNONYMS **morgue,** funeral parlor/home.

▶ **adjective** relating to burial or tombs.
– ORIGIN from Latin *mortuus* 'dead.'

Mo·sa·ic /mō'zā-ik/ ▶ **adjective** relating to or associated with the biblical prophet Moses.

mo·sa·ic /mō'zā-ik/ ▶ **noun** a picture or pattern produced by arranging together small pieces of stone, tile, or glass of different colors.
– DERIVATIVES **mo·sa·i·cist** /mō'zāəsist/ noun.
– ORIGIN French *mosaïque.*

Mo·selle /mō'zel/ (also **Mosel**) ▶ **noun** a light medium-dry white wine from the valley of the Moselle River.

mo·sey /'mōzē/ ▶ **verb** (**moseys, moseying, moseyed**) informal walk or move in a leisurely way.
– ORIGIN unknown.

mosh /mäsʜ/ ▶ **verb** informal dance to rock music in a violent way that involves jumping up and down and deliberately colliding with other dancers.
– ORIGIN perhaps from **MASH** or **MUSH**[1].

mosh pit ▶ **noun** informal an area where moshing occurs, especially in front of the stage at a rock concert.

Mos·lem /'mäzləm, 'mäs-/ ▶ **noun & adjective** variant spelling of **MUSLIM**.

mosque /mäsk/ ▶ **noun** a Muslim place of worship.
– ORIGIN French, from Arabic.

mos·qui·to /mə'skētō/ ▶ **noun** (pl. **mosquitoes**) a small fly, some kinds of which transmit diseases through the bite of the female.
– ORIGIN Spanish and Portuguese, 'little fly.'

mos·qui·to net ▶ **noun** a fine net hung across a door or window or around a bed to keep mosquitoes away.

moss /môs/ ▶ **noun** a small flowerless spreading green plant that grows in damp habitats and reproduces by means of spores.
– DERIVATIVES **moss·y** adjective.
– ORIGIN Old English.

most /mōst/ ▶ **determiner & pronoun 1** greatest in amount or degree. **2** the majority of. ▶ **adverb 1** to the greatest extent. **2** forming the superlative of adjectives and adverbs. **3** very.
– PHRASES **at (the) most** not more than. **for the most part** in most cases; usually. **make the most of** use something to the best advantage.
– ORIGIN Old English.

most·ly /'mōstlē/ ▶ **adverb 1** on the whole; mainly. **2** usually.

– SYNONYMS **1 mainly,** for the most part, on the whole, in the main, largely, chiefly, predominantly, principally, primarily. **2 usually,** generally, in general, as a rule, ordinarily, normally, customarily, typically, most of the time, almost always.

mote /mōt/ ▶ **noun** a speck.
– ORIGIN Old English.

mo·tel /mō'tel/ ▶ **noun** a roadside hotel for motorists.
– ORIGIN blend of **MOTOR** and **HOTEL**.

mo·tet /mō'tet/ ▶ **noun** a short piece of sacred choral music.
– ORIGIN Old French, 'little word.'

moth /môTH/ ▶ **noun** an insect resembling a butterfly but holding its wings flat when at rest and mainly active at night.
– ORIGIN Old English.

moth·ball /ˈmôTH,bôl/ ▶ **noun** a small ball of a strong-smelling substance such as naphthalene, placed among stored clothes to keep clothes moths away. ▶ **verb** put something into storage or on hold for an indefinite period: *plans to invest in four superstores have been mothballed.*

moth-eat·en /ˈmôTH ,ētn/ ▶ **adjective** damaged or apparently damaged by clothes moths; shabby or threadbare.

moth·er /ˈməT͟Hər/ ▶ **noun 1** a female parent. **2** (**Mother**) (especially as a title or form of address) the head of a female religious community. **3** informal an extreme or very large example of something: *the mother of all traffic jams.*

– SYNONYMS matriarch, materfamilias; informal mom, mommy, mama, ma; Brit. informal mum.

▶ **verb 1** bring up a child with care and affection. **2** look after someone kindly and protectively.

– SYNONYMS **look after,** care for, take care of, nurse, protect, tend, raise, rear, pamper, coddle, cosset, fuss over.

– DERIVATIVES **moth·er·hood** /-ˌho͝od/ noun **moth·er·less** adjective.
– ORIGIN Old English.

WORD LINKS
maternal *relating to a mother*
matricide *killing of one's mother*

moth·er·board /ˈməT͟Hərˌbôrd/ (also **mainboard** /ˈmānˌbôrd/) ▶ **noun** a printed circuit board containing the main components of a microcomputer.

moth·er coun·try ▶ **noun** a country in relation to its colonies.

Moth·er Goose ▶ **noun** the fictitious creator of a collection of nursery rhymes that was first published in London in the 1760s.

moth·er-in-law ▶ **noun** (pl. **mothers-in-law**) the mother of one's husband or wife.

moth·er·land /ˈməT͟Hərˌland/ ▶ **noun** a person's native country.

moth·er lode ▶ **noun** a principal vein of an ore or mineral.

moth·er·ly /ˈməT͟Hərlē/ ▶ **adjective** relating to or like a mother, especially in being caring, protective, and kind.

– SYNONYMS **maternal,** maternalistic, protective, caring, loving, affectionate, nurturing.

– DERIVATIVES **moth·er·li·ness** noun.

Moth·er Na·ture ▶ **noun** nature personified as a creative and controlling force.

moth·er-of-pearl ▶ **noun** a smooth pearly substance lining the shells of oysters and certain other mollusks.

Moth·er's Day ▶ **noun** a day of the year on which children honor their mothers (in Britain Mothering Sunday, and in North America and South Africa the second Sunday in May).

moth·er ship ▶ **noun** a large spacecraft or ship from which smaller craft are launched or maintained.

Moth·er Su·pe·ri·or ▶ **noun** the head of a community of nuns.

moth·er tongue ▶ **noun** a person's native language.

mo·tif /mōˈtēf/ ▶ **noun 1** a single or repeated image forming a design. **2** a theme that is repeated in an artistic, musical, or literary work.

– SYNONYMS **1 design,** pattern, decoration, figure, shape, device, emblem. **2 theme,** idea, concept, subject, topic, leitmotif.

– ORIGIN French.

mo·tile /ˈmōtl, ˈmōˌtīl/ ▶ **adjective** (of cells and single-celled organisms) capable of motion.
– DERIVATIVES **mo·til·i·ty** /mōˈtilətē/ noun.
– ORIGIN from Latin *motus* 'motion.'

mo·tion /ˈmōSHən/ ▶ **noun 1** the action of moving. **2** a movement or gesture. **3** a formal proposal put to a lawmaking body or committee.

– SYNONYMS **1 movement,** locomotion, progress, passage, transit, course, travel, orbit. **2 gesture,** movement, signal, sign, indication, wave, nod, gesticulation. **3 proposal,** proposition, recommendation.

▶ **verb** direct someone by making a gesture: *he motioned her toward the sofa.*

– SYNONYMS **gesture,** signal, direct, indicate, wave, beckon, nod.

– DERIVATIVES **mo·tion·less** adjective.
– PHRASES **go through the motions** do something with little effort or care.
– ORIGIN from Latin *movere* 'to move.'

WORD LINKS
kinetic *relating to motion*

mo·tion pic·ture ▶ **noun** a movie.

mo·tion sick·ness ▶ **noun** nausea caused by motion, especially by traveling in a motor vehicle, boat, or airplane.

mo·ti·vate /ˈmōtəˌvāt/ ▶ **verb 1** give someone a motive for doing something: *he was motivated by the desire for profit.* **2** stimulate someone's interest: *it is the teacher's job to motivate the child at school.*

– SYNONYMS **prompt,** drive, move, inspire, stimulate, influence, activate, impel, propel, push, spur (on), encourage, incentivize.

– DERIVATIVES **mo·ti·va·tor** /-ˌvātər/ noun.

mo·ti·va·tion /ˌmōtəˈvāSHən/ ▶ **noun 1** the reason or reasons behind someone's actions or behavior. **2** desire or willingness to do something; enthusiasm.

– SYNONYMS **motive,** motivating force, incentive, stimulus, stimulation, inspiration, inducement, incitement, spur.

– DERIVATIVES **mo·ti·va·tion·al** /-SHənl/ adjective.

mo·tive /ˈmōtiv/ ▶ **noun** a factor influencing a person to act in a particular way.

– SYNONYMS **reason,** motivation, motivating force, rationale, grounds, cause, basis.

▶ **adjective** producing physical or mechanical motion.
– DERIVATIVES **mo·tive·less** adjective.
– ORIGIN Latin *motivus.*

mo·tive pow·er ▶ **noun** the energy used to drive machinery.

mot juste /ˌmō ˈzhYst/ ▶ **noun** (pl. **mots justes** pronunc. same) (**the mot juste**) the most appropriate word or expression.
– ORIGIN French, 'appropriate word.'

mot·ley /ˈmätlē/ ▶ **adjective** made up of a variety of very different people or things: *a motley collection of cars.* ▶ **noun** a varied mixture.
– ORIGIN unknown.

mo·to·cross /ˈmōtōˌkrôs, -ˌkräs/ ▶ **noun** cross-country racing on motorcycles.

mo·tor /ˈmōtər/ ▶ **noun** a machine that supplies the power to drive a vehicle or other device. ▶ **adjective** **1** relating to motor vehicles. **2** giving or producing motion or action. **3** relating to muscular movement or the nerves activating it. ▶ **verb** travel in a car.
– ORIGIN Latin, 'mover,' from *movere* 'to move.'

mo·tor·bike /ˈmōtərˌbīk/ ▶ **noun** a motorcycle.

mo·tor·boat /ˈmōtərˌbōt/ ▶ **noun** a boat powered by a motor.

mo·tor·cade /ˈmōtərˌkād/ ▶ **noun** a procession of motor vehicles.
– ORIGIN from **MOTOR**, on the pattern of *cavalcade.*

mo·tor·car /ˈmōtərˌkär/ ▶ **noun** dated or Brit. an automobile.

mo·tor·cy·cle /ˈmōtərˌsīkəl/ ▶ **noun** a two-wheeled vehicle that is powered by a motor and has no pedals.
– DERIVATIVES **mo·tor·cy·cling** /-ˌsīk(ə)liNG/ noun **mo·tor·cy·clist** /-ˌsīk(ə)list/ noun.

mo·tor home ▶ **noun** a motor vehicle equipped like a trailer for living in, with kitchen facilities, beds, etc.

mo·tor·ist /ˈmōtərist/ ▶ **noun** the driver of a car.

mo·tor·ize /ˈmōtəˌrīz/ ▶ **verb** (usu. as adj. **motorized**) **1** equip a vehicle or device with a motor to operate or propel it. **2** equip troops with motor transport.
– DERIVATIVES **mo·tor·i·za·tion** /ˌmōtərəˈzāSHən/ noun.

mo·tor·man /ˈmōtərˌmən/ ▶ **noun** (pl. **motormen**) the driver of a subway train or streetcar.

mo·tor·mouth /ˈmōtərˌmouTH/ ▶ **noun** informal a person who talks rapidly and continuously.

mo·tor neu·ron di·sease ▶ **noun** a disease in which the nerve cells carrying messages to the muscles from the brain gradually deteriorate, causing muscle loss and eventual death.

mo·tor pool ▶ **noun** a group of vehicles maintained by the government or military for use by personnel.

mo·tor rac·ing ▶ **noun** the sport of racing in specially developed fast cars.

mo·tor ve·hi·cle ▶ **noun** a road vehicle powered by an internal combustion engine.

mo·tor·way /ˈmōtərˌwā/ ▶ **noun** Brit. a road designed for fast traffic; an expressway.

mot·tle /ˈmätl/ ▶ **verb** (usu. as adj. **mottled**) mark something with patches of a different color. ▶ **noun** a patch of color.
– ORIGIN probably from **MOTLEY**.

mot·to /ˈmätō/ ▶ **noun** (pl. **mottoes** or **mottos**) a short sentence or phrase expressing a belief or aim of a person or group.

> – SYNONYMS **slogan,** maxim, saying, proverb, aphorism, adage, saw, axiom, formula, catchphrase.

– ORIGIN Italian, 'word.'

moue /mo͞o/ ▶ **noun** a pout.
– ORIGIN French.

mould, etc. /mōld/ ▶ **noun & verb** British spelling of **MOLD**[1], **MOLD**[2], **MOLD**[3], etc.

mould·er /ˈmōldər/ ▶ **verb & noun** British spelling of **MOLDER**.

mould·ing /ˈmōldiNG/ ▶ **noun** British spelling of **MOLDING**.

mound /mound/ ▶ **noun** **1** a raised rounded mass of earth or other material. **2** a small hill. **3** a large pile or quantity of something.

> – SYNONYMS **1 heap,** pile, stack, mountain. **2 hillock,** hill, knoll, rise, hummock, hump.

▶ **verb** heap something up into a rounded pile.
– ORIGIN uncertain.

mount[1] /mount/ ▶ **verb** **1** climb up or onto something. **2** get up on an animal or bicycle to ride it. **3** (**be mounted**) be on horseback. **4** increase in size, number, or intensity. **5** organize and begin a course of action. **6** put or fix something in place or on a support. **7** set in or attach a picture to a backing.

> – SYNONYMS **1** *he mounted the stairs* **go up,** ascend, climb (up), scale. **2** *they mounted their horses* **get on to,** bestride, climb on to, leap on to, hop on to. **3** *the costs mount when you buy a home* **increase,** grow, rise, escalate, soar, spiral, shoot up, rocket, climb, accumulate, build up, multiply. **4** *the museum is mounting an exhibition* **put on,** present, install, organize, stage, set up, prepare, launch, set in motion.
> – ANTONYMS descend, dismount, fall.

▶ **noun** **1** (also **mounting**) something on which an object is mounted for support or display. **2** a horse used for riding.

> – SYNONYMS **setting,** backing, support, mounting, frame, stand.

– DERIVATIVES **mount·a·ble** adjective.
– PHRASES **mount guard** keep watch.
– ORIGIN Old French *munter.*

mount[2] ▶ **noun** old use or in place names a mountain or hill.
– ORIGIN Old English.

moun·tain /ˈmountn/ ▶ **noun** **1** a very high, steep hill. **2** a large pile or quantity.

> – SYNONYMS **1 peak,** summit; (**mountains**) range, massif, sierra. **2 lot**; informal heap, pile, stack, slew, lots, loads, tons, masses.

– PHRASES **move mountains** achieve spectacular and apparently impossible results.
– ORIGIN Old French *montaigne.*

moun·tain ash ▶ **noun** a rowan tree.

moun·tain bike ▶ **noun** a sturdy bicycle having multiple gears and broad tires with deep treads.

moun·tain·eer·ing /ˌmountnˈi(ə)riNG/ ▶ **noun** the sport or activity of climbing mountains.
– DERIVATIVES **moun·tain·eer** noun.

moun·tain goat ▶ **noun** a goat that lives on mountains, known for its agility.

moun·tain lau·rel ▶ **noun** a North American evergreen tree that bears clusters of white or pink flowers.

moun·tain li·on ▶ **noun** a cougar.

moun·tain·ous /ˈmountn-əs/ ▶ **adjective** **1** having many mountains. **2** huge; enormous.
– DERIVATIVES **moun·tain·ous·ly** adverb.

moun·tain sick·ness ▶ **noun** altitude sickness.

moun·tain·side /ˈmountn,sīd/ ▸ **noun** the sloping surface of a mountain.

Moun·tain time ▸ **noun** the standard time in a zone including the Rocky Mountain areas of the US and Canada.

moun·te·bank /ˈmounti,baNGk/ ▸ **noun** a person who deceives others.
– ORIGIN from Italian *monta in banco!* 'climb on the bench!,' referring to the raised platform used by people who sold patent medicines in public.

> **CHOOSE THE RIGHT WORD**
>
> See **QUACK**[2].

Moun·tie /ˈmountē/ ▸ **noun** informal a member of the Royal Canadian Mounted Police.

mount·ing /ˈmountiNG/ ▸ **noun 1** a backing, setting, or support for something. **2** the action of mounting something.

mourn /môrn/ ▸ **verb 1** feel deep sorrow following the death of someone. **2** feel regret or sadness about the loss of something.

> – SYNONYMS **1 grieve for,** sorrow over, lament for, weep for. **2 deplore,** bewail, bemoan, rue, regret.

– ORIGIN Old English.

> **CHOOSE THE RIGHT WORD**
>
> **mourn, bemoan, grieve, lament, rue, sorrow**
>
> Not everyone exhibits unhappiness in the same way. **Grieve** is the strongest of these verbs, implying deep mental anguish or suffering, often endured alone and in silence (*she grieved for years over the loss of her baby*). **Mourn** is more formal and often more public; although it implies deep emotion felt over a period of time, that emotion may be more ceremonial than sincere (*the people mourned the loss of their leader*). **Lament** comes from a Latin word meaning to wail or weep, and it therefore suggests a vocal or verbal expression of loss (*the shrieking women lamented their husbands' deaths*). **Bemoan** also suggests suppressed or inarticulate sounds of *grief*, often expressing regret or disapproval (*to bemoan one's fate*). **Sorrow** combines deep sadness with regret and often pertains to a less tragic loss than *grieve* or *mourn* (*sorrow over a lost love*), while **rue** has even stronger connotations of regret and repentance (*she rued the day she was born*).

mourn·er /ˈmôrnər/ ▸ **noun** a person who attends a funeral as a relative or friend of the dead person.

mourn·ful /ˈmôrnfəl/ ▸ **adjective** feeling, showing, or causing sadness or grief.
– DERIVATIVES **mourn·ful·ly** adverb **mourn·ful·ness** noun.

mourn·ing /ˈmôrniNG/ ▸ **noun 1** the expression of deep sorrow for someone who has died. **2** black clothes worn during a period of mourning.

> – SYNONYMS **grief,** grieving, sorrowing, lamentation.

mourn·ing dove ▸ **noun** a North and Central American dove with a long tail, a gray-brown back, and a plaintive call.

mouse /mous/ ▸ **noun** (pl. **mice**) **1** a small rodent with a pointed snout and a long thin tail. **2** a timid and quiet person. **3** (pl. also **mouses**) a small hand-held device that controls cursor movements on a computer screen. ▸ **verb 1** hunt for or catch mice. **2** informal use a mouse to move a cursor on a computer screen.
– DERIVATIVES **mous·er** noun.
– ORIGIN Old English.

mouse pad (also **mousepad**) ▸ **noun** a piece of rigid or slightly resilient material on which a computer mouse is moved.

mouse·trap /ˈmous,trap/ ▸ **noun** a trap for catching mice, traditionally baited with cheese.

mous·sa·ka /mo͞oˈsäkə/ ▸ **noun** a Greek dish of ground lamb layered with eggplant and tomatoes and topped with a cheese sauce.
– ORIGIN Turkish, 'that which is fed liquid.'

mousse /mo͞os/ ▸ **noun 1** a light sweet or savory dish made with whipped cream and beaten egg white. **2** a foamy substance for styling the hair or applying to the skin.
– ORIGIN French, 'moss or froth.'

mousse·line /,mo͞osəˈlēn, -ˈslēn/ ▸ **noun 1** a fine fabric similar to muslin. **2** a light sweet or savory mousse.
– ORIGIN French.

mous·tache ▸ **noun** variant spelling of **MUSTACHE**.

mous·y /ˈmousē, -zē/ (also **mousey**) ▸ **adjective** (**mousier, mousiest**) **1** (of hair) light brown. **2** timid and quiet.

> – SYNONYMS **timid,** quiet, timorous, shy, self-effacing, diffident.

mouth ▸ **noun** /mouTH/ **1** the opening in the body through which food is taken and sounds are made. **2** an opening or entrance of a structure, container, etc. **3** the place where a river enters the sea. **4** informal impudent or excessive talk.

> – SYNONYMS **1 lips,** jaws, muzzle; informal trap, chops, kisser, puss. **2 entrance,** opening. **3 estuary,** delta, firth, outlet, outfall.

▸ **verb** /mouTH, mouTH/ **1** move the lips as if to form words. **2** say something in an insincere way. **3** (**mouth off**) informal express one's opinions in an unpleasantly loud or assertive way.
– ORIGIN Old English.

> **WORD LINKS**
>
> **oral** *relating to the mouth*

mouth·feel /ˈmouTH,fēl/ ▸ **noun** the physical sensations in the mouth produced by a particular food.

mouth·ful /ˈmouTH,fo͝ol/ ▸ **noun 1** a quantity of food or drink that fills or can be put in the mouth. **2** a long or complicated word or phrase.

mouth or·gan ▸ **noun** a harmonica.

mouth·part /ˈmouTH,pärt/ ▸ **noun** any of the projecting parts surrounding the mouth of an insect or similar creature and adapted for feeding.

mouth·piece /ˈmouTH,pēs/ ▸ **noun 1** a part of a musical instrument, telephone, or breathing apparatus that is designed to be put in or against the mouth. **2** chiefly derogatory a person or publication that expresses the views of another person or an organization.

mouth-to-mouth ▸ **adjective** (of artificial respiration) in which a person breathes into someone's lungs through their mouth.

mouth·wash /ˈmouTH,wôSH, -,wäSH/ ▸ **noun** an antiseptic liquid for rinsing the mouth or gargling.

mouth·wa·ter·ing /ˈmouTH,wôtəriNG/ ▸ **adjective 1** smelling or looking delicious. **2** very attractive or tempting.

mouth·y /ˈmouT͟Hē, ˈmouTHē/ ▶ adjective (**mouthier, mouthiest**) informal inclined to talk a lot, especially in an impudent way.

mov·a·ble /ˈmo͞ovəbəl/ (also **moveable**) ▶ adjective **1** capable of being moved. **2** (of a religious festival) occurring on a different date each year.

move /mo͞ov/ ▶ verb **1** go or cause to go in a specified direction or way. **2** change or cause to change position. **3** change one's home or place of work. **4** change from one state or activity to another. **5** take or cause to take action. **6** make progress: *aircraft design has moved forward a long way.* **7** arouse sympathy, sadness, or other feelings in: *he was genuinely moved by the tragedy.* **8** propose something for discussion and resolution at a meeting or lawmaking assembly.

– SYNONYMS **1 go,** walk, step, proceed, progress, advance, budge, stir, shift, change position. **2 carry,** transfer, shift, push, pull, lift, slide. **3 progress,** advance, develop, evolve, change, happen. **4 act,** take steps, do something, take measures; informal get moving. **5 relocate,** move house, move away/out, change address, go (away), decamp. **6 affect,** touch, impress, shake, upset, disturb. **7 inspire,** prompt, stimulate, motivate, provoke, influence, rouse, induce, incite. **8 propose,** submit, suggest, advocate, recommend, urge.

▶ noun **1** an instance of moving. **2** an action taken toward achieving a purpose: *my next move is to talk to Mark.* **3** a player's turn during a board game.

– SYNONYMS **1 movement,** motion, action, gesture. **2 relocation,** change of house/address, transfer, posting. **3 initiative,** step, action, measure, maneuver, tactic, stratagem. **4 turn,** go.

– PHRASES **get a move on** informal hurry up. **make a move** take action. **move in** (or **out**) start (or cease) living or working in a place.
– ORIGIN Latin *movere.*

move·ment /ˈmo͞ovmənt/ ▶ noun **1** an act or the process of moving. **2** a group of people who share the same aims or ideas: *the women's movement.* **3** a trend or development. **4** (**movements**) a person's activities during a particular period of time. **5** a main division of a musical work. **6** the moving parts of a mechanism, especially a clock or watch.

– SYNONYMS **1 motion,** move, gesture, sign, signal, action. **2 transportation,** shifting, conveyance, moving, transfer. **3 group,** party, faction, wing, lobby, camp. **4 campaign,** crusade, drive, push, initiative.

WORD LINKS

kinetic *relating to movement*

mov·er /ˈmo͞ovər/ ▶ noun **1** a person whose job is to remove and transport furniture from one building, especially a house, to another. **2** a person who instigates or organizes something: *a key mover in making this a successful conference.*

mov·ie /ˈmo͞ovē/ ▶ noun **1** a motion picture. **2** (**the movies**) a movie theater.

– SYNONYMS **film,** picture, motion picture, feature film; informal flick.

mov·ie·go·er /ˈmo͞ovēˌgōər/ ▶ noun a person who goes to the movies, especially regularly.
– DERIVATIVES **mov·ie·go·ing** /-ˌgō-iNG/ noun & adjective.

mov·ing /ˈmo͞oviNG/ ▶ adjective **1** in motion. **2** arousing sadness or sympathy.

– SYNONYMS **1 in motion,** operating, operational, working, on the move, active, movable, mobile. **2 touching,** poignant, heartwarming, heart-rending, affecting, emotional, inspiring, inspirational, stimulating, stirring.
– ANTONYMS stationary, fixed.

– DERIVATIVES **mov·ing·ly** adverb.

mov·ing side·walk ▶ noun a moving walkway, typically at an airport.

mow /mō/ ▶ verb (past part. **mowed** or **mown**) **1** cut down grass or a cereal crop. **2** (**mow someone down**) kill someone by gunfire or by knocking them down with a motor vehicle.

– SYNONYMS **cut,** trim, crop, clip, shear.

– DERIVATIVES **mow·er** noun.
– ORIGIN Old English.

mox·ie /ˈmäksē/ ▶ noun informal force of character, determination, or nerve.
– ORIGIN from *Moxie,* the proprietary name of a soft drink.

Mo·zam·bi·can /ˌmōzamˈbēkən/ ▶ noun a person from Mozambique. ▶ adjective relating to Mozambique.

moz·za·rel·la /ˌmätsəˈrelə/ ▶ noun a firm white Italian cheese made from buffalo's or cow's milk.
– ORIGIN Italian.

MP ▶ abbreviation **1** Member of Parliament. **2** military police.

MP3 ▶ noun a means of compressing a sound sequence into a very small file, used as a way of downloading audio files from the Internet.
– ORIGIN from *MPEG* (an encoding standard) + *Audio Layer-3.*

MPAA ▶ abbreviation Motion Picture Association of America.

mpg ▶ abbreviation miles per gallon.

mph ▶ abbreviation miles per hour.

MPV ▶ abbreviation multi-purpose vehicle.

Mr. /ˈmistər/ ▶ noun **1** a title used before a man's surname or full name. **2** a title used to address the male holder of an office.
– ORIGIN abbreviation of **MASTER**.

MRE ▶ abbreviation meal ready to eat, a precooked and prepackaged meal used by military personnel.

MRI ▶ abbreviation magnetic resonance imaging.

Mrs. /ˈmisəz, ˈmiz-, -əs/ ▶ noun a title used before a married woman's surname or full name.
– ORIGIN abbreviation of **MISTRESS**.

MRSA /ˈmərsə/ ▶ abbreviation methicillin-resistant *Staphylococcus aureus,* a bacterium with antibiotic resistance that is common in hospitals and some other public places.

Mrs. Grun·dy /ˈgrəndē/ ▶ noun a person with very conventional standards of proper moral behavior.
– ORIGIN a person repeatedly mentioned in T. Morton's comedy *Speed the Plough.*

MS ▶ abbreviation **1** manuscript. **2** Mississippi. **3** multiple sclerosis.

Ms. /miz/ ▶ noun a title used before the surname or full name of a married or unmarried woman (a neutral alternative to **Mrs.** or **Miss**).

MSc ▶ abbreviation Master of Science.

MS-DOS /ˌem ˌes ˈdäs, dôs/ ▶ **abbreviation** Computing, trademark Microsoft disk operating system.

MSG ▶ **abbreviation** monosodium glutamate.

Msgr ▶ **abbreviation 1** Monseigneur. **2** Monsignor.

MSRP ▶ **abbreviation** manufacturer's suggested retail price.

MST ▶ **abbreviation** Mountain Standard Time.

MT ▶ **abbreviation** Montana.

Mt. ▶ **abbreviation** (in place names) Mount. ▶ **symbol** the chemical element meitnerium.

much /məCH/ ▶ **determiner & pronoun** (**more, most**) a large amount.

– SYNONYMS **1** *is there much food?* **a lot of,** a great/good deal of, a great/large amount of, plenty of, ample, abundant, plentiful; informal lots of, loads of, heaps of, masses of, tons of, stacks of. **2** *he did much for our team* **a lot,** a great/good deal, plenty; informal lots, loads, heaps, masses, tons.
– ANTONYMS little.

▶ **adverb 1** to a great extent; a great deal. **2** often.

– SYNONYMS **1** *it didn't hurt much* **greatly,** to a great extent/degree, a great deal, a lot, considerably, appreciably. **2** *does he come here much?* **often,** frequently, many times, regularly, habitually, routinely, usually, normally, commonly; informal a lot.

– PHRASES **a bit much** informal rather excessive or unreasonable. (**as**) **much as** even though. **not much of a** not a good example of: *I'm not much of a gardener.* **so much the better** (or **worse**) that is even better (or worse). **too much** too difficult or exhausting to tolerate.
– ORIGIN Old English.

mu·ci·lage /ˈmyo͞os(ə)lij/ ▶ **noun 1** a thick bodily fluid. **2** a thick or sticky solution extracted from plants, used in medicines and adhesives.
– DERIVATIVES **mu·ci·lag·i·nous** /ˌmyo͞osəˈlajənəs/ adjective.
– ORIGIN Latin *mucilago* 'musty juice.'

muck /mək/ ▶ **noun 1** dirt or waste matter. **2** manure. **3** informal, chiefly Brit. something unpleasant or worthless.

– SYNONYMS **1 dirt,** grime, filth, mud, mess. **2 dung,** manure, excrement, droppings, ordure.

▶ **verb 1** (**muck something up**) informal spoil something. **2** (**muck around with**) informal interfere with. **3** (**muck something out**) remove manure from a stable.
– ORIGIN probably Scandinavian.

muck·rak·ing /ˈməkˌrākiNG/ ▶ **noun** the searching out and publicizing of scandal about famous people.
– ORIGIN coined by President Theodore Roosevelt in a speech referring to the man with the *muck rake* in Bunyan's *Pilgrim's Progress*.

muck·y /ˈməkē/ ▶ **adjective** (**muckier, muckiest**) covered with muck; dirty.

mu·co·sa /myo͞oˈkōzə/ ▶ **noun** (pl. **mucosae** /-zē, -ˌzī/) a mucous membrane.

mu·cous /ˈmyo͞okəs/ ▶ **adjective** relating to or covered with mucus.

mu·cous mem·brane ▶ **noun** a tissue that produces mucus, lining many body cavities and tubular organs.

mu·cus /ˈmyo͞okəs/ ▶ **noun** a slimy substance produced by the mucous membranes and glands of animals for lubrication, protection, etc.
– ORIGIN Latin.

mud /məd/ ▶ **noun 1** wet earth that is soft and sticky. **2** damaging information or allegations.

– SYNONYMS **dirt,** sludge, ooze, silt, clay, mire, soil.

– PHRASES **drag someone through the mud** slander or criticize someone publicly. **someone's name is mud** informal someone is in disgrace or unpopular.
– ORIGIN probably from German *mudde.*

mud·bank /ˈmədˌbaNGk/ ▶ **noun** a bank of mud on the bed of a river or the bottom of the sea.

mud·bath /ˈmədˌbaTH/ ▶ **noun 1** a very muddy place. **2** a bath in the mud of mineral springs, taken to relieve rheumatic complaints.

mud·dle /ˈmədl/ ▶ **verb 1** bring something into a disordered or confusing state. **2** confuse someone. **3** (**muddle something up**) confuse two or more things with each other. **4** (**muddle through**) cope fairly well.

– SYNONYMS **1 confuse,** mix up, jumble (up), disarrange, disorganize, disorder, mess up. **2 bewilder,** confuse, bemuse, perplex, puzzle, baffle, mystify.

▶ **noun** a confused or disordered state.

– SYNONYMS **mess,** confusion, jumble, tangle, chaos, disorder, disarray, disorganization.

– DERIVATIVES **mud·dled** adjective.
– ORIGIN perhaps from Dutch *modden* 'dabble in mud.'

mud·dle-head·ed ▶ **adjective** disorganized or confused.

mud·dy /ˈmədē/ ▶ **adjective** (**muddier, muddiest**) **1** covered in or full of mud. **2** not bright or clear.

– SYNONYMS **1 marshy,** boggy, swampy, waterlogged, squelchy, squishy, mucky, slimy, wet, soft. **2 dirty,** filthy, mucky, grimy, soiled. **3 murky,** cloudy, turbid.
– ANTONYMS clean, clear.

▶ **verb** (**muddies, muddying, muddied**) **1** make something muddy. **2** make something difficult to understand.

mud·flap /ˈmədflap/ ▶ **noun** a flap hung behind the wheel of a vehicle to protect against mud and stones thrown up from the road.

mud·flat /ˈmədˌflat/ ▶ **noun** a stretch of muddy land left uncovered at low tide.

mud·guard /ˈmədˌgärd/ ▶ **noun** a curved strip fitted over a wheel of a bicycle or motorcycle to protect against water and dirt thrown up from the road.

mud·pup·py /ˈmədˌpəpē/ ▶ **noun** a large aquatic salamander of the eastern US, reaching sexual maturity while retaining an immature body form with feathery external gills.

mud·slide /ˈmədˌslīd/ ▶ **noun** a mass of mud and other earthy material that is falling or has fallen down a slope.

mud·sling·ing ▶ **noun** informal the use of insults and accusations to damage an opponent's reputation.

mues·li /ˈm(y)o͞ozlē/ ▶ **noun** (pl. **mueslis**) a breakfast cereal consisting of oats, dried fruit, and nuts.
– ORIGIN Swiss German.

mu·ez·zin /m(y)o͞oˈezən, ˈmo͞oəzən/ ▶ **noun** a man who calls Muslims to prayer from the minaret of a mosque.
– ORIGIN from Arabic, 'proclaim.'

muff[1] /məf/ ▶ **noun** a short tube made of fur or other warm material into which the hands are placed for warmth.
– ORIGIN Dutch *mof.*

muff[2] informal ▶ **verb** handle something clumsily or badly.
– ORIGIN unknown.

muf·fin /'məfən/ ▸ **noun 1** a small spongy cake with a rounded top. **2** short for **English muffin**.
– ORIGIN unknown.

muf·fle /'məfəl/ ▸ **verb 1** wrap or cover someone or something for warmth. **2** make a sound quieter or less distinct by covering its source.

– SYNONYMS **1 wrap (up),** swathe, enfold, envelop, cloak. **2 deaden,** dull, dampen, mute, soften, quiet, mask, stifle, smother.

– ORIGIN from Old French *moufle* 'thick glove.'

muf·fler /'məf(ə)lər/ ▸ **noun 1** a scarf worn around the neck and face. **2** a device for deadening the sound of a drum or other instrument. **3** a silencer for a motor vehicle exhaust.

muf·ti¹ /'məftē/ ▸ **noun** (pl. **muftis**) a Muslim legal expert empowered to give rulings on religious matters.
– ORIGIN from Arabic, 'decide a point of law.'

mufti² ▸ **noun** dated civilian clothes when worn by a person who wears a uniform for their job.
– ORIGIN perhaps from **mufti¹**.

mug /məg/ ▸ **noun 1** a large cylindrical cup with a handle. **2** informal a person's face. ▸ **verb** (**mugs, mugging, mugged**) **1** attack and rob someone in a public place. **2** informal make faces in front of an audience or a camera.
– DERIVATIVES **mug·ger** noun.
– PHRASES **a mug's game** informal an activity likely to be unsuccessful or dangerous.
– ORIGIN probably Scandinavian.

mug·gy /'məgē/ ▸ **adjective** (**muggier, muggiest**) (of the weather) unpleasantly warm and humid.

– SYNONYMS **humid,** close, sultry, sticky, oppressive, airless, stifling, suffocating, stuffy.
– ANTONYMS fresh.

– ORIGIN from dialect *mug* 'mist, drizzle.'

Mu·ghal /'mo͞ogəl/ ▸ **noun** variant spelling of **Mogul**.

mug·shot /'məg,sHät/ ▸ **noun** informal a photograph of a person's face made for an official purpose, especially police records.

mug·wort /'məg,wərt, -,wôrt/ ▸ **noun** a plant with aromatic leaves that are dark green above and whitish below.
– ORIGIN Old English.

Mu·ham·mad·an /mō'hämədən, mə-, 'ham-/ (also **Mohammedan**) ▸ **noun & adjective** old-fashioned term for **Muslim** (not favored by Muslims).
– ORIGIN from the name of the Arab prophet and founder of Islam, *Muhammad*.

mu·ja·he·din /,mo͞ojəhi'dēn/ (also **mujaheddin, mujahideen**) ▸ **plural noun** Islamic guerrilla fighters.
– ORIGIN Persian and Arabic, 'people who fight a holy war.'

muk·luk /'mək,lək/ ▸ **noun** a high, soft sealskin boot worn in the American Arctic.
– ORIGIN from Yupik (an Eskimo language), 'bearded seal.'

mu·lat·to /m(y)o͝o'lätō, -'latō/ ▸ **noun** (pl. **mulattoes** or **mulattos**) offensive a person with one white and one black parent.
– ORIGIN Spanish *mulato* 'young mule, mulatto.'

mul·ber·ry /'məl,berē/ ▸ **noun** (pl. **mulberries**) **1** a dark red or white fruit resembling the loganberry. **2** a dark red or purple color.
– ORIGIN Latin *morum* 'mulberry.'

mulch /məlcH/ ▸ **noun** a mass of leaves, bark, or compost spread around or over a plant for protection or to enrich the soil. ▸ **verb** cover soil or the base of a plant with mulch.
– ORIGIN probably from dialect *mulch* 'soft.'

mule¹ /myo͞ol/ ▸ **noun 1** the offspring of a male donkey and a female horse, typically sterile. **2** informal a courier for illegal drugs. **3** historical a kind of spinning machine producing yarn on spindles.
– ORIGIN Latin *mulus, mula*.

mule² ▸ **noun** a slipper or light shoe without a back.
– ORIGIN French, 'slipper.'

mu·le·teer /,myo͞olə'tir/ ▸ **noun** a person who drives mules.

mul·ish /'myo͞olisH/ ▸ **adjective** stubborn (like a mule).

mull¹ /məl/ ▸ **verb** (**mull something over**) think about something at length.

– SYNONYMS *I'll have to mull it over before making a final decision* **ponder,** consider, think over/about, reflect on, contemplate, chew over; formal cogitate on.

– ORIGIN uncertain.

mull² ▸ **verb** (usu. as adj. **mulled**) warm a beverage, especially wine or cider, and add sugar and spices to it.
– ORIGIN unknown.

mull³ ▸ **noun** a thin, soft, plain muslin, used in bookbinding for joining the spine of a book to its cover.

mul·lah /'mələ, 'mo͝olə, 'mo͞olə/ ▸ **noun** a Muslim who is learned in Islamic theology and sacred law.
– ORIGIN Arabic.

mul·lein /'mələn/ ▸ **noun** a plant with woolly leaves and tall spikes of yellow flowers.
– ORIGIN Celtic.

mul·let /'mələt/ ▸ **noun** any of various sea fish that are caught for food.
– ORIGIN Greek *mullos*.

mul·li·ga·taw·ny /,məligə'tônē, -'tänē/ ▸ **noun** a spicy meat soup originally made in India.
– ORIGIN Tamil, 'pepper water.'

mul·lion /'məlyən/ ▸ **noun** a vertical bar between the panes of glass in a window.
– DERIVATIVES **mul·lioned** adjective.
– ORIGIN probably from Old French *moinel* 'middle.'

multi- ▸ **combining form** more than one; many: *multicultural*.
– ORIGIN from Latin *multus* 'much, many.'

mul·ti·cast /'məlti,kast, ,məlti'kast/ ▸ **verb** (past and past part. **multicast**) send data across a computer network to several users at the same time. ▸ **noun** a set of multicast data.

mul·ti·col·ored /,məlti'kələrd, ,məltī-/ (also **multicolor**) ▸ **adjective** having many colors.

– SYNONYMS **kaleidoscopic,** psychedelic, colorful, many-hued, jazzy, variegated.
– ANTONYMS monochrome.

mul·ti·cul·tur·al /,məltē'kəlcH(ə)rəl, ,məltī-/ ▸ **adjective** relating to or made up of several cultural or ethnic groups.
– DERIVATIVES **mul·ti·cul·tur·al·ism** noun **mul·ti·cul·tur·al·ist** noun & adjective.

mul·ti·dis·ci·pli·nar·y /,məlti'disəpli'nerē, ,məltī-/ ▸ **adjective** involving several academic disciplines or professional specializations.

mul·ti·fac·et·ed /ˌməltiˈfasətəd, ˌməltī-/ ▶ **adjective** having many facets or aspects.

mul·ti·far·i·ous /ˌmələt(ə)ˈfe(ə)rēəs/ ▶ **adjective** having many different kinds; very varied: *multifarious talents.*
– ORIGIN Latin *multifarius.*

mul·ti·form /ˈməltiˌfôrm/ ▶ **adjective** existing in many forms or kinds.

mul·ti·hull /ˈməltiˌhəl, ˈməltī-/ ▶ **noun** a boat with two or more, especially three, hulls.

mul·ti·lat·er·al /ˌməltiˈlatərəl/ ▶ **adjective** involving three or more participants, especially governments.
– DERIVATIVES **mul·ti·lat·er·al·ism** /-ˌlizəm/ noun **mul·ti·lat·er·al·ly** adverb.

mul·ti·lay·ered /ˈməltiˈlāərd, ˈməltī-/ ▶ **adjective** consisting of several or many layers.

mul·ti·lin·gual /ˌməltēˈliNGg(yə)wəl, ˌməltī-/ ▶ **adjective** in or using several languages.

mul·ti·me·di·a /ˈməltiˈmēdēə, ˈməltī-/ ▶ **adjective** using more than one medium of expression or communication. ▶ **noun** a system for linking sound and images to text on a computer screen.

mul·ti·mil·lion /ˈməltiˈmilyən, ˈməltī-/ ▶ **adjective** consisting of several million of a currency.

mul·ti·mil·lion·aire /ˌməltiˌmilyəˈner, ˌməltī-/ ▶ **noun** a person with assets worth several million dollars.

mul·ti·na·tion·al /ˌməltiˈnasHənl, ˌməltī-/ ▶ **adjective** **1** involving several countries or nationalities. **2** operating in several countries. ▶ **noun** a company operating in several countries.
– DERIVATIVES **mul·ti·na·tion·al·ly** adverb.

mul·ti·pack /ˈməltiˌpak, ˈməltī-/ ▶ **noun** a package containing a number of similar or identical products.

mul·ti·par·ty /ˈməltiˈpärtē, ˈməltī-/ ▶ **adjective** relating to or involving several political parties.

mul·ti·ple /ˈməltəpəl/ ▶ **adjective** **1** having or involving several or many people or things: *multiple occupancy.* **2** (of a disease or injury) affecting several parts of the body.

– SYNONYMS **numerous,** many, various, different, diverse, several, manifold.
– ANTONYMS single.

▶ **noun** a number that may be divided by another a certain number of times without a remainder.
– ORIGIN Latin *multiplus.*

mul·ti·ple-choice ▶ **adjective** (of a question on an exam) accompanied by several possible answers, from which the candidate must choose the correct one.

mul·ti·ple scle·ro·sis ▶ **noun** see SCLEROSIS.

mul·ti·plex /ˈməltəˌpleks/ ▶ **noun** a movie theater having several separate screens within one building. ▶ **adjective** **1** consisting of many elements in a complex relationship. **2** involving simultaneous transmission of several messages along a single channel of communication.
– ORIGIN Latin.

mul·ti·pli·cand /ˌməltəpliˈkand/ ▶ **noun** a quantity that is to be multiplied by another (the multiplier).

mul·ti·pli·ca·tion /ˌməltəpləˈkāsHən/ ▶ **noun** **1** the process of multiplying. **2** Mathematics the process of combining matrices, vectors, or other quantities under specific rules to obtain their product.

mul·ti·pli·ca·tion sign ▶ **noun** the sign ×, used to indicate that one quantity is to be multiplied by another.

mul·ti·pli·ca·tion ta·ble ▶ **noun** a list of multiples of a particular number, typically from 1 to 12.

mul·ti·plic·i·ty /ˌməltəˈplisətē/ ▶ **noun** (pl. **multiplicities**) a large number or variety.

mul·ti·pli·er /ˈməltəˌplīər/ ▶ **noun** **1** a quantity by which a given number (the multiplicand) is to be multiplied. **2** a device for increasing the intensity of an electric current, force, etc., to a measurable level.

mul·ti·ply[1] /ˈməltəˌplī/ ▶ **verb** (**multiplies, multiplying, multiplied**) **1** add a number to itself a specified number of times. **2** increase in number or quantity: *the problems facing the industry have multiplied alarmingly.* **3** (of an organism) increase in number by reproducing.

– SYNONYMS **increase,** grow, accumulate, proliferate, mount up, mushroom, snowball.
– ANTONYMS decrease.

– ORIGIN Latin *multiplicare.*

mul·ti·ply[2] /ˈməltəplē/ ▶ **adverb** in different ways or respects.

mul·ti·proc·ess·ing /ˌməltiˈpräsesiNG, ˌməltī-, -ˈpräsəsiNG/ (also **multiprogramming** /ˌməltiˈprōgramiNG, ˌməltī-/) ▶ **noun** the execution of more than one program or task by a computer at the same time.

mul·ti·proc·es·sor /ˌməltiˈpräsesər, -ˈpräsəsər/ ▶ **noun** a computer with more than one central processor.

mul·ti·pur·pose /ˌməltēˈpərpəs, ˌməltī-/ ▶ **adjective** having several purposes.

mul·ti·ra·cial /ˌməltiˈrāsHəl, ˌməlˌtī-/ ▶ **adjective** relating to or involving people of many races.

mul·ti·stage /ˈməltiˈstāj, ˌməltī-/ ▶ **adjective** **1** consisting of or involving several stages or processes. **2** (of a rocket) having at least two sections that contain their own motor and are jettisoned as their fuel runs out.

mul·ti·sto·ry /ˈməltiˌstôrē, ˈməltī-/ ▶ **adjective** (of a building) having several stories.

mul·ti·task /ˈməltiˌtask, ˈməltī-/ ▶ **verb** (usu. as n. **multitasking**) **1** (of a computer) execute more than one program or task at the same time. **2** (of a person) deal with more than one task at the same time.
– DERIVATIVES **mul·ti·task·er** noun.

mul·ti·track /ˈməltiˌtrak, ˈməltī-/ ▶ **adjective** relating to or made by the mixing of several separately recorded tracks of sound.

mul·ti·tude /ˈməltəˌt(y)o͞od/ ▶ **noun** **1** a large number of people or things. **2** (**the multitude**) ordinary people.
– ORIGIN Latin *multitudo.*

mul·ti·tu·di·nous /ˌməltəˈt(y)o͞odn-əs/ ▶ **adjective** **1** very large in number. **2** consisting of many parts or elements.

mul·ti·us·er /ˈməltēˈyo͞ozər, ˈməltī-/ ▶ **adjective** **1** (of a computer system) able to be used by a number of people simultaneously. **2** referring to a computer game in which several players interact simultaneously using the Internet or other communications.

mul·ti·va·lent /ˌməltiˈvālənt, ˌməltī-/ ▶ **adjective** having many interpretations, uses, or values.

mul·ti·verse /ˈməltiˌvərs/ ▶ **noun** a hypothetical space or realm consisting of a number of universes, of which our own universe is only one.

mum[1] /məm/ ▶ **noun** informal, chiefly Brit. one's mother.

mum² ▶ **adjective** (in phrase **keep mum**) informal say nothing so as not to reveal a secret.
– PHRASES **mum's the word** do not reveal a secret.
– ORIGIN imitating a sound made with closed lips.

mum³ ▶ **noun** a cultivated chrysanthemum.

mum·ble /ˈməmbəl/ ▶ **verb** say something indistinctly and quietly.

> – SYNONYMS **mutter,** murmur, talk under one's breath.

▶ **noun** something said quietly and indistinctly.
– ORIGIN from MUM².

mum·bo-jum·bo /ˈməmbō ˈjəmbō/ ▶ **noun** informal language or a ceremony that seems complicated but has no real meaning.
– ORIGIN from *Mumbo Jumbo,* the supposed name of an African idol.

mum·mer /ˈməmər/ ▶ **noun** an actor in a traditional English folk play.
– ORIGIN from Old French *momer* 'act in a mime.'

mum·mer·y /ˈməmərē/ ▶ **noun** (pl. **mummeries**) **1** a performance of a traditional English folk play. **2** ridiculous or excessive ceremonial procedures.

mum·mi·fy /ˈməməˌfī/ ▶ **verb** (**mummifies, mummifying, mummified**) **1** (especially in ancient Egypt) preserve a body by embalming and wrapping it. **2** dry up a body and so preserve it.
– DERIVATIVES **mum·mi·fi·ca·tion** /ˌməməfiˈkāshən/ noun.

mum·my¹ /ˈməmē/ ▶ **noun** (pl. **mummies**) informal, chiefly Brit. one's mother.
– ORIGIN uncertain.

mum·my² ▶ **noun** (pl. **mummies**) (especially in ancient Egypt) a body that has been preserved for burial by embalming and wrapping in cloth.
– ORIGIN Arabic, 'embalmed body.'

mumps /məmps/ ▶ **plural noun** (treated as sing.) an infectious disease spread by a virus, causing swelling of the salivary glands at the sides of the face.
– ORIGIN from former *mump* 'grimace.'

munch /mənch/ ▶ **verb** eat food with a steady and noticeable chewing action.
– ORIGIN imitating the sound of eating.

Mun·chau·sen's syn·drome /ˈmo͝onˌchouzənz, ˈmən-/ ▶ **noun** a mental disorder in which a person pretends to be severely ill so as to obtain medical attention.
– ORIGIN from Baron *Munchausen,* the hero of a book of fantastic tales.

munch·ies /ˈmənchēz/ ▶ **plural noun** informal **1** snacks or small items of food. **2** (**the munchies**) a sudden strong desire for food.

mun·dane /ˌmənˈdān/ ▶ **adjective 1** lacking interest or excitement: *his mundane, humdrum existence.* **2** relating to the physical world rather than a heavenly or spiritual one.

> – SYNONYMS **humdrum,** dull, boring, tedious, monotonous, tiresome, unexciting, uninteresting, uneventful, unremarkable, routine, ordinary.
> – ANTONYMS extraordinary.

– DERIVATIVES **mun·dane·ly** adverb **mun·dan·i·ty** /-ˈdānətē/ noun.
– ORIGIN from Latin *mundus* 'world.'

mung bean /məng/ ▶ **noun** a small round green bean grown in the tropics, chiefly as a source of bean sprouts.
– ORIGIN Hindi.

mu·nic·i·pal /myo͞oˈnisəpəl, myə-/ ▶ **adjective** relating to a town or city or its governing body.

> – SYNONYMS **civic,** civil, metropolitan, urban, city, town, borough, council.

– DERIVATIVES **mu·nic·i·pal·ly** adverb.
– ORIGIN from Latin *municipium* 'free city.'

mu·nic·i·pal·i·ty /myo͞oˌnisəˈpalətē, myə-/ ▶ **noun** (pl. **municipalities**) a town or city that has local government.

mu·nif·i·cent /myo͞oˈnifəsənt, myə-/ ▶ **adjective** very generous.
– DERIVATIVES **mu·nif·i·cence** noun **mu·nif·i·cent·ly** adverb.
– ORIGIN Latin *munificus.*

mu·ni·ments /ˈmyo͞onəmənts/ ▶ **plural noun** Law title deeds or other documents proving a person's right of ownership of land.
– ORIGIN from Latin *munimentum* 'defense,' later 'title deed.'

mu·ni·tions /myo͞oˈnishənz, myə-/ ▶ **plural noun** military weapons, ammunition, equipment, and stores.
– ORIGIN Latin, 'fortification.'

munt·jac /ˈməntˌjak/ ▶ **noun** a small SE Asian deer with a doglike bark and small tusks.
– ORIGIN Sundanese.

mu·on /ˈmyo͞oˌän/ ▶ **noun** Physics an unstable subatomic particle of the same class as an electron, but with a mass around 200 times greater.
– ORIGIN from the earlier name *mu-meson.*

mu·ral /ˈmyo͝orəl/ ▶ **noun** a picture or design painted directly on a wall. ▶ **adjective** relating to or resembling a wall.
– ORIGIN from Latin *murus* 'wall.'

mur·der /ˈmərdər/ ▶ **noun 1** the unlawful and deliberate killing of one person by another. **2** informal a very difficult or unpleasant situation or experience.

> – SYNONYMS **killing,** homicide, assassination, extermination, execution, slaughter, butchery, massacre, manslaughter; literary slaying.

▶ **verb 1** kill someone unlawfully and deliberately. **2** informal spoil by lack of skill: *couples were shuffling around to a band murdering Beatles songs.*

> – SYNONYMS **kill,** put to death, assassinate, execute, butcher, slaughter, massacre, wipe out; informal bump off, ice, waste; literary slay.

– PHRASES **get away with murder** informal succeed in doing whatever one chooses without being punished. **scream bloody murder** informal protest strongly and noisily.
– ORIGIN Old English.

mur·der·er /ˈmərdərər/ ▶ **noun** a person who commits murder.

> – SYNONYMS **killer,** assassin, serial killer, butcher; informal hit man, hired gun.

– DERIVATIVES **mur·der·ess** noun.

mur·der·ous /ˈmərdərəs/ ▶ **adjective 1** capable of or involving murder or extreme violence. **2** informal very difficult or unpleasant.

> – SYNONYMS **homicidal,** brutal, violent, savage, ferocious, fierce, vicious, bloodthirsty, barbarous, barbaric, fatal, lethal, deadly.

– DERIVATIVES **mur·der·ous·ly** adverb **mur·der·ous·ness** noun.

murk /mərk/ ▶ **noun** darkness or fog causing poor visibility.
– ORIGIN Old English.

murk·y /ˈmərkē/ ▸ adjective (murkier, murkiest) **1** dark and gloomy. **2** (of water) dirty or cloudy. **3** unclear so as to conceal dishonesty or immorality: *a Congressman with a murky past.*

> – SYNONYMS **1 dark,** gloomy, gray, leaden, dull, dim, overcast, cloudy, clouded, sunless, dismal, dreary, bleak. **2 dirty,** muddy, cloudy, turbid.
> – ANTONYMS bright, clear.

– DERIVATIVES **murk·i·ly** adverb **murk·i·ness** noun.

mur·mur /ˈmərmər/ ▸ verb **1** say something quietly. **2** make a low continuous sound. **3** complain in a subdued way.

> – SYNONYMS **mutter,** mumble, whisper, talk under one's breath, talk sotto voce.

▸ noun **1** something that is said quietly. **2** a low continuous background noise. **3** a complaint: *she paid for the meal without a murmur.* **4** a recurring sound heard in the heart through a stethoscope and usually indicating disease or damage.

> – SYNONYMS **1 whisper,** mutter, mumble, undertone. **2 hum,** buzz, drone.

– ORIGIN Latin.

Mur·phy's Law /ˈmərfēz/ ▸ noun a supposed law of nature, to the effect that anything that can go wrong will go wrong.

mur·rain /ˈmərən/ ▸ noun **1** an infectious disease affecting cattle. **2** old use a plague or crop blight.
– ORIGIN Old French *morine.*

Mus·ca·det /ˌməskəˈdā, -ˈde/ ▸ noun a dry white wine from the Loire region of France.
– ORIGIN French.

mus·cat /ˈməsˌkət, -ˌkat/ ▸ noun **1** a variety of grape with a musky scent. **2** a sweet or fortified white wine made from muscat grapes.
– ORIGIN from Provençal *musc* 'musk.'

mus·ca·tel /ˌməskəˈtel/ ▸ noun a sweet wine made from muscat grapes.

mus·cle /ˈməsəl/ ▸ noun **1** a band of tissue in the body that is able to contract so as to move or hold the position of a part of the body. **2** power, influence, or strength: *the plan is designed to increase Japan's financial muscle.*

> – SYNONYMS **1 strength,** power, brawn; informal beef, beefiness. **2** *financial muscle* **influence,** power, strength, might, force, forcefulness, weight; informal clout.

▸ verb **(muscle in/into)** informal interfere in another's affairs.

> – SYNONYMS **interfere,** force one's way in, impose oneself, encroach; informal horn in.

– DERIVATIVES **mus·cly** /ˈməs(ə)lē/ adjective.
– ORIGIN Latin *musculus.*

> **USAGE**
> Do not confuse **muscle** with **mussel**. **Muscle** means *the tissue that moves a body part* (*tone up your thigh muscles*), whereas a **mussel** is a kind of shellfish.

mus·cle-bound ▸ adjective having overdeveloped muscles.

mus·cle·man /ˈməsəlˌman/ ▸ noun (pl. **musclemen**) a large, strong man, especially a bodyguard or hired thug.

mus·co·va·do /ˌməskəˈvādō, -ˈvädō/ ▸ noun unrefined sugar made from sugarcane.
– ORIGIN from Portuguese *mascabado açúcar* 'sugar of the lowest quality.'

Mus·co·vite /ˈməskəˌvīt/ ▸ noun a person from Moscow. ▸ adjective relating to Moscow.

Mus·co·vy /ˈməskəvē/ ▸ noun old use Russia.
– ORIGIN Russian *Moskva* 'Moscow.'

mus·cu·lar /ˈməskyələr/ ▸ adjective **1** relating to the muscles. **2** having well-developed muscles.

> – SYNONYMS **strong,** brawny, muscly, well built, burly, strapping, sturdy, powerful, athletic; informal hunky, beefy.

– DERIVATIVES **mus·cu·lar·i·ty** /ˌməskyəˈle(ə)ritē/ noun **mus·cu·lar·ly** adverb.

mus·cu·lar dys·tro·phy ▸ noun an inherited condition in which the muscles gradually become weaker and waste away.

mus·cu·la·ture /ˈməskyələCHər, -ˌCHo͝or/ ▸ noun the muscular system or arrangement of muscles in a body or an organ.

mus·cu·lo·skel·e·tal /ˌməskyəlōˈskelətl/ ▸ adjective relating to or referring to the musculature and skeleton together.

muse[1] /myo͞oz/ ▸ noun **1 (Muse)** (in Greek and Roman mythology) each of nine goddesses who encouraged the arts and sciences. **2** a woman, or a force personified as one, who is the inspiration for a creative artist.
– ORIGIN Greek *mousa.*

muse[2] ▸ verb **1** be absorbed in thought. **2** say something to oneself in a thoughtful way.

> – SYNONYMS **ponder,** consider, think over/about, mull over, reflect on, contemplate, turn over in one's mind, chew over.

– ORIGIN Old French *muser* 'meditate, waste time.'

mu·se·um /myo͞oˈzēəm/ ▸ noun a building in which important or interesting objects are stored and exhibited.
– ORIGIN Greek *mouseion* 'seat of the Muses.'

mu·se·um piece ▸ noun an old-fashioned or useless person or object.

mush[1] /məSH/ ▸ noun **1** a soft, wet mass. **2** excessive sentimentality. ▸ verb crush or mash something to form a soft, wet mass.
– ORIGIN probably from **MASH.**

mush[2] ▸ exclamation a command urging on dogs that pull a dog sled.
– ORIGIN probably from French *marchez!* or *marchons!* 'advance!'

mush·room /ˈməSHˌro͞om, -ˌro͝om/ ▸ noun **1** a spore-producing body of a fungus, typically having the form of a domed cap at the top of a stalk and often edible. **2** a pale pinkish-brown color. ▸ verb increase or develop rapidly.
– ORIGIN Old French *mousseron.*

mush·room cloud ▸ noun a mushroom-shaped cloud of dust and debris formed after a nuclear explosion.

mush·y /ˈməSHē/ ▸ adjective (**mushier, mushiest**) **1** soft and pulpy. **2** excessively sentimental.
– DERIVATIVES **mush·i·ness** noun.

mu·sic /ˈmyo͞ozik/ ▸ noun **1** the art of combining vocal or instrumental sounds in a pleasing way. **2** the sound so produced. **3** the written or printed signs representing such sound.
– PHRASES **music to one's ears** something very pleasant to hear or learn.
– ORIGIN from Greek *mousikē tekhnē* 'art of the Muses.'

mu·si·cal /ˈmyo͞ozikəl/ ▸ **adjective** **1** relating to or accompanied by music. **2** fond of or skilled in music. **3** pleasant-sounding.

– SYNONYMS **tuneful,** melodic, melodious, harmonious, sweet-sounding, dulcet, euphonious, mellifluous.
– ANTONYMS discordant.

▸ **noun** a play or movie in which singing and dancing play an essential part.
– DERIVATIVES **mu·si·cal·i·ty** /ˌmyo͞oziˈkalətē/ noun **mu·si·cal·ly** adverb.

mu·si·cal chairs ▸ **plural noun** (treated as sing.) **1** a party game in which players compete for a decreasing number of chairs when the accompanying music is stopped. **2** informal a situation in which people frequently exchange jobs or positions.

mu·sic box ▸ **noun** a small box that plays a tune when the lid is opened.

mu·sic hall ▸ **noun** **1** a form of vaudeville entertainment, popular in Britain from about 1850 to 1918. **2** a theater where musical events are staged.

mu·si·cian /myo͞oˈzisʜən/ ▸ **noun** a person who plays a musical instrument or composes music.
– DERIVATIVES **mu·si·cian·ly** adjective **mu·si·cian·ship** /-ˌsʜip/ noun.

mu·si·col·o·gy /ˌmyo͞oziˈkäləjē/ ▸ **noun** the study of music as an academic subject.
– DERIVATIVES **mu·si·co·log·i·cal** /-kəˈläjikəl/ adjective **mu·si·col·o·gist** /-jist/ noun.

musk /məsk/ ▸ **noun** a strong-smelling substance produced by the male musk deer, used in making perfume.
– DERIVATIVES **musk·i·ness** noun **musk·y** adjective.
– ORIGIN Persian.

musk deer ▸ **noun** a small East Asian deer, the male of which produces musk.

mus·keg /ˈməsˌkeg/ ▸ **noun** a North American swamp or bog formed by an accumulation of decayed vegetation and sphagnum moss.
– ORIGIN from an American Indian language.

mus·ket /ˈməskit/ ▸ **noun** historical a light gun with a long barrel, typically fired from the shoulder.
– ORIGIN Italian *moschetto* 'crossbow bolt.'

mus·ket·eer /ˌməskəˈti(ə)r/ ▸ **noun** historical **1** a soldier armed with a musket. **2** a member of the household troops of the French king in the 17th and 18th centuries.

mus·ket·ry /ˈməskətrē/ ▸ **noun** **1** musket fire. **2** soldiers armed with muskets. **3** the art or technique of handling a musket.

musk ox ▸ **noun** a large heavily built goat-antelope with a thick shaggy coat, native to the tundra of North America and Greenland.

musk·rat /ˈməˌskrat/ ▸ **noun** a large North American rodent with a musky smell that lives partly in water and is valued for its fur.

Mus·lim /ˈməzləm, ˈmo͝oz-/ (also **Moslem**) ▸ **noun** a follower of Islam. ▸ **adjective** relating to Muslims or Islam.
– ORIGIN Arabic.

mus·lin /ˈməzlən/ ▸ **noun** a lightweight cotton cloth in a plain weave.
– ORIGIN from Italian *Mussolo* 'Mosul' (the place in Iraq where it was made).

muss /məs/ ▸ **verb** informal make something untidy or messy.
– ORIGIN probably from **MESS**.

mus·sel /ˈməsəl/ ▸ **noun** an edible shellfish with a dark brown or purplish-black shell, found in the sea or in fresh water.
– ORIGIN Latin *musculus* 'muscle.'

USAGE

On the confusion of **mussel** with **muscle**, see the note at **MUSCLE**.

must[1] /məst/ ▸ **modal verb** (past **had to** or in reported speech **must**) **1** be obliged to; should. **2** used to insist on something. **3** expressing an opinion about something that is very likely.

– SYNONYMS **ought to,** should, have (got) to, need to, be obliged to, be required to, be compelled to.

▸ **noun** informal something that should be done or bought.
– ORIGIN Old English.

must[2] ▸ **noun** grape juice before or during fermentation.
– ORIGIN from Latin *mustus* 'new.'

must- ▸ **combining form** used to form adjectives referring to things that are essential or highly recommended: *a must-read book*.

mus·tache /ˈməsˌtasʜ, məˈstasʜ/ (also **moustache**) ▸ **noun** a strip of hair left to grow above a man's upper lip.
– DERIVATIVES **mus·tached** adjective.
– ORIGIN French *moustache*.

mus·tang /ˈməsˌtaNG/ ▸ **noun** a small wild horse of the southwestern US.
– ORIGIN from a blend of Spanish *mestengo* and *mostrenco*, both meaning 'wild cattle.'

mus·tard /ˈməstərd/ ▸ **noun** **1** a hot-tasting yellow or brown paste made from the crushed seeds of a plant, eaten with meat. **2** a brownish-yellow color.
– ORIGIN Old French *moustarde*.

mus·tard gas ▸ **noun** a liquid whose vapor causes severe irritation and blistering, used in chemical weapons.

mus·ter /ˈməstər/ ▸ **verb** **1** achieve a feeling, attitude, or reaction: *with all the courage I could muster, I came to my decision*. **2** bring troops together, especially for inspection or military action. **3** (of people) gather together.

– SYNONYMS **1** *she mustered her courage* **summon (up),** screw up, call up, rally. **2 assemble,** mobilize, rally, raise, summon, gather, call up, call to arms, recruit, draft, conscript. **3 congregate,** assemble, gather (together), come together, collect, convene, mass, rally.

▸ **noun** a formal gathering of troops.
– PHRASES **pass muster** be accepted as satisfactory.
– ORIGIN Old French *moustrer*.

must-have informal ▸ **adjective** essential or highly desirable. ▸ **noun** an essential or highly desirable item.

must·n't /ˈməsənt/ ▸ **contraction** must not.

must-see ▸ **noun** informal something that should or must be seen, especially a remarkable sight or entertainment.

mus·ty /ˈməstē/ ▸ **adjective** (**mustier, mustiest**) **1** having a stale or moldy smell or taste. **2** not fresh or original; outdated.

– SYNONYMS **moldy,** stale, fusty, damp, dank, mildewy, smelly, stuffy, airless, unventilated.
– ANTONYMS fresh.

– DERIVATIVES **mus·ti·ness** noun.
– ORIGIN perhaps from former *moisty* 'moist.'

mu·ta·ble /'myo͞otəbəl/ ▸ **adjective** liable to change; changeable.
– DERIVATIVES **mu·ta·bil·i·ty** /ˌmyo͞otə'bilətē/ noun.
– ORIGIN Latin *mutabilis*.

mu·ta·gen /'myo͞otəjən/ ▸ **noun** a substance that causes genetic mutation.

mu·tant /'myo͞otnt/ ▸ **adjective** resulting from or showing the effect of a change in genetic structure. ▸ **noun** an organism that has undergone a change in genetic structure.

mu·tate /'myo͞oˌtāt/ ▸ **verb** change in form or nature; undergo mutation.

mu·ta·tion /myo͞o'tāsʜən/ ▸ **noun 1** a change in form or structure. **2** a change in the structure of a gene that results in a variant form and may be transmitted to subsequent generations. **3** a distinct form resulting from a change in genetic structure.

– SYNONYMS **1 alteration,** change, transformation, metamorphosis, transmutation. **2 mutant,** freak (of nature), deviant, monstrosity, monster.

– DERIVATIVES **mu·ta·tion·al** adjective.
– ORIGIN from Latin *mutare* 'to change.'

mu·ta·tis mu·tan·dis /m(y)o͞o'tätəs m(y)o͞o'tändəs, -'tātəs, -'tandəs/ ▸ **adverb** (used when comparing two or more cases) making necessary alterations while not affecting the main point.
– ORIGIN Latin, 'things being changed that have to be changed.'

mute /myo͞ot/ ▸ **adjective 1** not speaking or temporarily speechless. **2** lacking the power of speech. **3** (of a letter in a word) not pronounced.

– SYNONYMS **1 silent,** speechless, dumb, unspeaking, tight-lipped, taciturn; informal mum. **2 wordless,** silent, dumb, unspoken.
– ANTONYMS voluble, spoken.

▸ **noun 1** dated a person who is unable to speak. **2** a clamp placed over the bridge of a stringed instrument to deaden the resonance of the strings. **3** a pad or cone placed in the opening of a wind instrument.
▸ **verb 1** deaden or muffle the sound of something. **2** reduce the strength or intensity of: *his sharp wit was muted by good nature*.
– DERIVATIVES **mute·ly** adverb **mute·ness** noun.
– ORIGIN Latin *mutus*.

USAGE

To describe a person without the power of speech as **mute** (especially as in **deaf mute**) is today likely to cause offense. Since there are no accepted alternative terms in general use, the solution may be to use a longer description, such as *she is both deaf and unable to speak*.

muted /'myo͞otid/ ▸ **adjective 1** (of a sound or voice) quiet and soft. **2** (of color or lighting) not bright; subdued.

– SYNONYMS **1** *the muted hum of traffic* **muffled,** faint, indistinct, quiet, soft, low, distant, faraway. **2** *muted colors* **subdued,** pastel, delicate, subtle, understated, restrained.

mute swan ▸ **noun** the commonest Eurasian swan, having an orange-red bill with a black knob at the base.

mu·ti·late /'myo͞otlˌāt/ ▸ **verb 1** cause a severe and disfiguring injury to someone. **2** cause serious damage to something.

– SYNONYMS **1 disfigure,** maim, mangle, dismember, slash, hack up. **2 vandalize,** damage, slash, deface, violate, desecrate.

– DERIVATIVES **mu·ti·la·tion** /ˌmyo͞otl'āsʜən/ noun **mu·ti·la·tor** noun.
– ORIGIN Latin *mutilare* 'maim.'

mu·ti·neer /ˌmyo͞otn'i(ə)r/ ▸ **noun** a person who refuses to obey a person in authority.

mu·ti·nous /'myo͞otn-əs/ ▸ **adjective** tending to mutiny or be disobedient; rebellious.

– SYNONYMS **rebellious,** insubordinate, subversive, seditious, insurgent, insurrectionary, disobedient, restive.

– DERIVATIVES **mu·ti·nous·ly** adverb.

mu·ti·ny /'myo͞otn-ē/ ▸ **noun** (pl. **mutinies**) an open rebellion against authority, especially by soldiers or sailors against their officers.

– SYNONYMS **insurrection,** rebellion, revolt, riot, uprising, insurgence, insubordination.

▸ **verb** (**mutinies, mutinying, mutinied**) refuse to obey a person in authority.

– SYNONYMS **rise up,** rebel, revolt, riot, strike.

– ORIGIN from French *mutin* 'mutineer, rebellious.'

mutt /mət/ ▸ **noun** informal **1** a dog, especially a mongrel. **2** dated a stupid or incompetent person.
– ORIGIN abbreviation of **MUTTONHEAD**.

mut·ter /'mətər/ ▸ **verb 1** say something in a very quiet voice. **2** talk or grumble in secret or in private.

– SYNONYMS **1 murmur,** talk under one's breath, talk sotto voce, mumble, whisper. **2 grumble,** complain, grouse, carp, whine; informal moan, whinge.

▸ **noun** something said very quietly.
– ORIGIN imitating the sound.

mut·ton /'mətn/ ▸ **noun** the flesh of mature sheep used as food.
– ORIGIN Old French *moton*.

mut·ton·chops /'mətnˌcʜäps/ (also **muttonchop sideburns**) ▸ **plural noun** sideburns that are narrow at the top and broad and rounded at the bottom.

mut·ton·head /'mətnˌhed/ ▸ **noun** informal, old use or dated a stupid person.

mu·tu·al /'myo͞ocʜo͞oəl/ ▸ **adjective 1** experienced or done by two or more people equally: *a partnership based on mutual respect*. **2** (of two or more people) having the same specified relationship to each other. **3** shared by two or more people: *a mutual friend*. **4** (of an insurance company or other organization) owned by its members and dividing its profits between them.

– SYNONYMS **reciprocal,** reciprocated, requited, returned, common, joint, shared.

– DERIVATIVES **mu·tu·al·i·ty** /ˌmyo͞ocʜo͞o'alitē/ noun **mu·tu·al·ly** adverb.
– ORIGIN Old French *mutuel*.

mu·tu·al fund ▸ **noun** an investment program funded by shareholders that trades in diversified holdings and is professionally managed.

muu·muu /'mo͞oˌmo͞o/ ▸ **noun** a loose, brightly colored dress as traditionally worn by Hawaiian women.
– ORIGIN Hawaiian, 'cut off.'

mu·zak /'myo͞oˌzak/ ▸ **noun** trademark recorded light background music played in public places.
– ORIGIN alteration of **MUSIC**.

muz·zle /'məzəl/ ▸ **noun 1** the projecting part of an animal's face, including the nose and mouth. **2** a guard fitted over an animal's muzzle to stop it biting or feeding. **3** the open end of the barrel of a firearm. ▸ **verb 1** put a guard over an animal's muzzle. **2** prevent someone from expressing their opinions freely.
– ORIGIN Latin *musum*.

muz·zy /'məzē/ ▸ **adjective** (**muzzier, muzziest**) **1** dazed or confused. **2** blurred or indistinct: *a slightly muzzy picture*.
– DERIVATIVES **muz·zi·ly** adverb **muz·zi·ness** noun.
– ORIGIN unknown.

MVP ▸ **abbreviation** most valuable player, an award given in various sports to the best player on a team or in a league.

MW ▸ **abbreviation 1** medium wave. **2** megawatt(s).

my /mī/ ▸ **possessive determiner 1** belonging to or associated with the speaker. **2** used in various expressions of surprise.
– ORIGIN Old English.

my·al·gi·a /mī'alj(ē)ə/ ▸ **noun** pain in a muscle or group of muscles.
– DERIVATIVES **my·al·gic** /-jik/ adjective.
– ORIGIN from Greek *mus* 'muscle' + *algos* 'pain.'

my·ce·li·um /mī'sēlēəm/ ▸ **noun** (pl. **mycelia**) Botany a network of fine white filaments (hyphae) making up the main part of a fungus, usually invisible above ground.
– ORIGIN from Greek *mukēs* 'fungus.'

My·ce·nae·an /ˌmīsə'nēən, mī'sēnēən/ ▸ **adjective** relating to a late Bronze Age civilization in Greece represented by archaeological discoveries at Mycenae and other ancient cities of the Peloponnese.

my·col·o·gy /mī'käləjē/ ▸ **noun** the scientific study of fungi.
– DERIVATIVES **my·co·log·i·cal** /ˌmīkə'läjikəl/ adjective **my·col·o·gist** /-jist/ noun.
– ORIGIN from Greek *mukēs* 'fungus.'

my·e·lin /'mīələn/ ▸ **noun** a whitish fatty substance forming a sheath around many nerve fibers.
– ORIGIN from Greek *muelos* 'marrow.'

my·e·loid /'mīəˌloid/ ▸ **adjective** relating to bone marrow or the spinal cord.
– ORIGIN from Greek *muelos* 'marrow.'

my·e·lo·ma /ˌmīə'lōmə/ ▸ **noun** (pl. **myelomas**) a malignant tumor of the bone marrow.

my·nah /'mīnə/ (also **mynah bird**) ▸ **noun** a southern Asian or Australasian starling with a loud call, some kinds of which can mimic human speech.
– ORIGIN Hindi.

my·o·car·di·al in·farc·tion /ˌmīə'kärdēəl/ ▸ **noun** a heart attack.

my·o·car·di·um /ˌmīə'kärdēəm/ ▸ **noun** the muscular tissue of the heart.
– DERIVATIVES **my·o·car·di·al** /-dēəl/ adjective.
– ORIGIN from Greek *mus* 'muscle' + *kardia* 'heart.'

my·o·pi·a /mī'ōpēə/ ▸ **noun 1** nearsightedness. **2** failure or inability to foresee the future consequences of an action, decision, etc.
– DERIVATIVES **my·op·ic** /mī'äpik/ adjective.
– ORIGIN from Greek *muein* 'shut' + *ōps* 'eye.'

myr·i·ad /'mirēəd/ ▸ **noun 1** (also **myriads**) a countless or very great number of people or things: *myriads of insects danced around the light*. **2** (in classical times) a unit of ten thousand. ▸ **adjective** countless: *the myriad lights of the city*.
– ORIGIN Greek *murias*, from *murioi* '10,000.'

myr·i·a·pod /'mirēəˌpäd/ ▸ **noun** a centipede, millipede, or other insect having a long body with numerous leg-bearing segments.
– ORIGIN from Greek *murioi* '10,000' + *pous* 'foot.'

myr·mi·don /'mərməˌdän, -mədən/ ▸ **noun** a follower or subordinate of a powerful person, especially one who is willing to engage in dishonest activities.
– ORIGIN from Greek *Murmidones*, a warlike people of Thessaly who accompanied Achilles to Troy.

myrrh /mər/ ▸ **noun** a sweet-smelling resin obtained from certain trees and used in perfumes, medicines, and incense.
– ORIGIN Greek *murra*.

myr·tle /'mərtl/ ▸ **noun** an evergreen shrub with glossy leaves and white flowers followed by purple-black berries.
– ORIGIN Greek *murtos*.

my·self /mī'self, mə-/ ▸ **pronoun** (first person sing.) **1** (reflexive) used by a speaker to refer to himself or herself as the object of a verb or preposition when he or she is the subject of the clause: *I hurt myself*. **2** (emphatic) I or me personally: *I wrote it myself*.
– ORIGIN Old English.

mys·te·ri·ous /mi'sti(ə)rēəs/ ▸ **adjective 1** difficult or impossible to understand, explain, or identify: *he vanished in mysterious circumstances*. **2** deliberately not saying much about something that interests other people: *he was rather mysterious about you*.

> – SYNONYMS **1 puzzling,** strange, peculiar, curious, funny, odd, weird, queer, bizarre, mystifying, inexplicable, baffling, perplexing, arcane, esoteric, cryptic, obscure. **2 secretive,** inscrutable, impenetrable, enigmatic, reticent, evasive.

– DERIVATIVES **mys·te·ri·ous·ly** adverb **mys·te·ri·ous·ness** noun.

> **WORD TOOLKIT**
>
> See **SECRET**.

mys·ter·y /'mist(ə)rē/ ▸ **noun** (pl. **mysteries**) **1** something that is difficult or impossible to understand or explain. **2** the quality of being secret or difficult to explain: *much of her past is shrouded in mystery*. **3** a novel, play, or movie dealing with a puzzling crime. **4** (**mysteries**) the secret rites or ceremonies of an ancient religion. **5** chiefly Christian Theology a religious belief based on divine revelation. **6** an incident in the life of Jesus or of a saint as a focus of devotion in the Roman Catholic Church.

> – SYNONYMS **1 puzzle,** enigma, conundrum, riddle, secret, paradox, question mark, closed book. **2 secrecy,** obscurity, uncertainty.

– ORIGIN Greek *mustērion*.

> **CHOOSE THE RIGHT WORD**
>
> See **RIDDLE**[1].

mys·ter·y play ▸ **noun** a popular medieval play based on biblical stories or the lives of the saints.

mys·tic /'mistik/ ▸ **noun** a person who devotes their time to prayer and meditation in order to become closer to God and to reach truths beyond human understanding. ▸ **adjective** mystical.

– ORIGIN Greek *mustēs* 'initiated person.'

mys·ti·cal /'mistikəl/ ▶ **adjective 1** relating to mystics or mysticism. **2** having a spiritual significance that goes beyond human understanding. **3** inspiring a sense of spiritual mystery, awe, and fascination: *the mystical city of Kathmandu.*

– SYNONYMS **spiritual,** religious, transcendental, paranormal, other-worldly, supernatural, occult, metaphysical.

– DERIVATIVES **mys·ti·cal·ly** adverb.

mys·ti·cism /'mistəˌsizəm/ ▶ **noun 1** the belief that knowledge of God and truths beyond human understanding can be gained by prayer and meditation. **2** religious or spiritual belief that is not clearly defined.

mys·ti·fy /'mistəˌfī/ ▶ **verb** (**mystifies, mystifying, mystified**) **1** utterly bewilder: *I was mystified by his disappearance.* **2** make something seem obscure or mysterious.

– SYNONYMS **bewilder,** puzzle, perplex, baffle, confuse, confound, bemuse, throw; informal flummox, stump, bamboozle.

– DERIVATIVES **mys·ti·fi·ca·tion** /ˌmistəfi'kāsʜən/ noun **mys·ti·fy·ing** adjective.
– ORIGIN French *mystifier.*

mys·tique /mis'tēk/ ▶ **noun 1** a quality of mystery, glamour, and power surrounding a person or thing. **2** an air of secrecy surrounding an activity or subject, making it impressive or baffling to people not involved in it.
– ORIGIN French.

myth /miᴛʜ/ ▶ **noun 1** a traditional story about the early history of a people or explaining a natural or social phenomenon, typically involving supernatural beings or events. **2** a widely held but false belief. **3** a fictitious or imaginary person or thing.

– SYNONYMS **1 folk tale,** folk story, legend, fable, saga, lore, folklore. **2 misconception,** fallacy, old wives' tale, fairy story, fiction; informal cock and bull story.

– ORIGIN Greek *muthos.*

myth·i·cal /'miᴛʜikəl/ ▶ **adjective 1** occurring in or characteristic of myths or folk tales. **2** fictitious or imaginary.
– DERIVATIVES **myth·ic** /'miᴛʜik/ adjective **myth·i·cal·ly** /-ik(ə)lē/ adverb.

myth·o·log·i·cal /ˌmiᴛʜə'läjikəl/ ▶ **adjective** relating to or found in myths or mythology.
– DERIVATIVES **myth·o·log·i·cal·ly** /ˌmiᴛʜə'läjik(ə)lē/ adverb.

my·thol·o·gize /mi'ᴛʜäləˌjīz/ ▶ **verb** make someone or something the subject of a myth.

my·thol·o·gy /mi'ᴛʜäləjē/ ▶ **noun** (pl. **mythologies**) **1** a collection of myths. **2** a set of widely held but exaggerated or false stories or beliefs. **3** the study of myths.
– DERIVATIVES **my·thol·o·gist** noun.

myth·o·ma·ni·a /ˌmiᴛʜə'mānēə/ ▶ **noun** an abnormal tendency to exaggerate or tell lies.
– DERIVATIVES **myth·o·ma·ni·ac** /-'mānēˌak/ noun & adjective.

myth·o·poe·ia /ˌmiᴛʜə'pēə/ ▶ **noun** the making of a myth or myths.
– DERIVATIVES **myth·o·poe·ic** /-'pēik/ adjective **myth·o·po·et·ic** /ˌmiᴛʜəpō'etik/ adjective.
– ORIGIN Greek.

myx·o·ma·to·sis /mikˌsōmə'tōsəs/ ▶ **noun** a highly infectious and usually fatal disease of rabbits, spread by a virus and causing inflammation and discharge around the eyes.
– ORIGIN from Greek *muxa* 'slime, mucus.'

N[1] (also **n**) ▶ **noun** (pl. **Ns** or **N's**) the fourteenth letter of the alphabet.

N[2] ▶ **abbreviation 1** (used in recording moves in chess) knight. **2** (chiefly in place names) New. **3** Physics newton(s). **4** North or Northern. ▶ **symbol** the chemical element nitrogen.

n ▶ **abbreviation 1** nano- (10^{-9}). **2** Grammar neuter. **3** Grammar noun. ▶ **symbol** an unspecified or variable number.

'n' (also **'n**) ▶ **contraction** informal and (e.g., *rock 'n' roll*).

Na ▶ **symbol** the chemical element sodium.
– ORIGIN from Latin *natrium.*

n/a ▶ **abbreviation 1** not applicable. **2** not available.

NAACP /ˌen dəbəl ˌā sē ˈpē/ ▶ **abbreviation** National Association for the Advancement of Colored People.

naan ▶ **noun** variant spelling of **NAN**.

nab /nab/ ▶ **verb** (**nabs, nabbing, nabbed**) informal **1** catch someone doing something wrong. **2** take or grab something suddenly.
– ORIGIN unknown.

na·bob /ˈnābäb/ ▶ **noun 1** historical a Muslim official or governor under the Mogul empire. **2** a very rich or important person.
– ORIGIN Urdu.

na·celle /nəˈsel/ ▶ **noun** the streamlined outer casing of an aircraft engine.
– ORIGIN French.

na·cho /ˈnächō/ ▶ **noun** (pl. **nachos**) a tortilla chip topped with melted cheese, peppers, etc.
– ORIGIN perhaps from Mexican Spanish *Nacho*, familiar form of *Ignacio*, first name of the chef credited with creating the dish.

na·cre /ˈnākər/ ▶ **noun** mother-of-pearl.
– DERIVATIVES **na·cre·ous** /-krēəs/ adjective.
– ORIGIN French.

na·da /ˈnädə/ ▶ **pronoun** informal nothing.
– ORIGIN Spanish.

na·dir /ˈnādər, ˈnādi(ə)r/ ▶ **noun 1** the lowest or most unsuccessful point: *the nadir of my career.* **2** Astronomy the point in the sky directly opposite the zenith and below an observer.

– SYNONYMS **low point,** all-time low, bottom, rock bottom; informal the pits.
– ANTONYMS zenith.

– ORIGIN from Arabic, 'opposite to the zenith.'

NAFTA /ˈnaftə/ (also **Nafta**) ▶ **abbreviation** North American Free Trade Agreement.

nag[1] /nag/ ▶ **verb** (**nags, nagging, nagged**) **1** constantly ask someone to do something that they are reluctant to do. **2** (often as adj. **nagging**) be persistently painful or worrying to someone: *I was left with nagging doubts.*

– SYNONYMS **1 harass,** keep on at, go on at, badger, hound, plague, criticize, find fault with, grumble at, henpeck; informal hassle, ride. **2 trouble,** worry, bother, torment, niggle, prey on one's mind; informal bug.

▶ **noun** a persistent feeling of anxiety.
– ORIGIN perhaps Scandinavian or German.

nag[2] ▶ **noun** informal, often derogatory a horse, especially one that is old or in poor condition.
– ORIGIN unknown.

Na·hua·tl /ˈnäˌwätl/ ▶ **noun** (pl. same or **Nahuatls**) **1** a member of a group of peoples native to southern Mexico and Central America, including the Aztecs. **2** the language of the Nahuatl.
– ORIGIN Nahuatl.

nai·ad /ˈnāad, -əd, nī-/ ▶ **noun** (in classical mythology) a water nymph.
– ORIGIN Greek *Naias.*

na·if /nīˈēf, nä-/ ▶ **adjective** naive. ▶ **noun** a naive person.
– ORIGIN French.

nail /nāl/ ▶ **noun 1** a small metal spike with a broadened flat head, hammered in to join things together or to serve as a hook. **2** a thin hard layer covering the upper surface of the tip of the fingers and toes.

– SYNONYMS **tack,** pin, brad, hobnail, spike, staple, rivet.

▶ **verb 1** fasten something with a nail or nails. **2** informal catch someone, especially a suspected criminal. **3** (**nail someone down**) informal force someone to commit themselves to something: *I can't nail her down to a specific date.* **4** (**nail something down**) informal identify something precisely.

– SYNONYMS **fasten,** fix, attach, secure, affix, pin, tack, hammer.

– PHRASES **a nail in the coffin** an action or event likely to have a bad or destructive effect on someone or something.
– ORIGIN Old English.

nail-bit·er ▶ **noun** a situation causing great tension or anxiety.

nail file ▶ **noun** a small file or emery board for smoothing and shaping the fingernails and toenails.

nail pol·ish (Brit. also **nail varnish**) ▶ **noun** a glossy colored substance applied to the fingernails or toenails.

na·ive /nīˈēv/ (also **naïve**) ▶ **adjective 1** lacking experience, wisdom, or judgment. **2** (of art or an artist) produced in or using a simple, childlike style that deliberately rejects sophisticated techniques.

– SYNONYMS **innocent,** unsophisticated, artless, inexperienced, unworldly, trusting, gullible, credulous, immature, callow, raw, green; informal wet behind the ears.
– ANTONYMS worldly.

– DERIVATIVES **na·ive·ly** adverb.
– ORIGIN French, from Latin *nativus* 'native, natural.'

> **CHOOSE THE RIGHT WORD**
>
> See **GULLIBLE**.

na·ive·té /ˌnīˌēv(ə)'tā, nī'ēv(ə)ˌtā/ (also **naïveté**) ▸ **noun** lack of experience, wisdom, or judgment.

na·ked /'nākid/ ▸ **adjective 1** without clothes. **2** (of an object) without the usual covering or protection: *a naked light bulb*. **3** not hidden or concealed: *naked aggression*. **4** helpless or vulnerable.

> – SYNONYMS **nude,** bare, in the nude, stark naked, stripped, unclothed, undressed; informal without a stitch on, in one's birthday suit, in the raw/buff, in the altogether, buck naked.
> – ANTONYMS dressed.

– DERIVATIVES **na·ked·ly** adverb **na·ked·ness** noun.
– PHRASES **the naked eye** the normal power of the eye, without using a telescope, microscope, or other optical instrument.
– ORIGIN Old English.

> **CHOOSE THE RIGHT WORD**
>
> **naked, bald, bare, barren, nude**
>
> Someone who isn't wearing any clothes is **naked**; this adjective is usually associated with revealing a part or all of the body (*her naked shoulder; a naked man ran from the burning building*). A *naked* person who appears in a painting or photograph is called a **nude**, a euphemistic but more socially acceptable term referring to the unclothed human body. **Bare** can describe the branches of a tree as well as human limbs; it implies the absence of the conventional or appropriate covering (*a bare wooden floor; bare legs; four bare walls*). **Bald** also suggests a lack of covering, but it refers particularly to a lack of natural covering, especially hair (*a bald head*). **Barren** implies a lack of vegetation, and it also connotes destitution and fruitlessness (*a barren wasteland devoid of life*). A *bald* artist might paint a *nude* woman whose *bare* arms are extended against a *barren* winter landscape.

nam·by-pam·by /'nambē 'pambē/ ▸ **adjective** weak and ineffectual.
– ORIGIN from the name of *Ambrose* Philips, an English writer ridiculed for his bad poetry.

name /nām/ ▸ **noun 1** a word or words by which someone or something is known. **2** a famous person. **3** a reputation, especially a good one: *he made a name for himself in the theater*.

> – SYNONYMS **title,** designation, tag, nickname, sobriquet, epithet, label, honorific; informal moniker, handle; formal appellation, denomination, cognomen.

▸ **verb 1** give someone or something a name. **2** identify or mention by name: *the dead man has been named by police*. **3** specify a time, place, or sum of money.

> – SYNONYMS **1 call,** dub, label, style, term, title, baptize, christen. **2 nominate,** designate, select, pick, decide on, choose.

– PHRASES **call someone names** insult someone verbally. **have to one's name** have in one's possession. **in all but name** existing in practice but not formally recognized as such. **in someone's name 1** formally registered as belonging to or reserved for someone. **2** on behalf of someone. **in the name of** for the sake of. **name names** mention specific names, especially of people accused of wrongdoing. **the name of the game** informal the main purpose or most important aspect of a situation.
– ORIGIN Old English.

> **WORD LINKS**
>
> **onomastic** *relating to names*

name-call·ing ▸ **noun** abusive language or insults.
– DERIVATIVES **name-call·er** noun.

name·check /'nāmˌchek/ ▸ **noun** a public mention of someone's name, especially to express gratitude or for publicity purposes. ▸ **verb** publicly mention someone's name.

name day ▸ **noun** the feast day of a saint after whom a person is named.

name-drop·ping ▸ **noun** the casual mentioning of famous people as if one knows them, so as to impress others.

name·less /'nāmlis/ ▸ **adjective 1** having no name. **2** not identified by name; anonymous. **3** too horrific or unpleasant to be described.

name·ly /'nāmlē/ ▸ **adverb** that is to say.

> – SYNONYMS **that is (to say),** to be specific, specifically, viz., to wit, in other words.

name·plate /'nāmˌplāt/ ▸ **noun** a plate attached to something and bearing the name of the owner, occupier, or the thing itself.

name·sake /'nāmˌsāk/ ▸ **noun** a person or thing with the same name as another.
– ORIGIN from the phrase *for the name's sake*.

Na·mib·i·an /nə'mibēən/ ▸ **noun** a person from Namibia, a country in southern Africa. ▸ **adjective** relating to Namibia.

nan /nän/ (also **naan**) ▸ **noun** a type of soft, flat Indian bread.
– ORIGIN Urdu and Persian.

nan·a /'nanə/ (Brit. also **nanna**) ▸ **noun** informal one's grandmother.
– ORIGIN child's pronunciation of **NANNY**.

nan·cy /'nänˈsē/ (also **nance, nancy boy**) ▸ **noun** (pl. **nancies**) informal, derogatory an effeminate or homosexual man.
– ORIGIN familiar form of the name *Ann*.

nan·keen /nan'kēn/ ▸ **noun** a yellowish cotton cloth.
– ORIGIN named after the city of *Nanking* in China, where it was first made.

nan·ny /'nanē/ ▸ **noun** (pl. **nannies**) **1** a woman employed to look after a child in its own home. **2** (also **nanny goat**) a female goat. ▸ **adjective** interfering and overprotective: *our tax-bloated nanny state*. ▸ **verb** (**nannies, nannying, nannied**) (usu. as n. **nannying**) **1** work as a nanny. **2** treat someone in an overprotective way.
– ORIGIN familiar form of the name *Ann*.

nan·ny state ▸ **noun** the government viewed as overprotective or as interfering unduly with personal choice.

nano- ▸ **combining form 1** referring to a factor of one billionth (10^{-9}): *nanosecond*. **2** extremely small; submicroscopic: *nanotechnology*.
– ORIGIN from Greek *nanos* 'dwarf.'

nan·o·bot /'nanōˌbät/ ▸ **noun** a submicroscopic self-propelled machine, especially one that has some freedom of action and can reproduce.

nan·o·me·ter /ˈnanəˌmētər/ ▶ **noun** one billionth of a meter.

nan·o·scale /ˈnanəˌskāl, ˈnā-/ ▶ **adjective** of a size measurable in nanometers or microns.

nan·o·sec·ond /ˈnanəˌsekənd/ ▶ **noun** one billionth of a second.

nan·o·struc·ture /ˈnanəˌstrəkCHər, ˈnā-/ ▶ **noun** a structure, especially a semiconductor device, that has dimensions of a few nanometers.

nan·o·tech·nol·o·gy /ˌnanəˌtekˈnäləjē, ˌnanō-/ ▶ **noun** technology on an atomic or molecular scale, concerned with dimensions of less than 100 nanometers.

nan·o·tube /ˈnanəˌt(y)o͞ob/ ▶ **noun** Chemistry a cylindrical molecule of a fullerene.

nan·o·wire /ˈnanəˌwī(ə)r, ˈnā-/ ▶ **noun** an extremely thin wire made of semiconducting material, used in miniature transistors and some laser applications.

nap[1] /nap/ ▶ **noun** a short sleep, especially during the day.

– SYNONYMS **sleep,** catnap, siesta, doze, lie-down, rest; informal snooze, forty winks, shut-eye.

▶ **verb** (**naps, napping, napped**) have a nap.
– ORIGIN Old English.

nap[2] ▶ **noun** short raised hairs or threads on the surface of materials such as velvet or suede.
– ORIGIN Dutch or German *noppe*.

na·palm /ˈnāˌpä(l)m/ ▶ **noun** a highly flammable jellylike form of gasoline, used in firebombs and flamethrowers.
– ORIGIN from *naphthenic* and *palmitic acids* (compounds used in its manufacture).

nape /nāp/ ▶ **noun** the back of a person's neck.
– ORIGIN unknown.

naph·tha /ˈnafTHə, ˈnap-/ ▶ **noun** a flammable oil distilled from coal, shale, or petroleum.
– ORIGIN Greek.

naph·tha·lene /ˈnafTHəˌlēn, ˈnap-/ ▶ **noun** a white crystalline substance used in mothballs and for chemical manufacture.

nap·kin /ˈnapkin/ ▶ **noun 1** a square piece of cloth or paper used at a meal to wipe the fingers or lips and to protect clothes. **2** a sanitary napkin.
– ORIGIN Old French *nappe* 'tablecloth.'

Na·po·le·on·ic /nəˌpōlēˈänik/ ▶ **adjective** relating to or characteristic of the French emperor Napoleon I or his time.

nap·py /ˈnapē/ ▶ **adjective** informal, often offensive (of hair) frizzy.
– ORIGIN abbreviation of **NAPKIN**.

narc /närk/ ▶ **noun** informal a federal agent or police officer who enforces laws regarding the sale or use of illicit drugs.
– ORIGIN abbreviation of **NARCOTIC**.

nar·cis·sism /ˈnärsəˌsizəm/ ▶ **noun** excessive interest in or admiration of oneself and one's physical appearance.
– DERIVATIVES **nar·cis·sist** /ˈnärsəsist/ noun **nar·cis·sis·tic** /ˌnärsəˈsistik/ adjective.
– ORIGIN from *Narcissus*, a beautiful youth in Greek mythology who fell in love with his reflection in a pool.

nar·cis·sus /närˈsisəs/ ▶ **noun** (pl. **narcissi** /-ˈsisī, -sē/ or **narcissuses**) a daffodil with a flower that has white or pale outer petals and a shallow orange or yellow center.
– ORIGIN Greek *narkissos*.

nar·co·lep·sy /ˈnärkəˌlepsē/ ▶ **noun** a condition characterized by an extreme tendency to fall asleep at inappropriate times.
– DERIVATIVES **nar·co·lep·tic** /ˌnärkəˈleptik/ adjective & noun.
– ORIGIN from Greek *narkē* 'numbness.'

nar·co·sis /närˈkōsis/ ▶ **noun** a state of drowsiness or unconsciousness produced by drugs.
– ORIGIN from Greek *narkoun* 'make numb.'

nar·cot·ic /närˈkätik/ ▶ **noun 1** an addictive drug, especially an illegal one, that affects mood or behavior. **2** Medicine a drug that causes drowsiness or unconsciousness and relieves pain.

– SYNONYMS **drug,** sedative, opiate, painkiller, analgesic, palliative.

▶ **adjective** relating to narcotics.

– SYNONYMS **soporific,** sedative, calming, painkilling, pain-relieving, analgesic, anodyne.

nar·rate /ˈnarˌāt/ ▶ **verb 1** give an account of something. **2** provide a commentary for a movie, television program, etc.

– SYNONYMS **tell,** relate, recount, recite, describe, chronicle, report, present.

– DERIVATIVES **nar·ra·tion** /naˈrāSHən/ noun.
– ORIGIN Latin *narrare*.

nar·ra·tive /ˈnarətiv/ ▶ **noun 1** an account of connected events; a story. **2** the part of a fictional work that tells the story, as distinct from the dialogue.

– SYNONYMS **account,** chronicle, history, description, record, report, story, tale.

▶ **adjective** in the form of a narrative or relating to the narration of something.
– DERIVATIVES **nar·ra·tive·ly** adverb.

nar·ra·tor /ˈnaˌrātər/ ▶ **noun** a person who narrates something, especially a character who recounts the events of a novel.

– SYNONYMS **storyteller,** chronicler, commentator, presenter, author.
– ANTONYMS listener, audience.

nar·row /ˈnarō/ ▶ **adjective** (**narrower, narrowest**) **1** of small width in comparison to length. **2** limited in extent, amount, or scope: *a narrow range of skills.* **3** only just achieved: *a narrow escape.*

– SYNONYMS **1 slender,** slim, small, slight, attenuated, tapering, thin, tiny. **2 confined,** cramped, tight, restricted, limited, constricted, small, tiny, inadequate, insufficient.
– ANTONYMS wide, broad.

▶ **verb 1** become or make narrower. **2** (**narrow something down**) reduce the number of possibilities or options.

– SYNONYMS **reduce,** restrict, limit, decrease, diminish, taper, contract, shrink, constrict.
– ANTONYMS widen.

▶ **noun** (**narrows**) a narrow channel connecting two larger areas of water.
– DERIVATIVES **nar·row·ness** noun.
– ORIGIN Old English.

nar·row·cast /ˈnarōˌkast/ ▶ **verb** (past and past part. **narrowcast** or **narrowcasted**) transmit a television program, especially by cable, to a comparatively small or specialist audience.

nar·row gauge ▶ **noun** a railroad gauge that is narrower than the standard gauge of 4 ft. 8½ inches (1.435 meters).

nar·row·ly /ˈnerōlē/ ▸ **adverb** by only a small margin: *one bullet narrowly missed him.*

– SYNONYMS **(only) just,** barely, scarcely, hardly, by a hair's breadth; informal by a whisker.

nar·row-mind·ed ▸ **adjective** unwilling to listen to or accept the views of other people.

– SYNONYMS **intolerant,** illiberal, reactionary, conservative, parochial, provincial, insular, small-minded, petty, blinkered, inward-looking, hidebound, prejudiced, bigoted.
– ANTONYMS tolerant.

nar·thex /ˈnärᴛʜeks/ ▸ **noun** an antechamber or large porch in a church.
– ORIGIN Greek.

nar·whal /ˈnärwəl/ ▸ **noun** a small Arctic whale, the male of which has a long spirally twisted tusk.
– ORIGIN Danish *narhval,* perhaps from an Old Norse word meaning 'corpse,' with reference to the whale's skin color.

nar·y /ˈne(ə)rē/ ▸ **adjective** informal or dialect form of **NOT**.
– ORIGIN from *ne'er a* 'never a.'

NASA /ˈnasə/ ▸ **abbreviation** National Aeronautics and Space Administration.

na·sal /ˈnāzəl/ ▸ **adjective 1** relating to the nose. **2** (of a speech sound) produced by the breath passing through the nose, e.g., *m, n, ng.* **3** (of speech) having an intonation caused by the breath passing through the nose.
– DERIVATIVES **na·sal·ly** adverb.
– ORIGIN from Latin *nasus* 'nose.'

na·sal·ize /ˈnāzəˌlīz/ ▸ **verb** pronounce something nasally.
– DERIVATIVES **na·sal·i·za·tion** /ˌnāzəliˈzāsʜən/ noun.

nas·cent /ˈnāsənt, ˈnasənt/ ▸ **adjective** just coming into existence and beginning to develop: *the nascent economic recovery.*
– ORIGIN from Latin *nasci* 'be born.'

NASDAQ /ˈnazdak/ ▸ **abbreviation** National Association of Securities Dealers Automated Quotations, a computerized system for trading in securities.

nas·tur·tium /naˈstərsʜəm, nə-/ ▸ **noun** a trailing garden plant with round leaves and bright orange, yellow, or red flowers.
– ORIGIN Latin.

nas·ty /ˈnastē/ ▸ **adjective** (**nastier, nastiest**) **1** unpleasant or disgusting. **2** spiteful, violent, or bad-tempered. **3** dangerous or serious: *a nasty bang on the head.*

– SYNONYMS **1 unpleasant,** disagreeable, disgusting, vile, foul, abominable, revolting, repulsive, repellent, horrible, obnoxious, unsavory, loathsome, noxious, foul-smelling, smelly, stinking, rank, fetid, malodorous; informal ghastly, horrid, yucky, lousy; literary noisome. **2 unkind,** unpleasant, unfriendly, disagreeable, rude, spiteful, malicious, mean, vicious, malevolent, hurtful. **3** *a nasty accident* **serious,** dangerous, bad, awful, dreadful, terrible, severe, painful.
– ANTONYMS nice, pleasant.

▸ **noun** (pl. **nasties**) informal an unpleasant or harmful person or thing.
– DERIVATIVES **nas·ti·ly** adverb **nas·ti·ness** noun.
– ORIGIN unknown.

Nat. ▸ **abbreviation 1** national. **2** nationalist.

na·tal /ˈnātl/ ▸ **adjective** relating to the place or time of one's birth.
– ORIGIN Latin *natalis.*

na·tion /ˈnāsʜən/ ▸ **noun** a large group of people sharing the same culture, language, or history, and inhabiting a particular country or territory.

– SYNONYMS **country,** state, land, realm, kingdom, republic, people, race, tribe.

– ORIGIN Latin, from *nasci* 'be born.'

na·tion·al /ˈnasʜənəl/ ▸ **adjective 1** relating to or characteristic of a nation. **2** owned, controlled, or financially supported by the federal government.

– SYNONYMS **1** *national politics* **federal,** public, governmental, state. **2** *a national strike* **nationwide,** countrywide, general, widespread.
– ANTONYMS local, international.

▸ **noun** a citizen of a particular country: *French nationals.*

– SYNONYMS **citizen,** subject, native, resident, inhabitant, voter.

– DERIVATIVES **na·tion·al·ly** adverb.

na·tion·al debt ▸ **noun** the total amount of money that a country's government has borrowed.

Na·tion·al Guard ▸ **noun** the main reserve military force partly maintained by each state of the United States but also available for federal use.

na·tion·al·ism /ˈnasʜənəˌlizəm/ ▸ **noun 1** strong support for and pride in one's own country, often to an extreme degree. **2** belief in political independence for a particular country.

– SYNONYMS **patriotism,** allegiance, xenophobia, chauvinism, jingoism, flag-waving.

– DERIVATIVES **na·tion·al·ist** /ˈnasʜənəlist/ noun & adjective **na·tion·al·is·tic** /ˌnasʜənəˈlistik/ adjective.

na·tion·al·i·ty /ˌnasʜəˈnalitē/ ▸ **noun** (pl. **nationalities**) **1** the status of belonging to a particular nation. **2** an ethnic group forming a part of one or more political nations.

na·tion·al·ize /ˈnasʜənəˌlīz/ ▸ **verb** transfer an industry or business from private to government ownership or control.
– DERIVATIVES **na·tion·al·i·za·tion** /ˌnasʜənəliˈzāsʜən/ noun.

na·tion·al park ▸ **noun** an area of natural beauty or environmental importance that is protected by the national government and may be visited by the public.

na·tion·al serv·ice ▸ **noun** Brit a period of compulsory service in the armed forces during peacetime.

Na·tion·al So·cial·ism ▸ **noun** historical the political doctrine of the Nazi Party of Germany.

na·tion state ▸ **noun** a sovereign state most of whose citizens or subjects are united by factors such as a shared language or culture.

na·tion·wide /ˈnāsʜənˈwīd/ ▸ **adjective & adverb** throughout the whole nation.

– SYNONYMS **national,** countrywide, state, general, widespread, extensive.
– ANTONYMS local.

na·tive /ˈnātiv/ ▸ **noun 1** a person born in a specified place: *she's a native of Boston.* **2** a local inhabitant. **3** an animal or plant that lives or grows naturally in a place. **4** dated, offensive a non-white original inhabitant of a country as regarded by European colonists or travelers.

– SYNONYMS **inhabitant,** resident, local, citizen, national, countryman.
– ANTONYMS foreigner.

▸ **adjective 1** associated with a person's place of birth: *her native country.* **2** (of a plant or animal) living or growing naturally in a place. **3** relating to the original inhabitants of a place. **4** naturally in a person's character: *his native wit.*

– SYNONYMS **1** *native species* **indigenous,** original, local, domestic. **2** *native wit* **innate,** inborn, natural, inherent, intrinsic.

– ORIGIN Latin *nativus.*

USAGE

In sentences such as *she's a native of Boston* the use of the noun **native** is quite acceptable. When it is used to refer to nonwhite original inhabitants of a country, however, it has an old-fashioned feel and may cause offense.

WORD TOOLKIT

See **ORIGINAL**.

Na·tive A·mer·i·can ▸ **noun** a member of any of the peoples who were the original inhabitants of North and South America and the Caribbean Islands. ▸ **adjective** relating to Native Americans.

USAGE

Native American is now the accepted term in many contexts. See also **AMERICAN INDIAN**.

na·tive speak·er ▸ **noun** a person who has spoken the language in question from their earliest childhood.

na·tiv·i·ty /nə'tivitē, nā-/ ▸ **noun** (pl. **nativities**) **1** old use a person's birth. **2** (**the Nativity**) the birth of Jesus.

na·tiv·i·ty play ▸ **noun** a play performed at Christmas based on the events surrounding the birth of Jesus.

NATO /'nātō/ (also **Nato**) ▸ **abbreviation** North Atlantic Treaty Organization.

nat·ter /'natər/ informal ▸ **verb** chat casually. ▸ **noun** a casual and leisurely conversation.
– ORIGIN first meaning 'grumble, fret.'

nat·ty /'natē/ ▸ **adjective** (**nattier, nattiest**) informal smart and fashionable.
– DERIVATIVES **nat·ti·ly** adverb.
– ORIGIN perhaps related to **NEAT**.

nat·u·ral /'nacHərəl/ ▸ **adjective 1** existing in or obtained from nature; not made or caused by humans: *natural disasters such as earthquakes.* **2** in accordance with nature; normal or to be expected: *he died of natural causes.* **3** born with a particular skill or quality: *a natural leader.* **4** relaxed and unaffected. **5** (of a parent or child) related by blood. **6** old use illegitimate. **7** Music (of a note) not sharp or flat.

– SYNONYMS **1 unprocessed,** organic, pure, unrefined, additive-free, green. **2** *a natural occurrence* **normal,** ordinary, everyday, usual, regular, common, commonplace, typical, routine, standard, logical, understandable, (only) to be expected, predictable. **3** *a natural leader* **born,** instinctive, congenital, pathological. **4** *his natural instincts* **innate,** inborn, inherent, native, inherited, hereditary. **5** *she seemed very natural* **unaffected,** spontaneous, uninhibited, relaxed, unselfconscious, genuine, open, artless, guileless, unpretentious, unstudied.
– ANTONYMS abnormal, artificial, affected.

▸ **noun 1** a person with an inborn gift or talent for a particular task or activity. **2** an off-white color. **3** Music a natural note or a sign (♮) indicating one.
– DERIVATIVES **nat·u·ral·ness** noun.
– ORIGIN Middle English.

nat·u·ral gas ▸ **noun** flammable gas, consisting largely of methane, occurring naturally underground and used as fuel.

nat·u·ral his·to·ry ▸ **noun** the scientific study of animals or plants, especially as concerned with observation rather than carrying out experiments.

nat·u·ral·ism /'nacHərə,lizəm/ ▸ **noun** an artistic or literary movement or style based on the highly detailed and realistic portrayal of daily life.

nat·u·ral·ist /'nacHərəlist/ ▸ **noun 1** an expert in or student of natural history. **2** a person who practices naturalism in art or literature.

nat·u·ral·is·tic /,nacHərə'listik/ ▸ **adjective 1** closely imitating real life or nature. **2** based on the theory of naturalism in art or literature.
– DERIVATIVES **nat·u·ral·is·ti·cal·ly** adverb.

nat·u·ral·ize /'nacHərə,līz/ ▸ **verb 1** make someone who was not born in a particular country a citizen of that country. **2** establish a plant or animal in a region where it does not occur naturally. **3** alter an adopted foreign word so that it conforms more closely to the language that has adopted it.
– DERIVATIVES **nat·u·ral·i·za·tion** /,nacHərələ'zāsHən/ noun.

nat·u·ral law ▸ **noun 1** a body of unchanging moral principles regarded as common to all human beings and forming a basis for human behavior. **2** an observable law relating to natural phenomena.

nat·u·ral log·a·rithm ▸ **noun** a logarithm to the base *e* (2.71828 ...).

nat·u·ral·ly /'nacHərəlē/ ▸ **adverb 1** in a natural way. **2** of course.

– SYNONYMS **of course,** as might be expected, needless to say, obviously, clearly, it goes without saying.

nat·u·ral num·bers ▸ **plural noun** the sequence of whole numbers 1, 2, 3, etc., used for counting.

nat·u·ral re·sources ▸ **plural noun** naturally occurring substances such as coal or oil.

nat·u·ral sci·ence ▸ **noun** a branch of science that deals with the physical world, e.g., physics, chemistry, geology, biology.

nat·u·ral se·lec·tion ▸ **noun** the evolutionary process by which those animals and plants that are better adapted to their environment tend to survive and produce more offspring.

na·ture /'nācHər/ ▸ **noun 1** the physical world, including plants, animals, the landscape, and natural phenomena, as opposed to people or things made by people. **2** the inborn qualities or characteristics of a person or thing: *it's not in her nature to listen to advice.* **3** a kind, sort, or class: *topics of a religious nature.* **4** hereditary characteristics as a factor that determines someone's personality. Often contrasted with **NURTURE**.

– SYNONYMS **1 the natural world,** the environment, Mother Nature, Mother Earth, the universe, the cosmos, wildlife, the countryside, the land. **2 character,** personality, disposition, temperament, makeup, psyche. **3 kind,** sort, type, variety, category, class, genre, order, quality, complexion, stripe.

– DERIVATIVES **na·tured** adjective.
– PHRASES **in the nature of things** inevitable or inevitably.
– ORIGIN Latin *natura* 'birth, nature, quality,' from *nasci* 'be born.'

na·ture re·serve ▶ noun an area of land managed so as to preserve its plants, animals, and physical features.

na·ture trail ▶ noun a path through the countryside designed to draw attention to natural features.

na·tur·op·a·thy /ˌnācHəˈräpəTHē, ˌnā-/ ▶ noun a system of alternative medicine involving the treatment or prevention of diseases by diet, exercise, and massage rather than by using drugs.
– DERIVATIVES **na·tur·o·path** /ˈnācHərəˌpaTH, ˈnā-/ noun **na·tur·o·path·ic** /ˌnācHərəˈpaTHik, ˌnā-/ adjective.

naught /nôt/ ▶ pronoun the digit 0; zero.

– SYNONYMS **nil,** zero, nothing; Tennis love. informal zilch, zip, nada.

– ORIGIN Old English.

naugh·ty /ˈnôtē, nä-/ ▶ adjective (**naughtier, naughtiest**) **1** (especially of a child) disobedient; badly behaved. **2** informal mildly rude or indecent.

– SYNONYMS **1 badly behaved,** disobedient, bad, wayward, defiant, unruly, insubordinate, willful, delinquent, undisciplined, refractory, disruptive, mischievous, impish. **2 indecent,** risqué, rude, racy, vulgar, dirty, filthy, smutty, crude, coarse.
– ANTONYMS well behaved, clean.

– DERIVATIVES **naugh·ti·ly** adverb **naugh·ti·ness** noun.
– ORIGIN from **NAUGHT**: first meaning 'possessing nothing.'

nau·se·a /ˈnôzēə, -ZHə/ ▶ noun **1** a feeling of sickness and being about to vomit. **2** disgust or revulsion.

– SYNONYMS **sickness,** biliousness, queasiness, vomiting, retching.

– ORIGIN Greek *nausia* 'seasickness.'

nau·se·ate /ˈnôzēˌāt, - ZHēˌāt/ ▶ verb make someone feel sick or disgusted.

nau·seous /ˈnôSHəs, -ZHəs, -zēəs/ ▶ adjective **1** feeling sick. **2** causing a feeling of sickness.
– DERIVATIVES **nau·seous·ly** adverb.

nau·ti·cal /ˈnôtikəl/ ▶ adjective relating to sailors or navigation.

– SYNONYMS **maritime,** marine, naval, seafaring, seagoing, sailing.

– DERIVATIVES **nau·ti·cal·ly** /-ik(ə)lē/ adverb.
– ORIGIN Greek *nautikos*, from *nautēs* 'sailor.'

nau·ti·cal mile ▶ noun a unit used in measuring distances at sea, equal to 1,852 meters (approximately 6,076 feet).

nau·ti·lus /ˈnôtl-əs/ ▶ noun (pl. **nautiluses** or **nautili** /ˈnôtl-ī/) a swimming mollusk with a spiral shell and many short tentacles around the mouth.
– ORIGIN Greek *nautilos* 'sailor.'

Nav·a·jo /ˈnavəˌhō, ˈnä-/ (also **Navaho**) ▶ noun (pl. same or **Navajos**) **1** a member of an American Indian people of New Mexico and Arizona. **2** the language of the Navajo.
– ORIGIN from an American Indian word meaning 'fields adjoining a dry gully.'

na·val /ˈnāvəl/ ▶ adjective relating to a navy or navies.
– ORIGIN from Latin *navis* 'ship.'

nave[1] /nāv/ ▶ noun the central part of a church apart from the side aisles, chancel, and transepts.
– ORIGIN Latin *navis* 'ship.'

nave[2] ▶ noun the hub of a wheel.
– ORIGIN Old English.

na·vel /ˈnāvəl/ ▶ noun the small hollow in the center of a person's belly where the umbilical cord was cut at birth.
– ORIGIN Old English.

na·vel-gaz·ing ▶ noun self-satisfied concentration on oneself or a single issue.

na·vel or·ange ▶ noun a variety of orange having a navel-like hollow at the top containing a small secondary fruit.

nav·i·ga·ble /ˈnavigəbəl/ ▶ adjective **1** wide and deep enough to be used by boats and ships. **2** (of a website) easy to move around in.
– DERIVATIVES **nav·i·ga·bil·i·ty** /ˌnavəgəˈbilitē/ noun.

nav·i·gate /ˈnaviˌgāt/ ▶ verb **1** plan and direct the route of a ship, aircraft, or other form of transport. **2** sail or travel over a stretch of water or terrain. **3** guide a ship, boat, or vehicle over a particular route: *she navigated the car safely through the traffic.* **4** move around a website, the Internet, etc.

– SYNONYMS **steer,** pilot, guide, direct, captain; informal skipper.

– ORIGIN Latin *navigare* 'to sail.'

nav·i·ga·tion /ˌnaviˈgāSHən/ ▶ noun **1** the process or activity of navigating. **2** the movement of ships.
– DERIVATIVES **nav·i·ga·tion·al** adjective.

nav·i·ga·tor /ˈnaviˌgātər/ ▶ noun **1** a person who navigates a ship, aircraft, etc. **2** historical a person who explored by sea. **3** a browser program for accessing data on the Internet or another information system.

na·vy /ˈnāvē/ ▶ noun (pl. **navies**) **1** the branch of a country's armed services that carries out military operations at sea. **2** (also **navy blue**) a dark blue color.

– SYNONYMS **fleet,** flotilla, armada.

– ORIGIN Old French *navie* 'ship, fleet,' from Latin *navis* 'ship.'

na·vy yard ▶ noun a shipyard where naval vessels are built, repaired, and equipped.

na·wab /nəˈwäb/ ▶ noun **1** a native governor during the time of the Mogul empire. **2** a Muslim nobleman or person of high status.
– ORIGIN Urdu, from Arabic, 'deputy.'

nay /nā/ ▶ adverb **1** or rather: *it will take months, nay years.* **2** old use or dialect no. ▶ noun a negative answer.
– ORIGIN Old Norse.

nay·say·er /ˈnāˌsāər/ ▶ noun a person who denies or opposes something.
– DERIVATIVES **nay·say** /ˈnāˌsā/ verb (past and past participle **naysaid**).

Naz·a·rene /ˈnazəˌrēn/ ▶ noun **1** a native or inhabitant of the town of Nazareth in Israel. **2** (**the Nazarene**) Jesus. **3** a member of an early sect of Jewish Christians. ▶ adjective relating to Nazareth or Nazarenes.

Na·zi /ˈnätsē, ˈnat-/ ▶ noun (pl. **Nazis**) historical a member of the far-right National Socialist German Workers' Party.

– DERIVATIVES **Na·zism** /-ˌizəm/ noun.
– ORIGIN German, representing the pronunciation of *Nati-* in *Nationalsozialist*.

NB ▶ **abbreviation 1** New Brunswick. **2** (used to draw attention to what follows) take special notice.
– ORIGIN sense 2 from Latin *nota bene* 'note well!'

Nb ▶ **symbol** the chemical element niobium.

NC ▶ **abbreviation 1** network computer. **2** North Carolina.

NC-17 ▶ **symbol** no one 17 and under admitted, referring to movies classified as suitable only for people aged 18 and over.
– ORIGIN representing *no children (under) 17*.

NCO ▶ **abbreviation** noncommissioned officer.

ND ▶ **abbreviation** North Dakota.

Nd ▶ **symbol** the chemical element neodymium.

Nde·be·le /ˌəndəˈbelā, -ˈbēlē/ ▶ **noun** (pl. same or **Ndebeles**) a member of a people of Zimbabwe and NE South Africa.
– ORIGIN Nguni (a Bantu language).

NE ▶ **abbreviation 1** Nebraska. **2** northeast or northeastern.

Ne ▶ **symbol** the chemical element neon.

NEA ▶ **abbreviation 1** National Education Association. **2** National Endowment for the Arts. **3** Nuclear Energy Agency.

Ne·an·der·thal /nēˈandərTHôl/ ▶ **noun 1** (also **Neanderthal man**) an extinct human living in ice age Europe between *c.*120,000 and 35,000 years ago. **2** informal a man who is uncouth or who holds very old-fashioned views.
– ORIGIN from *Neanderthal*, a region in Germany where remains of Neanderthal man were found.

neap /nēp/ (also **neap tide**) ▶ **noun** a tide just after the first or third quarters of the moon when there is the least difference between high and low water.
– ORIGIN Old English.

Ne·a·pol·i·tan /ˌnēəˈpälitn/ ▶ **noun** a person from the Italian city of Naples. ▶ **adjective 1** relating to Naples. **2** (of ice cream) made in layers of different colors and flavors.

near /ni(ə)r/ ▶ **adverb 1** at or to a short distance in space or time. **2** almost: *a near perfect fit.* ▶ **preposition** (also **near to**) **1** at or to a short distance in space or time from. **2** close to a state or condition; verging on: *she was near tears.* ▶ **adjective 1** at a short distance away in space or time. **2** close to being: *a near disaster.* **3** closely related. **4** located on the side of a vehicle that is normally closest to the curb.

> – SYNONYMS **1 close,** nearby, (close/near) at hand, a stone's throw away, neighboring, within reach, accessible, handy, convenient; informal within spitting distance. **2 imminent,** in the offing, on its way, coming, impending, looming.
> – ANTONYMS far, distant.

▶ **verb** approach: *he was nearing retirement.*
– DERIVATIVES **near·ness** noun.
– ORIGIN Old Norse.

near·by /ˈni(ə)rˌbī/ ▶ **adjective & adverb** not far away.

> – SYNONYMS **not far away,** not far off, close at hand, close by, near, within reach, neighboring, local, accessible, convenient, handy.
> – ANTONYMS distant.

WORD TOOLKIT

nearby ...	neighboring ...	convenient ...
hospital	countries	location
park	islands	source
hotel	farms	parking
school	territory	route

Near East ▶ **noun** the countries of SW Asia between the Mediterranean and India (including the Middle East).
– DERIVATIVES **Near East·ern** adjective.

near·ly /ˈni(ə)rlē/ ▶ **adverb** very close to; almost.

> – SYNONYMS **almost,** just about, more or less, practically, virtually, all but, as good as, not far off, to all intents and purposes, not quite; informal pretty well.

– PHRASES **not nearly** nothing like; far from.

near miss ▶ **noun 1** a narrowly avoided collision or accident. **2** a bomb or shot that just misses its target.

near·sight·ed /ˈni(ə)rˌsītəd/ ▶ **adjective** unable to see things clearly unless they are close to the eyes.

near-term ▶ **adjective** short-term.

neat /nēt/ ▶ **adjective 1** tidy or carefully arranged. **2** done with or showing skill or efficiency: *a neat bit of deduction.* **3** (of a drink of liquor) not diluted or mixed with anything else. **4** informal excellent.

> – SYNONYMS **1 tidy,** orderly, well ordered, in (good) order, spick-and-span, uncluttered, shipshape, straight, trim. **2 smart,** spruce, dapper, trim, well groomed, well turned out; informal natty. **3** *his neat footwork* **skillful,** deft, dexterous, adroit, adept, expert, nimble, elegant, graceful, accurate; informal nifty. **4** *a neat solution* **clever,** ingenious, inventive, imaginative. **5** *neat gin* **undiluted,** straight, pure.
> – ANTONYMS untidy.

– DERIVATIVES **neat·ly** adverb **neat·ness** noun.
– ORIGIN French *net*, from Latin *nitidus* 'shining.'

neat·en /ˈnētn/ ▶ **verb** make something neat.

neath /nēTH/ ▶ **preposition** literary beneath.

neat's-foot oil ▶ **noun** oil obtained by boiling the feet of cattle, used to treat leather.
– ORIGIN from *neat*, an old word for a cow or ox.

Neb·u·chad·nez·zar /ˌneb(y)əkə(d)ˈnezər/ ▶ **noun** a very large wine bottle, equal in capacity to about twenty regular bottles.
– ORIGIN from *Nebuchadnezzar* II, king of Babylon in the 6th century BC.

neb·u·la /ˈnebyələ/ ▶ **noun** (pl. **nebulae** /-lē/ or **nebulas**) a cloud of gas or dust in outer space, visible in the night sky either as a bright patch or as a dark silhouette against other glowing matter.
– DERIVATIVES **neb·u·lar** /ˈnebyələr/ adjective.
– ORIGIN Latin, 'mist.'

neb·u·liz·er /ˈnebyəˌlīzər/ ▶ **noun** a device for producing a fine spray of liquid, used for inhaling a medicinal drug.
– DERIVATIVES **neb·u·lize** verb.

neb·u·lous /ˈnebyələs/ ▶ **adjective 1** in the form of a cloud or haze; hazy: *a nebulous glow.* **2** not clearly defined; vague: *nebulous concepts.*
– DERIVATIVES **neb·u·los·i·ty** /ˌnebyəˈläsitē/ noun.

nec·es·sar·i·ly /ˌnesəˈse(ə)rəlē/ ▶ **adverb** as a necessary result; unavoidably.

– SYNONYMS **as a consequence,** as a result, automatically, as a matter of course, certainly, incontrovertibly, inevitably, unavoidably, inescapably, of necessity.

nec·es·sar·y /ˈnesəˌserē/ ▶ **adjective 1** needing to be done, achieved, or present: *major structural changes are necessary.* **2** that must be; unavoidable: *a necessary consequence.*

– SYNONYMS **1 obligatory,** required, requisite, compulsory, mandatory, imperative, needed, essential, vital, indispensable, de rigueur; formal needful. **2** *a necessary consequence* **inevitable,** unavoidable, inescapable, inexorable.

▶ **noun (necessaries)** the basic requirements of life, such as food and warmth.
– ORIGIN Latin *necessarius.*

ne·ces·si·tate /nəˈsesəˌtāt/ ▶ **verb 1** make necessary: *the rain necessitated a change of plan.* **2** force someone to do something.

ne·ces·si·tous /nəˈsesitəs/ ▶ **adjective** formal lacking the basic requirements of life; poor.

ne·ces·si·ty /nəˈsesətē/ ▶ **noun** (pl. **necessities**) **1** the state or fact of being needed or essential. **2** a thing that is essential: *a good book is a necessity when traveling.* **3** a situation that requires a particular course of action: *a system born out of political necessity.*

– SYNONYMS **1 essential,** prerequisite, requisite, sine qua non; informal must-have. **2** *political necessity forced him to resign* **force of circumstance,** obligation, need, call, exigency, force majeure.

neck /nek/ ▶ **noun 1** the part of the body connecting the head to the rest of the body. **2** a narrow connecting or end part, such as the part of a bottle near the mouth. **3** the part of a violin, guitar, or other instrument that bears the fingerboard. **4** the length of a horse's head and neck as a measure of its lead in a race. ▶ **verb** informal kiss and caress passionately.
– PHRASES **get it in the neck** Brit. informal be severely criticized or punished. **neck and neck** level in a race or competition. **neck of the woods** informal a particular place. **up to one's neck in** informal heavily or busily involved in something.
– ORIGIN Old English, 'nape of the neck.'

neck·band /ˈnekˌband/ ▶ **noun** a strip of material around the neck of a garment.

neck·er·chief /ˈnekərˌCHif, -ˌCHēf/ ▶ **noun** a square of cloth worn around the neck.

neck·lace /ˈneklis/ ▶ **noun 1** an ornamental chain or string of beads, jewels, or links worn around the neck. **2** (in South Africa) a tire soaked with gasoline, placed around a victim's neck and set alight in order to burn them to death.

neck·line /ˈnekˌlīn/ ▶ **noun** the edge of a dress or top at or below the neck.

neck·tie /ˈnekˌtī/ ▶ **noun** a strip of material worn beneath a collar, tied in a knot at the front.

neck·wear /ˈnekˌwe(ə)r/ ▶ **noun** ties, scarves, and other items worn around the neck.

nec·ro·man·cy /ˈnekrəˌmansē/ ▶ **noun 1** prediction of the future by supposedly communicating with the dead. **2** witchcraft or black magic.
– DERIVATIVES **nec·ro·man·cer** noun **nec·ro·man·tic** /ˌnekrəˈmantik/ adjective.
– ORIGIN from Greek *nekros* 'corpse.'

nec·ro·phil·i·a /ˌnekrəˈfilēə/ ▶ **noun** sexual intercourse with or attraction toward dead bodies.
– DERIVATIVES **nec·ro·phil·i·ac** /-ˈfilēˌak/ noun.

nec·ro·pho·bi·a /ˌnekrəˈfōbēə/ ▶ **noun** extreme or irrational fear of death or dead bodies.

ne·crop·o·lis /neˈkräpəlis/ ▶ **noun** a cemetery, especially a large ancient one.
– ORIGIN from Greek *nekros* 'corpse' + *polis* 'city.'

nec·rop·sy /ˈnekräpsē/ ▶ **noun** (pl. **necropsies**) another term for **AUTOPSY**.

ne·cro·sis /neˈkrōsis/ ▶ **noun** the death of most or all of the cells in an organ or tissue due to disease or injury.
– DERIVATIVES **ne·crot·ic** /-ˈkrätik/ adjective.
– ORIGIN from Greek *nekros* 'corpse.'

nec·ro·tiz·ing /ˈnekrəˌtīziNG/ ▶ **adjective** causing or accompanied by necrosis.

nec·tar /ˈnektər/ ▶ **noun 1** a sugary fluid produced by flowers to encourage pollination by insects, made into honey by bees. **2** (in Greek and Roman mythology) the drink of the gods. **3** a delicious drink.
– ORIGIN Greek *nektar.*

nec·tar·ine /ˌnektəˈrēn/ ▶ **noun** a variety of peach with smooth skin.
– ORIGIN from **NECTAR**.

née /nā/ ▶ **adjective** born (used in giving a married woman's maiden name): *Mrs. Hargreaves, née Liddell.*
– ORIGIN French.

need /nēd/ ▶ **verb 1** want something because it is essential or very important: *I need help.* **2** used to express what should or must be done: *need I say more?*

– SYNONYMS **require,** be in need of, want, be crying out for, demand, call for, necessitate, entail, involve, lack, be without, be short of.

▶ **noun 1** circumstances in which something is necessary or must be done: *he was in need of medical care.* **2** a thing that is wanted or required: *his day-to-day needs.* **3** a state of being poor or in great difficulty: *children in need.*

– SYNONYMS **1** *there's no need to apologize* **necessity,** requirement, call, demand. **2** *basic human needs* **requirement,** necessity, want, requisite, prerequisite, desideratum. **3** *my hour of need* **difficulty,** trouble, distress, crisis, emergency, urgency, extremity.

– ORIGIN Old English.

need·ful /ˈnēdfəl/ ▶ **adjective** formal necessary.

nee·dle /ˈnēdl/ ▶ **noun 1** a very thin pointed piece of metal with a hole or eye for thread at the blunter end, used in sewing. **2** a long thin metal or plastic rod with a pointed end, used in knitting. **3** the pointed hollow end of a hypodermic syringe. **4** a stylus used to play records. **5** a thin pointer on a dial, compass, etc. **6** the thin, sharp, stiff leaf of a fir or pine tree. ▶ **verb** informal deliberately provoke or annoy someone.
– ORIGIN Old English.

nee·dle·point /ˈnēdlˌpoint/ ▶ **noun 1** closely stitched embroidery worked over canvas. **2** lace made by hand using a needle rather than bobbins.

need·less /ˈnēdlis/ ▶ **adjective** unnecessary; avoidable.

– SYNONYMS **unnecessary,** unneeded, uncalled for, gratuitous, pointless, superfluous, redundant, excessive.
– ANTONYMS necessary.

– DERIVATIVES **need·less·ly** adverb.
– PHRASES **needless to say** of course.

nee·dle·work /ˈnēdlˌwərk/ ▸ **noun** sewing or embroidery.

need·n't /ˈnēdnt/ ▸ **contraction** need not.

need·y /ˈnēdē/ ▸ **adjective** (**needier, neediest**) **1** lacking the necessities of life; very poor. **2** insecure and needing emotional support.

– SYNONYMS **poor,** deprived, disadvantaged, underprivileged, in need, hard up, poverty-stricken, impoverished, destitute, penniless, dirt poor; informal broke, strapped (for cash); dated needful.
– ANTONYMS wealthy.

– DERIVATIVES **need·i·ness** noun.

neem /nēm/ ▸ **noun** a tropical tree from which wood, oil, medicinal products, and insecticide are obtained.
– ORIGIN Sanskrit.

ne'er /ne(ə)r/ ▸ **contraction** literary or dialect never.

ne'er-do-well /ˈne(ə)r do͞o ˌwel/ ▸ **noun** a person who is lazy and irresponsible.

ne·far·i·ous /niˈfe(ə)rēəs/ ▸ **adjective** wicked or criminal.
– ORIGIN from Latin *nefas* 'wrong.'

ne·gate /nəˈgāt/ ▸ **verb** **1** prevent something from having an effect: *alcohol negates the effects of the drug.* **2** deny that something exists.
– ORIGIN Latin *negare* 'deny.'

ne·ga·tion /nəˈgāshən/ ▸ **noun** **1** the contradiction or denial of something. **2** the absence or opposite of something: *evil is not merely the negation of goodness.* **3** Mathematics replacement of positive by negative.

neg·a·tive /ˈnegətiv/ ▸ **adjective** **1** characterized by the absence rather than the presence of particular features: *a negative test result.* **2** expressing or implying denial, disagreement, or refusal. **3** not optimistic, encouraging, or desirable: *his negative attitude.* **4** (of a quantity) less than zero. **5** relating to, containing, or producing the kind of electric charge carried by electrons. **6** (of a photographic image) showing light and shade or colors reversed from those of the original. **7** Grammar stating that something is not the case.

– SYNONYMS **1 pessimistic,** defeatist, gloomy, critical, cynical, fatalistic, dismissive, unenthusiastic, apathetic, unresponsive. **2 harmful,** bad, adverse, damaging, detrimental, unfavorable, disadvantageous.
– ANTONYMS positive, optimistic, favorable.

▸ **noun** **1** a word or statement expressing denial or refusal. **2** a negative photographic image from which positive prints may be made.
– DERIVATIVES **neg·a·tive·ly** adverb **neg·a·tiv·i·ty** /ˌnegəˈtivitē/ noun.

neg·a·tive eq·ui·ty ▸ **noun** a situation in which the market value of a property is less than the outstanding amount of the mortgage secured on it.

ne·glect /niˈglekt/ ▸ **verb** **1** fail to give proper care or attention to: *she neglected her children.* **2** fail to do something: *he neglected to write to her.*

– SYNONYMS **1 fail to look after,** leave alone, abandon, ignore, pay no attention to, let slide, not attend to, be remiss about, be lax about, shirk. **2 fail,** omit, forget.
– ANTONYMS cherish, remember.

▸ **noun** the action of neglecting someone or something, or the state of being neglected.

– SYNONYMS **1 disrepair,** dilapidation, shabbiness, abandonment, disuse. **2 negligence,** dereliction (of duty), carelessness, laxity, slackness, irresponsibility.
– ANTONYMS care.

– ORIGIN Latin *neglegere* 'disregard.'

CHOOSE THE RIGHT WORD

neglect, disregard, ignore, overlook, slight

One of the most common reasons why people fail to arrive at work on time is that they **neglect** to set their alarm clocks, a verb that implies a failure to carry out some expected or required action, either intentionally or through carelessness. Some people, of course, choose to **disregard** their employer's rules pertaining to tardiness, which implies a voluntary, and sometimes deliberate, inattention. Others hear the alarm go off and simply **ignore** it, which suggests not only a deliberate decision to **disregard** something but a stubborn refusal to face the facts. No doubt they hope their employers will **overlook** their frequent late arrivals, which implies a failure to see or to take action, which can be either intentional or due to haste or lack of care (*to overlook minor errors*). But they also hope no one will **slight** them for their conduct when it comes to handing out raises and promotions, which means to **disregard** or **neglect** in a disdainful way.

ne·glect·ed /niˈglektid/ ▸ **adjective** **1** not properly looked after. **2** ignored or disregarded.

– SYNONYMS **1** *neglected animals* **uncared for,** abandoned, mistreated, maltreated. **2** *a neglected cottage* **derelict,** dilapidated, tumbledown, ramshackle, untended. **3** *a neglected masterpiece* **disregarded,** forgotten, overlooked, ignored, unrecognized, unnoticed, unsung, underrated.

ne·glect·ful /niˈglektfəl/ ▸ **adjective** failing to give proper care or attention to someone or something.

neg·li·gee /ˈnegləˌzhā/ ▸ **noun** a woman's dressing gown made of very thin fabric.
– ORIGIN French, 'given little thought or attention.'

neg·li·gence /ˈnegləjəns/ ▸ **noun** **1** failure to take proper care in doing something. **2** Law breach of a duty of care that results in damage.

neg·li·gent /ˈnegləjənt/ ▸ **adjective** failing to take proper care in doing something: *a negligent safety inspector.*

– SYNONYMS **neglectful,** remiss, careless, lax, irresponsible, inattentive, thoughtless, uncaring, unmindful, forgetful, slack, sloppy, derelict.
– ANTONYMS dutiful.

neg·li·gi·ble /ˈneglijəbəl/ ▸ **adjective** so small or unimportant that it is not worth considering.

– SYNONYMS **trivial,** trifling, insignificant, unimportant, of no account, minor, inconsequential, minimal, small, slight, infinitesimal, minuscule.
– ANTONYMS significant.

– DERIVATIVES **neg·li·gi·bly** /-blē/ adverb.
– ORIGIN from French *négliger* 'to neglect.'

ne·go·ti·a·ble /nəˈgōshəbəl/ ▸ **adjective** **1** able to be changed as a result of discussion: *the fee may be negotiable.* **2** (of a route) able to be traveled on; passable. **3** (of a document) able to be transferred or given to the legal ownership of another person.
– DERIVATIVES **ne·go·ti·a·bil·i·ty** /nəˌgōshəˈbilitē/ noun.

ne·go·ti·ate /nəˈgōsнēˌāt/ ▶ **verb** **1** try to reach an agreement or compromise by discussion. **2** obtain or bring about by discussion: *he negotiated a new contract.* **3** find a way over an obstacle or through a difficult path. **4** transfer a check, bill, etc., to the legal ownership of another person.

– SYNONYMS **1 discuss (terms),** talk, consult, confer, debate, compromise, bargain, haggle. **2 arrange,** broker, work out, thrash out, complete, close, conclude, agree on. **3 get around,** get past, get over, clear, cross, surmount, overcome, deal with, cope with.

– ORIGIN Latin *negotiari* 'do in the course of business.'

ne·go·ti·a·tion /nəˌgōsнēˈāsнən/ (also **negotiations**) ▶ **noun** discussion aimed at reaching an agreement or compromise.

– SYNONYMS **1 discussion(s),** talks, conference, debate, dialogue, consultation. **2 arrangement,** brokering, settlement, conclusion, completion.

ne·go·ti·a·tor /nəˈgōsнēˌātər/ ▶ **noun** a person who negotiates: *they brought in an impartial negotiator to help settle the dispute.*

– SYNONYMS **mediator,** arbitrator, moderator, go-between, middleman, intermediary, representative, spokesperson, broker.

Ne·gress /ˈnēgris/ ▶ **noun** dated a woman or girl of black African origin.

Ne·gro /ˈnēgrō/ ▶ **noun** (pl. **Negroes**) a member of a group of black peoples originally native to Africa.
– ORIGIN from Latin *niger* 'black.'

USAGE

The terms **Negro** and **Negress** are now almost always regarded as offensive; **black** and **African-American** are the preferred terms.

Ne·gro spir·it·u·al ▶ **noun** see **SPIRITUAL**.

neigh /nā/ ▶ **noun** a high whinnying sound made by a horse. ▶ **verb** make a high whinnying sound.
– ORIGIN imitating the sound.

neigh·bor /ˈnābər/ ▶ **noun** **1** a person living next door to or very near to another. **2** a person or place next to or near another. ▶ **verb** (usu. as adj. **neighboring**) be situated next to or very near: *neighboring countries.*

– SYNONYMS (as adj. **neighboring**) **adjacent,** adjoining, bordering, connecting, next-door, nearby, in the vicinity.
– ANTONYMS remote.

– ORIGIN Old English.

neigh·bor·hood /ˈnābərˌho͝od/ ▶ **noun** **1** a district within a town or city. **2** the area surrounding a place, person, or object.

– SYNONYMS **1 district,** area, locality, locale, quarter, community; informal neck of the woods, hood. **2 vicinity,** environs.

– PHRASES **in the neighborhood of** about; approximately.

neigh·bor·hood watch ▶ **noun** a program in which local groups of householders watch each other's homes to discourage burglary and other crimes.

neigh·bor·ly /ˈnābərlē/ ▶ **adjective** characteristic of a good neighbor: *most of the tenants here are pretty neighborly.*

– SYNONYMS **obliging,** helpful, friendly, kind, considerate, amicable, sociable, hospitable, companionable, civil, cordial.
– ANTONYMS unfriendly.

nei·ther /ˈnēTHər, ˈnī-/ ▶ **determiner & pronoun** not either. ▶ **adverb** **1** used to show that a negative statement is true of two things: *I am neither a liberal nor a conservative.* **2** used to show that a negative statement is also true of something else.
– ORIGIN Old English.

nel·ly /ˈnelē/ ▶ **noun** (pl. **nellies**) informal a silly person.
– ORIGIN from the woman's name *Nelly.*

nel·son /ˈnelsən/ ▶ **noun** a wrestling hold in which one arm is passed under the opponent's arm from behind and the hand is applied to the neck (**half nelson**), or both arms and hands are applied (**full nelson**).
– ORIGIN probably from the surname *Nelson.*

nem·a·tode /ˈnēməˌtōd/ ▶ **noun** a worm of a group with slender, unsegmented, cylindrical bodies, such as a roundworm or threadworm.
– ORIGIN from Greek *nēma* 'thread.'

ne·me·sia /nəˈmēzнə/ ▶ **noun** a plant related to the snapdragon, grown for its colorful funnel-shaped flowers.
– ORIGIN Latin.

nem·e·sis /ˈneməsis/ ▶ **noun** (pl. **nemeses** /-ˌsēz/) **1** the inescapable agent of someone's or something's downfall: *it was in New York that she first met her future husband and ultimately her nemesis.* **2** downfall caused by an unavoidable agent.
– ORIGIN Greek, 'retribution.'

neo- ▶ **combining form** **1** new: *neonate.* **2** a new or revived form of: *neoclassicism.*
– ORIGIN from Greek *neos* 'new.'

ne·o·clas·si·cal /ˌnēōˈklasikəl/ (also **neoclassic**) ▶ **adjective** relating to the revival of a classical style in the arts.
– DERIVATIVES **ne·o·clas·si·cism** /ˌnēōˈklasiˌsizəm/ noun **ne·o·clas·si·cist** noun & adjective.

ne·o·co·lo·ni·al·ism /ˌnēōkəˈlōnēəˌlizəm/ ▶ **noun** the use of economic, political, or cultural pressures to control or influence other countries.
– DERIVATIVES **ne·o·co·lo·ni·al** adjective **ne·o·co·lo·ni·al·ist** noun & adjective.

ne·o·con /ˌnēōˈkän/ ▶ **adjective** neoconservative, especially in advocating democratic capitalism. ▶ **noun** a neoconservative.

ne·o·con·serv·a·tive /ˌnēōkənˈsərvətiv/ ▶ **adjective** relating to an approach to politics, economics, etc., that represents a return to a traditional conservative viewpoint, in contrast to more radical or liberal schools of thought. ▶ **noun** a person with neoconservative views.

ne·o·dym·i·um /ˌnēōˈdimēəm/ ▶ **noun** a silvery-white metallic element of the lanthanide series.
– ORIGIN from **NEO-** + *didymium,* a mixture of the elements praseodymium and neodymium, from Greek *didumos* 'twin.'

ne·o-Im·pres·sion·ism ▶ **noun** an artistic movement that aimed to improve on Impressionism through a systematic approach to form and color.
– DERIVATIVES **ne·o-Im·pres·sion·ist** adjective & noun.

Ne·o·lith·ic /ˌnēəˈliTHik/ ▶ **adjective** relating to the later part of the Stone Age, when agriculture was introduced

and ground or polished stone weapons and implements were used.
– ORIGIN from **NEO-** + Greek *lithos* 'stone.'

ne·ol·o·gism /nēˈäləˌjizəm/ ▸ **noun** a newly coined word or expression.
– ORIGIN from **NEO-** + Greek *logos* 'word.'

ne·on /ˈnēän/ ▸ **noun** an inert gas that gives an orange glow when electricity is passed through it, used in fluorescent lighting. ▸ **adjective** very bright or fluorescent in color: *bold neon colors.*
– ORIGIN Greek, 'something new.'

ne·o·na·tal /ˌnēōˈnātl/ ▸ **adjective** relating to newborn children.
– DERIVATIVES **ne·o·na·tol·o·gy** /-nāˈtäləjē/ noun.

ne·o·nate /ˈnēəˌnāt/ ▸ **noun** a newborn child or mammal.
– ORIGIN from Greek *neos* 'new' + Latin *nasci* 'be born.'

ne·o-Na·zi ▸ **noun** (pl. **neo-Nazis**) a person with extreme racist or nationalist views. ▸ **adjective** relating to neo-Nazis.
– DERIVATIVES **ne·o-Na·zism** noun.

ne·o·pho·bi·a /ˌnēōˈfōbēə/ ▸ **noun** extreme or irrational fear or dislike of anything new or unfamiliar.
– DERIVATIVES **ne·o·pho·bic** /-bik/ adjective.

ne·o·phyte /ˈnēəˌfīt/ ▸ **noun 1** a person who is new to a subject, skill, or belief. **2** a novice in a religious order, or a newly ordained priest.
– ORIGIN from Greek *neophutos* 'newly planted.'

CHOOSE THE RIGHT WORD

See **NOVICE**.

ne·o·plasm /ˈnēəˌplazəm/ ▸ **noun** a new and abnormal growth of tissue in the body, especially a cancerous tumor.
– ORIGIN from **NEO-** + Greek *plasma* 'formation.'

ne·o·prene /ˈnēəˌprēn/ ▸ **noun** a synthetic substance resembling rubber.
– ORIGIN from **NEO-** + *prene*, of uncertain origin.

Nep·a·lese /ˌnepəˈlēz, -ˈlēs/ ▸ **noun** a person from Nepal. ▸ **adjective** relating to Nepal.

Ne·pal·i /nəˈpôlē, -ˈpälē/ ▸ **noun** (pl. **Nepalis**) **1** a person from Nepal. **2** the language of Nepal. ▸ **adjective** relating to Nepal or Nepali.

neph·ew /ˈnefyo͞o/ ▸ **noun** a son of a person's brother or sister.
– ORIGIN Latin *nepos* 'grandson, nephew.'

neph·rite /ˈnefrīt/ ▸ **noun** a pale green or white form of jade.
– ORIGIN from Greek *nephros* 'kidney' (with reference to its supposed ability to treat kidney disease).

ne·phri·tis /nəˈfrītis/ ▸ **noun** inflammation of the kidneys.
– ORIGIN from Greek *nephros* 'kidney.'

ne plus ul·tra /ˈnē ˌpləs ˈəltrə, ˈnā ˌplo͝os ˈo͝oltrə/ ▸ **noun** (**the ne plus ultra**) the perfect example of its kind: *the ne plus ultra of editors.*
– ORIGIN Latin, 'not further beyond,' the supposed inscription on the Pillars of Hercules (at the Strait of Gibraltar) banning ships from going further.

nep·o·tism /ˈnepəˌtizəm/ ▸ **noun** favoritism shown to relatives or friends, especially by giving them jobs.
– DERIVATIVES **nep·o·tis·tic** /ˌnepəˈtistik/ adjective.
– ORIGIN from Italian *nipote* 'nephew' (with reference to privileges given to the 'nephews' of popes, often their illegitimate sons).

Nep·tune /ˈnept(y)o͞on/ ▸ **noun** a planet of the solar system, eighth in order from the sun.
– DERIVATIVES **Nep·tu·ni·an** /nepˈt(y)o͞onēən/ adjective.

nep·tu·ni·um /nepˈt(y)o͞onēəm/ ▸ **noun** a rare radioactive metallic element produced from uranium.
– ORIGIN from *Neptune*, on the pattern of *uranium* (Neptune being the next planet beyond Uranus).

nerd /nərd/ ▸ **noun** informal a person who is obsessively interested in something and lacks social skills.
– DERIVATIVES **nerd·ish** adjective **nerd·y** adjective.
– ORIGIN unknown.

Ne·re·id /ˈni(ə)rēid/ ▸ **noun** Greek Mythology a sea nymph.

nerve /nərv/ ▸ **noun 1** a fiber or bundle of fibers in the body that transmits impulses of sensation between the brain or spinal cord and other parts of the body.
2 steadiness and courage in a demanding situation.
3 informal impudent or excessively bold behavior.
4 (**nerves**) a person's mental state; nervousness or anxiety.

– SYNONYMS **1** *the match will be a test of nerve* **confidence,** assurance, courage, bravery, determination, will power, spirit, grit; informal guts, moxie. **2** *he had the nerve to ask her out again* **audacity,** cheek, effrontery, gall, temerity, presumption, impudence, impertinence, arrogance; informal face, front, brass, chutzpah. **3** (**nerves**) *pre-wedding nerves* **anxiety,** tension, nervousness, stress, worry, cold feet, apprehension; informal butterflies (in one's stomach), the jitters, the heebie-jeebies.

▸ **verb** chiefly Brit. (**nerve oneself**) brace oneself for a demanding situation.
– PHRASES **get on someone's nerves** informal irritate someone.
– ORIGIN Latin *nervus*.

WORD LINKS

neural *relating to nerves in the body*

nerve cell ▸ **noun** a neuron.

nerve cen·ter ▸ **noun 1** the control center of an organization or operation. **2** a group of connected nerve cells performing a particular function.

nerve gas ▸ **noun** a poisonous gas that attacks the nervous system, causing death or disablement.

nerve·less /ˈnərvlis/ ▸ **adjective 1** lacking strength or feeling. **2** not nervous; confident.

nerve-rack·ing (also **nerve-wracking**) ▸ **adjective** causing stress or anxiety.

nerv·ous /ˈnərvəs/ ▸ **adjective 1** easily frightened or worried. **2** apprehensive or anxious: *he's nervous about speaking in public.* **3** relating to the nerves.

– SYNONYMS **anxious,** worried, apprehensive, on edge, edgy, tense, stressed, agitated, uneasy, restless, worked up, keyed up, overwrought, jumpy, on tenterhooks, highly strung, nervy, excitable, neurotic; informal jittery, twitchy, in a state, uptight, wired, trepidatious, squirrelly.
– ANTONYMS relaxed, calm.

– DERIVATIVES **ner·vous·ly** adverb **ner·vous·ness** noun.

nerv·ous break·down ▸ **noun** a period of mental illness resulting from severe depression or stress.

nerv·ous sys·tem ▶ **noun** the network of nerve cells and fibers that transmits nerve impulses between parts of the body.

nerv·ous wreck ▶ **noun** informal a person suffering from stress or emotional exhaustion.

nerv·y /ˈnərvē/ ▶ **adjective** (**nervier**, **nerviest**) bold or impudent.
– DERIVATIVES **nerv·i·ly** adverb **nerv·i·ness** noun.

-ness ▶ **suffix** forming nouns referring to: **1** a state or condition: *liveliness*. **2** something in a certain state: *wilderness*.
– ORIGIN Old English.

nest /nest/ ▶ **noun 1** a structure made by a bird for laying eggs and sheltering its young. **2** a place where an animal or insect breeds or shelters. **3** a place filled with undesirable people or things: *a nest of spies*. **4** a set of similar objects of graduated sizes, fitting together for storage. ▶ **verb 1** (of a bird or animal) use or build a nest. **2** fit an object or objects inside a larger one. **3** (often as adj. **nested**) (especially in computing) place something in a lower position in a hierarchy.
– DERIVATIVES **nest·er** noun.
– ORIGIN Old English.

nest egg ▶ **noun** a sum of money saved for the future.

nes·tle /ˈnesəl/ ▶ **verb 1** settle comfortably within or against something. **2** (of a place) lie in a sheltered position.

– SYNONYMS **snuggle,** cuddle, huddle, nuzzle, settle, burrow.

– ORIGIN Old English.

nest·ling /ˈnes(t)liNG/ ▶ **noun** a bird that is too young to leave the nest.

net¹ /net/ ▶ **noun 1** a material made of strands of twine or cord woven or knotted together to form open squares. **2** a piece or structure of net for catching fish, surrounding a goal, etc. **3** a fine fabric with a very open weave. **4** a means of catching or securing someone or something: *passengers and luggage go through several checks to make sure no one slips through the net*. **5** (**the Net**) the Internet. **6** a communications or computer network.

– SYNONYMS **netting,** mesh, tulle, fishnet, lace, openwork.

▶ **verb** (**nets, netting, netted**) **1** catch something in a net. **2** catch or obtain in a skillful way: *customs have netted large caches of drugs*. **3** (in sports) kick or hit (a ball or puck) into the net. **4** cover something with a net.

– SYNONYMS **catch,** capture, trap, snare; informal nab, bag, collar, bust.

– ORIGIN Old English.

net² ▶ **adjective 1** (of an amount, value, or price) remaining after tax, discounts, or expenses have been deducted. Often contrasted with **GROSS**. **2** (of a weight) not including that of the packaging. **3** (of an effect or result) remaining after other factors have been taken into account; overall.

– SYNONYMS **after tax,** after deductions, take-home, final.
– ANTONYMS gross.

▶ **verb** (**nets, netting, netted**) gain a sum of money as clear profit.

– SYNONYMS **earn,** make, clear, take home, bring in, pocket, realize.

– ORIGIN French *net* 'neat.'

neth·er /ˈneTHər/ ▶ **adjective** lower in position.
– DERIVATIVES **neth·er·most** /-ˌmōst/ adjective.
– ORIGIN Old English.

Neth·er·land·er /ˈneTHərˌlandər/ ▶ **noun** a person from the Netherlands.
– DERIVATIVES **Neth·er·land·ish** /ˈneTHərˌlandisH/ adjective.

neth·er re·gions ▶ **plural noun 1** hell; the underworld. **2** euphemistic a person's genitals and buttocks.

neth·er·world /ˈneTHərˌwərld/ ▶ **noun 1** the underworld; hell. **2** an area of activity that is hidden, underhanded, or poorly defined.

net prof·it ▶ **noun** the actual profit after working expenses have been paid.

ne·tsu·ke /ˈnetsəkē/ ▶ **noun** (pl. same or **netsukes**) a carved ornament of wood or ivory, formerly worn in Japan to suspend items from the sash of a kimono.
– ORIGIN Japanese.

net·ting /ˈnetiNG/ ▶ **noun** material made of net.

net·tle /ˈnetl/ ▶ **noun** a plant with jagged leaves covered with stinging hairs. ▶ **verb** annoy someone.
– PHRASES **grasp the nettle** Brit. tackle a difficulty boldly.
– ORIGIN Old English.

net·work /ˈnetˌwərk/ ▶ **noun 1** an arrangement of horizontal and vertical lines that cross each other. **2** a system of railroads, roads, etc., that connect with each other. **3** a group of broadcasting stations that connect to broadcast a program at the same time. **4** a number of interconnected computers or operations. **5** a group of people who keep in contact to exchange information.

– SYNONYMS **web,** lattice, net, matrix, mesh, crisscross, grid, maze, labyrinth, warren, tangle.

▶ **verb** interact with other people to exchange information and develop contacts.
– DERIVATIVES **net·work·er** noun.

neu·ral /ˈn(y)o͝orəl/ ▶ **adjective** relating to a nerve or the nervous system.
– DERIVATIVES **neu·ral·ly** adverb.

neu·ral·gia /n(y)o͝oˈraljə/ ▶ **noun** intense pain along a nerve, especially in the head or face.
– DERIVATIVES **neu·ral·gic** /-jik/ adjective.

neu·ral net·work (also **neural net**) ▶ **noun** a computer system modeled on the human brain and nervous system.

neur·as·the·ni·a /ˌn(y)o͝orəsˈTHēnēə/ ▶ **noun** a condition characterized by weariness, headaches, and irritability, associated chiefly with emotional disturbance.
– DERIVATIVES **neur·as·then·ic** /-ˈTHenik/ adjective & noun.

neu·ri·tis /n(y)o͝oˈrītis/ ▶ **noun** inflammation of a peripheral nerve or nerves.

neuro- ▶ **combining form** relating to nerves or the nervous system: *neurosurgery*.
– ORIGIN from Greek *neuron* 'nerve, sinew, tendon.'

neu·ro·chem·is·try /ˌn(y)o͝orəˈkeməstrē/ ▶ **noun** the branch of biochemistry concerned with the processes occurring in nerve tissue and the nervous system.
– DERIVATIVES **neu·ro·chem·i·cal** /-ˈkemikəl/ adjective **neu·ro·chem·ist** /-ˈkemist/ noun.

neu·ro·lep·tic /ˌn(y)o͝orəˈleptik/ ▶ **adjective** (of a drug) tending to lower nervous tension by reducing nerve functions.
– ORIGIN from **NEURO-** + Greek *lēpsis* 'seizing.'

neu·rol·o·gy /n(y)o͝oˈräləjē/ ▶ **noun** the branch of medicine and biology concerned with the nervous system.

– DERIVATIVES **neu·ro·log·ic** /-rəˈläjik/ adjective **neu·ro·log·i·cal** /-rəˈläjikəl/ adjective **neu·rol·o·gist** noun.

neu·ron /ˈn(y)o͝orän/ (also **neurone** /-rōn/) ▶ **noun** a specialized cell that transmits nerve impulses.
– DERIVATIVES **neu·ron·al** /ˈn(y)o͝orənl, n(y)o͝oˈrōnl/ adjective.
– ORIGIN Greek *neuron* 'sinew, tendon, nerve.'

neu·ro·sci·ence /ˌn(y)o͝orōˈsīəns/ ▶ **noun** science that deals with the structure or function of the nervous system and brain.
– DERIVATIVES **neu·ro·sci·en·tist** /-ˈsīəntist/ noun.

neu·ro·sis /n(y)o͝oˈrōsis/ ▶ **noun** (pl. **neuroses** /-ˌsēz/) a relatively mild mental disorder involving symptoms such as depression, anxiety, obsessive behavior, or hypochondria.

neu·ro·sur·ger·y /ˌn(y)o͝orōˈsərjərē/ ▶ **noun** surgery performed on the nervous system.
– DERIVATIVES **neu·ro·sur·geon** /ˈn(y)ərōˌsərjən/ noun **neu·ro·sur·gi·cal** /-jikəl/ adjective.

neu·rot·ic /n(y)o͝oˈrätik/ ▶ **adjective 1** having or relating to neurosis. **2** informal abnormally sensitive, anxious, or obsessive.

– SYNONYMS **highly strung,** oversensitive, nervous, tense, paranoid, obsessive, fixated, hysterical, overwrought, irrational.
– ANTONYMS stable, calm.

▶ **noun** a neurotic person.
– DERIVATIVES **neu·rot·ic·al·ly** adverb **neu·rot·i·cism** /-ˈrätəˌsizəm/ noun.

WORD TOOLKIT

See **APPREHENSIVE**.

neu·ro·tox·in /ˈn(y)o͝orōˌtäksin/ ▶ **noun** a poison that acts on the nervous system.

neu·ro·trans·mit·ter /ˌn(y)o͝orōˈtranzmitər/ ▶ **noun** a chemical substance released from a nerve fiber and bringing about the transfer of an impulse to another nerve, muscle, etc.

neu·ter /ˈn(y)o͞otər/ ▶ **adjective 1** Grammar (of a noun) not masculine or feminine. **2** (of an animal or plant) having no sexual or reproductive organs. ▶ **verb 1** castrate or spay a domestic animal. **2** take away the power of: *their only purpose is to neuter local democracy.*
– ORIGIN Latin, 'neither.'

neu·tral /ˈn(y)o͞otrəl/ ▶ **adjective 1** not supporting either side in a dispute or conflict; impartial. **2** deliberately not expressing or provoking strong feeling: *her tone was neutral, devoid of sentiment.* **3** pale gray, cream, or beige in color. **4** Chemistry neither acid nor alkaline; having a pH of about 7. **5** electrically neither positive nor negative.

– SYNONYMS **1 impartial,** unbiased, unprejudiced, objective, open-minded, nonpartisan, even-handed, disinterested, dispassionate, detached, nonaligned, unaffiliated, uninvolved. **2 inoffensive,** bland, unobjectionable, unexceptionable, anodyne, uncontroversial, safe, harmless, innocuous. **3 pale,** light, colorless, indeterminate, drab, insipid, nondescript, dull.
– ANTONYMS biased, provocative.

▶ **noun 1** a country or person that does not take sides in a conflict or dispute. **2** pale gray, cream, or beige. **3** a position of a gear mechanism in which the engine is disconnected from the driven parts.
– DERIVATIVES **neu·tral·i·ty** /n(y)o͞oˈtralitē/ noun **neu·tral·ly** adverb.
– ORIGIN Latin *neutralis* 'of neuter gender.'

WORD TOOLKIT

See **EQUITABLE**.

neu·tral·ize /ˈn(y)o͞otrəˌlīz/ ▶ **verb 1** prevent something from having an effect by counteracting it with something else: *never try to neutralize odors with air fresheners.* **2** make an acid or alkaline chemically neutral. **3** euphemistic kill or destroy someone or something.

– SYNONYMS **counteract,** offset, counterbalance, balance, cancel out, nullify, negate.

– DERIVATIVES **neu·tral·i·za·tion** /ˌn(y)o͞otrəliˈzāsʜən/ noun.

neu·tri·no /n(y)o͞oˈtrēnō/ ▶ **noun** (pl. **neutrinos**) Physics a subatomic particle with a mass close to zero and no electric charge.
– ORIGIN Italian.

neu·tron /ˈn(y)o͞oträn/ ▶ **noun** a subatomic particle of about the same mass as a proton but without an electric charge.
– ORIGIN from **NEUTRAL**.

neu·tron bomb ▶ **noun** a nuclear weapon that produces large numbers of neutrons, destroying life but not property.

neu·tron star ▶ **noun** a very dense star composed mainly of neutrons.

né·vé /nāˈvā/ ▶ **noun** compacted or hardened snow, especially as found on the upper part of a glacier.
– ORIGIN Swiss French, 'glacier.'

nev·er /ˈnevər/ ▶ **adverb 1** not ever. **2** not at all.
– PHRASES **never-never land** an imaginary perfect place. [the ideal country in J. M. Barrie's *Peter Pan.*] **well I never!** informal expressing great surprise.
– ORIGIN Old English.

nev·er-end·ing ▶ **adjective** (especially of something unpleasant) having or seeming to have no end.

– SYNONYMS **incessant,** continuous, ceaseless, constant, continual, perpetual, uninterrupted, unbroken, steady, unremitting, relentless, persistent, interminable, nonstop, endless, unending.

CHOOSE THE RIGHT WORD

See **ETERNAL**.

nev·er·more /ˌnevərˈmôr/ ▶ **adverb** literary never again.

nev·er·the·less /ˌnevər<u>th</u>əˈles/ ▶ **adverb** in spite of that.

– SYNONYMS **nonetheless,** even so, however, still, yet, in spite of that, despite that, be that as it may, notwithstanding.

ne·vus /ˈnēvəs/ ▶ **noun** (pl. **nevi** /-ˌvī/) a birthmark or a mole on the skin.
– ORIGIN Latin.

new /n(y)o͞o/ ▶ **adjective 1** not existing before; made, introduced, or discovered recently: *she was signing copies of her new book.* **2** not previously used or owned. **3** obtained or experienced recently: *her new coat.* **4** (**new to/at**) not familiar with or experienced at. **5** better than before; renewed or transformed: *the pills would make him a new man.*

– SYNONYMS **1 recent,** up to date, the latest, current, state-of-the-art, contemporary, advanced, cutting-edge, modern, avant-garde. **2 unused,** brand new, pristine, fresh. **3 different,** another, alternative, additional, extra, supplementary, further, unfamiliar, unknown, strange. **4 reinvigorated,** restored, revived, improved, refreshed, regenerated.
– ANTONYMS old, secondhand.

▶ **adverb** newly.
– DERIVATIVES **new·ness** noun.
– ORIGIN Old English.

WORD TOOLKIT

new ...	recent ...	contemporary ...
car	years	art
job	months	music
school	times	society
clothes	studies	issues
friends	research	design
member	events	writer
life	trip	literature
generation	success	architecture

New Age ▶ **noun** a movement concerned with alternative approaches to traditional Western culture, religion, medicine, etc.

new·bie /ˈn(y)o͞obē/ ▶ **noun** (pl. **newbies**) an inexperienced newcomer.

new·born /ˈn(y)o͞oˌbôrn/ ▶ **adjective** recently born. ▶ **noun** a newborn child.

new·com·er /ˈn(y)o͞oˌkəmər/ ▶ **noun 1** a person who has recently arrived. **2** a person who is new to an activity or situation.

– SYNONYMS **1 incomer,** immigrant, settler, stranger, outsider, foreigner, alien; informal new kid on the block, johnny-come-lately. **2 beginner,** novice, learner, trainee, apprentice, probationer; informal rookie, newbie, tenderfoot.

new·el /ˈn(y)o͞owəl/ ▶ **noun 1** (also **newel post**) a post at the top or bottom of a flight of stairs, supporting a handrail. **2** the central supporting pillar of a spiral staircase.
– ORIGIN Old French *nouel* 'knob.'

new·fan·gled /ˈn(y)o͞oˈfaNGgəld, -ˌfaNG-/ ▶ **adjective** derogatory new and different from what one is used to.
– ORIGIN from dialect *newfangle* 'liking what is new.'

new·found /ˈn(y)o͞oˌfound/ ▶ **adjective** recently found or discovered: *his newfound political consciousness.*

New·found·land /ˌn(y)o͞ofəndˈland, ˈn(y)o͞ofəndlənd, -ˌland/ ▶ **noun** a dog of a very large breed with a thick, coarse coat.
– ORIGIN named after *Newfoundland* in Canada.

New Guin·e·an /ˈginēən/ ▶ **noun** a person from New Guinea. ▶ **adjective** relating to New Guinea.

new·ly /ˈn(y)o͞olē/ ▶ **adverb 1** recently. **2** again; afresh: *confidence for the newly single.*

– SYNONYMS **recently,** only just, lately, freshly, not long ago.

new·ly·wed /ˈn(y)o͞olēˌwed/ ▶ **noun** a recently married person.

new man ▶ **noun** chiefly Brit. a man who rejects traditional male attitudes, often taking on childcare and housework.

new math ▶ **plural noun** (usu. treated as sing.) a system of teaching mathematics to children, with emphasis on investigation by them and on set theory.

new moon ▶ **noun** the phase of the moon when it is invisible from earth or first appears as a slender crescent.

news /n(y)o͞oz/ ▶ **noun 1** new or important information about recent events. **2** (**the news**) a broadcast or published news report. **3** (**news to**) informal information not previously known to someone.

– SYNONYMS **report,** story, account, announcement, press release, communication, communiqué, bulletin, intelligence, information, word, revelation, disclosure, exposé; informal scoop; literary tidings.

news a·gen·cy ▶ **noun** an organization that collects and distributes news items to the media.

news·cast /ˈn(y)o͞ozˌkast/ ▶ **noun** a broadcast news report.
– DERIVATIVES **news·cast·er** noun.

news con·fer·ence ▶ **noun** a press conference.

news·feed /ˈn(y)o͞ozˌfēd/ (also **news feed**) ▶ **noun 1** a service by which news items are provided on a regular or continuous basis for distribution or broadcasting. **2** a system by which data is transferred or exchanged between central computers to provide newsgroup access to networked users.

news·flash /ˈn(y)o͞ozˌflasH/ ▶ **noun** a short broadcast of important news that often interrupts other programs.

news·group /ˈn(y)o͞ozˌgro͞op/ ▶ **noun** a group of Internet users who exchange information online on a particular topic.

news·let·ter /ˈn(y)o͞ozˌletər/ ▶ **noun** a bulletin issued periodically to the members of a society or other organization.

news·man /ˈn(y)o͞ozˌman/ ▶ **noun** (pl. **newsmen**) a male reporter or journalist.

news·pa·per /ˈn(y)o͞ozˌpāpər/ ▶ **noun** a daily or weekly publication consisting of folded sheets and containing news, articles, and advertisements.

– SYNONYMS **paper,** journal, gazette, tabloid, broadsheet, periodical; informal rag.

new·speak /ˈn(y)o͞oˌspēk/ ▶ **noun** deliberately misleading and indirect language, used by politicians.
– ORIGIN an official language in George Orwell's novel *Nineteen Eighty-Four.*

news·print /ˈn(y)o͞ozˌprint/ ▶ **noun** cheap, low-quality printing paper used for newspapers.

news·read·er /ˈn(y)o͞ozˌrēdər/ ▶ **noun 1** Brit. a person who reads the news on radio or television. **2** a computer program for reading emails posted to newsgroups.

news·reel /ˈn(y)o͞ozˌrēl/ ▶ **noun** a short film of news and current affairs.

news·room /ˈn(y)o͞ozˌro͞om, -ˌro͝om/ ▶ **noun** the area in a newspaper or broadcasting office where news is processed.

news·stand /ˈn(y)o͞ozˌstand/ ▶ **noun** a stand for the sale of newspapers.

New Style ▶ **noun** the method of calculating dates using the Gregorian calendar.

news·wire /ˈn(y)o͞oz,wīr/ ▸ **noun** an electronically transmitted news service.

news·wor·thy /ˈn(y)o͞oz,wərT͟Hē/ ▸ **adjective** important enough to be mentioned as news.

WORD TOOLKIT

See **GROUNDBREAKING**.

news·y /ˈn(y)o͞ozē/ ▸ **adjective** informal full of news.

newt /n(y)o͞ot/ ▸ **noun** a small animal with a thin body and a long tail that can live in water or on land.
– ORIGIN from *an ewt* (from Old English *efeta* 'eft'), interpreted as *a newt*.

New Tes·ta·ment ▸ **noun** the second part of the Christian Bible, recording the life and teachings of Jesus and his earliest followers.

new·ton /ˈn(y)o͞otn/ ▸ **noun** Physics the SI unit of force.
– ORIGIN named after the English scientist Sir Isaac *Newton*.

New·to·ni·an /n(y)o͞oˈtōnēən/ ▸ **adjective** relating to or arising from the work of Sir Isaac Newton; behaving according to the principles of classical physics.

new wave ▸ **noun 1** a group of people who introduce new styles and ideas in art, movies, literature, etc. **2** a style of rock music popular in the late 1970s, deriving from punk.

New World ▸ **noun** North and South America in contrast to Europe, Asia, and Africa.

new year ▸ **noun 1** the calendar year just begun or about to begin. **2** the period immediately before and after December 31.

New Year's Day ▸ **noun** January 1.

New Year's Eve ▸ **noun** December 31.

New York as·ter ▸ **noun** a garden plant with numerous pinkish-lilac daisylike flowers that bloom in autumn.

New York·er /ˌn(y)o͞o ˈyôrkər/ ▸ **noun** a person from the state or city of New York.

New York min·ute /yôrk/ ▸ **noun** informal a very short time; a moment.

New Zea·land·er /ˌn(y)o͞o ˈzēləndər/ ▸ **noun** a person from New Zealand.

next /nekst/ ▸ **adjective 1** coming immediately after the present one in time, space, or order. **2** (of a day of the week) nearest (or the nearest but one) after the present.

– SYNONYMS **1 following,** succeeding, subsequent, ensuing, upcoming, to come. **2 neighboring,** adjacent, adjoining, next-door, bordering, connected, closest, nearest; formal contiguous, proximate.
– ANTONYMS previous.

▸ **adverb 1** immediately afterwards. **2** following in the specified order: *Joe was the next oldest after Martin*.

– SYNONYMS **afterward,** after, then, later, subsequently; formal thereafter.

▸ **noun** the next person or thing.
– PHRASES **next of kin** a person's closest living relative or relatives. **next to 1** beside. **2** following in order or importance. **3** almost. **the next world** (in some religious beliefs) the place where people go after death.
– ORIGIN Old English.

next door ▸ **adverb & adjective** in or to the next house or room.

nex·us /ˈneksəs/ ▸ **noun** (pl. same or **nexuses**) **1** a connection or series of connections: *the nexus between birth and privilege*. **2** a connected group. **3** a central or focal point.
– ORIGIN Latin.

NF ▸ **abbreviation** Newfoundland.

NFC ▸ **abbreviation** National Football Conference.

NFL ▸ **abbreviation** National Football League.

NGO ▸ **abbreviation** nongovernmental organization.

NH ▸ **abbreviation** New Hampshire.

Ni ▸ **symbol** the chemical element nickel.

ni·a·cin /ˈnīəsin/ ▸ **noun** another term for **NICOTINIC ACID**.

nib /nib/ ▸ **noun** the pointed end part of a pen, which distributes the ink.
– ORIGIN probably from Dutch *nib* or German *nibbe* 'beak.'

nib·ble /ˈnibəl/ ▸ **verb 1** take small bites out of something. **2** bite a part of the body gently. **3** gradually reduce: *the fringes of the region have been nibbled away by development*. ▸ **noun 1** an instance of nibbling. **2** a small piece of food bitten off. **3** (**nibbles**) informal small savory snacks.
– ORIGIN probably German or Dutch.

nib·let /ˈniblit/ ▸ **noun** a small piece of food.

nib·lick /ˈniblik/ ▸ **noun** Golf, dated an iron with a heavy head, used for playing out of bunkers.
– ORIGIN unknown.

nibs /nibz/ ▸ **noun** (**his nibs**) informal, dated a mock title used to refer to a man who thinks he is important.
– ORIGIN unknown.

Ni·Cad /ˈnīˌkad/ (also trademark **Nicad**) ▸ **noun** a battery or cell containing nickel, cadmium, and potassium hydroxide.
– ORIGIN blend of **NICKEL** and **CADMIUM**.

Nic·a·ra·guan /nikəˈrägwən/ ▸ **noun** a person from Nicaragua in Central America. ▸ **adjective** relating to Nicaragua.

nice /nīs/ ▸ **adjective 1** pleasant, agreeable, or attractive. **2** good-natured; kind. **3** fine or subtle: *a nice distinction*.

– SYNONYMS **1** *have a nice time* **enjoyable,** pleasant, agreeable, good, pleasurable, satisfying, entertaining, amusing; informal lovely, great. **2** *nice people* **pleasant,** likable, agreeable, personable, good-natured, congenial, amiable, affable, genial, friendly, charming, delightful, engaging, sympathetic, polite, courteous, well mannered, civil, kind, obliging, helpful. **3** *nice weather* **fine,** dry, sunny, warm, mild, clement. **4** *a nice distinction* **subtle,** fine, slight, delicate, precise.
– ANTONYMS unpleasant, nasty.

– DERIVATIVES **nice·ly** adverb **nice·ness** noun.
– ORIGIN early senses included 'stupid' and 'coy': from Latin *nescius* 'ignorant.'

ni·ce·ty /ˈnīsitē/ ▸ **noun** (pl. **niceties**) **1** a fine detail or distinction: *legal niceties are wasted on him*. **2** a detail of polite social behavior. **3** accuracy or precision.
– PHRASES **to a nicety** precisely.

niche /nicн, nēsн/ ▸ **noun 1** a shallow recess, especially one in a wall to display an ornament. **2** (**one's niche**) a position or role in life that suits someone: *he found his niche as a writer*. **3** a particular group seen as a potential market for a product: *targeting the urban youth niche*.

– SYNONYMS **1 recess,** alcove, nook, cranny, hollow, bay, cavity, pigeonhole. **2 position,** slot, place, vocation, calling, métier, station, job, level.

– ORIGIN French.

nick /nik/ ▶ **noun** a small cut or notch.

– SYNONYMS **cut,** scratch, incision, notch, chip, dent, indentation.

▶ **verb 1** make a small cut in something. **2** (**nick someone for**) informal cheat someone of something. **3** Brit. informal steal something. **4** Brit. informal arrest someone.

– SYNONYMS **cut,** scratch, graze, chip, dent.

– PHRASES **in the nick of time** only just in time.
– ORIGIN unknown.

nick·el /'nikəl/ ▶ **noun 1** a silvery-white metallic chemical element resembling iron, used in alloys. **2** a five-cent coin. ▶ **verb** (**nickels, nickeling, nickeled**) coat something with nickel.
– ORIGIN German *Kupfernickel* (the copper-colored ore from which nickel was first obtained).

nick·el-and-dime ▶ **verb** put a financial strain on someone by charging small amounts for many minor services. ▶ **adjective** of little importance; trivial.

nick·el·o·de·on /,nikə'lōdēən/ ▶ **noun** informal, dated a jukebox.
– ORIGIN from **NICKEL** + **MELODEON**.

nick·el sil·ver ▶ **noun** an alloy of nickel, zinc, and copper.

nick·el steel ▶ **noun** stainless steel containing chromium and nickel.

nick·name /'nik,nām/ ▶ **noun** an informal, often amusing name for a person or thing.

– SYNONYMS **pet name,** diminutive, endearment, tag, label, sobriquet, epithet; informal handle, moniker.

▶ **verb** give a nickname to someone or something.
– ORIGIN from *an eke-name* (*eke* meaning 'addition'), misinterpreted as *a neke name*.

ni·co·ti·a·na /ni,kōshē'änə, -'anə/ ▶ **noun** an ornamental plant related to tobacco, with tubular sweet-smelling flowers.

nic·o·tine /'nikə,tēn/ ▶ **noun** a toxic oily liquid found in tobacco.
– ORIGIN named after Jean *Nicot*, a diplomat who introduced tobacco to France.

nic·o·tine patch ▶ **noun** a patch containing nicotine, worn on the skin by a person trying to give up smoking.

nic·o·tin·ic ac·id /,nikə'tinik, -'tēnik/ ▶ **noun** a vitamin of the B complex, found in milk, wheat germ, meat, and other foods.

nic·ti·tat·ing mem·brane /'nikti,tātiNG/ ▶ **noun** a whitish membrane forming an inner eyelid in birds, reptiles, and some mammals.
– ORIGIN from Latin *nictare* 'to blink.'

niece /nēs/ ▶ **noun** a daughter of a person's brother or sister.
– ORIGIN Old French.

ni·el·lo /nē'elō/ ▶ **noun 1** a black compound of sulfur with silver, lead, or copper, used for filling in engraved designs in metals. **2** objects decorated with niello.
– ORIGIN Italian.

Nietzs·che·an /'nēCHēən/ ▶ **adjective** relating to the German philosopher Friedrich Wilhelm Nietzsche.

nif·ty /'niftē/ ▶ **adjective** (**niftier, niftiest**) informal particularly good, effective, or stylish.
– DERIVATIVES **nif·ti·ly** /-təlē/ adverb.
– ORIGIN unknown.

Ni·ge·ri·an /nī'ji(ə)rēən/ ▶ **noun** a person from Nigeria. ▶ **adjective** relating to Nigeria.

nig·gard /'nigərd/ ▶ **noun** a miserly person.
– ORIGIN Scandinavian.

nig·gard·ly /'nigərdlē/ ▶ **adjective** not generous; stingy: *I was kept on a niggardly allowance.*

nig·ger /'nigər/ ▶ **noun** offensive a black person.
– ORIGIN from Spanish *negro* 'black.'

USAGE

The word **nigger** is very offensive and should not be used.

nig·gle /'nigəl/ ▶ **verb 1** worry or annoy someone slightly but persistently. **2** criticize someone in a petty way. ▶ **noun** a minor worry or criticism.
– DERIVATIVES **nig·gling** /'nig(ə)liNG/ adjective **nig·gly** /'nig(ə)lē/ adjective.
– ORIGIN probably Scandinavian.

nigh /nī/ ▶ **adverb, preposition, & adjective 1** old use or literary near. **2** almost; nearly.
– ORIGIN Old English.

night /nīt/ ▶ **noun 1** the time from sunset to sunrise. **2** the darkness of night. **3** an evening until bedtime. **4** literary dusk; nightfall.

– SYNONYMS **nighttime,** (hours of) darkness, dark.
– ANTONYMS day.

▶ **adverb** (**nights**) informal at night.
– ORIGIN Old English.

WORD LINKS

nocturnal *occurring or active at night*

night·cap /'nīt,kap/ ▶ **noun 1** a hot or alcoholic drink taken at bedtime. **2** historical a cap worn in bed.

night·clothes /'nīt,klō(TH)z/ ▶ **plural noun** clothes worn in bed.

night·club /'nīt,kləb/ ▶ **noun** a club that is open at night, with a bar and music.

night·dress /'nīt,dres/ ▶ **noun** a nightgown.

night·fall /'nīt,fôl/ ▶ **noun** dusk.

– SYNONYMS **sunset,** sundown, dusk, twilight, evening, dark; literary eventide.
– ANTONYMS dawn.

night·gown /'nīt,goun/ ▶ **noun** a light, loose garment worn by a woman or girl in bed.

night·ie /'nītē/ ▶ **noun** informal a nightdress.

night·in·gale /'nītn,gāl, 'nītiNG-/ ▶ **noun** a small brownish thrush noted for its tuneful song, often heard at night.
– ORIGIN from **NIGHT** and an Old English word meaning 'sing.'

night·jar /'nīt,jär/ ▶ **noun** a gray-brown bird with a distinctive call, active at night.

night·life /'nīt,līf/ ▶ **noun** social activities or entertainment available at night.

night·light /'nīt,līt/ ▶ **noun** a lamp or candle providing a dim light during the night.

night·ly /ˈnītlē/ ▶ **adjective 1** happening or done every night. **2** happening or done during the night. ▶ **adverb** every night.

night·mare /ˈnītˌme(ə)r/ ▶ **noun 1** a frightening or unpleasant dream. **2** a very unpleasant or difficult experience or situation: *acne is every teenager's nightmare.*

– SYNONYMS **ordeal,** trial, hell, misery, agony, torture, murder, purgatory, disaster; informal the pits.

– DERIVATIVES **night·mar·ish** adjective.
– ORIGIN from an Old English word meaning 'male demon believed to have sex with sleeping women.'

night owl ▶ **noun** informal a person who enjoys staying up late at night.

night school ▶ **noun** evening classes provided for people who work during the day.

night·shirt /ˈnītˌsHərt/ ▶ **noun** a long, loose shirt worn in bed.

night·side /ˈnītˌsīd/ ▶ **noun** the side of a planet or moon facing away from the sun and therefore in darkness.

night soil ▶ **noun** human excrement collected at night from buckets, cesspools, and outhouses.

night·spot /ˈnītˌspät/ ▶ **noun** informal a nightclub.

night·stand /ˈnītˌstand/ (also **night table**) ▶ **noun** a small, low bedside table, typically with drawers.

night·stick /ˈnītˌstik/ ▶ **noun** a police officer's club or billy.

night·time /ˈnītˌtīm/ ▶ **noun** the time between evening and morning.

night watch·man ▶ **noun** (pl. **night watchmen**) a person who guards a building at night.

night·wear /ˈnītˌwe(ə)r/ ▶ **noun** clothing worn in bed.

NIH ▶ **abbreviation** National Institutes of Health.

ni·hil·ism /ˈnīəˌlizəm, ˈnē-/ ▶ **noun** the rejection of all religious and moral principles, often in the belief that life is meaningless.
– DERIVATIVES **ni·hil·ist** noun **ni·hil·is·tic** /ˌnīəˈlistik, ˌnēə-/ adjective.
– ORIGIN from Latin *nihil* 'nothing.'

-nik ▶ **suffix** (forming nouns) referring to a person associated with a specified thing: *beatnik.*
– ORIGIN from Russian and Yiddish.

Nik·kei in·dex /ˈnēkā/ (also **Nikkei average**) ▶ **noun** an index of figures indicating the relative price of shares on the Tokyo Stock Exchange.
– ORIGIN abbreviation of *Ni(hon) Kei(zai Shimbun)* 'Japanese Economic Journal.'

nil /nil/ ▶ **noun** nothing; zero.

– SYNONYMS **nothing,** none, nought, zero; Tennis love.

▶ **adjective** nonexistent.
– ORIGIN Latin.

nil de·spe·ran·dum /ˈnil ˌdespəˈrändəm/ ▶ **exclamation** do not despair.
– ORIGIN from Latin *nil desperandum Teucro duce* 'no need to despair with Teucer as your leader,' from Horace's *Odes* 1.vii.27.

Ni·lot·ic /nīˈlätik/ ▶ **adjective** relating to the Nile River or to the Nile region of Africa.

nim·ble /ˈnimbəl/ ▶ **adjective** (**nimbler, nimblest**) quick and agile in movement or thought.

– SYNONYMS **1 agile,** light, quick, lithe, skillful, deft, dexterous, adroit, sprightly, spry; informal nippy. **2** *a nimble mind* **quick,** alert, lively, astute, perceptive, penetrating, discerning, shrewd, sharp, intelligent, bright, smart, clever, brilliant; informal quick on the uptake.
– ANTONYMS clumsy.

– DERIVATIVES **nim·bly** adverb.
– ORIGIN Old English.

nim·bus /ˈnimbəs/ ▶ **noun** (pl. **nimbi** /-ˌbī, -bē/ or **nimbuses**) **1** a large gray rain cloud. **2** a luminous cloud or a halo surrounding a supernatural being or saint.
– ORIGIN Latin, 'cloud, aureole.'

Nim·by /ˈnimbē/ ▶ **noun** (pl. **Nimbys**) informal a person who objects to the siting of unpleasant developments in their neighborhood.
– DERIVATIVES **Nim·by·ism** /-izəm/ noun.
– ORIGIN from the initial letters of *not in my back yard.*

nin·com·poop /ˈninkəmˌpo͞op, ˈniNG-/ ▶ **noun** a foolish or stupid person.
– ORIGIN perhaps from the man's name *Nicholas.*

nine /nīn/ ▶ **cardinal number** one less than ten; 9. (Roman numeral: **ix** or **IX.**)
– PHRASES **to the nines** to a great or elaborate extent: *the women were dressed to the nines.*
– ORIGIN Old English.

nine·teen /nīnˈtēn, ˈnīnˌtēn/ ▶ **cardinal number** one more than eighteen; 19. (Roman numeral: **xix** or **XIX.**)
– DERIVATIVES **nine·teenth** /nīnˈtēnTH, ˈnīnˌtēnTH/ ordinal number.

nine·teenth hole ▶ **noun** humorous the bar in a golf clubhouse, as reached after a round of eighteen holes.

nine·ty /ˈnīntē/ ▶ **cardinal number** (pl. **nineties**) ten less than one hundred; 90. (Roman numeral: **xc** or **XC.**)
– DERIVATIVES **nine·ti·eth** /-tēiTH/ ordinal number.

nin·ja /ˈninjə/ ▶ **noun** a person skilled in ninjutsu (the Japanese technique of espionage).
– ORIGIN Japanese, 'spy.'

nin·jut·su /ninˈjo͝otso͞o/ ▶ **noun** the traditional Japanese art of stealth, camouflage, and sabotage, first developed for espionage and now popular as a martial art.
– ORIGIN Japanese, 'art or science of stealth.'

nin·ny /ˈninē/ ▶ **noun** (pl. **ninnies**) informal a foolish and weak person.
– ORIGIN perhaps from **INNOCENT.**

ninth /nīnTH/ ▶ **ordinal number 1** that is number nine in a sequence; 9th. **2** (**a ninth/one ninth**) each of nine equal parts into which something is divided. **3** a musical interval spanning nine consecutive notes in a scale.
– DERIVATIVES **ninth·ly** adverb.

ni·o·bi·um /nīˈōbēəm/ ▶ **noun** a silver-gray metallic chemical element.
– ORIGIN from *Niobe,* daughter of Tantalus in Greek mythology.

nip[1] /nip/ ▶ **verb** (**nips, nipping, nipped**) **1** pinch or bite someone or something sharply. **2** (of cold or frost) hurt or damage someone or something.

– SYNONYMS **bite,** nibble, peck, pinch, tweak.

▶ **noun 1** a sharp bite or pinch. **2** a feeling of sharp coldness.
– PHRASES **nip something in the bud** stop something at an early stage.
– ORIGIN probably German or Dutch.

nip² ▶ **noun** a small quantity or sip of liquor.
– ORIGIN probably from former *nipperkin* 'small measure.'

nip and tuck ▶ **adverb & adjective** closely contested; neck and neck. ▶ **noun** informal a cosmetic surgical operation.

nip·per /'nipər/ ▶ **noun 1** informal a child. **2** (**nippers**) pliers, pincers, or a similar tool.

nip·ple /'nipəl/ ▶ **noun 1** a small projection in the center of each breast, containing (in females) the outlets of the organs that produce milk. **2** a small projection on a machine from which oil or other fluid is dispensed.

nip·py /'nipē/ ▶ **adjective** (**nippier, nippiest**) informal **1** (of the weather) chilly. **2** inclined to nip or bite.
– DERIVATIVES **nip·pi·ly** adverb **nip·pi·ness** noun.

nir·va·na /nər'vänə, nir-/ ▶ **noun 1** the ultimate goal of Buddhism, a state in which there is no suffering or desire, and no sense of self. **2** a perfect or very happy state or place: *Toronto is a restaurant-goer's nirvana.*
– ORIGIN Sanskrit.

ni·sei /nē'sā, 'nēsā/ (also **Nisei**) ▶ **noun** (pl. same or **niseis**) a person born in the US or Canada whose parents were immigrants from Japan. Compare with **ISSEI** and **SANSEI**.

nit /nit/ ▶ **noun** informal the egg of a human head louse.
– ORIGIN Old English.

ni·ter /'nītər/ ▶ **noun** potassium nitrate; saltpeter.
– ORIGIN Greek *nitron.*

nit·pick·ing /'nit,pikiNG/ ▶ **noun** informal fussy fault-finding.
– DERIVATIVES **nit·pick** verb **nit·pick·er** noun.

ni·trate ▶ **noun** /'nītrāt/ a salt or ester of nitric acid. ▶ **verb** /,nī'trāt/ treat a substance with nitric acid.
– DERIVATIVES **ni·tra·tion** /nī'trāsHən/ noun.

ni·tric ac·id /'nītrik/ ▶ **noun** a very corrosive acid.

ni·tride /'nītrīd/ ▶ **noun** a compound of nitrogen with another element or group.

ni·tri·fy /'nītrə,fī/ ▶ **verb** (**nitrifies, nitrifying, nitrified**) convert ammonia or another nitrogen compound into nitrites or nitrates.
– DERIVATIVES **ni·tri·fi·ca·tion** /,nītrəfi'kāsHən/ noun.

ni·trite /'nītrīt/ ▶ **noun** a salt or ester of nitrous acid.

nitro- ▶ **combining form** relating to or containing nitric acid, nitrates, or nitrogen: *nitroglycerine.*

ni·tro·cel·lu·lose /,nītrō'selyə,lōs, -lōz/ ▶ **noun** a highly flammable material used to make explosives and celluloid.

ni·tro·gen /'nītrəjən/ ▶ **noun** a colorless, odorless gas forming about 78 percent of the earth's atmosphere.
– DERIVATIVES **ni·trog·e·nous** /nī'träjənəs/ adjective.
– ORIGIN French *nitrogène* (from **NITER**).

ni·tro·gen cy·cle ▶ **noun** the series of processes by which nitrogen from the air is converted into compounds that are deposited in the soil, absorbed by plants, and eaten by animals, then returned to the atmosphere when these organic substances decay.

ni·tro·gen di·ox·ide ▶ **noun** a reddish-brown poisonous gas formed when many metals dissolve in nitric acid.

ni·tro·gen fix·a·tion ▶ **noun** the chemical processes by which nitrogen in the atmosphere is absorbed into organic compounds.

ni·tro·glyc·er·in /,nītrō'glisərin/ (also **nitroglycerine** /,nītrō'glisərēn/) ▶ **noun** an explosive yellow liquid used in dynamite and in medicine as a vasodilator in the treatment of angina.

ni·trous /'nītrəs/ ▶ **adjective** relating to or containing nitrogen.

ni·trous ac·id ▶ **noun** a weak acid made by the action of acids on nitrites.

ni·trous ox·ide ▶ **noun** a gas with a sweetish smell, used as an anesthetic.

nit·ty-grit·ty /'nitē 'gritē/ ▶ **noun** informal the most important aspects or basic details of a matter.
– ORIGIN unknown.

nit·wit /'nit,wit/ ▶ **noun** informal a silly or foolish person.
– ORIGIN probably from **NIT** + **WIT¹**.

nix /niks/ informal ▶ **noun** nothing. ▶ **verb** put an end to or cancel something.
– ORIGIN German, variant of *nichts* 'nothing.'

NJ ▶ **abbreviation** New Jersey.

NM ▶ **abbreviation** New Mexico.

nm ▶ **abbreviation 1** nanometer. **2** (also **n.m.**) nautical mile.

NNE ▶ **abbreviation** north-northeast.

NNW ▶ **abbreviation** north-northwest.

No¹ ▶ **noun** variant spelling of **NOH**.

No² ▶ **symbol** the chemical element nobelium.

no /nō/ ▶ **determiner 1** not any. **2** quite the opposite of: *he's no fool.* **3** hardly any. ▶ **exclamation** used to refuse, deny, or disagree with something. ▶ **adverb** (with comparative) not at all.

– SYNONYMS **absolutely not,** of course not, under no circumstances, not at all, never; informal nope, no way, not a chance, not on your life; old use nay.
– ANTONYMS yes.

▶ **noun** (pl. **noes**) a vote or decision against something.
– PHRASES **no can do** informal I am unable to do it. **no way** informal certainly not; not at all.
– ORIGIN Old English.

no. ▶ **abbreviation** (pl. **nos**) number.
– ORIGIN from Latin *numero* 'by number.'

nob·ble /'näbəl/ ▶ **verb** Brit. informal **1** try to influence or thwart by underhanded methods: *an attempt to nobble the jury.* **2** tamper with a racehorse to prevent it from winning a race. **3** stop someone so as to talk to them. **4** steal something.
– ORIGIN probably from dialect *knobble, knubble* 'knock, strike with the knuckles.'

no·bel·i·um /nō'belēəm/ ▶ **noun** a very unstable chemical element made by high-energy collisions.
– ORIGIN named after Alfred *Nobel* (see **NOBEL PRIZE**).

No·bel Prize /'nōbel/ ▶ **noun** any of six international prizes awarded annually for outstanding work in physics, chemistry, physiology or medicine, literature, economics, and the promotion of peace.
– ORIGIN named after the Swedish chemist and engineer Alfred *Nobel.*

no·bil·i·ty /nō'bilitē/ ▶ **noun 1** the quality of being noble. **2** the aristocracy.

no·ble /'nōbəl/ ▶ **adjective** (**nobler, noblest**) **1** belonging to the aristocracy. **2** having admirable personal qualities or high moral principles: *fighting for a noble cause*. **3** impressive; magnificent.

– SYNONYMS **1 aristocratic,** blue-blooded, patrician, high-born, titled. **2 worthy,** righteous, good, honorable, virtuous, upright. **3 magnificent,** splendid, grand, impressive, stately, imposing, dignified, proud, striking, majestic.
– ANTONYMS humble, lowly.

▶ **noun 1** (especially in former times) a member of the aristocracy. **2** a former English gold coin.

– SYNONYMS **aristocrat,** nobleman, noblewoman, lord, lady, peer (of the realm), peeress, patrician; informal aristo.
– ANTONYMS commoner.

– DERIVATIVES **no·bly** adverb.
– ORIGIN Latin *nobilis* 'noted, high-born.'

no·ble gas ▶ **noun** any of the gases helium, neon, argon, krypton, xenon, and radon, which seldom or never combine with other elements to form compounds.

no·ble·man /'nōbəlmən/ (or **noblewoman** /'nōbəl,wo͝omən/) ▶ **noun** (pl. **noblemen** or **noblewomen**) a man (or woman) who belongs to the aristocracy.

no·ble rot ▶ **noun** a gray mold deliberately cultivated on grapes in order to perfect certain wines.

no·ble sav·age ▶ **noun** a representative of primitive mankind as idealized in Romantic literature.

no·blesse ▶ **noun** (in phrase **noblesse oblige** /nō'bles ō'blēzʜ/) noble or wealthy people should help those who are less fortunate.
– ORIGIN French, 'nobility obliges.'

no·bod·y /'nō,bädē, -bədē/ ▶ **pronoun** no person; no one. ▶ **noun** (pl. **nobodies**) an unimportant person.

no-brain·er ▶ **noun** informal something that involves little or no mental effort.

nock /näk/ Archery ▶ **noun** a notch at either end of a bow or at the end of an arrow, for receiving the string of the bow. ▶ **verb** fit an arrow to the string of the bow.
– ORIGIN perhaps from Dutch *nocke* 'point, tip.'

noc·tur·nal /näk'tərnl/ ▶ **adjective** done, occurring, or active at night.
– DERIVATIVES **noc·tur·nal·ly** adverb.
– ORIGIN from Latin *nocturnus* 'of the night.'

noc·turne /'näk,tərn/ ▶ **noun** a short musical composition of a romantic and dreamy nature.
– ORIGIN French.

nod /näd/ ▶ **verb** (**nods, nodding, nodded**) **1** lower and raise one's head slightly and briefly to show agreement or as a greeting or signal. **2** let one's head fall forward when drowsy or asleep. **3** (**nod off**) informal fall asleep.

– SYNONYMS **1 incline,** bob, bow, dip. **2 signal,** gesture, gesticulate, motion, sign, indicate.

▶ **noun 1** an act of nodding. **2** a gesture acknowledging something: *a feel-good musical with a nod to pantomime*.
– PHRASES **give someone/thing the nod 1** approve someone or something. **2** give someone a signal. **a nodding acquaintance** a slight acquaintance.
– ORIGIN perhaps German.

node /nōd/ ▶ **noun** technical **1** a point in a network at which lines cross or branch. **2** the part of a plant stem from which one or more leaves grow. **3** a small mass of distinct body tissue. **4** Physics & Mathematics a point at which the amplitude of vibration of a wave is zero.
– DERIVATIVES **nod·al** adjective.
– ORIGIN Latin *nodus* 'knot.'

nod·ule /'näjo͞ol/ ▶ **noun 1** a small swelling or cluster of cells in the body. **2** a swelling on a root of a plant of the pea family, containing nitrogen-fixing bacteria. **3** a small rounded lump of matter distinct from its surroundings.
– DERIVATIVES **nod·u·lar** adjective.
– ORIGIN Latin *nodulus* 'little knot.'

No·el /nō'el/ ▶ **noun** Christmas.
– ORIGIN French.

no-frills ▶ **adjective** without unnecessary extras, especially ones for comfort or decoration: *a no-frills airline*.

nog·gin /'nägin/ ▶ **noun** informal **1** a person's head. **2** dated a small quantity of liquor.
– ORIGIN unknown.

no-go ▶ **adjective** informal **1** not ready or not functioning properly. **2** impossible, hopeless, or forbidden: *no-go zones for cars*. ▶ **noun** a negative response; no.

no-good ▶ **adjective** informal (of a person) contemptible; worthless: *a no-good layabout*. ▶ **noun** a worthless or contemptible person.

Noh /nō/ (also **No**) ▶ **noun** traditional Japanese masked drama with dance and song.
– ORIGIN Japanese.

no-hit·ter ▶ **noun** Baseball a complete game in which a pitcher yields no hits to the opposing team.

noir /nwär/ ▶ **noun** a type of crime fiction or movie marked by a mood of cynicism, fatalism, and a lack of moral certainty.
– DERIVATIVES **noir·ish** /'nwärisʜ/ adjective.
– ORIGIN from **FILM NOIR**.

noise /noiz/ ▶ **noun 1** a loud or unpleasant sound or series of sounds. **2** (**noises**) conventional remarks without real meaning: *Clarissa made encouraging noises*. **3** disturbances that accompany and interfere with an electrical signal.

– SYNONYMS **sound,** din, hubbub, clamor, racket, uproar, tumult, commotion, pandemonium; informal hullabaloo.
– ANTONYMS silence.

▶ **verb** (usu. **be noised about**) dated talk about or make something known publicly.
– DERIVATIVES **noise·less** adjective.
– ORIGIN Old French.

noise pol·lu·tion ▶ **noun** harmful or annoying levels of noise.

noi·sette /nwä'zet/ ▶ **noun 1** a small round piece of meat. **2** a chocolate made with hazelnuts.
– ORIGIN French, 'little nut.'

noi·some /'noisəm/ ▶ **adjective** literary **1** having a very unpleasant smell. **2** very unpleasant.
– ORIGIN from **ANNOY**.

nois·y /'noizē/ ▶ **adjective** (**noisier, noisiest**) full of or making a lot of noise.

– SYNONYMS **1 raucous,** rowdy, strident, clamorous, vociferous, boisterous. **2 loud,** blaring, booming, deafening, thunderous, ear-splitting, piercing, cacophonous, tumultuous.
– ANTONYMS quiet, soft.

– DERIVATIVES **nois·i·ly** adverb **nois·i·ness** noun.

nol·lie /,nälē/ ▶ **noun** a skateboarding jump performed without the aid of a takeoff ramp, executed by pressing the foot down on the nose of the board.

no·lo con·ten·de·re /ˌnōlō kənˈtendərē/ ▸ **noun** (also **nolo**) Law a plea by which a defendant accepts conviction as though a guilty plea had been entered but does not admit guilt.

no·mad /ˈnōˌmad/ ▸ **noun** a member of a people that travels from place to place to find fresh pasture for its animals.
– DERIVATIVES **no·mad·ism** /ˈnōmaˌdizəm/ noun.
– ORIGIN Greek *nomas*.

no·mad·ic /nōˈmadik/ ▸ **adjective** having the life of a nomad; wandering.
– DERIVATIVES **no·mad·i·cal·ly** /nōˈmadiklē/ adverb.

no man's land ▸ **noun** an area between two opposing armies that is not controlled by either.

nom de guerre /ˌnäm də ˈger/ ▸ **noun** (pl. **noms de guerre** pronunc. same) a name used by a person to engage in combat.
– ORIGIN French, 'war name.'

nom de plume /ˌnäm də ˈplo͞om/ ▸ **noun** (pl. **noms de plume** pronunc. same) a name used by a writer instead of their real name; a pen name.
– ORIGIN French.

no·men·cla·ture /ˈnōmənˌklāCHər/ ▸ **noun 1** a system of names used in a particular field. **2** the selecting of names for things in a particular field. **3** formal a name or term given to someone or something.
– DERIVATIVES **no·men·cla·tur·al** /ˌnōmənˈklāCHərəl/ adjective.
– ORIGIN Latin *nomenclatura*.

nom·i·nal /ˈnäminəl/ ▸ **adjective 1** existing in name but not in reality: *nominal independence under military occupation*. **2** (of a sum of money) very small, but charged or paid as a sign that payment is necessary. **3** Grammar relating to or functioning as a noun.

– SYNONYMS **1 in name only,** titular, formal, official, theoretical, supposed, ostensible, so-called, self-styled. **2 token,** symbolic, minimal.
– ANTONYMS real, considerable.

– DERIVATIVES **nom·i·nal·ly** adverb.
– ORIGIN Latin *nominalis*.

nom·i·nal·ism /ˈnäminəˌlizəm/ ▸ **noun** Philosophy the theory that general terms or ideas are mere names without any corresponding reality. Often contrasted with **REALISM**.
– DERIVATIVES **nom·i·nal·ist** noun.

nom·i·nal val·ue ▸ **noun 1** the value that is stated on a coin, bill, etc. **2** the price of a share, bond, or stock when it was issued, rather than its current market value.

nom·i·nate /ˈnäməˌnāt/ ▸ **verb 1** put someone forward as a candidate for election or for an honor or award. **2** appoint someone to a job or position. **3** specify something formally.

– SYNONYMS **1 propose,** put forward, put up, submit, present, recommend, suggest, name. **2 appoint,** name, choose, decide on, select, designate, assign.

– DERIVATIVES **nom·i·na·tion** /ˌnäməˈnāSHən/ noun **nom·i·na·tor** noun.
– ORIGIN Latin *nominare* 'to name.'

nom·i·na·tive /ˈnämənətiv/ ▸ **noun** the grammatical case used for the subject of a verb.

nom·i·nee /ˌnäməˈnē/ ▸ **noun 1** a person who is nominated for an office, award, etc. **2** a person or company in whose name a company, stock, or bond is registered.

non- ▸ **prefix** expressing negation or absence; not: *nonrecognition*.
– ORIGIN Latin, 'not.'

USAGE

The prefixes (word beginnings) **non-** and **un-** both mean 'not,' but they tend to be used in slightly different ways. **Non-** is more neutral, while **un-** often suggests a particular bias or standpoint. For example, **unnatural** means that something is not natural in a bad way, whereas **nonnatural** simply means 'not natural'.

non·a·ge·nar·i·an /ˌnänəjəˈne(ə)rēən, ˌnōnə-/ ▸ **noun** a person between 90 and 99 years old.
– ORIGIN Latin *nonagenarius*.

non·a·gon /ˈnänəˌgän/ ▸ **noun** a plane figure with nine straight sides and nine angles.

non·al·co·hol·ic /ˌnänˌalkəˈhôlik, -ˈhälik/ ▸ **adjective** (of a drink) not containing alcohol.

non·a·ligned /ˌnänəˈlīnd/ ▸ **adjective** (of a country during the cold war) not allied to any of the major world powers.

non·al·ler·gen·ic /ˌnänalərˈjenik/ ▸ **adjective** not causing an allergic reaction.

non·be·ing /nänˈbēiNG/ ▸ **noun** the state of not being; nonexistence.

non·be·liev·er /ˌnänbəˈlēvər/ ▸ **noun** a person who does not believe in something, especially one who has no religious faith.

non·bel·lig·er·ent /ˌnänbəˈlijərənt/ ▸ **adjective** not engaged in a war or conflict.

nonce /näns/ ▸ **adjective** (of a word or expression) coined for one occasion.
– PHRASES **for the nonce** for the present; temporarily.
– ORIGIN wrong division of former *then anes* 'the one (purpose).'

non·cha·lant /ˌnänSHəˈlänt/ ▸ **adjective** casually calm and relaxed.

– SYNONYMS **calm,** composed, unconcerned, cool, imperturbable, casual, blasé, offhand, insouciant; informal laid-back.
– ANTONYMS anxious.

– DERIVATIVES **non·cha·lance** noun **non·cha·lant·ly** adverb.
– ORIGIN French, 'not being concerned.'

non·com /ˈnänˌkäm/ ▸ **noun** Military informal a noncommissioned officer.

non·com·bat·ant /ˌnänkəmˈbatnt/ ▸ **noun** a person who is not engaged in fighting during a war, especially a civilian or an army chaplain or doctor.

non·com·mis·sioned /ˌnankəˈmisHənd/ ▸ **adjective** (of a military officer) appointed from the lower ranks rather than holding a commission.

non·com·mit·tal /ˌnänkəˈmitl/ ▸ **adjective** not expressing an opinion.

– SYNONYMS **evasive,** equivocal, guarded, circumspect, reserved; informal cagey.

– DERIVATIVES **non·com·mit·tal·ly** adverb.

non·com·pli·ance /ˌnänkəmˈplīəns/ ▸ **noun** failure to act in accordance with a wish or command: *illegal noncompliance with safety procedures*.

non com·pos men·tis /ˌnän ˈkämpəs ˈmentis/ ▸ **adjective** mentally unbalanced or insane.
– ORIGIN Latin, 'not having control of one's mind.'

non·con·duc·tor /ˌnänkənˈdəktər/ ▶ **noun** a substance that does not conduct heat or electricity.
– DERIVATIVES **non·con·duct·ing** adjective.

non·con·form·ist /ˌnänkənˈfôrmist/ ▶ **noun 1** a person who does not follow accepted ideas or behavior. **2** (**Nonconformist**) a member of a Protestant Church who does not follow the beliefs of the established Church of England.

– SYNONYMS **dissenter,** protester, rebel, freethinker, individualist, free spirit, maverick, renegade, schismatic, apostate, heretic.

▶ **adjective** not following accepted ideas or behavior.
– DERIVATIVES **non·con·form·ism** /-ˌmizəm/ noun **non·con·form·i·ty** /ˌnänkənˈfôrmitē/ noun.

non·con·trib·u·to·ry /ˌnänkənˈtribyəˌtôrē/ ▶ **adjective** (of a pension) funded by regular payments by the employer, not the employee.

non·co·op·er·a·tion /ˌnänkōˌäpəˈrāsHən/ ▶ **noun** failure to cooperate, especially as a form of protest.

non·de·nom·i·na·tion·al /ˌnändəˌnäməˈnāsHənəl/ ▶ **adjective** open or acceptable to people of any recognized branch of Christianity.

non·de·script /ˌnändəˈskript/ ▶ **adjective** lacking distinctive or interesting features: *a nondescript suburban apartment block.*

– SYNONYMS **undistinguished,** unremarkable, featureless, unmemorable, ordinary, average, run-of-the-mill, mundane, uninteresting, uninspiring, colorless, bland.
– ANTONYMS distinctive.

– ORIGIN from **NON-** + former *descript* 'described, engraved.'

non·drink·er /nänˈdriNGkər/ ▶ **noun** a person who does not drink alcohol.

none /nən/ ▶ **pronoun 1** not any. **2** no one. ▶ **adverb** (**none the**) (with comparative) not at all: *none the wiser.*
– ORIGIN Old English.

USAGE

When you use **none of** with a plural noun or pronoun (such as *them*), or with a singular noun that refers to a group of people or things, you can correctly use either a singular or plural verb: *none of them is coming* or *none of them are coming; none of the family was present* or *none of the family were present.*

non·en·ti·ty /nänˈentitē/ ▶ **noun** (pl. **nonentities**) an unimportant person or thing.
– ORIGIN Latin *nonentitas* 'nonexistence.'

non·es·sen·tial /ˌnänəˈsencHəl/ ▶ **adjective** not absolutely necessary. ▶ **noun** a nonessential thing.

no·net /nōˈnet/ ▶ **noun 1** a group of nine people or things. **2** a musical composition for nine voices or instruments.
– ORIGIN Italian *nonetto.*

none·the·less /ˌnənT͟Həˈles/ (also **none the less**) ▶ **adverb** in spite of that; nevertheless.

non·e·vent /ˌnäniˈvent/ ▶ **noun** an event that is not as interesting or important as it was expected to be.

non·ex·ist·ent /ˌnänigˈzistənt/ ▶ **adjective** not existing or not real or present.

– SYNONYMS **imaginary,** imagined, unreal, fictional, fictitious, made up, invented, fanciful, mythical, illusory.
– ANTONYMS real.

– DERIVATIVES **non·ex·ist·ence** noun.

non·fer·rous /nänˈferəs/ ▶ **adjective** (of metal) other than iron or steel.

non·fic·tion /nänˈfiksHən/ ▶ **noun** prose writing that deals with real people, facts, or events.
– DERIVATIVES **non·fic·tion·al** adjective.

non·flam·ma·ble /nänˈflaməbəl/ ▶ **adjective** not catching fire easily.

USAGE

The terms **nonflammable** and **noninflammable** both mean 'not catching fire easily.' See the note at **INFLAMMABLE**.

non·func·tion·al /nänˈfəNGksHənəl/ ▶ **adjective 1** not having a particular function. **2** not in working order.

non·gov·ern·men·tal /ˌnängəvər(n)ˈmentl/ ▶ **adjective** not belonging to or associated with any government.

non·in·ter·fer·ence /ˌnänintərˈfi(ə)rəns/ ▶ **noun** failure or refusal to intervene, especially in political matters.

non·in·ter·ven·tion /ˌnänintərˈvencHən/ ▶ **noun** the policy of not becoming involved in the affairs of other countries.
– DERIVATIVES **non·in·ter·ven·tion·ist** adjective & noun.

non·in·va·sive /ˌnäninˈvāsiv/ ▶ **adjective** (of medical procedures) not involving the introduction of instruments into the body.

non·judg·men·tal /ˌnänjəjˈmentl/ ▶ **adjective** avoiding personal and moral judgments.

non·lin·e·ar /nänˈlinēər/ ▶ **adjective** not linear or arranged in a straight line.

non·mem·ber /ˈnänˌmembər/ ▶ **noun** a person, group, or country that is not a member of a particular organization.

non·met·al /ˌnänˈmetl/ ▶ **noun** an element or substance that is not a metal.
– DERIVATIVES **non·me·tal·lic** /ˌnänməˈtalik/ adjective.

non·na·tive ▶ **adjective 1** (of a person, animal, or plant) not native to a particular place. **2** (of a speaker) not having spoken the language in question from earliest childhood.

non·nat·u·ral ▶ **adjective** not produced by or involving natural processes.

non·ne·go·ti·a·ble ▶ **adjective 1** not open to discussion or modification. **2** not able to be transferred to the legal ownership of another person.

no-no ▶ **noun** (pl. **no-nos**) informal a thing that is not possible or acceptable.

no-non·sense ▶ **adjective** simple and straightforward; sensible.

non·op·er·a·tion·al /ˌnänäpəˈrāsHənl/ ▶ **adjective 1** not working or in use. **2** not involving active duties.

non·pa·reil /ˌnänpəˈrel/ ▶ **adjective** better than anyone or anything else; unrivaled: *he's a nonpareil storyteller.* ▶ **noun** a person or thing that is unrivaled in a particular area.
– ORIGIN French, 'not equal.'

non·par·ti·san /nänˈpärtizən/ ▶ **adjective** not biased or prejudiced in favor of a particular cause or political group.

non·pay·ment /ˌnänˈpāmənt/ ▶ **noun** failure to pay an amount of money that is owed.

non·per·son /ˌnänˈpərsən/ ▶ **noun** a person who is ignored or forgotten.

non·plussed /nänˈpləst/ ▶ **adjective** surprised and confused and not knowing how to react.
– ORIGIN from Latin *non plus* 'not more.'

non·pro·duc·tive /ˌnänprəˈdəktiv/ ▶ **adjective** not producing or able to produce something.
– DERIVATIVES **non·pro·duc·tive·ly** adverb.

non·pro·fes·sion·al /ˌnänprəˈfesHənəl/ ▶ **adjective** **1** relating to or holding a job that does not need advanced education or training. **2** engaged in an activity that is not one's main paid job: *nonprofessional actors.*
▶ **noun** a nonprofessional person.

non·prof·it /ˈnänˈpräfit/ ▶ **adjective** not making or intended to make a profit.

non·pro·lif·er·a·tion /ˌnänprəˌlifəˈrāsHən/ ▶ **noun** the prevention of an increase in the number of nuclear weapons that are produced.

non·res·i·dent /nänˈrezidənt/ ▶ **adjective** not living in a particular country or a place of work. ▶ **noun** a person not living in a particular place.

non·sense /ˈnänˌsens/ ▶ **noun** **1** words that make no sense. **2** foolish or unacceptable behavior. **3** something that one disagrees with or disapproves of.

> – SYNONYMS **1 rubbish,** gibberish, claptrap, balderdash, garbage; informal baloney, bosh, tripe, drivel, gobbledygook, mumbo-jumbo, poppycock, twaddle, guff, bilge, hogwash, piffle. **2 mischief,** misbehavior; informal tomfoolery, monkey business, shenanigans, malarkey.
> – ANTONYMS sense.

non·sen·si·cal /nänˈsensikəl/ ▶ **adjective** making no sense; ridiculous.
– DERIVATIVES **non·sen·si·cal·ly** /nänˈsensik(ə)lē/ adverb.

non se·qui·tur /ˌnän ˈsekwitər/ ▶ **noun** a conclusion that does not logically follow from the previous statement.
– ORIGIN Latin, 'it does not follow.'

non·slip /ˌnänˈslip/ ▶ **adjective** designed to prevent slipping.

non·smok·er /nänˈsmōkər/ ▶ **noun** a person who does not smoke tobacco.
– DERIVATIVES **non·smok·ing** adjective.

non·spe·cif·ic /ˌnänspəˈsifik/ ▶ **adjective** not detailed or exact; general.

non·spe·cif·ic u·re·thri·tis ▶ **noun** inflammation of the urethra due to infection by organisms other than those that cause gonorrhea.

non·stand·ard /ˈnänˈstandərd/ ▶ **adjective** **1** not average or usual. **2** (of language) not considered correct by most educated speakers.

non·start·er /ˈnänˈstärtər/ ▶ **noun** **1** a person or animal that fails to take part in a race. **2** informal something that has no chance of succeeding.

non·stick /ˈnänˈstik/ ▶ **adjective** (of a pan or surface) covered with a substance that prevents food from sticking to it during cooking.

non·stop /ˈnänˈstäp/ ▶ **adjective** **1** continuing without stopping. **2** having no stops on the way to a destination.

> – SYNONYMS **continuous,** constant, continual, incessant, ceaseless, uninterrupted, unbroken, never-ending, perpetual, round/around-the-clock, persistent, steady, unremitting, relentless, interminable.
> – ANTONYMS intermittent, occasional.

▶ **adverb** without stopping.

> – SYNONYMS **continuously,** continually, incessantly, ceaselessly, all the time, constantly, perpetually, persistently, steadily, relentlessly, interminably; informal 24-7.

non·tech·ni·cal /nänˈteknikəl/ ▶ **adjective** **1** not relating to or involving science or technology. **2** not using technical terms or requiring specialized knowledge.

non·tox·ic /nänˈtäksik/ ▶ **adjective** not poisonous or toxic.

> **WORD TOOLKIT**
> See **HARMLESS**.

non·u·ni·form /nänˈyo͞onəˌfôrm/ ▶ **adjective** not uniform or regular; varying.

non·un·ion /nänˈyo͞onyən/ ▶ **adjective** not belonging to or connected with a labor union.

non·ver·bal /nänˈvərbəl/ ▶ **adjective** not involving or using words or speech.

non·vi·o·lent /ˌnänˈvīələnt/ ▶ **adjective** **1** using peaceful means rather than force to bring about political or social change. **2** not involving violence: *nonviolent movies.*
– DERIVATIVES **non·vi·o·lence** noun.

non·white /ˌnänˈ(h)wīt/ ▶ **adjective** (of a person) not white or not of European origin. ▶ **noun** a nonwhite person.

noo·dle[1] /ˈno͞odl/ ▶ **noun** (usu. **noodles**) a very thin, long strip of pasta or a similar flour paste.
– ORIGIN German *Nudel.*

noo·dle[2] ▶ **noun** informal **1** a silly person. **2** a person's head.
– ORIGIN unknown.

noo·dle[3] ▶ **verb** informal improvise or play casually on a musical instrument.
– ORIGIN unknown.

nook /no͝ok/ ▶ **noun** a small corner or other place that is sheltered or hidden.
– PHRASES **every nook and cranny** every part of something.
– ORIGIN unknown.

nook·y /ˈno͝okē/ (also **nookie**) ▶ **noun** informal sexual activity or intercourse.
– ORIGIN perhaps from **NOOK**.

noon /no͞on/ ▶ **noun** twelve o'clock in the day; midday.

> – SYNONYMS **midday,** twelve o'clock, high noon, noonday, noontime, twelve hundred hours.

– ORIGIN from Latin *nona hora* 'ninth hour' (from sunrise).

noon·day /ˈno͞onˌdā/ ▶ **adjective** happening or appearing in the middle of the day.

no one ▶ **pronoun** no person; not a single person.

noon·time /ˈno͞onˌtīm/ (also literary **noontide** /ˈno͞onˌtīd/) ▶ **noun** noon.

noose /no͞os/ ▶ **noun** a loop with a knot that tightens as the rope or wire is pulled, used to hang people or trap animals.
– ORIGIN probably from Old French *nous.*

nope /nōp/ ▸ **exclamation** informal variant of **NO**.

nor /nôr/ ▸ **conjunction & adverb** and not; and not either.
– ORIGIN Old English.

nor' /nôr/ ▸ **abbreviation** (especially in compounds) north: *nor'west*.

NORAD ▸ **abbreviation** North American Aerospace Defence Command.

nor·a·dren·a·line /ˌnôrəˈdrenəlin/ ▸ **noun** a hormone that functions as a neurotransmitter and is also used as a drug to raise blood pressure.

Nor·dic /ˈnôrdik/ ▸ **adjective 1** relating to Scandinavia, Finland, and Iceland. **2** referring to a tall, blond type of person associated with northern Europe.
– ORIGIN French *nordique*.

Nor·dic ski·ing ▸ **noun** cross-country skiing and ski jumping.

Nor·dic walk·ing ▸ **noun** a sport or activity that involves walking across country with the aid of long poles resembling ski poles.

no·ri /ˈnôrē/ ▸ **noun** (in Japanese cuisine) seaweed, eaten fresh or dried in sheets.
– ORIGIN Japanese.

norm /nôrm/ ▸ **noun 1** (**the norm**) the usual or standard thing: *strikes were the norm*. **2** a required or acceptable standard: *the norms of good behavior*.

> – SYNONYMS **1** (**the norm**) **normal,** usual, the rule, standard, typical, average, par for the course, expected. **2** **standard,** convention, criterion, yardstick, benchmark, touchstone, rule, formula, pattern.

– ORIGIN Latin *norma* 'rule, carpenter's square.'

nor·mal /ˈnôrməl/ ▸ **adjective 1** usual, typical, or expected. **2** technical (of a line) intersecting a given line or surface at right angles.

> – SYNONYMS **1** **usual,** standard, ordinary, customary, conventional, habitual, accustomed, typical, common, regular, routine, traditional, commonplace, everyday. **2** **ordinary,** average, run-of-the-mill, middle-of-the-road, conventional, mainstream, garden-variety. **3** **sane,** in one's right mind, right in the head, of sound mind, compos mentis; informal all there.
> – ANTONYMS unusual, insane.

▸ **noun 1** the normal state or condition: *her temperature was above normal*. **2** technical a line at right angles to a given line or surface.
– DERIVATIVES **nor·mal·i·ty** /nôrˈmalitē/ (also **normalcy** /ˈnôrməlsē/) noun.

nor·mal dis·tri·bu·tion (also **Gaussian distribution**) ▸ **noun** Statistics a function that represents the distribution of a set of variables as a bell-shaped curve.

nor·mal·ize /ˈnôrməˌlīz/ ▸ **verb** bring or return to a normal or standard state.
– DERIVATIVES **nor·mal·i·za·tion** /ˌnôrmələˈzāSHən/ noun.

nor·mal·ly /ˈnôrməlē/ ▸ **adverb 1** in the usual way. **2** under normal or usual conditions.

> – SYNONYMS **1** *try to breathe normally* **naturally,** conventionally, properly, like everyone else. **2** *normally, it takes three or four years to complete the training* **usually,** ordinarily, as a rule, generally, in general, mostly, on the whole, typically, habitually.

Nor·man /ˈnôrmən/ ▸ **noun 1** a member of a people of Normandy in northern France who conquered England in 1066. **2** (also **Norman French**) the form of Old French spoken by the Normans. **3** a person from modern Normandy. ▸ **adjective 1** relating to the Normans or Normandy. **2** relating to the style of Romanesque architecture used in Britain under the Normans.

nor·ma·tive /ˈnôrmətiv/ ▸ **adjective** formal relating to or setting a standard or norm: *a normative theory of world politics*.

No·ro·vi·rus /ˈnôrəˌvīrəs/ ▸ **noun** any of a group of viruses that can cause acute gastroenteritis in humans.

Norse /nôrs/ ▸ **noun** an ancient or medieval form of Norwegian or a related Scandinavian language. ▸ **adjective** relating to Norse or ancient or medieval Norway or Scandinavia.
– DERIVATIVES **Norse·man** noun (pl. **Norsemen** /ˈnôrsmən/).
– ORIGIN Dutch *noordsch*.

north /nôrTH/ ▸ **noun 1** the direction in which a compass needle normally points, on the left-hand side of a person facing east. **2** the northern part of a place. ▸ **adjective 1** lying toward, near, or facing the north. **2** (of a wind) blowing from the north. ▸ **adverb** to or toward the north.
– DERIVATIVES **north·bound** /ˈnôrTHˌbound/ adjective & adverb.
– ORIGIN Old English.

North A·mer·i·can ▸ **noun** a person from North America, especially a citizen of the US or Canada. ▸ **adjective** relating to North America.

north·east /ˌnôrTHˈēst/ ▸ **noun** the direction or region halfway between north and east. ▸ **adjective 1** lying toward, near, or facing the northeast. **2** (of a wind) from the northeast. ▸ **adverb** to or toward the northeast.
– DERIVATIVES **north·east·ern** /-ˈēstərn/ adjective.

north·east·er·ly /ˌnôrTHˈēstərlē/ ▸ **adjective & adverb** in a northeastward position or direction. ▸ **noun** (pl. **northeasterlies**) a wind blowing from the northeast.

north·east·ward /ˌnôrTHˈēstwərd/ ▸ **adverb** (also **northeastwards**) toward the northeast. ▸ **adjective** in, toward, or facing the northeast.

north·er·ly /ˈnôrT͟Hərlē/ ▸ **adjective & adverb 1** facing or moving toward the north. **2** (of a wind) blowing from the north. ▸ **noun** (pl. **northerlies**) a north wind.

north·ern /ˈnôrT͟Hərn/ ▸ **adjective 1** situated in, directed toward, or facing the north. **2** (usu. **Northern**) relating to or typical of the north.
– DERIVATIVES **north·ern·most** /-ˌmōst/ adjective.

north·ern·er /ˈnôrT͟Hərnər/ ▸ **noun** a person from the north of a region or country.

north·ern lights ▸ **plural noun** the aurora borealis.

north·land /ˈnôrTHlənd, -ˌland/ ▸ **noun** (also **northlands**) literary the northern part of a country or region.

north-north·east ▸ **noun** the direction midway between north and northeast.

north-north·west ▸ **noun** the direction midway between north and northwest.

North Star ▸ **noun** the Polestar.

north·ward /ˈnôrTHwərd/ ▸ **adjective** in a northerly direction. ▸ **adverb** (also **northwards**) toward the north.
– DERIVATIVES **north·ward·ly** adjective & adverb.

north·west /ˌnôrTH'west/ ▸ **noun** the direction or region halfway between north and west. ▸ **adjective 1** lying toward or facing the northwest. **2** (of a wind) from the northwest. ▸ **adverb** to or toward the northwest.
– DERIVATIVES **north·west·ern** /-'westərn/ adjective.

north·west·er·ly /ˌnôrTH'westərlē/ ▸ **adjective & adverb** in a northwestward position or direction. ▸ **noun** (pl. **northwesterlies**) a wind blowing from the northwest.

north·west·ward /ˌnôrTH'westwərd/ ▸ **adverb** (also **northwestwards**) toward the northwest. ▸ **adjective** in, toward, or facing the northwest.

Nor·we·gian /nôr'wējən/ ▸ **noun 1** a person from Norway. **2** the language spoken in Norway. ▸ **adjective** relating to Norway.
– ORIGIN from Latin *Norvegia* 'Norway.'

nose /nōz/ ▸ **noun 1** the part of the face above the mouth, containing the nostrils and used in breathing and smelling. **2** the front part of an aircraft or other vehicle. **3** the sense of smell. **4** a natural talent for detecting something: *he has a nose for a good script.* **5** the characteristic smell of a wine. **6** an act of looking around somewhere.

– SYNONYMS **snout,** muzzle, proboscis, trunk; informal beak, conk, schnozz, hooter.

▸ **verb 1** move slowly forward: *they nosed out of the parking place.* **2** look around or pry into something. **3** (of an animal) thrust its nose against or into something.

– SYNONYMS **1 pry,** inquire, poke around/about, interfere (in), meddle (in), stick/poke one's nose in; informal snoop. **2 ease,** inch, edge, move, maneuver, steer, guide.

– PHRASES **by a nose** (of a victory) by a very narrow margin. **cut off one's nose to spite one's face** do something that is supposed to harm someone else but that also puts oneself at a disadvantage. **keep one's nose clean** informal stay out of trouble. **keep one's nose out of** refrain from interfering in another person's business. **put someone's nose out of joint** informal offend someone or hurt their pride. **turn one's nose up at** informal show distaste or contempt for. **under someone's nose** informal directly in front of someone, typically without being noticed by them.
– ORIGIN Old English.

WORD LINKS

nasal *relating to the nose*

nose·bleed /'nōzˌblēd/ ▸ **noun** an instance of bleeding from the nose.

nose cone ▸ **noun** the cone-shaped nose of a rocket or aircraft.

nose·dive /'nōzˌdīv/ ▸ **noun 1** a sudden dramatic decline: *my fortunes took a nosedive.* **2** a steep downward plunge by an aircraft. ▸ **verb 1** fall or decline suddenly: *prices nosedived after the market collapsed.* **2** (of an aircraft) make a nosedive.

no-see-um /nō 'sē əm/ ▸ **noun** a minute bloodsucking insect, especially a midge.

nose·gay /'nōzˌgā/ ▸ **noun** a small bunch of flowers.
– ORIGIN from **GAY** in the former sense 'ornament.'

nos·ey /'nōzē/ ▸ **adjective** variant spelling of **NOSY**.

nosh /näSH/ informal ▸ **noun** food. ▸ **verb** eat enthusiastically or greedily.
– ORIGIN Yiddish.

no-show ▸ **noun** a person who has made a reservation or appointment but neither keeps nor cancels it.

nos·tal·gia /nä'staljə, nə-/ ▸ **noun** wistful longing or affection for a happier or better time in the past: *touches of nostalgia for the 70s.*
– ORIGIN from Greek *nostos* 'return home' + *algos* 'pain.'

nos·tal·gic /nä'staljik, nə-/ ▸ **adjective** characterized by or exhibiting feelings of nostalgia.

– SYNONYMS **wistful,** sentimental, emotional, homesick, regretful, dewy-eyed, maudlin.

– DERIVATIVES **nos·tal·gi·cal·ly** /nä'staljik(ə)lē, nə-/ adverb.

nos·tril /'nästrəl/ ▸ **noun** either of two external openings of the nose through which air passes to the lungs.
– ORIGIN Old English, 'nose hole.'

nos·trum /'nästrəm/ ▸ **noun 1** a favorite method for improving something: *right-wing nostrums such as cutting public spending.* **2** a medicine that is prepared by an unqualified person and is not effective.
– ORIGIN Latin, 'something of our own making.'

nos·y /'nōzē/ (also **nosey**) ▸ **adjective** (**nosier, nosiest**) informal too inquisitive about other people's business.

– SYNONYMS **prying,** inquisitive, curious, spying, eavesdropping, intrusive; informal snooping.

– DERIVATIVES **nos·i·ly** adverb **nos·i·ness** noun.

not /nät/ ▸ **adverb 1** used to form or express a negative. **2** less than: *not ten feet away.*
– ORIGIN from **NOUGHT**.

no·ta·ble /'nōtəbəl/ ▸ **adjective** worthy of attention or notice.

– SYNONYMS **1 noteworthy,** remarkable, outstanding, important, significant, memorable, marked, striking, impressive, momentous, uncommon. **2 prominent,** well known, famous, famed, noted, of note.
– ANTONYMS unremarkable, unknown.

▸ **noun** a famous or important person.

– SYNONYMS **celebrity,** VIP, dignitary, luminary, star, big name, personage; informal celeb, bigwig.

no·ta·bly /'nōtəblē/ ▸ **adverb 1** in particular. **2** in a way that is noticeable or remarkable.

– SYNONYMS **1 in particular,** particularly, especially, primarily, principally, chiefly. **2 remarkably,** especially, exceptionally, singularly, particularly, peculiarly, distinctly, significantly, unusually, uncommonly, conspicuously.

no·ta·rize /'nōtəˌrīz/ ▸ **verb** have a signature on a document confirmed as legal by a notary.

no·ta·ry /'nōtərē/ (in full **notary public**) ▸ **noun** (pl. **notaries**) a person who is officially authorized to draw up and witness the signing of contracts and other documents.
– DERIVATIVES **no·tar·i·al** /nō'terēəl/ adjective.
– ORIGIN Latin *notarius* 'secretary.'

no·ta·tion /nō'tāSHən/ ▸ **noun 1** a system of written symbols used to represent numbers, amounts, or elements in a subject such as music or mathematics. **2** a note or annotation.
– DERIVATIVES **no·tate** /'nōˌtāt/ verb **no·ta·tion·al** /-nəl/ adjective.

notch /näCH/ ▸ **noun 1** a V-shaped cut or indentation on an edge or surface. **2** a point or level on a scale: *her opinion of him dropped a few notches.*

– SYNONYMS **nick,** cut, incision, score, scratch, slit, slot, groove.

▶ **verb 1** make notches in something. **2** score or achieve something.
– ORIGIN Old French *osche.*

note /nōt/ ▶ **noun 1** a brief written record of something, used as an aid to memory. **2** a short written message or document. **3** Brit. a banknote. **4** a single sound of a particular pitch and length made by a musical instrument or voice, or a symbol representing this. **5** a particular quality or tone: *there was a note of scorn in his voice.* **6** a bird's song or call. **7** a basic component of a perfume or flavor.

– SYNONYMS **1 record,** entry, reminder, comment, jotting. **2 message,** letter, line, missive; informal memo; formal memorandum, epistle. **3 annotation,** footnote, marginalia. **4 banknote,** bill; informal greenback. **5** *the note of hopelessness in her voice* **tone,** hint, indication, sign, element, suggestion, sense.

▶ **verb 1** pay attention to or notice something. **2** record something in writing.

– SYNONYMS **1 bear in mind,** be mindful of, consider, take notice of, register, be aware, take in, notice, observe, see, perceive. **2 write down,** put down, jot down, take down, scribble, enter, mark, record, register, pencil in.

– PHRASES **hit** (or **strike**) **the right** (or **wrong**) **note** say or do something in the right (or wrong) way. **of note** important. **take note** pay attention.
– ORIGIN from Latin *nota* 'a mark' and *notare* 'to mark.'

note·book /ˈnōtˌbo͝ok/ ▶ **noun 1** a small book for writing notes in. **2** a portable computer smaller than a laptop.

– SYNONYMS **notepad,** register, logbook, log, diary, journal, record; trademark Filofax.

not·ed /ˈnōtid/ ▶ **adjective** well known; famous.

– SYNONYMS **famous,** famed, well known, renowned, prominent, notable, important, eminent, great, acclaimed, celebrated, distinguished.
– ANTONYMS unknown.

note·pad /ˈnōtˌpad/ ▶ **noun 1** a pad of paper for writing notes on. **2** a pocket-sized personal computer in which text is input by writing with a stylus on the screen.

note·pa·per /ˈnōtˌpāpər/ ▶ **noun** paper for writing letters on.

note-per·fect ▶ **adjective** (of a musical performance or performer) technically perfect.

note·wor·thy /ˈnōtˌwərT͟Hē/ ▶ **adjective** interesting or significant.

– SYNONYMS **notable,** interesting, significant, important, remarkable, striking, memorable, unique, special, unusual.
– ANTONYMS unexceptional.

WORD TOOLKIT

See **GROUNDBREAKING**.

noth·ing /ˈnəTHiNG/ ▶ **pronoun 1** not anything. **2** something of no importance or concern. **3** naught; no amount.

– SYNONYMS **1** *all my efforts add up to nothing* **not a thing,** zero; informal zilch, zip, nada, diddly-squat. **2** *the share value fell to nothing* **zero,** naught, nil, o; Tennis love.

▶ **adverb** not at all.

– PHRASES **for nothing 1** without payment or charge. **2** to no purpose. **nothing but** only. **nothing doing** informal there is no chance of success. **sweet nothings** words of affection exchanged by lovers.
– ORIGIN Old English.

noth·ing·ness /ˈnəTHiNGnis/ ▶ **noun** the state of not existing or a state where nothing exists.

no·tice /ˈnōtis/ ▶ **noun 1** the fact of being aware of or paying attention to something: *his silence did not escape my notice.* **2** information or warning that something is going to happen: *interest rates may change without notice.* **3** a formal statement that someone is going to leave a job or end an agreement. **4** a sheet or placard put on display to give information. **5** a small announcement or advertisement published in a newspaper. **6** a short published review of a new movie, play, or book.

– SYNONYMS **1 sign,** announcement, advertisement, poster, placard, bill, handbill, flyer. **2 attention,** observation, awareness, consciousness, perception, regard, consideration, scrutiny; formal cognizance. **3** *advance notice of the price increase* **notification,** warning, information, news, word.

▶ **verb 1** become aware of: *I noticed the youths behaving suspiciously.* **2** (**be noticed**) be recognized as worthy of attention.

– SYNONYMS **observe,** note, see, discern, detect, spot, perceive, make out.
– ANTONYMS overlook.

– PHRASES **at short** (or **a moment's**) **notice** with little warning. **take** (**no**) **notice** (**of**) pay (no) attention (to).
– ORIGIN Latin *notitia.*

no·tice·a·ble /ˈnōtisəbəl/ ▶ **adjective** easily seen; clear or apparent.

– SYNONYMS **obvious,** evident, apparent, manifest, plain, clear, conspicuous, perceptible, discernible, detectable, observable, visible, appreciable, unmistakable, patent.
– ANTONYMS imperceptible.

– DERIVATIVES **no·tice·a·bly** /-blē/ adverb.

no·ti·fi·a·ble /ˌnōtəˈfīəbəl/ ▶ **adjective** (of an infectious disease) so serious that it must be reported to the health authorities.

no·ti·fy /ˈnōtəˌfī/ ▶ **verb** (**notifies, notifying, notified**) formally inform someone about something.

– SYNONYMS **inform,** tell, let someone know, advise, apprise, alert, warn.

– DERIVATIVES **no·ti·fi·ca·tion** /ˌnōtəfiˈkāSHən/ noun.
– ORIGIN Latin *notificare* 'make known.'

no·tion /ˈnōSHən/ ▶ **noun 1** a concept or belief. **2** a person's understanding of something. **3** an impulse or whim.

– SYNONYMS **idea,** impression, belief, opinion, view, concept, conception, understanding, feeling, suspicion, intuition, inkling.

– ORIGIN Latin, 'idea.'

no·tion·al /ˈnōSHənəl/ ▶ **adjective** based on an estimate or theory; hypothetical.
– DERIVATIVES **no·tion·al·ly** adverb.

no·to·ri·e·ty /ˌnōtəˈrīətē/ ▶ **noun** the state of being famous for a bad quality or action.

no·to·ri·ous /nəˈtôrēəs, nō-/ ▶ **adjective** famous for a bad quality or action.

– SYNONYMS **infamous,** scandalous, disreputable, of ill repute.

– DERIVATIVES **no·to·ri·ous·ly** adverb.
– ORIGIN Latin *notus* 'known.'

not·with·stand·ing /ˌnätwiTHˈstandiNG, -wiTH-/ ▸ **preposition** in spite of. ▸ **adverb** nevertheless.

nou·gat /ˈno͞ogit/ ▸ **noun** a candy made from sugar or honey, nuts, and egg white.
– ORIGIN Provençal *noga* 'nut.'

nought /nôt/ ▸ **noun** variant spelling of **NAUGHT**.

noun /noun/ ▸ **noun** a word (other than a pronoun) that refers to a person, place, or thing.
– ORIGIN Latin *nomen* 'name.'

nour·ish /ˈnərisH, ˈnə-risH/ ▸ **verb 1** provide someone or something with the food or other substances necessary for growth and health. **2** keep a feeling or belief in the mind for a long time.

– SYNONYMS **feed,** sustain, provide for, care for, nurture.

– ORIGIN Latin *nutrire*.

nour·ish·ing /ˈnərisHiNG, ˈnə-ri-/ ▸ **adjective** (of food) containing substances necessary for growth and health: *a simple but nourishing meal*.

– SYNONYMS **nutritious,** wholesome, good for you, nutritive, healthy, health-giving, beneficial.
– ANTONYMS unhealthy.

nour·ish·ment /ˈnərisHmənt, ˈnə-risH-/ ▸ **noun 1** the food or other substances necessary for growth, health, and good condition. **2** the action of nourishing someone or something.

– SYNONYMS **food,** nutriment, nutrients, nutrition, sustenance.

nou·veau riche /ˈno͞ovō ˈrēsH/ ▸ **noun** (treated as pl.) people who have recently become rich and who like to display their wealth in an obvious or tasteless way.
– ORIGIN French, 'new rich.'

nou·velle cui·sine /no͞oˈvel kwiˈzēn/ ▸ **noun** a modern style of cooking that avoids rich foods and emphasizes the presentation of the dishes.
– ORIGIN French, 'new cookery.'

Nov. ▸ **abbreviation** November.

no·va /ˈnōvə/ ▸ **noun** (pl. **novae** /-vē, -ˌvī/ or **novas**) a star that suddenly becomes very bright and then slowly returns to normal.
– ORIGIN from Latin *novus* 'new.'

nov·el[1] /ˈnävəl/ ▸ **noun** a story about imaginary people and events, long enough to fill a complete book.

– SYNONYMS **story,** tale, narrative, romance, novella.

– ORIGIN from Italian *novella storia* 'new story.'

nov·el[2] ▸ **adjective** new in an interesting or unusual way: *a novel approach to architecture*.

– SYNONYMS **new,** original, unusual, unconventional, unorthodox, different, fresh, imaginative, innovative, unfamiliar, surprising.
– ANTONYMS traditional.

– ORIGIN Latin *novus* 'new.'

WORD TOOLKIT

See **UNFAMILIAR**.

nov·el·ette /ˌnävəˈlet/ ▸ **noun** a short novel, especially a romantic novel regarded as poorly written.

nov·el·ist /ˈnävəlist/ ▸ **noun** a person who writes novels.
– DERIVATIVES **nov·el·is·tic** /ˌnävəˈlistik/ adjective.

nov·el·ize /ˈnävəˌlīz/ ▸ **verb** convert a story, screenplay, or play into a novel.
– DERIVATIVES **nov·el·i·za·tion** /ˌnävəliˈzāsHən/ noun.

no·vel·la /nōˈvelə/ ▸ **noun** a short novel or long short story.
– ORIGIN Italian.

nov·el·ty /ˈnävəltē/ ▸ **noun** (pl. **novelties**) **1** the quality of being new and unusual: *the novelty of being a married woman wore off*. **2** a new or unfamiliar thing. **3** a small and inexpensive toy or ornament.

– SYNONYMS **1 originality,** newness, freshness, unconventionality, innovation, unfamiliarity. **2 knick-knack,** trinket, bauble, toy, trifle, kickshaw, ornament.

▸ **adjective** intended to be amusingly unusual: *a novelty teapot*.

No·vem·ber /nōˈvembər, nə-/ ▸ **noun** the eleventh month of the year.
– ORIGIN from Latin *novem* 'nine' (November being originally the ninth month of the Roman year).

no·ve·na /nōˈvēnə/ ▸ **noun** (in the Roman Catholic Church) a form of worship consisting of special prayers or services on nine successive days.
– ORIGIN Latin.

nov·ice /ˈnävəs/ ▸ **noun 1** a person who is new to and lacks experience in a job or situation. **2** a person who has entered a religious order and is under probation, before taking vows. **3** Brit. a racehorse that has not yet won a major prize or reached a qualifying level of performance.

– SYNONYMS **beginner,** learner, newcomer, fledgling, trainee, probationer, student, pupil, apprentice, tyro, neophyte; informal rookie, newbie, tenderfoot, greenhorn.
– ANTONYMS expert, veteran.

– ORIGIN Latin *novicius*.

CHOOSE THE RIGHT WORD

novice, apprentice, beginner, neophyte, probationer

All of these nouns are used to describe someone who has not yet acquired the skills and experience needed to qualify for a trade, a career, a profession, or a sphere of life. **Beginner** is the most general and informal term, used to describe someone who has begun to acquire the necessary skills but has not yet mastered them (*violin lessons for beginners*). An **apprentice** is also a beginner, usually a young person, who is serving under a more experienced master or teacher to learn the skills of a trade or profession (*an apprentice to one of the great Renaissance painters*); in a broad sense, *apprentice* refers to any beginner whose efforts are unpolished. **Novice** implies that the person lacks training and experience (*a novice when it came to writing fiction*), while **neophyte** is a less negative term, suggesting that the person is eagerly learning the ways, methods, or principles of something (*he was a neophyte at this type of sailing*). A **probationer** is a beginner who is undergoing a trial period, during which he or she must prove an aptitude for a certain type of work or life (*she was a lowly probationer, with no privileges or status*).

no·vi·ti·ate /nō'visн(ē)ət, nə-/ (also **noviciate** pronunc. same) ▶ **noun 1** the period or state of being a novice in a religious order. **2** a religious novice.

no·vo·caine /'nōvə,kān/ (also trademark **Novocain**) ▶ **noun** another term for **PROCAINE**.

now /nou/ ▶ **adverb 1** at the present time. **2** at or from this precise moment. **3** under the present circumstances.

– SYNONYMS **1 at the moment,** at present, presently, at this moment in time, currently, nowadays, these days, today, in this day and age. **2 at once,** straightaway, right away, (right) this minute, this instant, immediately, instantly, directly; informal pronto, asap.

▶ **conjunction** as a result of the fact.
– PHRASES **now and again** (or **then**) from time to time.
– ORIGIN Old English.

now·a·days /'nouə,dāz/ ▶ **adverb** at the present time, in contrast with the past.

no·where /'nō,(h)we(ə)r/ ▶ **adverb** not anywhere. ▶ **pronoun** no place.
– PHRASES **from** (or **out of**) **nowhere** appearing or happening suddenly and unexpectedly. **get** (or **go**) **nowhere** make no progress. **nowhere near** not nearly.

no-win ▶ **adjective** (of a situation) in which success or a favorable outcome is impossible.

nox·ious /'näksнəs/ ▶ **adjective** harmful, poisonous, or very unpleasant.

– SYNONYMS **poisonous,** toxic, deadly, harmful, dangerous, unhealthy, unpleasant.
– ANTONYMS innocuous.

– ORIGIN from Latin *noxa* 'harm.'

noz·zle /'näzəl/ ▶ **noun** a spout used to control a jet of liquid or gas.
– ORIGIN from **NOSE**.

Np ▶ **symbol** the chemical element neptunium.

NRA ▶ **abbreviation** National Rifle Association.

NRC ▶ **abbreviation 1** National Research Council. **2** National Response Center. **3** Nuclear Regulatory Commission.

NS ▶ **abbreviation 1** (in calculating dates) New Style. **2** Nova Scotia.

ns ▶ **abbreviation** nanosecond.

n/s ▶ **abbreviation** (in personal advertisements) nonsmoker; nonsmoking.

NSU ▶ **abbreviation** Medicine nonspecific urethritis.

NSW ▶ **abbreviation** New South Wales.

NT ▶ **abbreviation 1** National Trust. **2** New Testament. **3** Northern Territory. **4** Northwest Territories.

-n't ▶ **contraction** not, used with auxiliary verbs (e.g., *can't*).

nth /enтн/ ▶ **adjective 1** referring to the last or latest item in a long series. **2** Mathematics referring to an unspecified term in a series.
– PHRASES **to the nth degree** to the utmost.

nu·ance /'n(y)o͞o,äns/ ▶ **noun** a subtle difference in meaning, expression, sound, etc.: *the nuances of facial expression.*

– SYNONYMS **distinction,** shade, gradation, refinement, degree, subtlety, nicety.

▶ **verb** (often as adj. **nuanced**) give subtle differences to: *an intricate and nuanced portrait.*
– ORIGIN French.

nub /nəb/ ▶ **noun 1** (**the nub**) the central point of a matter. **2** a small lump.
– DERIVATIVES **nub·by** adjective.
– ORIGIN probably from German *knubbe, knobbe* 'knob.'

Nu·bi·an /'n(y)o͞obēən/ ▶ **adjective** relating to Nubia, an ancient region corresponding to southern Egypt and northern Sudan. ▶ **noun 1** a person from Nubia. **2** the language of the Nubians.

nu·bile /'n(y)o͞o,bīl, -bəl/ ▶ **adjective** (of a girl or young woman) sexually attractive.
– DERIVATIVES **nu·bil·i·ty** /n(y)o͞o'bilitē/ noun.
– ORIGIN from Latin *nubilis* 'fit for marriage.'

nu·buck /'n(y)o͞o,bək/ ▶ **noun** leather that has been rubbed on the flesh side of the skin to give a suedelike effect.

nu·cle·ar /'n(y)o͞oklēər, -kli(ə)r/ ▶ **adjective 1** relating to the nucleus of an atom or cell. **2** using energy released in the fission (splitting) or fusion of atomic nuclei. **3** referring to or involving nuclear weapons.

nu·cle·ar fam·i·ly ▶ **noun** a couple and their children, regarded as a basic unit of society.

nu·cle·ar fuel ▶ **noun** a substance that will undergo nuclear fission (splitting) and can be used as a source of nuclear energy.

nu·cle·ar med·i·cine ▶ **noun** the branch of medicine that deals with the use of radioactive substances in research, diagnosis, and treatment.

nu·cle·ar op·tion ▶ **noun** the most drastic or extreme response possible.

nu·cle·ar phys·ics ▶ **plural noun** (treated as sing.) the science of atomic nuclei and the way in which they interact.

nu·cle·ar pow·er ▶ **noun** power generated by a nuclear reactor.

nu·cle·ar waste ▶ **noun** radioactive waste material, especially from the use or reprocessing of nuclear fuel.

nu·cle·ar win·ter ▶ **noun** a period of abnormal cold and darkness predicted to follow a nuclear war, caused by smoke and dust blocking the sun's rays.

nu·cle·ate ▶ **verb** /'n(y)o͞oklē,āt/ (usu. as adj. **nucleated**) form a nucleus. ▶ **adjective** /'n(y)o͞oklēət, -,āt/ chiefly Biology having a nucleus.
– DERIVATIVES **nu·cle·a·tion** /,n(y)o͞oklē'āsнən/ noun.

nu·cle·i /'n(y)o͞oklē,ī/ plural of **NUCLEUS**.

nu·cle·ic ac·id /n(y)o͞o'klē-ik/ ▶ **noun** a complex organic substance, especially DNA or RNA, that is present in all living cells.

nu·cle·on /'n(y)o͞oklē,än/ ▶ **noun** a proton or neutron (type of subatomic particle).

nu·cle·o·tide /'n(y)o͞oklēə,tīd/ ▶ **noun** a compound forming the basic structural unit of nucleic acids.

nu·cle·us /'n(y)o͞oklēəs/ ▶ **noun** (pl. **nuclei** /-klē,ī/) **1** the central and most important part of an object or group: *the family is the nucleus of Islamic society.* **2** Physics the positively charged central core of an atom, containing nearly all its mass. **3** Biology a structure present in most cells, containing the genetic material.

– SYNONYMS **core,** center, heart, kernel, nub, hub, middle, focus.

– ORIGIN Latin, 'kernel, inner part.'

nude /n(y)o͞od/ ▸ **adjective** wearing no clothes.

– SYNONYMS **naked,** stark naked, bare, unclothed, undressed, stripped; informal without a stitch on, in one's birthday suit, in the raw/buff, in the altogether, buck naked.
– ANTONYMS dressed.

▸ **noun** a painting, sculpture, or photograph of a naked human figure.
– DERIVATIVES **nu·di·ty** /'n(y)o͞odətē/ noun.
– ORIGIN Latin *nudus* 'plain, explicit.'

CHOOSE THE RIGHT WORD

See **NAKED**.

nudge /nəj/ ▸ **verb 1** prod someone with one's elbow to attract their attention. **2** touch or push something gently. **3** gently encourage someone to do something.

– SYNONYMS **prod,** elbow, dig, poke, jab, jog, push, touch.

▸ **noun** a light touch or push.

– SYNONYMS **prod,** dig (in the ribs), poke, jab, push.

– ORIGIN unknown.

nud·ist /'n(y)o͞odist/ ▸ **noun** a person who goes naked wherever possible.
– DERIVATIVES **nud·ism** /-ˌdizəm/ noun.

nu·ga·to·ry /'n(y)o͞ogəˌtôrē/ ▸ **adjective** formal having no purpose or value.
– ORIGIN Latin *nugatorius.*

nug·get /'nəgət/ ▸ **noun 1** a small lump of gold or other precious metal found in the earth. **2** a small but valuable fact. **3** a small piece of food, typically battered and fried.
– ORIGIN unknown.

nui·sance /'n(y)o͞osəns/ ▸ **noun** a cause of inconvenience or annoyance.

– SYNONYMS **annoyance,** inconvenience, bore, bother, irritation, trial, burden, pest; informal pain (in the neck), hassle, bind, drag, headache.

– ORIGIN Old French, 'hurt.'

nuke /n(y)o͞ok/ informal ▸ **noun** a nuclear weapon. ▸ **verb** attack or destroy something with nuclear weapons.

null /nəl/ ▸ **adjective 1** (in phrase **null and void**) having no legal force; invalid. **2** Mathematics having or associated with the value zero.
– ORIGIN Latin *nullus* 'none.'

nul·li·fy /'nələˌfī/ ▸ **verb** (**nullifies, nullifying, nullified**) **1** make something legally invalid. **2** cancel out the effect of something.

– SYNONYMS **annul,** render null and void, invalidate, repeal, reverse, rescind, revoke, cancel, neutralize, negate, counteract.

– DERIVATIVES **nul·li·fi·ca·tion** /ˌnələfə'kāsʜən/ noun.

nul·li·ty /'nəlitē/ ▸ **noun** (pl. **nullities**) **1** the state of being legally invalid. **2** an unimportant or worthless thing.

numb /nəm/ ▸ **adjective 1** (of a part of the body) having no sensation. **2** lacking the power to feel, think, or react: *the tragic events left us shocked and numb.*

– SYNONYMS **1 without feeling,** without sensation, dead, numbed, desensitized, frozen, anesthetized, insensible, insensate. **2 dazed,** stunned, stupefied, paralyzed, immobilized.

▸ **verb** make someone or something numb.

– SYNONYMS **1 deaden,** desensitize, anesthetize, immobilize, freeze. **2 daze,** stun, stupefy, paralyze, immobilize.

– DERIVATIVES **numb·ly** adverb **numb·ness** noun.
– ORIGIN from Germanic.

num·ber /'nəmbər/ ▸ **noun 1** a quantity or value expressed by a word, symbol, or figure. **2** a quantity or amount: *the exhibition attracted vast numbers of visitors.* **3** (**a number of**) several. **4** a song, dance, or other piece of music. **5** informal an item of clothing regarded with approval: *a little black number.* **6** a grammatical classification of words that depends on whether one or more people or things are being referred to.

– SYNONYMS **1 numeral,** integer, figure, digit, character. **2 quantity,** total, aggregate, tally, quota. **3 song,** piece, tune, track, dance.

▸ **verb 1** amount to a specified figure or quantity. **2** give a number to each thing in a series. **3** count things or people. **4** include as a member of a group: *she wanted to be numbered among the more fashionable novelists.*

– SYNONYMS **1 add up to,** amount to, total, come to. **2 include,** count, reckon, deem.

– PHRASES **by the numbers** following standard operating procedure. **have someone's number** informal understand a person's real motives or character. **someone's days are numbered** someone will not survive for much longer. **someone's number is up** informal someone is finished or certain to die. **without number** too many to count.
– ORIGIN Latin *numerus.*

WORD LINKS

numerical *relating to numbers*

num·ber crunch·er ▸ **noun** informal **1** a computer or program for performing complicated calculations. **2** often derogatory an accountant, statistician, or other person whose job involves dealing with large amounts of numerical data.

num·ber·less /'nəmbərləs/ ▸ **adjective** too many to be counted; innumerable.

num·ber one ▸ **noun 1** the most important person or thing in a particular area or activity. **2** informal oneself. ▸ **adjective** most important; top: *a number-one priority.*

numb·skull /'nəmˌskəl/ (also **numskull**) ▸ **noun** informal a stupid or foolish person.

nu·mer·al /'n(y)o͞om(ə)rəl/ ▸ **noun** a figure or symbol representing a number.

nu·mer·ate /'n(y)o͞om(ə)rət/ ▸ **adjective** having a good basic knowledge of arithmetic.
– DERIVATIVES **nu·mer·a·cy** /'n(y)o͞om(ə)rəsē/ noun.
– ORIGIN from Latin *numerus* 'a number.'

nu·mer·a·tion /ˌn(y)o͞omə'rāsʜən/ ▸ **noun** the action of calculating or giving a number to something.

nu·mer·a·tor /'n(y)o͞oməˌrātər/ ▸ **noun** Mathematics the number above the line in a fraction.

nu·mer·i·cal /n(y)o͞o'merikəl/ ▸ **adjective** relating to or expressed as a number or numbers.
– DERIVATIVES **nu·mer·ic** adjective **nu·mer·i·cal·ly** adverb.

nu·mer·ol·o·gy /ˌn(y)o͞omə'räləjē/ ▸ **noun** the study of the supposed magical power of numbers.
– DERIVATIVES **nu·mer·o·log·i·cal** /-rə'läjikəl/ adjective **nu·mer·ol·o·gist** /-jist/ noun.

nu·me·ro u·no /ˈn(y)o͞omərō ˈo͞onō/ ▶ **noun** (pl. **unos**) informal the best or most important person or thing, especially oneself.
– ORIGIN Italian, literally 'number one.'

nu·mer·ous /ˈn(y)o͞om(ə)rəs/ ▶ **adjective** **1** great in number; many. **2** consisting of many members.

– SYNONYMS **many,** a number of, a lot of, lots of, several, plenty of, countless, copious, an abundance of, frequent; informal umpteen.
– ANTONYMS few.

– DERIVATIVES **nu·mer·ous·ly** adverb.

nu·mi·nous /ˈn(y)o͞omənəs/ ▶ **adjective** having a strong religious or spiritual quality.
– ORIGIN from Latin *numen*.

nu·mis·mat·ics /ˌn(y)o͞oməzˈmatiks, -məs-/ ▶ **plural noun** (usu. treated as sing.) the study or collection of coins, paper currency, and medals.
– DERIVATIVES **nu·mis·mat·ic** adjective **nu·mis·ma·tist** /n(y)o͞oˈmizmətist, -ˈmis-/ noun.

num·skull ▶ **noun** variant spelling of **NUMBSKULL**.

nun /nən/ ▶ **noun** a member of a female religious community, typically one who has taken vows of poverty, chastity, and obedience.
– ORIGIN Latin *nonna*.

nun·ci·o /ˈnənsēˌō, ˈno͝on-/ ▶ **noun** (pl. **nuncios**) (in the Roman Catholic Church) an official representative of the pope in a foreign country.
– ORIGIN Latin *nuntius* 'messenger.'

nun·ner·y /ˈnən(ə)rē/ ▶ **noun** (pl. **nunneries**) a convent.

nup·tial /ˈnəpsHəl, -cHəl/ ▶ **adjective** relating to marriage or weddings. ▶ **noun** (**nuptials**) a wedding.
– ORIGIN from Latin *nuptiae* 'wedding.'

nurse /nərs/ ▶ **noun** **1** a person trained to care for sick or injured people. **2** dated a person employed to look after young children. ▶ **verb** **1** give medical and other care to a sick or injured person. **2** treat or hold carefully or protectively: *he nursed his small case on his lap*. **3** cling to a belief or feeling for a long time: *she nursed the hope that their relationship would improve*. **4** feed a baby at the breast.

– SYNONYMS **1 care for,** take care of, look after, tend, minister to. **2** *they nursed old grievances* **harbor,** foster, bear, have, hold (on to), retain.

– DERIVATIVES **nurs·ing** noun.
– ORIGIN Old French *nourice*, from Latin *nutrire* 'nourish.'

nurse·maid /ˈnərsˌmād/ ▶ **noun** dated a woman or girl employed to look after a young child or children.

nurse prac·ti·tion·er ▶ **noun** a registered nurse who is trained to treat minor ailments and perform many tasks ordinarily performed by a doctor.

nurs·er·y /ˈnərs(ə)rē/ ▶ **noun** (pl. **nurseries**) **1** a room in a house in which young children sleep or play. **2** a place where young children are cared for during the working day. **3** a place where young plants and trees are grown for sale or for planting elsewhere.

nurs·er·y·man /ˈnərs(ə)rēmən/ ▶ **noun** (pl. **nurserymen**) a person who works in or owns a plant or tree nursery.

nurs·er·y rhyme ▶ **noun** a simple traditional song or poem for children.

nurs·er·y school ▶ **noun** a school for young children, mainly between the ages of three and five.

nurs·ing home ▶ **noun** a small private institution providing accommodations and health care for elderly people.

nurs·ling /ˈnərsliNG/ ▶ **noun** dated a baby that is being breastfed.

nur·ture /ˈnərCHər/ ▶ **verb** **1** care for and protect someone or something while they are growing and developing. **2** have a long-standing hope, belief, or ambition.

– SYNONYMS **1 bring up,** care for, take care of, look after, tend, rear, raise. **2** *he nurtured my love of art* **encourage,** promote, stimulate, develop, foster, cultivate, boost, strengthen, fuel.
– ANTONYMS neglect.

▶ **noun** **1** the action of nurturing someone or something. **2** upbringing, education, and environment as a factor determining someone's personality. Often contrasted with **NATURE**.
– ORIGIN Old French *noureture* 'nourishment,' from Latin *nutrire* 'nourish, cherish.'

nut /nət/ ▶ **noun** **1** a fruit consisting of a hard shell around an edible kernel. **2** the hard kernel of such a fruit. **3** a small flat piece of metal or other material, typically square or hexagonal, with a threaded hole through the center for screwing onto a bolt. **4** informal a crazy or eccentric person. **5** informal a person who is extremely interested in or enthusiastic about something: *a football nut*. **6** informal a person's head. **7** a small lump of something hard or solid, especially coal. **8** (**nuts**) vulgar slang a man's testicles.

– SYNONYMS **1 maniac,** lunatic, madman, madwoman; informal loony, nutcase, head case, screwball. **2 enthusiast,** fan, devotee, aficionado; informal freak, fanatic, addict, buff.

– DERIVATIVES **nut·ty** adjective.
– PHRASES **nuts and bolts** informal the basic practical details of a subject or activity. **a tough** (or **hard**) **nut to crack** informal a difficult problem or an opponent that is hard to overcome.
– ORIGIN Old English.

nut·case /ˈnətˌkās/ ▶ **noun** informal a mad or foolish person.

nut·crack·er /ˈnətˌkrakər/ ▶ **noun** a device for cracking the shells of nuts.

nut·hatch /ˈnətˌhaCH/ ▶ **noun** a small gray-backed songbird that climbs down tree trunks head first.
– ORIGIN from a former word related to **HACK**[1], from the bird's habit of hacking at nuts with its beak.

nut·meg /ˈnətˌmeg/ ▶ **noun** a spice made from the seed of a tropical tree.
– ORIGIN partial translation of Old French *nois muguede* 'musky nut.'

nu·tra·ceu·ti·cal /ˌn(y)o͞otrəˈso͞otikəl/ ▶ **noun** a food containing health-giving additives.

nu·tri·a /ˈn(y)o͞otrēə/ ▶ **noun** the skin or fur of the coypu, a large rodent.
– ORIGIN Spanish, 'otter.'

nu·tri·ent /ˈn(y)o͞otrēənt/ ▶ **noun** a substance that provides nourishment essential for life, growth, and health.
– ORIGIN from Latin *nutrire* 'nourish.'

nu·tri·ment /ˈn(y)o͞otrəmənt/ ▶ **noun** the food or other substances necessary for growth and health.

nu·tri·tion /n(y)o͞oˈtrisHən/ ▶ **noun** **1** the process of taking in and absorbing nutrients. **2** the branch of

science concerned with this process.
– DERIVATIVES **nu·tri·tion·al** adjective **nu·tri·tion·ist** noun.
– ORIGIN Latin, from *nutrire* 'nourish.'

nu·tri·tious /n(y)o͞oˈtrisHəs/ ▶ **adjective** (of food) full of nutrients and so helping the body to grow or stay healthy.

– SYNONYMS **nourishing,** nutritive, wholesome, good for you, healthy, health-giving, beneficial.

– DERIVATIVES **nu·tri·tious·ly** adverb.

nu·tri·tive /ˈn(y)o͞otrətiv/ ▶ **adjective 1** relating to nutrition. **2** nutritious.

nuts /nəts/ ▶ **adjective** informal insane.

nut·shell /ˈnətˌsHel/ ▶ **noun** (in phrase **in a nutshell**) in the fewest possible words.

nux vom·i·ca /ˈnəks ˈvämikə/ ▶ **noun** a southern Asian tree with berrylike fruit and toxic seeds that contain strychnine.
– ORIGIN Latin, 'nut causing vomiting.'

nuz·zle /ˈnəzəl/ ▶ **verb** rub or push against gently with the nose and mouth: *the foal nuzzled at its mother*.
– ORIGIN from **NOSE**.

NV ▶ **abbreviation** Nevada.

NW ▶ **abbreviation 1** northwest. **2** northwestern.

N-word ▶ **noun** euphemistic the word 'nigger.'

NY ▶ **abbreviation** New York.

NYC ▶ **abbreviation** New York City.

ny·lon /ˈnīˌlän/ ▶ **noun 1** a tough, lightweight synthetic material that can be made into fabric, yarn, and many other products. **2** (**nylons**) nylon stockings or tights.
– ORIGIN an invented word.

nymph /nimf/ ▶ **noun 1** (in Greek and Roman mythology) a spirit of nature in the form of a beautiful young woman. **2** literary a beautiful young woman. **3** an immature form of an insect such as a dragonfly.
– DERIVATIVES **nymph·al** adjective.
– ORIGIN Greek *numphē* 'nymph, bride.'

nymph·et /nimˈfet, ˈnimfit/ ▶ **noun** an attractive and sexually mature young girl.

nym·pho /ˈnimˈfō/ ▶ **noun** (pl. **nymphos**) informal a nymphomaniac.

nym·pho·ma·ni·a /ˌnimfəˈmānēə/ ▶ **noun** uncontrollable or abnormally strong sexual desire in a woman.
– DERIVATIVES **nym·pho·ma·ni·ac** /-ˈmānēˌak/ noun.

NYSE ▶ **abbreviation** New York Stock Exchange.

nys·tag·mus /nəˈstagməs/ ▶ **noun** rapid involuntary movements of the eyes.
– ORIGIN Greek *nustagmos* 'nodding, drowsiness.'

NZ ▶ **abbreviation** New Zealand.

O¹ (also **o**) ▶ **noun** (pl. **Os** or **O's**) **1** the fifteenth letter of the alphabet. **2** (also **oh**) zero.

O² ▶ **symbol** the chemical element oxygen.

O³ /ō/ ▶ **exclamation 1** old-fashioned spelling of **OH**¹. **2** old use used before a name when addressing someone, as in a prayer or poem: *give peace in our time, O Lord.*

o' /ə, ō/ ▶ **preposition** short for **OF**, used to represent an informal pronunciation: *a cup o' coffee.*

oaf /ōf/ ▶ **noun** a stupid, rude, or clumsy man.
– DERIVATIVES **oaf·ish** adjective.
– ORIGIN from Old Norse, 'elf.'

oak /ōk/ ▶ **noun 1** a large tree that produces acorns and a hard wood used for building and furniture. **2** a smoky flavor characteristic of wine that has been aged in oak barrels.
– DERIVATIVES **oak·en** adjective (old use) **oak·y** adjective.
– ORIGIN Old English.

oak ap·ple ▶ **noun** a spongy growth that forms on oak trees, caused by wasp larvae.

oa·kum /ˈōkəm/ ▶ **noun** chiefly historical loose fiber obtained by untwisting old rope, used especially to fill in cracks in wooden ships.
– ORIGIN Old English, 'off-combings.'

oar /ôr/ ▶ **noun** a pole with a flat blade, used for rowing or steering a boat.
– PHRASES **put in one's oar** informal, chiefly Brit. give an opinion without being asked.
– ORIGIN Old English.

oar·lock /ˈôrˌläk/ ▶ **noun** a fitting on the side of a boat for holding an oar.

oars·man /ˈôrzmən/ (or **oarswoman**) ▶ **noun** (pl. **oarsmen** or **oarswomen**) a rower.

OAS ▶ **abbreviation** Organization of American States.

o·a·sis /ōˈāsis/ ▶ **noun** (pl. **oases** /ōˈāsēz/) **1** a fertile place in a desert where water rises to ground level. **2** a calm and pleasant area or period in the midst of a difficult or hectic place or situation.
– ORIGIN Greek.

oat /ōt/ ▶ **noun 1** a cereal plant grown in cool climates. **2** (**oats**) the edible grain of this plant.
– DERIVATIVES **oat·y** adjective.
– PHRASES **sow one's wild oats** (especially of a young man) have many casual sexual relationships while young.
– ORIGIN Old English.

oath /ōTH/ ▶ **noun** (pl. **oaths**) **1** a solemn promise about one's future actions or behavior. **2** a sworn declaration, such as the promise to tell the truth, made in a court of law. **3** a swear word.

> – SYNONYMS **1 vow,** pledge, promise, affirmation, word (of honor), guarantee. **2 swear word,** expletive, profanity, four-letter word, dirty word, obscenity, curse; formal imprecation.

– PHRASES **under oath** having sworn to tell the truth, especially in a court of law.
– ORIGIN Old English.

oat·meal /ˈōtˌmēl/ ▶ **noun 1** meal made from ground oats, used in breakfast cereals or other food. **2** a dish of this meal cooked with milk or water.

ob·bli·ga·to /ˌäbləˈgätō/ (also **obligato**) ▶ **noun** (pl. **obbligatos** or **obbligati** /-ˈgätē/) an accompanying instrumental part that is necessary to a piece of music and must not be left out of a performance.
– ORIGIN from Italian, 'obligatory.'

ob·du·rate /ˈäbd(y)ərit/ ▶ **adjective** stubbornly refusing to change one's mind.
– DERIVATIVES **ob·du·ra·cy** /-rəsē/ noun **ob·du·rate·ly** adverb.
– ORIGIN Latin *obduratus.*

> **CHOOSE THE RIGHT WORD**
>
> See **STUBBORN**.

o·be·ah /ˈōbēə/ ▶ **noun** a kind of magic or witchcraft practiced especially in the Caribbean.
– ORIGIN from an African language.

o·be·di·ent /ōˈbēdēənt/ ▶ **adjective** willing to do what one is told.

> – SYNONYMS **compliant,** biddable, acquiescent, good, law-abiding, deferential, governable, docile, submissive.
> – ANTONYMS rebellious.

– DERIVATIVES **o·be·di·ence** noun **o·be·di·ent·ly** adverb.
– ORIGIN from Latin *oboedire* 'obey.'

o·bei·sance /ōˈbāsəns, ōˈbē-/ ▶ **noun 1** deferential respect for someone. **2** a gesture expressing this, such as a bow.
– ORIGIN Old French *obeissance.*

> **CHOOSE THE RIGHT WORD**
>
> See **HONOR**.

ob·e·lisk /ˈäbəˌlisk/ ▶ **noun** a four-sided stone pillar that tapers to a point, set up as a monument or landmark.
– ORIGIN Greek *obeliskos* 'small pointed pillar.'

ob·e·lus /ˈäbələs/ ▶ **noun** (pl. **obeli** /-ˌlī/) a symbol (†) used in printed material as a reference mark or to indicate that a person is dead.
– ORIGIN Greek *obelos* 'pointed pillar,' also 'critical mark.'

o·bese /ōˈbēs/ ▶ **adjective** very fat.

> – SYNONYMS **fat,** overweight, corpulent, gross, stout, fleshy, heavy, portly, potbellied, bloated, flabby; informal porky, roly-poly, blubbery.
> – ANTONYMS thin.

– DERIVATIVES **o·be·si·ty** noun.
– ORIGIN Latin *obesus.*

o·bey /ō'bā/ ▶ **verb 1** do what one is told to do. **2** carry out an order. **3** behave in accordance with a general principle or natural law.

– SYNONYMS **1 do as one is told,** defer to, submit to, bow to. **2** *he refused to obey the order* **carry out,** perform, act on, execute, discharge, implement. **3** *rules have to be obeyed* **comply with,** adhere to, observe, abide by, act in accordance with, conform to, respect, follow, keep to, stick to.
– ANTONYMS defy, ignore.

– ORIGIN Old French *obeir.*

ob·fus·cate /'äbfə,skāt/ ▶ **verb** make something hard to understand.
– DERIVATIVES **ob·fus·ca·tion** /,äbfə'skāsʜən/ noun **ob·fus·ca·to·ry** /äb'fəskə,tôrē/ adjective.
– ORIGIN Latin *obfuscare* 'darken.'

o·bi /'ōbē/ ▶ **noun** (pl. **obis**) a broad sash worn around the waist of a Japanese kimono.
– ORIGIN Japanese, 'belt.'

o·bit /'ōbit, ō'bit/ ▶ **noun** informal an obituary.

ob·i·ter dic·tum /'ōbitər 'diktəm/ ▶ **noun** (pl. **dicta** /'diktə/) Law a judge's incidental expression of opinion.
– ORIGIN Latin *obiter* 'in passing' + *dictum* 'something that is said.'

o·bit·u·ar·y /ō'bicʜo͞o,erē/ ▶ **noun** (pl. **obituaries**) a short biography of a person, published in a newspaper soon after their death.
– ORIGIN Latin *obitus* 'death.'

ob·ject ▶ **noun** /'äbjəkt/ **1** a physical thing that can be seen and touched. **2** a person or thing to which an action or feeling is directed: *he hated being the object of public attention.* **3** a goal or purpose: *the object of the exercise was to shock the audience.* **4** Grammar a noun acted on by a transitive verb or by a preposition.

– SYNONYMS **1 thing,** article, item, entity, device, gadget. **2 target,** butt, focus, recipient, victim. **3 objective,** aim, goal, target, purpose, end, plan, point, ambition, intention, idea.

▶ **verb** /əb'jekt/ express disapproval or opposition: *residents objected to the noise.*

– SYNONYMS *they* ***objected to*** *the scheme* **protest about,** oppose, take exception to, take issue with, take a stand against, argue against, quarrel with, condemn, draw the line at, demur at, mind, complain about.
– ANTONYMS approve of, accept.

– DERIVATIVES **ob·jec·tor** /əb'jektər/ noun.
– PHRASES **no object** not influencing or restricting choices or decisions: *money is no object.*
– ORIGIN Latin *objectum* 'thing presented to the mind.'

ob·jec·ti·fy /əb'jektə,fī/ ▶ **verb** (**objectifies, objectifying, objectified**) **1** express something abstract in a concrete form: *good poetry objectifies feeling.* **2** treat someone merely as an object rather than a person.
– DERIVATIVES **ob·jec·ti·fi·ca·tion** /əb,jektəfi'kāsʜən/ noun.

ob·jec·tion /əb'jeksʜən/ ▶ **noun** an expression of disapproval or opposition.

– SYNONYMS **protest,** protestation, complaint, opposition, demurral, counterargument, disagreement, disapproval, dissent.

ob·jec·tion·a·ble /əb'jeksʜənəbəl/ ▶ **adjective** unpleasant or offensive.

ob·jec·tive /əb'jektiv/ ▶ **adjective 1** not influenced by personal feelings or opinions: *historians try to be objective.* **2** having actual existence outside the mind: *a matter of objective fact.* **3** Grammar relating to a case of nouns and pronouns used for the object of a transitive verb or a preposition.

– SYNONYMS **1 impartial,** unbiased, unprejudiced, nonpartisan, disinterested, neutral, uninvolved, even-handed, fair, dispassionate, detached. **2 factual,** actual, real, empirical, verifiable.
– ANTONYMS subjective, emotional.

▶ **noun 1** a goal or aim: *his main objective was to combat inflation.* **2** (also **objective lens**) the lens in a telescope or microscope nearest to the object observed.

– SYNONYMS **aim,** intention, purpose, target, goal, object, end, idea, plan, ambition.

– DERIVATIVES **ob·jec·tiv·i·ty** /,äbjek'tivitē/ noun.

ob·jec·tive·ly /əb'jektivlē/ ▶ **adverb** in an objective way.

– SYNONYMS *encourage people to look at the information objectively and see how it will affect them* **impartially,** without bias/prejudice, even-handedly, fairly, dispassionately, with an open mind, without fear or favor.

ob·ject les·son ▶ **noun** a striking practical example of what should or should not be done in a particular situation: *they responded to emergencies in a way that was an object lesson to us all.*

ob·jet d'art /,ôbzʜä 'där/ ▶ **noun** (pl. **objets d'art** pronunc. same) a small decorative or artistic object.
– ORIGIN French, 'object of art.'

ob·late /'äb,lāt, ,ō'blāt/ ▶ **adjective** Geometry (of a sphere-shaped body) flattened at each pole.
– ORIGIN Latin *oblatus* 'carried inversely.'

ob·la·tion /ə'blāsʜən/ ▶ **noun 1** a thing presented or offered to a god. **2** Christian Church the presentation of bread and wine to God in the service of Holy Communion.
– ORIGIN Latin.

ob·li·gate /'äbli,gāt/ ▶ **verb** (**be obligated**) have a moral or legal duty to do something: *the hospital is obligated to provide health care.*
– ORIGIN Latin *obligare.*

ob·li·ga·tion /,äbli'gāsʜən/ ▶ **noun 1** something a person must do because it is morally right or legally necessary; a duty or commitment: *I have an obligation to look after her.* **2** the state of having to do something because it is morally right or legally necessary: *they are under no obligation to stick to the scheme.* **3** a feeling of gratitude for a service or favor.

– SYNONYMS **1 commitment,** duty, responsibility, function, task, job, charge, onus, liability, requirement, debt. **2** *a sense of obligation* **duty,** compulsion, indebtedness, necessity, pressure, constraint.

ob·li·ga·to /,äbli'gätō/ ▶ **noun** variant spelling of **OBBLIGATO**.

o·blig·a·to·ry /ə'bligə,tôrē/ ▶ **adjective** required by a law, rule, or custom; compulsory.

– SYNONYMS **compulsory,** mandatory, prescribed, required, statutory, enforced, binding, requisite, necessary, imperative, de rigueur.
– ANTONYMS optional.

o·blige /ə'blīj/ ▶ **verb 1** compel someone to do something because it is a law, necessity, or duty: *he was obliged to do military service.* **2** do as someone asks in order to help or please them. **3** (**be obliged**) be indebted or grateful.

– SYNONYMS **1 compel,** force, require, make, bind, constrain. **2 do someone a favor,** accommodate, help, assist, indulge, humor. **3** *if anyone could tell me what's wrong with this file, I'd* ***be obliged*** **thankful,** grateful, appreciative, beholden, indebted, in someone's debt.

– ORIGIN Latin *obligare*.

o·blig·ing /ə'blījiNG/ ▶ **adjective** willing to help someone or do as they ask.

– SYNONYMS **helpful,** accommodating, cooperative, agreeable, amenable, generous, kind, decent.

– DERIVATIVES **o·blig·ing·ly** adverb.

o·blique /ə'blēk, ō'blēk/ ▶ **adjective 1** neither parallel nor at right angles; slanting. **2** not explicit or direct: *an oblique reference to the US.* **3** Geometry (of a line, plane figure, or surface) inclined at other than a right angle.

– SYNONYMS **1** *an oblique line* **slanting,** slanted, sloping, at an angle, angled, diagonal, askew, squint. **2** *an oblique reference* **indirect,** roundabout, circuitous, implicit, implied, elliptical, evasive.
– ANTONYMS straight, direct.

▶ **noun** Brit. another term for **SLASH** (sense 3 of the noun).

– SYNONYMS **slash,** solidus, backslash.

– DERIVATIVES **o·blique·ly** adverb **o·blique·ness** noun **o·bliq·ui·ty** /ə'blikwətē/ noun.
– ORIGIN Latin *obliquus*.

ob·lit·er·ate /ə'blitə,rāt/ ▶ **verb 1** destroy something completely. **2** completely cover: *clouds obliterated the moon.*

– SYNONYMS **1 destroy,** wipe out, annihilate, demolish; informal zap. **2 hide,** obscure, blot out, block, cover, screen.

– DERIVATIVES **ob·lit·er·a·tion** /ə,blitə'rāSHən/ noun.
– ORIGIN Latin *obliterare* 'strike out, erase.'

ob·liv·i·on /ə'blivēən/ ▶ **noun 1** the state of being unaware of what is happening around one. **2** the state of being forgotten: *his name will fade into oblivion.* **3** the state of being completely destroyed.
– ORIGIN Latin, from *oblivisci* 'forget.'

ob·liv·i·ous /ə'blivēəs/ ▶ **adjective** not aware of what is happening around one: *he was oblivious to his surroundings.*

– SYNONYMS **unaware,** unconscious, heedless, unmindful, insensible, ignorant, blind, deaf, impervious.
– ANTONYMS conscious.

– DERIVATIVES **ob·liv·i·ous·ly** adverb **ob·liv·i·ous·ness** noun.

ob·long /'äb,lôNG, -,läNG/ ▶ **adjective** having a rectangular shape. ▶ **noun** an oblong object or shape.
– ORIGIN Latin *oblongus* 'longish.'

ob·lo·quy /'äbləkwē/ ▶ **noun 1** strong public criticism. **2** disgrace brought about by strong public criticism.
– ORIGIN from Latin *obloqui* 'speak against.'

ob·nox·ious /əb'näkSHəs/ ▶ **adjective** extremely unpleasant.

– SYNONYMS **unpleasant,** disagreeable, nasty, offensive, objectionable, unsavory, revolting, repulsive, repellent, repugnant, disgusting, odious, vile, foul, loathsome, nauseating, sickening, hateful, insufferable, intolerable; informal horrible, horrid, ghastly, gross, yucky, God-awful.
– ANTONYMS delightful.

– DERIVATIVES **ob·nox·ious·ly** adverb **ob·nox·ious·ness** noun.
– ORIGIN from Latin *obnoxius* 'exposed to harm.'

o·boe /'ōbō/ ▶ **noun** a woodwind instrument of treble pitch, played with a double reed.
– DERIVATIVES **o·bo·ist** noun.
– ORIGIN Italian, or from French *hautbois*, from *haut* 'high' + *bois* 'wood.'

ob·scene /əb'sēn/ ▶ **adjective 1** (of the portrayal or description of sexual matters) offensive or disgusting according to accepted standards of morality or decency. **2** (especially of an amount of money) unacceptably large: *obscene pay increases.*

– SYNONYMS **1 pornographic,** indecent, smutty, dirty, filthy, X-rated, explicit, lewd, rude, vulgar, coarse, scatological; informal blue; euphemistic adult. **2 scandalous,** shocking, outrageous, immoral.

– DERIVATIVES **ob·scene·ly** adverb.
– ORIGIN Latin *obscaenus* 'ill-omened, hateful.'

ob·scen·i·ty /əb'senitē/ ▶ **noun** (pl. **obscenities) 1** obscene language or behavior. **2** an obscene act or word.

ob·scu·rant·ism /əb'skyoo͝rən,tizəm, äb-, ,äbskyə'ran-/ ▶ **noun** the practice of deliberately preventing the facts or full details of something from becoming known or understood.
– DERIVATIVES **ob·scu·rant·ist** noun & adjective.
– ORIGIN from Latin *obscurare* 'make dark.'

ob·scure /əb'skyoo͝r/ ▶ **adjective (obscurer, obscurest) 1** not discovered or known about; uncertain. **2** not well known: *a relatively obscure actor.* **3** not clearly expressed or easily understood: *obscure references to Proust.* **4** hard to see or make out.

– SYNONYMS **1 unclear,** uncertain, unknown, mysterious, hazy, vague, indeterminate. **2 abstruse,** oblique, opaque, cryptic, arcane, enigmatic, puzzling, perplexing, baffling, incomprehensible, impenetrable, elliptical. **3 little known,** unknown, unheard of, unsung, minor, unrecognized, forgotten.
– ANTONYMS clear, plain, famous.

▶ **verb** make something difficult to see or understand.

– SYNONYMS **1 hide,** conceal, cover, veil, shroud, screen, mask, cloak, block, obliterate, eclipse. **2 confuse,** complicate, obfuscate, cloud, blur, muddy.
– ANTONYMS reveal, clarify.

– DERIVATIVES **ob·scu·ra·tion** /,äbskyə'rāSHən/ noun **ob·scure·ly** adverb.
– ORIGIN Latin *obscurus* 'dark.'

ob·scu·ri·ty /əb'skyoo͝ritē/ ▶ **noun** (pl. **obscurities) 1** the state of being unknown or forgotten. **2** the quality of being hard to understand.

ob·se·quies /'äbsəkwēz/ ▶ **plural noun** funeral rites.
– ORIGIN Latin.

ob·se·qui·ous /əb'sēkwēəs/ ▶ **adjective** trying too hard to please someone; excessively obedient or respectful.
– DERIVATIVES **ob·se·qui·ous·ly** adverb **ob·se·qui·ous·ness** noun.
– ORIGIN from Latin *obsequium* 'compliance.'

CHOOSE THE RIGHT WORD

obsequious, servile, slavish, subservient

If you want to get ahead with your boss, you might trying being **obsequious**, which suggests an attitude of inferiority that may or may not be genuine, but that is assumed in order to placate a superior in hopes of getting what one wants (*a "goody two shoes" whose obsequious* behavior made everyone in the class cringe*). While **subservient** may connote similar behavior, it is more often applied to those who are genuinely subordinate or dependent and act accordingly (*a timid, subservient child who was terrified of making a mistake*). **Servile** is a stronger and more negative term, suggesting a cringing submissiveness (*the dog's servile obedience to her master*). **Slavish**, suggesting the status or attitude of a slave, is often used to describe strict adherence to a set of rules or a code of conduct (*a slavish adherence to the rules of etiquette*).

ob·serv·ance /əb'zərvəns/ ▶ **noun 1** the obeying of a law or rule, or the following of a custom. **2** (**observances**) acts performed for religious or ceremonial reasons.

ob·serv·ant /əb'zərvənt/ ▶ **adjective 1** quick to notice things. **2** following the rules of a religion.

– SYNONYMS **alert,** sharp-eyed, eagle-eyed, attentive, watchful; informal beady-eyed, on the ball.
– ANTONYMS inattentive.

ob·ser·va·tion /ˌäbzər'vāsʜən/ ▶ **noun 1** the action of watching someone or something closely: *he was brought into the hospital for observation.* **2** the ability to notice important or significant details: *she was famous for her powers of observation.* **3** a comment based on something one has seen, heard, or noticed.

– SYNONYMS **1 monitoring,** watching, scrutiny, survey, surveillance, attention, study. **2 remark,** comment, opinion, impression, thought, reflection.

– DERIVATIVES **ob·ser·va·tion·al** adjective.

ob·serv·a·to·ry /əb'zərvəˌtôrē/ ▶ **noun** (pl. **observatories**) a building housing a telescope or other scientific equipment for studying natural phenomena such as the stars and the weather.

ob·serve /əb'zərv/ ▶ **verb 1** notice someone or something. **2** watch carefully; monitor: *many patients were observed for long periods.* **3** make a remark. **4** obey a law or rule. **5** celebrate or take part in a festival or ritual.

– SYNONYMS **1 notice,** see, note, perceive, discern, spot. **2 watch,** look at, contemplate, view, survey, regard, keep an eye on, scrutinize, keep under surveillance, monitor; informal keep tabs on. **3 remark,** comment, say, mention, declare, announce, state; formal opine. **4 comply with,** abide by, keep, obey, adhere to, heed, honor, fulfill, respect, follow, consent to, accept.

– DERIVATIVES **ob·serv·a·ble** adjective.
– ORIGIN Latin *observare* 'to watch.'

ob·serv·er /əb'zərvər/ ▶ **noun** a person who watches or notices something.

– SYNONYMS **spectator,** onlooker, watcher, fly on the wall, viewer, witness, eyewitness.

ob·sess /əb'ses/ ▶ **verb 1** preoccupy someone to a troubling extent: *he was obsessed with thoughts of suicide.* **2** be constantly talking or worrying about something.
– ORIGIN Latin *obsidere* 'besiege.'

ob·sessed /əb'sest/ ▶ **adjective** preoccupied with something to a troubling extent.

– SYNONYMS **fixated,** possessed, haunted, consumed, infatuated, besotted; informal smitten, hung up.

ob·ses·sion /əb'sesʜən/ ▶ **noun 1** the state of being obsessed. **2** a person or thing that someone is unable to stop thinking about: *her career had become an obsession.*

– SYNONYMS **fixation,** passion, mania, compulsion, fetish, preoccupation, infatuation, phobia, complex, neurosis; informal bee in one's bonnet, hang-up, thing.

– DERIVATIVES **ob·ses·sion·al** adjective.

ob·ses·sive /əb'sesiv/ ▶ **adjective 1** thinking continually about someone or something: *he was obsessive about cleanliness.* **2** preoccupying a person's mind to a disturbing extent: *obsessive jealousy.*

– SYNONYMS **consuming,** all-consuming, compulsive, controlling, fanatical, neurotic, excessive; informal pathological.

– DERIVATIVES **ob·ses·sive·ly** /-'sesivlē/ adverb **ob·ses·sive·ness** /-'sesivnis/ noun.

ob·ses·sive–com·pul·sive ▶ **adjective** relating to a mental condition in which a person feels compelled to carry out certain actions over and over again.

ob·sid·i·an /əb'sidēən, äb-/ ▶ **noun** a dark glasslike volcanic rock formed when lava solidifies rapidly without crystallizing.
– ORIGIN Latin *obsidianus.*

ob·so·les·cent /ˌäbsə'lesənt/ ▶ **adjective** becoming obsolete.
– DERIVATIVES **ob·so·les·cence** noun.
– ORIGIN from Latin *obsolescere* 'fall into disuse.'

ob·so·lete /ˌäbsə'lēt/ ▶ **adjective** no longer produced or used; out of date.

– SYNONYMS **out of date,** outdated, outmoded, old-fashioned, passé, antiquated, antediluvian, anachronistic, superannuated, archaic, ancient, fossilized, extinct, defunct.
– ANTONYMS current, modern.

– ORIGIN Latin *obsoletus* 'grown old, worn out.'

ob·sta·cle /'äbstəkəl/ ▶ **noun** a thing that blocks one's way or makes it difficult to do or achieve something.

– SYNONYMS **barrier,** hurdle, stumbling block, obstruction, bar, block, impediment, hindrance, snag, catch, drawback, hitch, fly in the ointment, handicap, difficulty, problem, disadvantage.
– ANTONYMS advantage, aid.

– ORIGIN Latin *obstaculum.*

ob·ste·tri·cian /ˌäbstə'trisʜən/ ▶ **noun** a doctor qualified to practice in obstetrics.

ob·stet·rics /əb'stetriks, äb-/ ▶ **plural noun** the branch of medicine and surgery concerned with childbirth.
– DERIVATIVES **ob·stet·ric** adjective.
– ORIGIN from Latin *obstetrix* 'midwife.'

ob·sti·nate /'äbstənit/ ▶ **adjective 1** stubbornly refusing to change one's mind. **2** hard to deal with or overcome: *an obstinate problem.*

– SYNONYMS **stubborn,** pigheaded, mulish, self-willed, unyielding, inflexible, unbending, intransigent, intractable; old use contumacious.
– ANTONYMS compliant.

– DERIVATIVES **ob·sti·na·cy** /-nəsē/ noun **ob·sti·nate·ly** adverb.
– ORIGIN Latin *obstinatus.*

CHOOSE THE RIGHT WORD

See **STUBBORN**.

ob·strep·er·ous /əb'strepərəs, äb-/ ▶ **adjective** noisy and difficult to control.
– DERIVATIVES **ob·strep·er·ous·ly** adverb

ob·strep·er·ous·ness noun.
– ORIGIN from Latin *obstrepere* 'clamor against.'

ob·struct /əb'strəkt, äb-/ ▶ verb **1** be in the way of; block: *she was obstructing the entrance.* **2** make it difficult to achieve something: *they promised not to obstruct the peace process.*

> – SYNONYMS **1 block (up),** clog (up), cut off, choke, dam up; technical occlude. **2 impede,** hinder, interfere with, hamper, block, interrupt, hold up, stand in the way of, frustrate, slow down, delay, bring to a standstill, stop, halt.
> – ANTONYMS clear, facilitate.

– DERIVATIVES **ob·struc·tor** noun.
– ORIGIN Latin *obstruere.*

ob·struc·tion /əb'strəkshən, äb-/ ▶ noun **1** an obstacle or blockage. **2** the action of obstructing someone or something.

> – SYNONYMS **obstacle,** barrier, stumbling block, impediment, hindrance, difficulty, check, restriction, blockage, stoppage, congestion, bottleneck, holdup.

ob·struc·tion·ism /əb'strəkshə͵nizəm, äb-/ ▶ noun the practice of deliberately blocking or delaying the progress of lawmaking or other procedures.
– DERIVATIVES **ob·struc·tion·ist** noun & adjective.

ob·struc·tive /əb'strəktiv, äb-/ ▶ adjective deliberately causing difficulties or delays.

ob·tain /əb'tān, äb-/ ▶ verb **1** come into possession of; get. **2** formal be established or usual: *the standards that obtain in this school.*

> – SYNONYMS **get,** acquire, come by, secure, procure, pick up, gain, earn, achieve, attain; informal get (a) hold of, lay one's hands on, land.

– ORIGIN Latin *obtinere.*

> **CHOOSE THE RIGHT WORD**
>
> See **GET**.

ob·tain·a·ble /əb'tānəbəl, äb-/ ▶ adjective able to be obtained.

> – SYNONYMS **available,** to be had, in circulation, on the market, on offer, in season, at one's disposal, accessible; informal up for grabs, on tap.

ob·trude /əb'tro͞od/ ▶ verb **1** become obtrusive. **2** impose or force something on someone.
– ORIGIN Latin *obtrudere.*

ob·tru·sive /əb'tro͞osiv, äb-/ ▶ adjective noticeable in an unwelcome or unpleasant way.
– DERIVATIVES **ob·tru·sive·ly** adverb **ob·tru·sive·ness** noun.

ob·tuse /əb't(y)o͞os, äb-/ ▶ adjective **1** annoyingly insensitive or slow to understand. **2** (of an angle) more than 90° and less than 180°. **3** not sharp or pointed; blunt.

> – SYNONYMS **stupid,** foolish, slow-witted, slow, unintelligent, simple-minded; informal **dim,** dimwitted, dense, dumb, slow on the uptake, halfwitted, brain-dead, moronic, cretinous, thick.
> – ANTONYMS clever.

– DERIVATIVES **ob·tuse·ly** adverb **ob·tuse·ness** noun.
– ORIGIN Latin *obtusus.*

> **CHOOSE THE RIGHT WORD**
>
> See **STUPID**.

ob·verse /'äb͵vərs/ ▶ noun **1** the side of a coin or medal with the head or main design. **2** the opposite or counterpart of a fact or truth.
– ORIGIN Latin *obversus* 'turned toward.'

ob·vi·ate /'äbvē͵āt/ ▶ verb remove or prevent a need or difficulty.
– ORIGIN Latin *obviare.*

ob·vi·ous /'äbvēəs/ ▶ adjective easily seen or understood; clear.

> – SYNONYMS **clear,** plain, evident, apparent, patent, manifest, conspicuous, pronounced, prominent, distinct, noticeable, unmistakable, perceptible, visible, palpable; informal sticking out like a sore thumb.
> – ANTONYMS imperceptible.

– DERIVATIVES **ob·vi·ous·ly** adverb **ob·vi·ous·ness** noun.
– ORIGIN from Latin *ob viam* 'in the way.'

oc·a·ri·na /͵äkə'rēnə/ ▶ noun a small egg-shaped wind instrument with holes for the fingers.
– ORIGIN Italian, 'little goose' (referring to its shape).

Oc·cam's ra·zor /'äkəmz/ (also **Ockham's razor**) ▶ noun the principle that in explaining something no more assumptions should be made than are necessary.
– ORIGIN named after the English philosopher William of *Occam.*

oc·ca·sion /ə'kāzhən/ ▶ noun **1** a particular event, or the time at which it takes place. **2** a special event or celebration. **3** a suitable time for doing something: *this is not the occasion for a detailed analysis of the proposals.* **4** formal reason or justification: *we have occasion to rejoice.*

> – SYNONYMS **1 time,** instance, juncture, point, moment, experience, case. **2 event,** affair, function, celebration, party, get-together, gathering; informal do, bash.

▶ verb formal cause something.

> – SYNONYMS **cause,** give rise to, bring about, result in, lead to, prompt, create, engender.

– PHRASES **on occasion** from time to time. **rise to the occasion** perform well in response to a special situation.
– ORIGIN Latin, 'juncture, reason.'

oc·ca·sion·al /ə'kāzhənl/ ▶ adjective **1** occurring infrequently or irregularly. **2** produced on or intended for particular occasions: *occasional verse.*

> – SYNONYMS **infrequent,** intermittent, irregular, periodic, sometime, sporadic, odd.
> – ANTONYMS regular, frequent.

oc·ca·sion·al·ly /ə'kāzhənlē/ ▶ adverb once in a while: *I occasionally have wine with dinner.*

> – SYNONYMS **sometimes,** from time to time, (every) now and then, (every) now and again, at times, every so often, (every) once in a while, on occasion, periodically.
> – ANTONYMS often.

Oc·ci·dent /'äksidənt, -͵dent/ ▶ noun (**the Occident**) literary the countries of the West.
– ORIGIN from Latin *occidere* 'go down, set,' with reference to the setting of the sun.

oc·ci·den·tal /͵äksə'dentl/ literary ▶ adjective relating to the countries of the West. ▶ noun (**Occidental**) a person from the West.

oc·ci·put /'äksəpət/ ▶ noun Anatomy the back of the head.
– DERIVATIVES **oc·cip·i·tal** /äk'sipitl/ adjective.
– ORIGIN Latin, from *caput* 'head.'

Oc·ci·tan /'äksi,tan/ ▶ **noun** the medieval or modern language of Languedoc (southern France), including Provençal.
– ORIGIN French.

oc·clude /ə'klo͞od/ ▶ **verb** technical **1** close up or block an opening or passage. **2** (of a tooth) come into contact with another in the opposite jaw.
– ORIGIN Latin *occludere*.

oc·clud·ed front ▶ **noun** a weather front produced when a cold front catches up with a warm front, so that the warm air in between them is forced upward.

oc·clu·sion /ə'klo͞ozhən/ ▶ **noun** technical the process of blocking something up.
– DERIVATIVES **oc·clu·sive** /-siv/ adjective.

oc·cult /ə'kəlt/ ▶ **noun** (**the occult**) supernatural or magical powers, practices, or phenomena.

– SYNONYMS **the supernatural,** magic, black magic, witchcraft, necromancy, the black arts, occultism.

▶ **adjective 1** relating to the occult. **2** beyond ordinary knowledge or experience. **3** Medicine (of blood) abnormally present, but detectable only microscopically or by chemical testing.

– SYNONYMS **supernatural,** magic, magical, satanic, mystical, unearthly, esoteric, psychic.

– DERIVATIVES **oc·cult·ism** /-,tizəm/ noun **oc·cult·ist** /-tist/ noun.
– ORIGIN from Latin *occulere* 'conceal.'

oc·cu·pan·cy /'äkyəpənsē/ ▶ **noun 1** the action or fact of occupying a place. **2** the proportion of accommodations occupied or used.

oc·cu·pant /'äkyəpənt/ ▶ **noun 1** a person who occupies a place at a given time. **2** the holder of a job or office.

– SYNONYMS **resident,** inhabitant, owner, householder, tenant, leaseholder, lessee.

oc·cu·pa·tion /,äkyə'pāshən/ ▶ **noun 1** a job or profession. **2** a way of spending time. **3** the action of occupying a place or the state of being occupied: *the Roman occupation of Britain.*

– SYNONYMS **1 job,** profession, work, line of work, trade, employment, business, career, métier, calling. **2 pastime,** activity, hobby, pursuit, interest, entertainment, recreation. **3 conquest,** capture, invasion, seizure, annexation, colonization, subjugation.

oc·cu·pa·tion·al /,äkyə'pāshənl/ ▶ **adjective** relating to a job or profession: *an occupational disease.*
– DERIVATIVES **oc·cu·pa·tion·al·ly** adverb.

oc·cu·pa·tion·al haz·ard ▶ **noun** a risk arising as a consequence of a particular job or profession.

oc·cu·pa·tion·al ther·a·py ▶ **noun** a form of therapy that emphasizes the performance of activities required in daily life.
– DERIVATIVES **oc·cu·pa·tion·al ther·a·pist** noun.

oc·cu·pied /'äkyə,pīd/ ▶ **adjective 1** busy and active. **2** in use; not available.

– SYNONYMS **1** *tasks that kept her occupied all day* **busy,** working, at work, active; informal tied up, hard at it, on the go. **2** *all the tables were occupied* **in use,** full, engaged, taken.

oc·cu·py /'äkyə,pī/ ▶ **verb** (**occupies, occupying, occupied**) **1** live or work in a place. **2** fill or take up a space, time, or position. **3** keep someone busy and active: *he has occupied himself with research.* **4** enter and take control of a place, especially by military force.

– SYNONYMS **1 live in,** inhabit, lodge in, move into, people, populate, settle, tenant. **2 engage,** busy, distract, absorb, engross, hold, interest, involve, entertain. **3** *the region was occupied by Japan* **capture,** seize, conquer, invade, colonize, annex, subjugate.

– DERIVATIVES **oc·cu·pi·er** noun.
– ORIGIN Latin *occupare* 'seize.'

oc·cur /ə'kər/ ▶ **verb** (**occurs, occurring, occurred**) **1** happen; take place. **2** be found or present: *radon occurs in rocks such as granite.* **3** (**occur to**) come into someone's mind.

– SYNONYMS **1 happen,** take place, come about, transpire; informal go down. **2 be found,** be present, exist, appear, develop, manifest itself. **3** (**occur to**) **enter one's head,** cross one's mind, come/spring to mind, strike, dawn on, suggest itself.

– ORIGIN Latin *occurrere* 'go to meet, present itself.'

CHOOSE THE RIGHT WORD

See **HAPPEN**.

oc·cur·rence /ə'kərəns/ ▶ **noun 1** a thing that happens; an incident or event. **2** the fact or frequency of something happening or existing: *the occurrence of cancer increases with age.*

– SYNONYMS **1 event,** incident, happening, phenomenon, circumstance, episode. **2 existence,** instance, appearance, frequency, incidence, prevalence, rate; Statistics distribution.

OCD ▶ **abbreviation** obsessive-compulsive disorder.

o·cean /'ōshən/ ▶ **noun 1** a very large expanse of sea, specifically each of the Atlantic, Pacific, Indian, Arctic, and Antarctic Oceans. **2** (**the ocean**) the sea.
– ORIGIN Greek *ōkeanos* 'great stream encircling the earth's disc.'

o·cea·nar·i·um /,ōshə'ne(ə)rēəm/ ▶ **noun** (pl. **oceanariums** or **oceanaria** /-'ne(ə)rēə/) a large seawater aquarium.

o·ce·an·ic /,ōshē'anik/ ▶ **adjective** relating to the ocean.

o·cea·nog·ra·phy /,ōshə'nägrəfē/ ▶ **noun** the branch of science concerned with the study of the sea.
– DERIVATIVES **o·cea·nog·ra·pher** noun **o·cea·no·graph·ic** /-nə'grafik/ adjective.

oc·e·lot /'äsə,lät, 'ōsə-/ ▶ **noun** a medium-sized striped and spotted wild cat, native to South and Central America.
– ORIGIN French.

o·cher /'ōkər/ ▶ **noun** a type of earth that varies in color from light yellow to brown or red, used as a pigment.
– ORIGIN Greek *ōkhra.*

Ock·ham's ra·zor ▶ **noun** variant spelling of **OCCAM'S RAZOR**.

o'·clock /ə'kläk/ ▶ **adverb** used to specify the hour when telling the time.
– ORIGIN from *of the clock.*

OCR ▶ **abbreviation** optical character recognition.

Oct. ▶ **abbreviation** October.

octa- (also **oct-** before a vowel) ▶ **combining form** eight; having eight: *octahedron.*
– ORIGIN Greek *oktō* 'eight.'

oc·ta·gon /ˈäktəˌgän, -gən/ ▶ **noun** a plane figure with eight straight sides and eight angles.
– DERIVATIVES **oc·tag·o·nal** /äkˈtagənl/ adjective.

oc·ta·he·dron /ˌäktəˈhēdrən/ ▶ **noun** (pl. **octahedra** /-drə/ or **octahedrons**) a three-dimensional shape having eight plane faces, in particular eight equal triangular faces.
– DERIVATIVES **oc·ta·he·dral** /-drəl/ adjective.

oc·tane /ˈäktān/ ▶ **noun** a liquid hydrocarbon obtained in petroleum refining.

oc·tane num·ber (or **octane rating**) ▶ **noun** a figure indicating the quality of a fuel, based on a comparison with a standard mixture.

oc·tave /ˈäktəv, ˈäkˌtāv/ ▶ **noun 1** a series of eight musical notes occupying the interval between (and including) two notes, one having twice or half the pitch of the other. **2** the interval between two such notes, or the notes themselves sounding together. **3** a poem or stanza of eight lines; an octet.
– ORIGIN from Latin *octava dies* 'eighth day,' first referring to a period of eight days following and including a Church festival.

oc·ta·vo /äkˈtävō/ ▶ **noun** (pl. **octavos**) a size of book page that results from folding each printed sheet into eight leaves (sixteen pages).
– ORIGIN from Latin *in octavo* 'in an eighth.'

oc·tet /äkˈtet/ ▶ **noun 1** a group of eight musicians. **2** a musical composition for eight voices or instruments. **3** a group of eight lines of poetry.

octo- (also **oct-** before a vowel) ▶ **combining form** eight; having eight: *octopus*.
– ORIGIN Latin *octo* or Greek *oktō* 'eight.'

Oc·to·ber /äkˈtōbər/ ▶ **noun** the tenth month of the year.
– ORIGIN from Latin *octo* 'eight,' October being originally the eighth month of the Roman year.

oc·to·ge·nar·i·an /ˌäktəjəˈne(ə)rēən/ ▶ **noun** a person who is between 80 and 89 years old.
– ORIGIN from Latin *octoginta* 'eighty.'

oc·to·pus /ˈäktəpəs/ ▶ **noun** (pl. **octopuses**) a sea animal with a soft body and eight long tentacles with suckers.
– DERIVATIVES **oc·to·poid** /-ˌpoid/ adjective.
– ORIGIN Greek, from *oktō* 'eight' + *pous* 'foot.'

> **USAGE**
>
> The standard plural in English of **octopus** is **octopuses**, but as the word comes from Greek, the Greek plural form **octopodes** is still occasionally used. The plural form **octopi**, formed according to rules for Latin plurals, is incorrect.

oc·to·roon /ˌäktəˈro͞on/ ▶ **noun** dated, often offensive a person who is one-eighth black by descent.

oc·tu·ple /äkˈtəpəl, -ˈt(y)o͞opəl/ ▶ **adjective 1** consisting of eight parts or things. **2** eight times as many or as much.
– ORIGIN from Latin *octo* 'eight' + *-plus* (as in *duplus* 'double').

oc·tup·let /äkˈtəplit, -ˈt(y)o͞o-/ ▶ **noun** each of eight children born at one birth.

oc·u·lar /ˈäkyələr/ ▶ **adjective** relating to the eyes or vision.
– ORIGIN from Latin *oculus* 'eye.'

oc·u·list /ˈäkyəlist/ ▶ **noun** dated a person who specializes in the medical treatment of diseases or defects of the eye.
– ORIGIN from Latin *oculus* 'eye.'

oc·u·lus /ˈäkyələs/ ▶ **noun** (pl. **oculi** /-ˌlī, -ˌlē/) Architecture **1** a circular window. **2** an opening at the top of a dome.
– ORIGIN Latin, 'eye.'

OD informal ▶ **verb** (**OD's, OD'ing, OD'd**) take an overdose of a drug. ▶ **noun** an overdose.

o·da·lisque /ˈōdlˌisk/ ▶ **noun** historical a female slave or concubine in a harem.
– ORIGIN French.

odd /äd/ ▶ **adjective 1** unusual or unexpected; strange. **2** (of whole numbers such as 3 and 5) having one left over as a remainder when divided by two. **3** (in combination) in the region of: *fifty-odd years*. **4** occasional: *we have the odd drink together*. **5** spare or available: *an odd five minutes*. **6** separated from a pair or set: *an odd sock*.

> – SYNONYMS **1 strange,** peculiar, queer, funny, bizarre, eccentric, unconventional, outlandish, unusual, weird, curious, abnormal, puzzling, mystifying, baffling, unaccountable; informal wacky. **2** *odd jobs* **occasional,** casual, irregular, isolated, sporadic, periodic, miscellaneous, various, varied, sundry. **3** *an odd shoe* **mismatched,** unmatched, unpaired, single, lone, solitary, extra, leftover, spare.
> – ANTONYMS normal, ordinary, regular.

– DERIVATIVES **odd·ly** adverb **odd·ness** noun.
– PHRASES **odd one out** a person or thing differing in some way from the other members of a group or set. **odds and ends** various small items that are not part of a larger set.
– ORIGIN Old Norse.

odd·ball /ˈädˌbôl/ ▶ **noun** informal a strange or eccentric person.

odd·i·ty /ˈäditē/ ▶ **noun** (pl. **oddities**) **1** the quality of being strange. **2** a strange person or thing.

odd·ment /ˈädmənt/ ▶ **noun** an item or piece left over from a larger piece or set.

odds /ädz/ ▶ **plural noun 1** the ratio between the amounts placed as a bet and the money that would be received if the bet was won: *odds of 8–1*. **2** (**the odds**) the chances of something happening or being the case. **3** (**the odds**) the advantage thought to be possessed by one person compared to another; superiority in strength, power, or resources: *she clung to the lead against all the odds*.

> – SYNONYMS **likelihood,** probability, chances.

– PHRASES **at odds** in conflict or disagreement.

odds-on ▶ **adjective 1** (especially of a horse) rated as more likely than evens to win. **2** very likely to happen or succeed.

ode /ōd/ ▶ **noun** a poem addressed to a person or thing, or celebrating an event.
– ORIGIN Greek *ōidē* 'song.'

o·dif·er·ous /ōˈdifərəs/ ▶ **adjective** variant spelling of **ODORIFEROUS**.

o·di·ous /ˈōdēəs/ ▶ **adjective** extremely unpleasant; repulsive.

> – SYNONYMS **revolting,** repulsive, repellent, repugnant, disgusting, offensive, objectionable, vile, foul, abhorrent, loathsome, nauseating, sickening, hateful, detestable, abominable, monstrous, appalling, insufferable, intolerable, despicable, contemptible, unspeakable, atrocious, awful, terrible, dreadful, frightful, obnoxious, unpleasant,

disagreeable, nasty; informal ghastly, horrible, horrid, God-awful.
– ANTONYMS delightful.

– DERIVATIVES **o·di·ous·ly** adverb **o·di·ous·ness** noun.
– ORIGIN from Latin *odium* 'hatred.'

o·di·um /ˈōdēəm/ ▶ **noun** general or widespread hatred or disgust.
– ORIGIN Latin.

o·dom·e·ter /ōˈdämitər/ ▶ **noun** an instrument for measuring the distance traveled by a vehicle.
– ORIGIN French *odomètre*.

o·don·tol·o·gy /ˌōdänˈtäləjē/ ▶ **noun** the scientific study of the structure and diseases of teeth.
– DERIVATIVES **o·don·tol·o·gist** /-jist/ noun.
– ORIGIN from Greek *odous* 'tooth.'

o·dor /ˈōdər/ ▶ **noun 1** a distinctive smell. **2** a lingering quality or impression: *an odor of suspicion*.

– SYNONYMS **smell,** stench, stink, reek, aroma, bouquet, scent, perfume, fragrance.

– DERIVATIVES **o·dor·ous** adjective **o·dor·less** adjective.
– ORIGIN Latin *odor*.

WORD LINKS

olfactory *relating to odor*

o·dor·ant /ˈōdərənt/ ▶ **noun** a substance used to give a scent or smell to a product.

o·dor·if·er·ous /ˌōdəˈrifərəs/ ▶ **adjective** giving off a smell, especially an unpleasant one.
– ORIGIN from Latin *odorifer* 'odor-bearing.'

od·ys·sey /ˈädəsē/ ▶ **noun** (pl. **odysseys**) a long, eventful journey.

– SYNONYMS **journey,** voyage, trip, trek, travels, quest, crusade, pilgrimage.

– DERIVATIVES **od·ys·se·an** /ōˈdisēən, ädəˈsēən/ adjective.
– ORIGIN the title of a Greek epic poem attributed to Homer, describing the adventures of Odysseus.

OECD ▶ **abbreviation** Organization for Economic Cooperation and Development.

OED ▶ **abbreviation** Oxford English Dictionary.

Oed·i·pus com·plex /ˈedəpəs, ˈēdə-/ ▶ **noun** (in the theory of Sigmund Freud) the emotions aroused in a young child by an unconscious sexual desire for the parent of the opposite sex.
– DERIVATIVES **Oed·i·pal** adjective.
– ORIGIN from *Oedipus* in Greek mythology, who unknowingly killed his father and married his mother.

OEM ▶ **abbreviation** original equipment manufacturer.

oe·no·phile /ˈēnəˌfīl/ (also **enophile**) ▶ **noun** a connoisseur of wines.

o'er /ōr/ ▶ **adverb & preposition** old-fashioned or literary form of **OVER**.

oeu·vre /ˈœvrə/ ▶ **noun** the works of an artist, composer, author, etc., considered as a whole.
– ORIGIN French.

of /əv/ ▶ **preposition 1** expressing the relationship between a part and a whole. **2** belonging to; coming from. **3** expressing the relationship between a scale or measure and a value. **4** made from. **5** expressing the relationship between a direction and a point of reference. **6** expressing the relationship between a general category and something that belongs to such a category. **7** expressing time in relation to the following hour.
– ORIGIN Old English.

USAGE

Be careful not to write the word **of** instead of **have** in sentences such as *I could have told you*. For more information, see the note at **HAVE**.

off /ôf, äf/ ▶ **adverb 1** away from the place in question. **2** so as to be removed or separated. **3** starting a journey or race. **4** so as to finish or be discontinued. **5** (of an electrical appliance or power supply) not functioning or so as to stop functioning. **6** having a particular level of wealth: *badly off*.

– SYNONYMS **1 away,** absent, off duty, on leave, on vacation. **2 canceled,** postponed, called off.

▶ **preposition 1** moving away and often down from. **2** situated or leading in a direction away from. **3** so as to be removed, separated, or absent from. **4** having a temporary dislike of. ▶ **adjective 1** unsatisfactory or inadequate: *an off day*. **2** (of food) no longer fresh. **3** located on the side of a vehicle that is normally farthest away from the curb.

– SYNONYMS **rotten,** bad, stale, moldy, sour, rancid, turned, spoiled.

▶ **noun 1** (also **off side**) Cricket the half of the field toward which the batsman's feet are pointed when standing to receive the ball. The opposite of **LEG**. **2** Brit. informal the start of a race or journey.
▶ **verb** kill; murder.
– PHRASES **off and on** not regularly or all the time.
– ORIGIN Old English.

USAGE

The use of **off of** rather than **off** is best avoided in formal written English: you should write *the cup fell off the table* rather than *the cup fell off of the table*.

of·fal /ˈôfəl, ˈäfəl/ ▶ **noun** the internal organs of an animal used as food.
– ORIGIN probably from Dutch *afval*.

off·beat /ˈôfˌbēt, ˈäf-/ ▶ **adjective** unconventional; unusual.

– SYNONYMS **unconventional,** unorthodox, unusual, eccentric, idiosyncratic, strange, bizarre, weird, peculiar, odd, freakish, outlandish, out of the ordinary, Bohemian, alternative, left-field, zany, quirky; informal wacky, freaky, way-out, off the wall, kooky, oddball.
– ANTONYMS conventional.

▶ **noun** Music any of the normally unaccented beats in a bar.

off-col·or ▶ **adjective** slightly indecent or obscene.

– SYNONYMS **smutty,** dirty, rude, crude, suggestive, indecent, indelicate, risqué, racy, bawdy, naughty, blue, vulgar, ribald, coarse; informal raunchy; euphemistic adult.
– ANTONYMS well.

of·fend /əˈfend/ ▶ **verb 1** make someone feel upset, resentful, or annoyed. **2** be displeasing to: *the smell of cigarette ash offended him*. **3** commit an illegal act.

– SYNONYMS **1 upset,** give offense to, affront, hurt someone's feelings, insult, hurt, wound, slight. **2 break the law,** commit a crime, do wrong.

– ORIGIN Latin *offendere* 'strike against.'

of·fend·er /əˈfendər/ ▶ **noun** a person who commits an illegal act.

– SYNONYMS **wrongdoer,** criminal, lawbreaker, crook, villain, miscreant, felon, delinquent, malefactor, culprit, guilty party.

of·fense /ə'fens/ (Brit. **offence**) ▶ **noun 1** an act that breaks a law or rule. **2** a feeling of hurt or annoyance: *I didn't mean to give offense.* **3** the action of making a military attack. **4** the attacking players on a team.

– SYNONYMS **1 crime,** illegal act, misdemeanor, felony, infringement, violation, wrongdoing, sin. **2 annoyance,** resentment, indignation, displeasure, bad feeling, animosity.

CHOOSE THE RIGHT WORD

See **SIN**[1].

of·fen·sive /ə'fensiv/ ▶ **adjective 1** making someone feel upset, resentful, or annoyed. **2** involved in an attack, or meant for use in an attack: *an offensive weapon.* **3** relating to the team in possession of the ball or puck in a game.

– SYNONYMS **1 insulting,** rude, derogatory, disrespectful, personal, hurtful, upsetting, wounding, abusive. **2 unpleasant,** disagreeable, nasty, distasteful, objectionable, off-putting, dreadful, frightful, obnoxious, abominable, disgusting, repulsive, repellent, vile, foul, horrible, sickening, nauseating; informal ghastly, horrid, gross. **3 hostile,** attacking, aggressive, invading, incursive, combative, threatening, martial, warlike, belligerent, bellicose.
– ANTONYMS complimentary, pleasant, defensive.

▶ **noun 1** an attacking military campaign. **2** a forceful campaign to achieve something: *the need to launch an offensive against crime.*

– SYNONYMS **attack,** assault, onslaught, invasion, push, thrust, charge, raid, incursion, blitz, campaign.

– DERIVATIVES **of·fen·sive·ly** adverb **of·fen·sive·ness** noun.
– PHRASES **be on the offensive** be ready to act aggressively.

of·fer /'ôfər, 'äfər/ ▶ **verb 1** present something for someone to accept or reject as they wish. **2** express willingness to do something for someone: *he offered to fix the gate.* **3** provide: *the hotel offers direct access to a spa and pool.* **4** present something to God or another deity as an act of worship: *a monk offered prayers for their health and happiness.*

– SYNONYMS **1 put forward,** proffer, give, present, come up with, suggest, propose, advance, submit, tender. **2 volunteer,** step/come forward. **3 bid,** tender, put in a bid/offer of.
– ANTONYMS withdraw, refuse.

▶ **noun 1** an expression of readiness to do or give something. **2** an amount of money that someone is willing to pay for something. **3** a specially reduced price.

– SYNONYMS **1 proposal,** proposition, suggestion, submission, approach, overture. **2 bid,** tender, bidding price.

– PHRASES **open to offers** willing to do or sell something for a reasonable price.
– ORIGIN Latin *offerre* 'bestow, present.'

of·fer·ing /'ôf(ə)riNG, äf-/ ▶ **noun** something that is offered; a gift or contribution.

– SYNONYMS **contribution,** donation, gift, present, sacrifice, tribute.

of·fer·to·ry /'ôfər,tôrē, 'äfər-/ ▶ **noun** (pl. **offertories**) Christian Church **1** the offering of the bread and wine in the service of Holy Communion. **2** a collection of money made at a church service.
– ORIGIN Latin *offertorium.*

off·hand /'ôf'hand, 'äf-/ ▶ **adjective** offensively casual or cool in manner.

– SYNONYMS **casual,** careless, uninterested, indifferent, cool, nonchalant, blasé, insouciant, cavalier, glib, perfunctory, cursory, dismissive.

▶ **adverb** without previous thought or consideration: *I can't think of a better answer offhand.*

of·fice /'ôfis, 'äf-/ ▶ **noun 1** a room, set of rooms, or building in which business or clerical work is carried out. **2** a position of authority: *the office of director general.* **3** the holding of an official position: *the president took office in 1980.* **4** (**offices**) services done for other people: *the good offices of the rector.* **5** (also **Divine Office**) Christian Church the services of prayers and psalms said daily by Catholic priests or other clergy.

– SYNONYMS **1 place of work,** workplace, workroom. **2** *the company's Paris office* **branch,** division, section, bureau, department. **3** *the office of president* **post,** position, appointment, job, occupation, role, situation, function.

– ORIGIN Latin *officium* 'performance of a task.'

of·fi·cer /'ôfisər, 'äf-/ ▶ **noun 1** a person holding a position of authority in the armed forces. **2** a policeman or policewoman. **3** a person holding a position of authority in the government or a large organization.

– SYNONYMS **official,** functionary, executive.

of·fi·cial /ə'fisHəl/ ▶ **adjective 1** relating to an authority or public organization and its activities and responsibilities. **2** permitted or done by a person or group in a position of authority: *an official inquiry.*

– SYNONYMS **1 authorized,** approved, validated, authenticated, certified, accredited, endorsed, sanctioned, licensed, recognized, legitimate, legal, lawful, valid, bona fide, proper; informal kosher. **2 ceremonial,** formal, solemn, bureaucratic.
– ANTONYMS unauthorized, informal.

▶ **noun** a person holding public office or having official duties.

– SYNONYMS **officer,** executive, functionary, administrator, bureaucrat, mandarin, representative, agent; derogatory apparatchik.

– DERIVATIVES **of·fi·cial·dom** noun **of·fi·cial·ly** adverb.

of·fi·cial·ese /ə,fisHə'lēz/ ▶ **noun** formal or complicated language typical of that used in official documents.

of·fi·ci·ant /ə'fisHēənt/ ▶ **noun** a priest or minister who performs a religious service or ceremony.

of·fi·ci·ate /ə'fisHē,āt/ ▶ **verb 1** act as an official in charge of something, especially a sporting event. **2** perform a religious service or ceremony.

– SYNONYMS **be in charge of,** take charge of, preside over; oversee, superintend, supervise, conduct, run.

– DERIVATIVES **of·fi·ci·a·tion** /ə,fisHē'āsHən/ noun **of·fi·ci·a·tor** noun.
– ORIGIN Latin *officiare* 'perform divine service.'

of·fi·cious /ə'fisHəs/ ▶ **adjective** too ready to assert one's authority or interfere.

– SYNONYMS **self-important,** bumptious, self-assertive, overbearing, interfering, intrusive, meddlesome, meddling; informal bossy.

– DERIVATIVES **of·fi·cious·ly** adverb **of·fi·cious·ness** noun.

off·ing /'ôfiNG, 'äf-/ ▶ **noun** the more distant part of the sea in view.
– PHRASES **in the offing** likely to happen or appear soon.

off-key ▶ **adjective & adverb 1** Music not having the correct tone or pitch. **2** not suitable or appropriate.

off-la·bel ▶ **adjective** (of the use of a drug) prescribed in a way or for a condition not covered by the original FDA approval: *off-label treatments*.

off-lim·its ▶ **adjective** out of bounds.

off·line /'ôf'līn, 'äf-/ ▶ **adjective** not connected to a computer or external network.

off·load /'ôf,lōd, 'äf-/ ▶ **verb 1** unload a cargo. **2** get rid of something by passing it on to someone else.

off-peak ▶ **adjective & adverb** at a time when demand is less.

off·print /'ôf,print, 'äf-/ ▶ **noun** a printed copy of an article that originally appeared as part of a larger publication.

off-put·ting ▶ **adjective** unpleasant or disconcerting.

off-ramp ▶ **noun** an exit road from a main highway.

off-road ▶ **adjective** (of a vehicle or bicycle) for use on rough terrain rather than on public roads.

off-screen ▶ **adjective 1** not appearing on a movie or television screen: *an off-screen narrator*. **2** happening in real life rather than fictionally on-screen: *they were off-screen lovers*. ▶ **adverb 1** outside what can be seen on a movie or television screen: *the girl is looking off-screen*. **2** in real life rather than fictionally in a movie or on television: *happy endings rarely happen off-screen*.

off sea·son (also **off-season**) ▶ **noun** a time of year when people do not take part in a particular activity or when a business is quiet.

off·set /'ôf,set, 'äf-/ ▶ **verb** (**offsetting**; past and past part. **offset**) **1** counteract something by having an equal and opposite force or effect: *many costs can be offset by productivity savings*. **2** place something out of line. **3** transfer an impression by means of offset printing.

– SYNONYMS **counteract,** balance (out), even out/up, counterbalance, compensate for, make up for, neutralize, cancel (out).

▶ **noun 1** a consideration or amount that reduces or balances the effect of an opposite one. **2** the amount by which something is out of line. **3** a side shoot from a plant that can be used for propagation. **4** a method of printing in which ink is transferred from a plate or stone to a rubber surface and from that to the paper.

off·shoot /'ôf,sHo͞ot, 'äf-/ ▶ **noun 1** a side shoot on a plant. **2** a thing that develops from something else.

off·shore /'ôf'sHôr, 'äf-/ ▶ **adjective & adverb 1** situated at sea some distance from the shore. **2** (of the wind) blowing toward the sea from the land. **3** relating to the business of extracting oil or gas from the seabed. **4** made, situated, or registered abroad. **5** relating to a foreign country.

off·shor·ing /'ôf'sHôriNG, 'äf-/ ▶ **noun** the practice of basing some of a company's processes or services overseas, to take advantage of lower costs.

off·side /'ôf'sīd, 'äf-/ ▶ **adjective & adverb** (of a player in games such as soccer, football, or hockey) occupying a position on the field where playing the ball or puck is not allowed. ▶ **noun** (also **offsides**) **1** the fact of being offside. **2** the right side of a horse.

off-site (also **offsite**) ▶ **adjective & adverb** taking place or situated away from a particular site or premises.

off·spring /'ôf,spriNG, 'äf-/ ▶ **noun** (pl. same) a person's child or children, or the young of an animal.

– SYNONYMS **children,** family, progeny, young, brood, descendants, heirs, successors; informal kids.

off·stage /'ôf'stāj, 'äf-/ ▶ **adjective & adverb** (in a theater) not on the stage and so not visible to the audience.

off-white ▶ **noun** a white color with a gray or yellowish tinge.

oft /ôft, äft/ (also **oft-times**) ▶ **adverb** old use or literary often.
– ORIGIN Old English.

of·ten /'ôf(t)ən, 'äf-/ (also **oftentimes** /'ôf(t)ən,tīmz, 'äf-/) ▶ **adverb** (**oftener, oftenest**) **1** frequently. **2** in many cases.

– SYNONYMS **frequently,** oftentimes, many times, a lot, repeatedly, again and again, time after time, regularly, commonly, generally, ordinarily.
– ANTONYMS seldom.

o·gee /ō'jē/ ▶ **noun** Architecture an S-shaped line or molding.
– ORIGIN uncertain.

o·gee arch ▶ **noun** Architecture a pointed arch with two S-shaped curves meeting at the top.

o·gle /'ōgəl, ä-/ ▶ **verb** stare at someone in a lecherous way.
– DERIVATIVES **o·gler** noun.
– ORIGIN probably from German or Dutch.

o·gre /'ōgər/ ▶ **noun** (fem. **ogress** /'ōgris/) **1** (in folklore) a man-eating giant. **2** a cruel or terrifying person.
– DERIVATIVES **o·gre·ish** /'ōg(ə)risH/ (also **ogrish**) adjective.
– ORIGIN French.

OH ▶ **abbreviation** Ohio.

oh[1] /ō/ ▶ **exclamation** expressing surprise, disappointment, joy, acknowledgment, etc.

oh[2] ▶ **noun** variant spelling of **O**[1] (sense 2).

ohm /ōm/ ▶ **noun** the SI unit of electrical resistance. (Symbol: Ω)
– ORIGIN named after the German physicist G. S. *Ohm*.

oil /oil/ ▶ **noun 1** a thick, sticky liquid obtained from petroleum, used especially as a fuel or lubricant. **2** petroleum. **3** any of various thick liquids that cannot be dissolved in water and are obtained from animals or plants. **4** Chemistry any of a group of organic compounds of glycerol and fatty acids that are liquid at room temperature. **5** (also **oils**) oil paint. ▶ **verb** lubricate, coat, or treat something with oil.
– ORIGIN Old French *oile*, from Latin *oleum* 'oil, olive oil.'

oil·can /'oil,kan/ ▶ **noun** a can with a long nozzle used for applying oil to machinery.

oil·cloth /'oil,klôTH/ ▶ **noun** cotton fabric treated with oil to make it waterproof.

oil·er /'oilər/ ▶ **noun 1** an oil tanker. **2** a person who oils machinery. **3** informal an oil well. **4** (**oilers**) oilskin garments.

oil·field /'oil,fēld/ ▶ **noun** an area where oil is found beneath the ground or the seabed.

oil paint ▶ **noun** artists' paint made from ground pigment mixed with linseed or other oil.

oil paint·ing ▶ **noun** **1** the art of painting in oil paint. **2** a picture painted in oil paint.

oil palm ▶ **noun** a tropical West African palm whose fruit yields a kind of oil.

oil plat·form ▶ **noun** a structure positioned on the seabed to provide a stable base above water for drilling and servicing oil wells.

oil rig ▶ **noun** a structure with equipment for drilling and servicing an oil well.

oil·seed /ˈoil,sēd/ ▶ **noun** any of various seeds from crops from which oil is obtained, e.g., rape, peanut, or cotton.

oil·skin /ˈoil,skin/ ▶ **noun** **1** heavy cotton cloth waterproofed with oil. **2** (**oilskins**) a set of garments made of oilskin.

oil slick ▶ **noun** a film or layer of oil floating on an area of water.

oil·stone /ˈoil,stōn/ ▶ **noun** a fine-grained flat stone used with oil for sharpening chisels, planes, or other tools.

oil well ▶ **noun** a shaft bored in rock so as to extract oil.

oil·y /ˈoilē/ ▶ **adjective** (**oilier, oiliest**) **1** containing, covered with, or soaked in oil. **2** resembling oil. **3** (of a person) polite or flattering in an insincere and unpleasant way.

– SYNONYMS **1** *oily food* **greasy,** fatty, buttery, rich, oleaginous. **2** *he's an oily character* **unctuous,** ingratiating, fawning, smooth-talking, flattering, obsequious, sycophantic, insincere; informal smarmy, slimy.

– DERIVATIVES **oil·i·ness** noun.

oink /oiNGk/ ▶ **noun** the characteristic grunting sound made by a pig. ▶ **verb** (of a pig) grunt.
– ORIGIN imitating the sound.

oint·ment /ˈointmənt/ ▶ **noun** a smooth substance that is rubbed on the skin for medicinal purposes.

– SYNONYMS **lotion,** cream, salve, liniment, embrocation, rub, gel, balm, emollient, unguent.

– ORIGIN Old French *oignement*.

OJ ▶ **abbreviation** orange juice.

O·jib·wa /ōˈjib,wā, -wə/ ▶ **noun** (pl. same or **Ojibwas**) a member of an American Indian people of the area around Lake Superior.
– ORIGIN Ojibwa, said to mean 'puckered' (with reference to their moccasins).

OK[1] /ˈōˈkā/ (also **okay**) informal ▶ **exclamation** expressing agreement or acceptance. ▶ **adjective** **1** satisfactory, but not especially good. **2** permissible; allowed.

– SYNONYMS **1** *the movie was OK* **satisfactory,** all right, acceptable, competent, adequate, tolerable, passable, reasonable, decent, fair, not bad, average, middling, moderate, unremarkable, unexceptional; informal so-so, fair-to-middling. **2** *is it OK for me to come to the party?* **permissible,** allowable, acceptable, all right, in order, permitted, fitting, suitable, appropriate.
– ANTONYMS unsatisfactory.

▶ **adverb** in a satisfactory way.
▶ **noun** approval or permission.

– SYNONYMS *the squadron leader gave them the OK to launch* **authorization,** (seal of) approval, agreement, consent, assent, permission, endorsement, ratification, sanction, blessing, leave; informal the go-ahead, the green light, the thumbs up, say-so.

▶ **verb** (**OK's, OK'ing, OK'd**) approve or agree to something.
– ORIGIN probably an abbreviation of *orl korrect*, humorous form of *all correct*.

OK[2] ▶ **abbreviation** Oklahoma.

o·ka·pi /ōˈkäpē/ ▶ **noun** (pl. same or **okapis**) a large African mammal of the giraffe family, having a dark chestnut coat with stripes on the hindquarters and upper legs.
– ORIGIN a local word.

o·kay /ˈōˈkā/ ▶ **exclamation, adjective, adverb, noun, & verb** variant spelling of **OK**[1].

o·kra /ˈōkrə/ ▶ **noun** the long seed pods of a tropical plant, eaten as a vegetable.
– ORIGIN a West African word.

old /ōld/ ▶ **adjective** (**older, oldest**) **1** having lived for a long time. **2** made or built long ago. **3** possessed or used for a long time: *I gave my old clothes away*. **4** long-established or known. **5** former; previous: *they moved back to their old house*. **6** of a specified age. **7** informal expressing affection or contempt.

– SYNONYMS **1** *old people* **elderly,** aged, older, senior, advanced in years, venerable, in one's dotage, past one's prime, long in the tooth, grizzled, ancient, decrepit, senescent, senile; informal getting on, over the hill. **2** *old clothes* **worn,** shabby, threadbare, frayed, patched, tattered, moth-eaten, ragged; informal tatty. **3** *the old days* **bygone,** olden, past, former, previous, early, earlier, earliest; prehistoric, primitive. **4** *old cars* **antique,** veteran, vintage, classic. **5** *an old girlfriend* **former,** previous, earlier, past, ex-, one-time, sometime, erstwhile; formal quondam.
– ANTONYMS young, new, modern, current.

– DERIVATIVES **old·ish** adjective **old·ness** noun.
– PHRASES **of old** **1** in or belonging to the past. **2** for a long time. **the old days** a period in the past. **the old school** the traditional form or type: *a gentleman of the old school*.
– ORIGIN Old English.

WORD LINKS

geriatric *relating to old people*

old age ▶ **noun** the later part of normal life.

old boy net·work (also **old boys' network**) ▶ **noun** an informal system through which men use their positions of influence to help others who went to the same school or university.

old coun·try ▶ **noun** (**the old country**) the native country of a person who has gone to live abroad.

olde /ˈōld, ˈōldē/ ▶ **adjective** mock old-fashioned attractively old-fashioned; quaint.

old·en /ˈōldən/ ▶ **adjective** relating to former times.

Old Eng·lish ▶ **noun** the language of the Anglo-Saxons (up to about 1150).

Old Eng·lish sheep·dog ▶ **noun** a large breed of sheepdog with a shaggy blue-gray and white coat.

old-fash·ioned ▶ **adjective** **1** no longer current or modern; outdated. **2** (of a person or their views) favoring traditional styles, ideas, or customs.

– SYNONYMS **out of date,** outdated, dated, out of fashion, outmoded, unfashionable, passé, behind the times, antiquated, antediluvian, archaic,

obsolescent, obsolete, superannuated; informal old hat.
– ANTONYMS modern.

Old French ▶ **noun** the French language up to about 1400.

Old Glo·ry ▶ **noun** informal the US national flag.

old-growth ▶ **adjective** (of a tree or forested area) never felled, harvested, or cleared; mature: *old-growth forests*.

old guard ▶ **noun** the long-standing members of a group, who are typically unwilling to accept change.

old hand ▶ **noun** a very experienced person.

old hat ▶ **noun** informal something that is boringly familiar or outdated.

old·ie /ˈōldē/ ▶ **noun** informal an old song, movie, or television program that is still well-known or popular.

old la·dy ▶ **noun** informal a person's mother, wife, or female lover.

old maid ▶ **noun 1** derogatory a single woman regarded as too old for marriage. **2** a prim and fussy person.

old man ▶ **noun** informal a person's father, husband, or male lover.

old man's beard ▶ **noun** a wild clematis with gray fluffy hairs around the seeds.

old mas·ter ▶ **noun** a great artist of the past, especially of the 13th–17th centuries in Europe.

Old Norse ▶ **noun** the language of medieval Norway, Iceland, Denmark, and Sweden.

old salt ▶ **noun** informal an experienced sailor.

old·ster /ˈōl(d)stər/ ▶ **noun** informal an older person.

Old Style ▶ **noun** the former method of calculating dates using the Julian calendar.

Old Tes·ta·ment ▶ **noun** the first part of the Christian Bible, comprising the sacred writings of Judaism in thirty-nine books.

old-time ▶ **adjective** relating to or typical of the past.

old-tim·er ▶ **noun** informal a very experienced person.

old wives' tale ▶ **noun** a widely held traditional belief that is now thought to be unscientific or incorrect.

old wom·an ▶ **noun 1** informal a person's mother, wife, or female lover. **2** derogatory a fussy or timid person.

old-world ▶ **adjective** belonging to or associated with past times; quaint.

Old World ▶ **noun** Europe, Asia, and Africa, regarded as the part of the world known before the discovery of the Americas.

o·lé /ōˈlā/ ▶ **exclamation** bravo!
– ORIGIN Spanish.

o·le·ag·i·nous /ˌōlēˈajənəs/ ▶ **adjective 1** oily or greasy. **2** excessively flattering; obsequious: *oleaginous speeches praising government policies*.
– ORIGIN Latin *oleaginus* 'of the olive tree.'

o·le·an·der /ˈōlēˌandər/ ▶ **noun** an evergreen shrub of warm countries with clusters of white, pink, or red flowers.
– ORIGIN Latin.

o·le·o /ˈōlēō/ ▶ **noun** informal margarine.

ol·fac·tion /älˈfakshən, ōl-/ ▶ **noun** technical the sense of smell.

ol·fac·to·ry /älˈfakt(ə)rē, ōl-/ ▶ **adjective** relating to the sense of smell.
– ORIGIN from Latin *olfacere* 'to smell.'

ol·i·garch /ˈäliˌgärk, ˈōl-/ ▶ **noun** a ruler in a country governed by a small group of people.

ol·i·gar·chy /ˈäliˌgärkē, ˈōli-/ ▶ **noun** (pl. **oligarchies**) **1** a small group of people having control of a country. **2** a country governed by a small group of people.
– DERIVATIVES **ol·i·gar·chic** /ˌäliˈgärkik, ˌōli-/ adjective.
– ORIGIN from Greek *oligoi* 'few' + *arkhein* 'to rule.'

Ol·i·go·cene /ˈäligōˌsēn/ ▶ **adjective** Geology relating to the third epoch of the Tertiary period (35.4 to 23.3 million years ago), when the first primates appeared.
– ORIGIN from Greek *oligos* 'few' + *kainos* 'new.'

ol·i·gop·o·ly /ˌäliˈgäpəlē/ ▶ **noun** (pl. **oligopolies**) a state of limited competition, in which a market is shared by a small number of producers or sellers.
– DERIVATIVES **ol·i·gop·o·list** noun **ol·i·gop·o·lis·tic** /ˌäliˌgäpəˈlistik/ adjective.

ol·ive /ˈäliv/ ▶ **noun 1** a small oval fruit with a hard pit and bitter flesh, green when unripe and black when ripe. **2** the small evergreen tree that produces olives. **3** (also **olive green**) a grayish-green color. ▶ **adjective** (of a person's complexion) yellowish brown; sallow.
– ORIGIN Latin *oliva*.

ol·ive branch ▶ **noun** an offer to restore friendly relations.
– ORIGIN with reference to the story of Noah in the Book of Genesis, to whom a dove returned with an olive branch after the Flood.

ol·ive drab ▶ **noun** a dull olive-green color, used in some military uniforms.

ol·ive oil ▶ **noun** an oil obtained from olives, used in cooking and salad dressings.

Ol·mec /ˈälˌmek, ˈōl-/ ▶ **noun** (pl. same or **Olmecs**) **1** a member of a prehistoric people who lived on the Gulf of Mexico. **2** an unrelated people inhabiting this area during the 15th and 16th centuries.
– ORIGIN Nahuatl, 'inhabitants of the rubber country.'

O·lym·pi·ad /ōˈlimpēˌad, əˈlim-/ ▶ **noun 1** a staging of the Olympic Games. **2** a major international contest in a particular game, sport, or scientific subject.

O·lym·pi·an /əˈlimpēən, ōˈlim-/ ▶ **adjective 1** relating to the Olympic Games. **2** like a god, especially in being powerful or aloof: *an editorial filled with Olympian disdain for the president*. **3** associated with Mount Olympus in Greece, traditional home of the Greek gods. ▶ **noun 1** a competitor in the Olympic Games. **2** a person who is greatly admired or superior to others. **3** any of the twelve main Greek gods.

O·lym·pic /əˈlimpik, ōˈlim-/ ▶ **adjective** relating to the Olympic Games. ▶ **noun** (**the Olympics**) the Olympic Games.

O·lym·pic Games ▶ **plural noun 1** a sports festival held every four years in different countries, established in 1896. **2** an ancient Greek festival with athletic, literary, and musical competitions, held every four years at Olympia in Greece.

om /ōm/ ▶ **noun** Hinduism & Tibetan Buddhism a mystic syllable, considered the most sacred mantra.
– ORIGIN Sanskrit.

O·ma·ni /ōˈmänē/ ▶ **noun** a person from Oman in the Arabian peninsula. ▶ **adjective** relating to Oman.

OMB ▶ **abbreviation** (in the federal government) Office of Management and Budget.

om·buds·man /ˈämbədzmən, -ˌbo͝odz-/ ▸ **noun** (pl. **ombudsmen**) an official appointed to investigate people's complaints against an organization.
– ORIGIN Swedish, 'legal representative.'

o·me·ga /ōˈmāgə, ōˈmē-/ ▸ **noun 1** the last letter of the Greek alphabet (Ω, ω), represented as 'o'. **2** (usu. before another noun) the last of a series.

o·me·ga-3 fat·ty ac·id ▸ **noun** an unsaturated fatty acid of a kind occurring chiefly in fish oils.

om·e·let /ˈäm(ə)lit/ (also **omelette**) ▸ **noun** a dish of beaten eggs cooked in a frying pan and folded over, usually with a filling inside.
– ORIGIN French.

o·men /ˈōmən/ ▸ **noun 1** an event regarded as a sign of future good or bad luck. **2** indication of the future: *a bird of evil omen.*

– SYNONYMS **portent,** sign, signal, token, forewarning, warning, harbinger, presage, indication; literary foretoken.

– ORIGIN Latin.

CHOOSE THE RIGHT WORD

See **SIGN**.

o·mer·tà /ōˈme(ə)rtə, ˌômerˈtä/ ▸ **noun** the Mafia code of silence about criminal activity.
– ORIGIN Italian, 'humility.'

om·i·nous /ˈämənəs/ ▸ **adjective** giving the impression that something bad is going to happen: *the first ominous signs of mental torment soon emerged.*

– SYNONYMS **threatening,** menacing, baleful, forbidding, foreboding, fateful, sinister, black, dark, gloomy.
– ANTONYMS promising.

– DERIVATIVES **om·i·nous·ly** adverb **om·i·nous·ness** noun.
– ORIGIN Latin *ominosus.*

o·mis·sion /ōˈmisʜən/ ▸ **noun 1** the action of leaving something out. **2** something that has been left out or not done. **3** a failure to fulfill a duty.

– SYNONYMS **1 exclusion,** leaving out, deletion, elimination. **2 negligence,** neglect, dereliction, oversight, lapse, failure.

o·mit /ōˈmit/ ▸ **verb** (**omits, omitting, omitted**) **1** leave out or exclude someone or something. **2** fail to do: *he modestly omits to mention that he was a pole-vault champion.*

– SYNONYMS **1 leave out,** exclude, miss out, miss, cut, drop, skip. **2 forget,** neglect, overlook, fail.
– ANTONYMS include, remember.

– DERIVATIVES **o·mis·si·ble** /ōˈmisəbəl/ adjective.
– ORIGIN Latin *omittere* 'let go.'

omni- ▸ **combining form 1** all; of all things: *omniscient.* **2** in all ways or places: *omnipresent.*
– ORIGIN from Latin *omnis* 'all.'

om·ni·bus /ˈämnəˌbəs/ ▸ **noun 1** a book containing several works previously published separately. **2** dated a bus.
– ORIGIN Latin, 'for all.'

om·ni·com·pet·ent /ˌämniˈkämpətənt/ ▸ **adjective** able to deal with all matters.
– DERIVATIVES **om·ni·com·pet·ence** noun.

om·ni·di·rec·tion·al /ˌämniˌdiˈreksʜənl/ ▸ **adjective** Telecommunications receiving signals from or transmitting in all directions.

om·nip·o·tent /ämˈnipətənt/ ▸ **adjective** having unlimited or very great power.

– SYNONYMS **all-powerful,** almighty, supreme, preeminent; invincible.

– DERIVATIVES **om·nip·o·tence** noun.
– ORIGIN Latin *omnipotens.*

om·ni·pres·ent /ˌämnəˈpreznt/ ▸ **adjective 1** widely or constantly encountered: *omnipresent military checkpoints.* **2** (of God) present everywhere at the same time.
– DERIVATIVES **om·ni·pres·ence** noun.

om·nis·cient /ämˈnisʜənt/ ▸ **adjective** knowing everything.

– SYNONYMS **all-knowing,** all-wise, all-seeing.

– DERIVATIVES **om·nis·cience** noun **om·nis·cient·ly** adverb.
– ORIGIN Latin *omnisciens.*

om·ni·sex·u·al /ˌämniˈseksʜo͞oəl/ ▸ **adjective** relating to or engaging in sexual activity with all kinds of people.

om·ni·vore /ˈämnəˌvôr/ ▸ **noun** an animal that eats both plants and meat.

om·niv·o·rous /ämˈniv(ə)rəs/ ▸ **adjective 1** (of an animal) eating both plants and meat. **2** taking in or using whatever is available; not selective: *an omnivorous reader.*
– DERIVATIVES **om·niv·o·rous·ly** adverb.

ON ▸ **abbreviation** Ontario.

on /än, ôn/ ▸ **preposition 1** in contact with and supported by a surface. **2** onto. **3** in the possession of. **4** forming a noticeable part of the surface of: *a scratch on her arm.* **5** about; concerning. **6** as a member of a committee, jury, etc. **7** having the thing mentioned as a target, aim, or focus: *thousands marched on Washington.* **8** stored in or broadcast by. **9** in the course of a journey or while traveling in a vehicle. **10** indicating the day or time of an event. **11** engaged in. **12** regularly taking a drug or medicine. **13** paid for by. **14** added to. ▸ **adverb 1** in contact with and supported by a surface. **2** (of clothing) being worn. **3** further forward; with continued movement or action: *I drove on.* **4** (of an entertainment or event) taking place or being presented. **5** (of an electrical appliance or power supply) functioning. **6** on duty or on stage. ▸ **noun** (also **on side**) Cricket the leg side.
– PHRASES **on and on** continually; without stopping. **you're on** informal said when accepting a challenge or bet.
– ORIGIN Old English.

on·a·ger /ˈänəjər/ ▸ **noun** a wild ass native to northern Iran.
– ORIGIN Greek *onagros* 'wild ass.'

on-air ▸ **adjective** broadcasting: *his on-air antics helped breathe new life into the series.*

o·nan·ism /ˈōnəˌnizəm/ ▸ **noun** formal **1** masturbation. **2** sexual intercourse in which the penis is withdrawn before ejaculation.
– DERIVATIVES **o·nan·ist** noun **o·nan·is·tic** /ˌōnəˈnistik/ adjective.
– ORIGIN from *Onan* in the Bible (Book of Genesis, chapter 38).

once /wəns/ ▸ **adverb 1** on one occasion or for one time only. **2** in the past; formerly. **3** on even one occasion: *he never once complained.*

– SYNONYMS **1 on one occasion,** one time. **2** *they were friends once* **formerly,** previously, in the past, once upon a time, in days/times gone by, in the (good) old days, long ago.

▶ **conjunction** as soon as; when.

– SYNONYMS *he'll be all right once she's gone* **as soon as,** the moment, when, after.

– PHRASES **all at once** suddenly. **at once 1** immediately. **2** at the same time; simultaneously. **for once** (or **this once**) on this occasion only. **once and for all** (or **once for all**) now and for the last time; finally. **once** (or **every once**) **in a while** occasionally. **once or twice** a few times. **once upon a time** at some time in the past.

once-o·ver ▶ **noun** informal a rapid inspection, search, or piece of work.

on·co·gene /'änGkəˌjēn/ ▶ **noun** a gene that in certain circumstances can transform a cell into a tumor cell.
– DERIVATIVES **on·co·gen·ic** /ˌänGkə'jenik/ adjective.
– ORIGIN from Greek *onkos* 'mass.'

on·col·o·gy /än'käləjē, änG-/ ▶ **noun** the study and treatment of tumors.
– DERIVATIVES **on·co·log·i·cal** /ˌänkə'läjikəl, ˌänG-/ adjective **on·col·o·gist** noun.

on·com·ing /'änˌkəmiNG, 'ôn-/ ▶ **adjective** approaching from the front; moving toward one.

on·co·pro·tein /ˌänGkə'prōtē(ə)n/ ▶ **noun** a protein encoded by an oncogene that can cause the transformation of a cell into a tumor cell if introduced into it.
– ORIGIN from *onco-* 'of or relating to tumors' + **PROTEIN**.

one /wən/ ▶ **cardinal number 1** the lowest cardinal number; 1. (Roman numeral: **i** or **I**.) **2** a single person or thing. **3** single; sole. **4** identical; the same. **5** (before a person's name) a certain. **6** informal a noteworthy example of: *he was one smart-mouthed troublemaker.* ▶ **pronoun 1** used to refer to a person or thing previously mentioned or easily identified. **2** a person of a specified kind: *her loved ones.* **3** (third person sing.) used to refer to the speaker, or any person, as representing people in general.
– PHRASES **at one** in agreement or harmony. **be one up on** informal have an advantage over someone. **one and all** everyone. **one and only** unique; single. **one another** each other. **one by one** separately and following each other. **one day** at an unspecified time in the past or future. **one or two** informal a few.
– ORIGIN Old English.

USAGE

In modern English the use of **one** to mean 'anyone' or 'me and people in general' (*one must try one's best*) is chiefly restricted to formal situations and writing, and can be regarded as pompous or overformal. In informal and spoken contexts the normal alternative is **you** (*you have to do what you can, don't you?*).

one-armed ban·dit ▶ **noun** informal a slot machine operated by pulling a long handle at the side.

one-di·men·sion·al ▶ **adjective** not complex or deep; superficial.

one-horse race ▶ **noun** a contest in which one competitor is clearly better than all the others.

one-horse town ▶ **noun** informal a small town with few and poor facilities.

o·nei·ric /ō'nīrik/ ▶ **adjective** formal relating to dreams or dreaming.
– ORIGIN from Greek *oneiros* 'dream.'

one-lin·er ▶ **noun** informal a short joke or witty remark.

one-man band ▶ **noun 1** a street entertainer who plays many instruments at the same time. **2** a person who runs a business alone.

one·ness /'wən(n)is/ ▶ **noun 1** the state of being unified, whole, or in harmony: *the oneness of man and nature.* **2** the state of being one in number.

one-night stand (also **one-nighter** /'nītər/) ▶ **noun 1** informal a sexual relationship lasting only one night. **2** a single performance of a play or show in a particular place.

one-on-one ▶ **noun** informal a face-to-face encounter.

on·er·ous /'ōnərəs, 'änərəs/ ▶ **adjective** involving great effort and difficulty: *the onerous task of running a country.*
– ORIGIN Latin *onerosus.*

WORD TOOLKIT

See **ARDUOUS**.

one·self /wən'self/ ▶ **pronoun** (third person sing.) **1** (reflexive) used as the object of a verb or preposition when this is the same as the subject of the clause and the subject is 'one'. **2** (emphatic) used to emphasize that one does something individually or without help. **3** in one's normal state of body or mind.

one-shot ▶ **adjective** informal achieved with a single attempt or action.

one-sid·ed ▶ **adjective 1** giving only one point of view; biased. **2** (of a contest or conflict) not involving participants of equal ability.

– SYNONYMS **1 biased,** prejudiced, partisan, partial, slanted, distorted, unfair. **2 unequal,** uneven, unbalanced.
– ANTONYMS impartial, equal.

one-stop ▶ **adjective** (of a store or other business) capable of supplying all a customer's needs within a particular range of goods or services: *one-stop shopping.*

one-time ▶ **adjective** former.

one-to-one ▶ **adjective & adverb** referring to a situation in which two people come into direct contact or opposition. ▶ **noun** informal a face-to-face meeting or conversation.

one-track mind ▶ **noun** informal a mind preoccupied with one subject, especially sex.

one-trick po·ny ▶ **noun** informal a person or thing with only one special feature or talent.

one-two ▶ **noun 1** a pair of punches in quick succession with alternate hands. **2** chiefly Football a move in which a player plays a short pass to a teammate and moves forward to receive an immediate return pass.

one-up·man·ship /wən 'əpmənˌSHip/ (also **one-upsmanship**) ▶ **noun** informal the technique of gaining an advantage over someone else.

one-way ▶ **adjective** moving or allowing movement in one direction only.

on·go·ing /'änˌgōiNG, 'ôn-/ ▶ **adjective** continuing; still in progress.

– SYNONYMS **in progress,** under way, going on, continuing, proceeding.

on·ion /'ənyən/ ▶ **noun** a vegetable consisting of a bulb with a strong taste and smell.

– DERIVATIVES **on·ion·y** adjective.
– ORIGIN Old French *oignon.*

on·line /ˈänlīn, ˈôn-/ ▶ **adjective & adverb 1** controlled by or connected to a computer. **2** available on or carried out via the Internet: *online banking.* **3** in or into operation.

on·look·er /ˈänˌlo͝okər, ˈôn-/ ▶ **noun** a person who watches something without getting involved in it.

– SYNONYMS **eyewitness,** witness, observer, spectator, bystander; informal rubberneck.

– DERIVATIVES **on·look·ing** adjective.

on·ly /ˈōnlē/ ▶ **adverb 1** and no one or nothing more besides. **2** no longer ago than. **3** not until. **4** with the negative result that: *he turned, only to find his way blocked.*

– SYNONYMS **1 at most,** at best, just, no more than, hardly, barely, scarcely. **2 exclusively,** solely, purely.

▶ **adjective 1** alone of its or their kind; single or solitary. **2** alone deserving consideration.

– SYNONYMS **sole,** single, one (and only), solitary, lone, unique, exclusive.

▶ **conjunction** informal except that.
– PHRASES **only just 1** by a very small margin. **2** very recently. **only too** —— to an extreme or regrettable extent.
– ORIGIN Old English.

USAGE

The traditional view is that, to avoid confusion, you should place the adverb **only** next to the word or words whose meaning it restricts: *I have seen him only once* rather than *I have only seen him once.* In practice, people tend to state **only** as early as possible in the sentence, generally just before the main verb, and the result is usually clear.

on·o·mas·tic /ˌänəˈmastik/ ▶ **adjective** relating to the study of the history and origin of proper names.
– DERIVATIVES **on·o·mas·tics** noun.
– ORIGIN from Greek *onoma* 'name.'

on·o·mat·o·poe·ia /ˌänəˌmatəˈpēə, -ˌmätə-/ ▶ **noun** the use or formation of words that sound similar to the noise described (e.g., *cuckoo, sizzle*).
– DERIVATIVES **on·o·mat·o·poe·ic** /-ˈpē-ik/ (or **onomatopoetic** /-pōˈetik/) adjective **on·o·mat·o·poe·i·cal·ly** /-ˈpē-ik(ə)lē/ (or **onomatopoetically** /-pōˈetik(ə)lē/) adverb.
– ORIGIN Greek *onomatopoiia* 'word-making.'

on-ramp ▶ **noun** a lane for traffic entering a turnpike or highway.

on·rush /ˈänˌrəsʜ, ˈôn-/ ▶ **noun** a surging rush forward.
– DERIVATIVES **on·rush·ing** adjective.

on-screen ▶ **adjective & adverb 1** shown or appearing in a movie or television program: *on-screen violence.* **2** making use of or performed using a video screen: *on-screen editing facilities.*

on·set /ˈänˌset, ˈôn-/ ▶ **noun** the beginning of something, especially something unpleasant: *technology is effective in detecting the onset of heart disease.*

– SYNONYMS **start,** beginning, commencement, arrival, appearance, inception, day one, outbreak; informal kickoff.
– ANTONYMS end.

on·shore /ˈänˈsʜôr, ˈôn-/ ▶ **adjective & adverb 1** situated or occurring on land. **2** (of the wind) blowing from the sea toward the land.

on·side /ˈänˈsīd, ˈôn-/ ▶ **adjective & adverb** (of a player in soccer, hockey, etc.) occupying a position where playing the ball is allowed.

on-site (also **onsite**) ▶ **adjective & adverb** taking place or situated on a particular site or premises.

on·slaught /ˈänˌslôt, ˈôn-/ ▶ **noun 1** a fierce or destructive attack. **2** an overwhelmingly large quantity of people or things: *the onslaught of cars far exceeds capacity.*

– SYNONYMS **attack,** assault, offensive, advance, charge, blitz, bombardment, barrage.

– ORIGIN Dutch *aenslag.*

on·stage /ˈänˈstāj, ˈôn-/ ▶ **adjective & adverb** (in a theater) on the stage and so visible to the audience.

on·to /ˈänˌto͞o, ˈôn-/ ▶ **preposition** moving to a place on: *they went up onto the ridge.*
– PHRASES **be onto** informal **1** be close to discovering that someone has done something wrong. **2** have an idea that is likely to lead to an important discovery.

USAGE

It is important to maintain a distinction between the preposition **onto** or **on to** and the use of the adverb **on** followed by the preposition **to**: *she climbed onto* (sometimes *on to*) *the roof,* but *let's go on to* (never onto) *the next chapter.*

on·tol·o·gy /änˈtäləjē/ ▶ **noun** the branch of philosophy concerned with the nature of being.
– DERIVATIVES **on·to·log·i·cal** /ˌäntəˈläjikəl/ adjective **on·tol·o·gist** noun.

o·nus /ˈōnəs/ ▶ **noun** a duty or responsibility: *the onus is on you to spot mistakes.*

– SYNONYMS **burden,** responsibility, obligation, duty, weight, load.

– ORIGIN Latin, 'load or burden.'

on·ward /ˈänwərd, ˈôn-/ ▶ **adverb** (also **onwards**) **1** in a continuing forward direction; ahead. **2** so as to make progress. ▶ **adjective** moving forward.

on·yx /ˈäniks/ ▶ **noun** a semiprecious variety of agate with different colors in layers.
– ORIGIN Greek *onux* 'fingernail, onyx.'

oo·dles /ˈo͞odlz/ ▶ **plural noun** informal a very great number or amount.
– ORIGIN unknown.

o·o·lite /ˈōəˌlīt/ ▶ **noun** limestone consisting of rounded granules, each consisting of calcium carbonate surrounding a grain of sand.
– DERIVATIVES **o·o·lit·ic** /ˌōəˈlitik/ adjective.
– ORIGIN Latin *oolites* 'egg stone.'

oo·long /ˈo͞oˌlôɴɢ, -ˌläɴɢ/ ▶ **noun** a kind of dark-colored partly fermented China tea.
– ORIGIN Chinese, 'black dragon.'

oom·pah /ˈo͞omˌpä, ˈo͝om-/ ▶ **noun** informal the sound of deep-toned brass instruments in a band.
– ORIGIN imitating the sound.

oomph /o͝omf, o͞omf/ (also **umph**) ▶ **noun** informal the quality of being exciting, vigorous, or sexually attractive: *add oomph to your personal style.*
– ORIGIN uncertain.

oops /o͝ops, o͞ops/ ▶ **exclamation** informal used to show recognition of a mistake or minor accident.

ooze /o͞oz/ ▶ **verb 1** (of a fluid) slowly trickle or seep out.

2 give a powerful impression of: *she oozes sex appeal.*

– SYNONYMS **seep,** discharge, flow, exude, trickle, drip, dribble, drain, leak.

▶ **noun 1** wet mud or slime, especially that found at the bottom of a river, lake, or sea. **2** the sluggish flow of a fluid.
– DERIVATIVES **ooz·y** adjective.
– ORIGIN Old English, 'juice or sap.'

op /äp/ ▶ **noun** informal **1** a surgical operation. **2** (**ops**) military operations.

Op. (also **op.**) ▶ **abbreviation** Music (before a number given to each work of a composer) opus.

o·pac·i·ty /ōˈpasitē/ ▶ **noun 1** the state of being opaque or difficult to see through. **2** the quality of being difficult to understand.

o·pal /ˈōpəl/ ▶ **noun** a semitransparent gemstone in which many small points of shifting color can be seen.
– ORIGIN Latin *opalus.*

o·pal·es·cent /ˌōpəˈlesənt/ ▶ **adjective** showing many small points of shifting color: *opalescent eyes.*
– DERIVATIVES **o·pal·es·cence** noun.

o·pal·ine /ˈōpəˌlēn, -ˌlīn/ ▶ **adjective** showing many points of shifting color; opalescent.

o·paque /ōˈpāk/ ▶ **adjective** (**opaquer, opaquest**) **1** not able to be seen through; not transparent. **2** difficult or impossible to understand.

– SYNONYMS **1 nontransparent,** cloudy, filmy, blurred, smeared, misty. **2 obscure,** unclear, unfathomable, incomprehensible, unintelligible, impenetrable; informal as clear as mud.
– ANTONYMS transparent, clear.

– DERIVATIVES **o·paque·ly** adverb.
– ORIGIN Latin *opacus* 'darkened.'

op art ▶ **noun** a form of abstract art that gives the illusion of movement by its use of pattern and color.
– ORIGIN abbreviation of *optical art.*

op. cit. /ˈäp ˌsit/ ▶ **adverb** in the work already cited.
– ORIGIN from Latin *opere citato.*

OPEC /ˈōpek/ ▶ **abbreviation** Organization of the Petroleum Exporting Countries.

op-ed /ˈäped/ ▶ **adjective** referring to the page opposite the editorial page in a newspaper, devoted to commentary, feature articles, etc.

o·pen /ˈōpən/ ▶ **adjective 1** not closed, fastened, or restricted. **2** exposed to view or attack; not covered or protected. **3** (**open to**) likely to suffer from or be affected by: *the system is open to abuse.* **4** spread out, expanded, or unfolded. **5** admitting customers or visitors; available for business. **6** accessible or available. **7** frank and communicative. **8** not disguised or hidden: *his eyes showed open admiration.* **9** not finally decided. **10** (**open to**) making possible: *a message open to different interpretations.* **11** (of a string of a musical instrument) allowed to vibrate along its whole length. **12** (of an electric circuit) having a break in the conducting path.

– SYNONYMS **1 unlocked,** unlatched, off the latch, ajar, gaping, yawning. **2** *open countryside | open spaces* **unenclosed,** rolling, sweeping, wide open, exposed, spacious, uncrowded, uncluttered, undeveloped. **3** *the position is still open* **available,** free, vacant, unfilled; informal up for grabs. **4** *open to abuse* **vulnerable,** subject, susceptible, liable, exposed, an easy target for. **5** *she was very open* **frank,** candid, honest, forthcoming, communicative, forthright, direct, unreserved, plain-spoken, outspoken, blunt; informal upfront. **6** *open hostility* **overt,** manifest, conspicuous, plain, undisguised, unconcealed, clear, naked, blatant, flagrant, barefaced, brazen.
– ANTONYMS shut, closed.

▶ **verb 1** make or become open. **2** formally begin or establish: *he opened his own restaurant.* **3** make something available or more widely known. **4** (**open onto/into**) give access to. **5** (**open up**) become more frank or communicative. **6** break the conducting path of an electric circuit.

– SYNONYMS **1 unfasten,** unlock, unbolt, throw wide. **2 unwrap,** undo, untie. **3 spread out,** unfold, unfurl, unroll, straighten out. **4 begin,** start, commence, initiate, set in motion, get going, get under way, get off the ground; informal kick off.
– ANTONYMS close, shut.

▶ **noun 1** (**the open**) outdoors or in the countryside. **2** (**Open**) a competition with no restrictions on who may compete.
– DERIVATIVES **o·pen·a·ble** adjective **o·pen·ness** noun.
– PHRASES **in open court** in a court of law, before the judge and the public. **in** (or **into**) **the open** not concealed or secret. **open-and-shut** not disputed; straightforward. **open up** (or **open fire**) begin shooting.
– ORIGIN Old English.

WORD LINKS

agoraphobia *fear of open spaces*

o·pen air ▶ **noun** a free or unenclosed space outdoors. ▶ **adjective** (**open-air**) positioned or taking place out of doors.

– SYNONYMS **outdoor,** out-of-doors, outside, alfresco.

o·pen book ▶ **noun** a person or thing that is easily understood or interpreted.

o·pen-end·ed ▶ **adjective** having no limit decided in advance.

o·pen en·roll·ment ▶ **noun** the unrestricted enrollment of students at schools, colleges, or universities of their choice.

o·pen·er /ˈōp(ə)nər/ ▶ **noun 1** a device for opening something. **2** the first of a series of games, cultural events, etc.
– PHRASES **for openers** informal to start with.

o·pen-hand·ed ▶ **adjective 1** (of a blow) delivered with the palm of the hand. **2** giving freely; generous.

o·pen-heart·ed ▶ **adjective** friendly and kind.

o·pen-heart sur·ger·y ▶ **noun** surgery in which the heart is exposed and the blood made to bypass it.

o·pen house ▶ **noun 1** a place or situation in which all visitors are welcome. **2** a day when members of the public are invited to visit a place or institution to which they do not normally have access.

o·pen·ing /ˈōp(ə)niNG/ ▶ **noun 1** a space or gap that allows access or passage. **2** a beginning. **3** a ceremony at which a building, show, etc., is declared to be open. **4** an opportunity or available job: *there are few openings for an ex-football player.*

– SYNONYMS **1 hole,** gap, aperture, space, orifice, vent, crack, slit, chink, fissure, cleft, crevice, interstice. **2 beginning,** start, commencement, outset; informal kickoff. **3 vacancy,** position, post, job, opportunity.

▶ **adjective** coming at the beginning; initial.

– SYNONYMS **first,** initial, introductory, preliminary, maiden, inaugural.
– ANTONYMS final, closing.

o·pen let·ter ▶ **noun** a letter addressed to a particular person but intended for publication in a newspaper or journal.

o·pen·ly /ˈōpənlē/ ▶ **adverb** in a frank, honest, or public way.

– SYNONYMS **1 publicly,** blatantly, flagrantly, overtly. **2 frankly,** candidly, explicitly, honestly, sincerely, forthrightly, freely.

o·pen mar·ket ▶ **noun** a situation in which people or companies can trade without restrictions.

o·pen mar·riage ▶ **noun** a marriage in which both partners agree that each may have other sexual partners.

o·pen-mind·ed ▶ **adjective** willing to consider new ideas.

– SYNONYMS **unbiased,** unprejudiced, neutral, objective, disinterested, tolerant, liberal, permissive, broad-minded.
– ANTONYMS prejudiced, narrow-minded.

o·pen-necked ▶ **adjective** (of a shirt) worn with the collar unbuttoned and without a tie.

o·pen-pit ▶ **adjective** (of mining) in which coal or ore is extracted from a level near the earth's surface, rather than from shafts.

o·pen-plan ▶ **adjective** (of a room or building) having few or no dividing walls.

o·pen sea·son ▶ **noun 1** the annual period when restrictions on the killing of certain types of wildlife are lifted. **2** a period when all restrictions on a particular activity or product are abandoned or ignored.

o·pen se·cret ▶ **noun** a supposed secret that is in fact known to many people.

o·pen-source ▶ **adjective** referring to computer software for which the original source code is made freely available.

o·pen-toed ▶ **adjective** (of a shoe) not covering the toes.

o·pen·work /ˈōpənˌwərk/ ▶ **noun** ornamental work in cloth, leather, etc., with regular patterns of openings and holes.

o·pe·ra¹ /ˈäp(ə)rə/ ▶ **noun 1** a dramatic work set to music for singers and musicians. **2** a building in which operas are performed.
– ORIGIN Italian.

o·pe·ra² plural of **OPUS**.

op·er·a·ble /ˈäp(ə)rəbəl/ ▶ **adjective 1** able to be used. **2** able to be treated by a surgical operation.

o·pe·ra buf·fa /ˈäp(ə)rə ˈbo͞ofə, ˌōperä ˈbo͞ofä/ ▶ **noun** (pl. **opere buffe** /ˈäpərā ˈbo͞ofā, ˈōpeˌrā/) a comic opera, especially in Italian.
– ORIGIN Italian.

op·er·a glass·es ▶ **plural noun** small binoculars for use at the opera or theater.

op·er·a house ▶ **noun** a theater designed for the performance of opera.

op·er·and /ˈäpəˌrand/ ▶ **noun** Mathematics the quantity on which an operation is to be done.
– ORIGIN Latin *operandum* 'thing to be operated on.'

o·pe·ra se·ri·a /ˈäp(ə)rə ˈsi(ə)rēə, ˈōpeˌrä ˈserēˌä/ ▶ **noun** (pl. **opere serie** /ˈäpərā ˈsi(ə)rēā, ˈōpeˌrā ˈserēˌā/) an opera, especially one of the 18th century in Italian, on a serious theme.
– ORIGIN Italian.

op·er·ate /ˈäpəˌrāt/ ▶ **verb 1** (of a machine, process, or system) be in action; function. **2** control a machine, process, or business. **3** (of an organization) carry on its activities in a particular way or from a particular place: *they operate from a New York office*. **4** (of an armed force) carry on military activities in a particular place. **5** be in effect: *a powerful law operates in politics*. **6** perform a surgical operation.

– SYNONYMS **1 work,** run, use, handle, control, manage, drive, steer, maneuver, function, go, perform. **2 direct,** control, manage, run, handle, be in control/charge of.

– ORIGIN Latin *operari*.

op·er·at·ic /ˌäpəˈratik/ ▶ **adjective 1** relating to opera. **2** melodramatic or exaggerated: *she wrung her hands in operatic despair*.
– DERIVATIVES **op·er·at·i·cal·ly** /-ik(ə)lē/ adverb.

op·er·at·ing prof·it ▶ **noun** a gross profit before expenses are deducted.

op·er·at·ing room ▶ **noun** a room in which surgical operations are performed.

op·er·at·ing sys·tem ▶ **noun** the low-level software that supports a computer's basic functions.

op·er·at·ing ta·ble ▶ **noun** a table on which a patient is placed during a surgical operation.

op·er·a·tion /ˌäpəˈrāsʜən/ ▶ **noun 1** the action or process of operating: *we have a lot of security measures in operation*. **2** an act of surgery performed on a patient to remove or repair a damaged body part. **3** an organized action involving a number of people: *a rescue operation*. **4** a business organization. **5** Mathematics a process in which a number, quantity, expression, etc., is altered according to formal rules.

– SYNONYMS **1 functioning,** working, running, performance, action. **2** *a military operation* **action,** exercise, undertaking, enterprise, maneuver, campaign. **3 business,** enterprise, company, firm.

op·er·a·tion·al /ˌäpəˈrāsʜənl/ ▶ **adjective 1** being used or ready for use. **2** relating to the functioning of an organization.

– SYNONYMS **running,** up and running, working, functioning, operative, in operation, in use, in action, in working order, serviceable, functional.

– DERIVATIVES **op·er·a·tion·al·ly** adverb.

op·er·a·tive /ˈäp(ə)rətiv, ˈäpəˌrātiv/ ▶ **adjective** **1** functioning or having effect. **2** (of a word) having the most importance in a phrase. **3** relating to surgery.

– SYNONYMS **running,** up and running, working, functioning, operational, in operation, in use, in action, in effect.

▶ **noun 1** a worker. **2** a private detective or secret agent.

– SYNONYMS **1 machinist,** operator, mechanic, engineer, worker, workman, (factory) hand. **2 agent,** secret/undercover agent, spy, mole, plant.

– DERIVATIVES **op·er·a·tive·ly** adverb.

op·er·a·tor /ˈäpəˌrātər/ ▶ **noun 1** a person who operates equipment or a machine. **2** a person who works at the switchboard of a telephone exchange. **3** a person or company that runs a business. **4** informal a person who acts in a clever or manipulative way: *a smooth operator.* **5** a mathematical symbol or function referring to an operation (e.g., ×, +).

op·er·et·ta /ˌäpəˈretə/ ▶ **noun** a short opera on a light or humorous theme.
– ORIGIN Italian, 'little opera.'

o·phid·i·an /ōˈfidēən/ ▶ **adjective** literary resembling or typical of a snake: *a soft, ophidian hiss.*
– ORIGIN Greek *ophis* 'snake.'

oph·thal·mi·a /äfˈᴛʜalmēə, äp-/ ▶ **noun** inflammation of the eye, especially conjunctivitis.
– ORIGIN from Greek *ophthalmos* 'eye.'

oph·thal·mic /äfˈᴛʜalmik, äp-/ ▶ **adjective** relating to the eye and its diseases.

oph·thal·mol·o·gy /ˌäfᴛʜə(l)ˈmäləjē, ˌäp-/ ▶ **noun** the study and treatment of disorders and diseases of the eye.
– DERIVATIVES **oph·thal·mo·log·i·cal** /-məˈläjikəl/ adjective **oph·thal·mol·o·gist** noun.

oph·thal·mo·scope /äfˈᴛʜalməˌskōp, äp-/ ▶ **noun** an instrument for inspecting the retina and other parts of the eye.
– DERIVATIVES **oph·thal·mo·scop·ic** /ˌäfᴛʜalməˈskäpik, ˌäp-/ adjective **oph·thal·mos·co·py** /ˌäfᴛʜəlˈmäskəpē, ˌäp-/ noun.

o·pi·ate /ˈōpēət, -ˌāt/ ▶ **noun 1** a drug containing or related to opium. **2** something that causes a false sense of contentment: *movies are the opiate of the people.* ▶ **adjective** relating to or containing opium.
– DERIVATIVES **o·pi·at·ed** adjective.

o·pine /ōˈpīn/ ▶ **verb** formal state something as one's opinion.
– ORIGIN Latin *opinari* 'think, believe.'

o·pin·ion /əˈpinyən/ ▶ **noun 1** a personal view not necessarily based on fact or knowledge. **2** the views of people in general: *public opinion.* **3** an estimate of quality or worth: *he had a high opinion of himself.* **4** a formal statement of advice by an expert or professional.

– SYNONYMS **belief,** thought(s), idea, way of thinking, feeling, mind, view, point of view, viewpoint, standpoint, assessment, estimation, judgment, conviction.

– PHRASES **a matter of opinion** something not capable of being proven either way.
– ORIGIN Latin.

CHOOSE THE RIGHT WORD

opinion, belief, conviction, persuasion, sentiment, view

When you give your **opinion** on something, you offer a conclusion or a judgment that, although it may be open to question, seems true or probable to you at the time (*she was known for her strong opinions on women in the workplace*). A **view** is an opinion that is affected by your personal feelings or biases (*his views on life were essentially optimistic*), while a **sentiment** is a more or less settled opinion that may still be colored by emotion (*her sentiments on aging were shared by many other women approaching fifty*). A **belief** differs from an opinion or a view in that it is not necessarily the creation of the person who holds it; the emphasis here is on the mental acceptance of an idea, a proposition, or a doctrine and on the assurance of its truth (*religious beliefs; his belief in the power of the body to heal itself*). A **conviction** is a firmly-held and unshakable belief whose truth is not doubted (*she could not be swayed in her convictions*), while a **persuasion** (in this sense) is a strong belief that is unshakable because you want to believe that it's true rather than because there is evidence proving it so (*she was of the persuasion that he was innocent*).

o·pin·ion·at·ed /əˈpinyəˌnātid/ ▶ **adjective** tending to state one's views forcefully and to be unwilling to change them.

o·pin·ion poll ▶ **noun** the questioning of a small sample of people in order to assess wider public opinion.

o·pi·oid /ˈōpēˌoid/ ▶ **noun** a compound resembling opium. ▶ **adjective** relating to opioids.

o·pi·um /ˈōpēəm/ ▶ **noun** an addictive drug prepared from the juice of a poppy, used to alter mood or behavior and in medicine as a painkiller.
– ORIGIN Greek *opion* 'poppy juice.'

o·pos·sum /(ə)ˈpäsəm/ ▶ **noun** an American marsupial mammal with a tail that it can use for grasping.
– ORIGIN Algonquian, 'white dog.'

opp. ▶ **abbreviation** opposite.

op·po·nent /əˈpōnənt/ ▶ **noun 1** a person who opposes or competes with another in a contest, argument, or fight. **2** a person who disagrees with a proposal or practice.

– SYNONYMS **1 rival,** adversary, competitor, enemy, antagonist, combatant, contender, challenger; literary foe. **2 critic,** objector, dissenter.
– ANTONYMS ally, supporter.

– ORIGIN from Latin *opponere* 'set against.'

op·por·tune /ˌäpərˈt(y)o͞on/ ▶ **adjective 1** (of a time) especially convenient or appropriate for something: *he chose an opportune moment to get away.* **2** done or occurring at an especially convenient or appropriate time.
– DERIVATIVES **op·por·tune·ly** adverb.
– ORIGIN Latin *opportunus.*

CHOOSE THE RIGHT WORD

See **TIMELY**.

op·por·tun·ist /ˌäpərˈt(y)o͞onist/ ▶ **noun** a person who takes advantage of opportunities when they arise, regardless of whether or not they are right to do so. ▶ **adjective** taking advantage of opportunities when they arise; opportunistic.
– DERIVATIVES **op·por·tun·ism** /-ˌnizəm/ noun.

op·por·tun·is·tic /ˌäpərt(y)o͞oˈnistik/ ▶ **adjective 1** taking advantage of opportunities when they arise, especially in a selfish way. **2** (of an infection) occurring when the immune system is depressed.
– DERIVATIVES **op·por·tun·is·ti·cal·ly** /-ik(ə)lē/ adverb.

op·por·tu·ni·ty /ˌäpərˈt(y)o͞onitē/ ▶ **noun** (pl. **opportunities**) **1** a favorable time or set of circumstances for doing something. **2** a chance for employment or promotion: *job opportunities.*

– SYNONYMS **chance,** time, occasion, moment, opening, option, window, possibility, scope, freedom; informal shot, break.

op·pos·a·ble /əˈpōzəbəl/ ▶ **adjective** (of the thumb of a primate mammal) capable of facing and touching the other digits on the same hand.

op·pose /əˈpōz/ ▶ **verb 1** (also **be opposed to**) disagree with and try to prevent or resist: *Ross was rabidly* *opposed to the plan*. **2** (as adj. **opposing**) opposite. **3** (as adj. **opposed**) (of two or more things) contrasting or conflicting. **4** compete with or fight someone.

– SYNONYMS **1 be against,** object to, be hostile to, disagree with, disapprove of, resist, take a stand against, put up a fight against, fight, counter, challenge, take issue with. **2** (as adj. **opposing**) *the brothers fought on opposing sides in the war* **rival,** opposite, enemy, competing. **3** (as adj. **opposing**) *two opposing points of view* **conflicting,** contrasting, opposite, incompatible, irreconcilable, contradictory, clashing, at variance, at odds, opposed.
– ANTONYMS support.

– DERIVATIVES **op·pos·er** noun.
– ORIGIN Latin *opponere* 'set against.'

op·po·site /'äpəzit/ ▶ **adjective 1** situated on the other or further side; facing. **2** completely different. **3** being the other of a contrasted pair: *the opposite ends of the price range*. **4** (of angles) between opposite sides of the intersection of two lines.

– SYNONYMS **1 facing,** face to face with, across from. **2 conflicting,** contrasting, incompatible, irreconcilable, contradictory, at variance, at odds, differing. **3 rival,** opposing, competing, enemy.

▶ **noun** a person or thing that is completely different from or the reverse of another.

– SYNONYMS **reverse,** converse, antithesis, contrary, polar opposite.
– ANTONYMS same.

▶ **adverb** in an opposite position.
▶ **preposition** in a position opposite to.
– DERIVATIVES **op·po·site·ly** adverb.
– ORIGIN Latin *oppositus*.

CHOOSE THE RIGHT WORD

opposite, contradictory, antithetical, contrary, reverse

All of these adjectives are usually applied to abstractions and are used to describe ideas, statements, qualities, forces, etc., that are so far apart as to seem irreconcilable. **Opposite** refers to ideas or things that are symmetrically opposed in position, direction, or character—in other words, that are set against each other in such a way that the contrast or conflict between them is highlighted (*they sat opposite one another at the table*). **Contradictory** goes a little further, implying that if one of two opposing statements, propositions, or principles is true, the other must be false (*he assured us the fee would be under $500; his partner gave us contradictory information, saying costs could go as high as $800*). Two contradictory elements are mutually exclusive; for example, *alive* and *dead* are contradictory terms because logically they cannot be applied to the same thing. **Antithetical** implies that the two things being contrasted are diametrically opposed—as far apart or as different from each other as is possible (*they debated the antithetical theories of creationism and evolution*). **Contrary** adds connotations of conflict or antagonism (*the group's discussion was hindered by his contrary remarks*). **Reverse** applies to that which moves or faces in the opposite direction (*he scribbled something on the reverse side of her business card*).

op·po·site num·ber ▶ **noun** a person's counterpart in another organization.

op·po·site sex ▶ **noun** (**the opposite sex**) women in relation to men or vice versa.

op·po·si·tion /ˌäpəˈzisHən/ ▶ **noun 1** resistance or disagreement: *there was considerable opposition to the plan*. **2** a group of opponents. **3** (**the opposition**) the political party that is opposed to the one in office. **4** a contrast or complete opposite.

– SYNONYMS **1 resistance,** hostility, antagonism, antipathy, objection, dissent, disapproval. **2 opponent(s),** opposing side, competition, rival(s), adversary.
– ANTONYMS agreement.

– DERIVATIVES **op·po·si·tion·al** adjective **op·po·si·tion·ist** adjective & noun.

op·press /ə'pres/ ▶ **verb 1** treat or govern someone in a very harsh and unfair way. **2** make someone feel distressed or anxious.

– SYNONYMS **persecute,** tyrannize, crush, repress, subjugate, subdue, keep down, rule with a rod of iron, rule with an iron fist.

– DERIVATIVES **op·pres·sor** noun.
– ORIGIN Old French *oppresser*.

op·pres·sion /ə'presHən/ ▶ **noun** prolonged cruel or unjust treatment or control.

– SYNONYMS **persecution,** abuse, ill-treatment, tyranny, repression, suppression, subjugation, cruelty, brutality, injustice.
– ANTONYMS freedom.

op·pres·sive /ə'presiv/ ▶ **adjective 1** harsh and demanding strict obedience: *an oppressive dictatorship*. **2** causing anxiety or distress. **3** (of weather) hot and humid.

– SYNONYMS **1 harsh,** cruel, brutal, repressive, tyrannical, despotic, draconian, ruthless, merciless, pitiless. **2 muggy,** close, heavy, hot, humid, sticky, airless, stuffy, stifling, sultry.
– ANTONYMS lenient, fresh.

– DERIVATIVES **op·pres·sive·ly** adverb **op·pres·sive·ness** noun.

op·pro·bri·ous /ə'prōbrēəs/ ▶ **adjective** formal expressing criticism or scorn.
– DERIVATIVES **op·pro·bri·ous·ly** adverb.

op·pro·bri·um /ə'prōbrēəm/ ▶ **noun** formal **1** criticism or scorn. **2** public disgrace arising from bad behavior.
– ORIGIN Latin, 'infamy.'

opt /äpt/ ▶ **verb** make a choice: *the couple opted for a traditional marriage*.

– SYNONYMS **choose,** select, pick, decide, elect; (**opt for**) go for, settle on.

– PHRASES **opt out** choose not to participate in something.
– ORIGIN Latin *optare* 'choose, wish.'

op·tic /'äptik/ ▶ **adjective** relating to the eye or vision.
▶ **noun** Brit. trademark a device fastened to the neck of an inverted bottle for measuring out liquor.
– ORIGIN Greek *optikos*.

op·ti·cal /'äptikəl/ ▶ **adjective** relating to vision, light, or optics.
– DERIVATIVES **op·ti·cal·ly** adverb.

op·ti·cal char·ac·ter rec·og·ni·tion ▶ **noun** the identification of printed characters using photoelectric devices and computer software.

op·ti·cal fi·ber ▶ **noun** a thin glass fiber through which light can be transmitted.

op·ti·cal il·lu·sion ▶ **noun** a thing that deceives the eye by appearing to be something that it is not.

op·ti·cian /äpˈtisʜən/ ▶ **noun** a person qualified to make and supply eyeglasses and contact lenses.

op·tic nerve ▶ **noun** each of the pair of nerves transmitting impulses from the eyes to the brain.

op·tics /ˈäptiks/ ▶ **plural noun** (usu. treated as sing.) the branch of science concerned with vision and the behavior of light.

op·ti·mal /ˈäptəməl/ ▶ **adjective** best or most favorable.
– DERIVATIVES **op·ti·mal·i·ty** /ˌäptəˈmalitē/ noun **op·ti·mal·ly** adverb.

op·ti·mism /ˈäptəˌmizəm/ ▶ **noun 1** hopefulness and confidence about the future or success of something. **2** Philosophy the belief that this world is the best of all possible worlds.
– ORIGIN French *optimisme*.

op·ti·mist /ˈäptəˌmist/ ▶ **noun** a person who is hopeful and confident about the future.

op·ti·mis·tic /ˌäptəˈmistik/ ▶ **adjective** hopeful and confident about the future.

– SYNONYMS **1 positive,** confident, hopeful, sanguine, bullish, buoyant, upbeat. **2 encouraging,** promising, reassuring, favorable.
– ANTONYMS pessimistic, depressing.

– DERIVATIVES **op·ti·mis·ti·cal·ly** /-ik(ə)lē/ adverb.

WORD TOOLKIT

See **CONFIDENT**.

op·ti·mize /ˈäptəˌmīz/ ▶ **verb** make the best use of a situation or resource.
– DERIVATIVES **op·ti·mi·za·tion** /ˌäptəməˈzāsʜən/ noun **op·ti·miz·er** noun.

op·ti·mum /ˈäptəməm/ ▶ **adjective** most likely to lead to a favorable outcome: *the units combine high quality with optimum performance*.

– SYNONYMS **best,** most favorable, most advantageous, ideal, perfect, prime, optimal.

▶ **noun** (pl. **optima** /-mə/ or **optimums**) the most favorable conditions for growth or success.
– ORIGIN from Latin, 'best thing.'

op·tion /ˈäpsʜən/ ▶ **noun 1** a thing that is or may be chosen. **2** the freedom or right to choose: *she was given the option of resigning or being fired*. **3** a right to buy or sell something at a specified price within a set time.

– SYNONYMS **choice,** preference, alternative, selection, possibility.

– PHRASES **keep** (or **leave**) **one's options open** not commit oneself.

op·tion·al /ˈäpsʜənl/ ▶ **adjective** available to be chosen but not compulsory.

– SYNONYMS **voluntary,** noncompulsory, elective, discretionary.
– ANTONYMS compulsory.

– DERIVATIVES **op·tion·al·i·ty** /ˌäpsʜəˈnalitē/ noun **op·tion·al·ly** adverb.

op·tom·e·trist /äpˈtämitrist/ ▶ **noun** a person who practices optometry.

op·tom·e·try /äpˈtämitrē/ ▶ **noun** the occupation of measuring eyesight, prescribing corrective lenses, and detecting eye disease.

opt-out ▶ **noun** an instance of choosing not to participate in something: *opt-outs from key parts of the treaty*.

op·u·lent /ˈäpyələnt/ ▶ **adjective** expensive and luxurious.

– SYNONYMS **luxurious,** sumptuous, palatial, lavishly appointed, rich, splendid, magnificent, grand, fancy; informal plush, swank, swish.
– ANTONYMS spartan.

– DERIVATIVES **op·u·lence** noun **op·u·lent·ly** adverb.
– ORIGIN Latin *opulens* 'wealthy, splendid.'

o·pus /ˈōpəs/ ▶ **noun** (pl. **opuses** or **opera** /ˈäp(ə)rə/) **1** a musical composition or set of compositions. **2** an artistic work.
– ORIGIN Latin, 'work.'

OR ▶ **abbreviation** Oregon.

or[1] /ôr/ ▶ **conjunction 1** used to link alternatives. **2** introducing a word that means the same as a preceding word or phrase, or that explains it. **3** otherwise.
– ORIGIN Old English.

or[2] ▶ **noun** gold or yellow, as a conventional heraldic color.
– ORIGIN French.

-or ▶ **suffix 1** forming nouns referring to a person or thing performing the action of a verb: *escalator*. **2** forming nouns referring to a state: *terror*.
– ORIGIN Latin.

or·a·cle /ˈôrəkəl/ ▶ **noun 1** (in ancient Greece or Rome) a priest or priestess who acted as a channel for advice or prophecy from the gods. **2** an authority that is always correct.
– ORIGIN Latin *oraculum*.

o·rac·u·lar /ôˈrakyələr/ ▶ **adjective 1** relating to an oracle. **2** hard to interpret. **3** having the authority of an oracle.

o·ral /ˈôrəl/ ▶ **adjective 1** spoken rather than written. **2** relating to the mouth. **3** done or taken by the mouth.

– SYNONYMS **spoken,** verbal, unwritten, vocal, uttered.
– ANTONYMS written.

▶ **noun** a spoken exam or test.
– DERIVATIVES **o·ral·ly** adverb.
– ORIGIN Latin *oralis*.

USAGE

On the confusion of **oral** and **aural**, see the note at **AURAL**.

o·ral his·to·ry ▶ **noun** the collection and study of historical information drawn from the speaker's personal memories.

o·ral·ism /ˈôrəˌlizəm/ ▶ **noun** the teaching of deaf people to communicate by the use of speech and lip-reading rather than sign language.
– DERIVATIVES **o·ral·ist** adjective & noun.

or·ange /ôˈrinzʜ, ˈär-/ ▶ **noun 1** a large round citrus fruit with a tough reddish-yellow rind. **2** a bright reddish-yellow color. ▶ **adjective** reddish yellow.
– DERIVATIVES **or·ang·ey** (also **orangy**) adjective.
– ORIGIN Old French *orenge*.

or·ange·ade /ˌôrənjˈād, ˌär-/ ▶ **noun** a soft drink flavored with orange.

or·ange pe·koe /ˈpēˌkō/ ▶ **noun** a type of black tea made from young leaves.
– ORIGIN *pekoe* from a Chinese dialect word meaning 'white down.'

or·ange rough·y /ˈrəfē/ ▶ **noun** a widespread edible fish whose reddish body turns orange after being exposed to air.

or·ange·ry /ˈôrənjrē, ˈär-/ ▸ **noun** (pl. **orangeries**) a type of large conservatory where orange trees are grown.

or·ange stick ▸ **noun** a thin pointed stick for manicuring the fingernails.

o·rang·u·tan /əˈrang(g)əˌtan/ (also **orangutang** /ōˈrang(g)əˌtang/) ▸ **noun** a large ape with long red hair, native to forests in Borneo and Sumatra.
– ORIGIN Malay, 'forest person.'

o·rate /ôˈrāt, ˈôrˌāt/ ▸ **verb** make a speech, especially a long or pompous one.

o·ra·tion /ôˈrāshən/ ▸ **noun** a formal speech made on a public occasion.
– ORIGIN from Latin *orare* 'speak, pray.'

or·a·tor /ˈôrətər, ˈär-/ ▸ **noun** a skillful public speaker.
– DERIVATIVES **or·a·to·ri·al** /ˌôrəˈtôrēəl/ adjective.

or·a·to·ri·o /ˌôrəˈtôrēˌō, ˌär-/ ▸ **noun** (pl. **oratorios**) a large-scale musical work on a religious theme for orchestra and voices.
– ORIGIN Italian.

or·a·to·ry[1] /ˈôrəˌtôrē, ˈär-/ ▸ **noun** (pl. **oratories**) a small chapel for private worship.

or·a·to·ry[2] ▸ **noun** powerful and persuasive public speaking.
– DERIVATIVES **or·a·tor·i·cal** /ˌôrəˈtôrikəl/ adjective.

orb /ôrb/ ▸ **noun 1** a spherical object or shape. **2** a golden globe with a cross on top, carried by a monarch on ceremonial occasions.
– ORIGIN Latin *orbis* 'ring.'

or·bit /ˈôrbit/ ▸ **noun 1** the regularly repeated elliptical course of a planet, moon, spacecraft, etc., around a star or planet. **2** an area of activity or influence: *they brought many friends within the orbit of our lives.* **3** the path of an electron around an atomic nucleus. **4** Anatomy the eye socket.

– SYNONYMS **circuit,** course, path, track, trajectory, rotation, revolution.

▸ **verb** (**orbits, orbiting, orbited**) move in orbit around a star or planet.

– SYNONYMS **circle,** go around/round, revolve around, travel around, circumnavigate.

– DERIVATIVES **or·bit·er** noun.
– ORIGIN Latin *orbita* 'course, track.'

or·bit·al /ˈôrbitl/ ▸ **adjective** relating to an orbit or orbits.
– DERIVATIVES **or·bit·al·ly** adverb.

or·bit·al sand·er ▸ **noun** a sander in which the sanding surface has a minute circular motion without rotating relative to the object being worked on.

or·ca /ˈôrkə/ ▸ **noun** a killer whale.
– ORIGIN French *orque* or Latin *orca.*

or·chard /ˈôrchərd/ ▸ **noun** a piece of enclosed land planted with fruit trees.
– ORIGIN Old English.

or·ches·tra /ˈôrkistrə, -ˌkestrə/ ▸ **noun 1** (treated as sing. or pl.) a large group of musicians with string, woodwind, brass, and percussion sections. **2** (also **orchestra pit**) the part of a theater where the orchestra plays, typically in front of the stage and on a lower level. **3** the ground floor seats in a theater. **4** the semicircular space in front of an ancient Greek theater stage where the chorus danced and sang.

– SYNONYMS **ensemble,** group; informal band, combo.

– DERIVATIVES **or·ches·tral** /ôrˈkestrəl/ adjective **or·ches·tral·ly** adverb.
– ORIGIN Greek *orkhēstra,* from *orkheisthai* 'to dance.'

or·ches·trate /ˈôrkiˌstrāt/ ▸ **verb 1** adapt a musical composition so that it can be performed by an orchestra. **2** organize a complicated event or situation carefully or secretly: *a nationwide campaign orchestrated by conservationists.*

– SYNONYMS **organize,** arrange, plan, set up, mobilize, mount, stage, mastermind, coordinate, direct.

– DERIVATIVES **or·ches·tra·tion** /ˌôrkəˈstrāshən/ noun **or·ches·tra·tor** /-ˌstrātər/ noun.

or·chid /ˈôrkid/ ▸ **noun** a plant of a large family with complex showy flowers.
– DERIVATIVES **or·chi·da·ceous** /ˌôrkiˈdāshəs/ adjective.
– ORIGIN Greek *orkhis* 'testicle' (because of the shape of the tuber).

or·dain /ôrˈdān/ ▸ **verb 1** make someone a priest or minister. **2** order something officially: *the king ordained that the courts should be revived.* **3** (of God or fate) decide something in advance.

– SYNONYMS **1 confer holy orders on,** admit to the priesthood, appoint, anoint, consecrate. **2 determine,** predestine, preordain, predetermine, prescribe, designate.

– ORIGIN Latin *ordinare.*

or·deal /ôrˈdēl/ ▸ **noun 1** a prolonged painful or unpleasant experience. **2** an ancient test of guilt or innocence in which the accused person was subjected to severe pain, survival of which was taken as divine proof of their innocence.

– SYNONYMS **trial,** hardship, suffering, nightmare, trauma, hell, torture, torment, agony.

– ORIGIN Old English.

or·der /ˈôrdər/ ▸ **noun 1** the arrangement of people or things according to a particular sequence or method: *I filed the cards in alphabetical order.* **2** a state in which everything is in its right place. **3** a state in which the laws and rules regulating public behavior are followed: *a breakdown of law and order.* **4** an instruction that must be obeyed; a command. **5** a request for something to be made, supplied, or served. **6** the set procedure followed in a meeting, court of law, or religious service. **7** quality or nature: *poetry of the highest order.* **8** a social class or system. **9** a rank in the Christian ministry. **10** (**orders** or **holy orders**) the rank of an ordained minister of the Church. **11** a society of monks, nuns, or friars living under the same rule. **12** (**Order**) Brit. an institution founded by a king or queen to honor good conduct: *the Order of the Garter.* **13** Biology a main category into which animals and plants are divided that ranks below class and above family. **14** any of the five classical styles of architecture (Doric, Ionic, Corinthian, Tuscan, and Composite).

– SYNONYMS **1** *alphabetical order* **sequence,** arrangement, organization, codification, classification, system, series, succession. **2** *some semblance of order* **tidiness,** neatness, orderliness, method, symmetry, uniformity, regularity, routine. **3** *the police managed to keep order* **peace,** control, law and order, calm. **4** *in good order* **condition,** state, repair, shape, situation. **5** *I had to obey orders* **command,** instruction, directive, direction, decree, edict, injunction, dictate. **6** *the lower orders of society* **class,** level, rank, grade, caste. **7** *a religious order* **community,** brotherhood, sisterhood. **8** *the Benevolent and Protective Order of Elks* **organization,**

association, society, fellowship, fraternity, lodge, guild, league, union, club.
– ANTONYMS chaos.

▶ **verb** **1** give a command: *she ordered me to leave.* **2** request that something be made, supplied, or served: *I ordered a steak.* **3** arrange something methodically.

– SYNONYMS **1 instruct,** tell, command, direct, charge, require, enjoin, ordain, decree, rule. **2 request,** apply for, book, reserve, requisition. **3 organize,** arrange, sort out, lay out, group, classify, categorize, catalog.

– PHRASES **in order 1** in the right condition for operation or use. **2** appropriate in the circumstances. **in order for** (or **that**) so that. **in order to** with the purpose of doing. **of the order of** approximately. **on order** (of goods) requested but not yet received. **the order of the day 1** the current situation. **2** the day's business to be considered in a meeting, etc. **out of order** not working properly or at all.
– ORIGIN Latin *ordo* 'row, series.'

or·der·ly /'ôrdərlē/ ▶ **adjective** **1** neatly and methodically arranged. **2** well behaved.

– SYNONYMS **1 neat,** tidy, well ordered, in order, trim, in apple-pie order, shipshape. **2 organized,** efficient, methodical, systematic, coherent, structured, logical. **3 well behaved,** law-abiding, disciplined, peaceful, peaceable.
– ANTONYMS untidy, unruly.

▶ **noun** (pl. **orderlies**) **1** a hospital worker responsible for cleaning and other nonmedical tasks. **2** a soldier who carries orders or performs minor tasks for an officer.
– DERIVATIVES **or·der·li·ness** noun.

or·der of mag·ni·tude ▶ **noun** **1** a level in a system of classifying things by size, typically where each level is higher by a factor of ten. **2** relative size or quantity.

or·di·nal /'ôrdn-əl/ ▶ **adjective** relating to order in a series.
– ORIGIN Latin *ordinalis.*

or·di·nal num·ber ▶ **noun** a number defining a thing's position in a series, such as 'first' or 'second.'

or·di·nance /'ôrdn-əns/ ▶ **noun** formal **1** an official order. **2** a religious rite.
– ORIGIN Old French *ordenance.*

or·di·nand /'ôrdn,and/ ▶ **noun** a person who is training to be ordained as a priest or minister.
– ORIGIN Latin *ordinandus.*

or·di·nar·y /'ôrdn,erē/ ▶ **adjective** **1** having no distinctive features; normal or usual. **2** not interesting or exceptional: *a very ordinary piece of work.*

– SYNONYMS **1 usual,** normal, standard, typical, common, customary, habitual, everyday, regular, routine, day-to-day, quotidian. **2 average,** run-of-the-mill, typical, middle-of-the-road, conventional, humdrum, unremarkable, unexceptional, pedestrian, prosaic, workaday; informal garden-variety.
– ANTONYMS unusual.

▶ **noun** (pl. **ordinaries**) **1** what is commonplace or standard: *a level of skill well above the ordinary.* **2** (**Ordinary**) those parts of a Roman Catholic service, especially the Mass, that do not vary from day to day. **3** a rule or book laying down the order of divine service. **4** Heraldry any of the simplest main emblems or devices used in coats of arms.
– DERIVATIVES **or·di·nar·i·ly** adverb **or·di·nar·i·ness** noun.
– PHRASES **out of the ordinary** unusual.
– ORIGIN Latin *ordinarius* 'orderly.'

or·di·nate /'ôrdnit, -,āt/ ▶ **noun** Mathematics a straight line from a point on a graph drawn parallel to the vertical axis and meeting the other; the *y*-coordinate.
– ORIGIN from Latin *linea ordinata applicata* 'line applied parallel.'

or·di·na·tion /,ôrdn'āshən/ ▶ **noun** the action of ordaining someone as a priest or minister.

ord·nance /'ôrdnəns/ ▶ **noun** **1** large guns mounted on wheels. **2** military weapons, ammunition, and equipment. **3** a branch of the armed forces dealing with military supplies.
– ORIGIN variant of **ORDINANCE**.

Or·do·vi·cian /,ôrdə'vishən/ ▶ **adjective** Geology relating to the second period of the Paleozoic era (about 510 to 439 million years ago), when the first vertebrates appeared.
– ORIGIN from *Ordovices*, the Latin name of an ancient British tribe in North Wales.

or·dure /'ôrjər/ ▶ **noun** excrement or dung.
– ORIGIN Old French.

ore /ôr/ ▶ **noun** a naturally occurring material from which a metal or valuable mineral can be extracted.
– ORIGIN Old English, 'unwrought metal.'

ø·re /'ərə/ ▶ **noun** (pl. same) a monetary unit of Denmark and Norway, equal to one hundredth of a krone.
– ORIGIN Danish and Norwegian.

ö·re /'ərə/ ▶ **noun** (pl. same) a monetary unit of Sweden, equal to one hundredth of a krona.
– ORIGIN Swedish.

o·reg·a·no /ə'regə,nō/ ▶ **noun** a sweet-smelling plant whose leaves are used as an herb in cooking.
– ORIGIN Spanish.

org. ▶ **abbreviation** **1** organic. **2** organization or organized.

or·gan /'ôrgən/ ▶ **noun** **1** a part of an animal or plant that is adapted for a particular function, for example the heart or kidneys. **2** a large musical keyboard instrument with rows of pipes supplied with air from bellows. **3** a smaller keyboard instrument producing similar sounds electronically. **4** a newspaper or journal that puts forward the views of a political party or movement.

– SYNONYMS **newspaper,** paper, journal, periodical, magazine, voice, mouthpiece.

– DERIVATIVES **or·gan·ist** noun.
– ORIGIN Greek *organon* 'tool, sense organ.'

or·gan·dy /'ôrgəndē/ (also **organdie**) ▶ **noun** a fine, translucent, stiff cotton muslin.
– ORIGIN French *organdi.*

or·gan·elle /,ôrgə'nel/ ▶ **noun** Biology a specialized structure within a cell.
– ORIGIN Latin *organella* 'little tool.'

or·gan grind·er ▶ **noun** a street musician who plays a barrel organ.

or·gan·ic /ôr'ganik/ ▶ **adjective** **1** relating to or obtained from living matter. **2** not involving or produced with artificial chemicals such as fertilizers: *organic farming.* **3** (of a chemical compound) containing carbon and chiefly or ultimately of biological origin. **4** relating to or affecting an organ or organs of the body. **5** (of the parts of a whole) fitting together in a harmonious way. **6** (of development or change) continuous or natural.

– SYNONYMS **1** *organic matter* **living,** live, animate, biological. **2** *organic vegetables* **natural,** chemical-free, pesticide-free, bio-. **3** *an organic whole* structured, organized, coherent, integrated, coordinated, ordered, harmonious.

▶ **noun** (usu. **organics**) **1** a food produced by organic farming. **2** an organic compound.
– DERIVATIVES **or·gan·i·cal·ly** /-ik(ə)lē/ adverb.

WORD TOOLKIT

organic ...	biological ...	living ...
food	weapons	organisms
vegetables	warfare	creatures
waste	father/mother	cells
fertilizer	diversity	people
chemistry	clock	plants

or·gan·ism /ˈôrgəˌnizəm/ ▶ **noun 1** an individual animal, plant, or other life form. **2** a whole made up of interdependent parts.

– SYNONYMS **living thing,** being, creature, animal, plant, life form.

or·gan·i·za·tion /ˌôrgəniˈzāsʜən/ ▶ **noun 1** an organized group of people with a particular purpose, e.g., a business. **2** the action of organizing something. **3** a systematic arrangement or approach.

– SYNONYMS **1 planning,** arrangement, coordination, organizing, running, management. **2 structure,** arrangement, plan, pattern, order, form, format, framework, composition. **3 institution,** body, group, company, concern, firm, business, corporation, conglomerate, consortium, syndicate, agency, association, society; informal outfit.

– DERIVATIVES **or·gan·i·za·tion·al** /-sʜənl/ adjective **or·gan·i·za·tion·al·ly** /-sʜən-lē/ adverb.

or·gan·ize /ˈôrgəˌnīz/ ▶ **verb 1** arrange something in a systematic way: *the book is organized into nine thematic chapters.* **2** make arrangements or preparations for an event or activity: *social programs are organized by the school.* **3** form people into a labor union or other political group.

– SYNONYMS **1 order,** arrange, sort, assemble, marshal, put straight, group, classify, collate, categorize, catalog, codify. **2 arrange,** coordinate, sort out, put together, fix up, set up, lay on, orchestrate, see to, mobilize.

– DERIVATIVES **or·gan·iz·er** noun.
– ORIGIN Latin *organizare*.

or·ga·no·phos·phate /ˌôrgənəˈfäsˌfāt, ôrˌganō-/ ▶ **noun** any of a group of organic compounds whose molecules contain phosphates, especially a pesticide of this kind.

or·gan·za /ôrˈganzə/ ▶ **noun** a thin, stiff, transparent fabric made of silk or a synthetic yarn.
– ORIGIN uncertain.

or·gasm /ˈôrˌgazəm/ ▶ **noun** the climax of sexual excitement, when feelings of sexual pleasure are most intense. ▶ **verb** have an orgasm.
– DERIVATIVES **or·gas·mic** /ôrˈgazmik/ adjective.
– ORIGIN Greek *orgasmos*.

or·gi·as·tic /ˌôrjēˈastik/ ▶ **adjective** relating to or like an orgy.

or·gy /ˈôrjē/ ▶ **noun** (pl. **orgies**) **1** a wild party involving a great deal of drinking and indiscriminate sexual activity. **2** an instance of engaging in a particular activity to an extreme or excessive degree: *an orgy of spending.*
– ORIGIN Greek *orgia* 'secret rites or revels.'

o·ri·el /ˈôrēəl/ ▶ **noun** a large upper-story bay with a window (an **oriel window**), supported by brackets or projections from the wall.
– ORIGIN Old French *oriol* 'gallery.'

o·ri·ent ▶ **noun** /ˈôrēˌənt/ (**the Orient**) literary the countries of the East, especially east Asia. ▶ **adjective** /ˈôrēˌənt/ literary oriental. ▶ **verb** /ˈôrēˌent/ **1** align or position something in relation to the points of a compass or other specified positions. **2** (**orient oneself**) find one's position in relation to unfamiliar surroundings. **3** tailor or adapt something to particular needs or circumstances: *magazines oriented to the business community.*

– SYNONYMS **1** *you need time to orient yourself* **acclimatize,** familiarize, adjust, accustom, find one's feet, get one's bearings. **2 aim,** direct, pitch, design, intend. **3 align,** place, position, arrange.

– ORIGIN from Latin *oriens* 'rising or east.'

o·ri·en·tal /ˌôrēˈentl/ ▶ **adjective** relating to or from the Far East. ▶ **noun** often offensive a person of Far Eastern descent.
– DERIVATIVES **o·ri·en·tal·ism** /ˌôrēˈen(t)lˌizəm/ noun **o·ri·en·tal·ist** noun **o·ri·en·tal·ly** adverb.

USAGE

The term **oriental** is now regarded as old-fashioned and potentially offensive as a term referring to people from the Far East. **Asian** and more specific terms such as **East Asian**, **Chinese**, and **Japanese** are preferred.

o·ri·en·ta·tion /ˌôrēənˈtāsʜən/ ▶ **noun 1** the action of orienting someone or something. **2** the relative position or direction of something. **3** a person's basic attitude, beliefs, or feelings about something: *a bill outlawing job discrimination on the basis of sexual orientation.*
– DERIVATIVES **o·ri·en·ta·tion·al** adjective.

o·ri·en·teer·ing /ˌôriənˈti(ə)rɪɴɢ/ ▶ **noun** a competitive sport in which runners have to find their way across rough country with the aid of a map and compass.
– DERIVATIVES **o·ri·en·teer** noun & verb.

or·i·fice /ˈôrəfis/ ▶ **noun** an opening, particularly one in the body such as a nostril.
– ORIGIN French.

o·ri·ga·mi /ˌôrəˈgämē/ ▶ **noun** the Japanese art of folding paper into decorative shapes and figures.
– ORIGIN Japanese.

or·i·gin /ˈôrəjən/ ▶ **noun 1** the point or place where something begins: *the origin of the universe.* **2** a person's social background or ancestry: *his Italian origins.* **3** Mathematics a fixed point from which coordinates are measured.

– SYNONYMS **1 beginning,** start, genesis, birth, dawning, dawn, emergence, creation, source, basis, cause, root(s), derivation, provenance. **2 descent,** ancestry, parentage, pedigree, lineage, line (of descent), heritage, birth, extraction, family, roots.

– ORIGIN Latin *origo*, from *oriri* 'to rise.'

o·rig·i·nal /əˈrijənl/ ▶ **adjective 1** existing from the beginning; first or earliest: *a Tudor fireplace with original oak beams.* **2** produced by an artist, author, etc.; not a copy. **3** new and different from what has been done before; inventive: *an unusual and original idea.*

– SYNONYMS **1 indigenous,** aboriginal, native, first, earliest, early, ur-. **2 authentic,** genuine, actual, true, bona fide. **3 innovative,** creative, imaginative, inventive, new, novel, fresh, unusual,

– SYNONYMS unconventional, unorthodox, groundbreaking, pioneering, unique, distinctive.

▶ **noun** the earliest form of something, from which copies can be made.

– SYNONYMS **prototype,** source, master.

WORD TOOLKIT

original ...	native ...	indigenous ...
version	language	people
idea	land	culture
design	country	groups
meaning	tongue	species
members	speakers	tribe
owner	habitat	plants
equipment	American	religions

CHOOSE THE RIGHT WORD

See **CREATIVE**.

o·rig·i·nal·i·ty /əˌrijəˈnalitē/ ▶ **noun 1** the ability to think independently or creatively. **2** the quality of being new or inventive.

o·rig·i·nal·ly /əˈrijənl-ē/ ▶ **adverb** in the beginning; at first: *the conference was originally scheduled for November.*

– SYNONYMS **at first,** in the beginning, to begin with, initially, in the first place, at the outset.

o·rig·i·nal sin ▶ **noun** (in Christian theology) the tendency to be sinful that is thought to be present in all human beings as a consequence of Adam and Eve's disobedience.

o·rig·i·nate /əˈrijəˌnāt/ ▶ **verb 1** begin in a particular place or situation: *the word originated as a marketing term.* **2** create or initiate something.

– SYNONYMS **1 arise,** have its origin, begin, start, stem, spring, emerge, emanate. **2 invent,** create, devise, think up, dream up, conceive, formulate, form, develop, produce, mastermind, pioneer.

– DERIVATIVES **o·rig·i·na·tion** /əˌrijəˈnāSHən/ noun **o·rig·i·na·tor** noun.

O-ring ▶ **noun** a pliable ring with a circular cross section used to seal joints between pipes, etc.

o·ri·ole /ˈôrēˌōl/ ▶ **noun** a brightly colored bird with a musical call.

– ORIGIN Latin *oriolus.*

or·i·son /ˈôrisən, -zən, ˈär-/ ▶ **noun** literary a prayer.

– ORIGIN Old French *oreison.*

or·mo·lu /ˈôrməˌlo͞o/ ▶ **noun** a gold-colored alloy of copper, zinc, and tin used in decoration.

– ORIGIN from French *or moulu* 'powdered gold.'

or·na·ment /ˈôrnəmənt/ ▶ **noun 1** an object designed to make something look more attractive but usually having no practical purpose. **2** decorative items as a whole. **3** (**ornaments**) Music embellishments made to a melody.

– SYNONYMS **1 knick-knack,** trinket, bauble, gewgaw; informal kickshaw. **2 decoration,** adornment, embellishment, ornamentation, trimming, accessories, frills.

▶ **verb** make something more attractive by adding decorative items: *large rooms ornamented with marble and gilt columns.*

– DERIVATIVES **or·na·men·ta·tion** /ˌôrnəmenˈtāSHən/ noun.

– ORIGIN Latin *ornamentum.*

or·na·men·tal /ˌôrnəˈmentl/ ▶ **adjective** acting or intended as an ornament; decorative.

– SYNONYMS **decorative,** fancy, ornate, ornamented, attractive.

▶ **noun** a plant grown for its attractive appearance.

– DERIVATIVES **or·na·men·tal·ly** adverb.

or·nate /ôrˈnāt/ ▶ **adjective** elaborately or highly decorated.

– SYNONYMS **elaborate,** decorated, embellished, adorned, ornamented, rococo, fancy, fussy, ostentatious, showy; informal flashy.

– ANTONYMS plain.

– DERIVATIVES **or·nate·ly** adverb **or·nate·ness** noun.

– ORIGIN from Latin *ornare* 'adorn.'

or·ner·y /ˈôrn(ə)rē/ ▶ **adjective** informal bad-tempered.

– ORIGIN representing a dialect pronunciation of **ORDINARY**.

or·ni·thol·o·gy /ˌôrnəˈTHäləjē/ ▶ **noun** the scientific study of birds.

– DERIVATIVES **or·ni·tho·log·i·cal** /ˌôrniTHəˈläjikəl/ adjective **or·ni·thol·o·gist** noun.

– ORIGIN from Greek *ornis* 'bird.'

or·ni·thop·ter /ˌôrnəˈTHäptər/ ▶ **noun** chiefly historical a flying machine with flapping wings.

– ORIGIN French *ornithoptère.*

o·ro·tund /ˈôrəˌtənd/ ▶ **adjective 1** (of a person's voice) resonant and impressive. **2** (of writing or style) pompous.

– ORIGIN from Latin *ore rotundo* 'with rounded mouth.'

or·phan /ˈôrfən/ ▶ **noun** a child whose parents are dead. ▶ **verb** (**be orphaned**) (of a child) be made an orphan.

– ORIGIN from Greek *orphanos* 'bereaved.'

or·phan·age /ˈôrfənij/ ▶ **noun** a residential institution where orphans are cared for.

or·pi·ment /ˈôrpəmənt/ ▶ **noun** a bright yellow mineral formerly used as a dye and artist's pigment.

– ORIGIN Latin *auripigmentum.*

or·rer·y /ˈôrərē/ ▶ **noun** (pl. **orreries**) a clockwork model of the solar system.

– ORIGIN named after the fourth Earl of *Orrery*, for whom one was made.

or·ris /ˈôris/ (also **orris root**) ▶ **noun** a preparation made from the fragrant root of a kind of iris, used in perfumery.

– ORIGIN alteration of **IRIS**.

ortho- ▶ **combining form 1** straight; rectangular; upright: *orthodontics.* **2** correct: *orthography.*

– ORIGIN from Greek *orthos* 'straight, right.'

or·tho·don·tics /ˌôrTHəˈdäntiks/ ▶ **plural noun** (treated as sing.) the treatment of irregularities in the teeth and jaws.

– DERIVATIVES **or·tho·don·tic** adjective **or·tho·don·tist** /-tist/ noun.

– ORIGIN from Greek *odous* 'tooth.'

or·tho·dox /ˈôrTHəˌdäks/ ▶ **adjective 1** following traditional or generally accepted beliefs: *orthodox medical treatment.* **2** conventional or normal. **3** (**Orthodox**) relating to Orthodox Judaism or the Orthodox Church.

– SYNONYMS **1 conventional,** mainstream, conformist, established, traditional, traditionalist, prevalent, popular, conservative, received. **2** *an orthodox Muslim* **observant,** devout, strict.

– ANTONYMS unconventional.

– ORIGIN Greek *orthodoxos.*

Or·tho·dox Church ▸ **noun** any of the ancient branches of the Christian Church that originated in eastern Europe and the Middle East and that do not accept the authority of the Pope of Rome.

Or·tho·dox Ju·da·ism ▸ **noun** a branch of Judaism that teaches that the requirements of Jewish law and traditional custom regarding religious and everyday life must be strictly followed.

or·tho·dox·y /'ôrTHəˌdäksē/ ▸ **noun** (pl. **orthodoxies**) **1** traditional or generally accepted theories, beliefs, or practices. **2** the state of being orthodox. **3** the whole community of Orthodox Jews or Orthodox Christians.

or·thog·ra·phy /ôr'THägrəfē/ ▸ **noun** (pl. **orthographies**) the conventional spelling system of a language.
– DERIVATIVES **or·tho·graph·ic** /ˌôrTHə'grafik/ adjective.

or·tho·pe·dics /ˌôrTHə'pēdiks/ (Brit. **orthopaedics**) ▸ **plural noun** (treated as sing.) the branch of medicine concerned with the correction of deformities caused by disease of or damage to bones or joints.
– DERIVATIVES **or·tho·pe·dic** adjective.
– ORIGIN from Greek *paideia* 'rearing of children.'

or·thot·ics /ôr'THätiks/ ▸ **plural noun** (treated as sing.) the branch of medicine concerned with the design and fitting of mechanical devices such as braces or splints.
– DERIVATIVES **or·thot·ic** adjective & noun.

or·to·lan /'ôrtl-ən/ ▸ **noun** a small songbird formerly eaten as a delicacy.
– ORIGIN Provençal, 'gardener' (because the bird frequents gardens).

Or·well·i·an /ôr'welēən/ ▸ **adjective** relating to the work of the British novelist George Orwell, especially the totalitarian government depicted in *Nineteen Eighty-Four*.

o·ryx /'ôriks/ ▸ **noun** a large antelope with long horns, found in arid regions of Africa and Arabia.
– ORIGIN Greek *orux* 'stonemason's pickax' (because of its pointed horns).

OS ▸ **abbreviation 1** (in calculating dates) Old Style. **2** Computing operating system. **3** Ordinary Seaman. **4** (as a size of clothing) outsize.

Os ▸ **symbol** the chemical element osmium.

Os·car /'äskər/ ▸ **noun** trademark the nickname for a gold statuette given as an Academy Award.
– ORIGIN one explanation claims that the statuette reminded an executive director of the Academy of Motion Picture Arts and Sciences of her uncle Oscar.

os·cil·late /'äsəˌlāt/ ▸ **verb 1** move or swing back and forth in a regular rhythm. **2** waver between extremes of opinion or emotion: *he was oscillating between fear and bravery.*

– SYNONYMS **1 swing to and fro,** swing back and forth, sway. **2 waver,** swing, fluctuate, alternate, seesaw, yo-yo, vacillate.

– DERIVATIVES **os·cil·la·tion** /ˌäsə'lāSHən/ noun **os·cil·la·tor** noun **os·cil·la·to·ry** /ə'siləˌtôrē/ adjective.
– ORIGIN Latin *oscillare* 'to swing.'

os·cil·lo·scope /ə'siləˌskōp/ ▸ **noun** a device for showing changes in electrical current as a display on the screen of a cathode ray tube.

OSHA /'ōSHə/ ▸ **abbreviation** Occupational Safety and Health Administration.

o·sier /'ōZHər/ ▸ **noun** a small willow tree with long flexible shoots used in making baskets.
– ORIGIN Old French.

os·mi·um /'äzmēəm/ ▸ **noun** a hard, dense silvery-white metallic element.
– ORIGIN from Greek *osmē* 'smell' (from the strong smell of one of its oxides).

os·mo·reg·u·la·tion /ˌäzmōˌregyə'lāSHən/ ▸ **noun** Biology the control of water content and salt concentration in the body of an organism.

os·mo·sis /äz'mōsis, äs-/ ▸ **noun 1** a process by which molecules of a solvent pass through a semipermeable membrane from a less concentrated solution into a more concentrated one. **2** the gradual absorbing of ideas or information.
– DERIVATIVES **os·mot·ic** /-mätik/ adjective.
– ORIGIN Greek *ōsmos* 'a push.'

os·prey /'äsprā, -prē/ ▸ **noun** (pl. **ospreys**) a large fish-eating bird of prey with a brown back and white underside.
– ORIGIN apparently from Latin *ossifraga*, from *os* 'bone' + *frangere* 'to break.'

OSS ▸ **abbreviation** Office of Strategic Services, a US intelligence organization during World War II.

os·se·ous /'äsēəs/ ▸ **adjective** chiefly Zoology & Medicine consisting of or turned into bone.
– ORIGIN Latin *osseus* 'bony.'

os·si·cle /'äsikəl/ ▸ **noun** a very small bone, especially one of those that transmit sounds within the middle ear.
– ORIGIN Latin *ossiculum* 'little bone.'

os·si·fy /'äsəˌfī/ ▸ **verb** (**ossifies, ossifying, ossified**) **1** turn into bone or bony tissue. **2** (usu. as adj. **ossified**) stop developing: *ossified political institutions.*
– DERIVATIVES **os·si·fi·ca·tion** /ˌäsəfi'kāSHən/ noun.
– ORIGIN from Latin *os* 'bone.'

os·su·ar·y /'äSHo͞oˌerē, 'äs(y)o͞o-/ ▸ **noun** (pl. **ossuaries**) a container or room for the bones of dead people.
– ORIGIN from Latin *os* 'bone.'

os·ten·si·ble /ä'stensəbəl, ə'sten-/ ▸ **adjective** apparently true, but not necessarily so.
– DERIVATIVES **os·ten·si·bly** /-blē/ adverb.
– ORIGIN Latin *ostensibilis*.

os·ten·ta·tion /ˌästən'tāSHən/ ▸ **noun** a showy display of wealth, knowledge, etc., that is intended to impress other people.
– ORIGIN from Latin *ostendere* 'stretch out to view.'

os·ten·ta·tious /ˌästən'tāSHəs/ ▸ **adjective** expensive or showy in a way that is intended to impress other people: *ostentatious gold jewelry.*

– SYNONYMS **showy,** conspicuous, flamboyant, gaudy, brash, vulgar, loud, extravagant, fancy, ornate, rococo; informal flash, flashy, bling-bling, over the top, OTT, glitzy.
– ANTONYMS restrained.

– DERIVATIVES **os·ten·ta·tious·ly** adverb.

osteo- ▸ **combining form** relating to the bones: *osteoporosis.*
– ORIGIN from Greek *osteon* 'bone.'

os·te·o·ar·thri·tis /ˌästēōär'THrītis/ ▸ **noun** a condition in which cartilage in the joints deteriorates, causing pain and stiffness.

os·te·ol·o·gy /ˌästē'äləjē/ ▸ **noun** the study of the skeleton and bony structures.
– DERIVATIVES **os·te·o·log·i·cal** /ˌästēə'läjikəl/ adjective **os·te·ol·o·gist** noun.

os·te·o·my·e·li·tis /ˌästēōˌmīə'lītis/ ▸ **noun** inflammation of bone or bone marrow.

os·te·op·a·thy /ˌästēˈäpəᴛʜē/ ▸ **noun** a system of complementary medicine involving the manipulation of the bones and muscles.
– DERIVATIVES **os·te·o·path** /ˈästēəˌpaᴛʜ/ noun **os·te·o·path·ic** /ˌästēəˈpaᴛʜik/ adjective.

os·te·o·pe·ni·a /ˌästēōˈpēnēə/ ▸ **noun** reduced bone mass that is less severe than osteoporosis.

os·te·o·po·ro·sis /ˌästēōpəˈrōsis/ ▸ **noun** a medical condition in which the bones become brittle and fragile, typically as a result of hormonal changes, or lack of calcium or vitamin D.
– ORIGIN from Greek *poros* 'passage, pore.'

os·ti·na·to /ˌästiˈnätō/ ▸ **noun** (pl. **ostinatos** or **ostinati** /-tē/) a continually repeated musical phrase or rhythm.
– ORIGIN from Italian, 'obstinate.'

os·tler /ˈäslər/ (also **hostler** /ˈ(h)äslər/) ▸ **noun** historical a man employed at an inn to look after customers' horses.
– ORIGIN Old French *hostelier* 'innkeeper.'

os·tra·cize /ˈästrəˌsīz/ ▸ **verb** exclude someone from a society or group; refuse to meet or speak to someone.

– SYNONYMS **exclude,** shun, spurn, cold-shoulder, reject, ignore, snub, blackball, blacklist. informal freeze out.

– DERIVATIVES **os·tra·cism** /-ˌsizəm/ noun.
– ORIGIN Greek *ostrakizein*, from *ostrakon* 'shell or piece of broken pottery' (on which names were written in voting to banish unpopular citizens).

os·trich /ˈästricʜ/ ▸ **noun 1** a large flightless swift-running African bird with a long neck and long legs. **2** a person who refuses to accept unpleasant truths.
– ORIGIN sense 1 from Old French *ostriche*; sense 2 from the popular belief that ostriches bury their heads in the sand if pursued.

Os·tro·goth /ˈästrəˌgäᴛʜ/ ▸ **noun** a member of the eastern branch of the Goths, who conquered Italy in the 5th–6th centuries AD.
– ORIGIN Latin *Ostrogothi* 'East Goths.'

OT ▸ **abbreviation 1** occupational therapist; occupational therapy. **2** Old Testament.

o·ta·ku /ōˈtäko͞o/ ▸ **plural noun** (in Japan) young people who are highly skilled in or obsessed with computer technology to the detriment of their social skills.
– ORIGIN Japanese, literally 'your house,' alluding to the reluctance of such young people to leave the house.

OTC ▸ **abbreviation 1** over the counter. **2** (in the UK) Officers' Training Corps.

oth·er /ˈəᴛʜər/ ▸ **adjective & pronoun 1** used to refer to a person or thing that is different from one already mentioned or known: *other people found her difficult.* **2** additional: *one other word of advice.* **3** alternative of two: *the other side of the page.* **4** those not already mentioned.

– SYNONYMS **1 alternative,** different, distinct, separate, various. **2 more,** further, additional, extra, fresh, new, added, supplementary.

– PHRASES **the other day** (or **night**, **week**, etc.) a few days (or nights, weeks, etc.) ago.
– ORIGIN Old English.

oth·er half ▸ **noun** (**one's other half**) informal one's wife, husband, or partner.

oth·er·ness /ˈəᴛʜərnis/ ▸ **noun** the quality or fact of being different.

oth·er·wise /ˈəᴛʜərˌwīz/ ▸ **adverb 1** in different circumstances; or else. **2** in other respects. **3** in a different way. **4** alternatively. ▸ **adjective** in a different state or situation.

oth·er wom·an ▸ **noun** the mistress of a married man.

oth·er-world·ly ▸ **adjective 1** relating to an imaginary or spiritual world. **2** not aware of the realities of life; unworldly.

o·ti·ose /ˈōsʜēˌōs, ˈōtēˌōs/ ▸ **adjective** serving no practical purpose; pointless.
– ORIGIN Latin *otiosus*.

o·ti·tis /ōˈtītis/ ▸ **noun** inflammation of part of the ear, especially the middle ear (**otitis media**).
– ORIGIN from Greek *ous* 'ear.'

ot·ter /ˈätər/ ▸ **noun** a fish-eating mammal with a long body, dense fur, and webbed feet, living partly in water and partly on land.
– ORIGIN Old English.

Ot·to·man /ˈätəmən/ ▸ **adjective** historical **1** relating to the Turkish dynasty of Osman I (Othman I), founded in about 1300. **2** relating to the Ottoman Empire, the Turkish empire ruled by the successors of Osman I. **3** Turkish. ▸ **noun** (pl. **Ottomans**) a Turk, especially of the Ottoman period.
– ORIGIN Arabic.

ot·to·man /ˈätəmən/ ▸ **noun** (pl. **ottomans**) a low upholstered seat without a back or arms that can also be used as a box or chest, the seat being hinged to form a lid.

ou·bli·ette /ˌo͞oblēˈet/ ▸ **noun** a secret dungeon that can only be accessed through a trapdoor in its ceiling.
– ORIGIN French, from *oublier* 'forget.'

ouch /oucʜ/ ▸ **exclamation** used to express pain.

ought /ôt/ ▸ **modal verb** (3rd sing. present and past **ought**) **1** used to indicate duty or correctness. **2** used to indicate something that is probable. **3** used to indicate a desirable or expected state. **4** used to give or ask advice.
– ORIGIN Old English.

USAGE

The correct way of forming negative sentences with **ought** is *he ought not to have gone*. Uses such as *he didn't ought to have gone* and *he hadn't ought to have gone* are found in dialect but are not acceptable in standard modern English.

ought·n't /ˈôtnt/ ▸ **contraction** ought not.

Oui·ja board /ˈwējə, -jē/ ▸ **noun** trademark a board with letters, numbers, and other signs around its edge, to which a pointer moves, supposedly in answer to questions at a seance.
– ORIGIN from French *oui* 'yes' + German *ja* 'yes.'

ounce /ouns/ ▸ **noun 1** a unit of weight of one sixteenth of a pound avoirdupois (approximately 28 grams). **2** a unit of one twelfth of a pound troy, equal to 480 grains (approximately 31 grams). **3** a very small amount: *a girl without an ounce of ambition.*
– ORIGIN Latin *uncia* 'twelfth part.'

our /ou(ə)r, är/ ▸ **possessive determiner 1** belonging to or connected with the speaker and one or more other people. **2** belonging to or associated with people in general. **3** used in formal contexts by a writer, editor, or monarch to refer to something associated with himself or herself.
– ORIGIN Old English.

Our Fa·ther ▶ **noun 1** God. **2** the Lord's Prayer.

Our La·dy ▶ **noun** the Virgin Mary.

Our Lord ▶ **noun** God or Jesus.

ours /'ou(ə)rz, ärz/ ▶ **possessive pronoun** used to refer to something belonging to or connected with the speaker and one or more other people.

> USAGE
>
> There is no apostrophe: the spelling should be **ours** not *our's*.

our·self /ou(ə)r'self, är-/ ▶ **pronoun** (first person pl.) used instead of 'ourselves,' typically when 'we' refers to people in general.

> USAGE
>
> The standard reflexive pronoun (a word such as 'myself' or 'himself') corresponding to **we** and **us** is **ourselves**, as in *we enjoyed ourselves*. The singular form **ourself** is sometimes used, but it is not widely accepted in standard English.

our·selves /ou(ə)r'selvz, är-/ ▶ **pronoun** (first person pl.) **1** used as the object of a verb or preposition when this is the same as the subject of the clause and the subject is the speaker and one or more other people considered together. **2** (emphatic) we or us personally.

oust /oust/ ▶ **verb** force out of a job or position of power: *three directors have been ousted from the board.*

> – SYNONYMS **expel,** drive out, force out, eject, get rid of, depose, topple, unseat, overthrow, bring down, overturn, dismiss, dislodge.

– ORIGIN Old French *ouster* 'take away.'

> CHOOSE THE RIGHT WORD
>
> See **EJECT**.

oust·er /'oustər/ ▶ **noun** dismissal or expulsion from a position.

out /out/ ▶ **adverb 1** moving away from a place, especially from one that is enclosed to one that is open. **2** away from one's home or place of work. **3** outdoors. **4** so as to be revealed, heard, or known. **5** at or to an end: *the romance fizzled out.* **6** at a specified distance away from the target. **7** to sea, away from the land. **8** (of the tide) falling or at its lowest level. **9** no longer in prison. **10** (of a light or fire) so as to be extinguished or no longer burning. ▶ **preposition** through to the outside. ▶ **adjective 1** not at home or one's place of work. **2** made public or available. **3** open about one's homosexuality. **4** not possible or worth considering. **5** no longer existing or current. **6** unconscious. **7** mistaken. **8** (of the ball in tennis, squash, etc.) outside the playing area. **9** Baseball no longer batting. ▶ **verb** informal reveal that someone is homosexual.

– PHRASES **out for** intent on having: *he was out for revenge.* **out of 1** from. **2** not having a stock or supply of something. **out to do** trying hard to do something: *they were out to impress.*

– ORIGIN Old English.

> USAGE
>
> It is better to write **out of** rather than simply **out** in sentences such as *he threw it out of the window.*

out- ▶ **prefix 1** to the point of surpassing or going beyond: *outperform.* **2** external; separate; from outside: *outbuildings.* **3** away from: *outpost.*

out·age /'outij/ ▶ **noun** a period when a power supply or other service is not available.

out-and-out ▶ **adjective** in every way; complete: *an out-and-out lie.*

out·back /'out,bak/ ▶ **noun (the outback)** the remote inland area of Australia that has very few inhabitants.

out·bid /,out'bid/ ▶ **verb (outbids, outbidding;** past and past part. **outbid)** bid more for something than someone else.

out·board /'out,bô(ə)rd/ ▶ **adjective & adverb** on, toward, or near the outside of a ship or aircraft. ▶ **noun 1** an outboard motor. **2** a boat with an outboard motor.

out·board mo·tor ▶ **noun** a portable motor that can be attached to the outside of a boat.

out·bound /'out'bound/ ▶ **adjective & adverb** traveling from a place rather than arriving in it.

out·break /'out,brāk/ ▶ **noun** a sudden or violent occurrence of war, disease, etc.

> – SYNONYMS **1 eruption,** flare-up, upsurge, rash, wave, spate, burst, flurry. **2 start,** beginning, commencement, onset.

out·build·ing /'out,bildiNG/ ▶ **noun** a smaller building near to but separate from a main building.

out·burst /'out,bərst/ ▶ **noun 1** a sudden release of strong emotion: *an angry outburst from the director.* **2** a sudden violent occurrence of something: *outbursts of fighting.*

> – SYNONYMS **eruption,** explosion, flare-up, storm, outpouring, burst, surge, fit, paroxysm, spasm.

out·cast /'out,kast/ ▶ **noun** a person rejected by their society or social group.

> – SYNONYMS **pariah,** persona non grata, reject, outsider.

out·class /,out'klas/ ▶ **verb** be far better than someone or something.

out·come /'out,kəm/ ▶ **noun** the result or consequence of an action or event: *his remarks did not affect the outcome of the trial.*

> – SYNONYMS **result,** end result, net result, consequence, upshot, conclusion, end product; informal **payoff.**

out·crop /'out,kräp/ ▶ **noun** a part of a rock formation that is visible above the surface of the ground.

out·cry /'out,krī/ ▶ **noun** (pl. **outcries**) a strong expression of public disapproval.

> – SYNONYMS **protest,** protestation, complaints, objections, furor, hue and cry, fuss, uproar, opposition, dissent; informal **hullabaloo, ruction(s),** stink.

out·dat·ed /,out'dātid/ ▶ **adjective** no longer used or fashionable.

> – SYNONYMS **old-fashioned,** out of date, outmoded, out of fashion, unfashionable, dated, passé, old, behind the times, antiquated; informal **old hat, square.**
> – ANTONYMS modern.

out·dis·tance /,out'distəns/ ▶ **verb** leave a competitor or pursuer far behind.

out·do /ˌout'do͞o/ ▶ **verb** (**outdoes** /ˌout'dəz/, **outdoing** /ˌout'do͞oiNG/; past **outdid** /ˌout'did/; past part. **outdone** /ˌout'dən/) be better than someone else.

– SYNONYMS **surpass,** outshine, overshadow, eclipse, outclass, outmaneuver, put in the shade, upstage, exceed, transcend, top, cap, beat, better; informal be a cut above.

out·door /'out'dôr/ ▶ **adjective 1** done, situated, or used outdoors. **2** fond of being outdoors.

– SYNONYMS **open-air,** out-of-doors, outside, alfresco.
– ANTONYMS indoor.

out·doors /ˌout'dôrz/ ▶ **adverb** in or into the open air. ▶ **noun** any area outside buildings or shelter.

out·doors·man /out'dôrzmən/ ▶ **noun** (pl. **outdoorsmen**; fem. **outdoorswoman** /-ˌwo͝omən/ pl. **outdoorswomen**) a person who spends a lot of time outdoors or doing outdoor activities.

out·er /'outər/ ▶ **adjective 1** outside; external. **2** further from the center or the inside.

– SYNONYMS **1 outside,** outermost, outward, exterior, external, surface. **2 outlying,** distant, remote, faraway, far-flung, furthest.
– ANTONYMS inner.

▶ **noun** Brit. the division of a target furthest from the bullseye.

out·er·most /'outərˌmōst/ ▶ **adjective** furthest from the center.

out·er space ▶ **noun** the universe beyond the earth's atmosphere.

out·er·wear /'outərˌwe(ə)r/ ▶ **noun** clothing worn over other clothes, especially outdoors.

out·fall /'outˌfôl/ ▶ **noun** the place where a river, drain, or sewer empties into the sea, a river, or a lake.

out·field /'outˌfēld/ ▶ **noun** the outer part of a baseball field.

out·fight /ˌout'fīt/ ▶ **verb** (past and past participle **outfought**) fight better than and beat (an opponent).

out·fit /'outˌfit/ ▶ **noun 1** a set of clothes worn together. **2** informal a group of people working together as a business, team, etc.

– SYNONYMS **1 costume,** suit, uniform, ensemble, clothes, clothing, dress, garb; informal getup, gear. **2 organization,** enterprise, company, firm, business, group, body, team; informal setup.

▶ **verb** (**outfits, outfitting, outfitted**) provide someone with a set of clothes, equipment, etc.

out·fit·ter /'outˌfitər/ (also **outfitters**) ▶ **noun** a store that sells clothing and equipment, especially for outdoor activities.

out·flank /ˌout'flaNGk/ ▶ **verb 1** move around the side of an enemy, especially so as to attack them from behind. **2** outwit someone.

out·flow /'outˌflō/ ▶ **noun** a large amount of something that moves or is transferred out of a place.

out·fox /ˌout'fäks/ ▶ **verb** informal defeat someone by being more clever or cunning than they are.

out·gas /ˌout'gas/ ▶ **verb** (**outgases, outgassing, outgassed**) release or give off a substance as a gas or vapor.

out·go·ing /'outˌgōiNG/ ▶ **adjective 1** friendly and confident. **2** leaving a job or position. **3** going out or away from a place.

– SYNONYMS **1 extrovert,** uninhibited, unreserved, demonstrative, affectionate, warm, sociable, gregarious, convivial, lively, expansive. **2 departing,** retiring, leaving.
– ANTONYMS introverted, incoming.

▶ **noun** Brit. (**outgoings**) money that has to be spent regularly.

out·grow /ˌout'grō/ ▶ **verb** (past **outgrew** /ˌout'gro͞o/; past part. **outgrown** /ˌout'grōn/) **1** grow too big for something. **2** stop doing or having an interest in something as one matures: *she had outgrown her collection of china kittens.* **3** grow faster or taller than someone or something else.

out·growth /'outˌgrōTH/ ▶ **noun 1** something that grows out of something else. **2** a natural development or result.

out·gun /ˌout'gən/ ▶ **verb** (**outguns, outgunning, outgunned**) have more or better weapons than another person or group.

out·house /'outˌhous/ ▶ **noun** a small building containing a toilet, typically with no plumbing.

out·ing /'outiNG/ ▶ **noun 1** a short trip taken for pleasure. **2** informal an occasion when a competitor takes part in a sporting event, or an actor appears in a movie, play, etc.: *an actress in her first screen outing.* **3** the practice of revealing someone's homosexuality.

– SYNONYMS **trip,** excursion, jaunt, expedition, day out, tour, drive, ride, run; informal spin, junket.

out·land·ish /out'landisH/ ▶ **adjective** extremely unusual or unconventional; bizarre.

– SYNONYMS **weird,** queer, far out, eccentric, unconventional, unorthodox, funny, bizarre, unusual, strange, peculiar, odd, curious; informal offbeat, off the wall, way-out, wacky, freaky, kinky, oddball.
– ANTONYMS ordinary.

– ORIGIN Old English, 'not native.'

out·last /ˌout'last/ ▶ **verb** last longer than: *the kind of beauty that will outlast youth.*

out·law /'outˌlô/ ▶ **noun 1** a person who has broken the law, especially one who has escaped captivity or is in hiding. **2** historical a person who has been deprived of legal rights or protection.

– SYNONYMS **fugitive,** bandit, robber.

▶ **verb 1** make something illegal: *secondary picketing has been outlawed.* **2** historical deprive someone of legal rights or protection.

– SYNONYMS **ban,** bar, prohibit, forbid, make illegal, proscribe.
– ANTONYMS permit.

– DERIVATIVES **out·law·ry** /-ˌlôrē/ noun.

out·lay /'outˌlā/ ▶ **noun** an amount of money spent.

out·let /'outˌlet/ ▶ **noun 1** a pipe or hole through which water or gas may escape. **2** a point from which goods are sold or distributed: *a fast-food outlet.* **3** a retail store offering discounted merchandise. **4** a means of expressing one's talents, energy, or emotions: *boxing provided a perfect outlet for his aggression.* **5** the mouth of a river. **6** an electrical output socket.

– SYNONYMS **1 vent,** way out, outfall, opening, channel, conduit, duct. **2 market,** shop, store.

out·li·er /'outˌlīər/ ▶ **noun 1** a thing that is separate or detached from a main body or system. **2** a younger rock formation among older rocks.

out·line /ˈout,līn/ ▶ **noun 1** a drawing or diagram showing the shape of an object. **2** the contours or outer edges of an object. **3** a brief description of the main points of something.

– SYNONYMS **1 silhouette,** profile, shape, contour(s), form, lines. **2 rough idea,** thumbnail sketch, rundown, summary, synopsis, résumé, précis, gist, bare bones.

▶ **verb 1** draw or define the outer edge or shape of something. **2** give a summary of: *she outlined the case briefly.*

– SYNONYMS **rough out,** sketch out, draft, summarize, précis.

out·live /,outˈliv/ ▶ **verb** live or last longer than someone or something else.

out·look /ˈout,lo͝ok/ ▶ **noun 1** a person's point of view or attitude to life. **2** a view. **3** what is likely to happen in the future.

– SYNONYMS **1 point of view,** viewpoint, way of thinking, perspective, attitude, standpoint, stance, frame of mind. **2 view,** vista, prospect, panorama. **3 prospects,** future, expectations, prognosis.

out·ly·ing /ˈout,lī-iNG/ ▶ **adjective** situated far from a center.

out·man /,outˈman/ ▶ **verb** (**outmans, outmanning, outmanned**) (usu. as adj. **outmanned**) **1** outnumber: *the rebels are outmanned.* **2** overpower with skill or physical strength.

out·ma·neu·ver /,outməˈno͞ovər/ ▶ **verb** evade or gain an advantage over an opponent by using skill and cunning.

out·match /,outˈmaCH/ ▶ **verb** be better than someone or something else.

out·mod·ed /,outˈmōdid/ ▶ **adjective** old-fashioned.

out·num·ber /,outˈnəmbər/ ▶ **verb** be more numerous than: *women outnumbered men by three to one.*

out-of-bod·y ex·pe·ri·ence ▶ **noun** a sensation of being outside one's body, typically of observing oneself from a distance.

out of date ▶ **adjective 1** old-fashioned. **2** no longer valid.

– SYNONYMS **1 old-fashioned,** outmoded, outdated, dated, old, passé, behind the times, obsolete, antiquated, anachronistic, antediluvian; informal old hat. **2 expired,** lapsed, invalid, void.
– ANTONYMS fashionable, valid, current.

out·pace /,outˈpās/ ▶ **verb** go, rise, or improve faster than someone or something else.

out·pa·tient /ˈout,pāSHənt/ ▶ **noun** a patient who goes to a hospital for treatment without staying overnight.

out·per·form /,outpərˈfôrm/ ▶ **verb** perform better than someone or something else.

out·place·ment /ˈoutplāsmənt/ ▶ **noun** the action of helping workers who have been laid off find new employment.

out·play /,outˈplā/ ▶ **verb** play better than another person or team.

out·post /ˈout,pōst/ ▶ **noun 1** a small military camp at a distance from the main army. **2** a remote part of a country or empire.

out·pour·ing /ˈout,pôriNG/ ▶ **noun 1** something that streams out rapidly. **2** an outburst of strong emotion: *an outpouring of grief.*

out·put /ˈout,po͝ot/ ▶ **noun 1** the amount of something produced. **2** the process of producing something. **3** the power, energy, etc., supplied by a device or system. **4** Electronics a place where power or information leaves a system.

– SYNONYMS **production,** yield, product, productivity, work, result.

▶ **verb** (**outputting**; past and past part. **output** or **outputted**) (of a computer) produce data.

out·rage /ˈout,rāj/ ▶ **noun 1** an extremely strong reaction of anger, shock, or indignation. **2** an extremely cruel, wicked, or shocking act: *some of the worst terrorist outrages.*

– SYNONYMS **1 indignation,** fury, anger, rage, wrath, annoyance; literary ire. **2 scandal,** offense, insult, affront, disgrace, atrocity.

▶ **verb** make someone feel extremely angry, shocked, or indignant.

– SYNONYMS **enrage,** infuriate, incense, anger, scandalize, offend, affront, shock.

– ORIGIN Old French, from Latin *ultra* 'beyond.'

out·ra·geous /outˈrājəs/ ▶ **adjective 1** shockingly bad or unacceptable: *an outrageous waste of time and money.* **2** very unusual and slightly shocking: *her outrageous costumes.*

– SYNONYMS **1 shocking,** disgraceful, scandalous, atrocious, appalling, dreadful, insufferable, intolerable. **2 exaggerated,** improbable, preposterous, ridiculous, unwarranted.

– DERIVATIVES **out·ra·geous·ly** adverb **out·ra·geous·ness** noun.

out·ran /,outˈran/ past of **OUTRUN**.

out·rank /,outˈraNGk/ ▶ **verb 1** have a higher rank than someone else. **2** be better or more important than something else.

ou·tré /o͞oˈtrā/ ▶ **adjective** unusual and startling.
– ORIGIN French, 'exceeded.'

out·reach /ˈout,rēCH/ ▶ **noun** an organization's involvement with the community, especially in the context of social welfare.

out·rid·er /ˈout,rīdər/ ▶ **noun** a person in a vehicle or on horseback who escorts or guards another vehicle.

out·rig·ger /ˈout,rigər/ ▶ **noun 1** a spar or framework projecting from or over a boat's side. **2** a float fixed parallel to a canoe or other boat to help keep it stable. **3** a boat fitted with an outrigger.

out·right /ˈout,rīt/ ▶ **adverb 1** altogether: *unions rejected the offer outright.* **2** in an open and direct way. **3** immediately or instantly.

– SYNONYMS **1 completely,** entirely, wholly, totally, categorically, absolutely, utterly, flatly, unreservedly, out of hand. **2 explicitly,** directly, frankly, candidly, bluntly, plainly, to someone's face, straight up. **3 instantly,** instantaneously, immediately, at once, straightaway, then and there, on the spot.

▶ **adjective 1** complete and total: *an outright ban.* **2** open and direct: *an outright refusal.*

– SYNONYMS **1 complete,** absolute, out-and-out, downright, utter, sheer, categorical. **2 definite,** unequivocal, unmistakable, clear.

out·run /ˌout'rən/ ▶ **verb** (**outruns, outrunning;** past **outran** /ˌout'ran/; past part. **outrun**) **1** run or travel faster or farther than someone or something else. **2** go beyond or exceed something.

out·sell /ˌout'sel/ ▶ **verb** (past and past part. **outsold**) be sold in greater quantities than another product.

out·set /'outˌset/ ▶ **noun** the start or beginning.

– SYNONYMS **start,** starting point, beginning, inception; informal the word go.
– ANTONYMS end.

out·shine /ˌout'SHīn/ ▶ **verb** (past and past part. **outshone** /ˌout'SHôn/) **1** shine more brightly than something else. **2** be much better than: *his technical expertise far outshone that of his rivals.*

out·shoot /ˌout'SHo͞ot/ ▶ **verb** (past and past participle **outshot**) **1** shoot better than (someone else). **2** Sports make or take more shots than (another player or team).

out·side /'out'sīd/ ▶ **noun 1** the external side or surface of something. **2** the external appearance of someone or something. **3** the side of a bend or curve where the edge is longer.

– SYNONYMS **exterior,** case, skin, shell, covering, facade.

▶ **adjective 1** situated on or near the outside. **2** not of or belonging to a particular group, organization, etc.: *outside contractors.* **3** (in soccer, etc.) referring to positions nearer to the sides of the field.

– SYNONYMS **1 exterior,** external, outer, outdoor, out-of-doors. **2 independent,** freelance, consultant, external.

▶ **preposition & adverb 1** situated or moving beyond the boundaries of something. **2** (in football, soccer, etc.) closer to the side of the field than. **3** beyond the limits or scope of something. **4** not being a member of a particular group.

– SYNONYMS **outdoors,** out of doors, alfresco.
– ANTONYMS inside.

– PHRASES **at the outside** at the most. **an outside chance** a remote possibility.

out·side in·ter·est ▶ **noun** an interest not connected with one's work or studies.

out·sid·er /ˌout'sīdər/ ▶ **noun 1** a person who does not belong to a particular group. **2** a competitor thought to have little chance of success.

– SYNONYMS **stranger,** visitor, foreigner, alien, interloper, immigrant, incomer, newcomer.

out·size /ˌout'sīz/ ▶ **adjective** (also **outsized**) exceptionally large.

out·skirts /'outˌskərts/ ▶ **plural noun** the outer parts of a town or city.

– SYNONYMS **edges,** fringes, margins, suburbs, suburbia, environs, borders, periphery.

out·smart /ˌout'smärt/ ▶ **verb** defeat or get the better of someone by being clever or cunning.

– SYNONYMS **outwit,** outmaneuver, trick, get the better of; informal pull a fast one on, put one over on.

out·sold /ˌout'sōld/ past and past participle of **OUTSELL.**

out·sole /'outˌsōl/ ▶ **noun** the outer sole of a boot or shoe.

out·source /'outˌsôrs/ ▶ **verb 1** obtain goods from an outside supplier. **2** arrange for work to be done outside one's own company.

out·spo·ken /ˌout'spōkən/ ▶ **adjective** (of a person or utterance) frank and direct.

– SYNONYMS **forthright,** direct, candid, frank, straightforward, open, straight from the shoulder, plain-spoken, blunt.

– DERIVATIVES **out·spok·en·ness** noun.

out·spread /ˌout'spred/ ▶ **adjective** extended or stretched out as far as possible.

out·stand·ing /ˌout'standiNG, 'out-/ ▶ **adjective 1** exceptionally good. **2** clearly noticeable. **3** not yet dealt with or paid.

– SYNONYMS **1 excellent,** marvelous, fine, magnificent, superb, wonderful, superlative, exceptional, preeminent, renowned, celebrated; informal great, terrific, tremendous, super; Brit. informal brilliant. **2 to be done,** undone, unfinished, incomplete, remaining, pending. **3 unpaid,** unsettled, owing, owed, to be paid, payable, due, overdue, delinquent.

– DERIVATIVES **out·stand·ing·ly** adverb.

out·sta·tion /'outˌstāSHən/ ▶ **noun** a branch of an organization situated far from its headquarters.

out·stay /ˌout'stā/ ▶ **verb** stay somewhere for longer than the expected or permitted time.

out·stretched /ˌout'strecHt, ˌout'strecHd/ ▶ **adjective** extended or stretched out.

out·strip /ˌout'strip/ ▶ **verb** (**outstrips, outstripping, outstripped**) **1** move faster than and overtake someone or something else. **2** exceed or go beyond: *demand is outstripping supply.* **3** be better than: *the company outstripped its competitors.*

out·ta /'outə/ (also **outa**) ▶ **preposition** an informal contraction of "out of," used in representing colloquial speech: *we'd better get outta here.*

out·take /'outˌtāk/ ▶ **noun** a scene or sequence filmed or recorded for a movie or program but not included in the final version.

out·vote /ˌout'vōt/ ▶ **verb** defeat someone or something by winning a larger number of votes.

out·ward /'outwərd/ ▶ **adjective 1** of, on, or from the outside. **2** going out or away from a place.

– SYNONYMS **external,** surface, superficial, seeming, apparent, ostensible.
– ANTONYMS inward.

▶ **adverb** (also **outwards**) toward the outside.

– DERIVATIVES **out·ward·ly** adverb.

out·weigh /ˌout'wā/ ▶ **verb** be heavier, greater, or more significant than: *the advantages greatly outweigh the disadvantages.*

– SYNONYMS **be greater than,** exceed, be superior to, prevail over, override, supersede, offset, cancel out, outbalance, compensate for.

out·wit /ˌout'wit/ ▶ **verb** (**outwits, outwitting, outwitted**) defeat or gain an advantage over someone as a result of greater cleverness or ingenuity.

– SYNONYMS **outsmart,** outmaneuver, trick, get the better of; informal pull a fast one on, put one over on.

out·work /'outˌwərk/ ▶ **noun** an outer section of a fortification.

– DERIVATIVES **out·work·er** noun.

ou·zo /'o͞ozō/ ▶ **noun** an anise-flavored Greek liqueur.

– ORIGIN modern Greek.

o·va /ˈōvə/ plural of **OVUM**.

o·val /ˈōvəl/ ▸ **adjective** having a rounded and slightly elongated outline; egg-shaped. ▸ **noun 1** an oval object or design. **2** an oval sports field or track.
– ORIGIN from Latin *ovum* 'egg.'

O·val Of·fice ▸ **noun** the office of the US president in the White House.

o·var·i·an /ōˈve(ə)rēən/ ▸ **adjective** relating to the ovaries.

o·va·ry /ˈōv(ə)rē/ ▸ **noun** (pl. **ovaries**) **1** a female reproductive organ in which eggs or ova are produced. **2** the base of the reproductive organ of a flower, containing one or more ovules.
– ORIGIN from Latin *ovum* 'egg.'

o·vate /ˈōˌvāt/ ▸ **adjective** oval; egg-shaped.
– ORIGIN Latin *ovatus*.

o·va·tion /ōˈvāsHən/ ▸ **noun** a long and enthusiastic round of applause.

> – SYNONYMS **applause,** round of applause, cheers, bravos, acclaim, standing ovation; informal (big) hand.

– ORIGIN Latin, from *ovare* 'exult.'

ov·en /ˈəvən/ ▸ **noun 1** an enclosed compartment in which food is cooked or heated. **2** a small furnace or kiln.
– ORIGIN Old English.

ov·en·proof /ˈəvənˌpro͞of/ ▸ **adjective** suitable for use in an oven.

ov·en-read·y ▸ **adjective** (of food) sold as a prepared dish, ready for cooking in an oven.

o·ver /ˈōvər/ ▸ **preposition 1** extending upward from or above. **2** above so as to cover or protect. **3** expressing movement or a route across. **4** beyond and falling or hanging from. **5** expressing length of time. **6** at a higher level, layer, or intensity than. **7** higher or more than. **8** expressing authority or control. **9** on the subject of.

> – SYNONYMS **1 above,** on top of, atop, covering. **2 more than,** above, in excess of, upwards of.
> – ANTONYMS under.

▸ **adverb 1** expressing movement or a route across an area. **2** beyond and falling or hanging from a point. **3** in or to the place indicated. **4** expressing action and result: *the car flipped over.* **5** finished. **6** expressing repetition of a process.

> – SYNONYMS **1 overhead,** past, by. **2 at an end,** finished, ended, no more, a thing of the past; informal finito.

▸ **noun** Cricket a sequence of six balls bowled by a bowler from one end of the field.
– PHRASES **be over** be no longer affected by something. **over and above** in addition to.
– ORIGIN Old English.

over- ▸ **prefix 1** excessively: *overambitious.* **2** completely: *overjoyed.* **3** upper; outer; extra: *overcoat.* **4** over; above: *overcast.*

o·ver·a·chieve /ˌōvərəˈcHēv/ ▸ **verb 1** do better than expected. **2** be excessively dedicated to the achievement of success.
– DERIVATIVES **o·ver·a·chieve·ment** noun **o·ver·a·chiev·er** noun.

o·ver·act /ˌōvərˈakt/ ▸ **verb** act a role in a play or movie in an exaggerated way.

o·ver·ac·tive /ˌōvərˈaktiv/ ▸ **adjective** more active than is normal or desirable.
– DERIVATIVES **o·ver·ac·tiv·i·ty** /ˌōvərakˈtivətē/ noun.

o·ver·all /ˈōvərˌäl/ ▸ **adjective** taking everything into account; total.

> – SYNONYMS **total,** all-inclusive, gross, final, inclusive, complete, entire, blanket.

▸ **adverb** taken as a whole.

> – SYNONYMS **generally (speaking),** in general, altogether, all in all, on balance, on average, for the most part, in the main, on the whole, by and large.

▸ **noun** (**overalls**) a garment consisting of pants with a front flap over the chest held up by straps over the shoulders.

o·ver·am·bi·tious /ˌōvəramˈbisHəs/ ▸ **adjective** too ambitious.

o·ver·arch /ˌōvərˈärcH/ ▸ **verb 1** form an arch over something. **2** (as adj. **overarching**) covering or dealing with everything: *a single overarching principle.*

o·ver·arm /ˈōvərˌärm/ ▸ **adjective & adverb** done with the arm moving above the level of the shoulder.

o·ver·ate /ˌōvərˈet/ past of **OVEREAT**.

o·ver·awe /ˌōvərˈô/ ▸ **verb** impress someone so much that they are silent or nervous.

o·ver·bal·ance /ˌōvərˈbaləns/ ▸ **verb** fall or cause to fall due to loss of balance.

o·ver·bear·ing /ˌōvərˈbe(ə)riNG/ ▸ **adjective** trying to impose one's views or control other people in a forceful and unpleasant way.

> – SYNONYMS **domineering,** dominating, autocratic, tyrannical, despotic, high-handed; informal bossy.

o·ver·bite /ˈōvərˌbīt/ ▸ **noun** the overlapping of the lower teeth by the upper.

o·ver·blown /ˌōvərˈblōn/ ▸ **adjective 1** made to seem more important or impressive than is really the case: *an overblown action thriller.* **2** (of a flower) past its prime.

> – SYNONYMS **florid,** grandiose, pompous, flowery, overwrought, pretentious, high-flown; informal highfalutin.

o·ver·board /ˈōvərˌbôrd/ ▸ **adverb** from a ship into the water.
– PHRASES **go overboard 1** be very enthusiastic. **2** react in an extreme way.

o·ver·book /ˌōvərˈbo͝ok/ ▸ **verb** accept more reservations for a flight or hotel than there is room for.

o·ver·bur·den /ˌōvərˈbərdn/ ▸ **verb** give someone or something more work or pressure than it is possible to deal with.

o·ver·came /ˌōvərˈkām/ past of **OVERCOME**.

o·ver·ca·pac·i·ty /ˌōvərkəˈpasitē/ ▸ **noun** a situation in which an industry or factory cannot sell as much as it is designed to produce.

o·ver·cast /ˈōvərˌkast, ˌōvərˈkast/ ▸ **adjective** (of the sky or weather) cloudy; dull.

> – SYNONYMS **cloudy,** sunless, dark, gray, black, leaden, heavy, dull, murky.
> – ANTONYMS bright.

o·ver·cau·tious /ˌōvərˈkôsHəs/ ▸ **adjective** excessively cautious.

o·ver·charge /ˌōvərˈcHärj/ ▸ **verb** charge someone too high a price for something.

o·ver·class /ˈōvərˌklas/ ▸ **noun** often derogatory a privileged, wealthy, or powerful section of society.

o·ver·coat /ˈōvərˌkōt/ ▶ **noun** **1** a long warm coat. **2** a top layer of paint or varnish.

o·ver·come /ˌōvərˈkəm/ ▶ **verb** (past **overcame** /ˌōvərˈkām/; past part. **overcome**) **1** succeed in dealing with a problem. **2** defeat an opponent. **3** (of an emotion) overwhelm: *she was overcome with excitement.*

– SYNONYMS **1 conquer,** defeat, beat, prevail over, control, get/bring under control, master, get the better of; informal lick, best. **2 overwhelm,** move, affect, render speechless.

o·ver·com·mit /ˌōvərkəˈmit/ ▶ **verb** (**overcommits, overcommitting, overcommitted**) (**overcommit oneself**) undertake to do more than one is capable of doing.

o·ver·com·pen·sate /ˌōvərˈkämpənˌsāt/ ▶ **verb** do something that is too extreme in an attempt to correct a problem.
– DERIVATIVES **o·ver·com·pen·sa·tion** /ˈōvərˌkämpənˈsāsʜən/ noun.

o·ver·con·fi·dent /ˌōvərˈkänfidənt/ ▶ **adjective** excessively confident.
– DERIVATIVES **o·ver·con·fi·dence** noun.

o·ver·cook /ˌōvərˈko͝ok/ ▶ **verb** cook food for too long.

o·ver·crowd·ed /ˌōvərˈkroudid/ ▶ **adjective** filled with more people or things than is usual or comfortable.
– DERIVATIVES **o·ver·crowd·ing** noun.

o·ver·de·ter·mine /ˌōvərdiˈtərmən/ ▶ **verb** formal determine or account for something in more than one way or with more conditions than are necessary.
– DERIVATIVES **o·ver·de·ter·mi·na·tion** /ˌōvərdiˌtərməˈnāsʜən/ noun.

o·ver·de·vel·op /ˌōvərdəˈveləp/ ▶ **verb** (**overdevelops, overdeveloping, overdeveloped**) develop something too much.
– DERIVATIVES **o·ver·de·vel·op·ment** noun.

o·ver·do /ˌōvərˈdo͞o/ ▶ **verb** (**overdoes** /ˌōvərˈdəz/, **overdoing** /ˌōvərˈdo͞oiɴɢ/, **overdid** /ˌōvərˈdid/; past part. **overdone** /ˌōvərˈdən/) **1** do something excessively or in an exaggerated way. **2** use too much of: *I'd overdone the garlic in the curry.* **3** (**overdo it/things**) exhaust oneself. **4** (as adj. **overdone**) overcooked.

o·ver·dose /ˈōvərˌdōs/ ▶ **noun** an excessive and dangerous dose of a drug. ▶ **verb** take an overdose.
– DERIVATIVES **o·ver·dos·age** noun.

o·ver·draft /ˈōvərˌdraft/ ▶ **noun** a deficit in a bank account caused by drawing more money than the account holds.

o·ver·dram·a·tize /ˌōvərˈdraməˌtīz, -ˈdrämə-/ ▶ **verb** react to or portray something in an excessively dramatic way.
– DERIVATIVES **o·ver·dra·mat·ic** /-drəˈmatik/ adjective.

o·ver·drawn /ˌōvərˈdrôn/ ▶ **adjective** **1** (of a bank account) in a state in which more money has been taken out than the account holds. **2** having an overdrawn bank account.

o·ver·dressed /ˌōvərˈdrest, ˌōvərˈdresd/ ▶ **adjective** wearing clothes that are too elaborate or formal for a particular occasion.

o·ver·drive /ˈōvərˌdrīv/ ▶ **noun** **1** a mechanism in a motor vehicle providing an extra gear above the usual top gear. **2** a state of great or excessive activity: *my heart had gone into overdrive.*
– DERIVATIVES **o·ver·driv·en** /ˈōvərˌdrivən/ adjective.

o·ver·due /ˌōvərˈd(y)o͞o/ ▶ **adjective** not having arrived, happened, or been done at the expected or required time.

– SYNONYMS **1 late,** behind schedule, behind time, delayed, tardy. **2 unpaid,** unsettled, owing, owed, payable, due, outstanding, delinquent, undischarged.
– ANTONYMS early, punctual.

o·ver·ea·ger /ˌōvərˈēgər/ ▶ **adjective** excessively eager.

o·ver·eat /ˌōvərˈēt/ ▶ **verb** (past **overate** /ˌōvərˈāt/; past part. **overeaten**) eat too much.

o·ver·e·lab·o·rate /ˌōvəriˈlab(ə)rit/ ▶ **adjective** excessively elaborate.

o·ver·e·mo·tion·al /ˌōvəriˈmōsʜənl/ ▶ **adjective** excessively emotional.

o·ver·em·pha·size /ˌōvərˈemfəˌsīz/ ▶ **verb** place excessive emphasis or importance on something.
– DERIVATIVES **o·ver·em·pha·sis** /ˌōvərˈemfəˌsis/ noun.

o·ver·en·thu·si·as·tic /ˌōvərenˌᴛʜo͞ozēˈastik/ ▶ **adjective** excessively enthusiastic.
– DERIVATIVES **o·ver·en·thu·si·asm** /ˌōvərenˌᴛʜo͞ozēˌazəm/ noun.

o·ver·es·ti·mate /ˌōvərˈestəˌmāt/ ▶ **verb** estimate as better or greater than in reality: *has the record company overestimated the popularity of these new stars?* ▶ **noun** an excessively high estimate.
– DERIVATIVES **o·ver·es·ti·ma·tion** /ˈōvərˌestəˈmāsʜən/ noun.

o·ver·ex·cit·ed /ˌōvərikˈsītid/ ▶ **adjective** too excited to behave sensibly.
– DERIVATIVES **o·ver·ex·cit·a·ble** adjective **o·ver·ex·cite·ment** noun.

o·ver·ex·ert /ˌōvərigˈzərt/ ▶ **verb** (**overexert oneself**) exhaust oneself by making too much physical effort.
– DERIVATIVES **o·ver·ex·er·tion** /ˌōvərigˈzərsʜən/ noun.

o·ver·ex·pose /ˌōvərikˈspōz/ ▶ **verb** **1** subject photographic film to too much light. **2** (as adj. **overexposed**) seen too much on television, in the newspapers, etc.
– DERIVATIVES **o·ver·ex·po·sure** /-ikˈspōzʜər/ noun.

o·ver·ex·tend /ˌōvərikˈstend/ ▶ **verb** **1** involve someone in excessive work or financial commitments: *the major chains overextended themselves in the 1980s.* **2** make something too long.

o·ver·fa·mil·iar /ˌōvərfəˈmilyər/ ▶ **adjective** **1** too well known. **2** behaving or speaking in an inappropriately informal way.
– DERIVATIVES **o·ver·fa·mil·i·ar·i·ty** /-fəˌmilēˈaritē/ noun.

o·ver·feed /ˌōvərˈfēd/ ▶ **verb** (past and past part. **overfed** /ˌōvərˈfed/) feed someone or something too much.

o·ver·fill /ˌōvərˈfil/ ▶ **verb** put more into a container than there is room for.

o·ver·fish /ˌōvərˈfisʜ/ ▶ **verb** take too many fish from the sea or a river or lake, greatly reducing the stock.

o·ver·flow /ˌōvərˈflō/ ▶ **verb** **1** flow over the brim of a container. **2** be excessively full or crowded. **3** (**overflow with**) be very full of an emotion.

– SYNONYMS **spill over,** flow over, brim over, well over, flood.

▶ **noun** **1** the overflowing of a liquid. **2** the people or things that do not fit into a particular space. **3** (also **overflow pipe**) an outlet for excess water.

– SYNONYMS **surplus,** excess, extra, remainder, overspill.

o·ver·fly /ˌōvərˈflī/ ▸ **verb** (**overflies**; past **overflew**; past participle **overflown**) fly over a place or territory.
– DERIVATIVES **o·ver·flight** /ˈōvərˌflīt/ noun.

o·ver·gar·ment /ˈōvərˌgärmənt/ ▸ **noun** an item of clothing worn over others.

o·ver·gen·er·al·ize /ˌōvərˈjen(ə)rəˌlīz/ ▸ **verb** express something in a way that is too general.

o·ver·gen·er·ous /ˌōvərˈjen(ə)rəs/ ▸ **adjective** excessively generous.

o·ver·graze /ˌōvərˈgrāz/ ▸ **verb** graze grassland too heavily.

o·ver·ground /ˈōvərˌground/ ▸ **adverb & adjective** on or above the ground.

o·ver·grown /ˌōvərˈgrōn/ ▸ **adjective 1** covered with plants that have been allowed to grow wild. **2** having grown too large.

o·ver·growth /ˈōvərˌgrōTH/ ▸ **noun** excessive growth of something.

o·ver·hand /ˈōvərˌhand/ ▸ **adjective & adverb** (of a throw or stroke with a racket) made with the hand passing above the level of the shoulder.

o·ver·hang /ˌōvərˈhaNG/ ▸ **verb** (past and past part. **overhung** /ˌōvərˈhəNG/) hang outward over something. ▸ **noun** a part that hangs outward over something.

o·ver·haul /ˌōvərˈhôl/ ▸ **verb 1** examine and repair equipment or machinery. **2** analyze and improve a system or process.

– SYNONYMS **service,** maintain, repair, mend, fix up, rebuild, renovate, recondition, refit, refurbish.

▸ **noun** a thorough examination of machinery or a system, with repairs or changes made if necessary.

o·ver·head /ˈōvərˈhed/ ▸ **adverb** above the head.

– SYNONYMS *the sky overhead* **above,** high up, in the sky, on high, above your head.
– ANTONYMS below.

▸ **adjective 1** situated above the head. **2** (of a garage door) opened by being raised and pushed back into a horizontal position. **3** (of a driving mechanism) above the object driven.

– SYNONYMS *overhead lines* **aerial,** elevated, raised, suspended, overhanging.
– ANTONYMS surface, underground.

▸ **noun 1** the regular expenses involved in running a business or organization, such as rent, electricity, wages, etc. **2** a transparency for use with an overhead projector.

– SYNONYMS **running costs,** operating costs, fixed costs, expenses.

o·ver·head pro·jec·tor ▸ **noun** a device that projects an enlarged image of a transparency by means of an overhead mirror.

o·ver·hear /ˌōvərˈhi(ə)r/ ▸ **verb** (past and past part. **overheard** /ˌōvərˈhərd/) hear someone or something accidentally or secretly.

o·ver·heat /ˌōvərˈhēt/ ▸ **verb 1** make or become too hot. **2** (of a country's economy) show marked inflation when increased demand results in rising prices.

o·ver·hung /ˌōvərˈhəNG/ past and past participle of **OVERHANG**.

o·ver·hype /ˌōvərˈhīp/ ▸ **verb** informal make exaggerated claims about the good qualities of a product, idea, or event, in order to get public attention.

o·ver·in·dulge /ˌōvərinˈdəlj/ ▸ **verb 1** have too much of something enjoyable. **2** give in to someone's wishes too readily.
– DERIVATIVES **o·ver·in·dul·gence** noun **o·ver·in·dul·gent** adjective.

o·ver·in·flat·ed /ˌōvərinˈflātid/ ▸ **adjective 1** (of a price or value) excessive. **2** exaggerated: *overinflated claims.* **3** filled with too much air.

o·ver·joyed /ˌōvərˈjoid/ ▸ **adjective** very happy.

– SYNONYMS **ecstatic,** euphoric, thrilled, elated, delighted, on cloud nine, in seventh heaven, jubilant, rapturous, jumping for joy, delirious, blissful, in raptures, as pleased as Punch; informal over the moon, on top of the world, tickled pink, as happy as a clam.
– ANTONYMS unhappy.

o·ver·kill /ˈōvərˌkil/ ▸ **noun** too much of something: *the heavy security has raised concerns of overkill.*

o·ver·lad·en /ˌōvərˈlādn/ ▸ **adjective** carrying too large a load.

o·ver·laid /ˌōvərˈlād/ past and past participle of **OVERLAY**[1].

o·ver·lain /ˌōvərˈlān/ past participle of **OVERLIE**.

o·ver·land /ˈōvərˌland/ ▸ **adjective & adverb** by land.

o·ver·lap /ˌōvərˈlap/ ▸ **verb** (**overlaps, overlapping, overlapped**) **1** extend over something so as to partly cover it. **2** (of two events) occur at the same time for part of their duration. **3** cover part of the same area of interest or responsibility: *the union's commitments overlapped with those of NATO.* ▸ **noun 1** an overlapping part or amount. **2** a common area of interest or responsibility.

o·ver·large /ˌōvərˈlärj/ ▸ **adjective** too large.

o·ver·lay[1] /ˌōvərˈlā/ ▸ **verb** (past and past part. **overlaid** /ˌōvərˈlād/) **1** coat the surface of something. **2** (of a quality or feeling) become more noticeable than a previous one: *the concern in his voice was overlaid with annoyance.* ▸ **noun** /ˈōvərˌlā/ **1** a covering. **2** a transparent sheet over artwork or a map, giving additional detail.

o·ver·lay[2] past of **OVERLIE**.

o·ver·leaf /ˈōvərˌlēf/ ▸ **adverb** on the other side of the page.

o·ver·lie /ˌōvərˈlī/ ▸ **verb** (**overlies, overlying** /ˈōvərˈlī-iNG/, **overlay** /ˌōvərˈlā/; past part. **overlain** /ˌōvərˈlān/) lie on top of something.

o·ver·load /ˌōvərˈlōd/ ▸ **verb 1** load something too heavily. **2** put too great a demand on: *the staff is heavily overloaded with work.*

– SYNONYMS **strain,** overtax, overwork, overuse, swamp, overwhelm.

▸ **noun** an excessive amount.

o·ver·lock /ˌōvərˈläk/ ▸ **verb** prevent fraying of an edge of cloth by oversewing it.
– DERIVATIVES **o·ver·lock·er** noun.

o·ver·long /ˈōvərˈlôNG, -ˈläNG/ ▸ **adjective & adverb** too long.

o·ver·look /ˈōvərˈlo͝ok/ ▸ **verb 1** fail to notice: *she's overlooked one important fact.* **2** choose to ignore a fault or wrongdoing. **3** have a view of something from above.

– SYNONYMS **1 fail to notice,** fail to spot, miss. **2 disregard,** neglect, ignore, pass over, forget, take no notice of, make allowances for, turn a blind eye to, excuse, pardon, forgive. **3 have a view of,** look over/across, look on to, look out on.

CHOOSE THE RIGHT WORD

See **NEGLECT**.

o·ver·lord /'ōvər,lôrd/ ▶ **noun** a person who rules or controls many people.

o·ver·ly /'ōvərlē/ ▶ **adverb** excessively; too.

o·ver·ly·ing /'ōvər'lī-ɪɴɢ/ present participle of **OVERLIE**.

o·ver·man /,ōvər'man/ ▶ **verb** (**overmans, overmanning, overmanned**) provide an organization with more employees than necessary.

o·ver·man·tel /'ōvər,mantl/ ▶ **noun** an ornamental structure over a mantelpiece.

o·ver·mas·ter /,ōvər'mastər/ ▶ **verb** literary overcome someone or something.

o·ver·much /'ōvər'məcʜ/ ▶ **adverb, determiner, & pronoun** too much.

o·ver·night /'ōvər'nīt/ ▶ **adverb 1** for the duration of a night. **2** during a night. **3** very quickly. ▶ **adjective 1** done, happening, or for use overnight. **2** very quick; instant: *Tom became an overnight celebrity.* ▶ **verb 1** stay in a place overnight. **2** ship something for delivery the next day.
– DERIVATIVES **o·ver·night·er** noun.

o·ver·op·ti·mis·tic /,ōvər,optə'mistik/ ▶ **adjective** having a feeling of optimism about something that is unlikely to be justified.

o·ver·paint /,ōvər'pānt/ ▶ **verb** cover something with paint.

o·ver·pass /'ōvər,pas/ ▶ **noun** a bridge by which a road or railroad passes over another.

o·ver·pay /,ōvər'pā/ ▶ **verb** (past and past part. **overpaid**) pay someone too much.
– DERIVATIVES **o·ver·pay·ment** noun.

o·ver·play /,ōvər'plā/ ▶ **verb** give too much importance or emphasis to something.
– PHRASES **overplay one's hand** spoil one's chance of success by being too confident.

o·ver·pop·u·lat·ed /,ōvər'päpyə,lātid/ ▶ **adjective** (of an area or city) having too many people living in it.
– DERIVATIVES **o·ver·pop·u·la·tion** /'ōvər,päpyə'lāsʜən/ noun.

o·ver·pow·er /,ōvər'pou(-ə)r/ ▶ **verb 1** defeat someone with superior strength. **2** have an overwhelming effect on: *he was overpowered by the fumes.*

– SYNONYMS **overwhelm,** get the better of, overthrow, subdue, suppress, subjugate, repress, bring someone to their knees.

o·ver·pow·er·ing /,ōvər'pou(-ə)rɪɴɢ/ ▶ **adjective** extremely strong.

– SYNONYMS **1** *overpowering disappointment* **overwhelming,** oppressive, unbearable, unendurable, intolerable, shattering. **2** *an overpowering smell* **stifling,** suffocating, strong, pungent, powerful; nauseating, offensive, acrid, fetid.

o·ver·priced /,ōvər'prīsd/ ▶ **adjective** too expensive.

o·ver·print ▶ **verb** /,ōvər'print/ print additional matter on a stamp or other surface already bearing print: *menus will be overprinted with company logos.*

o·ver·pro·duce /,ōvərprə'd(y)o͞os/ ▶ **verb 1** produce too much of something. **2** record or produce a song or movie in an excessively elaborate way.
– DERIVATIVES **o·ver·pro·duc·tion** /-'dəksʜən/ noun.

o·ver·pro·tec·tive /,ōvərprə'tektiv/ ▶ **adjective** excessively protective.

o·ver·qual·i·fied /,ōvər'kwôlə,fīd/ ▶ **adjective** too highly qualified.

o·ver·ran /,ōvər'ran/ past of **OVERRUN**.

o·ver·rate /,ōvər'rāt/ ▶ **verb** (often as adj. **overrated**) have too high an opinion of someone or something.

o·ver·reach /,ōvər'rēcʜ/ ▶ **verb** (**overreach oneself**) fail as a result of being too ambitious or trying too hard.

o·ver·re·act /,ōvər-rē'akt/ ▶ **verb** react to something more strongly or emotionally than is justified.
– DERIVATIVES **o·ver·re·ac·tion** /-rē'aksʜən/ noun.

o·ver·ride /,ōvər'rīd/ ▶ **verb** (past **overrode** /,ōvər'rōd/; past part. **overridden** /,ōvər'ridn/) **1** use one's authority to reject or cancel another's decision or order. **2** be more important than: *teachers' professionalism should override personal feelings.* **3** interrupt the action of an automatic device.

– SYNONYMS **1 disallow,** overrule, countermand, veto, quash, overturn, overthrow, cancel, reverse, rescind, revoke, repeal. **2 outweigh,** supersede, take precedence over, take priority over, cancel out, outbalance.

▶ **noun** a device on a machine for overriding an automatic process.

o·ver·rid·ing /,ōvər'rīdɪɴɢ/ ▶ **adjective** more important than any other considerations.

– SYNONYMS **most important,** top, first (and foremost), predominant, principal, primary, paramount, chief, main, major, foremost, central, key.

o·ver·ripe /,ōvər'rīp/ ▶ **adjective** too ripe.

o·ver·rule /,ōvər'ro͞ol/ ▶ **verb** use one's superior authority to reverse or disallow another's decision or order.

– SYNONYMS **countermand,** cancel, reverse, rescind, repeal, revoke, disallow, override, veto, quash, overturn, overthrow.

o·ver·run /,ōvər'rən/ ▶ **verb** (**overruns, overrunning, overran** /,ōvər'ran/; past part. **overrun**) **1** spread over or occupy a place in large numbers. **2** go beyond a set time, cost, or limit.

– SYNONYMS **invade,** storm, occupy, swarm into, surge into, inundate, overwhelm.

o·ver·seas /'ōvər'sēz/ ▶ **adverb** in or to a foreign country. ▶ **adjective** relating to a foreign country.

o·ver·see /,ōvər'sē/ ▶ **verb** (**oversees, overseeing, oversaw** /,ōvər'sô/; past part. **overseen**) supervise a person or their work.

– SYNONYMS **supervise,** superintend, be in charge/control of, be responsible for, look after, keep an eye on, inspect, administer, organize, manage, direct, preside over.

– DERIVATIVES **o·ver·se·er** /'ōvər,si(ə)r, -,sēər/ noun.

o·ver·sell /ˌōvərˈsel/ ▶ **verb** (past and past part. **oversold** /ˌōvərˈsōld/) **1** exaggerate the quality or worth of someone or something. **2** sell more of something than is available.

o·ver·sen·si·tive /ˌōvərˈsensitiv/ ▶ **adjective** excessively sensitive.
– DERIVATIVES **o·ver·sen·si·tiv·i·ty** /ˌōvərˌsensiˈtivitē/ noun.

o·ver·sexed /ˌōvərˈsekst/ ▶ **adjective** having unusually strong sexual desires.

o·ver·shad·ow /ˌōvərˈsʜadō/ ▶ **verb 1** appear more important or successful than: *he was overshadowed by his brilliant brother*. **2** cast gloom over something. **3** tower above and cast a shadow over something.

– SYNONYMS **outshine,** eclipse, surpass, exceed, outclass, outstrip, outdo, upstage; informal be head and shoulders above.

o·ver·shirt /ˈōvərˌsʜərt/ ▶ **noun** a loose shirt worn over other clothes.

o·ver·shoe /ˈōvərˌsʜo͞o/ ▶ **noun** a protective shoe worn over a normal shoe.

o·ver·shoot /ˌōvərˈsʜo͞ot/ ▶ **verb** (past and past part. **overshot**) **1** accidentally go past an intended stopping or turning point. **2** exceed a financial target or limit.

o·ver·sight /ˈōvərˌsīt/ ▶ **noun** an unintentional failure to notice or do something.

– SYNONYMS **1 mistake,** error, omission, lapse, slip, blunder; informal slip-up, boo-boo, goof. **2** *the omission was due to oversight* **carelessness,** inattention, negligence, forgetfulness.

o·ver·sim·pli·fy /ˌōvərˈsimpləˌfī/ ▶ **verb** (**oversimplifies, oversimplifying, oversimplified**) simplify something so much that an inaccurate impression is given.
– DERIVATIVES **o·ver·sim·pli·fi·ca·tion** /ˈōvərˌsimpləfiˈkāsʜən/ noun.

o·ver·sized /ˈōvərˈsīzd/ (also **oversize**) ▶ **adjective** bigger than the usual size.

o·ver·skirt /ˈōvərˌskərt/ ▶ **noun** an outer skirt, worn over the skirt of a dress.

o·ver·sleep /ˌōvərˈslēp/ ▶ **verb** (past and past part. **overslept** /ˌōvərˈslept/) sleep longer or later than one intended.

o·ver·sold /ˌōvərˈsōld/ past and past participle of **OVERSELL**.

o·ver·spe·cial·ize /ˌōvərˈspesʜəˌlīz/ ▶ **verb** concentrate too much on one aspect of something.
– DERIVATIVES **o·ver·spe·cial·iz·a·tion** /ˌōvərˌspesʜəliˈzāsʜən/ noun.

o·ver·spend /ˌōvərˈspend/ ▶ **verb** (past and past part. **overspent**) spend too much.

o·ver·spill /ˈōvərˌspil/ ▶ **noun** Brit. part of the population of a city or town moving from an overcrowded area to live elsewhere.

o·ver·staffed /ˌōvərˈstaft/ ▶ **adjective** having more employees than are necessary.

o·ver·state /ˌōvərˈstāt/ ▶ **verb** state something too strongly; exaggerate something.
– DERIVATIVES **o·ver·state·ment** noun.

o·ver·stay /ˌōvərˈstā/ ▶ **verb** stay longer than an allowed or expected time.

o·ver·steer /ˌōvərˈsti(ə)r/ ▶ **verb** (of a vehicle) turn more sharply than is desirable.

o·ver·step /ˌōvərˈstep/ ▶ **verb** (**oversteps, overstepping, overstepped**) go beyond a set or accepted limit.
– PHRASES **overstep the mark** behave in an unacceptable way.

o·ver·stim·u·late /ˌōvərˈstimyəˌlāt/ ▶ **verb** stimulate someone or something excessively.
– DERIVATIVES **o·ver·stim·u·la·tion** /ˈōvərˌstimyəˈlāsʜən/ noun.

o·ver·stock /ˌōvərˈstäk/ ▶ **verb** stock something with more of something than is necessary or required. ▶ **noun** a supply or quantity that exceeds demand.

o·ver·strain /ˌōvərˈstrān/ ▶ **verb** place too much strain on someone or something.

o·ver·stress /ˌōvərˈstres/ ▶ **verb 1** cause too much stress to someone or something. **2** lay too much emphasis on something.

o·ver·stretch /ˈōvərˌstrecʜ/ ▶ **verb 1** make excessive demands on: *classes are large and facilities are overstretched*. **2** stretch something too much.

o·ver·stuffed /ˌōvərˈstəft/ ▶ **adjective 1** (of a container) excessively full. **2** (of furniture) covered completely with padded upholstery.

o·ver·sub·scribed /ˌōvərsəbˈskrībd/ ▶ **adjective 1** (of something for sale) applied for in greater quantities than are available. **2** chiefly Brit. (of a course, college, etc.) having more applications than available places.

o·ver·sup·ply /ˈōvərsəˌplī/ ▶ **noun** (pl. **oversupplies**) an excessive supply of something. ▶ **verb** (**oversupplies, oversupplying, oversupplied**) supply with too much or too many of something: *the country was oversupplied with lawyers*.

o·vert /ōˈvərt, ˈōvərt/ ▶ **adjective** done or shown openly: *an overt act of aggression*.

– SYNONYMS **undisguised,** unconcealed, plain (to see), clear, conspicuous, obvious, noticeable, manifest, patent, open, blatant.
– ANTONYMS covert.

– DERIVATIVES **o·vert·ly** adverb **o·vert·ness** noun.
– ORIGIN Old French, 'opened.'

o·ver·take /ˌōvərˈtāk/ ▶ **verb** (past **overtook** /ˌōvərˈto͝ok/; past part. **overtaken**) **1** catch up with and pass someone while traveling in the same direction. **2** become greater or more successful than someone or something. **3** suddenly affect: *weariness overtook him*.

– SYNONYMS **1 pass,** go past, pull ahead of. **2 outstrip,** surpass, overshadow, eclipse, outshine, outclass, exceed, top, cap. **3 befall,** happen to, come upon, hit, strike, overwhelm, overcome.

o·ver·tax /ˌōvərˈtaks/ ▶ **verb 1** make excessive demands on a person's strength or abilities. **2** require people to pay too much tax.

o·ver·throw /ˌōvərˈTHrō/ ▶ **verb** (past **overthrew** /ˌōvərˈTHro͞o/; past part. **overthrown**) **1** forcibly remove someone from power. **2** put an end to something through force.

– SYNONYMS **oust,** remove, bring down, topple, depose, displace, unseat, defeat, conquer.

▶ **noun** the forcible removal of someone from power.

– SYNONYMS **removal,** ousting, defeat, fall, collapse, demise.

o·ver·time /ˈōvərˌtīm/ ▶ **noun 1** time worked in addition to one's normal working hours. **2** extra time played at the end of a game that is tied. ▶ **adverb** in addition to normal working hours.

o·ver·tired /ˌōvər'tīrd/ ▶ **adjective** excessively tired; exhausted.

o·ver·tone /'ōvərˌtōn/ ▶ **noun 1** a subtle additional quality or implication: *the decision had political overtones.* **2** a musical tone that is a part of the harmonic series above a fundamental note and may be heard with it.

– SYNONYMS **connotation,** hidden meaning, implication, association, undercurrent, undertone, echo, vibrations, hint, suggestion, insinuation, intimation, suspicion, feeling, nuance.

o·ver·top /ˌōvər'täp/ ▶ **verb** (**overtops, overtopping, overtopped**) be higher or taller than someone or something.

o·ver·train /ˌōvər'trān/ ▶ **verb 1** (especially of an athlete) train too hard or for too long. **2** subject to excessive training.

o·ver·ture /'ōvərchər, -ˌchŏŏr/ ▶ **noun 1** an orchestral piece at the beginning of a musical work. **2** an independent orchestral composition in one movement. **3** (**overtures**) approaches made with the aim of opening negotiations or establishing a relationship: *he began making overtures to merchant banks.* **4** an introduction to something more substantial.

– SYNONYMS **1 preliminary,** prelude, introduction, lead-in, precursor, start, beginning. **2 opening move,** approach, advances, feeler, signal.

– ORIGIN Old French, 'aperture.'

o·ver·turn /ˌōvər'tərn/ ▶ **verb 1** turn over and come to rest upside down. **2** abolish or reverse a decision, system, etc.

– SYNONYMS **1 capsize,** turn turtle, keel over, tip over, topple over, upset, turn over, knock over, upend. **2 cancel,** reverse, rescind, repeal, revoke, countermand, disallow, override, overrule, veto, quash, overthrow.

o·ver·use ▶ **verb** /ˌōvər'yŏŏz/ use something too much. ▶ **noun** /'ōvər'yŏŏs/ excessive use.

o·ver·val·ue /ˌōvər'valyŏŏ/ ▶ **verb** (**overvalues, overvaluing, overvalued**) **1** overestimate the importance of something. **2** fix the value of something, especially a currency at too high a level.

– DERIVATIVES **o·ver·val·u·a·tion** /'ōvərˌvalyŏŏ'āshən/ noun.

o·ver·view /'ōvərˌvyŏŏ/ ▶ **noun** a general summary or survey.

o·ver·ween·ing /'ōvər'wēniNG/ ▶ **adjective** (especially of a quality) excessive: *overweening pride.*

– ORIGIN from Old English, 'think or suppose.'

o·ver·weight /'ōvər'wāt/ ▶ **adjective** above a normal, desirable, or permitted weight.

– SYNONYMS **fat,** obese, stout, plump, portly, chubby, potbellied, flabby; informal tubby.

o·ver·whelm /ˌōvər'(h)welm/ ▶ **verb 1** have a strong emotional effect on: *she was overwhelmed by guilt.* **2** give someone too much of something. **3** defeat someone or something completely. **4** cover something completely with a huge mass of water.

– SYNONYMS **1 trounce,** rout, beat hollow, conquer, crush; informal thrash, lick, wipe the floor with. **2 overcome,** move, stir, affect, touch, strike, dumbfound, shake, leave speechless; informal bowl over, knock sideways.

– ORIGIN from Old English, 'engulf or submerge.'

o·ver·whelm·ing /ˌōvər'(h)welmiNG/ ▶ **adjective 1** very great in amount. **2** very strong.

– SYNONYMS **1** *an overwhelming number of players were unavailable* **very large,** enormous, immense, inordinate, massive, huge. **2** *the overwhelming desire to laugh* **very strong,** powerful, uncontrollable, irrepressible, irresistible, overpowering, compelling.

o·ver·win·ter /'ōvər'win(t)ər/ ▶ **verb 1** spend the winter in a particular place. **2** (of an insect, plant, etc.) survive through the winter.

o·ver·work /'ōvər'wərk/ ▶ **verb 1** work or cause to work too hard. **2** use a word or idea too much and so make it less effective. ▶ **noun** excessive work.

o·ver·write /ˌōvər'rīt/ ▶ **verb** (past **overwrote** /ˌōvər'rōt/; past part. **overwritten** /ˌōvər'ritn/) **1** write on top of other writing. **2** destroy computer data by entering new data in its place. **3** write something too elaborately.

o·ver·wrought /'ōvə'rôt/ ▶ **adjective 1** in a state of nervous excitement or anxiety. **2** (of a piece of writing or a work of art) too elaborate.

– SYNONYMS **tense,** agitated, nervous, on edge, edgy, keyed up, worked up, highly strung, neurotic, overexcited, beside oneself, distracted, distraught, frantic, hysterical; informal in a state, in a tizzy, uptight, wound up.

– ANTONYMS calm.

o·ver·zeal·ous /'ōvər'zeləs/ ▶ **adjective** excessively enthusiastic.

o·vi·duct /'ōviˌdəkt/ ▶ **noun** the tube through which an ovum (female reproductive cell) passes from an ovary.

– ORIGIN from Latin *ovum* 'egg.'

o·vine /'ōˌvīn/ ▶ **adjective** relating to sheep.

– ORIGIN Latin *ovinus.*

o·vip·a·rous /ō'vipərəs/ ▶ **adjective** (of an animal such as a bird) producing young by means of eggs that are hatched after they have been laid by the parent. Compare with **VIVIPAROUS.**

o·vi·pos·i·tor /ˌōvə'päzitər/ ▶ **noun** a tubular organ through which a female insect or fish deposits eggs.

– ORIGIN from Latin *ovum* 'egg' + *ponere* 'to place.'

o·void /'ōˌvoid/ ▶ **adjective 1** egg-shaped. **2** (of a plane figure) oval. ▶ **noun** an oval or egg-shaped object or shape.

– ORIGIN Latin *ovoides.*

ov·u·late /'ōvyəˌlāt, 'äv-/ ▶ **verb** (of a woman or female animal) discharge ova (reproductive cells) from the ovary.

– DERIVATIVES **ov·u·la·tion** /ˌōvyə'lāshən, ˌäv-/ noun.

ov·ule /'ōvyŏŏl, 'äv-/ ▶ **noun** the part of the ovary of seed plants that becomes the seed after fertilization.

– DERIVATIVES **ov·u·lar** /-lər/ adjective.

– ORIGIN Latin *ovulum* 'little egg.'

o·vum /'ōvəm/ ▶ **noun** (pl. **ova** /'ōvə/) a mature female reproductive cell that can divide to develop into an embryo if fertilized by a male cell.

– ORIGIN Latin, 'egg.'

ow /ou/ ▶ **exclamation** used to express sudden pain.

– ORIGIN natural exclamation.

owe /ō/ ▶ **verb 1** be required to pay money or goods to someone in return for something received. **2** be morally obliged to do or give something to: *you owe me an* *apology*. **3** (**owe something to**) have something because of: *I owe my life to you*.

– SYNONYMS **be in debt (to),** be indebted (to), be in arrears (to), be under an obligation (to).

– ORIGIN Old English.

ow·ing /'ō-iNG/ ▶ **adjective** (of money) yet to be paid.

– SYNONYMS **unpaid,** to be paid, payable, due, overdue, undischarged, owed, outstanding, in arrears, delinquent.

– PHRASES **owing to** because of.

owl /oul/ ▶ **noun** a bird of prey with large eyes, a hooked beak, and a hooting call, active at night.
– ORIGIN Old English.

owl·et /'oulit/ ▶ **noun** a young or small owl.

owl·ish /'oulisH/ ▶ **adjective 1** like an owl, especially in appearing to be wise or solemn. **2** (of glasses) resembling the large round eyes of an owl.
– DERIVATIVES **owl·ish·ly** adverb.

own /ōn/ ▶ **adjective & pronoun 1** (with a possessive) belonging or relating to the person specified: *I saw it with my own eyes*. **2** done or produced by the person specified. **3** particular to the person or thing specified; individual.

– SYNONYMS **personal,** individual, particular, private, personalized, unique.

▶ **verb 1** possess something. **2** (**own up**) admit to having done something wrong or embarrassing. **3** formal admit or acknowledge that something is the case.

– SYNONYMS **1 possess,** keep, hold, be the owner of, have to/in one's name. **2** (**own up**) **confess,** admit, acknowledge; informal come clean.

– PHRASES **come into its** (or **one's**) **own** become fully effective. **hold one's own** remain in a strong position in a demanding situation.
– ORIGIN Old English.

own·er /'ōnər/ ▶ **noun** a person who owns something.

– SYNONYMS **possessor,** holder, proprietor, homeowner, freeholder, landlord, landlady.

own·er·ship /'ōnər,sHip/ ▶ **noun** the act, state, or right of possessing something.

– SYNONYMS **possession,** freehold, proprietorship, title.

own goal ▶ **noun** (in soccer) a goal scored when a player accidentally hits the ball into their own team's goal.

ox /äks/ ▶ **noun** (pl. **oxen**) **1** a cow or bull. **2** a castrated bull, used for pulling heavy loads.
– ORIGIN Old English.

ox·al·ic ac·id /äk'salik/ ▶ **noun** a poisonous acid found in rhubarb leaves and other plants.
– ORIGIN from Greek *oxalis* 'wood sorrel.'

ox·bow /'äks,bō/ ▶ **noun** a loop formed by a horseshoe bend in a river.
– ORIGIN first referring to the U-shaped collar of an ox-yoke.

ox·bow lake ▶ **noun** a curved lake formed from a horseshoe bend in a river where the main stream has cut across the neck and no longer flows around the loop of the bend.

Ox·bridge /'äks,brij/ ▶ **noun** chiefly Brit. Oxford and Cambridge universities regarded together.

ox·en /'äksən/ plural of **ox**.

ox·eye dai·sy ▶ **noun** a daisy that has large white flowers with yellow centers.

ox·ford /'äksfərd/ ▶ **noun** a type of lace-up shoe with a low heel.
– ORIGIN named after the city of *Oxford*.

ox·i·dant /'äksidənt/ ▶ **noun** Chemistry a substance that brings about oxidation.

ox·i·da·tion /,äksi'dāsHən/ ▶ **noun** Chemistry the process of oxidizing or the result of being oxidized.
– DERIVATIVES **ox·i·da·tive** /'äksi,dātiv/ adjective.

ox·ide /'äk,sīd/ ▶ **noun** a compound of oxygen with another element or group.

ox·i·dize /'äksi,dīz/ ▶ **verb 1** combine or cause to combine with oxygen. **2** Chemistry cause a substance to undergo a reaction in which electrons are lost to another substance or molecule. The opposite of **REDUCE**.
– DERIVATIVES **ox·i·di·za·tion** /,äksidi'zāsHən/ noun **ox·i·diz·er** noun.

ox·tail /'äks,tāl/ ▶ **noun** the tail of an ox (used in making soup).

ox·y·a·cet·y·lene /,äksēə'setl-in, -,ēn/ ▶ **adjective** (of welding or cutting techniques) using a very hot flame produced by mixing acetylene and oxygen.

ox·y·co·done /,äksē'kō,dōn, ,äksē'kō,dän/ (also trademark **OxyContin** /,äksē'käntin/) ▶ **noun** a synthetic painkilling drug similar to morphine.

ox·y·gen /'äksəjən/ ▶ **noun** a colorless, odorless, gaseous chemical element, forming about 20 percent of the earth's atmosphere and essential to life.
– ORIGIN from French *principe oxygène* 'acidifying constituent' (because at first it was believed to be the essential component of acids).

ox·y·gen·ate /'äksəjə,nāt/ ▶ **verb** (often as adj. **oxygenated**) supply or enrich with oxygen: *oxygenated blood*.
– DERIVATIVES **ox·y·gen·a·tion** /,äksəjə'nāsHən/ noun **ox·y·gen·a·tor** noun.

ox·y·gen bar ▶ **noun** a place where people pay to inhale pure oxygen for its reputedly therapeutic effects.

ox·y·gen mask ▶ **noun** a mask placed over the nose and mouth and connected to an oxygen supply, used when the body is not able to gain enough oxygen by breathing air.

ox·y·mo·ron /,äksə'môr,än/ ▶ **noun** a figure of speech in which apparently contradictory terms appear together (e.g., *a deafening silence*).
– DERIVATIVES **ox·y·mo·ron·ic** /-mə'ränik/ adjective.
– ORIGIN from Greek *oxumōros* 'pointedly foolish.'

ox·y·to·cin /,äksə'tōsən/ ▶ **noun** a hormone released by the pituitary gland that in women causes contraction of the uterus during labor and stimulates the flow of milk into the breasts.
– ORIGIN from Greek *oxutokia* 'sudden delivery.'

o·yez /'ō'yā, 'ō'yez/ (also **oyes**) ▶ **exclamation** a call given by a town crier or court official to ask for silence before an announcement.
– ORIGIN Old French, 'hear!'

oys·ter /'oistər/ ▶ **noun 1** a shellfish with two hinged oval shells, several kinds of which are farmed for food or pearls. **2** a shade of grayish white.
– PHRASES **the world is your oyster** you have a wide range of opportunities available to you. [from Shakespeare's *Merry Wives of Windsor* (II. ii. 5).]
– ORIGIN Greek *ostreon*.

oys·ter·catch·er /ˈoistər,kaCHər/ ▸ **noun** a wading bird with black or black-and-white plumage and a strong orange-red bill, feeding chiefly on shellfish.

oys·ter mush·room ▸ **noun** an edible fungus with a grayish-brown oval cap.

Oz /äz/ ▸ **noun & adjective** Brit. & Austral. informal Australia or Australian.
– ORIGIN from the abbreviation of *Australia*.

oz. ▸ **abbreviation** ounce(s).
– ORIGIN Italian *onza* 'ounce.'

o·zone /ˈō,zōn/ ▸ **noun** a strong-smelling, toxic form of oxygen, formed by electrical discharges or ultraviolet light.
– ORIGIN Greek *ozein* 'to smell.'

o·zone hole ▸ **noun** an area of the ozone layer where the ozone is greatly reduced, due to CFCs and other pollutants.

o·zone lay·er ▸ **noun** a layer in the earth's stratosphere containing a high concentration of ozone, which absorbs most of the ultraviolet radiation reaching the earth from the sun.

Pp

P[1] (also **p**) ▸ **noun** (pl. **Ps** or **P's**) the sixteenth letter of the alphabet.

P[2] ▸ **abbreviation** (on road signs and street plans) parking. ▸ **symbol** the chemical element phosphorus.

p ▸ **abbreviation 1** page. **2** Brit. penny or pence.

P2P ▸ **abbreviation** peer-to-peer, an Internet network that enables a group of users to access and copy files from each other's hard drives.

PA ▸ **abbreviation 1** Pennsylvania. **2** public address. **3** personal assistant.

Pa ▸ **abbreviation** pascal(s). ▸ **symbol** the chemical element protactinium.

pa /pä/ ▸ **noun** informal a person's father.
– ORIGIN abbreviation of **PAPA**.

p.a. ▸ **abbreviation** per annum.

pab·lum /'pabləm/ (also **pabulum** /'pabyələm/) ▸ **noun** literary bland intellectual matter or entertainment: *predictable pop pablum*.
– ORIGIN Latin, 'food, fodder.'

PAC /pak/ ▸ **abbreviation 1** Pan-Africanist Congress. **2** political action committee.

pa·ca /'päkə, 'pakə/ ▸ **noun** a large South American rodent that has a reddish-brown coat with rows of white spots.
– ORIGIN Tupi.

pace[1] /pās/ ▸ **noun 1** a single step taken when walking or running. **2** speed in walking, running, or moving. **3** the speed or rate at which something happens or develops: *the pace of change*. **4** a way in which a horse is trained to run or walk.

– SYNONYMS **1 step,** stride. **2 gait,** walk, march, tread. **3 speed,** rate, velocity, tempo.

▸ **verb 1** walk up and down in a small area, typically as an expression of anxiety. **2** (**pace something out**) measure a distance by walking it and counting the number of steps taken. **3** set the speed or rate at which something happens or develops: *they paced their drinking throughout the week*. **4** lead another runner in a race in order to establish a competitive speed. **5** (**pace oneself**) do something at a controlled and steady rate.

– SYNONYMS **walk,** step, stride, march, pound.

– PHRASES **keep pace with** progress at the same speed as. **put someone through their paces** make someone demonstrate their abilities. **stand** (or **stay**) **the pace** be able to keep up with others.
– ORIGIN Latin *passus* 'stretch (of the leg).'

pace[2] /'pā,sē, 'pä,chā/ ▸ **preposition** with due respect to someone.
– ORIGIN Latin, 'in peace.'

pace·mak·er /'pās,mākər/ ▸ **noun 1** an artificial device for stimulating and regulating the heart muscle. **2** another term for **PACESETTER**.

pace·set·ter /'pās,setər/ ▸ **noun 1** a runner or other competitor who sets the pace at the beginning of a race or other competition. **2** a person or organization viewed as taking the lead or setting a standard for others: *Alaska is the pacesetter when it comes to salaries for teachers*.
– DERIVATIVES **pace·set·ting** adjective & noun.

pach·y·derm /'pakə,dərm/ ▸ **noun** a very large mammal with thick skin, especially an elephant, rhinoceros, or hippopotamus.
– ORIGIN from Greek *pakhus* 'thick' + *derma* 'skin.'

pa·cif·ic /pə'sifik/ ▸ **adjective 1** peaceful or pacifying: *a pacific gesture*. **2** (**Pacific**) relating to the Pacific Ocean. ▸ **noun** (**the Pacific**) the Pacific Ocean.
– DERIVATIVES **pa·cif·i·cal·ly** /-(ə)lē/ adverb.
– ORIGIN Latin *pacificus* 'peacemaking.'

Pa·cif·ic time ▸ **noun** the standard time in a zone including the Pacific coastal region of the US and Canada.

pac·i·fi·er /'pasə,fīər/ ▸ **noun** a rubber or plastic nipple for a baby to suck on.

pac·i·fism /'pasə,fizəm/ ▸ **noun** the belief that disputes should be settled peacefully and that war and violence are always wrong.
– DERIVATIVES **pac·i·fist** noun & adjective.

pac·i·fy /'pasə,fī/ ▸ **verb** (**pacifies, pacifying, pacified**) **1** make someone less angry or upset. **2** bring peace to a country or groups in conflict.

– SYNONYMS **placate,** appease, calm (down), conciliate, propitiate, assuage, mollify, soothe.
– ANTONYMS enrage.

– DERIVATIVES **pa·cif·i·ca·tion** /,pasifi'kāshən/ noun.
– ORIGIN Latin *pacificare*.

CHOOSE THE RIGHT WORD

pacify, appease, conciliate, mollify, placate, propitiate

You might try to **pacify** a crying baby, to **appease** a demanding boss, to **mollify** a friend whose feelings have been hurt, and to **placate** an angry crowd. While all of these verbs have something to do with quieting people who are upset, excited, or disturbed, each involves taking a slightly different approach. *Pacify* suggests soothing or calming (*the mother made soft cooing noises in an attempt to pacify her child*). *Appease* implies that you've given in to someone's demands or made concessions in order to please (*she said she would visit his mother just to appease him*), while *mollify* stresses minimizing anger or hurt feelings by taking positive action (*her flattery failed to mollify him*). *Placate* suggests changing a hostile or angry attitude to a friendly or favorable one, usually with a more complete or long-lasting effect than *appease* (*they were able to placate their enemies by offering to support them*). You can **propitiate** a superior or someone who has the power to injure you by allaying or forestalling their anger (*they were able to propitiate the trustees by *holding a dinner party in their honor*). **Conciliate** implies the use of arbitration or compromise to settle a dispute or to win someone over (*the company made every effort to conciliate its angry competitor*).

pack[1] /pak/ ▶ **noun 1** a cardboard or paper container and the items inside it. **2** a collection of related documents. **3** a group of animals that live and hunt together. **4** chiefly derogatory a group of similar things or people: *the reports were a pack of lies*. **5** (**the pack**) the main body of competitors following the leader in a race. **6** Rugby a team's forwards. **7** (**Pack**) an organized group of Cub Scouts or Brownies. **8** a rucksack. **9** a hot or cold pad of absorbent material, used for treating an injury.

– SYNONYMS **1 packet,** container, package, box, carton, parcel. **2 group,** herd, troop, crowd, mob, band, party, set, gang, rabble, horde, throng, huddle, mass, assembly, gathering, host; informal crew, bunch.

▶ **verb 1** fill a suitcase or bag with clothes and other items needed for travel. **2** place something in a container for transport or storage. **3** be capable of being folded up for transport or storage: *a tent that packs away compactly*. **4** cram a large number of things into something. **5** cover, surround, or fill something. **6** informal carry a gun: *he drove downtown packing an automatic*.

– SYNONYMS **1 fill,** load, stow, store, bundle, stuff, cram. **2 wrap (up),** package, parcel, swathe, swaddle, encase, envelop, bundle. **3 throng,** crowd, fill, cram, jam, squash into, squeeze into.

– DERIVATIVES **pack·a·ble** adjective **pack·er** noun.

– PHRASES **pack a punch 1** be capable of hitting with skill or force. **2** have a powerful effect. **pack something in** informal give up an activity or job. **pack someone off** informal send someone somewhere without much notice. **send someone packing** informal dismiss someone abruptly.

– ORIGIN German *pak*.

pack[2] ▶ **verb** fill a jury or committee with people likely to support a particular verdict or decision.

– ORIGIN probably from former *pact* 'enter into an agreement with.'

pack·age /ˈpakij/ ▶ **noun 1** an object or group of objects wrapped in paper or packed in a box. **2** the box or bag in which things are packed. **3** (also **package deal**) a set of proposals or terms offered or agreed as a whole. **4** informal a package tour. **5** a collection of related computer programs or sets of instructions.

– SYNONYMS **1 parcel,** packet, box, carton. **2 collection,** bundle, combination, range, complement, raft, platform.

▶ **verb 1** put something into a box or wrapping. **2** present in a favorable way: *school science is packaged to appeal to boys*. **3** combine various products for sale as one unit.

– SYNONYMS **wrap,** gift-wrap, pack, box, seal.

– DERIVATIVES **pack·aged** adjective **pack·ag·er** noun.

pack·age tour ▶ **noun** a vacation organized by a travel agent, the price of which includes arrangements for transportation and accommodations.

pack·ag·ing /ˈpakijiNG/ ▶ **noun** materials used to wrap or protect goods.

pack an·i·mal ▶ **noun 1** an animal used to carry heavy loads. **2** an animal that lives and hunts in a pack.

packed /pakd/ ▶ **adjective** very crowded.

– SYNONYMS **crowded,** full, filled (to capacity), crammed, jammed, solid, teeming, seething, swarming; informal jam-packed, chock-full, chock-a-block, full to the gunwales, bursting at the seams.

pack·et /ˈpakit/ ▶ **noun 1** a paper or cardboard container. **2** Computing a block of data transmitted across a network.

– SYNONYMS **pack,** carton, container, case, package.

▶ **verb** (**packets, packeting, packeted**) wrap something up in a packet.

– ORIGIN from **PACK**[1].

pack·et boat ▶ **noun** dated a boat traveling at regular intervals between two ports, originally carrying mail and later taking passengers.

pack·horse /ˈpakˌhôrs/ ▶ **noun** a horse used to carry loads.

pack ice ▶ **noun** a mass of ice floating in the sea, formed by smaller pieces freezing together.

pack·ing /ˈpakiNG/ ▶ **noun** material used to protect fragile goods in transit.

pack rat ▶ **noun 1** a ratlike rodent that accumulates a mound of sticks and debris in its nest. **2** a person who saves unnecessary objects or hoards things.

pact /pakt/ ▶ **noun** a formal agreement between people or parties.

– SYNONYMS **agreement,** treaty, entente, protocol, deal, settlement, armistice, truce.

– ORIGIN Latin *pactum* 'something agreed.'

pad[1] /ˈpad/ ▶ **noun 1** a thick piece of soft or absorbent material. **2** the fleshy underpart of an animal's foot or of a human finger. **3** a protective guard worn over a part of the body by an athlete. **4** a number of sheets of blank paper fastened together at one edge. **5** a flat-topped structure or area used for helicopter takeoff and landing or for rocket-launching. **6** informal a person's home.

– SYNONYMS **1 dressing,** pack, wad. **2 notebook,** notepad, writing pad, scratch pad.

▶ **verb** (**pads, padding, padded**) (often as adj. **padded**) **1** fill or cover something with a pad or padding. **2** make a speech or piece of writing longer by adding unnecessary material.

– SYNONYMS (as adj. **padded**) *a padded envelope* **cushioned,** insulated, lined, quilted, stuffed.

– ORIGIN uncertain.

pad[2] ▶ **verb** (**pads, padding, padded**) walk with steady steps making a soft, dull sound.

– SYNONYMS **creep,** sneak, steal, tiptoe, pussyfoot.

– ORIGIN German *padden*.

pad·ding /ˈpadiNG/ ▶ **noun 1** soft material used to pad or stuff something. **2** unnecessary material added to a speech or piece of writing to make it longer.

– SYNONYMS **1 cushioning,** stuffing, packing, filling, lining. **2 verbiage,** wordiness.

pad·dle[1] /ˈpadl/ ▶ **noun 1** a short pole with a broad blade at one or both ends, used to move a small boat through the water. **2** an implement or part of a machine shaped like a paddle, used for stirring or mixing. **3** each of the boards fitted around the outside edge of a paddle wheel or mill wheel.

– SYNONYMS **oar,** scull, blade.

▶ **verb 1** move a boat with a paddle or paddles. **2** (of a bird or other animal) swim with short fast strokes.

– SYNONYMS **row,** pull, scull.

– DERIVATIVES **pad·dler** noun.
– ORIGIN unknown.

pad·dle² Brit. ▶ **verb** walk with bare feet in shallow water.

– SYNONYMS **splash (around/about),** dabble, wade.

▶ **noun** an act of paddling.
– DERIVATIVES **pad·dler** noun.
– ORIGIN uncertain.

pad·dle·boat /ˈpadl,bōt/ ▶ **noun** a boat powered by steam and propelled by paddle wheels.

pad·dle wheel ▶ **noun** a large steam-driven wheel with paddles around its edge, attached to the side or stern of a ship and moving the ship as it turns.

pad·dock /ˈpadək/ ▶ **noun 1** a small field or enclosure for horses. **2** an enclosure next to a racetrack where horses or cars are displayed before a race.
– ORIGIN unknown.

Pad·dy /ˈpadē/ ▶ **noun** (pl. **Paddies**) informal, chiefly offensive an Irishman.
– ORIGIN informal form of the Irish man's name *Padraig*.

pad·dy /ˈpadē/ ▶ **noun** (pl. **paddies**) **1** (also **paddy field**) a field where rice is grown. **2** rice before threshing or still in the husk.
– ORIGIN Malay.

pad·dy wag·on ▶ **noun** informal a police van.
– ORIGIN from **PADDY**, perhaps because formerly many American police officers were of Irish descent.

pad·lock /ˈpad,läk/ ▶ **noun** a detachable lock hanging by a hinged hook on the object fastened. ▶ **verb** secure something with a padlock.
– ORIGIN *pad-* is of unknown origin.

pa·dre /ˈpädrā/ ▶ **noun** informal a chaplain in the armed services.
– ORIGIN from Italian, Spanish, and Portuguese 'father, priest.'

pa·dro·ne /pəˈdrōnā, pəˈdrōnē/ ▶ **noun** a patron or master, especially a Mafia boss.
– ORIGIN Italian.

pae·an /ˈpēən/ ▶ **noun** a song of praise or triumph.
– ORIGIN Greek *paian* 'hymn of thanksgiving to Apollo.'

pa·el·la /päˈāyä, pəˈelə/ ▶ **noun** a Spanish dish of rice, saffron, chicken, seafood, and vegetables, cooked in a large shallow pan.
– ORIGIN Catalan.

pa·gan /ˈpāgən/ ▶ **noun** a person who holds religious beliefs other than those of the main world religions.

– SYNONYMS **heathen,** infidel, idolater, idolatress.

▶ **adjective** relating to pagans or their beliefs.

– SYNONYMS **heathen,** ungodly, irreligious, infidel, idolatrous.

– DERIVATIVES **pa·gan·ism** /-,nizəm/ noun.
– ORIGIN Latin *paganus* 'villager,' later 'civilian' (i.e. a person who was not a 'soldier' in Christ's army).

page¹ /pāj/ ▶ **noun 1** one side of a leaf of a book, magazine, or newspaper, or the material on it. **2** both sides of such a leaf considered as a single unit. **3** a section of data displayed on a computer screen at one time. **4** a particular event considered as part of a longer history: *the vote will form a page in the world's history*.

– SYNONYMS **folio,** sheet, side, leaf.

▶ **verb** (**page through**) **1** look through the pages of a book, magazine, etc. **2** move through and display information on a computer screen one page at a time.
– ORIGIN Latin *pagina*.

page² ▶ **noun 1** a boy or young man employed in a hotel or club to run errands, open doors, etc. **2** a young boy attending a bride at a wedding. **3** historical a boy who entered the service of a knight while training to be a knight himself.

– SYNONYMS **1 errand boy/girl,** messenger (boy/girl), bellboy, bellhop, bellman, runner. **2 attendant,** pageboy, train-bearer.

▶ **verb** summon someone over a public address system or by means of a pager.

– SYNONYMS **call (for),** summon, send for.

– ORIGIN Old French.

pag·eant /ˈpajənt/ ▶ **noun 1** a public entertainment consisting of a procession of people in elaborate costumes, or an outdoor performance of a historical scene. **2** (also **beauty pageant**) a beauty contest.

– SYNONYMS **parade,** procession, cavalcade, tableau, spectacle, extravaganza, show.

– ORIGIN unknown.

pag·eant·ry /ˈpajəntrē/ ▶ **noun** elaborate display or ceremony.

– SYNONYMS **spectacle,** display, ceremony, magnificence, pomp, splendor, grandeur, show; informal razzle-dazzle, razzmatazz.

page·boy /ˈpāj,boi/ ▶ **noun 1** a page in a hotel or attending a bride at a wedding. **2** a woman's hairstyle consisting of a shoulder-length bob with the ends rolled under.

pag·er /ˈpājər/ ▶ **noun** a small radio device that bleeps or vibrates to inform the bearer that someone wishes to contact them or that it has received a short text message.

page-turn·er ▶ **noun** informal an exciting book.
– DERIVATIVES **page-turn·ing** adjective.

pag·i·nate /ˈpajə,nāt/ ▶ **noun** give numbers to the pages of a book, journal, document, etc.
– DERIVATIVES **pag·i·na·tion** /,pajəˈnāsʜən/ noun.

pa·go·da /pəˈgōdə/ ▶ **noun** a Hindu or Buddhist temple, typically having a tower with several tiers.
– ORIGIN Portuguese *pagode*.

paid /pād/ past and past participle of **PAY**.

paid-up ▶ **adjective 1** (of a member of an organization) with all subscriptions paid in full. **2** committed to a cause or group: *a fully paid-up postmodernist*.

pail /pāl/ ▶ **noun** a bucket.
– ORIGIN uncertain.

pain /pān/ ▶ **noun 1** a very unpleasant feeling caused by illness or injury. **2** mental suffering or distress. **3** (**pains**) great care or trouble. **4** (also **pain in the neck** or vulgar slang **pain in the ass**) informal an annoying or boring person or thing.

– SYNONYMS **1** *she endured great pain* **suffering,** agony, torture, torment. **2** *a pain in the stomach* **ache,** aching, soreness, throbbing, sting, twinge, stab, pang, discomfort, irritation. **3** *the pain of losing a loved one* **sorrow,** grief, heartache, heartbreak, sadness, unhappiness, distress, misery, despair, agony, torment, torture. **4** (**pains**) *he took pains to hide his feelings* **care,** effort, bother, trouble.

▶ **verb** cause pain to someone.

– SYNONYMS **sadden,** grieve, distress, trouble, perturb, oppress, cause anguish to.

– PHRASES **on** (or **under**) **pain of** the punishment for wrongdoing being: *we must not, on pain of death, utter a sound.*

– ORIGIN Latin *poena* 'penalty, pain.'

USAGE

Do not confuse **pain** with **pane**. **Pain** means 'an unpleasant feeling caused by illness or injury' (*agonizing stomach pains*), whereas **pane** means 'a sheet of glass' (*a window pane*).

WORD LINKS

analgesic *pain-relieving drug*
anesthetic *drug that stops someone feeling pain*

pained /pānd/ ▶ **adjective** showing annoyance or distress: *a pained expression came over his face.*

pain·ful /'pānfəl/ ▶ **adjective 1** affected with or causing pain. **2** informal very bad: *their attempts at reggae are painful.*

– SYNONYMS **1 sore,** hurting, tender, aching, throbbing. **2 disagreeable,** unpleasant, nasty, distressing, upsetting, sad, traumatic, miserable, heartbreaking, agonizing, harrowing.

– DERIVATIVES **pain·ful·ly** adverb **pain·ful·ness** noun.

pain·kil·ler /'pān,kilər/ ▶ **noun** a medicine for relieving pain.

– DERIVATIVES **pain·kill·ing** adjective.

pain·less /'pānləs/ ▶ **adjective 1** not causing pain. **2** involving little effort or stress.

– SYNONYMS **1 pain-free,** without pain. **2 easy,** trouble-free, straightforward, simple, uncomplicated; informal child's play.
– ANTONYMS painful, difficult.

– DERIVATIVES **pain·less·ly** adverb **pain·less·ness** noun.

pains·tak·ing /'pānz,tākiNG, 'pān,stākiNG/ ▶ **adjective** very careful and thorough.

– SYNONYMS **careful,** meticulous, thorough, assiduous, attentive, conscientious, punctilious, scrupulous, rigorous.
– ANTONYMS slapdash.

– DERIVATIVES **pains·tak·ing·ly** adverb.

paint /pānt/ ▶ **noun 1** a colored substance that is spread over a surface to give a thin decorative or protective coating. **2** dated cosmetic makeup.

– SYNONYMS **coloring,** color, tint, dye, stain, pigment, emulsion, gloss.

▶ **verb 1** apply paint to something. **2** apply a liquid to a surface with a brush. **3** produce a picture with paint. **4** give a description of: *the city isn't as bad as it's painted.*

– SYNONYMS **1 color,** decorate, whitewash, airbrush, daub, smear. **2 portray,** picture, paint a picture/portrait of, depict, represent.

– PHRASES **be like watching paint dry** be very boring. **paint oneself into a corner** leave oneself no means of escape or room to maneuver. **paint the town red** informal go out and enjoy oneself in a lively way.

– ORIGIN from Latin *pingere* 'to paint.'

paint·ball /'pānt,bôl/ ▶ **noun** a combat game in which participants shoot capsules of paint at each other with air guns.

paint·box /'pānt,bäks/ ▶ **noun** a box holding a palette of dry paints for painting pictures.

paint·brush /'pānt,brəsH/ ▶ **noun** a brush for applying paint.

paint·ed la·dy ▶ **noun 1** a butterfly with mainly orange-brown wings and darker markings. **2** a Victorian house, the exterior of which is painted in three or more colors to accentuate the architectural features.

paint·er[1] /'pāntər/ ▶ **noun 1** an artist who paints pictures. **2** a person who paints buildings.

paint·er[2] ▶ **noun** a rope attached to the bow of a boat for tying it to a quay.

– ORIGIN uncertain.

paint·er·ly /'pāntərlē/ ▶ **adjective 1** relating to or like a painter; artistic. **2** (of a painting) characterized by qualities of color, brushstroke, and texture rather than of line.

paint·ing /'pāntiNG/ ▶ **noun 1** the action of painting. **2** a painted picture.

– SYNONYMS **picture,** illustration, portrayal, depiction, representation, image, portrait, landscape, artwork, canvas, oil, watercolor.

paint·work /'pānt,wərk/ ▶ **noun** chiefly Brit. painted surfaces in a building or on a vehicle.

pair /pe(ə)r/ ▶ **noun 1** a set of two things used together or regarded as a unit. **2** an article consisting of two joined or corresponding parts: *a pair of jeans.* **3** two people or animals that are related or considered together. **4** two opposing members of a parliament who agree to be absent for a particular vote, leaving the relative position of the parties unaffected.

– SYNONYMS **set,** brace, couple, duo, two, twosome, team, yoke.

▶ **verb 1** join or put together to form a pair: *a cardigan paired with a matching skirt.* **2** (**pair off/up**) form a romantic or sexual relationship.

– SYNONYMS **match,** put together, couple, combine, yoke.

– ORIGIN Latin *par* 'equal.'

pai·sa /'pīsä/ ▶ **noun** (pl. **paise** /-sā/) a unit of money of India, Pakistan, and Nepal, equal to one hundredth of a rupee.

– ORIGIN Hindi.

pais·ley /'pāzlē/ ▶ **noun** an intricate pattern on fabric, consisting of curved shapes resembling feathers.

– ORIGIN named after the town of *Paisley* in Scotland.

Pai·ute /'pī(y)o͞ot, pī'(y)o͞ot/ ▶ **noun** (pl. same or **Paiutes**) a member of either of two American Indian peoples (the **Southern Paiute** and the **Northern Paiute**) of the western US.

– ORIGIN Spanish *Payuchi, Payuta.*

pa·ja·mas /pə'jäməz, -jaməz/ (Brit. **pyjamas**) ▶ **plural noun 1** a set of loose-fitting pants and shirt worn in bed. **2** a loose pair of pants with a drawstring waist, worn by both sexes in some Asian countries.

– ORIGIN from the Persian words for 'leg' + 'clothing.'

Pak·i /'pakē/ ▶ **noun** (pl. **Pakis**) informal, offensive, chiefly Brit. a Pakistani person.

Pak·i·sta·ni /,pakə'stanē, ,päki'stänē/ ▶ **noun** (pl. **Pakistanis**) a person from Pakistan. ▶ **adjective** relating to Pakistan.

pa·ko·ra /pə'kôrə/ ▶ **noun** (in Indian cooking) a piece of battered and deep-fried vegetable or meat.

– ORIGIN Hindi, referring to a dish of vegetables in gram flour.

pal /pal/ informal ▶ **noun** a friend. ▶ **verb** (**pals, palling, palled**) (**pal around**) spend time with a friend.
– ORIGIN Romany, 'brother, mate.'

pal·ace /'palis/ ▶ **noun** a large, impressive building forming the official residence of a sovereign, president, archbishop, etc.

– SYNONYMS **castle,** château, mansion, stately home, royal estate.

– ORIGIN Old French *paleis.*

pal·ace coup ▶ **noun** the nonviolent overthrow of a sovereign or government by senior officials within the ruling group.

pal·a·din /'palədin/ ▶ **noun 1** literary a brave, chivalrous knight. **2** historical any of the twelve most famous warriors of Charlemagne's court.
– ORIGIN French.

palaeo-, etc. ▶ **combining form** British spelling of **PALEO-**, etc.

pal·an·quin /ˌpalən'kēn/ ▶ **noun** (in India and the East) a seat with a canopy, carried on poles and used as a form of transport for one passenger.
– ORIGIN Portuguese *palanquim.*

pal·at·a·ble /'palətəbəl/ ▶ **adjective 1** pleasant to taste. **2** pleasant or acceptable to someone.

– SYNONYMS **1 edible,** tasty, appetizing, delicious, mouthwatering, toothsome, succulent; informal scrumptious, yummy. **2 pleasant,** acceptable, agreeable, to one's liking.
– ANTONYMS disagreeable.

– DERIVATIVES **pal·at·a·bil·i·ty** /ˌpalətə'bilətē/ noun.

pal·a·tal /'palətl/ ▶ **adjective 1** relating to the palate. **2** Phonetics (of a speech sound) made by placing the blade of the tongue against or near the hard palate (e.g., *y* in *yes*).

pal·ate /'palit/ ▶ **noun 1** the roof of the mouth, separating the cavities of the mouth and nose in vertebrates. **2** a person's ability to distinguish between and appreciate different flavors: *a cocktail created for the discerning palates of the international jet set.*
– ORIGIN Latin *palatum.*

USAGE

On the confusion of **palate** with **palette** or **pallet**, see the note at **PALLET²**.

pa·la·tial /pə'lāsʜəl/ ▶ **adjective** resembling a palace, especially in being impressively spacious or grand.

– SYNONYMS **luxurious,** magnificent, sumptuous, splendid, grand, opulent, lavish, stately, fancy, upscale, upmarket; informal plush, swanky, posh, ritzy, swish.
– ANTONYMS modest.

– DERIVATIVES **pa·la·tial·ly** adverb.

pa·lat·i·nate /pə'latnˌāt, -ˌit/ ▶ **noun** historical a territory under the jurisdiction of a palatine official or feudal lord.

pal·a·tine /'paləˌtīn/ ▶ **adjective** chiefly historical **1** (of an official or feudal lord) having local authority that elsewhere belongs only to a king or queen. **2** (of a territory) subject to such authority.
– ORIGIN French.

pa·lav·er /pə'lavər, -'läv-/ ▶ **noun** informal a lengthy or boring fuss about something; an unnecessarily long-drawn-out process.
– ORIGIN Portuguese *palavra* 'word.'

pa·laz·zo /pə'lätsō/ ▶ **noun** (pl. **palazzos** or **palazzi** /-'lätsē/) a large, grand building, especially in Italy.
– ORIGIN Italian, 'palace.'

pa·laz·zo pants ▶ **plural noun** women's loose wide-legged pants.

pale¹ /pāl/ ▶ **adjective 1** of a light shade or color. **2** (of a person's face) having little color, through shock, fear, illness, etc. **3** not very good or impressive: *a pale imitation of the real thing.*

– SYNONYMS **1 white,** pallid, pasty, wan, colorless, anemic, washed out, peaked, ashen, sickly; informal like death warmed over. **2 light,** pastel, muted, subtle, soft, faded, bleached, washed out. **3 dim,** faint, weak, feeble.
– ANTONYMS ruddy, dark.

▶ **verb 1** become pale in one's face. **2** seem or become less good or important: *his version of the song pales in comparison to the original.*

– SYNONYMS **turn white,** turn pale, blanch, lose color.

– DERIVATIVES **pale·ly** adverb **pale·ness** noun.
– ORIGIN Old French.

pale² ▶ **noun 1** a wooden stake used with others to form a fence. **2** a boundary or limit. **3** old use or historical an area within set boundaries or subject to a particular jurisdiction.
– PHRASES **beyond the pale** outside the boundaries of acceptable behavior.
– ORIGIN Old French *pal.*

pale·face /'pālˌfās/ ▶ **noun** informal, derogatory a name supposedly used by North American Indians for a white person.

paleo- (Brit. **palaeo-**) ▶ **combining form** older or ancient: *Paleolithic.*
– ORIGIN from Greek *palaios* 'ancient.'

Pa·le·o·cene /'pālēəˌsēn/ ▶ **adjective** Geology relating to the earliest epoch of the Tertiary period (about 65 to 56.5 million years ago), a time of rapid development of mammals.
– ORIGIN from Greek *palaios* 'ancient' + *kainos* 'new.'

pa·le·og·ra·phy /ˌpālē'ägrəfē/ ▶ **noun** the study of ancient writing systems and manuscripts.
– DERIVATIVES **pa·le·og·ra·pher** /-fər/ noun **pa·le·o·graph·ic** /ˌpālēə'grafik/ adjective.

Pa·le·o·lith·ic /ˌpālēə'liᴛʜik/ ▶ **adjective** Archaeology relating to the early phase of the Stone Age, up to the end of the glacial period.
– ORIGIN from Greek *palaios* 'ancient' + *lithos* 'stone.'

pa·le·on·tol·o·gy /ˌpālēˌən'täləjē/ ▶ **noun** the branch of science concerned with fossil animals and plants.
– DERIVATIVES **pa·le·on·to·log·i·cal** /ˌpālēˌäntə'läjikəl/ adjective **pa·le·on·tol·o·gist** /-jist/ noun.
– ORIGIN from Greek *palaios* 'ancient' + *onta* 'beings.'

Pa·le·o·zo·ic /ˌpālēə'zōik/ ▶ **adjective** Geology relating to the era between the Precambrian eon and the Mesozoic era, about 570 to 245 million years ago, which ended with the rise to dominance of the reptiles.
– ORIGIN from Greek *palaios* 'ancient' + *zōē* 'life.'

Pal·es·tin·i·an /ˌpalə'stinēən/ ▶ **adjective** relating to Palestine. ▶ **noun** a member of the native Arab population of Palestine.

pal·ette /ˈpalit/ ▶ **noun 1** a thin board on which an artist lays and mixes paints. **2** the range of colors used by an artist.
– ORIGIN French, 'little shovel.'

> **USAGE**
>
> On the confusion of **palette**, **palate**, and **pallet**, see the note at **PALLET**[2].

pal·ette knife ▶ **noun** a thin steel blade with a handle for mixing paints or for applying or removing paint.

pal·i·mo·ny /ˈpalə,mōnē/ ▶ **noun** informal financial support given by one member of an unmarried couple to the other after separation.
– ORIGIN from **PAL** + **ALIMONY**.

pal·imp·sest /ˈpalimp,sest/ ▶ **noun 1** a parchment or other surface on which writing has been applied over earlier writing that has been erased. **2** something altered or used again but still bearing visible traces of its earlier form: *the house is a palimpsest of the taste of successive owners.*
– ORIGIN from Greek *palin* 'again' + *psēstos* 'rubbed smooth.'

pal·in·drome /ˈpalin,drōm/ ▶ **noun** a word or sequence of words that reads the same backward as forward, e.g., *madam*.
– DERIVATIVES **pal·in·drom·ic** /,palinˈdrämik, ˈdrō-/ adjective.
– ORIGIN from Greek *palindromos* 'running back again.'

pal·ing /ˈpāliNG/ ▶ **noun 1** a fence made from stakes. **2** a stake used in such a fence.

pal·i·sade /,paləˈsād/ ▶ **noun** a fence of stakes or iron railings forming an enclosure or defense.
– ORIGIN French *palissade.*

pall[1] /pôl/ ▶ **noun 1** a dark cloud of smoke or dust. **2** a cloth spread over a coffin, hearse, or tomb. **3** a general atmosphere of gloom or fear: *the murder had cast a pall of terror over the village.*

> – SYNONYMS **cloud,** covering, cloak, shroud, layer, blanket.

– ORIGIN Latin *pallium* 'covering, cloak.'

pall[2] ▶ **verb** become less appealing or interesting as a result of being too familiar: *the thrill of flouting her father's wishes began to pall.*
– ORIGIN shortening of **APPALL**.

Pal·la·di·an /pəˈlādēən/ ▶ **adjective** referring to a neoclassical style of architecture based on that of the Italian architect Andrea Palladio.

pal·la·di·um /pəˈlādēəm/ ▶ **noun** a rare silvery-white metallic element resembling platinum.
– ORIGIN from *Pallas*, an asteroid discovered just before the element.

pall·bear·er /ˈpôl,be(ə)rər/ ▶ **noun** a person helping to carry or escorting a coffin at a funeral.

pal·let[1] /ˈpalit/ ▶ **noun** a straw mattress or makeshift bed.
– ORIGIN Old French *paillete.*

pal·let[2] ▶ **noun** a portable platform on which goods can be moved, stacked, and stored.
– DERIVATIVES **pal·let·ize** /ˈpalə,tīz/ verb.
– ORIGIN French, 'little blade.'

> **USAGE**
>
> Do not confuse **pallet** with **palate** or **palette**. A **pallet** is 'a portable platform for moving goods' or 'a makeshift bed,' **palate** means 'the roof of the mouth' or 'a person's ability to distinguish between different flavors,' and a **palette** is 'an artist's board for mixing paints.'

pal·liasse /,palˈyas, ˈpal,yas/ ▶ **noun** a straw mattress.
– ORIGIN French *paillasse.*

pal·li·ate /ˈpalē,āt/ ▶ **verb 1** make the symptoms of a disease less severe without curing it. **2** cause something bad to seem less serious: *there is no way to palliate his offense.*
– DERIVATIVES **pal·li·a·tion** /,palēˈāSHən/ noun.
– ORIGIN Latin *palliare* 'to cloak.'

pal·li·a·tive /ˈpalē,ātiv, ˈpalēətiv/ ▶ **adjective 1** (of a medicine or medical care) relieving pain without curing the condition that is causing it. **2** (of an action) intended to make a problem less severe without dealing with its underlying cause. ▶ **noun** a palliative medicine or remedy.

pal·lid /ˈpalid/ ▶ **adjective 1** pale, especially because of poor health. **2** weak or insipid: *a pallid ray of winter sun.*

> – SYNONYMS **1 pale,** white, pasty, wan, colorless, anemic, washed out, peaked, ashen, gray, drained, sickly, sallow; informal like death warmed over.
> **2 insipid,** uninspired, colorless, uninteresting, unexciting, unimaginative, lifeless, sterile, bland.

– ORIGIN Latin *pallidus* 'pale.'

pal·lor /ˈpalər/ ▶ **noun** an unhealthy pale appearance.
– ORIGIN Latin.

pal·ly /ˈpalē/ ▶ **adjective** informal having a close, friendly relationship.

palm[1] /pä(l)m/ ▶ **noun 1** (also **palm tree**) an evergreen tree with a crown of very long feathered or fan-shaped leaves, growing in warm regions. **2** a leaf of a palm tree awarded as a prize or viewed as a symbol of victory.
– ORIGIN Latin *palma* 'palm (of a hand),' its leaf being likened to a spread hand.

palm[2] ▶ **noun** the inner surface of the hand between the wrist and fingers. ▶ **verb 1** hide a small object in the hand, especially as part of a trick. **2** (**palm something off**) sell or get rid of something dishonestly, especially by misrepresenting its quality or worth. **3** (**palm someone off**) Brit. informal persuade someone to accept something that is unwanted or has little value.
– PHRASES **in the palm of one's hand** under one's control or influence. **read someone's palm** tell someone's fortune by looking at the lines on their palm.
– ORIGIN Latin *palma.*

pal·mate /ˈpal,māt, ˈpä(l)-/ ▶ **adjective** shaped like an open hand with a number of sections resembling fingers: *palmate leaves.*

pal·met·to /pä(l)ˈmetō, pal-/ ▶ **noun** (pl. **palmettos**) an American palm with large fan-shaped leaves.
– ORIGIN Spanish *palmito* 'small palm.'

palm·is·try /ˈpä(l)məstrē/ ▶ **noun** the supposed interpretation of a person's character or prediction of their future by examining their hand.
– DERIVATIVES **palm·ist** noun.

Palm Sun·day ▶ **noun** the Sunday before Easter, on which Jesus's entry into Jerusalem is celebrated by processions in which palm tree branches are carried.

palm·top /ˈpä(l)m,täp/ ▶ **noun** a computer small and light enough to be held in one hand.

palm·y /ˈpä(l)mē/ ▶ **adjective** (**palmier**, **palmiest**) comfortable and prosperous: *the palmy days of the 1970s.*

pal·o·mi·no /ˌpalə'mēnō/ ▶ **noun** (pl. **palominos**) a pale golden or tan-colored horse with a white mane and tail.
– ORIGIN Latin American Spanish, from Spanish, 'young pigeon.'

palp /palp/ ▶ **noun** each of a pair of long segmented feelers near the mouth of some insects and crustaceans.
– ORIGIN Latin *palpus*.

pal·pa·ble /'palpəbəl/ ▶ **adjective 1** able to be touched or felt. **2** (of a feeling or atmosphere) so intense that one seems to experience it as a physical sensation: *a palpable sense of loss*.

– SYNONYMS **1 tangible,** touchable. **2 perceptible,** visible, noticeable, discernible, detectable, observable, unmistakable, transparent, obvious, clear, plain (to see), evident, apparent, manifest, staring one in the face, written all over someone.
– ANTONYMS imperceptible.

– DERIVATIVES **pal·pa·bly** adverb.
– ORIGIN Latin *palpabilis*.

WORD TOOLKIT

See **PERCEPTIBLE**.

pal·pate /'palˌpāt/ ▶ **verb** examine a part of the body by touch, especially for medical purposes.
– DERIVATIVES **pal·pa·tion** /pal'pāsʜən/ noun.

pal·pi·tate /'palpiˌtāt/ ▶ **verb 1** (of the heart) beat rapidly or irregularly. **2** shake or tremble.
– ORIGIN Latin *palpitare* 'tremble, throb.'

pal·pi·ta·tion /ˌpalpi'tāsʜən/ ▶ **noun 1** throbbing or trembling. **2** (**palpitations**) a noticeably rapid, strong, or irregular heartbeat.

pal·sy /'pôlzē/ ▶ **noun** (pl. **palsies**) dated paralysis, especially when accompanied by involuntary shaking of the limbs. ▶ **verb** (**be palsied**) suffer from palsy.
– ORIGIN Old French *paralisie*, from Latin *paralysis*.

pal·try /'pôltrē/ ▶ **adjective** (**paltrier, paltriest**) **1** (of an amount) very small. **2** petty or trivial.

– SYNONYMS **small,** meager, trifling, insignificant, negligible, inadequate, insufficient, derisory, pitiful, pathetic, miserable, niggardly, beggarly; informal measly, piddling.
– ANTONYMS considerable.

– DERIVATIVES **pal·tri·ness** noun.
– ORIGIN probably from dialect *pelt* 'rubbish.'

WORD TOOLKIT

See **INCONSEQUENTIAL**.

pam·pas ▶ **noun** (treated as sing. or pl.) large treeless plains in South America.
– ORIGIN Quechua, 'plain.'

pam·pas grass /'pampəs/ ▶ **noun** a tall South American grass with silky flowering plumes.

pam·per /'pampər/ ▶ **verb** lavish care and attention on someone; spoil someone.

– SYNONYMS **spoil,** indulge, overindulge, cosset, mollycoddle, coddle, baby, wait on someone hand and foot.

– ORIGIN probably from German or Dutch, first meaning 'cram with food.'

pam·phlet /'pamflit/ ▶ **noun** a small booklet or leaflet containing information about a particular subject.

– SYNONYMS **brochure,** leaflet, booklet, circular, mailer, folder.

▶ **verb** (**pamphlets, pamphleting, pamphleted**) distribute pamphlets to people.
– ORIGIN from *Pamphilet*, the name given to a 12th-century Latin love poem *Pamphilus, seu de Amore*.

pam·phlet·eer /ˌpamfli'ti(ə)r/ ▶ **noun** a person who writes pamphlets, especially ones that deal with political issues.
– DERIVATIVES **pam·phlet·eer·ing** noun.

pan¹ /pan/ ▶ **noun 1** a metal container for cooking food in. **2** a bowl fitted at either end of a pair of scales. **3** a shallow bowl in which gravel and mud are shaken and washed by people looking for gold. **4** a hollow in the ground in which water collects or in which salt is deposited after evaporation. **5** a part of the lock that held the priming in old types of gun. **6** a steel drum.

– SYNONYMS **saucepan,** pot, frying pan, skillet, roasting pan, roaster, baking sheet.

▶ **verb** (**pans, panning, panned**) **1** informal criticize someone or something severely. **2** (**pan out**) informal end up or conclude: *he's happy with the way the deal panned out*. **3** wash gravel in a pan to separate out gold.
– ORIGIN Old English.

pan² ▶ **verb** (**pans, panning, panned**) swing a video or film camera on a horizontal plane to give a panoramic effect or follow a subject.

– SYNONYMS **swing (around),** sweep, move, turn.

▶ **noun** a panning movement.
– ORIGIN abbreviation of **PANORAMA**.

pan- ▶ **combining form** including everything or everyone, especially the whole of a continent, people, etc.: *pan-African*.
– ORIGIN Greek.

pan·a·ce·a /ˌpanə'sēə/ ▶ **noun** a solution or remedy for all difficulties or diseases.
– ORIGIN Greek *panakeia*.

pa·nache /pə'nasʜ, -'näsʜ/ ▶ **noun** an impressively confident and stylish way of doing something.

– SYNONYMS **flamboyance,** confidence, self-assurance, style, flair, elan, dash, verve, zest, spirit, brio, vivacity, gusto, liveliness, vitality, energy; informal pizzazz, oomph, zip, zing.

– ORIGIN French, 'plume of feathers.'

pan·a·ma /'panəˌmä, -ˌmô/ ▶ **noun** a man's wide-brimmed hat of strawlike material, originally made from the leaves of a tropical palm tree.
– ORIGIN named after the country of *Panama*.

Pan·a·ma·ni·an /ˌpanə'mānēən/ ▶ **noun** a person from Panama. ▶ **adjective** relating to Panama.

pan·a·tel·a /ˌpanə'telə/ ▶ **noun** a long thin cigar.
– ORIGIN Latin American Spanish *panatela* 'long thin biscuit.'

pan·cake /'panˌkāk/ ▶ **noun 1** a thin, flat cake of batter, fried and turned in a pan. **2** theatrical makeup consisting of a flat solid layer of compressed powder.

pan·cet·ta /pan'cʜetə/ ▶ **noun** Italian cured belly of pork.
– ORIGIN Italian, 'little belly.'

pan·chro·mat·ic /ˌpankrō'matik/ ▶ **adjective** (of black-and-white photographic film) sensitive to all visible colors of the spectrum.

pan·cre·as /'paNGkrēəs, 'pankrēəs/ ▶ **noun** (pl. **pancreases**) a large gland behind the stomach that

produces digestive enzymes and releases them into the duodenum.
– DERIVATIVES **pan·cre·at·ic** /-krē'atik/ adjective.
– ORIGIN from Greek *pan* 'all' + *kreas* 'flesh.'

pan·cre·a·ti·tis /ˌpaNGkrēə'tītis, ˌpan-/ ▶ **noun** inflammation of the pancreas.

pan·da /'pandə/ ▶ **noun 1** (also **giant panda**) a large black-and-white bearlike mammal native to bamboo forests in China. **2** (also **red panda**) a raccoonlike Himalayan mammal with thick reddish-brown fur and a bushy tail.
– ORIGIN Nepali.

pan·da·nus /pan'dānəs, -'danəs/ ▶ **noun** a tropical tree or shrub with a twisted stem and long, narrow spiny leaves from which fiber is obtained.
– ORIGIN Malay.

pan·dem·ic /pan'demik/ ▶ **adjective** (of a disease) widespread over a whole country or large part of the world. ▶ **noun** an outbreak of such a disease.
– ORIGIN from Greek *pan* 'all' + *dēmos* 'people.'

pan·de·mo·ni·um /ˌpandə'mōnēəm/ ▶ **noun** a state of wild and noisy disorder or confusion; uproar.
– ORIGIN first meaning 'the place of all demons,' in Milton's *Paradise Lost*: from Greek *pan* 'all' + *daimōn* 'demon.'

pan·der /'pandər/ ▶ **verb** (**pander to**) satisfy or indulge someone's desires or tastes, especially when these are unreasonable or distasteful: *newspapers are pandering to people's baser instincts.* ▶ **noun** dated a pimp.
– ORIGIN from *Pandare*, a character in Chaucer's *Troilus and Criseyde* who acts as a lovers' go-between.

pan·dit /'pandit, 'pən-/ (also **pundit** pronunc. same) ▶ **noun** a Hindu scholar learned in Sanskrit and Hindu philosophy and religion.
– ORIGIN from Sanskrit, 'learned.'

Pan·do·ra's box /pan'dôrəz/ ▶ **noun** a process that once begun creates many complicated problems.
– ORIGIN from *Pandora* in Greek mythology, who was sent to earth with a jar or box of evils and contrary to instructions opened it, letting the evils escape.

pane /pān/ ▶ **noun 1** a single sheet of glass in a window or door. **2** a sheet or page of stamps.
– ORIGIN Latin *pannus* 'piece of cloth.'

USAGE

On the confusion of **pane** and **pain**, see the note at **PAIN**.

pa·neer /pə'ni(ə)r/ ▶ **noun** a type of milk curd cheese used in Indian and Iranian cooking.
– ORIGIN Hindi or Persian, 'cheese.'

pan·e·gyr·ic /ˌpanə'jirik/ ▶ **noun** a speech or piece of writing in praise of someone or something.
– ORIGIN from Greek *panēgurikos* 'of public assembly.'

pan·el /'panl/ ▶ **noun 1** a distinct, usually rectangular section of a door, vehicle, item of clothing, etc. **2** a flat board on which instruments or controls are fixed. **3** a small group of people brought together to investigate, discuss, or decide on something. **4** a jury, or a list of available jurors.

– SYNONYMS **1 console,** dashboard, instruments, controls, dials. **2 group,** team, body, committee, board.

– DERIVATIVES **pan·eled** adjective.
– ORIGIN Latin *pannus* 'piece of cloth.'

pan·el·ing /'panəliNG/ (Brit. **panelling**) ▶ **noun** wooden panels as a decorative wall covering.

pan·el·ist /'panəlist/ (Brit. **panellist**) ▶ **noun** a member of a panel taking part in a game show or discussion.

pan·el truck ▶ **noun** a small enclosed delivery truck; a van.

pan-fry ▶ **verb** fry food in a pan in shallow fat.

pang /paNG/ ▶ **noun** a sudden sharp pain or painful emotion: *pangs of remorse.*
– ORIGIN perhaps an alteration of **PRONG**.

Pan·gloss·i·an /pan'glôsēən, -'gläs-/ ▶ **adjective** literary unrealistically optimistic.
– ORIGIN from *Pangloss*, the tutor and philosopher in Voltaire's *Candide*.

pan·go·lin /'paNGgəlin, paNG'gōlin/ ▶ **noun** an insect-eating mammal whose body is covered with horny overlapping scales.
– ORIGIN Malay, 'roller' (from the animal's habit of rolling into a ball).

pan·han·dle /'panˌhandl/ ▶ **noun** a narrow strip of territory projecting from the main territory of one state into another. ▶ **verb** informal beg in the street.
– DERIVATIVES **pan·han·dler** noun.

pan·ic /'panik/ ▶ **noun 1** sudden uncontrollable fear or anxiety. **2** frenzied hurry to do something.

– SYNONYMS **alarm,** anxiety, fear, fright, trepidation, dread, terror, hysteria, apprehension; informal flap, fluster, cold sweat.
– ANTONYMS calm.

▶ **verb** (**panics**, **panicking**, **panicked**) feel sudden uncontrollable fear or anxiety, or make someone feel this: *the crowd panicked and stampeded for the exit.*

– SYNONYMS **1 be alarmed,** be scared, be afraid, be hysterical, lose one's nerve, get worked up; informal run around like a chicken with its head cut off. **2 frighten,** alarm, scare, unnerve.

– DERIVATIVES **pan·ick·y** adjective.
– ORIGIN from the name of the Greek god *Pan*, noted for causing terror.

pan·ic at·tack ▶ **noun** a sudden overwhelming feeling of acute anxiety, making someone unable to function normally.

pan·ic but·ton ▶ **noun** a button for summoning help in an emergency.

pan·i·cle /'panikəl/ ▶ **noun** a loose branching cluster of flowers, as in oats.
– ORIGIN Latin *panicula*.

pan·ic room ▶ **noun** another term for **SAFE ROOM**.

pa·ni·ni /pə'nēnē/ ▶ **noun** (pl. same or **paninis**) a sandwich made with a baguette or with Italian bread, typically toasted.
– ORIGIN Italian, 'bread roll.'

pan·jan·drum /pan'jandrəm/ ▶ **noun** a pompous, self-important person in a position of authority.
– ORIGIN from *Grand Panjandrum*, an invented phrase in a nonsense verse by Samuel Foote.

panne /pan/ (also **panne velvet**) ▶ **noun** a glossy fabric resembling velvet, with a flattened pile.
– ORIGIN French.

pan·nier /'panyər, 'panēər/ ▶ **noun 1** a bag or box fitted on either side of the rear wheel of a bicycle or

motorcycle. **2** a basket, especially each of a pair carried by a donkey or mule.
– ORIGIN Old French *panier*.

pan·o·ply /ˈpanəplē/ ▶ **noun** a large or impressive collection or display of something.
– ORIGIN from Greek *pan* 'all' + *hopla* 'weapons, armor.'

pan·op·tic /paˈnäptik/ ▶ **adjective** showing or seeing the whole of something at one view.
– ORIGIN Greek *panoptos* 'seen by all.'

pan·o·ram·a /ˌpanəˈramə, -ˈrämə/ ▶ **noun 1** an unbroken view of the whole region surrounding an observer. **2** a complete survey of a subject or sequence of events: *a full panorama of 20th-century art*.

– SYNONYMS **view,** vista, prospect, scenery, landscape, seascape, cityscape, skyline.

– ORIGIN from Greek *pan* 'all' + *horama* 'view.'

pan·o·ram·ic /ˌpanəˈramik/ ▶ **adjective** with an unbroken view.

– SYNONYMS **sweeping,** wide, extensive, scenic, commanding.

– DERIVATIVES **pan·o·ram·i·cal·ly** /-ˈramik(ə)lē/ adverb.

pan·pipes /ˈpanˌpīps/ ▶ **plural noun** a musical instrument made from a row of short pipes fixed together.
– ORIGIN from the name of the Greek god *Pan*.

pan·sex·u·al /panˈsekshōōəl/ ▶ **adjective** another term for **OMNISEXUAL**.

pan·sy /ˈpanzē/ ▶ **noun 1** a plant of the viola family, with brightly colored flowers. **2** informal, derogatory an effeminate or homosexual man.
– ORIGIN French *pensée* 'thought, pansy.'

pant /pant/ ▶ **verb 1** breathe with short, quick breaths, typically as a result of physical exertion. **2** (**pant for**) long for something.

– SYNONYMS **breathe heavily,** breathe hard, huff and puff, gasp, heave, wheeze.

▶ **noun** a short, quick breath.
– ORIGIN Old French *pantaisier* 'be agitated, gasp.'

pan·ta·loons /ˌpantəˈlōōnz/ ▶ **plural noun 1** women's baggy pants gathered at the ankles. **2** historical men's close-fitting breeches fastened below the calf or at the foot.
– ORIGIN from *Pantalone*, a character in Italian comic theater represented as a foolish old man wearing pantaloons.

pan·tech·ni·con /panˈteknikən, -ˌkän/ ▶ **noun** Brit. a large van for transporting furniture.
– ORIGIN from Greek *pan* 'all' + *tekhnikon* 'piece of art,' originally the name of a London market selling artistic work, later converted into a furniture warehouse.

pan·the·ism /ˈpanTHēˌizəm/ ▶ **noun 1** the belief that God is present in all things in the universe. **2** the worship or tolerance of many gods.
– DERIVATIVES **pan·the·ist** noun **pan·the·is·tic** /ˌpanTHēˈistik/ adjective.

pan·the·on /ˈpanTHēˌän, -THēən/ ▶ **noun 1** all the gods of a people or religion. **2** an ancient temple dedicated to all the gods. **3** a collection of famous or important people: *the pantheon of powerful Washington journalists*.
– ORIGIN from Greek *pan* 'all' + *theion* 'holy.'

pan·ther /ˈpanTHər/ ▶ **noun 1** a leopard, especially a black one. **2** a cougar.
– ORIGIN Greek *panthēr*.

pant·ies /ˈpantēz/ ▶ **plural noun** informal underpants worn by women and girls.

pan·tile /ˈpanˌtīl/ ▶ **noun** a roof tile curved to form an S-shaped section, fitted to overlap its neighbor.
– ORIGIN from **PAN**[1] + **TILE**.

pan·to·graph /ˈpantəˌgraf/ ▶ **noun 1** an instrument for copying a plan or drawing on a different scale by a system of hinged and jointed rods. **2** a jointed framework conveying a current to an electric train or trolley car from overhead wires.

pan·to·mime /ˈpantəˌmīm/ ▶ **noun 1** an entertainment in which performers express meaning through gestures. **2** Brit. a theatrical entertainment involving music, topical jokes, and slapstick comedy, usually produced around Christmas. **3** a ridiculous or confused action or situation.
– ORIGIN Greek *pantomimos* 'imitator of all,' first meaning 'actor using mime.'

pan·to·then·ic ac·id /ˌpantəˈTHenik/ ▶ **noun** a vitamin of the B complex, found in rice, bran, and other foods, and essential for the oxidation of fats and carbohydrates.
– ORIGIN from Greek *pantothen* 'from every side' (referring to its widespread occurrence).

pan·try /ˈpantrē/ ▶ **noun** (pl. **pantries**) a small room or cupboard in which food, dishes, and utensils are kept.
– ORIGIN from Old French *paneter* 'baker.'

pants /pants/ ▶ **plural noun 1** an outer garment covering the body from the waist to the ankles, with a separate part for each leg; trousers. **2** chiefly Brit. underpants.

– SYNONYMS **trousers,** slacks, jeans, khakis, leggings, shorts, clamdiggers, palazzo pants; informal cords.

▶ **adjective** (**pant**) relating to pants: *her pant pockets*.
– PHRASES **fly** (or **drive**) **by the seat of one's pants** informal rely on instinct rather than logic or knowledge. **scare** (or **bore**, etc.) **the pants off** informal make someone extremely scared (or bored, etc.). **wear the pants** informal be the dominant partner in a relationship.
– ORIGIN abbreviation of **PANTALOONS**.

pant·suit /ˈpantˌsōōt/ (also **pants suit**) ▶ **noun** a pair of pants and a matching jacket worn by women.

pant·y·hose /ˈpantēˌhōz/ ▶ **plural noun** women's thin nylon tights.

pan·zer /ˈpanzər/ ▶ **noun** a German armored military unit.
– ORIGIN German, 'coat of mail.'

pap /pap/ ▶ **noun 1** bland soft or semiliquid food suitable for babies or invalids. **2** books, magazines, television programs, or other forms of entertainment that require no intellectual effort.
– DERIVATIVES **pap·py** adjective.
– ORIGIN probably from Latin *pappare* 'eat.'

pa·pa /ˈpäpə/ ▶ **noun** dated one's father.
– ORIGIN French.

pa·pa·cy /ˈpāpəsē/ ▶ **noun** (pl. **papacies**) the position or period of office of the pope.
– ORIGIN Latin *papa* 'pope.'

pa·pal /ˈpāpəl/ ▶ **adjective** relating to the pope or the papacy.
– DERIVATIVES **pa·pal·ly** adverb.

pa·pa·raz·zo /ˌpäpəˈrätsō/ ▶ **noun** (pl. **paparazzi** /-ˈrätsē/) a freelance photographer who pursues celebrities to get photographs of them.
– ORIGIN Italian, the name of a character in Fellini's film *La Dolce Vita*.

pa·paw /pə'pô, 'pôpô/ ▸ **noun** variant spelling of **PAWPAW**.

pa·pa·ya /pə'pīə/ ▸ **noun** a tropical fruit with edible orange flesh and small black seeds.
– ORIGIN Spanish and Portuguese.

pa·per /'pāpər/ ▸ **noun 1** material manufactured in thin sheets from the pulp of wood or other fibrous substances, used for writing or printing on or as wrapping material. **2** (**papers**) sheets of paper covered with writing or printing; documents. **3** an essay or thesis. **4** a newspaper. **5** a government report or policy document.

– SYNONYMS **1 newspaper,** journal, gazette, periodical, tabloid, broadsheet, daily, weekly; informal rag. **2 document,** certificate, letter, file, deed, record, archive; (**papers**) paperwork, documentation; identification, identity card, ID, credentials. **3 essay,** article, monograph, theme, thesis, work, dissertation, treatise, study, report, analysis.

▸ **verb 1** cover a wall with wallpaper. **2** (**paper something over**) disguise an awkward problem instead of resolving it.
▸ **adjective** officially recorded but having no real existence or use: *a paper profit*.
– DERIVATIVES **pa·per·less** adjective **pa·per·y** adjective.
– PHRASES **on paper 1** in writing. **2** in theory rather than in reality.
– ORIGIN Old French *papir*, from Latin *papyrus* (see **PAPYRUS**).

pa·per·back /'pāpər,bak/ ▸ **noun** a book bound in stiff paper or flexible cardboard.

pa·per·boy /'pāpər,boi/ (or **paper girl** /'pāpər,gərl/) ▸ **noun** a boy (or girl) who delivers newspapers to people's homes.

pa·per clip ▸ **noun** a piece of bent wire or plastic used for holding several sheets of paper together.

pa·per mon·ey ▸ **noun** money in the form of banknotes.

pa·per route ▸ **noun 1** a job of regularly delivering newspapers. **2** the route taken to do this.

pa·per-thin ▸ **adjective** very thin or insubstantial.

pa·per ti·ger ▸ **noun** a person or thing that appears threatening but is actually weak or ineffectual.

pa·per trail ▸ **noun** the total amount of written evidence of someone's activities.

pa·per·weight /'pāpər,wāt/ ▸ **noun** a small, heavy object for keeping loose papers in place.

pa·per·work /'pāpər,wərk/ ▸ **noun** routine work involving written documents.

pa·pier mâ·ché /,pāpər mə'shā, pä'p(y)ā/ ▸ **noun** a mixture of paper and glue that is easily molded but becomes hard when dry.
– ORIGIN French, 'chewed paper.'

pa·pil·la /pə'pilə/ ▸ **noun** (pl. **papillae** /-'pil,ē, -'pil,ī/) a small rounded protuberance on a part of the body or on a plant.
– DERIVATIVES **pap·il·lar·y** /'papə,lerē/ adjective.
– ORIGIN Latin, 'nipple.'

pap·il·lo·ma /,papə'lōmə/ ▸ **noun** (pl. **papillomas** or **papillomata** /-mətə/) a small, usually benign wartlike growth.

pap·il·lon /,päpē'yôn/ ▸ **noun** a breed of toy dog with ears suggesting the form of a butterfly.
– ORIGIN French, 'butterfly.'

pa·pist /'pāpist/ chiefly derogatory ▸ **noun** a Roman Catholic.
▸ **adjective** Roman Catholic.

pa·poose /pa'po͞os, pə-/ ▸ **noun** often offensive a young North American Indian child.
– ORIGIN Algonquian.

pap·ri·ka /pə'prēkə, pa-/ ▸ **noun** a deep orange-red powdered spice made from certain varieties of sweet pepper.
– ORIGIN Hungarian.

Pap test /pap/ ▸ **noun** a test to detect cancer of the cervix or uterus using a specimen from the neck of the uterus spread on a microscope slide (**Pap smear**).
– ORIGIN named after the American scientist George N. *Papanicolaou*.

Pap·u·an /'päpo͞oən, 'papyo͞oən/ ▸ **noun 1** a person from Papua or Papua New Guinea. **2** a group of languages spoken in Papua New Guinea and neighboring islands.
▸ **adjective** relating to Papua or its languages.

pap·ule /'pap,yo͞ol/ ▸ **noun** a small pimple or swelling on the skin, often forming part of a rash.
– ORIGIN Latin *papula*.

pa·py·rus /pə'pīrəs/ ▸ **noun** (pl. **papyri** /-'pīrī/ or **papyruses**) **1** a material made in ancient Egypt from the stem of a kind of water plant, used for writing or painting on. **2** the plant from which papyrus was obtained.
– ORIGIN Greek *papuros*.

par /pär/ ▸ **noun 1** Golf the number of strokes a first-class player should normally require for a particular hole or course. **2** Stock Exchange the face value of a share or other security. ▸ **verb** (**pars, parring, parred**) Golf play a hole in a score equal to par.
– PHRASES **above** (or **below** or **under**) **par** above (or below) the usual or expected level. **on par with** equal to. **par for the course** what is normal or expected in any given circumstances.
– ORIGIN Latin, 'equal, equality.'

par·a[1] /'parə/ ▸ **noun** informal a paratrooper.

par·a[2] /'pärə/ ▸ **noun** (pl. same or **paras**) a unit of money of Bosnia, Montenegro, and Serbia, equal to one hundredth of a dinar.
– ORIGIN Turkish, 'money.'

para- (also **par-**) ▸ **prefix 1** beside; adjacent to: *parallel*. **2** beyond or distinct from, but comparable to: *paramilitary*.
– ORIGIN from Greek *para* 'beside, beyond.'

par·a·ble /'parəbəl/ ▸ **noun** a simple story used to illustrate a moral or spiritual lesson.

– SYNONYMS **allegory,** moral tale, fable.

– ORIGIN Latin *parabola* 'comparison.'

pa·rab·o·la /pə'rabələ/ ▸ **noun** (pl. **parabolas** or **parabolae** /-lē, -lī/) a symmetrical open plane curve of the kind formed by the intersection of a cone with a plane parallel to its side.
– DERIVATIVES **par·a·bol·ic** /,parə'bälik/ adjective.
– ORIGIN Latin.

par·a·chute /'parə,sho͞ot/ ▸ **noun** a cloth canopy that allows a person or heavy object attached to it to descend slowly through the air when dropped from a high position. ▸ **verb 1** drop from an aircraft by parachute. **2** chiefly Brit. appoint someone in an emergency or from outside the existing management structure: *he was parachuted in as chief executive in May*.
– DERIVATIVES **par·a·chut·ist** noun.

– ORIGIN from French *para-* 'protection against' + *chute* 'fall.'

pa·rade /pə'rād/ ▶ **noun 1** a public procession. **2** a formal march or gathering of troops for inspection or display. **3** a series or succession: *the parade of celebrities who troop onto his show.* **4** a boastful or obvious display of something.

– SYNONYMS **1 procession,** march, cavalcade, motorcade, spectacle, display, pageant, review, tattoo. **2 promenade,** walkway, esplanade, boardwalk, mall.

▶ **verb 1** walk, march, or display something in a parade. **2** display something in order to impress other people or attract attention: *he enjoyed being able to parade his knowledge.* **3** (**parade as**) appear to be something that is not the case: *these untruths parading as history.*

– SYNONYMS **1 march,** process, file, troop. **2 strut,** swagger, stride, sashay. **3 display,** exhibit, make a show of, flaunt, show (off), demonstrate.

– ORIGIN French, 'a showing.'

pa·rade ground ▶ **noun** a place where troops gather for parade.

par·a·did·dle /'parə,didl/ ▶ **noun** Music a simple drum roll consisting of four even strokes.
– ORIGIN imitating the sound.

par·a·digm /'parə,dīm/ ▶ **noun** a typical example, pattern, or model of something: *society's paradigm of the 'ideal woman.'*
– DERIVATIVES **par·a·dig·mat·ic** /,parədig'matik/ adjective **par·a·dig·mat·i·cal·ly** adverb.
– ORIGIN Greek *paradeigma.*

par·a·digm shift ▶ **noun** a fundamental change in approach or in the assumptions underlying something.

par·a·dise /'parə,dīs/ ▶ **noun 1** (in some religions) heaven as the place where the good live after death. **2** the Garden of Eden. **3** an ideal or very beautiful place or state: *the surrounding countryside is a walker's paradise.*

– SYNONYMS **1 heaven,** the promised land, the Elysian Fields. **2 Utopia,** Shangri-La, Eden, idyll. **3 bliss,** heaven (on earth), ecstasy, delight, joy, happiness.
– ANTONYMS hell.

– DERIVATIVES **par·a·dis·al** /,parə'dīsəl/ adjective **par·a·di·si·a·cal** /,parədi'sīəkəl/ adjective.
– ORIGIN Old French *paradis.*

par·a·dox /'parə,däks/ ▶ **noun 1** a statement that sounds absurd or seems to contradict itself but may in fact be true. **2** a person or thing that combines contradictory features or qualities.

– SYNONYMS **contradiction,** self-contradiction, inconsistency, incongruity, conflict, enigma, puzzle, conundrum.

– DERIVATIVES **par·a·dox·i·cal** /,parə'däksikəl/ adjective **par·a·dox·i·cal·ly** adverb.
– ORIGIN Greek *paradoxon* 'contrary opinion.'

CHOOSE THE RIGHT WORD

See **RIDDLE**[1].

par·af·fin /'parəfin/ ▶ **noun 1** (also **paraffin wax**) a flammable waxy solid obtained from petroleum or shale and used for sealing and waterproofing and in candles. **2** (also **paraffin oil** or **liquid paraffin**) Brit. a liquid fuel made in a similar way, especially kerosene.
– ORIGIN German.

par·a·glid·ing /'parə,glīdiNG/ ▶ **noun** a sport in which a person glides through the air attached to a wide parachute after jumping from or being hauled to a height.
– DERIVATIVES **par·a·glide** verb **par·a·glid·er** noun.

par·a·gon /'parə,gän, -gən/ ▶ **noun** a person or thing seen as perfect, or as a perfect example of a particular quality: *he was a paragon of blond male beauty.*
– ORIGIN Italian *paragone* 'touchstone.'

par·a·graph /'parə,graf/ ▶ **noun** a distinct section of a piece of writing, beginning on a new line and often indented.

– SYNONYMS **section,** division, part, portion, segment, passage, clause.

– ORIGIN French *paragraphe.*

par·a·graph mark ▶ **noun** a symbol (usually ¶) used to mark a new paragraph or as a reference mark.

Par·a·guay·an /,parə'gwīən, -'gwā-/ ▶ **noun** a person from Paraguay. ▶ **adjective** relating to Paraguay.

par·a·keet /'parə,kēt/ (also **parrakeet**) ▶ **noun** a small parrot with mainly green plumage and a long tail.
– ORIGIN Old French *paroquet,* Italian *parrocchetto,* and Spanish *periquito.*

par·a·le·gal /,parə'lēgəl/ ▶ **noun** a person trained in certain legal matters but not fully qualified as a lawyer.

par·al·lax /'parə,laks/ ▶ **noun 1** the apparent difference in the position of an object when viewed from different positions, e.g., through the viewfinder and the lens of a camera. **2** Astronomy the angular difference in the apparent positions of a star observed from opposite sides of the earth's orbit.
– DERIVATIVES **par·al·lac·tic** /,parə'laktik/ adjective.
– ORIGIN Greek *parallaxis* 'a change.'

par·al·lel /'parə,lel, -ləl/ ▶ **adjective 1** (of lines, planes, or surfaces) side by side and having the same distance continuously between them. **2** occurring or existing at the same time or in a similar way: *a parallel universe.*

– SYNONYMS **1 aligned,** side by side, equidistant. **2 similar,** analogous, comparable, corresponding, like, equivalent, matching.
– ANTONYMS divergent, different.

▶ **noun 1** a person or thing that is similar or comparable to another. **2** a similarity or comparison: *there are interesting parallels between the 1960s and the 1940s.* **3** (also **parallel of latitude**) each of the imaginary parallel circles of latitude on the earth's surface. **4** Printing two parallel lines (‖) used as a reference mark for footnotes.

– SYNONYMS **1 counterpart,** analog, equivalent, match, twin, duplicate, mirror. **2 similarity,** likeness, resemblance, analogy, correspondence, comparison, equivalence, symmetry.
– ANTONYMS divergence, difference.

▶ **verb** (**parallels, paralleling, paralleled**) **1** run or lie parallel to something. **2** be similar or corresponding to: *changes in 20th century art have paralleled changes in society.*
– DERIVATIVES **par·al·lel·ism** noun.
– PHRASES **in parallel 1** taking place at the same time and having some connection. **2** (of electrical components or circuits) connected to common points at each end, so that the current is divided between them.
– ORIGIN Greek *parallēlos.*

par·al·lel bars ▶ **plural noun** a pair of parallel rails on posts, used in gymnastics.

par·al·lel im·ports ▶ **plural noun** goods imported by unlicensed distributors for sale at less than the manufacturer's official retail price.

par·al·lel·o·gram /ˌparəˈleləˌgram/ ▶ **noun** a plane figure with four straight sides and opposite sides parallel.

Par·a·lym·pics /ˌparəˈlimpiks/ ▶ **plural noun** (usu. treated as sing.) an international athletic competition for athletes with disabilities.
– DERIVATIVES **Par·a·lym·pic** adjective.
– ORIGIN blend of *paraplegic* and *Olympics*.

pa·ral·y·sis /pəˈraləsis/ ▶ **noun** (pl. **paralyses** /-sēz/) **1** the loss of the ability to move part or most of the body. **2** inability to act or function.

> – SYNONYMS **1 immobility,** powerlessness, incapacity; Medicine paraplegia, quadriplegia. **2 shutdown,** immobilization, stoppage, gridlock, standstill, blockage.

– ORIGIN Greek *paralusis*.

par·a·lyt·ic /ˌparəˈlitik/ ▶ **adjective** relating to paralysis.
– DERIVATIVES **par·a·lyt·i·cal·ly** adverb.

par·a·lyze /ˈparəˌlīz/ (Brit. also **paralyse**) ▶ **verb 1** cause a person or part of the body to become partly or wholly incapable of movement. **2** prevent someone or something from functioning: *the regional capital was paralyzed by a general strike*.

> – SYNONYMS **1 disable,** cripple, immobilize, incapacitate; (**paralyzed**) Medicine paraplegic, quadriplegic. **2 bring to a standstill,** immobilize, bring to a halt, freeze, cripple, disable.

par·a·me·ci·um /ˌparəˈmēsʜ(ē)əm, -sēəm/ ▶ **noun** (pl. **paramecia** /ˌparəˈmēsʜ(ē)ə, -sēə/) a single-celled freshwater animal that has a slipperlike shape.
– ORIGIN Latin.

par·a·med·ic /ˌparəˈmedik/ ▶ **noun** a person who is trained to do medical work, especially emergency first aid, but is not a fully qualified doctor.
– DERIVATIVES **par·a·med·i·cal** adjective.

pa·ram·e·ter /pəˈramitər/ ▶ **noun 1** a limit or boundary that dictates the scope of a particular process or activity: *the parameters within which the media work*. **2** technical a numerical or other measurable factor forming one of a set that defines a system or sets the conditions of its operation. **3** Mathematics a quantity that is fixed for the case in question but may vary in other cases.

> – SYNONYMS **framework,** variable, limit, boundary, limitation, restriction, criterion, guideline.

– DERIVATIVES **par·a·met·ric** /ˌparəˈmetrik/ adjective **par·a·met·ric·al·ly** adverb.
– ORIGIN from Greek *para-* 'beside' + *metron* 'measure.'

par·a·mil·i·tar·y /ˌparəˈmiliˌterē/ ▶ **adjective** organized on similar lines to a military force. ▶ **noun** (pl. **paramilitaries**) a member of a paramilitary organization.

par·a·mount /ˈparəˌmount/ ▶ **adjective 1** more important than anything else: *the safety of the staff is paramount*. **2** having supreme power.

> – SYNONYMS **most important,** supreme, chief, overriding, predominant, foremost, prime, primary, principal, main, key, central; informal number-one.

– DERIVATIVES **par·a·mount·cy** /-sē/ noun.
– ORIGIN from Old French *par* 'by' + *amont* 'above.'

par·a·mour /ˈparəˌmo͝or/ ▶ **noun** old use a person's lover, especially the illicit lover of someone who is married.
– ORIGIN from Old French *par amour* 'by love.'

par·a·noi·a /ˌparəˈnoiə/ ▶ **noun 1** a mental condition characterized by delusions of persecution, unfounded jealousy, or exaggerated self-importance. **2** unjustified suspicion and mistrust of other people.
– DERIVATIVES **par·a·noi·ac** /-ˈnoi-ak, -ˈnoi-ik/ (also **paranoic** /-ˈnoi-ik/) adjective & noun **par·a·noi·a·cal·ly** adverb.
– ORIGIN Latin, from Greek *para* 'irregular' + *noos* 'mind.'

par·a·noid /ˈparəˌnoid/ ▶ **adjective 1** relating to or suffering from paranoia. **2** unreasonably or obsessively anxious, suspicious, or mistrustful: *he was paranoid about being overcharged*.

> – SYNONYMS **suspicious,** mistrustful, anxious, fearful, insecure, obsessive.

par·a·nor·mal /ˌparəˈnôrməl/ ▶ **adjective** beyond the scope of normal scientific understanding.
– DERIVATIVES **par·a·nor·mal·ly** adverb.

par·a·pet /ˈparəpit/ ▶ **noun 1** a low protective wall along the edge of a roof, bridge, or balcony. **2** a protective wall or bank along the top of a military trench.
– ORIGIN French, or from Italian *parapetto*, 'chest-high wall.'

par·a·pher·na·lia /ˌparəfə(r)ˈnālyə/ ▶ **noun** (treated as sing. or pl.) miscellaneous items, especially the equipment needed for a particular activity.

> – SYNONYMS **equipment,** stuff, things, apparatus, kit, implements, tools, utensils, material(s), appliances, accoutrements, appurtenances, odds and ends, bits and pieces; informal gear.

– ORIGIN Latin, first meaning 'property owned by a married woman.'

par·a·phrase /ˈparəˌfrāz/ ▶ **verb** express the meaning of something written or spoken using different words.

> – SYNONYMS **reword,** rephrase, express differently, rewrite, gloss.

▶ **noun** a rewording of something written or spoken.

par·a·ple·gi·a /ˌparəˈplēj(ē)ə/ ▶ **noun** paralysis of the legs and lower body.
– DERIVATIVES **par·a·ple·gic** /-jik/ adjective & noun.
– ORIGIN Greek, from *paraplēssein* 'strike at the side.'

par·a·psy·chol·o·gy /ˌparəsīˈkäləjē/ ▶ **noun** the study of mental phenomena that cannot be explained by scientific knowledge, such as hypnosis or telepathy.
– DERIVATIVES **par·a·psy·cho·log·i·cal** /-ˌsīkəˈläjikəl/ adjective **par·a·psy·chol·o·gist** /-jist/ noun.

par·a·quat /ˈparəˌkwät/ ▶ **noun** a poisonous fast-acting weedkiller.
– ORIGIN from **PARA-** + **QUATERNARY**.

par·a·sail·ing /ˈparəˌsālinɢ/ ▶ **noun** the sport of gliding through the air wearing an open parachute while being towed by a motorboat.
– DERIVATIVES **par·a·sail** /ˈparəˌsāl/ noun & verb.

par·a·site /ˈparəˌsīt/ ▶ **noun 1** an animal or plant that lives in or on another animal or plant from which it obtains food. **2** derogatory a person who lives off or exploits other people.

> – SYNONYMS **hanger-on,** leech, passenger; informal freeloader, sponger, scrounger; N. Amer. informal mooch.

– DERIVATIVES **par·a·sit·ism** /ˈparəsiˌtizəm, -ˌsī-/ noun.
– ORIGIN Greek *parasitos* 'person eating at another's table.'

par·a·sit·ic /ˌparəˈsitik/ ▶ **adjective 1** (of an animal or plant) living in or on another animal or plant. **2** resulting from infestation by a parasite: *a parasitic disease*. **3** derogatory (of a person) habitually relying on or exploiting other people.
– DERIVATIVES **par·a·sit·i·cal** adjective **par·a·sit·i·cal·ly** adverb.

par·a·si·tize /ˈparəsiˌtīz, -sī-/ ▶ **verb** live in or on another animal or plant as a parasite.

par·a·si·tol·o·gy /ˌparəsiˈtäləjē, -sī-/ ▶ **noun** the study of parasitic animals and plants.
– DERIVATIVES **par·a·si·tol·o·gist** /-jist/ noun.

par·a·sol /ˈparəˌsôl, -ˌsäl/ ▶ **noun** a light umbrella used to give shade from the sun.
– ORIGIN Italian *parasole*.

par·a·sym·pa·thet·ic /ˌparəˌsimpəˈTHetik/ ▶ **adjective** relating to a system of nerves arising from the brain and the lower end of the spinal cord and supplying the internal organs, blood vessels, and glands.

par·a·thy·roid /ˌparəˈTHīˌroid/ ▶ **noun** a gland next to the thyroid that produces a hormone that regulates calcium levels in a person's body.

par·a·troops /ˈparəˌtro͞ops/ ▶ **plural noun** troops equipped to be dropped by parachute from aircraft.
– DERIVATIVES **par·a·troop·er** noun.

par·boil /ˈpärˌboil/ ▶ **verb** partly cook something by boiling it.
– ORIGIN Latin *perbullire* 'boil thoroughly.'

par·cel /ˈpärsəl/ ▶ **noun 1** an object or collection of objects wrapped in paper in order to be carried or sent by post. **2** a quantity or amount of something: *a parcel of land*.

> – SYNONYMS **package,** packet, pack, bundle, box, case, bale.

▶ **verb** (**parcels, parceling, parceled**) **1** make something into a parcel by wrapping it. **2** (**parcel something out**) divide something into portions and then share it between people.

> – SYNONYMS **pack (up),** package, wrap (up), gift-wrap, tie up, bundle up.

– ORIGIN Old French *parcelle*.

parch /pärCH/ ▶ **verb** make something dry through intense heat.
– ORIGIN unknown.

parched /pärCHt/ ▶ **adjective 1** extremely dry. **2** extremely thirsty.

> – SYNONYMS **1 (bone) dry,** dried up/out, arid, desiccated, dehydrated, baked, burned, scorched, withered, shriveled. **2** thirsty, dehydrated, dry; informal gasping.

parch·ment /ˈpärCHmənt/ ▶ **noun 1** a stiff material made from the skin of a sheep or goat, formerly used for writing on. **2** (also **parchment paper**) stiff translucent paper treated to resemble parchment.
– ORIGIN Old French *parchemin*.

pard·ner ▶ **noun** variant spelling of **PARTNER**, used to represent US dialect speech: *howdy, pardner!*

par·don /ˈpärdn/ ▶ **noun 1** the action of forgiving someone for a mistake or offense. **2** an official cancellation of the legal consequences of an offense. **3** Christian Church, historical an indulgence.

> – SYNONYMS **1 forgiveness,** absolution. **2 reprieve,** amnesty, exoneration, release, acquittal, discharge.

▶ **verb 1** forgive or excuse a person, mistake, or offense. **2** give an offender an official pardon.

> – SYNONYMS **1 forgive,** absolve. **2 exonerate,** acquit, reprieve; informal let off.
> – ANTONYMS blame, punish.

▶ **exclamation** used to ask a speaker to repeat something because one did not hear or understand it.
– DERIVATIVES **par·don·a·ble** adjective.
– ORIGIN Latin *perdonare* 'concede.'

> **CHOOSE THE RIGHT WORD**
>
> See **ABSOLVE**.

par·don·er /ˈpärdn-ər/ ▶ **noun** historical a person licensed to sell papal pardons or indulgences.

pare /pe(ə)r/ ▶ **verb 1** trim something by cutting away its outer edges. **2** (often **pare something away/down**) reduce or diminish something in a number of small successive stages: *the company's domestic operations were pared down*.
– ORIGIN Old French *parer*.

par·ent /ˈpe(ə)rənt, ˈpar-/ ▶ **noun 1** a father or mother. **2** an animal or plant from which younger ones are derived. **3** an organization that owns or controls a number of smaller organizations. **4** old use a forefather or ancestor. ▶ **verb** (often as n. **parenting**) be or act as a parent to someone: *institutions cannot provide good parenting*.
– DERIVATIVES **pa·ren·tal** /pəˈrentl/ adjective **pa·ren·tal·ly** /pəˈrentl-ē/ adverb **par·ent·hood** /-ˌho͝od/ noun.
– ORIGIN from Latin *parere* 'bring forth.'

par·ent·age /ˈpe(ə)rəntij, ˈpar-/ ▶ **noun** the identity and origins of one's parents.

> – SYNONYMS **origins,** extraction, birth, family, ancestry, lineage, heritage, pedigree, descent, blood, stock, roots.

pa·ren·the·sis /pəˈrenTHəsis/ ▶ **noun** (pl. **parentheses** /-ˌsēz/) **1** a word or phrase inserted as an explanation or afterthought, in writing usually marked off by parentheses, dashes, or commas. **2** (**parentheses**) a pair of round brackets () used to include such a word or phrase.
– ORIGIN Greek.

par·en·thet·ic·al /ˌparənˈTHetikəl/ (also **parenthetic**) ▶ **adjective** added as an explanation or afterthought.
– DERIVATIVES **par·en·thet·i·cal·ly** adverb.

par ex·cel·lence /ˌpär ˌeksəˈläns/ ▶ **adjective** (after a noun) better or more than all others of the same kind: *a designer par excellence*.
– ORIGIN French, 'by excellence.'

par·fait /pärˈfā/ ▶ **noun 1** a rich cold dessert made with whipped cream, eggs, and fruit. **2** a dessert consisting of layers, especially of ice cream, meringue, and fruit, served in a tall glass.
– ORIGIN from French, 'perfect.'

par·he·li·on /pärˈhēlēən, -ˈhēlyən/ ▶ **noun** (pl. **parhelia** /-ˈhēlēə/) a bright spot in the sky on either side of the sun, formed by the refraction of sunlight through ice crystals high in the atmosphere.
– ORIGIN from Greek *para-* 'beside' + *hēlios* 'sun.'

pa·ri·ah /pəˈrīə/ ▶ **noun 1** an outcast: *they were treated as social pariahs*. **2** historical a member of a low caste or of no caste in southern India.
– ORIGIN from a Tamil word meaning 'hereditary drummers.'

pa·ri·e·tal /pə'rīətəl/ ▸ **adjective** relating to the walls of a body cavity.
– ORIGIN from Latin *paries* 'wall.'

pa·ri·e·tal bone ▸ **noun** a bone forming the central side and upper back part of each side of the skull.

pa·ri·e·tal lobe ▸ **noun** either of the paired lobes of the brain at the top of the head.

par·i·mu·tu·el /ˌparə 'myoo͞chəo͞əl/ ▸ **noun** a form of betting in which gamblers backing the first three places divide the losers' stakes.
– ORIGIN French, literally 'mutual stake.'

par·ings /'pe(ə)riNGz/ ▸ **plural noun** thin strips pared off from something.

par·ish /'parisH/ ▸ **noun 1** (in the Christian Church) a small administrative district with its own church and clergy. **2** (in Louisiana) a territorial division corresponding to a county in other states. **3** (also **civil parish**) Brit. the smallest unit of local government in rural areas.

– SYNONYMS **1 district,** community. **2 parishioners,** churchgoers, congregation, fold, flock, community.

– ORIGIN Old French *paroche.*

WORD LINKS

parochial *relating to a parish*

par·ish·ion·er /pə'risHənər/ ▸ **noun** a person who lives in a particular church parish.

Pa·ri·sian /pə'rizHən, -'rē-, -'rizē-/ ▸ **adjective** relating to Paris. ▸ **noun** a person from Paris.

Pa·ri·si·enne /pəˌrēzē'en/ ▸ **noun** a Parisian girl or woman.

par·i·ty /'paritē/ ▸ **noun 1** the state of being equal or equivalent: *the euro's slide to parity with the dollar.* **2** Mathematics the fact of being an even or an odd number.
– ORIGIN Latin *paritas.*

park /pärk/ ▸ **noun 1** a large public green area in a town or city, where people go to walk, relax, play games, etc. **2** a large area of land kept in its natural state for public recreational use. **3** an area devoted to a particular purpose: *an industrial park.* **4** chiefly Brit. a large area of woodland and pasture attached to a country house.

– SYNONYMS **1** public garden, recreation ground, playground. **2 parkland,** wilderness area, protected area, nature preserve/reserve, game preserve/reserve.

▸ **verb 1** stop and leave a vehicle somewhere for a period of time. **2** informal leave something in a convenient place until required. **3** (**park oneself**) informal sit down.

– SYNONYMS **1 leave,** position, stop, pull up, pull over. **2 put (down),** place, deposit, leave, stick, dump; informal plonk.

– ORIGIN Old French *parc.*

par·ka /'pärkə/ ▸ **noun** a large, insulated windproof jacket with a hood.
– ORIGIN Russian.

park·ing ga·rage ▸ **noun** a multilevel building in which cars or other vehicles are left temporarily.

park·ing lot ▸ **noun** an area where cars or other vehicles are left temporarily.

park·ing me·ter ▸ **noun** a machine next to a parking space in a street, into which coins are inserted to pay for parking a vehicle.

park·ing tick·et ▸ **noun** a notice informing a driver of a fine for parking illegally.

Par·kin·son's dis·ease /'pärkinsənz/ ▸ **noun** a progressive disease of the brain and nervous system marked by involuntary trembling, muscular rigidity, and slow, imprecise movement.
– DERIVATIVES **Par·kin·son·ism** /'pärkinsənˌizəm/ noun.
– ORIGIN named after the English surgeon James *Parkinson.*

Par·kin·son's law ▸ **noun** the idea that work expands so as to fill the time available for its completion.
– ORIGIN named after the English writer Cyril Northcote *Parkinson.*

park·land /'pärkˌland/ (also **parklands**) ▸ **noun** open land consisting of fields and scattered groups of trees.

park·way /'pärkˌwā/ ▸ **noun** a highway or main road with trees, grass, etc., planted alongside.

par·lance /'pärləns/ ▸ **noun** a way of using words associated with a particular subject: *medical parlance.*
– ORIGIN Old French, from *parler* 'speak.'

par·lay /'pärˌlā, -lē/ ▸ **verb** (**parlay something into**) turn an asset, situation, etc., into something much better or more valuable: *a banker who parlayed a sizable inheritance into a financial empire.* ▸ **noun** a bet placed on a series of events, the winnings and stake from each being placed on the next.
– ORIGIN from French *paroli* 'cumulative series of bets.'

par·ley /'pärlē/ ▸ **noun** (pl. **parleys**) a meeting between opponents or enemies to discuss terms for a truce. ▸ **verb** (**parleys, parleying, parleyed**) hold a parley.
– ORIGIN perhaps from Old French *parlee* 'spoken.'

CHOOSE THE RIGHT WORD

See **CONVERSATION**.

par·lia·ment /'pärləmənt/ ▸ **noun 1** (**Parliament**) (in the UK) the highest lawmaking body, consisting of the king or queen, the House of Lords, and the House of Commons. **2** a similar body in other countries.

– SYNONYMS **legislature,** assembly, chamber, house, congress, senate, diet.

– ORIGIN Old French *parlement* 'speaking.'

par·lia·men·tar·i·an /ˌpärləmen'te(ə)rēən/ ▸ **noun 1** a member of parliament who is experienced in parliamentary procedures and debates. **2** historical a supporter of Parliament in the English Civil War; a Roundhead. ▸ **adjective** relating to parliament or parliamentarians.

par·lia·men·ta·ry /ˌpärlə'mentərē/ ▸ **adjective** relating to, enacted by, or suitable for a parliament.

– SYNONYMS **legislative,** lawmaking, governmental, congressional, democratic, elected.

par·lor /'pärlər/ (Brit. **parlour**) ▸ **noun 1** dated a sitting room. **2** a store or business providing particular goods or services: *an ice-cream parlor.* **3** a room or building equipped for milking cows.
– ORIGIN Old French *parlur* 'place for speaking.'

par·lor game ▸ **noun** an indoor game, especially a word game.

par·lous /'pärləs/ ▸ **adjective** old use or humorous dangerously uncertain; precarious: *the parlous state of the economy.*
– ORIGIN from **PERILOUS**.

Par·ma ham /'pärmə/ ▸ **noun** a strongly flavored Italian cured ham, eaten uncooked and thinly sliced.
– ORIGIN named after the Italian city of *Parma*.

Par·me·san /'pärmə,zän/ ▸ **noun** a hard, dry Italian cheese used chiefly in grated form.
– ORIGIN from Italian *Parmigiano* 'of Parma.'

pa·ro·chi·al /pə'rōkēəl/ ▸ **adjective 1** relating to a parish. **2** having a narrow outlook or range: *parochial attitudes*.

> – SYNONYMS **narrow-minded,** small-minded, provincial, small-town, conservative; informal jerkwater.
> – ANTONYMS broad-minded.

– DERIVATIVES **pa·ro·chi·al·ism** /-,izəm/ noun.
– ORIGIN Latin *parochialis*.

pa·ro·chi·al school ▸ **noun** a private school operated and supported by a particular church or parish, especially a Catholic one.

par·o·dy /'parədē/ ▸ **noun** (pl. **parodies**) **1** a piece of writing or music that deliberately copies the style of another, exaggerating it in order to be funny or ironical. **2** an imitation of something that falls far short of the real thing.

> – SYNONYMS **1 satire,** burlesque, lampoon, pastiche, caricature, imitation; informal spoof, takeoff, sendup. **2 distortion,** travesty, misrepresentation, perversion, corruption.

▸ **verb** (**parodies, parodying, parodied**) produce a parody of something.
– DERIVATIVES **pa·rod·ic** /pə'rädik/ adjective **par·o·dist** /-dist/ noun.
– ORIGIN Greek *parōidia* 'burlesque poem or song.'

> **CHOOSE THE RIGHT WORD**
>
> See **CARICATURE**.

pa·role /pə'rōl/ ▸ **noun 1** the temporary or permanent release of a prisoner before the end of a sentence, on condition that they behave well. **2** historical a prisoner of war's word of honor not to escape or, if released, to return to custody under certain specified conditions.
▸ **verb** release a prisoner on parole.
– DERIVATIVES **pa·rol·ee** /-,rō'lē/ noun.
– ORIGIN Old French, 'word.'

pa·rot·id /pə'rätid/ ▸ **adjective** relating to a pair of large salivary glands situated just in front of each ear.
– ORIGIN Greek.

par·ox·ysm /'parək,sizəm, pə'räk-/ ▸ **noun** a sudden attack or outburst: *a paroxysm of weeping*.
– DERIVATIVES **par·ox·ys·mal** /,parək'sizməl, pə,räk-/ adjective.
– ORIGIN Greek *paroxusmos*.

par·quet /pär'kā/ ▸ **noun** flooring composed of wooden blocks arranged in a geometric pattern.
– DERIVATIVES **par·quet·ry** /'pärkitrē/ noun.
– ORIGIN French, 'small compartment.'

parr /pär/ ▸ **noun** (pl. same) a young salmon or trout up to two years old.
– ORIGIN unknown.

par·ri·cide /'parə,sīd/ ▸ **noun 1** the killing of a parent or other near relative. **2** a person who commits parricide.
– DERIVATIVES **par·ri·cid·al** /,parə'sīdl/ adjective.
– ORIGIN Latin *parricidium*.

par·rot /'parət/ ▸ **noun** a mainly tropical bird with brightly colored plumage and a strong hooked bill, some kinds of which are able to mimic human speech.
▸ **verb** (**parrots, parroting, parroted**) repeat something mechanically.
– ORIGIN probably from French dialect *perrot*, from the man's name *Pierre* 'Peter.'

par·rot·fish /'parət,fisн/ ▸ **noun** (pl. same or **parrotfishes**) a brightly colored sea fish with a parrotlike beak.

par·ry /'parē/ ▸ **verb** (**parries, parrying, parried**) **1** ward off a weapon or attack. **2** say something to avoid answering a question directly.

> – SYNONYMS **1** *he parried the blow* **ward off,** fend off, deflect, block. **2** *I parried her questions* **evade,** sidestep, avoid, dodge, field.

▸ **noun** (pl. **parries**) an act of parrying.
– ORIGIN probably from French *parer* 'ward off.'

parse /pärs/ ▸ **verb** divide a sentence into parts and describe the grammar of each word or part.
– ORIGIN perhaps from Old French *pars* 'parts.'

par·sec /'pär,sek/ ▸ **noun** a unit of astronomical distance equal to about 3.25 light years.
– ORIGIN blend of **PARALLAX** and **SECOND**[2].

Par·see /pär'sē, 'pärsē/ ▸ **noun** a descendant of a group of Zoroastrian Persians who fled to India during the 7th–8th centuries.
– ORIGIN from a Persian word meaning 'Persian.'

par·si·mo·ny /'pärsə,mōnē/ ▸ **noun** extreme unwillingness to spend money or use resources.
– DERIVATIVES **par·si·mo·ni·ous** /,pärsə'mōnēəs/ adjective.
– ORIGIN Latin *parsimonia, parcimonia*.

pars·ley /'pärslē/ ▸ **noun** an herb with crinkly or flat leaves, used for seasoning or garnishing food.
– ORIGIN Greek *petroselinon*.

pars·nip /'pärsnip/ ▸ **noun** a long tapering cream-colored root vegetable.
– ORIGIN Old French *pasnaie*.

par·son /'pärsən/ ▸ **noun 1** dated, informal any member of the clergy, especially a Protestant one. **2** (in the Church of England) a parish priest.

> – SYNONYMS **priest,** minister, clergyman, vicar, rector, cleric, chaplain, pastor, curate; informal reverend, padre.

– ORIGIN Latin *persona* 'person,' later 'rector.'

par·son·age /'pärsənij/ ▸ **noun** a church house provided for a parson.

par·son's nose ▸ **noun** informal the piece of fatty flesh at the rump of a cooked fowl.

part /pärt/ ▸ **noun 1** a piece or section that is combined with others to make up a whole. **2** some but not all of something. **3** a specified fraction of a whole: *a twentieth part*. **4** a role played by an actor or actress. **5** a person's contribution to something. **6** (**parts**) informal a region: *they wanted to know why he was loitering in these parts*. **7** a measure allowing comparison between the amounts of different ingredients used in a mixture: *a mix of one part cement to five parts ballast*. **8** a melody or other constituent of harmony given to a particular voice or instrument. **9** a line of scalp revealed by combing the hair away from it on either side.

> – SYNONYMS **1 piece,** amount, portion, proportion, percentage, fraction; informal slice, chunk. **2** *car parts* **component,** bit, constituent, element, module, unit. **3** *body parts* **organ,** limb, member. **4** *the third part of the book* **section,** division, volume, chapter, act,

scene, installment. **5** *another part of the country* **district,** neighborhood, quarter, section, area, region. **6** *the part of Juliet* **role,** character. **7** *he played a key part in ending the revolt* **involvement,** role, function, hand, responsibility, capacity, participation, contribution; informal bit.
– ANTONYMS whole.

▶ **verb 1** move apart or divide to leave a central space: *her lips parted in a smile.* **2** (also **be parted**) leave someone's company. **3** (**part with**) give up possession of.

– SYNONYMS **1 separate,** divide, split, move apart. **2 leave each other,** part company, say goodbye/farewell, say one's goodbyes/farewells, go one's separate ways, take one's leave. **3** (**part with**) **give away, give up,** relinquish, forgo, surrender, hand over.
– ANTONYMS join, meet.

▶ **adverb** partly: *part jazz, part blues.*

– PHRASES **be part and parcel of** be an essential element of. **for my** (or **his, her,** etc.) **part** as far as I am (or he, she, etc., is) concerned. **in part** to some extent. **on the part of** used to say that someone is responsible for something. **part company** go in different directions or end a relationship. **take part** join in an activity. **take the part of** give support to someone in a dispute.

– ORIGIN Latin *pars*; the verb is from Latin *partire* 'divide, share.'

CHOOSE THE RIGHT WORD

See **FRAGMENT**.

par·take /pär'tāk/ ▶ **verb** (past **partook** /pär'to͝ok/; past part. **partaken**) formal **1** (**partake of**) eat or drink something. **2** (**partake in**) participate in an activity.
– ORIGIN from earlier *partaker* 'person who takes a part.'

par·terre /pär'te(ə)r/ ▶ **noun** a group of flower beds laid out in a formal pattern.
– ORIGIN French.

part ex·change ▶ **noun** Brit. a way of buying something in which one gives an article that one already owns as part of the payment for a more expensive one, paying the balance in money.

par·the·no·gen·e·sis /ˌpärᴛʜənō'jenəsis/ ▶ **noun** Biology reproduction from an ovum without fertilization, especially in some invertebrate animals and lower plants.
– DERIVATIVES **par·the·no·ge·net·ic** /-jə'netik/ adjective.
– ORIGIN from Greek *parthenos* 'virgin' + *genesis* 'creation.'

Par·thi·an shot /'pärᴛʜēən/ ▶ **noun** another term for **PARTING SHOT**.
– ORIGIN from the practice among horsemen from the ancient Asian kingdom of Parthia of shooting arrows backwards while fleeing.

par·tial /'pärsʜəl/ ▶ **adjective 1** existing only in part; incomplete. **2** favoring one side in a dispute above the other; biased. **3** (**partial to**) having a liking for.

– SYNONYMS **1** *a partial recovery* **incomplete,** limited, qualified, imperfect, fragmentary, unfinished. **2** *a very partial view of the situation* **biased,** prejudiced, partisan, one-sided, slanted, skewed, colored, unbalanced. **3** (**partial to**) *I'm partial to hotdogs and beer* **like,** love, enjoy, be fond of, be keen on, have a soft spot for, have a taste for, have a penchant for.
– ANTONYMS complete, unbiased.

– DERIVATIVES **par·ti·al·i·ty** /ˌpärsʜē'alitē/ noun.

par·tial·ly /'pärsʜəlē/ ▶ **adverb** in part; to some extent: *the plan was only partially successful.*

– SYNONYMS **somewhat,** to a limited extent, to a certain extent, partly, in part, up to a point, slightly.
– ANTONYMS wholly.

par·tic·i·pant /pär'tisəpənt/ ▶ **noun** a person who takes part in something.

– SYNONYMS **participator,** contributor, party, member, entrant, competitor, player, contestant, candidate.

par·tic·i·pate /pär'tisəˌpāt/ ▶ **verb** take part in an activity or event.

– SYNONYMS **take part,** join, engage, get involved, share, play a part, play a role, contribute, partake, have a hand in.

– DERIVATIVES **par·tic·i·pa·tive** /-ˌpātiv, -pətiv/ adjective **par·tic·i·pa·tor** /-ˌpātər/ noun **par·tic·i·pa·to·ry** /-pəˌtôrē/ adjective.
– ORIGIN Latin *participare* 'share in.'

par·tic·i·pa·tion /pärˌtisə'pāsʜən/ ▶ **noun** the action of taking part in an activity or event: *your participation is appreciated.*

– SYNONYMS **involvement,** part, contribution, association.

par·ti·ci·ple /'pärtəˌsipəl/ ▶ **noun** Grammar a word formed from a verb and used as an adjective or noun (*burned* as in *burned toast*; *breeding* as in *good breeding*) or used to make compound verb forms (*going* as in *is going*; *been* as in *has been*).
– DERIVATIVES **par·ti·cip·i·al** /ˌpärtə'sipēəl/ adjective.
– ORIGIN from Latin *participium* 'sharing.'

par·ti·cle /'pärtikəl/ ▶ **noun 1** a minute piece of a substance. **2** Physics a component of the physical world smaller than an atom, e.g., an electron or proton. **3** Grammar an adverb or preposition that has comparatively little meaning, e.g., *in, up, off,* or *over,* used with verbs to make phrasal verbs.

– SYNONYMS **(tiny) bit,** (tiny) piece, speck, spot, fragment, sliver, splinter, iota.

– ORIGIN Latin *particula* 'little part.'

par·ti·cle·board /'pärtikəlˌbôrd/ ▶ **noun** another term for **CHIPBOARD**.

par·ti·col·ored /'pärti'kələrd/ ▶ **adjective** having two or more different colors.

par·tic·u·lar /pə(r)'tikyələr/ ▶ **adjective 1** relating to an individual member of a group or class. **2** more than is usual; special: *he had dressed with particular care.* **3** insisting that something should be correct or suitable in every detail; fastidious: *she is very particular about cleanliness.*

– SYNONYMS **1 specific,** individual, certain, distinct, separate, definite, precise. **2 special,** exceptional, unusual, uncommon, notable, noteworthy, remarkable, unique. **3 fussy,** fastidious, finicky, discriminating, selective; informal persnickety, choosy, picky.
– ANTONYMS general, indiscriminate.

▶ **noun** a detail.

– SYNONYMS **detail,** item, point, element, fact, circumstance, feature.

– PHRASES **in particular** especially.
– ORIGIN Latin *particularis*.

par·tic·u·lar·ism /pə(r)ˈtikyələˌrizəm/ ▶ **noun** **1** exclusive attachment to one's own group, party, or nation. **2** the principle of leaving each state in an empire or federation free to govern itself.

par·tic·u·lar·i·ty /pə(r)ˌtikyəˈlaritē/ ▶ **noun** (pl. **particularities**) **1** the quality of being individual. **2** attention to detail in the treatment of something. **3** (**particularities**) small details.

par·tic·u·lar·ize /pə(r)ˈtikyələˌrīz/ ▶ **verb** formal treat something individually or in detail.
– DERIVATIVES **par·tic·u·lar·i·za·tion** /pə(r)ˌtikyələˌrīˈzāsHən/ noun.

par·tic·u·lar·ly /pə(r)ˈtikyələrlē/ ▶ **adverb** **1** more than is usual; especially or very. **2** in particular; specifically.

– SYNONYMS **1 especially,** specially, exceptionally, unusually, remarkably, outstandingly, uncommonly, uniquely. **2 specifically,** explicitly, expressly, in particular, especially, specially.

par·tic·u·late /pärˈtikyəlit, -ˌlāt/ ▶ **adjective** relating to or in the form of minute particles. ▶ **noun** (**particulates**) matter in the form of minute particles.
– ORIGIN from Latin *particula* 'particle.'

part·ing /ˈpärtiNG/ ▶ **noun** a leave-taking or departure.

– SYNONYMS *an emotional parting* **farewell,** leave-taking, goodbye, adieu, departure.

part·ing shot ▶ **noun** a cutting remark made by someone as they are leaving.

par·ti·san /ˈpärtəzən/ ▶ **noun** **1** a strong supporter of a party, cause, or person. **2** a member of an armed group fighting secretly against an occupying force.

– SYNONYMS **guerrilla,** freedom fighter, resistance fighter, underground fighter, irregular.

▶ **adjective** prejudiced in favor of a particular cause, party, or person.

– SYNONYMS **biased,** prejudiced, one-sided, discriminatory, partial, sectarian, factional.
– ANTONYMS neutral.

– DERIVATIVES **par·ti·san·ship** /-ˌSHip/ noun.
– ORIGIN Italian *partigiano*.

par·ti·tion /pärˈtisHən, pər-/ ▶ **noun** **1** a light interior wall or other structure dividing a space into parts. **2** the division of something into parts, especially a country.

– SYNONYMS **1 division,** partitioning, separation, break-up. **2 screen,** divider, dividing wall, barrier, panel.

▶ **verb** **1** divide into parts: *an agreement was reached to partition the country.* **2** divide a room with a partition.

– SYNONYMS **1 divide,** separate, split up, break up. **2 subdivide,** divide (up), separate, section off, screen off.

– DERIVATIVES **par·ti·tion·ist** /-ist/ noun.
– ORIGIN from Latin *partiri* 'divide into parts.'

par·ti·tive /ˈpärtitiv/ ▶ **adjective** (of a grammatical construction) indicating that only a part of a whole is referred to (e.g., *a slice of bacon, some of the children*). ▶ **noun** a noun or pronoun used as the first term in a partitive construction (e.g., *slice, some*).

part·ly /ˈpärtlē/ ▶ **adverb** to some extent; not completely.

– SYNONYMS **in part,** partially, somewhat, a little, up to a point, in some measure, slightly, to some extent.
– ANTONYMS wholly.

part·ner /ˈpärtnər/ ▶ **noun** **1** a person who takes part in an undertaking with another or others, especially in a business with shared risks and profits. **2** either of two people doing something as a pair. **3** either member of a couple in a marriage or a romantic or sexual relationship.

– SYNONYMS **1 colleague,** associate, coworker, fellow worker, collaborator, comrade, teammate. **2 accomplice,** confederate, accessory, collaborator, fellow conspirator, helper; informal sidekick. **3 spouse,** husband, wife, life partner, lover, girlfriend, boyfriend, fiancé, fiancée, significant other, live-in lover, mate; informal better half, other half.

▶ **verb** be the partner of someone.
– ORIGIN Old French *parcener*.

part·ner·ship /ˈpärtnərˌsHip/ ▶ **noun** **1** the state of being a partner or partners. **2** an association of two or more people as partners.

– SYNONYMS **1 cooperation,** association, collaboration, coalition, alliance, union, affiliation, connection. **2 company,** association, consortium, syndicate, firm, business, organization.

part of speech ▶ **noun** a category in which a word is placed according to its grammatical function, e.g., noun, pronoun, adjective, verb.

par·took /pärˈto͝ok/ past of **PARTAKE**.

par·tridge /ˈpärtrij/ ▶ **noun** (pl. same or **partridges**) a short-tailed game bird with mainly brown plumage.
– ORIGIN Latin *perdix*.

part song ▶ **noun** a song with three or more voice parts, typically without musical accompaniment.

part-time ▶ **adjective & adverb** for only part of the usual working day or week.

par·tu·ri·ent /pärˈt(y)o͝orēənt/ ▶ **adjective** technical about to give birth; in labor.

par·tu·ri·tion /ˌpärcHo͝oˈrisHən/ ▶ **noun** formal or technical the action of giving birth; childbirth.
– ORIGIN from Latin *parturire* 'be in labor.'

part·way /ˈpärtˌwā, ˈpärtˈwā/ ▶ **adverb** part of the way.

par·ty /ˈpärtē/ ▶ **noun** (pl. **parties**) **1** a social gathering of invited guests. **2** a political organization that puts forward candidates for election for local or national office. **3** a group of people taking part in an activity or trip. **4** a person or group forming one side in an agreement or dispute. **5** informal, dated a person of a particular type: *an old party came in to clean.*

– SYNONYMS **1 social gathering,** function, get-together, celebration, reunion, festivity, reception, soirée, social; informal bash, do. **2 group,** company, body, gang, band, crowd, pack, contingent; informal bunch, crew, load. **3 faction,** group, bloc, camp, caucus, alliance.

▶ **verb** (**parties, partying, partied**) informal enjoy oneself by going out socially and typically also drinking and dancing.
– PHRASES **be party** (or **a party**) **to** be involved in.
– ORIGIN Old French *partie*.

par·ty line ▶ **noun** **1** a policy or policies officially adopted by a political party. **2** a telephone line shared by two or more subscribers.

par·ty pol·i·tics ▶ **plural noun** (treated as sing. or pl.) politics that relate to political parties rather than to the good of the general public.

par·ty poop·er ▶ **noun** informal a person who spoils other people's fun.

par·ty wall ▶ **noun** a wall shared by two adjoining buildings or rooms.

par·ve·nu /ˈpärvəˌn(y)o͞o/ ▶ **noun** chiefly derogatory a person from a humble background who has recently become rich or famous.
– ORIGIN from French, 'arrived.'

par·vo·vi·rus /ˈpärvōˌvīrəs/ ▶ **noun** any of a class of very small viruses causing contagious disease in dogs and other animals.
– ORIGIN from Latin *parvus* 'small.'

pas·cal /päˈskäl/ ▶ **noun** the SI unit of pressure, equal to one newton per square meter.
– ORIGIN named after the French scientist Blaise *Pascal.*

pas·chal /ˈpaskəl/ ▶ **adjective 1** relating to Easter. **2** relating to the Jewish Passover.
– ORIGIN from Latin *pascha* 'feast of Passover.'

pas de deux /ˌpä də ˈdo͞o/ ▶ **noun** (pl. same) Ballet a dance for a couple.
– ORIGIN French, 'step of two.'

pa·sha /ˈpäsнə, ˈpasнə, pəˈsнä/ (also **pacha** pronunc. same) ▶ **noun** historical the title of a Turkish officer of high rank.
– ORIGIN Turkish.

pash·mi·na /pəsнˈmēnə/ ▶ **noun** a shawl made from fine-quality goat's wool.
– ORIGIN Persian, 'wool, down.'

Pash·to /ˈpəsнtō/ ▶ **noun** the official language of Afghanistan, also spoken in northern Pakistan.
– ORIGIN the name in Pashto.

pa·so do·ble /ˌpäsō ˈdōblā/ ▶ **noun** (pl. **paso dobles**) a fast-paced ballroom dance based on a Latin American marching style.
– ORIGIN Spanish, 'double step.'

pasque·flow·er /ˈpaskˌflou(-ə)r/ ▶ **noun** a spring-flowering plant with purple flowers.
– ORIGIN French *passe-fleur*; later associated with former *pasque* 'Easter.'

pass[1] /pas/ ▶ **verb 1** move or go onward, past, through, or across. **2** change from one state or condition to another: *those who have just passed from middle-aged to elderly.* **3** transfer something to someone. **4** kick, hit, or throw the ball to a teammate. **5** (of time) go by. **6** occupy or spend time. **7** be done or said: *not another word passed between them.* **8** come to an end. **9** be successful in an exam, test, or course. **10** declare something to be satisfactory. **11** approve or put into effect a proposal or law by voting. **12** formally state a judgment or sentence. **13** choose not to do or have something that is offered: *we'll pass on dessert and just have coffee.* **14** (**pass something up**) choose not to take up an opportunity. **15** discharge urine or feces from the body.

– SYNONYMS **1** *the traffic passing through the village* **go,** proceed, move, progress, make your way, travel. **2** *a car passed him* **overtake,** go past/by, pull ahead of, leave behind. **3** *pass me the salt* **hand,** let someone have, give. **4** *her estate passed to her grandson* **be transferred,** go, be left, be bequeathed, be handed down/on, be passed on; Law devolve. **5** *time passed* **elapse,** go by, advance, wear on, roll by, tick by. **6** *he passed the time reading* **occupy,** spend, fill, use (up), employ, while away. **7** *the storm passed* **come to an end,** fade (away), blow over, run its course, die out/down, finish, end, cease. **8** *he passed the exam* **be successful in,** succeed in, get through; informal sail through, scrape through. **9** *the senate passed the bill* **approve,** vote for, accept, ratify, adopt, agree to, authorize, endorse, legalize, enact; informal OK. **10** (**pass something up**) *I should never have passed up my chance to go to Rome* **turn down,** reject, refuse, decline, give up, forgo, let pass, miss (out on); informal give something a miss.
– ANTONYMS fail, reject.

▶ **noun 1** an act of passing. **2** a success in an exam. **3** an official document authorizing the holder to go somewhere or use something. **4** (also **a pretty pass**) an undesirable situation: *things came to such a pass that mothers feared for their daughters' safety.* **5** a single scan through a set of computer data or a program.

– SYNONYMS *you must show your pass* **permit,** warrant, authorization, license.

– DERIVATIVES **pass·er** noun.
– PHRASES **make a pass at** informal make a sexual approach to someone. **pass as/for** be accepted as. **pass away/on** (of a person) die. **pass off** happen in a specified, usually satisfactory, way. **pass something off** lightly dismiss an awkward remark. **pass someone/thing off as** present someone or something in a way that gives a false impression. **pass out** become unconscious. **pass someone over** ignore someone's claims to be promoted. **pass something over** avoid mentioning or considering something.
– ORIGIN Old French *passer.*

pass[2] ▶ **noun** a route over or through mountains.
– ORIGIN from **PACE**[1], influenced by **PASS**[1].

pass·a·ble /ˈpasəbəl/ ▶ **adjective 1** just good enough to be accepted. **2** (of a route) able to be traveled along or on.

– SYNONYMS **1 adequate,** all right, acceptable, satisfactory, not (too) bad, average, tolerable, fair, mediocre, middling, ordinary, indifferent, unremarkable, unexceptional; informal OK, so-so. **2 navigable,** traversable, negotiable, open, clear.

– DERIVATIVES **pass·a·bly** adverb.

pas·sage /ˈpasij/ ▶ **noun 1** the action of passing: *the feeling will fade with the passage of time.* **2** a way through something. **3** a journey by sea or air. **4** the right to pass through somewhere: *a permit for safe passage.* **5** a short section from a written work or musical composition.

– SYNONYMS **1 passing,** progress, advance, course, march, flow. **2 corridor,** hall, hallway. **3 alley,** alleyway, passageway, lane, path, footpath, track, thoroughfare. **4 journey,** voyage, crossing, transit, trip. **5 extract,** excerpt, quotation, quote.

pas·sage·way /ˈpasijˌwā/ ▶ **noun** a corridor or other narrow passage between buildings or rooms.

pass·book /ˈpasˌbo͝ok/ ▶ **noun** a book issued by a bank to an account holder, recording amounts deposited and withdrawn.

pas·sé /paˈsā/ ▶ **adjective** no longer fashionable; out of date.
– ORIGIN French, 'gone by.'

pas·sen·ger /ˈpasinjər/ ▶ **noun** a person traveling in a vehicle, ship, or aircraft other than the driver, pilot, or crew.

– SYNONYMS **traveler,** commuter, rider, fare.

– ORIGIN from Old French *passager* 'passing, transitory.'

pas·sen·ger pi·geon ▶ **noun** an extinct long-tailed North American pigeon, noted for its long migrations in huge flocks.

pas·ser·by /ˈpasər,bī/ ▶ **noun** (pl. **passersby** /ˈpasərz,bī/) a person who happens to be walking past something or someone.

pas·ser·ine /ˈpasərin, -,rīn/ ▶ **adjective** referring to birds of a large group distinguished by having feet adapted for perching and including all songbirds.
– ORIGIN from Latin *passer* 'sparrow.'

pas·sim /ˈpasim/ ▶ **adverb** (of references) at various places throughout a written work.
– ORIGIN Latin, 'everywhere.'

pass·ing /ˈpasiNG/ ▶ **adjective 1** done quickly and casually. **2** (of a resemblance or similarity) slight.

– SYNONYMS **1 fleeting,** transient, transitory, ephemeral, brief, short-lived, temporary, momentary. **2 hasty,** rapid, hurried, brief, quick, cursory, superficial, casual, perfunctory, desultory.

▶ **noun 1** the end of something. **2** euphemistic a person's death.

– SYNONYMS **1 passage,** course, progress, advance. **2 death,** demise, passing away, end, loss.

– PHRASES **in passing** while doing or saying something else; briefly.

pas·sion /ˈpasHən/ ▶ **noun 1** very strong emotion. **2** intense sexual love. **3** an intense enthusiasm for something: *the English have a passion for gardens.* **4** (**the Passion**) the suffering and death of Jesus.

– SYNONYMS **1 intensity,** enthusiasm, fervor, eagerness, zeal, vigor, fire, energy, spirit, fanaticism. **2 love,** desire, ardor, lust, lasciviousness, lustfulness. **3 fascination,** love, mania, obsession, preoccupation, fanaticism, fixation, compulsion, appetite, addiction; informal thing.
– ANTONYMS apathy.

– DERIVATIVES **pas·sion·less** adjective.
– ORIGIN Latin.

pas·sion·ate /ˈpasHənit/ ▶ **adjective** having or showing intense emotion, sexual love, or enthusiasm: *a passionate belief in freedom.*

– SYNONYMS **1 intense,** impassioned, ardent, fervent, vehement, fiery, heated, emotional, heartfelt, excited. **2 very keen,** very enthusiastic, addicted; informal mad, crazy, hooked. **3 amorous,** ardent, hot-blooded, loving, sexy, sensual, erotic, lustful; informal steamy, hot, turned on.
– ANTONYMS apathetic, cool.

– DERIVATIVES **pas·sion·ate·ly** adverb.

pas·sion·flow·er /ˈpasHən,flou(-ə)r/ ▶ **noun** a climbing plant with a flower whose parts are said to suggest objects associated with Jesus's Crucifixion.

pas·sion fruit ▶ **noun** the edible purple fruit of some species of passionflower.

Pas·sion play ▶ **noun** a play about Jesus's crucifixion.

pas·sive /ˈpasiv/ ▶ **adjective 1** accepting or allowing what happens or what others do, without reacting or resisting: *he takes on a passive role in the story.* **2** Grammar (of verbs) in which the subject undergoes the action of the verb (e.g., *they were killed* as opposed to the active form *he killed them*). **3** (of a circuit or device) containing no source of energy or electromotive force. **4** Chemistry (of a metal) unreactive because of a thin inert surface layer of oxide.

– SYNONYMS **1 inactive,** nonactive, nonparticipative, uninvolved. **2 submissive,** acquiescent, unresisting, compliant, docile.
– ANTONYMS active, resistant.

▶ **noun** a passive form of a verb.
– DERIVATIVES **pas·sive·ly** adverb **pas·sive·ness** noun **pas·siv·i·ty** /paˈsivitē/ noun.
– ORIGIN Latin *passivus*.

pas·sive re·sist·ance ▶ **noun** nonviolent opposition to authority, especially a refusal to cooperate with legal requirements.

pas·sive smok·ing ▶ **noun** breathing in smoke from other people's cigarettes, cigars, or pipes.

pass·key /ˈpas,kē/ ▶ **noun 1** a key given only to people who are officially allowed access. **2** a master key.

Pass·o·ver /ˈpas,ōvər/ ▶ **noun** the major Jewish spring festival, commemorating the liberation of the Israelites from slavery in Egypt.
– ORIGIN from *pass over*, with reference to the exemption of the Israelites from the death of their firstborn (Book of Exodus, chapter 12).

pass·port /ˈpas,pôrt/ ▶ **noun 1** an official government document certifying the holder's identity and citizenship and entitling them to travel abroad. **2** a thing that enables someone to do or achieve something: *qualifications are a passport to success.*

pass·word /ˈpas,wərd/ ▶ **noun 1** a secret word or phrase used to gain entry to somewhere. **2** a series of letters and/or numbers allowing someone to use a computer system.

past /past/ ▶ **adjective 1** gone by in time and no longer existing: *the danger is now past.* **2** belonging to a former time. **3** (of time) occurring before and leading up to the present: *he's been unwell for the past six months.* **4** (of a tense of a verb) expressing an action that has happened or a state that used to exist.

– SYNONYMS **1 gone by,** bygone, former, previous, old, of old, olden, long-ago. **2 last,** recent, preceding. **3 previous,** former, foregoing, erstwhile, one-time, sometime, ex-.
– ANTONYMS present, future.

▶ **noun 1** a past period or the events in it. **2** a person's or thing's history or earlier life: *the country's colorful past.* **3** a past tense or form of a verb.

– SYNONYMS **history,** background, past life, life story.

▶ **preposition 1** beyond in time or space. **2** in front of or from one side to the other of. **3** beyond the scope, limits, or power of: *I was long past caring.*

▶ **adverb 1** so as to pass from one side to the other. **2** used to indicate the passage of time.
– PHRASES **not put it past** believe someone to be capable of doing something wrong or rash. **past it** informal, chiefly Brit. too old to be any good at anything.
– ORIGIN from *passed*, past participle of PASS[1].

pas·ta /ˈpästə/ ▶ **noun** dough formed into various shapes (e.g., spaghetti, lasagna), cooked as part of a dish or in boiling water.
– ORIGIN Italian, 'paste.'

paste /pāst/ ▶ **noun 1** a thick, soft, moist substance. **2** a savory spread: *salmon paste.* **3** a glue made from water and starch. **4** a hard glassy substance used in making imitation gems.

– SYNONYMS **1 purée,** pulp, mush, spread, pâté. **2 adhesive,** glue, mucilage.

▶ **verb 1** coat or stick something with paste. **2** Computing insert a section of data into a document. **3** informal beat or defeat someone severely.

– SYNONYMS **stick,** glue, fix, affix.

– ORIGIN Latin *pasta* 'paste.'

paste·board /ˈpās(t)ˌbôrd/ ▶ **noun** thin board made by pasting together sheets of paper.

pas·tel /paˈstel/ ▶ **noun 1** a crayon made of powdered pigments bound with gum or resin. **2** a picture drawn with pastels. **3** a pale shade of a color. ▶ **adjective** (of a color) pale.

– SYNONYMS **pale,** soft, light, delicate, muted.
– ANTONYMS dark, bright.

– DERIVATIVES **pas·tel·list** (also **pastelist**) noun.
– ORIGIN Italian *pastello.*

pas·tern /ˈpastərn/ ▶ **noun** the part of a horse's or other animal's foot between the fetlock and the hoof.
– ORIGIN Old French *pasturon.*

paste-up ▶ **noun** a document prepared for copying or printing by pasting various sections on a backing.

pas·teur·ize /ˈpasCHəˌrīz/ ▶ **verb** make milk or other food safe to eat by heating it to destroy most of the microorganisms in it.
– DERIVATIVES **pas·teur·i·za·tion** /ˌpasCHəriˈzāSHən/ noun.
– ORIGIN named after the French chemist Louis *Pasteur.*

pas·tiche /paˈstēSH, pä-/ ▶ **noun** an artistic work in a style that imitates that of another work, artist, or period.
– DERIVATIVES **pas·ti·cheur** /pasˈtēSHər/ noun.
– ORIGIN Italian *pasticcio.*

past·ie /ˈpāstē/ ▶ **noun** variant spelling of **PASTY**[1].

pas·tille /paˈstēl/ ▶ **noun** a small candy or lozenge.
– ORIGIN Latin *pastillus* 'little loaf, lozenge.'

pas·time /ˈpasˌtīm/ ▶ **noun** an activity done regularly for enjoyment; a hobby.

– SYNONYMS **hobby,** leisure activity, leisure pursuit, recreation, game, amusement, diversion, entertainment, interest.

– ORIGIN from **PASS**[1] + **TIME.**

pas·tis /päˈstēs/ ▶ **noun** (pl. same) an anise-flavored aperitif.
– ORIGIN French.

past mas·ter ▶ **noun** a person who is skilled in an activity.

pas·tor /ˈpastər/ ▶ **noun** a minister in charge of a Christian church or congregation.

– SYNONYMS **priest,** minister, parson, clergyman, cleric, chaplain, vicar, rector, curate; informal reverend, padre.

– ORIGIN Latin, 'shepherd.'

pas·to·ral /ˈpastərəl, pasˈtôrəl/ ▶ **adjective 1** relating to or portraying country life: *the property is located in a beautiful pastoral setting.* **2** relating to the farming or grazing of sheep or cattle. **3** (in the Christian Church) relating to the giving of spiritual guidance by the clergy.

– SYNONYMS **1 rural,** country, rustic, agricultural, bucolic; literary Arcadian. **2 priestly,** clerical, ecclesiastical, ministerial.
– ANTONYMS urban, lay.

▶ **noun** a literary work portraying an idealized version of country life.
– DERIVATIVES **pas·to·ral·ism** /ˈpastərəˌlizəm/ noun.

pas·to·rale /ˌpastəˈräl, -ˈral/ ▶ **noun** (pl. **pastorales** or **pastorali** /-ˈrälē/) **1** a slow instrumental composition in compound time. **2** a simple musical play with a rural subject.
– ORIGIN Italian, literally 'pastoral.'

past par·ti·ci·ple ▶ **noun** the form of a verb that is used in forming perfect and passive tenses and sometimes as an adjective, e.g., *looked* in *have you looked?, lost* in *lost property.*

past per·fect ▶ **noun** Grammar a tense of verbs expressing an action completed prior to some past point of time, in English exemplified by *he had gone.*

pas·tra·mi /pəˈsträmē/ ▶ **noun** highly seasoned smoked beef.
– ORIGIN Yiddish.

pas·try /ˈpāstrē/ ▶ **noun** (pl. **pastries**) **1** a dough of flour, fat, and water, used as a base and covering in baked dishes such as pies. **2** a cake consisting of sweet pastry with a cream, jam, or fruit filling.
– ORIGIN from **PASTE.**

pas·tur·age /ˈpasCHərij/ ▶ **noun 1** land used for grazing cattle or sheep. **2** the occupation of pasturing cattle or sheep.

pas·ture /ˈpasCHər/ ▶ **noun** land covered with grass, suitable for grazing cattle or sheep.

– SYNONYMS **grassland,** grass, grazing, meadow, field; literary lea.

▶ **verb** put animals to graze in a pasture.
– PHRASES **new pastures** (or **pastures new**) somewhere offering new opportunities. [from 'Tomorrow to fresh woods and pastures new' (Milton's *Lycidas*).] **put someone out to pasture** force someone to retire.
– ORIGIN Latin *pastura* 'grazing.'

past·y[1] /ˈpastē/ (also **pastie**) ▶ **noun** (pl. **pasties**) Brit. a folded pastry case filled with meat and vegetables.
– ORIGIN Old French *pastee.*

past·y[2] /ˈpāstē/ ▶ **adjective** (**pastier, pastiest**) (of a person's skin) unhealthily pale.

pat[1] /pat/ ▶ **verb** (**pats, patting, patted**) **1** tap someone or something quickly and gently with the flat of the hand. **2** mold or position something with gentle taps.

– SYNONYMS **tap,** touch, clap.

▶ **noun 1** an act of patting. **2** a compact mass of a soft substance.

– SYNONYMS **tap,** touch, clap.

– PHRASES **a pat on the back** an expression of congratulation or encouragement.
– ORIGIN probably imitating the sound.

pat[2] ▶ **adjective** too quick and easy and not convincing: *there are no pat answers to these questions.*
– PHRASES **have something down pat** have something memorized perfectly.
– ORIGIN related to **PAT**[1].

Pat·a·go·ni·an /ˌpatəˈgōnēən/ ▶ **noun** a person from the South American region of Patagonia. ▶ **adjective** relating to Patagonia.

patch /paCH/ ▶ **noun 1** a piece of material used to mend a hole or strengthen a weak point. **2** a small area that is different from its surroundings. **3** a small plot of land: *a cabbage patch.* **4** informal a brief period of time: *she's going through a bad patch.* **5** a shield worn over a sightless or injured eye. **6** an adhesive piece of material containing a drug and worn on the skin so that the drug may be gradually absorbed. **7** a temporary electrical or telephone connection. **8** a small piece of code inserted to correct or improve a computer program.

– SYNONYMS **1 blotch,** mark, spot, smudge, smear, stain, streak, blemish. **2 plot,** area, lot, piece, strip, tract, parcel, bed. **3 period,** time, spell, phase, stretch.

▶ **verb 1** mend, strengthen, or protect something with a patch. **2** (**patch someone/thing up**) informal treat an injured person or repair something temporarily. **3** (**patch something up**) informal settle a quarrel or dispute. **4** (**patch something together**) make something hastily. **5** connect someone by a temporary electrical, radio, or telephonic connection.

– SYNONYMS **mend,** repair, sew up, stitch up, cover, reinforce.

– DERIVATIVES **patch·er** noun.
– ORIGIN perhaps from Old French dialect *pieche* 'piece.'

patch·ou·li /pəˈCHo͞olē/ ▶ **noun** a scented oil obtained from a SE Asian shrub, used in perfumery, insecticides, and medicine.
– ORIGIN Tamil.

patch pock·et ▶ **noun** a pocket made of a separate piece of cloth sewn onto the outside of a garment.

patch test ▶ **noun** an allergy test in which a range of substances are applied to the skin in light scratches or under a patch.

patch·work /ˈpaCH,wərk/ ▶ **noun 1** needlework in which small pieces of cloth in different designs are sewn together to form a larger piece of fabric. **2** a thing composed of many different elements: *a patchwork of educational courses.*
– DERIVATIVES **patch·worked** adjective.

patch·y /ˈpaCHē/ ▶ **adjective** (**patchier, patchiest**) **1** existing or happening in small, isolated areas: *patchy fog.* **2** not complete or even throughout: *his memory of what happened was patchy.*
– DERIVATIVES **patch·i·ly** adverb **patch·i·ness** noun.

pate /pāt/ ▶ **noun** old use or humorous a person's head.
– ORIGIN unknown.

pâ·té /päˈtā/ ▶ **noun** a rich savory paste made from finely ground or mashed meat, fish, or other ingredients.
– ORIGIN French.

pâ·té de foie gras /päˈtā də ˌfwä ˈgrä/ ▶ **noun** fuller form of **FOIE GRAS**.

pa·tel·la /pəˈtelə/ ▶ **noun** (pl. **patellae** /-lē/) the kneecap.
– DERIVATIVES **pa·tel·lar** /-ˈtelər/ adjective.
– ORIGIN Latin, 'small dish.'

pat·en /ˈpatn/ ▶ **noun** a plate for holding the bread during the Eucharist (Holy Communion).
– ORIGIN Greek *patanē* 'a plate.'

pat·ent ▶ **noun** /ˈpatnt/ a government license giving a person or body the sole right to make, use, or sell an invention for a set period. ▶ **adjective 1** /ˈpātnt, ˈpat-/ easily recognizable; obvious: *she smiled with patent insincerity.* **2** /ˈpatnt/made and marketed under a patent.

– SYNONYMS **1 obvious,** clear, plain, evident, manifest, conspicuous, blatant, barefaced, flagrant. **2 proprietary,** patented, licensed, branded.

▶ **verb** /ˈpatnt/ obtain a patent for an invention.
– DERIVATIVES **pat·ent·a·ble** adjective **pat·ent·ly** /ˈpatntlē, ˈpā-/ adverb.
– ORIGIN from Latin *patere* 'lie open.'

pat·ent·ee /ˌpatnˈtē/ ▶ **noun** a person or body that obtains or holds a patent.

pat·ent leath·er ▶ **noun** glossy varnished leather.

pat·ent med·i·cine ▶ **noun** a medicine made and sold under a patent and available without prescription.

pa·ter /ˈpātər, ˈpä-, ˈpa-/ ▶ **noun** Brit. informal, dated father.
– ORIGIN Latin.

pa·ter·fa·mil·i·as /ˌpātərfəˈmilēəs, ˌpä-/ ▶ **noun** (pl. **patresfamilias** /ˌpātrēzfə-, ˌpä-/) the male head of a family.
– ORIGIN Latin, 'father of the family.'

pa·ter·nal /pəˈtərnl/ ▶ **adjective 1** relating to or like a father. **2** related through the father.
– DERIVATIVES **pa·ter·nal·ly** adverb.

pa·ter·nal·ism /pəˈtərnlˌizəm/ ▶ **noun** the policy of people in authority protecting those who are governed or employed by them, but also restricting their freedom or responsibilities.
– DERIVATIVES **pa·ter·nal·ist** noun & adjective **pa·ter·nal·is·tic** /-ˌtərnlˈistik/ adjective.

pa·ter·ni·ty /pəˈternitē/ ▶ **noun 1** the state of being a father. **2** a person's descent from a father.

pa·ter·ni·ty suit ▶ **noun** a court case held to establish the identity of a child's father.

pa·ter·nos·ter /ˈpätərˌnästər, ˈpatər-/ ▶ **noun** (in the Roman Catholic Church) the Lord's Prayer.
– ORIGIN from Latin *pater noster* 'our father,' the first words of the Lord's Prayer.

path /paTH/ ▶ **noun 1** a way or track laid down for walking or made by continual treading. **2** the direction in which a person or thing moves. **3** a course of action: *a chosen career path.*

– SYNONYMS **1 footpath,** pathway, track, trail, bridle path, lane, towpath. **2 route,** way, course, direction, orbit, trajectory. **3 course of action,** route, road, avenue, line, approach, tack.

– ORIGIN Old English.

path. ▶ **abbreviation 1** pathological. **2** pathology.

path-break·ing ▶ **adjective** pioneering; innovative.

pa·thet·ic /pəˈTHetik/ ▶ **adjective 1** arousing pity. **2** informal completely inadequate.

– SYNONYMS **1 pitiful,** piteous, moving, touching, poignant, plaintive, wretched, heart-rending, sad. **2 feeble,** woeful, sorry, poor, weak, pitiful, lamentable, deplorable, contemptible.

– DERIVATIVES **pa·thet·i·cal·ly** adverb.
– ORIGIN Greek *pathētikos* 'sensitive.'

pa·thet·ic fal·la·cy ▶ **noun** (in art and literature) the depiction of inanimate things or animals as having human feelings.

path·find·er /ˈpaTHˌfīndər/ ▶ **noun** a person who goes ahead and discovers or shows others a way.

patho- ▶ **combining form** relating to disease: *pathology.*
– ORIGIN from Greek *pathos* 'suffering, disease.'

path·o·gen /ˈpaTHəjən, -ˌjen/ ▶ **noun** a microorganism that can cause disease.
– DERIVATIVES **path·o·gen·ic** /ˌpaTHəˈjenik/ adjective.

path·o·log·i·cal /ˌpaTHəˈläjikəl/ (also **pathologic**) ▶ **adjective 1** relating to or caused by a disease. **2** informal possessing a quality to an extreme or uncontrollable degree: *a pathological liar.* **3** relating to pathology.

– SYNONYMS **1 morbid,** diseased. **2 compulsive,** obsessive, inveterate, habitual, persistent, chronic, hardened, confirmed.

– DERIVATIVES **path·o·log·i·cal·ly** adverb.

pa·thol·o·gy /pəˈᴛʜäləjē/ ▶ **noun 1** the branch of medicine concerned with the causes and effects of diseases. **2** the typical behavior of a disease.
– DERIVATIVES **pa·thol·o·gist** noun.

pa·thos /ˈpāˌᴛʜäs, -ˌᴛʜôs/ ▶ **noun** a quality that arouses pity or sadness.
– ORIGIN Greek, 'suffering.'

path·way /ˈpaᴛʜˌwā/ ▶ **noun** a path or its course.

pa·tience /ˈpāsʜəns/ ▶ **noun 1** the ability to accept delay, trouble, or suffering without becoming angry or upset. **2** Brit. solitaire (card game).

– SYNONYMS **1 forbearance,** tolerance, restraint, equanimity, understanding, indulgence. **2 perseverance,** persistence, endurance, tenacity, application, doggedness, staying power.

– ORIGIN Latin *patientia.*

pa·tient /ˈpāsʜənt/ ▶ **adjective** able to accept delay, trouble, or suffering without becoming angry or upset: *supporters have been patient and understanding.*

– SYNONYMS **1 forbearing,** uncomplaining, long-suffering, resigned, stoical, calm, imperturbable, tolerant, accommodating, indulgent. **2 persevering,** persistent, tenacious, dogged, determined.

▶ **noun** a person receiving or registered to receive medical treatment.
– DERIVATIVES **pa·tient·ly** adverb.

pat·i·na /pəˈtēnə/ ▶ **noun 1** a green or brown film on the surface of old bronze. **2** a sheen on wooden furniture produced by age and polishing.
– DERIVATIVES **pat·i·nat·ed** /ˈpatnˌātid/ adjective **pat·i·na·tion** /ˌpatnˈāsʜən/ noun.
– ORIGIN Latin, 'shallow dish.'

pat·i·o /ˈpatēˌō/ ▶ **noun** (pl. **patios**) **1** a paved outdoor area adjoining a house. **2** a roofless inner courtyard in a Spanish or Spanish-American house.
– ORIGIN Spanish.

pat·i·o door ▶ **noun** a large glass sliding door leading to a patio or balcony.

pa·tis·se·rie /pəˈtisərē/ ▶ **noun 1** a store where pastries and cakes are sold. **2** pastries and cakes.
– ORIGIN French.

pat·ois /ˈpaˌtwä, ˈpä-/ ▶ **noun** (pl. same) the local dialect of a region, especially one with low status in relation to the standard language of the country.
– ORIGIN French, 'rough speech.'

pa·tres·fa·mil·i·as /ˌpatrēzfəˈmilēəs, ˌpä-/ plural of **PATERFAMILIAS.**

pa·tri·arch /ˈpātrēˌärk/ ▶ **noun 1** the male head of a family or tribe. **2** a biblical figure regarded as a father of the human race, such as Abraham, Isaac, or Jacob. **3** a powerful or respected older man. **4** a high-ranking bishop in certain Christian churches. **5** the head of an independent Orthodox Church.
– DERIVATIVES **pa·tri·ar·chal** /ˌpātrēˈärkəl/ adjective **pa·tri·arch·ate** /ˈpātrēˌärkit/ noun.
– ORIGIN Greek *patriarkhēs.*

pa·tri·arch·y /ˈpātrēˌärkē/ ▶ **noun** (pl. **patriarchies**) **1** a system of society in which men hold most or all of the power. **2** a form of social organization in which the father or eldest male is the head of the family.

pa·tri·cian /pəˈtrisʜən/ ▶ **noun 1** an aristocrat. **2** a member of the nobility in ancient Rome. ▶ **adjective** relating to or typical of aristocrats; upper-class.
– ORIGIN Latin *patricius* 'having a noble father.'

pat·ri·cide /ˈpatrəˌsīd/ ▶ **noun 1** the killing of a father by his child. **2** a person who kills their father.
– ORIGIN Latin *patricidium.*

pat·ri·lin·e·al /ˌpatrəˈlinēəl/ ▶ **adjective** relating to or based on relationship to the father or descent through the male line.
– ORIGIN Latin *pater, patr-* 'father' + **LINEAL.**

pat·ri·mo·ny /ˈpatrəˌmōnē/ ▶ **noun** (pl. **patrimonies**) **1** property inherited from a person's father or male ancestor. **2** valued things passed down from previous generations; heritage.
– ORIGIN Latin *patrimonium.*

pa·tri·ot /ˈpātrēət/ ▶ **noun** a person who strongly supports their country and is prepared to defend it.
– DERIVATIVES **pa·tri·ot·ism** /-ˌtizəm/ noun.
– ORIGIN Latin *patriota* 'fellow countryman.'

pa·tri·ot·ic /ˌpātrēˈätik/ ▶ **adjective** devoted to and vigorously supporting one's country.

– SYNONYMS **nationalistic,** loyalist, loyal, chauvinistic, jingoistic, flag-waving.
– ANTONYMS traitorous.

– DERIVATIVES **pa·tri·ot·i·cal·ly** adverb.

pa·tris·tic /pəˈtristik/ ▶ **adjective** relating to the early Christian theologians or their writings.
– ORIGIN German *patristisch.*

pa·trol /pəˈtrōl/ ▶ **noun 1** a person or group that keeps watch over an area by walking or traveling around it at regular intervals. **2** the action of patrolling an area. **3** a unit of six to eight Scouts or Guides forming part of a troop.

– SYNONYMS **1** *ships on patrol in the straits* **guard,** watch, vigil. **2 squad,** detachment, party, force.

▶ **verb** (**patrols, patrolling, patrolled**) keep watch over an area by regularly walking or traveling around it.

– SYNONYMS **guard,** keep watch on, police, make the rounds (of), stand guard (over), defend, safeguard.

– DERIVATIVES **pa·trol·ler** noun.
– ORIGIN from French *patrouiller* 'paddle in mud.'

pa·trol·man /pəˈtrōlmən/ ▶ **noun** (pl. **patrolmen**) a patrolling police officer.

pa·tron /ˈpātrən/ ▶ **noun 1** a person who gives financial or other support to a person, organization, or cause. **2** a regular customer of a restaurant, hotel, or store.

– SYNONYMS **1 sponsor,** backer, benefactor, contributor, subscriber, donor, philanthropist, promoter, friend, supporter; informal angel. **2 customer,** client, consumer, user, visitor, guest; informal regular.

– DERIVATIVES **pa·tron·ess** /ˈpātrənis/ noun.
– ORIGIN Latin *patronus* 'protector of clients, defender.'

pa·tron·age /ˈpatrənij, ˈpā-/ ▶ **noun 1** support given by a patron: *the arts could no longer depend on private patronage.* **2** the system by which a powerful person gives a job or privilege to someone in return for their support. **3** the regular customers attracted by a restaurant, hotel, or store. **4** a patronizing way of behaving.

– SYNONYMS **1 sponsorship,** backing, funding, financing, assistance, support. **2 custom,** trade, business.

pa·tron·ize /ˈpātrəˌnīz, ˈpa-/ ▶ verb **1** (often as adj. **patronizing**) treat someone in a way that suggests they are inferior. **2** be a regular customer of a restaurant, hotel, or store.

– SYNONYMS **1** *don't patronize me!* **talk down to,** look down on, condescend to, treat like a child. **2** (as adj. **patronizing**) *your patronizing mother just told me how "adequate" my dress is* **condescending,** supercilious, superior, imperious, scornful; informal uppity, high and mighty. **3** *they patronized local merchants* **use,** buy from, shop at, be a customer/client of, deal with, frequent, support.

pa·tron saint ▶ noun the protecting or guiding saint of a person or place.

pat·ro·nym·ic /ˌpatrəˈnimik/ ▶ noun a name derived from the name of a father or ancestor, e.g., *Johnson, O'Brien.*
– ORIGIN Greek *patrōnumikos.*

pat·sy /ˈpatsē/ ▶ noun (pl. **patsies**) informal a person who is easily taken advantage of.
– ORIGIN unknown.

pat·ten /ˈpatn/ ▶ noun historical a shoe with a raised sole or set on an iron ring, worn to raise the feet above wet ground.
– ORIGIN Old French *patin.*

pat·ter[1] /ˈpatər/ ▶ verb **1** make a repeated light tapping sound. **2** run with quick light steps. ▶ noun a repeated light tapping sound.
– ORIGIN from **PAT**[1].

pat·ter[2] ▶ noun **1** rapid continuous talk, such as that used by a comedian. **2** the jargon of a group or profession: *the patter of an urban street culture.*
– ORIGIN from **PATERNOSTER** (from the rapid and mechanical way in which the prayer was often said).

pat·tern /ˈpatərn/ ▶ noun **1** a repeated decorative design. **2** a regular form or order in which a series of things occur: *a change in working patterns.* **3** a model, design, or set of instructions for making something. **4** an example for others to follow. **5** a sample of cloth or wallpaper.

– SYNONYMS **1 design,** decoration, motif, device, marking. **2 system,** order, arrangement, form, method, structure, scheme, plan, format. **3 model,** example, blueprint, criterion, standard, norm, yardstick, touchstone, benchmark.

▶ verb **1** decorate something with a pattern. **2** (**pattern something on/after**) use something as a model for something else: *the characters are not patterned on real people.*
– ORIGIN from **PATRON** in the former sense 'something serving as a model.'

pat·ty /ˈpatē/ ▶ noun (pl. **patties**) **1** a small flat cake of minced food, especially meat. **2** a flat, round chocolate-covered mint candy. **3** Brit. a small meat pie or turnover.
– ORIGIN French *pâté.*

pau·ci·ty /ˈpôsitē/ ▶ noun the presence of something in only small or insufficient quantities or amounts: *a paucity of information.*
– ORIGIN from Latin *paucus* 'few.'

Pau·line /ˈpôˌlīn, -ˌlēn/ ▶ adjective relating to St. Paul.

paunch /pônch, pänch/ ▶ noun a belly or abdomen that is large or sticks out.
– DERIVATIVES **paunch·y** adjective.
– ORIGIN Old French *paunche.*

pau·per /ˈpôpər/ ▶ noun **1** a very poor person. **2** historical a person who received public charity.
– DERIVATIVES **pau·per·ism** /-ˌrizəm/ noun **pau·per·ize** /-ˌrīz/ verb.
– ORIGIN from Latin, 'poor.'

pause /pôz/ ▶ verb stop temporarily: *he paused for a moment, as if he was going to say more.*

– SYNONYMS **stop,** break off, take a break, adjourn, rest, wait, hesitate; informal take a breather.

▶ noun **1** a temporary stop in action or speech. **2** a mark (𝄐) over a musical note or rest that is to be lengthened by an unspecified amount.

– SYNONYMS **break,** interruption, lull, respite, breathing space, gap, interlude, adjournment, rest, wait, hesitation; informal letup, breather.

– PHRASES **give pause to someone** (or **give someone pause for thought**) cause someone to stop and think before doing something.
– ORIGIN Greek *pausis.*

pa·vane /pəˈvän/ (also **pavan**) ▶ noun a stately dance in slow duple time, popular in the 16th and 17th centuries.
– ORIGIN French.

pave /pāv/ ▶ verb cover a piece of ground with stones, concrete, asphalt, or bricks.
– DERIVATIVES **pav·er** noun **pav·ing** noun.
– PHRASES **pave the way for** create the circumstances to enable something to happen.
– ORIGIN Old French *paver.*

pave·ment /ˈpāvmənt/ ▶ noun **1** the hard surface of a road or street. **2** Geology a horizontal expanse of bare rock with cracks or joints. **3** British term for **SIDEWALK**.
– ORIGIN Latin *pavimentum* 'trodden down floor.'

pa·vil·ion /pəˈvilyən/ ▶ noun **1** a summer house or other decorative shelter in a park or large garden. **2** a large tent used at a show or fair. **3** a temporary display stand or other structure at a trade exhibition.
– ORIGIN Old French *pavillon.*

Pav·lov·i·an /pavˈlōvēən, -ˈläv-/ ▶ adjective relating to trained reflexes as described by the Russian physiologist Ivan P. Pavlov, famous for training dogs to respond instantly to various stimuli.

paw /pô/ ▶ noun **1** an animal's foot having claws and pads. **2** informal a person's hand. ▶ verb **1** feel or scrape something with a paw or hoof. **2** informal touch or handle someone or something clumsily or sexually.
– ORIGIN Old French *poue.*

pawl /pôl/ ▶ noun a pivoted bar or lever whose free end engages with the teeth of a cogwheel or ratchet, allowing it to move or turn in one direction only.
– ORIGIN perhaps from German and Dutch *pal.*

pawn[1] /pôn/ ▶ noun **1** a chess piece of the smallest size and value. **2** a person used by others for their own purposes.
– ORIGIN Old French *poun.*

pawn[2] ▶ verb place an object with a pawnbroker as security for money lent.
– PHRASES **in pawn** (of an object) held as security by a pawnbroker.
– ORIGIN from Old French *pan* 'pledge, security.'

pawn·brok·er /ˈpônˌbrōkər/ ▶ noun a person licensed to lend money in exchange for an article left with them, which they can sell if the borrower fails to pay the money back.

Paw·nee /pôˈnē/ ▶ noun (pl. same or **Pawnees**) a member of an American Indian confederacy now living mainly in Oklahoma.

– ORIGIN from a North American Indian language.

pawn·shop /'pôn,sHäp/ ▸ **noun** a pawnbroker's store.

paw·paw /'pôpô/ (also **papaw** /pə'pô, 'pôpô/) ▸ **noun** **1** a papaya (fruit). **2** an edible yellow fruit from a North American tree related to the custard apple.
– ORIGIN Spanish and Portuguese *papaya*.

pay /pā/ ▸ **verb** (past and past part. **paid**) **1** give someone money owed to them for work, goods, or as a debt. **2** be profitable or advantageous. **3** suffer as a result of an action: *someone's got to pay for all that grief.* **4** give someone attention, respect, or a compliment. **5** make a call or visit to someone. **6** give what is due or deserved to someone.

> – SYNONYMS **1** *I want to pay him for his work* **reward,** reimburse, recompense, remunerate. **2** *Tom must pay a few more dollars* **spend,** pay out; informal lay out, shell out, fork out/over, cough up, ante up, pony up. **3** *he paid his debts* **discharge,** settle, pay off, clear. **4** *crime doesn't pay* **be profitable,** make money, make a profit; **be advantageous to,** benefit, be of advantage to, be beneficial to. **5** *he will pay for his mistakes* **suffer,** be punished, atone, pay the penalty/price.

▸ **noun** money paid for work.

> – SYNONYMS **salary,** wages, payment, earnings, remuneration, fee, reimbursement, income, revenue, stipend, emolument.

– DERIVATIVES **pay·er** noun.
– PHRASES **in the pay of** employed by. **pay someone back** take revenge on someone. **pay dearly** suffer for wrongdoing or failure. **pay one's last respects** show respect toward a dead person by attending their funeral. **pay off** informal yield good results. **pay someone off 1** dismiss someone with a final payment. **2** pay someone not to do something: *he offered to pay her off to drop the case.* **pay something out** let out a rope by slackening it. **pay through the nose** informal pay much more than a fair price.
– ORIGIN Old French *payer* 'appease.'

pay·a·ble /'pāəbəl/ ▸ **adjective** **1** that must be paid. **2** able to be paid.

> – SYNONYMS **due,** owed, owing, outstanding, unpaid, overdue, delinquent.

pay·back /'pā,bak/ ▸ **noun** **1** profit from an investment equal to the initial amount invested. **2** informal an act of revenge.

pay·check /'pā,cHek/ ▸ **noun** a check for salary or wages made out to an employee.

pay·day /'pā,dā/ ▸ **noun** a day on which someone is paid their wages.

pay dirt ▸ **noun** **1** ground containing ore in sufficient quantity to be profitably extracted. **2** informal profit or reward: *the gig pays three hundred bucks a week—looks like I just hit pay dirt.*

pay·ee /pā'ē/ ▸ **noun** a person to whom money is paid or to be paid.

pay·load /'pā,lōd/ ▸ **noun** **1** passengers and cargo as the part of a vehicle's load that earns money. **2** an explosive warhead carried by an aircraft or missile. **3** the load carried by a spacecraft.

pay·mas·ter /'pā,mastər/ ▸ **noun** **1** a person who pays another and therefore controls them. **2** an official who pays troops or workers.

pay·ment /'pāmənt/ ▸ **noun** **1** the action of paying or the process of being paid. **2** an amount paid.

> – SYNONYMS **1 remittance,** settlement, discharge, clearance. **2 installment,** premium. **3 salary,** wages, pay, earnings, fees, remuneration, reimbursement, income, stipend, emolument.

pay·off /'pā,ôf/ ▸ **noun** informal **1** a payment, especially as a bribe or on leaving a job. **2** the return on investment or on a bet. **3** a final outcome.

pay·o·la /pā'ōlə/ ▸ **noun** the practice of bribing someone in return for the unofficial promotion of a product.
– ORIGIN from **PAY** + *-ola* as in *Victrola*, a make of gramophone (the term first referred to the bribery of a disc jockey to promote a record).

pay·out /'pā,out/ ▸ **noun** a large payment of money.

pay-per-view ▸ **noun** a television service in which viewers have to pay a fee to watch a particular program.

pay·phone /'pā,fōn/ ▸ **noun** a public telephone operated by coins or by a credit or prepaid card.

pay·roll /'pā,rōl/ ▸ **noun** a list of a company's employees and the amount of money they are to be paid.

Pb ▸ **symbol** the chemical element lead.
– ORIGIN from Latin *plumbum*.

pb ▸ **abbreviation** paperback.

PBS ▸ **abbreviation** Public Broadcasting Service.

PC ▸ **abbreviation** **1** personal computer. **2** (also **pc**) politically correct; political correctness.

PCB ▸ **abbreviation** **1** Electronics printed circuit board. **2** Chemistry polychlorinated biphenyl, a poisonous compound formed as waste in some industrial processes.

PCV ▸ **abbreviation** Brit. passenger-carrying vehicle.

PD ▸ **abbreviation** **1** Police Department: *the Chicago PD.* **2** public domain: *PD software.*

Pd ▸ **symbol** the chemical element palladium.

PDA ▸ **abbreviation** personal digital assistant, a basic palmtop computer.

PDF ▸ **noun** Computing **1** a file format for capturing and sending electronic documents in exactly the intended format. **2** a file in this format.
– ORIGIN abbreviation of *Portable Document Format*.

PDQ ▸ **abbreviation** informal pretty damn quick.

PDT ▸ **abbreviation** Pacific Daylight Time.

PE ▸ **abbreviation** physical education.

pea /pē/ ▸ **noun** **1** a round green seed eaten as a vegetable. **2** the climbing plant that has pods containing peas.
– ORIGIN Old English.

peace /pēs/ ▸ **noun** **1** freedom from noise or anxiety; tranquility. **2** freedom from or the ending of war. **3** (**the peace**) an action such as a handshake, signifying Christian unity and performed during the Eucharist (Holy Communion).

> – SYNONYMS **1 quiet,** silence, peace and quiet, hush, stillness, still. **2 serenity,** peacefulness, tranquility, calm, calmness, composure, ease, contentment, rest, repose. **3 treaty,** truce, ceasefire, armistice.
> – ANTONYMS noise, war.

– PHRASES **at peace 1** free from anxiety or distress. **2** euphemistic dead. **hold one's peace** remain silent. **keep**

the **peace** refrain or prevent others from disturbing civil order. **make (one's) peace** re-establish friendly relations with someone.
– ORIGIN Latin *pax*.

peace·a·ble /ˈpēsəbəl/ ▶ **adjective 1** inclined to avoid conflict. **2** free from conflict; peaceful.
– DERIVATIVES **peace·a·bly** adverb.

Peace Corps ▶ **noun** an organization that enables young people to work as volunteers in developing countries.

peace div·i·dend ▶ **noun** a sum of public money available for other purposes when spending on defense is reduced.

peace·ful /ˈpēsfəl/ ▶ **adjective 1** free from noise or anxiety: *her peaceful mood vanished.* **2** not involving war or violence. **3** inclined to avoid conflict; peaceable.

– SYNONYMS **1 tranquil,** calm, restful, quiet, still, relaxing, serene, composed, placid, at ease, untroubled, unworried. **2 harmonious,** on good terms, amicable, friendly, cordial, nonviolent.
– ANTONYMS noisy.

– DERIVATIVES **peace·ful·ly** adverb **peace·ful·ness** noun.

peace·keep·ing /ˈpēsˌkēpiNG/ ▶ **noun** the practice of using an international military force to maintain a truce.
– DERIVATIVES **peace·keep·er** noun.

peace·mak·er /ˈpēsˌmākər/ ▶ **noun** a person who brings about peace.

– SYNONYMS **arbitrator,** arbiter, mediator, negotiator, conciliator, go-between, intermediary.

– DERIVATIVES **peace·mak·ing** noun.

peace·nik /ˈpēsˌnik/ ▶ **noun** informal, often derogatory a member of a pacifist movement.

peace of·fer·ing ▶ **noun** a gift that is given in an attempt to re-establish friendly relations.

peace pipe ▶ **noun** a tobacco pipe offered and smoked as a token of peace among North American Indians.

peace·time /ˈpēsˌtīm/ ▶ **noun** a period when a country is not at war.

peach[1] /pēCH/ ▶ **noun 1** a round fruit with juicy yellow flesh, downy red and yellow skin, and a stone inside. **2** a pinkish-orange color. **3** informal an exceptionally good or attractive person or thing: *it was another peach of a day.*
– DERIVATIVES **peach·y** adjective.
– ORIGIN Old French *pesche*.

peach[2] ▶ **verb** (**peach on**) informal inform on.
– ORIGIN related to **IMPEACH**.

pea·cock /ˈpēˌkäk/ ▶ **noun** a large male bird of the pheasant family, having very long tail feathers with eyelike markings that can be fanned out in display.
– ORIGIN Old English.

pea·cock blue ▶ **noun** a greenish-blue color like that of a peacock's neck.

pea·fowl /ˈpēˌfoul/ ▶ **noun** a peacock or peahen.

pea green ▶ **noun** a bright green color.

pea·hen /ˈpēˌhen/ ▶ **noun** a female peafowl, which has mainly brown plumage and a shorter tail than a peacock.

pea jack·et (also **pea coat**) ▶ **noun** a short double-breasted overcoat of coarse woolen cloth.
– ORIGIN Dutch *pijjakker*.

peak /pēk/ ▶ **noun 1** the pointed top of a mountain. **2** a mountain with a pointed top. **3** the point of highest activity, achievement, intensity, etc.: *he was at his peak as a cricketer.*

– SYNONYMS **1 summit,** top, crest, pinnacle, cap. **2 mountain,** hill, height. **3 height,** high point, pinnacle, summit, top, climax, culmination, apex, zenith, acme.

▶ **verb** reach a highest point or maximum.

– SYNONYMS **reach its height,** climax, culminate.

▶ **adjective** characterized by maximum activity or demand.

– SYNONYMS **maximum,** greatest, busiest, highest.

– ORIGIN probably from dialect *picked* 'pointed.'

peak·ed /ˈpēˌkid/ ▶ **adjective** pale from illness or exhaustion.

peak load ▶ **noun** the maximum of electrical power demand.

peal /pēl/ ▶ **noun 1** a loud ringing of a bell or bells. **2** a loud repeated or resounding sound of thunder or laughter. **3** a set of bells. ▶ **verb** (of a bell or sound) ring or resound loudly.
– ORIGIN shortening of **APPEAL**.

pea·nut /ˈpēnət/ ▶ **noun 1** the oval edible seed of a plant native to South America, whose seeds develop in underground pods. **2** (**peanuts**) informal a very small sum of money.

pea·nut but·ter ▶ **noun** a spread made from ground roasted peanuts.

pear /pe(ə)r/ ▶ **noun** a yellow or green edible fruit that is narrow at the stalk and widens toward the bottom.
– ORIGIN Old English, from Latin *pirum*.

pearl /pərl/ ▶ **noun 1** a small, hard, shiny white or bluish-gray ball formed inside the shell of an oyster or other mollusk and having great value as a gem. **2** a highly valued person or thing: *pearls of wisdom.* **3** a very pale bluish gray or white color.
– PHRASES **cast pearls before swine** offer valuable things to people who do not appreciate them. [with reference to the Gospel of Matthew, chapter 7.]
– ORIGIN Old French *perle*.

pearl bar·ley ▶ **noun** barley reduced to small round grains by grinding.

pearled /pərld/ ▶ **adjective** literary decorated with or wearing pearls.

pearl·es·cent /pərˈlesənt/ ▶ **adjective** having a soft glow resembling that of mother-of-pearl.

pearl·y /ˈpərlē/ ▶ **adjective** (**pearlier, pearliest**) resembling a pearl in luster or color. ▶ **noun** (**pearlies**) (also **pearly whites**) informal a person's teeth.

Pearl·y Gates ▶ **plural noun** informal the gates of heaven.
– ORIGIN from the Book of Revelation in the Bible.

pear-shaped ▶ **adjective** having hips that are disproportionately wide in relation to the upper part of the body.

peas·ant /ˈpezənt/ ▶ **noun 1** a poor farmer or farm laborer of low social status. **2** informal an ignorant, rude, or unsophisticated person.
– DERIVATIVES **peas·ant·ry** noun.
– ORIGIN Old French *paisent*.

pea·shoot·er /ˈpēˌSHo͞otər/ ▶ **noun** a toy weapon consisting of a small tube out of which dried peas are blown.

pea soup ▸ **noun** **1** a thick soup made from dried split peas. **2** informal a thick, yellowish fog.

pea-souper ▸ **noun** chiefly Brit. a very thick fog.

peat /pēt/ ▸ **noun** partly decomposed vegetable matter forming a deposit on acidic, boggy ground, dried for use in gardening and as fuel.
– DERIVATIVES **peat·y** adjective.
– ORIGIN Anglo-Latin *peta*.

peat moss ▸ **noun** a large moss that grows on boggy ground and decays to form peat deposits, which are used as compost.

peb·ble /'pebəl/ ▸ **noun** a small stone made smooth and round by the action of water or sand.
– DERIVATIVES **peb·bly** adjective.
– ORIGIN Old English.

pec /pek/ ▸ **noun** informal a pectoral muscle.

pe·can /pə'kän, 'pē,kan/ ▸ **noun** a smooth pinkish-brown nut with a kernel similar to a walnut, obtained from a tree of the southern US.
– ORIGIN from an American Indian language.

pec·ca·dil·lo /,pekə'dilō/ ▸ **noun** (pl. **peccadilloes** or **peccadillos**) a minor fault.
– ORIGIN Spanish.

pec·ca·ry /'pekərē/ ▸ **noun** (pl. **peccaries**) a piglike mammal found from the southwestern US to Paraguay.
– ORIGIN Carib.

peck[1] /pek/ ▸ **verb** **1** (of a bird) strike or bite something with its beak. **2** kiss someone lightly and briefly. **3** (**peck at**) informal eat food without enthusiasm. **4** type something slowly and laboriously. ▸ **noun** **1** an act of pecking. **2** a quick, light kiss.
– ORIGIN unknown.

peck[2] ▸ **noun** a measure of capacity for dry goods, equal to a quarter of a bushel.
– ORIGIN Old French *pek*.

peck·er /'pekər/ ▸ **noun** vulgar slang a penis.
– PHRASES **keep your pecker up** informal, chiefly Brit. remain cheerful.

peck·ing or·der ▸ **noun** a strict order of importance among members of a group.

peck·ish /'pekish/ ▸ **adjective** informal, chiefly Brit. hungry.

pec·o·ri·no /pekə'rēnō/ ▸ **noun** an Italian cheese made from ewes' milk.
– ORIGIN from Italian, 'of ewes.'

pec·tin /'pektin/ ▸ **noun** a soluble jellylike substance present in ripe fruits, used to set jams and jellies.
– ORIGIN from Greek *pektos* 'congealed.'

pec·to·ral /'pektərəl/ ▸ **adjective** relating to or worn on the breast or chest. ▸ **noun** a pectoral muscle.
– ORIGIN Latin *pectoralis*.

pec·to·ral mus·cle ▸ **noun** each of four large paired muscles that cover the front of the ribcage.

pec·u·la·tion /,pekyə'lāshən/ ▸ **noun** formal embezzlement of public funds.
– ORIGIN from Latin *peculari* 'embezzle.'

pe·cu·liar /pə'kyo͞olyər/ ▸ **adjective** **1** different to what is normal or expected; strange. **2** (**peculiar to**) belonging exclusively to. **3** particular; special: *the peculiar difficulties faced by West African women*.

> – SYNONYMS **1 strange,** unusual, odd, funny, curious, bizarre, weird, eccentric, queer, abnormal, unconventional, outlandish, anomalous, out of the ordinary, unexpected, offbeat. **2** *customs peculiar to the area* **distinctive,** exclusive, unique, characteristic, distinct, individual, typical, special.
> – ANTONYMS ordinary.

– DERIVATIVES **pe·cu·liar·ly** adverb.
– ORIGIN Latin *peculiaris* 'of private property.'

pe·cu·li·ar·i·ty /pə,kyo͞olē'aritē/ ▸ **noun** (pl. **pecularities**) **1** an unusual or distinctive feature or habit. **2** the state of being strange or odd.

pe·cu·ni·ar·y /pi'kyo͞onē,erē/ ▸ **adjective** formal relating to money.
– ORIGIN Latin *pecuniarius*.

ped·a·gogue /'pedə,gäg/ ▸ **noun** formal or humorous a teacher.
– ORIGIN Greek *paidagōgos*, referring to a slave who accompanied a child to school.

ped·a·go·gy /'pedə,gäjē, -,gōjē/ ▸ **noun** the profession or theory of teaching.
– DERIVATIVES **ped·a·gog·ic** /,pedə'gäjik/ (also **pedagogical**) adjective.

ped·al[1] /'pedl/ ▸ **noun** **1** each of a pair of foot-operated levers for powering a bicycle or other vehicle. **2** a foot-operated throttle, brake, or clutch control. **3** a foot-operated lever on a piano, organ, etc., for sustaining or softening the tone. ▸ **verb** (**pedals, pedaling, pedaled**) work the pedals of a bicycle or other vehicle to move along.
– DERIVATIVES **ped·al·er** (Brit. **pedaller**) noun.
– ORIGIN Latin *pedalis* 'a foot in length.'

> **USAGE**
>
> Do not confuse the words **pedal** and **peddle**. **Pedal** is a noun referring to a foot-operated lever, as on a bicycle; as a verb it means 'work the pedals of a bicycle' (*we pedaled along the road*). **Peddle** is a verb meaning 'sell goods or promote an idea' (*she peddled a ridiculous view of the past*).

ped·al[2] /'pēdl/ ▸ **adjective** chiefly Medicine & Zoology relating to the foot or feet.
– ORIGIN Latin *pedalis*.

ped·al push·ers ▸ **plural noun** women's calf-length pants.

ped·ant /'pednt/ ▸ **noun** a person who is excessively concerned with minor detail or with displaying academic learning.

> – SYNONYMS **dogmatist,** purist, literalist, formalist, quibbler, hair-splitter; informal nit-picker.

– DERIVATIVES **ped·ant·ry** noun.
– ORIGIN French *pédant*.

pe·dan·tic /pə'dantik/ ▸ **adjective** excessively concerned with minor detail or with displaying academic learning.

> – SYNONYMS **finicky,** fussy, fastidious, dogmatic, purist, hair-splitting, quibbling; informal nitpicking, pernickety.

– DERIVATIVES **pe·dan·ti·cal·ly** /-tik(ə)lē/ adverb.

ped·dle /'pedl/ ▸ **verb** **1** sell goods by going from place to place. **2** sell an illegal drug or stolen item. **3** promote an idea persistently or widely.

> – SYNONYMS **sell,** hawk, tout, trade, deal in, traffic in.

– ORIGIN from PEDDLER.

> **USAGE**
>
> On the confusion between **pedal** and **peddle**, see the note at PEDAL[1].

ped·dler /ˈpedlər, ˈpedl-ər/ (also **pedlar**) ▸ **noun 1** a traveling trader who sells small goods. **2** a person who sells illegal drugs or stolen goods. **3** a person who promotes an idea or view persistently.
– ORIGIN perhaps from dialect *ped* 'pannier.'

ped·er·as·ty /ˈpedəˌrastē/ ▸ **noun** sexual intercourse between a man and a boy.
– DERIVATIVES **ped·er·ast** /ˈpedəˌrast/ noun **ped·er·as·tic** /ˌpedəˈrastik/ adjective.
– ORIGIN Greek *paiderastia.*

ped·es·tal /ˈpedəstl/ ▸ **noun 1** the base or support on which a statue or column is mounted. **2** the supporting column of a washbasin or toilet pan.

– SYNONYMS **plinth,** base, support, mount, stand, pillar, column.

– PHRASES **put someone on a pedestal** admire someone greatly and uncritically.
– ORIGIN Italian *piedestallo.*

pe·des·tri·an /pəˈdestrēən/ ▸ **noun** a person walking rather than traveling in a vehicle.

– SYNONYMS **walker,** person on foot.

▸ **adjective** not exciting or interesting: *a pedestrian task.*

– SYNONYMS **dull,** boring, tedious, monotonous, unremarkable, uninspired, unimaginative, unexciting, routine, commonplace, ordinary, everyday, run-of-the-mill, mundane, humdrum.
– ANTONYMS exciting.

– DERIVATIVES **pe·des·tri·an·ly** adverb.
– ORIGIN from Latin *pedester* 'going on foot.'

pe·des·tri·an·ize /pəˈdestrēəˌnīz/ ▸ **verb** make a street or area accessible only to pedestrians.
– DERIVATIVES **pe·des·tri·an·i·za·tion** /pəˌdestrēəniˈzāsʜən/ noun.

pe·di·at·rics /ˌpēdēˈatriks/ (Brit. **paediatrics**) ▸ **plural noun** (treated as sing.) the branch of medicine concerned with children and their diseases.
– DERIVATIVES **pe·di·at·ric** /-ˈatrik/ adjective **pe·di·a·tri·cian** /ˌpēdēəˈtrisʜən/ noun.
– ORIGIN from Greek *pais* 'child' + *iatros* 'physician.'

ped·i·cure /ˈpediˌkyo͝or/ ▸ **noun** a cosmetic treatment of the feet and toenails.
– DERIVATIVES **ped·i·cur·ist** noun.
– ORIGIN French.

ped·i·gree /ˈpedəˌgrē/ ▸ **noun 1** the record of an animal's origins, showing that all the animals from which it is descended are of the same breed. **2** a person's family background or ancestry. **3** the history or origin of a person or thing: *the scheme has a long pedigree.*

– SYNONYMS **1 ancestry,** lineage, line, descent, genealogy, extraction, parentage, bloodline, family tree. **2** (as adj.) *a pedigree cat* **purebred,** full-blooded, thoroughbred.

– ORIGIN from Old French *pé de grue* 'crane's foot,' a mark used to show succession in pedigrees.

ped·i·ment /ˈpedəmənt/ ▸ **noun** the triangular upper part above the entrance to a classical building.
– ORIGIN perhaps from PYRAMID.

pe·dom·e·ter /pəˈdämitər/ ▸ **noun** an instrument for estimating the distance traveled on foot by recording the number of steps taken.
– ORIGIN from Latin *pes* 'foot.'

pe·do·phile /ˈpedəˌfīl, ˈpēdə-/ (Brit. **paedophile**) ▸ **noun** a person who is sexually attracted to children.
– DERIVATIVES **pe·do·phil·i·a** /ˌpedəˈfilēə, ˌpēdə-/ noun **pe·do·phil·i·ac** /-ˈfilēˌak/ adjective & noun.
– ORIGIN from Greek *pais* 'child.'

pe·dun·cle /ˈpēˌdənɢkəl, pəˈdənɢkəl/ ▸ **noun 1** Botany the stalk carrying a flower or fruit. **2** Zoology a stalklike connecting structure.
– DERIVATIVES **pe·dun·cu·late** /pəˈdənɢkyəˌlāt, -lit/ adjective.
– ORIGIN Latin *pedunculus.*

pee /pē/ informal ▸ **verb** (**pees, peeing, peed**) urinate. ▸ **noun 1** an act of urinating. **2** urine.
– ORIGIN from the initial letter of PISS.

peek /pēk/ ▸ **verb 1** look quickly or furtively. **2** stick out slightly so as to be just visible: *his socks were so full of holes his toes peeked through.*

– SYNONYMS **1 peep,** look; informal take a gander, have a squint. **2 appear,** show, peep (out).

▸ **noun** a quick or furtive look.

– SYNONYMS **look,** peep, glance, glimpse.

– ORIGIN unknown.

peek·a·boo /ˈpēkəˌbo͞o/ ▸ **adjective** (of an item of clothing) made of transparent fabric or having a pattern of small holes.

peel /pēl/ ▸ **verb 1** remove the outer covering or skin from a fruit or vegetable. **2** (of a surface or object) lose parts of its outer layer or covering in small pieces. **3** (**peel something away/off**) remove a thin outer covering. **4** (**peel off**) leave a group by veering away.

– SYNONYMS **1 pare,** skin, hull, shell, shuck. **2 flake (off),** come off, fall off, strip off.

▸ **noun** the outer skin or rind of a fruit or vegetable.

– SYNONYMS **rind,** skin, covering, zest.

– DERIVATIVES **peel·a·ble** adjective **peel·ings** plural noun.
– ORIGIN Latin *pilare* 'to strip hair from.'

peel·er /ˈpēlər/ ▸ **noun** a knife or device for peeling fruit and vegetables.

peen /pēn/ ▸ **noun** the rounded or wedge-shaped end of a hammer head opposite the face.
– ORIGIN probably Scandinavian.

peep[1] /pēp/ ▸ **verb 1** look quickly and furtively. **2** (**peep out**) come slowly or partially into view.

– SYNONYMS **peek,** look, sneak a peek/look, glance; informal squint.

▸ **noun 1** a quick or furtive look. **2** a glimpse of something: *a peep of gold earring.*

– SYNONYMS **peek,** look, glance; informal squint.

peep[2] ▸ **noun** a weak or brief high-pitched sound. ▸ **verb** make a peep.
– PHRASES **not a peep** not the slightest sound or complaint.
– ORIGIN imitating the sound.

peep·er /ˈpēpər/ ▸ **noun 1** a person who looks quickly or furtively. **2** (**peepers**) informal a person's eyes.

peep·hole /ˈpēpˌhōl/ ▸ **noun** a small hole in a door through which callers may be identified.

peep·ing Tom ▸ **noun** a person who gains sexual pleasure from secretly watching people undress or have sex.
– ORIGIN the name of the tailor said to have watched Lady Godiva ride naked through Coventry.

peep show ▸ **noun** a form of entertainment in which pictures are viewed through a lens or hole set into a box.

peer[1] /pi(ə)r/ ▶ **verb 1** look with difficulty or concentration. **2** be just visible: *the towers peer over the roofs.*

– SYNONYMS **look closely,** squint, gaze, stare.

– ORIGIN uncertain.

peer[2] ▶ **noun 1** a member of the nobility in Britain or Ireland, comprising the ranks of duke, marquess, earl, viscount, and baron. **2** a person of the same age, status, or ability as another specified person: *his astute management is better than any of his peers.*

– SYNONYMS **1 aristocrat,** lord, lady, noble, nobleman, noblewoman. **2 equal,** fellow, contemporary.

– PHRASES **without peer** better than all others; unrivaled.
– ORIGIN Old French.

peer·age /ˈpi(ə)rij/ ▶ **noun 1** the title and rank of peer or peeress. **2** (**the peerage**) peers as a group.

peer·ess /ˈpi(ə)ris/ ▶ **noun 1** a woman holding the rank of a peer in her own right. **2** the wife or widow of a peer.

peer group ▶ **noun** a group of people of approximately the same age, status, and interests.

peer·less /ˈpi(ə)rlis/ ▶ **adjective** better than all others; unrivaled.

peer-to-peer ▶ **adjective** Computing denoting a network in which each computer can act as a server for the others, allowing shared access to files and peripherals without the need for a central server.

peeve /pēv/ informal ▶ **verb** annoy or irritate someone: *he was peeved at being left out.*

– SYNONYMS **irritate,** annoy, vex, anger, irk, gall, pique, put out, nettle; informal aggravate, rile, tee off, tick off, needle, get to, bug, get someone's goat, get/put someone's back up.

▶ **noun** a cause of annoyance.
– ORIGIN from **PEEVISH**.

peev·ish /ˈpēvisн/ ▶ **adjective** easily annoyed; irritable.
– DERIVATIVES **peev·ish·ly** adverb **peev·ish·ness** noun.
– ORIGIN unknown.

peg /peg/ ▶ **noun 1** a short projecting pin or bolt used for hanging things on, securing something in place, or marking a position. **2** Brit. a clothespin. **3** informal a person's leg.

– SYNONYMS **pin,** nail, dowel.

▶ **verb** (**pegs, pegging, pegged**) **1** fix, attach, or mark something with a peg or pegs. **2** fix a price, rate, or amount at a particular level. **3** (**peg away**) informal work hard over a long period.

– SYNONYMS **1 fix,** pin, attach, fasten, secure. **2 set,** hold, fix, limit, freeze, keep down, hold down.

– PHRASES **a square peg in a round hole** a person in a situation unsuited to their abilities or character. **take** (or **bring**) **someone down a peg or two** make someone less arrogant.
– ORIGIN probably German.

peg·board /ˈpeg,bôrd/ ▶ **noun** a board with a regular pattern of small holes for pegs.

peg leg ▶ **noun** informal an artificial leg.

peign·oir /,pānˈwär/ ▶ **noun** a woman's light bathrobe or negligee.
– ORIGIN French.

pe·jo·ra·tive /pəˈjôrətiv, ˈpejə,rātiv/ ▶ **adjective** (of a word or phrase) expressing contempt or disapproval.
– DERIVATIVES **pe·jo·ra·tive·ly** adverb.
– ORIGIN French *péjoratif.*

Pe·king duck /,pēˈkiNG, ,pā-/ ▶ **noun** a Chinese dish consisting of strips of roast duck served with shredded vegetables and a sweet sauce.

Pe·king·ese (also **Pekinese**) ▶ **noun** /ˈpēkə,nēz, -,nēs/ (pl. same) a small dog of a short-legged breed with long hair and a snub nose. ▶ **adjective** /,pēkiNGˈēz, -ˈēs/ relating to Beijing (Peking).

pe·lag·ic /pəˈlajik/ ▶ **adjective** technical **1** relating to the open sea. **2** (chiefly of fish) inhabiting the upper layers of the open sea.
– ORIGIN Greek *pelagikos.*

pel·ar·go·ni·um /,pelärˈgōnēəm/ ▶ **noun** a garden plant with red, pink, or white flowers.
– ORIGIN Latin.

pelf /pelf/ ▶ **noun** literary money, especially when gained dishonestly.
– ORIGIN Old French *pelfre* 'spoils.'

pel·i·can /ˈpelikən/ ▶ **noun** a large waterbird with a long bill and a pouch hanging from its throat.
– ORIGIN Greek *pelekan.*

pe·lisse /pəˈlēs/ ▶ **noun** historical a woman's long cloak with armholes or sleeves.
– ORIGIN French.

pel·la·gra /pəˈlagrə, -ˈlāgrə, -ˈlägrə/ ▶ **noun** a disease that results from a lack of a vitamin, causing inflamed skin, diarrhea, and mental disturbance.
– ORIGIN Italian.

pel·let /ˈpelit/ ▶ **noun 1** a small, rounded, compressed mass of a substance. **2** a piece of small shot or other lightweight bullet. ▶ **verb** (**pellets, pelleting, pelleted**) form a substance into pellets.
– DERIVATIVES **pel·let·ize** /ˈpeli,tīz/ verb.
– ORIGIN Old French *pelote* 'metal ball.'

pell-mell /ˈpel ˈmel/ ▶ **adjective & adverb** in a confused, rushed, or disorderly way.
– ORIGIN French *pêle-mêle.*

pel·lu·cid /pəˈlo͞osid/ ▶ **adjective** literary **1** transparent or semitransparent. **2** easily understood: *pellucid answers.*
– ORIGIN Latin *pellucidus.*

pe·lo·ta /pəˈlōtə/ ▶ **noun** a Basque or Spanish ball game played in a walled court with basketlike rackets.
– ORIGIN Spanish, 'ball.'

pel·o·ton /ˈpelə,tän/ ▶ **noun** the main group of cyclists in a race.
– ORIGIN French, 'small ball.'

pelt[1] /pelt/ ▶ **verb 1** hurl missiles at someone or something. **2** (**pelt down**) (chiefly of rain) fall very heavily. **3** run very quickly.
– PHRASES (**at**) **full pelt** Brit. as fast as possible.
– ORIGIN unknown.

pelt[2] ▶ **noun** the skin of an animal with the fur, wool, or hair still on it.
– ORIGIN Latin *pellis* 'skin.'

pel·vic gir·dle ▶ **noun** (in vertebrates) the enclosing structure formed by the pelvis.

pel·vis /ˈpelvis/ ▶ **noun** (pl. **pelvises** or **pelves** /-vēz/) the large bony frame at the base of the spine to which the lower limbs are attached.
– DERIVATIVES **pel·vic** /ˈpelvik/ adjective.
– ORIGIN Latin, 'basin.'

pen¹ /pen/ ▸ **noun 1** an instrument for writing or drawing with ink. **2** an electronic device used with a writing surface to enter commands into a computer. ▸ **verb** (**pens, penning, penned**) write or compose something.

– SYNONYMS **write,** compose, draft, dash off; write down, jot down, set down, take down, scribble.

– ORIGIN Latin *penna* 'feather' (pens were originally made from a quill feather).

pen² ▸ **noun 1** a small enclosure for farm animals. **2** a covered dock for a submarine or other warship.

– SYNONYMS **enclosure,** fold, pound, compound, stockade, sty, coop, corral.

▸ **verb** (**pens, penning, penned**) **1** put or keep an animal in a pen. **2** (**pen someone up/in**) confine someone in a restricted space.

– SYNONYMS **confine,** coop, cage, shut, box, lock, trap, imprison, incarcerate.

– ORIGIN Old English.

pen³ ▸ **noun** a female swan.
– ORIGIN unknown.

pe·nal /ˈpēnəl/ ▸ **adjective 1** relating to the punishment of offenders under the legal system. **2** chiefly Brit. very severe: *penal rates of interest.*
– ORIGIN from Latin *poena* 'pain, penalty.'

pe·nal·ize /ˈpenəlˌīz, ˈpē-/ ▸ **verb 1** give a penalty or punishment to someone who has broken the law or a rule. **2** make an action punishable by law. **3** put in an unfavorable position: *single people are often penalized by hotels by being charged a supplement.*

– SYNONYMS **1 punish,** discipline. **2 handicap,** disadvantage, discriminate against.
– ANTONYMS reward.

– DERIVATIVES **pe·nal·i·za·tion** /ˌpenəliˈzāsʜən, ˌpē-/ noun.

pe·nal ser·vi·tude ▸ **noun** imprisonment with hard labor.

pen·al·ty /ˈpenltē/ ▸ **noun** (pl. **penalties**) **1** a punishment for breaking a law, rule, or contract. **2** a disadvantage suffered as a result of an action or situation: *feeling cold is one of the penalties of old age.* **3** a penalty kick or shot.

– SYNONYMS **punishment,** sanction, fine, forfeit, sentence.
– ANTONYMS reward.

pen·al·ty ar·e·a (also **penalty box**) ▸ **noun** Soccer the rectangular area marked out in front of each goal, within which a foul by a defender involves the award of a penalty kick.

pen·al·ty box ▸ **noun** Ice Hockey an enclosure alongside the rink where players who have been assessed penalties must remain while they serve out their penalties.

pen·al·ty kick ▸ **noun 1** Soccer a free shot at the goal awarded to the attacking team after a foul within the penalty area. **2** Rugby a place kick awarded to a team after an offense by an opponent.

pen·ance /ˈpenəns/ ▸ **noun 1** punishment inflicted on oneself to show that one is sorry for wrongdoing: *he had done public penance for those hasty words.* **2** (chiefly in the Roman Catholic and Orthodox Church) a religious act in which a person confesses their sins to a priest and is asked to perform a religious duty before being given formal forgiveness. **3** a religious duty that a priest asks a person to do to show repentance for a sin.

– SYNONYMS **atonement,** expiation, amends, punishment, penalty.

– ORIGIN Latin *paenitentia* 'repentance.'

pence /pens/ Brit. plural of **PENNY** (used for sums of money).

pen·chant /ˈpencʜənt/ ▸ **noun** a strong liking for or tendency to do something: *a penchant for champagne.*

– SYNONYMS **liking,** fondness, preference, taste, appetite, partiality, love, passion, weakness, inclination, bent, proclivity, predilection, predisposition.

– ORIGIN French, 'leaning, inclining.'

pen·cil /ˈpensəl/ ▸ **noun** an instrument for writing or drawing, typically consisting of a thin stick of graphite enclosed in a wooden case. ▸ **verb** (**pencils, penciling, penciled**) **1** write, draw, or color something with a pencil. **2** (**pencil something in**) arrange or note something down provisionally.
– ORIGIN Old French *pincel* 'paintbrush.'

pen·cil push·er ▸ **noun** informal an office worker who deals with routine paperwork.

pen·cil skirt ▸ **noun** a very narrow straight skirt.

pend·ant /ˈpendənt/ ▸ **noun 1** a piece of jewelry that hangs from a necklace chain. **2** a light designed to hang from the ceiling. ▸ **adjective** hanging downward.
– ORIGIN from Old French, 'hanging.'

pend·ent /ˈpendənt/ ▸ **adjective** literary hanging down or overhanging.

pend·ing /ˈpendiɴɢ/ ▸ **adjective 1** awaiting decision or settlement. **2** about to happen.

– SYNONYMS **1 unresolved,** undecided, unsettled, up in the air, ongoing, outstanding; informal on the back burner. **2 imminent,** impending, about to happen, forthcoming, on the way, coming, approaching, looming, near, on the horizon, in the offing.

▸ **preposition** until something happens.
– ORIGIN anglicized spelling of French *pendant* 'hanging.'

pen·du·lous /ˈpenjələs, ˈpendyə-/ ▸ **adjective** hanging down; drooping.

pen·du·lum /ˈpenjələm, ˈpendyə-/ ▸ **noun** a weight hung from a fixed point so that it can swing freely, especially one regulating the mechanism of a clock.
– DERIVATIVES **pen·du·lar** /-lər/ adjective.
– ORIGIN Latin, 'thing hanging down.'

pe·ne·plain /ˈpēnəˌplān/ ▸ **noun** a level land surface produced by erosion over a long period.
– ORIGIN from Latin *paene* 'almost.'

pen·e·trate /ˈpeniˌtrāt/ ▸ **verb 1** go into or through something, especially with force or effort. **2** understand something complex. **3** gain access to an organization, place, or system, especially in an underhanded way: *our network had been penetrated by foreign agents.* **4** (of a company) begin to sell its products in a new market or area. **5** (of a man) insert the penis into the vagina or anus of a sexual partner.

– SYNONYMS **1 pierce,** puncture, enter, perforate, stab, gore. **2 permeate,** pervade, fill, imbue, suffuse, seep through, saturate. **3 register,** sink in, become clear, fall into place; informal click.

– DERIVATIVES **pen·e·tra·ble** /ˈpenitrəbəl/ adjective **pen·e·tra·tive** /ˈpeniˌtrātiv/ adjective **pen·e·tra·tor** noun.
– ORIGIN Latin *penetrare* 'go into.'

pen·e·trat·ing /ˈpeniˌtrātiNG/ ▶ **adjective** **1** able to make a way through or into something. **2** (of a sound) clearly heard through or above other sounds. **3** (of a person's eyes or expression) piercingly intense. **4** having or showing clear insight.

– SYNONYMS **1** *a penetrating wind* **cold,** cutting, biting, keen, sharp, harsh, raw, freezing, chill, bitter. **2** *a penetrating voice* **shrill,** strident, piercing, ear-splitting. **3** *her penetrating gaze* **intent,** searching, piercing, probing, sharp, keen. **4** *a penetrating analysis* **perceptive,** insightful, keen, sharp, intelligent, clever, smart, incisive, trenchant, astute.
– ANTONYMS mild, soft.

pen·e·tra·tion /ˌpeniˈtrāSHən/ ▶ **noun** **1** the action of penetrating. **2** the extent to which a product is recognized and bought by customers in a particular market: *the company achieved remarkable market penetration.* **3** understanding of complex matters.

pen·guin /ˈpeNGgwin, ˈpengwin/ ▶ **noun** a flightless black and white seabird of the southern hemisphere, with wings used as flippers.
– ORIGIN unknown.

pen·i·cil·lin /ˌpenəˈsilən/ ▶ **noun** an antibiotic produced naturally by certain blue molds and now usually made synthetically.
– ORIGIN from Latin *penicillum* 'paintbrush' (from the shape of the fruiting bodies on the mold).

pen·in·su·la /pəˈninsələ/ ▶ **noun** a long, narrow piece of land projecting out into a sea or lake.
– DERIVATIVES **pen·in·su·lar** adjective.
– ORIGIN Latin.

pe·nis /ˈpēnis/ ▶ **noun** (pl. **penises** or **penes** /-nēz/) the male organ that is used for sexual intercourse and urinating.
– DERIVATIVES **pe·nile** /ˈpēnəl, -nīl/ adjective.
– ORIGIN Latin, 'tail.'

pen·i·tent /ˈpenitnt/ ▶ **adjective** feeling sorrow and regret for having done wrong. ▶ **noun** a person who repents their sins or does a religious duty required by a priest.
– DERIVATIVES **pen·i·tence** noun **pen·i·ten·tial** /ˌpenəˈtenSHəl/ adjective **pen·i·tent·ly** adverb.
– ORIGIN from Latin *paenitere* 'repent.'

WORD TOOLKIT

See **APOLOGETIC**.

pen·i·ten·tia·ry /ˌpenəˈtenSHərē/ ▶ **noun** (pl. **penitentiaries**) a prison for people convicted of serious crimes.

pen·knife /ˈpenˌnīf/ ▶ **noun** (pl. **penknives**) a small knife with a blade that folds into the handle.

pen·light /ˈpenˌlīt/ ▶ **noun** a small flashlight shaped like a pen.

pen·man /ˈpenˌmən/ ▶ **noun** (pl. **penmen**) **1** a person with a specified ability in handwriting. **2** historical a person employed to write or copy documents; a clerk.

pen·man·ship /ˈpenmənˌSHip/ ▶ **noun** **1** the art or skill of writing by hand. **2** a person's handwriting.

pen name ▶ **noun** a name used by a writer instead of their real name.

pen·nant /ˈpenənt/ ▶ **noun** **1** a long, narrow pointed flag, especially one flown by a ship and used for signaling. **2** a flag identifying a sports team, club, etc.
– ORIGIN blend of **PENDANT** and **PENNON**.

pen·ne /ˈpenā/ ▶ **plural noun** pasta in the form of short wide tubes.
– ORIGIN Italian, 'quills.'

pen·ni·less /ˈpenēlis/ ▶ **adjective** having no money; very poor.

pen·non /ˈpenən/ ▶ **noun** less common term for **PENNANT**.
– ORIGIN Old French.

Penn·syl·va·nia Dutch (also **Pennsylvania German**) ▶ **noun** a dialect of High German spoken in parts of Pennsylvania.
– ORIGIN German *Deutsch* 'German.'

Penn·syl·va·nian /ˌpensəlˈvānyən, -ˈvānēən/ ▶ **adjective** **1** relating to the state of Pennsylvania. **2** Geology relating to or denoting the later part of the Carboniferous period in North America. ▶ **noun** a native or inhabitant of Pennsylvania.

pen·ny /ˈpenē/ ▶ **noun** (pl. **pennies** (for separate coins); **pence** /pens/ (for a sum of money)) **1** a one-cent coin. **2** a British bronze coin worth one hundredth of a pound. **3** a former British coin worth one twelfth of a shilling and 240th of a pound.
– PHRASES **in for a penny, in for a pound** used to say that since one has started something one may as well spend as much time or money as is necessary to complete it. **not a penny** no money at all. **penny wise and pound foolish** economical in small matters but extravagant in large ones.
– ORIGIN Old English.

pen·ny-far·thing ▶ **noun** chiefly Brit. an early type of bicycle with a very large front wheel and a small rear wheel.

pen·ny-pinch·ing ▶ **adjective** unwilling to spend money; stingy. ▶ **noun** unwillingness to spend money; stinginess.
– DERIVATIVES **pen·ny-pinch·er** noun.

pen·ny·roy·al /ˈpenēˌroiəl/ ▶ **noun** a small-leaved plant of the mint family, used in herbal medicine.
– ORIGIN from Old French *puliol real* 'royal thyme.'

pen·ny stock ▶ **noun** Stock Exchange a common stock valued at less than one dollar.

pen·ny·wort /ˈpenēwərt, -ˌwôrt/ ▶ **noun** a plant with small rounded leaves, growing in crevices or marshy places.

pe·nol·o·gy /pēˈnäləjē/ ▶ **noun** the study of the punishment of crime and of prison management.
– DERIVATIVES **pe·no·log·i·cal** /ˌpēnəˈläjikəl/ adjective **pe·nol·o·gist** noun.
– ORIGIN from Latin *poena* 'penalty.'

pen pal ▶ **noun** a person with whom one becomes friendly by exchanging letters.

pen·sée /ˌpänˈsā/ ▶ **noun** a thought written down in a concise or witty form.
– ORIGIN French.

pen·sion[1] /ˈpenSHən/ ▶ **noun** **1** a regular payment made to retired people and to some widows and disabled people, either by the government or from an investment fund. **2** historical a regular payment made to a favorite of a monarch or to an artist or scholar.

– SYNONYMS **retirement (benefits),** superannuation, Social Security, allowance, benefit, support, welfare.

▶ **verb** (**pension someone off**) dismiss someone from employment and pay them a pension.
– DERIVATIVES **pen·sion·a·ble** adjective **pen·sion·er** noun.
– ORIGIN Latin, 'payment.'

pen·sion² /pänsē'ōn/ ▶ **noun** a small hotel or guest house in France and other European countries.
– ORIGIN French.

pen·si·o·ne /pänsē'ōnā/ ▶ **noun** (pl. **pensioni** /-'ōnē/) a small hotel or guest house in Italy.
– ORIGIN Italian.

pen·sive /'pensiv/ ▶ **adjective** engaged in deep or serious thought.

– SYNONYMS **thoughtful,** reflective, contemplative, meditative, introspective, ruminative, absorbed, preoccupied, deep/lost in thought, brooding.

– DERIVATIVES **pen·sive·ly** adverb **pen·sive·ness** noun.
– ORIGIN Old French *pensif*.

WORD TOOLKIT

See **WISTFUL**.

pen·ste·mon /pen'stēmən, 'penstəmən/ ▶ **noun** a North American plant with snapdragonlike flowers.
– ORIGIN Latin.

pent /pent/ ▶ **adjective** chiefly literary another term for **PENT-UP**.

penta- ▶ **combining form** five; having five: *pentagon*.
– ORIGIN Greek *pente* 'five.'

pen·ta·cle /'pentəkəl/ ▶ **noun** a pentagram.
– ORIGIN Latin *pentaculum*.

pen·tad /'pen,tad/ ▶ **noun** a group or set of five.

pen·ta·gon /'pentə,gän/ ▶ **noun 1** a plane figure with five straight sides and five angles. **2** (**the Pentagon**) the headquarters of the US Department of Defense, near Washington DC.
– DERIVATIVES **pen·tag·o·nal** /pen'tagənəl/ adjective.

pen·ta·gram /'pentə,gram/ ▶ **noun** a five-pointed star drawn using a continuous line, often used as a mystic and magical symbol.

pen·tam·e·ter /pen'tamitər/ ▶ **noun** a line of verse consisting of five metrical feet.

pen·tan·gle /'pen,taNGgəl/ ▶ **noun** a pentagram.
– ORIGIN perhaps from Latin *pentaculum* 'pentacle.'

pen·ta·prism /'pentə,prizəm/ ▶ **noun** a five-sided prism that deviates light from any direction, used chiefly in camera viewfinders.

Pen·ta·teuch /'pentə,t(y)o͞ok/ ▶ **noun** the first five books of the Old Testament and Hebrew Scriptures (Genesis, Exodus, Leviticus, Numbers, and Deuteronomy).
– ORIGIN Greek.

pen·tath·lon /pen'taTH(ə),län/ ▶ **noun** an athletic contest consisting of five different events for each competitor, in particular (**modern pentathlon**) a contest involving fencing, shooting, swimming, riding, and cross-country running.
– DERIVATIVES **pen·tath·lete** /pen'taTHlēt/ noun.
– ORIGIN Greek.

pen·ta·ton·ic /,pentə'tänik/ ▶ **adjective** relating to or consisting of a musical scale of five notes.

Pen·te·cost /'pentə,kôst, -,käst/ ▶ **noun 1** the Christian festival celebrating the coming of the Holy Spirit to the disciples of Jesus after his Ascension. **2** the Jewish festival of Shavuoth, held on the fiftieth day after the second day of Passover.
– ORIGIN from Greek *pentēkostē hēmera* 'fiftieth day.'

Pen·te·cos·tal /,pentə'kôstl, -'kästl/ ▶ **adjective 1** relating to a Christian movement that emphasizes the gifts of the Holy Spirit, such as 'speaking in tongues' and healing of the sick. **2** relating to the Christian festival of Pentecost.
– DERIVATIVES **Pen·te·cos·tal·ism** /-,izəm/ noun **Pen·te·cos·tal·ist** adjective & noun.

pent·house /'pent,hous/ ▶ **noun** an apartment on the top floor of a tall building.
– ORIGIN Old French *apentis* 'outhouse,' changed by association with *house*.

Pen·to·thal /'pentə,THôl, -,THäl/ ▶ **noun** trademark an anesthetic and sedative drug.

pent-up ▶ **adjective** not expressed or released: *pent-up anger*.
– ORIGIN former past participle of **PEN²**.

pe·nul·ti·mate /pe'nəltəmit/ ▶ **adjective** last but one in a series; second to the last.
– ORIGIN from Latin *paene* 'almost' + *ultimus* 'last.'

pe·num·bra /pe'nəmbrə/ ▶ **noun** (pl. **penumbrae** /-brē, -brī/ or **penumbras**) the partially shaded outer region of the shadow cast by an object.
– DERIVATIVES **pe·num·bral** /-brəl/ adjective.
– ORIGIN from Latin *paene* 'almost' + *umbra* 'shadow.'

pe·nu·ri·ous /pə'n(y)o͝orēəs/ ▶ **adjective** formal **1** having no money; very poor. **2** unwilling to spend money; stingy.
– DERIVATIVES **pe·nu·ri·ous·ly** adverb.

pen·u·ry /'penyərē/ ▶ **noun** the state of having no money; great poverty.
– ORIGIN Latin *penuria*.

pe·on /'pē,än, 'pēən/ ▶ **noun** an unskilled Spanish-American farm worker.
– ORIGIN from Portuguese *pea-o* and Spanish *peón*.

pe·o·ny /'pēənē/ ▶ **noun** a plant grown for its large white, pink, or red flowers.
– ORIGIN Greek *Paiōn*, the physician of the gods.

peo·ple /'pēpəl/ ▶ **plural noun 1** human beings in general or as a whole. **2** (**the people**) the ordinary citizens of a country. **3** (pl. **peoples**) (treated as sing. or pl.) the members of a particular nation, community, or ethnic group. **4** (**one's people**) one's employees or supporters. **5** (**one's people**) dated one's relatives.

– SYNONYMS **1 human beings,** persons, individuals, humans, mortals, living souls, personages, [men, women, and children]; informal folk. **2 citizens,** subjects, electors, voters, taxpayers, residents, inhabitants, public, citizenry, nation, population, populace. **3 the common people,** the proletariat, the masses, the populace, the rank and file; derogatory the hoi polloi, the great unwashed; informal, derogatory the proles, the plebs. **4 race,** ethnic group, tribe, clan, nation. **5 family,** parents, relatives, relations, folk, kinfolk, kinsfolk, flesh and blood, nearest and dearest; informal folks.

▶ **verb** inhabit a place: *a mountain region peopled by warring clans*.

– SYNONYMS **populate,** settle (in), colonize, inhabit, live in, occupy.

– ORIGIN Latin *populus* 'populace.'

WORD LINKS

ethnic *relating to a people*
anthropology *study of people*

pep /pep/ informal ▶ **verb** (**peps, pepping, pepped**) (**pep someone/thing up**) make someone or something more

lively or interesting. ▶ **noun** liveliness or energy.
– DERIVATIVES **pep·py** adjective.
– ORIGIN abbreviation of **PEPPER**.

pep·lum /'pepləm/ ▶ **noun** a short flared strip of fabric attached at the waist of a woman's jacket, dress, or blouse.
– ORIGIN Greek *peplos* 'woman's outer tunic or shawl.'

pep·per /'pepər/ ▶ **noun 1** a hot-tasting powder made from peppercorns, used to flavor food. **2** the fruit of a tropical American plant, of which sweet peppers and chili peppers are varieties. ▶ **verb 1** season food with pepper. **2** cover or fill with a large amount of scattered items: *the script is peppered with four-letter words.* **3** hit someone or something repeatedly with small missiles or gunshot.

– SYNONYMS **1 sprinkle,** fleck, dot, spot, stipple. **2 bombard,** pelt, shower, rain down on, strafe, rake, blitz.

– DERIVATIVES **pep·per·y** adjective.
– ORIGIN Greek *peperi.*

pep·per·corn /'pepər,kôrn/ ▶ **noun** the dried berry of a climbing vine, used whole as a spice or crushed or ground to make pepper.

pep·per·mint /'pepər,mint/ ▶ **noun 1** a plant of the mint family that produces aromatic leaves and oil, used as a flavoring in food. **2** a candy flavored with peppermint oil.

pep·per·o·ni /,pepə'rōnē/ ▶ **noun** beef and pork sausage seasoned with pepper.
– ORIGIN Italian *peperone* 'chilli.'

pep·per spray ▶ **noun** an aerosol spray containing oils obtained from cayenne pepper that irritate the eyes, used to disable an attacker.

pep pill ▶ **noun** informal a pill containing a stimulant drug.

pep·sin /'pepsin/ ▶ **noun** the chief digestive enzyme in the stomach, which breaks down proteins.
– ORIGIN from Greek *pepsis* 'digestion.'

pep talk ▶ **noun** informal a talk intended to make someone feel braver or more enthusiastic.

pep·tic /'peptik/ ▶ **adjective** relating to digestion.
– ORIGIN Greek *peptikos* 'able to digest.'

pep·tic ul·cer ▶ **noun** an ulcer in the lining of the stomach or small intestine.

pep·tide /'peptīd/ ▶ **noun** a chemical compound consisting of two or more linked amino acids.
– ORIGIN German *Peptid.*

per /pər/ ▶ **preposition 1** for each. **2** by means of.
– PHRASES **as per** in accordance with. **as per usual** as usual.
– ORIGIN Latin, 'through, by means of.'

per- ▶ **prefix 1** through; all over: *pervade.* **2** completely; very: *perfect.* **3** Chemistry having the maximum proportion of a particular element in combination: *peroxide.*

per. ▶ **abbreviation 1** percentile. **2** period. **3** person.

per·ad·ven·ture /,pərəd'vencHər, ,per-/ ▶ **adverb** old use perhaps. ▶ **noun** uncertainty or doubt.
– ORIGIN from Old French *per* (or *par*) *auenture* 'by chance.'

per·am·bu·late /pə'rambyə,lāt/ ▶ **verb** formal, chiefly Brit. walk or travel from place to place.
– DERIVATIVES **per·am·bu·la·tion** /pə,rambyə'lāsHən/ noun **per·am·bu·la·to·ry** /-lə,tôrē/ adjective.
– ORIGIN Latin *perambulare* 'walk about.'

per·am·bu·la·tor /pə'rambyə,lātər/ ▶ **noun** dated a baby carriage.

per an·num /pər 'anəm/ ▶ **adverb** for each year.
– ORIGIN Latin.

per·cale /pər'kāl, -'kal/ ▶ **noun** a closely woven fine cotton fabric.
– ORIGIN French.

per cap·i·ta /pər 'kapitə/ ▶ **adverb & adjective** for each person.
– ORIGIN Latin, 'by heads.'

per·ceive /pər'sēv/ ▶ **verb 1** become aware of something through the senses. **2** come to realize: *her mouth fell open as she perceived the truth.* **3** regard in a particular way: *the couple were perceived as arrogant.*

– SYNONYMS **1 see,** discern, detect, catch sight of, spot, observe, notice; literary espy. **2 regard,** look on, view, consider, think of, judge, deem.

– DERIVATIVES **per·ceiv·a·ble** adjective **per·ceiv·er** noun.
– ORIGIN Latin *percipere* 'seize, understand.'

per·cent /pər'sent/ ▶ **adverb** by a specified amount in or for every hundred. ▶ **noun** one part in every hundred.

per·cent·age /pər'sentij/ ▶ **noun 1** a rate, number, or amount in each hundred. **2** any proportion or share in relation to a whole: *camera phones are making up a huge percentage of all cell phone sales.* **3** a share in the profits of something, granted as a commission.

per·cen·tile /pər'sen,tīl/ ▶ **noun** Statistics each of 100 equal groups into which a large group of people can be divided, according to their place on a scale measuring a particular value.

per·cept /'pərsept/ ▶ **noun** Philosophy an object of perception; something that is perceived.
– ORIGIN Latin *perceptum* 'something perceived.'

per·cep·ti·ble /pər'septəbəl/ ▶ **adjective** able to be seen or noticed: *a perceptible decline in public confidence.*
– DERIVATIVES **per·cep·ti·bly** /-blē/ adverb.

WORD TOOLKIT

perceptible ...	palpable ...	appreciable ...
shift	tension	difference
nod	fear	effect
form	presence	increase
risk	relief	number
bias	excitement	extent
rise	desire	degree
noise	anger	benefit
movement	sensation	quantity

per·cep·tion /pər'sepsHən/ ▶ **noun 1** the ability to see, hear, or become aware of something through the senses. **2** the process of perceiving something. **3** a way of understanding or interpreting something: *the public perception of him seems distorted.* **4** intuitive understanding; insight.

– SYNONYMS **1 impression,** idea, conception, notion, thought, belief. **2 insight,** perceptiveness, understanding, intelligence, intuition, incisiveness.

– ORIGIN Latin.

per·cep·tive /pər'septiv/ ▶ **adjective** having or showing sensitive insight.

– SYNONYMS **insightful,** discerning, sensitive, intuitive, observant, penetrating, intelligent, clever,

canny, keen, sharp, astute, shrewd, quick, smart, acute; informal on the ball.
– ANTONYMS obtuse.

– DERIVATIVES **per·cep·tive·ly** adverb **per·cep·tive·ness** noun.

per·cep·tu·al /pər'sepCHōōəl/ ▶ **adjective** relating to the ability to perceive things through the senses.
– DERIVATIVES **per·cep·tu·al·ly** adverb.

perch[1] /pərCH/ ▶ **noun 1** an object on which a bird rests or roosts. **2** a high or narrow seat or resting place.
▶ **verb 1** sit, rest, or place somewhere. **2** (**be perched**) (of a building) be situated above or on the edge of something.

– SYNONYMS **1** *three swallows perched on the telegraph wire* **sit,** rest, alight, settle, land, roost. **2** *she perched her glasses on her nose* **put,** place, set, rest, balance. **3** *the church **is perched** on a hill* **be located,** be situated, be positioned, be sited, stand.

– DERIVATIVES **perch·er** noun.
– ORIGIN from Latin *pertica* 'measuring rod, pole.'

perch[2] ▶ **noun** (pl. same or **perches**) a freshwater fish with a spiny fin on its back and dark vertical bars on the body.
– ORIGIN Greek *perkē*.

per·chance /pər'CHans/ ▶ **adverb** old use or literary by some chance; perhaps.
– ORIGIN from Old French *par cheance* 'by chance.'

per·che·ron /'pərSHə,rän, 'pərCHə-/ ▶ **noun** a powerful breed of gray or black horse, used for pulling loads.
– ORIGIN French (the animal was originally bred in le *Perche* in northern France).

per·cip·i·ent /pər'sipēənt/ ▶ **adjective** having a sensitive understanding; perceptive.
– DERIVATIVES **per·cip·i·ence** noun **per·cip·i·ent·ly** adverb.

per·co·late /'pərkə,lāt/ ▶ **verb 1** (of a liquid or gas) filter through a porous surface or substance. **2** (of information or ideas) spread gradually through a group of people: *this attitude is starting to percolate down to the masses.* **3** prepare coffee in a percolator.
– DERIVATIVES **per·co·la·tion** /,pərkə'lāSHən/ noun.
– ORIGIN Latin *percolare* 'strain through.'

per·co·la·tor /'pərkə,lātər/ ▶ **noun** a machine for making coffee, consisting of a pot in which boiling water is circulated through a small chamber that holds the ground beans.

per·cuss /pər'kəs/ ▶ **verb** gently tap a part of the body as part of a medical diagnosis.

per·cus·sion /pər'kəSHən/ ▶ **noun 1** musical instruments that are played by being struck or shaken, such as drums or cymbals. **2** the striking of one solid object with or against another.
– DERIVATIVES **per·cus·sion·ist** /-ist/ noun **per·cus·sive** /-'kəsiv/ adjective.
– ORIGIN Latin.

per·cus·sion cap ▶ **noun** full form of **CAP**[1] (sense 6 of the noun).

per di·em /pər 'dēəm/ ▶ **adverb & adjective** for each day.
– ORIGIN Latin.

per·di·tion /pər'disHən/ ▶ **noun 1** (in Christian belief) a state of eternal damnation into which a sinful person who has not repented passes after death. **2** complete and utter ruin: *the spending plan dooms the state to fiscal perdition.*
– ORIGIN Latin.

per·dur·a·ble /pər'd(y)ŏŏrəbəl/ ▶ **adjective** literary enduring continuously; permanent.

père /pe(ə)r/ ▶ **noun** used after a French surname to distinguish a father from a son of the same name.
– ORIGIN French, 'father.'

per·e·gri·na·tion /,perigrə'nāsHən/ ▶ **noun** literary a long or rambling journey: *a secret diary of their boozy peregrinations.*
– DERIVATIVES **per·e·gri·nate** /'perigrə,nāt/ verb (old use).
– ORIGIN from Latin *peregrinari* 'travel abroad.'

per·e·grine /'perəgrin/ ▶ **noun** a powerful falcon with a bluish-gray back and wings and pale underparts.
– ORIGIN Latin, 'pilgrim falcon.'

per·emp·to·ry /pə'remptərē/ ▶ **adjective 1** insisting on immediate attention or obedience, especially in an abrupt way: *she had come to dread his peremptory orders.* **2** Law not open to appeal or challenge; final.
– DERIVATIVES **per·emp·to·ri·ly** adverb.
– ORIGIN Latin *peremptorius* 'deadly, decisive.'

per·en·ni·al /pə'renēəl/ ▶ **adjective 1** lasting or doing something for a long time or forever: *his perennial distrust of the media.* **2** (of a plant) living for several years.

– SYNONYMS **lasting,** enduring, abiding, long-lasting, long-lived, perpetual, continuing, continual, recurring.
– ANTONYMS ephemeral.

▶ **noun** a plant that lives for several years.
– DERIVATIVES **per·en·ni·al·ly** adverb.
– ORIGIN from Latin *perennis* 'lasting the year through.'

pe·re·stroi·ka /,perə'stroikə/ ▶ **noun** the economic and political reforms established in the former Soviet Union during the 1980s.
– ORIGIN Russian, 'restructuring.'

per·fect ▶ **adjective** /'pərfikt/ **1** having all the required elements or qualities: *she strove to be the perfect wife.* **2** free from any flaws or defects. **3** complete; absolute: *they were perfect strangers to him.* **4** Grammar (of a tense) describing a completed action or a state in the past, formed in English with *have* or *has* and the past participle, as in *they have eaten.* **5** Mathematics (of a number) equal to the sum of its positive divisors, e.g., the number 6, whose divisors (1, 2, 3) also add up to 6.

– SYNONYMS **1 ideal,** model, faultless, flawless, consummate, exemplary, best, ultimate, textbook. **2 flawless,** mint, as good as new, pristine, immaculate, optimum, prime, peak; informal tip-top, A1. **3 exact,** precise, accurate, faithful, true, on the money, spot on. **4 absolute,** complete, total, real, out-and-out, thorough, downright, utter.

▶ **verb** /pər'fekt/ make something perfect or as good as possible: *she perfected her English by tuning in to American television.*

– SYNONYMS **improve,** polish (up), hone, refine, brush up, fine-tune.

– DERIVATIVES **per·fect·er** /pər'fektər/ noun **per·fect·i·ble** /pər'fektəbəl/ adjective.
– ORIGIN Latin *perfectus* 'completed.'

per·fec·tion /pər'feksHən/ ▶ **noun 1** the state of being excellent, complete, or flawless: *all the food was cooked to perfection.* **2** the action of making something perfect.

– SYNONYMS **the ideal,** a paragon, the last word, the ultimate; informal the tops, the bee's knees.

per·fec·tion·ist /pər'feksHə,nist/ ▶ **noun** a person who refuses to be satisfied with something unless it is perfect.
– DERIVATIVES **per·fec·tion·ism** noun.

per·fect·ly /'pərfik(t)lē/ ▶ **adverb 1** in a perfect way. **2** completely; absolutely (used for emphasis).

per·fect pitch ▶ **noun** the ability to recognize the pitch of a note or produce any given note.

per·fer·vid /pər'fərvid/ ▶ **adjective** literary intensely passionate or enthusiastic.
– ORIGIN from Latin *per-* 'utterly' + *fervidus* 'glowing hot, fiery.'

per·fid·i·ous /pər'fidēəs/ ▶ **adjective** literary deceitful and untrustworthy.
– DERIVATIVES **per·fid·i·ous·ly** adverb **per·fid·i·ous·ness** noun.

per·fi·dy /'pərfidē/ ▶ **noun** literary the state of being deceitful and untrustworthy.
– ORIGIN Latin *perfidia*.

per·fo·rate /'pərfə,rāt/ ▶ **verb** pierce and make a hole or holes in something.
– DERIVATIVES **per·fo·ra·tion** /,pərfə'rāsHən/ noun **per·fo·ra·tor** noun.
– ORIGIN Latin *perforare* 'pierce through.'

per·force /pər'fôrs/ ▶ **adverb** formal necessarily; inevitably.
– ORIGIN from Old French *par force* 'by force.'

per·form /pər'fôrm/ ▶ **verb 1** carry out or complete an action or function. **2** function or do something to a specified standard: *the car performs well at low speeds.* **3** present entertainment to an audience.

– SYNONYMS **1 carry out,** do, execute, discharge, conduct, implement; informal pull off. **2 function,** work, operate, run, go, respond, behave, act. **3 stage,** put on, present, mount, act, produce. **4 play,** sing, appear.

– DERIVATIVES **per·form·a·ble** adjective.
– ORIGIN Old French *parfournir*.

per·for·mance /pər'fôrməns/ ▶ **noun 1** the action of performing a task or function. **2** an act of performing a play, concert, song, etc. **3** the standard of functioning achieved by a machine or product. **4** informal an act that involves a great deal of time and effort, often when exaggerated or unnecessary: *she stayed behind, making a performance of wiping her shoes.*

– SYNONYMS **1 show,** production, showing, presentation, staging, concert, recital; informal gig. **2 rendition,** interpretation, playing, acting. **3 carrying out,** execution, discharge, completion, fulfillment. **4 functioning,** working, operation, running, behavior, response.

per·for·mance art ▶ **noun** an art form that combines visual art with dramatic performance.

per·form·er /pər'fôrmər/ ▶ **noun** a person who performs.

– SYNONYMS **actor, actress,** artiste, artist, entertainer, trouper, player, musician, singer, dancer, comic, comedian, comedienne.

per·form·ing arts ▶ **plural noun** forms of creative activity that are performed in front of an audience, such as drama, music, and dance.

per·fume /'pər,fyo͞om, ,pər'fyo͞om/ ▶ **noun 1** a fragrant liquid used to give a pleasant smell to one's body. **2** a pleasant smell.

– SYNONYMS **1 scent,** fragrance, eau de toilette, toilet water, cologne, eau de cologne. **2 smell,** scent, fragrance, aroma, bouquet, nose.

▶ **verb 1** give a pleasant smell to something. **2** put perfume or a sweet-smelling ingredient on or into something.
– DERIVATIVES **per·fumed** adjective.
– ORIGIN French *parfum*.

per·fum·er·y /pər'fyo͞omərē/ ▶ **noun** (pl. **perfumeries**) **1** the process of producing and selling perfumes. **2** a store that sells perfumes.
– DERIVATIVES **per·fum·er** noun.

per·func·to·ry /pər'fəNGktərē/ ▶ **adjective** carried out with very little effort or interest: *they exchanged a perfunctory handshake.*
– DERIVATIVES **per·func·to·ri·ly** /-'fəNGktərəlē/ adverb.
– ORIGIN Latin *perfunctorius* 'careless.'

per·fuse /pər'fyo͞oz/ ▶ **verb** literary spread a liquid, color, quality, etc., throughout something; permeate.
– DERIVATIVES **per·fu·sion** /-zHən/ noun.
– ORIGIN Latin *perfundere* 'pour through.'

per·go·la /'pərgələ/ ▶ **noun** an arched structure forming a framework for climbing plants.
– ORIGIN Latin *pergula* 'projecting roof.'

per·haps /pər'(h)aps/ ▶ **adverb 1** expressing uncertainty or possibility. **2** used when making a polite request or suggestion.

– SYNONYMS **maybe,** for all you know, it could be, it may be, it's possible, possibly, conceivably.

– ORIGIN from **PER** + former *hap* 'luck.'

peri- ▶ **prefix** around; about: *perimeter.*
– ORIGIN Greek *peri* 'about, around.'

per·i·anth /'perē,anTH/ ▶ **noun** the outer part of a flower, consisting of the calyx (sepals) and corolla (petals).
– ORIGIN from Greek *peri* 'around' + *anthos* 'flower.'

per·i·car·di·um /,peri'kärdēəm/ ▶ **noun** (pl. **pericardia** /-'kärdēə/) the membrane enclosing the heart.
– DERIVATIVES **per·i·car·di·al** /-'kärdēəl/ adjective.
– ORIGIN Latin.

per·i·carp /'peri,kärp/ ▶ **noun** the part of a fruit formed from the wall of the ripened ovary.
– ORIGIN from Greek *peri-* 'around' + *karpos* 'fruit.'

per·i·dot /'peri,dät/ ▶ **noun** a green semiprecious stone.
– ORIGIN French.

per·i·do·tite /'peridə,tīt, pə'ridə,tīt/ ▶ **noun** a dense rock that is rich in magnesium and iron, thought to be the main constituent of the earth's mantle.

per·i·gee /'perə,jē/ ▶ **noun** the point in the orbit of the moon or a satellite at which it is nearest to the earth. The opposite of **APOGEE**.
– ORIGIN from Greek *peri-* 'around' + *gē* 'earth.'

per·i·he·li·on /,perə'hēlyən, -'hēlēən/ ▶ **noun** (pl. **perihelia** /-'hēlyə, -'hēlēə/) the point in the orbit of a planet, asteroid, or comet at which it is closest to the sun. The opposite of **APHELION**.
– ORIGIN from Greek *peri-* 'around' + *hēlios* 'sun.'

per·il /'perəl/ ▶ **noun 1** a situation of serious and immediate danger. **2** the risks or difficulties of a situation or activity.

– SYNONYMS **danger,** jeopardy, risk, hazard, menace, threat.
– ANTONYMS safety.

– PHRASES **at one's peril** at one's own risk. **in peril of** very likely to suffer from; at risk of.
– ORIGIN Latin *periculum* 'danger.'

per·il·ous /'perələs/ ▶ adjective full of danger or risk.
– DERIVATIVES **per·il·ous·ly** adverb **per·il·ous·ness** noun.

pe·rim·e·ter /pə'rimitər/ ▶ noun **1** the outermost parts or boundary of an area or object: *I drove around the perimeter of the parking lot.* **2** the continuous line forming the boundary of a closed geometrical figure.

– SYNONYMS **boundary,** border, limits, bounds, edge, margin, fringe(s), periphery.
– ANTONYMS center.

– ORIGIN from Greek *peri-* 'around' + *metron* 'measure.'

per·i·na·tal /ˌperə'nātl/ ▶ adjective relating to the time immediately before and after a birth.
– DERIVATIVES **per·i·na·tal·ly** adverb.

per·i·ne·um /ˌperə'nēəm/ ▶ noun (pl. **perinea** /ˌperə'nēə/) the area between the anus and the scrotum or vulva.
– DERIVATIVES **per·i·ne·al** /-'nēəl/ adjective.
– ORIGIN Greek *perinaion.*

pe·ri·od /'pi(ə)rēəd/ ▶ noun **1** a length or portion of time. **2** a portion of time with particular characteristics: *the early medieval period.* **3** a major division of geological time, forming part of an era. **4** a punctuation mark (.) used at the end of a sentence or an abbreviation. **5** a lesson in a school. **6** (also **menstrual period**) a monthly flow of blood and other material from the lining of the uterus, occurring in women between puberty and the menopause who are not pregnant. **7** Physics the interval of time between recurrences of a phenomenon.

– SYNONYMS **1 time,** spell, interval, stretch, term, span, phase, bout; informal patch. **2 era,** age, epoch, eon, time, days, years.

▶ adjective belonging to or typical of a past historical time: *period furniture.*
– ORIGIN Greek *periodos* 'orbit, recurrence, course.'

pe·ri·od·ic /ˌpi(ə)rē'ädik/ ▶ adjective appearing or occurring at intervals.

– SYNONYMS **regular,** at fixed intervals, recurrent, recurring, repeated, cyclical, seasonal, occasional, intermittent, sporadic, odd.

– DERIVATIVES **pe·ri·o·dic·i·ty** /ˌpi(ə)rēə'disitē/ noun.

pe·ri·od·i·cal /ˌpi(ə)rē'ädikəl/ ▶ adjective occurring or appearing at intervals. ▶ noun a magazine or newspaper published at regular intervals.

– SYNONYMS **journal,** magazine, newspaper, paper, review, newsletter, digest, gazette, organ; informal mag.

– DERIVATIVES **pe·ri·od·i·cal·ly** adverb.

pe·ri·od·i·cal ci·ca·da ▶ noun an American cicada whose nymphs emerge from the soil every seventeen years in the north (**seventeen-year locust**) or every thirteen years in the south.

pe·ri·od·ic ta·ble ▶ noun a table of the chemical elements arranged in order of atomic number, usually in rows, with elements having similar atomic structure appearing in vertical columns.

per·i·o·don·tics /ˌperēə'däntiks/ ▶ plural noun (treated as sing.) the branch of dentistry concerned with the structures surrounding and supporting the teeth.
– DERIVATIVES **per·i·o·don·tal** /-'däntl/ adjective.
– ORIGIN from **PERI-** + Greek *odous, odont-* 'tooth' + *ics.*

pe·ri·od piece ▶ noun an object or work that is set in or typical of an earlier historical period.

per·i·pa·tet·ic /ˌperipə'tetik/ ▶ adjective **1** traveling from place to place. **2** Brit. (of a teacher) working in more than one school or college.
– DERIVATIVES **per·i·pa·tet·i·cal·ly** adverb.
– ORIGIN Greek *peripatētikos* 'walking up and down.'

pe·riph·er·al /pə'rifərəl/ ▶ adjective **1** relating to or situated on the outer limits of something. **2** of secondary importance: *she saw their problems as peripheral to her own.* **3** (of a device) able to be attached to and used with a computer.

– SYNONYMS **secondary,** subsidiary, incidental, tangential, marginal, minor, unimportant, ancillary.
– ANTONYMS central.

▶ noun a device that is able to be attached to and used with a computer.
– DERIVATIVES **pe·riph·er·al·i·ty** /-ˌrifə'ralitē/ noun **pe·riph·er·al·ly** adverb.

pe·riph·er·al nerv·ous sys·tem ▶ noun the nervous system outside the brain and spinal cord.

pe·riph·er·al vi·sion ▶ noun side vision; what is seen on the side by the eye when looking straight ahead.

pe·riph·er·y /pə'rifərē/ ▶ noun (pl. **peripheries**) **1** the outer limits or edge of an area or object. **2** a part of a subject, group, or area of activity that is of secondary importance: *she's content to stay on the periphery of music.*
– ORIGIN Greek *periphereia* 'circumference.'

pe·riph·ra·sis /pə'rifrəsis/ ▶ noun (pl. **periphrases** /-ˌsēz/) the use of indirect and roundabout language.
– DERIVATIVES **per·i·phras·tic** /ˌperə'frastik/ adjective.
– ORIGIN from Greek *peri-* 'around' + *phrazein* 'declare.'

per·i·scope /'perəˌskōp/ ▶ noun a tube attached to a set of mirrors or prisms, by which an observer in a submerged submarine or behind an obstacle can see things that are otherwise out of sight.

per·ish /'perisʜ/ ▶ verb **1** literary die, especially in a violent or sudden way. **2** literary be completely ruined or destroyed. **3** chiefly Brit. (of rubber, food, etc.) rot or decay.

– SYNONYMS **1 die,** lose one's life, be killed, fall, be lost; informal buy it. **2 go bad,** spoil, rot, decay, decompose.

– PHRASES **perish the thought** informal used to say that a suggestion or idea is ridiculous or unwelcome.
– ORIGIN Latin *perire* 'pass away.'

per·ish·a·ble /'perisʜəbəl/ ▶ adjective (of food) likely to rot quickly. ▶ noun (**perishables**) perishable foods.

per·i·stal·sis /ˌperə'stôlsis, -'stal-/ ▶ noun the contraction and relaxation of the muscles of the intestines, creating movements that push the contents of the intestines forward.
– DERIVATIVES **per·i·stal·tic** /-'stôltik/ adjective.
– ORIGIN from Greek *peristallein* 'wrap around.'

per·i·style /'perəˌstīl/ ▶ noun a row of columns surrounding a courtyard or internal garden or edging a veranda or porch.
– ORIGIN from Greek *peri-* 'around' + *stulos* 'pillar.'

per·i·to·ne·um /ˌperitn'ēəm/ ▶ noun (pl. **peritoneums** or **peritonea** /-'nēə/) the membrane lining the cavity of the abdomen and covering the abdominal organs.
– DERIVATIVES **per·i·to·ne·al** /-'ēəl/ adjective.
– ORIGIN Latin.

per·i·to·ni·tis /ˌperitnˈītis/ ▶ **noun** inflammation of the peritoneum.

per·i·wig /ˈperiˌwig/ ▶ **noun** a wig of a kind worn in the 17th and 18th centuries.
– ORIGIN from **PERUKE**.

per·i·win·kle[1] /ˈperiˌwiNGkəl/ ▶ **noun** a plant with flat five-petaled flowers and glossy leaves.
– ORIGIN Latin *pervinca*.

per·i·win·kle[2] ▶ **noun** another term for **WINKLE**.
– ORIGIN unknown.

per·jure /ˈpərjər/ ▶ **verb 1** (**perjure oneself**) deliberately tell a lie in a court of law after one has sworn to tell the truth. **2** (as adj. **perjured**) (of evidence) involving deliberate untruth.
– DERIVATIVES **per·jur·er** noun.
– ORIGIN Latin *perjurare* 'swear falsely.'

per·ju·ry /ˈpərjərē/ ▶ **noun** the offense of deliberately telling a lie in a court of law when having sworn to be truthful.

perk[1] /pərk/ ▶ **verb** (**perk up** or **perk someone/thing up**) become or make more cheerful or lively.
– ORIGIN perhaps from Old French *percher* 'to perch.'

perk[2] ▶ **noun** informal a benefit, especially one that a person receives from their job.

– SYNONYMS **fringe benefit,** advantage, bonus, extra, plus; informal freebie.

– ORIGIN abbreviation of **PERQUISITE**.

perk[3] ▶ **verb** informal (of coffee) percolate.

perk·y /ˈpərkē/ ▶ **adjective** (**perkier**, **perkiest**) cheerful and lively.

– SYNONYMS **cheerful,** lively, vivacious, bubbly, effervescent, bouncy, spirited, cheery, merry, buoyant, exuberant, jaunty, frisky, sprightly, spry, bright, sunny, jolly; informal full of beans, bright-eyed and bushy-tailed, chirpy, chipper, peppy.

– DERIVATIVES **perk·i·ly** adverb **perk·i·ness** noun.

per·lite /ˈpərlīt/ ▶ **noun** a form of obsidian (volcanic rock) consisting of glassy globules, used as insulation or in a mixture with plant compost.
– ORIGIN French.

perm /pərm/ ▶ **noun** (also **permanent wave**) a method of setting the hair in curls and treating it with chemicals so that the style lasts for several months. ▶ **verb** set the hair in a perm.

per·ma·cul·ture /ˈpərməˌkəlCHər/ ▶ **noun** the development of agricultural ecosystems that are intended to be sustainable and self-sufficient.
– ORIGIN blend of **PERMANENT** and **AGRICULTURE**.

per·ma·frost /ˈpərməˌfrôst, -ˌfräst/ ▶ **noun** a thick layer beneath the surface of the soil that remains frozen throughout the year.

per·ma·nent /ˈpərmənənt/ ▶ **adjective** lasting or intending to last for a long time or forever: *he had never settled down in a permanent job.*

– SYNONYMS **lasting,** enduring, indefinite, continuing, constant, perpetual, indelible, irreparable, irreversible, lifelong, perennial, established, standing, long-term, stable, secure.
– ANTONYMS temporary.

– DERIVATIVES **per·ma·nence** noun **per·ma·nen·cy** noun.
– ORIGIN from Latin *permanere* 'remain to the end.'

per·ma·nent·ly /ˈpərmənəntlē/ ▶ **adverb 1** forever. **2** continually; always.

– SYNONYMS **1** *the attack left her permanently disabled* **forever,** for all time, for good, irreversibly, incurably, irreparably, indelibly; informal for keeps. **2** *I was permanently hungry* **continually,** constantly, perpetually, always.

per·ma·nent wave ▶ **noun** see **PERM**.

per·ma·nent way ▶ **noun** Brit. the finished foundation of a railroad together with the track.

per·man·ga·nate /pərˈmaNGgəˌnāt/ ▶ **noun** a salt of manganese, oxygen, and another element such as potassium, used as an oxidizing agent in some tanning preparations and disinfectants.

per·me·a·ble /ˈpərmēəbəl/ ▶ **adjective** allowing liquids or gases to pass through.
– DERIVATIVES **per·me·a·bil·i·ty** /ˌpərmēəˈbilitē/ noun.

per·me·ate /ˈpərmēˌāt/ ▶ **verb** spread throughout something: *the aroma of soup permeated the air.*
– DERIVATIVES **per·me·a·tion** /ˌpərmēˈāSHən/ noun.
– ORIGIN Latin *permeare* 'pass through.'

Per·mi·an /ˈpərmēən/ ▶ **adjective** Geology relating to the last period of the Paleozoic era, about 290 to 245 million years ago, a time when reptiles increased rapidly in number.
– ORIGIN from *Perm*, a Russian province with deposits from this period.

per·mis·si·ble /pərˈmisəbəl/ ▶ **adjective** allowable; permitted.
– DERIVATIVES **per·mis·si·bil·i·ty** /-ˌmisəˈbilitē/ noun.

per·mis·sion /pərˈmiSHən/ ▶ **noun** the action of officially allowing something; authorization.

– SYNONYMS **authorization,** consent, leave, authority, sanction, license, dispensation, assent, agreement, approval, blessing, clearance; informal the go-ahead, the green light, say-so.
– ANTONYMS ban.

CHOOSE THE RIGHT WORD

See **LIBERTY**.

per·mis·sive /pərˈmisiv/ ▶ **adjective** allowing or characterized by freedom of behavior, especially in sexual matters: *the permissive society of the 60s.*
– DERIVATIVES **per·mis·sive·ly** adverb **per·mis·sive·ness** noun.

permit ▶ **verb** /pərˈmit/ (**permits, permitting, permitted**) **1** officially allow someone to do something. **2** (also formal **permit of**) make possible: *the parking lot was too rutted to permit ball games.*

– SYNONYMS **allow,** let, authorize, give permission, sanction, grant, license, consent to, assent to, agree to; informal give the go-ahead to, give the green light to.
– ANTONYMS forbid.

▶ **noun** /ˈpərmit/ an official document allowing someone to do something.

– SYNONYMS **authorization,** license, pass, ticket, warrant, passport, visa.

– ORIGIN Latin *permittere*.

per·mu·ta·tion /ˌpərmyo͝oˈtāSHən/ ▶ **noun 1** each of several possible ways in which things can be ordered or arranged. **2** Mathematics the action of changing the arrangement of a set of items.

– DERIVATIVES **per·mu·ta·tion·al** adjective **per·mu·tate** verb.
– ORIGIN from Latin *permutare* 'change completely.'

per·mute /pərˈmyo͞ot/ (also **permutate** /ˈpərmyo͞oˌtāt/) ▶ **verb** technical alter the sequence of a set or group of things.

per·ni·cious /pərˈnisHəs/ ▶ **adjective** having a harmful effect, especially in a gradual or subtle way: *the pernicious influences of the mass media*.
– DERIVATIVES **per·ni·cious·ly** adverb **per·ni·cious·ness** noun.
– ORIGIN Latin *perniciosus* 'destructive.'

per·ni·cious a·ne·mi·a ▶ **noun** a deficiency in the production of red blood cells through a lack of vitamin B_{12}.

pe·ro·gi ▶ **noun** variant spelling of **PIROGI**.

per·o·ra·tion /ˌperəˈrāsHən/ ▶ **noun** the concluding part of a speech; the summing up.
– ORIGIN Latin *perorare* 'speak at length.'

per·ox·ide /pəˈräksīd/ ▶ **noun 1** Chemistry a compound containing two oxygen atoms bonded together. **2** hydrogen peroxide, a chemical used as a bleach for the hair. ▶ **verb** bleach hair with peroxide.

per·pen·dic·u·lar /ˌpərpənˈdikyələr/ ▶ **adjective 1** at an angle of 90° to a given line, plane, or surface, or to the ground. **2** (**Perpendicular**) referring to the latest stage of English Gothic architecture (late 14th to mid 16th centuries), characterized by large windows with vertical tracery. ▶ **noun** a straight line at an angle of 90° to a given line, plane, or surface.
– DERIVATIVES **per·pen·dic·u·lar·i·ty** /-ˌdikyəˈlaritē/ noun **per·pen·dic·u·lar·ly** adverb.
– ORIGIN Latin *perpendicularis*.

per·pe·trate /ˈpərpəˌtrāt/ ▶ **verb** carry out a bad or illegal act.
– DERIVATIVES **per·pe·tra·tion** /ˌpərpəˈtrāsHən/ noun **per·pe·tra·tor** noun.
– ORIGIN Latin *perpetrare* 'perform.'

USAGE

Do not confuse **perpetrate** and **perpetuate**. **Perpetrate** means 'carry out a bad or illegal act' (*a crime has been perpetrated against a sovereign state*), whereas **perpetuate** means 'make something continue for a considerable time' (*a monument to perpetuate the memory of those killed in the war*).

per·pet·u·al /pərˈpecHo͞oəl/ ▶ **adjective 1** never ending or changing. **2** so frequent as to seem continual: *their perpetual money worries*.

– SYNONYMS **1 constant,** permanent, uninterrupted, continuous, unremitting, unending, everlasting, eternal, unceasing, without end, persistent, lasting, abiding. **2 interminable,** incessant, ceaseless, endless, relentless, unrelenting, persistent, continual, continuous, nonstop, never-ending, repeated, unremitting, around-the-clock, unabating; informal eternal.
– ANTONYMS temporary, intermittent.

– DERIVATIVES **per·pet·u·al·ly** adverb.
– ORIGIN Latin *perpetualis*.

per·pet·u·al mo·tion ▶ **noun** the motion of a hypothetical machine that, once activated, would run forever unless subject to an external force or to wear.

per·pet·u·ate /pərˈpecHo͞oˌāt/ ▶ **verb** make something continue for a considerable time.

– SYNONYMS **keep alive,** keep going, preserve, conserve, sustain, maintain, continue, extend.

– DERIVATIVES **per·pet·u·a·tion** /pərˌpecHo͞oˈāsHən/ noun **per·pet·u·a·tor** noun.
– ORIGIN Latin *perpetuare* 'make permanent.'

USAGE

On the difference between **perpetuate** and **perpetrate**, see the note at **PERPETRATE**.

per·pe·tu·i·ty /ˌpərpiˈt(y)o͞oitē/ ▶ **noun** (pl. **perpetuities**) **1** the state or quality of lasting forever. **2** a bond or other security with no fixed maturity date.
– PHRASES **in** (or **for**) **perpetuity** forever.

per·plex /pərˈpleks/ ▶ **verb** make someone feel baffled or very puzzled.

– SYNONYMS **puzzle,** baffle, mystify, bemuse, bewilder, confound, confuse, nonplus, disconcert; informal flummox.

– ORIGIN from Latin *perplexus* 'entangled.'

per·plex·i·ty /pərˈpleksitē/ ▶ **noun** (pl. **perplexities**) **1** the state of being puzzled. **2** a puzzling thing.

per·qui·site /ˈpərkwəzit/ ▶ **noun** formal a benefit or right enjoyed as a result of one's job or position.
– ORIGIN Latin *perquisitum* 'acquisition.'

per se /pər ˈsā/ ▶ **adverb** by or in itself or themselves.
– ORIGIN Latin.

per·se·cute /ˈpərsəˌkyo͞ot/ ▶ **verb 1** treat someone in a cruel or unfair way, especially because of their race or beliefs. **2** persistently harass someone.

– SYNONYMS **1 oppress,** abuse, victimize, ill-treat, mistreat, maltreat, torment, torture. **2 harass,** hound, plague, badger, harry, intimidate, pick on, pester; informal hassle.

– DERIVATIVES **per·se·cu·tor** noun.
– ORIGIN Latin *persequi* 'follow with hostility.'

per·se·cu·tion /ˌpərsəˈkyo͞osHən/ ▶ **noun 1** cruel or unfair treatment. **2** persistent harassment.

– SYNONYMS **1** *victims of religious persecution* **oppression,** victimization, ill-treatment, mistreatment, abuse, discrimination. **2** *the persecution she endured at school* **harassment,** hounding, intimidation, bullying.

per·se·vere /ˌpərsəˈvi(ə)r/ ▶ **verb** continue in a course of action in spite of difficulty or lack of success: *he persevered with subjects that he found disagreeable*.

– SYNONYMS **persist,** continue, carry on, go on, keep on, keep going, struggle on, hammer away, be persistent, keep at it, not take no for an answer, be tenacious, plod on, plow on; informal soldier on, hang on, plug away, stick to one's guns, stick it out, hang in there.
– ANTONYMS give up.

– DERIVATIVES **per·se·ver·ance** /ˌpərsəˈvi(ə)rəns/ noun.
– ORIGIN Latin *perseverare* 'abide by strictly.'

Per·sian /ˈpərzHən/ ▶ **noun 1** a person from Persia (now Iran). **2** the language of ancient Persia or modern Iran. **3** a long-haired breed of domestic cat. ▶ **adjective** relating to Persia or Iran.

Per·sian car·pet ▶ **noun** a carpet or rug with a traditional Persian design incorporating stylized symbolic designs.

Per·sian lamb ▶ **noun** the silky, tightly curled fleece of the karakul (an Asian sheep), used to make clothing.

per·si·flage /ˈpərsəˌfläzн/ ▶ **noun** formal light mockery or banter.
– ORIGIN from French *persifler* 'to banter.'

per·sim·mon /pərˈsimən/ ▶ **noun** an edible fruit resembling a large tomato, with very sweet flesh.
– ORIGIN Algonquian.

per·sist /pərˈsist/ ▶ **verb 1** continue doing something in spite of difficulty or opposition: *the minority of drivers who persist in drinking.* **2** continue to exist.

– SYNONYMS **1** *he persisted with his questioning* **persevere,** continue, carry on, go on, keep on, keep going, hammer away, keep at it; informal soldier on, plug away. **2** *the dry weather persists* **continue,** hold, carry on, last, keep on, remain, linger, stay, endure.
– ANTONYMS give up, stop.

– ORIGIN Latin *persistere* 'continue steadfastly.'

per·sist·ence /pərˈsistəns/ ▶ **noun** the fact of continuing to do something in spite of difficulty or opposition.

– SYNONYMS **perseverance,** tenacity, determination, staying power, endurance, doggedness, stamina; informal stickability; formal pertinacity.

per·sist·ent /pərˈsistənt/ ▶ **adjective 1** continuing to do something in spite of difficulty or opposition. **2** continuing or recurring for a long time.

– SYNONYMS **1 tenacious,** determined, resolute, dogged, tireless, indefatigable, insistent, unrelenting; formal pertinacious. **2 constant,** continuous, continuing, continual, nonstop, never-ending, steady, uninterrupted, unbroken, interminable, incessant, endless, unending, unrelenting. **3** *a persistent cough* **chronic,** nagging, frequent, repeated, habitual.
– ANTONYMS irresolute, intermittent.

– DERIVATIVES **per·sist·ent·ly** adverb.

per·sist·ent veg·e·ta·tive state ▶ **noun** a condition in which a patient is kept alive by medical means but displays no sign of higher brain function.

per·snick·et·y /pərˈsnikitē/ ▶ **adjective** informal **1** placing excessive emphasis on minor details; fussy. **2** requiring a precise or careful approach.
– ORIGIN unknown.

per·son /ˈpərsən/ ▶ **noun** (pl. **people** /ˈpēpəl/ or **persons**) **1** a human being regarded as an individual. **2** a human being's body: *a bottle of wine concealed on his person.* **3** Grammar a category used to classify pronouns or verb forms according to whether they indicate the speaker (**first person**), the person spoken to (**second person**), or a third party (**third person**).

– SYNONYMS **human being,** individual, man, woman, human, being, living soul, mortal, creature; informal type, sort.

– PHRASES **in person** with the presence or action of the person specified.
– ORIGIN Latin *persona* 'actor's mask, character in a play.'

USAGE

The words **people** and **persons** are not used in exactly the same way. **People** is by far the most common and is used in ordinary writing (*a group of people*). However, **persons** is now found chiefly in official or formal writing: *this vehicle is authorized to carry twenty persons.*

-person ▶ **combining form** used as a neutral alternative to *-man* in nouns referring to role or status: *salesperson.*

per·so·na /pərˈsōnə/ ▶ **noun** (pl. **personas** or **personae** /-ˈsōnē/) **1** the aspect of a person's character that is presented to others: *her public persona.* **2** a role or character adopted by an author or actor.
– ORIGIN Latin, 'mask, character in a play.'

per·son·a·ble /ˈpərsənəbəl/ ▶ **adjective** having a pleasant appearance and character.
– DERIVATIVES **per·son·a·bly** /-blē/ adverb.

per·son·age /ˈpərsənij/ ▶ **noun** an important or high-ranking person.
– ORIGIN Old French.

per·son·al /ˈpərsənəl/ ▶ **adjective 1** relating or belonging to a particular person. **2** done by a particular person rather than someone else: *a personal appearance.* **3** concerning a person's private rather than professional life. **4** referring to a person's character or appearance in an offensive way: *he had the gall to make personal remarks.* **5** relating to a person's body. **6** Grammar relating to one of the three persons.

– SYNONYMS **1 distinctive,** characteristic, unique, individual, idiosyncratic. **2 in person,** in the flesh, actual, live, physical. **3 private,** intimate. **4 derogatory,** disparaging, belittling, insulting, rude, disrespectful, offensive, pejorative.

▶ **noun** (**personals**) advertisements or messages in the personal column of a newspaper.

per·son·al as·sis·tant ▶ **noun** a secretary or administrative assistant working for one particular person.

per·son·al col·umn ▶ **noun** a section of a newspaper containing private advertisements or messages.

per·son·al com·pu·ter ▶ **noun** a microcomputer designed for use by one person.

per·son·al i·den·ti·fi·ca·tion num·ber ▶ **noun** a number allocated to a person and used with a bank card to validate electronic transactions.

per·son·al·i·ty /ˌpərsəˈnalitē/ ▶ **noun** (pl. **personalities**) **1** the characteristics or qualities that form a person's character. **2** lively or interesting personal qualities: *she's always had loads of personality.* **3** a celebrity.

– SYNONYMS **1 character,** nature, disposition, temperament, makeup, psyche. **2 charisma,** magnetism, character, charm, presence. **3 celebrity,** VIP, star, superstar, big name, somebody, leading light, luminary, notable; informal celeb.

per·son·al·i·ty dis·or·der ▶ **noun** Psychiatry a deeply ingrained pattern of behavior causing long-term difficulties in relationships or in functioning in society.

per·son·al·ize /ˈpərsənəˌlīz/ ▶ **verb 1** design or produce something to meet someone's individual requirements. **2** mark something to show that it belongs to a particular person. **3** cause an issue or argument to become concerned with personalities or feelings: *the media's tendency to personalize politics.*
– DERIVATIVES **per·son·al·i·za·tion** /ˌpərsənəliˈzāsнən/ noun.

per·son·al·ly /ˈpərsənəlē/ ▶ **adverb 1** in person. **2** from one's own viewpoint.

– SYNONYMS **1 in person,** oneself. **2 for my part,** for myself, as far as I am concerned, from my own point of view, subjectively.

– PHRASES **take something personally** interpret a remark or action as directed against oneself and be upset by it.

per·son·al pro·noun ▸ **noun** each of the pronouns in English (*I, you, he, she, it, we, they, me, him, her, us,* and *them*) that show person, gender, number, and case.

USAGE

I, **we**, **they**, **he**, and **she** are **subjective** personal pronouns, which means they are used as the subject of a sentence, often coming before the verb (*she lives in Paris*). **Me**, **us**, **them**, **him**, and **her** are **objective** personal pronouns, which means that they are used as the object of a verb or preposition (*John hates me*). This explains why it is wrong to use *me* in *John and me went to the store*: the personal pronoun is in the subject position, so it must be **I**.

Where a personal pronoun is used alone, the situation is more difficult. Some people say that statements such as *she's younger than me* are wrong and that the correct form is *she's younger than I*. This is based on the fact that **than** is a conjunction and so the personal pronoun is still in the subject position even though there is no verb (in full it would be *she's younger than I am*). Yet for most people the supposed 'correct' form does not sound natural and it is mainly found in very formal writing; it is usually perfectly acceptable to say *she's younger than me*.

per·son·al pro·per·ty ▸ **noun** Law all of someone's property except land and buildings. Compare with **REAL PROPERTY**.

per·son·al·ty /ˈpərsənəltē/ ▸ **noun** Law a person's personal property. Compare with **REALTY**.

per·so·na non gra·ta /pərˈsōnə nän ˈgrätə/ ▸ **noun** (pl. **personae non gratae** /pərˈsōnē nän ˈgrätē/) a person who is not welcome somewhere because they have done something unacceptable.
– ORIGIN Latin.

per·son·ate /ˈpərsəˌnāt/ ▸ **verb** formal pretend to be someone else, especially for fraudulent purposes.
– DERIVATIVES **per·son·a·tion** /ˌpərsəˈnāsʜən/ noun.

per·son·i·fi·ca·tion /pərˌsänəfiˈkāsʜən/ ▸ **noun** a person who represents or embodies a quality or concept: *he is the personification of heroism.*

– SYNONYMS **embodiment,** incarnation, epitome, quintessence, essence, type, symbol, soul, model, exemplification, exemplar, image, representation.

per·son·i·fy /pərˈsänəˌfī/ ▸ **verb** (**personifies, personifying, personified**) **1** represent a quality or concept by a figure in human form: *dramas in which vices and virtues were personified.* **2** give a personal nature or human characteristics to something nonhuman.

per·son·nel /ˌpərsəˈnel/ ▸ **plural noun** people who work for an organization or one of the armed forces.

– SYNONYMS **staff,** employees, workforce, workers, labor force, manpower, human resources.

– ORIGIN from French, 'personal.'

per·son·nel car·ri·er ▸ **noun** an armored vehicle for transporting troops.

per·spec·tive /pərˈspektiv/ ▸ **noun 1** the art of representing three-dimensional objects on a two-dimensional surface so as to convey the impression of height, width, depth, and relative distance. **2** a particular point of view. **3** understanding of the relative importance of things: *we must keep a sense of perspective about what he's done.*

– SYNONYMS **outlook,** view, viewpoint, point of view, standpoint, position, stand, stance, angle, slant, attitude.

– DERIVATIVES **per·spec·tiv·al** /-tivəl/ adjective.
– ORIGIN from Latin *perspectiva ars* 'science of optics.'

per·spi·ca·cious /ˌpərspiˈkāsʜəs/ ▸ **adjective** quickly gaining insight into and understanding of things.
– DERIVATIVES **per·spi·ca·cious·ly** adverb **per·spi·cac·i·ty** /-ˈkasitē/ noun.
– ORIGIN from Latin *perspicax* 'seeing clearly.'

CHOOSE THE RIGHT WORD

See **KEEN**[1].

per·spic·u·ous /pərˈspikyo͞owəs/ ▸ **adjective 1** clearly expressed and easily understood; lucid. **2** expressing things clearly.
– DERIVATIVES **per·spi·cu·i·ty** /ˌpərspiˈkyo͞oitē/ noun **per·spic·u·ous·ly** adverb.
– ORIGIN Latin *perspicuus* 'transparent, clear.'

per·spi·ra·tion /ˌpərspəˈrāsʜən/ ▸ **noun 1** sweat. **2** the process of sweating.

per·spire /pərˈspīr/ ▸ **verb** give out sweat through the pores of the skin.
– ORIGIN Latin *perspirare*, from *spirare* 'breathe.'

per·suade /pərˈswād/ ▸ **verb** use reasoning or argument to make someone do or believe something: *he persuaded her to go out with him.*

– SYNONYMS **1 prevail on,** talk into, coax, convince, get, induce, win over, bring around, influence, sway; informal sweet-talk. **2 cause,** lead, move, dispose, incline.
– ANTONYMS dissuade, deter.

– DERIVATIVES **per·suad·a·ble** adjective **per·suad·er** noun.
– ORIGIN Latin *persuadere*.

CHOOSE THE RIGHT WORD

See **CONVINCE**.

per·sua·sion /pərˈswāzʜən/ ▸ **noun 1** the process of persuading someone or of being persuaded. **2** a belief or set of beliefs: *writers of all political persuasions.* **3** a group or sect holding a particular religious belief.

– SYNONYMS **1 coaxing,** urging, inducement, encouragement; informal sweet-talking. **2 group,** grouping, sect, denomination, party, camp, side, faction, school of thought, belief, creed, faith.

CHOOSE THE RIGHT WORD

See **OPINION**.

per·sua·sive /pərˈswāsiv, -ziv/ ▸ **adjective 1** good at persuading someone to do or believe something. **2** providing sound reasons or arguments: *an informative and persuasive speech.*

– SYNONYMS **convincing,** compelling, effective, telling, forceful, powerful, eloquent, impressive, sound, cogent, valid, strong, plausible, credible.
– ANTONYMS unconvincing.

– DERIVATIVES **per·sua·sive·ly** adverb **per·sua·sive·ness** noun.

pert /pərt/ ▸ **adjective 1** attractively lively or cheeky. **2** (especially of a part of the body) attractively small and well shaped. **3** impudent or cheeky.
– DERIVATIVES **pert·ly** adverb **pert·ness** noun.
– ORIGIN from Latin *apertus* 'opened.'

per·tain /pərˈtān/ ▸ **verb 1** (**pertain to**) be relevant or appropriate to: *matters pertaining to the organization* *of government.* **2** formal be in effect or existence at a particular place or time.

– SYNONYMS **1** *developments* ***pertaining to*** *the economy* **concern,** relate to, connected with, relevant to, apply to, refer to, have a bearing on, affect, involve, touch on. **2 exist,** be the case, prevail.

– ORIGIN Latin *pertinere* 'extend to.'

per·ti·na·cious /ˌpərtn'āsнəs/ ▶ **adjective** formal persistent and determined.
– DERIVATIVES **per·ti·na·cious·ly** adverb **per·ti·nac·i·ty** /-'asitē/ noun.
– ORIGIN Latin *pertinax* 'holding fast.'

CHOOSE THE RIGHT WORD

See **STUBBORN**.

per·ti·nent /'pərtn-ənt/ ▶ **adjective** relevant or appropriate: *she asked a lot of pertinent questions.*

– SYNONYMS **relevant,** to the point, apposite, appropriate, suitable, applicable, material, germane.
– ANTONYMS irrelevant.

– DERIVATIVES **per·ti·nence** noun **per·ti·nent·ly** adverb.
– ORIGIN from Latin *pertinere* 'extend to.'

per·turb /pər'tərb/ ▶ **verb 1** make someone anxious or unsettled. **2** alter the normal or regular state or path of a system, moving object, etc.

– SYNONYMS **worry,** upset, disturb, unsettle, concern, trouble, disquiet, disconcert, discomfit, unnerve, alarm, bother; informal rattle.
– ANTONYMS reassure.

– ORIGIN Latin *perturbare.*

per·tur·ba·tion /ˌpərtər'bāsнən/ ▶ **noun 1** anxiety or uneasiness. **2** an alteration in the normal or regular state or path of a system, moving object, etc.

per·tus·sis /pər'təsis/ ▶ **noun** medical term for **WHOOPING COUGH**.
– ORIGIN Latin, from *tussis* 'a cough.'

pe·ruke /pə'ro͞ok/ ▶ **noun** old use a wig or periwig.
– ORIGIN French *perruque.*

pe·ruse /pə'ro͞oz/ ▶ **verb** formal read or examine something thoroughly or carefully.
– DERIVATIVES **pe·rus·al** noun **pe·rus·er** noun.
– ORIGIN perhaps from **PER-** + **USE**.

USAGE

The verb **peruse** means 'read something thoroughly and carefully.' It is sometimes taken to mean 'read through something quickly,' but this is a mistake.

Pe·ru·vi·an /pə'ro͞ovēən/ ▶ **noun** a person from Peru. ▶ **adjective** relating to Peru.

perv /pərv/ (also **perve**) ▶ **noun** informal a sexual pervert.
– DERIVATIVES **perv·y** adjective.

per·vade /pər'vād/ ▶ **verb** spread or be present throughout: *a smell of cabbage pervaded the air.*

– SYNONYMS **permeate,** spread through, fill, suffuse, imbue, penetrate, filter through, infuse, inform.

– ORIGIN Latin *pervadere* 'go or come through.'

per·va·sive /pər'vāsiv/ ▶ **adjective** spreading widely through an area or group of people; widespread: *ageism is pervasive in our society.*

– SYNONYMS **prevalent,** pervading, extensive, ubiquitous, omnipresent, universal, widespread, general.

– DERIVATIVES **per·va·sive·ly** adverb **per·va·sive·ness** noun.

per·verse /pər'vərs/ ▶ **adjective 1** showing a deliberate desire to behave in a way that other people find difficult or unacceptable. **2** contrary to what is accepted or expected. **3** sexually perverted.

– SYNONYMS **1 awkward,** contrary, difficult, unreasonable, uncooperative, unhelpful, obstructive, stubborn, obstinate. **2 illogical,** irrational, wrongheaded.

– DERIVATIVES **per·verse·ly** adverb **per·verse·ness** noun **per·ver·si·ty** /-'vərsitē/ noun (pl. **perversities**).

CHOOSE THE RIGHT WORD

See **STUBBORN**.

per·ver·sion /pər'vərzнən/ ▶ **noun 1** the action of perverting something. **2** abnormal or unacceptable sexual behavior.

– SYNONYMS **1 distortion,** misrepresentation, travesty, twisting, corruption, misuse. **2 deviance,** abnormality, depravity.

per·vert ▶ **verb** /pərˌvərt/ **1** change the original form or meaning of something so that it is no longer what it should be. **2** lead someone away from doing what is right, natural, or acceptable.

– SYNONYMS **distort,** warp, corrupt, subvert, twist, bend, abuse, divert.

▶ **noun** /'pərˌvərt/ a person whose sexual behavior is abnormal and unacceptable.

– SYNONYMS **deviant,** degenerate; informal perv, dirty old man, sicko.

– ORIGIN Latin *pervertere* 'turn about.'

per·vert·ed /pər'vərtid/ ▶ **adjective** sexually abnormal or unacceptable.

– SYNONYMS **unnatural,** deviant, warped, twisted, abnormal, unhealthy, depraved, perverse, aberrant, debased, degenerate; informal sick, kinky.

per·vi·ous /'pərvēəs/ ▶ **adjective** allowing water to pass through; permeable.
– ORIGIN Latin *pervius* 'having a passage through.'

Pe·sach /'pāˌsäk/ ▶ **noun** the Passover festival.
– ORIGIN from Hebrew.

pe·se·ta /pə'sātə/ ▶ **noun** (until the introduction of the euro in 2002) the basic unit of money of Spain.
– ORIGIN Spanish, 'little weight.'

pes·ky /'peskē/ ▶ **adjective** (**peskier, peskiest**) informal annoying.
– ORIGIN perhaps related to **PEST**.

pe·so /'pāsō/ ▶ **noun** (pl. **pesos**) the basic unit of money of several Latin American countries and of the Philippines.
– ORIGIN Spanish, 'weight.'

pes·sa·ry /'pesərē/ ▶ **noun** (pl. **pessaries**) **1** a small solid block of a medical preparation designed to dissolve after being inserted into the vagina, used to treat an infection or as a contraceptive. **2** a device inserted into the vagina to support the uterus.
– ORIGIN Latin *pessarium.*

pes·si·mism /'pesəˌmizəm/ ▶ **noun 1** lack of hope or confidence in the future. **2** Philosophy a belief that this

world is as bad as it could be or that evil will ultimately triumph over good.
– ORIGIN from Latin *pessimus* 'worst.'

pes·si·mist /'pesə,mist/ ▶ **noun** a person who lacks hope or confidence in the future.

– SYNONYMS **defeatist,** fatalist, prophet of doom, alarmist, cynic, skeptic, misery, killjoy, Cassandra; informal doom (and gloom) merchant, wet blanket.
– ANTONYMS optimist.

pes·si·mis·tic /,pesə'mistik/ ▶ **adjective** lacking hope or confidence in the future.

– SYNONYMS **gloomy,** negative, cynical, defeatist, downbeat, bleak, fatalistic, depressed.
– ANTONYMS optimistic.

– DERIVATIVES **pes·si·mis·ti·cal·ly** /,pesə'mistik(ə)lē/ adverb.

pest /pest/ ▶ **noun 1** a destructive animal or insect that attacks crops, food, or livestock. **2** informal an annoying person or thing.

– SYNONYMS **nuisance,** annoyance, irritant, thorn in one's flesh/side, trial, menace, trouble, problem, worry, bother; informal pain in the neck, headache.

– ORIGIN French *peste* or Latin *pestis* 'plague.'

pes·ter /'pestər/ ▶ **verb** trouble or annoy someone with persistent requests or interruptions.

– SYNONYMS **badger,** hound, harass, plague, annoy, bother, harry, worry; informal hassle, bug.

– ORIGIN French *empestrer* 'encumber.'

pes·ti·cide /'pestə,sīd/ ▶ **noun** a substance for destroying insects or other pests.

pes·tif·er·ous /pe'stifərəs/ ▶ **adjective 1** literary carrying infection and disease. **2** humorous annoying.
– ORIGIN Latin *pestifer* 'bringing pestilence.'

pes·ti·lence /'pestələns/ ▶ **noun** old use a deadly epidemic disease, especially bubonic plague.
– ORIGIN Latin *pestilentia*.

pes·ti·lent /'pestələnt/ ▶ **adjective 1** deadly. **2** informal, dated annoying.

pes·ti·len·tial /,pestə'lenCHəl/ ▶ **adjective 1** relating to or tending to cause infectious diseases. **2** very widespread and troublesome: *pestilential weeds.* **3** informal annoying.

pes·tle /'pestl, 'pesəl/ ▶ **noun** a heavy implement with a rounded end, used for crushing and grinding substances in a mortar.
– ORIGIN Latin *pistillum*.

pes·to /'pestō/ ▶ **noun** a sauce of crushed basil leaves, pine nuts, garlic, Parmesan cheese, and olive oil, served with pasta.
– ORIGIN Italian.

PET /pet/ ▶ **abbreviation 1** polyethylene terephthalate. **2** positron emission tomography.

pet[1] /pet/ ▶ **noun 1** an animal or bird kept for companionship or pleasure. **2** a person treated with special favor or affection: *the teacher's pet.* ▶ **adjective 1** relating to or kept as a pet. **2** treated with special attention or arousing particularly strong feelings: *my pet hate.*

– SYNONYMS **1 tame,** domesticated, housebroken, companion. **2 favorite,** favored, cherished, particular, special, personal.

▶ **verb** (**pets, petting, petted**) **1** stroke or pat an animal. **2** caress someone sexually.

– SYNONYMS **1 stroke,** caress, fondle, pat, tickle. **2 cuddle,** embrace, caress, kiss; informal neck, make out, smooch, canoodle.

– ORIGIN unknown.

pet[2] ▶ **noun** a fit of sulking or bad temper.
– ORIGIN unknown.

PETA /pētə/ ▶ **abbreviation** People for the Ethical Treatment of Animals.

peta- ▶ **combining form** referring to a factor of one quadrillion (10^{15}).
– ORIGIN alteration of **PENTA-**.

pet·al /'petl/ ▶ **noun** each of the segments forming the outer part of a flower.
– ORIGIN Greek *petalon* 'leaf.'

pe·tard /pi'tärd/ ▶ **noun** historical a small bomb made of a metal or wooden box filled with powder.
– PHRASES **be hoist with** (or **by**) **one's own petard** find that one's schemes to cause trouble for other people backfire on one. [from Shakespeare's *Hamlet* (III. iv. 207); *hoist* is in the sense 'lifted and removed.']
– ORIGIN French, from *péter* 'break wind.'

pe·ter /'pētər/ ▶ **verb** (usu. **peter out**) gradually come to an end: *the storm had petered out.*

– SYNONYMS (**peter out**) **fizzle out,** fade (away), die away/out, dwindle, diminish, taper off, tail off, trail away/off, wane, ebb, melt away, evaporate, disappear.

– ORIGIN unknown.

Pe·ter Pan /,pētər 'pan/ ▶ **noun** a person who continues to have youthful characteristics, or one who is immature, especially one who is averse to growing up.
– ORIGIN the hero of J. M. Barrie's play of the same name.

peth·i·dine /'peTHi,dēn, 'peTHə,dēn/ ▶ **noun** a painkiller used especially for women giving birth.

pé·til·lant /,pāti'yän/ ▶ **adjective** (of wine) slightly sparkling.
– ORIGIN French.

pet·i·ole /'petē,ōl/ ▶ **noun** the stalk that joins a leaf to a stem.
– ORIGIN Latin *petiolus* 'little foot, stalk.'

pet·it bour·geois /'petē boŏr'ZHwä, pə'tē/ ▶ **adjective** characteristic of the lower middle class, especially in being conventional and conservative. ▶ **noun** (pl. **petits bourgeois** pronunc. same) a petit bourgeois person.
– ORIGIN French, 'little citizen.'

pe·tite /pə'tēt/ ▶ **adjective** (of a woman) attractively small and slim.
– ORIGIN French, feminine of *petit* 'small.'

CHOOSE THE RIGHT WORD

See **SMALL**.

pe·tite bour·geoi·sie /pə'tēt ,boŏrZHwä'zē/ (also **petit bourgeoisie**) ▶ **noun** the lower middle class.
– ORIGIN French, 'little townsfolk.'

pe·tit four /'petē 'fôr/ ▶ **noun** (pl. **petits fours** /'petē 'fôrz/) a very small fancy cake, cookie, or candy.
– ORIGIN French, 'little oven.'

pe·ti·tion /pə'tiSHən/ ▶ **noun 1** a formal written appeal or request concerning a particular cause, signed by many people and presented to an authority. **2** an appeal or prayer to a deity or someone in authority. **3** Law an application to a court for a writ, judicial action, etc.: *a divorce petition.*

– SYNONYMS **appeal,** round robin, letter, request, entreaty, application, plea.

▶ **verb** make or present a petition to: *they petitioned the government for a total ban on pesticide use.*

– SYNONYMS **appeal to,** request, ask, call on, entreat, beg, implore, plead with, apply to, press, urge.

– DERIVATIVES **pe·ti·tion·er** noun.
– ORIGIN Latin.

pe·tit mal /ˈpetē ˈmäl/ ▶ **noun** a mild form of epilepsy with only very brief spells of unconsciousness. Compare with **GRAND MAL.**
– ORIGIN French, 'little sickness.'

pe·tit point /ˈpetē ˌpoint/ ▶ **noun** embroidery on canvas, using small diagonal stitches.
– ORIGIN French, 'little stitch.'

pet name ▶ **noun** a name used to express affection or familiarity.

pet·rel /ˈpetrəl/ ▶ **noun** a black-and-white seabird that typically flies far from land.
– ORIGIN from the name of St. *Peter*, because of the bird's habit of flying low with legs dangling, and so appearing to walk on the water (as St. Peter did in the Gospel of Matthew).

pe·tri dish /ˈpētrē/ ▶ **noun** a shallow transparent dish with a flat lid, used in laboratories for the culture of microorganisms.
– ORIGIN named after the German bacteriologist Julius R. *Petri.*

pet·ri·fy /ˈpetrəˌfī/ ▶ **verb** (**petrifies, petrifying, petrified**) **1** make someone so frightened that they are unable to move: *the thought of speaking in public petrified her.* **2** change organic matter into stone by encrusting or replacing its original substance with a mineral deposit.
– DERIVATIVES **pet·ri·fac·tion** /ˌpetrəˈfakSHən/ noun **pet·ri·fi·ca·tion** /ˌpetrəfiˈkāSHən/ noun.
– ORIGIN from Latin *petra* 'rock.'

pet·ro·chem·i·cal /ˌpetrōˈkemikəl/ ▶ **adjective** relating to the chemical properties and processing of petroleum and natural gas. ▶ **noun** a chemical obtained from petroleum and natural gas.
– ORIGIN from **PETROLEUM.**

pet·ro·dol·lar /ˈpetrōˌdälər/ ▶ **noun** a unit of currency used for calculating the money earned by a country from the export of petroleum.

pet·ro·glyph /ˈpetrəˌglif/ ▶ **noun** a rock carving.
– ORIGIN from Greek *petros* 'rock' + *glyphē* 'carving.'

pe·trog·ra·phy /pəˈträgrəfē/ ▶ **noun** the study of the composition and properties of rocks.
– DERIVATIVES **pe·trog·ra·pher** noun **pet·ro·graph·ic** /ˌpetrəˈgrafik/ adjective.

pet·rol /ˈpetrəl/ ▶ **noun** chiefly Brit. gasoline.

pet·ro·la·tum /ˌpetrəˈlātəm/ ▶ **noun** another term for **PETROLEUM JELLY.**
– ORIGIN Latin, from **PETROL.**

pe·tro·le·um /pəˈtrōlēəm/ ▶ **noun** a hydrocarbon oil found in layers of rock and extracted and refined to produce fuels including gasoline, paraffin, and diesel oil.
– ORIGIN Latin, from *petra* 'rock' + *oleum* 'oil.'

pe·tro·le·um jel·ly ▶ **noun** a translucent solid substance obtained from petroleum, used as a lubricant or ointment.

pe·trol·o·gy /pəˈträləjē/ ▶ **noun** the study of the origin, structure, and composition of rocks.
– DERIVATIVES **pet·ro·log·i·cal** /ˌpetrəˈläjikəl/ adjective **pe·trol·o·gist** /-jist/ noun.

pet·ti·coat /ˈpetēˌkōt/ ▶ **noun** a woman's light, loose undergarment in the form of a skirt or dress.
– ORIGIN from former *petty coat* 'small coat.'

pet·ti·fog /ˈpetēˌfôg, ˈpetēˌfäg/ ▶ **verb** (**pettifogs, pettifogging, pettifogged**) old use quibble about trivial points.
– DERIVATIVES **pet·ti·fog·ger·y** /ˌpetēˈfôgərē, -ˈfäg-/ noun.

pet·ti·fog·ging /ˈpetēˌfôgiNG, -ˌfäg-/ ▶ **adjective** petty or trivial.
– ORIGIN from **PETTY** + former *fogger* 'underhand dealer.'

pet·tish /ˈpetiSH/ ▶ **adjective** childishly sulky.
– DERIVATIVES **pet·tish·ly** adverb.

pet·ty /ˈpetē/ ▶ **adjective** (**pettier, pettiest**) **1** of little importance; trivial. **2** (of a person's behavior) small-minded. **3** of secondary or lesser importance, rank, or scale: *petty theft.*

– SYNONYMS **1 trivial,** trifling, minor, insignificant, paltry, unimportant, inconsequential, footling, negligible; informal piffling. **2 small-minded,** mean, shabby, spiteful.
– ANTONYMS important, magnanimous.

– DERIVATIVES **pet·ti·ly** adverb **pet·ti·ness** noun.
– ORIGIN from the pronunciation of French *petit* 'small.'

WORD TOOLKIT

See **INCONSEQUENTIAL.**

pet·ty bour·geois ▶ **noun** variant of **PETIT BOURGEOIS.**

pet·ty bour·geoi·sie ▶ **noun** variant of **PETITE BOURGEOISIE.**

pet·ty cash ▶ **noun** a small amount of money kept in an office for minor payments.

pet·ty of·fi·cer ▶ **noun** a rank of noncommissioned officer in the navy, above seaman and below chief petty officer.

pet·u·lant /ˈpeCHələnt/ ▶ **adjective** childishly sulky or bad-tempered.

– SYNONYMS **peevish,** bad-tempered, querulous, pettish, fretful, irritable, sulky, tetchy, crotchety, testy, fractious; informal grouchy, cranky.
– ANTONYMS good-humored.

– DERIVATIVES **pet·u·lance** noun **pet·u·lant·ly** adverb.
– ORIGIN Latin *petulans* 'impudent.'

pe·tu·nia /pəˈt(y)o͞onyə/ ▶ **noun** a South American plant with white, purple, or red funnel-shaped flowers.
– ORIGIN from an American Indian word meaning 'tobacco' (to which these plants are related).

pew /pyo͞o/ ▶ **noun** (in a church) a long bench with a back.
– ORIGIN Old French *puye* 'balcony.'

pew·ter /ˈpyo͞otər/ ▶ **noun** a gray alloy of tin with copper and antimony (formerly, tin and lead).
– ORIGIN Old French *peutre.*

pe·yo·te /pāˈyōtē/ ▶ **noun 1** a small cactus native to Mexico and the southern US. **2** a hallucinogenic drug prepared from this, containing mescaline.
– ORIGIN Nahuatl.

PFC (also **Pfc.**) ▶ **abbreviation** Private First Class.

pfen·nig /ˈfenig/ ▶ **noun** (pl. same or **pfennigs**) a former unit of money of Germany, equal to one hundredth of a mark.
– ORIGIN German, related to **PENNY**.

pfft /ft/ ▶ **exclamation** used to represent a dull abrupt sound like that of a small impact or explosion.
– PHRASES **go pfft** informal fail to work properly or at all.

PG ▶ **abbreviation** parental guidance (a movie rating indicating that some parents may find certain material in the movie unsuitable for their children).

PG-13 ▶ **symbol** a movie rating indicating that some material may be inappropriate for children under 13.

pH ▶ **noun** Chemistry a figure expressing how acid or alkaline a substance is (7 is neutral, lower values are more acid, and higher values are more alkaline).
– ORIGIN from *p* representing German *Potenz* 'power' + *H*, the symbol for hydrogen.

pha·e·ton /ˈfā-itn/ ▶ **noun** historical a light, open four-wheeled horse-drawn carriage.
– ORIGIN from *Phaethōn*, son of the sun god Helios in Greek mythology, who was allowed to drive the chariot of the sun for a day.

phage /fāj/ ▶ **noun** a kind of virus that acts as a parasite of bacteria, infecting them and reproducing inside them.
– ORIGIN short for *bacteriophage*, from **BACTERIUM** + Greek *phagein* 'eat.'

phag·o·cyte /ˈfagəˌsīt/ ▶ **noun** a type of body cell that surrounds and absorbs bacteria and other small particles.
– DERIVATIVES **phag·o·cyt·ic** /ˌfagəˈsitik/ adjective.
– ORIGIN from Greek *phago-* 'eating' + *kutos* 'vessel.'

pha·lan·ge·al /fəˈlanjēəl/ ▶ **adjective** Anatomy relating to a phalanx or the phalanges.

pha·lanx /ˈfālaNGks, ˈfal-/ ▶ **noun** (pl. **phalanxes**) **1** a group of similar people or things: *the phalanx of waiting reporters*. **2** a body of troops or police officers in close formation. **3** (pl. **phalanges** /fəˈlanjēz, fāˈlanjēz/) Anatomy a bone of the finger or toe.
– ORIGIN Greek.

phal·lic /ˈfalik/ ▶ **adjective** relating to or resembling a penis, especially when erect.

phal·lo·cen·tric /ˌfalōˈsentrik/ ▶ **adjective** focused on the penis as a symbol of male dominance.

phal·lus /ˈfaləs/ ▶ **noun** (pl. **phalli** /ˈfalī, -lē/ or **phalluses**) **1** a penis, especially when erect. **2** a representation of an erect penis as a symbol of fertility or potency.
– ORIGIN Greek *phallos*.

Phan·er·o·zo·ic /ˌfanərəˈzōik/ ▶ **adjective** Geology relating to the eon covering the whole of time since the beginning of the Cambrian period, and comprising the Paleozoic, Mesozoic, and Cenozoic eras.

phan·tasm /ˈfantazəm/ ▶ **noun** literary a thing that exists only in the imagination.
– DERIVATIVES **phan·tas·mal** /fanˈtazməl/ adjective.
– ORIGIN Greek *phantasma*.

phan·tas·ma·go·ri·a /fanˌtazməˈgôrēə/ ▶ **noun** a sequence of real or imaginary images like that seen in a dream.
– DERIVATIVES **phan·tas·ma·gor·ic** /-gôrik/ adjective **phan·tas·ma·gor·i·cal** /-gôrikəl/ adjective.
– ORIGIN probably from French *fantasmagorie*.

phan·tom /ˈfantəm/ ▶ **noun 1** a ghost. **2** a thing that exists only in the imagination.

– SYNONYMS **ghost**, apparition, spirit, specter, wraith; informal spook.

▶ **adjective** apparently real but not actually so: *a phantom conspiracy*.
– ORIGIN Greek *phantasma*.

phan·tom limb ▶ **noun** a sensation experienced by a person who has had a limb amputated that the limb is still there.

phan·tom preg·nan·cy ▶ **noun** a condition in which signs of pregnancy are present in a woman who is not pregnant.

phar·aoh /ˈfarˌō, ˈfe(ə)rˌō, ˈfāˌrō/ ▶ **noun** a ruler in ancient Egypt.
– DERIVATIVES **phar·a·on·ic** /ˌfarāˈänik, ˌfe(ə)r-/ adjective.
– ORIGIN Greek *Pharaō*, from an Egyptian word meaning 'great house.'

Phar·i·see /ˈfarəsē/ ▶ **noun 1** a member of an ancient Jewish sect noted for following traditional and written Jewish law very strictly. **2** a self-righteous or hypocritical person.
– DERIVATIVES **Phar·i·sa·ic** /ˌfarəˈsāik/ adjective **Phar·i·sa·i·cal** /ˌfarəˈsāikəl/ adjective.
– ORIGIN Greek *Pharisaios*.

phar·ma·ceu·ti·cal /ˌfärməˈsōōtikəl/ ▶ **adjective** relating to medicinal drugs. ▶ **noun** a manufactured medicinal drug.
– DERIVATIVES **phar·ma·ceu·ti·cal·ly** adverb.
– ORIGIN from Greek *pharmakon* 'drug.'

phar·ma·cist /ˈfärməsist/ ▶ **noun** a person qualified to prepare and dispense medicinal drugs.

phar·ma·col·o·gy /ˌfärməˈkäləjē/ ▶ **noun** the branch of science concerned with the uses, effects, and action of drugs.
– DERIVATIVES **phar·ma·co·log·ic** /ˌfärməkəˈläjik/ adjective **phar·ma·co·log·i·cal** /-ˈläjikəl/ adjective **phar·ma·col·o·gist** noun.
– ORIGIN from Greek *pharmakon* 'drug.'

phar·ma·co·pe·ia /ˌfärməkəˈpēə/ ▶ **noun 1** a book containing a list of medicinal drugs with directions for their use. **2** a stock of medicinal drugs.
– ORIGIN Greek *pharmakopoiia* 'art of preparing drugs.'

phar·ma·cy /ˈfärməsē/ ▶ **noun** (pl. **pharmacies**) **1** a place where medicinal drugs are prepared or sold. **2** the science or practice of preparing and dispensing medicinal drugs.
– ORIGIN Old French *farmacie*, from Greek *pharmakon* 'drug.'

pharm·ing /ˈfärmiNG/ ▶ **noun 1** the genetic modification of plants and animals so that they produce substances that can be used as pharmaceuticals. **2** a criminal activity in which Internet users are redirected to a website that has been set up to steal identity information.

pha·ryn·ge·al /fəˈrinj(ē)əl, ˌfarinˈjēəl/ ▶ **adjective** relating to the pharynx.

phar·ynx /ˈfariNGks/ ▶ **noun** (pl. **pharynges** /fəˈrinjēz/) the cavity behind the nose and mouth, connecting them to the esophagus.
– ORIGIN Greek *pharunx*.

phase /fāz/ ▶ **noun 1** a distinct period or stage in a process of change or development: *the final phases of the war*. **2** each of the forms in which the moon or a planet appears, according to the amount that is lit up. **3** Physics the stage that a regularly varying quantity (e.g., an alternating electric current) has reached in relation to zero or another chosen value.

– SYNONYMS **stage,** period, chapter, episode, part, step.

▶ **verb 1** carry something out in gradual stages. **2** (**phase something in/out**) gradually introduce or withdraw something: *the changes will be phased in over 10 years.*
– PHRASES **in** (or **out of**) **phase** working (or not working) together in the correct or a harmonious way.
– ORIGIN French.

phat·ic /'fatik/ ▶ **adjective** (of words) used for general social interaction rather than to convey information or ask questions.
– ORIGIN Greek *phatos* 'spoken.'

PhD ▶ **abbreviation** Doctor of Philosophy.
– ORIGIN from Latin *philosophiae doctor.*

pheas·ant /'fezənt/ ▶ **noun** a large long-tailed game bird, the male of which has brightly colored plumage.
– ORIGIN Greek *phasianos* 'bird of Phasis,' a river in the Caucasus from which the bird is said to have spread westwards.

phen·cy·cli·dine /fen'sīkli,dēn, -'sik-/ ▶ **noun** a drug used in veterinary medicine as an anesthetic and in hallucinogenic drugs such as angel dust.

phe·no·bar·bi·tal /,fēnō'bärbi,tôl/ ▶ **noun** a sedative drug used to treat epilepsy.

phe·nol /'fē,nôl, -,näl/ ▶ **noun** a poisonous white crystalline solid obtained from coal tar. Also called **CARBOLIC ACID.**
– DERIVATIVES **phe·no·lic** /fi'nälik/ adjective.
– ORIGIN French *phène* 'benzene.'

phe·nom·e·nal /fə'nämənəl/ ▶ **adjective 1** remarkable or outstanding: *the town expanded at a phenomenal rate.* **2** able to be perceived by the senses: *the phenomenal world.*

– SYNONYMS **remarkable,** exceptional, extraordinary, marvelous, miraculous, wonderful, outstanding, unprecedented; informal fantastic, terrific, tremendous, stupendous.

– DERIVATIVES **phe·nom·e·nal·ly** adverb.

phe·nom·e·nol·o·gy /fi,nämə'näləjē/ ▶ **noun** Philosophy **1** the study of phenomena (things that can be observed) as distinct from that of the nature of being (ontology). **2** an approach that concentrates on the study of consciousness and the objects of direct experience.
– DERIVATIVES **phe·nom·e·no·log·i·cal** /-,nämənə'läjikəl/ adjective **phe·nom·e·nol·o·gist** /-'näləjist/ noun.

phe·nom·e·non /fə'nämə,nän, -nən/ ▶ **noun** (pl. **phenomena** /fə'nämənə/) **1** a fact or situation that is observed to exist or happen: *natural phenomena such as clouds or the wind.* **2** a remarkable person or thing: *the band was a pop phenomenon for their sales figures alone.* **3** Philosophy the object of a person's perception.

– SYNONYMS **1 occurrence,** event, happening, fact, situation, circumstance, experience, case, incident, episode. **2 marvel,** sensation, wonder, prodigy.

– ORIGIN Greek *phainomenon* 'thing appearing to view.'

USAGE

The singular form is **phenomenon** and the plural form is **phenomena**. Do not use **phenomena** as if it were a singular form; say *this is a strange phenomenon* not *this is a strange phenomena.*

phe·no·type /'fēnə,tīp/ ▶ **noun** Biology the observable characteristics of an individual determined by its genetic makeup and the environment.
– ORIGIN from Greek *phainein* 'to show.'

phen·yl /'fenəl, 'fē-/ ▶ **noun** Chemistry the radical $-C_6H_5$, obtained from benzene.
– ORIGIN French *phényle.*

pher·o·mone /'ferə,mōn/ ▶ **noun** a chemical substance produced by an animal and causing a response in others of its species.
– ORIGIN from Greek *pherein* 'convey' + **HORMONE.**

phew /fyōō/ ▶ **exclamation** informal expressing relief.
– ORIGIN in imitation of puffing.

phi·al /'fīəl/ ▶ **noun** another term for **VIAL.**
– ORIGIN Greek *phialē* 'broad flat container.'

phil·a·del·phus /,filə'delfəs/ ▶ **noun** a mock orange (shrub).
– ORIGIN Latin, from Greek *philadelphos* 'loving one's brother.'

phi·lan·der /fə'landər/ ▶ **verb** (of a man) have many casual sexual relationships with women.
– ORIGIN from an earlier meaning 'man, husband,' from Greek *philandros* 'fond of men.'

phi·lan·der·er /fə'landərər/ ▶ **noun** a man who has many casual sexual relationships with women.

– SYNONYMS **womanizer,** Casanova, Don Juan, Lothario, flirt, ladies' man, playboy; informal **stud,** ladykiller.

phil·an·throp·ic /,filən'THräpik/ ▶ **adjective** (of a person or organization) helping other people, especially by giving money to good causes.

– SYNONYMS *a philanthropic millionaire* **charitable,** generous, benevolent, humanitarian, public-spirited, altruistic, magnanimous, unselfish, kind.
– ANTONYMS selfish, mean.

– DERIVATIVES **phil·an·throp·i·cal·ly** /-(ə)lē/ adverb.

phi·lan·thro·pist /fə'lanTHrəpist/ ▶ **noun** a person who helps other people, especially by giving money to good causes.

phi·lan·thro·py /fə'lanTHrəpē/ ▶ **noun** the practice of helping other people, especially by giving money to good causes.
– ORIGIN from Greek *philanthrōpos* 'man-loving.'

phi·lat·e·ly /fə'latl-ē/ ▶ **noun** the collection and study of postage stamps.
– DERIVATIVES **phil·a·tel·ic** /,filə'telik/ adjective **phi·lat·e·list** /-ist/ noun.
– ORIGIN from Greek *philo-* 'loving' + *ateleia* 'exemption from payment,' used to mean a franking mark or postage stamp exempting the recipient from payment.

-phile ▶ **combining form** referring to a person or thing having a liking for a particular thing: *bibliophile.*
– ORIGIN from Greek *philos* 'loving.'

phil·har·mon·ic /,filər'mänik, ,filhär-/ ▶ **adjective** (in the names of orchestras) devoted to music.

-philia ▶ **combining form** referring to a liking for something, especially an abnormal love for or inclination toward something: *pedophilia.*
– ORIGIN from Greek *philia* 'fondness.'

phi·lip·pic /fə'lipik/ ▶ **noun** a bitter verbal attack.
– ORIGIN from Greek *philippikos,* the name given to Demosthenes' speeches against Philip II of Macedon, and Cicero's against Mark Antony.

Phil·ip·pine /ˈfiləˌpēn/ ▸ **adjective** relating to the Philippines.

Phil·is·tine /ˈfiləˌstēn, -ˌstīn/ ▸ **noun 1** a member of a people of ancient Palestine who came into conflict with the Israelites. **2** (**philistine**) a person who is hostile toward or uninterested in culture and the arts.

> – SYNONYMS **1** *my only mistake was thinking I could share something culturally uplifting with you philistines* **barbarian,** boor, yahoo, materialist. **2** (as adj.) *a romantic visionary, persecuted by a philistine establishment* **uncultured,** lowbrow, uncultivated, uncivilized, uneducated, unenlightened, commercial, materialist, bourgeois, ignorant, crass, boorish, barbarian.

– DERIVATIVES **phil·is·tin·ism** /ˈfiləstēˌnizəm, fəˈlistə-/ noun.
– ORIGIN Greek *Philistinos*.

Phil·lips /ˈfiləps/ ▸ **adjective** trademark referring to a screw with a cross-shaped slot for turning, or a corresponding screwdriver.
– ORIGIN the name of the American manufacturer Henry F. *Phillips*.

phil·o·den·dron /ˌfiləˈdendrən/ ▸ **noun** (pl. **philodendrons** or **philodendra** /-drə/) a tropical American climbing plant grown as a greenhouse or indoor plant.
– ORIGIN from Greek *philos* 'loving' + *dendron* 'tree.'

phi·lol·o·gy /fəˈläləjē/ ▸ **noun** the study of the structure and historical development of languages.
– DERIVATIVES **phil·o·log·i·cal** /ˌfiləˈläjikəl/ adjective **phi·lol·o·gist** noun.
– ORIGIN Greek *philologia*.

phi·los·o·pher /fəˈläsəfər/ ▸ **noun** a person engaged or learned in philosophy.

> – SYNONYMS **thinker,** theorist, theoretician, scholar, intellectual, sage.

phil·o·soph·i·cal /ˌfiləˈsäfikəl/ ▸ **adjective 1** relating to the study of philosophy. **2** calm in difficult circumstances.

> – SYNONYMS **1 theoretical,** metaphysical. **2 thoughtful,** reflective, pensive, meditative, contemplative, introspective. **3 stoical,** self-possessed, serene, dispassionate, phlegmatic, long-suffering, resigned.

– DERIVATIVES **phil·o·soph·ic** adjective **phil·o·soph·i·cal·ly** adverb.

phi·los·o·phize /fəˈläsəˌfīz/ ▸ **verb** talk about serious issues, especially in a boring or pompous way.

phi·los·o·phy /fəˈläsəfē/ ▸ **noun** (pl. **philosophies**) **1** the study of the fundamental nature of knowledge, reality, and existence. **2** the theories of a particular philosopher. **3** a theory or attitude that guides a person's behavior. **4** the study of the theoretical basis of a branch of knowledge or experience: *the philosophy of science*.

> – SYNONYMS **1 thinking,** thought, reasoning, logic. **2 beliefs,** credo, ideology, ideas, thinking, theories, doctrine, principles, views, outlook.

– ORIGIN Greek *philosophia* 'love of wisdom.'

phil·ter /ˈfiltər/ ▸ **noun** a love potion.
– ORIGIN Greek *philtron*.

phish·ing /ˈfisHiNG/ ▸ **noun** a type of Internet fraud in which a person impersonates a reputable company in order to persuade others to reveal personal information, such as passwords and credit card numbers, online.
– ORIGIN respelling of **FISHING** (see **FISH**[1]).

phle·bi·tis /fləˈbītis/ ▸ **noun** inflammation of the walls of a vein.
– ORIGIN from Greek *phleps* 'vein.'

phle·bot·o·my /fləˈbätəmē/ ▸ **noun** (pl. **phlebotomies**) the surgical opening or puncture of a vein to withdraw blood or introduce a fluid.
– DERIVATIVES **phle·bot·o·mist** noun.

phlegm /flem/ ▸ **noun 1** a thick substance produced by the mucous membranes of the nose and throat, especially when one has a cold. **2** (in medieval science and medicine) one of the four bodily humors, believed to be associated with a calm or apathetic temperament. **3** calmness of temperament.
– DERIVATIVES **phlegm·y** adjective.
– ORIGIN Greek *phlegma* 'inflammation.'

phleg·mat·ic /flegˈmatik/ ▸ **adjective** calm and unemotional.
– DERIVATIVES **phleg·mat·i·cal·ly** adverb.

phlo·em /ˈflōˌem/ ▸ **noun** the tissue in plants that conducts nutrients downward from the leaves.
– ORIGIN from Greek *phloos* 'bark.'

phlo·gis·ton /flōˈjistän, -tən/ ▸ **noun** a substance supposed by 18th-century chemists to exist in all combustible bodies, and to be released in combustion.

phlox /fläks/ ▸ **noun** a plant with clusters of colorful scented flowers.
– ORIGIN Greek, 'flame.'

-phobe ▸ **combining form** referring to a person having a fear or dislike of a specified thing: *technophobe*.
– ORIGIN from Greek *phobos* 'fear.'

pho·bi·a /ˈfōbēə/ ▸ **noun** an extreme or irrational fear of something.

> – SYNONYMS **fear,** dread, horror, terror, aversion, antipathy, revulsion; informal hang-up.

– DERIVATIVES **pho·bic** /ˈfōbik/ adjective & noun.

-phobia ▸ **combining form** extreme or irrational fear or dislike of a specified thing: *arachnophobia*.
– DERIVATIVES **-phobic** combining form.

phoe·be /ˈfēbē/ ▸ **noun** a mainly gray-brown or blackish American tyrant flycatcher.

Phoe·ni·cian /fəˈnēsHən/ ▸ **noun** a member of an ancient people living in Phoenicia in the eastern Mediterranean. ▸ **adjective** relating to Phoenicia.

phoe·nix /ˈfēniks/ ▸ **noun** (in classical mythology) a bird that periodically burned itself on a funeral pyre and was born again from the ashes.
– ORIGIN Greek *phoinix*.

phone /fōn/ ▸ **noun** a telephone.

> – SYNONYMS **telephone,** cell phone, cellular phone, mobile phone, cordless phone; informal horn, blower.

▸ **verb** make a telephone call to someone.

> – SYNONYMS **call,** telephone, ring (up); informal call up, give someone a ring/buzz.

-phone ▸ **combining form 1** referring to an instrument using or connected with sound: *megaphone*. **2** referring to a person who uses a specified language: *francophone*.
– ORIGIN from Greek *phōnē* 'sound, voice.'

phone book ▸ **noun** a telephone directory.

phone card ▸ **noun** another term for **CALLING CARD** (sense 2).

phone-in ▸ **noun** another term for **CALL-IN**.

phone jack ▸ **noun** a socket designed to receive the plug from a telephone, fax machine, etc.

pho·neme /ˈfōnēm/ ▸ **noun** any of the distinct units of sound that distinguish one word from another, e.g., *p*, *b*, *d*, and *t* in *pad*, *pat*, *bad*, and *bat*.
– ORIGIN Greek *phōnēma* 'sound, speech.'

pho·net·ic /fəˈnetik/ ▸ **adjective 1** relating to speech sounds. **2** (of a system of spelling) closely matching the sounds represented.
– DERIVATIVES **pho·net·i·cal·ly** adverb.
– ORIGIN Greek *phōnētikos*.

pho·net·ics /fəˈnetiks/ ▸ **plural noun** (treated as sing.) the study and classification of speech sounds.

pho·ney /ˈfōnē/ ▸ **adjective & noun** variant spelling of PHONY.

phon·ic /ˈfänik/ ▸ **adjective** relating to speech sounds.

phon·ics /ˈfäniks/ ▸ **plural noun** (treated as sing.) a method of teaching people to read by associating letters or groups of letters with particular sounds.

pho·no /ˈfōnō/ ▸ **adjective** referring to a type of plug used with audio and video equipment, in which one conductor is cylindrical and the other is a central prong that extends beyond it.
– ORIGIN abbreviation of PHONOGRAPH.

phono- ▸ **combining form** relating to sound: *phonograph*.
– ORIGIN from Greek *phōnē* 'sound, voice.'

pho·no·graph /ˈfōnəˌgraf/ ▸ **noun 1** old use a record player. **2** historical an early form of gramophone.
– DERIVATIVES **pho·no·graph·ic** /ˌfōnəˈgrafik/ adjective.

pho·nol·o·gy /fəˈnäləjē, fō-/ ▸ **noun** the system of relationships between the basic speech sounds of a language.
– DERIVATIVES **pho·no·log·i·cal** /ˌfōnəˈläjikəl/ adjective.

pho·ny /ˈfōnē/ (also **phoney**) informal ▸ **adjective** (**phonier**, **phoniest**) not genuine.

– SYNONYMS **bogus,** false, fake, fraudulent, counterfeit, forged, imitation, affected, insincere; informal pretend.
– ANTONYMS authentic.

▸ **noun** (pl. **phonies**) a person or thing that is not genuine.

– SYNONYMS **1 impostor,** sham, fake, fraud, charlatan; informal con artist. **2 fake,** imitation, counterfeit, forgery.

– DERIVATIVES **pho·ni·ness** noun.
– ORIGIN unknown.

phoo·ey /ˈfo͞oē/ informal ▸ **exclamation** used to express scorn or disbelief. ▸ **noun** nonsense.
– ORIGIN imitating the sound of a scornful exclamation.

phos·gene /ˈfäsjēn/ ▸ **noun** a poisonous gas formerly used in warfare.
– ORIGIN from Greek *phōs* 'light.'

phos·phate /ˈfäsfāt/ ▸ **noun** Chemistry a salt or ester of phosphoric acid.

phos·phine /ˈfäsfēn/ ▸ **noun** a foul-smelling gas formed from phosphorus and hydrogen.

phos·phor /ˈfäsfər/ ▸ **noun 1** a synthetic fluorescent or phosphorescent substance. **2** old-fashioned term for PHOSPHORUS.

phos·pho·res·cence /ˌfäsfəˈresəns/ ▸ **noun** light given out by a substance without burning or heat, or with so little heat that it cannot be felt.
– DERIVATIVES **phos·pho·resce** verb **phos·pho·res·cent** adjective.

phos·phor·ic /fäsˈfôrik/ ▸ **adjective** relating to or containing phosphorus.

phos·phor·ic ac·id ▸ **noun** a crystalline acid obtained by treating phosphates with sulfuric acid.

phos·pho·rus /ˈfäsfərəs/ ▸ **noun** a poisonous nonmetallic chemical element in the form of a yellowish waxy solid that ignites spontaneously in air and glows in the dark.
– DERIVATIVES **phos·pho·rous** adjective.
– ORIGIN Greek *phōsphoros*.

pho·to /ˈfōtō/ ▸ **noun** (pl. **photos**) a photograph.

photo- ▸ **combining form 1** relating to light. **2** relating to photography.
– ORIGIN sense 1 from Greek *phōs* 'light.'

pho·to·cell /ˈfōtōˌsel/ ▸ **noun** short for PHOTOELECTRIC CELL.

pho·to·chem·is·try /ˌfōtōˈkeməstrē/ ▸ **noun** the branch of chemistry concerned with the chemical effects of light.
– DERIVATIVES **pho·to·chem·i·cal** /ˌfōtōˈkemikəl/ adjective.

pho·to·chro·mic /ˌfōtəˈkrōmik/ ▸ **adjective** (of glass, lenses, etc.) undergoing a reversible change in color when exposed to bright light.

pho·to·cop·i·er /ˈfōtəˌkäpēər/ ▸ **noun** a machine for making photocopies.

pho·to·cop·y /ˈfōtəˌkäpē/ ▸ **noun** (pl. **photocopies**) a photographic copy of something produced by a process involving the action of light on a specially prepared surface.

– SYNONYMS **copy,** duplicate, reproduction, facsimile; trademark Xerox, photostat.

▸ **verb** (**photocopies, photocopying, photocopied**) make a photocopy of something.

– SYNONYMS **copy,** duplicate, xerox, photostat, reproduce.

– DERIVATIVES **pho·to·cop·i·a·ble** adjective.

pho·to·e·lec·tric /ˌfōtōiˈlektrik/ ▸ **adjective** involving the emission of electrons from a surface by the action of light.

pho·to·e·lec·tric cell ▸ **noun** a device using a photoelectric effect to generate current.

pho·to fin·ish ▸ **noun** a close finish of a race in which the winner can be identified only from a photograph of competitors crossing the line.

pho·to·gen·ic /ˌfōtəˈjenik/ ▸ **adjective 1** looking attractive in photographs. **2** Biology producing or giving out light.

pho·to·graph /ˈfōtəˌgraf/ ▸ **noun** a picture made with a camera, in which an image is focused onto film and then made visible and permanent by chemical treatment.

– SYNONYMS **picture,** photo, snap, snapshot, shot, print, still, transparency.

▸ **verb** take a photograph of someone or something.
– DERIVATIVES **pho·tog·ra·pher** /fəˈtägrəfər/ noun.

pho·to·graph·ic /ˌfōtəˈgrafik/ ▸ **adjective 1** relating to photographs or photography. **2** extremely detailed and accurate.

– SYNONYMS **1** *a photographic record* **pictorial,** graphic, in photographs. **2** *a photographic memory* **detailed,** exact, precise, accurate, vivid.

pho·to·graph·ic mem·o·ry /ˌfōtəˈgrafik/ ▸ **noun** an ability to remember information or visual images in great detail.

pho·tog·ra·phy /fəˈtägrəfē/ ▸ **noun** the taking and processing of photographs.

pho·to·gra·vure /ˌfōtəgrəˈvyo͝or/ ▸ **noun** a printing process in which the type or image is produced from a photographic negative transferred to a metal plate and etched in.
– ORIGIN French, 'photo-engraving.'

pho·to·jour·nal·ism /ˌfōtōˈjərnəˌlizəm/ ▸ **noun** the taking and publishing of photographs as a means of communicating news.
– DERIVATIVES **pho·to·jour·nal·ist** noun.

pho·to·mon·tage /ˌfōtōmänˈtäzʜ/ ▸ **noun** a picture consisting of a number of separate photographs placed together or overlapping.

pho·ton /ˈfōtän/ ▸ **noun** Physics a particle representing a quantum of light or other electromagnetic radiation.
– DERIVATIVES **pho·ton·ic** adjective.

pho·to op·por·tu·ni·ty (also **photo op**) ▸ **noun** an occasion on which famous people pose for photographers by arrangement.

pho·to·re·al·ism /ˈfōtōˈrēəˌlizəm/ ▸ **noun** a style of art and sculpture characterized by a very detailed and unidealized portrayal of ordinary life.
– DERIVATIVES **pho·to·re·al·ist** noun & adjective **pho·to·re·al·is·tic** /ˌfōtōˌrēəˈlistik/ adjective.

pho·to·re·cep·tor /ˌfōtōriˈseptər/ ▸ **noun** a structure in an animal or plant that responds to light.

pho·to·sen·si·tive /ˌfōtəˈsensitiv/ ▸ **adjective** responding to light.
– DERIVATIVES **pho·to·sen·si·tiv·i·ty** /-ˌsensəˈtivitē/ noun.

pho·to·stat /ˈfōtōˌstat/ ▸ **noun** trademark **1** a type of machine for making photocopies on special paper. **2** a copy made by a photostat. ▸ **verb** (**photostats, photostatting, photostatted**) copy something with a photostat.

pho·to·syn·the·sis /ˌfōtōˈsinᴛʜəsis/ ▸ **noun** the process by which green plants use sunlight to form nutrients from carbon dioxide and water.
– DERIVATIVES **pho·to·syn·the·size** /ˌfōtōˈsinᴛʜəˌsīz/ verb **pho·to·syn·thet·ic** /-ˌsinˈᴛʜetik/ adjective.

pho·tot·ro·pism /ˌfōtəˈtrōpizəm, fōˈtätrəˌpizəm/ ▸ **noun** the turning of a plant or other organism either toward or away from a source of light.
– DERIVATIVES **pho·to·trop·ic** /ˌfōtəˈtrōpik, -ˈträpik/ adjective.

pho·to·vol·ta·ic /ˌfōtəvōlˈtāik, ˌfōtōväl-/ ▸ **adjective** relating to the production of electric current at the junction of two substances exposed to light.

phras·al verb ▸ **noun** a verb combined with an adverb or preposition to give a new meaning that cannot be worked out from the individual parts, e.g., *break down* or *see to*.

phrase /frāz/ ▸ **noun 1** a small group of words forming a unit within a clause. **2** Music a group of notes forming a distinct unit within a longer passage. **3** a group of words that have a particular meaning when used together.

– SYNONYMS **expression,** construction, term, turn of phrase, idiom, saying.

▸ **verb 1** put into a particular form of words: *it's important to phrase the question correctly.* **2** (often as n. **phrasing**) divide music into phrases in a particular way.

– SYNONYMS **express,** put into words, put, word, formulate, couch, frame.

– DERIVATIVES **phras·al** adjective.
– PHRASES **turn of phrase** a particular or characteristic manner of expression.
– ORIGIN Greek *phrasis*.

phrase book ▸ **noun** a book listing useful expressions in a foreign language and their translations.

phra·se·ol·o·gy /ˌfrāzēˈäləjē/ ▸ **noun** (pl. **phraseologies**) a particular or characteristic way in which words are used: *legal phraseology*.

phre·nol·o·gy /freˈnäləjē/ ▸ **noun** chiefly historical the study of the shape and size of a person's skull as a supposed indication of their character.
– DERIVATIVES **phre·nol·o·gist** noun.
– ORIGIN from Greek *phrēn* 'mind.'

Phryg·i·an /ˈfrijēən/ ▸ **noun** a person from Phrygia, an ancient region of west central Asia Minor (the western peninsula of Asia). ▸ **adjective** relating to Phrygia.

phthi·sis /ˈᴛʜīsis, ˈtī-/ ▸ **noun** old use tuberculosis or a similar disease.
– ORIGIN Greek.

phy·la /ˈfīlə/ plural of **PHYLUM**.

phy·lac·ter·y /fiˈlaktərē/ ▸ **noun** (pl. **phylacteries**) a small leather box containing biblical passages written in Hebrew, worn by Jewish men at morning prayer.
– ORIGIN Greek *phulaktērion* 'amulet.'

phyl·lo /ˈfēlō/ ▸ **noun** variant spelling of **FILO**.

phyl·lo·qui·none /ˌfilōˈkwinōn, -kwiˈnōn/ ▸ **noun** vitamin K_1, a compound found in cabbage, spinach, and other leafy green vegetables, and essential for blood-clotting.
– ORIGIN from Greek *phullon* 'leaf' + **QUINONE**.

phyl·lox·e·ra /fiˈläksərə, ˌfilәkˈsi(ə)rə/ ▸ **noun** an insect that is a pest of vines.
– ORIGIN from Greek *phullon* 'leaf' + *xēros* 'dry.'

phy·lum /ˈfīləm/ ▸ **noun** (pl. **phyla** /-lə/) a category in the classification of animals and plants that ranks above class and below kingdom.
– ORIGIN Greek *phulon* 'race.'

phys·ic /ˈfizik/ ▸ **noun** old use medicinal drugs or medical treatment.
– ORIGIN Latin *physica*.

phys·i·cal /ˈfizikəl/ ▸ **adjective 1** relating to the body as opposed to the mind. **2** relating to things that can be seen, heard, or touched. **3** involving bodily contact or activity: *a physical relationship.* **4** relating to physics or the operation of natural forces.

– SYNONYMS **1 bodily,** corporeal, corporal, carnal, fleshly, nonspiritual. **2 manual,** laboring, blue-collar. **3 material,** concrete, tangible, palpable, solid, substantial, real, actual, visible.
– ANTONYMS mental, spiritual.

▸ **noun** a medical examination to establish how healthy or fit a person is.
– DERIVATIVES **phys·i·cal·i·ty** /ˌfiziˈkalitē/ noun **phys·i·cal·ly** adverb.

phys·i·cal chem·is·try ▸ **noun** the branch of chemistry concerned with the application of the techniques and theories of physics to the study of chemical systems.

phys·i·cal ed·u·ca·tion ▸ **noun** instruction in physical exercise and games, especially in schools.

phys·i·cal ge·og·ra·phy ▶ **noun** the branch of geography concerned with natural features.

phys·i·cal sci·ences ▶ **plural noun** the sciences concerned with the study of inanimate natural objects, including physics, chemistry, and astronomy.

phys·i·cal ther·a·py ▶ **noun** the treatment of disease or injury by physical methods such as massage and exercise.
– DERIVATIVES **phys·i·cal ther·a·pist** noun.

phy·si·cian /fiˈzisʜən/ ▶ **noun** a person qualified to practice medicine.

> – SYNONYMS **doctor,** medical practitioner, general practitioner, GP, clinician, specialist, consultant; informal doc, medic, quack.

phys·ics /ˈfiziks/ ▶ **plural noun** (treated as sing.) **1** the branch of science concerned with the nature and properties of matter and energy. **2** the physical properties and nature of something.
– DERIVATIVES **phys·i·cist** /ˈfizəsist/ noun.
– ORIGIN Latin *physica* 'natural things.'

phys·i·og·no·my /ˌfizēˈä(g)nəmē/ ▶ **noun** (pl. **physiognomies**) a person's facial features or expression, especially when seen as an indication of character.
– ORIGIN Greek *phusiognōmonia*.

phys·i·ol·o·gy /ˌfizēˈäləjē/ ▶ **noun 1** the branch of biology concerned with the normal functions of living organisms and their parts. **2** the way in which a living organism or bodily part functions.
– DERIVATIVES **phys·i·o·log·i·cal** /ˌfizēəˈläjikəl/ adjective **phys·i·ol·o·gist** noun.

phys·i·o·ther·a·py /ˌfizēōˈᴛʜerəpē/ ▶ **noun** British term for **PHYSICAL THERAPY**.
– DERIVATIVES **phys·i·o·ther·a·pist** noun.

phy·sique /fiˈzēk/ ▶ **noun** the form, size, and development of a person's body.

> – SYNONYMS **body,** build, figure, frame, anatomy, shape, form, proportions; muscles, musculature; informal vital statistics, bod.

– ORIGIN French, 'physical' (used as a noun).

phy·to·chem·i·cal /ˌfītōˈkemikəl/ ▶ **noun** any of a group of compounds found in plants that are believed to have beneficial effects.
– ORIGIN from Greek *phuton* 'a plant.'

phy·to·es·tro·gen /ˌfītōˈestrəjən/ ▶ **noun** a substance found in certain plants which can produce effects like that of the hormone estrogen when ingested.

phy·to·plank·ton /ˌfītōˈplaɴɢktən/ ▶ **noun** plankton consisting of microscopic plants.
– ORIGIN from Greek *phuton* 'a plant.'

PI ▶ **abbreviation** private investigator.

pi /pī/ ▶ **noun 1** the sixteenth letter of the Greek alphabet (Π, π), represented as 'p'. **2** the numerical value of the ratio of the circumference of a circle to its diameter (approximately 3.14159).
– ORIGIN Greek: sense 2 from the initial letter of *periphereia* 'circumference.'

pi·a /ˈpīə, ˈpēə/ (in full **pia mater** /ˈpīə ˈmātər, ˈpēə ˈmätər/) ▶ **noun** the delicate innermost membrane enveloping the brain and spinal cord.
– ORIGIN Latin, (in full) 'tender mother.'

pi·a·nism /ˈpēəˌnizəm/ ▶ **noun** skill or artistry in playing the piano or composing music for the piano.
– DERIVATIVES **pi·a·nis·tic** /ˌpēəˈnistik/ adjective.

pi·a·nis·si·mo /ˌpēəˈnisiˌmō/ ▶ **adverb & adjective** Music very soft or softly.
– ORIGIN Italian, 'softest.'

pi·an·o[1] /pēˈanō/ ▶ **noun** (pl. **pianos**) a large keyboard musical instrument with metal strings that are struck by hammers when the keys are pressed.
– DERIVATIVES **pi·an·ist** /ˈpēənist, pēˈanist/ noun.
– ORIGIN Italian, abbreviation of **PIANOFORTE**.

pi·an·o[2] /pēˈänō, pēˈanō/ ▶ **adverb & adjective** Music soft or softly.
– ORIGIN Italian, 'soft.'

pi·an·o·forte /pēˌanōˈfôrtā, pēˈanōˌfôrt/ ▶ **noun** formal term for **PIANO**[1].
– ORIGIN from Italian *piano e forte* 'soft and loud.'

pi·a·no·la /ˌpēəˈnōlə/ ▶ **noun** trademark a piano equipped to be played automatically with a roll of perforated paper that controls the movement of the keys to produce a tune.

pi·as·ter /pēˈastər/ (also **piastre**) ▶ **noun** a unit of money of several Middle Eastern countries.
– ORIGIN from Italian *piastra d'argento* 'plate of silver.'

pi·az·za /pēˈätsə, pēˈazə/ ▶ **noun** a public square or marketplace, especially in Italy.
– ORIGIN Italian.

pic /pik/ ▶ **noun** informal a photograph or movie.

pi·ca /ˈpīkə/ ▶ **noun** Printing **1** a unit of type size and line length equal to 12 points (about ⅙ inch or 4.2 mm). **2** a size of letter in typewriting, with 10 characters to the inch (about 3.9 to the centimeter).
– ORIGIN Latin.

pi·ca·dor /ˈpikəˌdôr/ ▶ **noun** (in bullfighting) a person on horseback who goads the bull with a lance.
– ORIGIN Spanish.

pic·a·resque /ˌpikəˈresk/ ▶ **adjective** relating to fiction dealing with the adventures of a dishonest but appealing hero.
– ORIGIN from Spanish *pícaro* 'rogue.'

pic·a·yune /ˌpikiˈyo͞on/ informal ▶ **adjective** of little value or importance. ▶ **noun** an unimportant person or thing.
– ORIGIN French *picaillon*, referring to a copper coin from Piedmont.

pic·ca·lil·li /ˈpikəˌlilē/ ▶ **noun** (pl. **piccalillies** or **piccalillis**) an Indian relish made of chopped vegetables, mustard, and hot spices.
– ORIGIN probably from a blend of **PICKLE** and **CHILI**.

pic·co·lo /ˈpikəˌlō/ ▶ **noun** (pl. **piccolos**) a small flute an octave higher than the ordinary one.
– ORIGIN Italian, 'small flute.'

pick[1] /pik/ ▶ **verb 1** (also **pick something up**) take hold of something and move it: *he picked a match out of the ash tray.* **2** remove a flower or fruit from where it is growing. **3** choose someone or something from a number of alternatives. **4** remove unwanted matter from one's nose or teeth with a finger or a pointed instrument.

> – SYNONYMS **1** *I got a job picking apples* **harvest,** gather (in), collect, pluck. **2** *pick the time that suits you best* **choose,** select, single out, opt for, elect, decide on, settle on, fix on, name, nominate, identify. **3** *he tried to pick a fight* **provoke,** start, cause, incite, instigate, prompt.

▶ **noun 1** an act of selecting something. **2** (**the pick of**) informal the best person or thing in a particular group.

– SYNONYMS **1** *take your pick from our extensive menu* **choice,** selection, option, decision; preference, favorite. **2** (**the pick of**) *he was the pick of the bunch* **best,** finest, choice, choicest, cream, flower, crème de la crème, elite.

– DERIVATIVES **pick·er** noun.
– PHRASES **pick and choose** select only the best from among a number of alternatives. **pick at 1** repeatedly pull at something with one's fingers. **2** eat food in small amounts. **pick someone's brain** informal obtain information by questioning someone who is better informed about a subject. **pick a fight** provoke an argument or fight. **pick holes in** find fault with. **pick a lock** open a lock with an instrument other than the proper key. **pick someone/thing off** shoot one of a group from a distance. **pick on** single someone out for unfair treatment. **pick someone/thing out 1** distinguish someone or something from among a group. **2** play a tune slowly or with difficulty on a guitar or similar instrument. **pick over** (or **pick through**) sort through a number of items carefully. **pick someone's pockets** steal something from a person's pocket. **pick up** improve or increase. **pick someone/thing up 1** go to collect someone or something. **2** informal casually strike up a relationship with someone with a sexual purpose in mind. **3** return to an earlier point or topic. **4** obtain, acquire, or learn something: *he had picked up a little Russian from his father.* **5** become aware of or sensitive to something. **6** detect or receive a signal or sound. **pick one's way** walk slowly and carefully.
– ORIGIN unknown.

pick² (also **pickax** /ˈpikˌaks/) ▶ **noun 1** a tool consisting of a curved iron bar with one or both ends pointed, fixed at right angles to its handle, used for breaking up hard ground or rock. **2** a plectrum.
– ORIGIN variant of PIKE².

pick·a·nin·ny /ˈpikəˌninē/ ▶ **noun** (pl. **pickaninnies**) offensive a small black child.
– ORIGIN from Spanish *pequeño* or Portuguese *pequeno* 'little.'

pick·ax /ˈpikˌaks/ (also **pickaxe**) ▶ **noun** another term for PICK². ▶ **verb** break or strike with a pickax.

pick·et /ˈpikit/ ▶ **noun 1** a person or group of people standing outside a workplace with the aim of persuading other people not to work during a strike. **2** a soldier or small group of troops sent out to watch for the enemy. **3** a pointed wooden stake driven into the ground.

– SYNONYMS **1 demonstrator,** striker, protester. **2 demonstration,** picket line, blockade, boycott, strike.

▶ **verb** (**pickets, picketing, picketed**) act as a picket outside a workplace.
– ORIGIN French *piquet* 'pointed stake,' first meaning a pointed stake, on which a soldier had to stand on one foot as a military punishment.

pick·ings /ˈpikiNGz/ ▶ **plural noun** profits or gains, especially those made easily or dishonestly.

pick·le /ˈpikəl/ ▶ **noun 1** a small cucumber preserved in vinegar, brine, or a similar solution. **2** liquid used to preserve food or other perishable items. **3** (**a pickle**) informal a difficult situation. ▶ **verb 1** preserve food in vinegar, brine, or a similar solution. **2** (as adj. **pickled**) informal, dated drunk.
– ORIGIN Dutch or German *pekel*.

pick-me-up ▶ **noun** informal a thing that makes one feel more energetic or cheerful.

pick·pock·et /ˈpikˌpäkət/ ▶ **noun** a person who steals from people's pockets.

pick·up /ˈpikˌəp/ ▶ **noun 1** (also **pickup truck**) a small truck with an enclosed cab and open back. **2** an act of picking up or collecting a person or goods. **3** informal a casual encounter with someone, with a view to having a sexual relationship. **4** an improvement in an economic indicator. **5** the cartridge of a record player, carrying the stylus. **6** a device on an electric guitar that converts sound vibrations into electrical signals for amplification.

– SYNONYMS **improvement,** recovery, revival, upturn, upswing, rally, resurgence, renewal, turnaround.

pick·y /ˈpikē/ ▶ **adjective** (**pickier, pickiest**) informal fussy: *a picky eater.*

pic·nic /ˈpikˌnik/ ▶ **noun** a packed meal eaten outdoors, or an occasion when such a meal is eaten. ▶ **verb** (**picnics, picnicking, picnicked**) have or take part in a picnic.
– DERIVATIVES **pic·nick·er** noun.
– PHRASES **be no picnic** informal be difficult or unpleasant.
– ORIGIN French *pique-nique*.

pico- ▶ **combining form** referring to a factor of one million millionth (10^{-12}): *picosecond.*
– ORIGIN from Spanish *pico*, 'beak, little bit.'

pi·cot /ˈpēkō/ ▶ **noun** a small loop or series of loops in lace or embroidery, typically used to decorate a border.
– ORIGIN French, 'small peak or point.'

Pict /pikt/ ▶ **noun** a member of an ancient people living in northern Scotland in Roman times.
– ORIGIN Latin *Picti*, perhaps from *pingere* 'to paint or tattoo.'

pic·to·graph /ˈpiktəˌgraf/ (also **pictogram** /-ˌgram/) ▶ **noun 1** a picture or symbol representing a word or phrase. **2** a pictorial representation of statistics on a chart, graph, or computer screen.
– DERIVATIVES **pic·to·graph·ic** /ˌpiktəˈgrafik/ adjective.
– ORIGIN from Latin *pingere* 'to paint.'

pic·to·ri·al /pikˈtôrēəl/ ▶ **adjective** relating to or using pictures. ▶ **noun** a newspaper or magazine that has pictures as a main feature.
– DERIVATIVES **pic·to·ri·al·ly** adverb.
– ORIGIN Latin *pictorius*.

pic·ture /ˈpikCHər/ ▶ **noun 1** a painting, drawing, or photograph. **2** an image on a television screen. **3** a movie. **4** (**the pictures**) the movies. **5** an impression formed from an account or description of something: *a full picture of the disaster had not yet emerged.*

– SYNONYMS **1 painting, drawing,** sketch, watercolor, print, canvas, portrait, illustration, depiction, likeness, representation, image. **2 photograph,** photo, snap, snapshot, shot, frame, exposure, still, print. **3 concept,** idea, impression, image, vision, visualization, notion. **4 personification,** embodiment, epitome, essence, quintessence, soul, model.

▶ **verb 1** represent someone or something in a picture. **2** form a mental image of; visualize: *she pictured him waiting and smiled.*

– SYNONYMS **1 depict,** portray, show, represent, draw, sketch, photograph, paint. **2 visualize,** see (in one's mind's eye), imagine, remember.

– PHRASES (as) **pretty as a picture** very pretty. **in the picture** informal informed about something.
– ORIGIN Latin *pictura*, from *pingere* 'to paint.'

pic·ture-post·card ▶ **adjective** (of a view) prettily picturesque.

pic·tur·esque /ˌpikCHəˈresk/ ▶ **adjective** attractive in a quaint or charming way: *miles of picturesque beaches*.

– SYNONYMS **attractive,** pretty, beautiful, lovely, scenic, charming, quaint, pleasing, delightful.
– ANTONYMS ugly.

– DERIVATIVES **pic·tur·esque·ly** adverb **pic·tur·esque·ness** noun.

WORD TOOLKIT

See **GRAPHIC**.

pic·ture win·dow ▶ **noun** a large window consisting of one pane of glass.

pid·dle /ˈpidl/ ▶ **verb** informal **1** urinate. **2** (**piddle around/about**) spend time in unimportant activities.
– ORIGIN probably from **PISS** and **PUDDLE**.

pid·dling /ˈpidliNG/ (also **piddly**) ▶ **adjective** informal ridiculously small or unimportant.

– SYNONYMS **trivial,** trifling, petty, meager, inadequate, insufficient, paltry, derisory, pitiful, miserable, puny, niggardly, mere, tiny, insignificant, unimportant, inconsequential; informal measly, pathetic, piffling, nickel-and-dime, mingy.

pidg·in /ˈpijən/ ▶ **noun** a simplified form of a language with elements taken from local languages, used for communication between people not sharing a common language.
– ORIGIN Chinese alteration of English *business*.

pie /pī/ ▶ **noun** a baked dish of fruit, or meat and vegetables, encased in or topped with pastry.
– PHRASES **pie in the sky** informal a pleasant future event or idea that is very unlikely to happen.
– ORIGIN probably the same word as former *pie* 'magpie,' the combinations of ingredients being compared to objects collected by a magpie.

pie·bald /ˈpīˌbôld/ ▶ **adjective** (of a horse) having irregular patches of two colors, typically black and white. ▶ **noun** a piebald horse.
– ORIGIN from *pie* in *magpie* + *bald* in the former sense 'streaked with white.'

piece /pēs/ ▶ **noun 1** a portion separated from the whole. **2** an item used in constructing something or forming part of a set: *a piece of luggage*. **3** a musical or written work. **4** a figure or token used to make moves in a board game. **5** a coin of specified value. **6** informal a firearm.

– SYNONYMS **1 bit,** slice, chunk, segment, section, lump, hunk, wedge, slab, block, cake, bar, stick, length. **2 component,** part, bit, constituent, element, section, unit, module. **3 item,** article, specimen. **4 share,** portion, slice, quota, part, percentage, amount, quantity, ration, fraction. **5 work (of art),** artwork, artifact, composition, opus. **6 article,** item, story, report, essay, feature, review, column.

▶ **verb** (**piece something together**) assemble something from individual parts.
– PHRASES **go to pieces** become so upset that one cannot function normally. **in one piece** not harmed or damaged. **(all) of a piece (with something)** (entirely) consistent (with something). **say one's piece** give one's opinion.
– ORIGIN Old French.

CHOOSE THE RIGHT WORD

See **FRAGMENT**.

pièce de ré·sis·tance /pēˈes də ˌrəziˈstäns, -rāziˈstäNS/ ▶ **noun** the most important or impressive feature of something: *the garden was her pièce de résistance*.
– ORIGIN French, 'piece (i.e. means) of resistance.'

piece·meal /ˈpēsˌmēl/ ▶ **adjective & adverb** done in stages over a period of time.
– ORIGIN from **PIECE** + an Old English word meaning 'measure, quantity taken at one time.'

piece·work /ˈpēsˌwərk/ ▶ **noun** work paid for according to the amount produced.

pie chart ▶ **noun** a diagram in which a circle is divided into sectors that each represent a proportion of the whole.

pied /pīd/ ▶ **adjective** having two or more different colors.
– ORIGIN first meaning 'black and white like a magpie.'

pied-à-terre /pēˌyād ə ˈter/ ▶ **noun** (pl. **pieds-à-terre** pronunc. same) a small apartment or house kept for occasional use, one's permanent home being elsewhere.
– ORIGIN French, 'foot to earth.'

pied·mont /ˈpēdmänt/ ▶ **noun** a gentle slope leading from the base of mountains to a region of flat land.

Pied Pip·er /ˈpīd ˈpīpər/ ▶ **noun** a person who entices others to follow them in a course of action, especially one with disastrous results.
– ORIGIN from the piper in German legend who rid the town of Hamelin of rats by enticing them away with his music, and when refused the promised payment lured away the town's children.

pie-eyed ▶ **adjective** informal very drunk.

pier /pi(ə)r/ ▶ **noun 1** a structure leading out to sea and used as a landing stage for boats or as a place of entertainment. **2** a pillar supporting an arch or a bridge. **3** a wall between windows or other adjoining openings.

– SYNONYMS **jetty,** quay, wharf, dock, landing stage.

– ORIGIN Latin *pera*.

pierce /pi(ə)rs/ ▶ **verb 1** make a hole in or through something with a sharp object. **2** force a way through: *a shrill voice pierced the air*.

– SYNONYMS **penetrate,** puncture, perforate, prick, spike, stab, drill, bore.

– DERIVATIVES **pierc·er** noun.
– ORIGIN Old French *percer*.

pierc·ing /ˈpi(ə)rsiNG/ ▶ **adjective 1** (of a voice or sound) extremely high, loud, or shrill. **2** (of the wind) very cold. **3** (of eyes or a look) appearing to see through someone; searching.

– SYNONYMS **1** *a piercing shriek* **shrill,** ear-splitting, high-pitched, penetrating, strident. **2** *the piercing wind* **bitter,** biting, cutting, penetrating, sharp, keen, stinging, raw; freezing, frigid, glacial, arctic, chill. **3** *his piercing gaze* **searching,** probing, penetrating, sharp, keen, shrewd.

Pi·er·rot /ˌpēəˈrō/ ▶ **noun** a male character in French pantomime, with a sad white-painted face, a loose white costume, and a pointed hat.
– ORIGIN French, familiar form of the man's name *Pierre* 'Peter.'

pi·e·ty /ˈpī-itē/ ▸ **noun** (pl. **pieties**) **1** the quality of being deeply religious. **2** a conventional belief that is accepted without thinking.

– SYNONYMS **devoutness,** devotion, piousness, holiness, godliness, reverence, faith, spirituality.

– ORIGIN Latin *pietas* 'dutifulness.'

pi·e·zo /pīˈēzō, pēˈäzō/ ▸ **adjective** piezoelectric.

pi·e·zo·e·lec·tric /pēˌāzōˌilekˈtrik, pīˌēz-/ ▸ **adjective** relating to electric polarization produced in certain crystals by the application of mechanical stress.
– ORIGIN from Greek *piezein* 'press, squeeze.'

pif·fle /ˈpifəl/ ▸ **noun** informal nonsense.
– ORIGIN uncertain.

pif·fling /ˈpifliNG/ ▸ **adjective** informal trivial; unimportant.

pig /pig/ ▸ **noun 1** a domesticated mammal with sparse bristly hair and a flat snout, kept for its meat. **2** informal a greedy, dirty, or unpleasant person. **3** informal, derogatory a police officer. **4** an oblong mass of iron or lead from a smelting furnace.

– SYNONYMS **hog,** boar, sow, porker, swine, piglet.

▸ **verb** (**pigs, pigging, pigged**) informal (often **pig out**) gorge oneself with food.
– DERIVATIVES **pig·let** /ˈpiglit/ noun.
– PHRASES **make a pig of oneself** informal overeat. **a pig in a poke** something that is bought without first being seen.
– ORIGIN probably from an Old English word meaning 'acorn' or 'pig bread.'

WORD LINKS

porcine *relating to pigs*

pi·geon /ˈpijən/ ▸ **noun** a fat bird with a small head and a cooing voice.
– ORIGIN Old French *pijon* 'young bird.'

pi·geon·hole /ˈpijənˌhōl/ ▸ **noun 1** each of a set of small compartments where letters or messages may be left for people. **2** a category into which someone or something is placed. ▸ **verb** place in a particular category, especially a restrictive one: *I was pigeonholed as a 'youth writer.'*

pi·geon-toed ▸ **adjective** having the toes or feet turned inward.

pig·ger·y /ˈpigərē/ ▸ **noun** (pl. **piggeries**) **1** a farm or enclosure where pigs are kept. **2** greed or unpleasantness, regarded as characteristic of pigs.

pig·gish /ˈpigisH/ ▸ **adjective** greedy, dirty, or unpleasant.

pig·gy /ˈpigē/ ▸ **noun** (pl. **piggies**) a child's word for a pig. ▸ **adjective** resembling a pig, especially in features or appetite.

pig·gy·back /ˈpigēˌbak/ ▸ **noun** a ride on someone's back and shoulders. ▸ **adverb** on the back and shoulders of another person. ▸ **verb** link to or take advantage of an existing system or body of work: *they have piggybacked their own networks onto the system.*

pig·gy bank ▸ **noun** a container for saving money, shaped like a pig.

pig·head·ed /ˈpigˌhedid/ ▸ **adjective** stupidly obstinate.

pig i·ron ▸ **noun** crude iron as first obtained from a smelting furnace.

pig·ment /ˈpigmənt/ ▸ **noun 1** a natural substance that gives animal or plant tissue its color. **2** a substance used for coloring or painting.

– SYNONYMS **coloring,** color, tint, dye, stain.

– DERIVATIVES **pig·men·tar·y** /-ˌterē/ adjective **pig·men·ta·tion** /ˌpigmənˈtāsHən/ noun.
– ORIGIN Latin *pigmentum.*

pig·ment·ed /ˈpigˌməntid, ˌpigˈməntid/ ▸ **adjective** colored with or as if with pigment.

pig·my ▸ **noun** variant spelling of **PYGMY**.

pig·pen /ˈpigˌpen/ ▸ **noun 1** a pen or enclosure for pigs. **2** a very dirty or untidy house or room.

pig·skin /ˈpigˌskin/ ▸ **noun 1** leather made from the hide of a pig. **2** informal a football.

pig·sty /ˈpigˌstī/ ▸ **noun** (pl. **pigsties**) **1** an enclosure for a pig or pigs. **2** a very dirty or untidy house or room.

pig·tail /ˈpigˌtāl/ ▸ **noun** a braided length of hair worn singly at the back or on each side of the head.
– DERIVATIVES **pig·tailed** adjective.

pike[1] /pīk/ ▸ **noun** (pl. same) a predatory freshwater fish with a long body and sharp teeth.
– ORIGIN from **PIKE**[2] (because of the fish's pointed jaw).

pike[2] ▸ **noun** historical a weapon with a pointed metal head on a long wooden shaft.
– ORIGIN French *pique.*

pike[3] ▸ **noun** a jackknife position in diving or gymnastics.
– ORIGIN unknown.

pike[4] ▸ **noun** short for **TURNPIKE**.
– PHRASES **come down the pike** appear on the scene; come to someone's notice.

pik·er /ˈpīkər/ ▸ **noun** informal **1** a gambler who makes only small bets. **2** a miserly or cautious person.

pike·staff /ˈpīkˌstaf/ ▸ **noun** historical the wooden shaft of a pike.
– PHRASES **(as) plain as a pikestaff** very obvious. [alteration of *as plain as a packstaff*, the staff being that of a pedlar, on which he rested his pack of wares.]

pi·laf /pəˈläf, ˈpēläf/ (also **pilau** /-ˈlô, -lou/, **pulao** /-lô, -lou/) ▸ **noun** a Middle Eastern or Indian dish of spiced rice, often with vegetables or meat added.
– ORIGIN Turkish.

pi·las·ter /pəˈlastər/ ▸ **noun** a rectangular column incorporated within and projecting slightly from a wall.
– ORIGIN Latin *pilastrum.*

Pi·la·tes /piˈlätēz/ ▸ **noun** a system of exercises designed to improve physical strength, flexibility, and posture, and to enhance mental awareness.
– ORIGIN named after Joseph *Pilates*, its German inventor.

pil·chard /ˈpilcHərd/ ▸ **noun** a small edible sea fish of the herring family.
– ORIGIN unknown.

pile[1] /pīl/ ▸ **noun 1** a heap of things laid or lying one on top of another. **2** informal a large amount. **3** a large imposing building.

– SYNONYMS **1 heap,** stack, mound, pyramid, mass, collection, accumulation, assemblage, stockpile, hoard. **2 lot,** mountain, reams, abundance; informal load, heap, mass, slew, stack, ton, oodles.

▸ **verb 1** place things one on top of the other. **2** (**pile up**) form a pile or very large quantity. **3** (**pile into/out of**) get into or out of a vehicle in a disorganized way. **4** (**pile something on**) informal exaggerate something for effect.

– SYNONYMS **1 heap,** stack, load, fill, charge. **2** (**pile up**) **accumulate,** amass, grow, mount up, build up, multiply, escalate, soar, spiral, rocket, increase. **3** (**pile into/out of**) *we piled into the car* **crowd,** clamber, pack, squeeze, scramble, struggle.

– ORIGIN Latin *pila* 'pillar, pier.'

pile² ▶ **noun** a heavy stake or post driven into the ground as a foundation or support for a structure.
– ORIGIN Old English.

pile³ ▶ **noun** the soft projecting surface of a carpet or a fabric, consisting of the cut ends of many small threads.

– SYNONYMS **nap,** fibers, threads.

– ORIGIN Latin *pilus* 'hair.'

pile driv·er ▶ **noun** a machine for driving piles into the ground.

piles /pīlz/ ▶ **plural noun** hemorrhoids.
– ORIGIN probably from Latin *pila* 'ball.'

pile·up /'pīl,əp/ ▶ **noun 1** a crash involving several vehicles. **2** a large collection of something.

– SYNONYMS **crash,** collision, accident, wreck, smash.

pil·fer /'pilfər/ ▶ **verb** steal things of little value.
– DERIVATIVES **pil·fer·age** noun.
– ORIGIN Old French *pelfrer* 'to pillage.'

pil·grim /'pilgrəm/ ▶ **noun 1** a person who journeys to a holy place for religious reasons. **2** (**Pilgrim**) a member of a group of English Puritans who sailed in the *Mayflower* and founded Plymouth in 1620.

– SYNONYMS **traveler,** wayfarer, haji, worshiper, devotee, believer.

– ORIGIN Provençal *pelegrin.*

pil·grim·age /'pilgrəmij/ ▶ **noun 1** a pilgrim's journey to a holy place. **2** a journey to a place of interest or importance.

– SYNONYMS **journey,** expedition, mission, hajj, visit, trek, trip, odyssey.

CHOOSE THE RIGHT WORD

See **JOURNEY**.

pill /pil/ ▶ **noun 1** a small round mass of solid medicine for swallowing whole. **2** (**the pill**) a contraceptive pill.

– SYNONYMS **tablet,** capsule, pellet, lozenge, pastille.

– PHRASES **a bitter pill** something that is unpleasant but must be accepted. **sweeten the pill** chiefly Brit. make an unpleasant necessity easier to accept.
– ORIGIN Latin *pilula* 'little ball.'

pil·lage /'pilij/ ▶ **verb** rob a place or steal something with violence, especially in wartime.

– SYNONYMS **1** *the abbey was pillaged* **ransack,** rob, plunder, raid, sack, devastate, lay waste, ravage, loot. **2** *columns pillaged from an ancient tomb* **steal,** pilfer, take, purloin, loot; informal swipe, rob, nab, rip off, heist, lift, 'liberate', 'borrow', filch.

▶ **noun** the action of pillaging a place or property.
– DERIVATIVES **pil·lag·er** noun.
– ORIGIN Old French.

pil·lar /'pilər/ ▶ **noun 1** a tall vertical structure used as a support for a building or as an ornament. **2** a person or thing providing reliable support: *he was a pillar of his local community.*

– SYNONYMS **1 column,** post, support, upright, pier, pile, prop, stanchion, obelisk. **2 stalwart,** mainstay, bastion, leading light, worthy, backbone, supporter, upholder, champion.

– DERIVATIVES **pil·lared** adjective.
– PHRASES **from pillar to post** from one place to another in an unsatisfactory way.
– ORIGIN Latin *pila* 'pillar.'

pill·box /'pil,bäks/ ▶ **noun 1** a woman's hat with straight sides, a flat top, and no brim. **2** a small round box for holding pills. **3** a small, partly underground, concrete fort.

pil·lion /'pilyən/ ▶ **noun** a seat for a passenger behind a motorcyclist.
– ORIGIN Irish *pillín* 'small cushion.'

pil·lo·ry /'pilərē/ ▶ **noun** (pl. **pillories**) a wooden framework with holes for the head and hands, in which offenders were formerly imprisoned and exposed to public abuse. ▶ **verb** (**pillories, pillorying, pilloried**) **1** attack or ridicule someone publicly. **2** put someone in a pillory.
– ORIGIN Old French *pilori.*

pil·low /'pilō/ ▶ **noun** a rectangular cloth bag stuffed with soft material, used to support the head when lying down or sleeping. ▶ **verb** support the head on something soft.
– DERIVATIVES **pil·low·y** adjective.
– ORIGIN Latin *pulvinus* 'cushion.'

pil·low·case /'pilō,kās/ ▶ **noun** a removable cloth cover for a pillow.

pil·low talk ▶ **noun** intimate conversation between lovers in bed.

pi·lot /'pīlət/ ▶ **noun 1** a person who operates the flying controls of an aircraft. **2** a person with local knowledge who is qualified to take charge of a ship entering or leaving a harbor. **3** something done or produced as a test before introducing it more widely: *a pilot for a Channel 4 sitcom.*

– SYNONYMS **1 airman, airwoman,** flyer, aviator, captain; informal skipper; dated aviatrix. **2 navigator,** helmsman, steersman, coxswain. **3 trial,** sample, experiment. **4** (as adj.) *a pilot project* **experimental,** exploratory, trial, test, sample, preliminary.

▶ **verb** (**pilots, piloting, piloted**) **1** act as a pilot of an aircraft or ship. **2** test a scheme, program, etc., before introducing it more widely.

– SYNONYMS **navigate,** guide, maneuver, steer, control, direct, captain, fly, drive, sail; informal skipper.

– DERIVATIVES **pi·lot·age** noun.
– ORIGIN Latin *pilotus.*

pi·lot light ▶ **noun 1** a small gas burner kept alight permanently to light a larger burner when needed. **2** an electric indicator light or control light.

pi·lot whale ▶ **noun** a black toothed whale with a square bulbous head.

Pil·sner /'pilznər/ ▶ **noun** a lager beer with a strong hop flavor, originally brewed at Pilsen (Plzeň) in the Czech Republic.

PIM ▶ **abbreviation** personal information manager.

pi·mien·to /pə'm(y)entō/ (also **pimento** /pə'mentō/) ▶ **noun** (pl. **pimientos**) a red sweet pepper.
– ORIGIN Spanish.

pimp /pimp/ ▶ **noun** a man who controls prostitutes and arranges clients for them, taking a percentage of their

earnings in return. ▶ **verb** **1** act as a pimp. **2** informal make something, especially a car, more showy or impressive.
– ORIGIN unknown.

pim·per·nel /ˈpimpərˌnel, -pərnəl/ ▶ **noun** a low-growing plant with bright five-petaled flowers.
– ORIGIN Old French *pimpernelle*.

pim·ple /ˈpimpəl/ ▶ **noun** a small hard inflamed spot on the skin.
– DERIVATIVES **pim·pled** adjective **pim·ply** adjective.
– ORIGIN related to an Old English word meaning 'break out in pustules.'

PIN /pin/ (also **PIN number**) ▶ **abbreviation** personal identification number.

pin /pin/ ▶ **noun** **1** a thin piece of metal with a sharp point at one end and a round head at the other, used for fastening pieces of cloth, paper, etc. **2** a metal projection from an electric plug or an integrated circuit. **3** a small brooch or badge. **4** a steel rod used to join the ends of fractured bones while they heal. **5** Golf a stick with a flag placed in a hole to mark its position. **6** a metal peg in a hand grenade that prevents it from exploding. **7** (in bowling) one of a set of bottle-shaped wooden pieces arranged in an upright position at the end of a lane. **8** (**pins**) informal legs.

– SYNONYMS **1 tack,** safety pin, nail, staple, fastener. **2 bolt,** peg, rod, rivet, dowel. **3 badge,** brooch.

▶ **verb** (**pins, pinning, pinned**) **1** attach or fasten something with a pin or pins. **2** hold someone firmly so they are unable to move. **3** (**pin someone down**) force someone to be specific about their intentions. **4** (**pin someone down**) restrict the actions of an enemy by firing at them. **5** (**pin something on**) place blame or responsibility on someone.

– SYNONYMS **1 attach,** fasten, affix, fix, join, secure, clip, nail. **2 hold,** press, pinion. **3** (**pin someone down**) *she tried to pin him down to a plan* **constrain,** pressure, tie down, nail down. **4** (**pin someone down**) *our troops can pin down the enemy* **confine,** trap, hem in, corner, close in, shut in, pen in. **5** (**pin something on**) *they pinned the crime on him* **blame for,** hold responsible for, attribute to, ascribe to, lay something at someone's door; informal stick on.

– PHRASES **pin one's hopes on** rely heavily on.
– ORIGIN Latin *pinna* 'point, tip, edge.'

pin·a·fore /ˈpinəˌfôr/ ▶ **noun** **1** a collarless, sleeveless dress worn over a blouse or sweater. **2** Brit. a loose sleeveless piece of clothing worn over other clothes to keep them clean.
– ORIGIN from **PIN** + **AFORE**.

pin·ball /ˈpinˌbôl/ ▶ **noun** a game in which small metal balls are shot across a sloping board to strike targets.

pince-nez /ˈpansˌnā, ˈpins/ ▶ **noun** (treated as sing. or pl.) a pair of glasses with a nose clip instead of earpieces.
– ORIGIN French, 'that pinches the nose.'

pin·cer /ˈpinsər/ ▶ **noun** **1** (**pincers**) a tool made of two pieces of metal with blunt inward-curving jaws, used for gripping and pulling things. **2** a front claw of a lobster or similar type of shellfish.
– ORIGIN from Old French *pincier* 'to pinch.'

pin·cer move·ment ▶ **noun** an attack in which an army approaches the enemy from two sides at the same time.

pinch /pinCH/ ▶ **verb** **1** grip flesh tightly between the finger and thumb. **2** (of a shoe) hurt a foot by being too tight. **3** informal steal something. **4** informal arrest someone.

– SYNONYMS **nip,** tweak, squeeze, grasp, compress.

▶ **noun** **1** an act of pinching. **2** an amount of an ingredient that can be held between the fingers and thumb: *a pinch of salt*.

– SYNONYMS **1 nip,** tweak, squeeze. **2 bit,** touch, dash, spot, trace, soupçon, speck, taste; informal smidgen, tad.

– PHRASES **in a pinch** if absolutely necessary. **feel the pinch** experience financial hardship.
– ORIGIN Old French *pincier* 'to pinch.'

pinch-hit ▶ **verb** **1** Baseball bat in place of another player, typically at a critical point in the game. **2** informal act as a substitute for someone, especially in an emergency: *last year I briefly pinch-hit for a movie critic on leave*.

pin·cush·ion /ˈpinˌko͝oSHən/ ▶ **noun** a small pad for holding pins.

pine[1] /pīn/ ▶ **noun** (also **pine tree**) an evergreen coniferous tree having clusters of long needle-shaped leaves.
– ORIGIN Latin *pinus*.

pine[2] ▶ **verb** **1** (often **pine away**) feel very distressed or weak because one misses someone so much. **2** (**pine for**) miss or long for: *some members still pine for the old days*.

– SYNONYMS **1 fade,** waste away, weaken, decline, languish, wilt, sicken. **2** (**pine for**) **long for,** yearn for, ache for, sigh for, hunger for, thirst for, itch for, carry a torch for, miss, mourn.

– ORIGIN Old English.

pin·e·al gland /ˈpinēəl, ˈpī-/ (also **pineal body**) ▶ **noun** a small gland at the back of the skull within the brain, producing a hormonelike substance in some mammals.
– ORIGIN from Latin *pinea* 'pine cone.'

pine·ap·ple /ˈpīˌnapəl/ ▶ **noun** a large tropical fruit with juicy yellow flesh surrounded by a tough skin and topped with a tuft of leaves.
– ORIGIN from **PINE**[1] + **APPLE**.

pine cone ▶ **noun** the conical or rounded woody fruit of a pine tree.

pine mar·ten ▶ **noun** a dark brown weasellike mammal that lives in trees.

pine nut ▶ **noun** the edible seed of various pine trees.

pine sis·kin /ˈsiskin/ ▶ **noun** a North American finch with dark-streaked plumage, a notched tail, and touches of yellow on its wings and tail.
– ORIGIN Dutch *siseken*.

pine·y /ˈpīnē/ (also **piny**) ▶ **adjective** relating to, resembling, or full of pines.

ping /piNG/ ▶ **noun** an abrupt high-pitched ringing sound. ▶ **verb** make an abrupt high-pitched ringing sound.
– ORIGIN imitating the sound.

ping-pong /ˈpiNG ˌpôNG, -ˌpäNG/ (also trademark **Ping-Pong**) ▶ **noun** informal table tennis.
– ORIGIN imitating the sound of a bat striking a ball.

pin·head /ˈpinˌhed/ ▶ **noun** **1** the flattened head of a pin. **2** informal a stupid person.

pin·hole /ˈpinˌhōl/ ▶ **noun** a very small hole.

pin·ion[1] /ˈpinyən/ ▶ **noun** the outer part of a bird's wing including the flight feathers. ▶ **verb** **1** tie or hold someone by the arms or legs. **2** cut off the pinion of a bird to prevent it from flying.
– ORIGIN Old French *pignon*.

pin·ion² ▶ **noun** a small gear or spindle that engages with a large gear.
– ORIGIN French *pignon*.

pink¹ /piNGk/ ▶ **adjective 1** of a color between red and white. **2** informal, often derogatory left-wing. **3** relating to homosexuals: *the pink economy*.

– SYNONYMS **rose,** rosy, rosé, pale red, salmon, coral, flushed, blushing.

▶ **noun 1** pink color or material. **2** (**the pink**) informal the best condition: *he's in the pink of health*.
– DERIVATIVES **pink·ish** adjective **pink·y** adjective.
– ORIGIN from **PINK²**.

pink² ▶ **noun** a plant with sweet-smelling pink or white flowers and narrow gray-green leaves.
– ORIGIN uncertain.

pink³ ▶ **verb** cut a zigzag edge on something.
– ORIGIN perhaps from German *pinken* 'strike, peck.'

pink⁴ ▶ **verb** Brit. (of a vehicle engine) make rattling sounds as a result of over-rapid combustion in the cylinders.
– ORIGIN imitating the sound.

pink·ie /ˈpiNGkē/ (also **pinky**) ▶ **noun** (pl. **pinkies**) informal the little finger.
– ORIGIN partly from Dutch *pink*.

pink·ing shears ▶ **plural noun** scissors with a serrated blade, used to cut a zigzag edge in fabric.

pink·o /ˈpiNGkō/ ▶ **noun** (pl. **pinkos** or **pinkoes**) informal, derogatory a left-wing or liberal person.

pink slip informal ▶ **noun** a notice of dismissal from employment. ▶ **verb** (**pink-slip**) dismiss someone from employment.

pin mon·ey ▶ **noun** a small sum of money for spending on items that are not essential.
– ORIGIN first referring to an allowance to a woman from her husband for personal expenses.

pin·na /ˈpinə/ ▶ **noun** (pl. **pinnae** /ˈpinē/) the external part of the ear; the auricle.
– ORIGIN Latin.

pin·nace /ˈpinis/ ▶ **noun** chiefly historical a small boat forming part of the equipment of a larger ship.
– ORIGIN French *pinace*.

pin·na·cle /ˈpinəkəl/ ▶ **noun 1** the most successful point: *the pinnacle of his career*. **2** a high pointed piece of rock. **3** a small pointed turret on a roof.

– SYNONYMS **1 height,** peak, high point, top, apex, zenith, acme. **2 peak,** needle, crag, tor.
– ANTONYMS nadir.

– ORIGIN Latin *pinnaculum*.

pin·nate /ˈpināt, -it/ ▶ **adjective** Botany & Zoology having leaflets or other parts arranged on either side of a stem or axis.
– ORIGIN Latin *pinnatus* 'feathered.'

PIN num·ber ▶ **noun** see **PIN**.

Pi·not /ˈpēnō, pēˈnō/ ▶ **noun** any of several varieties of wine grape, which are either red (**Pinot Noir** /nwär/) or white (**Pinot Blanc** /bläNGk/).
– ORIGIN French.

pin·point /ˈpinˌpoint/ ▶ **verb** find or identify exactly: *it is difficult to pinpoint a single cause for violence like this*.

– SYNONYMS **identify,** determine, distinguish, discover, find, locate, detect, track down, spot, diagnose, recognize, pin down, home in on.

▶ **noun** a tiny dot or point.
▶ **adjective** absolutely precise.

– SYNONYMS *pinpoint accuracy* **precise,** exact, strict, absolute, complete, scientific.

pin·prick /ˈpinˌprik/ ▶ **noun 1** a prick caused by a pin. **2** a cause of minor irritation.

pins and nee·dles ▶ **plural noun** (treated as sing.) a tingling sensation in a limb recovering from numbness.

pin·stripe /ˈpinˌstrīp/ ▶ **noun** a very narrow stripe in cloth, used especially for suits.
– DERIVATIVES **pin·striped** adjective.

pint /pīnt/ ▶ **noun 1** a unit of liquid or dry capacity equal to one half of a quart. **2** chiefly Brit. informal a pint of beer.
– ORIGIN Old French *pinte*.

pin·tail /ˈpinˌtāl/ ▶ **noun** a duck with a long pointed tail.

pin·to /ˈpintō/ ▶ **noun** (pl. **pintos**) a piebald horse.
– ORIGIN from Spanish, 'mottled.'

pin·to bean ▶ **noun** a medium-sized speckled variety of kidney bean.

pint-sized (also **pint-size**) ▶ **adjective** informal very small.

pin-tuck ▶ **noun** a very narrow ornamental tuck in an item of clothing.

pin·up /ˈpinˌəp/ ▶ **noun** a poster featuring a sexually attractive person.

pin·wheel /ˈpinˌ(h)wēl/ ▶ **noun 1** a child's toy consisting of a stick with colored vanes that twirl in the wind. **2** something shaped or rotating like a pinwheel.

Pin·yin /ˈpinˈyin/ ▶ **noun** the standard system for transliterating Chinese characters into the Roman alphabet.
– ORIGIN Chinese, 'spell-sound.'

pi·ña co·la·da /ˈpēnyə kəˈlädə/ ▶ **noun** a cocktail made with rum, pineapple juice, and coconut.
– ORIGIN Spanish, 'strained pineapple.'

pi·ña·ta /pēnˈyätə/ ▶ **noun** (especially in Spanish-speaking communities) a papier mâché figure of an animal, hung in the air at festivals so that children can smash it with sticks and share the contents.

pi·ñon /ˈpinyən, ˌpinˈyōn/ (also **pinyon**) ▶ **noun 1** a small pine tree with edible seeds, native to Mexico and the southwestern US. **2** (also **piñon nut**) a pine nut from this tree.

pi·on /ˈpīˌän/ ▶ **noun** Physics a meson (subatomic particle) with a mass around 270 times that of the electron.
– ORIGIN from the earlier name *pi-meson*.

pi·o·neer /ˌpīəˈni(ə)r/ ▶ **noun 1** a person who explores or settles in a new region. **2** a person who develops new ideas or techniques.

– SYNONYMS **1 settler,** colonist, colonizer, frontiersman, explorer. **2 developer,** innovator, trailblazer, groundbreaker, founding father, architect, creator.

▶ **verb** develop or be the first to use: *the company pioneered the use of the computer in the courtroom*.

– SYNONYMS **introduce,** develop, launch, instigate, initiate, spearhead, institute, establish, found.

– ORIGIN French *pionnier* 'foot soldier.'

pi·ous /ˈpīəs/ ▶ **adjective 1** deeply religious. **2** pretending to be good or religious so as to impress. **3** (of a hope) sincere but unlikely to be fulfilled.

– SYNONYMS **religious,** devout, God-fearing, churchgoing, holy, godly, saintly, reverent, righteous.
– ANTONYMS irreligious.

– DERIVATIVES **pi·ous·ly** adverb **pi·ous·ness** noun.
– ORIGIN Latin *pius* 'dutiful.'

pip[1] /pip/ ▸ **noun** a small hard seed in a fruit.
– ORIGIN abbreviation of **PIPPIN**.

pip[2] ▸ **noun 1** Brit. a star indicating rank on the shoulder of an army officer's uniform. **2** any of the spots on a playing card, dice, or domino.
– ORIGIN unknown.

pip[3] ▸ **noun** a disease of poultry or other birds causing thick mucus in the throat.
– ORIGIN Dutch *pippe*.

pip[4] ▸ **verb** (of a young bird) crack (the shell of the egg) when hatching.

pipe /pīp/ ▸ **noun 1** a tube used to carry water, gas, oil, etc. **2** a device for smoking tobacco, consisting of a narrow tube that opens into a small bowl in which the tobacco is burned. **3** a wind instrument consisting of a single tube with holes along its length that are covered by the fingers to produce different notes. **4** one of the tubes by which notes are produced in an organ. **5** (**pipes**) bagpipes.

– SYNONYMS **tube,** conduit, hose, main, duct, line, channel, pipeline, drain.

▸ **verb 1** convey something through a pipe. **2** transmit music, a program, or a signal by wire or cable. **3** play a tune on a pipe. **4** sing or say something in a high, shrill voice. **5** decorate food, clothing, or furnishings with piping.

– SYNONYMS **feed,** siphon, channel, run, convey.

– PHRASES **pipe down** informal be less noisy. **pipe up** say something suddenly. **put that in your pipe and smoke it** informal said to emphasize that someone will have to accept a particular situation, even if it is unwelcome.
– ORIGIN from Latin *pipare* 'to peep, chirp.'

pipe-clay ▸ **noun** a fine white clay, used for making tobacco pipes or for whitening leather.

pipe clean·er ▸ **noun** a piece of wire covered with fiber, used to clean a tobacco pipe.

piped-in mu·sic ▸ **noun** prerecorded background music played through loudspeakers.

pipe dream ▸ **noun** a hope or scheme that will never be realized.
– ORIGIN referring to a dream experienced when smoking an opium pipe.

pipe·line /ˈpīpˌlīn/ ▸ **noun** a long pipe for carrying oil, gas, or water over a long distance. ▸ **verb** carry oil, gas, or water by a pipeline.
– PHRASES **in the pipeline** in the process of being developed.

pipe or·gan ▸ **noun** an organ using pipes instead of or as well as reeds.

pip·er /ˈpīpər/ ▸ **noun** a person who plays a pipe or bagpipes.
– PHRASES **pay the piper** bear the consequences of an action or activity that one has enjoyed.

pi·pette /pīˈpet/ ▸ **noun** a narrow tube used in a laboratory for handling small quantities of liquid, the liquid being drawn into the tube by suction.
– ORIGIN French, 'little pipe.'

pip·ing /ˈpīpiNG/ ▸ **noun 1** lengths of pipe. **2** lines of icing or whipped cream, used to decorate cakes and desserts. **3** thin cord covered in fabric and inserted along a seam or hem for decoration.
– PHRASES **piping hot** (of food or water) very hot. [with reference to the whistling sound made by very hot liquid or food.]

pip·i·strelle /ˌpipəˈstrel, ˈpipəˌstrel/ ▸ **noun** a small insect-eating bat.
– ORIGIN French.

pip·it /ˈpipit/ ▸ **noun** a songbird of open country, typically having brown streaky plumage.
– ORIGIN probably imitating its call.

pip·pin /ˈpipin/ ▸ **noun** a red and yellow dessert apple.
– ORIGIN Old French *pepin* 'seed of a fruit.'

pip·squeak /ˈpipˌskwēk/ ▸ **noun** informal an insignificant person.

pi·quant /ˈpēkənt, -känt/ ▸ **adjective 1** having a pleasantly sharp or spicy taste. **2** stimulating or interesting: *legal arguments punctuated by piquant asides.*

– SYNONYMS **1** *a piquant sauce* **spicy,** tangy, peppery, hot, tasty, flavorsome, savory, pungent, sharp, tart, zesty, strong, salty. **2** *a piquant story* **intriguing,** stimulating, interesting, fascinating, colorful, exciting, lively, spicy, provocative, racy; informal juicy.
– ANTONYMS bland, dull.

– DERIVATIVES **pi·quan·cy** noun **pi·quant·ly** adverb.
– ORIGIN French, 'stinging, pricking.'

pique /pēk/ ▸ **noun** irritation or resentment arising from hurt pride.

– SYNONYMS **irritation,** annoyance, resentment, anger, displeasure, indignation, petulance, ill humor, vexation, exasperation, disgruntlement, discontent.

▸ **verb** (**piques, piquing, piqued**) **1** arouse someone's interest. **2** (**be piqued**) feel irritated or resentful.

– SYNONYMS **1** *his curiosity was piqued* **stimulate,** arouse, rouse, provoke, whet, awaken, excite, kindle, stir, galvanize. **2** *she was piqued by his neglect* **irritate,** annoy, bother, vex, displease, upset, offend, affront, anger, gall, irk, nettle; informal peeve, aggravate, miff, rile, tick off, tee off, bug, needle, get someone's back up, get someone's goat.

– ORIGIN French *piquer* 'prick, irritate.'

pi·qué /pēˈkā, pi-/ ▸ **noun** stiff cotton fabric woven in a ribbed or raised pattern.
– ORIGIN French, 'backstitched.'

pi·quet /piˈkā, ˈket/ ▸ **noun** a trick-taking card game for two players.
– ORIGIN French.

pi·ra·cy /ˈpīrəsē/ ▸ **noun 1** the practice of attacking and robbing ships at sea. **2** the use or reproduction of a movie, recording, or other material without permission and in order to make a profit.

pi·ra·nha /pəˈränə/ ▸ **noun** a freshwater fish with very sharp teeth.
– ORIGIN Portuguese.

pi·rate /ˈpīrət/ ▸ **noun 1** a person who attacks and robs ships at sea. **2** a person who reproduces the work of another for profit without permission.

– SYNONYMS **raider,** hijacker, freebooter, marauder; historical privateer, buccaneer; old use corsair.

▸ **adjective 1** (of a movie, recording, or other material) that has been reproduced and used for profit without permission: *pirate videos.* **2** (of an organization) broadcasting without official permission: *a pirate radio station.*

▶ **verb 1** reproduce (another's work) for profit without permission. **2** dated rob or plunder a ship.

– SYNONYMS **steal,** copy, plagiarize, poach, appropriate, bootleg; informal crib, lift, rip off.

– DERIVATIVES **pi·rat·ic** /pī'ratik, pi-/ adjective.
– ORIGIN Greek *peiratēs.*

pi·ro·gi /pi'rōgē/ (also **perogi**) ▶ **noun** (pl. same or **pirogies**) a dough dumpling stuffed with a filling such as potato or cheese.

pi·rogue /pi'rōg/ ▶ **noun** (in Central America and the Caribbean) a long narrow canoe made from a single tree trunk.
– ORIGIN French.

pir·ou·ette /ˌpiro͞o'et/ ▶ **noun** (especially in ballet) an act of spinning on one foot. ▶ **verb** spin around on one foot.
– ORIGIN French, 'spinning top.'

pis·ca·to·ri·al /ˌpiskə'tôrēəl/ (also **piscatory** /'piskəˌtôrē/) ▶ **adjective** formal relating to fishing.
– ORIGIN from Latin *piscator* 'fisherman.'

Pis·ces /'pīsēz, 'pisēz/ ▶ **noun 1** a constellation and the twelfth sign of the zodiac (the Fish or Fishes), which the sun enters about February 20. **2** (**a Pisces**) a person born when the sun is in this sign.
– DERIVATIVES **Pis·ce·an** /-sēən/ noun & adjective.
– ORIGIN Latin, 'fishes.'

pis·ci·cul·ture /'pisiˌkəlchər/ ▶ **noun** the controlled breeding and rearing of fish.
– ORIGIN from Latin *piscis* 'fish.'

pis·cine /'pīsēn, 'pisīn/ ▶ **adjective** relating to fish.

pis·civ·o·rous /pi'sivərəs/ ▶ **adjective** (of an animal) feeding on fish.
– DERIVATIVES **pis·ci·vore** /'pisiˌvôr/ noun.

piss /pis/ vulgar slang ▶ **verb** urinate. ▶ **noun 1** urine. **2** an act of urinating.
– DERIVATIVES **piss·er** noun.
– PHRASES **piss off** chiefly Brit. go away. **piss someone off** annoy someone. **piss something away** waste something.
– ORIGIN Old French *pisser.*

pissed /pist/ ▶ **adjective** vulgar slang **1** (also **pissed off**) very annoyed. **2** chiefly Brit. drunk.

pis·tach·i·o /pə'stashēˌō/ ▶ **noun** (pl. **pistachios**) the edible pale green seed of an Asian tree.
– ORIGIN Greek *pistakion.*

piste /pēst/ ▶ **noun** a ski trail of compacted snow.
– ORIGIN French, 'racetrack.'

pis·til /'pistl/ ▶ **noun** the female organs of a flower, comprising the stigma, style, and ovary.
– ORIGIN Latin *pistillum* 'pestle.'

pis·tol /'pistl/ ▶ **noun** a small gun designed to be held in one hand.

– SYNONYMS **handgun,** gun, revolver, sidearm; six-shooter; informal piece, gat, rod, shooting iron, derringer, Saturday night special.

– ORIGIN French *pistole.*

pis·tol-whip ▶ **verb** (**pistol-whips, pistol-whipping, pistol-whipped**) hit or beat someone with the butt of a pistol.

pis·ton /'pistn/ ▶ **noun 1** a disk or short cylinder fitting closely inside a tube in which it moves up and down, used especially in an internal combustion engine to make other parts of the engine move. **2** a valve in a brass instrument that is pressed down to alter the pitch of a note.
– ORIGIN Italian *pestone* 'large pestle.'

pit[1] /pit/ ▶ **noun 1** a large hole in the ground. **2** a mine or quarry for coal, gravel, etc. **3** a hollow or indentation in a surface. **4** a sunken area in a workshop floor allowing access to a car's underside. **5** an area at the side of a track where race cars are serviced and refueled. **6** a part of a theater where an orchestra plays. **7** a part of the floor of an exchange in which a particular stock or commodity is traded. **8** historical an enclosure in which animals were made to fight as a form of entertainment. **9** (**the pits**) informal a very bad place or situation. **10** (**the pit**) literary hell.

– SYNONYMS **1 hole,** trough, hollow, excavation, cavity, crater, pothole. **2 coal mine,** colliery, quarry, shaft.

▶ **verb** (**pits, pitting, pitted**) **1** make a hollow in the surface of something. **2** (**pit someone/thing against**) test someone or something in a contest or struggle against: *pit your wits against the world champions.*

– SYNONYMS **mark,** pockmark, pock, scar, dent, indent.

– DERIVATIVES **pit·ted** adjective.
– PHRASES **the pit of one's stomach** the lower part of the abdomen, regarded as the seat of strong feelings, especially anxiety.
– ORIGIN Old English, from Latin *puteus* 'well, shaft.'

pit[2] ▶ **noun** the stone of a fruit. ▶ **verb** (**pits, pitting, pitted**) remove the stone from fruit.
– ORIGIN probably from Dutch.

pi·ta /'pētə/ (also **pita bread**) ▶ **noun** a type of flat bread that can be split open to hold a filling.
– ORIGIN modern Greek, 'cake or pie.'

pit-a-pat /'pit ə ˌpat/ (also **pitapat**) ▶ **adverb** with a sound like quick light taps.
– ORIGIN imitating the sound.

pit bull (in full **pit bull terrier**) ▶ **noun** a fierce American type of bull terrier.

pitch[1] /pich/ ▶ **noun 1** the extent to which a sound or tone is high or low. **2** a particular level of intensity. **3** Baseball a legal delivery of the ball by the pitcher. **4** particular words used to sell or promote something. **5** the steepness of a roof. **6** the movement up and down of the front of a ship or aircraft.

– SYNONYMS **1** *her voice rose in pitch* **tone,** key, modulation, frequency. **2** *her anger reached such a pitch that she screamed* **level,** intensity, point, degree, height, extent. **3** *a sales pitch* **patter,** talk; informal spiel, line. **4** *the pitch of the roof* **gradient,** grade, slope, slant, angle, tilt, incline.

▶ **verb 1** Baseball throw (the ball) for the batter to try to hit. **2** throw or fall heavily or roughly. **3** set one's voice or a piece of music at a particular pitch. **4** set or aim at a particular level, target, or audience: *he should pitch his talk at a suitable level.* **5** set up and fix something in position. **6** (of the front of a moving ship or aircraft) move up and down. **7** (**pitch in**) informal join in enthusiastically with a task or activity. **8** (as adj. **pitched**) (of a roof) sloping.

– SYNONYMS **1** *she pitched the crumpled note into the fire* **throw,** toss, fling, hurl, cast, lob, flip; informal chuck, sling, heave. **2** *he pitched overboard* **fall,** tumble, topple, plunge, plummet. **3** *they pitched* *their tents* **put up,** set up, erect, raise. **4** *the boat pitched* **lurch,** toss, plunge, roll, reel, sway, rock, list.

– PHRASES **make a pitch** make an attempt at or bid for something.
– ORIGIN uncertain.

pitch² ▶ **noun** a sticky black substance that hardens on cooling, made from tar or turpentine and used for waterproofing.
– ORIGIN Old English.

pitch-black (also **pitch-dark**) ▶ **adjective** completely dark.

pitch·blende /ˈpicн,blend/ ▶ **noun** a mineral found in dark pitchlike masses and containing radium.
– ORIGIN German *Pechblende*.

pitched bat·tle /picнt ˈbatl/ ▶ **noun** a fierce fight involving a large number of people.

pitch·er¹ /ˈpicнər/ ▶ **noun** a large jug.
– ORIGIN Old French *pichier* 'pot.'

pitch·er² ▶ **noun** Baseball the player who throws the ball for the batter to hit.

pitch·er plant ▶ **noun** a plant with a deep pitcher-shaped pouch containing fluid in which insects are trapped and absorbed.

pitch·fork /ˈpicн,fôrk/ ▶ **noun** a farm tool with a long handle and sharp metal prongs, used for lifting hay. ▶ **verb 1** lift something with a pitchfork. **2** thrust suddenly into an unexpected and difficult situation: *he was pitchforked into the job for six months.*
– ORIGIN from former *pickfork*, influenced by PITCH¹.

pitch-per·fect ▶ **adjective** exactly right in tone, mood, or pitch: *a pitch-perfect performance.*

pitch pine ▶ **noun** a pine tree with hard, heavy, resinous wood.

pitch·y /ˈpicнē/ ▶ **adjective** (**pitchier, pitchiest**) resembling pitch, especially in being sticky or dark.

pit·e·ous /ˈpitēəs/ ▶ **adjective** deserving or arousing pity: *piteous cries.*
– DERIVATIVES **pit·e·ous·ly** adverb **pit·e·ous·ness** noun.
– ORIGIN Old French *piteus*.

pit·fall /ˈpit,fôl/ ▶ **noun 1** a hidden or unsuspected danger or difficulty: *the pitfalls of setting up an office at home.* **2** a covered pit used to trap animals.

– SYNONYMS **hazard,** danger, risk, peril, difficulty, catch, snag, stumbling block, drawback.

pith /piтн/ ▶ **noun 1** spongy white tissue lining the rind of citrus fruits. **2** spongy tissue in the stems and branches of many plants. **3** the essential part of something: *puzzling over the pith of the problem.* **4** conciseness and clarity in expressing a point.
– ORIGIN Old English.

pith hel·met ▶ **noun** a head covering made from the dried pith of a tropical plant, used for protection from the sun.

pith·y /ˈpiтнē/ ▶ **adjective** (**pithier, pithiest**) **1** (of language or style) concise and expressing a point clearly. **2** (of a fruit or plant) containing much pith.

– SYNONYMS **succinct,** terse, concise, compact, short (and sweet), brief, condensed, to the point, epigrammatic, crisp, significant, meaningful, telling.
– ANTONYMS verbose.

– DERIVATIVES **pith·i·ly** adverb **pith·i·ness** noun.

pit·i·a·ble /ˈpitēəbəl/ ▶ **adjective 1** deserving or arousing pity. **2** ridiculously poor or small.
– DERIVATIVES **pit·i·a·bly** /-əblē/ adverb.

pit·i·ful /ˈpitifəl/ ▶ **adjective 1** deserving or arousing pity. **2** very small or poor; inadequate.

– SYNONYMS **1 distressing,** sad, piteous, pitiable, pathetic, heart-rending, moving, touching, tear-jerking, plaintive, poignant, forlorn, poor, sorry, wretched, miserable. **2 paltry,** miserable, meager, trifling, negligible, pitiable, derisory; informal pathetic, measly. **3 dreadful,** awful, terrible, appalling, lamentable, hopeless, feeble, pitiable, woeful, inadequate, deplorable, laughable; informal pathetic, useless, lousy, abysmal, dire.

– DERIVATIVES **pit·i·ful·ly** adverb **pit·i·ful·ness** noun.

pit·i·less /ˈpitēlis/ ▶ **adjective** showing no pity; harsh or cruel.

– SYNONYMS **merciless,** unmerciful, ruthless, cruel, heartless, remorseless, hard-hearted, cold-hearted, harsh, callous, severe, unsparing, unforgiving, unfeeling, uncaring, unsympathetic, uncharitable.
– ANTONYMS merciful.

– DERIVATIVES **pit·i·less·ly** adverb **pit·i·less·ness** noun.

pi·ton /ˈpētän/ ▶ **noun** a peg or spike driven into a crack to support a climber or a rope.
– ORIGIN French, 'eye bolt.'

pit stop ▶ **noun 1** (in auto racing) a stop in the pits for servicing and refueling. **2** a brief rest during a journey.

pit·tance /ˈpitns/ ▶ **noun** a very small or inadequate amount of money.
– ORIGIN Old French *pitance* 'pity, pittance.'

pit·ter-pat·ter /ˈpitər ˈpatər/ ▶ **noun** a sound of quick light steps or taps. ▶ **adverb** with a sound of quick light steps or taps.

pi·tu·i·tar·y gland /pəˈt(y)o͞oə,terē/ (also **pituitary body**) ▶ **noun** a pea-sized gland attached to the base of the brain, important in controlling growth and development.
– ORIGIN Latin *pituitarius* 'secreting phlegm.'

pit·y /ˈpitē/ ▶ **noun** (pl. **pities**) **1** a feeling of sorrow and sympathy caused by the sufferings of others. **2** a cause for regret or disappointment: *what a pity we can't be friends.*

– SYNONYMS **1 compassion,** commiseration, condolence, sympathy, fellow feeling, understanding. **2** *it's a pity you can't go* **shame,** misfortune.
– ANTONYMS indifference.

▶ **verb** (**pities, pitying, pitied**) feel pity for someone.

– SYNONYMS **feel sorry for,** feel for, sympathize with, empathize with, commiserate with, take pity on, be moved by, bleed for.

– ORIGIN Old French *pite* 'compassion.'

piv·ot /ˈpivət/ ▶ **noun 1** the central point, pin, or shaft on which a mechanism turns or balances. **2** a person or thing playing a central part in an activity or organization.

– SYNONYMS **fulcrum,** axis, axle, swivel, pin, shaft, hub, spindle, hinge, kingpin.

▶ **verb** (**pivots, pivoting, pivoted**) **1** turn on a central point. **2** (**pivot on**) depend on: *success pivots on the performance of the sales force.*

– SYNONYMS **1 rotate,** turn, swivel, revolve, spin. **2** *it all pivoted on his response* **depend on,** hinge on, turn on, center on, hang on, rely on, rest on, revolve around.

– DERIVATIVES **piv·ot·a·ble** adjective.
– ORIGIN French.

piv·ot·al /ˈpivətl/ ▶ **adjective 1** of central importance; vital: *Japan's pivotal role in the world economy*. **2** fixed or turning on a pivot.

– SYNONYMS **central,** crucial, vital, critical, focal, essential, key, decisive.

pix·el /ˈpiksəl/ ▶ **noun** any of the tiny areas of light on a display screen that make up an image.
– ORIGIN abbreviation of *picture element*.

pix·el·ate /ˈpiksəlāt/ (also **pixellate** or **pixilate**) ▶ **verb 1** divide an image into pixels, for display or for storage in a digital format. **2** display a person's image as a small number of large pixels in order to disguise their identity.
– DERIVATIVES **pix·el·a·tion** /ˌpiksəˈlāsʜən/ noun.

pix·ie /ˈpiksē/ (also **pixy**) ▶ **noun** (pl. **pixies**) a supernatural being in folklore.

– SYNONYMS **elf,** fairy, sprite, imp, brownie, puck, leprechaun.

– DERIVATIVES **pix·ie·ish** adjective.
– ORIGIN unknown.

pix·il·at·ed /ˈpiksəˌlātid/ (Brit. **pixillated**) ▶ **adjective** informal crazy; confused.

piz·za /ˈpētsə/ ▶ **noun** a dish consisting of a flat, round base of dough baked with a topping of tomatoes, cheese, and other ingredients.
– ORIGIN Italian, 'pie.'

piz·zazz /pəˈzaz/ (also **pizazz** or **pzazz**) ▶ **noun** informal a combination of liveliness and style.
– ORIGIN said to have been invented by Diana Vreeland, fashion editor of *Harper's Bazaar* in the 1930s.

piz·ze·ri·a /ˌpētsəˈrēə/ ▶ **noun** a pizza restaurant.
– ORIGIN Italian.

piz·zi·ca·to /ˌpitsiˈkätō/ ▶ **adverb & adjective** plucking the strings of a violin or other stringed instrument with the finger.
– ORIGIN Italian, 'pinched.'

PJs ▶ **abbreviation** pajamas.

pkg. ▶ **abbreviation** (pl. **pkgs.**) package.

pl. ▶ **abbreviation 1** (also **Pl.**) place. **2** plural.

plac·ard /ˈplakärd, -ərd/ ▶ **noun** a sign for public display, either fixed on a wall or carried during a demonstration. ▶ **verb** cover something with placards.
– ORIGIN Old French *placquart*.

pla·cate /ˈplākāt/ ▶ **verb** make someone less angry or hostile.

– SYNONYMS **pacify,** calm, appease, mollify, soothe, win over, conciliate, propitiate, make peace with, humor.
– ANTONYMS provoke.

– DERIVATIVES **pla·ca·to·ry** /-kəˌtôrē, ˈplakə-/ adjective.
– ORIGIN Latin *placare*.

CHOOSE THE RIGHT WORD

See **PACIFY**.

place /plās/ ▶ **noun 1** a particular position or area; a location. **2** a portion of space occupied by or set aside for someone or something: *Jack had saved her a place*. **3** a vacancy or available position. **4** informal a person's home. **5** a position in a sequence: *I finished in second place*. **6** the position of a figure in a decimal number. **7** (in place names) a square or short street.

– SYNONYMS **1** *an ideal place for dinner* **location,** site, spot, setting, position, situation, area, region, locale, venue. **2** *foreign places* **country,** state, area, region, town, city. **3** *a place was reserved for her* **seat,** chair, space. **4** *I offered him a place in the company* **job,** position, post, appointment, situation, employment. **5** *a place of her own* **home,** house, flat, apartment, pied-à-terre, accommodations, property, rooms, quarters; informal **pad**; formal **residence,** abode, dwelling.

▶ **verb 1** put in a particular position or situation: *enemy officers were placed under arrest*. **2** find an appropriate place or role for someone or something. **3** allocate a specified position in a sequence to. **4** remember where one has seen someone or something. **5** arrange for an order, bet, etc., to be carried out.

– SYNONYMS **1** *books were placed on the table* **put (down),** set (down), lay, deposit, position, plant, rest, stand, station, situate, leave; informal stick, dump, park, plonk, plunk, plop. **2** *a survey placed the company 13th for achievement* **rank,** order, grade, class, classify, put. **3** *Joe couldn't quite place her* **identify,** recognize, remember, put a name to, pin down, locate, pinpoint.

– DERIVATIVES **plac·er** noun.
– PHRASES **go places** informal be increasingly successful. **in place** established and working or ready. **in place of** instead of. **keep someone in his** (or **her**) **place** keep someone from becoming too self-important. **out of place 1** not in the proper position. **2** in a situation where one does not fit in. **put someone in his** (or **her**) **place** make someone feel less proud or arrogant. **take place** happen; occur. **take the place of** replace someone or something.
– ORIGIN Old French.

pla·ce·bo /pləˈsēbō/ ▶ **noun** (pl. **placebos**) **1** a medicine given to a patient to make them feel better psychologically rather than for any physical effect. **2** a substance that has no medicinal effect, used as a control in testing new drugs.
– ORIGIN Latin, 'I shall be acceptable or pleasing.'

place·kick /ˈplāsˌkik/ Football ▶ **noun** a kick made after the ball is first placed on the ground. ▶ **verb** take a place kick.
– DERIVATIVES **place·kick·er** noun.

place·ment /ˈplāsmənt/ ▶ **noun** the action of placing someone or something.

pla·cen·ta /pləˈsentə/ ▶ **noun** (pl. **placentae** /-tē/ or **placentas**) an organ that forms in the uterus of a pregnant mammal and that supplies blood and nourishment to the fetus through the umbilical cord.
– DERIVATIVES **pla·cen·tal** /pləˈsentl/ adjective.
– ORIGIN Latin.

plac·id /ˈplasid/ ▶ **adjective 1** not easily upset or excited. **2** with little movement or activity; calm: *the placid waters of the lake*.

– SYNONYMS **1 even-tempered,** calm, tranquil, equable, unexcitable, serene, mild, composed, self-possessed, poised, easygoing, levelheaded, steady, unruffled, unperturbed, phlegmatic; informal unflappable. **2 quiet,** calm, tranquil, still, peaceful, undisturbed, restful, sleepy.
– ANTONYMS excitable.

– DERIVATIVES **pla·cid·i·ty** /pləˈsiditē/ noun **plac·id·ly** adverb.
– ORIGIN Latin *placidus*.

plack·et /ˈplakit/ ▶ **noun 1** an opening in an item of clothing, covering fastenings or for access to a pocket. **2** a flap of material used to strengthen such an opening.
– ORIGIN from **PLACARD** in the former sense 'garment worn under an open coat.'

pla·gia·rize /ˈplājəˌrīz/ ▶ **verb** take the work or idea of someone else and pass it off as one's own.

– SYNONYMS **copy,** pirate, steal, poach, appropriate; informal rip off, crib.

– DERIVATIVES **pla·gia·rism** /ˈplājəˌrizəm/ noun **pla·gia·rist** noun **pla·gia·riz·er** /ˈplājəˌrīzər/ noun.
– ORIGIN from Latin *plagiarius* 'kidnapper.'

plague /plāg/ ▶ **noun 1** a contagious disease spread by bacteria and causing fever and delirium. **2** an unusually large quantity of destructive insects or animals.

– SYNONYMS **1 pandemic,** epidemic, disease, sickness; dated contagion; old use pestilence. **2 infestation,** invasion, swarm.

▶ **verb** (**plagues, plaguing, plagued**) **1** cause continual trouble to: *he grew up in a neighborhood plagued by crime*. **2** pester someone continually.

– SYNONYMS **1 afflict,** trouble, torment, beset, dog, curse, bedevil. **2 pester,** harass, badger, bother, torment, harry, hound, trouble, nag, molest; informal hassle, bug.

– ORIGIN Latin *plaga* 'stroke, wound.'

plaice /plās/ ▶ **noun** (pl. same) an edible brown marine flatfish with orange spots.
– ORIGIN Old French *plaiz*.

plaid /plad/ ▶ **noun** fabric woven in a checkered or tartan design.
– ORIGIN Scottish Gaelic *plaide* 'blanket.'

plain /plān/ ▶ **adjective 1** not decorated or elaborate; simple or ordinary: *good plain food*. **2** without a pattern or in only one color. **3** without identification; unmarked: *a plain envelope*. **4** easy to see or understand; clear. **5** (of language) clearly expressed, without the use of difficult terms. **6** (of a woman or girl) not beautiful or attractive. **7** sheer; simple: *the problem was plain exhaustion*. **8** (of a knitting stitch) made by putting the needle through the front of the stitch from left to right. Compare with **PURL**[1].

– SYNONYMS **1 obvious,** clear, evident, apparent, manifest, unmistakable. **2 intelligible,** comprehensible, understandable, clear, lucid, simple, straightforward, user-friendly. **3 candid,** frank, outspoken, forthright, direct, honest, truthful, blunt, bald, unequivocal; informal upfront. **4 simple,** ordinary, unadorned, homely, basic, modest, unsophisticated, restrained. **5 unattractive,** unprepossessing, ugly, homely, ordinary. **6 sheer,** pure, downright, out-and-out.
– ANTONYMS obscure, fancy, attractive.

▶ **adverb** informal used for emphasis: *that's plain stupid*.
▶ **noun** a large area of flat land with few trees.

– SYNONYMS **grassland,** flatland, prairie, savannah, steppe, tundra, pampas, veld, plateau.

– DERIVATIVES **plain·ly** adverb **plain·ness** noun.
– ORIGIN Latin *planus* 'flat, plain.'

plain·clothes /ˈplānˌklōᴛʜz/ ▶ **plural noun** ordinary clothes rather than uniform, especially when worn by police officers.

plain·song /ˈplānˌsôɴɢ, -säɴɢ/ (also **plainchant**) ▶ **noun** unaccompanied medieval church music sung by a number of voices together.

plain-spo·ken ▶ **adjective** outspoken; blunt.

plaint /plānt/ ▶ **noun 1** Law, Brit. an accusation or charge. **2** chiefly literary a complaint or lament.
– ORIGIN Old French *plainte*.

plain·tiff /ˈplāntif/ ▶ **noun** a person who brings a case against another in a court of law. Compare with **DEFENDANT**.
– ORIGIN Old French *plaintif* 'plaintive.'

plain·tive /ˈplāntiv/ ▶ **adjective** sounding sad and mournful.

– SYNONYMS **mournful,** sad, pathetic, pitiful, melancholy, sorrowful, unhappy, wretched, woeful, forlorn.

– DERIVATIVES **plain·tive·ly** adverb **plain·tive·ness** noun.
– ORIGIN Old French.

WORD TOOLKIT

See **WISTFUL**.

plait /plāt, plat/ ▶ **noun** a single length of hair, rope, or other material made up of three or more interlaced strands. ▶ **verb** form hair or other material into a plait or plaits.
– ORIGIN Old French *pleit* 'a fold.'

plan /plan/ ▶ **noun 1** a detailed proposal for doing or achieving something. **2** an intention or decision about what one is going to do. **3** a scheme for making regular payments toward a pension, insurance policy, etc. **4** a map or diagram. **5** a scale drawing of a horizontal section of a building.

– SYNONYMS **1 scheme,** idea, proposal, proposition, project, program, system, method, strategy, stratagem, formula, recipe. **2 intention,** aim, idea, objective, object, goal, target, ambition. **3 map,** diagram, chart, blueprint, plat, drawing, sketch, impression.

▶ **verb** (**plans, planning, planned**) **1** decide on and arrange something in advance. **2** (**plan for**) make preparations for. **3** make a plan of something to be made or built.

– SYNONYMS **1 organize,** arrange, work out, outline, map out, prepare, formulate, frame, develop, devise. **2 intend,** aim, propose, mean, hope. **3 design,** draw up a plan for, sketch out, plat, map out.

– ORIGIN French.

CHOOSE THE RIGHT WORD

See **INTEND**.

pla·nar /ˈplānər/ ▶ **adjective** Mathematics relating to or in the form of a plane.

plan·chette /planˈsʜet/ ▶ **noun** a small board on casters and fitted with a vertical pencil, used in seances to convey supposed messages from spirits.
– ORIGIN French, 'small plank.'

plane[1] /plān/ ▶ **noun 1** a level of existence or thought: *many believe there is a higher plane of existence*. **2** technical a flat surface on which a straight line joining any two points would wholly lie.

– SYNONYMS **level,** degree, standard, stratum, dimension.

▶ **adjective 1** completely level or flat. **2** relating to two-dimensional surfaces or magnitudes.
▶ **verb 1** (especially of a bird) soar without moving the wings; glide. **2** (of a boat, surfboard, etc.) skim over the surface of water.

– SYNONYMS **1** *seagulls planed overhead* **soar,** glide, float, drift, wheel. **2** *boats planed across the water* **skim,** glide.

– ORIGIN Latin *planum* 'flat surface.'

plane² ▶ **noun** an airplane.

– SYNONYMS **airplane,** aircraft, airliner, jet, flying machine, ship.

WORD LINKS

aeronautics *science of flight*

plane³ (also **planer**) ▶ **noun** a tool consisting of a block with a projecting steel blade, used to smooth a wooden surface by paring shavings from it. ▶ **verb** smooth a surface with a plane.
– ORIGIN Latin *plana.*

plane⁴ (also **plane tree**) ▶ **noun** a tall spreading tree with maplelike leaves and a peeling bark.
– ORIGIN Old French.

plan·et /'planit/ ▶ **noun 1** a large round object in space that orbits around a star. **2** (**the planet**) the earth.
– DERIVATIVES **plan·e·tar·y** /'plani,terē/ adjective **plan·e·tol·o·gy** /,plani'täləjē/ noun.
– ORIGIN Greek *planētēs* 'wanderer, planet.'

plan·e·tar·i·um /,plani'te(ə)rēəm/ ▶ **noun** (pl. **planetariums** or **planetaria** /-'te(ə)rēə/) a building in which images of stars, planets, and constellations are projected onto a domed ceiling.
– ORIGIN Latin.

plan·et·oid /'plani,toid/ ▶ **noun** another term for **ASTEROID.**

plan·gent /'planjənt/ ▶ **adjective** literary (of a sound) resonant and mournful.
– DERIVATIVES **plan·gen·cy** noun **plan·gent·ly** adverb.
– ORIGIN from Latin *plangere* 'to lament.'

plank /plaNGk/ ▶ **noun 1** a long, flat piece of timber, used in flooring. **2** a fundamental part of a political or other program: *crime reduction is a central plank of the manifesto.*
– DERIVATIVES **planked** adjective.
– PHRASES **walk the plank** be forced by pirates to walk blindfolded along a plank over the side of a ship to one's death in the sea.
– ORIGIN Latin *planca* 'board.'

plank·ing /'plaNGkiNG/ ▶ **noun** planks used for flooring or as part of a boat.

plank·ton /'plaNGktən/ ▶ **noun** small and microscopic organisms living in the sea or fresh water.
– DERIVATIVES **plank·tic** adjective **plank·ton·ic** /-'tänik/ adjective.
– ORIGIN from Greek *planktos* 'wandering.'

planned e·con·o·my ▶ **noun** another term for **COMMAND ECONOMY.**

plan·ner /'planər/ ▶ **noun 1** a person who controls or plans urban development: *city planners.* **2** a person who plans their activities thoroughly. **3** a book or chart with information that is an aid to planning: *my day planner.*

pla·nning /'planiNG/ ▶ **noun 1** the process of making plans for something. **2** the control of development in cities and towns by local government.

plant /plant/ ▶ **noun 1** a living organism that grows in the ground, having roots with which it absorbs substances and leaves in which it makes nutrients by photosynthesis. **2** a place where an industrial or manufacturing process takes place. **3** machinery used in an industrial or manufacturing process. **4** a person placed in a group as a spy. **5** a thing put among someone's belongings to make them appear guilty of wrongdoing.

– SYNONYMS **1 flower,** vegetable, herb, shrub, bush, weed; (**plants**) vegetation, greenery, flora. **2 factory,** works, facility, refinery, mill. **3 machinery,** machines, equipment, apparatus, appliances, gear. **4 spy,** informant, informer, secret agent, mole, infiltrator, operative; informal spook.

▶ **verb 1** place a seed, bulb, or plant in the ground so that it can grow. **2** place or fix someone or something in a specified position. **3** establish an idea in someone's mind. **4** secretly place a bomb somewhere. **5** put or hide something among someone's belongings to make them appear guilty of wrongdoing. **6** send someone to join a group to act as a spy.

– SYNONYMS **1 sow,** scatter. **2 place,** put, set, position, situate, settle; informal plonk. **3** *she planted the idea in his mind* **instill,** implant, put, place, introduce, fix, establish, lodge.

– DERIVATIVES **plant·let** /-lit/ noun.
– ORIGIN from Latin *planta* 'sprout, cutting' and *plantare* 'plant, fix in place.'

Plan·tag·e·net /plan'tajənit/ ▶ **noun** a member of the English royal dynasty that ruled from 1154 until 1485.
– ORIGIN from Latin *planta genista* 'sprig of broom,' said to be worn as a crest by Geoffrey, count of Anjou, the father of Henry II.

plan·tain¹ /'plantən/ ▶ **noun** a low-growing plant, with a rosette of leaves and green flowers.
– ORIGIN Old French.

plan·tain² ▶ **noun** a type of banana that is harvested green and cooked as a vegetable.
– ORIGIN Spanish *plá(n)tano* 'plane tree.'

plan·tar /'plantər/ ▶ **adjective** Anatomy relating to the sole of the foot.

plan·ta·tion /plan'tāSHən/ ▶ **noun 1** a large estate on which crops such as coffee, sugar, and tobacco are grown. **2** an area in which trees have been planted.

plant·er /'plantər/ ▶ **noun 1** a manager or owner of a plantation. **2** a decorative container in which plants are grown.

plaque /plak/ ▶ **noun 1** an ornamental tablet fixed to a wall in commemoration of a person or event. **2** a sticky deposit on teeth that encourages the growth of bacteria.
– ORIGIN French.

plash /plaSH/ ▶ **noun** a splashing sound. ▶ **verb** make or hit with a splash.
– DERIVATIVES **plash·y** adjective.
– ORIGIN probably imitating the sound.

plas·ma /'plazmə/ ▶ **noun 1** the colorless fluid part of blood, lymph, or milk, in which corpuscles or fat globules are suspended. **2** Physics a gas of positive ions and free electrons with little or no overall electric charge.
– DERIVATIVES **plas·mat·ic** /plaz'matik/ adjective **plas·mic** /-mik/ adjective.
– ORIGIN Greek.

plas·ma screen ▶ **noun** a flat display screen that uses an array of cells containing a gas plasma to produce different colors in each cell.

plas·ter /ˈplastər/ ▸ **noun 1** a soft mixture of lime with sand or cement and water for spreading on walls and ceilings to form a smooth hard surface when dried. **2** (also **plaster of Paris**) a hard white substance made by adding water to powdered gypsum, used for setting broken bones and making sculptures and casts. ▸ **verb 1** cover a wall or ceiling with plaster. **2** coat thickly with a substance: *a face plastered in heavy makeup.* **3** make hair lie flat by dampening it. **4** display widely and prominently: *her story was plastered all over the December issue.*

– SYNONYMS **1 spread,** smother, smear, cake, coat, bedaub. **2 flatten (down),** smooth down, slick down.

– DERIVATIVES **plas·ter·er** noun.
– ORIGIN Latin *plastrum.*

plas·ter·board /ˈplastərˌbôrd/ ▸ **noun** board made of plaster set between two sheets of heavy paper, used to line interior walls and ceilings.

plas·tered /ˈplastərd/ ▸ **adjective** informal very drunk.

plas·tic /ˈplastik/ ▸ **noun 1** a material produced by chemical processes that can be molded into shape while soft and then set into a rigid or slightly elastic form. **2** informal credit cards or other plastic cards that can be used as money. ▸ **adjective 1** made of plastic. **2** easily shaped or molded. **3** artificial or false: *a sales rep with a plastic smile.* **4** relating to molding or modeling in three dimensions: *the plastic arts.*

– SYNONYMS **1 soft,** pliable, pliant, flexible, malleable, workable, moldable; informal bendy. **2 artificial,** false, fake, bogus, insincere; informal phony, pretend.

– DERIVATIVES **plas·ti·cal·ly** /-(ə)lē/ adverb **plas·tic·i·ty** /plaˈstisitē/ noun.
– ORIGIN Greek *plastikos.*

plas·tic ex·plo·sive ▸ **noun** a puttylike explosive capable of being molded by hand.

plas·ti·cine /ˈplastəˌsēn/ ▸ **noun** trademark a soft modeling material.

plas·ti·cize /ˈplastəˌsīz/ ▸ **verb 1** treat or coat something with plastic. **2** make something plastic or able to be molded.
– DERIVATIVES **plas·ti·ci·za·tion** /ˌplastəsiˈzāshən/ noun **plas·ti·ciz·er** noun.

plas·tick·y /ˈplastikē/ ▸ **adjective 1** resembling plastic. **2** artificial or of poor quality.

plas·tic sur·ger·y ▸ **noun** surgery performed to repair or reconstruct parts of the body damaged by injury or for cosmetic reasons.

plas·tique /plaˈstēk/ ▸ **noun** plastic explosive.
– ORIGIN French, ‘plastic.’

plate /plāt/ ▸ **noun 1** a flat dish from which food is eaten or served. **2** bowls, cups, and other utensils made of gold or silver. **3** a thin, flat piece of metal used to join or strengthen something or forming part of a machine. **4** a small, flat piece of metal with a name or other writing on it, fixed to a wall or door. **5** a sheet of metal or other material with an image of type or illustrations on it, from which multiple copies are printed. **6** a printed photograph or illustration in a book. **7** Baseball short for **HOME PLATE**. **8** a thin, flat structure in a plant or animal. **9** each of the several rigid pieces of the earth's crust and upper mantle that together make up the earth's surface.

– SYNONYMS **1 dish,** platter, salver; historical trencher; old use charger. **2 plateful,** helping, portion, serving. **3 panel,** sheet, slab. **4 plaque,** sign, tablet. **5 picture,** print, illustration, photograph, photo.

▸ **verb 1** cover a metal object with a thin coating of a different metal. **2** put food on a plate before a meal.

– SYNONYMS **cover,** coat, overlay, laminate, gild.

– DERIVATIVES **plat·er** noun **plat·ing** noun.
– PHRASES **on a plate** informal with little or no effort. **on one's plate** occupying one's time or energy.
– ORIGIN from Old French *plat* ‘platter’ or *plate* ‘sheet of metal.’

pla·teau /plaˈtō/ ▸ **noun** (pl. **plateaux** /-ˈtōz/ or **plateaus**) **1** an area of fairly level high ground. **2** a period of little or no change following a period of activity or progress.

– SYNONYMS **upland,** mesa, highland, tableland.

▸ **verb** (**plateaus, plateauing, plateaued**) reach a period of little or no change following activity or progress: *after making a huge jump in the rankings his game has really plateaued.*
– ORIGIN French.

plate glass ▸ **noun** thick fine-quality glass used for store windows and doors.

plate·let /ˈplāt-lit/ ▸ **noun** a small disk-shaped cell fragment without a nucleus, found in large numbers in blood and involved in clotting.

plat·en /ˈplatn/ ▸ **noun 1** a cylindrical roller in a typewriter against which the paper is held. **2** a plate in a small letterpress printing press that presses the paper against the type.
– ORIGIN French *platine* ‘flat piece.’

plate tec·ton·ics ▸ **noun** another term for **TECTONICS**.

plat·form /ˈplatfôrm/ ▸ **noun 1** a raised level surface on which people or things can stand. **2** a raised structure along the side of a railroad track where passengers get on and off trains. **3** a raised structure standing in the sea from which oil or gas wells can be drilled. **4** the declared policy of a political party or group: *seeking election on a platform of low taxes.* **5** an opportunity for the expression or exchange of views. **6** a very thick sole on a shoe. **7** a standard for the hardware of a computer system that determines the kinds of software it can run.

– SYNONYMS **1 stage,** dais, rostrum, podium, stand. **2 program,** manifesto, policies, principles, party line.

– ORIGIN French *plateforme* ‘ground plan.’

plat·i·num /ˈplatn-əm/ ▸ **noun** a precious silvery-white metallic chemical element used in jewelry and in some electrical and laboratory equipment. ▸ **adjective** grayish-white or silvery.
– ORIGIN Spanish *platina.*

plat·i·num blonde ▸ **adjective** (of hair) silvery-blond.

plat·i·tude /ˈplatiˌt(y)o͞od/ ▸ **noun** a remark or statement that has been used too often to be interesting or thoughtful.

– SYNONYMS **cliché,** truism, commonplace, old chestnut, banality.

– DERIVATIVES **plat·i·tu·di·nous** /ˌplatiˈt(y)o͞odn-əs/ adjective.
– ORIGIN French.

Pla·ton·ic /pləˈtänik/ ▸ **adjective 1** relating to the ancient Greek philosopher Plato or his ideas. **2** (**platonic**) (of love or friendship) intimate and affectionate but not sexual.
– DERIVATIVES **pla·ton·i·cal·ly** adverb.

Pla·to·nism /ˈplātnˌizəm/ ▸ **noun** the philosophy of Plato, especially his theories on the relationship between abstract ideas or entities and their corresponding objects or forms in the material world.
– DERIVATIVES **Pla·to·nist** noun & adjective.

pla·toon /pləˈto͞on/ ▸ **noun** a subdivision of a company of soldiers, usually commanded by a lieutenant and divided into two or more sections.
– ORIGIN French *peloton* 'platoon,' literally 'small ball.'

plat·ter /ˈplatər/ ▸ **noun 1** a large flat serving dish. **2** a selection of food served on a platter: *a seafood platter*.

– SYNONYMS **plate,** dish, salver, tray; old use charger.

– PHRASES **on a (silver) platter** informal with little or no effort.
– ORIGIN Old French *plater*.

plat·y·pus /ˈplatəpəs, -ˌpo͝os/ (also **duck-billed platypus**) ▸ **noun** (pl. **platypuses**) an egg-laying Australian mammal with a ducklike bill and webbed feet, living partly on land and partly in water.
– ORIGIN from Greek *platupous* 'flat-footed.'

plau·dits /ˈplôdits/ ▸ **plural noun** enthusiastic approval; praise.

– SYNONYMS **praise,** acclaim, commendation, congratulations, accolades, compliments, cheers, applause, tributes.
– ANTONYMS criticism.

– ORIGIN from Latin *plaudite* 'applaud!'

plau·si·ble /ˈplôzəbəl/ ▸ **adjective 1** seeming reasonable or probable. **2** skilled at producing persuasive arguments: *a plausible liar*.

– SYNONYMS **credible,** believable, reasonable, likely, possible, conceivable, imaginable, convincing, persuasive.
– ANTONYMS unlikely.

– DERIVATIVES **plau·si·bil·i·ty** /ˌplôzəˈbilitē/ noun **plau·si·bly** adverb.
– ORIGIN from Latin *plaudere* 'applaud.'

play /plā/ ▸ **verb 1** take part in games or other activities for enjoyment. **2** take part in a sport or contest. **3** compete against another player or team. **4** take a specified position on a sports team: *he played goalie*. **5** act the role of a character in a play or movie. **6** perform on a musical instrument or perform a piece of music. **7** move a piece or display a playing card in one's turn in a game. **8** make a CD, tape, or record produce sounds. **9** be cooperative: *he needs financial backing, but the banks won't play*. **10** move lightly and quickly; flicker: *a smile played about her lips*.

– SYNONYMS **1 amuse oneself,** entertain oneself, enjoy oneself, have fun, relax, occupy oneself, frolic, romp, cavort; informal mess around. **2 take part in,** participate in, be involved in, compete in, do. **3 compete against,** take on, meet. **4 act the part of,** take the role of, appear as, portray, perform.

▸ **noun 1** games and other activities that one takes part in for enjoyment. **2** a dramatic work written for the stage or to be broadcast. **3** the progress of an athletic match: *bad weather stopped play*. **4** a move or maneuver in a sport or game. **5** the state of being active or effective: *luck came into play*. **6** freedom of movement in a mechanism. **7** constantly changing movement: *the play of light across the surface*.

– SYNONYMS **1 amusement,** relaxation, recreation, diversion, leisure, enjoyment, pleasure, fun. **2 drama,** theatrical work, piece, comedy, tragedy, production, performance.

– DERIVATIVES **play·a·ble** adjective.
– PHRASES **make great play of** chiefly Brit. draw attention to something in an exaggerated way. **make a play for** informal attempt to attract someone or gain something. **play around** (or **about**) behave in a casual or irresponsible way. **play along** pretend to cooperate with someone. **play something by ear 1** perform music without having seen a score. **2** (**play it by ear**) informal proceed according to circumstances rather than following rules or a plan. **play something down** disguise the importance of something. **play fast and loose** behave irresponsibly or immorally. **play for time** use excuses or unnecessary activities to gain time. **play into someone's hands** give someone an advantage without meaning to do so. **play someone off against another** cause someone to compete with or oppose another for one's own advantage. **play on** exploit someone's weak point. **a play on words** a pun. **play** (or **play it**) **safe** avoid taking risks. **play up to** humor or flatter someone. **play something up** emphasize the extent or importance of something. **play with** treat someone inconsiderately for one's own amusement. **play with fire** take foolish risks.
– ORIGIN Old English, 'to exercise.'

play-act·ing ▸ **noun** behavior that is exaggerated for pretense.

play·back /ˈplāˌbak/ ▸ **noun** the replaying of previously recorded sound or moving images.

play·bill /ˈplāˌbil/ ▸ **noun 1** a poster announcing a theatrical performance. **2** a theater program.

play·boy /ˈplāˌboi/ ▸ **noun** a wealthy man who spends his time enjoying himself.

– SYNONYMS **socialite,** man about town, ladies' man, womanizer, philanderer, rake, roué, pleasure-seeker; informal ladykiller.

play-by-play ▸ **noun** a detailed running commentary on an athletic contest.

play·er /ˈplāər/ ▸ **noun 1** a person taking part in a sport or game. **2** a person who plays a musical instrument. **3** a device for playing compact discs, tapes, or records. **4** a person who is influential in an area of activity: *a major player in political circles*. **5** an actor.

– SYNONYMS **1 participant,** contestant, competitor, contender, sportsman, sportswoman. **2 musician,** performer, artist, virtuoso, instrumentalist. **3 actor, actress,** performer, thespian, entertainer, artiste, trouper.

play·er pi·an·o ▸ **noun** a piano fitted with an apparatus that enables it to be played automatically.

play·ful /ˈplāfəl/ ▸ **adjective 1** fond of playing; full of fun. **2** made or done in fun; not serious: *a playful punch on the arm*.

– SYNONYMS **1 frisky,** lively, full of fun, frolicsome, high-spirited, exuberant, mischievous, impish; informal full of beans. **2 lighthearted,** humorous, jocular, teasing, jokey, facetious, frivolous, flippant.
– ANTONYMS serious.

– DERIVATIVES **play·ful·ly** adverb **play·ful·ness** noun.

play·ground /ˈplāˌground/ ▸ **noun** an outdoor area provided for children to play on.

play·group /ˈplāˌgro͞op/ ▸ **noun** a regular play session for preschool children.

play·house /ˈplāˌhous/ ▶ **noun 1** a theater. **2** a toy house for children to play in.

play·ing card ▶ **noun** each of a set of rectangular pieces of card with numbers and symbols on one side, used to play various games.

play·ing field ▶ **noun** a field used for outdoor team games.

play·list /ˈplāˌlist/ ▶ **noun** a list of songs or pieces of music chosen to be broadcast on a radio station.

play·mak·er /ˈplāˌmākər/ ▶ **noun** a player in a team game who leads attacks or brings teammates into attacking positions.

play·mate /ˈplāˌmāt/ ▶ **noun** a friend with whom a child plays.

play·off /ˈplāˌôf/ ▶ **noun 1** an additional match played to decide the outcome of a contest. **2** (**playoffs**) a series of contests played to determine the winner of a championship, as between the leading teams in different divisions or leagues.

play·pen /ˈplāˌpen/ ▶ **noun** a small portable enclosure in which a baby or small child can play safely.

play·thing /ˈplāˌTHiNG/ ▶ **noun 1** a person who is treated as amusing but unimportant. **2** a toy.

play·time /ˈplāˌtīm/ ▶ **noun** a period in the school day when children are allowed to go outside and play.

play·wright /ˈplāˌrīt/ ▶ **noun** a person who writes plays.

pla·za /ˈplazə, ˈpläzə/ ▶ **noun 1** a public square or similar open space in a town or city. **2** a shopping center.
– ORIGIN Spanish, 'place.'

plc (also **PLC**) ▶ **abbreviation** Brit. public limited company.

plea /plē/ ▶ **noun 1** a request made in an urgent and emotional way. **2** a formal statement made by or on behalf of a person charged with an offense in a court of law. **3** a claim that one should not be blamed for or have to do something because of particular circumstances.
– SYNONYMS **appeal,** entreaty, supplication, petition, request, call.
– ORIGIN Old French *plait, plaid* 'agreement, discussion.'

plea bar·gain·ing ▶ **noun** Law an arrangement between a prosecutor and a person charged with an offense in which the latter pleads guilty to a lesser charge in the expectation of a less severe sentence.

plead /plēd/ ▶ **verb** (past and past part. **pleaded** or **pled**) **1** make an urgent and emotional request. **2** present an excuse for doing or not doing something. **3** argue in support of: *he visited the country to plead his cause.* **4** state formally in a court of law whether one is guilty or not guilty of the offense with which one is charged. **5** Law give a reason or a point of law as an accusation or defense.
– SYNONYMS **1** *he pleaded with her to stay* **beg,** implore, entreat, appeal to, ask. **2** *she pleaded ignorance* **claim,** use as an excuse, assert, allege, argue.
– DERIVATIVES **plead·er** noun.
– ORIGIN Old French *plaidier* 'go to law.'

USAGE

In a law court a person can **plead guilty** or **plead not guilty**. The phrase **plead innocent** is not a legal term, although it is found in general use.

plead·ing /ˈplēdiNG/ ▶ **adjective** earnestly appealing. ▶ **noun** (usu. **pleadings**) a formal statement of a case presented by each party in a lawsuit.
– DERIVATIVES **plead·ing·ly** adverb.

pleas·ant /ˈplezənt/ ▶ **adjective 1** enjoyable, pleasing, or attractive: *a pleasant town on a river.* **2** friendly and likable.
– SYNONYMS **1 enjoyable,** pleasurable, nice, agreeable, entertaining, amusing, delightful, charming; informal lovely, great. **2 friendly,** charming, agreeable, amiable, nice, delightful, sweet, genial, cordial, good-natured, personable, hospitable, polite.
– DERIVATIVES **pleas·ant·ly** adverb **pleas·ant·ness** noun.
– ORIGIN Old French *plaisant.*

pleas·ant·ry /ˈplezntrē/ ▶ **noun** (pl. **pleasantries**) **1** a conventional remark made as part of a polite conversation. **2** a mildly amusing joke.

please /plēz/ ▶ **verb 1** make someone feel happy and satisfied. **2** wish or desire: *do as you please.* **3** (**please oneself**) do as one wishes, without considering anyone else.
– SYNONYMS **1 make happy,** give pleasure to, delight, charm, amuse, entertain, divert, satisfy, gratify, humor. **2 like,** want, wish, desire, see fit, think fit, choose, will, prefer.
– ANTONYMS annoy.

▶ **adverb** used in polite requests or questions, or to accept an offer.
– ORIGIN Old French *plaisir.*

pleased /plēzd/ ▶ **adjective 1** feeling or showing pleasure and satisfaction. **2** (**pleased to do**) willing or glad to do something.
– SYNONYMS **happy,** glad, delighted, gratified, grateful, thankful, content, contented, satisfied, thrilled; informal over the moon, on cloud nine.
– ANTONYMS unhappy.

pleas·ing /ˈplēziNG/ ▶ **adjective** pleasant, satisfying, or attractive.
– SYNONYMS **1 good,** agreeable, pleasant, pleasurable, satisfying, gratifying, great. **2 friendly,** amiable, pleasant, agreeable, affable, nice, genial, likable, charming, engaging, delightful; informal lovely.
– DERIVATIVES **pleas·ing·ly** adverb.

pleas·ur·a·ble /ˈplezHərəbəl/ ▶ **adjective** pleasing; enjoyable.
– DERIVATIVES **pleas·ur·a·bly** /-blē/ adverb.

pleas·ure /ˈplezHər/ ▶ **noun 1** a feeling of happy satisfaction and enjoyment. **2** an enjoyable event or activity. **3** sexual satisfaction.
– SYNONYMS **happiness,** delight, joy, gladness, glee, satisfaction, gratification, contentment, enjoyment, amusement, fun, entertainment, relaxation, recreation, diversion.

▶ **adjective** intended for entertainment rather than business: *pleasure boats.*
▶ **verb** arouse someone sexually.
– PHRASES **at someone's pleasure** formal as and when someone wishes.
– ORIGIN from Old French *plaisir* 'to please.'

pleat /plēt/ ▶ **noun** a fold in fabric or an item of clothing, held by stitching the top or side. ▶ **verb** fold or form fabric into pleats.

– ORIGIN from **PLAIT**.

pleb /pleb/ ▸ **noun** informal, derogatory a lower-class person.
– DERIVATIVES **pleb·by** adjective.
– ORIGIN abbreviation of **PLEBEIAN**.

plebe /plēb/ ▸ **noun** informal a newly entered cadet or freshman, especially at a military academy.

ple·be·ian /pli'bēən/ ▸ **adjective** lower-class or unsophisticated: *I've got very plebeian tastes.* ▸ **noun 1** a lower-class person. **2** (in ancient Rome) a commoner.
– ORIGIN from Latin *plebs* 'the common people.'

pleb·i·scite /'plebə,sīt/ ▸ **noun** a vote made by all the members of an electorate on an important public issue.
– DERIVATIVES **ple·bis·ci·tar·y** /plə'bisi,terē/ adjective.
– ORIGIN French *plébiscite*.

plec·trum /'plektrəm/ ▸ **noun** (pl. **plectrums** or **plectra**) a thin flat piece of plastic or tortoiseshell used to pluck the strings of a guitar or similar musical instrument.
– ORIGIN Greek *plēktron* 'something with which to strike.'

pled /pled/ past and past participle of **PLEAD**.

pledge /plej/ ▸ **noun 1** a solemn promise to do something. **2** something valuable given as a guarantee that a debt will be paid or a promise kept. **3** (**the pledge**) a solemn vow not to drink alcohol. **4** a thing given as a token of love, favor, or loyalty.

– SYNONYMS **promise,** vow, undertaking, word, commitment, assurance, oath, guarantee.

▸ **verb 1** solemnly promise to do or give something. **2** give something valuable as a guarantee on a loan.

– SYNONYMS **promise,** vow, undertake, swear, commit oneself, declare, affirm.

– ORIGIN Old French *plege* 'person acting as surety for another.'

Pleis·to·cene /'plīstə,sēn/ ▸ **adjective** Geology relating to the first epoch of the Quaternary period (from 1.64 million to about 10,000 years ago), a time that included the ice ages and the appearance of humans.
– ORIGIN from Greek *pleistos* 'most' + *kainos* 'new.'

ple·na·ry /'plenərē/ ▸ **adjective 1** full; absolute: *plenary powers.* **2** (of a meeting at a conference or assembly) to be attended by all participants. ▸ **noun** a meeting attended by all participants at a conference or assembly.
– ORIGIN Latin *plenus* 'full.'

plen·i·po·ten·ti·ar·y /,plenəpə'tenshē,erē, -'tenshərē/ ▸ **noun** (pl. **plenipotentiaries**) a person given full power by a government to act on its behalf. ▸ **adjective 1** having full power to take independent action. **2** (of power) absolute.
– ORIGIN from Latin *plenus* 'full' + *potentia* 'power.'

plen·i·tude /'pleni,t(y)o͞od/ ▸ **noun** formal a large amount of something; an abundance.
– ORIGIN Old French.

plen·te·ous /'plentēəs/ ▸ **adjective** literary plentiful; abundant.

plen·ti·ful /'plentəfəl/ ▸ **adjective** existing in great quantities; abundant: *countries with plentiful supplies of oil.*

– SYNONYMS **abundant,** copious, ample, profuse, rich, lavish, generous, bountiful, bumper, prolific; informal galore.
– ANTONYMS scarce.

– DERIVATIVES **plen·ti·ful·ly** adverb.

CHOOSE THE RIGHT WORD

See **PREVALENT**.

plen·ty /'plentē/ ▸ **pronoun** a large amount or quantity, or as much as is needed.

– SYNONYMS *we've got plenty of games* **a lot of,** many, a great deal of, a plethora of, enough and to spare, no lack of, a wealth of; informal loads of, heaps of, stacks of, masses of, oodles of.

▸ **noun** a situation in which food and other necessities are available in large quantities.

– SYNONYMS **prosperity,** affluence, wealth, opulence, comfort, luxury, abundance.

▸ **adverb** informal used to emphasize the degree or extent of something: *she has plenty more ideas.*
– ORIGIN Old French *plente*.

ple·num /'plenəm, 'plēnəm/ ▸ **noun 1** an assembly of all the members of a group or committee. **2** Physics a space completely filled with matter, or the whole of space regarded in such a way.
– ORIGIN Latin, 'full space.'

ple·o·nasm /'plēə,nazəm/ ▸ **noun** the use of more words than are necessary to express meaning (e.g., *I saw her with my own eyes*).
– DERIVATIVES **ple·o·nas·tic** /,plēə'nastik/ adjective.
– ORIGIN Greek *pleonasmos*.

pleth·o·ra /'plethərə/ ▸ **noun** an excessive amount: *a plethora of complaints.*

– SYNONYMS **excess,** abundance, superabundance, surplus, glut, surfeit, profusion, enough and to spare.
– ANTONYMS dearth.

– ORIGIN Latin.

pleu·ra /'plo͝orə/ ▸ **noun** (pl. **pleurae** /'plo͝orē/) each of a pair of membranes covering the lungs.
– DERIVATIVES **pleu·ral** adjective.
– ORIGIN Greek, 'side of the body, rib.'

pleu·ri·sy /'plo͝orəsē/ ▸ **noun** inflammation of the membranes around the lungs, causing pain during breathing.

Plex·i·glas /'pleksi,glas/ (also **plexiglas** or **plexiglass**) ▸ **noun** trademark a tough transparent plastic used as a substitute for glass.

plex·us /'pleksəs/ ▸ **noun** (pl. same or **plexuses**) **1** a network of nerves or vessels in the body. **2** an intricate network or weblike formation.
– ORIGIN Latin, 'plaited formation.'

pli·a·ble /'plīəbəl/ ▸ **adjective 1** easily bent; flexible. **2** easily influenced: *pliable teenage minds.*

– SYNONYMS **1 flexible,** pliant, bendable, supple, workable, plastic; informal bendy. **2 malleable,** impressionable, flexible, adaptable, biddable, pliant, tractable, suggestible, persuadable.
– ANTONYMS rigid.

– DERIVATIVES **pli·a·bil·i·ty** /,plīə'bilitē/ noun.
– ORIGIN French.

CHOOSE THE RIGHT WORD

See **FLEXIBLE**.

pli·ant /'plīənt/ ▸ **adjective** easily bent or influenced; pliable.
– DERIVATIVES **pli·an·cy** noun **pli·ant·ly** adverb.

CHOOSE THE RIGHT WORD

See **FLEXIBLE**.

pli·é /plē'ā/ ▸ **noun** Ballet a movement in which a dancer bends the knees and straightens them again, having the feet turned out and heels firmly on the ground.
– ORIGIN French, 'bent.'

pli·ers /'plīərz/ ▸ **plural noun** pincers with parallel flat jaws, used for gripping small objects or bending wire.
– ORIGIN from French *plier* 'to bend.'

plight¹ /plīt/ ▸ **noun** a dangerous or difficult situation.

– SYNONYMS **predicament,** difficult situation, dire straits, trouble, difficulty, bind; informal tight corner, tight spot, hole, pickle, jam, fix.

– ORIGIN Old French *plit* 'fold.'

plight² ▸ **verb** old use **1** solemnly promise faith or loyalty. **2** (**be plighted to**) be engaged to be married to.
– ORIGIN Old English.

plim·soll /'plimsəl, -sōl/ (also **plimsole**) ▸ **noun** Brit. a light rubber-soled canvas sports shoe.
– ORIGIN probably from the resemblance of the side of the sole to a *Plimsoll line*, a marking on a ship's side showing the limit of legal submersion under various conditions.

plink /pliNGk/ ▸ **verb** make a short, sharp, metallic ringing sound. ▸ **noun** a short, sharp, metallic ringing sound.
– DERIVATIVES **plink·y** adjective.
– ORIGIN imitating the sound.

plinth /plinTH/ ▸ **noun 1** a heavy base supporting a statue or vase. **2** the lower square slab at the base of a column.
– ORIGIN Greek *plinthos* 'tile, brick, squared stone.'

Pli·o·cene /'plīə,sēn/ ▸ **adjective** Geology relating to the last epoch of the Tertiary period (5.2 to 1.64 million years ago), when the first hominids appeared.
– ORIGIN from Greek *pleiōn* 'more' + *kainos* 'new.'

PLO ▸ **abbreviation** Palestine Liberation Organization.

plod /pläd/ ▸ **verb** (**plods, plodding, plodded**) **1** walk slowly with heavy steps. **2** work slowly but determinedly at a dull task.

– SYNONYMS **trudge,** walk heavily, clump, stomp, tramp, lumber, slog.

▸ **noun** a slow, heavy walk.
– DERIVATIVES **plod·der** noun.
– ORIGIN probably imitating the sound of a heavy walk.

plonk /läNGk/ informal ▸ **verb 1** set something down heavily or carelessly. **2** play unskillfully on a musical instrument. ▸ **noun** a sound like that of something being set down heavily.
– ORIGIN imitating the sound.

plop /pläp/ ▸ **noun** a sound like that of a small solid object dropping into water. ▸ **verb** (**plops, plopping, plopped**) fall or drop with a plop.
– ORIGIN imitating the sound.

plo·sive /'plōsiv/ ▸ **adjective** referring to a consonant (e.g., *d* or *p*) that is produced by stopping the flow of air from the mouth with the lips, teeth, or palate and then suddenly releasing it.
– ORIGIN from **EXPLOSIVE**.

plot /plät/ ▸ **noun 1** a secret plan to do something illegal or wrong. **2** the main sequence of events in a play, novel, or movie. **3** a small piece of ground marked out for building, gardening, etc. **4** a graph showing the relation between two variables.

– SYNONYMS **1 conspiracy,** intrigue, stratagem, plan, machinations. **2 storyline,** story, scenario, action, thread, narrative. **3 piece of ground,** patch, area, tract, lot, acreage, plat.

▸ **verb** (**plots, plotting, plotted**) **1** secretly make plans to carry out something illegal or wrong. **2** invent the plot of a play, novel, or movie. **3** mark a route or position on a chart or graph.

– SYNONYMS **1 plan,** scheme, arrange, organize, contrive. **2 conspire,** scheme, intrigue, connive. **3 mark,** chart, map.

– DERIVATIVES **plot·less** adjective **plot·ter** noun.
– ORIGIN Old English, 'small piece of ground'; sense 1 is associated with Old French *complot* 'dense crowd, secret project.'

CHOOSE THE RIGHT WORD

plot, cabal, conspiracy, intrigue, machination

If you come up with a secret plan to do something, especially with evil or mischievous intent, it's called a **plot** (*a plot to seize control of the company*). If you get other people or groups involved in your plot, it's called a **conspiracy** (*a conspiracy to overthrow the government*). **Cabal** usually applies to a small group of political conspirators (*a cabal of right-wing extremists*), while **machination** (usually plural) suggests deceit and cunning in devising a plot intended to harm someone (*the machinations of the would-be assassins*). An **intrigue** involves more complicated scheming or maneuvering than a plot and often employs underhanded methods in an attempt to gain one's own ends (*she had a passion for intrigue, particularly where romance was involved*).

plough, etc. /plou/ ▸ **noun & verb** British spelling of **PLOW**, etc.

plov·er /'pləvər, 'plō-/ ▸ **noun** a wading bird with a short bill.
– ORIGIN Old French.

plow /plou/ (Brit. **plough**) ▸ **noun** a large farming implement with one or more blades fixed in a frame, drawn over soil to turn it over and cut furrows. ▸ **verb 1** turn up earth with a plow. **2** (**plow through/into**) (of a vehicle) move in a fast or uncontrolled way through or into someone or something. **3** move forward or progress with difficulty: *the students are plowing through grammar exercises*. **4** (**plow something in**) invest money in a business.

– SYNONYMS **1 till,** furrow, harrow, cultivate, work. **2 crash,** smash, career, plunge, bulldoze, hurtle, cannon.

– DERIVATIVES **plow·a·ble** adjective **plow·man** /'ploumən/ noun (pl. **plowmen**).
– ORIGIN Old English.

plow·share /'plou,SHe(ə)r/ ▸ **noun** the main cutting blade of a plow.

ploy /ploi/ ▸ **noun** a cunning plan or action intended to gain an advantage.

– SYNONYMS **ruse,** tactic, move, device, stratagem, scheme, trick, gambit, plan, maneuver, dodge, subterfuge.

– ORIGIN unknown.

pluck /plək/ ▸ **verb 1** take hold of something and quickly remove it from its place. **2** pull out a hair, feather, etc. **3** pull the feathers from a bird's carcass to prepare it for cooking. **4** catch hold of: *she plucked at his sleeve.*

5 sound a stringed musical instrument with the finger or a plectrum.

– SYNONYMS **1 remove,** pick, pull, extract. **2 pull,** tug, clutch, snatch, grab, catch, tweak, jerk; informal yank. **3 strum,** pick, thrum, twang.

▶ **noun 1** spirited and determined courage. **2** the heart, liver, and lungs of an animal as food.

– SYNONYMS **courage,** bravery, nerve, daring, spirit, grit; informal guts, moxie.

– PHRASES **pluck up courage** summon up enough courage to do something frightening.
– ORIGIN Old English.

pluck·y /ˈpləkē/ ▶ **adjective** (**pluckier, pluckiest**) determined and brave in the face of difficulties.
– DERIVATIVES **pluck·i·ly** adverb **pluck·i·ness** noun.

plug /pləg/ ▶ **noun 1** a piece of solid material fitting tightly into and blocking a hole. **2** a device consisting of an insulated casing with metal pins that fit into holes in a socket to make an electrical connection. **3** informal an electrical socket. **4** informal a piece of publicity promoting a product or event. **5** a piece of tobacco cut from a larger cake for chewing.

– SYNONYMS **1 stopper,** bung, cork. **2 advertisement,** promotion, commercial, recommendation, mention, good word; informal hype, push.

▶ **verb** (**plugs, plugging, plugged**) **1** block or fill in a hole or gap. **2** (**plug something in**) connect an electrical appliance by means of a socket. **3** (**plug into**) gain access to an information system or area of activity. **4** informal promote a product or event by mentioning it publicly: *during the show she plugged her new record.* **5** informal shoot or hit someone or something. **6** (**plug away**) informal proceed steadily with a task.

– SYNONYMS **1 stop,** seal, close, block, fill. **2 publicize,** promote, advertise, mention, bang the drum for, draw attention to; informal hype, push.

– DERIVATIVES **plug·ger** noun.
– ORIGIN Dutch and German *plugge.*

plug-in ▶ **noun** a module or piece of software that can be added to an existing computer system to give extra features.

plum /pləm/ ▶ **noun 1** a soft oval fruit with purple, reddish, or yellow skin, containing a flattish pit. **2** a reddish-purple color. ▶ **adjective** informal highly desirable: *a plum job.*
– ORIGIN Latin *prunum.*

plum·age /ˈplo͞omij/ ▶ **noun** a bird's feathers.
– ORIGIN Old French.

plumb[1] /pləm/ ▶ **verb 1** explore or experience fully or to extremes: *using the Bible to plumb the spiritual depths of the human heart.* **2** measure the depth of water. **3** test an upright surface to determine the vertical.

– SYNONYMS **explore,** probe, delve into, search, examine, investigate, fathom, penetrate, understand.

▶ **noun** a lead ball or other heavy object attached to a line for finding the depth of water or determining the verticality of an upright surface.
▶ **adverb** informal **1** exactly: *plumb in the center.* **2** extremely or completely.

– SYNONYMS **right,** exactly, precisely, directly, dead, straight; informal bang.

▶ **adjective** vertical.
– ORIGIN Latin *plumbum* 'lead.'

plumb[2] ▶ **verb** install and connect water and drainage pipes.
– ORIGIN from **PLUMBER.**

plum·ba·go /pləmˈbāgō/ ▶ **noun** (pl. **plumbagos**) an evergreen shrub or climber with gray or blue flowers.
– ORIGIN from Latin *plumbum* 'lead.'

plumb·er /ˈpləmər/ ▶ **noun** a person who installs and repairs the pipes and fittings of water supply, sanitation, or heating systems.
– ORIGIN Old French *plommier* 'person working with lead.'

plumb·ing /ˈpləmiNG/ ▶ **noun 1** the system of pipes, tanks, and fittings required for the water supply, heating, and sanitation in a building. **2** the occupation of a plumber.

plumb line ▶ **noun** a line with a heavy weight attached to it, used to find the depth of water or to check that something is vertical.

plume /plo͞om/ ▶ **noun 1** a long, soft feather or arrangement of feathers. **2** a long spreading cloud of smoke or vapor. ▶ **verb 1** (as adj. **plumed**) decorated with feathers. **2** (of smoke or vapor) spread out in a plume.
– ORIGIN Latin *pluma* 'down.'

plum·met /ˈpləmit/ ▶ **verb** (**plummets, plummeting, plummeted**) **1** fall or drop straight down at high speed. **2** decrease rapidly in value or amount: *foreign sales have plummeted.*

– SYNONYMS **plunge,** dive, drop, fall, hurtle, nosedive, tumble.
– ANTONYMS soar.

▶ **noun 1** a steep and rapid fall or drop. **2** a plumb line or weight.
– ORIGIN from Old French *plommet* 'small sounding lead.'

plump[1] /pləmp/ ▶ **adjective 1** rather fat. **2** full and rounded in shape.

– SYNONYMS **fat,** chubby, rotund, ample, round, stout, portly, overweight; informal tubby, roly-poly, pudgy, zaftig, corn-fed.
– ANTONYMS thin.

▶ **verb** (**plump something up**) make a cushion or pillow full and rounded.
– DERIVATIVES **plump·ish** adjective **plump·ness** noun.
– ORIGIN related to Dutch *plomp,* German *plump* 'blunt, obtuse.'

plump[2] ▶ **verb 1** set or sit down heavily and suddenly. **2** (**plump for**) make a definite choice: *offered drinks, he plumped for brandy.* ▶ **adverb** informal with a sudden or heavy fall: *she fell plump backwards.*
– ORIGIN uncertain.

plum pud·ding ▶ **noun** a rich suet pudding containing raisins, currants, and spices.

plum to·ma·to ▶ **noun** an oval variety of tomato.

plun·der /ˈpləndər/ ▶ **verb** steal goods from a place by force, especially during war or rioting.

– SYNONYMS **1 pillage,** loot, rob, raid, ransack, rifle, strip, sack. **2 steal,** seize, thieve, pilfer, embezzle.

▶ **noun 1** goods obtained illegally and by force. **2** the forcible theft of goods.

– SYNONYMS **booty,** loot, stolen goods, spoils, ill-gotten gains; informal swag.

– DERIVATIVES **plun·der·er** noun.
– ORIGIN German *plündern,* 'rob of household goods.'

plunge /plənj/ ▶ **verb 1** fall or move suddenly and uncontrollably. **2** jump or dive quickly and energetically. **3** (**plunge in**) begin a course of action without much thought. **4** (**be plunged into**) suddenly be brought into a specified condition or state: *the area was plunged into darkness.* **5** push or thrust something quickly.

– SYNONYMS **1 plummet,** nosedive, drop, fall, tumble, descend. **2 dive,** jump, throw oneself, immerse oneself. **3 charge,** hurtle, career, plow, tear; informal barrel. **4 thrust,** stab, sink, stick, ram, drive, push, shove, force.

▶ **noun 1** an act of plunging. **2** a sudden and marked fall in value or amount: *a 75% plunge in profits.*
– PHRASES **take the plunge** informal decide on a course of action that one feels nervous about.
– ORIGIN Old French *plungier* 'thrust down.'

plunge pool ▶ **noun** a deep basin at the foot of a waterfall formed by the action of the falling water.

plung·er /'plənjər/ ▶ **noun 1** a part of a device that can be pushed down. **2** a rubber cup on a long handle, used to clear blocked pipes by means of suction.

plunk /pləNGk/ informal ▶ **verb 1** play a keyboard or pluck a stringed instrument in a heavy-handed way. **2** put something down heavily. ▶ **noun** the sound of a stringed instrument being plucked.
– ORIGIN probably imitating the sound.

plu·per·fect /ˌplo͞o'pərfikt/ ▶ **noun** Grammar another term for **PAST PERFECT**.
– ORIGIN from Latin *plus quam perfectum* 'more than perfect.'

plu·ral /'plo͝orəl/ ▶ **adjective 1** more than one in number. **2** Grammar (of a word or form) referring to more than one. **3** containing diverse elements: *a plural society.* ▶ **noun** Grammar a plural word or form.
– DERIVATIVES **plu·ral·ly** adverb.
– ORIGIN Latin *pluralis.*

plu·ral·ism /'plo͝orəˌlizəm/ ▶ **noun 1** a political system of power-sharing among a number of political parties. **2** the existence or toleration in society of a number of different ethnic groups, cultures, and beliefs. **3** the holding of more than one ecclesiastical office or position at the same time by one person.
– DERIVATIVES **plu·ral·ist** noun & adjective **plu·ral·is·tic** /-'listik/ adjective.

plu·ral·i·ty /plo͝o'ralitē/ ▶ **noun** (pl. **pluralities**) **1** the state of being plural or more than one. **2** a large number of people or things. **3** the number of votes cast for a candidate who receives more than any other but does not receive an absolute majority.

plu·ral·ize /'plo͝orəˌlīz/ ▶ **verb 1** make something more numerous. **2** give a plural form to a word.
– DERIVATIVES **plu·ral·i·za·tion** /ˌplo͝orəli'zāSHən/ noun.

plus /pləs/ ▶ **preposition 1** with the addition of. **2** informal together with.

– SYNONYMS **as well as,** together with, along with, in addition to, and, added to, not to mention.
– ANTONYMS minus.

▶ **adjective 1** (after a number or amount) at least: *companies put losses at $500,000 plus.* **2** (after a grade) better than: *B-plus.* **3** (before a number) above zero: *plus 60 degrees centigrade.* **4** having a positive electric charge.
▶ **noun 1** (also **plus sign**) the symbol +, indicating addition or a positive value. **2** informal an advantage.

– SYNONYMS **advantage,** good point, asset, pro, benefit, bonus, attraction; informal perk.
– ANTONYMS disadvantage.

▶ **conjunction** informal furthermore; also.
– ORIGIN Latin, 'more.'

plus ça change /'plo͞o sä'SHÄNZH/ ▶ **exclamation** used to acknowledge that certain things remain essentially unchanged.
– ORIGIN from French *plus ça change, plus c'est la même chose* 'the more it changes, the more it stays the same.'

plus fours /pləs fôrz/ ▶ **plural noun** men's short baggy trousers that fit closely below the knee, formerly worn for hunting and golf.
– ORIGIN so named because the overhang at the knee added four inches of material.

plush /pləSH/ ▶ **noun** a rich fabric of silk, cotton, or wool, with a long, soft nap. ▶ **adjective** informal expensively luxurious.

– SYNONYMS **luxurious,** luxury, deluxe, sumptuous, opulent, magnificent, rich, expensive, fancy, upmarket, upscale; informal posh, classy, swish, swank.
– ANTONYMS austere.

– DERIVATIVES **plush·y** adjective.
– ORIGIN former French *pluche.*

plus-size ▶ **adjective** (of a woman or women's clothing) of a larger size than normal; outsize.

Plu·to /'plo͞otō/ ▶ **noun** the most remote known planet of the solar system, ninth in order from the sun.
– DERIVATIVES **Plu·to·ni·an** /plo͞o'tōnēən/ adjective.

plu·toc·ra·cy /plo͞o'täkrəsē/ ▶ **noun** (pl. **plutocracies**) **1** government by wealthy people. **2** a society governed by wealthy people. **3** a ruling class whose power is based on their wealth.
– DERIVATIVES **plu·to·crat·ic** /ˌplo͞otə'kratik/ adjective.
– ORIGIN from Greek *ploutos* 'wealth' + *kratos* 'strength, authority.'

plu·to·crat /'plo͞otəˌkrat/ ▶ **noun** often derogatory a person who is powerful because they are wealthy.

plu·ton·ic /plo͞o'tänik/ ▶ **adjective** (of igneous rock) formed by solidification at considerable depth beneath the earth's surface.

plu·to·ni·um /plo͞o'tōnēəm/ ▶ **noun** a radioactive metallic element used as a fuel in nuclear reactors and as an explosive in atomic weapons.
– ORIGIN from **PLUTO**.

plu·vi·al /'plo͞ovēəl/ ▶ **adjective** technical relating to rainfall.
– ORIGIN Latin *pluvialis.*

ply[1] /plī/ ▶ **noun** (pl. **plies**) **1** a thickness or layer of a folded or laminated material. **2** each of a number of multiple layers or strands of which something is made.

– SYNONYMS **layer,** thickness, strand, sheet, leaf.

– ORIGIN French *pli* 'fold.'

ply[2] ▶ **verb** (**plies, plying, plied**) **1** work steadily with a tool or at one's job. **2** (of a ship or vehicle) travel regularly over a route. **3** (**ply someone with**) provide someone with food or drink in an insistent way. **4** (**ply someone with**) repeatedly ask someone questions.

– SYNONYMS **1 engage in,** carry on, pursue, conduct, practice. **2 travel,** shuttle, go back and forth. **3** *she plied me with fresh pastries* **provide,** supply, shower. **4** *he plied her with questions* **bombard,** assail, pester, plague, harass; informal hassle.

– ORIGIN shortening of **APPLY**.

ply·wood /ˈplīˌwo͝od/ ▸ **noun** thin strong board consisting of two or more layers of wood glued together.

PM ▸ **abbreviation** **1** post-mortem. **2** prime minister.

Pm ▸ **symbol** the chemical element promethium.

p.m. ▸ **abbreviation** after noon.
– ORIGIN from Latin *post meridiem.*

PMS ▸ **abbreviation** premenstrual syndrome.

pneu·mat·ic /n(y)o͞oˈmatik/ ▸ **adjective** containing or operated by air or gas under pressure: *a pneumatic drill.*
– DERIVATIVES **pneu·mat·i·cal·ly** /n(y)o͞oˈmadək(ə)lē/ adverb.
– ORIGIN Greek *pneumatikos.*

pneu·mat·ics /n(y)o͞oˈmatiks/ ▸ **plural noun** (treated as sing.) the science of the mechanical properties of gases.

pneu·mo·coc·cus /ˌn(y)o͞omōˈkäkəs/ ▸ **noun** (pl. **pneumococci** /-ˈkäksī, -ˈkäksē/) a bacterium associated with pneumonia and some forms of meningitis.
– DERIVATIVES **pneu·mo·coc·cal** adjective.

pneu·mo·nia /n(y)o͞oˈmōnēə, -ˈmōnyə/ ▸ **noun** an infection causing inflammation of one or both lungs.
– DERIVATIVES **pneu·mon·ic** /n(y)o͞oˈmänik/ adjective.
– ORIGIN from Greek *pneumōn* 'lung.'

PO ▸ **abbreviation** **1** postal order. **2** Post Office.

Po ▸ **symbol** the chemical element polonium.

poach[1] /pōCH/ ▸ **verb** cook food by simmering it in a small amount of liquid.
– ORIGIN Old French *pochier* 'poach, enclose in a bag.'

poach[2] ▸ **verb** **1** take game or fish illegally from private or protected areas. **2** take or obtain in an unfair or underhanded way: *they tried to poach passengers by offering better seats.*
– ORIGIN probably related to **POKE**[1].

poach·er[1] /ˈpōCHər/ ▸ **noun** a pan for poaching eggs or other food.

poach·er[2] ▸ **noun** a person who poaches game or fish.

PO box ▸ **noun** a numbered box in a post office where mail for a person or organization is kept until collected.

po·chard /ˈpōCHərd/ ▸ **noun** a diving duck, the male of which has a reddish-brown head.
– ORIGIN unknown.

pock /päk/ ▸ **noun** a pockmark.
– DERIVATIVES **pocked** adjective.
– ORIGIN Old English.

pock·et /ˈpäkət/ ▸ **noun** **1** a small bag sewn into or on clothing, used for carrying small articles. **2** a small group or area that is set apart or different from its surroundings: *the advancing forces encountered only pockets of resistance.* **3** informal a person's financial resources: *gifts to suit every pocket.* **4** a pouchlike storage compartment in a suitcase, car door, etc. **5** an opening at the corner or on the side of a billiard table into which balls are struck.

– SYNONYMS **1 pouch,** compartment. **2 area,** patch, region, cluster.

▸ **adjective** of a suitable size for carrying in a pocket.

– SYNONYMS **small,** little, miniature, mini, compact, concise, abridged, portable.

▸ **verb** (**pockets, pocketing, pocketed**) **1** put something into one's pocket. **2** take something belonging to someone else. **3** earn or win money: *he pocketed $1000 for a few hours' work.* **4** Billiards drive a ball into a pocket.

– SYNONYMS **1 acquire,** obtain, gain, get, secure, win, make, earn. **2 steal,** appropriate, purloin, misappropriate, embezzle.

– DERIVATIVES **pock·et·a·ble** adjective.
– PHRASES **in someone's pocket** dependent on someone financially and therefore under their influence. **out of** (or **in**) **pocket** having lost (or gained) money.
– ORIGIN Old French *pokete* 'little bag.'

pock·et·book /ˈpäkətˌbo͝ok/ ▸ **noun** a wallet, purse, or handbag.

pock·et·knife /ˈpäkətˌnīf/ ▸ **noun** (pl. **pocketknives**) a penknife.

pock·et mon·ey ▸ **noun** a small amount of money for minor expenses.

pock·et ve·to ▸ **noun** an indirect veto of a legislative bill by retaining the bill unsigned until it is too late for it to be dealt with during the legislative session.

pock·et watch ▸ **noun** a watch on a chain, intended to be carried in a jacket or vest pocket.

pock·mark /ˈpäkˌmärk/ ▸ **noun** **1** a hollow scar or mark on the skin left by a pustule or pimple. **2** a hollow mark on a surface. ▸ **verb** cover something with hollow scars or marks.

pod[1] /päd/ ▸ **noun** **1** a long seed case of a pea, bean, or related plant. **2** a self-contained or detachable unit on an aircraft or spacecraft.

– SYNONYMS **shell,** husk, hull, case, shuck.

▸ **verb** (**pods, podding, podded**) **1** remove peas or beans from their pods before cooking. **2** (of a plant) form pods.
– ORIGIN unknown.

pod[2] ▸ **noun** a small group of whales or similar sea mammals.
– ORIGIN unknown.

p.o.'d /ˌpēˈōd/ ▸ **abbreviation** informal pissed off: *what was he p.o.'d about?*

pod·cast /pädkast/ ▸ **noun** a multimedia digital file made available on the Internet for downloading to a personal computer, portable media player, etc.
– DERIVATIVES **pod·cast·er** noun **pod·cast·ing** noun.

po·di·a·try /pəˈdīətrē/ ▸ **noun** another term for **CHIROPODY**.
– DERIVATIVES **po·di·a·trist** /-trəst/ noun.
– ORIGIN from Greek *pous* 'foot' + *iatros* 'physician.'

po·di·um /ˈpōdēəm/ ▸ **noun** (pl. **podiums** or **podia** /-dēə/) a small platform on which a person stands when giving a speech or conducting an orchestra.

– SYNONYMS **platform,** stage, dais, rostrum, stand.

– ORIGIN Greek *podion* 'little foot.'

po·em /ˈpōəm, ˈpōim, pōm/ ▸ **noun** a piece of imaginative writing that combines elements of both speech and song, that is usually metaphorical, and that often exhibits meter and/or rhyme.

– SYNONYMS **verse,** rhyme, lyric, piece of poetry.

– ORIGIN Greek *poiēma* 'fiction, poem.'

po·e·sy /ˈpōəzē, -sē/ ▸ **noun** old use or literary poetry.
– ORIGIN Greek *poēsis, poiēsis* 'making, poetry.'

po·et /ˈpōət, ˈpōit/ ▸ **noun** **1** a person who writes poems. **2** a person possessing special powers of imagination or expression.
– DERIVATIVES **po·et·ess** noun.

po·et·as·ter /ˈpōət,astər/ ▶ **noun** a person who writes very bad poetry.

po·et·ic /pōˈetik/ (also **poetical** /pōˈetikəl/) ▶ **adjective** relating to or resembling poetry.

– SYNONYMS **expressive,** figurative, symbolic, flowery, artistic, imaginative, creative.

– DERIVATIVES **po·et·i·cal·ly** /-ik(ə)lē/ adverb.

po·et·i·cize /pōˈetə,sīz/ ▶ **verb 1** make something poetic. **2** write or speak poetically.
– DERIVATIVES **po·et·i·cism** /-,sizəm/ noun.

po·et·ic jus·tice ▶ **noun** suitable or deserved punishment or reward.

po·et·ic li·cense ▶ **noun** freedom to depart from the facts of a matter or from the accepted rules of language for artistic effect.

po·et·ics /pōˈetiks/ ▶ **plural noun** (treated as sing.) the study of linguistic techniques in poetry and literature.

po·et lau·re·ate /ˈlôrēət/ ▶ **noun** (pl. **poets laureate**) a poet appointed to an honorary representative position in a state, country, or locality.

po·et·ry /ˈpōətrē, ˈpōitrē/ ▶ **noun 1** poems as a whole or as a form of literature. **2** a quality of beauty or emotional intensity: *the sheer poetry of her tennis.*

– SYNONYMS **poems,** verse, versification, rhyme.

po·go /ˈpōgō/ ▶ **verb** (**pogoes, pogoing, pogoed**) informal jump up and down as if on a pogo stick as a form of dancing to rock music.

po·go stick ▶ **noun** a toy for bouncing around on, consisting of a spring-loaded pole with a handle at the top and a bar to stand on near the bottom.

po·grom /ˈpōgrəm, pəˈgräm/ ▶ **noun** an organized massacre of an ethnic group, originally that of Jews in Russia or eastern Europe.
– ORIGIN Russian, ‘devastation.’

poign·ant /ˈpoinyənt/ ▶ **adjective** arousing a feeling of sadness or regret: *a poignant moment's silence for the dead football player.*

– SYNONYMS **touching,** moving, sad, affecting, pitiful, pathetic, plaintive.

– DERIVATIVES **poign·an·cy** noun **poign·ant·ly** adverb.
– ORIGIN from Old French *poindre* ‘to prick.’

poin·set·ti·a /poinˈset(ē)ə/ ▶ **noun** a small shrub with large showy scarlet modified leaves (bracts) surrounding the small yellow flowers.
– ORIGIN named after the American diplomat and botanist Joel R. *Poinsett.*

point /point/ ▶ **noun 1** the tapered, sharp end of a tool, weapon, or other object. **2** a particular place or moment. **3** an item, detail, or idea in a discussion, written work, etc. **4** (**the point**) the most important or relevant part of what is being discussed. **5** the advantage or purpose of something. **6** a particular feature or quality. **7** a unit of scoring or of measuring value, achievement, or extent. **8** a very small dot or mark on a surface. **9** a decimal point. **10** (in geometry) something having position but not spatial extent, magnitude, dimension, or direction. **11** each of thirty-two directions marked at equal distances around a compass. **12** a narrow piece of land jutting out into the sea. **13** Printing a unit of measurement for type sizes and spacing (in the UK and US 0.351 mm, in Europe 0.376 mm). **14** (**points**) a set of electrical contacts in the distributor of a motor vehicle.

– SYNONYMS **1** *the point of a needle* **tip,** (sharp) end, extremity, prong, spike, tine, nib, barb. **2** *a meeting point* **place,** position, location, site, spot. **3** *this point in her life* **time,** stage, juncture, period, phase. **4** *an important point* **detail,** item, fact, thing, argument, consideration, factor, element, subject, issue, topic, question, matter. **5** (**the point**) *get to the point* **heart of the matter,** essence, nub, core, crux; informal nitty-gritty. **6** *what's the point of it all?* **purpose,** aim, object, objective, goal, intention, use, sense, value, advantage. **7** *he had his good points* **attribute,** characteristic, feature, trait, quality, property, aspect, side. **8** *the tension had reached such a high point* **level,** degree, stage, pitch, extent. **9** *points of light* **pinpoint,** dot, spot, speck.

▶ **verb 1** direct someone's attention in a particular direction by extending one's finger. **2** direct or aim something. **3** face in or indicate a particular direction: *a sign pointing left.* **4** (**point something out**) make someone aware of something. **5** (**point to**) indicate that something is likely to happen. **6** (**point something up**) reveal the true nature or importance of something. **7** give a sharp point to something. **8** fill in the joints of brickwork or tiling with mortar or cement.

– SYNONYMS **1 aim,** direct, level, train, focus. **2** (**point something out**) *the flaws in the plan have already been pointed out* **identify,** show, draw attention to, indicate, specify, detail, mention. **3** (**point to**) *the evidence pointed to his guilt* **indicate,** suggest, evidence, signal, signify, denote.

– PHRASES **a case in point** an example that illustrates what is being discussed. **make a point of** make a special effort to do something. **on the point of** on the verge of. **take someone's point** accept that what someone is saying is valid. **up to a point** to some extent.
– ORIGIN from Old French *pointe* or *point.*

point-blank ▶ **adjective & adverb 1** (of a shot or missile) fired from very close to its target. **2** in a blunt way, without explanation.

point·ed /ˈpointid/ ▶ **adjective 1** having a sharpened or tapered tip or end. **2** (of a remark or look) directed toward a particular person and expressing a clear message.

– SYNONYMS **1 sharp,** spiky, spiked, tapering, barbed. **2 cutting,** biting, incisive, trenchant, acerbic, caustic, scathing, venomous, sarcastic.

– DERIVATIVES **point·ed·ly** adverb.

point·er /ˈpointər/ ▶ **noun 1** a long, thin piece of metal on a scale or dial that moves to give a reading. **2** a rod used for pointing to features on a map or chart. **3** a hint or tip. **4** a breed of dog that on scenting game stands rigid looking toward it. **5** Computing a cursor or a link.

– SYNONYMS **1 indicator,** needle, arrow, hand. **2 indication,** indicator, clue, hint, sign, signal, evidence. **3 tip,** hint, suggestion, guideline, recommendation.

poin·til·lism /ˈpwantē,yizəm, ˈpointl,izəm/ ▶ **noun** a technique of neo-Impressionist painting using tiny dots of various pure colors, which become blended in the viewer's eye.
– DERIVATIVES **poin·til·list** noun & adjective.
– ORIGIN from French *pointiller* ‘mark with dots.’

point·ing /ˈpointiNG/ ▶ **noun** mortar or cement used to fill the joints of brickwork or tiling.

point·less /ˈpointlis/ ▶ **adjective** having little or no sense or purpose.

– SYNONYMS **senseless,** futile, useless, hopeless, unavailing, unproductive, aimless, idle, worthless, valueless.
– ANTONYMS valuable.

– DERIVATIVES **point·less·ly** adverb **point·less·ness** noun.

point man ▸ noun **1** the soldier at the head of a patrol. **2** (especially in a political context) a person at the forefront of an activity or endeavor.

point of de·par·ture ▸ noun the starting point of a line of thought or course of action.

point of or·der ▸ noun (pl. **points of order**) a query in a formal debate or meeting as to whether correct procedure is being followed.

point of view ▸ noun (pl. **points of view**) **1** a particular attitude or opinion. **2** the position from which something or someone is observed.

point spread ▸ noun a forecast of the number of points by which one sports team is expected to defeat another, used for betting purposes.

point-to-point ▸ noun (pl. **point-to-points**) Brit. an amateur cross-country steeplechase for horses used in hunting.

point·y /ˈpointē/ ▸ adjective (**pointier**, **pointiest**) informal having a pointed tip or end.

poise /poiz/ ▸ noun **1** a graceful and elegant way of holding the body. **2** calmness and confidence: *he had a moment to think, to recover his poise.*

– SYNONYMS **1 grace,** gracefulness, elegance, balance, control. **2 composure,** equanimity, self-possession, aplomb, self-assurance, self-control, sangfroid, dignity, presence of mind; informal cool.

▸ verb **1** be or cause to be balanced or suspended. **2** (**be poised to do**) be ready and prepared to do something. **3** (as adj. **poised**) calm and elegant or confident.

– SYNONYMS **1** *she was poised on one foot* **balance,** hold (oneself) steady, be suspended, remain motionless, hang, hover. **2** *he was poised for action* **prepare oneself,** ready oneself, brace oneself, gear oneself up, stand by.

– ORIGIN Old French *pois.*

poi·son /ˈpoizən/ ▸ noun **1** a substance that causes death or injury when swallowed or absorbed by a living organism. **2** a destructive influence: *the poison of fear.*

– SYNONYMS **toxin,** venom.

▸ verb **1** harm or kill a person or animal with poison. **2** contaminate something with poison. **3** have a destructive or harmful effect on: *the bad professors who poisoned the minds of a generation.*

– SYNONYMS **pollute,** contaminate, infect, taint, spoil.

– DERIVATIVES **poi·son·er** noun.
– ORIGIN Old French, 'magic potion.'

WORD LINKS

toxicology *study of poisons*

poi·son i·vy ▸ noun a North American climbing plant that produces an irritant oil in its leaves.

poi·son·ous /ˈpoiz(ə)nəs/ ▸ adjective **1** (of an animal) producing poison. **2** (of a plant or substance) causing or capable of causing death or illness if taken into the body. **3** very unpleasant or spiteful.

– SYNONYMS **1 venomous,** deadly. **2 toxic,** noxious, deadly, fatal, lethal, mortal. **3 malicious,** malevolent, hostile, spiteful, bitter, venomous, malign.
– ANTONYMS harmless.

– DERIVATIVES **poi·son·ous·ly** adverb.

poi·son pill ▸ noun a tactic used by a company threatened with an unwelcome takeover bid to make itself unattractive to the bidder.

poke[1] /pōk/ ▸ verb **1** prod someone or something with a finger or a sharp object. **2** make a hole by jabbing or prodding. **3** (**poke around**) look or search around. **4** push or stick out: *she poked her tongue out at him.*

– SYNONYMS **1 prod,** jab, dig, elbow, nudge, shove, jolt, stab, stick. **2** *leave the cable* ***poking out*** **stick out,** jut out, protrude, project, extend.

▸ noun an act of poking.

– SYNONYMS **prod,** jab, dig, elbow, nudge.

– PHRASES **poke fun at** tease or make fun of. **poke one's nose into** informal take an unwelcome interest in.
– ORIGIN uncertain.

poke[2] ▸ noun a bag or small sack.

pok·er[1] /ˈpōkər/ ▸ noun a metal rod with a handle, used for prodding and stirring an open fire.

pok·er[2] ▸ noun a card game in which the players bet on the value of the hands dealt to them, sometimes using bluffing.
– ORIGIN perhaps related to German *pochen* 'to brag,' *Pochspiel* 'bragging game.'

pok·er face ▸ noun an emotionless expression that hides one's true feelings.

poke·weed /ˈpōkˌwēd/ ▸ noun a North American plant with red stems, spikes of cream flowers, and purple berries.

pok·ey /ˈpōkē/ ▸ noun (usu. **the pokey**) informal prison.

pok·y /ˈpōkē/ (also **pokey**) ▸ adjective (**pokier**, **pokiest**) **1** annoyingly slow or dull. **2** (of a room or building) uncomfortably small and cramped.

– SYNONYMS **1 slow,** plodding, dawdling, sluggish, sluggardly. **2 small,** little, tiny, cramped, confined, restricted, boxy.

– ORIGIN from **POKE**[1] (in the former sense 'confine').

po·lar /ˈpōlər/ ▸ adjective **1** relating to the North or South Poles of the earth or the areas around them. **2** having an electrical or magnetic field. **3** completely opposite in type.

– SYNONYMS **opposite,** opposed, dichotomous, extreme, contrary, contradictory, antithetical.

po·lar bear ▸ noun a large white arctic bear that lives mainly on the pack ice.

po·lar·i·ty /pōˈlaritē, pə-/ ▸ noun (pl. **polarities**) **1** the state of having poles or opposites. **2** the direction of a magnetic or electric field.

po·lar·ize /ˈpōləˌrīz/ ▸ verb **1** divide into two groups with sharply contrasting opinions: *the nation's media are polarized in the controversy.* **2** Physics restrict the vibrations of a transverse wave, especially light, to one direction. **3** give magnetic or electric polarity to something.
– DERIVATIVES **po·lar·i·za·tion** /ˌpōlərəˈzāsʜən/ noun.

Po·lar·oid /ˈpōləˌroid/ ▸ noun trademark **1** a composite material that polarizes the light passing through it, produced in thin plastic sheets and used in sunglasses. **2** a type of camera that produces a finished print rapidly after each exposure. **3** a photograph taken with a Polaroid camera.

pol·der /ˈpōldər/ ▶ **noun** a piece of land reclaimed from the sea or a river, especially in the Netherlands.
– ORIGIN Dutch.

Pole /pōl/ ▶ **noun** a person from Poland.

pole[1] /pōl/ ▶ **noun 1** a long, thin rounded piece of wood or metal, used as a support. **2** a fishing rod.

– SYNONYMS **post,** pillar, stanchion, stake, support, prop, stick, paling, staff.

▶ **verb** move a boat along with a pole.
– ORIGIN Old English.

pole[2] ▶ **noun 1** either of the two locations (**North Pole** or **South Pole**) at opposite ends of the earth's axis. **2** each of two opposing qualities or ideas: *these discs represent the opposite poles of rave culture*. **3** each of the two opposite points of a magnet at which magnetic forces are strongest. **4** the positive or negative terminal of an electric cell or battery.
– PHRASES **be poles apart** have nothing in common.
– ORIGIN Greek *polos* 'pivot, axis, sky.'

pole·ax /ˈpōlˌaks/ (also **poleaxe**) ▶ **verb 1** knock down or stun someone with a heavy blow. **2** shock someone greatly: *she was poleaxed by the news*. ▶ **noun 1** a battleaxe. **2** a butcher's ax used to slaughter animals.
– ORIGIN from **POLL** + **AX**.

pole build·ing ▶ **noun** a quickly constructed building in which vertical poles are secured in the ground to serve as both the foundation and framework.

pole·cat /ˈpōlˌkat/ ▶ **noun 1** a weasellike mammal with dark brown fur and an unpleasant smell. **2** a skunk.
– ORIGIN perhaps from Old French *pole* 'chicken' + **CAT**.

pole danc·ing ▶ **noun** erotic dancing that involves swinging around a fixed pole.
– DERIVATIVES **pole danc·er** noun.

po·lem·ic /pəˈlemik/ ▶ **noun 1** a strong verbal or written attack: *a polemic against liberalism*. **2** (also **polemics**) the practice of engaging in fierce discussion. ▶ **adjective** (also **polemical** /pəˈlemikəl/) relating to fierce discussion.
– DERIVATIVES **po·lem·i·cist** /pəˈleməsist/ noun **po·lem·i·cize** /pəˈleməˌsīz/ verb.
– ORIGIN Greek *polemos* 'war.'

po·len·ta /pōˈlentə/ ▶ **noun** (in Italian cooking) a paste or dough made from cornmeal, which is boiled and then fried or baked.
– ORIGIN Latin, 'pearl barley.'

pole po·si·tion ▶ **noun** the most favorable position at the start of an automobile race.
– ORIGIN from the use of *pole* in horse racing to mean the starting position next to the inside boundary fence.

pole·star /ˈpōlˌstär/ ▶ **noun** the North Star.

pole vault ▶ **noun** an athletic event in which competitors attempt to vault over a high bar with the aid of a long flexible pole.

po·lice /pəˈlēs/ ▶ **noun** (treated as pl.) **1** an official civic organization responsible for preventing and solving crime and maintaining public order. **2** the members of a police force.

– SYNONYMS **police force,** police officers, policemen, policewomen. informal the cops, the boys in blue, [city's] finest, the fuzz, the heat, the law.

▶ **verb 1** maintain law and order in an area. **2** ensure that a law, rule, agreement, etc., is obeyed.

– SYNONYMS **1 guard,** watch over, protect, defend, patrol. **2 enforce,** regulate, oversee, supervise, monitor, observe, check.

– ORIGIN Latin *politia* 'policy, government.'

po·lice·man /pəˈlēsmən/ (or **policewoman** /pəˈlēsˌwo͝omən/) ▶ **noun** (pl. **policemen** or **policewomen**) a member of a police force.

po·lice of·fi·cer ▶ **noun** a policeman or policewoman.

– SYNONYMS **policeman, policewoman,** patrolman, (state) trooper. informal **cop, uniform;** Brit. informal **bobby.**

po·lice state ▶ **noun** a state in which the police are required by the government to keep secret watch over and control citizens' activities.

po·lice sta·tion ▶ **noun** a building housing a local police force.

pol·i·cy[1] /ˈpäləsē/ ▶ **noun** (pl. **policies**) **1** a course of action adopted or proposed by a political party, business, or other organization. **2** a principle that influences one's behavior: *his was a policy of live and let live*.

– SYNONYMS *government policy* **plans,** approach, code, system, guidelines, theory, line, position, stance.

– ORIGIN Greek *politeia* 'citizenship.'

pol·i·cy[2] ▶ **noun** (pl. **policies**) a contract of insurance.
– DERIVATIVES **pol·i·cy·hold·er** noun.
– ORIGIN French *police* 'bill of lading, contract of insurance.'

pol·i·cy wonk ▶ **noun** full form of **WONK**.

po·li·o /ˈpōlēˌō/ ▶ **noun** short for **POLIOMYELITIS**.

po·li·o·my·e·li·tis /ˌpōlēōˌmīəˈlītis/ ▶ **noun** an infectious disease that affects the central nervous system and can cause temporary or permanent paralysis.
– ORIGIN from Greek *polios* 'gray' + *muelos* 'marrow.'

Pol·ish /ˈpōlisʜ/ ▶ **noun** the language of Poland. ▶ **adjective** relating to Poland.

pol·ish /ˈpälisʜ/ ▶ **verb 1** make the surface of something smooth and shiny by rubbing. **2** improve or refine: *she's got to polish up her French for the job*. **3** (**polish something off**) finish or consume something quickly.

– SYNONYMS **1 shine,** wax, buff, rub up/down, gloss, burnish. **2** ***polish up your essay*** **perfect,** refine, improve, hone, enhance, brush up, revise, edit, correct, rewrite, go over, touch up.

▶ **noun 1** a substance rubbed on something to make it smooth and shiny. **2** an act of polishing something. **3** smoothness or glossiness produced by polishing. **4** the quality of being skillful, elegant, or refined: *she has the confidence and polish of a veteran gymnast*.

– SYNONYMS **sophistication,** refinement, urbanity, suaveness, elegance, style, grace, finesse; informal class.

– DERIVATIVES **pol·ish·er** noun.
– ORIGIN Latin *polire*.

CHOOSE THE RIGHT WORD

polish, gloss, luster, sheen
All of these words refer to a smooth, shining, or bright surface that reflects light. If this surface is produced by rubbing or friction, the correct word is **polish** (*the*

car's mirrorlike polish was the result of regular waxing and buffing). **Gloss**, on the other hand, suggests the hard smoothness associated with lacquered, varnished, or enameled surfaces (*a high-gloss paint*). **Luster** is associated with the light reflected from the surfaces of certain materials, such as silk or pearl (*a green stone with a brilliant luster*). **Sheen** describes a glistening or radiant brightness that is also associated with specific materials (*her hair had a rich, velvety sheen*).

pol·ished /ˈpälisʜt/ ▶ **adjective 1** shiny as a result of being rubbed. **2** accomplished and skillful.

– SYNONYMS **1** *a polished table* **shiny,** glossy, gleaming, lustrous, glassy, waxed, buffed, burnished. **2** *a polished performance* **expert,** accomplished, masterly, skillful, adept, adroit, dexterous, consummate, superlative, superb.
– ANTONYMS dull, inexpert.

po·lit·bu·ro /ˈpälət͵byo͝orō, ˈpō-/ ▶ **noun** (pl. **politburos**) the chief policy-making committee of a communist party, especially that of the former Soviet Union.
– ORIGIN from Russian *politicheskoe byuro* 'political bureau.'

po·lite /pəˈlīt/ ▶ **adjective** (**politer, politest**) **1** respectful and considerate toward other people; courteous. **2** cultured or well bred: *polite society*.

– SYNONYMS **1 well mannered,** civil, courteous, respectful, well behaved, well bred, gentlemanly, ladylike, genteel, gracious, tactful, diplomatic. **2 civilized,** refined, cultured, sophisticated, urbane.
– ANTONYMS rude.

– DERIVATIVES **po·lite·ly** adverb **po·lite·ness** noun.
– ORIGIN Latin *politus* 'polished, made smooth.'

pol·i·tesse /͵päləˈtes/ ▶ **noun** formal politeness.
– ORIGIN French.

pol·i·tic /ˈpälə͵tik/ ▶ **adjective 1** (of an action) sensible and wise in the circumstances. **2** (also **politick**) old use (of a person) prudent and shrewd.

– SYNONYMS **wise,** prudent, sensible, shrewd, astute, judicious, expedient, advantageous, beneficial, profitable.
– ANTONYMS unwise.

▶ **verb** (also **politick**) (**politics** or **politicks, politicking, politicked**) (usu. as n. **politicking**) often derogatory take part in political activity.
– ORIGIN Greek *politikos*.

po·lit·i·cal /pəˈlitikəl/ ▶ **adjective 1** relating to the government or public affairs of a country. **2** related to or interested in politics. **3** chiefly derogatory concerned with power or status within an organization rather than matters of principle: *they are paying the price for years of political infighting*.

– SYNONYMS **governmental,** government, constitutional, ministerial, parliamentary, diplomatic, legislative, administrative.

– DERIVATIVES **po·lit·i·cal·ly** /-ik(ə)lē/ adverb.

po·lit·i·cal cor·rect·ness ▶ **noun** the avoidance of language or behavior considered to be discriminatory or offensive to certain groups of people.

po·lit·i·cal·ly cor·rect /pəˈlitik(ə)lē/ (or **incorrect**) ▶ **adjective** showing (or failing to show) political correctness.

po·lit·i·cal pris·on·er ▶ **noun** a person imprisoned for their political beliefs or actions.

po·lit·i·cal sci·ence ▶ **noun** the study of political activity and behavior.

pol·i·ti·cian /͵päləˈtisʜən/ ▶ **noun** a person who is involved in politics as a job, as either a holder of or a candidate for an elected office.

– SYNONYMS **legislator,** representative, senator, congressman, congresswoman, statesman, stateswoman, member of Parliament, MP, minister; informal politico, pol.

po·lit·i·cize /pəˈlitə͵sīz/ ▶ **verb 1** make someone politically aware; involve someone in politics. **2** make an issue or activity political in nature.
– DERIVATIVES **po·lit·i·ci·za·tion** /pə͵litəsiˈzāsʜən/ noun.

pol·i·tick ▶ **verb** variant spelling of **POLITIC**.

po·lit·i·co /pəˈlitikō/ ▶ **noun** (pl. **politicos**) informal, chiefly derogatory a politician.
– ORIGIN Spanish and Italian, 'politic' or 'political person.'

pol·i·tics /ˈpälə͵tiks/ ▶ **plural noun** (usu. treated as sing.) **1** the activities associated with governing a country or area, and with the political relations between countries. **2** the political beliefs of a person or organization. **3** activities aimed at gaining power within an organization: *office politics*. **4** the principles relating to or underlying a sphere or activity, especially when concerned with power and status.

pol·i·ty /ˈpälətē/ ▶ **noun** (pl. **polities**) **1** a particular form of government. **2** a state as having a distinct political existence.
– ORIGIN Greek *politeia* 'citizenship, government.'

pol·ka /ˈpō(l)kə/ ▶ **noun** a lively dance for couples in duple time.
– ORIGIN Czech *půlka* 'half-step.'

pol·ka dot ▶ **noun** each of a number of round dots repeated to form a regular pattern.

poll /pōl/ ▶ **noun 1** the process of voting in an election. **2** a record of the number of votes cast. **3** dialect a person's head.

– SYNONYMS **1 vote,** ballot, show of hands, referendum, plebiscite, election. **2 survey,** opinion poll, market research, census.

▶ **verb 1** record the opinion or vote of a number of people. **2** (of a candidate in an election) receive a specified number of votes. **3** Telecommunications & Computing check the status of a device, especially as part of a repeated cycle. **4** cut the horns off a young cow.

– SYNONYMS **1 canvass,** survey, ask, question, interview, ballot. **2 get,** gain, register, record, return.

– ORIGIN perhaps from German.

pol·lack /ˈpälək/ (also **pollock**) ▶ **noun** (pl. same or **pollacks**) an edible greenish-brown fish of the cod family.
– ORIGIN perhaps from Celtic.

pol·lard /ˈpälərd/ ▶ **verb** cut off the top and branches of a tree to encourage new growth. ▶ **noun** a pollarded tree.
– ORIGIN from **POLL**.

pol·len /ˈpälən/ ▶ **noun** a powdery substance produced by the male part of a flower, containing the fertilizing agent.
– ORIGIN Latin, 'fine powder.'

pol·len count ▶ **noun** a measure of the amount of pollen in the air.

pol·li·nate /ˈpälə,nāt/ ▸ **verb** carry pollen to a flower or plant and so fertilize it.
– DERIVATIVES **pol·li·na·tion** /ˌpäləˈnāsHən/ noun **pol·li·na·tor** /-ˌnātər/ noun.

pol·lock ▸ **noun** variant spelling of POLLACK.

poll·ster /ˈpōlstər/ ▸ **noun** a person who carries out or analyzes opinion polls.

pol·lu·tant /pəˈlo͞otnt/ ▸ **noun** a substance that creates unpleasant or harmful effects in the air, soil, or water.

pol·lute /pəˈlo͞ot/ ▸ **verb 1** add harmful or unpleasant substances to soil, air, or water. **2** spoil or harm: *a society polluted by racism.*

– SYNONYMS **contaminate,** taint, poison, foul, dirty, soil, infect.
– ANTONYMS purify.

– DERIVATIVES **pol·lut·er** noun.
– ORIGIN Latin *polluere.*

pol·lu·tion /pəˈlo͞osHən/ ▸ **noun** the presence in the air, soil, or water of a substance with unpleasant or harmful effects.

– SYNONYMS **contamination,** impurity, dirt, filth, infection.

Pol·ly·an·na /ˌpälēˈanə/ ▸ **noun** an excessively cheerful or optimistic person.
– ORIGIN the name of the optimistic heroine created by the American author Eleanor H. Porter.

po·lo /ˈpōlō/ ▸ **noun** a game similar to hockey, played on horseback with a long-handled mallet.
– ORIGIN from a word in Tibetan language meaning 'ball.'

pol·o·naise /ˌpäləˈnāz, ˌpō-/ ▸ **noun** a slow stately dance of Polish origin in triple time. ▸ **adjective** (of a dish) garnished with chopped hard-boiled egg yolk, breadcrumbs, and parsley.
– ORIGIN from French, 'Polish.'

po·lo·ni·um /pəˈlōnēəm/ ▸ **noun** a rare radioactive metallic element.
– ORIGIN from Latin *Polonia* 'Poland' (the native country of Marie Curie, the element's co-discoverer).

po·lo shirt ▸ **noun** a casual short-sleeved shirt with a collar and two or three buttons at the neck.

pol·ter·geist /ˈpōltər,gīst/ ▸ **noun** a supernatural being supposedly responsible for throwing objects around.
– ORIGIN from German *poltern* 'create a disturbance' + *Geist* 'ghost.'

pol·troon /pälˈtro͞on/ ▸ **noun** old use a coward.
– ORIGIN Italian *poltrone.*

pol·y /ˈpälē/ ▸ **noun** (pl. **polys**) informal **1** polyethylene. **2** polytechnic.

poly- ▸ **combining form** many; much: *polychrome.*
– ORIGIN from Greek *polus* 'much,' *polloi* 'many.'

pol·y·am·ide /ˌpälēˈamīd/ ▸ **noun** a polymer of a type that includes many synthetic fibers such as nylon.

pol·y·an·dry /ˈpälē,andrē/ ▸ **noun** the practice of having more than one husband at the same time.
– DERIVATIVES **pol·y·an·drous** /ˌpälēˈandrəs/ adjective.
– ORIGIN from Greek *anēr* 'male.'

pol·y·an·thus /ˌpälēˈanTHəs/ ▸ **noun** (pl. same) a flowering garden plant that is a hybrid of the wild primrose.
– ORIGIN from Greek *anthos* 'flower.'

pol·y·car·bon·ate /ˌpäliˈkärbə,nāt, -nət/ ▸ **noun** a synthetic resin of a type that includes many molding materials and films.

pol·y·chro·mat·ic /ˌpälikrōˈmatik/ ▸ **adjective** having several colors; multicolored.

pol·y·chrome /ˈpäli,krōm/ ▸ **adjective** painted, printed, or decorated in several colors. ▸ **noun** varied coloring.
– DERIVATIVES **pol·y·chro·my** /ˈpäli,krōmē/ noun.
– ORIGIN from Greek *khrōma* 'color.'

pol·y·cot·ton /ˈpälē,kätn/ ▸ **noun** fabric made from a mixture of cotton and polyester fiber.

pol·y·es·ter /ˈpälē,estər/ ▸ **noun** a synthetic resin of a type that is used chiefly to make textile fibers.

pol·y·eth·yl·ene /ˌpälēˈeTHəlēn/ ▸ **noun** a tough, light, synthetic resin used for plastic bags, food containers, and other packaging.

po·lyg·a·my /pəˈligəmē/ ▸ **noun** the practice of having more than one wife or husband at the same time.
– DERIVATIVES **po·lyg·a·mist** noun **po·lyg·a·mous** adjective.
– ORIGIN from Greek *polugamos* 'often marrying.'

pol·y·glot /ˈpäli,glät/ ▸ **adjective** knowing, using, or written in several languages. ▸ **noun** a person who knows or uses several languages.
– ORIGIN Greek *poluglōttos* 'many-tongued.'

pol·y·gon /ˈpäli,gän/ ▸ **noun** a plane figure with three or more straight sides and angles.
– DERIVATIVES **po·lyg·o·nal** /pəˈligənl/ adjective.

pol·y·graph /ˈpäli,graf/ ▸ **noun** a machine that records changes in a person's physiological characteristics, such as pulse and breathing rates, used especially as a lie detector.

po·lyg·y·ny /pəˈlijənē/ ▸ **noun** the practice of having more than one wife at the same time.
– DERIVATIVES **po·lyg·y·nous** /pəˈlijənəs/ adjective.
– ORIGIN from Greek *gunē* 'woman.'

pol·y·he·dron /ˌpäliˈhēdrən/ ▸ **noun** (pl. **polyhedra** /-ˈhēdrə/ or **polyhedrons**) a solid figure with many plane faces, typically more than six.
– DERIVATIVES **pol·y·he·dral** /-ˈhēdrəl/ adjective.

pol·y·math /ˈpäli,maTH/ ▸ **noun** a person with a wide knowledge of many different subjects.
– DERIVATIVES **pol·y·math·ic** /ˌpäliˈmaTHik/ adjective.
– ORIGIN from Greek *polumathēs* 'having learned much.'

pol·y·mer /ˈpäləmər/ ▸ **noun** a substance with a molecular structure formed from many identical small molecules bonded together.
– DERIVATIVES **pol·y·mer·ic** /ˌpäləˈmerik/ adjective.
– ORIGIN from Greek *polumeros* 'having many parts.'

pol·y·mer·ase /pəˈlimə,rās, -,rāz/ ▸ **noun** an enzyme that brings about the formation of a particular polymer, especially DNA or RNA.

po·lym·er·ize /pəˈlimə,rīz, ˈpäləmə,rīz/ ▸ **verb** combine or cause to combine to form a polymer.
– DERIVATIVES **po·lym·er·i·za·tion** /pə,limərəˈzāsHən, ˌpäləmərə-/ noun.

pol·y·mor·phism /ˌpäliˈmôr,fizəm/ ▸ **noun** the occurrence of something in several different forms.
– DERIVATIVES **pol·y·mor·phic** /-ˈmôrfik/ adjective **pol·y·mor·phous** /-ˈmôrfəs/ adjective.

Pol·y·ne·sian /ˌpäləˈnēzHən/ ▸ **noun 1** a person from Polynesia, a large group of Pacific islands including New Zealand, Hawaii, and Samoa. **2** a group of languages spoken in Polynesia. ▸ **adjective** relating to Polynesia.

pol·y·no·mi·al /ˌpäləˈnōmēəl/ ▶ **noun** Mathematics an expression consisting of several terms, especially terms containing different powers of the same variable.
– ORIGIN from **POLY-**, on the pattern of *binomial*.

pol·y·nos·ic /ˌpäliˈnäsik/ ▶ **noun** a rayon-and-polyester yarn with a soft finish, used mainly in clothing.

pol·yp /ˈpäləp/ ▶ **noun 1** a simple sea creature that remains fixed in the same place, such as coral. **2** Medicine a small growth protruding from a mucous membrane.
– ORIGIN Greek *polupous* 'cuttlefish, polyp.'

pol·y·pep·tide /ˌpäliˈpepˌtīd/ ▶ **noun** a peptide consisting of many amino acids bonded together in a chain, e.g., in a protein.

pol·y·phar·ma·cy /ˌpälēˈfärməsē/ ▶ **noun** (pl. **polypharmacies**) the simultaneous use of multiple drugs to treat a single illness or condition.

pol·y·phon·ic /ˌpäliˈfänik/ ▶ **adjective 1** having many sounds or voices. **2** (especially of vocal music) in two or more parts, each having a melody of its own.
– ORIGIN from Greek *phōnē* 'voice, sound.'

po·lyph·o·ny /pəˈlifənē/ ▶ **noun** (pl. **polyphonies**) the combination in harmony of a number of musical parts, each forming an individual melody.

pol·y·ploid /ˈpäliˌploid/ ▶ **adjective** (of a cell or nucleus) containing more than two matching sets of chromosomes.

pol·y·pro·pyl·ene /ˌpäliˈprōpəˌlēn/ ▶ **noun** a synthetic resin that is a polymer of propylene.

pol·yp·tych /ˈpälipˌtik/ ▶ **noun** a painting, especially an altarpiece, consisting of more than three panels joined by hinges or folds.
– ORIGIN from Greek *poluptukhos* 'having many folds.'

pol·y·rhythm /ˈpäliˌri<u>TH</u>əm/ ▶ **noun** Music the use of two or more different rhythms simultaneously.
– DERIVATIVES **pol·y·rhyth·mic** /ˌpäliˈri<u>TH</u>mik/ adjective.

pol·y·sac·cha·ride /ˌpäliˈsakəˌrīd/ ▶ **noun** a carbohydrate (e.g., starch or cellulose) whose molecules consist of long chains of monosaccharide units.

pol·y·sty·rene /ˌpäliˈstīrēn/ ▶ **noun** a light synthetic material used especially as packaging.
– ORIGIN blend of **POLYMER** + **STYRENE**.

pol·y·syl·lab·ic /ˌpälisəˈlabik/ ▶ **adjective** having more than one syllable.

pol·y·tech·nic /ˌpäliˈteknik/ ▶ **noun** a college offering courses in many subjects, especially vocational or technical subjects.

pol·y·the·ism /ˈpäliTHēˌizəm/ ▶ **noun** the belief in or worship of more than one god.
– DERIVATIVES **pol·y·the·ist** /-ˌTHēist/ noun **pol·y·the·is·tic** /ˌpäliTHēˈistik/ adjective.
– ORIGIN from Greek *polutheos* 'of many gods.'

pol·y·thene /ˈpäləTHēn/ ▶ **noun** Brit. another term for **POLYETHYLENE**.
– ORIGIN shortened form of *polyethylene*.

pol·y·un·sat·u·rat·ed /ˌpälēənˈsacHəˌrātid/ ▶ **adjective** referring to fats whose molecules contain several double or triple bonds, believed to be less healthy in the diet than monounsaturated fats.
– DERIVATIVES **pol·y·un·sat·u·rates** /ˌpälēənˈsacHərits/ plural noun.

pol·y·u·re·thane /ˌpäliˈyo͝orəˌTHān/ ▶ **noun** a synthetic resin used in paints and varnishes.
– ORIGIN blend of **POLYMER** + **URETHANE**.

pol·y·va·lent /ˌpäliˈvālənt/ ▶ **adjective** having many different functions, forms, or aspects.

pol·y·vi·nyl chlo·ride /ˌpäliˈvīnl/ ▶ **noun** full form of **PVC**.

po·made /pōˈmād, -ˈmäd/ ▶ **noun** a scented oil or cream for making the hair smooth and glossy.
– DERIVATIVES **po·mad·ed** adjective.
– ORIGIN French *pommade*.

po·man·der /pōˈmandər, ˈpōˌmandər/ ▶ **noun** a ball or perforated container of mixed sweet-smelling substances used to perfume a room or cupboard.
– ORIGIN from Latin *pomum de ambra* 'apple of ambergris.'

pome·gran·ate /ˈpäm(ə)ˌgranit, ˈpəm-/ ▶ **noun** a round tropical fruit with a tough golden-orange skin and sweet red flesh containing many seeds.
– ORIGIN from Latin *pomum granatum* 'apple having many seeds.'

pom·e·lo /ˈpäməˌlō, ˈpəm-/ ▶ **noun** (pl. **pomelos**) a large citrus fruit similar to a grapefruit, with a thick yellow skin and bitter pulp.
– ORIGIN unknown.

Pom·er·a·ni·an /ˌpäməˈrānēən/ ▶ **noun** a small breed of dog with long silky hair and a pointed muzzle.
– ORIGIN from *Pomerania*, a region of central Europe.

pom·mel /ˈpäməl, ˈpəməl/ ▶ **noun 1** the upward curving or projecting front part of a saddle. **2** a rounded knob on the end of the handle of a sword, dagger, or old-fashioned gun.
– ORIGIN Old French *pomel*.

pommes frites /ˌpäm ˈfrēt/ ▶ **plural noun** very thin French fries.
– ORIGIN French.

pomp /pämp/ ▶ **noun 1** the impressive clothes, music, and traditions that are part of a grand public ceremony. **2** (also **pomps**) old use a showy display of something, intended to impress other people.

> – SYNONYMS **ceremony,** solemnity, ritual, display, spectacle, pageantry, show, ostentation, splendor, grandeur, magnificence, majesty, stateliness, glory; informal razzmatazz.

– ORIGIN Greek *pompē* 'procession.'

pom·pa·dour /ˈpämpəˌdôr, -ˌdo͝or, pôNpäˈdo͝or/ ▶ **noun** a hairstyle in which the hair is turned back off the forehead in a roll.
– ORIGIN named after Madame de *Pompadour*, the mistress of Louis XV of France.

pom·pom /ˈpämˌpäm/ (also **pompon**) ▶ **noun 1** a small woolen ball attached to a garment for decoration. **2** a cluster of brightly colored strands of yarn or plastic, waved in pairs by cheerleaders. **3** a dahlia, chrysanthemum, or aster with small tightly clustered petals.
– ORIGIN French *pompon* 'tuft, topknot.'

pom-pom ▶ **noun** a large-caliber British machine gun, in service since 1930.
– ORIGIN imitating the sound of the discharge.

pomp·ous /ˈpämpəs/ ▶ **adjective** affectedly solemn or self-important.

> – SYNONYMS **self-important,** overbearing, sententious, grandiose, affected, pretentious, puffed up, haughty, proud, conceited, supercilious, condescending, patronizing.

– DERIVATIVES **pom·pos·i·ty** /päm'päsətē/ noun **pomp·ous·ly** adverb.

ponce /'pônsā/ Brit. informal ▶ **noun 1** a man who lives off a prostitute's earnings. **2** derogatory an effeminate man. ▶ **verb** (**ponce about/around**) behave in a way that wastes time or looks affected or foolish.
– DERIVATIVES **pon·cey** (also **poncy**) adjective.
– ORIGIN perhaps from POUNCE[1].

pon·cho /'pänchō/ ▶ **noun** (pl. **ponchos**) a garment made of a large piece of woolen cloth with a slit in the middle for the head.
– ORIGIN Latin American Spanish.

pond /pänd/ ▶ **noun 1** a fairly small area of still water. **2** (**the pond**) humorous the Atlantic Ocean.
– ORIGIN alteration of POUND[3].

pon·der /'pändər/ ▶ **verb** consider something carefully.

– SYNONYMS **think about,** contemplate, consider, review, reflect on, mull over, meditate on, muse on, dwell on.

– ORIGIN Latin *ponderare* 'weigh.'

pon·der·a·ble /'pändərəbəl/ ▶ **adjective** literary worthy of consideration; thought-provoking.

pon·der·o·sa /,pändə'rōsə/ (also **ponderosa pine**) ▶ **noun** a tall North American pine tree, grown for its wood and as an ornamental.
– ORIGIN feminine of Latin *ponderosus* 'massive.'

pon·der·ous /'pändərəs/ ▶ **adjective 1** slow and clumsy because of great weight. **2** tediously solemn or long-winded: *the play's ponderous dialogue*.

– SYNONYMS **1** *a ponderous procession* **slow,** awkward, lumbering, cumbersome, ungainly, graceless. **2** *a ponderous speech* **labored,** laborious, lifeless, plodding, pedestrian, boring, dull, tedious, monotonous.
– ANTONYMS light, lively.

– DERIVATIVES **pon·der·ous·ly** adverb.
– ORIGIN Latin *ponderosus*.

pond·weed /'pänd,wēd/ ▶ **noun** a plant that grows in still or running water.

pons /pänz/ ▶ **noun** (pl. **pontes** /'pän,tēz/) the part of the brainstem that links the medulla oblongata and the thalamus.
– ORIGIN Latin, 'bridge.'

pon·tiff /'päntəf/ ▶ **noun** the Pope.
– ORIGIN Latin *pontifex* 'high priest.'

pon·tif·i·cal /pän'tifikəl/ ▶ **adjective 1** relating to the Pope; papal. **2** speaking as if one's own opinions are always correct; pompously dogmatic.
– DERIVATIVES **pon·tif·i·cal·ly** adverb.

pon·tif·i·cate ▶ **verb** /pän'tifi,kāt/ **1** express one's opinions in a pompous and overbearing or dogmatic way. **2** (in the Roman Catholic Church) officiate as bishop, especially at Mass.

– SYNONYMS **hold forth,** expound, declaim, preach, lay down the law, sound off, lecture; informal mouth off.

▶ **noun** /-kət/ (also **Pontificate**) (in the Roman Catholic Church) the office or period of office of pope or bishop.
– DERIVATIVES **pon·tif·i·ca·tor** /-,kātər/ noun.

pon·toon /,pän'tōōn/ ▶ **noun 1** a flat-bottomed boat or hollow metal cylinder used with others to support a temporary bridge or floating landing stage. **2** a bridge or landing stage supported by pontoons.
– ORIGIN French *ponton*.

po·ny /'pōnē/ ▶ **noun** (pl. **ponies**) a horse of a small breed, especially one below 15 hands (58 inches).
– ORIGIN probably from French *poulenet* 'small foal.'

po·ny·tail /'pōnē,tāl/ ▶ **noun** a hairstyle in which the hair is drawn back and tied at the back of the head.

poo ▶ **exclamation & noun** variant spelling of POOH.

pooch /pōōch/ ▶ **noun** informal a dog.
– ORIGIN unknown.

poo·dle /'pōōdl/ ▶ **noun 1** a breed of dog with a curly coat that is usually clipped. **2** Brit. a person who is too ready to do what someone else tells them to do.
– ORIGIN German *Pudelhund*, from *puddeln* 'splash in water.'

pooh /pōō, pŏŏ/ (also **poo**) informal ▶ **exclamation** expressing impatience or contempt. ▶ **noun** excrement.

pooh-bah /'pōō ,bä/ ▶ **noun** a pompous or self-important person who has a great deal of influence or holds many posts at the same time.
– ORIGIN named after a character in W. S. Gilbert's *The Mikado*.

pooh-pooh /'pōō ,pōō, pōō 'pōō/ ▶ **verb** informal dismiss an idea or suggestion as being foolish or impractical.

pool[1] /pōōl/ ▶ **noun 1** a small area of still water. **2** (also **swimming pool**) an artificial pool for swimming in. **3** a small, shallow patch of liquid lying on a surface: *a pool of blood*. **4** a deep place in a river.

– SYNONYMS **1** *pools of water* **puddle,** pond, lake; literary mere. **2** *the hotel has a pool* **swimming pool,** baths, lap pool, natatorium.

– ORIGIN Old English.

pool[2] ▶ **noun 1** a shared supply of vehicles, people, goods, or funds that is available when needed. **2** the total amount of players' stakes in gambling or sweepstakes. **3** a game played on a billiard table using 16 balls. **4** an arrangement between competing commercial organizations to fix prices and share business so as to eliminate competition.

– SYNONYMS **1** *a pool of skilled labor* **supply,** reserve(s), reservoir, fund, store, bank, stock, cache. **2** *a pool of money for emergencies* **fund,** reserve, kitty, pot, bank, purse.

▶ **verb** put money or other resources into a common fund to be used by a number of people: *they pooled their wages and bought food*.

– SYNONYMS **combine,** group, join, unite, merge, share.

– ORIGIN French *poule* 'stake, kitty.'

pool·room /'pōōl,rōōm, -,rŏŏm/ ▶ **noun** (also **pool hall**) a commercial establishment where pool or billiard games are played.

pool·side /'pōōl,sīd/ ▶ **noun** the area immediately next to a swimming pool.

poop[1] /pōōp/ (also **poop deck**) ▶ **noun** a raised deck at the stern of a ship, especially a sailing ship.
– ORIGIN Latin *puppis* 'stern.'

poop[2] ▶ **verb** (often as adj. **pooped**) informal **1** exhaust someone. **2** (**poop out**) stop functioning.

poop[3] informal ▶ **noun** excrement. ▶ **verb** defecate.

poop[4] ▶ **noun** informal up-to-date or inside information.

pooped /pōōpd/ ▶ **adjective** informal exhausted.

– ORIGIN unknown.

poor /po͝or, pôr/ ▶ **adjective** **1** not having enough money to live at a comfortable or normal standard. **2** of a low standard or quality: *poor working conditions.* **3** (**poor in**) lacking in: *an acid soil that is poor in nutrients.* **4** deserving pity or sympathy: *he's driven the poor woman away.*

> – SYNONYMS **1 poverty-stricken,** penniless, impoverished, impecunious, needy, destitute, dirt poor. informal hard up, strapped; formal penurious. **2 substandard,** bad, deficient, defective, faulty, imperfect, inferior, unsatisfactory, shoddy, crude, inadequate, unacceptable; informal crummy, rotten. **3 meager,** scanty, scant, paltry, reduced, modest, sparse, spare, deficient, insubstantial, skimpy, lean; informal measly, stingy. **4 unfortunate,** unlucky, unhappy, hapless, wretched, luckless, ill-fated, ill-starred.
> – ANTONYMS rich.

– PHRASES **the poor man's ——** an inferior or cheaper substitute for the thing specified: *herring roe—the poor man's caviar.* **poor relation** a person or thing that is considered less good than others of the same type. **take a poor view of** regard someone or something with disapproval.
– ORIGIN Old French *poure.*

poor·house /ˈpo͝orˌhous, ˈpôr-/ ▶ **noun** historical an institution where paupers were maintained with public funds.

poor·ly /ˈpo͝orlē, ˈpôr-/ ▶ **adverb** in a poor way: *schools that were performing poorly.*

> – SYNONYMS **badly,** imperfectly, incompetently, crudely, shoddily, inadequately.

▶ **adjective** chiefly Brit. unwell.

> – SYNONYMS **ill,** unwell, not very well, ailing, indisposed, out of sorts, under par, peaked. informal under the weather.

poor white ▶ **noun** derogatory a white person, especially in the southern US, who lacks money, education, or social status.

POP /päp/ ▶ **abbreviation** **1** Computing point of presence, referring to the location at which equipment supporting access to the Internet is situated. **2** point of purchase, referring to products or promotions located adjacent to a retail checkout or cashier.

pop[1] /päp/ ▶ **verb** (**pops, popping, popped**) **1** make or cause to make a sudden short explosive sound. **2** go or come quickly or unexpectedly. **3** quickly put something somewhere: *he popped a candy into his mouth.* **4** (of a person's eyes) open wide and appear to bulge. **5** informal take or inject a drug.

> – SYNONYMS **1 go bang,** go off, crack, snap, burst, explode. **2** *I might pop around later* **go**; drop in, stop by, visit. **3** *pop a lid over the pot* **put,** place, slip, throw, slide, stick, set, lay, position.

▶ **noun** **1** a sudden short explosive sound. **2** informal a sweet carbonated soft drink. **3** Baseball a ball hit high but not deep, providing an easy catch.

> – SYNONYMS **bang,** crack, snap, explosion, report.

– PHRASES **have** (or **take**) **a pop at** informal attack. **pop the question** informal propose marriage.
– ORIGIN imitating the sound.

pop[2] ▶ **noun** (also **pop music**) popular modern commercial music, typically with a strong melody and beat. ▶ **adjective** **1** relating to pop music. **2** often derogatory (especially of a scientific or academic subject) presented in a way that the general public will easily understand: *pop psychology.*

pop[3] ▶ **noun** informal term for **FATHER**.
– ORIGIN abbreviation of **POPPA**.

po·pa·dom ▶ **noun** variant spelling of **POPPADOM**.

pop art ▶ **noun** art that uses styles and images from modern popular culture.

pop·corn /ˈpäpˌkôrn/ ▶ **noun** corn kernels that swell up and burst open when heated and are then eaten as a snack.

pope /pōp/ ▶ **noun** (**the Pope**) the Bishop of Rome as head of the Roman Catholic Church.
– ORIGIN Greek *papas* 'bishop, patriarch.'

pop·er·y /ˈpōpərē/ ▶ **noun** derogatory, chiefly old use Roman Catholicism.

pop-eyed ▶ **adjective** informal having bulging or staring eyes.

pop·gun /ˈpäpˌgən/ ▶ **noun** a child's toy gun that shoots a harmless pellet or cork.

pop·in·jay /ˈpäpənˌjā/ ▶ **noun** dated a conceited person who is extremely concerned with their clothes and appearance.
– ORIGIN Old French *papingay* 'parrot.'

pop·ish /ˈpōpisн/ ▶ **adjective** derogatory Roman Catholic.

pop·lar /ˈpäplər/ ▶ **noun** a tall, slender tree with soft wood.
– ORIGIN Latin *populus.*

pop·lin /ˈpäplən/ ▶ **noun** a cotton fabric with a finely ribbed surface.
– ORIGIN former French *papeline.*

pop·lit·e·al /päpˈlitēəl, ˌpäpləˈtēəl/ ▶ **adjective** relating to or situated in the hollow at the back of the knee.
– ORIGIN Latin *popliteus.*

pop·pa /ˈpäpə/ ▶ **noun** informal term for **FATHER**.
– ORIGIN alteration of **PAPA**.

pop·pa·dom /ˈpäpədəm/ (also **poppadum** or **popadom**) ▶ **noun** (in Indian cooking) a large thin circular piece of unleavened spiced bread made from ground lentils and fried in oil until crisp.
– ORIGIN Tamil.

pop·per /ˈpäpər/ ▶ **noun** informal **1** a pan or utensil for popping corn. **2** a small vial of amyl nitrite that is inhaled, making a popping sound when opened.

pop·py /ˈpäpē/ ▶ **noun** a plant with showy red, pink, or orange flowers and large seed capsules, including species that produce drugs such as opium and codeine.
– ORIGIN Old English.

pop·py·cock /ˈpäpēˌkäk/ ▶ **noun** informal nonsense.
– ORIGIN Dutch dialect *pappekak,* literally 'soft dung.'

Pop·si·cle /ˈpäpˌsikəl/ ▶ **noun** trademark a piece of flavored ice or ice cream on a stick.

pop·u·lace /ˈpäpyələs/ ▶ **noun** (treated as sing. or pl.) the general public.

> – SYNONYMS **population,** inhabitants, residents, natives, community, country, (general) public, people, nation, common people, masses, multitude, rank and file; informal John Q. Public; derogatory hoi polloi, rabble, riffraff.

– ORIGIN Italian *popolaccio* 'common people.'

pop·u·lar /ˈpäpyələr/ ▸ **adjective 1** liked or admired by many people or by a particular group: *one of the most popular girls in the school*. **2** intended for or suited to the taste or means of the general public: *the popular press*. **3** (of a belief or attitude) widely held among the general public. **4** (of political activity) carried on by the people as a whole: *a popular revolt*.

> – SYNONYMS **1 well liked,** sought-after, in demand, commercial, marketable, fashionable, in vogue, all the rage, hot; informal in, cool, big. **2 nonspecialist,** nontechnical, amateur, lay person's, general, middle-of-the-road, accessible, simplified, understandable, mass-market. **3 widespread,** general, common, current, prevailing, standard, ordinary, conventional.

– DERIVATIVES **pop·u·lar·i·ty** /ˌpäpyəˈlaritē/ noun **pop·u·lar·ly** adverb.
– ORIGIN Latin *popularis*, from *populus* 'people.'

pop·u·lar front ▸ **noun** a political party or coalition representing left-wing elements.

pop·u·lar·ize /ˈpäpyələˌrīz/ ▸ **verb 1** make something popular: *his books have done much to popularize the sport*. **2** present something scientific or academic in a way that the general public will find interesting and understandable.
– DERIVATIVES **pop·u·lar·i·za·tion** /ˌpäpyələrəˈzāsʜən/ noun **pop·u·lar·iz·er** noun.

pop·u·late /ˈpäpyəˌlāt/ ▸ **verb 1** live in a place and form its population: *the island is populated by scarcely 40,000 people*. **2** cause people to settle in a place. **3** add data to a computer database.

> – SYNONYMS **inhabit,** occupy, people, settle, colonize.

– ORIGIN Latin *populare* 'supply with people.'

pop·u·la·tion /ˌpäpyəˈlāsʜən/ ▸ **noun 1** all the inhabitants of a place. **2** a particular group within this: *the country's immigrant population*. **3** Biology a community of animals or plants that interbreed.

> – SYNONYMS **inhabitants,** residents, people, citizens, public, community, populace, society, natives, occupants.

pop·u·list /ˈpäpyələst/ ▸ **adjective** intended to appeal to or represent the interests and views of ordinary people. ▸ **noun** a member of a political party that seeks to appeal to or represent the interests and views of ordinary people.
– DERIVATIVES **pop·u·lism** /-ˌlizəm/ noun.

pop·u·lous /ˈpäpyələs/ ▸ **adjective** having a large population.

> – SYNONYMS **densely populated,** congested, crowded, packed, teeming.
> – ANTONYMS deserted.

pop-up ▸ **adjective 1** (of a book or greeting card) containing folded pictures that rise up to form a three-dimensional scene or figure when opened. **2** (of a computer menu or other feature) able to be superimposed on the screen being worked on and suppressed rapidly. ▸ **noun 1** a pop-up computer menu or other feature. **2** an Internet browser window that appears without having been requested, especially one containing an advertisement. **3** Baseball another term for **POP**[1] (sense 3 of the noun).

por·bea·gle /ˈpôrˌbēgəl/ ▸ **noun** a large shark found chiefly in the open seas of the North Atlantic and in the Mediterranean.
– ORIGIN Cornish dialect.

por·ce·lain /ˈpôrs(ə)lən/ ▸ **noun 1** a type of fine translucent china. **2** articles made of porcelain.
– ORIGIN Italian *porcellana* 'cowrie shell, china.'

porch /pôrcʜ/ ▸ **noun** a covered shelter projecting from the entrance of a building.
– ORIGIN Old French *porche*.

por·cine /ˈpôrˌsīn/ ▸ **adjective** relating to or resembling a pig or pigs.
– ORIGIN from Latin *porcus* 'pig.'

por·ci·ni /pôrˈcʜēnē/ ▸ **plural noun** ceps (edible wild mushrooms).
– ORIGIN Italian, 'little pigs.'

por·cu·pine /ˈpôrkyəˌpīn/ ▸ **noun** a large rodent with protective spines or quills on the body and tail.
– ORIGIN from Latin *porcus* 'pig' + *spina* 'thorn.'

pore[1] /pôr/ ▸ **noun** a tiny opening in the skin or other surface through which gases, liquids, or microscopic particles may pass.
– ORIGIN Greek *poros*.

pore[2] ▸ **verb** (**pore over/through**) study or read something with close attention.
– ORIGIN perhaps related to **PEER**[1].

> **USAGE**
> Do not confuse **pore** and **pour**. **Pore** is used with **over** or **through** and means 'study or read something closely' (*I spend hours poring over cookbooks*), while **pour** means 'flow in a steady stream' (*water poured off the roof*).

pork /pôrk/ ▸ **noun** the flesh of a pig used as food.
– ORIGIN Latin *porcus* 'pig.'

pork bar·rel ▸ **noun** informal referring to the use of government funds for projects designed to win votes.
– ORIGIN from the farmers' practice of keeping a reserve supply of meat in a barrel, later meaning 'a supply of money.'

pork·er /ˈpôrkər/ ▸ **noun 1** a young pig raised and fattened for food. **2** informal, derogatory a fat person.

pork·pie hat ▸ **noun** a hat with a flat crown and a brim turned up all around.

pork·y /ˈpôrkē/ informal ▸ **adjective** (**porkier, porkiest**) fat. ▸ **noun** (pl. **porkies**) (also **porky pie**) Brit. rhyming slang a lie.

porn /pôrn/ (also **porno**) informal ▸ **noun** pornography. ▸ **adjective** pornographic.

por·no·graph·ic /ˌpôrnəˈgrafik/ ▸ **adjective** designed to cause sexual excitement.

> – SYNONYMS *pornographic magazines* **obscene,** indecent, dirty, smutty, filthy, erotic, titillating, sexy, risqué, X-rated, adult.

por·nog·ra·phy /pôrˈnägrəfē/ ▸ **noun** photographs, writing, movies, etc., intended to cause sexual excitement.
– DERIVATIVES **por·nog·ra·pher** noun.
– ORIGIN Greek *pornographos* 'writing about prostitutes.'

po·rous /ˈpôrəs/ ▸ **adjective** (of a rock or other material) having tiny spaces through which liquid or air may pass.

> – SYNONYMS **permeable,** penetrable, absorbent, spongy.
> – ANTONYMS impermeable.

– DERIVATIVES **po·ros·i·ty** /pəˈräsətē, pôrˈäs-/ noun.
– ORIGIN from Latin *porus* 'pore.'

por·phyr·i·a /pôr'fi(ə)rēə/ ▶ **noun** a rare hereditary disease in which the body fails to break down hemoglobin properly, causing mental disturbance, extreme sensitivity to light, and excretion of dark pigments in the urine.
– ORIGIN from *porphyrin* (a pigment made by breakdown of hemoglobin).

por·phy·ry /'pôrfərē/ ▶ **noun** (pl. **porphyries**) a hard reddish igneous rock containing crystals of feldspar.
– ORIGIN Greek *porphuritēs*.

por·poise /'pôrpəs/ ▶ **noun** a small toothed whale with a blunt rounded snout.
– ORIGIN Old French *porpois*.

por·ridge /'pôrij/ ▶ **noun** chiefly British term for **OATMEAL** (sense 2).
– ORIGIN alteration of **POTTAGE**.

por·rin·ger /'pôrənjər/ ▶ **noun** historical a small bowl, often with a handle, used for soup or similar food.
– ORIGIN Old French *potager*.

port[1] /pôrt/ ▶ **noun 1** a harbor. **2** a town or city with a harbor.

– SYNONYMS **harbor,** docks, marina, haven, seaport.

– PHRASES **port of call** a place where a ship or person stops on a journey.
– ORIGIN Latin *portus* 'harbor.'

port[2] (also **port wine**) ▶ **noun** a sweet dark red fortified wine from Portugal.
– ORIGIN shortened form of *Oporto*, a port in Portugal from which the wine is shipped.

port[3] ▶ **noun** the side of a ship or aircraft that is on the left when one is facing forward. The opposite of **STARBOARD**. ▶ **verb** turn a ship or its helm to the port side.
– ORIGIN probably originally the side turned toward the port or quayside for loading.

port[4] ▶ **noun 1** an opening in the side of a ship for boarding or loading. **2** a porthole. **3** an opening for the passage of steam, liquid, or gas. **4** an opening in the body of an aircraft or in a wall or armored vehicle through which a gun may be fired. **5** a socket in a computer network into which a device can be plugged.
– ORIGIN Latin *porta* 'gate.'

port[5] ▶ **verb 1** Computing transfer software from one system or machine to another. **2** Military carry a weapon diagonally across and close to the body with the barrel or blade near the left shoulder. ▶ **noun 1** Military the position required by an order to port a weapon. **2** Computing a transfer of software from one system or machine to another.
– ORIGIN from French *porter* 'carry' or Old French *port* 'bearing, gait.'

port·a·ble /'pôrtəbəl/ ▶ **adjective 1** able to be easily carried or moved. **2** (of a loan or pension) capable of being transferred. **3** Computing (of software) able to be ported.

– SYNONYMS **transportable,** movable, mobile, wireless, lightweight, compact, handy, convenient.

– DERIVATIVES **port·a·bil·i·ty** /,pôrtə'bilətē/ noun.

por·tage /'pôrtij/ ▶ **noun 1** the carrying of a boat or its cargo overland between two navigable waterways. **2** a place at which this is necessary. ▶ **verb** carry a boat or its cargo in this way.
– ORIGIN French.

por·tal /'pôrtl/ ▶ **noun 1** a large and imposing doorway, gate, or gateway. **2** an Internet site providing a directory of links to other sites.
– ORIGIN Latin *porta*.

por·tal vein ▶ **noun** a vein carrying blood to the liver from the spleen, stomach, pancreas, and intestines.

por·ta·men·to /,pôrtə'men,tō/ ▶ **noun** (pl. **portamentos** or **portamenti** /-tē/) Music a slide from one note to another, especially in singing or playing the violin.
– ORIGIN Italian, 'carrying.'

port·cul·lis /pôrt'kələs/ ▶ **noun** a strong, heavy grating that can be lowered to block a gateway to a castle.
– ORIGIN from Old French *porte coleice* 'sliding door.'

por·tend /pôr'tend/ ▶ **verb** be a sign or warning that something important or disastrous is likely to happen.

– SYNONYMS **presage,** augur, foreshadow, foretell, prophesy, be a sign, warn, be an omen, indicate, herald, signal, bode, promise, threaten, signify, spell, denote.

– ORIGIN Latin *portendere*.

por·tent /'pôr,tent/ ▶ **noun** a sign or warning that something important or disastrous is likely to happen: *many birds are regarded as portents of death*.
– ORIGIN Latin *portentum*.

por·ten·tous /pôr'tentəs/ ▶ **adjective 1** important as a sign or warning of what is likely to happen; of great significance: *this portentous year in their history*. **2** done in a pompous or excessively solemn way.
– DERIVATIVES **por·ten·tous·ly** adverb **por·ten·tous·ness** noun.

por·ter[1] /'pôrtər/ ▶ **noun 1** a person employed to carry luggage and other loads. **2** an attendant in a railroad sleeping car. **3** dark brown bitter beer brewed from charred or browned malt.

– SYNONYMS **carrier,** bearer, redcap, skycap.

– DERIVATIVES **por·ter·age** /'pôrtərij/ noun.
– ORIGIN Old French *porteour*.

por·ter[2] ▶ **noun** chiefly Brit. an employee in charge of the entrance of a hotel, apartment complex, or other large building.
– ORIGIN Old French *portier*.

por·ter·house steak /'pôrtər,hous/ ▶ **noun** a choice steak cut from the thick end of a sirloin.
– ORIGIN from *porterhouse*, formerly an establishment where porter and other drinks and sometimes steaks were served.

port·fo·li·o /pôrt'fōlē,ō/ ▶ **noun** (pl. **portfolios**) **1** a thin, flat case for carrying drawings, maps, etc. **2** a set of pieces of creative work intended to demonstrate a person's ability. **3** a range of investments held by a person or organization. **4** the position and duties of a government minister.
– ORIGIN Italian *portafogli*.

port·hole /'pôrt,hōl/ ▶ **noun 1** a small window on the outside of a ship or aircraft. **2** historical an opening for firing a cannon through.

por·ti·co /'pôrti,kō/ ▶ **noun** (pl. **porticoes** or **porticos**) a roof supported by columns at regular intervals, built over the entrance to a building.
– ORIGIN Latin *porticus* 'porch.'

por·tion /'pôrsнən/ ▶ **noun 1** a part or a share. **2** an amount of food suitable for or served to one person. **3** old use a person's destiny or fate. **4** old use a dowry.

– SYNONYMS **1 part,** piece, bit, section, segment. **2 share,** quota, ration, allocation, tranche. **3 helping,** serving, plateful, slice, piece.

▶ **verb** divide something into portions and distribute it.
– ORIGIN Latin, from *pro portione* 'in proportion.'

CHOOSE THE RIGHT WORD

See **FRAGMENT**.

Port·land ce·ment /'pôrtlənd/ ▶ **noun** cement made from limestone and clay that hardens under water.

port·ly /'pôrtlē/ ▶ **adjective** (**portlier, portliest**) (especially of a man) rather fat.

– SYNONYMS **stout,** plump, fat, overweight, heavy, corpulent, fleshy, potbellied, well padded, rotund, stocky, bulky; informal tubby, roly-poly, beefy, porky, corn-fed.
– ANTONYMS slim.

– DERIVATIVES **port·li·ness** noun.
– ORIGIN from Old French *port* 'bearing, gait.'

port·man·teau /pôrt'mantō/ ▶ **noun** (pl. **portmanteaus** or **portmanteaux** /-tōz/) a large traveling bag made of stiff leather and opening into two equal parts. ▶ **adjective** consisting of two or more aspects or qualities: *a portmanteau movie*.
– ORIGIN French *portemanteau*.

port·man·teau word ▶ **noun** a word blending the sounds and combining the meanings of two others, e.g., *brunch* from *breakfast* and *lunch*.

por·trait /'pôrtrət, -ˌtrāt/ ▶ **noun 1** a painting, drawing, or photograph of a person, especially one depicting only the face or head and shoulders. **2** a written or filmed description.

– SYNONYMS **1 picture,** likeness, painting, drawing, photograph, image. **2 description,** portrayal, representation, depiction, impression, account, profile.

▶ **adjective** referring to a format for printed material that is higher than it is wide. Compare with **LANDSCAPE**.
– DERIVATIVES **por·trait·ist** noun **por·trai·ture** /'pôrtricнər, -ˌcнo͝or/ noun.
– ORIGIN Old French *portraire* 'portray.'

por·tray /pôr'trā/ ▶ **verb 1** show or describe in a work of art or literature: *the suburban couples portrayed in this movie*. **2** describe in a particular way: *the book portrayed him as a relentless careerist*. **3** (of an actor) play the part of someone in a movie or play.

– SYNONYMS **1 paint,** draw, sketch, picture, depict, represent, illustrate, render, show. **2 describe,** depict, characterize, delineate, put into words. **3 play,** act the part of, take the role of, represent, appear as.

– DERIVATIVES **por·tray·er** noun.
– ORIGIN Old French *portraire*.

por·tray·al /pôr'trā(ə)l/ ▶ **noun** a depiction or representation of something.

– SYNONYMS **description,** representation, characterization, depiction, delineation, evocation, interpretation.

Por·tu·guese /'pôrcнəˌgēz/ ▶ **noun** (pl. same) **1** a person from Portugal. **2** the language of Portugal and Brazil. ▶ **adjective** relating to Portugal.

Por·tu·guese man-of-war ▶ **noun** a floating sea creature like a jellyfish, with long stinging tentacles.

pose /pōz/ ▶ **verb 1** present or be a problem, danger, question, etc. **2** raise a question or matter for consideration. **3** (**pose as**) pretend to be: *two women posing as social workers forced their way into the house*. **4** behave in a way intended to impress other people. **5** sit or stand in a particular position in order to be photographed, painted, or drawn.

– SYNONYMS **1** *the sheer number of visitors is posing a threat to the area* **constitute,** present, offer. **2** *the question posed earlier* **raise,** ask, put, submit, advance, propose. **3 (pose as) pretend to be,** impersonate, pass oneself off as, masquerade as; formal personate. **4 posture,** attitudinize, put on airs; informal show off.

▶ **noun 1** a position taken up in order to be painted, drawn, or photographed. **2** a way of behaving adopted in order to impress other people or give a false impression.

– SYNONYMS **1 posture,** position, stance, attitude. **2 act,** affectation, show, display, front, airs.

– ORIGIN Old French *poser*.

pos·er /'pōzər/ ▶ **noun 1** a person who behaves or dresses in a way intended to impress other people. **2** a puzzling question or problem.

– SYNONYMS **1 exhibitionist,** poseur, posturer, fake; informal show-off. **2 difficult question,** problem, puzzle, mystery, riddle, conundrum; informal dilemma.

po·seur /pō'zər/ ▶ **noun** another term for **POSER** (sense 1).
– ORIGIN French.

po·sey /'pōzē/ (also **posy**) ▶ **adjective** informal trying to impress other people; pretentious.

posh /päsн/ informal ▶ **adjective 1** very elegant or luxurious. **2** chiefly Brit. upper-class.

– SYNONYMS **1 smart,** stylish, fancy, high-class, fashionable, chic, upmarket, upscale, luxurious, luxury, exclusive; informal classy, plush, flash, swish, swank, tony. **2 upper-class,** aristocratic.

– DERIVATIVES **posh·ly** adverb **posh·ness** noun.
– ORIGIN perhaps from former slang *posh* 'a dandy'; there is no evidence for the well-known theory that *posh* is formed from the initials of *port out starboard home* (referring to the more comfortable accommodation, out of the heat of the sun, on ships between England and India).

pos·it /'päzit/ ▶ **verb** (**posits, positing, posited**) put something forward as a fact or as a basis for argument.
– ORIGIN Latin, 'placed.'

po·si·tion /pə'zisнən/ ▶ **noun 1** a place where someone or something is located or has been put. **2** the correct place. **3** a way in which someone or something is placed or arranged: *he raised himself to a sitting position*. **4** a situation: *the company's financial position is grim*. **5** a person's place or level of importance in relation to other people: *she finished in second position*. **6** high rank or social standing. **7** a job. **8** a point of view or attitude: *the party's position on abortion*. **9** a place where part of a military force is posted.

– SYNONYMS **1 location,** place, situation, spot, site, locality, setting, area, whereabouts, bearings. **2 posture,** stance, attitude, pose. **3 situation,** state, condition, circumstances, predicament, plight. **4 status,** place, level, rank, standing, stature, prestige, reputation. **5 job,** post, situation, appointment, opening, vacancy, placement. **6 viewpoint,** opinion, outlook, attitude, stand, standpoint, stance, perspective, thinking, policy, feelings.

▶ **verb** put or arrange in a particular position: *she positioned herself near the fireplace.*

– SYNONYMS **put,** place, locate, situate, set, site, stand, station, plant, stick; informal **plonk, plunk, park.**

– DERIVATIVES **po·si·tion·al** /pəˈzisʜənl/ adjective **po·si·tion·al·ly** adverb.

– ORIGIN Latin, from *ponere* 'to place.'

pos·i·tive /ˈpäzətiv, ˈpäztiv/ ▶ **adjective 1** characterized by the presence rather than the absence of distinguishing features: *a positive test result.* **2** expressing or implying confirmation, agreement, or permission. **3** constructive, optimistic, or confident: *a positive outlook on life.* **4** with no possibility of doubt; certain. **5** (of a quantity) greater than zero. **6** relating to, containing, or producing the kind of electric charge opposite to that carried by electrons. **7** (of a photographic image) showing light and shade or colors true to the original. **8** (of an adjective or adverb) expressing the basic degree of a quality. Contrasted with **COMPARATIVE** and **SUPERLATIVE**.

– SYNONYMS **1 affirmative,** favorable, good, enthusiastic, supportive, constructive, useful, productive, helpful, worthwhile, beneficial. **2 optimistic,** hopeful, confident, cheerful, sanguine, buoyant; informal upbeat. **3** *positive economic signs* **good,** promising, favorable, encouraging, heartening, propitious, auspicious. **4 definite,** certain, reliable, concrete, tangible, clear-cut, explicit, firm, decisive, real, actual. **5 convinced,** sure, confident, satisfied.
– ANTONYMS negative, pessimistic.

▶ **noun** a positive quality, attribute, or image.

– DERIVATIVES **pos·i·tive·ness** noun **pos·i·tiv·i·ty** /ˌpäzəˈtivətē/ noun.

– ORIGIN from Old French *positif* or Latin *positivus.*

pos·i·tive·ly /ˈpäzətivlē, ˈpäztivlē, ˌpäzəˈtivlē/ ▶ **adverb 1** with certainty. **2** extremely.

– SYNONYMS **1** *I could not positively identify the voice* **confidently,** definitely, firmly, categorically, with certainty, conclusively. **2** *he was positively livid* **absolutely,** extremely, utterly, downright, simply, virtually; informal plain.

pos·i·tiv·ism /ˈpäzətivˌizəm, ˈpäztiv-/ ▶ **noun** a system of philosophy recognizing only that which can be scientifically verified or logically proved.

– DERIVATIVES **pos·i·tiv·ist** noun & adjective **pos·i·tiv·is·tic** /ˌpäzətəˈvistik/ adjective.

pos·i·tron /ˈpäzəˌträn/ ▶ **noun** Physics a subatomic particle with the same mass as an electron and a numerically equal but positive charge.

pos·se /ˈpäsē/ ▶ **noun 1** historical a group of men summoned by a sheriff to enforce the law. **2** informal a group of people: *a posse of medical students.*

– ORIGIN from Latin, 'be able,' later 'power.'

pos·sess /pəˈzes/ ▶ **verb 1** have as property; own. **2** (also **be possessed of**) have as an ability, quality, or characteristic: *he did not possess a sense of humor.* **3** (of a demon or spirit) have complete power over someone. **4** (of an emotion, idea, etc.) dominate someone's mind.

– SYNONYMS **1 own,** have (to one's name), be in possession of. **2 have,** be blessed with, be endowed with, enjoy, boast. **3 take control of,** take over, bewitch, enchant, enslave.

– DERIVATIVES **pos·ses·sor** noun.

– ORIGIN from Latin *possidere* 'occupy, hold.'

pos·ses·sion /pəˈzesʜən/ ▶ **noun 1** the state of having or owning something: *the book came into his possession.* **2** a thing owned: *my most precious possession.* **3** the state of being possessed by a demon, emotion, etc. **4** (in sports) temporary control of the ball by a player or team.

– SYNONYMS **1 ownership,** control, hands, keeping, care, custody, charge. **2** *she packed her possessions* **belongings,** things, property, worldly goods, goods and chattels, personal effects, stuff, bits and pieces; informal gear, junk.

pos·ses·sive /pəˈzesiv/ ▶ **adjective 1** demanding someone's total attention and love. **2** unwilling to share one's possessions with other people. **3** Grammar expressing possession.

– SYNONYMS **proprietorial,** overprotective, controlling, dominating, jealous, clingy.

– DERIVATIVES **pos·ses·sive·ly** adverb **pos·ses·sive·ness** noun.

pos·ses·sive pro·noun ▶ **noun** Grammar a pronoun showing possession, e.g., *mine.*

pos·si·bil·i·ty /ˌpäsəˈbilətē/ ▶ **noun** (pl. **possibilities**) **1** a thing that is possible. **2** the state of being possible. **3** (**possibilities**) general qualities of a promising nature: *the house had possibilities.*

– SYNONYMS **1 chance,** likelihood, probability, potentiality, hope, risk, hazard, danger, fear. **2 option,** alternative, choice, course of action, solution. **3 potential,** promise, prospects.

pos·si·ble /ˈpäsəbəl/ ▶ **adjective 1** capable of existing, happening, or being done. **2** that may be so, but that is not certain: *the possible cause of the plane crash.*

– SYNONYMS **1 feasible,** practicable, viable, attainable, achievable, workable, within reach; informal on, doable. **2 likely,** plausible, imaginable, believable, potential, probable, credible, tenable.
– ANTONYMS impossible, unlikely.

▶ **noun** a possible candidate for a job or member of a team.

– ORIGIN Latin *possibilis.*

pos·si·bly /ˈpäsəblē/ ▶ **adverb 1** perhaps. **2** in accordance with what is possible: *I try to do the job as well as I possibly can.*

– SYNONYMS **1 perhaps,** maybe, it is possible, for all you know. **2 conceivably,** under any circumstances, by any means.

pos·sum /ˈpäsəm/ ▶ **noun 1** an Australasian marsupial that lives in trees. **2** informal an opossum.

– PHRASES **play possum** pretend to be unconscious, asleep, or unaware of something in order to trick someone.

– ORIGIN shortening of **OPOSSUM**.

post[1] /pōst/ ▶ **noun 1** a long, strong, upright piece of timber or metal used as a support or a marker. **2** (**the post**) a starting post or winning post in a race. **3** a message sent to an Internet bulletin board or newsgroup.

– SYNONYMS **pole,** stake, upright, shaft, prop, support, picket, strut, pillar, stanchion, baluster.

▶ **verb 1** display a notice in a public place. **2** announce or publish something: *the company posted a $460,000 loss.* **3** send a message to an Internet bulletin board or newsgroup. **4** achieve or record a particular score or result.

– SYNONYMS **1 affix,** attach, fasten, display, pin up, put up, stick up. **2 announce,** report, make known, publish.

– ORIGIN Latin *postis* 'doorpost.'

post[2] ▶ **noun 1** an official service or system that delivers letters and parcels. **2** letters and parcels delivered. **3** a single collection or delivery of mail. ▶ **verb 1** send a letter or parcel via the postal system. **2** (in bookkeeping) enter an item in a ledger.
– PHRASES **keep someone posted** keep someone informed of the latest developments or news.
– ORIGIN French *poste* 'station, stand.'

post[3] ▶ **noun 1** a place where someone is on duty or where an activity is carried out. **2** a job.

– SYNONYMS **1 assigned position,** station, place, base. **2 job,** position, appointment, situation, place, vacancy, opening.

▶ **verb 1** station a soldier, police officer, etc., in a particular place. **2** send someone to a place to take up a job.

– SYNONYMS **1 put on duty,** mount, station. **2 send,** assign, dispatch, consign.

– ORIGIN Italian *posto.*

post- ▶ **prefix** after in time or order: *post-date.*
– ORIGIN Latin *post* 'after, behind.'

post·age /'pōstij/ ▶ **noun 1** the sending of letters and parcels by mail. **2** the amount required to send something by mail.

post·age stamp ▶ **noun** an adhesive stamp stuck on a letter or parcel to show the amount of postage paid.

post·al /'pōstəl/ ▶ **adjective** relating to the post office or the mail.
– PHRASES **go postal** become crazed or violent, especially as a result of stress.

post·al code ▶ **noun** another term for **POSTCODE**.

post·bel·lum /pōst'beləm/ ▶ **adjective** occurring or existing after a war, in particular the American Civil War.
– ORIGIN from Latin *post* 'after' + *bellum* 'war.'

post·card /'pōst,kärd/ ▶ **noun** a card for sending a message by mail without an envelope.

post·code /'pōst,kōd/ ▶ **noun** Brit. a group of letters and numbers added to a mailing address to assist the sorting of mail.

post·co·i·tal /,pōst'kōətl/ ▶ **adjective** occurring or done after sex.
– DERIVATIVES **post·co·i·tal·ly** adverb.

post·date /pōst'dāt/ ▶ **verb 1** put a date later than the actual one on a document or check. **2** occur or come at a later date than: *Stonehenge was believed to postdate these structures.*

post·doc·tor·al /pōst'däktərəl/ ▶ **adjective** (of research) undertaken after the completion of a doctorate.

post·er /'pōstər/ ▶ **noun** a large printed picture or notice used for decoration or advertisement.

– SYNONYMS **notice,** placard, bill, sign, advertisement, playbill.

post·er child (or **poster boy** or **poster girl**) ▶ **noun** a person who epitomizes or represents a specified quality, cause, etc.: *he has become a poster boy for the antiglobalization movement.*

pos·te·ri·or /pä'sti(ə)rēər, pō-/ ▶ **adjective 1** chiefly Anatomy further back in position; at or nearer the rear or hind end. The opposite of **ANTERIOR**. **2** formal coming after in time or order; later. ▶ **noun** humorous a person's buttocks.
– ORIGIN Latin, from *posterus* 'following.'

pos·ter·i·ty /pä'steritē/ ▶ **noun** all future generations of people.
– ORIGIN from Latin *posterus* 'following.'

pos·tern /'pōstərn, 'päs-/ ▶ **noun** old use a back or side entrance.
– ORIGIN Old French *posterne.*

pos·ter paint ▶ **noun** a thick opaque paint used for posters and children's paintings.

post·fem·i·nist /pōst'femənist/ ▶ **adjective** moving beyond or rejecting some of the earlier ideas of feminism as out of date.

post·grad·u·ate /pōst'grajōōit/ ▶ **adjective** relating to study undertaken after completing a first degree. ▶ **noun** a person engaged in postgraduate study.

post·haste /'pōst'hāst/ ▶ **adverb** with great speed.
– ORIGIN from the direction 'haste, post, haste,' formerly given on letters.

post hoc /'pōst 'häk/ ▶ **adjective & adverb** occurring or done after the event: *a post hoc justification for the changes.*

post·hu·mous /'päschəməs, päst'(h)yōōməs/ ▶ **adjective** happening, awarded, or appearing after the person involved has died: *he was granted a posthumous pardon.*
– DERIVATIVES **post·hu·mous·ly** adverb.
– ORIGIN Latin *postumus* 'last.'

pos·til·ion /pə'stilyən, pō-/ (also **postillion**) ▶ **noun** chiefly historical the rider of the leading nearside horse of a team or pair drawing a coach, when there is no coachman.
– ORIGIN French *postillon.*

post-Im·pres·sion·ism ▶ **noun** a late 19th-century and early 20th-century style of art in which emphasis was placed on the emotions of the artist, as expressed by color, line, and shape.
– DERIVATIVES **post-Im·pres·sion·ist** noun & adjective.

post·in·dus·tri·al /,pōstin'dəstrēəl/ ▶ **adjective** (of an economy or society) no longer relying on heavy industry.

post·ing /'pōsting/ ▶ **noun** a message sent to an Internet bulletin board or newsgroup.

post·lude /'pōs(t),lōōd/ ▶ **noun** a concluding piece of music.
– ORIGIN from **POST-**, on the pattern of *prelude.*

post·man /'pōstmən/ (or **postwoman** /'pōstwōōmən/) ▶ **noun** (pl. **postmen** or **postwomen**) a mail carrier.

post·mark /'pōst,märk/ ▶ **noun** an official mark stamped on a letter or parcel, giving the date of mailing and canceling the postage stamp. ▶ **verb** stamp a letter or parcel with a postmark.

post·mas·ter /'pōst,mastər/ (or **postmistress** /'pōst,mistris/) ▶ **noun** a person in charge of a post office.

post·mod·ern·ism /pōst'mädər,nizəm/ ▶ **noun** a style and movement in the arts characterized by distrust of theories and ideologies and by the deliberate mixing of different styles.
– DERIVATIVES **post·mod·ern** adjective **post·mod·ern·ist** noun & adjective **post·mod·er·ni·ty** /,pōstmə'dərnətē/ noun.

post·mor·tem /pōst'môrtəm/ ▶ **noun 1** an examination of a dead body to establish the cause of death. **2** an

analysis of an event made after it has happened: *an election postmortem*. ▶ **adjective** happening after death.
– ORIGIN Latin, 'after death.'

post·na·tal /pōst'nātl/ ▶ **adjective** happening in or relating to the period after childbirth.

post·nup·tial /pōst'nəpsʜəl, -cʜəl/ ▶ **adjective** after marriage.

post of·fice ▶ **noun 1** the public department or corporation responsible for postal services and (in some countries) telecommunications. **2** a building where postal business is carried out.

post·op·er·a·tive /pōst'äp(ə)rətiv/ ▶ **adjective** relating to the period following a surgical operation.

post·paid /pōst'pād/ ▶ **adjective & adverb** (with reference to a letter or parcel) on which postage has already been paid.

post·par·tum /pōst'pärtəm/ ▶ **adjective** relating to the period following childbirth or the birth of young.
– ORIGIN from Latin *post partum* 'after childbirth.'

post·pone /pōst'pōn/ ▶ **verb** arrange for something to take place at a time later than that first planned.

– SYNONYMS **put off,** put back, delay, defer, hold over, reschedule, adjourn, shelve; informal put on ice, put on the back burner.

– DERIVATIVES **post·pone·ment** noun.
– ORIGIN Latin *postponere*.

CHOOSE THE RIGHT WORD

postpone, adjourn, defer, delay, suspend

All of these verbs have to do with putting things off. **Defer** is the broadest in meaning; it suggests putting something off until a later time (*defer payment; defer a discussion*). If you **postpone** an event or activity, you put it off intentionally, usually until a definite time in the future (*we postponed the party until the next weekend*). If you **adjourn** an activity, you postpone its completion until another day or place; *adjourn* is usually associated with meetings or other formal gatherings that are brought to an end and then resumed (*the judge adjourned the hearing until the following morning*). If you **delay** something, you postpone it because of obstacles (*delayed by severe thunderstorms and highway flooding*) or because you are reluctant to do it (*delay going to the dentist*). **Suspend** suggests stopping an activity for a while, usually for a reason (*forced to suspend work on the bridge until the holiday weekend was over*).

post·pos·i·tive /ˌpōst'päzətiv/ ▶ **adjective** (of a word) placed after the word that it relates to.

post·pran·di·al /pōst'prandēəl/ ▶ **adjective** formal or humorous during or relating to the period after a meal.
– ORIGIN from Latin *prandium* 'a meal.'

post-punk ▶ **noun** a style of rock music inspired by punk but less aggressive in performance and musically more experimental.

post·script /'pōs(t)ˌskript/ ▶ **noun** an additional remark at the end of a letter, following the signature.
– ORIGIN Latin *postscriptum*.

post·sea·son /'pōs(t)ˌsēzən/ ▶ **adjective** after the end of the regular season for a particular sport. ▶ **noun** the period following the regular season.

post-trau·mat·ic stress dis·or·der ▶ **noun** a condition of persistent stress occurring as a result of injury or severe psychological shock.

pos·tu·lant /'päscʜələnt/ ▶ **noun** a person who wishes to enter a religious order.

pos·tu·late ▶ **verb** /'päscʜəˌlāt/ suggest or assume that something exists or is true, as a basis for a theory or discussion. ▶ **noun** /'päscʜələt/ a thing that is postulated.
– DERIVATIVES **pos·tu·la·tion** /ˌpäscʜə'lāsʜən/ noun.
– ORIGIN Latin *postulare* 'ask.'

pos·ture /'päscʜər/ ▶ **noun 1** a particular position of the body. **2** the usual way in which a person holds their body: *muscle tension can be the result of bad posture*. **3** an approach or attitude toward something: *labor unions adopted a more militant posture in wage negotiations*.

– SYNONYMS **1 position,** pose, attitude, stance, carriage, bearing, deportment, comportment. **2 attitude,** standpoint, point of view, viewpoint, opinion, position, stance.

▶ **verb** behave in a way that is intended to impress or mislead other people.

– SYNONYMS **pose,** strike an attitude, attitudinize, strut; informal show off.

– DERIVATIVES **pos·tur·al** adjective.
– ORIGIN Latin *positura* 'position.'

post·war /'pōst'wär/ ▶ **adjective** occurring or existing after a war.

po·sy[1] /'pōzē/ ▶ **noun** (pl. **posies**) a small bunch of flowers.
– ORIGIN first meaning 'motto or line of verse inscribed inside a ring': from **POESY**.

po·sy[2] ▶ **adjective** variant spelling of **POSEY**.

pot[1] /pät/ ▶ **noun 1** a rounded or cylindrical container used for storage or cooking. **2** a container designed to hold a particular thing: *a lobster pot*. **3** (**the pot**) the total sum of the bets made on a round in poker and other card games. **4** Billiards a shot in which a player strikes a ball into a pocket. ▶ **verb** (**pots, potting, potted**) **1** plant something in a flowerpot. **2** preserve food in a sealed pot or jar. **3** Billiards strike a ball into a pocket. **4** informal hit or kill someone or something by shooting.
– PHRASES **go to pot** informal deteriorate as a result of neglect.
– ORIGIN Old English.

pot[2] ▶ **noun** informal marijuana.
– ORIGIN probably from Mexican Spanish *potiguaya* 'cannabis leaves.'

po·ta·ble /'pōtəbəl/ ▶ **adjective** formal (especially of water) safe to drink.
– DERIVATIVES **po·ta·bil·i·ty** /ˌpōtə'bilətē/ noun.
– ORIGIN from Latin *potare* 'to drink.'

po·tage /pô'täzʜ/ ▶ **noun** thick soup.
– ORIGIN French.

po·tag·er /'pätijər/ ▶ **noun** a kitchen garden.
– ORIGIN from French *jardin potager* 'garden providing vegetables for the pot.'

pot·ash /'pätˌasʜ/ ▶ **noun** an alkaline potassium compound, used especially in making fertilizers.
– ORIGIN from *pot-ashes*, because first obtained from a solution made from ashes that was evaporated in an iron pot.

po·tas·si·um /pə'tasēəm/ ▶ **noun** a soft silvery-white reactive metallic element.
– ORIGIN from **POTASH**.

po·tas·si·um hy·drox·ide ▶ **noun** a strongly alkaline white compound used in many industrial processes, e.g., soap manufacture.

po·tas·si·um ni·trate ▸ **noun** a white crystalline salt used in fertilizer, as a meat preservative, and as a constituent of gunpowder.

po·ta·tion /pō'tāsʜən/ ▸ **noun** old use or humorous **1** the action of drinking alcohol. **2** an alcoholic drink.
– ORIGIN Latin, from *potare* 'to drink.'

po·ta·to /pə'tātō/ ▸ **noun** (pl. **potatoes**) a starchy plant tuber that is cooked and eaten as a vegetable.
– ORIGIN Spanish *patata* 'sweet potato,' from Taino (an extinct Caribbean language).

pot-au-feu /ˌpôt ō 'fœ/ ▸ **noun** (pl. same) a French soup of meat and vegetables cooked in a large pot.
– ORIGIN French, 'pot on the fire.'

pot·bel·ly /'pätˌbelē/ ▸ **noun** a large protruding stomach.

pot·boil·er /'pätˌboilər/ ▸ **noun** informal a book, movie, etc., produced purely to earn money quickly by appealing to popular taste.

pot-bound /pät bound/ ▸ **adjective** (of a plant) having roots that fill the flowerpot, leaving no room for them to expand.

po·teen /pə'tēn, -'cʜēn/ ▸ **noun** (in Ireland) whiskey that is made illicitly.
– ORIGIN from Irish *fuisce poitín* 'little pot of whiskey.'

po·tent /'pōtnt/ ▸ **adjective 1** having great power, influence, or effect: *a potent drug.* **2** (of a male) able to achieve an erection or to reach an orgasm.

– SYNONYMS **1 powerful,** strong, mighty, formidable, influential, dominant. **2 forceful,** convincing, cogent, compelling, persuasive, powerful, strong.
– ANTONYMS weak.

– DERIVATIVES **po·ten·cy** noun (pl. **potencies**) **po·tent·ly** adverb.
– ORIGIN from Latin *posse* 'be powerful, be able.'

po·ten·tate /'pōtnˌtāt/ ▸ **noun** a monarch or ruler.
– ORIGIN Latin *potentatus* 'dominion.'

po·ten·tial /pə'tencʜəl/ ▸ **adjective** having the capacity to develop into something in the future: *a potential problem.*

– SYNONYMS **possible**, likely, prospective, future, probable.

▸ **noun 1** qualities or abilities that may be developed and lead to future success or usefulness: *he showed great potential as an actor.* **2** (often **potential for/to do**) the possibility of something happening or of someone doing something in the future. **3** Physics the difference in voltage between two points in an electric field or circuit.

– SYNONYMS **possibilities,** potentiality, prospects, promise, capability, capacity.

– DERIVATIVES **po·ten·ti·al·i·ty** /pəˌtencʜē'alətē/ noun **po·ten·tial·ly** adverb.
– ORIGIN from Latin *potentia* 'power.'

WORD TOOLKIT

See **LATENT**.

po·ten·tial dif·fer·ence ▸ **noun** Physics the difference of electrical potential between two points.

po·ten·tial en·er·gy ▸ **noun** Physics energy possessed by a body as a result of its position or state. Compare with **KINETIC ENERGY**.

po·ten·ti·ate /pə'tencʜēˌāt/ ▸ **verb** increase the power or effect of a drug, physiological reaction, etc.

po·ten·til·la /ˌpōtn'tilə/ ▸ **noun** a small shrub with yellow or red flowers.
– ORIGIN from Latin *potent-* 'being powerful' (with reference to its herbal qualities).

po·ten·ti·om·e·ter /pəˌtencʜē'ämətər/ ▸ **noun** an instrument for measuring or adjusting an electromotive force.

poth·er /'päᴛʜər/ ▸ **noun** a commotion or fuss.
– ORIGIN unknown.

pot·hole /'pätˌhōl/ ▸ **noun 1** a deep underground cave formed by water eroding the rock. **2** a hole in a road surface. ▸ **verb** (usu. as n. **potholing**) Brit. explore underground potholes as a pastime.
– DERIVATIVES **pot·holed** adjective **pot·hol·er** noun.
– ORIGIN from dialect *pot* 'pit.'

po·tion /'pōsʜən/ ▸ **noun** a liquid with healing, magical, or poisonous properties.

– SYNONYMS **concoction,** mixture, brew, elixir, drink, medicine, tonic, philter.

– ORIGIN Latin, 'drink.'

pot·latch /'pätˌlacʜ/ ▸ **noun** (among some North American Indian peoples) a ceremonial feast at which possessions are given away or destroyed as an indication of wealth.
– ORIGIN from an American Indian language.

pot·luck /'pät'lək/ ▸ **noun 1** the chance that whatever is available will prove to be good or acceptable. **2** a meal or party to which each of the guests contributes a dish.

pot pie ▸ **noun 1** a meat and vegetable pie baked in a deep dish. **2** a stew with dumplings.

pot·pour·ri /ˌpōpə'rē, ˌpōpŏŏ'rē/ ▸ **noun** (pl. **potpourris**) **1** a mixture of dried petals and spices placed in a bowl to perfume a room. **2** a mixture of things.
– ORIGIN French, 'rotten pot,' first meaning 'stew made of different kinds of meat.'

pot roast ▸ **noun** a piece of meat cooked slowly in a covered pot.

pot·sherd /'pätˌsʜərd/ ▸ **noun** a piece of broken pottery.
– ORIGIN from **POT**[1] + **SHERD**.

pot·shot /'pätˌsʜät/ ▸ **noun** a shot aimed unexpectedly or at random.
– ORIGIN first meaning a *shot* at an animal intended for the *pot*, i.e. for food, rather than for display (which would require skilled shooting).

pot·tage /'pätij/ ▸ **noun** old use soup or stew.
– ORIGIN Old French *potage* 'that which is put into a pot.'

pot·ted /'pätid/ ▸ **adjective 1** grown or preserved in a pot. **2** informal intoxicated by drink or drugs.

pot·ter /'pätər/ ▸ **noun** a person who makes pottery.

pot·ter's wheel ▸ **noun** a flat revolving disk on which wet clay is shaped into pots, bowls, etc.

pot·ter·y /'pätərē/ ▸ **noun** (pl. **potteries**) **1** articles made of clay baked in a kiln. **2** the craft of making such articles. **3** a factory or workshop where such articles are made.

– SYNONYMS **ceramics,** crockery, earthenware, terracotta, stoneware, china, porcelain.

pot·ting shed ▸ **noun** a shed used for potting plants and storing garden tools and supplies.

pot·ty[1] /'pätē/ ▸ **adjective** (**pottier, pottiest**) informal, chiefly Brit. **1** foolish; crazy. **2** extremely enthusiastic about

someone or something.
– DERIVATIVES **pot·ti·ness** noun.
– ORIGIN unknown.

pot·ty[2] ▸ **noun** (pl. **potties**) a container for a child to urinate or defecate into.

pouch /poucн/ ▸ **noun 1** a small flexible bag, typically carried in a pocket or attached to a belt. **2** a pocket of skin in an animal's body, especially that in which marsupials carry their young.

– SYNONYMS **bag**, purse, sack, sac, pocket.

– DERIVATIVES **pouched** adjective **pouch·y** adjective.
– ORIGIN Old French *poche* 'bag.'

pouf[1] /po͞of/ ▸ **noun** variant spelling of **POUFFE**.

pouf[2] ▸ **noun 1** a part of a dress in which a large mass of material has been gathered so that it stands away from the body. **2** a bouffant hairstyle.
– ORIGIN French.

pouffe /po͞of/ (also **pouf**) ▸ **noun** a large, firm cushion used as a seat or stool.
– ORIGIN French.

poult /pōlt/ ▸ **noun** a young domestic fowl being raised for food.
– ORIGIN from **PULLET**.

poul·tice /'pōltəs/ ▸ **noun** a soft moist mass, traditionally of flour, bran, and herbs, applied to the skin to reduce inflammation.
– ORIGIN from Latin *puls* 'pottage, pap.'

poul·try /'pōltrē/ ▸ **noun** chickens, turkeys, ducks, and geese.
– ORIGIN Old French *pouletrie*.

pounce[1] /pouns/ ▸ **verb 1** spring or swoop suddenly so as to seize or attack someone or something. **2** take swift advantage of a mistake or sign of weakness: *the press pounced on his words.*

– SYNONYMS **jump**, spring, leap, dive, lunge, swoop, attack.

▸ **noun** an act of pouncing.
– ORIGIN uncertain.

pounce[2] ▸ **noun** a fine powder formerly used to prevent ink from spreading on paper or to prepare parchment for writing.
– ORIGIN French *poncer*.

pound[1] /pound/ ▸ **noun 1** a unit of weight equal to 16 oz avoirdupois (0.4536 kg), or 12 oz troy (0.3732 kg). **2** (also **pound sterling**) (pl. **pounds sterling**) the basic unit of money of the UK, equal to 100 pence. **3** the basic monetary unit of several Middle Eastern countries, equal to 100 piasters.
– DERIVATIVES **pound·er** noun.
– PHRASES **one's pound of flesh** something that one is owed but, if given, would cause suffering or trouble to the person who owes it. [with reference to Shakespeare's *Merchant of Venice*.]
– ORIGIN Old English, from Latin *libra pondo*, referring to a Roman 'pound weight' of 12 ounces.

pound[2] ▸ **verb 1** strike or hit heavily and repeatedly. **2** beat or throb with a strong regular rhythm. **3** walk or run with heavy steps. **4** (**pound something out**) produce a document or piece of music with heavy strokes on a keyboard or instrument. **5** crush or grind something into a powder or paste.

– SYNONYMS **1** *the men pounded him with their fists* **beat**, strike, hit, batter, thump, pummel, punch, rain blows on, belabor, hammer; informal bash, clobber, wallop. **2** *waves pounded the seafront* **beat against**, crash against, batter, dash against, lash, buffet. **3** *her heart was pounding* **throb**, thump, thud, hammer, pulse, race. **4** *I heard him pounding along the gangway* **stomp**, stamp, clomp, clump, tramp, lumber. **5** *pound the cloves with salt* **crush**, grind, pulverize, mash, pulp.

– ORIGIN Old English.

pound[3] ▸ **noun** a place where stray dogs or illegally parked vehicles may officially be taken and kept until claimed.

– SYNONYMS **enclosure**, compound, pen, yard, corral.

– ORIGIN uncertain.

pound·age /'poundij/ ▸ **noun 1** weight. **2** Brit. a charge made for every pound weight of something, or for every pound sterling in value.

pound cake ▸ **noun** a rich cake originally made with a pound of each chief ingredient.

pound sign ▸ **noun 1** the sign (#), representing a pound as a unit of weight or mass. **2** the sign (£), representing a British pound sterling.

pour /pôr/ ▸ **verb 1** flow or cause to flow in a steady stream. **2** (of rain) fall heavily. **3** prepare and serve a drink. **4** come or go in a steady stream: *people poured out of the train.* **5** (**pour something out**) express one's feelings freely.

– SYNONYMS **1 stream**, flow, run, gush, course, jet, spurt, surge, spill. **2 tip**, splash, spill, decant; informal slosh, slop. **3 rain hard**, teem down, pelt down, rain cats and dogs. **4 crowd**, throng, swarm, stream, flood.

– DERIVATIVES **pour·er** noun.
– ORIGIN unknown.

USAGE

On the confusion of **pour** and **pore**, see the note at **PORE**[2].

pous·sin /po͝o'sen, -'sɑɴ/ ▸ **noun** a chicken killed young for eating.
– ORIGIN French.

pout /pout/ ▸ **verb** push one's lips forward as an expression of sulky annoyance or in order to make oneself look sexually attractive. ▸ **noun** a pouting expression.
– DERIVATIVES **pout·y** adjective.
– ORIGIN perhaps related to Swedish dialect *puta* 'be inflated.'

pout·er /'poutər/ ▸ **noun** a kind of pigeon that is able to puff up its crop to a considerable extent.

pov·er·ty /'pävərtē/ ▸ **noun 1** the state of being extremely poor. **2** the state of being inadequate in quality or amount: *the poverty of her imagination.*

– SYNONYMS **1 destitution**, pennilessness, penury, impoverishment, neediness, hardship, impecuniousness, indigence. **2 scarcity**, deficiency, dearth, shortage, paucity, absence, lack, inadequacy.
– ANTONYMS wealth, abundance.

– ORIGIN Old French *poverte*.

pov·er·ty-strick·en ▸ **adjective** extremely poor.

POW ▸ **abbreviation** prisoner of war.

pow·der /'poudər/ ▸ **noun 1** fine dry particles produced by the grinding, crushing, or disintegration of a solid

substance. **2** a cosmetic in this form for use on the face. **3** dated a medicine in this form. **4** gunpowder. ▶ **verb** **1** sprinkle or cover something with powder. **2** (often as adj. **powdered**) make something into a powder: *powdered milk*.
– PHRASES **keep one's powder dry** remain cautious and ready for a possible emergency.
– ORIGIN Old French *poudre*.

pow·der blue ▶ **noun** a soft, pale blue.

pow·der keg ▶ **noun** **1** a situation that may suddenly become dangerous or violent. **2** a barrel of gunpowder.

pow·der puff ▶ **noun** a soft pad for applying powder to the face.

pow·der room ▶ **noun** euphemistic a women's lavatory in a public building.

pow·der·y /ˈpoudərē/ ▶ **adjective** consisting of or resembling powder.

– SYNONYMS *a powdery substance floated through the air* **fine,** dry, fine-grained, powderlike, dusty, chalky, floury, sandy, crumbly, friable.

pow·er /ˈpou(-ə)r/ ▶ **noun** **1** the ability to do something or act in a particular way: *the power of speech*. **2** the ability to control or influence people or events. **3** the right or authority to do something: *police have the power to seize equipment*. **4** political authority or control. **5** physical strength or force. **6** a country viewed in terms of its international influence and military strength: *a world power*. **7** capacity or performance of an engine or other device. **8** energy that is produced by mechanical, electrical, or other means. **9** Physics the rate of doing work, measured in watts or horse power. **10** Mathematics the product obtained when a number is multiplied by itself a certain number of times.

– SYNONYMS **1 ability,** capacity, capability, potential, potentiality, faculty. **2 control,** command, authority, dominance, supremacy, ascendancy, mastery, influence, sway, leverage; informal clout, teeth. **3 authority,** right, authorization. **4 state,** country, nation. **5 strength,** might, force, vigor, energy. **6 forcefulness,** powerfulness, strength, force, cogency, persuasiveness. **7 driving force,** horsepower, acceleration, torque; informal oomph. **8 energy,** electricity.
– ANTONYMS weakness.

▶ **verb** **1** supply a device with mechanical or electrical energy. **2** (**power something up/down**) switch a device on or off. **3** move with speed or force.
– DERIVATIVES **pow·ered** adjective.
– PHRASES **the powers that be** the authorities.
– ORIGIN Old French *poeir*.

WORD LINKS

megalomania *obsession with power*

CHOOSE THE RIGHT WORD

See **JURISDICTION**.

pow·er·boat /ˈpou(-ə)rˌbōt/ ▶ **noun** a fast motorboat.
– DERIVATIVES **pow·er·boat·ing** noun.

pow·er brok·er ▶ **noun** a person who influences the balance of political or economic power.

pow·er·ful /ˈpou(-ə)rfəl/ ▶ **adjective** **1** having great power. **2** having a strong effect: *powerful anti-war images*.

– SYNONYMS **1 strong,** muscular, muscly, sturdy, strapping, robust, brawny, burly, athletic, manly, well built, solid; informal beefy. **2 intoxicating,** hard, strong, stiff, potent. **3 violent,** forceful, hard, mighty. **4 intense,** keen, fierce, strong, irresistible, overpowering, overwhelming. **5 influential,** strong, important, dominant, commanding, formidable. **6 cogent,** compelling, convincing, persuasive, forceful, potent.
– ANTONYMS weak, gentle.

– DERIVATIVES **pow·er·ful·ly** adverb.

pow·er·house /ˈpou(-ə)rˌhous/ ▶ **noun** a person or thing having great energy or power.

pow·er·less /ˈpou(-ə)rləs/ ▶ **adjective** without ability, influence, or power.

– SYNONYMS **impotent,** helpless, ineffectual, ineffective, useless, defenseless, vulnerable.

– DERIVATIVES **pow·er·less·ly** adverb **pow·er·less·ness** noun.

pow·er line ▶ **noun** a cable carrying electrical power.

pow·er of at·tor·ney ▶ **noun** the authority to act for another person in particular legal or financial matters.

pow·er pack ▶ **noun** **1** a unit that stores and supplies electrical power. **2** a transformer for converting an alternating current to a direct current at a different voltage.

pow·er plant ▶ **noun** a power station.

pow·er play ▶ **noun** **1** tactics exhibiting or intended to increase a person's power or influence. **2** tactics in a team sport involving the concentration of players at a particular point. **3** Ice Hockey a situation in which a team has a numerical advantage over its opponents while one or more players is serving a penalty.

pow·er pop ▶ **noun** a style of pop music characterized by a strong melody line, heavy use of guitars, and simple rhythm.

pow·er rat·ing ▶ **noun** **1** the amount of electrical power required for a particular device. **2** a numerical representation of a sports team's strength for betting purposes.

pow·er sta·tion ▶ **noun** a building where electrical power is generated.

pow·er steer·ing ▶ **noun** steering aided by power from the vehicle's engine.

pow·wow /ˈpouˌwou/ ▶ **noun** **1** informal a meeting for discussion. **2** a North American Indian ceremony involving feasting and dancing. ▶ **verb** informal meet to discuss something.
– ORIGIN from a word in a North American Indian language meaning 'magician.'

pox /päks/ ▶ **noun** **1** any disease caused by a virus and producing a rash of pus-filled pimples that leave pockmarks on healing. **2** (**the pox**) informal syphilis. **3** (**the pox**) historical smallpox.
– ORIGIN from *pocks*, plural of **POCK**.

pp ▶ **abbreviation** **1** (**pp.**) pages. **2** (also **p.p.**) per procurationem (used when signing a letter on someone else's behalf). **3** Music pianissimo.
– ORIGIN sense 2 from Latin, 'through the agency of.'

ppm ▶ **abbreviation** **1** part(s) per million. **2** page(s) per minute, a measure of the speed of a computer printer.

PPS ▶ **abbreviation** post (additional) postscript.

PPV ▸ **abbreviation** pay-per-view.

PR ▸ **abbreviation** **1** proportional representation. **2** public relations.

Pr ▸ **symbol** the chemical element praseodymium.

prac·ti·ca·ble /ˈpraktikəbəl/ ▸ **adjective** able to be done or put into effect successfully: *it was not practicable to call her as a witness.*

– SYNONYMS **realistic,** feasible, possible, viable, reasonable, sensible, workable, achievable; informal doable.

– DERIVATIVES **prac·ti·ca·bil·i·ty** /ˌpraktikəˈbilətē/ noun **prac·ti·ca·bly** adverb.

prac·ti·cal /ˈpraktikəl/ ▸ **adjective** **1** relating to the actual doing or use of something rather than theory: *the candidate should have practical management experience.* **2** likely to be effective or successful: *practical solutions to transport problems.* **3** suitable for a particular purpose. **4** realistic or sensible in one's approach to a situation. **5** skilled at making or doing things. **6** almost complete; virtual: *it was a practical certainty that he would raise more money.*

– SYNONYMS **1 empirical,** hands-on, actual. **2 feasible,** practicable, realistic, viable, workable, possible, reasonable, sensible; informal doable. **3 functional,** sensible, utilitarian. **4 realistic,** sensible, down-to-earth, businesslike, commonsensical, hardheaded, no-nonsense; informal hard-nosed.
– ANTONYMS theoretical.

▸ **noun** Brit. an exam or lesson in which theories and procedures are applied to making or doing something.
– ORIGIN from Greek *praktikos* 'concerned with action.'

prac·ti·cal·i·ty /ˌpraktiˈkalətē/ ▸ **noun** (pl. **practicalities**) **1** the quality or state of being practical. **2** (**practicalities**) the aspects of a situation that involve action or experience rather than theories or ideas.

prac·ti·cal joke ▸ **noun** a trick played on someone to make them look foolish.

prac·ti·cal·ly /ˈpraktik(ə)lē/ ▸ **adverb** **1** virtually; almost. **2** in a practical way.

– SYNONYMS **1 almost,** very nearly, virtually, just about, all but, more or less, as good as, to all intents and purposes; informal pretty well. **2 realistically,** sensibly, reasonably, rationally, matter-of-factly.

prac·ti·cal nurse ▸ **noun** a nurse who has completed a training course of a lower standard than a registered nurse.

prac·tice /ˈpraktəs/ ▸ **noun** **1** the use or application of an idea or method, as opposed to the theories relating to it: *putting policy into practice.* **2** the usual way of doing something. **3** the work, business, or place of work of a doctor, dentist, or lawyer. **4** the action of doing something repeatedly so as to become more skillful in it: *math improves with practice.*

– SYNONYMS **1 application,** exercise, use, operation, implementation, execution. **2 custom,** procedure, policy, convention, tradition. **3 training,** rehearsal, repetition, preparation, dummy run, run-through; informal dry run. **4 profession,** career, business, work. **5 business,** firm, office, company; informal outfit.

▸ **verb** (Brit. **practise**) **1** do something repeatedly in order to become skillful in it: *I need to practice my French.* **2** carry out an activity or custom regularly. **3** work in a particular profession: *she began to practice law.* **4** observe the teaching and rules of a religion.

– SYNONYMS **1 rehearse,** run through, go over/through, work on/at, polish, perfect, refine. **2 train,** rehearse, prepare, go through one's paces. **3 carry out,** perform, observe, follow. **4 work in,** pursue a career in, engage in.

– ORIGIN Latin *practicare* 'perform, carry out.'

prac·ticed /ˈpraktəst/ (Brit. **practised**) ▸ **adjective** expert in something as the result of much experience.

– SYNONYMS **expert,** experienced, seasoned, skilled, skillful, accomplished, proficient, talented, able, adept.

prac·tise ▸ **verb** British spelling of **PRACTICE** (verb).

prac·ti·tion·er /prakˈtisʜənər/ ▸ **noun** a person who practices a particular profession or activity.

prae·tor /ˈprētər/ (also **pretor**) ▸ **noun** each of two ancient Roman magistrates ranking below consul.
– DERIVATIVES **prae·to·ri·an** /prēˈtôrēən/ adjective & noun.
– ORIGIN Latin.

prae·to·ri·an guard ▸ **noun** (in ancient Rome) the bodyguard of the emperor.

prag·mat·ic /pragˈmatik/ ▸ **adjective** **1** dealing with things in a realistic and practical way. **2** relating to philosophical pragmatism.

– SYNONYMS **practical,** matter-of-fact, sensible, down-to-earth, commonsensical, businesslike, hardheaded, no-nonsense; informal hard-nosed.
– ANTONYMS impractical.

– DERIVATIVES **prag·mat·i·cal·ly** /-ik(ə)lē/ adverb.
– ORIGIN Greek *pragmatikos* 'relating to fact.'

prag·ma·tism /ˈpragməˌtizəm/ ▸ **noun** **1** a realistic and practical attitude or approach. **2** a philosophical approach that evaluates theories in terms of the success of their practical application.
– DERIVATIVES **prag·ma·tist** noun.

prai·rie /ˈpre(ə)rē/ ▸ **noun** a large open area of grassland.
– ORIGIN French.

prai·rie dog ▸ **noun** a type of rodent that lives in burrows in the grasslands of North America.

praise /prāz/ ▸ **verb** **1** express warm approval of or admiration for: *he praised the work being done by the security forces.* **2** express respect and gratitude toward God or a god.

– SYNONYMS **commend,** applaud, pay tribute to, speak highly of, compliment, congratulate, sing the praises of, rave about.
– ANTONYMS criticize.

▸ **noun** **1** the expression of approval or admiration. **2** the expression of respect and gratitude as an act of worship.

– SYNONYMS **approval,** acclaim, admiration, approbation, plaudits, congratulations, commendation, accolade, compliment, a pat on the back, eulogy.
– ANTONYMS criticism.

– PHRASES **praise someone/thing to the skies** praise someone or something very highly or enthusiastically.
– ORIGIN Old French *preisier* 'to prize, praise.'

praise·wor·thy /ˈprāzˌwərTHē/ ▸ **adjective** deserving approval and admiration.

– SYNONYMS **commendable,** admirable, laudable, worthy (of admiration), meritorious, estimable, excellent, exemplary.

– DERIVATIVES **praise·wor·thi·ly** adverb **praise·wor·thi·ness** noun.

pra·line /ˈpräˌlēn/ ▸ **noun** a smooth substance made from nuts boiled in sugar, used as a filling for chocolates.
– ORIGIN named after Marshal de Plessis-*Praslin*, the French soldier whose cook invented it.

pram /pram/ ▸ **noun** Brit. a four-wheeled vehicle for a baby, pushed by a person on foot.
– ORIGIN from **PERAMBULATOR**.

prance /prans/ ▸ **verb 1** move quickly with exaggerated steps. **2** (of a horse) move with high springy steps.
– SYNONYMS **cavort,** dance, jig, trip, caper, jump, leap, spring, bound, skip, hop, frisk, romp, frolic.
– ORIGIN unknown.

pran·di·al /ˈprandēəl/ ▸ **adjective** formal during or relating to a meal.
– ORIGIN from Latin *prandium* 'meal.'

prang /praNG/ Brit. informal ▸ **verb** crash a motor vehicle or aircraft. ▸ **noun** a collision or crash.
– ORIGIN imitating the sound.

prank /praNGk/ ▸ **noun** a practical joke or mischievous act.
– SYNONYMS **(practical) joke,** trick, escapade, stunt, caper, jape, game, hoax; informal lark, leg-pull.
– DERIVATIVES **prank·ish** adjective.
– ORIGIN unknown.

prank·ster /ˈpraNGkstər/ ▸ **noun** a person who is fond of playing pranks.

pra·se·o·dym·i·um /ˌprāzēōˈdimēəm/ ▸ **noun** a silvery-white metallic chemical element of the lanthanide series.
– ORIGIN Latin.

prate /prāt/ ▸ **verb** talk too much in a foolish or boring way.
– ORIGIN from Dutch or German *praten*.

prat·fall /ˈpratˌfôl/ ▸ **noun** informal **1** a fall onto one's buttocks. **2** an embarrassing mistake.

prat·tle /ˈpratl/ ▸ **verb** talk too much in a foolish or trivial way. ▸ **noun** foolish or trivial talk.
– ORIGIN German *pratelen*.

prawn /prôn/ ▸ **noun** an edible shellfish that resembles a large shrimp.
– ORIGIN unknown.

prax·is /ˈpraksəs/ ▸ **noun 1** practice, as distinguished from theory. **2** accepted practice or custom, especially in religion.
– ORIGIN Greek, 'doing.'

pray /prā/ ▸ **verb 1** say a prayer to God or a god. **2** wish or hope strongly for: *after days of rain, we were praying for sun*. ▸ **adverb** formal or old use please: *pray continue*.
– ORIGIN Old French *preier*.

prayer /pre(ə)r/ ▸ **noun 1** a request for help or expression of thanks addressed to God or a god. **2** (**prayers**) a religious service at which people gather to pray together. **3** an earnest hope or wish.

prayer·ful /ˈpre(ə)rfəl/ ▸ **adjective 1** relating to praying or prayers. **2** tending to pray; devout.
– DERIVATIVES **prayer·ful·ly** adverb.

prayer wheel ▸ **noun** a small revolving cylinder inscribed with or containing prayers, used by Tibetan Buddhists.

pray·ing man·tis ▸ **noun** see **MANTIS**.

PRC ▸ **abbreviation** People's Republic of China.

pre- ▸ **prefix** before: *prearrange*.
– ORIGIN from Latin *prae-*.

preach /prēCH/ ▸ **verb 1** give a religious talk to a gathering of people. **2** strongly recommend a course of action: *my parents always preached tolerance*. **3** (**preach at**) give moral advice to someone in a pompous way.
– SYNONYMS **1 give a sermon,** sermonize, evangelize, spread the gospel. **2 proclaim,** teach, spread, propagate, expound. **3 advocate,** recommend, advise, urge, teach, counsel.
– DERIVATIVES **preach·er** noun.
– ORIGIN Old French *prechier*.

WORD LINKS

homiletic *relating to preaching*

preach·y /ˈprēCHē/ ▸ **adjective** giving moral advice in a pompous or overbearing way.

pre·am·ble /ˈprēˌambəl/ ▸ **noun** an opening statement; an introduction.
– ORIGIN from Latin *praeambulus* 'going before.'

pre·am·pli·fi·er /prēˈampləˌfīər/ (also **preamp**) ▸ **noun** an electronic device that amplifies a very weak signal and transmits it to a main amplifier.

pre·ar·range /ˌprēəˈrānj/ ▸ **verb** arrange or agree upon something in advance.

Pre·cam·bri·an /prēˈkambrēən, -kām-/ ▸ **adjective** Geology relating to the earliest period of the earth's history, ending about 570 million years ago, a time when living organisms first appeared.

pre·can·cer·ous /prēˈkansərəs/ ▸ **adjective** (of a cell or medical condition) likely to develop into cancer if untreated.

pre·car·i·ous /priˈke(ə)rēəs/ ▸ **adjective 1** likely to fall or to cause someone to fall. **2** not safe or stable; uncertain: *the country's precarious financial position*.
– SYNONYMS **insecure,** uncertain, unpredictable, risky, hazardous, dangerous, unsafe, unstable, unsteady, shaky; informal dicey, iffy; old use parlous.
– ANTONYMS safe.
– DERIVATIVES **pre·car·i·ous·ly** adverb **pre·car·i·ous·ness** noun.
– ORIGIN Latin *precarius* 'obtained by entreaty.'

pre·cast /ˈprēˈkast/ ▸ **adjective** (especially of concrete) cast in its final shape before positioning.

pre·cau·tion /priˈkôSHən/ ▸ **noun 1** something done in advance to avoid problems or danger: *the best ways to foil hackers is to take a few simple precautions*. **2** (**precautions**) informal contraception.
– SYNONYMS **safeguard,** preventive measure, safety measure, insurance; informal backstop.
– DERIVATIVES **pre·cau·tion·ar·y** /-ˌnerē/ adjective.
– ORIGIN Latin.

pre·cede /priˈsēd/ ▸ **verb 1** come before in time, order, or position: *read the chapters that precede the recipes*. **2** go in front or ahead of someone.
– SYNONYMS **1 go before,** come before, lead up to, pave the way for, herald, introduce, usher in. **2 go ahead of,** go in front of, lead the way.
– ANTONYMS follow.

– DERIVATIVES **pre·ced·ing** adjective.
– ORIGIN Latin *praecedere*.

prec·e·dence /ˈpresədəns, priˈsēdns/ ▶ **noun** the state of coming before other people or things in order or importance: *his desire for power took precedence over everything*.

– SYNONYMS **seniority,** superiority, ascendancy, supremacy; (**take precedence over**) take priority over, outweigh, prevail over, come before.

prec·e·dent ▶ **noun** /ˈpresid(ə)nt/ **1** an earlier event or action that acts as an example to be followed in a similar situation. **2** a previous legal case or decision that may or must be followed in subsequent similar cases.

– SYNONYMS **model,** exemplar, example, pattern, paradigm, criterion, yardstick, standard.

▶ **adjective** /priˈsēd(ə)nt/ coming before in time, order, or importance.

pre·cept /ˈprēˌsept/ ▶ **noun 1** a general rule regulating behavior or thought. **2** a writ or warrant.
– ORIGIN Latin *praeceptum* 'something advised.'

pre·cep·tor /ˈprēˌseptər, priˈseptər/ ▶ **noun** (fem. **preceptress** /ˈprēˌseptris/) a teacher or instructor.

pre·ces·sion /prəˈsesʜən/ ▶ **noun 1** the slow movement of the axis of a spinning body around another axis. **2** the earlier occurrence of the equinoxes each year.
– DERIVATIVES **pre·cess** /prēˈses, ˈprēˌses/ verb **pre·ces·sion·al** /priˈsesʜənl/ adjective.
– ORIGIN from Latin *praecedere* 'go before.'

pre·cinct /ˈprēˌsiɴɢkt/ ▶ **noun 1** one of the districts into which a city or town is divided for elections or policing purposes. **2** the area within the walls or boundaries of a place. **3** an enclosed area around a cathedral, church, or college.

– SYNONYMS **district,** zone, sector, quarter, area.

– ORIGIN Latin *praecinctum*.

pre·ci·os·i·ty /ˌpresʜēˈäsətē/ ▶ **noun** affectation or pretentiousness in language or art.

pre·cious /ˈpresʜəs/ ▶ **adjective 1** very valuable. **2** greatly loved or treasured: *my daughter's very precious to me*. **3** ironic considerable: *a precious lot you know!* **4** sophisticated in an affected or exaggerated way.

– SYNONYMS **1 valuable,** costly, expensive, invaluable, priceless. **2 valued,** cherished, treasured, prized, favorite, dear, beloved, special. **3 affected,** pretentious; informal la-di-da.

– DERIVATIVES **pre·cious·ly** adverb **pre·cious·ness** noun.
– PHRASES **precious little** (or **few**) informal very little (or few).
– ORIGIN Latin *pretiosus*.

pre·cious met·al ▶ **noun** a valuable metal such as gold, silver, or platinum.

pre·cious stone ▶ **noun** a very attractive and valuable piece of mineral, used in jewelry.

prec·i·pice /ˈpresəpəs/ ▶ **noun** a tall and very steep rock face or cliff.

– SYNONYMS **cliff (face),** rock face, sheer drop, crag, bluff, escarpment.

– ORIGIN Latin *praecipitium* 'abrupt descent.'

pre·cip·i·tant /priˈsipətənt/ ▶ **noun** a cause of an action or event.

pre·cip·i·tate ▶ **verb** /priˈsipəˌtāt/ **1** cause something undesirable to happen suddenly or prematurely. **2** cause to move suddenly and with force: *the ladder broke, precipitating them down into a heap*. **3** Chemistry cause a substance to be deposited in solid form from a solution. **4** cause moisture in the atmosphere to condense and fall as rain, snow, sleet, or hail.

– SYNONYMS **bring about,** bring on, cause, lead to, give rise to, instigate, trigger, spark, touch off, provoke, hasten, speed up, accelerate.

▶ **adjective** /priˈsipətət/ done or occurring suddenly or without careful consideration.

– SYNONYMS **hasty,** overhasty, rash, hurried, rushed, impetuous, impulsive, precipitous, incautious, imprudent, injudicious, ill-advised, reckless.

▶ **noun** /priˈsipətət, -əˌtāt/ Chemistry a substance precipitated from a solution.
– DERIVATIVES **pre·cip·i·tate·ly** /priˈsipətətlē/ adverb **pre·cip·i·ta·tor** /priˈsipəˌtātər/ noun.
– ORIGIN Latin *praecipitare* 'throw headlong.'

pre·cip·i·ta·tion /priˌsipəˈtāsʜən/ ▶ **noun 1** rain, snow, sleet, or hail. **2** Chemistry the action of precipitating a substance from a solution. **3** old use sudden and unthinking action.

pre·cip·i·tous /priˈsipətəs/ ▶ **adjective 1** dangerously high or steep. **2** (of a change to a worse situation) sudden and dramatic. **3** done suddenly and without consideration; precipitate.

– SYNONYMS **1 steep,** sheer, perpendicular, abrupt, sharp, vertical. **2 sudden,** rapid, swift, abrupt, headlong, speedy, quick, fast.

– DERIVATIVES **pre·cip·i·tous·ly** adverb.

pré·cis /prāˈsē, ˈprāsē/ (also **precis**) ▶ **noun** (pl. same) a summary of a written work or speech. ▶ **verb** (**précises, précising, précised**) make a summary of a piece of writing or a speech.
– ORIGIN from French, 'precise.'

pre·cise /priˈsīs/ ▶ **adjective 1** expressed in a detailed and accurate way: *precise directions*. **2** very attentive to detail. **3** exact; particular: *at that precise moment the car stopped*.

– SYNONYMS **1 exact,** accurate, correct, specific, detailed, explicit, careful, meticulous, strict, rigorous. **2** *at that precise moment* **exact,** particular, actual, specific, distinct.
– ANTONYMS inaccurate.

– DERIVATIVES **pre·cise·ness** noun.
– ORIGIN Old French *prescis*.

USAGE

Precise does not mean exactly the same thing as **accurate**. **Accurate** means 'correct in all details,' while **precise** contains an idea of trying to specify details exactly: if you say 'It's 4:04 and 12 seconds' you are being *precise*, but not necessarily *accurate* (your watch might be slow).

pre·cise·ly /priˈsīslē/ ▶ **adverb 1** exactly (used to emphasize the complete accuracy or truth of a statement). **2** in exact terms; without vagueness.

– SYNONYMS **1** *at 2:00 precisely, the phone rang* **exactly,** sharp, on the dot, promptly; informal on the button, on the nose, bang (on). **2** *fertilization can be timed precisely* **accurately,** exactly; clearly, distinctly, strictly.

pre·ci·sion /priˈsizʜən/ ▶ **noun** the quality or fact of being precise.

– SYNONYMS **exactness,** accuracy, exactitude, correctness, care, meticulousness, scrupulousness, punctiliousness, rigor.

▶ **adjective** very accurate: *a precision instrument.*

pre·clude /pri'klo͞od/ ▶ **verb** prevent something from happening or someone from doing something.

– SYNONYMS **prevent,** make it impossible for, rule out, stop, prohibit, debar, bar, hinder, impede, inhibit, exclude.

– DERIVATIVES **pre·clu·sion** /-'klo͞ozʜən/ noun.
– ORIGIN Latin *praecludere* 'shut off, impede.'

CHOOSE THE RIGHT WORD

See **PROHIBIT**.

pre·co·cious /pri'kōsʜəs/ ▶ **adjective** (of a child) having developed certain abilities or ways of behaving at an earlier age than usual.
– DERIVATIVES **pre·co·cious·ly** adverb **pre·co·cious·ness** noun **pre·coc·i·ty** /pri'käsətē/ noun.
– ORIGIN from Latin *praecox*, from *praecoquere* 'ripen fully.'

pre·cog·ni·tion /ˌprēkäg'nisʜən/ ▶ **noun** knowledge of an event before it happens, especially through supposed paranormal means.
– DERIVATIVES **pre·cog·ni·tive** /prē'kägnətiv/ adjective.

pre·con·ceived /ˌprēkən'sēvd/ ▶ **adjective** (of an idea or opinion) formed before full knowledge or evidence is available.

pre·con·cep·tion /ˌprēkən'sepsʜən/ ▶ **noun** an idea or opinion that is formed before full knowledge or evidence is available.

– SYNONYMS **preconceived idea,** presupposition, assumption, presumption, prejudgment, prejudice.

pre·con·di·tion /ˌprēkən'disʜən/ ▶ **noun** something that must exist or happen before other things can happen or be done.

pre·cook /prē'ko͝ok/ ▶ **verb** cook something in advance.

pre·cur·sor /'prēˌkərsər, pri'kər-/ ▶ **noun** a person or thing that comes before another of the same kind: *the game was a precursor of baseball.*
– DERIVATIVES **pre·cur·so·ry** adjective.
– ORIGIN Latin *praecursor*.

pre·da·cious /pri'dāsʜəs/ (also **predaceous**) ▶ **adjective** (of an animal) predatory.

pre·date /prē'dāt/ ▶ **verb** exist or occur at a date earlier than something.

pre·da·tion /pri'dāsʜən/ ▶ **noun** the preying of one animal on others.
– ORIGIN Latin.

pred·a·tor /'predətər/ ▶ **noun 1** an animal that hunts and kills other animals for food. **2** a person who exploits others: *a sexual predator.*

pred·a·to·ry /'predəˌtôrē/ ▶ **adjective 1** (of an animal) hunting and killing other animals for food. **2** (of a person) exploiting other people.

– SYNONYMS **1 predacious,** carnivorous, hunting. **2 exploitative,** wolfish, rapacious, manipulative.

pre·dawn /prē'dôn/ ▶ **adjective** relating to or taking place before dawn.

pre·de·cease /ˌprēdi'sēs/ ▶ **verb** formal die before another person.

pred·e·ces·sor /'predəˌsesər, 'prē-/ ▶ **noun 1** a person who held a job or office before the current holder. **2** a thing that has been followed or replaced by another: *the chapel was built on the site of its predecessor.*

– SYNONYMS **1 forerunner,** precursor, antecedent. **2 ancestor,** forefather, forebear, antecedent.
– ANTONYMS successor, descendant.

– ORIGIN Latin *praedecessor*.

pre·des·ti·na·tion /prēˌdestə'nāsʜən/ ▶ **noun** the Christian belief that everything has been decided or planned in advance by God.

pre·des·tine /prē'destin/ ▶ **verb** (usu. as adj. **predestined**) (of God or fate) decide in advance that something will happen or that someone will have a particular fate.

pre·de·ter·mine /ˌprēdi'tərmən/ ▶ **verb** establish or decide something in advance.
– DERIVATIVES **pre·de·ter·mi·na·tion** /-ˌtərmə'nāsʜən/ noun.

pre·de·ter·min·er /ˌprēdi'tərmənər/ ▶ **noun** Grammar a word or phrase that occurs before a determiner, for example *both* or *a lot of*.

pre·dic·a·ment /pri'dikəmənt/ ▶ **noun** a difficult or embarrassing situation.

– SYNONYMS **difficulty,** mess, plight, quandary, muddle, dilemma; informal hole, fix, jam, pickle.

– ORIGIN Latin *praedicamentum* 'something predicated.'

pred·i·cate ▶ **noun** /'predikət/ **1** Grammar the part of a sentence or clause containing a verb and stating something about the subject (e.g., *went home* in *John went home*). **2** Logic something that is declared or denied concerning an argument of a proposition. ▶ **verb** /'predəˌkāt/ **1** (**predicate something on**) found or base something on: *the oil's low price is predicated on tax exemptions.* **2** declare or assert something as true or existing.
– DERIVATIVES **pred·i·ca·tion** /ˌpredə'kāsʜən/ noun.
– ORIGIN from Latin *praedicare* 'make known beforehand, declare.'

pred·i·ca·tive /'predəˌkātiv, -ikətiv/ ▶ **adjective** Grammar (of an adjective or noun) forming part or the whole of the predicate and coming after a verb, for example *old* in *the dog is old*. Contrasted with **ATTRIBUTIVE**.
– DERIVATIVES **pred·i·ca·tive·ly** adverb.

pre·dict /pri'dikt/ ▶ **verb** state that an event will happen in the future.

– SYNONYMS **forecast,** foretell, prophesy; old use augur.

– DERIVATIVES **pre·dic·tive** adjective **pre·dic·tor** noun.
– ORIGIN Latin *praedicere* 'make known beforehand, declare.'

pre·dict·a·ble /pri'diktəbəl/ ▶ **adjective 1** able to be predicted. **2** always behaving or occurring in the way expected and therefore boring.

– SYNONYMS **foreseeable,** to be expected, anticipated, likely, foreseen, unsurprising, reliable; informal inevitable.

– DERIVATIVES **pre·dict·a·bil·i·ty** /-ˌdiktə'bilətē/ noun **pre·dict·a·bly** adverb.

pre·dic·tion /pri'diksʜən/ ▶ **noun 1** a thing predicted; a forecast. **2** the action of predicting something.

– SYNONYMS **forecast,** prophecy, prognosis, prognostication.

pre·di·gest /ˌprēdīˈjest, ˌprēdə-/ ▶ **verb 1** (of an animal) treat food by a process similar to digestion to make it more easily digestible when subsequently eaten. **2** simplify information so that it is easier to absorb.

pre·di·lec·tion /ˌpredlˈeksʜən, ˌprēdl-/ ▶ **noun** a preference or special liking for something.
– ORIGIN from Latin *praediligere* 'prefer.'

pre·dis·pose /ˌprēdiˈspōz/ ▶ **verb** make someone likely to do, be, or think something: *certain people are predisposed to become drug abusers.*

pre·dis·po·si·tion /ˌprēˌdispəˈzisʜən/ ▶ **noun** a liability or tendency to do, be, or think something.

– SYNONYMS **1** *a predisposition to heart disease* **susceptibility,** proneness, tendency, liability, inclination, vulnerability. **2** *their political predispositions* **preference,** predilection, inclination, leaning, bent.

pre·dom·i·nant /priˈdämənənt/ ▶ **adjective 1** present as the main element: *the bird's predominant color was white.* **2** having the greatest control or power.
– DERIVATIVES **pre·dom·i·nance** noun.

pre·dom·i·nant·ly /priˈdämənəntlē/ ▶ **adverb** mainly; for the most part.

– SYNONYMS **mainly,** mostly, for the most part, chiefly, principally, primarily, in the main, on the whole, largely, by and large, typically, generally, usually.

pre·dom·i·nate /priˈdäməˌnāt/ ▶ **verb 1** be the main element in something: *small-scale producers predominate in the south.* **2** have control or power.

pre·dom·i·nate·ly /priˈdämənətlē/ ▶ **adverb** mainly; for the most part.

pre·ec·lamp·sia /ˌprē-iˈklampsēə/ ▶ **noun** a condition in pregnancy characterized especially by high blood pressure.
– DERIVATIVES **pre·ec·lamp·tic** /-ˈklamptik/ adjective & noun.

pree·mie /ˈprēmē/ ▶ **noun** (pl. **preemies**) informal a baby born prematurely.

pre·em·i·nent /prēˈemənənt/ ▶ **adjective** better than all others; outstanding.
– DERIVATIVES **pre-em·i·nence** noun **pre-em·i·nent·ly** adverb.

pre-empt /prēˈempt/ ▶ **verb 1** take action in order to prevent something from happening. **2** prevent someone from saying something by speaking first.
– DERIVATIVES **pre-empt·ive** adjective **pre-empt·or** noun.

pre-emp·tion /prēˈempsʜən/ ▶ **noun 1** the action of preventing something from happening. **2** the buying of goods or shares before the opportunity is offered to others.
– ORIGIN from Latin *praeemere* 'buy in advance.'

preen /prēn/ ▶ **verb 1** (of a bird) tidy and clean its feathers with its beak. **2** make oneself look attractive and then admire one's appearance. **3** (**preen oneself**) congratulate or pride oneself: *he's preening himself on having such a pretty girlfriend.*
– ORIGIN probably from Latin *ungere* 'anoint.'

pre·ex·ist /ˌprē-igˈzist/ ▶ **verb** (usu. as adj. **preexisting**) exist before or from an earlier time.
– DERIVATIVES **pre·ex·ist·ence** noun **pre·ex·ist·ent** adjective.

pre·fab /prēˈfab, ˈprēˌfab/ ▶ **noun** informal a prefabricated building.

pre·fab·ri·cat·ed /prēˈfabriˌkātid/ ▶ **adjective** (of a building) made in sections that can be easily assembled on site.
– DERIVATIVES **pre·fab·ri·ca·tion** /-ˌfabrəˈkāsʜən/ noun.

pref·ace /ˈprefəs/ ▶ **noun 1** an introduction to a book, stating its subject, scope, or aims. **2** a preliminary explanation.

– SYNONYMS **introduction,** foreword, preamble, prologue, prelude, front matter; informal intro.

▶ **verb 1** (**preface something with/by**) begin a speech or event with or by doing something. **2** provide a book with a preface.

– SYNONYMS **precede,** introduce, begin, open, start.

– DERIVATIVES **pref·a·to·ry** /ˈprefəˌtôrē/ adjective.
– ORIGIN Old French.

pre·fect /ˈprēˌfekt/ ▶ **noun** a chief officer, magistrate, or regional governor in certain countries.
– DERIVATIVES **pre·fec·to·ri·al** /ˌprēˌfekˈtôrēəl/ adjective.
– ORIGIN Latin *praefectus.*

pre·fec·ture /ˈprēˌfekcʜər/ ▶ **noun 1** a district governed by a prefect. **2** the office or residence of a prefect.
– DERIVATIVES **pre·fec·tur·al** /prēˈfekcʜərəl/ adjective.

pre·fer /priˈfər/ ▶ **verb** (**prefers, preferring, preferred**) **1** like someone or something better than another or others: *I prefer Greece to Spain.* **2** put forward a formal accusation for consideration by a court of law. **3** old use promote someone to an important position.

– SYNONYMS **like better,** would rather (have), would sooner (have), favor, be more partial to, choose, select, pick, opt for, go for.

– ORIGIN Latin *praeferre* 'bear or carry before.'

pref·er·a·ble /ˈpref(ə)rəbəl/ ▶ **adjective** more desirable or suitable.

– SYNONYMS **better,** best, more desirable, more suitable, advantageous, superior, preferred, recommended.

– DERIVATIVES **pref·er·a·bil·i·ty** /ˌpref(ə)rəˈbilətē/ noun.

pref·er·a·bly /ˈpref(ə)rəblē/ ▶ **adverb** ideally; if possible.

– SYNONYMS **ideally,** if possible, for preference, from choice.

pref·er·ence /ˈpref(ə)rəns/ ▶ **noun 1** a greater liking for one alternative over another or others. **2** a thing preferred. **3** favor shown to one person over another or others: *preference is given to those who make a donation.*

– SYNONYMS **1 liking,** partiality, fondness, taste, inclination, leaning, bent, penchant, predisposition. **2 priority,** favor, precedence, preferential treatment.

pref·er·en·tial /ˌprefəˈrencʜəl/ ▶ **adjective** favoring a particular person or group: *he was giving his son-in-law preferential treatment.*
– DERIVATIVES **pref·er·en·tial·ly** adverb.

pre·fer·ment /priˈfərmənt/ ▶ **noun** promotion or appointment to a job or office.

pre·ferred stock ▶ **noun** stock that entitles the holder to a fixed dividend, whose payment takes priority over that of common-stock dividends.

pre·fig·ure /prēˈfigyər/ ▶ **verb** be an early indication or version of: *the fall of Jericho was thought to prefigure the Last Judgment.*
– DERIVATIVES **pre·fig·u·ra·tion** /prēˌfigyəˈrāsʜən/ noun.

pre·fix /ˈprēˌfiks/ ▶ **noun 1** a word, letter, or number placed before another. **2** a letter or group of letters placed at the beginning of a word to alter its meaning (e.g., *non-*, *re-*). **3** a title placed before a name (e.g., *Mr.*). ▶ **verb** add letters or numbers to the beginning of a word or number.

pre·game /prēˈgām/ ▶ **adjective** in or relating to the period before a sporting event.

preg·nan·cy /ˈpregnənsē/ ▶ **noun** (pl. **pregnancies**) the condition or period of being pregnant.

preg·nant /ˈpregnənt/ ▶ **adjective 1** (of a woman or female animal) having a child or young developing in the uterus. **2** full of meaning; significant: *a pregnant pause.*

– SYNONYMS **1 expecting,** expectant, carrying a child, with child; informal in the family way. **2 meaningful,** significant, suggestive, expressive, charged.

– ORIGIN Latin *praegnans.*

pre·heat /prēˈhēt/ ▶ **verb** heat something beforehand.

pre·hen·sile /prēˈhensəl, -ˌsīl/ ▶ **adjective** (chiefly of an animal's limb or tail) capable of grasping things.
– ORIGIN from Latin *prehendere* 'to grasp.'

pre·his·tor·ic /ˌprē(h)iˈstôrik/ ▶ **adjective** relating to the period before written records.

WORD TOOLKIT

prehistoric ...	ancient ...	primordial ...
man	Greece	slime
creatures	city	ooze
cave paintings	history	sea
fish	Egyptians	swamp
ancestors	cultures	jungle
monster	civilization	germ cells

pre·his·to·ry /prēˈhist(ə)rē/ ▶ **noun 1** the period of time before written records. **2** the early stages of the development of something: *the prehistory of capitalism.*
– DERIVATIVES **pre·his·to·ri·an** /-ˈstôrēən/ noun.

pre·in·dus·tri·al /ˌprē-inˈdəstrēəl/ ▶ **adjective** before the development of industries on a large scale.

pre·judge /prēˈjəj/ ▶ **verb** make a judgment about someone or something without having all the necessary information.

prej·u·dice /ˈprejədəs/ ▶ **noun 1** an opinion that is not based on reason or actual experience: *widespread prejudice against foreigners.* **2** dislike or unjust behavior based on this. **3** chiefly Law harm that may result from an action or judgment.

– SYNONYMS **1 preconceived idea,** preconception. **2 bigotry,** bias, partiality, intolerance, discrimination, unfairness, inequality.

▶ **verb 1** influence someone so that they have a biased or unfair opinion: *the statement might prejudice the jury.* **2** have a harmful effect on a situation.

– SYNONYMS **1 bias,** influence, sway, predispose, make partial, color. **2 damage,** be detrimental to, be prejudicial to, injure, harm, hurt, spoil, impair, undermine, compromise.

– PHRASES **without prejudice** Law without adversely affecting any existing right or claim.
– ORIGIN Latin *praejudicium.*

prej·u·diced /ˈprejədəst/ ▶ **adjective** having or showing a dislike or distrust that is derived from prejudice.

– SYNONYMS **biased,** bigoted, discriminatory, partisan, intolerant, narrow-minded, unfair, unjust, inequitable.
– ANTONYMS impartial.

prej·u·di·cial /ˌprejəˈdishəl/ ▶ **adjective** harmful to someone or something.

pre·kin·der·gar·ten /prēˈkindərˌgärtn, -ˌgärdn/ ▶ **noun** day care with some educational content for children younger than five.

pre·lap·sar·i·an /ˌprēlapˈse(ə)rēən/ ▶ **adjective** chiefly literary before the Fall of Man, when humans lapsed into a state of sin; innocent and unspoiled.
– ORIGIN from **PRE-** + Latin *lapsus* 'a fall.'

prel·ate /ˈprelət/ ▶ **noun** formal a bishop or other high-ranking Christian priest.
– ORIGIN Latin *praelatus* 'civil dignitary.'

pre·lim·i·nar·y /priˈliməˌnerē/ ▶ **adjective** happening before or done in preparation for a main action or event: *preliminary talks.*

– SYNONYMS **preparatory,** introductory, initial, opening, early, exploratory.
– ANTONYMS final.

▶ **noun** (pl. **preliminaries**) **1** an action or event that comes before or is done in preparation for something. **2** a preliminary round in a sports competition.

– SYNONYMS **introduction,** preamble, preface, opening remarks, formalities.

– ORIGIN from Latin *prae* 'before' + *limen* 'threshold.'

pre·lit·er·ate /prēˈlitərət/ ▶ **adjective** relating to a society or culture that has not developed the use of writing.

prel·ude /ˈprelˌ(y)o͞od, ˈprāˌl(y)o͞od/ ▶ **noun 1** an action or event acting as an introduction to something more important: *the talks should be the prelude to a final agreement.* **2** a piece of music acting as an introduction to a longer work.

– SYNONYMS **preliminary,** overture, opening, preparation, introduction, lead-in, precursor.

▶ **verb** act as an introduction to something.
– ORIGIN from Latin *praeludere* 'play beforehand.'

pre·mar·i·tal /prēˈmaritl/ ▶ **adjective** happening before marriage.

pre·ma·ture /ˌprēməˈchŏŏr, -ˈt(y)ŏŏr/ ▶ **adjective 1** happening or done before the proper time: *the sun can cause premature aging.* **2** (of a baby) born before the normal length of pregnancy is completed.

– SYNONYMS **1 untimely,** too early, before time, unseasonable. **2 rash,** overhasty, hasty, precipitate, impulsive, impetuous; informal previous.
– ANTONYMS overdue.

– DERIVATIVES **pre·ma·ture·ly** adverb **pre·ma·tu·ri·ty** /-ˈchŏŏritē, -ˈt(y)ŏŏr-/ noun.
– ORIGIN Latin *praematurus* 'very early.'

pre·med·i·ca·tion /ˌprēˌmedəˈkāshən/ ▶ **noun** medication given in preparation for an operation or other treatment.

pre·med·i·tat·ed /priˈmedəˌtātid, prē-/ ▶ **adjective** (of an action, especially a crime) planned in advance.

– SYNONYMS **planned,** intentional, deliberate, preplanned, calculated, cold-blooded, conscious, prearranged.
– ANTONYMS spontaneous.

– DERIVATIVES **pre·med·i·ta·tion** /-ˌmedəˈtāshən/ noun.

pre·men·stru·al /prēˈmenstr(o͞o)əl/ ▶ **adjective** occurring or experienced before a menstrual period.

pre·men·stru·al syn·drome ▶ noun a complex of symptoms (including emotional tension and fluid retention) experienced by some women before a menstrual period.

pre·mier /prēˈm(y)i(ə)r, ˈprēmēər, ˈprēˌmi(ə)r/ ▶ adjective first in importance, order, or position.

– SYNONYMS **leading,** foremost, chief, principal, head, ranking, top-ranking, top, prime, primary, first, highest, preeminent, senior, outstanding.

▶ noun a prime minister or other head of government.

– SYNONYMS **head of government,** prime minister, PM, president, chancellor.

– ORIGIN Latin *primarius* 'principal.'

pre·miere /prēˈmyer, -ˈmi(ə)r/ ▶ noun the first performance of a play or musical work or the first showing of a movie.

– SYNONYMS **first performance,** first night, opening night, debut.

▶ verb present the premiere of a play, musical work, or movie.

– ORIGIN French *première.*

pre·mier·ship /prēˈm(y)irˌsʜip, ˈprēmēər-, ˈprēˌmi(ə)r-/ ▶ noun the office or position of a prime minister or other head of government.

prem·ise /ˈpremis/ ▶ noun a statement or idea that forms the basis for a theory, argument, or line of reasoning.

– SYNONYMS **proposition,** assumption, hypothesis, thesis, presupposition, supposition, presumption, assertion.

▶ verb (**premise something on**) base an argument, theory, etc., on something.

– ORIGIN Old French *premisse.*

prem·is·es /ˈpreməsəz/ ▶ plural noun a building, together with its land and outbuildings, occupied by a business.

– SYNONYMS **building(s),** property, site, office, establishment.

pre·mi·um /ˈprēmēəm/ ▶ noun (pl. **premiums**) **1** an amount paid for an insurance policy. **2** a sum added to a basic price or other payment.

– SYNONYMS **1 (regular) payment,** installment. **2 surcharge,** additional payment, extra.

▶ adjective (of a product) superior and more expensive: *premium beers.*

– PHRASES **at a premium 1** scarce and in demand. **2** above the usual price. **put** (or **place**) **a premium on** regard something as particularly important.

– ORIGIN Latin *praemium* 'booty, reward.'

pre·mo·lar /prēˈmōlər/ ▶ noun a tooth between the canines and molar teeth.

pre·mo·ni·tion /ˌprēməˈnisʜən, ˌprem-/ ▶ noun a strong feeling that something is about to happen.

– SYNONYMS **foreboding,** presentiment, intuition, (funny) feeling, hunch, suspicion, feeling in one's bones.

– DERIVATIVES **pre·mon·i·to·ry** /prēˈmänəˌtôrē/ adjective.

– ORIGIN from Latin *praemonere* 'forewarn.'

pre·na·tal /prēˈnātl/ ▶ adjective before birth.

– DERIVATIVES **pre·na·tal·ly** adverb.

pre·nup /prēˈnəp/ ▶ noun informal a prenuptial agreement.

pre·nup·tial /prēˈnəpsʜəl, -cʜəl/ ▶ adjective before marriage.

pre·nup·tial a·gree·ment ▶ noun an agreement made by a couple before they marry concerning the ownership of their respective assets should the marriage fail.

pre·oc·cu·pa·tion /ˌprēˌäkyəˈpāsʜən/ ▶ noun **1** the state of thinking about something continuously and ignoring everything else. **2** a matter that fills someone's mind completely.

– SYNONYMS **obsession,** fixation, concern, passion, enthusiasm, hobbyhorse; informal bee in one's bonnet.

pre·oc·cu·py /prēˈäkyəˌpī/ ▶ verb (**preoccupies, preoccupying, preoccupied**) fill someone's mind completely, so that they ignore everything else: *her mother was preoccupied with paying the bills* | (as adj. **preoccupied**) *she seemed a bit preoccupied.*

– SYNONYMS (as adj. **preoccupied**) **lost in thought,** deep in thought, oblivious, pensive, distracted, absorbed, engrossed, involved, wrapped up, concerned.

pre·or·dain /ˌprēôrˈdān/ ▶ verb decide or determine something beforehand.

prep /prep/ informal ▶ verb prepare; make ready. ▶ noun preparation.

– ORIGIN abbreviation of **PREPARATION.**

pre·pack·aged /prēˈpakijd/ ▶ adjective (of goods) packed or wrapped before they are sold.

pre·paid /prēˈpād/ past and past participle of **PREPAY.**

prep·a·ra·tion /ˌprepəˈrāsʜən/ ▶ noun **1** the action of preparing or the state of being prepared: *the preparation of a draft contract.* **2** something done to get ready for something else. **3** a substance that has been prepared for use as a medicine, cosmetic, or food.

– SYNONYMS **1** *preparations for the party* **arrangements,** planning, plans, groundwork, spadework, provision. **2 devising,** drawing up, construction, composition, development. **3 mixture,** compound, concoction, solution, medicine, potion.

pre·par·a·tive /prēˈpe(ə)rətiv, -ˈpar-/ ▶ adjective done in order to prepare for something; preparatory.

pre·par·a·to·ry /priˈpe(ə)rəˌtôrē, -ˈparə-, ˈprep(ə)rə-/ ▶ adjective done in order to prepare for something.

pre·par·a·to·ry school ▶ noun a private school that prepares students for college or university.

pre·pare /priˈpe(ə)r/ ▶ verb **1** make something ready for use. **2** make something from other parts, ingredients, or substances. **3** make or get ready to do or deal with something. **4** (**be prepared to do**) be willing to do.

– SYNONYMS **1** *I want you to prepare a report* **get ready,** put together, draw up, produce, arrange, assemble, construct, compose, formulate. **2** *the meal was easy to prepare* **cook,** make, get, concoct; informal fix, rustle up. **3** *preparing for war* **get ready,** make preparations, arrange things, make provision. **4** *athletes preparing for the Olympics* **train,** get into shape, practice, get ready, warm up, limber up. **5** *prepare yourself for a shock* **brace,** ready, tense, steel, steady. **6** (**be prepared to do**) *I'm not prepared to cut the price* **willing,** ready, disposed, (favorably) inclined, of a mind, minded.

– DERIVATIVES **pre·par·er** noun.

– ORIGIN Latin *praeparare.*

pre·par·ed·ness /prəˈpe(ə)r(ə)dnis/ ▶ noun a state of readiness, especially for war.

pre·pay /prē'pā/ ▶ **verb** (past and past part. **prepaid**) pay for something in advance.
– DERIVATIVES **pre·pay·ment** noun.

pre·plan /'prē'plan/ ▶ **verb** plan something in advance.

pre·pon·der·ance /pri'pändərəns/ ▶ **noun** the state of being greater in number: *the preponderance of women among older people*.

pre·pon·der·ant /pri'pändərənt/ ▶ **adjective** greater in number or importance.
– DERIVATIVES **pre·pon·der·ant·ly** adverb.

pre·pon·der·ate /pri'pändə,rāt/ ▶ **verb** be greater in number or importance: *the advantages preponderate over this apparent disadvantage*.
– ORIGIN Latin *praeponderare* 'weigh more.'

prep·o·si·tion /,prepə'zisHən/ ▶ **noun** Grammar a word used with a noun or pronoun to show place, position, time, or method.
– DERIVATIVES **prep·o·si·tion·al** adjective.

> **USAGE**
>
> A preposition (a word such as *from*, *to*, *on*, *after*, etc.) usually comes before a noun or pronoun and gives information about how, when, or where something has happened (*she arrived after dinner*). Some people believe that a preposition should never come at the end of a sentence, as in *where do you come from?*, and that you should say *from where do you come?* instead. However, this can result in English that sounds very awkward and unnatural, and is not a rule that has to be followed as long as the meaning of what you are saying is clear.

pre·pos·sess·ing /,prēpə'zesiNG/ ▶ **adjective** attractive or appealing in appearance: *he was not a prepossessing sight*.

pre·pos·ter·ous /pri'päst(ə)rəs/ ▶ **adjective** completely ridiculous or outrageous.

> – SYNONYMS **absurd,** ridiculous, foolish, stupid, ludicrous, outrageous, farcical, laughable, comical, risible, nonsensical, senseless, insane; informal crazy.
> – ANTONYMS sensible.

– DERIVATIVES **pre·pos·ter·ous·ly** adverb **pre·pos·ter·ous·ness** noun.
– ORIGIN Latin *praeposterus* 'reversed, absurd.'

prep·py /'prepē/ (also **preppie**) informal ▶ **adjective** (**preppier**, **preppiest**) typical of a student at an expensive preparatory school, especially with reference to their neat style of dress. ▶ **noun** (pl. **preppies**) **1** a student attending an expensive preparatory school. **2** a person with a preppy style.

pre·pran·di·al /prē'prandēəl/ ▶ **adjective** formal or humorous done or taken before dinner.
– ORIGIN from Latin *prandium* 'a meal.'

pre·pro·duc·tion /,prēprə'dəksHən/ ▶ **noun** work done on a product, movie, or broadcast program before full-scale production begins.

pre·pro·gram /prē'prō,gram, -grəm/ ▶ **verb** (**preprograms, preprogramming, preprogrammed**) program a computer in advance for ease of use.

prep school ▶ **noun** a preparatory school.

pre·pu·ber·tal /prē'pyo͞obərtl/ ▶ **adjective** another term for **PREPUBESCENT**.
– DERIVATIVES **pre·pu·ber·ty** noun.

pre·pu·bes·cent /,prēpyo͞o'besənt/ ▶ **adjective** relating to or in the period before puberty.

pre·puce /'prē,pyo͞os/ ▶ **noun 1** technical term for **FORESKIN**. **2** the fold of skin surrounding the clitoris.
– ORIGIN French *prépuce*.

pre·quel /'prēkwəl, -kwil/ ▶ **noun** a story or movie containing events that happen before those of an existing work.
– ORIGIN from **PRE-** + **SEQUEL**.

Pre-Raph·a·el·ite /'rafēə,līt, -rāfē-, -'räfē-/ ▶ **noun** a member of a group of English 19th-century artists who painted in the style of Italian artists from before the time of Raphael. ▶ **adjective 1** relating to the Pre-Raphaelites. **2** (of a woman) resembling one depicted in a Pre-Raphaelite painting, typically in having long auburn hair and pale skin.
– DERIVATIVES **Pre-Raph·a·el·it·ism** /-,līt,izəm/ noun.

pre·re·cord /,prēri'kôrd/ ▶ **verb** (often as adj. **prerecorded**) record sound or film in advance.

pre·req·ui·site /prē'rekwəzət/ ▶ **noun** a thing that must exist or happen before something else can exist or happen: *an education is a prerequisite for getting a well-paid job*.

> – SYNONYMS **(necessary) condition,** precondition, essential, requirement, requisite, necessity, sine qua non; informal must.

▶ **adjective** required before something else can exist or happen.

> – SYNONYMS **necessary,** required, called for, essential, requisite, obligatory, compulsory.
> – ANTONYMS unnecessary.

pre·rog·a·tive /pri'rägətiv, pə'räg-/ ▶ **noun** a right or privilege belonging to a particular person or group: *owning a car used to be the prerogative of the rich*.

> – SYNONYMS **entitlement,** right, privilege, advantage, due, birthright.

– ORIGIN Latin *praerogativa* 'verdict of the people chosen to vote first in the assembly.'

Pres. ▶ **abbreviation** President.

pres·age /'presij, pri'sāj/ ▶ **verb** be a sign or warning of an event that is about to happen. ▶ **noun** a sign or warning of an event that is about to happen; an omen.
– ORIGIN Latin *praesagire* 'forebode.'

pres·by·ter /'prezbitər, 'pres-/ ▶ **noun 1** formal (in Presbyterian Churches) an elder. **2** historical an elder or minister of the Christian Church.
– DERIVATIVES **pres·byt·er·al** /prez'bitərəl, pres-/ adjective **pres·by·te·ri·al** /,prezbi'ti(ə)rēəl, ,pres-/ adjective.
– ORIGIN Greek *presbuteros* 'elder.'

Pres·by·te·ri·an /,prezbə'tirēən, ,pres-/ ▶ **adjective** relating to a Protestant Church or branch governed by elders, all of equal rank. ▶ **noun** a member of a Presbyterian Church.
– DERIVATIVES **Pres·by·te·ri·an·ism** /,prezbə'tirēə,nizəm, ,pres-/ noun.

pres·by·ter·y /'prezbə,terē, 'pres-, -bətrē/ ▶ **noun** (pl. **presbyteries**) **1** (treated as sing. or pl.) a group of Church elders. **2** the house of a Roman Catholic parish priest. **3** the eastern part of a church near the altar.

pre·school /'prē'sko͞ol/ ▶ **adjective** relating to the time before a child is old enough to go to school. ▶ **noun** a school for children younger than those attending elementary school.

pre·scient /'presH(ē)ənt, 'prē-/ ▶ **adjective** having knowledge of events before they take place.

– DERIVATIVES **pre·science** noun **pre·scient·ly** adverb.
– ORIGIN from Latin *praescire* 'know beforehand.'

pre·scribe /pri'skrīb/ ▸ **verb 1** recommend and authorize the use of a medicine or treatment. **2** (often as adj. **prescribed**) state authoritatively that something should be done: *doing things in the prescribed way.*

– SYNONYMS **1 advise,** recommend, advocate, suggest. **2 stipulate,** lay down, dictate, order, direct, specify, determine.

– ORIGIN Latin *praescribere* 'direct in writing.'

USAGE

On the confusion between **prescribe** and **proscribe**, see the note at **PROSCRIBE**.

pre·scrip·tion /pri'skripsʜən/ ▸ **noun 1** a doctor's written instruction authorizing a patient to be issued with a medicine or treatment. **2** the action of prescribing a medicine or treatment. **3** an authoritative recommendation.

pre·scrip·tive /pri'skriptiv/ ▸ **adjective 1** relating to the enforcement of a rule or method. **2** (of a right, title, etc.) legally established by long usage.
– DERIVATIVES **pre·scrip·tiv·ism** /-'skriptə,vizəm/ noun **pre·scrip·tiv·ist** /-vist/ noun & adjective.
– ORIGIN Latin *praescriptivus* 'relating to a legal exception.'

pre·sea·son /'prē'sēzən/ ▸ **adjective** before the start of the season for a particular sport.

pres·ence /'prezəns/ ▸ **noun 1** the state or fact of being present. **2** a person's impressive manner or appearance. **3** a person or thing that is present but not seen. **4** a group of soldiers or police stationed in a particular place: *the US would maintain a presence in the region.*

– SYNONYMS **1** *the presence of a train was indicated electrically* **existence,** being there. **2** *I requested the presence of a nurse* **attendance,** appearance. **3** *a woman of great presence* **aura,** charisma, personality, magnetism.
– ANTONYMS absence.

– PHRASES **presence of mind** the ability to remain calm and take quick, sensible action in a difficult situation.
– ORIGIN Latin *praesentia* 'being at hand.'

pres·ent[1] /'prezənt/ ▸ **adjective 1** being or occurring in a particular place. **2** existing or occurring now. **3** Grammar (of a tense or participle) expressing an action now going on or a condition now existing.

– SYNONYMS **1 in attendance,** here, there, near, nearby, at hand, available. **2 in existence,** detectable, occurring, existing, extant, current.
– ANTONYMS absent.

▸ **noun 1** (**the present**) the period of time now occurring. **2** Grammar a present tense or form of a verb.

– SYNONYMS **now,** today, the present time, the here and now, modern times.
– ANTONYMS past, future.

– PHRASES **at present** now. **for the present** for now; temporarily. **these presents** Law, formal this document.
– ORIGIN Latin *praesens* 'being at hand.'

pres·ent[2] /pri'zent/ ▸ **verb 1** give something to someone formally or at a ceremony. **2** offer for acceptance or consideration: *he stopped and presented his passport.* **3** formally introduce someone to someone else. **4** put a show or exhibition before the public. **5** introduce and appear in a television or radio show. **6** be the cause of a problem. **7** give a particular impression to others: *the EU presented a united front over the crisis.* **8** (**present oneself**) appear at or attend a formal occasion.

– SYNONYMS **1 hand over,** give (out), confer, bestow, award, grant, accord. **2 submit,** set forth, put forward, offer, tender, table. **3 introduce,** make known, acquaint someone with. **4 host,** introduce, compère; informal emcee, MC. **5 represent,** describe, portray, depict.

– PHRASES **present arms** hold a rifle vertically in front of the body as a salute.
– ORIGIN Latin *praesentare* 'place before.'

pres·ent[3] /'prezənt/ ▸ **noun** a thing given to someone as a gift.

– SYNONYMS **gift,** donation, offering, contribution, gratuity, tip, handout.

– ORIGIN Old French.

CHOOSE THE RIGHT WORD

present, bonus, donation, gift, gratuity, lagniappe, largesse

What's the difference between a birthday **present** and a Christmas **gift**? Both words refer to something given as an expression of friendship, affection, esteem, etc. But *gift* is a more formal term, suggesting something of monetary value that is formally bestowed on an individual, group, or institution (*a gift to the university*). *Present*, on the other hand, implies something of less value that is an expression of goodwill (*a housewarming present; a present for the teacher*). **Largesse** is a somewhat pompous term for a very generous gift that is conferred in an ostentatious or condescending way, often on many recipients (*the king's largesse; the largesse of our government*). A **gratuity** is associated with tipping and other forms of voluntary compensation for special attention or service above and beyond what is included in a charge (*known for her generous gratuities, the duchess enjoyed watching the waiters compete with each other to serve her*), while a **lagniappe** is a Southern word, used chiefly in Louisiana and southeast Texas, for either a gratuity or a small gift given to a customer along with a purchase. If you give money or anything else as a gift to a philanthropic, charitable, or religious organization, it is known as a **donation** (*donations for the poor*). But if your employer gives you money at the end of the year in addition to your regular salary, it isn't a Christmas gift; it's a Christmas **bonus**.

pre·sent·a·ble /pri'zentəbəl/ ▸ **adjective** clean, well-dressed, or decent enough to be seen in public.

pres·en·ta·tion /,prē,zen'tāsʜən, ,prezən-, ,prēzən-/ ▸ **noun 1** the action of showing or giving something to someone. **2** the way in which something is presented: *the presentation of food is designed to stimulate your appetite.* **3** a talk or meeting at which a new product, idea, or piece of work is shown to an audience.

– SYNONYMS **1 awarding,** presenting, bestowal, granting. **2 appearance,** arrangement, packaging, layout. **3 demonstration,** talk, lecture, address, speech, show, exhibition, display, introduction, launch, unveiling.

– DERIVATIVES **pres·en·ta·tion·al** adjective **pres·en·ta·tion·al·ly** adverb.

pre·sen·ti·ment /pri'zentəmənt/ ▸ **noun** a feeling that something undesirable is going to happen.
– ORIGIN from former French *présentiment*.

pres·ent·ly /'prezəntlē/ ▸ **adverb 1** after a short time; soon. **2** at the present time; now.

– SYNONYMS **1 soon,** shortly, momentarily, quite soon, in a short time, in a little while, at any moment/minute/second, before long; informal in a sec. **2 at present,** currently, at the/this moment.

pres·ent par·ti·ci·ple ▶ **noun** Grammar the form of a verb, ending in *-ing*, that is used in forming tenses describing continuous action (e.g., *I'm thinking*), as a noun (e.g., *good thinking*), and as an adjective (e.g., *running water*).

pres·er·va·tion /ˌprezərˈvāsʜən/ ▶ **noun 1** the action of preserving something. **2** the degree to which something has been preserved: *the chapel is in a poor state of preservation.*

– SYNONYMS **1 conservation,** protection, care. **2 continuation,** conservation, maintenance, upholding, sustaining, perpetuation.

pres·er·va·tion·ist /ˌprezərˈvāsʜənəst/ ▶ **noun** a person who supports the preservation of historic buildings or works of art.

pre·serv·a·tive /priˈzərvətiv/ ▶ **noun** a substance used to prevent food or other materials from decaying. ▶ **adjective** preventing something from decaying.

pre·serve /priˈzərv/ ▶ **verb 1** keep something in its original or existing state. **2** keep a quality, situation, memory, etc., in existence: *a fight to preserve local democracy.* **3** keep something safe from harm. **4** treat food or other material to prevent it from decaying.

– SYNONYMS **1 conserve,** protect, maintain, care for, look after. **2 continue (with),** conserve, keep going, maintain, uphold, sustain, perpetuate, prolong. **3 guard,** protect, keep, defend, safeguard, shelter, shield.
– ANTONYMS attack, abandon.

▶ **noun 1** (usu. **preserves**) food made with fruit boiled in sugar, such as jam or marmalade. **2** something regarded as reserved for a particular person or group: *jobs that used to be the preserve of men.* **3** a place where game is protected and kept for private hunting.

– SYNONYMS **1** *jobs that are no longer the preserve of men* **domain,** area, field, sphere, orbit, realm, province, territory; informal turf, bailiwick. **2 sanctuary,** (game) reserve, reservation.

– DERIVATIVES **pre·serv·a·ble** adjective **pre·serv·er** noun.
– ORIGIN Latin *praeservare.*

pre·set /prēˈset/ ▶ **verb** (**presets, presetting, preset**) set the controls of a device at a certain level before using it. ▶ **noun** a control or level that is set or adjusted before use.

pre·shrunk /prēˈsʜrəNGk/ ▶ **adjective** (of a fabric or an item of clothing) shrunk during manufacture to prevent further shrinking when in use.

pre·side /priˈzīd/ ▶ **verb 1** (**preside over**) be in charge of a situation. **2** be in charge of a meeting, court, etc.

– SYNONYMS (**preside over**) **be in charge of,** be responsible for, head, manage, administer, control, direct, chair, conduct, officiate at, lead, govern, rule, command, supervise, oversee; informal head up.

– ORIGIN Latin *praesidere.*

pres·i·den·cy /ˈprez(ə)dənsē, ˈprezəˌdensē/ ▶ **noun** (pl. **presidencies**) **1** the office or position of president. **2** the period of time that a president is in office.

pres·i·dent /ˈprez(ə)dənt, ˈprezəˌdent/ ▶ **noun 1** the elected head of a republic. **2** the head of a society or similar organization. **3** the head of a bank or business.
– DERIVATIVES **pres·i·den·tial** /ˌprezəˈdencʜəl/ adjective.
– ORIGIN from Latin *praesidere* 'preside.'

pres·i·dent-e·lect ▶ **noun** (pl. **presidents-elect**) a person who has been elected president but has not yet taken office.

pre·sid·i·um /priˈsidēəm, -ˈzid-/ (also **praesidium**) ▶ **noun** a standing executive committee in a communist country.
– ORIGIN Russian *prezidium.*

press¹ /pres/ ▶ **verb 1** move into contact with something by using steady physical force. **2** apply pressure to something to flatten or shape it. **3** push something to operate a device. **4** move along by pushing. **5** forcefully put forward an opinion or claim. **6** make strong efforts to persuade someone to do something. **7** (**press on/ahead**) continue to do something. **8** extract juice or oil by crushing or squeezing fruit, vegetables, etc. **9** (of time) be short.

– SYNONYMS **1** *press the paper down firmly* **push (down),** depress, hold down, force, thrust, squeeze, compress. **2** *his shirt was pressed* **iron,** smooth out, flatten. **3** *she pressed the child to her bosom* **clasp,** hold close, hug, cuddle, squeeze, clutch, grasp, embrace. **4** *the crowd pressed around* **cluster,** gather, converge, congregate, flock, swarm, crowd. **5** *the government pressed its claim* **plead,** urge, advance, present, submit, put forward. **6** *they pressed him to agree* **urge,** put pressure on, pressurize, force, push, coerce, dragoon, steamroller, browbeat; informal lean on, put the screws on, twist someone's arm, railroad, bulldoze. **7** *they pressed for a ban* **call,** ask, clamor, push, campaign, demand.

▶ **noun 1** (**the press**) (treated as sing. or pl.) newspapers or journalists as a whole. **2** a device for crushing, flattening, or shaping something. **3** a printing press. **4** coverage in newspapers and magazines: *the government has had bad press for years.* **5** a closely packed mass of people or things.

– SYNONYMS (**the press**) **the media,** the newspapers, journalism, reporters, the fourth estate.

– DERIVATIVES **pres·ser** noun.
– PHRASES **be pressed for** have very little of something, especially time. **go to press** go to be printed.
– ORIGIN Latin *pressare* 'keep pressing.'

press² ▶ **verb** historical force someone to serve in the army or navy.
– PHRASES **press someone/thing into service** put someone or something to a specified use as a temporary measure.
– ORIGIN Latin *praestare* 'provide.'

press con·fer·ence ▶ **noun** a meeting held with journalists in order to make an announcement or answer questions.

press gang ▶ **noun** historical a group of men employed to force other men to serve in the army or navy. ▶ **verb** (**press-gang**) force someone to do something: *we press-ganged Simon into playing.*

press·ing /ˈpresiNG/ ▶ **adjective 1** requiring urgent action. **2** expressing something strongly.

– SYNONYMS **1 urgent,** critical, crucial, acute, desperate, serious, grave, life-and-death. **2 important,** high-priority, critical, crucial, unavoidable.

▶ **noun** a record or other object made by molding material under pressure.

press·man /'pres,mən, ,man/ ▶ **noun** (pl. **pressmen**) chiefly Brit. a journalist.

press re·lease ▶ **noun** an official statement issued to journalists.

pres·sure /'presHər/ ▶ **noun 1** the steady force brought to bear on an object by something in contact with it. **2** the use of persuasion or intimidation to make someone do something. **3** a feeling of stress caused by having many demands on one's time or resources: *she resigned due to the pressure of work*. **4** the force per unit area applied by a fluid against a surface.

– SYNONYMS **1 force,** load, stress, thrust, compression, weight. **2 persuasion,** intimidation, coercion, compulsion, duress, harassment, nagging, badgering. **3 strain,** stress, tension, trouble, difficulty, burden; informal hassle.

▶ **verb** try to persuade or force someone to do something.

– SYNONYMS **coerce,** pressurize, push, persuade, force, bulldoze, hound, nag, badger, browbeat, bully, intimidate, dragoon, twist someone's arm; informal railroad, lean on, hustle.

– ORIGIN Latin *pressura*.

pres·sure cook·er ▶ **noun** an airtight pot in which food can be cooked quickly under steam pressure.

pres·sure group ▶ **noun** a group that tries to influence government policy and public opinion in the interest of a particular cause.

pres·sur·ize /'presHə,rīz/ ▶ **verb 1** keep the air pressure in an aircraft cabin the same as it is at ground level. **2** try to persuade or force someone to do something.
– DERIVATIVES **pres·sur·i·za·tion** /,presHərə'zāsHən/ noun.

pres·ti·dig·i·ta·tion /,prestə,dijə'tāsHən/ ▶ **noun** formal magic tricks performed as entertainment.
– DERIVATIVES **pres·ti·dig·i·ta·tor** /-'dijə,tātər/ noun.
– ORIGIN French.

pres·tige /pres'tēzH, -'tēj/ ▶ **noun** respect and admiration resulting from achievements or high quality: *her prestige in Europe was tremendous*.

– SYNONYMS **status,** standing, kudos, cachet, stature, reputation, repute, renown, honor, esteem, importance, prominence, distinction.

– ORIGIN French, 'illusion, glamour.'

pres·tig·ious /pre'stijəs, -'stē-/ ▶ **adjective** having or bringing respect and admiration.

– SYNONYMS **reputable,** distinguished, respected, high-status, esteemed, eminent, highly regarded, renowned, influential.
– ANTONYMS disreputable, obscure.

pres·to /'prestō/ ▶ **adverb & adjective** Music in a quick tempo.
▶ **exclamation** suggesting that something has been done so easily that it seems to be magic.
– ORIGIN Italian, 'quick, quickly.'

pre·stressed /prē'strest/ ▶ **adjective** (of concrete) strengthened by means of rods or wires inserted under tension before setting.

pre·sum·a·bly /pri'zo͞oməblē/ ▶ **adverb** as may be supposed; probably.

pre·sume /pri'zo͞om/ ▶ **verb 1** suppose that something is probably the case. **2** be bold enough to do something that one does not have the right to do: *don't presume to give me orders in my own house*. **3** (**presume on/upon**) take advantage of someone's friendship or good nature.

– SYNONYMS **1 assume,** suppose, surmise, imagine, take it, expect. **2 dare,** venture, have the effrontery, be so bold as, go so far as, take the liberty of.

– DERIVATIVES **pre·sum·a·ble** adjective.
– ORIGIN Latin *praesumere* 'anticipate.'

pre·sump·tion /pri'zəmpsHən/ ▶ **noun 1** an act of presuming something to be the case. **2** an idea that is presumed to be true. **3** disrespectful or excessively bold behavior.

pre·sump·tive /pri'zəmptiv/ ▶ **adjective 1** presumed in the absence of further information. **2** behaving with disrespectful boldness; presumptuous.
– DERIVATIVES **pre·sump·tive·ly** adverb.

pre·sump·tu·ous /pri'zəmpcH(o͞o)əs/ ▶ **adjective** behaving with disrespectful boldness.

– SYNONYMS **brazen,** audacious, forward, familiar, impertinent, insolent, impudent, rude.

– DERIVATIVES **pre·sump·tu·ous·ly** adverb **pre·sump·tu·ous·ness** noun.

CHOOSE THE RIGHT WORD

See **BOLD**.

pre·sup·pose /,prēsə'pōz/ ▶ **verb 1** depend on something in order to exist or be true. **2** assume something to be the case.
– DERIVATIVES **pre·sup·po·si·tion** /,prē,səpə'zisHən/ noun.

pre·tend /pri'tend/ ▶ **verb 1** make it appear that something is the case when in fact it is not: *she turned the pages and pretended to read*. **2** (of a child) play an imaginative game. **3** give the appearance of feeling an emotion or having a quality. **4** (**pretend to**) claim to have a quality or title.

– SYNONYMS **put on an act,** act, play-act, put it on, dissemble, sham, feign, fake, dissimulate, make believe, put on a false front, posture, go through the motions, make as if.

▶ **adjective** informal imaginary; make-believe.

– SYNONYMS **mock,** fake, sham, simulated, artificial, false, pseudo; informal phony.

– ORIGIN Latin *praetendere* 'stretch forth, claim.'

pre·tend·er /pri'tendər/ ▶ **noun** a person who claims to have a right to a title or position.

pre·tense /'prē,tens, pri'tens/ ▶ **noun 1** an attempt to make something that is not the case appear true: *his anger was masked by a pretense that all was well*. **2** affected and pretentious behavior. **3** (**pretense to**) a claim to have or be something.

– SYNONYMS **1 make-believe,** acting, faking, play-acting, posturing, deception, trickery. **2 show,** semblance, affectation, appearance, outward appearance, impression, guise, facade.
– ANTONYMS honesty.

pre·ten·sion /pri'tencHən/ ▶ **noun 1** (often **pretensions**) a claim to a quality: *an aging rocker with literary pretensions*. **2** the action of trying to appear more important or better than one actually is.

pre·ten·tious /pri'tencHəs/ ▶ **adjective** attempting to impress others by pretending to be more important or better than one actually is.

– SYNONYMS **affected,** ostentatious, showy, pompous, overblown, high-sounding, flowery, grandiose; informal pseudo.

– DERIVATIVES **pre·ten·tious·ly** adverb **pre·ten·tious·ness** noun.

pret·er·it /'pretərit/ (also **preterite**) Grammar ▶ **adjective** expressing a past action or state. ▶ **noun** a simple past tense or form.
– ORIGIN Latin *praeteritus*.

pre·term /prē'tərm/ ▶ **adjective & adverb** after a pregnancy significantly shorter than normal: *babies born during preterm labor*.

pre·ter·nat·u·ral /ˌprētər'nacʜ(ə)rəl/ ▶ **adjective** beyond what is normal or natural.
– DERIVATIVES **pre·ter·nat·u·ral·ly** adverb.
– ORIGIN from Latin *praeter* 'past, beyond.'

pre·text /'prēˌtekst/ ▶ **noun** a false reason used to justify an action.
– ORIGIN Latin *praetextus* 'outward display.'

pre·tor /'prētər/ ▶ **noun** variant spelling of **PRAETOR**.

pre·treat /prē'trēt/ ▶ **verb** treat something with a chemical before use.
– DERIVATIVES **pre·treat·ment** noun.

pret·ti·fy /'pritəˌfī/ ▶ **verb** (**prettifies, prettifying, prettified**) make something appear pretty.
– DERIVATIVES **pret·ti·fi·ca·tion** /ˌpritəfə'kāsʜən/ noun.

pret·ty /'pritē/ ▶ **adjective** (**prettier, prettiest**) **1** (of a woman or girl) attractive in a delicate way. **2** pleasant in appearance: *a pretty dress*. **3** informal used to express displeasure: *a pretty state of affairs*.

– SYNONYMS **attractive,** good-looking, nice-looking, personable, fetching, prepossessing, appealing, charming, delightful, cute; Scottish bonny; old use fair, comely.
– ANTONYMS plain, ugly.

▶ **adverb** informal to a certain extent; fairly.

– SYNONYMS **quite,** rather, somewhat, fairly.

▶ **noun** (pl. **pretties**) informal a pretty object.
– DERIVATIVES **pret·ti·ly** adverb **pret·ti·ness** noun.
– PHRASES **be sitting pretty** informal be in a favorable position. **a pretty penny** informal a large sum of money.
– ORIGIN Old English, 'cunning,' later 'clever, pleasing.'

pret·zel /'pretsəl/ ▶ **noun** a crisp or soft bread baked in the shape of a knot or stick and flavored with salt.
– ORIGIN German.

pre·vail /pri'vāl/ ▶ **verb 1** be widespread or current: *a friendly atmosphere prevailed among the crowds*. **2** be more powerful: *it is hard for logic to prevail over emotion*. **3** (**prevail on**) persuade someone to do something.

– SYNONYMS **1 exist,** be present, be the case, occur, be prevalent, be in force. **2 win,** triumph, be victorious, carry the day, come out on top, succeed, rule, reign.

– ORIGIN Latin *praevalere* 'have greater power.'

pre·vail·ing /pri'vāliɴɢ/ ▶ **adjective** most common or frequent.

– SYNONYMS *prevailing attitudes* **current,** existing, prevalent, usual, common, general, widespread.

pre·vail·ing wind ▶ **noun** a wind from the predominant or most usual direction.

prev·a·lent /'prevələnt/ ▶ **adjective** widespread in a particular area at a particular time.

– SYNONYMS **widespread,** frequent, usual, common, current, popular, general.
– ANTONYMS rare.

– DERIVATIVES **prev·a·lence** noun.
– ORIGIN from Latin *praevalere* (see **PREVAIL**).

CHOOSE THE RIGHT WORD

prevalent, prevailing, abundant, plentiful, rife, copious, common

Wildflowers might be **prevalent** in the mountains during the spring months, but a particular type of wildflower might be the **prevailing** one. *Prevalent*, in other words, implies widespread occurrence or acceptance in a particular place or time (*a prevalent belief during the nineteenth century*), while *prevailing* suggests that something exists in such quantity that it surpasses or leads all others in acceptance, usage, or belief (*the prevailing theory about the evolution of man*). Wildflowers might also be **abundant** in the valleys—a word that, unlike *prevalent* and *prevailing*, is largely restricted to observations about a place and may suggest oversupply (*an abundant harvest; indications of decay were abundant*). **Plentiful**, on the other hand, refers to a large or full supply without the connotations of oversupply (*a country where jobs were plentiful*). If wildflowers are **rife**, it means that they are not only *prevalent* but spreading rapidly (*speculation was rife among the soldiers*); if they're **copious**, it means they are being produced in such quantity that they constitute a rich or flowing abundance (*weep copious tears*). What often happens, with wildflowers as well as with other beautiful things, is that they become so abundant they are regarded as **common**, a word meaning usual or ordinary (*the common cold*). Like *prevalent*, *common* can apply to a time as well as a place (*an expression common during the Depression*). But neither *abundant* nor *common* connotes dominance as clearly as *prevalent* does.

pre·var·i·cate /pri'variˌkāt/ ▶ **verb** avoid giving a direct answer to a question.
– DERIVATIVES **pre·var·i·ca·tion** /priˌvari'kāsʜən/ noun **pre·var·i·ca·tor** noun.
– ORIGIN Latin *praevaricari* 'walk crookedly, deviate.'

pre·vent /pri'vent/ ▶ **verb 1** stop something from happening or arising. **2** stop someone from doing something.

– SYNONYMS **stop,** avert, nip in the bud, foil, inhibit, thwart, prohibit, forbid.
– ANTONYMS allow.

– DERIVATIVES **pre·vent·a·ble** adjective **pre·vent·er** noun **pre·ven·tion** /pri'vencʜən/ noun.
– ORIGIN Latin *praevenire* 'precede, hinder.'

pre·ven·tive /pri'ventiv/ (also **preventative**) ▶ **adjective** designed to prevent something from happening. ▶ **noun** a medicine or other treatment intended to prevent disease or poor health.

pre·view /'prēˌvyo͞o/ ▶ **noun 1** a viewing or display of something before it becomes generally available. **2** a publicity article or trailer of a forthcoming movie, book, etc. ▶ **verb** provide or have a preview of a product, movie, etc.
– DERIVATIVES **pre·view·er** noun.

pre·vi·ous /'prēvēəs/ ▶ **adjective 1** coming before in time or order. **2** informal too hasty in acting.

– SYNONYMS *the previous commissioner retired after more than 40 years of service* **foregoing,** preceding; old, earlier, prior, former, ex-, past, last, sometime, one-time, erstwhile; formal quondam.
– ANTONYMS next.

– PHRASES **previous to** before.
– ORIGIN Latin *praevius* 'going before.'

pre·vi·ous·ly /ˈprēvēəslē/ ▸ **adverb** at an earlier time.

– SYNONYMS *previously, only the outermost doors were locked at night* **formerly,** earlier (on), before, hitherto, at one time, in the past.

pre·war /prēˈwôr/ ▸ **adjective** occurring or existing before a war.

prey /prā/ ▸ **noun 1** an animal hunted and killed by another for food. **2** a person who is easily exploited or harmed. **3** a person prone to experiencing distressing emotions.

– SYNONYMS **1 quarry,** kill. **2 victim,** target, dupe; informal sucker.
– ANTONYMS predator.

▸ **verb** (**prey on**) **1** hunt and kill another animal for food. **2** take advantage of someone. **3** cause constant distress to: *the problem had begun to prey on my mind.*
– ORIGIN Old French *preie.*

pri·ap·ic /prīˈapik, -ˈāpik/ ▸ **adjective 1** relating to male sexuality. **2** relating to an erect penis.
– DERIVATIVES **pri·a·pism** /ˈprīəˌpizəm/ noun.
– ORIGIN from Greek *Priapos,* a god of fertility.

price /prīs/ ▸ **noun 1** the amount of money for which something is bought or sold. **2** something unwelcome that has to be done or given in order to achieve an aim: *some inequality would be a fair price to pay for a society where there is no poverty.* **3** the odds in betting.

– SYNONYMS **1 cost,** charge, fee, fare, amount, sum; informal damage. **2 consequence,** result, cost, penalty, toll, sacrifice, downside, drawback, disadvantage, minus.

▸ **verb** decide the price of something.
– PHRASES **at any price** no matter what is involved. **at a price** at a high cost. **what price something?** what has become of or what is the chance of something?
– ORIGIN Old French *pris.*

price·less /ˈprīsləs/ ▸ **adjective 1** very valuable or precious. **2** informal very amusing.

– SYNONYMS **invaluable,** beyond price, irreplaceable, expensive, costly.
– ANTONYMS worthless, cheap.

price tag ▸ **noun** the cost of something.

pric·ey /ˈprīsē/ ▸ **adjective** (**pricier, priciest**) informal expensive.

prick /prik/ ▸ **verb 1** make a small hole in something with a sharp point. **2** feel as though a sharp point or points were sticking into one. **3** cause mental or emotional discomfort to: *her conscience pricked her when she lied.*

– SYNONYMS **pierce,** puncture, stab, perforate, spike, penetrate, jab.

▸ **noun 1** an act of pricking someone or something. **2** a sharp pain, hole, or mark caused by pricking. **3** vulgar slang a man's penis. **4** vulgar slang a stupid or unpleasant man.

– SYNONYMS **jab,** sting, pinprick, stab, pinhole, wound.

– DERIVATIVES **prick·er** noun.
– PHRASES **kick against the pricks** hurt oneself by continuing to resist something that cannot be changed. [with reference to Acts of the Apostles, chapter 9.] **prick up one's ears 1** (of a horse or dog) make the ears stand erect when alert. **2** (of a person) suddenly begin to pay attention.
– ORIGIN Old English.

prick·le /ˈprikəl/ ▸ **noun 1** a small thorn on a plant or a short spine on an animal. **2** a tingling or mildly painful feeling on the skin. ▸ **verb** have a tingling feeling on the skin.
– ORIGIN Old English.

prick·ly /ˈprik(ə)lē/ ▸ **adjective** (**pricklier, prickliest**) **1** covered in prickles. **2** having or causing a prickling feeling. **3** easily offended.

– SYNONYMS **spiky,** spiked, thorny, barbed, spiny, bristly.

prick·ly heat ▸ **noun** an itchy skin rash experienced in hot moist weather.

prick·ly pear ▸ **noun** a cactus that produces prickly, pear-shaped fruits.

pride /prīd/ ▸ **noun 1** deep pleasure or satisfaction gained from achievements, qualities, or possessions. **2** a cause or source of deep pleasure or satisfaction: *the swimming pool was the pride of the village.* **3** a feeling of self-respect. **4** an excessively high opinion of oneself. **5** a group of lions forming a social unit.

– SYNONYMS **1 self-esteem,** dignity, honor, self-respect. **2 pleasure,** joy, delight, gratification, fulfillment, satisfaction, sense of achievement. **3 arrogance,** vanity, self-importance, hubris, conceitedness, egotism, snobbery.
– ANTONYMS shame, humility.

▸ **verb** (**pride oneself on**) be especially proud of a quality or skill.
– DERIVATIVES **pride·ful** /-fəl/ adjective.
– PHRASES **pride of place** the most noticeable position.
– ORIGIN Old English.

CHOOSE THE RIGHT WORD

pride, arrogance, conceit, egotism, self-esteem, vainglory, vanity

If you take **pride** in yourself or your accomplishments, it means that you believe in your own worth, merit, or superiority—whether or not that belief is justified (*she took pride in her accomplishments*). When your opinion of yourself is exaggerated, you're showing **conceit**, a word that combines *pride* with self-obsession. If you like to be noticed and admired for your appearance or achievements, you're revealing your **vanity**, and if you show off or boast about your accomplishments, you're likely to be accused of **vainglory**, a somewhat literary term for a self-important display of power, skill, or influence. **Arrogance** is an overbearing pride combined with disdain for others (*his arrogance led him to assume that everyone else would obey his orders*), while **egotism** implies self-centeredness or an excessive preoccupation with yourself (*blinded by egotism to the suffering of others*). While no one wants to be accused of *arrogance* or *egotism*, there's a lot to be said for **self-esteem**, which may suggest undue pride but is more often used to describe a healthy belief in oneself and respect for one's worth as a person (*she suffered from low self-esteem*).

prie-dieu /prē ˈdyə(r), -ˈdyœ/ ▸ **noun** (pl. **prie-dieux** pronunc. same) a piece of furniture used for prayer, consisting of a kneeling surface and a narrow upright front with a rest for the elbows or for books.
– ORIGIN French, 'pray God.'

priest /prēst/ ▸ **noun 1** an ordained minister of the Catholic, Orthodox, or Anglican Church, authorized to perform certain ceremonies. **2** a person who performs ceremonies in a non-Christian religion.

– SYNONYMS **clergyman,** clergywoman, minister, cleric, pastor, vicar, rector, parson, churchman, churchwoman, father, curate. informal reverend, padre.

– DERIVATIVES **priest·hood** /ˈprēstˌho͝od, ˈprēˌsto͝od/ noun **priest·ly** adjective.
– ORIGIN Old English.

WORD LINKS

clerical, sacerdotal *relating to priests*

priest·ess /ˈprēstis/ ▶ **noun** a female priest of a non-Christian religion.

prig /prig/ ▶ **noun** a person who behaves as if they are morally superior to others.
– DERIVATIVES **prig·gish** adjective.
– ORIGIN unknown.

prim /prim/ ▶ **adjective** (**primmer, primmest**) very formal and correct and disapproving of anything improper or rude.

– SYNONYMS **demure,** formal, stuffy, strait-laced, prudish, prissy, mimsy, priggish, puritanical. informal starchy.

– DERIVATIVES **prim·ly** adverb **prim·ness** noun.
– ORIGIN probably from Old French *prin*, 'excellent, delicate.'

pri·ma bal·le·ri·na /ˈprēmə/ ▶ **noun** the chief female dancer in a ballet or ballet company.
– ORIGIN Italian.

pri·ma·cy /ˈprīməsē/ ▶ **noun** the fact of being primary or most important.
– ORIGIN Latin *primatia*.

pri·ma don·na /ˌprimə ˈdänə, ˌprēmə/ ▶ **noun 1** the chief female singer in an opera or opera company. **2** a very temperamental and self-important person.
– ORIGIN Italian, 'first lady.'

pri·ma fa·ci·e /ˌprīmə ˈfāsʜə, ˈfāsʜē, ˈfāsʜēˌē/ ▶ **adjective & adverb** Law accepted as correct until proved otherwise.
– ORIGIN Latin.

pri·mal /ˈprīməl/ ▶ **adjective 1** at a very primitive or early stage of development; primeval. **2** Psychology relating to feelings or behavior believed to form the origins of emotional life: *primal fears*.
– ORIGIN Latin *primalis*.

pri·ma·ri·ly /prīˈme(ə)rəlē/ ▶ **adverb** for the most part; mainly.

– SYNONYMS **1 first and foremost,** firstly, essentially, in essence, fundamentally, principally, predominantly. **2 mostly,** for the most part, chiefly, mainly, in the main, on the whole, largely, principally, predominantly.

pri·ma·ry /ˈprīˌmerē, ˈprīm(ə)rē/ ▶ **adjective 1** of chief importance; principal. **2** earliest in time or order. **3** relating to education for children between the ages of about five and eleven.

– SYNONYMS **main,** chief, key, prime, central, principal, foremost, first, most important, predominant, paramount; informal number-one.
– ANTONYMS secondary.

▶ **noun** (pl. **primaries**) a preliminary election to appoint delegates to a party conference or to select candidates for an election.
– ORIGIN Latin *primarius*.

pri·ma·ry care ▶ **noun** health care received by people making an initial approach to a doctor or nurse for treatment.

pri·ma·ry col·or ▶ **noun** any of a group of colors from which all others can be obtained by mixing.

pri·ma·ry in·dus·try ▶ **noun** an industry concerned with obtaining or providing raw materials, such as mining or agriculture.

pri·mate /ˈprīˌmāt, ˈprīmət/ ▶ **noun 1** a mammal of an order including monkeys, apes, and humans. **2** (in the Christian Church) an archbishop.
– ORIGIN from Latin *primas* 'of the first rank.'

pri·ma·tol·o·gy /ˌprīməˈtäləjē/ ▶ **noun** the branch of zoology concerned with monkeys and other primates.
– DERIVATIVES **pri·ma·tol·o·gist** noun.

prime[1] /prīm/ ▶ **adjective 1** most important; main. **2** of the highest quality; excellent. **3** (of a number) that can be divided only by itself and one (e.g., 2, 3, 5, 7).

– SYNONYMS **1 main,** chief, key, primary, central, principal, foremost, first, most important, paramount, major; informal number-one. **2 top-quality,** top, best, first-class, superior, choice, select, finest; informal tip-top, A1.
– ANTONYMS secondary, inferior.

▶ **noun 1** a time of greatest vigor or success in a person's life. **2** a prime number.

– SYNONYMS **heyday,** peak, pinnacle, high point/spot, zenith, flower, bloom, flush.

– ORIGIN from Latin *prima hora* 'first hour.'

prime[2] ▶ **verb 1** prepare someone for a situation by giving them relevant information. **2** make something, especially a firearm or bomb, ready for use or action. **3** cover a surface with primer. **4** pour or spray liquid into a pump to make it operate more easily.

– SYNONYMS **brief,** fill in, prepare, advise, instruct, coach, drill, train.

– PHRASES **prime the pump** stimulate the growth or success of something with funding.
– ORIGIN probably from Latin *primus* 'first.'

prime min·is·ter ▶ **noun** the head of the elected government in some countries, such as the UK and Canada.

prime mov·er ▶ **noun** a person who originates a plan or project.

prim·er[1] /ˈprīmər/ ▶ **noun** a substance painted on a surface as a base coat.

prim·er[2] ▶ **noun** a book providing a basic introduction to a subject or used for teaching reading.
– ORIGIN from Latin *primarius liber* 'primary book' and *primarium manuale* 'primary manual.'

prime rate ▶ **noun** the lowest rate of interest at which money may be borrowed commercially.

prime time ▶ **noun** the time at which a radio or television audience is expected to be greatest.

pri·me·val /prīˈmēvəl/ ▶ **adjective 1** relating to the earliest time in history. **2** (of behavior or emotion) not based on reason; instinctive.
– ORIGIN Latin *primaevus*.

prim·i·tive /ˈprimətiv/ ▶ **adjective 1** relating to the earliest times in history or stages in development of something: *primitive mammals*. **2** referring to a simple form of society that has not yet developed writing or industry. **3** offering a very basic level of comfort or convenience. **4** (of behavior or emotion) not based on reason; instinctive.

– SYNONYMS **1 ancient,** earliest, first, prehistoric, primordial, primeval. **2 crude,** simple, rough (and ready), basic, rudimentary, makeshift.
– ANTONYMS modern, sophisticated.

▶ **noun 1** a person belonging to a primitive society. **2** a painter who deliberately uses a simple, naive style that rejects conventional techniques.
– DERIVATIVES **prim·i·tive·ly** adverb **prim·i·tive·ness** noun.
– ORIGIN Latin *primitivus* 'first of its kind.'

prim·i·tiv·ism /ˈprimətiv,izəm/ ▶ **noun 1** a belief in the value of what is simple and unsophisticated, expressed especially through art or literature. **2** instinctive and unreasoning behavior.
– DERIVATIVES **prim·i·tiv·ist** noun & adjective.

pri·mo·gen·i·ture /,prīmōˈjeni,CHər, -,CHo͝or/ ▶ **noun 1** the state of being the firstborn child. **2** the system by which the firstborn child, especially the eldest son, inherits all his parents' property.
– ORIGIN Latin *primogenitura*.

pri·mor·di·al /prīˈmôrdēəl/ ▶ **adjective** existing at or from the beginning of time; primeval.
– ORIGIN Latin *primordialis* 'first of all.'

WORD TOOLKIT

See **PREHISTORIC**.

pri·mor·di·al soup ▶ **noun** a solution rich in organic compounds from which life on earth is supposed to have originated.

primp /primp/ ▶ **verb** make minor adjustments to one's hair, clothes, or makeup.
– ORIGIN related to **PRIM**.

prim·rose /ˈprim,rōz/ ▶ **noun 1** a plant of European woodlands with pale yellow flowers. **2** a pale yellow color.
– PHRASES **primrose path** the pursuit of pleasure, especially when bringing undesirable consequences. [with reference to Shakespeare's *Hamlet* I. iii. 50.]
– ORIGIN probably related to Latin *prima rosa* 'first rose.'

prim·u·la /ˈprimyələ/ ▶ **noun** a plant of a genus that includes primroses, cowslips, and polyanthus.
– ORIGIN from Latin *primula veris* 'little first thing.'

prince /prins/ ▶ **noun 1** a son or other close male relative of a monarch. **2** a male monarch of a small country. **3** (in some European countries) a nobleman.

– SYNONYMS **ruler,** sovereign, monarch, crowned head.

– DERIVATIVES **prince·dom** /-dəm/ noun.
– ORIGIN from Latin *princeps* 'first, chief, sovereign.'

Prince Charm·ing ▶ **noun** a handsome and honorable young male lover.
– ORIGIN from French *Roi Charmant*, 'King Charming,' the title of a fairy tale.

prince con·sort ▶ **noun** the husband of a reigning queen who is himself a prince.

prince·ling /ˈprinsliNG/ ▶ **noun 1** the ruler of a small or unimportant country. **2** a young prince.

prince·ly /ˈprinslē/ ▶ **adjective 1** relating to or suitable for a prince. **2** (of a sum of money) generous.

Prince of Dark·ness ▶ **noun** the Devil.

Prince of Wales ▶ **noun** a title granted to the heir apparent to the British throne (usually the eldest son of the monarch).

prin·cess /ˈprinsəs, ˈprin,ses, prinˈses/ ▶ **noun 1** a daughter or other close female relative of a monarch. **2** the wife or widow of a prince. **3** a female monarch of a small country.

prin·ci·pal /ˈprinsəpəl/ ▶ **adjective** most important; main.

– SYNONYMS **main,** chief, primary, leading, foremost, first, most important, predominant, dominant, preeminent, highest, top; informal number-one.
– ANTONYMS minor.

▶ **noun 1** the most important person in an organization or group. **2** the head of a school. **3** a sum of money lent or invested, on which interest is paid. **4** a person for whom another acts as a representative. **5** Law a person directly responsible for a crime.

– SYNONYMS **head teacher,** headmaster, headmistress, head, dean, rector, master, mistress, chancellor, vice chancellor, president, provost, warden.

– DERIVATIVES **prin·ci·pal·ship** /-,SHip/ noun.
– ORIGIN Latin *principalis* 'first, original.'

USAGE

Do not confuse **principal** and **principle**. **Principal** is usually an adjective meaning 'main or most important' (*the country's principal cities*), whereas **principle** is a noun that usually means 'a truth or general law used as the basis for something' (*the basic principles of democracy*).

prin·ci·pal·i·ty /,prinsəˈpalətē/ ▶ **noun** (pl. **principalities**) a country ruled by a prince.

prin·ci·pal·ly /ˈprinsəp(ə)lē/ ▶ **adverb** for the most part; chiefly.

– SYNONYMS **mainly,** mostly, chiefly, for the most part, in the main, on the whole, largely, predominantly, primarily.

prin·ci·ple /ˈprinsəpəl/ ▶ **noun 1** a truth or general law that is used as a basis for a theory or system of belief: *the basic principles of democracy*. **2** (usu. **principles**) a rule or belief governing a person's behavior. **3** morally correct behavior: *a man of principle*. **4** a general scientific theorem or natural law. **5** a fundamental quality or basis of something. **6** Chemistry an active or characteristic constituent of a substance.

– SYNONYMS **1 truth,** concept, idea, theory, fundamental, essential, precept, rule, law. **2 doctrine,** belief, creed, credo, code, ethic. **3 morals,** morality, ethics, ideals, standards, integrity, virtue, probity, honor, decency, conscience, scruples.

– PHRASES **in principle** in theory. **on principle** because of one's beliefs about what is right and wrong.
– ORIGIN Latin *principium* 'source.'

prin·ci·pled /ˈprinsəpəld/ ▶ **adjective** (of actions or behavior) based on one's beliefs about what is right and wrong.

– SYNONYMS **moral,** ethical, virtuous, righteous, upright, upstanding, honorable, honest.

print /print/ ▶ **verb 1** produce books, newspapers, etc., by a process involving the transfer of words or images to paper. **2** produce words or an image by printing. **3** produce a paper copy of information stored on a computer. **4** produce a photographic print from a negative. **5** write words clearly without joining the letters. **6** transfer a colored design onto fabric or another surface.

> – SYNONYMS **1 publish,** issue, release, circulate, run off, copy, reproduce. **2 imprint,** impress, stamp, mark.

▶ **noun 1** the printed words appearing in a book, newspaper, etc. **2** a mark where something has pressed or touched a surface: *paw prints*. **3** a printed picture or design. **4** a photograph printed on paper from a negative or transparency. **5** a copy of a motion picture on film. **6** a piece of fabric with a colored design.

> – SYNONYMS **1 type,** printing, letters, lettering, characters, typeface, font. **2 impression,** handprint, fingerprint, footprint. **3 picture,** engraving, etching, lithograph, woodcut. **4 photograph,** photo, snap, snapshot, picture, still, enlargement, reproduction, copy.

– DERIVATIVES **print·a·ble** adjective.
– PHRASES **in print 1** (of a book) available from the publisher. **2** in published form. **out of print** (of a book) no longer available from the publisher.
– ORIGIN Old French *preinte* 'pressed.'

print·ed cir·cuit ▶ **noun** an electronic circuit based on thin strips of a conductor on an insulating board.

print·er /'printər/ ▶ **noun 1** a person or business involved in printing. **2** a machine for printing, especially one linked to a computer.

print·ing /'printiNG/ ▶ **noun 1** the production of books, newspapers, etc. **2** all the copies of a book printed at one time. **3** handwriting in which the letters are written separately.

print·ing press ▶ **noun** a machine for printing from type or plates.

print·mak·er /'print,mākər/ ▶ **noun** a person who creates and prints pictures or designs from plates or blocks.
– DERIVATIVES **print·mak·ing** noun.

print·out /'print,out/ ▶ **noun** a page of printed material from a computer's printer.

print run ▶ **noun** the number of copies of a book, magazine, etc., printed at one time.

pri·on /'prē,än/ ▶ **noun** a protein particle believed to be the cause of certain brain diseases, such as BSE.
– ORIGIN by rearrangement of elements from *pro(teinaceous) in(fectious particle)*.

pri·or[1] /'prīər/ ▶ **adjective** coming before in time, order, or importance: *the government denied having any prior knowledge of the attack.*

> – SYNONYMS **earlier,** previous, preceding, advance, preexisting.
> – ANTONYMS subsequent.

– PHRASES **prior to** before.
– ORIGIN Latin, 'former, elder.'

prior[2] ▶ **noun** (fem. **prioress** /'prīərəs/) **1** (in an abbey) the person next in rank below an abbot (or abbess). **2** the head of a house of friars (or nuns).
– ORIGIN from Latin, 'former, elder.'

pri·or·i·tize /prī'ôrə,tīz, 'prīərə-/ ▶ **verb 1** treat something as most important. **2** decide the order of importance of items or tasks.
– DERIVATIVES **pri·or·i·ti·za·tion** /,prī,ôrətə'zāSHən/ noun.

pri·or·i·ty /prī'ôrətē/ ▶ **noun** (pl. **priorities**) **1** the condition of being treated as more important: *safety should take priority over any other matter.* **2** a thing regarded as more important than others.

> – SYNONYMS **1 precedence,** preference, preeminence, predominance, primacy. **2 prime concern,** main consideration, most important thing.

pri·or re·straint ▶ **noun** Law suppression of material before it is published or broadcast, on the grounds that it is libelous or harmful.

pri·o·ry /'prīərē/ ▶ **noun** (pl. **priories**) a monastery or nunnery governed by a prior or prioress.

prise ▶ **verb** variant spelling of **PRIZE**[2].

prism /'prizəm/ ▶ **noun 1** a transparent object with triangular ends that breaks light up into the colors of the rainbow. **2** a solid geometric figure whose two ends are parallel and of the same size and shape, and whose sides are parallelograms.
– ORIGIN Greek *prisma* 'thing sawn.'

pris·mat·ic /priz'matik/ ▶ **adjective 1** relating to or in the shape of a prism. **2** (of colors) formed or distributed by a prism.

pris·on /'prizən/ ▶ **noun** a building in which criminals or people awaiting trial are confined.

> – SYNONYMS *the prisons upstate are just as crowded* **jail,** jailhouse, penitentiary, correctional facility, penal institution; informal clink, slammer, can, pen, hoosegow, the big house, joint, stir, pokey, cooler; **(be in prison)** informal be inside, do time, be behind bars.

– ORIGIN Old French *prisun*.

pris·on camp ▶ **noun** a camp where prisoners of war or political prisoners are kept.

pris·on·er /'priz(ə)nər/ ▶ **noun 1** a person found guilty of a crime and sent to prison. **2** a person captured and kept confined. **3** a person trapped by a situation: *he was a prisoner of his own fame.*

> – SYNONYMS **1 convict,** detainee, inmate; informal jailbird, con, yardbird. **2 prisoner of war,** POW, internee, captive, hostage.

– PHRASES **take no prisoners** be ruthless in attempting to achieve one's objectives.

pris·on·er of con·science ▶ **noun** a person imprisoned for their political or religious views.

pris·on·er of war ▶ **noun** a person captured and imprisoned by the enemy in war.

pris·sy /'prisē/ ▶ **adjective** (**prissier, prissiest**) excessively concerned with behaving in a respectable way.
– DERIVATIVES **pris·si·ly** adverb **pris·si·ness** noun.
– ORIGIN perhaps from **PRIM** and **SISSY**.

pris·tine /'pris,tēn, pri'stēn/ ▶ **adjective 1** in its original condition; unspoiled: *two miles of pristine beaches.* **2** clean and fresh as if new.

> – SYNONYMS **immaculate,** perfect, in mint condition, as new, spotless, unspoiled.
> – ANTONYMS dirty, spoiled.

– DERIVATIVES **pris·tine·ly** adverb.
– ORIGIN Latin *pristinus* 'former.'

> **WORD TOOLKIT**
>
> See **IMPECCABLE**.

pri·va·cy /'prīvəsē/ ▶ **noun** a state in which one is not watched or disturbed by others.

– SYNONYMS **seclusion,** solitude, isolation.

pri·vate /ˈprīvit/ ▶ **adjective 1** for or belonging to one particular person or group only. **2** (of thoughts or feelings) not to be revealed to others. **3** not revealing thoughts and feelings to others. **4** (of a place) free from people who may overhear or interrupt. **5** (of a service or industry) provided by a person or commercial business rather than the government. **6** working for oneself rather than for the government or an organization. **7** not connected with one's work or official position: *the president visited the country in a private capacity.*

– SYNONYMS **1** *his private plane* **personal,** own, special, exclusive. **2** *private talks* **confidential,** secret, classified, privileged, unofficial, off the record; informal hush-hush. **3** *private thoughts* **intimate,** personal, secret, innermost, undisclosed, unspoken, unvoiced. **4** *a very private man* **reserved,** introverted, self-contained, reticent, retiring, unsociable, withdrawn, solitary, reclusive, secretive. **5** *they found a private place in which to talk* **secluded,** undisturbed, out of the way, remote, isolated. **6** *private industry* **independent,** nongovernmental, privatized, commercial, private-enterprise.
– ANTONYMS public, open, official.

▶ **noun 1** (also **private soldier**) a soldier of the lowest rank in the army. **2** (**privates**) informal private parts; genitals.

– SYNONYMS **soldier,** GI, trooper.

– DERIVATIVES **pri·vate·ly** adverb.
– PHRASES **in private** with no one else present.
– ORIGIN Latin *privatus* 'withdrawn from public life.'

pri·vate en·ter·prise ▶ **noun** business or industry managed by independent companies rather than by the government.

pri·va·teer /ˌprīvəˈtir/ ▶ **noun** historical a privately owned armed ship, authorized by a government for use in war.

pri·vate eye ▶ **noun** informal a private investigator.

pri·vate in·ves·ti·ga·tor (also **private detective**) ▶ **noun** a detective who is not a police officer and who carries out investigations for private clients.

pri·vate life ▶ **noun** a person's personal relationships, interests, etc., as distinct from their work or public life.

pri·vate parts ▶ **plural noun** euphemistic a person's genitals.

pri·vate school ▶ **noun 1** a school supported by a private organization or individuals. **2** Brit. an independent school that is wholly financed by fees paid by students.

pri·vate sec·re·tar·y ▶ **noun 1** a secretary who deals with the personal matters of their employer. **2** a civil servant acting as an assistant to a senior government official.

pri·vate sec·tor ▶ **noun** the part of a country's economy not under direct government control.

pri·va·tion /prīˈvāsHən/ ▶ **noun** a state in which essentials such as food are lacking.
– ORIGIN Latin.

pri·va·tize /ˈprīvəˌtīz/ ▶ **verb** transfer a business or industry from public to private ownership.
– DERIVATIVES **pri·va·ti·za·tion** /ˌprīvətəˈzāsHən/ noun.

priv·et /ˈprivit/ ▶ **noun** a shrub with small dark green leaves.
– ORIGIN unknown.

priv·i·lege /ˈpriv(ə)lij/ ▶ **noun 1** a special right or advantage granted or available to a particular person or group. **2** an opportunity to do something regarded as a special honor: *she had the privilege of giving the opening lecture.* **3** the rights and advantages of rich and powerful people: *a young man of wealth and privilege.*

– SYNONYMS **1 advantage,** benefit, prerogative, entitlement, right, concession, freedom, liberty. **2 honor,** pleasure.

– ORIGIN Latin *privilegium* 'bill or law affecting an individual.'

priv·i·leged /ˈpriv(ə)lijd/ ▶ **adjective 1** having a special right or advantage. **2** (of information) legally protected from being made public.

– SYNONYMS **1 wealthy,** rich, affluent, prosperous, elite, advantaged. **2 confidential,** private, secret, restricted, classified, not for publication, off the record, inside; informal hush-hush.
– ANTONYMS underprivileged, disadvantaged.

priv·y /ˈprivē/ ▶ **adjective** (**privy to**) sharing in the knowledge of something secret. ▶ **noun** (pl. **privies**) a toilet in a small shed outside a house.
– DERIVATIVES **priv·i·ly** adverb.
– ORIGIN Old French *prive* 'private,' also 'private place.'

prix fixe /ˈprē ˈfēks, ˈfiks/ ▶ **noun** a meal of several courses costing a fixed price.
– ORIGIN French, 'fixed price.'

prize¹ /prīz/ ▶ **noun 1** something given as a reward to a winner or to recognize an outstanding achievement. **2** something of great value that is worth struggling to achieve: *the prize will be victory in the election.*

– SYNONYMS **award,** reward, trophy, medal, cup, winnings, purse, honor.

▶ **adjective 1** having been or likely to be awarded a prize. **2** outstanding of its kind.

– SYNONYMS **1 champion,** prize-winning, award-winning, top, best. **2 utter,** complete, total, absolute, real, perfect.

▶ **verb** value highly: *the berries were prized for their healing properties.*
– ORIGIN Old French *preisier* 'praise.'

prize² /prīz/ (also **prise**) ▶ **verb 1** force something open or apart. **2** (**prize something out of/from**) obtain something from someone with difficulty.

prized /prīzd/ ▶ **adjective** highly valued: *the bicycle was her most prized possession.*

– SYNONYMS **treasured,** precious, cherished, much loved, beloved, valued, esteemed, highly regarded.

prize·fight /ˈprīzˌfīt/ ▶ **noun** a boxing match for prize money.
– DERIVATIVES **prize·fight·er** noun.

pro¹ /prō/ ▶ **noun** (pl. **pros**) informal a professional. ▶ **adjective** professional.

pro² ▶ **noun** (pl. **pros**) (usu. in phrase **pros and cons**) an advantage or argument in favor of something. ▶ **preposition & adverb** in favor of.
– ORIGIN Latin, 'for, on behalf of.'

pro-¹ ▶ **prefix 1** in favor of; supporting: *pro-choice.* **2** referring to movement forward, out, or away: *propel.* **3** acting as a substitute for: *proconsul.*
– ORIGIN Latin *pro* 'in front of, instead of, because of.'

pro-² ▶ **prefix** before in time or order: *proactive.*
– ORIGIN Greek *pro.*

pro·ac·tive /prō'aktiv/ ▶ **adjective** creating or controlling a situation rather than just responding to it.
– DERIVATIVES **pro·ac·tive·ly** adverb.

pro-am /'prō 'am/ ▶ **adjective** (of a sports event) involving both professionals and amateurs.

prob·a·bi·lis·tic /ˌpräbəbə'listik/ ▶ **adjective** based on a theory of probability; involving chance.

prob·a·bil·i·ty /ˌpräbə'bilətē/ ▶ **noun** (pl. **probabilities**) **1** the extent to which something is likely to happen or be the case: *rain will make the probability of postponement even greater*. **2** a probable or the most probable event.

– SYNONYMS **likelihood,** prospect, expectation, chance(s), odds, possibility.

– PHRASES **in all probability** most probably.

prob·a·ble /'präbəbəl/ ▶ **adjective** likely to happen or be the case.

– SYNONYMS **likely,** odds-on, expected, anticipated, predictable; informal in the cards, a safe bet.
– ANTONYMS unlikely.

▶ **noun** a person likely to become or do something.
– ORIGIN Latin *probabilis*.

prob·a·bly /'präbəblē, 'präblē/ ▶ **adverb** almost certainly.

– SYNONYMS **in all likelihood,** in all probability, as likely as not, ten to one, the chances are, doubtless.

pro·bate /'prōˌbāt/ ▶ **noun 1** the official process of proving that a will is valid. **2** a verified copy of a will with a certificate as handed to the executors.
– ORIGIN Latin *probatum* 'something proved.'

pro·ba·tion /prō'bāsʜən/ ▶ **noun 1** the release of an offender from detention or prison on condition that they behave well and report regularly to a supervisor. **2** a period of training and testing a person in a new job or role.

– SYNONYMS **trial,** trial period, apprenticeship, training.

– DERIVATIVES **pro·ba·tion·ar·y** /-ˌnerē/ adjective.

CHOOSE THE RIGHT WORD

See **NOVICE**.

pro·ba·tion·er /prō'bāsʜənər/ ▶ **noun 1** a person serving a period of probation in a job or role. **2** an offender on probation from detention or prison.

pro·ba·tion of·fi·cer ▶ **noun** a person who supervises offenders on probation.

probe /prōb/ ▶ **noun 1** a thorough investigation: *a probe into political corruption*. **2** a blunt-ended surgical instrument for exploring a wound or part of the body. **3** a small measuring or testing device, especially an electrode. **4** an unmanned exploratory spacecraft.

– SYNONYMS **investigation,** inquiry, examination, inquest, study.

▶ **verb 1** investigate something thoroughly. **2** explore or examine something with the hands or an instrument.

– SYNONYMS **1 prod,** poke, dig into, delve into, explore, feel around in, examine. **2 investigate,** inquire into, look into, go into, study, examine, explore.

– DERIVATIVES **prob·er** noun **prob·ing** adjective.
– ORIGIN from Latin *proba* 'examination.'

pro·bi·ot·ic /ˌprōbī'ätik/ ▶ **noun** a substance that stimulates the growth of beneficial microorganisms, especially the natural bacteria in the intestines.

pro·bi·ty /'prōbitē/ ▶ **noun** the quality of having strong moral principles; honesty and good character.

– SYNONYMS **integrity,** honesty, uprightness, decency, morality, rectitude, goodness, virtue.
– ANTONYMS untrustworthiness.

– ORIGIN Latin *probitas*.

prob·lem /'präbləm/ ▶ **noun 1** a thing that is difficult to deal with or understand. **2** a question that can be resolved by using logical thought or mathematics.

– SYNONYMS **1 difficulty,** worry, complication, snag, hitch, drawback, stumbling block, obstacle, hiccup, setback, catch, dilemma, quandary; informal headache, fly in the ointment. **2 nuisance,** bother; informal drag, pain, hassle. **3 puzzle,** question, poser, riddle, conundrum; informal brain-teaser.

– ORIGIN Greek *problēma*.

prob·lem·at·ic /ˌpräblə'matik/ ▶ **adjective** difficult to deal with or understand; presenting a problem.

– SYNONYMS **difficult,** troublesome, tricky, awkward, controversial, ticklish, complicated, complex, knotty.
– ANTONYMS easy, straightforward.

– DERIVATIVES **prob·lem·at·i·cal** adjective **prob·lem·at·i·cal·ly** adverb.

prob·lem·a·tize /'präbləməˌtīz/ ▶ **verb** make something into or regard something as a problem.

pro bo·no /ˌprō 'bônō, 'bōnō/ ▶ **adverb & adjective** referring to legal work undertaken without charge.
– ORIGIN Latin.

pro·bos·cis /prə'bäsəs, -'bäskəs/ ▶ **noun** (pl. **probosces** /-'bäsēz/ or **proboscises**) **1** the long flexible nose of a mammal, such as an elephant's trunk. **2** an elongated sucking organ or mouthpart of an insect or worm.
– ORIGIN Greek *proboskis* 'means of obtaining food.'

pro·bos·cis mon·key ▶ **noun** a monkey native to the forests of Borneo, the male of which has a large dangling nose.

pro·caine /'prōˌkān/ ▶ **noun** a synthetic compound used as a local anesthetic.
– ORIGIN from **PRO-**[1] (denoting substitution) + *-caine* (from **COCAINE**).

pro·car·y·ote ▶ **noun** variant spelling of **PROKARYOTE**.

pro·ce·dure /prə'sējər/ ▶ **noun 1** an established or official way of doing something. **2** a series of actions carried out in a certain way. **3** a surgical operation.

– SYNONYMS **course of action,** method, system, strategy, way, approach, formula, mechanism, technique, routine, drill, practice.

– DERIVATIVES **pro·ce·dur·al** adjective **pro·ce·dur·al·ly** adverb.
– ORIGIN French *procédure*.

pro·ceed /prə'sēd, prō-/ ▶ **verb 1** begin a course of action. **2** do something after something else: *she got up and proceeded to cook us breakfast*. **3** (of an action) continue. **4** move forward. **5** start a lawsuit against someone.

– SYNONYMS **1 begin,** make a start, get going, move. **2 go,** make one's way, advance, move, progress, carry on, continue, press on, push on.
– ANTONYMS stop.

– ORIGIN Latin *procedere*.

pro·ceed·ings /prəˈsēdiNGz, prō-/ ▶ **plural noun 1** an event or a series of activities with a set procedure. **2** action taken in a court of law to settle a dispute. **3** a report of a set of meetings or a conference.

– SYNONYMS **1 events,** activities, action, happenings, goings-on. **2 report,** transactions, minutes, account, story, record(s). **3 legal action,** litigation, suit, lawsuit, case, prosecution.

pro·ceeds /ˈprōˌsēdz/ ▶ **plural noun** money obtained from an event or activity.

– SYNONYMS **profits,** earnings, receipts, returns, take, income, revenue, profit, yield; Sports gate.

proc·ess[1] /ˈpräˌses, ˈpräsəs, ˈprō-/ ▶ **noun 1** a series of actions or steps taken toward achieving a particular end. **2** a natural series of changes: *the aging process.* **3** a summons to appear in a court of law. **4** a natural projection or growth on the body or in an organism.

– SYNONYMS **1 procedure,** operation, action, activity, exercise, business, job, task, undertaking. **2** *a new manufacturing process* **method,** system, technique, means.

▶ **verb 1** deal with by means of an established procedure: *an administrator is needed to process applications.* **2** treat raw material, food, etc., in order to change or preserve it. **3** operate on data by means of a computer program.

– SYNONYMS **deal with,** attend to, see to, sort out, handle, take care of.

– ORIGIN Latin *processus* 'progression, course.'

proc·ess[2] /prəˈses/ ▶ **verb** (of people or vehicles) move forward in an orderly way.
– ORIGIN from **PROCESSION**.

pro·ces·sion /prəˈseSHən/ ▶ **noun 1** a number of people or vehicles moving forward in an orderly way. **2** the action of moving forward in an orderly way. **3** a large number of people or things coming one after the other.

– SYNONYMS **parade,** march, cavalcade, motorcade, cortège, column, file.

pro·ces·sion·al /prəˈseSHənl/ ▶ **adjective** relating to a religious or ceremonial procession. ▶ **noun** a book of litanies and hymns used in Christian religious processions.

proc·es·sor /ˈpräsˌesər, ˈpräsəsər, ˈprō-/ ▶ **noun 1** a machine that processes something. **2** a central processing unit in a computer.

pro-choice /prōˈCHois/ ▶ **adjective** supporting the right of a woman to choose to have an abortion.

pro·claim /prəˈklām, prō-/ ▶ **verb 1** announce something officially or publicly. **2** declare someone officially or publicly to be: *he proclaimed James as King of England.* **3** show clearly; be a sign of: *his high forehead proclaimed his strength of mind.*

– SYNONYMS **declare,** announce, pronounce, state, make known, give out, advertise, publish, broadcast, trumpet.

– ORIGIN Latin *proclamare* 'cry out.'

CHOOSE THE RIGHT WORD

See **ANNOUNCE**.

proc·la·ma·tion /ˌpräkləˈmāSHən/ ▶ **noun** a public or official announcement: *the Church issued a proclamation denouncing the movie.*

– SYNONYMS **declaration,** announcement, pronouncement, statement, notification, broadcast, assertion, profession, protestation, decree, order, edict, ruling.

pro·cliv·i·ty /prōˈklivətē, prə-/ ▶ **noun** (pl. **proclivities**) a tendency to do something regularly; an inclination.

– SYNONYMS **inclination,** tendency, leaning, disposition, proneness, propensity, bent, bias, penchant, predisposition, predilection, partiality, liking, preference, taste, fondness.

– ORIGIN Latin *proclivitas.*

pro·con·sul /prōˈkänsəl/ ▶ **noun 1** a governor or deputy consul of a colony. **2** a governor of a province in ancient Rome.

pro·cras·ti·nate /prəˈkrastəˌnāt, prō-/ ▶ **verb** delay or postpone action.

– SYNONYMS **delay,** put off doing something, postpone action, defer action, play for time, dawdle; informal dilly-dally.

– DERIVATIVES **pro·cras·ti·na·tion** /prəˌkrastəˈnāSHən, prō-/ noun **pro·cras·ti·na·tor** /-ˌnātər/ noun.
– ORIGIN Latin *procrastinare* 'defer till the morning.'

pro·cre·ate /ˈprōkrēˌāt/ ▶ **verb** produce young; reproduce.
– DERIVATIVES **pro·cre·a·tion** /ˌprōkrēˈāSHən/ noun **pro·cre·a·tive** /-krēˌātiv/ adjective.
– ORIGIN Latin *procreare* 'generate, bring forth.'

Pro·crus·te·an /prəˈkrəstēən, prō-/ ▶ **adjective** literary enforcing uniformity regardless of natural variation or individuality.
– ORIGIN from *Procrustes,* a robber in Greek mythology who fitted victims to a bed by stretching or cutting off parts of them.

proc·tol·o·gy /präkˈtäləjē/ ▶ **noun** the branch of medicine concerned with the anus and rectum.
– DERIVATIVES **proc·to·log·i·cal** /ˌpräktəˈläjikəl/ adjective **proc·tol·o·gist** noun.
– ORIGIN from Greek *prōktos* 'anus.'

proc·tor /ˈpräktər/ ▶ **noun** a person who monitors students during an examination.
– ORIGIN contraction of **PROCURATOR**.

proc·u·ra·tor /ˈpräkyəˌrātər/ ▶ **noun** an agent representing others in a court of law.
– ORIGIN Latin *procurator* 'administrator, finance agent.'

pro·cure /prəˈkyo͝or, prō-/ ▶ **verb 1** get or obtain something. **2** Law persuade or cause someone to do something. **3** provide a prostitute for someone.
– DERIVATIVES **pro·cur·a·ble** adjective **pro·cure·ment** noun **pro·cur·er** noun.
– ORIGIN Latin *procurare* 'take care of, manage.'

CHOOSE THE RIGHT WORD

See **GET**.

prod /präd/ ▶ **verb** (**prods, prodding, prodded**) **1** poke someone or something with a finger or pointed object. **2** persuade someone who is reluctant or slow to do something.

– SYNONYMS **1 poke,** jab, stab, dig, nudge, elbow. **2 spur,** stimulate, prompt, push, galvanize, persuade, urge, remind.

▶ **noun 1** a poke. **2** a reminder to do something. **3** a pointed implement used to drive cattle.
– ORIGIN perhaps from **POKE**[1] and dialect *brod* 'to goad, prod.'

prod·i·gal /'prädigəl/ ▶ **adjective 1** using money or resources in a wasteful way. **2** (**prodigal with**) having lavish amounts of something.

– SYNONYMS **wasteful,** extravagant, spendthrift.
– ANTONYMS thrifty.

▶ **noun 1** a wasteful and extravagant person. **2** (also **prodigal son**) a person who leaves home and lives a wasteful and extravagant life but returns repentant.
– DERIVATIVES **prod·i·gal·i·ty** /ˌprädə'galətē/ noun **prod·i·gal·ly** adverb.
– ORIGIN Latin *prodigalis*; noun sense 2 with reference to the Gospel of Luke, chapter 15.

pro·di·gious /prə'dijəs/ ▶ **adjective** impressively large.
– DERIVATIVES **pro·di·gious·ly** adverb.
– ORIGIN Latin *prodigiosus*.

prod·i·gy /'prädəjē/ ▶ **noun** (pl. **prodigies**) **1** a young person with exceptional abilities. **2** an outstanding example of a quality: *his book is a prodigy of information gathering*.

– SYNONYMS **genius,** mastermind, virtuoso, wunderkind; informal whiz kid, whiz.

– ORIGIN Latin *prodigium* 'portent.'

pro·duce ▶ **verb** /prə'd(y)o͞os, prō-/ **1** make, manufacture, or create something. **2** cause to happen or exist: *a report has concluded that richer colleges produce better results*. **3** show or provide something for inspection or use. **4** administer the financial and managerial aspects of a movie or broadcast or the staging of a play. **5** supervise the making of a musical recording.

– SYNONYMS **1 manufacture,** make, construct, build, fabricate, put together, assemble, turn out, create, mass-produce. **2 yield,** grow, give, supply, provide, furnish, bear. **3 give birth to,** bear, deliver, bring forth, bring into the world. **4 create,** fashion, turn out, compose, write, pen, paint. **5 pull out,** extract, fish out, present, offer, proffer, show. **6 cause,** bring about, give rise to, occasion, generate, lead to, result in, provoke, precipitate, spark, trigger. **7 stage,** put on, mount, present, exhibit.

▶ **noun** /'präd(y)o͞os, 'prō-/ things that have been produced or grown: *fresh produce from the garden*.

– SYNONYMS **food,** foodstuff(s), products, crops, harvest.

– DERIVATIVES **pro·duc·i·ble** adjective.
– ORIGIN Latin *producere* 'bring forth, extend, produce.'

pro·duc·er /prə'd(y)o͞osər, prō-/ ▶ **noun 1** a person, company, or country that makes, grows, or supplies something. **2** a person responsible for the financial and managerial aspects of a movie or broadcast or the staging of a play.

– SYNONYMS **1** *a car producer* **manufacturer,** maker, builder, constructor. **2** *coffee producers* **grower,** farmer. **3** *the producer of the show* **impresario,** manager, administrator, promoter, director.

prod·uct /'prädəkt/ ▶ **noun 1** an article or substance manufactured for sale. **2** a result of an action or process: *the arrests were the product of a lengthy investigation*. **3** a substance produced during a natural, chemical, or manufacturing process. **4** Mathematics a quantity obtained by multiplying quantities together.

– SYNONYMS **1 commodity,** artifact; (**products**) goods, wares, -ware, merchandise, produce. **2 result,** consequence, outcome, effect, upshot.

– ORIGIN Latin *productum* 'something produced.'

pro·duc·tion /prə'dəkshən, prō-/ ▶ **noun 1** the action of producing something or the process of being produced. **2** the amount of something produced. **3** a movie, play, or music recording viewed in terms of the way it is made or staged: *a new production of "Hamlet."*

– SYNONYMS **1 manufacture,** making, construction, building, fabrication, assembly, creation, mass production. **2 creation,** origination, fashioning, composition, writing. **3 output,** yield, productivity. **4 performance,** staging, presentation, show, piece, play.

pro·duc·tion line ▶ **noun** an assembly line in a factory.

pro·duc·tive /prə'dəktiv, prō-/ ▶ **adjective 1** producing or able to produce large amounts of goods or crops. **2** achieving or producing a significant amount or result: *a long and productive career*.

– SYNONYMS **1 prolific,** inventive, creative. **2 useful,** constructive, profitable, fruitful, valuable, effective, worthwhile, helpful. **3 fertile,** fruitful, rich, fecund.

– DERIVATIVES **pro·duc·tive·ly** adverb **pro·duc·tive·ness** noun.

pro·duc·tiv·i·ty /ˌprōˌdək'tivətē, ˌprädək-, prəˌdək-/ ▶ **noun 1** the state of being productive. **2** the efficiency with which things are produced: *workers boosted productivity by 30 percent*.

– SYNONYMS **efficiency,** work rate, output, yield, production.

prod·uct place·ment ▶ **noun** a practice in which companies pay for their products to be featured in movies and television programs.

pro·fane /prə'fān, prō-/ ▶ **adjective 1** not holy or religious; secular. **2** not showing respect for God or holy things. **3** (of language) blasphemous or obscene.

– SYNONYMS **1** *subjects both sacred and profane* **secular,** lay, non-religious. **2** *profane language* **obscene,** blasphemous, indecent, foul, vulgar, crude, filthy, dirty, coarse, rude, offensive.
– ANTONYMS decorous.

▶ **verb** treat something holy with disrespect.

– SYNONYMS *invaders profaned our temples* **desecrate,** violate, defile.

– DERIVATIVES **prof·a·na·tion** /ˌpräfə'nāshən, ˌprō-/ noun.
– ORIGIN Latin *profanus* 'outside the temple, not sacred.'

pro·fan·i·ty /prə'fanətē, prō-/ ▶ **noun** (pl. **profanities**) **1** behavior that shows a lack of respect for God or holy things. **2** a swear word.

– SYNONYMS **1 swear word,** oath, expletive, curse, obscenity, four-letter word, dirty word, blasphemy, swearing, foul language, bad language, cursing. **2** *acts of profanity* **sacrilege,** blasphemy, ungodliness, impiety, irreverence, disrespect.

pro·fess /prə'fes, prō-/ ▶ **verb 1** claim, often falsely, that something is true or the case: *she lied, cheated, and then professed her undying love*. **2** state openly that one has a particular feeling, opinion, etc. **3** belong to a particular religion.

– SYNONYMS **1 declare,** announce, proclaim, assert, state, affirm, maintain, protest, avow. **2 claim,** pretend, purport, affect, make out.

– ORIGIN Latin *profiteri* 'declare publicly.'

pro·fessed /prə'fest, prō-/ ▶ **adjective 1** (of a quality or feeling) claimed openly but often falsely. **2** openly declared to be: *a professed liberal*.

– SYNONYMS **1 claimed,** supposed, ostensible, self-styled, apparent, pretended, purported. **2 declared,** sworn, confirmed, self-confessed.

– DERIVATIVES **pro·fess·ed·ly** /prəˈfesədlē, -ˈfestlē/ adverb.

pro·fes·sion /prəˈfesHən/ ▶ **noun 1** an occupation that involves training and a formal qualification. **2** (treated as sing. or pl.) a group of people working in a profession: *the legal profession.* **3** a claim that is often false. **4** a declaration of belief in a religion.

– SYNONYMS **career,** occupation, calling, vocation, métier, line of work, job, business, trade, craft.

pro·fes·sion·al /prəˈfesHənl/ ▶ **adjective 1** relating or belonging to a profession. **2** engaged in a sport or other activity as a paid occupation rather than as an amateur. **3** appropriate to a professional person; competent or skillful.

– SYNONYMS **1 white-collar,** nonmanual, graduate, qualified, chartered. **2 paid,** salaried. **3 expert,** accomplished, skillful, masterly, fine, polished, skilled, proficient, competent, able, businesslike, deft. **4** *he always behaved in a professional way* **appropriate,** fitting, proper, honorable, ethical.
– ANTONYMS amateur, amateurish.

▶ **noun 1** a person who is engaged or qualified in a profession. **2** a person who is very skilled in a particular activity.

– SYNONYMS **expert,** virtuoso, old hand, master, maestro, past master; informal pro, ace.

– DERIVATIVES **pro·fes·sion·al·ize** /prəˈfesHənlˌīz/ verb **pro·fes·sion·al·ly** adverb.

pro·fes·sion·al·ism /prəˈfesHənlˌizəm/ ▶ **noun** the competence or skill expected of a professional.

pro·fes·sor /prəˈfesər/ ▶ **noun 1** a college or university teacher. **2** a university academic of the highest rank. **3** a person who openly declares their faith.
– DERIVATIVES **pro·fes·so·ri·al** /ˌpräfəˈsôrēəl/ adjective **pro·fes·sor·ship** /-ˌSHip/ noun.
– ORIGIN Latin.

prof·fer /ˈpräfər/ ▶ **verb** offer something to someone for acceptance.
– ORIGIN Old French *proffrir.*

pro·fi·cient /prəˈfisHənt/ ▶ **adjective** competent or skilled in doing or using something: *she's proficient in Urdu.*

– SYNONYMS **skilled,** skillful, expert, accomplished, competent, masterly, adept, adroit, deft, dexterous, able, professional; informal crack, ace, mean.
– ANTONYMS incompetent.

– DERIVATIVES **pro·fi·cien·cy** noun **pro·fi·cient·ly** adverb.
– ORIGIN from Latin *proficere* 'to advance.'

pro·file /ˈprōˌfīl/ ▶ **noun 1** an outline of something, especially a face, as seen from one side. **2** a descriptive article about someone. **3** the extent to which a person or organization attracts public notice: *her high profile as a pop star.*

– SYNONYMS **1 outline,** silhouette, side view, contour, shape, form, lines. **2 description,** account, study, portrait, rundown, sketch, outline.

▶ **verb 1** describe someone in an article. **2 (be profiled)** appear in outline.
– DERIVATIVES **pro·fil·er** noun.
– PHRASES **in profile** as seen from one side. **keep a low profile** try not to attract attention.
– ORIGIN from former Italian *profilo* 'a drawing or border.'

pro·fil·ing /ˈprōˌfīliNG/ ▶ **noun** the analysis of a person's psychological and behavioral characteristics.

prof·it /ˈpräfit/ ▶ **noun 1** a financial gain, especially the difference between the amount earned and the costs involved in producing, buying, or operating something. **2** the advantage or benefit gained from something.

– SYNONYMS **1 financial gain,** return(s), yield, proceeds, earnings, winnings, surplus; informal pay dirt, bottom line. **2 advantage,** benefit, value, use, good; informal mileage.
– ANTONYMS loss, disadvantage.

▶ **verb (profits, profiting, profited)** benefit, especially financially: *the only people to profit from the episode were the lawyers.*

– SYNONYMS **1 make money,** earn; informal rake it in, clean up, make a fast buck, make a killing. **2 benefit,** be advantageous to, be of use to, do someone good, help, be of service to, serve.
– ANTONYMS lose.

– DERIVATIVES **prof·it·less** adjective.
– ORIGIN Latin *profectus* 'progress, profit.'

prof·it·a·ble /ˈpräfitəbəl/ ▶ **adjective 1** (of a business or activity) making a profit. **2** beneficial; useful: *he'd had a profitable day.*

– SYNONYMS **1 moneymaking,** profit-making, paying, lucrative, commercial, successful, gainful. **2 beneficial,** useful, advantageous, valuable, productive, worthwhile, rewarding, fruitful, illuminating, informative, well spent.

– DERIVATIVES **prof·it·a·bil·i·ty** /ˌpräfitəˈbilətē/ noun **prof·it·a·bly** adverb.

prof·it and loss ac·count ▶ **noun** an account to which incomes and gains are added and expenses and losses taken away, so as to show the net profit or loss.

prof·it·eer·ing /ˌpräfəˈti(ə)riNG/ ▶ **noun** the making of an excessive profit in an unfair or dishonest way.
– DERIVATIVES **prof·it·eer** /ˌpräfəˈti(ə)r/ noun.

pro·fit·er·ole /prəˈfitəˌrōl/ ▶ **noun** a small hollow pastry filled with cream and covered with chocolate sauce.
– ORIGIN French, 'small profit.'

prof·it mar·gin ▶ **noun** the difference between the cost of producing something and the price for which it is sold.

prof·it-shar·ing ▶ **noun** a system in which the people who work for a company receive a direct share of its profits.

prof·li·gate /ˈpräfligət, -ləˌgāt/ ▶ **adjective 1** recklessly extravagant or wasteful. **2** indulging excessively in physical pleasures; licentious. ▶ **noun** a licentious or wasteful person.
– DERIVATIVES **prof·li·ga·cy** /ˈpräfligəsē/ noun.
– ORIGIN Latin *profligatus* 'dissolute.'

pro for·ma /prō ˈfôrmə/ ▶ **adverb & adjective** as a matter of form or politeness. ▶ **noun** a standard document or form.
– ORIGIN Latin.

pro·found /prəˈfound, prō-/ ▶ **adjective (profounder, profoundest) 1** very great or intense: *profound feelings of disquiet.* **2** showing great knowledge or insight. **3** demanding deep study or thought. **4** old use very deep.

– SYNONYMS **1 heartfelt,** intense, keen, extreme, acute, severe, sincere, earnest, deep, deep-seated, overpowering, overwhelming. **2 far-reaching,** radical, extensive, sweeping, exhaustive, thoroughgoing. **3 wise,** learned, intelligent,

scholarly, discerning, penetrating, perceptive, astute, thoughtful, insightful.
– ANTONYMS superficial.

– DERIVATIVES **pro·found·ly** adverb.
– ORIGIN Latin *profundus*.

pro·fun·di·ty /prəˈfəndətē/ ▶ **noun** (pl. **profundities**) **1** great depth of insight or knowledge. **2** intensity of a state, quality, or emotion.

pro·fuse /prəˈfyo͞os, prō-/ ▶ **adjective** done or appearing in large quantities; abundant: *I offered my profuse apologies*.

– SYNONYMS **1** *profuse apologies* **copious,** prolific, abundant, liberal, unstinting, fulsome, effusive, extravagant, lavish, gushing. **2** *profuse blooms* **luxuriant,** plentiful, copious, abundant, lush, rich, exuberant, riotous, teeming, rank, rampant.
– ANTONYMS meager, sparse.

– DERIVATIVES **pro·fuse·ly** adverb.
– ORIGIN Latin *profusus* 'lavish, spread out.'

pro·fu·sion /prəˈfyo͞ozʜən, prō-/ ▶ **noun** a large quantity of something; an abundance.

pro·gen·i·tor /prəˈjenətər, prō-/ ▶ **noun 1** an ancestor or parent. **2** a person who originates a cultural or intellectual movement.
– DERIVATIVES **pro·gen·i·to·ri·al** /-ˌjenəˈtôrēəl/ adjective.
– ORIGIN Latin.

prog·e·ny /ˈpräjənē/ ▶ **noun** (treated as sing. or pl.) the offspring of a person or animal.
– ORIGIN Old French *progenie*.

pro·ges·ter·one /prōˈjestəˌrōn, prə-/ ▶ **noun** a hormone that stimulates the uterus to prepare for pregnancy.

pro·ges·to·gen /prōˈjestəjən/ ▶ **noun** a hormone that maintains pregnancy and prevents further ovulation, used in oral contraceptives.

prog·na·thous /ˈprägnəᴛʜəs, prägˈnā-/ ▶ **adjective** (of a jaw or chin) projecting.
– ORIGIN from **PRO-**[2] + Greek *gnathos* 'jaw.'

prog·no·sis /prägˈnōsəs/ ▶ **noun** (pl. **prognoses** /-ˌsēz/) a forecast, especially of the likely course of a medical condition.
– ORIGIN Greek.

prog·nos·tic /prägˈnästik/ ▶ **adjective** predicting the likely course of a medical condition.
– DERIVATIVES **prog·nos·ti·cal·ly** /-ik(ə)lē/ adverb.

prog·nos·ti·cate /prägˈnästəˌkāt/ ▶ **verb** make a forecast about a future event.
– DERIVATIVES **prog·nos·ti·ca·tion** /prägˌnästəˈkāsʜən/ noun **prog·nos·ti·ca·tor** /-ˌkātər/ noun.

pro·gram /ˈprōˌgram, -grəm/ (Brit. **programme**) ▶ **noun 1** a planned series of events. **2** a radio or television broadcast. **3** a set of related measures or activities with a long-term aim: *a program of reforms*. **4** a sheet or booklet giving details of a performance or event. **5** (Brit. **program**) a series of coded software instructions to control the operation of a computer or other machine.

– SYNONYMS **1 schedule,** agenda, calendar, timetable, order (of the day), lineup. **2 scheme,** plan, package, strategy, initiative, proposal. **3 broadcast,** production, show, presentation, transmission, performance. **4 course,** syllabus, curriculum.

▶ **verb** (**programs, programming, programmed**; or **programing, programed**) **1** (Brit. **program**) provide a computer with a program. **2** cause a person or animal to behave in a predetermined way. **3** arrange something according to a plan or schedule.

– SYNONYMS **arrange,** organize, schedule, slate, plan, map out, timetable, line up.

– DERIVATIVES **pro·gram·ma·ble** /ˈprōˌgraməbəl, prōˈgram-/ adjective **pro·gram·mer** noun.
– ORIGIN Greek *programma*.

pro·gram·mat·ic /ˌprōgrəˈmatik/ ▶ **adjective** relating to a program, schedule, or method.
– DERIVATIVES **pro·gram·mat·i·cal·ly** /-ik(ə)lē/ adverb.

prog·ress ▶ **noun** /ˈprägrəs, ˈprägˌres, ˈprōˌgres/ **1** forward movement toward a destination. **2** development toward an improved or more advanced condition: *some states had made significant progress in nuclear technology*.

– SYNONYMS **1 (forward) movement,** advance, going, headway, passage. **2 development,** advance, advancement, headway, step forward, improvement, growth.

▶ **verb** /prəˈgres/ **1** move toward a destination. **2** develop toward a more advanced condition.

– SYNONYMS **1 go,** make one's way, move, proceed, advance, go on, continue, make headway, work one's way. **2 develop,** make progress, advance, make headway, move on, get on, gain ground, improve, get better, come on, come along, make strides.
– ANTONYMS regress.

– ORIGIN Latin *progressus* 'an advance.'

pro·gres·sion /prəˈgresʜən/ ▶ **noun 1** a gradual movement or development toward a destination or a more advanced state. **2** a number of things in a series. **3** a sequence of numbers following a mathematical rule.

– SYNONYMS **1 progress,** advancement, movement, passage, development, evolution, growth. **2 succession,** series, sequence, string, stream, chain, train, row, cycle.

– DERIVATIVES **pro·gres·sion·al** adjective.

pro·gres·sive /prəˈgresiv/ ▶ **adjective 1** happening or developing gradually: *a progressive decline in popularity*. **2** favoring social reform or original thinking. **3** (of tax) at a rate increasing with the sum taxed. **4** (of a lens) allowing an infinite number of focusing distances for near, intermediate, and far vision.

– SYNONYMS **1 continuing,** continuous, ongoing, gradual, step-by-step, cumulative. **2 modern,** liberal, advanced, forward-thinking, enlightened, pioneering, reforming, reformist, radical; informal go-ahead.
– ANTONYMS conservative.

▶ **noun 1** a person who favors social reform. **2** (**progressives**) progressive lenses, or eyeglasses with such lenses.
– DERIVATIVES **pro·gres·sive·ly** adverb **pro·gres·sive·ness** noun.

pro·hib·it /prəˈhibit, prō-/ ▶ **verb** (**prohibits, prohibiting, prohibited**) **1** formally forbid someone from doing something by law or a rule. **2** make impossible; prevent: *the budget agreement had prohibited any tax cuts*.

– SYNONYMS **1 forbid,** ban, bar, proscribe, make illegal, outlaw, disallow, veto. **2 prevent,** stop, rule out, preclude, make impossible.
– ANTONYMS allow.

– DERIVATIVES **pro·hib·i·to·ry** /-ˌtôrē/ adjective.
– ORIGIN Latin *prohibere* 'keep in check.'

CHOOSE THE RIGHT WORD

prohibit, ban, disallow, enjoin, forbid, hinder, interdict, preclude

There are a number of ways to prevent something from happening. You can **prohibit** it, which assumes that you have legal or other authority and are willing to back up your prohibition with force (*prohibit smoking*); or you can simply **forbid** it and hope that you've got the necessary clout (*forbid teenagers to stay out after midnight*). **Ban** carries a little more weight—both legal and moral—and **interdict** suggests that church or civil authorities are behind the idea. To **enjoin** (in this sense) is to prohibit by legal injunction (*the truckers were enjoined from striking*), which practically guarantees that you'll get what you want. A government or some other authority may **disallow** an act it might otherwise have permitted (*the IRS disallowed the deduction*), but anyone with a little gumption can **hinder** an activity by putting obstacles in its path (*hinder the thief's getaway by tripping him on his way out the door*). Of course, the easiest way to prohibit something is to **preclude** it, which means stopping it before it even gets started.

pro·hi·bi·tion /ˌprō(h)əˈbisʜən/ ▶ **noun 1** the action of formally forbidding something. **2** an order that forbids something. **3** (**Prohibition**) the prevention by law of the manufacture and sale of alcohol in the US from 1920 to 1933.

– SYNONYMS **ban,** bar, veto, embargo, boycott, injunction, moratorium, interdict.

– DERIVATIVES **Pro·hi·bi·tion·ist** noun.

pro·hib·i·tive /prəˈhibitiv, prō-/ ▶ **adjective 1** forbidding or preventing something. **2** (of a price) so high as to prevent something from being done or bought.
– DERIVATIVES **pro·hib·i·tive·ly** adverb.

proj·ect ▶ **noun** /ˈpräjˌekt, -ikt/ **1** an enterprise that is carefully planned to achieve a particular aim. **2** a piece of research work by a student. **3** a government-subsidized housing development.

– SYNONYMS **1 scheme,** plan, program, enterprise, undertaking, venture, proposal, idea, concept. **2 assignment,** piece of work, task.

▶ **verb** /prəˈjekt, prōˈjekt/ **1** estimate or forecast something on the basis of present trends. **2** plan a scheme. **3** stick out beyond something else. **4** throw or send something forward or outward. **5** cause light, shadow, or an image to fall on a surface. **6** present a particular image or impression: *he strives to project an image of youth*. **7** (**project something onto**) think that another person has the same feelings or emotions as oneself, especially unconsciously.

– SYNONYMS **1 forecast,** predict, expect, estimate, calculate, reckon. **2 stick out,** jut (out), protrude, extend, stand out, bulge out. **3 cast,** throw, send, shed, shine.

– ORIGIN Latin *projectum* 'something prominent.'

CHOOSE THE RIGHT WORD

See **BULGE**.

pro·jec·tile /prəˈjektl, -ˌtīl/ ▶ **noun** a missile fired or thrown at a target. ▶ **adjective 1** relating to a projectile. **2** propelled with great force.

pro·jec·tion /prəˈjeksʜən/ ▶ **noun 1** an estimate or forecast based on present trends. **2** a thing that sticks out from something. **3** the projecting of an image or sound. **4** the presentation of someone or something in a particular way: *the legal profession's projection of an image of altruism*. **5** a method for representing part of the surface of a solid object on a flat surface, used especially for making maps.

– SYNONYMS **1 forecast,** prediction, prognosis, expectation, estimate. **2 outcrop,** outgrowth, overhang, ledge, shelf, prominence, protrusion, protuberance.

– DERIVATIVES **pro·jec·tive** /prəˈjektiv/ adjective **pro·jec·tion·ist** noun.

pro·jec·tor /prəˈjektər/ ▶ **noun** a device for projecting slides or film onto a screen.

pro·kar·y·ote /prōˈkarēˌōt/ (also **procaryote**) ▶ **noun** Biology a single-celled organism with neither a distinct nucleus with a membrane nor other specialized structures. Compare with **EUKARYOTE**.

pro·lapse /prōˈlaps, ˈprōˌlaps/ ▶ **noun 1** a condition in which a part or organ of the body has slipped forward or down. **2** a part or organ that has slipped forward or down.
– DERIVATIVES **pro·lapsed** adjective.
– ORIGIN from Latin *prolabi* 'slip forward.'

prole /prōl/ ▶ **noun** informal, derogatory a working-class person.
– ORIGIN from **PROLETARIAT**.

pro·le·gom·e·non /ˌprōləˈgäməˌnän, -nən/ ▶ **noun** (pl. **prolegomena** /-nə/) a critical or discursive introduction to a book.
– ORIGIN Greek.

pro·le·tar·i·an /ˌprōliˈte(ə)rēən/ ▶ **adjective** relating to workers or working-class people. ▶ **noun** a working-class person.
– ORIGIN Latin *proletarius*, referring to a person without wealth, who served the state only by producing offspring.

pro·le·tar·i·at /ˌprōliˈte(ə)rēət/ ▶ **noun** (treated as sing. or pl.) workers or working-class people.

pro-life /prōˈlīf/ ▶ **adjective** opposing abortion and euthanasia.
– DERIVATIVES **pro-lif·er** noun.

pro·lif·er·ate /prəˈlifəˌrāt/ ▶ **verb 1** increase rapidly in number: *the rave clubs that proliferated in the late Eighties*. **2** (of a cell or organism) reproduce rapidly.

– SYNONYMS **increase,** grow, multiply, rocket, mushroom, snowball, burgeon, spread, expand, run riot.
– ANTONYMS decrease, dwindle.

– DERIVATIVES **pro·lif·er·a·tion** /prəˌlifəˈrāsʜən/ noun **pro·lif·er·a·tive** /-ˌrātiv/ adjective.
– ORIGIN from Latin *prolificus*.

pro·lif·ic /prəˈlifik/ ▶ **adjective 1** producing much fruit or foliage or many offspring. **2** (of an artist, author, or composer) producing many works. **3** present in large quantities; plentiful.

– SYNONYMS **1 plentiful,** abundant, bountiful, profuse, copious, luxuriant, rich, lush, fruitful. **2 productive,** fertile, creative, inventive.
– ANTONYMS meager.

– DERIVATIVES **pro·lif·i·cal·ly** /-ik(ə)lē/ adverb.
– ORIGIN Latin *prolificus*.

CHOOSE THE RIGHT WORD

See **FERTILE**.

pro·lix /prō'liks/ ▶ **adjective** (of speech or writing) long and boring.
– DERIVATIVES **pro·lix·i·ty** /-'liksətē/ noun.
– ORIGIN Latin *prolixus* 'poured forth, extended.'

pro·logue /'prō,lôg, -,läg/ ▶ **noun 1** an introductory section or scene in a book, play, or musical work. **2** an event or action leading to another.
– ORIGIN Greek *prologos*.

pro·long /prə'lông, -'läng/ ▶ **verb** cause to last longer: *the council prolonged the deadline to March 9th*.

– SYNONYMS **lengthen,** extend, drag out, draw out, protract, spin out, carry on, continue, keep up, perpetuate.
– ANTONYMS shorten.

– DERIVATIVES **pro·lon·ga·tion** /prō,lông'gāshən, prə-/ noun.
– ORIGIN Latin *prolongare*.

pro·longed /prə'lôngd, -'längd/ ▶ **adjective** continuing for a long time; lengthy.

prom /präm/ ▶ **noun** a formal dance at a high school or college.

prom·e·nade /,prämə'nād, -'näd/ ▶ **noun 1** a paved public walk along a seafront. **2** a leisurely walk taken for social reasons. ▶ **verb** take a leisurely walk for social reasons.
– DERIVATIVES **prom·e·nad·er** noun.
– ORIGIN French.

Pro·me·the·an /prə'mēthēən/ ▶ **adjective** daring or skillful like Prometheus, a minor god in Greek mythology who stole fire from the gods and gave it to the human race.

pro·me·thi·um /prō'mēthēəm/ ▶ **noun** an unstable radioactive metallic chemical element of the lanthanide series.
– ORIGIN named after *Prometheus* (see **PROMETHEAN**).

prom·i·nence /'prämənəns/ ▶ **noun 1** the state of being important, famous, or noticeable. **2** a thing that projects or sticks out.

– SYNONYMS **1 fame,** celebrity, eminence, importance, distinction, greatness, prestige, stature, standing. **2** *the press gave prominence to the reports* **wide coverage,** importance, precedence, weight, a high profile, top billing.

prom·i·nent /'prämənənt/ ▶ **adjective 1** important; famous. **2** projecting or sticking out from something. **3** particularly noticeable: *the statue occupies a prominent position in the Sculpture Garden*.

– SYNONYMS **1 important,** well known, leading, eminent, distinguished, notable, noteworthy, noted, illustrious, celebrated, famous, renowned, major-league. **2 jutting (out),** protruding, projecting, protuberant, standing out, sticking out, proud, bulging. **3 conspicuous,** noticeable, obvious, unmistakable, eye-catching, pronounced, salient, striking, dominant, obtrusive.
– ANTONYMS unimportant, inconspicuous.

– DERIVATIVES **prom·i·nent·ly** adverb.
– ORIGIN from Latin *prominere* 'jut out.'

pro·mis·cu·ous /prə'miskyo͞oəs/ ▶ **adjective 1** having many sexual partners. **2** not selective in approach; indiscriminate: *a promiscuous mixing of styles*.
– DERIVATIVES **prom·is·cu·i·ty** /,prämə'skyo͞oitē, prə,mis'kyo͞o-/ noun **prom·is·cu·ous·ly** adverb.
– ORIGIN Latin *promiscuus* 'indiscriminate.'

prom·ise /'präməs/ ▶ **noun 1** an assurance that one will do something or that something will happen. **2** indications of future excellence or success: *he showed some promise as an actor*. **3** a sign that something is likely to happen.

– SYNONYMS **1 word (of honor),** assurance, pledge, vow, guarantee, oath, bond, undertaking, agreement, commitment, contract. **2 potential,** ability, talent, aptitude, possibility.

▶ **verb 1** assure someone that one will do something or that something will happen. **2** make something seem likely: *it promised to be a night to remember*.

– SYNONYMS **1 give one's word,** swear, pledge, vow, undertake, give an undertaking, guarantee, warrant, contract, give an assurance, commit oneself. **2 indicate,** lead someone to expect, point to, be a sign of, betoken, give hope of, augur, herald, portend, presage.

– ORIGIN Latin *promissum*.

Prom·ised Land ▶ **noun 1** the land of Canaan, promised to Abraham and his descendants in the Bible (Book of Genesis, chapter 12). **2** (**the promised land**) a place or situation where great happiness is expected.

prom·is·ee /,prämə'sē/ ▶ **noun** Law a person to whom a promise is made.

prom·is·ing /'präməsing/ ▶ **adjective** showing signs of future excellence or success.

– SYNONYMS **1 good,** encouraging, favorable, hopeful, auspicious, propitious, bright, rosy, heartening. **2 talented,** gifted, budding, up-and-coming, rising, coming, in the making.
– ANTONYMS unfavorable.

– DERIVATIVES **prom·is·ing·ly** adverb.

prom·i·sor /'präməsər/ ▶ **noun** Law a person who makes a promise.

prom·is·so·ry note /'prämə,sôrē/ ▶ **noun** a signed document containing a written promise to pay a stated sum.

pro·mo /'prōmō/ ▶ **noun** (pl. **promos**) informal a promotional film, video, etc.

prom·on·to·ry /'prämən,tôrē/ ▶ **noun** (pl. **promontories**) a point of high land jutting out into the sea or a lake.
– ORIGIN Latin *promontorium*.

pro·mote /prə'mōt/ ▶ **verb 1** support or actively encourage a cause, venture, or aim. **2** publicize a product or celebrity. **3** appoint someone to a higher position or rank. **4** transfer a sports team to a higher division.

– SYNONYMS **1 upgrade,** give promotion to, elevate, advance, move up. **2 encourage,** further, advance, foster, develop, contribute to, boost, stimulate. **3 advertise,** publicize, give publicity to, beat/bang the drum for, market, merchandise; informal push, plug, hype.
– ANTONYMS demote, obstruct.

– ORIGIN Latin *promovere* 'move forward.'

pro·mot·er /prə'mōtər/ ▶ **noun 1** the organizer of a sporting event or theatrical production. **2** a supporter of a cause or aim.

pro·mo·tion /prə'mōshən/ ▶ **noun 1** activity that supports or encourages something: *the promotion of human rights*. **2** the publicizing of a product or celebrity. **3** (**promotions**) the activity or business of publicizing a product or celebrity. **4** the action of promoting someone or something to a higher position or rank.

– SYNONYMS **1 upgrading,** preferment, elevation, advancement, step up (the ladder). **2 encouragement,** furtherance, furthering, advancement, contribution to, fostering, boosting, stimulation. **3 advertising,** marketing, publicity, propaganda; informal hard sell, plug, hype.

– DERIVATIVES **pro·mo·tion·al** adjective.

prompt /prämpt/ ▶ **verb 1** cause something to happen. **2** (**prompt someone to/to do**) cause someone to do something. **3** encourage a hesitating speaker to say something. **4** supply a forgotten word or line to an actor.

– SYNONYMS **1 induce,** make, move, motivate, lead, dispose, persuade, incline, encourage, stimulate, prod, impel, spur on, inspire. **2 give rise to,** bring about, cause, occasion, result in, lead to, elicit, produce, precipitate, trigger, spark, provoke. **3 remind,** cue, feed, help out, jog someone's memory.
– ANTONYMS deter.

▶ **noun 1** an act of prompting a speaker or actor. **2** a word or phrase used to prompt an actor. **3** a word or symbol that appears on a computer screen to show that input is required.

▶ **adjective** done or acting without delay.

– SYNONYMS **quick,** swift, rapid, speedy, fast, expeditious, direct, immediate, instant, early, punctual, in good time, on time.
– ANTONYMS slow, late.

▶ **adverb** Brit. exactly or punctually: *lunch is at 12 o'clock prompt.*

– SYNONYMS **exactly,** precisely, sharp, on the dot, dead, punctually; informal on the button, on the nose, bang on.

– DERIVATIVES **prompt·ness** noun.
– ORIGIN Latin *promptus* 'brought to light,' also 'ready.'

prompt·er /'prämptər/ ▶ **noun** a person who prompts the actors during a play.

prompt·ly /'prämptlē/ ▶ **adverb 1** punctually: *William arrived promptly at 7:30.* **2** without delay: *I expect the matter to be dealt with promptly.*

– SYNONYMS **1 punctually,** on time; informal on the button, on the nose, on the dot, bang on. **2 without delay,** straightaway, right away, at once, immediately, now, as soon as possible, quickly, swiftly, rapidly, speedily, fast; informal pronto, ASAP.
– ANTONYMS late.

prom·ul·gate /'prämәl,gāt, prō'mәl-/ ▶ **verb 1** make something widely known. **2** put a law or decree into effect by an official announcement.
– DERIVATIVES **prom·ul·ga·tion** /,prämәl'gāsʜәn, ,prōmәl-/ noun **prom·ul·ga·tor** noun.
– ORIGIN Latin *promulgare* 'expose to public view.'

CHOOSE THE RIGHT WORD

See **ANNOUNCE**.

pro·nate /'prō,nāt/ ▶ **verb** technical **1** put or hold (a hand, foot, or limb) with the palm or sole turned downward. Compare with **SUPINATE**. **2** walk or run with most of the weight on the outside of the feet.
– DERIVATIVES **pro·na·tion** /'prō,nāsʜәn/ noun.

prone /prōn/ ▶ **adjective 1** (**prone to/to do**) likely or liable to suffer from, do, or experience something unpleasant or undesirable. **2** lying flat, especially face downward.

– SYNONYMS **1 susceptible,** vulnerable, subject, open, liable, given, predisposed, likely, disposed, inclined, apt. **2 lying face down,** on one's stomach/front, lying flat, lying down, horizontal, prostrate.

– DERIVATIVES **prone·ness** noun.
– ORIGIN Latin *pronus* 'leaning forward.'

prong /prôɴɢ/ ▶ **noun 1** each of two or more projecting pointed parts on a fork or other article. **2** each of the separate parts of an attack, argument, or scheme.
– ORIGIN perhaps related to German *prange* 'pinching instrument.'

prong·horn /'prôɴɢ,hôrn/ (also **pronghorn antelope**) ▶ **noun** a fast-running North American mammal resembling but unrelated to an antelope.
– ORIGIN named for the pronged horns on the males of the species.

pro·nom·i·nal /prō'nämәnl/ ▶ **adjective** relating to or acting as a pronoun.
– DERIVATIVES **pro·nom·i·nal·ly** adverb.

pro·noun /'prō,noun/ ▶ **noun** a word used instead of a noun to indicate someone or something already mentioned or known, e.g., *I, she, this.*

pro·nounce /prә'nouns/ ▶ **verb 1** make the sound of a word or part of a word. **2** declare or announce something in a formal or solemn way. **3** (**pronounce on**) pass judgment or make a decision on.

– SYNONYMS **1 say,** enunciate, articulate, utter, voice, sound, vocalize, get one's tongue around. **2 declare,** proclaim, judge, rule, decree, ordain.

– DERIVATIVES **pro·nounce·a·ble** adjective **pro·nounc·er** noun.
– ORIGIN Latin *pronuntiare.*

pro·nounced /prә'nounst/ ▶ **adjective** very noticeable.

– SYNONYMS **noticeable,** marked, strong, conspicuous, striking, distinct, prominent, unmistakable, obvious.
– ANTONYMS slight.

– DERIVATIVES **pro·nounc·ed·ly** /-'nounsәdlē, -'nounstlē/ adverb.

pro·nounce·ment /prә'nounsmәnt/ ▶ **noun** a formal public statement.

pron·to /'präntō/ ▶ **adverb** informal promptly; quickly.
– ORIGIN Spanish.

pro·nun·ci·a·tion /prә,nәnsē'āsʜәn/ ▶ **noun** the way in which a word is pronounced.

USAGE

Pronunciation should be pronounced with **-nun-** as the second syllable, and not as though it were spelled **-noun-**.

proof /pro͞of/ ▶ **noun 1** evidence that proves that a fact or statement is true. **2** the action of proving that something is true. **3** a series of stages in the solving of a mathematical or philosophical problem. **4** a copy of a printed page used for making corrections before final printing. **5** a trial photographic print. **6** a standard used to measure the strength of distilled alcoholic liquor.

– SYNONYMS **evidence,** verification, corroboration, demonstration, authentication, confirmation, certification, documentation.

▶ **adjective** (in combination) able to resist: *bulletproof.*

– SYNONYMS **resistant,** immune, unaffected, impervious.

▶ **verb 1** make a proof of a printed work. **2** proofread

something. **3** make something waterproof.
– ORIGIN Old French *proeve*.

proof pos·i·tive ▶ **noun** final or absolute proof of something.

proof·read /ˈpro͞ofˌrēd/ ▶ **verb** read printer's proofs and mark any errors.
– DERIVATIVES **proof·read·er** noun.

proof spir·it ▶ **noun** a mixture of alcohol and water used as a standard of strength of distilled alcoholic liquor.

prop[1] /präp/ ▶ **noun 1** a pole or beam used as a temporary support. **2** a source of support or assistance.

– SYNONYMS **1 pole,** post, support, upright, brace, buttress, stay, strut. **2 mainstay,** pillar, anchor, support, cornerstone.

▶ **verb** (**props, propping, propped**) **1** support something with a prop. **2** lean something against something else. **3** (**prop someone/thing up**) support or help someone or something that would otherwise fail.

– SYNONYMS **1 lean,** rest, stand, balance. **2** *this post is **propping** the wall **up*** **hold up,** shore up, buttress, support, brace, underpin. **3** *they **prop up** failing industries* **subsidize,** underwrite, fund, finance.

– ORIGIN probably from Dutch *proppe* 'support (for vines).'

prop[2] ▶ **noun** a portable object used on the set of a play or movie.
– ORIGIN abbreviation of **PROPERTY**.

prop[3] ▶ **noun** informal an aircraft propeller.

prop·a·gan·da /ˌpräpəˈgandə/ ▶ **noun** information that is often biased or misleading, used to promote a political cause or point of view.

– SYNONYMS **information,** promotion, advertising, publicity, disinformation; informal hype.

– ORIGIN from Latin *congregatio de propaganda fide* 'congregation for propagation of the faith.'

prop·a·gan·dist /ˌpräpəˈgandist/ chiefly derogatory ▶ **noun** a person who spreads propaganda. ▶ **adjective** consisting of or spreading propaganda.
– DERIVATIVES **prop·a·gan·dize** /ˌpräpəˈganˌdīz/ verb.

prop·a·gate /ˈpräpəˌgāt/ ▶ **verb 1** produce a new plant naturally from the parent stock. **2** promote an idea or knowledge widely. **3** transmit motion, light, sound, etc., in a particular direction.
– DERIVATIVES **prop·a·ga·tion** /ˌpräpəˈgāsʜən/ noun.
– ORIGIN Latin *propagare* 'multiply from layers or shoots.'

prop·a·ga·tor /ˈpräpəˌgātər/ ▶ **noun 1** a covered, heated container of earth or compost, used for germinating seedlings. **2** a person who spreads an idea or knowledge.

pro·pane /ˈprōˌpān/ ▶ **noun** a flammable gas present in natural gas and used as bottled fuel.

pro·pel /prəˈpel/ ▶ **verb** (**propels, propelling, propelled**) **1** drive or push someone or something forward. **2** send or force into a particular situation: *his doctorate propelled him into prominence*.

– SYNONYMS **1 move,** power, push, drive. **2 throw,** thrust, toss, fling, hurl, pitch, send, shoot.

– ORIGIN Latin *propellere* 'to drive forward.'

pro·pel·lant /prəˈpelənt/ ▶ **noun 1** a compressed gas that forces out the contents of an aerosol. **2** a substance used to provide thrust in a rocket engine. ▶ **adjective** capable of propelling something.

pro·pel·ler /prəˈpelər/ (also **propellor**) ▶ **noun** a revolving shaft with two or more angled blades, for propelling a ship or aircraft.

pro·pen·si·ty /prəˈpensətē/ ▶ **noun** (pl. **propensities**) a tendency to behave in a particular way.
– ORIGIN from Latin *propensus* 'inclined.'

prop·er /ˈpräpər/ ▶ **adjective 1** truly what something is said or regarded to be; genuine. **2** (after a noun) according to the precise meaning of the term: *the World Cup proper*. **3** suitable, right, or correct: *an artist needs the proper tools*. **4** respectable, especially excessively so. **5** (**proper to**) belonging particularly to: *the degree of certainty proper to mathematics*.

– SYNONYMS **1 real,** genuine, actual, true, bona fide; informal kosher. **2 right,** correct, accepted, conventional, established, official, regular, acceptable, appropriate, suitable, apt. **3 formal,** conventional, correct, orthodox, polite, respectable, seemly.
– ANTONYMS wrong, improper.

▶ **adverb** Brit. informal or dialect thoroughly.
– ORIGIN Latin *proprius* 'one's own, special.'

prop·er frac·tion ▶ **noun** a fraction that is less than one, with the numerator less than the denominator.

prop·er·ly /ˈpräpərlē/ ▶ **adverb 1** in a proper way. **2** in the precise sense. **3** informal, chiefly Brit. completely.

prop·er noun (also **proper name**) ▶ **noun** a name for a particular person, place, or organization, having an initial capital letter. Often contrasted with **COMMON NOUN**.

prop·er·tied /ˈpräpərtēd/ ▶ **adjective** owning property and land.

prop·er·ty /ˈpräpərtē/ ▶ **noun** (pl. **properties**) **1** a thing or things belonging to someone. **2** a building and the land belonging to it. **3** Law the right to possess, use, or dispose of something; ownership. **4** a characteristic or quality: *a perfumed oil with calming properties*.

– SYNONYMS **1 possessions,** belongings, things, effects, stuff, goods; informal gear. **2 real estate,** building(s), premises, house(s), land, holdings. **3 quality,** attribute, characteristic, feature, power, trait, hallmark.

– ORIGIN Latin *proprietas*.

proph·e·cy /ˈpräfəsē/ ▶ **noun** (pl. **prophecies**) **1** a prediction of a future event. **2** the power of prophesying the future.

– SYNONYMS **prediction,** forecast, prognostication, prognosis, divination.

– ORIGIN Greek *prophēteia*.

proph·e·sy /ˈpräfəˌsī/ ▶ **verb** (**prophesies, prophesying, prophesied**) predict a future event.

– SYNONYMS **predict,** foretell, forecast, foresee, prognosticate.

USAGE

The words **prophesy** and **prophecy** are often confused. **Prophesy** is the spelling that should be used for the verb (*how can I prophesy the coming of a God in which I do not believe?*), whereas **prophecy** is the correct spelling for the noun (*a bleak prophecy of war*).

proph·et /ˈpräfit/ ▶ **noun** (fem. **prophetess** /ˈpräfətəs/) **1** (in some religions) a person believed to have been sent by God to teach people about his intentions.

2 a person who predicts the future. **3** a person who promotes or supports a new belief or theory.

– SYNONYMS **forecaster,** seer, soothsayer, fortune teller, clairvoyant, oracle.

– ORIGIN Greek *prophētēs* 'spokesman.'

pro·phet·ic /prəˈfetik/ ▶ **adjective** **1** accurately predicting the future. **2** relating to a prophet or prophecy.
– DERIVATIVES **pro·phet·i·cal** adjective **pro·phet·i·cal·ly** /-ik(ə)lē/ adverb.

pro·phy·lac·tic /ˌprōfəˈlaktik/ ▶ **adjective** intended to prevent disease. ▶ **noun** **1** a medicine or course of action that is intended to prevent disease. **2** a condom.
– ORIGIN Greek *prophulaktikos*.

pro·phy·lax·is /ˌprōfəˈlaksəs/ ▶ **noun** action taken to prevent disease.
– ORIGIN Greek *phulaxis* 'act of guarding.'

pro·pin·qui·ty /prəˈpiNGkwətē/ ▶ **noun** nearness in time or space; proximity.
– ORIGIN Latin *propinquitas*.

pro·pi·ti·ate /prəˈpisHēˌāt/ ▶ **verb** win or regain the favor of a person, god, or spirit.
– DERIVATIVES **pro·pi·ti·a·tion** /prəˌpisHēˈāsHən/ noun **pro·pi·ti·a·to·ry** /-ˈpisHēəˌtôrē/ adjective.
– ORIGIN Latin *propitiare* 'make favorable.'

CHOOSE THE RIGHT WORD

See **PACIFY**.

pro·pi·tious /prəˈpisHəs/ ▶ **adjective** giving or indicating a good chance of success; favorable: *it was a propitious moment for a global telephone network*.
– DERIVATIVES **pro·pi·tious·ly** adverb **pro·pi·tious·ness** noun.

CHOOSE THE RIGHT WORD

See **TIMELY**.

prop·o·lis /ˈpräpələs/ ▶ **noun** a substance collected by honeybees from tree buds for constructing and varnishing honeycombs.
– ORIGIN Greek, 'suburb,' also 'bee glue.'

pro·po·nent /prəˈpōnənt/ ▶ **noun** a person who supports a theory, proposal, or project.

– SYNONYMS **advocate,** champion, supporter, booster, promoter, protagonist, campaigner.

– ORIGIN from Latin *proponere* 'put forward.'

pro·por·tion /prəˈpôrsHən/ ▶ **noun** **1** a part, share, or number considered in relation to a whole. **2** the relationship of one thing to another in terms of size or quantity; a ratio. **3** the correct or pleasing relationship of things or between the parts of a whole: *keep the size of the vase and the size of the flowers in your arrangement in proportion*. **4** (**proportions**) dimensions; size.

– SYNONYMS **1 part,** portion, amount, quantity, bit, piece, percentage, fraction, section, segment, share. **2 ratio,** distribution, relative amount/number, relationship. **3 balance,** symmetry, harmony, correspondence, correlation, agreement. **4** *men of huge* ***proportions*** **size,** dimensions, magnitude, measurements, mass, volume, bulk, expanse, extent.

▶ **verb** formal adjust something so as to have a particular or suitable relationship to something else.
– DERIVATIVES **pro·por·tioned** adjective.
– PHRASES **in** (or **out of**) **proportion** regarded without (or with) exaggeration. **sense of proportion** the ability to judge the relative importance of things.
– ORIGIN Latin.

pro·por·tion·al /prəˈpôrsHənl/ ▶ **adjective** corresponding in size or amount to something else.

– SYNONYMS **corresponding,** comparable, in proportion, pro rata, commensurate, equivalent, consistent.
– ANTONYMS disproportionate.

– DERIVATIVES **pro·por·tion·al·i·ty** /prəˌpôrsHəˈnalətē, pərˌpôrsHəˈnalədē/ noun **pro·por·tion·al·ly** adverb.

pro·por·tion·al rep·re·sen·ta·tion ▶ **noun** an electoral system in which parties gain seats in proportion to the number of votes cast for them.

pro·por·tion·ate /prəˈpôrsHənət/ ▶ **adjective** another term for **PROPORTIONAL**.

– SYNONYMS **corresponding,** comparable, in proportion, pro rata, commensurate, equivalent, consistent.
– ANTONYMS disproportionate.

– DERIVATIVES **pro·por·tion·ate·ly** adverb.

pro·pos·al /prəˈpōzəl/ ▶ **noun** **1** a plan or suggestion put forward for consideration. **2** the action of proposing something. **3** an offer of marriage.

– SYNONYMS **scheme,** plan, idea, project, program, motion, proposition, suggestion, submission.

pro·pose /prəˈpōz/ ▶ **verb** **1** put forward an idea or plan for consideration. **2** nominate someone for an office or position. **3** put forward a motion to a lawmaking body or committee. **4** plan or intend to do something. **5** make an offer of marriage to someone.

– SYNONYMS **1 put forward,** suggest, submit, advance, offer, present, move, come up with, nominate, recommend. **2 intend,** mean, plan, have in mind, aim.

– DERIVATIVES **pro·pos·er** noun.
– ORIGIN Latin *proponere* 'put forward.'

CHOOSE THE RIGHT WORD

See **INTEND**.

prop·o·si·tion /ˌpräpəˈzisHən/ ▶ **noun** **1** a statement expressing a judgment or opinion. **2** a proposed scheme or plan. **3** a problem or task to be dealt with: *keeping weight off for life is a difficult proposition*. **4** Mathematics a formal statement of a theorem or problem.

– SYNONYMS **1 proposal,** scheme, plan, project, idea, program. **2 task,** job, undertaking, venture, activity, affair.

▶ **verb** informal **1** make an offer or suggestion to someone. **2** ask someone to have sex.
– DERIVATIVES **prop·o·si·tion·al** adjective.

pro·pound /prəˈpound/ ▶ **verb** put forward an idea or theory for consideration.
– DERIVATIVES **pro·pound·er** noun.
– ORIGIN Latin *proponere* 'put forward.'

pro·pri·e·tar·y /p(r)əˈprīˌiˌterē/ ▶ **adjective** **1** relating to an owner or ownership. **2** behaving as if one owned something or someone: *he looked around with a proprietary air*. **3** (of a product) marketed under a registered trade name.
– ORIGIN from Latin *proprietarius* 'proprietor.'

pro·pri·e·tar·y name ▶ **noun** a name of a product or service registered as a trademark.

pro·pri·e·tor /p(r)əˈprīətər/ ▸ **noun** (fem. **proprietress** /p(r)əˈprīətrəs/) **1** the owner of a business. **2** a holder of property.

– SYNONYMS **owner,** possessor, holder, householder, master, mistress, landowner, landlord, landlady, store owner, shopkeeper.

pro·pri·e·to·ri·al /p(r)əˌprīəˈtôrēəl/ ▸ **adjective** behaving as if one owned someone or something; possessive: *he draped his arm across her shoulders in a proprietorial way.*
– DERIVATIVES **pro·pri·e·to·ri·al·ly** /p(r)əˌprīəˈtôrēəlē/ adverb.

pro·pri·e·ty /p(r)əˈprīətē/ ▸ **noun** (pl. **proprieties**) **1** correctness of behavior or morals. **2** (**proprieties**) the generally accepted details or rules of behavior. **3** the quality of being appropriate or right: *they questioned the propriety of investments made by the council.*

– SYNONYMS **decorum,** respectability, decency, correctness, good manners, courtesy, politeness, rectitude.
– ANTONYMS indecorum.

– ORIGIN Latin *proprietas* 'property.'

props /präps/ ▸ **plural noun** informal respect or credit due to a person: *Erika gets props for the great work she did on the music.*

pro·pul·sion /prəˈpəlsʜən/ ▸ **noun** the action of propelling or driving something forward.
– DERIVATIVES **pro·pul·sive** /-siv/ adjective **pro·pul·sive·ly** adverb.

pro·pyl·ene /ˈprōpəˌlēn/ ▸ **noun** a hydrocarbon gas obtained by cracking petroleum, used for making plastics and other chemicals.

pro ra·ta /prō ˈrātə, ˈrätə, ˈratə/ ▸ **adjective** proportional. ▸ **adverb** proportionally.
– ORIGIN Latin, 'according to the rate.'

pro·rate /prōˈrāt, ˈprōˌrāt/ ▸ **verb** allocate, distribute, or assess pro rata: *bonuses are prorated over the life of a player's contract.*

pro·rogue /p(r)əˈrōg/ ▸ **verb** (**prorogues, proroguing, prorogued**) discontinue a session of a parliament without dissolving it.
– DERIVATIVES **pro·ro·ga·tion** /ˌprōrəˈgāsʜən/ noun.
– ORIGIN Latin *prorogare* 'prolong, extend.'

pro·sa·ic /prōˈzāik/ ▸ **adjective 1** (of language) not imaginative or original. **2** ordinary, dull, or mundane: *a prosaic travel experience.*

– SYNONYMS **ordinary,** everyday, commonplace, conventional, straightforward, routine, run-of-the-mill; **unimaginative,** uninspired, uninspiring, matter-of-fact, dull, dreary, humdrum, mundane, pedestrian, tame, plodding.
– ANTONYMS interesting, imaginative, inspired.

– DERIVATIVES **pro·sa·i·cal·ly** /-ik(ə)lē/ adverb.

pro·sce·ni·um /prəˈsēnēəm, prō-/ ▸ **noun** (pl. **prosceniums** or **proscenia** /-nēə/) **1** the part of a stage in front of the curtain. **2** (also **proscenium arch**) an arch that frames the opening between the stage and the auditorium.
– ORIGIN Greek *proskēnion.*

pro·sciut·to /prəˈsʜōōtō/ ▸ **noun** raw cured Italian ham.
– ORIGIN Italian.

pro·scribe /prōˈskrīb/ ▸ **verb 1** officially forbid something. **2** criticize or condemn someone or something. **3** historical outlaw someone.
– DERIVATIVES **pro·scrip·tion** /-ˈskripsʜən/ noun **pro·scrip·tive** /-ˈskriptiv/ adjective.
– ORIGIN Latin *proscribere* 'publish by writing.'

USAGE

The words **proscribe** and **prescribe** are often confused. **Proscribe** means 'officially forbid something' (*strikes remained proscribed in the armed forces*), whereas **prescribe** means either 'issue a medical prescription' or 'state authoritatively that something should be done' (*these rights can only be interfered with in circumstances prescribed by law*).

prose /prōz/ ▸ **noun** ordinary written or spoken language. ▸ **verb** talk in a boring way.
– ORIGIN from Latin *prosa oratio* 'straightforward discourse.'

pros·e·cute /ˈpräsiˌkyōōt/ ▸ **verb 1** take legal action against someone or with respect to an offense. **2** continue a course of action with a view to completing it.

– SYNONYMS **charge,** take to court, take legal action against, sue, try, bring to trial, put on trial, put in the dock, impeach, indict.
– ANTONYMS defend.

– DERIVATIVES **pros·e·cut·a·ble** adjective.
– ORIGIN Latin *prosequi* 'pursue, accompany.'

pros·e·cu·tion /ˌpräsiˈkyōōsʜən/ ▸ **noun 1** the process of taking legal action against someone. **2** (**the prosecution**) (treated as sing. or pl.) the party prosecuting someone in a lawsuit. **3** the continuation of a course of action.

pros·e·cu·tor /ˈpräsiˌkyōōtər/ ▸ **noun 1** a person, especially a public official, who takes legal action against someone. **2** a lawyer who conducts the case against a person accused of a crime.
– DERIVATIVES **pros·e·cu·to·ri·al** /ˌpräsikyəˈtôrēəl/ adjective.

pros·e·lyte /ˈpräsəˌlīt/ ▸ **noun** a person who has converted from one opinion, religion, or party to another.
– DERIVATIVES **pros·e·lyt·ism** /-ləˌtizəm/ noun.
– ORIGIN Greek *prosēluthos* 'stranger, convert.'

pros·e·lyt·ize /ˈpräsələˌtīz/ ▸ **verb** convert someone from one religion, belief, or opinion to another.
– DERIVATIVES **pros·e·lyt·iz·a·tion** /ˌpräsələtiˈzāsʜən/ noun **pros·e·lyt·iz·er** noun.

pros·o·dy /ˈpräsədē, ˈpräzədē/ ▸ **noun 1** the patterns of rhythm and sound used in poetry. **2** the theory or study of these patterns, or the rules governing them. **3** the patterns of stress and intonation in a language.
– DERIVATIVES **pro·sod·ic** /prəˈsädik, -zädik/ adjective **pros·o·dist** /ˈpräsədist, ˈpräz-/ noun.
– ORIGIN Greek *prosōidia* 'song sung to music, tone of a syllable.'

pros·pect /ˈpräsˌpekt/ ▸ **noun 1** the possibility or likelihood of a future event occurring: *there was no prospect of a reconciliation.* **2** a mental picture of a future or expected event. **3** (**prospects**) chances for success. **4** a person regarded as likely to be successful: *he was seen as a leading medal prospect for the Olympics.* **5** a wide view of landscape.

– SYNONYMS **likelihood,** hope, expectation, chance, odds, probability, possibility, promise, outlook, lookout.

▸ **verb** (**prospect for**) search for mineral deposits, especially by means of drilling and excavation.

– SYNONYMS **search,** look, explore, survey, scout, hunt, dowse.

– DERIVATIVES **pros·pec·tor** noun.
– ORIGIN Latin *prospectus* 'view.'

pro·spec·tive /prə'spektiv/ ▶ **adjective** likely to happen or be something in the future: *a prospective buyer.*

– SYNONYMS **potential,** possible, probable, likely, future, eventual, -to-be, soon-to-be, in the making, intending, aspiring, would-be.

– DERIVATIVES **pro·spec·tive·ly** adverb.

pro·spec·tus /prə'spektəs/ ▶ **noun** (pl. **prospectuses**) a printed booklet advertising a school or university or giving details of a stock offering.

– SYNONYMS **brochure,** syllabus, curriculum, catalog, program, list, schedule.

– ORIGIN Latin, 'view, prospect.'

pros·per /'präspər/ ▶ **verb** succeed or flourish, especially financially.

– SYNONYMS **flourish,** thrive, do well, bloom, blossom, burgeon, progress, do all right for oneself, get ahead, get on (in the world), be successful; informal go places.
– ANTONYMS fail.

– ORIGIN Latin *prosperare.*

pros·per·i·ty /prä'speritē/ ▶ **noun** the state of being rich and successful.

– SYNONYMS **success,** affluence, wealth, ease, plenty.
– ANTONYMS hardship, failure.

pros·per·ous /'präspərəs/ ▶ **adjective** rich and successful.

– SYNONYMS **1 thriving,** flourishing, successful, strong, vigorous, profitable, lucrative, expanding, booming, burgeoning. **2 affluent,** wealthy, rich, moneyed, well off, well-to-do; informal in the money.
– ANTONYMS ailing, poor.

– DERIVATIVES **pros·per·ous·ly** adverb.

pros·ta·glan·din /ˌprästə'glandin/ ▶ **noun** any of a group of compounds with various biological effects, such as causing contractions of the uterus.

pros·tate /'präsˌtāt/ ▶ **noun** a gland that surrounds the neck of the bladder in male mammals and produces a component of semen.
– DERIVATIVES **pros·tat·ic** /prä'statik/ adjective.
– ORIGIN Greek *prostatēs* 'one that stands before.'

pros·the·sis /präs'THēsis/ ▶ **noun** (pl. **prostheses** /-sēz/) an artificial body part.
– ORIGIN Greek.

pros·thet·ics /präs'THetiks/ ▶ **plural noun 1** artificial body parts. **2** pieces of flexible material applied to actors' faces to change their appearance. **3** (treated as sing.) the branch of medicine concerned with making and fitting artificial body parts.
– DERIVATIVES **pros·thet·ic** /-'THetik/ adjective **pros·the·tist** /'präsTHətist/ noun.

pros·ti·tute /'prästəˌt(y)o͞ot/ ▶ **noun** a person who has sex with people for money.

– SYNONYMS whore, call girl, courtesan; informal hooker, hustler, lady of the night/evening, working girl.

▶ **verb** (often **prostitute oneself**) **1** do something unworthy or corrupt for the sake of money or personal advantage: *he decided that he would no longer prostitute his talent to win popularity.* **2** offer someone or work as a prostitute.

– SYNONYMS **betray,** sacrifice, sell, sell out, debase, degrade, demean, devalue, cheapen, lower, shame, misuse.

– DERIVATIVES **pros·ti·tu·tion** /ˌprästə't(y)o͞oSHən/ noun.
– ORIGIN Latin *prostituere* 'expose publicly, offer for sale.'

pros·trate /'präsˌtrāt/ ▶ **adjective 1** lying stretched out on the ground with the face downward. **2** completely overcome with distress or exhaustion. **3** (of a plant) growing along the ground.

– SYNONYMS **1 prone,** lying flat, lying down, stretched out, spread-eagle, sprawling, horizontal, recumbent. **2** *prostrate with grief* **overwhelmed,** overcome, overpowered, stunned, dazed; speechless, helpless.
– ANTONYMS upright.

▶ **verb 1** (**prostrate oneself**) throw oneself flat on the ground, especially as an act of worship. **2** (**be prostrated**) be completely overcome with stress or exhaustion.

– SYNONYMS (**prostrate oneself**) **throw oneself down,** lie down, stretch oneself out, throw oneself at someone's feet.

– DERIVATIVES **pros·tra·tion** /prä'strāSHən/ noun.
– ORIGIN Latin *prosternere* 'throw down.'

pro·sum·er /prō'so͞omər/ ▶ **noun 1** an amateur who purchases equipment suitable for professional use. **2** a well-informed and proactive consumer.

pros·y /'prōzē/ ▶ **adjective** (of speech or writing) dull and unimaginative.

prot·ac·tin·i·um /ˌprōˌtak'tinēəm/ ▶ **noun** a rare radioactive metallic chemical element.

pro·tag·o·nist /prō'tagənist, prə-/ ▶ **noun 1** the leading character in a play, movie, or novel. **2** an important person in a real situation. **3** an active supporter of a cause or idea.
– ORIGIN Greek *prōtagōnistēs.*

pro·te·a /'prōtēə/ ▶ **noun** a chiefly South African shrub with large conelike flowerheads surrounded by brightly colored modified leaves (bracts).
– ORIGIN from *Proteus* (see **PROTEAN**, with reference to the many species of the genus.

pro·te·an /'prōtēən, prō'tēən/ ▶ **adjective** tending or able to change or adapt; variable or versatile.
– ORIGIN from the Greek sea god *Proteus*, who was able to change shape at will.

pro·tect /prə'tekt/ ▶ **verb 1** keep safe from harm or injury: *he tried to protect her from the attack.* **2** shield a country's own industry from foreign competition by taxing imported goods. **3** (as adj. **protected**) (of a threatened plant or animal species) safeguarded through laws against collecting or hunting.

– SYNONYMS **keep safe,** keep from harm, guard, defend, shield, save, safeguard, preserve, cushion, insulate, shelter, screen, keep, look after.
– ANTONYMS expose, harm.

– ORIGIN Latin *protegere* 'cover in front.'

pro·tect·ant /prə'tektənt/ ▶ **noun** a substance that provides protection, for example against ultraviolet radiation.

pro·tec·tion /prə'tekSHən/ ▶ **noun 1** the action of protecting or the state of being protected: *the vehicle provides protection against anti-personnel mines.* **2** a thing that protects someone or something. **3** the payment of money to criminals to prevent them from attacking oneself or one's property.

– SYNONYMS **1 defense,** security, safeguard, safety, sanctuary, shelter, refuge, immunity, indemnity. **2 safekeeping,** care, charge, guardianship, support, aegis, patronage. **3 barrier,** buffer, shield, screen, cushion, bulwark, armor, insulation.

pro·tec·tion·ism /prəˈteksнəˌnizəm/ ▶ **noun** the theory or practice of shielding a country's own industries from foreign competition by taxing imports.
– DERIVATIVES **pro·tec·tion·ist** noun & adjective.

pro·tec·tive /prəˈtektiv/ ▶ **adjective 1** intended to protect someone or something from harm or injury. **2** having a strong wish to protect someone from harm or injury.

– SYNONYMS **1 protecting,** covering, insulated, impermeable, -proof, -resistant. **2 solicitous,** careful, caring, defensive, paternal, maternal, overprotective, possessive.

– DERIVATIVES **pro·tec·tive·ly** adverb **pro·tec·tive·ness** noun.

pro·tec·tive or·der ▶ **noun** a court order instructing a person to stop abusing or harassing a particular individual.

pro·tec·tor /prəˈtektər/ ▶ **noun 1** a person or thing that protects someone or something. **2** (**Protector**) historical a regent in charge of a kingdom when the monarch is away, ill, or too young to reign.

– SYNONYMS **1 defender,** preserver, guardian, champion, patron, custodian. **2 guard,** shield, buffer, cushion, pad, screen.

– DERIVATIVES **pro·tect·ress** /ˈprōtektres/ noun.

pro·tec·tor·ate /prəˈtektərət/ ▶ **noun 1** a country that is controlled and protected by another. **2** (**Protectorate**) historical the position or period of office of a Protector, in particular that of Oliver Cromwell and his son Richard as heads of state in England 1653–59.

pro·té·gé /ˈprōtəˌzнā, ˌprōtəˈzнā/ ▶ **noun** (fem. **protégée** pronunc. same) a person who is guided and supported by an older and more experienced person.
– ORIGIN French, 'protected.'

pro·tein /ˈprōˌtē(ə)n/ ▶ **noun** any of a group of organic compounds forming part of body tissues and forming an important part of the diet.
– ORIGIN from Greek *prōteios* 'primary.'

pro tem /prō ˈtem/ ▶ **adverb & adjective** for the time being.
– ORIGIN from Latin *pro tempore.*

Prot·er·o·zo·ic /ˌprōtərəˈzōik/ ▶ **adjective** Geology relating to the later part of the Precambrian eon (about 2,500 to 570 million years ago), in which the earliest forms of life evolved.
– ORIGIN from Greek *proteros* 'former' + *zōē* 'life.'

pro·test ▶ **noun** /ˈprōˌtest/ **1** a statement or action expressing disapproval or objection. **2** an organized public demonstration objecting to an official policy or course of action.

– SYNONYMS **1 objection,** complaint, challenge, dissent, demurral, remonstration, fuss, outcry. **2 demonstration,** rally, vigil, sit-in, occupation, stoppage, strike, walkout, mutiny, picket, boycott; informal demo.

▶ **verb** /prəˈtest, prōˈtest, ˈprōˌtest/ **1** express an objection to what someone has said or done. **2** take part in a public protest. **3** state strongly in response to an accusation or criticism: *she has always protested her innocence.*

– SYNONYMS **1 object,** express opposition, dissent, take issue, take a stand, put up a fight, take exception, complain, express disapproval, disagree, make a fuss, speak out; informal kick up a fuss. **2 insist on,** maintain, assert, affirm, announce, proclaim, declare, profess, avow.

– DERIVATIVES **pro·test·er** /ˈprōˌtestər, prəˈtes-/ (also **protestor**) noun.
– ORIGIN Latin *protestari* 'assert formally.'

Prot·es·tant /ˈprätəstənt/ ▶ **noun** a member or follower of any of the Western Christian Churches that are separate from the Roman Catholic Church. ▶ **adjective** relating or belonging to any of the Protestant Churches.
– DERIVATIVES **Prot·es·tant·ism** /ˈprätəstəntˌizəm/ noun.
– ORIGIN Protestants are so called after the declaration (Latin *protestatio*) of Martin Luther and his supporters dissenting from the anti-Reformation decision of the Diet of Spires.

Prot·es·tant eth·ic (also **Protestant work ethic**) ▶ **noun** another term for **WORK ETHIC**.

prot·es·ta·tion /ˌprätəˈstāsнən, ˌprōˌtesˈtā-/ ▶ **noun 1** a strong declaration that something is or is not the case. **2** an objection or protest.

pro·ti·um /ˈprōtēəm, ˈprōsн(ē)əm/ ▶ **noun** Chemistry the common, stable isotope of hydrogen.
– ORIGIN Latin.

proto- ▶ **combining form 1** original; primitive: *prototype.* **2** first: *protozoan.*
– ORIGIN from Greek *prōtos.*

pro·to·col /ˈprōtəˌkôl, -ˌkäl/ ▶ **noun 1** the official system of rules governing affairs of state or diplomatic occasions. **2** the accepted code of behavior in a particular situation. **3** the original draft of a diplomatic document, especially of the terms of a treaty. **4** a formal record of scientific experimental observations. **5** Computing a set of rules governing the exchange or transmission of data between devices.

– SYNONYMS **etiquette,** convention, formalities, custom, the rules, procedure, ritual, decorum, the done thing.

– ORIGIN Greek *prōtokollon* 'first page.'

pro·ton /ˈprōˌtän/ ▶ **noun** Physics a subatomic particle with a positive electric charge, occurring in all atomic nuclei.
– ORIGIN Greek, 'first thing.'

pro·to·plasm /ˈprōtəˌplazəm/ ▶ **noun** the material comprising the living part of a cell, including the cytoplasm and nucleus.
– DERIVATIVES **pro·to·plas·mic** /ˌprōtəˈplazmik/ adjective.
– ORIGIN Greek *prōtoplasma.*

pro·to·type /ˈprōtəˌtīp/ ▶ **noun 1** a first or preliminary version of a device or vehicle from which other versions are developed or copied. **2** the first or typical form of something.

– SYNONYMS **original,** master, template, pattern, sample.

– DERIVATIVES **pro·to·typ·i·cal** /ˌprōtəˈtipikəl/ adjective **pro·to·typ·i·cal·ly** /ˌprōtəˈtipik(ə)lē/ adverb.

pro·to·zo·an /ˌprōtəˈzōən/ ▶ **noun** a single-celled microscopic animal such as an amoeba.
– ORIGIN from Greek *protos* 'first' + *zōion* 'animal.'

pro·tract /prəˈtrakt, prō-/ ▶ **verb** (often as adj. **protracted**) make something longer than expected or normal.

– SYNONYMS **1** *the opposition will try to protract the discussion* **prolong,** lengthen, extend, draw out, drag out, spin out, stretch out, string out. **2** (as adj. **protracted**) *a protracted dispute* **prolonged,** extended, long-drawn-out, lengthy, long.
– ANTONYMS curtail, shorten.

– ORIGIN Latin *protrahere*.

pro·trac·tion /prəˈtrakSHən, prō-/ ▶ **noun** the action of prolonging something or the state of being prolonged.

pro·trac·tor /ˈprōˌtraktər/ ▶ **noun** an instrument for measuring angles, typically in the form of a flat semicircle marked with degrees along the curved edge.

pro·trude /prəˈtro͞od, prō-/ ▶ **verb** extend or stick out beyond or above a surface.

– SYNONYMS **stick out,** jut (out), project, extend, stand out, bulge out, poke out.

– ORIGIN Latin *protrudere* 'to thrust forward.'

CHOOSE THE RIGHT WORD

See **BULGE**.

pro·tru·sion /prəˈtro͞oZHən, prō-/ ▶ **noun 1** something that protrudes or sticks out. **2** the action of protruding.

pro·tu·ber·ance /prəˈt(y)o͞ob(ə)rəns, prō-/ ▶ **noun** a thing that protrudes or sticks out.

pro·tu·ber·ant /prəˈt(y)o͞ob(ə)rənt, prō-/ ▶ **adjective** sticking out or bulging.
– ORIGIN from Latin *protuberare* 'swell out.'

proud /proud/ ▶ **adjective 1** feeling pride or satisfaction in one's own achievements or those of someone close to one. **2** causing pride: *his proudest moment was when his son married Mandy*. **3** having or showing a high opinion of oneself. **4** having self-respect or dignity: *I was too proud to go home*.

– SYNONYMS **1 pleased,** glad, happy, delighted, thrilled, satisfied, gratified. **2** *a proud moment* **pleasing,** gratifying, satisfying, cheering, heartwarming, happy, glorious. **3 arrogant,** conceited, vain, self-important, full of oneself, overbearing, bumptious, presumptuous, overweening, haughty, high and mighty; informal bigheaded, too big for one's boots/britches, stuck-up.
– ANTONYMS ashamed, humble.

– DERIVATIVES **proud·ly** adverb.
– PHRASES **do someone proud** informal **1** make someone feel pleased or satisfied. **2** treat or entertain someone very well.
– ORIGIN Old French *prud* 'valiant.'

prove /pro͞ov/ ▶ **verb** (past part. **proved** or **proven** /ˈpro͞ovən/) **1** demonstrate by evidence or argument that something is true or exists. **2** show or be seen to be: *the scheme has proved a great success*. **3** (**prove oneself**) demonstrate one's abilities or courage. **4** Law establish the genuineness and validity of a will. **5** subject a gun to a testing process. **6** (of bread dough) rise through the action of yeast.

– SYNONYMS **show (to be true),** demonstrate, substantiate, corroborate, verify, validate, authenticate, confirm.
– ANTONYMS disprove.

– DERIVATIVES **prov·a·ble** adjective **prov·er** noun.
– ORIGIN Latin *probare* 'test, approve, demonstrate.'

USAGE

Prove has two past participles, **proved** and **proven**. You can correctly use either in sentences such as *this hasn't been proved yet* or *this hasn't been proven yet*. However, you should always use **proven** when the word is an adjective coming before the noun: *a proven talent* (not *a proved talent*).

prov·e·nance /ˈprävənəns/ ▶ **noun 1** the origin or earliest known history of something. **2** a record of ownership of a work of art or an antique.
– ORIGIN French.

Pro·ven·çal /ˌprävənˈsäl, ˌprō-/ ▶ **adjective** relating to Provence in southern France. ▶ **noun 1** a person from Provence. **2** the language of Provence.

pro·ven·çale /ˌprävənˈsäl, ˌprō-/ ▶ **adjective** (after a noun) cooked in a sauce made with tomatoes, garlic, and herbs.
– ORIGIN from French *à la provençale* 'in the Provençal style.'

prov·en·der /ˈprävəndər/ ▶ **noun** animal fodder.
– ORIGIN Old French *provendre*.

pro·verb /ˈpräˌvərb/ ▶ **noun** a short saying that states a general truth or piece of advice.

– SYNONYMS **saying,** adage, saw, maxim, axiom, motto, aphorism, epigram.

– ORIGIN Latin *proverbium*.

CHOOSE THE RIGHT WORD

See **SAYING**.

pro·ver·bi·al /prəˈvərbēəl/ ▶ **adjective 1** referred to in a proverb or saying. **2** well known, especially so as to be stereotypical: *he was the proverbial, consummate showman*.
– DERIVATIVES **pro·ver·bi·al·ly** adverb.

pro·vide /prəˈvīd/ ▶ **verb 1** make something available for use; supply something. **2** (**provide someone with**) equip or supply someone with something useful or necessary. **3** (**provide for**) make adequate preparation or arrangements for: *new qualifications must provide for changes in technology*. **4** state something in a will or other legal document.

– SYNONYMS **1 supply,** give, come up with, produce, deliver, donate, contribute; informal fork out, lay out. **2** (**provide someone with**) *he was provided with tools* **equip with,** furnish with, issue, supply with, fit out with, rig out with, arm with, provision with; informal fix up with. **3** (**provide for**) **feed,** nurture, nourish, support, maintain, keep, sustain.

– ORIGIN Latin *providere* 'foresee, attend to.'

pro·vid·ed /prəˈvīdid/ ▶ **conjunction** on the condition or understanding that.

– SYNONYMS **if,** on condition that, provided that, presuming (that), assuming (that), as long as, with/on the understanding that.

prov·i·dence /ˈprävəˌdens, -dəns/ ▶ **noun** the protective care of God or of nature as a spiritual power.

prov·i·dent /ˈprävədənt, -ˌdent/ ▶ **adjective** careful in preparing for the future.
– DERIVATIVES **prov·i·dent·ly** adverb.

CHOOSE THE RIGHT WORD

See **ECONOMICAL**.

prov·i·den·tial /ˌprävəˈdenCHəl/ ▶ **adjective 1** happening by chance at a favorable time; opportune: *it was providential that he was on call to provide free legal advice.* **2** involving divine foresight or intervention.
– DERIVATIVES **prov·i·den·tial·ly** adverb.

pro·vid·er /prəˈvīdər/ ▶ **noun** a person or thing that provides something.

– SYNONYMS **supplier,** donor, giver, contributor, source.

pro·vid·ing /prəˈvīdiNG/ ▶ **conjunction** on the condition or understanding that.

– SYNONYMS **if,** on condition that, provided that, presuming (that), assuming (that), as long as, with/on the understanding that.

prov·ince /ˈprävins/ ▶ **noun 1** a chief administrative division of a country or empire. **2** (**the provinces**) the whole of a country outside the capital, especially when regarded as unsophisticated or narrow-minded. **3** (**one's province**) one's particular area of knowledge, interest, or responsibility.

– SYNONYMS **1 territory,** region, state, department, canton, area, district, sector, zone, division. **2** (**the provinces**) **the regions,** the rest of the country, rural areas/districts, the countryside; informal the sticks, the boondocks, the boonies, the middle of nowhere. **3** (**one's province**) **domain,** area, department, responsibility, sphere, world, realm, field, discipline, territory; informal bailiwick.

– ORIGIN Latin *provincia* 'charge, province.'

pro·vin·cial /prəˈvinSHəl/ ▶ **adjective 1** relating to a province or the provinces. **2** unsophisticated or narrow-minded.

– SYNONYMS **1 local,** small-town, rural, country, outlying, backwoods; informal one-horse. **2 unsophisticated,** parochial, insular, narrow-minded, inward-looking, suburban, small-town; informal corn-fed.
– ANTONYMS cosmopolitan, sophisticated.

▶ **noun 1** an inhabitant of a province. **2** an inhabitant of the regions outside the capital city of a country.
– DERIVATIVES **pro·vin·cial·ism** /prəˈvinCHəˌlizəm/ noun **pro·vin·ci·al·i·ty** /prəˌvinSHēˈalətē/ noun **pro·vin·cial·ly** adverb.

prov·ing ground ▶ **noun** an area or situation in which a person or thing is tested or proved.

pro·vi·sion /prəˈviZHən/ ▶ **noun 1** the action of providing or supplying something. **2** something supplied or provided. **3** (**provisions**) supplies of food, drink, or equipment, especially for a journey. **4** a condition or requirement in a legal document. **5** (**provision for/against**) arrangements for future events or requirements: *people must make provision for their retirement.*

– SYNONYMS **1** *limited provision for young children* **facilities,** services, amenities, resource(s), arrangements. **2** (**provisions**) **supplies,** food and drink, stores, groceries, foodstuff(s), rations. **3 term,** requirement, specification, stipulation.

▶ **verb** supply someone or something with provisions.

pro·vi·sion·al /prəˈviZHənl/ ▶ **adjective 1** arranged or existing for the present, possibly to be changed later. **2** (**Provisional**) relating to the unofficial wings of the Irish Republican Army and Sinn Fein.

– SYNONYMS **interim,** temporary, transitional, changeover, stopgap, short-term, fill-in, acting, working.
– ANTONYMS permanent, definite.

▶ **noun** (**Provisional**) a member of the unofficial wing of the Irish Republican Army or Sinn Fein.
– DERIVATIVES **pro·vi·sion·al·i·ty** /prəˌviZHəˈnalətē/ noun **pro·vi·sion·al·ly** /-ZHənl-ē/ adverb.

pro·vi·so /prəˈvīzō/ ▶ **noun** (pl. **provisos**) a condition attached to an agreement.

– SYNONYMS **condition,** stipulation, provision, clause, rider, qualification, restriction, caveat.

– ORIGIN from Latin *proviso quod* 'it being provided that.'

pro·vi·ta·min /prōˈvītəmən/ ▶ **noun** a substance that is converted into a vitamin within an organism.

prov·o·ca·tion /ˌprävəˈkāSHən/ ▶ **noun 1** action or speech that makes someone angry or arouses a strong reaction. **2** the action of provoking someone.

– SYNONYMS **goading,** prodding, incitement, harassment, pressure, teasing, taunting, torment; informal hassle, aggravation.

pro·voc·a·tive /prəˈväkətiv/ ▶ **adjective 1** deliberately causing annoyance or anger. **2** intended to arouse sexual desire or interest.

– SYNONYMS **annoying,** irritating, maddening, galling, insulting, offensive, inflammatory, incendiary; informal aggravating.

– DERIVATIVES **pro·voc·a·tive·ly** adverb **pro·voc·a·tive·ness** noun.

pro·voke /prəˈvōk/ ▶ **verb 1** arouse a strong or unwelcome reaction or emotion in someone: *the decision provoked a storm of protest.* **2** deliberately make someone annoyed or angry. **3** make someone do or feel something, especially by arousing their anger.

– SYNONYMS **1 arouse,** produce, evoke, cause, give rise to, excite, spark, touch off, kindle, generate, engender, instigate, result in, lead to, bring on, precipitate, prompt, trigger. **2 goad,** spur, prick, sting, prod, incite, rouse, stimulate. **3 annoy,** anger, enrage, irritate, rub the wrong way, madden, nettle; informal aggravate, rile, needle, get/put someone's back up.
– ANTONYMS allay, appease.

– ORIGIN Latin *provocare* 'to challenge.'

pro·vo·lo·ne /ˌprōvəˈlōnē, ˈprōvəˌlōn/ ▶ **noun** an Italian soft smoked cheese.
– ORIGIN Italian.

pro·vost /ˈprōˌvōst/ ▶ **noun 1** a senior administrative officer in certain colleges and universities. **2** Brit. the head of certain university colleges and private schools. **3** the head of a chapter in a cathedral.
– ORIGIN Old English.

pro·vost mar·shal ▶ **noun** the officer in charge of military police in camp or on active service.

prow /prou/ ▶ **noun** the pointed front part of a ship; the bow.
– ORIGIN Old French *proue*.

prow·ess /ˈprou-əs, ˈprōəs/ ▶ **noun 1** skill or expertise in a particular activity or field. **2** bravery in battle.

– SYNONYMS **skill,** expertise, mastery, ability, capability, capacity, talent, aptitude, dexterity, proficiency, finesse; informal know-how.
– ANTONYMS inability, ineptitude.

– ORIGIN Old French *proesce.*

prowl /proul/ ▸ **verb** move about in a stealthy or restless way, especially in search of prey.

– SYNONYMS **steal,** slink, skulk, sneak, stalk, creep; informal snoop.

– DERIVATIVES **prowl·er** noun.
– PHRASES **on the prowl** moving around in a stealthy way.
– ORIGIN unknown.

prox·i·mal /ˈpräksəməl/ ▸ **adjective** chiefly Anatomy situated nearer to the center of the body or the point of attachment. The opposite of **DISTAL**.
– DERIVATIVES **prox·i·mal·ly** adverb.

prox·i·mate /ˈpräksəmit/ ▸ **adjective** closest in space, time, or relationship.
– ORIGIN Latin *proximatus* 'drawn near.'

prox·im·i·ty /präkˈsimətē/ ▸ **noun** nearness in space, time, or relationship.

prox·y /ˈpräksē/ ▸ **noun** (pl. **proxies**) **1** the authority to represent someone else, especially in voting. **2** a person authorized to act on behalf of someone else.

– SYNONYMS **deputy,** representative, substitute, delegate, agent, surrogate, stand-in, go-between.

– ORIGIN from former *procuracy,* 'the position or office of a procurator.'

Pro·zac /ˈprōˌzak/ ▸ **noun** trademark fluoxetine, a drug that is taken to treat depression.
– ORIGIN an invented name.

prude /pro͞od/ ▸ **noun** a person who is easily shocked by matters relating to sex or nudity.

– SYNONYMS **puritan,** prig, killjoy, moralist; informal goody-goody, bluenose.

– DERIVATIVES **prud·er·y** /ˈpro͞odərē/ noun.
– ORIGIN French *prudefemme* 'good woman and true.'

pru·dent /ˈpro͞odnt/ ▸ **adjective** acting with or showing care and thought for the future.

– SYNONYMS **1 wise,** well judged, sensible, politic, judicious, shrewd, sage, sagacious, farsighted, canny. **2 cautious,** careful, provident, circumspect, thrifty, economical.
– ANTONYMS unwise, extravagant.

– DERIVATIVES **pru·dence** noun **pru·dent·ly** adverb.
– ORIGIN Latin *prudens.*

CHOOSE THE RIGHT WORD

See **ECONOMICAL**.

pru·den·tial /pro͞oˈdenCHəl/ ▸ **adjective** involving or showing care and forethought, especially in business.
– DERIVATIVES **pru·den·tial·ly** adverb.

prud·ish /ˈpro͞odiSH/ ▸ **adjective** easily shocked by matters relating to sex or nudity.

– SYNONYMS *it's unusual to find someone so young and yet so prudish* **puritanical,** priggish, prim, moralistic, censorious, strait-laced, Victorian, stuffy; informal goody-goody.
– ANTONYMS permissive.

prune[1] /pro͞on/ ▸ **noun** a dried plum with a black, wrinkled appearance.
– ORIGIN Greek *prounon* 'plum.'

prune[2] ▸ **verb 1** trim a tree, shrub, or bush by cutting away dead or overgrown branches or stems. **2** make smaller by removing unwanted parts: *staff numbers have been pruned.*

– SYNONYMS **1 cut back,** trim, clip, shear, shorten, thin, shape. **2 reduce,** cut (back/down), pare (down), slim down, trim, downsize, ax, shrink; informal slash.
– ANTONYMS increase.

▸ **noun** an instance of pruning something.
– DERIVATIVES **prun·er** noun.
– ORIGIN Old French *proignier.*

pru·ri·ent /ˈpro͝orēənt/ ▸ **adjective** having or encouraging too great an interest in sexual matters.

– SYNONYMS **salacious,** licentious, voyeuristic, lascivious, lecherous, lustful, lewd, libidinous.

– DERIVATIVES **pru·ri·ence** noun **pru·ri·ent·ly** adverb.
– ORIGIN from Latin *prurire* 'itch, long, be wanton.'

pru·ri·tus /pro͝oˈrītəs/ ▸ **noun** severe itching of the skin.
– DERIVATIVES **pru·rit·ic** /-ˈritik/ adjective.
– ORIGIN Latin, 'itching.'

Prus·sian /ˈprəSHən/ ▸ **noun** a person from the former German kingdom of Prussia. ▸ **adjective** relating to Prussia.

Prus·sian blue ▸ **noun** a deep blue pigment.

prus·sic ac·id /ˈprəsik/ ▸ **noun** old-fashioned term for **HYDROCYANIC ACID**.
– ORIGIN from French *prussique* 'relating to Prussian blue.'

pry[1] /prī/ ▸ **verb** (**pries, prying, pried**) inquire too intrusively into a person's private affairs.

– SYNONYMS **be inquisitive,** poke about/around, ferret about/around, spy, be a busybody; informal stick/poke one's nose in/into, be nosy, snoop.

– DERIVATIVES **pry·ing** adjective & noun.
– ORIGIN unknown.

pry[2] ▸ **verb** (**pries, prying, pried**) use force to move or open something, or to separate something from something else.
– ORIGIN from **PRISE**.

PS ▸ **abbreviation 1** police sergeant. **2** postscript. **3** public school.

psalm /sä(l)m/ ▸ **noun** a religious song or hymn, in particular any of those contained in the Book of Psalms in the Bible.
– DERIVATIVES **psalm·ist** noun.
– ORIGIN Greek *psalmos* 'song sung to harp music.'

psal·ter /ˈsôltər/ ▸ **noun** a copy of the Book of Psalms in the Bible.
– ORIGIN Greek *psaltērion* 'stringed instrument.'

psal·ter·y /ˈsôltərē/ ▸ **noun** (pl. **psalteries**) an ancient and medieval musical instrument like a dulcimer but played by plucking the strings.

PSAT ▸ **abbreviation** Preliminary Scholastic Aptitude Test.

pse·phol·o·gy /sēˈfäləjē/ ▸ **noun** the statistical study of elections and trends in voting.
– DERIVATIVES **pse·phol·o·gist** noun.
– ORIGIN from Greek *psēphos* 'pebble, vote.'

pseud /so͞od/ ▸ **noun** Brit. informal a person who tries to impress others by pretending to have knowledge, especially about art or literature.

pseu·do /ˈso͞odō/ ▸ **adjective** informal not genuine; fake, pretentious, or insincere.

pseudo- (also **pseud-** before a vowel) ▶ **combining form** false; not genuine: *pseudonym*.
– ORIGIN from Greek *pseudēs* 'false.'

pseu·do·e·phed·rine /ˌso͞odōəˈfedrin/ ▶ **noun** a drug used as a nasal decongestant.

pseu·do·nym /ˈso͞odn-im/ ▶ **noun** a false name, especially one used by an author.

– SYNONYMS **pen name,** nom de plume, assumed name, alias, sobriquet, stage name, nom de guerre.

– ORIGIN from Greek *pseudēs* 'false' + *onoma* 'name.'

pseu·don·y·mous /so͞oˈdänəməs/ ▶ **adjective** writing or written under a false name.
– DERIVATIVES **pseu·do·nym·i·ty** /ˌso͞odnˈimətē/ noun **pseu·don·y·mous·ly** adverb.

pseu·do·sci·ence /ˌso͞odōˈsīəns/ ▶ **noun** beliefs or practices mistakenly regarded as being based on scientific methods.
– DERIVATIVES **pseu·do·sci·en·tif·ic** /-ˌsīənˈtifik/ adjective.

p.s.i. ▶ **abbreviation** pounds per square inch.

psil·o·cy·bin /ˌsīləˈsībin/ ▶ **noun** a substance that causes hallucinations, found in certain toadstools.
– ORIGIN from Greek *psilos* 'bald' + *kubē* 'head.'

psit·ta·cine /ˈsitəˌsīn/ Ornithology ▶ **adjective** relating to birds of the parrot family. ▶ **noun** a bird of the parrot family.
– ORIGIN from Greek *psittakos* 'parrot.'

psit·ta·co·sis /ˌsitəˈkōsəs/ ▶ **noun** a contagious disease of birds, which can be passed (especially from parrots) to human beings as a form of pneumonia.

pso·ri·a·sis /səˈrīəsəs/ ▶ **noun** a skin disease marked by red, itchy, scaly patches.
– DERIVATIVES **pso·ri·at·ic** /ˌsôrēˈatik/ adjective.
– ORIGIN Greek, from *psōrian* 'to itch.'

PST ▶ **abbreviation** Pacific Standard Time.

psych /sīk/ ▶ **verb** informal **1** (**psych someone up**) mentally prepare someone for a difficult task or occasion: *we had to psych ourselves up for the race*. **2** (**psych someone out**) intimidate an opponent or rival by appearing very confident or aggressive.

psy·che /ˈsīkē/ ▶ **noun** the human soul, mind, or spirit.
– ORIGIN Greek *psukhē* 'breath, life, soul.'

psych·e·de·lia /ˌsīkəˈdēlyə/ ▶ **noun** music, culture, or art based on the experiences produced by psychedelic drugs.

psy·che·del·ic /ˌsīkəˈdelik/ ▶ **adjective 1** (of drugs) producing hallucinations. **2** (of rock music) experimental and having drug-related lyrics. **3** having an intense, bright color or a swirling abstract pattern.
– DERIVATIVES **psy·che·del·i·cal·ly** /-ik(ə)lē/ adverb.
– ORIGIN from Greek *psyche* 'soul' + *dēlos* 'clear, manifest.'

psy·chi·a·trist /səˈkīətrist, sī-/ ▶ **noun** a doctor specializing in the diagnosis and treatment of mental illness.

– SYNONYMS **psychotherapist,** psychoanalyst, analyst; informal shrink.

psy·chi·a·try /səˈkīətrē, sī-/ ▶ **noun** the branch of medicine concerned with the study and treatment of mental disorders.
– DERIVATIVES **psy·chi·at·ric** /ˌsīkēˈatrik/ adjective **psy·chi·at·ri·cal·ly** /-ik(ə)lē/ adverb.
– ORIGIN from Greek *psukhē* 'soul, mind' + *iatreia* 'healing.'

psy·chic /ˈsīkik/ ▶ **adjective 1** relating to abilities or phenomena that cannot be explained by natural laws, especially involving telepathy or clairvoyance. **2** (of a person) appearing or considered to be telepathic or clairvoyant. **3** relating to the soul or mind.

– SYNONYMS **1 supernatural,** paranormal, otherworldly, metaphysical, extrasensory, magic(al), mystic(al), occult. **2 clairvoyant,** telepathic.

▶ **noun** a person considered or claiming to have psychic powers; a medium.

– SYNONYMS **clairvoyant,** fortune teller, medium, spiritualist, telepath, mind-reader.

– DERIVATIVES **psy·chi·cal** /ˈsīkikəl/ adjective **psy·chi·cal·ly** /ˈsīkik(ə)lē/ adverb.

psy·cho /ˈsīkō/ ▶ **noun** (pl. **psychos**) informal a psychopath.

psycho- ▶ **combining form** relating to the mind or psychology: *psychometrics*.
– ORIGIN from Greek *psukhē* 'breath, soul, mind.'

psy·cho·ac·tive /ˌsīkōˈaktiv/ ▶ **adjective** affecting the mind.

psy·cho·a·nal·y·sis /ˌsīkōəˈnaləsəs/ ▶ **noun** a method of treating mental disorders by investigating the conscious and unconscious elements in the mind and bringing repressed fears and conflicts into the conscious mind.
– DERIVATIVES **psy·cho·an·a·lyst** /ˌsīkōˈanl-əst/ noun **psy·cho·an·a·lyt·ic** /ˌsīkōˌanlˈitik/ adjective.

psy·cho·an·a·lyze /ˌsīkōˈanlˌīz/ ▶ **verb** treat someone using psychoanalysis.

psy·cho·bab·ble /ˈsīkōˌbabəl/ ▶ **noun** informal, derogatory jargon used in popular psychology.

psy·cho·dra·ma /ˌsīkōˈdrämə, -ˈdramə/ ▶ **noun 1** a form of psychotherapy in which patients act out events from their past. **2** a play, movie, or novel in which psychological elements are the main interest.

psy·cho·ki·ne·sis /ˌsīkōkəˈnēsis/ ▶ **noun** the supposed ability to move objects by mental effort alone.
– DERIVATIVES **psy·cho·ki·net·ic** /-ˈnetik/ adjective.

psy·cho·log·i·cal /ˌsīkəˈläjəkəl/ ▶ **adjective 1** relating to or affecting the mind. **2** relating to psychology.

– SYNONYMS **1 mental,** emotional, inner, cognitive. **2 (all) in the mind,** psychosomatic, emotional, subjective, subconscious, unconscious.
– ANTONYMS physical.

– DERIVATIVES **psy·cho·log·i·cal·ly** /-ik(ə)lē/ adverb.

psy·cho·log·i·cal war·fare ▶ **noun** actions intended to reduce an opponent's confidence.

psy·chol·o·gy /sīˈkäləjē/ ▶ **noun 1** the scientific study of the human mind and its functions. **2** the mental characteristics or attitude of a person.

– SYNONYMS **mind,** mindset, thought processes, way of thinking, mentality, psyche, attitude(s), make-up, character, temperament; informal what makes someone tick.

– DERIVATIVES **psy·chol·o·gist** noun.

psy·cho·met·rics /ˌsīkəˈmetriks/ ▶ **plural noun** (treated as sing.) the science of measuring mental abilities and processes.
– DERIVATIVES **psy·cho·met·ric** adjective.

psy·cho·path /ˈsīkəˌpaTH/ ▶ **noun** a person suffering from a serious mental disorder that causes them to commit violent or antisocial acts.

– DERIVATIVES **psy·cho·path·ic** /ˌsīkəˈpaTHik/ adjective.

psy·cho·pa·thol·o·gy /ˌsīkōpəˈTHäləjē, -paTHˈäl-/ ▶ **noun 1** the scientific study of mental disorders. **2** mental or behavioral disorder.
– DERIVATIVES **psy·cho·path·o·log·i·cal** /-paTHōˈläjikəl/ adjective.

psy·chop·a·thy /sīˈkäpəTHē/ ▶ **noun** mental illness or disorder.

psy·cho·sex·u·al /ˌsīkōˈsekSHōōəl/ ▶ **adjective** relating to or involving the psychological aspects of a person's sexual feelings.
– DERIVATIVES **psy·cho·sex·u·al·ly** adverb.

psy·cho·sis /sīˈkōsəs/ ▶ **noun** (pl. **psychoses** /-ˌsēz/) a mental disorder in which a person's perception of reality is severely distorted.

psy·cho·so·cial /ˌsīkōˈsōSHəl/ ▶ **adjective** relating to the way in which social factors and individual thought and behavior are connected or linked.
– DERIVATIVES **psy·cho·so·cial·ly** adverb.

psy·cho·so·mat·ic /ˌsīkōsəˈmatik/ ▶ **adjective 1** (of a physical illness) caused or made worse by a mental factor such as stress. **2** relating to the way in which the mind and body affect each other.
– DERIVATIVES **psy·cho·so·mat·i·cal·ly** /-ik(ə)lē/ adverb.

psy·cho·sur·ger·y /ˌsīkōˈsərjərē/ ▶ **noun** brain surgery used to treat severe mental disorder.
– DERIVATIVES **psy·cho·sur·gi·cal** /-ˈsərjikəl/ adjective.

psy·cho·ther·a·py /ˌsīkōˈTHerəpē/ ▶ **noun** the treatment of mental disorder by psychological rather than medical means.
– DERIVATIVES **psy·cho·ther·a·peu·tic** /-ˌTHerəˈpyōōtik/ adjective **psy·cho·ther·a·pist** noun.

psy·chot·ic /sīˈkätik/ ▶ **adjective** relating to or having a mental disorder in which a person's perception of reality is severely distorted. ▶ **noun** a person with such a disorder.
– DERIVATIVES **psy·chot·i·cal·ly** /-ik(ə)lē/ adverb.

WORD TOOLKIT

psychotic ...	demented ...	crazed ...
disorder	old man	fan
episode	soul	gunman
killer	minds	animal
rage	comedy	genius

psy·cho·tro·pic /ˌsīkəˈtrōpik, -ˈträpik/ ▶ **adjective** (of drugs) affecting a person's mental state.

PT ▶ **abbreviation** physical therapy.

Pt ▶ **abbreviation 1** Part. **2** (**pt**) pint. **3** (in scoring) point. **4** Printing point (as a unit of measurement). **5** (**Pt.**) Point (on maps). **6** (**pt**) port (a side of a ship or aircraft). ▶ **symbol** the chemical element platinum.

p.t. ▶ **abbreviation 1** past tense. **2** post town. **3** pro tempore. **4** part time.

PTA ▶ **abbreviation** Parent–Teacher Association.

ptar·mi·gan /ˈtärməgən/ ▶ **noun** a grouse of northern mountains and the Arctic, whose gray and black plumage changes to white in winter.
– ORIGIN Scottish Gaelic *tàrmachan*.

pter·o·dac·tyl /ˌterəˈdaktəl/ ▶ **noun** a pterosaur (extinct flying reptile) of the late Jurassic period, with a long slender head and neck.
– ORIGIN from Greek *pteron* 'wing' + *daktulos* 'finger.'

pter·o·saur /ˈterəˌsôr/ ▶ **noun** an extinct flying reptile of the Jurassic and Cretaceous periods.
– ORIGIN from Greek *pteron* 'wing' + *sauros* 'lizard.'

PTO ▶ **abbreviation 1** Parent–Teacher Organization. **2** chiefly Brit. please turn over.

Ptol·e·ma·ic /ˌtäləˈmā-ik/ ▶ **adjective 1** relating to the 2nd-century Greek astronomer Ptolemy. **2** relating to the Ptolemies, rulers of Egypt 304–30 BC.

Ptol·e·ma·ic sys·tem (also **Ptolemaic theory**) ▶ **noun** the former theory that the earth is the stationary center of the universe. Compare with **COPERNICAN SYSTEM**.

pto·maine /ˈtōˌmān, tōˈmān/ ▶ **noun** any of a group of organic compounds with an unpleasant taste and smell formed in decaying animal and vegetable matter.
– ORIGIN from Greek *ptōma* 'corpse.'

PTSD ▶ **abbreviation** post-traumatic stress disorder.

Pu ▶ **symbol** the chemical element plutonium.

pub /pəb/ ▶ **noun 1** chiefly Brit. a tavern or bar. **2** Austral. a hotel.

– SYNONYMS **bar,** tavern, lounge. informal watering hole. historical saloon.

– ORIGIN abbreviation of **PUBLIC HOUSE**.

pube /pyōōb/ ▶ **noun** vulgar slang a pubic hair.

pu·ber·ty /ˈpyōōbərtē/ ▶ **noun** the period during which adolescents reach sexual maturity and become able to have children.

– SYNONYMS **adolescence,** pubescence, youth, teenage years, teens.

– DERIVATIVES **pu·ber·tal** /-bərtl/ adjective.
– ORIGIN Latin *pubertas*, from *puber* 'adult.'

pu·bes ▶ **noun 1** /ˈpyōōbēz, pyōōbz/(pl. same) the lower part of the abdomen at the front of the pelvis, covered with hair from puberty. **2** /ˈpyōōbēz/ plural of **PUBIS**. **3** /pyōōbz/ vulgar slang plural of **PUBE**.
– ORIGIN Latin, 'pubic hair, genitals.'

pu·bes·cent /pyōōˈbesənt/ ▶ **adjective 1** relating to a person at or approaching the age of puberty. **2** Botany & Zoology covered with short, soft hair; downy.
– DERIVATIVES **pu·bes·cence** noun.
– ORIGIN from Latin *pubescere* 'reach puberty.'

pu·bic /ˈpyōōbik/ ▶ **adjective** relating to the pubes or pubis.

pu·bis /ˈpyōōbəs/ ▶ **noun** (pl. **pubes** /-bēz/) either of a pair of bones forming the two sides of the pelvis.
– ORIGIN from Latin *os pubis* 'bone of the pubes.'

pub·lic /ˈpəblik/ ▶ **adjective 1** relating to or available to the people as a whole: *a campaign to raise public awareness of the problem.* **2** relating to or involved in the affairs of the community, especially in government or entertainment: *a public figure.* **3** intended to be seen or heard by people in general: *a public apology.* **4** provided by the government rather than an independent commercial company.

– SYNONYMS **1 state,** national, constitutional, civic, civil, official, social, municipal, nationalized. **2 popular,** general, common, communal, collective, shared, joint, universal, widespread. **3 prominent,** well known, important, leading, eminent, distinguished, celebrated, household, famous. **4 open (to the public),** communal, available, free, unrestricted.
– ANTONYMS private, secret.

▶ **noun 1** (**the public**) (treated as sing. or pl.) ordinary people in society in general. **2** a group of people with a shared interest or activity: *the moviegoing public.*

– SYNONYMS **1 people,** citizens, subjects, electors, electorate, voters, taxpayers, residents, inhabitants, citizenry, population, populace, community, society, country, nation. **2 audience,** spectators, followers, following, fans, devotees, admirers.

– DERIVATIVES **pub·lic·ly** adverb.
– PHRASES **go public 1** reveal details about something that was previously secret or private. **2** become a public company. **in public** when other people are present. **the public eye** the state of being well known to people in general, especially through the media.
– ORIGIN Latin *publicus.*

WORD LINKS

agoraphobia *fear of public places*

pub·lic ad·dress sys·tem ▶ **noun** a system of microphones, amplifiers, and loudspeakers used to amplify speech or music.

pub·li·can /'pəblikən/ ▶ **noun 1** chiefly Brit. a person who owns or manages a bar. **2** Austral. a person who owns or manages a hotel. **3** (in ancient Roman and biblical times) a tax collector.
– ORIGIN Latin *publicanus.*

pub·li·ca·tion /ˌpəbli'kāsʜən/ ▶ **noun 1** the action or process of publishing something. **2** a published book or journal.

– SYNONYMS **1 book,** volume, title, opus, tome, newspaper, paper, magazine, periodical, newsletter, bulletin, journal, report. **2 issuing,** publishing, printing, distribution.

pub·lic de·fend·er ▶ **noun** Law a lawyer employed by the government in a criminal trial to represent a defendant who is unable to afford legal assistance.

pub·lic en·e·my ▶ **noun 1** a notorious wanted criminal. **2** a person or thing regarded as the greatest threat to a group or community.

pub·lic house ▶ **noun** Brit. formal term for **PUB**.

pub·li·cist /'pəbləsist/ ▶ **noun** a person responsible for publicizing a product or celebrity.

pub·lic·i·ty /pə'blisətē/ ▶ **noun 1** attention given to someone or something by the media. **2** information that is given out about a product, person, company, etc., in order to advertise or promote them.

– SYNONYMS **1 public attention,** media attention, exposure, glare, limelight, spotlight. **2 promotion,** advertising, propaganda, boost, push; informal hype, ballyhoo, buildup, plug.

pub·li·cize /'pəbləˌsīz/ ▶ **verb 1** make widely known: *their attempts to publicize the dangers of pesticides.* **2** advertise or promote something.

– SYNONYMS **1 make known,** make public, announce, broadcast, spread, promulgate, disseminate, circulate, air. **2 advertise,** promote, build up, talk up, push, beat the drum for, boost; informal hype, plug.
– ANTONYMS conceal, suppress.

CHOOSE THE RIGHT WORD

See **ANNOUNCE**.

pub·lic nui·sance ▶ **noun 1** an act that is illegal because it interferes with the rights of the public generally. **2** informal an unpleasant or dangerous person or group.

pub·lic pros·e·cu·tor ▶ **noun** a district attorney.

pub·lic re·la·tions ▶ **plural noun** (treated as sing.) the business of creating and maintaining a good public image for an organization or well-known person.

pub·lic school ▶ **noun 1** (chiefly in North America) a school supported by public funds. **2** (in the UK) a private fee-paying secondary school.

pub·lic sec·tor ▶ **noun** the part of an economy that is controlled by the government.

pub·lic serv·ant ▶ **noun** a person who works for the government.

pub·lic-spir·it·ed ▶ **adjective** showing a willingness to do things that will help other people in society.

pub·lic trans·por·ta·tion ▶ **noun** buses, trains, and other forms of transport that are available to the public, charge set fares, and run on fixed routes.

pub·lic u·til·i·ty ▶ **noun** an organization supplying the community with electricity, gas, water, or sewerage.

pub·lish /'pəblisʜ/ ▶ **verb 1** prepare and issue a book, newspaper, piece of music, etc., for public sale. **2** print something in a book, newspaper, or journal so as to make it generally known. **3** formally announce or read an edict or marriage banns.

– SYNONYMS **1 issue,** bring out, produce, print. **2 make known,** make public, publicize, announce, broadcast, issue, put out, distribute, spread, promulgate, disseminate, circulate, air.

– DERIVATIVES **pub·lish·a·ble** adjective **pub·lish·ing** noun.
– ORIGIN Latin *publicare* 'make public.'

pub·lish·er /'pəblisʜər/ ▶ **noun 1** a company or person that prepares and issues books, newspapers, journals, or music for sale. **2** a newspaper proprietor.

puce /pyo͞os/ ▶ **noun** a dark red or purple-brown color.
– ORIGIN French, 'flea, flea-color.'

puck¹ /pək/ ▶ **noun** a black disk made of hard rubber, used in ice hockey.
– ORIGIN unknown.

puck² ▶ **noun** a mischievous or evil spirit.
– ORIGIN Old English.

puck·er /'pəkər/ ▶ **verb** tightly gather or contract into wrinkles or small folds: *she puckered her lips.*

– SYNONYMS **wrinkle,** crinkle, crease, furrow, crumple, rumple, ruck up, scrunch up, ruffle, screw up, shrivel.

▶ **noun** a wrinkle or small fold.

– SYNONYMS **wrinkle,** crinkle, crumple, furrow, line, fold.

– ORIGIN probably from **POKE²** and **POCKET**.

puck·ish /'pəkisʜ/ ▶ **adjective** playful and mischievous.

pud·ding /'po͝odiɴɢ/ **1** a dessert with a creamy consistency. **2** chiefly Brit. a dessert, especially a cooked one. **3** chiefly Brit. the dessert course of a meal. **4** a sweet or savory steamed dish made with flour. **5** Brit. the intestines of a pig or sheep stuffed with oatmeal, spices, and meat and boiled.
– DERIVATIVES **pud·ding·y** adjective.
– ORIGIN probably from Old French *boudin* 'black pudding.'

pud·dle /ˈpədl/ ▶ **noun 1** a small pool of liquid, especially of rainwater on the ground. **2** clay and sand mixed with water and used as a watertight covering or lining for embankments or canals. ▶ **verb 1** cover with or form puddles. **2** (usu. as n. **puddling**) historical stir molten iron with iron oxide in a furnace, to produce wrought iron.
– ORIGIN Old English, 'small ditch.'

pu·den·dum /pyo͞oˈdendəm/ ▶ **noun** (pl. **pudenda** /-ˈdendə/) the external genitals, especially those of a woman.
– ORIGIN from Latin *pudenda membra* 'parts to be ashamed of.'

pudg·y /ˈpəjē/ ▶ **adjective** (**pudgier**, **pudgiest**) informal fat or flabby.
– ORIGIN unknown.

pueb·lo /ˈpweblō/ ▶ **noun** (pl. **pueblos**) **1** a town or village in Spain, Latin America, or the southwestern US, especially an American Indian settlement. **2** (**Pueblo**) (pl. same or **Pueblos**) a member of any of various American Indian peoples living in pueblos, chiefly in New Mexico and Arizona.
– ORIGIN Spanish, 'people.'

pu·er·ile /ˈpyo͝o(ə)rəl, ˈpyo͝orˌīl/ ▶ **adjective** childishly silly and trivial.

– SYNONYMS **childish,** immature, infantile, juvenile, babyish, silly, inane, fatuous, foolish.
– ANTONYMS mature.

– DERIVATIVES **pu·er·il·i·ty** /pyo͝o(ə)ˈrilətē/ noun (pl. **puerilities**).
– ORIGIN from Latin *puer* 'child, boy.'

pu·er·per·al fe·ver /pyo͞oˈərpərəl/ ▶ **noun** fever caused by infection of the uterus after childbirth.
– ORIGIN from Latin *puer* 'child, boy' + *parus* 'bearing.'

Puer·to Ri·can /ˌpôrtə ˈrēkən, ˌpwertə/ ▶ **noun** a person from Puerto Rico. ▶ **adjective** relating to Puerto Rico.

puff /pəf/ ▶ **noun 1** a small amount of air or smoke blown from somewhere. **2** an act of drawing quickly on a pipe, cigarette, or cigar. **3** a light pastry case, typically filled with cream or jam. **4** informal (usu. **puff piece**) an overly complimentary review or advertisement.

– SYNONYMS **1 gust,** blast, flurry, rush, draft, waft, breeze, breath. **2 pull;** informal drag, toke.

▶ **verb 1** breathe in repeated short gasps. **2** move with short, noisy puffs of air or steam: *a train puffed steadily across the bridge.* **3** smoke a pipe, cigarette, or cigar. **4** (**puff out/up** or **puff something out/up**) swell or cause to swell: *he puffed his chest out.*

– SYNONYMS **1 breathe heavily,** pant, blow, gasp. **2 smoke,** draw on, drag on, inhale.

– DERIVATIVES **puff·er** noun.
– ORIGIN imitating the sound.

puff ad·der ▶ **noun** a large African viper that inflates the upper part of its body and hisses loudly when threatened.

puff·ball /ˈpəfˌbôl/ ▶ **noun** a fungus that produces a large round fruiting body that bursts when ripe to release a cloud of spores.

puff·er·fish /ˈpəfərˌfisʜ/ ▶ **noun** (pl. same or **pufferfishes**) a fish with a spiny body that can inflate itself like a balloon when threatened.

puff·er·y /ˈpəfərē/ ▶ **noun** exaggerated or false praise.

puf·fin /ˈpəfən/ ▶ **noun** a seabird of the North Atlantic with a large head and a massive brightly colored triangular bill.
– ORIGIN probably from **PUFF**.

puff pas·try ▶ **noun** light flaky pastry.

puff·y /ˈpəfē/ ▶ **adjective** (**puffier**, **puffiest**) **1** softly rounded: *puffy clouds.* **2** (of a part of the body) swollen and soft.

– SYNONYMS **swollen,** puffed up, distended, enlarged, inflated, dilated, bloated, engorged, bulging.

– DERIVATIVES **puff·i·ness** noun.

WORD TOOLKIT

puffy ...	swollen ...	bloated ...
eyes	glands	bureaucracy
clouds	lips	corpse
face	ankles	ego
sleeves	feet	belly
cotton ball	river	budget

pug /pəg/ ▶ **noun** a small dog with a broad flat nose and deeply wrinkled face.
– ORIGIN perhaps German.

pu·gi·list /ˈpyo͞ojəlist/ ▶ **noun** chiefly humorous a boxer.
– DERIVATIVES **pu·gi·lism** /-ˌlizəm/ noun **pu·gi·lis·tic** /ˌpyo͞ojəˈlistik/ adjective.
– ORIGIN Latin *pugil* 'boxer.'

pug·na·cious /pəgˈnāsʜəs/ ▶ **adjective** eager or quick to argue, quarrel, or fight.

– SYNONYMS **combative,** aggressive, antagonistic, belligerent, quarrelsome, argumentative, hostile, truculent.
– ANTONYMS peaceable.

– DERIVATIVES **pug·nac·i·ty** /ˌpəgˈnasətē/ noun.
– ORIGIN from Latin *pugnare* 'to fight.'

pug nose ▶ **noun** a short nose with an upturned tip.

pu·is·sance /ˈpwisəns, ˈpwē-, pyo͞oˈisəns/ ▶ **noun 1** a show jumping competition that tests a horse's ability to jump large, high obstacles. **2** old use or literary great power or skill.
– DERIVATIVES **pu·is·sant** /ˈpwisənt, ˈpwēsənt, ˈpyo͞oəsənt/ adjective (old use or literary).
– ORIGIN Old French, from Latin *posse* 'be able.'

pu·ja /ˈpo͞ojə/ ▶ **noun** a Hindu ceremonial offering.
– ORIGIN Sanskrit, 'worship.'

puke /pyo͞ok/ ▶ **verb & noun** informal vomit.
– DERIVATIVES **puk·ey** adjective.
– ORIGIN probably imitating the sound.

puk·ka /ˈpəkə/ (also **pukkah**) ▶ **adjective** informal **1** authentic or genuine. **2** socially acceptable. **3** informal excellent.
– ORIGIN Hindi, 'cooked, ripe, substantial.'

pu·lao /pəˈlou, pəˈlō, ˈpərlo͞o/ ▶ **noun** variant spelling of **PILAF**.

pul·chri·tude /ˈpəlkrəˌt(y)o͞od/ ▶ **noun** literary beauty.
– DERIVATIVES **pul·chri·tu·di·nous** /ˌpəlkrəˈt(y)o͞odn-əs/ adjective.
– ORIGIN from Latin *pulcher* 'beautiful.'

pule /pyo͞ol/ ▶ **verb** (often as adj. **puling**) literary cry feebly or in a complaining way.
– ORIGIN probably imitating the sound.

pull /po͝ol/ ▶ **verb 1** apply force to someone or something so as to move them toward oneself or the origin of the force. **2** remove by pulling: *she pulled a handkerchief* *from her pocket.* **3** strain a muscle or ligament. **4** attract as a customer: *a DJ who is expected to pull in the crowds.* **5** move steadily: *the bus pulled away.* **6** move oneself with effort or against resistance: *she tried to pull away from him.* **7** (**pull at/on**) inhale deeply while drawing on a cigarette. **8** informal cancel an event or withdraw an advertisement. **9** informal bring out a weapon for use. **10** deliberately slow the speed of a horse to make it lose a race.

– SYNONYMS **1 tug,** haul, drag, draw, tow, heave, jerk, wrench; informal yank. **2** *she pulled a muscle* **strain,** sprain, wrench, tear. **3 attract,** draw, bring in, pull in, lure, seduce, entice, tempt.
– ANTONYMS push.

▶ **noun 1** an act of pulling. **2** a force, influence, or attraction: *the pull of her home town was a strong one.* **3** a deep drink of something, or an act of taking a deep breath from a cigarette, pipe, etc.

– SYNONYMS **1 tug,** jerk, heave; informal yank. **2 attraction,** draw, lure, magnetism, fascination, appeal, allure.

– DERIVATIVES **pull·er** noun.
– PHRASES **pull back** retreat or withdraw. **pull something down** demolish a building. **pull someone/thing in 1** succeed in securing or obtaining something. **2** informal arrest someone. **pull someone's leg** deceive someone playfully. **pull something off** informal succeed in achieving or winning something difficult. **pull out** withdraw or retreat. **pull the plug on** informal prevent something from happening or continuing. **pull (one's) punches** be less forceful, severe, or critical than one could be. **pull strings** make use of one's influence to gain an advantage. **pull through** get through an illness or other difficult situation. **pull oneself together** regain one's self-control. **pull up** (of a vehicle) come to a halt. **pull someone up** make someone stop or pause. **pull one's weight** do one's fair share of work.
– ORIGIN Old English, 'pluck, snatch.'

pul·let /'po͝olət/ ▶ **noun** a young hen, especially one less than one year old.
– ORIGIN Old French *poulet.*

pul·ley /'po͝olē/ ▶ **noun** (pl. **pulleys**) a wheel with a grooved rim around which a rope, chain, or belt passes, used to raise heavy weights.
– ORIGIN Old French *polie.*

Pull·man /'po͝olmən/ ▶ **noun** (pl. **Pullmans**) a luxurious railroad car.
– ORIGIN named after its American designer George M. *Pullman.*

pull·out /'po͝ol,out/ ▶ **adjective** (of a section of a magazine or newspaper) designed to be detached and kept. ▶ **noun 1** a pullout section of a magazine or newspaper. **2** a withdrawal from military involvement or a commercial venture.

pull·o·ver /'po͝ol,ōvər/ ▶ **noun** a knitted garment put on over the head and covering the top half of the body.

pul·lu·late /'pəlyə,lāt/ ▶ **verb 1** reproduce or spread so as to become abundant. **2** be filled with life and activity.
– ORIGIN Latin *pullulare* 'to sprout.'

pul·mo·nar·y /'po͝olmə,nerē, 'pəl-/ ▶ **adjective** relating to the lungs.
– ORIGIN from Latin *pulmo* 'lung.'

pulp /pəlp/ ▶ **noun 1** a soft, wet mass of crushed or pounded material. **2** the soft fleshy part of a fruit. **3** a soft, wet mass of fibers obtained from rags or wood, used in making paper.

– SYNONYMS **1 mush,** mash, paste, purée, slop, slush, mulch. **2 flesh,** marrow, meat.

▶ **verb 1** crush something into a pulp. **2** withdraw a publication from the market and recycle the paper.

– SYNONYMS **mash,** purée, cream, crush, press, liquidize.

▶ **adjective** referring to popular or sensational books or magazines, often regarded as being badly written: *pulp fiction.*
– DERIVATIVES **pulp·y** adjective.
– ORIGIN Latin *pulpa.*

pul·pit /'po͝ol,pit, 'pəl-, -pət/ ▶ **noun** a raised enclosed platform in a church or chapel from which the preacher gives a sermon.
– ORIGIN Latin *pulpitum* 'scaffold, platform.'

pul·sar /'pəl,sär/ ▶ **noun** an object in outer space, thought to be a rapidly rotating neutron star, that gives off regular rapid pulses of radio waves.
– ORIGIN from *pulsating star.*

pul·sate /'pəl,sāt/ ▶ **verb 1** expand and contract with strong regular movements. **2** produce a regular throbbing sensation or sound. **3** (as adj. **pulsating**) very exciting: *a pulsating semi-final.*
– DERIVATIVES **pul·sa·tion** /,pəl'sāshən/ noun.
– ORIGIN Latin *pulsare* 'throb, pulse.'

pulse[1] /pəls/ ▶ **noun 1** the regular throbbing of the arteries as blood is sent through them. **2** each successive throb of the arteries. **3** a single vibration or short burst of sound, electric current, or light. **4** a musical beat or other regular rhythm. **5** the center of activity in a particular area or field: *those close to the economic pulse.*

– SYNONYMS **1 heartbeat,** heart rate. **2 rhythm,** beat, tempo, pounding, throb, throbbing, thudding, drumming.

▶ **verb 1** pulsate. **2** convert a wave or beam into a series of pulses.

– SYNONYMS **throb,** pulsate, vibrate, beat, pound, thud, thump, drum, reverberate, echo.

– ORIGIN Latin *pulsus* 'beating.'

pulse[2] ▶ **noun** the edible seeds of certain plants of the pea family, e.g., lentils.
– ORIGIN Latin *puls* 'porridge of meal or pulse.'

pul·ver·ize /'pəlvə,rīz/ ▶ **verb 1** crush something into fine particles. **2** informal defeat utterly: *he pulverized the opposition.*

– SYNONYMS **1 grind,** crush, pound, powder, mill, press, pulp, mash; technical comminute. **2** *he pulverized the opposition* See **TROUNCE.**

– DERIVATIVES **pul·ver·iz·er** noun.
– ORIGIN Latin *pulverizare,* from *pulvis* 'dust.'

pu·ma /'p(y)o͞omə/ ▶ **noun** another term for **COUGAR.**
– ORIGIN Quechua.

pum·ice /'pəməs/ ▶ **noun** a light and porous form of solidified lava, used to remove hard skin.
– ORIGIN Old French *pomis.*

pum·mel /'pəməl/ ▶ **verb** (**pummels, pummeling, pummeled**) strike someone or something repeatedly with the fists.

– SYNONYMS **batter,** pound, belabor, beat, punch, strike, hit, thump; informal clobber, wallop, bash, whack, beat the living daylights out of, belt, lay into.

– ORIGIN variant of **POMMEL.**

pump[1] /pəmp/ ▶ **noun** a mechanical device using suction or pressure to raise or move liquids, compress gases, or force air into inflatable objects. ▶ **verb 1** force liquid or gas to move by using a pump or by means of something that works like a pump: *the heart pumps blood around the body.* **2** (of liquid) flow as if being forced by a pump. **3** fill something with liquid or gas. **4** move or cause to move vigorously up and down: *we had to pump the handle like mad.* **5** (**pump something out**) produce something in large quantities or amounts: *carnival bands pumping out music.* **6** informal try to obtain information from someone by persistent questioning. **7** (as adj. **pumped up**) informal very enthusiastic or excited.

– SYNONYMS **1 force,** drive, push, inject, suck, draw. **2 spurt,** spout, squirt, jet, surge, spew, gush, stream, flow, pour, spill, well, cascade. **3 inflate,** blow up, fill up, swell, enlarge, distend, expand, dilate, puff up.

– PHRASES **pump iron** informal exercise with weights.
– ORIGIN related to Dutch *pomp* 'ship's pump.'

pump[2] ▶ **noun** a lightweight women's shoe, with a low-cut upper and a medium heel.
– ORIGIN unknown.

pump-ac·tion ▶ **adjective** referring to a firearm capable of firing several shots in succession without reloading, in which a new round is brought into the chamber by a slide action in line with the barrel.

pum·per·nick·el /ˈpəmpərˌnikəl/ ▶ **noun** a dark, dense German bread made from whole-grain rye.
– ORIGIN German, originally meaning 'lout, bumpkin.'

pump·kin /ˈpəm(p)kən, ˈpəNGkən/ ▶ **noun 1** a large rounded orange-yellow fruit with a thick rind and edible flesh. **2** Brit. another term for SQUASH[2].
– ORIGIN former French *pompon.*

pun /pən/ ▶ **noun** a joke playing on the different meanings of a word or exploiting the fact that there are words of the same sound and different meanings. ▶ **verb** (**puns, punning, punned**) make a pun.
– DERIVATIVES **pun·ster** /ˈpənstər/ noun.
– ORIGIN uncertain.

punch[1] /pənCH/ ▶ **verb 1** strike someone or something with the fist. **2** press a button or key on a machine.

– SYNONYMS **hit,** strike, thump, jab, smash; informal sock, slug, bop, boff.

▶ **noun 1** a blow with the fist. **2** informal effectiveness or impact: *photos give their argument an extra visual punch.*

– SYNONYMS **blow,** hit, knock, thump, box, jab, clip; informal sock, slug, bop, boff.

– DERIVATIVES **punch·er** noun.
– PHRASES **beat someone to the punch** informal anticipate or forestall someone's actions.
– ORIGIN variant of POUNCE[1].

punch[2] ▶ **noun 1** a device or machine for making holes in paper, leather, metal, etc. **2** a tool or machine for stamping a design on a material. ▶ **verb** pierce a hole in paper, leather, metal, etc.

– SYNONYMS **perforate,** puncture, pierce, prick, hole, spike, skewer.

– ORIGIN perhaps an abbreviation of PUNCHEON, or from PUNCH[1].

punch[3] ▶ **noun** a drink made from fruit juices, spices, etc., and usually wine or liquor.
– ORIGIN apparently from a Sanskrit word meaning 'five, five kinds of' (because the drink had five ingredients).

punch·bowl /ˈpənCHˌbōl/ ▶ **noun 1** a deep bowl for mixing and serving punch. **2** chiefly Brit. a deep round hollow in a hilly area.

punch·card /ˈpənCHˌkärd/ ▶ **noun** a perforated card used to control the operation of a machine or (formerly) to program computers.

punch-drunk ▶ **adjective** confused or dazed as a result of a series of heavy blows to the head.

pun·cheon /pənCHən/ ▶ **noun 1** a short post, especially one used for supporting the roof in a coal mine. **2** another term for PUNCH[2].
– ORIGIN Old French *poinchon.*

punching bag ▶ **noun** a stuffed suspended bag used for punching as exercise or training, especially by boxers.

punch·line /ˈpənCHˌlīn/ ▶ **noun** the final part of a joke or story, providing the humor or climax.

punch-up ▶ **noun** informal, chiefly Brit. a brawl.

punch·y /ˈpənCHē/ ▶ **adjective** (**punchier, punchiest**) **1** having an immediate impact; forceful. **2** another term for PUNCH-DRUNK.

punc·til·i·o /ˌpəNGkˈtilēˌō/ ▶ **noun** (pl. **punctilios**) **1** a fine or trivial point of behavior or procedure. **2** punctilious behavior.
– ORIGIN Italian *puntiglio* and Spanish *puntillo* 'small point.'

punc·til·i·ous /ˌpəNGkˈtilēəs/ ▶ **adjective** showing great attention to detail or correct behavior.
– DERIVATIVES **punc·til·i·ous·ly** adverb **punc·til·i·ous·ness** noun.

punc·tu·al /ˈpəNGkCHo͞oəl/ ▶ **adjective** happening at or keeping to the arranged time.

– SYNONYMS **on time,** prompt, on schedule, in (good) time; informal on the dot.
– ANTONYMS late.

– DERIVATIVES **punc·tu·al·i·ty** /ˌpəNGkCHo͞oˈalitē/ noun **punc·tu·al·ly** adverb.
– ORIGIN Latin *punctualis,* from *punctum* 'a point.'

punc·tu·ate /ˈpəNGkCHo͞oˌāt/ ▶ **verb 1** occur or interrupt at intervals throughout: *the country's history has been punctuated by coups.* **2** put punctuation marks in a piece of writing.

– SYNONYMS **break up,** interrupt, intersperse, pepper, sprinkle, scatter.

– ORIGIN Latin *punctuare* 'bring to a point.'

punc·tu·a·tion /ˌpəNGkCHo͞oˈāSHən/ ▶ **noun** the marks, such as period, comma, and parentheses, used in writing to separate sentences and their parts and to make meaning clear.

punc·ture /ˈpəNGkCHər/ ▶ **noun** a small hole caused by a sharp object, especially one in a tire.

– SYNONYMS **1 hole,** perforation, rupture, cut, gash, slit, leak. **2 flat tire**; informal flat.

▶ **verb 1** make a puncture in something. **2** destroy a mood, feeling, etc.

– SYNONYMS **prick,** pierce, stab, rupture, perforate, cut, slit, deflate.

– ORIGIN Latin *punctura.*

pun·dit /ˈpəndit/ ▶ **noun 1** an expert who frequently gives opinions about a subject in public. **2** variant spelling of PANDIT.

– SYNONYMS **expert,** authority, specialist, doyen/doyenne, master, guru, sage, savant; informal buff, whiz.

– DERIVATIVES **pun·dit·ry** noun.
– ORIGIN from a Sanskrit word meaning 'learned.'

pun·gent /ˈpənjənt/ ▶ **adjective 1** having a sharply strong taste or smell. **2** (of remarks or humor) sharp and strongly worded.

> – SYNONYMS **strong,** powerful, pervasive, penetrating, sharp, acid, sour, biting, bitter, tart, vinegary, tangy, aromatic, spicy, piquant, peppery, hot, garlicky.
> – ANTONYMS bland, mild.

– DERIVATIVES **pun·gen·cy** noun **pun·gent·ly** adverb.
– ORIGIN from Latin *pungere* 'to prick.'

WORD TOOLKIT

pungent ...	aromatic ...	spicy ...
smell	herbs	Thai food
odor	oil	sauce
aroma	wine	burrito
smoke	candle	sausage
cheeses	rice	soup

Pu·nic /ˈpyo͞onik/ ▶ **adjective** relating to ancient Carthage. ▶ **noun** the language of ancient Carthage.
– ORIGIN Latin *Punicus*, from Greek *Phoinix* 'Phoenician.'

pun·ish /ˈpənisʜ/ ▶ **verb 1** cause someone to experience something unpleasant as a result of a criminal or wrongful act. **2** treat harshly or unfairly: *a rise in prescription charges would punish the poor*.

> – SYNONYMS **discipline,** penalize, correct, sentence, teach someone a lesson; informal come down on (like a ton of bricks); dated chastise.

– DERIVATIVES **pun·ish·a·ble** adjective.
– ORIGIN Latin *punire*.

pun·ish·ing /ˈpənisʜiɴɢ/ ▶ **adjective** arduous and demanding: *a punishing schedule*.

> – SYNONYMS **arduous,** demanding, taxing, strenuous, rigorous, stressful, trying, heavy, difficult, tough, exhausting, tiring, grueling.
> – ANTONYMS easy.

pun·ish·ment /ˈpənisʜmənt/ ▶ **noun 1** an unpleasant experience imposed on someone as a result of a criminal or wrongful act. **2** the action of punishing someone. **3** harsh or rough treatment.

> – SYNONYMS **penalty,** sanction, penance, discipline, forfeit, sentence.

WORD LINKS

penal, **punitive** *relating to punishment*

pu·ni·tive /ˈpyo͞onətiv/ ▶ **adjective 1** imposing or intended as punishment. **2** (of a tax or other charge) extremely high.

> – SYNONYMS **penal,** disciplinary, corrective.

– DERIVATIVES **pu·ni·tive·ly** adverb **pu·ni·tive·ness** noun.

Pun·ja·bi /ˌpənˈjäbē, po͝on-/ (also **Panjabi** /ˌpən-/) ▶ **noun** (pl. **Punjabis**) **1** a person from Punjab, a region of NW India and Pakistan. **2** the language of Punjab. ▶ **adjective** relating to Punjab.

punk /pəɴɢk/ ▶ **noun 1** (also **punk rock**) a loud, fast form of rock music characterized by aggressive lyrics and behavior. **2** (also **punk rocker**) an admirer or player of punk music, typically having colored spiked hair and clothing decorated with safety pins and zippers. **3** informal a worthless person; a thug or criminal. ▶ **adjective** relating to punk rock and its admirers.
– DERIVATIVES **punk·ish** adjective **punk·y** adjective.
– ORIGIN perhaps, in some senses, related to former *punk* 'prostitute,' also to **SPUNK**.

pun·kah /ˈpəɴɢkə/ ▶ **noun** chiefly historical (in India) a large cloth fan on a frame suspended from the ceiling, worked by a cord or electrically.
– ORIGIN Sanskrit, 'wing.'

punt[1] /pənt/ ▶ **noun** a long, narrow, flat-bottomed boat, square at both ends and propelled with a long pole. ▶ **verb** travel in a punt.
– DERIVATIVES **punt·er** noun.
– ORIGIN Latin *ponto*, referring to a flat-bottomed ferry boat.

punt[2] ▶ **verb 1** Football, etc. kick the ball after it has dropped from the hands and before it reaches the ground. **2** Football (of an offensive team) turn possession over to the defensive team by punting the ball after failing to make a first down. **3** delay in answering or taking action. ▶ **noun** a kick of this kind.
– DERIVATIVES **punt·er** noun.
– ORIGIN probably from dialect *punt*, 'push forcibly.'

punt[3] ▶ **verb 1** (in some gambling card games) lay a stake against the bank. **2** Brit. informal bet on or make a risky investment in something. ▶ **noun** Brit. informal a bet.
– DERIVATIVES **punt·er** noun.
– ORIGIN French *ponte* 'player against the bank.'

pu·ny /ˈpyo͞onē/ ▶ **adjective** (**punier**, **puniest**) **1** physically small and weak. **2** not impressive in quality, amount, or size: *their puny efforts*.

> – SYNONYMS **1 small,** weak, feeble, slight, undersized, stunted, underdeveloped; informal weedy. **2 pitiful,** pitiable, miserable, sorry, meager, paltry; informal pathetic, measly.
> – ANTONYMS sturdy.

– DERIVATIVES **pu·ni·ly** adverb **pu·ni·ness** noun.
– ORIGIN Old French *puisne* 'junior or inferior person.'

pup /pəp/ ▶ **noun 1** a young dog. **2** a young wolf, seal, rat, or other mammal. **3** dated an impudent or arrogant boy or young man. ▶ **verb** (**pups**, **pupping**, **pupped**) give birth to a pup or pups.
– ORIGIN from **PUPPY**.

pu·pa /ˈpyo͞opə/ ▶ **noun** (pl. **pupae** /-ˌpē, -ˌpī/) an insect in its inactive stage of development between larva and adult, e.g., a chrysalis.
– DERIVATIVES **pu·pal** adjective.
– ORIGIN Latin, 'girl, doll.'

pu·pate /ˈpyo͞oˌpāt/ ▶ **verb** (of an insect) become a pupa.
– DERIVATIVES **pu·pa·tion** /pyo͞oˈpāsʜən/ noun.

pu·pil[1] /ˈpyo͞opəl/ ▶ **noun** a person, especially a schoolchild, who is taught by someone; a student.

> – SYNONYMS **1 student,** scholar, schoolchild, schoolboy, schoolgirl. **2 disciple,** follower, student, protégé, apprentice, trainee, novice.
> – ANTONYMS teacher.

– ORIGIN from Latin *pupillus* 'little boy' and *pupilla* 'little girl.'

pu·pil[2] ▶ **noun** the dark circular opening in the center of the iris of the eye, which controls the amount of light reaching the retina.
– ORIGIN Latin *pupilla* 'little doll' (from the tiny reflected images visible in the eye).

pup·pet /ˈpəpət/ ▶ **noun 1** a model of a person or animal that can be moved either by strings or by a hand inside it. **2** a person under someone else's control.

– SYNONYMS **1 marionette,** sock puppet, finger puppet. **2 pawn,** tool, instrument, cat's paw, poodle, mouthpiece, stooge.

– DERIVATIVES **pup·pet·eer** /ˌpəpəˈtir/ noun **pup·pet·ry** noun.

– ORIGIN later form of the British term *poppet* 'a pretty or endearing child.'

pup·py /ˈpəpē/ ▶ **noun** (pl. **puppies**) **1** a young dog. **2** informal, dated a conceited or arrogant young man.

– DERIVATIVES **pup·py·ish** adjective.

– ORIGIN perhaps from Old French *poupee* 'doll, toy.'

pup·py love ▶ **noun** intense but short-lived feelings of love for someone, associated with adolescents.

pup tent ▶ **noun** a small triangular tent with room for one or two people.

pur·blind /ˈpərˌblīnd/ ▶ **adjective** literary **1** lacking awareness or understanding. **2** partially sighted.

– ORIGIN from **PURE** 'utterly' + **BLIND**.

pur·chase /ˈpərchəs/ ▶ **verb** buy something.

– SYNONYMS **buy,** acquire, obtain, pick up, procure, pay for, invest in; informal get (a) hold of, score.
– ANTONYMS sell.

▶ **noun 1** the action of buying something. **2** a thing bought. **3** firm contact or grip. **4** a pulley or similar device for moving heavy objects.

– SYNONYMS **1 acquisition,** buy, investment, order. **2 grip,** grasp, hold, foothold, toehold, anchorage, support, traction, leverage.
– ANTONYMS sale.

– DERIVATIVES **pur·chas·a·ble** adjective **pur·chas·er** noun.

– ORIGIN Old French *pourchacier* 'seek to obtain or bring about.'

pur·dah /ˈpərdə/ ▶ **noun** the practice in certain Muslim and Hindu societies of screening women from men or strangers by means of a curtain or clothes that completely conceal their bodies.

– ORIGIN from Urdu and Persian, 'veil, curtain.'

pure /pyo͝or/ ▶ **adjective 1** not mixed with any other substance or material: *the jacket was pure wool.* **2** free of contamination. **3** innocent or morally good. **4** complete; nothing but: *a shout of pure anger.* **5** theoretical rather than practical: *pure mathematics.* **6** (of a sound) perfectly in tune and with a clear tone.

– SYNONYMS **1 unadulterated,** undiluted, sterling, solid, unalloyed. **2 clean,** clear, fresh, sparkling, unpolluted, uncontaminated, untainted. **3 virtuous,** moral, good, righteous, honorable, reputable, wholesome, clean, honest, upright, upstanding, exemplary, innocent, chaste, unsullied, undefiled; informal squeaky clean. **4 sheer,** utter, absolute, out-and-out, complete, total, perfect.
– ANTONYMS impure, polluted.

– ORIGIN Latin *purus*.

pure·bred /ˈpyo͝orˌbred/ ▶ **adjective** (of an animal) bred from parents of the same breed or variety.

pu·rée /pyo͝oˈrā, -ˈrē/ ▶ **noun** a thick smooth substance made of crushed or liquidized fruit or vegetables. ▶ **verb** (**purées, puréeing, puréed**) make a purée of fruit or vegetables.

– ORIGIN French, 'purified.'

pure·ly /ˈpyo͝orlē/ ▶ **adverb** entirely; exclusively: *the purpose of the meeting was purely to give information.*

– SYNONYMS **entirely,** wholly, exclusively, solely, only, just, merely.

pure play ▶ **noun 1** a company whose products are available only through the Internet. **2** a company that focuses exclusively on one particular market or commodity.

pur·ga·tion /ˌpərˈgāshən/ ▶ **noun 1** purification. **2** emptying of the bowels brought about by laxatives.

– ORIGIN Latin, from *purgare* 'purify.'

pur·ga·tive /ˈpərgətiv/ ▶ **adjective** having a strong laxative effect. ▶ **noun** a laxative.

pur·ga·to·ry /ˈpərgəˌtôrē/ ▶ **noun** (pl. **purgatories**) **1** (in Catholic belief) a place or state of suffering inhabited by the souls of sinners who are atoning for their sins before going to heaven. **2** extreme distress or mental anguish.

– SYNONYMS **torment,** torture, misery, suffering, affliction, anguish, agony, woe, an ordeal, a nightmare, hell.
– ANTONYMS paradise.

– DERIVATIVES **pur·ga·to·ri·al** /ˌpərgəˈtôrēəl/ adjective.

– ORIGIN Latin *purgatorium*.

purge /pərj/ ▶ **verb 1** rid of unwanted or undesirable things: *years of analysis had purged him of anger.* **2** remove a group of people considered to be undesirable from an organization. **3** empty one's bowels, especially as a result of taking a laxative. **4** Law atone for or wipe out contempt of court.

– SYNONYMS **1 cleanse,** clear, purify, rid, empty, strip, scour. **2 remove,** get rid of, eliminate, clear out, sweep out, expel, eject, evict, dismiss, sack, oust, ax, depose, root out, weed out.

▶ **noun 1** an act of removing a group of people from an organization. **2** dated a laxative.

– SYNONYMS **removal,** elimination, expulsion, ejection, exclusion, eviction, dismissal.

– ORIGIN Latin *purgare* 'purify.'

pu·ri /ˈpo͝orē/ ▶ **noun** (pl. **puris**) (in Indian cooking) a small, round piece of unleavened bread that puffs up when deep-fried.

– ORIGIN Sanskrit.

pu·ri·fy /ˈpyo͝orəˌfī/ ▶ **verb** (**purifies, purifying, purified**) make something pure by removing harmful, dirty, or unwanted substances.

– SYNONYMS **clean,** cleanse, refine, decontaminate, filter, clear, freshen, deodorize, sanitize, disinfect, sterilize.

– DERIVATIVES **pu·ri·fi·ca·tion** /ˌpyo͝orəfiˈkāshən/ noun **pu·ri·fi·er** noun.

Pu·rim /ˈpo͝orim, po͝oˈrēm/ ▶ **noun** a Jewish festival held in spring to commemorate the defeat of Haman's plot to massacre the Jews.

– ORIGIN Hebrew, plural of *pūr* 'lot.'

pur·ist /ˈpyo͝orist/ ▶ **noun** a person who insists on following traditional rules, especially in language or style.

– DERIVATIVES **pur·ism** /ˈpyo͝orˌizəm/ noun.

pu·ri·tan /ˈpyo͝oritn/ ▶ **noun 1** (**Puritan**) a member of a group of English Protestants in the 16th and 17th centuries who sought to simplify and regulate forms of worship. **2** a person with strict moral beliefs who is critical of self-indulgent behavior. ▶ **adjective 1** (**Puritan**) relating to the Puritans. **2** characteristic of a puritan.

– DERIVATIVES **pu·ri·tan·ism** /ˈpyo͝oritəˌnizəm/ (also **Puritanism**) noun.

pu·ri·tan·i·cal /ˌpyo͝oriˈtanikəl/ ▸ **adjective** having a very strict or critical attitude toward self-indulgent behavior.

– SYNONYMS **moralistic,** puritan, strait-laced, stuffy, prudish, prim, priggish, narrow-minded, censorious, austere, severe, ascetic, abstemious; informal goody-goody, starchy.
– ANTONYMS permissive.

pu·ri·ty /ˈpyo͝oritē/ ▸ **noun** the state of being pure.

– SYNONYMS **1 cleanness,** freshness, cleanliness. **2 virtue,** morality, goodness, righteousness, piety, honor, honesty, integrity, innocence.

purl[1] /pərl/ ▸ **adjective** (of a knitting stitch) made by putting the needle through the front of the stitch from right to left. Compare with **PLAIN** (sense 8 of the adjective). ▸ **verb** knit with a purl stitch.
– ORIGIN uncertain.

purl[2] ▸ **verb** literary (of a stream or river) flow with a swirling movement and a continuous murmuring sound.
– ORIGIN probably imitating the sound.

pur·lieu /ˈpərl(y)o͞o/ ▸ **noun** (pl. **purlieus**) **1** (**purlieus**) the area near or surrounding a place. **2** a person's usual haunts.
– ORIGIN probably from Old French *puralee* 'a walk round to settle boundaries.'

pur·lin /ˈpərlən/ ▸ **noun** a horizontal beam along the length of a roof, supporting the rafters.
– ORIGIN perhaps French.

pur·loin /pərˈloin/ ▸ **verb** formal or humorous steal something.
– ORIGIN Old French *purloigner* 'put away.'

pur·ple /ˈpərpəl/ ▸ **noun 1** a color between red and blue. **2** (**the purple**) the scarlet official dress of a cardinal. ▸ **adjective** of a color between red and blue.
– DERIVATIVES **pur·plish** adjective **pur·ply** adjective.
– ORIGIN from Greek *porphura*, referring to molluscs from which a crimson dye was obtained, also to cloth dyed with this.

Pur·ple Heart ▸ **noun** a US military decoration for members of the armed forces wounded or killed in action.

pur·ple pas·sage ▸ **noun** an extremely ornate or elaborate passage in a literary work.

pur·ple prose ▸ **noun** prose that is too ornate.

pur·port ▸ **verb** /pərˈpôrt/ appear or claim to be someone or do something: *she is not the person she purports to be.* ▸ **noun** /ˈpərˌpôrt/ **1** the meaning of something. **2** the purpose of something.
– DERIVATIVES **pur·port·ed** adjective **pur·port·ed·ly** adverb.
– ORIGIN Latin *proportare.*

pur·pose /ˈpərpəs/ ▸ **noun 1** the reason for which something is done or for which something exists. **2** determination.

– SYNONYMS **1** *the purpose of his visit* **motive,** motivation, grounds, occasion, reason, point, basis, justification. **2** *their purpose was to subvert the economy* **intention,** aim, object, objective, goal, plan, ambition, aspiration. **3** *the original purpose of the porch* **function,** role, use. **4** *there was a sense of purpose in her step as she set off* **determination,** resolution, resolve, steadfastness, single-mindedness, enthusiasm, ambition, motivation, commitment, conviction, dedication.

▸ **verb** formal have something as one's aim or intention.
– PHRASES **on purpose** intentionally.
– ORIGIN Old French *porpos.*

CHOOSE THE RIGHT WORD

See **INTEND**.

pur·pose·ful /ˈpərpəsfəl/ ▸ **adjective 1** having or showing determination. **2** having a useful purpose.

– SYNONYMS **determined,** resolute, steadfast, single-minded, committed.
– ANTONYMS aimless.

– DERIVATIVES **pur·pose·ful·ly** adverb **pur·pose·ful·ness** noun.

pur·pose·less /ˈpərpəslis/ ▸ **adjective** done with or having no purpose.
– DERIVATIVES **pur·pose·less·ly** adverb **pur·pose·less·ness** noun.

pur·pose·ly /ˈpərpəslē/ ▸ **adverb** deliberately; on purpose.

– SYNONYMS **deliberately,** intentionally, on purpose, willfully, knowingly, consciously.

pur·pos·ive /ˈpərpəsiv, pərˈpō-/ ▸ **adjective** having or done with a purpose.
– DERIVATIVES **pur·pos·ive·ly** adverb **pur·pos·ive·ness** noun.

purr /pər/ ▸ **verb 1** (of a cat) make a low continuous sound in the throat, especially when happy or contented. **2** (of a vehicle or engine) move or run smoothly while making a similar sound. ▸ **noun** a purring sound.
– ORIGIN imitating the sound.

purse /pərs/ ▸ **noun 1** a handbag. **2** a small pouch for carrying money. **3** money available for spending; funds. **4** a sum of money given as a prize in a sporting contest.

– SYNONYMS **1 wallet,** change purse, billfold. **2 handbag,** pocketbook, shoulder bag, clutch (purse/bag). **3 prize,** reward, winnings, stake(s).

▸ **verb** pucker one's lips into a tight, round shape.

– SYNONYMS **press together,** compress, tighten, pucker, pout.

– PHRASES **hold the purse strings** have control of expenditure.
– ORIGIN Latin *bursa.*

purs·er /ˈpərsər/ ▸ **noun** a ship's officer who keeps the accounts, especially on a passenger vessel.

purse seine ▸ **noun** a large seine (fishing net) that may be drawn into the shape of a bag, used for catching fish swimming in shoals.

purs·lane /ˈpərslən, -ˌslān/ ▸ **noun** a small plant with fleshy leaves that grows in damp or marshy areas.
– ORIGIN Old French *porcelaine.*

pur·su·ance /pərˈso͞oəns/ ▸ **noun** formal the carrying out of a plan or action.

pur·su·ant /pərˈso͞oənt/ ▸ **adverb** (**pursuant to**) formal in accordance with a law or legal resolution.
– ORIGIN Old French.

pur·sue /pərˈso͞o/ ▸ **verb** (**pursues, pursuing, pursued**) **1** follow in order to catch or attack: *police officers pursued the car along I-95.* **2** try to achieve a goal. **3** engage in or continue with an activity or course of action: *he took a degree before pursuing his professional sports career.* **4** continue to investigate or discuss something.

– SYNONYMS **1 follow,** run after, chase, hunt, stalk, track, trail, hound. **2 strive for,** work toward, seek, search for, aim at/for, aspire to. **3 engage in,** be occupied in, practice, follow, conduct, ply, take up, undertake, carry on with, continue, proceed with, apply oneself to.

– DERIVATIVES **pur·su·er** noun.
– ORIGIN Old French *pursuer*.

pur·suit /pər'so͞ot/ ▶ **noun 1** the action of pursuing someone or something. **2** a leisure or sporting activity.

– SYNONYMS *a range of leisure pursuits* **activity,** hobby, pastime, diversion, recreation, amusement, occupation.

pu·ru·lent /'pyo͝or(y)ələnt/ ▶ **adjective** consisting of, containing, or discharging pus.
– ORIGIN Latin *purulentus*.

pur·vey /pər'vā/ ▶ **verb** formal provide or supply food or drink as one's business.
– DERIVATIVES **pur·vey·or** noun.
– ORIGIN Old French *purveier* 'foresee.'

pur·view /'pər,vyo͞o/ ▶ **noun** formal **1** the scope of the influence or concerns of something: *such crimes are not within the purview of the tribunal.* **2** a range of experience or thought.
– ORIGIN from Old French *purveu* 'foreseen.'

pus /pəs/ ▶ **noun** a thick yellowish or greenish liquid produced in infected tissue.
– ORIGIN Latin.

push /po͝osh/ ▶ **verb 1** apply force to someone or something so as to move them away from oneself or from the source of the force. **2** move one's body or a part of it forcefully into a particular position: *she pushed her hands into her pockets.* **3** move forward by using force: *he pushed his way through the crowd.* **4** drive oneself or urge someone to greater effort. **5** (**push for**) make persistent demands for something: *some legislators are pushing for tighter border controls.* **6** informal promote the use, sale, or acceptance of something. **7** informal sell a drug illegally. **8** (**be pushed**) informal have very little of something, especially time. **9** (**be pushing**) informal be nearly a particular age: *she's pushing forty.*

– SYNONYMS **1 shove,** thrust, propel, send, drive, force, prod, poke, nudge, elbow, shoulder, ram, squeeze, jostle. **2 press,** depress, hold down, squeeze, operate, activate. **3 urge,** press, pressure, pressurize, force, coerce, dragoon, browbeat; informal lean on, twist someone's arm.
– ANTONYMS pull.

▶ **noun 1** an act of pushing. **2** a great effort: *one last push for success.*

– SYNONYMS **1 shove,** thrust, nudge, bump, jolt, prod, poke. **2** *the army's eastward push* **advance,** drive, thrust, charge, attack, assault, onslaught, onrush, offensive.

– DERIVATIVES **push·er** noun.
– PHRASES **push ahead** proceed with or continue a course of action. **push off** exert pressure so as to move a boat out from shore or away from another vessel. **when push comes to shove** informal when one has no choice but to act or make a decision.
– ORIGIN Old French *pousser*.

push·cart /'po͝osh,kärt/ ▶ **noun** a small cart that is pushed or drawn by hand.

push·o·ver /'po͝osh,ōvər/ ▶ **noun** informal **1** a person who is easy to influence or defeat. **2** a thing that is easily done.

push-start ▶ **verb** start a motor vehicle by pushing it in order to make the engine turn.

push·up /'po͝osh,əp/ ▶ **noun** an exercise in which a person lies facing the floor and raises their body by pressing down on their hands.

push·y /'po͝oshē/ ▶ **adjective** (**pushier**, **pushiest**) too self-assertive or ambitious.

– SYNONYMS **assertive,** overbearing, domineering, aggressive, forceful, forward, thrusting, ambitious, overconfident, cocky; informal bossy.

– DERIVATIVES **push·i·ness** noun.

pu·sil·lan·i·mous /,pyo͞osə'lanəməs/ ▶ **adjective** timid or cowardly.
– DERIVATIVES **pu·sil·la·nim·i·ty** /-lə'nimətē/ noun.
– ORIGIN from Latin *pusillus* 'very small' + *animus* 'mind.'

puss[1] /po͝os/ ▶ **noun** informal **1** a cat. **2** a girl or young woman: *a glamour puss.*
– ORIGIN probably from German *pūs* or Dutch *poes*.

puss[2] ▶ **noun** informal a person's face or mouth.

pus·sy /'po͝osē/ ▶ **noun** (pl. **pussies**) **1** informal a cat. **2** vulgar slang a woman's genitals. **3** vulgar slang women considered sexually. **4** vulgar slang sexual intercourse with a woman. **5** informal a weak, cowardly, or effeminate man.

pus·sy·cat /'po͝osē,kat/ ▶ **noun** informal **1** a cat. **2** a mild-tempered or easy-going person.

pus·sy·foot /'po͝osē,fo͝ot/ ▶ **verb** (**pussyfoots**, **pussyfooting**, **pussyfooted**) act very cautiously.

pus·sy wil·low ▶ **noun** a willow with soft fluffy catkins that appear before the leaves.

pus·tule /'pəschoo͞l, 'pəst(y)o͞ol/ ▶ **noun** a small blister or pimple containing pus.
– DERIVATIVES **pus·tu·lar** adjective.
– ORIGIN Latin *pustula*.

put /po͝ot/ ▶ **verb** (**puts**, **putting**, **put**) **1** move to or place in a particular position. **2** express something in a particular way. **3** (**put something on**) make someone or something subject to something. **4** give a value, figure, or limit to something. **5** bring into a particular state or condition: *she tried to put me at ease.* **6** (of a ship) proceed in a particular direction: *the boat put out to sea.* **7** throw a shot or weight as an athletic sport.

– SYNONYMS **1** *he put down his cup* **place,** set, lay, deposit, position, leave, plant, locate, situate, settle, install; informal stick, dump, park, plunk, plonk, pop. **2** *to put it bluntly, we've been framed* **express,** word, phrase, frame, formulate, render, convey, state. **3** (**put something on**) *don't* **put** *the blame* **on** *me* **lay on,** pin on, place on, fix on; attribute to, impute to, assign to, allocate to, ascribe to. **4** *he put the cost at $8,000* **estimate,** calculate, reckon, gauge, assess, evaluate, value, judge, measure, compute, fix, set, peg; informal guesstimate.

▶ **noun** a throw of the shot or weight as a sport.
– PHRASES **be put upon** informal be taken advantage of as a result of one's good nature. **put about** (of a ship) turn on the opposite tack. **put someone down** informal criticize someone. **put something down 1** suppress a rebellion, coup, or riot by force. **2** kill a sick, old, or injured animal. **3** pay a sum as a deposit. **put something down to** attribute something to. **put one's hands together** applaud. **put someone off 1** cause someone to feel dislike or lose enthusiasm. **2** distract someone. **put something off** postpone something. **put something on 1** present or provide a play, service, etc. **2** become heavier by a particular amount. **3** adopt a particular

expression, accent, etc. **put someone out** inconvenience, upset, or annoy someone. **put something out** dislocate a joint. **put one over on** informal deceive someone into accepting something that is not true. **put someone through 1** subject someone to an unpleasant experience. **2** connect someone by telephone to another person or place. **put something to** offer or submit something to someone for consideration: *he put the proposal to his daughter*. **put someone up 1** give someone temporary accommodations. **2** propose someone for election or adoption. **put something up** present, provide, or offer something: *the sponsors are putting up $5,000*. **put someone up to** informal encourage someone to do something wrong or unwise. **put up with** tolerate or endure: *I'm too tired to put up with any nonsense*.
– ORIGIN Old English.

pu·ta·tive /ˈpyo͞otətiv/ ▶ **adjective** generally considered or believed to be: *the putative father of her children*.
– DERIVATIVES **pu·ta·tive·ly** adverb.
– ORIGIN from Latin *putare* 'think.'

put-down ▶ **noun** informal a humiliating or critical remark.

pu·tre·fy /ˈpyo͞otrəˌfī/ ▶ **verb** (**putrefies, putrefying, putrefied**) decay or rot and produce a very unpleasant smell.
– DERIVATIVES **pu·tre·fac·tion** /ˌpyo͞otrəˈfakshən/ noun.
– ORIGIN Latin *putrefacere*.

pu·tres·cent /pyo͞oˈtresənt/ ▶ **adjective** becoming putrid; rotting.

pu·trid /ˈpyo͞otrid/ ▶ **adjective 1** decaying or rotting and giving off a very unpleasant smell. **2** informal very unpleasant.

> – SYNONYMS **decomposing,** decaying, rotting, rotten, bad, foul, fetid, rank, putrefied, putrescent, rancid, moldy.

– ORIGIN from Latin *putrere* 'to rot.'

putsch /po͝och/ ▶ **noun** a violent attempt to overthrow a government.
– ORIGIN Swiss German, 'thrust, blow.'

putt /pət/ ▶ **verb** (**putts, putting, putted**) strike a golf ball gently so that it rolls into or near a hole. ▶ **noun** a stroke of this kind.
– ORIGIN Scots form of PUT.

put·ta·nes·ca /ˌpo͝otəˈneskə, ˌpo͝otnˈeskə/ ▶ **noun** a pasta sauce made with tomatoes, garlic, olives, anchovies, etc.
– ORIGIN Italian, from *puttana* 'a prostitute' (the sauce is said to have been devised by prostitutes as one which could be cooked quickly between clients' visits).

put·tee /ˌpəˈtē/ ▶ **noun** a long strip of cloth wound around the leg from ankle to knee for protection and support.
– ORIGIN Hindi, 'band, bandage.'

put·ter¹ /ˈpətər/ ▶ **noun** a golf club designed for putting.

put·ter² ▶ **noun** the rapid intermittent sound of a small gasoline engine. ▶ **verb** move with or make such a sound.
– ORIGIN imitating the sound.

put·ter³ ▶ **verb 1** occupy oneself by doing minor, pleasant tasks in a relaxed way. **2** move or go in a casual, unhurried way.
– ORIGIN from dialect *pote* 'to push, kick, or poke.'

put·ting green /ˈpətiNG/ ▶ **noun** a smooth area of short grass surrounding a hole on a golf course.

put·to /ˈpo͞otō/ ▶ **noun** (pl. **putti** /ˈpo͞otē/) a representation of a naked child, especially a cherub or a cupid in Renaissance art.
– ORIGIN Italian, 'boy.'

put·ty /ˈpətē/ ▶ **noun** a paste that is easily pressed into shape and gradually hardens as it sets, used for sealing glass in window frames, filling holes in wood, etc.
– PHRASES **be (like) putty in someone's hands** be easily manipulated by someone.
– ORIGIN French *potée*, 'potful.'

putz /ˈpəts, ˈpo͝ots/ ▶ **noun** informal a stupid person.
– ORIGIN Yiddish, 'penis.'

puz·zle /ˈpəzəl/ ▶ **verb 1** make someone feel confused as a result of being difficult to understand: *I was very puzzled by his reply*. **2** think hard about something that is difficult to understand: *he puzzled over this problem for years*.

> – SYNONYMS **baffle,** perplex, bewilder, confuse, bemuse, mystify, nonplus; informal flummox, stump, beat.

▶ **noun 1** a game, toy, or problem designed to test mental skills or knowledge. **2** a person or thing that is difficult to understand.

> – SYNONYMS **enigma,** mystery, paradox, conundrum, poser, riddle, problem.

– DERIVATIVES **puz·zle·ment** noun **puz·zler** noun.
– ORIGIN unknown.

> **CHOOSE THE RIGHT WORD**
>
> See RIDDLE¹.

puz·zling /ˈpəz(ə)liNG/ ▶ **adjective** confusing and difficult to understand: *his explanation was rather puzzling*.

> – SYNONYMS **baffling,** perplexing, bewildering, confusing, complicated, unclear, mysterious, enigmatic.

PVA ▶ **abbreviation** polyvinyl acetate, a synthetic resin used in paints and glues.

PVC ▶ **abbreviation** polyvinyl chloride, a tough synthetic resin used for a wide variety of products including pipes and floor coverings.

PVS ▶ **abbreviation** Medicine persistent vegetative state.

Pvt. ▶ **abbreviation** (in the US Army and in company names) private.

PWR ▶ **abbreviation** pressurized-water reactor.

PX ▶ **abbreviation** post exchange.

pyg·my /ˈpigmē/ (also **pigmy**) ▶ **noun** (pl. **pygmies**) **1** (**Pygmy**) a member of certain peoples of very short stature in equatorial Africa. **2** chiefly derogatory a very small person or thing. **3** a person who is lacking in a particular respect: *intellectual pygmies*. ▶ **adjective** very small; dwarf.
– ORIGIN Greek *pugmaios* 'dwarf.'

py·ja·mas /pəˈjäməz, -ˈjaməz/ ▶ **plural noun** British spelling of PAJAMAS.

py·lon /ˈpīˌlän, -lən/ ▶ **noun** (also **electricity pylon**) a tall towerlike metal structure for carrying power lines.
– ORIGIN Greek *pulōn* 'gateway' (first referring to the gateway of an ancient Egyptian temple).

py·lo·rus /pīˈlôrəs, pə-/ ▶ **noun** (pl. **pylori** /-ˈlôrˌī, -ˈlôrē/) the opening from the stomach into the small intestine.
– DERIVATIVES **py·lor·ic** /pīˈlôrik, pə-/ adjective.
– ORIGIN Greek *pulouros* 'gatekeeper.'

py·ra·can·tha /ˌpīrəˈkanTHə/ ▶ **noun** a thorny evergreen shrub with white flowers and bright red or yellow berries.

– ORIGIN Latin, from Greek *pur* 'fire' + *akantha* 'thorn.'

pyr·a·mid /'pirə,mid/ ▶ **noun 1** a huge stone structure with a square or triangular base and sloping sides that meet in a point at the top, especially one built as a royal tomb in ancient Egypt. **2** Geometry a polyhedron of which one face is a polygon and the other faces are triangles with a common vertex. **3** a pyramid-shaped thing or pile of things.
– DERIVATIVES **py·ram·i·dal** /pi'ramidl/ adjective.
– ORIGIN Greek *puramis*.

pyr·a·mid scheme ▶ **noun** a system of selling goods in which agency rights are sold to an increasing number of distributors at successively lower levels.

pyre /pīr/ ▶ **noun** a large pile of wood on which a dead body is placed and burned as part of a funeral ceremony.
– ORIGIN Greek *pur* 'fire.'

py·re·thrum /pī'rēᴛʜrəm, -'reᴛʜrəm/ ▶ **noun 1** a plant of the daisy family, typically with brightly colored flowers. **2** an insecticide made from the dried flowers of these plants.
– ORIGIN Greek *purethron* 'feverfew.'

py·ret·ic /pī'retik/ ▶ **adjective** feverish or causing fever.
– ORIGIN from Greek *puretos* 'fever.'

Py·rex /'pī,reks/ ▶ **noun** trademark a hard heat-resistant type of glass.

py·rex·i·a /pī'reksēə/ ▶ **noun** raised body temperature; fever.
– ORIGIN Greek *purexis*.

pyr·i·dox·ine /,piri'däk,sēn/ ▶ **noun** vitamin B_6, a compound present chiefly in cereals, liver oils, and yeast.
– ORIGIN from *pyrid(ine)* (a liquid chemical) + *oxy(gen)*.

py·rite /'pī,rīt/ (also **iron pyrites** or **pyrites** /pə'rītēz, pī-/) ▶ **noun** a shiny yellow mineral that is a compound of iron and sulfur.
– ORIGIN from Greek *puritēs* 'of fire.'

pyro- ▶ **combining form** relating to fire: *pyromania*.
– ORIGIN from Greek *pur* 'fire.'

py·ro·clas·tic /,pīrō'klastik/ ▶ **adjective** Geology relating to rock fragments or ash erupted by a volcano, especially as a hot, dense, destructive flow.
– ORIGIN from Greek *klastos* 'broken in pieces.'

py·rog·ra·phy /pī'rägrəfē/ ▶ **noun** the art or technique of decorating wood or leather by burning a design on the surface with a heated metallic point.

py·ro·ma·ni·a /,pīrō'mānēə/ ▶ **noun** an obsessive desire to set fire to things.
– DERIVATIVES **py·ro·ma·ni·ac** /-'mānē,ak/ noun.

py·ro·tech·nic /,pīrə'teknik/ ▶ **adjective 1** relating to fireworks. **2** brilliant or spectacular.
– DERIVATIVES **py·ro·tech·ni·cal** adjective.

py·ro·tech·nics /,pīrə'tekniks/ ▶ **plural noun 1** a firework display. **2** (treated as sing.) the art of making fireworks or staging firework displays. **3** a spectacular performance or display: *vocal pyrotechnics*.

pyr·rhic /'pirik/ ▶ **adjective** (of a victory) won at too great a cost to have been worthwhile for the victor.
– ORIGIN named after *Pyrrhus*, a king of Epirus whose victory over the Romans in 279 BC incurred heavy losses.

Py·thag·o·re·an /pi,ᴛʜagə'rēən, pī-/ ▶ **adjective** relating to the Greek philosopher and mathematician Pythagoras (*c.*580–500 BC) or his philosophy.

Py·thag·o·re·an the·o·rem ▶ **noun** the theorem that the square of the hypotenuse of a right triangle is equal in area to the sum of the squares of the other two sides.

py·thon /'pī,ᴛʜän, 'pīᴛʜən/ ▶ **noun** a large nonvenomous snake that kills its prey by squeezing and crushing it.
– ORIGIN Greek *Puthōn*, a huge serpent killed by Apollo.

pyx /piks/ (also **pix**) ▶ **noun** Christian Church the container in which the consecrated bread used in the service of Holy Communion is kept.
– ORIGIN Greek *puxis* 'box.'

p·zazz /pə'zaz/ ▶ **noun** variant spelling of PIZZAZZ.

Qq

Q[1] (also **q**) ▶ **noun** (pl. **Qs** or **Q's**) the seventeenth letter of the alphabet.

Q[2] ▶ **abbreviation 1** queen (used especially in card games and chess). **2** question.

Qa·ba·lah /kə'bälə/ ▶ **noun** variant spelling of **KABBALAH.**

Qa·tar·i /'kätärē, kə'tärē/ ▶ **noun** (pl. **Qataris**) a person from Qatar, a country in the Persian Gulf. ▶ **adjective** relating to Qatar.

QC ▶ **abbreviation 1** quality control. **2** Quebec.

QED ▶ **abbreviation** quod erat demonstrandum, used to state that something proves the truth of one's claim.
– ORIGIN Latin, 'which was to be demonstrated.'

qi /CHē/ ▶ **noun** variant spelling of **CHI.**

qi·gong /ˌCHē'gäNG, -'gôNG/ ▶ **noun** a Chinese system of physical exercises and breathing control related to t'ai chi.
– ORIGIN Chinese.

QT ▶ **noun** (in phrase **on the QT**) informal secretly.
– ORIGIN abbreviation of *quiet*.

qt. ▶ **abbreviation** quart(s).

qty. ▶ **abbreviation** quantity.

qua /kwä/ ▶ **conjunction** formal in the capacity of; as being.
– ORIGIN Latin.

quack[1] /kwak/ ▶ **noun** the harsh sound made by a duck. ▶ **verb** make a quack.
– ORIGIN imitating the sound.

quack[2] ▶ **noun 1** an unqualified person who dishonestly claims to have medical knowledge. **2** informal a doctor perceived as one who prescribes wrong, useless, or harmful treatments.
– DERIVATIVES **quack·er·y** noun.
– ORIGIN abbreviation of earlier *quacksalver*, from Dutch, probably from former *quacken* 'prattle' + *salf* 'salve.'

CHOOSE THE RIGHT WORD

quack, charlatan, dissembler, fake, impostor, mountebank

There are many different ways to describe a **fake**, a colloquial term for anyone who knowingly practices deception or misrepresentation. Someone who sells a special tonic that claims to do everything from curing the common cold to making hair grow on a bald man's head is called a **quack**, a term that refers to any fraudulent practitioner of medicine or law. **Mountebank** sometimes carries implications of quackery, but more often it refers to a self-promoting person who resorts to cheap tricks or undignified efforts to win attention (*political mountebanks*). A **charlatan** is usually a writer, speaker, preacher, professor, or some other "expert" who tries to conceal his or her lack of skill or knowledge by resorting to pretentious displays (*supposedly a leading authority in his field, he turned out to be nothing but a charlatan*). An individual who tries to pass himself or herself off as someone else is an **impostor** (*an impostor who bore a close physical resemblance to the king*), although this term can also refer to anyone who assumes a title or profession that is not his or her own. Although all of these deceivers are out to fool people, it is the **dissembler** who is primarily interested in concealing his or her true motives or evil purpose (*he is a dissembler who weaves a tangled web of lies*).

quad /kwäd/ ▶ **noun 1** a quadrangle. **2** a quadruplet.

quad·ran·gle /'kwäˌdraNGgəl/ ▶ **noun 1** a square or rectangular courtyard enclosed by buildings. **2** a four-sided geometrical figure, especially a square or rectangle.
– DERIVATIVES **quad·ran·gu·lar** /kwä'draNGgyələr/ adjective.
– ORIGIN from Latin *quadri-* 'four' + *angulus* 'corner, angle.'

quad·rant /'kwädrənt/ ▶ **noun 1** each of four parts of a circle, plane, object, etc., divided by two lines or planes at right angles. **2** historical an instrument for measuring altitude in astronomy and navigation.
– ORIGIN Latin *quadrans* 'quarter.'

quad·ra·phon·ic /ˌkwädrə'fänik/ (also **quadrophonic**) ▶ **adjective** (of sound reproduction) transmitted through four channels.
– DERIVATIVES **qua·draph·o·ny** /kwä'dräfənē/ noun.

quad·rate /'kwäˌdrāt, -rət/ ▶ **adjective** roughly square or rectangular.
– ORIGIN from Latin *quadrare* 'make square.'

quad·rat·ic /kwä'dratik/ ▶ **adjective** Mathematics involving the second and no higher power of an unknown quantity or variable.

quad·ren·ni·al /kwä'drenēəl/ ▶ **adjective** lasting for or recurring every four years.
– ORIGIN from Latin *quadri-* 'four' + *annus* 'year.'

quadri- ▶ **combining form** four; having four: *quadriplegia*.
– ORIGIN Latin.

quad·ri·ceps /'kwädrəˌseps/ ▶ **noun** (pl. same) a large muscle at the front of the thigh.
– ORIGIN from Latin, 'four-headed.'

quad·ri·lat·er·al /ˌkwädrə'latərəl/ ▶ **noun** a four-sided figure. ▶ **adjective** having four straight sides.

quad·rille[1] /kwä'dril, k(w)ə-/ ▶ **noun** a square dance performed by four couples.
– ORIGIN Spanish *cuadrilla* or Italian *quadriglia* 'troop, company.'

quad·rille[2] ▶ **noun** a trick-taking card game for four players, fashionable in the 18th century.
– ORIGIN French.

quad·ril·lion /kwä'drilyən/ ▶ **cardinal number 1** a thousand raised to the power of five (10^{15}). **2** (also **quadrillions**) informal a very large number or amount.

– DERIVATIVES **quad·ril·lionth** /kwä'drilyənTH/ ordinal number.

quad·ri·par·tite /ˌkwädrə'pärtīt/ ▸ **adjective 1** consisting of four parts. **2** shared by or involving four parties.

quad·ri·ple·gi·a /ˌkwädrə'plēj(ē)ə/ ▸ **noun** paralysis of all four limbs.
– DERIVATIVES **quad·ri·ple·gic** /-'plējik/ adjective & noun.

quad·roon /kwä'dro͞on/ ▸ **noun** offensive a person who has one parent who is black and the other who has one black parent and one white one.
– ORIGIN Spanish *cuarterón*.

quad·ro·phon·ic /ˌkwädrə'fänik/ ▸ **adjective** variant spelling of **QUADRAPHONIC**.

quad·ru·ped /'kwädrəˌped/ ▸ **noun** an animal that has four feet, especially a mammal.
– DERIVATIVES **quad·ru·pe·dal** /ˌkwädrə'pedl, kwä'dro͞opədl/ adjective.
– ORIGIN from Latin *quadru-* 'four' + *pes* 'foot.'

quad·ru·ple /kwä'dro͞opəl/ ▸ **adjective 1** consisting of four parts or elements. **2** four times as much or as many. **3** (of time in music) having four beats in a bar. ▸ **verb** multiply or be multiplied by four. ▸ **noun** a quadruple number or amount.
– ORIGIN Latin *quadruplus*.

quad·ru·plet /kwä'dro͞oplit/ ▸ **noun** each of four children born at one birth.

quad·ru·pli·cate /kwä'dro͞opləkit/ ▸ **adjective** consisting of four parts.
– PHRASES **in quadruplicate** in four copies.
– ORIGIN from Latin *quadruplicare* 'to quadruple.'

quaff /kwäf/ ▸ **verb** drink something heartily.
– DERIVATIVES **quaff·a·ble** adjective **quaff·er** noun.
– ORIGIN probably imitating the sound.

quag·ga /'kwagə/ ▸ **noun** an extinct South African zebra with a yellowish-brown coat with darker stripes.
– ORIGIN probably from Khoikhoi.

quag·mire /'kwagˌmīr/ ▸ **noun 1** a soft boggy area of land that gives way underfoot. **2** a complex or difficult situation: *a quagmire of unresolved issues*.
– ORIGIN from former *quag* 'a marshy place' + **MIRE**.

quail[1] /kwāl/ ▸ **noun** (pl. same or **quails**) a small short-tailed game bird, typically with brown plumage.
– ORIGIN Old French *quaille*.

quail[2] ▸ **verb** feel or show fear or worry.
– ORIGIN unknown.

quaint /kwānt/ ▸ **adjective** attractively unusual or old-fashioned.

> – SYNONYMS **1 picturesque,** charming, sweet, attractive, old-fashioned, old-world. **2 unusual,** curious, eccentric, quirky, bizarre, whimsical, unconventional; informal offbeat.
> – ANTONYMS ugly.

– DERIVATIVES **quaint·ly** adverb **quaint·ness** noun.
– ORIGIN Old French *cointe* 'wise.'

quake /kwāk/ ▸ **noun** informal an earthquake. ▸ **verb 1** shudder with fear. **2** (especially of the earth) shake or tremble.

> – SYNONYMS **shake,** tremble, quiver, shudder, sway, rock, wobble, move, heave, convulse.

– ORIGIN Old English.

> **CHOOSE THE RIGHT WORD**
>
> See **SHAKE**.

Quak·er /'kwākər/ ▸ **noun** a member of the Religious Society of Friends, a Christian movement that is strongly opposed to war and violence and that meets without any formal ceremony.
– DERIVATIVES **Quak·er·ism** /-izəm/ noun.
– ORIGIN from **QUAKE**, perhaps with reference to the founder's direction to his followers to 'tremble at the Word of the Lord.'

qual·i·fi·ca·tion /ˌkwäləfə'kāSHən/ ▸ **noun 1** a pass of an exam or an official completion of a course. **2** the action of qualifying or the fact of becoming qualified: *England needs to beat Poland to ensure qualification for the World Cup finals.* **3** a quality that makes someone suitable for a job or activity. **4** an official requirement. **5** a statement that restricts the meaning of another.

> – SYNONYMS **1 certificate,** diploma, degree, license, document, warrant. **2 modification,** limitation, reservation, stipulation, alteration, amendment, revision, moderation, mitigation, condition, proviso, caveat.

qual·i·fied /'kwäləˌfīd/ ▸ **adjective** certified or licensed as able to practice a particular profession or activity.

> – SYNONYMS *qualified mechanics* **certified,** certificated, chartered, licensed, professional.
> – ANTONYMS wholehearted.

qual·i·fi·er /'kwäləˌfīər/ ▸ **noun 1** a person or team that qualifies for a competition or its final rounds. **2** a match or contest to decide which people or teams qualify for a competition or its final rounds. **3** Grammar a word or phrase, especially an adjective, used to describe another word, especially a noun.

qual·i·fy /'kwäləˌfī/ ▸ **verb** (**qualifies, qualifying, qualified**) **1** meet the necessary standard or conditions to be entitled to do or receive something: *it's the best chance in years for the team to qualify for a major tournament.* **2** certify or license someone as able to practice a particular profession or activity. **3** make someone competent or knowledgeable enough to do something: *I'm not qualified to write on the subject.* **4** add restrictions to a statement to limit its meaning. **5** Grammar (of a word or phrase) describe another word in a particular way in order to restrict its meaning (e.g., in *the open door*, *open* is an adjective qualifying *door*).

> – SYNONYMS **1 be eligible,** meet the requirements, be entitled, be permitted. **2 be certified,** be licensed, pass, graduate, succeed. **3 authorize,** empower, allow, permit, license. **4 modify,** limit, restrict, make conditional, moderate, temper, modulate, mitigate.

– ORIGIN Latin *qualificare*.

qual·i·ta·tive /'kwäləˌtātiv/ ▸ **adjective** relating to or measured by quality.
– DERIVATIVES **qual·i·ta·tive·ly** adverb.

qual·i·ta·tive a·nal·y·sis ▸ **noun** Chemistry the identification of the constituents present in a substance.

qual·i·ty /'kwälətē/ ▸ **noun** (pl. **qualities**) **1** the standard of how good something is as measured against other similar things: *an improvement in product quality.* **2** general excellence. **3** a distinctive feature or characteristic: *strong leadership qualities.* **4** old use high social standing.

> – SYNONYMS **1 standard,** grade, class, caliber, condition, character, nature, form, rank, value, level. **2 excellence,** superiority, merit, worth, value, virtue, caliber, distinction. **3 feature,** trait,

attribute, characteristic, point, aspect, facet, side, property.

▶ **adjective** informal of good quality; excellent: *he's a quality player.*
– ORIGIN Latin *qualitas.*

qual·i·ty con·trol ▶ **noun** a system of maintaining quality in manufactured products by testing a sample to see if it meets the required standard.

qual·i·ty time ▶ **noun** time spent in giving one's full attention to one's child or partner, in order to strengthen the relationship.

qualm /kwä(l)m, kwô(l)m/ ▶ **noun 1** a feeling of doubt or unease, especially about one's behavior: *he had no qualms about divorcing her.* **2** old use a brief faint or sick feeling.
– ORIGIN perhaps related to an Old English word meaning 'pain.'

quan·da·ry /ˈkwänd(ə)rē/ ▶ **noun** (pl. **quandaries**) a state of uncertainty over what to do in a difficult situation.
– ORIGIN perhaps partly from Latin *quando* 'when.'

quan·ta /ˈkwäntə/ plural of **QUANTUM**.

quan·ti·fy /ˈkwäntəˌfī/ ▶ **verb** (**quantifies, quantifying, quantified**) express or measure the quantity of: *the method used to quantify how much acid rain it takes to damage ecosystems.*
– DERIVATIVES **quan·ti·fi·a·ble** /ˈkwäntəˌfīəbəl/ adjective **quan·ti·fi·ca·tion** /ˌkwäntəfiˈkāsʜən/ noun **quan·ti·fi·er** /ˈkwäntəˌfīər/ noun.

quan·ti·ta·tive /ˈkwäntəˌtātiv/ ▶ **adjective** relating to or measured by quantity.
– DERIVATIVES **quan·ti·ta·tive·ly** adverb.

quan·ti·ta·tive a·nal·y·sis ▶ **noun** Chemistry the measurement of the quantities of particular constituents present in a substance.

quan·ti·ty /ˈkwäntətē/ ▶ **noun** (pl. **quantities**) **1** a certain amount or number of something. **2** the aspect of something that is measurable in number, amount, size, or weight: *wages depended on quantity of output.* **3** a considerable number or amount.

– SYNONYMS **amount,** total, aggregate, sum, quota, mass, weight, volume, bulk.

– ORIGIN Latin *quantitas.*

quan·tize /ˈkwänˌtīz/ ▶ **verb** Physics apply quantum theory to; in particular, restrict the number of possible values of a quantity or states of a system.
– DERIVATIVES **quan·ti·za·tion** /ˌkwäntəˈzāsʜən/ noun **quan·tiz·er** noun.

quan·tum /ˈkwäntəm/ ▶ **noun** (pl. **quanta** /ˈkwäntə/) **1** Physics a distinct quantity of energy corresponding to that involved in the absorption or emission of energy by an atom. **2** a share or portion.
– ORIGIN Latin.

quan·tum com·put·er ▶ **noun** a hypothetical computer that makes use of the quantum states of subatomic particles to store information.

quan·tum dot ▶ **noun** Physics a nanoscale particle of semiconducting material that can be embedded in cells or organisms for various experimental purposes, such as labeling proteins.

quan·tum leap (also **quantum jump**) ▶ **noun** a sudden large increase or advance.

quan·tum me·chan·ics ▶ **plural noun** (treated as sing.) the branch of physics concerned with describing the behavior of subatomic particles in terms of quanta.

quan·tum the·o·ry ▶ **noun** a theory of matter and energy based on the idea of quanta.

quar·an·tine /ˈkwôrənˌtēn/ ▶ **noun** a state or period of isolation for people or animals that have or may have a disease. ▶ **verb** put a person or animal in quarantine.
– ORIGIN Italian *quarantina* 'forty days.'

quark[1] /kwärk/ ▶ **noun** Physics any of a group of subatomic particles that carry a fractional electric charge and are believed to be building blocks of protons, neutrons, and other particles.
– ORIGIN term invented by the American physicist Murray Gell-Mann.

quark[2] ▶ **noun** a type of low-fat curd cheese.
– ORIGIN German, 'curd, curds.'

quar·rel[1] /ˈkwôrəl, ˈkwä-/ ▶ **noun 1** an angry argument or disagreement. **2** a reason for disagreement: *his quarrel is with those who exaggerate the benefits of the project.*

– SYNONYMS **argument,** disagreement, squabble, fight, dispute, wrangle, clash, altercation, feud, vendetta; Brit. row; informal tiff, run-in, spat.
– ANTONYMS agreement.

▶ **verb** (**quarrels, quarreling, quarreled**) **1** have a quarrel. **2** (**quarrel with**) disagree with.

– SYNONYMS **1 argue,** fight, disagree, fall out, differ, be at odds, bicker, squabble, cross swords. **2** *you can't quarrel with the verdict* **fault,** criticize, object to, oppose, take exception to, attack, take issue with, impugn, contradict, dispute, controvert; informal knock.
– ANTONYMS agree.

– ORIGIN Latin *querella* 'complaint.'

quar·rel[2] ▶ **noun** historical a short heavy square-headed arrow or bolt for a crossbow.
– ORIGIN Old French.

quar·rel·some /ˈkwôrəlsəm, ˈkwä-/ ▶ **adjective** tending or likely to quarrel.

– SYNONYMS **argumentative,** disputatious, confrontational, captious, pugnacious, combative, antagonistic, bellicose, belligerent, cantankerous, choleric.
– ANTONYMS peaceable.

quar·ry[1] /ˈkwôrē, ˈkwä-/ ▶ **noun** (pl. **quarries**) an area of the earth's surface that has been dug open so that stone or other materials can be obtained. ▶ **verb** (**quarries, quarrying, quarried**) take stone or other materials from a quarry.
– DERIVATIVES **quar·ri·er** noun.
– ORIGIN Old French *quarriere.*

quar·ry[2] ▶ **noun** (pl. **quarries**) **1** an animal being hunted. **2** a person or thing being chased or looked for.

– SYNONYMS **prey,** victim, object, goal, target, kill, game, prize.

– ORIGIN Old French *couree* 'parts of a deer given to the hounds.'

quar·ry[3] ▶ **noun** (pl. **quarries**) **1** (also **quarry tile**) an unglazed floor tile. **2** a diamond-shaped pane in a lattice window.
– ORIGIN from **QUARREL**[2], which originally referred to a lattice windowpane.

quart /kwôrt/ ▶ **noun** a unit of liquid capacity equal to a quarter of a gallon or two pints, equivalent to approximately 0.94 liter (or 1.13 liters in the UK).
– ORIGIN from Latin *quarta pars* 'fourth part.'

quar·ter /ˈkwôrtər/ ▶ **noun** **1** each of four equal parts into which something is divided. **2** a period of three months, used especially in reference to financial transactions. **3** a school term of 12 weeks. **4** a period of fifteen minutes; a quarter of an hour: *a quarter past nine*. **5** one fourth of a pound weight, equal to 4 ounces avoirdupois. **6** a part of a town or city with a specific character or use: *the business quarter*. **7** (**quarters**) rooms or lodgings. **8** a US or Canadian coin worth 25 cents. **9** one fourth of a hundredweight (US 25 lb or Brit. 28 lb). **10** a person, group, or area regarded as the source of something: *help came from an unexpected quarter*. **11** mercy shown to an opponent: *they gave the enemy no quarter*. **12** (**quarters**) the haunches or hindquarters of a horse. **13** the direction of one of the points of the compass.

– SYNONYMS **1 district,** area, region, part, side, neighborhood, precinct, locality, sector, zone, ghetto, community, enclave. **2 source,** direction, place, location. **3** *the servants' quarters* **accommodations,** rooms, chambers, home, lodgings; informal pad, digs; formal abode, residence, domicile. **4** *riot squads gave no quarter* **mercy,** leniency, clemency, compassion, pity, charity, sympathy, tolerance.

▶ **verb** **1** divide something into quarters. **2** (**be quartered**) be lodged somewhere. **3** historical cut the body of an executed person into four parts. **4** range over an area in all directions.

– SYNONYMS **accommodate,** house, board, lodge, put up, take in, install, shelter; Military billet.

– ORIGIN Latin *quartarius* 'fourth part of a measure.'

quar·ter·back /ˈkwôrtərˌbak/ ▶ **noun** Football a player stationed behind the center who directs a team's offensive play.

quar·ter·deck /ˈkwôrtərˌdek/ ▶ **noun** the part of a ship's upper deck near the stern, traditionally reserved for officers or for ceremonial use.

quar·ter·fi·nal /ˈkwôrtərˌfīnl/ ▶ **noun** a match or round of a tournament preceding the semifinal.
– DERIVATIVES **quar·ter·fi·nal·ist** /ˈkwôrtərˌfīnl-ist/ noun.

quar·ter-hour ▶ **noun** **1** (also **quarter of an hour**) a period of fifteen minutes. **2** a point of time fifteen minutes before or after a full hour of the clock.

quar·ter·ly /ˈkwôrtərlē/ ▶ **adjective & adverb** produced or occurring once every quarter of a year. ▶ **noun** (pl. **quarterlies**) a publication produced four times a year.

quar·ter·mas·ter /ˈkwôrtərˌmastər/ ▶ **noun** **1** a regimental officer in charge of providing accommodations and supplies. **2** a naval petty officer responsible for steering and signals.

quar·ter note ▶ **noun** a musical note having the time value of half a half note, represented by a solid dot with a plain stem.

quar·tet /kwôrˈtet/ (also **quartette**) ▶ **noun** **1** a group of four people playing music or singing together. **2** a composition for a quartet. **3** a set of four people or things.
– ORIGIN Italian *quartetto*.

quar·tile /ˈkwôrˌtīl, ˈkwôrtl/ ▶ **noun** Statistics each of four equal groups into which a population can be divided according to the distribution of values of a particular variable.
– ORIGIN Latin *quartilis*.

quar·to /ˈkwôrtō/ ▶ **noun** (pl. **quartos**) a page or paper size resulting from folding a sheet into four leaves, typically 10 inches × 8 inches (254 × 203 mm).
– ORIGIN from Latin *in quarto* 'in the fourth (of a sheet).'

quartz /kwôrts/ ▶ **noun** a hard mineral consisting of silica, typically occurring as colorless or white hexagonal prisms.
– ORIGIN German *Quarz*.

quartz clock (or **watch**) ▶ **noun** a clock (or watch) regulated by vibrations of an electrically driven quartz crystal.

quartz·ite /ˈkwôrtˌsīt/ ▶ **noun** a compact, hard, granular rock consisting mainly of quartz.

qua·sar /ˈkwāˌzär/ ▶ **noun** a massive and extremely remote object in space that emits huge amounts of energy.
– ORIGIN from *quasi-stellar* radio source.

quash /kwôsʜ, kwäsʜ/ ▶ **verb** **1** officially reject a legal decision as invalid. **2** put an end to; suppress: *rumors of job losses were quashed*.

– SYNONYMS **1 cancel,** reverse, rescind, repeal, revoke, retract, countermand, withdraw, overturn, overrule. **2 stop,** put an end to, stamp out, crush, put down, check, curb, nip in the bud, squash, suppress, stifle.

– ORIGIN Old French *quasser* 'annul.'

quasi- /ˌkwāˌzī, ˌkwäzē-/ ▶ **combining form** **1** seemingly: *quasi-scientific*. **2** being partly or almost: *quasicrystalline*.
– ORIGIN Latin, 'as if, almost.'

quas·sia /ˈkwäsʜ(ē)ə/ ▶ **noun** a South American shrub or small tree whose wood, bark, or root yields a bitter medicinal tonic and insecticide.
– ORIGIN named after Graman *Quassi*, the Surinamese slave who discovered its medicinal properties.

quat·er·nar·y /ˈkwätərˌnerē/ ▶ **adjective** **1** fourth in order or rank. **2** (**Quaternary**) Geology relating to the most recent period in the Cenozoic era, from about 1.64 million years ago to the present.
– ORIGIN Latin *quaternarius*.

quat·rain /ˈkwäˌtrān/ ▶ **noun** a stanza of four lines, typically with alternate rhymes.
– ORIGIN French.

quat·re·foil /ˈkatərˌfoil, ˈkatrə-/ ▶ **noun** an ornamental design of four lobes or leaves, resembling a clover leaf.
– ORIGIN from Old French *quatre* 'four' + *foil* 'leaf.'

quat·tro·cen·to /ˌkwätrōˈcʜentō/ ▶ **noun** the 15th century as a period of Italian art or architecture.
– ORIGIN Italian, '400' (shortened from *milquattrocento* '1400').

qua·ver /ˈkwāvər/ ▶ **verb** (of a voice) tremble. ▶ **noun** a tremble in a voice.
– DERIVATIVES **qua·ver·y** adjective.
– ORIGIN probably from an Old English word related to QUAKE.

quay /kē, k(w)ā/ ▶ **noun** a platform lying alongside or projecting into water for loading and unloading ships.
– ORIGIN Old French *kay*.

quay·side /ˈkēˌsīd, ˈk(w)ā-/ ▶ **noun** a quay and the area around it.

quea·sy /ˈkwēzē/ ▶ **adjective** (**queasier, queasiest**) **1** feeling sick; nauseous. **2** slightly nervous or uneasy.

– SYNONYMS **nauseous,** bilious, sick, ill, unwell, poorly, green around the gills.

– DERIVATIVES **quea·si·ly** adverb **quea·si·ness** noun.
– ORIGIN perhaps related to Old French *coisier* 'to hurt.'

Quech·ua /ˈkeCHwə/ ▸ **noun** (pl. same or **Quechuas**) **1** a member of an American Indian people of Peru and neighboring countries. **2** the language of the Quechua.
– DERIVATIVES **Quech·uan** adjective & noun.
– ORIGIN Quechua, 'temperate valleys.'

queen /kwēn/ ▸ **noun** **1** the female ruler of an independent country, especially one who inherits the position by birth. **2** (also **queen consort**) a king's wife. **3** the best or most important woman or thing in a field of activity or group. **4** a playing card bearing a picture of a queen, ranking next below a king. **5** the most powerful chess piece, able to move in any direction. **6** a reproductive female in a colony of ants, bees, wasps, or termites. **7** informal, often derogatory a homosexual man, especially an effeminate or flamboyant one.

– SYNONYMS **monarch,** sovereign, ruler, head of state, Crown, Her Majesty.

▸ **verb** **1** (**queen it**) (of a woman) act in an unpleasantly superior way. **2** Chess convert a pawn into a queen when it reaches the opponent's end of the board.
– DERIVATIVES **queen·dom** /-dəm/ noun **queen·ly** /ˈkwēnlē/ adjective **queen·ship** /-ˌSHip/ noun.
– ORIGIN Old English.

Queen Anne ▸ **adjective** referring to a style of English furniture or architecture characteristic of the early 18th century.

Queen Anne's lace ▸ **noun** the uncultivated form of the carrot, with broad round heads of tiny white flowers that resemble lace.

queen bee ▸ **noun** **1** the single reproductive female in a colony of honeybees. **2** informal a dominant woman in a group.

queen moth·er ▸ **noun** the widow of a king and mother of the current sovereign.

queen post ▸ **noun** either of two upright timbers between the tie beam and main rafters of a roof truss.

Queens·ber·ry Rules /ˈkwēnzˌberē/ ▸ **plural noun** the standard rules of boxing.
– ORIGIN named after the 9th Marquess of *Queensberry*, who supervised the preparation of the rules.

Queen's Eng·lish ▸ **noun** the English language as correctly written and spoken in Britain.

queen-sized (also **queen-size**) ▸ **adjective** (of a bed) of a larger size than the standard but smaller than king-sized.

queer /kwi(ə)r/ ▸ **adjective** **1** strange; odd. **2** informal, derogatory (of a man) homosexual. **3** informal, dated slightly ill.

– SYNONYMS **odd,** strange, unusual, funny, peculiar, curious, bizarre, weird, uncanny, freakish, eerie, unnatural, abnormal, anomalous; informal spooky.
– ANTONYMS normal.

▸ **noun** informal, derogatory a homosexual man.
▸ **verb** informal spoil or ruin something.
– DERIVATIVES **queer·ish** adjective **queer·ly** adverb **queer·ness** noun.
– PHRASES **queer someone's pitch** Brit. informal spoil someone's plans or chances of doing something.
– ORIGIN perhaps from German *quer* 'oblique, perverse.'

USAGE

The word **queer** was first used to mean 'homosexual' in the early 20th century: it was originally, and often still is, a deliberately offensive and aggressive term when used by heterosexual people. In recent years, however, many gay people have taken the word **queer** and deliberately used it in place of **gay** or **homosexual**, in an attempt, by using the word positively, to deprive it of its negative power.

quell /kwel/ ▸ **verb** **1** put an end to a rebellion or other disorder. **2** stop or reduce a strong or unpleasant feeling: *I hurried to quell her fears.*

– SYNONYMS **1 put an end to,** put a stop to, stop, crush, put down, check, crack down on, curb, nip in the bud, squash, quash, subdue, suppress, overcome. **2 calm,** soothe, pacify, settle, quieten, silence, allay, assuage, mitigate, moderate.

– ORIGIN Old English, 'kill.'

quench /kwenCH/ ▸ **verb** **1** satisfy thirst by drinking. **2** satisfy a desire. **3** extinguish a fire. **4** stop or reduce a strong feeling. **5** rapidly cool hot metal.
– DERIVATIVES **quench·er** noun.
– ORIGIN Old English.

que·nelle /kəˈnel/ ▸ **noun** a small ball of ground meat or fish.
– ORIGIN French.

quer·u·lous /ˈkwer(y)ələs/ ▸ **adjective** complaining in a petulant or irritable way.
– DERIVATIVES **quer·u·lous·ly** adverb **quer·u·lous·ness** noun.
– ORIGIN Latin *querulus*.

que·ry /ˈkwi(ə)rē/ ▸ **noun** (pl. **queries**) **1** a question expressing doubt or asking for information. **2** chiefly Printing a question mark.

– SYNONYMS **1 question,** inquiry. **2 doubt,** uncertainty, question (mark), reservation.

▸ **verb** (**queries, querying, queried**) **1** ask a question to express doubt or obtain information. **2** put a query or queries to someone.

– SYNONYMS **1 ask,** inquire, question. **2 challenge,** question, dispute, doubt, have suspicions about, distrust.
– ANTONYMS accept.

– ORIGIN from Latin *quaerere* 'ask, seek.'

que·sa·dil·la /ˌkāsəˈdēyə/ ▸ **noun** a hot tortilla with a spicy cheese filling.
– ORIGIN Spanish.

quest /kwest/ ▸ **noun** **1** a long or difficult search: *the quest for a better life.* **2** (in medieval romance) an expedition by a knight to accomplish a specific task.

– SYNONYMS **1 search,** hunt, pursuance. **2 expedition,** journey, voyage, trek, travels, odyssey, adventure, exploration, search, crusade, mission, pilgrimage.

▸ **verb** search for something.
– DERIVATIVES **quest·er** (also **questor**) noun.
– ORIGIN Old French *queste*.

ques·tion /ˈkwesCHən/ ▸ **noun** **1** a sentence worded or expressed so as to obtain information. **2** a doubt as to whether something is true or valid. **3** a problem that needs to be resolved. **4** a matter that depends on conditions: *it's only a question of time before something changes.* **5** the raising of a doubt or objection: *he obeyed without question.*

– SYNONYMS **1 inquiry,** query, interrogation. **2 doubt,** dispute, argument, debate, uncertainty, reservation. **3 issue,** matter, topic, business, problem, concern, debate, argument, dispute, controversy.
– ANTONYMS answer, certainty.

▸ **verb** **1** ask someone questions. **2** express doubt about or object to something.

– SYNONYMS **1 interrogate,** cross-examine, cross-question, quiz, interview, debrief, examine; informal grill, pump. **2 query,** challenge, dispute, cast aspersions on, doubt, suspect.

– DERIVATIVES **ques·tion·er** noun.
– PHRASES **come** (or **bring**) **into question** become (or raise) an issue for further consideration or discussion. **in question 1** being considered. **2** in doubt. **no question of** no possibility of. **out of the question** not possible.
– ORIGIN Old French.

WORD LINKS

interrogative *relating to questions*

ques·tion·a·ble /ˈkwesCHənəbəl/ ▶ **adjective 1** open to doubt. **2** likely to be dishonest or morally wrong: *questionable financial deals.*

– SYNONYMS **suspicious,** suspect, dubious, irregular, odd, strange, murky, dark, unsavory, disreputable; informal funny, fishy, shady, iffy.

– DERIVATIVES **ques·tion·a·bly** /-əblē/ adverb.

ques·tion mark ▶ **noun** a punctuation mark (?) indicating a question.

ques·tion·naire /ˌkwesCHəˈne(ə)r/ ▶ **noun** a set of questions, usually with a choice of answers, written for a survey or statistical study.
– ORIGIN French.

quet·zal /ketˈsäl/ ▶ **noun** a long-tailed tropical American bird with iridescent green plumage.
– ORIGIN from an Aztec word meaning 'brightly colored tail feather.'

queue /kyo͞o/ ▶ **noun 1** chiefly Brit. a line of people or vehicles awaiting their turn for something or to continue. **2** Computing a list of data items, commands, etc., stored so as to be retrievable in a definite order.

– SYNONYMS **row,** line, column, file, chain, string, procession.

▶ **verb** (**queues, queuing** or **queueing, queued**) chiefly Brit. wait in line.
– ORIGIN French, 'tail.'

quib·ble /ˈkwibəl/ ▶ **noun 1** a minor objection or criticism. **2** old use a pun.

– SYNONYMS *I have just one quibble* **criticism,** objection, complaint, protest, argument, exception, grumble, grouse, cavil; informal niggle, moan, gripe, beef, grouch.

▶ **verb** argue about a trivial matter.

– SYNONYMS *no one quibbled with the title* **object to,** find fault with, complain about, cavil at, split hairs over, criticize, fault, poke holes in; informal nitpick (over/about).

– ORIGIN from former *quib* 'a petty objection.'

quiche /kēSH/ ▶ **noun** a dish made with eggs, milk, and various savory fillings, baked in a pie crust.
– ORIGIN French.

quick /kwik/ ▶ **adjective 1** moving fast. **2** lasting or taking a short time: *a quick worker.* **3** with little or no delay; prompt. **4** able to think, learn, or notice things promptly; intelligent. **5** (of temper) easily roused.

– SYNONYMS **1 fast,** swift, rapid, speedy, brisk, smart, lightning, whirlwind, whistle-stop, breakneck; informal nippy, zippy; literary fleet. **2 hasty,** hurried, cursory, perfunctory, desultory, superficial, brief. **3 sudden,** instantaneous, instant, immediate, abrupt, precipitate. **4 intelligent,** bright, clever, gifted, able, astute, sharp-witted, smart, alert, sharp, perceptive; informal brainy, on the ball.
– ANTONYMS slow, long.

▶ **noun 1** (**the quick**) the tender flesh below the growing part of a fingernail or toenail. **2** (as pl. n. **the quick**) old use people who are living.
– DERIVATIVES **quick·ness** noun.
– PHRASES **a quick one** informal a rapidly consumed alcoholic drink. **cut someone to the quick** upset someone very much: *his laughter cut us to the quick.* **quick with child** old use at a stage of pregnancy when the fetus can be felt to move.
– ORIGIN Old English, 'alive, animated, alert.'

quick·en /ˈkwikən/ ▶ **verb 1** make or become quicker. **2** stimulate or be stimulated: *my interest quickened.* **3** old use reach a stage in pregnancy when the fetus can be felt to move.

– SYNONYMS **1 speed up,** accelerate, step up, hasten, hurry (up). **2 stimulate,** excite, arouse, rouse, stir up, activate, whet, inspire, kindle.

quick-fire ▶ **adjective 1** unhesitating and rapid. **2** (of a gun) firing shots in rapid succession.

quick fix ▶ **noun** a solution that is implemented quickly but that is not good enough for the long term.

quick·ie /ˈkwikē/ informal ▶ **noun 1** a rapidly consumed alcoholic drink. **2** a brief act of sex. ▶ **adjective** done or made quickly.

quick·lime /ˈkwikˌlīm/ ▶ **noun** a white caustic alkaline substance consisting of calcium oxide, obtained by heating limestone.

quick·ly /ˈkwiklē/ ▶ **adverb 1** with haste or speed: *he walked quickly.* **2** immediately: *you'd better leave quickly.* **3** briefly; without care or attention: *he quickly inspected it.*

– SYNONYMS **1 fast,** swiftly, briskly, rapidly, speedily, at full tilt, at a gallop, on the double, posthaste, hotfoot; informal like (greased) lightning, hell-bent for leather, like blazes, like the wind, lickety-split. **2 immediately,** directly, at once, straightaway, right away, instantly, forthwith, momentarily; informal like a shot, ASAP, PDQ, pronto. **3 briefly,** fleetingly, briskly, hastily, hurriedly, cursorily, perfunctorily.

quick march ▶ **noun** a brisk military march.

quick·sand /ˈkwikˌsand/ ▶ **noun** (also **quicksands**) loose wet sand that sucks in anything resting on it.

quick·set /ˈkwikˌset/ ▶ **noun** Brit. hedging, especially of hawthorn, grown from cuttings.

quick·sil·ver /ˈkwikˌsilvər/ ▶ **noun** liquid mercury. ▶ **adjective** moving or changing rapidly and unexpectedly.

quick·step /ˈkwikˌstep/ ▶ **noun** a fast foxtrot (dance) in 4/4 time.

quick stud·y ▶ **noun** a person who adapts quickly and easily to a new job, situation, etc.: *he proved to be a quick study and a fearless entrepreneur.*

quick-tem·pered ▶ **adjective** easily angered.

quick-wit·ted ▶ **adjective** able to think or respond quickly.

quid[1] /kwid/ ▶ **noun** (pl. same) Brit. informal one pound sterling.
– PHRASES **quids in** Brit. informal profiting or likely to profit from something.
– ORIGIN unknown.

quid[2] ▶ **noun** a lump of chewing tobacco.
– ORIGIN variant of CUD.

quid·di·ty /'kwidətē/ ▶ **noun** (pl. **quiddities**) the essential nature of a person or thing.
– ORIGIN Latin *quidditas*.

quid pro quo /'kwid ˌprō 'kwō/ ▶ **noun** (pl. **quid pro quos**) a favor given in return for something.
– ORIGIN Latin, 'something for something.'

qui·es·cent /kwē'esnt, kwī-/ ▶ **adjective** in a state or period of inactivity.
– DERIVATIVES **qui·es·cence** noun **qui·es·cent·ly** adverb.
– ORIGIN from Latin *quiescere* 'be still.'

qui·et /'kwīət/ ▶ **adjective** (**quieter**, **quietest**) **1** making little or no noise. **2** free from activity, disturbance, or excitement. **3** without being disturbed or interrupted: *a quiet drink*. **4** discreet, moderate, or restrained: *we wanted a quiet wedding*. **5** (of a person) calm and shy.

– SYNONYMS **1 silent,** still, hushed, noiseless, soundless, mute, dumb, speechless. **2 soft,** low, muted, muffled, faint, hushed, whispered, suppressed. **3 peaceful,** sleepy, tranquil, calm, still, restful.
– ANTONYMS loud, busy.

▶ **noun** absence of noise or disturbance.

– SYNONYMS **silence,** still, hush, restfulness, calm, tranquility, serenity, peace.

▶ **verb** make or become quiet.
– DERIVATIVES **qui·et·ness** noun.
– PHRASES **keep quiet** say nothing or keep something secret. **on the quiet** informal secretly or without attracting attention.
– ORIGIN from Latin *quies* 'repose, quiet.'

USAGE

Do not confuse **quiet** and **quite**. **Quiet** means 'making little or no noise' (*he spoke in a quiet voice*), whereas **quite** means 'moderately' or 'completely,' as in *it's quite warm* or *I quite agree*.

qui·et·en /'kwīətn/ ▶ **verb** chiefly Brit. make or become quiet and calm.

qui·et·ly /'kwīətlē/ ▶ **adverb 1** with little or no noise: *she quietly entered the room*. **2** with low volume: *he spoke quietly*.

– SYNONYMS **1 silently,** noiselessly, soundlessly, inaudibly. **2 softly,** faintly, in a low voice, in a whisper, in a murmur, under one's breath, in an undertone, sotto voce.

qui·e·tude /'kwīəˌt(y)o͞od/ ▶ **noun** a state of calmness and quiet.

qui·e·tus /'kwīētəs/ ▶ **noun** (pl. **quietuses**) literary death or a cause of death, regarded as a release from life.
– ORIGIN from Latin *quietus est* 'he is quit.'

quill /kwil/ ▶ **noun 1** a main wing or tail feather of a bird. **2** the hollow shaft of a feather. **3** a pen made from a main wing or tail feather of a bird. **4** a spine of a porcupine, hedgehog, etc.
– ORIGIN probably from German *quiele*.

quilt /kwilt/ ▶ **noun 1** a warm bed covering made of padding enclosed between layers of fabric and kept in place by lines of decorative stitching. **2** a bedspread with decorative stitching.

– SYNONYMS **comforter,** cover(s), coverlet, duvet; Brit. eiderdown.

▶ **verb** (usu. as adj. **quilted**) stitch padding between layers of fabric to form a quilt or item of clothing.
– DERIVATIVES **quilt·er** noun **quilt·ing** noun.
– ORIGIN Old French *cuilte*.

quince /kwins/ ▶ **noun** the hard, acid, pear-shaped fruit of a tree originally from Asia.
– ORIGIN Old French *cooin*.

quin·cen·ten·ar·y /ˌkwinsen'tenərē, kwin'sentəˌnerē/ ▶ **noun** (pl. **quincentenaries**) a five-hundredth anniversary.
– DERIVATIVES **quin·cen·ten·ni·al** /ˌkwinsen'tenēəl/ noun & adjective.
– ORIGIN from Latin *quinque* 'five.'

quin·cunx /'kwinˌkəNGks/ ▶ **noun** (pl. **quincunxes**) an arrangement of five objects with four at the corners of a square or rectangle and the fifth at its center.
– DERIVATIVES **quin·cun·cial** /ˌkwin'kənSHəl/ adjective.
– ORIGIN Latin, 'five twelfths.'

qui·nine /'kwīˌnīn/ ▶ **noun** a bitter compound present in cinchona bark, formerly used to treat malaria.
– ORIGIN Quechua, 'bark.'

qui·none /'kwinōn/ ▶ **noun** any of a class of organic chemical compounds related to benzene but having two hydrogen atoms replaced by oxygen.
– ORIGIN from Spanish *quina* 'cinchona bark.'

quin·quen·ni·al /kwiNG'kwenēəl/ ▶ **adjective** lasting for or recurring every five years.
– DERIVATIVES **quin·quen·ni·al·ly** adverb.
– ORIGIN from Latin *quinque* 'five' + *annus* 'year.'

quin·sy /'kwinzē/ ▶ **noun** inflammation of the throat, especially an abscess near the tonsils.
– ORIGIN Greek *kunankhē* 'canine quinsy.'

quint /kwint/ ▶ **noun** a quintuplet.

quin·ta /'kwintə/ ▶ **noun 1** (in Spain, Portugal, and Latin America) a large country house. **2** a wine-growing estate, especially in Portugal.
– ORIGIN Spanish and Portuguese.

quin·tal /kwintl/ ▶ **noun 1** a unit of weight equal to a hundredweight (112 lb) or, formerly, 100 lb. **2** a unit of weight equal to 100 kg.
– ORIGIN Latin *quintale*.

quin·tes·sence /kwin'tesəns/ ▶ **noun 1** the most perfect or typical example of a quality or type: *he's emerged as the quintessence of cool*. **2** a refined essence or extract of a substance.
– ORIGIN from Latin *quinta essentia* 'fifth essence,' from the former belief that a fifth substance existed in addition to the four elements, which pervaded all things.

quin·tes·sen·tial /ˌkwintə'senCHəl/ ▶ **adjective** representing the most perfect or typical example of a quality or type.

– SYNONYMS **typical,** prototypical, stereotypical, archetypal, classic, model, standard, stock, representative, conventional; ideal, consummate, exemplary, best, ultimate.

– DERIVATIVES **quin·tes·sen·tial·ly** adverb.

quin·tet /kwin'tet/ ▶ **noun 1** a group of five people playing music or singing together. **2** a composition for a quintet. **3** a set of five people or things.
– ORIGIN Italian *quintetto*.

quin·til·lion /kwin'tilyən/ ▶ **cardinal number** a thousand raised to the power of six (10^{18}).
– DERIVATIVES **quin·til·lionth** /-yənTH/ ordinal number.

quin·tu·ple /kwin't(y)o͞opəl, -'təpəl/ ▸ **adjective** **1** consisting of five parts or elements. **2** five times as much or as many. **3** (of time in music) having five beats in a bar. ▸ **verb** multiply or be multiplied by five. ▸ **noun** a quintuple number or amount.
– ORIGIN Latin *quintuplus*.

quin·tu·plet /kwin'təplət, -'t(y)o͞oplət/ ▸ **noun** each of five children born at one birth.

quip /kwip/ ▸ **noun** a witty remark.

– SYNONYMS **joke,** witticism, jest, pun, pleasantry, bon mot; informal one-liner, gag, wisecrack, funny.

▸ **verb** (**quips, quipping, quipped**) make a witty remark.
– DERIVATIVES **quip·ster** /-stər/ noun.
– ORIGIN perhaps from Latin *quippe* 'indeed.'

quire /kwīr/ ▸ **noun** **1** 24 or 25 sheets of paper; one twentieth of a ream. **2** four sheets of paper folded to form eight leaves, as in medieval manuscripts.
– ORIGIN Old French *quaier*.

quirk /kwərk/ ▸ **noun** **1** a peculiar aspect of a person's behavior. **2** a strange thing that happens by chance: *a quirk of fate*. **3** a sudden twist or curve.

– SYNONYMS **1 idiosyncrasy,** peculiarity, oddity, eccentricity, foible, whim, vagary, habit, characteristic, trait, fad. **2 chance,** fluke, freak, anomaly, twist.

– ORIGIN unknown.

quirk·y /'kwərkē/ ▸ **adjective** (**quirkier, quirkiest**) having peculiar or unexpected habits or qualities: *a quirky sense of humor*.

– SYNONYMS **eccentric,** idiosyncratic, unconventional, unorthodox, unusual, strange, bizarre, peculiar, zany; informal wacky, way-out, offbeat.
– ANTONYMS conventional.

– DERIVATIVES **quirk·i·ly** adverb **quirk·i·ness** noun.

WORD TOOLKIT

See **ECCENTRIC**.

quirt /kwərt/ ▸ **noun** a short-handled riding whip with a braided leather lash.
– ORIGIN Spanish *cuerda* 'cord' or Mexican Spanish *cuarta* 'whip.'

quis·ling /'kwizliNG/ ▸ **noun** a traitor collaborating with an occupying enemy force.
– ORIGIN from Major Vidkun *Quisling*, who ruled Norway during World War II on behalf of the German occupying forces.

quit /kwit/ ▸ **verb** (**quits, quitting, quitted** or **quit**) **1** leave a place, especially permanently. **2** resign from a job. **3** informal stop doing something.

– SYNONYMS **1 leave,** vacate, exit, depart from. **2 resign from,** leave, give up, hand in one's notice; informal pack (it) in. **3 give up,** stop, discontinue, drop, abandon, abstain from; informal pack in, leave off.

– PHRASES **be quit of** be rid of someone or something.
– ORIGIN Old French *quiter*.

quite /kwīt/ ▸ **adverb** **1** to a certain extent; moderately. **2** to the greatest extent or degree; completely: *I quite agree*.

– SYNONYMS **1 completely,** entirely, totally, wholly, absolutely, utterly, thoroughly, altogether. **2 fairly,** rather, somewhat, relatively, comparatively, moderately, reasonably; informal pretty.

▸ **exclamation** (also **quite so**) expressing agreement.
– PHRASES **quite a ——** a remarkable or impressive person or thing.
– ORIGIN from **QUIT**.

USAGE

For an explanation of the difference between **quite** and **quiet**, see the note at **QUIET**.

quits /kwits/ ▸ **adjective** on equal terms because a debt or score has been settled.
– PHRASES **call it quits 1** decide to stop doing something. **2** agree that terms are now equal.
– ORIGIN perhaps from Latin *quietus est* 'he is quit,' used as a receipt.

quit·ter /'kwitər/ ▸ **noun** informal a person who gives up easily.

quiv·er¹ /'kwivər/ ▸ **verb** shake or vibrate with a slight rapid movement.

– SYNONYMS **1 tremble,** shake, shiver, quaver, quake, shudder. **2 flutter,** flap, beat, agitate, vibrate.

▸ **noun** a quivering movement or sound.
– DERIVATIVES **quiv·er·y** adjective.
– ORIGIN from an Old English word meaning 'nimble, quick.'

CHOOSE THE RIGHT WORD

See **SHAKE**.

quiv·er² ▸ **noun** an archer's case for carrying arrows.
– ORIGIN Old French *quiveir*.

qui vive /ˌkē 'vēv/ ▸ **noun** (in phrase **on the qui vive**) on the alert or lookout.
– ORIGIN French, '(long) live who?,' i.e., 'on whose side are you?,' used as a sentry's challenge.

quix·ot·ic /kwik'sätik/ ▸ **adjective** unselfish and idealistic to an impractical extent: *the quixotic desire to do good*.

– SYNONYMS **idealistic,** romantic, visionary, Utopian, extravagant, starry-eyed, unrealistic, unworldly; impracticable, unworkable, impossible.

– DERIVATIVES **quix·ot·i·cal·ly** /-ik(ə)lē/ adverb **quix·o·tism** /'kwiksəˌtizəm/ noun.
– ORIGIN from Don *Quixote*, hero of a book by the Spanish writer Cervantes.

WORD TOOLKIT

quixotic ...	**idealistic ...**	**visionary ...**
attempt	youth	leadership
quest	dream	leader
campaign	rhetoric	work
gesture	student	artist
venture	belief	thinker
pursuit	philosophy	poet
mission	generation	architect

quiz /kwiz/ ▸ **noun** (pl. **quizzes**) **1** a game or competition involving a set of questions as a test of knowledge. **2** informal, chiefly Brit. a period of questioning.

– SYNONYMS **test,** exam, pop quiz, questionnaire.

▸ **verb** (**quizzes, quizzing, quizzed**) question someone.

– SYNONYMS **question,** interrogate, cross-examine, cross-question, interview; informal grill, pump.

– ORIGIN uncertain.

quiz·mas·ter /'kwizˌmastər/ ▸ **noun** a person in charge of a quiz, especially someone who hosts a quiz show.

quiz show ▶ **noun** a television or radio program in which people compete in a quiz, usually for cash or other prizes.

quiz·zi·cal /ˈkwizəkəl/ ▶ **adjective** showing mild or amused puzzlement.

– SYNONYMS **inquiring,** questioning, curious; puzzled, perplexed, baffled, mystified; amused, mocking, teasing.

– DERIVATIVES **quiz·zi·cal·i·ty** /ˌkwiziˈkalətē/ noun **quiz·zi·cal·ly** adverb.

quoin /k(w)oin/ ▶ **noun 1** an external angle of a wall or building. **2** a cornerstone.
– DERIVATIVES **quoin·ing** noun.
– ORIGIN from **COIN**, in the former senses 'cornerstone' and 'wedge.'

quoit /k(w)oit/ ▶ **noun 1** a ring thrown in a game with the aim of landing it over an upright peg. **2** (**quoits**) (treated as sing.) a game of throwing quoits.
– ORIGIN probably French.

quon·dam /ˈkwändəm, -ˌdam/ ▶ **adjective** formal that once was; former.
– ORIGIN Latin, 'formerly.'

Quon·set /ˈkwänsət/ (usu. **Quonset hut**) ▶ **noun** trademark a prefabricated building with a semicylindrical corrugated roof.

quo·rum /ˈkwôrəm/ ▶ **noun** (pl. **quorums**) the minimum number of members that must be present at a meeting to make its business valid.
– ORIGIN Latin, 'of whom.'

quo·ta /ˈkwōtə/ ▶ **noun 1** a limited quantity of a product that may be produced, exported, or imported. **2** a share that a person or group is entitled to receive or has to contribute: *her weekly quota of articles is two for newspapers and one for a magazine*. **3** a fixed number of a group allowed to do something, e.g., immigrants entering a country.

– SYNONYMS **share,** allocation, allowance, ration, portion, slice, percentage.

– ORIGIN from Latin *quota pars* 'how great a part.'

quot·a·ble /ˈkwōtəbəl/ ▶ **adjective** suitable for or worth quoting.
– DERIVATIVES **quot·a·bil·i·ty** /ˌkwōtəˈbilətē/ noun.

quo·ta·tion /ˌkwōˈtāsʜən/ ▶ **noun 1** a passage or remark repeated by someone other than the person who originally said or wrote it. **2** a short musical passage or visual image taken from one piece of music or work of art and used in another. **3** the action of quoting from a speech, artistic work, etc. **4** a formal statement of the estimated cost of a job or service. **5** a registration granted to a company enabling their shares to be officially listed and traded on a stock exchange.

– SYNONYMS **1 extract,** quote, citation, excerpt, passage. **2 estimate,** quote, price, tender, bid, costing.

quo·ta·tion mark ▶ **noun** each of a set of punctuation marks, single (' ') or double (" "), used to mark the beginning and end of a title or quotation, or to set off a word or phrase regarded as slang or jargon.

quote /kwōt/ ▶ **verb 1** repeat or copy out a passage or remark by another person. **2** (**quote something as**) mention something as an example to support a point: *the figures were quoted as more evidence for the failure of our schools*. **3** give someone an estimate for a job or service. **4** (**quote someone/thing at/as**) name someone or something at specified odds. **5** give a company a listing on a stock exchange.

– SYNONYMS **1 recite,** repeat, reproduce, retell, echo. **2 mention,** cite, refer to, name, instance, allude to, point out.

▶ **noun 1** a quotation. **2** (**quotes**) quotation marks.

– SYNONYMS see **QUOTATION**.

– PHRASES **quote —— unquote** informal used in speech to indicate the start and end of a quotation: *the second sentence of the statement says, quote, There has never been a better time to invest, unquote*.
– ORIGIN Latin *quotare* 'mark with numbers.'

quoth /kwōᴛʜ/ ▶ **verb** old use or humorous said (used only in first and third person singular before the subject).
– ORIGIN Germanic.

quo·tid·i·an /kwōˈtidēən/ ▶ **adjective 1** happening every day; daily. **2** ordinary or everyday.
– ORIGIN Latin *quotidianus*.

quo·tient /ˈkwōsʜənt/ ▶ **noun 1** Mathematics a result obtained by dividing one quantity by another. **2** a degree or amount of a specified quality: *my coolness quotient evaporated on the spot*.
– ORIGIN from Latin *quotiens* 'how many times.'

Qu·r'an /kəˈrän, -ˈran/ (also **Quran**) ▶ **noun** Arabic spelling of **KORAN**.

q.v. ▶ **abbreviation** used to direct a reader to another part of a written work for further information.
– ORIGIN from Latin *quod vide*, 'which see.'

qwer·ty /ˈkwərtē/ ▶ **adjective** referring to the standard layout on English-language typewriters and keyboards, having *q, w, e, r, t,* and *y* as the first keys on the top row of letters.

R[1] (also r) ▶ **noun** (pl. **Rs** or **R's**) the eighteenth letter of the alphabet.
– PHRASES **the three Rs** reading, writing, and arithmetic, regarded as the fundamentals of learning.

R[2] ▶ **abbreviation 1** rand. **2** (®) registered as a trademark. **3** (**R.**) River. **4** roentgen(s). **5** rook (in chess). **6** Baseball (on scorecards) run(s). **7** Brit. Regina or Rex.

r ▶ **abbreviation 1** radius. **2** right.

R & B ▶ **abbreviation 1** rhythm and blues. **2** a kind of pop music with a vocal style derived from soul.

R & D ▶ **abbreviation** research and development.

R & R ▶ **abbreviation** informal rest and recreation.

RA ▶ **abbreviation 1** (in the UK) Royal Academician or Royal Academy. **2** (in the UK) Royal Artillery.

Ra ▶ **symbol** the chemical element radium.

rab·bet /ˈrabit/ ▶ **noun** a step-shaped recess cut into wood, to which the edge or tongue of another piece may be joined. ▶ **verb** (**rabbets, rabbeting, rabbeted**) **1** make a rabbet in. **2** join or fix with a rabbet.
– ORIGIN from Old French *rabbat* 'abatement, recess.'

rab·bi /ˈrabˌī/ ▶ **noun** (pl. **rabbis**) **1** a Jewish scholar or teacher, especially of Jewish law. **2** a Jewish religious leader.
– DERIVATIVES **rab·bin·ate** /ˈrabənət, -ˌnāt/ noun.
– ORIGIN from a Hebrew word meaning 'my master.'

rab·bin·ic /rəˈbinik, ra-/ ▶ **adjective** relating to rabbis or to Jewish law or teachings.
– DERIVATIVES **rab·bin·i·cal** /rəˈbinikəl, ra-/ adjective.

rab·bit /ˈrabit/ ▶ **noun 1** a burrowing mammal with long ears and a short tail. **2** a hare. **3** the fur of the rabbit. ▶ **verb** (**rabbits, rabbiting, rabbited**) (usu. as n. **rabbiting**) hunt rabbits.
– DERIVATIVES **rab·bit·y** adjective.
– ORIGIN probably from Old French.

rab·bit punch ▶ **noun** a sharp chop with the edge of the hand to the back of the neck.

rab·ble /ˈrabəl/ ▶ **noun 1** a disorderly crowd. **2** (**the rabble**) ordinary people regarded as common or uncouth.
– ORIGIN perhaps related to dialect *rabble* 'to gabble.'

rab·ble-rous·er ▶ **noun** a person who stirs up popular opinion, especially for political reasons.

Rab·e·lai·sian /ˌrabəˈlāzHən/ ▶ **adjective** relating to or like the French satirist François Rabelais or his writings, especially in being very imaginative and full of earthy humor.

rab·id /ˈrabəd, ˈrā-/ ▶ **adjective 1** extreme; fanatical: *rabid football fans.* **2** relating to or affected with rabies.
– DERIVATIVES **rab·id·ly** adverb.

ra·bies /ˈrābēz/ ▶ **noun** a dangerous disease of dogs and other mammals, caused by a virus that can be transmitted through an animal's saliva to humans, causing madness and convulsions.
– ORIGIN Latin.

rac·coon /raˈko͞on, rə-/ (also **racoon**) ▶ **noun** a grayish-brown American mammal with a black face and a ringed tail.
– ORIGIN from an Algonquian dialect word.

race[1] /rās/ ▶ **noun 1** a competition between runners, horses, vehicles, etc., to see which is fastest over a set course. **2** a situation in which people compete to be first to achieve something: *the race for governor.* **3** a strong current flowing through a narrow channel. **4** a water channel, especially one in a mill or mine. **5** a smooth ring-shaped groove or guide for a ball bearing or roller bearing.

> – SYNONYMS **1 contest,** competition, event, heat, trial(s). **2** *the race for naval domination* **rivalry,** competition, contention, quest.

▶ **verb 1** compete in a race. **2** have a race with someone. **3** prepare and enter an animal or car for races. **4** move or progress swiftly: *I raced into the house.* **5** (of machinery) operate at excessive speed.

> – SYNONYMS **1 compete,** contend, run, be pitted against. **2 hurry,** dash, rush, run, sprint, bolt, charge, career, shoot, hurtle, fly, speed, zoom; informal tear, belt.

– DERIVATIVES **rac·er** noun.
– ORIGIN Old Norse, 'current.'

race[2] ▶ **noun 1** each of the major divisions of humankind, having distinct physical characteristics. **2** racial origin or distinction. **3** a group of people sharing the same culture, language, etc.; an ethnic group. **4** a group of people or things with a shared feature: *a race of intelligent computers.* **5** Biology a subdivision of a species.

> – SYNONYMS **1 ethnic group,** origin, bloodline, stock. **2 people,** nation.

– ORIGIN French.

> **USAGE**
>
> Some people feel that the word **race** should be avoided, because of its associations with the now discredited theories of 19th-century anthropologists and physiologists about supposed racial superiority. Terms such as **people**, **community**, or **ethnic group** are less likely to cause offense.

race·car /ˈrāsˌkär/ ▶ **noun** a car built for racing.

race·course /ˈrāsˌkôrs/ ▶ **noun** a racetrack.

race·horse /ˈrāsˌhôrs/ ▶ **noun** a horse bred and trained for racing.

ra·ceme /rāˈsēm, rə-/ ▶ **noun** a flower cluster with the separate flowers attached by short stalks along a central stem, the lower flowers developing first. Compare with **CYME**.
– ORIGIN Latin *racemus* 'bunch of grapes.'

race re·la·tions ▸ plural noun relations between members of different races within a country.

race·track /ˈrās,trak/ ▸ noun **1** a ground or track for horse or dog racing. **2** a track for motor racing.

race·way /ˈrās,wā/ ▸ noun **1** a racetrack. **2** a water channel, especially an artificial one in which fish are reared. **3** a pipe or channel enclosing electric wires.

ra·cial /ˈrāsнəl/ ▸ adjective **1** relating to race. **2** relating to differences or relations between races.

– SYNONYMS **ethnic,** ethnological, race-related, cultural, national, tribal, genetic.

– DERIVATIVES **ra·cial·ly** adverb.

ra·cial·ism /ˈrāsнə,lizəm/ ▸ noun racism.
– DERIVATIVES **ra·cial·ist** noun & adjective.

ra·cial·ize /ˈrāsнə,līz/ ▸ verb make something racial or racist in nature or outlook.

rac·ing /ˈrāsiɴɢ/ ▸ noun a sport that involves competing in races. ▸ adjective moving swiftly.

ra·ci·no /rəˈsēnō/ ▸ noun a building complex or grounds having a racetrack and gambling facilities traditionally associated with a casino.

rac·ism /ˈrā,sizəm/ ▸ noun **1** the belief that each race has certain qualities or abilities, giving rise to the view that some races are better than others. **2** discrimination against or hostility toward other races.
– DERIVATIVES **rac·ist** noun & adjective.

rack[1] /rak/ ▸ noun **1** a framework for holding or storing things. **2** a bar with cogs or teeth that fit into a wheel or pinion. **3** a triangular frame for positioning pool balls. **4** a single game of pool. **5** (**the rack**) historical an instrument of torture consisting of a frame on which the victim was tied by the wrists and ankles and stretched.

– SYNONYMS **frame,** framework, stand, holder, trestle, support, shelf.

▸ verb **1** (also **wrack**) cause great pain or distress to someone. **2** place something in or on a rack. **3** (**rack something up**) accumulate or achieve a score or amount.

– SYNONYMS **torment,** afflict, torture, agonize, harrow, plague, persecute, trouble, worry.

– PHRASES **rack** (or **wrack**) **one's brains** think very hard.
– ORIGIN from Dutch *rec*, German *rek* 'horizontal bar or shelf.'

USAGE

The words **rack** and **wrack** are often confused. The noun is always spelled **rack** (*a magazine rack*). The verb can be spelled **rack** or **wrack**, but only when it means *cause great pain to someone* (*he was racked/wracked with guilt*) or in the phrase **rack** (or **wrack**) **one's brains**.

rack[2] ▸ noun a cut of meat, especially lamb, including the front ribs.
– ORIGIN unknown.

rack[3] ▸ noun (in phrase **go to rack and ruin**) gradually fall into a bad condition.
– ORIGIN Old English, 'vengeance.'

rack[4] ▸ verb draw off wine, beer, etc., from the sediment in the barrel.
– ORIGIN Provençal *arracar*.

rack-and-pin·ion ▸ adjective (of a mechanism) using a fixed bar with cogs or teeth that fit into a smaller cog.

rack·et[1] /ˈrakit/ (also **racquet**) ▸ noun a bat consisting of an oval or round frame with strings stretched across it, used in tennis, badminton, and squash.
– ORIGIN French *raquette*.

rack·et[2] ▸ noun **1** a loud unpleasant noise. **2** informal a dishonest scheme for obtaining money: *a protection racket*. **3** informal a person's line of business.

– SYNONYMS **1 noise,** din, hubbub, clamor, uproar, tumult, commotion, rumpus, pandemonium; Brit. row; informal hullabaloo. **2 fraud,** swindle; informal scam, rip-off, con job.

▸ verb (**rackets, racketing, racketed**) make a loud unpleasant noise.
– DERIVATIVES **rack·et·y** adjective.
– ORIGIN perhaps imitating a loud noise.

rack·et·eer /,rakiˈti(ə)r/ ▸ noun a person who makes money from dishonest activities.
– DERIVATIVES **rack·et·eer·ing** noun.

rac·on·teur /,rak,änˈtər, -ən-/ ▸ noun a person who tells stories in an interesting way.
– ORIGIN French.

ra·coon ▸ noun variant spelling of RACCOON.

rac·quet /ˈrakit/ ▸ noun variant spelling of RACKET[1].

rac·quet·ball /ˈrakit,bôl/ ▸ noun a game played with a rubber ball and a short-handled racket in a four-walled court.

rac·y /ˈrāsē/ ▸ adjective (**racier, raciest**) lively or exciting, especially in a sexual way.

– SYNONYMS **risqué,** suggestive, naughty, sexy, spicy, ribald; indecorous, indecent, immodest, off-color, dirty, rude, smutty, crude, salacious; informal raunchy, blue; euphemistic adult.
– ANTONYMS prim.

– DERIVATIVES **rac·i·ly** adverb **rac·i·ness** noun.

rad[1] /rad/ ▸ abbreviation radian(s).

rad[2] ▸ adjective informal excellent or impressive.

ra·dar /ˈrā,där/ ▸ noun a system for detecting the position and speed of aircraft, ships, etc., by sending out pulses of radio waves that are reflected off the object back to the source.
– ORIGIN from *radio detection and ranging*.

ra·dar gun ▸ noun a hand-held radar device used by traffic police to estimate a vehicle's speed.

ra·dar trap ▸ noun an area of road in which radar is used by the police to detect speeding vehicles.

ra·di·al /ˈrādēəl/ ▸ adjective **1** relating to or arranged in lines coming out from a central point to the edge of a circle: *radial markings resembling spokes*. **2** (of a tire) in which the layers of fabric have their cords running at right angles to the circumference of the tire. ▸ noun a radial tire.
– DERIVATIVES **ra·di·al·ly** adverb.
– ORIGIN from Latin *radius* 'spoke, ray.'

ra·di·al sym·me·try ▸ noun chiefly Biology symmetry about a central axis, as in a starfish.

ra·di·an /ˈrādēən/ ▸ noun an angle of 57.3 degrees, equal to that at the center of a circle formed by an arc equal in length to the radius.

ra·di·ant /ˈrādēənt/ ▸ adjective **1** shining or glowing brightly. **2** showing great joy, love, or health: *a radiant smile*. **3** (of electromagnetic energy, especially heat) transmitted by radiation, rather than conduction or convection. **4** (of an appliance) emitting radiant energy for cooking or heating.

– SYNONYMS **1 shining,** bright, illuminated, brilliant, gleaming, glowing, ablaze, luminous, lustrous, incandescent, dazzling, shimmering. **2 joyful,** elated, thrilled, overjoyed, jubilant, rapturous, ecstatic, euphoric, in seventh heaven, on cloud nine, delighted, very happy; informal on top of the world, over the moon.
– ANTONYMS dark, gloomy.

– DERIVATIVES **ra·di·ance** noun **ra·di·ant·ly** adverb.

CHOOSE THE RIGHT WORD

See **BRIGHT**.

ra·di·ate /ˈrādēˌāt/ ▸ **verb 1** (with reference to light, heat, or other energy) send out or be sent out in rays or waves. **2** show a strong feeling or quality: *she radiated an aura of ambition.* **3** spread out from a central point: *rows of cells radiated from a central hall.*

– SYNONYMS **1 emit,** give off, discharge, diffuse, scatter, shed, cast. **2 shine,** beam, emanate, pour. **3 fan out,** spread out, branch out/off, extend, issue.

– DERIVATIVES **ra·di·a·tive** /-ˌātiv/ adjective.
– ORIGIN Latin *radiare*.

ra·di·a·tion /ˌrādēˈāsʜən/ ▸ **noun 1** the action or process of radiating. **2** energy sent out as electromagnetic waves or subatomic particles.

ra·di·a·tion sick·ness ▸ **noun** illness caused when a person is exposed to X-rays, gamma rays, or other radiation.

ra·di·a·tion ther·a·py ▸ **noun** the treatment of cancer or other disease using X-rays or similar radiation.

ra·di·a·tor /ˈrādēˌātər/ ▸ **noun 1** a thing that radiates light, heat, or sound. **2** a heating device consisting of a metal case through which hot water circulates, or one heated by electricity or oil. **3** a cooling device in a vehicle or aircraft engine consisting of a bank of thin tubes in which circulating water is cooled by the surrounding air.

rad·i·cal /ˈradikəl/ ▸ **adjective 1** relating to the basic nature of something; fundamental: *she made radical changes in her life.* **2** supporting complete political or social reform. **3** departing from tradition; innovative or progressive. **4** Mathematics relating to the root of a number or quantity.

– SYNONYMS **1 thorough,** complete, total, comprehensive, exhaustive, sweeping, far-reaching, wide-ranging, extensive, profound, major. **2 fundamental,** basic, deep-seated, essential, structural. **3 revolutionary,** progressive, reformist, revisionist, progressivist, extreme, fanatical, militant.
– ANTONYMS superficial, minor, conservative.

▸ **noun 1** a person who supports radical political or social reform. **2** Chemistry a group of atoms behaving as a unit in certain compounds.
– DERIVATIVES **rad·i·cal·ism** /-ˌlizəm/ noun **rad·i·cal·ize** /ˈradikəˌlīz/ verb **rad·i·cal·ly** adverb.
– ORIGIN Latin *radicalis*.

rad·i·cal chic ▸ **noun** superficial and purely fashionable support for radical left-wing views.

rad·i·cal sign ▸ **noun** Mathematics the sign √, which indicates the square root of the number following (or a higher root indicated by a raised numeral before the symbol).

ra·dic·chi·o /raˈdēkēˌō, rə-/ ▸ **noun** (pl. **radicchios**) a variety of chicory with dark red leaves.
– ORIGIN Italian.

rad·i·cle /ˈradikəl/ ▸ **noun** the part of a plant embryo that develops into the primary root.
– ORIGIN Latin *radicula* 'little root.'

ra·di·i /ˈrādēˌī/ plural of **RADIUS**.

ra·di·o /ˈrādēˌō/ ▸ **noun** (pl. **radios**) **1** the sending and receiving of electromagnetic waves carrying sound messages. **2** broadcasting in sound: *she's written plays for radio.* **3** a broadcasting station or channel. **4** a device for receiving radio programs or for sending and receiving radio messages. ▸ **verb** (**radioes, radioing, radioed**) **1** send a message by radio. **2** communicate with a person or place by radio.
– ORIGIN abbreviation of **RADIOTELEPHONE**.

radio- ▸ **combining form 1** referring to radio waves or broadcasting: *radiogram.* **2** connected with rays, radiation, or radioactivity: *radiography.*

ra·di·o·ac·tive /ˌrādēōˈaktiv/ ▸ **adjective** emitting ionizing radiation or particles.
– DERIVATIVES **ra·di·o·ac·tive·ly** adverb.

ra·di·o·ac·tiv·i·ty /ˌrādēōakˈtivətē/ ▸ **noun 1** the emission of ionizing radiation or particles, caused when atomic nuclei disintegrate spontaneously. **2** radioactive particles.

ra·di·o as·tron·o·my ▸ **noun** the branch of astronomy concerned with radio emissions from stars and other celestial objects.

ra·di·o·car·bon /ˌrādēōˈkärbən/ ▸ **noun** a radioactive isotope of carbon used in carbon dating.

ra·di·o·car·bon dat·ing ▸ **noun** another term for **CARBON DATING**.

ra·di·o·con·trolled ▸ **adjective** controllable from a distance by radio.

ra·di·o·gram /ˈrādēōˌgram/ ▸ **noun** Brit. dated a combined radio and record player.
– ORIGIN from **RADIO-** + **GRAMOPHONE**.

ra·di·o·graph /ˈrādēōˌgraf/ ▸ **noun** an image produced on a sensitive plate or film by X-rays or other radiation.
– DERIVATIVES **ra·di·o·graph·ic** adjective.

ra·di·og·ra·phy /ˌrādēˈägrəfē/ ▸ **noun** the process of taking radiographs to assist in medical examinations.
– DERIVATIVES **ra·di·og·ra·pher** /ˌrādēˈägrəfər/ noun.

ra·di·o·i·so·tope /ˌrādēōˈīsəˌtōp/ ▸ **noun** a radioactive isotope.

ra·di·ol·o·gy /ˌrādēˈäləjē/ ▸ **noun** the science of X-rays and similar radiation, especially as used in medicine.
– DERIVATIVES **ra·di·o·log·ic** /ˌrādēəˈläjik/ adjective **ra·di·o·log·i·cal** /ˌrādēəˈläjikəl/ adjective **ra·di·ol·o·gist** /-jist/ noun.

ra·di·om·e·ter /ˌrādēˈämitər/ ▸ **noun** an instrument for detecting or measuring radiation.
– DERIVATIVES **ra·di·om·e·try** /-trē/ noun.

ra·di·o·met·ric /ˌrādēəˈmetrik/ ▸ **adjective** relating to the measurement of radioactivity.

ra·di·o·nu·clide /ˌrādēōˈn(y)o͞oˌklīd/ ▸ **noun** a radioactive isotope.

ra·di·o·phon·ic /ˌrādēōˈfänik/ ▸ **adjective** relating to sound that is produced electronically.

ra·di·o·tel·e·phone /ˌrādēōˈteləfōn/ ▸ **noun** a telephone using radio transmission.

ra·di·o tel·e·scope ▸ **noun** an instrument used to detect radio emissions from space.

ra·di·o·ther·a·py /ˌrādēōˈTHerəpē/ ▸ **noun** radiation therapy.
– DERIVATIVES **ra·di·o·ther·a·pist** noun.

ra·di·o wave ▸ **noun** an electromagnetic wave having a frequency in the range 10^4 to 10^{11} or 10^{12} hertz.

rad·ish /ˈradiSH/ ▸ **noun** the small, hot-tasting, red root of a plant that is eaten raw as a salad vegetable.
– ORIGIN Latin *radix* 'root.'

ra·di·um /ˈrādēəm/ ▸ **noun** a reactive, radioactive metallic chemical element.
– ORIGIN from Latin *radius* 'ray.'

ra·di·us /ˈrādēəs/ ▸ **noun** (pl. **radii** /ˈrādēˌī/ or **radiuses**) **1** a straight line from the center to the circumference of a circle or sphere. **2** a specified distance from a center in all directions: *hydrants within a two-mile radius.* **3** the thicker and shorter of the two bones in the human forearm.
– ORIGIN Latin, 'spoke, ray.'

ra·don /ˈrāˌdän/ ▸ **noun** a chemical element that is a rare radioactive gas.
– ORIGIN from **RADIUM**, on the pattern of *argon*.

RAF ▸ **abbreviation** (in the UK) Royal Air Force.

raf·fi·a /ˈrafēə/ ▸ **noun** fiber from the leaves of a tropical palm tree, used for making hats, baskets, etc.
– ORIGIN Malagasy.

raff·ish /ˈrafiSH/ ▸ **adjective** slightly disreputable, but in an attractive way.
– ORIGIN from **RIFFRAFF**.

raf·fle /ˈrafəl/ ▸ **noun** a lottery with goods rather than money as prizes.

– SYNONYMS **lottery,** (prize) drawing, lotto, sweepstakes.

▸ **verb** offer something as a prize in a raffle.
– ORIGIN Old French.

raft[1] /raft/ ▸ **noun 1** a flat structure of pieces of timber fastened together, used as a boat or floating platform. **2** a small inflatable boat. ▸ **verb** travel or transport on a raft.
– DERIVATIVES **raft·ing** noun.
– ORIGIN Old Norse, 'rafter.'

raft[2] ▸ **noun** a large amount: *she speaks a raft of languages.*
– ORIGIN perhaps Scandinavian.

raft·er[1] /ˈraftər/ ▸ **noun** a beam forming part of the internal framework of a roof.
– DERIVATIVES **raft·ered** adjective.
– ORIGIN Old English.

raft·er[2] ▸ **noun** a person who travels by raft.

rag[1] /rag/ ▸ **noun 1** a piece of old cloth. **2** (**rags**) old or tattered clothes. **3** informal a low-quality newspaper. ▸ **verb** (**rags, ragging, ragged**) give a decorative effect to a painted surface by applying paint with a rag.
– ORIGIN probably from **RAGGED** or **RAGGY**.

rag[2] ▸ **noun** Brit. a program of entertainments organized by students to raise money for charity. ▸ **verb** (**rags, ragging, ragged**) **1** (usu. **rag on someone**) tease or make fun of someone. **2** rebuke someone harshly.
– ORIGIN unknown.

rag[3] ▸ **noun** a piece of ragtime music.

ra·ga /ˈrägə/ (also **rag** /räg/) ▸ **noun** (in Indian classical music) each of the six basic musical modes that express different moods in certain characteristic progressions.
– ORIGIN Sanskrit, 'color, musical tone.'

rag·a·muf·fin /ˈragəˌməfən/ ▸ **noun 1** a person in ragged, dirty clothes. **2** (also **raggamuffin**) a person who performs or likes ragga dance music.
– ORIGIN probably from **RAG**[1].

rag doll ▸ **noun** a soft doll made from pieces of cloth.

rage /rāj/ ▸ **noun 1** violent uncontrollable anger. **2** (in combination) anger or aggression associated with conflict arising from a particular situation: *air rage.* **3** a very popular person or thing: *remember when bell-bottoms were the rage?* **4** a strong desire: *a rage for order and purity.*

– SYNONYMS **1 fury,** anger, wrath, outrage, indignation, temper, spleen; formal ire. **2 craze,** passion, fashion, taste, trend, vogue, fad, mania; informal thing.

▸ **verb 1** feel or express violent anger. **2** continue with great force or intensity: *the battle raged for six hours.*

– SYNONYMS **be angry,** be furious, be enraged, be incensed, seethe, be beside oneself, rave, storm, fume, spit; informal be livid, be wild, be steamed up.

– DERIVATIVES **ra·ger** noun.
– PHRASES **all the rage** temporarily very popular or fashionable.
– ORIGIN Old French.

rag·ga /ˈragə/ ▸ **noun** a style of dance music in which a DJ improvises lyrics over a backing track.
– ORIGIN from **RAGAMUFFIN**, because of the scruffy clothing worn by its followers.

rag·ga·muf·fin /ˈragəˌməfən/ ▸ **noun** variant spelling of **RAGAMUFFIN**.

rag·ged /ˈragid/ ▸ **adjective 1** (of cloth or clothes) old and torn. **2** wearing ragged clothes. **3** having a rough or irregular surface or edge. **4** not steady or uniform: *her breath came in ragged gasps.* **5** exhausted or stressed.

– SYNONYMS **1 tattered,** torn, ripped, frayed, worn (out), threadbare, scruffy, shabby; informal tatty. **2 jagged,** craggy, rugged, uneven, rough, irregular, indented.

– DERIVATIVES **rag·ged·ly** adverb **rag·ged·y** adjective.
– PHRASES **run someone ragged** exhaust someone.
– ORIGIN Scandinavian.

rag·gle-tag·gle /ˈragəl ˌtagəl/ ▸ **adjective** untidy and scruffy.
– ORIGIN probably from **RAGTAG**.

rag·gy /ˈragē/ ▸ **adjective** informal ragged or shabby.
– ORIGIN Scandinavian.

rag·lan /ˈraglən/ ▸ **adjective** having or referring to sleeves that continue in one piece up to the neck of a garment.
– ORIGIN named after Lord *Raglan*, a British commander in the Crimean War.

ra·gout /raˈgo͞o/ ▸ **noun** a spicy stew of meat and vegetables.
– ORIGIN French.

rag·pick·er /ˈragˌpikər/ ▸ **noun** chiefly historical a person who collects and sells rags.

rag rug ▸ **noun** a rug made from small strips of fabric hooked into or pushed through a material such as hessian.

rag·tag /ˈragˌtag/ ▸ **adjective** untidy, disorganized, or very varied: *a ragtag group of idealists.*
– ORIGIN from **RAG**[1] + **TAG**[1].

rag·time /ˈragˌtīm/ ▶ **noun** an early form of jazz with a syncopated melody, played especially on the piano.
– ORIGIN probably referring to the 'ragged' rhythm.

rag trade ▶ **noun** informal the clothing or fashion industry.

rag·weed /ˈragˌwēd/ ▶ **noun** a North American plant of the daisy family, whose pollen is a major cause of hay fever.

rag·wort /ˈragˌwərt, -ˌwôrt/ ▶ **noun** a yellow-flowered plant with ragged leaves.

rah /rä/ ▶ **exclamation** informal a cheer of encouragement or approval.
– ORIGIN shortening of **HURRAH**.

rai /rī/ ▶ **noun** a style of music blending Arabic and Algerian folk elements with Western rock.
– ORIGIN perhaps from an Arabic phrase found in the songs meaning 'that's the thinking, here is the view.'

raid /rād/ ▶ **noun 1** a sudden attack on an enemy or on a building to commit a crime. **2** a surprise visit by police to arrest suspects or seize illegal goods.

– SYNONYMS **1 attack,** assault, descent, blitz, incursion, sortie, onslaught, storming. **2 robbery,** burglary, holdup, break-in; informal stickup, heist.

▶ **verb 1** make a raid on a place. **2** take something from a place in a secretive way: *she crept downstairs to raid the pantry.*

– SYNONYMS **1 attack,** assault, set upon, descend on, swoop on, storm, rush. **2 rob,** hold up, break into, plunder, steal from, pillage, loot, ransack; informal stick up.

– ORIGIN Scots variant of **ROAD** in the early senses 'journey on horseback,' 'attack.'

raid·er /ˈrādər/ ▶ **noun** a person who attacks an enemy or a building to commit a crime.

– SYNONYMS **robber,** burglar, thief, housebreaker, plunderer, pillager, looter, marauder, attacker, assailant, invader.

rail[1] /rāl/ ▶ **noun 1** a bar or bars fixed on upright supports or attached to a wall or ceiling, forming part of a fence or used to hang things on. **2** each of the two metal bars laid on the ground to form a railroad track. **3** railroads as a means of transport. ▶ **verb 1** provide or enclose something with a rail or rails. **2** convey goods by rail.
– PHRASES **go off the rails** informal begin behaving in an odd or unacceptable way. **on the rails 1** informal functioning normally. **2** (of a racehorse or jockey) in a position on the racetrack nearest the inside fence.
– ORIGIN Old French *reille* 'iron rod.'

rail[2] ▶ **verb** (**rail against/at**) complain or protest strongly about something.
– ORIGIN French *railler*.

rail[3] ▶ **noun** a secretive gray and brown waterside bird.
– ORIGIN Old French *raille*.

rail car ▶ **noun** a railroad car.

rail·head /ˈrālˌhed/ ▶ **noun** a point at which a railroad ends.

rail·ing /ˈrāliNG/ ▶ **noun** a fence made of rails.

– SYNONYMS **fence,** fencing, rail(s), palisade, balustrade, banister.

rail·ler·y /ˈrālərē/ ▶ **noun** good-humored teasing.
– ORIGIN from French *railler* 'complain strongly about.'

rail·road /ˈrālˌrōd/ ▶ **noun 1** a track made of rails along which trains run. **2** a system of such tracks with the trains, organization, and staff required to run it. ▶ **verb** informal **1** rush or force someone into doing something. **2** cause a measure to be approved quickly by putting pressure on a group: *the bill was railroaded through the Senate.*

rail·road tie ▶ **noun** each of the wooden or concrete beams on which a railroad track rests.

rail·way /ˈrālˌwā/ ▶ **noun** chiefly Brit. a railroad.

rai·ment /ˈrāmənt/ ▶ **noun** old use or literary clothing.
– ORIGIN shortening of former *arrayment*, from **ARRAY**.

rain /rān/ ▶ **noun 1** the condensed moisture of the atmosphere falling in drops. **2** (**rains**) falls of rain. **3** a large quantity of things falling or descending: *a rain of blows.*

– SYNONYMS **1 rainfall,** precipitation, raindrops, drizzle, shower, rainstorm, cloudburst, torrent, downpour, deluge, storm. **2** *a rain of hot ash* **shower,** deluge, flood, torrent, avalanche, flurry, storm, hail.

▶ **verb 1** (**it rains, it is raining, it rained**) rain falls. **2** (**be rained out**) (of an event) be canceled or interrupted because of rain. **3** fall or cause to fall in large quantities.

– SYNONYMS **1 pour (down),** pelt down, teem down, beat down, drizzle. **2** *bombs rained on the city* **fall,** hail, drop, shower.

– PHRASES **be as right as rain** be perfectly fit and well. **rain cats and dogs** rain heavily.
– ORIGIN Old English.

WORD LINKS

pluvial *relating to rain*

rain·bow /ˈrānˌbō/ ▶ **noun** an arch of colors seen in the sky, caused by the refraction and dispersion of the sun's light by water droplets in the atmosphere.

rain·bow co·a·li·tion ▶ **noun** a political alliance of different groups, representing ethnic and other minorities.

rain·bow trout ▶ **noun** a large trout with reddish sides, native to western North America and introduced elsewhere.

rain check ▶ **noun** a ticket given for later use when an outdoor event is rained off.
– PHRASES **take a rain check** refuse an offer but imply that one may take it up later.

rain·coat /ˈrānˌkōt/ ▶ **noun** a coat made from waterproofed or water-resistant fabric.

rain date ▶ **noun** an alternative date for an event in case of bad weather.

rain·drop /ˈrānˌdräp/ ▶ **noun** a single drop of rain.

rain·fall /ˈrānˌfôl/ ▶ **noun** the quantity of rain falling within an area in a given time.

rain·for·est /ˈrānˌfôrəst/ ▶ **noun** a dense forest found in tropical areas with consistently heavy rainfall.

rain gauge ▶ **noun** a device for collecting and measuring the amount of rain that falls.

rain·mak·er /ˈrānˌmākər/ ▶ **noun** informal a person who generates income for a business by brokering deals or attracting clients or funds.

rain·proof /ˈrānˌpro͞of/ ▶ **adjective** (especially of a building or garment) impervious to rain.

rain·storm /ˈrānˌstôrm/ ▶ **noun** a storm with heavy rain.

rain·swept /ˈrān,swept/ ▶ **adjective** frequently or recently exposed to rain and wind.

rain·wa·ter /ˈrān,wôtər, -,wätər/ ▶ **noun** water that has fallen as rain.

rain·wear /ˈrān,we(ə)r/ ▶ **noun** waterproof or water-resistant clothes for wearing in the rain.

rain·y /ˈrānē/ ▶ **adjective** (**rainier, rainiest**) having a great deal of rain.

– SYNONYMS **wet,** showery, drizzly, damp, inclement.
– ANTONYMS dry, fine.

– PHRASES **a rainy day** a time in the future when money may be needed.

raise /rāz/ ▶ **verb 1** lift or move someone or something upward or into an upright position. **2** increase the amount, level, or strength of: *she had to raise her voice to be heard.* **3** cause to be heard, felt, or considered: *doubts have been raised.* **4** collect or bring together money or resources. **5** bring up a child. **6** breed or grow animals or plants. **7** abandon a blockade, embargo, etc. **8** bring someone back from death. **9** (**raise something to**) Mathematics multiply a quantity to a specified power.

– SYNONYMS **1 lift (up),** hold aloft, elevate, uplift, hoist, haul up, hitch up. **2 increase,** put up, push up, up, mark up, inflate; informal hike (up), jack up, bump up. **3 amplify,** louden, magnify, intensify, boost, lift, increase. **4 get,** obtain, acquire, accumulate, amass, collect, fetch, net, make. **5 bring up,** air, present, table, propose, submit, advance, suggest, put forward. **6 give rise to,** occasion, cause, produce, engender, elicit, create, result in, lead to, prompt. **7 bring up,** rear, nurture, educate.
– ANTONYMS lower, reduce.

▶ **noun** an increase in salary.
– DERIVATIVES **rais·er** noun.
– PHRASES **raise hell** informal make a noisy disturbance. **raise the roof** make a great deal of noise, especially by cheering.
– ORIGIN Old Norse.

raised ranch ▶ **noun** a style of house similar to a ranch, but with a split level.

rai·sin /ˈrāzən/ ▶ **noun** a partially dried grape.
– DERIVATIVES **rai·sin·y** adjective.
– ORIGIN Old French, 'grape.'

rai·son d'ê·tre /rāˈzôN ˈdetr(ə)/ ▶ **noun** (pl. **raisons d'être** /rāˈzôn(z)/) the most important reason or purpose for someone's or something's existence.
– ORIGIN French, 'reason for being.'

rai·ta /ˈrītə/ ▶ **noun** an Indian side dish of spiced yogurt containing chopped cucumber or other vegetables.
– ORIGIN Hindi.

Raj /räj/ ▶ **noun** (**the Raj**) historical the period of British rule in India.
– ORIGIN Hindi, 'reign.'

ra·jah /ˈräjə, ˈräzhə/ (also **raja**) ▶ **noun** historical an Indian king or prince.
– ORIGIN from Hindi or Sanskrit.

Raj·put /ˈräj,po͞ot, ˈräzh-/ ▶ **noun** a member of a Hindu military caste.
– ORIGIN from the Sanskrit words for 'king' + 'son.'

rake[1] /rāk/ ▶ **noun** a tool consisting of a pole with metal prongs at the end, used for drawing together leaves, cut grass, etc., or smoothing soil or gravel. ▶ **verb 1** draw together leaves or grass or smooth soil with a rake. **2** scratch something with a long sweeping movement. **3** search through something. **4** pull or drag through something with a sweeping movement: *I raked a comb through my hair.* **5** sweep the air with gunfire or a beam of light.

– SYNONYMS **1** *he raked the leaves into a pile* **scrape up,** collect, gather. **2** *she raked the gravel* **smooth (out),** level, even out, flatten, comb. **3** *I raked through my pockets* **rummage,** search, hunt, sift, rifle.

– DERIVATIVES **rak·er** noun.
– PHRASES **rake something in** informal make a lot of money.
– ORIGIN Old English or Old Norse.

rake[2] ▶ **noun** a fashionable or wealthy man who leads an immoral life.
– ORIGIN from former *rakehell* in the same sense.

rake[3] ▶ **verb** set something at a sloping angle. ▶ **noun** the angle at which something slopes.
– ORIGIN probably from German *ragen* 'to project.'

rake-off ▶ **noun** informal a share of the profits from a deal, especially one that is underhanded or illegal.

ra·ki /rəˈkē, ˈrakē, ˈräkē/ ▶ **noun** a strong alcoholic drink made in eastern Europe or the Middle East.
– ORIGIN Turkish.

rak·ish /ˈrākish/ ▶ **adjective 1** dashing, jaunty, or slightly disreputable: *a cap set at a rakish angle.* **2** (of a boat or car) smart and streamlined.
– DERIVATIVES **rak·ish·ly** adverb.

ral·len·tan·do /,rälənˈtändō, ,ralənˈtandō/ ▶ **adverb & adjective** Music another term for **RITARDANDO**.
– ORIGIN Italian, 'slowing down.'

ral·ly /ˈralē/ ▶ **verb** (**rallies, rallying, rallied**) **1** (with reference to troops) bring or come together again so as to continue fighting. **2** bring or come together as support or for united action: *my family rallied around.* **3** recover in health, spirits, or composure: *he floundered for a moment, then rallied again.* **4** (of share, currency, or commodity prices) increase after a fall. **5** drive in a motor rally.

– SYNONYMS **1 regroup,** reassemble, re-form, reunite, convene, mobilize. **2 recover,** improve, get better, pick up, revive, bounce back, perk up, look up, turn a corner.

▶ **noun** (pl. **rallies**) **1** a mass meeting held as a protest or in support of a cause. **2** a long-distance race for motor vehicles over roads or rough country. **3** an open-air event for people who own a particular kind of vehicle. **4** a quick or marked recovery: *the market staged a late rally.* **5** (in tennis and other racket sports) an exchange of several strokes between players.

– SYNONYMS **1 (mass) meeting,** gathering, assembly, demonstration, march; informal demo. **2 recovery,** upturn, improvement, comeback, resurgence.

– DERIVATIVES **ral·ly·ist** noun.
– ORIGIN French *rallier.*

ral·ly·ing /ˈralēiNG/ ▶ **noun** the action or sport of participating in a motor rally. ▶ **adjective** having the effect of calling people to action: *a rallying cry.*

RAM /ram/ ▶ **abbreviation** Computing random-access memory.

ram /ram/ ▶ **noun 1** an uncastrated adult male sheep. **2** a battering ram. **3** a striking or plunging device in some machines. ▶ **verb** (**rams, ramming, rammed**) **1** roughly force something into place. **2** strike or be struck with force.

– SYNONYMS **1 force,** thrust, plunge, stab, push, sink, dig, stick, cram, jam, stuff. **2 hit,** strike, crash into, collide with, impact, smash into, butt.

– DERIVATIVES **ram·mer** noun.
– ORIGIN Old English.

Ram·a·dan /ˈrämə̩dän, ˈramə̩dan/ (also **Ramadhan**) ▶ **noun** the ninth month of the Muslim year, during which Muslims fast from dawn to sunset.
– ORIGIN Arabic, 'be hot' (the fasting period was originally supposed to be in one of the hot months).

ram·ble /ˈrambəl/ ▶ **verb 1** walk for pleasure in the countryside. **2** talk or write in an unfocused way for a long time: *he rambled on about Norman archways.* **3** (of a plant) grow over walls, fences, etc.

– SYNONYMS **1 walk,** hike, tramp, trek, backpack. **2 chatter,** babble, prattle, blather, gabble, jabber, twitter, rattle.

▶ **noun** a walk taken for pleasure in the countryside.
– DERIVATIVES **ram·bler** noun.
– ORIGIN probably related to Dutch *rammelen* 'wander about on heat' (referring to an animal), also to **RAM**.

ram·bling /ˈramb(ə)liNG/ ▶ **adjective 1** (of writing or speech) straying from one subject to another. **2** (of a building or path) spreading or winding irregularly in various directions.

– SYNONYMS **1** *a rambling speech* **long-winded,** verbose, wordy, prolix, disjointed, disconnected. **2** *a big old rambling house* **sprawling,** spreading, labyrinthine, mazelike.
– ANTONYMS concise, compact.

Ram·bo /ˈrambō/ ▶ **noun** an extremely tough and aggressive man.
– ORIGIN the hero of the novel *First Blood* (1972), and the films *First Blood* (1982) and *Rambo: First Blood Part II* (1985).

ram·bunc·tious /ramˈbəNGkSHəs/ ▶ **adjective** informal uncontrollably exuberant.
– ORIGIN unknown.

ram·bu·tan /ramˈbo͞otn/ ▶ **noun** the red, plum-sized fruit of a tropical tree, with soft spines and a slightly sour taste.
– ORIGIN Malay.

ram·e·kin /ˈramikən/ ▶ **noun** a small dish for baking and serving an individual portion of food.
– ORIGIN French *ramequin.*

ra·men /ˈrämən/ ▶ **plural noun** (in oriental cuisine) quick-cooking noodles.
– ORIGIN Japanese.

ram·ie /ˈramē, ˈrā-/ ▶ **noun** a vegetable fiber from a tropical Asian plant, used in making textiles.
– ORIGIN Malay.

ram·i·fi·ca·tion /̩raməfəˈkāSHən/ ▶ **noun 1** (**ramifications**) complex consequences of an action or event: *the ramifications of global environmental changes.* **2** a subdivision of a complex structure or process.

– SYNONYMS **consequence,** result, aftermath, outcome, effect, upshot, development, implication.

ram·i·fy /ˈramə̩fī/ ▶ **verb** (**ramifies, ramifying, ramified**) chiefly technical form parts that branch out.
– ORIGIN Latin *ramificare.*

ram·jet /ˈram̩jet/ ▶ **noun** a type of jet engine in which the air drawn in for combustion is compressed solely by the forward motion of the aircraft.

ramp /ramp/ ▶ **noun 1** a sloping surface joining two different levels. **2** a movable set of steps for entering or leaving an aircraft. **3** an inclined road leading to or from a main highway.

– SYNONYMS **slope,** bank, incline, gradient, rise, drop.

▶ **verb 1** (**ramp something up**) increase the level or amount of something: *the company plans to ramp up production of TVs.* **2** (as adj. **ramped**) provided with a ramp.
– ORIGIN Old French *ramper* 'creep, crawl.'

ram·page ▶ **verb** /̩ramˈpāj/ rush around in a wild and violent way.

– SYNONYMS **riot,** run amok, go berserk, storm, charge, tear.

▶ **noun** /ˈram̩pāj/ a period of wild and violent behavior.
– ORIGIN perhaps from **RAMP** and **RAGE**.

ramp·ant /ˈrampənt/ ▶ **adjective 1** flourishing or spreading in an uncontrolled way: *rampant inflation.* **2** unrestrained or wild: *rampant sex.* **3** (after a noun) Heraldry (of an animal) shown standing on its left hind foot with its forefeet in the air.

– SYNONYMS **uncontrolled,** unrestrained, unchecked, unbridled, out of control, out of hand, widespread, rife, spreading.
– ANTONYMS controlled.

– DERIVATIVES **ramp·ant·ly** adverb.
– ORIGIN Old French, 'crawling.'

ram·part /ˈram̩pärt/ ▶ **noun** a defensive wall of a castle or city, having a broad top with a walkway.
– ORIGIN French *rempart.*

ram·rod /ˈram̩räd/ ▶ **noun 1** a rod for ramming down the charge of a muzzle-loading firearm. **2** used to describe a person's erect posture: *he stood ramrod straight.*

ram·shack·le /ˈram̩SHakəl/ ▶ **adjective** in a very bad condition.
– ORIGIN ultimately from **RANSACK**.

ran /ran/ past of **RUN**.

ranch /ranCH/ ▶ **noun 1** a large farm where cattle or other animals are bred. **2** (also **ranch house**) a single-story house. ▶ **verb** run a ranch.
– ORIGIN Spanish *rancho* 'group of people eating together.'

ranch dress·ing ▶ **noun** a type of thick white salad dressing made with sour cream or buttermilk.

ranch·er /ˈranCHər/ ▶ **noun 1** a person who owns or runs a ranch. **2** a ranch house.

ran·che·ro /ranˈCHerō/ ▶ **noun** (pl. **rancheros**) a person who farms or works on a ranch, especially in the southwestern US and Mexico.
– ORIGIN Spanish, from *rancho* (see **RANCH**).

ran·cid /ˈransid/ ▶ **adjective 1** (of fatty or oily foods) stale and smelling or tasting unpleasant. **2** highly unpleasant.

– SYNONYMS **putrid,** turned, rank, sour, foul, rotten, bad; gamy, fetid.
– ANTONYMS fresh.

– DERIVATIVES **ran·cid·i·ty** /ranˈsidətē/ noun.
– ORIGIN Latin *rancidus* 'stinking.'

ran·cor /ˈraNGkər/ (Brit. **rancour**) ▶ **noun** bitter feeling or resentment.
– DERIVATIVES **ran·cor·ous** adjective.
– ORIGIN Latin *rancor* 'rankness,' later 'bitter grudge.'

rand /rand, ränd, ränt/ ▶ **noun** the basic unit of money of South Africa.
– ORIGIN from *the Rand*, a goldfield district near Johannesburg.

ran·dom /ˈrandəm/ ▸ **adjective** done or happening without a deliberate order, purpose, or decision: *the trees had been planted in a random pattern.*

– SYNONYMS **unsystematic,** unmethodical, arbitrary, unplanned, chance, casual, indiscriminate, nonspecific, haphazard, stray, erratic, hit-or-miss.
– ANTONYMS systematic.

– DERIVATIVES **ran·dom·ly** adverb **ran·dom·ness** noun.
– PHRASES **at random** without thinking or planning in advance.
– ORIGIN Old French *randon* 'great speed.'

ran·dom ac·cess ▸ **noun** the process of storing or finding information on a computer without having to access items in a fixed sequence.

ran·dom·ize /ˈrandəˌmīz/ ▸ **verb** (usu. as adj. **randomized**) technical make a random selection in an experiment, trial, etc.

rand·y /ˈrandē/ ▸ **adjective** (**randier**, **randiest**) informal, chiefly Brit. sexually aroused or excited.
– ORIGIN perhaps from former Dutch *randen* 'to rant.'

rang /raNG/ past of **RING**².

range /rānj/ ▸ **noun 1** the area of variation between limits on a particular scale: *the car's outside my price range.* **2** a set of different things of the same general type. **3** the scope or extent of a person's or thing's abilities or capacity: *he has shown his range in a number of roles.* **4** the distance within which something is able to operate or be effective. **5** a line of mountains or hills. **6** a large area of open land for grazing or hunting. **7** an area used as a testing ground for military equipment or for shooting practice. **8** a large cooking stove with several burners and an oven.

– SYNONYMS **1 extent,** limit, reach, span, scope, compass, sweep, area, field, orbit, ambit, horizon, latitude. **2 row,** chain, sierra, ridge, massif. **3 assortment,** variety, diversity, mixture, collection, array, selection, choice.

▸ **verb 1** vary between specified limits. **2** arrange people or things in a row or rows or in a particular way. **3** (**range someone against** or **be ranged against**) set oneself or be set in opposition to: *Japan ranged herself against the European nations.* **4** travel over a wide area. **5** cover a wide number of different topics.

– SYNONYMS **1 vary,** fluctuate, differ, extend, stretch, reach, go, run, cover. **2 roam,** wander, travel, journey, rove, traverse, walk, hike, trek.

– ORIGIN Old French, 'row, rank.'

CHOOSE THE RIGHT WORD

range, compass, gamut, latitude, reach, scope, sweep

To say that someone has a wide **range** of interests implies that these interests are not only extensive but varied. Another way of expressing the same idea would be to say that the person's interests run the **gamut** from TV quiz shows to nuclear physics, a word that suggests a graduated scale or series running from one extreme to another. **Compass** implies a range of knowledge or activity that falls within very definite limits reminiscent of a circumference (*within the compass of her abilities*), while **sweep** suggests more of an arc-shaped range of motion or activity (*the sweep of the searchlight*) or a continuous extent or stretch (*a broad sweep of lawn*). **Latitude** and **scope** both emphasize the idea of freedom, although *scope* implies great freedom within prescribed limits (*the scope of the investigation*), while *latitude* means freedom from such limits (*she was granted more latitude than usual in interviewing the disaster victims*). Even someone who has a wide *range* of interests and a broad *scope* of authority, however, will sooner or later come up against something that is beyond his or her **reach**, which suggests the furthest limit of effectiveness or influence.

range·find·er /ˈrānjˌfīndər/ ▸ **noun** an instrument for estimating the distance of an object.

rang·er /ˈrānjər/ ▸ **noun 1** a keeper of a park, forest, or area of countryside. **2** a member of a body of armed men.

rang·y /ˈrānjē/ ▸ **adjective** (of a person) tall and slim with long limbs.

– SYNONYMS **long-legged,** long-limbed, leggy, tall; slender, slim, lean, thin, gangly, lanky, spindly, skinny, spare.
– ANTONYMS squat.

rank¹ /raNGk/ ▸ **noun 1** a position within the armed forces or an organization. **2** high social standing. **3** a line or row of people or things positioned side by side. **4** (**ranks**) the members of a group: *the ranks of the unemployed.* **5** (**the ranks**) members of the armed forces who are not commissioned officers. **6** each of the eight rows of eight squares running from side to side across a chessboard. Compare with **FILE**¹.

– SYNONYMS **1 position,** level, grade, echelon, class, status, standing. **2 high standing,** blue blood, high birth, nobility, aristocracy. **3 row,** line, file, column, string, train, procession.

▸ **verb 1** give someone or something a rank within a grading system: *rank the samples in order of preference.* **2** hold a specified rank: *he now ranks third in the US.* **3** arrange things in a row or rows.

– SYNONYMS **1 classify,** class, categorize, rate, grade, bracket, group, designate, list. **2 line up,** align, order, arrange, dispose, set out, array, range.

– PHRASES **break rank** (or **ranks**) fail to support a group to which you belong. **close ranks** unite so as to defend common interests. **pull rank** use your senior position to take advantage of someone. **rank and file** the ordinary members of an organization.
– ORIGIN Old French *ranc.*

rank² ▸ **adjective 1** smelling very unpleasant. **2** complete and utter: *a rank amateur.* **3** (of vegetation) growing too thickly.

– SYNONYMS **1 abundant,** lush, luxuriant, dense, profuse, vigorous, overgrown; informal jungly. **2 offensive,** nasty, revolting, sickening, obnoxious, foul, fetid, rancid, putrid. **3** *rank stupidity* **downright,** utter, out-and-out, absolute, complete, sheer, blatant, arrant, thorough, unqualified.

– ORIGIN Old English, 'proud, rebellious, sturdy.'

rank·ing /ˈraNGkiNG/ ▸ **noun** a position on a scale of importance or achievement. ▸ **adjective** having a specified rank: *high-ranking officers.*

ran·kle /ˈraNGkəl/ ▸ **verb 1** (of a comment or fact) cause continuing annoyance or resentment. **2** annoy or irritate someone.

– SYNONYMS **annoy,** upset, anger, irritate, offend, affront, displease, provoke, irk, vex, pique, nettle, gall; informal rile, miff, peeve, aggravate, tick off.

– ORIGIN Old French *rancler* 'fester.'

ran·sack /ˈranˌsak, ranˈsak/ ▸ **verb 1** go hurriedly through a place stealing things and causing damage.

2 search something in a thorough and harmful way.

– SYNONYMS 1 **plunder,** pillage, raid, rob, loot, sack, strip, despoil, ravage, devastate. 2 scour, rifle through, comb, search, turn upside down.

– ORIGIN Old Norse.

ran·som /ˈransəm/ ▶ **noun** a sum of money demanded or paid for the release of a captive.

– SYNONYMS **payoff,** payment, sum, price.

▶ **verb 1** obtain the release of someone by paying a ransom. **2** hold a captive and demand payment for their release.

– PHRASES **hold someone to ransom** chiefly Brit. force someone to do something by threatening damaging action. **a king's ransom** a huge amount of money.

– ORIGIN Old French *ransoun*.

rant /rant/ ▶ **verb** speak or shout in an angry or uncontrolled way.

– SYNONYMS **shout,** sound off, hold forth, go on, fulminate, spout, bluster; informal mouth off.

▶ **noun** a spell of ranting.

– DERIVATIVES **rant·er** noun.

– ORIGIN Dutch *ranten* 'talk nonsense, rave.'

rap /rap/ ▶ **verb (raps, rapping, rapped) 1** hit a hard surface several times. **2** hit someone or something sharply. **3** informal criticize someone severely. **4** say sharply: *he rapped out an order*. **5** perform rap music.

– SYNONYMS **hit,** knock, strike, smack, bang; informal whack, thwack, bash, wallop.

▶ **noun 1** a quick, sharp knock or blow. **2** a type of popular music of African-American origin in which words are spoken rapidly and rhythmically over an instrumental backing. **3** informal a criminal charge: *a murder rap*.

– DERIVATIVES **rap·per** noun.

– PHRASES **take the rap** informal be punished or blamed for something.

– ORIGIN probably Scandinavian.

ra·pa·cious /rəˈpāsнəs/ ▶ **adjective** very greedy or grasping.

– DERIVATIVES **ra·pa·cious·ly** adverb **ra·pa·cious·ness** noun **ra·pac·i·ty** /rəˈpasətē/ noun.

– ORIGIN from Latin *rapere* 'seize.'

CHOOSE THE RIGHT WORD

See **GREEDY**.

rap·a·my·cin /ˌrapəˈmīsin/ ▶ **noun** an antibiotic used as an immunosuppressant, especially to prevent organ rejection in transplants.

rape[1] /rāp/ ▶ **verb** (of a man) force someone to have sex with him against their will. ▶ **noun 1** the crime of raping someone. **2** the spoiling or destruction of a place: *the rape of the countryside*.

– ORIGIN Latin *rapere* 'seize.'

rape[2] ▶ **noun** a plant with bright yellow flowers, especially a variety (**oilseed rape**) grown for its oil-rich seed.

– ORIGIN Latin *rapum, rapa* 'turnip.'

rape·seed /ˈrāpˌsēd/ ▶ **noun** seeds of the rape plant, used to make oil.

rap·id /ˈrapid/ ▶ **adjective 1** happening in a short time: *several shots fired in rapid succession*. **2** (of an action) very fast.

– SYNONYMS **quick,** fast, swift, speedy, express, expeditious, brisk, lightning, meteoric, whirlwind, sudden, instantaneous, instant, immediate.
– ANTONYMS slow.

▶ **noun** (usu. **rapids**) a part of a river where the water flows very fast, often over rocks.

– DERIVATIVES **ra·pid·i·ty** /rəˈpidətē/ noun **rap·id·ly** adverb.

– ORIGIN Latin *rapidus*.

ra·pi·er /ˈrāpēər/ ▶ **noun** a thin, light sharp-pointed sword used for thrusting.

– ORIGIN French *rapière*.

rap·ine /ˈrapən, -īn/ ▶ **noun** literary the violent seizure of property.

– ORIGIN Old French.

rap·ist /ˈrāpist/ ▶ **noun** a man who commits rape.

rap·pel /rəˈpel/ ▶ **verb (rappels, rappelling, rappelled)** climb down a steep rock face using a rope coiled around the body and attached at a higher point.

– ORIGIN French.

rap·port /raˈpôr, rə-/ ▶ **noun** a close relationship in which people understand each other and communicate well.

– SYNONYMS **affinity,** close relationship, (mutual) understanding, bond, empathy, sympathy, accord.

– ORIGIN French.

rap·por·teur /ˌraˌpôrˈtər/ ▶ **noun** a person appointed by an organization to report on its meetings.

– ORIGIN French.

rap·proche·ment /ˌrapˌrōsнˈmäɴ, -ˌrôsн-/ ▶ **noun** a renewal of friendly relations between countries or groups.

– ORIGIN French.

rap·scal·lion /rapˈskalyən/ ▶ **noun** old use a mischievous person.

– ORIGIN perhaps from **RASCAL**.

rapt /rapt/ ▶ **adjective 1** completely fascinated and absorbed: *they listened with rapt attention*. **2** literary filled with an intense and pleasant emotion.

– SYNONYMS **fascinated,** enthralled, spellbound, captivated, riveted, gripped, mesmerized, enchanted, entranced, bewitched; transported, enraptured, thrilled, ecstatic.
– ANTONYMS inattentive.

– DERIVATIVES **rapt·ly** adverb.

– ORIGIN Latin *raptus* 'seized.'

rap·tor /ˈraptər/ ▶ **noun** a bird of prey.

– DERIVATIVES **rap·to·ri·al** /rapˈtôrēəl/ adjective.

– ORIGIN Latin, 'plunderer.'

rap·ture /ˈrapcнər/ ▶ **noun 1** great pleasure or joy. **2 (raptures)** expressions of great pleasure or enthusiasm.

– SYNONYMS **1 ecstasy,** bliss, exaltation, euphoria, elation, joy, enchantment, delight, happiness, pleasure. **2** *I went into raptures over the music and performance* **enthuse,** rhapsodize, rave, gush, wax lyrical.

– ORIGIN from Latin *raptura* 'seizing,' influenced by **RAPT**.

CHOOSE THE RIGHT WORD

rapture, bliss, ecstasy, euphoria, transport
Happiness is one thing; **bliss** is another, suggesting a state of utter joy and contentment (*marital bliss*). **Ecstasy** is even more extreme, describing a trancelike state in which one loses consciousness of one's surroundings (*the ecstasy of young love*). Although **rapture** originally

referred to being raised or lifted out of oneself by divine power, nowadays it is used in much the same sense as *ecstasy* to describe an elevated sensation of bliss (*she listened in speechless rapture to her favorite soprano*). **Transport** applies to any powerful emotion by which one is carried away (*a transport of delight*). When happiness is carried to an extreme or crosses over into mania, it is called **euphoria**. *Euphoria* may outwardly resemble *ecstasy* or *rapture*; but upon closer examination, it is usually found to be exaggerated and out of proportion (*the euphoria that came over him whenever he touched alcohol*).

rap·tur·ous /ˈrapCHərəs/ ▶ **adjective** feeling or expressing great pleasure or enthusiasm.
– DERIVATIVES **rap·tur·ous·ly** adverb.

ra·ra a·vis /ˌre(ə)rə ˈāvis, ˌrärə ˈäwis/ ▶ **noun** another term for **RARE BIRD**.
– ORIGIN Latin.

rare[1] /re(ə)r/ ▶ **adjective** (**rarer, rarest**) **1** not occurring or found very often: *a rare genetic disorder*. **2** unusually good.

– SYNONYMS **1 infrequent,** scarce, sparse, few and far between, occasional, limited, isolated, odd, unaccustomed. **2 unusual,** recherché, uncommon, thin on the ground, unfamiliar, atypical. **3 exceptional,** outstanding, unparalleled, peerless, matchless, unique, unrivaled, beyond compare.
– ANTONYMS common, commonplace.

– ORIGIN Latin *rarus*.

rare[2] ▶ **adjective** (**rarer, rarest**) (of red meat) lightly cooked, so that the inside is still red.
– ORIGIN Old English, 'half-cooked.'

rare bird ▶ **noun** an exceptional or unusual person or thing.

rare·bit /ˈre(ə)rbit/ (also **Welsh rarebit** or **Welsh rabbit**) ▶ **noun** a dish of melted cheese on toast.
– ORIGIN first recorded as *Welsh rabbit*; the term *rabbit* is unexplained.

rare earth ▶ **noun** any of a group of chemically similar metallic elements including the lanthanide elements together with (usually) scandium and yttrium.

rar·e·fied /ˈrerəˌfīd/ ▶ **adjective 1** (of air) of lower pressure than usual; thin. **2** distant from the lives and concerns of ordinary people; esoteric: *rarefied scholarly pursuits*.
– ORIGIN from Latin *rareficare* 'make rare.'

rare·ly /ˈre(ə)rlē/ ▶ **adverb** not often; seldom.

– SYNONYMS **seldom,** infrequently, hardly (ever), scarcely.
– ANTONYMS often.

rar·ing /ˈre(ə)riNG/ ▶ **adjective** informal very eager to do something: *she was raring to go*.

– SYNONYMS **eager,** keen, enthusiastic, impatient, longing, desperate; informal dying, itching.

– ORIGIN from *rare*, dialect variant of **ROAR** or **REAR**[2].

rar·i·ty /ˈre(ə)ritē/ ▶ **noun** (pl. **rarities**) **1** a rare or unusual thing. **2** the state or quality of being rare.

– SYNONYMS **1 infrequency,** scarcity. **2 curiosity,** oddity, collector's item, rare bird, wonder, nonpareil, one of a kind.

ras·cal /ˈraskəl/ ▶ **noun 1** a mischievous or impudent person. **2** a dishonest man.

– SYNONYMS **scallywag,** imp, monkey, mischief-maker; informal scamp, tyke, horror, monster.

– DERIVATIVES **ras·cal·i·ty** /rasˈkalətē/ noun **ras·cal·ly** adjective.
– ORIGIN from Old French *rascaille* 'rabble.'

rash[1] /rasH/ ▶ **adjective** acting or done without careful consideration: *a rash decision*.

– SYNONYMS **reckless,** impulsive, impetuous, hotheaded, daredevil, madcap, hasty, foolhardy, incautious, precipitate, careless, heedless, thoughtless, unthinking, imprudent, foolish.
– ANTONYMS prudent.

– DERIVATIVES **rash·ly** adverb **rash·ness** noun.
– ORIGIN Germanic.

rash[2] ▶ **noun 1** an area of red spots or patches on a person's skin. **2** a series of unwelcome things happening within a short time: *a rash of strikes*.

– SYNONYMS **1 spots,** eruption, hives. **2** *a rash of articles in the press* **series,** succession, spate, wave, flood, deluge, torrent, outbreak, epidemic, flurry.

– ORIGIN probably related to Old French *rasche* 'sores, scurf.'

rash·er /ˈrasHər/ ▶ **noun** chiefly Brit. a thin slice of bacon.
– ORIGIN unknown.

rasp /rasp/ ▶ **verb 1** make a harsh, grating sound: *cicadas rasped in the surrounding pines*. **2** say something in a harsh, grating tone. **3** (of a rough object) scrape something. **4** file something with a rasp. ▶ **noun 1** a coarse file for use on metal or other hard material. **2** a harsh, grating noise.
– DERIVATIVES **rasp·y** adjective.
– ORIGIN Old French *rasper*.

rasp·ber·ry /ˈrazˌberē, -b(ə)rē/ ▶ **noun** (pl. **raspberries**) **1** an edible reddish-pink soft fruit related to the blackberry. **2** informal a sound made with the tongue and lips, expressing scorn or contempt.
– ORIGIN unknown.

Ras·ta /ˈrastə/ ▶ **noun & adjective** informal short for **RASTAFARIAN**.

Ras·ta·far·i·an /ˌrastəˈfe(ə)rēən, -ˈfärēən/ ▶ **adjective** relating to a religious movement of Jamaican origin believing that Haile Selassie (the former emperor of Ethiopia) was the Messiah and that black people are the chosen people. ▶ **noun** a member of the Rastafarian movement.
– DERIVATIVES **Ras·ta·far·i·an·ism** noun.
– ORIGIN from *Ras Tafari*, the name by which Haile Selassie was known.

Ras·ta·man /ˈrastəˌman/ ▶ **noun** (pl. **Rastamen**) informal a male Rastafarian.

ras·ter /ˈrastər/ ▶ **noun** a rectangular pattern of parallel scanning lines followed by the electron beam on a television screen or computer monitor.
– ORIGIN German, 'screen.'

rat /rat/ ▶ **noun 1** a long-tailed rodent resembling a large mouse, often considered a serious pest. **2** informal an unpleasant person, especially one who is deceitful or disloyal. **3** informal an informant. **4** informal a person who is associated with or often visits a particular place: *a mall rat*. ▶ **verb** (**rats, ratting, ratted**) **1** (**rat on**) informal inform on someone. **2** (**rat on**) informal break an agreement or promise. **3** hunt or kill rats.
– ORIGIN Old English.

rat·a·ble /ˈrātəbəl/ ▶ **adjective** variant spelling of **RATEABLE**.

rat-a-tat /ˈrat ə ˌtat/ (also **rat-a-tat-tat** /ˌrat ə ˌtat ˈtat/) ▶ **noun** a rapping sound, as of knocking on a door, or the sound of gunfire.
– ORIGIN imitating the sound.

ra·ta·touille /ˌratəˈto͞o-ē, ˌräˌtä-/ ▶ **noun** a dish consisting of onions, zucchini, tomatoes, eggplant, and peppers, stewed in oil.
– ORIGIN French.

rat·bag /ˈratˌbag/ ▶ **noun** informal an unpleasant or disliked person.

ratch·et /ˈraCHit/ ▶ **noun** a device consisting of a bar or wheel with a set of angled teeth in which a cog, tooth, or pivoted bar fits, allowing motion in one direction only. ▶ **verb** (**ratchets, ratcheting, ratcheted**) **1** (**ratchet something up/down**) make something rise (or fall) as a step in an inevitable process: *the bank ratcheted up interest rates again*. **2** operate something by means of a ratchet.
– ORIGIN French *rochet*.

rate /rāt/ ▶ **noun 1** a measure, quantity, or frequency measured against another quantity or measure: *the island has the lowest crime rate in the world*. **2** the speed with which something moves or happens. **3** a fixed price paid or charged for something. **4** the amount of a charge or payment expressed as a percentage of another amount, or as a basis of calculation: *our current interest rates are very competitive*.

– SYNONYMS **1 percentage,** ratio, proportion, scale, standard. **2 speed,** pace, tempo, velocity. **3 charge,** price, cost, tariff, fare, fee, remuneration, payment.

▶ **verb 1** give a standard or value to something according to a particular scale. **2** consider to be of a certain quality or standard: *scouts rate him as the No. 1 player overall*. **3** be worthy of or merit something. **4** informal have a high opinion of someone or something.

– SYNONYMS **1 assess,** evaluate, appraise, judge, weigh up, estimate, gauge. **2 merit,** deserve, warrant, be worthy of.

– PHRASES **at any rate** whatever happens or may have happened. **at this rate** if things continue in this way.
– ORIGIN Latin *rata*.

rate·a·ble /ˈrātəbəl/ (also **ratable**) ▶ **adjective** able to be rated or estimated.

rate of ex·change ▶ **noun** another term for **EXCHANGE RATE**.

rath·er /ˈraT͟Hər/ ▶ **adverb 1** (**would rather**) would prefer: *I'd rather you didn't tell him*. **2** to a certain extent; quite. **3** used to correct something you have said or to be more precise: *I walked, or rather limped, home*. **4** instead of.

– SYNONYMS **1 sooner,** by preference, by choice, more readily. **2 quite,** a bit, a little, fairly, slightly, somewhat, relatively, comparatively; informal pretty.

▶ **exclamation** Brit. dated used to emphasize that you agree with or accept something.
– ORIGIN Old English, 'earlier, sooner.'

rat·i·fy /ˈratəˌfī/ ▶ **verb** (**ratifies, ratifying, ratified**) give formal consent to an agreement, making it officially valid.

– SYNONYMS **confirm,** approve, sanction, endorse, agree to, accept, uphold, authorize, formalize, sign.

– DERIVATIVES **rat·i·fi·ca·tion** /ˌratəfəˈkāSHən/ noun.
– ORIGIN from Latin *ratus* 'fixed.'

rat·ing /ˈrātiNG/ ▶ **noun 1** a classification or ranking based on quality, standard, or performance. **2** (**ratings**) the estimated audience size of a television or radio program.

– SYNONYMS **grade,** classification, ranking, position, category, assessment, evaluation, mark, score.

ra·tio /ˈrāSHō, ˈrāSHēˌō/ ▶ **noun** (pl. **ratios**) the quantitative relationship between two amounts showing the number of times one value contains or is contained within the other.

– SYNONYMS **proportion,** relationship, rate, percentage, fraction, correlation.

– ORIGIN Latin, 'reckoning.'

ra·ti·oc·i·na·tion /ˌratēˌōsəˈnāSHən/ ▶ **noun** formal the formation of judgments by logic; reasoning.
– DERIVATIVES **ra·ti·oc·i·nate** /ˌratēˈōsəˌnāt, ˌraSHē-/ verb **ra·ti·oc·i·na·tive** /-ˈōsəˌnātiv, -ˈäs-/ adjective.
– ORIGIN Latin *ratiocinari* 'deliberate, calculate.'

ra·tion /ˈraSHən, ˈrā-/ ▶ **noun 1** a fixed amount of food, fuel, or a similar commodity, officially allowed to each person during a shortage. **2** (**rations**) a regular allowance of food supplied to members of the armed forces.

– SYNONYMS **1 allowance,** allocation, quota, share, portion, helping. **2** *the garrison ran out of rations* **supplies,** provisions, food, stores.

▶ **verb 1** limit the supply of a commodity to fixed rations. **2** (**ration someone to**) allow someone to have only a fixed amount of a commodity.

– SYNONYMS **control,** limit, restrict, conserve.

– ORIGIN Latin, 'reckoning, ratio.'

ra·tion·al /ˈraSHənl, ˈraSHnəl/ ▶ **adjective 1** based on reason or logic: *a rational explanation*. **2** able to think sensibly or logically. **3** having the capacity to reason. **4** Mathematics (of a number or quantity) able to be expressed as a ratio of whole numbers.

– SYNONYMS **logical,** reasoned, sensible, reasonable, realistic, cogent, intelligent, shrewd, common-sense, sane, sound.

– DERIVATIVES **ra·tion·al·i·ty** /ˌraSHəˈnalətē/ noun **ra·tion·al·ly** adverb.

ra·tion·ale /ˌraSHəˈnal/ ▶ **noun** a set of reasons for a course of action or a belief.

– SYNONYMS **reason(s),** thinking, logic, grounds, sense.

ra·tion·al·ism /ˈraSHənlˌizəm, ˈraSHnəˌlizəm/ ▶ **noun** the belief that opinions and actions should be based on reason and knowledge rather than on religious belief or emotions.
– DERIVATIVES **ra·tion·al·ist** noun.

ra·tion·al·ize /ˈraSHənlˌīz, ˈraSHnəˌlīz/ ▶ **verb 1** try to find a logical reason for an action or attitude: *rationalize your fear by thinking about it positively*. **2** make a company or industry more efficient by disposing of unwanted staff or equipment.

– SYNONYMS **1 justify,** explain (away), account for, defend, vindicate, excuse. **2 streamline,** reorganize, modernize, update, trim, hone, simplify, downsize, prune.

– DERIVATIVES **ra·tion·al·i·za·tion** /ˌraSHənl-əˈzāSHən, ˌraSHnələ-/ noun **ra·tion·al·iz·er** noun.

rat race ▶ **noun** informal a way of life that is a fiercely competitive struggle for wealth or power.

rat·tan /ra'tan, rə-/ ▶ **noun** the thin, pliable stems of a tropical climbing palm, used to make furniture.
– ORIGIN Malay.

rat·tle /'ratl/ ▶ **verb 1** make or cause to make a rapid series of short, sharp knocking sounds. **2** move with a knocking sound. **3** informal make someone nervous or irritated. **4** (**rattle something off**) say or produce something quickly and easily: *he rattled off some safety tips*. **5** (**rattle on/away**) talk rapidly and at length.

– SYNONYMS **1 clatter,** clank, knock, clunk, clink, jangle, tinkle. **2 unnerve,** disconcert, disturb, fluster, shake, perturb, throw, discomfit; informal faze.

▶ **noun 1** a rattling sound. **2** a device or toy that makes a rattling sound.
– DERIVATIVES **rat·tly** adjective.
– ORIGIN related to Dutch and German *ratelen*.

rat·tler /'ratl-ər, 'ratlər/ ▶ **noun** informal a rattlesnake.

rat·tle·snake /'ratl,snāk/ ▶ **noun** an American viper with a series of horny rings on the tail that produce a rattling sound.

rat·tle·trap /'ratl,trap/ ▶ **noun** informal an old or rickety vehicle.

rat·tling /'ratl-ing, 'ratling/ ▶ **adjective** informal, dated very: *a rattling good story*.

rat·trap /'rat,trap/ ▶ **noun 1** a trap for catching rats. **2** informal a shabby or squalid building or establishment.

rat·ty /'ratē/ ▶ **adjective 1** resembling or like a rat. **2** informal in bad condition; shabby.

rau·cous /'rôkəs/ ▶ **adjective 1** (of a sound) loud and harsh. **2** noisy or rowdy: *a raucous late-night dinner*.

– SYNONYMS **1 harsh,** strident, screeching, piercing, shrill, grating, discordant, dissonant, noisy, loud, cacophonous. **2 rowdy,** noisy, boisterous, roisterous, wild.
– ANTONYMS soft, quiet.

– DERIVATIVES **rau·cous·ly** adverb **rau·cous·ness** noun.
– ORIGIN Latin *raucus* 'hoarse.'

raunch /rônch,ränch/ ▶ **noun** informal explicit earthiness or sexuality.

raun·chy /'rônchē, 'rän-/ ▶ **adjective** (**raunchier, raunchiest**) informal earthy and sexually explicit.
– DERIVATIVES **raunch·i·ly** adverb **raunch·i·ness** noun.
– ORIGIN unknown.

rav·age /'ravij/ ▶ **verb** cause severe damage to someone or something.

– SYNONYMS **lay waste,** devastate, ruin, destroy, wreak havoc on.

▶ **noun** (**ravages**) the destructive effects of something.
– ORIGIN French *ravager*.

rave /rāv/ ▶ **verb 1** talk in a wild or angry way. **2** speak or write very enthusiastically about: *critics raved about his technique*.

– SYNONYMS **1 rant,** rage, lose one's temper, storm, fume, shout; informal fly off the handle, hit the roof, flip one's wig. **2 enthuse,** go into raptures, wax lyrical, rhapsodize, sing the praises of, acclaim, eulogize, extol; informal ballyhoo.
– ANTONYMS criticize.

▶ **noun** informal **1** a very enthusiastic review. **2** a very large party or similar event with dancing to loud, fast electronic music.
– ORIGIN probably from Old French *raver*.

rav·el /'ravəl/ ▶ **verb** (**ravels, raveling, raveled**) **1** (**ravel something out**) untangle something. **2** confuse or complicate a situation.
– ORIGIN probably from Dutch *ravelen* 'fray out, tangle.'

ra·ven /'rāvən/ ▶ **noun** a large black crow. ▶ **adjective** (of hair) black and glossy.
– ORIGIN Old English.

rav·en·ing /'ravəning/ ▶ **adjective** (especially of a wild animal) very hungry and searching for food.

rav·en·ous /'ravənəs/ ▶ **adjective** very hungry.
– DERIVATIVES **rav·en·ous·ly** adverb.
– ORIGIN from Old French *raviner* 'to ravage.'

rav·er /'rāvər/ ▶ **noun** informal **1** a person who regularly goes to raves. **2** a person who talks wildly or incoherently.

rave-up ▶ **noun** Brit. informal a lively, noisy party.

ra·vine /rə'vēn/ ▶ **noun** a deep, narrow gorge with steep sides.
– ORIGIN French, 'violent rush.'

rav·ing /'rāving/ ▶ **noun** (**ravings**) wild talk that makes no sense.▶ **adjective & adverb** informal used for emphasis: *she was no raving beauty*.

ra·vi·o·li /,ravē'ōlē/ ▶ **plural noun** small pasta cases filled with cheese, ground meat, etc.
– ORIGIN Italian.

rav·ish /'ravish/ ▶ **verb 1** (**be ravished**) literary be filled with great pleasure: *ravished by a sunny afternoon, she had agreed without thinking*. **2** dated rape someone. **3** old use seize and carry off someone by force.
– ORIGIN Old French *ravir*.

rav·ish·ing /'ravishing/ ▶ **adjective** very beautiful or delightful: *a ravishing film star*.
– DERIVATIVES **rav·ish·ing·ly** adverb.

raw /rô/ ▶ **adjective 1** (of food) uncooked. **2** (of a material or substance) not processed or finished: *turn under the raw edges of the fabric*. **3** (of data) not organized or evaluated. **4** (of the skin) red and painful from being rubbed or scraped. **5** (of a person's nerves) very sensitive. **6** (of an emotion or quality) strong and undisguised: *raw masculinity*. **7** (of the weather) cold and damp. **8** new to an activity or job and therefore lacking experience.

– SYNONYMS **1 uncooked,** fresh, natural. **2 unprocessed,** untreated, unrefined, crude, natural. **3 inexperienced,** new, untrained, untried, untested, callow, green; informal wet behind the ears. **4 sore,** red, painful, tender, chafed.
– ANTONYMS cooked, processed.

– DERIVATIVES **raw·ly** adverb **raw·ness** noun.
– PHRASES **in the raw 1** in its true state. **2** informal naked. **a raw deal** informal unfair or harsh treatment.
– ORIGIN Old English.

raw·hide /'rô,hīd/ ▶ **noun** stiff leather that has not been tanned.

raw ma·te·ri·al ▶ **noun** a basic material from which a product is made.

ray[1] /rā/ ▶ **noun 1** a line of light coming from the sun or any luminous object. **2** the straight line in which radiation travels to a given point. **3** (**rays**) a specified form of nonluminous radiation: *ultraviolet rays*. **4** a slight indication of a welcome quality: *a ray of hope*.

– SYNONYMS **beam,** shaft, stream, streak, flash, glimmer, flicker, spark.

– ORIGIN Old French *rai*.

ray² ▶ **noun** a broad flat fish with winglike pectoral fins and a long thin tail.
– ORIGIN Latin *raia*.

ray·on /'rā,än/ ▶ **noun** a synthetic fiber or fabric made from viscose.
– ORIGIN invented name.

raze /rāz/ ▶ **verb** completely destroy a building, town, etc.

– SYNONYMS **destroy,** demolish, tear down, pull down, knock down, level, flatten, bulldoze, wipe out, lay waste.

– ORIGIN Old French *raser* 'shave closely.'

CHOOSE THE RIGHT WORD

See **DESTROY**.

ra·zor /'rāzər/ ▶ **noun** an implement with a sharp blade, used to shave hair from the face or body. ▶ **verb** cut hair with a razor.
– ORIGIN Old French *rasor*.

ra·zor·back /'rāzər,bak/ ▶ **noun 1** a pig of a half-wild breed common in the southern US, with the back formed into a high, narrow ridge. **2** (also **razorback ridge**) a steep-sided, narrow ridge of land.

ra·zor·bill /'rāzər,bil/ ▶ **noun** a black-and-white auk (seabird) with a deep bill.

ra·zor clam ▶ **noun** a burrowing mollusk with a long straight shell.

ra·zor wire ▶ **noun** metal wire with sharp edges or studded with small sharp blades, used as a barrier.

razz /raz/ ▶ **verb** informal tease someone playfully.
– ORIGIN from **RASPBERRY**.

raz·zle /,razəl/ ▶ **noun** (in phrase **on the razzle**) Brit. informal out celebrating or enjoying oneself.
– ORIGIN from **RAZZLE-DAZZLE**.

raz·zle-daz·zle /,razəl 'dazəl/ ▶ **noun** informal exciting or noisy activity, intended to attract attention.
– ORIGIN from **DAZZLE**.

razz·ma·tazz /'razmə,taz/ (also **razzamatazz**) ▶ **noun** informal another term for **RAZZLE-DAZZLE**.
– ORIGIN probably from **RAZZLE-DAZZLE**.

Rb ▶ **symbol** the chemical element rubidium.

RC ▶ **abbreviation 1** Red Cross. **2** Electronics resistance/capacitance (or resistor/capacitor). **3** Roman Catholic.

Rd. ▶ **abbreviation** Road (used in street names).

RDA ▶ **abbreviation** recommended daily (or dietary) allowance.

RDS ▶ **abbreviation** respiratory distress syndrome.

Re ▶ **symbol** the chemical element rhenium.

re¹ /rā, rē/ ▶ **preposition 1** in the matter of (used in headings or to introduce a reference). **2** about; concerning.
– ORIGIN Latin.

re² ▶ **noun** Music the second note of a major scale, coming after 'do' and before 'mi.'
– ORIGIN the first syllable of *resonare*, a word taken from a Latin hymn.

re- ▶ **prefix 1** once more; anew: *reactivate*. **2** with return to a previous state: *restore*.
– ORIGIN Latin.

USAGE

Words formed with the prefix (word beginning) **re-** are usually spelled without a hyphen (*react*). However, if the word to which **re-** is attached begins with **e**, then a hyphen is used to make it clear (*re-examine, re-enter*). You should also use a hyphen when the word formed with **re-** would be exactly the same as a word that already exists; use **re-cover** to mean 'cover again' and **recover** to mean 'get well again.'

're ▶ **abbreviation** informal are (usually after *you, we*, and *they*).

reach /rēCH/ ▶ **verb 1** stretch out an arm to touch or grasp something. **2** be able to touch something with an outstretched arm or leg. **3** arrive at a place. **4** achieve or extend to a specified point, level, or state: *unemployment reached a peak in 1933*. **5** succeed in achieving: *I hope we will be able to reach agreement*. **6** make contact with someone.

– SYNONYMS **1 extend,** stretch, outstretch, thrust, stick, hold. **2 arrive at,** get to, come to, end up at. **3** *the temperature reached 75°* **attain,** get to, rise to, fall to, sink to, drop to; informal hit. **4** *the senators reached an agreement* **achieve,** work out, draw up, put together, negotiate, thrash out, hammer out. **5 contact,** get in touch with, get through to, get, speak to; informal get (a) hold of.

▶ **noun 1** an act of reaching. **2** the distance to which someone can stretch out their arm. **3** the extent to which someone or something has power, influence, or the ability to do something: *college was out of her reach*. **4** (often **reaches**) a continuous extent of water, especially a stretch of river between two bends.

– SYNONYMS **1 grasp,** range, stretch, capabilities, capacity. **2 jurisdiction,** authority, influence, power, scope, range, compass, ambit.

– DERIVATIVES **reach·a·ble** adjective.
– ORIGIN Old English.

CHOOSE THE RIGHT WORD

See **RANGE**.

re·ac·quaint /,rēə'kwānt/ ▶ **verb** (**reacquaint someone/oneself with**) make someone familiar or acquainted with again: *she came here to reacquaint herself with existing customers*.

re·act /rē'akt/ ▶ **verb 1** respond to something in a particular way: *he reacted angrily to the news of his dismissal*. **2** suffer from harmful effects after eating, breathing, or touching a substance. **3** interact and undergo a chemical or physical change.

– SYNONYMS **respond,** act in response, reply, answer, behave.

re·ac·tance /rē'aktəns/ ▶ **noun** Physics the nonresistive component of impedance in an alternating-current circuit, arising from inductance and/or capacitance.

re·ac·tant /rē'aktənt/ ▶ **noun** Chemistry a substance that takes part in and undergoes change during a chemical reaction.

re·ac·tion /rē'akSHən/ ▶ **noun 1** something done or experienced as a result of an event or situation: *her first reaction was one of relief*. **2** (**reactions**) a person's ability to respond to an event. **3** a response by the body to a drug or substance to which someone is allergic. **4** a way of thinking or behaving that is deliberately different from that of the past: *a reaction against austerity*. **5** opposition to political or social progress: *the forces of reaction*. **6** a process in which substances interact causing chemical or physical change. **7** Physics a force exerted in opposition to an applied force.

– SYNONYMS **1 response,** answer, reply, rejoinder, retort, riposte; informal comeback. **2 backlash,** counteraction.

re·ac·tion·ar·y /rē'aksнə,nerē/ ▶ **adjective** opposing political or social progress or reform.

– SYNONYMS **right-wing,** conservative, traditionalist, conventional, diehard.
– ANTONYMS radical, progressive.

▶ **noun** (pl. **reactionaries**) a person holding reactionary views.

re·ac·ti·vate /rē'aktivāt/ ▶ **verb** bring something back into action.
– DERIVATIVES **re·ac·ti·va·tion** /rē,akti'vāsнən/ noun.

re·ac·tive /rē'aktiv/ ▶ **adjective 1** showing a response to a stimulus. **2** acting in response to a situation rather than creating or controlling it. **3** having a tendency to react chemically.
– DERIVATIVES **re·ac·tiv·i·ty** /,rē,ak'tivətē/ noun.

re·ac·tor /rē'aktər/ ▶ **noun 1** (also **nuclear reactor**) a structure or piece of equipment in which suitable material can be made to undergo a controlled nuclear reaction, so releasing nuclear energy. **2** a container or device in which substances are made to react chemically.

read /rēd/ ▶ **verb** (past and past part. **read** /red/) **1** look at and understand the meaning of written or printed matter by interpreting its characters or symbols. **2** speak written or printed words aloud. **3** have a particular wording: *the placard read 'We want justice.'* **4** discover information by reading: *I read about the course in the paper*. **5** habitually read a particular newspaper or magazine. **6** understand or interpret the nature or significance of: *he didn't dare look away in case this was read as a sign of weakness*. **7** (**read something into**) think that something has a meaning or significance that it may not possess. **8** (**read up on**) gain information about a subject by reading. **9** chiefly Brit. study an academic subject at a university. **10** look at and record the figure indicated on a measuring instrument. **11** present a bill or other measure before a lawmaking body. **12** (of a computer) copy or transfer data. **13** hear and understand the words of someone speaking on a radio transmitter.

– SYNONYMS **1 peruse,** study, scrutinize, look through, pore over, run one's eye over, cast an eye over, leaf through, scan. **2 understand,** make out, make sense of, decipher, interpret, construe. **3 register,** record, display, show, indicate.

▶ **noun 1** informal a book that is interesting or enjoyable to read. **2** a period or act of reading.
– PHRASES **read between the lines** look for or find a meaning that is not explicitly stated. **read someone's mind** know what someone else is thinking.
– ORIGIN Old English; early senses included 'advise' and 'interpret a riddle or dream.'

WORD LINKS

literacy *ability to read*
illiteracy *inability to read*

read·a·ble /'rēdəbəl/ ▶ **adjective 1** able to be read or deciphered. **2** easy or enjoyable to read.

– SYNONYMS **1** *the inscription is perfectly readable* **legible,** decipherable, clear, intelligible, comprehensible. **2** *her novels are immensely readable* **enjoyable,** entertaining, interesting, absorbing, gripping, enthralling, engrossing; informal unputdownable.
– ANTONYMS illegible.

read·er /'rēdər/ ▶ **noun 1** a person who reads. **2** a person who assesses the quality of manuscripts submitted for publication. **3** a book containing extracts of another book or books for teaching purposes. **4** a device that produces a readable image from microfiche or microfilm on a screen.
– DERIVATIVES **read·er·ly** adjective.

read·er·ship /'rēdər,sнip/ ▶ **noun** (treated as sing. or pl.) the readers of a publication as a group.

read·i·ly /'redl-ē/ ▶ **adverb 1** without hesitation; willingly. **2** without difficulty; easily.

– SYNONYMS **1 willingly,** unhesitatingly, ungrudgingly, gladly, happily, eagerly. **2 easily,** without difficulty.

read·i·ness /'redēnis/ ▶ **noun 1** willingness to do something: *their readiness to accept change*. **2** the state of being fully prepared for something.

– SYNONYMS **1 willingness,** eagerness, keenness, enthusiasm, alacrity. **2 preparedness,** preparation.

read·ing /'rēdiɴɢ/ ▶ **noun 1** the action or skill of reading. **2** an instance of something being read to an audience. **3** a way of interpreting something: *his reading of the situation was justified*. **4** a figure recorded on a measuring instrument. **5** a stage of debate in a legislature through which a bill must pass before it can become law.

– SYNONYMS **1 perusal,** study, scanning. **2 learning,** scholarship, education, erudition. **3 recital,** recitation, performance. **4 lesson,** passage, excerpt. **5 interpretation,** understanding, explanation, analysis, construction.

read·ing age ▶ **noun** a child's reading ability, measured by comparing it with the average ability of children of a particular age.

re·ad·just /,rēə'jəst/ ▶ **verb 1** set or adjust something again. **2** adjust or adapt to a changed situation or environment.
– DERIVATIVES **re·ad·just·ment** noun.

read-on·ly mem·o·ry /rēd/ ▶ **noun** Computing memory read at high speed but not capable of being changed by program instructions.

read·out /'rēd,out/ ▶ **noun** a visual record or display of the output from a computer or scientific instrument.

read-write /'rēd 'rīt/ ▶ **adjective** Computing capable of reading existing data and accepting alterations or further input.

read·y /'redē/ ▶ **adjective** (**readier, readiest**) **1** prepared for an activity or situation. **2** made suitable and available for immediate use: *dinner's ready*. **3** easily available or obtained; within reach. **4** (**ready to**/**for**) willing to do or having a desire for. **5** immediate, quick, or prompt: *his ready wit*.

– SYNONYMS **1 prepared,** equipped, all set, organized, primed; informal fit, psyched (up), geared up. **2 completed,** finished, prepared, organized, done, arranged, fixed. **3** *he's always ready to help* **willing,** prepared, pleased, inclined, disposed, eager, keen, happy, glad; informal game. **4** *a ready supply of food* **(easily) available,** accessible, handy, close/near at hand, on hand, convenient, within reach, near, at one's fingertips; informal on tap. **5** *a ready answer*

prompt, quick, swift, speedy, fast, immediate, unhesitating.

▶ **noun** (**readies** or **the ready**) Brit. informal available money; cash.
▶ **verb** (**readies, readying, readied**) prepare someone or something for an activity or purpose.

– SYNONYMS **prepare,** organize, gear up; informal psych up.

– PHRASES **at the ready** prepared or available for immediate use. **make ready** prepare.
– ORIGIN Old English.

read·y-made ▶ **adjective** **1** made to a standard size or specification rather than to order. **2** easily available: *ready-made answers.*

read·y-mixed ▶ **adjective** (of concrete, paint, food, etc.) having some or all of the constituents already mixed together.

read·y mon·ey ▶ **noun** money in the form of cash that is immediately available.

read·y reck·on·er ▶ **noun** a book, table, etc., listing standard numerical calculations or other kinds of information.

read·y-to-wear ▶ **adjective** (of clothes) sold through stores rather than made to order for an individual customer.

re·af·firm /ˌrēəˈfərm/ ▶ **verb** **1** state something again. **2** confirm the validity of something already established.
– DERIVATIVES **re·af·fir·ma·tion** /ˌrēˌafərˈmāsʜən/ noun.

re·a·gent /rēˈājənt/ ▶ **noun** a substance or mixture used to cause a chemical reaction, used especially to test for the presence of another substance.

re·al[1] /ˈrē(ə)l/ ▶ **adjective** **1** actually existing or occurring; not imagined or supposed. **2** not artificial; genuine: *real diamonds.* **3** worthy of the description; proper: *he's my idea of a real man.* **4** significant; serious: *a real danger of war.* **5** adjusted for changes in the value of money: *real incomes had fallen by 30 percent.* **6** Mathematics (of a number or quantity) having no imaginary part.

– SYNONYMS **1 actual,** true, factual, nonfictional, historical, material, physical, tangible, concrete. **2 genuine,** authentic, bona fide, proper, true; informal kosher. **3 sincere,** genuine, true, unfeigned, heartfelt. **4 complete,** utter, thorough, absolute, total, prize, perfect.
– ANTONYMS imaginary, false.

▶ **adverb** informal really; very.
– DERIVATIVES **real·ness** noun.
– ORIGIN Latin *realis.*

re·al[2] /rāˈäl/ ▶ **noun** **1** the basic unit of money of Brazil since 1994, equal to 100 centavos. **2** a former coin and unit of money of various Spanish-speaking countries.
– ORIGIN Spanish and Portuguese, 'royal.'

real es·tate ▶ **noun** property in the form of land or buildings.

re·a·lign /ˌrēəˈlīn/ ▶ **verb** **1** change or restore something to a different or former position or state. **2** (**realign oneself with**) change one's opinions so as to share those of another person, group, etc.
– DERIVATIVES **re·a·lign·ment** noun.

re·al·ism /ˈrēəˌlizəm/ ▶ **noun** **1** the practice of accepting a situation as it is and dealing with it accordingly. **2** (in art or literature) the representation of things in a way that is accurate and true to life. **3** Philosophy the theory that abstract ideas have their own existence, independent of the mind. Often contrasted with **NOMINALISM**.

– SYNONYMS **1 pragmatism,** practicality, common sense, levelheadedness. **2 authenticity,** accuracy, fidelity, truthfulness, verisimilitude.

– DERIVATIVES **re·al·ist** noun & adjective.

re·al·is·tic /ˌrēəˈlistik/ ▶ **adjective** **1** having a sensible and practical idea of what can be achieved or expected. **2** representing things in a way that is accurate and true to life.

– SYNONYMS **1 practical,** pragmatic, matter-of-fact, down-to-earth, sensible, commonsensical, rational, levelheaded; informal no-nonsense. **2 achievable,** attainable, feasible, practicable, reasonable, sensible, workable; informal doable. **3 authentic,** accurate, true to life, lifelike, truthful, faithful, natural, naturalistic.
– ANTONYMS unrealistic.

– DERIVATIVES **re·al·is·ti·cal·ly** /-ik(ə)lē/ adverb.

re·al·i·ty /rēˈalətē/ ▶ **noun** (pl. **realities**) **1** the state of things as they actually exist, as opposed to how one might like them to be: *he refuses to face reality.* **2** a thing that is actually experienced or seen: *the harsh realities of life in a farming community.* **3** the state or quality of having existence or substance.

– SYNONYMS **1 the real world,** real life, actuality, corporeality. **2 fact,** actuality, truth. **3 authenticity,** verisimilitude, fidelity, truthfulness, accuracy.
– ANTONYMS fantasy.

▶ **adjective** referring to television programs based on real people or situations, intended to be entertaining rather than informative: *reality TV.*

re·al·i·za·tion /ˌrē(ə)ləˈzāsʜən/ ▶ **noun** **1** an act of becoming fully aware of something as a fact: *a growing realization of the danger.* **2** the achievement of something desired or anticipated: *the realization of our dreams.*

– SYNONYMS **1 awareness,** understanding, comprehension, consciousness, appreciation, recognition, discernment. **2 fulfillment,** achievement, accomplishment, attainment.

re·al·ize /ˈrē(ə)ˌlīz/ ▶ **verb** **1** become fully aware of as a fact; understand clearly. **2** achieve something desired or anticipated. **3** be sold for or make a particular amount. **4** convert property, shares, etc., into money by selling them. **5** (**be realized**) (of something one is afraid will happen) happen: *their worst fears were realized.* **6** give actual or physical form to something.

– SYNONYMS **1** *he realized his mistake at once* **register,** perceive, understand, grasp, comprehend, see, recognize, take in. **2** *he finally realized his lifelong ambition* **fulfill,** achieve, accomplish, make happen, bring to fruition, bring about/off, actualize. **3** *the company realized significant profits* **make,** clear, gain, earn, return, produce. **4** *the goods realized $3000* **be sold for,** fetch, go for, make, net.

– DERIVATIVES **re·al·i·za·ble** /ˌrēəˈlīzəbəl/ adjective.

real life ▶ **noun** life as it is lived in reality, as distinct from a fictional or ideal world.

re·al·ly /ˈrē(ə)lē/ ▶ **adverb** **1** in reality; in actual fact. **2** very; thoroughly.

– SYNONYMS **1 in (actual) fact,** actually, in reality, in truth. **2 genuinely,** truly, certainly, honestly, undoubtedly, unquestionably.

▶ **exclamation** expressing interest, surprise, or protest.

realm /relm/ ▶ **noun 1** literary or Law a kingdom. **2** a field of activity or interest: *the realm of chemistry.*

– SYNONYMS **1 kingdom,** country, land, state, nation, territory, dominion, empire, monarchy, principality. **2** *the realm of academia* **domain,** sphere, area, field, world, province.

– ORIGIN Old French *reaume.*

re·al·po·li·tik /rāˈälˌpōliˌtēk/ ▶ **noun** politics based on practical considerations rather than moral or ideological principles.
– ORIGIN German, 'practical politics.'

real prop·er·ty ▶ **noun** Law property consisting of land or buildings. Compare with **PERSONAL PROPERTY.**

real time ▶ **noun** the actual time during which something occurs. ▶ **adjective** (**real-time**) (of a computer system) in which input data is processed extremely fast so that it is available virtually immediately as feedback to the process from which it is coming, e.g., in a missile guidance system.

re·al·tor /ˈrē(ə)ltər, -ˌtôr, ˈrē(ə)lətər/ ▶ **noun** a person who acts as an agent for the sale and purchase of buildings and land; a real estate agent.

re·al·ty /ˈrē(ə)ltē/ ▶ **noun** Law a person's real property. Compare with **PERSONALTY.**

ream[1] /rēm/ ▶ **noun 1** 500 (formerly 480) sheets of paper. **2** (**reams**) a large quantity of something, especially paper.
– ORIGIN Old French *raime.*

ream[2] ▶ **verb** widen a bore or hole with a special tool.
– DERIVATIVES **ream·er** noun.
– ORIGIN unknown.

re·an·a·lyze /rēˈanlˌīz/ ▶ **verb** carry out a further analysis of something.
– DERIVATIVES **re·a·nal·y·sis** /ˌrēəˈnaləsəs/ noun.

re·an·i·mate /rēˈanəˌmāt/ ▶ **verb** bring someone back to life or consciousness.
– DERIVATIVES **re·an·i·ma·tion** /ˌrēˌanəˈmāsʜən/ noun.

reap /rēp/ ▶ **verb 1** cut or gather a crop or harvest. **2** receive something as a result of one's own or others' actions: *the company is poised to reap the benefits of this investment.*

– SYNONYMS **1 harvest,** cut, pick, gather, garner. **2 receive,** obtain, get, derive, acquire, secure, realize.

– ORIGIN Old English.

reap·er /ˈrēpər/ ▶ **noun 1** a person or machine that harvests a crop. **2** (**the Reaper** or **the Grim Reaper**) a representation of death as a cloaked skeleton holding a large scythe.

re·ap·pear /ˌrēəˈpi(ə)r/ ▶ **verb** appear again.
– DERIVATIVES **re·ap·pear·ance** /ˌrēəˈpi(ə)rəns/ noun.

re·ap·point /ˌrēəˈpoint/ ▶ **verb** appoint someone again to a position they previously held.
– DERIVATIVES **re·ap·point·ment** noun.

re·ap·praise /ˌrēəˈprāz/ ▶ **verb** appraise something again or differently.
– DERIVATIVES **re·ap·prais·al** noun.

rear[1] /ri(ə)r/ ▶ **noun 1** the back part of something. **2** (also **rear end**) informal a person's buttocks.

– SYNONYMS **back (part),** hind part, end, tail (end), back (end); Nautical stern.

▶ **adjective** at the back.

– SYNONYMS **back,** end, rearmost, hind, last.
– ANTONYMS front.

– PHRASES **bring up the rear 1** be at the very end of a line. **2** come last in a race.
– ORIGIN Old French *rere.*

rear[2] ▶ **verb 1** bring up and care for offspring. **2** breed or cultivate animals or plants. **3** (of an animal) raise itself upright on its hind legs. **4** (of a building, mountain, etc.) extend or appear to extend to a great height. **5** (**rear up**) show anger or irritation.

– SYNONYMS **1 bring up,** raise, care for, look after, nurture, parent. **2 breed,** raise, keep, grow, cultivate. **3** *houses reared up on either side* **rise,** tower, soar, loom.

– ORIGIN Old English, 'set upright, construct.'

rear ad·mir·al ▶ **noun** a rank of naval officer, above captain and below vice admiral.

rear·guard /ˈri(ə)rˌgärd/ ▶ **noun 1** the soldiers at the rear of a body of troops, especially those protecting a retreating army. **2** a reactionary or conservative group in an organization.

rear·guard ac·tion ▶ **noun** a defensive action carried out by a retreating army.

re·arm /rēˈärm/ ▶ **verb** provide with or obtain a new supply of weapons.
– DERIVATIVES **re·ar·ma·ment** /rēˈärməmənt/ noun.

rear·most /ˈri(ə)rˌmōst/ ▶ **adjective** furthest back.

re·ar·range /ˌrēəˈrānj/ ▶ **verb** arrange something again in a different way.
– DERIVATIVES **re·ar·range·ment** noun.

re·ar·rest /ˌrēəˈrest/ ▶ **verb** arrest someone again.

rear·view mir·ror /ˈri(ə)rˌvyo͞o/ ▶ **noun** a mirror fixed inside the windshield of a vehicle, enabling the driver to see the vehicle or road behind.

rear·ward /ˈri(ə)rwərd/ ▶ **adjective** directed toward the back. ▶ **adverb** (also **rearwards**) toward the back.

rear-wheel drive ▶ **noun** a transmission system that provides power to the rear wheels of a motor vehicle.

rea·son /ˈrēzən/ ▶ **noun 1** a cause, explanation, or justification. **2** good or obvious cause to do something: *we have reason to celebrate.* **3** the power to think, understand, and form judgments logically. **4** (**one's reason**) one's sanity. **5** what is right, practical, or possible: *I'll answer anything, within reason.*

– SYNONYMS **1 cause,** ground(s), basis, rationale, motive, explanation, justification, defense, vindication, excuse, apologia. **2 rationality,** logic, cognition, reasoning, intellect, thought, understanding; formal ratiocination. **3 sanity,** mind, mental faculties, senses, wits; informal marbles.

▶ **verb 1** think, understand, and form judgments logically. **2** (**reason something out**) find a solution to a problem by considering possible options. **3** (**reason with**) persuade someone by using logical argument.

– SYNONYMS **1 calculate,** conclude, reckon, think, judge, deduce, infer, surmise; informal figure. **2** (**reason something out**) *we finally reasoned out the cryptic message in chapter twelve* **work out,** think through, make sense of, get to the bottom of, puzzle out; informal figure out. **3** (**reason with**) *she tried to reason with her husband* **talk around,** bring around, persuade, prevail on, convince.

– DERIVATIVES **rea·soned** adjective.

– PHRASES **by reason of** formal because of. **listen to reason** be persuaded to act sensibly. **it stands to reason** it is obvious or logical.
– ORIGIN Old French *reisun*.

WORD LINKS

rational *relating to reason*

rea·son·a·ble /ˈrēz(ə)nəbəl/ ▶ **adjective 1** fair and sensible. **2** as much as is appropriate or fair in a particular situation: *they have had a reasonable time to reply*. **3** fairly good; average. **4** not too expensive.

– SYNONYMS **1 sensible,** rational, logical, fair, just, equitable, intelligent, wise, levelheaded, practical, realistic, sound, valid, commonsensical, tenable, plausible, credible, believable. **2 practicable,** sensible, appropriate, suitable. **3 fairly good,** acceptable, satisfactory, average, adequate, fair, tolerable, passable; informal OK. **4 inexpensive,** affordable, moderate, low, cheap, within one's means.

– DERIVATIVES **rea·son·a·ble·ness** noun **rea·son·a·bly** adverb.

re·as·sem·ble /ˌrēəˈsembəl/ ▶ **verb** put something back together.
– DERIVATIVES **re·as·sem·bly** /-blē/ noun.

re·as·sert /ˌrēəˈsərt/ ▶ **verb** state or declare something again.
– DERIVATIVES **re·as·ser·tion** /ˌrēəˈsərsʜən/ noun.

re·as·sess /ˌrēəˈses/ ▶ **verb** consider or assess someone or something again, in the light of new or different factors.
– DERIVATIVES **re·as·sess·ment** noun.

re·as·sign /ˌrēəˈsīn/ ▶ **verb** assign someone or something again or differently.
– DERIVATIVES **re·as·sign·ment** noun.

re·as·sure /ˌrēəˈsʜo͝or/ ▶ **verb** make someone feel less worried or afraid.

– SYNONYMS **put someone's mind at rest,** encourage, hearten, buoy up, cheer up, comfort, soothe.
– ANTONYMS alarm.

– DERIVATIVES **re·as·sur·ance** noun **re·as·sur·ing** adjective.

re·at·tach /ˌrēəˈtaᴄʜ/ ▶ **verb** attach something again.
– DERIVATIVES **re·at·tach·ment** noun.

re·a·wak·en /ˌrēəˈwākən/ ▶ **verb** awaken again.

re·bal·ance /rēˈbaləns/ ▶ **verb** restore the correct balance to someone or something.

re·bar /ˈrēˌbär/ ▶ **noun** reinforcing steel, especially as rods in concrete.

re·bar·ba·tive /rəˈbärbətiv/ ▶ **adjective** formal unattractive and unpleasant or offensive.
– ORIGIN French *rébarbatif*, from Old French *se rebarber* 'face each other aggressively' (literally 'beard to beard').

re·bate ▶ **noun** /ˈrēˌbāt/ **1** a partial refund to someone who has paid too much for tax, rent, etc. **2** a deduction or discount on a sum of money due.

– SYNONYMS **partial refund,** partial repayment, discount, deduction, reduction.

▶ **verb** /ˈrēˌbāt, riˈbāt/ pay money back as a rebate.
– ORIGIN from Old French *rebatre* 'beat back.'

re·bec /ˈrēˌbek, ˈrebˌek/ ▶ **noun** a medieval three-stringed instrument played with a bow.
– ORIGIN French.

reb·el ▶ **noun** /ˈrebəl/ a person who rebels.

– SYNONYMS **1 revolutionary,** insurgent, insurrectionist, mutineer, guerrilla, terrorist, freedom fighter. **2 nonconformist,** dissenter, dissident, maverick. **3** (as adj.) *rebel troops* **rebellious,** insurgent, revolutionary, mutinous. **4** (as adj.) *rebel clergymen* **defiant,** disobedient, insubordinate, subversive, rebellious, nonconformist, maverick.
– ANTONYMS loyalist, conformist.

▶ **verb** /riˈbel/ (**rebels, rebelling, rebelled**) **1** fight against or refuse to obey an established government or ruler. **2** resist authority, control, or accepted behavior.

– SYNONYMS **1** *the citizens rebelled* **revolt,** mutiny, riot, rise up, take up arms. **2** *teenagers rebelling against their parents* **defy,** disobey, kick against, challenge, oppose, resist.

– ORIGIN Old French *rebelle*, from Latin *bellum* 'war.'

re·bel·lion /riˈbelyən/ ▶ **noun 1** an act of rebelling against an established government or ruler. **2** defiance of authority or control.

– SYNONYMS **1 revolt,** uprising, insurrection, mutiny, revolution, insurgence. **2 defiance,** disobedience, insubordination, subversion, resistance.
– ANTONYMS compliance.

re·bel·lious /riˈbelyəs/ ▶ **adjective** rebelling or showing a desire to rebel.

– SYNONYMS **1 rebel,** insurgent, mutinous, revolutionary. **2 defiant,** disobedient, insubordinate, unruly, mutinous, obstreperous, recalcitrant, intractable.
– ANTONYMS loyal, obedient.

– DERIVATIVES **re·bel·lious·ly** adverb **re·bel·lious·ness** noun.

WORD TOOLKIT

See **UNRULY**.

re·birth /rēˈbərᴛʜ, ˈrēˌbərᴛʜ/ ▶ **noun 1** the process of being reincarnated or born again. **2** a period of new life, growth, or activity: *the rebirth of a defeated nation*.

re·birth·ing /rēˈbərᴛʜiɴɢ/ ▶ **noun** a form of therapy involving controlled breathing intended to imitate the traumatic experience of being born.

re·boot /rēˈbo͞ot/ ▶ **verb** boot a computer system again.

re·born /rēˈbôrn/ ▶ **adjective 1** brought back to life or activity. **2** newly converted to a personal faith in Jesus; born-again.

re·bound ▶ **verb** /riˈbound, ˈrēˌbound/ **1** bounce back after hitting a hard surface. **2** recover in value, amount, or strength. **3** (**rebound on**) have an unexpected and unpleasant consequence for: *his tricks are rebounding on him*.

– SYNONYMS **1 bounce (back),** spring back, ricochet, boomerang. **2 backfire,** misfire, come back on.

▶ **noun** /ˈrēˌbound/ **1** a ball or shot that rebounds. **2** Basketball the act of gaining possession of a rebounding ball. **3** an instance of recovering in value, amount, or strength: *shares rose sharply in anticipation of an economic rebound*.
– PHRASES **on the rebound** while still distressed after the ending of a romantic relationship.
– ORIGIN Old French *rebondir*.

re·brand /rēˈbrand/ ▶ **verb** change the corporate image of a company or organization.

re·buff /ri'bəf/ ▶ **verb** reject someone or something in an abrupt or ungracious way: *they rebuffed his attempt to negotiate a new deal*.

– SYNONYMS **reject,** turn down, spurn, refuse, decline, snub, slight, dismiss, brush off.
– ANTONYMS accept.

▶ **noun** an abrupt or unkind rejection.

– SYNONYMS **rejection,** snub, slight, refusal, spurning; informal brush-off, kick in the teeth, slap in the face.

– ORIGIN former French *rebuffer*.

re·build /rē'bild/ ▶ **verb** (past and past part. **rebuilt**) build something again.

re·buke /ri'byo͞ok/ ▶ **verb** criticize or reprimand someone sharply.

– SYNONYMS **reprimand,** reproach, scold, admonish, reprove, chastise, upbraid, berate, take to task; informal tell off, chew out; formal castigate.

▶ **noun** a sharp criticism.

– SYNONYMS **reprimand,** reproach, scolding, admonition; informal telling-off, chewing-out, dressing-down.
– ANTONYMS praise.

– ORIGIN Old French *rebuker* 'beat down.'

CHOOSE THE RIGHT WORD

rebuke, admonish, censure, reprimand, reproach, scold

All of these verbs mean to criticize or express disapproval, but which one you use depends on how upset you are. If you want to go easy on someone, you can **admonish** or **reproach**, both of which indicate mild and sometimes kindly disapproval. To *admonish* is to warn or counsel someone, usually because a duty has been forgotten or might be forgotten in the future (*admonish her about leaving the key in the lock*), while *reproach* also suggests mild criticism aimed at correcting a fault or pattern of misbehavior (*he was reproached for his lack of attention in class*). If you want to express your disapproval formally or in public, use **censure** or **reprimand**. You can *censure* someone either directly or indirectly (*the judge censured the lawyer for violating courtroom procedures; a newspaper article that censured "deadbeat dads"*), while *reprimand* suggests a direct confrontation (*reprimanded by his parole officer for leaving town without reporting his whereabouts*).
If you're irritated enough to want to express your disapproval quite harshly and at some length, you can **scold** (*to scold a child for jaywalking*). **Rebuke** is the harshest word of this group, meaning to criticize sharply or sternly, often in the midst of some action (*rebuke a carpenter for walking across an icy roof*).

re·bus /'rēbəs/ ▶ **noun** (pl. **rebuses**) a puzzle in which words are represented by combinations of pictures and letters.
– ORIGIN Latin, 'by things.'

re·but /ri'bət/ ▶ **verb** (**rebuts, rebutting, rebutted**) claim or prove that evidence or an accusation is false.
– ORIGIN Old French *rebuter*.

CHOOSE THE RIGHT WORD

See **REFUTE**.

re·but·tal /ri'bətl/ ▶ **noun** an act of rebutting evidence or an accusation.

– SYNONYMS **refutation,** denial, countering, invalidation, negation, contradiction.

rec /rek/ ▶ **noun** informal recreation: (as adj.) *the rec center*.
– ORIGIN abbreviation.

rec. ▶ **abbreviation 1** record; recorder; recording. **2** recipe. **3** receipt. **4** (in prescriptions) fresh.
– ORIGIN sense 4 from Latin *recens*.

re·cal·ci·trant /ri'kalsətrənt/ ▶ **adjective** obstinately uncooperative or disobedient.

– SYNONYMS **uncooperative,** intractable, insubordinate, defiant, rebellious, willful, wayward, headstrong, self-willed, contrary, perverse, difficult, awkward; formal refractory.
– ANTONYMS amenable.

– DERIVATIVES **re·cal·ci·trance** noun **re·cal·ci·trant·ly** adverb.
– ORIGIN from Latin *recalcitrare* 'kick out with the heels.'

re·cal·cu·late /rē'kalkyə,lāt/ ▶ **verb** calculate something again or differently.
– DERIVATIVES **re·cal·cu·la·tion** /,rē,kalkyə'lāsʜən/ noun.

re·call ▶ **verb** /ri'kôl/ **1** remember something. **2** cause one to remember or think of someone or something. **3** officially order to return: *the ambassador was recalled from Peru*. **4** (of a manufacturer) request all the purchasers of a product to return it, as a result of the discovery of a fault. **5** select an athlete as a member of a team from which they have previously been dropped, or bring an inactive player back to an active status. **6** call up stored computer data.

– SYNONYMS **1 remember,** recollect, call to mind, think back on/to, reminisce about. **2 remind someone of,** bring to mind, call up, conjure up, evoke. **3 call back,** order home, withdraw.
– ANTONYMS forget.

▶ **noun** /'rē,kôl, ri'kôl, rē'kôl/ **1** the action of remembering or the ability to remember. **2** an act of officially recalling someone or something.

– SYNONYMS **recollection,** remembrance, memory.

– PHRASES **beyond recall** in such a way that restoration to the original state is impossible.

re·cant /ri'kant/ ▶ **verb** state that one no longer holds an opinion or belief.
– DERIVATIVES **re·can·ta·tion** /,rē,kan'tāsʜən/ noun.
– ORIGIN Latin *recantare* 'revoke,' from *cantare* 'sing, chant.'

re·cap /rē'kap/ ▶ **verb** (**recaps, recapping, recapped**) recapitulate. ▶ **noun** a recapitulation.

re·ca·pit·u·late /,rēkə'picʜə,lāt/ ▶ **verb** summarize and state again the main points of a speech, argument, etc.
– ORIGIN Latin *recapitulare* 'go through heading by heading,' from *capitulum* 'chapter.'

re·ca·pit·u·la·tion /,rēkə,picʜə'lāsʜən/ ▶ **noun 1** an act of recapitulating something. **2** Music a part of a movement in which themes from the exposition are repeated.

re·cap·ture /rē'kapcʜər/ ▶ **verb 1** capture a person or animal that has escaped. **2** recover something taken or lost. **3** experience a past time, event, or feeling again: *the programs give viewers a chance to recapture their own childhoods*. ▶ **noun** an act of recapturing someone or something.

re·cast /rē'kast/ ▶ **verb** (past and past part. **recast**) **1** present something in a different form or style: *his thesis has been recast for the general reader*. **2** give roles in a play, movie, or television show to different actors. **3** cast metal again or differently.

rec·ce /'rekē/ Brit. informal ▶ **noun** an act of reconnoitering a place or area. ▶ **verb** (**recces**, **recceing**, **recced**) reconnoiter a place or area.

re·cede /ri'sēd/ ▶ **verb** **1** move back or further away. **2** gradually diminish: *her panic receded*. **3** (of a man's hair) stop growing at the temples and above the forehead. **4** (as adj. **receding**) (of a facial feature) sloping backward: *a receding chin*.

– SYNONYMS **1 retreat,** go back/down/away, withdraw, ebb, subside. **2 diminish,** lessen, dwindle, fade, abate, subside.
– ANTONYMS advance, grow.

– ORIGIN Latin *recedere* 'go back.'

re·ceipt /ri'sēt/ ▶ **noun** **1** the action of receiving something or the fact of its being received. **2** a written statement confirming that something has been paid for or received. **3** (**receipts**) an amount of money received over a period by an organization.
– ORIGIN Old French *receite*.

re·ceiv·a·ble /ri'sēvəbəl/ ▶ **adjective** able to be received. ▶ **plural noun** (**receivables**) amounts owed to a business, regarded as assets.

re·ceive /ri'sēv/ ▶ **verb** **1** be given, presented with, or paid: *they received a $100,000 advance*. **2** accept or take delivery of something sent or offered. **3** form an idea or impression from an experience. **4** suffer, experience, or meet with: *the event received wide press coverage*. **5** (as adj. **received**) widely accepted as true or correct. **6** entertain someone as a guest. **7** admit someone as a member: *hundreds of converts were received into the Church*. **8** detect or pick up broadcast signals. **9** (in tennis and similar games) be the player to whom the server serves the ball. **10** buy or accept goods known to be stolen. **11** serve as a container for something.

– SYNONYMS **1 be given,** be presented with, be awarded, be sent, be in receipt of, get, obtain, gain, acquire, be paid. **2 hear,** listen to, respond to, react to. **3 experience,** sustain, undergo, meet with, suffer, bear.
– ANTONYMS give, send.

– PHRASES **be at** (or **on**) **the receiving end** informal be subjected to something unpleasant.
– ORIGIN Old French *receivre*.

re·ceiv·er /ri'sēvər/ ▶ **noun** **1** a person or thing that receives something. **2** a piece of radio or television equipment converting broadcast signals into sound or images. **3** a telephone handset, in particular the part that converts electrical signals into sounds. **4** Football a player who catches a pass or kick. **5** a person appointed to manage the financial affairs of a bankrupt business.

re·ceiv·er·ship /ri'sēvər,sʜip/ ▶ **noun** the state of being managed financially by a receiver.

re·cent /'rēsənt/ ▶ **adjective** **1** having happened or been done lately; belonging to a period of time not long ago. **2** (**Recent**) Geology another term for **Holocene**.

– SYNONYMS **new,** the latest, current, fresh, modern, late, contemporary, up to date, up to the minute.
– ANTONYMS old.

– ORIGIN Latin *recens*.

WORD TOOLKIT

See **new**.

re·cent·ly /'rēsəntlē/ ▶ **adverb** in the recent past: *they recently installed a new flagpole*.

– SYNONYMS **not long ago,** a little while back, just now, newly, freshly, of late, lately, latterly.

re·cep·ta·cle /ri'septikəl/ ▶ **noun** **1** an object or space used to contain something. **2** Botany the base of a flower or flowerhead.
– ORIGIN Latin *receptaculum*.

re·cep·tion /ri'sepsʜən/ ▶ **noun** **1** the action or process of receiving someone or something. **2** the way in which someone or something is received: *an enthusiastic reception*. **3** a formal social occasion held to welcome someone or celebrate an event. **4** the area in a hotel, office, etc., where visitors are greeted. **5** the quality with which broadcast signals are received.

– SYNONYMS **1 response,** reaction, treatment. **2 party,** function, social occasion, celebration, get-together, gathering, soirée; informal do.

– ORIGIN Latin, from *recipere* 'receive.'

re·cep·tion·ist /ri'sepsʜənist/ ▶ **noun** a person who greets and deals with clients and visitors to an office, hotel, doctor's office, etc.

re·cep·tive /ri'septiv/ ▶ **adjective** **1** able or willing to receive something. **2** willing to consider new suggestions and ideas.

– SYNONYMS **open-minded,** responsive, amenable, well disposed, flexible, approachable, accessible.
– ANTONYMS unresponsive.

– DERIVATIVES **re·cep·tiv·i·ty** /,rē,sep'tivətē/ noun.

re·cep·tor /ri'septər/ ▶ **noun** an organ or cell in the body that responds to external stimuli such as light or heat and transmits signals to a sensory nerve.

re·cess /'rē,ses, ri'ses/ ▶ **noun** **1** a small space set back in a wall or into a surface. **2** a hollow space inside something. **3** (**recesses**) remote, secluded, or secret places. **4** a break between sessions of a congress, court of law, etc. **5** a break between school classes.

– SYNONYMS **1 alcove,** bay, niche, nook, corner. **2 break,** adjournment, interlude, interval, rest, holiday, vacation.

▶ **verb** (often as adj. **recessed**) set a fixture back into a wall or surface.
– ORIGIN Latin *recessus*.

re·ces·sion /ri'sesʜən/ ▶ **noun** a temporary economic decline during which trade and industrial activity are reduced.

– SYNONYMS **downturn,** depression, slump, slowdown.
– ANTONYMS boom.

– DERIVATIVES **re·ces·sion·ar·y** /-,nerē/ adjective.

re·ces·sion·al /ri'sesʜənl, ri'sesʜnəl/ ▶ **noun** a hymn sung while the clergy and choir withdraw after a service.

re·ces·sive /ri'sesiv/ ▶ **adjective** (of a gene) appearing in offspring only if a contrary gene is not also inherited. Compare with **dominant**.

re·charge /rē'cʜärj/ ▶ **verb** charge a battery or a battery-operated device again.
– DERIVATIVES **re·charge·a·ble** adjective **re·charg·er** noun.

re·check /rē'cʜek/ ▶ **verb** check something again.

re·cher·ché /rə,sʜer'sʜā, rə'sʜer,sʜā/ ▶ **adjective** too unusual or obscure to be easily understood.
– ORIGIN French, 'carefully sought out.'

re·chris·ten /rē'krisən/ ▶ **verb** give a new name to someone or something.

re·cid·i·vist /ri'sidəvist/ ▶ **noun** a person who repeatedly commits crimes and is not discouraged by being punished.
– DERIVATIVES **re·cid·i·vism** /-ˌvizəm/ noun.
– ORIGIN French *récidiver*.

rec·i·pe /'resəˌpē/ ▶ **noun 1** a list of ingredients and instructions for preparing a dish. **2** something likely to lead to a particular outcome: *high interest rates are a recipe for disaster*.

– SYNONYMS *a recipe for success* **formula,** prescription, blueprint.

– ORIGIN Latin, 'receive!' (originally used as an instruction in medical prescriptions).

re·cip·i·ent /ri'sipēənt/ ▶ **noun** a person who receives something.

re·cip·ro·cal /ri'siprəkəl/ ▶ **adjective 1** given, felt, or done in return: *he showed no reciprocal interest*. **2** (of an agreement or arrangement) affecting two parties equally. **3** Grammar (of a pronoun or verb) expressing mutual action or relationship (e.g., *each other*; *they kissed*).

– SYNONYMS **mutual,** common, shared, give-and-take, joint, corresponding, complementary.

▶ **noun** Mathematics the quantity obtained by dividing the number one by a given quantity.
– DERIVATIVES **re·cip·ro·cal·ly** /-ək(ə)lē/ adverb.
– ORIGIN Latin *reciprocus*.

re·cip·ro·cate /ri'siprəˌkāt/ ▶ **verb** respond to a gesture, action, or emotion with a corresponding one.

– SYNONYMS **requite,** return, give back.

– DERIVATIVES **re·cip·ro·ca·tion** /riˌsiprə'kāshən/ noun.

rec·i·proc·i·ty /ˌresə'präsətē/ ▶ **noun** the practice of exchanging things with other parties to the benefit or advantage of both.

re·cir·cu·late /rē'sərkyəˌlāt/ ▶ **verb** circulate something again.
– DERIVATIVES **re·cir·cu·la·tion** /rēˌsərkyə'lāshən/ noun.

re·cit·al /ri'sītl/ ▶ **noun 1** the performance of a program of music by a soloist or small group. **2** a long account of a series of connected things: *a recital of Adam's failures*.

– SYNONYMS **1 performance,** concert, recitation, reading. **2 report,** account, listing, catalog, litany.

– DERIVATIVES **re·cit·al·ist** noun.

rec·i·ta·tive /ˌres(ə)tə'tēv/ ▶ **noun** the narrative and dialogue passages in an opera or oratorio, sung in a way that reflects the rhythms of ordinary speech.

re·cite /ri'sīt/ ▶ **verb 1** repeat a poem or passage aloud from memory in front of an audience. **2** state a series of names, facts, etc., in order.

– SYNONYMS **1 quote,** say, speak, read aloud, declaim, deliver, render. **2 recount,** list, detail, reel off, relate, enumerate.

– DERIVATIVES **rec·i·ta·tion** /ˌresi'tāshən/ noun **re·cit·er** noun.
– ORIGIN Latin *recitare* 'read out.'

reck·less /'rekləs/ ▶ **adjective** without thought or care for the consequences of an action.

– SYNONYMS **rash,** careless, thoughtless, heedless, precipitate, impetuous, impulsive, irresponsible, foolhardy, devil-may-care.
– ANTONYMS cautious.

– DERIVATIVES **reck·less·ly** adverb **reck·less·ness** noun.
– ORIGIN Old English.

reck·on /'rekən/ ▶ **verb 1** be of the opinion; think: *I reckon he'll win*. **2** include in: *he reckoned Hugh among his friends*. **3** (**be reckoned**) be considered to be: *their goalkeeper was reckoned to be the best in the world*. **4** calculate something. **5** (**reckon with** or **without**) take (or fail to take) something into account. **6** (**reckon on**) rely on or expect: *no one had reckoned on a strike*.

– SYNONYMS **1 think,** believe, be of the opinion, suppose, assume. **2 include,** consider, regard as, look on as, judge, think of as, count, deem, rate. **3 calculate,** compute, work out, figure, count (up), add up, total, tally; Brit. tot up. **4** (**reckon with** or **without**) **take into account,** take into consideration, bargain for/on, anticipate, foresee, be prepared for, consider.

– PHRASES **to be reckoned with** not to be ignored or underestimated.
– ORIGIN Old English, 'recount, tell.'

reck·on·ing /'rekəniNG/ ▶ **noun 1** the action of calculating or estimating something. **2** an opinion or judgment. **3** punishment or retribution for one's actions.

– SYNONYMS **calculation,** estimation, computation, working out, addition, count.

re·claim /ri'klām/ ▶ **verb 1** recover possession of something. **2** make wasteland or land formerly under water usable for growing crops.

– SYNONYMS **1 get back,** claim back, recover, retrieve, recoup. **2 save,** rescue, redeem, salvage.

▶ **noun** the action of reclaiming something.
– DERIVATIVES **rec·la·ma·tion** /ˌreklə'māshən/ noun.

re·clas·si·fy /rē'klasəˌfī/ ▶ **verb** (**reclassifies, reclassifying, reclassified**) classify someone or something differently.
– DERIVATIVES **re·clas·si·fi·ca·tion** /rēˌklasəfə'kāshən/ noun.

re·cline /ri'klīn/ ▶ **verb 1** lean or lie back in a relaxed position. **2** (of a seat) have a back able to move into a sloping position.

– SYNONYMS **lie,** lie down/back, lean back, relax, loll, lounge, sprawl, stretch out.

– DERIVATIVES **re·clin·a·ble** adjective.
– ORIGIN Latin *reclinare*.

re·clin·er /ri'klīnər/ ▶ **noun** an upholstered armchair that can be tilted backward, especially one with a footrest.

rec·luse /'rekˌlo͞os, ri'klo͞os, 'rekˌlo͞oz/ ▶ **noun** a person who avoids other people and lives a solitary life.

– SYNONYMS **hermit,** ascetic, eremite, loner, lone wolf; historical anchorite.

– ORIGIN from Old French *reclus* 'shut up.'

re·clu·sive /ri'klo͞osiv, -ziv/ ▶ **adjective** tending to avoid the company of other people: *a reclusive former rock star*.

rec·og·ni·tion /ˌrekig'nishən/ ▶ **noun 1** the action of recognizing or the process of being recognized. **2** appreciation or acknowledgment of something. **3** (also **diplomatic recognition**) formal acknowledgment by a country that another country has the status of an independent nation.

– SYNONYMS **1 identification,** recollection, remembrance. **2 acknowledgment,** acceptance, admission, confession. **3 appreciation,** gratitude, thanks, congratulations, credit, commendation, acclaim, acknowledgment.

re·cog·ni·zance /ri'kägnəzəns, -'känəzəns/ ▶ **noun** Law a bond by which a person undertakes before a court or magistrate to observe a particular condition, especially to appear when summoned.

rec·og·nize /'rekig,nīz, 'rekə(g),nīz/ ▶ **verb 1** identify or know someone or something from having come across them before. **2** accept or acknowledge the existence, validity, or legality of: *he was recognized as an international authority.* **3** show official appreciation of: *his work was recognized by an honorary degree from Albertus Magnus.*

– SYNONYMS **1 identify,** place, know, put a name to, remember, recall, recollect. **2 acknowledge,** accept, admit, concede, confess, realize. **3 pay tribute to,** appreciate, be grateful for, acclaim, commend.

– DERIVATIVES **rec·og·niz·a·ble** adjective.
– ORIGIN Latin *recognoscere*, from *cognoscere* 'to learn.'

re·coil /ri'koil/ ▶ **verb 1** suddenly spring back or flinch in fear, horror, or disgust. **2** spring back as a result of the force of impact or elasticity. **3** (of a gun) move abruptly backward as a reaction on firing a bullet or shell. **4** (**recoil on**) (of an action) have an unwelcome result or effect on the person responsible.

– SYNONYMS **1 draw back,** jump back, pull back, flinch, shy away, shrink (back), blench. **2 feel revulsion,** feel disgust, shrink from, wince at.

▶ **noun** the action of recoiling.
– ORIGIN Old French *reculer* 'move back.'

CHOOSE THE RIGHT WORD

See **WINCE**.

rec·ol·lect[1] /,rekə'lekt/ ▶ **verb** remember something.

– SYNONYMS **remember,** recall, call to mind, think of, think back to, reminisce about.
– ANTONYMS forget.

re·col·lect[2] /,rēkə'lekt/ ▶ **verb 1** collect something again. **2** (**recollect oneself**) manage to control one's feelings.

rec·ol·lec·tion /,rekə'leksHən/ ▶ **noun 1** the action of remembering, or the ability to remember. **2** a memory.

– SYNONYMS **memory,** recall, remembrance, impression, reminiscence.

re·com·bi·nant /rē'kämbənənt, ri-/ ▶ **adjective** relating to genetic material formed by recombination.

re·com·bi·na·tion /rē,kəmbə'nāsHən/ ▶ **noun 1** the process of recombining. **2** the rearrangement of genetic material, especially by exchange between chromosomes or by the artificial joining of DNA segments from different organisms.

re·com·bine /,rēkəm'bīn/ ▶ **verb** combine again or differently.

re·com·mence /,rēkə'mens/ ▶ **verb** begin again.

rec·om·mend /,rekə'mend/ ▶ **verb 1** state that someone or something is good or would be suitable for a purpose or role. **2** advise as a course of action: *he recommended that I leave the country.* **3** make appealing or desirable: *the house had much to recommend it.*

– SYNONYMS **1 advocate,** endorse, commend, suggest, put forward, propose, nominate, put up, speak favorably of, put in a good word for, vouch for; informal plug. **2 advise,** counsel, urge, exhort, enjoin, prescribe, argue for, back, support.

– DERIVATIVES **rec·om·mend·a·ble** adjective.

rec·om·men·da·tion /,rekəmən'dāsHən, -,men-/ ▶ **noun 1** a suggestion or proposal as to the best course of action. **2** the action of recommending.

– SYNONYMS **1 advice,** counsel, guidance, suggestion, proposal. **2 commendation,** endorsement, good word, testimonial, tip; informal plug.

re·com·mis·sion /,rēkə'misHən/ ▶ **verb** commission something again.

rec·om·pense /'rekəm,pens/ ▶ **verb 1** compensate or make amends to someone for loss or harm suffered. **2** pay or reward someone for effort or work. ▶ **noun** compensation or reward.
– ORIGIN Latin *recompensare*.

re·con informal ▶ **noun** /'rē,kän, ri'kän/ short for **RECONNAISSANCE**. ▶ **verb** /ri'kän/ (**recons, reconning, reconned**) short for **RECONNOITER**.

rec·on·cile /'rekən,sīl/ ▶ **verb 1** restore friendly relations between people. **2** make apparently incompatible things able to exist together without problems or conflict: *an attempt to reconcile freedom with commitment.* **3** (**reconcile someone to**) make someone accept an unwelcome or unpleasant situation.

– SYNONYMS **1 reunite,** bring (back) together, pacify, appease, placate, mollify; formal conciliate. **2** *reconciling his religious beliefs with his career* **make compatible,** harmonize, square, make congruent, balance. **3 settle,** resolve, sort out, smooth over, iron out, mend, remedy, heal, rectify; informal patch up. **4** *they had to* ***reconcile themselves to*** *drastic losses* **accept,** resign oneself to, come to terms with, learn to live with, get used to, make the best of.

– DERIVATIVES **rec·on·cil·a·ble** adjective.
– ORIGIN Latin *reconciliare*.

rec·on·cil·i·a·tion /,rekən,silē'āsHən/ ▶ **noun 1** the end of a disagreement and the return to friendly relations. **2** the action of reconciling.

rec·on·dite /'rekən,dīt, ri'kän-/ ▶ **adjective** not known about or understood by many people.
– ORIGIN Latin *reconditus* 'hidden, put away.'

re·con·di·tion /,rēkən'disHən/ ▶ **verb 1** condition something again. **2** overhaul or repair an engine or other piece of equipment.

re·con·fig·ure /,rēkən'figyər/ ▶ **verb** configure something differently.
– DERIVATIVES **re·con·fig·u·ra·tion** /,rēkən,figyə'rāsHən/ noun.

re·con·nais·sance /ri'känəzəns, -səns/ ▶ **noun** military observation of an area carried out to locate an enemy or gain information.
– ORIGIN French.

re·con·nect /,rēkə'nekt/ ▶ **verb** connect someone or something again.
– DERIVATIVES **re·con·nec·tion** /,rēkə'neksHən/ noun.

re·con·noi·ter /,rēkə'noitər, ,rek-/ (Brit. **reconnoitre**) ▶ **verb** make a military observation of an area.

– SYNONYMS **survey,** explore, scout (out), find out the lay of the land, investigate, examine, scrutinize, inspect, observe, take a look at, patrol; informal check out.

▶ **noun** an act of reconnoitering an area.
– ORIGIN former French.

re·con·sid·er /ˌrēkən'sidər/ ▸ **verb** consider something again, with a view to changing a decision that has been made.

– SYNONYMS **rethink,** review, revise, re-evaluate, reassess, have second thoughts, change one's mind.

– DERIVATIVES **re·con·sid·er·a·tion** /ˌrēkənˌsidə'rāsʜən/ noun.

re·con·sti·tute /rē'känstəˌt(y)o͞ot/ ▸ **verb 1** change the form and organization of an institution. **2** restore dried food to its original state by adding water. **3** reconstruct something.

– DERIVATIVES **re·con·sti·tu·tion** /ˌrēˌkänstə't(y)o͞osʜən/ noun.

re·con·struct /ˌrēkən'strəkt/ ▸ **verb 1** construct something again. **2** re-enact or form an impression of a past event from the evidence available.

– SYNONYMS **rebuild,** remake, recreate, restore, reassemble, remodel, revamp, renovate.

– DERIVATIVES **re·con·struc·tion** /ˌrēkən'strəksʜən/ noun **re·con·struc·tive** /-tiv/ adjective.

re·con·vene /ˌrēkən'vēn/ ▸ **verb** come or bring together again for a meeting or activity.

re·con·vert /ˌrēkən'vərt/ ▸ **verb** change something back to a former state.

– DERIVATIVES **re·con·ver·sion** /-'vərzʜən/ noun.

rec·ord ▸ **noun** /'rekərd/ **1** a piece of evidence or information forming a permanent account of something that has happened, been said, etc. **2** a thin plastic disk carrying recorded sound in grooves on each surface, for reproduction by a record player. **3** the previous behavior or performance of a person or thing: *the team preserved their unbeaten home record.* **4** the best performance or most remarkable event of its kind that has been officially recognized. **5** (also **criminal record**) a list of a person's previous criminal convictions.

– SYNONYMS **1 account,** document, data, file, dossier, evidence, report, annals, archive, chronicle, minutes, transactions, proceedings, transcript, certificate, deed, register, log. **2** recording, album, LP, single.

▸ **verb** /ri'kôrd/ **1** put in writing or some other permanent form for later reference: *they were asked to keep a diary and record everything they ate or drank.* **2** convert sound, a broadcast, etc., into permanent form to be reproduced later.

– SYNONYMS **1 write down,** take down, note, jot down, put down on paper, document, enter, log, register. **2 indicate,** register, show, display. **3 film,** photograph, tape, tape-record, video-record, videotape.

– DERIVATIVES **re·cord·a·ble** /rə'kôrdəbəl, rē-/ adjective **re·cord·ist** /ri'kôrdist/ noun.

– PHRASES **for the record** so that the true facts are recorded or known. **on record** officially measured and noted. **on** (or **off**) **the record** made (or not made) as an official statement. **put** (or **set**) **the record straight** correct a mistaken belief.

– ORIGIN Latin *recordari* 'remember.'

rec·ord-break·ing ▸ **adjective** beating a record or best-ever achievement.

– DERIVATIVES **rec·ord-break·er** noun.

re·cord·er /ri'kôrdər/ ▸ **noun 1** a device for recording sound, pictures, or data. **2** a person who keeps records. **3** a simple woodwind instrument without keys, played by blowing air through a shaped mouthpiece.

re·cord·ing /ri'kôrdiɴɢ/ ▸ **noun 1** a piece of music or film that has been recorded. **2** the process of recording something.

rec·ord play·er ▸ **noun** a device for playing records, with a turntable and a stylus that picks up sound from the groove.

re·count[1] /ri'kount/ ▸ **verb** tell someone about an event or experience.

– SYNONYMS **tell,** relate, narrate, describe, report, relay, convey, communicate, impart.

– ORIGIN Old French *reconter* 'tell again.'

re·count[2] ▸ **verb** /rē'kount, 'rē-/ count something again. ▸ **noun** /'rēˌkount/ an act of counting something again.

re·coup /ri'ko͞op/ ▸ **verb** get back an amount of money that has been spent or lost.

– DERIVATIVES **re·coup·a·ble** adjective **re·coup·ment** noun.

– ORIGIN French *recouper* 'retrench, cut back.'

re·course /'rēˌkôrs, ri'kôrs/ ▸ **noun 1** a source of help in a difficult situation. **2** (**recourse to**) the use of someone or something as a source of help.

– SYNONYMS **1** *surgery may be the only recourse* **option,** possibility, alternative, resort, way out, hope, remedy, choice, expedient. **2** *we had recourse to the national committee for additional funding* **resort to,** make use of, avail oneself of, turn to, call on, look to, fall back on.

– ORIGIN Latin *recursus.*

re·cov·er /ri'kəvər/ ▸ **verb 1** return to a normal state of health, mind, or strength. **2** find or regain possession or control of: *he recovered his balance.* **3** regain or secure money by legal means or the making of profits. **4** remove or extract a substance from waste material for recycling or reuse.

– SYNONYMS **1 get better,** improve, rally, recuperate, convalesce, revive, be on the mend, get back on one's feet, pick up, heal, bounce back, pull through. **2 retrieve,** regain, get back, recoup, reclaim, repossess, recapture. **3 salvage,** save, rescue, retrieve.
– ANTONYMS deteriorate.

– DERIVATIVES **re·cov·er·a·ble** /ri'kəvərəbəl/ adjective.

– ORIGIN Old French *recoverer*, from Latin *recuperare* 'get again.'

re-cov·er /rē 'kəvər, 'rē-/ ▸ **verb** put a new cover or covering on something.

re·cov·er·y /ri'kəvərē/ ▸ **noun** (pl. **recoveries**) an act or the process of recovering.

– SYNONYMS **1 improvement,** recuperation, convalescence, rally, revival. **2 retrieval,** repossession, reclamation, recapture.
– ANTONYMS relapse.

re·cov·er·y po·si·tion ▸ **noun** Brit. a position used to prevent an unconscious person from choking, the body being placed face downward and slightly to the side, supported by the bent limbs.

rec·re·ant /'rekrēənt/ old use ▸ **adjective 1** cowardly. **2** disloyal. ▸ **noun** a recreant person.

– ORIGIN Old French, 'surrendering.'

re·cre·ate /ˌrēkrē'āt/ ▸ **verb** make or do something again.

rec·re·a·tion[1] /ˌrekrē'āsʜən/ ▸ **noun** enjoyable leisure activity.

– SYNONYMS **1 pleasure,** leisure, relaxation, fun, enjoyment, entertainment, amusement, diversion.

2 **pastime**, hobby, leisure activity.
– ANTONYMS work.

– DERIVATIVES **rec·re·a·tion·al** adjective.
– ORIGIN Latin, from *recreare* 'create again.'

rec·re·a·tion[2] /ˌrēkrēˈāsʜən/ ▶ **noun** the action of recreating something.

re·crim·i·na·tion /riˌkriməˈnāsʜən/ ▶ **noun** (usu. **recriminations**) an accusation made in response to one from someone else.
– ORIGIN Latin, from *recriminari* 'accuse in return.'

re·cru·des·cence /ˌrēkroo͞ˈdesns/ ▶ **verb** formal a renewed outbreak or occurrence of something.
– DERIVATIVES **re·cru·des·cent** adjective.
– ORIGIN from Latin *recrudescere* 'become raw again.'

re·cruit /riˈkroo͞t/ ▶ **verb 1** enlist someone in the armed forces. **2** enroll someone as a member or worker in an organization. **3** informal persuade someone to do or help with something.

– SYNONYMS **1 enlist**, draft, call up, conscript. **2 muster**, form, raise, mobilize. **3 hire**, employ, take on, enroll, sign up, engage.
– ANTONYMS demobilize.

▶ **noun** a newly recruited person.

– SYNONYMS **1 conscript**, draftee; informal yardbird. **2 newcomer**, trainee, initiate, joiner, beginner, novice; informal rookie, newbie.

– DERIVATIVES **re·cruit·er** noun **re·cruit·ment** noun.
– ORIGIN former French *recrute*.

rec·tal /ˈrektəl/ ▶ **adjective** relating to the rectum.
– DERIVATIVES **rec·tal·ly** adverb.

rec·tan·gle /ˈrekˌtaɴɢgəl/ ▶ **noun** a plane figure with four straight sides and four right angles.
– DERIVATIVES **rec·tan·gu·lar** /rekˈtaɴɢgyələr/ adjective.
– ORIGIN Latin *rectangulum*, from *rectus* 'straight' + *angulus* 'an angle.'

rec·ti·fi·er /ˈrektəˌfīər/ ▶ **noun** an electrical device converting an alternating current into a direct one by allowing it to flow in one direction only.

rec·ti·fy /ˈrektəˌfī/ ▶ **verb** (**rectifies**, **rectifying**, **rectified**) **1** put something right. **2** convert alternating current to direct current.

– SYNONYMS **correct**, (put) right, sort out, deal with, amend, remedy, repair, fix, make good, resolve, settle; informal patch up.

– DERIVATIVES **rec·ti·fi·a·ble** adjective **rec·ti·fi·ca·tion** /ˌrektəfiˈkāsʜən/ noun.
– ORIGIN Latin *rectificare*, from *rectus* 'right.'

rec·ti·lin·e·ar /ˌrektəˈlinēər/ ▶ **adjective** contained by, consisting of, or moving in a straight line or lines.
– ORIGIN from Latin *rectus* 'straight' + *linea* 'line.'

rec·ti·tude /ˈrektəˌt(y)oo͞d/ ▶ **noun** morally correct behavior.
– ORIGIN Old French, from Latin *rectus* 'right.'

rec·to /ˈrektō/ ▶ **noun** (pl. **rectos**) a right-hand page of an open book, or the front of a loose document. Contrasted with **VERSO**.
– ORIGIN Latin, 'on the right.'

rec·tor /ˈrektər/ ▶ **noun 1** (in an Anglican Church) a member of the clergy in charge of a parish. **2** (in the Roman Catholic Church) a priest in charge of a church or a religious institution. **3** the head of certain universities, colleges, and schools.
– DERIVATIVES **rec·to·ri·al** /rekˈtôrēəl/ adjective **rec·tor·ship** /-ˌsʜip/ noun.
– ORIGIN Latin, 'ruler.'

rec·to·ry /ˈrektərē/ ▶ **noun** (pl. **rectories**) a rector's house.

rec·tum /ˈrektəm/ ▶ **noun** (pl. **rectums** or **recta** /-tə/) the final section of the large intestine, ending at the anus.
– ORIGIN from Latin *rectum intestinum* 'straight intestine.'

re·cum·bent /riˈkəmbənt/ ▶ **adjective 1** lying down. **2** (of a plant) growing close to the ground.
– DERIVATIVES **re·cum·ben·cy** noun.
– ORIGIN from Latin *recumbere* 'recline.'

re·cu·per·ate /riˈkoo͞pəˌrāt/ ▶ **verb 1** recover from illness or physical exertion. **2** regain something lost.

– SYNONYMS **1 get better**, recover, convalesce, get well, regain one's strength/health, get over something. **2** *he recuperated the money* **get back**, regain, recover, recoup, retrieve, reclaim, repossess, redeem.

– DERIVATIVES **re·cu·per·a·tion** /riˌkoo͞pəˈrāsʜən/ noun **re·cu·per·a·tive** /riˈkoo͞pəˌrātiv/ adjective.
– ORIGIN Latin *recuperare* 'regain.'

re·cur /riˈkər/ ▶ **verb** (**recurs**, **recurring**, **recurred**) **1** happen again or repeatedly. **2** (of a thought, image, etc.) come back to one's mind.

– SYNONYMS **happen again**, reoccur, repeat (itself), come back, return, reappear.

– DERIVATIVES **re·cur·rence** /riˈkərəns, -ˈkə-rəns/ noun.
– ORIGIN Latin *recurrere*, from *currere* 'run.'

re·cur·rent /riˈkərənt, -ˈkə-rənt/ ▶ **adjective** happening often or repeatedly.
– DERIVATIVES **re·cur·rent·ly** adverb.

WORD TOOLKIT

recurrent ...	repeated ...	intermittent ...
theme	attempts	rain
dream	calls	treatment
nightmare	use	periods
role	warnings	fever
motif	exposure	symptoms
images	appeals	electricity
injury	assurances	flashes

re·cur·sion /riˈkərʒʜən/ ▶ **noun** chiefly Mathematics & Linguistics the repeated application of a procedure or rule to successive results of the process.
– DERIVATIVES **re·cur·sive** /riˈkərsiv/ adjective.

re·cuse /riˈkyoo͞z/ ▶ **verb** (**recuse oneself**) (of a judge) excuse oneself from a case because of a possible lack of impartiality.

re·cy·cle /rēˈsīkəl/ ▶ **verb 1** convert waste into reusable material. **2** use something again.

– SYNONYMS **reuse**, reprocess, reclaim, recover, salvage.

– DERIVATIVES **re·cy·cla·ble** /rēˈsīk(ə)ləbəl/adjective & noun **re·cy·cler** /-k(ə)lər/ noun.

red /red/ ▶ **adjective** (**redder**, **reddest**) **1** of the color of blood, fire, or rubies. **2** (of a person's face) red due to embarrassment, anger, or heat. **3** (of hair or fur) of a reddish-brown color. **4** (of wine) made from dark grapes and colored by their skins. **5** informal, chiefly derogatory communist or socialist.

– SYNONYMS **1 scarlet**, vermilion, ruby, cherry, cerise, cardinal, carmine, crimson, maroon, magenta, burgundy, claret. **2 flushed**, blushing, pink, rosy, florid, ruddy. **3** auburn, Titian, chestnut, carroty, ginger.

▶ **noun 1** red color or material. **2** informal, chiefly derogatory a communist or socialist.
– DERIVATIVES **red·dish** adjective **red·dy** adjective **red·ly** adverb **red·ness** noun.
– PHRASES **in the red** having spent more than is in one's bank account. **the red planet** Mars. **see red** informal suddenly become very angry.
– ORIGIN Old English.

re·dact /ri'dakt/ ▶ **verb** edit something for publication.
– DERIVATIVES **re·dac·tion** /ri'daksHən/ noun **re·dac·tor** noun.
– ORIGIN Latin *redigere* 'bring back.'

red blood cell ▶ **noun** less technical term for **ERYTHROCYTE**.

red-blood·ed ▶ **adjective** (of a man) full of strength and energy; virile.

red-brick ▶ **adjective** chiefly Brit. (of a British university) founded in the late 19th or early 20th century and often with buildings of red brick rather than stone, so being distinct from the older universities.

red·cap /'red,kap/ ▶ **noun 1** a railroad porter. **2** Brit. informal a member of the military police.

red card ▶ **noun** (especially in soccer) a red card shown by the referee to a player being sent off the field.

red car·pet ▶ **noun** a long, narrow red carpet for an important visitor to walk along.

red cell ▶ **noun** less technical term for **ERYTHROCYTE**.

red·coat /'red,kōt/ ▶ **noun** historical a British soldier.

Red Cres·cent ▶ **noun** a national branch in Muslim countries of the International Movement of the Red Cross and the Red Crescent.

Red Cross ▶ **noun** the International Movement of the Red Cross and the Red Crescent, an organization bringing relief to victims of war or natural disaster.

red deer ▶ **noun** a deer with a rich red-brown summer coat that turns brownish-gray in winter, the male having large antlers.

red·den /'redn/ ▶ **verb 1** make or become red. **2** blush.

red dwarf ▶ **noun** Astronomy a small, old, relatively cool star.

re·dec·o·rate /rē'dekə,rāt/ ▶ **verb** decorate something again or differently.
– DERIVATIVES **re·dec·o·ra·tion** /,rē,dekə'rāsHən/ noun.

re·deem /ri'dēm/ ▶ **verb 1** make up for the faults or bad aspects of: *a poor debate redeemed by an outstanding speech*. **2** (**redeem oneself**) make up for one's poor performance or behavior in the past. **3** save someone from sin, error, or evil. **4** repay or clear a debt: *owners were unable to redeem their mortgages*. **5** exchange a coupon for goods or money. **6** gain or regain possession of something in exchange for payment. **7** fulfill a pledge or promise.

– SYNONYMS **1 save,** deliver from sin, absolve. **2 retrieve,** regain, recover, get back, reclaim, repossess, buy back. **3 exchange,** convert, trade in, cash in.

– DERIVATIVES **re·deem·a·ble** adjective.
– ORIGIN Latin *redimere* 'buy back.'

re·deem·er /ri'dēmər/ ▶ **noun 1** a person who redeems someone or something. **2** (**the Redeemer**) Jesus.

re·de·fine /,rēdi'fīn/ ▶ **verb** define something again or differently.
– DERIVATIVES **re·def·i·ni·tion** /,rē,defə'nisHən/ noun.

re·demp·tion /ri'dempsHən/ ▶ **noun 1** the action of redeeming or the process of being redeemed. **2** a thing that saves someone from error or evil.
– DERIVATIVES **re·demp·tive** /ri'demptiv/ adjective.

re·de·ploy /,rēdə'ploi/ ▶ **verb** move troops, employees, or resources to a new place or task.
– DERIVATIVES **re·de·ploy·ment** noun.

re·de·sign /,rēdi'zīn/ ▶ **verb** design something again or differently. ▶ **noun** the action or process of redesigning.

re·de·vel·op /,rēdi'veləp/ ▶ **verb 1** develop something again or differently. **2** construct new buildings in an area, especially after demolishing the existing buildings.
– DERIVATIVES **re·de·vel·op·er** noun **re·de·vel·op·ment** noun.

red-faced ▶ **adjective** embarrassed or ashamed.

red flag ▶ **noun 1** a warning of danger. **2** the symbol of socialist revolution.

red gi·ant ▶ **noun** a very large luminous star with a low surface temperature.

red-hand·ed ▶ **adjective** in or just after the act of doing something wrong.

– SYNONYMS **in the act,** in flagrante delicto; informal with one's hand in the cookie jar.

red·head /'red,hed/ ▶ **noun** a person, especially a woman, with red hair.
– DERIVATIVES **red-head·ed** adjective.

red heat ▶ **noun** the temperature or state of something so hot that it gives off red light.

red her·ring ▶ **noun** a clue or piece of information that is misleading or distracting.
– ORIGIN so named from the practice of using the scent of a dried smoked herring in training hounds.

red-hot ▶ **adjective 1** so hot as to glow red. **2** extremely exciting or of great interest. **3** very passionate.

red-hot pok·er ▶ **noun** a plant with tall erect spikes of tubular flowers, the upper ones of which are red and the lower ones yellow.

re·di·al /rē'dīl/ ▶ **verb** (**redials, redialing, redialed**) dial a telephone number again.

re·did /rē'did/ past of **REDO**.

red ink ▶ **noun** used in reference to financial deficit or debt: *a project that has left the state awash in red ink*.

re·di·rect /,rēdə'rekt, -,dī-/ ▶ **verb** direct something to a new or different place or purpose.
– DERIVATIVES **re·di·rec·tion** /-'reksHən/ noun.

re·dis·cov·er /,rēdis'kəvər/ ▶ **verb** discover something forgotten or ignored again.
– DERIVATIVES **re·dis·cov·er·y** noun.

re·dis·tri·bute /,rēdə'strib,yōōt/ ▶ **verb** distribute something again or in a different way.
– DERIVATIVES **re·dis·tri·bu·tion** /,rē,distrə'byōōsHən/ noun **re·dis·trib·u·tive** /-'stribyətiv/ adjective.

red-let·ter day ▶ **noun** an important or memorable day.
– ORIGIN from the practice of highlighting a festival in red on a calendar.

red light ▶ **noun** a red light instructing moving vehicles to stop.

red-light dis·trict ▶ noun an area with many brothels, strip clubs, etc.
– ORIGIN from the use of a red light as the sign of a brothel.

red·line /ˈred,līn/ ▶ verb informal **1** drive with a car's engine at its maximum rpm. **2** refuse a loan or insurance to someone because they live in an area considered to be a bad financial risk.
– ORIGIN from the use of *red* as a limit marker, in sense 2 a limit marked out by ringing part of a map.

red meat ▶ noun meat that is red when raw, e.g., beef or lamb.

red mul·let ▶ noun a food fish with long, thin growths (barbels) on the chin, living in warmer seas.

red·neck /ˈred,nek/ ▶ noun informal, derogatory a working-class white person from the southern US, especially one with politically conservative views.

re·do /rēˈdo͞o/ ▶ verb (**redoes** /rēˈdəz/, **redoing** /rēˈdo͞oiNG/; past **redid** /rēˈdid/; past part. **redone** /rēˈdən/) do something again or differently.

red·o·lent /ˈredl-ənt/ ▶ adjective **1** (**redolent of/with**) strongly suggesting or making one think of something: *names redolent of history and tradition.* **2** (**redolent of/with**) literary strongly smelling of something. **3** old use or literary fragrant.

– SYNONYMS **evocative,** suggestive, reminiscent.

– DERIVATIVES **red·o·lence** noun.
– ORIGIN from Latin *redolere* 'give out a strong smell.'

re·dou·ble /rēˈdəbəl/ ▶ verb make or become greater, more intense, or more numerous: *we will redouble our efforts.*

re·doubt /riˈdout/ ▶ noun a temporary or additional fortification.
– ORIGIN French *redoute.*

re·doubt·a·ble /riˈdoutəbəl/ ▶ adjective often humorous (of a person) worthy of respect or fear, especially as an opponent.
– DERIVATIVES **re·doubt·a·bly** /-blē/ adverb.
– ORIGIN from Old French *redouter* 'to fear.'

re·dound /riˈdound/ ▶ verb (**redound to**) formal contribute greatly to a person's credit or honor.
– ORIGIN Latin *redundare* 'surge.'

re·dox /ˈrē,däks/ ▶ adjective Chemistry involving the process of both oxidation and reduction.
– ORIGIN blend.

red pep·per ▶ noun a ripe sweet pepper, red in color and eaten as a vegetable.

re·draft /rēˈdraft/ ▶ verb draft a document again in a different way.

re·draw /rēˈdrô/ ▶ verb (past **redrew** /rēˈdro͞o/; past part. **redrawn** /rēˈdrôn/) draw or draw up again or in a different way: *strategists will have to redraw their plans.*

re·dress /riˈdres, ˈrē,dres/ ▶ verb put an undesirable or unfair situation right.

– SYNONYMS **rectify,** correct, right, compensate for, make amends for, remedy, make good.

▶ noun compensation for a grievance or an unjust act: *redress for victims of discrimination.*

– SYNONYMS **compensation,** reparation, restitution, recompense, repayment, amends.

– PHRASES **redress the balance** restore equality in a situation.
– ORIGIN Old French *redresser.*

red salm·on ▶ noun the sockeye salmon.

red snap·per ▶ noun a reddish edible marine fish.

red squir·rel ▶ noun a small squirrel with a reddish coat.

red·start /ˈred,stärt/ ▶ noun a small songbird of the warbler family.
– ORIGIN from **RED** + **START** in the former sense 'tail.'

red tape ▶ noun time-consuming or complicated official rules and procedures.
– ORIGIN so named because of the red or pink tape used to tie up official documents.

re·duce /riˈd(y)o͞os/ ▶ verb **1** make or become smaller or less in amount, degree, or size. **2** (**reduce someone/thing to**) bring someone or something to a particular state or action: *she had been reduced to near poverty.* **3** (**reduce something to**) change something to a simpler or more basic form. **4** boil a sauce or other liquid so that it becomes thicker and more concentrated. **5** Chemistry cause a substance to combine chemically with hydrogen. **6** Chemistry cause a substance to undergo a reaction in which electrons are gained from another substance or molecule. The opposite of **OXIDIZE.**

– SYNONYMS **1 lessen,** make smaller, lower, decrease, diminish, minimize, shrink, narrow, cut, curtail, contract, shorten, downsize; informal chop. **2 bring down,** make cheaper, lower, mark down, slash, discount. **3** *he* ***reduced*** *her* ***to*** *tears* **bring to,** bring to the point of, drive to.
– ANTONYMS increase.

– DERIVATIVES **re·duc·er** noun **re·duc·i·ble** adjective.
– PHRASES **reduced circumstances** a state of poverty after one has been relatively wealthy. **reduce someone to the ranks** demote a non-commissioned officer to an ordinary soldier.
– ORIGIN Latin *reducere* 'bring or lead back.'

re·duc·ti·o ad ab·sur·dum /rəˈdəktē,ō ,ad əbˈsərdəm, -ˈdəksHē,ō/ ▶ noun a method of proving that an argument or theory is false by showing that its logical consequence is absurd or contradictory.
– ORIGIN Latin, 'reduction to the absurd.'

re·duc·tion /riˈdəksHən/ ▶ noun **1** the action of reducing something. **2** the amount by which something is reduced. **3** a smaller copy of a picture or photograph. **4** a thick and concentrated liquid or sauce.

– SYNONYMS **1 lessening,** lowering, decrease, diminution, cut, cutback, downsizing. **2 discount,** deduction, cut.

re·duc·tion·ism /riˈdəksHə,nizəm/ ▶ noun often derogatory the analysis or explanation of something complex in terms of its simplest or most basic elements.
– DERIVATIVES **re·duc·tion·ist** noun & adjective.

re·duc·tive /riˈdəktiv/ ▶ adjective **1** often derogatory tending to present a subject or problem in an oversimplified form. **2** relating to chemical reduction.
– DERIVATIVES **re·duc·tive·ly** adverb **re·duc·tive·ness** noun.

re·dun·dant /riˈdəndənt/ ▶ adjective **1** not or no longer needed or useful: *many of the old skills had become redundant.* **2** Brit. (of a person) no longer employed because there is no more work available.

– SYNONYMS **unnecessary,** not required, unneeded, superfluous.

– DERIVATIVES **re·dun·dan·cy** noun (pl. **redundancies**) **re·dun·dant·ly** adverb.

– ORIGIN first meaning 'abundant'; from Latin *redundare* 'surge.'

re·du·pli·cate /ri'd(y)o͞opli,kāt, 'rē-/ ▸ **verb** repeat or copy something so as to form another of the same kind.
– DERIVATIVES **re·du·pli·ca·tion** /ri,d(y)o͞opli'kāsʜən, ,rē-/ noun.

re·dux /rē'dəks, 'rē'dəks/ ▸ **adjective** (after a noun) revived or restored.
– ORIGIN Latin, from *reducere* 'bring back.'

red·wing /'red,wiɴɢ/ ▸ **noun** a small thrush of northern Europe, having orange-red patches on its sides.

red·wood /'red,wo͝od/ ▸ **noun** a giant coniferous tree with reddish wood, native to California and Oregon.

re-ech·o ▸ **verb** echo again or repeatedly.

reed /rēd/ ▸ **noun 1** a tall, slender-leaved plant with a hollow stem, growing in water or on marshy ground. **2** a piece of thin cane or metal that vibrates in a current of air to produce the sound of various musical instruments, as in the mouthpiece of a clarinet or at the base of some organ pipes. **3** a wind instrument played with a reed.
– DERIVATIVES **reed·ed** adjective.
– ORIGIN Old English.

re-e·dit ▸ **verb** edit something again.

reed or·gan ▸ **noun** a keyboard instrument similar to a harmonium, in which air is drawn upward past metal reeds.

re-ed·u·cat·e ▸ **verb** educate or train someone to behave or think differently.
– DERIVATIVES **re-ed·u·ca·tion** noun.

reed·y /'rēdē/ ▸ **adjective** (**reedier, reediest**) **1** (of a sound or voice) high and thin in tone. **2** full of or edged with reeds. **3** (of a person) tall and thin.

reef /rēf/ ▸ **noun 1** a ridge of jagged rock or coral just above or below the surface of the sea. **2** a vein of gold or other ore. **3** each of several strips across a sail that can be taken in or rolled up to reduce the area exposed to the wind. ▸ **verb** take in one or more reefs of a sail.
– ORIGIN Old Norse, 'rib.'

reef·er /'rēfər/ ▸ **noun** informal a marijuana cigarette.
– ORIGIN perhaps related to Mexican Spanish *grifo* 'smoker of marijuana.'

reek /rēk/ ▸ **verb 1** have a very unpleasant smell. **2** (**reek of**) suggest something unpleasant or undesirable: *the whole thing reeks of hypocrisy.* ▸ **noun** a very unpleasant smell.
– ORIGIN Old English.

reel /rēl/ ▸ **noun 1** a cylinder on which film, wire, thread, etc., can be wound. **2** a part of a movie. **3** a lively Scottish folk dance. ▸ **verb 1** (**reel something in**) bring something toward one by turning a reel. **2** (**reel something off**) say or recite something rapidly and with ease. **3** stagger or lurch violently. **4** feel shocked or bewildered: *workers are still reeling at the news that the factory is to close.*

> – SYNONYMS **1 stagger,** lurch, sway, rock, stumble, totter, wobble, teeter. **2 go round (and around/round),** whirl, spin, revolve, swirl, twirl, turn, swim.

– ORIGIN Old English.

re-e·lect ▸ **verb** elect someone to a further term of office.
– DERIVATIVES **re-e·lec·tion** noun.

reel-to-reel ▸ **adjective** (of a tape recorder) in which the tape passes between two reels mounted separately rather than within a cassette.

re-e·merge ▸ **verb** emerge again; begin to exist or become prominent once more.
– DERIVATIVES **re-e·mer·gence** noun **re-e·mer·gent** adjective.

re-em·pha·size ▸ **verb** emphasize something again.
– DERIVATIVES **re-em·pha·sis** noun.

re-en·act ▸ **verb 1** act out a past event. **2** bring a law into effect again when the original statute has been repealed or has expired.
– DERIVATIVES **re-en·act·ment** noun.

re-en·gin·eer ▸ **verb 1** redesign a machine. **2** restructure a company or its operations.

re-en·list /,rē-ən'list/ ▸ **verb** enlist again in the armed forces.
– DERIVATIVES **re-en·list·er** noun.

re-en·ter ▸ **verb** enter again: *women who wish to re-enter the labor market.*
– DERIVATIVES **re-en·trance** noun.

re-entrant ▸ **adjective** (of an angle) pointing inward. The opposite of **SALIENT**.

re-en·try /rē 'entrē/ ▸ **noun** (pl. **re-entries**) **1** the action or process of re-entering. **2** the return of a spacecraft or missile into the earth's atmosphere.

reeve[1] /rēv/ ▸ **noun** historical a local official, in particular the chief magistrate of a town or district in Anglo-Saxon England.
– ORIGIN Old English.

reeve[2] ▸ **noun** a female ruff (bird).
– ORIGIN unknown.

re-ex·am·ine ▸ **verb 1** examine something again or further. **2** Law examine one's own witness again, after cross-examination by the opposing counsel.
– DERIVATIVES **re-ex·am·i·na·tion** noun.

re-export /rē'ek,spôrt, rē-ek'spôrt/ ▸ **verb** export imported goods, typically after further processing or manufacture. ▸ **noun** the action of re-exporting goods.

ref /ref/ ▸ **noun** informal (in sports) a referee.

ref. ▸ **abbreviation 1** reference. **2** refer to.

re·face /rē'fās/ ▸ **verb** put a new facing on a building.

re·fec·tion /ri'feksʜən/ ▸ **noun** literary or old use **1** the process of refreshing oneself by eating or drinking. **2** a light meal.
– ORIGIN Latin, from *reficere* 'refresh, renew.'

re·fec·to·ry /ri'fekt(ə)rē/ ▸ **noun** (pl. **refectories**) a large room in an educational or religious institution in which people eat meals together.

re·fer /ri'fər/ ▸ **verb** (**refers, referring, referred**) **1** (**refer to**) write or speak about; mention. **2** (**refer to**) (of a word or phrase) describe someone or something. **3** (**refer to**) consult a source of information. **4** (**refer someone/thing to**) pass a person or matter to an authority or specialist for a decision. **5** (**refer someone to**) direct the attention of someone to something.

> – SYNONYMS **1** (**refer to**) *he referred to errors in the article* **mention,** allude to, touch on, speak of/about, talk of/about, write about, comment on, point out, call attention to. **2** (**refer to**) *the name refers to a native village* **denote,** describe, indicate, mean, signify, designate. **3** (**refer to**) *the doctor referred to his notes* **consult,** turn to, look at, have recourse to. **4** (**refer someone/thing to**) *the matter has been referred to my insurers* **pass,** direct, hand on/over, send on, transfer, entrust, assign.

– DERIVATIVES **ref·er·a·ble** /ˈref(ə)rəbəl, riˈfər-/ adjective **re·fer·rer** noun.
– ORIGIN Latin *referre* 'carry back.'

ref·er·ee /ˌrefəˈrē/ ▸ **noun 1** an official who supervises a game or match to ensure that players keep to the rules. **2** a person appointed to examine and assess an academic work submitted for publication.

– SYNONYMS **umpire,** judge, adjudicator, arbitrator; informal ref.

▸ **verb** (**referees, refereeing, refereed**) act as referee of something.

ref·er·ence /ˈref(ə)rəns/ ▸ **noun 1** the action of referring to something. **2** a note in a book or article giving the source of a particular piece of information. **3** a letter from a previous employer giving information about someone's ability or reliability, used when applying for a new job. **4** a person providing such a letter.

– SYNONYMS **1 mention,** allusion, quotation, comment, remark. **2 source,** citation, authority, credit. **3 testimonial,** recommendation, character reference, credentials.

▸ **verb 1** provide a book or article with references. **2** mention or refer to someone or something.
– PHRASES **with** (or **in**) **reference to** in relation to.

ref·er·ence li·brar·y ▸ **noun** a library in which the books are to be consulted in the building rather than borrowed.

ref·er·ence point ▸ **noun** a basis or standard for assessment or comparison.

ref·er·en·dum /ˌrefəˈrendəm/ ▸ **noun** (pl. **referendums** or **referenda** /-də/) a general vote by a country's electorate on a single political question that has been referred to them for a direct decision.

– SYNONYMS **(popular) vote,** ballot, poll, plebiscite.

– ORIGIN Latin, 'something to be referred.'

ref·er·ent /ˈref(ə)rənt/ ▸ **noun** Linguistics the thing that a word or phrase refers to or stands for.

ref·er·en·tial /ˌrefəˈrenCHəl/ ▸ **adjective** containing or taking the form of a reference or references.

re·fer·ral /riˈfərəl/ ▸ **noun** the action of referring someone or something to a specialist or higher authority.

re·ferred pain ▸ **noun** pain felt in a part of the body other than its actual source.

re·fi /rēˈfī/ ▸ **verb** (**refies, refied, refying**) refinance (a mortgage). ▸ **adjective** relating to refinancing and the refinancing market: *the refi boom is over.*
– ORIGIN shortening.

re·fill ▸ **verb** /rēˈfil/ fill a container again. ▸ **noun** /ˈrēˌfil/ an act of refilling a container, or a glass that is refilled.
– DERIVATIVES **re·fill·a·ble** adjective.

re·fi·nance /ˌrēfəˈnans, rēˈfīˌnans/ ▸ **verb** finance something again, typically with new loans at a lower rate of interest.

re·fine /riˈfīn/ ▸ **verb 1** remove impurities or unwanted elements from something. **2** make minor changes to something so as to improve it: *he gradually refined his technique.*

– SYNONYMS **1 purify,** filter, distill, process, treat. **2 improve,** perfect, polish (up), hone, fine-tune.

– DERIVATIVES **re·fin·er** noun.

re·fined /riˈfīnd/ ▸ **adjective 1** with impurities or unwanted elements having been removed by processing. **2** well educated, polite, and having good taste and manners.

– SYNONYMS **1 purified,** processed, treated. **2 cultivated,** cultured, polished, elegant, sophisticated, urbane, polite, gracious, well bred. **3 discriminating,** discerning, fastidious, exquisite, impeccable, fine.
– ANTONYMS crude, coarse.

re·fine·ment /riˈfīnmənt/ ▸ **noun 1** the process of refining. **2** an improvement brought about by the making of small changes. **3** the quality of being well educated, polite, and having good taste and manners.

re·fin·er·y /riˈfīnərē/ ▸ **noun** (pl. **refineries**) an industrial establishment where a substance is refined.

re·fin·ish /rēˈfiniSH/ ▸ **verb** apply a new finish to a surface or object.

re·fit /rēˈfit/ ▸ **verb** (**refits, refitting, refitted**) replace or repair machinery, equipment, and fittings in a ship, building, etc. ▸ **noun** an act of refitting something.

re·flate /riˈflāt/ ▸ **verb** (of a government) increase an economy's level of output.
– DERIVATIVES **re·fla·tion** /riˈflāSHən/ noun **re·fla·tion·ar·y** /riˈflāSHəˌnerē/ noun.

re·flect /riˈflekt/ ▸ **verb 1** throw back heat, light, or sound without absorbing it. **2** (of a mirror or shiny surface) show an image of: *he could see himself reflected in Keith's glasses.* **3** represent in a realistic or appropriate way: *the letters reflect all aspects of his life.* **4** (**reflect well/badly on**) bring about a good or bad impression of someone or something. **5** (**reflect on**) think deeply or carefully about.

– SYNONYMS **1 mirror,** send back, throw back, echo. **2 indicate,** show, display, demonstrate, be evidence of, evince, reveal, betray. **3 think,** consider, review, mull over, ponder, contemplate, deliberate, ruminate, meditate, muse, brood; formal cogitate.

– ORIGIN Latin *reflectere* 'bend back.'

re·flect·ance /riˈflektəns/ ▸ **noun** Physics a property of a surface equal to the proportion of the light shining on it that it reflects or scatters.

re·flect·ing tel·e·scope ▸ **noun** a telescope in which a mirror is used to collect and focus light.

re·flec·tion /riˈflekSHən/ ▸ **noun 1** the phenomenon of light, heat, sound, etc., being reflected. **2** an image formed by reflection. **3** a consequence or result of something: *healthy skin is a reflection of good health.* **4** a source of shame or blame: *his behavior was no reflection on his wife.* **5** serious thought or consideration.

– SYNONYMS **1 image,** likeness. **2 indication,** display, demonstration, manifestation, expression, evidence. **3 thought,** consideration, contemplation, deliberation, pondering, rumination, meditation, musing; formal cogitation.

re·flec·tive /riˈflektiv/ ▸ **adjective 1** providing or produced by reflection. **2** thoughtful.
– DERIVATIVES **re·flec·tive·ly** adverb **re·flec·tiv·i·ty** /riˌflekˈtivətē, ˌrēˌflek-/ noun.

re·flec·tor /riˈflektər/ ▸ **noun 1** a piece of material that reflects light, e.g., a piece of red glass or plastic on the back of a motor vehicle or bicycle. **2** an object or device that reflects radio waves, sound, or other waves. **3** a reflecting telescope.

re·flex /ˈrēˌfleks/ ▸ **noun 1** an action or movement performed without conscious thought as a response to something. **2** a thing that reproduces the essential features or qualities of something else: *politics was no more than a reflex of economics.* ▸ **adjective 1** performed as a reflex. **2** (of an angle) more than 180°.
– ORIGIN Latin *reflexus* 'a bending back.'

re·flex cam·er·a ▸ **noun** a camera with a focusing screen on which the image given by the lens is reflected by an angled mirror, so that the scene viewed is the same as that photographed.

re·flex·ion /riˈflekSHən/ ▸ **noun** old-fashioned spelling of **REFLECTION**.

re·flex·ive /riˈfleksiv/ ▸ **adjective 1** Grammar (of a pronoun) referring back to the subject of the clause in which it is used, e.g., *myself*. **2** Grammar (of a verb or clause) having a reflexive pronoun as its object (e.g., *wash oneself*). **3** performed without conscious thought; reflex.
– DERIVATIVES **re·flex·ive·ly** adverb **re·flex·iv·i·ty** /riˌflekˈsivətē, ˌrēˌflek/ noun.

re·flex·ol·o·gy /ˌrēˌflekˈsäləjē/ ▸ **noun** a system of massage used to relieve tension and treat illness, based on the theory that there are points on the feet, hands, and head linked to every part of the body.
– DERIVATIVES **re·flex·ol·o·gist** noun.

re·flux /ˈrēˌfləks/ ▸ **noun 1** technical the flowing back of a liquid, especially that of a fluid in the body. **2** Chemistry the process of boiling a liquid so that any vapor is liquefied and returned to the stock of liquid.

re·fo·cus /rēˈfōkəs/ ▸ **verb** (**refocuses, refocusing, refocused** or **refocusses, refocussing, refocussed**) **1** adjust the focus of a lens or one's eyes. **2** focus attention or resources on something new or different.

re·for·est·a·tion /rēˌfôrəˈstāSHən, -ˈfärə-/ ▸ **noun** the process of planting new trees in an area of land that was formerly a forest.
– DERIVATIVES **re·for·est** /rēˈfôrəst, -ˈfärəst/ verb.

re·form /riˈfôrm/ ▸ **verb 1** make changes in something in order to improve it: *a copyright law that needs to be reformed.* **2** abandon an immoral or criminal lifestyle, or make someone do this.

– SYNONYMS **1 improve,** better, ameliorate, correct, rectify, restore, revise, refine, adapt, revamp, redesign, reconstruct, reorganize. **2 mend one's ways,** change for the better, turn over a new leaf.

▸ **noun** the action or process of reforming something: *a major reform of the tax system.*

– SYNONYMS **improvement,** amelioration, refinement, rectification, restoration, adaptation, revision, redesign, revamp, reconstruction, reorganization.

– DERIVATIVES **re·form·er** noun.
– ORIGIN Latin *reformare* 'form or shape again.'

re·for·mat /rēˈfôrˌmat/ ▸ **verb** (**reformats, reformatting, reformatted**) chiefly Computing give a new format to something.

ref·or·ma·tion /ˌrefərˈmāSHən/ ▸ **noun 1** the action or process of reforming. **2** (**the Reformation**) a 16th-century movement for the reform of the Roman Catholic Church, ending in the establishment of the Reformed and Protestant Churches.

re·form·a·to·ry /riˈfôrməˌtôrē/ ▸ **noun** (pl. **reformatories**) (especially in names) a prison: *Illinois State Reformatory.*

Re·formed Church ▸ **noun** a Church that has accepted the principles of the Reformation, especially a Calvinist Church (as distinct from a Lutheran one).

re·form·ist /riˈfôrmist/ ▸ **adjective** supporting or recommending gradual political or social reform. ▸ **noun** a person who supports or recommends such a policy.
– DERIVATIVES **re·form·ism** /-ˌmizəm/ noun.

re·form school ▸ **noun** historical an institution to which young offenders were sent as an alternative to prison.

re·for·mu·late /rēˈfôrmyəˌlāt/ ▸ **verb** formulate something again or differently.
– DERIVATIVES **re·for·mu·la·tion** /rēˌfôrmyəˈlāSHən/ noun.

re·fract /riˈfrakt/ ▸ **verb** (of water, air, or glass) make a ray of light change direction when it enters at an angle.
– ORIGIN Latin *refringere* 'break up.'

re·fract·ing tel·e·scope ▸ **noun** a telescope that uses a lens to collect and focus the light.

re·frac·tion /riˈfrakSHən/ ▸ **noun** the fact or phenomenon of light changing direction when it enters water, air, or glass at an angle.

re·frac·tive /riˈfraktiv/ ▸ **adjective** relating to or involving refraction.
– DERIVATIVES **re·frac·tive·ly** adverb.

re·frac·tive in·dex ▸ **noun** the ratio of the velocity of light in a vacuum to its velocity in a specified medium.

re·frac·tor /riˈfraktər/ ▸ **noun 1** a lens or other object that causes refraction. **2** a refracting telescope.

re·frac·to·ry /riˈfraktərē/ ▸ **adjective 1** formal stubborn or difficult to control. **2** (of a disease or medical condition) not responding to treatment. **3** technical heat-resistant; hard to melt or fuse.
– DERIVATIVES **re·frac·to·ri·ness** noun.
– ORIGIN Latin *refractarius* 'stubborn.'

re·frain[1] /riˈfrān/ ▸ **verb** (**refrain from**) stop oneself from doing something.

– SYNONYMS **abstain,** desist, hold back, stop oneself, forbear, avoid; informal swear off.

– ORIGIN Latin *refrenare*, from *frenum* 'bridle.'

re·frain[2] ▸ **noun** a repeated line or section in a poem or song, typically at the end of each verse.
– ORIGIN from Latin *refringere* 'break up' (because the refrain 'broke' the sequence).

re·fresh /riˈfresH/ ▸ **verb 1** give new strength or energy to someone. **2** revise or update skills, knowledge, or information. **3** prompt someone's memory by going over previous information.

– SYNONYMS **1 reinvigorate,** revitalize, revive, rejuvenate, restore, energize, enliven, perk up, brace, freshen, wake up, breathe new life into; informal buck up. **2** *refresh your memory* **jog,** stimulate, prompt, prod.

re·fresh·er /riˈfresHər/ ▸ **noun** a course or activity intended to update or improve one's skills or knowledge.

re·fresh·ing /riˈfresHiNG/ ▸ **adjective 1** giving new energy or strength. **2** welcome because new or different: *a refreshing change of pace.*

– SYNONYMS **1 invigorating,** revitalizing, reviving, bracing, fortifying, enlivening, stimulating, exhilarating, energizing. **2** *a refreshing change of direction* **welcome,** stimulating, fresh, new, imaginative, innovative.

– DERIVATIVES **re·fresh·ing·ly** adverb.

re·fresh·ment /ri'fresʜmənt/ ▶ **noun 1** a light snack or drink. **2** the giving of fresh strength or energy.

– SYNONYMS (**refreshments**) **food and drink,** snacks, tidbits, eatables; informal nosh, goodies, nibbles, eats, grub.

re·frig·er·ant /ri'frijərənt/ ▶ **noun** a substance used for cooling things. ▶ **adjective** causing cooling or refrigeration.

re·frig·er·ate /ri'frijə,rāt/ ▶ **verb** chill food or drink in order to preserve it.
– DERIVATIVES **re·frig·er·a·tion** /ri,frijə'rāsʜən/ noun.
– ORIGIN Latin *refrigerare* 'make cool.'

re·frig·er·a·tor /ri'frijə,rātər/ ▶ **noun** an appliance or compartment in which food and drink is stored at a low temperature.

re·fu·el /rē'fyo͞o(ə)l/ ▶ **verb** (**refuels, refueling, refueled**) supply or be supplied with more fuel.

ref·uge /'ref,yo͞oj, -,yo͞ozʜ/ ▶ **noun 1** a place or state of safety from danger or trouble: *he took refuge in the French embassy.* **2** a place that provides a temporary home for those in need of protection or shelter: *a refuge for mountain gorillas.*

– SYNONYMS **1 shelter,** protection, safety, security, asylum, sanctuary. **2 place of safety,** shelter, haven, sanctuary, sanctum, retreat, hideout, den, hiding place.

– ORIGIN Latin *refugium.*

ref·u·gee /,refyo͝o'jē, 'refyo͝o,jē/ ▶ **noun** a person who has been forced to leave their country in order to escape war, persecution, or natural disaster.

– SYNONYMS *collecting blankets for the refugees* **asylum seeker,** fugitive, displaced person, exile, émigré.

re·ful·gent /ri'fo͝oljənt, -'fəl-/ ▶ **adjective** literary shining very brightly.
– DERIVATIVES **re·ful·gence** noun **re·ful·gent·ly** adverb.
– ORIGIN from Latin *refulgere* 'shine out.'

re·fund ▶ **verb** /ri'fənd, 'rē,fənd/ pay a sum of money back to someone.

– SYNONYMS **repay,** give back, return, pay back, reimburse, compensate, recompense, remunerate, indemnify.

▶ **noun** /'rē,fənd/ a repayment of a sum of money: *a full refund.*

– SYNONYMS **repayment,** reimbursement, compensation, rebate.

– DERIVATIVES **re·fund·a·ble** adjective.
– ORIGIN Latin *refundere* 'pour back.'

re·fur·bish /ri'fərbisʜ/ ▶ **verb** renovate and redecorate a building or room: *the airfield plans to refurbish its museum.*

– SYNONYMS **renovate,** recondition, rehabilitate, revamp, overhaul, restore, redecorate, upgrade, refit; informal do up.

– DERIVATIVES **re·fur·bish·ment** noun.

re·fus·al /ri'fyo͞ozəl/ ▶ **noun 1** an act of refusing to do something. **2** an expression of unwillingness to accept or grant an offer or request.

– SYNONYMS **nonacceptance,** no, rejection, rebuff; informal thumbs down.

ref·use[1] /ri'fyo͞oz/ ▶ **verb 1** state that one is unwilling to do something: *he refused their invitation.* **2** state that one is unwilling to grant or accept something offered or requested: *the city refused planning permission.* **3** (of a horse) be unwilling to jump a fence or other obstacle.

– SYNONYMS **1 decline,** turn down, say no to, reject, spurn, rebuff; informal pass up. **2 withhold,** deny; informal give thumbs down to.
– ANTONYMS accept.

– DERIVATIVES **re·fus·er** noun.
– ORIGIN Old French *refuser.*

ref·use[2] /'ref,yo͞os, -,yo͞oz/ ▶ **noun** matter thrown away as worthless.

– SYNONYMS *piles of refuse* **trash,** garbage, rubbish, waste, litter; debris, detritus; informal dreck, junk.

– ORIGIN perhaps from Old French *refusé* 'refused.'

re·fuse·nik /ri'fyo͞oznik/ ▶ **noun 1** a Jew in the former Soviet Union who was refused permission to emigrate to Israel. **2** a person who refuses to follow orders or obey the law as a protest.

re·fute /ri'fyo͞ot/ ▶ **verb 1** prove a statement, theory, or person to be wrong: *these claims have not been convincingly refuted.* **2** deny a statement or accusation: *a spokesman totally refuted the allegation of bias.*

– SYNONYMS **1 disprove,** prove wrong, rebut, explode, debunk, discredit, invalidate; informal shoot full of holes. **2 deny,** reject, repudiate, rebut, contradict.

– DERIVATIVES **re·fut·a·ble** adjective **ref·u·ta·tion** /,refyo͝o'tāsʜən/ noun.
– ORIGIN Latin *refutare* 'repel, rebut.'

USAGE

Strictly speaking, **refute** means 'prove a statement or theory to be wrong' (*attempts to refute Einstein's theory*). However, it is often now used to mean simply 'deny a statement or accusation' (*I absolutely refute the charges made against me*): although some people object to this use, it is widely accepted in standard English.

re·gain /ri'gān/ ▶ **verb 1** get something back after losing control or possession of it: *government troops regained the capital.* **2** get back to a place or position: *they regained dry land.*

– SYNONYMS **recover,** get back, win back, recoup, retrieve, repossess, take back, retake, recapture, reconquer.

re·gal /'rēgəl/ ▶ **adjective** relating to or fit for a monarch, especially in being magnificent or dignified: *his regal forebears.*

– SYNONYMS **royal,** kingly, queenly, princely, majestic.

– DERIVATIVES **re·gal·i·ty** noun **re·gal·ly** adverb.
– ORIGIN Latin *regalis.*

re·gale /ri'gāl/ ▶ **verb 1** entertain someone with conversation. **2** supply someone with generous amounts of food or drink.
– ORIGIN French *régaler.*

re·ga·li·a /ri'gālyə/ ▶ **plural noun** (treated as sing. or pl.) **1** objects such as a crown and scepter, symbolizing

royalty and used at coronations or other occasions. **2** the distinctive clothing and objects of an office, activity, or group, worn at formal occasions: *full yachting regalia*.
– ORIGIN Latin, 'royal privileges.'

re·gard /ri'gärd/ ▶ **verb 1** think of in a particular way: *he regarded London as his base*. **2** look at someone or something in a particular way. **3** old use pay attention to someone or something.

– SYNONYMS **1 consider,** look on, view, see, think of, judge, deem, estimate, assess, reckon, rate. **2 look at,** contemplate, eye, gaze at, stare at, observe, view, study, scrutinize.

▶ **noun 1** care or concern: *she rescued him without regard for herself*. **2** high opinion; respect. **3** a steady look. **4** (**regards**) best wishes.

– SYNONYMS **1 consideration,** care, concern, thought, notice, heed, attention. **2** *doctors are held in high regard* **esteem,** respect, admiration, approval, honor, estimation. **3 (fixed) look,** gaze, stare, observation, contemplation, study, scrutiny. **4** *he sends his* ***regards*** **best wishes,** greetings, respects, compliments.

– PHRASES **as regards** concerning. **in this** (or **that**) **regard** in connection with the point previously mentioned. **with** (or **in**) **regard to** as concerns.
– ORIGIN Old French *regarder* 'to watch.'

re·gard·ing /ri'gärdiNG/ ▶ **preposition** about; concerning.

– SYNONYMS **concerning,** as regards, with/in regard to, with respect to, with reference to, relating to, respecting, re, about, apropos, on the subject of, in connection with, vis-à-vis.

re·gard·less /ri'gärdləs/ ▶ **adverb** despite the current situation: *they were determined to carry on regardless*.

– SYNONYMS **anyway,** anyhow, in any case, nevertheless, nonetheless, despite everything, even so, all the same, in any event, come what may.

– PHRASES **regardless of** without care or concern for.

re·gat·ta /ri'gätə, ri'gatə/ ▶ **noun** a sporting event consisting of a series of boat or yacht races.
– ORIGIN Italian, 'a fight or contest.'

re·gen·cy /'rējənsē/ ▶ **noun** (pl. **regencies**) **1** the office or period of government by a regent. **2** (**the Regency**) the period when George, Prince of Wales, acted as regent in Britain (1811–20). ▶ **adjective** (**Regency**) relating to the neoclassical style of British architecture and furniture popular during the late 18th and early 19th centuries.

re·gen·er·ate ▶ **verb** /ri'jenə,rāt/ **1** bring new and more vigorous life to an area, industry, or institution. **2** grow new tissue. ▶ **adjective** /ri'jenərət/ reborn, especially in a spiritual sense.
– DERIVATIVES **re·gen·er·a·tion** /ri,jenə'rāsHən, ,rē-/ noun **re·gen·er·a·tive** /ri'jenərətiv, -,rātiv/ adjective **re·gen·er·a·tor** /-,rātər/ noun.

re·gent /'rējənt/ ▶ **noun** a person appointed to rule a country because the monarch is too young or unfit to rule, or is absent. ▶ **adjective** (after a noun) acting as regent: *Prince Regent*.
– ORIGIN from Latin *regere* 'to rule.'

reg·gae /'regā, 'rāgā/ ▶ **noun** a style of popular music with a strong beat, originating in Jamaica.
– ORIGIN perhaps from Jamaican English *rege-rege* 'quarrel, row.'

reg·i·cide /'rejə,sīd/ ▶ **noun 1** the killing of a king. **2** a person who kills a king.
– DERIVATIVES **reg·i·cid·al** /,rejə'sīdl/ adjective.
– ORIGIN from Latin *rex* 'king.'

re·gime /ri'zHēm, rā-/ ▶ **noun 1** a government, especially one that strictly controls a country. **2** an ordered way of doing something; a system: *our approach is to simplify the licensing regime*. **3** a regimen.

– SYNONYMS **1 government,** administration, leadership, rule, authority, control, command. **2 system,** arrangement, scheme, policy, method, course, plan, program.

– ORIGIN French.

reg·i·men /'rejəmən, 'rezH-/ ▶ **noun** a course of diet, exercise, or medical treatment that is followed to improve one's health.
– ORIGIN Latin.

reg·i·ment ▶ **noun** /'rejəmənt/ **1** a permanent unit of an army, typically divided into several smaller units. **2** a large number of people or things. ▶ **verb** /'rejə,ment/ organize according to a strict system: *every aspect of their life is strictly regimented*.
– DERIVATIVES **reg·i·men·ta·tion** /,rejəmən'tāsHən, -,men-/ noun.
– ORIGIN Latin *regimentum* 'rule.'

reg·i·men·tal /,rejə'mentl/ ▶ **adjective** relating to an army regiment. ▶ **noun** (**regimentals**) military uniform, especially that of a particular regiment.
– DERIVATIVES **reg·i·men·tal·ly** /-'mentl-ē/ adverb.

Re·gi·na /rə'jēnə/ ▶ **noun** a reigning queen (used following a name).
– ORIGIN Latin, 'queen.'

re·gion /'rējən/ ▶ **noun 1** an area of a country or the world having particular characteristics: *the equatorial regions*. **2** an administrative district of a city, state, or country. **3** a part of the body.

– SYNONYMS **district,** province, territory, division, area, section, sector, zone, belt, quarter.

– PHRASES **in the region of** approximately.
– ORIGIN Latin, 'direction, district.'

re·gion·al /'rējənl, 'rējnəl/ ▶ **adjective** relating to or typical of a region.

– SYNONYMS **1 geographical,** territorial. **2 local,** provincial, district, parochial, zonal.
– ANTONYMS national.

– DERIVATIVES **re·gion·al·ize** /'rējənl,īz, 'rējnə,līz/ verb **re·gion·al·ly** /'rējənl-ē, 'rējnəlē/ adverb.

re·gion·al·ism /'rējənl,izəm, 'rējnə-/ ▶ **noun 1** loyalty to one's own region in cultural and political terms, rather than to central government. **2** a feature of language specific to a particular region.
– DERIVATIVES **re·gion·al·ist** noun & adjective.

reg·is·ter /'rejəstər/ ▶ **noun 1** an official list or record. **2** a record of attendance, for example of students in a class. **3** the level and style of a piece of writing or speech, varying according to the situation in which it is used. **4** a particular part of the range of a voice or musical instrument. **5** a sliding device controlling a set of organ pipes, or a set of organ pipes controlled by such a device. **6** (in electronic devices) a location in a store of data.

– SYNONYMS **1 list,** roll, roster, index, directory, catalog, inventory. **2 record,** chronicle, log, ledger, archive, annals, files.

▶ **verb 1** enter someone or something in a register. **2** put one's name on an official list. **3** officially report one's arrival as a guest at a hotel or a departing passenger at an airport. **4** express an opinion or emotion. **5** (of an emotion) show in a person's face or gestures. **6** become aware of: *he had not even registered her presence.* **7** (of an instrument) detect and show a reading automatically.

– SYNONYMS **1 record,** enter, file, lodge, write down, submit, report, note, minute, log. **2 enroll,** put one's name down, enlist, sign on/up, apply. **3 indicate,** read, record, show. **4 display,** show, express, exhibit, betray, reveal.

– DERIVATIVES **reg·is·tra·ble** /-st(ə)rəbəl/ adjective.
– ORIGIN Latin *registrum.*

reg·is·tered mail ▶ **noun** a postal service in which the sender can claim compensation if the item sent is damaged, late, or lost.

reg·is·tered nurse ▶ **noun** a nurse who has graduated from a college or a school of nursing. Compare with **PRACTICAL NURSE.**

reg·is·trant /'rejəstrənt/ ▶ **noun** a person who registers for something.

reg·is·trar /'rejəˌsträr/ ▶ **noun 1** an official responsible for keeping official records. **2** the chief administrative officer in a college or university.

reg·is·tra·tion /ˌrejə'strāsʜən/ ▶ **noun 1** the action of registering or recording someone or something. **2** a certificate that attests to the registering of a person, a motor vehicle, etc. **3** (also **registration number**) the series of letters and figures identifying a motor vehicle, displayed on a license plate.

reg·is·try /'rejəstrē/ ▶ **noun** (pl. **registries**) **1** a place where official records are kept. **2** the registration of someone or something.

reg·nant /'regnənt/ ▶ **adjective 1** reigning; ruling. **2** formal currently having the greatest influence; dominant.
– ORIGIN from Latin *regnare* 'to reign.'

re·gress ▶ **verb** /ri'gres/ **1** return to a former or less advanced state. **2** return mentally to a former stage of life or a supposed previous life.

– SYNONYMS **revert,** retrogress, relapse, lapse, backslide, slip back; deteriorate, decline, worsen, degenerate; informal go downhill.
– ANTONYMS progress.

▶ **noun** /'rēˌgres/ a return to a former or less advanced state.
– ORIGIN Latin *regredi* 'go back, return.'

re·gres·sion /ri'gresʜən/ ▶ **noun 1** a return to a former or less advanced state. **2** the action of returning mentally to an earlier stage of life or a supposed previous life.

re·gres·sive /ri'gresiv/ ▶ **adjective 1** returning to a former or less advanced state. **2** (of a tax) taking a proportionally greater amount from people with lower incomes.
– DERIVATIVES **re·gres·sive·ly** adverb **re·gres·sive·ness** noun.

re·gret /ri'gret/ ▶ **verb** (**regrets, regretting, regretted**) feel or express sorrow or disappointment about something one has done or which one should have done.

– SYNONYMS **1 be sorry about,** feel contrite about, feel remorse for, rue, repent of. **2 mourn,** grieve for/over, weep over, sigh over, lament, bemoan.
– ANTONYMS welcome.

▶ **noun 1** a feeling of sorrow or disappointment: *she expressed her regret at Ann's death.* **2** (often **one's regrets**) used in polite expressions of apology or sadness.

– SYNONYMS **1 remorse,** contrition, repentance, compunction, ruefulness, self-reproach, pangs of conscience. **2 sadness,** sorrow, disappointment, unhappiness, grief.

– ORIGIN Old French *regreter* 'lament the dead.'

re·gret·ful /ri'gretfəl/ ▶ **adjective** feeling or showing regret.
– DERIVATIVES **re·gret·ful·ness** noun.

re·gret·ful·ly /ri'gretfəlē/ ▶ **adverb 1** in a regretful way. **2** it is regrettable or undesirable that.

USAGE

The main sense of **regretfully** is 'in a regretful way' (*he sighed regretfully*). However, it is now also used to mean 'it is regrettable or undesirable that' (*regretfully, mounting costs forced the branch to close*), although some people object to this use.

re·gret·ta·ble /ri'gretəbəl/ ▶ **adjective** giving rise to regret; undesirable.

– SYNONYMS **unfortunate,** unwelcome, sorry, woeful, disappointing, reprehensible, deplorable, disgraceful.

– DERIVATIVES **re·gret·ta·bly** /-blē/ adverb.

re·group /rē'grōōp/ ▶ **verb** gather into organized groups again, typically after being attacked or defeated.
– DERIVATIVES **re·group·ment** noun.

re·grow /rē'grō/ ▶ **verb** (past **regrew** /rē'grōō/; past part. **regrown** /rē'grōn/) grow or cause to grow again.
– DERIVATIVES **re·growth** /rē'grōтʜ/ noun.

reg·u·lar /'regyələr, 'reg(ə)lər/ ▶ **adjective 1** following or arranged in a pattern, especially with the same space between one thing and the next: *the association holds regular meetings.* **2** doing the same thing often: *regular worshipers.* **3** done or happening frequently. **4** following or controlled by an accepted standard: *the buying and selling of shares through regular channels.* **5** usual or customary. **6** Grammar (of a word) following the normal pattern of inflection. **7** (of food or clothing) of average size. **8** belonging to the permanent professional armed forces of a country. **9** of an ordinary kind. **10** (of a geometrical figure) having all sides and all angles equal. **11** (of a member of the Christian clergy) belonging to a religious or monastic order. **12** informal, dated rightly so called; absolute: *this place is a regular fisherman's paradise.*

– SYNONYMS **1 uniform,** even, consistent, constant, unchanging, unvarying, fixed. **2 frequent,** repeated, continual, recurrent, periodic, constant, perpetual, numerous. **3 usual,** normal, customary, habitual, routine, typical, accustomed, established.
– ANTONYMS erratic, occasional, unusual.

▶ **noun** a regular customer, member of a team, etc.
– DERIVATIVES **reg·u·lar·i·ty** /ˌregyə'laritē/ noun (pl. **regularities**) **reg·u·lar·ly** adverb.
– ORIGIN Latin *regularis.*

reg·u·lar ca·non ▶ **noun** see **CANON**[2].

reg·u·lar·ize /'regyələˌrīz/ ▶ **verb 1** make something regular. **2** place a temporary or provisional arrangement on an official or correct basis.
– DERIVATIVES **reg·u·lar·i·za·tion** /ˌregyələrə'zāsʜən/ noun.

reg·u·late /'regyəˌlāt/ ▶ **verb 1** control or maintain the rate or speed of a machine or process. **2** control something, especially a business activity, by means of rules.

– SYNONYMS **1 control,** adjust, balance, set, synchronize. **2 police,** supervise, monitor, be responsible for, control, manage, direct, govern.

– DERIVATIVES **reg·u·la·tive** /-ˌlātiv/ adjective **reg·u·la·tor** noun **reg·u·la·to·ry** /ˈregyələˌtôrē/ adjective.

reg·u·la·tion /ˌreg(y)əˈlāsʜən/ ▸ noun **1** a rule or order made and enforced by an authority. **2** the action of regulating something.

– SYNONYMS **1 rule,** order, directive, act, law, bylaw, statute, dictate, decree. **2 control,** policing, supervision, superintendence, monitoring, governance, management, administration, responsibility.

▸ adjective informal in accordance with expectations or conventions: *regulation blond hair.*

re·gur·gi·tate /riˈgərjəˌtāt/ ▸ verb **1** bring swallowed food up again to the mouth. **2** repeat information without analyzing or understanding it.

– DERIVATIVES **re·gur·gi·ta·tion** /riˌgərjəˈtāsʜən/ noun.

– ORIGIN Latin *regurgitare.*

re·hab /ˈrēˌhab/ ▸ noun a course of rehabilitative treatment, especially for drug addiction or injury. ▸ verb (**rehabs, rehabbing, rehabbed**) rehabilitate or restore.

re·ha·bil·i·tate /ˌrē(h)əˈbiləˌtāt/ ▸ verb **1** prepare someone who has been injured, ill, in prison, or addicted to drugs to resume normal life by training and therapy. **2** restore someone to their former status or reputation after being out of favor. **3** restore something to a former condition.

– SYNONYMS **1 reintegrate,** readapt; informal rehab. **2 reinstate,** restore, bring back, pardon, absolve, exonerate, forgive; formal exculpate. **3 recondition,** restore, renovate, refurbish, revamp, overhaul, redevelop, rebuild, reconstruct.

– DERIVATIVES **re·ha·bil·i·ta·tion** /-ˌbiləˈtāsʜən/ noun **re·ha·bil·i·ta·tive** /-ˌtātiv/ adjective.

– ORIGIN Latin *rehabilitare.*

re·hash /rēˈhasʜ/ ▸ verb reuse old ideas or material without significant change or improvement. ▸ noun a reuse of old ideas or material.

re·hears·al /riˈhərsəl/ ▸ noun **1** a trial performance of a play or other work for later public performance. **2** the action of rehearsing.

– SYNONYMS **practice,** trial performance, read-through, run-through, drill, training, coaching; informal dry run.

re·hearse /riˈhərs/ ▸ verb **1** practice a play, piece of music, or other work for later public performance. **2** state a list of points that have been made many times before.

– SYNONYMS **1 prepare,** practice, read through, run through/over, go over. **2 train,** drill, prepare, coach. **3 list,** enumerate, itemize, detail, spell out, catalog, recite, repeat, go over, run through, recap.

– ORIGIN Old French *rehercier* 'repeat aloud.'

re·heat /rēˈhēt/ ▸ verb heat something again.

re·house /rēˈhouz/ ▸ verb provide someone with new housing.

re·hy·drate /rēˈhīˌdrāt/ ▸ verb absorb or cause to absorb moisture after dehydration.

– DERIVATIVES **re·hy·dra·tion** /ˌrēhīˈdrāsʜən/ noun.

re·i·fy /ˈrēəˌfī/ ▸ verb (**reifies, reifying, reified**) formal make something abstract more real or physical.

– DERIVATIVES **re·i·fi·ca·tion** /ˌrēəfəˈkāsʜən/ noun.

– ORIGIN from Latin *res* 'thing.'

reign /rān/ ▸ verb **1** rule as monarch. **2** be the dominant quality or aspect: *chaos reigned.* **3** (as adj. **reigning**) (of an athlete or team) currently holding a particular title.

– SYNONYMS **1 be king/queen,** sit on the throne, wear the crown, be supreme, rule. **2 prevail,** exist, be present, be the case, occur, be rife, be rampant, be the order of the day.

▸ noun **1** the period of rule of a monarch. **2** the period during which someone or something is best or most important.

– SYNONYMS **rule,** sovereignty, monarchy, dominion, control.

– ORIGIN Old French *reignier.*

USAGE

On the confusion of **reign** and **rein**, see the note at **REIN**.

rei·ki /ˈrākē/ ▸ noun a healing technique based on the belief that the therapist can channel energy into the patient by means of touch, to activate the natural healing processes of the patient's body.

– ORIGIN Japanese, 'universal life energy.'

re·im·burse /ˌrē-imˈbərs/ ▸ verb repay money to a person who has spent or lost it.

– DERIVATIVES **re·im·burs·a·ble** adjective **re·im·burse·ment** noun.

– ORIGIN Latin *imbursare* 'put in a purse.'

rein /rān/ ▸ noun **1** a long, narrow strap attached at one end to a horse's bit, used in pairs to control a horse. **2** (**reins**) the power to direct and control: *a new manager will soon take over the reins.* ▸ verb **1** control a horse by pulling on its reins. **2** keep under control; restrain: *he has failed to rein in his own security forces.*

– SYNONYMS **restrain,** check, curb, constrain, hold back/in, keep under control, regulate, restrict, control, curtail, limit.

– PHRASES (**a**) **free rein** freedom of action. **keep a tight rein on** exercise strict control over.

– ORIGIN Old French *rene.*

USAGE

The phrase **a free rein**, which comes from the meaning of allowing a horse to move freely without being controlled by reins, is often misinterpreted and wrongly spelled as *a free reign*.

re·in·car·nate /ˌrē-inˈkärˌnāt/ ▸ verb cause someone to be born again in another body.

re·in·car·na·tion /ˌrē-inkärˈnāsʜən/ ▸ noun **1** the rebirth of a soul in a new body. **2** a person in whom a soul is believed to have been reborn.

rein·deer /ˈrānˌdi(ə)r/ ▸ noun (pl. same or **reindeers**) a deer with large branching antlers, native to the northern tundra and subarctic regions.

– ORIGIN Old Norse.

re·in·fect /ˌrē-inˈfekt/ ▸ verb infect someone or something again.

– DERIVATIVES **re·in·fec·tion** /-ˈfeksʜən/ noun.

re·in·force /ˌrē-inˈfôrs/ ▸ verb **1** strengthen or support an object. **2** strengthen or intensify a feeling, idea, etc. **3** strengthen a military force with additional personnel or equipment.

– SYNONYMS **1 strengthen,** fortify, bolster up, shore up, buttress, prop up, underpin, brace, support, boost. **2 augment,** increase, add to, supplement, boost, top up.

– DERIVATIVES **re·in·forc·er** noun.
– ORIGIN French *renforcer*.

re·in·forced con·crete ▶ **noun** concrete in which metal bars or wire are embedded to strengthen it.

re·in·force·ment /ˌrē-inˈfôrsmənt/ ▶ **noun 1** the action of reinforcing something. **2** (**reinforcements**) extra personnel sent to strengthen an army or similar force.

– SYNONYMS **1 strengthening,** fortification, bolstering, shoring up, buttressing. **2** *we need reinforcements* **additional troops,** auxiliaries, reserves, support, backup, help.

re·in·stall /ˌrē-inˈstôl/ (Brit. **reinstal**) ▶ **verb** install again (used especially of software). ▶ **noun** a reinstallation of software.
– DERIVATIVES **re·in·stal·la·tion** /ˌrē-instəˈlāsʜən/ noun **re·in·stall·er** noun.

re·in·state /ˌrē-inˈstāt/ ▶ **verb** restore someone or something to a former position or state.

– SYNONYMS **restore,** put back, bring back, reinstitute, reinstall, re-establish.

– DERIVATIVES **re·in·state·ment** noun.

re·in·sure /ˌrē-inˈsʜo͝or/ ▶ **verb** (of an insurer) transfer all or part of a risk to another insurer to provide protection against the risk of the first insurance.
– DERIVATIVES **re·in·sur·ance** noun **re·in·sur·er** noun.

re·in·te·grate /rēˈintəˌgrāt/ ▶ **verb 1** restore distinct elements into a whole. **2** integrate someone back into society.
– DERIVATIVES **re·in·te·gra·tion** /ˌrēintəˈgrāsʜən/ noun.

re·in·ter·pret /ˌrē-inˈtərprət/ ▶ **verb** (**reinterprets, reinterpreting, reinterpreted**) interpret something in a new or different light.
– DERIVATIVES **re·in·ter·pre·ta·tion** noun.

re·in·tro·duce /ˌrē-intrəˈd(y)o͞os/ ▶ **verb 1** bring something into effect again. **2** put a species of animal or plant back into a place where it once lived.
– DERIVATIVES **re·in·tro·duc·tion** /-ˈdəksʜən/ noun.

re·in·vent /ˌrē-inˈvent/ ▶ **verb** change something so much that it appears entirely new.
– DERIVATIVES **re·in·ven·tion** /-ˈvencʜən/ noun.
– PHRASES **reinvent the wheel** waste a great deal of time or effort in creating something that already exists.

re·in·vest /ˌrē-inˈvest/ ▶ **verb** put the profit on a previous investment back into the same scheme.
– DERIVATIVES **re·in·vest·ment** noun.

re·in·vig·or·ate /ˌrē-inˈvigəˌrāt/ ▶ **verb** give new energy or strength to someone or something.
– DERIVATIVES **re·in·vig·or·a·tion** /ˌrē-inˌvigəˈrāsʜən/ noun.

re·is·sue /rēˈisʜo͞o/ ▶ **verb** (**reissues, reissuing, reissued**) make a new supply or different form of a book, record, or other product available for sale. ▶ **noun** a new issue of a product.

re·it·er·ate /rēˈitəˌrāt/ ▶ **verb** say something again or repeatedly.

– SYNONYMS **repeat,** restate, recapitulate, recap, go over, rehearse.

– DERIVATIVES **re·it·er·a·tion** /rēˌitəˈrāsʜən/ noun.
– ORIGIN Latin *reiterare* 'go over again.'

re·ject ▶ **verb** /riˈjekt/ **1** dismiss as unsatisfactory or faulty: *union negotiators rejected a 1.5 percent pay increase.* **2** refuse to consider or agree to something. **3** fail to show proper affection or concern for someone. **4** (of the body) show a damaging immune response to a transplanted organ or tissue.

– SYNONYMS **1 turn down,** refuse, decline, say no to, spurn; informal pass up, give the thumbs down to. **2 rebuff,** spurn, shun, snub, cast off/aside, discard, abandon, desert, turn one's back on, cold-shoulder; informal give someone the brush-off.
– ANTONYMS accept, welcome.

▶ **noun** /ˈrēˌjekt/ a rejected person or thing.

– SYNONYMS **second,** discard, misshape, faulty item, castoff.

– DERIVATIVES **re·jec·tion** /riˈjeksʜən/ noun.
– ORIGIN Latin *reicere* 'throw back.'

CHOOSE THE RIGHT WORD

See **REFUTE**.

re·jig /rēˈjig/ ▶ **verb** (**rejigs, rejigging, rejigged**) rearrange something.

re·joice /riˈjois/ ▶ **verb** feel or show great joy.

– SYNONYMS **1** *they rejoiced when she returned* **be happy,** be glad, be delighted, celebrate, make merry; informal be over the moon. **2** *he* ***rejoiced in*** *their success* **delight in,** enjoy, revel in, glory in, relish, savor.
– ANTONYMS mourn.

– ORIGIN Old French *rejoir*.

re·join[1] /rēˈjoin, ˈrē-/ ▶ **verb 1** return to a companion, organization, or route that one has left. **2** join things together again.

– SYNONYMS **return to,** be reunited with, join again, reach again, regain.

re·join[2] /riˈjoin/ ▶ **verb** say something in reply; retort.
– ORIGIN Old French *rejoindre*.

re·join·der /riˈjoindər/ ▶ **noun** a sharp or witty reply.

re·ju·ve·nate /riˈjo͞ovəˌnāt/ ▶ **verb** make someone or something appear or feel younger, better, or more lively.

– SYNONYMS **revive,** revitalize, regenerate, breathe new life into, revivify, reanimate, resuscitate, refresh, reawaken; informal give a shot in the arm to, pep up, buck up.

– DERIVATIVES **re·ju·ve·na·tion** /riˌjo͞ovəˈnāsʜən/ noun **re·ju·ve·na·tor** noun.
– ORIGIN from Latin *juvenis* 'young.'

re·kin·dle /rēˈkindəl/ ▶ **verb 1** revive a past feeling, relationship, or interest. **2** relight a fire.

re·laid /rēˈlād, ˈrē-/ past and past participle of **RELAY**[2].

re·lapse ▶ **verb** /riˈlaps, ˈrēˌlaps/ **1** (of a sick or injured person) become ill again after a period of improvement. **2** (**relapse into**) return to a worse or less active state.

– SYNONYMS **deteriorate,** degenerate, lapse, slip back, slide back, regress, revert, retrogress.
– ANTONYMS improve.

▶ **noun** /ˈrēˌlaps/ a return to poor health after a temporary improvement.
– ORIGIN Latin *relabi* 'slip back.'

re·late /riˈlāt/ ▶ **verb 1** give an account of something. **2** make or show a connection between. **3** (**relate to**) have to do with; concern. **4** (**relate to**) feel sympathy for. **5** (**be related**) be connected by blood or marriage.

– SYNONYMS **1** *he related many stories* **tell,** recount, narrate, report, describe, recite, rehearse. **2** *many drowning accidents are related to alcohol use* **connect with,** associate with, link with, ally with, couple with. **3** (**relate to**) *the charges relate to offenses committed in August* **apply to,** concern, pertain to, have a bearing on, involve. **4** (**relate to**) *she cannot relate to her stepfather* **identify with,** get on (well) with, feel sympathy with, have a rapport with, empathize with, understand; informal hit it off with.

– DERIVATIVES **re·lat·er** (also **relator**) noun.
– ORIGIN Latin *referre* 'bring back.'

re·lat·ed /ri'lātid/ ▸ **adjective** belonging to the same family, group, or type; connected.

– SYNONYMS **connected,** interconnected, associated, linked, allied, corresponding, analogous, parallel, comparable, equivalent.

– DERIVATIVES **re·lat·ed·ness** noun.

re·la·tion /ri'lāsʜən/ ▸ **noun 1** the way in which two or more people or things are connected or related. **2** (**relations**) the way in which two or more people or groups feel about and behave toward each other. **3** a relative by blood or marriage. **4** (**relations**) formal sex or a sexual relationship. **5** the action of telling a story.

– SYNONYMS **1 connection,** relationship, association, link, tie-in, correlation, correspondence, parallel. **2** *our relations with Europe* **dealings,** communication, relationship, connections, contact, interaction. **3 relative,** family member, kinsman, kinswoman; (**relations**) family, kin, kith and kin, kindred.

– DERIVATIVES **re·la·tion·al** adjective.
– PHRASES **in relation to** in connection with.

re·la·tion·ship /ri'lāsʜənˌsʜip/ ▸ **noun 1** the way in which two or more people or things are connected, or the state of being connected: *the relationship between art and architecture*. **2** the way in which two or more people or groups feel about and behave toward each other. **3** a loving and sexual association between two people.

– SYNONYMS **1 connection,** relation, association, link, correlation, correspondence, parallel. **2 family ties,** kinship, affinity, common ancestry. **3 romance,** affair, love affair, liaison, amour, fling.

rel·a·tive /'relətiv/ ▸ **adjective 1** considered in relation or in proportion to something else. **2** existing only in comparison to something else. **3** Grammar (of a pronoun, determiner, or adverb) referring to an earlier noun, sentence, or clause (e.g., *who* in *a contestant who qualified in the first round*). **4** Grammar (of a clause) connected to a main clause by a relative pronoun, determiner, or adverb.

– SYNONYMS **1** *the food required is relative to body weight* **proportionate,** in proportion, commensurate, corresponding. **2** *the relative importance of each factor* **comparative,** respective, comparable.
– ANTONYMS disproportionate.

▸ **noun 1** a person connected by blood or marriage. **2** a species related to another.

– SYNONYMS **relation,** member of the family, kinsman, kinswoman; (**relatives**) family, kin, kith and kin, kindred.

– PHRASES **relative to 1** compared with or in relation to. **2** about; concerning.

rel·a·tive a·tom·ic mass ▸ **noun** the ratio of the average mass of one atom of an element to one twelfth of the mass of an atom of carbon-12.

rel·a·tive hu·mid·i·ty ▸ **noun** the amount of water vapor present in air expressed as a percentage of the amount needed for saturation at the same temperature.

rel·a·tive·ly /'relətivlē/ ▸ **adverb** in relation, comparison, or proportion to something else: *the room was relatively clean*.

rel·a·tive mo·lec·u·lar mass ▸ **noun** the ratio of the average mass of one molecule of an element or compound to one twelfth of the mass of an atom of carbon-12.

rel·a·tiv·ism /'relətəˌvizəm/ ▸ **noun** the belief that knowledge, truth, and morality exist in relation to culture, society, or historical context, and are not always the same.
– DERIVATIVES **rel·a·tiv·ist** noun.

rel·a·tiv·i·ty /ˌrelə'tivətē/ ▸ **noun 1** the state of being relative in comparison to something else. **2** Physics a description of matter, energy, space, and time according to Einstein's theories based on the importance of relative motion and the principle that the speed of light is constant for all observers.

rel·a·tiv·ize /'relətəˌvīz/ ▸ **verb** make or treat something as relative to or dependent on something else.
– DERIVATIVES **rel·a·tiv·i·za·tion** /ˌrelətəvə'zāsʜən/ noun.

re·launch /rē'lôncʜ, -'läncʜ/ ▸ **verb** launch a product again or in a different form. ▸ **noun** an instance of relaunching a product.

re·lax /ri'laks/ ▸ **verb 1** make or become less tense, anxious, or rigid. **2** rest from work or engage in a leisure activity. **3** make a rule or restriction less strict.

– SYNONYMS **1 rest,** loosen up, ease up/off, slow down, de-stress, unbend, unwind, put one's feet up, take it easy; informal chill (out), hang loose, decompress. **2 loosen,** slacken, unclench, weaken, lessen. **3 moderate,** temper, ease, loosen, lighten, dilute, weaken, reduce, decrease; informal let up on.
– ANTONYMS tense, tighten.

– ORIGIN Latin *relaxare*.

re·lax·ant /ri'laksənt/ ▸ **noun** a drug that causes relaxation or reduces tension. ▸ **adjective** causing relaxation.

re·lax·a·tion /riˌlak'sāsʜən, rē-/ ▸ **noun 1** the state of being free from tension and worry. **2** the action of making something less strict.

– SYNONYMS **recreation,** enjoyment, amusement, entertainment, fun, pleasure, leisure.

re·lay[1] ▸ **noun** /'rēˌlā/ **1** a group of people or animals performing a task for a period of time and then replaced by a similar group. **2** a race between teams of runners, each team member in turn covering part of the total distance. **3** an electrical device that opens or closes a circuit in response to a current in another circuit. **4** a device to receive, reinforce, and transmit a signal again. ▸ **verb** /ri'lā, 'rēˌlā/ **1** receive and pass on information or a message. **2** broadcast something by means of a relay.

– SYNONYMS **pass on,** hand on, transfer, repeat, communicate, send, transmit, circulate.

– ORIGIN Old French *relayer*.

re·lay² /'rē,lā/ ▸ **verb** (past and past part. **relaid** /'rē,lād/) lay something again or differently.

re·lease /ri'lēs/ ▸ **verb 1** set someone free from imprisonment or confinement. **2** free someone from a duty. **3** allow to move freely: *she released his arm and pushed him aside.* **4** allow information to be generally available. **5** make a movie or recording available to the public. **6** make property, money, or a right available to someone else.

– SYNONYMS **1 free,** set free, turn loose, let go/out, liberate, discharge. **2 untie,** undo, unfasten, loose, let go, unleash. **3 make public,** make known, issue, put out, publish, broadcast, circulate, launch, distribute.
– ANTONYMS imprison.

▸ **noun 1** the action of releasing or freeing someone or something. **2** a movie or recording released to the public. **3** a handle or catch that releases part of a mechanism.
– DERIVATIVES **re·leas·a·ble** adjective **re·leas·er** noun.
– ORIGIN Old French *relesser*.

rel·e·gate /'relə,gāt/ ▸ **verb** place someone or something in a less important rank or position.

– SYNONYMS **downgrade,** demote, lower, put down, move down.
– ANTONYMS upgrade, promote.

– DERIVATIVES **rel·e·ga·tion** /,relə'gāsʜən/ noun.
– ORIGIN Latin *relegare* 'send away.'

re·lent /ri'lent/ ▸ **verb 1** finally agree to something after first refusing it. **2** become less severe or intense.

– SYNONYMS **1 change one's mind,** do a U-turn, backpedal, back down, give way/in, capitulate, do an about-face; informal do a one-eighty. **2 ease,** slacken, let up, abate, drop, die down, lessen, decrease, subside, weaken, tail off.

– ORIGIN from Latin *re-* 'back' + *lentare* 'to bend.'

re·lent·less /ri'lentləs/ ▸ **adjective 1** never stopping or becoming weaker: *the relentless pursuit of wealth.* **2** refusing to give up; determined or strict.

– SYNONYMS **1 persistent,** unfaltering, unremitting, unflagging, untiring, unwavering, dogged, single-minded, tireless, indefatigable. **2 harsh,** cruel, remorseless, unrelenting, merciless, pitiless, implacable, inexorable, unforgiving, unbending, unyielding.

– DERIVATIVES **re·lent·less·ly** adverb **re·lent·less·ness** noun.

rel·e·vant /'reləvənt/ ▸ **adjective** closely connected or appropriate to the current matter.

– SYNONYMS **pertinent,** applicable, apposite, material, apropos, to the point, germane.

– DERIVATIVES **rel·e·vance** noun **rel·e·van·cy** noun **rel·e·vant·ly** adverb.
– ORIGIN from Latin *relevare* 'raise up.'

re·li·a·ble /ri'līəbəl/ ▸ **adjective** able to be depended on or trusted.

– SYNONYMS **dependable,** trustworthy, good, safe, authentic, faithful, genuine, sound, true, loyal, unfailing; humorous trusty.
– ANTONYMS unreliable.

– DERIVATIVES **re·li·a·bil·i·ty** /ri,līə'bilətē/ noun **re·li·a·bly** /-blē/ adverb.

re·li·ance /ri'līəns/ ▸ **noun** dependence on or trust in someone or something.

– SYNONYMS **1 dependence,** need. **2 trust,** confidence, faith, belief, conviction.

– DERIVATIVES **re·li·ant** adjective.

rel·ic /'relik/ ▸ **noun 1** an interesting object that has survived from the past. **2** a person or thing that has survived from the past but is now outdated. **3** a part of a holy person's body or belongings kept and treated as holy after their death.

– SYNONYMS **artifact,** historical object, antiquity, remnant, vestige, remains.

– ORIGIN from Latin *reliquiae* 'remains.'

rel·ict /'relikt/ ▸ **noun 1** an organism or other thing that has survived from an earlier period. **2** old use a widow.
– ORIGIN from Latin *relictus* 'left behind.'

re·lief /ri'lēf/ ▸ **noun 1** a feeling of reassurance and relaxation following release from anxiety or distress: *the rise in profits was greeted with relief.* **2** a cause of relief. **3** the action of removing or reducing pain, distress, or discomfort. **4** a temporary break in a tense or boring situation. **5** financial or practical assistance given to people in need or difficulty: *famine relief.* **6** a person or group replacing others who have been on duty. **7** the action of lifting a siege on a town. **8** the quality of being more noticeable than surrounding objects: *the sun threw the peaks into relief.* **9** a way of cutting a design into wood, stone, etc., so that parts of it stand out from the surface.

– SYNONYMS **1 respite,** remission, interruption, variation, diversion; informal letup. **2 alleviation,** relieving, palliation, soothing, easing, lessening, mitigation. **3 help,** aid, assistance, charity, succor. **4 replacement,** substitute, deputy, reserve, cover, stand-in, supply, locum, understudy.

– ORIGIN from Latin *relevare* 'raise again, alleviate.'

re·lief map ▸ **noun** a map that shows hills and valleys by shading rather than by contour lines alone.

re·lieve /ri'lēv/ ▸ **verb 1** reduce or remove pain, distress, or difficulty. **2** cause someone to stop feeling distressed or anxious. **3** take over from someone who is on duty. **4** (**relieve someone of**) take a responsibility from someone. **5** make less boring or monotonous: *the bird's body is black, relieved only by white under the tail.* **6** bring military support for a besieged place. **7** (**relieve oneself**) formal or euphemistic urinate or defecate.

– SYNONYMS **1** *this helps relieve pain* **alleviate,** mitigate, ease, counteract, dull, reduce. **2** (as adj. **relieved**) *I'll be relieved when it's over* **glad,** thankful, grateful, pleased, happy, reassured. **3** *the helpers relieved us* **replace,** take over from, stand in for, fill in for, substitute for, deputize for, cover for. **4** *this relieves the teacher of a heavy load* **free,** release, exempt, excuse, absolve, let off.
– ANTONYMS aggravate.

– DERIVATIVES **re·liev·er** noun.
– ORIGIN Old French *relever*.

CHOOSE THE RIGHT WORD

See **ALLEVIATE**.

re·light /rē'līt, 'rē-/ ▸ **verb** (past and past part. **relighted** or **relit** /-'lit/) light something again.

re·li·gion /ri'lijən/ ▸ **noun 1** the belief in and worship of a God or gods. **2** a particular system of faith and worship. **3** a pursuit or interest that is very important to someone.

– SYNONYMS **faith,** belief, worship, creed, church, sect, denomination, cult.

– ORIGIN Latin *religio* 'obligation, reverence.'

WORD LINKS

divinity, theology *study of religion*

re·li·gi·os·i·ty /ri͵lijēˈäsətē/ ▸ **noun** the state of being excessively religious.
– DERIVATIVES **re·li·gi·ose** /riˈlijē͵ōs/ adjective.

re·li·gious /riˈlijəs/ ▸ **adjective 1** relating to or believing in a religion. **2** treated as very important or done with great care: *a boy with an almost religious devotion to fishing.*

– SYNONYMS **1 devout,** pious, reverent, godly, God-fearing, churchgoing. **2 spiritual,** theological, scriptural, doctrinal, ecclesiastical, church, holy, divine, sacred. **3 scrupulous,** conscientious, meticulous, punctilious, strict, rigorous.
– ANTONYMS atheistic, secular.

▸ **noun** (pl. same) a monk or nun.
– DERIVATIVES **re·li·gious·ly** adverb **re·li·gious·ness** noun.

re·lin·quish /riˈlinGkwisH/ ▸ **verb** willingly give something up.

– SYNONYMS **1 renounce,** resign, give up/away, hand over, let go of. **2 leave,** resign from, stand down from, bow out of, give up; informal quit.
– ANTONYMS retain.

– DERIVATIVES **re·lin·quish·ment** noun.
– ORIGIN Latin *relinquere.*

CHOOSE THE RIGHT WORD

relinquish, abandon, cede, surrender, waive, yield

Of all these verbs meaning to let go or give up, **relinquish** is the most general. It can imply anything from simply releasing one's grasp (*she relinquished the wheel*) to giving up control or possession reluctantly (*after the defeat, he was forced to relinquish his command*). **Surrender** also implies giving up, but usually after a struggle or show of resistance (*the villagers were forced to surrender to the guerrillas*). **Yield** is a milder synonym for *surrender*, implying some concession, respect, or even affection on the part of the person who is surrendering (*she yielded to her mother's wishes and stayed home*). **Waive** means to give up voluntarily a right or claim to something (*she waived her right to have a lawyer present*), while **cede** is to give up by legal transfer or according to the terms of a treaty (*the French ceded the territory that is now Louisiana*). If one *relinquishes* something finally and completely, often because of weariness or discouragement, the correct word is **abandon** (*they were told to abandon all hope of being rescued*).

rel·i·quar·y /ˈrelə͵kwerē/ ▸ **noun** (pl. **reliquaries**) a container for holy relics.

rel·ish /ˈrelisH/ ▸ **noun 1** great enjoyment. **2** a pleasant feeling of looking forward to something: *he was waiting with relish for her promised visit.* **3** a condiment eaten with plain food to add flavor.

– SYNONYMS **1 enjoyment,** gusto, delight, pleasure, glee, appreciation, enthusiasm. **2 condiment,** sauce, dressing.
– ANTONYMS distaste.

▸ **verb 1** enjoy something greatly. **2** look forward to something with pleasure.

– SYNONYMS **enjoy,** delight in, love, adore, take pleasure in, rejoice in, appreciate, savor, revel in, luxuriate in, glory in.
– ANTONYMS dislike.

– ORIGIN Old French *reles* 'remainder.'

re·live /rēˈliv, ˈrē-/ ▸ **verb** live through an experience or feeling again in one's imagination.

re·load /rēˈlōd/ ▸ **verb** load something, especially a gun, again.

re·lo·cate /rēˈlō͵kāt, ͵rēlōˈkāt/ ▸ **verb** move to a new place and establish one's home or business there.
– DERIVATIVES **re·lo·ca·tion** /͵rēlōˈkāsHən/ noun.

re·luc·tance /riˈləktəns/ ▸ **noun** unwillingness to do something.

– SYNONYMS **unwillingness,** disinclination, hesitation, wavering, vacillation, doubts, second thoughts, misgivings.

re·luc·tant /riˈləktənt/ ▸ **adjective** unwilling and hesitant.

– SYNONYMS **unwilling,** disinclined, unenthusiastic, resistant, opposed, hesitant, loath.
– ANTONYMS willing, eager.

– DERIVATIVES **re·luc·tant·ly** adverb.
– ORIGIN from Latin *reluctari* 'struggle against.'

re·ly /riˈlī/ ▸ **verb** (**relies, relying, relied**) (**rely on**) **1** have complete trust or confidence in someone or something. **2** be dependent on: *the charity has to rely on public donations.*

– SYNONYMS **depend on,** count on, bank on, be confident of, be sure of, have faith in, trust in; informal swear by, figure on.

– ORIGIN Old French *relier* 'bind together.'

REM /rem/ ▸ **abbreviation** rapid eye movement, referring to a kind of sleep that occurs at intervals during the night and is characterized by rapid eye movement and more dreaming.

re·made /rēˈmād, ˈrē-/ past and past participle of **REMAKE.**

re·main /riˈmān/ ▸ **verb 1** stay in the same place or condition during further time. **2** continue to have a particular quality or fill a particular role. **3** be left over or outstanding after others or other parts have been dealt with or used: *a more difficult problem remains.*

– SYNONYMS **1 continue,** endure, last, abide, carry on, persist, stay around, survive, live on. **2 stay,** stay behind, stay put, wait behind, be left, hang on; informal hang around. **3** *he remained calm* **continue to be,** stay, keep.

– ORIGIN Latin *remanere.*

re·main·der /riˈmāndər/ ▸ **noun 1** a part, number, or quantity that is left over. **2** a part that is still to come: *the remainder of the year.* **3** the number that is left over when one quantity does not exactly divide another. **4** a copy of a book left unsold when demand has fallen.

– SYNONYMS **rest,** balance, residue, others, remnant(s), leftovers, surplus, extra, excess.

▸ **verb** put an unsold book on sale at a reduced price.

re·mains /riˈmānz/ ▸ **plural noun 1** things remaining. **2** historical or archaeological relics. **3** a person's body after death.

– SYNONYMS **1 remainder,** residue, rest, remnant(s), leftovers, scraps, debris, detritus. **2 antiquities,** relics, artifacts. **3 corpse,** body, carcass, bones; Medicine cadaver.

CHOOSE THE RIGHT WORD

See **BODY.**

re·make ▸ **verb** /rē'māk, 'rē-/ (past and past part. **remade** /rē'mād, 'rē-/) make something again or differently.
▸ **noun** /'rē,māk/ a movie or piece of music that has been filmed or recorded anew and re-released.

re·mand /ri'mand/ Law ▸ **verb** place a person charged with a crime on bail or in custody to await their trial.
▸ **noun** the process of remanding someone to await trial.
– ORIGIN Latin *remandare* 'commit again.'

re·mark /ri'märk/ ▸ **verb 1** say something as a comment; mention something. **2** notice someone or something.

> – SYNONYMS **comment,** say, observe, mention, reflect; formal opine.

▸ **noun 1** a comment. **2** the fact of being noticed or commented on: *the landscape was not worthy of remark.*

> – SYNONYMS **comment,** statement, utterance, observation, reflection.

– ORIGIN French *remarquer* 'note again.'

re·mark·a·ble /ri'märkəbəl/ ▸ **adjective** worthy of attention; extraordinary or striking.

> – SYNONYMS **extraordinary,** exceptional, outstanding, notable, striking, memorable, unusual, conspicuous, momentous.
> – ANTONYMS ordinary.

– DERIVATIVES **re·mark·a·bly** /-blē/ adverb.

> **WORD TOOLKIT**
>
> See **EXCEPTIONAL**.

re·mar·ry /rē'marē/ ▸ **verb** (**remarries, remarrying, remarried**) marry again.
– DERIVATIVES **re·mar·riage** /rē'marij/ noun.

re·mas·ter /rē'mastər/ ▸ **verb** make a new or improved master of a sound recording.

re·match /'rē,macн/ ▸ **noun** a second match or game between two sports teams or players.

re·me·di·al /ri'mēdēəl/ ▸ **adjective 1** intended to set right or cure something: *an obligation to take remedial action in case animals are suffering.* **2** provided or intended for children with learning difficulties.

re·me·di·a·tion /ri,mēdē'āsнən/ ▸ **noun 1** the action of setting something right, in particular environmental damage. **2** the giving of remedial teaching or therapy to children with learning difficulties.
– DERIVATIVES **re·me·di·ate** /ri'mēdē,āt/ verb.

rem·e·dy /'remədē/ ▸ **noun** (pl. **remedies**) **1** a medicine or treatment for a disease or injury. **2** a way of setting right or improving an undesirable situation. **3** a means of gaining legal amends for a wrong.

> – SYNONYMS **1 treatment,** cure, medicine, medication, medicament, drug. **2 solution,** answer, cure, fix, antidote, panacea.

▸ **verb** (**remedies, remedying, remedied**) set right an undesirable situation.

> – SYNONYMS **put right,** set right, rectify, solve, sort out, straighten out, resolve, correct, repair, mend, fix.

– DERIVATIVES **re·me·di·a·ble** /ri'mēdēəbəl/ adjective.
– ORIGIN Latin *remedium.*

re·mem·ber /ri'membər/ ▸ **verb 1** have in or bring to one's mind someone or something from the past. **2** keep something necessary in mind: *remember to mail the letters.* **3** bear someone in mind by making them a gift or by mentioning them in prayer: *he remembered the boy in his will.* **4** (**remember someone to**) pass on greetings from one person to another.

> – SYNONYMS **1 recall,** call to mind, recollect, think of, reminisce about, look back on. **2 memorize,** retain, learn by heart, get down pat. **3 bear in mind,** be mindful of, take into account. **4 commemorate,** pay tribute to, honor, salute, pay homage to.
> – ANTONYMS forget.

– ORIGIN Latin *rememorari* 'call to mind.'

re·mem·brance /ri'membrəns/ ▸ **noun 1** the action of remembering. **2** a memory. **3** a thing kept or given as a reminder of someone.

> – SYNONYMS **1 recollection,** reminiscence, recall. **2 commemoration,** memory, recognition.

re·mind /ri'mīnd/ ▸ **verb 1** cause someone to remember something. **2** (**remind someone of**) cause someone to think of someone or something because they are similar in some way.

> – SYNONYMS **1 jog someone's memory,** prompt. **2 (remind someone of) make someone think of,** cause someone to remember, put someone in mind of, call to mind, evoke.

re·mind·er /ri'mīndər/ ▸ **noun 1** a thing that causes someone to remember something. **2** chiefly Brit. a letter sent to remind someone to pay a bill.

rem·i·nisce /,remə'nis/ ▸ **verb** think or talk contentedly about the past.

rem·i·nis·cence /,remə'nisəns/ ▸ **noun 1** a story told by a person about a past event that they remember. **2** the enjoyable recollection of past events.
– ORIGIN from Latin *reminisci* 'remember.'

rem·i·nis·cent /,remə'nisənt/ ▸ **adjective 1** tending to remind one of someone or something; similar: *the leaves have a fresh taste reminiscent of cucumber.* **2** with one's mind full of memories.

> – SYNONYMS *the painting is **reminiscent of** an early Picasso* **similar to,** comparable with, evocative of, suggestive of, redolent of.

– DERIVATIVES **rem·i·nis·cent·ly** adverb.

re·miss /ri'mis/ ▸ **adjective** lacking care or attention to duty.

> – SYNONYMS **negligent,** neglectful, irresponsible, careless, thoughtless, heedless, derelict, lax, slack, slipshod, lackadaisical; informal sloppy.
> – ANTONYMS careful.

– ORIGIN from Latin *remittere* 'slacken.'

re·mis·sion /ri'misнən/ ▸ **noun 1** the cancellation of a debt, charge, or penalty. **2** a temporary period during which a serious illness becomes less severe. **3** formal forgiveness of sins.

re·mit ▸ **noun** /ri'mit, 'rē,mit/ chiefly Brit. the area of activity that a person or organization controls or is officially responsible for: *food labeling falls within the remit of the Food Standards Agency.*

> – SYNONYMS **area of responsibility,** sphere, orbit, scope, ambit, province, brief, instructions, orders; informal bailiwick.

▸ **verb** /ri'mit/ (**remits, remitting, remitted**) **1** send money in payment. **2** cancel a debt or punishment. **3** refer a matter for decision to an authority. **4** forgive a sin.

> – SYNONYMS **1 send,** dispatch, forward, hand over, pay. **2 pardon,** forgive, excuse.

– ORIGIN Latin *remittere* 'send back, restore.'

re·mit·tance /ri'mitns/ ▶ **noun 1** a sum of money sent in payment. **2** the action of sending payment.

re·mix ▶ **verb** /rē'miks, 'rē-/ **1** mix something again. **2** produce a different version of a musical recording by altering the balance of the separate tracks. ▶ **noun** /'rē,miks/ a remixed musical recording.
– DERIVATIVES **re·mix·er** noun.

rem·nant /'remnənt/ ▶ **noun 1** a small remaining part or quantity. **2** a piece of cloth left when the greater part has been used or sold.

– SYNONYMS **remains,** remainder, leftovers, residue, rest.

– ORIGIN Old French *remenant*.

CHOOSE THE RIGHT WORD

See **TRACE**[1].

re·mod·el /rē'mädl/ ▶ **verb (remodels, remodeling, remodeled) 1** change the structure or form of something. **2** shape an object again or differently.

re·mon·strance /ri'mänstrəns/ ▶ **noun** a strongly critical protest.

re·mon·strate /ri'män,strāt, 'remən-/ ▶ **verb** make a strongly critical protest.

– SYNONYMS **protest,** complain, object, take issue, argue, expostulate.

– DERIVATIVES **re·mon·stra·tion** /ri,män'strāsʜən, ,remən-/ noun.
– ORIGIN Latin *remonstrare* 'demonstrate.'

rem·o·ra /'remərə, ri'môrə/ ▶ **noun** a slender sea fish that attaches itself to large fish by means of a sucker on top of the head.
– ORIGIN Latin, 'hindrance' (because of the former belief that the fish slowed down ships).

re·morse /ri'môrs/ ▶ **noun** deep regret or guilt for a wrong that one has done.

– SYNONYMS **regret,** guilt, contrition, repentance, shame.

– ORIGIN Latin *remorsus*.

re·morse·ful /ri'môrsfəl/ ▶ **adjective** filled with deep regret or guilt.

– SYNONYMS **sorry,** regretful, contrite, repentant, penitent, guilt-ridden, conscience-stricken, chastened, self-reproachful.
– ANTONYMS unrepentant.

– DERIVATIVES **re·morse·ful·ly** adverb.

re·morse·less /ri'môrsləs/ ▶ **adjective 1** (of something unpleasant) never ending or improving; relentless. **2** without regret or guilt.
– DERIVATIVES **re·morse·less·ly** adverb **re·morse·less·ness** noun.

re·mort·gage /rē'môrgij/ ▶ **verb** take out another or a different mortgage on a property. ▶ **noun** a different or additional mortgage.

re·mote /ri'mōt/ ▶ **adjective (remoter, remotest) 1** far away in space or time. **2** situated far from the main cities or towns. **3** distantly related. **4** having very little connection: *the theory seems rather remote from everyday experience.* **5** (of a chance or possibility) unlikely to occur. **6** aloof and unfriendly. **7** (of an electronic device) operating or operated by means of radio or infrared signals. **8** Computing (of a device) that can only be accessed by means of a network.

– SYNONYMS **1 isolated,** far-off, faraway, distant, out of the way, off the beaten track, secluded, lonely, inaccessible, in the backwoods; informal in the middle of nowhere. **2** *a remote possibility* **unlikely,** improbable, doubtful, dubious, faint, slight, slim, small, slender. **3 aloof,** distant, detached, withdrawn, unforthcoming, unapproachable, unresponsive, unfriendly, unsociable, introspective, introverted; informal standoffish.
– ANTONYMS close.

▶ **noun** a remote control device.
– DERIVATIVES **re·mote·ly** adverb **re·mote·ness** noun.
– ORIGIN Latin *remotus* 'removed.'

re·mote con·trol ▶ **noun 1** control of a device from a distance by means of signals transmitted from a radio or electronic device. **2** a device that controls another device in this way.
– DERIVATIVES **re·mote-con·trolled** adjective.

re·mou·lade /,rāmə'läd, -mōō-/ ▶ **noun** a salad or seafood dressing made with hard-boiled egg yolks, oil, vinegar, and seasoning.
– ORIGIN French.

re·mount ▶ **verb** /rē'mount, 'rē-/ **1** get on a horse or vehicle again. **2** attach something to a new frame or setting. **3** organize or begin a course of action again. ▶ **noun** /'rē,mount/ a fresh horse for a rider.

re·mov·al /ri'mōōvəl/ ▶ **noun 1** the act of removing something, especially something unwanted. **2** the dismissal of someone from a job or office.

– SYNONYMS **1 taking away,** withdrawal, abolition; move, transfer, relocation. **2 dismissal,** ejection, expulsion, ousting, deposition; informal sacking, firing.

re·move /ri'mōōv/ ▶ **verb 1** take something off or away from the position occupied. **2** abolish or get rid of something. **3** dismiss someone from a job. **4 (be removed from)** be very different from. **5** (as adj. **removed**) separated by a particular number of steps of descent: *his second cousin once removed.*

– SYNONYMS **1 take off,** take away, move, take out, pull out, withdraw, detach, undo, unfasten, disconnect. **2 abolish,** withdraw, eliminate, get rid of, do away with, stop, cut; informal ax. **3 dismiss,** discharge, get rid of, eject, expel, oust, depose, unseat; informal sack, fire, kick out.
– ANTONYMS attach, insert.

▶ **noun** the extent to which people or things are separated or remote from each other: *he kept himself at a certain remove from the confrontations.*
– DERIVATIVES **re·mov·a·ble** adjective **re·mov·er** noun.
– ORIGIN Latin *removere*.

re·mu·ner·ate /ri'myōōnə,rāt/ ▶ **verb** pay someone for services rendered or work done.
– DERIVATIVES **re·mu·ner·a·tive** /-rətiv, -,rātiv/ adjective.
– ORIGIN Latin *remunerari* 'reward, recompense.'

re·mu·ner·a·tion /ri,myōōnə'rāsʜən/ ▶ **noun** money paid for work or a service.

Ren·ais·sance /'renə,säns, -,zäns/ ▶ **noun 1** the revival of European art and literature under the influence of classical styles in the 14th–16th centuries. **2 (renaissance)** a revival of or renewed interest in something.

– SYNONYMS **(renaissance)** *rail travel is enjoying a renaissance* **revival,** renewal, resurrection, reawakening, re-emergence, rebirth, reappearance, resurgence.

– ORIGIN French, 'rebirth.'

Ren·ais·sance man ▶ **noun** a person with a wide range of talents or interests.

re·nal /'rēnl/ ▶ **adjective** relating to the kidneys.
– ORIGIN Latin *renalis*.

re·name /rē'nām, 'rē-/ ▶ **verb** give a new name to someone or something.

re·nas·cent /ri'nasənt, -'nāsənt/ ▶ **adjective** becoming active again.
– DERIVATIVES **re·nas·cence** noun.
– ORIGIN from Latin *renasci* 'be born again.'

rend /rend/ ▶ **verb** (past and past part. **rent**) literary **1** tear something to pieces. **2** cause great distress to someone.
– ORIGIN Old English.

rend·er /'rendər/ ▶ **verb 1** provide a service, help, etc. **2** present something for inspection, consideration, or payment. **3** cause to be or become: *I was rendered speechless*. **4** perform or represent musically or artistically: *the children in the painting are very sensitively rendered*. **5** translate something into another language. **6** literary hand something over. **7** melt down fat so as to separate out its impurities. **8** cover stone or brick with a coat of plaster.

– SYNONYMS **1 make,** cause to be/become, leave, turn. **2 give,** provide, supply, furnish, contribute. **3 act,** perform, play, depict, portray, interpret, represent, draw, paint, execute.

– DERIVATIVES **ren·der·er** noun.
– ORIGIN Old French *rendre*.

rend·er·ing /'rendəriNG/ ▶ **noun 1** a performance of a piece of music or a role in a play. **2** a translation. **3** a first coat of plaster.

ren·dez·vous /'rändi,vo͞o, -dā-/ ▶ **noun** (pl. same /-vo͞o/ or /-vo͞oz/) **1** a meeting at an agreed time and place. **2** a meeting place.

– SYNONYMS **meeting,** appointment, assignation; informal date; literary tryst.

▶ **verb** (**rendezvouses** /-,vo͞oz/, **rendezvousing** /-,vo͞oiNG/, **rendezvoused** /-,vo͞od/) meet at an agreed time and place.

– SYNONYMS **meet,** come together, gather, assemble.

– ORIGIN French *rendez-vous!* 'present yourselves!'

ren·di·tion /ren'disHən/ ▶ **noun 1** a way that something is rendered, performed, or represented, especially a performance of a dramatic role or a musical work: *a quick rendition of 'Happy Birthday.'* **2** a translation. **3** (also **extraordinary rendition**) the sending of a foreign criminal or terrorist suspect to be interrogated in a country with less rigorous controls on the treatment of prisoners.

ren·e·gade /'reni,gād/ ▶ **noun** a person who deserts and betrays an organization, country, or set of principles.

– SYNONYMS **traitor,** defector, deserter, turncoat, rebel, mutineer.

▶ **adjective** having treacherously changed allegiance.

– SYNONYMS **1 treacherous,** traitorous, disloyal, treasonous, rebel, mutinous. **2 apostate,** heretic, heretical, dissident.
– ANTONYMS loyal.

– ORIGIN Spanish *renegado*.

re·nege /ri'neg, -'nig/ ▶ **verb** go back on a promise or contract.

– SYNONYMS **default on,** fail to honor, go back on, break, back out of, withdraw from, retreat from, backtrack on, break one's word/promise.
– ANTONYMS honor.

– ORIGIN Latin *renegare*.

re·ne·go·ti·ate /,rēnə'gōsHē,āt/ ▶ **verb** negotiate something again in order to change the original agreed terms.
– DERIVATIVES **re·ne·go·ti·a·ble** /-'gōsH(ē)əbəl/ adjective **re·ne·go·ti·a·tion** /-,gōsHē'āsHən, -,gōsē-/ noun.

re·new /ri'n(y)o͞o/ ▶ **verb 1** begin something again after an interruption. **2** (usu. as adj. **renewed**) give fresh life or intensity to: *a renewed interest in exercise*. **3** extend the period for which a license, subscription, or contract is valid. **4** replace something broken or worn out.

– SYNONYMS **1 resume,** return to, take up again, come back to, begin again, restart, recommence, continue (with), carry on (with). **2 reaffirm,** repeat, reiterate, restate. **3 revive,** regenerate, revitalize, reinvigorate, restore, resuscitate. **4 renovate,** restore, refurbish, revamp, remodel, modernize; informal do up.

– DERIVATIVES **re·new·al** noun **re·new·er** noun.

re·new·a·ble /ri'n(y)o͞oəbəl/ ▶ **adjective 1** capable of being renewed. **2** (of energy or its source) not exhausted when used.
– DERIVATIVES **re·new·a·bil·i·ty** /ri,n(y)o͞oə'bilətē/ noun.

ren·min·bi /'ren'min'bē/ ▶ **noun** (pl. same) **1** the system of currency of China. **2** a yuan.
– ORIGIN Chinese.

ren·net /'renit/ ▶ **noun** a substance made from curdled milk from the stomach of a calf, used in curdling milk for cheese.
– ORIGIN probably related to **RUN**.

re·nounce /ri'nouns/ ▶ **verb 1** formally state that one has given up a claim, right, or possession. **2** state publicly that one no longer has a particular belief or supports a particular cause. **3** abandon a bad habit or way of life.

– SYNONYMS **1 give up,** relinquish, abandon, surrender, waive, forgo, desist from, keep off; informal say goodbye to. **2 reject,** repudiate, deny, abandon, wash one's hands of, turn one's back on, disown, spurn, shun.

– DERIVATIVES **re·nounce·a·ble** adjective **re·nounce·ment** noun **re·nounc·er** noun.
– ORIGIN Old French *renoncer*.

ren·o·vate /'renə,vāt/ ▶ **verb** restore something old to a good state of repair.

– SYNONYMS **modernize,** restore, refurbish, revamp, recondition, rehabilitate, update, upgrade, refit; informal do up.

– DERIVATIVES **ren·o·va·tion** /,renə'vāsHən/ noun **ren·o·va·tor** noun.
– ORIGIN Latin *renovare* 'make new again.'

re·nown /ri'noun/ ▶ **noun** the state of being famous and respected: *born to a family of political renown*.

– SYNONYMS **fame,** distinction, eminence, illustriousness, prominence, repute, reputation, prestige, acclaim, celebrity, notability.

– ORIGIN from Old French *renomer* 'make famous.'

re·nowned /ri'nound/ ▶ **adjective** known or talked about by many people; famous: *a renowned Indian filmmaker*.

– SYNONYMS **famous,** well known, celebrated, famed, eminent, distinguished, acclaimed, illustrious, prominent, great, esteemed.
– ANTONYMS unknown.

rent[1] /rent/ ▶ **noun 1** a tenant's regular payment to a landlord for the use of property or land. **2** a payment for the rental of equipment.

– SYNONYMS **rental,** fee, lease.

▶ **verb 1** pay someone for the use of something. **2** let someone use something in return for payment.

– SYNONYMS **1 hire,** lease, charter. **2 let,** lease, hire, charter.

– DERIVATIVES **rent·a·ble** adjective **rent·er** noun.
– ORIGIN Old French *rente*.

rent[2] ▶ **noun** a large tear in a piece of fabric.
– ORIGIN from **REND**.

rent[3] past and past participle of **REND**.

ren·tal /ˈrentl/ ▶ **noun 1** the action of renting something. **2** a rented house or car. **3** an amount paid or received as rent. ▶ **adjective** relating to or available for rent.

re·num·ber /rēˈnəmbər/ ▶ **verb** change the number or numbers given to something.

re·nun·ci·a·tion /riˌnənsēˈāsʜən/ ▶ **noun** the formal giving up of a claim, belief, or course of action.

re·oc·cu·py /rēˈäkyəˌpī/ ▶ **verb** (**reoccupies, reoccupying, reoccupied**) occupy a place or position again.
– DERIVATIVES **re·oc·cu·pa·tion** /ˌrēˌäkyəˈpāsʜən/ noun.

re·oc·cur /rēəˈkər/ ▶ **verb** (**reoccurs, reoccurring, reoccurred**) occur again or repeatedly.
– DERIVATIVES **re·oc·cur·rence** /rēəˈkərəns/ noun.

re·of·fend /ˌrēəˈfend/ ▶ **verb** commit a further offense.
– DERIVATIVES **re·of·fend·er** noun.

re·o·pen /rēˈōpən/ ▶ **verb** open again: *the house was reopened to the public.*

re·or·der /rēˈôrdər/ ▶ **verb 1** order goods again. **2** arrange something again or differently. ▶ **noun** a repeated order for goods.

re·or·gan·ize /rēˈôrgəˌnīz/ ▶ **verb** change the way in which something is organized.
– DERIVATIVES **re·or·gan·i·za·tion** /ˌrēˌôrgənəˈzāsʜən/ noun **re·or·gan·iz·er** noun.

re·or·i·ent /rēˈôrēˌent/ ▶ **verb 1** change the focus or direction of something. **2** (**reorient oneself**) find one's position again in relation to one's surroundings.
– DERIVATIVES **re·o·ri·en·tate** /-ēənˌtāt/ verb **re·o·ri·en·ta·tion** /ˌrēˌôrēənˈtāsʜən/ noun.

rep[1] /rep/ informal ▶ **noun** a representative.

rep[2] ▶ **noun** informal **1** repertory. **2** a repertory theater or company.

rep[3] (also **repp**) ▶ **noun** a fabric with a ribbed surface, used in curtains and upholstery.
– ORIGIN French *reps*.

rep[4] ▶ **noun** (in weight training) a repetition of a set of exercises.

rep[5] ▶ **noun** informal short for **REPUTATION**.

Rep. ▶ **abbreviation 1** (in the federal or a state legislature) Representative. **2** Republic. **3** a Republican.

re·pack·age /rēˈpakij/ ▶ **verb** package or present something again or differently.

re·paid /rēˈpād/ past and past participle of **REPAY**.

re·paint /rēˈpānt/ ▶ **verb** cover something with a new coat of paint.

re·pair[1] /riˈpe(ə)r/ ▶ **verb 1** restore something damaged, worn, or faulty to a good condition. **2** set right a breakdown in relations.

– SYNONYMS **1 mend,** fix, put/set right, restore, overhaul, renovate; informal patch up. **2 rectify,** make good, put right, correct, make up for, make amends for, compensate for, redress.

▶ **noun 1** the action of repairing something. **2** a part that has been repaired. **3** the relative condition of something: *the cottages were in good repair.*

– SYNONYMS **1 restoration,** mending, overhaul, renovation. **2 mend,** darn, patch. **3** *in good repair* **condition,** working order, state, shape, fettle.

– DERIVATIVES **re·pair·a·ble** adjective **re·pair·er** noun.
– ORIGIN Latin *reparare*.

re·pair[2] ▶ **verb** (**repair to**) formal or humorous go to a place.
– ORIGIN Old French *repairer*.

re·pair·man /riˈpe(ə)rˌman, -mən/ ▶ **noun** (pl. **repairmen**) a person who repairs vehicles, machinery, or appliances.

rep·a·ra·ble /ˈrep(ə)rəbəl/ ▶ **adjective** able to be repaired or rectified.

rep·a·ra·tion /ˌrepəˈrāsʜən/ ▶ **noun 1** the making of amends for a wrong: *sinners who make reparation for their sins.* **2** (**reparations**) compensation for war damage paid by a defeated country or faction.
– DERIVATIVES **re·par·a·tive** /riˈparətiv/ adjective.
– ORIGIN Latin.

rep·ar·tee /ˌrepərˈtē, ˌrepˌärˈtē, -ˈtā/ ▶ **noun** conversation characterized by quick, witty comments or replies.
– ORIGIN from French *repartie* 'replied promptly.'

re·past /riˈpast, ˈrēˌpast/ ▶ **noun** formal a meal.
– ORIGIN Old French.

re·pa·tri·ate /rēˈpātrēˌāt, rēˈpa-/ ▶ **verb** send someone back to their own country.
– DERIVATIVES **re·pa·tri·a·tion** /ˌrēˌpātrēˈāsʜən, ˌrēˌpa-/ noun.
– ORIGIN Latin *repatriare* 'return to one's country.'

re·pay /rēˈpā/ ▶ **verb** (past and past part. **repaid**) **1** pay back a loan that is owed to someone. **2** do or give something as reward for a favor or kindness received.

– SYNONYMS **1 reimburse,** refund, pay back, recompense, compensate, remunerate, settle up with. **2** *he repaid her kindness* **reciprocate,** return, requite, reward.

– DERIVATIVES **re·pay·a·ble** adjective **re·pay·ment** noun.

re·peal /riˈpēl/ ▶ **verb** officially cancel a law or congressional act.

– SYNONYMS **cancel,** abolish, reverse, rescind, revoke, annul, quash.
– ANTONYMS enact.

▶ **noun** the action of repealing a law or congressional act.

– SYNONYMS **cancellation,** abolition, reversal, rescinding, annulment.

– ORIGIN Old French *repeler*.

re·peat /riˈpēt/ ▶ **verb 1** say something again. **2** do something again or more than once. **3** (**repeat itself**) occur again in the same way: *I don't intend to let history repeat itself.* **4** (of food) be tasted again after being swallowed, as a result of indigestion.

– SYNONYMS **1 say again,** restate, reiterate, go/run through again, recapitulate, recap. **2 recite,** quote, parrot, regurgitate, echo. **3 do again,** redo, replicate, duplicate.

▶ **noun 1** something that occurs or is done again. **2** a repeated broadcast of a television or radio program. **3** a musical passage that is to be repeated.

– SYNONYMS **repetition,** replication, duplicate.

▶ **adjective** happening, done, or used more than once: *a repeat performance.*
– DERIVATIVES **re·peat·a·ble** adjective **re·peat·er** noun.
– ORIGIN Latin *repetere.*

re·peat·ed /riˈpētid/ ▶ **adjective** recurring again and again; frequent: *his repeated complaints about the noise.*

– SYNONYMS **recurrent,** frequent, persistent, continual, incessant, constant, regular, periodic, numerous, (very) many.
– ANTONYMS occasional.

re·peat·ed·ly /riˈpētidlē/ ▶ **adverb** more than once; frequently: *he tried repeatedly to hit that low note.*

– SYNONYMS **frequently,** often, again and again, over and over (again), time and (time) again, many times, persistently, recurrently, constantly, continually, regularly, oftentimes.

re·peat·ing dec·i·mal ▶ **noun** a decimal fraction in which a figure or group of figures is repeated indefinitely, as in *0.333 ....*

re·pel /riˈpel/ ▶ **verb** (**repels, repelling, repelled**) **1** drive or force an attack or attacker back or away. **2** make someone feel disgust or horror. **3** (of a substance) be able to keep something out or be unable to mix with something: *boots with leather uppers to repel moisture.* **4** (of a magnetic pole or electric field) force away something similarly magnetized or charged.

– SYNONYMS **1 fight off,** repulse, drive back, force back, beat back, hold off, ward off, fend off, keep at bay. **2 revolt,** disgust, repulse, sicken, nauseate, turn someone's stomach; informal turn off, gross out.
– ANTONYMS attract.

– DERIVATIVES **re·pel·ler** noun.
– ORIGIN Latin *repellere.*

re·pel·lent /riˈpelənt/ (also **repellant**) ▶ **adjective** **1** able to repel a particular thing: *water-repellent nylon.* **2** disgusting or distasteful.

– SYNONYMS **1 impermeable,** impervious, resistant, -proof. **2 revolting,** repulsive, disgusting, repugnant, sickening, nauseating, stomach-turning, vile, nasty, foul, awful, horrible, dreadful, terrible, obnoxious, loathsome, offensive, objectionable, abhorrent, despicable, reprehensible, contemptible, odious, hateful; informal ghastly, horrid, gross; literary noisome.

▶ **noun** **1** a substance that deters insects or other pests. **2** a substance used to treat something to make it repel water.
– DERIVATIVES **re·pel·lence** noun **re·pel·len·cy** noun **re·pel·lent·ly** adverb.

re·pent /riˈpent/ ▶ **verb** feel or express sincere regret or remorse about something bad or wrong that one has done.

– SYNONYMS **feel remorse,** regret, be sorry, rue, reproach oneself, be ashamed, feel contrite, be penitent, be remorseful.

– DERIVATIVES **re·pent·ance** noun **re·pent·er** noun.
– ORIGIN Old French *repentir.*

re·pent·ant /riˈpentnt/ ▶ **adjective** feeling or expressing sincere regret or remorse about something bad or wrong that one has done.

– SYNONYMS **penitent,** contrite, regretful, rueful, remorseful, apologetic, chastened, ashamed, shamefaced.
– ANTONYMS impenitent.

re·per·cus·sions /ˌrēpərˈkəsнənz, ˌrep-/ ▶ **plural noun** the consequences of an event or action: *the political repercussions of the scandal.*

– SYNONYMS **consequences,** results, effects, outcome, reverberations, backlash, aftermath, fallout.

– ORIGIN from Latin *repercutere* 'cause to rebound, push back.'

rep·er·toire /ˈrepə(r)ˌtwär/ ▶ **noun** the plays, operas, or other items known or regularly performed by a performer or company.

– SYNONYMS **collection,** range, repertory, list, store, stock, repository, supply.

– ORIGIN French.

rep·er·to·ry /ˈrepə(r)ˌtôrē/ ▶ **noun** (pl. **repertories**) **1** the performance by a company of the plays, operas, or ballets in its repertoire at regular short intervals. **2** another term for **REPERTOIRE.**
– ORIGIN Latin *repertorium* 'catalog, storehouse.'

rep·er·to·ry the·a·ter ▶ **noun** a theatrical company that performs plays from its repertoire for regular, short periods of time, moving on from one play to another.

rep·e·ti·tion /ˌrepəˈtisнən/ ▶ **noun** **1** the action of repeating something. **2** a thing that has been said or done before.

– SYNONYMS **1 reiteration,** restatement, retelling. **2 repetitiousness,** repetitiveness, tautology.

rep·e·ti·tious /ˌrepəˈtisнəs/ ▶ **adjective** having too much repetition; repetitive.

– SYNONYMS **recurring,** recurrent, repeated, unvaried, unchanging, routine, mechanical, automatic, monotonous, boring.
– ANTONYMS varied.

– DERIVATIVES **rep·e·ti·tious·ly** adverb **rep·e·ti·tious·ness** noun.

re·pet·i·tive /riˈpetətiv/ ▶ **adjective** repeated many times or too much.

– SYNONYMS **recurring,** recurrent, repeated, unvaried, unchanging, routine, mechanical, automatic, monotonous, boring.
– ANTONYMS varied.

– DERIVATIVES **re·pet·i·tive·ly** adverb **re·pet·i·tive·ness** noun.

re·pet·i·tive strain in·ju·ry ▶ **noun** a condition in which prolonged repetitive action causes pain or weakening in the tendons and muscles involved.

re·phrase /rēˈfrāz/ ▶ **verb** express something in an alternative way.

re·pine /riˈpīn/ ▶ **verb** literary be discontented; fret.

re·place /riˈplās/ ▶ **verb** **1** take the place of someone or something. **2** provide a substitute for something that is faulty, old, or damaged. **3** remove from a role and substitute with someone or something different: *he was replaced by a lightweight who knew nothing about the case.* **4** put something back in the place it occupied before.

– SYNONYMS **1 take the place of,** succeed, take over from, supersede, stand in for, substitute for, deputize for; informal step into someone's shoes/boots. **2 put back,** return, restore. **3 substitute,** exchange, change, swap.

– DERIVATIVES **re·place·a·ble** adjective **re·plac·er** noun.

CHOOSE THE RIGHT WORD

replace, displace, supersede, supplant

When a light bulb burns out, you **replace** it, meaning that you substitute something new or functioning for what is lost, destroyed, or worn out. If something that is obsolete or ineffective is replaced by something that is superior, more up-to-date, or more authoritative, the correct verb is **supersede** (*the computer superseded the electric typewriter*). In contrast, **displace** suggests that someone or something has been ousted or dislodged forcibly, without necessarily implying that it was inferior or ineffective (*a growing number of workers were being displaced by machines*). **Supplant** is more restricted in meaning; it suggests displacement by force, fraud, or innovation (*the democratic government had been supplanted by a power-hungry tyrant*). It can also mean to uproot or wipe out (*the English immigrants gradually supplanted the island's native inhabitants*).

re·place·ment /ri'plāsmənt/ ▶ **noun 1** the action of replacing someone or something. **2** a person or thing that takes the place of another.

– SYNONYMS **substitute,** stand-in, fill-in, locum, understudy, relief, cover, proxy, surrogate.

re·plant /rē'plant, 'rē-/ ▶ **verb 1** plant a tree or other plant in a new pot or site. **2** provide an area with new plants.

re·play /rē'plā, 'rē-/ ▶ **noun 1** an instance of playing a recording again. **2** a match or contest that is played again because the previous game was a draw. **3** an event that closely follows the pattern of a previous event. ▶ **verb 1** play back a recording. **2** play a match or contest again.

re·plen·ish /ri'plenisн/ ▶ **verb 1** fill something up again. **2** restore a stock or supply to a former level.

– SYNONYMS **1 refill,** top up, fill up, recharge, freshen. **2 stock up,** restock, restore, replace.
– ANTONYMS empty.

– DERIVATIVES **re·plen·ish·er** noun **re·plen·ish·ment** noun.
– ORIGIN Old French *replenir*.

re·plete /ri'plēt/ ▶ **adjective 1** (**replete with**) filled or well supplied with: *a courtyard replete with cacti*. **2** very full with food.
– DERIVATIVES **re·ple·tion** /ri'plēsнən/ noun.
– ORIGIN from Latin *replere* 'fill up.'

rep·li·ca /'replikə/ ▶ **noun** an exact copy or model of something, especially one on a smaller scale.

– SYNONYMS **copy,** model, duplicate, reproduction, dummy, imitation, facsimile.

– ORIGIN Italian.

rep·li·cate ▶ **verb** /'repli,kāt/ **1** make an exact copy of something. **2** (**replicate itself**) (of genetic material or a living organism) reproduce or give rise to a copy of itself. **3** repeat an experiment to obtain a consistent result. ▶ **noun** /-kit/ a close or exact copy; a replica.
– DERIVATIVES **rep·li·ca·ble** /'replikəbəl/ adjective **rep·li·ca·tion** /,repli'kāsнən/ noun **rep·li·ca·tor** /'repli,kātər/ noun.
– ORIGIN Latin *replicare*.

re·ply /ri'plī/ ▶ **verb** (**replies, replying, replied**) **1** say or write something as an answer to something. **2** respond with a similar action: *they replied to the shelling with a mortar attack*.

– SYNONYMS **respond,** answer, write back, rejoin, retort, riposte, counter, come back.

▶ **noun** (pl. **replies**) **1** a spoken or written answer. **2** the action of answering or responding to someone or something.

– SYNONYMS **answer,** response, rejoinder, retort, riposte; informal **comeback.**

– DERIVATIVES **re·pli·er** noun.
– ORIGIN Old French *replier*.

re·po /'rē,pō/ informal ▶ **noun** (pl. **repos**) **1** another term for **REPURCHASE AGREEMENT**. **2** a car or other item that has been repossessed. ▶ **verb** (**repo's, repo'd, repoing**) repossess (a car or other item) when a buyer defaults on payments.

re·pop·u·late /rē'päpyə,lāt/ ▶ **verb 1** introduce a population into an area previously deserted. **2** populate or fill again: *probiotics repopulate your gut with healthy bacteria*.
– DERIVATIVES **re·pop·u·la·tion** /,rē,päpyə'lāsнən/ noun.

re·port /ri'pôrt/ ▶ **verb 1** give a spoken or written account of something. **2** cover an event or situation as a journalist. **3** (**be reported**) be said or rumored. **4** make a formal complaint about someone or something. **5** present oneself as having arrived somewhere or as ready to do something: *he had to report to the boss at 9 a.m.* **6** (**report to**) be responsible to a supervisor or manager.

– SYNONYMS **1 communicate,** announce, divulge, disclose, reveal, relay, describe, narrate, delineate, detail, document, give an account of, make public, publish, broadcast, proclaim, publicize. **2** *his son reported him to the police* **inform on**; informal tell on, squeal on, rat on. **3** *I reported for duty* **present oneself,** arrive, turn up, clock in; informal show up.

▶ **noun 1** an account given of a matter after investigation or consideration. **2** a description of an event or situation. **3** a teacher's written assessment of a student's work and progress. **4** a sudden loud noise, especially of gunfire.

– SYNONYMS **1 account,** record, minutes, proceedings, transcript. **2 news,** information, word, intelligence. **3 story,** account, article, piece, item, column, feature, bulletin, dispatch, communiqué. **4 rumor,** whisper; informal buzz. **5 bang,** crack, explosion, boom.

– DERIVATIVES **re·port·a·ble** adjective.
– ORIGIN Latin *reportare* 'bring back.'

re·port·age /rə'pôrtij, ,repôr'täzн/ ▶ **noun 1** the reporting of news by the media. **2** factual, journalistic writing in a book.

re·port card ▶ **noun 1** a teacher's written assessment of a student's work and progress. **2** an evaluation of performance: *legislators fared poorly in a recent report card*.

re·port·ed speech ▶ **noun** a speaker's words reported with the required changes of person and tense (e.g., *he said that he would go*, based on *I will go*). Contrasted with **DIRECT SPEECH**.

re·port·er /ri'pôrtər/ ▶ **noun** a person who reports news for a newspaper or broadcasting company.

– SYNONYMS **journalist,** correspondent, newsman, newswoman, columnist; informal hack, stringer.

rep·or·to·ri·al /,repə(r)'tôrēəl, ,rē-/ ▶ **adjective** of or characteristic of newspaper reporters: *reportorial ambition and curiosity*.

re·pose[1] /ri'pōz/ ▶ **noun 1** a state of rest or tranquility. **2** the state of being calm and composed. ▶ **verb** formal

1 lie down and rest. **2** be situated or kept in a particular place.
– ORIGIN Old French *reposer*.

re·pose² ▸ **verb** (**repose something in**) place one's confidence or trust in.
– ORIGIN from POSE.

re·po·si·tion /ˌrēpəˈzisHən/ ▸ **verb 1** alter the position of someone or something. **2** change the image of a company, product, etc., to target a different market.

re·pos·i·to·ry /riˈpäzəˌtôrē/ ▸ **noun** (pl. **repositories**) **1** a place or container for storage. **2** a person or thing that is full of information or a particular quality: *the lighthouse keeper is a repository of local history*.
– ORIGIN Latin *repositorium*.

re·pos·sess /ˌrēpəˈzes/ ▸ **verb** retake possession of something when a buyer fails to make the required payments.
– DERIVATIVES **re·pos·ses·sion** /-ˈzesHən/ noun **re·pos·ses·sor** noun.

re·pot /rēˈpät, ˈrē-/ ▸ **verb** (**repots, repotting, repotted**) put a plant in another pot.

re·pous·sé /rəˌpo͞oˈsā/ ▸ **adjective** (of metalwork) hammered into relief from the reverse side.
– ORIGIN French, 'pushed back.'

repp /rep/ ▸ **noun** variant spelling of REP³.

rep·re·hend /ˌrepriˈhend/ ▸ **verb** reprimand someone.
– DERIVATIVES **rep·re·hen·sion** /-ˈhencHən/ noun.
– ORIGIN Latin *reprehendere* 'seize, check, rebuke.'

rep·re·hen·si·ble /ˌrepriˈhensəbəl/ ▸ **adjective** wrong or bad and deserving condemnation.

> – SYNONYMS **deplorable,** disgraceful, discreditable, despicable, blameworthy, culpable, wrong, bad, shameful, dishonorable, inexcusable, unforgivable, indefensible, unjustifiable.
> – ANTONYMS praiseworthy.

– DERIVATIVES **rep·re·hen·si·bil·i·ty** /-ˌhensəˈbilətē/ noun **rep·re·hen·si·bly** /-blē/ adverb.

rep·re·sent /ˌrepriˈzent/ ▸ **verb 1** be entitled or appointed to act and speak on behalf of someone. **2** be an elected member of a lawmaking body for a constituency or party. **3** constitute; amount to: *this figure represents eleven percent of total sales*. **4** be a specimen or typical example of something. **5** (**be represented**) be present to a particular degree: *abstract art is well represented in this exhibition*. **6** portray in a particular way: *they were represented as being in need of protection*. **7** depict a subject in a work of art. **8** be a symbol of something.

> – SYNONYMS **1 appear for,** act for, speak on behalf of. **2 stand for,** symbolize, personify, epitomize, typify, embody, illustrate, exemplify. **3 depict,** portray, render, picture, delineate, show, illustrate.

– ORIGIN Latin *repraesentare*.

rep·re·sen·ta·tion /ˌrepriˌzenˈtāsHən, -zən-/ ▸ **noun 1** the action or an instance of representing someone or something. **2** an image, model, or other depiction of something. **3** (**representations**) statements made to an authority to express an opinion or register a protest.

> – SYNONYMS **1 portrayal,** depiction, delineation, presentation, rendition. **2 likeness,** painting, drawing, picture, illustration, sketch, image, model, figure, statue.

rep·re·sen·ta·tion·al /ˌrepriˌzenˈtāsHənl/ ▸ **adjective 1** relating to representation. **2** relating to art that shows the physical appearance of things.
– DERIVATIVES **rep·re·sen·ta·tion·al·ly** /ˌrepriˌzenˈtāsHənl-ē/ adverb.

rep·re·sen·ta·tive /ˌrepriˈzentətiv/ ▸ **adjective 1** typical of a class or group. **2** containing typical examples of many or all types: *a representative sample*. **3** (of a lawmaking body) consisting of people chosen to act and speak on behalf of a wider group. **4** serving as a portrayal or symbol of something.

> – SYNONYMS **1 typical,** archetypal, characteristic, illustrative, indicative. **2 symbolic,** emblematic.
> – ANTONYMS atypical.

▸ **noun 1** a person chosen to act and speak on behalf of another or others. **2** an agent of a firm who visits potential clients to sell its products. **3** an example of a class or group.

> – SYNONYMS **1 spokesperson,** spokesman, spokeswoman, agent, official, mouthpiece. **2 salesman,** commercial traveler, agent, negotiator; informal rep. **3 deputy,** substitute, stand-in, proxy, delegate, ambassador, emissary.

– DERIVATIVES **rep·re·sent·a·tive·ly** adverb **rep·re·sent·a·tive·ness** noun.

re·press /riˈpres/ ▸ **verb 1** use force to control or stop: *the regime continues to repress political parties*. **2** prevent or restrict the expression or development of something. **3** try not to allow a thought or feeling to enter one's conscious mind.

> – SYNONYMS **1 suppress,** quell, quash, subdue, put down, crush, extinguish, stamp out, defeat, contain. **2 oppress,** subjugate, keep down, tyrannize. **3 restrain,** hold back/in, suppress, keep in check, control, curb, stifle, bottle up; informal button up, keep the lid on.
> – ANTONYMS express.

– DERIVATIVES **re·press·er** noun **re·press·i·ble** /-əbəl/ adjective.
– ORIGIN Latin *reprimere* 'press back, check.'

re·pressed /riˈprest/ ▸ **adjective 1** (of a thought or feeling) not acknowledged; kept unconscious in one's mind. **2** tending to suppress one's feelings and desires.

re·pres·sion /riˈpresHən/ ▸ **noun** the action of repressing, or the state of being repressed.

> – SYNONYMS **1** *the repression of the protests* **suppression,** quashing, subduing, crushing, stamping out. **2** *political repression* **oppression,** subjugation, suppression, tyranny, authoritarianism, despotism. **3** *the repression of sexual urges* **restraint,** suppression, control, curbing, stifling.

re·pres·sive /riˈpresiv/ ▸ **adjective** severely restricting personal freedom; oppressive.

> – SYNONYMS **oppressive,** authoritarian, despotic, tyrannical, dictatorial, fascist, autocratic, totalitarian, undemocratic.

– DERIVATIVES **re·pres·sive·ly** adverb **re·pres·sive·ness** noun.

re·prieve /riˈprēv/ ▸ **verb 1** cancel the punishment of someone. **2** chiefly Brit. abandon or postpone plans to close something: *the threatened mines could be reprieved*.

> – SYNONYMS **pardon,** spare, give/grant amnesty to; informal let off (the hook).

▸ **noun 1** the cancellation of a punishment. **2** a brief delay before something undesirable happens.

> – SYNONYMS **pardon,** stay of execution, amnesty.

– ORIGIN Old French *reprendre*.

rep·ri·mand /ˈreprəˌmand/ ▸ **noun** a formal expression of disapproval; a rebuke.

– SYNONYMS **rebuke,** reproach, scolding, admonition; informal telling-off, chewing-out, dressing-down.

▸ **verb** formally tell someone that they have done something wrong.

– SYNONYMS **rebuke,** reproach, scold, admonish, reprove, chastise, upbraid, berate, take to task, castigate; informal tell off, chew out.
– ANTONYMS praise.

– ORIGIN French *réprimande.*

CHOOSE THE RIGHT WORD

See **REBUKE**.

re·print ▸ **verb** /rēˈprint, ˈrē-/ print something again or in a revised form. ▸ **noun** /ˈrēˌprint/ **1** an act of reprinting. **2** a copy of a book or other material that has been reprinted.

re·pris·al /riˈprīzəl/ ▸ **noun** a violent or aggressive act done in return for a similar act.

– SYNONYMS **retaliation,** counter-attack, comeback, revenge, vengeance, retribution, requital; informal a taste of one's own medicine.

– ORIGIN Old French *reprisaille.*

re·prise /riˈprēz, -ˈprīz/ ▸ **noun 1** a repeated passage in music. **2** a repeat of something: *Mets fans had hoped for a reprise of the last Series.* ▸ **verb** repeat a piece of music or a performance.
– ORIGIN French, 'taken up again.'

re·proach /riˈprōCH/ ▸ **verb 1** express one's disapproval of or disappointment with someone. **2** (**reproach someone with**) accuse someone of. ▸ **noun** an expression of disapproval or disappointment.
– DERIVATIVES **re·proach·a·ble** adjective.
– PHRASES **above** (or **beyond**) **reproach** so perfect as to be beyond criticism.
– ORIGIN Old French *reprochier.*

CHOOSE THE RIGHT WORD

See **REBUKE**.

re·proach·ful /riˈprōCHfəl/ ▸ **adjective** expressing disapproval or disappointment.

– SYNONYMS **disapproving,** reproving, critical, censorious, disparaging, withering, accusatory, admonitory.
– ANTONYMS approving.

– DERIVATIVES **re·proach·ful·ly** adverb.

rep·ro·bate /ˈreprəˌbāt/ ▸ **noun** a person who behaves in an immoral way.
– DERIVATIVES **rep·ro·ba·tion** /ˌreprəˈbāSHən/ noun.
– ORIGIN from Latin *reprobare* 'disapprove.'

re·proc·ess /rēˈpräsˌes, -ˈpräsəs, -ˈprō-/ ▸ **verb** process something again or differently in order to reuse it.

re·pro·duce /ˌrēprəˈd(y)o͞os/ ▸ **verb 1** produce a copy of something. **2** produce something similar to something else in a different situation. **3** (of an organism) produce offspring.

– SYNONYMS **1 copy,** duplicate, replicate, photocopy, xerox, photostat, print. **2 repeat,** replicate, recreate, redo, simulate, imitate, emulate, mimic. **3 breed,** procreate, propagate, multiply, proliferate.

– DERIVATIVES **re·pro·duc·er** noun **re·pro·duc·i·ble** adjective.

re·pro·duc·tion /ˌrēprəˈdəksHən/ ▸ **noun 1** the action of reproducing. **2** a copy of a work of art, especially a print made of a painting.

– SYNONYMS **1 print,** copy, reprint, duplicate, facsimile, photocopy; trademark Xerox. **2 breeding,** procreation, propagation, proliferation.

▸ **adjective** made to imitate the style of an earlier period or particular craftsman: *reproduction furniture.*
– DERIVATIVES **re·pro·duc·tive** /-ˈdəktiv/ adjective.

re·proof /riˈpro͞of/ ▸ **noun** a criticism or rebuke.
– ORIGIN from Old French *reprover* 'reprove.'

re·prove /riˈpro͞ov/ ▸ **verb** rebuke or reprimand someone.
– ORIGIN Old French *reprover.*

rep·tile /ˈreptəl, ˈrepˌtīl/ ▸ **noun** a cold-blooded vertebrate animal of a class that includes snakes, lizards, crocodiles, turtles, and tortoises, typically having a dry scaly skin and laying soft-shelled eggs.
– DERIVATIVES **rep·til·i·an** /repˈtilēən, -ˈtilyən/ adjective & noun.
– ORIGIN from Latin *reptilis* 'crawling.'

re·pub·lic /riˈpəblik/ ▸ **noun** a state in which power is held by the people and their elected representatives, and that has a president rather than a monarch.
– ORIGIN Latin *respublica.*

re·pub·li·can /riˈpəblikən/ ▸ **adjective 1** belonging to or typical of a republic. **2** supporting the principles of a republic. **3** (**Republican**) supporting the Republican Party. ▸ **noun 1** a person in favor of republican government. **2** (**Republican**) a member or supporter of the Republican Party.
– DERIVATIVES **re·pub·li·can·ism** /-ˌnizəm/ noun.

Re·pub·li·can Par·ty ▸ **noun** one of the two main US political parties (the other being the Democratic Party), favoring a conservative stance, limited central government, and a strong national defense.

re·pu·di·ate /riˈpyo͞odēˌāt/ ▸ **verb 1** refuse to accept something. **2** deny the truth or validity of: *he repudiated allegations that he was a shirker.* **3** chiefly Law refuse to fulfill an agreement, obligation, or debt. **4** old use disown or divorce one's wife.

– SYNONYMS **1 reject,** renounce, disown, abandon, give up, turn one's back on, cast off, lay aside, wash one's hands of; formal forswear; literary forsake. **2 deny,** refute, contradict, controvert, rebut, dispute, dismiss, brush aside; formal gainsay.
– ANTONYMS embrace.

– DERIVATIVES **re·pu·di·a·tion** /riˌpyo͞odēˈāsHən/ noun **re·pu·di·a·tor** noun.
– ORIGIN from Latin *repudiatus* 'divorced, cast off.'

re·pug·nance /riˈpəgnəns/ ▸ **noun** intense disgust.
– DERIVATIVES **re·pug·nan·cy** noun.
– ORIGIN from Latin *repugnare* 'oppose.'

re·pug·nant /riˈpəgnənt/ ▸ **adjective** unpleasant and completely unacceptable.

– SYNONYMS **abhorrent,** revolting, repulsive, repellent, disgusting, offensive, objectionable, vile, foul, nasty, loathsome, sickening, nauseating, hateful, detestable, execrable, abominable, monstrous, appalling, unsavory, unpalatable.
– ANTONYMS pleasant.

re·pulse /riˈpəls/ ▸ **verb 1** drive back an attacking enemy by force. **2** reject or refuse to accept an offer or the person making it. **3** cause someone to feel intense distaste or disgust. ▸ **noun 1** the action of driving

back an attack. **2** a rejection or refusal of an offer or approach.
– ORIGIN Latin *repellere*.

re·pul·sion /ri'pəlsHən/ ▶ **noun 1** a feeling of intense distaste or disgust. **2** Physics a force under the influence of which objects tend to move away from each other, e.g., through having the same magnetic polarity.

re·pul·sive /ri'pəlsiv/ ▶ **adjective 1** arousing intense distaste or disgust. **2** Physics relating to repulsion between objects.

– SYNONYMS **disgusting,** revolting, foul, nasty, obnoxious, sickening, nauseating, stomach-churning, vile; informal ghastly, gross, horrible; literary noisome.
– ANTONYMS attractive.

– DERIVATIVES **re·pul·sive·ly** adverb **re·pul·sive·ness** noun.

re·pur·chase a·gree·ment ▶ **noun** Finance a contract in which the vendor of a security agrees to repurchase it from the buyer at an agreed price.

re·pur·pose /rē'pərpəs/ ▶ **verb** adapt something for use in a different purpose.

rep·u·ta·ble /'repyətəbəl/ ▶ **adjective** having a good reputation.

– SYNONYMS **well thought of,** highly regarded, respected, respectable, of (good) repute, prestigious, established, reliable, dependable, trustworthy.
– ANTONYMS untrustworthy.

– DERIVATIVES **rep·u·ta·bly** /-blē/ adverb.

rep·u·ta·tion /ˌrepyə'tāsHən/ ▶ **noun 1** the beliefs or opinions that are generally held about someone or something. **2** a high public opinion of someone or something: *they have damaged the reputation of public service broadcasting*.

– SYNONYMS **name,** good name, character, repute, standing, stature, position, renown, esteem, prestige.

re·pute /ri'pyo͞ot/ ▶ **noun 1** the opinion generally held of someone or something. **2** the state of being highly regarded. ▶ **verb 1** (**be reputed**) be generally regarded as having done something or as having particular characteristics. **2** (as adj. **reputed**) generally believed to exist.

– SYNONYMS **1** (**be reputed**) *they are reputed to be very rich* **thought,** said, reported, rumored, believed, held, considered, deemed, alleged. **2** (as adj. **reputed**) *the reputed flatness of the country* **supposed,** putative.

– DERIVATIVES **re·put·ed·ly** adverb.
– ORIGIN from Latin *reputare* 'think over.'

re·quest /ri'kwest/ ▶ **noun 1** an act of asking politely or formally for something. **2** a thing that is asked for politely or formally.

– SYNONYMS **1 appeal,** entreaty, plea, petition, application, demand, call, solicitation. **2 requirement,** wish, desire, choice.

▶ **verb** politely or formally ask for something or ask someone to do something.

– SYNONYMS **ask for,** appeal for, call for, seek, solicit, plead for, beg for, apply for, put in for, demand, petition for, sue for, implore, entreat; literary beseech.

– DERIVATIVES **re·quest·er** noun.
– ORIGIN from Latin *requirere* 'require.'

req·ui·em /'rekwēəm, 'rā-/ ▶ **noun 1** (especially in the Roman Catholic Church) a Mass for the souls of the dead. **2** a musical composition setting parts of such a Mass.
– ORIGIN Latin.

re·quire /ri'kwīr/ ▶ **verb 1** need something for a purpose. **2** instruct or expect someone to do something. **3** specify as compulsory: *the minimum car insurance required by law*. **4** (**require something of**) regard an action or quality as due from someone because of the position they hold.

– SYNONYMS **1 need,** have need of, be short of, want, desire, lack, miss. **2 necessitate,** demand, call for, involve, entail, take. **3 demand,** insist on, call for, ask for, expect. **4 order,** instruct, command, enjoin, oblige, compel, force.

– ORIGIN Latin *requirere*.

re·quire·ment /ri'kwīrmənt/ ▶ **noun 1** something required; a need. **2** something that is compulsory.

– SYNONYMS **need,** necessity, prerequisite, stipulation, demand, want, essential.

req·ui·site /'rekwəzət/ ▶ **adjective** made necessary by particular circumstances or regulations: *some lack the requisite skills to succeed*. ▶ **noun** a thing that is necessary for a purpose.
– ORIGIN Latin *requisitus* 'searched for, deemed necessary.'

req·ui·si·tion /ˌrekwə'zisHən/ ▶ **noun 1** an official order enabling property or materials to be taken and used. **2** the taking of goods for military or public use. **3** a formal written demand that something should be done or put into operation.

– SYNONYMS **1 order,** request, call, application, claim, demand. **2 appropriation,** commandeering, seizure, confiscation, expropriation.

▶ **verb** demand the use or supply of something by an official order.

– SYNONYMS **1 commandeer,** appropriate, take over, take possession of, occupy, seize, confiscate, expropriate. **2 request,** order, call for, demand.

re·quite /ri'kwīt/ ▶ **verb** formal give or do something suitable in return for a favor, love, kindness, etc.
– DERIVATIVES **re·quit·al** noun.
– ORIGIN from **RE-** + former *quite* 'behave.'

re·ran /rē'ran/ past of **RERUN**.

re·read /rē'rēd/ ▶ **verb** (past and past part. **reread** /rē'red/) read a written work or passage again.

rere·dos /'rerəˌdäs, 'ri(ə)rə-/ ▶ **noun** (pl. same) an ornamental screen at the back of an altar in a church.
– ORIGIN Old French *areredos*.

re·re·lease /ˌrē-ri'lēs/ ▶ **verb** release a recording or movie again. ▶ **noun** a re-released recording or movie.

re·route /rē'ro͞ot, rē'rout/ ▶ **verb** send someone or something by or along a different route.

re·run /rē'rən/ ▶ **verb** (**reruns**, **rerunning**, **reran** /rē'ran/; past part. **rerun**) show, stage, or perform something again. ▶ **noun** an event or program that is run again.

re·sale /'rēˌsāl/ ▶ **noun** the sale of a thing previously bought.
– DERIVATIVES **re·sale·a·ble** (also **resalable**) adjective.

re·sat /rē'sat/ past and past participle of **RESIT**.

re·sched·ule /rē'skejo͞o(ə)l/ ▶ **verb 1** change the time of a planned event. **2** arrange a new scheme of repayments of a debt.

re·scind /ri'sind/ ▸ **verb** formally cancel a law, order, or agreement.

– SYNONYMS **revoke,** repeal, cancel, reverse, overturn, overrule, annul, nullify, void, invalidate, quash, abolish; formal abrogate.
– ANTONYMS enforce.

– DERIVATIVES **re·scind·a·ble** adjective.
– ORIGIN Latin *rescindere.*

re·scis·sion /ri'sizʜən/ ▸ **noun** formal the official canceling of a law, order, or agreement.

res·cue /'reskyo͞o/ ▸ **verb** (**rescues, rescuing, rescued**) save someone or something from a dangerous or difficult situation.

– SYNONYMS **1 save,** free, set free, release, liberate, deliver. **2 retrieve,** recover, salvage.

▸ **noun** an act of rescuing someone or something.

– SYNONYMS **saving,** rescuing, release, freeing, liberation, deliverance.

– DERIVATIVES **res·cu·a·ble** adjective **res·cu·er** noun.
– ORIGIN Old French *rescoure.*

re·seal /rē'sēl/ ▸ **verb** seal something again.
– DERIVATIVES **re·seal·a·ble** adjective.

re·search ▸ **noun** /'rē,sərcʜ, ri'sərcʜ/ the systematic study of materials and sources in order to establish facts and reach new conclusions.

– SYNONYMS **investigation,** experimentation, testing, analysis, fact-finding, examination, scrutiny.

▸ **verb 1** carry out research into a subject. **2** discover or check information for a book, program, etc.

– SYNONYMS **investigate,** study, inquire into, look into, probe, explore, analyze, examine, scrutinize.

– DERIVATIVES **re·search·er** noun.
– ORIGIN from former French *recercher.*

re·search and de·vel·op·ment ▸ **noun** (in industry) work directed toward new ideas and improvement of products and processes.

re·se·lect /,rēse'lekt/ ▸ **verb** select someone or something again or differently.
– DERIVATIVES **re·se·lec·tion** /,rēsel'eksʜən/ noun.

re·sell /rē'sel/ ▸ **verb** (past and past part. **resold**) sell something one has bought to someone else.
– DERIVATIVES **re·sell·er** noun.

re·sem·blance /ri'zembləns/ ▸ **noun 1** the fact of looking like or being similar to someone or something: *he bears a strong resemblance to his mother.* **2** a way in which things are alike.

– SYNONYMS **similarity,** likeness, similitude, correspondence, congruence, conformity, comparability, parallel.
– ANTONYMS dissimilarity.

CHOOSE THE RIGHT WORD

See **LIKENESS**.

re·sem·ble /ri'zembəl/ ▸ **verb** be similar to someone or something in appearance or qualities.

– SYNONYMS **look like,** be similar to, remind someone of, take after, approximate to, smack of, correspond to, echo, mirror, parallel.
– ANTONYMS differ from.

– ORIGIN Old French *resembler.*

re·sent /ri'zent/ ▸ **verb** feel bitter or angry toward someone or something.

– SYNONYMS **begrudge,** feel aggrieved at/about, feel bitter about, grudge, be resentful of, take exception to, object to, take amiss, take offense at.
– ANTONYMS welcome.

– ORIGIN from former French *resentir.*

re·sent·ful /ri'zentfəl/ ▸ **adjective** feeling bitter or angry about something, especially unfair treatment.

– SYNONYMS **aggrieved,** indignant, irritated, piqued, put out, in high dudgeon, dissatisfied, disgruntled, discontented, offended, bitter, jaundiced, envious, jealous; informal miffed, peeved, sore.

– DERIVATIVES **re·sent·ful·ly** adverb **re·sent·ful·ness** noun.

re·sent·ment /ri'zentmənt/ ▸ **noun** bitterness or anger at unfair treatment.

– SYNONYMS **bitterness,** indignation, irritation, pique, dissatisfaction, disgruntlement, discontentment, acrimony, rancor.

res·er·va·tion /,rezər'vāsʜən/ ▸ **noun 1** an expression of doubt qualifying overall approval of a plan or statement: *some generals voiced reservations about making air strikes.* **2** an area of land set aside for occupation by North American Indians or Australian Aboriginals. **3** the action of reserving something. **4** an arrangement in which something is reserved.

– SYNONYMS **1 doubt,** qualm, scruple; (**reservations**) misgivings, skepticism, unease, hesitation, objection. **2 reserve,** enclave, sanctuary, territory, homeland.

re·serve /ri'zərv/ ▸ **verb 1** keep something for future use. **2** arrange for a seat, ticket, etc., to be kept for a particular person. **3** retain or hold a right or entitlement. **4** hold back from delivering a decision without proper consideration or evidence: *I'll reserve my views on his ability until he's played again.*

– SYNONYMS **1 put aside,** set aside, keep (back), save, hold back, keep in reserve, earmark, retain. **2 book,** order, arrange for, secure, engage, hire.

▸ **noun 1** a supply of something available for use if required. **2** funds kept available by a bank, company, or government. **3** a military force withheld from action to protect others, or additional to the regular forces and available in an emergency. **4** an extra player on a team, serving as a possible substitute. **5** (**the reserves**) the second-choice team. **6** an area of land set aside for occupation by a native people. **7** a protected area for wildlife. **8** a lack of warmth or openness: *he smiled and some of her natural reserve melted.*

– SYNONYMS **1 stock,** store, supply, stockpile, pool, hoard, cache, fund. **2 reinforcements,** extras, auxiliaries. **3 national park,** sanctuary, preserve, reservation. **4 shyness,** diffidence, timidity, taciturnity, inhibition, reticence, detachment, aloofness, distance, remoteness. **5** *she trusted him without reserve* **reservation,** qualification, condition, limitation, hesitation, doubt.

– DERIVATIVES **re·serv·a·ble** adjective.
– ORIGIN Latin *reservare* 'keep back.'

re·serve bank ▸ **noun** a regional bank operating under and implementing the policies of the Federal Reserve.

re·serve cur·ren·cy ▸ **noun** a strong currency widely used in international trade that a central bank is prepared to hold as part of its foreign exchange reserves.

re·served /ri'zərvd/ ▸ **adjective** **1** slow to reveal emotion or opinions. **2** kept specially for a particular person.

– SYNONYMS **1 uncommunicative,** reticent, unforthcoming, aloof, cool, undemonstrative, unsociable, unfriendly, quiet, silent, taciturn, withdrawn, secretive, shy, retiring, diffident, timid, introverted; informal standoffish. **2 booked,** taken, spoken for, prearranged.
– ANTONYMS outgoing.

– DERIVATIVES **re·serv·ed·ly** adverb **re·serv·ed·ness** noun.

re·serve price ▸ **noun** the price set as the lowest acceptable by the seller for an item sold at auction.

re·serv·ist /ri'zərvist/ ▸ **noun** a member of a military reserve force.

res·er·voir /'rezə(r),vwär, -,v(w)ôr/ ▸ **noun** **1** a large lake used as a source of water supply. **2** a place where fluid collects, especially in rock strata or in the body. **3** a container or part of a machine designed to hold fluid. **4** a supply or source of something: *the country's vast reservoir of computer scientists.*

– SYNONYMS **1 lake,** pool, pond, basin. **2 receptacle,** container, holder, tank. **3 stock,** store, stockpile, reserve(s), supply, bank, pool.

– ORIGIN French.

re·set /rē'set/ ▸ **verb** (**resets, resetting, reset**) **1** set something again or differently. **2** set a counter, timer, etc., to zero.
– DERIVATIVES **re·set·ta·ble** adjective.

re·set·tle /rē'setl/ ▸ **verb** settle or cause to settle in a different place.
– DERIVATIVES **re·set·tle·ment** noun.

re·shape /rē'sHāp/ ▸ **verb** shape or form something differently or again.

re·shuf·fle /rē'sHəfəl/ ▸ **verb** **1** change around the positions of members of a team, especially government officials. **2** rearrange something. ▸ **noun** an act of reshuffling.

re·side /ri'zīd/ ▸ **verb** **1** live in a particular place. **2** (of a right or legal power) belong to a person or body. **3** (**reside in**) (of a quality) be present in: *intelligence and judgment reside in old men.*

– SYNONYMS **1 live,** lodge, stay, occupy, inhabit; formal dwell, be domiciled. **2 be vested in,** be bestowed on, be conferred on, be in the hands of.

res·i·dence /'rez(ə)dəns, 'rezə,dens/ ▸ **noun** **1** the fact of living somewhere. **2** a person's home. **3** the official house of a government official.

– SYNONYMS **home,** house, address, quarters, lodgings; informal pad; formal dwelling, abode, domicile.

– PHRASES **artist** (or **writer**) **in residence** an artist or writer who is based for a set period within a college or other institution and is available for teaching purposes.

res·i·den·cy /'rez(ə)dənsē, 'rezə,densē/ ▸ **noun** (pl. **residencies**) **1** the fact of living in a place. **2** a residential post held by an artist or writer. **3** a period of specialized medical training in a hospital.

res·i·dent /'rez(ə)dənt, 'rezə,dent/ ▸ **noun** **1** a person who lives somewhere on a long-term basis. **2** a medical graduate engaged in specialized practice under supervision in a hospital. **3** a bird, butterfly, or other animal of a species that does not migrate.

– SYNONYMS **inhabitant,** local, citizen, native, householder, homeowner, occupier, tenant; humorous denizen.

▸ **adjective** **1** living somewhere on a long-term basis. **2** having living quarters at one's place of work. **3** attached to and working regularly for a particular institution.
– ORIGIN from Latin *residere* 'remain.'

res·i·den·tial /,rezə'dencHəl/ ▸ **adjective** **1** designed for people to live in. **2** (of a job, course, etc.) requiring someone to live in a particular place. **3** (of an area) occupied by private houses.
– DERIVATIVES **res·i·den·tial·ly** adverb.

re·sid·u·a /ri'zijo͞oə/ plural of **RESIDUUM**.

re·sid·u·al /ri'zijooəl/ ▸ **adjective** remaining after the greater part or quantity has gone or been removed. ▸ **noun** a quantity remaining after the greater part has gone or been removed.
– DERIVATIVES **re·sid·u·al·ly** adverb.

res·i·due /'rezə,d(y)o͞o/ ▸ **noun** **1** a small amount of something that remains after the main part has gone or been taken or used. **2** Law the part of an estate that is left after the payment of charges, debts, and bequests. **3** a substance that remains after a process such as combustion or evaporation.

– SYNONYMS **remainder,** rest, remnant(s), surplus, extra, excess, remains, leftovers.

– ORIGIN Latin *residuum.*

re·sid·u·um /ri'zijo͞oəm/ ▸ **noun** (pl. **residua** /-'zijo͞oə/) technical a chemical residue.
– ORIGIN Latin.

re·sign /ri'zīn/ ▸ **verb** **1** voluntarily leave a job or position of office. **2** (**be resigned**) accept that something undesirable cannot be avoided.

– SYNONYMS **1** *the executive director resigned* **leave,** give notice, stand down, step down; informal quit, pack (it) in. **2** *three state senators resigned their seats* **give up,** leave, vacate, renounce, relinquish, surrender. **3** *we **resigned ourselves to** a long wait* **reconcile oneself to,** become resigned to, come to terms with, accept.

– ORIGIN Latin *resignare* 'unseal, cancel.'

res·ig·na·tion /,rezig'nāsHən/ ▸ **noun** **1** an act of resigning from a job. **2** a letter stating one's intention to resign. **3** acceptance of something undesirable that cannot be avoided: *he confronted old age with his usual resignation.*

– SYNONYMS *he accepted his fate with resignation* **patience,** forbearance, stoicism, fortitude, fatalism, acceptance.

re·signed /ri'zīnd/ ▸ **adjective** full of resignation and acceptance.

– SYNONYMS *he gave a resigned sigh* **patient,** long-suffering, uncomplaining, forbearing, stoical, philosophical, fatalistic.

re·sil·ient /ri'zilyənt/ ▸ **adjective** **1** able to recoil or spring back into shape after bending, stretching, or being compressed. **2** (of a person) able to recover quickly from difficult conditions.

– SYNONYMS **1 flexible,** pliable, supple, durable, hard-wearing, stout, strong, sturdy, tough. **2 strong,** tough, hardy, quick to recover, buoyant, irrepressible.

– DERIVATIVES **re·sil·ience** noun **re·sil·ient·ly** adverb.
– ORIGIN from Latin *resilire* 'leap back.'

CHOOSE THE RIGHT WORD

See **FLEXIBLE**.

res·in /'rezən/ ▸ **noun 1** a sticky substance produced by some trees. **2** a synthetic polymer used as the basis of plastics, adhesives, varnishes, etc.
– DERIVATIVES **res·in·ous** adjective.
– ORIGIN Latin *resina*.

re·sist /ri'zist/ ▸ **verb 1** withstand the action or effect of something. **2** try to prevent something by action or argument. **3** stop oneself from having or doing something tempting: *I couldn't resist taking a peek*. **4** struggle or fight back when attacked.

– SYNONYMS **1 withstand,** be proof against, combat, weather, endure, be resistant to, keep out. **2 oppose,** fight against, object to, defy, kick against, obstruct. **3 refrain from,** abstain from, forbear from, desist from, not give in to, restrain oneself from.

– DERIVATIVES **re·sist·er** noun **re·sist·i·ble** adjective.
– ORIGIN Latin *resistere*.

re·sist·ance /ri'zistəns/ ▸ **noun 1** the action of resisting. **2** the ability not to be affected by something undesirable. **3** the impeding or stopping effect that one material thing has on another: *air resistance was reduced by streamlining*. **4** the degree to which a material or device opposes the passage of an electric current. **5** (also **resistance movement**) a secret organization that fights against authority in an occupied country.

– SYNONYMS **1 opposition,** hostility, struggle, fight, battle, stand, defiance. **2 immunity,** defenses.

– PHRASES **the path of least resistance** the easiest course of action.

re·sist·ant /ri'zistənt/ ▸ **adjective 1** unaffected by something undesirable: *people are more* ***resistant to*** *infection if they have an adequate diet*. **2** opposed to or against something or someone: *she is very* ***resistant to*** *change*.

– SYNONYMS **1 impervious to,** immune, invulnerable to, proof against, unaffected by. **2 opposed to,** averse to, hostile to, inimical to, against; informal anti.
– ANTONYMS vulnerable.

re·sis·tive /ri'zistiv/ ▸ **adjective 1** technical able to resist something. **2** relating to electrical resistance.
– DERIVATIVES **re·sis·tiv·i·ty** /ri,zis'tivətē/ noun.

re·sis·tor /ri'zistər/ ▸ **noun** a device that resists the passage of an electric current.

re·sit /rē'sit/ Brit. ▸ **verb** (**resits, resitting, resat**) take an exam again after failing. ▸ **noun** an exam that is taken again for this reason.

re·size /rē'sīz/ ▸ **verb** alter the size of something, especially a computer window or image.

re·skill /rē'skil/ ▸ **verb** teach someone new skills.

re·sold /rē'sōld/ past and past participle of **RESELL**.

res·o·lute /'rezə,lo͞ot, -lət/ ▸ **adjective** admirably purposeful and determined.

– SYNONYMS **determined,** purposeful, resolved, adamant, single-minded, firm, unswerving, unwavering, steadfast, staunch, stalwart, unfaltering, indefatigable, tenacious, strong-willed, unshakable.
– ANTONYMS half-hearted.

– DERIVATIVES **res·o·lute·ly** adverb **res·o·lute·ness** noun.
– ORIGIN Latin *resolutus* 'loosened, paid.'

WORD TOOLKIT

See **STAUNCH**[1].

res·o·lu·tion /,rezə'lo͞osʜən/ ▸ **noun 1** a firm decision. **2** a formal expression of opinion or intention agreed on by a lawmaking body. **3** the quality of being resolute or determined. **4** the resolving of a problem or dispute. **5** the process of separating something into its component parts. **6** the degree of detail visible in a photographic or television image. **7** the smallest interval between adjacent objects that is measurable by a telescope or other scientific instrument.

– SYNONYMS **1 intention,** decision, intent, aim, plan, commitment, pledge, promise. **2 motion,** proposal, proposition. **3 determination,** purpose, purposefulness, resolve, single-mindedness, firmness, willpower, strength of character. **4 solution,** answer, end, settlement, conclusion.

re·solve /ri'zälv, -'zôlv/ ▸ **verb 1** settle or find a solution to a problem. **2** decide firmly on a course of action. **3** (of a lawmaking body) take a decision by a formal vote. **4** (**resolve something into**) separate something into its component parts. **5** (of something seen at a distance) turn into a different form when seen more clearly. **6** (of optical or photographic equipment) separate or distinguish between objects that are close together.

– SYNONYMS **1 settle,** sort out, solve, fix, straighten out, deal with, put right, rectify; informal hammer out, thrash out. **2 determine,** decide, make up one's mind. **3 vote,** rule, decide formally, agree.

▸ **noun** firm determination to do something.

– SYNONYMS **determination,** purpose, resolution, single-mindedness; informal guts.

– DERIVATIVES **re·solv·a·ble** adjective **re·solv·er** noun.
– ORIGIN Latin *resolvere*.

re·solv·ing pow·er ▸ **noun** the ability of an optical instrument or type of film to distinguish small or closely adjacent images.

res·o·nance /'rezənəns/ ▸ **noun 1** the quality in a sound of being deep, clear, and reverberating. **2** the power to suggest images, emotions, or a quality. **3** Physics the reinforcement or prolongation of sound by reflection from a surface or by the vibration of an adjacent object at the same time.

res·o·nant /'rezənənt/ ▸ **adjective 1** (of sound) deep, clear, and continuing to reverberate. **2** (of a room, musical instrument, or hollow body) tending to reinforce or prolong sounds. **3** (**resonant with**) filled or resounding with a sound. **4** suggesting images, emotions, or a quality: *a name resonant with Hollywood glamour*.
– DERIVATIVES **res·o·nant·ly** adverb.
– ORIGIN from Latin *resonare* 'sound again, resound.'

res·o·nate /'rezn,āt/ ▸ **verb** produce or be filled with a deep, clear reverberating sound.
– DERIVATIVES **res·o·na·tor** noun.

re·sort /ri'zôrt/ ▸ **noun 1** a place visited for vacations or recreation. **2** a strategy or course of action. **3** the adoption of a course of action in a difficult situation: *achieving desired outcomes without resort to war*.

– SYNONYMS **1** *a seaside resort* **vacation spot,** tourist center, vacationland; retreat; spa; informal tourist trap. **2** *strike action is our last resort* **option,** alternative, choice, possibility, hope, measure, step, recourse, expedient.

▶ **verb** (**resort to**) adopt a course of action, especially an undesirable one, so as to resolve a difficult situation.

– SYNONYMS **fall back on,** have recourse to, turn to, make use of, use, avail oneself of.

– PHRASES **as a first** (or **last** or **final**) **resort** before anything else is attempted (or when all else has failed).

– ORIGIN Old French *resortir* 'come or go out again.'

re·sound /ri'zound/ ▶ **verb 1** fill or be filled with a ringing, booming, or echoing sound. **2** (as adj. **resounding**) emphatic; definite: *a resounding success.* **3** (of fame, success, etc.) be much talked about.

– SYNONYMS **1 echo,** reverberate, ring, boom, thunder, rumble, resonate. **2** (as adj. **resounding**) **enormous,** huge, very great, tremendous, terrific, colossal, emphatic, outstanding, remarkable, phenomenal.

re·source /'rē,sôrs, 'rē'zôrs, ri'sôrs, ri'zôrs/ ▶ **noun 1** (**resources**) a stock or supply of materials or assets that can be drawn on when required. **2** (**resources**) a country's means of supporting itself or becoming wealthier, as represented by its minerals, land, and other assets. **3** a source of help or information: *the database could be used as a teaching resource.* **4** a strategy adopted in a difficult situation. **5** (**resources**) personal qualities that help one to cope in a difficult situation.

– SYNONYMS **1 facility,** amenity, aid, help, support. **2 initiative,** resourcefulness, enterprise, ingenuity, inventiveness. **3** *we lack* ***resources*** **assets,** funds, wealth, money, capital, supplies, materials, stores, stocks, reserves.

▶ **verb** provide someone or something with resources.

– ORIGIN from Old French dialect *resourdre* 'rise again, recover.'

re·source·ful /ri'sôrsfəl, -'zôrs-/ ▶ **adjective** able to find quick and clever ways to overcome difficulties.

– SYNONYMS **ingenious,** enterprising, inventive, creative, clever, talented, able, capable.

– DERIVATIVES **re·source·ful·ly** adverb **re·source·ful·ness** noun.

CHOOSE THE RIGHT WORD

See **CREATIVE**.

re·spect /ri'spekt/ ▶ **noun 1** a feeling of admiration for someone or something because of their qualities or achievements. **2** a particular aspect or point. **3** (**respects**) polite greetings. **4** consideration for the feelings or rights of others.

– SYNONYMS **1 esteem,** regard, high opinion, admiration, reverence, deference, honor. **2** *the report was accurate in every respect* **aspect,** regard, feature, way, sense, particular, point, detail. **3** (**respects**) **regards,** compliments, greetings, best/good wishes.
– ANTONYMS contempt.

▶ **verb 1** feel or have respect for someone or something. **2** avoid harming or interfering with something. **3** agree to recognize and observe a law or rule.

– SYNONYMS **1 esteem,** admire, think highly of, have a high opinion of, look up to, revere, honor. **2 show consideration for,** have regard for, observe, be mindful of, be heedful of. **3 abide by,** comply with, follow, adhere to, conform to, act in accordance with, obey, observe, keep (to).
– ANTONYMS despise, disobey.

– DERIVATIVES **re·spect·er** noun.

– PHRASES **with respect to** (or **in respect of**) as regards; with reference to.

– ORIGIN Latin *respectus.*

re·spect·a·ble /ri'spektəbəl/ ▶ **adjective 1** regarded by society to be proper, correct, and good. **2** adequate or acceptable; fairly good.

– SYNONYMS **1 reputable,** upright, honest, honorable, trustworthy, decent, good, well bred, clean-living. **2 fairly good,** decent, fair-sized, reasonable, moderately good, large, sizable, considerable.
– ANTONYMS disreputable.

– DERIVATIVES **re·spect·a·bil·i·ty** /ri,spektə'bilətē/ noun **re·spect·a·bly** adverb.

re·spect·ful /ri'spektfəl/ ▶ **adjective** feeling or showing respect or consideration.

– SYNONYMS **deferential,** reverent, dutiful, polite, well mannered, civil, courteous, gracious.
– ANTONYMS rude.

– DERIVATIVES **re·spect·ful·ly** adverb **re·spect·ful·ness** noun.

re·spect·ing /ri'spektiNG/ ▶ **preposition** with reference to.

re·spec·tive /ri'spektiv/ ▶ **adjective** belonging or relating separately to each of two or more people or things: *they chatted about their respective lives.*

– SYNONYMS **separate,** personal, own, particular, individual, specific, special.

re·spec·tive·ly /ri'spektivlē/ ▶ **adverb** separately and in the order already mentioned.

re·spell /rē'spel/ ▶ **verb** (past and past part. **respelled** or chiefly Brit. **respelt**) spell a word differently, especially to show how to pronounce it.

res·pi·ra·tion /,respə'rāSHən/ ▶ **noun 1** the action of breathing. **2** a single breath. **3** the processes in living organisms involving the production of energy, typically with the intake of oxygen and the release of carbon dioxide.

res·pi·ra·tor /'respə,rātər/ ▶ **noun 1** a device worn over the face to prevent the inhalation of smoke or other harmful substances. **2** a device that enables someone to breathe artificially.

res·pi·ra·to·ry /'respərə,tôrē, ri'spīrə-/ ▶ **adjective** relating to breathing.

res·pi·ra·to·ry tract ▶ **noun** the passage formed by the mouth, nose, throat, and lungs, through which air passes during breathing.

re·spire /ri'spī(ə)r/ ▶ **verb 1** breathe. **2** (of a plant) carry out the process of respiration.

– DERIVATIVES **res·pi·ra·ble** adjective.

– ORIGIN Latin *respirare* 'breathe out.'

res·pite /'respət, ri'spīt/ ▶ **noun** a short period of rest or relief from something difficult or unpleasant.

– SYNONYMS **rest,** break, breathing space, interval, lull, pause, time out, relief; informal breather, letup.

– ORIGIN Old French *respit.*

re·splend·ent /ri'splendənt/ ▶ **adjective** attractive and colorful in an impressive way.

– DERIVATIVES **re·splend·ence** noun **re·splend·ent·ly** adverb.

– ORIGIN from Latin *resplendere* 'shine out.'

CHOOSE THE RIGHT WORD

See **BRIGHT**.

re·spond /ri'spänd/ ▶ **verb 1** say something in reply. **2** do something as a reaction to someone or something.

– SYNONYMS **1 answer,** reply, write back, come back, rejoin, retort, riposte, counter. **2 react,** reciprocate, retaliate.

– DERIVATIVES **re·spond·er** noun.
– ORIGIN Latin *respondere* 'answer, offer in return.'

re·spond·ent /ri'spändənt/ ▶ **noun 1** Law a person against whom a petition is filed, especially one in an appeal or a divorce case. **2** a person who responds to a questionnaire or an advertisement.

re·sponse /ri'späns/ ▶ **noun 1** a spoken or written answer. **2** a reaction to something. **3** technical a physical reaction to a stimulus or situation.

– SYNONYMS **1 answer,** reply, rejoinder, retort, riposte; informal comeback. **2 reaction,** reply, retaliation; informal comeback.
– ANTONYMS question.

re·spon·si·bil·i·ty /ri,spänsə'bilətē/ ▶ **noun** (pl. **responsibilities**) **1** the state of being responsible for someone or something. **2** the opportunity or ability to act independently and make decisions without authorization. **3** a thing that one is required to do as part of a job or legal obligation.

– SYNONYMS **1 duty,** task, function, job, role, onus. **2 blame,** fault, guilt, culpability, liability, accountability, answerability. **3 trustworthiness,** (common) sense, maturity, reliability, dependability. **4** *managerial responsibility* **authority,** control, power, leadership.

re·spon·si·ble /ri'spänsəbəl/ ▶ **adjective 1** having a duty to do something, or having control over or care for someone. **2** being the cause of something and so able to be blamed or credited for it: *the president is ultimately responsible for this situation.* **3** capable of being trusted. **4** (of a job or position) involving important duties or decisions or control over others. **5** (**responsible to**) having to report to a senior person.

– SYNONYMS **1 in charge of,** in control of, at the helm of, accountable for, liable for. **2 accountable,** answerable, to blame, guilty, culpable, blameworthy, at fault, in the wrong. **3 trustworthy,** sensible, mature, reliable, dependable, levelheaded, stable.
– ANTONYMS irresponsible.

– DERIVATIVES **re·spon·si·ble·ness** noun **re·spon·si·bly** /-blē/ adverb.
– ORIGIN from Latin *respondere* 'answer, offer in return.'

re·spon·sive /ri'spänsiv/ ▶ **adjective 1** responding readily and with interest. **2** in response; answering.

– SYNONYMS **reactive,** receptive, open to suggestions, amenable, flexible, forthcoming.

– DERIVATIVES **re·spon·sive·ly** adverb **re·spon·sive·ness** noun.

rest[1] /rest/ ▶ **verb 1** stop work or activity in order to relax or recover strength. **2** place or be placed so as to stay in a specified position. **3** (**rest on**) depend or be based on. **4** (**rest something in/on**) place trust, hope, or confidence in or on. **5** (**rest with**) be the responsibility of or belong to: *the final say rests with the city council.* **6** (of an issue) be left without further investigation or discussion.

– SYNONYMS **1** *he needed to rest* **relax,** ease up/off, let up, slow down, have/take a break, unbend, unwind, take it easy, put one's feet up; informal take five, have/take a breather, chill out. **2** *her hands rested on the rail* **lie,** be laid, repose, be placed, be positioned, be supported by. **3** *she rested her basket on the ground* **support,** prop (up), lean, lay, set, stand, position, place, put.

▶ **noun 1** the state or a period of resting. **2** an object that is used to hold or support something. **3** Music an interval of silence of a specified duration.

– SYNONYMS **1 relaxation,** repose, leisure, time off; informal lie-down. **2 break,** breathing space, interval, interlude, intermission, time off/out, respite, lull, pause; informal breather. **3 stand,** base, holder, support, rack, frame, shelf.

– PHRASES **rest one's case** conclude one's presentation of evidence and arguments in a lawsuit.
– ORIGIN Old English.

rest[2] ▶ **noun 1** the remaining part of something. **2** (treated as pl.) the remaining people or things; the others.

– SYNONYMS **remainder,** residue, balance, others, remnant(s), surplus, excess.

▶ **verb** remain or be left in a specified condition: *rest assured we will do everything we can.*
– ORIGIN from Latin *restare* 'remain.'

re·start ▶ **verb** /rē'stärt/ start again. ▶ **noun** /'rē,stärt/ a new start or beginning.

re·state /rē'stāt/ ▶ **verb** state something again or differently.

res·tau·rant /'rest(ə)rənt, 'restə,ränt, 'res,tränt/ ▶ **noun** a place where people pay to sit and eat meals that are cooked on the premises.
– ORIGIN French.

res·tau·ra·teur /,restərə'tər/ ▶ **noun** a person who owns and manages a restaurant.
– ORIGIN French.

USAGE

Although **restaurateur** is related to *restaurant*, it is not spelled with an *n*.

rest·ful /'restfəl/ ▶ **adjective** having a quiet and soothing quality.

– SYNONYMS **relaxing,** quiet, calm, tranquil, soothing, peaceful, leisurely, undisturbed, untroubled.
– ANTONYMS exciting.

– DERIVATIVES **rest·ful·ly** adverb.

WORD TOOLKIT

See **SLEEPY**.

rest home ▶ **noun** an institution where old or frail people live and are cared for.

res·ti·tu·tion /,restə't(y)o͞osʜən/ ▶ **noun 1** the restoration of something lost or stolen to its proper owner. **2** payment to compensate for injury or loss. **3** the restoration of something to its original state.

– SYNONYMS **1** *restitution of the land seized* **return,** restoration, handing back, surrender. **2** *restitution for the damage caused* **compensation,** recompense, reparation, damages, indemnification, reimbursement, repayment, remuneration, redress.

– DERIVATIVES **res·ti·tu·tive** /ˈrestə,t(y)o͞otiv/ adjective.
– ORIGIN Latin.

res·tive /ˈrestiv/ ▶ **adjective** unable to keep still or unwilling to submit to control: *the republic's restive minorities*.
– DERIVATIVES **res·tive·ly** adverb **res·tive·ness** noun.
– ORIGIN Old French.

rest·less /ˈrestləs/ ▶ **adjective 1** unable to rest or relax as a result of anxiety or boredom. **2** offering no physical or emotional rest: *a restless night*.

– SYNONYMS **1 uneasy,** ill at ease, fidgety, edgy, tense, worked up, nervous, nervy, agitated, anxious; informal jumpy, jittery, twitchy, uptight. **2** *a restless night* **sleepless,** wakeful, fitful, broken, disturbed, troubled, unsettled.

– DERIVATIVES **rest·less·ly** adverb **rest·less·ness** noun.

re·stock /rēˈstäk/ ▶ **verb** replenish a store with fresh stock or supplies.

res·to·ra·tion /ˌrestəˈrāsʜən/ ▶ **noun 1** the action of returning something to a former condition, place, or owner. **2** the process of repairing or renovating a building, work of art, etc. **3** the reinstatement of a previous practice, right, or situation. **4** the return of a monarch to a throne, a head of state to government, or a regime to power. **5** (**the Restoration**) the re-establishment of Charles II as King of England in 1660, or the period following this.

– SYNONYMS **1 reinstatement,** reinstitution, re-establishment, reimposition, return. **2 repair,** renovation, mending, refurbishment, reconditioning, rehabilitation, rebuilding, reconstruction; informal rehab.

re·stor·a·tive /riˈstôrətiv/ ▶ **adjective** having the ability to restore health, strength, or well-being. ▶ **noun** a medicine or drink that restores health, strength, or well-being.
– DERIVATIVES **re·stor·a·tive·ly** adverb.

re·store /riˈstôr/ ▶ **verb 1** bring back a previous practice, right, or situation. **2** return to a former condition, place, or owner: *he was restored to full favor*. **3** repair or renovate a building, work of art, etc.

– SYNONYMS **1 reinstate,** bring back, reinstitute, reimpose, reinstall, re-establish. **2** *he restored it to its rightful owner* **return,** give back, hand back. **3 repair,** fix, mend, refurbish, recondition, rehabilitate, renovate, revamp, rebuild; informal do up. **4 reinvigorate,** revitalize, revive, refresh, energize, freshen.

– DERIVATIVES **re·stor·a·ble** adjective **re·stor·er** noun.
– ORIGIN Latin *restaurare* 'rebuild, restore.'

re·strain /riˈstrān/ ▶ **verb 1** keep someone or something under control or within limits. **2** prevent someone from moving or acting as they wish. **3** control a strong emotion.

– SYNONYMS **control,** check, hold in check, curb, suppress, repress, contain, rein back/in, smother, stifle, bottle up; informal keep the lid on.

– DERIVATIVES **re·strain·a·ble** adjective **re·strain·er** noun.
– ORIGIN Latin *restringere* 'tie back.'

re·strained /riˈstrānd/ ▶ **adjective 1** reserved or unemotional. **2** not highly decorated or brightly colored.

– SYNONYMS **1 self-controlled,** sober, steady, unemotional, undemonstrative. **2 muted,** soft, discreet, subtle, quiet, unobtrusive, unostentatious, understated, tasteful.
– ANTONYMS impetuous.

re·straint /riˈstrānt/ ▶ **noun 1** a rule, measure, or fact that limits or controls: *the financial restraints of the budget*. **2** the action of restraining someone or something. **3** a device that limits or prevents freedom of movement. **4** unemotional or controlled behavior.

– SYNONYMS **1 constraint,** check, control, restriction, limitation, curtailment, rein, brake, deterrent. **2 self-control,** self-discipline, control, moderation, judiciousness. **3 subtlety,** taste, discretion, discrimination.

re·strict /riˈstrikt/ ▶ **verb 1** put a limit on something; keep something under control. **2** prevent someone from moving or acting as they wish.

– SYNONYMS **1 limit,** keep within bounds, regulate, control, moderate, cut down, curtail. **2 hinder,** interfere with, impede, hamper, obstruct, block, check, curb.

– ORIGIN Latin *restringere* 'tie back.'

re·strict·ed /riˈstriktid/ ▶ **adjective 1** limited in extent, number, or scope. **2** not revealed or made public for reasons of national security.

– SYNONYMS **1 cramped,** confined, constricted, small, narrow, tight. **2 limited,** controlled, regulated, reduced.

re·stric·tion /riˈstriksʜən/ ▶ **noun 1** a limiting rule, measure, or condition. **2** the limitation or control of someone or something, or the state of being restricted.

– SYNONYMS **limitation,** constraint, control, regulation, check, curb, reduction, diminution, curtailment.

re·stric·tive /riˈstriktiv/ ▶ **adjective** limiting or controlling freedom of action or movement.
– DERIVATIVES **re·stric·tive·ly** adverb **re·stric·tive·ness** noun.

re·string /rēˈstrinɢ, ˈrē-/ ▶ **verb** (past and past part. **restrung**) fit new strings to a musical instrument or sports racket.

rest·room /ˈrestˌro͞om, -ˌro͝om/ ▶ **noun** a lavatory in a public building.

re·struc·ture /rēˈstrəkcʜər/ ▶ **verb 1** organize something differently. **2** convert a debt into another debt that is repayable at a later time.

re·struc·tur·ing /rēˈstrəkcʜəriɴɢ/ ▶ **noun** a reorganization of a company with a view to achieving greater efficiency and profit.

re·style ▶ **verb** /rēˈstīl/ **1** give something a new shape or layout. **2** give a new description or name to someone or something. ▶ **noun** /ˈrēstīl/ an instance of restyling something.

re·sult /riˈzəlt/ ▶ **noun 1** a thing that is caused or produced by something else; an outcome. **2** a quantity or another item of information obtained by experiment or calculation. **3** a final score, mark, or placing in a sporting event or exam. **4** a satisfactory or favorable outcome: *determination and persistence guarantee results*. **5** the outcome of a business's trading over a particular period, expressed as a statement of profit or loss.

– SYNONYMS **consequence,** outcome, upshot, sequel, effect, reaction, repercussion.
– ANTONYMS cause.

▶ **verb 1** happen because of something else: *differences between species could* ***result from*** *their habitat*. **2** (**result in**) have a specified outcome: *the shooting resulted in five deaths*.

– SYNONYMS **1 follow,** ensue, develop, stem, spring, arise, derive, proceed; (**result from**) be caused by, be brought about by, be produced by, originate in. **2** (**result in**) **end in,** culminate in, lead to, trigger, cause, bring about, occasion, effect, give rise to, produce.

– ORIGIN Latin *resultare* 'spring back, result.'

re·sult·ant /ri'zəltnt/ ▶ **adjective** happening or produced as a result.

re·sume /ri'zo͞om/ ▶ **verb 1** begin again or continue after a pause or interruption. **2** return to a seat or place.

– SYNONYMS **restart,** recommence, begin again, start again, reopen, renew, return to, continue with, carry on with.
– ANTONYMS suspend, abandon.

– ORIGIN Latin *resumere* 'take back.'

ré·su·mé /'rezə,mā, ,rezə'mā/ ▶ **noun 1** a summary of a person's education, qualifications, and previous jobs, sent with a job application; a curriculum vitae. **2** a summary of something.

– SYNONYMS **summary,** précis, synopsis, abstract, outline, abridgment, overview.

– ORIGIN from French, 'resumed.'

re·sump·tion /ri'zəmpsʜən/ ▶ **noun** the action of beginning something again after an interruption.

– SYNONYMS **restart,** recommencement, reopening, continuation, renewal, return, revival.

re·sup·ply /,rēsə'plī/ ▶ **verb** (**resupplies, resupplying, resupplied**) provide with or obtain a fresh supply.

re·sur·face /rē'sərfəs/ ▶ **verb 1** put a new coating on a surface. **2** come back up to the surface of deep water. **3** arise or become evident again: *the old animosities have resurfaced.*

re·sur·gent /ri'sərjənt/ ▶ **adjective** becoming stronger, or more active or popular again.
– DERIVATIVES **re·sur·gence** noun.
– ORIGIN from Latin *resurgere* 'rise again.'

res·ur·rect /,rezə'rekt/ ▶ **verb 1** restore a dead person to life. **2** revive something inactive, disused, or forgotten.

– SYNONYMS **revive,** restore, regenerate, revitalize, breathe new life into, reinvigorate, resuscitate, rejuvenate, re-establish, relaunch.

res·ur·rec·tion /,rezə'rekSHən/ ▶ **noun 1** the action of resurrecting or reviving someone or something. **2** (**the Resurrection**) (in Christian belief) the time when Jesus rose from the dead.
– ORIGIN Latin.

re·sus·ci·tate /ri'səsə,tāt/ ▶ **verb 1** revive someone from unconsciousness. **2** make something active again.
– DERIVATIVES **re·sus·ci·ta·tion** /ri,səsə'tāsʜən/ noun **re·sus·ci·ta·tive** /-,tātiv/ adjective **re·sus·ci·ta·tor** /-,tātər/ noun.
– ORIGIN Latin *resuscitare* 'raise again.'

re·tail /'rē,tāl/ ▶ **noun** the sale of goods to the general public (rather than to a wholesaler). ▶ **verb 1** sell goods to the public. **2** (**retail at/for**) be sold by retail for a specified price. **3** describe the details of an incident to others.
– DERIVATIVES **re·tail·er** noun.
– ORIGIN Old French *retaillier*.

re·tain /ri'tān/ ▶ **verb 1** continue to have or own something. **2** absorb and continue to hold a substance. **3** keep something in place. **4** keep someone as an employee. **5** obtain the services of an attorney with a preliminary payment.

– SYNONYMS **keep (possession of),** keep (a) hold of, hang on to, maintain, preserve, conserve.

– DERIVATIVES **re·tain·a·ble** adjective.
– ORIGIN Latin *retinere* 'hold back.'

re·tain·er /ri'tānər/ ▶ **noun 1** a thing that holds something in place. **2** a fee paid in advance to an attorney to obtain their services. **3** a servant who has worked for someone for a long time.

re·tain·ing wall ▶ **noun** a wall that holds back earth or water on one side of it.

re·take /rē'tāk, 'rē-/ ▶ **verb** (past **retook** /rē'to͝ok/; past part. **retaken**) **1** take a test or exam again. **2** regain possession or control of something. ▶ **noun 1** a test or exam that is retaken. **2** an instance of filming a scene or recording a piece of music again.

re·tal·i·ate /ri'talē,āt/ ▶ **verb** make an attack in return for a similar attack.

– SYNONYMS **fight back,** hit back, respond, react, reply, reciprocate, counterattack, get back at someone, pay someone back; informal get one's own back.

– DERIVATIVES **re·tal·i·a·tion** /ri,talē'āsʜən/ noun **re·tal·i·a·tive** /ri'talē,ātiv, -ēətiv/ adjective **re·tal·i·a·tor** /-,ātər/ noun **re·tal·i·a·to·ry** /ri'talēə,tôrē/ adjective.
– ORIGIN Latin *retaliare* 'return in kind.'

re·tard ▶ **verb** /ri'tärd/ hold back the development or progress of someone or something.

– SYNONYMS **delay,** slow down/up, hold back/up, postpone, detain, decelerate, hinder, impede, check.
– ANTONYMS accelerate.

▶ **noun** /'rē,tärd/ offensive a person who has a mental disability.
– DERIVATIVES **re·tar·da·tion** /,rē,tär'dāsʜən, ri-/ noun **re·tard·er** noun.
– ORIGIN Latin *retardare*.

re·tar·dant /ri'tärdnt/ ▶ **adjective** preventing or inhibiting: *fire-retardant polymers.* ▶ **noun** a fabric or substance that prevents or inhibits the outbreak of fire.

re·tard·ed /ri'tärdid/ ▶ **adjective** chiefly offensive less advanced in mental, physical, or social development than is usual for one's age.

retch /recʜ/ ▶ **verb** make the sound and movement of vomiting. ▶ **noun** an instance of retching.
– ORIGIN from a Germanic word meaning 'spittle.'

re·tell /rē'tel/ ▶ **verb** (past and past part. **retold** /rē'tōld/) tell a story again or differently.

re·ten·tion /ri'tencʜən/ ▶ **noun 1** the action of keeping or holding something or the fact of being retained. **2** failure to remove a substance from the body.

re·ten·tive /ri'tentiv/ ▶ **adjective 1** (of a person's memory) good at storing facts and impressions. **2** (of a substance) able to absorb and hold moisture.
– DERIVATIVES **re·ten·tive·ly** adverb **re·ten·tive·ness** noun **re·ten·tiv·i·ty** /,rē,ten'tivətē, ri-/ noun.

re·think /rē'ᴛʜiNGk/ ▶ **verb** (past and past part. **rethought**) consider a policy or course of action again. ▶ **noun** an instance of rethinking.

ret·i·cent /'retəsənt/ ▶ **adjective** not revealing one's thoughts or feelings readily.

– SYNONYMS **uncommunicative,** unforthcoming, unresponsive, tight-lipped, quiet, taciturn, silent, reserved.
– ANTONYMS expansive.

– DERIVATIVES **ret·i·cence** noun **ret·i·cent·ly** adverb.
– ORIGIN from Latin *reticere* 'remain silent.'

re·tic·u·lat·ed /ri'tikyə,lātid/ ▶ **adjective** arranged or marked like a net or network.
– ORIGIN Latin *reticulatus.*

re·tic·u·la·tion /ri,tikyə'lāsʜən/ ▶ **noun** a pattern or arrangement of interlacing lines resembling a net.

ret·i·cule /'reti,kyo͞ol/ ▶ **noun** chiefly historical a woman's small handbag, closed with a drawstring.
– ORIGIN French.

re·tie /rē'tī/ ▶ **verb** (**reties, retying, retied**) tie something again.

ret·i·na /'retn-ə/ ▶ **noun** (pl. **retinas** or **retinae** /'retn,ē, 'retn,ī/) a layer at the back of the eyeball containing cells that are sensitive to light and from which impulses are sent to the brain.
– DERIVATIVES **ret·i·nal** /'retn-əl/ adjective.
– ORIGIN Latin.

ret·i·nol /'retnôl, -,ōl/ ▶ **noun** vitamin A.

ret·i·nop·a·thy /,retn'äpəᴛʜē/ ▶ **noun** disease of the retina of the eye that results in impairment or loss of vision.

ret·i·nue /'retn,(y)o͞o/ ▶ **noun** a group of advisers or assistants accompanying an important person.
– ORIGIN from Old French *retenir* 'keep back, retain.'

re·tire /ri'tīr/ ▶ **verb 1** leave one's job and stop working, especially because one has reached a particular age. **2** Baseball put out a batter or side. **3** leave a place, especially so as to go somewhere more private: *it was Mr. Theil's habit to retire to his sitting room and stay there.* **4** go to bed. **5** (of a jury) leave the courtroom to decide the verdict of a trial.

– SYNONYMS **1 give up work,** stop work, stop working, pack it in, call it quits. **2 withdraw,** go away, exit, leave, take oneself off, absent oneself. **3 go to bed,** call it a day; informal turn in, hit the hay/sack.

– DERIVATIVES **re·tir·ee** /ri,tī'rē/ noun **re·tired** adjective.
– ORIGIN French *retirer* 'draw back.'

re·tire·ment /ri'tīrmənt/ ▶ **noun 1** the action or fact of retiring. **2** the period of one's life after retiring from work. **3** the state of being private; seclusion.

re·tire·ment plan ▶ **noun** another term for **PENSION**[1] (sense 1 of the noun).

re·tir·ing /ri'tīriɴɢ/ ▶ **adjective** tending to avoid other people; shy.

– SYNONYMS **shy,** diffident, self-effacing, unassuming, unassertive, reserved, reticent, quiet, timid, modest.
– ANTONYMS incoming, outgoing.

re·ti·tle /rē'tītl/ ▶ **verb** give a different title to a book, play, movie, etc.

re·told /rē'tōld/ past and past participle of **RETELL.**

re·took /rē'to͝ok/ past of **RETAKE.**

re·tool /rē'to͞ol/ ▶ **verb 1** equip (a factory) with new or adapted tools. **2** alter the form or character of: *he has a little time to retool his candidacy.*

re·tort[1] /ri'tôrt/ ▶ **verb** say something sharp or witty in answer to a remark or accusation.

– SYNONYMS **answer,** reply, respond, return, counter, riposte, retaliate.

▶ **noun** a sharp or witty reply.

– SYNONYMS **answer,** reply, response, counter, rejoinder, riposte, retaliation; informal comeback.

– ORIGIN Latin *retorquere* 'twist back.'

re·tort[2] ▶ **noun 1** a container or furnace for carrying out a chemical process on a large or industrial scale. **2** historical a glass container with a long neck, used in distilling liquids and other chemical operations.
– ORIGIN Latin *retorta.*

re·touch /rē'təᴄʜ/ ▶ **verb** improve a painting, photograph, or other image by making slight additions or alterations.
– DERIVATIVES **re·touch·er** noun.

re·trace /rē'trās/ ▶ **verb 1** go back over the same route that one has just taken. **2** discover and follow a route taken by someone else. **3** trace something back to its source or beginning.

re·tract /ri'trakt/ ▶ **verb 1** withdraw a statement or accusation because it is not supported by evidence. **2** go back on an agreement or promise. **3** draw or be drawn back.

– SYNONYMS **1 take back,** withdraw, recant, disavow, disclaim, repudiate, renounce, reverse, revoke, rescind, go back on, backtrack on; formal **abjure.**
2 pull in, pull back, draw in.

– DERIVATIVES **re·tract·a·ble** adjective **re·trac·tion** /ri'traksʜən/ noun **re·trac·tor** noun.
– ORIGIN Latin *retrahere* 'draw back.'

re·trac·tile /ri'traktəl, -,tīl/ ▶ **adjective** capable of being retracted or drawn back: *retractile claws.*

re·train /rē'trān/ ▶ **verb** teach or learn new skills.

re·trans·mit /,rētrans'mit, -tranz-/ ▶ **verb** (**retransmits, retransmitting, retransmitted**) transmit data, a radio signal, or a broadcast again or onto another receiver.
– DERIVATIVES **re·trans·mis·sion** /-'misʜən/ noun.

re·tread /rē'tred/ ▶ **verb 1** (past **retrod** /rē'träd/; past part. **retrodden** /rē'trädn/) go back over a path or one's steps. **2** (past and past part. **retreaded**) put a new tread on a worn tire. ▶ **noun** a tire that has been given a new tread.

re·treat /ri'trēt/ ▶ **verb 1** (of an army) withdraw from an attack on enemy forces. **2** move away or back. **3** go to a quiet or secluded place. **4** change one's mind as a result of criticism or difficulty.

– SYNONYMS **withdraw,** retire, draw back, pull back/out, fall back, give way, give ground.
– ANTONYMS advance.

▶ **noun 1** an act of retreating. **2** a quiet or secluded place. **3** a place where a person goes for a time in order to be quiet and pray or meditate. **4** a military musical ceremony carried out at sunset.

– SYNONYMS **1 withdrawal,** retirement, pullback, flight. **2 refuge,** haven, sanctuary, hideaway, hideout, hiding place.

– ORIGIN Latin *retrahere* 'draw back.'

re·trench /ri'trenᴄʜ/ ▶ **verb** reduce costs or spending in response to economic difficulty.
– DERIVATIVES **re·trench·ment** noun.
– ORIGIN French *retrancher* 'cut out.'

re·tri·al /rē'trīəl, 'rē,trīəl/ ▶ **noun** a second or further trial on the same issues and with the same parties.

ret·ri·bu·tion /ˌretrəˈbyo͞osʜən/ ▸ **noun** severe punishment in revenge for a wrong or criminal act.

– SYNONYMS **punishment,** penalty, one's just deserts, revenge, reprisal, requital, retaliation, vengeance, an eye for an eye (and a tooth for a tooth), tit for tat, nemesis.

– DERIVATIVES **re·trib·u·tive** /riˈtribyətiv/ adjective **re·trib·u·to·ry** /riˈtribyəˌtôrē/ adjective.
– ORIGIN Latin.

re·trieve /riˈtrēv/ ▸ **verb 1** get or bring something back. **2** (of a dog) find and bring back game that has been shot. **3** find or extract information stored in a computer. **4** make a difficult situation better.

– SYNONYMS **get back,** bring back, recover, recapture, regain, recoup, salvage, rescue.

– DERIVATIVES **re·triev·a·ble** adjective **re·triev·al** noun.
– ORIGIN Old French *retrover* 'find again.'

re·triev·er /riˈtrēvər/ ▸ **noun** a dog of a breed used for finding and bringing back game that has been shot.

ret·ro /ˈretrō/ ▸ **adjective** imitative of a style from the recent past. ▸ **noun** retro clothes, music, or style.
– ORIGIN French.

retro- ▸ **combining form 1** back or backward: *retrogression.* **2** behind: *retrorocket.*
– ORIGIN Latin *retro* 'backward.'

ret·ro·ac·tive /ˌretrōˈaktiv/ ▸ **adjective** (especially of a law) taking effect from a date in the past.
– DERIVATIVES **ret·ro·ac·tive·ly** adverb.

re·trod /rēˈträd/ past of **RETREAD** (sense 1 of the verb).

re·trod·den /rēˈträdn/ past participle of **RETREAD** (sense 1 of the verb).

ret·ro·fit /ˌretrōˈfit/ ▸ **verb** (**retrofits, retrofitting, retrofitted**) fit something with a component or accessory not fitted during manufacture. ▸ **noun** an act of fitting a component or accessory to something after manufacture.
– ORIGIN from **RETROACTIVE** and **REFIT.**

ret·ro·fu·tur·ist·ic (also **retrofuturist**) ▸ **adjective** of or resembling a futuristic style or aesthetic from an earlier era; having both retro and futuristic elements.

ret·ro·grade /ˈretrəˌgrād/ ▸ **adjective 1** directed or moving backward. **2** going back to an earlier and worse situation: *reconsidering these concepts would be a retrograde step.* **3** (of the order of something) reversed. **4** chiefly Astronomy (of the apparent motion of a planet) in a reverse direction from normal (from east to west).

– SYNONYMS **for the worse,** regressive, retrogressive, negative, downhill, backward(s), unwelcome.

▸ **verb** go back in position or time.
– DERIVATIVES **ret·ro·gra·da·tion** /ˌretrōgrāˈdāsʜən/ noun.
– ORIGIN Latin *retrogradus.*

ret·ro·gres·sion /ˌretrəˈgresʜən/ ▸ **noun** the process of returning to an earlier state, especially a worse one.
– DERIVATIVES **ret·ro·gres·sive** /-ˈgresiv/ adjective.

ret·ro·rock·et /ˈretrōˌräkit/ ▸ **noun** a small auxiliary rocket on a spacecraft or missile, fired in the direction of travel to slow it down.

ret·ro·spect /ˈretrəˌspekt/ ▸ **noun** (in phrase **in retrospect**) when looking back on a past event; with hindsight.

– SYNONYMS *in retrospect, we can see that more guards should have been installed at the front gate* **looking back,** on reflection, in hindsight.

– DERIVATIVES **ret·ro·spec·tion** /ˌretrəˈspeksʜən/ noun.

ret·ro·spec·tive /ˌretrəˈspektiv/ ▸ **adjective 1** looking back on or dealing with past events. **2** (of an exhibition) showing the development of an artist's work over a period of time. **3** (of a statute or legal decision) taking effect from a date in the past. ▸ **noun** an exhibition showing the development of an artist's work over time.
– DERIVATIVES **ret·ro·spec·tive·ly** adverb.

ret·rous·sé /rəˌtro͞oˈsā, ˌretro͞o-/ ▸ **adjective** (of a person's nose) turned up at the tip.
– ORIGIN French, 'tucked up.'

ret·ro·vi·rus /ˌretrōˈvīrəs, ˈretrōˌvīrəs/ ▸ **noun** any of a group of RNA viruses that insert a DNA copy of their genetic material into the host cell in order to replicate, e.g., HIV.
– DERIVATIVES **ret·ro·vi·ral** adjective.
– ORIGIN from the initial letters of *reverse transcriptase* + **VIRUS.**

ret·si·na /retˈsēnə/ ▸ **noun** a Greek white wine flavored with resin.
– ORIGIN modern Greek.

re·tune /rēˈt(y)o͞on/ ▸ **verb** tune a radio, musical instrument, etc., again or differently.

re·turn /riˈtərn/ ▸ **verb 1** come or go back to a place. **2** (**return to**) go back to a particular state or activity. **3** give, send, or put back: *she returned the spider to the garden.* **4** feel, say, or do the same feeling, action, etc., in response: *she didn't return my phone calls.* **5** (in tennis) hit or send the ball back to an opponent. **6** (of a judge or jury) state a verdict in response to a formal request. **7** yield or make a profit. **8** (of voters) elect a person or party to office.

– SYNONYMS **1 go back,** come back, arrive back, come home. **2 recur,** reoccur, repeat itself, reappear. **3 give back,** hand back, pay back, repay, restore, put back, replace, reinstall, reinstate.
– ANTONYMS leave.

▸ **noun 1** an act or the action of returning. **2** a profit from an investment. **3** (also **return match** or **game**) a second sporting contest between the same opponents. **4** a piece of merchandise that has been returned because it is no longer wanted. **5** an official report submitted in response to a formal demand: *census returns.*

– SYNONYMS **1 recurrence,** reoccurrence, repeat, reappearance. **2 replacement,** restoration, reinstatement, restitution. **3 yield,** profit, gain, revenue, interest, dividend.

– DERIVATIVES **re·turn·a·ble** adjective **re·turn·er** noun.
– PHRASES **many happy returns** a greeting to someone on their birthday.
– ORIGIN Old French *returner.*

re·turn·ee /riˌtərˈnē/ ▸ **noun 1** a person who returns to their own country from abroad. **2** a person who returns to work after a long absence.

re·ty·ing /rēˈtīiɴɢ/ present participle of **RETIE.**

re·type /rēˈtīp/ ▸ **verb** type words again, especially to correct a mistake.

re·u·ni·fy /rēˈyo͞onəˌfī/ ▸ **verb** (**reunifies, reunifying, reunified**) restore political unity to a place or group.
– DERIVATIVES **re·u·ni·fi·ca·tion** /ˌrēˌyo͞onəfiˈkāsʜən/ noun.

re·un·ion /rēˈyo͞onyən/ ▸ **noun 1** the action of coming or bringing together again after a period of separation. **2** a social gathering of people who have not seen each other for some time.

re·u·nite /ˌrēyo͞oˈnīt/ ▶ **verb** bring or come together again after a period of separation.

re·use ▶ **verb** /rēˈyo͞oz/ use something again or more than once. ▶ **noun** /reˈyo͞os/ the action of using something again.
– DERIVATIVES **re·us·a·ble** /rēˈyo͞ozəbəl/ adjective.

rev /rev/ informal ▶ **noun** (**revs**) the number of revolutions of an engine per minute. ▶ **verb** (**revs, revving, revved**) increase the running speed of an engine by pressing the accelerator.

Rev. ▶ **abbreviation** Reverend.

re·val·ue /rēˈvalyo͞o/ ▶ **verb** (**revalues, revaluing, revalued**) **1** assess the value of something again. **2** adjust the official value of a currency in relation to other currencies.
DERIVATIVES **re·val·u·a·tion** /rēˌvalyo͞oˈāsʜən/ noun.

re·vamp ▶ **verb** /rēˈvamp/ alter something so as to improve its appearance.

– SYNONYMS **renovate,** redecorate, refurbish, remodel, refashion, redesign, restyle; informal do up, give something a facelift, give something a makeover.

▶ **noun** /ˈrēˌvamp/ an act of improving the appearance of something.

re·vanch·ism /rəˈvänˌsʜizəm/ ▶ **noun** a policy of retaliation, especially to recover lost territory.
– DERIVATIVES **re·vanch·ist** adjective & noun.
– ORIGIN from French *revanche* 'revenge.'

re·veal[1] /riˈvēl/ ▶ **verb 1** make information that was previously unknown or secret known to others. **2** cause or allow to be seen: *the clouds were breaking up to reveal a clear blue sky.*

– SYNONYMS **1 disclose,** make known, make public, broadcast, publicize, circulate, divulge, tell, let slip/drop, give away/out, blurt out, release, leak, bring to light, lay bare, unveil; informal let on. **2 show,** display, exhibit, unveil, uncover.
– ANTONYMS conceal, hide.

– DERIVATIVES **re·veal·er** noun.
– ORIGIN Latin *revelare.*

re·veal[2] ▶ **noun** either side surface of an opening in a wall for a door or window.
– ORIGIN from Old French *revaler* 'to lower.'

re·veal·ing /riˈvēliɴɢ/ ▶ **adjective 1** making interesting information known to others. **2** (of an item of clothing) allowing much of the wearer's body to be seen.
– DERIVATIVES **re·veal·ing·ly** adverb.

rev·eil·le /ˈrevəlē/ ▶ **noun** a signal sounded on a bugle or drum to wake personnel in the armed forces.
– ORIGIN from French *réveillez!* 'wake up!'

rev·el /ˈrevəl/ ▶ **verb** (**revels, reveling, reveled**) **1** enjoy oneself with others in a lively and noisy way. **2** (**revel in**) gain great pleasure from.

– SYNONYMS **1 celebrate,** make merry; informal party, live it up, whoop it up, paint the town red. **2** (**revel in**) **enjoy,** delight in, love, like, adore, take pleasure in, relish, lap up, savor; informal get a kick out of.

▶ **noun** (**revels**) lively and noisy celebrations.

– SYNONYMS **celebration,** festivity, jollification, merrymaking, party; informal rave, shindig, blast, bash, wingding.

– DERIVATIVES **rev·el·er** noun.
– ORIGIN Old French *reveler* 'rise up in rebellion.'

rev·e·la·tion /ˌrevəˈlāsʜən/ ▶ **noun 1** the revealing of something previously secret or unknown. **2** a surprising and previously unknown fact: *revelations about his personal life.* **3** the revealing of knowledge to humans by God. **4** (**Revelation** or informal **Revelations**) the last book of the New Testament, describing God's revelation of the future to St. John.

– SYNONYMS **disclosure,** announcement, report, admission, confession, divulging, giving away/out, leak, betrayal, publicizing.

– DERIVATIVES **rev·e·la·tion·al** adjective.

re·vel·a·to·ry /ˈrevələˌtôrē, riˈvel-/ ▶ **adjective** revealing something previously unknown.

rev·el·ry /ˈrevəlrē/ ▶ **noun** (pl. **revelries**) lively and noisy celebrations.

– SYNONYMS **celebration(s),** parties, festivity, jollification, merrymaking, carousal, roistering, fun and games; informal partying.

rev·e·nant /ˈrevəˌnäɴ, -nənt/ ▶ **noun** a person who has returned, especially supposedly from the dead.
– ORIGIN from French, 'coming back.'

re·venge /riˈvenj/ ▶ **noun** harmful action taken in return for an injury or wrong: *he would some day take his revenge on reporters.*

– SYNONYMS **retaliation,** retribution, vengeance, reprisal, recrimination, an eye for an eye (and a tooth for a tooth), redress.
– ANTONYMS forgiveness.

▶ **verb 1** (**revenge oneself** or **be revenged**) take harmful action against someone for an injury or wrong done to oneself. **2** take revenge on behalf of someone else for a wrong or injury.

– SYNONYMS **avenge,** exact retribution for, take reprisals for, get redress for, make someone pay for; informal get one's own back for.

– ORIGIN Old French *revencher.*

re·venge·ful /riˈvenjfəl/ ▶ **adjective** eager for revenge.

rev·e·nue /ˈrevəˌn(y)o͞o/ ▶ **noun 1** the income received by an organization. **2** a country's or state's annual income, received especially from taxes, from which public expenses are met.

– SYNONYMS **income,** takings, receipts, proceeds, earnings, profit(s), gain, yield, take, gate.
– ANTONYMS expenditure.

– ORIGIN from Latin *revenire* 'return.'

re·ver·ber·ate /riˈvərbəˌrāt/ ▶ **verb 1** (of a loud noise) be repeated as an echo. **2** have continuing serious effects: *the effects of his suicide reverberated around the globe.*

– SYNONYMS **resound,** echo, resonate, ring, boom, rumble.

– DERIVATIVES **re·ver·ber·ant** /-rənt/ adjective **re·ver·ber·a·tion** /riˌvərbəˈrāsʜən/ noun.
– ORIGIN Latin *reverberare* 'strike again.'

re·vere /riˈvi(ə)r/ ▶ **verb** respect or admire someone or something deeply.

– SYNONYMS **respect,** admire, think highly of, esteem, venerate, look up to, be in awe of.
– ANTONYMS despise.

– ORIGIN Latin *revereri.*

CHOOSE THE RIGHT WORD

revere, admire, adore, idolize, venerate, worship
We might **admire** someone who walks a tightrope between two skyscrapers, **idolize** a rock star, **adore** our

mothers, and **revere** a person like Martin Luther King, Jr. Each of these verbs conveys the idea of regarding someone or something with respect and honor, but they differ considerably in terms of the feelings they connote. *Admire* suggests a feeling of delight and enthusiastic appreciation (*admire the courage of the mountain climber*), while *adore* implies the tenderness and warmth of unquestioning love (*he adored babies*). *Idolize* is an extreme form of adoration, suggesting a slavish, helpless love, (*he idolized the older quarterback*). We *revere* individuals and institutions that command our respect for their accomplishments or attributes (*he revered his old English professor*). **Venerate** and **worship** are usually found in religious contexts (*venerate saints and worship God*) but both words may be used in other contexts as well. *Venerate* is usually associated with dignity and advanced age (*venerate the old man who had founded the company more than 50 years ago*), while *worship* connotes an excessive and uncritical respect (*the young girls who waited outside the stage door worshiped the ground he walked on*).

rev·er·ence /ˈrev(ə)rəns/ ▶ **noun 1** deep respect or admiration for someone or something. **2** (**His/Your Reverence**) a title given to a member of the clergy, especially a priest in Ireland.

– SYNONYMS **high esteem,** high regard, great respect, honor, veneration, homage, admiration, appreciation, deference.
– ANTONYMS scorn.

▶ **verb** respect or admire someone or something deeply.

CHOOSE THE RIGHT WORD

See **HONOR**.

rev·er·end /ˈrev(ə)rənd, ˈrevərnd/ ▶ **adjective** a title or form of address to members of the Christian clergy.
▶ **noun** informal a clergyman.

rev·er·ent /ˈrev(ə)rənt, ˈrevərnt/ ▶ **adjective** showing deep respect.

– SYNONYMS **reverential,** respectful, admiring, devoted, devout, awed, deferential.

– DERIVATIVES **rev·er·en·tial** /ˌrevəˈrenCHəl/ adjective **rev·er·ent·ly** adverb.

rev·er·ie /ˈrevərē/ ▶ **noun** a daydream.
– ORIGIN Old French, 'rejoicing, revelry.'

re·vers /riˈvi(ə)r, -ˈve(ə)r/ ▶ **noun** (pl. same) the turned-back edge of a garment revealing the underside, especially at the lapel.
– ORIGIN French, 'reverse.'

re·ver·sal /riˈvərsəl/ ▶ **noun 1** a change to an opposite direction, position, or course of action. **2** an adverse change of fortune.

– SYNONYMS **1 turnaround,** turnabout, about-face, volte-face, change of heart, U-turn, backtracking. **2 swap,** exchange, change, interchange, switch. **3 alteration,** overturning, overthrow, disallowing, overriding, overruling, veto, revocation. **4 setback,** upset, failure, misfortune, mishap, disaster, blow, disappointment, adversity, hardship, affliction, vicissitude, defeat.

re·verse /riˈvərs/ ▶ **verb 1** move backward. **2** make something the opposite of what it was: *the damage done to the ozone layer may be reversed*. **3** turn something the other way around or up or inside out. **4** cancel or annul a judgment by a lower court or authority. **5** (of an engine) work in an opposite direction from normal.

– SYNONYMS **1 back,** move back/backward(s). **2 turn upside down,** turn over, upend, invert, turn back to front. **3 swap,** change (around), exchange, switch (around), transpose. **4 alter,** change, overturn, overthrow, disallow, override, overrule, veto, revoke.

▶ **adjective 1** going in or turned toward the opposite direction. **2** operating or behaving in a way opposite to that which is usual or expected.

– SYNONYMS **backward(s),** inverted, transposed, opposite.

▶ **noun 1** a complete change of direction or action. **2** (**the reverse**) the opposite to that previously stated. **3** a setback or defeat. **4** the opposite side or face to the observer. **5** the side of a coin or medal bearing the value or secondary design. **6** reverse gear.

– SYNONYMS **1 opposite,** contrary, converse, inverse, antithesis. **2 setback,** reversal, upset, failure, misfortune, mishap, disaster, blow, disappointment, adversity, hardship, affliction, vicissitude, defeat. **3 other side,** back, underside, flip side.
– ANTONYMS front.

– PHRASES **reverse the charges** make the person who receives a telephone call responsible for paying for it.
– ORIGIN Latin *revertere* 'turn back.'

CHOOSE THE RIGHT WORD

See **OPPOSITE**.

re·verse en·gi·neer·ing ▶ **noun** the reproduction of another manufacturer's product after detailed examination of how it is made.

re·verse gear ▶ **noun** a gear making a vehicle or piece of machinery move or work backward.

re·vers·i·ble /riˈvərsəbəl/ ▶ **adjective 1** able to be returned to an original state or position: *the rise in crime is reversible*. **2** (of a garment or fabric) able to be turned inside out and worn or used with either side visible.
– DERIVATIVES **re·vers·i·bil·i·ty** /riˌvərsəˈbilətē/ noun **re·vers·i·bly** adverb.

re·ver·sion /riˈvərZHən/ ▶ **noun 1** a return to a previous state, practice, or belief. **2** Biology the action of an organism returning to a former or ancestral type. **3** the legal right, especially of the original owner, to possess or succeed to property when the present possessor dies or a lease ends.
– DERIVATIVES **re·ver·sion·ar·y** /-ˌnerē/ adjective.

re·vert /riˈvərt/ ▶ **verb** (**revert to**) **1** return to a previous state, condition, or subject. **2** Biology (of an organism) return to a former or ancestral type. **3** (of property) legally return to the original owner.

– SYNONYMS **return,** go back, change back, default, relapse.

– ORIGIN Latin *revertere* 'turn back.'

re·vet·ment /riˈvetmənt/ ▶ **noun 1** a retaining wall of masonry that supports or protects a rampart, wall, etc. **2** a barricade of earth or sandbags providing protection from a blast or to prevent aircraft from overrunning when landing.
– ORIGIN French *revêtement*.

re·view /riˈvyo͞o/ ▶ **noun 1** a formal assessment of something with the intention of making changes if necessary. **2** a critical assessment of a book, play, or other work. **3** a report on a past event. **4** Law a reconsideration of a judgment, sentence, etc. by a higher court or authority. **5** a ceremonial display and formal inspection of military or naval forces.

– SYNONYMS **1 analysis,** evaluation, assessment, appraisal, examination, investigation, inquiry, probe, inspection, study. **2 reconsideration,** reassessment, re-evaluation, reappraisal. **3 criticism,** critique, write-up, assessment, commentary.

▶ **verb 1** assess something formally with the intention of making changes if necessary. **2** write a review of a play, book, or other work. **3** Law submit a sentence, case, etc., for reconsideration by a higher court or authority. **4** view something again.

– SYNONYMS **1 survey,** study, research, consider, analyze, examine, scrutinize, explore, look into, probe, investigate, inspect, assess, evaluate, appraise, weigh up; informal size up. **2 reconsider,** re-examine, reassess, re-evaluate, reappraise, rethink.

– DERIVATIVES **re·view·a·ble** adjective.
– ORIGIN from former French *reveue*.

re·view·er /ri'vyo͞oər/ ▶ **noun** a person who writes critical appraisals of books, plays, etc.

– SYNONYMS **critic,** commentator, judge, observer, pundit, analyst.

re·vile /ri'vīl/ ▶ **verb** criticize someone in an abusive or scornful way.

– SYNONYMS **criticize,** censure, condemn, attack, inveigh against, rail against, lambaste, denounce; slander, libel, malign, vilify, besmirch, abuse; informal knock, slam, pan, crucify, roast, bad-mouth, pummel; formal excoriate.
– ANTONYMS praise.

– ORIGIN Old French *reviler*.

CHOOSE THE RIGHT WORD

See **SCOLD**.

re·vise /ri'vīz/ ▶ **verb 1** reconsider and alter an opinion or judgment in the light of further evidence. **2** examine and amend a piece of writing.

– SYNONYMS **1 reconsider,** review, re-examine, reassess, re-evaluate, reappraise, rethink, change, alter, modify. **2 amend,** correct, edit, rewrite, redraft, rephrase, rework.

▶ **noun** Printing a proof including corrections made in an earlier proof.

– DERIVATIVES **re·vis·er** noun.
– ORIGIN Latin *revisere* 'look at again.'

re·vi·sion /ri'vizʜən/ ▶ **noun 1** the action of revising something. **2** a revised edition or form of something.

– SYNONYMS **1 alteration,** adaptation, editing, rewriting, redrafting, correction, updating. **2 reconsideration,** review, re-examination, reassessment, re-evaluation, reappraisal, rethink, change, modification.

– DERIVATIVES **re·vi·sion·ar·y** /-ˌnerē/ adjective.

re·vi·sion·ism /ri'vizʜəˌnizəm/ ▶ **noun** often derogatory the reconsideration or modification of accepted theories or principles.
– DERIVATIVES **re·vi·sion·ist** noun & adjective.

re·vis·it /rē'vizit/ ▶ **verb (revisits, revisiting, revisited) 1** come back to or visit a place again. **2** consider a situation again or from a different perspective.

re·vi·tal·ize /rē'vītlˌīz/ ▶ **verb** give new life and vitality to someone or something.

– SYNONYMS **reinvigorate,** re-energize, boost, regenerate, revive, revivify, rejuvenate, reanimate, resuscitate, refresh, stimulate, breathe new life into; informal give a shot in the arm to, pep up, buck up.

– DERIVATIVES **re·vi·tal·i·za·tion** /rēˌvītl-ə'zāsʜən/ noun.

re·viv·al /ri'vīvəl/ ▶ **noun 1** an improvement in the condition, strength, or popularity of something: *an economic revival*. **2** a new production of a play that has not been performed for some time. **3** a reawakening of religious faith brought about by evangelistic meetings.

– SYNONYMS **1 improvement,** rallying, turn for the better, upturn, upswing, resurgence. **2 comeback,** re-establishment, reintroduction, restoration, reappearance, resurrection, rebirth.
– ANTONYMS downturn.

re·viv·al·ism /ri'vīvəˌlizəm/ ▶ **noun 1** the promotion of a revival of religious faith. **2** a tendency or desire to revive a former custom or practice.
– DERIVATIVES **re·viv·al·ist** noun & adjective.

re·vive /ri'vīv/ ▶ **verb 1** make someone conscious, healthy, or strong again. **2** restore interest in or the popularity of: *this style was revived in the 1970s*. **3** improve the condition of something.

– SYNONYMS **1 resuscitate,** bring around, bring back to consciousness, administer CPR to; informal give the kiss of life to. **2 reinvigorate,** revitalize, refresh, energize, reanimate. **3** *reviving old traditions* **reintroduce,** re-establish, restore, resurrect, bring back.

– DERIVATIVES **re·viv·a·ble** adjective **re·viv·er** noun.
– ORIGIN Latin *revivere*.

re·viv·i·fy /rē'vivəˌfī/ ▶ **verb (revivifies, revivifying, revivified)** give new life or strength to someone or something.
– DERIVATIVES **re·viv·i·fi·ca·tion** /ˌrēˌvivəfə'kāsʜən/ noun.

re·voke /ri'vōk/ ▶ **verb** officially cancel a decree or decision.

– SYNONYMS **cancel,** repeal, rescind, reverse, annul, nullify, void, invalidate, countermand, retract, withdraw, overrule, override; formal abrogate.

– DERIVATIVES **rev·o·ca·ble** /'revəkəbəl, ri'vōkəbəl/ adjective **rev·o·ca·tion** /ˌrevə'kāsʜən, riˌvō-/ noun.
– ORIGIN Latin *revocare* 'call back.'

re·volt /ri'vōlt/ ▶ **verb 1** take violent action against a government or ruler. **2** refuse to acknowledge someone or something as having authority: *the new chefs began to revolt against classic haute cuisine*. **3** make someone feel disgust.

– SYNONYMS **1 rebel,** rise up, take to the streets, riot, mutiny. **2 disgust,** sicken, nauseate, turn someone's stomach, put off, offend; informal turn off, gross out.

▶ **noun 1** an attempt to overthrow a government or ruler by violent action. **2** a refusal to continue to obey something: *a revolt over tax increases*.

– SYNONYMS **rebellion,** revolution, insurrection, mutiny, uprising, riot, insurgence, coup (d'état).

– ORIGIN French *révolter*.

re·volt·ing /ri'vōltiɴɢ/ ▶ **adjective** causing disgust: *a number of revolting items in their refrigerator*.

– SYNONYMS **disgusting,** sickening, nauseating, stomach-turning, repulsive, repugnant, hideous,

nasty, foul, offensive; informal ghastly, horrid, gross.
– ANTONYMS attractive, pleasant.

rev·o·lu·tion /ˌrevəˈlo͞osнən/ ▶ **noun 1** a forcible overthrow of a government or social order, in favor of a new system. **2** a great and far-reaching change: *marketing underwent a revolution*. **3** movement in orbit or in a circular course around a central point. **4** a complete circular movement around a central point.

– SYNONYMS **1 rebellion,** revolt, insurrection, mutiny, uprising, rising, riot, insurgence, coup (d'état). **2 dramatic change,** sea change, metamorphosis, transformation, innovation, reorganization, restructuring; informal shake-up, shakedown. **3 turn,** rotation, circle, spin, orbit, circuit, lap.

– DERIVATIVES **rev·o·lu·tion·ist** noun.
– ORIGIN Latin.

rev·o·lu·tion·ar·y /ˌrevəˈlo͞osнəˌnerē/ ▶ **adjective 1** involving or causing great change: *a revolutionary new drug*. **2** engaged in or relating to political revolution.

– SYNONYMS **1 new,** novel, original, unusual, unconventional, unorthodox, newfangled, innovatory, modern, state-of-the-art, futuristic, pioneering. **2 rebellious,** rebel, insurgent, rioting, mutinous, renegade.

▶ **noun** (pl. **revolutionaries**) a person who starts or supports a political revolution.

– SYNONYMS **rebel,** insurgent, mutineer, insurrectionist, agitator.

rev·o·lu·tion·ize /ˌrevəˈlo͞osнəˌnīz/ ▶ **verb** change something greatly or completely.

– SYNONYMS **transform,** shake up, turn upside down, restructure, reorganize, transmute, metamorphose; humorous transmogrify.

re·volve /riˈvälv, riˈvôlv/ ▶ **verb 1** move in a circle around a central point. **2** (**revolve around/about**) move in a circular orbit around. **3** (**revolve around**) treat as the most important aspect: *her life revolved around her husband*.

– SYNONYMS **1 go around/round,** turn around/round, rotate, spin. **2 circle,** travel, orbit.

– ORIGIN Latin *revolvere* 'roll back.'

re·volv·er /riˈvälvər, -ˈvôl-/ ▶ **noun** a pistol with revolving chambers enabling several shots to be fired without reloading.

re·volv·ing door ▶ **noun** an entrance to a large building in which four partitions turn about a central point.

re·vue /riˈvyo͞o/ ▶ **noun** a theatrical show with short sketches, songs, and dances, typically dealing satirically with topical issues.
– ORIGIN French, 'review.'

re·vul·sion /riˈvəlsнən/ ▶ **noun** a feeling of disgust and horror.

– SYNONYMS **disgust,** repulsion, abhorrence, repugnance, nausea, horror, aversion, abomination, distaste.
– ANTONYMS delight.

– ORIGIN Latin.

re·ward /riˈwôrd/ ▶ **noun 1** a thing given in recognition of service, effort, or achievement. **2** a fair return for good or bad behavior: *a slap on the face was the reward for his crude remark*. **3** a sum of money offered for helping to find a criminal or handing in lost property.

– SYNONYMS **award,** honor, decoration, bonus, premium, bounty, present, gift, payment, recompense, prize; informal payoff.

▶ **verb 1** give a reward to someone to show appreciation of their service, qualities, or achievements. **2** (**be rewarded**) receive what one deserves.

– SYNONYMS **recompense,** pay, remunerate.
– ANTONYMS punish.

– ORIGIN Old French *reguard* 'regard, heed.'

re·ward·ing /riˈwôrdiNG/ ▶ **adjective** providing satisfaction.

– SYNONYMS **satisfying,** gratifying, pleasing, fulfilling, enriching, illuminating, worthwhile, productive, fruitful.

– DERIVATIVES **re·ward·ing·ly** adverb.

re·wind /rēˈwīnd/ ▶ **verb** (past and past part. **rewound** /rēˈwound/) wind a film or tape back to the beginning. ▶ **noun** a mechanism for rewinding a film or tape.
– DERIVATIVES **re·wind·er** noun.

re·wire /rēˈwīr/ ▶ **verb** provide a building, device, or vehicle with new electric wiring.
– DERIVATIVES **re·wir·a·ble** adjective.

re·word /rēˈwərd/ ▶ **verb** put something into different words.

re·work /rēˈwərk/ ▶ **verb** change something in order to improve or update it.

re·wound /rēˈwound/ past and past participle of **REWIND**.

re·writ·a·ble /rēˈrītəbəl/ ▶ **adjective** Computing (of a storage device) enabling previously recorded data to be overwritten.

re·write /rēˈrīt/ ▶ **verb** (past **rewrote** /rēˈrōt/; past part. **rewritten** /rēˈritn/) write something again so as to change or improve it. ▶ **noun** an instance of rewriting something.

Reye's syn·drome /rīz, rāz/ ▶ **noun** a life-threatening metabolic disorder in young children, involving encephalitis and liver failure.
– ORIGIN named after Ralph D. K. *Reye*, Australian pediatrician.

Rf ▶ **symbol** the chemical element rutherfordium.

RFD ▶ **abbreviation** rural free delivery.

RFID ▶ **abbreviation** radio frequency identification, denoting technologies that use radio waves to identify people or objects carrying encoded microchips.

RFP ▶ **abbreviation** request for proposal, a detailed specification of goods or services required by an organization, sent to potential contractors or suppliers.

Rg ▶ **symbol** the chemical element roentgenium.

Rh ▶ **abbreviation** rhesus (factor).

r.h. ▶ **abbreviation** right hand.

rhap·so·dize /ˈrapsəˌdīz/ ▶ **verb** express great enthusiasm about someone or something.

rhap·so·dy /ˈrapsədē/ ▶ **noun** (pl. **rhapsodies**) **1** an expression of great joy or enthusiasm: *rhapsodies of praise*. **2** a musical composition that is full of feeling and is not regular in form. **3** (in ancient Greece) an epic poem of a suitable length for recitation at one time.
– DERIVATIVES **rhap·sod·ic** /rapˈsädik/ adjective.
– ORIGIN Greek *rhapsōidia*.

rhe·a /rēə/ ▶ **noun** a large flightless bird of South American grasslands, resembling a small ostrich with grayish-brown plumage.
– ORIGIN from *Rhea*, the mother of Zeus in Greek mythology.

rhe·ni·um /'rēnēəm/ ▶ **noun** a rare silvery-white metallic element.
– ORIGIN from Latin *Rhenus* 'Rhine.'

rhe·ol·o·gy /rē'äləjē/ ▶ **noun** the branch of physics concerned with the deformation and flow of matter.
– DERIVATIVES **rhe·o·log·i·cal** /ˌrēə'läjikəl/ adjective **rhe·ol·o·gist** noun.
– ORIGIN from Greek *rheos* 'stream.'

rhe·o·stat /'rēəˌstat/ ▶ **noun** an instrument used to control the current in an electrical circuit by varying the amount of resistance in it.
– DERIVATIVES **rhe·o·stat·ic** /ˌrēə'statik/ adjective.
– ORIGIN from Greek *rheos* 'stream.'

rhe·sus fac·tor /'rēsəs/ ▶ **noun** a substance in red blood cells that can cause disease in a newborn baby whose blood contains the factor (i.e., is **rhesus positive**) while the mother's blood does not (i.e., is **rhesus negative**).
– ORIGIN from **RHESUS MONKEY**, in which the substance was first observed.

rhe·sus mon·key ▶ **noun** a small brown macaque with red skin on the face and rump, native to southern Asia.
– ORIGIN Greek *Rhēsos*, a mythical king of Thrace.

rhet·o·ric /'retərik/ ▶ **noun** **1** the art of effective or persuasive speaking or writing. **2** persuasive or impressive language that is insincere or meaningless: *I was sick of empty nationalist rhetoric.*

– SYNONYMS **1 oratory,** eloquence, command of language, way with words. **2 wordiness,** verbosity, grandiloquence, bombast, pomposity, extravagant language, purple prose, turgidity; informal hot air.

– ORIGIN from Greek *rhētorikē tekhnē* 'art of rhetoric.'

rhe·tor·i·cal /rə'tôrikəl/ ▶ **adjective** **1** relating to rhetoric. **2** (of a statement) intended to persuade or impress. **3** (of a question) asked for effect or to make a statement rather than to obtain an answer.

– SYNONYMS **1** *a rhetorical device* **stylistic,** oratorical, linguistic, verbal. **2 extravagant,** grandiloquent, high-flown, bombastic, grandiose, pompous, pretentious, overblown, turgid, flowery; informal highfalutin.

– DERIVATIVES **rhe·tor·i·cal·ly** adverb.

rhet·o·ri·cian /ˌretə'rishən/ ▶ **noun** **1** an expert in the art of effective or persuasive speaking or writing. **2** a speaker whose words are intended to impress or persuade.

rheum /ro͞om/ ▶ **noun** chiefly literary a watery fluid that collects in or drips from the nose or eyes.
– DERIVATIVES **rheum·y** adjective.
– ORIGIN Greek *rheuma* 'stream.'

rheu·mat·ic /ro͝o'matik/ ▶ **adjective** relating to or having rheumatism. ▶ **noun** a person with rheumatism.
– DERIVATIVES **rheu·ma·tick·y** adjective (informal).
– ORIGIN first referring to infection characterized by a watery fluid (see **RHEUM**).

rheu·mat·ic fe·ver ▶ **noun** an acute fever marked by inflammation and pain in the joints, caused by a bacterial infection.

rheu·ma·tism /'ro͞oməˌtizəm/ ▶ **noun** any disease marked by inflammation and pain in the joints, muscles, or fibrous tissue.
– ORIGIN from Greek *rheuma* 'stream' (the disease was believed to be caused by the internal flow of 'watery' humors).

rheu·ma·toid /'ro͞oməˌtoid/ ▶ **adjective** relating to or resembling rheumatism.

rheu·ma·toid ar·thri·tis ▶ **noun** a disease that gradually worsens, causing inflammation in the joints and painful swelling and immobility.

rheu·ma·tol·o·gy /ˌro͞omə'täləjē/ ▶ **noun** the study of rheumatism, arthritis, and other disorders of the joints, muscles, and ligaments.
– DERIVATIVES **rheu·ma·to·log·i·cal** /ˌro͞omətl'äjikəl/ adjective **rheu·ma·tol·o·gist** noun.

rhine·stone /'rīnˌstōn/ ▶ **noun** an imitation diamond.
– ORIGIN translating French *caillou du Rhin* 'pebble of the Rhine.'

rhi·ni·tis /rī'nītis/ ▶ **noun** inflammation of the mucous membrane of the nose, caused by infection with a virus or an allergic reaction.
– ORIGIN from Greek *rhis* 'nose.'

rhi·no /'rīnō/ ▶ **noun** (pl. same or **rhinos**) informal a rhinoceros.

rhi·noc·er·os /rī'näs(ə)rəs/ ▶ **noun** (pl. same or **rhinoceroses**) a large plant-eating mammal with one or two horns on the nose and thick folded skin, native to Africa and South Asia.
– ORIGIN from Greek *rhis* 'nose' + *keras* 'horn.'

rhi·no·plas·ty /'rīnōˌplastē/ ▶ **noun** (pl. **rhinoplasties**) plastic surgery performed on the nose.

rhi·zome /'rīˌzōm/ ▶ **noun** a horizontal underground plant stem bearing both roots and shoots.
– ORIGIN Greek *rhizōma*.

Rho·de·sian /rō'dēzhən/ ▶ **noun** a person from Rhodesia (now Zimbabwe). ▶ **adjective** relating to Rhodesia.

Rhodes Schol·ar·ship /rōdz/ ▶ **noun** any of several scholarships awarded annually for study at Oxford University by students from certain Commonwealth countries, the US, and Germany.
– DERIVATIVES **Rhodes schol·ar** noun.
– ORIGIN named after the South African statesman and founder of the scholarships Cecil *Rhodes*.

rho·di·um /'rōdēəm/ ▶ **noun** a hard, dense silvery-white metallic element.
– ORIGIN from Greek *rhodon* 'rose.'

rho·do·den·dron /ˌrōdə'dendrən/ ▶ **noun** a shrub with large clusters of colorful trumpet-shaped flowers and large evergreen leaves.
– ORIGIN from Greek *rhodon* 'rose' + *dendron* 'tree.'

rhom·bi /'rämˌbī, -ˌbē/ plural of **RHOMBUS**.

rhom·bo·he·dron /ˌrämbō'hēdrən/ ▶ **noun** (pl. **rhombohedra** /-drə/ or **rhombohedrons**) a solid figure whose faces are six equal rhombuses.
– DERIVATIVES **rhom·bo·he·dral** /ˌrämbō'hēdrəl/ adjective.

rhom·boid /'rämˌboid/ ▶ **adjective** having or resembling the shape of a rhombus. ▶ **noun** a parallelogram in which adjacent sides are unequal.
– DERIVATIVES **rhom·boi·dal** /räm'boidl/ adjective.

rhom·bus /'rämbəs/ ▶ **noun** (pl. **rhombuses** or **rhombi** /-ˌbī, -ˌbē/) a quadrilateral whose sides all have the same length.
– ORIGIN Greek *rhombos* 'thing that can be spun round, a rhombus.'

rhu·barb /ˈro͞oˌbärb/ ▶ **noun 1** the thick reddish or green leaf stalks of a plant, which are cooked and eaten as a fruit. **2** informal, dated a heated dispute.
– ORIGIN Latin *rheubarbarum*, *rhabarbarum* 'foreign rhubarb.'

rhum·ba ▶ **noun** variant spelling of **RUMBA**.

rhyme /rīm/ ▶ **noun 1** a word that has the same sound or ends with the same sound as another. **2** similarity of sound between words or the endings of words. **3** a short poem with rhyming lines.

– SYNONYMS **poem,** verse, ode; **(rhymes)** poetry, doggerel.

▶ **verb 1** (of a word, syllable, or line) have or end with the same sound as another. **2** (**rhyme something with**) put a word together with another word that has a similar sound. **3** literary compose poetry.
– DERIVATIVES **rhym·er** noun.
– PHRASES **rhyme or reason** logical explanation: *there's no rhyme or reason to it.*
– ORIGIN Greek *rhuthmos* 'rhythm.'

rhyme·ster /ˈrīmstər/ ▶ **noun** a person who composes simple or inferior rhymes.

rhym·ing slang ▶ **noun** a type of slang that replaces words with rhyming words or phrases, typically with the rhyming element omitted (e.g., *butcher's*, short for *butcher's hook*, meaning 'look').

rhy·thm /ˈriT͟Həm/ ▶ **noun 1** a strong, regular repeated pattern of music, sound, or movement. **2** a particular pattern formed by musical rhythm: *a slow waltz rhythm.* **3** the measured flow of words and phrases in verse or prose as determined by the length of and stress on syllables. **4** a regularly recurring sequence of events or processes: *the twice daily rhythms of the tides.*

– SYNONYMS **1 beat,** cadence, tempo, time, pulse. **2 meter,** measure, pattern.

– DERIVATIVES **rhythm·less** adjective.
– ORIGIN Greek *rhuthmos*.

rhy·thm and blues ▶ **noun** popular music of US black origin, arising from a combination of blues with jazz rhythms.

rhyth·mic /ˈriT͟Hmik/ ▶ **adjective 1** having or relating to rhythm. **2** occurring regularly.
– DERIVATIVES **rhyth·mi·cal** adjective **rhyth·mi·cal·ly** /-ik(ə)lē/ adverb **rhyth·mic·i·ty** /ˌriT͟Hˈmisətē/ noun.

rhy·thm meth·od ▶ **noun** a method of birth control in which sex is restricted to the times of a woman's menstrual cycle when ovulation is least likely to occur.

rhy·thm sec·tion ▶ **noun** the part of a pop or jazz group supplying the rhythm, in particular the bass, drums, and sometimes piano, other keyboards, or guitar.

RI ▶ **abbreviation** Rhode Island.

ri·a /ˈrēə/ ▶ **noun** a long narrow inlet formed by the partial submerging of a river valley by the sea.
– ORIGIN Spanish, 'estuary.'

ri·al /rēˈôl, rēˈäl/ (also **riyal**) ▶ **noun 1** the basic unit of money of Iran and Oman. **2** (usu. **riyal**) the basic unit of money of Saudi Arabia, Qatar, and Yemen.
– ORIGIN Arabic.

rib /rib/ ▶ **noun 1** each of a series of thin bones attached in pairs to the spine and curving around to protect the chest and its organs. **2** a curved structure that supports a vault. **3** a curved strut forming part of the framework of a ship's hull. **4** a vein of a leaf or an insect's wing. **5** a combination of alternate plain and purl knitting stitches producing a ridged, slightly elastic fabric. ▶ **verb** (**ribs, ribbing, ribbed**) **1** mark with or form into ridges: *the road was ribbed with furrows of slush.* **2** informal tease someone good-naturedly.
– ORIGIN Old English.

rib·ald /ˈribəld, ˈribˌôld, ˈrīˌbôld/ ▶ **adjective** referring to sex in an amusingly coarse way.
– ORIGIN from Old French *riber* 'indulge in licentious pleasures.'

rib·ald·ry /ˈribəldrē, ˈrī-/ ▶ **noun** coarse humorous talk or behavior.

ribbed /ribd/ ▶ **adjective 1** having a pattern of raised bands. **2** (of a vault or other structure) strengthened with ribs.

rib·bing /ˈribiNG/ ▶ **noun 1** a riblike structure or pattern. **2** informal good-natured teasing.

rib·bon /ˈribən/ ▶ **noun 1** a long, narrow strip of fabric, used for tying something or for decoration. **2** a ribbon of a special color or design awarded as a prize or worn to indicate the holding of an honor. **3** something that is long and narrow in shape. **4** a narrow band of inked material on a spool, used to produce the characters in some typewriters and computer printers.
– DERIVATIVES **rib·boned** adjective.
– PHRASES **cut** (or **tear**) **something to ribbons** severely damage something.
– ORIGIN from former *riband* 'a ribbon.'

rib·by /ˈribē/ ▶ **adjective** having prominent ribs.

rib·cage /ˈribˌkāj/ ▶ **noun** the bony frame formed by the ribs.

ri·bo·fla·vin /ˌrībəˈflāvin, ˈrībəˌflā-/ ▶ **noun** vitamin B_2, a compound essential for energy production and present in milk, liver, and green vegetables.
– ORIGIN from *ribose* (a sugar found in DNA) + Latin *flavus* 'yellow.'

ri·bo·nu·cle·ic ac·id /ˌrībōn(y)o͝oˈklē-ik, -ˈklā-ik/ ▶ **noun** see **RNA**.
– ORIGIN from *ribose* (a sugar found in DNA) + **NUCLEIC ACID**.

rib-tick·ler ▶ **noun** informal a very amusing joke or story.

rice /rīs/ ▶ **noun** the grains of a cereal plant that is grown for food on wet land in warm countries. ▶ **verb** force cooked potatoes or other vegetables through a sieve or similar utensil.
– DERIVATIVES **ric·er** noun.
– ORIGIN Old French *ris*.

rice pa·per ▶ **noun** thin edible paper made from the flattened and dried pith of a shrub, used in oriental painting and in baking cookies and cakes.

rich /riCH/ ▶ **adjective 1** having a great deal of money or assets. **2** (of a country or region) having valuable natural resources or a successful economy. **3** made of expensive materials: *rich mahogany furniture.* **4** existing in plentiful quantities; abundant. **5** having or producing something in large amounts: *fruits rich in vitamins.* **6** (of food) containing much fat, sugar, etc. **7** (of a color, sound, or smell) pleasantly deep and strong. **8** (of soil or land) fertile. **9** (of the mixture in an internal-combustion engine) containing a high proportion of fuel. **10** informal (of a remark) causing ironic amusement or indignation.

– SYNONYMS **1 wealthy,** affluent, moneyed, well off, well-to-do, prosperous; informal loaded, well heeled, made of money. **2 sumptuous,** opulent, luxurious, lavish, gorgeous, splendid, magnificent,

costly, expensive, fancy, palatial; informal plush, swish, swank. **3** *a garden rich in flowers* **well stocked,** well provided, abounding, crammed, packed, teeming, bursting. **4** *a rich supply* **plentiful,** abundant, copious, ample, profuse, lavish, liberal, generous. **5 fertile,** productive, fruitful, fecund. **6 creamy,** fatty, heavy, full-flavored. **7** *rich colors* **strong,** deep, full, intense, vivid, brilliant.
– ANTONYMS poor, plain.

– DERIVATIVES **rich·ness** noun.
– ORIGIN Old English, 'powerful, wealthy.'

rich·es /'ricHiz/ ▶ **plural noun 1** material wealth. **2** valuable natural resources.

– SYNONYMS **money,** wealth, funds, cash, means, assets, capital, resources; informal bread, loot, (big) bucks.

rich·ly /'ricHlē/ ▶ **adverb 1** in a rich way. **2** fully: *a richly deserved vacation.*

– SYNONYMS **1 sumptuously,** opulently, luxuriously, lavishly, gorgeously, splendidly, magnificently. **2** *the reward she richly deserves* **fully,** amply, well, thoroughly, completely, wholly, totally, entirely, absolutely, utterly.

Rich·ter scale /'riktər/ ▶ **noun** a scale for expressing the magnitude of an earthquake.
– ORIGIN named after the American geologist Charles F. *Richter.*

ri·cin /'rīsən, 'ris-/ ▶ **noun** a highly toxic protein obtained from the seeds of the castor oil plant.
– ORIGIN from Latin *Ricinus communis* (referring to the castor oil plant).

rick /rik/ ▶ **noun** a stack of hay, cereal, or straw, especially one built into a regular shape.
– ORIGIN Old English.

rick·ets /'rikits/ ▶ **noun** (treated as sing. or pl.) a disease of children caused by a lack of vitamin D, in which the bones become softened and distorted.
– ORIGIN perhaps from Greek *rhakhitis,* from *rhakhis* 'spine.'

rick·ett·si·a /ri'ketsēə/ ▶ **noun** (pl. **rickettsiae** /-sē,ē, -sē,ī/ or **rickettsias**) any of a group of very small bacteria of which some cause typhus and similar diseases in humans.
– DERIVATIVES **rick·ett·si·al** adjective.
– ORIGIN named after Howard Taylor *Ricketts,* American pathologist.

rick·et·y /'rikitē/ ▶ **adjective** poorly made and likely to collapse.

– SYNONYMS **shaky,** unsteady, unsound, unsafe, tumbledown, broken-down, dilapidated, ramshackle.

– DERIVATIVES **rick·et·i·ness** noun.

rick·rack /'rik,rak/ ▶ **noun** braided trimming in a zigzag pattern, used on clothes.
– ORIGIN unknown.

rick·shaw /'rik,sHô/ ▶ **noun** a light two-wheeled hooded vehicle drawn by one or more people, used in Asian countries.
– ORIGIN Japanese, 'person-strength-vehicle.'

ric·o·chet /'rikə,sHā, -,sHet/ ▶ **verb** (**ricochets** /'rikə,sHāz, -,sHets/, **ricocheting** /-,sHā-iNG, -,sHetiNG/, **ricocheted** /-,sHād, -,sHetid/) (of a bullet or other fast moving object) rebound off a surface. ▶ **noun 1** a shot or hit that rebounds off a surface. **2** the action of rebounding off a surface.
– ORIGIN French.

ri·cot·ta /ri'kätə/ ▶ **noun** a soft white unsalted Italian cheese.
– ORIGIN Italian, 'cooked again.'

ric·tus /'riktəs/ ▶ **noun** a fixed grimace or grin.
– DERIVATIVES **ric·tal** adjective.
– ORIGIN Latin, 'open mouth.'

rid /rid/ ▶ **verb** (**rids, ridding, rid**) **1** (**rid someone/thing of**) make someone or something free of an unwanted person or thing. **2** (**be** (or **get**) **rid of**) be or make oneself free of someone or something that is unwanted or annoying.

– SYNONYMS **1** *ridding the building of asbestos* **clear,** free, purge, empty, strip. **2** (**get rid of**) *we must get rid of some stuff* **dispose of,** throw away/out, clear out, discard, scrap, dump, bin, jettison, expel, eliminate; informal trash, chuck, ditch, junk.

– ORIGIN Old Norse.

rid·dance /'ridns/ ▶ **noun** (in phrase **good riddance**) said to express relief at being rid of someone or something.

rid·den /'ridn/ past participle of **RIDE** ▶ **adjective** (in combination) full of a particular thing: *guilt-ridden.*

rid·dle[1] /'ridl/ ▶ **noun 1** a question or statement that is worded in such a way that one needs to think hard to find its answer or meaning. **2** a puzzling person or thing.

– SYNONYMS **puzzle,** conundrum, brain-teaser, problem, question, poser, enigma, mystery.

– DERIVATIVES **rid·dler** noun.
– ORIGIN Old English.

CHOOSE THE RIGHT WORD

riddle, conundrum, enigma, mystery, paradox, puzzle

All of these terms imply something baffling or challenging. A **mystery** is anything that is incomprehensible to human reason, particularly if it invites speculation (*the mystery surrounding her sudden disappearance*). An **enigma** is a statement whose meaning is hidden under obscure or ambiguous allusions, so that we can only guess at its significance; it can also refer to a person of puzzling or contradictory character (*he remained an enigma throughout his long career*). A **riddle** is a mystery involving contradictory statements, with a hidden meaning designed to be guessed at (*the old riddle about how many college graduates it takes to change a light bulb*). **Conundrum** applies specifically to a riddle phrased as a question, the answer to which usually involves a pun or a play on words, such as "What is black and white and read all over?"; *conundrum* can also refer to any puzzling or difficult situation. A **paradox** is a statement that seems self-contradictory or absurd, but in reality expresses a possible truth (*Francis Bacon's well-known paradox, "The most corrected copies are commonly the least correct"*). A **puzzle** is not necessarily a verbal statement, but it presents a problem with a particularly baffling solution or tests one's ingenuity or skill in coming up with a solution (*a crossword puzzle*).

rid·dle[2] ▶ **verb 1** make many holes in someone or something. **2** fill with something undesirable: *my foot is now riddled with arthritis.* **3** pass a substance through a large coarse sieve. ▶ **noun** a large coarse sieve.
– ORIGIN Old English.

ride /rīd/ ▶ **verb** (past **rode**; past part. **ridden**) **1** sit on and control the movement of a horse, bicycle, or motorcycle. **2** (usu. **ride in/on**) travel in a vehicle or on a horse.

3 travel over an area on horseback or on a bicycle or motorcycle. **4** be carried or supported by: *surfers rode the waves.* **5** sail or float: *a ship rode at anchor in the dock.* **6** (**ride on**) depend on. **7** (**ride something out**) come safely through a difficult situation. **8** (**ride up**) (of an item of clothing) gradually move upward out of its proper position. **9** yield to a blow so as to reduce its impact. **10** (**be ridden**) be full of or dominated by: *people ridden by ill health.*

– SYNONYMS **1 sit on,** mount, control, manage, handle. **2 travel,** move, proceed, drive, cycle, trot, canter, gallop.

▶ **noun 1** an act of riding. **2** a roller coaster, merry-go-round, etc., ridden at a fair or amusement park. **3** a path for horse riding.

– SYNONYMS **trip,** journey, drive, run, excursion, outing, jaunt, lift; informal spin.

– DERIVATIVES **ride·a·ble** (also **ridable**) adjective.
– PHRASES **be riding for a fall** informal be acting in a reckless way that invites failure. **let something ride** take no immediate action over something. **ride high** be successful. **a rough** (or **easy**) **ride** a difficult (or easy) time. **take someone for a ride** informal deceive someone.
– ORIGIN Old English.

rid·er /ˈrīdər/ ▶ **noun 1** a person who rides a horse, bicycle, motorcycle, etc. **2** a condition added to something already agreed.
– DERIVATIVES **rid·er·less** adjective.

ridge /rij/ ▶ **noun 1** a long narrow hilltop or mountain range. **2** a narrow raised strip on a surface. **3** Meteorology a long, narrow region of high pressure. **4** the edge formed where the two sloping sides of a roof meet at the top. ▶ **verb** (often as adj. **ridged**) form something into ridges.
– DERIVATIVES **ridg·y** adjective.
– ORIGIN Old English, 'spine, crest.'

ridge tent ▶ **noun** a tent with a central ridge supported by a pole or frame at each end.

rid·i·cule /ˈridiˌkyo͞ol/ ▶ **noun** the use of language to make fun of someone or something in an unkind way: *he became an object of ridicule among his own aides.*

– SYNONYMS **mockery,** derision, laughter, scorn, scoffing, jeering.
– ANTONYMS respect.

▶ **verb** mock or make fun of someone or something.

– SYNONYMS **mock,** deride, laugh at, heap scorn on, jeer at, make fun of, scoff at, satirize, caricature, parody.

ri·dic·u·lous /riˈdikyələs/ ▶ **adjective** very silly or unreasonable; absurd.

– SYNONYMS **laughable,** absurd, ludicrous, risible, comical, funny, hilarious, amusing, farcical, silly, stupid, idiotic, preposterous.
– ANTONYMS sensible.

– DERIVATIVES **ri·dic·u·lous·ly** adverb **ri·dic·u·lous·ness** noun.
– ORIGIN Latin *ridiculus* 'laughable.'

rid·ing /ˈrīdiNG/ ▶ **noun** the sport or activity of riding horses.

rid·ing crop ▶ **noun** a short flexible whip with a loop for the hand, used when riding horses.

rid·ing hab·it ▶ **noun** a woman's riding dress, consisting of a skirt and a double-breasted jacket.

Ries·ling /ˈrēzliNG, ˈrēs-/ ▶ **noun** a dry white wine made from a variety of grape grown especially in Germany and Austria.
– ORIGIN German.

rife /rīf/ ▶ **adjective 1** (especially of something undesirable) widespread: *drug addiction is rife.* **2** (**rife with**) full of something, especially something undesirable.

– SYNONYMS **widespread,** general, common, universal, extensive, ubiquitous, endemic, inescapable.

– ORIGIN Old English.

CHOOSE THE RIGHT WORD

See **PREVALENT**.

riff /rif/ ▶ **noun** a short repeated phrase in popular music or jazz. ▶ **verb** play riffs.
– ORIGIN from **RIFFLE**.

rif·fle /ˈrifəl/ ▶ **verb 1** turn over the pages of a book or document quickly and casually. **2** (**riffle through**) search quickly through. ▶ **noun** an act of turning over pages or searching through something.
– ORIGIN perhaps from **RUFFLE**, influenced by **RIPPLE**.

riff·raff /ˈrifˌraf/ ▶ **noun** people who are considered disreputable or socially unacceptable.

– SYNONYMS **rabble,** good-for-nothings, undesirables, the lowest of the low, scum; informal peasants.
– ANTONYMS elite.

– ORIGIN from Old French *rif et raf* 'one and all, every bit.'

ri·fle[1] /ˈrīfəl/ ▶ **noun 1** a gun having a long spirally grooved barrel to make a bullet spin and thereby increase accuracy over a long distance. **2** (**rifles**) troops armed with rifles. ▶ **verb 1** (usu. as adj. **rifled**) make spiral grooves in a gun or its barrel or bore. **2** hit or kick a ball hard and straight.
– ORIGIN from French *rifler* 'graze, scratch.'

rifle[2] ▶ **verb 1** search through something hurriedly to find or steal something. **2** steal something.

– SYNONYMS **1 rummage,** search, hunt, forage. **2 ransack,** plunder, loot, raid, rob, steal from, burgle, burglarize.

– ORIGIN Old French *rifler* 'graze, plunder.'

ri·fle·man /ˈrīfəlmən/ ▶ **noun** (pl. **riflemen**) a soldier armed with a rifle.

ri·fle range ▶ **noun** a place for practicing shooting with rifles.

ri·fling /ˈrīf(ə)liNG/ ▶ **noun** spiral grooves on the inside of a rifle barrel.

rift /rift/ ▶ **noun 1** a crack, split, or break. **2** a serious break in friendly relations.

– SYNONYMS **1 crack,** split, breach, fissure, fracture, cleft, crevice, opening. **2 disagreement,** estrangement, breach, split, schism, quarrel, falling-out, conflict, feud; Brit. row.

– ORIGIN Scandinavian.

rift val·ley ▶ **noun** a steep-sided valley formed by subsidence of the earth's surface between nearly parallel faults.

rig[1] /rig/ ▶ **verb** (**rigs, rigging, rigged**) **1** provide a boat with sails and rigging. **2** assemble and adjust the equipment of a sailboat, aircraft, etc., in readiness for operation. **3** set up a device or structure, often in a makeshift way: *he'd rigged up a sort of tent.* **4** (**rig someone out**) dress someone in a particular outfit.

– SYNONYMS **1 equip,** fit out, supply, furnish, provide, arm. **2** *he will* **rig up** *a shelter* **set up,** erect, assemble, put together, whip up, improvise, contrive; informal knock together. **3 dress,** clothe, attire, robe, garb, get up; informal doll up.

▶ **noun 1** the arrangement of a boat's sails and rigging. **2** equipment or a device for a particular purpose: *a lighting rig.* **3** an oil rig or drilling rig. **4** a person's costume or outfit. **5** a truck.
– DERIVATIVES **rigged** adjective.
– ORIGIN perhaps Scandinavian.

rig² ▶ **verb** (**rigs, rigging, rigged**) manage or arrange in a dishonest way so as to gain an advantage: *the results of the elections had been rigged.*

– SYNONYMS **manipulate,** engineer, distort, misrepresent, pervert, tamper with, falsify, fake; informal fix.

– ORIGIN unknown.

rig·a·to·ni /ˌrigəˈtōnē/ ▶ **plural noun** pasta in the form of short hollow fluted tubes.
– ORIGIN Italian.

rig·ger /ˈrigər/ ▶ **noun 1** (in combination) a ship rigged in a particular way: *a square-rigger.* **2** a person who erects and maintains scaffolding or cranes. **3** a person who works on or helps to build an oil rig.

rig·ging /ˈrigiNG/ ▶ **noun 1** the system of ropes or chains supporting a ship's masts and controlling or setting the yards and sails. **2** the ropes and wires supporting the structure of a hang-glider or parachute.

right /rīt/ ▶ **adjective 1** on, toward, or relating to the side of a person or thing that is to the east when the person or thing is facing north. **2** morally good, justified, or acceptable. **3** factually correct. **4** most appropriate. **5** in a satisfactory, sound, or normal condition. **6** relating to a right-wing person or group.

– SYNONYMS **1 right-hand;** Nautical starboard; Heraldry dexter. **2** *it wouldn't be right to do that* **just,** fair, equitable, proper, good, upright, righteous, virtuous, moral, ethical, principled, honorable, honest, lawful, legal. **3** *Mr. Hubert had the right answer* **correct,** unerring, accurate, exact, precise, valid. **4** *the right person for the job* **suitable,** appropriate, fitting, apposite, apt, correct, proper, desirable, preferable, ideal. **5** *you've come at the right time* **opportune,** advantageous, favorable, convenient, good, lucky, fortunate.
– ANTONYMS wrong, left.

▶ **adverb 1** on or to the right side. **2** to the furthest extent or degree; completely. **3** exactly; directly. **4** in a correct or satisfactory way. **5** informal without delay; immediately.

– SYNONYMS **1** *the car spun right off the track* **completely,** fully, totally, absolutely, utterly, thoroughly, quite. **2** *right in the middle of the village* **exactly,** precisely, directly, immediately, just, squarely, dead; informal (slam) bang, smack, plumb. **3** *I think I heard right* **correctly,** accurately, perfectly.
– ANTONYMS wrong, badly.

▶ **noun 1** that which is morally right. **2** a moral or legal entitlement to have or do something. **3** (**rights**) the authority to perform, publish, or film a particular work or event. **4** (**the right**) the right-hand part, side, or direction. **5** a right turn. **6** a person's right fist, or a blow given with it. **7** (often **the Right**) (treated as sing. or pl.) a group or political party favoring conservative views.

– SYNONYMS **1** *the difference between right and wrong* **goodness,** righteousness, virtue, integrity, propriety, probity, morality, truth, honesty, honor, justice, fairness, equity. **2** *you have every right to be angry* **entitlement,** prerogative, privilege, liberty, authority, power, license, permission, dispensation, leave, due.
– ANTONYMS wrong.

▶ **verb 1** return someone or something to a normal or upright position. **2** return to a normal or correct condition: *righting the economy demanded cuts in defense spending.* **3** make amends for a wrong.

– SYNONYMS **remedy,** rectify, retrieve, fix, resolve, sort out, settle, square, straighten out, correct, repair, mend, redress.

– DERIVATIVES **right·er** noun **right·ish** adjective **right·most** /ˈrītˌmōst/ adjective **right·ness** noun **right·ward** /ˈrītwərd/ adjective & adverb **right·wards** /ˈrītwərdz/ adverb.
– PHRASES **by rights** if things were fair or correct. **in one's own right** as a result of one's own qualifications or efforts. **put** (or **set**) **someone right** tell someone the true facts of a situation. **put** (or **set**) **something to rights** return something to its correct or normal state. **right** (or **straight**) **away** immediately. **right on** informal **1** expressing support, approval, or encouragement. **2** (**right-on**) informal precisely correct: *I think the Japanese have it the most right-on.* **3** (**right-on**) Brit. informal, often derogatory in keeping with fashionable liberal or left-wing opinions and values.
– ORIGIN Old English.

right an·gle ▶ **noun** an angle of 90°, as in a corner of a square.
– DERIVATIVES **right-an·gled** adjective.
– PHRASES **at right angles to** forming an angle of 90° with.

right-click ▶ **verb** press the right-hand button on a computer mouse. ▶ **noun** an act of right-clicking.

right·eous /ˈrīCHəs/ ▶ **adjective 1** morally right or justifiable: *righteous indignation about pay and conditions.* **2** (of a person) morally good; virtuous.

– SYNONYMS **good,** virtuous, upright, upstanding, decent, ethical, principled, moral, honest, honorable, blameless.
– ANTONYMS wicked.

– DERIVATIVES **right·eous·ly** adverb **right·eous·ness** noun.

right field ▶ **noun** Baseball **1** the part of the outfield to the right of center field from the perspective of home plate. **2** the position of the defensive player stationed in right field.

right·ful /ˈrītfəl/ ▶ **adjective 1** having a legal or moral right to something. **2** rightly claimed; appropriate: *helping the sport reach its rightful place in the Olympics.*

– SYNONYMS **1 legal,** lawful, legitimate, real, true, proper, correct, recognized, genuine, authentic, acknowledged, approved, valid, bona fide; informal legit, kosher. **2 deserved,** merited, due, just, right, fair, proper, fitting, appropriate, suitable.
– ANTONYMS wrongful.

– DERIVATIVES **right·ful·ly** adverb **right·ful·ness** noun.

right hand ▶ **noun 1** the region or direction on the right side of someone or something. **2** the most important position next to someone. ▶ **adjective 1** on or toward the right side. **2** done with or using the right hand.

right-hand·ed ▶ **adjective 1** (of a person) using the right hand more naturally than the left. **2** done with the right hand. **3** turning to the right; toward the right. **4** (of a screw) that is to be turned clockwise.

right-hand·er /'handər/ ▸ **noun 1** a right-handed person. **2** a blow struck with a person's right hand.

right-hand man ▸ **noun** a person's chief assistant.

right·ism /'rīt,izəm/ ▸ **noun** the political views or policies of the right.
– DERIVATIVES **right·ist** /'rītist/ noun & adjective.

right·ly /'rītlē/ ▸ **adverb 1** in accordance with what is true, morally right, or just. **2** with good reason.

right-mind·ed (also **right-thinking**) ▸ **adjective** having views and principles that most people approve of.

right of way ▸ **noun 1** the legal right to pass along a specific route through another's property. **2** a public path through another's property. **3** the right of a vehicle or ship to go before another.

Right Rev·er·end ▸ **adjective** a title given to a bishop, especially in the Anglican Church.

right side ▸ **noun** the side of something intended to be at the top or front.
– PHRASES **on the right side of 1** in favor with. **2** rather less than a specified age.

right-size /'rīt,sīz/ ▸ **verb** convert something to an appropriate size, especially by reducing staff levels in an organization.

rights of·fer·ing ▸ **noun** an issue of shares offered at a special price by a company to its existing shareholders.

right-to-die ▸ **adjective** relating to or advocating the right to refuse extraordinary measures intended to prolong someone's life when they are terminally ill or comatose.

right-to-life ▸ **adjective** another term for **PRO-LIFE**.

right whale ▸ **noun** a whale with a large head and a deeply curved jaw, of Arctic and temperate waters.

right wing ▸ **noun 1** the conservative or reactionary section of a political party or system. **2** the right side of a sports team on the field or of an army.
– DERIVATIVES **right-wing·er** noun.
– ORIGIN see **LEFT WING**.

rig·id /'rijid/ ▸ **adjective 1** unable to bend or be forced out of shape. **2** not able to be changed or adapted: *rigid rules governing the production of certain wines*. **3** stiff and unmoving, especially with fear.

> – SYNONYMS **1 stiff,** hard, taut, firm, inflexible, unbendable, unyielding, inelastic. **2** *a rigid routine* **fixed,** set, firm, inflexible, invariable, hard and fast, cast-iron, strict, stringent, rigorous, uncompromising, intransigent.
> – ANTONYMS flexible.

– DERIVATIVES **ri·gid·i·fy** /rə'jidə,fī/ verb (**rigidifies, rigidifying, rigidified**) **ri·gid·i·ty** /rə'jidətē/ noun **rig·id·ly** adverb.
– ORIGIN Latin *rigidus*.

rig·ma·role /'rig(ə)mə,rōl/ ▸ **noun 1** a lengthy and complicated procedure. **2** a long, rambling story.
– ORIGIN probably from former *ragman roll*, referring to a legal document recording a list of offences.

rig·or /'rigər/ (Brit. **rigour**) ▸ **noun 1** the quality of being thorough or severe: *his analysis is lacking in rigor*. **2** (**rigors**) demanding or extreme conditions.
– ORIGIN Latin *rigor* 'stiffness.'

rig·or mor·tis /,rigər 'môrtəs/ ▸ **noun** stiffening of the joints and muscles a few hours after death, lasting from one to four days.
– ORIGIN Latin, 'stiffness of death.'

rig·or·ous /'rigərəs/ ▸ **adjective 1** very thorough or accurate. **2** (of a rule or system) strictly applied or followed. **3** strictly following a belief or system. **4** harsh and demanding: *rigorous military training*.

> – SYNONYMS **1 meticulous,** conscientious, punctilious, careful, scrupulous, painstaking, exact, precise, accurate, particular, strict. **2 strict,** stringent, rigid, inflexible, draconian, intransigent, uncompromising. **3** *rigorous conditions* **harsh,** severe, bleak, extreme, demanding.
> – ANTONYMS slapdash, lax.

– DERIVATIVES **rig·or·ous·ly** adverb **rig·or·ous·ness** noun.

rijst·ta·fel /'rī,stäfəl/ ▸ **noun** a meal of SE Asian food consisting of a selection of spiced rice dishes.
– ORIGIN Dutch.

rile /rīl/ ▸ **verb** informal annoy or irritate someone.
– ORIGIN from **ROIL**.

Ri·ley /'rīlē/ ▸ **noun** (in phrase **the life of Riley**) informal a luxurious or carefree existence.
– ORIGIN unknown.

rill /ril/ ▸ **noun** a small stream.
– ORIGIN probably German.

rim /rim/ ▸ **noun 1** the upper or outer edge of something circular. **2** (also **wheel rim**) the outer edge of a wheel, on which the tire is fitted. **3** a stain or deposit left on a surface by dirty water.

> – SYNONYMS **edge,** brim, lip, border, side, margin, brink, boundary, perimeter, circumference, limits, periphery.

▸ **verb** (**rims, rimming, rimmed**) provide or mark with a rim: *a lake rimmed by glaciers*.
– DERIVATIVES **rim·less** adjective.
– ORIGIN Old English, 'a border, coast.'

> **CHOOSE THE RIGHT WORD**
>
> See **BORDER**.

rime /rīm/ ▸ **noun** technical & literary hoar frost. ▸ **verb** literary cover something with hoar frost.
– DERIVATIVES **rim·y** adjective.
– ORIGIN Old English.

rind /rīnd/ ▸ **noun** the tough skin of some fruit, or the hard outer edge of cheese or bacon.

> – SYNONYMS **skin,** peel, zest, integument.

– DERIVATIVES **rind·ed** adjective **rind·less** adjective.
– ORIGIN Old English.

ring[1] /riNG/ ▸ **noun 1** a small circular metal band worn on a finger. **2** a circular band, object, or mark. **3** an enclosed space in which a sport, performance, or show takes place. **4** a group of people or things arranged in a circle. **5** a group of people involved in a shared activity, especially one that is illegal or secret: *a drug ring*. **6** a number of atoms bonded together to form a closed loop in a molecule.

> – SYNONYMS **1 circle,** band, halo, disk/disc. **2 arena,** enclosure, amphitheater, bowl. **3 gang,** syndicate, cartel, mob, band, circle, organization, association, society, alliance, league.

▸ **verb 1** surround someone or something. **2** chiefly Brit. draw a circle around something.

> – SYNONYMS **surround,** circle, encircle, enclose, hem in, confine, seal off.

– DERIVATIVES **ringed** adjective.

– PHRASES **run rings around** informal outclass or outwit easily.
– ORIGIN Old English.

ring² ▶ **verb** (past **rang**; past part. **rung**) **1** make or cause to make a clear resounding sound. **2** (**ring with**) be filled or resound with a sound. **3** telephone someone. **4** call for attention by sounding a bell. **5** sound the hour or a peal on a bell or bells. **6** (of the ears) be filled with a buzzing or humming sound due to a blow or loud noise. **7** convey a specified impression or quality: *her honesty rings true*. **8** (**ring something up**) record an amount on a cash register.

– SYNONYMS **1 chime,** sound, peal, toll, clang, bong; literary knell. **2 resound,** reverberate, resonate, echo. **3 telephone,** phone (up), call (up); informal give someone a buzz/ring.

▶ **noun 1** an act of ringing. **2** a resounding sound or tone. **3** informal a telephone call: *give me a ring*. **4** a quality conveyed by something heard: *the tale had a ring of truth*. **5** a set of bells, especially church bells.
– PHRASES **ring down** (or **up**) **the curtain 1** lower (or raise) a theater curtain. **2** mark the end (or beginning) of something.
– ORIGIN Old English.

ring bind·er ▶ **noun** a loose-leaf binder with ring-shaped clasps that can be opened to pass through holes in the paper.

ring·er /ˈriNGər/ ▶ **noun 1** a person or device that rings. **2** informal another term for **DEAD RINGER**. **3** informal an athlete or horse fraudulently substituted for another in a competition.

ring fin·ger ▶ **noun** the finger next to the little finger of the left hand, on which the wedding ring is worn.

ring·ing /ˈriNGiNG/ ▶ **adjective 1** having a clear resounding tone or sound. **2** (of a statement) forceful and completely clear.
– DERIVATIVES **ring·ing·ly** adverb.

ring·lead·er /ˈriNGˌlēdər/ ▶ **noun** a person who leads others in crime or causing trouble.

ring·let /ˈriNGlit/ ▶ **noun** a corkscrew-shaped curl of hair.
– DERIVATIVES **ring·let·ted** (also **ringleted**) adjective.

ring·mas·ter /ˈriNGˌmastər/ ▶ **noun** the person who directs a circus performance.

ring mold ▶ **noun** a ring-shaped open-topped container used for making molds and cakes.

ring road ▶ **noun** Brit. a bypass encircling a town.

ring·side /ˈriNGˌsīd/ ▶ **noun** the area beside a boxing ring or circus ring.
– DERIVATIVES **ring·sid·er** noun.

ring·side seat ▶ **noun** a very good position from which to observe something.

ring·tone /ˈriNGˌtōn/ ▶ **noun** a sound made by a cell phone when an incoming call is received.

ring·worm /ˈriNGˌwərm/ ▶ **noun** a skin disease occurring in small circular itchy patches, caused by various fungi and affecting chiefly the scalp or feet.

rink /riNGk/ ▶ **noun 1** (also **ice rink**) an enclosed area of ice for skating, ice hockey, or curling. **2** (also **roller rink**) a smooth enclosed floor for roller skating. **3** (also **bowling rink**) the strip of a lawn bowling green used for a match. **4** a team in curling or lawn bowling.
– ORIGIN perhaps from Old French *renc* 'rank.'

rinse /rins/ ▶ **verb 1** wash something with clean water to remove soap or dirt. **2** (often **rinse something off/out**) remove soap or dirt by rinsing.

– SYNONYMS **wash (out),** clean, cleanse, bathe, dip, drench, splash, swill, sluice.

▶ **noun 1** an act of rinsing. **2** a liquid for conditioning or coloring the hair. **3** an antiseptic liquid for cleaning the mouth.
– DERIVATIVES **rins·er** noun.
– ORIGIN Old French *rincer*.

Ri·o·ja /rēˈōhä/ ▶ **noun** a wine produced in La Rioja, Spain.

ri·ot /ˈrīət/ ▶ **noun 1** a violent public disturbance by a crowd of people. **2** a large or varied display or combination: *the garden was a riot of color*. **3** (**a riot**) informal a highly amusing or entertaining person or thing.

– SYNONYMS **disorder,** disturbance, lawlessness, upheaval, uproar, commotion, free-for-all, uprising, insurrection.

▶ **verb** take part in a riot.

– SYNONYMS **(go on the) rampage,** run wild, run amok, run riot, go berserk; informal raise hell.

– DERIVATIVES **ri·ot·er** noun.
– PHRASES **read someone the Riot Act** give someone a severe warning or reprimand. [from the name of a former act partly read out to disperse rioters.] **run riot 1** behave in a violent and uncontrolled way. **2** spread uncontrollably.
– ORIGIN Old French *riote* 'debate.'

ri·ot·ous /ˈrīətəs/ ▶ **adjective 1** involving uncontrolled behavior, especially in celebration of something: *a riotous party*. **2** having a vivid, varied appearance. **3** involving public disorder.

– SYNONYMS **1 unruly,** rowdy, disorderly, uncontrollable, unmanageable, undisciplined, uproarious, tumultuous, violent, wild, lawless, anarchic. **2 boisterous,** lively, loud, noisy, unrestrained, uninhibited, uproarious; informal rambunctious.
– ANTONYMS peaceful.

– DERIVATIVES **ri·ot·ous·ly** adverb **ri·ot·ous·ness** noun.

RIP ▶ **abbreviation** rest in peace (used on graves).
– ORIGIN from Latin *requiescat* (or (plural) *requiescant*) *in pace*.

rip¹ /rip/ ▶ **verb** (**rips, ripping, ripped**) **1** tear or pull something forcibly away from something or someone. **2** make a tear or hole in something. **3** move forcefully and rapidly: *a fire ripped through the building*. **4** (**rip someone off**) informal cheat someone. **5** (**rip something off**) informal steal or copy something.

– SYNONYMS **tear,** pull, wrench, snatch, drag, pluck; informal yank.

▶ **noun** a long tear or cut.
– DERIVATIVES **rip·per** noun.
– PHRASES **let rip** informal **1** do something without restraint. **2** express oneself forcefully or angrily.
– ORIGIN unknown.

rip² (also **rip tide**) ▶ **noun** a stretch of fast-flowing and rough water caused by the meeting of currents.
– ORIGIN perhaps from **RIP¹**.

ri·par·i·an /riˈpe(ə)rēən, rī-/ ▶ **adjective** relating to or situated on the banks of a river.
– ORIGIN from Latin *riparius*.

rip·cord /ˈripˌkôrd/ ▶ **noun** a cord that is pulled to open a parachute.

ripe /rīp/ ▶ **adjective** **1** (of fruit or grain) ready for harvesting and eating. **2** (of a cheese or wine) full-flavored and mature. **3** (**ripe for**) having reached a fitting time for: *land ripe for development*. **4** (**ripe with**) full of something.

– SYNONYMS **1 mature,** full grown, fully developed. **2** *ripe for development* **ready,** fit, suitable, right. **3** *the time is ripe* **opportune,** advantageous, favorable, auspicious, good, right.
– ANTONYMS immature.

– DERIVATIVES **ripe·ly** adverb **ripe·ness** noun.
– PHRASES **ripe old age** a person's age that is very old.
– ORIGIN Old English.

WORD TOOLKIT

ripe ...	succulent ...	moist ...
tomatoes	leaves	cake
berries	flavor	chicken
peaches	morsels	salmon
cheese	roast	bread

rip·en /'rīpən/ ▶ **verb** become or make ripe or ready for eating.

– SYNONYMS **mature,** mellow, develop.

CHOOSE THE RIGHT WORD

See **MATURE**.

rip-off ▶ **noun** informal **1** an article that is greatly overpriced. **2** a poor-quality copy of something.

ri·poste /ri'pōst/ ▶ **noun** **1** a quick clever reply to a critical or insulting remark. **2** a quick return thrust in fencing.

– SYNONYMS **retort,** counter, rejoinder, sally, return, answer, reply, response; informal comeback.

▶ **verb** make a quick clever reply to an insult or criticism.
– ORIGIN French.

rip·ple /'ripəl/ ▶ **noun** **1** a small wave or series of waves. **2** a sound or feeling that spreads through a person, group, or place: *a ripple of laughter went around the hall*. **3** a type of ice cream with wavy lines of colored flavored syrup running through it. **4** a small periodic variation in voltage. ▶ **verb** **1** form or move with a series of small waves. **2** (of a sound or feeling) spread through a person, group, or place.
– DERIVATIVES **rip·ply** adjective.
– ORIGIN unknown.

rip-roar·ing ▶ **adjective** full of energy and excitement.

rip·saw /'rip,sô/ ▶ **noun** a coarse saw for cutting wood along the grain.

rip·stop /'rip,stäp/ ▶ **noun** nylon fabric that is woven so that a tear will not spread.

RISC /risk/ ▶ **noun** reduced instruction set computer; computing based on a form of microprocessor designed to perform a limited set of operations very quickly.
– ORIGIN from *reduced instruction set computer* (or *computing*).

rise /rīz/ ▶ **verb** (past **rose** /rōz/; past part. **risen** /'rizən/) **1** come or go up. **2** get up from lying, sitting, or kneeling. **3** increase in number, size, intensity, or quality: *house prices had risen*. **4** (of land) slope upward. **5** (of the sun, moon, or stars) appear above the horizon. **6** reach a higher social or professional position. **7** (**rise above**) succeed in not being restricted by: *try to rise above prejudice*. **8** (**rise to**) respond well to a challenging situation. **9** (often **rise up**) rebel against authority. **10** (of a river) have its source in a particular place.

– SYNONYMS **1 climb,** come up, arise, ascend, mount, soar. **2 loom,** tower, soar. **3 go up,** increase, soar, shoot up, surge, leap, jump, rocket, escalate, spiral. **4 get higher,** grow, increase, become louder, swell, intensify. **5 stand up,** get to one's feet, get up, jump up, leap up, stir, bestir oneself.
– ANTONYMS fall, descend, drop.

▶ **noun** **1** an act of rising. **2** an increase in number, size, amount, or degree. **3** an upward slope or hill. **4** the vertical height of a step or slope.

– SYNONYMS **1 increase,** hike, leap, upsurge, upswing, climb. **2 raise,** increase, increment. **3 slope,** incline, hill, elevation, acclivity.

– PHRASES **get a rise out of** informal provoke an angry or irritated response from. **on the rise** **1** increasing. **2** becoming more successful. **rise and shine** informal wake up and get out of bed promptly. **rise from the dead** come to life again.
– ORIGIN Old English, 'make an attack,' 'get out of bed.'

ris·er /'rīzər/ ▶ **noun** **1** a person who usually gets out of bed at a particular time of the morning: *an early riser*. **2** a vertical section between the treads of a staircase. **3** a vertical pipe for the upward flow of liquid or gas.

ris·i·ble /'rizəbəl/ ▶ **adjective** causing laughter; ridiculous.
– DERIVATIVES **ris·i·bil·i·ty** /,rizə'bilətē/ noun **ris·i·bly** /-blē/ adverb.
– ORIGIN Latin *risibilis*.

ris·ing /'rīziNG/ ▶ **noun** a rebellion or revolt. ▶ **adjective** approaching a specified age.

risk /risk/ ▶ **noun** **1** a situation that could be dangerous or have an undesirable outcome: *outdoor activities carry an element of risk*. **2** the possibility that something unpleasant will happen. **3** a person or thing regarded as a likely source of danger or harm: *gloss paint can pose a fire risk*.

– SYNONYMS **1 chance,** uncertainty, unpredictability, instability, insecurity. **2 possibility,** chance, probability, likelihood, danger, peril, threat, menace, prospect.

▶ **verb** **1** expose someone or something to danger, harm, or loss. **2** act in such a way as to make an undesirable outcome possible: *children risk serious injury as a result of strenuous gymnastics training*. **3** take a risk by engaging in a particular activity.

– SYNONYMS **endanger,** jeopardize, imperil, hazard, gamble (with), chance, put at risk, put on the line.

– PHRASES **at one's** (**own**) **risk** taking responsibility for one's own safety or possessions. **run** (or **take**) **a risk** (or **risks**) act in such a way as to make an undesirable outcome possible.
– ORIGIN Italian *risco* 'danger.'

risk cap·i·tal ▶ **noun** another term for **VENTURE CAPITAL**.

risk·y /'riskē/ ▶ **adjective** (**riskier**, **riskiest**) involving the possibility of danger, failure, or loss.

– SYNONYMS **dangerous,** hazardous, perilous, unsafe, insecure, precarious, touch-and-go, treacherous, uncertain, unpredictable; informal dicey.

– DERIVATIVES **risk·i·ly** adverb **risk·i·ness** noun.

ri·sot·to /ri'zôtō, -'sôtō/ ▶ **noun** (pl. **risottos**) an Italian dish of rice cooked in stock with ingredients such as meat or seafood.
– ORIGIN Italian.

ris·qué /ri'skā/ ▸ **adjective** referring to sex in an indecent or slightly shocking way.

– SYNONYMS **ribald,** rude, bawdy, racy, earthy, indecent, vulgar, dirty, smutty, crude, coarse, obscene, lewd, X-rated, suggestive, improper, naughty, locker-room; informal blue, off color, raunchy; euphemistic adult.

– ORIGIN French.

ris·sole /ri'sōl, 'ris,ōl/ ▸ **noun** chiefly Brit. a small cake or ball of meat and spices, coated in breadcrumbs and fried.
– ORIGIN French.

ri·tar·dan·do /,rētär'dändō, ,ri-/ ▸ **adverb & adjective** Music with a gradual decrease of speed.
– ORIGIN Italian.

rite /rīt/ ▸ **noun 1** a religious or other solemn ceremony or act. **2** a set of customary practices typical of a Church or a part of it: *the celebration of the full Roman rite.*

– SYNONYMS **ceremony,** ritual, ceremonial, custom, service, observance, liturgy, worship, office.

– PHRASES **rite of passage** a ceremony or event, e.g., marriage, marking an important stage in someone's life.
– ORIGIN Latin *ritus* '(religious) usage.'

rit·u·al /'ricHōōəl/ ▸ **noun 1** a religious or solemn ceremony involving a series of actions performed according to a set order. **2** a set order of performing such a ceremony. **3** a series of actions done regularly and without variation: *it became a ritual to take her out every week to the hairdresser.*

– SYNONYMS **ceremony,** rite, act, practice, custom, tradition, convention, formality, protocol.

▸ **adjective** relating to or done as a ritual.

– SYNONYMS **ceremonial,** prescribed, set, conventional, traditional, formal.

– DERIVATIVES **rit·u·al·ly** adverb.

rit·u·al·is·tic /,ricHōōə'listik/ ▸ **adjective** relating to or followed as part of a religious or other ritual: *a ritualistic act of worship.*
– DERIVATIVES **rit·u·al·is·ti·cal·ly** adverb **rit·u·al·ism** /'ricHōōə,lizəm/ noun.

rit·u·al·ize /'ricHōōə,līz/ ▸ **verb** make something into a ritual by following a pattern of actions or behavior.
– DERIVATIVES **rit·u·al·i·za·tion** /,ricHōōələ'zāsHən/ noun.

ritz·y /'ritsē/ ▸ **adjective** (**ritzier, ritziest**) informal expensively stylish.
– ORIGIN from *Ritz*, a proprietary name of luxury hotels.

ri·val /'rīvəl/ ▸ **noun 1** a person or thing competing with another for the same objective or to be better than the other. **2** a person or thing equal to another in quality: *she has no rivals as a female rock singer.*

– SYNONYMS **opponent,** opposition, challenger, competitor, contender, adversary, antagonist, enemy; literary foe.
– ANTONYMS ally.

▸ **verb** (**rivals, rivaling, rivaled**) be equal or comparable to: *a weekly TV ad budget that rivals that of any Broadway musical.*

– SYNONYMS **match,** compare with, compete with, vie with, equal, emulate, measure up to, touch; informal hold a candle to.

– DERIVATIVES **ri·val·rous** /'rīvəlrəs/ adjective.
– ORIGIN Latin *rivalis*, first meaning 'person using the same stream as another.'

ri·val·ry /'rīvəlrē/ ▸ **noun** (pl **rivalries**) a situation in which two people or groups are competing for the same thing.

– SYNONYMS **competition,** contention, opposition, conflict, feuding; informal keeping up with the Joneses.

rive /rīv/ ▸ **verb** (past **rived** /rīvd/; past part. **riven** /'rivən/) (usu. **be riven**) literary tear apart or split.
– ORIGIN Old Norse.

riv·er /'rivər/ ▸ **noun 1** a large natural flow of water traveling along a channel to the sea, a lake, or another river. **2** a large quantity of a flowing liquid.

– SYNONYMS **1 stream,** brook, creek, watercourse, rivulet, tributary. **2** *a river of molten lava* **stream,** torrent, flood, deluge, cascade.

– PHRASES **sell someone down the river** informal betray someone. [with reference to the sale of a troublesome slave to a plantation owner on the lower Mississippi, where conditions were worse.]
– ORIGIN Old French.

WORD LINKS

fluvial *relating to rivers*
riparian *relating to or situated on the banks of a river*

riv·er·bank /'rivər,baNGk/ ▸ **noun** the bank of a river.

riv·er·bed /'rivər,bed/ ▸ **noun** the bed or channel in which a river flows.

riv·er·boat /'rivər,bōt/ ▸ **noun** a boat designed for use on rivers.

riv·er·ine /'rivə,rīn, -,rēn/ ▸ **adjective** technical or literary relating to or situated on a river or riverbank.

riv·er·side /'rivər,sīd/ ▸ **noun** the ground along a riverbank.

riv·et /'rivit/ ▸ **noun** a short metal pin or bolt for holding together two metal plates, its headless end being beaten out or pressed down when in place.
▸ **verb** (**rivets, riveting, riveted**) **1** join metal plates with a rivet or rivets. **2** hold someone's interest or attention completely: *moviegoers have been riveted by great car chases for years* | (as adj. **riveting**) *the final chapter was riveting.*

– SYNONYMS (as adj. **riveting**) **fascinating,** gripping, engrossing, intriguing, absorbing, captivating, enthralling, compelling, spellbinding, mesmerizing; informal unputdownable.
– ANTONYMS boring.

– DERIVATIVES **riv·et·er** noun.
– ORIGIN Old French.

riv·i·er·a /,rivē'e(ə)rə, ri'vye(ə)rə/ ▸ **noun** a coastal region with a subtropical climate and vegetation, especially that of southern France and northern Italy.
– ORIGIN Italian, 'seashore.'

riv·u·let /'riv(y)ələt/ ▸ **noun** a very small stream.
– ORIGIN from former French *riveret* 'small river.'

ri·yal /rē'(y)ôl, rē'(y)äl/ ▸ **noun** variant spelling of RIAL.

RN ▸ **abbreviation 1** registered nurse. **2** (in the UK) Royal Navy.

Rn ▸ **symbol** the chemical element radon.

RNA ▸ **noun** ribonucleic acid, a substance in living cells that carries instructions from DNA for controlling the synthesis of proteins.

roach[1] /rōch/ ▸ **noun** informal **1** a cockroach. **2** the butt of a marijuana cigarette.

roach[2] ▸ **noun** (pl. same) a common freshwater fish of the carp family.
– ORIGIN Old French *roche*.

road /rōd/ ▸ **noun 1** a wide way between places, especially one with a hard surface for vehicles to travel on. **2** a way to achieving a particular outcome: *he's well on the road to recovery*. **3** (usu. **roads**) a partly sheltered stretch of water near the shore in which ships can ride at anchor.

– SYNONYMS **1 street,** thoroughfare, roadway, avenue, boulevard, highway, lane. **2** *the road to recovery* **way,** path, route, course.

– DERIVATIVES **road·less** adjective.
– PHRASES **one for the road** informal a final alcoholic drink before leaving. **on the road 1** on a long journey or series of journeys. **2** (of a car) able to be driven.
– ORIGIN Old English, 'journey on horseback, foray.'

road·bed /'rōd,bed/ ▸ **noun 1** material laid down to form a road, or on which railroad tracks are laid. **2** the part of a road on which vehicles travel.

road·block /'rōd,bläk/ ▸ **noun** a barrier put across a road by the police or army to stop and examine traffic.

road hog ▸ **noun** informal a motorist who makes it difficult for others to pass.

road·hold·ing /'rōd,hōldiNG/ ▸ **noun** chiefly Brit. the ability of a moving vehicle to remain stable, especially when cornering at high speeds.

road·house /'rōd,hous/ ▸ **noun** a tavern or restaurant on a country road.

road·ie /'rōdē/ ▸ **noun** informal a person employed by a touring pop or rock group to set up and maintain equipment.

road·kill /'rōd,kil/ ▸ **noun** animals killed on the road by a vehicle.

road·map /'rōd,map/ ▸ **noun 1** a map showing the roads of an area. **2** a document setting out the procedure for achieving a goal: *a roadmap for peace*.

road pric·ing ▸ **noun** the practice of charging motorists to use busy roads at certain times, especially to relieve congestion.

road rage ▸ **noun** violent anger arising from conflict with the driver of another motor vehicle.

road·run·ner /'rōd,rənər/ ▸ **noun** a slender fast-running bird of the cuckoo family, found chiefly in arid country from the southern US to Central America.
– ORIGIN probably a calque from Spanish *correcamino*.

road·show /'rōd,SHō/ ▸ **noun 1** each of a series of radio or television programs broadcast on location from different places. **2** a touring political or promotional campaign.

road·side /'rōd,sīd/ ▸ **noun** the strip of land beside a road.

road·stead /'rōd,sted/ ▸ **noun** another term for **ROAD** (sense 3).

road·ster /'rōdstər/ ▸ **noun** an open-top car with two seats.

road test ▸ **noun 1** a test of the performance of a vehicle or engine on the road. **2** a test of a driver's competence, required for obtaining a driver's license. **3** a test of equipment carried out in working conditions. ▸ **verb** (**road-test**) **1** test a vehicle or engine on the road. **2** try out something under working conditions, especially before it is made generally available: *we road-tested a new laptop computer*.

road·way /'rōd,wā/ ▸ **noun 1** a road. **2** the part of a road intended for vehicles, in contrast to a sidewalk or median.

road·work /'rōd,wərk/ ▸ **plural noun** repairs to roads or to pipes or cables under roads.

road·wor·thy /'rōd,wər<u>TH</u>ē/ ▸ **adjective** (of a vehicle) fit to be used on the road.
– DERIVATIVES **road·wor·thi·ness** noun.

roam /rōm/ ▸ **verb 1** travel aimlessly over a wide area. **2** (of the eyes or hands) pass lightly over something without stopping.

– SYNONYMS **wander,** rove, ramble, drift, walk, traipse, range, travel, tramp, trek; informal **cruise.**

– DERIVATIVES **roam·er** noun.
– ORIGIN unknown.

roam·ing /'rōmiNG/ ▸ **noun** the use of or ability to use a cell phone outside of its network area.

roan /rōn/ ▸ **adjective** (of a horse or cow) having a coat that is mainly bay, chestnut, or black mixed with another color, typically white. ▸ **noun** a roan animal.
– ORIGIN Old French.

roar /rôr/ ▸ **noun 1** a long, deep sound such as that made by a lion, natural force, or engine. **2** a loud, deep sound uttered by a person, especially as an expression of pain, anger, or amusement. ▸ **verb 1** make a roar. **2** laugh loudly. **3** move, act, or happen fast or decisively: *Korean stocks roared back, closing with a gain of almost five percent*.

– SYNONYMS **bellow,** yell, shout, thunder, bawl, howl, scream, cry, bay; informal **holler.**

– ORIGIN Old English.

roar·ing /'rôriNG/ ▸ **adjective** informal complete: *a roaring success*.

– SYNONYMS **blazing,** burning, flaming.

– DERIVATIVES **roar·ing·ly** adverb.
– PHRASES **do a roaring trade** informal, chiefly Brit. do very good business. **the roaring forties** stormy ocean areas between latitudes 40° and 50° south. **the roaring twenties** the prosperous years of the 1920s.

roast /rōst/ ▸ **verb 1** cook meat or vegetables in an oven or over a fire. **2** process coffee beans, nuts, etc., in intense heat. **3** make or become very warm. **4** informal criticize or reprimand someone severely. **5** informal offer a mocking tribute to someone. ▸ **adjective** (of food) having been roasted. ▸ **noun 1** a cut of meat that has been roasted or that is intended for roasting. **2** the process of roasting something, especially coffee. **3** an outdoor party at which food is roasted: *a pig roast*. **4** a banquet to honor a person with good-natured ridicule.
– DERIVATIVES **roast·er** noun.
– ORIGIN Old French *rostir*.

roast·ing /'rōstiNG/ informal ▸ **adjective** very hot and dry. ▸ **noun** a severe criticism or reprimand.

rob /räb/ ▸ **verb** (**robs, robbing, robbed**) **1** take property unlawfully from a person or place by force or threat of force. **2** (**rob someone of**) deprive someone of something needed, deserved, or important. **3** informal overcharge someone.

– SYNONYMS **1 steal from,** burglarize, burgle, hold up, break into, raid, loot, plunder, pillage; informal mug. **2 cheat,** swindle, defraud; informal do out of, con out of.

– PHRASES **rob Peter to pay Paul** deprive one person of something in order to pay another. [probably with reference to the saints *Peter* and *Paul*.]
– ORIGIN Old French *rober*.

rob·ber /ˈräbər/ ▸ **noun** a person who commits robbery.

– SYNONYMS **burglar,** thief, housebreaker, mugger, shoplifter, raider, looter.

rob·ber·y /ˈräb(ə)rē/ ▸ **noun** (pl. **robberies**) **1** the action of robbing a person or place. **2** informal blatant overcharging.

– SYNONYMS **burglary,** theft, stealing, housebreaking, shoplifting, embezzlement, fraud, holdup, raid; informal mugging, stickup, heist.

robe /rōb/ ▸ **noun 1** a loose outer garment reaching to the ankles, often worn on formal or ceremonial occasions as an indication of the wearer's rank, office, or profession. **2** a bathrobe.

– SYNONYMS **1 cloak,** kaftan, wrap, wrapper, mantle, cape. **2** *ceremonial robes* **garb,** vestments, regalia, finery.

▸ **verb** dress someone or oneself in a robe.
– ORIGIN Old French, 'garment, booty.'

rob·in /ˈräbən/ ▸ **noun 1** (also **American robin**) a large North American thrush with an orange-red breast. **2** a small European songbird with a red breast and brown back and wings.
– ORIGIN Old French, familiar form of the man's name *Robert*.

ro·bot /ˈrōˌbät, ˈrōbət/ ▸ **noun** a machine capable of carrying out a complex series of actions automatically, especially one programmable by a computer.

– SYNONYMS **machine,** automaton, android; informal bot, droid.

– DERIVATIVES **ro·bot·ize** /ˈrōbəˌtīz/ verb.
– ORIGIN Czech *robota* 'forced labor'; the term was coined in K. Čapek's play *R.U.R.* 'Rossum's Universal Robots.'

ro·bot·ic /rōˈbätik/ ▸ **adjective 1** relating to robots. **2** mechanical, stiff, or unemotional.
– DERIVATIVES **ro·bot·i·cal·ly** /-ik(ə)lē/ adverb.

ro·bot·ics /rōˈbätiks/ ▸ **plural noun** (treated as sing.) the branch of technology concerned with the design, construction, and use of robots.

ro·bust /rōˈbəst, ˈrōˌbəst/ ▸ **adjective 1** able to withstand heavy use; sturdy. **2** strong and healthy. **3** determined and forceful: *a robust approach to reform*. **4** (of wine or food) strong and rich in flavor or smell.

– SYNONYMS **1 strong,** vigorous, sturdy, tough, powerful, solid, rugged, hardy, strapping, healthy, (fighting) fit, hale and hearty. **2 durable,** resilient, tough, hard-wearing, long-lasting, sturdy, strong.
– ANTONYMS frail, fragile.

– DERIVATIVES **ro·bust·ly** adverb **ro·bust·ness** noun.
– ORIGIN Latin *robustus* 'firm and hard.'

ro·bus·ta /rōˈbəstə/ ▸ **noun** a type of coffee bean from a West African species of coffee plant, used especially in making instant coffee.
– ORIGIN Latin.

rock[1] /räk/ ▸ **noun 1** the hard mineral material of the earth's crust. **2** a mass of rock projecting out of the ground or water. **3** a boulder. **4** Geology any natural material with a distinctive composition of minerals. **5** informal a diamond or other precious stone.

– SYNONYMS **boulder,** stone, pebble.

– PHRASES **on the rocks** informal **1** in difficulties and likely to fail. **2** (of a drink) served undiluted and with ice cubes.
– ORIGIN Latin *rocca*.

rock[2] ▸ **verb 1** move gently to and fro or from side to side. **2** shake violently, especially because of an earthquake or explosion. **3** shock or distress greatly: *the company was rocked by the resignation of its chairman*. **4** informal dance to or play rock music. **5** (often as adj. **rocking**) informal (of a place) be exciting or full of social activity.

– SYNONYMS **1 move to and fro,** sway, seesaw, roll, pitch, plunge, toss, lurch. **2 stun,** shock, stagger, astonish, startle, surprise, shake, take aback, throw, unnerve, disconcert.

▸ **noun 1** rock music. **2** rock and roll music. **3** a rocking movement.
– ORIGIN Old English.

rock·a·bil·ly /ˈräkəˌbilē/ ▸ **noun** a type of popular music combining rock and roll and country music.
– ORIGIN from **ROCK AND ROLL** and **HILLBILLY**.

rock and roll (also **rock 'n' roll**) ▸ **noun** a type of popular dance music originating in the 1950s, having a heavy beat and simple melodies.

rock-bot·tom ▸ **adjective** at the lowest possible level.

rock climb·ing ▸ **noun** the sport or pastime of climbing rock faces, especially with ropes and special equipment.

rock crys·tal ▸ **noun** transparent quartz, typically in the form of colorless hexagonal crystals.

rock dove ▸ **noun** a mainly blue-gray pigeon found on cliffs, the ancestor of domestic and wild pigeons.

rock·er /ˈräkər/ ▸ **noun 1** a person who performs or enjoys rock music. **2** a rocking chair. **3** a curved bar or similar support on which something such as a chair can rock. **4** a rocking device forming part of a mechanism.
– PHRASES **off one's rocker** informal mad.

rock·et[1] /ˈräkit/ ▸ **noun 1** a cylindrical missile or spacecraft propelled to a great height or distance by a stream of burning gases. **2** a firework or signal propelled in this way. ▸ **verb** (**rockets, rocketing, rocketed**) **1** increase very rapidly and suddenly. **2** move or progress very rapidly: *he rocketed to national stardom*. **3** attack something with rocket-propelled missiles.
– ORIGIN Italian *rocchetto* 'small distaff (for spinning).'

rock·et[2] ▸ **noun** another term for **ARUGULA**.
– ORIGIN French *roquette*.

rock·et·ry /ˈräkətrē/ ▸ **noun** the branch of science and technology concerned with rockets.

rock·et sci·ence ▸ **noun** humorous something very difficult to understand.
– DERIVATIVES **rock·et sci·en·tist** noun.

rock face ▸ **noun** a vertical surface of bare rock.

rock gar·den ▸ **noun** a heaped arrangement of rocks with soil between them, planted with rock plants.

rock·ing chair ▸ **noun** a chair mounted on rockers or springs.

rock·ing horse ▸ **noun** a model of a horse mounted on rockers or springs for a child to ride on.

rock music ▸ **noun** a form of popular music with a strong beat, played on electric guitars, drums, etc.

rock pool ▸ **noun** a pool of water among rocks along a shoreline.

rock salt ▶ **noun** common salt occurring naturally as a mineral.

rock-sol·id ▶ **adjective** completely firm or stable.

rock wool ▶ **noun** inorganic material made into matted fiber, used especially for insulation or soundproofing.

rock·y[1] /'räkē/ ▶ **adjective** (**rockier**, **rockiest**) **1** consisting of rock. **2** full of rocks.

– SYNONYMS **stony,** pebbly, shingly, rough, bumpy, craggy, mountainous.

rock·y[2] ▶ **adjective** (**rockier, rockiest**) unsteady or unstable.

– SYNONYMS **unsteady,** shaky, unstable, wobbly, tottery, rickety.
– ANTONYMS steady, stable.

ro·co·co /rə'kōkō, ˌrōkə'kō/ ▶ **adjective 1** relating to an elaborately ornate style of European furniture or architecture of the 18th century. **2** (of music or literature) highly or excessively ornate. ▶ **noun** the rococo style of architecture, furniture, etc.
– ORIGIN French.

rod /räd/ ▶ **noun 1** a thin straight bar, especially of wood or metal. **2** a fishing rod. **3** (**the rod**) the use of a stick for caning or flogging someone. **4** one of two types of light-sensitive cell in the retina of the eye, responsible mainly for monochrome vision in poor light. Compare with **CONE**.

– SYNONYMS **bar,** stick, pole, baton, staff, shaft, strut, rail, spoke.

– ORIGIN Old English.

rode /rōd/ past of **RIDE**.

ro·dent /'rōdnt/ ▶ **noun** a mammal of a large group including rats, mice, and squirrels and distinguished by strong constantly growing incisors.
– ORIGIN from Latin *rodere* 'gnaw.'

ro·den·ti·cide /rō'dentəˌsīd/ ▶ **noun** a poison used to kill rodents.

ro·de·o /'rōdēˌō, rə'dāō/ ▶ **noun** (pl. **rodeos**) **1** a contest or entertainment in which cowboys show their skill at riding broncos, roping calves, etc. **2** a competitive display of other skills, such as motorcycle riding.
– ORIGIN Spanish.

roe[1] /rō/ ▶ **noun 1** (also **hard roe**) the mass of eggs contained in the ovaries of a female fish or shellfish, especially when ripe and used as food. **2** (**soft roe**) the ripe testes of a male fish, especially when used as food.
– ORIGIN related to German, Dutch *roge*.

roe[2] (also **roe deer**) ▶ **noun** (pl. same or **roes**) a small deer with a reddish summer coat that turns grayish in winter.
– ORIGIN Old English.

roe·buck /'rōˌbək/ ▶ **noun** a male roe deer.

roent·gen /'rentgən, 'rənt-, -jən/ ▶ **noun** a unit of quantity of ionizing radiation.
– ORIGIN named after the German physicist Wilhelm Conrad *Röntgen*.

roent·gen·i·um /rent'genēəm, rənt-, -'je-/ ▶ **noun** a radioactive element produced artificially.
– ORIGIN named after Wilhelm Conrad *Röntgen* (see **ROENTGEN**).

ro·gan josh /'rōgən 'jäsн/ ▶ **noun** an Indian dish of curried meat in a rich tomato-based sauce.
– ORIGIN Urdu.

rog·er /'räjər/ ▶ **exclamation** your message has been received (used in radio communication). ▶ **verb** Brit. vulgar slang (of a man) have sex with someone.
– ORIGIN from the man's name *Roger*; the verb is from the former noun sense 'penis.'

rogue /rōg/ ▶ **noun 1** a dishonest or immoral man. **2** a mischievous but likable person.

– SYNONYMS **scoundrel,** rascal, good-for-nothing, wretch, villain, criminal, lawbreaker; informal crook.

▶ **adjective 1** (of an elephant or other large wild animal) destructive and living apart from the herd. **2** behaving in a faulty, unpredictable, or dangerous way: *a rogue state*.
– ORIGIN probably from Latin *rogare* 'beg, ask.'

rogue di·al·ing ▶ **noun** the illicit use of software to command a computer to call premium-rate telephone numbers over the Internet.

ro·guer·y /'rōgərē/ ▶ **noun** (pl. **rogueries**) dishonest, immoral, or mischievous behavior.

rogues' gal·ler·y ▶ **noun** informal a collection of photographs of known criminals, used by police to identify suspects.

ro·guish /'rōgisн/ ▶ **adjective** playfully mischievous: *a roguish smile*.
– DERIVATIVES **ro·guish·ly** adverb **ro·guish·ness** noun.

roil /roil/ ▶ **verb 1** make a liquid muddy by disturbing the sediment. **2** (of a liquid) move in a turbulent way.
– ORIGIN perhaps from Old French *ruiler* 'mix mortar.'

roist·er /'roistər/ ▶ **verb** enjoy oneself or celebrate in a noisy or boisterous way.
– DERIVATIVES **roist·er·er** noun **roist·er·ous** adjective.
– ORIGIN from French *rustre* 'ruffian.'

role /rōl/ ▶ **noun 1** an actor's part in a play, movie, etc. **2** a person's or thing's function in a particular situation: *religion plays a vital role in society*.

– SYNONYMS **1 part,** character. **2 capacity,** position, function, job, post, office, duty, responsibility.

– ORIGIN from former French *roule* 'roll,' first referring to the roll of paper on which an actor's part was written.

USAGE

Do not confuse **role** with **roll**. **Role** means 'a part played by an actor,' whereas **roll** mainly means 'move by turning over and over' or 'a rolling movement' (*a roll of the dice*).

role mod·el ▶ **noun** a person whom others look to as an example to be imitated.

role-play·ing (also **role-play**) ▶ **noun** the acting out of a particular role, either consciously (as a technique in psychotherapy or training) or unconsciously (in accordance with the expectations of society).

Rolf·ing /'rôlfiNG/ ▶ **noun** a deep massage technique aimed at releasing muscular tension by manipulating connective tissue.
– ORIGIN named after the American physiotherapist Ida P. *Rolf*.

roll /rōl/ ▶ **verb 1** move by turning over and over on an axis. **2** move forward on wheels or with a smooth, wavelike motion: *the fog rolled across the fields*. **3** (of a moving ship, aircraft, or vehicle) sway from side to side. **4** (of a machine or device) begin operating. **5** (often **roll something up**) turn something flexible over and over on itself to form a cylindrical or round shape. **6** (**roll up**) curl up tightly. **7** flatten something by passing a roller over it or by passing it between rollers. **8** (of a loud, deep sound) resound or reverberate. **9** pronounce a consonant, typically an *r*, with a trill.

– SYNONYMS **1 turn over and over,** spin, rotate, revolve, wheel, trundle, bowl. **2 flow,** run, course, stream, pour, trickle. **3 wind,** coil, fold, curl, twist. **4 rock,** sway, reel, list, pitch, plunge, lurch, toss.

▶ **noun 1** a cylinder formed by rolling flexible material. **2** a rolling movement. **3** a gymnastic exercise in which the body is rolled into a tucked position and turned in a forward or backward circle. **4** a long, deep, reverberating sound. **5** (in drumming) a sustained, rapid alternation of single or double strokes of each stick. **6** a very small loaf of bread. **7** an official list or register of names.

– SYNONYMS **1 cylinder,** tube, scroll, reel, spool, bobbin. **2 turn,** rotation, revolution, spin, whirl. **3** *a roll of thunder* **rumble,** reverberation, echo, boom, clap, crack. **4 list,** register, directory, record, file, index, catalog, inventory.

– PHRASES **a roll in the hay** informal an act of sex. **be rolling in it** (or **money**) informal be very rich. **on a roll** informal experiencing a prolonged spell of success or good luck. **roll in** informal **1** be received in large amounts. **2** arrive in a casual way in spite of being late. **roll of honor** a list of people whose deeds are honored, especially a list of those who have died in battle. **roll something out** officially launch a new product. **roll something over** extend a financial arrangement. **roll up** informal arrive. **roll up one's sleeves** prepare to work or fight.
– ORIGIN Old French *roller.*

roll·back /ˈrōlˌbak/ ▶ **noun 1** a reduction or decrease. **2** a reversion to a previous state or situation: *they opposed a rollback to Stalinism.* **3** Computing the process of restoring a database or program to a previous state, typically to recover from an error. ▶ **verb** Computing restore a database to a previous state.

roll bar ▶ **noun** a metal bar running up the sides and across the top of a vehicle, protecting the occupants if the car overturns.

roll call ▶ **noun** the reading aloud of a list of names to establish who is present.

rolled gold ▶ **noun** gold in the form of a thin coating applied to a nonprecious metal by rolling.

rolled oats ▶ **plural noun** oats that have had the husks removed and been crushed.

roll·er /ˈrōlər/ ▶ **noun 1** a rotating cylinder used to move, flatten, or spread something. **2** a small cylinder on which hair is rolled to produce curls. **3** a long swelling wave that appears to roll steadily toward the shore.

roll·er·ball /ˈrōlərˌbôl/ ▶ **noun 1** a ballpoint pen using thinner ink than other such pens. **2** Computing an input device containing a ball that is moved with the fingers to control the cursor.

roll·er bear·ing ▶ **noun** a bearing similar to a ball bearing but using small rollers instead of balls.

Roll·er·blade /ˈrōlərˌblād/ ▶ **noun** trademark a skate with wheels fixed in a single line. ▶ **verb** skate using Rollerblades.
– DERIVATIVES **roll·er·blad·er** noun **roll·er·blad·ing** noun.

roll·er coast·er ▶ **noun** a fairground attraction consisting of a light railroad track with many tight turns and steep slopes, on which people ride in small open cars.

roll·er rink ▶ **noun** see **RINK** (sense 2).

roll·er skate ▶ **noun** each of a pair of boots having four or more small wheels and used for gliding across a hard surface.
– DERIVATIVES **roll·er skat·er** noun **roll·er skat·ing** noun.

rol·lick·ing /ˈräliking/ ▶ **adjective** lively and amusing in a high-spirited way.
– ORIGIN perhaps from **ROMP** and **FROLIC**.

roll·ing /ˈrōling/ ▶ **adjective 1** (of land) extending in a series of gently rounded hills. **2** done in regular stages over a period of time: *a rolling program of reforms.*

roll·ing pin ▶ **noun** a cylinder for rolling out dough.

roll·ing stock ▶ **noun** locomotives, cars, or other vehicles used on a railroad.

roll·ing stone ▶ **noun** a person who is unwilling to settle for long in one place.
– PHRASES **a rolling stone gathers no moss** proverb a person who does not settle in one place will not accumulate wealth, status, responsibilities, or commitments.

roll neck ▶ **noun** a high loosely turned-over collar.

roll-on ▶ **adjective** (of a deodorant or cosmetic) applied by means of a rotating ball in the neck of the container.

roll·out /ˈrōlˌout/ ▶ **noun 1** the unveiling of a new aircraft or spacecraft. **2** the official launch of a new product or service. **3** Football a play in which the quarterback runs toward the sideline before attempting to pass or advance.

roll·o·ver /ˈrōlˌōvər/ ▶ **noun** the extension or transfer of a debt or other financial arrangement: *the plan does not allow for rollover of outstanding loans.*

roll·top desk /ˈrōlˌtäp/ ▶ **noun** a writing desk with a semicircular flexible cover sliding in curved grooves.

roll-up ▶ **noun** an article of food rolled up and sometimes with a filling: *ham roll-ups.*

ro·ly-po·ly /ˈrōlē ˈpōlē/ ▶ **adjective** informal round and plump. ▶ **noun** (also **roly-poly pudding**) Brit. a pudding made of a sheet of suet pastry covered with jam or fruit, formed into a roll, and steamed or baked.
– ORIGIN from **ROLL**.

ROM /räm/ ▶ **abbreviation** Computing read-only memory.

ro·maine /rōˈmān/ ▶ **noun** a variety of lettuce with crisp narrow leaves.
– ORIGIN French.

Ro·man /ˈrōmən/ ▶ **adjective 1** relating to the ancient city of Rome or its empire or people. **2** relating to the modern city of Rome. **3** referring to the alphabet used for writing Latin, English, and most European languages. **4** (**roman**) (of type) of a plain upright kind used in ordinary print. ▶ **noun 1** an inhabitant of Rome. **2** (**roman**) roman type.

ro·man-à-clef /rōˌmän ä ˈklā/ ▶ **noun** (pl. **romans-à-clef** pronunc. same) a novel in which real people or events appear with invented names.
– ORIGIN French, 'novel with a key.'

Ro·man can·dle ▶ **noun** a firework giving off flaming colored balls and sparks.

Ro·man Cath·o·lic ▶ **adjective** relating to the Roman Catholic Church. ▶ **noun** a member of the Roman Catholic Church.
– DERIVATIVES **Ro·man Ca·thol·i·cism** noun.

Ro·man Cath·o·lic Church ▶ **noun** the part of the Christian Church that has the Pope as its head.

Ro·mance /rō'mans, 'rō,mans/ ▶ **noun** the group of languages descended from Latin, such as French, Spanish, Portuguese, and Italian.
– ORIGIN from Latin *Romanicus* 'Roman.'

ro·mance /rō'mans, 'rō,mans/ ▶ **noun 1** a pleasurable feeling of excitement and wonder associated with love. **2** a love affair. **3** a book or movie dealing with love in a sentimental or idealized way. **4** a quality or feeling of mystery, excitement, and remoteness from everyday life: *the romance of the past.* **5** a medieval story dealing with the adventures of knights.

– SYNONYMS **1 love affair,** relationship, liaison, courtship, attachment, amour. **2 story,** tale, legend, fairy tale. **3 mystery,** glamour, excitement, exoticism, mystique, appeal, allure, charm.

▶ **verb 1** try to win someone's love. **2** informal seek someone's custom or attention: *he's being romanced by the big boys in New York.* **3** deal with something in an idealized way.
– DERIVATIVES **ro·manc·er** noun.
– ORIGIN from **ROMANCE**.

Ro·man Em·pire ▶ **noun** the empire under Roman rule established in 27 BC and divided into two parts in AD 395.

Ro·man·esque /,rōmə'nesk/ ▶ **adjective** relating to a style of architecture prevalent in Europe *c.*900–1200, with massive vaulting and round arches.
– ORIGIN French.

Ro·ma·ni·an /rō'mānēən, ro͝o-/ (also **Rumanian** /ro͝o'mānēən, -nyən/) ▶ **noun 1** a person from Romania. **2** the language of Romania. ▶ **adjective** relating to Romania.

ro·man·ize /'rōmə,nīz/ ▶ **verb** put written words into the Roman alphabet or into roman type.
– DERIVATIVES **ro·man·i·za·tion** /,rōmənə'zāshən/ noun.

Ro·man law ▶ **noun** the law code of the ancient Romans forming the basis of civil law in many countries today.

Ro·man nose ▶ **noun** a nose with a high bridge.

Ro·man num·er·al ▶ **noun** any of the letters representing numbers in the ancient Roman system: I = 1, V = 5, X = 10, L = 50, C = 100, D = 500, M = 1,000.

Ro·ma·no /rə'mänō/ ▶ **noun** a strong-tasting hard cheese, originally made in Italy.
– ORIGIN Italian, literally 'Roman.'

ro·man·tic /rō'mantik, rə-/ ▶ **adjective 1** relating to or likely to lead to love or romance: *a romantic dinner for two.* **2** showing or regarding life in an idealized and unrealistic way: *Buffalo Bill is largely responsible for our romantic view of the Old West.* **3** (**Romantic**) relating to the artistic and literary movement of romanticism.

– SYNONYMS **1 loving,** amorous, passionate, tender, affectionate; informal lovey-dovey. **2 sentimental,** hearts-and-flowers; informal sappy, slushy, schmaltzy. **3 idyllic,** picturesque, fairy-tale, beautiful, lovely, charming, pretty. **4 idealistic,** unrealistic, fanciful, impractical, head-in-the-clouds, starry-eyed, utopian, rose-tinted.
– ANTONYMS unsentimental, realistic.

▶ **noun 1** a person who is emotional and has an unrealistic view of life or love. **2** (**Romantic**) a writer or artist of the Romantic movement.

– SYNONYMS **idealist,** sentimentalist, dreamer, fantasist.
– ANTONYMS realist.

– DERIVATIVES **ro·man·ti·cal·ly** /-ik(ə)lē/ adverb.

ro·man·ti·cism /rō'mantə,sizəm, rə-/ ▶ **noun** a literary and artistic movement that began in the late 18th century and emphasized creative inspiration and individual feeling.
– DERIVATIVES **ro·man·ti·cist** noun.

ro·man·ti·cize /rō'mantə,sīz, rə-/ ▶ **verb** deal with or describe in an idealized or unrealistic way: *folklore romanticizes pirates, who made their living by murder and robbery.*
– DERIVATIVES **ro·man·ti·ci·za·tion** /rō,mantəsə'zāshən, rə-/ noun.

Rom·a·ny /'rämənē, 'rō-/ ▶ **noun** (pl. **Romanies**) **1** the language of the Gypsies. **2** a Gypsy.
– ORIGIN from Romany *Rom* 'man, husband.'

rom·com /'räm,käm/ ▶ **noun** informal (in movies or television) a romantic comedy.

Ro·me·o /'rōmē,ō/ ▶ **noun** (pl. **Romeos**) an attractive, passionate male lover.
– ORIGIN the hero of Shakespeare's *Romeo and Juliet.*

romp /rämp, rômp/ ▶ **verb 1** play around roughly and energetically. **2** informal achieve or win something easily. **3** informal engage in sexual activity.

– SYNONYMS **play,** frolic, frisk, gambol, skip, prance, caper, cavort.

▶ **noun 1** a spell of romping. **2** a lighthearted movie or other work. **3** informal an easy victory.
– ORIGIN perhaps from **RAMP**.

romp·er suit /'rämpər, 'rôm-/ (also **rompers** /'rämpər, 'rôm-/) ▶ **noun** a young child's one-piece outer garment.

ron·deau /'rändō, rän'dō/ ▶ **noun** (pl. **rondeaux** pronunc. same or /-dōz, 'dōz/) a poem of ten or thirteen lines with only two rhymes throughout and with the opening words used twice as a refrain.
– ORIGIN French.

ron·do /'rändō, rän'dō/ ▶ **noun** (pl. **rondos**) a musical form with a recurring leading theme, often found in the final movement of a sonata or concerto.
– ORIGIN Italian.

rönt·gen ▶ **noun** variant spelling of **ROENTGEN**.

roo /ro͞o/ ▶ **noun** Austral. informal a kangaroo.

rood /ro͞od/ ▶ **noun 1** a crucifix, especially one in a church. **2** chiefly Brit. a former measure of land area equal to a quarter of an acre.
– ORIGIN Old English.

rood screen ▶ **noun** a screen of wood or stone separating the nave from the chancel of a church.

roof /ro͞of, ro͝of/ ▶ **noun** (pl. **roofs**) **1** the structure forming the upper covering of a building or vehicle. **2** the top inner surface of a covered area or space. **3** the upper limit or level of prices or wages. ▶ **verb** cover a building with a roof.
– DERIVATIVES **roof·er** noun **roof·less** adjective.
– PHRASES **go through the roof** informal (of prices or figures) reach very high levels. **hit** (or **go through**) **the roof** informal suddenly become very angry. **the roof of the mouth** the palate.
– ORIGIN Old English.

roof·ing /'ro͞ofing, 'ro͝of-/ ▶ **noun** material for constructing the roof of a building.

roof·line /'ro͞of,līn, 'ro͝of-/ ▶ **noun** the design or proportions of the roof of a building or vehicle.

roof rack ▶ **noun** a framework for carrying luggage or equipment on the roof of a vehicle.

roof·top /ˈro͞ofˌtäp, ˈro͝of-/ ▸ **noun** the outer surface of a building's roof.

rook[1] /ro͝ok/ ▸ **noun** a crow with black plumage and a bare face, nesting in colonies in treetops. ▸ **verb** informal swindle or overcharge someone.
– ORIGIN Old English.

rook[2] ▸ **noun** a chess piece, typically with its top in the shape of a battlement, that can move in any direction along a rank or file on which it stands.
– ORIGIN Arabic.

rook·er·y /ˈro͝okərē/ ▸ **noun** (pl. **rookeries**) **1** a collection of rooks' nests high in a clump of trees. **2** a breeding colony of birds (especially seabirds), seals, or turtles.

rook·ie /ˈro͝okē/ ▸ **noun** informal a new recruit or member, especially in the army or police or a sports team.
– ORIGIN perhaps from **RECRUIT**.

room /ro͞om, ro͝om/ ▸ **noun** **1** a part of a building enclosed by walls, floor, and ceiling. **2** empty space that can be occupied or where something can be done: *there was no room to move*. **3** opportunity or scope: *there's room for improvement in kayak design*.

– SYNONYMS **1 space,** headroom, legroom, area, expanse, extent. **2** *there's very little room for maneuver* **scope,** opportunity, capacity, leeway, latitude, freedom.

▸ **verb** share a room or apartment, especially at a college or similar institution.
– ORIGIN Old English.

room·ie /ˈro͞omē, ˈro͝omē/ ▸ **noun** informal a roommate.

room·ing house ▸ **noun** a private house providing rented accommodations.

room·mate /ˈro͞omˌmāt, ˈro͝om-/ ▸ **noun** **1** a person occupying the same room as another. **2** a person occupying the same apartment or house as another.

room serv·ice ▸ **noun** provision of food and drink to hotel guests in their rooms.

room tem·per·a·ture ▸ **noun** a comfortable indoor temperature, generally taken as about 70°F.

room·y /ˈro͞omē, ˈro͝omē/ ▸ **adjective** (**roomier, roomiest**) having plenty of room; spacious.

– SYNONYMS **spacious,** capacious, sizable, generous, big, large, extensive, voluminous, ample; formal commodious.
– ANTONYMS cramped.

– DERIVATIVES **room·i·ness** noun.

roost /ro͞ost/ ▸ **noun** a place where birds or bats regularly settle to rest. ▸ **verb** (of a bird or bat) settle or gather for rest.
– ORIGIN Old English.

roost·er /ˈro͞ostər, ˈro͝ostər/ ▸ **noun** a male domestic fowl; a cock.

root[1] /ro͞ot, ro͝ot/ ▸ **noun** **1** a part of a plant normally below ground, which acts as a support and collects water and nutrients. **2** the part of a bodily organ or structure such as a hair that is embedded in tissue. **3** the basic cause, source, or origin: *money is the root of all evil*. **4** (**roots**) a person's family, ethnic, or cultural origins. **5** a form from which words have been made by adding prefixes or suffixes or by other modification. **6** Mathematics a number or quantity that when multiplied by itself one or more times gives a specified number or quantity.

– SYNONYMS **1 source,** origin, cause, reason, basis, foundation, bottom, seat. **2** *his Irish **roots*** **origins,** beginnings, family, birth, heritage.

▸ **verb** **1** (of a plant or cutting) establish roots. **2** establish deeply and firmly. **3** (**be rooted**) stand completely still through fear or amazement. **4** (**root something out/up**) find and get rid of something.

– SYNONYMS **1** *vegetarianism is rooted in Indian culture* **embed,** fix, establish, entrench, ingrain. **2** (**be rooted**) *Neil was rooted to the spot* **frozen,** riveted, paralyzed, glued, fixed. **3** (**root something out/up**) *a campaign to root out corruption* **eradicate,** eliminate, weed out, destroy, wipe out, stamp out, abolish, end, put a stop to.

– DERIVATIVES **root·less** adjective.
– PHRASES **at root** basically; fundamentally. **put down roots** begin to have a settled life in a place. **root and branch** Brit. (of a process or operation) thorough or radical. **take root** become established.
– ORIGIN Old English.

root[2] ▸ **verb** **1** (of an animal) turn up the ground with its snout in search of food. **2** search through something; rummage. **3** (**root for**) informal support a person or team enthusiastically.

– SYNONYMS **rummage,** hunt, search, rifle, delve, forage, dig, poke.

– ORIGIN Old English.

root beer ▸ **noun** a carbonated drink made from an extract of the roots and bark of certain plants.

root ca·nal ▸ **noun** **1** the pulp-filled cavity in the root of a tooth. **2** a procedure to replace infected pulp in a root canal with an inert material.

root mean square ▸ **noun** Mathematics the square root of the arithmetic mean of the squares of a set of values.

root sign ▸ **noun** Mathematics the radical sign.

root·stock /ˈro͞otˌstäk, ˈro͝ot-/ ▸ **noun** **1** a rhizome. **2** a plant onto which another variety is grafted.

root·sy /ˈro͞otsē, ˈro͝ot-/ ▸ **adjective** informal (of music) not commercialized and emphasizing its traditional or ethnic origins.

root veg·e·ta·ble ▸ **noun** a carrot or other vegetable that grows as the root of a plant.

rope /rōp/ ▸ **noun** **1** a length of thick cord made by twisting together strands of hemp, nylon, etc. **2** a quantity of objects strung together: *a rope of pearls*. **3** (**the ropes**) the ropes enclosing a boxing or wrestling ring. **4** (**the ropes**) informal the established way of doing something: *I showed her the ropes*.

– SYNONYMS **cord,** cable, line, hawser, string.

▸ **verb** **1** catch or tie someone or something with rope. **2** (**rope someone in/into**) persuade someone to take part in something.
– PHRASES **on the ropes** **1** Boxing forced against the ropes by the opponent's attack. **2** in a state of near collapse.
– ORIGIN Old English.

rope lad·der ▸ **noun** two long ropes connected by short crosspieces, used as a ladder.

rop·y /ˈrōpē/ (also **ropey**) ▸ **adjective** (**ropier, ropiest**) **1** resembling a rope. **2** Brit. informal poor in quality or health.
– DERIVATIVES **rop·i·ly** adverb **rop·i·ness** noun.

Roque·fort /ˈrōkfərt/ ▸ **noun** trademark a soft blue cheese made from ewes' milk.
– ORIGIN from *Roquefort*-sur-Soulzon, a village in southern France.

ror·qual /ˈrôrkwəl, -ˌkwôl/ ▸ **noun** a whale of a small group with pleated skin on the underside, e.g., the blue whale.
– ORIGIN Norwegian *røyrkval* 'fin whale.'

Ror·schach test /ˈrôrˌshäk/ ▸ **noun** a test used in psychoanalysis, in which a standard set of symmetrical ink blots is presented to a person, who is asked to describe what they suggest or resemble.
– ORIGIN named after the Swiss psychiatrist Hermann *Rorschach*.

ro·sa·ce·a /rōˈzāsh(ē)ə/ ▸ **noun** a condition in which some facial blood vessels enlarge, giving the cheeks and nose a flushed appearance.
– ORIGIN short for Latin *acne rosacea* 'rose-colored acne.'

ro·sa·ceous /rōˈzāshəs/ ▸ **adjective** relating to plants of the rose family.

ro·sa·ry /ˈrōzərē/ ▸ **noun** (pl. **rosaries**) **1** (in the Roman Catholic Church) a form of devotion in which five (or fifteen) sets of ten Hail Marys are repeated. **2** a string of beads for keeping count of prayers said.
– ORIGIN Latin *rosarium* 'rose garden.'

rose[1] /rōz/ ▸ **noun 1** a sweet-smelling flower that grows on a prickly bush. **2** a perforated cap attached to a shower, the spout of a watering can, or the end of a hose to produce a spray. **3** a warm pink or light crimson color.
– PHRASES **come up roses** (of a situation) develop in a very favorable way. **come up** (or **out**) **smelling like roses** keep one's good reputation after involvement in a difficult situation.
– ORIGIN Latin *rosa*.

rose[2] past of **RISE**.

ro·sé /rōˈzā/ ▸ **noun** deep pink wine colored by only brief contact with red grape skins.
– ORIGIN French, 'pink.'

ro·se·ate /ˈrōzēət, -ˌāt/ ▸ **adjective** literary rose-colored.

rose·bud /ˈrōzˌbəd/ ▸ **noun** the bud of a rose.

rose-col·ored (also **rose-tinted**) ▸ **adjective** (of a person's viewpoint) unrealistic and naive: *such thinking is the ultimate in rose-colored analysis*.

rose hip ▸ **noun** fuller form of **HIP**[2].

rose·mar·y /ˈrōzˌme(ə)rē/ ▸ **noun** an evergreen shrub of southern Europe, the leaves of which are used as an herb in cooking.
– ORIGIN from Latin *ros* 'dew' + *marinus* 'of the sea.'

rose of Shar·on /ˈsharən, ˈshe(ə)r-/ ▸ **noun 1** a hardy hibiscus with pink or lavender flowers. **2** a low-growing St. John's wort with dense foliage and large golden-yellow flowers.
– ORIGIN from *Sharon*, a fertile coastal plain in Israel.

ro·sette /rōˈzet/ ▸ **noun 1** a rose-shaped decoration made of ribbon, worn by supporters of a team or political party or awarded as a prize. **2** a design or object resembling a rose.
– ORIGIN French, 'little rose.'

rose wa·ter ▸ **noun** scented water made with rose petals.

rose win·dow ▸ **noun** a circular window in a church with tracery radiating in a roselike pattern.

rose·wood /ˈrōzˌwo͝od/ ▸ **noun** a close-grained timber of a tropical tree, used for making furniture and musical instruments.

Rosh Ha·sha·nah /ˌrōsh (h)əˈshōnə, ˌräsh, -ˈshänə/ (also **Rosh Hashana**) ▸ **noun** the Jewish New Year festival.
– ORIGIN Hebrew, 'head of the year.'

Ro·si·cru·cian /ˌrōzəˈkro͞oshən, ˌräzə-/ ▸ **noun** a member of a secretive 17th- and 18th-century society devoted to the study of alchemy and the occult. ▸ **adjective** relating to the Rosicrucians.
– DERIVATIVES **Ro·si·cru·cian·ism** /-ˌnizəm/ noun.
– ORIGIN from the Latin form of the name of Christian *Rosenkreuz*, legendary founder of the movement.

ros·in /ˈräzən/ ▸ **noun** a kind of resin produced by distilling oil of turpentine, used for treating the bows of stringed instruments. ▸ **verb** (**rosins**, **rosining**, **rosined**) rub or treat something with rosin.
– ORIGIN Latin *rosina*.

ros·ter /ˈrästər, ˈrô-/ ▸ **noun 1** a list of people's names together with the jobs they have to do at a particular time. **2** a list of athletes available for team selection.

– SYNONYMS **schedule,** list, lineup, register, agenda, calendar.

▸ **verb** put a person's name on a roster.
– ORIGIN Dutch *rooster* 'list.'

ros·trum /ˈrästrəm, ˈrô-/ ▸ **noun** (pl. **rostra** /ˈrästrə, ˈrô-/ or **rostrums**) **1** a raised platform on which a person stands to make a public speech, play music, or conduct an orchestra. **2** a platform for supporting a movie or television camera.
– ORIGIN Latin, 'beak'; the word first referred to an orator's platform in ancient Rome, which was decorated with the beak-like projections from captured warships.

ros·y /ˈrōzē/ ▸ **adjective** (**rosier**, **rosiest**) **1** (especially of a person's skin) pink. **2** promising or hopeful: *he painted a rosy picture of the future*.

– SYNONYMS **1 pink,** roseate, reddish, glowing, healthy, fresh, radiant, blooming, blushing, flushed, ruddy. **2 promising,** optimistic, auspicious, hopeful, encouraging, favorable, bright, golden.
– ANTONYMS pale, bleak.

– DERIVATIVES **ros·i·ly** adverb **ros·i·ness** noun.

rot /rät/ ▸ **verb** (**rots**, **rotting**, **rotted**) **1** (of organic matter) decompose by the action of bacteria and fungi; decay. **2** gradually get worse: *the education system has been allowed to rot*.

– SYNONYMS **1 decay,** decompose, disintegrate, crumble, perish. **2 go bad,** go off, spoil, molder, putrefy, fester. **3 deteriorate,** degenerate, decline, decay, go to seed, go downhill; informal go to pot, go to the dogs.

▸ **noun 1** the process of decaying. **2** rotten or decayed matter. **3** a disease that causes tissue decay, especially in plants. **4** informal, chiefly Brit. nonsense; rubbish: *don't talk rot*.

– SYNONYMS **decay,** decomposition, mold, mildew, blight, canker.

– ORIGIN Old English.

Ro·ta·ry /ˈrōtərē/ ▸ **noun** a worldwide charitable society of business and professional people organized into local Rotary clubs.
– DERIVATIVES **Ro·tar·i·an** /rōˈte(ə)rēən/ noun & adjective.

ro·ta·ry /ˈrōtərē/ ▸ **adjective 1** revolving around a center or axis. **2** having a rotating part or parts: *a rotary mower*.

ro·tate /ˈrōˌtāt/ ▸ **verb 1** move in a circle around a central point or axis. **2** pass to each member of a group in a regularly recurring order: *the job of chairing the meeting* *rotates.* **3** grow different crops one after the other on the same area of land.

– SYNONYMS **1 revolve,** go around/round, turn (around/round), spin, gyrate, whirl, twirl, swivel, circle, pivot. **2 alternate,** take turns, change, switch, interchange, exchange, swap.

– DERIVATIVES **ro·tat·a·ble** /ˈrōˌtātəbəl, rōˈtāt-/ adjective **ro·ta·tor** /ˈrōˌtātər/ noun **ro·ta·to·ry** /ˈrōtəˌtôrē/ adjective.
– ORIGIN Latin *rotare* 'turn in a circle.'

ro·ta·tion /rōˈtāsʜən/ ▶ **noun 1** the action of rotating around a central point. **2** the action or system of changing people or things in a repeated sequence: *crop rotation.* **3** a complete circular movement around a central point.

– SYNONYMS **1 revolving,** turning, spinning, gyration, circling. **2 turn,** revolution, orbit, spin. **3 sequence,** succession, alternation, cycle.

– DERIVATIVES **ro·ta·tion·al** adjective **ro·ta·tion·al·ly** adverb.

ROTC /ˈrätsē/ ▶ **abbreviation** Reserve Officers' Training Corps.

rote /rōt/ ▶ **noun** regular repetition of something to be learned: *a poem learned by rote.*
– ORIGIN unknown.

rot·gut /ˈrätˌgət/ ▶ **noun** informal poor-quality alcoholic drink.

ro·ti /ˈrōtē/ ▶ **noun** (pl. **rotis**) (in Indian cooking) bread, especially a flat round bread cooked on a griddle.
– ORIGIN Hindi.

ro·tis·ser·ie /rōˈtisərē/ ▶ **noun 1** a rotating spit for roasting and barbecuing meat. **2** a restaurant specializing in roasted or barbecued meat.
– ORIGIN French.

ro·tor /ˈrōtər/ ▶ **noun 1** the rotating part of a turbine, electric motor, or other device. **2** a hub with a number of blades spreading out from it that is rotated to provide the lift for a helicopter.

ro·to·till·er /ˈrōtəˌtilər/ ▶ **noun** trademark a machine with rotating blades for breaking up or tilling the soil.
– DERIVATIVES **ro·to·till** verb.

rot·ten /ˈrätn/ ▶ **adjective 1** rotting or decaying: *rotten meat.* **2** morally or politically corrupt: *he's rotten to the core.* **3** informal very bad or unpleasant.

– SYNONYMS **1 decaying,** moldy, bad, decomposing, spoiled, putrid, rancid, festering, fetid, far gone. **2 corrupt,** unprincipled, dishonest, dishonorable, unscrupulous, untrustworthy, immoral; informal crooked.
– ANTONYMS fresh.

▶ **adverb** informal very much: *your mother spoiled you rotten.*
– DERIVATIVES **rot·ten·ness** noun.
– ORIGIN Old Norse.

Rott·wei·ler /ˈrätˌwīlər, ˈrôtˌvīlər/ ▶ **noun** a large powerful black-and-tan breed of dog.
– ORIGIN from *Rottweil,* a town in SW Germany.

ro·tund /rōˈtənd, ˈrōˌtənd/ ▶ **adjective** having a large and rounded body or shape.
– DERIVATIVES **ro·tun·di·ty** /-ˈtəndətē/ noun **ro·tund·ly** adverb.
– ORIGIN Latin *rotundus.*

ro·tun·da /rōˈtəndə/ ▶ **noun** a round building or room, especially one with a dome.
– ORIGIN from Italian *rotonda camera* 'round chamber.'

rou·ble /ˈro͞obəl/ ▶ **noun** variant spelling of **RUBLE**.

rou·é /ro͞oˈā/ ▶ **noun** a man who leads an immoral life.
– ORIGIN French, 'broken on a wheel,' referring to the instrument of torture thought to be deserved by such a person.

rouge /ro͞ozʜ/ ▶ **noun** a red powder or cream used as a cosmetic for coloring the cheeks. ▶ **verb** color the cheeks with rouge. ▶ **adjective** (of wine) red.
– ORIGIN French, 'red.'

rough /rəf/ ▶ **adjective 1** having an uneven or irregular surface; not smooth or level. **2** not gentle or careful; violent: *rough treatment.* **3** (of weather or the sea) wild and stormy. **4** not finished tidily; plain and basic: *rough wooden tables.* **5** not worked out or correct in every detail; approximate: *a rough guess.* **6** harsh in sound or taste. **7** not sophisticated or cultured. **8** informal difficult and unpleasant.

– SYNONYMS **1 uneven,** irregular, bumpy, stony, rocky, rugged, rutted, pitted. **2 coarse,** bristly, scratchy, prickly, shaggy, hairy, bushy. **3 dry,** leathery, weather-beaten, chapped, calloused, scaly. **4 gruff,** hoarse, harsh, rasping, husky, throaty, gravelly. **5 violent,** aggressive, belligerent, pugnacious, boisterous, rowdy, disorderly, unruly, riotous. **6 boorish,** loutish, oafish, brutish, coarse, crude, uncouth, vulgar, unrefined, unladylike, ungentlemanly, uncultured. **7 turbulent,** stormy, squally, tempestuous, violent, heavy, choppy. **8 preliminary,** hasty, quick, sketchy, cursory, basic, crude, rudimentary, raw, unpolished, incomplete, unfinished. **9 approximate,** inexact, imprecise, vague, estimated; informal ballpark.
– ANTONYMS smooth, gentle, calm, exact.

▶ **noun 1** a basic, preliminary state: *we'll ask the designer for some roughs to start with.* **2** chiefly Brit. a violent person. **3** (on a golf course) the area of longer grass around the fairway and the green.

– SYNONYMS **sketch,** draft, outline, mock-up.

▶ **verb 1** (**rough something out**) make a basic, preliminary version of something. **2** make something uneven. **3** (**rough it**) informal live in discomfort with only basic necessities. **4** (**rough someone up**) informal beat someone up.
– DERIVATIVES **rough·ness** noun.
– PHRASES **in the rough** in a natural state. **rough and ready 1** basic but effective. **2** not sophisticated or refined. **rough edges** small flaws in something that is otherwise satisfactory. **rough justice** treatment that is not fair or in accordance with the law.
– ORIGIN Old English.

rough·age /ˈrəfij/ ▶ **noun** fiber in vegetables, cereals, and fruit that cannot be digested and which helps food and waste products to pass through the gut.

rough and tum·ble ▶ **noun** a situation without rules or organization.
– ORIGIN boxing slang.

rough·cast /ˈrəfˌkast/ ▶ **noun** plaster of lime, cement, and gravel, used on outside walls. ▶ **adjective** coated with roughcast. ▶ **verb** coat a wall with roughcast.

rough·en /ˈrəfən/ ▶ **verb** make or become rough.

rough-hewn ▶ **adjective** (of a person) unsophisticated or uncouth.

rough·house informal ▶ **noun** /ˈrəfˌhous/ a violent disturbance. ▶ **verb** /ˈrəfˌhous, -ˌhouz/ act or treat in a rough, violent way.

rough·ly /ˈrəflē/ ▶ **adverb 1** in a rough or harsh way. **2** not exactly; approximately.

rough·neck /ˈrəfˌnek/ ▸ **noun** informal **1** a rough, uncouth person. **2** an oil-rig worker.

rough·shod /ˈrəfˌsʜäd/ ▸ **adjective** (in phrase **ride roughshod over**) fail to consider a person's wishes or feelings.
– ORIGIN first referring to a horse having shoes with nail heads projecting to prevent slipping.

rough trade ▸ **noun** informal male homosexual prostitution, especially when involving brutality or sadism.

rou·lade /ro͞oˈläd/ ▸ **noun** a piece of meat, sponge cake, or other food, spread with a filling and rolled up.
– ORIGIN French.

rou·lette /ro͞oˈlet/ ▸ **noun** a gambling game in which a ball is dropped onto a revolving wheel with numbered compartments, the players betting on the number at which the ball will come to rest.
– ORIGIN French, 'small wheel.'

round /round/ ▸ **adjective 1** shaped like a circle, cylinder, or sphere. **2** having a curved shape: *round red cheeks.* **3** (of a person's shoulders) bent forward. **4** (of a voice or musical tone) rich and mellow. **5** (of a number) expressed in convenient units rather than exactly, for example to the nearest whole number. **6** frank and truthful: *she berated him in round terms.*

– SYNONYMS **circular,** spherical, globular, cylindrical.

▸ **noun 1** a circular piece or shape. **2** a route by which a number of people or places are visited or inspected in turn: *hospital ward rounds.* **3** a regularly recurring sequence of activities. **4** each of a sequence of sessions in a process, especially in a sports contest. **5** a single division of a boxing or wrestling match. **6** a set of drinks bought for all the members of a group. **7** the amount of ammunition needed to fire one shot. **8** a song for three or more unaccompanied voices or parts, each singing the same theme but starting one after another. **9** a thick disk of beef cut from the haunch for a roast.

– SYNONYMS **1 ball,** sphere, globe, orb, circle, disk/disc, ring, hoop. **2** *a policeman on his* ***rounds*** **circuit,** beat, route, tour. **3** *their lives were a daily round of housework and laundry* **succession,** sequence, series, cycle. **4** *the first round of the tournament* **stage,** level, heat, game, bout, contest.

▸ **adverb** chiefly Brit. variant of **AROUND** (adverb).
▸ **preposition** chiefly Brit. variant of **AROUND** (preposition).
▸ **verb 1** pass and go around something. **2** make a figure less exact but more convenient for calculations: *round the weight up to the nearest ounce.* **3** make or become round in shape.

– SYNONYMS **go around/round,** travel around/round, skirt, circumnavigate, orbit.

– DERIVATIVES **round·ish** adjective **round·ness** noun.
– PHRASES **in the round 1** (of theater) with the audience placed on at least three sides of the stage. **2** (of sculpture) standing free, rather than carved in relief. **3** fully and thoroughly. **round something off 1** smooth the edges of something. **2** complete something in a satisfying or suitable way. **round someone/thing up** drive or collect people or animals together.
– ORIGIN Old French.

WORD TOOLKIT

See **CIRCULAR**.

round·a·bout /ˈroundəˌbout/ ▸ **adjective 1** not following a direct route; circuitous. **2** not saying what is meant clearly and directly.

– SYNONYMS **circuitous,** indirect, meandering, serpentine, tortuous, oblique, circumlocutory.
– ANTONYMS direct.

▸ **noun** Brit. **1** a merry-go-round. **2** a road junction at which traffic moves in one direction around a central island to reach one of the roads converging on it.

round·ed /ˈroundid/ ▸ **adjective 1** round or curved. **2** well developed in all aspects; balanced: *a rounded human being.*

roun·del /ˈroundl/ ▸ **noun 1** a small disk, especially a decorative medallion. **2** a circular identifying mark painted on military aircraft.
– ORIGIN Old French *rondel.*

Round·head /ˈroundˌhed/ ▸ **noun** historical a member or supporter of the Parliamentary party in the English Civil War.
– ORIGIN with reference to their short-cropped hair.

round·house /ˈroundˌhous/ ▸ **noun 1** a railroad locomotive maintenance shed built around a turntable. **2** informal a blow given with a wide sweep of the arm.

round·ly /ˈroundlē/ ▸ **adverb 1** in an emphatic or blunt way. **2** so as to form a circular shape.

– SYNONYMS **1 vehemently,** emphatically, fiercely, forcefully, severely, plainly, frankly, candidly. **2 utterly,** completely, thoroughly, decisively, conclusively, heavily, soundly.

round rob·in ▸ **noun 1** a tournament in which each competitor plays in turn against every other. **2** a petition, especially one with signatures written in a circle to conceal the order of writing.

round ta·ble ▸ **noun** (usu. before another noun) a meeting at which parties meet on equal terms for discussion.

round-the-clock ▸ **adjective** lasting all day and all night: *round-the-clock surveillance.*

round trip ▸ **noun** a journey to a place and back again.

round·up /ˈroundˌəp/ ▸ **noun 1** a gathering together of people or things. **2** a summary of facts or events.

round·worm /ˈroundˌwərm/ ▸ **noun** a parasitic worm found in the intestines of some mammals.

rouse /rouz/ ▸ **verb 1** bring or come out of sleep. **2** cause someone to move or take interest after being inactive. **3** stir up or arouse: *his evasiveness roused my curiosity.*

– SYNONYMS **1 wake (up),** awaken, arouse. **2 wake up,** awake, come to, get up, rise, bestir oneself. **3 stir up,** excite, galvanize, electrify, stimulate, inspire, move, inflame, agitate, goad, provoke, prompt, whip up.

– ORIGIN probably from Old French.

rous·ing /ˈrouziɴɢ/ ▸ **adjective** exciting; stirring: *a rousing speech.*

– SYNONYMS **stirring,** inspiring, exciting, stimulating, moving, electrifying, invigorating, energizing, exhilarating.

– DERIVATIVES **rous·ing·ly** adverb.

roust /roust/ ▸ **verb** informal make someone get up or start moving.
– ORIGIN perhaps from **ROUSE**.

roust·a·bout /ˈroustəˌbout/ ▸ **noun** an unskilled or casual worker, especially a laborer on an oil rig or in a circus.
– ORIGIN from **ROUST**.

rout[1] /rout/ ▶ **noun 1** a decisive defeat. **2** a disorderly retreat of defeated troops.

– SYNONYMS **defeat,** beating, retreat, flight; informal licking, hammering, thrashing, pasting, drubbing.
– ANTONYMS victory.

▶ **verb** defeat someone decisively and force them to retreat.

– SYNONYMS **defeat,** beat, conquer, vanquish, crush, put to flight, drive off, scatter; informal lick, hammer, clobber, thrash.

– ORIGIN Old French *rute*.

rout[2] ▶ **verb** cut a groove in a hard surface.
– ORIGIN from ROOT[2].

route /ro͞ot, rout/ ▶ **noun 1** a way taken in getting from a starting point to a destination. **2** a method or process that leads to a particular result: *a fast-track route to a coaching career*.

– SYNONYMS **way,** course, road, path, direction.

▶ **verb** (**routes, routing, routed**) send someone or something along a particular course.
– ORIGIN Old French *rute* 'road.'

rout·er[1] /ˈroutər/ ▶ **noun** a power tool with a rotating shaped cutter, used in carpentry for making grooves, decorative moldings, etc.

rout·er[2] /ˈro͞otər, ˈroutər/ ▶ **noun** a device that forwards data packets to the appropriate parts of a computer network.

rou·tine /ro͞oˈtēn/ ▶ **noun 1** a sequence of actions regularly followed. **2** a set sequence in a dance or comedy act.

– SYNONYMS **1 procedure,** practice, pattern, drill, regime, program, schedule, plan. **2 act,** performance, number, turn, piece; informal spiel, patter.

▶ **adjective 1** performed as part of a regular procedure: *a routine inspection*. **2** without variety; dull.

– SYNONYMS **1 standard,** regular, customary, normal, usual, ordinary, typical, everyday. **2 boring,** tedious, monotonous, humdrum, run-of-the-mill, pedestrian, predictable, hackneyed, unimaginative, unoriginal, banal, trite.
– ANTONYMS unusual.

– DERIVATIVES **rou·tine·ly** adverb.
– ORIGIN French.

rout·ing code ▶ **noun 1** a numeric code that directs telephone calls or Internet traffic. **2** the magnetically encoded numbers on a check.

rou·tin·ize /ro͞oˈtēˌnīz, ˈro͞otnˌīz/ ▶ **verb** make something into a matter of routine; subject to a routine.
– DERIVATIVES **rou·tin·i·za·tion** /-ˌtēnəˈzāsʜən, ˌro͞otn-ə-/ noun.

roux /ro͞o/ ▶ **noun** (pl. same) Cooking a mixture of fat (especially butter) and flour used in making sauces.
– ORIGIN from French *beurre roux* 'browned butter.'

rove /rōv/ ▶ **verb 1** travel constantly without a fixed destination; wander. **2** (of a person's eyes) look around in all directions.
– DERIVATIVES **rov·er** noun.
– ORIGIN perhaps from dialect *rave* 'to stray.'

row[1] /rō/ ▶ **noun** a number of people or things in a line.

– SYNONYMS **1 line,** column, file, queue, procession, chain, string, succession. **2 tier,** line, rank, bank.

– PHRASES **in a row** informal one after the other; in succession.
– ORIGIN Old English.

row[2] /rō/ ▶ **verb 1** propel a boat with oars. **2** row a boat as a sport. ▶ **noun** a spell of rowing.
– DERIVATIVES **row·er** noun.
– ORIGIN Old English.

row[3] /rou/ chiefly Brit. ▶ **noun 1** an angry quarrel. **2** a serious dispute. **3** a loud noise or uproar. ▶ **verb** have an angry quarrel.
– ORIGIN unknown.

row·an /ˈrōən/ ▶ **noun** a small tree with white flowers and red berries.
– ORIGIN Scandinavian.

row·boat /ˈrōˌbōt/ (Brit. **rowing boat**) ▶ **noun** a small boat propelled by oars.

row·dy /ˈroudē/ ▶ **adjective** (**rowdier, rowdiest**) noisy and disorderly.

– SYNONYMS **unruly,** disorderly, riotous, undisciplined, uncontrollable, ungovernable, disruptive, obstreperous, out of control, rough, wild, boisterous, uproarious, noisy, loud; informal rambunctious.
– ANTONYMS peaceful.

▶ **noun** (pl. **rowdies**) a rowdy person.
– DERIVATIVES **row·di·ly** /ˈroudl-ē/ adverb **row·di·ness** noun **row·dy·ism** /-ˌizəm/ noun.
– ORIGIN unknown.

WORD TOOLKIT

rowdy ...	boisterous ...	lively ...
behavior	laughter	debate
crowd	applause	discussion
bunch	children	music
bar	celebration	atmosphere
drunks	comedy	dance
sailors	cheers	game

row·el /ˈrou(ə)l/ ▶ **noun** a spiked revolving disk at the end of a spur.
– ORIGIN Old French *roele*.

row house /rō / ▶ **noun** any of a row of houses joined by common side walls.

row·ing ma·chine ▶ **noun** an exercise machine with a handle to pull to simulate rowing a boat.

roy·al /ˈroiəl/ ▶ **adjective 1** relating to or having the status of a king or queen or a member of their family. **2** of a quality or size suitable for a king or queen; splendid. **3** informal real; complete: *she's a royal pain in the butt*.

– SYNONYMS **regal,** kingly, queenly, princely, sovereign.

▶ **noun** informal a member of the royal family.
– DERIVATIVES **roy·al·ly** adverb.
– ORIGIN Old French *roial*.

roy·al blue ▶ **noun** a deep, vivid blue.

roy·al·ist /ˈroiəlist/ ▶ **noun** a person who supports the principle of rule by a king or queen.
– DERIVATIVES **roy·al·ism** /-ˌizəm/ noun.

roy·al jel·ly ▶ **noun** a substance produced by honeybee workers and fed by them to larvae that are being raised as potential queen bees.

roy·al·ty /ˈroiəltē/ ▶ **noun** (pl. **royalties**) **1** people of royal blood or status. **2** the status or power of a king or queen: *the insignia of royalty*. **3** a sum paid for the use of a patent or to an author or composer for each copy of a work sold or for each public performance.

RPI ▶ **abbreviation** retail price index.

rpm ▶ **abbreviation** revolutions per minute.

RR ▶ **abbreviation** **1** railroad. **2** rural route.

RSI ▶ **abbreviation** repetitive strain injury.

RSS ▶ **noun** Computing really simple syndication, a system for the distribution or syndication of Internet content from an online publisher to Web users.

RSVP ▶ **abbreviation** répondez s'il vous plaît; please reply (used at the end of invitations).
– ORIGIN French.

rte. ▶ **abbreviation** route.

RTF ▶ **abbreviation** Computing rich text format.

Ru ▶ **symbol** the chemical element ruthenium.

RU-486 ▶ **noun** trademark for **MIFEPRISTONE**.

rub /rəb/ ▶ **verb** (**rubs, rubbing, rubbed**) **1** move back and forth over a surface while pressing against it. **2** apply with a rubbing action. **3** (**rub something down**) dry, smooth, or clean something by rubbing. **4** (**rub something in/into**) work an ingredient into a mixture by breaking and blending it with the fingertips.

– SYNONYMS **1** *Sally rubbed her arm* **massage,** knead, stroke, pat. **2** *my shoes rub badly* **chafe,** scrape, pinch. **3** *she rubbed some cream on her nose* **apply,** smear, spread, work in.

▶ **noun** **1** an act of rubbing. **2** an ointment for rubbing into the skin. **3** (**the rub**) the central or most important difficulty.
– PHRASES **rub one's hands** show satisfaction. **rub it in** (or **rub someone's nose in something**) informal forcefully draw someone's attention to an embarrassing fact. **rub off** be transferred: *she hoped that some of his confidence would rub off on her.* **rub shoulders with** associate or come into contact with someone. **rub someone the wrong way** irritate someone.
– ORIGIN perhaps from German *rubben.*

ru·ba·to /ro͞o'bätō/ ▶ **noun** (pl. **rubatos** or **rubati** /-'bätē/) Music temporary disregard for strict tempo to allow an expressive quickening or slackening.
– ORIGIN Italian, 'robbed.'

rub·ber[1] /'rəbər/ ▶ **noun** **1** a tough elastic substance made from the latex of a tropical tree or synthetically. **2** informal a condom. **3** Brit. a rubber eraser.
– DERIVATIVES **rub·ber·ize** verb **rub·ber·y** adjective.
– ORIGIN from **RUB**.

rub·ber[2] ▶ **noun** **1** a contest consisting of a series of matches between the same sides in certain games. **2** (in Davis Cup tennis) a match forming part of a contest ('tie') between two nations. **3** Bridge a unit of play in which one side scores bonus points for winning the best of three games. **4** Baseball an oblong piece of rubber embedded in the pitcher's mound, on which the pitcher must keep one foot while delivering the ball.
– ORIGIN unknown.

rub·ber band ▶ **noun** a loop of rubber for holding things together.

rub·ber bul·let ▶ **noun** a bullet made of rubber, used in riot control.

rub·ber·neck /'rəbər,nek/ informal ▶ **verb** turn one's head to stare at something in a foolish way. ▶ **noun** a person who stares in a foolish way.
– DERIVATIVES **rub·ber·neck·er** noun.

rub·ber plant ▶ **noun** an evergreen tree with large dark green shiny leaves, native to SE Asia and formerly grown as a source of rubber.

rub·ber stamp ▶ **noun** **1** a hand-held device for stamping dates, addresses, etc., on a surface. **2** an instance of automatic approval given without proper consideration. ▶ **verb** (**rubber-stamp**) approve something automatically without proper consideration.

rub·ber tree ▶ **noun** a tree that produces the latex from which rubber is manufactured, native to the Amazonian rainforest.

rub·bing /'rəbiNG/ ▶ **noun** an impression of a design on brass or stone, made by placing a sheet of paper over it and rubbing it with chalk, wax, or a pencil.

rub·bing al·co·hol ▶ **noun** denatured alcohol, typically perfumed, used as an antiseptic or in massage.

rub·bish /'rəbisH/ ▶ **noun** **1** waste material; refuse or litter. **2** unimportant or inferior material. **3** ridiculous or foolish talk or ideas; nonsense.

– SYNONYMS **1 refuse,** trash, garbage, waste, litter, scrap, detritus, debris, dross; informal dreck, junk. **2 nonsense,** gibberish, claptrap, garbage; informal baloney, tripe, drivel, bilge, bunk, piffle, twaddle, poppycock, gobbledygook.

▶ **verb** Brit. informal criticize and reject as worthless. ▶ **adjective** Brit. informal very bad.
– ORIGIN Old French *rubbous.*

rub·ble /'rəbəl/ ▶ **noun** rough fragments of stone, brick, concrete, etc., especially as the debris from the demolition of buildings.

– SYNONYMS **debris,** remains, ruins, wreckage.

– DERIVATIVES **rub·bly** adjective.
– ORIGIN perhaps from Old French *robe* 'spoils.'

rube /ro͞ob/ ▶ **noun** informal a country bumpkin.
– ORIGIN abbreviation of the man's name *Reuben.*

Rube Gold·berg /'gōld,bərg/ ▶ **adjective** unnecessarily or comically complex in design.
– ORIGIN from US cartoonist *Ruben Goldberg,* whose illustrations depicted such complex devices.

ru·bel·la /ro͞o'belə/ ▶ **noun** a disease transmitted by a virus and with symptoms like mild measles; German measles.
– ORIGIN Latin, 'reddish things.'

Ru·bi·con /'ro͞obə,kän/ ▶ **noun** a point of no return.
– ORIGIN a stream in NE Italy marking the ancient boundary between Italy and Gaul; by leading his army across it, Julius Caesar caused a civil war.

ru·bi·cund /'ro͞obə,kənd/ ▶ **adjective** having a reddish complexion.
– ORIGIN Latin *rubicundus.*

ru·bid·i·um /ro͞o'bidēəm/ ▶ **noun** a rare soft silvery reactive metallic element.
– ORIGIN from Latin *rubidus* 'red.'

ru·ble /'ro͞obəl/ (also chiefly Brit. **rouble**) ▶ **noun** the basic unit of money of Russia and some other former republics of the Soviet Union.
– ORIGIN Russian.

ru·bric /'ro͞obrik/ ▶ **noun** **1** a heading on a document. **2** a set of instructions or rules. **3** a direction as to how a church service should be conducted.
– ORIGIN first referring to material written in red for emphasis: from Latin *rubrica terra* 'red earth or ochre as writing material.'

ru·by /ˈro͞obē/ ▸ **noun** (pl. **rubies**) **1** a precious stone that is typically deep red in color. **2** a deep red color.
– ORIGIN Latin *rubinus*.

ruche /ro͞osH/ ▸ **noun** a frill or pleat of fabric.
– DERIVATIVES **ruched** adjective **ruch·ing** noun.
– ORIGIN French.

ruck·sack /ˈrəkˌsak, ˈro͝ok-/ ▸ **noun** a bag with two shoulder straps that allow it to be carried on the back.
– ORIGIN German.

ruck·us /ˈrəkəs/ ▸ **noun** an argument or commotion.
– ORIGIN perhaps related to **RUCTION** and **RUMPUS**.

ruc·tion /ˈrəksHən/ ▸ **noun** informal a disturbance or quarrel.
– ORIGIN perhaps from **INSURRECTION**.

rud·beck·i·a /ro͞odˈbekēə, ˌrəd-/ ▸ **noun** a North American plant of the daisy family, with yellow or orange flowers and a dark cone-shaped center.
– ORIGIN named after the Swedish botanist Olaf *Rudbeck*.

rud·der /ˈrədər/ ▸ **noun 1** a flat hinged upright piece at the back of a boat, used for steering. **2** an upright airfoil pivoted from the tailplane of an aircraft, used for steering.
– ORIGIN Old English, 'paddle, oar.'

rud·der·less /ˈrədərləs/ ▸ **adjective** lacking a clear sense of one's aims or direction.

rud·dy /ˈrədē/ ▸ **adjective** (**ruddier, ruddiest**) **1** (of a person's face) having a healthy red color. **2** reddish in color.

> – SYNONYMS **rosy,** red, pink, roseate, rubicund, healthy, glowing, fresh, flushed, blushing, florid.
> – ANTONYMS pale.

– DERIVATIVES **rud·di·ness** noun.
– ORIGIN Old English.

rude /ro͞od/ ▸ **adjective 1** offensively impolite or bad-mannered. **2** referring to sex or bodily functions in an offensive way. **3** very abrupt: *the war came as a rude awakening*. **4** dated roughly made or done. **5** old use ignorant and uneducated.

> – SYNONYMS **1 ill-mannered,** bad-mannered, impolite, discourteous, uncivil, impertinent, insolent, impudent, disparaging, abusive, curt, brusque, offhand. **2 vulgar,** coarse, smutty, dirty, filthy, crude, lewd, obscene, risqué; informal blue.
> – ANTONYMS polite.

– DERIVATIVES **rude·ly** adverb **rude·ness** noun **ru·der·y** /-ərē/ noun.
– ORIGIN Latin *rudis* 'not wrought or cultivated.'

ru·di·ment /ˈro͞odəmənt/ ▸ **noun 1** (**rudiments**) the basic facts of a subject. **2** (**rudiments**) a basic or primitive form of something. **3** Biology an undeveloped or immature part or organ.

> – SYNONYMS **(rudiments) basics,** fundamentals, essentials, foundations; informal nuts and bolts, ABCs.

– ORIGIN Latin *rudimentum*.

ru·di·men·ta·ry /ˌro͞odəˈment(ə)rē/ ▸ **adjective 1** involving only the basic facts or elements: *a rudimentary education*. **2** not highly or fully developed: *a rudimentary stage of evolution*.

> – SYNONYMS **1 basic,** elementary, fundamental, essential. **2 primitive,** crude, simple, unsophisticated, rough (and ready), makeshift. **3 vestigial,** undeveloped, incomplete.

– DERIVATIVES **ru·di·men·ta·ri·ly** /-menˈte(ə)rəlē, -ˈment(ə)rəlē/ adverb.

rue¹ /ro͞o/ ▸ **verb** (**rues, rueing** or **ruing, rued**) bitterly regret a past event or action.

> – SYNONYMS **regret,** be sorry about, feel remorseful about, repent of, reproach oneself for, deplore, lament, bemoan, bewail.

– ORIGIN Old English.

> **CHOOSE THE RIGHT WORD**
>
> See **MOURN**.

rue² ▸ **noun** an evergreen shrub with bitter strong-scented leaves that are used in herbal medicine.
– ORIGIN Greek *rhutē*.

rue·ful /ˈro͞ofəl/ ▸ **adjective** expressing regret: *a rueful smile*.

> – SYNONYMS **regretful,** apologetic, sorry, remorseful, shamefaced, sheepish, hangdog, contrite, repentant, penitent, conscience-stricken, self-reproachful, sorrowful, sad.

– DERIVATIVES **rue·ful·ly** adverb **rue·ful·ness** noun.

ruff¹ /rəf/ ▸ **noun 1** a projecting starched frill worn around the neck, especially in Elizabethan and Jacobean times. **2** a ring of feathers or hair around the neck of a bird or mammal. **3** (pl. same or **ruffs**) a wading bird, the male of which has a large ruff and ear tufts in the breeding season.
– ORIGIN probably from **ROUGH**.

ruff² ▸ **verb** (in bridge and whist) play a trump in a trick that was led in a different suit. ▸ **noun** an act of playing such a trump.
– ORIGIN Old French *rouffle*.

ruf·fi·an /ˈrəfēən/ ▸ **noun** a violent or lawless person.

> – SYNONYMS **thug,** lout, hooligan, hoodlum, vandal, delinquent, rowdy, scoundrel, villain, rogue, bully, brute; informal tough (guy), bruiser.

– DERIVATIVES **ruf·fi·an·ism** /-ˌnizəm/ noun **ruf·fi·an·ly** adjective.
– ORIGIN Old French.

ruf·fle /ˈrəfəl/ ▸ **verb 1** disrupt the smooth surface of something. **2** irritate or upset someone. **3** (as adj. **ruffled**) gathered into a frill.

> – SYNONYMS **1 disarrange,** tousle, dishevel, rumple, mess up; informal muss up. **2 disconcert,** unnerve, fluster, agitate, upset, disturb, discomfit, put off, perturb, unsettle; informal faze, throw, get to.
> – ANTONYMS smooth.

▸ **noun** a gathered frill on a garment.
– ORIGIN unknown.

ru·fi·yaa /ˈro͞ofēˌyä/ ▸ **noun** (pl. same) the basic unit of money of the Maldives.
– ORIGIN Maldivian.

ru·fous /ˈro͞ofəs/ ▸ **adjective** (especially of an animal or bird) reddish brown in color.
– ORIGIN Latin *rufus* 'red, reddish.'

rug /rəg/ ▸ **noun 1** a small carpet. **2** informal, humorous a toupee.
– PHRASES **pull the rug out from under someone** abruptly withdraw support from someone.
– ORIGIN probably Scandinavian.

rug·by /ˈrəgbē/ (also **rugby football**) ▸ **noun** a team game played with an oval ball that may be kicked, carried, and passed by hand, in which points are won by scoring a try or by kicking the ball over the crossbar of the opponents' goal.

– ORIGIN named after *Rugby* School in England, where it was first played.

rug·ged /ˈrəgid/ ▶ **adjective 1** having a rocky and uneven surface. **2** (of clothing or equipment) strong and capable of withstanding rough handling. **3** having or requiring toughness and determination: *a stubborn, rugged individualist.* **4** (of a man) having attractively strong features.

> – SYNONYMS **1 rough,** uneven, bumpy, rocky, stony, pitted. **2 robust,** durable, sturdy, strong, tough, resilient. **3 well built,** burly, strong, muscular, muscly, brawny, strapping, tough, hardy, robust, sturdy, solid; informal hunky. **4** *his rugged features* **strong,** craggy, rough-hewn, manly, masculine.
> – ANTONYMS smooth, delicate.

– DERIVATIVES **rug·ged·ly** adverb **rug·ged·ness** noun.
– ORIGIN probably of Scandinavian origin.

ru·in /ˈro͞oin/ ▶ **noun 1** the physical destruction or collapse of something. **2** the remains of a building that has decayed or suffered much damage. **3** a severe downfall or decline: *such action can only result in the utter ruin of our nation.* **4** the complete loss of a person's money and other assets.

> – SYNONYMS **1 disintegration,** decay, disrepair, dilapidation, destruction, demolition, devastation. **2** *the* **ruins** *of a church* **remains,** remnants, fragments, rubble, debris, wreckage. **3 downfall,** collapse, defeat, undoing, failure. **4 bankruptcy,** insolvency, penury, destitution, poverty.

▶ **verb 1** destroy or severely damage a building or other structure. **2** have a very damaging effect on: *the expressway has ruined village life.* **3** make someone very poor or bankrupt.

> – SYNONYMS **1 destroy,** devastate, lay waste, ravage, raze, demolish, wreck, wipe out, flatten. **2 spoil,** wreck, blight, shatter, dash, scotch, mess up, sabotage; informal screw up. **3 bankrupt,** make insolvent, impoverish, pauperize, wipe out, break, cripple, bring someone to their knees.

– ORIGIN Latin *ruina.*

ru·in·a·tion /ˌro͞oəˈnāsʜən/ ▶ **noun** the action of ruining someone or something or the state of being ruined.

ru·ined /ˈro͞oind/ ▶ **adjective** in a state of decay: *a ruined castle.*

> – SYNONYMS **derelict,** dilapidated, tumbledown, ramshackle, decrepit, falling to pieces, crumbling, decaying, disintegrating, in ruins.

ru·in·ous /ˈro͞oənəs/ ▶ **adjective 1** disastrous or destructive. **2** costing far more than a person can afford. **3** (of a building) in ruins.

> – SYNONYMS **1 disastrous,** devastating, catastrophic, calamitous, crippling, crushing, damaging, destructive, harmful, costly. **2 extortionate,** exorbitant, excessive, sky-high, outrageous, inflated; informal steep.

– DERIVATIVES **ru·in·ous·ly** adverb.

rule /ro͞ol/ ▶ **noun 1** a regulation or statement controlling behavior or procedure within a particular area of activity. **2** (**the rule**) the normal or usual state of things. **3** control of a country or people. **4** a code of practice and discipline for a religious community. **5** a ruler for measuring things. **6** a thin printed line or dash.

> – SYNONYMS **1** *health and safety rules* **regulation,** ruling, directive, order, law, statute, ordinance. **2** *moderation is the golden rule* **principle,** precept, standard, axiom, truth, maxim. **3** *lateness was the general rule* **procedure,** practice, protocol, convention, norm, routine, custom, habit. **4** *Punjab came under British rule* **government,** jurisdiction, command, power, dominion, control, administration, sovereignty, leadership.

▶ **verb 1** control or govern a people or country. **2** state with legal authority that something is the case. **3** have a powerful and restricting influence on: *her whole life was ruled by fear.* **4** informal be very good or the best. **5** make parallel lines on paper.

> – SYNONYMS **1 govern,** preside over, control, lead, dominate, run, head, administer. **2 reign,** be on the throne, be in power, govern. **3 decree,** order, pronounce, judge, adjudge, ordain, decide, determine, find.

– PHRASES **as a rule** usually, but not always. **rule of thumb** a broadly accurate guide or principle, based on practice rather than theory. **rule something out/in** exclude (or include) something as a possibility. **rule the roost** be in complete control.
– ORIGIN Old French *reule.*

rul·er /ˈro͞olər/ ▶ **noun 1** a person who rules a people or country. **2** a straight strip of rigid material, marked at regular intervals and used to draw straight lines or measure distances.

> – SYNONYMS **leader,** sovereign, monarch, potentate, king, queen, emperor, empress, prince, princess, crowned head, head of state, president, premier, governor.
> – ANTONYMS subject.

rul·ing /ˈro͞olɪɴɢ/ ▶ **noun** a decision or statement made by someone in authority.

> – SYNONYMS **judgment,** decision, adjudication, finding, verdict, pronouncement, resolution, decree, injunction.

▶ **adjective** in control; governing.

> – SYNONYMS **1 governing,** controlling, commanding, supreme. **2 main,** chief, principal, major, dominating, consuming; informal number-one.

rum /rəm/ ▶ **noun** an alcoholic liquor distilled from sugarcane residues or molasses.
– ORIGIN perhaps from former *rumbullion.*

Ru·ma·ni·an /ro͝oˈmānēən, -nyən/ ▶ **adjective & noun** variant spelling of **ROMANIAN.**

rum·ba /ˈrəmbə, ˈro͝om-, ˈro͞om-/ (also **rhumba**) ▶ **noun 1** a rhythmic dance with Spanish and African elements, originating in Cuba. **2** a ballroom dance based on the Cuban rumba.
– ORIGIN Latin American Spanish.

rum·ble /ˈrəmbəl/ ▶ **verb** make or move with a continuous deep sound. ▶ **noun 1** a continuous deep sound like distant thunder. **2** informal a street fight between rival gangs.
– DERIVATIVES **rum·bler** noun.
– ORIGIN probably from Dutch *rommelen, rummelen.*

rum·ble strip ▶ **noun** one of a series of raised strips set in a road to warn drivers to slow down or to indicate that they have deviated from their lane.

ru·mi·nant /ˈro͞omənənt/ ▶ **noun** a mammal of a type that chews the cud, such as cattle, sheep, or deer.
▶ **adjective** relating to mammals that chew the cud.
– ORIGIN from Latin *ruminari* 'chew over again.'

ru·mi·nate /ˈro͞oməˌnāt/ ▶ **verb 1** think deeply about something. **2** (of a cow, sheep, etc.) chew the cud.

– DERIVATIVES **ru·mi·na·tion** /ˌro͞oməˈnāsHən/ noun **ru·mi·na·tive** /-ˌnātiv/ adjective.

rum·mage /ˈrəmij/ ▶ **verb** search for something in an unmethodical way.

– SYNONYMS **search,** hunt, root about/around, ferret about/around, fish about/around, dig, delve, go through, explore, sift through, rifle through.

▶ **noun** an act of rummaging.

– ORIGIN from Old French *arrumer* 'stow in a hold (of a ship).'

rum·mage sale ▶ **noun** a sale of various secondhand goods, especially for charity.

rum·my /ˈrəmē/ ▶ **noun** a card game in which the players try to form sets and sequences of cards.

– ORIGIN unknown.

ru·mor /ˈro͞omər/ (Brit. **rumour**) ▶ **noun** a story spread among a number of people that is unconfirmed and may be false.

– SYNONYMS **gossip,** hearsay, talk, tittle-tattle, speculation, word, report, story, whisper; informal the grapevine, the word on the street, the buzz.

▶ **verb** (**be rumored**) be spread as a rumor.

– ORIGIN Latin *rumor* 'noise.'

rump /rəmp/ ▶ **noun 1** the hind part of the body of a mammal or the lower back of a bird. **2** a small or unimportant part left over from something larger.

– ORIGIN probably Scandinavian.

rum·ple /ˈrəmpəl/ ▶ **verb** make something untidy or disheveled.

– DERIVATIVES **rum·pled** adjective.

– ORIGIN Dutch *rompel* 'wrinkle.'

rum·pus /ˈrəmpəs/ ▶ **noun** (pl. **rumpuses**) a noisy disturbance.

– ORIGIN uncertain.

run /rən/ ▶ **verb** (**runs, running, ran** /ran/; past part. **run**) **1** move fast using the legs. **2** move or pass something in a particular direction: *Helen ran her fingers through her hair*. **3** move forcefully or fast: *the tanker ran aground*. **4** be in charge of people or an organization. **5** continue, operate, or proceed: *everything's running according to plan*. **6** function or cause to function. **7** pass into or reach a specified state or level: *inflation is running at 11 percent*. **8** (of a liquid) flow. **9** send out a liquid. **10** (**run in**) (of a quality) be common in members of a family. **11** stand as a candidate in an election. **12** enter or be entered in a race. **13** (of dye or color) dissolve and spread when wet. **14** (of a bus, train, etc.) make a regular journey on a particular route. **15** transport someone in a car. **16** publish or be published in a newspaper or magazine. **17** smuggle goods. **18** (of a stocking or pair of tights) develop a vertical strip of unraveling.

– SYNONYMS **1** *she ran across the road* **sprint,** race, dart, rush, dash, hasten, hurry, scurry, scamper, gallop, jog, trot. **2** *the robbers turned and ran* **flee,** take flight, make off, take off, take to one's heels, bolt, make one's getaway, escape; informal beat it, clear off/out, scram, leg it. **3** *the road runs the length of the valley* **extend,** stretch, reach, continue. **4** *water ran from the eaves* **flow,** pour, stream, gush, flood, cascade, roll, course, glide, spill, trickle, drip, dribble, leak. **5** *he runs a mail-order company* **be in charge of,** manage, direct, control, head, govern, supervise, superintend, oversee, organize, coordinate. **6** *it's expensive to run a car* **maintain,** keep, own, possess, have, use, operate. **7** *I left the engine running* **operate,** function, work, go.

▶ **noun 1** an act or spell of running. **2** a running pace. **3** a journey or route. **4** a short trip in a car. **5** a spell or stretch of something: *a run of bad luck*. **6** an enclosed area in which animals or birds may run freely in the open. **7** a course or track made or regularly used: *a ski run*. **8** (**the run of**) free and unrestricted use of or access to somewhere. **9** (**the run**) the average or usual type: *she stood out from the general run of Harvard women*. **10** a rapid series of musical notes. **11** a sequence of cards of the same suit. **12** Baseball a point scored by the batter returning to the home plate after touching the bases. **13** a vertical strip of unraveled fabric in stockings or tights. **14** (**the runs**) informal diarrhea.

– SYNONYMS **1 jog,** sprint, dash, gallop, trot. **2 route,** journey, circuit, round, beat. **3 drive,** ride, turn, trip, excursion, outing, jaunt; informal spin, tootle. **4 series,** succession, sequence, string, streak, spate. **5 enclosure,** pen, coop. **6** *a ski run* **slope,** trail, track, piste.

– DERIVATIVES **run·na·ble** adjective.

– PHRASES **be run off one's feet** be very busy. **give someone/thing a (good) run for their money** provide someone or something with challenging competition. **have a (good) run for one's money** receive reward or enjoyment in return for one's efforts. **on the run 1** escaping from arrest. **2** while running or moving. **run across** meet or find by chance. **run after** informal pursue persistently. **run along** informal go away. **run away 1** escape from a person, place, or situation. **2** try to avoid facing up to danger or difficulty. **run away with 1** be out of the control of: *her imagination was running away with her*. **2** win a competition or prize easily. **run before one can walk** attempt something difficult before one has grasped the basic skills. **run something by** (or **past**) tell someone about something to find out their opinion. **run something down** (or **run down**) **1** gradually lose or cause to lose power. **2** reduce or be reduced in size or resources. **3** get worse or cause to get worse in quality. **run someone/thing down 1** knock someone or something down with a vehicle. **2** criticize someone or something. **run someone in** informal arrest someone. **run into 1** collide with. **2** meet someone by chance. **3** experience a problem. **run something off 1** produce a copy on a machine. **2** write or recite something quickly and with little effort. **run on** continue without stopping. **run out 1** use up or be used up. **2** become no longer valid. **run over** (of a container or its contents) overflow. **run someone/thing over** knock someone or something down with a vehicle. **run through** (or **over**) go over quickly or briefly as a rehearsal or reminder. **run to 1** extend to or reach an amount or size. **2** show a tendency toward. **run something up 1** allow a bill, score, etc., to build up. **2** make something quickly or hurriedly. **3** raise a flag. **run up against** experience or meet a problem.

– ORIGIN Old English.

run·a·bout /ˈrənəˌbout/ ▶ **noun** a small car or light aircraft, especially one used for short journeys.

run·a·round /ˈrənəˌround/ ▶ **noun** informal (in phrase **give someone the runaround**) treat someone badly by misleading them or failing to do or provide something.

run·a·way /ˈrənəˌwā/ ▶ **noun** a person who has run away from their home or an institution.

– SYNONYMS **fugitive,** refugee, truant, absconder, deserter.

▶ **adjective 1** (of an animal or vehicle) running out of

control. **2** happening or done quickly or uncontrollably: *the runaway success of his first novel.*

run·down /ˈrənˌdoun/ ▶ **noun** a brief analysis or summary.

– SYNONYMS **summary,** synopsis, précis, run-through, recap, review, overview, briefing, sketch, outline; informal lowdown.

▶ **adjective** (**run-down**) **1** in a poor or neglected state. **2** tired and rather unwell, especially through overwork.

– SYNONYMS **1 dilapidated,** tumbledown, ramshackle, derelict, crumbling, neglected, uncared-for. **2 unwell,** ill, poorly, unhealthy, peaked, tired, drained, exhausted, worn out, below par, washed out; informal under the weather, off one's feed/oats.

rune /ro͞on/ ▶ **noun 1** a letter of an ancient Germanic alphabet used especially in Scandinavia. **2** a symbol with mysterious or magical significance.
– DERIVATIVES **ru·nic** adjective.
– ORIGIN Old English, 'secret, mystery.'

rung[1] /rəNG/ ▶ **noun 1** a horizontal bar on a ladder to stand on. **2** a level or rank in society, a profession, etc.: *a youth on a low rung at the Foreign Office.* **3** a strengthening crosspiece in the structure of a chair.
– ORIGIN Old English.

rung[2] past participle of RING[2].

run-in ▶ **noun** informal a disagreement or fight.

run·nel /ˈrənl/ ▶ **noun 1** a gutter. **2** a brook or stream.
– ORIGIN dialect *rindle.*

run·ner /ˈrənər/ ▶ **noun 1** a person or animal that runs. **2** a rod, groove, blade, or roller on which something slides. **3** a messenger or collector, especially for a bookmaker. **4** a shoot of a plant that grows along the ground and can take root at points along its length. **5** a long, narrow rug.

– SYNONYMS **1 athlete,** sprinter, hurdler, racer, jogger. **2 messenger,** courier, errand boy/girl; informal gofer.

run·ner bean ▶ **noun** a climbing bean plant with scarlet flowers and long green edible pods.

run·ner-up ▶ **noun** (pl. **runners-up**) a competitor or team taking second place in a contest.

run·ning /ˈrəniNG/ ▶ **adjective 1** (of water) flowing naturally or supplied through pipes and taps. **2** producing liquid or pus. **3** continuous or recurring: *a running joke.* **4** done while running. **5** (after a noun) in succession: *the third week running.*

– SYNONYMS **1 flowing,** gushing, rushing, moving. **2 in succession,** in a row, in sequence, consecutively, straight, together.

– PHRASES **in** (or **out of**) **the running** in (or no longer in) with a chance of success.

run·ning bat·tle ▶ **noun** a battle that does not occur at a fixed location.

run·ning board ▶ **noun** a footboard extending along the side of a vehicle.

run·ning com·men·ta·ry ▶ **noun** a spoken description of events, given as they occur.

run·ning head ▶ **noun** a heading printed at the top of each page of a book or chapter.

run·ning mate ▶ **noun** an election candidate for the lesser of two linked political offices.

run·ning re·pairs ▶ **plural noun** Brit. minor or temporary repairs carried out on machinery while it is in use.

run·ning stitch ▶ **noun** a simple needlework stitch consisting of a line of small even stitches that run back and forth through the cloth.

run·ning to·tal ▶ **noun** a total that is continually adjusted to take account of further items.

run·ny /ˈrənē/ ▶ **adjective** (**runnier, runniest**) **1** more liquid in consistency than is usual or expected. **2** (of a person's nose) producing thin mucus.

– SYNONYMS **liquid,** liquefied, fluid, melted, molten, watery, thin.
– ANTONYMS solid, thick.

WORD TOOLKIT

runny ...	molten ...	watery ...
nose	metal	soup
eyes	rock	beer
cheese	lava	coffee
eggs	lead	oatmeal
mascara	glass	mustard
paste	globule	discharge

run·off /ˈrənˌôf/ ▶ **noun 1** a further contest after a clear winner has not emerged in a previous one. **2** rainfall or other liquid that drains away from the surface of an area.

run-of-the-mill ▶ **adjective** lacking unusual or special aspects; ordinary.

– SYNONYMS **ordinary,** average, middle-of-the-road, commonplace, humdrum, mundane, standard, nondescript, characterless, conventional, unremarkable, unexceptional, uninteresting, dull, boring, routine, bland, lackluster, (common) garden-variety; informal nothing special, nothing to write home about, a dime a dozen.
– ANTONYMS exceptional.

runt /rənt/ ▶ **noun** a small pig or other animal, especially the smallest in a litter.
– DERIVATIVES **runt·ish** adjective **runt·y** adjective.
– ORIGIN unknown.

run-through ▶ **noun 1** a rehearsal. **2** a brief summary.

run-up ▶ **noun 1** a period of preparation before an important event. **2** an act of running briefly to gain momentum before bowling, performing a jump, etc.

run·way /ˈrənˌwā/ ▶ **noun 1** a strip of hard ground along which aircraft take off and land. **2** a catwalk in a fashion show.

ru·pee /ro͞oˈpē, ˈro͞oˌpē/ ▶ **noun** the basic unit of money of India, Pakistan, Sri Lanka, and some other countries.
– ORIGIN Sanskrit, 'wrought silver.'

rup·ture /ˈrəpCHər/ ▶ **verb 1** break or burst suddenly. **2** (**be ruptured** or **rupture oneself**) suffer a hernia in the abdomen. **3** disturb good relations.

– SYNONYMS **break,** fracture, crack, breach, burst, split; informal bust.

▶ **noun 1** a sudden breaking or bursting of something. **2** a hernia in the abdomen.

– SYNONYMS **break,** fracture, crack, breach, burst, split, fissure.

– ORIGIN Latin *ruptura.*

ru·ral /ˈro͝orəl/ ▶ **adjective** relating to or typical of the countryside rather than the town.

– SYNONYMS **country,** rustic, bucolic, pastoral, agricultural, agrarian.
– ANTONYMS urban.

– DERIVATIVES **ru·ral·i·ty** /ro͞oˈralitē/ noun **ru·ral·ize** verb **ru·ral·ly** adverb.
– ORIGIN Latin *ruralis.*

Ru·ri·ta·ni·an /ˌro͞oriˈtānēən/ ▶ **adjective** relating to or typical of romantic adventure or its setting.
– ORIGIN from *Ruritania,* the imaginary setting for the novels written by the English novelist Anthony Hope.

ruse /ro͞oz, ro͞os/ ▶ **noun** an action intended to deceive someone; a trick.

– SYNONYMS **ploy,** stratagem, tactic, scheme, trick, gambit, dodge, subterfuge, machination, wile.

– ORIGIN from Old French *ruser* 'use trickery.'

rush¹ /rəsh/ ▶ **verb 1** move or act with urgent haste. **2** deliver or produce something with urgent haste. **3** deal with hurriedly: *panic measures were rushed through the legislature.* **4** (of air or a liquid) flow strongly. **5** try to attack or capture a person or place suddenly.

– SYNONYMS **1** *she rushed home* **hurry,** dash, run, race, sprint, bolt, dart, gallop, career, charge, shoot, hurtle, fly, speed, zoom, scurry, scuttle, scamper, hasten; informal tear, belt, pelt, scoot, zip, whip, hotfoot it. **2** *water rushed along gutters* **gush,** pour, surge, stream, course, cascade. **3** *the mob rushed the police* **attack,** charge, storm.

▶ **noun 1** a sudden quick movement or flow: *there was a rush for the door.* **2** a flurry of hasty activity. **3** a sudden strong demand for a product. **4** a sudden intense feeling. **5** informal a sudden thrill experienced after taking certain drugs. **6** (**rushes**) the first prints made of a movie after a period of shooting.

– SYNONYMS **1** *Tim made a rush for the exit* **dash,** run, sprint, dart, bolt, charge, scramble. **2** *the lunch rush* **hustle and bustle,** commotion, hubbub, stir. **3** *I made a sudden rush at him* **charge,** onslaught, attack, assault.

– ORIGIN Old French *ruser* 'drive back.'

rush² ▶ **noun** a marsh or waterside plant with slender pith-filled leaves, some kinds of which are used for matting, baskets, etc.
– DERIVATIVES **rush·y** adjective.
– ORIGIN Old English.

rushed /rəsht/ ▶ **adjective** done with great haste: *a rushed job.*

– SYNONYMS **hasty,** fast, speedy, quick, swift, rapid, hurried.

rush hour ▶ **noun** a time at the start and end of the working day when traffic is at its heaviest.

rush·light /ˈrəshˌlīt/ ▶ **noun** historical a candle made by dipping the pith of a rush in tallow.

rusk /rəsk/ ▶ **noun** a dry slice of rebaked bread, especially one eaten by babies.
– ORIGIN Spanish or Portuguese *rosca* 'twist, coil, roll of bread.'

rus·set /ˈrəsət/ ▶ **adjective** reddish brown. ▶ **noun 1** a reddish-brown color. **2** a variety of dessert apple with a slightly rough greenish-brown skin.
– DERIVATIVES **rus·set·y** adjective.
– ORIGIN Old French *rousset.*

Rus·sian /ˈrəshən/ ▶ **noun 1** a person from Russia. **2** the language of Russia. ▶ **adjective** relating to Russia.

Rus·sian doll ▶ **noun** each of a set of brightly painted hollow wooden dolls that fit inside each other.

Rus·sian Or·tho·dox Church ▶ **noun** the national Church of Russia.

Rus·sian rou·lette ▶ **noun** a dangerous game of chance in which a person loads a bullet into one chamber of a revolver, spins the cylinder, and then pulls the trigger while pointing the gun at their own head.

Russ·ki /ˈrəskē, ˈro͞oskē/ (also **Russky**) ▶ **noun** (pl. **Russkis** or **Russkies**) informal, chiefly derogatory a Russian.

rust /rəst/ ▶ **noun 1** a reddish-brown flaky coating of iron oxide that is formed on iron or steel by the action of water and oxygen. **2** a disease of plants caused by a fungus, which results in reddish or brownish patches. **3** a reddish-brown color. ▶ **verb** be affected with rust.

– SYNONYMS **corrode,** oxidize, tarnish.

– DERIVATIVES **rust·less** adjective.
– ORIGIN Old English.

rust belt ▶ **noun** informal (especially in the American Midwest and NE states) a region where heavy industry is in decline and the population is falling.

rust buck·et ▶ **noun** informal a vehicle or ship that is old and badly rusted.

rus·tic /ˈrəstik/ ▶ **adjective 1** relating to or typical of the country, especially in being attractively simple or unsophisticated: *hearty rustic dishes.* **2** (of furniture) made of rough branches or timber.

– SYNONYMS **1 rural,** country, pastoral, bucolic, agricultural, agrarian; literary Arcadian. **2 plain,** simple, homey, homely, unsophisticated, rough, crude.
– ANTONYMS urban.

▶ **noun** often derogatory an unsophisticated country person.

– SYNONYMS **peasant,** countryman, countrywoman, bumpkin, yokel, country cousin; informal hillbilly, hayseed, hick.

– DERIVATIVES **rus·ti·cal·ly** /-ik(ə)lē/ adverb **rus·tic·i·ty** /rəˈstisətē/ noun.
– ORIGIN Latin *rusticus.*

rus·ti·cate /ˈrəstiˌkāt/ ▶ **verb 1** go to, live in, or spend time in the country. **2** (usu. as adj. **rusticated**) shape masonry in large blocks with sunken joints and a roughened surface.
– DERIVATIVES **rus·ti·ca·tion** /ˌrəstiˈkāshən/ noun.
– ORIGIN from Latin *rusticus* 'rustic.'

rus·tle /ˈrəsəl/ ▶ **verb 1** make or move with a soft crackling sound like that caused by the movement of dry leaves. **2** round up and steal cattle, horses, or sheep. **3** (**rustle something up**) informal produce food or a drink quickly.

– SYNONYMS **1 swish,** whoosh, whisper, sigh. **2 steal,** thieve, take, abduct, kidnap.

▶ **noun** a rustling sound.
– DERIVATIVES **rus·tler** noun.
– ORIGIN imitating the sound.

rust·proof /ˈrəstˌpro͞of/ ▶ **adjective** not able to be corroded by rust. ▶ **verb** make something rustproof.

rust·y /ˈrəstē/ ▶ **adjective** (**rustier, rustiest**) **1** affected by rust. **2** rust-colored; reddish-brown. **3** (of knowledge or a skill) less good than it used to be because of lack of practice.

– SYNONYMS **1** *rusty wire* **rusted,** rust-covered, corroded, oxidized, tarnished, discolored. **2** *a rusty* *color* **reddish-brown,** chestnut, auburn, tawny, russet, coppery, Titian, red. **3** *my French is a little rusty* **out of practice,** below par, deficient, weak, unpracticed.

– DERIVATIVES **rust·i·ly** adverb **rust·i·ness** noun.

rut[1] /rət/ ▶ **noun 1** a long deep track made by the repeated passage of the wheels of vehicles. **2** a pattern of behavior that has become dull but is hard to change: *here's me, stuck in a rut with Roger after all these years.*

– SYNONYMS **1 furrow,** groove, trough, ditch, hollow, pothole, crater. **2 boring routine,** humdrum existence, groove, dead end.

– DERIVATIVES **rut·ted** adjective **rut·ty** adjective.
– ORIGIN probably from Old French *rute* 'road.'

rut[2] ▶ **noun** an annual period of sexual activity in deer and some other mammals, during which the males fight each other for access to the females. ▶ **verb** (**ruts, rutting, rutted**) be in such a period of activity.
– ORIGIN Old French.

ru·ta·ba·ga /'ro͞otə,bāgə, 'ro͝ot-/ ▶ **noun** a round yellow root vegetable related to the turnip.

ru·the·ni·um /ro͞o'thēnēəm/ ▶ **noun** a hard silvery-white metallic chemical element.
– ORIGIN from *Ruthenia*, a region of central Europe.

ruth·er·for·di·um /,rəTHər'fôrdēəm/ ▶ **noun** a very unstable chemical element made by high-energy atomic collisions.
– ORIGIN named after the New Zealand physicist Ernest *Rutherford*.

ruth·less /'ro͞oTHləs/ ▶ **adjective** having or showing no pity or sympathy; hard and selfish.

– SYNONYMS **merciless,** pitiless, cruel, heartless, hard-hearted, cold-hearted, cold-blooded, harsh, callous.
– ANTONYMS merciful.

– DERIVATIVES **ruth·less·ly** adverb **ruth·less·ness** noun.
– ORIGIN from the old-fashioned word *ruth* 'pity.'

RV ▶ **abbreviation** recreational vehicle.

R·V·er /'är'vēər/ ▶ **noun** a user of a recreational vehicle.

Rwan·dan /ro͝o'ändən, rə'wändən/ (also **Rwandese** /-dēz, -dēs/) ▶ **noun** a person from Rwanda, a country in central Africa. ▶ **adjective** relating to Rwanda.

rye /rī/ ▶ **noun 1** a cereal plant resembling wheat, that grows in poor soils. **2** whiskey in which much of the grain used in distilling it is fermented rye.
– ORIGIN Old English.

rye bread ▶ **noun** a dense, chewy bread made with rye flour.

rye·grass /'rī,gras/ ▶ **noun** a grass used for fodder and lawns.
– ORIGIN unknown.

Ss

S[1] (also **s**) ▸ **noun** (pl. **Ss** or **S's**) the nineteenth letter of the alphabet.

S[2] ▸ **abbreviation 1** (chiefly in Catholic use) Saint. **2** siemens. **3** small (as a clothes size). **4** South or Southern. ▸ **symbol** the chemical element sulfur.

s ▸ **abbreviation 1** second or seconds. **2** shilling or shillings.

's ▸ **contraction** informal **1** is: *she's an editor.* **2** has: *he's just gone.* **3** us: *let's be honest.* **4** does: *what's he want?*

-'s ▸ **suffix 1** showing possession in singular nouns, also in plural nouns not ending in *-s*: *John's car | the children's school.* **2** forming the plural of a letter or symbol: *9's.*

S&H ▸ **abbreviation** shipping and handling.

SA ▸ **abbreviation 1** Salvation Army. **2** South Africa. **3** South America. **4** South Australia.

sab·ba·tar·i·an /ˌsabəˈte(ə)rēən/ ▸ **noun** a person who strictly observes the sabbath.
– DERIVATIVES **sab·ba·tar·i·an·ism** /-ˌnizəm/ noun.

sab·bath /ˈsabəTH/ ▸ **noun** (often **the Sabbath**) a day intended for religious worship and rest from work, kept by Jews from Friday evening to Saturday evening, and by most Christians on Sunday.
– ORIGIN from Hebrew, 'to rest.'

sab·bat·i·cal /səˈbatikəl/ ▸ **noun** a period of paid leave granted to a college or university teacher for study or travel. ▸ **adjective** relating to a sabbatical.
– ORIGIN from Greek *sabbatikos* 'of the sabbath.'

sa·ber /ˈsābər/ (Brit. **sabre**) ▸ **noun 1** a heavy cavalry sword with a curved blade and a single cutting edge. **2** a light fencing sword with a tapering, typically curved blade.
– ORIGIN French.

sa·ber-rat·tling ▸ **noun** the display or threat of military force.

sa·ber·tooth /ˈsābərˌto͞oTH/ (also **saber-toothed tiger**) ▸ **noun** a large extinct member of the cat family with huge curved upper canine teeth.

sa·ble /ˈsābəl/ ▸ **noun 1** a marten with a short tail and dark brown fur, native to Japan and Siberia. **2** the fur of the sable. ▸ **adjective** literary or Heraldry black.
– ORIGIN Old French.

sab·ot /saˈbō, ˈsabō/ ▸ **noun** a kind of simple wooden shoe resembling a clog.
– ORIGIN French.

sab·o·tage /ˈsabəˌtäZH/ ▸ **verb** deliberately destroy, damage, or hinder: *they might try and sabotage the deal.*

> – SYNONYMS **vandalize,** wreck, damage, destroy, incapacitate, obstruct, disrupt, spoil, ruin, undermine; informal throw a monkey wrench in the works.

▸ **noun** the action of sabotaging something.

> – SYNONYMS **vandalism,** wrecking, destruction, damage, obstruction, disruption; informal a monkey wrench in the works.

– ORIGIN from French *saboter* 'kick with sabots, destroy.'

sab·o·teur /ˌsabəˈtər/ ▸ **noun** a person who sabotages something.
– ORIGIN French.

sa·bra /ˈsäbrə/ ▸ **noun** a Jew born in Israel (or before 1948 in Palestine).
– ORIGIN Hebrew, 'opuntia fruit' (opuntias being common in parts of Israel).

sa·bre, etc. /ˈsābər/ ▸ **noun** British spelling of **SABER**, etc.

SAC /sak/ ▸ **abbreviation** Strategic Air Command.

sac /sak/ ▸ **noun** a hollow, flexible structure in the body or a plant, resembling a bag or pouch and containing air or liquid.
– ORIGIN Latin *saccus* 'sack, bag.'

sac·cha·rin /ˈsak(ə)rən/ ▸ **noun** a synthetic substance used as a low-calorie sweetener.
– ORIGIN Greek *sakkharon* 'sugar.'

sac·cha·rine /ˈsak(ə)rin, -rēn, -rīn/ ▸ **adjective** very sweet or sentimental: *horribly saccharine sitcoms.* ▸ **noun** saccharin.

sac·er·do·tal /ˌsasərˈdōtl, ˌsakər-/ ▸ **adjective** relating to priests or the priesthood.
– ORIGIN Latin *sacerdotalis.*

sa·chem /ˈsāCHəm/ ▸ **noun 1** (among some American Indian peoples) a chief. **2** informal a boss or leader.
– ORIGIN Narragansett, a North American Indian language.

sa·chet /saˈSHā/ ▸ **noun** a small perfumed bag used to scent clothes in a drawer or closet.
– ORIGIN French, 'little bag.'

sack[1] /sak/ ▸ **noun 1** a large bag made of strong fabric, paper, or plastic, used for storing and carrying goods. **2** (**the sack**) informal dismissal from employment: *he got the sack for swearing.* **3** (**the sack**) informal bed.

> – SYNONYMS **1 bag,** pouch, pocket, pack. **2** (**the sack**) **dismissal,** discharge, redundancy; informal the boot, the ax, the heave-ho, the push.

▸ **verb** informal dismiss someone from employment.

> – SYNONYMS **dismiss,** discharge, lay off, make redundant, let go, throw out; informal fire, give someone the sack, give someone their walking papers.

– DERIVATIVES **sack·a·ble** adjective **sack·ful** /ˈsakˌfo͝ol/ noun.
– PHRASES **hit the sack** informal go to bed.
– ORIGIN Greek *sakkos* 'sack, sackcloth.'

sack[2] ▸ **verb** (in historical contexts) plunder and destroy a town or building. ▸ **noun** the plundering and destruction of a place.
– ORIGIN from French *mettre à sac* 'put to sack' which perhaps first referred to filling a sack with plunder.

sack[3] ▶ **noun** historical a white wine formerly imported into Britain from Spain.
– ORIGIN from French *vin sec* 'dry wine.'

sack·but /'sak,bət/ ▶ **noun** an early form of trombone used in Renaissance music.
– ORIGIN French *saquebute*.

sack·cloth /'sak,klôTH, -,kläTH/ ▶ **noun** a coarse fabric woven from flax or hemp.
– PHRASES **sackcloth and ashes** an expression of extreme sorrow or remorse. [with reference to the wearing of sackcloth and having ashes sprinkled on the head as a sign of deep regret for having done wrong.]

sack·ing /'sakiNG/ ▶ **noun** coarse material for making sacks; sackcloth.

sack lunch ▶ **noun** a lunch packed in a paper bag and carried to work, school, etc.

sa·cra /'sakrə, 'sā-/ plural of **SACRUM**.

sa·cral /'sakrəl, 'sā-/ ▶ **adjective 1** Anatomy relating to the sacrum in the lower back. **2** relating to sacred rites or symbols.

sac·ra·ment /'sakrəmənt/ ▶ **noun 1** (in the Christian Church) a religious ceremony in which the participants receive the grace of God, such as Holy Communion. **2** (also **the Blessed Sacrament** or **the Holy Sacrament**) (in Roman Catholic use) the consecrated bread and wine used in Holy Communion.
– DERIVATIVES **sac·ra·men·tal** /,sakrə'mentl/ adjective.
– ORIGIN Latin *sacramentum* 'solemn oath.'

sa·cred /'sākrid/ ▶ **adjective 1** connected with God or a god and treated as holy. **2** (of a text) containing the doctrines of a religion. **3** religious rather than secular: *sacred music*. **4** regarded as too valuable to be interfered with: *nothing is sacred, no name is beyond reach*.

– SYNONYMS **1 holy,** hallowed, blessed, consecrated, sanctified. **2 religious,** spiritual, devotional, church, ecclesiastical.
– ANTONYMS secular, profane.

– DERIVATIVES **sa·cred·ly** adverb **sa·cred·ness** noun.
– ORIGIN from Latin *sacer* 'holy.'

sa·cred cow ▶ **noun** an idea, custom, or institution regarded as being above criticism (with reference to the Hindu belief that the cow is a sacred animal).

sac·ri·fice /'sakrə,fīs/ ▶ **noun 1** an act of killing an animal or person or giving up a possession as an offering to a god or goddess. **2** an animal, person, or object offered to a god or goddess. **3** an act of giving up something you value for the sake of something more important: *parents make sacrifices to give their children an education*.

– SYNONYMS **1 offering,** gift, oblation. **2 surrender,** giving up, abandonment, renunciation, forfeiture.

▶ **verb** offer or give up someone or something as a sacrifice.

– SYNONYMS **1 offer up,** immolate. **2 give up,** forgo, abandon, renounce, relinquish, cede, surrender, forfeit.

– DERIVATIVES **sac·ri·fi·cial** /,sakrə'fisHəl/ adjective.
– ORIGIN Latin *sacrificium*.

sac·ri·lege /'sakrəlij/ ▶ **noun** the treating of something sacred or highly valued with great disrespect.

– SYNONYMS **desecration,** profanity, blasphemy, irreverence, disrespect.

– DERIVATIVES **sac·ri·le·gious** /,sakrə'lijəs/ adjective.
– ORIGIN Latin *sacrilegium*.

sac·ris·tan /'sakristən/ ▶ **noun** a person in charge of a church sacristy.

sac·ris·ty /'sakristē/ ▶ **noun** (pl. **sacristies**) a room in a church where a priest prepares for a service, and where things used in worship are kept.
– ORIGIN Latin *sacristia*.

sac·ro·sanct /'sakrō,saNG(k)t/ ▶ **adjective** regarded as too important or valuable to be changed or questioned: *the protection of free speech by the constitution is sacrosanct*.
– DERIVATIVES **sac·ro·sanc·ti·ty** /,sakrō'saNG(k)titē/ noun.
– ORIGIN Latin *sacrosanctus*.

sac·rum /'sakrəm, 'sā-/ ▶ **noun** (pl. **sacra** /'sakrə, 'sā-/ or **sacrums**) Anatomy a triangular bone in the lower back situated between the two hipbones of the pelvis.
– ORIGIN from Latin *os sacrum* 'sacred bone.'

SAD ▶ **abbreviation** seasonal affective disorder, depression that is associated with late autumn and winter and thought to be caused by a lack of light.

sad /sad/ ▶ **adjective** (**sadder, saddest**) **1** feeling sorrow; unhappy. **2** causing or characterized by sorrow or regret: *the sad story of his life*. **3** informal very inadequate or unfashionable; pathetic.

– SYNONYMS **1 unhappy,** sorrowful, depressed, downcast, miserable, down, despondent, wretched, glum, gloomy, doleful, melancholy, mournful, woebegone, forlorn, heartbroken; informal blue, down in the mouth, down in the dumps. **2 tragic,** unhappy, miserable, wretched, sorry, pitiful, pathetic, heartbreaking, heart-rending. **3 unfortunate,** regrettable, sorry, deplorable, lamentable, pitiful, shameful, disgraceful.
– ANTONYMS happy, cheerful.

– ORIGIN Old English 'sated, weary.'

SADD ▶ **abbreviation** Students Against Drunk Driving.

sad·den /'sadn/ ▶ **verb** make someone unhappy.

– SYNONYMS **depress,** dispirit, deject, dishearten, grieve, discourage, upset, get down.

sad·dle /'sadl/ ▶ **noun 1** a seat with a raised ridge at the front and back, fastened on the back of a horse for riding. **2** a seat on a bicycle or motorcycle. **3** a low part of a hill or mountain ridge between two higher points. **4** a cut of meat consisting of the two loins. ▶ **verb 1** put a saddle on a horse. **2** (**be saddled with**) be burdened with: *he's saddled with debts of $2 million*.

– SYNONYMS **burden,** encumber, land, impose something on.

– PHRASES **in the saddle 1** on horseback. **2** in a position of control or responsibility.
– ORIGIN Old English.

sad·dle·back /'sadl,bak/ ▶ **noun 1** a hill with a ridge along the top that dips in the middle. **2** a pig of a black breed with a white stripe across the back.

sad·dle·bag /'sadl,bag/ ▶ **noun** a bag attached to a saddle.

sad·dle horse ▶ **noun** a horse kept for riding only.

sad·dler /'sadlər/ ▶ **noun** a person who makes, repairs, or deals in equipment for horses.

sad·dler·y /'sadlərē, -əlrē/ ▶ **noun** (pl. **saddleries**) **1** saddles, bridles, and other equipment for horses. **2** the making or repairing of such equipment. **3** a saddler's premises.

sad·dle soap ▶ **noun** a kind of soft soap used for cleaning leather.

sad·dle·sore /ˈsadlˌsôr/ ▶ **noun** a sore on a horse's back, caused by an ill-fitting saddle. ▶ **adjective** chafed by riding on a saddle.

sad·dle stitch ▶ **noun** **1** a stitch of thread or a wire staple passed through the fold of a magazine or booklet. **2** (in needlework) a decorative stitch made with long stitches on the upper side of the cloth alternated with short stitches on the underside.

Sad·du·cee /ˈsajəˌsē, ˈsadyə-/ ▶ **noun** a member of an ancient Jewish sect that denied the resurrection of the dead and the existence of spirits, and that emphasized acceptance of the written Law rather than oral tradition.
– ORIGIN Hebrew, 'descendant of Zadok' (high priest in the time of kings David and Solomon).

sa·dhu /ˈsädo͞o/ ▶ **noun** Indian a holy man or wise man.
– ORIGIN Sanskrit.

sa·dism /ˈsāˌdizəm/ ▶ **noun** the desire to gain sexual or other pleasure from hurting or humiliating other people.
– DERIVATIVES **sa·dist** noun **sa·dis·tic** /səˈdistik/ adjective **sa·dis·ti·cal·ly** /səˈdistik(ə)lē/ adverb.
– ORIGIN French *sadisme*, from the name of the French writer the Marquis de *Sade*.

sad·ly /ˈsadlē/ ▶ **adverb** **1** in a sad way. **2** it is sad or regrettable that: *sadly, I never spoke to Jenny again.*

sad·ness /ˈsadnis/ ▶ **noun** the state of being sad.

> – SYNONYMS **unhappiness,** sorrow, dejection, depression, misery, despondency, wretchedness, gloom, gloominess, melancholy.

sa·do·mas·o·chism /ˌsādōˈmasəˌkizəm, ˌsadō-/ ▶ **noun** sexual activity or psychological tendency that combines sadism and masochism.
– DERIVATIVES **sa·do·mas·o·chist** noun **sa·do·mas·o·chis·tic** /ˈˌsādōˌmasəˈkistik, ˌsadō-/ adjective.

sad sack ▶ **noun** informal an inept, blundering person.

sa·fa·ri /səˈfärē/ ▶ **noun** (pl. **safaris**) an expedition to observe or hunt animals in their natural habitat.
– ORIGIN Kiswahili.

safe /sāf/ ▶ **adjective** **1** protected from danger or risk. **2** not leading to harm; not risky: *a safe investment providing regular income.* **3** providing security or protection: *keep your valuables in a safe place.* **4** (of a statement, verdict, etc.) based on good reasons or evidence and not likely to be wrong.

> – SYNONYMS **1 secure,** protected, sheltered, guarded, out of harm's way. **2 unharmed,** unhurt, uninjured, unscathed, all right, fine, well, in one piece, out of danger, safe and sound. **3 cautious,** circumspect, prudent, careful, unadventurous, conservative. **4 harmless,** innocuous, nontoxic, nonpoisonous.
> – ANTONYMS dangerous, harmful.

▶ **noun** a strong fireproof cabinet with a complex lock, used for storing valuables.
– DERIVATIVES **safe·ly** adverb.
– PHRASES **safe and sound** with no harm done; uninjured. **to be on the safe side** so as to avoid the risk of something bad happening.
– ORIGIN Old French *sauf.*

safe con·duct ▶ **noun** the official protection of someone from arrest or harm when passing through an area.

safe de·pos·it box (also **safety deposit box**) ▶ **noun** a metal box for valuables in a bank or hotel.

safe·guard /ˈsāfˌgärd/ ▶ **noun** a measure taken to protect or prevent something.

> – SYNONYMS **protection,** defense, buffer, provision, security, cover, insurance.

▶ **verb** protect against something undesirable: *a program to safeguard the future of endangered species.*

> – SYNONYMS **protect,** preserve, conserve, save, secure, shield, guard, keep safe.
> – ANTONYMS jeopardize.

safe house ▶ **noun** a house in a secret location, used by spies or criminals in hiding.

safe·keep·ing /ˈsāfˈkēpiNG/ ▶ **noun** the keeping of something in a safe place.

safe pe·ri·od ▶ **noun** the time during and near a woman's menstrual period when conception is least likely.

safe room ▶ **noun** a room that is safe from attack, from which security operations can be directed.

safe sex (also **safer sex**) ▶ **noun** sexual activity in which people take precautions to protect themselves against sexually transmitted diseases.

safe·ty /ˈsāftē/ ▶ **noun** the condition of being safe: *the survivors were airlifted to safety.*

> – SYNONYMS **1 welfare,** well-being, protection, security. **2 shelter,** sanctuary, refuge.

▶ **adjective** designed to prevent injury or damage: *a safety barrier.*

safe·ty belt ▶ **noun** another term for **SEAT BELT**.

safe·ty catch ▶ **noun** a device that prevents a gun being fired or a machine being operated accidentally.

safe·ty cur·tain ▶ **noun** a fireproof curtain that can be lowered between the stage and the main part of a theater to prevent the spread of fire.

safe·ty glass ▶ **noun** glass that has been toughened or laminated so that it is less likely to splinter when broken.

safe·ty match ▶ **noun** a match that can be lit only by striking it on a special surface, such as that on the side of a matchbox.

safe·ty net ▶ **noun** **1** a net placed to catch an acrobat in case of a fall. **2** a safeguard against hardship or risk: *a safety net of measures to protect vulnerable children.*

safe·ty pin ▶ **noun** a pin with a point that is bent back to the head and is held in a guard when closed.

safe·ty ra·zor ▶ **noun** a razor with a guard to reduce the risk of cutting the skin.

safe·ty valve ▶ **noun** **1** a valve that opens automatically to relieve excessive pressure. **2** a means of releasing feelings of tension or stress in a harmless way.

Saf·fir-Simp·son scale /ˌsafiər ˈsimpsən/ ▶ **noun** a scale used for classifying hurricanes that form in the Atlantic and northern Pacific Oceans east of the International Date Line.

saf·flow·er /ˈsafˌlou(-ə)r/ ▶ **noun** an orange-flowered plant resembling a thistle, with seeds that are used to produce an edible oil.
– ORIGIN from Arabic, 'yellow.'

saf·fron /ˈsafrən/ ▶ **noun** an orange-yellow spice and food coloring made from the dried stigmas of a crocus.
– ORIGIN Arabic.

sag /sag/ ▶ **verb** (**sags, sagging, sagged**) **1** sink downward gradually under weight or pressure. **2** hang down loosely or unevenly. **3** (often as adj. **sagging**) weaken or decline: *the company is trying to boost sagging sales.*

– SYNONYMS **1 sink,** slump, loll, flop, crumple. **2 dip,** droop, bulge, bag.

▶ **noun** an instance of sagging.
– DERIVATIVES **sag·gy** adjective.
– ORIGIN probably related to German *sacken,* Dutch *zakken* 'subside.'

sa·ga /ˈsägə/ ▶ **noun 1** a long story describing heroic adventures, especially a medieval Norse or Icelandic one. **2** a long, involved story or series of incidents.

– SYNONYMS **1 epic,** legend, (folk) tale, romance, narrative, myth. **2 story,** tale, yarn.

– ORIGIN Old Norse, 'narrative.'

sa·ga·cious /səˈgāsHəs/ ▶ **adjective** having or showing good judgment; wise.
– DERIVATIVES **sa·ga·cious·ly** adverb **sa·gac·i·ty** /səˈgasitē/ noun.
– ORIGIN from Latin *sagax* 'wise.'

sage[1] /sāj/ ▶ **noun** a Mediterranean plant with grayish-green leaves that are used as an herb in cooking.
– ORIGIN Latin *salvia* 'healing plant.'

sage[2] ▶ **noun** a very wise man.

– SYNONYMS **wise man,** philosopher, scholar, guru, prophet, mystic.

▶ **adjective** very wise.
– DERIVATIVES **sage·ly** adverb.
– ORIGIN Old French.

sage·brush /ˈsājˌbrəsH/ ▶ **noun 1** a shrubby aromatic North American plant of the daisy family. **2** semi-arid scrub dominated by sagebrush.

Sag·it·tar·i·us /ˌsajiˈte(ə)rēəs/ ▶ **noun 1** a constellation and the ninth sign of the zodiac (the Archer), which the sun enters about November 22. **2** (**a Sagittarius**) a person born when the sun is in this sign.
– DERIVATIVES **Sag·it·ta·ri·an** /-ˈte(ə)rēən/ noun & adjective.
– ORIGIN Latin, 'archer.'

sa·go /ˈsāgō/ ▶ **noun** flour or starchy granules obtained from a palm tree, often cooked with milk to make a pudding.
– ORIGIN Malay.

sa·gua·ro /səˈ(g)wärō/ ▶ **noun** (pl. **saguaros**) a giant cactus whose branches are shaped like a candelabrum, native to Mexico and the southwestern US.
– ORIGIN from Mexican Spanish.

Sa·har·an /səˈharən, -ˈhe(ə)rən, -ˈhärən/ ▶ **adjective** relating to the Sahara Desert in North Africa.

Sa·hel·i·an /səˈhālēən, -ˈhēlēən, -ˈhelēən/ ▶ **adjective** relating to the Sahel, a semiarid region bordering the southern Sahara Desert in North Africa.

sa·hib /ˈsä(h)ib/ ▶ **noun** Indian a polite way of addressing a man.
– OR IGIN Arabic, 'friend, lord.'

said /sed/ past and past participle of **SAY** ▶ **adjective** referring to someone or something already mentioned: *the said agreement.*

sail /sāl/ ▶ **noun 1** a piece of material spread on a mast to catch the wind and propel a boat or ship. **2** a trip in a sailboat or ship. **3** a wind-catching structure attached to the arm of a windmill. ▶ **verb 1** travel in a sailboat as a sport or pastime. **2** travel in any ship or boat. **3** begin a voyage. **4** navigate or control a boat or ship. **5** move smoothly or confidently: *she sailed into the room.* **6** (**sail through**) informal achieve something easily.

– SYNONYMS **1 voyage,** travel, navigate, cruise. **2 set sail,** put to sea, leave, weigh anchor. **3 steer,** pilot, captain; informal skipper. **4 glide,** drift, float, flow, sweep, skim, coast, flit, scud.

– PHRASES **sail close to the wind 1** behave or operate in a risky way. **2** sail as nearly against the wind as possible. **under sail** with the sails hoisted.
– ORIGIN Old English.

sail·board /ˈsālˌbôrd/ ▶ **noun** a board with a mast and a sail, used in windsurfing.
– DERIVATIVES **sail·board·er** noun **sail·board·ing** noun.

sail·boat /ˈsālˌbōt/ (Brit. **sailing boat**) ▶ **noun** a boat propelled by sails.

sail·cloth /ˈsālˌklôTH, -ˌkläTH/ ▶ **noun 1** canvas or other strong fabric used for making sails. **2** a similar strong fabric used for making clothes.

sail·fish /ˈsālˌfisH/ ▶ **noun** (pl. same or **sailfishes**) an edible marine fish with a high sail-like fin on its back.

sail·or /ˈsālər/ ▶ **noun 1** a person who works as a member of the crew of a ship or boat. **2** a person who sails as a sport or pastime. **3** (**a good/bad sailor**) a person who rarely (or often) becomes seasick.

– SYNONYMS **seaman,** seafarer, mariner, yachtsman, yachtswoman, hand; informal old salt, tar.

sail·or suit ▶ **noun** a boy's blue and white suit resembling the traditional uniform of a sailor.

sail·plane /ˈsālˌplān/ ▶ **noun** a glider designed to fly for long distances.

saint /sānt/ ▶ **noun 1** a very good or holy person who Christians believe will go to heaven after they die. **2** a very good or holy person who is officially declared to be a saint by the Christian Church after they die. **3** informal a very kind or patient person.
– DERIVATIVES **saint·hood** /-ˌho͝od/ noun.
– ORIGIN from Latin *sanctus* 'holy.'

St. Ber·nard ▶ **noun** a breed of very large dog originally kept to rescue travelers by the monks of the hospice on the Great St. Bernard, a pass across the Alps.

saint·ed /ˈsāntid/ ▶ **adjective** very good or kind, like a saint.

St. El·mo's fire /ˈelmōz/ ▶ **noun** a luminous electrical discharge sometimes seen on a ship or aircraft during a storm.
– ORIGIN regarded as a sign of protection given by *St. Elmo,* the patron saint of sailors.

St. John's wort ▶ **noun** an herbaceous plant or shrub with yellow flowers.
– ORIGIN because some species come into flower near the feast day of St. John the Baptist (24 June).

saint·ly /ˈsāntlē/ ▶ **adjective** very holy or good.

– SYNONYMS **holy,** godly, pious, religious, devout, spiritual, virtuous, righteous, good, pure.
– ANTONYMS ungodly.

– DERIVATIVES **saint·li·ness** noun.

St. Vi·tus's dance /ˈvītəsiz/ ▶ **noun** old-fashioned term for **SYDENHAM'S CHOREA**.
– ORIGIN because a visit to the shrine of *St. Vitus* was believed to alleviate the disease.

saith /seTH, ˈsāiTH/ old-fashioned third person singular present of **SAY**.

sake[1] /sāk/ ▶ noun **(for the sake of) 1** so as to achieve (something); in the interest of: *they moved to the coast for the sake of her health.* **2** out of consideration for or to help (someone).

– SYNONYMS **1** *for the sake of clarity* **purpose(s),** reason(s). **2** *for her son's sake* **benefit,** advantage, good, well-being, welfare.

– PHRASES **for old times' sake** in memory of former times. **for God's/goodness sake** expressing impatience or desperation.
– ORIGIN Old English, 'contention, crime.'

sa·ke[2] /ˈsäkē/ ▶ noun a Japanese alcoholic drink made from fermented rice.
– ORIGIN Japanese.

sa·laam /səˈläm/ ▶ noun a gesture of greeting or respect in Arabic-speaking and Muslim countries, consisting of a low bow with the hand or fingers touching the forehead. ▶ verb make a gesture of salaam.
– ORIGIN from Arabic, 'peace be upon you.'

sal·a·ble /ˈsāləbəl/ ▶ adjective variant spelling of **SALEABLE.**

sa·la·cious /səˈlāsʜəs/ ▶ adjective having or showing too much interest in sexual matters.
– DERIVATIVES **sa·la·cious·ly** adverb.
– ORIGIN from Latin *salax.*

sal·ad /ˈsaləd/ ▶ noun a cold dish of mixed raw vegetables.
– PHRASES **one's salad days** the period when one is young and inexperienced. [from Shakespeare's *Antony and Cleopatra.*]
– ORIGIN Old French *salade.*

sal·ad dress·ing ▶ noun see **DRESSING** (sense 1).

sa·lade ni·çoise /səˈläd nēˈswäz/ ▶ noun (pl. **salades niçoises** pronunc. same) a salad made typically from hard-boiled eggs, tuna, black olives, and tomatoes.
– ORIGIN French, 'salad from Nice.'

sal·a·man·der /ˈsaləˌmandər/ ▶ noun **1** a long-tailed amphibian resembling a newt, typically with bright markings. **2** a mythical lizardlike creature said to live in fire.
– ORIGIN Greek *salamandra.*

sa·la·mi /səˈlämē/ ▶ noun (pl. same or **salamis**) a type of spicy preserved sausage.
– ORIGIN Italian.

sal·a·ried /ˈsalərēd/ ▶ adjective earning or offering a salary: *a salaried job.*

sal·a·ry /ˈsalərē/ ▶ noun (pl. **salaries**) a fixed regular payment made by an employer to an employee, especially a professional or white-collar worker.

– SYNONYMS **pay,** wages, earnings, payment, remuneration, fee(s), stipend, income.

– ORIGIN Latin *salarium,* first meaning a Roman soldier's allowance to buy salt.

sale /sāl/ ▶ noun **1** the exchange of something for money: *cars for sale at reasonable prices.* **2 (sales)** the activity or profession of selling. **3** a period in which goods are sold at reduced prices. **4** a public event at which goods are sold or auctioned.

– SYNONYMS **1 selling,** dealing, trading. **2 deal,** transaction, bargain.
– ANTONYMS purchase.

– ORIGIN Old English.

sale·a·ble /ˈsāləbəl/ (also **salable**) ▶ adjective fit or able to be sold.
– DERIVATIVES **sale·a·bil·i·ty** /ˌsāləˈbilitē/ noun.

sales·clerk ▶ noun a store assistant.

sales·girl /ˈsālzˌgərl/ ▶ noun a female store assistant.

sales·man /ˈsālzmən/ (or **saleswoman** /ˈsālzˌwo͝omən/) ▶ noun (pl. **salesmen** or **saleswomen**) a person whose job involves selling or promoting goods.
– DERIVATIVES **sales·man·ship** /-ˌsʜip/ noun.

sales·per·son /ˈsālzˌpərsən/ ▶ noun (pl. **salespeople** /-ˌpēpəl/ or **salespersons**) a salesman or saleswoman.

sales·room /ˈsālzˌro͞om, -ˌro͝om/ ▶ noun a room in which auctions are held.

sales tax ▶ noun a tax on sales or on the receipts from sales.

sal·i·cyl·ic ac·id /ˌsaləˈsilik/ ▶ noun a bitter substance present in certain plants, used in making aspirin and dyes.
– ORIGIN from Latin *salix* 'willow' (because originally derived from willow bark).

sa·li·ent /ˈsālyənt, -lēənt/ ▶ adjective **1** most important: *the salient points of the case.* **2** (of an angle) pointing outward. The opposite of **RE-ENTRANT.** ▶ noun **1** a piece of land or section of fortification that juts out to form an angle. **2** an outward bulge in a military line.
– DERIVATIVES **sa·li·ence** noun **sa·li·en·cy** noun.
– ORIGIN from Latin *salire* 'to leap.'

sa·line /ˈsāˌlēn, -ˌlīn/ ▶ adjective **1** containing salt. **2** chiefly Medicine (of a solution) containing sodium chloride and/or other salts, especially in the same concentration as in the body. ▶ noun a saline solution.
– DERIVATIVES **sa·lin·i·ty** /səˈlinitē/ noun **sal·i·ni·za·tion** /ˌsalənəˈzāsʜən/ noun.
– ORIGIN from Latin *sal* 'salt.'

Sa·lish /ˈsālisʜ/ ▶ noun (pl. same) a member of a group of American Indian peoples of the northwestern US and the west coast of Canada.
– DERIVATIVES **Sa·lish·an** /-ən/ adjective.
– ORIGIN a local name, literally 'Flatheads.'

sa·li·va /səˈlīvə/ ▶ noun a watery liquid produced by glands in the mouth, helping chewing, swallowing, and digestion.
– DERIVATIVES **sal·i·var·y** /ˈsaləˌverē/ adjective.
– ORIGIN Latin.

sal·i·vate /ˈsaləˌvāt/ ▶ verb **1** produce saliva. **2** show great delight at the sight or prospect of something: *companies are salivating over the promise of the new technology.*
– DERIVATIVES **sal·i·va·tion** /ˌsaləˈvāsʜən/ noun.
– ORIGIN Latin *salivare.*

sal·low /ˈsalō/ ▶ adjective (of a person's face or complexion) yellowish or pale brown in color.
– ORIGIN Old English, 'dusky.'

sal·ly /ˈsalē/ ▶ noun (pl. **sallies**) **1** a sudden charge out of a place surrounded by an enemy. **2** a witty or lively reply. ▶ verb **(sallies, sallying, sallied)** set out: *they sallied forth to battle with disease.*
– ORIGIN French *saillie.*

salm·on /ˈsamən/ ▶ noun (pl. same or **salmons**) a large fish with edible pink flesh, that matures in the sea and migrates to freshwater streams to spawn.
– ORIGIN Latin *salmo.*

sal·mo·nel·la /ˌsalməˈnelə/ ▶ noun **1** a bacterium that occurs mainly in the gut and can cause food poisoning. **2** food poisoning caused by this bacterium.

– ORIGIN named after the American veterinary surgeon Daniel E. *Salmon*.

salm·on pink ▶ **noun** a pale orange-pink color.

sa·lon /sə'län, sa'lôɴ/ ▶ **noun 1** a place where a hairdresser, beautician, or fashion designer carries out their work. **2** a reception room in a large house. **3** chiefly historical a regular gathering of writers, artists, etc., held in a fashionable household.
– ORIGIN French.

sa·loon /sə'lo͞on/ ▶ **noun 1** dated a bar, especially one associated with the American West of the 19th century. **2** a large public lounge on a ship.
– ORIGIN French *salon*.

sa·lo·pettes /ˌsalə'pets/ ▶ **plural noun** padded pants with a high waist and shoulder straps, worn for skiing.
– ORIGIN French *salopette*.

sal·sa /'sälsə/ ▶ **noun 1** a type of Latin American dance music incorporating elements of jazz and rock. **2** a dance performed to this music. **3** a spicy tomato condiment or dip.
– ORIGIN Spanish, 'sauce.'

sal·si·fy /'salsəfē, -ˌfī/ ▶ **noun** a plant with a long edible root like that of a parsnip.
– ORIGIN French *salsifis*.

SALT /sôlt/ ▶ **abbreviation** Strategic Arms Limitation Talks.

salt /sôlt/ ▶ **noun 1** (also **common salt** or **table salt**) sodium chloride, a white substance in the form of crystals used for seasoning or preserving food. **2** any chemical compound formed by the reaction of an acid with a base, with the hydrogen of the acid replaced by a metal or equivalent group. ▶ **adjective** containing or treated with salt: *salt water*. ▶ **verb 1** season or preserve something with salt. **2** sprinkle a road or path with salt to melt snow or ice. **3** (**salt something away**) informal secretly put money away for future use.
– DERIVATIVES **salt·less** adjective **salt·ness** noun.
– PHRASES **rub salt into the wound** make a painful experience even more distressing. **the salt of the earth** a very kind, honest, or reliable person. [with reference to the Gospel of Matthew, chapter 5.] **take something with a grain of salt** be aware that something may be exaggerated. **worth one's salt** good or competent at one's job.
– ORIGIN Old English.

salt-and-pep·per ▶ **adjective** speckled with a mixture of dark and light shades.

salt·box /'sôltˌbäks/ ▶ **noun** a style of house with two or three stories in the front and one fewer in the back, with a deeply pitched roof.

salt·bush /'sôltˌbo͝osн/ ▶ **noun** a salt-tolerant plant, sometimes planted on saline soils to provide grazing.

salt·cel·lar /'sôltˌselər/ (also **salt cellar**) ▶ **noun 1** a dish or other container for serving or storing salt. **2** a salt shaker.
– ORIGIN *cellar* is from Old French *salier* 'salt box.'

salt flats ▶ **plural noun** areas of flat land covered with a layer of salt.

sal·tire /'salˌtīr, 'sôl-/ ▶ **noun** Heraldry an X-shaped cross.
– ORIGIN Old French *saultoir* 'stirrup cord, stile, saltire.'

salt lick ▶ **noun 1** a place where animals go to lick salt from the ground. **2** a block of salt provided for animals to lick.

salt marsh ▶ **noun** an area of coastal grassland that is regularly flooded by seawater.

salt pan ▶ **noun** a shallow container or hollow in the ground in which salt water evaporates to leave a deposit of salt.

salt·pe·ter /sôlt'pētər/ (Brit. **saltpetre**) ▶ **noun** potassium nitrate or (**Chile saltpeter**) sodium nitrate.
– ORIGIN Latin *salpetra*.

salt shak·er ▶ **noun** a container with a perforated lid for sprinkling salt.

salt·wa·ter /'sôltˌwôtər, -ˌwätər/ ▶ **adjective** relating to or found in salt water; living in the sea.

salt·y /'sôltē/ ▶ **adjective** (**saltier, saltiest**) **1** tasting of or containing salt. **2** (of language or humor) racy or coarse: *recounting salty anecdotes*.

– SYNONYMS **salt,** salted, saline, briny, brackish.

– DERIVATIVES **salt·i·ly** adverb **salt·i·ness** noun.

sa·lu·bri·ous /sə'lo͞obrēəs/ ▶ **adjective 1** good for the health; healthy. **2** (of a place) clean, well kept and pleasant.

– SYNONYMS **pleasant,** agreeable, nice, select, high-class, upscale, upmarket; informal posh, classy, swish.

– DERIVATIVES **sa·lu·bri·ous·ly** adverb **sa·lu·bri·ty** /-britē/ noun.
– ORIGIN from Latin *salus* 'health.'

sa·lu·ki /sə'lo͞okē/ ▶ **noun** (pl. **salukis**) a tall, slender breed of dog with a silky coat and large drooping ears.
– ORIGIN Arabic.

sal·u·tar·y /'salyəˌterē/ ▶ **adjective 1** (of something unpleasant) beneficial because providing an opportunity to learn from experience: *the cut and thrust over pricing proved a salutary experience for the company*. **2** dated health-giving.
– ORIGIN from Latin *salus* 'health.'

sal·u·ta·tion /ˌsalyə'tāsнən/ ▶ **noun** formal a greeting.

sa·lute /sə'lo͞ot/ ▶ **noun 1** a gesture of respect or acknowledgment. **2** a movement, typically a raising of a hand to the head, made as a formal gesture of respect by a member of a military or similar force. **3** the firing of a gun or guns as a formal or ceremonial sign of respect or celebration.

– SYNONYMS **tribute,** testimonial, homage, honor, celebration (of), acknowledgment (of).

▶ **verb 1** make a formal salute to a member of a military or similar force. **2** greet someone with a gesture. **3** express admiration and respect for: *we salute his genius*.

– SYNONYMS **pay tribute to,** pay homage to, honor, celebrate, acknowledge, take one's hat off to.

– ORIGIN from Latin *salutare* 'greet, pay one's respects to.'

Sal·va·dor·ean /ˌsalvə'dôrēən/ ▶ **noun** a person from El Salvador, a country in Central America. ▶ **adjective** relating to El Salvador.

sal·vage /'salvij/ ▶ **verb 1** rescue a ship or its cargo from loss at sea. **2** save from possible loss, harm, or failure: *his latest stunt will do nothing to salvage his reputation*.

– SYNONYMS **rescue,** save, recover, retrieve, reclaim.

▶ **noun 1** the rescue of a ship or its cargo from loss at sea. **2** cargo, property, or other items that have been saved from loss or harm. **3** Law payment made or due to a person who has salvaged a ship or its cargo.
– DERIVATIVES **sal·vage·a·ble** adjective **sal·vag·er** noun.
– ORIGIN from Latin *salvare* 'to save.'

sal·va·tion /sal'vāsнən/ ▶ **noun 1** the saving or protection of someone or something from harm or ruin. **2** (**one's salvation**) a means of being saved from harm or ruin: *his only salvation was to outwit the enemy.* **3** (in Christian belief) deliverance from sin and its consequences, believed to be brought about by faith in Jesus.

– SYNONYMS **1 lifeline,** means of escape, savior. **2 redemption,** deliverance.
– ANTONYMS damnation, ruin.

– ORIGIN from Latin *salvare* 'to save.'

sal·va·tion·ist /sal'vāsHənist/ ▶ **noun** (**Salvationist**) a member of the Salvation Army, a Christian evangelical organization. ▶ **adjective 1** relating to salvation in Christian belief. **2** (**Salvationist**) relating to the Salvation Army.

salve /sav, säv/ ▶ **noun 1** an ointment used to help the skin to heal. **2** something that helps to reduce distress, guilt, etc.: *shopping is the perfect salve for my wounded ego.* ▶ **verb** do something to feel less guilty: *charity salves our conscience.*
– ORIGIN Old English.

sal·ver /'salvər/ ▶ **noun** a tray, typically one made of silver and used on formal occasions.
– ORIGIN French *salve* 'tray for presenting food to the king.'

sal·vi·a /'salvēə/ ▶ **noun** a plant of a large group that includes sage, especially one grown for its bright scarlet flowers.
– ORIGIN Latin, 'sage.'

sal·vo /'sal,vō/ ▶ **noun** (pl. **salvos** or **salvoes**) **1** a simultaneous firing of artillery or other guns in a battle. **2** a sudden vigorous or aggressive series of acts: *a salvo of accusations.*
– ORIGIN Italian *salva* 'salutation.'

sal vo·la·ti·le /,sal və'latl-ē/ ▶ **noun** a scented solution of ammonium carbonate in alcohol, used as smelling salts.
– ORIGIN Latin, 'volatile salt.'

SAM /sam/ ▶ **abbreviation** surface-to-air missile.

Sa·mar·i·tan /sə'maritn, -'me(ə)r-/ ▶ **noun 1** (**good Samaritan**) a charitable or helpful person. **2** a member of a people inhabiting Samaria, an ancient city and region of Palestine, in biblical times.
– ORIGIN sense 1 is with reference to the story of the man from ancient Samaria who helped a man in need whom others had passed by, in the Gospel of Luke.

sa·mar·i·um /sə'me(ə)rēəm/ ▶ **noun** a hard silvery-white metallic chemical element of the lanthanide series.
– ORIGIN named after a Russian official called *Samarsky.*

sam·ba /'sambə, 'säm-/ ▶ **noun** a Brazilian dance of African origin. ▶ **verb** (**sambas, sambaing** /-bə,iNG/, **sambaed** /-bəd/) dance the samba.
– ORIGIN Portuguese.

sam·bal /'sämbäl/ ▶ **noun** (in oriental cooking) a spicy vegetable or fruit relish.
– ORIGIN Malay.

sam·bu·ca /sam'bo͞okə/ ▶ **noun** an Italian anise-flavored liqueur.
– ORIGIN Italian.

same /sām/ ▶ **adjective 1** (**the same**) exactly alike; not different or changed. **2** (**this/that same**) referring to a person or thing just mentioned: *that same year I went to Boston.*

– SYNONYMS **1** (**the same**) *we stayed at the same hotel* **identical,** selfsame, very same. **2** (**the same**) *they had the same symptoms* **matching,** identical, alike, carbon-copy, twin, indistinguishable, interchangeable, corresponding, equivalent, parallel, like, comparable, similar, homogeneous. **3** (**the same**) *they provide the same menu worldwide* **unchanging,** unvarying, unvaried, consistent, uniform.
– ANTONYMS another, different.

▶ **pronoun** (**the same**) **1** the same thing as previously mentioned. **2** identical people or things.
▶ **adverb** in the same way.
– DERIVATIVES **same·ness** noun.
– PHRASES **all** (or **just**) **the same** in spite of this; even so.
– ORIGIN Old Norse.

WORD TOOLKIT

See **IDENTICAL**.

Sa·mi /'sāmē/ ▶ **plural noun** the people of Lapland in northern Scandinavia.
– ORIGIN Lappish (the language of the Lapps).

USAGE

Sami is the term by which the Lapps themselves prefer to be known.

sam·ite /'samīt, 'sā-/ ▶ **noun** historical a rich silk fabric interwoven with gold and silver threads.
– ORIGIN Old French *samit.*

sam·iz·dat /'sämiz,dät, səmyiz'dät/ ▶ **noun** (especially in the former Soviet Union) the secret copying and distribution of literature banned by the government.
– ORIGIN Russian, 'self-publishing house.'

Sa·mo·an /sə'mōən/ ▶ **noun 1** a person from Samoa. **2** the Polynesian language of Samoa. ▶ **adjective** relating to Samoa.

sa·mo·sa /sə'mōsə/ ▶ **noun** a triangular fried Indian pastry containing spiced vegetables or meat.
– ORIGIN Persian and Urdu.

sam·o·var /'samə,vär/ ▶ **noun** a decorated Russian urn used to heat water for tea.
– ORIGIN Russian, 'self-boiler.'

Sam·o·yed /'samə,yed, sə'moiyid/ ▶ **noun 1** a white Arctic breed of dog. **2** a member of a group of mainly nomadic peoples of northern Siberia.
– ORIGIN Russian *samoed.*

sam·pan /'sam,pan/ ▶ **noun** a small boat propelled with an oar at the stern, used in the Far East.
– ORIGIN from Chinese words meaning 'three' and 'board.'

sam·phire /'sam,fīr/ ▶ **noun** an edible fleshy-leaved plant that grows on rocks near the sea.
– ORIGIN from French *herbe de Saint Pierre* 'St. Peter's herb.'

sam·ple /'sampəl/ ▶ **noun 1** a small part or quantity intended to show what the whole is like. **2** a specimen of a substance taken for scientific testing or analysis. **3** a sound created by sampling.

– SYNONYMS **1 specimen,** example, snippet, swatch, taste. **2 cross section,** sampling, selection.

▶ **verb 1** take a sample or samples of something. **2** experience something briefly to see what it is like: *we finally got a chance to sample the New Orleans nightlife.* **3** (often as n. **sampling**) record or extract a small piece of music or sound digitally for use in a different piece of music.

– SYNONYMS **try (out),** taste, test, put to the test, appraise, evaluate; informal check out.

– ORIGIN Old French *essample* 'example.'

sam·pler /'samplər/ ▶ **noun 1** a piece of embroidery worked in various stitches to demonstrate a person's skill. **2** a representative collection or example of something. **3** an electronic device for sampling music and sound.

sam·u·rai /'samə,rī/ ▶ **noun** (pl. same) historical a member of a military class in Japan.
– ORIGIN Japanese.

San /sän/ ▶ **noun** (pl. same) **1** a member of the Bushmen (a number of aboriginal peoples) of southern Africa. **2** the languages spoken by the San.
– ORIGIN Nama, 'aboriginals, settlers.'

san·a·to·ri·um /,sanə'tôrēəm/ ▶ **noun** (pl. **sanatoriums** or **sanatoria** /-rēə/) another term for **SANITARIUM**.
– ORIGIN Latin.

San·cerre /säN'ser/ ▶ **noun** a light white wine produced in Sancerre, in the Loire region of France.

sanc·ti·fy /'saNG(k)tə,fī/ ▶ **verb** (**sanctifies, sanctifying, sanctified**) **1** make or declare something holy; consecrate. **2** make official or binding by a religious ceremony: *their love is sanctified by the sacrament of marriage*. **3** free someone or something from sin.
– DERIVATIVES **sanc·ti·fi·ca·tion** /-fi'kāSHən/ noun.
– ORIGIN Latin *sanctificare*.

sanc·ti·mo·ni·ous /,saNG(k)tə'mōnēəs/ ▶ **adjective** derogatory making a show of being morally better than other people.

– SYNONYMS **self-righteous,** holier-than-thou, pious, moralizing, smug, superior, priggish, hypocritical, insincere; informal goody-goody.

– DERIVATIVES **sanc·ti·mo·ni·ous·ly** adverb **sanc·ti·mo·ni·ous·ness** noun **sanc·ti·mo·ny** /'saNG(k)tə,mōnē/ noun.
– ORIGIN from Latin *sanctimonia* 'sanctity.'

sanc·tion /'saNG(k)SHən/ ▶ **noun 1** a threatened penalty or punishment for disobeying a law or rule. **2** (**sanctions**) measures taken by a country to try to force another to do or obey something. **3** official permission or approval.

– SYNONYMS **1 penalty,** punishment, deterrent, restriction, embargo, ban, prohibition, boycott. **2 authorization,** consent, leave, permission, authority, dispensation, assent, acquiescence, agreement, approval, endorsement, blessing; informal the thumbs up, the OK, the green light.
– ANTONYMS prohibition.

▶ **verb 1** give official permission for: *the scheme was sanctioned by the court*. **2** impose a penalty on someone or something.

– SYNONYMS **authorize,** permit, allow, endorse, approve, accept, back, support; informal OK.
– ANTONYMS prohibit.

– DERIVATIVES **sanc·tion·a·ble** adjective.
– ORIGIN from Latin *sancire* 'ratify.'

sanc·ti·ty /'saNG(k)titē/ ▶ **noun 1** the state or quality of being holy. **2** the state of being highly valued and worthy of great respect: *the sanctity of human life*.
– ORIGIN from Latin *sanctus* 'holy.'

sanc·tu·ar·y /'saNG(k)CHōō,erē/ ▶ **noun** (pl. **sanctuaries**) **1** a place or state of safety or protection: *they fled abroad, where they were offered sanctuary*. **2** a nature reserve. **3** a place where injured or unwanted animals are cared for. **4** a holy place. **5** the part of the chancel of a church containing the high altar.

– SYNONYMS **1 refuge,** haven, oasis, shelter, retreat, hideaway. **2 safety,** protection, shelter, immunity, asylum. **3 reserve,** wildlife reserve, park.

– ORIGIN Latin *sanctuarium*.

sanc·tum /'saNG(k)təm/ ▶ **noun** (pl. **sanctums**) **1** a sacred or holy place. **2** a room to which a person can go for privacy and quiet: *the inner sanctum of the library*.
– ORIGIN Latin.

Sanc·tus /'saNG(k)təs/ ▶ **noun** (in the Christian Church) a hymn beginning *Sanctus, sanctus, sanctus* (Holy, holy, holy) forming a set part of the Mass.
– ORIGIN Latin.

sand /sand/ ▶ **noun 1** a substance consisting of very fine particles resulting from the erosion of rocks, found on beaches, riverbeds, the seabed, and deserts. **2** (**sands**) a wide area of sand. ▶ **verb 1** smooth something with sandpaper or a sander. **2** sprinkle something with sand.
– ORIGIN Old English.

san·dal /'sandl/ ▶ **noun** a shoe with a partly open upper or straps attaching the sole to the foot.
– DERIVATIVES **san·daled** adjective.
– ORIGIN Greek *sandalon* 'wooden shoe.'

san·dal·wood /'sandl,wōōd/ ▶ **noun** the sweet-smelling wood of an Indian or SE Asian tree.
– ORIGIN *sandal* from Latin *sandalum*.

sand·bag /'san(d),bag/ ▶ **noun** a bag of sand, used for protection against floods or explosions. ▶ **verb** (**sandbags, sandbagging, sandbagged**) **1** protect or reinforce something with sandbags. **2** informal cause severe harm or damage to: *they saw their marriage sandbagged by problems*.
– DERIVATIVES **sand·bag·ger** noun.

sand·bank /'san(d),baNGk/ ▶ **noun** a buildup of sand forming a raised bank in the sea or a river.

sand·bar /'san(d),bär/ ▶ **noun** a long, narrow sandbank.

sand·blast /'san(d),blast/ ▶ **verb** roughen or clean something with a jet of sand driven by compressed air or steam.
– DERIVATIVES **sand·blast·er** noun.

sand·board /'san(d),bôrd/ ▶ **noun** a long, narrow board, often a modified snowboard, used for sliding down sand dunes.
– DERIVATIVES **sand·board·er** noun **sand·board·ing** noun.

sand·box /'san(d),bäks/ ▶ **noun** a shallow box or hollow containing sand for children to play in.

sand·cas·tle /'san(d),kasəl/ ▶ **noun** a model of a castle built out of sand.

sand·er /'sandər/ ▶ **noun** a power tool used for smoothing a surface.

sand·er·ling /'sandərliNG/ ▶ **noun** a small sandpiper, typically seen running after waves on the beach.
– ORIGIN unknown.

sand·fly /'san(d),flī/ ▶ **noun** (pl. **sandflies**) a small biting fly of tropical and subtropical regions that transmits a number of diseases.

San·di·nis·ta /,sandə'nēstə/ ▶ **noun** a member of a left-wing Nicaraguan political organization, in power from 1979 until 1990.
– ORIGIN named after a similar organization founded by the nationalist leader Augusto César *Sandino*.

sand·man /ˈsan(d)ˌman/ ▸ **noun** (**the sandman**) (in stories) a man supposed to make children sleep by sprinkling sand in their eyes.

sand mar·tin ▸ **noun** a small swallow with dark brown and white plumage, which digs nest holes in sandy banks near water.

sand·pa·per /ˈsan(d)ˌpāpər/ ▸ **noun** paper with sand or another rough substance stuck to it, used for smoothing surfaces. ▸ **verb** smooth something with sandpaper.
– DERIVATIVES **sand·pa·per·y** adjective.

sand·pi·per /ˈsan(d)ˌpīpər/ ▸ **noun** a wading bird with a long bill and long legs, found in coastal areas.

sand·pit /ˈsan(d)ˌpit/ ▸ **noun** a quarry from which sand is excavated.

sand·stone /ˈsan(d)ˌstōn/ ▸ **noun** red, yellow, or brown rock consisting of sand or quartz grains cemented together.

sand·storm /ˈsan(d)ˌstôrm/ ▸ **noun** a strong wind in a desert carrying clouds of sand.

sand·wich /ˈsan(d)wicн/ ▸ **noun** two pieces of bread with a filling between them. ▸ **verb 1** place in a restricted space between two other people or things: *the house was sandwiched between a store and a clinic.* **2** (**sandwich things together**) squeeze two things together.
– ORIGIN named after the English nobleman the 4th Earl of *Sandwich*, said to have eaten sandwiches so as to stay at the gambling table.

sand·wich board ▸ **noun** a pair of advertisement boards connected by straps by which they are hung over a person's shoulders.

sand·y /ˈsandē/ ▸ **adjective** (**sandier**, **sandiest**) **1** covered in or consisting of sand. **2** light yellowish brown.

sane /sān/ ▸ **adjective 1** having a normal mind; not mad. **2** reasonable or sensible: *a sane discussion of important issues.*

> – SYNONYMS **1 of sound mind,** in one's right mind, compos mentis, lucid, rational, balanced, normal; informal all there. **2 sensible,** practical, realistic, prudent, reasonable, rational, levelheaded, commonsensical.
> – ANTONYMS mad, foolish.

– DERIVATIVES **sane·ly** adverb.
– ORIGIN Latin *sanus* 'healthy.'

sang /sanɢ/ past of **SING**.

sang·froid /sängˈfrwä/ ▸ **noun** the ability to stay calm in difficult circumstances.
– ORIGIN French, 'cold blood.'

San·gio·vese /ˌsanjōˈvāzē/ ▸ **noun** an Italian red wine made from a variety of black wine grape.
– ORIGIN Italian.

san·gri·a /sanɢˈgrēə/ ▸ **noun** a Spanish drink of red wine, lemonade, fruit, and spices.
– ORIGIN Spanish, 'bleeding.'

san·gui·nar·y /ˈsanɢgwəˌnerē/ ▸ **adjective** chiefly literary involving or causing much bloodshed.

san·guine /ˈsanɢgwin/ ▸ **adjective 1** cheerfully confident about the future. **2** (in medieval medicine) having a predominance of blood among the bodily humors, supposedly marked by a ruddy complexion and an optimistic disposition.

> – SYNONYMS **optimistic,** hopeful, buoyant, positive, confident, cheerful, bullish; informal upbeat.
> – ANTONYMS gloomy.

– ORIGIN from Latin *sanguis* 'blood.'

> **WORD TOOLKIT**
>
> See **CONFIDENT**.

San·hed·rin /sanˈhedrən, -ˈhēdrin, sän- / ▸ **noun** the highest court of justice and the supreme council in ancient Jerusalem.
– ORIGIN Hebrew.

san·i·tar·i·um /ˌsaniˈte(ə)rēəm/ ▸ **noun** (pl. **sanitariums** or **sanitaria** /-ˈte(ə)rēə/) a place for the care of people who are recovering from an illness or who are chronically ill.

san·i·tar·y /ˈsaniˌterē/ ▸ **adjective 1** relating to sanitation: *a sanitary engineer.* **2** hygienic and clean. **3** referring to sanitary napkins and tampons.
– ORIGIN from Latin *sanitas* 'health.'

> **CHOOSE THE RIGHT WORD**
>
> **sanitary, antiseptic, healthful, hygienic, salubrious, sterile**
>
> Americans thrive on cleanliness and the eradication of germs. They try to keep their homes **sanitary**, a term that goes beyond cleanliness to imply that measures have been taken to guard against infections or disease. They demand that their communities provide schools and workplaces that are **hygienic**—in other words, that adhere to the rules or standards promoting public health. But it would be almost impossible to duplicate the conditions found in a hospital, where everything that comes in contact with patients must be **sterile** or free of germs entirely. Most Americans want to make their environment **healthful**, which means conducive to the health or soundness of the body, but they are not interested in making it **antiseptic**, a word that is similar in meaning to *sterile* but implies preventing infections by destroying germs that are already present (*an antiseptic solution*). Many Americans, as they grow older, choose to move to a more **salubrious** climate, a word that means health-giving and applies primarily to an air quality that is invigorating and that avoids harsh extremes.

san·i·tary nap·kin (Brit. **sanitary towel**) ▸ **noun** a pad worn by women to absorb blood during a menstrual period.

san·i·ta·tion /ˌsaniˈtāsнən/ ▸ **noun** arrangements to protect public health, especially the provision of clean drinking water and the disposal of sewage.

san·i·tize /ˈsaniˌtīz/ ▸ **verb 1** make something hygienic. **2** (often as adj. **sanitized**) derogatory make more acceptable by removing inappropriate or unpleasant material: *sanitized versions of raunchy CDs.*
– DERIVATIVES **san·i·tiz·er** noun.

san·i·ty /ˈsanitē/ ▸ **noun 1** the condition of being mentally healthy. **2** reasonable and rational behavior.

> – SYNONYMS **1 mental health,** reason, rationality, stability, lucidity, sense, wits, mind. **2 sense,** good sense, common sense, wisdom, prudence, rationality.

sank /sanɢk/ past of **SINK**[1].

sans /sanz/ ▸ **preposition** literary without: *she plays her role sans accent.*
– ORIGIN Old French *sanz*.

sans-cu·lotte /ˌsanz k(y)o͝oˈlät/ ▸ **noun** an extreme republican or revolutionary.
– ORIGIN French, 'without knee breeches' (first referring to a lower-class Parisian republican in the French Revolution).

san·sei /'sänsā/ ▶ **noun** (pl. same) a person born in the US or Canada whose grandparents were immigrants from Japan. Compare with **NISEI** and **ISSEI**.

San·skrit /'san,skrit/ ▶ **noun** an ancient language of India, still used as a language of religion and scholarship.
– ORIGIN from Sanskrit, 'composed, elaborated.'

sans ser·if /,san(z) 'serəf/ ▶ **noun** a style of type without serifs (small projections on the letters).

San·ta Claus /'santə ,klôz/ (also informal **Santa**) ▶ **noun** an imaginary figure said to bring presents for children at Christmas.
– ORIGIN Dutch *Sante Klaas* 'St. Nicholas.'

sap¹ /sap/ ▶ **noun** the fluid that circulates in plants, consisting chiefly of water with nutrients.

– SYNONYMS **juice**, secretion, fluid, liquid.

▶ **verb** (**saps, sapping, sapped**) **1** gradually weaken a person's strength or power. **2** (**sap someone of**) drain someone of strength or power: *they were sapped of stamina and their self-belief.*

– SYNONYMS **erode**, wear away/down, deplete, reduce, lessen, undermine, drain, bleed.

– ORIGIN Old English.

sap² ▶ **noun** historical a tunnel or trench dug to conceal the approach of an attacker to a fortified place.
– ORIGIN from Italian *zappa* 'spade, spadework.'

sap³ ▶ **noun** informal a foolish person.
– ORIGIN abbreviation of *sapskull* 'person with a head like sapwood' (soft layers of new wood in a tree).

sap·id /'sapid/ ▶ **adjective** having a strong and pleasant taste.
– ORIGIN Latin *sapidus*.

sa·pi·ent /'sāpēənt/ ▶ **adjective** formal wise or intelligent.
– ORIGIN from Latin *sapere* 'be wise.'

sap·ling /'sapliNG/ ▶ **noun** a young, slender tree.

sap·o·dil·la /,sapə'dilə/ ▶ **noun** **1** a large evergreen tropical American tree with hard wood and a milky latex that is used to make chewing gum. **2** the sweet brownish bristly fruit of the sapodilla.
– ORIGIN Spanish *zapotillo*.

sa·pon·i·fy /sə'pänə,fī/ ▶ **verb** (**saponifies, saponifying, saponified**) turn fat or oil into soap by reaction with an alkali.
– DERIVATIVES **sa·pon·i·fi·ca·tion** /sə,pänəfi'kāSHən/ noun.
– ORIGIN from Latin *sapo* 'soap.'

sap·per /'sapər/ ▶ **noun** a military engineer who lays or detects and disarms mines.
– ORIGIN from **SAP²**.

sap·phic /'safik/ ▶ **adjective** **1** (**Sapphic**) relating to the ancient Greek poet Sappho, or her poetry expressing love and affection for women. **2** formal or humorous relating to lesbians.

sap·phire /'saf,ī(ə)r/ ▶ **noun** **1** a transparent blue precious stone. **2** a bright blue color.
– ORIGIN Greek *sappheiros*, probably referring to lapis lazuli.

sap·py /'sapē/ ▶ **adjective** (**sappier, sappiest**) **1** informal excessively sentimental. **2** (of a plant) containing a lot of sap.

sap·ro·phyte /'saprə,fīt/ ▶ **noun** a plant, fungus, or microorganism that lives on decaying matter.
– DERIVATIVES **sap·ro·phyt·ic** /,saprə'fitik/ adjective.
– ORIGIN from Greek *sapros* 'putrid' + *phuton* 'plant.'

sap·wood /'sap,wo͝od/ ▶ **noun** the soft outer layers of new wood between the heartwood and the bark of a tree.

sar·a·band /'sarə,band/ (also **sarabande**) ▶ **noun** a slow, stately Spanish dance in triple time.
– ORIGIN Spanish and Italian *zarabanda*.

Sar·a·cen /'sarəsən/ ▶ **noun** an Arab or Muslim at the time of the Crusades.
– ORIGIN Greek *Sarakēnos*.

sa·ra·pe ▶ **noun** variant of **SERAPE**.

sar·casm /'sär,kazəm/ ▶ **noun** a way of using words that say the opposite of what one means, in order to mock someone.

– SYNONYMS **irony**, derision, mockery, ridicule, scorn.

– ORIGIN Greek *sarkasmos*.

sar·cas·tic /sär'kastik/ ▶ **adjective** using words that say the opposite of what one means, in order to mock someone.

– SYNONYMS **ironic**, sardonic, derisive, scornful, contemptuous, mocking, caustic, scathing, trenchant, acerbic.

– DERIVATIVES **sar·cas·ti·cal·ly** /-ik(ə)lē/ adverb.

sar·co·ma /sär'kōmə/ ▶ **noun** (pl. **sarcomas** or **sarcomata** /-mətə/) a cancerous tumor of a kind found chiefly in connective tissue.
– ORIGIN Greek *sarkōma*.

sar·coph·a·gus /sär'käfəgəs/ ▶ **noun** (pl. **sarcophagi** /-,jī/) a stone coffin.
– ORIGIN from Greek *sarkophagos* 'flesh-consuming.'

sar·dine /sär'dēn/ ▶ **noun** a young pilchard or other young or small herringlike fish.
– ORIGIN Latin *sardina*.

Sar·din·i·an /sär'dinēən/ ▶ **noun** **1** a person from Sardinia. **2** the language of Sardinia. ▶ **adjective** relating to Sardinia.

sar·don·ic /sär'dänik/ ▶ **adjective** showing a mocking or cynical attitude.

– SYNONYMS **mocking**, cynical, scornful, derisive, sneering, scathing, caustic, trenchant, cutting, acerbic.

– DERIVATIVES **sar·don·i·cal·ly** /-ik(ə)lē/ adverb **sar·don·i·cism** /-'dänə,sizəm/ noun.
– ORIGIN French *sardonique*.

sar·don·yx /sär'däniks/ ▶ **noun** onyx (a semiprecious stone) in which white layers alternate with yellow or reddish ones.
– ORIGIN Greek *sardonux*.

sar·gas·so /sär'gasō/ (also **sargassum** /sär'gasəm/) ▶ **noun** a brown seaweed with fronds that contain sacs filled with air, typically floating in large masses.
– ORIGIN Portuguese *sargaço*.

sarge /särj/ ▶ **noun** informal sergeant.

sa·ri /'särē/ (also **saree**) ▶ **noun** (pl. **saris** or **sarees**) an item of clothing consisting of a length of cotton or silk draped around the body, worn by women from the Indian subcontinent.
– ORIGIN Hindi.

sa·rin /sä'rēn/ ▶ **noun** a nerve gas developed during World War II.
– ORIGIN German.

sa·rong /sə'rôNG, -'räNG/ ▶ **noun** an item of clothing consisting of a long piece of cloth wrapped around the body and tucked at the waist or under the armpits.
– ORIGIN Malay, 'sheath.'

SARS /särz/ (also **Sars**) ▶ **abbreviation** severe acute respiratory syndrome.

sar·sa·pa·ril·la /ˌsärs(ə)pə'rilə, ˌsaspə-/ ▶ **noun 1** a preparation of the dried roots of a tropical plant, used as a flavoring. **2** a sweet drink flavored with sarsaparilla.
– ORIGIN Spanish *zarzaparilla*.

sar·sen /'särsən/ ▶ **noun** a sandstone boulder of a kind used to construct Stonehenge and other prehistoric monuments in southern England.
– ORIGIN probably from **SARACEN**.

sar·to·ri·al /sär'tôrēəl/ ▶ **adjective** relating to clothes or a person's style of dress: *their sartorial splendor has been emulated around the world*.
– DERIVATIVES **sar·to·ri·al·ly** adverb.
– ORIGIN from Latin *sartor* 'tailor.'

SASE ▶ **abbreviation** self-addressed stamped envelope.

sash[1] /sasH/ ▶ **noun** a long strip of cloth worn over one shoulder or around the waist.
– ORIGIN Arabic, 'muslin, turban.'

sash[2] ▶ **noun** a frame holding the glass in a window.
– ORIGIN from **CHASSIS**.

sa·shay /sa'sHā/ ▶ **verb** informal walk in a confident way, swinging the hips from side to side.
– ORIGIN from French *chassé* 'chased.'

sa·shi·mi /sä'sHēmē/ ▶ **noun** a Japanese dish of small pieces of raw fish eaten with soy sauce and horseradish paste.
– ORIGIN Japanese.

sash win·dow ▶ **noun** a window with one or two sashes (frames of glass) that can be slid up or down to open it.

Sas·quatch /'saskwäcH, -kwacH/ ▶ **noun** another name for **BIGFOOT**.
– ORIGIN Salish.

sass /sas/ informal ▶ **noun** disrespectful behavior; impertinence. ▶ **verb** be impertinent or rude to (someone).
– ORIGIN variant of **SAUCE**.

sas·sa·fras /'sasəˌfras/ ▶ **noun** an extract of the aromatic leaves or bark of a North American tree, used in medicines and perfumes.
– ORIGIN Spanish *sasafrás*.

Sas·se·nach /'sasəˌnak/ Scottish & Irish derogatory ▶ **noun** an English person. ▶ **adjective** English.
– ORIGIN Scottish Gaelic *Sasunnoch* or Irish *Sasanach*.

sas·sy /'sasē/ ▶ **adjective** (**sassier**, **sassiest**) informal lively, confident, or impudent.
– DERIVATIVES **sas·si·ness** noun.
– ORIGIN from **SAUCY**.

SAT ▶ **abbreviation** trademark (formerly and variously 'Scholastic Assessment Test' and 'Scholastic Aptitude Test') a test of a student's academic skills, used for admission to US colleges.

sat /sat/ past and past participle of **SIT**.

Sa·tan /'sātn/ ▶ **noun** the Devil.
– ORIGIN Hebrew, 'adversary.'

sa·tan·ic /sə'tanik, sā'-/ ▶ **adjective 1** relating to or typical of Satan, especially in being evil. **2** connected with satanism.

– SYNONYMS **diabolical,** fiendish, devilish, demonic, ungodly, hellish, infernal, wicked, evil, sinful.
– ANTONYMS godly.

sa·tan·ism /'sātnˌizəm/ ▶ **noun** the worship of Satan.
– DERIVATIVES **sa·tan·ist** noun & adjective.

sa·tay /'säˌtā/ (also **saté**) ▶ **noun** a SE Asian dish consisting of small pieces of meat broiled on a skewer and served with spiced peanut sauce.
– ORIGIN Malay and Indonesian.

satch·el /'sacHəl/ ▶ **noun** a shoulder bag with a long strap and typically closed by a flap.
– ORIGIN Old French *sachel*.

sate /sāt/ ▶ **verb 1** satisfy a desire fully. **2** supply with as much as or more than is desired: *the child slept, sated with food*.
– ORIGIN Old English, 'become sated or weary.'

sa·teen /sa'tēn/ ▶ **noun** a cotton fabric with a glossy surface.
– ORIGIN from **SATIN**.

sat·el·lite /'satlˌīt/ ▶ **noun 1** an artificial object placed in orbit around the earth or another planet to collect information or for communication. **2** a natural object orbiting a planet. **3** (usu. before another noun) a country, community, or organization dependent on or controlled by a larger or more powerful one: *satellite offices in London and New York*.
– ORIGIN Latin *satelles* 'attendant.'

sat·el·lite dish ▶ **noun** a bowl-shaped aerial with which signals are transmitted to or received from a communications satellite.

sat·el·lite tel·e·vi·sion ▶ **noun** television in which the signals are broadcast via satellite.

sa·ti /ˌsə'tē, 'səˌtē/ (also **suttee** pronunc. same) ▶ **noun** the former Hindu practice of a widow throwing herself onto her husband's funeral pyre.
– ORIGIN Sanskrit, 'faithful wife.'

sa·ti·ate /'sāsHēˌāt/ ▶ **verb** give someone as much as or more than they want.
– DERIVATIVES **sa·ti·a·tion** /ˌsāsHē'āsHən/ noun.
– ORIGIN Latin *satiare*.

sa·ti·e·ty /sə'tīətē/ ▶ **noun** the feeling or state of being fully satisfied.

sat·in /'satn/ ▶ **noun** a smooth, glossy fabric, usually of silk. ▶ **adjective** having a smooth, glossy surface or finish.
– DERIVATIVES **sat·in·y** adjective.
– ORIGIN from an Arabic word meaning 'of *Tsinkiang*,' a town in China.

sat·in·wood /'satnˌwo͝od/ ▶ **noun** the glossy yellowish wood of a tropical tree, used in making furniture.

sat·ire /'saˌtīr/ ▶ **noun 1** the use of humor, irony, or exaggeration as a form of mockery or criticism. **2** a play, novel, etc., using satire.

– SYNONYMS **parody,** burlesque, caricature, irony, lampoon, skit; informal spoof, takeoff, sendup.

– DERIVATIVES **sat·i·rist** /'satərist/ noun.
– ORIGIN Latin *satira* 'poetic medley.'

sa·tir·i·cal /sə'ti(ə)rikəl/ (also **satiric** /-'ti(ə)rik/) ▶ **adjective** using humor, irony, or exaggeration to mock or criticize.

– SYNONYMS **mocking,** ironic, sardonic, critical, irreverent, disparaging, disrespectful.

– DERIVATIVES **sa·tir·i·cal·ly** adverb.

sat·i·rize /ˈsatəˌrīz/ ▶ **verb** mock or criticize by using humor, irony, or exaggeration: *the movie satirized the idea of national superiority.*

– SYNONYMS **mock,** ridicule, deride, make fun of, parody, lampoon, caricature, take off, criticize.

sat·is·fac·tion /ˌsatisˈfakSHən/ ▶ **noun 1** the state of being pleased because one's needs have been met or one has achieved something. **2** Law the payment of a debt or fulfillment of a duty or claim. **3** something due to one to make up for an injustice: *the work will stop if they don't get satisfaction.*

– SYNONYMS **contentment,** content, pleasure, gratification, fulfillment, enjoyment, happiness, pride.

sat·is·fac·to·ry /ˌsatisˈfakt(ə)rē/ ▶ **adjective** acceptable, but not outstanding or perfect.

– SYNONYMS **adequate,** all right, acceptable, good enough, sufficient, reasonable, competent, fair, decent, average, passable, fine, in order, up to scratch, up to the mark.

– DERIVATIVES **sat·is·fac·to·ri·ly** adverb.

sat·is·fied /ˈsatisˌfīd/ ▶ **adjective** contented; pleased: *satisfied customers.*

sat·is·fy /ˈsatisˌfī/ ▶ **verb (satisfies, satisfying, satisfied) 1** please someone by meeting their expectations, needs, or desires: *I've never been satisfied with my job.* **2** fulfill a desire, demand, or need. **3** provide someone with adequate information about or proof of something. **4** meet or comply with a condition or duty: *he had ceased to satisfy the conditions for residence.*

– SYNONYMS **1 fulfill,** gratify, meet, fill, indulge, appease, assuage, quench, slake, satiate. **2 convince,** assure, reassure, put someone's mind at rest. **3 comply with,** meet, fulfill, answer, conform to, measure up to, come up to.
– ANTONYMS frustrate.

– ORIGIN Latin *satisfacere* 'to content.'

sat·phone /ˈsatˌfōn/ ▶ **noun** a telephone that transmits its signal via a communications satellite.

sa·trap /ˈsāˌtrap, ˈsa-/ ▶ **noun 1** a subordinate or local ruler. **2** a provincial governor in the ancient Persian empire.
– ORIGIN Latin *satrapa.*

sat·su·ma /satˈsōōmə, ˈsatsəˌmä/ ▶ **noun** a variety of tangerine with a loose skin.
– ORIGIN named after the former Japanese province of *Satsuma.*

sat·u·rate ▶ **verb** /ˈsacHəˌrāt/ **1** soak someone or something thoroughly with water or other liquid. **2** fill a market with so many products that demand is fully satisfied and no more products can be sold. **3** Chemistry cause a substance to combine with, dissolve, or hold the greatest possible quantity of another substance.

– SYNONYMS **1 soak,** drench, wet through. **2 flood,** glut, oversupply, overfill, overload.

▶ **noun** /-rət/ a saturated fat.
– ORIGIN Latin *saturare* 'fill, glut.'

sat·u·rat·ed /ˈsacHəˌrātid/ ▶ **adjective 1** (of fats) having only single bonds between carbon atoms in their molecules and as a result being less easily processed by the body. **2** Chemistry (of a solution) containing the largest possible amount of the substance dissolved in it. **3** (of color) bright and rich.

– SYNONYMS **1 soaked,** soaking (wet), wet through, sopping (wet), sodden, dripping, wringing wet, drenched, soaked to the skin. **2 waterlogged,** flooded, boggy, awash.
– ANTONYMS dry.

sat·u·ra·tion /ˌsacHəˈrāSHən/ ▶ **noun** the state of being so full that nothing else can be added: *a bid for market saturation.* ▶ **adjective** to the fullest extent: *saturation coverage by the press of police shootings.*

sat·u·ra·tion point ▶ **noun** the stage beyond which no more can be absorbed or accepted.

Sat·ur·day /ˈsatərˌdā, -dē/ ▶ **noun** the day of the week before Sunday and following Friday.
– ORIGIN from Latin *Saturni dies* 'day of Saturn.'

Sat·urn /ˈsatərn/ ▶ **noun** a planet of the solar system, sixth in order from the sun and circled by broad flat rings.
– DERIVATIVES **Sa·tur·ni·an** /səˈtərnēən/ adjective.

Sat·ur·na·li·a /ˌsatərˈnālēə, -nālyə/ ▶ **noun** (treated as sing. or pl.) **1** the ancient Roman festival of the god Saturn in December, a period of wild celebration. **2 (saturnalia)** literary a period or spell of wild celebration or self-indulgence.
– DERIVATIVES **sat·ur·na·li·an** adjective.
– ORIGIN Latin, 'matters relating to Saturn.'

sat·ur·nine /ˈsatərˌnīn/ ▶ **adjective 1** gloomy or serious. **2** (of looks) dark and moody.
– ORIGIN from Latin *Saturninus* 'of Saturn' (associated with slowness and gloom by astrologers).

sa·tyr /ˈsatər, ˈsātər/ ▶ **noun 1** (in Greek Mythology) a lustful, drunken woodland god, represented as a man with a horse's ears and tail or (in Roman myth) with a goat's ears, tail, legs, and horns. **2** a man with strong sexual desires.
– DERIVATIVES **sa·tyr·ic** /səˈtirik/ adjective.
– ORIGIN Greek *saturos.*

sauce /sôs/ ▶ **noun 1** a liquid substance served with food to add moistness and flavor. **2** informal, chiefly Brit. impudent language or behavior; impudence.

– SYNONYMS **gravy,** jus, dressing, dip, condiment, ketchup.

▶ **verb 1** provide with a sauce: *the noodles are sauced with a fish curry.* **2** informal, chiefly Brit. be impertinent or impudent to someone.
– ORIGIN Old French.

sauce·boat /ˈsôsˌbōt/ ▶ **noun** a long, narrow vessel for serving sauce or gravy.

sauce·pan /ˈsôsˌpan/ ▶ **noun** a deep cooking pan with a long handle and a lid.

sau·cer /ˈsôsər/ ▶ **noun** a shallow dish with a central circular hollow, on which a cup is placed.
– ORIGIN Old French *saussier* 'sauce boat.'

sau·cy /ˈsôsē/ ▶ **adjective (saucier, sauciest)** informal **1** sexually suggestive in a lighthearted way: *saucy postcards.* **2** impudent.
– DERIVATIVES **sau·ci·ly** adverb **sau·ci·ness** noun.

Sau·di /ˈsoudē, ˈsô-/ ▶ **noun** (pl. **Saudis**) a person from Saudi Arabia, or a member of its ruling dynasty. ▶ **adjective** relating to Saudi Arabia or its ruling dynasty.
– DERIVATIVES **Sau·di A·ra·bi·an** noun & adjective.

sau·er·kraut /ˈsou(ə)rˌkrout/ ▶ **noun** a German dish of chopped pickled cabbage.
– ORIGIN German.

sau·na /ˈsônə, ˈsou-/ ▸ **noun 1** a small room used as a hot-air or steam bath for cleaning and refreshing the body. **2** a session in a sauna.
– ORIGIN Finnish.

saun·ter /ˈsôntər/ ▸ **verb** walk in a slow, relaxed way.

– SYNONYMS **stroll,** amble, wander, meander, walk; informal mosey, tootle; formal promenade.

▸ **noun** a leisurely stroll.
– ORIGIN unknown.

sau·ri·an /ˈsôrēən/ ▸ **adjective** relating to or like a lizard.
– ORIGIN from Greek *sauros* 'lizard.'

sau·ro·pod /ˈsôrəˌpäd/ ▸ **noun** a very large plant-eating dinosaur with a long neck and tail and a small head.
– ORIGIN from Greek *sauros* 'lizard' + *pous* 'foot.'

sau·sage /ˈsôsij/ ▸ **noun 1** a short tube of raw minced meat encased in a skin, that is broiled or fried before eating. **2** a tube of spicy minced meat that is cooked or preserved and eaten cold in slices. **3** a cylindrical object.
– ORIGIN Old French *saussiche*.

sau·té /sôˈtā, sō-/ (also **saute**) ▸ **adjective** fried quickly in a little hot fat. ▸ **noun** a dish of sautéed food. ▸ **verb** (**sautés, sautéing, sautéed** /-ˈtād/ or **sautéd**) fry food quickly in a little hot fat.
– ORIGIN French, 'jumped.'

Sau·ternes /sōˈtərn, sô-/ ▸ **noun** a sweet white wine from Sauternes in the Bordeaux region of France.

Sau·vi·gnon /ˌsōvinˈyôN, -vēˈnyôN/ (also **Sauvignon Blanc**) ▸ **noun** a white wine made from the Sauvignon variety of grape.
– ORIGIN French.

sav·age /ˈsavij/ ▸ **adjective 1** fierce and violent. **2** cruel or highly damaging: *a savage attack on the president.* **3** primitive; uncivilized.

– SYNONYMS **1 vicious,** brutal, cruel, sadistic, ferocious, fierce, violent, barbaric, bloodthirsty, merciless, pitiless. **2 fierce,** blistering, scathing, searing, stinging, devastating, withering, virulent, vitriolic. **3 untamed,** wild, feral, undomesticated.
– ANTONYMS mild, tame.

▸ **noun 1** a member of a people regarded as primitive and uncivilized. **2** a brutal or vicious person.

– SYNONYMS **brute,** beast, monster, barbarian, sadist, animal.

▸ **verb 1** (especially of a dog) attack someone or something ferociously. **2** criticize someone or something harshly.

– SYNONYMS **maul,** attack, lacerate, claw, bite, tear to pieces.

– DERIVATIVES **sav·age·ly** adverb **sav·age·ry** /-rē/ noun.
– ORIGIN Old French *sauvage* 'wild.'

sa·van·na /səˈvanə/ (also **savannah**) ▸ **noun** a grassy plain in tropical and subtropical regions, with few trees.
– ORIGIN Spanish *sabana*.

sa·vant /saˈvänt, sə-/ ▸ **noun** a very knowledgeable person.
– ORIGIN French, 'knowing.'

save[1] /sāv/ ▸ **verb 1** rescue someone or something from harm or danger. **2** prevent someone from dying. **3** store or keep something for future use. **4** keep data in a computer. **5** avoid the need to use up or spend: *computers save time.* **6** avoid something or prevent someone from doing or experiencing something: *this approach saves wear and tear on the books.* **7** (in Christian use) protect a person's soul from damnation. **8** Baseball (of a relief pitcher) finish a game while preserving a leading score. **9** chiefly Soccer & Hockey prevent an opponent from scoring a goal or point.

– SYNONYMS **1 rescue,** set free, free, liberate, deliver, redeem. **2 preserve,** keep, protect, safeguard, salvage, retrieve, reclaim, rescue. **3 put aside,** set aside, put by, keep, conserve, retain, store, hoard, stockpile; informal squirrel away. **4 prevent,** avoid, forestall, spare, stop, obviate, avert.

▸ **noun 1** Baseball an instance of a relief pitcher saving a game. **2** chiefly Soccer & Hockey an act of preventing an opponent from scoring.
– PHRASES **save one's breath** not bother to say something pointless. **save someone's skin** (or **neck** or **bacon**) rescue someone from difficulty.
– ORIGIN Latin *salvare*.

save[2] ▸ **preposition & conjunction** formal or literary except; other than.
– ORIGIN from Latin *salvus* 'safe.'

sav·er /ˈsāvər/ ▸ **noun 1** a person who regularly saves money through a bank or recognized scheme. **2** something that prevents a resource from being used up: *a space-saver.*

sav·ing /ˈsāviNG/ ▸ **noun 1** a reduction in use of a resource such as money or time. **2** (**savings**) money saved.

– SYNONYMS **1 reduction,** cut, decrease, economy. **2** (**savings**) **nest egg,** capital, assets, funds, resources, reserves.

▸ **adjective** (in combination) preventing waste of a resource: *energy-saving.*
▸ **preposition** not including; except.

sav·ing grace ▸ **noun** a good quality that makes up for the faults of someone or something.

sav·ings ac·count ▸ **noun** a bank account that earns interest.

sav·ings and loan (also **savings and loan association**) ▸ **noun** an institution that pays interest on money deposited and lends money to savers.

sav·ings bank ▸ **noun** a bank that pays interest on deposits into savings accounts.

sav·ings bond ▸ **noun** a bond issued by the government and sold to the general public.

sav·ior /ˈsāvyər/ (Brit. **saviour**) ▸ **noun 1** a person who saves someone or something from danger or harm. **2** (**the/our Savior**) (in Christianity) God or Jesus.

– SYNONYMS **rescuer,** liberator, deliverer, champion, protector, redeemer.

– ORIGIN Old French *sauveour*.

sav·oir faire /ˌsavwär ˈfe(ə)r/ ▸ **noun** the ability to act appropriately in social situations.
– ORIGIN French, 'know how to do.'

sa·vor /ˈsāvər/ (Brit. **savour**) ▸ **verb 1** taste food or drink and enjoy it to the full. **2** enjoy or appreciate to the full: *I wanted to savor every moment.* **3** (**savor of**) have a suggestion or trace of an undesirable quality.

– SYNONYMS **relish,** enjoy, appreciate, delight in, revel in, luxuriate in.

▸ **noun 1** a characteristic taste or smell. **2** a trace, especially of something undesirable.

– SYNONYMS **smell,** aroma, fragrance, scent, perfume, bouquet; **taste,** flavor, tang.

– ORIGIN Old French.

sa·vor·y[1] /'sāv(ə)rē/ ▶ **noun** a plant of the mint family, used as an herb in cooking.
– ORIGIN Latin *satureia*.

sa·vor·y[2] (Brit. **savoury**) ▶ **adjective 1** (of food) salty or spicy rather than sweet. **2** morally wholesome or acceptable: *the less savory aspects of the story*.

– SYNONYMS **salty,** spicy, tangy, piquant.
– ANTONYMS sweet.

▶ **noun** (pl. **savories**) chiefly Brit. a savory snack.

– SYNONYMS **canapé,** hors d'oeuvre, appetizer, tidbit.

sa·voy /sə'voi/ ▶ **noun** a cabbage of a variety with wrinkled leaves.
– ORIGIN from *Savoy*, an area of SE France.

sav·vy /'savē/ informal ▶ **noun** common sense or shrewdness. ▶ **adjective** (**savvier, savviest**) having common sense; shrewd. ▶ **verb** (**savvies, savvying, savvied**) know or understand something.
– ORIGIN black and pidgin English imitating Spanish *sabe usted* 'you know.'

saw[1] /sô/ ▶ **noun 1** a hand tool for cutting wood or other hard materials, having a long, thin toothed blade. **2** a mechanical power-driven cutting tool with a toothed rotating disk or moving band. ▶ **verb** (past part. **sawed** or **sawn**) **1** cut or make something with a saw. **2** cut something roughly. **3** make rapid movements like those of a saw.
– ORIGIN Old English.

saw[2] past of SEE[1].

saw[3] ▶ **noun** a proverb or wise saying.
– ORIGIN Old English.

saw·buck /'sô,bək/ ▶ **noun 1** a sawhorse. **2** informal a $10 bill.
– ORIGIN Dutch *zaagbok*, from *zaag* 'saw' + *bok* 'vaulting horse.'

saw·dust /'sô,dəst/ ▶ **noun** powdery particles of wood produced by sawing.

sawed-off (also **sawn-off**) ▶ **adjective 1** (of a gun) having had the barrel shortened for ease of handling and a wider field of fire. **2** informal (of an item of clothing) having been cut short.

saw·fish /'sô,fisH/ ▶ **noun** (pl. same or **sawfishes**) a large tropical fish with a long flattened snout bearing large blunt teeth along each side.

saw·fly /'sô,flī/ ▶ **noun** (pl. **sawflies**) an insect related to the wasps, with a sawlike tube used in laying eggs in plant tissue.

saw·horse /'sô,hôrs/ ▶ **noun** a frame or trestle that supports wood for sawing.

saw·mill /'sô,mil/ ▶ **noun** a factory in which logs are sawn by machine.

sawn /sôn/ past participle of SAW[1].

saw·tooth /'sô,to͞oTH/ (also **sawtoothed**) ▶ **adjective** shaped like the teeth of a saw.

saw·yer /'sôyər/ ▶ **noun** a person who saws timber.

sax /saks/ ▶ **noun** informal a saxophone.
– DERIVATIVES **sax·ist** noun.

sax·i·frage /'saksə,frij, -frāj/ ▶ **noun** a low-growing plant of rocky or stony ground, bearing small white, yellow, or red flowers.
– ORIGIN Latin *saxifraga*.

Sax·on /'saksən/ ▶ **noun 1** a member of a Germanic people that conquered and settled in much of southern England in the 5th–6th centuries. **2** a person from modern Saxony in Germany. **3** (**Old Saxon**) the language of the ancient Saxons. ▶ **adjective 1** relating to the Anglo-Saxons or their period of dominance in England (5th–11th centuries). **2** relating to modern Saxony.
– ORIGIN Greek *Saxones*.

sax·o·phone /'saksə,fōn/ ▶ **noun** a member of a family of metal wind instruments with a reed like a clarinet, used especially in jazz.
– DERIVATIVES **sax·o·phon·ic** /,saksə'fänik/ adjective **sax·o·phon·ist** /-,fōnist/ noun.
– ORIGIN named after the Belgian instrument-maker Adolphe *Sax*.

say /sā/ ▶ **verb** (**says** /sez/, **saying** /'sāiNG/, **said** /sed/) **1** speak words so as to convey information, an opinion, an instruction, etc. **2** (of a piece of writing or a symbol) convey information or instructions. **3** (of a clock or watch) indicate a time. **4** (**be said**) be claimed or reported. **5** (**say something for**) present a consideration in favor of or excusing: *he had nothing to say for himself*. **6** suggest as an example, possibility, or a basis for a theory: *let's say the fine is $79*.

– SYNONYMS **1 speak,** utter, voice, pronounce. **2 declare,** state, announce, remark, observe, mention, comment, note, add. **3 recite,** repeat, utter, deliver, perform. **4 indicate,** show, read.

▶ **noun** an opportunity to state one's opinion or to influence events.

– SYNONYMS **influence,** sway, weight, voice, input.

– DERIVATIVES **say·a·ble** adjective **say·er** noun.
– PHRASES **go without saying** be obvious. **say the word** give permission or instructions. **there is no saying** it is impossible to know. **when all is said and done** when everything is taken into account.
– ORIGIN Old English.

say·ing /'sāiNG/ ▶ **noun** a short, well-known expression containing advice or wisdom.

– SYNONYMS **proverb,** maxim, aphorism, axiom, expression, phrase, formula, slogan, catchphrase.

CHOOSE THE RIGHT WORD

saying, adage, aphorism, apothegm, epigram, epigraph, maxim, proverb

"Once burned, twice shy" is an old **saying** about learning from your mistakes. In fact, *sayings*—a term used to describe any current or habitual expression of wisdom or truth—are a dime a dozen. **Proverbs**—sayings that are well known and often repeated, usually expressing metaphorically a truth based on common sense or practical experience—are just as plentiful (*her favorite proverb was "A stitch in time saves nine"*). An **adage** is a time-honored and widely known proverb, such as "Where's there's smoke, there's fire." A **maxim** offers a rule of conduct or action in the form of a proverb, such as "Neither a borrower nor a lender be." **Epigram** and **epigraph** are often confused, but their meanings are quite separate. An *epigram* is a terse, witty, or satirical statement that often relies on a paradox for its effect (*Oscar Wilde's well-known epigram that "The only way to get rid of temptation is to yield to it"*). An *epigraph*, on the other hand, is a brief quotation used to introduce a piece of writing (*he used a quote from T. S. Eliot as the epigraph to his new novel*). An **aphorism** requires a little more thought than an *epigram*, since it aims to be profound rather than witty (*she'd just *finished reading a book of Mark Twain's aphorisms*). An **apothegm** is a pointed and often startling aphorism, such as Samuel Johnson's remark that "Patriotism is the last refuge of a scoundrel."

say-so ▶ **noun** informal the power to decide or allow something: *an owner can only close an area with the say-so of the council*.

Sb ▶ **symbol** the chemical element antimony.
– ORIGIN from Latin *stibium*.

SBA ▶ **abbreviation** Small Business Administration.

SBS ▶ **abbreviation 1** sick building syndrome. **2** Special Boat Service.

SC ▶ **abbreviation** South Carolina.

Sc ▶ **symbol** the chemical element scandium.

scab /skab/ ▶ **noun 1** a dry protective crust that forms over a cut or wound during healing. **2** mange or a similar skin disease in animals. **3** a plant disease caused by a fungus, in which rough patches develop. **4** informal, derogatory a person who refuses to take part in a strike.
– DERIVATIVES **scabbed** adjective **scab·by** adjective.
– ORIGIN Old Norse.

scab·bard /ˈskabərd/ ▶ **noun 1** a sheath for the blade of a sword or dagger. **2** a sheath for a gun or tool.
– ORIGIN Old French *escalberc*.

sca·bies /ˈskābēz/ ▶ **noun** a contagious skin disease marked by itching and small raised red spots, caused by a mite.
– ORIGIN Latin, from *scabere* 'to scratch.'

sca·bi·ous /ˈskābēəs/ ▶ **noun** a plant with blue, pink, or white pincushion-shaped flowers.
– ORIGIN from Latin *scabiosa herba* 'rough, scabby plant.'

scab·rous /ˈskabrəs/ ▶ **adjective 1** indecent or sordid: *scabrous Hollywood gossip*. **2** rough and covered with scabs.
– ORIGIN Latin *scabrosus*.

scads /skadz/ ▶ **plural noun** informal a large number or quantity.
– ORIGIN unknown.

scaf·fold /ˈskafəld, -ˌfōld/ ▶ **noun 1** a raised wooden platform formerly used for public executions. **2** a structure made using scaffolding. ▶ **verb** attach scaffolding to a building.
– DERIVATIVES **scaf·fold·er** noun.
– ORIGIN Old French *eschaffaut*.

scaf·fold·ing /ˈskafəldiNG, -ˌfōl-/ ▶ **noun 1** a temporary structure made of wooden planks and metal poles, used while building, repairing, or cleaning a building. **2** the materials used in scaffolding.

scal·a·ble /ˈskāləbəl/ (also **scaleable**) ▶ **adjective 1** able to be climbed. **2** able to be changed in size or scale. **3** technical able to be graded according to a scale.
– DERIVATIVES **scal·a·bil·i·ty** /ˌskāləˈbilitē/ noun.

sca·lar /ˈskālər/ Mathematics & Physics ▶ **adjective** having only magnitude, not direction. ▶ **noun** a quantity having only magnitude, not direction.
– ORIGIN Latin *scalaris*.

scal·a·wag /ˈskaləˌwag/ (also **scallywag**) ▶ **noun** informal a mischievous person; a rascal.

scald /skôld/ ▶ **verb 1** burn someone or something with very hot liquid or steam. **2** heat a liquid to near boiling point. **3** dip something briefly in boiling water. ▶ **noun** a burn caused by hot liquid or steam.
– ORIGIN Latin *excaldare*.

scale[1] /skāl/ ▶ **noun 1** each of the small overlapping plates protecting the skin of fish and reptiles. **2** a thick dry flake of skin. **3** limescale in a kettle, boiler, etc. **4** tartar formed on teeth. ▶ **verb 1** remove scale or scales from something. **2** (often as n. **scaling**) (especially of the skin) form or flake off in scales.
– ORIGIN Old French *escale*.

scale[2] ▶ **noun 1** (usu. **scales**) an instrument or device for weighing. **2** either of the dishes on a simple scale balance.
– PHRASES **tip the scales** (or **balance**) be the deciding factor.
– ORIGIN Old Norse, 'bowl.'

scale[3] ▶ **noun 1** a range of values forming a standard system for measuring or grading something: *a pay scale*. **2** a measuring instrument with a series of marks at regular intervals. **3** relative size or extent: *he operated on a grand scale*. **4** a ratio of size in a map, model, drawing, or plan. **5** an arrangement of the notes in a system of music in ascending or descending order of pitch.

– SYNONYMS **1** *we are at opposite ends of the social scale* **hierarchy,** ladder, ranking, pecking order, order, spectrum. **2** *no one foresaw the scale of the disaster* **extent,** size, scope, magnitude, dimensions, range, breadth, degree. **3** *the scale of the map is too small to show details* **ratio,** proportion, relative size.

▶ **verb 1** climb up or over something high and steep. **2** (**scale something back/down** or **up**) reduce (or increase) something in size, number, or extent. **3** (usu. as adj. **scaled**) represent in measurements that are in proportion to the size of the original: *a strictly scaled depiction of Scotland's regions*.

– SYNONYMS **climb,** ascend, clamber up, scramble up, shinny (up), mount.

– PHRASES **to scale** reduced or enlarged in proportion to something.
– ORIGIN Latin *scala* 'ladder.'

scale in·sect ▶ **noun** a small bug that produces a shieldlike scale and spends its life attached to a single plant.

sca·lene /skāˈlēn/ ▶ **adjective** (of a triangle) having sides unequal in length.
– ORIGIN Greek *skalēnos* 'unequal.'

scal·lion /ˈskalyən/ ▶ **noun** a long-necked onion with a small bulb, especially a green onion.
– ORIGIN Old French *scaloun*.

scal·lop /ˈskäləp, ˈskal-/ ▶ **noun 1** an edible shellfish with two hinged fan-shaped shells. **2** each of a series of small curves resembling the edge of a scallop shell, forming a decorative edging. ▶ **verb** (**scallops, scalloping, scalloped**) (usu. as adj. **scalloped**) decorate something with a series of small curves.
– ORIGIN Old French *escalope*.

scal·ly·wag /ˈskalēˌwag/ ▶ **noun** variant spelling of SCALAWAG.
– ORIGIN unknown.

scalp /skalp/ ▶ **noun 1** the skin covering the top and back of the head. **2** historical the scalp with the hair cut away from an enemy's head as a battle trophy, a former practice among American Indians. ▶ **verb 1** historical take the scalp of an enemy. **2** informal resell a ticket for a popular event at a price higher than the official one.
– DERIVATIVES **scalp·er** noun.
– ORIGIN probably Scandinavian.

scal·pel /'skalpəl/ ▶ noun a knife with a small sharp blade, used by a surgeon.
– ORIGIN Latin *scalpellum* 'small chisel.'

scal·y /'skālē/ ▶ adjective **1** covered in scales. **2** (of skin) dry and flaking.

– SYNONYMS **dry,** flaky, scurfy, rough, scabrous.

scam /skam/ informal ▶ noun a dishonest scheme; a fraud. ▶ verb (**scams, scamming, scammed**) swindle someone.
– DERIVATIVES **scam·mer** noun.
– ORIGIN unknown.

scamp /skamp/ ▶ noun informal a mischievous person, especially a child.
– DERIVATIVES **scamp·ish** adjective.
– ORIGIN probably from Dutch *schampen* 'slip away.'

scamp·er /'skampər/ ▶ verb run with quick light steps, especially through fear or excitement. ▶ noun an act of scampering.
– ORIGIN probably from **SCAMP**.

scam·pi /'skampē/ ▶ noun (treated as sing. or pl.) a dish consisting of the tails of a kind of large shrimp, typically fried in butter and garlic and topped with breadcrumbs.
– ORIGIN Italian.

scan /skan/ ▶ verb (**scans, scanning, scanned**) **1** look over something quickly in order to find relevant features or information. **2** move a detector or electromagnetic beam across someone or something, especially to obtain an image. **3** convert a document or picture into digital form for storage or processing on a computer. **4** analyze the meter of a line of verse. **5** (of verse) follow metrical principles.

– SYNONYMS **1 study,** examine, scrutinize, inspect, survey, search, scour, sweep, watch. **2 glance through,** look through, have a look at, run/cast one's eye over, flick through, browse through, leaf through, thumb through.

▶ noun **1** an act of scanning. **2** a medical examination using a scanner. **3** an image obtained by scanning.
– DERIVATIVES **scan·na·ble** adjective.
– ORIGIN Latin *scandere* 'climb' (later 'scan verses').

scan·dal /'skandl/ ▶ noun **1** behavior or a situation regarded as wrong or unacceptable and causing general outrage. **2** outrage or gossip arising from such behavior: *the media's craving for scandal.*

– SYNONYMS **1 gossip,** rumor(s), slander, libel, aspersions, muckraking; informal dirt. **2** *it's a scandal that the hospital has closed* **disgrace,** outrage, sin, (crying) shame.

– ORIGIN Latin *scandalum* 'cause of offense.'

scan·dal·ize /'skandl,īz/ ▶ verb shock or horrify someone by acting in an immoral or unacceptable way.

scan·dal·mon·ger /'skandl,məNGgər, -,mäNGgər/ ▶ noun a person who spreads rumors or spiteful gossip.

scan·dal·ous /'skandl-əs/ ▶ adjective **1** causing general outrage by being wrong or unacceptable. **2** (of a situation) disgracefully bad.

– SYNONYMS **1 disgraceful,** shocking, outrageous, monstrous, criminal, wicked, shameful, appalling, deplorable, inexcusable, intolerable, unforgivable, unpardonable. **2 discreditable,** disreputable, dishonorable, improper, unseemly, sordid. **3 scurrilous,** malicious, slanderous, libelous, defamatory.

– DERIVATIVES **scan·dal·ous·ly** adverb.

Scan·di·na·vi·an /,skandə'nāvēən/ ▶ adjective relating to Scandinavia. ▶ noun **1** a person from Scandinavia. **2** the northern branch of the Germanic languages, comprising Danish, Norwegian, Swedish, Icelandic, and Faeroese.

scan·di·um /'skandēəm/ ▶ noun a soft silvery-white metallic chemical element.
– ORIGIN Latin.

scan·ner /'skanər/ ▶ noun **1** a machine that examines the body through the use of radiation, ultrasound, etc., used to aid diagnosis. **2** a device that scans documents and converts them into digital data.

scan·sion /'skansʜən/ ▶ noun **1** the action of scanning a line of verse to determine its rhythm. **2** the rhythm of a line of verse.

scant /skant/ ▶ adjective **1** not enough; hardly any: *he paid scant attention to the needs of his wife.* **2** only just reaching the amount specified: *she weighed a scant two pounds.*

– SYNONYMS **little,** little or no, minimal, limited, negligible, meager, insufficient, inadequate.
– ANTONYMS abundant, ample.

– DERIVATIVES **scant·ly** adverb.
– ORIGIN Old Norse, 'short.'

scant·y /'skantē/ ▶ adjective (**scantier, scantiest**) too little in quantity or amount.

– SYNONYMS **1 meager,** scant, minimal, limited, modest, restricted, sparse, tiny, small, paltry, negligible, scarce, in short supply, few and far between; informal measly, piddling, mingy, pathetic. **2 skimpy,** revealing, short, brief, low-cut.
– ANTONYMS ample, plentiful.

▶ plural noun (**scanties**) informal women's skimpy panties.
– DERIVATIVES **scant·i·ly** adverb.

scape·goat /'skāp,gōt/ ▶ noun **1** a person who is blamed for the wrongdoings or mistakes of others. **2** (in the Bible) a goat sent into the wilderness after the Jewish chief priest had symbolically laid the sins of the people on it.

– SYNONYMS **whipping boy;** informal fall guy, patsy.

▶ verb blame someone for the wrongdoings or mistakes of others.
– ORIGIN from former *scape* 'escape' + **GOAT**.

scap·u·la /'skapyələ/ ▶ noun (pl. **scapulae** /-,lē/ or **scapulas**) technical term for **SHOULDER BLADE**.
– ORIGIN Latin.

scap·u·lar /'skapyələr/ ▶ adjective relating to the shoulder or shoulder blade. ▶ noun a short cloak worn by monks, covering the shoulders.

scar /skär/ ▶ noun **1** a mark left on the skin or within body tissue after a wound or burn has healed. **2** a lasting effect left following an unpleasant experience. **3** a mark left at the point where a leaf or other part has separated from a plant.

– SYNONYMS **1 mark,** blemish, disfigurement, discoloration, pockmark, pit, lesion, cicatrix. **2** *psychological scars* **trauma,** damage, injury.

▶ verb (**scars, scarring, scarred**) **1** mark someone or something with a scar or scars. **2** have a lasting and unpleasant effect on: *he was so traumatized by his childhood that he was scarred for life.*

– SYNONYMS **disfigure,** mark, blemish, discolor, mar, spoil.

– ORIGIN Greek *eskhara* 'scab.'

scar·ab /ˈskarəb/ ▶ **noun 1** a large dung beetle, treated as sacred in ancient Egypt. **2** an ancient Egyptian gem in the form of a scarab.
– ORIGIN Greek *skarabeios*.

scarce /ske(ə)rs/ ▶ **adjective 1** (of a resource) available in quantities that are too small to meet the demand for it. **2** occurring in small numbers or quantities; rare.

– SYNONYMS **in short supply,** scant, scanty, inadequate, lacking, meager, sparse, hard to come by, at a premium, few and far between, rare.
– ANTONYMS plentiful.

– PHRASES **make oneself scarce** informal leave a place, especially so as to avoid a difficult situation.
– ORIGIN Old French *escars*.

scarce·ly /ˈske(ə)rslē/ ▶ **adverb 1** only just. **2** only a very short time before. **3** used to suggest that something is unlikely: *they could scarcely all be wrong*.

– SYNONYMS **1 hardly,** barely, only just. **2 rarely,** seldom, infrequently, not often, hardly ever; informal once in a blue moon.

scar·ci·ty /ˈskersitē/ ▶ **noun** insufficiency of supply: *the scarcity of affordable housing*.

– SYNONYMS **shortage,** dearth, lack, undersupply, insufficiency, paucity, poverty, deficiency, inadequacy, unavailability, absence.

scare /ske(ə)r/ ▶ **verb 1** frighten or become frightened: *just seeing those needles scared me to death*. **2** (**scare someone away/off**) drive or keep someone away by fear.

– SYNONYMS **frighten,** startle, alarm, terrify, unnerve, worry, intimidate, terrorize, cow; informal freak out, spook.

▶ **noun 1** a sudden attack of fright. **2** a period of general anxiety or alarm: *a bomb scare*.

– SYNONYMS **fright,** shock, start, turn, jump.

– ORIGIN Old Norse.

scare·crow /ˈske(ə)rˌkrō/ ▶ **noun** an object made to resemble a person, set up to scare birds away from a field where crops are growing.

scared /ske(ə)rd/ ▶ **adjective** feeling or showing fear or nervousness.

– SYNONYMS **frightened,** afraid, fearful, nervous, panicky, terrified; informal in a cold sweat, spooked.

scared·y-cat /ˈske(ə)rdē ˌkat/ ▶ **noun** informal a timid person.

scare·mon·ger /ˈske(ə)rˌməNGgər, -ˌmäNGgər/ ▶ **noun** a person who spreads frightening rumors.
– DERIVATIVES **scare·mon·ger·ing** noun.

scare quotes ▶ **plural noun** quotation marks used around a word or phrase for emphasis or to express doubt.

scarf[1] /skärf/ ▶ **noun** (pl. **scarves** /skärvz/ or **scarfs**) a length or square of fabric worn around the neck or head.
– DERIVATIVES **scarfed** /skärft/ (also **scarved** /skärvd/) adjective.
– ORIGIN probably from Old French *escharpe* 'pilgrim's pouch.'

scarf[2] ▶ **verb** join the ends of two pieces of wood or metal by beveling or notching them so that they fit together. ▶ **noun** a joint made by scarfing.
– ORIGIN Old Norse.

scarf[3] ▶ **verb** informal eat or drink hungrily or enthusiastically: *he scarfed down the waffles*.
– ORIGIN variant of **SCOFF**[2].

scar·i·fy /ˈskarəˌfī/ ▶ **verb** (**scarifies, scarifying, scarified**) **1** make shallow cuts in the skin. **2** break up the surface of soil or a road or sidewalk. **3** break up and remove matted vegetation from a lawn. **4** criticize someone harshly.
– DERIVATIVES **scar·i·fi·ca·tion** /-fiˈkāSHən/ noun **scar·i·fi·er** noun.
– ORIGIN Old French *scarifier*.

scar·la·ti·na /ˌskärləˈtēnə/ ▶ **noun** another term for **SCARLET FEVER**.
– ORIGIN Latin.

scar·let /ˈskärlit/ ▶ **noun** a bright red color.
– ORIGIN Latin *scarlata* 'brightly colored cloth.'

scar·let fe·ver ▶ **noun** an infectious disease that particularly affects children, caused by bacteria and marked by fever and a scarlet rash.

scar·let wom·an ▶ **noun** chiefly humorous a woman known for having many sexual relationships.

scarp /skärp/ ▶ **noun** a very steep bank or slope; an escarpment.
– ORIGIN Italian *scarpa*.

scarp·er /ˈskärpər/ ▶ **verb** Brit. informal run away.
– ORIGIN probably from Italian *scappare* 'to escape.'

Scart /skärt/ (also **SCART**) ▶ **noun** a 21-pin socket used to connect video equipment.
– ORIGIN from French *Syndicat des Constructeurs des Appareils Radiorécepteurs et Téléviseurs*, the committee which designed the connector.

scarves /skärvz/ plural of **SCARF**[1].

scar·y /ˈske(ə)rē/ ▶ **adjective** (**scarier, scariest**) informal causing fear; frightening.

– SYNONYMS **frightening,** terrifying, hair-raising, spine-chilling, blood-curdling, eerie, sinister; informal creepy, spine-tingling, spooky.

– DERIVATIVES **scar·i·ly** adverb.

scat[1] /skat/ ▶ **verb** (**scats, scatting, scatted**) informal go away; leave.
– ORIGIN perhaps from **SCATTER**.

scat[2] ▶ **noun** improvised jazz singing in which the voice is used to imitate an instrument. ▶ **verb** (**scats, scatting, scatted**) sing using the voice to imitate an instrument.
– ORIGIN probably imitating the sound.

scath·ing /ˈskā<u>TH</u>iNG/ ▶ **adjective** harshly critical or scornful.

– SYNONYMS **withering,** blistering, searing, devastating, fierce, ferocious, savage, severe, stinging, biting, cutting, virulent, vitriolic, scornful, bitter, harsh.
– ANTONYMS mild.

– DERIVATIVES **scath·ing·ly** adverb.
– ORIGIN from Old Norse, 'harm, injure.'

scat·o·log·i·cal /ˌskatlˈäjikəl/ ▶ **adjective** concerned or obsessed with excrement and excretion.
– DERIVATIVES **sca·tol·o·gy** /skəˈtäləjē/ noun.
– ORIGIN from Greek *skōr* 'dung.'

scat·ter /ˈskatər/ ▶ **verb 1** throw a number of things in various random directions. **2** (of a group of people or animals) separate and move off in different directions. **3** (**be scattered**) occur or be found at various places rather than all together: *more than 73,000 cell phone masts are scattered across the landscape*.

– SYNONYMS **1 spread,** sprinkle, distribute, strew, disseminate, sow, throw, toss, fling. **2 disperse,**

break up, disband, separate, dissolve.
– ANTONYMS gather, assemble.

– ORIGIN probably from SHATTER.

CHOOSE THE RIGHT WORD

scatter, broadcast, diffuse, dispel, disperse, disseminate, dissipate

If you **scatter** something, you throw it about in different directions, often using force (*the wind scattered leaves around the yard*). **Disperse** implies a scattering that completely breaks up a mass or assemblage and spreads the units far and wide (*the crowd dispersed as soon as the storm arrived; the ships were so widely dispersed that they couldn't see each other*). To **dispel** is to scatter or to drive away something that obscures, confuses, or bothers (*to dispel her fears*), while to **diffuse** is to lessen the intensity of something by spreading it out over a broader area (*the curtains diffused the bright sunlight pouring in the window*). **Dissipate** suggests that something has completely dissolved, disintegrated, or vanished (*early-morning mist dissipated by the sun*). **Broadcast** originally meant to scatter seed, but it is also used figuratively to mean make public (*the news of the president's defeat was broadcast the next morning*). **Disseminate** also means to publish or make public, but it implies a wider audience and usually a longer duration. You can spend a lifetime *disseminating* knowledge, in other words, but you would *broadcast* the news of the birth of your first grandchild.

scat·ter·brained /ˈskatərˌbrānd/ ▸ **adjective** disorganized and unable to concentrate on things.

scat·ter·gun /ˈskatərˌgən/ ▸ **noun** a shotgun. ▸ **adjective** another term for SCATTERSHOT.

scat·ter·ing /ˈskatəriNG/ (also **scatter**) ▸ **noun** a small amount or number of things spread over an area: *a scattering of chairs and tables on the sidewalk*.

scat·ter·shot /ˈskatərˌSHät/ ▸ **adjective** (also **scattergun**) covering a broad range in an unsystematic way: *the scattershot approach to selecting material*.

scav·enge /ˈskavənj/ ▸ **verb 1** search for and collect anything usable from rubbish. **2** (of an animal or bird) search for and eat dead animals.

– SYNONYMS **search,** hunt, look, forage, rummage, root about/around, grub about/around.

– ORIGIN from SCAVENGER.

scav·eng·er /ˈskavənjər/ ▸ **noun 1** an animal that feeds on dead animals or waste material. **2** a person who searches for and collects usable items from rubbish.
– ORIGIN first referring to an official who collected *scavage*, a toll on foreign merchants' goods, later a person who kept the streets clean: from Old French *escauwer* 'inspect.'

sce·nar·i·o /səˈne(ə)rēˌō, -ˈnär-/ ▸ **noun** (pl. **scenarios**) **1** a suggested sequence of events: *in the worst-case scenario, he could be looking at assault charges*. **2** a written outline of a movie, novel, play, etc., giving details of the plot and individual scenes.

– SYNONYMS **1 situation,** chain of events, course of events. **2 plot,** outline, storyline, framework, screenplay, script.

– ORIGIN Italian.

scene /sēn/ ▸ **noun 1** the place where an incident occurs or occurred. **2** a view or landscape as seen by a spectator. **3** an incident or situation of a particular kind: *scenes of violence*. **4** a sequence of continuous action in a play, movie, opera, book, etc. **5** a public display of emotion or anger: *she was loath to make a scene in the office*. **6** a specified area of activity or interest: *the literary scene*. **7** the scenery used in a play or opera.

– SYNONYMS **1 location,** site, place, position, spot, locale. **2 background,** setting, context, milieu, backdrop. **3 incident,** event, episode, happening, proceeding. **4 view,** vista, outlook, panorama, landscape, scenery. **5** *she made a scene* **fuss,** exhibition of oneself, performance, tantrum, commotion, disturbance, row; informal to-do. **6** *the political scene* **arena,** stage, sphere, world, milieu, realm. **7 clip,** section, segment, part, sequence, extract.

– PHRASES **behind the scenes** out of public view. **come** (or **appear** or **arrive**) **on the scene** arrive; appear.
– ORIGIN Greek *skēnē* 'tent, stage.'

scen·er·y /ˈsēn(ə)rē/ ▸ **noun 1** the natural features of a landscape considered in terms of their appearance. **2** the painted background used to represent a place on a stage or movie set.

– SYNONYMS **1 landscape,** countryside, country, terrain, setting, surroundings, environment. **2 set,** setting, backdrop.

– PHRASES **chew the scenery** informal (of an actor) overact.

sce·nic /ˈsēnik/ ▸ **adjective 1** relating to impressive or beautiful natural scenery: *the scenic route*. **2** relating to theatrical scenery.

– SYNONYMS **picturesque,** pretty, attractive, beautiful, charming, impressive, striking, spectacular, breathtaking, panoramic.

– DERIVATIVES **sce·ni·cal·ly** /-ik(ə)lē/ adverb.

scent /sent/ ▸ **noun 1** a distinctive smell, especially one that is pleasant. **2** pleasant-smelling liquid worn on the skin; perfume. **3** a trail indicated by the smell of an animal.

– SYNONYMS **1 smell,** fragrance, aroma, perfume, savor, odor. **2 perfume,** fragrance, cologne, eau de cologne, eau de toilette, toilet water, body spray. **3** (as adj. **scented**) **perfumed,** fragranced, fragrant, sweet-smelling, aromatic. **4 spoor,** trail, track.

▸ **verb 1** give a pleasant scent to something. **2** find or recognize something by the sense of smell. **3** sense that something exists or is about to happen: *the general scented victory last night*.

– SYNONYMS **smell,** nose out, detect, pick up, sense.

– ORIGIN from Latin *sentire* 'perceive, smell.'

scep·ter /ˈseptər/ (Brit. **sceptre**) ▸ **noun** a staff carried by a king or queen on ceremonial occasions.
– DERIVATIVES **scep·tered** adjective.
– ORIGIN Greek *skēptron*.

scep·tic, etc. /ˈskeptik/ ▸ **noun** British spelling of SKEPTIC, etc.

scha·den·freu·de /ˈSHädənˌfroidə/ ▸ **noun** pleasure that someone gains from another person's misfortune.
– ORIGIN German.

sched·ule /ˈskejo͞ol, -jəl/ ▸ **noun 1** a plan that lists the intended tasks, events, and times needed to achieve something. **2** a timetable. **3** chiefly Law an appendix to a formal document or statute.

– SYNONYMS **plan,** program, timetable, scheme, agenda, diary, calendar, itinerary.

▸ **verb** arrange or plan for something to happen or for someone to do something.

– SYNONYMS **arrange,** organize, plan, program, slate, set up, line up.

– DERIVATIVES **sched·ul·er** noun.
– PHRASES **on** (or **to** or **according to**) **schedule** on time; as planned.
– ORIGIN Latin *schedula* 'slip of paper.'

sched·uled /ˈskeˌjo͞old, -əld/ ▶ **adjective 1** forming part of or included on a schedule. **2** (of an airline or flight) forming part of a regular service rather than specially chartered.

sched·uled caste ▶ **noun** the official name given in India to the caste considered 'untouchable' in orthodox Hindu scriptures and practice, officially regarded as socially disadvantaged.

sche·ma /ˈskēmə/ ▶ **noun** (pl. **schemata** /-mətə/ or **schemas**) technical an outline of a plan or theory.
– ORIGIN Greek *skhēma* 'form, figure.'

sche·mat·ic /skəˈmatik, skē-/ ▶ **adjective 1** (of a diagram) outlining the main features of something; simplified. **2** following a fixed pattern or plan: *the plot feels manipulative and schematic.*
– DERIVATIVES **sche·mat·i·cal·ly** /-ik(ə)lē/ adverb.

sche·ma·tize /ˈskēməˌtīz/ ▶ **verb** arrange or represent something in a schematic or simplified form.

scheme /skēm/ ▶ **noun 1** a systematic plan for achieving a particular aim. **2** a secret or underhanded plan; a plot. **3** an ordered system or pattern: *a classical rhyme scheme.*

– SYNONYMS **1 plan,** project, program, strategy, stratagem, tactic. **2 plot,** intrigue, conspiracy, ruse, ploy, stratagem, maneuver, subterfuge, machinations; informal racket, scam.

▶ **verb** make plans in an underhanded way; plot.

– SYNONYMS **plot,** conspire, intrigue, connive, maneuver, plan.

– DERIVATIVES **schem·er** noun.
– ORIGIN Greek *skhēma* 'form, figure.'

schem·ing /ˈskēmiNG/ ▶ **adjective** given to or involved in making secret and underhanded plans: *he finally saw his scheming wife for what she really was.*

– SYNONYMS **cunning,** crafty, calculating, devious, conniving, wily, sly, tricky, artful.
– ANTONYMS ingenuous, honest.

scher·zo /ˈskertsō/ ▶ **noun** (pl. **scherzos** or **scherzi** /-tsē/) a lively, light, or playful musical composition, typically comprising a movement in a symphony or sonata.
– ORIGIN Italian, 'jest.'

schil·ling /ˈSHiliNG/ ▶ **noun** (until the introduction of the euro in 2002) the basic unit of money of Austria.
– ORIGIN German *Schilling*.

schism /ˈs(k)izəm/ ▶ **noun 1** a split between strongly opposed groups within an organization, caused by differences of opinion or belief. **2** the formal separation of a Church into two Churches owing to differences in belief.

– SYNONYMS **division,** split, rift, breach, rupture, break, separation, severance, chasm, gulf, disagreement.

– DERIVATIVES **schis·mat·ic** /s(k)izˈmatik/ adjective & noun.
– ORIGIN Greek *skhisma* 'cleft.'

schist /SHist/ ▶ **noun** a coarse-grained metamorphic rock that consists of layers of different minerals.
– ORIGIN from Greek *skhistos* 'split.'

schis·to·so·mi·a·sis /ˌSHistōsəˈmīəsis/ ▶ **noun** another term for **BILHARZIA**.
– ORIGIN from *schistosome*, referring to the worm that causes bilharzia, from Greek *skhistos* 'divided' + *sōma* 'body.'

schiz·oid /ˈskitˌsoid/ ▶ **adjective 1** referring to a personality type characterized by emotional coldness, eccentric behavior, and withdrawal into a fantasy world. **2** informal mad or crazy. ▶ **noun** a person with a schizoid personality.

schiz·o·phre·ni·a /ˌskitsəˈfrēnēə, -ˈfrenēə/ ▶ **noun** a long-term mental disorder whose symptoms include a disintegration in the process of thinking and withdrawal from reality into fantasy.
– ORIGIN from Greek *skhizein* 'to split' + *phrēn* 'mind.'

schiz·o·phren·ic /ˌskitsəˈfrenik/ ▶ **adjective 1** having schizophrenia. **2** informal having inconsistent or contradictory elements. ▶ **noun** a person with schizophrenia.

schle·miel /SHləˈmēl/ (also **shlemiel**) ▶ **noun** informal a stupid, awkward, or unlucky person.
– ORIGIN from Yiddish *shlemiel*.

schlep /SHlep/ (also **schlepp**) informal ▶ **verb** (**schleps, schlepping. schlepped**) **1** haul or carry something heavy or awkward. **2** go or move reluctantly or with effort. ▶ **noun** a boring or difficult journey.
– ORIGIN Yiddish, 'drag.'

schlock /SHläk/ ▶ **noun** informal cheap or inferior goods or material; rubbish.
– DERIVATIVES **schlock·y** adjective.
– ORIGIN probably from Yiddish words meaning 'an apoplectic stroke' and 'wretch, untidy person.'

schmaltz /SHmälts, SHmôlts/ ▶ **noun** informal excessive sentimentality.
– DERIVATIVES **schmaltz·y** adjective.
– ORIGIN German *Schmalz* 'dripping, lard.'

schmooze /SHmo͞oz/ informal ▶ **verb 1** chat, especially at a social event. **2** talk in a friendly way to someone in order to gain an advantage.
– DERIVATIVES **schmooz·er** noun **schmooz·y** adjective.
– ORIGIN Yiddish.

schmuck /SHmək/ ▶ **noun** informal a stupid or worthless person.
– ORIGIN Yiddish, 'penis.'

schnapps /SHnäps, SHnaps/ ▶ **noun** a strong alcoholic drink resembling gin.
– ORIGIN German *Schnaps* 'dram of liquor.'

schnau·zer /ˈSHnouzər/ ▶ **noun** a German breed of dog with a close wiry coat and heavy whiskers around the muzzle.
– ORIGIN German.

schnit·zel /ˈSHnitsəl/ ▶ **noun** a thin slice of veal or other pale meat, coated in breadcrumbs and fried.
– ORIGIN German, 'slice.'

schol·ar /ˈskälər/ ▶ **noun 1** a person who studies a particular subject in detail; an academic. **2** a college student holding a scholarship.

– SYNONYMS **academic,** intellectual, learned person, man/woman of letters, authority, expert; informal egghead.

– ORIGIN Latin *scholaris*.

schol·ar·ly /ˈskälərlē/ ▶ **adjective 1** relating to serious academic study. **2** devoted to academic studies; learned.

– SYNONYMS **learned,** educated, erudite, academic, well read, intellectual, literary, highbrow.
– ANTONYMS uneducated, illiterate.

schol·ar·ship /ˈskälərˌSHip/ ▶ **noun 1** serious academic study. **2** a grant made to support a student's education, awarded on the basis of achievement.

– SYNONYMS **1 learning,** knowledge, erudition, education, academic study. **2 grant,** award, endowment.

CHOOSE THE RIGHT WORD

See **KNOWLEDGE**.

scho·las·tic /skəˈlastik/ ▶ **adjective 1** relating to schools and education. **2** relating to medieval scholasticism. ▶ **noun** a follower of medieval scholasticism.

scho·las·ti·cism /skəˈlastiˌsizəm/ ▶ **noun** the system of theology and philosophy taught in medieval European universities, based mainly on Aristotle's philosophy and logic and the works of early Christian religious writers.

school[1] /sko͞ol/ ▶ **noun 1** an institution for educating children. **2** a day's work at school. **3** any institution at which instruction is given in a particular subject. **4** a department or faculty of a university. **5** informal a college or university. **6** a group of artists, writers, or philosophers who share similar ideas or methods.

– SYNONYMS **1 college,** academy, alma mater. **2 department,** faculty, division.

▶ **verb 1** formal send someone to school. **2** train in a particular skill or activity: *he schooled her in horsemanship.*

– SYNONYMS **train,** teach, tutor, coach, instruct, drill.

– PHRASES **school of thought** a particular way of thinking.
– ORIGIN Greek *skholē* 'leisure, philosophy, lecture-place.'

WORD LINKS

scholastic *relating to schools*

school[2] ▶ **noun** a large group of fish or sea mammals.
– ORIGIN German or Dutch *schōle.*

school board ▶ **noun** a local board or authority responsible for providing and maintaining schools.

school·boy /ˈsko͞olˌboi/ (or **schoolgirl**) ▶ **noun** a boy (or girl) attending school.

school·child /ˈsko͞olˌCHīld/ ▶ **noun** (pl. **schoolchildren** /ˈsko͞olˌCHildrən/) a child attending school.

school·days /ˈsko͞olˌdāz/ ▶ **plural noun** the period in someone's life when they attended school.

school·house /ˈsko͞olˌhous/ ▶ **noun** a building used as a school, especially in a small community.

school·ing /ˈsko͞oliNG/ ▶ **noun** education received at school.

school·marm /ˈsko͞olˌmä(r)m/ ▶ **noun** old use a schoolmistress, especially one who is prim and strict.

school·mas·ter /ˈsko͞olˌmastər/ (or **schoolmistress** /ˈsko͞olˌmistris/) ▶ **noun** chiefly Brit. a teacher in a school.

school·mate /ˈsko͞olˌmāt/ ▶ **noun** informal a fellow student.

school·room /ˈsko͞olˌro͞om, -ˌro͝om/ ▶ **noun** a room in which a class of students is taught.

school·teach·er /ˈsko͞olˌtēCHər/ ▶ **noun** a person who teaches in a school.

school vouch·er ▶ **noun** a government-funded voucher redeemable for tuition fees at a school other than the public school that a student could attend free.

school·work /ˈsko͞olˌwərk/ ▶ **noun** work assigned to students by their teachers in school.

schoon·er /ˈsko͞onər/ ▶ **noun 1** a sailing ship with two or more masts, typically with a mainmast that is larger than the the mast nearer the front. **2** a large glass for beer or ale.
– ORIGIN perhaps from dialect *scun* 'skim along.'

schot·tische /ˈSHätiSH/ ▶ **noun** a dance resembling a slow polka.
– ORIGIN from German *der schottische Tanz* 'the Scottish dance.'

schuss /SHo͞os, SHo͝os/ ▶ **noun** a straight downhill run on skis. ▶ **verb** make a straight downhill run on skis.
– ORIGIN German, 'shot.'

schwa /SHwä/ ▶ **noun** Phonetics an unstressed vowel (as in *a* moment *a*go), represented by the symbol /ə/ in the International Phonetic Alphabet.
– ORIGIN from German, from Hebrew *šĕwā'*.

sci·at·ic /sīˈatik/ ▶ **adjective 1** relating to the hip. **2** affecting the sciatic nerve. **3** suffering from sciatica.
– ORIGIN Greek *iskhiadikos* 'relating to the hips.'

sci·at·i·ca /sīˈatikə/ ▶ **noun** pain affecting the back, hip, and outer side of the leg, caused by pressure on the sciatic nerve root in the lower back.

sci·at·ic nerve ▶ **noun** a major nerve extending from the lower end of the spinal cord down the back of the thigh.

sci·ence /ˈsīəns/ ▶ **noun 1** the systematic study of the structure and behavior of the physical and natural world through observation and experiment. **2** an organized body of knowledge on any subject.

– SYNONYMS *the science of criminology* **subject,** discipline, field, branch of knowledge, body of knowledge, area of study.

– ORIGIN Latin *scientia.*

sci·ence fic·tion ▶ **noun** fiction set typically in the future and dealing with imagined scientific, technological, or social developments.

sci·ence park ▶ **noun** an area devoted to scientific research or the development of science-based industries.

sci·en·tif·ic /ˌsīənˈtifik/ ▶ **adjective 1** relating to or based on science. **2** done in a methodical or organized way.

– SYNONYMS **1 technological,** technical, evidence-based, empirical. **2 systematic,** methodical, organized, ordered, rigorous, exact, precise, accurate, mathematical.

– DERIVATIVES **sci·en·tif·i·cal·ly** /-ik(ə)lē/ adverb.

sci·en·tist /ˈsīəntist/ ▶ **noun** a person who has expert knowledge of one or more of the natural or physical sciences.

Sci·en·tol·o·gy /ˌsīənˈtäləjē/ ▶ **noun** trademark a religious system based on the seeking of self-knowledge and spiritual fulfillment through courses of study and training.
– DERIVATIVES **Sci·en·tol·o·gist** noun.
– ORIGIN from Latin *scientia* 'knowledge.'

sci-fi /'sī 'fī/ ▶ **noun** informal short for **SCIENCE FICTION**.

scil·la /'silə/ ▶ **noun** a plant with small blue star- or bell-shaped flowers and glossy leaves.
– ORIGIN Greek *skilla* 'sea onion.'

scim·i·tar /'simətər, -ˌtär/ ▶ **noun** a short sword with a curved blade that broadens toward the point, first used in Eastern countries.
– ORIGIN French *cimeterre* or Italian *scimitarra*.

scin·til·la /sin'tilə/ ▶ **noun** a tiny trace or amount: *not a scintilla of doubt*.
– ORIGIN Latin, 'spark.'

scin·til·late /'sin(t)lˌāt/ ▶ **verb** give off flashes of light; sparkle.
– DERIVATIVES **scin·til·lant** /-ənt/ adjective & noun **scin·til·la·tion** /ˌsin(t)l'āsʜən/ noun.
– ORIGIN Latin *scintillare* 'to sparkle.'

scin·til·lat·ing /'sin(t)lˌātiɴɢ/ ▶ **adjective 1** very clever, skillful, or exciting: *a scintillating performance*. **2** sparkling brightly.

– SYNONYMS **brilliant,** dazzling, exciting, exhilarating, stimulating, sparkling, lively, vivacious, vibrant, animated, effervescent, witty, clever.
– ANTONYMS dull, boring.

sci·on /'sīən/ ▶ **noun 1** a young shoot or twig of a plant that is cut off to create a new plant. **2** a descendant of an important or famous family.
– ORIGIN Old French *ciun* 'shoot, twig.'

scis·sor /'sizər/ ▶ **verb 1** cut something with scissors. **2** move the legs back and forward in a way that resembles the action of scissors.

scis·sors /'sizərz/ ▶ **plural noun** (also **a pair of scissors**) a tool for cutting cloth and paper, consisting of two crossing blades pivoted in the middle. ▶ **adjective** (also **scissor**) (of an action) in which two things cross each other or open and close like a pair of scissors: *a scissor kick*.
– ORIGIN Latin *cisorium* 'cutting instrument.'

scle·ra /'skli(ə)rə/ ▶ **noun** the white outer layer of the eyeball.
– ORIGIN Latin.

scle·ro·der·ma /ˌskli(ə)rə'dərmə, ˌskler-/ ▶ **noun** a medical condition in which the skin and connective tissue hardens and contracts.

scle·ro·sis /sklə'rōsis/ ▶ **noun 1** abnormal hardening of body tissue. **2** (in full **multiple sclerosis**) a disease involving damage to the sheaths of nerve cells in the brain and spinal cord, leading to partial or complete paralysis.
– ORIGIN Greek *sklērōsis*.

scle·rot·ic /sklə'rätik/ ▶ **adjective 1** Medicine relating to or having sclerosis. **2** unable to adapt; rigid: *sclerotic management*.

scoff[1] /skôf, skäf/ ▶ **verb** speak about someone or something in a scornful way.

– SYNONYMS *they **scoffed at** her article* mock, deride, ridicule, sneer at, jeer at, laugh at, dismiss, belittle; informal pooh-pooh.

– DERIVATIVES **scoff·er** noun.
– ORIGIN perhaps Scandinavian.

scoff[2] ▶ **verb** informal eat something quickly and greedily.
– ORIGIN from Dutch *schoft* 'quarter of a day, meal.'

scold /skōld/ ▶ **verb** angrily tell someone that they have done something wrong.

– SYNONYMS **rebuke,** reprimand, reproach, reprove, admonish, chastise, chide, upbraid, berate, haul over the coals; informal tell off, dress down, give someone an earful, bawl out, give someone hell, chew out; formal castigate.
– ANTONYMS praise.

▶ **noun** old use a woman who nags or grumbles constantly.
– ORIGIN probably from Old Norse, 'person who writes and recites epic poems.'

CHOOSE THE RIGHT WORD

scold, berate, chide, revile, upbraid, vituperate

A mother might **scold** a child who misbehaves, which means to rebuke in an angry, irritated, and often nagging way, whether or not such treatment is justified. **Chide** is a more formal term than *scold*, and it usually implies disapproval for specific failings (*she was chided by her teacher for using "less" instead of "fewer"*), while **berate** suggests a prolonged scolding, usually aimed at a pattern of behavior or way of life rather than a single misdeed and often combined with scorn or contempt for the person being criticized (*he berated his parents for being too protective and ruining his social life*). **Upbraid** also implies a lengthy expression of displeasure or criticism, but usually with more justification than scold and with an eye toward encouraging better behavior in the future (*the tennis coach upbraided her players for missing so many serves*). **Revile** and **vituperate** are reserved for very strong or even violent displays of anger. To *revile* is to use highly abusive and contemptuous language (*revile one's opponent in the press*), while *vituperate* connotes even more violence in the attack (*the angry hockey players were held apart by their teammates, but they continued to vituperate each other with the foulest possible language*).

CHOOSE THE RIGHT WORD

See **REBUKE**.

sco·li·o·sis /ˌskōlē'ōsis/ ▶ **noun** Medicine abnormal lateral curvature of the spine.
– ORIGIN Greek *skolios* 'bent.'

sconce /skäns/ ▶ **noun** a candle holder attached to a wall with an ornamental bracket.
– ORIGIN Old French *esconse* 'lantern.'

scone /skōn, skän/ ▶ **noun** a small plain cake made from flour, fat, and milk.
– ORIGIN perhaps from Dutch *schoonbroot* 'fine bread.'

scoop /sko͞op/ ▶ **noun 1** a utensil resembling a spoon, having a short handle and a deep bowl. **2** the bowl-shaped part of a digging machine or dredger. **3** informal a piece of news published by a newspaper or broadcast by a television or radio station before its rivals know about it.

– SYNONYMS **spoon,** ladle, dipper.

▶ **verb 1** pick something up with a scoop. **2** create a hollow in something. **3** pick up in a swift, smooth movement. **4** informal win a prize. **5** informal publish a news story before a rival.

– SYNONYMS **1** *a hole was **scooped out** in the floor* **hollow out,** gouge out, dig, excavate. **2** *cut the tomatoes in half and **scoop out** the flesh* **remove,** take out, spoon out, scrape out. **3** *she **scooped up** armfuls of clothes* **pick up,** gather up, lift, take up, snatch, grab.

– ORIGIN German *schōpe* 'waterwheel bucket.'

scoop neck ▶ **noun** a deeply curved wide neckline on a woman's garment.

scoot /sko͞ot/ ▶ **verb** informal go or leave somewhere quickly.
– ORIGIN unknown.

scoot·er /ˈsko͞otər/ ▶ **noun 1** (also **motor scooter**) a light two-wheeled motorcycle. **2** a child's toy consisting of a footboard mounted on two wheels and a long steering handle, moved by pushing one foot against the ground. ▶ **verb** travel or ride on a scooter.

scope[1] /skōp/ ▶ **noun 1** the opportunity or possibility for doing something: *there is clearly scope for development in the future.* **2** the range of the area or subject matter that something deals with: *these matters are beyond the scope of this book.*

– SYNONYMS **1 opportunity,** freedom, latitude, leeway, capacity, room (to maneuver). **2 extent,** range, breadth, reach, sweep, span, area, sphere, realm, compass, orbit, ambit, terms of reference, remit.

– ORIGIN Greek *skopos* 'target.'

CHOOSE THE RIGHT WORD
See **RANGE**.

scope[2] ▶ **noun** informal a telescope, microscope, or other device having a name ending in *-scope.*

-scope ▶ **combining form** referring to an instrument for observing or examining: *telescope.*
– ORIGIN from Greek *skopein* 'look at.'

scor·bu·tic /skôrˈbyo͞otik/ ▶ **adjective** relating to or affected with scurvy.
– ORIGIN from Latin *scorbutus* 'scurvy.'

scorch /skôrCH/ ▶ **verb 1** burn or become burned on the surface or edges. **2** (as adj. **scorched**) dried out and withered as a result of extreme heat. **3** informal move very fast: *a car scorching along the highway.*

– SYNONYMS **1 burn,** sear, singe, char, blacken, discolor. **2 dry up,** parch, wither, shrivel, desiccate.

▶ **noun** the burning of the surface of something.
– ORIGIN perhaps related to Old Norse, 'be shriveled.'

scorched earth pol·i·cy ▶ **noun** a military strategy of burning or destroying all crops and other resources that might be of use to an invading enemy force.

scorch·er /ˈskôrCHər/ ▶ **noun** informal a day or period of very hot weather.

scorch·ing /ˈskôrCHiNG/ ▶ **adjective** very hot: *the scorching July sun.*

– SYNONYMS **hot,** red-hot, blazing, flaming, fiery, burning, blistering, searing; informal boiling, baking, sizzling.
– ANTONYMS freezing, mild.

score /skôr/ ▶ **noun 1** the number of points, goals, runs, etc., achieved by a person or side in a game. **2** (pl. same) a group or set of twenty. **3** (**scores of**) a large number of. **4** the written music for a composition, showing all the vocal and instrumental parts. **5** (**the score**) informal the real situation or facts: *I'm not thick, I know the score.* **6** a notch or line cut into a surface.

– SYNONYMS **1 result,** outcome, total, tally, count. **2 rating,** grade, mark, percentage.

▶ **verb 1** gain a point, goal, run, etc., in a game. **2** orchestrate or arrange a piece of music. **3** cut or scratch a mark on a surface. **4** (**score something out/through**) delete part of a piece of writing by drawing a line through it. **5** be worth a number of points. **6** record the score during a game. **7** informal succeed in obtaining illegal drugs. **8** informal succeed in attracting a sexual partner.

– SYNONYMS **1 get,** gain, chalk up, achieve, make, record, rack up, notch up; informal **bag. 2 arrange,** set, adapt, orchestrate, write, compose. **3 scratch,** cut, notch, incise, scrape, nick, gouge. **4** (**score something out/through**) **cross out,** strike out, delete, put a line through, obliterate.

– DERIVATIVES **score·less** adjective **scor·er** noun.
– PHRASES **settle a score** take revenge on someone.
– ORIGIN Old Norse, 'notch, tally, twenty.'

score·board /ˈskôrˌbôrd/ ▶ **noun** a large board on which the score in a game or match is displayed.

score·card /ˈskôrˌkärd/ ▶ **noun 1** (also **scoresheet** /ˈskôrˌSHēt/) a card or sheet of paper in which scores are recorded. **2** a card listing the names and positions of players in a team.

scorn /skôrn/ ▶ **noun** a strong feeling that someone or something is worthless; contempt.

– SYNONYMS **contempt,** derision, disdain, mockery, sneering.
– ANTONYMS admiration, respect.

▶ **verb 1** express contempt for someone or something. **2** reject in a scornful way: *I have never scorned newspapers as many people do.*

– SYNONYMS **1 deride,** treat with contempt, mock, scoff at, sneer at, jeer at, laugh at. **2 spurn,** rebuff, reject, ignore, shun, snub.
– ANTONYMS admire, respect.

– ORIGIN Old French *escarn.*

CHOOSE THE RIGHT WORD
See **DESPISE**.

scorn·ful /ˈskôrnfəl/ ▶ **adjective** showing that one feels someone or something is worthless; contemptuous.

– SYNONYMS **contemptuous,** derisive, withering, mocking, sneering, jeering, scathing, snide, disparaging, supercilious, disdainful.
– ANTONYMS admiring.

– DERIVATIVES **scorn·ful·ly** adverb.

Scor·pi·o /ˈskôrpēˌō/ ▶ **noun 1** the eighth sign of the zodiac (the Scorpion), which the sun enters about October 23. **2** (**a Scorpio**) a person born when the sun is in this sign.
– DERIVATIVES **Scor·pi·an** /-pēən/ noun & adjective.
– ORIGIN Latin.

scor·pi·on /ˈskôrpēən/ ▶ **noun** a creature related to spiders, with pincers and a poisonous sting at the end of its tail.
– ORIGIN Greek *skorpios.*

scor·zo·ne·ra /ˌskôrzəˈni(ə)rə/ ▶ **noun** the purple-brown root of a plant of the daisy family, eaten as a vegetable.
– ORIGIN Italian.

Scot /skät/ ▶ **noun 1** a person from Scotland. **2** a member of a Gaelic people that migrated from Ireland to Scotland around the late 5th century.
– ORIGIN Latin *Scottus.*

Scotch /skäCH/ ▶ **noun** (also **Scotch whiskey**) whiskey made in Scotland. ▶ **adjective** old-fashioned term for

Scottish.
– ORIGIN from **Scottish.**

scotch /skäch/ ▶ **verb** decisively put an end to: *they were quick to scotch talk of a disagreement.*
– ORIGIN perhaps related to **skate**[1].

Scotch broth ▶ **noun** a traditional Scottish soup made from meat stock with pearl barley and vegetables.

Scotch pine ▶ **noun** a pine tree widely grown for timber and other products.

Scotch tape ▶ **noun** trademark transparent adhesive tape. ▶ **verb** fasten or stick something with transparent adhesive tape.

Scotch whis·key ▶ **noun** another term for **Scotch.**

scot-free ▶ **adverb** without suffering any punishment or injury: *the people who kidnapped her will get off scot-free.*
– ORIGIN from former *scot* 'a tax.'

Scots /skäts/ ▶ **adjective** another term for **Scottish.** ▶ **noun** the form of English used in Scotland.

Scots·man /'skätsmən/ (or **Scotswoman** /'skäts,wo͝omən/) ▶ **noun** (pl. **Scotsmen** or **Scotswomen**) a person from Scotland.

Scot·ti·cism /'skäti,sizəm/ ▶ **noun** a characteristically Scottish word or phrase.

Scot·tie /'skätē/ ▶ **noun** informal a Scottish terrier.

Scot·tish /'skätish/ ▶ **adjective** relating to Scotland or its people. ▶ **noun** (as pl. n. **the Scottish**) the people of Scotland.
– DERIVATIVES **Scot·tish·ness** noun.

Scot·tish ter·ri·er ▶ **noun** a small rough-haired breed of terrier.

scoun·drel /'skoundrəl/ ▶ **noun** a person who takes advantage of or deceives others; a rogue.

> – SYNONYMS **rogue,** rascal, miscreant, good-for-nothing, reprobate; cheat, swindler, fraudster, trickster, charlatan; informal villain, rat, louse, swine, dog, skunk, heel, wretch, scumbag, rat fink; dated cad; old use blackguard, knave.

– DERIVATIVES **scoun·drel·ly** adjective.
– ORIGIN unknown.

scour[1] /skou(ə)r/ ▶ **verb 1** clean something by rubbing it with a detergent or something rough. **2** (of running water) wear away rock to form a channel or pool.

> – SYNONYMS **scrub,** rub, clean, polish, buff, shine, burnish, grind, abrade.

– DERIVATIVES **scour·er** noun.
– ORIGIN Old French *escurer.*

scour[2] ▶ **verb** search a place thoroughly.

> – SYNONYMS **search,** comb, hunt through, rummage through, look high and low in, ransack, turn upside-down.

– ORIGIN unknown.

scourge /skərj/ ▶ **noun 1** a cause of great trouble or suffering: *the plague was the scourge of the Middle Ages.* **2** historical a whip used to punish people.

> – SYNONYMS **affliction,** bane, curse, plague, menace, evil, misfortune, burden, blight, cancer, canker.

▶ **verb 1** cause great suffering to someone or something. **2** historical whip someone as a punishment.
– ORIGIN Old French *escorge.*

scout /skout/ ▶ **noun 1** a person sent ahead of a main force to gather information about the enemy. **2** (also **Scout**) a member of the Boy Scouts or Girl Scouts, organizations that aim to develop character through outdoor and other activities. **3** a talent scout. **4** an instance of searching somewhere to gather information.

> – SYNONYMS **1 lookout,** spy. **2 reconnaissance,** reconnoiter, survey, exploration, search; informal recce.

▶ **verb 1** search a place in order to discover something. **2** explore or examine so as to gather information: *they are keen to scout out business opportunities.* **3** act as a talent scout.

> – SYNONYMS **1** *I* ***scouted around*** *for some logs* **search,** look, hunt, ferret around, root around. **2** *a patrol was sent to* ***scout out*** *the area* **reconnoiter,** explore, inspect, investigate, spy out, survey, scan, study; informal check out, case.

– DERIVATIVES **scout·ing** noun.
– ORIGIN Old French *escouter* 'listen.'

scout·mas·ter /'skout,mastər/ ▶ **noun** the adult in charge of a group of Boy Scouts.

scow /skou/ ▶ **noun** a flat-bottomed boat for transporting cargo to and from ships in harbor.
– ORIGIN Dutch *schouw* 'ferry boat.'

scowl /skoul/ ▶ **noun** an angry or bad-tempered expression. ▶ **verb** frown in an angry or bad-tempered way.

> – SYNONYMS **glower,** frown, glare, grimace, lour, look daggers.
> – ANTONYMS smile.

– ORIGIN probably Scandinavian.

scrab·ble /'skrabəl/ ▶ **verb 1** grope around with the fingers to find or hold onto something. **2** move quickly and awkwardly; scramble. ▶ **noun** (**Scrabble**) trademark a board game in which players build up words from small lettered squares or tiles.
– ORIGIN Dutch *schrabbelen.*

scrag·gly /'skrag(ə)lē/ (also **scraggy** /'skragē/) ▶ **adjective 1** thin and bony. **2** ragged or untidy in appearance.

scram /skram/ ▶ **verb** (**scrams, scramming, scrammed**) informal go away or leave quickly.
– ORIGIN probably from **scramble.**

scram·ble /'skrambəl/ ▶ **verb 1** move or make one's way quickly and awkwardly, using the hands as well as the feet. **2** make or become jumbled or confused. **3** put a broadcast transmission or telephone conversation into a form that can only be understood if received by a decoding device. **4** cook beaten eggs with a little liquid in a pan. **5** informal act in a hurried or undignified way: *firms scrambled to win contracts.* **6** (of fighter aircraft) take off immediately in an emergency or for action.

> – SYNONYMS **1 clamber,** climb, shinny, crawl, claw one's way, scrabble, struggle. **2 muddle,** confuse, mix up, jumble (up), disarrange, disorganize, disorder, disturb, mess up.

▶ **noun 1** an act of scrambling up or over something. **2** a hasty or undignified struggle to achieve or get something.

> – SYNONYMS **1 clamber,** climb. **2** *the scramble for a seat* **struggle,** jostle, scrimmage, scuffle, tussle, free-for-all, jockeying, competition, race.

– ORIGIN imitating the sound.

scram·bler /ˈskramb(ə)lər/ ▶ **noun** a device for scrambling a broadcast transmission or telephone conversation.
– DERIVATIVES **scram·bling** noun.

scrap[1] /skrap/ ▶ **noun 1** a small piece or amount of something, especially one that is left over after the rest has been used. **2** waste metal and other material that can be reprocessed. **3** (**scraps**) bits of uneaten food left after a meal.

– SYNONYMS **1 fragment,** piece, bit, snippet, oddment, remnant, morsel, sliver. **2** *not a scrap of evidence* **bit,** shred, speck, iota, particle, ounce, jot. **3 waste,** garbage, trash, rubbish, refuse, debris; informal junk.

▶ **verb** (**scraps, scrapping, scrapped**) **1** abolish or cancel a plan, policy, or law. **2** remove something from use so as to convert it to scrap metal.

– SYNONYMS **1** *campaigners called for the plans to be scrapped* **abandon,** drop, abolish, withdraw, do away with, put an end to, cancel, ax; informal ditch, dump, junk. **2** *old cars due to be scrapped* **throw away,** throw out, dispose of, get rid of, discard, dispense with, bin, decommission, break up, demolish; informal trash, chuck, ditch, dump, junk.
– ANTONYMS keep.

– ORIGIN Old Norse.

scrap[2] informal ▶ **noun** a brief or minor fight or quarrel.
▶ **verb** (**scraps, scrapping, scrapped**) have a brief or minor fight or quarrel.
– DERIVATIVES **scrap·per** noun.
– ORIGIN perhaps from **SCRAPE**.

scrap·book /ˈskrapˌbo͝ok/ ▶ **noun** a book of blank pages for sticking cuttings, drawings, or pictures in.

scrap·book·ing /ˈskrapˌbo͝okiNG/ ▶ **noun** the activity or hobby of keeping a scrapbook.

scrape /skrāp/ ▶ **verb 1** drag or pull a hard or sharp implement across a surface or object to remove dirt or waste matter. **2** damage something by rubbing against a rough or hard surface. **3** just manage to achieve, succeed, or pass: *he now scrapes a living from a roadside stand.* **4** (**scrape something together/up**) collect or accumulate something with difficulty. **5** (**scrape by/along**) manage to live with difficulty.

– SYNONYMS **1 rub,** scratch, scour, grind, sand, sandpaper, abrade, file. **2 grate,** creak, rasp, scratch. **3 graze,** scratch, scuff, rasp, skin, cut, lacerate, bark, chafe.

▶ **noun 1** an act or sound of scraping. **2** an injury or mark caused by scraping. **3** informal an embarrassing or difficult situation that one has caused oneself.

– SYNONYMS **1 grating,** creaking, rasp, scratch. **2 graze,** scratch, abrasion, cut, laceration, wound.

– DERIVATIVES **scrap·er** noun.
– PHRASES **scrape the barrel** (or **the bottom of the barrel**) informal be forced to use the last and poorest resources because nothing else is available.
– ORIGIN Old English, 'scratch with the fingernails.'

scrap·heap /ˈskrapˌhēp/ ▶ **noun** a pile of things that have been thrown away as rubbish.
– PHRASES **on the scrapheap** rejected as no longer wanted or useful.

scrap·ie /ˈskrāpē/ ▶ **noun** a disease of sheep involving the central nervous system, in which the animals suffer from a lack of coordination.
– ORIGIN from **SCRAPE**.

scrap·py[1] /ˈskrapē/ ▶ **adjective** (**scrappier, scrappiest**) disorganized, untidy, or incomplete.
– DERIVATIVES **scrap·pi·ly** adverb **scrap·pi·ness** noun.

scrap·py[2] ▶ **adjective** (**scrappier, scrappiest**) inclined to fight; aggressive and quarrelsome.
– DERIVATIVES **scrap·pi·ly** adverb **scrap·pi·ness** noun.

scrap·yard /ˈskrapˌyärd/ ▶ **noun** a place where waste metal and other material is collected before being discarded or recycled.

scratch /skraCH/ ▶ **verb 1** make a long mark or wound on a surface with something sharp. **2** rub a part of one's body with one's fingernails to relieve itching. **3** cross out writing. **4** cancel or abandon a plan or project. **5** withdraw from a competition. **6** make a living or achieve something with difficulty: *he was just scratching a living from the black market.* **7** (as n. **scratching**) the technique, used in rap music, of stopping a record by hand and moving it back and forward to give a rhythmic scratching effect. **8** (of a bird or mammal) rake the ground with the beak or claws in search of food.

– SYNONYMS **scrape,** abrade, graze, score, scuff, skin, cut, lacerate, bark, chafe.

▶ **noun 1** a mark or wound made by scratching. **2** an act or spell of scratching. **3** informal a slight wound or injury.

– SYNONYMS **abrasion,** graze, scrape, cut, laceration, wound, mark, line.

▶ **adjective** put together from whatever is available: *we were a scratch team at best.*
– DERIVATIVES **scratch·er** noun.
– PHRASES **from scratch** from the very beginning. **scratch the surface** deal with a matter only in the most superficial way. **up to scratch** up to the required standard; satisfactory.
– ORIGIN uncertain.

scratch card ▶ **noun** a card with a section or sections coated in a waxy substance that may be scraped away to reveal whether a prize has been won.

scratch·y /ˈskraCHē/ ▶ **adjective** (**scratchier, scratchiest**) **1** rough in texture and causing scratching. **2** (of a voice or sound) rough; grating.

scrawl /skrôl/ ▶ **verb** write in a hurried, careless way.
▶ **noun** hurried, careless handwriting.
– ORIGIN probably from **CRAWL**.

scrawn·y /ˈskrônē/ ▶ **adjective** (**scrawnier, scrawniest**) unattractively thin and bony.

– SYNONYMS **skinny,** thin, as thin as a rail, skin-and-bones, gaunt, bony, angular, gawky, scraggy.
– ANTONYMS fat.

– ORIGIN from dialect *scranny.*

scream /skrēm/ ▶ **verb 1** make a long, loud, piercing cry or sound expressing strong emotion or pain. **2** move very rapidly, especially with a loud, high-pitched sound. **3** present in an urgent or obvious way: *the headlines screamed 'he offered me sex.'*

– SYNONYMS **shriek,** screech, yell, howl, bawl, yelp, squeal, wail, squawk.

▶ **noun 1** a long, loud, piercing cry or sound. **2** (**a scream**) informal a very funny person or thing.

– SYNONYMS **shriek,** screech, yell, howl, bawl, yelp, squeal, wail, squawk.

– DERIVATIVES **scream·er** noun.
– ORIGIN perhaps Dutch.

scream·ing·ly /ˈskrēmiNGlē/ ▶ **adverb** to a very great extent; extremely: *screamingly funny television.*

scree /skrē/ ▶ noun a mass of small loose stones that form or cover a slope on a mountain.
– ORIGIN probably from Old Norse, 'landslip.'

screech /skrēCH/ ▶ verb 1 make a loud, harsh cry. 2 move fast with a loud, harsh sound. ▶ noun a loud, harsh cry or sound.
– DERIVATIVES **screech·er** noun **screech·y** adjective.
– ORIGIN imitating the sound.

screech owl ▶ noun a small American owl with a screeching call and distinctive ear tufts.

screed /skrēd/ ▶ noun 1 a long speech or piece of writing. 2 a layer of material applied to level a floor or other surface.
– ORIGIN probably from **SHRED**.

screen /skrēn/ ▶ noun 1 an upright partition used to divide a room, give shelter, or conceal something. 2 a thing that shelters or conceals: *his jeep was parked behind a screen of trees.* 3 the flat front surface of a television or monitor, on which images and data are displayed. 4 a blank surface on which movies are projected. 5 (often **the screen**) movies or television: *a star of stage and screen.*

> – SYNONYMS 1 **partition,** divider, windbreak. 2 **display,** monitor, visual display unit. 3 **mesh,** net, netting. 4 **buffer,** protection, shield, shelter, guard.

▶ verb 1 conceal, protect, or shelter with a screen: *her hair swung across to screen her face.* 2 show a movie or video or broadcast a television program. 3 protect someone from something dangerous or unpleasant. 4 test someone to find out whether or not they have a disease. 5 investigate someone to assess their suitability for a job.

> – SYNONYMS 1 **partition,** divide, separate, curtain. 2 **conceal,** hide, veil, shield, shelter, shade, protect. 3 **show,** broadcast, transmit, televise, put on, air. 4 *all blood is screened for the virus* **check,** test, examine, investigate, vet; informal check out.

– DERIVATIVES **screen·er** noun **screen·ful** /-ˌfo͝ol/ noun.
– ORIGIN Old French *escren.*

screen·play /ˈskrēnˌplā/ ▶ noun the script of a movie, including acting instructions and scene directions.

screen-print ▶ verb force ink onto a surface through a prepared piece of fine material such as silk or nylon so as to create a picture or pattern. ▶ noun (**screen print**) a picture or design produced by screen-printing.

screen sav·er ▶ noun a computer program that replaces an unchanging screen display with a moving image to prevent damage to the phosphor.

screen test ▶ noun a filmed test to assess whether an actor is suitable for a movie or television role. ▶ verb (**screen-test**) give a screen test to an actor.

screen·writ·er /ˈskrēnˌrītər/ ▶ noun a person who writes a screenplay for a movie.
– DERIVATIVES **screen·writ·ing** noun.

screw /skro͞o/ ▶ noun 1 a metal pin with a spiral thread running around it and a slotted head, used to join things together by being turned and pressed in. 2 a cylinder with a spiral ridge or thread running around the outside that can be turned to seal an opening, apply pressure, adjust position, etc. 3 (also **screw propeller**) a ship's or aircraft's propeller. 4 informal, derogatory a prison guard. 5 vulgar slang an act of having sex.

> – SYNONYMS 1 **bolt,** fastener. 2 **screw propeller,** propeller, rotor.

▶ verb 1 fasten or tighten something with a screw or screws. 2 turn something so as to attach or remove it by means of a spiral thread. 3 informal cheat or swindle someone. 4 vulgar slang have sex with someone.

> – SYNONYMS 1 **tighten,** turn, twist, wind. 2 **fasten,** secure, fix, attach. 3 **extort,** force, extract, wrest, wring, squeeze; informal bleed.

– PHRASES **have one's head screwed on (the right way)** informal have common sense. **have a screw loose** informal be slightly eccentric or mentally disturbed. **screw someone up** informal make someone emotionally disturbed. **screw something up** 1 crush something into a tight mass. 2 informal make something go wrong.
– ORIGIN Old French *escroue* 'female screw, nut.'

screw·ball /ˈskro͞oˌbôl/ informal ▶ noun a mad or eccentric person. ▶ adjective 1 crazy; absurd. 2 referring to a movie style of fast-moving comedy involving eccentric characters or ridiculous situations.

screw·driv·er /ˈskro͞oˌdrīvər/ ▶ noun 1 a tool with a shaped tip that fits into the head of a screw to turn it. 2 a cocktail made from vodka and orange juice.

screw·y /ˈskro͞oē/ ▶ adjective (**screwier, screwiest**) informal rather odd or eccentric.

scrib·ble /ˈskribəl/ ▶ verb 1 write or draw something carelessly or hurriedly. 2 informal write for a living or as a hobby.

> – SYNONYMS **scrawl,** scratch, dash off, jot (down), doodle, sketch.

▶ noun a piece of writing or a picture produced carelessly or hurriedly.

> – SYNONYMS **scrawl,** squiggle(s), jottings, doodle, doodlings.

– DERIVATIVES **scrib·bler** noun.
– ORIGIN Latin *scribillare.*

scribe /skrīb/ ▶ noun 1 historical a person who copied out documents. 2 informal, often humorous a writer, especially a journalist. 3 historical a Jewish record-keeper or, later, a professional religious and legal expert. 4 (also **scriber**) a pointed instrument used for making marks to guide a saw or in signwriting. ▶ verb 1 literary write something. 2 mark something with a pointed instrument.
– DERIVATIVES **scrib·al** adjective.
– ORIGIN Latin *scriba.*

scrim /skrim/ ▶ noun strong, coarse fabric used for heavy-duty lining or upholstery.
– ORIGIN unknown.

scrim·mage /ˈskrimij/ ▶ noun 1 a confused struggle or fight. 2 Football offensive play begun with the ball on the ground between the offensive and defensive lines with its longest axis at right angles to the goal line. 3 chiefly Football a practice session in which a simulated game is played.
– ORIGIN from **SKIRMISH**.

scrimp /skrimp/ ▶ verb be very careful with money; economize.
– ORIGIN Scots, 'meager.'

scrim·shaw /ˈskrimˌSHô/ ▶ noun decorative work consisting of carved designs on the bones and teeth of marine mammals or on similar materials.
– ORIGIN unknown.

scrip /skrip/ ▶ noun 1 a certificate that demonstrates ownership of stocks, shares, and bonds, especially a certificate relating to an issue of additional shares to shareholders in proportion to the shares they already hold. 2 such certificates as a whole.
– ORIGIN short for *subscription receipt.*

script /skript/ ▸ noun **1** the written part of a play, movie, or television or radio broadcast. **2** handwriting as distinct from print. **3** writing using a particular alphabet: *Cyrillic script.*

– SYNONYMS **1 text,** screenplay, libretto, score, lines, dialogue, words. **2 handwriting,** writing, hand.

▸ verb write a script for a play, movie, or television or radio broadcast.
– ORIGIN Latin *scriptum.*

scrip·tur·al /ˈskripCHərəl/ ▸ adjective relating to the Bible.

scrip·ture /ˈskripCHər/ (also **scriptures**) ▸ noun **1** the sacred writings of Christianity contained in the Bible. **2** the sacred writings of a religion other than Christianity.
– ORIGIN Latin *scriptura* 'writings.'

script·writ·er /ˈskriptˌrītər/ ▸ noun a person who writes a script for a play, movie, or television or radio broadcast.
– DERIVATIVES **script·writ·ing** noun.

scrive·ner /ˈskriv(ə)nər/ ▸ noun historical a person who made a living by writing out documents; a clerk or scribe.
– ORIGIN Old French *escrivein.*

scrof·u·la /ˈskrôfyələ, ˈskräf-/ ▸ noun historical a disease characterized by swollen glands, probably a form of tuberculosis.
– DERIVATIVES **scrof·u·lous** adjective.
– ORIGIN from Latin *scrofa* 'breeding sow' (said to be subject to the disease).

scroll /skrōl/ ▸ noun **1** a roll of parchment or paper for writing or painting on. **2** an ornamental design or carving resembling a partly unrolled scroll of parchment. ▸ verb move displayed writing or graphics on a computer screen in order to view different parts of them.
– DERIVATIVES **scroll·a·ble** adjective **scroll·er** noun.
– ORIGIN from former *scrow* 'roll.'

scroll bar ▸ noun a long, thin section at the edge of a computer display by which material can be scrolled using a mouse.

scrolled /skrōld/ ▸ adjective having an ornamental design or carving resembling a scroll.

scroll·work /ˈskrōlˌwərk/ ▸ noun decoration consisting of spiral lines or patterns.

Scrooge /skro͞oj/ ▸ noun a person who is stingy with money.
– ORIGIN from Ebenezer *Scrooge* in Charles Dickens's story *A Christmas Carol.*

scro·tum /ˈskrōtəm/ ▸ noun (pl. **scrota** or **scrotums**) the pouch of skin containing the testicles.
– DERIVATIVES **scro·tal** /ˈskrōtl/ adjective.
– ORIGIN Latin.

scrounge /skrounj/ ▸ verb informal try to get something from someone without having to pay or work for it.

– SYNONYMS **beg,** borrow; informal cadge, sponge, bum, touch someone for, mooch.

– DERIVATIVES **scroung·er** noun.
– ORIGIN from dialect *scrunge* 'steal.'

scrub[1] /skrəb/ ▸ verb (**scrubs, scrubbing, scrubbed**) **1** rub someone or something hard so as to clean them. **2** (**scrub up**) thoroughly clean one's hands and arms before performing surgery. **3** informal cancel or abandon something.

– SYNONYMS **1 brush,** scour, rub, clean, cleanse, wash. **2 abandon,** scrap, drop, cancel, call off, ax; informal ditch, dump, junk.

▸ noun **1** an act of scrubbing. **2** a cosmetic lotion used to remove dead cells and cleanse the skin. **3** (**scrubs**) hygienic clothing worn by surgeons during operations.
– ORIGIN probably from German or Dutch *schrobben, schrubben.*

scrub[2] ▸ noun **1** vegetation consisting mainly of brushwood or stunted trees. **2** land covered with brushwood or stunted trees. ▸ adjective referring to a shrubby or small form of a plant: *scrub oak.*
– DERIVATIVES **scrub·by** adjective.
– ORIGIN from **SHRUB.**

scrub·ber /ˈskrəbər/ ▸ noun **1** a brush for scrubbing. **2** a device that uses water or a solution for purifying gases.

scrub·land /ˈskrəbˌland/ ▸ noun (also **scrublands**) land consisting of brushwood or stunted trees.

scruff /skrəf/ ▸ noun the back of a person's or animal's neck.
– ORIGIN from dialect *scuff.*

scruff·y /ˈskrəfē/ ▸ adjective (**scruffier, scruffiest**) shabby and untidy or dirty.

– SYNONYMS **shabby,** worn, down at the heels, ragged, tattered, mangy, dirty, untidy, unkempt, bedraggled, messy, disheveled, ill-groomed; informal tatty.
– ANTONYMS smart.

– DERIVATIVES **scruff·i·ly** /-əlē/ adverb **scruff·i·ness** noun.

scrum /skrəm/ Rugby ▸ noun an ordered formation of players in which the forwards of each team push against each other with heads down and the ball is thrown in. ▸ verb (**scrums, scrumming, scrummed**) form or take part in a scrum.
– ORIGIN shortening of *scrummage.*

scrump·tious /ˈskrəm(p)SHəs/ ▸ adjective informal very delicious or attractive.
– ORIGIN unknown.

scrunch /skrənCH/ ▸ verb **1** make a loud crunching noise. **2** crush or squeeze something into a tight mass. ▸ noun a loud crunching noise.
– ORIGIN probably imitating the sound.

scrunch·ie /ˈskrənCHē/ (also **scrunchy**) ▸ adjective making a loud crunching noise when crushed. ▸ noun (pl. **scrunchies**) a circular band of fabric-covered elastic used for fastening the hair.

scru·ple /ˈskro͞opəl/ ▸ noun **1** (usu. **scruples**) a feeling of doubt as to whether an action is morally right. **2** historical a unit of weight equal to 20 grains.

– SYNONYMS (**scruples**) *I had no scruples about eavesdropping* **qualms,** compunction, hesitation, reservations, second thoughts, doubt(s), misgivings, uneasiness, reluctance.

▸ verb hesitate to do something that one thinks may be wrong: *she doesn't scruple to ask her parents for money.*
– ORIGIN from Latin *scrupus* 'anxiety, rough pebble.'

scru·pu·lous /ˈskro͞opyələs/ ▸ adjective **1** very careful and thorough. **2** very concerned to avoid doing wrong.

– SYNONYMS **careful,** meticulous, painstaking, thorough, assiduous, sedulous, attentive, conscientious, punctilious, searching, close, rigorous, strict.
– ANTONYMS careless.

– DERIVATIVES **scru·pu·los·i·ty** /ˌskro͞opyəˈläsitē/ noun **scru·pu·lous·ly** adverb **scru·pu·lous·ness** noun.

scru·ti·nize /ˈskro͞otnˌīz/ ▶ **verb** examine someone or something closely and thoroughly.

– SYNONYMS **examine,** inspect, survey, study, look at, peruse, investigate, explore, probe, inquire into, go into, check.

scru·ti·ny /ˈskro͞otn-ē/ ▶ **noun** (pl. **scrutinies**) close and critical observation or examination.
– ORIGIN Latin *scrutinium*.

scry /skrī/ ▶ **verb** (**scries, scrying, scried**) foretell the future with a crystal ball.
– ORIGIN from **DESCRY**.

SCSI /ˈskəzē/ ▶ **abbreviation** small computer system interface.

scu·ba /ˈsko͞obə/ ▶ **noun** self-contained underwater breathing apparatus; a portable breathing apparatus for divers, consisting of cylinders of compressed air attached to a mouthpiece or mask.
– ORIGIN from the initial letters of *self-contained underwater breathing apparatus*.

scu·ba div·ing ▶ **noun** the sport or pastime of swimming underwater using a scuba.

scud /skəd/ ▶ **verb** (**scuds, scudding, scudded**) move fast because driven by the wind: *clouds scudded across the sky*. ▶ **noun** literary clouds or spray driven by the wind.
– ORIGIN perhaps from *scut* 'the short tail of a hare, rabbit, or deer,' reflecting the sense 'race like a hare.'

scuff /skəf/ ▶ **verb 1** scrape a shoe or other object against something. **2** mark a surface by scraping it. **3** drag one's feet when walking. ▶ **noun** a mark made by scraping a surface or object.
– ORIGIN perhaps imitating the sound.

scuf·fle /ˈskəfəl/ ▶ **noun** a short, confused fight or struggle. ▶ **verb 1** take part in a scuffle. **2** move in a hurried way, making a rustling or shuffling sound.
– ORIGIN probably Scandinavian.

scull /skəl/ ▶ **noun 1** each of a pair of small oars used by a single rower. **2** an oar placed over the back of a boat and moved from side to side to propel it. **3** a light, narrow boat propelled with a scull or a pair of sculls. ▶ **verb** propel a boat with sculls.
– DERIVATIVES **scul·ler** noun.
– ORIGIN unknown.

scul·ler·y /ˈskəl(ə)rē/ ▶ **noun** (pl. **sculleries**) a small kitchen or room at the back of a house used for washing dishes and other dirty household work.
– ORIGIN Old French *escuelerie*.

scul·lion /ˈskəlyən/ ▶ **noun** old use a servant given the most menial tasks in a kitchen.
– ORIGIN perhaps influenced by **SCULLERY**.

sculpt /skəlpt/ ▶ **verb** make a sculpture of someone or something.

sculp·tor /ˈskəlptər/ ▶ **noun** (fem. **sculptress**) an artist who makes sculptures.

sculp·ture /ˈskəlpCHər/ ▶ **noun 1** the art of making three-dimensional figures and shapes by carving stone or wood or casting metal. **2** a work made by carving stone or wood or casting metal.

– SYNONYMS **carving,** statue, statuette, figure, figurine, effigy, bust, head, model.

▶ **verb 1** make something by carving stone or wood or casting metal. **2** (as adj. **sculptured**) having strong, smooth curves: *sculptured bodies doing pushups*.
– DERIVATIVES **sculp·tur·al** /ˈskəlpCHərəl/ adjective.
– ORIGIN from Latin *sculpere* 'carve.'

scum /skəm/ ▶ **noun 1** a layer of dirt or froth on the surface of a liquid. **2** informal a worthless or hated person or group of people.

– SYNONYMS **film,** layer, covering, froth, filth, dross, dirt.

▶ **verb** (**scums, scumming, scummed**) cover the surface of a liquid with a layer of dirt or froth.
– DERIVATIVES **scum·my** adjective.
– ORIGIN German or Dutch *schūm*.

scum·bag /ˈskəmˌbag/ ▶ **noun** informal a hated or unpleasant person.

scum·ble /ˈskəmbəl/ Art ▶ **verb** give a softer or duller effect to a painting or color by applying a very thin coat of paint. ▶ **noun** a very thin coat of paint applied to a painting or color.
– ORIGIN perhaps from **SCUM**.

scup·per[1] /ˈskəpər/ ▶ **noun** a hole in a ship's side to allow water to run away from the deck.
– ORIGIN perhaps from Old French *escopir* 'to spit.'

scup·per[2] ▶ **verb** chiefly Brit. **1** informal prevent from working or succeeding; thwart: *the unions scuppered the plan*. **2** sink a ship deliberately.
– ORIGIN unknown.

scurf /skərf/ ▶ **noun** flakes on the surface of the skin, occurring especially as dandruff.
– DERIVATIVES **scurf·y** adjective.
– ORIGIN from Old English, 'cut to shreds.'

scur·ril·ous /ˈskərələs/ ▶ **adjective** rude and insulting, and intended to damage someone's reputation: *a scurrilous attack*.

– SYNONYMS **defamatory,** slanderous, libelous, scandalous, insulting, offensive, abusive, malicious; informal bitchy.

– DERIVATIVES **scur·ril·i·ty** /skəˈrilitē/ noun (pl. **scurrilities**).
– ORIGIN Latin *scurrilus*.

scur·ry /ˈskərē/ ▶ **verb** (**scurries, scurrying, scurried**) move hurriedly with short, quick steps. ▶ **noun** a situation of hurried and confused movement.
– ORIGIN from **HURRY**.

scur·vy /ˈskərvē/ ▶ **noun** a disease caused by a lack of vitamin C, characterized by bleeding gums and the opening of previously healed wounds. ▶ **adjective** (**scurvier, scurviest**) old use worthless or contemptible.
– ORIGIN from **SCURF**.

scut·tle[1] /ˈskətl/ ▶ **noun** a metal container with a lid and a handle, used to store coal for a domestic fire.
– ORIGIN Latin *scutella* 'dish.'

scuttle[2] ▶ **verb** run with short, quick steps. ▶ **noun** an act or sound of scuttling.
– ORIGIN probably from **SCUD**.

scuttle[3] ▶ **verb 1** deliberately cause a scheme to fail. **2** sink one's own ship deliberately. ▶ **noun** an opening with a lid in a ship's deck or side.
– ORIGIN perhaps from Spanish *escotilla* 'hatchway.'

scut·tle·butt /ˈskətlˌbət/ ▶ **noun** informal rumor; gossip.
– ORIGIN first referring to a water butt on the deck of a ship: from *scuttled butt*.

scuzz·y /ˈskəzē/ ▶ **adjective** (**scuzzier, scuzziest**) informal disgustingly dirty or unpleasant.

– DERIVATIVES **scuzz** /skəz/ noun.
– ORIGIN probably from *disgusting*.

scythe /sīTH/ ▶ noun a tool used for cutting crops such as grass or wheat, with a long curved blade at the end of a long pole. ▶ verb **1** cut crops with a scythe. **2** move through something rapidly and forcefully.
– ORIGIN Old English.

Scyth·i·an /ˈsiTHēən/ ▶ noun a person from Scythia, an ancient region of SE Europe and Asia. ▶ adjective relating to Scythia.

SD ▶ abbreviation South Dakota.

SDI ▶ abbreviation Strategic Defense Initiative.

SE ▶ abbreviation **1** southeast. **2** southeastern.

Se ▶ symbol the chemical element selenium.

sea /sē/ ▶ noun **1** the large continuous area of salt water that covers most of the earth's surface and surrounds its landmasses. **2** a vast expanse or quantity: *a sea of faces.* **3** a particular area of sea: *the Black Sea.*

– SYNONYMS **1 ocean,** waves; informal **the drink;** literary the (briny) deep. **2 expanse,** stretch, area, tract, sweep, carpet, mass.

– DERIVATIVES **sea·ward** /ˈsēwərd/ adjective & adverb **sea·wards** /ˈsēwərdz/ adverb.
– PHRASES **at sea 1** sailing on the sea. **2** confused; uncertain. **one's sea legs** one's ability to keep one's balance and not feel seasick on board a ship.
– ORIGIN Old English.

sea a·nem·o·ne ▶ noun a sea creature with a tube-shaped body that bears a ring of stinging tentacles around the mouth.

sea bass /bas/ ▶ noun a sea fish with a spiny fin on its back, resembling the freshwater perch.

sea·bed /ˈsēˌbed/ ▶ noun the ground under the sea; the ocean floor.

sea·bird /ˈsēˌbərd/ ▶ noun a bird that lives near the sea or coast.

sea·board /ˈsēˌbôrd/ ▶ noun a region bordering the sea; the coastline.

sea·bor·gi·um /sēˈbôrgēəm/ ▶ noun a very unstable chemical element made by high-energy atomic collisions.
– ORIGIN named after the American nuclear chemist Glenn *Seaborg*.

sea·borne /ˈsēˌbôrn/ ▶ adjective transported or traveling by sea.

sea bream ▶ noun a sea fish that resembles the freshwater bream.

sea breeze ▶ noun **1** a breeze blowing toward the land from the sea. **2** a cocktail consisting of vodka, grapefruit juice, and cranberry juice.

sea change ▶ noun a great and very noticeable change in a situation.
– ORIGIN from Shakespeare's *The Tempest*.

sea cow ▶ noun a manatee or similar mammal that lives in the sea.

sea cu·cum·ber ▶ noun a sea creature having a thick wormlike body with tentacles around the mouth.

sea dog ▶ noun informal an old or experienced sailor.

sea·far·ing /ˈsēˌfe(ə)riNG/ ▶ adjective (of a person) regularly traveling by sea. ▶ noun travel by sea.
– DERIVATIVES **sea·far·er** noun.

sea·food /ˈsēˌfo͞od/ ▶ noun shellfish and sea fish as food.

sea·front /ˈsēˌfrənt/ ▶ noun the part of a coastal town next to and facing the sea.

sea·go·ing /ˈsēˌgōiNG/ ▶ adjective **1** (of a ship) suitable for voyages on the sea. **2** relating to travel by sea.

sea green ▶ noun a pale bluish-green color.

sea·gull /ˈsēˌgəl/ ▶ noun a gull.

sea·horse /ˈsēˌhôrs/ ▶ noun a small sea fish that swims upright and has a head that resembles that of a horse.

sea·kale /ˈsēˌkāl/ ▶ noun a coastal plant of the cabbage family, grown for its edible shoots.

SEAL /sēl/ (also **Seal**) ▶ noun a member of an elite force within the US Navy.
– ORIGIN abbreviation of 'sea, air, land.'

seal¹ /sēl/ ▶ noun **1** a device or substance used to join two things together or to prevent anything from passing between them. **2** a piece of wax or lead with a design stamped into it, attached to a document as a guarantee that it is genuine. **3** a confirmation or guarantee: *the scheme has the government's seal of approval.*

– SYNONYMS **1 sealant,** adhesive, mastic. **2 emblem,** symbol, insignia, badge, crest.

▶ verb **1** fasten or close something securely. **2** (**seal something off**) isolate an area by preventing people from entering or leaving it: *police sealed off the block.* **3** make definite; finalize: *the consortium said they hoped to seal a deal within two weeks.* **4** apply a coating to a surface to prevent something from passing through it. **5** fix a seal to a document to show that it is genuine.

– SYNONYMS **1 stop up,** seal up, cork, stopper, plug, make watertight. **2** (**seal something off**) **close off,** shut off, cordon off, fence off, isolate. **3 clinch,** secure, settle, conclude, complete, finalize, confirm.

– DERIVATIVES **seal·a·ble** adjective.
– PHRASES **my lips are sealed** I will not discuss or reveal something. **put** (or **set**) **the seal on** finally confirm or complete something.
– ORIGIN Old French *seel*.

seal² ▶ noun a fish-eating mammal that lives in the sea, with flippers and a streamlined body. ▶ verb (usu. as n. **sealing**) hunt for seals.
– ORIGIN Old English.

seal·ant /ˈsēlənt/ ▶ noun material used to make something airtight or watertight.

sea lav·en·der ▶ noun another term for STATICE.

seal·er¹ /ˈsēlər/ ▶ noun a device or substance used to make something airtight or watertight.

seal·er² ▶ noun a ship or person engaged in hunting seals.

sea lev·el ▶ noun the level of the sea's surface, used in calculating the height of geographical features such as hills.

seal·ing wax ▶ noun a mixture of shellac and rosin with turpentine, used to make seals.

sea li·on ▶ noun a large seal of the Pacific Ocean, the male of which has a mane on the neck and shoulders.

seal·skin /ˈsēlˌskin/ ▶ noun the skin or prepared fur of a seal, used for making clothes.

seam /sēm/ ▶ noun **1** a line where two pieces of fabric are sewn together. **2** a line where the edges of two pieces of wood or other material touch each other. **3** an underground layer of a mineral such as coal or gold. **4** a supply of something valuable: *they've got a rich seam of experienced players.*

– SYNONYMS **1 join,** stitching, joint. **2 layer,** stratum, vein, lode.

▶ **verb** join things with a seam.
– ORIGIN Old English.

sea·man /ˈsēmən/ ▶ **noun** (pl. **seamen**) a sailor, especially one below the rank of officer.

– SYNONYMS **sailor,** seafarer, mariner, boatman, hand, merchant seaman.
– ANTONYMS landlubber.

– DERIVATIVES **sea·man·like** /-ˌlīk/ adjective **sea·man·ship** /-ˌsʜip/ noun.

seam·less /ˈsēmlis/ ▶ **adjective** smooth and without seams or obvious joins.
– DERIVATIVES **seam·less·ly** adverb.

seam·stress /ˈsēmstris/ ▶ **noun** a woman who sews, especially as a job.
– ORIGIN from old-fashioned *seamster* 'tailor, seamstress.'

seam·y /ˈsēmē/ ▶ **adjective** (**seamier, seamiest**) immoral and unpleasant; sordid.

se·ance /ˈsāˌäns/ ▶ **noun** a meeting at which people attempt to make contact with the spirits of people who are dead.
– ORIGIN French.

sea·plane /ˈsēˌplān/ ▶ **noun** an aircraft with floats or skis instead of wheels, designed to land on and take off from water.

sea·port /ˈsēˌpôrt/ ▶ **noun** a town or city with a harbor for seagoing ships.

sear /si(ə)r/ ▶ **verb 1** burn or scorch something with a sudden intense heat. **2** (of pain) be experienced as a sudden burning sensation. **3** brown food quickly at a high temperature.

– SYNONYMS **1 scorch,** burn, singe, char, dry up, wither. **2 flash-fry,** seal, brown.

▶ **adjective** variant spelling of **SERE**.
– ORIGIN Old English.

search /sərcʜ/ ▶ **verb 1** try to find someone or something by looking carefully and thoroughly. **2** examine thoroughly in order to find something or someone. **3** (as adj. **searching**) investigating very thoroughly. **4** look for information in a computer network or database by using a search engine.

– SYNONYMS **1** *I searched for the key in my handbag* **hunt,** look, seek, forage, look high and low, ferret about, root about, rummage. **2** *he searched the house* **look through,** scour, go through, sift through, comb, turn upside down, ransack, rifle through. **3** *the guards searched him for weapons* **examine,** inspect, check, frisk. **4** (as adj. **searching**) *searching questions* **penetrating,** piercing, probing, keen, shrewd, sharp, intent.

▶ **noun** an act of searching.

– SYNONYMS **hunt,** look, quest, examination, exploration.

– DERIVATIVES **search·a·ble** adjective **search·er** noun.
– PHRASES **search me!** informal I do not know.
– ORIGIN Old French *cerchier*.

search en·gine ▶ **noun** a computer program that searches for and identifies specified items in a database, used especially for searching the Internet.

search·light /ˈsərcʜˌlīt/ ▶ **noun** a powerful outdoor electric light with a beam that can be turned in the required direction.

search par·ty ▶ **noun** a group of people organized to look for someone or something.

search war·rant ▶ **noun** a legal document authorizing a police officer or other official to enter and search a place.

sea salt ▶ **noun** salt produced by the evaporation of seawater.

sea·scape /ˈsēˌskāp/ ▶ **noun** a view or picture of an area of sea.

sea·shell /ˈsēˌsʜel/ ▶ **noun** the shell of a marine shellfish.

sea·shore /ˈsēˌsʜôr/ ▶ **noun** an area of sandy or rocky land next to the sea.

sea·sick /ˈsēˌsik/ ▶ **adjective** suffering from nausea caused by the motion of a ship at sea.
– DERIVATIVES **sea·sick·ness** noun.

sea·side /ˈsēˌsīd/ ▶ **noun** a beach area or vacation resort.

– SYNONYMS **coast,** shore, seashore, beach, sand, sands.

sea·son /ˈsēzən/ ▶ **noun 1** each of the four divisions of the year (spring, summer, autumn, and winter) marked by particular weather patterns and daylight hours. **2** a period of the year with particular weather or when a particular activity is done: *the football season.* **3** (**the season**) the time of year traditionally marked by fashionable upper-class social events.

– SYNONYMS **period,** time, time of year, spell, term.

▶ **verb 1** add salt, herbs, or spices to food. **2** (as adj. **seasoned**) used to particular conditions; experienced. **3** make more lively or interesting: *his conversation is seasoned with punchlines.* **4** keep wood so as to dry it for use as firewood or lumber.

– SYNONYMS **1 flavor,** add salt and pepper to, salt, spice. **2** (as adj. **seasoned**) *a seasoned traveler* **experienced,** practiced, well versed, knowledgeable, established, veteran, hardened.

– PHRASES **in season 1** (of a fruit, vegetable, or other food) ready to eat and in good condition at a particular time of year. **2** (of a female mammal) ready to mate.
– ORIGIN Old French *seson*.

sea·son·a·ble /ˈsēzənəbəl/ ▶ **adjective** usual for or appropriate to a particular season of the year.

CHOOSE THE RIGHT WORD

See **TIMELY**.

sea·son·al /ˈsēzənəl/ ▶ **adjective 1** relating to or typical of a particular season of the year. **2** changing according to the season.
– DERIVATIVES **sea·son·al·i·ty** /ˌsēzəˈnalitē/ noun **sea·son·al·ly** adverb.

sea·son·al af·fec·tive dis·or·der ▶ **noun** full form of **SAD**.

sea·son·ing /ˈsēzəniɴɢ/ ▶ **noun** salt, herbs, or spices added to food to improve the flavor.

– SYNONYMS **flavoring,** salt and pepper, herbs, spice(s), condiments.

sea·son tick·et ▶ **noun** a ticket allowing travel within a particular period or admission to a series of events.

sea squirt ▶ **noun** a sea animal that has a baglike body with openings through which water flows in and out.

seat /sēt/ ▶ **noun 1** a thing made or used for sitting on. **2** the part of a chair for sitting on. **3** a sitting place for a passenger in a vehicle or for a member of an audience. **4** a person's buttocks. **5** a place in an elected legislature or council. **6** a place where someone or something is based or something is carried out: *the town is the island's seat of government*. **7** the way in which a person sits on a horse. **8** a part of a machine that supports or guides another part.

– SYNONYMS **1 chair,** bench, stool; (**seats**) seating. **2 headquarters,** base, center, nerve center, hub, heart, location, site. **3 residence,** ancestral home, mansion.

▶ **verb 1** arrange for someone to sit somewhere. **2** (of a place) have sufficient seats for a specified number of people. **3** (**seat oneself** or **be seated**) sit down.

– SYNONYMS **1 position,** put, place, ensconce, install, settle. **2 have room for,** contain, take, sit, hold, accommodate.

– DERIVATIVES **seat·ing** noun **seat·less** adjective.
– ORIGIN Old Norse.

seat belt ▶ **noun** a belt used to secure someone in the seat of a motor vehicle or aircraft.

sea ur·chin ▶ **noun** a sea animal that has a shell covered in spines.

sea wall ▶ **noun** a wall built to prevent the sea from flowing over an area of land.

sea·wa·ter /ˈsēˌwôtər, -ˌwätər/ ▶ **noun** water in or taken from the sea.

sea·way /ˈsēˌwā/ ▶ **noun** a waterway or channel used by seagoing ships.

sea·weed /ˈsēˌwēd/ ▶ **noun** large algae growing in the sea or on rocks at the edge of the sea.

sea·wor·thy /ˈsēˌwərT͟Hē/ ▶ **adjective** (of a boat) in a good enough condition to sail on the sea.
– DERIVATIVES **sea·wor·thi·ness** noun.

se·ba·ceous /səˈbāsHəs/ ▶ **adjective** technical **1** relating to a sebaceous gland. **2** relating to oil or fat.
– ORIGIN Latin *sebaceus*.

se·ba·ceous gland ▶ **noun** a gland in the skin that produces an oily substance to lubricate the skin and hair.

seb·or·rhe·a /ˌsebəˈrēə/ (Brit. **seborrhoea**) ▶ **noun** Medicine excessive discharge of sebum from the sebaceous glands.

se·bum /ˈsēbəm/ ▶ **noun** an oily substance produced by the sebaceous glands.
– ORIGIN Latin, 'grease.'

SEC ▶ **abbreviation** Securities and Exchange Commission.

sec[1] /sek/ ▶ **abbreviation** secant.

sec[2] ▶ **noun** informal a second or a very short space of time.

sec[3] ▶ **adjective** (of wine) dry.
– ORIGIN French, from Latin *siccus*.

sec. ▶ **abbreviation** second(s).

se·cant /ˈsēˌkant, -kənt/ ▶ **noun 1** Mathematics (in a right triangle) the ratio of the hypotenuse to the shorter side adjacent to an acute angle. **2** Geometry a straight line that cuts a curve in two or more parts.
– ORIGIN from Latin *secare* 'to cut.'

se·cede /siˈsēd/ ▶ **verb** withdraw formally from membership of a federation of states or other alliance.
– DERIVATIVES **se·ced·er** noun.
– ORIGIN Latin *secedere* 'withdraw.'

se·ces·sion /səˈsesHən/ ▶ **noun** the action of withdrawing from a federation or other alliance.

se·clude /siˈklo͞od/ ▶ **verb** keep someone or oneself away from other people.
– ORIGIN Latin *secludere*.

se·clud·ed /siˈklo͞odid/ ▶ **adjective 1** (of a place) not seen or visited by many people; sheltered and private. **2** (of a person's life) having little contact with other people.

– SYNONYMS **sheltered,** private, concealed, hidden, unfrequented, sequestered, tucked away, remote, isolated, off the beaten track.

se·clu·sion /siˈklo͞ozHən/ ▶ **noun** the state of being private and away from other people.

sec·ond[1] /ˈsekənd/ ▶ **ordinal number 1** that is number two in a sequence; 2nd. **2** lower in position, rank, or importance: *New York is second only to Los Angeles for air pollution*. **3** (**seconds**) goods of less than perfect quality. **4** (**seconds**) informal a second helping of food at a meal. **5** secondly (used to introduce a second point). **6** a person who assists a contestant in a boxing match or duel.

– SYNONYMS **1** *the second day of the trial* **next,** following, subsequent. **2** *he keeps a second pair of glasses in his office* **additional,** extra, alternative, another, spare, backup, fallback, alternate. **3** *he was demoted to the second level* **secondary,** lower, subordinate, subsidiary, lesser, inferior.
– ANTONYMS first.

▶ **verb 1** formally support a proposal, nomination, etc., before it is voted on or discussed further. **2** express agreement with someone or something.

– SYNONYMS **support,** vote for, back, approve, endorse.

– DERIVATIVES **sec·ond·er** noun.
– ORIGIN Latin *secundus* 'following, second.'

sec·ond[2] /ˈsekənd/ ▶ **noun 1** the unit of time in the SI system, equal to one-sixtieth of a minute. **2** informal a very short time. **3** (also **arc second** or **second of arc**) a measurement of an angle equal to one sixtieth of a minute.

– SYNONYMS **moment,** bit, little while, instant, flash; informal sec, jiffy.

– ORIGIN from Latin *secunda minuta* 'second minute.'

sec·ond[3] /siˈkänd/ ▶ **verb** Brit. temporarily transfer an employee to another position or role.
– DERIVATIVES **se·cond·ment** noun.
– ORIGIN from French *en second* 'in the second rank (of officers).'

sec·ond·ar·y /ˈsekənˌderē/ ▶ **adjective 1** coming after, less important than, or resulting from someone or something that is first or most important: *a secondary road*. **2** relating to education for children from the age of eleven to sixteen or eighteen.

– SYNONYMS **1 less important,** subordinate, lesser, minor, peripheral, incidental, subsidiary, ancillary. **2 accompanying,** attendant, concomitant, consequential, resulting, resultant.
– ANTONYMS primary, main.

– DERIVATIVES **sec·ond·ar·i·ly** /-ˌderəlē/ adverb.

sec·ond·ar·y col·or ▶ **noun** a color that is a result of mixing two primary colors.

sec·ond·ar·y sex·u·al char·ac·ter·is·tics ▶ **plural noun** physical characteristics developed at puberty that distinguish between the sexes but are not involved in reproduction.

sec·ond best ▶ **adjective** next after the best. ▶ **noun** a less adequate or less desirable alternative.

sec·ond class ▶ **noun** **1** a set of people or things grouped together as the second best. **2** the second-best accommodations on an aircraft, train, or ship. ▶ **adjective & adverb** relating to the second class.

Sec·ond Com·ing ▶ **noun** (in Christian belief) the prophesied return of Jesus to Earth at the Last Judgment.

sec·ond cous·in ▶ **noun** see **COUSIN**.

sec·ond-de·gree ▶ **adjective** **1** (of burns) that cause blistering but not permanent scars. **2** Law (of a crime, especially a murder) less serious than a first-degree crime.

sec·ond-gen·er·a·tion ▶ **adjective** **1** referring to the children of parents who have emigrated from one country to another. **2** of a more advanced stage of technology than previous models or systems.

sec·ond-guess ▶ **verb** predict someone's actions or thoughts by guessing.

sec·ond·hand /ˈsekən(d)ˈhand/ ▶ **adjective & adverb** **1** (of goods) having had a previous owner; not new. **2** accepted on another person's authority and not from original investigation: *authors have had to make do with secondhand information.*

– SYNONYMS **1** *secondhand clothes* **used,** old, worn, pre-owned, nearly new, handed-down, hand-me-down, castoff. **2** *secondhand information* **indirect,** derivative; vicarious. **3** *I ignore anything I hear secondhand* **indirectly**; informal on the grapevine.
– ANTONYMS new, direct, directly.

– PHRASES **at second hand** on the basis of what others have said rather than direct observation or experience.

sec·ond hand ▶ **noun** an extra hand in some watches and clocks that moves around to indicate the seconds.

sec·ond in com·mand ▶ **noun** the officer next in authority to the commanding or chief officer.

– SYNONYMS **assistant,** attendant, helper, aide, supporter, auxiliary, second in command, number two, deputy, understudy; informal sidekick.

sec·ond lieu·ten·ant ▶ **noun** a rank of officer in the US Army, Air Force, and Marine Corps above chief warrant officer and below first lieutenant.

sec·ond·ly /ˈsekən(d)lē/ ▶ **adverb** in the second place; second.

– SYNONYMS **furthermore,** also, moreover, second, in the second place, next.

sec·ond name ▶ **noun** Brit. a surname.

sec·ond na·ture ▶ **noun** something that one does very easily or naturally because one has done it so often or is particularly suited to it.

sec·ond per·son ▶ **noun** see **PERSON** (sense 3).

sec·ond-rate ▶ **adjective** poor in quality.
– DERIVATIVES **sec·ond-rat·er** noun.

sec·ond read·ing ▶ **noun** a second presentation of a bill to a lawmaking assembly.

sec·ond sight ▶ **noun** the supposed ability to predict future events or to know what is happening in a different place.

sec·ond string ▶ **noun** (often in phrase **a second string to one's bow**) an alternative resource or course of action in case another one fails.

sec·ond thoughts ▶ **plural noun** a change of opinion or decision after considering something again.

sec·ond wind /wind/ ▶ **noun** fresh energy that enables one to continue with an activity after being tired.

se·cre·cy /ˈsēkrəsē/ ▶ **noun** the action of keeping something secret or the state of being kept secret.

– SYNONYMS **confidentiality,** privacy, mystery, concealment, stealth.

se·cret /ˈsēkrit/ ▶ **adjective** **1** kept from or not known or seen by others. **2** fond of keeping secrets; secretive.

– SYNONYMS **1** *a secret plan* **confidential,** top secret, classified, undisclosed, unknown, private, under wraps; informal hush-hush. **2** *a secret drawer in the table* **hidden,** concealed, disguised, camouflaged. **3** *a secret campaign to infiltrate drug operations on the east coast* **clandestine,** covert, undercover, underground, surreptitious, stealthy, cloak-and-dagger, furtive, conspiratorial.
– ANTONYMS public, open.

▶ **noun** **1** something that others do not know about. **2** a method of achieving something that is not generally known: *the secret of a happy marriage is compromise.* **3** something that is not fully understood; a mystery: *the secrets of the universe.*
– ORIGIN Latin *secretus* 'separate, set apart.'

WORD TOOLKIT

secret ...	arcane ...	mysterious ...
agent	knowledge	man/woman
ballot	language	circumstances
society	rules	death
location	art	disappearance
life	ritual	illness
meeting	symbols	power
information	matters	forces
admirer	science	figure

se·cret a·gent ▶ **noun** a spy acting for a country.

sec·re·taire /ˌsekriˈte(ə)r/ ▶ **noun** a small writing desk.
– ORIGIN French, 'secretary.'

sec·re·tar·i·at /ˌsekriˈte(ə)rēət/ ▶ **noun** a governmental administrative office or department.

sec·re·tar·y /ˈsekriˌterē/ ▶ **noun** (pl. **secretaries**) **1** a person employed to deal with letters and telephone calls, make arrangements, and keep records. **2** an official of a society or other organization who deals with its correspondence and keeps its records. **3** an official in charge of a government department: *the defense secretary is in Cairo.* **4** a writing desk with shelves on top of it.
– DERIVATIVES **sec·re·tar·i·al** /-ˈte(ə)rēəl/ adjective.
– ORIGIN Latin *secretarius* 'confidential officer.'

sec·re·tar·y bird ▶ **noun** a slender long-legged African bird of prey, having a crest resembling a quill pen stuck behind the ear.

sec·re·tary gen·er·al ▶ **noun** (pl. **secretaries general**) the chief administrator of some organizations.

sec·re·tar·y of state ▶ **noun** the head of the State Department, responsible for foreign affairs.

se·crete[1] /si'krēt/ ▶ **verb** (of a cell, gland, or organ) produce and discharge a substance.
– DERIVATIVES **se·cre·tor** /-tər/ noun **se·cre·to·ry** /-tərē/ adjective.

secrete[2] ▶ **verb** conceal or hide something.
– ORIGIN from the former verb *secret* 'keep secret.'

se·cre·tion /si'krēsнən/ ▶ **noun 1** a process by which substances are produced and discharged from a cell, gland, or organ for a particular function in the organism or for excretion. **2** a substance discharged by this process.
– ORIGIN Latin, 'separation.'

se·cre·tive /'sēkritiv/ ▶ **adjective** inclined to keep information secret or to hide one's feelings and intentions.

– SYNONYMS **uncommunicative,** secret, unforthcoming, playing one's cards close to one's chest, reticent, tight-lipped.
– ANTONYMS open, communicative.

– DERIVATIVES **se·cre·tive·ly** adverb **se·cre·tive·ness** noun.

se·cret·ly /'sēkritlē/ ▶ **adverb** in secret.

– SYNONYMS *they met secretly for a year* **in secret,** in private, privately, behind closed doors, under cover, furtively, stealthily, on the QT, covertly.

se·cret po·lice ▶ **noun** (treated as pl.) a police force working in secret against a government's political opponents.

se·cret sauce ▶ **noun** informal a special feature or technique kept secret by an organization and regarded as being the chief factor in its success.

se·cret serv·ice ▶ **noun 1** a government department concerned with spying. **2** (**Secret Service**) a branch of the Treasury Department dealing with counterfeiting and providing protection for the president.

se·cret so·ci·e·ty ▶ **noun** an organization whose members are sworn to secrecy about its activities.

sect /sekt/ ▶ **noun** a group of people with different religious beliefs from those of a larger group to which they belong.

– SYNONYMS **group,** cult, denomination, order, splinter group, faction, camp.

– ORIGIN Latin *secta* 'following, faction.'

sec·tar·i·an /sek'te(ə)rēən/ ▶ **adjective 1** relating to a religious sect or sects. **2** resulting from the differences that exist between members of different sects: *sectarian killings*.

– SYNONYMS **factional,** separatist, partisan, doctrinaire, dogmatic, illiberal, intolerant, bigoted, narrow-minded.

▶ **noun** a member of a sect.
– DERIVATIVES **sec·tar·i·an·ism** /-ˌnizəm/ noun.

sec·tion /'seksнən/ ▶ **noun 1** any of the parts into which something is divided or from which it is made up. **2** a distinct group within a larger body of people or things: *eco-warriors enjoyed widespread support from large sections of the population.* **3** the shape resulting from cutting a solid by or along a plane. **4** a representation of the internal structure of something as if it has been cut through. **5** a thin slice of plant or animal tissue prepared for examination with a microscope. **6** a separation by surgical cutting.

– SYNONYMS **1 part,** bit, portion, segment, compartment, module, element, unit. **2 passage,** subsection, chapter, subdivision, clause. **3 department,** area, division.

▶ **verb 1** divide something into sections. **2** divide something by surgical cutting.
– ORIGIN Latin.

CHOOSE THE RIGHT WORD

See **FRAGMENT**.

sec·tion·al /'seksнənl/ ▶ **adjective** of or relating to a section. ▶ **noun** a sofa made in sections that can be used separately as chairs.
– DERIVATIVES **sec·tion·al·ize** /-ˌīz/ verb **sec·tion·al·ly** adverb.

sec·tor /'sektər/ ▶ **noun 1** an area or part that is distinct from others. **2** a distinct part of an economy, society, or field of activity: *the government aimed to reassure the commercial sector.* **3** a subdivision of an area for military operations. **4** a part of a circle between two lines drawn from its center to its circumference.

– SYNONYMS **1 district,** quarter, section, zone, region, area, belt. **2 part,** branch, arm, division, area, department, field, sphere.

– DERIVATIVES **sec·tor·al** /-rəl/ adjective.
– ORIGIN Latin, 'cutter.'

sec·u·lar /'sekyələr/ ▶ **adjective 1** not religious or spiritual. **2** (of Christian clergy) not belonging to or living in a monastic or other order.

– SYNONYMS **nonreligious,** lay, temporal, civil, worldly, earthly, profane.
– ANTONYMS sacred, religious.

– DERIVATIVES **sec·u·lar·ism** /-ˌrizəm/ noun **sec·u·lar·ist** /-rist/ noun **sec·u·lar·ize** /-ˌrīz/ verb **sec·u·lar·ly** adverb.
– ORIGIN Latin *saecularis* 'relating to an age or period.'

se·cure /si'kyŏŏr/ ▶ **adjective 1** likely to continue or to remain safe: *the days of secure staff jobs are over.* **2** fixed or fastened so as not to give way, become loose, or be lost. **3** feeling confident and free from fear or anxiety. **4** protected against attack or other criminal activity. **5** (of a prison or similar establishment) having measures in place to prevent the escape of inmates.

– SYNONYMS **1 fastened,** fixed, secured, done up, closed, shut, locked. **2 safe,** protected, safe and sound, out of harm's way, in safe hands, invulnerable, undamaged, unharmed. **3** *his position as leader was secure* **certain,** assured, settled, stable, not at risk. **4 unworried,** at ease, relaxed, happy, confident.
– ANTONYMS loose, insecure.

▶ **verb 1** protect someone or something from danger or threat. **2** fix or fasten something securely. **3** succeed in obtaining: *he has secured a place on the ballot.* **4** guarantee a loan by having the right to take possession of property or goods if the borrower is unable to repay the money.

– SYNONYMS **1 fasten,** close, shut, lock, bolt, chain, seal. **2 obtain,** acquire, gain, get, get (a) hold of, come by; informal land.

– DERIVATIVES **se·cure·ly** adverb.
– ORIGIN Latin *securus*.

CHOOSE THE RIGHT WORD

See **GET**.

se·cu·ri·ty /si'kyŏŏritē/ ▶ **noun** (pl. **securities**) **1** the state of being or feeling secure: *long-term job security*. **2** the safety of a state or organization against criminal activity such as terrorism. **3** something that is promised as a guarantee that a loan will be repaid. **4** a certificate proving ownership of stocks or bonds.

– SYNONYMS **1 safety,** protection. **2 safety measures,** safeguards, surveillance, defense, policing. **3 guarantee,** collateral, surety, pledge, bond.

se·cu·ri·ty blan·ket ▶ **noun** a blanket or other familiar object that is a comfort to someone, typically a child.

se·dan /si'dan/ ▶ **noun 1** an enclosed chair carried between two horizontal poles, used especially in the 17th and 18th centuries. **2** a car for four or more people.
– ORIGIN perhaps from Latin *sella* 'saddle.'

se·date[1] /si'dāt/ ▶ **adjective 1** slow, calm, and relaxed. **2** serious, quiet, and rather dull: *sedate small-town life*.

– SYNONYMS **1 slow,** steady, dignified, unhurried, relaxed, measured, leisurely, slow-moving, easy, gentle. **2 calm,** placid, tranquil, quiet, uneventful, staid, boring, dull.
– ANTONYMS fast, exciting.

– DERIVATIVES **se·date·ly** adverb **se·date·ness** noun.
– ORIGIN from Latin *sedare* 'settle.'

sedate[2] ▶ **verb** give someone a drug to make them calm or fall asleep.

– SYNONYMS **tranquilize,** put under sedation, drug.

se·da·tion /si'dāsʜən/ ▶ **noun** the giving of a sedative drug to someone to calm them or make them sleep.
– ORIGIN Latin.

sed·a·tive /'sedətiv/ ▶ **noun** a drug that makes someone calm or sleepy. ▶ **adjective** making someone calm or sleepy.

sed·en·tar·y /'sedn,terē/ ▶ **adjective 1** (of work or a way of life) involving much sitting and little exercise. **2** tending to sit down a lot; taking little exercise: *healthy but sedentary young men*. **3** (of an animal or people) tending to stay in the same place for much of the time.

– SYNONYMS **sitting,** seated, desk-bound; inactive.
– ANTONYMS active.

– ORIGIN Latin *sedentarius*.

sedge /sej/ ▶ **noun** a grasslike plant with triangular stems and small flowers, growing in wet ground.
– ORIGIN Old English.

sed·i·ment /'sedəmənt/ ▶ **noun 1** matter that settles to the bottom of a liquid. **2** material carried in particles by water or wind and deposited on the land surface or seabed.

– SYNONYMS **dregs,** grounds, lees, residue, deposit, silt.

▶ **verb** settle or deposit as sediment.
– DERIVATIVES **sed·i·men·ta·tion** /,sedəmən'tāsʜən/ noun.
– ORIGIN Latin *sedimentum* 'settling.'

sed·i·men·ta·ry /,sedə'mentərē/ ▶ **adjective** Geology (of rock) formed from sediment deposited by water or wind.

se·di·tion /si'disʜən/ ▶ **noun** actions or speech that encourage rebellion against the authority of a government or ruler.

– SYNONYMS **rabble-rousing,** subversion, troublemaking, provocation; rebellion, insurrection, mutiny, insurgence, civil disorder.

– ORIGIN Latin, from *sed-* 'apart' + *itio* 'going.'

se·di·tious /si'disʜəs/ ▶ **adjective** inciting or causing people to rebel against the authority of a government or ruler: *a seditious speech*.

– SYNONYMS **rabble-rousing,** provocative, inflammatory, subversive, troublemaking; rebellious, mutinous, insurgent.

se·duce /si'd(y)ōōs/ ▶ **verb 1** tempt someone into sexual activity. **2** persuade someone to do something unwise: *she was almost seduced into believing him*.

– SYNONYMS **1 attract,** allure, lure, tempt, entice, beguile, inveigle, manipulate. **2 have one's way with,** take advantage of.

– DERIVATIVES **se·duc·er** noun **se·duc·tion** /si'dəksʜən/ noun.
– ORIGIN Latin *seducere* 'lead aside or away.'

CHOOSE THE RIGHT WORD

See **TEMPT**.

se·duc·tive /si'dəktiv/ ▶ **adjective** tempting and attractive.

– SYNONYMS **tempting,** inviting, enticing, alluring, beguiling, attractive.

– DERIVATIVES **se·duc·tive·ly** adverb **se·duc·tive·ness** noun.

se·duc·tress /si'dəktris/ ▶ **noun** a woman who seduces someone, especially into sexual activity.

sed·u·lous /'sejələs/ ▶ **adjective** showing dedication and great care or effort.
– DERIVATIVES **sed·u·lous·ly** adverb.
– ORIGIN Latin *sedulus* 'zealous.'

CHOOSE THE RIGHT WORD

See **BUSY**.

se·dum /'sēdəm/ ▶ **noun** a plant of a large group having fleshy leaves and small star-shaped flowers.
– ORIGIN Latin.

see[1] /sē/ ▶ **verb** (**sees** /sēz/, **seeing** /'sē-iɴɢ/; past **saw** /sô/; past part. **seen** /sēn/) **1** become aware of someone or something with the eyes. **2** experience or witness an event or situation. **3** form an opinion or conclusion after thinking or from information. **4** view as a possibility. **5** consult a specialist or professional. **6** meet someone regularly as a boyfriend or girlfriend. **7** (**see to**) deal with something. **8** meet someone one knows socially or by chance. **9** regard in a particular way: *he saw himself as a good teacher*. **10** give someone an interview or consultation. **11** guide or take someone somewhere: *don't bother seeing me out*. **12** (**see that**) ensure that.

– SYNONYMS **1** *he saw her running across the road* **discern,** detect, perceive, spot, notice, catch sight of, glimpse, make out, pick out, distinguish, spy; literary behold, espy, descry. **2** *I saw a documentary about it last week* **watch,** look at, view, catch. **3** *would you like to see the house?* **inspect,** view, look around, tour, survey, examine, scrutinize. **4** *I must go and see what Victor is up to* **find out,** discover, learn, ascertain, determine, establish. **5** *see that no harm comes to him* **ensure,** make sure/certain, see to it, take care, mind. **6** *I finally saw what she meant*

understand, grasp, comprehend, follow, realize, appreciate, recognize, work out, fathom; informal get, latch on to, figure out. **7** *I see trouble ahead* **foresee,** predict, forecast, prophesy, anticipate, envisage. **8** *you'd better see a doctor* **consult,** confer with, talk to, have recourse to, call in, turn to. **9** *he's seeing someone else now* **go out with,** date, take out, be involved with; informal go steady with; dated court. **10** (**see to**) *I'll see to the dogs as soon as we finish lunch* **attend to,** deal with, see about, take care of, look after, sort out, organize, arrange.

– PHRASES **see about** deal with something. **see someone off** accompany a person who is leaving to their point of departure. **see someone out** accompany a person to the door upon their leaving. **see something out** come to the end of a period of time or undertaking. **see through** realize someone's or something's true nature. **see someone through** support someone during a difficult period. **see something through** carry on with an undertaking until it is completed.
– ORIGIN Old English.

see² ▶ **noun** the district or position of a bishop or archbishop, centered on a cathedral church.
– ORIGIN Latin *sedes* 'seat.'

seed /sēd/ ▶ **noun** **1** a flowering plant's unit of reproduction, capable of developing into another such plant. **2** the beginning of a feeling, process, or condition: *the conversation sowed a seed of doubt in his mind.* **3** any of a number of stronger competitors in a sports tournament who have been given a position in an ordered list to ensure that they do not play each other in the early rounds. **4** old use a man's semen. **5** old use (chiefly in the Bible) a person's offspring or descendants.

– SYNONYMS **pip,** stone, kernel.

▶ **verb** **1** sow land with seeds. **2** produce or drop seeds. **3** remove the seeds from vegetables or fruit. **4** make a competitor a seed in a sports tournament.
– DERIVATIVES **seed·less** adjective.
– PHRASES **go** (or **run**) **to seed** **1** (of a plant) stop flowering as the seeds develop. **2** deteriorate, especially as a result of neglect: *he had gone to seed after his wife left him.*
– ORIGIN Old English, related to **sow¹**.

seed·bed /ˈsēd,bed/ ▶ **noun** a bed of fine soil in which seedlings are germinated.

seed corn ▶ **noun** good-quality corn kept for seed.

seed head ▶ **noun** a flowerhead when it is producing seeds.

seed leaf ▶ **noun** a cotyledon.

seed·ling /ˈsēdliNG/ ▶ **noun** a young plant raised from seed.

seed mon·ey (also **seed capital**) ▶ **noun** money provided to start up a project.

seed pearl ▶ **noun** a very small pearl.

seed po·ta·to ▶ **noun** a potato intended for replanting to produce a new plant.

seed·y /ˈsēdē/ ▶ **adjective** (**seedier, seediest**) **1** sordid or immoral: *his seedy affair with a soft-porn starlet.* **2** shabby, dirty, and unpleasant: *a seedy bar.* **3** dated unwell.

– SYNONYMS **1** *the seedy world of prostitution* **sordid,** disreputable, seamy, sleazy, squalid, unsavory. **2** *a seedy part of town* **dilapidated,** tumbledown, ramshackle, decrepit, run-down, shabby, dingy, slummy, insalubrious, squalid; informal crummy.
– ANTONYMS high-class.

– DERIVATIVES **seed·i·ly** adverb **seed·i·ness** noun.

see·ing /ˈsē-iNG/ ▶ **conjunction** because; since.

seek /sēk/ ▶ **verb** (past and past part. **sought**) **1** try to find or obtain: *she may decide to seek alternative employment.* **2** (**seek someone/thing out**) search for and find someone or something. **3** ask for: *we are seeking legal advice.* **4** (**seek to do**) try or want to do: *they had never sought to interfere with her freedom.*

– SYNONYMS **1** **search for,** try to find, look for, be after, hunt for. **2** **ask for,** request, solicit, call for, appeal for, apply for. **3** **try,** attempt, endeavor, strive, work, do one's best.

– DERIVATIVES **seek·er** noun.
– ORIGIN Old English.

seem /sēm/ ▶ **verb** **1** give the impression of being: *she seemed annoyed.* **2** (**cannot seem to do**) appear to be unable to do something, despite having tried.

– SYNONYMS **appear (to be),** have the appearance/air of being, give the impression of being, look, sound, come across as, strike someone as.

– ORIGIN from an Old Norse word meaning 'appropriate, fitting.'

seem·ing /ˈsēmiNG/ ▶ **adjective** appearing to be real or true; apparent.
– DERIVATIVES **seem·ing·ly** adverb.

seem·ly /ˈsēmlē/ ▶ **adjective** in keeping with good taste or correct behavior.
– DERIVATIVES **seem·li·ness** noun.
– ORIGIN Old Norse, 'fitting.'

seen /sēn/ past participle of **SEE¹**.

seep /sēp/ ▶ **verb** (of a liquid) flow or leak slowly through or into something.

– SYNONYMS **ooze,** trickle, exude, drip, dribble, flow, leak, drain, bleed, filter, percolate, soak.

– DERIVATIVES **seep·age** /ˈsēpij/ noun.
– ORIGIN perhaps a dialect form of an Old English word meaning 'to soak.'

seer /ˈsēər, si(ə)r/ ▶ **noun** a person who is supposedly able to see visions of the future.

seer·suck·er /ˈsi(ə)r,səkər/ ▶ **noun** a fabric with a puckered surface.
– ORIGIN from a Persian phrase meaning 'milk and sugar' (with reference to the alternating stripes in which the fabric was originally woven).

see·saw /ˈsē,sô/ ▶ **noun** **1** a long plank balanced on a fixed support, on each end of which children sit and move up and down by pushing the ground with their feet. **2** a situation characterized by repeated changes from one state or condition to another: *the emotional seesaw of a first love affair.* ▶ **verb** repeatedly change from one state or condition to another and back again.
– ORIGIN from **SAW¹**.

seethe /sēT͟H/ ▶ **verb** **1** be filled with strong but unexpressed anger. **2** be crowded with people or things. **3** (of a liquid) boil or churn as if boiling.

– SYNONYMS **1** **be angry,** be furious, be enraged, rage, be incensed, be beside oneself, boil, rant, fume; informal be livid, foam at the mouth. **2** **teem,** swarm, boil, swirl, churn, surge, bubble, heave.

– ORIGIN Old English.

see-through ▶ **adjective** transparent or translucent.

seg·ment ▶ **noun** /ˈsegmənt/ **1** each of the parts into which something is divided. **2** Geometry a part of a circle cut off by a chord, or a part of a sphere cut off by a plane not passing through the center.

– SYNONYMS **piece,** bit, section, part, portion, division, slice, wedge.

▶ **verb** /ˈseg,ment, segˈment/ divide something into segments.
– DERIVATIVES **seg·men·tal** adjective **seg·men·ta·tion** /,segmənˈtāsʜən/ noun.
– ORIGIN Latin *segmentum.*

CHOOSE THE RIGHT WORD

See **FRAGMENT**.

seg·re·gate /ˈsegri,gāt/ ▶ **verb 1** set apart from the rest or from each other: *disabled people should not be segregated from the rest of society.* **2** separate people along racial, sexual, or religious lines.

– SYNONYMS **separate,** set apart, keep apart, isolate, quarantine, partition, divide, discriminate against.
– ANTONYMS integrate.

– ORIGIN Latin *segregare* 'separate from the flock.'

seg·re·ga·tion /,segriˈgāsʜən/ ▶ **noun 1** the action of segregating or the state of being segregated. **2** the enforced separation of different racial groups in a country, community, or place.
– DERIVATIVES **seg·re·ga·tion·al** /-sʜənl/ adjective **seg·re·ga·tion·ist** /-ist/ adjective & noun.

se·gue /ˈsegwā, ˈsā-/ ▶ **verb (segues** /ˈsegwāz, ˈsā-/, **segueing** /ˈsegwā-ɪɴɢ, ˈsā-/ or **seguing** /ˈsegwɪɴɢ, ˈsā-/, **segued** /ˈsegwād, ˈsā-/) (in music, movies, television, etc.) move without interruption from one song, melody, or scene to another. ▶ **noun** an instance of this.
– ORIGIN Italian, 'follows.'

sei·cen·to /sāˈcʜen,tō/ ▶ **noun** the style of Italian art and literature of the 17th century.
– ORIGIN Italian, '600' (shortened from *mille seicento* '1600').

sei·gneur /sānˈyər/ ▶ **noun** a feudal lord; a lord of a medieval manor.
– DERIVATIVES **sei·gneu·ri·al** /-ˈyərēəl/ adjective.
– ORIGIN Old French.

seine /sān, sen/ ▶ **noun** a fishing net that hangs vertically in the water with floats at the top and weights at the bottom edge, the ends being drawn together to encircle the fish. ▶ **verb** fish with a seine.
– ORIGIN Greek *sagēnē.*

seis·mic /ˈsīzmik/ ▶ **adjective 1** relating to earthquakes or other vibrations of the earth and its crust. **2** very great in size or effect: *seismic shifts in the global economy.*
– DERIVATIVES **seis·mi·cal·ly** /-ik(ə)lē/ adverb **seis·mic·i·ty** /sīzˈmisitē/noun.
– ORIGIN from Greek *seismos* 'earthquake.'

seis·mo·graph /ˈsīzmə,graf/ ▶ **noun** an instrument that measures and records details of earthquakes, such as force and duration.

seis·mol·o·gy /sīzˈmäləjē/ ▶ **noun** the branch of science concerned with earthquakes.
– DERIVATIVES **seis·mo·log·i·cal** /,sīzməˈläjikəl/ adjective **seis·mol·o·gist** noun.

seis·mom·e·ter /sīzˈmämitər/ ▶ **noun** another term for **SEISMOGRAPH**.

seize /sēz/ ▶ **verb 1** take hold of someone or something suddenly and forcibly. **2** take possession of something by force. **3** (of the police or another authority) officially take possession of: *customs officers seized drugs with a street value of over $300 million.* **4** take an opportunity eagerly and decisively. **5** (**seize on**) take eager advantage of. **6** (often **seize up**) (of a machine or part in a machine) become jammed.

– SYNONYMS **1 grab,** grasp, snatch, take (a) hold of, clutch, grip. **2 capture,** take, overrun, occupy, conquer, take over. **3 confiscate,** impound, commandeer, requisition, appropriate, expropriate, sequestrate. **4 kidnap,** abduct, take captive, take prisoner, take hostage, hijack; informal snatch.
– ANTONYMS release.

– ORIGIN Latin *sacire,* in the phrase *ad proprium sacire* 'claim as one's own.'

sei·zure /ˈsēzʜər/ ▶ **noun 1** the action of seizing. **2** a sudden attack of illness, especially a stroke or an epileptic fit.

– SYNONYMS **1 capture,** takeover, annexation, invasion, occupation. **2 confiscation,** appropriation, expropriation, sequestration. **3 kidnap/kidnapping,** abduction, hijack/hijacking. **4 convulsion,** fit, spasm, paroxysm.

sel·dom /ˈseldəm/ ▶ **adverb** not often; rarely.

– SYNONYMS **rarely,** infrequently, hardly (ever), scarcely (ever); informal once in a blue moon.
– ANTONYMS often.

– ORIGIN Old English.

se·lect /səˈlekt/ ▶ **verb** carefully choose someone or something as being the best or most suitable.

– SYNONYMS **choose,** pick (out), single out, opt for, decide on, settle on, sort out, take, adopt.

▶ **adjective 1** carefully chosen as being among the best. **2** used by or consisting of wealthy or sophisticated people: *a select area of Boston.*

– SYNONYMS **1 choice,** prime, hand-picked, top-quality, first-class; informal top-flight. **2 exclusive,** elite, privileged, wealthy; informal posh.
– ANTONYMS inferior.

– DERIVATIVES **se·lect·a·ble** adjective.
– ORIGIN Latin *seligere* 'choose.'

se·lect com·mit·tee ▶ **noun** a small legislative committee appointed for a special purpose.

se·lec·tion /səˈleksʜən/ ▶ **noun 1** the action of selecting. **2** a thing or number of things that have been chosen from a wider group. **3** a range of things from which a choice may be made: *a wide selection of hot and cold dishes.*

– SYNONYMS **1 choice,** pick, option, preference. **2 range,** array, diversity, variety, assortment, mixture. **3 anthology,** assortment, collection, assemblage, miscellany, medley.

se·lec·tive /səˈlektiv/ ▶ **adjective 1** relating to or involving selection. **2** tending to choose carefully: *he's very selective in his reading.* **3** affecting some things and not others: *modern pesticides are selective in effect.*

– SYNONYMS **discerning,** discriminating, exacting, demanding, particular; informal choosy, picky.
– ANTONYMS indiscriminate.

– DERIVATIVES **se·lec·tive·ly** adverb **se·lec·tiv·i·ty** /səlekˈtivitē/ noun.

se·lec·tive serv·ice ▶ **noun** service in the armed forces under conscription.

se·lec·tor /sə'lektər/ ▶ **noun** a device for selecting a particular gear or other setting of a machine or device.

se·le·ni·um /sə'lēnēəm/ ▶ **noun** a gray crystalline nonmetallic chemical element with semiconducting properties.
– ORIGIN Greek *selēnē* 'moon.'

self /self/ ▶ **noun** (pl. **selves** /selvz/) **1** a person's essential being that distinguishes them from other people. **2** a person's particular nature or personality: *he was back to his old self.* ▶ **pronoun** (pl. **selves**) oneself. ▶ **adjective** (of a trim, woven design, etc.) of the same material or color as the rest of the item.
– ORIGIN Old English.

self- ▶ **combining form 1** relating to or directed toward oneself or itself: *self-hatred.* **2** by one's own efforts; by its own action: *self-adjusting.* **3** on, in, for, or relating to oneself or itself: *self-adhesive.*

self-ab·sorbed ▶ **adjective** preoccupied with one's own emotions, interests, or situation.
– DERIVATIVES **self-ab·sorp·tion** noun.

self-a·buse /ə'byo͞os/ ▶ **noun 1** behavior that causes damage or harm to oneself. **2** dated masturbation.

self-ad·dressed ▶ **adjective** (of an envelope) addressed to oneself.

self-ad·he·sive ▶ **adjective** sticking without needing to be moistened.

self-ad·just·ing ▶ **adjective** (chiefly of machinery) adjusting itself to meet changing requirements.

self-ag·gran·dize·ment ▶ **noun** the action of increasing one's own power or importance.
– DERIVATIVES **self-ag·gran·diz·ing** adjective.

self-ap·point·ed ▶ **adjective** having taken on a position or role without the agreement of other people.

self-as·sem·bly ▶ **noun** the construction of a piece of furniture from materials sold in kit form.
– DERIVATIVES **self-as·sem·ble** verb.

self-as·ser·tion ▶ **noun** the quality of being confident or forceful in the expression of one's opinions.
– DERIVATIVES **self-as·ser·tive** adjective **self-as·ser·tive·ness** noun.

self-as·sess·ment ▶ **noun** the process of judging oneself or one's actions or performance.

self-as·sur·ance ▶ **noun** confidence in one's own abilities or character.
– DERIVATIVES **self-as·sured** adjective.

self-a·ware·ness ▶ **noun** conscious knowledge and understanding of one's own character, feelings, and motives.
– DERIVATIVES **self-a·ware** adjective.

self-cen·sor·ship ▶ **noun** the exercising of control over what one says and does.

self-cen·tered ▶ **adjective** preoccupied with oneself and one's own feelings or needs.

> – SYNONYMS **egocentric**, egotistic, self-absorbed, self-obsessed, self-seeking, self-serving, narcissistic, vain, inconsiderate, thoughtless; informal looking after number one.

– DERIVATIVES **self-cen·tered·ness** noun.

self-col·ored ▶ **adjective 1** of a single uniform color. **2** (of a trim or accessory) of the same color as the rest of the item.

self-con·fessed ▶ **adjective** openly admitting to having certain characteristics: *a self-confessed alcoholic.*

self-con·fi·dence ▶ **noun** a feeling of trust in one's abilities, qualities, and judgment.

> – SYNONYMS **self-assurance,** assurance, confidence, composure, aplomb, poise, sangfroid.

– DERIVATIVES **self-con·fi·dent** adjective **self-con·fi·dent·ly** adverb.

self-con·grat·u·la·tion ▶ **noun** too much pride in one's achievements or qualities.
– DERIVATIVES **self-con·grat·u·la·to·ry** adjective.

self-con·scious ▶ **adjective 1** nervous, awkward, or embarrassed as a result of being worried about how one appears to other people. **2** done deliberately and with full awareness of the effect produced.

> – SYNONYMS **embarrassed,** uncomfortable, uneasy, ill at ease, nervous, awkward, shy, diffident, timid.
> – ANTONYMS confident.

– DERIVATIVES **self-con·scious·ly** adverb **self-con·scious·ness** noun.

self-con·sis·tent ▶ **adjective** not having conflicting parts or aspects; consistent.
– DERIVATIVES **self-con·sis·ten·cy** noun.

self-con·tained ▶ **adjective 1** complete, or having all that is needed, in itself. **2** not depending on or influenced by other people.

self-con·tra·dic·tion ▶ **noun** inconsistency between aspects or parts of a whole.

self-con·trol ▶ **noun** the ability to control one's emotions or behavior in difficult situations.
– DERIVATIVES **self-con·trolled** adjective.

self-de·cep·tion ▶ **noun** the tendency to deceive oneself into believing that a false or unfounded feeling, idea, or situation is true.

self-de·feat·ing ▶ **adjective** (of an action or policy) preventing rather than achieving a desired result.

self-de·fense ▶ **noun** the defending of oneself or one's interests, especially through the use of physical force, which is permitted in certain cases as an answer to a charge of violent crime.
– DERIVATIVES **self-de·fen·sive** adjective.

self-de·ni·al ▶ **noun** the action of going without or not doing something that one desires to have or do.
– DERIVATIVES **self-de·ny·ing** adjective.

self-dep·re·cat·ing ▶ **adjective** modest about or critical of oneself.
– DERIVATIVES **self-dep·re·ca·tion** noun **self-dep·re·ca·to·ry** adjective.

self-de·struct ▶ **verb** (of a device) destroy itself by exploding or disintegrating automatically, having been preset to do so.

self-de·struc·tive ▶ **adjective** causing harm to oneself.
– DERIVATIVES **self-de·struc·tion** noun **self-de·struc·tive·ly** adverb.

self-de·ter·mi·na·tion ▶ **noun 1** the process by which a country gains independence and forms its own government and political system. **2** the right or ability of a person to control their own life.

self-di·rect·ed ▶ **adjective 1** (of an emotion, statement, or activity) directed at oneself. **2** (of an activity) under one's own control.
– DERIVATIVES **self-di·rec·tion** noun.

self-dis·ci·pline ▶ noun the ability to control one's feelings and overcome one's weaknesses.
– DERIVATIVES **self-dis·ci·plined** adjective.

self-doubt ▶ noun lack of confidence in oneself and one's abilities.

self-ed·u·cat·ed ▶ adjective educated largely through one's own efforts, rather than by formal instruction.
– DERIVATIVES **self-ed·u·ca·tion** noun.

self-ef·fac·ing ▶ adjective not seeking to attract attention to oneself or one's abilities or achievements.
– DERIVATIVES **self-ef·face·ment** noun.

self-em·ployed ▶ adjective working for oneself as a freelance or the owner of a business rather than for an employer.
– DERIVATIVES **self-em·ploy·ment** noun.

self-es·teem ▶ noun confidence in one's own worth or abilities.

– SYNONYMS **self-respect**, pride, dignity, self-regard, faith in oneself; morale, self-confidence, confidence, self-assurance.

CHOOSE THE RIGHT WORD

See **PRIDE**.

self-e·val·u·a·tion ▶ noun another term for **SELF-ASSESSMENT**.

self-ev·i·dent ▶ adjective not needing to be demonstrated or explained; obvious.

self-ex·am·i·na·tion ▶ noun **1** the study of one's own behavior and motivations. **2** the examination of one's own body for any signs of illness.

self-ex·plan·a·to·ry ▶ adjective not needing explanation; clearly understood.

self-ex·pres·sion ▶ noun the expression of one's feelings or thoughts, especially in writing, art, music, or dance.

self-fer·tile ▶ adjective (of a plant) capable of self-fertilization.

self-fer·ti·li·za·tion ▶ noun the fertilization of plants and some invertebrate animals by their own pollen or sperm.
– DERIVATIVES **self-fer·ti·lize** verb.

self-fi·nanc·ing ▶ adjective (of an organization or enterprise) having or generating enough income to finance itself.
– DERIVATIVES **self-fi·nanced** adjective.

self-ful·fill·ing ▶ adjective (of a prediction) bound to become true because people expect it to and so act in a way that will make it happen.

self-gov·ern·ing ▶ adjective (of a former colony or dependency) administering its own affairs.
– DERIVATIVES **self-gov·ern·ment** noun.

self-harm ▶ noun deliberate injury to oneself, typically as a sign of psychological or psychiatric disorder.
▶ verb commit self-harm.
– DERIVATIVES **self-harm·er** noun.

self-help ▶ noun the use of one's own efforts and resources to achieve things without relying on other people.

self·hood /ˈselfˌho͝od/ ▶ noun the quality that forms a person's individual character.

self-im·age ▶ noun the idea one has of one's abilities, appearance, and personality.

self-im·por·tance ▶ noun an exaggerated sense of one's own value or importance.
– DERIVATIVES **self-im·por·tant** adjective.

self-im·prove·ment ▶ noun the improvement of one's knowledge, status, or character by one's own efforts.

self-in·duced ▶ adjective brought about by oneself.

self-in·dul·gent ▶ adjective allowing oneself to do or have what one wants, especially to an excessive extent.
– DERIVATIVES **self-in·dul·gence** noun.

self-in·flict·ed ▶ adjective (of a wound or other harm) caused by oneself.

self-in·ter·est ▶ noun one's personal interest or advantage, especially when pursued without concern for other people.
– DERIVATIVES **self-in·ter·est·ed** adjective.

self-in·volved ▶ adjective wrapped up in oneself or one's own thoughts.

self·ish /ˈselfiSH/ ▶ adjective concerned mainly with one's own needs or wishes at the expense of consideration for other people.

– SYNONYMS **egocentric**, egotistic, self-centered, self-absorbed, self-obsessed, self-seeking, wrapped up in oneself, mean, greedy; informal looking after number one.
– ANTONYMS unselfish, altruistic.

– DERIVATIVES **self·ish·ly** adverb **self·ish·ness** noun.

self·less /ˈselfləs/ ▶ adjective concerned more with the needs and wishes of other people than with one's own.

– SYNONYMS **unselfish**, altruistic, considerate, compassionate, kind, noble, generous, magnanimous, ungrudging.
– ANTONYMS selfish, inconsiderate.

– DERIVATIVES **self·less·ly** adverb **self·less·ness** noun.

self-lim·it·ing ▶ adjective (of a disease or condition) ultimately resolving itself without medical treatment.

self-love ▶ noun care or concern for one's own well-being and happiness.

self-made ▶ adjective having become successful or rich by one's own efforts.

self-med·i·cate ▶ verb treat oneself with medicine without seeking any medical supervision.
– DERIVATIVES **self-med·i·ca·tion** noun.

self-mo·ti·vat·ed ▶ adjective motivated to do something because of one's own enthusiasm or interest, without needing pressure from others.
– DERIVATIVES **self-mo·ti·va·tion** noun.

self-mu·ti·la·tion ▶ noun deliberate injury to one's own body.

self-o·pin·ion·at·ed ▶ adjective having too high a regard for one's own opinions and unwilling to listen to those of other people.

self-per·pet·u·at·ing ▶ adjective able to continue indefinitely without the assistance of anything or anyone else.

self-pit·y ▶ noun excessive concern with and unhappiness over one's own troubles.
– DERIVATIVES **self-pit·y·ing** adjective.

self-po·lic·ing ▶ noun the process of keeping order or maintaining control within a community without being accountable to an outside authority.

self-pol·li·na·tion ▶ **noun** the pollination of a flower by pollen from the same plant.
– DERIVATIVES **self-pol·li·nate** verb.

self-por·trait ▶ **noun** a portrait by an artist of himself or herself.

self-pos·sessed ▶ **adjective** calm, confident, and in control of one's feelings.
– DERIVATIVES **self-pos·ses·sion** noun.

self-pres·er·va·tion ▶ **noun** the protection of oneself from harm or death, regarded as a basic instinct in human beings and animals.

self-pro·claimed ▶ **adjective** describing oneself as something, without the agreement or approval of other people: *self-proclaimed experts.*

self-pro·pelled ▶ **adjective** moving or able to move without external propulsion.
– DERIVATIVES **self-pro·pel·ling** adjective.

self-re·al·i·za·tion ▶ **noun** fulfillment of one's own potential.

self-ref·er·en·tial ▶ **adjective** (especially of a literary or other creative work) making references to itself, its author or creator, or their other work.

self-re·gard ▶ **noun 1** consideration for oneself. **2** too much pride in oneself; vanity.
– DERIVATIVES **self-re·gard·ing** adjective.

self-reg·u·lat·ing ▶ **adjective** regulating itself without intervention from external organizations, systems, etc.
– DERIVATIVES **self-reg·u·la·tion** noun **self-reg·u·la·to·ry** adjective.

self-re·li·ance ▶ **noun** reliance on one's own powers and resources rather than those of other people.
– DERIVATIVES **self-re·li·ant** adjective.

self-re·spect ▶ **noun** pride and confidence in oneself.
– DERIVATIVES **self-re·spect·ing** adjective.

self-re·straint ▶ **noun** self-control.

self-right·eous ▶ **adjective** certain that one is totally correct or morally superior to other people.

> – SYNONYMS **sanctimonious,** holier-than-thou, pious, self-satisfied, smug, priggish, complacent, moralizing, superior, hypocritical; informal goody-goody.
> – ANTONYMS humble.

– DERIVATIVES **self-right·eous·ly** adverb **self-right·eous·ness** noun.

self-ris·ing flour ▶ **noun** flour that contains baking powder.

self-rule ▶ **noun** government of a country, state, or region by its own people.

self-sac·ri·fice ▶ **noun** the giving up of one's own interests or wishes in order to help other people.
– DERIVATIVES **self-sac·ri·fic·ing** adjective.

self·same /ˈselfˌsām/ ▶ **adjective** (**the selfsame**) the very same.

self-sat·is·fied ▶ **adjective** smugly pleased with oneself.
– DERIVATIVES **self-sat·is·fac·tion** noun.

self-seed ▶ **verb** (of a plant) propagate itself by the seed it produces, without human intervention.
– DERIVATIVES **self-seed·er** noun.

self-seek·ing ▶ **adjective** chiefly British term for **SELF-SERVING.**
– DERIVATIVES **self-seek·er** noun.

self-se·lect ▶ **verb** choose for oneself. ▶ **adjective** allowing users to select.
– DERIVATIVES **self-se·lec·tion** noun.

self-serv·ice ▶ **adjective** (of a store or restaurant) in which customers choose goods for themselves and pay at a checkout.

self-serv·ing ▶ **adjective** concerned with one's own welfare and interests rather than those of other people.
– DERIVATIVES **self-serv·er** noun.

self-start·er ▶ **noun** an ambitious person who acts on their own initiative.

self-styled ▶ **adjective** using a description or title that one has given oneself: *self-styled experts.*

self-suf·fi·cient ▶ **adjective 1** able to support oneself or produce what one needs without outside help. **2** emotionally and intellectually independent.
– DERIVATIVES **self-suf·fi·cien·cy** noun.

self-sup·port·ing ▶ **adjective 1** having the resources to be able to survive without outside help. **2** staying up or upright without being supported by something else.

self-sus·tain·ing ▶ **adjective** able to continue in a healthy state without outside help.
– DERIVATIVES **self-sus·tained** adjective.

self-tap·ping ▶ **adjective** (of a screw) able to cut a thread in the material into which it is inserted.

self-taught ▶ **adjective** having gained knowledge or skill by reading or experience rather than through formal teaching or training.

self-tim·er ▶ **noun** a mechanism in a camera that introduces a delay between the operation of the shutter release and the opening of the shutter, enabling the photographer to be included in the photograph.

self-willed ▶ **adjective** determined to have one's own way, without concern for the wishes of other people.

self-worth ▶ **noun** self-esteem.

sell /sel/ ▶ **verb** (past and past part. **sold**) **1** hand over something in exchange for money. **2** offer goods or property for sale. **3** (of goods) be bought in particular amounts or for a particular price: *the book didn't sell well.* **4** (**sell out**) sell all of one's stock of something. **5** (**sell up**) sell all of one's property or assets. **6** persuade someone that something has particular good qualities. **7** (**sell out**) abandon one's principles because it is expedient to do so. **8** (**sell someone out**) betray someone for one's own financial or material benefit.

> – SYNONYMS **put up for sale,** put on the market, auction (off), trade in, deal in, retail, market, traffic in, peddle, hawk.
> – ANTONYMS buy.

– DERIVATIVES **sell·a·ble** adjective.
– PHRASES **sell someone/thing short** fail to recognize or describe the true value of someone or something.
– ORIGIN Old English.

sell-by date ▶ **noun 1** a date marked on packaged food indicating the recommended time by which it should be sold. **2** informal a time after which something or someone is no longer considered desirable or effective.

sell·er /ˈselər/ ▶ **noun 1** a person who sells something. **2** a product that sells in a particular way.

> – SYNONYMS **vendor,** dealer, retailer, trader, merchant, agent, hawker, peddler, purveyor, supplier.
> – ANTONYMS buyer.

sell·ing point ▶ **noun** a feature of a product for sale that makes it attractive to customers.

sell-off ▶ **noun** a sale of business assets at a low price, carried out in order to dispose of them rather than as part of normal trading.

sell·out /'sel,out/ ▶ **noun 1** the selling of the whole stock of something. **2** an event for which all tickets are sold. **3** a sale of a business or company. **4** a betrayal.

selt·zer /'seltsər/ (also **seltzer water**) ▶ **noun** soda water.
– ORIGIN from German *Selterser*.

sel·vage /'selvij/ (chiefly Brit. also **selvedge**) ▶ **noun** an edge produced on woven fabric during manufacture that prevents it from unraveling.
– ORIGIN from **SELF** + **EDGE**.

selves /selvz/ plural of **SELF**.

se·man·tic /sə'mantik/ ▶ **adjective** relating to the meaning of words and sentences.
– DERIVATIVES **se·man·ti·cal·ly** /-ik(ə)lē/ adverb.
– ORIGIN Greek *sēmantikos* 'significant.'

se·man·tics /sə'mantiks/ ▶ **plural noun** (usu. treated as sing.) **1** the branch of linguistics concerned with meaning. **2** the meaning of a word, phrase, sentence, or piece of writing.

sem·a·phore /'semə,fôr/ ▶ **noun 1** a system of sending messages by holding one's arms or two flags or poles in certain positions that represent letters of the alphabet. **2** a device for sending messages in this way, consisting of an upright with movable parts. ▶ **verb** send a message by semaphore or by signals resembling semaphore.
– ORIGIN French *sémaphore*.

sem·blance /'sembləns/ ▶ **noun** the outward appearance or apparent form of something.

– SYNONYMS **(outward) appearance**, air, show, facade, front, veneer, guise, pretense.

– ORIGIN from Old French *sembler* 'seem.'

se·men /'sēmən/ ▶ **noun** the fluid containing spermatozoa that is produced by men and male animals.
– ORIGIN Latin, 'seed.'

se·mes·ter /sə'mestər/ ▶ **noun** a half-year term in a school or college.
– ORIGIN from Latin *semestris* 'six-monthly.'

sem·i /'semī/ ▶ **noun** (pl. **semis**) informal **1** a tractor-trailer. **2** a semifinal.

semi- ▶ **prefix 1** half: *semicircular*. **2** partly; in some degree: *semiconscious*.
– ORIGIN Latin.

sem·i·au·to·mat·ic /,semē,ôtə'matik, ,sem,ī-/ ▶ **adjective 1** partially automatic. **2** (of a firearm) able to load bullets automatically but not fire continuously.

sem·i·cir·cle /'semē,sərkəl, 'sem,ī-/ ▶ **noun** a half of a circle or of its circumference.
– DERIVATIVES **sem·i·cir·cu·lar** /,semē'sərkyələr, ,semī'sərkyələr/ adjective.

sem·i·cir·cu·lar ca·nals ▶ **plural noun** a system of three fluid-filled bony channels in the inner ear, involved in sensing and maintaining balance.

sem·i·co·lon /'semi,kōlən, 'sem,ī-/ ▶ **noun** a punctuation mark (;) indicating a longer pause than that indicated by a comma.

sem·i·con·duc·tor /'semēkən,dəktər, 'sem,ī-/ ▶ **noun** a solid, e.g., silicon, whose capacity to conduct electricity is limited but increases with temperature.
– DERIVATIVES **sem·i·con·duct·ing** adjective.

sem·i·con·scious /,semē'känsHəs, ,sem,ī-/ ▶ **adjective** partially conscious.

sem·i·dou·ble /,semē'dəbəl, ,sem,ī-/ ▶ **adjective** (of a flower) intermediate between single and double, with the additional petals not completely concealing the center of the flower.

sem·i·fi·nal /,semē'fīnl, ,sem,ī-/ ▶ **noun** (in sports) a match or round immediately preceding the final.
– DERIVATIVES **sem·i·fi·nal·ist** noun.

sem·i·flu·id /,semē'flo͞o-id, ,sem,ī-/ ▶ **adjective** having a thick consistency between solid and liquid.

sem·i·liq·uid /,semē'likwid, ,sem,ī-/ ▶ **adjective** another term for **SEMIFLUID**.

sem·i·nal /'semənl/ ▶ **adjective 1** (of a work, event, or idea) strongly influencing later developments. **2** referring to semen. **3** relating to the seed of a plant.
– DERIVATIVES **sem·i·nal·ly** adverb.
– ORIGIN Latin *seminalis*, from *semen* 'seed.'

sem·i·nar /'semə,när/ ▶ **noun 1** a conference or other meeting for discussion or training. **2** a college class in which a small group of students meet to discuss topics with a teacher.

– SYNONYMS **1 conference**, symposium, meeting, convention, forum, summit. **2 study group**, workshop, tutorial, class.

– ORIGIN German, from Latin *seminarium* 'seed plot.'

sem·i·nar·y /'semə,nerē/ ▶ **noun** (pl. **seminaries**) a college that prepares students to be priests, ministers, or rabbis.
– DERIVATIVES **sem·i·nar·i·an** /,semə'ne(ə)rēən/ noun.
– ORIGIN Latin *seminarium* 'seed plot,' from *semen* 'seed.'

se·mi·ol·o·gy /,sēmē'äləjē, ,semē-, ,sēm,ī- / ▶ **noun** another term for **SEMIOTICS**.
– DERIVATIVES **se·mi·o·log·i·cal** /-ə'läjikəl/ adjective **se·mi·ol·o·gist** noun.
– ORIGIN from Greek *sēmeion* 'sign.'

se·mi·ot·ics /,sēmē'ätiks, ,semē-, ,sem,ī-/ ▶ **plural noun** (treated as sing.) the study of signs and symbols and their use or interpretation.
– DERIVATIVES **se·mi·ot·ic** adjective **se·mi·o·ti·cian** /,semēə'tisHən, ,sēmēə-/ noun.
– ORIGIN from Greek *sēmeiotikos* 'of signs.'

sem·i·per·me·a·ble /,semē'pərmēəbəl, ,sem,ī-/ ▶ **adjective** (of a cell membrane) allowing small molecules to pass through but not large ones.

sem·i·pre·cious /,semē'presHəs, ,sem,ī-/ ▶ **adjective** referring to minerals that can be used as gems but are considered to be less valuable than precious stones.

sem·i·pro·fes·sion·al /,semēprə'fesHənl, ,sem,ī-/ ▶ **adjective** receiving payment for an activity but not relying entirely on it for a living. ▶ **noun** a person who is engaged in an activity on such a basis.

sem·i·re·tired /,semēri'tī(ə)rd, ,semī-/ ▶ **adjective** having retired from employment but continuing to work part-time or occasionally.
– DERIVATIVES **sem·i·re·tire·ment** /-'tī(ə)rmənt/ noun.

sem·i·skilled /,semē'skild, ,sem,ī-/ ▶ **adjective** (of work or a worker) needing or having some, but not extensive, training.

sem·i·sol·id /,semē'sälid, ,sem,ī-/ ▶ **adjective** having a very thick, sticky consistency; slightly thicker than semifluid.

Sem·ite /ˈsemīt/ ▸ **noun** a member of a people speaking a Semitic language, in particular the Jews and Arabs.
– ORIGIN from Greek *Sēm* 'Shem,' son of Noah in the Bible, from whom these people are traditionally descended.

Se·mit·ic /səˈmitik/ ▸ **noun** a family of languages that includes Hebrew, Arabic, and Aramaic. ▸ **adjective** relating to these languages or their speakers.

sem·i·tone /ˈsemēˌtōn, ˈsemˌī-/ ▸ **noun** chiefly British term for **HALF STEP**.

sem·i·trail·er /ˈsemēˌtrālər, ˈsemˌī-/ ▸ **noun 1** a trailer having wheels at the back but supported at the front by a towing vehicle. **2** a tractor trailer.

sem·o·li·na /ˌseməˈlēnə/ ▸ **noun** the hard grains left after the milling of flour, used in puddings and in pasta.
– ORIGIN Italian *semolino*.

sem·pi·ter·nal /ˌsempəˈtərnl/ ▸ **adjective** literary eternal and unchanging; everlasting.
– ORIGIN Latin *sempiternus*.

Sem·tex /ˈsemˌteks/ ▸ **noun** a type of plastic explosive.
– ORIGIN probably a blend of *Semtin* (a village in the Czech Republic near the place of production) and **EXPLOSIVE**.

Sen. ▸ **abbreviation 1** Senate. **2** Senator. **3** Senior.

sen·ate /ˈsenit/ ▸ **noun 1** a lawmaking or governing body, especially the smaller upper assembly in the US, US states, France, and other countries. **2** the governing body of a college or university. **3** the state council of the ancient Roman republic and empire.
– ORIGIN Latin *senatus*, from *senex* 'old man.'

sen·a·tor /ˈsenitər/ ▸ **noun** a member of a senate.
– DERIVATIVES **sen·a·to·ri·al** /ˌsenəˈtôrēəl/ adjective **sen·a·tor·ship** /-ˌship/ noun.

send /send/ ▸ **verb** (past and past part. **sent**) **1** cause something to go or be taken to a destination. **2** order or instruct someone to go somewhere. **3** move something sharply or quickly. **4** cause to be in a particular state: *the traffic nearly sent me crazy*.

> – SYNONYMS **1** *they sent a message to HQ* **dispatch**, post, mail, email, consign, forward, transmit, convey, communicate, broadcast, radio. **2** *we* ***sent for*** *a doctor* **call**, summon, ask for, request, order. **3** *the pump* ***sent out*** *a jet of steam* **propel**, project, eject, deliver, discharge, spout, fire, shoot, release, throw, fling, cast, hurl. **4** *you're sending me crazy* **make**, drive, turn.
> – ANTONYMS receive.

– DERIVATIVES **send·er** noun.
– PHRASES **send for 1** order someone to come. **2** order something by mail. **send word** send a message to someone.
– ORIGIN Old English.

send-off ▸ **noun** a gathering of people to wish good luck to someone who is leaving.

> – SYNONYMS **farewell**, goodbye, adieu, leave-taking, departure.

send·up /ˈsendˌəp/ ▸ **noun** informal an exaggerated imitation of someone or something, done in order to make fun of them.

Sen·e·ga·lese /ˌsenəgəˈlēz, -ˈlēs/ ▸ **noun** (pl. **Senegalese**) a person from Senegal, a country on the coast of West Africa. ▸ **adjective** relating to Senegal.

se·nes·cence /səˈnesəns/ ▸ **noun** the process by which a living thing gradually deteriorates with age.
– DERIVATIVES **se·nes·cent** adjective.
– ORIGIN Latin *senescere*, from *senex* 'old.'

sen·e·schal /ˈsenəshəl/ ▸ **noun 1** the steward of a noble's or monarch's house in medieval times. **2** chiefly historical a governor or other administrative or judicial officer.
– ORIGIN Latin *seniscalus*.

se·nile /ˈsēˌnīl, ˈsen-/ ▸ **adjective** having the weaknesses or diseases of old age, especially a loss of mental abilities.

> – SYNONYMS **doddering**, decrepit, senescent, infirm, feeble; (mentally) confused, having Alzheimer's (disease), having senile dementia; informal gaga.

– DERIVATIVES **se·nil·i·ty** /siˈnilitē/ noun.
– ORIGIN Latin *senilis*, from *senex* 'old man.'

se·nile de·men·tia ▸ **noun** severe mental deterioration in old age, with loss of memory and lack of control of bodily functions.

sen·ior /ˈsēnyər/ ▸ **adjective 1** relating to older people. **2** high or higher in rank or status. **3** relating to the final of four years of high school or college. **4** (after a name) referring to the elder of two with the same name in a family.

> – SYNONYMS **1 older**, elder. **2 superior**, higher-ranking, more important, ranking.
> – ANTONYMS junior, subordinate.

▸ **noun 1** a person who is a specified number of years older than someone else: *she was two years his senior*. **2** a student in the fourth and final year of high school or college. **3** (in sports) a competitor of above a certain age or of the highest status. **4** a senior citizen.
– DERIVATIVES **sen·ior·i·ty** /sēnˈyôritē, -ˈyär-/ noun.
– ORIGIN Latin, from *senex* 'old.'

sen·ior cit·i·zen ▸ **noun** an elderly person, especially one who is retired.

sen·ior mo·ment ▸ **noun** humorous a temporary mental lapse.

sen·na /ˈsenə/ ▸ **noun** a laxative prepared from the dried pods of the cassia tree.
– ORIGIN Arabic.

sen·sate /ˈsenˌsāt/ ▸ **adjective** becoming aware of things through the senses.

sen·sa·tion /senˈsāshən/ ▸ **noun 1** a physical feeling resulting from something that happens to or comes into contact with the body. **2** the ability to have such feelings. **3** a general awareness or impression not caused by anything that can be seen or defined: *the eerie sensation that she was being watched*. **4** a widespread reaction of interest and excitement, or a person or thing causing it.

> – SYNONYMS **1 feeling**, sense, perception, impression. **2 commotion**, stir, uproar, furor, scandal, impact; informal splash, to-do.

sen·sa·tion·al /senˈsāshənl/ ▸ **adjective 1** causing or intending to cause great public interest and excitement. **2** informal very impressive or attractive.

> – SYNONYMS **1 shocking**, scandalous, fascinating, exciting, thrilling, interesting, dramatic, momentous, historic, newsworthy. **2 overdramatized**, melodramatic, exaggerated, sensationalist, graphic, explicit, lurid; informal shock-horror, juicy. **3 gorgeous**, stunning, wonderful, superb, excellent, first-class; informal great, terrific,

tremendous, fantastic, fabulous, out of this world, smashing.
– ANTONYMS dull, unremarkable.

– DERIVATIVES **sen·sa·tion·al·ly** adverb.

sen·sa·tion·al·ism /sen'sāshənl,izəm/ ▶ **noun** (in the media) the use of exciting or shocking stories or language at the expense of accuracy, in order to arouse public interest or excitement.
– DERIVATIVES **sen·sa·tion·al·ist** noun & adjective **sen·sa·tion·al·is·tic** /sen,sāshənl'istik/ adjective.

sen·sa·tion·al·ize /sen'sāshənl,īz/ ▶ **verb** present information in an exaggerated way in order to make it seem more interesting or exciting.

sense /sens/ ▶ **noun 1** any of the faculties of sight, smell, hearing, taste, and touch, by which the body becomes aware of external things. **2** a feeling that something is the case. **3** (**sense of**) awareness of or sensitivity to: *a sense of direction*. **4** a sensible and practical attitude to situations or problems. **5** reason or purpose; good judgment: *there's no sense in standing in the rain*. **6** a meaning of a word or expression or the way in which a word or expression can be interpreted.

– SYNONYMS **1 feeling,** faculty, awareness, sensation, recognition, perception. **2 appreciation,** awareness, understanding, comprehension. **3 wisdom,** common sense, wit, reason, intelligence, judgment, brain(s), sagacity; informal gumption, horse sense, savvy, smarts. **4 purpose,** point, use, value, advantage, benefit. **5 meaning,** definition, denotation, nuance, drift, gist, thrust, tenor, message.
– ANTONYMS stupidity.

▶ **verb 1** become aware of something by a sense or senses. **2** be vaguely aware of something. **3** (of a machine or similar device) detect something.

– SYNONYMS **detect,** feel, observe, notice, recognize, pick up, be aware of, distinguish, make out, perceive, discern, divine, intuit; informal catch on to.

– PHRASES **come to one's senses 1** regain consciousness. **2** think and behave reasonably or sensibly again. **make sense** be understandable, justifiable, or sensible. **make sense of** manage to understand something.
– ORIGIN Latin *sensus* 'faculty of feeling, thought, meaning,' from *sentire* 'feel.'

sen·sei /'sen,sā, sen'sā/ ▶ **noun** (pl. same) (in martial arts) a teacher.
– ORIGIN Japanese, from *sen* 'previous' + *sei* 'birth.'

sense·less /'sensləs/ ▶ **adjective 1** lacking meaning, purpose, or common sense. **2** unconscious.

– SYNONYMS **pointless,** futile, useless, needless, meaningless, absurd, foolish, insane, stupid, idiotic, mindless, illogical.
– ANTONYMS wise.

– DERIVATIVES **sense·less·ly** adverb **sense·less·ness** noun.

sense or·gan ▶ **noun** an organ of the body that responds to external stimuli by sending impulses to the brain.

sen·si·bil·i·ty /,sensə'bilitē/ ▶ **noun** (pl. **sensibilities**) **1** the ability to appreciate and respond to complex emotions, especially as expressed in art and literature. **2** (**sensibilities**) a person's feelings that are liable to be easily shocked or offended.

sen·si·ble /'sensəbəl/ ▶ **adjective 1** having or showing common sense. **2** practical and functional rather than decorative. **3** (**sensible of/to**) formal or dated aware of: *I am very sensible to your concerns*.

– SYNONYMS **practical,** realistic, responsible, reasonable, commonsensical, rational, logical, sound, no-nonsense, levelheaded, down-to-earth, wise.
– ANTONYMS foolish.

– DERIVATIVES **sen·si·bly** /-blē/ adverb.

sen·si·tive /'sensitiv/ ▶ **adjective 1** quick to detect, respond to, or be affected by slight changes or influences. **2** appreciating the feelings of other people. **3** easily offended or upset. **4** (of a subject or issue) needing careful handling because likely to cause offense or controversy. **5** (of information) kept secret to avoid endangering national security.

– SYNONYMS **1** *she's sensitive to changes in temperature* **responsive to,** reactive to, sensitized to, aware of, conscious of, susceptible to, affected by, vulnerable to. **2 delicate,** fragile, tender, sore. **3 tactful,** careful, thoughtful, diplomatic, delicate, subtle, kid-glove. **4 touchy,** oversensitive, hypersensitive, easily offended, thin-skinned, defensive, paranoid, neurotic. **5 difficult,** delicate, tricky, awkward, problematic, ticklish, controversial, emotive.
– ANTONYMS insensitive, resilient.

– DERIVATIVES **sen·si·tive·ly** adverb **sen·si·tive·ness** noun.
– ORIGIN Latin *sensitivus*, from *sentire* 'feel.'

sen·si·tive plant ▶ **noun** a tropical American plant of the pea family, whose leaves bend down when touched.

sen·si·tiv·i·ty /,sensi'tivitē/ ▶ **noun** (pl. **sensitivities**) **1** the quality or condition of being sensitive. **2** (**sensitivities**) a person's feelings that might be easily offended or hurt.

– SYNONYMS **1 responsiveness,** sensitiveness, reactivity, susceptibility. **2 tact,** diplomacy, delicacy, subtlety, understanding. **3 touchiness,** oversensitivity, hypersensitivity, defensiveness. **4 delicacy,** trickiness, awkwardness, ticklishness.

sen·si·tize /'sensi,tīz/ ▶ **verb** make someone or something sensitive to or aware of something.
– DERIVATIVES **sen·si·ti·za·tion** /,sensiti'zāshən/ noun **sen·si·tiz·er** noun.

sen·sor /'sensər/ ▶ **noun** a device that detects or measures a physical property.

sen·so·ry /'sensərē/ ▶ **adjective** relating to sensation or the senses.
– DERIVATIVES **sen·so·ri·ly** /-rəlē/ adverb.

sen·su·al /'senshooəl/ ▶ **adjective** relating to the physical senses as a source of pleasure, especially sexual pleasure.

– SYNONYMS **1 physical,** carnal, bodily, fleshly, animal. **2 passionate,** sexual, physical, tactile, hedonistic.
– ANTONYMS spiritual.

– DERIVATIVES **sen·su·al·ist** noun **sen·su·al·i·ty** /,senshoo'alitē/ noun **sen·su·al·ly** adverb.

USAGE

Strictly speaking there is a difference between **sensual** and **sensuous**. **Sensual** is used in relation to pleasure experienced through the senses, especially sexual pleasure, while **sensuous** is a more neutral term, meaning 'relating to the senses rather than the intellect.'

sen·su·ous /'senshooəs/ ▶ **adjective 1** relating to or affecting the senses rather than the intellect.

2 attractive or pleasing physically, especially sexually.

– SYNONYMS **1 rich,** sumptuous, luxurious. **2 voluptuous,** sexy, seductive, luscious, lush, ripe.

– DERIVATIVES **sen·su·ous·ly** adverb **sen·su·ous·ness** noun.
– ORIGIN from Latin *sensus* 'sense.'

sent[1] /sent/ past and past participle of **SEND**.

sent[2] ▶ **noun** a unit of money of Estonia, equal to one hundredth of a kroon.
– ORIGIN respelling of **CENT**.

sen·tence /'sentns/ ▶ **noun 1** a set of words that is complete in itself, conveying a statement, question, exclamation, or command. **2** the punishment given to someone found guilty by a court.

– SYNONYMS **1 judgment,** ruling, decision, verdict. **2** *a long sentence* **punishment,** prison term; informal time, stretch.

▶ **verb** declare in a court that a person found guilty is to receive a particular punishment.

– SYNONYMS **condemn,** doom, punish, convict.

– ORIGIN from Latin *sententia* 'opinion.'

sen·ten·tious /sen'tenchəs/ ▶ **adjective** given to making pompous comments on moral issues.
– DERIVATIVES **sen·ten·tious·ly** adverb **sen·ten·tious·ness** noun.
– ORIGIN from Latin *sententia* 'opinion.'

sen·tient /'sench(ē)ənt/ ▶ **adjective** able to perceive or feel things.
– DERIVATIVES **sen·tience** noun.
– ORIGIN from Latin *sentire* 'to feel.'

sen·ti·ment /'sen(t)əmənt/ ▶ **noun 1** a view, opinion, or feeling. **2** exaggerated and self-indulgent feelings of tenderness, sadness, or nostalgia.

– SYNONYMS **1 view,** feeling, attitude, thought, opinion, belief. **2 sentimentality,** emotion, tenderness, softness; informal schmaltz.

– ORIGIN Latin *sentimentum*, from *sentire* 'feel.'

CHOOSE THE RIGHT WORD

See **OPINION**.

sen·ti·men·tal /ˌsen(t)ə'men(t)l/ ▶ **adjective 1** connected with or caused by feelings of tenderness, sadness, or nostalgia: *he had a sentimental attachment to the place.* **2** having or causing such feelings in a way that is exaggerated or self-indulgent: *a sentimental love song.*

– SYNONYMS **1 nostalgic,** emotional, affectionate, loving, tender. **2 mawkish,** overemotional, romantic, hearts-and-flowers; informal schmaltzy, sappy, corny.

– DERIVATIVES **sen·ti·men·tal·ism** /ˌsen(t)ə'men(t)lˌizəm/ noun **sen·ti·men·tal·ist** noun **sen·ti·men·tal·i·ty** /ˌsen(t)əmen'talitē, -mən-/ noun **sen·ti·men·tal·ly** adverb.

sen·ti·men·tal·ize /ˌsen(t)ə'men(t)lˌīz/ ▶ **verb** present or treat something in a sentimental way.

sen·ti·men·tal val·ue ▶ **noun** the value of an object that comes from its personal or emotional associations rather than its material worth.

sen·ti·nel /'sentn-əl/ ▶ **noun** a soldier or guard whose job is to stand and keep watch.
– ORIGIN Italian *sentinella*.

sen·try /'sentrē/ ▶ **noun** (pl. **sentries**) a soldier stationed to keep guard or to control access to a place.
– ORIGIN perhaps from former *centrinel*, from **SENTINEL**.

sen·try box ▶ **noun** a structure with an open front, providing shelter for a standing sentry.

se·ñor /sān'yôr, sen-/ ▶ **noun** a title or form of address for a Spanish-speaking man, corresponding to *Mr.* or *sir*.

se·ño·ra /sān'yôrə, sen-/ ▶ **noun** a title or form of address for a Spanish-speaking woman, corresponding to *Mrs.* or *madam*.

se·ño·ri·ta /ˌsānyə'rētə, ˌsen-/ ▶ **noun** a title or form of address for a Spanish-speaking unmarried woman, corresponding to *Miss*.

se·pal /'sēpəl/ ▶ **noun** each of the leaflike parts of a flower that surround the petals, enclosing them when the flower is in bud.
– ORIGIN from Greek *skepē* 'covering.'

sep·a·ra·ble /'sep(ə)rəbəl/ ▶ **adjective** able to be separated or treated separately.
– DERIVATIVES **sep·a·ra·bil·i·ty** /ˌsep(ə)rə'bilitē/ noun.

sep·a·rate ▶ **adjective** /'sep(ə)rit/ **1** forming or seen as a unit apart or by itself; not joined or united with others. **2** different; distinct.

– SYNONYMS **1** *the infirmary was separate from the school* **set apart,** detached, cut off, segregated, isolated, free-standing, self-contained. **2** *his personal life was separate from his job* **unconnected,** unrelated, different, distinct, discrete, detached, divorced, disconnected, independent.

▶ **verb** /'sepəˌrāt/ **1** move or come apart. **2** form a distinction or boundary between: *a footpath separated their yard from the shore.* **3** stop living together as a couple. **4** divide into component parts: *the milk had separated into curds and whey.* **5** extract or remove something for use or because it is unwanted. **6** distinguish between or from others; consider individually: *it is impossible to separate belief from emotion.*

– SYNONYMS **1 disconnect,** detach, disengage, uncouple, split, sunder, sever. **2 partition,** divide, stand between, come between, keep apart, isolate, section off. **3 split up,** break up, part, become estranged, divorce.
– ANTONYMS unite, join.

▶ **noun** /'sep(ə)rit/ (**separates**) individual items of clothing designed to be worn in different combinations.
– DERIVATIVES **sep·a·rate·ness** noun **sep·a·ra·tor** /'sepəˌrātər/ noun.
– ORIGIN from Latin *separare*.

sep·a·rate·ly /'sep(ə)ritlē/ ▶ **adverb** individually; without others: *I'll have to interview you all separately.*

– SYNONYMS **individually,** one by one, one at a time, singly, severally, apart, independently, alone, by oneself, on one's own.

sep·a·ra·tion /ˌsepə'rāshən/ ▶ **noun 1** the action of separating or the state of being separated. **2** the state in which a husband and wife remain married but live apart.

– SYNONYMS **1 disconnection,** splitting, division, breaking-up. **2 break-up,** split, estrangement, divorce.

sep·a·ra·tist /'sep(ə)rətist/ ▶ **noun** a person who supports the separation of a particular group from a larger body on the basis of ethnic origin, religion, etc. ▶ **adjective** relating to such separation or people who support it.
– DERIVATIVES **sep·a·ra·tism** /'sep(ə)rəˌtizəm/ noun.

Se·phar·di /sə'färdē/ ▸ **noun** (pl. **Sephardim** /-'färdim, -ˌfär'dēm/) a Jew of Spanish or Portuguese descent. Compare with **ASHKENAZI**.
– DERIVATIVES **Se·phar·dic** /-dik/ adjective.
– ORIGIN Hebrew, from the name of a country mentioned in the Bible (Obadiah 20) and taken to be Spain.

se·pi·a /'sēpēə/ ▸ **noun 1** a reddish-brown color, associated particularly with early photographs. **2** a brown pigment prepared from cuttlefish ink, used in drawing and in watercolors.
– ORIGIN Greek, 'cuttlefish.'

se·poy /'sēˌpoi/ ▸ **noun** historical an Indian soldier serving under British or other European orders.
– ORIGIN Urdu and Persian, 'soldier.'

sep·pu·ku /'sepo͞oˌko͞o, sə'po͞oko͞o/ ▸ **noun** another term for **HARA-KIRI**.
– ORIGIN Japanese, from words meaning 'to cut' and 'abdomen.'

sep·sis /'sepsis/ ▸ **noun** the presence in tissues of harmful bacteria, typically through infection of a wound.
– ORIGIN Greek, from *sēpein* 'make rotten.'

Sept. ▸ **abbreviation** September.

sep·ta /'septə/ plural of **SEPTUM**.

sep·tal /'septl/ ▸ **adjective** relating to a septum or septa.

Sep·tem·ber /sep'tembər/ ▸ **noun** the ninth month of the year.
– ORIGIN from Latin *septem* 'seven' (being originally the seventh month of the Roman year).

sep·tet /sep'tet/ ▸ **noun** a group of seven people playing music or singing together.
– ORIGIN from Latin *septem* 'seven.'

sep·tic /'septik/ ▸ **adjective** (of a wound or a part of the body) infected with bacteria.

> – SYNONYMS **infected**, festering, suppurating, putrid, putrefying, poisoned; Medicine purulent.

– ORIGIN Greek *sēptikos*, from *sēpein* 'make rotten.'

> **USAGE**
>
> Do not confuse **septic** with **skeptic**. **Septic** means 'infected with bacteria' (*a septic finger*), whereas **skeptic** means 'a person who tends to question or doubt accepted opinions' (*numerous skeptics poured scorn on his claim*).

sep·ti·ce·mi·a /ˌsepti'sēmēə/ (Brit. **septicaemia**) ▸ **noun** blood poisoning caused by bacteria.

sep·tic tank ▸ **noun** an underground tank in which sewage is allowed to decompose through the action of bacteria before draining away into the ground.

sep·tu·a·ge·nar·i·an /ˌsepˌto͞oəjə'ne(ə)rēən/ ▸ **noun** a person who is between 70 and 79 years old.
– ORIGIN Latin *septuagenarius*.

Sep·tu·a·gint /'septo͞oəˌjint/ ▸ **noun** a Greek version of the Hebrew Bible (or Old Testament), including the Apocrypha, produced in the 3rd and 2nd centuries BC.
– ORIGIN from Latin *septuaginta* 'seventy,' because of the tradition that it was produced by seventy-two translators working independently.

sep·tum /'septəm/ ▸ **noun** (pl. **septa** /-tə/) a partition separating two cavities in the body, such as that between the nostrils.
– ORIGIN Latin.

sep·tup·let /sep'təplit, sep't(y)o͞o-/ ▸ **noun** each of seven children born at one birth.

sep·ul·cher /'sepəlkər/ (Brit. **sepulchre**) ▸ **noun** a stone tomb or monument in which a dead person is laid or buried.
– ORIGIN Latin *sepulcrum* 'burial place.'

se·pul·chral /sə'pəlkrəl/ ▸ **adjective 1** gloomy and solemn: *a speech delivered in sepulchral tones*. **2** relating to a tomb or burial.
– DERIVATIVES **se·pul·chral·ly** adverb.

se·quel /'sēkwəl/ ▸ **noun 1** a book, movie, or television program that continues the story or develops the theme of an earlier one. **2** something that takes place after or as a result of an earlier event.

> – SYNONYMS **continuation**, further episode, follow-up.

– ORIGIN Latin *sequella*, from *sequi* 'follow.'

se·que·la /si'kwelə/ ▸ **noun** (pl. **sequelae** /-'kwelē, -'kwelī/) a medical condition that is the consequence of a previous disease or injury.
– ORIGIN Latin, from *sequi* 'follow.'

se·quence /'sēkwəns/ ▸ **noun 1** a particular order in which related things follow each other. **2** a set of related things that follow each other in a particular order. **3** a part of a movie or television program dealing with one particular event or topic. **4** Music a repetition of a phrase or melody at a higher or lower pitch.

> – SYNONYMS **1 succession**, order, course, series, chain, train, progression, chronology, pattern, flow. **2 excerpt**, clip, extract, section.

▸ **verb 1** arrange something in a sequence. **2** play or record music with a sequencer.
– ORIGIN Latin *sequentia*, from *sequi* 'follow.'

se·quenc·er /'sēkwənsər/ ▸ **noun** an electronic device for storing sequences of musical notes, chords, or rhythms and transmitting them to an electronic musical instrument.

se·quen·tial /si'kwencʜəl/ ▸ **adjective** forming or following in a logical order or sequence.
– DERIVATIVES **se·quen·tial·ly** adverb.

se·ques·ter /sə'kwestər/ ▸ **verb 1** isolate or hide away: *he sequestered himself in his studio*. **2** another term for **SEQUESTRATE**.
– ORIGIN Latin *sequestrare* 'commit for safekeeping.'

se·ques·trate /'sēkwiˌstrāt, 'sek-, sə'kwesˌtrāt/ ▸ **verb 1** take legal possession of assets until a debt has been paid or other claims have been met. **2** take forcible possession of something.
– DERIVATIVES **se·ques·tra·tion** /ˌsēkwi'strāsʜən, ˌsek-/ noun **se·ques·tra·tor** noun.

se·quin /'sēkwin/ ▸ **noun** a small shiny disk sewn onto clothing for decoration.
– DERIVATIVES **sequined** (also **sequinned**) adjective.
– ORIGIN from Italian *zecchino*, first referring to a former Venetian gold coin.

se·quoi·a /sə'k(w)oi-ə/ ▸ **noun** a redwood tree, especially the California redwood.
– ORIGIN named after *Sequoya*, a Cherokee Indian scholar.

se·ra /'si(ə)rə/ plural of **SERUM**.

se·ragl·io /sə'rälyō/ ▸ **noun** (pl. **seraglios**) **1** the women's rooms in a Muslim house or palace. **2** a harem.
– ORIGIN Italian *serraglio*.

se·ra·pe /sə'räpē/ (also **sarape**) ▸ **noun** a shawl or blanket worn as a cloak by people from Latin America.
– ORIGIN Mexican Spanish.

ser·aph /ˈserəf/ ▶ **noun** (pl. **seraphim** /ˈserəˌfim/ or **seraphs**) a type of angel associated with light and purity.
– DERIVATIVES **se·raph·ic** /səˈrafik/ adjective **se·raph·i·cal·ly** /səˈrafik(ə)lē/ adverb.
– ORIGIN Hebrew.

Serb /sərb/ ▶ **noun** a person from Serbia.

Ser·bi·an /ˈsərbēən/ ▶ **noun 1** the language of the Serbs. **2** a Serb. ▶ **adjective** relating to Serbia.

Ser·bo-Cro·at /ˈsərbō ˈkrōˌät, ˈkrōt/ (also **Serbo-Croatian** /krōˈāsʜən/) ▶ **noun** the language spoken in Serbia, Croatia, and elsewhere in the former Yugoslavia.

sere /si(ə)r/ (also **sear**) ▶ **adjective** literary (of a plant) withered.

ser·e·nade /ˌserəˈnād/ ▶ **noun** a piece of music sung or played in the open air at night, especially by a man under the window of the woman he loves. ▶ **verb** entertain someone with a serenade.
– DERIVATIVES **ser·e·nad·er** noun.
– ORIGIN Italian *serenata*.

ser·en·dip·i·ty /ˌserənˈdipitē/ ▶ **noun** the occurrence of events by chance in a beneficial or lucky way: *many cancer drugs have been discovered through serendipity*.
– DERIVATIVES **ser·en·dip·i·tous** /-ˈdipitəs/ adjective **ser·en·dip·i·tous·ly** adverb.
– ORIGIN coined by the English politician Horace Walpole from *The Three Princes of Serendip*, a fairy tale in which the heroes were always making fortunate discoveries (*Serendip* was a former name for Sri Lanka).

se·rene /səˈrēn/ ▶ **adjective** calm, peaceful, and untroubled; tranquil.

> – SYNONYMS **calm,** composed, tranquil, peaceful, placid, untroubled, relaxed, at ease, unperturbed, unruffled, unworried, centered; informal together, unflappable.
> – ANTONYMS agitated.

– DERIVATIVES **se·rene·ly** adverb **se·ren·i·ty** /səˈrenitē/ noun.
– ORIGIN Latin *serenus*.

serf /sərf/ ▶ **noun** (in the feudal system) an agricultural laborer who was tied to working on a particular estate.
– DERIVATIVES **serf·dom** /-dəm/ noun.
– ORIGIN Latin *servus* 'slave.'

serge /sərj/ ▶ **noun** a hard-wearing woolen or worsted fabric.
– ORIGIN Old French *sarge*.

ser·geant /ˈsärjənt/ ▶ **noun 1** a rank of noncommissioned officer in the army or air force, above corporal. **2** a police officer ranking below a lieutenant.
– ORIGIN Old French *sergent*.

ser·geant-at-arms (also Brit. **serjeant-at-arms**) ▶ **noun** (pl. **sergeants-at-arms**) an official of a lawmaking body whose duties include maintaining order and security.

ser·geant ma·jor ▶ **noun** a high-ranking noncommissioned officer in the US Army or Marine Corps, above master sergeant and below warrant officer.

se·ri·al /ˈsi(ə)rēəl/ ▶ **adjective 1** consisting of or taking place in a series. **2** repeatedly committing the same offense or following a characteristic behavior pattern: *a serial killer*. **3** Computing (of a device) involving the transfer of data as a single sequence of bits. ▶ **noun** a story or play published or broadcast in regular instalments.
– DERIVATIVES **se·ri·al·i·ty** /ˌsi(ə)rēˈalitē/ noun **se·ri·al·ly** adverb.

se·ri·al·ism /ˈsi(ə)rēəˌlizəm/ ▶ **noun** a technique of musical composition using the twelve notes of the chromatic scale (one that rises or falls by half steps) in a fixed order that is subject to change only in specific ways.
– DERIVATIVES **se·ri·al·ist** adjective & noun.

se·ri·al·ize /ˈsi(ə)rēəˌlīz/ ▶ **verb 1** publish or broadcast a story or play in regular instalments. **2** arrange something in a series.
– DERIVATIVES **se·ri·al·i·za·tion** /ˌsi(ə)rēələˈzāsʜən/ noun.

se·ri·al num·ber ▶ **noun** an identification number showing the position of a manufactured item in a series.

se·ries /ˈsi(ə)rēz/ ▶ **noun** (pl. same) **1** a number of similar or related things coming one after another. **2** a sequence of related television or radio programs. **3** Geology a range of rock strata corresponding to an epoch in time: *the Pliocene series*. **4** Mathematics a set of quantities constituting a progression or having values determined by a common relation.

> – SYNONYMS **succession,** sequence, string, chain, run, round, spate, wave, rash, course, cycle, row.

– PHRASES **in series** (of electrical components or circuits) arranged so that the current passes through each in turn.
– ORIGIN Latin, 'row, chain.'

ser·if /ˈserəf/ ▶ **noun** a slight projection finishing off a stroke of a letter, as in T contrasted with T.
– ORIGIN perhaps from Dutch *schreef* 'dash, line.'

se·ri·o·com·ic /ˌsi(ə)rē-ōˈkämik/ (also **serio-comic**) ▶ **adjective** combining serious and comic elements.

se·ri·ous /ˈsi(ə)rēəs/ ▶ **adjective 1** dangerous or very bad: *serious injury*. **2** needing or showing careful consideration or action: *marriage is a serious matter*. **3** solemn or sensible. **4** sincere and in earnest. **5** informal substantial in size, number, or quality: *every minute is costing you serious money*.

> – SYNONYMS **1 solemn,** earnest, grave, somber, unsmiling, stern, grim, humorless, stony, dour, poker-faced, long-faced. **2 important,** significant, momentous, weighty, far-reaching, consequential. **3 intellectual,** highbrow, heavyweight, deep, profound, literary, learned, scholarly; informal heavy. **4** *a serious injury* **severe,** grave, bad, critical, acute, terrible, dire, dangerous, grievous. **5 sincere,** earnest, genuine, wholehearted, committed, resolute, determined.
> – ANTONYMS lighthearted, trivial, minor.

– DERIVATIVES **se·ri·ous·ness** noun.
– ORIGIN Latin *serius*.

se·ri·ous·ly /ˈsi(ə)rēəslē/ ▶ **adverb 1** in a serious way. **2** very; extremely: *he's seriously rich*.

ser·mon /ˈsərmən/ ▶ **noun 1** a talk on a religious or moral subject, especially one given during a church service. **2** informal a long or boring reprimand.

> – SYNONYMS **address,** homily, talk, speech, lecture.

– DERIVATIVES **ser·mon·ic** /sərˈmänik/ adjective.
– ORIGIN Latin, 'discourse, talk.'

ser·mon·ize /ˈsərməˌnīz/ ▶ **verb** give a long talk about morals to someone.

se·rol·o·gy /siˈräləjē/ ▶ **noun** the scientific study or examination of blood serum.
– DERIVATIVES **se·ro·log·ic** /ˌsi(ə)rəˈläjik/ adjective **se·ro·log·i·cal** adjective **se·rol·o·gist** noun.

se·ro·pos·i·tive /ˌsi(ə)rōˈpäzitiv/ (or **seronegative** /ˌsi(ə)rōˈnegətiv/) ▶ **adjective** giving a positive (or negative) result in a test of blood serum, especially for the presence of a virus.

ser·o·to·nin /ˌserəˈtōnən, ˌsi(ə)r-/ ▶ **noun** a compound in blood that constricts the blood vessels and brings about the transfer of impulses from one nerve to another.
– ORIGIN from **SERUM** + **TONIC**.

se·rous /ˈsi(ə)rəs/ ▶ **adjective** relating to, resembling, or producing serum.

ser·pent /ˈsərpənt/ ▶ **noun** literary a large snake.
– ORIGIN from Latin *serpere* 'to creep.'

ser·pen·tine /ˈsərpənˌtēn, -ˌtīn/ ▶ **adjective** like a serpent or snake, especially in being winding or twisting. ▶ **noun** a dark green mineral that is often mottled or spotted like a snake's skin.

WORD TOOLKIT

serpentine ...	meandering ...	winding ...
lines	river	road
tail	path	staircase
canyon	thoughts	driveway
curves	narrative	corridor

ser·ra·no /səˈränō/ ▶ **noun** a small, red or yellow, very hot chili that is used fresh or dried in Mexican cooking.

ser·rat·ed /ˈserˌātid, səˈrātid/ ▶ **adjective** having a jagged edge like the teeth of a saw.
– ORIGIN Latin *serratus*.

ser·ra·tion /seˈrāsʜən/ ▶ **noun** a tooth or point of a jagged edge.

ser·ried /ˈserēd/ ▶ **adjective** (of rows of people or things) standing close together.
– ORIGIN probably from French *serré* 'close together.'

se·rum /ˈsi(ə)rəm/ ▶ **noun** (pl. **sera** /ˈsi(ə)rə/ or **serums**) the thin amber-colored liquid that separates out when blood has clotted.
– ORIGIN Latin, 'whey.'

serv·ant /ˈsərvənt/ ▶ **noun 1** a person employed to perform domestic duties in a household or for a person. **2** a person providing support or service for an organization or person: *he was a great servant of the community*.

– SYNONYMS **attendant,** domestic, maid, housemaid, retainer, flunky, minion, slave, lackey, drudge; informal skivvy.

– ORIGIN Old French, 'person serving.'

serve /sərv/ ▶ **verb 1** perform duties or provide a service for: *the hospital serves a large area of Central New York*. **2** be employed as a member of the armed forces. **3** spend a period in office, in an apprenticeship, or in prison. **4** present someone with food or drink. **5** attend to a customer in a store. **6** fulfill a purpose. **7** treat in a specified way: *homeowners wonder if they are being fairly served*. **8** (of food or drink) be enough for a specified number of people. **9** Law formally deliver a summons or writ to the person to whom it is addressed. **10** (in tennis and other racket sports) hit the ball or shuttlecock to begin play for each point of a game. **11** (of a male breeding animal) mate with a female.

– SYNONYMS **1 work for,** obey, do the bidding of. **2** *this job serves the community* **benefit,** help, assist, aid, make a contribution to. **3** *he served a six-month apprenticeship* **carry out,** perform, do, fulfill, complete, discharge, spend. **4 present,** give out, distribute, dish up, provide, supply. **5 attend to,** deal with, see to, assist, help, look after. **6** *a saucer serving as an ashtray* **act as,** function as, do duty.

▶ **noun** an act of serving in tennis, badminton, etc.
– PHRASES **if (my) memory serves (me)** if I remember correctly. **serve someone right** be someone's deserved punishment or bad luck.
– ORIGIN Latin *servire*.

serv·er /ˈsərvər/ ▶ **noun 1** a person or thing that serves. **2** a computer or program that controls or supplies information to a computer network.

serv·ice /ˈsərvis/ ▶ **noun 1** the action of serving, helping, or providing: *he complained about the poor service in the hotel*. **2** a period of employment with an organization. **3** assistance or advice given to customers. **4** a ceremony of religious worship that follows a set form. **5** a system supplying a public need such as transportation, or utilities such as water. **6** a department or organization run by the government: *the parks service*. **7** (**the services**) the armed forces. **8** (often in phrase **in service**) employment as a servant. **9** a set of matching dishes used for serving a particular meal. **10** (in tennis, badminton, etc.) a serve. **11** a regular inspection and maintenance of a vehicle or other machine.

– SYNONYMS **1 work,** employment, labor. **2** *he has done us a service* **favor,** kindness, good turn, helping hand. **3 ceremony,** ritual, rite, sacrament. **4 overhaul,** check, maintenance, servicing, repair. **5** *a range of local services* **amenity,** facility, resource, utility. **6 (armed) forces,** military, army, navy, air force.

▶ **verb 1** perform regular maintenance or repair work on a vehicle or machine. **2** provide a service or services for someone. **3** pay interest on a debt. **4** (of a male animal) mate with a female animal.

– SYNONYMS **overhaul,** check, go over, maintain, repair.

– PHRASES **in** (or **out of**) **service** available (or not available) for use.
– ORIGIN Latin *servitium* 'slavery.'

serv·ice·a·ble /ˈsərvəsəbəl/ ▶ **adjective 1** usable or in working order. **2** useful and hard-wearing rather than attractive.

– SYNONYMS **1 in working order,** working, functioning, operational, usable, workable, viable. **2 functional,** utilitarian, sensible, practical, hard-wearing, durable, tough, robust.

– DERIVATIVES **serv·ice·a·bil·i·ty** /ˌsərvəsəˈbilitē/ noun.

serv·ice ar·e·a ▶ **noun 1** a roadside area where services are available to motorists. **2** the area in which a subscriber can use their cell phone.

serv·ice charge ▶ **noun 1** a charge added to a bill for service in a restaurant. **2** a charge made for other services, such as maintenance on a leased property.

serv·ice in·dus·try ▶ **noun** a business that provides a service for a customer rather than manufacturing goods.

serv·ice·man /ˈsərvəsˌmən, -ˌman/ (or **servicewoman** /ˈsərvəsˌwo͝omən/) ▶ **noun** (pl. **servicemen** or **servicewomen**) **1** a person serving in the armed forces. **2** a person providing maintenance for machinery.

serv·ice pack ▶ **noun** a periodically released update to software from a manufacturer, consisting of requested enhancements and fixes for known bugs.

serv·ice pro·vid·er ▶ **noun** a company that provides access to the Internet for its subscribers.

serv·ice road ▶ **noun** a minor road running parallel to a main road and giving access to houses, stores, or businesses.

serv·ice sta·tion ▶ **noun** a garage selling gasoline and oil and sometimes offering vehicle maintenance.

ser·vi·ette /ˌsərvēˈet/ ▶ **noun** chiefly Brit. a table napkin.
– ORIGIN Old French.

ser·vile /ˈsərvəl, -ˌvīl/ ▶ **adjective 1** excessively willing to serve or please others. **2** relating to a slave or slaves.
– DERIVATIVES **ser·vile·ly** adverb **ser·vil·i·ty** /sərˈvilitē/ noun.
– ORIGIN Latin *servilis*.

CHOOSE THE RIGHT WORD

See **OBSEQUIOUS**.

serv·ing /ˈsərviNG/ ▶ **noun** a quantity of food suitable for or served to one person.

ser·vi·tude /ˈsərviˌt(y)o͞od/ ▶ **noun** the state of being a slave or of being under the complete control of someone more powerful.
– ORIGIN Latin *servitudo*.

serv·let /ˈsərvlit/ ▶ **noun** Computing a small, server-resident program that typically runs automatically in response to user input.

ser·vo·mech·an·ism /ˈsərvōˌmekəˌnizəm/ ▶ **noun** a powered mechanism producing motion or forces at a higher level of energy than the input level, e.g., in the brakes and steering of large motor vehicles.

ser·vo·mo·tor /ˈsərvōˌmōtər/ ▶ **noun** the element in a servomechanism that provides mechanical motion.

ses·a·me /ˈsesəmē/ ▶ **noun** a tall plant of tropical and subtropical areas, grown for its oil-rich seeds.
– PHRASES **o·pen ses·a·me** a free or unrestricted means of entering or accessing something. [from the magic words spoken in the tale of Ali Baba and the Forty Thieves.]
– ORIGIN Greek *sēsamon*, *sēsamē*.

ses·qui·pe·da·li·an /ˌseskwəpəˈdālyən/ ▶ **adjective** formal **1** (of a word) having many syllables; long. **2** full of long words; long-winded.
– ORIGIN from Latin *sesquipedalis* 'a foot and a half long.'

ses·sile /ˈsesəl, -īl/ ▶ **adjective** technical **1** (of an organism, e.g., a barnacle) fixed in one place; immobile. **2** (of a plant or animal structure) attached directly by its base without a stalk or similar structure.
– ORIGIN Latin *sessilis*.

ses·sion /ˈsesHən/ ▶ **noun 1** a period devoted to a particular activity: *a training session*. **2** a meeting of a council, court, or lawmaking body to carry out its business. **3** a period during which council and other meetings are regularly held. **4** an academic year.

– SYNONYMS **1 meeting,** sitting, assembly, caucus, conclave. **2 period,** time, term.

– DERIVATIVES **ses·sion·al** adjective.
– ORIGIN Latin.

ses·sion mu·si·cian ▶ **noun** a freelance musician hired to play on recording sessions.

ses·tet /sesˈtet/ ▶ **noun** the last six lines of a sonnet.
– ORIGIN Italian *sestetto*.

set[1] /set/ ▶ **verb** (**sets, setting, set**) **1** put, lay, or stand something in a specified place or position. **2** decide on or fix a time, value, or limit. **3** give someone a task. **4** prepare a table for a meal by placing utensils, dishes, etc., on it. **5** adjust a device as required. **6** harden into a solid, semisolid, or fixed state. **7** put or bring into a specified state: *the hostages were set free*. **8** cause to start doing something: *the incident set me thinking*. **9** establish something as an example or record. **10** arrange damp hair into the required style. **11** put a broken or dislocated bone or limb into the correct position for healing. **12** (of the sun or moon) appear to move toward and below the earth's horizon. **13** arrange type or written material for printing as required. **14** (of blossom or a tree) form into or produce fruit.

– SYNONYMS **1** *Beth set the bag on the table* **put (down),** place, lay, deposit, position, settle, leave, stand, plant; informal stick, dump, park, plonk, pop. **2** *they set a date for the election* **arrange,** schedule, fix (on), decide on, settle on, choose, agree on, determine, designate, appoint, name, specify, stipulate. **3** *he set us some work* **assign,** allocate, give, allot. **4** *set the table* **lay,** prepare, arrange. **5** *he set his watch* **adjust,** regulate, synchronize, calibrate, put right, correct. **6** *the adhesive will set in an hour* **solidify,** harden, stiffen, thicken, gel, cake, congeal, coagulate, clot.

– PHRASES **set about** start doing something in an energetic or determined way. **set someone apart** make someone seem superior to others. **set something aside 1** keep something for a particular purpose. **2** formally cancel a legal decision or order. **set someone back** informal cost someone a particular amount of money. **set something down** record something in writing. **set forth** dated begin a journey. **set something forth** state something in writing or speech. **set in** (of something unwelcome) begin and seem likely to continue. **set off** begin a journey. **set something off 1** cause a bomb or alarm to go off. **2** make something more attractive by being placed near to something else. **set on** attack someone violently. **set out 1** begin a journey. **2** intend to do something. **set something out** arrange or display something. **set sail 1** begin a voyage. **2** hoist the sails of a boat. **set to** begin doing something in an energetic way. **set something to music** provide music for a written work. **set something up 1** place or erect something in position. **2** establish a business or other organization. **set someone up 1** establish someone in a particular enterprise or role. **2** informal make an innocent person appear guilty.
– ORIGIN Old English.

set[2] ▶ **noun 1** a number of things or people grouped together as similar or forming a unit. **2** a group of people with shared interests or occupations: *the literary set*. **3** the way in which something is set or positioned: *that cold set of his jaw*. **4** a radio or television receiver. **5** (in tennis and other games) a group of games counting as a unit toward a match. **6** a collection of scenery, stage furniture, etc., used for a scene in a play, movie, etc. **7** (in jazz or popular music) a sequence of songs or pieces forming part or all of a live show or recording. **8** Mathematics a collection of distinct entities satisfying specified conditions and regarded as a unit. **9** a cutting, young plant, or bulb used to produce new plants: *an onion set*.

– SYNONYMS **1 series,** collection, group, batch, arrangement, array, assortment, selection. **2 group,** circle, crowd, crew, band, fraternity, company, ring, camp, school, clique, faction; informal gang, bunch.

– ORIGIN partly from Old French *sette*, partly from **SET[1]**.

set[3] ▶ **adjective 1** fixed or arranged in advance. **2** firmly fixed and unchanging: *set ideas about race and* *culture*. **3** having a fixed wording. **4** ready or likely to do something: *we're all set for tonight!* **5** (**set on**) determined to do something.

– SYNONYMS **1 fixed,** established, scheduled, specified, appointed, arranged, settled, decided, agreed, predetermined, hard and fast, unvarying, unchanging, invariable, rigid, inflexible. **2 ready,** prepared, organized, equipped, primed; informal geared up, psyched up.
– ANTONYMS variable, unprepared.

set-a·side ▶ **noun 1** the policy of taking land out of production to reduce crop surpluses. **2** a portion of funds or other resources reserved for a particular purpose.

set·back /ˈset,bak/ ▶ **noun** a problem that prevents or holds up progress.

– SYNONYMS **problem,** difficulty, hitch, complication, upset, blow; informal glitch, hiccup.
– ANTONYMS breakthrough.

set piece ▶ **noun** a part of a novel, movie, play, piece of music, etc., that is arranged in a recognized or elaborate way to create a particular effect.

set play ▶ **noun** Sport a prearranged maneuver carried out from a restart by the team who have the advantage.

set point ▶ **noun** (in tennis and other sports) a point that if won by one of the players will also win them a set.

set square ▶ **noun** a right-angled triangular plate for drawing lines, especially at 90°, 45°, 60°, or 30°.

set·tee /seˈtē/ ▶ **noun** a long upholstered seat for more than one person, typically with a back and arms.
– ORIGIN perhaps from *settle* 'a wooden bench.'

set·ter /ˈsetər/ ▶ **noun** a breed of large dog with long hair, trained to stand rigid when scenting game.

set the·o·ry ▶ **noun** the branch of mathematics concerned with the properties and applications of sets.

set·ting /ˈsetiNG/ ▶ **noun 1** the way or place in which something is set: *the islands offer a perfect setting for a family vacation*. **2** a piece of metal in which a precious stone or gem is fixed to form a piece of jewelry. **3** a piece of vocal or choral music composed for particular words. **4** (also **place setting**) a complete set of dishes and utensils for one person at a meal.

– SYNONYMS **surroundings,** position, situation, environment, background, backdrop, spot, place, location, locale, site, scene.

set·tle /ˈsetl/ ▶ **verb 1** reach agreement on something disputed. **2** decide or arrange something finally: *they hadn't settled on a date for the wedding*. **3** make one's home in a new place. **4** (often **settle down**) adopt a more steady or secure life. **5** become or make calmer or quieter. **6** sit or place so as to be comfortable or secure: *she settled her bag on her shoulder*. **7** sink or fall slowly downward: *dust from the mill had settled on the roof*. **8** (often **settle in**) begin to feel comfortable in a new situation. **9** pay a debt or bill. **10** (**settle for**) accept something less than satisfactory. **11** (**settle down to**) begin to concentrate on an activity. **12** (**settle something on**) give money or property to someone through a legal document such as a will.

– SYNONYMS **1 resolve,** sort out, clear up, end, fix, work out, iron out, set right, reconcile; informal patch up. **2 put in order,** sort out, tidy up, arrange, organize, order, clear up, straighten out. **3 decide on,** set, fix, agree on, name, establish, arrange, choose, pick. **4** *I've settled the bill* **pay,** square, clear. **5 make one's home,** set up home, take up residence, put down roots, establish oneself, live, move to. **6** *a drink will settle your nerves* **calm,** quiet, soothe, relax. **7 land,** come to rest, alight, perch.
– ORIGIN Old English, 'to seat, place.'

set·tle·ment /ˈsetlmənt/ ▶ **noun 1** the action of settling. **2** an official agreement intended to settle a dispute or conflict. **3** a place where people establish a community. **4** a legal arrangement by which a person gives money or property to someone else: *a divorce settlement*.

– SYNONYMS **1 agreement,** deal, arrangement, conclusion, resolution, understanding, pact. **2 community,** colony, outpost, encampment, post, village.

set·tler /ˈsetl-ər, ˈsetlər/ ▶ **noun** a person who establishes a community in a new area.

– SYNONYMS **colonist,** frontiersman, pioneer, immigrant, newcomer, incomer.

set·tlor /ˈsetl-ər, ˈsetlər/ ▶ **noun** a person who makes a legal arrangement to transfer property to establish a trust.

set-to ▶ **noun** (pl. **set-tos**) informal a fight or argument.

set-top box ▶ **noun** a device that converts a digital television signal to an analog one, so that it can be viewed on a conventional set.

set·up /ˈset,əp/ ▶ **noun** informal **1** the way in which something is organized. **2** an organization. **3** a scheme intended to trick someone or make it appear that they have done something wrong.

sev·en /ˈsevən/ ▶ **cardinal number** one more than six; 7. (Roman numeral: **vii** or **VII**.)
– DERIVATIVES **sev·en·fold** /ˈsevən,fōld/ adjective & adverb.
– PHRASES **the seven deadly sins** (in Christian tradition) the sins of pride, covetousness, lust, anger, gluttony, envy, and sloth. **the seven seas** all the oceans of the world (the Arctic, Antarctic, North Pacific, South Pacific, North Atlantic, South Atlantic, and Indian Oceans). **the seven-year itch** a tendency to be unfaithful, supposed to arise after seven years of marriage.
– ORIGIN Old English.

Sev·en Sis·ters (**the Seven Sisters**) **1** Astronomy the star cluster of the Pleiades. **2** a group of seven women's (or formerly women's) colleges in the eastern US having high academic and social prestige.

sev·en·teen /,sevənˈtēn, ˈsevən,tēn/ ▶ **cardinal number** one more than sixteen; 17. (Roman numeral: **xvii** or **XVII**.)
– DERIVATIVES **sev·en·teenth** /,sevənˈtēnTH, ˈsevən,tēnTH/ adjective & noun.

sev·en·teen-year lo·cust ▶ **noun** the nymph of the northern species of the periodical cicada. See **PERIODICAL CICADA**.

sev·enth /ˈsevənTH/ ▶ **ordinal number 1** that is number seven in a sequence; 7th. **2** (**a seventh/one seventh**) each of seven equal parts into which something is divided. **3** a musical interval spanning seven consecutive notes in a scale.

Sev·enth-Day Ad·vent·ist ▶ **noun** a member of a strict Protestant sect that preaches that Jesus is about to return to earth and that observes Saturday as the sabbath.

sev·en·ty /'sevəntē/ ▶ **cardinal number** (pl. **seventies**) ten less than eighty; 70. (Roman numeral: **lxx** or **LXX**.)
– DERIVATIVES **sev·en·ti·eth** /-tēəTH/ ordinal number.

sev·en·ty-eight ▶ **noun** an old phonograph record designed to be played at 78 rpm.

sev·er /'sevər/ ▶ **verb 1** cut something off or into pieces. **2** put an end to a connection or relationship.

– SYNONYMS **1 cut off,** chop off, detach, separate, amputate. **2 cut (through),** rupture, split, pierce. **3 break off,** discontinue, suspend, end, cease, dissolve.
– ANTONYMS join.

– ORIGIN Old French *severer*.

sev·er·al /'sev(ə)rəl/ ▶ **determiner & pronoun** more than two but not many. ▶ **adjective** separate or respective: *the two levels of government sorted out their several responsibilities.*

– SYNONYMS **some,** a number of, a few, various, assorted.

– DERIVATIVES **sev·er·al·ly** adverb.
– ORIGIN Old French.

sev·er·ance /'sev(ə)rəns/ ▶ **noun 1** the ending of a connection or relationship. **2** the state of being separated or cut off.

sev·er·ance pay ▶ **noun** money paid to an employee upon dismissal or discharge from employment.

se·vere /sə'vi(ə)r/ ▶ **adjective 1** (of something bad or difficult) very great; intense. **2** strict or harsh: *severe penalties for hackers.* **3** very plain in style or appearance.

– SYNONYMS **1 acute,** very bad, serious, grave, critical, dire, dangerous, life-threatening. **2** *severe storms* **fierce,** violent, strong, powerful, intense, forceful. **3 cold,** freezing, icy, arctic, harsh, bitter. **4** *severe criticism* **harsh,** scathing, sharp, strong, fierce, savage, devastating, withering. **5** *a severe expression* **stern,** dour, grim, forbidding, disapproving, unsmiling, unfriendly, somber, stony, cold, frosty. **6 plain,** simple, austere, spartan, unadorned, stark, clinical, uncluttered, minimalist, functional.
– ANTONYMS minor, gentle, mild.

– DERIVATIVES **se·vere·ly** adverb **se·ver·i·ty** /-'veritē/ noun.
– ORIGIN Latin *severus*.

CHOOSE THE RIGHT WORD

severe, ascetic, austere, stern, strict, unmitigated

A storm, a hairdo, and a punishment may all be described as **severe**, which means harsh or uncompromising, without a hint of softness, mildness, levity, or indulgence. **Austere**, on the other hand, primarily applies to people, their habits, their way of life, and the environments they create; it implies coldness, stark simplicity, and restraint (*an austere room with only a table and chair*). **Ascetic** implies extreme self-denial and self-discipline, in some cases to the point of choosing what is painful or disagreeable (*he had an ascetic approach to life and rejected all creature comforts*). **Strict** literally means bound or stretched tight; in extended use, it means strenuously exact (*a strict curfew; strict obedience*). **Stern** combines harshness and authority with strictness or severity (*a stern judge*). **Unmitigated** means unmodified and unsoftened in any way (*a streak of unmitigated bad luck*).

se·viche ▶ **noun** variant spelling of **CEVICHE**.

Se·ville or·ange /sə'vil/ ▶ **noun** a bitter orange used for marmalade.
– ORIGIN from the Spanish city of *Seville*.

Sè·vres /'sevrə/ ▶ **noun** a type of elaborately decorated fine porcelain.
– ORIGIN from *Sèvres* in Paris.

sew /sō/ ▶ **verb** (past part. **sewn** or **sewed**) **1** join or repair something by making stitches with a needle and thread or a sewing machine. **2** (**sew something up**) informal bring something to a favorable conclusion.

– SYNONYMS **stitch,** tack, seam, hem, embroider.

– ORIGIN Old English.

sew·age /'sōōij/ ▶ **noun** waste water and excrement that is carried away in sewers.
– ORIGIN from **SEWER**[1].

sew·age treat·ment plant (also **sewage plant**) ▶ **noun** a place where sewage is treated.

sew·er[1] /'sōōər/ ▶ **noun** an underground pipe for carrying off drainage water and waste matter.
– ORIGIN Old French *seuwiere* 'channel to drain the overflow from a fish pond.'

sew·er[2] /'sōər/ ▶ **noun** a person who sews.

sew·er·age /'sōōərij/ ▶ **noun 1** the provision of drainage by sewers. **2** another term for **SEWAGE**.

sew·ing ma·chine ▶ **noun** a machine with a mechanically driven needle for sewing cloth.

sewn /sōn/ past participle of **SEW**.

sex /seks/ ▶ **noun 1** either of the two main categories (male and female) into which humans and most other living things are divided on the basis of their reproductive functions. **2** sexual intercourse. **3** the fact of being male or female. **4** the group of all members of either sex: *her efforts to improve the condition of her sex.*

– SYNONYMS **1 sexual intercourse,** lovemaking, making love, sexual relations, mating, copulation; formal fornication, coitus. **2 gender.**

▶ **verb 1** (**sex something up**) informal present something in a more interesting or lively way. **2** (**sex someone up**) informal have sex with someone. **3** determine the sex of an animal.
– DERIVATIVES **sex·er** noun.
– ORIGIN Latin *sexus*.

USAGE

On the difference between the words **sex** and **gender**, see the note at **GENDER**.

WORD LINKS

carnal *relating to sexual activity*

sex·a·ge·nar·i·an /ˌseksəjə'ne(ə)rēən/ ▶ **noun** a person between 60 and 69 years old.
– ORIGIN Latin *sexagenarius*.

sex ap·peal ▶ **noun** the quality of being attractive in a sexual way.

sex change ▶ **noun** a change in a person's physical sexual characteristics by surgery and hormone treatment.

sex chro·mo·some ▶ **noun** a chromosome concerned in determining the sex of an organism (in mammals the X and Y chromosomes).

sexed /sekst/ ▶ **adjective** having specified sexual appetites: *highly sexed men.*

sex hor·mone ▶ **noun** a hormone affecting sexual development or reproduction, such as estrogen or testosterone.

sex·ism /ˈsekˌsizəm/ ▶ **noun** prejudice or discrimination, typically against women, on the basis of a person's sex.
– DERIVATIVES **sex·ist** adjective & noun.

sex kit·ten ▶ **noun** informal a young woman who is very sexually attractive.

sex·less /ˈseksləs/ ▶ **adjective 1** not sexually attractive or active. **2** neither male nor female.

sex life ▶ **noun** a person's sexual activity and relationships considered as a whole.

sex ob·ject ▶ **noun** a person regarded purely in terms of their sexual attractiveness or availability.

sex·ol·o·gy /sekˈsäləjē/ ▶ **noun** the study of people's sexual behavior.
– DERIVATIVES **sex·o·log·i·cal** /ˌseksəˈläjikəl/ adjective **sex·ol·o·gist** noun.

sex·ploi·ta·tion /ˌseksploiˈtāsʜən/ ▶ **noun** informal the commercial exploitation of sex, sexual attractiveness, or sexually explicit material.

sex·pot /ˈseksˌpät/ ▶ **noun** informal a sexy person.

sex sym·bol ▶ **noun** a person famous for their sexual attractiveness.

sex·tant /ˈsekstənt/ ▶ **noun** an instrument for measuring the angular distances between objects, used for navigation and surveying.
– ORIGIN first referring to the sixth part of a circle: from Latin *sextans* 'sixth part.'

sex·tet /sekˈstet/ ▶ **noun 1** a group of six people playing music or singing together. **2** a composition for a sextet. **3** a set of six.
– ORIGIN from Latin *sex* 'six.'

sex·ton /ˈsekstən/ ▶ **noun** a person who looks after a church and churchyard, sometimes acting as bell-ringer and formerly as gravedigger.
– ORIGIN Old French *segrestein.*

sex tour·ism ▶ **noun** the organization of vacations abroad with the aim of taking advantage of the lack of restrictions on sexual activity and prostitution in some countries.

sex·tu·ple /sekˈst(y)o͞opəl, -ˈtəpəl/ ▶ **adjective 1** consisting of six parts. **2** six times as much or as many.
– ORIGIN Latin *sextuplus.*

sex·tu·plet /sekˈstəplit, -ˈst(y)o͞oplət/ ▶ **noun** each of six children born at one birth.

sex·u·al /ˈseksʜo͞oəl/ ▶ **adjective 1** relating to sex or to physical attraction or intimate contact between people or animals. **2** relating to the two sexes or to gender. **3** (of reproduction) involving the fusion of male and female cells.
– DERIVATIVES **sex·u·al·ize** /ˈseksʜo͞oəˌlīz/ verb **sex·u·al·ly** adverb.

sex·u·al ha·rass·ment ▶ **noun** the making of unwanted sexual advances or obscene remarks to a person, especially at work.

sex·u·al in·ter·course ▶ **noun** sexual contact in which a man puts his erect penis into a woman's vagina.

sex·u·al·i·ty /ˌseksʜo͞oˈalitē/ ▶ **noun** (pl. **sexualities**) **1** a person's capacity for sexual feelings. **2** a person's sexual preference.

> – SYNONYMS **1 sensuality,** sexiness, seductiveness, eroticism, physicality, sexual appetite, passion, desire, lust. **2 sexual orientation,** sexual preference, leaning, persuasion.

sex·u·al o·ri·en·ta·tion ▶ **noun** a person's sexual attraction toward members of the same, opposite, or both genders: *a draft ordinance that would prohibit discrimination on the basis of sexual orientation.*

sex work·er ▶ **noun** euphemistic a prostitute.

sex·y /ˈseksē/ ▶ **adjective** (**sexier, sexiest**) **1** sexually attractive or exciting. **2** sexually aroused. **3** informal exciting or appealing: *a sexy marketing buzzword.*

> – SYNONYMS **1 sexually attractive,** seductive, desirable, alluring; informal foxy, hot. **2 erotic,** sexually explicit, titillating, naughty, X-rated, rude, pornographic, crude; informal raunchy, steamy; euphemistic adult.

– DERIVATIVES **sex·i·ly** adverb **sex·i·ness** noun.

sez /sez/ ▶ **verb** nonstandard spelling of "says," used in representing uneducated speech: *"Oh Lordy!" sez de man.*

SF ▶ **abbreviation** science fiction.

SFX ▶ **abbreviation** special effects.
– ORIGIN *FX* representing a pronunciation of *effects.*

SG ▶ **abbreviation** Physics specific gravity.

Sg ▶ **symbol** the chemical element seaborgium.

SGML ▶ **abbreviation** Computing Standard Generalized Markup Language, a system for encoding electronic texts so that they can be displayed in any format.

shab·by /ˈsʜabē/ ▶ **adjective** (**shabbier, shabbiest**) **1** in poor condition because of long use or neglect. **2** dressed in old or worn clothes. **3** mean and unfair: *a shabby trick.*

> – SYNONYMS **1 run-down,** scruffy, dilapidated, in disrepair, ramshackle, tumbledown, dingy. **2 scruffy,** old, worn out, threadbare, ragged, frayed, tattered, battered, faded, moth-eaten, the worse for wear; informal tatty, raggedy. **3 mean,** unkind, unfair, shameful, shoddy, unworthy, contemptible, despicable, discreditable, ignoble; informal rotten.
> – ANTONYMS smart.

– DERIVATIVES **shab·bi·ly** adverb **shab·bi·ness** noun.
– ORIGIN from Germanic.

shack /sʜak/ ▶ **noun** a roughly built hut or cabin.

> – SYNONYMS **hut,** cabin, shanty, lean-to, shed, hovel.

▶ **verb** (**shack up with**) informal live with someone as a lover.
– ORIGIN perhaps from Mexican or Nahuatl.

shack·le /ˈsʜakəl/ ▶ **noun 1** (**shackles**) a pair of metal rings connected by a chain, used to fasten a prisoner's wrists or ankles together. **2** (**shackles**) something that restricts freedom: *the human need to be free of the shackles of oppression.* **3** a metal link closed by a bolt, used to secure a chain or rope to something.

> – SYNONYMS (**shackles**) **chains,** fetters, irons, leg irons, manacles, handcuffs.

▶ **verb 1** chain someone with shackles. **2** restrain or limit someone or something.

> – SYNONYMS **1 chain,** fetter, manacle, secure, tie (up), bind, tether, hobble, put in chains, clap in irons, handcuff. **2 restrain,** restrict, limit, constrain,

handicap, hamstring, hamper, hinder, impede, obstruct, inhibit.

– ORIGIN Old English.

shad /shad/ ▶ **noun** (pl. same or **shads**) an edible herringlike sea fish.

– ORIGIN Old English.

shad·dock /ˈshadək/ ▶ **noun** another term for **POMELO**.

– ORIGIN named after Captain *Shaddock*, who introduced it to the West Indies.

shade /shād/ ▶ **noun 1** an area that is dark and cool because it is sheltered from direct sunlight. **2** a form of a color with regard to how light or dark it is: *various shades of blue*. **3** a slightly different variety of something. **4** a lampshade. **5** (**shades**) informal sunglasses. **6** literary a ghost.

– SYNONYMS **1 shadow,** shadiness, shelter, cover. **2 color,** hue, tone, tint, tinge. **3 nuance,** gradation, degree, difference, variation, variety, nicety, subtlety, undertone, overtone. **4 little,** bit, trace, touch, modicum, tinge; informal tad, smidgen. **5 blind,** curtain, screen, cover, covering, awning, canopy.
– ANTONYMS light.

▶ **verb 1** screen someone or something from direct light. **2** block all or some of the light coming from something. **3** represent a darker area in a picture with pencil or a block of color. **4** pass or change gradually: *outrage began to shade into dismay*.

– SYNONYMS **cast a shadow over,** shadow, shelter, cover, screen.

– DERIVATIVES **shade·less** adjective **shad·er** noun.

– PHRASES **a shade** a slight amount: *I felt a shade anxious*. **shades of ——** similar to or reminiscent of. **put someone/thing in the shade** be much better or more impressive than someone or something.

– ORIGIN Old English.

shad·ing /ˈshādiNG/ ▶ **noun 1** the representation of light and shade on a drawing or map. **2** a very slight variation in something.

shad·ow /ˈshadō/ ▶ **noun 1** a dark area or shape produced by an object coming between light rays and a surface. **2** partial or complete darkness. **3** a feeling of sadness or gloom. **4** the slightest trace: *without a shadow of a doubt*. **5** a weak or less good version: *she was a shadow of her former self*. **6** a position of less importance: *he lived in the shadow of his father*. **7** a person who constantly accompanies or secretly follows another.

– SYNONYMS **1 silhouette,** outline, shape, contour, profile. **2 shade,** darkness, twilight, gloom.

▶ **verb 1** cast a shadow over someone or something. **2** follow and observe someone secretly. **3** accompany an employee in their daily activities to gain experience of a job.

– SYNONYMS **follow,** trail, track, stalk, pursue; informal tail, keep tabs on.

▶ **adjective** Brit. referring to a government minister's counterpart in the opposition party.

– DERIVATIVES **shad·ow·er** noun **shad·ow·less** adjective.

– ORIGIN Old English.

shad·ow·box /ˈshadō,bäks/ ▶ **verb** box against an imaginary opponent as a form of training. ▶ **noun** (also **shadow box**) a case with compartments for displaying small collectible or decorative objects.

shad·ow e·con·o·my ▶ **noun** illicit economic activity existing alongside a country's official economy.

shad·ow·land /ˈshadō,land/ (also **shadowlands**) ▶ **noun** literary a place or situation that is vague or that exists on the boundaries of other places or states.

shad·ow·y /ˈshadōē/ ▶ **adjective** (**shadowier, shadowiest**) **1** full of shadows. **2** not well known; full of mystery: *the shadowy world of computer hacking*.

– DERIVATIVES **shad·ow·i·ness** noun.

shad·y /ˈshādē/ ▶ **adjective** (**shadier, shadiest**) **1** situated in or full of shade. **2** giving shade from the sun. **3** informal seeming to be dishonest or illegal.

– SYNONYMS **1 shaded,** shadowy, dim, dark, sheltered, leafy. **2 suspicious,** suspect, questionable, dubious, irregular, underhanded/underhand; informal fishy, murky.
– ANTONYMS bright, honest.

– DERIVATIVES **shad·i·ness** noun.

shaft /shaft/ ▶ **noun 1** a long, narrow part forming the handle of a tool or club, the body of a spear or arrow, or similar object. **2** a ray of light or bolt of lightning. **3** a long, narrow passage giving access to a mine, accommodating a lift, or providing ventilation. **4** each of the pair of poles between which a horse is harnessed to a vehicle. **5** a cylindrical rotating rod for the transmission of mechanical power in a machine. **6** the part of a column between the base and capital. **7** a sudden flash of a quality or feeling: *a shaft of inspiration*. **8** a witty or hurtful remark.

– SYNONYMS **1 pole,** stick, rod, staff, shank, handle, stem. **2** *a shaft of light* **ray,** beam, gleam, streak, pencil. **3 tunnel,** passage, hole, bore, duct, well, flue, vent.

▶ **verb 1** (of light) shine in beams. **2** informal treat someone harshly or unfairly.

– DERIVATIVES **shaft·ed** adjective.

– ORIGIN Old English.

shag[1] /shag/ ▶ **noun 1** a thick, tangled hairstyle. **2** coarse cut tobacco. ▶ **adjective 1** (of a carpet or rug) having a long, rough pile. **2** (of pile on a carpet) long and rough.

– ORIGIN Old English.

shag[2] ▶ **noun** a cormorant (seabird) with greenish-black plumage and a long curly crest.

– ORIGIN perhaps from **SHAG**[1], with reference to the bird's 'shaggy' crest.

shag[3] Brit. vulgar slang ▶ **verb** (**shags, shagging, shagged**) have sex with someone. ▶ **noun** an act of sex.

– DERIVATIVES **shag·ger** noun.

– ORIGIN unknown.

shag·gy /ˈshagē/ ▶ **adjective** (**shaggier, shaggiest**) **1** (of hair or fur) long, thick, and untidy. **2** having shaggy hair or fur.

– SYNONYMS **hairy,** bushy, thick, woolly; tangled, tousled, unkempt, disheveled, untidy; formal hirsute.
– ANTONYMS sleek.

– DERIVATIVES **shag·gi·ly** adverb **shag·gi·ness** noun.

– PHRASES **shaggy-dog story** a long, rambling story or joke, amusing only because it is pointless.

sha·green /shəˈgrēn/ ▶ **noun 1** sharkskin used for decoration or for cleaning or polishing hard surfaces. **2** a kind of leather that has not been tanned, with a rough surface.

– ORIGIN from **CHAGRIN** in the sense 'rough skin.'

shah /shä/ ▶ **noun** historical a title of the former king of Iran.

– ORIGIN Persian, 'king.'

shake /shāk/ ▶ **verb** (past **shook**; past part. **shaken**) **1** move quickly and jerkily up and down or to and fro.

2 tremble uncontrollably with strong emotion. **3** make a threatening gesture with: *he shook his fist*. **4** remove something by shaking. **5** shock or astonish someone. **6** get rid of or put an end to: *old habits he couldn't shake off*.

> – SYNONYMS **1 vibrate,** tremble, quiver, quake, shiver, shudder, wobble, rock, sway, convulse. **2 jiggle,** joggle, jerk, agitate; informal wiggle, waggle. **3 brandish,** wave, flourish, swing, wield. **4 upset,** distress, disturb, unsettle, disconcert, discompose, unnerve, throw off balance, agitate, fluster, shock, alarm, scare, worry; informal rattle.

▶ **noun 1** an act of shaking. **2** an amount sprinkled from a container. **3** informal a milkshake. **4** (**the shakes**) informal a fit of trembling.

> – SYNONYMS **tremor,** trembling, quivering, quake, shiver, shudder, wobble.

– PHRASES **in two shakes (of a lamb's tail)** informal very quickly. **no great shakes** informal not very good. **shake down** settle down. **shake hands (with someone)** hold someone's right hand in one's own when meeting or leaving them, to congratulate them, or to show agreement. **shake on it** informal confirm an agreement by shaking hands. **shake someone up** stir someone into action. **shake something up** make major changes to an organization or system.
– ORIGIN Old English.

> **CHOOSE THE RIGHT WORD**
>
> **shake, quake, quiver, shiver, shudder, tremble**
>
> Does a cool breeze make you **shiver**, **quiver**, **shudder**, or **tremble**? All of these verbs describe vibrating, wavering, or oscillating movements that, in living creatures, are often involuntary expressions of strain or discomfort. **Shake**, which refers to abrupt forward-and-backward, side-to-side, or up-and-down movements, is different from the others in that it can be done to a person or object as well as by one (*shake a can of paint; shake visibly while lifting a heavy load*). *Tremble* applies specifically to the slight and rapid shaking motion the human body makes when it is nervous, frightened, or uneasy (*his hands trembled when he picked up the phone*). To *shiver* is to make a similar movement with the entire body, but the cause is usually cold or fear (*shiver in the draft from an open door*). *Quiver* suggests a rapid and almost imperceptible vibration resulting from disturbed or irregular surface tension; it refers more often to things (*the leaves quivered in the breeze*), although people may quiver when they're under emotional tension (*her lower lip quivered and her eyes were downcast*). *Shudder* suggests a more intense shaking, usually in response to something horrible or revolting (*shudder at the thought of eating uncooked meat*). **Quake** implies a violent upheaval or shaking, similar to what occurs during an earthquake (*the boy's heart quaked at his father's approach*).

shake·down /ˈsʜākˌdoun/ ▶ **noun** informal **1** a thorough search. **2** a major change or restructuring. **3** an act of swindling someone. **4** a makeshift bed.

shake·out /ˈsʜākˌout/ ▶ **noun** informal an upheaval or reorganization of a business, market, or organization due to competition and typically involving streamlining and layoffs.

shak·er /ˈsʜākər/ ▶ **noun 1** a container for mixing ingredients by shaking them. **2** a container with a pierced top from which a powdered substance such as flour is poured by shaking. **3** (**Shaker**) a member of an American Christian sect living simply in celibate mixed communities. ▶ **adjective** (**Shaker**) referring to a style of elegant but functional furniture traditionally produced by Shakers.

Shake·spear·e·an /sʜākˈspi(ə)rēən/ (also **Shakespearian**) ▶ **adjective** relating to the English dramatist William Shakespeare. ▶ **noun** an expert in or student of Shakespeare's works.

shake-up ▶ **noun** informal a major reorganization.

shak·o /ˈsʜakō, ˈsʜā-/ ▶ **noun** (pl. **shakos**) a cylindrical military hat with a peak and a plume or pompom.
– ORIGIN Hungarian *csákó süveg* 'peaked cap.'

Shak·ti /ˈsʜəktē/ ▶ **noun** Hinduism female creative power or divine energy.
– ORIGIN Sanskrit.

shak·y /ˈsʜākē/ ▶ **adjective** (**shakier, shakiest**) **1** shaking or trembling. **2** not steady or stable. **3** likely to fail or falter: *after a shaky start the team made superb efforts*.

> – SYNONYMS **1 unsteady,** unstable, rickety, wobbly. **2 faint,** dizzy, lightheaded, giddy, weak, wobbly, in shock. **3 unreliable,** untrustworthy, questionable, dubious, doubtful, tenuous, suspect, flimsy, weak; informal iffy.
> – ANTONYMS steady, stable.

– DERIVATIVES **shak·i·ly** adverb **shak·i·ness** noun.

shale /sʜāl/ ▶ **noun** soft rock formed from compressed mud or clay, that can be split into thin layers.
– DERIVATIVES **shal·y** (also **shaley**) adjective.
– ORIGIN probably from German *Schale*.

shall /sʜal/ ▶ **modal verb** (3rd sing. present **shall**) **1** used with *I* and *we* to express the future tense. **2** expressing a strong statement, intention, or order. **3** used in questions to make offers or suggestions.
– ORIGIN Old English.

> **USAGE**
>
> The traditional rule is that when forming the future tense, **shall** should be used with **I** and **we** (*I shall be late*), while **will** should be used with **you**, **he**, **she**, **it**, and **they** (*he will not be there*). However, when telling someone what to do or showing determination, this rule is reversed: **will** is used with **I** and **we** (*I will not tolerate this*), and **shall** is used with **you**, **he**, **she**, **it**, and **they** (*you shall go to school*). Nowadays, people do not follow these rules so strictly and are more likely to use the shortened forms **I'll**, **she'll**, etc., especially when speaking.

shal·lot /sʜəˈlät, ˈsʜalət/ ▶ **noun** a small vegetable of the onion family.
– ORIGIN Old French *eschaloigne*, *scaloun* 'scallion.'

shal·low /ˈsʜalō/ ▶ **adjective 1** having a short distance between the top and the bottom; not deep. **2** not thinking or thought out seriously or in detail: *a shallow analysis of society*.

> – SYNONYMS **superficial,** trivial, facile, insubstantial, lightweight, empty, trifling, surface, skin-deep, frivolous, foolish, silly.
> – ANTONYMS profound.

▶ **noun** (**shallows**) a shallow area of water.
– DERIVATIVES **shal·low·ly** adverb **shal·low·ness** noun.
– ORIGIN related to **SHOAL²**.

sha·lom /sʜäˈlōm, sʜə-/ ▶ **exclamation** said by Jews at meeting or parting.
– ORIGIN Hebrew, 'peace.'

shalt /sʜalt/ old-fashioned second person singular of **SHALL**.

sham /sHam/ ▶ **noun 1** a thing that is not as good or as genuine as it seems to be: *our current free health service is a sham.* **2** a person who pretends to be something that they are not.

– SYNONYMS **pretense,** fake, act, simulation, fraud, lie, counterfeit, humbug.

▶ **adjective** not genuine; false.

– SYNONYMS **fake,** pretended, feigned, simulated, false, artificial, bogus, insincere, affected, make-believe; informal pretend, put-on, phony.
– ANTONYMS genuine.

▶ **verb** (**shams, shamming, shammed**) pretend or pretend to be: *people who are shamming insanity.*

– SYNONYMS **pretend,** fake, malinger; informal put it on.

– ORIGIN perhaps from **SHAME**.

sha·man /ˈsHämən, ˈsHā-/ ▶ **noun** (pl. **shamans**) (especially among some peoples of northern Asia and North America) a person who is believed to be able to contact good and evil spirits.
– DERIVATIVES **sha·man·ic** /sHəˈmanik/ adjective **sha·man·ism** /-ˌnizəm/ noun **sha·man·is·tic** /ˌsHäməˈnistik, ˌsHā-/ adjective.
– ORIGIN Tungus (a language of Siberia).

sham·ble /ˈsHambəl/ ▶ **verb** walk in a slow, shuffling, awkward way. ▶ **noun** a slow, shuffling walk.
– ORIGIN probably from dialect *shamble* 'ungainly.'

sham·bles /ˈsHambəlz/ ▶ **plural noun 1** informal a state of complete disorder. **2** old use a butcher's slaughterhouse.

– SYNONYMS **1 chaos,** muddle, jumble, confusion, disorder, havoc. **2 mess,** pigsty; informal disaster area.

– ORIGIN first meaning 'meat market': from Latin *scamellum* 'little bench.'

shame /sHām/ ▶ **noun 1** a feeling of humiliation or distress arising from one's awareness that one has done something wrong or foolish. **2** loss of respect; dishonor: *the incident had brought shame on his family.* **3** a cause of shame or dishonor. **4** a cause for regret or disappointment: *what a shame Ellie won't be here.*

– SYNONYMS **1 guilt,** remorse, contrition. **2 humiliation,** embarrassment, indignity, loss of face, mortification, disgrace, dishonor, discredit, ignominy, disrepute, infamy, scandal. **3** *it's a shame she never married* **pity,** sad thing, bad luck; informal crime, sin.
– ANTONYMS pride, honor.

▶ **verb** make someone feel ashamed.

– SYNONYMS **1 disgrace,** dishonor, discredit, blacken, drag through the mud. **2 humiliate,** embarrass, humble, take down a peg or two, cut down to size; informal show up.
– ANTONYMS honor.

– PHRASES **put someone to shame** make someone feel ashamed by being much better than them.
– ORIGIN Old English.

shame·faced /ˈsHāmˌfāst/ ▶ **adjective** showing shame.

– SYNONYMS **ashamed,** abashed, sheepish, guilty, contrite, sorry, remorseful, repentant, penitent, regretful, rueful, apologetic; informal with one's tail between one's legs.
– ANTONYMS unrepentant.

– DERIVATIVES **shame·fac·ed·ly** /-ˌfāsidlē, -ˌfāstlē/ adverb **shame·fac·ed·ness** /-ˌfāsidnis/ noun.

shame·ful /ˈsHāmfəl/ ▶ **adjective** causing or worthy of shame or disgrace: *a shameful secret.*

– SYNONYMS **1 disgraceful,** deplorable, despicable, contemptible, discreditable, unworthy, reprehensible, shabby, shocking, scandalous, outrageous, abominable, atrocious, appalling, inexcusable, unforgivable. **2 embarrassing,** mortifying, humiliating, ignominious.
– ANTONYMS admirable.

– DERIVATIVES **shame·ful·ly** adverb **shame·ful·ness** noun.

shame·less /ˈsHāmlis/ ▶ **adjective** not feeling ashamed, even though one has done something wrong or foolish.

– SYNONYMS **flagrant,** blatant, barefaced, overt, brazen, undisguised, unconcealed, unabashed, unashamed, unblushing, unrepentant.

– DERIVATIVES **shame·less·ly** adverb **shame·less·ness** noun.

sham·my /ˈsHamē/ ▶ **noun** (pl. **shammies**) informal a chamois leather.

sham·poo /sHamˈpo͞o/ ▶ **noun 1** a liquid soap for washing the hair. **2** a similar liquid for cleaning a carpet, car, etc. **3** an act of washing with shampoo. ▶ **verb** (**shampoos, shampooing, shampooed**) wash or clean something with shampoo.
– ORIGIN Hindi, 'to press.'

sham·rock /ˈsHamˌräk/ ▶ **noun** a cloverlike plant with three rounded leaves on each stem, the national emblem of Ireland.
– ORIGIN Irish *seamróg.*

shang·hai /ˈsHaNGˈhī/ ▶ **verb** (**shanghais, shanghaiing** /-ˌhī-iNG/, **shanghaied** /-ˌhīd/) **1** informal force or trick someone into doing something. **2** historical force someone to join a ship's crew.
– ORIGIN from *Shanghai,* a Chinese seaport.

Shan·gri-La /ˈsHaNGgri ˈlä/ ▶ **noun** a very pleasant or unspoiled place.
– ORIGIN named after a Tibetan Utopia in James Hilton's novel *Lost Horizon.*

shank /sHaNGk/ ▶ **noun 1** the lower part of a person's leg. **2** the lower part of an animal's foreleg, especially as a cut of meat. **3** the shaft or stem of a tool, spoon, etc. **4** the band of a ring rather than the setting.
– DERIVATIVES **shanked** adjective.
– ORIGIN Old English.

shan't /sHant/ ▶ **contraction** shall not.

shan·tung /sHanˈtəNG/ ▶ **noun** a type of soft silk with a coarse surface.
– ORIGIN from *Shantung* in China, where it was first made.

shant·y[1] /ˈsHantē/ ▶ **noun** (pl. **shanties**) a small roughly built shack.
– ORIGIN perhaps from Canadian French *chantier* 'lumberjack's cabin.'

shant·y[2] ▶ **noun** (pl. **shanties**) variant spelling of **CHANTEY**.
– ORIGIN probably from French *chantez!* 'sing!'

shan·ty·town ▶ **noun** a settlement in or near a city where poor people live in makeshift houses or shacks.

shape /sHāp/ ▶ **noun 1** the outward form of someone or something as produced by their outline. **2** a geometric figure such as a rectangle. **3** a piece of material or paper made or cut in a particular form. **4** the correct or original form of something: *the wheels are out of shape and not perfectly circular.* **5** organized or well-defined structure or arrangement. **6** a particular condition or state: *the house was in poor shape.* **7** good physical condition.

– SYNONYMS **1 form,** appearance, configuration, structure, contours, lines, outline, silhouette, profile. **2 guise,** likeness, semblance, form, appearance, image. **3 condition,** health, trim, fettle, order.

▶ **verb 1** give a shape to something. **2** determine the nature of. **3** develop in a particular way: *it was shaping up to be another bleak year.* **4** (**shape up**) improve one's fitness, performance, or behavior.

– SYNONYMS **1 form,** fashion, make, mold, model. **2** *events that shaped the course of her life* **determine,** form, influence, affect.

– DERIVATIVES **shaped** adjective **shap·er** noun.
– PHRASES **lick** (or **knock**) **someone/thing into shape** take forceful action to improve someone or something. **take shape** develop into something more definite or organized.
– ORIGIN Old English.

shape·less /ˈSHāplis/ ▶ **adjective** lacking a definite or attractive shape.

– SYNONYMS **1 formless,** amorphous, unformed, indefinite. **2 baggy,** saggy, ill-fitting, oversized, unstructured, badly cut.

– DERIVATIVES **shape·less·ly** adverb **shape·less·ness** noun.

shape·ly /ˈSHāplē/ ▶ **adjective** (**shapelier, shapeliest**) having an attractive or well-proportioned shape: *shapely legs.*

– SYNONYMS **well proportioned,** curvaceous, voluptuous, full-figured, attractive, sexy; informal curvy.

– DERIVATIVES **shape·li·ness** noun.

shape-shift·er ▶ **noun** an imaginary being who is able to change their physical form when they want to.
– DERIVATIVES **shape-shift·ing** noun & adjective.

shard /SHärd/ ▶ **noun** a sharp piece of broken pottery, metal, glass, etc.
– ORIGIN Old English, 'gap, notch, shard.'

share /SHe(ə)r/ ▶ **noun 1** a part of a larger amount that is divided among or contributed by a number of people. **2** any of the equal parts into which a company's capital is divided, which can be bought by people in return for a proportion of the profits. **3** an amount regarded as normal or acceptable: *the new system had more than its fair share of problems.* **4** a person's contribution to an activity.

– SYNONYMS **portion,** part, division, quota, allowance, ration, allocation; informal cut, slice.

▶ **verb 1** have or give a share of something. **2** possess or use jointly with others: *they shared an apartment.* **3** (**share in**) participate in an activity. **4** tell someone about something.

– SYNONYMS **1 split,** divide, go halves on; informal go fifty-fifty on. **2 apportion,** divide up, allocate, portion out, measure out, carve up; informal divvy up. **3 participate,** take part, play a part, be involved, have a hand.

– DERIVATIVES **share·a·ble** (also **sharable**) adjective **shar·er** noun.
– ORIGIN Old English.

share·crop·per /ˈSHe(ə)r,kräpər/ ▶ **noun** a tenant farmer who gives a part of each crop as rent.

share·hold·er /ˈSHe(ə)r,hōldər/ ▶ **noun** a stockholder.
– DERIVATIVES **share·hold·ing** noun.

share·ware /ˈSHe(ə)r,we(ə)r/ ▶ **noun** computer software that is available free of charge and often distributed informally for users to evaluate.

sha·ri·a /SHäˈrēə/ ▶ **noun** Islamic law, based on the teachings of the Koran and the traditions of Muhammad.
– ORIGIN Arabic.

shark[1] /SHärk/ ▶ **noun** a large sea fish with a triangular fin on its back, many kinds of which prey on other animals.
– ORIGIN unknown.

shark[2] ▶ **noun** informal a person who exploits or swindles others.
– ORIGIN perhaps from German *Schurke* 'worthless rogue.'

shark·skin /ˈSHärk,skin/ ▶ **noun** a stiff, slightly shiny synthetic fabric.

sharp /SHärp/ ▶ **adjective 1** having a cutting or piercing edge or point. **2** tapering to a point or edge. **3** sudden and rapid. **4** (of a feeling or emotion) sudden and intense. **5** quick to understand, notice, or respond. **6** (of a food, taste, or smell) strong and slightly bitter. **7** (of a person or remark) critical or hurtful. **8** clear and definite: *the mood is in sharp contrast to last year's summit.* **9** (of a sound) sudden and penetrating. **10** quick to take advantage, especially in a dishonest way. **11** making a sudden change of direction. **12** informal smart and stylish. **13** (after a noun) (of a note or key) higher by a half step than a specified note or key: *F sharp.*

– SYNONYMS **1** *a sharp knife* **keen,** razor-edged, sharpened, well honed. **2** *a sharp increase* **sudden,** abrupt, unexpected, rapid, steep. **3** *a sharp pain* **intense,** acute, severe, agonizing, excruciating, stabbing, shooting, searing. **4** *she was sharp and witty* **astute,** intelligent, bright, incisive, keen, quick-witted, shrewd, canny, perceptive, smart, quick; informal on the ball, quick on the uptake, heads-up. **5** *a sharp taste* **tangy,** piquant, acidic, acid, sour, tart, pungent, vinegary. **6** *sharp words* **harsh,** bitter, cutting, caustic, scathing, barbed, spiteful, hurtful, unkind, cruel, malicious.
– ANTONYMS blunt, mild.

▶ **adverb 1** precisely: *the meeting starts at 7:30 sharp.* **2** suddenly or abruptly.

– SYNONYMS **precisely,** exactly, prompt, promptly, punctually; informal on the dot, on the nose, on the button.

▶ **noun 1** a musical note raised a half step above natural pitch, shown by the sign ♯. **2** an object with a sharp point. **3** a card sharp.
– DERIVATIVES **sharp·ish** adjective **sharp·ly** adverb **sharp·ness** noun.
– ORIGIN Old English.

CHOOSE THE RIGHT WORD

See **KEEN**[1].

sharp·en /ˈSHärpən/ ▶ **verb** make or become sharp.

– SYNONYMS **hone,** whet, strop, grind, file.

– DERIVATIVES **shar·pen·er** noun.

sharp·er /ˈSHärpər/ ▶ **noun** informal a swindler, especially at cards; a card sharp.

sharp·shoot·er /ˈSHärp,SHo͞otər/ ▶ **noun** a person skilled in shooting.

sharp-tongued ▶ **adjective** using harsh or critical language.

sharp-wit·ted ▶ adjective intelligent and quick to notice things.

shat /sʜat/ past and past participle of **SHIT**.

shat·ter /ˈsʜatər/ ▶ verb **1** break suddenly and violently into pieces. **2** damage or destroy: *he broke her heart and shattered her dreams*. **3** upset someone greatly.

– SYNONYMS **1 smash,** break, splinter, crack, fracture, fragment, disintegrate. **2 destroy,** wreck, ruin, dash, crush, devastate, demolish, torpedo, scotch.

– DERIVATIVES **shat·ter·er** noun.
– ORIGIN uncertain.

shave /sʜāv/ ▶ verb **1** remove hair from the face or body by cutting it off close to the skin with a razor. **2** cut a thin slice or slices from something. **3** reduce by a small amount: *21 percent was shaved off the research budget*. **4** pass very close to something.

– SYNONYMS **1 cut off,** crop, trim, barber. **2 plane,** pare, whittle, scrape, shear.

▶ noun an act of shaving.
– ORIGIN Old English.

shav·en /ˈsʜāvən/ ▶ adjective (of a part of the body) shaved.

shav·er /ˈsʜāvər/ ▶ noun **1** an electric razor. **2** informal, dated a young lad.

Sha·vi·an /ˈsʜāvēən/ ▶ adjective relating to or in the style of the Irish dramatist George Bernard Shaw. ▶ noun an admirer of Shaw or his work.
– ORIGIN from *Shavius*, the Latin form of *Shaw*.

shav·ing /ˈsʜāviNG/ ▶ noun a thin strip cut off a surface.

Sha·vu·ot /sʜəˈvo͞oˌōt, ˌsʜävo͞oˈōt, sʜəˈvo͞oəs/ ▶ noun a major Jewish festival held fifty days after the second day of Passover.
– ORIGIN Hebrew.

shawl /sʜôl/ ▶ noun a large piece of fabric worn by women over the shoulders or head or wrapped around a baby.
– DERIVATIVES **shawled** adjective.
– ORIGIN Urdu and Persian.

Shaw·nee /sʜôˈnē/ ▶ noun (pl. same or **Shawnees**) a member of an American Indian people now living chiefly in Oklahoma.
– ORIGIN the name in Delaware (an American Indian language).

she /sʜē/ ▶ pronoun (third person sing.) **1** used to refer to a woman, girl, or female animal previously mentioned or easily identified. **2** used to refer to a ship, country, or other thing regarded as female. ▶ noun a female; a woman.
– ORIGIN Old English.

s/he /ˈsʜē ər ˈhē, ˈsʜēˈhē/ ▶ pronoun a written representation of "he or she" used as a neutral alternative to indicate someone of either sex.

sheaf /sʜēf/ ▶ noun (pl. **sheaves** /sʜēvz/) **1** a bundle of papers. **2** a bundle of grain stalks tied together after reaping. ▶ verb tie grain stalks into bundles.
– ORIGIN Old English.

shear /sʜi(ə)r/ ▶ verb (past part. **shorn** or **sheared**) **1** cut the wool off a sheep or other animal. **2** cut off hair or wool with scissors or shears. **3** (**be shorn of**) have something taken away: *he was shorn of nearly $2 billion*. **4** break off because of a structural strain. ▶ noun a strain produced by pressure in the structure of a substance, so that each layer slides over the next.
– DERIVATIVES **shear·er** noun.
– ORIGIN Old English.

USAGE

Do not confuse **shear** and **sheer**. **Shear** means 'cut the wool off a sheep.' As a verb, **sheer** means 'change course quickly' (*the boat sheered off*); **sheer** is also an adjective meaning 'nothing but; absolute' (*sheer hard work*).

shears /sʜi(ə)rz/ (also **a pair of shears**) ▶ plural noun a cutting instrument resembling a very large pair of scissors.

shear·wa·ter /ˈsʜi(ə)rˌwôtər, -ˌwätər/ ▶ noun a long-winged seabird related to the petrels.

sheath /sʜēᴛʜ/ ▶ noun (pl. **sheaths** /sʜē<u>ᴛʜ</u>z, sʜēᴛʜs/) **1** a cover for the blade of a knife or sword. **2** a condom. **3** a close-fitting covering or protective structure. **4** (also **sheath dress**) a close-fitting dress.

– SYNONYMS **covering,** cover, case, casing, sleeve, scabbard.

– ORIGIN Old English.

sheathe /sʜē<u>ᴛʜ</u>/ ▶ verb **1** put a knife or sword into a sheath. **2** cover in a close-fitting or protective covering: *her legs were sheathed in black stockings*.

sheath·ing /ˈsʜē<u>ᴛʜ</u>iNG/ ▶ noun a protective casing or covering.

sheaves /sʜēvz/ plural of **SHEAF**.

she·bang /sʜəˈbaNG/ ▶ noun (in phrase **the whole shebang**) informal the whole thing; everything.
– ORIGIN unknown.

she·been /sʜəˈbēn/ ▶ noun (especially in Ireland, Scotland, and South Africa) a place that sells alcoholic drink illegally.
– ORIGIN Anglo-Irish *síbín*.

shed[1] /sʜed/ ▶ noun **1** a simple building used for storage or to shelter animals. **2** a larger structure, typically with one or more sides open, for storing vehicles or machinery.

– SYNONYMS **hut,** lean-to, outhouse, outbuilding, cabin, shack, woodshed, toolshed.

– ORIGIN probably from **SHADE**.

shed[2] ▶ verb (**sheds, shedding, shed**) **1** get rid of: *exercise helps you shed pounds*. **2** cast or give off light. **3** allow leaves, hair, skin, etc., to fall off naturally. **4** take off clothes. **5** be able to repel water.

– SYNONYMS **1 drop,** scatter, spill. **2 throw off,** cast off, discard, slough off, molt. **3 take off,** remove, discard, climb out of, slip out of; informal peel off. **4** *the moon shed a faint light* **cast,** radiate, emit, give out.

– DERIVATIVES **shed·der** noun.
– PHRASES **shed tears** cry.
– ORIGIN Old English, 'divide, scatter.'

she'd /sʜēd/ ▶ contraction she had; she would.

she-dev·il ▶ noun a malicious or spiteful woman.

sheen /sʜēn/ ▶ noun a soft shine on a surface.

– SYNONYMS **shine,** luster, gloss, patina, burnish, polish, shimmer.

– DERIVATIVES **sheen·y** adjective.
– ORIGIN probably from **SHINE**.

CHOOSE THE RIGHT WORD

See **POLISH**.

sheep /shēp/ ▸ **noun** (pl. same) a grass-eating mammal with a thick woolly coat, kept in flocks for its wool or meat.
– DERIVATIVES **sheep·like** /-ˌlīk/ adjective.
– PHRASES **like sheep** (of people) easily led or influenced.
– ORIGIN Old English.

sheep dip ▸ **noun 1** a liquid in which sheep are dipped to clean and disinfect their wool. **2** a place where sheep are dipped in this liquid.

sheep·dog /ˈshēpˌdôg, -ˌdäg/ ▸ **noun 1** a dog trained to guard and herd sheep. **2** a breed of dog suitable for guarding and herding sheep.

sheep·ish /ˈshēpish/ ▸ **adjective** embarrassed as a result of having done something foolish.

– SYNONYMS **embarrassed,** uncomfortable, hangdog, self-conscious; shamefaced, ashamed, abashed, mortified, chastened, remorseful, contrite, apologetic, penitent, repentant.

– DERIVATIVES **sheep·ish·ly** adverb **sheep·ish·ness** noun.

sheep·shank /ˈshēpˌshangk/ ▸ **noun** a knot made in a rope to shorten it temporarily.

sheep·skin /ˈshēpˌskin/ ▸ **noun 1** a sheep's skin with the wool on, made into a garment or rug. **2** informal a diploma.

sheer[1] /shi(ə)r/ ▸ **adjective 1** nothing but; absolute: *sheer hard work*. **2** (of a cliff, wall, etc.) vertical or almost vertical. **3** (of a fabric) very thin and almost transparent.

– SYNONYMS **1 utter,** complete, absolute, total, thorough, pure, downright, out-and-out, unqualified, unmitigated, unalloyed. **2 steep,** abrupt, sharp, precipitous, vertical. **3 thin,** fine, gauzy, diaphanous, transparent, see-through, flimsy, filmy, translucent.

▸ **adverb** vertically; perpendicularly.
– DERIVATIVES **sheer·ly** adverb **sheer·ness** noun.
– ORIGIN probably from **SHINE**.

USAGE

On the confusion of **sheer** and **shear**, see the note at **SHEAR**.

sheer[2] ▸ **verb 1** (especially of a boat) swerve or change course quickly. **2** avoid or move away from an unpleasant topic.
– ORIGIN perhaps from German *scheren* 'to shear.'

sheet[1] /shēt/ ▸ **noun 1** a large rectangular piece of cotton or other fabric, used on a bed to lie on or under. **2** a broad flat piece of metal or glass. **3** a rectangular piece of paper. **4** a wide expanse or moving mass of water, ice, flame, etc.

– SYNONYMS **1** *a sheet of glass* **pane,** panel, slab, plate, piece. **2** *she put a fresh sheet in the typewriter* **page,** leaf, folio. **3** *a sheet of ice* **layer,** covering, stratum, blanket, coat, film, skin. **4** *a sheet of water* **expanse,** area, stretch, sweep.

▸ **verb 1** cover something with a sheet of cloth. **2** (of rain) fall heavily.
– ORIGIN Old English.

sheet[2] ▸ **noun** a rope attached to the lower corner of a sail, to hold and adjust it.
– PHRASES **two** (or **three**) **sheets to the wind** informal drunk.
– ORIGIN Old English, 'lower corner of a sail.'

sheet·ing /ˈshēting/ ▸ **noun** material formed into or used as a sheet.

sheet light·ning ▸ **noun** lightning seen as a broad area of light in the sky.

sheet met·al ▸ **noun** metal formed into thin sheets.

sheet mu·sic ▸ **noun** music published on loose sheets of paper and not bound into a book.

sheikh /shēk, shāk/ (also **shaykh** or **sheik**) ▸ **noun 1** the leader of an Arab tribe, family, or village. **2** a leader in a Muslim community or organization.
– DERIVATIVES **sheikh·dom** /-dəm/ noun.
– ORIGIN Arabic, 'old man, sheikh.'

shei·la /ˈshēlə/ ▸ **noun** Austral./NZ informal a girl or woman.
– ORIGIN unknown.

shek·el /ˈshekəl/ ▸ **noun 1** the basic unit of money of modern Israel. **2** (**shekels**) informal money; wealth.
– ORIGIN Hebrew.

shel·duck /ˈshelˌdək/ ▸ **noun** (pl. same or **shelducks**) a large gooselike duck with brightly colored plumage.
– ORIGIN probably from dialect *sheld* 'black and white' + **DUCK[1]**.

shelf /shelf/ ▸ **noun** (pl. **shelves**) **1** a flat length of wood or other rigid material fixed horizontally to a wall or forming part of a piece of furniture and used to display or store things. **2** a ledge of rock or protruding strip of land.
– PHRASES **off the shelf** taken from existing stock, not made to order.
– ORIGIN German *schelf*.

shelf life ▸ **noun** the length of time for which an item is expected to remain able to be eaten, used, or sold.

shell /shel/ ▸ **noun 1** the hard protective outer case of an animal such as a snail, shellfish, or turtle. **2** the outer covering of an egg, nut kernel, or seed. **3** a metal case filled with explosives, to be fired from a large gun. **4** a hollow case, especially one used as a container for fireworks, cartridges, etc. **5** an outer structure or framework of a building or vehicle. **6** a light racing boat. **7** (also **shell program**) a program that provides an interface between the user and the operating system.

– SYNONYMS **1 pod,** hull, husk. **2 body,** case, casing, framework, hull, fuselage, hulk.

▸ **verb 1** fire explosive shells at something. **2** remove the shell or pod from a nut or seed. **3** (**shell something out**) informal pay an amount of money.

– SYNONYMS **1 pod,** hull, husk, shuck. **2 bombard,** fire on, attack, bomb, blitz.

– DERIVATIVES **shell-less** adjective **shell-like** /-ˌlīk/ adjective **shell·y** /ˈshelē/ adjective.
– PHRASES **come out of one's shell** stop being shy.
– ORIGIN Old English.

she'll /shēl/ ▸ **contraction** she will; she shall.

shel·lac /shəˈlak/ ▸ **noun** lac resin melted into thin flakes, used for making varnish. ▸ **verb** (**shellacks, shellacking, shellacked**) **1** varnish something with shellac. **2** informal defeat someone decisively.
– ORIGIN from **SHELL** + **LAC**.

shell·fire /ˈshelˌfīr/ ▸ **noun** bombardment by explosive shells.

shell·fish /ˈsHelˌfisH/ ▸ **noun** a creature such as a crab or oyster that has a shell and lives in water, especially an edible one.

shell shock ▸ **noun** dated a mental disorder that can affect soldiers who have been in battle.
– DERIVATIVES **shell-shocked** adjective.

Shel·ta /ˈsHeltə/ ▸ **noun** an ancient secret language used by Irish and Welsh tinkers and Gypsies, based on altered Irish or Gaelic words.
– ORIGIN unknown.

shel·ter /ˈsHeltər/ ▸ **noun 1** a place giving protection from bad weather or danger. **2** a place providing food and accommodations for homeless people. **3** protection from something unpleasant or dangerous: *he waited in the shelter of a rock*.

> – SYNONYMS **1 protection,** cover, shade, safety, security, refuge. **2 sanctuary,** refuge, home, haven, safe house.
> – ANTONYMS exposure.

▸ **verb 1** provide someone or something with shelter. **2** take cover from bad weather or danger. **3** (as adj. **sheltered**) protected from the more unpleasant aspects of life.

> – SYNONYMS **1 protect,** shield, screen, cover, shade, defend, cushion, guard, insulate, cocoon. **2** (as adj. **sheltered**) *the plants need a sheltered spot in the garden* **shady,** shaded, protected, still, tranquil. **3 take shelter,** take refuge, take cover; informal hole up. **4** (as adj. **sheltered**) *she led a sheltered life* **protected,** cloistered, isolated, secluded, cocooned, insulated, secure, safe, quiet.
> – ANTONYMS expose.

– ORIGIN perhaps from a former spelling of **SHIELD**.

shelve[1] /sHelv/ ▸ **verb 1** place something on a shelf. **2** decide not to continue with; cancel or postpone: *the company shelved plans for a big pay raise for its CEO*. **3** fit something with shelves.

> – SYNONYMS **postpone,** put off, delay, defer, put back, reschedule, hold over/off, put to one side, table, suspend, stay, mothball; informal put on ice, put on the back burner.

– DERIVATIVES **shelv·er** noun.
– ORIGIN from *shelves*, plural of **SHELF**.

shelve[2] ▸ **verb** (of ground) slope downward.
– ORIGIN perhaps from **SHELF**.

shelves /sHelvz/ plural of **SHELF**.

shelv·ing /ˈsHelviNG/ ▸ **noun** shelves as a whole.

she·nan·i·gans /sHəˈnanəgənz/ ▸ **plural noun** informal **1** secret or dishonest activity. **2** high-spirited or mischievous behavior.
– ORIGIN unknown.

shep·herd /ˈsHepərd/ ▸ **noun 1** a person who looks after sheep. **2** a member of the clergy regarded as providing spiritual care and guidance for a congregation. ▸ **verb 1** guide or direct somewhere: *she shepherded them through the door*. **2** look after sheep.

> – SYNONYMS **usher,** steer, herd, lead, take, escort, guide, conduct, marshal, walk.

– DERIVATIVES **shep·herd·ess** /ˈsHepərdis/ noun.
– ORIGIN Old English.

shep·herd's pie ▸ **noun** a dish of minced meat under a layer of mashed potato.

sher·bet /ˈsHərbit/ ▸ **noun** a frozen dessert made with fruit juice; sorbet.
– ORIGIN Arabic, 'drink.'

sherd /sHərd/ ▸ **noun** another term for **POTSHERD**.
– ORIGIN from **SHARD**.

sher·iff /ˈsHerif/ ▸ **noun** an elected officer in a county or town, responsible for keeping the peace.
– ORIGIN Old English, 'shire reeve.'

Sher·pa /ˈsHərpə/ ▸ **noun** (pl. same or **Sherpas**) a member of a Himalayan people living on the borders of Nepal and Tibet.
– ORIGIN Tibetan, 'inhabitant of an Eastern country.'

sher·ry /ˈsHerē/ ▸ **noun** (pl. **sherries**) a fortified wine originally from southern Spain.
– ORIGIN from Spanish *vino de Xeres* 'Xeres wine' (Xeres being the former name of the city of *Jerez de la Frontera*).

she's /sHēz/ ▸ **contraction** she is; she has.

Shet·land po·ny /ˈsHetlənd/ ▸ **noun** a small breed of pony with a rough coat.

shew /sHō/ ▸ **verb** old-fashioned variant of **SHOW**.

Shi·a /ˈsHēˌä/ (also **Shi'a**) ▸ **noun** (pl. same or **Shias**) **1** one of the two main branches of Islam, the other being Sunni. **2** a Muslim who follows the Shia branch of Islam.
– ORIGIN Arabic, 'party (of Ali).'

shi·at·su /sHēˈätso͞o/ ▸ **noun** a Japanese therapy in which pressure is applied with the hands to points on the body.
– ORIGIN Japanese, 'finger pressure.'

shib·bo·leth /ˈsHibəliTH, -ˌleTH/ ▸ **noun** a long-standing belief or principle that many people regard as outdated or no longer important: *the conflict challenged a series of military shibboleths*.
– ORIGIN Hebrew, 'ear of corn'; first meaning in English 'a word which a foreigner is unable to pronounce' (according to the Book of Judges, the word was used as a test of nationality because it was difficult to pronounce).

shied /sHīd/ past and past participle of **SHY**[2].

shield /sHēld/ ▸ **noun 1** a broad piece of armor held for protection against blows or missiles. **2** a person or thing that provides protection. **3** a sporting trophy consisting of an engraved metal plate mounted on a piece of wood. **4** a drawing or model of a shield used for displaying a coat of arms. **5** a police officer's badge.

> – SYNONYMS **protection,** guard, defense, cover, screen, shelter.

▸ **verb 1** protect someone or something from something dangerous, unpleasant, or risky. **2** prevent from being seen: *the runners were shielded from view by the tunnel*. **3** enclose machinery or a source of sound, light, or radiation to protect the user.

> – SYNONYMS **protect,** guard, defend, cover, screen, shade, shelter.
> – ANTONYMS expose.

– ORIGIN Old English.

shift /sHift/ ▸ **verb 1** move or change from one position or direction to another: *the warming Gulf Stream could shift away from the UK*. **2** transfer responsibility, blame, or power to someone else. **3** change gear in a vehicle. **4** informal sell goods quickly or in large quantities. **5** Brit. informal move quickly.

> – SYNONYMS **1 move,** transfer, transport, switch, relocate, reposition, rearrange. **2** *the wind shifted* **veer,** alter, change, turn.

▸ **noun 1** a slight change in position, direction, or tendency: *a shift in public opinion*. **2** a period of time worked by a group of workers who start work as another group finishes. **3** a straight dress without a waist. **4** a key used to switch between two sets of characters or functions on a keyboard. **5** a gear lever or gear-changing mechanism. **6** old use a clever or crafty plan.

– SYNONYMS **1 change,** alteration, adjustment, variation, modification, revision, reversal, U-turn. **2 stint,** stretch, spell.

– DERIVATIVES **shift·er** noun.
– ORIGIN Old English, 'arrange, divide.'

shift·less /'SHiftlis/ ▶ **adjective** lazy and lacking ambition.

– SYNONYMS **lazy,** idle, indolent, slothful, lethargic, feckless, good-for-nothing, worthless.

– DERIVATIVES **shift·less·ness** noun.

shift·y /'SHiftē/ ▶ **adjective** (**shiftier, shiftiest**) informal appearing untrustworthy or dishonest.

– SYNONYMS **devious,** evasive, slippery, duplicitous, deceitful, untrustworthy.
– ANTONYMS honest.

– DERIVATIVES **shift·i·ly** adverb **shift·i·ness** noun.

Shih Tzu /'SHē 'dzōō/ ▶ **noun** a dog of a breed with long, silky, erect hair and short legs.
– ORIGIN from Chinese *shizi* 'lion.'

shi·i·ta·ke /SHē'täkē, SHē-ē'täke/ ▶ **noun** an edible mushroom grown in Japan and China.
– ORIGIN Japanese.

Shi·ite /'SHē,īt/ (also **Shi'ite**) ▶ **noun** a follower of the Shia branch of Islam. ▶ **adjective** relating to the Shia branch of Islam.
– DERIVATIVES **Shi·ism** /'SHē,izəm/ noun.

shik·sa /'SHiksə/ ▶ **noun** derogatory (in Jewish use) a non-Jewish girl or woman.
– ORIGIN Hebrew, 'detested thing.'

shill /SHil/ informal ▶ **noun** an accomplice of a hawker, gambler, or swindler who acts as an enthusiastic customer to entice or encourage others. ▶ **verb** act or work as such a person.
– ORIGIN unknown.

shil·le·lagh /SHə'lālē/ ▶ **noun** (in Ireland) a wooden cudgel.
– ORIGIN named after the Irish town of *Shillelagh.*

shil·ling /'SHiliNG/ ▶ **noun 1** a former British coin and unit of money equal to one twentieth of a pound or twelve pence. **2** the basic unit of money of Kenya, Tanzania, and Uganda.
– ORIGIN Old English.

shil·ly-shal·ly /'SHilē ,SHalē/ ▶ **verb** (**shilly-shallies, shilly-shallying, shilly-shallied**) be unable to make up one's mind.
– ORIGIN from *shill I, shall I?*

shim /SHim/ ▶ **noun** a washer or thin strip of material used in machinery to fill a space between parts or reduce wear. ▶ **verb** (**shims, shimming, shimmed**) fill up a space with a shim.
– ORIGIN unknown.

shim·mer /'SHimər/ ▶ **verb** shine with a soft wavering light.

– SYNONYMS **glint,** glisten, twinkle, sparkle, flash, gleam, glow, glimmer, wink.

▶ **noun** a soft wavering light or reflected light.

– SYNONYMS **glint,** twinkle, sparkle, flash, gleam, glow, glimmer, luster, glitter.

– DERIVATIVES **shim·mer·y** adjective.
– ORIGIN Old English.

shim·my /'SHimē/ ▶ **verb** (**shimmies, shimmying, shimmied**) **1** walk or move with a smooth swaying motion. **2** shake or vibrate abnormally. **3** dance the shimmy. ▶ **noun** (pl. **shimmies**) a kind of ragtime dance in which the dancer shakes or sways the whole body.
– ORIGIN unknown.

shin /SHin/ ▶ **noun 1** the front of the leg below the knee. **2** a cut of beef from the lower part of a cow's leg. ▶ **verb** (**shins, shinning, shinned**) (**shin up/down**) climb quickly up or down by gripping with the arms and legs.
– ORIGIN Old English.

shin·bone /'SHin,bōn/ ▶ **noun** the tibia.

shin·dig /'SHin,dig/ ▶ **noun** informal **1** a large, lively party. **2** a noisy disturbance or quarrel.
– ORIGIN probably from **SHIN** and **DIG**.

shine /SHīn/ ▶ **verb** (past and past part. **shone** or **shined**) **1** give out or reflect light. **2** point a torch or other light in a particular direction. **3** (of a person's eyes) be bright with an emotion. **4** be very good at something: *she shines at comedy.* **5** (**shine through**) (of a quality or skill) be clearly evident. **6** (past and past part. **shined**) polish something.

– SYNONYMS **1 beam,** gleam, radiate, glow, glint, glimmer, sparkle, twinkle, glitter, glisten, shimmer, flash. **2 excel,** stand out. **3 polish,** burnish, buff, rub up, brush, clean.

▶ **noun 1** a quality of brightness produced by reflected light. **2** an act of polishing.

– SYNONYMS **polish,** gleam, gloss, luster, sheen, patina.

– PHRASES **take the shine off** make something seem less good or exciting. **take a shine to** informal develop a liking for someone.
– ORIGIN Old English.

shin·er /'SHīnər/ ▶ **noun** informal a black eye.

shin·gle¹ /'SHiNGgəl/ ▶ **noun 1** a tile of asphalt composite, wood, metal, or slate used on walls or roofs. **2** dated a woman's short haircut, tapering from the back of the head to the nape of the neck. **3** a signboard, especially one outside a lawyer's or doctor's office: *Ol' Doc Green hung out his shingle in 1902.* ▶ **verb 1** roof or clad something with shingles. **2** dated cut hair in a shingle.
– ORIGIN probably from Latin *scindula* 'a split piece of wood.'

shingle² ▶ **noun** a mass of small rounded pebbles, especially on a seashore.
– DERIVATIVES **shin·gly** /-g(ə)lē/ adjective.
– ORIGIN unknown.

shin·gles /'SHiNGgəlz/ ▶ **plural noun** (treated as sing.) a disease caused by a virus, in which painful blisters form along the path of a nerve or nerves.
– ORIGIN from Latin *cingulum* 'girdle.'

shin·ny¹ /'SHinē/ ▶ **verb** (**shinnies, shinnied**) another term for **SHIN**: *he loved to shinny up that tree.*

shin·ny² (also **shinny hockey**) ▶ **noun** an informal form of ice hockey played especially by children, on the street or on ice, often with a ball or other object in place of a puck: *we used to play shinny on the canal with tin cans.*
– ORIGIN variant of **SHINTY**.

shin splints ▶ **plural noun** (treated as sing. or pl.) pain in the shin and lower leg caused by prolonged running on hard surfaces.

Shin·to /ˈsʜin,tō/ ▶ **noun** a Japanese religion involving the worship of ancestors and nature spirits.
– DERIVATIVES **Shin·to·ism** /-izəm/ noun **Shin·to·ist** /-ist/ noun.
– ORIGIN Chinese, 'way of the gods.'

shin·ty /ˈsʜin(t)ē/ ▶ **noun** a Scottish game resembling field hockey.

shin·y /ˈsʜīnē/ ▶ **adjective** (**shinier, shiniest**) reflecting light because very smooth, clean, or polished.

– SYNONYMS **glossy,** bright, glassy, polished, gleaming, satiny, lustrous.
– ANTONYMS matte.

– DERIVATIVES **shin·i·ly** adverb **shin·i·ness** noun.

ship /sʜip/ ▶ **noun 1** a large boat for transporting people or goods by sea. **2** a sailboat with a bowsprit and three or more square-rigged masts.

– SYNONYMS **boat,** vessel, craft.

▶ **verb** (**ships, shipping, shipped**) **1** transport people or goods on a ship or by other means. **2** make a product available for sale. **3** (of a boat) take in water over the side. **4** take oars from the oarlocks and lay them inside a boat. **5** (of a sailor) be employed on a ship.

– SYNONYMS **deliver,** send, dispatch, transport, carry, distribute.

– DERIVATIVES **ship·load** /ˈsʜip,lōd/ noun **ship·per** noun.
– PHRASES **when someone's ship comes in** when someone's fortune is made.
– ORIGIN Old English.

WORD LINKS

maritime, nautical *relating to ships*

-ship ▶ **suffix** forming nouns referring to. **1** a quality or condition: *companionship*. **2** status or office: *citizenship*. **3** a skill: *workmanship*. **4** the members of a group: *membership*.
– ORIGIN Old English.

ship·board /ˈsʜip,bôrd/ ▶ **adjective** used or occurring on board a ship.

ship·build·er /ˈsʜip,bildər/ ▶ **noun** a person or company that designs and builds ships.
– DERIVATIVES **ship·build·ing** noun.

ship·mate /ˈsʜip,māt/ ▶ **noun** a fellow member of a ship's crew.

ship·ment /ˈsʜipmənt/ ▶ **noun 1** the action of transporting goods. **2** a quantity of goods shipped.

ship·ping /ˈsʜipiɴɢ/ ▶ **noun 1** ships as a whole. **2** the transport of goods.

ship·shape /ˈsʜip,sʜāp/ ▶ **adjective** in good order; neat and clean.

ship·wreck /ˈsʜip,rek/ ▶ **noun 1** the sinking or breaking up of a ship at sea. **2** a ship that has sunk or been destroyed at sea. ▶ **verb** (**be shipwrecked**) **1** be left somewhere after one's ship has sunk or been destroyed. **2** (of a ship) suffer a shipwreck.

ship·wright /ˈsʜip,rīt/ ▶ **noun** a shipbuilder.

ship·yard /ˈsʜip,yärd/ ▶ **noun** a place where ships are built and repaired.

Shi·raz /sʜiˈräz/ ▶ **noun** a red wine made from a variety of black wine grape.
– ORIGIN from the city of *Shiraz* in Iran.

shire /sʜī(ə)r/ ▶ **noun 1** Brit. a county in England. **2** (**the Shires**) the rural areas of the English Midlands, regarded as strongholds of traditional country life. **3** Austral. a rural area with its own elected council.
– ORIGIN Old English, 'care, official charge, county.'

shire horse ▶ **noun** a heavy powerful breed of horse, used for pulling loads.

shirk /sʜərk/ ▶ **verb** avoid or neglect work or a duty.

– SYNONYMS **evade,** dodge, avoid, get out of, sidestep, shrink from, shun, skip, neglect; informal duck (out of), book (out of), cop out of, cut.

– DERIVATIVES **shirk·er** noun.
– ORIGIN perhaps from German *Schurke* 'scoundrel.'

shirr /sʜər/ ▶ **verb** (usu. as adj. **shirred**) **1** gather fabric by means of drawn or elastic threads in parallel rows. **2** bake an egg without its shell.
– ORIGIN unknown.

shirt /sʜərt/ ▶ **noun 1** an item of clothing for the upper body, with a collar and sleeves and buttons down the front. **2** a similar top of light material without full fastenings, worn for sports and leisure: *a polo shirt*.
– DERIVATIVES **shirt·ed** adjective.
– PHRASES **keep your shirt on** informal stay calm. **lose one's shirt** informal lose all one's money.
– ORIGIN Old English.

shirt·dress ▶ **noun** a dress with a collar and button fastening in the style of a shirt, without a seam at the waist.

shirt·front /ˈsʜərt,frənt/ ▶ **noun** the breast of a shirt, in particular the part that shows when a suit is worn.

shirt·sleeve /ˈsʜərt,slēv/ ▶ **noun** the sleeve of a shirt.
– DERIVATIVES **shirt·sleeved** adjective.
– PHRASES **in (one's) shirtsleeves** wearing a shirt without a jacket over it.

shirt·tail ▶ **noun** the curved part of a shirt that comes below the waist.

shirt·waist /ˈsʜərt,wāst/ ▶ **noun 1** a woman's blouse that resembles a shirt. **2** (also **shirtwaister**) a shirt dress with a seam at the waist.

shish ke·bab /ˈsʜisʜ kə,bäb/ ▶ **noun** a dish of pieces of meat and vegetables cooked and served on skewers.
– ORIGIN Turkish *şiş kebap*.

shit /sʜit/ vulgar slang ▶ **verb** (**shits, shitting, shitted** or **shit** or **shat** /sʜat/) **1** pass feces from the body. **2** (**shit oneself**) be very frightened. ▶ **noun 1** feces. **2** something worthless; rubbish. **3** an unpleasant or disliked person. ▶ **exclamation** expressing disgust or annoyance.
– DERIVATIVES **shit·ty** adjective.
– ORIGIN Old English, 'diarrhea.'

shit·load /ˈsʜit,lōd/ ▶ **noun** vulgar slang a large amount or number: *I have a shitload of work to do this week*.

Shi·va /ˈsʜēvə/ (also **Siva**) (in Indian religion) a god regarded by some as the supreme being and by others as one of a supreme triad, and associated with the powers of reproduction and dissolution.
– ORIGIN from Sanskrit *Śiva*, literally 'the auspicious one.'

shiv·er[1] /ˈsʜivər/ ▶ **verb** shake slightly and uncontrollably from cold, fear, or excitement.

– SYNONYMS **tremble,** quiver, shake, shudder, quake.

▶ **noun 1** a brief trembling movement. **2** (**the shivers**) a spell of shivering from fear or cold.

– SYNONYMS **shudder,** twitch, start.

– DERIVATIVES **shiv·er·y** adjective.
– ORIGIN perhaps from an Old English word meaning 'jaw.'

> **CHOOSE THE RIGHT WORD**
>
> See **SHAKE**.

shiv·er² ▶ **noun** a splinter or fragment of a material such as glass. ▶ **verb** break into splinters or fragments.
– ORIGIN from a Germanic word meaning 'to split.'

Sho·ah /ˈSHōə, SHōˈä/ ▶ **noun** (in Jewish use) the Holocaust.
– ORIGIN modern Hebrew, 'catastrophe.'

shoal¹ /SHōl/ ▶ **noun** a large number of fish swimming together. ▶ **verb** (of fish) swim together in a shoal.
– ORIGIN probably from Dutch *schōle* 'troop.'

shoal² ▶ **noun 1** an area of shallow water. **2** a submerged sandbank that is visible at low tide. ▶ **verb** (of water) become shallower.
– ORIGIN Old English.

shock¹ /SHäk/ ▶ **noun 1** a sudden upsetting or surprising event or experience: *her illness has come as a great shock to all of us.* **2** an unpleasant feeling of surprise and distress. **3** a serious medical condition associated with a fall in blood pressure, caused by loss of blood, severe injury, or sudden emotional stress. **4** a violent shaking movement caused by an impact, explosion, or earthquake. **5** an electric shock.

> – SYNONYMS **1 blow,** upset, surprise, revelation, bolt from the blue, rude awakening, eye-opener. **2 fright,** scare, start; informal turn. **3 trauma,** collapse, breakdown, post-traumatic stress disorder. **4 vibration,** reverberation, shake, jolt, impact, blow.

▶ **verb 1** make someone feel very surprised and upset. **2** make someone feel outraged or disgusted. **3** cause someone to be in a state of medical shock.

> – SYNONYMS **appall,** horrify, outrage, scandalize, disgust, traumatize, distress, upset, disturb, stun, rock, shake.
> – ANTONYMS delight.

– DERIVATIVES **shock·a·ble** adjective.
– ORIGIN French *choc.*

shock² ▶ **noun** an untidy or thick mass of hair.

> – SYNONYMS **mass,** mane, mop, thatch, head, bush, tangle, cascade.

– ORIGIN uncertain.

shock³ ▶ **noun** a group of sheaves of grain placed upright and supporting each other to allow the grain to dry and ripen.
– ORIGIN perhaps from Dutch, German *schok*.

shock ab·sorb·er ▶ **noun** a device for absorbing jolts and vibrations, especially on a vehicle.

shock·er /ˈSHäkər/ ▶ **noun** informal a thing that shocks, especially through being unacceptable or sensational.

shock·ing /ˈSHäkiNG/ ▶ **adjective 1** causing great surprise or disgust. **2** Brit. informal very bad.

> – SYNONYMS **appalling,** horrifying, horrific, dreadful, awful, terrible, scandalous, outrageous, disgraceful, abominable, atrocious, disgusting, distressing, upsetting, disturbing, startling.

– DERIVATIVES **shock·ing·ly** adverb.

shock·ing pink ▶ **noun** a very bright shade of pink.

shock·proof /ˈSHäk,proof/ ▶ **adjective 1** designed to resist damage when dropped or knocked: *a shockproof watch.* **2** not easily shocked: *her shockproof attitude toward ignorance.*

shock tac·tics ▶ **plural noun** the use of sudden violent or extreme action to shock someone into doing something.

shock ther·a·py (also **shock treatment**) ▶ **noun** treatment of certain mental illnesses by giving controlled electric shocks to the brain.

shock troops ▶ **plural noun** troops trained to carry out sudden attacks.

shock wave ▶ **noun** a moving wave of very high pressure caused by an explosion or by something traveling faster than sound.

shod /SHäd/ past and past participle of **SHOE**.

shod·dy /ˈSHädē/ ▶ **adjective** (**shoddier, shoddiest**) **1** badly made or done. **2** dishonest or underhanded: *a shoddy political deal.*

> – SYNONYMS **poor-quality,** inferior, second-rate, tawdry, jerry-built, cheapjack, gimcrack; informal tatty.

– DERIVATIVES **shod·di·ly** adverb **shod·di·ness** noun.
– ORIGIN unknown.

shoe /SHoo/ ▶ **noun 1** a covering for the foot with a stiff sole, ending just below the ankle. **2** a horseshoe. **3** a socket on a camera for fitting a flash unit. **4** a brake shoe. ▶ **verb** (**shoes, shoeing, shod**) **1** fit a horse with a shoe or shoes. **2** (**be shod**) be wearing shoes of a specified kind: *his large feet were shod in moccasins.*
– PHRASES **be** (or **put oneself**) **in someone else's shoes** imagine oneself in another person's situation.
– ORIGIN Old English.

shoe·box /ˈSHoo,bäks/ ▶ **noun** informal a very small room or space.

shoe·horn /ˈSHoo,hôrn/ ▶ **noun** a curved piece of metal or plastic, used for easing one's heel into a shoe. ▶ **verb** force into a space that is too small: *seven lecturers shoehorned into an office designed for one person.*

shoe·lace /ˈSHoo,lās/ ▶ **noun** a cord or leather strip passed through holes or hooks on opposite sides of a shoe and pulled tight to fasten it.

shoe·mak·er /ˈSHoo,mākər/ ▶ **noun** a person who makes footwear as a profession.

shoe·shine /ˈSHoo,SHīn/ ▶ **noun** an act of polishing someone's shoes.
– DERIVATIVES **shoe·shin·er** noun.

shoe·string /ˈSHoo,striNG/ ▶ **noun 1** a shoelace. **2** informal a small or inadequate amount of money: *living on a shoestring.*

shoe tree ▶ **noun** a shaped block put into a shoe when it is not being worn to keep it in shape.

sho·gun /ˈSHōgən/ ▶ **noun** (formerly, in Japan) a hereditary commander-in-chief of the army.
– DERIVATIVES **sho·gun·ate** /-gənit, -gə,nāt/ noun.
– ORIGIN Japanese.

shone /SHän/ past and past participle of **SHINE**.

shoo /SHoo/ ▶ **exclamation** used to drive away an animal or person. ▶ **verb** (**shoos, shooing, shooed**) drive a person or animal away by saying 'shoo' or otherwise acting in a discouraging way.

shoo-in ▶ **noun** informal a person or thing that is certain to succeed or win.

shook /SHook/ past of **SHAKE**

shoot /SHoot/ ▶ **verb** (past and past part. **shot** /SHät/) **1** kill or wound a person or animal with a bullet or arrow. **2** fire a missile from a weapon. **3** move suddenly and rapidly: *the car shot forward.* **4** glance at or say something to someone quickly or abruptly. **5** film or photograph a scene, movie, etc. **6** (in sports) kick, hit, or throw the ball or puck in an attempt to score a goal. **7** (as adj. **shooting**) (of a pain) sudden and piercing. **8** (of a boat) sweep swiftly down or under rapids, a waterfall, or a bridge. **9** (of a plant) send out buds or shoots.

– SYNONYMS **1 gun down,** mow down, pick off, hit, wound, injure, kill. **2 fire,** open fire, snipe, let fly, bombard, shell, discharge, launch. **3 race,** speed, flash, dash, rush, hurtle, streak, whiz, zoom, career, fly; informal belt, tear, zip, whip, hightail it, barrel. **4 film,** photograph, record.

▶ **noun 1** a new part growing from the main trunk or stem of a tree or other plant. **2** an occasion of taking photographs professionally or making a movie or video: *a fashion shoot.* **3** an occasion when a group of people hunt and shoot game for sport. **4** Brit. land used for shooting game. **5** variant spelling of **CHUTE**[1].

– SYNONYMS **sprout,** bud, runner, tendril, offshoot, cutting.

– PHRASES **shoot the breeze** informal have a casual conversation. **shoot oneself in the foot** informal accidentally make a situation worse for oneself. **shoot one's mouth off** informal talk boastfully or too freely. **the whole shooting match** informal everything. **shoot up** informal inject oneself with a narcotic drug.
– ORIGIN Old English.

shoot·er /'sHo͞otər/ ▶ **noun 1** a person who uses a gun. **2** informal a gun. **3** (in basketball) a player whose role is to attempt to score goals.

shoot·ing gal·ler·y ▶ **noun 1** a room or fairground booth for shooting at targets. **2** informal a place used for taking drugs, especially by injection.

shoot·ing range ▶ **noun** an area provided with targets for the controlled practice of shooting.

shoot·ing star ▶ **noun** a small, rapidly moving meteor that burns up on entering the earth's atmosphere.

shoot-out ▶ **noun 1** a gun battle that continues until one side is killed or defeated. **2** Soccer a tiebreaker decided by each side taking a specified number of penalty kicks.

shop /sHäp/ ▶ **noun 1** a building or part of a building where goods or services are sold; a store. **2** a place where things are manufactured or repaired; a workshop. **3** informal an act of going shopping.

– SYNONYMS **1 store,** retail outlet, mart, boutique, emporium. **2 factory,** plant, workshop, workroom, works, mill.

▶ **verb** (**shops, shopping, shopped**) **1** go to a store or stores to buy goods. **2** (**shop around**) look for the best available price or rate for something.
– PHRASES **talk shop** discuss work matters with a colleague when one is not at work.
– ORIGIN Old French *eschoppe* 'lean-to booth.'

shop·a·hol·ic /ˌsHäpə'hôlik, -'hälik/ ▶ **noun** informal a person with an uncontrollable urge to go shopping.

shop class ▶ **noun** a class in which practical skills such as carpentry or metalwork are taught.

shop floor ▶ **noun** the part of a factory where things are made or assembled.

shop·keep·er /'sHäpˌkēpər/ ▶ **noun** the owner and manager of a store.

shop·lift·ing /'sHäpˌliftiNG/ ▶ **noun** the theft of goods from a store by someone pretending to be a customer.
– DERIVATIVES **shop·lift** verb **shop·lift·er** noun.

shop·per /'sHäpər/ ▶ **noun** a person who is shopping.

shop·ping /'sHäpiNG/ ▶ **noun 1** the buying of goods from stores. **2** goods bought from stores.

shop·ping cen·ter ▶ **noun** a group of stores situated together, sometimes under one roof.

shop stew·ard ▶ **noun** a person elected by workers in a factory to represent them in dealings with management.

shop·worn /'sHäpˌwôrn/ ▶ **adjective** (of an article) dirty or damaged from being displayed or handled in a store.

shore[1] /sHôr/ ▶ **noun 1** the land along the edge of a sea, lake, or large river. **2** (also **shores**) literary a foreign country: *distant shores.*

– SYNONYMS **seashore,** beach, sand(s), shoreline, coast; literary littoral.

– DERIVATIVES **shore·ward** adjective & adverb **shore·wards** adverb.
– PHRASES **on shore** ashore; on land.
– ORIGIN Dutch, German *schōre.*

shore[2] ▶ **verb** (**shore something up**) **1** support or strengthen something weak or in difficulties: *the company will cut its investment program to shore up its shaky finances.* **2** support something with a prop or beam. ▶ **noun** a prop or beam set up against something to support it.
– DERIVATIVES **shor·ing** noun.
– ORIGIN Dutch, German *schore* 'prop.'

shore leave ▶ **noun** leisure time spent ashore by a sailor.

shore·line /'sHôrˌlīn/ ▶ **noun** the line along which the sea or other large body of water meets the land.

shorn /sHôrn/ past participle of **SHEAR.**

short /sHôrt/ ▶ **adjective 1** of a small length in space or time. **2** (of a person) small in height. **3** smaller than is usual or expected. **4** (**short of/on**) not having enough of something. **5** not available in sufficient quantities; scarce. **6** rude and abrupt. **7** (of a ball in sports) traveling a small distance, or not far enough. **8** (of odds in betting) reflecting a high level of probability. **9** (of a vowel) pronounced in a way that takes a shorter time than a long vowel in the same position (e.g., in standard English the vowel sound in *good*). **10** (of pastry) containing a high proportion of fat to flour and therefore crumbly.

– SYNONYMS **1** *a short time* **brief,** fleeting, short-lived, momentary, passing, lightning, quick, rapid, cursory. **2** *short people* **small,** little, petite, tiny, diminutive, elfin; Scottish wee; informal pint-sized, knee-high to a grasshopper. **3** *a short report* **concise,** brief, succinct, to the point, compact, pithy, abridged, abbreviated, condensed. **4** (**short of/on**) *we are short of nurses* **deficient in,** lacking, in need of, low on, missing; informal strapped for, minus. **5** *money is a bit short* **scarce,** scant, meager, sparse, insufficient, deficient, inadequate, lacking. **6** *he was rather short with her* **curt,** sharp, abrupt, blunt, brusque, terse, offhand.
– ANTONYMS tall, long, plentiful.

▶ **adverb** not as far as the point aimed at: *you pitch the ball short.*
▶ **noun** a short movie as opposed to a feature film.
▶ **verb** experience a short circuit.
– DERIVATIVES **short·ish** adjective **short·ness** noun.
– PHRASES **be caught short** be put at a disadvantage.

bring (or **pull**) **someone up short** make someone stop or pause abruptly. **for short** as an abbreviation or nickname. **in short** to sum up; briefly. **in short order** immediately; rapidly: *the debt will be totally paid off in short order*. **in the short run** (or **term**) in the near future. **in short supply** (of a commodity) scarce. **make short work of** achieve, eat, or drink something quickly. **run short** not have enough of something. **short for** an abbreviation or nickname for. **short of 1** less than. **2** not reaching as far as. **3** without going so far as doing something extreme. **a short one** a drink of beer or liquor served in a measure smaller than usual. **stop short** stop suddenly.
– ORIGIN Old English.

short·age /ˈsʜôrtij/ ▶ **noun** a situation in which there is not enough of something needed.

– SYNONYMS **scarcity,** dearth, poverty, insufficiency, deficiency, inadequacy, famine, lack, deficit, shortfall.
– ANTONYMS abundance.

short·bread /ˈsʜôrtˌbred/ ▶ **noun** a crisp, rich, crumbly type of cookie made with butter, flour, and sugar.

short·cake /ˈsʜôrtˌkāk/ ▶ **noun** a small circular sponge cake or cake made of biscuit dough that is served with fruit and whipped cream as a dessert.

short·change ▶ **verb 1** cheat someone by giving them less than the correct change. **2** treat unfairly by withholding something deserved: *women have been shortchanged by our education system*.

short cir·cuit ▶ **noun** a faulty connection in an electrical circuit in which the current flows along a shorter route than it should. ▶ **verb** (**short-circuit**) **1** cause or suffer a short circuit. **2** shorten a process by using a more direct but irregular method.

short·com·ing /ˈsʜôrtˌkəmiɴɢ/ ▶ **noun** a failure to meet a certain standard; a fault or weakness: *the shortcomings of the legal system*.

– SYNONYMS **fault,** defect, flaw, imperfection, deficiency, limitation, failing, drawback, weakness, weak point.
– ANTONYMS strength.

short·cut ▶ **noun 1** an alternative route that is shorter than the one usually taken. **2** a way of achieving something that is quicker than usual.

short·en /ˈsʜôrtn/ ▶ **verb** make or become shorter.

– SYNONYMS **abbreviate,** abridge, condense, contract, compress, reduce, shrink, diminish, cut (down), trim, pare (down), prune, curtail, truncate.
– ANTONYMS lengthen.

short·en·ing /ˈsʜôrtniɴɢ, ˈsʜôrtn-iɴɢ/ ▶ **noun** fat used for making pastry.

short·fall /ˈsʜôrtˌfôl/ ▶ **noun** a situation in which there is less of something than is required or expected.

short fuse ▶ **noun** informal a quick temper.

short·hand /ˈsʜôrtˌhand/ ▶ **noun 1** a method of rapid writing by means of abbreviations and symbols, used for recording what someone is saying. **2** a short and simple way of expressing or referring to something: *she learned that 'HS' is military shorthand for mustard gas*.

short-hand·ed ▶ **adjective** not having enough or the usual number of staff.

short haul ▶ **noun** a relatively short distance in terms of travel or the transport of goods.

short·horn /ˈsʜôrtˌhôrn/ ▶ **noun** a breed of cattle with short horns.

short·list /ˈsʜôrtˌlist/ ▶ **noun** a list of selected candidates from which a final choice is made. ▶ **verb** put someone or something on a shortlist.

short-lived /ˈlivd, ˈlīvd/ ▶ **adjective** lasting only a short time.

short·ly /ˈsʜôrtlē/ ▶ **adverb 1** in a short time; soon. **2** abruptly or sharply.

– SYNONYMS **soon,** presently, momentarily, in a little while, at any moment, in a minute, in next to no time, before long, by and by; informal anon, any time now, in a sec, in a jiffy.

short or·der ▶ **noun** an order or dish of food that can be quickly prepared and served.
– PHRASES **in short order** see **SHORT**.

short-range ▶ **adjective 1** able to be used or be effective only over short distances. **2** relating to a period of future time that is near to the present: *a short-range weather forecast*.

shorts /sʜôrts/ ▶ **plural noun 1** short pants that reach to the knees or thighs. **2** men's underpants.

short shrift ▶ **noun** abrupt and unsympathetic treatment: *he gave short shrift to admirers who praised his courage*.
– ORIGIN first meaning 'little time allowed for making confession between being condemned and punished'; from **SHRIVE**.

short·sight·ed /ˈsʜôrtˈsītid/ ▶ **adjective 1** not thinking carefully about the consequences of something. **2** Brit. nearsighted.
– DERIVATIVES **short·sight·ed·ly** adverb **short·sight·ed·ness** noun.

short-staffed ▶ **adjective** not having enough or the usual number of staff.

short·stop /ˈsʜôrtˌstäp/ ▶ **noun** Baseball a fielder positioned between second and third base.

short-tem·pered ▶ **adjective** having a tendency to lose one's temper quickly.

short-term ▶ **adjective** occurring over or relating to a short period of time: *it might be a wise short-term investment*.

short-term·ism /ˈtərmizəm/ ▶ **noun** a policy of gaining profit or benefit in the near future without concern for more far-reaching effects.

short·wave ▶ **noun 1** a radio wave of a wavelength between about 10 and 100 meters (and a frequency of about 3 to 30 megahertz). **2** broadcasting using a wavelength between about 10 and 100 meters.

short-wind·ed /ˈwindid/ ▶ **adjective** out of breath, or tending to run out of breath quickly.

short·y /ˈsʜôrtē/ (also **shortie**) ▶ **noun** (pl. **shorties**) informal **1** a short person. **2** a short dress, nightdress, or raincoat.

Sho·sho·ne /sʜōˈsʜōnē/ ▶ **noun** (pl. same or **Shoshones**) a member of an American Indian people living chiefly in Wyoming, Idaho, and Nevada.
– ORIGIN unknown.

shot[1] /sʜät/ ▶ **noun 1** the firing of a gun or cannon. **2** a hit, stroke, or kick of the ball in sports, especially as an attempt to score. **3** a person with a specified level of ability in shooting: *he was an excellent shot*. **4** a photograph. **5** informal an attempt to do something. **6** a film sequence photographed continuously by one camera. **7** (also **lead shot**) tiny lead pellets used in a single charge or cartridge in a shotgun. **8** (pl. same) a ball of stone or metal fired from a large gun or cannon. **9** a heavy ball thrown by a shot-putter. **10** the launch of a rocket: *a moon shot*. **11** informal a small drink of liquor. **12** informal an injection of a drug or vaccine.

– SYNONYMS **1 report,** crack, bang, blast; (**shots**) gunfire, firing. **2** *the winning shot* **stroke,** hit, strike, kick, throw. **3 marksman,** markswoman, shooter. **4 photograph,** photo, snap, snapshot, picture, print, slide, still.

– PHRASES **give it one's best shot** informal do the best that one can. **like a shot** informal without hesitation. **a shot in the arm** informal a source of encouragement.
– ORIGIN Old English.

shot² past and past participle of **SHOOT** ▶ **adjective** **1** (of cloth) woven with a warp and weft of different colors, giving a contrasting effect when looked at from different angles. **2** interspersed with a different color: *dark hair shot with silver*. **3** informal ruined or worn out.
– PHRASES **shot through with** filled with a quality or feature.

shot glass ▶ **noun** a small glass for serving liquor.

shot·gun /ˈsʜätˌgən/ ▶ **noun** a gun for firing small shot at short range.

shot·gun wed·ding (also **shotgun marriage**) ▶ **noun** informal an enforced or hurried wedding, especially because the bride is pregnant.

shot put ▶ **noun** an athletic contest in which a very heavy round ball is thrown as far as possible.
– DERIVATIVES **shot-put·ter** noun **shot-put·ting** noun.

should /sʜŏŏd/ ▶ **modal verb** (3rd sing. **should**) **1** used to indicate what is right or ought to be done. **2** used to indicate what is probable. **3** formal used to state what would happen if something else was the case: *if you should change your mind, I'll be at the hotel*.
– ORIGIN past of **SHALL**.

shoul·der /ˈsʜōldər/ ▶ **noun** **1** the joint between the upper arm or forelimb and the main part of the body. **2** a cut of meat from the upper foreleg and shoulder blade of an animal. **3** a steep sloping side of a mountain. ▶ **verb** **1** put something heavy over one's shoulder or shoulders to carry it. **2** take on a responsibility. **3** push someone or something out of one's way with one's shoulder.

– SYNONYMS **1 take on (oneself),** undertake, accept, assume, bear, carry. **2 push,** shove, thrust, jostle, force, bulldoze, bundle.

– DERIVATIVES **shoul·dered** adjective.
– PHRASES **put one's shoulder to the wheel** set to work in a determined way. **shoulder arms** hold a rifle against the right side of the body, barrel upward. **shoulder to shoulder** side by side or acting together.
– ORIGIN Old English.

shoul·der bag ▶ **noun** a bag with a long strap that is hung over the shoulder.

shoul·der blade ▶ **noun** either of the large, flat triangular bones at the top of the back; the scapula.

shoul·der pad ▶ **noun** a pad sewn into the shoulder of a jacket, dress, etc., to provide shape or give protection.

shoul·der strap ▶ **noun** **1** a narrow strip of material going over the shoulder from front to back of a dress or top. **2** a long strap attached to a bag for carrying it over the shoulder.

should·n't /ˈsʜŏŏdnt/ ▶ **contraction** should not.

shout /sʜout/ ▶ **verb** **1** speak or call out very loudly. **2** (**shout at**) speak angrily and loudly to someone. **3** (**shout someone down**) prevent someone from speaking or being heard by shouting.

– SYNONYMS **yell,** cry (out), call (out), roar, howl, bellow, bawl, raise one's voice; informal holler.
– ANTONYMS whisper.

▶ **noun** a loud cry or call.

– SYNONYMS **yell,** cry, call, roar, howl, bellow, bawl; informal holler.

– ORIGIN perhaps from **SHOOT**.

shout-out ▶ **noun** informal a message of congratulation, support, or appreciation.

shove /sʜəv/ ▶ **verb** **1** push someone or something roughly. **2** put something somewhere carelessly or roughly. **3** (**shove off**) informal go away. **4** (**shove off**) push away from the shore in a boat.

– SYNONYMS **push,** thrust, propel, drive, force, ram, knock, elbow, shoulder, jostle.

▶ **noun** a strong push.
– ORIGIN Old English.

shov·el /ˈsʜəvəl/ ▶ **noun** a tool resembling a spade with a broad blade and upturned sides, used for moving earth, snow, etc. ▶ **verb** (**shovels, shoveling, shoveled**) **1** move earth, snow, etc., with a shovel. **2** (**shovel something down/in**) informal eat food quickly and in large quantities.
– ORIGIN Old English.

shov·el·er /ˈsʜəv(ə)lər/ (also **shoveller**) ▶ **noun** a duck with a long, broad bill.

show /sʜō/ ▶ **verb** (past part. **shown** or **showed**) **1** be or make visible: *wrinkles were starting to show on her face*. **2** offer something to be inspected or viewed. **3** display a quality, emotion, or characteristic. **4** be evidence of or prove something. **5** make someone understand something by explaining it or doing it oneself. **6** lead or guide. **7** (also **show up**) informal arrive for an appointment. **8** present an image of: *a postcard showing Mount Etna*. **9** treat someone in a particular way.

– SYNONYMS **1 be visible,** be seen, be in view, be obvious. **2 display,** exhibit, put on show, put on display, put on view. **3** *he showed his frustration* **manifest,** exhibit, reveal, convey, communicate, make known, express, make plain, make obvious, disclose, evince, betray. **4** *recent events show this to be true* **prove,** demonstrate, confirm, substantiate, corroborate, verify, bear out. **5** *I'll show you how to make a daisy chain* **demonstrate,** explain, describe, illustrate, teach, instruct. **6** *she showed them to their seats* **escort,** accompany, take, conduct, lead, usher, guide, direct. **7** *they never showed* **turn up,** appear, arrive, come, get here/there, put in an appearance, materialize.
– ANTONYMS conceal.

▶ **noun** **1** a theatrical performance, especially a musical. **2** a light entertainment program on television or radio. **3** an event or competition involving the public display of animals, plants, or products. **4** an impressive or attractive sight or display. **5** a display of a quality or feeling. **6** an outward display intended to give a false impression. **7** a ridiculous display: *don't make a show of yourself*. **8** informal a project or organization: *I run the show*.

– SYNONYMS **1 program,** broadcast, presentation, production. **2 exhibition,** exhibit, display, fair, exposition, festival, parade. **3 display,** array, sight, spectacle. **4 appearance,** outward appearance, image, pretense, (false) front, guise, pose, affectation, semblance.

– PHRASES **for show** for the sake of appearance rather than use. **get the show on the road** informal begin a project or enterprise. **show one's hand** reveal one's plans. **show off** try to impress others by talking about one's abilities or possessions. **show something off** display something that one is proud of. **show of hands** a vote carried out by the raising of hands. **show oneself** (or **one's face**) appear in public. **show someone around** point out interesting features in a place or building to someone. **show someone/thing up 1** reveal someone or something as being bad or at fault. **2** informal embarrass or humiliate someone.
– ORIGIN Old English, 'look at, inspect.'

show biz /'shō,biz/ ▶ **noun** informal show business.
– DERIVATIVES **show·biz·zy** adjective.

show·boat /'shō,bōt/ ▶ **noun 1** a river steamboat on which theatrical performances are given. **2** informal a show-off; an exhibitionist. ▶ **verb** informal show off: (as adj. **showboating**) *a lot of showboating politicians.*
– DERIVATIVES **show·boat·er** noun.

show busi·ness ▶ **noun** the world of movies, television, pop music, and the theater as a profession or industry.

show·case /'shō,kās/ ▶ **noun 1** an occasion for presenting someone or something favorably to the public. **2** a glass case for displaying articles in a store or museum. ▶ **verb** put on display: *he made a short film to showcase his directing talents.*

show·down /'shō,doun/ ▶ **noun** a final test or confrontation intended to settle a dispute.

– SYNONYMS **confrontation,** clash, face-off.

show·er /'shou(-ə)r/ ▶ **noun 1** a brief fall of rain or snow. **2** a mass of small things falling at once. **3** a large number of things arriving at the same time: *a shower of awards.* **4** a piece of equipment that creates a spray of water under which a person stands to wash. **5** an act of washing in a shower. **6** a party at which presents are given to a woman who is about to get married or have a baby.

– SYNONYMS **1 fall,** drizzle, sprinkling, flurry. **2 volley,** hail, salvo, barrage.

▶ **verb 1** fall or cause to fall in a shower. **2** (**shower someone with** or **shower something on**) give a large number of things to someone. **3** wash oneself in a shower.

– SYNONYMS **1 rain,** fall, hail. **2 deluge,** flood, inundate, swamp, overwhelm, snow under.

– ORIGIN Old English.

show·er·proof /'shou(-ə)r,prōōf/ ▶ **adjective** (of a raincoat or jacket) able to keep out light rain.

show·er·y /'shou(-ə)rē/ ▶ **adjective** with frequent showers of rain.

show·girl /'shō,gərl/ ▶ **noun** an actress who sings and dances in a musical or variety show.

show·ground /'shō,ground/ ▶ **noun** an area of land on which a show takes place.

show·ing /'shō-iNG/ ▶ **noun 1** a presentation of a movie or television program. **2** a performance of a particular quality: *poor opinion poll showings.*

show jump·ing ▶ **noun** the competitive sport of riding horses over a course of fences and other obstacles in an arena.
– DERIVATIVES **show jump·er** noun.

show·man /'shōmən/ ▶ **noun** (pl. **showmen**) **1** the manager or presenter of a circus, fair, etc. **2** a person who is skilled at entertaining people or gaining their attention.
– DERIVATIVES **show·man·ship** /-,ship/ noun.

shown /shōn/ past participle of **SHOW**.

show-off ▶ **noun** informal a person who tries to impress others by talking about their own abilities or possessions.

– SYNONYMS **exhibitionist,** extrovert, poser, poseur, swaggerer, self-publicist.

show·piece /'shō,pēs/ ▶ **noun 1** an outstanding example of something: *the harbor is one of the showpieces of the city.* **2** an item of work put on exhibition or display.

show·place /'shō,plās/ ▶ **noun** a beautiful or interesting place that attracts many visitors.

show·room /'shō,rōōm, -,rŏŏm/ ▶ **noun** a room used to display cars, furniture, or other goods for sale.

show-stop·per ▶ **noun** informal something that is very impressive, striking, or appealing.
– DERIVATIVES **show-stop·ping** adjective.

show tri·al ▶ **noun** a trial that is held in public to produce a preordained verdict and to influence or satisfy public opinion, rather than to ensure that justice is done.

show·y /'shō-ē/ ▶ **adjective** (**showier, showiest**) very bright or colorful and attracting much attention.

– SYNONYMS **ostentatious,** flamboyant, gaudy, garish, brash, vulgar, loud, fancy, ornate; informal flash, flashy.
– ANTONYMS restrained.

– DERIVATIVES **show·i·ly** adverb **show·i·ness** noun.

shrank /shrangk/ past of **SHRINK**.

shrap·nel /'shrapnəl/ ▶ **noun** small metal fragments thrown out by the explosion of a shell, bomb, etc.
– ORIGIN named after the British soldier General Henry *Shrapnel*, inventor of shells that explode with a shower of shrapnel.

shred /shred/ ▶ **noun 1** a strip of material that has been torn, cut, or scraped from something larger. **2** a very small amount: *not a shred of evidence.*

– SYNONYMS **1 tatter,** ribbon, rag, fragment, sliver, snippet, remnant. **2 scrap,** bit, speck, particle, ounce, jot, crumb, fragment, grain, drop, trace.

▶ **verb** (**shreds, shredding, shredded**) tear or cut something into shreds.

– SYNONYMS **grate,** cut up, tear up.

– ORIGIN Old English.

shred·der /'shredər/ ▶ **noun 1** a machine or other device for shredding something, especially documents. **2** informal a snowboarder.

shrew /shrōō/ ▶ **noun 1** a small mammal resembling a mouse, with a long pointed snout and tiny eyes. **2** a bad-tempered woman.
– ORIGIN Old English.

shrewd /shrōōd/ ▶ **adjective** having or showing sharp powers of judgment; astute: *he's a shrewd businessman who knows how to make money.*

– SYNONYMS **astute,** sharp, smart, intelligent, clever, canny, perceptive; informal on the ball.
– ANTONYMS stupid.

– DERIVATIVES **shrewd·ly** adverb **shrewd·ness** noun.

– ORIGIN from **SHREW** in the former sense 'evil person or thing.'

CHOOSE THE RIGHT WORD

See **KEEN**[1].

shrew·ish /ˈSHrōōisH/ ▶ **adjective** (of a woman) bad-tempered or nagging.
– DERIVATIVES **shrew·ish·ly** adverb **shrew·ish·ness** noun.

shriek /SHrēk/ ▶ **verb** make a high-pitched piercing cry or sound.

– SYNONYMS **scream,** screech, squeal, squawk, roar, howl, shout, yelp.

▶ **noun** a high-pitched piercing cry or sound.

– SYNONYMS **scream,** screech, squeal, squawk, roar, howl, shout, yelp.

– DERIVATIVES **shriek·er** noun.
– ORIGIN imitating the sound.

shrike /SHrīk/ ▶ **noun** a songbird with a hooked bill that often impales its prey on thorns.
– ORIGIN imitating its call.

shrill /SHril/ ▶ **adjective** **1** (of a voice or sound) high-pitched and piercing. **2** (of a complaint or demand) loud and forceful.

– SYNONYMS **high-pitched,** piercing, high, sharp, ear-piercing, ear-splitting, penetrating.

▶ **verb** make a high-pitched piercing noise.
– DERIVATIVES **shrill·ness** noun **shril·ly** adverb.
– ORIGIN Germanic.

shrimp /SHrimp/ ▶ **noun** **1** (pl. same or **shrimps**) a small edible shellfish with ten legs. **2** informal, derogatory a small weak person. ▶ **verb** (often as n. **shrimping**) fish for shrimp.
– DERIVATIVES **shrimp·er** noun.
– ORIGIN probably from German *schrempen* 'to wrinkle.'

shrine /SHrīn/ ▶ **noun** **1** a place regarded as holy because it is connected to a holy person or event. **2** a place or receptacle containing a religious statue or holy object. **3** a place regarded as notable because it is associated with a particular person or thing: *the room was a shrine to middle-class taste*.
– ORIGIN Old English, 'cabinet, chest.'

shrink /SHriNGk/ ▶ **verb** (past **shrank** /SHraNGk/; past part. **shrunk** /SHrəNGk/ or (especially as adj.) **shrunken** /ˈSHrəNGkən/) **1** become or make smaller in size or amount. **2** (of clothes or material) become smaller as a result of being washed in water that is too hot. **3** move back or away in fear or disgust. **4** (**shrink from**) be unwilling to do: *I don't shrink from my responsibilities*.

– SYNONYMS **1 get smaller,** contract, diminish, lessen, reduce, decrease, dwindle, decline, fall off. **2 recoil,** shy away, flinch, be averse, be afraid, hesitate.
– ANTONYMS expand, increase.

▶ **noun** informal a psychiatrist.
– DERIVATIVES **shrink·a·ble** adjective.
– ORIGIN Old English; the noun is from *headshrinker*.

shrink·age /ˈSHriNGkij/ ▶ **noun** **1** the process of shrinking or the amount by which something has shrunk. **2** an allowance made for reduction in the takings of a business due to theft or wastage.

shrink·ing vi·o·let ▶ **noun** informal a very shy person.

shrink-wrap ▶ **verb** package an object in clinging plastic film. ▶ **noun** (**shrink wrap**) clinging plastic film used to package an object.

shrive /SHrīv/ ▶ **verb** (past **shrove** /SHrōv/; past part. **shriven** /ˈSHrivən/) old use (of a priest) hear a person's confession, give them a religious duty, and declare them free from sin.
– ORIGIN Old English.

shriv·el /ˈSHrivəl/ ▶ **verb** (**shrivels, shriveling, shriveled**) wrinkle and shrink through loss of moisture.

– SYNONYMS **wither,** shrink, wilt, dry up, dehydrate, parch, frazzle.

– ORIGIN perhaps Scandinavian.

shroud /SHroud/ ▶ **noun** **1** a length of cloth in which a dead person is wrapped for burial. **2** a thing that surrounds or hides someone or something: *a shroud of mist often envelops the island*. **3** (**shrouds**) a set of ropes supporting the mast or topmast of a sailboat.

– SYNONYMS **covering,** cover, cloak, mantle, blanket, layer, cloud, veil, winding sheet.

▶ **verb** surround so as to cover or hide: *his early life is shrouded in mystery*.

– SYNONYMS **cover,** envelop, veil, cloak, blanket, screen, conceal, hide, mask, obscure.

– ORIGIN Old English, 'garment, clothing.'

shrove /SHrōv/ past of **SHRIVE**.

Shrove Tues·day /SHrōv/ ▶ **noun** the day before Ash Wednesday.

shrub /SHrəb/ ▶ **noun** a woody plant that is smaller than a tree and divided into separate stems at or near the ground.
– DERIVATIVES **shrub·by** adjective.
– ORIGIN Old English.

shrub·ber·y /ˈSHrəb(ə)rē/ ▶ **noun** (pl. **shrubberies**) **1** shrubs collectively. **2** an area planted with shrubs.

shrug /SHrəg/ ▶ **verb** (**shrugs, shrugging, shrugged**) **1** raise one's shoulders slightly and briefly as a sign that one does not know or care about something. **2** (**shrug something off**) dismiss something as unimportant. ▶ **noun** **1** an act of shrugging one's shoulders. **2** a woman's close-fitting cardigan or jacket, cut short at the front and back so that only the arms and shoulders are covered.
– ORIGIN unknown.

shrunk /SHrəNGk/ (also **shrunken**) past participle of **SHRINK**.

shtick /SHtik/ ▶ **noun** informal **1** a performer's routine or gimmick. **2** a person's talent or typical behavior: *he has developed a distinctive courtroom shtick*.
– ORIGIN German *Stück* 'piece.'

shuck /SHək/ ▶ **verb** **1** remove the husks or shells from corn or shellfish. **2** informal get rid of something. **3** informal take off an item of clothing. ▶ **noun** **1** the husk of an ear of corn. **2** the shell of an oyster, scallop, or clam.
– ORIGIN unknown.

shucks /SHəks/ ▶ **exclamation** informal used to express surprise, regret, etc.

shud·der /ˈSHədər/ ▶ **verb** tremble or shake violently, especially as a result of fear or disgust.

– SYNONYMS **shake,** shiver, tremble, quiver.

▶ **noun** an act of shuddering.

– SYNONYMS **shake,** shiver, tremor, trembling, quivering, vibration.

– DERIVATIVES **shud·der·y** adjective.
– ORIGIN Dutch *schüderen*.

CHOOSE THE RIGHT WORD

See **SHAKE**.

shuf·fle /ˈSHəfəl/ ▶ **verb 1** walk without lifting the feet completely from the ground. **2** move restlessly while sitting or standing. **3** rearrange a deck of cards by sliding them over each other quickly. **4** rearrange people or things. **5** (**shuffle through**) look through a number of things hurriedly.

– SYNONYMS **1 shamble,** hobble, limp, drag one's feet. **2 mix (up),** rearrange, jumble (up), reorganize.

▶ **noun 1** a shuffling walk or sound. **2** an act of shuffling a deck of cards. **3** a rearrangement of people or things; a reshuffle. **4** a dance performed with a quick dragging movement of the feet.
– DERIVATIVES **shuf·fler** noun.
– ORIGIN perhaps from German *schuffeln* 'walk clumsily,' also 'deal dishonestly, shuffle cards.'

shuf·fle·board /ˈSHəfəlˌbôrd/ ▶ **noun** a game played by pushing disks with a long-handled cue over a marked surface.

shun /SHən/ ▶ **verb** (**shuns, shunning, shunned**) avoid, ignore, or reject: *he shunned fashionable society.*

– SYNONYMS **avoid,** steer clear of, give a wide berth to, have nothing to do with; informal freeze out, give the cold shoulder to.
– ANTONYMS welcome.

– ORIGIN Old English, 'hate, shrink back in fear.'

shunt /SHənt/ ▶ **verb 1** slowly push or pull a railroad vehicle or vehicles from one set of tracks to another. **2** push or shove someone or something. **3** divert to a less important place or position: *amateurs were gradually being shunted to filing jobs.* ▶ **noun 1** an act of shunting. **2** an electrical conductor joining two points of a circuit. **3** Surgery an alternative path for the flow of blood or other body fluid.
– DERIVATIVES **shunt·er** noun.
– ORIGIN perhaps from **SHUN**.

shush /SHŏŏSH, SHəSH/ ▶ **exclamation** be quiet. ▶ **noun 1** an utterance of 'shush.' **2** a soft swishing or rustling sound. ▶ **verb 1** tell or signal someone to be silent. **2** move with a soft swishing or rustling sound.
– ORIGIN imitating the sound.

shut /SHət/ ▶ **verb** (**shuts, shutting, shut**) **1** move something into position to block an opening. **2** (**shut someone/thing in/out**) keep someone or something in or out by closing a door, gate, etc. **3** prevent access to a place or along a route. **4** stop operating for business: *we shut the store for lunch.* **5** close a book, curtains, etc.

– SYNONYMS **close,** pull to, push to, slam, fasten, put the lid on, lock, secure.
– ANTONYMS open.

– PHRASES **be** (or **get**) **shut of** informal be (or get) rid of. **shut down** stop operating or opening for business. **shut something off** stop something from flowing or working. **shut something out** prevent oneself from thinking about something. **shut up** informal stop talking.
– ORIGIN Old English, 'put a bolt in position to hold fast.'

shut·down /ˈSHətˌdoun/ ▶ **noun** an act of closing a factory or of turning off a machine.

shut-eye ▶ **noun** informal sleep.

shut-in ▶ **noun 1** a person confined indoors, especially as a result of physical or mental disability. **2** a state or period in which an oil or gas well has available but unused capacity.

shut·out /ˈSHətˌout/ ▶ **noun** a competition or game in which the losing side fails to score.

shut·ter /ˈSHətər/ ▶ **noun 1** each of a pair of hinged panels fixed inside or outside a window that can be closed for security or to keep out the light. **2** a device that opens and closes to expose the film in a camera. ▶ **verb** close the shutters of a window or building.

shut·tle /ˈSHətl/ ▶ **noun 1** a form of transportation that travels regularly between two places. **2** (in weaving) a bobbin used for carrying the weft thread across the cloth between the warp threads. **3** a bobbin carrying the lower thread in a sewing machine. ▶ **verb** travel or transport someone or something regularly between places.

– SYNONYMS **commute,** run, ply, go/travel back and forth, ferry.

– ORIGIN Old English, 'dart, missile.'

shut·tle·cock /ˈSHətlˌkäk/ ▶ **noun** a light cone-shaped object consisting of a rounded piece of cork with feathers attached, or a similar object made of plastic, struck with rackets in badminton.

shut·tle di·plo·ma·cy ▶ **noun** negotiations conducted by a person who travels between two or more countries that are reluctant to hold direct discussions.

shy[1] /SHī/ ▶ **adjective** (**shyer, shyest**) **1** nervous or timid in the company of other people. **2** (**shy about/of**) slow or reluctant to do something. **3** (in combination) having a specified dislike: *camera-shy.* **4** (**shy of**) informal less than; short of: *the car weighs just shy of 3,000 pounds.*

– SYNONYMS **bashful,** diffident, timid, reserved, introverted, retiring, self-effacing, withdrawn.
– ANTONYMS confident.

▶ **verb** (**shies, shying, shied**) **1** (usu. **shy away from**) avoid something through nervousness or lack of confidence. **2** (of a horse) suddenly turn aside in fright.

– SYNONYMS (**shy away from**) **flinch at,** recoil at, hang back from, be reluctant about, balk at, have misgivings about.

– DERIVATIVES **shy·ly** adverb **shy·ness** noun.
– ORIGIN Old English.

shy[2] ▶ **verb** (**shies, shying, shied**) throw something at a target.
– ORIGIN unknown.

shy·ster /ˈSHīstər/ ▶ **noun** informal a dishonest or deceitful person, especially a lawyer.
– ORIGIN said to be from *Scheuster*, the name of a lawyer.

SI ▶ **abbreviation** Système International, the international system of units of measurement based on the meter, kilogram, second, ampere, kelvin, candela, and mole.

Si ▶ **symbol** the chemical element silicon.

Si·a·mese /ˌsīəˈmēz/ ▶ **noun** (pl. same) **1** (also **Siamese cat**) a breed of cat that has short pale fur with a darker face, ears, feet, and tail. **2** dated a person from Siam (now Thailand) in SE Asia. ▶ **adjective** dated relating to Thailand.

Siam·ese twins ▶ **plural noun** twins whose bodies are joined at birth.
– ORIGIN with reference to the *Siamese* men Chang and Eng, who were joined in this way.

USAGE

The technical term is **conjoined twins**.

sib /sib/ ▶ noun a brother or sister; a sibling.
– ORIGIN from Old English, 'related by birth or descent.'

Si·be·ri·an /sī'bi(ə)rēən/ ▶ noun a person from Siberia. ▶ adjective relating to Siberia.

sib·i·lant /'sibələnt/ ▶ adjective making a soft hissing sound. ▶ noun a speech sound made with a hissing effect, for example *s*, *sh*.
– DERIVATIVES **sib·i·lance** noun.
– ORIGIN from Latin *sibilare* 'hiss.'

sib·ling /'sibliNG/ ▶ noun a brother or sister.
– ORIGIN Old English, 'relative.'

sib·yl /'sibəl/ ▶ noun (in ancient Greece and Rome) a woman supposedly able to pass on the messages and prophecies of a god.
– DERIVATIVES **sib·yl·line** /'sibəˌlīn, -ˌlēn/ adjective.
– ORIGIN Greek *Sibulla*.

sic[1] /sik/ ▶ adverb (after a copied or quoted word that appears odd or wrong) written exactly as it stands in the original.
– ORIGIN Latin, 'so, thus.'

sic[2] (also **sick**) ▶ verb (**sics, sicced, siccing,** or **sicks, sicked, sicking**) **1** set a dog or other animal on someone or something. **2** informal set someone to pursue, keep watch on, or accompany someone else.
– ORIGIN dialect form of **SEEK**.

Si·cil·ian /si'silyən/ ▶ noun a person from Sicily. ▶ adjective relating to Sicily.

sick[1] /sik/ ▶ adjective **1** affected by physical or mental illness. **2** feeling nauseous and wanting to vomit. **3** (**sick of**) bored by or annoyed with someone or something because one has had too much of them. **4** informal (of humor) dealing with unpleasant subjects in a cruel or upsetting way. **5** informal behaving in an abnormal or cruel way.

> – SYNONYMS **1 ill,** unwell, poorly, ailing, indisposed, out of sorts; informal under the weather, laid up. **2 nauseous,** queasy, bilious, green around the gills. **3** (**sick of**) *I'm sick of this music* **fed up with,** bored with, tired of, weary of. **4 macabre,** tasteless, ghoulish, morbid, black, gruesome, perverted, cruel.
> – ANTONYMS well.

▶ noun Brit. informal vomit.
▶ verb (**sick something up**) Brit. informal bring something up by vomiting.
– PHRASES **be sick 1** be ill. **2** vomit.
– ORIGIN Old English.

sick[2] ▶ verb variant spelling of **SIC**[2].
– ORIGIN dialect variant of **SEEK**.

sick·bay /'sikˌbā/ ▶ noun a room or building in a school or on a ship that is set aside for sick people.

sick·bed /'sikˌbed/ ▶ noun the bed of a person who is ill.

sick build·ing syn·drome ▶ noun a condition affecting office workers, including headaches and breathing problems, which is said to be caused by factors such as poor ventilation.

sick·en /'sikən/ ▶ verb **1** make someone feel disgusted or appalled: *the stench sickened him* | (as adj. **sickening**) *ooh, that smell is sickening*. **2** become ill.

> – SYNONYMS **1 nauseate,** make sick, turn someone's stomach, disgust, revolt, repel, appall; informal gross out. **2** (as adj. **sickening**) **nauseating,** stomach-turning, repulsive, revolting, disgusting, offensive, off-putting, distasteful, obscene, gruesome, grisly; informal gross. **3 fall ill,** become infected, be stricken.

– DERIVATIVES **sick·en·ing·ly** adverb.

sick·le /'sikəl/ ▶ noun a farming tool with a short handle and a semicircular blade, used for cutting cereals or grass.
– ORIGIN Latin *secula*.

sick leave ▶ noun permission to be absent from work because of illness.

sick·le-cell a·ne·mi·a (also **sickle-cell disease**) ▶ noun a severe hereditary form of anemia in which the red blood cells are distorted into a crescent shape at low oxygen levels.

sick·ly /'siklē/ ▶ adjective (**sicklier, sickliest**) **1** often ill; in poor health. **2** showing or causing poor health. **3** (of flavor, color, etc.) so bright or sweet as to be unpleasant or make one feel sick. **4** excessively sentimental.

> – SYNONYMS **1 unhealthy,** in poor health, delicate, frail, weak. **2 pale,** wan, pasty, sallow, pallid, ashen, anemic. **3 sentimental,** mawkish, cloying, sugary, syrupy, saccharine; informal sappy, schmaltzy, cheesy, corny.
> – ANTONYMS healthy.

– DERIVATIVES **sick·li·ness** noun.

sick·ness /'siknis/ ▶ noun **1** the state of being ill. **2** a particular type of illness or disease. **3** nausea or vomiting.

> – SYNONYMS **1 illness,** disease, ailment, infection, malady, infirmity; informal bug, virus. **2 nausea,** biliousness, queasiness, vomiting, retching; informal throwing up, puking.

sick·o /'sikō/ ▶ noun (pl. **sickos**) informal a perverted person.

sick·room /'sikˌrōōm/ ▶ noun a room occupied by or set apart for people who are unwell.

side /sīd/ ▶ noun **1** a position to the left or right of an object, place, or central point. **2** either of the two halves into which something can be divided: *she lay on her side of the bed*. **3** an upright or sloping surface of a structure or object that is not the top, bottom, front, or back. **4** each of the flat surfaces of a solid object. **5** either of the two surfaces of something flat and thin, e.g., paper. **6** a part or area near the edge of something. **7** a person or group opposing another or others in a dispute or contest. **8** a sports team. **9** a particular aspect: *he had a disagreeable side*. **10** either of the two faces of a record or of the corresponding parts of a cassette tape. **11** Geometry each of the lines forming the boundary of a plane rectilinear figure. **12** a person's line of descent as traced through either their father or mother.

> – SYNONYMS **1** *they were standing on the side of the road* **edge,** border, verge, boundary, margin, rim, fringe(s), flank, bank, perimeter, extremity, periphery, limit(s). **2** *the east side of the city* **district,** quarter, area, region, part, neighborhood, sector, zone. **3** *one side of the paper* **surface,** face. **4** *his side of the argument* **point of view,** viewpoint, perspective, opinion, standpoint, position, outlook, slant, angle, aspect, facet. **5** *the losing side in the war* **faction,** camp, bloc, party, wing. **6** *the players on their side* **team,** squad, lineup.
> – ANTONYMS center, end.

▶ adjective additional or less important: *a side dish*.

> – SYNONYMS **subordinate,** secondary, minor, peripheral, incidental, subsidiary.
> – ANTONYMS front, central.

▶ verb (**side with/against**) support or oppose one person or group in a conflict or dispute.

– SYNONYMS **support,** take someone's part, stand by, back, be loyal to, defend, champion, ally oneself with.

– DERIVATIVES **sid·ed** adjective **side·ward** /sīdwərd/ adjective & adverb **side·wards** /sīdwərdz/ adverb.

– PHRASES **on the side 1** informal in addition to one's regular job. **2** informal as a secret additional sexual relationship. **3** (of food) served separately from the main dish. **side by side** close together and facing the same way. **side on** on, from, or toward the side. **take sides** support one person or cause against another.

– ORIGIN Old English.

side·arm ▶ **noun** a weapon worn at a person's side, such as a pistol or other small firearm (or, formerly, a sword or bayonet).

side·band /ˈsīdˌband/ ▶ **noun** Telecommunications one of two frequency bands on either side of the carrier wave, containing the modulated signal.

side·bar /ˈsīdˌbär/ ▶ **noun 1** a short piece of additional information placed alongside a main article in a newspaper or magazine. **2** a courtroom discussion between the lawyers and the judge held out of earshot of the jury.

side·board /ˈsīdˌbôrd/ ▶ **noun 1** a flat-topped piece of furniture with cupboards and drawers, used for storing dishes, glasses, etc. **2** (**sideboards**) Brit. sideburns.

side·burns /ˈsīdˌbərnz/ ▶ **plural noun** a strip of hair growing down each side of a man's face in front of his ears.

– ORIGIN reversal of the name of the American General Ambrose *Burnside*, who had sideburns.

side·car /ˈsīdˌkär/ ▶ **noun** a small, low vehicle attached to the side of a motorcycle for carrying passengers.

side ef·fect ▶ **noun** a secondary, typically undesirable effect of a drug or medical treatment.

side·kick /ˈsīdˌkik/ ▶ **noun** informal a person's assistant.

side·light /ˈsīdˌlīt/ ▶ **noun 1** (**sidelights**) a ship's navigation lights. **2** a narrow pane of glass alongside a door or larger window.

side·line /ˈsīdˌlīn/ ▶ **noun 1** an activity done in addition to a person's main job. **2** either of the two lines forming the boundaries of the longer sides of a football field, basketball court, etc. **3** (**the sidelines**) a position of observing a situation rather than being directly involved in it. ▶ **verb 1** prevent a player from playing in a team or game. **2** remove from an influential position: *our committee has been sidelined and excluded from decision-making.*

side·long /ˈsīdˌlôNG/ ▶ **adjective & adverb** (especially of a look) to or from one side; sideways.

side·man /ˈsīdˌman/ ▶ **noun** (pl. **sidemen**) a supporting musician in a jazz band or rock group.

si·de·re·al /sīˈdi(ə)rēəl/ ▶ **adjective** relating to the distant stars or their apparent positions in the sky.

– ORIGIN from Latin *sidus* 'star.'

si·de·re·al time ▶ **noun** Astronomy time reckoned from the motion of the earth (or a planet) relative to the distant stars (rather than with respect to the sun).

side road ▶ **noun** a minor road joining or branching from a main road.

side·sad·dle ▶ **adverb** (of a woman rider) sitting with both feet on the same side of the horse.

side·show /ˈsīdˌSHō/ ▶ **noun 1** a small show or stall at an exhibition, fair, or circus. **2** a minor incident or issue that diverts attention from the main subject.

side·split·ting ▶ **adjective** informal very amusing.

side·step /ˈsīdˌstep/ ▶ **verb** (**sidesteps, sidestepping, sidestepped**) **1** avoid someone or something by stepping sideways. **2** avoid dealing with or discussing: *he neatly sidestepped the questions about riots.* ▶ **noun** a step to one side to avoid someone or something.

side street ▶ **noun** a minor street.

side·swipe /ˈsīdˌswīp/ ▶ **verb** strike something, especially a motor vehicle, with a glancing blow. ▶ **noun** a critical remark made while discussing another matter.

side·track /ˈsīdˌtrak/ ▶ **verb** distract someone from an urgent or important issue.

– SYNONYMS **distract,** divert, deflect, draw away.

side-view mir·ror ▶ **noun** a mirror projecting from the side of a vehicle, enabling the driver to see vehicles approaching alongside.

side·walk /ˈsīdˌwôlk/ ▶ **noun** a paved path for pedestrians at the side of a road.

side·ways /ˈsīdˌwāz/ (also **sidewise** /ˈsīdˌwīz/) ▶ **adverb & adjective 1** to, toward, or from the side. **2** not conventional; alternative: *a sideways look at life.*

– SYNONYMS **1** *I slid off sideways* **to the side,** laterally. **2** *the expansion slots are mounted sideways* **edgewise,** edgeways, side first, end on. **3** *he looked sideways at her* **obliquely,** indirectly, sidelong; covertly, furtively, surreptitiously, slyly. **4** *sideways force* **lateral,** sideward, on the side, side to side. **5** *a sideways look* **indirect,** oblique, sidelong, surreptitious, furtive, covert, sly.

side·wind·er /ˈsīdˌwīndər/ ▶ **noun** a burrowing rattlesnake of North American deserts that moves sideways by throwing its body into S-shaped curves.

sid·ing /ˈsīdiNG/ ▶ **noun 1** cladding material for the outside of a building. **2** a short track beside and opening onto a main railroad line, where trains are shunted or left.

si·dle /ˈsīdl/ ▶ **verb** walk in a stealthy or uncertain way.

– ORIGIN from former *sideling* 'sidelong.'

SIDS /sidz/ ▶ **abbreviation** sudden infant death syndrome (technical term for **CRIB DEATH**).

siege /sēj/ ▶ **noun 1** a military operation in which enemy forces try to capture a town or building by surrounding it and cutting off essential supplies. **2** a similar operation by a police team to force an armed person to surrender.

– PHRASES **lay siege to** begin a siege of a place. **under siege** under constant pressure or attack: *the farmed salmon industry is under siege.*

– ORIGIN Old French *sege* 'seat.'

siege men·tal·i·ty ▶ **noun** a defensive or paranoid attitude based on the belief that others are hostile toward one.

sie·mens /ˈsēmənz/ ▶ **noun** Physics the SI unit of conductance.

– ORIGIN named after the German-born British engineer Sir Charles William *Siemens.*

si·en·na /sēˈenə/ ▶ **noun** a kind of earth used as a pigment in painting, normally yellowish-brown (**raw sienna**) or deep reddish-brown when roasted (**burnt sienna**).

– ORIGIN from Italian *terra di Sienna* 'earth of *Siena*' (an Italian city).

si·er·ra /sē'erə/ ▶ **noun** (in Spanish-speaking countries or the western US) a long jagged mountain chain.
– ORIGIN Spanish.

Si·er·ra Le·o·ne·an /sē,erə lē'ōnēən/ ▶ **noun** a person from Sierra Leone, a country in West Africa. ▶ **adjective** relating to Sierra Leone.

si·es·ta /sē'estə/ ▶ **noun** an afternoon rest or nap, especially one taken regularly in hot countries.
– ORIGIN Spanish.

sieve /siv/ ▶ **noun** a utensil consisting of a wire or plastic mesh held in a frame, used for straining solids from liquids or separating coarser particles from finer ones. ▶ **verb** put a substance through a sieve.
– ORIGIN Old English.

sie·vert /'sēvərt/ ▶ **noun** Physics the SI unit of dose equivalent, equal to an effective dose of a joule of energy per kilogram of recipient mass.
– ORIGIN named after the Swedish physicist Rolf M. *Sievert* (1896–1966).

sift /sift/ ▶ **verb 1** put a fine or loose substance through a sieve so as to remove lumps or large particles. **2** examine something thoroughly to sort out what is important or useful.

– SYNONYMS **1 sieve,** strain, screen, filter. **2** *we sift out unsuitable applications* **separate out,** filter out, sort out, weed out, get rid of, remove. **3** *sifting through the data* **search,** look, examine, inspect, scrutinize.

– DERIVATIVES **sift·er** noun.
– ORIGIN Old English.

sigh /sī/ ▶ **verb 1** let out a long, deep breath expressing sadness, relief, tiredness, etc. **2** (**sigh for**) literary long for someone or something.

– SYNONYMS **1 breathe (out),** exhale, groan, moan. **2 rustle,** whisper, murmur.

▶ **noun** an act of sighing.
– ORIGIN Old English.

sight /sīt/ ▶ **noun 1** the faculty of seeing. **2** the action of seeing: *I hate the sight of blood.* **3** the area or distance within which someone can see or something can be seen. **4** a thing that is seen. **5** (**sights**) places of interest to tourists and other visitors. **6** (**a sight**) informal a ridiculous or unattractive person or thing. **7** (also **sights**) a device that one looks through to aim a gun or to see with a telescope or similar instrument.

– SYNONYMS **1 eyesight,** vision, eyes. **2 view,** glimpse, glance, look. **3 landmark,** place of interest, monument, spectacle, marvel, wonder.

▶ **verb 1** manage to see or glimpse: *two suspicious men had been sighted in the area.* **2** take aim by looking through the sights of a gun.

– SYNONYMS **glimpse,** catch sight of, see, spot, spy, make out, pick out, notice, observe.

– DERIVATIVES **sight·er** noun **sight·ing** noun.
– PHRASES **at first sight** on the first impression. **catch sight of** manage to glimpse. **in sight** close to being achieved. **in** (or **within**) **sight of 1** so as to see or be seen from. **2** close to achieving. **in** (or **within**) **one's sights** within the scope of one's ambitions or expectations. **lose sight of** fail to consider, be aware of, or remember. **on** (or **at**) **sight** as soon as someone or something has been seen. **raise** (or **lower**) **one's sights** increase (or lower) one's expectations. **set one's sights on** hope strongly to achieve. **a sight ——** informal considerably: *she is a sight cleverer than Sarah.* **a sight for sore eyes** informal a person or thing that one is very pleased or relieved to see.
– ORIGIN Old English.

USAGE

For an explanation of the difference between **sight** and **site**, see the note at **SITE**.

WORD LINKS

optical, **visual** *relating to sight*

sight·ed /'sītid/ ▶ **adjective 1** having the ability to see; not blind. **2** having a specified kind of sight: *keen-sighted.*

sight·less /'sītlis/ ▶ **adjective** unable to see; blind.

sight line ▶ **noun** an imaginary line from someone's eye to what is seen.

sight-read /'sīt,rēd/ ▶ **verb** read a musical score and perform it without preparation.

sight·see·ing /'sīt,sēiNG/ ▶ **noun** the activity of visiting places of interest.
– DERIVATIVES **sight·se·er** noun.

sign /sīn/ ▶ **noun 1** a thing whose presence or occurrence indicates that something exists, is happening, or may happen: *dark circles under the eyes are a sign of stress.* **2** a signal, gesture, or notice giving information or an instruction. **3** a symbol or word used to represent something in algebra, music, or other subjects. **4** each of the twelve equal sections into which the zodiac is divided.

– SYNONYMS **1 indication,** signal, symptom, pointer, suggestion, intimation, mark, manifestation, demonstration, token. **2 warning,** omen, portent, threat, promise. **3 notice,** board, placard, signpost. **4 symbol,** figure, emblem, device, logo, character.

▶ **verb 1** write one's name on a letter, document, etc., in order to show that one has written it or that one authorizes its contents. **2** recruit an athlete, musician, etc., by signing a contract with them. **3** use gestures to give information or instructions.

– SYNONYMS **1 write one's name on/to,** autograph, initial, countersign. **2 endorse,** validate, agree to, approve, ratify, adopt. **3 write,** inscribe, pen.

– DERIVATIVES **sign·er** noun.
– PHRASES **sign off** conclude a letter, broadcast, or other message. **sign on** commit oneself to a job or other undertaking. **sign someone on** employ someone. **sign up** commit oneself to a job, course of study, etc.
– ORIGIN Latin *signum* 'mark, token.'

CHOOSE THE RIGHT WORD

See **EMBLEM**.

CHOOSE THE RIGHT WORD

sign, augury, indication, manifestation, omen, signal, symptom, token

What's the difference between a **sign** and a **signal**? The former (in this sense) is a general term for anything that gives evidence of an event, a mood, a quality of character, a mental or physical state, or a trace of something (*a sign of approaching rain; a sign of good breeding; a sign that someone has entered the house*). While a *sign* may be involuntary or even unconscious, a *signal* is always voluntary and is usually deliberate. A ship that shows signs of distress may or may not be in trouble; but one that sends a distress *signal* is definitely in need of help.

Indication, like *sign*, is a comprehensive term for anything that serves to indicate or point out (*he gave no indication that he was lying*). A **manifestation** is an outward or perceptible indication of something (*the letter was a manifestation of his guilt*), and a **symptom** is an indication of a diseased condition (*a symptom of pneumonia*). An object that proves the existence of something abstract is called a **token** (*she gave him a locket as a token of her love*). **Omen** and **augury** both pertain to foretelling future events, with *augury* being the general term for a prediction of the future and *omen* being a definite sign foretelling good or evil (*they regarded the stormy weather as a bad omen*).

sign·age /'sīnij/ ▶ **noun** commercial or public display signs.

sig·nal[1] /'signəl/ ▶ **noun** **1** a gesture, action, or sound giving information or an instruction. **2** a sign of a particular situation: *pain is a warning signal, telling you that something is wrong*. **3** an electrical impulse or radio wave transmitted or received. **4** a device that uses lights or a movable arm, used to tell drivers to stop or beware on a road or railroad.

– SYNONYMS **1 gesture,** gesticulation, sign, wave, cue, indication, warning, prompt, reminder. **2 indication,** sign, symptom, hint, pointer, clue, demonstration, evidence, proof.

▶ **verb** (**signals, signaling, signaled**) give information or an instruction to someone by means of a signal.

– SYNONYMS **1 gesture,** gesticulate, sign, indicate, motion, wave, beckon, nod. **2** *his death signals the end of an era* **mark,** signify, mean, indicate, be a sign of, be evidence of.

– DERIVATIVES **sig·nal·er** noun.
– ORIGIN Latin *signum* 'mark, token.'

CHOOSE THE RIGHT WORD

See **SIGN**.

sig·nal[2] ▶ **adjective** striking in extent, seriousness, or importance.
– DERIVATIVES **sig·nal·ly** adverb.
– ORIGIN Italian *segnalato* 'distinguished.'

sig·nal-to-noise ra·tio ▶ **noun** the ratio of the strength of an electrical or other signal carrying information to that of unwanted interference, generally given in decibels.

sig·na·to·ry /'signəˌtôrē/ ▶ **noun** (pl. **signatories**) a person, organization, state, or country that has signed an agreement.
– ORIGIN from Latin *signare* 'to sign.'

sig·na·ture /'signəCHər, -ˌCHo͝or/ ▶ **noun** **1** a person's name written in a distinctive way, used in signing a document, letter, etc. **2** the action of signing something. **3** a distinctive product or quality by which someone or something can be recognized: *the chef produced the pâté that was his signature*. **4** Music a key signature or time signature.
– ORIGIN from Latin *signare* 'to sign.'

sig·na·ture tune ▶ **noun** a piece of music used to introduce a particular television or radio program; theme tune.

sign·board /'sīnˌbôrd/ ▶ **noun** a board displaying the name or logo of a business or product.

sig·net /'signit/ ▶ **noun** historical a small seal, especially one set in a ring, used to authorize an official document.
– ORIGIN Latin *signetum*.

sig·net ring ▶ **noun** a ring with letters or a design set into it.

sig·nif·i·cance /sig'nifikəns/ ▶ **noun** **1** the quality of being significant; importance. **2** the meaning of something: *he took in the full significance of Peter's remarks*.

– SYNONYMS **importance,** import, consequence, seriousness, gravity, weight, magnitude.

– ORIGIN Latin *significantia*, from *significare* 'indicate.'

sig·nif·i·cant /sig'nifikənt/ ▶ **adjective** **1** important or large enough to be noticed. **2** having a particular meaning: *it's significant that he set the story in Italy*. **3** having a meaning that is not stated directly: *a significant look*.

– SYNONYMS **1 notable,** noteworthy, remarkable, important, of consequence, momentous. **2 large,** considerable, sizable, appreciable, conspicuous, obvious, sudden. **3 meaningful,** expressive, eloquent, suggestive, knowing, telling.

– DERIVATIVES **sig·nif·i·cant·ly** adverb.

sig·nif·i·cant fig·ure ▶ **noun** Mathematics each of the digits of a number that are used to express it to the required degree of accuracy.

sig·nif·i·cant oth·er ▶ **noun** a person with whom someone has an established romantic or sexual relationship.

sig·ni·fy /'signəˌfī/ ▶ **verb** (**signifies, signifying, signified**) **1** be an indication of something. **2** be a symbol of something. **3** make a feeling or intention known. **4** be of importance: *the locked door doesn't necessarily signify*.

– SYNONYMS **mean,** denote, designate, represent, symbolize, stand for.

– DERIVATIVES **sig·ni·fi·ca·tion** /ˌsignəfi'kāSHən/ noun.
– ORIGIN Latin *significare*.

sign·ing /'sīniNG/ ▶ **noun** **1** an event at which an author signs copies of their book to gain publicity and sales. **2** sign language.

sign lan·guage ▶ **noun** a system of communication used among and with deaf people, consisting of gestures and signs made by the hands and face.

si·gnor /sēn'yôr/ ▶ **noun** a title or form of address for an Italian-speaking man, corresponding to *Mr.* or *sir*.

si·gno·ra /sēn'yôrə/ ▶ **noun** a title or form of address for an Italian-speaking married woman, corresponding to *Mrs.* or *madam*.

si·gno·ri·na /ˌsēnyə'rēnə/ ▶ **noun** a title or form of address for an Italian-speaking unmarried woman, corresponding to *Miss*.

sign·post /'sīnˌpōst/ ▶ **noun** a sign on a post, giving information such as the direction and distance to a nearby town. ▶ **verb** chiefly Brit. mark a place or a feature with a signpost or signposts.

si·ka /'sēkə/ ▶ **noun** a deer with a grayish coat that turns yellowish-brown with white spots in summer, native to Japan and SE Asia.
– ORIGIN Japanese.

Sikh /sēk/ ▶ **noun** a member of a religion (**Sikhism** /'sēkizəm/) that has one God and was founded in the Punjab in the 15th century by Guru Nanak. ▶ **adjective** relating to Sikhs or Sikhism.
– ORIGIN Punjabi, 'disciple.'

si·lage /'sīlij/ ▶ **noun** grass or other green crops that are stored in airtight conditions without first being dried,

used as animal feed in the winter.
– ORIGIN from Spanish *ensilar* 'put into a silo.'

si·lence /'sīləns/ ▶ **noun 1** complete lack of sound. **2** a situation in which someone refuses or fails to speak: *he withdrew into sullen silence.*

– SYNONYMS **1 quietness,** quiet, still, stillness, hush, tranquility, peace, peacefulness. **2 failure to speak,** dumbness, muteness, reticence, taciturnity.
– ANTONYMS noise, loquacity.

▶ **verb 1** prevent someone from speaking. **2** make something silent.

– SYNONYMS **1 quiet,** hush, still, muffle, quieten. **2 gag,** muzzle, censor.

– ORIGIN Latin *silentium.*

si·lenc·er /'sīlənsər/ ▶ **noun** a device for reducing the noise made by a mechanism, especially a gun.

si·lent /'sīlənt/ ▶ **adjective 1** not making or accompanied by any sound. **2** not speaking or not spoken aloud: *a silent prayer.* **3** (of a movie) without an accompanying soundtrack. **4** (of a letter) written but not pronounced, e.g., *b* in *doubt.*

– SYNONYMS **1 quiet,** still, hushed, noiseless, soundless, inaudible. **2 speechless,** quiet, unspeaking, dumb, mute, taciturn, uncommunicative, tight-lipped. **3 unspoken,** wordless, tacit, unvoiced, unexpressed, implied, implicit, understood.
– ANTONYMS audible, loquacious.

– DERIVATIVES **si·lent·ly** adverb.

si·lent part·ner ▶ **noun** a partner who invests money in a business but is not involved in running it.

sil·hou·ette /ˌsilo͞o'et/ ▶ **noun 1** the dark shape and outline of someone or something visible against a lighter background. **2** a representation of someone or something that shows them as a black shape on a light background.

– SYNONYMS **outline,** contour(s), profile, form, shape.

▶ **verb** show as a silhouette: *the castle was silhouetted against the sky.*

– SYNONYMS **outline,** define.

– ORIGIN named after the French author and politician Étienne de *Silhouette.*

sil·i·ca /'silikə/ ▶ **noun** silicon dioxide, a hard colorless compound that occurs as quartz and in sandstone and many other rocks.
– DERIVATIVES **si·li·ceous** /sə'lisHəs/ adjective.
– ORIGIN from Latin *silex* 'flint.'

sil·i·ca gel ▶ **noun** hydrated silica in a hard granular form that absorbs moisture from the air.

sil·i·cate /'siləˌkāt, -kit/ ▶ **noun** a compound of silica combined with a metal oxide.

sil·i·con /'siləˌkän, -kən/ ▶ **noun** a gray nonmetallic chemical element with semiconducting properties, used in making electronic circuits.
– ORIGIN from Latin *silex* 'flint.'

USAGE

Do not confuse **silicon** with **silicone**. **Silicon** is a chemical element used in electronic circuits and microchips, while **silicone** is the material used in cosmetic implants.

sil·i·con chip ▶ **noun** a microchip.

sil·i·cone /'siləˌkōn/ ▶ **noun** a synthetic resin made from silicon, used to make cosmetic implants, plastic, paints, etc.

sil·i·co·sis /ˌsilə'kōsis/ ▶ **noun** a lung disease caused by breathing dust containing silica.

silk /silk/ ▶ **noun 1** a fine, soft fiber produced by silkworms. **2** thread or fabric made from silk. **3** (**silks**) clothes made from silk, worn by a jockey.
– ORIGIN Latin *sericus*, from Greek *Sēres*, the name given to the inhabitants of the Far Eastern countries from which silk first came overland to Europe.

silk·en /'silkən/ ▶ **adjective 1** smooth, soft, and shiny like silk: *her silken hair.* **2** made of silk.

silk·screen /'silkˌskrēn/ ▶ **noun** a piece of fine material used in screen printing. ▶ **verb** print, decorate, or reproduce something using a silkscreen.

silk·worm /'silkˌwərm/ ▶ **noun** a caterpillar that spins a silk cocoon from which silk fiber is obtained.

silk·y /'silkē/ ▶ **adjective** (**silkier, silkiest**) **1** smooth, soft, and shiny like silk. **2** (of a person's voice) smooth and gentle or persuasive.
– DERIVATIVES **silk·i·ly** adverb **silk·i·ness** noun.

sill /sil/ ▶ **noun 1** a shelf or slab of stone, wood, or metal at the foot of a window or doorway. **2** a horizontal piece of metal that forms part of the frame of a vehicle. **3** Geology a sheet of igneous rock intruded between and parallel with existing strata. Compare with **DIKE**[1].
– ORIGIN Old English.

sil·ly /'silē/ ▶ **adjective** (**sillier, silliest**) showing a lack of common sense or judgment; foolish.

– SYNONYMS **1 foolish,** stupid, inane, featherbrained, birdbrained, frivolous, immature, childish, empty-headed, scatterbrained; informal dotty, scatty. **2 unwise,** imprudent, thoughtless, foolish, stupid, unintelligent, rash, reckless, foolhardy, irresponsible, harebrained; informal crazy, balmy, daft. **3** *he brooded about silly things* **trivial,** trifling, petty, small, insignificant, unimportant.
– ANTONYMS sensible.

▶ **noun** (pl. **sillies**) informal a silly person.
– DERIVATIVES **sil·li·ness** noun.
– ORIGIN first in the sense 'happy,' later 'innocent, feeble, ignorant': from dialect *seely*, from Germanic.

WORD TOOLKIT

See **FOOLISH**.

si·lo /'sīlō/ ▶ **noun** (pl. **silos**) **1** a tall tower on a farm, used to store grain. **2** a pit or other airtight structure in which green crops are stored as silage. **3** an underground chamber in which a guided missile is kept ready for firing.
– ORIGIN Spanish.

silt /silt/ ▶ **noun** fine sand, clay, or other material carried by running water and deposited as a sediment. ▶ **verb** (usu. **silt up** or **silt something up**) fill or block something with silt.
– DERIVATIVES **sil·ta·tion** /sil'tāsHən/ noun **silt·y** adjective.
– ORIGIN probably Scandinavian; related to **SALT**.

Si·lu·ri·an /si'lo͝orēən, sī-/ ▶ **adjective** Geology referring to the third period of the Paleozoic era (about 439 to 409 million years ago), when the first fish and land plants appeared.
– ORIGIN from *Silures*, the Latin name of a people of ancient Wales.

sil·ver /'silvər/ ▶ **noun 1** a precious grayish-white metallic chemical element. **2** a shiny gray-white color like that of silver. **3** coins made from silver or from a metal that

resembles silver. **4** silver dishes, containers, or cutlery. ▶ **verb 1** coat or plate something with silver. **2** literary give a silvery appearance to: *the dome was silvered with frost.* **3** (of a person's hair) turn gray or white.
– DERIVATIVES **sil·ver·i·ness** noun **sil·ver·y** adjective.
– PHRASES **be born with a silver spoon in one's mouth** be born into a wealthy upper-class family. **the silver screen 1** a movie screen. **2** motion pictures.
– ORIGIN Old English.

sil·ver birch ▶ **noun** a birch tree with silver-gray bark.

sil·ver·fish /ˈsilvərˌfisʜ/ ▶ **noun** (pl. same or **silverfishes**) a small silvery wingless insect that lives in buildings.

sil·ver ju·bi·lee ▶ **noun** the twenty-fifth anniversary of an important event.

sil·ver med·al ▶ **noun** a medal made of or colored silver, awarded for second place in a race or competition.

sil·ver plate ▶ **noun 1** a thin layer of silver applied as a coating to another metal. **2** plates, dishes, etc., made of or plated with silver.

sil·ver·smith /ˈsilvərˌsmiᴛʜ/ ▶ **noun** a person who makes silver articles.
– DERIVATIVES **sil·ver·smith·ing** noun.

sil·ver tongue ▶ **noun** an ability to be eloquent and persuasive in speaking.
– DERIVATIVES **sil·ver-tongued** adjective.

sil·ver·ware /ˈsilvərˌwer/ ▶ **noun 1** dishes, containers, or cutlery made of or coated with silver. **2** eating and serving utensils made of any material.

sil·vi·cul·ture /ˈsilviˌkəlcʜər/ ▶ **noun** the growing and cultivation of trees.
– DERIVATIVES **sil·vi·cul·tur·al** /ˌsilviˈkəlcʜərəl/ adjective.
– ORIGIN from Latin *silva* 'wood.'

SIM /sim/ (also **SIM card**) ▶ **noun** subscriber identification module, a smart card inside a cell phone, carrying an identification number unique to the user, storing personal data, and preventing operation of the phone if removed.
– ORIGIN from the initial letters of *subscriber identification module*.

sim·i·an /ˈsimēən/ ▶ **adjective** relating to or resembling apes or monkeys. ▶ **noun** an ape or monkey.
– ORIGIN from Latin *simia* 'ape.'

sim·i·lar /ˈsimələr/ ▶ **adjective 1** like something else in appearance, character, etc., but not exactly the same: *a soft cheese similar to Brie.* **2** (of geometrical figures) having the same angles and proportions, though of different sizes.

– SYNONYMS **alike,** like, much the same, comparable, corresponding, equivalent, parallel, analogous, kindred.
– ANTONYMS different, dissimilar.

– ORIGIN Latin *similaris*, from *similis* 'like.'

USAGE

It is not good English to say **similar as** (*I've had similar problems as yourself*); use **similar to** instead (*I've had problems similar to yours*).

sim·i·lar·i·ty /ˌsiməˈlaritē/ ▶ **noun** (pl. **similarities**) **1** the state or fact of being similar. **2** (usu. **similarities**) a similar feature or aspect.

– SYNONYMS *the similarity between John and his daughter* **resemblance,** likeness, comparability, correspondence, parallel, equivalence, uniformity.

sim·i·lar·ly /ˈsimələrlē/ ▶ **adverb** in a similar way: *the two vases are similarly flawed at the base.*

– SYNONYMS **likewise,** comparably, correspondingly, equivalently, in the same way, identically.

sim·i·le /ˈsiməlē/ ▶ **noun** a figure of speech in which one thing is compared to another of a different kind (e.g., *our team was solid as a rock*).
– ORIGIN Latin, from *similis* 'like.'

si·mil·i·tude /siˈmiləˌt(y)o͞od/ ▶ **noun** the quality or state of being similar.

CHOOSE THE RIGHT WORD

See **LIKENESS**.

SIMM /sim/ ▶ **abbreviation** Computing single inline memory module.

sim·mer /ˈsimər/ ▶ **verb 1** stay or keep just below boiling point while bubbling gently. **2** be filled with anger or another strong emotion that is only just kept under control. **3** (**simmer down**) become calmer and quieter.

– SYNONYMS **1 boil gently,** cook gently, bubble, stew, poach. **2 seethe,** fume, smolder.

▶ **noun** a state or temperature just below boiling point.
– ORIGIN from dialect *simper* in the same sense.

si·mo·ny /ˈsīmənē, ˈsi-/ ▶ **noun** chiefly historical the buying or selling of pardons and other Church privileges.
– ORIGIN from *Simon* Magus in the Bible, who offered money to the Apostles.

sim·pa·ti·co /simˈpätiˌkō/ ▶ **adjective** (of a person) likable and easy to get along with; having or characterized by shared attributes or interests.
– ORIGIN Italian and Spanish.

sim·per /ˈsimpər/ ▶ **verb** smile in a coy or affected way. ▶ **noun** a coy or affected smile.
– DERIVATIVES **sim·per·ing** adjective.
– ORIGIN unknown.

CHOOSE THE RIGHT WORD

See **SMILE**.

sim·ple /ˈsimpəl/ ▶ **adjective** (**simpler, simplest**) **1** easily understood or done. **2** plain and basic or uncomplicated in form, nature, or design: *a simple white blouse.* **3** of low or ordinary status: *she's a simple country girl.* **4** of very low intelligence. **5** consisting of a single element; not compound. **6** (of interest) payable on the sum loaned only. Compare with **COMPOUND**[1]. **7** (of a leaf or stem) not divided.

– SYNONYMS **1 straightforward,** easy, uncomplicated, uninvolved, undemanding, elementary; informal child's play, a cinch, a piece of cake, like falling off a log. **2 clear,** plain, lucid, straightforward, unambiguous, understandable, comprehensible, accessible; informal user-friendly. **3 plain,** unadorned, basic, unsophisticated, no-frills, classic, understated, uncluttered, restrained. **4 unpretentious,** unsophisticated, ordinary, unaffected, unassuming, natural, straightforward.
– ANTONYMS difficult, complex, ornate.

▶ **noun** chiefly historical an herb with healing properties, or a medicine made from one.
– DERIVATIVES **sim·ple·ness** noun.
– ORIGIN Latin *simplus*.

sim·ple frac·ture ▶ **noun** an injury in which a broken bone does not pierce the skin.

sim·ple·mind·ed /ˈsimpəlˈmīndid/ ▸ **adjective** having or showing very little intelligence or judgment.
– DERIVATIVES **sim·ple·mind·ed·ly** adverb **sim·ple·mind·ed·ness** noun.

sim·ple·ton /ˈsimpəltən/ ▸ **noun** a foolish or unintelligent person.

sim·plex /ˈsimpleks/ ▸ **adjective** technical made up of a single part or structure.
– ORIGIN Latin, 'single.'

sim·plic·i·ty /simˈplisitē/ ▸ **noun** the quality or condition of being simple.

– SYNONYMS **1 straightforwardness,** ease. **2 clarity,** plainness, lucidity, intelligibility, comprehensibility, accessibility. **3 austerity,** plainness, spareness, clean lines. **4 plainness,** modesty, naturalness.
– ANTONYMS complexity.

sim·pli·fy /ˈsimpləˌfī/ ▸ **verb** (**simplifies, simplifying, simplified**) make something easier to do or understand.

– SYNONYMS **make simpler,** clarify, put into words of one syllable, streamline; informal **dumb down.**
– ANTONYMS complicate.

– DERIVATIVES **sim·pli·fi·ca·tion** /ˌsimpləfiˈkāsʜən/ noun.

sim·plis·tic /simˈplistik/ ▸ **adjective** treating complex issues and problems as simpler than they really are.
– DERIVATIVES **sim·plis·ti·cal·ly** adverb.

sim·ply /ˈsimplē/ ▸ **adverb 1** in a simple way. **2** merely; just. **3** absolutely; completely.

– SYNONYMS **1 straightforwardly,** directly, clearly, plainly, intelligibly, lucidly, unambiguously. **2 plainly,** soberly, unfussily, without clutter, classically. **3 merely,** just, purely, solely, only.

sim·u·la·crum /ˌsimyəˈlākrəm, -ˈlak-/ ▸ **noun** (pl. **simulacra** /-ˈlākrə, -ˈlakrə/ or **simulacrums**) **1** an image or representation of someone or something. **2** an unsatisfactory copy or substitute.
– ORIGIN Latin.

sim·u·late /ˈsimyəˌlāt/ ▸ **verb 1** imitate the appearance or nature of: *red ocher intended to simulate blood.* **2** use a computer to create conditions resembling those in real life. **3** pretend to feel an emotion.

– SYNONYMS **1 feign,** pretend, fake, affect, put on. **2 replicate,** reproduce, imitate, mimic.

– DERIVATIVES **sim·u·la·tion** /ˌsimyəˈlāsʜən/ noun.
– ORIGIN Latin *simulare* 'copy, represent.'

sim·u·la·tor /ˈsimyəˌlātər/ ▸ **noun** a machine that imitates the controls and conditions of a real vehicle, process, etc., used for training or testing.

si·mul·cast /ˈsīməlˌkast/ ▸ **noun** a broadcast of the same program on radio and television at the same time, or on two or more channels at the same time. ▸ **verb** broadcast a program in this way.
– ORIGIN blend of **SIMULTANEOUS** and **BROADCAST**.

si·mul·ta·ne·ous /ˌsīməlˈtānēəs/ ▸ **adjective** happening, operating, or done at the same time.

– SYNONYMS **concurrent,** happening at the same time, contemporaneous, coinciding, coincident, synchronized.
– ANTONYMS separate.

– DERIVATIVES **si·mul·ta·ne·i·ty** /ˌsīməltəˈnēitē/ noun.
– ORIGIN from Latin *simul* 'at the same time.'

si·mul·ta·ne·ous e·qua·tions ▸ **plural noun** equations involving two or more unknowns that are to have the same values in each equation.

si·mul·ta·ne·ous·ly /ˌsīməlˈtānēəslē/ ▸ **adverb** at the same time: *Alison and Frank spoke simultaneously.*

– SYNONYMS **at the same time,** at one and the same time, at once, concurrently, (all) together, in unison, in concert, in chorus.

sin[1] /sin/ ▸ **noun 1** an act considered to break a religious or moral law. **2** an act regarded as a serious offense.

– SYNONYMS **1 wrong,** act of wickedness, transgression, crime, offense, misdeed; old use trespass. **2 wickedness,** wrongdoing, evil, immorality, iniquity, vice, crime.
– ANTONYMS virtue.

▸ **verb** (**sins, sinning, sinned**) commit a sin.

– SYNONYMS **transgress,** do wrong, misbehave, err, go astray; old use **trespass.**

– PHRASES **live in sin** informal, dated (of an unmarried couple) live together.
– ORIGIN Old English.

CHOOSE THE RIGHT WORD

sin, crime, fault, indiscretion, offense, transgression, vice

If you've ever driven through a red light or chewed with your mouth open, you've committed an **offense**, which is a broad term covering any violation of the law or of standards of propriety and taste. A **sin**, on the other hand, is an act that specifically violates a religious, ethical, or moral standard (*to marry someone of another faith was considered a sin*). **Transgression** is a weightier and more serious word for *sin*, suggesting any violation of an agreed-upon set of rules (*their behavior was clearly a transgression of the terms set forth in the treaty*). A **crime** is any act forbidden by law and punishable upon conviction (*a crime for which he was sentenced to death*). A **vice** has less to do with violating the law and more to do with habits and practices that debase a person's character (*alcohol was her only vice*). **Fault** and **indiscretion** are gentler words, although they may be used as euphemisms for *sin* or *crime*. A *fault* is an unsatisfactory feature in someone's character (*she is exuberant to a fault*), while *indiscretion* refers to an unwise or improper action (*speaking to the media was an indiscretion for which she was chastised*). In recent years, however, *indiscretion* has become a euphemism for such sins as adultery, as if to excuse such behavior by attributing it to a momentary lapse of judgment (*his indiscretions were no secret*).

sin[2] /sīn/ ▸ **abbreviation** sine.

sin bin ▸ **noun** informal (in sports) a box or bench to which offending players can be sent as a penalty during a game.

since /sins/ ▸ **preposition** in the period between a time in the past and the present. ▸ **conjunction 1** during or in the time after. **2** for the reason that; because. ▸ **adverb 1** from the time mentioned until the present. **2** ago.
– ORIGIN Old English.

sin·cere /sinˈsi(ə)r/ ▸ **adjective** (**sincerer, sincerest**) showing genuine feelings; free from deceit or pretense.

– SYNONYMS **1 heartfelt,** wholehearted, profound, deep, true, honest, earnest, fervent. **2 honest,** genuine, truthful, direct, frank, candid; informal straight, on the level, upfront, on the up and up.

– ORIGIN Latin *sincerus* 'clean, pure.'

sin·cere·ly /sinˈsi(ə)rlē/ ▸ **adverb** in a sincere or genuine way: *we sincerely hope you'll be better soon.*

– SYNONYMS **genuinely,** honestly, really, truly, truthfully, wholeheartedly, earnestly.

sin·cer·i·ty /sin'seritē/ ▶ **noun** the quality of being genuine and truthful: *there's no reason to doubt her sincerity.*

– SYNONYMS **genuineness,** honesty, truthfulness, integrity, directness, openness, candor.

sine /sīn/ ▶ **noun** (in a right triangle) the ratio of the side opposite a particular acute angle to the hypotenuse.
– ORIGIN Latin *sinus* 'curve.'

si·ne·cure /'sīnə,kyo͝or, 'si-/ ▶ **noun** a position for which the holder is paid but which involves little or no work.
– ORIGIN from Latin *sine cura* 'without care.'

si·ne qua non /,sini ,kwä 'nōn, ,sini ,kwä 'nän/ ▶ **noun** a thing that is absolutely essential.
– ORIGIN Latin, 'without which not.'

sin·ew /'sinyo͞o/ ▶ **noun** a piece of tough fibrous tissue that joins muscle to bone; a tendon or ligament.
– DERIVATIVES **sin·ew·y** adjective.
– ORIGIN Old English.

sin·fo·ni·a /,sinfə'nēə/ ▶ **noun** Music **1** a symphony. **2** (in baroque music) an orchestral piece used as an introduction to an opera, cantata, or suite. **3** a small symphony orchestra.
– ORIGIN Italian.

sin·fo·niet·ta /,sinfən'yetə/ ▶ **noun** Music **1** a short or simple symphony. **2** a small symphony orchestra.
– ORIGIN Italian.

sin·ful /'sinfəl/ ▶ **adjective 1** wicked and immoral. **2** disgraceful: *a sinful waste.*

– SYNONYMS **immoral,** wicked, (morally) wrong, evil, bad, iniquitous, ungodly, irreligious, sacrilegious.
– ANTONYMS virtuous.

– DERIVATIVES **sin·ful·ly** adverb **sin·ful·ness** noun.

sing /siNG/ ▶ **verb** (past **sang**; past part. **sung**) **1** make musical sounds with the voice in the form of a song or tune. **2** (of a bird) make characteristic tuneful whistling and twittering sounds. **3** make a high-pitched whistling sound.

– SYNONYMS **1 chant,** trill, intone, croon, chorus. **2 trill,** warble, chirp, cheep.

– DERIVATIVES **sing·a·ble** adjective.
– PHRASES **sing the praises of** express enthusiastic approval or admiration of.
– ORIGIN Old English.

sing. ▶ **abbreviation** singular.

sing·a·long /'siNGə,lôNG, 'siNGə,läNG/ ▶ **noun** an informal occasion when people sing together in a group.

Sin·ga·po·re·an /,siNGə'pôrēən/ ▶ **noun** a person from Singapore. ▶ **adjective** relating to Singapore.

singe /sinj/ ▶ **verb** (**singes, singeing, singed**) burn the surface of something lightly.

– SYNONYMS **scorch,** burn, sear, char.

▶ **noun** a slight burn.
– ORIGIN Old English.

sing·er /'siNGər/ ▶ **noun** a person who sings, especially professionally.

– SYNONYMS **vocalist,** songster, songstress, soloist, chorister, cantor.

Sin·gha·lese /,siNGgə'lēz, -'lēs/ ▶ **noun & adjective** variant spelling of **SINHALESE**.

sin·gle /'siNGgəl/ ▶ **adjective 1** only one; not one of several. **2** consisting of one part. **3** not involved in an established romantic or sexual relationship. **4** designed or suitable for one person: *a single bed.* **5** regarded as distinct or separate from others in a group: *alcohol is the single most important cause of violence.* **6** even one: *they didn't receive a single reply.*

– SYNONYMS **1 sole,** one, lone, solitary, unaccompanied, alone. **2 individual,** separate, particular, distinct. **3 unmarried,** unwed, unattached, free.
– ANTONYMS double, multiple.

▶ **noun 1** a single person or thing. **2** a short record or CD featuring one main song. **3** (**singles**) a game or competition for individual players.
▶ **verb** (**single someone/thing out**) choose someone or something from a group for special treatment.

– SYNONYMS **select,** pick out, choose, decide on, target, earmark, mark out, separate out, set apart.

– DERIVATIVES **sin·gle·ness** noun.
– ORIGIN Latin *singulus.*

sin·gle bond ▶ **noun** a chemical bond in which one pair of electrons is shared between two atoms.

sin·gle-breast·ed ▶ **adjective** (of a jacket or coat) fastened by one row of buttons at the center of the front.

sin·gle com·bat ▶ **noun** fighting between two people.

sin·gle cur·ren·cy ▶ **noun 1** a currency used by all the members of an economic federation. **2** (also **single European currency**) the currency (the euro) that replaced the national currencies of twelve member countries of the European Union in 2002.

sin·gle file ▶ **noun** a line of people or things arranged one behind another.

sin·gle-hand·ed ▶ **adverb & adjective** done without help from other people.

– SYNONYMS **by oneself,** alone, on one's own, solo, unaided, unassisted, without help.

– DERIVATIVES **sin·gle-hand·ed·ly** adverb.

sin·gle-lens re·flex ▶ **adjective** referring to a reflex camera in which the lens that forms the image on the film also provides the image in the viewfinder.

sin·gle malt ▶ **noun** malt whiskey that has been produced by one distillery and is not blended with any other malt whiskey.

sin·gle mar·ket ▶ **noun** an association of countries that have few or no restrictions on the movement of goods, money, or people within the association.

sin·gle-mind·ed ▶ **adjective** concentrating with determination on one particular aim.

– SYNONYMS **determined,** committed, unswerving, unwavering, resolute, purposeful, devoted, dedicated, uncompromising, tireless, tenacious, persistent, dogged.
– ANTONYMS half-hearted.

– DERIVATIVES **sin·gle-mind·ed·ly** adverb **sin·gle-mind·ed·ness** noun.

sin·gle par·ent ▶ **noun** a person bringing up a child or children without a partner.

sin·gle·ton /'siNGgəltən/ ▶ **noun 1** a single person or thing of the kind under consideration. **2** informal a person who is not in a long-term relationship. **3** (in card games) a card that is the only one of its suit in a hand.

sin·gle trans·fer·a·ble vote ▶ **noun** an electoral system of proportional representation in which a person's vote can be transferred to a further choice of candidate.

sin·gly /'siNGglē/ ▶ **adverb** one by one: *people, please enter singly into the hallway.*

– SYNONYMS **one by one,** one at a time, one after the other, individually, separately.
– ANTONYMS together.

sing·song /'siNG,sôNG/ ▶ **adjective** (of a person's voice) having a repeated rising and falling rhythm. ▶ **noun** Brit. informal an informal occasion when people sing together in a group.

sin·gu·lar /'siNGgyələr/ ▶ **adjective 1** Grammar (of a word or form) referring to just one person or thing. **2** very good or great; remarkable. **3** strange or eccentric.

– SYNONYMS **remarkable,** extraordinary, exceptional, outstanding, signal, notable, noteworthy.

▶ **noun** Grammar the singular form of a word.
– DERIVATIVES **sin·gu·lar·ly** adverb.
– ORIGIN Latin *singularis.*

sin·gu·lar·i·ty /,siNGgyə'laritē/ ▶ **noun** (pl. **singularities**) the state, fact, quality, or condition of being singular; a peculiarity or odd trait.

Sin·ha·lese /,sinhə'lēz, -'lēs/ (also **Singhalese** /,siNGgə-/, **Sinhala** /'sinhələ/) ▶ **noun** (pl. same) **1** a member of an Indian people now forming the majority of the population of Sri Lanka. **2** the language spoken by the Sinhalese. ▶ **adjective** relating to the Sinhalese.
– ORIGIN from Sanskrit, 'Sri Lanka.'

sin·is·ter /'sinistər/ ▶ **adjective 1** giving the impression that something harmful or evil will happen or is happening: *a dark building with a sinister air.* **2** old use & Heraldry on or toward the bearer's left-hand side of a coat of arms. The opposite of **DEXTER**.

– SYNONYMS **1 menacing,** threatening, forbidding, baleful, frightening, alarming, disturbing, ominous. **2 evil,** wicked, criminal, nefarious, villainous; informal shady.
– ANTONYMS innocent.

– DERIVATIVES **sin·is·ter·ly** adverb.
– ORIGIN Latin, 'left.'

sink[1] /siNGk/ ▶ **verb** (past **sank** /saNGk/ or **sunk** /səNGk/; past part. **sunk**) **1** go down below the surface of liquid. **2** (with reference to a ship) go or cause to go to the bottom of the sea. **3** drop downward. **4** lower oneself or drop down gently: *she sank back onto her pillow.* **5** gradually decrease in amount or intensity. **6** (**sink in**) (of words or facts) become fully understood or realized. **7** (**sink something into**) force something sharp through a surface: *the dog sank its teeth into her arm.* **8** insert something beneath a surface. **9** pass into a particular state or condition: *she sank into sleep.* **10** (**sink something in/into**) put money or resources into.

– SYNONYMS **1 submerge,** founder, capsize, go down, be engulfed. **2 scuttle. 3 fall,** drop, descend, plunge, plummet, slump. **4 embed,** insert, drive, plant.
– ANTONYMS float, rise.

– PHRASES **a sinking feeling** an unpleasant feeling caused by the realization that something unpleasant or undesirable has happened or will happen. **sink or swim** fail or succeed by one's own efforts.
– ORIGIN Old English.

sink[2] ▶ **noun 1** a fixed basin with a water supply and outflow pipe. **2** a sinkhole. ▶ **adjective** Brit. (of a school or housing estate) in a socially deprived area.
– ORIGIN from **SINK**[1].

sink·er /'siNGkər/ ▶ **noun** a weight used to keep a fishing line beneath the water.

sink·hole /'siNGk,hōl/ ▶ **noun** a cavity in the ground caused by water erosion and providing a route for surface water to disappear underground.

sink·ing fund ▶ **noun** a fund formed by regularly setting aside money in order to pay off a particular debt.

sin·ner /'sinər/ ▶ **noun** a person who sins.

– SYNONYMS **wrongdoer,** evildoer, transgressor, miscreant, offender, criminal; old use trespasser.

Sino- /'sīnō/ ▶ **combining form** Chinese; Chinese and ...: *Sino-American.*
– ORIGIN from Latin *Sinae.*

si·nol·o·gy /sī'näləjē/ ▶ **noun** the study of Chinese language, history, and culture.
– DERIVATIVES **si·nol·o·gist** noun.

sin·ter /'sin(t)ər/ ▶ **noun** a hard substance that is deposited from mineral springs. ▶ **verb** make a powdered material form a solid mass by heating and compressing it.
– ORIGIN German, 'cinder.'

sin·u·ous /'sinyo͞oəs/ ▶ **adjective 1** having many curves and turns. **2** lithe and supple.

– SYNONYMS **1** *a sinuous river* **winding,** windy, serpentine, curving, twisting, meandering, snaking, zigzag, curling, coiling. **2** *sinuous grace* **lithe,** supple, graceful, loose-limbed, lissom.
– ANTONYMS straight, awkward.

– DERIVATIVES **sin·u·os·i·ty** /,sinyo͞o'äsitē/ noun **sin·u·ous·ly** adverb.
– ORIGIN Latin *sinuosus,* from *sinus* 'a bend.'

si·nus /'sīnəs/ ▶ **noun** a hollow space within a bone or other tissue, especially one in the bones of the face or skull that connects with the inside of the nose.
– ORIGIN Latin, 'a recess, bend.'

si·nus·i·tis /,sīnə'sītis/ ▶ **noun** inflammation of a sinus that connects with the inside of the nose.

Sioux /so͞o/ ▶ **noun** (pl. same) a member of a North American Indian people of the northern Mississippi valley area.
– ORIGIN from Ojibwa (an American Indian language).

sip /sip/ ▶ **verb** (**sips, sipping, sipped**) drink something by taking small mouthfuls.

– SYNONYMS **drink,** taste, sample, nip.

▶ **noun** a small mouthful of liquid.

– SYNONYMS **mouthful,** swallow, drink, drop, dram, nip; informal swig.

– DERIVATIVES **sip·per** noun.
– ORIGIN perhaps from former *sup* 'take drink or liquid food by sips or spoonfuls.'

si·phon /'sīfən/ (also **syphon**) ▶ **noun** a tube used to convey liquid upward from a container and then down to a lower level, using the different fluid pressures at the tube openings to maintain the flow. ▶ **verb 1** draw off or convey liquid by means of a siphon. **2** take small amounts of money from a source over a period of time, especially illicitly.

– DERIVATIVES **si·phon·age** /-nij/ noun **si·phon·ic** /sīˈfänik/ adjective.
– ORIGIN Greek, 'pipe.'

sir /sər/ (also **Sir**) ▸ **noun 1** a polite form of address to a man. **2** used to address a man at the beginning of a formal letter. **3** used as a title before the first name of a knight or baronet.
– ORIGIN from SIRE.

sire /sīr/ ▸ **noun 1** the male parent of an animal. **2** literary a father or other male ancestor. **3** old use a respectful form of address to someone of high social status, especially a king. ▸ **verb 1** be the male parent of an animal. **2** literary be the father of a child.
– ORIGIN Old French.

si·ren /ˈsīrən/ ▸ **noun 1** a device that makes a long, loud signal or warning sound. **2** Greek Mythology each of a group of female creatures whose singing lured unwary sailors onto rocks. **3** a woman whose sexual attractiveness is regarded as dangerous to men.
– ORIGIN Greek *Seirēn*, first referring to an imaginary type of snake.

sir·loin /ˈsərloin/ ▸ **noun** good-quality beef cut from the upper part of the loin.
– ORIGIN Old French, 'above the loin.'

si·roc·co /səˈräkō/ ▸ **noun** (pl. **siroccos**) a hot wind blowing from North Africa to southern Europe.
– ORIGIN Arabic, 'east wind.'

sis /sis/ ▸ **noun** informal sister.

si·sal /ˈsisəl, ˈsī-/ ▸ **noun** fiber made from the leaves of a tropical Mexican plant, used especially for ropes or matting.
– ORIGIN named after the Mexican port of *Sisal*.

sis·sy /ˈsisē/ (also **cissy**) informal ▸ **noun** (pl. **sissies**) a weak or effeminate person. ▸ **adjective** (**sissier, sissiest**) weak or effeminate.
– DERIVATIVES **sis·si·fied** /ˈsisəˌfīd/ adjective.
– ORIGIN from SIS.

sis·ter /ˈsistər/ ▸ **noun 1** a woman or girl in relation to other children of her parents. **2** a female friend or fellow member of a group or organization. **3** (often **Sister**) a member of a religious order of women. **4** (often **Sister**) Brit. a senior female nurse. ▸ **adjective** belonging to the same group or type as something else: *a sister company*.
– DERIVATIVES **sis·ter·ly** adjective.
– ORIGIN Old English.

sis·ter·hood /ˈsistərˌho͝od/ ▸ **noun 1** the relationship between sisters. **2** a feeling of closeness and loyalty to a group of women or all women. **3** a group of women linked by a shared interest, belief, trade, etc.

sis·ter-in-law ▸ **noun** (pl. **sisters-in-law**) **1** the sister of one's wife or husband. **2** the wife of one's brother or brother-in-law.

Sis·y·phe·an /ˌsisəˈfēən/ ▸ **adjective** (of a task) unending.
– ORIGIN from *Sisyphus* in Greek mythology who was condemned to the never-ending task of rolling a large stone to the top of a hill, from which it always rolled down again.

sit /sit/ ▸ **verb** (**sits, sitting**; past and past part. **sat**) **1** be or put in a position in which one's weight is supported by one's buttocks and one's back is upright. **2** be or remain in a particular position or state: *the fridge was sitting in a pool of water*. **3** (of an animal) rest with the hind legs bent and the body close to the ground. **4** (of a legislature, committee, or court of law) be carrying on its business. **5** serve as a member of a council, jury, or other official body. **6** (of a table or room) have enough seats for: *the dining room sat 200 people*. **7** (**sit for**) pose for an artist or photographer.

– SYNONYMS **1 take a seat,** sit down, be seated, perch, ensconce oneself, flop; informal take a load off (one's feet). **2 be placed,** be positioned, be situated, be set, rest, stand, perch. **3 be in session,** meet, be convened. **4** *she sits on the tribunal* **serve on,** have a seat on, be a member of.
– ANTONYMS stand.

▸ **noun** a period of sitting.
– PHRASES **sit in for** temporarily carry out someone else's duties. **sit something out** not take part in something. **sit tight** informal **1** remain firmly in one's place. **2** hold back from taking action.
– ORIGIN Old English.

si·tar /siˈtär/ ▸ **noun** a large Indian lute with a long neck.
– DERIVATIVES **si·tar·ist** noun.
– ORIGIN from the Persian words for 'three' and 'string.'

sit·com /ˈsitˌkäm/ ▸ **noun** a television or radio series in which the same set of characters are involved in amusing situations.
– ORIGIN abbreviation of SITUATION COMEDY.

sit-down ▸ **adjective 1** (of a meal) eaten sitting at a table. **2** (of a protest) in which demonstrators occupy their workplace or sit down on the ground in a public place. ▸ **noun** a period of sitting down.

site /sīt/ ▸ **noun 1** an area of ground on which something is or will be located. **2** a place where a particular event or activity is happening or has happened. **3** a website.

– SYNONYMS **location,** place, position, situation, locality, whereabouts.

▸ **verb** build or locate something in a particular place.

– SYNONYMS **place,** put, position, situate, locate.

– ORIGIN Latin *situs* 'local position.'

USAGE

Do not confuse **site** and **sight**. As a noun, **site** means 'a place where something is located or has happened' (*the site of the battle*), while **sight** chiefly means 'the ability to see' (*he lost his sight as a baby*).

sit-in ▸ **noun** a form of protest in which demonstrators occupy a place until their demands are met.

Sit·ka /ˈsitkə/ ▸ **noun** a fast-growing North American spruce tree, grown for its strong lightweight wood.
– ORIGIN named after the town of *Sitka* in Alaska.

sit·ter /ˈsitər/ ▸ **noun 1** a person who poses for an artist or photographer. **2** a person who looks after children, pets, or a house while the parents or owners are away.

sit·ting /ˈsitiNG/ ▸ **noun 1** a period of being seated. **2** a period of time when a group of people are served a meal. **3** a period of time during which a committee, parliament, or court of law is carrying out its normal business. ▸ **adjective 1** in a seated position. **2** (of an elected representative) currently present or in office.

sit·ting duck ▸ **noun** informal a person or thing with no protection against attack.

sit·ting room ▸ **noun** a room for sitting and relaxing in.

sit·u·ate /ˈsicho͞oˌāt/ ▸ **verb 1** put in a particular place or context. **2** (**be situated**) be in a particular situation or set of circumstances: *she is now comfortably situated*.
– ORIGIN Latin *situare* 'place,' from *situs* 'site.'

sit·u·a·tion /ˌsicho͞oˈāsHən/ ▸ **noun 1** a set of circumstances that exist at a particular time and in a particular place: *the political situation in Russia*. **2** the location and surroundings of a place. **3** formal a job.

– SYNONYMS **1 circumstances,** state of affairs, affairs, state, condition, case, predicament, plight. **2 location,** position, spot, site, setting, environment. **3 post,** position, job, employment.

– DERIVATIVES **sit·u·a·tion·al** adjective.

sit·u·a·tion com·e·dy ▸ **noun** full form of SITCOM.

sit·u·a·tion·ism /ˌsicho͞oˈāsHəˌnizəm/ ▸ **noun** a radical cultural and political movement of the mid 20th century that rejected conventional politics and aimed to transform attitudes to all aspects of everyday life.
– DERIVATIVES **sit·u·a·tion·ist** noun & adjective.

sit-up ▸ **noun** an exercise designed to strengthen the abdominal muscles, in which a person sits up from a horizontal position without using the arms.

sitz bath /sits/ ▸ **noun** a bath in which only the buttocks and hips are immersed in water.
– ORIGIN partial translation of German *Sitzbad*, from *sitzen* 'sit' + *Bad* 'bath.'

six /siks/ ▸ **cardinal number** one more than five; 6. (Roman numeral: **vi** or **VI**.)
– DERIVATIVES **six·fold** /ˈsiksˌfōld/ adjective & adverb.
– PHRASES **at sixes and sevens** in a state of confusion or disorganization. **six of one, (and) half a dozen of the other** a situation in which there is not much difference between two alternatives.
– ORIGIN Old English.

six-gun ▸ **noun** another term for SIX-SHOOTER.

six-pack ▸ **noun 1** a pack of six cans of beer. **2** informal a man's set of well-developed abdominal muscles.

six·pence /ˈsiksˌpens, -pəns/ ▸ **noun** Brit. a small coin worth six old pence (2½ p), withdrawn in 1980.

six-shoot·er ▸ **noun** a revolver with six chambers.

six·teen /sikˈstēn, ˈsikˌstēn/ ▸ **cardinal number** one more than fifteen; 16. (Roman numeral: **xvi** or **XVI**.)
– DERIVATIVES **six·teenth** /sikˈstēnTH, ˈsikˌstēnTH/ ordinal number.

six·teenth note ▸ **noun** a musical note having the time value of a sixteenth of a whole note or half an eighth note, represented by a solid dot with a two-hooked stem.

sixth /siksTH/ ▸ **ordinal number 1** that is number six in a sequence; 6th. **2** (**a sixth/one sixth**) each of six equal parts into which something is divided. **3** a musical interval spanning six consecutive notes in a scale.

sixth sense ▸ **noun** a supposed ability to know things by intuition or instinct rather than by sight, smell, hearing, etc.

six·ty /ˈsikstē/ ▸ **cardinal number** (pl. **sixties**) ten more than fifty; 60. (Roman numeral: **lx** or **LX**.)
– DERIVATIVES **six·ti·eth** /-iTH/ ordinal number.

six·ty-four thou·sand dol·lar ques·tion (usu. **$64,000 question**) ▸ **noun** informal something that is not known and on which a great deal depends.
– ORIGIN first as *sixty-four dollar question*, from a question posed for the top prize in a broadcast quiz show.

siz·a·ble /ˈsīzəbəl/ (also **sizeable**) ▸ **adjective** fairly large.

– SYNONYMS **large,** substantial, considerable, respectable, significant, goodly.
– ANTONYMS small.

size[1] /sīz/ ▸ **noun 1** the overall measurements or extent of something. **2** each of a series of standard measurements in which articles are made or sold.

– SYNONYMS **dimensions,** measurements, proportions, magnitude, largeness, area, expanse, breadth, width, length, height, depth.

▸ **verb 1** group or sort items according to their size. **2** (**size someone/thing up**) form a judgment of someone or something.

– SYNONYMS *having **sized up** the competition, I knew I would win* **assess,** appraise, get the measure of, judge, take stock of, evaluate.

– DERIVATIVES **sized** adjective.
– ORIGIN Old French *sise*.

size[2] ▸ **noun** a sticky solution used to glaze paper, stiffen textiles, and prepare plastered walls for papering. ▸ **verb** treat something with size.
– ORIGIN perhaps the same word as SIZE[1].

size·ism /ˈsīzˌizəm/ ▸ **noun** prejudice or discrimination against people on the grounds of their size.
– DERIVATIVES **size·ist** adjective.

siz·zle /ˈsizəl/ ▸ **verb 1** (of food) make a hissing sound when frying or roasting. **2** (as adj. **sizzling**) informal very hot or exciting.

– SYNONYMS **crackle,** fizzle, sputter, hiss, spit.

▸ **noun** the sound of food sizzling.
– DERIVATIVES **siz·zler** noun.
– ORIGIN imitating the sound.

SK ▸ **abbreviation** Saskatchewan.

ska /skä/ ▸ **noun** a style of fast popular music originating in Jamaica in the 1960s.
– ORIGIN unknown.

skank /skaNGk/ ▸ **noun** a dance performed to reggae music, characterized by rhythmically bending forward, raising the knees, and extending the hands palms-downward. ▸ **verb** play reggae music or dance in this style.
– ORIGIN unknown.

skank·y /ˈskaNGkē/ ▸ **adjective** informal very unpleasant.

skate[1] /skāt/ ▸ **noun** an ice skate or roller skate. ▸ **verb 1** glide on ice skates or roller skates. **2** ride on a skateboard. **3** (**skate over/around**) pass over or refer only briefly to a subject or problem.
– DERIVATIVES **skat·er** noun **skat·ing** noun.
– ORIGIN Dutch *schaats*.

skate[2] ▸ **noun** (pl. same or **skates**) an edible sea fish with a flattened diamond-shaped body.
– ORIGIN Old Norse.

skate·board /ˈskātˌbôrd/ ▸ **noun** a short, narrow board with two small wheels fixed to the bottom of either end, on which a person can ride. ▸ **verb** ride on a skateboard.
– DERIVATIVES **skate·board·er** noun **skate·board·ing** noun.

skate·park /ˈskātˌpärk/ ▸ **noun** an area set aside and equipped for skateboarding.

ske·dad·dle /skiˈdadl/ ▸ **verb** informal leave hurriedly.
– ORIGIN unknown.

skeet /skēt/ (also **skeet shooting**) ▸ **noun** a shooting sport in which a clay target is thrown from a trap.
– ORIGIN apparently an alteration of SHOOT.

skein /skān/ ▸ **noun 1** a length of thread or yarn, loosely coiled and knotted. **2** a flock of wild geese or swans in flight.
– ORIGIN Old French *escaigne*.

skel·e·tal /ˈskelətl/ ▶ **adjective 1** relating to a skeleton. **2** extremely thin. **3** existing only in outline or as a framework: *a skeletal plot for a novel.*
– DERIVATIVES **skel·e·tal·ly** adverb.

skel·e·ton /ˈskelitn/ ▶ **noun 1** a framework of bone, cartilage, or other rigid material supporting or containing the body of an animal. **2** a supporting framework or basic structure: *the concrete skeleton of an unfinished building.* ▶ **adjective** referring to an essential or minimum number of people or things: *a skeleton staff.*
– DERIVATIVES **skel·e·ton·ize** /-ˌīz/ verb.
– PHRASES **skeleton in the closet** an embarrassing or shocking fact that someone wishes to keep secret.
– ORIGIN Greek, from *skeletos* 'dried up.'

skel·e·ton key ▶ **noun** a key designed to fit many locks.

skep·tic /ˈskeptik/ (Brit. **sceptic**) ▶ **noun 1** a person who tends to question or doubt accepted opinions. **2** a person who doubts the truth of Christianity and other religions; an atheist.

– SYNONYMS **cynic,** doubter, unbeliever, doubting Thomas.

– ORIGIN Greek *skeptikos.*

USAGE

Do not confuse **skeptic** with **septic**. See the note at **SEPTIC**.

skep·ti·cal /ˈskeptikəl/ ▶ **adjective** not easily convinced; having doubts.

– SYNONYMS **dubious,** doubtful, doubting, cynical, distrustful, suspicious, disbelieving, unconvinced.
– ANTONYMS certain, convinced.

– DERIVATIVES **skep·ti·cal·ly** /-ik(ə)lē/ adverb.

skep·ti·cism /ˈskeptəˌsizəm/ ▶ **noun** doubt about the truth of something.

– SYNONYMS **doubt,** disbelief, cynicism, distrust, suspicion, incredulity.

sketch /skecH/ ▶ **noun 1** a rough or unfinished drawing or painting. **2** a short, funny, self-contained scene in a comedy show. **3** a brief written or spoken account or description of something.

– SYNONYMS **drawing,** outline, draft, diagram, design, plan; informal rough.

▶ **verb 1** make a sketch of someone or something. **2** give a brief account or description of: *he sketched out his business plan.*

– SYNONYMS **draw,** make a drawing of, pencil, rough out, outline.

– DERIVATIVES **sketch·er** noun.
– ORIGIN Italian *schizzo.*

sketch·book /ˈskecHˌbo͝ok/ (also **sketch pad**) ▶ **noun** a pad of drawing paper for sketching on.

sketch·y /ˈskecHē/ ▶ **adjective** (**sketchier, sketchiest**) not thorough or detailed.

– SYNONYMS **incomplete,** patchy, fragmentary, scrappy, cursory, perfunctory, scanty, vague, inadequate, insufficient.
– ANTONYMS detailed.

– DERIVATIVES **sketch·i·ly** adverb **sketch·i·ness** noun.

skew /skyo͞o/ ▶ **verb 1** suddenly change direction or move at an angle. **2** change or influence something so that it is not accurate, normal, or fair. ▶ **noun 1** a slant. **2** a bias toward one particular group or subject: *the paper had a working-class skew.*
– DERIVATIVES **skew·ness** noun.
– ORIGIN from Old French *eschiver* 'eschew.'

skew·bald /ˈskyo͞oˌbôld/ ▶ **adjective** (of a horse) with irregular patches of white and another color, typically a shade of brown. ▶ **noun** a skewbald horse.
– ORIGIN from former *skewed* 'skewbald,' on the pattern of *piebald.*

skew·er /ˈskyo͞oər/ ▶ **noun** a long piece of wood or metal used for holding pieces of food together during cooking. ▶ **verb** hold something in place or pierce something with a skewer or other pointed object.
– ORIGIN unknown.

ski /skē/ ▶ **noun** (pl. **skis**) **1** each of a pair of long, narrow pieces of wood, metal, or plastic attached to boots for traveling over snow. **2** a similar device attached beneath a vehicle or aircraft. ▶ **verb** (**skis, skiing, skied**) travel over snow on skis.
– DERIVATIVES **ski·a·ble** adjective **ski·er** noun **ski·ing** noun.
– ORIGIN Norwegian.

skid /skid/ ▶ **verb** (**skids, skidding, skidded**) **1** (of a vehicle) slide sideways on slippery ground or as a result of stopping or turning too quickly. **2** slip or slide. ▶ **noun 1** an act of skidding. **2** a runner attached to the underside of an aircraft for use when landing on snow or grass. **3** a braking device consisting of a wooden or metal shoe that prevents a wheel from revolving.
– PHRASES **hit the skids** informal begin a rapid decline. **on the skids** informal in a bad state; failing.
– ORIGIN perhaps related to **SKI**.

skid row /rō/ ▶ **noun** informal a run-down part of a town inhabited by homeless people, drug addicts, and alcoholics.

skiff /skif/ ▶ **noun** a light rowboat, usually for one person.
– ORIGIN Italian *schifo.*

ski jump ▶ **noun** a steep slope leveling off before a sharp drop to allow a skier to leap through the air.

ski lift ▶ **noun** a system used to carry skiers up a slope to the top of a run, consisting of moving seats attached to an overhead cable.

skill /skil/ ▶ **noun 1** the ability to do something well. **2** a particular ability: *practical skills such as cooking.*

– SYNONYMS **expertise,** accomplishment, skillfulness, mastery, talent, deftness, dexterity, prowess, competence, artistry.
– ANTONYMS incompetence.

– ORIGIN Old Norse, 'knowledge.'

skilled /skild/ ▶ **adjective 1** having or showing skill. **2** (of work) requiring special skills.

– SYNONYMS **experienced,** trained, qualified, proficient, practiced, accomplished, expert, skillful, adept, adroit, deft, dexterous, able, good, competent; informal crack, crackerjack.
– ANTONYMS inexperienced.

skil·let /ˈskilit/ ▶ **noun** a frying pan.
– ORIGIN perhaps from Latin *scutella* 'dish, platter.'

skill·ful /ˈskilfəl/ (Brit. **skilful**) ▶ **adjective** having or showing skill.
– DERIVATIVES **skill·ful·ly** adverb **skill·ful·ness** noun.

skill set ▶ **noun** a person's range of skills or abilities.

skim /skim/ ▶ **verb** (**skims, skimming, skimmed**) **1** remove a substance from the surface of a liquid. **2** move quickly and lightly over or on a surface or through the air.

3 read through something quickly, noting only the important points. **4** (**skim over**) deal with a subject briefly or superficially. **5** throw a flat stone so that it bounces several times on the surface of water. **6** (usu. as n. **skimming**) fraudulently copy credit or debit card details with an electronic device.

– SYNONYMS **1** *skim off the fat* **remove,** scoop off, separate. **2 glide,** move lightly, slide, sail, skate. **3** *she* ***skimmed through*** *the paper* **glance through,** flick through, flip through, leaf through, thumb through, read quickly, scan, run one's eye over.

– ORIGIN Old French *escumer*.

ski mask ▸ **noun** a protective covering for the head and face, with holes for the eyes, nose, and mouth.

skim·mer /'skimər/ ▸ **noun 1** a utensil, device, or craft for removing a substance from the surface of water or other liquid. **2** a vessel such as a hydroplane that has little or no displacement when traveling. **3** a long-winged seabird that feeds by flying low with the lower half of its beak skimming through the water. **4** a flat, broad-brimmed straw hat. **5** informal a fitted dress, often sleeveless and with a flared skirt. **6** a broad-bodied dragonfly found at ponds and swamps.
– ORIGIN Old French *escumer*.

skim milk (also **skimmed milk**) ▸ **noun** milk from which the cream has been removed.

skimp /skimp/ ▸ **verb** spend less money or use less of something than is really necessary in an attempt to economize: *don't skimp on vacation insurance*.
– ORIGIN unknown.

skimp·y /'skimpē/ ▸ **adjective** (**skimpier, skimpiest**) **1** providing or consisting of less than is necessary; meager. **2** (of clothes) small and not covering much of the body.

skin /skin/ ▸ **noun 1** the thin layer of tissue forming the natural outer covering of the body of a person or animal. **2** the skin of a dead animal used as material for clothing or other items. **3** the peel or outer layer of a fruit or vegetable. **4** an outer layer.

– SYNONYMS **1 hide,** pelt, fleece. **2 peel,** rind. **3 film,** layer, membrane, crust, covering, coating.

▸ **adjective** informal referring to pornography: *the skin trade*. ▸ **verb** (**skins, skinning, skinned**) **1** remove the skin from something. **2** graze a part of one's body.

– SYNONYMS **1 peel,** pare. **2 graze,** scrape, abrade, bark, rub raw, chafe.

– DERIVATIVES **skin·less** adjective.
– PHRASES **by the skin of one's teeth** by a very narrow margin; only just. **get under someone's skin** informal annoy someone greatly. **have a thick** (or **thin**) **skin** be insensitive (or oversensitive) to criticism or insults. **have skin in the game** informal have a personal investment in an organization or undertaking and therefore a vested interest in its success. **it's no skin off my** (or **his,** etc.) **nose** someone is not annoyed or upset about something.
– ORIGIN Old English.

WORD LINKS

cutaneous *relating to the skin*
dermatology *branch of medicine concerning the skin*

skin·care /'skin,ke(ə)r/ ▸ **noun** the use of cosmetics to care for the skin.

skin-deep ▸ **adjective** not deep or lasting; superficial.

skin-div·ing ▸ **noun** the activity of swimming under water without a diving suit, typically using scuba equipment and flippers.
– DERIVATIVES **skin-div·er** noun.

skin flick (also **skinflick**) ▸ **noun** informal a pornographic movie.

skin·flint /'skin,flint/ ▸ **noun** informal a very miserly person.

skin·head /'skin,hed/ ▸ **noun** a young man of a group with close-cropped hair, especially one who is aggressive and openly racist.

skin·ny /'skinē/ ▸ **adjective** (**skinnier, skinniest**) **1** very thin. **2** (of a piece of clothing) tight-fitting.

– SYNONYMS **thin,** underweight, scrawny, bony, gaunt, emaciated, skeletal, wasted, pinched, spindly, gangly; informal anorexic.

– DERIVATIVES **skin·ni·ness** noun.

skin·ny-dip ▸ **verb** informal swim naked.

skin test ▸ **noun** a test to discover whether an immune reaction occurs when a substance is applied to or injected into the skin.

skin·tight /'skin'tīt/ ▸ **adjective** (of a piece of clothing) very close-fitting.

skip /skip/ ▸ **verb** (**skips, skipping, skipped**) **1** move along lightly, stepping from one foot to the other with a little jump. **2** jump repeatedly over a rope that is held at both ends and turned over the head and under the feet. **3** leave out or move quickly over a section of something being read or watched. **4** not have or do something that one should have or do: *try not to skip breakfast*.

– SYNONYMS **1 caper,** prance, trip, dance, bound, bounce, gambol. **2 omit,** leave out, miss out, dispense with, pass over, skim over, disregard; informal give something a miss.

▸ **noun** a skipping movement.
– ORIGIN probably Scandinavian.

ski pants ▸ **plural noun** women's stretch pants with tapering legs and an elastic stirrup under each foot.

skip·jack /'skip,jak/ ▸ **noun** (also **skipjack tuna**) a small tuna with dark horizontal stripes.
– ORIGIN from **SKIP** + **JACK**[1] (with reference to the fish's habit of jumping out of the water).

ski pole ▸ **noun** either of two lightweight poles held by a skier to help them balance or move along.

skip·per /'skipər/ informal ▸ **noun 1** the captain of a ship, boat, or aircraft. **2** the captain of a sports team. ▸ **verb** be the captain of a ship, boat, aircraft, or sports team.
– ORIGIN Dutch or German *schipper*, from *schip* 'ship.'

skirl /skərl/ ▸ **noun** a shrill sound, especially that made by bagpipes. ▸ **verb** (of bagpipes) make a shrill sound.
– ORIGIN probably Scandinavian.

skir·mish /'skərmisн/ ▸ **noun** a brief period of unplanned fighting. ▸ **verb** take part in a skirmish.
– DERIVATIVES **skir·mish·er** noun.
– ORIGIN Old French *eskirmir*.

skirt /skərt/ ▸ **noun 1** a woman's outer garment that hangs from the waist and covers part or all of the legs. **2** the part of a coat or dress that hangs below the waist. **3** a surface that conceals or protects the wheels or underside of a vehicle or aircraft. **4** dated, informal women regarded as sexually desirable. ▸ **verb** (also **skirt around**) **1** go around or past the edge of something. **2** avoid dealing with: *they are both skirting the issue*.

> – SYNONYMS **1 go around,** walk around, circle. **2 border,** edge, flank, line. **3** *he skirted the subject* **avoid,** evade, sidestep, dodge, pass over, gloss over; informal **duck.**

– ORIGIN Old Norse, 'shirt.'

skirt·ing /'skərtiNG/ (also **skirting board**) ▶ **noun** chiefly Brit. a baseboard.

skit /skit/ ▶ **noun** a short comedy sketch or piece of humorous writing, especially one that makes fun of someone or something by imitating them.
– ORIGIN related to former *skit* 'move lightly and quickly.'

skit·ter /'skitər/ ▶ **verb** move lightly and quickly.
– ORIGIN perhaps from dialect *skite* 'move quickly.'

skit·ter·y /'skitərē/ ▶ **adjective** restless; skittish.

skit·tish /'skitisH/ ▶ **adjective 1** (of a horse) excitable or easily frightened and therefore difficult to control. **2** playful and unpredictable.
– DERIVATIVES **skit·tish·ly** adverb **skit·tish·ness** noun.
– ORIGIN perhaps related to **SKIT**.

skit·tle /'skitl/ ▶ **noun 1** (**skittles**) (treated as sing.) a game played with wooden pins set up at the end of an alley to be bowled down with a wooden ball. **2** a pin used in the game of skittles. **3** (also **table skittles**) a game played with similar pins set up on a board to be knocked down by swinging a suspended ball.
– ORIGIN unknown.

skiv·vies /'skivēz/ ▶ **plural noun** trademark an undershirt and underpants as a set, or just the underpants.

sku·a /'skyōōə/ ▶ **noun** a large predatory seabird that pursues other birds to make them regurgitate fish.
– ORIGIN Faroese.

skul·dug·ger·y /skəl'dəgərē/ (also **skullduggery**) ▶ **noun** underhanded or dishonest behavior.
– ORIGIN alteration of Scots *sculduddery*.

skulk /skəlk/ ▶ **verb** hide or move around in a stealthy or furtive way.
– DERIVATIVES **skulk·er** noun.
– ORIGIN Scandinavian.

skull /skəl/ ▶ **noun 1** the bone framework that surrounds and protects the brain of a person or animal. **2** informal a person's head or brain.

> – SYNONYMS cranium.

– PHRASES **skull and crossbones** a representation of a skull with two thigh bones crossed below it, used formerly by pirates and now as a warning symbol.
– ORIGIN unknown.

> **WORD LINKS**
>
> **cranial** *relating to the skull*

skull·cap /'skəl,kap/ ▶ **noun** a small close-fitting cap without a peak.

skunk /skəNGk/ ▶ **noun** a black-and-white striped American mammal able to spray foul-smelling liquid at attackers.
– ORIGIN Abnaki (an American Indian language).

sky /skī/ ▶ **noun** (pl. **skies**) **1** the region of the upper atmosphere seen from the earth. **2** literary heaven.

> – SYNONYMS literary the heavens, the firmament, the ether, the (wide) blue yonder.

▶ **verb** (**skies, skying, skied**) informal hit a ball high into the air.
– DERIVATIVES **sky·ward** /'skīwərd/ adjective & adverb **sky·wards** /'skīwərdz/ adverb.
– PHRASES **the sky is the limit** there is practically no limit.
– ORIGIN Old Norse, 'cloud.'

> **WORD LINKS**
>
> **celestial** *relating to the sky*

sky blue ▶ **noun** a bright, clear blue.

sky·box /'skī,bäks/ ▶ **noun** a luxurious enclosed seating area located high in a sports arena.

sky·cap /'skī,kap/ ▶ **noun** a porter at an airport.

sky·div·ing /'skī,dīviNG/ ▶ **noun** the sport of jumping from an aircraft and performing acrobatic maneuvers in the air before landing by parachute.
– DERIVATIVES **sky·div·er** noun.

sky-high ▶ **adverb & adjective** very high.

sky·lark /'skī,lärk/ ▶ **noun** a common Old World lark that sings while rising slowly high into the air. ▶ **verb** behave in a playful or mischievous way.

sky·light /'skī,līt/ ▶ **noun** a window set in a roof or ceiling.

sky·line /'skī,līn/ ▶ **noun** an outline of land and buildings seen against the sky.

sky mar·shal ▶ **noun** an undercover armed guard who travels on commercial airlines, trained to take action in the event of a hijack or other terrorist action.

sky·rock·et /'skī,räkit/ ▶ **verb** (**skyrockets, skyrocketing, skyrocketed**) informal (of a price or amount) increase very quickly.

sky·scrap·er /'skī,skrāpər/ ▶ **noun** a very tall building.

sky·walk /'skī,wôk/ ▶ **noun** an enclosed overhead walkway between buildings.

sky·way /'skī,wā/ ▶ **noun 1** a route used by aircraft. **2** (also **skywalk** /'skī,wôk/) a covered overhead walkway between buildings.

slab /slab/ ▶ **noun 1** a large, thick, flat piece of stone, concrete, or other hard material. **2** a thick slice or piece of food.

> – SYNONYMS **piece,** block, hunk, chunk, lump, cake, tablet, brick, panel, plate, sheet.

– ORIGIN unknown.

slack /slak/ ▶ **adjective 1** not taut or held tightly in position; loose. **2** (of business or trade) not busy; quiet. **3** careless or lazy: *slack accounting procedures.* **4** (of a tide) neither ebbing nor flowing.

> – SYNONYMS **1 limp,** loose. **2 sagging,** flabby, flaccid, loose, saggy. **3 sluggish,** slow, quiet, slow-moving, flat, depressed, stagnant. **4 lax,** negligent, careless, slapdash, slipshod; informal sloppy.
> – ANTONYMS taut, firm.

▶ **noun 1** the part of a rope or line that is not held taut. **2** (**slacks**) casual trousers.
▶ **verb 1** make slower or less intense: *the horse slacked his pace.* **2** (**slack off/up**) become slower or less intense.

> – SYNONYMS **idle,** shirk, be lazy, be indolent, waste time, lounge about; informal **goof off.**

– DERIVATIVES **slack·en** verb **slack·ly** adverb **slack·ness** noun.
– PHRASES **take** (or **pick**) **up the slack 1** improve the use of resources in a business. **2** pull on the loose part of a rope to make it taut.
– ORIGIN Old English, 'inclined to be lazy, unhurried.'

slack·er /ˈslakər/ ▶ **noun** informal a person who is lazy and avoids work.

slack wa·ter ▶ **noun** the state of the tide when it is turning.

slag /slag/ ▶ **noun** stony waste matter that is left when metal has been separated from ore by smelting or refining. ▶ **verb** (**slags, slagging, slagged**) (usu. **slag someone off**) Brit. informal criticize someone in a rude or unpleasant way.
– ORIGIN German *slagge.*

slag heap ▶ **noun** a large pile of waste material from a mine or industrial site.

slain /slān/ past participle of SLAY.

slake /slāk/ ▶ **verb** satisfy a desire, one's thirst, etc.
– ORIGIN Old English, 'become less eager.'

slaked lime ▶ **noun** calcium hydroxide, a soluble substance produced by combining quicklime with water.

sla·lom /ˈsläləm/ ▶ **noun** a skiing, canoeing, or sailing race following a winding course marked out by poles. ▶ **verb** move or race in a winding path, avoiding obstacles.
– ORIGIN Norwegian, 'sloping track.'

slam¹ /slam/ ▶ **verb** (**slams, slamming, slammed**) **1** shut something forcefully and loudly. **2** push, put, or hit with great force: *she slammed down the phone.* **3** put into action suddenly or forcefully: *I slammed on the brakes.* **4** informal criticize someone or something severely.

– SYNONYMS *the car **slammed into** a post* **crash into,** smash into, collide with, plow into, run into, bump into, hit, strike, ram, impact.

▶ **noun** a loud bang caused by the forceful shutting of something.
▶ **adverb** (also **slam bang**) informal suddenly and forcefully.
– ORIGIN probably Scandinavian.

slam² ▶ **noun** Bridge the bidding and winning of a grand slam (all thirteen tricks) or a small slam (twelve tricks).
– ORIGIN perhaps from former *slampant* 'trickery.'

slam-dance ▶ **verb** a form of dancing to rock music in which the dancers deliberately collide with one another.

slam dunk ▶ **noun** **1** Basketball a shot thrust down through the basket. **2** informal a foregone conclusion or certainty. ▶ **verb** (**slam-dunk**) Basketball thrust the ball down through the basket.

slam·mer /ˈslamər/ ▶ **noun** **1** informal prison. **2** (also **tequila slammer**) a cocktail made with tequila and champagne or another fizzy drink, which is covered, slammed on the table, and then drunk in one swallow.

slan·der /ˈslandər/ ▶ **noun** **1** the action or crime of making untrue statements that damage a person's reputation. Compare with LIBEL. **2** a statement of this kind. ▶ **verb** make untrue and damaging statements about someone.
– DERIVATIVES **slan·der·er** noun.
– ORIGIN Old French *esclandre.*

slan·der·ous /ˈslandərəs/ ▶ **adjective** untrue and damaging to a person's reputation.

– SYNONYMS **defamatory,** denigratory, disparaging, libelous, pejorative, false, misrepresentative, scurrilous, scandalous, malicious.

slang /slaNG/ ▶ **noun** very informal words and phrases that are more common in speech than in writing and are used by a particular group of people.
– DERIVATIVES **slang·y** adjective.
– ORIGIN unknown.

slant /slant/ ▶ **verb** **1** slope or lean in a particular direction. **2** present information from a particular angle, especially in an unfair way.

– SYNONYMS **1 slope,** tilt, incline, be at an angle, tip, lean, dip, pitch, shelve, list, bank. **2 bias,** distort, twist, skew, weight.

▶ **noun** **1** a sloping position. **2** a point of view: *a new slant on science.*

– SYNONYMS **1 slope,** incline, tilt, gradient, grade, pitch, angle, camber. **2 point of view,** viewpoint, standpoint, stance, angle, perspective, approach, view, attitude, position, bias, spin.

▶ **adjective** at an angle; sloping.
– DERIVATIVES **slant·wise** /ˈslantˌwīz/ adjective & adverb.
– ORIGIN Scandinavian.

slant top desk ▶ **noun** a writing desk with drawers and a sloping top that opens downward to form a writing surface.

slap /slap/ ▶ **verb** (**slaps, slapping, slapped**) **1** hit someone or something with the palm of the hand or a flat object. **2** hit against something with a slapping sound. **3** (**slap something on**) put something on a surface quickly, carelessly, or forcefully. **4** (**slap something on**) informal impose a fine or other penalty on.

– SYNONYMS **smack,** strike, hit, cuff, clip, spank; informal whack.

▶ **noun** a blow with the palm of the hand.

– SYNONYMS **smack,** blow, cuff, clip, spank; informal whack.

▶ **adverb** (also **slap bang**) informal suddenly and forcefully.
– PHRASES **slap in the face** an unexpected rejection. **slap on the back** an instance of congratulating or praising someone. **slap on the wrist** a mild reprimand.
– ORIGIN probably imitating the sound.

slap·dash /ˈslapˌdasH/ ▶ **adjective & adverb** done too hurriedly and carelessly.

slap·hap·py /ˈslapˌhapē/ (also **slap-happy**) ▶ **adjective** informal **1** casual or flippant in a cheerful and often irresponsible way. **2** (of an action or operation) unmethodical; poorly thought out. **3** dazed or stupefied from happiness or relief.

slap·stick /ˈslapˌstik/ ▶ **noun** comedy based on deliberately clumsy actions and embarrassing events.
– ORIGIN first referring to a device consisting of two pieces of wood joined at one end, used by clowns to make a loud slapping sound.

slash /slasH/ ▶ **verb** **1** cut someone or something with a forceful sweeping movement. **2** informal reduce a price, quantity, or amount greatly.

– SYNONYMS **1 cut,** gash, slit, lacerate, knife. **2 reduce,** cut, lower, bring down, mark down.

▶ **noun** **1** a cut made with a sweeping stroke. **2** a bright patch or flash of color or light. **3** a slanting stroke (/) used chiefly between alternatives and in fractions and ratios.

– SYNONYMS **cut,** gash, slit, laceration, incision, wound.

– DERIVATIVES **slash·er** noun.
– ORIGIN Old French *esclachier* 'break in pieces.'

slash-and-burn ▶ **adjective** (of agriculture) in which vegetation is cut down and burned off before new seeds are sown.

slat /slat/ ▶ **noun** each of a series of thin, narrow pieces of wood or other material, arranged so as to overlap or fit

into each other.
– DERIVATIVES **slat·ted** adjective.
– ORIGIN Old French *esclat* 'splinter.'

slate /slāt/ ▸ **noun 1** a gray, green, or bluish-purple rock easily split into smooth, flat plates, used as roofing material. **2** a plate of slate formerly used in schools for writing on. **3** a bluish-gray color. **4** a list of candidates for election to a post or office. ▸ **verb 1** schedule or plan something. **2** cover a roof with slates.
– DERIVATIVES **slat·er** noun.
– ORIGIN Old French *esclate* 'splinter.'

slath·er /ˈslaT͟Hər/ ▸ **verb** informal spread or smear a substance thickly or liberally.
– ORIGIN unknown.

slat·tern /ˈslatərn/ ▸ **noun** dated a dirty, untidy woman.
– DERIVATIVES **slat·tern·ly** adjective.
– ORIGIN unknown.

slaugh·ter /ˈslôtər/ ▸ **noun 1** the killing of farm animals for food. **2** the killing of a large number of people in a cruel or violent way.

– SYNONYMS **massacre,** (mass) murder, (mass) killing, (mass) execution, extermination, carnage, bloodshed, bloodletting, bloodbath; literary slaying.

▸ **verb 1** kill animals for food. **2** kill many people in a cruel or violent way. **3** informal defeat an opponent thoroughly.

– SYNONYMS **1 kill,** butcher, cull, put down. **2 massacre,** murder, butcher, kill, exterminate, wipe out, put to death, execute; literary slay.

– DERIVATIVES **slaugh·ter·er** noun.
– ORIGIN Old Norse, 'butcher's meat.'

slaugh·ter·house /ˈslôtərˌhous/ ▸ **noun** a place where animals are killed for food.

Slav /släv/ ▸ **noun** a member of a group of peoples in central and eastern Europe who speak Slavic languages.
– ORIGIN Greek *Sklabos*.

slave /slāv/ ▸ **noun 1** a person who is the legal property of another and is forced to obey them. **2** a person who is strongly influenced by or controlled by something: *she was no slave to fashion.*

– SYNONYMS **servant,** lackey, drudge; historical serf, vassal.
– ANTONYMS master.

▸ **verb** work excessively hard.

– SYNONYMS **toil,** labor, sweat, work like a Trojan/dog, work one's fingers to the bone; informal sweat blood.

– ORIGIN Latin *sclava* 'Slavonic captive.'

WORD LINKS

servile *like a slave*

slave driv·er ▸ **noun** informal a person who makes others work very hard.

slave la·bor ▸ **noun** work that is demanding and very poorly paid.

slav·er[1] /ˈslāvər/ ▸ **noun 1** a person dealing in or owning slaves. **2** a ship used for transporting slaves.

slav·er[2] /ˈslavər/ ▸ **verb 1** let saliva run from the mouth. **2** show excessive desire or admiration: *the press corps is slavering over the idea of a real election battle.* ▸ **noun** saliva running from the mouth.
– ORIGIN probably from German.

slav·er·y /ˈslāvərē/ ▸ **noun 1** the state of being a slave. **2** the practice or system of owning slaves.

– SYNONYMS **enslavement,** servitude, serfdom, bondage, captivity.
– ANTONYMS freedom.

slave trade ▸ **noun** the buying, transporting, and selling of people, especially black Africans, as slaves.

Slav·ic /ˈslävik/ ▸ **noun** the group of languages that includes Russian, Polish, Czech, Bulgarian, and Serbo-Croat. ▸ **adjective** relating to Slavic or the Slavs.

slav·ish /ˈslāvisH/ ▸ **adjective 1** following or copying something without trying to be original: *he's a slavish follower of White House policy.* **2** obeying someone in a servile way.
– DERIVATIVES **slav·ish·ly** adverb.

CHOOSE THE RIGHT WORD

See **OBSEQUIOUS**.

Sla·von·ic /sləˈvänik/ ▸ **noun & adjective** another term for **SLAVIC**.

slaw /slô/ ▸ **noun** coleslaw.
– ORIGIN Dutch *sla*.

slay /slā/ ▸ **verb** (past **slew** /slo͞o/; past part. **slain** /slān/) **1** old use or literary kill a person or animal in a violent way. **2** murder someone.
– DERIVATIVES **slay·er** noun.
– ORIGIN Old English.

sleaze /slēz/ ▸ **noun** informal **1** immoral or dishonest behavior or activities, especially in politics or business. **2** a dishonest or immoral person.
– ORIGIN from **SLEAZY**.

slea·zy /ˈslēzē/ ▸ **adjective** (**sleazier, sleaziest**) **1** dishonest or immoral. **2** (of a place) dirty and seedy.

– SYNONYMS **1 corrupt,** immoral, ignoble, dishonorable. **2 squalid,** seedy, seamy, sordid, insalubrious.

– DERIVATIVES **slea·zi·ly** adverb **slea·zi·ness** noun.
– ORIGIN unknown.

sled /sled/ ▸ **noun** a vehicle on runners for traveling over snow or ice, either pushed, pulled, or allowed to slide downhill. ▸ **verb** (**sleds, sledding, sledded**) ride on a sled.
– ORIGIN German *sledde*.

sledge[1] /slej/ ▸ **noun** a sledgehammer. ▸ **verb** (as n. **sledging**) Cricket offensive remarks made by a fielder to a batsman in order to break their concentration.
– ORIGIN Old English.

sledge[2] chiefly Brit. ▸ **noun & verb** British term for **SLED**.
– ORIGIN Dutch *sleedse*.

sledge·ham·mer /ˈslejˌhamər/ ▸ **noun** a large, heavy hammer used for breaking rocks, driving in posts, etc. ▸ **adjective** very powerful, forceful, or unsubtle: *sledgehammer blows.*

sleek /slēk/ ▸ **adjective 1** (of hair or fur) smooth and glossy. **2** wealthy and smart in appearance. **3** elegant and streamlined: *a sleek black car.*

– SYNONYMS **1 smooth,** glossy, shiny, shining, lustrous, silken, silky. **2 streamlined,** elegant, graceful.
– ANTONYMS scruffy.

▸ **verb** make hair smooth and glossy.
– DERIVATIVES **sleek·ly** adverb **sleek·ness** noun.
– ORIGIN from **SLICK**.

sleep /slēp/ ▶ **noun 1** a state of rest in which the eyes are closed, the muscles are relaxed, the nervous system is inactive, and the mind is unconscious. **2** a gummy substance found in the corners of the eyes after sleep.

– SYNONYMS **nap,** doze, siesta, catnap; informal snooze, forty winks, shut-eye; literary slumber.

▶ **verb** (past and past part. **slept**) **1** be asleep. **2** (**sleep something off**) recover from something by going to sleep. **3** (**sleep in**) remain asleep or in bed later than usual in the morning. **4** provide a specified number of people with beds or bedrooms. **5** (**sleep with**) have sex or be in a sexual relationship with someone. **6** (**sleep around**) have many casual sexual partners.

– SYNONYMS **be asleep,** doze, take a nap, take a siesta, catnap; informal snooze, get some shut-eye; literary slumber.
– ANTONYMS wake up.

– DERIVATIVES **sleep·less** adjective.
– PHRASES **put something to sleep** kill an animal painlessly.
– ORIGIN Old English.

WORD LINKS

sedative, **soporific** *causing sleep*

sleep·er /ˈslēpər/ ▶ **noun 1** a sleeping car or a train carrying sleeping cars. **2** a movie, book, or play that suddenly achieves success after first attracting little attention.

sleep·er cell ▶ **noun** a secretive group with suspected links to a terrorist organization that is planning or believed capable of carrying out an attack.

sleep·ing bag ▶ **noun** a warm padded bag to sleep in, especially when camping.

sleep·ing car ▶ **noun** a railroad car provided with beds or berths.

sleep·ing pill ▶ **noun** a tablet of a drug that helps a person to sleep.

sleep·ing sick·ness ▶ **noun** a tropical disease transmitted by the bite of the tsetse fly, causing extreme tiredness.

sleep·o·ver /ˈslēpˌōvər/ ▶ **noun** a night spent by children or young people at a friend's house.

sleep·walk /ˈslēpˌwôk/ ▶ **verb** walk around while asleep.
– DERIVATIVES **sleep·walk·er** noun.

sleep·y /ˈslēpē/ ▶ **adjective** (**sleepier**, **sleepiest**) **1** needing or ready for sleep. **2** (of a place) without much activity.

– SYNONYMS **1 drowsy,** tired, somnolent, heavy-eyed; informal dopey. **2 quiet,** peaceful, tranquil, placid, slow-moving, dull, boring.
– ANTONYMS awake, alert.

– DERIVATIVES **sleep·i·ly** adverb **sleep·i·ness** noun.

WORD TOOLKIT

sleepy ...	**tranquil ...**	**restful ...**
town	setting	sleep
backwater	atmosphere	night
seaside	beauty	slumber
hamlet	oasis	holiday
suburb	existence	break
morning	lake	weekend
summer	garden	activities

sleet /slēt/ ▶ **noun** rain containing some ice, or snow melting as it falls. ▶ **verb** (**it sleets**, **it is sleeting**, **it sleeted**) sleet falls.
– DERIVATIVES **sleet·y** adjective.
– ORIGIN Germanic.

sleeve /slēv/ ▶ **noun 1** the part of a piece of clothing that wholly or partly covers the arm. **2** a protective cover for a record. **3** a protective or connecting tube fitting over a rod, spindle, or smaller tube.
– DERIVATIVES **sleeved** adjective **sleeve·less** adjective.
– PHRASES **up one's sleeve** kept secret and ready for use when needed.
– ORIGIN Old English.

sleigh /slā/ ▶ **noun** a sled drawn by horses or reindeer.
– DERIVATIVES **sleigh·ing** noun.
– ORIGIN Dutch *slee*.

sleigh bell ▶ **noun** a tinkling bell attached to the harness of a sleigh horse.

sleight /slīt/ ▶ **noun** (in phrase **sleight of hand**) **1** skillful use of the hands, typically in performing conjuring tricks. **2** the use of cunning to deceive people.
– ORIGIN from Old Norse, 'sly.'

slen·der /ˈslendər/ ▶ **adjective** (**slenderer**, **slenderest**) **1** thin in a graceful and attractive way. **2** barely enough: *a slender majority.*

– SYNONYMS **1 slim,** lean, willowy, svelte, lissom, graceful, slight, thin, skinny. **2 faint,** remote, tenuous, fragile, slim, small, slight.
– ANTONYMS plump, strong.

– DERIVATIVES **slen·der·ly** adverb **slen·der·ness** noun.
– ORIGIN unknown.

slept /slept/ past and past participle of **SLEEP**.

sleuth /slo͞oᴛʜ/ informal ▶ **noun** a detective. ▶ **verb** (usu. as n. **sleuthing**) carry out a search or investigation.
– ORIGIN from Old Norse, 'track.'

slew[1] /slo͞o/ ▶ **verb** turn or slide violently or uncontrollably. ▶ **noun** a violent or uncontrollable turn or slide.
– ORIGIN unknown.

slew[2] past of **SLAY**.

slew[3] ▶ **noun** informal a large number or quantity: *he won a slew of awards for his film.*
– ORIGIN Irish *sluagh*.

slice /slīs/ ▶ **noun 1** a thin, broad piece of food cut from a larger portion. **2** a portion or share. **3** (in sports) a stroke or shot that makes the ball spin to one side.

– SYNONYMS **1 piece,** portion, slab, wedge, sliver, wafer. **2 share,** part, portion, percentage, proportion, allocation; informal cut.

▶ **verb 1** cut something into slices. **2** cut something with a sharp implement. **3** move easily and quickly: *a missile sliced through the air.* **4** (in sports) hit the ball at a slight angle so that it spins and curves as it travels.

– SYNONYMS **cut,** carve, divide.

– DERIVATIVES **slic·er** noun.
– ORIGIN Old French *esclice* 'splinter.'

slice-and-dice ▶ **adjective** informal involving the quick rearrangement of elements; able to be analyzed in a number of different ways.

slick /slik/ ▶ **adjective 1** done or operating in an impressively smooth and efficient way: *a slick piece of software.* **2** self-confident but shallow or insincere. **3** smooth, wet, and slippery or glossy: *his face was slick with sweat.*

– SYNONYMS **1 efficient,** smooth, smooth-running, polished, well organized, well run, streamlined.

2 **glib,** polished, assured, self-assured, smooth-talking, plausible; informal smarmy.

▶ **noun 1** an oil slick. **2** an application or amount of a glossy or oily substance.

▶ **verb** make hair smooth and glossy with water, oil, or cream.

– SYNONYMS **smooth,** plaster, sleek, grease, oil, gel.

– DERIVATIVES **slick·ly** adverb **slick·ness** noun.

– ORIGIN probably from an Old Norse word meaning 'smooth.'

slick·er /'slikər/ ▶ **noun 1** a raincoat. **2** informal a cheat or swindler.

slide /slīd/ ▶ **verb** (past and past part. **slid**) **1** move along a smooth surface while remaining in contact with it. **2** move smoothly, quickly, or without being noticed. **3** change gradually to a worse condition or lower level: *shares in the company slid to a ten-year low.*

– SYNONYMS **glide,** slip, slither, skim, skate, skid, slew.

▶ **noun 1** a structure with a smooth sloping surface for children to slide down. **2** a smooth stretch of ice or packed snow for sliding on. **3** an act of sliding. **4** a rectangular piece of glass on which an object is placed to be viewed under a microscope. **5** a small piece of photographic film set in a frame and viewed with a projector.

– ORIGIN Old English.

slid·er /'slīdər/ ▶ **noun 1** a North American freshwater turtle with a red or yellow patch on the side of the head. **2** Baseball a pitch that breaks slightly as it nears home plate. **3** a knob or lever that is moved horizontally or vertically to control a variable, such as the volume of a radio; a computer icon that mimics such a knob or lever.

slide rule ▶ **noun** a ruler with a sliding central strip, marked with logarithmic scales and used for making calculations.

slid·ing scale ▶ **noun** a scale of fees, wages, etc., that varies according to particular conditions.

slight /slīt/ ▶ **adjective 1** small in degree: *a slight increase in inflation.* **2** not sturdy and strongly built. **3** rather trivial or superficial.

– SYNONYMS **1 small,** tiny, minute, negligible, insignificant, minimal, remote, slim, faint. **2 slim,** slender, delicate, dainty, fragile.
– ANTONYMS large, plump.

▶ **verb** insult someone by treating them without proper respect.

– SYNONYMS **insult,** snub, rebuff, spurn, give someone the cold shoulder, take no notice of, scorn, ignore.

▶ **noun** an insult.

– SYNONYMS **insult,** affront, snub, rebuff; informal put-down, slap in the face.

– DERIVATIVES **slight·ness** noun.

– ORIGIN Old Norse, 'smooth.'

WORD TOOLKIT

See **MINOR**.

CHOOSE THE RIGHT WORD

See **NEGLECT**.

slight·ly /'slītlē/ ▶ **adverb** to a small degree.

– SYNONYMS *beat the egg whites until they're slightly stiff* **a little,** a bit, somewhat, moderately, faintly, vaguely, a shade.
– ANTONYMS very.

slim /slim/ ▶ **adjective** (**slimmer, slimmest**) **1** thin in a graceful way; slender. **2** small in width and long and narrow in shape. **3** very small: *a slim chance of success.*

– SYNONYMS **1 slender,** lean, thin, willowy, sylphlike, svelte, lissom, slight, trim. **2** *a slim chance* **slight,** small, slender, faint, remote.
– ANTONYMS fat.

▶ **verb** (**slims, slimming, slimmed**) **1** make or become thinner, especially by dieting. **2** (usu. **slim down**) reduce a business to a smaller size to make it more efficient.

– SYNONYMS **lose weight,** diet, go on a diet, slenderize.

– DERIVATIVES **slim·mer** noun **slim·ness** noun.

– ORIGIN German or Dutch.

slime /slīm/ ▶ **noun** an unpleasantly moist, soft, and slippery substance. ▶ **verb** cover something with slime.

– ORIGIN Old English.

slim·line /'slim,līn/ ▶ **adjective** slender in design.

slim·y /'slīmē/ ▶ **adjective** (**slimier, slimiest**) **1** covered by or resembling slime. **2** informal flattering in an unpleasantly insincere way.

– SYNONYMS **slippery,** slithery, greasy, sticky, viscous; informal slippy.

sling[1] /sliNG/ ▶ **verb** (past and past part. **slung** /sləNG/) **1** hang or carry loosely: *he had a huge bag slung over his shoulder.* **2** informal throw something casually. **3** hurl something from a sling or similar weapon.

– SYNONYMS **1 hang,** suspend, string, swing. **2 throw,** toss, fling, hurl, cast, pitch, lob, flip; informal chuck, heave.

▶ **noun 1** a flexible loop of fabric used to support or raise a hanging weight. **2** a weapon in the form of a strap or loop, used to hurl stones or other small missiles.

– DERIVATIVES **sling·er** noun.

– ORIGIN probably from German.

sling[2] ▶ **noun** a sweetened drink of liquor, especially gin, and water.

– ORIGIN unknown.

sling·shot /'sliNG,SHät/ ▶ **noun** a forked stick with an elastic strap fastened to the two prongs, used for shooting small stones.

slink /sliNGk/ ▶ **verb** (past and past part. **slunk** /sləNGk/) move smoothly and quietly in a stealthy way. ▶ **noun** an act of slinking.

– ORIGIN Old English, 'crawl, creep.'

slink·y /'sliNGkē/ ▶ **adjective** (**slinkier, slinkiest**) informal **1** (of an item of clothing) fitting closely to the curves of the body. **2** moving in a graceful and sensuous way: *slinky models sashayed down the catwalk.*

slip[1] /slip/ ▶ **verb** (**slips, slipping, slipped**) **1** lose one's balance or footing and slide for a short distance. **2** move or place quietly, quickly, or stealthily: *we slipped out by the back door.* **3** (usu. **slip up**) make a careless error. **4** accidentally slide or move out of position or from someone's grasp: *the paper slipped from his fingers.* **5** fail to grip or make proper contact with a surface. **6** gradually become worse. **7** escape or get free from something. **8** fail to be remembered by someone's mind.

9 release the clutch of a motor vehicle slightly or for a moment. **10** Knitting move a stitch to the other needle without knitting it.

– SYNONYMS **1 slide,** skid, slither, fall (over), lose one's balance, lose one's footing, tumble. **2 creep,** steal, sneak, slide, sidle, slope, slink, tiptoe. **3 (slip up) make a mistake,** blunder, get something wrong, miscalculate, make an error, err; informal make a boo-boo, goof (up).

▶ **noun 1** an act of slipping. **2** a minor or careless mistake. **3** a loose-fitting undergarment worn under a dress or skirt. **4** a space in which to dock a boat or ship.

– SYNONYMS **1 false step,** slide, skid, fall, tumble. **2 mistake,** error, blunder, gaffe, oversight, miscalculation, omission, lapse; informal slip-up, boo-boo, goof, blooper, howler.

– DERIVATIVES **slip·page** /'slipij/ noun.
– PHRASES **give someone the slip** informal avoid or escape from someone. **let something slip** reveal something accidentally in conversation. **slip of the tongue** (or **the pen**) a minor mistake in speech (or writing).
– ORIGIN probably from German *slippen*.

CHOOSE THE RIGHT WORD

See **MISTAKE**.

slip² ▶ **noun 1** a small piece of paper for writing on or that gives printed information. **2** a cutting taken from a plant for grafting or planting.
– PHRASES **a slip of a thing/boy/girl** a small, slim young person.
– ORIGIN probably from Dutch or German *slippe* 'cut, strip.'

slip³ ▶ **noun** a creamy mixture of clay, water, and typically a pigment, used for decorating earthenware.
– ORIGIN uncertain.

slip·case /'slip,kās/ ▶ **noun** a close-fitting case open at one side or end for an object such as a book.

slip·cov·er /'slip,kəvər/ ▶ **noun 1** a detachable fitted cover for a chair or sofa. **2** a jacket for a book.

slip knot ▶ **noun** a knot that can be undone by a pull, or that can slide along the rope on which it is tied.

slip-on ▶ **adjective** (of shoes or clothes) having no fastenings and able to be put on and taken off quickly.

slipped disk (also **slipped disc**) ▶ **noun** an instance of the inner material of a disk between the bones of the spine protruding through the outer coat, pressing on nearby nerves and causing pain.

slip·per /'slipər/ ▶ **noun** a comfortable slip-on shoe that is worn indoors.
– DERIVATIVES **slip·pered** adjective.

slip·per·y /'slipərē/ ▶ **adjective 1** difficult to hold firmly or stand on through being smooth, wet, or slimy. **2** (of a person) not able to be relied on or trusted.

– SYNONYMS **1 slithery,** greasy, oily, icy, glassy, smooth, slimy, wet; informal slippy. **2 sneaky,** sly, devious, crafty, cunning, tricky, evasive, scheming, unreliable, untrustworthy; informal shady, shifty.

– DERIVATIVES **slip·per·i·ness** noun.
– PHRASES **slippery slope** a course of action very likely to lead to something undesirable: *she was on the slippery slope to alcoholism*.

slip·per·y elm ▶ **noun** a North American elm tree with a slimy inner bark that is used in herbal medicine.

slip·shod /'slip,shäd/ ▶ **adjective** careless, thoughtless, or disorganized.

– SYNONYMS **careless,** lackadaisical, slapdash, disorganized, haphazard, hit-or-miss, untidy, messy, unsystematic, casual, negligent, neglectful, lax, slack; informal sloppy, slaphappy.
– ANTONYMS meticulous.

– ORIGIN first meaning 'wearing loose shoes or slippers.'

slip stitch ▶ **noun** (in sewing) a loose stitch used to join layers of fabric, invisible from the outside of the garment.

slip·stream /'slip,strēm/ ▶ **noun 1** a current of air or water driven back by a revolving propeller or jet engine. **2** the partial vacuum created behind a moving vehicle. ▶ **verb** (especially in motor racing) follow in the slipstream of a vehicle to assist in overtaking it.

slip-up ▶ **noun** informal a mistake.

slip·way /'slip,wā/ ▶ **noun** a slope leading into water, used for launching and landing boats and ships or for building and repairing them.

slit /slit/ ▶ **noun** a long, narrow cut or opening.

– SYNONYMS **1 cut,** incision, split, slash, gash. **2 opening,** gap, chink, crack, aperture, slot.

▶ **verb** (**slits, slitting, slit**) **1** make a slit in something. **2** (past and past part. **slitted**) narrow one's eyes into slits; squint.

– SYNONYMS **cut,** slash, split open, slice open.

– ORIGIN Old English.

slith·er /'sli*th*ər/ ▶ **verb 1** move smoothly over a surface with a twisting motion. **2** slide unsteadily on a loose or slippery surface.

– SYNONYMS **slide,** slip, glide, wriggle, crawl, skid.

▶ **noun 1** a sliding or twisting movement. **2** a small, narrow piece of something; a sliver.
– DERIVATIVES **slith·er·y** adjective.
– ORIGIN from **SLIDE**.

sliv·er /'slivər/ ▶ **noun** a small, narrow piece cut or split off a larger piece.

– SYNONYMS **splinter,** shard, chip, flake, shred, scrap, shaving, paring, piece, fragment.

▶ **verb** cut or break something into slivers.
– ORIGIN from dialect *slive* 'cleave.'

sliv·o·vitz /'slivə,vits/ ▶ **noun** a type of plum brandy made chiefly in the former Yugoslavia and in Romania.
– ORIGIN Serbo-Croat.

slob /släb/ informal ▶ **noun** a lazy and untidy person.

– SYNONYMS **layabout,** good-for-nothing, sluggard, laggard; informal slacker, couch potato.

▶ **verb** behave in a lazy and untidy way.
– DERIVATIVES **slob·bish** adjective **slob·by** adjective.
– ORIGIN Irish *slab* 'mud.'

slob·ber /'släbər/ ▶ **verb 1** have saliva dripping from the mouth. **2** (**slobber over**) show excessive enthusiasm for someone or something.

– SYNONYMS **drool,** slaver, dribble, salivate.

▶ **noun** excessive saliva dripping from the mouth.
– DERIVATIVES **slob·ber·y** adjective.
– ORIGIN probably from Dutch *slobberen* 'walk through mud, feed noisily.'

sloe /slō/ ▶ **noun 1** the small bluish-black fruit of the blackthorn, with a sharp sour taste. **2** another term for **BLACKTHORN**.
– ORIGIN Old English.

sloe-eyed ▸ adjective having attractive dark almond-shaped eyes.

slog /släg/ informal ▸ verb (**slogs, slogging, slogged**) **1** work hard over a period of time. **2** walk or move with difficulty or effort. **3** hit something forcefully but wildly. ▸ noun a spell of difficult, tiring work or traveling.
– DERIVATIVES **slog·ger** noun.
– ORIGIN unknown.

slo·gan /'slōgən/ ▸ noun a short, memorable phrase used in advertising or associated with a political party or other group.

> – SYNONYMS **catchphrase,** catchline, sound bite, motto, jingle; informal tag line.

– ORIGIN from Scottish Gaelic *sluagh* 'army' + *gairm* 'shout.'

slo-mo /'slō 'mō/ ▸ noun short for SLOW MOTION.

sloop /slo͞op/ ▸ noun a type of sailboat with one mast.
– ORIGIN Dutch *sloep.*

slop /släp/ ▸ verb (**slops, slopping, slopped**) **1** (of a liquid) spill over the edge of a container. **2** apply something casually or carelessly. **3** feed slops to an animal, especially a pig. ▸ noun (**slops**) **1** waste water that has to be emptied by hand. **2** unappetizing semiliquid food. **3** semiliquid kitchen refuse, often used as animal food.
– ORIGIN probably from SLIP[3].

slope /slōp/ ▸ noun **1** a surface with one end or side at a higher level than another. **2** a part of the side of a hill or mountain.

> – SYNONYMS **tilt,** pitch, slant, angle, gradient, grade, incline, inclination, fall, camber.

▸ verb (of a surface) be at an angle so that one end is higher than another.

> – SYNONYMS **1 tilt,** slant, incline, lean, drop/fall away, descend, shelve, camber, rise, ascend, climb. **2** (as adj. **sloping**) *a sloping floor* **slanting,** leaning, inclined, angled, cambered, tilted.

– ORIGIN uncertain.

slop·py /'släpē/ ▸ adjective (**sloppier, sloppiest**) **1** careless and disorganized: *the organization's sloppy management is hindering its work.* **2** slovenly. **3** (of a substance) containing too much liquid; watery. **4** (of a piece of clothing) casual and loose-fitting. **5** informal excessively sentimental.

> – SYNONYMS **1 runny,** watery, liquid, mushy; informal gloppy. **2 careless,** slapdash, slipshod, disorganized, untidy, slack, slovenly; informal slaphappy.

– DERIVATIVES **slop·pi·ly** adverb **slop·pi·ness** noun.

slosh /släsн/ ▸ verb **1** (of liquid in a container) move around with a splashing sound. **2** move through liquid with a splashing sound. **3** pour liquid clumsily. ▸ noun an act or sound of splashing.
– DERIVATIVES **slosh·y** adjective.
– ORIGIN from SLUSH.

sloshed /släsнt/ ▸ adjective informal drunk.

slot /slät/ ▸ noun **1** a long, narrow opening into which something may be placed or fitted. **2** a place given to someone or something in an arrangement or scheme: *her show is taking its rightful place in the Saturday evening slot.*

> – SYNONYMS **1 aperture,** slit, crack, hole, opening. **2 time,** spot, period, niche, space; informal window.

▸ verb (**slots, slotting, slotted**) **1** place or be placed into a slot. **2** (**slot in/into**) fit easily into a new role or situation.

> – SYNONYMS **insert,** slide, fit, put, place.

– DERIVATIVES **slot·ted** adjective.
– ORIGIN Old French *esclot.*

sloth /slôтн, slätн, slōтн/ ▸ noun **1** reluctance to work or make an effort; laziness. **2** a slow-moving tropical American mammal that hangs upside down from branches.

> – SYNONYMS **laziness,** idleness, indolence, slothfulness, inactivity, inertia, sluggishness, shiftlessness, apathy, listlessness, lassitude, lethargy, languor.
> – ANTONYMS industriousness.

– DERIVATIVES **sloth·ful** adjective.
– ORIGIN Old English.

slot ma·chine ▸ noun a coin-operated gambling machine that generates combinations of symbols, with certain combinations winning money for the player.

slouch /slouсн/ ▸ verb stand, move, or sit in a lazy, drooping way. ▸ noun a lazy, drooping way of standing or sitting.
– DERIVATIVES **slouch·y** adjective.
– PHRASES **be no slouch** informal be good or fast at something.
– ORIGIN unknown.

slouch hat ▸ noun a hat with a wide, flexible brim.

slough[1] /slou, slo͞o/ ▸ noun **1** a swamp. **2** a situation in which there is no progress or activity.
– ORIGIN Old English.

slough[2] /sləf/ ▸ verb **1** (of an animal, especially a snake) shed an old skin. **2** (**slough something off**) get rid of something that is unwanted.
– ORIGIN perhaps from German *sluwe* 'husk, peel.'

Slo·vak /'slōväk, -vak/ ▸ noun **1** a person from Slovakia. **2** the language of Slovakia.

Slo·va·ki·an /slō'väkēən/ ▸ noun a person from Slovakia. ▸ adjective relating to Slovakia.

Slo·vene /'slōvēn/ ▸ noun **1** a person from Slovenia. **2** the language of Slovenia.
– DERIVATIVES **Slo·ve·ni·an** /slō'vēnēən/ noun & adjective.

slov·en·ly /'sləvənlē, 'slä-/ ▸ adjective **1** untidy and dirty. **2** excessively casual; careless.

> – SYNONYMS **1 scruffy,** untidy, messy, unkempt, ill-groomed, disheveled, bedraggled, rumpled, frowzy. **2 careless,** slapdash, slipshod, haphazard, hit-or-miss, untidy, messy, negligent, lax, lackadaisical, slack; informal sloppy, slaphappy.
> – ANTONYMS tidy, careful.

– DERIVATIVES **slov·en·li·ness** noun.

slow /slō/ ▸ adjective **1** moving or capable of moving only at a low speed. **2** taking a long time. **3** not quick to understand, think, or learn. **4** (of a clock or watch) showing a time earlier than the correct time. **5** showing little activity: *sales were slow.* **6** (of photographic film) needing long exposure. **7** (of an oven) giving off heat gently.

> – SYNONYMS **1 unhurried,** leisurely, steady, sedate, measured, ponderous, sluggish, plodding. **2 lengthy,** time-consuming, long-drawn-out, protracted, prolonged, gradual. **3 stupid,** unintelligent, obtuse; informal dense, dim, thick, slow on the uptake, dumb, dopey.
> – ANTONYMS fast, quick.

▶ **verb** (often **slow down/up**) **1** reduce one's speed or the speed of a vehicle or process. **2** work or live less actively or intensely.

– SYNONYMS **1** *the traffic forced him to* ***slow down*** **reduce speed,** go slower, decelerate, brake. **2** *this would* ***slow up*** *our progress* **hold back,** hold up, delay, retard, set back, check, curb.
– ANTONYMS accelerate.

– DERIVATIVES **slow·ness** noun.
– ORIGIN Old English.

USAGE

Slow is normally used as an adjective (*a slow learner*). It is also used as an adverb in certain situations, including compounds such as **slow-acting** and in the expression **go slow**. However, it is not the best style to use **slow** as an adverb in other ways (e.g. *he drives too slow*): in these cases, you should use **slowly** instead.

CHOOSE THE RIGHT WORD

See **STUPID**.

slow cook·er ▶ **noun** a large electric pot used for cooking food very slowly.

slow·down /ˈslō,doun/ ▶ **noun** a reduction in speed or activity, especially economic activity.

slow·ly /ˈslōlē/ ▶ **adverb** at a slow speed; not quickly.

– SYNONYMS **1** *Tom walked off slowly* **unhurriedly,** without hurrying, steadily, at a leisurely pace, at a snail's pace. **2** *her health is improving slowly* **gradually,** bit by bit, little by little, slowly but surely, step by step.
– ANTONYMS quickly.

slow mo·tion ▶ **noun** the action of showing film or video more slowly than it was made or recorded, so that the action appears much slower than in real life.

slow·poke /ˈslō,pōk/ ▶ **noun** informal a person who acts or moves slowly, especially in an annoying or inconvenient way.

slow-worm ▶ **noun** a small snakelike lizard without legs.
– ORIGIN Old English.

SLR ▶ **abbreviation 1** self-loading rifle. **2** single-lens reflex.

sludge /sləj/ ▶ **noun 1** thick, soft, wet mud. **2** semisolid industrial waste.
– DERIVATIVES **sludg·y** adjective.
– ORIGIN uncertain.

slug[1] /sləg/ ▶ **noun 1** a small mollusk that resembles a snail without a shell. **2** a small amount of an alcoholic drink. **3** a bullet. ▶ **verb** (**slugs, slugging, slugged**) gulp a drink, especially an alcoholic one.
– ORIGIN probably Scandinavian.

slug[2] informal ▶ **verb** (**slugs, slugging, slugged**) **1** hit someone hard. **2** (**slug it out**) settle a dispute or contest by fighting or competing fiercely. ▶ **noun** a hard blow.
– ORIGIN unknown.

slug·gard /ˈsləgərd/ ▶ **noun** a lazy, inactive person.
– DERIVATIVES **slug·gard·ly** adjective.
– ORIGIN from former *slug* 'be lazy or slow.'

slug·ger /ˈsləgər/ ▶ **noun 1** a person who throws hard punches. **2** a baseball player who consistently hits for power, especially home runs and doubles.

slug·gish /ˈsləgisн/ ▶ **adjective 1** slow-moving or inactive. **2** lacking energy or alertness.

– SYNONYMS **lethargic,** listless, lacking in energy, lifeless, inactive, slow, torpid, enervated.
– ANTONYMS vigorous.

– DERIVATIVES **slug·gish·ly** adverb **slug·gish·ness** noun.

sluice /slo͞os/ ▶ **noun 1** (also **sluice gate**) a sliding gate or other device for controlling the flow of water. **2** (also **sluiceway**) an artificial channel for carrying off surplus water. **3** an act of rinsing with water. ▶ **verb** wash or rinse someone or something with water.
– ORIGIN Old French *escluse*.

slum /sləm/ ▶ **noun 1** a run-down and overcrowded area of a city or town inhabited by very poor people. **2** a house or building that is unfit to be lived in.

– SYNONYMS **hovel**; (**slums**) ghetto, shanty town.

▶ **verb** (**slums, slumming, slummed**) (**slum it**) informal accept conditions that are worse than those one is used to.
– DERIVATIVES **slum·mer** noun **slum·my** adjective.
– ORIGIN unknown.

slum·ber /ˈsləmbər/ literary ▶ **verb** be asleep. ▶ **noun** a sleep.
– DERIVATIVES **slum·ber·ous** /-bərəs/ (also **slumbrous** /-brəs/) adjective.
– ORIGIN from Scots and northern English *sloom*.

slump /sləmp/ ▶ **verb 1** sit, lean, or fall heavily and limply. **2** decline greatly or over a prolonged period: *prices slumped due to sluggish demand.*

– SYNONYMS **1 sit heavily,** flop, collapse, sink. **2 fall,** plummet, tumble, collapse, drop; informal crash, nosedive.

▶ **noun 1** a sudden or severe drop in the price or value of something. **2** a prolonged period of abnormally low economic activity. **3** a period of poor performance.

– SYNONYMS **1 fall,** drop, tumble, downturn, downswing, slide, decline, decrease; informal nosedive. **2 recession,** decline, depression, slowdown.
– ANTONYMS rise, boom.

– ORIGIN probably from Norwegian *slumpe* 'to fall.'

slung /sləɴɢ/ past and past participle of **SLING**[1].

slunk /sləɴɢk/ past and past participle of **SLINK**.

slur /slər/ ▶ **verb** (**slurs, slurring, slurred**) **1** speak words in an unclear way, with the sounds running into one another. **2** perform a group of musical notes so that each runs smoothly into the next. **3** make damaging or false statements about someone.

– SYNONYMS **mumble,** speak unclearly, garble.

▶ **noun 1** an insult or accusation intended to damage someone's reputation. **2** an act of speaking indistinctly. **3** a curved line indicating that musical notes are to be performed so that each runs into the next.

– SYNONYMS **insult,** slight, slander, smear, allegation, imputation.

– ORIGIN unknown.

slurp /slərp/ ▶ **verb** eat or drink something with a loud sucking sound. ▶ **noun** an act or sound of slurping.
– ORIGIN Dutch *slurpen*.

slur·ry /ˈslərē/ ▶ **noun** (pl. **slurries**) a semiliquid mixture of manure, cement, or coal and water.
– ORIGIN unknown.

slush /sləsн/ ▶ **noun 1** partially melted snow or ice. **2** informal excessive sentiment in novels, movies, etc. ▶ **verb** make a soft splashing sound.
– DERIVATIVES **slush·y** adjective.
– ORIGIN uncertain.

slush fund ▶ **noun** a reserve of money used for underhanded or dishonest purposes, especially political bribery.
– ORIGIN from nautical slang, referring to money collected to buy luxuries, from the sale of watery food known as *slush*.

slut /slət/ ▶ **noun** a woman who has many sexual partners.
– DERIVATIVES **slut·tish** adjective **slut·ty** adjective.
– ORIGIN unknown.

sly /slī/ ▶ **adjective** (**slyer, slyest**) **1** having a cunning and deceitful nature. **2** (of a remark, glance, or expression) suggesting that one has secret knowledge that may be damaging or embarrassing: *slip the doorman a note with a sly grin*. **3** (of an action) done secretly.

– SYNONYMS **1 cunning,** crafty, clever, wily, artful, tricky, scheming, devious, underhanded/underhand, sneaky. **2 roguish,** mischievous, impish, playful, wicked, arch, knowing. **3 surreptitious,** furtive, stealthy, covert.
– ANTONYMS open, straightforward.

– DERIVATIVES **sly·ly** adverb **sly·ness** noun.
– PHRASES **on the sly** in a secret way.
– ORIGIN Old Norse, 'cunning.'

SM ▶ **abbreviation 1** sadomasochism. **2** Sergeant Major.

Sm ▶ **symbol** the chemical element samarium.

smack[1] /smak/ ▶ **noun 1** a sharp blow given with the palm of the hand. **2** a loud, sharp sound. **3** a loud kiss.

– SYNONYMS **slap,** blow, cuff, clip, spank; informal whack.

▶ **verb 1** hit someone or something sharply with the palm of the hand. **2** hit or smash something into something else. **3** part the lips noisily.

– SYNONYMS **slap,** strike, hit, cuff, clip, spank; informal whack.

▶ **adverb** informal **1** exactly; precisely: *the hotel is slap in the middle of town*. **2** in a sudden and violent way: *storming out of her room, she ran slap into Luke*.

– SYNONYMS **exactly,** precisely, straight, right, directly, squarely, dead, plumb; informal slam bang, smack dab.

– ORIGIN Dutch *smacken*.

smack[2] ▶ **verb** (**smack of**) **1** seem to contain or involve something wrong or undesirable: *such writing smacks of racism*. **2** taste of something. ▶ **noun** (**a smack of**) a taste or suggestion of something.
– ORIGIN Old English.

smack[3] ▶ **noun** informal heroin.
– ORIGIN probably from a Yiddish word meaning 'a sniff.'

smack[4] ▶ **noun** Brit. a sailboat with one mast, used for fishing.
– ORIGIN Dutch *smak*.

smack·er /'smakər/ (also **smackeroo** /ˌsmakə'ro͞o/) ▶ **noun** informal **1** a loud kiss. **2** dated one dollar.

small /smôl/ ▶ **adjective 1** not large in size, amount, or number. **2** not great in strength, importance, or power: *a small voice*. **3** not fully grown or developed; young. **4** (of a business or its owner) operating on a modest scale: *a small farmer*.

– SYNONYMS **1 little,** tiny, short, petite, diminutive, elfin, miniature, mini, minute, toy, baby, undersized, poky, cramped; Scottish wee; informal teeny, teensy, teeny-weeny, teensy-weensy, tiddly, pint-sized. **2 slight,** minor, unimportant, trifling, trivial, insignificant, inconsequential, negligible, inappreciable; informal piffling.
– ANTONYMS big, large.

▶ **noun** (**smalls**) Brit. informal underwear.
▶ **adverb** into small pieces.
– DERIVATIVES **small·ness** noun.
– PHRASES **feel** (or **look**) **small** feel (or look) foolish or unimportant. **the small of the back** the part of a person's back where the spine curves in at the level of the waist. **the small screen** television.
– ORIGIN Old English.

CHOOSE THE RIGHT WORD

small, diminutive, little, miniature, minute, petite, tiny

Why do we call a house **small** and a woman **petite**? *Small* and **little** are used interchangeably to describe people or things of reduced dimensions, but *small* is preferred when describing something concrete that is of less than the usual size, quantity, value, or importance (*a small matter to discuss; a small room; a small price to pay*). *Little* more often refers to concepts (*through little fault of his own; an issue of little importance*) or to a more drastic reduction in scale (*a little shopping cart just like the one her mother used*). **Diminutive** and *petite* intensify the meaning of *small*, particularly with reference to women's figures that are very trim and compact (*with her diminutive figure, she had to shop in stores that specialized in petite sizes*). **Tiny** is used to describe what is extremely small, often to the point where it can be seen only by looking closely (*a tiny flaw in the material; a tiny insect*), while **minute** not only describes what is seen with difficulty but may also refer to a very small amount of something (*minute traces of gunpowder on his glove*). **Miniature** applies specifically to a copy, a model, or a representation of something on a very small scale (*a child's mobile consisting of miniature farm animals*).

small arms ▶ **plural noun** portable firearms.

small change ▶ **noun 1** coins of low value. **2** something trivial.

small claims court ▶ **noun** a local court in which claims for small sums of money can be heard and decided quickly and cheaply, without using a lawyer.

small fry ▶ **plural noun 1** unimportant people or things. **2** young or small fish.

small in·tes·tine ▶ **noun** the part of the intestine that runs between the stomach and the large intestine.

small-mind·ed ▶ **adjective** having a narrow outlook; petty.

small·pox /'smôlˌpäks/ ▶ **noun** a serious disease spread by a virus, with fever and blisters that leave permanent scars.

small print ▶ **noun** important details or conditions in an agreement or contract that are printed in small type so that they are not easily noticed.

small-scale ▶ **adjective** of limited size or extent.

small talk ▶ **noun** polite conversation about unimportant matters.

small-time ▶ **adjective** informal unimportant; minor.

smarm·y /'smärmē/ ▶ **adjective** (**smarmier, smarmiest**) informal friendly or flattering in an insincere or excessive way.

– SYNONYMS **unctuous,** ingratiating, slick, oily, greasy, obsequious, sycophantic, fawning; informal slimy.

– DERIVATIVES **smarm·i·ly** adverb **smarm·i·ness** noun.

smart /smärt/ ▶ **adjective** **1** informal intelligent. **2** informal quick-witted and clever. **3** clever in an impudent or sarcastic way. **4** clean, tidy, and stylish. **5** (of a place) fashionable and upmarket. **6** attractive and new in appearance: *smart bathroom furniture*. **7** quick; brisk: *I set off at a smart pace.*

– SYNONYMS **1 well dressed,** well turned out, stylish, chic, fashionable, modish, elegant, dapper; informal natty, snappy. **2** *a smart restaurant* **fashionable,** stylish, high-class, exclusive, chic, fancy, upscale, upmarket, high-toned; informal trendy, classy, swanky, swank, swish. **3 clever,** bright, intelligent, quick-witted, shrewd, astute, perceptive; informal brainy, quick on the uptake. **4** *a smart pace* **brisk,** quick, fast, rapid, lively, energetic, vigorous; informal cracking.
– ANTONYMS scruffy, stupid.

▶ **verb** **1** feel a sharp, stinging pain. **2** feel upset and annoyed.

– SYNONYMS **1 sting,** burn, tingle, prickle, hurt. **2** *she smarted at the accusation* **feel hurt,** feel upset, take offense, feel aggrieved, feel indignant, be put out.

▶ **noun** **1** a sharp, stinging pain. **2** (**smarts**) informal intelligence or shrewdness.
– DERIVATIVES **smart·ly** adverb **smart·ness** noun.
– PHRASES **look smart** chiefly Brit. be quick.
– ORIGIN Old English.

smart al·eck /'alik/ (also **smart alec**) ▶ **noun** informal a person who is irritating because they behave as if they know everything.

smart-ass ▶ **noun** informal another term for SMART ALECK.

smart bomb ▶ **noun** a radio-controlled or laser-guided bomb, often with a built-in computer.

smart card ▶ **noun** a plastic card on which information is stored in electronic form, used for financial transactions.

smart dust ▶ **noun** a collection of very small computerized sensors capable of wireless communication, designed to act as a dispersed network.

smart·en /'smärtn/ ▶ **verb** (**smarten up**) make or become smarter.

smart growth ▶ **noun** planned economic and community development that attempts to curb urban sprawl and worsening environmental conditions.

smart·phone /'smärtˌfōn/ ▶ **noun** a cell phone that incorporates a palmtop computer.

smart·y /'smärtē/ ▶ **noun** (pl. **smarties**) informal a person who behaves as if they know everything.

smart·y-pants ▶ **noun** another term for SMARTY.

smash /smasʜ/ ▶ **verb** **1** break violently into pieces. **2** hit or collide forcefully. **3** crash and severely damage a vehicle. **4** (in sports) hit the ball very hard. **5** completely defeat, destroy, or put an end to: *police smashed a major crime network*.

– SYNONYMS **1 break,** shatter, splinter, crack; informal bust. **2** *he smashed into a wall* **crash into,** smack into, slam into, plow into, run into, bump into, hit, strike, ram, collide with, impact.

▶ **noun** **1** an act or sound of smashing. **2** (also **smash hit**) informal a very successful song, movie, or show.

– SYNONYMS **crash,** collision, accident, wreck; informal pile-up.

– ORIGIN probably imitating the sound.

smashed /smasʜt/ ▶ **adjective** informal very drunk.

smash·ing /'smasʜiɴɢ/ ▶ **adjective** Brit. informal excellent; wonderful.

smat·ter·ing /'smatəriɴɢ/ ▶ **noun** **1** a small amount. **2** a slight knowledge of a language or subject.

– SYNONYMS **bit,** little, modicum, touch, soupçon, rudiments, basics; informal smidgen, smidge, tad.

– ORIGIN unknown.

smear /smi(ə)r/ ▶ **verb** **1** coat or mark someone or something with a greasy or sticky substance. **2** blur or smudge something. **3** damage a person's reputation by false accusations.

– SYNONYMS **1 spread,** rub, daub, slap, cover, coat, smother, plaster. **2 smudge,** streak, mark. **3 sully,** tarnish, blacken, drag through the mud, damage, defame, malign, slur, slander, libel.

▶ **noun** **1** a greasy or sticky mark. **2** a false accusation. **3** a sample thinly spread on a slide for examination under a microscope.

– SYNONYMS **1 streak,** smudge, daub, dab, spot, patch, blotch, mark; informal splotch. **2 accusation,** lie, untruth, slur, slander, libel, defamation.

– DERIVATIVES **smear·y** adjective.
– ORIGIN Old English.

smell /smel/ ▶ **noun** **1** the faculty of sensing things by means of the organs in the nose. **2** something sensed by the nose; a scent or odor. **3** an act of smelling.

– SYNONYMS **1 odor,** aroma, fragrance, scent, perfume, bouquet, nose. **2 stink,** stench, reek.

▶ **verb** (past and past part. **smelt** or **smelled**) **1** sense the scent or odor of someone or something. **2** sniff at something in order to find out its smell. **3** have a particular scent or odor: *the room smelled of dampness*. **4** have a strong or unpleasant odor. **5** sense or suspect that something exists or is about to happen: *I can smell trouble*.

– SYNONYMS **1 scent,** sniff, get a sniff/whiff of, detect. **2 stink,** reek.

– DERIVATIVES **smell·er** noun.
– PHRASES **smell a rat** informal suspect a trick.
– ORIGIN unknown.

WORD LINKS

olfactory *relating to the sense of smell*

smell·ing salts ▶ **plural noun** chiefly historical a chemical mixed with perfume, sniffed by someone who feels faint.

smell·y /'smelē/ ▶ **adjective** (**smellier**, **smelliest**) having a strong or unpleasant smell.

– SYNONYMS **foul-smelling,** stinking, reeking, rank, fetid, malodorous, pungent; literary noisome.

– DERIVATIVES **smell·i·ness** noun.

smelt[1] /smelt/ ▶ **verb** extract metal from its ore by a process involving heating and melting.
– DERIVATIVES **smelt·er** noun.
– ORIGIN Dutch, German *smelten*.

smelt[2] past and past participle of SMELL.

smelt[3] ▶ **noun** (pl. same or **smelts**) a small silvery fish that lives both in fresh water and the sea.
– ORIGIN Old English.

smid·gen /ˈsmijin/ (also **smidgeon** or **smidgin**) ▶ **noun** informal a tiny amount of something.
– ORIGIN perhaps from Scots *smitch* in the same sense.

smi·lax /ˈsmīlaks/ ▶ **noun 1** a climbing shrub with hooks and tendrils, grown as ornamentals or for their sarsaparilla-yielding roots. **2** a climbing asparagus with decorative foliage.

smile /smīl/ ▶ **verb 1** form the features of the face into a pleased, friendly, or amused expression, with the corners of the mouth turned up. **2 (smile at/on)** be favorable to: *luck was smiling on them as they carried out their plan.*

– SYNONYMS **beam,** grin (from ear to ear), smirk, simper, leer.
– ANTONYMS frown.

▶ **noun** an act of smiling.

– SYNONYMS **beam,** grin, smirk, simper, leer.

– ORIGIN perhaps Scandinavian.

CHOOSE THE RIGHT WORD

smile, grin, simper, smirk

The facial expression created by turning the corners of the mouth upward is commonly known as a **smile**. It can convey a wide range of emotion, from pleasure, approval, or amusement to insincerity and disinterest (*his complaint was met with a blank smile*). A **grin** is a wide smile that suggests spontaneous cheerfulness, warmth, pleasure, or amusement (*her teasing provoked an affectionate grin*). But *grin* may also describe a ferocious baring of the teeth or an angry grimace (*the grin of a skeleton*). A **simper**, on the other hand, is an expression of smugness and self-righteousness (*her simper of superiority*) as well as a silly or affected smile (*she curtsied with a girlish simper*). **Smirk** also implies an affected or self-conscious smile, but one that expresses derision or hostility (*to trick someone and then smirk as he makes a fool of himself*).

smil·ey /ˈsmīlē/ ▶ **adjective** informal smiling; cheerful. ▶ **noun** (pl. **smileys**) a symbol that represents a smiling face, formed by the characters :-) and used in emails and similar electronic communications.

smirch /smərCH/ ▶ **verb 1** make someone or something dirty. **2** damage a person's reputation.
– ORIGIN uncertain.

smirk /smərk/ ▶ **verb** smile in a smug or silly way.

– SYNONYMS **sneer,** simper, snigger, leer, grin.

▶ **noun** a smug or silly smile.
– DERIVATIVES **smirk·er** noun **smirk·y** adjective.
– ORIGIN Old English.

CHOOSE THE RIGHT WORD

See note at **SMILE**.

smite /smīt/ ▶ **verb** (past **smote** /smōt/; past part. **smitten** /ˈsmitn/) **1 (be smitten)** be affected severely by a disease or feeling. **2 (be smitten)** be strongly attracted to someone or something. **3** literary hit someone or something with a hard blow. **4** old use defeat or conquer an opponent.

– SYNONYMS **1 (be smitten)** *he was smitten with cholera* **struck down,** laid low, suffering, affected, afflicted. **2 (be smitten)** *Vince had been smitten with Tess for years* **infatuated,** besotted, in love, obsessed, head over heels, enamored, captivated, enchanted, under someone's spell; informal bowled over, swept off one's feet.

– ORIGIN Old English, 'to smear, blemish.'

smith /smiTH/ ▶ **noun 1** a person who works in metal. **2** a blacksmith. ▶ **verb** treat metal by heating, hammering, and forging it.
– ORIGIN Old English.

smith·er·eens /ˌsmiT͟Həˈrēnz/ ▶ **plural noun** informal small pieces.
– ORIGIN probably from Irish *smidirín*.

smith·y /ˈsmiTHē/ ▶ **noun** (pl. **smithies**) a blacksmith's workshop.
– ORIGIN Old Norse.

smit·ten /ˈsmitn/ past participle of **SMITE**.

smock /smäk/ ▶ **noun 1** a loose dress or blouse with the upper part closely gathered in smocking. **2** a loose garment worn to protect one's clothes. ▶ **verb** decorate a dress or blouse with smocking.
– ORIGIN Old English.

smock·ing /ˈsmäkiNG/ ▶ **noun** decoration on a garment created by gathering a section of the material into tight pleats and holding them together with a pattern of parallel stitches.

smog/ smäg/ ▶ **noun** fog or haze intensified by smoke or other pollution in the atmosphere.
– DERIVATIVES **smog·gy** adjective.
– ORIGIN blend of **SMOKE** and **FOG**.

smoke /smōk/ ▶ **noun 1** a visible vapor in the air, produced by a burning substance. **2** an act of smoking tobacco. **3** informal a cigarette or cigar.

– SYNONYMS **fumes,** exhaust, gas, vapor, smog.

▶ **verb 1** give out smoke. **2** breathe the smoke of a cigarette, pipe, etc., in and out. **3** cure or preserve meat or fish by hanging it in smoke. **4 (smoke someone/thing out)** drive someone or something out of a place by using smoke. **5** (as adj. **smoked**) (of glass) treated so as to darken it.

– SYNONYMS **1 smolder;** old use reek. **2 puff on,** draw on, pull on, inhale; informal drag on.

– DERIVATIVES **smok·a·ble** adjective **smoke·less** /ˈsmōkləs/ adjective **smok·er** noun.
– PHRASES **go up in smoke** informal **1** be destroyed by fire. **2** (of a plan) come to nothing. **where there's smoke, there's fire** there is always a reason for a rumor.
– ORIGIN Old English.

smoke alarm ▶ **noun** a device that detects and gives a warning of the presence of smoke.

smoke-free ▶ **adjective 1** without smoke: *a smoke-free environment.* **2** where smoking is not permitted: *a smoke-free train.*

smoke·screen /ˈsmōkˌskrēn/ ▶ **noun 1** something intended to disguise someone's real intentions or activities. **2** a cloud of smoke created to conceal military operations.

smoke·stack /ˈsmōkˌstak/ ▶ **noun** a chimney or funnel for discharging smoke from a locomotive, ship, or factory.

smok·ing gun ▶ **noun** a piece of evidence that proves without doubt that someone is guilty of wrongdoing.

smok·ing jack·et ▶ **noun** a man's comfortable jacket, formerly worn while smoking after dinner.

smok·y /ˈsmōkē/ (also **smokey**) ▶ **adjective** (**smokier, smokiest**) **1** producing or filled with smoke. **2** having the taste or smell of smoked food. **3** resembling smoke in color or appearance: *smoky gray eyeshadows.*

– SYNONYMS **smoke-filled,** sooty, smoggy, hazy, foggy, murky, thick.

– DERIVATIVES **smok·i·ly** adverb **smok·i·ness** noun.

smol·der /ˈsmōldər/ (Brit. **smoulder**) ▶ **verb 1** burn slowly with smoke but no flame. **2** feel intense and barely concealed anger, hatred, lust, etc.
– ORIGIN Dutch *smeulen.*

smolt /smōlt/ ▶ **noun** a young salmon or trout after the parr stage (two years old), when it migrates to the sea for the first time.
– ORIGIN unknown.

smooch /smo͞oCH/ informal ▶ **verb** kiss and cuddle amorously. ▶ **noun** a spell of kissing and cuddling.
– DERIVATIVES **smooch·er** noun **smooch·y** adjective.
– ORIGIN imitating the sound.

smooth /smo͞oTH/ ▶ **adjective 1** having an even and regular surface. **2** (of a liquid) without lumps. **3** (of movement) without jerks. **4** happening without problems: *the organizers deserve thanks for the smooth running of the festival.* **5** charming in very confident or flattering way. **6** (of a flavor) not harsh or bitter.

– SYNONYMS **1 even,** level, flat, plane, unwrinkled, glassy, glossy, silky, polished. **2 creamy,** fine, velvety. **3 calm,** still, tranquil, undisturbed, unruffled, even, flat, like a millpond. **4 steady,** regular, uninterrupted, unbroken, easy, effortless, trouble-free. **5 suave,** urbane, sophisticated, polished, debonair, courteous, gracious, persuasive, glib, slick, smooth-tongued; informal smarmy.
– ANTONYMS uneven, rough.

▶ **verb 1** make something smooth. **2** deal successfully with a problem: *these disputes were smoothed over.*

– SYNONYMS **1 flatten,** level (out/off), even out/off, press, roll, iron, plane. **2 ease,** facilitate, expedite, help, assist, aid, pave the way for.
– ANTONYMS roughen, hinder.

– DERIVATIVES **smooth·ly** adverb **smooth·ness** noun.
– ORIGIN Old English.

smooth·bore /ˈsmo͞oTHˌbôr/ ▶ **noun** a gun with a barrel that is not rifled.

smooth·ie /ˈsmo͞oTHē/ ▶ **noun 1** a thick, smooth drink of fresh fruit puréed with milk, yogurt, or ice cream. **2** informal a charming and confident man who is often not sincere.

smooth-talk·ing ▶ **adjective** informal using very persuasive or flattering language.
– DERIVATIVES **smooth-talk·er** noun.

smor·gas·bord /ˈsmôrgəsˌbôrd/ ▶ **noun** a buffet offering a variety of meats, salads, hors d'oeuvres, etc.
– ORIGIN Swedish.

smote /smōt/ past of **SMITE**.

smoth·er /ˈsməTHər/ ▶ **verb 1** suffocate someone by covering the nose and mouth. **2** (**smother someone/thing in/with**) cover someone or something entirely with something. **3** prevent from developing or being expressed: *she smothered a sigh.* **4** make someone feel overwhelmed by treating them too protectively. **5** put out a fire by covering it.

– SYNONYMS **1 suffocate,** asphyxiate, stifle, choke. **2 extinguish,** put out, snuff out, douse, stamp out. **3 smear,** daub, spread, cover, plaster. **4** *she smothered a giggle* **stifle,** muffle, strangle, suppress, hold back, fight back, swallow, conceal.

– ORIGIN Old English.

smoul·der /ˈsmōldər/ ▶ **verb** British spelling of **SMOLDER**.

SMS ▶ **abbreviation** Short Message (or Messaging) Service, a system that enables cell-phone users to send and receive text messages. ▶ **noun** a message sent or received using SMS.

SMTP ▶ **abbreviation** Simple Mail Transfer (or Transport) Protocol, a standard for the transmission of email on a computer network.

smudge /sməj/ ▶ **verb** make or become blurred or smeared.

– SYNONYMS **streak,** mark, dirty, soil, blotch, blacken, smear, blot, daub, stain; informal splotch.

▶ **noun** a blurred or smeared mark.

– SYNONYMS **streak,** smear, mark, stain, blotch, blob, dab; informal splotch.

– DERIVATIVES **smudg·y** adjective.
– ORIGIN unknown.

smug /sməg/ ▶ **adjective** (**smugger, smuggest**) pleased with oneself in an irritating way; self-satisfied.

– SYNONYMS **self-satisfied,** conceited, complacent, superior, pleased with oneself.

– DERIVATIVES **smug·ly** adverb **smug·ness** noun.
– ORIGIN German *smuk* 'pretty.'

WORD TOOLKIT

See **CONCEITED**.

smug·gle /ˈsməgəl/ ▶ **verb 1** move goods illegally into or out of a country. **2** take someone or something secretly to or from a place.
– DERIVATIVES **smug·gler** noun **smug·gling** noun.
– ORIGIN German *smuggelen.*

smut /smət/ ▶ **noun 1** a small flake of soot or dirt. **2** indecent or obscene talk, writing, or pictures. **3** a disease of cereal crops caused by a fungus, in which affected parts change to black powder.
– ORIGIN from German *schmutzen* 'make dirty or corrupt.'

smut·ty /ˈsmətē/ ▶ **adjective** (**smuttier, smuttiest**) **1** indecent or obscene. **2** dirty or sooty.

Sn ▶ **symbol** the chemical element tin.
– ORIGIN from Latin *stannum* 'tin.'

snack /snak/ ▶ **noun** a small quantity of food eaten between meals or instead of a meal.

– SYNONYMS **light meal,** sandwich, refreshments, nibbles, tidbit(s); informal bite (to eat).

▶ **verb** eat a snack.
– ORIGIN Dutch.

snack bar ▶ **noun** a place where snacks or quickly prepared light meals are sold.

snaf·fle /ˈsnafəl/ ▶ **verb** Brit. informal take something quickly or secretly for oneself. ▶ **noun** a simple bit on a horse's bridle, used with a single set of reins.
– ORIGIN probably German or Dutch.

sna·fu /snaˈfo͞o/ ▶ **noun** informal a situation that is confused, disorganized, or that has gone wrong.
– ORIGIN from the initial letters of *situation normal: all fouled* (or *fucked*) *up.*

snag /snag/ ▶ **noun 1** an unexpected difficulty or drawback. **2** a sharp or jagged projection. **3** a small tear in fabric.

– SYNONYMS **complication,** difficulty, catch, hitch, obstacle, pitfall, problem, setback, disadvantage, drawback.

▶ verb (**snags, snagging, snagged**) **1** catch or tear something on a sharp projection. **2** informal manage to get or obtain something.

– SYNONYMS **catch,** hook, tear.

– DERIVATIVES **snag·gy** adjective.
– ORIGIN probably Scandinavian.

snag·gle-toothed /ˈsnagəl,to͞otʜt/ ▶ adjective having irregular or projecting teeth.
– ORIGIN from **SNAG**.

snail /snāl/ ▶ noun a slow-moving mollusk with a spiral shell into which it can withdraw its whole body.
– PHRASES **snail's pace** a very slow speed or rate of progress.
– ORIGIN Old English.

snail mail ▶ noun informal the ordinary postal service as opposed to email.

snake /snāk/ ▶ noun a reptile with a long, slender limbless body, many kinds of which have a venomous bite.

– SYNONYMS serpent.

▶ verb move or extend with the twisting motion of a snake.

– SYNONYMS *the road snakes inland* **twist,** wind, meander, zigzag, curve.

– PHRASES **snake in the grass** a person who pretends to be friendly but is secretly working against someone.
– ORIGIN Old English.

snake·bite /ˈsnāk,bīt/ ▶ noun Brit. a drink consisting of draft cider and lager in equal proportions.

snake charm·er ▶ noun an entertainer who appears to make snakes move by playing music.

snake·head /ˈsnāk,hed/ ▶ noun a member of a Chinese criminal network chiefly involved in smuggling illegal immigrants.
– ORIGIN translation of Chinese *shetou*.

snake·skin /ˈsnāk,skin/ ▶ noun the skin of a snake.

snak·y /ˈsnākē/ (also **snakey**) ▶ adjective (**snakier, snakiest**) **1** long and winding. **2** cold and cunning.

snap /snap/ ▶ verb (**snaps, snapping, snapped**) **1** break with a sharp cracking sound. **2** open or close with a brisk movement or sharp sound. **3** (of an animal) make a sudden bite. **4** (**snap someone/thing up**) quickly obtain someone or something that is desirable or in short supply. **5** suddenly lose one's self-control. **6** say something quickly and irritably. **7** (**snap out of**) informal get out of a bad mood by a sudden effort. **8** take a snapshot of someone or something.

– SYNONYMS **1 break,** fracture, splinter, split, crack; informal bust. **2 bark,** snarl, growl, retort; informal jump down someone's throat.

▶ noun **1** an act or sound of snapping. **2** a snapshot. **3** a crisp, brittle cookie. **4** a children's card game in which players compete to call 'snap' as soon as two cards of the same type are exposed.

– SYNONYMS **photograph,** picture, photo, shot, snapshot, print, slide.

▶ adjective done or taken on the spur of the moment: *a snap decision*.
– ORIGIN probably from Dutch or German *snappen* 'seize.'

snap·drag·on /ˈsnap,dragən/ ▶ noun a plant with brightly colored flowers that have a mouthlike opening.

snap fas·ten·er ▶ noun a small fastener with two parts that fit together when pressed.

snap-lock ▶ adjective (of a device or part) that fastens automatically when pushed into position.

snap·per /ˈsnapər/ ▶ noun an edible sea fish noted for snapping its toothed jaws.

snap·ping tur·tle ▶ noun a large American freshwater turtle with a long neck and strong hooked jaws.

snap·pish /ˈsnapisʜ/ ▶ adjective informal irritable; snappy.
– DERIVATIVES **snap·pish·ly** adverb **snap·pish·ness** noun.

snap·py /ˈsnapē/ ▶ adjective (**snappier, snappiest**) informal **1** irritable and sharp. **2** cleverly brief and to the point: *a comedy loaded with snappy dialogue*. **3** neat and stylish: *a snappy dresser*.
– DERIVATIVES **snap·pi·ly** adverb.
– PHRASES **make it snappy** do it quickly.

snap·shot /ˈsnap,sʜät/ ▶ noun an informal photograph, taken quickly.

snare /sne(ə)r/ ▶ noun **1** a trap for catching small animals, consisting of a loop of wire or cord that pulls tight. **2** something likely to lure someone into harm or trouble. **3** (also **snare drum**) a drum with a length of wire, gut, or hide stretched across the head to make a rattling sound.

– SYNONYMS **trap,** gin, wire, net, noose.

▶ verb catch someone or something in a snare or trap.

– SYNONYMS **trap,** catch, net, bag, ensnare, hook.

– ORIGIN Old Norse; sense 3 is probably from German or Dutch, 'harp string.'

snarl[1] /snärl/ ▶ verb **1** growl with bared teeth. **2** say something aggressively. ▶ noun an act or sound of snarling.
– DERIVATIVES **snarl·y** adjective.
– ORIGIN Germanic.

snarl[2] ▶ verb (**snarl something up**) **1** tangle something up. **2** hinder something. ▶ noun a knot or tangle.
– ORIGIN from **SNARE**.

snarl-up ▶ noun Brit. informal **1** a traffic jam. **2** a muddle.

snatch /snacʜ/ ▶ verb **1** grab something in a rude or eager way. **2** informal steal something or kidnap someone suddenly. **3** quickly take when the chance presents itself: *I snatched a few hours' sleep*.

– SYNONYMS **1 grab,** seize, take hold of, take, pluck, grasp at, clutch at. **2 steal,** take, thieve, make off with; informal swipe, nab, lift. **3 kidnap,** abduct, take as hostage.

▶ noun **1** an act of snatching. **2** a fragment of music or talk.
– DERIVATIVES **snatch·er** noun.
– ORIGIN perhaps from **SNACK**.

snaz·zy /ˈsnazē/ ▶ adjective (**snazzier, snazziest**) informal smart and stylish.
– ORIGIN unknown.

sneak /snēk/ ▶ verb (past and past part. **sneaked** or informal **snuck** /snək/) **1** move or take in a stealthy or secretive way. **2** do or achieve in a stealthy way: *she sneaked a glance at her watch*.

– SYNONYMS **creep,** slink, steal, slip, slide, sidle, tiptoe, pad.

▶ **noun** informal a person who behaves in a secretive and underhanded way.
▶ **adjective** acting or done secretly or unofficially: *a sneak preview.*
– ORIGIN perhaps from former *snike* 'to creep.'

sneak·er /ˈsnēkər/ ▶ **noun** a soft shoe worn for sports or casual occasions.

sneak·ing /ˈsnēkiNG/ ▶ **adjective** (of a feeling) remaining in one's mind.

– SYNONYMS **1 secret,** private, hidden, concealed, unvoiced, unexpressed. **2** *a sneaking suspicion* **niggling,** nagging, insidious, lingering, persistent.

sneak·y /ˈsnēkē/ ▶ **adjective** (**sneakier, sneakiest**) secretive in a sly or guilty way.

– SYNONYMS **sly,** crafty, cunning, wily, scheming, devious, deceitful, underhanded/underhand.

– DERIVATIVES **sneak·i·ly** adverb **sneak·i·ness** noun.

sneer /sni(ə)r/ ▶ **noun** a scornful or mocking smile, remark, or tone.

– SYNONYMS **1 smirk,** snigger. **2 jeer,** jibe, insult; informal dig.

▶ **verb** smile or speak in a scornful or mocking way.

– SYNONYMS **1 smirk,** snigger, curl one's lip. **2 scoff,** laugh, scorn, disdain, be contemptuous, mock, ridicule, deride, jeer, jibe.

– ORIGIN uncertain.

sneeze /snēz/ ▶ **verb** suddenly expel air from the nose and mouth due to irritation of the nostrils. ▶ **noun** an act or the sound of sneezing.
– DERIVATIVES **sneez·er** noun **sneez·y** adjective.
– PHRASES **not to be sneezed at** informal not to be rejected without careful consideration.
– ORIGIN Old English.

snick·er /ˈsnikər/ ▶ **verb 1** give a smothered scornful laugh. **2** (of a horse) make a gentle high-pitched neigh.
▶ **noun** an act of snickering; a gentle high-pitched neigh.
– ORIGIN imitating the sound.

snide /snīd/ ▶ **adjective** disrespectful or mocking in an indirect way.

– SYNONYMS **disparaging,** derogatory, deprecating, insulting, mocking, taunting, sneering, scornful, derisive, sarcastic, spiteful, nasty, mean, contemptuous.

– DERIVATIVES **snide·ly** adverb **snide·y** adjective.
– ORIGIN unknown.

WORD TOOLKIT

See **DISMISSIVE**.

sniff /snif/ ▶ **verb 1** draw in air audibly through the nose. **2** (**sniff something out**) informal discover something by investigation. **3** (**sniff around/round**) informal investigate something secretly.

– SYNONYMS **1** *she sniffed and blew her nose* **inhale,** breathe in, snuffle. **2** *Sandra sniffed the socks and grimaced* **smell,** scent, get a whiff of. **3** (**sniff something out**) **detect,** find, discover, bring to light, track down, dig up, root out, uncover, unearth.

▶ **noun 1** an act or sound of sniffing. **2** informal a hint or sign: *they're off at the first sniff of trouble.* **3** informal a slight chance.

– SYNONYMS **1** *she gave a loud sniff* **snuffle,** snort, inhalation. **2** *a sniff of fresh air* **smell,** scent, whiff, lungful.

– DERIVATIVES **sniff·er** noun.
– PHRASES **not to be sniffed at** informal worth having or considering.
– ORIGIN imitating the sound.

sniff·er dog ▶ **noun** a dog trained to find drugs or explosives by smell.

snif·fle /ˈsnifəl/ ▶ **verb** sniff slightly or repeatedly, typically because of a cold or fit of crying. ▶ **noun 1** an act of sniffling. **2** (also **the sniffles**) a slight head cold.
– DERIVATIVES **snif·fly** adjective.
– ORIGIN imitating the sound.

snif·fy /ˈsnifē/ ▶ **adjective** (**sniffier, sniffiest**) informal scornful; contemptuous.
– DERIVATIVES **sniff·i·ly** adverb.

snif·ter /ˈsniftər/ ▶ **noun** a footed glass that is wide at the bottom and tapers to the top, used especially for brandy.
– ORIGIN uncertain.

snip /snip/ ▶ **verb** (**snips, snipping, snipped**) cut something with scissors using small, quick strokes.

– SYNONYMS **1** *she snipped my bangs* **cut,** clip, trim. **2** *snip off the faded flowers* **cut off,** trim (off), clip, prune, chop off, sever, detach, remove, take off.

▶ **noun 1** an act of snipping. **2** a small piece that has been cut off. **3** (**snips**) hand shears for cutting metal.

– SYNONYMS **1** *make snips along the edge* **cut,** slit, snick, nick, notch, incision. **2** *snips of wallpaper* **scrap,** snippet, cutting, shred, remnant, fragment, sliver, bit, piece.

– ORIGIN from German, 'small piece.'

snipe /snīp/ ▶ **verb** (usu. **snipe at**) **1** shoot at someone from a hiding place at long range. **2** criticize someone or something in a sly or petty way. ▶ **noun** (pl. same or **snipes**) a wading bird with brown plumage and a long straight bill.
– DERIVATIVES **snip·er** noun.
– ORIGIN probably Scandinavian.

snip·pet /ˈsnipit/ ▶ **noun** a small piece or brief extract.

– SYNONYMS **piece,** bit, scrap, fragment, particle, shred, excerpt, extract.

snip·py /ˈsnipē/ ▶ **adjective** informal curt or sharp.

snitch /sniCH/ informal ▶ **verb 1** steal something. **2** inform on someone. ▶ **noun** an informer.
– ORIGIN unknown.

sniv·el /ˈsnivəl/ ▶ **verb** (**snivels, sniveling, sniveled**) **1** cry and sniffle. **2** complain in a whining or tearful way.

– SYNONYMS **sniffle,** snuffle, whimper, whine, weep, cry; informal blubber.

▶ **noun** a spell of sniveling.
– DERIVATIVES **sniv·el·er** noun.
– ORIGIN from Old English, 'mucus.'

snob /snäb/ ▶ **noun 1** a person who greatly respects upper-class or rich people and who looks down on people of a lower class. **2** a person who believes that their tastes in a particular area are superior to others: *a wine snob.*
– DERIVATIVES **snob·ber·y** /-bərē/ noun (pl. **snobberies**) **snob·bism** /-ˌbizəm/ noun **snob·by** adjective (**snobbier, snobbiest**).
– ORIGIN uncertain.

snob·bish /ˈsnäbisн/ ▶ **adjective** relating to or typical of a snob: *his snobbish contempt for the lower classes.*

– SYNONYMS **elitist,** superior, supercilious, arrogant, condescending, pretentious, affected; informal snooty, high and mighty, la-di-da, stuck-up; Brit. informal toffee-nosed.

– DERIVATIVES **snob·bish·ly** adverb.

snood /snŏŏd/ ▶ **noun 1** an ornamental hairnet or pouch worn over the hair at the back of a woman's head. **2** a wide ring of knitted material worn as a hood or scarf.
– ORIGIN Old English.

snook /snŏŏk/ ▶ **noun** (in phrase **cock a snook at**) informal, chiefly Brit. **1** openly show contempt or a lack of respect for someone or something. **2** place one's hand so that the thumb touches one's nose and the fingers are spread out, as a gesture of contempt.
– ORIGIN unknown.

snook·er /ˈsnŏŏkər/ ▶ **noun 1** a game played with cue sticks on a billiard table, in which the players use a white cue ball to pocket the other balls in a set order. **2** a position in a game of snooker or pool in which a player cannot make a direct shot at any permitted ball. ▶ **verb 1** (in snooker and pool) put an opponent in a position in which they cannot make a direct shot at any permitted ball. **2** (**be snookered**) informal be tricked or deceived: *they get snookered into signing away their paychecks.*
– ORIGIN unknown.

snoop /snŏŏp/ informal ▶ **verb** look around or investigate secretly to try to find out private information.

– SYNONYMS **pry,** spy, be a busybody, poke one's nose into, root about, ferret about; informal be nosy.

▶ **noun** an act of snooping.
– DERIVATIVES **snoop·er** noun.
– ORIGIN Dutch *snoepen* 'eat on the sly.'

snoot·y /ˈsnŏŏtē/ ▶ **adjective** (**snootier, snootiest**) informal treating people as if they are socially inferior; snobbish.
– DERIVATIVES **snoot·i·ly** adverb **snoot·i·ness** noun.
– ORIGIN from **SNOUT**.

snooze /snŏŏz/ informal ▶ **noun** a short, light sleep. ▶ **verb** sleep lightly and briefly.
– DERIVATIVES **snooz·er** noun **snooz·y** adjective.
– ORIGIN unknown.

snooze but·ton ▶ **noun** a control on a clock that sets an alarm to repeat after a short interval.

snore /snôr/ ▶ **noun** a snorting sound in a person's breathing while they are asleep. ▶ **verb** make a snorting sound while asleep.
– DERIVATIVES **snor·er** noun.
– ORIGIN probably imitating the sound.

snor·kel /ˈsnôrkəl/ ▶ **noun** a tube for a swimmer to breathe through while under water. ▶ **verb** (**snorkels, snorkeling, snorkeled**) (often as n. **snorkeling**) swim using a snorkel.
– DERIVATIVES **snor·kel·er** noun.
– ORIGIN German *Schnorchel.*

snort /snôrt/ ▶ **noun 1** an explosive sound made by the sudden forcing of breath through the nose. **2** informal an amount of cocaine that is breathed in through the nose. **3** informal a measure of an alcoholic drink. ▶ **verb 1** make a snort, especially to express anger or mockery. **2** informal inhale cocaine.
– DERIVATIVES **snort·er** noun.
– ORIGIN probably imitating the sound.

snot /snät/ ▶ **noun** informal **1** mucus in the nose. **2** an unpleasant person.
– ORIGIN probably from Dutch, German.

snot·ty /ˈsnätē/ ▶ **adjective** (**snottier, snottiest**) informal **1** full of or covered with mucus from the nose. **2** having a superior or arrogant attitude.
– DERIVATIVES **snot·ti·ly** adverb **snot·ti·ness** noun.

snout /snout/ ▶ **noun 1** the projecting nose and mouth of an animal. **2** the projecting front or end of something such as a pistol.
– DERIVATIVES **snout·ed** adjective.
– ORIGIN Dutch, German *snūt.*

snow /snō/ ▶ **noun 1** frozen water vapor in the atmosphere that falls in light white flakes. **2** (**snows**) falls of snow. **3** a mass of flickering white spots on a television or radar screen, caused by interference or a poor signal. ▶ **verb 1** (**it snows, it is snowing, it snowed**) snow falls. **2** (**be snowed in/up**) be unable to leave somewhere due to heavy snow. **3** (**be snowed under**) be overwhelmed with a large quantity of something, especially work.
– DERIVATIVES **snow·less** adjective.
– ORIGIN Old English.

snow·ball /ˈsnō͵bôl/ ▶ **noun 1** a ball of packed snow. **2** a cocktail containing advocaat and lemonade. ▶ **verb 1** increase rapidly in size, intensity, or importance: *my enthusiasm quickly snowballed.* **2** throw snowballs at someone.

snow·bird /ˈsnō͵bərd/ ▶ **noun 1** informal a person who moves from Canada or a northern US state to a warmer southern US state in the winter. **2** a kind of junco with gray or brown upper parts and a white belly.

snow blind·ness ▶ **noun** temporary blindness caused by the glare of light reflected by a large expanse of snow.

snow·board /ˈsnō͵bôrd/ ▶ **noun** a board resembling a short, broad ski, used for sliding downhill on snow.
– DERIVATIVES **snow·board·er** noun **snow·board·ing** noun.

snow·bound /ˈsnō͵bound/ ▶ **adjective 1** prevented from traveling or going out by snow. **2** (of a place) cut off because of snow.

snow·capped ▶ **adjective** (of the top of a mountain) covered with snow.

snow·drift /ˈsnō͵drift/ ▶ **noun** a bank of deep snow heaped up by the wind.

snow·drop /ˈsnō͵dräp/ ▶ **noun** a plant that bears drooping white flowers during late winter.

snow·fall /ˈsnō͵fôl/ ▶ **noun 1** a fall of snow. **2** the quantity of snow falling within a particular area in a given time.

snow·field /ˈsnō͵fēld/ ▶ **noun** a permanent wide expanse of snow in mountainous or polar regions.

snow·flake /ˈsnō͵flāk/ ▶ **noun** each of the many feathery ice crystals that fall as snow.

snow goose ▶ **noun** a goose that breeds in Arctic Canada and Greenland, having white plumage with black wing tips.

snow job ▶ **noun** informal an attempt to deceive or persuade someone, especially by using flattery.

snow leop·ard ▶ **noun** a rare large cat that has pale gray fur patterned with dark blotches and rings, living in mountainous parts of central Asia.

snow·line /ˈsnō͵līn/ ▶ **noun** the altitude above which some snow remains on the ground throughout the year.

snow·man /ˈsnōˌman/ ▶ **noun** (pl. **snowmen**) a model of a human figure created with compressed snow.

snow·mo·bile /ˈsnōmōˌbēl/ ▶ **noun** a motor vehicle with runners or caterpillar tracks for traveling over snow.

snow pea ▶ **noun** a variety of pea with an edible pod.

snow·plow /ˈsnōˌplou/ (Brit. **snowplough**) ▶ **noun** **1** a device or vehicle for clearing roads of snow. **2** an act of turning the points of one's skis inward in order to slow down or turn.

snow·shoe /ˈsnōˌsʜo͞o/ ▶ **noun** a flat device resembling a tennis racket, which is attached to the sole of a boot and used for walking on snow.

snow·storm /ˈsnōˌstôrm/ ▶ **noun** a heavy fall of snow accompanied by a high wind.

snow·y /ˈsnōē/ ▶ **adjective** (**snowier**, **snowiest**) **1** covered with snow. **2** (of weather or a period of time) characterized by snowfall. **3** like snow, especially in being pure white.

snow·y owl ▶ **noun** a large northern owl, the male being entirely white.

snub /snəb/ ▶ **verb** (**snubs**, **snubbing**, **snubbed**) ignore or reject someone or something scornfully.

– SYNONYMS **rebuff,** spurn, cold-shoulder, ignore, insult, slight; informal stiff, freeze out.

▶ **noun** an act of snubbing someone or something.

– SYNONYMS **rebuff,** slap in the face; informal brush-off, put-down.

▶ **adjective** (of a person's nose) short and turned up at the end.
– ORIGIN Old Norse, 'chide.'

snuck /snək/ informal past and past participle of **SNEAK**.

snuff[1] /snəf/ ▶ **verb** **1** put out a candle. **2** (**snuff something out**) abruptly put an end to something. ▶ **noun** the charred part of a candle wick.
– ORIGIN unknown.

snuff[2] ▶ **noun** powdered tobacco that is sniffed up the nostril. ▶ **verb** inhale or sniff at something.
– PHRASES **up to snuff** informal **1** up to the required standard. **2** in good health.
– ORIGIN probably an abbreviation of Dutch *snuftabak*; the verb is from Dutch *snuffen* 'to snuffle.'

snuff·er /ˈsnəfər/ ▶ **noun** a small hollow metal cone on the end of a handle, used to put out a candle by smothering the flame.

snuf·fle /ˈsnəfəl/ ▶ **verb** **1** breathe noisily through a partially blocked nose. **2** (of an animal) make repeated sniffing sounds. ▶ **noun** **1** a snuffling sound. **2** (also **the snuffles**) informal a cold.
– DERIVATIVES **snuf·fly** adjective.
– ORIGIN probably from German and Dutch *snuffelen*.

snuff mov·ie ▶ **noun** informal a pornographic movie or video recording of an actual murder.

snug /snəg/ ▶ **adjective** (**snugger**, **snuggest**) **1** warm and cozy. **2** close-fitting.

– SYNONYMS **1 cozy,** comfortable, warm, sheltered, secure; informal comfy. **2 tight,** skintight, close-fitting, figure-hugging.
– ANTONYMS loose.

▶ **noun** Brit. a small, cozy bar in a pub or small hotel.
– DERIVATIVES **snug·ly** adverb **snug·ness** noun.
– ORIGIN probably from German or Dutch.

snug·gle /ˈsnəgəl/ ▶ **verb** settle into a warm, comfortable position.

– SYNONYMS **nestle,** curl up, huddle (up), cuddle up, nuzzle, settle.

– ORIGIN from **SNUG**.

so[1] /sō/ ▶ **adverb** **1** to such a great extent. **2** extremely; very much. **3** to the same extent: *he isn't so bad as you'd think*. **4** referring back to something previously mentioned. **5** similarly: *times have changed and so have I*. **6** in the way described or demonstrated; thus. ▶ **conjunction** **1** therefore. **2** (**so that**) with the result or aim that. **3** and then. **4** introducing a question or concluding statement. **5** in the same way.
– PHRASES **and so on** (or **forth**) and similar things; et cetera. **or so** approximately. **so long!** informal goodbye. **so much as** even: *without so much as a word*.
– ORIGIN Old English.

so[2] ▶ **noun** variant of **SOL**[1].

So. ▶ **abbreviation** South.

soak /sōk/ ▶ **verb** **1** make or become thoroughly wet by leaving or remaining in liquid. **2** (of a liquid) penetrate or spread through completely: *the rain soaked their hair*. **3** (**soak something up**) absorb a liquid. **4** (**soak something up**) expose oneself to something beneficial or enjoyable: *soak up the Mediterranean sun*. **5** (**soak oneself in**) involve oneself deeply in a particular experience.

– SYNONYMS **1 dip,** immerse, steep, submerge, douse, marinate, souse. **2 drench,** wet through, saturate. **3** *water soaked through the carpet* **permeate,** penetrate, impregnate, percolate, seep, spread. **4 absorb,** suck up, blot, mop up.

▶ **noun** **1** an act or period of soaking. **2** informal a heavy drinker.
– ORIGIN Old English.

soak·ing /ˈsōkiɴɢ/ (also **soaking wet**) ▶ **adjective** very wet.

– SYNONYMS **drenched,** wet (through), soaked (through), sodden, soggy, waterlogged, saturated, sopping, dripping, wringing.
– ANTONYMS parched.

so-and-so ▶ **noun** (pl. **so-and-sos**) informal **1** a person or thing whose name the speaker does not know or need to specify. **2** an unpleasant or disliked person (used instead of an offensive word): *a nosy so-and-so*.

soap /sōp/ ▶ **noun** **1** a substance used with water for washing and cleaning, made of natural oils or fats combined with an alkali, and typically perfumed. **2** informal a soap opera. ▶ **verb** wash someone or something with soap.
– ORIGIN Old English.

soap·box /ˈsōpˌbäks/ ▶ **noun** **1** a box or crate used as a stand when making a speech in public. **2** an opportunity for someone to express their views publicly: *I tend to get up on my soapbox about this issue*.

soap op·er·a ▶ **noun** a television or radio drama serial dealing with daily events in the lives of the same group of characters.
– ORIGIN so named because such serials were originally sponsored in the US by soap manufacturers.

soap pow·der ▶ **noun** powdered detergent for washing clothes.

soap·stone /ˈsōpˌstōn/ ▶ **noun** a soft rock consisting largely of the mineral talc.

soap·suds /ˈsōpˌsədz/ ▶ **plural noun** another term for **SUDS**.

soap·y /ˈsōpē/ ▶ **adjective** (**soapier, soapiest**) **1** containing or covered with soap. **2** like soap.

soar /sôr/ ▶ **verb 1** fly or rise high into the air. **2** maintain height in the air by gliding. **3** increase rapidly above the usual level.

– SYNONYMS **1 rise,** ascend, climb. **2 glide,** plane, float, hover. **3 increase,** escalate, shoot up, spiral, rocket; informal go through the roof, skyrocket.
– ANTONYMS plummet.

– ORIGIN Old French *essorer*.

So·a·ve /ˈswävā/ ▶ **noun** a dry white Italian wine.
– ORIGIN named after the village of *Soave* in northern Italy.

SOB ▶ **abbreviation** son of a bitch.

sob /säb/ ▶ **verb** (**sobs, sobbing, sobbed**) **1** cry making loud gasping noises. **2** say something while sobbing.

– SYNONYMS **weep,** cry, snivel, whimper; informal blubber.

▶ **noun** an act or sound of sobbing.
– ORIGIN perhaps Dutch or German.

so·ber /ˈsōbər/ ▶ **adjective** (**soberer, soberest**) **1** not affected by alcohol; not drunk. **2** serious and sensible or thoughtful. **3** (of a color) not bright or conspicuous.

– SYNONYMS **1 clear-headed,** teetotal, abstinent, dry; informal on the wagon. **2 serious,** solemn, sensible, staid, sedate, quiet, dignified, grave, levelheaded, down-to-earth. **3 somber,** subdued, restrained, austere, severe, drab, plain, dark.
– ANTONYMS drunk.

▶ **verb 1** (usu. **sober up** or **sober someone up**) become or make sober after being drunk. **2** (often as adj. **sobering**) make or become serious: *a sobering thought*.
– DERIVATIVES **so·ber·ly** adverb.
– ORIGIN Latin *sobrius*.

so·bri·e·ty /səˈbrīətē, sō-/ ▶ **noun** the state of being sober.

so·bri·quet /ˈsōbriˌkā, -ˌket/ (also **soubriquet**) ▶ **noun** a person's nickname.
– ORIGIN French.

sob sto·ry ▶ **noun** informal a story intended to arouse sympathy.

Soc. ▶ **abbreviation 1** Socialist. **2** Society.

so·ca /ˈsōkə/ ▶ **noun** calypso music with elements of soul, originally from Trinidad.
– ORIGIN blend of **SOUL** and **CALYPSO**.

so-called ▶ **adjective** called by the name or term specified (often in the speaker's view, inappropriately): *her so-called friends*.

– SYNONYMS **supposed,** alleged, presumed, inappropriately named, ostensible, reputed, self-styled.

soc·cer /ˈsäkər/ ▶ **noun** a game played by two teams of eleven players with a round ball that may not be handled during play except by the goalkeepers, the object being to score goals by kicking or heading the ball into the opponents' goal.
– ORIGIN shortening of *Assoc.* from *Association Football*.

so·cia·ble /ˈsōsʜəbəl/ ▶ **adjective 1** liking to talk to and join in activities with other people. **2** friendly and welcoming: *a very sociable little village*.

– SYNONYMS **friendly,** amicable, affable, companionable, gregarious, cordial, warm, genial.
– ANTONYMS unfriendly.

– DERIVATIVES **so·cia·bil·i·ty** /ˌsōsʜəˈbilitē/ noun **so·cia·bly** adverb.
– ORIGIN Latin *sociabilis*, from *sociare* 'unite.'

so·cial /ˈsōsʜəl/ ▶ **adjective 1** relating to society and its organization. **2** needing the company of other people; suited to living in communities. **3** relating to or designed for activities in which people meet each other for pleasure. **4** (of birds, insects, or mammals) breeding or living in colonies or organized communities.

– SYNONYMS **1 communal,** community, collective, general, popular, civil, public, civic. **2 recreational,** leisure, entertainment.

▶ **noun** an informal social gathering organized by the members of a club or group.

– SYNONYMS **party,** gathering, function, get-together, celebration; informal do.

– DERIVATIVES **so·ci·al·i·ty** /ˌsōsʜēˈalitē/ noun **so·cial·ly** /ˈsōsʜəlē/ adverb.
– ORIGIN Latin *socialis* 'allied,' from *socius* 'friend.'

so·cial climb·er ▶ **noun** derogatory a person who is anxious to gain a higher social status.

so·cial con·tract (also **social compact**) ▶ **noun** an unspoken agreement among the members of a society to cooperate for the benefit of everyone, for example by sacrificing some individual freedom in return for government protection.

so·cial de·moc·ra·cy ▶ **noun** a socialist system of government achieved by democratic means.

so·cial·ism /ˈsōsʜəˌlizəm/ ▶ **noun** a political and economic theory of social organization that holds that a country's land, transportation, natural resources, and chief industries should be owned or controlled by the community as a whole.
– DERIVATIVES **so·cial·ist** noun & adjective **so·cial·is·tic** /ˌsōsʜəˈlistik/ adjective.

so·cial·ite /ˈsōsʜəˌlīt/ ▶ **noun** a person who mixes in fashionable society.

so·cial·ize /ˈsōsʜəˌlīz/ ▶ **verb 1** mix socially with other people. **2** make someone behave in a way that is acceptable to society.

– SYNONYMS **interact,** converse, be sociable, mix, mingle, get together, meet, fraternize, consort; informal hobnob, hang out.

– DERIVATIVES **so·cial·i·za·tion** /ˌsōsʜəliˈzāsʜən/ noun.

so·cial mar·ket e·con·o·my (also **social market**) ▶ **noun** an economic system based on a free market operating together with a welfare state to protect people who are unable to sell their labor, such as the elderly or unemployed.

so·cial net·work·ing ▶ **noun** the use of a dedicated website to communicate informally with other members of the site, by posting messages, photographs, etc.

so·cial re·al·ism ▶ **noun** the realistic portrayal in art of contemporary life, as a means of commenting on the social or political situation.

so·cial sci·ence ▶ **noun 1** the scientific study of human society and social relationships. **2** a subject within this field, such as economics.

So·cial Se·cu·ri·ty ▶ **noun** a federal insurance program that provides benefits to retired persons, the unemployed, and the disabled.

so·cial ser·vi·ces ▶ **plural noun** services provided by the government for the community, such as education and medical care.

so·cial stud·ies ▶ **plural noun** (treated as sing.) the study of human society.

so·cial work ▶ **noun** work carried out by people trained to help improve the conditions of people who are poor, old, or socially deprived.
– DERIVATIVES **so·cial work·er** noun.

so·ci·e·ty /səˈsīətē/ ▶ **noun** (pl. **societies**) **1** all the people living together in a more or less ordered community. **2** a particular community of people living in a country or region, and having shared customs, laws, and organizations. **3** (also **high society**) people who are fashionable, wealthy, and influential, viewed as a distinct social group. **4** an organization or club formed for a particular purpose or activity. **5** the situation of being in the company of other people: *she shunned the society of others.*

– SYNONYMS **1 the community,** the (general) public, the people, the population, civilization, humankind, mankind, the world at large. **2** *an industrial society* **culture,** community, civilization, nation. **3 high society,** polite society, the upper classes, the gentry, the elite, the smart set, the beau monde; informal the upper crust. **4 club,** association, group, circle, institute, guild, lodge, league, union, alliance. **5 company,** companionship, fellowship, friendship.

– DERIVATIVES **so·ci·e·tal** /səˈsīitl/ adjective.
– ORIGIN Latin *societas*, from *socius* 'companion.'

WORD LINKS

sociology *study of society*

so·ci·o·bi·ol·o·gy /ˌsōsēōˌbīˈäləjē/ ▶ **noun** the scientific study of the biological aspects of social behavior in animals and humans.
– DERIVATIVES **so·ci·o·bi·o·log·i·cal** /-ˌbīəˈläjikəl/ adjective **so·ci·o·bi·ol·o·gist** noun.

so·ci·o·cul·tur·al /ˌsōsēōˈkəlCHərəl/ ▶ **adjective** combining social and cultural factors.

so·ci·o·ec·o·nom·ic /ˌsōsēōˌēkəˈnämik, -ekə-/ ▶ **adjective** relating to the interaction of social and economic factors.

so·ci·ol·o·gy /ˌsōsēˈäləjē/ ▶ **noun** the study of the structure and functioning of human society.
– DERIVATIVES **so·ci·o·log·i·cal** /ˌsōsēōˈläjikəl/ adjective **so·ci·ol·o·gist** noun.

so·ci·o·path /ˈsōsēōˌpaTH/ ▶ **noun** a person with a personality disorder showing itself in extreme antisocial attitudes and behavior.
– DERIVATIVES **so·ci·o·path·ic** /ˌsōsēōˈpaTHik/ adjective.

so·ci·o·po·lit·i·cal /ˌsōsēōpəˈlitikəl/ ▶ **adjective** combining social and political factors.

sock /säk/ ▶ **noun 1** a knitted garment for the foot and lower part of the leg. **2** informal a hard blow. ▶ **verb** informal hit someone or something hard.
– PHRASES **put a sock in it** informal stop talking. **sock it to** informal make a forceful impression on someone.
– ORIGIN Greek *sukkhos* 'comic actor's shoe.'

sock·et /ˈsäkit/ ▶ **noun 1** a hollow in which something fits or revolves. **2** an electrical device into which a plug or light bulb is fitted.
– ORIGIN Old French *soket* 'small ploughshare.'

sock·eye /ˈsäkˌī/ ▶ **noun** a North Pacific salmon that is an important food fish.
– ORIGIN Salish, 'fish of fishes.'

So·crat·ic /səˈkratik/ ▶ **adjective** relating to the ancient Greek philosopher Socrates or his ideas.

sod /säd/ ▶ **noun 1** grass-covered ground; turf. **2** a piece of turf.
– ORIGIN Dutch or German *sode.*

so·da /ˈsōdə/ ▶ **noun 1** a carbonated soft drink. **2** (also **soda water**) carbonated water (originally made with sodium bicarbonate). **3** sodium carbonate.
– ORIGIN Latin.

so·da bread ▶ **noun** bread in which baking soda is used as the raising agent.

so·da foun·tain ▶ **noun 1** a device dispensing soda water or soft drinks. **2** a cafe or counter selling soft drinks, ice creams, etc.

sod·den /ˈsädn/ ▶ **adjective 1** soaked through. **2** (in combination) having drunk too much of an alcoholic drink: *whiskey-sodden.*
– ORIGIN from SEETHE, first meaning 'boiled.'

so·di·um /ˈsōdēəm/ ▶ **noun** a soft silver-white metallic chemical element of which common salt and soda are compounds.
– ORIGIN from SODA.

so·di·um bi·car·bon·ate ▶ **noun** a soluble white powder used chiefly in fire extinguishers and effervescent drinks and as a raising agent in baking.

so·di·um chlo·ride ▶ **noun** the chemical name for common salt.

so·di·um hy·drox·ide ▶ **noun** a strongly alkaline white compound used in many industrial processes; caustic soda.

so·di·um-va·por lamp (also **sodium lamp**) ▶ **noun** a lamp in which an electrical discharge in sodium vapor gives a yellow light.

sod·om·ite /ˈsädəˌmīt/ ▶ **noun** a person who engages in sodomy.

sod·om·y /ˈsädəmē/ ▶ **noun** anal or oral sex.
– DERIVATIVES **sod·om·ize** /ˈsädəˌmīz/ verb.
– ORIGIN from Latin *peccatum Sodomiticum* 'sin of Sodom' (after the Book of Genesis chapter 19, which implies that the men of the town of Sodom in ancient Palestine practiced homosexual rape).

so·fa /ˈsōfə/ ▶ **noun** a long upholstered seat with a back and arms, for two or more people.

– SYNONYMS **couch,** settee, divan, chaise longue, chesterfield.

– ORIGIN French.

so·fa bed ▶ **noun** a sofa that can be converted into a bed.

sof·fit /ˈsäfit/ ▶ **noun** the underside of an arch, a balcony, overhanging eaves, etc.
– ORIGIN Italian *soffitto.*

soft /sôft/ ▶ **adjective 1** easy to mold, cut, compress, or fold. **2** not rough or coarse in texture. **3** quiet and gentle. **4** (of light or color) not harsh. **5** sympathetic or lenient; not strict or strict enough. **6** informal (of a job or way of life) needing little effort. **7** informal foolish. **8** (**soft on**) informal having romantic feelings for someone. **9** (of a drink) not alcoholic. **10** (of a drug) not likely to cause addiction. **11** (of water) free from mineral salts. **12** (of a group within a political party) willing to compromise. **13** (also **soft-core**) (of pornography) suggestive but not explicit.

– SYNONYMS **1 mushy,** squashy, pulpy, squishy, doughy, spongy, springy, elastic, pliable, pliant; informal gooey. **2 swampy,** marshy, boggy, muddy, squelchy. **3 smooth,** velvety, fleecy, downy, furry, silky, silken. **4 dim,** low, faint, subdued, muted, subtle. **5 quiet,** low, gentle, faint, muted, subdued, muffled, hushed, whispered. **6 lenient,** easygoing, tolerant, forgiving, forbearing, indulgent, liberal, lax.
– ANTONYMS hard, firm, harsh.

– DERIVATIVES **soft·ish** adjective **soft·ly** adverb **soft·ness** noun.
– PHRASES **have a soft spot for** be fond of. **a soft** (or **easy**) **touch** informal a person who is easily persuaded or imposed on.
– ORIGIN Old English.

soft·back /ˈsôf(t)ˌbak/ ▶ **adjective & noun** another term for **PAPERBACK**.

soft·ball /ˈsôf(t)ˌbôl/ ▶ **noun** a form of baseball played on a smaller field with a larger, softer ball.

soft-boiled ▶ **adjective** (of an egg) lightly boiled, leaving the yolk soft or liquid.

soft·cov·er /ˈsôf(t)ˌkəvər/ ▶ **adjective & noun** another term for **PAPERBACK**.

soft·en /ˈsôfən/ ▶ **verb 1** make or become soft or softer. **2** (often **soften someone up**) make someone more likely to do something.

– SYNONYMS *the compensation should soften the blow* **ease,** alleviate, relieve, soothe, take the edge off, cushion, lessen, diminish, blunt, deaden.

– DERIVATIVES **soft·en·er** noun.

soft fo·cus ▶ **noun** deliberate slight blurring or lack of definition in a photograph or movie.

soft·heart·ed /ˈsôftˈhärtid/ ▶ **adjective** kind, caring and sympathetic.

soft·ie /ˈsôftē/ (also **softy**) ▶ **noun** (pl. **softies**) informal a weak or softhearted person.

soft pal·ate /ˈpalit/ ▶ **noun** the fleshy, flexible part toward the back of the roof of the mouth.

soft-ped·al ▶ **verb** play down the unpleasant aspects of something. ▶ **noun** (**soft pedal**) a pedal on a piano that can be pressed to soften the tone.

soft rock ▶ **noun** a style of rock music with a less persistent beat and more emphasis on lyrics and melody than hard rock.

soft sell ▶ **noun** the selling of something in a gentle and persuasive way.

soft-soap ▶ **verb** informal use flattery to persuade someone to do something.

soft-spo·ken ▶ **adjective** speaking or said with a gentle, quiet voice.

soft tar·get ▶ **noun** a person or thing that is relatively unprotected or vulnerable.

soft·ware /ˈsôftˌwe(ə)r/ ▶ **noun** programs and other operating information used by a computer.

soft·wood /ˈsôftˌwo͝od/ ▶ **noun** the wood from conifers as opposed to that of broadleaved trees.

soft·y ▶ **noun** variant spelling of **SOFTIE**.

sog·gy /ˈsägē/ ▶ **adjective** (**soggier**, **soggiest**) very wet and soft.

– SYNONYMS **mushy,** squashy, pulpy, slushy, squelchy, swampy, marshy, boggy, soaking, wet, saturated, drenched.

– DERIVATIVES **sog·gi·ly** adverb **sog·gi·ness** noun.
– ORIGIN from dialect *sog* 'a swamp.'

soh /sō/ ▶ **noun** variant of **SOL**[1].

soi-di·sant /ˌswä dēˈzän(t)/ ▶ **adjective** using a description or title that one has given oneself; self-styled: *a soi-disant novelist.*
– ORIGIN French, from *soi* 'oneself' + *disant* 'saying.'

soi·gné /swänˈyā/ ▶ **adjective** (fem. **soignée** pronunc. same) elegant and well groomed.
– ORIGIN French, from *soigner* 'take care of.'

soil[1] /soil/ ▶ **noun 1** the upper layer of earth in which plants grow. **2** the territory of a particular nation.

– SYNONYMS **1 earth,** dirt, clay, ground, loam. **2 territory,** land, region, country, domain, dominion.

– ORIGIN Old French.

soil[2] ▶ **verb 1** make something dirty. **2** damage someone's reputation.

– SYNONYMS **dirty,** stain, smear, smudge, spoil, foul.

▶ **noun** waste matter, especially sewage.
– ORIGIN Old French *soiller*.

soi·rée /swäˈrā/ ▶ **noun** an evening social gathering, typically in a private house, for conversation or music.
– ORIGIN French, from *soir* 'evening.'

so·journ /ˈsōjərn/ literary ▶ **noun** a temporary stay.

– SYNONYMS **stay,** visit, stop, stopover, vacation.

▶ **verb** stay somewhere temporarily.

– SYNONYMS **stay,** live, put up, stop (over), vacation, lodge, room, board.

– DERIVATIVES **so·journ·er** noun.
– ORIGIN from Old French *sojourner*.

sol[1] /sōl/ ▶ **noun** Music the fifth note of a major scale, coming after 'fa' and before 'la.'
– ORIGIN the first syllable of *solve*, taken from a Latin hymn.

sol[2] /säl, sōl/ ▶ **noun** Chemistry a liquid containing a colloid in suspension.
– ORIGIN abbreviation of **SOLUTION**.

sol[3] /sōl, sôl/ ▶ **noun** (pl. **soles** /ˈsōlāz, ˈsôles/) the basic unit of money of Peru.
– ORIGIN Spanish, 'sun.'

sol·ace /ˈsälis/ ▶ **noun** comfort or consolation given in a time of difficulty or sadness.

– SYNONYMS **comfort,** consolation, cheer, support, relief.

▶ **verb** give solace to someone.
– ORIGIN Old French *solas*.

so·lar /ˈsōlər/ ▶ **adjective** relating to the sun or its rays, or using the sun's energy.
– ORIGIN from Latin *sol* 'sun.'

so·lar bat·ter·y (also **solar cell**) ▶ **noun** a device that converts the sun's radiation into electricity.

so·lar e·clipse ▶ **noun** an eclipse in which the sun is hidden by the moon.

so·lar en·er·gy ▸ **noun** energy in the form of radiation given off by the sun.

so·lar flare ▸ **noun** a brief eruption of intense high-energy radiation from the sun's surface.

so·lar·i·um /sə'le(ə)rēəm, sō-/ ▸ **noun** (pl. **solariums** or **solaria** /-'le(ə)rēə/) **1** a room equipped with sunlamps or sunbeds. **2** a room with large areas of glass to let in sunlight.
– ORIGIN Latin, 'sundial, place for sunning oneself.'

so·lar·ize /'sōləˌrīz/ ▸ **verb** Photography change the relative darkness of a part of an image by overexposure to light.

so·lar pan·el ▸ **noun** a panel designed to absorb the sun's rays as a source of energy for generating electricity or heating.

so·lar plex·us /'pleksəs/ ▸ **noun** a network of nerves at the pit of the stomach.

so·lar pow·er ▸ **noun** power obtained by controlling and using the energy of the sun's rays.

so·lar sys·tem ▸ **noun** the sun together with the planets, asteroids, comets, etc., in orbit around it.

so·lar wind ▸ **noun** a continuous flow of charged particles from the sun, spreading throughout the solar system.

so·lar year ▸ **noun** the time between one spring or autumn equinox and the next, or between one winter or summer solstice and the next (365 days, 5 hours, 48 minutes, and 46 seconds).

sold /sōld/ past and past participle of **SELL**.

sol·der /'sädər/ ▸ **noun** an alloy, especially one based on lead and tin, that is heated and melted and used to join pieces of metal together. ▸ **verb** join pieces of metal with solder.
– ORIGIN Old French *soudure*.

sol·der·ing i·ron ▸ **noun** an electrical tool for melting and applying solder.

sol·dier /'sōljər/ ▸ **noun** **1** a person who serves in an army. **2** (also **common soldier** or **private soldier**) a private in an army.

– SYNONYMS **fighter,** GI, trooper, serviceman, servicewoman, warrior.

▸ **verb** **1** serve as a soldier. **2** (**soldier on**) informal continue doing something in spite of difficulty.
– DERIVATIVES **sol·dier·ly** adjective.
– PHRASES **soldier of fortune** a professional soldier hired to serve in a foreign army.
– ORIGIN Old French.

WORD LINKS

military *relating to soldiers*

sole[1] /sōl/ ▸ **noun** **1** the underside of a person's foot. **2** the section forming the underside of a piece of footwear. **3** the underside of a tool or implement such as a plane. ▸ **verb** replace the sole on a shoe.
– ORIGIN Latin *solea* 'sandal, sill.'

sole[2] ▸ **noun** (pl. same) an edible flatfish.
– ORIGIN Latin *solea* (see **SOLE**[1]), named from its shape.

sole[3] ▸ **adjective** **1** one and only. **2** belonging or restricted to one person or group.

– SYNONYMS **only,** one, single, solitary, lone, unique, exclusive.

– ORIGIN Latin *sola*, feminine of *solus* 'alone.'

sol·e·cism /'säləˌsizəm, 'sō-/ ▸ **noun** **1** a grammatical mistake. **2** an instance of bad manners or incorrect behavior.
– ORIGIN Greek *soloikismos*.

sole·ly /'sōl(l)ē/ ▸ **adverb** not involving anyone or anything else; only.

– SYNONYMS **only,** simply, purely, just, merely, uniquely, exclusively, entirely, wholly, alone.

sol·emn /'säləm/ ▸ **adjective** **1** formal and dignified. **2** not cheerful; serious. **3** deeply sincere: *a solemn oath*.

– SYNONYMS **1 dignified,** ceremonial, stately, formal, majestic, imposing, splendid, magnificent, grand. **2 serious,** grave, sober, somber, unsmiling, stern, grim, dour, humorless. **3 sincere,** earnest, honest, genuine, firm, heartfelt, wholehearted, sworn.
– ANTONYMS frivolous, lighthearted.

– DERIVATIVES **sol·emn·ly** adverb.
– ORIGIN Latin *sollemnis* 'customary.'

so·lem·ni·ty /sə'lemnitē/ ▸ **noun** (pl. **solemnities**) **1** the state or quality of being solemn. **2** (**solemnities**) formal, dignified rites or ceremonies.

sol·em·nize /'säləmˌnīz/ ▸ **verb** **1** perform a ceremony, especially that of marriage. **2** mark an occasion with a formal ceremony.
– DERIVATIVES **sol·em·ni·za·tion** /ˌsäləmni'zāsʜən/ noun.

so·le·noid /'sōləˌnoid/ ▸ **noun** a cylindrical coil of wire that becomes magnetic when an electric current is passed through it.
– ORIGIN from Greek *sōlēn* 'channel, pipe.'

sole·plate /'sōlˌplāt/ ▸ **noun** **1** a metal plate forming the base of an electric iron, jigsaw, or other machine. **2** a horizontal timber at the base of a wall frame.

sol-fa /ˌsōl 'fä/ ▸ **noun** short for **TONIC SOL-FA**.

so·lic·it /sə'lisit/ ▸ **verb** (**solicits, soliciting, solicited**) **1** ask for or try to obtain something from someone: *he called a meeting to solicit their views*. **2** (of a prostitute) approach someone and offer sex for money.

– SYNONYMS **1 ask for,** request, seek, apply for, put in for, call for, beg for, plead for. **2 ask,** approach, appeal to, lobby, petition, importune, call on, press.

– DERIVATIVES **so·lic·i·ta·tion** /səˌlisə'tāsʜən/ noun.
– ORIGIN Latin *sollicitare* 'agitate.'

so·lic·i·tor /sə'lisitər/ ▸ **noun** **1** a person who contacts businesses to sell them supplies, services, or advertising. **2** the chief law officer of a city, town, or government department. **3** Brit. a lawyer qualified to deal with conveyancing, draw up wills, advise clients and instruct barristers, and represent clients in lower courts. Compare with **BARRISTER**.

so·lic·i·tor gen·er·al ▸ **noun** (pl. **solicitors general**) the law officer directly below the attorney general in the US Department of Justice.

so·lic·i·tous /sə'lisitəs/ ▸ **adjective** showing interest or concern about a person's well-being.

– SYNONYMS **concerned,** caring, considerate, attentive, mindful, thoughtful, interested, anxious, worried.

– DERIVATIVES **so·lic·i·tous·ly** adverb **so·lic·i·tous·ness** noun.

WORD TOOLKIT

See **HUMANE**.

so·lic·i·tude /sə'lisi,t(y)o͞od/ ▶ **noun** care or concern for someone or something.

sol·id /'sälid/ ▶ **adjective** (**solider, solidest**) **1** firm and stable in shape; not liquid or fluid. **2** strongly built or made. **3** not hollow or having spaces or gaps. **4** consisting of the same substance throughout. **5** (of time) continuous: *two solid hours of entertainment*. **6** able to be relied on: *solid evidence*. **7** Geometry three-dimensional.

– SYNONYMS **1 hard,** rock-hard, rigid, firm, solidified, set, frozen, compact, compressed, dense. **2** *solid gold* **pure,** unadulterated, genuine. **3 well built,** sound, substantial, strong, sturdy, durable, stout. **4 well founded,** valid, sound, logical, authoritative, convincing, cogent. **5** *solid support* **unanimous,** united, consistent, undivided.
– ANTONYMS liquid, flimsy, untenable.

▶ **noun 1** a solid substance or object. **2** (**solids**) food that is not liquid. **3** a three-dimensional body or geometric figure.
– DERIVATIVES **so·lid·i·ty** /sə'liditē/ noun **sol·id·ly** adverb **sol·id·ness** noun.
– ORIGIN Latin *solidus*.

sol·i·dar·i·ty /,sälə'de(ə)ritē/ ▶ **noun** unity and mutual support resulting from shared interests, feelings, or opinions.

– SYNONYMS **unanimity,** unity, agreement, team spirit, accord, harmony, consensus; formal concord.

sol·i·di /'säli,dī/ plural of **SOLIDUS**.

so·lid·i·fy /sə'lidə,fī/ ▶ **verb** (**solidifies, solidifying, solidified**) make or become hard or solid.

– SYNONYMS **harden,** set, thicken, stiffen, congeal, cake, freeze, ossify, fossilize, petrify.
– ANTONYMS liquefy.

– DERIVATIVES **so·lid·i·fi·ca·tion** /sə,lidəfi'kāshən/ noun.

sol·id state ▶ **adjective** (of an electronic device) using solid semiconductors, e.g., transistors, as opposed to valves.

sol·i·dus /'sälidəs/ ▶ **noun** (pl. **solidi** /-,dī/) another term for **SLASH** (sense 3 of the noun).
– ORIGIN Latin, 'solid.'

so·lil·o·quy /sə'liləkwē/ ▶ **noun** (pl. **soliloquies**) a speech in a play in which a character speaks their thoughts aloud when alone on stage.
– DERIVATIVES **so·lil·o·quize** /-,kwīz/ verb.
– ORIGIN from Latin *solus* 'alone' + *loqui* 'speak.'

sol·ip·sism /'sälip,sizəm/ ▶ **noun 1** the view that the self is all that can be known to exist. **2** the quality of being selfish.
– DERIVATIVES **sol·ip·sist** noun **sol·ip·sis·tic** /,sälip'sistik/ adjective.
– ORIGIN from Latin *solus* 'alone' + *ipse* 'self.'

sol·i·taire /'sälə,te(ə)r/ ▶ **noun 1** any of various card games for one person, played by trying to use up all one's cards by forming certain sequences. **2** a single diamond or other gem in a piece of jewelry.
– ORIGIN French.

sol·i·tar·y /'sälə,terē/ ▶ **adjective 1** done or existing alone. **2** (of a place) secluded or isolated. **3** single: *not a solitary shred of evidence*.

– SYNONYMS **1 lonely,** unaccompanied, by oneself, on one's own, lonesome, alone, friendless, unsociable, withdrawn, reclusive. **2 isolated,** remote, lonely, out of the way, in the back of beyond, outlying, off the beaten track, in the backwoods, secluded. **3 single,** lone, sole, only, one, individual.
– ANTONYMS sociable.

▶ **noun** (pl. **solitaries**) **1** a person who lives alone for personal or religious reasons. **2** informal solitary confinement.
– DERIVATIVES **sol·i·tar·i·ness** noun.
– ORIGIN Latin *solitarius*, from *solus* 'alone.'

sol·i·tar·y con·fine·ment ▶ **noun** the isolating of a prisoner in a separate cell as a punishment.

sol·i·tude /'sälə,t(y)o͞od/ ▶ **noun 1** the state of being alone. **2** a lonely or uninhabited place.

– SYNONYMS **loneliness,** solitariness, isolation, seclusion, privacy, peace.

CHOOSE THE RIGHT WORD

solitude, alienation, desolation, disaffection, estrangement, lonesomeness, solitude

Loneliness, which refers to a lack of companionship and is often associated with unhappiness, should not be confused with **solitude**, which is the state of being alone or cut off from all human contact (*the solitude of the lighthouse keeper*). You can be in the midst of a crowd of people and still experience *loneliness*, but not *solitude*, since you are not physically alone. Similarly, if you enjoy being alone, you can have solitude without loneliness. **Lonesomeness** is more intense than *loneliness*, suggesting the downheartedness you may experience when a loved one is absent (*she experienced lonesomeness following the death of her dog*). **Desolation** is more intense still, referring to a state of being utterly alone or forsaken (*the widow's desolation*). *Desolation* can also indicate a state of ruin or barrenness (*the desolation of the volcanic islands*). **Alienation**, **disaffection**, and **estrangement** have less to do with being or feeling alone and more to do with emotions that change over time. *Alienation* is a word that suggests a feeling of unrelatedness, especially a feeling of distance from your social or intellectual environment (*alienation from society*). *Disaffection* suggests that you now feel indifference or even distaste toward someone of you were once fond of (*a wife's growing disaffection for her husband*), while *estrangement* is a voluntary disaffection that can result in complete separation and strong feelings of dislike or hatred (*a daughter's estrangement from her parents*).

sol·mi·za·tion /,sälmi'zāshən, sōl-/ ▶ **noun** a system of associating each note of a musical scale with a particular syllable (typically the sequence do, re, mi, fa, sol, la, ti), especially to teach singing.
– ORIGIN French, from *sol*'soh' + *mi* (see **MI**).

so·lo /'sōlō/ ▶ **noun** (pl. **solos**) **1** a song, dance, or piece of music for one performer. **2** a flight undertaken by a single pilot. **3** (also **solo whist**) a card game resembling whist in which the players make bids and the highest bidder plays against the others.▶ **adjective & adverb** for or done by one person.

– SYNONYMS **unaccompanied,** alone, on one's own, single-handed(ly), by oneself, unescorted, unattended, unaided, independent(ly).
– ANTONYMS accompanied.

▶ **verb** (**soloes, soloing, soloed**) perform a solo.
– ORIGIN Latin *solus* 'alone.'

so·lo·ist /'sōlōist/ ▶ **noun** a musician or singer who performs a solo.

Sol·o·mon's seal ▶ **noun** a plant with arching stems bearing a double row of broad leaves and drooping green and white flowers.

sol·stice /'sōlstis/ ▶ **noun** each of the two times in the year, respectively at midsummer and midwinter, when the sun reaches its highest or lowest point in the sky at noon, marked by the longest and shortest days.
– ORIGIN Latin *solstitium*, from *sol* 'sun' + *sistere* 'stop.'

sol·u·ble /'sälyəbəl/ ▶ **adjective 1** (of a substance) able to be dissolved, especially in water. **2** (of a problem) able to be solved.
– DERIVATIVES **sol·u·bil·i·ty** /ˌsälyə'bilitē/ noun.
– ORIGIN Latin *solubilis*.

sol·ute /'sälˌyōōt/ ▶ **noun** the minor component in a solution, dissolved in the solvent.

so·lu·tion /sə'lōōsʜən/ ▶ **noun 1** a means of solving a problem. **2** the correct answer to a puzzle. **3** a mixture formed when a substance (the solute) is dissolved in a liquid (the solvent). **4** the process of dissolving or the state of being dissolved.

> – SYNONYMS **1 answer,** result, resolution, key, explanation. **2 mixture,** blend, emulsion, compound.

– ORIGIN Latin, from *solvere* 'loosen.'

solve /sälv, sôlv/ ▶ **verb** find an answer to, explanation for, or way of dealing with a problem or mystery.

> – SYNONYMS **answer,** resolve, work out, puzzle out, fathom, decipher, decode, clear up, straighten out, get to the bottom of, unravel, explain; informal figure out, crack.

– DERIVATIVES **solv·a·ble** adjective **solv·er** noun.
– ORIGIN Latin *solvere* 'loosen, unfasten.'

sol·vent /'sälvənt/ ▶ **adjective 1** having more money than one owes. **2** able to dissolve other substances. ▶ **noun 1** a liquid that can dissolve other substances. **2** the liquid in which another substance is dissolved to form a solution.
– DERIVATIVES **sol·ven·cy** noun.

sol·vent a·buse ▶ **noun** the deliberate inhalation of the intoxicating fumes of certain solvents such as glue.

so·ma /'sōmə/ ▶ **noun 1** Biology the parts of an organism other than the reproductive cells. **2** the body as distinct from the soul or mind.
– ORIGIN Greek, 'body.'

So·ma·li /sə'mälē, sō-/ ▶ **noun** (pl. **Somalis**) **1** a person from Somalia. **2** a member of a mainly Muslim people of Somalia. **3** the language of the Somali. ▶ **adjective** relating to Somalia.
– DERIVATIVES **So·ma·li·an** adjective & noun.

so·mat·ic /sə'matik, sō-/ ▶ **adjective** relating to the body, especially as distinct from the mind.
– ORIGIN Greek *sōmatikos*.

som·ber /'sämbər/ (Brit. **sombre**) ▶ **adjective 1** dark or dull. **2** serious and sad.

> – SYNONYMS **1 dark,** drab, dull, dingy, restrained, sober, funereal. **2 solemn,** earnest, serious, grave, sober, unsmiling, gloomy, sad, mournful, melancholy, lugubrious, cheerless.
> – ANTONYMS bright, cheerful.

– DERIVATIVES **som·ber·ly** adverb **som·ber·ness** noun.
– ORIGIN French, from Latin *sub* 'under' + *umbra* 'shade.'

som·bre·ro /säm'bre(ə)rō/ ▶ **noun** (pl. **sombreros**) a broad-brimmed hat, typically worn in Mexico and the southwestern US.
– ORIGIN Spanish.

some /səm/ ▶ **determiner 1** an unspecified amount or number of. **2** referring to an unknown or unspecified person or thing. **3** (used with a number) approximately. **4** a considerable amount or number of. **5** a certain small amount or number of. **6** expressing admiration: *that was some goal*. ▶ **pronoun 1** an unspecified number or amount of people or things. **2** a certain small number or amount of people or things.
– ORIGIN Old English.

some·bod·y /'səmbədē, 'səmˌbädē/ ▶ **pronoun** someone.

some·day /'səmˌdā/ ▶ **adverb** at some time in the future.

some·how /'səmˌhou/ ▶ **adverb 1** by one means or another. **2** for an unknown or unspecified reason.

> – SYNONYMS **one way or another,** no matter how, by hook or by crook, come what may, come hell or high water, by fair means or foul.

some·one /'səmˌwən/ ▶ **pronoun 1** an unknown or unspecified person. **2** an important or famous person.

some·place /'səmˌplās/ ▶ **adverb & pronoun** informal somewhere.

som·er·sault /'səmərˌsôlt/ ▶ **noun** an acrobatic movement in which a person turns head over heels in the air or on the ground and finishes on their feet. ▶ **verb** perform a somersault.
– ORIGIN Old French *sombresault*.

some·thing /'səmˌᴛʜiɴɢ/ ▶ **pronoun 1** an unspecified or unknown thing. **2** an unspecified or unknown amount or degree. ▶ **adverb** informal used for emphasis: *my back hurts something terrible*.

some·time /'səmˌtīm/ ▶ **adverb** at some unspecified or unknown time. ▶ **adjective** former: *the sometime editor of the paper*.

some·times /'səmˌtīmz/ ▶ **adverb** occasionally.

> – SYNONYMS **occasionally,** from time to time, now and then, every so often, once in a while, on occasion, at times, off and on.

some·what /'səmˌ(h)wät/ ▶ **adverb** to some extent; rather.

> – SYNONYMS **1** *matters have improved somewhat* **a little,** a bit, to some extent, (up) to a point, in some measure; informal some, kind of, sort of. **2** *a somewhat longer book* **slightly,** relatively, comparatively, moderately, fairly, rather, quite, marginally.
> – ANTONYMS greatly.

some·where /'səmˌ(h)we(ə)r/ ▶ **adverb 1** in or to an unspecified or unknown place. **2** used to indicate an approximate amount. ▶ **pronoun** some unspecified place.
– PHRASES **get somewhere** informal make progress.

som·me·lier /ˌsəməl'yā/ ▶ **noun** a waiter who serves wine.
– ORIGIN French, 'butler.'

som·nam·bu·lism /säm'nambyəˌlizəm/ ▶ **noun** sleepwalking.
– DERIVATIVES **som·nam·bu·lant** adjective **som·nam·bu·list** noun **som·nam·bu·lis·tic** /-ˌnambyə'listik/ adjective.
– ORIGIN from Latin *somnus* 'sleep' + *ambulare* 'to walk.'

som·no·lent /'sämnələnt/ ▶ **adjective 1** sleepy. **2** causing sleepiness.
– DERIVATIVES **som·no·lence** noun **som·no·lent·ly** adverb.
– ORIGIN from Latin *somnus* 'sleep.'

son /sən/ ▶ **noun 1** a boy or man in relation to his parents. **2** a male descendant. **3** (**the Son** or **the Son of Man**)

Jesus. **4** (also **my son**) a form of address for a boy or younger man.
– ORIGIN Old English.

so·nar /'sō,när/ ▶ **noun 1** a system for detecting objects under water based on the emission and reflection of sound pulses. **2** a device used in this system.
– ORIGIN from *so(und) na(vigation and) r(anging)*, on the pattern of *radar*.

so·na·ta /sə'nätə/ ▶ **noun** a piece of classical music for a solo instrument, often with a piano accompaniment.
– ORIGIN Italian, 'sounded.'

song /sôNG/ ▶ **noun 1** a poem or other set of words set to music. **2** singing: *they broke into song*. **3** the musical sounds made by some birds, whales, and insects. **4** literary a poem.

– SYNONYMS **air,** strain, ditty, chant, number, track, melody, tune.

– PHRASES **for a song** informal very cheaply. **a song and dance** informal a fuss.
– ORIGIN Old English.

song·bird /'sôNG,bərd/ ▶ **noun** a bird with a musical song.

song cy·cle ▶ **noun** a set of related songs forming a single musical work.

song·smith /'sôNG,smiTH/ ▶ **noun** informal a writer of popular songs.

song·ster /'sôNGstər/ ▶ **noun** (fem. **songstress**) a person who sings.

song·writ·er /'sôNG,rītər/ ▶ **noun** a writer of songs or the music for them.

son·ic /'sänik/ ▶ **adjective** relating to or using sound waves.
– DERIVATIVES **son·i·cal·ly** /-ik(ə)lē/ adverb.
– ORIGIN from Latin *sonus* 'sound.'

son·ic boom ▶ **noun** an explosive noise caused by the shock wave from an aircraft or other object traveling faster than the speed of sound.

son·ics /'säniks/ ▶ **plural noun** musical sounds artificially produced or reproduced.

son-in-law ▶ **noun** (pl. **sons-in-law**) the husband of one's daughter.

son·net /'sänit/ ▶ **noun** a poem of fourteen lines using any of a number of fixed rhyme schemes.
– ORIGIN Italian *sonetto* 'little sound.'

son·ny /'sənē/ ▶ **noun** informal a familiar form of address to a boy or young man.

son·o·gram /'sänə,gram/ ▶ **noun 1** a graph showing the distribution of energy at different frequencies in a sound. **2** a visual image produced from an ultrasound examination.
– DERIVATIVES **son·o·graph·ic** /,sänə'grafik/ adjective **so·nog·ra·phy** /sə'nägrəfē/ noun.
– ORIGIN from Latin *sonus* 'sound.'

so·no·rous /sə'nôrəs, 'sänərəs/ ▶ **adjective 1** (of a sound) deep and full. **2** (of speech) using grand or impressive language.

– SYNONYMS **resonant,** rich, full, round, booming, deep, clear, mellow, strong, resounding, reverberant.

– DERIVATIVES **so·nor·i·ty** /sə'nôritē/ noun **so·no·rous·ly** adverb.
– ORIGIN from Latin *sonor* 'sound.'

soon /so͞on/ ▶ **adverb 1** in or after a short time. **2** early. **3** used to indicate a preference: *I'd just as soon Tim did it*.

– SYNONYMS **shortly,** presently, in the near future, before long, in a little while, in a minute, in a moment; informal in a sec.

– DERIVATIVES **soon·ish** adverb.
– PHRASES **no sooner than** at the very moment that. **sooner or later** eventually.
– ORIGIN Old English.

USAGE

The phrase **no sooner** should be followed by **than** rather than **when** in standard English: *we had no sooner arrived than we had to leave*, not *we had no sooner arrived when we had to leave*. This is because **sooner** is a comparative form, and comparative forms should be followed by **than**.

soot /so͝ot/ ▶ **noun** a black powdery or flaky substance produced when an organic substance such as coal is burned.
– ORIGIN Old English.

sooth /so͞oTH/ ▶ **noun** old use truth.
– PHRASES **in sooth** truly.
– ORIGIN Old English.

soothe /so͞oTH/ ▶ **verb 1** gently calm a person or their fears. **2** relieve pain or discomfort.

– SYNONYMS **1 calm (down),** pacify, comfort, hush, quiet (down), settle (down), appease, mollify. **2** (as adj. **soothing**) *soothing music* **relaxing,** restful, calm, calming, tranquil, peaceful. **3 ease,** alleviate, relieve, take the edge off, allay, lessen, reduce.
– ANTONYMS agitate, aggravate.

– DERIVATIVES **sooth·er** noun.
– ORIGIN Old English, 'verify,' from **SOOTH**.

sooth·say·er /'so͞oTH,sāər/ ▶ **noun** a person supposed to be able to foresee the future.
– DERIVATIVES **sooth·say·ing** noun.

soot·y /'so͝otē/ ▶ **adjective** (**sootier**, **sootiest**) covered with or colored like soot.

SOP ▶ **abbreviation** standard operating procedure.

sop /säp/ ▶ **noun** a thing of no great value given or done in an attempt to appease someone who is angry or disappointed. ▶ **verb** (**sops**, **sopping**, **sopped**) (**sop something up**) soak up liquid.
– ORIGIN Old English.

soph. ▶ **abbreviation** sophomore.

soph·ism /'säfizəm/ ▶ **noun** a clever but false argument, especially one used to deceive other people.
– ORIGIN Greek *sophisma* 'clever device.'

soph·ist /'säfist/ ▶ **noun** a person who uses clever but false arguments.
– DERIVATIVES **so·phis·tic** /sə'fistik/ adjective **so·phis·ti·cal** /sə'fistikəl/ adjective.

so·phis·ti·cate ▶ **noun** /sə'fistə,kit, -kāt/ a person having experience and taste in matters of fashion and culture. ▶ **verb** /sə'fistə,kāt/ make someone or something more sophisticated.
– ORIGIN Latin *sophisticare* 'tamper with.'

so·phis·ti·cat·ed /sə'fisti,kātid/ ▶ **adjective 1** having or showing experience and taste in matters of culture or fashion. **2** (of a machine, system, or technique) highly developed and complex. **3** appealing to sophisticated people.

– SYNONYMS **1** *a sophisticated woman* **worldly,** worldly-wise, experienced, cosmopolitan, urbane, cultured, cultivated, polished, refined. **2** *sophisticated techniques* **advanced,** state-of-the-art, the latest, up-to-the-minute, cutting-edge, complex.
– ANTONYMS crude, naive.

CHOOSE THE RIGHT WORD

See **URBANE**.

so·phis·ti·ca·tion /səˌfistiˈkāsʜən/ ▶ **noun** the quality or fact of having experience and taste in matters of fashion and culture.

– SYNONYMS **worldliness,** experience, urbanity, culture, polish, refinement, elegance, style, poise, finesse, savoir faire.

soph·ist·ry /ˈsäfəstrē/ ▶ **noun** (pl. **sophistries**) **1** the use of clever false arguments, especially to deceive other people. **2** a clever but false argument.

soph·o·more /ˈsäf(ə)ˌmôr/ ▶ **noun** a second-year high-school or college student.
– ORIGIN probably from *sophum, sophom* (former variants of **SOPHISM**).

soph·o·mor·ic /ˌsäf(ə)ˈmôrik/ ▶ **adjective 1** relating to or characteristic of a sophomore. **2** pretentious or juvenile: *sophomoric humor.*

sop·o·rif·ic /ˌsäpəˈrifik/ ▶ **adjective** causing drowsiness or sleep. ▶ **noun** a drug or other substance that causes drowsiness or sleep.
– ORIGIN from Latin *sopor* 'sleep.'

sop·ping /ˈsäpiɴɢ/ (also **sopping wet**) ▶ **adjective** wet through.

sop·py /ˈsäpē/ ▶ **adjective** (**soppier, soppiest**) informal **1** sentimental in a silly or self-indulgent way. **2** rather weak and feeble.
– DERIVATIVES **sop·pi·ly** adverb **sop·pi·ness** noun.
– ORIGIN first meaning 'soaked with water': from **SOP**.

so·pran·o /səˈpranō/ ▶ **noun** (pl. **sopranos**) the highest singing voice. ▶ **adjective** (of an instrument) of a high or the highest pitch in its family: *a soprano saxophone.*
– ORIGIN Italian, from *sopra* 'above.'

sor·bet /sôrˈbā, ˈsôrbit/ ▶ **noun** a frozen dessert consisting of fruit juice or purée in a sugar syrup.
– ORIGIN French, from an Arabic word meaning 'to drink.'

sor·cer·er /ˈsôrsərər/ ▶ **noun** (fem. **sorceress** /ˈsôrsəris/) a person believed to practice magic; a wizard.
– DERIVATIVES **sor·cer·y** /ˈsôrsərē/ noun.
– ORIGIN Old French *sorcier.*

sor·did /ˈsôrdid/ ▶ **adjective 1** dishonest or immoral; morally distasteful: *the truth about his sordid past.* **2** dirty or squalid.

– SYNONYMS **1 sleazy,** seedy, seamy, unsavory, tawdry, cheap, disreputable, discreditable, ignominious, shameful, wretched, despicable. **2 squalid,** slummy, dirty, filthy, shabby, scummy; informal scuzzy.
– ANTONYMS respectable.

– DERIVATIVES **sor·did·ly** adverb **sor·did·ness** noun.
– ORIGIN Latin *sordidus.*

WORD TOOLKIT

See **DIRTY**.

sore /sôr/ ▶ **adjective 1** painful or aching. **2** informal upset and angry. **3** great; urgent: *we're in sore need of him.*

– SYNONYMS **1 painful,** hurting, aching, throbbing, smarting, stinging, inflamed, sensitive, tender, raw, wounded, injured. **2 upset,** angry, annoyed, cross, disgruntled, dissatisfied, irritated; informal aggravated, miffed, peeved, ticked off.

▶ **noun** a raw or painful place on the body.
▶ **adverb** old use extremely: *sore afraid.*
– DERIVATIVES **sore·ness** noun.
– PHRASES **sore point** an issue about which someone feels distressed or annoyed. **stand** (or **stick**) **out like a sore thumb** be quite obviously different.
– ORIGIN Old English.

sore·ly /ˈsôrlē/ ▶ **adverb** extremely; greatly.

sor·ghum /ˈsôrgəm/ ▶ **noun** a cereal native to warm regions, grown for grain and animal feed.
– ORIGIN Italian *sorgo.*

so·ror·i·ty /səˈrôritē, -ˈrä-/ ▶ **noun** (pl. **sororities**) a society for female students in a college or university.
– ORIGIN from Latin *soror* 'sister.'

sor·rel[1] /ˈsôrəl/ ▶ **noun** an edible plant of the dock family with arrow-shaped leaves and a bitter flavor.
– ORIGIN Old French *sorele.*

sor·rel[2] ▶ **noun 1** a light reddish-brown color. **2** a horse with a sorrel coat.
– ORIGIN Old French *sorel.*

sor·row /ˈsärō, ˈsôrō/ ▶ **noun 1** deep distress caused by loss or disappointment. **2** a cause of sorrow.

– SYNONYMS **1 sadness,** unhappiness, misery, despondency, regret, despair, desolation, heartache, grief. **2** *the sorrows of life* **trouble,** difficulty, problem, woe, affliction, trial, tribulation, misfortune.
– ANTONYMS joy.

▶ **verb** feel sorrow.
– ORIGIN Old English.

CHOOSE THE RIGHT WORD

See **MOURN**.

sor·row·ful /ˈsärəfəl, ˈsôrō-/ ▶ **adjective 1** feeling or showing sorrow. **2** causing sorrow.
– DERIVATIVES **sor·row·ful·ly** adverb.

sor·ry /ˈsärē, ˈsô-/ ▶ **adjective** (**sorrier, sorriest**) **1** feeling distress or pity through sympathy with someone else's misfortune. **2** feeling or expressing regret. **3** in a poor or pitiful state. **4** unpleasant and regrettable: *a sorry business.*

– SYNONYMS **1 regretful,** apologetic, remorseful, contrite, repentant, rueful, penitent, guilty, shamefaced, ashamed. **2** *he felt sorry for her* **full of pity,** sympathetic, compassionate, moved, concerned. **3** *I was sorry to hear about the accident* **sad,** sorrowful, distressed.
– ANTONYMS glad, unrepentant.

– DERIVATIVES **sor·ri·ness** noun.
– ORIGIN Old English, 'pained, distressed.'

sort /sôrt/ ▶ **noun 1** a category of people or things with a common feature or features. **2** informal a person with a particular nature: *he was a friendly sort.*

– SYNONYMS **type,** kind, variety, class, category, style, form, genre, species, breed, make, model, brand.

▶ **verb 1** arrange systematically in groups: *he sorted the contents of the desk into two piles.* **2** (often **sort something out**) separate something from a mixed group. **3** (**sort something out**) resolve a problem or difficulty. **4** (**sort someone out**) informal deal with a troublesome person.

> – SYNONYMS **1 classify,** class, group, organize, arrange, order, grade, catalog. **2** *the problem was soon* ***sorted out*** **resolve,** settle, solve, fix, work out, straighten out, deal with, put right, set right, rectify, iron out.

– DERIVATIVES **sort·er** noun.
– PHRASES **of a sort** (or **of sorts**) of a somewhat unusual or inferior kind. **out of sorts** slightly unwell or unhappy. **sort of** informal to some extent.
– ORIGIN Old French *sorte.*

> **USAGE**
>
> The expression **these sort of**, as in *I don't want to answer these sort of questions*, does not follow traditional grammar and should be avoided in formal writing. This is because **these** is plural and normally agrees with a plural noun; the preferred usage is *these sorts of questions*. See also the note at **KIND**[1].

sort·ie /ˌsôrˈtē, ˈsôrtē/ ▶ **noun 1** an attack made by troops coming out from a position of defense. **2** a flight by a single aircraft on a military operation. **3** a short trip.
– ORIGIN French, from *sortir* 'go out.'

SOS ▶ **noun 1** an international signal of extreme distress, used especially by ships at sea. **2** an urgent appeal for help.
– ORIGIN letters chosen as being easily transmitted and recognized in Morse code; popularly taken as an abbreviation of *save our souls*.

so-so ▶ **adjective** neither very good nor very bad.

> – SYNONYMS **mediocre,** indifferent, average, middle-of-the-road, middling, moderate, ordinary, adequate, fair, uninspired, undistinguished, unexceptional, unremarkable, run-of-the-mill, lackluster; informal no great shakes.

sot /sät/ ▶ **noun** a person who is regularly drunk.
– DERIVATIVES **sot·tish** adjective.
– ORIGIN Latin *sottus* 'foolish person.'

sot·to vo·ce /ˈsätō ˈvōchē/ ▶ **adverb & adjective** in a quiet voice.
– ORIGIN from Italian *sotto* 'under' + *voce* 'voice.'

sou /so͞o/ ▶ **noun** dated, informal a very small amount of money.
– ORIGIN French, first referring to a former French coin of low value.

sou·brette /so͞oˈbret/ ▶ **noun** a pert maidservant or similar minor female role in a comedy.
– ORIGIN Provençal *soubret* 'coy.'

sou·bri·quet ▶ **noun** variant spelling of **SOBRIQUET**.

souf·flé /so͞oˈflā/ ▶ **noun** a light, spongy baked dish made by mixing egg yolks and another ingredient such as cheese or fruit with stiffly beaten egg whites.
– ORIGIN French, 'blown.'

sought /sôt/ past and past participle of **SEEK**.
– PHRASES **sought af·ter** in great demand.

souk /so͞ok/ ▶ **noun** an Arab market.
– ORIGIN Arabic.

soul /sōl/ ▶ **noun 1** the spiritual element of a person, believed to be immortal. **2** a person's moral or emotional nature. **3** emotional or intellectual energy or power: *their performance lacked soul.* **4** a person regarded as a perfect example of a particular quality: *she's the soul of discretion.* **5** an individual person: *I'll never tell a soul.* **6** (also **soul music**) a kind of music that incorporates elements of gospel music and rhythm and blues, popularized by black Americans.

> – SYNONYMS **1 spirit,** psyche, (inner) self. **2 feeling,** emotion, passion, animation, intensity, warmth, energy, vitality, spirit.

– ORIGIN Old English.

soul-des·troy·ing ▶ **adjective** unbearably dull and repetitive.

soul food ▶ **noun** food traditionally associated with black people of the southern US.

soul·ful /ˈsōlfəl/ ▶ **adjective** expressing deep and usually sorrowful feeling.
– DERIVATIVES **soul·ful·ly** adverb **soul·ful·ness** noun.

soul·less /ˈsōlˌlis/ ▶ **adjective 1** lacking character and individuality: *soulless postwar apartment blocks.* **2** (of an activity) dull and uninspiring. **3** lacking human feelings.

soul·mate /ˈsōlˌmāt/ ▶ **noun** a person ideally suited to another.

soul-search·ing ▶ **noun** close examination of one's emotions and motives.

sound[1] /sound/ ▶ **noun 1** vibrations that travel through air or water and are sensed by the ear. **2** a thing that can be heard. **3** music, speech, and sound effects accompanying a movie or broadcast. **4** an idea or impression given by words: *you've had a hard day, by the sound of it.*

> – SYNONYMS **1 noise,** din, racket, resonance, reverberation. **2 utterance,** cry, word, noise, peep.
> – ANTONYMS silence.

▶ **verb 1** make a sound. **2** make a sound to show or warn of something. **3** give a particular impression: *the job sounds great.* **4** (**sound off**) express one's opinions loudly or forcefully.

> – SYNONYMS **1 make a noise,** resonate, resound, reverberate, go off, ring, chime, ping. **2** *sound the horn* **blow,** blast, toot, ring, use, operate, activate, set off. **3 appear,** look (like), seem, give every indication of being, strike someone as.

– DERIVATIVES **sound·less** adjective.
– ORIGIN Latin *sonus.*

> **WORD LINKS**
>
> **acoustic**, **sonic** *relating to sound*

sound[2] ▶ **adjective 1** in good condition. **2** based on reason or good judgment. **3** financially secure. **4** competent or reliable. **5** (of sleep) deep and unbroken. **6** severe or thorough: *a sound thrashing.*

> – SYNONYMS **1 healthy,** in good condition/shape, fit, hale and hearty, in fine fettle, undamaged, unimpaired. **2 well built,** solid, substantial, strong, sturdy, durable, stable, intact. **3 well founded,** valid, reasonable, logical, weighty, authoritative, reliable. **4 solvent,** debt-free, in the black, creditworthy, secure. **5 reliable,** dependable, trustworthy, fair, good. **6** *a doze that deepened into a sound sleep* **deep,** undisturbed, uninterrupted, untroubled, peaceful.
> – ANTONYMS unhealthy, unsafe.

▶ **adverb** in a sound way.

– DERIVATIVES **sound·ly** adverb **sound·ness** noun.
– ORIGIN Old English.

sound³ ▶ verb **1** find out the depth of water in the sea, a lake, etc., by means of a line or pole or using sound echoes. **2** (**sound someone out**) question someone discreetly or cautiously about their opinions or feelings. **3** examine the bladder or another part of the body with a long surgical probe.
– DERIVATIVES **sound·er** noun.
– ORIGIN Old French *sonder*.

sound⁴ ▶ noun a narrow stretch of water forming an inlet or connecting two larger areas of water.
– ORIGIN Old Norse, 'swimming, strait.'

sound-and-light ▶ adjective referring to a nighttime entertainment held at a historic monument or building, telling its history by the use of lighting effects and recorded sound.

sound bar·ri·er ▶ noun the point at which an aircraft reaches the speed of sound, causing reduced control, an explosive noise, and various other effects.

sound bite ▶ noun a short, memorable extract from a speech or interview.

sound·board /ˈsoun(d)ˌbôrd/ (also **sounding board**) ▶ noun a thin board over which the strings of a piano or similar instrument are positioned to increase the sound produced.

sound·box /ˈsoundˌbäks/ ▶ noun the hollow chamber that forms the body of a stringed instrument and makes the sound resonate.

sound·check /ˈsoun(d)ˌCHek/ ▶ noun a test of sound equipment before a musical performance or recording.

sound ef·fect ▶ noun a sound other than speech or music made artificially for use in a play, movie, etc.

sound·ing /ˈsoundiNG/ ▶ noun **1** the action of sounding the depth of water. **2** a measurement taken by sounding. **3** (**soundings**) information or evidence found out before taking action.

sound·ing board ▶ noun **1** a person or group with whom new ideas or opinions are discussed to test their validity or likelihood of success. **2** a board over or behind a pulpit or stage to reflect a speaker's voice forward. **3** a soundboard.

sound·ing line ▶ noun a weighted line used to measure the depth of water under a boat.

sound·proof /ˈsoun(d)ˌpro͞of/ ▶ adjective preventing sound getting in or out. ▶ verb make something soundproof.

sound·scape /ˈsoun(d)ˌskāp/ ▶ noun a piece of music considered in terms of the different sounds of which it is composed.

sound sys·tem ▶ noun a set of equipment for reproducing and amplifying sound.

sound·track /ˈsoun(d)ˌtrak/ ▶ noun the sound accompaniment to a movie.

sound wave ▶ noun a wave of alternate compression and reduction in density by which sound travels through air or water.

soup /so͞op/ ▶ noun a savory liquid dish made by boiling meat, fish, or vegetables in stock or water. ▶ verb (**soup something up**) informal **1** increase the power and efficiency of an engine or other machine. **2** make something more elaborate or impressive.
– PHRASES **in the soup** informal in trouble.
– ORIGIN Old French *soupe* 'broth (poured on slices of bread).'

soup·çon /so͞opˈsôN/ ▶ noun a very small amount of something.
– ORIGIN French, from Latin *suspectio* 'suspicion.'

soup kitch·en ▶ noun a place where free food is served to homeless or destitute people.

soup·y /ˈso͞opē/ ▶ adjective (**soupier, soupiest**) **1** having the appearance or consistency of soup. **2** informal foolishly sentimental.

sour /ˈsou(ə)r/ ▶ adjective **1** having a sharp taste like lemon or vinegar. **2** tasting or smelling unpleasant as a result of fermentation or staleness. **3** resentful, bitter, or angry.

> – SYNONYMS **1 acid,** acidic, tart, bitter, sharp, vinegary, pungent. **2 bad,** off, turned, curdled, rancid, fetid. **3 embittered,** resentful, jaundiced, bitter, cross, crabby, crotchety, cantankerous, bad-tempered, disagreeable, unpleasant; informal grouchy.
> – ANTONYMS sweet, fresh.

▶ verb make or become sour.

> – SYNONYMS **spoil,** mar, damage, harm, impair, upset, poison, blight.

▶ noun a cocktail made by mixing liquor with lemon or lime juice.
– DERIVATIVES **sour·ly** adverb **sour·ness** noun.
– PHRASES **go** (or **turn**) **sour** become less pleasant; turn out badly. **sour grapes** an attitude in which someone pretends to despise or dislike something because they cannot have it themselves. [with allusion to Aesop's fable *The Fox and the Grapes*.]
– ORIGIN Old English.

source /sôrs/ ▶ noun **1** a place, person, or thing from which something originates. **2** a person, book, or document that provides information or evidence. **3** the spring or other place from which a river or stream begins.

> – SYNONYMS **1 spring,** wellspring, wellhead, origin. **2 origin,** derivation, starting point, start, beginning, fountainhead, root, author, originator.

▶ verb get something from a particular place: *the milk is sourced from local farms*.
– ORIGIN Old French *sourse*.

source·book /ˈsôrsˌbo͝ok/ ▶ noun a collection of writings and articles on a particular subject, especially one used as a basic introduction to that subject.

sour cream ▶ noun cream deliberately made sour by the addition of certain bacteria.

sour·dough /ˈsou(ə)rˌdō/ ▶ noun bread made from fermenting dough, originally that left over from a previous baking.

sour·puss /ˈsou(ə)rˌpo͝os/ ▶ noun informal a bad-tempered or grumpy person.

sour·sop /ˈsou(ə)rˌsäp/ ▶ noun a large acidic custard apple with white fibrous flesh.

sou·sa·phone /ˈso͞ozəˌfōn/ ▶ noun a form of tuba with a wide end that points forward above the player's head.
– ORIGIN named after the American composer J. P. *Sousa*.

souse /sous/ ▶ verb **1** soak or drench something with liquid. **2** (as adj. **soused**) (of gherkins, fish, etc.) pickled or marinaded: *soused herring*. **3** (as adj. **soused**) informal drunk. ▶ noun liquid used for pickling.

– ORIGIN Old French *sous* 'pickle.'

sou·tane /sōō'tän/ ▶ **noun** a type of cassock worn by Roman Catholic priests.
– ORIGIN Italian *sottana*.

south /souTH/ ▶ **noun 1** the direction toward the point of the horizon 90° clockwise from east. **2** the southern part of a place. ▶ **adjective 1** lying toward, near, or facing the south. **2** (of a wind) blowing from the south. ▶ **adverb** to or toward the south.
– DERIVATIVES **south·bound** /'souTH,bound/ adjective & adverb.
– ORIGIN Old English.

South Af·ri·can ▶ **noun** a person from South Africa. ▶ **adjective** relating to South Africa.

South A·mer·i·can ▶ **noun** a person from South America. ▶ **adjective** relating to South America.

south·east /,souTH'ēst/ ▶ **noun** the direction or region halfway between south and east. ▶ **adjective 1** lying toward, near, or facing the southeast. **2** (of a wind) from the southeast. ▶ **adverb** to or toward the southeast.
– DERIVATIVES **south·east·ern** adjective.

south·east·er·ly /,souTH'ēstərlē/ ▶ **adjective & adverb** in a southeastward position or direction. ▶ **noun** a wind blowing from the southeast.

south·east·ward /,souTH'ēstwərd/ ▶ **adverb** (also **southeastwards**) toward the southeast. ▶ **adjective** in, toward, or facing the southeast.

south·er·ly /'səT͟Hərlē/ ▶ **adjective & adverb 1** facing or moving toward the south. **2** (of a wind) blowing from the south. ▶ **noun** (pl. **southerlies**) a south wind.

south·ern /'səT͟Hərn/ ▶ **adjective 1** situated in, directed toward, or facing the south. **2** (usu. **Southern**) relating to or typical of the south.
– DERIVATIVES **south·ern·most** /-,mōst/ adjective.

south·ern·er /'səT͟Hərnər/ ▶ **noun** a person from the south of a region or country.

South·ern Lights ▶ **plural noun** the aurora australis.

south·paw /'souTH,pô/ ▶ **noun 1** informal a left-handed person. **2** a left-handed boxer who leads with the right hand.

south-south·east ▶ **noun** the direction halfway between south and southeast.

south-south·west ▶ **noun** the direction halfway between south and southwest.

south·ward /'souTHwərd/ ▶ **adjective** in a southerly direction. ▶ **adverb** (also **southwards**) toward the south.

south·west /,souTH'west/ ▶ **noun** the direction or region halfway between south and west. ▶ **adjective 1** lying toward or facing the southwest. **2** (of a wind) from the southwest. ▶ **adverb** to or toward the southwest.
– DERIVATIVES **south·west·ern** adjective.

south·west·er·ly /,souTH'westərlē/ ▶ **adjective & adverb** in a southwestward position or direction. ▶ **noun** (pl. **southwesterlies**) a wind blowing from the southwest.

south·west·ward /,souTH'westwərd/ ▶ **adverb** (also **southwestwards**) toward the southwest. ▶ **adjective** in, toward, or facing the southwest.

sou·ve·nir /,sōōvə'ni(ə)r/ ▶ **noun** a thing that is kept as a reminder of a person, place, or event.

– SYNONYMS **memento,** keepsake, reminder, memorial, trophy.

– ORIGIN French.

sou'·west·er /,sou'westər/ ▶ **noun** a waterproof hat with a broad brim or flap covering the back of the neck.

sov·er·eign /'säv(ə)rən/ ▶ **noun 1** a king or queen who is the supreme ruler of a country. **2** a former British gold coin worth one pound sterling.

– SYNONYMS **ruler,** monarch, potentate, overlord, king, queen, emperor, empress, prince, princess.

▶ **adjective 1** possessing supreme power. **2** (of a nation or its affairs) acting or done independently.

– SYNONYMS **autonomous,** independent, self-governing, self-determining, nonaligned, free.

– ORIGIN Old French *soverain*.

sov·er·eign·ty /'säv(ə)rəntē/ ▶ **noun** (pl. **sovereignties**) **1** supreme power or authority. **2** a self-governing country.

– SYNONYMS **1 power,** rule, supremacy, dominion, jurisdiction, ascendancy, domination, authority, control. **2 autonomy,** independence, self-rule, self-government, home rule, self-determination, freedom.

CHOOSE THE RIGHT WORD

See **JURISDICTION**.

so·vi·et /'sōvēit, -,et/ ▶ **noun 1** (**Soviet**) a citizen of the former Soviet Union. **2** an elected council in the former Soviet Union. ▶ **adjective** (**Soviet**) relating to the former Soviet Union.
– DERIVATIVES **So·vi·et·ism** /-,tizəm/ noun **So·vi·et·ize** /-,tīz/ verb.
– ORIGIN Russian *sovet* 'council.'

So·vi·et·ol·o·gist /,sōvēi'täləjist/ ▶ **noun** an expert on the former Soviet Union.

sow[1] /sō/ ▶ **verb** (past **sowed**; past part. **sown** or **sowed**) **1** plant seed by scattering it on or in the earth. **2** spread or introduce something unwelcome: *the new policy has sown confusion and doubt*.

– SYNONYMS **plant,** scatter, disperse, strew, broadcast, seed.

– DERIVATIVES **sow·er** noun.
– ORIGIN Old English.

sow[2] /sou/ ▶ **noun** an adult female pig.
– ORIGIN Old English.

soy /soi/ ▶ **noun** another term for **SOYBEAN**. ▶ **adjective** made from soybeans: *soy burgers*.

soy·bean /'soi,bēn/ (also **soya bean** /'soiə/) ▶ **noun** an edible bean that is high in protein.
– ORIGIN Malay.

soy·meal /'soi,mēl/ ▶ **noun** a high-protein foodstuff made from soybeans, used in livestock feeds and as a raw ingredient in some processed foods.

soy milk /soi/ (also **soya milk** /soiə/) ▶ **noun** a liquid made from soybean flour in water, used as a substitute for milk.

soy sauce /soi/ ▶ **noun** a sauce made with fermented soybeans, used in Chinese and Japanese cooking.
– ORIGIN Chinese.

SP ▶ **abbreviation 1** starting price. **2** service pack.

spa /spä/ ▶ **noun 1** a place or resort with a mineral spring that is considered to have health-giving properties. **2** a place offering a range of health and beauty treatments.

3 (also **spa bath** or **pool**) a bath containing hot aerated water.
– ORIGIN from *Spa*, a town in Belgium noted for its mineral springs.

space /spās/ ▸ **noun 1** a continuous area or expanse that is free or unoccupied. **2** the dimensions of height, depth, and width within which all things exist and move. **3** (also **outer space**) the physical universe beyond the earth's atmosphere. **4** an interval of time (indicating that it is short): *forty men died in the space of two days.* **5** a blank between typed or written words or characters. **6** the freedom to live and develop as one wishes.

– SYNONYMS **1 room,** capacity, latitude, margin, leeway, play, elbow room, clearance. **2 area,** expanse, stretch, sweep, tract. **3 gap,** interval, opening, aperture, cavity, niche, interstice. **4 blank,** gap, box. **5 period,** span, time, duration, stretch, course, interval, gap. **6 outer space,** deep space, the universe, the galaxy, the solar system.

▸ **verb 1** position things at a distance from one another. **2** (**be spaced out**) informal be in a state of great happiness or confusion, especially from taking drugs.

– SYNONYMS **position,** arrange, range, array, spread, lay out, set.

– DERIVATIVES **spac·er** noun **spac·ing** noun.
– ORIGIN Latin *spatium*.

space age ▸ **noun** (**the space age**) the era that started when the exploration of space became possible. ▸ **adjective** (**space-age**) very modern; technologically advanced.

space bar ▸ **noun** a long key on a typewriter or computer keyboard for making a space.

space ca·det ▸ **noun** informal a person regarded as being out of touch with reality.

space cap·sule ▸ **noun** a small spacecraft or the part of a larger one that contains the instruments or crew, designed to be returned to earth.

space·craft /ˈspāsˌkraft/ ▸ **noun** (pl. same or **spacecrafts**) a vehicle used for traveling in space.

space heat·er ▸ **noun** a self-contained appliance, usually electric, for heating an enclosed room.
– DERIVATIVES **space heat·ing** noun.

space·man /ˈspāsˌman, -mən/ ▸ **noun** (pl. **spacemen**) a male astronaut.

space probe ▸ **noun** an unmanned spacecraft used for exploration.

space·ship /ˈspā(s)ˌsʜip/ ▸ **noun** a manned spacecraft.

space shut·tle ▸ **noun** a rocket-launched spacecraft able to land like an unpowered aircraft, used to make repeated journeys between earth and craft orbiting the earth.

space sta·tion ▸ **noun** a large artificial satellite used as a long-term base for manned operations in space.

space·suit /ˈspāsˌsoot/ ▸ **noun** a sealed and pressurized suit designed to allow an astronaut to survive in space.

space–time ▸ **noun** Physics the concepts of time and three-dimensional space regarded as forming a four-dimensional continuum.

space·walk /ˈspāsˌwôk/ ▸ **noun** a period of activity by an astronaut outside a spacecraft.
– DERIVATIVES **space·walk·er** noun.

spac·ey /ˈspāsē/ (also **spacy**) ▸ **adjective** (**spacier, spaciest**) informal **1** out of touch with reality. **2** (of popular music) drifting and unworldly.

spa·cial ▸ **adjective** variant spelling of **SPATIAL**.

spa·cious /ˈspāsʜəs/ ▸ **adjective** (of a room or building) having plenty of space.

– SYNONYMS **roomy,** capacious, commodious, voluminous, sizable, generous.
– ANTONYMS cramped.

– DERIVATIVES **spa·cious·ly** adverb **spa·cious·ness** noun.

spade /spād/ ▸ **noun** a tool with a rectangular metal blade and a long handle, used for digging. ▸ **verb** dig or move earth with a spade.
– PHRASES **call a spade a spade** speak plainly and frankly.
– ORIGIN Old English.

spades /spādz/ ▸ **noun** one of the four suits in a deck of playing cards, represented by an upside-down black heart shape with a small stalk.
– PHRASES **in spades** informal in large amounts or to a high degree.
– ORIGIN Italian *spade* 'swords.'

spade·work /ˈspādˌwərk/ ▸ **noun** hard or routine work done to prepare for something.

spa·dix /ˈspādiks/ ▸ **noun** (pl. **spadices** /-dəsēz/) Botany a spike of tiny flowers closely arranged around a fleshy stem and typically enclosed in a spathe (large modified leaf).
– ORIGIN Greek, 'palm branch.'

spa·ghet·ti /spəˈgetē/ ▸ **plural noun** pasta made in long strands.
– ORIGIN Italian, 'little strings.'

spa·ghet·ti bo·lo·gnese /ˌbōlənˈyēz, -ˈyāz/ ▸ **noun** a dish of spaghetti with a sauce of ground beef, tomato, onion, and herbs.
– ORIGIN Italian, 'spaghetti of Bologna.'

spa·ghet·ti west·ern ▸ **noun** informal a western (movie) filmed in Europe by an Italian director.

spake /spāk/ old use past of **SPEAK**.

spam /spam/ ▸ **noun 1** email that has not been requested, sent to large numbers of Internet users. **2** (**Spam**) trademark a canned meat product made mainly from ham. ▸ **verb** (**spams, spamming, spammed**) send email that has not been requested to large numbers of Internet users.
– DERIVATIVES **spam·mer** noun.
– ORIGIN probably from *spiced ham*; the Internet sense probably derives from a sketch in the British 'Monty Python' comedy show, in which every item on a cafe's menu includes spam.

span /span/ ▸ **noun 1** the length of time for which something lasts: *he scored twice within a span of four minutes.* **2** the full extent of something from end to end. **3** a part of a bridge between the uprights supporting it. **4** a wingspan of a bird or aircraft. **5** (also **handspan**) the maximum distance between the tips of the thumb and little finger.

– SYNONYMS **1 extent,** length, width, reach, stretch, spread, distance, range. **2 period,** space, time, duration, course, interval.

▸ **verb** (**spans, spanning, spanned**) **1** extend from side to side of something. **2** extend across a period of time or a range of subjects: *their interests span almost all the conventional disciplines.*

– SYNONYMS **1 bridge,** cross, traverse, pass over. **2 last,** cover, extend, spread over.

– ORIGIN Old English.

span·dex /ˈspandeks/ ▶ **noun** a type of stretchy synthetic fabric.
– ORIGIN from **EXPAND**.

span·drel /ˈspandrəl/ ▶ **noun** Architecture the roughly triangular space between the curve of an arch and the ceiling or framework above.
– ORIGIN perhaps from Old French *espaundre* 'expand.'

span·gle /ˈspaNGgəl/ ▶ **noun 1** a small thin piece of glittering material, used to decorate an item of clothing; a sequin. **2** a spot of bright color or light. ▶ **verb** (usu. as adj. **spangled**) cover an item of clothing with spangles.
– DERIVATIVES **span·gly** adjective.
– ORIGIN Dutch *spange* 'buckle.'

Span·iard /ˈspanyərd/ ▶ **noun** a person from Spain.

span·iel /ˈspanyəl/ ▶ **noun** a breed of dog with a long, silky coat and drooping ears.
– ORIGIN Old French *espaigneul* 'Spanish (dog).'

Span·ish /ˈspanisH/ ▶ **noun** the main language of Spain and of much of Central and South America. ▶ **adjective** relating to Spain or Spanish.
– DERIVATIVES **Span·ish·ness** noun.

Span·ish fly ▶ **noun** a toxic preparation of the dried bodies of a kind of beetle, sometimes used as an aphrodisiac.

Span·ish gui·tar ▶ **noun** the standard six-stringed acoustic guitar, used especially for classical and folk music.

Span·ish om·e·let ▶ **noun** an omelet containing chopped vegetables, served open rather than folded.

Span·ish on·ion ▶ **noun** a large onion with a mild flavor.

spank /spaNGk/ ▶ **verb** slap someone on the buttocks with the open hand or a flat object, especially as a punishment. ▶ **noun** a slap or series of slaps on the buttocks.
– ORIGIN uncertain.

spank·ing /ˈspaNGkiNG/ ▶ **adjective 1** lively; brisk: *a spanking pace.* **2** informal impressive or pleasing. ▶ **noun** a series of spanks on the buttocks.

span·ner /ˈspanər/ ▶ **noun** chiefly Brit. a wrench (tool).
– ORIGIN from German *spannen* 'draw tight.'

spar¹ /spär/ ▶ **noun** a thick, strong pole used as a mast or yard on a ship.
– ORIGIN from Old French *esparre* or Old Norse.

spar² ▶ **verb** (**spars, sparring, sparred**) **1** make the motions of boxing without landing heavy blows, as a form of training. **2** argue with someone without hostility. ▶ **noun** a period of sparring.
– ORIGIN Old English, 'strike out.'

spar³ ▶ **noun** a crystalline transparent or semitransparent mineral that is easily split.
– ORIGIN German.

spare /spe(ə)r/ ▶ **adjective 1** not currently being used or needed: *the spare bedroom was filled with boxes.* **2** (of time) not taken up by one's usual work or activities. **3** with no excess fat; thin. **4** elegantly simple: *her clothes are smart and spare in style.*

– SYNONYMS **1 extra,** supplementary, additional, second, other, alternate, alternative, emergency, reserve, backup, relief, substitute. **2 surplus,** superfluous, excess, leftover, redundant, unnecessary, unwanted; informal going begging. **3** *your spare time* **free,** leisure, unoccupied. **4 slender,** lean, willowy, svelte, lissom, thin, skinny, gaunt, lanky, spindly.

▶ **noun** an item kept in case another of the same type is lost, broken, or worn out.
▶ **verb 1** give something that one has enough of to someone. **2** make free or available: *can you spare me a moment?* **3** hold back from killing or harming someone. **4** protect someone from something unpleasant.

– SYNONYMS **1 afford,** manage, part with, give, provide, do without. **2 pardon,** let off, forgive, have mercy on, reprieve, release, free.

– DERIVATIVES **spare·ly** adverb **spare·ness** noun.
– PHRASES **spare no expense** be prepared to pay any amount. **to spare** left over.
– ORIGIN Old English, 'not plentiful, meager.'

spare·ribs ▶ **plural noun** trimmed ribs of pork.
– ORIGIN probably from German *ribbesper*.

spare tire ▶ **noun 1** an extra tire carried in a motor vehicle in case of a puncture. **2** informal a roll of fat around a person's waist.

spar·ing /ˈspe(ə)riNG/ ▶ **adjective** using or giving only a little of something: *sparing use of hair sprays.*

– SYNONYMS **thrifty,** economical, frugal, careful, prudent, cautious.
– ANTONYMS lavish, extravagant.

– DERIVATIVES **spar·ing·ly** adverb.

CHOOSE THE RIGHT WORD

See **ECONOMICAL**.

spark /spärk/ ▶ **noun 1** a small fiery particle produced by burning or caused by friction. **2** a flash of light produced by an electrical discharge. **3** an electrical discharge that ignites the explosive mixture in an internal-combustion engine. **4** a small amount of an intense feeling: *a tiny spark of anger.* **5** a sense of liveliness and excitement.

– SYNONYMS **flash,** glint, twinkle, flicker, flare.

▶ **verb 1** produce sparks. **2** ignite a fire. **3** (also **spark off**) cause to happen: *the announcement sparked off protests.*

– SYNONYMS *their comments sparked immediate anger* **cause,** give rise to, occasion, bring about, start, precipitate, prompt, trigger, provoke, stimulate, stir up.

– DERIVATIVES **spark·y** adjective.
– ORIGIN Old English.

spar·kle /ˈspärkəl/ ▶ **verb 1** shine brightly with flashes of light. **2** (as adj. **sparkling**) (of drink) fizzy. **3** be lively and witty.

– SYNONYMS **1** *her earrings sparkled* **glitter,** glint, glisten, twinkle, flash, shimmer, shine, gleam. **2** (as adj. **sparkling**) *sparkling wine* **effervescent,** fizzy, carbonated, aerated.

▶ **noun 1** a glittering flash of light. **2** liveliness and wit.

– SYNONYMS **glitter,** glint, twinkle, flicker, shimmer, flash, shine.

– DERIVATIVES **spar·kly** adjective.

spar·kler /ˈspärk(ə)lər/ ▶ **noun** a hand-held firework that gives out sparks.

spark plug ▶ **noun** a device for firing the explosive mixture in an internal combustion engine.

spar·row /ˈsparō/ ▶ **noun** a small bird with brown and gray plumage.
– ORIGIN Old English.

spar·row hawk /ˈsparō ˌhôk/ ▶ **noun** a small hawk that preys on small birds.

sparse /spärs/ ▶ **adjective** present in small amounts or numbers and often thinly scattered: *Australia's relatively sparse animal population.*

– SYNONYMS **scant,** scanty, scattered, scarce, infrequent, few and far between, meager, paltry, limited, in short supply.
– ANTONYMS abundant.

– DERIVATIVES **sparse·ly** adverb **sparse·ness** noun **spar·si·ty** /ˈspärsitē/ noun.
– ORIGIN Latin *sparsus.*

Spar·tan /ˈspärtn/ ▶ **adjective 1** relating to Sparta, a city-state in ancient Greece. **2** (**spartan**) not comfortable or luxurious; basic: *spartan barracklike hotels.*

– SYNONYMS (**spartan**) **austere,** harsh, hard, frugal, rigorous, strict, severe, ascetic, self-denying, abstemious, bleak, bare, plain.
– ANTONYMS luxurious.

▶ **noun** a citizen of Sparta.

spasm /ˈspazəm/ ▶ **noun 1** a sudden and uncontrollable tightening of a muscle. **2** a sudden brief spell of an activity or feeling.

– SYNONYMS **1** *a muscle spasm* **contraction,** convulsion, cramp; twitch, jerk, tic, shudder, shiver, tremor. **2** *a spasm of coughing* **fit,** paroxysm, attack, burst, bout, seizure, outburst.

– ORIGIN Greek *spasmos.*

spas·mod·ic /spazˈmädik/ ▶ **adjective** occurring or done in brief, irregular bursts: *spasmodic fighting.*
– DERIVATIVES **spas·mod·i·cal·ly** /-ik(ə)lē/ adverb.

spas·tic /ˈspastik/ ▶ **adjective 1** relating to or affected by muscle spasm. **2** relating to cerebral palsy, which makes it difficult for a person to control their muscles and movements. ▶ **noun** offensive **1** a person with cerebral palsy. **2** informal an incompetent person.
– DERIVATIVES **spas·ti·cal·ly** adverb **spas·tic·i·ty** /spaˈstisitē/ noun.
– ORIGIN Greek *spastikos* 'pulling.'

USAGE

You should not use the word **spastic** as a noun, because many people feel it is offensive; say *person with cerebral palsy* instead.

spat[1] /spat/ past and past participle of **SPIT**[1].

spat[2] ▶ **noun** a cloth covering formerly worn by men over the ankles and shoes.
– ORIGIN from *spatterdash,* a long legging formerly worn when riding.

spat[3] ▶ **noun** informal a petty quarrel.
– ORIGIN uncertain.

spate /spāt/ ▶ **noun 1** a large number of similar things coming quickly one after the other. **2** chiefly Brit. a sudden flood in a river.

– SYNONYMS **series,** succession, run, cluster, string, rash, epidemic, outbreak, wave, flurry.

– ORIGIN unknown.

spathe /spāT͟H/ ▶ **noun** Botany a large bract (modified leaf) enclosing the flower cluster of certain plants.
– ORIGIN Greek, 'broad blade.'

spa·tial /ˈspāsHəl/ (also **spacial**) ▶ **adjective** relating to space: *a map showing spatial distribution of species of birds.*
– DERIVATIVES **spa·ti·al·i·ty** /ˌspāsHēˈalitē/ noun **spa·tial·ly** adverb.
– ORIGIN from Latin *spatium* 'space.'

spat·ter /ˈspatər/ ▶ **verb** cover someone or something with drops or spots of a liquid or substance. ▶ **noun** a spray or splash of a liquid or substance.
– ORIGIN from Dutch, German *spatten* 'burst, spout.'

spat·u·la /ˈspacHələ/ ▶ **noun 1** an implement with a broad flat blunt blade, used for mixing or spreading food, plaster, paint, etc. **2** a kitchen utensil with a long handle and a broad flat square or rectangular blade, sometimes slotted, used for flipping and lifting pancakes, etc.
– ORIGIN Latin.

spat·u·late /ˈspacHələt/ ▶ **adjective** having a broad rounded end.

spawn /spôn/ ▶ **verb 1** (of a fish, frog, etc.) release or deposit eggs. **2** give rise to: *overeating has spawned a weight-loss industry that reaps $40 billion per year.* ▶ **noun** the eggs of fish, frogs, etc.
– DERIVATIVES **spawn·er** noun.
– ORIGIN Old French *espaundre* 'to shed roe.'

spay /spā/ ▶ **verb** sterilize a female animal by removing the ovaries.
– ORIGIN Old French *espeer* 'cut with a sword.'

speak /spēk/ ▶ **verb** (**speaks, speaking, spoke**; past part. **spoken**) **1** say something. **2** (**speak to**) talk to someone in order to pass on information, advise them, etc. **3** communicate in or be able to communicate in a specified language: *my mother spoke Russian.* **4** (**speak up**) speak more loudly. **5** (**speak out/up**) express one's opinions frankly and publicly. **6** (**speak for**) express the views or position of another person. **7** be evidence of: *the islands speak of history.* **8** (**speak to**) appeal or relate to someone. **9** make a speech.

– SYNONYMS **1 talk,** converse, communicate, chat, have a word, gossip, commune, say something; informal chew the fat. **2 say,** utter, state, declare, voice, express, pronounce, articulate, enunciate, verbalize. **3 give a speech,** talk, lecture, hold forth; informal spout, sound off.

– PHRASES **speak in tongues** speak in an unknown language during religious worship. **speak one's mind** express one's opinions frankly. **speak volumes** express a great deal without using words.
– ORIGIN Old English.

speak·eas·y /ˈspēkˌēzē/ ▶ **noun** (pl. **speakeasies**) informal (during Prohibition) a secret illegal drinking club.

speak·er /ˈspēkər/ ▶ **noun 1** a person who speaks. **2** a person who speaks a particular language. **3** a person who makes a speech. **4** (**Speaker**) the officer in charge of proceedings in a legislative assembly. **5** a loudspeaker.

– SYNONYMS **speech-maker,** lecturer, talker, orator, spokesperson, spokesman, spokeswoman, reader, commentator, broadcaster, narrator.

speak·er·phone /ˈspēkərˌfōn/ ▶ **noun** a telephone with a loudspeaker and microphone, which does not need to be held in the hand.

speak·ing /ˈspēkiNG/ ▶ **adjective 1** used for or engaged in speech. **2** able to speak a particular language.
– PHRASES **on speaking terms** polite or friendly toward someone, especially after an argument.

spear /spi(ə)r/ ▸ **noun 1** a weapon with a pointed metal tip set on a long shaft. **2** a stem of asparagus or broccoli. ▸ **verb** pierce or hit someone or something with a spear or other pointed object.
– ORIGIN Old English.

spear·head /ˈspi(ə)rˌhed/ ▸ **verb** lead a campaign, activity, or attack. ▸ **noun** a person or group that leads a campaign, activity, or attack.

spear·mint /ˈspi(ə)rˌmint/ ▸ **noun** the common garden mint, used in cooking as an herb and as a flavoring.

spec[1] /spek/ ▸ **noun** (in phrase **on spec**) informal in the hope of success but without any specific preparation or plan.
– ORIGIN short for *speculation*.

spec[2] informal ▸ **noun** a detailed working description; a specification. ▸ **verb** (**specs, speccing, specced**) construct something to a specified standard.

spe·cial /ˈspesʜəl/ ▸ **adjective 1** better, greater, or otherwise different from what is usual: *they make a special effort at Christmas.* **2** organized or intended for a particular purpose. **3** belonging or particular to a specific person or thing: *we want to preserve the town's special character.* **4** (of education) for children with particular needs, especially those with learning difficulties.

– SYNONYMS **1 exceptional,** unusual, remarkable, out of the ordinary, outstanding, unique. **2 distinctive,** distinct, individual, particular, specific, peculiar. **3 momentous,** significant, memorable, important, historic, red-letter.
– ANTONYMS ordinary, general.

▸ **noun 1** something designed or organized for a particular occasion or purpose. **2** a dish not on a restaurant's regular menu but served on a particular day.
– DERIVATIVES **spe·cial·ness** noun.
– ORIGIN Latin *specialis*.

spe·cial ef·fects ▸ **plural noun** illusions created for movies and television by camerawork, computer graphics, etc.

Spe·cial For·ces ▸ **plural noun** an elite force within the US Army specializing in guerrilla warfare and counterinsurgency.

spe·cial·ist /ˈspesʜəlist/ ▸ **noun** a person who is highly skilled or knowledgeable in a particular field.

– SYNONYMS **expert,** authority, pundit, professional, connoisseur, master, maestro; informal **buff**.

▸ **adjective** relating to or involving detailed knowledge within a field.
– DERIVATIVES **spe·cial·ism** /-ˌlizəm/ noun.

spe·ci·al·i·ty /ˌspesʜēˈalitē/ ▸ **noun** (pl. **specialities**) chiefly British term for SPECIALTY.

spe·cial·ize /ˈspesʜəˌlīz/ ▸ **verb 1** concentrate on and become expert in a particular skill or area: *he could specialize in neurosurgery.* **2** focus on providing a particular product or service. **3** (**be specialized**) (of an organ or part) be adapted or set apart to serve a special function.
– DERIVATIVES **spe·cial·i·za·tion** /ˌspesʜəliˈzāsʜən/ noun.

spe·cial·ly /ˈspesʜəlē/ ▸ **adverb 1** for a special purpose. **2** informal in particular; chiefly.

USAGE

For an explanation of the difference between **specially** and **especially**, see the note at ESPECIALLY.

spe·cial needs ▸ **plural noun** particular educational requirements of children with learning difficulties, a physical disability, or emotional and behavioral difficulties.

spe·cial·ty /ˈspesʜəltē/ ▸ **noun** (pl. **specialties**) **1** a pursuit, area of study, or skill to which someone has devoted themselves and in which they are expert. **2** a product for which a person or region is famous. **3** a branch of medicine or surgery.

– SYNONYMS **strength,** strong point, forte, métier, strong suit, pièce de résistance, claim to fame.

spe·ci·a·tion /ˌspēsʜēˈāsʜən, ˌspēsē-/ ▸ **noun** Biology the formation of new and distinct species in the course of evolution.

spe·cie /ˈspēsʜē, -sē/ ▸ **noun** money in the form of coins rather than notes.
– ORIGIN from Latin *in specie* 'in kind,' from *species* 'form, kind.'

spe·cies/ ˈspēsēz, -sʜēz/ ▸ **noun** (pl. same) **1** a group of living organisms consisting of similar individuals capable of breeding with each other. **2** a kind or sort: *they reject this species of feminism.*

– SYNONYMS **type,** kind, sort, breed, strain, variety, class, classification, category.

– ORIGIN Latin, 'appearance, form.'

spe·cies bar·ri·er ▸ **noun** the natural mechanisms that prevent a virus, disease, etc., from spreading from one species to another.

spe·cif·ic /spəˈsifik/ ▸ **adjective 1** clearly defined or identified. **2** precise and clear. **3** (**specific to**) belonging or relating only to: *the term is specific to Canada.* **4** relating to species or a species.

– SYNONYMS **1 particular,** specified, fixed, set, determined, distinct, definite. **2 detailed,** explicit, express, clear-cut, unequivocal, precise, exact.
– ANTONYMS general, vague.

▸ **noun** (**specifics**) precise details.
– DERIVATIVES **spe·cif·i·cal·ly** adverb **spec·i·fic·i·ty** /ˌspesəˈfisitē/ noun.
– ORIGIN Latin *specificus*.

spec·i·fi·ca·tion /ˌspesəfiˈkāsʜən/ ▸ **noun 1** the action of identifying something precisely or of stating a precise requirement. **2** (usu. **specifications**) a detailed description of the design and materials used to make something. **3** a standard of workmanship and materials required to be met in a piece of work.

– SYNONYMS *a shelter built to their specifications* **instruction,** guideline, parameter, stipulation, requirement, condition, order, detail.

spe·cif·ic grav·i·ty ▸ **noun** technical the ratio of the density of a substance to a standard density, usually that of water or air.

spec·i·fy /ˈspesəˌfī/ ▸ **verb** (**specifies, specifying, specified**) state or identify clearly and definitely: *the company can't specify a delivery date.*

– SYNONYMS **state,** name, identify, define, set out, itemize, detail, list, enumerate, spell out, stipulate, lay down.

– DERIVATIVES **spec·i·fi·a·ble** adjective **spec·i·fi·er** noun.

spec·i·men /ˈspesəmən/ ▸ **noun 1** an animal, plant, object, etc., used as an example of its species or type for scientific study or display. **2** a sample for medical testing, especially of urine. **3** a typical example of something. **4** informal a person or animal of a specific type: *this odd female specimen.*

– SYNONYMS **sample,** example, model, instance, illustration, demonstration.

– ORIGIN Latin, 'pattern, model.'

spe·cious /ˈspēsHəs/ ▶ **adjective 1** seeming reasonable or plausible, but actually wrong: *a specious argument.* **2** misleading in appearance.
– DERIVATIVES **spe·cious·ly** adverb **spe·cious·ness** noun.
– ORIGIN Latin *speciosus* 'fair, plausible.'

speck /spek/ ▶ **noun** a tiny spot or particle. ▶ **verb** mark something with small spots.
– ORIGIN Old English.

speck·le /ˈspekəl/ ▶ **noun** a small spot or patch of color. ▶ **verb** (often as adj. **speckled**) mark with speckles: *a speckled brown egg.*
– ORIGIN Dutch *spekkel.*

specs /ˈspeks/ ▶ **plural noun** informal a pair of spectacles.

spec·ta·cle /ˈspektəkəl/ ▶ **noun** a visually impressive performance or display.

– SYNONYMS **1 display,** show, pageantry, performance, exhibition, pomp and circumstance, extravaganza, spectacular. **2 sight,** vision, scene, prospect, picture.

– PHRASES **make a spectacle of oneself** draw attention to oneself by behaving in a ridiculous way in public.
– ORIGIN Latin *spectaculum* 'public show.'

spec·ta·cles /ˈspektəkəlz/ ▶ **plural noun** a pair of eyeglasses.
– DERIVATIVES **spec·ta·cled** adjective.

spec·tac·u·lar /spekˈtakyələr/ ▶ **adjective** very impressive, striking, or dramatic.

– SYNONYMS **impressive,** magnificent, splendid, dazzling, sensational, stunning, dramatic, outstanding, memorable, unforgettable, striking, picturesque, eye-catching, breathtaking, glorious; informal out of this world.
– ANTONYMS dull, unimpressive.

▶ **noun** a large-scale and impressive performance or event.
– DERIVATIVES **spec·tac·u·lar·ly** adverb.

spec·tate /ˈspektāt/ ▶ **verb** watch an event; be a spectator.

spec·ta·tor /ˈspekˌtātər/ ▶ **noun** a person who watches at a show, game, or other event.

– SYNONYMS **watcher,** viewer, observer, onlooker, bystander, witness.

– ORIGIN Latin.

spec·ter /ˈspektər/ (Brit. **spectre**) ▶ **noun 1** a ghost. **2** a possible unpleasant or dangerous situation.

– SYNONYMS **ghost,** phantom, apparition, spirit, wraith, presence; informal spook.

– ORIGIN French.

spec·tra /ˈspektrə/ plural of SPECTRUM.

spec·tral[1] /ˈspektrəl/ ▶ **adjective** relating to or like a specter or ghost.
– DERIVATIVES **spec·tral·ly** adverb.

spec·tral[2] ▶ **adjective** relating to spectra or the spectrum.
– DERIVATIVES **spec·tral·ly** adverb.

spec·tre ▶ **noun** British spelling of SPECTER.

spec·tro·graph /ˈspektrəˌgraf/ ▶ **noun** a device for photographing or otherwise recording spectra.
– DERIVATIVES **spec·tro·graph·ic** /ˌspektrəˈgrafik/ adjective.

spec·trom·e·ter /spekˈträmitər/ ▶ **noun** a device used for recording and measuring spectra, especially as a method of analysis.
– DERIVATIVES **spec·tro·met·ric** /ˌspektrəˈmetrik/ adjective **spec·trom·e·try** /spekˈträmətrē/ noun.

spec·tro·scope /ˈspektrəˌskōp/ ▶ **noun** a device for producing and recording spectra for examination.

spec·tros·co·py /spekˈträskəpē/ ▶ **noun** the branch of science concerned with the investigation and measurement of spectra produced when matter interacts with or emits electromagnetic radiation.
– DERIVATIVES **spec·tro·scop·ic** /ˌspektrəˈskäpik/ adjective **spec·tros·co·pist** /-pist/ noun.

spec·trum /ˈspektrəm/ ▶ **noun** (pl. **spectra** /-trə/) **1** a band of colors produced by separating light into elements with different wavelengths, e.g., in a rainbow. **2** the entire range of wavelengths of electromagnetic radiation (such as light and radio waves). **3** the components of a sound or other phenomenon arranged according to frequency, energy, etc. **4** a range of beliefs, ideas, qualities, etc.: *the idea could gain support across the political spectrum.*
– ORIGIN Latin, 'image, apparition.'

spec·u·la /ˈspəkyələ/ plural of SPECULUM.

spec·u·late /ˈspekyəˌlāt/ ▶ **verb 1** form a theory or opinion without firm evidence. **2** invest in stocks, property, or other ventures in the hope of making a profit but with the risk of loss.

– SYNONYMS **1 conjecture,** theorize, hypothesize, guess, surmise, wonder, muse. **2 gamble,** venture, wager, invest, play the market.

– DERIVATIVES **spec·u·la·tion** /ˌspekyəˈlāsHən/ noun **spec·u·la·tor** /-ˌlātər/ noun.
– ORIGIN Latin *speculari* 'observe.'

spec·u·la·tive /ˈspekyəˌlātiv, -lətiv/ ▶ **adjective 1** based on theory or guesswork rather than knowledge. **2** (of an investment) involving a high risk of loss.

– SYNONYMS **1 conjectural,** suppositional, theoretical, hypothetical, tentative, unproven, unfounded, groundless, unsubstantiated. **2 risky,** hazardous, unsafe, uncertain, unpredictable; informal chancy.

– DERIVATIVES **spec·u·la·tive·ly** adverb **spec·u·la·tive·ness** noun.

spec·u·lum /ˈspekyələm/ ▶ **noun** (pl. **specula** /-lə/) Medicine a metal instrument that is used to widen an opening or passage in the body to allow inspection.
– ORIGIN Latin, 'mirror.'

sped /sped/ past and past participle of SPEED.

speech /spēcH/ ▶ **noun 1** the expression of thoughts and feelings using spoken language. **2** a formal talk delivered to an audience. **3** a sequence of lines written for one character in a play.

– SYNONYMS **1 speaking,** talking, verbal communication, conversation, dialogue, discussion. **2 diction,** elocution, articulation, enunciation, pronunciation, delivery, words. **3 talk,** address, lecture, discourse, oration, presentation, sermon. **4 language,** parlance, tongue, idiom, dialect, vernacular; informal lingo.

– ORIGIN Old English.

WORD LINKS

oral, phonetic, phonic *relating to speech*

speech·i·fy /ˈspēcHəˌfī/ ▸ **verb** (**speechifies, speechifying, speechified**) deliver a speech in a boring or pompous way.
– DERIVATIVES **speech·i·fi·er** noun.

speech·less /ˈspēcHlis/ ▸ **adjective** unable to speak, especially as a result of shock or strong emotion.

– SYNONYMS **lost for words,** dumbstruck, struck dumb, tongue-tied, inarticulate, mute, dumb, voiceless, silent.

– DERIVATIVES **speech·less·ly** adverb **speech·less·ness** noun.

speech rec·og·ni·tion ▸ **noun** the process of enabling a computer to identify and respond to the sounds produced in human speech.

speech ther·a·py ▸ **noun** treatment to help people with speech and language problems.
– DERIVATIVES **speech ther·a·pist** noun.

speed /spēd/ ▸ **noun 1** the rate at which someone or something moves or operates: *the car has a top speed of 147 mph.* **2** a fast rate of movement or action. **3** each of the possible gear ratios of a bicycle. **4** the light-gathering power of a camera lens. **5** the sensitivity of photographic film to light. **6** informal an amphetamine drug.

– SYNONYMS **1 rate,** pace, tempo, momentum, velocity; informal lick. **2 rapidity,** swiftness, promptness, alacrity, briskness, haste, hurry; old use celerity.
– ANTONYMS slowness.

▸ **verb** (past and past part. **sped** /sped/ or **speeded**) **1** move quickly. **2** (**speed up**) move or work more quickly. **3** (also **speed something up**) cause something to happen more quickly. **4** (of a motorist) travel at a speed greater than the legal limit. **5** old use make prosperous or successful: *may God speed you.*

– SYNONYMS **1 hurry,** rush, dash, race, sprint, career, shoot, hurtle, fly, zoom, hasten; informal tear, belt, pelt. **2** (**speed up**) **hurry up,** accelerate, go faster, get a move on, put a spurt on, pick up speed; informal step on it. **3** *a vacation will speed his recovery* **hasten,** accelerate, advance, further, promote, boost, stimulate, aid, assist, facilitate.
– ANTONYMS slow, hinder.

– DERIVATIVES **speed·er** noun.
– PHRASES **up to speed** informal fully informed or up to date.
– ORIGIN Old English.

speed·boat /ˈspēdˌbōt/ ▸ **noun** a motorboat designed for high speed.

speed bump (Brit. also **speed hump**) ▸ **noun** a ridge set in a road to control the speed of vehicles.

speed cam·era ▸ **noun** a roadside camera designed to catch speeding vehicles.

speed dat·ing (trademark **SpeedDating**) ▸ **noun** an organized activity in which a person has short conversations with a series of people to see if they like each other enough to begin a relationship.

speed di·al ▸ **noun** a function on some telephones that allows numbers to be entered into a memory and dialed with the push of a single button. ▸ **verb** (**speed-dial**) dial a telephone number by using a speed dial function.

speed lim·it ▸ **noun** the maximum speed at which a vehicle may legally travel on a particular stretch of road.

speed·om·e·ter /spəˈdämitər/ ▸ **noun** an instrument on a vehicle's dashboard that indicates its speed.

speed·ster /ˈspēdstər/ ▸ **noun** informal a person or thing that operates well at high speed.

speed·way /ˈspēdˌwā/ ▸ **noun 1** a stadium or track used for automobile or motorcycle racing. **2** Brit. a form of motorcycle racing in which the riders race laps around an oval dirt track.

speed·well /ˈspēdˌwel/ ▸ **noun** a small creeping plant with blue or pink flowers.

speed·y /ˈspēdē/ ▸ **adjective** (**speedier, speediest**) **1** done or occurring quickly. **2** moving or able to move quickly.

– SYNONYMS **fast,** swift, quick, rapid, expeditious, prompt, immediate, brisk, hasty, hurried, precipitate, rushed.
– ANTONYMS slow.

– DERIVATIVES **speed·i·ly** adverb **speed·i·ness** noun.

spe·le·ol·o·gy /ˌspēlēˈäləjē/ ▸ **noun** the study or exploration of caves.
– DERIVATIVES **spe·le·o·log·i·cal** /ˌspēlēəˈläjikəl/ adjective **spe·le·ol·o·gist** noun.
– ORIGIN from Greek *spēlaion* 'cave.'

spell[1] /spel/ ▸ **verb** (past and past part. **spelled** or chiefly Brit. **spelt**) **1** write or name the letters that form a word in the correct order. **2** (of letters) form a word. **3** be a sign of; lead to: *the plans would spell disaster.* **4** (**spell something out**) explain something clearly: *allow us to spell out the plan in detail.*

– SYNONYMS **1 signal,** signify, mean, amount to, add up to, constitute. **2** (**spell something out**) **explain,** make clear, clarify, specify, detail.

– ORIGIN Old French *espeller.*

spell[2] ▸ **noun 1** a form of words thought to have magical power. **2** a very attractive or fascinating quality: *those who fell under the spell of his undeniable charm.*

– SYNONYMS **1** *the witch recited a spell* **charm,** incantation, magic formula, hex, curse; (**spells**) magic, sorcery, witchcraft. **2** *she surrendered to his spell* **influence,** charm, magnetism, charisma, magic.

– ORIGIN Old English, 'narration.'

spell[3] ▸ **noun** a short period of time.

– SYNONYMS **1 period,** time, interval, season, stretch, run, patch. **2 bout,** fit, attack.

▸ **verb** allow someone to rest briefly by taking over from them in an activity.
– ORIGIN unknown.

spell·bind /ˈspelˌbīnd/ ▸ **verb** (past and past part. **spellbound** /ˈspelˌbound/) hold someone's complete attention: *the singer held the audience spellbound.*

– SYNONYMS **enthrall,** fascinate, entrance, bewitch, captivate, rivet, transfix, grip, enchant, mesmerize, hypnotize.

– DERIVATIVES **spell·bind·er** noun.

spell·check·er /ˈspelˌcHekər/ ▸ **noun** a computer program that checks the spelling of words in a computer document.
– DERIVATIVES **spell·check** verb & noun.

spell·er /ˈspelər/ ▸ **noun 1** a person who spells with a specified ability: *a good speller.* **2** a book for teaching spelling. **3** another term for **SPELLCHECKER**.

spell·ing /ˈspeliNG/ ▶ **noun** **1** the way in which a word is spelled. **2** a person's ability to spell.

spell·ing bee ▶ **noun** a spelling competition.

spelt /spelt/ ▶ **noun** an old kind of wheat with bearded ears and spikelets that each contain two narrow grains, used especially in health foods.

spe·lunk·ing /spiˈləNGkiNG/ ▶ **noun** the exploration of caves, especially as a hobby.
– DERIVATIVES **spe·lunk·er** /-kər/ noun.
– ORIGIN from obsolete *spelunk* 'cave.'

spend /spend/ ▶ **verb** (past and past part. **spent**) **1** pay out money to buy or hire goods or services. **2** use or use up energy or resources. **3** pass time in a specified way: *she spent a lot of time traveling.*

– SYNONYMS **1 pay out,** expend, disburse; informal lay out, blow, splurge. **2 pass,** occupy, fill, take up, while away.

– DERIVATIVES **spend·a·ble** adjective **spend·er** noun.
– ORIGIN Latin *expendere* 'pay out.'

spend·thrift /ˈspen(d)ˌTHrift/ ▶ **noun** a person who spends money in an extravagant and irresponsible way.

– SYNONYMS **profligate,** prodigal, squanderer, waster; informal big spender.
– ANTONYMS miser.

▶ **adjective** extravagant or wasteful.

– SYNONYMS **profligate,** improvident, wasteful, extravagant, prodigal.
– ANTONYMS frugal.

spent /spent/ past and past participle of **SPEND** ▶ **adjective** used up; exhausted.

– SYNONYMS **used up,** consumed, exhausted, finished, depleted, drained; informal burned/burnt out.

sperm /spərm/ ▶ **noun** (pl. same or **sperms**) **1** semen. **2** a spermatozoon (male sex cell).
– ORIGIN Greek *sperma* 'seed.'

sper·ma·cet·i /ˌspərməˈsetē/ ▶ **noun** a white waxy substance obtained from an organ in the head of the sperm whale, formerly used in candles and ointments.
– ORIGIN from Latin *sperma* 'sperm' + *ceti* 'of a whale,' from the belief that it was whale spawn.

sper·ma·to·zo·on /ˌspərmətəˈzōən, spərˌma-/ ▶ **noun** (pl. **spermatozoa** /-ˈzōə/) the male sex cell of an animal, which fertilizes the ovum (female reproductive cell).
– ORIGIN from Greek *sperma* 'seed' + *zōion* 'animal.'

sperm count ▶ **noun** the number of spermatozoa in a measured amount of semen, used as an indication of a man's fertility.

sper·mi·cide /ˈspərməˌsīd/ ▶ **noun** a substance that kills sperm, used as a contraceptive.
– DERIVATIVES **sper·mi·cid·al** /ˌspərməˈsīdl/ adjective.

sperm whale ▶ **noun** a toothed whale with a massive head, feeding largely on squid.
– ORIGIN from **SPERMACETI**.

spew /spyo͞o/ ▶ **verb** **1** pour out or discharge rapidly and in large quantities: *a fax machine spewed out information.* **2** informal vomit.

– SYNONYMS **1 emit,** discharge, eject, expel, belch/pour out. **2** *he wanted to spew* See **VOMIT**.

▶ **noun** informal vomit.
– DERIVATIVES **spew·er** noun.
– ORIGIN Old English.

SPF ▶ **abbreviation** sun protection factor.

sphag·num /ˈsfagnəm, ˈspag-/ ▶ **noun** a type of moss that grows on bogs.
– ORIGIN Latin.

sphere /sfi(ə)r/ ▶ **noun** **1** a round solid figure in which every point on the surface is at an equal distance from the center. **2** an area of activity, interest, or expertise: *political reforms to match those in the economic sphere.* **3** a particular section of society.

– SYNONYMS **1 globe,** ball, orb, bubble. **2** *his sphere of influence* **area,** field, compass, orbit, range, scope, extent. **3 domain,** realm, province, field, area, territory, arena, department.

– ORIGIN Greek *sphaira* 'ball.'

spher·i·cal /ˈsfi(ə)rikəl, ˈsfer-/ ▶ **adjective** shaped like a sphere.
– DERIVATIVES **spher·i·cal·ly** adverb.

sphe·roid /ˈsfi(ə)rˌoid/ ▶ **noun** an object that is roughly the same shape as a sphere.
– DERIVATIVES **sphe·roi·dal** /sfiˈroidl/ adjective.

spher·ule /ˈsfi(ə)r(y)o͞ol, ˈsfer-/ ▶ **noun** a small sphere.
– DERIVATIVES **spher·u·lar** /-yo͞olər/ adjective.

sphinc·ter /ˈsfiNGktər/ ▶ **noun** a ring of muscle that surrounds an opening such as the anus, and can be tightened to close it.
– ORIGIN Greek *sphinktēr*.

sphinx /sfiNGks/ ▶ **noun** an ancient Egyptian stone figure with a lion's body and a human or animal head.
– ORIGIN Greek, first referring to a winged monster in Greek mythology with a woman's head and a lion's body, who set a riddle and killed those who could not solve it.

sphyg·mo·ma·nom·e·ter /ˌsfigmōməˈnämitər/ ▶ **noun** an instrument for measuring blood pressure, consisting of an inflatable rubber cuff that is fitted around the arm and connected to a column of mercury next to a graduated scale.
– ORIGIN from Greek *sphugmos* 'pulse.'

spic /spik/ ▶ **noun** informal, offensive a Spanish-speaking person from Central or South America or the Caribbean.
– ORIGIN perhaps from *speak the* in 'no speak the English.'

spice /spīs/ ▶ **noun** **1** a strong-tasting vegetable substance used to flavor food. **2** something that adds interest and excitement: *shared highs and lows can add spice to your relationship.*

– SYNONYMS **1 seasoning,** flavoring, condiment. **2 excitement,** interest, color, piquancy, zest, an edge.

▶ **verb** **1** flavor something with spice. **2** (**spice something up**) make something more exciting or interesting.
– ORIGIN Old French *espice*.

spick-and-span ▶ **adjective** neat, clean, and well looked after.
– ORIGIN from Old Norse words meaning 'chip' and 'new.'

spic·ule /ˈspikˌyo͞ol/ ▶ **noun** chiefly Zoology a small needlelike object or structure.
– ORIGIN Latin *spicula* 'little ear of grain.'

spic·y /ˈspīsē/ ▶ **adjective** (**spicier, spiciest**) **1** strongly flavored with spice. **2** mildly indecent: *spicy jokes.*

– SYNONYMS **hot,** tangy, peppery, piquant, spiced, highly seasoned, pungent.
– ANTONYMS bland.

– DERIVATIVES **spic·i·ly** adverb **spic·i·ness** noun.

WORD TOOLKIT

See **PUNGENT**.

spi·der /ˈspīdər/ ▸ **noun 1** an eight-legged arachnid (insectlike creature), most kinds of which spin webs in which to capture insects. **2** a long-legged rest for a billiard cue that can be placed over a ball without touching it.
– ORIGIN Old English.

spi·der crab ▸ **noun** a crab with long, thin legs and a compact pear-shaped body.

spi·der mite ▸ **noun** a plant-feeding mite resembling a tiny spider.

spi·der mon·key ▸ **noun** a South American monkey with very long limbs and a long tail that it can use for grasping.

spi·der plant ▸ **noun** a plant having long, narrow leaves with a central yellow stripe, popular as a house plant.

spi·der·y /ˈspīdərē/ ▸ **adjective** long and thin, like a spider's legs: *spidery writing.*

spiel /spēl, sʜpēl/ ▸ **noun** informal an elaborate and insincere speech made to persuade someone to buy or believe something.
– ORIGIN German, 'a game.'

spiff·y /ˈspifē/ ▸ **adjective** (**spiffier**, **spiffiest**) informal smart or stylish.
– DERIVATIVES **spif·fi·ly** adverb.
– ORIGIN unknown.

spig·ot /ˈspigət/ ▸ **noun 1** a faucet. **2** a small peg or plug, especially for putting into the vent of a cask. **3** the plain end of a section of a pipe fitting into the socket of the next one.
– ORIGIN perhaps from Provençal *espigou.*

spike[1] /spīk/ ▸ **noun 1** a thin pointed piece of metal or wood. **2** each of several metal points set into the sole of a sports shoe to prevent slipping. **3** a sharp increase: *a spike in demand.*

– SYNONYMS **prong,** pin, barb, point, skewer, stake, spit.

▸ **verb 1** impale on or pierce with something sharp: *she spiked another oyster.* **2** form something into or cover something with sharp points. **3** informal secretly add alcohol or a drug to drink or food. **4** put an end to a plan or undertaking. **5** increase and then decrease sharply: *oil prices would spike and then fall again.*
– ORIGIN perhaps from German, Dutch *spiker*; sense 4 of the verb comes from the editorial practice of rejecting submitted news stories by filing them on a metal spike.

spike[2] ▸ **noun** Botany a flower cluster formed of many flowerheads attached directly to a long stem.
– ORIGIN Latin *spica* 'ear of corn.'

spike·nard /ˈspīkˌnärd/ ▸ **noun** historical an expensive perfumed ointment made from the rhizome (underground stem) of a Himalayan plant.
– ORIGIN from Latin *spica* 'spike' + Greek *nardos* 'spikenard.'

spik·y /ˈspīkē/ ▸ **adjective** (**spikier**, **spikiest**) **1** like a spike or spikes or having many spikes: *short spiky hair.* **2** informal easily annoyed; irritable.
– DERIVATIVES **spik·i·ly** adverb **spik·i·ness** noun.

WORD TOOLKIT

spiky ...	barbed ...	jagged ...
hair	wire	edge
haircut	sutures	rocks
leaves	tail	scar
grass	arrow	metal
fins	whip	glass

spill[1] /spil/ ▸ **verb** (past and past part. **spilled** or **spilt**) **1** flow or cause to flow over the edge of a container. **2** move or empty out from a place: *students began to spill out of the building.* **3** informal reveal private or personal information.

– SYNONYMS **1 knock over,** tip over, upset, overturn. **2 overflow,** brim over, run over, pour, slop, slosh, splash, leak.

▸ **noun 1** an instance of a liquid spilling or the quantity spilled. **2** a fall from a horse or bicycle.
– DERIVATIVES **spill·age** /ˈspilij/ noun **spill·er** noun.
– PHRASES **spill the beans** informal reveal secret information. **spill blood** kill or wound people.
– ORIGIN Old English, 'kill, waste, shed blood.'

spill[2] ▸ **noun** a thin strip of wood or paper used for lighting a fire.
– ORIGIN probably from Dutch or German.

spill·o·ver /ˈspilˌōvər/ ▸ **noun 1** a thing that overflows or has spread into another area. **2** (usu. before another noun) an unexpected result or effect of something.

spill·way /ˈspilˌwā/ ▸ **noun** a passage for surplus water from a dam.

spin /spin/ ▸ **verb** (**spins**, **spinning**, **spun** /spən/) **1** turn around quickly. **2** (of a person's head) have a feeling of dizziness. **3** (of a ball) move through the air with a revolving motion. **4** draw out and twist the fibers of wool, cotton, etc., to convert them into yarn. **5** (of a spider or a silkworm or other insect) produce a web, silk, or cocoon by forcing out a fine thread from a special gland. **6** (**spin something out**) make something last as long as possible.

– SYNONYMS **1 revolve,** rotate, turn, go around, whirl, twirl, gyrate. **2** *she spun around to face him* **whirl,** wheel, turn, swing, twist, swivel, pivot.

▸ **noun 1** a spinning motion. **2** informal a brief trip in a vehicle for pleasure. **3** a favorable slant given to a news story.

– SYNONYMS **1 rotation,** revolution, turn, whirl, twirl, gyration. **2 slant,** angle, twist, bias. **3 trip,** jaunt, outing, excursion, journey, drive, ride, run, turn; informal tootle.

– DERIVATIVES **spin·ner** noun.
– PHRASES **spin a yarn** tell a far-fetched story.
– ORIGIN Old English.

spi·na bif·i·da /ˈspīnə ˈbifidə/ ▸ **noun** a condition present from birth in which part of the spinal cord is exposed through a gap in the backbone, and which can cause paralysis and other problems.
– ORIGIN from Latin *spina* 'backbone, thorn' + *bifidus* 'doubly split.'

spin·ach /ˈspinicʜ/ ▸ **noun** a vegetable with large dark green leaves.
– ORIGIN probably from Old French *espinache.*

spi·nal /ˈspīnl/ ▸ **adjective** relating to the spine.
– DERIVATIVES **spi·nal·ly** adverb.

spi·nal col·umn ▸ **noun** the spine.

spi·nal cord ▶ **noun** the cylindrical bundle of nerve fibers in the spine that connects all parts of the body to the brain.

spin·dle /ˈspindl/ ▶ **noun 1** a slender rounded rod with tapered ends, used in spinning wool, flax, etc., by hand. **2** a rod serving as an axis that revolves or on which something revolves.
– ORIGIN Old English.

spin·dly /ˈspin(d)lē/ ▶ **adjective** long or tall and thin.

– SYNONYMS **1 lanky,** thin, skinny, lean, spare, gangling, gangly, scrawny, bony, rangy, angular. **2** *spindly chairs* **rickety,** flimsy, wobbly, shaky.
– ANTONYMS stocky.

spin doc·tor ▶ **noun** informal a spokesperson for a political party or politician employed to present events in a favorable way to the media.

spin·drift /ˈspin,drift/ ▶ **noun 1** spray blown from the crests of waves by the wind. **2** driving snow.
– ORIGIN from former *spoon* 'run before wind or sea' + **DRIFT.**

spine /spīn/ ▶ **noun 1** a series of vertebrae (bones) extending from the skull to the small of the back, enclosing the spinal cord; the backbone. **2** the part of a book that encloses the inner edges of the pages. **3** a central or strengthening feature: *Norway's mountainous spine.* **4** a hard pointed projection found on certain plants (e.g., cacti) and animals (e.g., hedgehogs).

– SYNONYMS **1 backbone,** spinal column, back. **2 needle,** quill, bristle, barb, spike, prickle, thorn.

– ORIGIN Latin *spina* 'thorn, backbone.'

WORD LINKS

vertebral *relating to the spine*

spine-chill·er ▶ **noun** a story or movie that causes terror and excitement.
– DERIVATIVES **spine-chill·ing** adjective.

spine·less /ˈspīnlis/ ▶ **adjective 1** lacking courage and determination. **2** (of an animal) having no backbone; invertebrate. **3** (of an animal or plant) lacking spines.

– SYNONYMS **weak,** weak-willed, feeble, soft, ineffectual, cowardly, timid, faint-hearted, pusillanimous, craven, lily-livered, chicken-hearted; informal wimpish, wimpy, gutless.
– ANTONYMS bold, brave, strong-willed.

– DERIVATIVES **spine·less·ly** adverb **spine·less·ness** noun.

spin·et /ˈspinit/ ▶ **noun** a type of small harpsichord popular in the 18th century.
– ORIGIN Italian *spinetta* 'virginal, spinet.'

spine-tin·gling ▶ **adjective** informal thrilling or pleasurably frightening.

spin·i·fex /ˈspinə,feks/ ▶ **noun** a grass with spiny flowerheads that break off and are blown about, occurring from east Asia to Australia.
– ORIGIN Latin.

spin·na·ker /ˈspinəkər/ ▶ **noun** a large three-cornered sail set in front of the mainsail of a racing yacht when the wind is coming from behind.
– ORIGIN probably from *Sphinx*, the yacht first using such a sail.

spin·ner·et /,spinəˈret/ ▶ **noun** an organ through which the silk, gossamer, or thread of spiders, silkworms, and certain other insects is produced.

spin·ning jen·ny ▶ **noun** historical a machine for spinning with more than one spindle at a time.

spin·ning wheel ▶ **noun** a machine for spinning yarn or thread with a spindle driven by a wheel attached to a crank or treadle.

spin-off ▶ **noun 1** a product or benefit produced during or after the main activity. **2** a book, movie, television program, etc., based on another book, movie, program, etc.

spin·ster /ˈspinstər/ ▶ **noun** chiefly derogatory a single woman beyond the usual age for marriage.
– DERIVATIVES **spin·ster·hood** /-,ho͝od/ noun **spin·ster·ish** adjective.
– ORIGIN first meaning 'woman who spins.'

spin·y /ˈspīnē/ ▶ **adjective** (**spinier, spiniest**) full of or covered with prickles.
– DERIVATIVES **spin·i·ness** noun.

spin·y ant·eat·er ▶ **noun** another term for **ECHIDNA.**

spi·ra·cle /ˈspirəkəl, ˈspī-/ ▶ **noun** an external opening used for breathing in certain insects, fish, and other animals.
– DERIVATIVES **spi·rac·u·lar** /spiˈrakyələr, spī-/ adjective.
– ORIGIN Latin *spiraculum.*

spi·rae·a /spīˈrēə/ ▶ **noun** chiefly Brit. variant spelling of **SPIREA.**

spi·ral /ˈspīrəl/ ▶ **adjective** winding in a continuous curve around a central point or axis.

– SYNONYMS **coiled,** helical, curling, winding, twisting.

▶ **noun 1** a spiral curve, shape, or pattern. **2** a continuous increase or decrease in prices, wages, etc., that gradually gets faster: *a downward spiral of crippling debt.*

– SYNONYMS **coil,** curl, twist, whorl, scroll, helix, corkscrew.

▶ **verb** (**spirals, spiraling, spiraled**) **1** move in a spiral course. **2** show a continuous and rapid increase or decrease.

– SYNONYMS **coil,** wind, swirl, twist, snake.

– DERIVATIVES **spi·ral·ly** adverb.
– ORIGIN Latin *spiralis.*

spi·ral-bound ▶ **adjective** (of a book or notepad) bound with a spiral wire threaded through a row of holes along one edge.

spire /spī(ə)r/ ▶ **noun** a tall pointed structure on the top of a church tower or other building.
– ORIGIN Old English, 'tall plant stem.'

spi·re·a /spīˈrēə/ (also **spiraea**) ▶ **noun** a shrub with clusters of small white or pink flowers.
– ORIGIN Greek *speiraia.*

spir·it /ˈspirit/ ▶ **noun 1** the part of a person that consists of their character and feelings rather than their body, often believed to survive after their body is dead. **2** a ghost or other supernatural being. **3** the typical or dominant character, quality, or mood: *they shared her spirit of adventure.* **4** (**spirits**) a person's mood. **5** courage, energy, and determination. **6** the real meaning of something as opposed to its strict interpretation: *the rule had been broken in spirit if not in letter.* **7** chiefly Brit. strong distilled alcoholic drink, such as rum. **8** purified distilled alcohol, such as methylated spirit.

– SYNONYMS **1 soul,** psyche, inner self, mind. **2 ghost,** phantom, specter, apparition, presence. **3 mood,** frame/state of mind, humor, temper,

morale, esprit de corps. **4 ethos,** essence, atmosphere, mood, feeling, climate. **5 enthusiasm,** energy, verve, vigor, dynamism, dash, sparkle, exuberance, gusto, fervor, zeal, fire, passion; informal get-up-and-go.
– ANTONYMS body, flesh.

▶ **verb** (**spirits, spiriting, spirited**) (**spirit someone/thing away**) take someone or something away rapidly and secretly.
– PHRASES **when the spirit moves someone** when someone feels inclined to do something.
– ORIGIN Latin *spiritus* 'breath, spirit.'

spir·it·ed /'spiritid/ ▶ **adjective 1** full of energy, enthusiasm, and determination. **2** having a specified character: *a generous-spirited man.*

– SYNONYMS **lively,** energetic, enthusiastic, vigorous, dynamic, passionate; informal peppy, feisty, gutsy.
– ANTONYMS apathetic, lifeless.

– DERIVATIVES **spir·it·ed·ly** adverb **spir·it·ed·ness** noun.

spir·it gum ▶ **noun** a quick-drying solution of gum, used by actors to attach false hair to their faces.

spir·it·less /'spiritlis/ ▶ **adjective** lacking courage, energy, or determination.
– DERIVATIVES **spir·it·less·ly** adverb **spir·it·less·ness** noun.

spir·it lev·el ▶ **noun** see **LEVEL** (sense 6 of the noun).

spir·it·u·al /'spiricHo͞oəl/ ▶ **adjective 1** relating to the human spirit as opposed to material or physical things: *I'm responsible for his spiritual welfare.* **2** relating to religion or religious belief.

– SYNONYMS **1 inner,** mental, psychological, incorporeal, nonmaterial. **2 religious,** sacred, divine, holy, devotional.
– ANTONYMS physical, secular.

▶ **noun** (also **Negro spiritual**) a religious song of a kind associated with black Christians of the southern US.
– DERIVATIVES **spir·it·u·al·i·ty** /ˌspiricHo͞o'alitē/ noun **spir·it·u·al·ize** /'spiricHo͞oəˌlīz/ verb **spir·it·u·al·ly** adverb.

spir·it·u·al·ism /'spiricHo͞oəˌlizəm/ ▶ **noun** the belief that it is possible to communicate with the spirits of the dead, especially through mediums.
– DERIVATIVES **spir·it·u·al·ist** noun **spir·it·u·al·is·tic** /ˌspiricHo͞oə'listik/ adjective.

spi·ro·gy·ra /ˌspīrə'jīrə/ ▶ **noun** a type of algae consisting of long green threads.
– ORIGIN from Greek *speira* 'coil' + *guros* 'round.'

spit[1] /spit/ ▶ **verb** (**spits, spitting, spat** /spat/ or **spit**) **1** force saliva, food, or liquid from the mouth. **2** say something in a hostile way. **3** (of a fire or food being cooked) give out small bursts of sparks or hot fat.

– SYNONYMS **expectorate**; informal hawk, gob.

▶ **noun 1** saliva. **2** an act of spitting.

– SYNONYMS **spittle,** saliva, sputum, slobber, dribble.

– DERIVATIVES **spit·ter** noun.
– PHRASES **be the spitting image of** informal look exactly like. [perhaps from the idea of a person apparently being formed from the spit of another, so similar are they.] **spit and polish** thorough cleaning and polishing. **spit blood** feel or express strong anger. **spit it out** informal say it quickly; stop hesitating.
– ORIGIN Old English.

spit[2] ▶ **noun 1** a thin metal rod pushed through meat in order to hold and turn it while it is roasted. **2** a narrow point of land projecting into the sea.
– ORIGIN Old English.

spit·ball /'spitˌbôl/ ▶ **noun 1** a ball of chewed paper used as a missile. **2** Baseball an illegal pitch made with a ball moistened with saliva or another substance to make it move erratically. ▶ **verb** informal throw out a suggestion for discussion: *I'm just spitballing a few ideas.*
– DERIVATIVES **spit·ball·er** noun.

spite /spīt/ ▶ **noun** a desire to hurt, annoy, or offend someone.

– SYNONYMS **malice,** malevolence, ill will, vindictiveness, meanness, nastiness; informal bitchiness, cattiness.

▶ **verb** deliberately hurt, annoy, or offend someone.

– SYNONYMS **upset,** hurt, wound.
– ANTONYMS please.

– PHRASES **in spite of 1** without being affected by. **2** without regard for. **in spite of oneself** although one did not want or expect to do so.
– ORIGIN Old French *despit* 'contempt.'

spite·ful /'spītfəl/ ▶ **adjective** deliberately hurtful; malicious.

– SYNONYMS **malicious,** malevolent, vindictive, vengeful, mean, nasty, hurtful, mischievous, cruel, unkind; informal bitchy, catty.
– ANTONYMS benevolent.

– DERIVATIVES **spite·ful·ly** adverb **spite·ful·ness** noun.

CHOOSE THE RIGHT WORD

See **VINDICTIVE**.

spit·fire /'spitˌfīr/ ▶ **noun** a person with a fierce temper.

spit·tle /'spitl/ ▶ **noun** saliva; spit.
– ORIGIN from dialect *spattle.*

spit·toon /spi'to͞on/ ▶ **noun** a container for spitting into.

splash /splasH/ ▶ **verb 1** (with reference to a liquid) fall or cause to fall in scattered drops: *wine splashed onto the bed.* **2** make someone or something wet with scattered drops. **3** move around in water, causing it to fly about. **4** (**splash down**) (of a spacecraft) land on the sea. **5** display a story or photograph very noticeably in a newspaper or magazine.

– SYNONYMS **1 sprinkle,** spatter, splatter, spray, shower, wash, squirt, slosh, slop. **2 wash,** break, lap, pound. **3 paddle,** wade, wallow.

▶ **noun 1** an instance or sound of splashing. **2** a small quantity of liquid that has splashed onto a surface. **3** a small quantity of liquid added to a drink. **4** a bright patch of color. **5** informal a noticeable or sensational news story.
– DERIVATIVES **splash·y** adjective (**splashier, splashiest**).
– PHRASES **make a splash** informal attract a great deal of attention.
– ORIGIN from **PLASH**.

splash·down /'splasHˌdoun/ ▶ **noun** the moment at which a spacecraft lands on the sea.

splat /splat/ informal ▶ **noun** a sound of something soft and wet or heavy striking a surface. ▶ **verb** (**splats, splatting, splatted**) hit or land with a splat.
– ORIGIN from **SPLATTER**.

splat·ter /'splatər/ ▶ **verb** splash someone or something with a sticky or thick liquid. ▶ **noun** a splash of a sticky or thick liquid. ▶ **adjective** informal (of a film) featuring many violent and gruesome deaths.
– ORIGIN imitating the sound.

splay /splā/ ▶ **verb** spread or be spread out or further apart: *he stood with his legs splayed out.* ▶ **adjective** turned outward or widened: *she sat splay-legged.*
– ORIGIN from DISPLAY.

splay-foot·ed ▶ **adjective** having a broad flat foot turned outward.

spleen /splēn/ ▶ **noun 1** an organ in the abdomen that is involved in the production and removal of blood cells and forms part of the immune system. **2** bad temper; spite.
– ORIGIN Greek *splēn*; sense 2 comes from the former belief that bad temper originated in the spleen.

splen·did /'splendid/ ▶ **adjective 1** magnificent; very impressive. **2** informal excellent; very good.

– SYNONYMS **1 magnificent,** sumptuous, grand, imposing, superb, spectacular, resplendent, rich, lavish, ornate, gorgeous, glorious, dazzling, handsome, beautiful; informal plush, swish. **2 excellent,** wonderful, marvelous, superb, glorious, lovely, delightful, first-class; informal super, great, amazing, fantastic, terrific, tremendous; Brit. informal smashing, brilliant.
– ANTONYMS simple, modest, inferior.

– DERIVATIVES **splen·did·ly** adverb.
– ORIGIN Latin *splendidus*.

splen·dif·er·ous /splen'difərəs/ ▶ **adjective** informal, humorous very good; splendid.

splen·dor /'splendər/ (Brit. **splendour**) ▶ **noun** magnificent and impressive quality or appearance: *the splendor of Mount Everest.*

– SYNONYMS **magnificence,** sumptuousness, grandeur, resplendence, richness, glory, majesty.
– ANTONYMS simplicity.

sple·net·ic /splə'netik/ ▶ **adjective** bad-tempered or spiteful.
– ORIGIN Latin *spleneticus*.

splen·ic /'splēnik, 'sple-/ ▶ **adjective** relating to the spleen.

splice /splīs/ ▶ **verb 1** join a rope or ropes by weaving the strands together at the ends. **2** join pieces of wood, film, or tape at the ends. ▶ **noun** a place where film, rope, etc., has been spliced together.
– DERIVATIVES **splic·er** noun.
– ORIGIN probably from Dutch *splissen*.

spliff /splif/ ▶ **noun** informal a marijuana cigarette.
– ORIGIN unknown.

spline /splīn/ ▶ **noun** a rectangular key fitting into grooves in the hub and shaft of a wheel. ▶ **verb** secure a part with a spline.
– ORIGIN perhaps from SPLINTER.

splint /splint/ ▶ **noun** a strip of rigid material for supporting a broken bone when it has been set. ▶ **verb** secure a broken limb with a splint or splints.
– ORIGIN Dutch, German *splinte* 'metal plate or pin.'

splin·ter /'splin(t)ər/ ▶ **noun** a small, thin sharp piece of wood, glass, etc., broken off from a larger piece.

– SYNONYMS **sliver,** chip, shard, fragment, shred.

▶ **verb 1** break into splinters. **2** (of a group) divide into smaller separate groups: *the company splintered into seven regional operating companies.*

– SYNONYMS **shatter,** smash, break into smithereens, fracture, split, crack, disintegrate.

– DERIVATIVES **splin·ter·y** adjective.
– ORIGIN Dutch.

splin·ter group ▶ **noun** a small organization that has broken away from a larger one.

split /split/ ▶ **verb (splits, splitting, split) 1** break into parts by force. **2** divide into parts or groups: *once again the family was split up.* **3** (often **split up**) end a marriage or other relationship. **4** informal leave a place, especially suddenly. **5** (**be splitting**) informal (of a person's head) be suffering from a bad headache.

– SYNONYMS **1 break,** cut, burst, snap, crack, splinter, fracture, rupture, come apart. **2 tear,** rip, slash, slit. **3 share,** divide up, distribute, dole out, parcel out, carve up, slice up, apportion. **4 fork,** divide, branch, diverge. **5** *the band* ***split up*** *last year* **break up,** separate, part, part company, go their separate ways.
– ANTONYMS join, unite, converge.

▶ **noun 1** a tear or crack. **2** an instance of splitting or dividing: *a 75–25 split of the proceeds.* **3** a division between members of a group or an end of a relationship: *a split in the ruling party.* **4** (**the splits**) (in gymnastics and dance) an act of leaping in the air or sitting down with the legs straight and at right angles to the body.

– SYNONYMS **1 crack,** fissure, cleft, crevice, break, fracture, breach. **2 rip,** tear, cut, rent, slash, slit. **3 division,** rift, breach, schism, rupture, separation, estrangement. **4 break-up,** split-up, separation, parting, estrangement, rift.
– ANTONYMS merger.

– DERIVATIVES **split·ter** noun.
– PHRASES **split the difference** take the average of two proposed amounts. **split one's sides** informal laugh heartily or uncontrollably.
– ORIGIN Dutch *splitten* '(of a storm or rock) break up a ship.'

split end ▶ **noun** a tip of a person's hair that has split from dryness or ill-treatment.

split in·fin·i·tive ▶ **noun** a sentence consisting of the infinitive of a verb with an adverb or other word placed between *to* and the verb, e.g., *she seems to really like it.*

USAGE

Many people still think that splitting infinitives (putting a word between *to* and the verb) is wrong. They think that it is better to say *she used secretly to admire him* rather than *she used to secretly admire him*, although this sometimes sounds awkward or gives a different emphasis to what is being said. For this reason, the rule about not splitting infinitives is not followed so strictly today, although it is best not to split them in formal writing.

split-lev·el ▶ **adjective 1** (of a room or building) having the floor divided into different levels. **2** (of a range) having the oven and stovetop in separate units.

split pea ▶ **noun** a pea dried and split in half for cooking.

split screen ▶ **noun** a movie, television, or computer screen on which two or more separate images are displayed.

split sec·ond ▶ **noun** a very brief moment of time. ▶ **adjective** (**split-second**) very rapid or accurate: *split-second timing.*

splits·ville /'splits,vil/ (also **Splitsville**) ▶ **noun** informal the termination of a relationship, especially a romantic one: *her parents are headed for Splitsville.*

splosh /spläsн/ informal ▶ **verb** move with a soft splashing sound. ▶ **noun** a splash.
– ORIGIN imitating the sound.

splotch /spläcH/ informal ▶ **noun** a spot, splash, or smear of something. ▶ **verb** mark something with a spot, splash or smear.
– DERIVATIVES **splotch·y** adjective.
– ORIGIN perhaps from SPOT and former *plotch* 'blotch.'

splurge /splərj/ informal ▶ **verb** spend extravagantly: *this is a good place to splurge on extravagant materials.* ▶ **noun** a sudden spell of spending money extravagantly.
– ORIGIN uncertain.

splut·ter /'splətər/ ▶ **verb 1** make a series of short explosive spitting or choking sounds. **2** say something in a rapid and unclear way. ▶ **noun** a spluttering sound.
– DERIVATIVES **splut·ter·er** noun.
– ORIGIN imitating the sound.

spoil /spoil/ ▶ **verb** (past and past part. **spoiled** or (chiefly Brit.) **spoilt**) **1** make less good or enjoyable: *I am not going to let her spoil my day.* **2** harm a child's character by not treating them strictly enough. **3** treat someone with great or excessive kindness. **4** (of food) become unfit for eating. **5** (**be spoiling for**) be very eager for: *Cooper was spoiling for a fight.*

– SYNONYMS **1 damage,** ruin, impair, blemish, disfigure, blight, deface, harm, destroy, wreck. **2** *rain spoiled my plans* **upset,** mess up, ruin, wreck, undo, sabotage, scotch, torpedo; informal muck up, screw up, do for. **3 overindulge,** pamper, indulge, mollycoddle, cosset, wait on someone hand and foot. **4 go bad,** go rancid, turn, go sour, rot, decompose, decay, perish.
– ANTONYMS improve, enhance.

▶ **noun** (**spoils**) stolen goods.
– ORIGIN Latin *spoliare.*

spoil·age /'spoilij/ ▶ **noun** the decay of food and other perishable goods.

spoil·er /'spoilər/ ▶ **noun 1** a part fitted to a car in order to improve roadholding at high speeds. **2** a flap on an aircraft wing that can be raised to create drag and so reduce speed. **3** a news story published with the intention of reducing the impact of a similar item published in a rival paper. **4** a part of the storyline of a book, movie, etc., the knowledge of which would reveal too much to someone who has not yet read the book or viewed the movie.

spoil·sport /'spoil,spôrt/ ▶ **noun** a person who spoils the pleasure of others.

– SYNONYMS **killjoy,** dog in the manger, misery; informal wet blanket, party pooper.

spoils sys·tem ▶ **noun** the practice of a successful political party giving public office to its supporters.

spoke[1] /spōk/ ▶ **noun 1** each of the bars or wire rods connecting the center of a wheel to its rim. **2** each of the metal rods in an umbrella to which the material is attached.
– ORIGIN Old English.

spoke[2] past of SPEAK.

spo·ken /'spōkən/ past participle of SPEAK ▶ **adjective** (in combination) speaking in a specified way: *a soft-spoken man.*

– SYNONYMS **verbal,** oral, vocal, unwritten, word-of-mouth.

– PHRASES **be spoken for 1** be already claimed or reserved. **2** already have a romantic relationship.

spoke·shave /'spōk,sHāv/ ▶ **noun** a small plane with a handle on each side of its blade, used for shaping curved surfaces.

spokes·man /'spōksmən/ (or **spokeswoman** /'spōks,wo͝omən/) ▶ **noun** (pl. **spokesmen** or **spokeswomen**) a person who makes statements on behalf of a group.

– SYNONYMS **representative,** voice, mouthpiece, agent, official; informal spin doctor.

spokes·per·son /'spōks,pərsən/ ▶ **noun** (pl. **spokespersons** or **spokespeople** /-,pēpəl/) a spokesman or spokeswoman.

– SYNONYMS **representative,** voice, mouthpiece, agent, official; informal spin doctor.

spo·li·a·tion /,spōlē'āsHən/ ▶ **noun 1** the action of destroying or ruining something. **2** the action of plundering a place.

spon·dee /'spändē/ ▶ **noun** a foot (unit of poetic meter) consisting of two long (or stressed) syllables.
– ORIGIN from Greek *spondeios pous* 'metrical foot relating to a ritual offering of drink.'

spon·dy·li·tis /,spändə'lītis/ ▶ **noun** arthritis in the backbone, especially (**ankylosing spondylitis**) a form in which the vertebrae (bones) become fused.
– ORIGIN from Latin *spondylus* 'vertebra.'

sponge /spənj/ ▶ **noun 1** an invertebrate sea creature with a soft porous body. **2** a piece of a light absorbent substance used for washing, as padding, etc. ▶ **verb** (**sponges, sponging** or **spongeing, sponged**) **1** wipe or clean someone or something with a wet sponge or cloth. **2** (usu. **sponge off**) informal obtain money or food from others without giving anything in return.
– DERIVATIVES **sponge·like** /'spənj,līk/ adjective.
– ORIGIN Greek *spongos.*

sponge cake ▶ **noun** a very light cake made with eggs, sugar, and flour but little or no fat.

spong·er /'spənjər/ ▶ **noun** informal a person who lives by obtaining money or food from others.

spon·gi·form /'spənji,fôrm/ ▶ **adjective** technical having a porous structure or consistency like that of a sponge.

spon·gy /'spənjē/ ▶ **adjective** (**spongier, spongiest**) like a sponge in being porous, absorbent, or compressible.
– DERIVATIVES **spon·gi·ness** noun.

spon·sor /'spänsər/ ▶ **noun 1** a person or organization that pays for or contributes to the costs of an event or a radio or television program in return for advertising. **2** a person who promises to give money to a charity after another person has participated in a fund-raising activity. **3** a person who introduces and supports a proposal for a new law. **4** a person taking official responsibility for the actions of another. **5** a godparent at a child's baptism.

– SYNONYMS **backer,** patron, promoter, benefactor, supporter, contributor.

▶ **verb** be a sponsor for a person, event, or fund-raising activity.

– SYNONYMS **finance,** fund, subsidize, back, promote, support, contribute to; informal bankroll.

– DERIVATIVES **spon·sor·ship** /-,sHip/ noun.
– ORIGIN Latin.

spon·ta·ne·ous /spän'tānēəs/ ▶ **adjective 1** done or occurring as a result of an unplanned impulse: *the crowd broke into spontaneous applause.* **2** open, natural, and uninhibited. **3** (of a process or event) happening naturally, without being made to do so.

– SYNONYMS **1 unplanned,** unpremeditated, impulsive, impromptu, spur-of-the-moment, unprompted; informal off-the-cuff. **2 natural,** uninhibited, relaxed, unselfconscious, unaffected.

– DERIVATIVES **spon·ta·ne·i·ty** /ˌspäntəˈnēitē, -ˈnā-/ noun **spon·ta·ne·ous·ly** adverb.

– ORIGIN Latin *spontaneus.*

WORD TOOLKIT

spontaneous ...	involuntary ...	unintentional ...
applause	manslaughter	injury
reaction	movement	humor
outpouring	unemployment	irony
uprising	servitude	bias
rupture	commitment	death
combustion	treatment	poisoning
mutation	spasm	mistake

spon·ta·ne·ous com·bus·tion ▶ **noun** the burning of organic matter caused by chemical changes within the substance itself.

spoof /spo͞of/ informal ▶ **noun 1** a humorous imitation of something in which its typical features are exaggerated: *a spoof of Bond films.* **2** a trick played on someone as a joke. ▶ **verb 1** imitate something while exaggerating its typical features. **2** trick someone.

– DERIVATIVES **spoof·er** noun **spoof·er·y** /ˈspo͞ofərē/ noun.

– ORIGIN coined by the English comedian Arthur Roberts.

spook /spo͝ok/ informal ▶ **noun 1** a ghost. **2** a spy. ▶ **verb** frighten someone or something.

– ORIGIN Dutch.

spook·y /ˈspo͝okē/ ▶ **adjective** (**spookier, spookiest**) informal sinister or ghostly.

– SYNONYMS **eerie,** sinister, ghostly, uncanny, weird, unearthly, mysterious; informal creepy, scary.

– DERIVATIVES **spook·i·ly** adverb **spook·i·ness** noun.

spool /spo͞ol/ ▶ **noun** a cylindrical device on which thread, film, etc., can be wound. ▶ **verb 1** wind or be wound onto a spool. **2** Computing send data for printing or processing on a peripheral device to an intermediate store.

– ORIGIN Old French *espole* or German *spōle*; sense 2 of the verb is from the initial letters of *simultaneous peripheral operation online.*

spoon /spo͞on/ ▶ **noun** an implement consisting of a small shallow bowl on a long handle, used for eating, stirring, and serving food. ▶ **verb 1** transfer food with a spoon. **2** informal, dated (of a couple) kiss and cuddle amorously.

– DERIVATIVES **spoon·ful** /-ˌfo͝ol/ noun.

– ORIGIN Old English, 'chip of wood.'

spoon·bill /ˈspo͞onˌbil/ ▶ **noun** a tall wading bird having a long bill with a very broad flat tip.

spoon·er·ism /ˈspo͞onəˌrizəm/ ▶ **noun** an error in speech in which the initial sounds or letters of two or more words are accidentally swapped around, as in *you have hissed the mystery lectures.*

– ORIGIN named after the English scholar Revd W. A. *Spooner,* who was said to have made such errors.

spoon-feed ▶ **verb 1** provide someone with so much help or information that they do not need to think for themselves. **2** feed a baby with a spoon.

spoor /spo͝or, spô(ə)r/ ▶ **noun** the track or scent of an animal.

– ORIGIN Dutch *spor.*

spo·rad·ic /spəˈradik/ ▶ **adjective** occurring at irregular intervals or only in a few places: *sporadic fighting broke out.*

– SYNONYMS **occasional,** infrequent, irregular, periodic, scattered, patchy, isolated, odd, intermittent, spasmodic, fitful, desultory, erratic, unpredictable.
– ANTONYMS frequent, continuous.

– DERIVATIVES **spo·rad·i·cal·ly** /-ik(ə)lē/ adverb.

– ORIGIN Greek *sporadikos.*

spore /spôr/ ▶ **noun** a tiny reproductive cell produced by plants without vascular systems (such as mosses and algae), fungi, etc.

– ORIGIN Greek *spora* 'sowing, seed.'

spor·ran /ˈspärən, ˈspôr-/ ▶ **noun** a small pouch worn around the waist so as to hang in front of the kilt as part of men's Scottish Highland dress.

– ORIGIN Scottish Gaelic *sporan.*

sport /spôrt/ ▶ **noun 1** an activity involving physical effort and skill in which a person or team competes against another or others. **2** informal a person who behaves in a good or specified way when teased or defeated: *go on, be a sport!* **3** success or pleasure derived from an activity such as hunting. **4** dated entertainment; fun. **5** Biology an animal or plant that is markedly different from the parent type as a result of mutation.

– SYNONYMS **game,** physical recreation.

▶ **verb 1** wear or display a distinctive item. **2** literary play in a lively way.

– SYNONYMS **wear,** have on, dress in, show off, parade, flaunt.

– DERIVATIVES **sport·er** noun.

– PHRASES **the sport of kings** horse racing.

– ORIGIN from DISPORT.

sport coat ▶ **noun** another term for SPORTS JACKET.

sport·ing /ˈspôrtiNG/ ▶ **adjective 1** connected with or interested in sports. **2** fair and generous toward others.

– SYNONYMS **sportsmanlike,** generous, considerate, fair.

– DERIVATIVES **sport·ing·ly** adverb.

sport·ing chance ▶ **noun** a reasonable chance of winning or succeeding.

spor·tive /ˈspôrtiv/ ▶ **adjective** playful; light-hearted.

sports car /spôrts/ ▶ **noun** a low-built fast car.

sports·cast /ˈspôrtsˌkast/ ▶ **noun** a broadcast of sports news or a sports event.

– DERIVATIVES **sports·cast·er** noun **sports·cast·ing** noun.

sports jack·et /spôrts/ ▶ **noun** a man's informal jacket resembling a suit jacket.

sports·man /ˈspôrtsmən/ (or **sportswoman** /ˈspôrtsˌwo͝omən/) ▶ **noun** (pl. **sportsmen** or **sportswomen**) **1** a person who takes part in a sport, especially as a professional. **2** a person who behaves in a fair and generous way toward others.

– DERIVATIVES **sports·man·like** /-ˌlīk/ adjective **sports·man·ship** /-ˌSHip/ noun.

sports·per·son /ˈspôrtsˌpərsən/ ▶ **noun** (pl. **sportspersons** or **sportspeople** /-ˌpēpəl/) a sportsman or sportswoman.

sport·ster /ˈspôrtstər/ ▶ **noun** a sports car.

sports·wear /ˈspôrtsˌwe(ə)r/ ▶ **noun** clothes worn for sport or for casual use.

sport u·til·i·ty ve·hi·cle ▶ **noun** a high-performance four-wheel-drive vehicle.

sport·y /ˈspôrtē/ ▶ **adjective** (**sportier**, **sportiest**) informal **1** fond of or good at sports. **2** (of clothing) suitable for sport or casual wear. **3** (of a car) compact and with fast acceleration.

– SYNONYMS **athletic,** fit, active, energetic.

– DERIVATIVES **sport·i·ness** noun.

spot /spät/ ▶ **noun 1** a small round mark on a surface. **2** a pimple. **3** a particular place, point, or position: *an ideal picnic spot*. **4** a place for an individual item in a show. **5** informal, chiefly Brit. a small amount: *have a spot of tea*.

– SYNONYMS **1 mark,** patch, dot, fleck, smudge, smear, stain, blotch, splash; informal splotch. **2 pimple,** pustule, blackhead, boil, blemish; informal zit. **(spots)** acne, rash. **3 place,** site, position, situation, setting, location, venue.

▶ **verb** (**spots, spotting, spotted**) **1** notice or recognize someone or something that is difficult to find or that one is searching for. **2** mark something with spots. **3** (**it spots, it is spotting, it spotted**) light rain falls.

– SYNONYMS **see,** notice, observe, catch sight of, detect, make out, discern, recognize, identify, locate; literary espy, descry.

– PHRASES **on the spot 1** immediately. **2** at the scene of an event. **put someone on the spot** informal force someone into a situation in which they must respond or act. **spot on** informal completely accurate or accurately.

– ORIGIN perhaps from Dutch *spotte*.

spot check ▶ **noun** a test made without warning on a person or thing selected at random. ▶ **verb** (**spot-check**) make a random check on someone or something without warning.

spot·less /ˈspätlis/ ▶ **adjective 1** absolutely clean. **2** without any mistakes or moral faults; perfect: *the defendant has a spotless record*.

– SYNONYMS **clean,** pristine, immaculate, shining, shiny, gleaming, spick and span.
– ANTONYMS filthy.

– DERIVATIVES **spot·less·ly** adverb **spot·less·ness** noun.

spot·light /ˈspätˌlīt/ ▶ **noun 1** a lamp projecting a narrow, intense beam of light directly onto a place or person. **2** (**the spotlight**) intense public attention.

– SYNONYMS **attention,** glare of publicity, limelight, public eye.

▶ **verb** (past and past part. **spotlighted** or **spotlit** /-lit/) **1** light up someone or something with a spotlight. **2** direct attention to a problem or situation.

spot·ted /ˈspätid/ ▶ **adjective** marked or decorated with spots.

– SYNONYMS **spotty,** dotted, polka-dot, freckled, mottled.

spot·ted dick ▶ **noun** Brit. a suet pudding containing currants.

spot·ter /ˈspätər/ ▶ **noun 1** (usu. in combination) a person who observes or looks for a particular thing as a hobby or job: *a talent spotter*. **2** a pilot or aircraft employed in spotting enemy positions.

spot·ty /ˈspätē/ ▶ **adjective** (**spottier, spottiest**) **1** marked with or having spots. **2** of uneven quality.

spous·al /ˈspouzəl/ ▶ **adjective** Law relating to marriage or to a husband or wife.

spouse /spous/ ▶ **noun** a husband or wife.

– SYNONYMS **partner,** husband, wife, mate, consort; informal other half, better half.

– ORIGIN Latin *sponsus*.

spout /spout/ ▶ **noun 1** a projecting tube or lip through or over which liquid can be poured from a container. **2** a stream of liquid flowing out with great force.

– SYNONYMS **nozzle,** lip.

▶ **verb 1** send out or flow forcibly in a stream: *water spouted from a pipe*. **2** express one's views in a lengthy or emphatic way.

– SYNONYMS **1 spurt,** gush, spew, erupt, shoot, squirt, spray, discharge, emit, belch. **2** *he spouted about morality* **hold forth,** sound off, go on; informal mouth off.

– DERIVATIVES **spout·ed** adjective **spout·er** noun.

– ORIGIN from an Old Norse word meaning 'to spit.'

sprain /sprān/ ▶ **verb** wrench the ligaments of a joint so as to cause pain and swelling. ▶ **noun** the result of wrenching a joint.

– ORIGIN unknown.

sprang /spraNG/ past of **SPRING**.

sprat /sprat/ ▶ **noun** a small edible sea fish of the herring family.

– ORIGIN Old English.

sprawl /sprôl/ ▶ **verb 1** sit, lie, or fall with the limbs spread out in an awkward way. **2** (often as adj. **sprawling**) spread out irregularly over a large area: *a sprawling city*.

– SYNONYMS **stretch out,** lounge, loll, slump, flop, slouch.

▶ **noun 1** the disorganized expansion of an urban or industrial area into the nearby countryside. **2** a relaxed or awkward position with the limbs spread out.

– ORIGIN Old English, 'move the limbs convulsively.'

spray[1] /sprā/ ▶ **noun 1** liquid sent through the air in tiny drops. **2** a liquid that can be forced out of an aerosol or other container in a spray.

– SYNONYMS **1 shower,** sprinkle, jet, squirt, mist, spume, foam, froth, spindrift. **2 aerosol,** vaporizer, atomizer, sprinkler.

▶ **verb 1** apply liquid in a spray. **2** cover or treat someone or something with a spray. **3** (of liquid) be sent through the air in a spray. **4** scatter over an area or object with force: *the gunmen sprayed bullets at all three cars*.

– SYNONYMS **1 sprinkle,** dribble, drizzle, water, soak, douse, drench. **2 spout,** jet, gush, spurt, shoot, squirt.

– DERIVATIVES **spray·er** noun.

– ORIGIN from Dutch *spraeyen* 'sprinkle.'

spray[2] ▶ **noun 1** a stem or small branch of a tree or plant, bearing flowers and leaves. **2** a bunch of cut flowers arranged in an attractive way.

– ORIGIN Old English.

spray gun ▶ **noun** a device resembling a gun that is used to spray a liquid such as paint under pressure.

spray-paint ▶ **verb** paint an image or message on to a surface with a spray, or paint a surface with a spray.

spread /spred/ ▶ **verb** (past and past part. **spread**) **1** open something out so as to increase its surface area, width, or length. **2** stretch out limbs, hands, fingers, or wings so that they are far apart. **3** extend or distribute over a large or increasing area: *rain will spread southeast during the day*. **4** reach or cause to reach more and more people:

panic spread among the crowd. **5** apply a substance in an even layer.

– SYNONYMS **1 lay out,** open out, unfurl, unroll, roll out, straighten out, fan out, stretch out, extend. **2** *the landscape spread out below* **extend,** stretch, sprawl. **3 scatter,** strew, disperse, distribute. **4 circulate,** broadcast, put about, publicize, propagate, repeat. **5 travel,** move, be borne, sweep, diffuse, reproduce, be passed on, be transmitted. **6 smear,** daub, plaster, apply, rub.

▶ **noun 1** the action of spreading over an area. **2** the extent, width, or area covered by something. **3** the range of something: *a wide spread of ages.* **4** a soft paste that can be spread on bread. **5** an article or advertisement covering several columns or pages of a newspaper or magazine. **6** informal a large and impressive meal. **7** a large farm or ranch.

– SYNONYMS **1 expansion,** proliferation, dissemination, diffusion, transmission, propagation. **2 span,** width, extent, stretch, reach.

– DERIVATIVES **spread·a·ble** adjective **spread·er** noun.
– ORIGIN Old English.

spread bet·ting ▶ **noun** a form of betting in which money is won or lost according to the degree by which the score or result of a sporting event varies from the spread of expected values quoted by the bookmaker.

spread-ea·gle ▶ **verb** (**be spread-eagled**) be stretched out with the arms and legs spread wide.

spread·sheet /ˈspred,shēt/ ▶ **noun** a computer program in which figures arranged in a grid can be manipulated and used in calculations.

spree /sprē/ ▶ **noun** a spell of unrestrained activity: *a shopping spree.*

– SYNONYMS **bout,** orgy; informal binge, splurge.

– ORIGIN unknown.

sprig /sprig/ ▶ **noun 1** a small stem bearing leaves or flowers, taken from a bush or plant. **2** a descendant or younger member of a family or social class. **3** a small molded decoration applied to a piece of pottery before firing.
– DERIVATIVES **sprigged** adjective.
– ORIGIN German *sprick.*

spright·ly /ˈsprītlē/ ▶ **adjective** (**sprightlier, sprightliest**) (especially of an old person) lively; energetic.

– SYNONYMS **spry,** lively, agile, nimble, energetic, active, vigorous, spirited, animated, vivacious, frisky.
– ANTONYMS doddery, lethargic.

– DERIVATIVES **spright·li·ness** noun.
– ORIGIN from **SPRITE**.

spring /spriNG/ ▶ **verb** (past **sprang** /sprаNG/ or **sprung** /sprəNG/; past part. **sprung**) **1** move suddenly or rapidly upward or forward. **2** (**spring from**) originate or arise from: *his short film sprang from a midlife crisis.* **3** move or do suddenly: *the door sprang open.* **4** (**spring up**) suddenly develop or appear. **5** (as adj. **sprung**) (of a vehicle or item of furniture) having springs. **6** (**spring something on**) present something suddenly or unexpectedly to someone. **7** informal bring about the escape or release of a prisoner.

– SYNONYMS **1 leap,** jump, bound, vault, hop. **2** (**spring from**) **originate from,** have its origins in, derive from, arise in, stem from, emanate from, evolve from.

▶ **noun 1** the ability to spring back strongly; elastic quality. **2** the season after winter and before summer. **3** a spiral metal coil that can be pressed or pulled but returns to its former shape when released. **4** a sudden jump upward or forward. **5** a place where water wells up from an underground source.

– SYNONYMS **springiness,** bounce, resilience, elasticity, flexibility, stretch, stretchiness, give.

– DERIVATIVES **spring·less** adjective **spring·like** /-,līk/ adjective.
– PHRASES **spring a leak** (of a boat or container) develop a leak.
– ORIGIN Old English.

WORD LINKS

vernal *relating to the season of spring*

spring·board /ˈspriNG,bôrd/ ▶ **noun 1** a flexible board from which a diver or gymnast may jump in order to push off more strongly. **2** a thing that starts off an activity or enterprise: *a book can be a springboard for discussions with children about their own lives.*

spring·bok /ˈspriNG,bäk/ ▶ **noun 1** a southern African gazelle that leaps when disturbed. **2** (**the Springboks**) the South African international rugby union team.
– ORIGIN Afrikaans.

spring chick·en ▶ **noun 1** informal a young person: *I'm no spring chicken.* **2** a young chicken for eating (originally available only in spring).

spring clean·ing ▶ **noun** a thorough cleaning of a house or room. ▶ **verb** (**spring-clean**) clean a house or room thoroughly.

spring·er span·iel /ˈspriNGər/ ▶ **noun** a small spaniel of a breed originally used to drive game birds out of cover.

spring-load·ed ▶ **adjective** containing a compressed or stretched spring pressing one part against another.

spring on·ion ▶ **noun** chiefly Brit. a green onion; a scallion.

spring roll ▶ **noun** an Asian snack or appetizer consisting of rice paper filled with vegetables and sometimes meat, rolled into a cylinder and deep-fried.

spring·tail /ˈspriNG,tāl/ ▶ **noun** a minute wingless insect that uses a springlike organ under the abdomen to leap when disturbed.

spring tide /ˈspriNG ,tīd/ ▶ **noun** a tide just after a new or full moon, when there is the greatest difference between high and low water.

spring·time /ˈspriNG,tīm/ ▶ **noun** the season of spring.

spring·y /ˈspriNGē/ ▶ **adjective** (**springier, springiest**) **1** springing back quickly when squeezed or stretched. **2** (of movements) light and confident.
– DERIVATIVES **spring·i·ly** adverb **spring·i·ness** noun.

sprin·kle /ˈspriNGkəl/ ▶ **verb 1** scatter or pour small drops or particles over an object or surface. **2** distribute something randomly throughout: *the city is sprinkled with factories producing computers.*

– SYNONYMS **splash,** trickle, drizzle, spray, shower, drip, scatter, strew, dredge, dust.

▶ **noun** a small amount that is sprinkled over something.
– ORIGIN perhaps from Dutch *sprenkelen.*

sprin·kler /ˈspriNGk(ə)lər/ ▶ **noun 1** a device for watering lawns. **2** an automatic fire extinguisher installed in a ceiling.

sprin·kling /ˈspriNGk(ə)liNG/ ▶ **noun** a small, thinly distributed amount of something.

sprint /sprint/ ▶ **verb** run at full speed over a short distance.

– SYNONYMS **run,** race, rush, dash, bolt, fly, charge, shoot, speed; informal hotfoot it, leg it.
– ANTONYMS stroll.

▶ **noun 1** an act of sprinting. **2** a short, fast race.
– DERIVATIVES **sprint·er** noun.
– ORIGIN from Swedish *spritta.*

sprit /sprit/ ▶ **noun** a small pole reaching diagonally from a mast to the upper outer corner of a sail.
– ORIGIN Old English, 'punting pole.'

sprite /sprīt/ ▶ **noun 1** an elf or fairy. **2** a computer graphic that can be moved on-screen and otherwise manipulated as a single entity.
– ORIGIN a shortening of **SPIRIT**.

sprit·sail /ˈsprit,sāl, -səl/ ▶ **noun** a sail that is extended diagonally from the mast by a small pole reaching to the upper outer corner.

spritz /sprits/ ▶ **verb** spray liquid in quick short bursts at or onto something. ▶ **noun** an act of spraying a short burst of liquid.
– ORIGIN German *spritzen* 'to squirt.'

spritz·er /ˈspritsər/ ▶ **noun** a mixture of wine and soda water.
– ORIGIN German, 'a splash.'

sprock·et /ˈspräkit/ ▶ **noun 1** each of several projections on the rim of a wheel that fit into the links of a chain or holes in film, tape, or paper. **2** (also **sprocket wheel**) a wheel with sprockets.
– ORIGIN unknown.

sprout /sprout/ ▶ **verb 1** (of a plant) produce shoots. **2** start to grow something, especially hair. **3** appear or develop in large numbers: *multiplexes are sprouting up around the country.*

– SYNONYMS **1 germinate,** put/send out shoots, bud. **2 spring,** come up, grow, develop, appear.

▶ **noun 1** a shoot of a plant. **2** a Brussels sprout.
– ORIGIN Germanic.

spruce[1] /sprōōs/ ▶ **adjective** neat and smart.

– SYNONYMS **neat,** well groomed, well turned out, well dressed, smart, trim, dapper; informal natty, snazzy.
– ANTONYMS disheveled.

▶ **verb** (**spruce someone/thing up**) make someone or something neater.

– SYNONYMS **smarten up,** tidy up, clean, groom; informal do up, gussy up.

– ORIGIN perhaps from **SPRUCE**[2] in the former sense 'Prussian.'

spruce[2] ▶ **noun** a conical coniferous tree that has hanging cones.
– ORIGIN from former *Pruce* 'Prussia.'

sprue /sprōō/ ▶ **noun 1** a channel through which metal or plastic is poured into a mold. **2** a piece of metal or plastic that has solidified in a sprue.
– ORIGIN unknown.

sprung /sprəNG/ past participle and past of **SPRING**.

spry /sprī/ ▶ **adjective** (**spryer, spryest,** or **sprier, spriest**) (especially of an old person) lively.

– SYNONYMS **sprightly,** lively, agile, nimble, spirited, animated, vivacious, frisky, active.
– ANTONYMS doddery, lethargic.

– ORIGIN unknown.

spud /spəd/ ▶ **noun** informal a potato.
– ORIGIN unknown.

spu·man·te /spəˈmäntē, spyə-/ ▶ **noun** an Italian sparkling white wine.
– ORIGIN Italian, 'sparkling.'

spume /spyōōm/ literary ▶ **noun** froth or foam that is found on waves. ▶ **verb** form froth or foam.
– ORIGIN Latin *spuma.*

spun /spən/ past and past participle of **SPIN**.

spunk /spəNGk/ ▶ **noun** informal courage and determination.
– DERIVATIVES **spunk·y** adjective (**spunkier, spunkiest**).
– ORIGIN perhaps from **SPARK** and former *funk* 'spark.'

spur /spər/ ▶ **noun 1** a device with a small spike or a spiked wheel, worn on a rider's heel for urging a horse forward. **2** a thing that encourages an act or activity: *wars act as a spur to invention.* **3** a projection from a mountain. **4** a short branch road or railroad line. **5** Botany a slender tubular projection from the base of a flower.

– SYNONYMS **stimulus,** incentive, encouragement, inducement, impetus, motivation.
– ANTONYMS disincentive.

▶ **verb** (**spurs, spurring, spurred**) **1** encourage someone to do something or cause something to speed up: *governments should be providing incentives to spur economic growth.* **2** urge a horse forward with spurs.

– SYNONYMS **stimulate,** encourage, prompt, prod, impel, motivate, move, galvanize, inspire, drive.
– ANTONYMS discourage.

– PHRASES **on the spur of the moment** on an impulse; without thinking.
– ORIGIN Old English.

spurge /spərj/ ▶ **noun** a plant or shrub with milky latex and small greenish flowers.
– ORIGIN Old French *espurge.*

spur gear ▶ **noun** a gearwheel with teeth projecting parallel to the wheel's axis.

spu·ri·ous /ˈspyŏŏrēəs/ ▶ **adjective 1** not being what it seems to be; false. **2** (of reasoning) apparently but not actually correct.

– SYNONYMS **bogus,** fake, false, fraudulent, sham, artificial, imitation, simulated, feigned; informal phony.
– ANTONYMS genuine.

– DERIVATIVES **spu·ri·ous·ly** adverb **spu·ri·ous·ness** noun.
– ORIGIN Latin *spurius* 'false.'

spurn /spərn/ ▶ **verb** reject someone or something with contempt.

– SYNONYMS **reject,** rebuff, scorn, turn down, treat with contempt, disdain, look down one's nose at; informal turn one's nose up at.
– ANTONYMS welcome, accept.

– ORIGIN Old English.

spurt /spərt/ ▶ **verb 1** gush out in a sudden stream. **2** move with a sudden burst of speed.

– SYNONYMS **squirt,** shoot, jet, erupt, gush, pour, stream, pump, surge, spew, course, well, spring, burst, spout.

▶ **noun 1** a sudden gushing stream. **2** a sudden burst of activity or speed.

– SYNONYMS **squirt,** jet, gush, stream, rush, surge, flood, cascade, torrent.

– ORIGIN unknown.

sput·nik /ˈspətnik, ˈspo͝ot-/ ▶ **noun** each of a series of Soviet artificial satellites, the first of which was the first to be placed in orbit.
– ORIGIN Russian, 'fellow traveller.'

sput·ter /ˈspətər/ ▶ **verb 1** make a series of soft explosive sounds. **2** say something in a rapid and unclear way; splutter. ▶ **noun** a sputtering sound.
– ORIGIN Dutch *sputteren*.

spu·tum /ˈspyo͞otəm/ ▶ **noun** a mixture of saliva and mucus coughed up from the throat or lungs.
– ORIGIN Latin.

spy /spī/ ▶ **noun** (pl. **spies**) **1** a person employed to collect and report secret information on an enemy or competitor. **2** a person or device that observes people secretly.

– SYNONYMS **agent,** mole, plant; informal spook.

▶ **verb** (**spies, spying, spied**) **1** be able to see; notice: *he could spy a figure in the distance*. **2** (**spy on**) watch someone secretly. **3** work as a spy. **4** (**spy something out**) collect information about something before deciding how to act.

– SYNONYMS **1 notice,** observe, see, spot, sight, catch sight of, glimpse, make out, discern, detect. **2** (**spy on**) *investigators spied on them* **observe,** keep under surveillance, eavesdrop on, watch, bug.

– ORIGIN from Old French *espier* 'espy.'

spy·glass /ˈspīˌglas/ ▶ **noun** a small telescope.

spy·ware /ˈspīˌwe(ə)r/ ▶ **noun** software that enables someone to gather information about another's computer activities by transmitting data secretly from their hard drive.

sq. ▶ **abbreviation** square.

SQL ▶ **abbreviation** Structured Query Language, a computer language used for database manipulation.

squab /skwäb/ ▶ **noun** a young pigeon that is yet to leave the nest.
– ORIGIN unknown.

squab·ble /ˈskwäbəl/ ▶ **noun** a quarrel about an unimportant matter.

– SYNONYMS **quarrel,** disagreement, row, argument, dispute, wrangle, clash, altercation; informal tiff, set-to, run-in, scrap.

▶ **verb** quarrel about an unimportant matter.

– SYNONYMS **quarrel,** row, argue, bicker, disagree; informal scrap.

– ORIGIN uncertain.

squad /skwäd/ ▶ **noun** (treated as sing. or pl.) **1** a division of a police force dealing with a particular type of crime: *the vice squad*. **2** a group of athletes from which a team is chosen. **3** a small number of soldiers assembled for drill or given a particular task.

– SYNONYMS **1 team,** crew, gang, force. **2 detachment,** detail, unit, platoon, battery, troop, patrol, squadron, commando.

– ORIGIN Italian *squadra* 'square.'

squad car ▶ **noun** a police patrol car.

squad·ron /ˈskwädrən/ ▶ **noun 1** an operational unit in an air force. **2** a main division of an armored or cavalry regiment. **3** a group of warships on a particular duty.
– ORIGIN Italian *squadra* 'square.'

squal·id /ˈskwälid/ ▶ **adjective 1** very dirty and unpleasant. **2** highly immoral or dishonest: *a squalid attempt to buy votes*.

– SYNONYMS **1 dirty,** filthy, dingy, grubby, grimy, wretched, miserable, mean, seedy, shabby, sordid, insalubrious. **2 improper,** sordid, unseemly, unsavory, sleazy, cheap, base, low, corrupt, dishonest, dishonorable, disreputable, discreditable, contemptible, shameful.
– ANTONYMS clean.

– ORIGIN Latin *squalidus*.

squall /skwôl/ ▶ **noun 1** a sudden violent gust of wind or localized storm. **2** a loud cry. ▶ **verb** (of a baby or small child) cry noisily and continuously.
– DERIVATIVES **squal·ly** adjective.
– ORIGIN probably from SQUEAL.

squal·or /ˈskwälər/ ▶ **noun** the state of being dirty and unpleasant.

– SYNONYMS **dirt,** filth, grubbiness, grime, muck, foulness, poverty, wretchedness, shabbiness, neglect, decay, dilapidation, sordidness; informal scruffiness, crumminess, grunge.
– ANTONYMS cleanliness, pleasantness, smartness.

squan·der /ˈskwändər/ ▶ **verb** waste money, time, or an opportunity in a reckless or foolish way.

– SYNONYMS **waste,** throw away, misuse, misspend, fritter away, spend like water; informal blow, run through, splurge, pour down the drain.
– ANTONYMS save.

– ORIGIN unknown.

square /skwe(ə)r/ ▶ **noun 1** a plane figure with four equal straight sides and four right angles. **2** an open four-sided area surrounded by buildings. **3** an area within a military barracks or camp that is used for drill. **4** the product of a number multiplied by itself. **5** an L-shaped or T-shaped instrument used for obtaining or testing right angles. **6** informal, dated an old-fashioned or boringly conventional person.

– SYNONYMS **piazza,** plaza, quadrangle.

▶ **adjective 1** having the shape of a square. **2** having or forming a right angle. **3** (of a unit of measurement) equal to the area of a square whose side is of the unit specified: *1,500 square meters of land*. **4** (after a noun) referring to the length of each side of a square shape or object: *the room was ten meters square*. **5** at right angles. **6** (of two or more things) level or parallel. **7** broad and solid in shape. **8** fair and honest: *she'd been as square with him as anybody could be*. **9** informal, dated old-fashioned or boringly conventional.

– SYNONYMS **level,** even, drawn, equal, tied; informal even-steven(s).

▶ **adverb** directly; straight.
▶ **verb 1** make something square or rectangular. **2** (as adj. **squared**) marked out in squares. **3** multiply a number by itself. **4** (**square with**) agree or be consistent with: *do those claims square with the facts?* **5** settle a bill or debt. **6** make the score of a match or game even. **7** informal pay someone money in order to obtain their cooperation. **8** bring the shoulders into a position in which they appear square and broad.
– DERIVATIVES **square·ness** noun **squar·er** noun **squar·ish** adjective.
– PHRASES **back to square one** informal back to where one started. **a square deal** see DEAL[1]. **a square peg in a round hole** see PEG. **square up 1** take up the position of a person about to fight. **2** (**square up to**) tackle a difficulty with determination.
– ORIGIN Old French *esquare*.

square dance ▶ **noun** a country dance that starts with four couples facing one another in a square.

square knot ▶ **noun** a type of double knot that holds very securely but can be easily undone.

square·ly /ˈskwe(ə)rlē/ ▶ **adverb 1** not at an angle; directly. **2** without any doubt; firmly: *he put the blame squarely on your shoulders.*

square meal ▶ **noun** a large and satisfying meal.

square meas·ure ▶ **noun** a unit of measurement relating to area.

square-rigged ▶ **adjective** (of a sailing ship) having the main sails at right angles to the length of the ship.

square root ▶ **noun** a number that produces a specified quantity when multiplied by itself.

squash[1] /skwäsʜ, skwôsʜ/ ▶ **verb 1** crush or squeeze something so that it becomes flat, soft, or out of shape. **2** force someone or something into a restricted space. **3** put an end to: *he squashed reports that the firm had changed its mind.*

> – SYNONYMS **1 crush,** squeeze, mash, pulp, flatten, compress, distort, pound, trample. **2 force,** ram, thrust, push, cram, jam, stuff, pack, squeeze, wedge.

▶ **noun 1** a state of being squashed. **2** (also **squash rackets**) a game in which two players use rackets to hit a small rubber ball against the walls of a closed court.
– DERIVATIVES **squash·y** adjective.
– ORIGIN from **QUASH**.

squash[2] ▶ **noun** (pl. same or **squashes**) a gourd with flesh that can be cooked and eaten as a vegetable.
– ORIGIN from a North American Indian language.

squat /skwät/ ▶ **verb** (**squats, squatting, squatted**) **1** crouch or sit with the knees bent and the heels close to the buttocks or thighs. **2** unlawfully occupy an uninhabited building or area of land. ▶ **adjective** (**squatter, squattest**) short and wide or broad. ▶ **noun 1** a squatting position. **2** a building occupied unlawfully.
– DERIVATIVES **squat·ter** noun.
– ORIGIN Old French *esquatir* 'flatten.'

squat thrust ▶ **noun** an exercise in which the legs are thrust backward to their full extent from a squatting position with the hands on the floor.

squaw /skwô/ ▶ **noun** offensive an American Indian woman or wife.
– ORIGIN from a North American Indian language.

squawk /skwôk/ ▶ **verb 1** (of a bird) make a loud, harsh noise. **2** say something in a loud, shrill tone.

> – SYNONYMS *a pheasant squawked* **screech,** squeal, shriek, scream, croak, crow, caw, cluck, cackle, hoot, cry, call.

▶ **noun** an act of squawking.

> – SYNONYMS *the gull gave a squawk* **screech,** squeal, shriek, scream, croak, crow, caw, cluck, cackle, hoot, cry, call.

– DERIVATIVES **squawk·er** noun.
– ORIGIN imitating the sound.

squeak /skwēk/ ▶ **noun 1** a short, high-pitched sound or cry. **2** a single communication or sound: *I didn't hear a squeak from him.*

> – SYNONYMS **1** *the vole's squeak* **peep,** cheep, tweet, squeal, yelp, whimper. **2** *the squeak of the hinge* **screech,** creak, scrape, grate, rasp, jar, groan.

▶ **verb 1** make a squeak. **2** say something in a high-pitched tone. **3** informal only just manage to succeed or to achieve something: *the bill squeaked through with just six votes to spare.*

> – SYNONYMS **1 peep,** cheep, tweet, squeal, yelp, whimper. **2** *the hinges of the gate squeaked* **screech,** creak, scrape, grate, rasp, groan.

– DERIVATIVES **squeak·er** noun **squeak·y** adjective (**squeakier, squeakiest**).
– ORIGIN imitating the sound.

squeak·y clean ▶ **adjective** informal **1** completely clean. **2** morally correct; very virtuous.

squeal /skwēl/ ▶ **verb 1** make a long, high-pitched cry or noise. **2** say something in a high-pitched tone. **3** (often **squeal on**) informal inform on someone. **4** informal complain about something. ▶ **noun** a long, high-pitched cry or noise.
– DERIVATIVES **squeal·er** noun.
– ORIGIN imitating the sound.

squeam·ish /ˈskwēmisʜ/ ▶ **adjective 1** easily disgusted or made to feel sick. **2** having very firm moral views.

> – SYNONYMS *I'm too squeamish to gut fish | are you squeamish about a little blood?* **easily nauseated,** nervous; (**squeamish about**) put off by, not able to stand the sight of.

– DERIVATIVES **squeam·ish·ly** adverb **squeam·ish·ness** noun.
– ORIGIN Old French *escoymos*.

squee·gee /ˈskwēˌjē/ ▶ **noun** a scraping tool with a rubber-edged blade, used for cleaning windows. ▶ **verb** (**squeegees, squeegeeing, squeegeed**) clean something with a squeegee.
– ORIGIN from **SQUEEZE**.

squeeze /skwēz/ ▶ **verb 1** firmly press something from opposite or all sides. **2** extract liquid or a soft substance from something by squeezing. **3** (**squeeze in/into/through**) manage to get into or through a restricted space. **4** (**squeeze someone/thing in**) manage to find time for someone or something. **5** obtain by pressure, force, etc.: *a series of con games designed to squeeze money out of the government.*

> – SYNONYMS **1 compress,** press, crush, squash, pinch, nip, grasp, grip, clutch. **2 extract,** press, force, express. **3 force,** thrust, cram, ram, jam, stuff, pack, wedge, press, push, squash, crush, crowd, force one's way.

▶ **noun 1** an act of squeezing or the state of being squeezed. **2** a hug. **3** a small amount of liquid that is squeezed out. **4** a strong financial demand or pressure: *a squeeze on profits.* **5** (usu. **main squeeze**) informal a person's girlfriend or boyfriend.

> – SYNONYMS **1 press,** pinch, nip, grasp, grip, clutch, hug. **2 crush,** jam, squash, congestion.

– DERIVATIVES **squeez·a·ble** adjective **squeez·er** noun.
– PHRASES **put the squeeze on** informal pressure someone into doing something.
– ORIGIN unknown.

squeeze·box ▶ **noun** informal an accordion or concertina.

squelch /skwelcʜ/ ▶ **verb 1** make a soft sucking sound such as that made by treading in thick mud. **2** informal forcefully silence someone or put an end to something. ▶ **noun** a squelching sound.
– DERIVATIVES **squelch·y** adjective.
– ORIGIN imitating the sound.

squib /skwib/ ▶ **noun 1** a small firework that hisses before exploding. **2** a short piece of satirical writing.
– ORIGIN unknown.

squid /skwid/ ▸ **noun** (pl. same or **squids**) a mollusk that lives in the sea, with a long body, eight arms, and two long tentacles.
– ORIGIN unknown.

squig·gle /ˈskwigəl/ ▸ **noun** a short line that curls and loops irregularly.
– DERIVATIVES **squig·gly** adjective.
– ORIGIN perhaps from **SQUIRM** and **WIGGLE** or **WRIGGLE**.

squill /skwil/ ▸ **noun 1** (also **sea squill**) a Mediterranean plant with broad leaves and white flowers. **2** a small plant resembling a hyacinth, with clusters of violet-blue or blue-striped flowers.
– ORIGIN Greek *skilla*.

squint /skwint/ ▸ **verb 1** look at someone or something with partly closed eyes. **2** partly close the eyes. **3** have an eye that looks in a different direction to the other eye. ▸ **noun 1** a permanent condition in which one eye does not look in the same direction as the other. **2** informal a quick look.
– DERIVATIVES **squint·y** adjective.
– ORIGIN perhaps from Dutch *schuinte* 'slant.'

squire /ˈskwīr/ ▸ **noun 1** a country gentleman, especially the chief landowner in an area. **2** historical a young nobleman acting as an attendant to a knight before becoming a knight himself. ▸ **verb** (of a man) accompany or escort a woman.
– ORIGIN Old French *esquier* 'esquire.'

squire·ar·chy /ˈskwīrärkē/ ▸ **noun** (pl. **squirearchies**) country landowners as a group.
– ORIGIN from **SQUIRE**, on the pattern of words such as *hierarchy*.

squirm /skwərm/ ▸ **verb 1** wriggle or twist the body from side to side, especially from nervousness or discomfort. **2** be embarrassed or ashamed.

> – SYNONYMS **1 wriggle,** wiggle, writhe, twist, slither, fidget, twitch, toss and turn. **2 wince,** shudder.

▸ **noun** a wriggling movement.
– DERIVATIVES **squirm·y** adjective.
– ORIGIN probably from **WORM**.

squir·rel /ˈskwər(ə)l/ ▸ **noun** an agile rodent with a bushy tail that lives in trees. ▸ **verb** (**squirrels, squirreling, squirreled**) (**squirrel something away**) hide or keep money or valuables in a safe place.
– ORIGIN Old French *esquireul*.

squir·rel·ly /ˈskwər(ə)lē/ ▸ **adjective 1** relating to or resembling a squirrel. **2** informal restless or nervous.

squirt /skwərt/ ▸ **verb 1** force out liquid in a thin jet from a small opening. **2** wet someone or something with a jet of liquid.

> – SYNONYMS **1 spurt,** shoot, spray, jet, erupt, gush, rush, pump, surge, stream, spew, well, issue, emanate. **2 splash,** spray, shower, sprinkle.

▸ **noun 1** a thin jet of liquid. **2** informal a weak or insignificant person.
– ORIGIN imitating the sound.

squish /skwisʜ/ ▸ **verb 1** make a soft squelching sound. **2** informal squash something. ▸ **noun** a soft squelching sound.
– DERIVATIVES **squish·y** adjective.
– ORIGIN imitating the sound.

Sr ▸ **symbol** the chemical element strontium.

Sr. ▸ **abbreviation** senior (in names): *E. T. Krebs, Sr.*

SRAM /ˈesˌram/ ▸ **abbreviation** Electronics static random-access memory.

Sri Lan·kan /ˌsrē ˈlänɢkən, ˌsʜrē, ˈlaɴɢkən/ ▸ **noun** a person from Sri Lanka. ▸ **adjective** relating to Sri Lanka.

SRO ▸ **abbreviation 1** standing room only. **2** single room occupancy.

SS[1] ▸ **abbreviation 1** Saints. **2** steamship. **3** social security. **4** Baseball shortstop.

SS[2] ▸ **noun** the Nazi special police force.
– ORIGIN short for German *Schutzstaffel* 'defense squadron.'

SSA ▸ **abbreviation 1** Social Security Act. **2** Social Security Administration.

SSE ▸ **abbreviation** south-southeast.

SSRI ▸ **abbreviation** selective serotonin reuptake inhibitor, any of a group of antidepressant drugs that prevent the uptake of serotonin in the brain.

SST ▸ **abbreviation** supersonic transport.

SSW ▸ **abbreviation** south-southwest.

St. ▸ **abbreviation 1** Saint. **2** Street.

stab /stab/ ▸ **verb** (**stabs, stabbing, stabbed**) **1** thrust a knife or other pointed weapon into someone. **2** make a short, forceful movement with a pointed object: *I stabbed at my salad in irritation*. **3** (of a pain) cause a sudden sharp feeling.

> – SYNONYMS **knife,** run through, skewer, spear, gore, spike, impale.

▸ **noun 1** an act of stabbing. **2** a sudden sharp feeling or pain. **3** (**a stab at**) informal an attempt to do something.

> – SYNONYMS **1** *a stab of pain* **twinge,** pang, throb, spasm, cramp, prick. **2 attempt,** try, endeavor, effort; informal go, shot, crack.

– DERIVATIVES **stab·ber** noun.
– PHRASES **stab someone in the back** betray someone.
– ORIGIN unknown.

sta·bil·i·ty /stəˈbilitē/ ▸ **noun** the state of being stable, steady, or unchanging.

> – SYNONYMS **1 firmness,** solidity, steadiness. **2 balance (of mind),** (mental) health, sanity, reason. **3 strength,** durability, lasting nature, permanence.

sta·bi·lize /ˈstābəˌlīz/ ▸ **verb** make or become stable, steady, or unchanging.
– DERIVATIVES **sta·bi·li·za·tion** /ˌstābəliˈzāsʜən/ noun.

sta·bi·liz·er /ˈstābəˌlīzər/ ▸ **noun 1** a device used to stabilize a ship or aircraft. **2** a substance preventing the breakdown of emulsions in food or paint. **3** a mood stabilizer.

sta·ble[1] /ˈstābəl/ ▸ **adjective** (**stabler, stablest**) **1** not likely to give way or overturn; firmly fixed. **2** not likely to change or fail: *a stable relationship*. **3** not worsening in health after an injury or operation. **4** not easily upset or disturbed; sane and sensible. **5** not liable to undergo chemical decomposition or radioactive decay.

> – SYNONYMS **1 firm,** solid, steady, secure. **2 well balanced,** well adjusted, of sound mind, compos mentis, sane, normal, rational, reasonable, sensible. **3** *a stable relationship* **secure,** solid, strong, steady, firm, sure, steadfast, established, enduring, lasting.
> – ANTONYMS unstable.

– DERIVATIVES **sta·bly** /-b(ə)lē/ adverb.
– ORIGIN Latin *stabilis*.

stable² ▶ **noun** **1** a building for housing horses. **2** a place where racehorses are kept and trained. **3** an organization or place that produces particular types of people or things: *the magazine is from the same stable as "Vogue."* ▶ **verb** put or keep a horse in a stable.
– ORIGIN Old French *estable* 'stable, pigsty.'

sta·ble·mate /ˈstābəlˌmāt/ ▶ **noun** **1** a horse from the same stable as another. **2** a person or product from the same organization or background as another.

sta·bling /ˈstāb(ə)liNG/ ▶ **noun** accommodations for horses.

stac·ca·to /stəˈkätō/ ▶ **adverb & adjective** Music with each sound or note sharply separated from the others. ▶ **noun** (pl. **staccatos**) **1** Music a staccato passage or performance. **2** a series of short detached sounds or words.
– ORIGIN Italian, 'detached.'

stack /stak/ ▶ **noun** **1** a neat pile of objects. **2** a rectangular or cylindrical pile of hay, straw, etc. **3** informal a large quantity of something. **4** a chimney.

– SYNONYMS **heap,** pile, mound, mountain, pyramid, tower.

▶ **verb** **1** arrange things in a stack. **2** fill or cover a place with stacks of things. **3** cause aircraft to fly at different altitudes while waiting to land. **4** shuffle or arrange a deck of cards dishonestly. **5** (**be stacked against/in favor of**) (of a situation) be very likely to produce an unfavorable or favorable outcome for: *the odds were stacked against Fiji in the World Cup.*

– SYNONYMS **1 heap (up),** pile (up), assemble, put together, collect. **2 load,** fill (up), pack, charge, stuff, cram, stock.

– DERIVATIVES **stack·a·ble** adjective **stack·er** noun.
– ORIGIN Old Norse, 'haystack.'

sta·di·um /ˈstādēəm/ ▶ **noun** (pl. **stadiums** or **stadia** /-dēə/) a sports arena with tiers of seats for spectators.

– SYNONYMS **arena,** field, ground, track, course, racetrack, racecourse, speedway, velodrome.

– ORIGIN Greek *stadion* 'racing track.'

staff /staf/ ▶ **noun** **1** (treated as sing. or pl.) the employees of an organization. **2** (treated as sing. or pl.) a group of officers assisting a commanding officer. **3** a long stick used as a support or weapon. **4** a rod or scepter held as a sign of office or authority. **5** Music a stave.

– SYNONYMS **1 employees,** workers, workforce, personnel, human resources, manpower, labor. **2 stick,** stave, pole, rod.

▶ **verb** provide an organization with staff.

– SYNONYMS **man,** people, crew, work, operate.

– PHRASES **the staff of life** a basic food, especially bread.
– ORIGIN Old English.

staff·er /ˈstafər/ ▶ **noun** a member of a staff, especially of a newspaper.

staff of·fi·cer ▶ **noun** a military officer serving on the staff of a headquarters or government department.

staff ser·geant ▶ **noun** a rank of noncommissioned officer in the US armed forces, just above sergeant.

stag /stag/ ▶ **noun** **1** a fully adult male deer. **2** a social gathering attended by men only. **3** a person who attends a social gathering without a partner. ▶ **adverb** without a partner at a social gathering: *we decided to go stag.*
– ORIGIN from an Old Norse word meaning 'male bird.'

stag bee·tle ▶ **noun** a large dark beetle, the male of which has large branched jaws resembling antlers.

stage /stāj/ ▶ **noun** **1** a part, period, or point in a process: *she was in the early stages of pregnancy.* **2** a raised floor or platform on which actors, entertainers, or speakers perform. **3** (**the stage**) the theater as a profession or form of entertainment. **4** a part of a journey. **5** an area of public activity: *his aim is to put Latin American art back on the world stage.* **6** a floor or level of a structure. **7** each of two or more sections of a rocket or spacecraft that are jettisoned in turn when their fuel is exhausted. **8** Electronics a part of a circuit containing a single amplifying transistor or valve.

– SYNONYMS **1 phase,** period, juncture, step, point, level. **2 part,** section, portion, stretch, leg, lap, circuit. **3 platform,** dais, stand, rostrum, podium.

▶ **verb** **1** present a performance of a play or other show. **2** organize and participate in a public event. **3** cause something dramatic or unexpected to happen.
– DERIVATIVES **stage·a·ble** adjective.
– PHRASES **set the stage for** prepare the conditions for something to happen.
– ORIGIN Old French *estage* 'dwelling.'

stage·coach /ˈstājˌkōCH/ ▶ **noun** a closed horse-drawn vehicle formerly used to carry passengers and often mail along a regular route.

stage·craft /ˈstājˌkraft/ ▶ **noun** skill in writing or staging plays.

stage di·rec·tion ▶ **noun** an instruction in a play script indicating the position or tone of an actor, or specifying sound effects, lighting, etc.

stage door ▶ **noun** an actors' and workmen's entrance from the street to the backstage area of a theater.

stage fright ▶ **noun** nervousness before or during a performance.

stage·hand /ˈstājˌhand/ ▶ **noun** a person dealing with scenery or props during a play.

stage-man·age ▶ **verb** **1** arrange and control carefully to create a particular effect: *he stage-managed his image with astounding success.* **2** be the stage manager of a play or other production.
– DERIVATIVES **stage man·age·ment** noun.

stage man·ag·er ▶ **noun** the person responsible for lighting and other technical arrangements for a stage play.

stage name ▶ **noun** a name used by an actor for professional purposes.

stage-struck ▶ **adjective** having a passionate wish to become an actor.

stage whis·per ▶ **noun** a loud whisper by an actor on stage, intended to be heard by the audience.

stage·y ▶ **adjective** variant spelling of **STAGY**.

stag·fla·tion /ˌstagˈflāSHən/ ▶ **noun** high inflation combined with high unemployment and stagnant demand in a country's economy.
– ORIGIN from *stagnation* and *inflation.*

stag·ger /ˈstagər/ ▶ **verb** **1** walk or move unsteadily, as if about to fall. **2** astonish someone greatly. **3** spread payments, events, etc., over a period of time. **4** arrange objects or parts so that they are not in line.

– SYNONYMS **1 lurch,** reel, sway, teeter, totter, stumble. **2 amaze,** astound, astonish, surprise, stun, confound, daze, take aback; informal flabbergast, knock for a loop.

▸ noun an act of staggering.
– ORIGIN Old Norse.

stag·ing /ˈstājiNG/ ▸ noun **1** a way of staging a play or similar production. **2** a temporary platform for working or standing on.

stag·ing ar·e·a (also **staging point** or **staging post**) ▸ noun a stopping place or assembly point en route to a destination.

stag·nant /ˈstagnənt/ ▸ adjective **1** (of water or air) completely still and often having an unpleasant smell. **2** showing little activity: *a stagnant economy.*

– SYNONYMS **1 still,** motionless, standing, stale, dirty, brackish. **2 inactive,** sluggish, slow-moving, static, flat, depressed, moribund, dead, dormant.
– ANTONYMS flowing.

– ORIGIN from Latin *stagnare* 'form a pool of standing water.'

stag·nate /ˈstagˌnāt/ ▸ verb **1** stop developing; become inactive: *while the economy has stagnated, individual savings have increased.* **2** (of water or air) become still or stagnant.
– DERIVATIVES **stag·na·tion** /stagˈnāSHən/ noun.

stag party ▸ noun an all-male celebration, especially one held for a man about to be married.

stag·y /ˈstājē/ (also **stagey**) ▸ adjective excessively theatrical or exaggerated.
– DERIVATIVES **stag·i·ly** adverb **stag·i·ness** noun.

staid /stād/ ▸ adjective respectable, serious, and unadventurous.

– SYNONYMS **sedate,** respectable, serious, steady, conventional, traditional, unadventurous, set in one's ways, sober, formal, stuffy, stiff; informal starchy, stick-in-the-mud.
– ANTONYMS frivolous.

– ORIGIN former past participle of **STAY**[1].

stain /stān/ ▸ verb **1** mark or discolor something with something that is difficult to remove. **2** damage the reputation of someone or something. **3** color something with a dye or chemical.

– SYNONYMS **1 discolor,** soil, mark, spot, spatter, splatter, smear, splash, smudge, begrime. **2 color,** tint, dye, paint.

▸ noun **1** a discolored patch or dirty mark that is difficult to remove. **2** a thing that damages a person's reputation: *I left the court without a stain on my character.* **3** a dye or chemical used to color materials.

– SYNONYMS **1 mark,** spot, blotch, smudge, smear. **2 blemish,** taint, blot, smear, slur, stigma.

– DERIVATIVES **stain·a·ble** adjective **stain·er** noun.
– ORIGIN from Old French *desteindre* 'tinge with a different color.'

stained glass ▸ noun colored glass used to form pictures or designs, typically used for church windows.

stain·less /ˈstānlis/ ▸ adjective unmarked by or resistant to stains.

stain·less steel ▸ noun a form of steel containing chromium, resistant to tarnishing and rust.

stair /ste(ə)r/ ▸ noun **1** each of a set of fixed steps. **2** (**stairs**) a set of fixed steps leading from one floor of a building to another.
– ORIGIN from a Germanic word meaning 'climb.'

stair·case /ˈste(ə)rˌkās/ (also **stairway**) ▸ noun a set of stairs and its surrounding structure.

stair·climb·er /ˈste(ə)rˌklīmər/ ▸ noun an exercise machine on which the user simulates the action of climbing a staircase.

stair·lift /ˈste(ə)rˌlift/ ▸ noun a lift in the form of a chair that can be raised or lowered at the edge of a staircase.

stair·way /ˈste(ə)rˌwā/ ▸ noun a set of steps or stairs and its surrounding walls or structure.

stair·well /ˈste(ə)rˌwel/ ▸ noun a shaft in which a staircase is built.

stake[1] /stāk/ ▸ noun **1** a strong post with a point at one end, driven into the ground to support a tree, form part of a fence, etc. **2** (**the stake**) historical a wooden post to which a person was tied before being burned alive.

– SYNONYMS **post,** pole, stick, spike, upright, support, cane.

▸ verb **1** support a plant with a stake. **2** (**stake something out**) state one's position or assert one's rights forcefully. **3** (**stake someone/thing out**) informal keep a place or person under secret observation.
– PHRASES **stake a claim** assert one's right to something.
– ORIGIN Old English.

stake[2] ▸ noun **1** a sum of money gambled. **2** a share or interest in a business or situation. **3** (**stakes**) prize money. **4** (**stakes**) a competitive situation: *one step ahead in the fashion stakes.*

– SYNONYMS **1 bet,** wager, ante. **2 share,** interest, investment, involvement, concern.

▸ verb gamble money or something of value.

– SYNONYMS **bet,** wager, lay, put on, gamble, risk.

– PHRASES **at stake 1** at risk. **2** in question.
– ORIGIN perhaps from **STAKE**[1].

stake·hold·er /ˈstākˌhōldər/ ▸ noun a person with an interest or concern in a business or similar venture.
▸ adjective (of an organization or system) in which all those people involved are seen as having an interest in its success: *a stakeholder economy.*
– DERIVATIVES **stake·hold·ing** noun & adjective.

stake-out ▸ noun informal a period of secret observation.

sta·lac·tite /stəˈlakˌtīt/ ▸ noun a tapering structure hanging from the roof of a cave, formed of calcium salts deposited by dripping water.
– ORIGIN from Greek *stalaktos* 'dripping.'

sta·lag·mite /stəˈlagˌmīt/ ▸ noun a tapering column rising from the floor of a cave, formed of calcium salts deposited by dripping water.
– ORIGIN from Greek *stalagma* 'a drop.'

stale /stāl/ ▸ adjective (**staler, stalest**) **1** (of food) no longer fresh or pleasant to eat. **2** no longer new and interesting: *their marriage had gone stale.* **3** (of a person) no longer performing well because of having done something for too long.

– SYNONYMS **1 old,** past its best, off, dry, hard, musty, moldy, rancid. **2 stuffy,** musty, fusty, stagnant. **3 overused,** hackneyed, tired, worn out, overworked, played out, threadbare, banal, clichéd, trite, unimaginative, uninspired, flat; informal old hat.
– ANTONYMS fresh.

▸ verb make or become stale.
– DERIVATIVES **stale·ly** /ˈstā(l)lē/ adverb **stale·ness** noun.
– ORIGIN probably from Old French *estaler* 'to halt.'

stale·mate /ˈstālˌmāt/ ▶ **noun 1** a situation in which further progress by opposing sides seems impossible. **2** Chess a position counting as a draw, in which a player is not in check but can only move into check.

– SYNONYMS **deadlock,** impasse, standoff, gridlock.

▶ **verb** cause a situation to reach stalemate.
– ORIGIN from Old French *estale* 'position' + **MATE²**.

Sta·lin·ism /ˈstäləˌnizəm/ ▶ **noun** the ideology and policies adopted by the Soviet Communist Party leader and head of state Joseph Stalin, based on dictatorial state control and the pursuit of communism.
– DERIVATIVES **Sta·lin·ist** noun & adjective.

stalk¹ /stôk/ ▶ **noun 1** the main stem of a plant. **2** the attachment or support of a leaf, flower, or fruit. **3** a slender support or stem of an object.
– DERIVATIVES **stalk·like** /-ˌlīk/ adjective **stalk·y** adjective.
– ORIGIN probably from an Old English word meaning 'rung of a ladder, long handle.'

stalk² ▶ **verb 1** follow someone or something stealthily. **2** harass someone with unwanted and obsessive attention. **3** stride in a proud, stiff, or angry way. **4** chiefly literary move silently or threateningly through a place: *fear stalks the streets.*

– SYNONYMS **1 trail,** follow, shadow, track, go after, hunt; informal tail. **2 strut,** stride, march, flounce, storm, stomp, sweep.

– DERIVATIVES **stalk·er** noun.
– ORIGIN Old English.

stalk·ing horse ▶ **noun** a person or thing that is used to disguise a person's real intentions.
– ORIGIN first referring to a horse used by a hunter to hide behind until within easy range of wildfowl.

stall /stôl/ ▶ **noun 1** a stand, booth, or compartment for the sale of goods in a market. **2** an individual compartment for an animal in a stable or cowshed. **3** a stable or cowshed. **4** a compartment for one person in a set of toilets or shower cubicles. **5** (also **starting stall**) a compartment in which a horse is held before the start of a race. **6** a seat in the choir or chancel of a church, enclosed at the back and sides.

– SYNONYMS **1 stand,** table, counter, booth, kiosk. **2 pen,** coop, sty, corral, enclosure, compartment.

▶ **verb 1** (of a motor vehicle or its engine) stop running. **2** stop making progress. **3** be vague or indecisive in order to gain time to deal with something: *she was stalling for time.* **4** (of an aircraft) be moving too slowly to allow it to be controlled effectively.

– SYNONYMS **1 delay,** play for time, procrastinate, hedge, drag one's feet, filibuster, stonewall. **2 hold off,** stave off, keep at bay, evade, avoid.

– ORIGIN Old English.

stal·lion /ˈstalyən/ ▶ **noun** an adult male horse that has not been castrated.
– ORIGIN Old French *estalon*.

stal·wart /ˈstôlwərt/ ▶ **adjective 1** loyal, reliable, and hard-working. **2** dated sturdy and strongly built.

– SYNONYMS **staunch,** loyal, faithful, committed, devoted, dedicated, dependable, reliable.
– ANTONYMS disloyal.

▶ **noun** a loyal and reliable supporter or member of an organization.
– ORIGIN from Old English words meaning 'place' and 'worth.'

sta·men /ˈstāmin/ ▶ **noun** the male fertilizing organ of a flower, typically consisting of a pollen-containing anther on a very thin stalk.
– ORIGIN Latin, 'warp in an upright loom, thread.'

stam·i·na /ˈstamənə/ ▶ **noun** the ability to keep up physical or mental effort over a long period.

– SYNONYMS **endurance,** staying power, energy, toughness, determination, tenacity, perseverance, grit.

– ORIGIN from Latin, plural of **STAMEN** in the sense 'threads spun by the Fates.'

stam·mer /ˈstamər/ ▶ **verb** speak or say something with difficulty, repeating the first letters of words and often pausing.

– SYNONYMS **stutter,** stumble over one's words, hesitate, falter, pause, splutter.

▶ **noun** a tendency to stammer.
– DERIVATIVES **stam·mer·er** noun.
– ORIGIN Old English, related to **STUMBLE**.

stamp /stamp/ ▶ **verb 1** bring the foot down heavily on the ground or an object. **2** walk with heavy, forceful steps. **3** press a device against something in order to leave a mark or pattern. **4** (**stamp something out**) put an end to something by taking decisive action. **5** (**stamp something on**) fix something in the mind: *the date was stamped on his memory.* **6** stick a postage stamp on a letter or parcel.

– SYNONYMS **1 trample,** step, tread, tramp, stomp, stump, clump, crush, squash, flatten. **2 imprint,** print, impress, punch, inscribe, emboss. **3** (**stamp something out**) **put an end to,** end, stop, crush, put down, curb, quell, suppress, extinguish, stifle, abolish, get rid of, eliminate, eradicate, destroy, wipe out.

▶ **noun 1** a small piece of paper that is stuck to a letter or parcel to show that postage has been paid. **2** an instrument for stamping a pattern or mark. **3** a mark or pattern made by a stamp. **4** a distinctive impression or quality: *the whole project has the stamp of authority.* **5** a particular class or type: *he went around with men of his own stamp.* **6** an act of stamping the foot.

– SYNONYMS **mark,** hallmark, sign, seal, sure sign, smack, savor, air.

– DERIVATIVES **stamp·er** noun.
– ORIGIN Germanic.

stamp duty ▶ **noun** a duty that must be paid in order for certain documents to be legally recognized.

stam·pede /stamˈpēd/ ▶ **noun 1** a sudden panicked or excited rush of a group of people or animals. **2** a situation in which a large number of people are trying to respond to something at once: *he tried in vain to stem the stampede toward modernism.*

– SYNONYMS **charge,** panic, rush, flight, rout.

▶ **verb 1** (of animals or people) rush in a sudden mass panic. **2** rush someone into doing something: *she claimed to have been stampeded into making wrong decisions.*

– SYNONYMS **bolt,** charge, flee, take flight, race, rush, career, run.

– DERIVATIVES **stam·ped·er** noun.
– ORIGIN Spanish *estampida* 'crash, uproar.'

stamp·ing ground ▶ **noun** chiefly British term for **STOMPING GROUND**.

stance /stans/ ▶ **noun 1** the way in which someone stands. **2** an attitude toward something; a standpoint.

– SYNONYMS **1 posture,** body position, pose, attitude. **2 attitude,** opinion, standpoint, position, approach, policy, line.

– ORIGIN French.

stanch /stônCH, stänCH/ (Brit. also **staunch**) ▸ **verb** stop or restrict the flow of something, especially blood from a wound.

– SYNONYMS **stem,** stop, halt, check, curb; Brit. staunch.

stan·chion /ˈstanCHən/ ▸ **noun** an upright bar, post, or frame forming a support or barrier.

– ORIGIN Old French *stanchon*.

stand /stand/ ▸ **verb** (past and past part. **stood** /sto͝od/) **1** be in or rise to an upright position, supported by the feet. **2** place or be situated in a particular position. **3** remain valid. **4** withstand an experience without being damaged. **5** tolerate or like. **6** move in a standing position to a specified place: *I stood aside to let him enter*. **7** be in a particular state or condition: *since grandad's death the house had stood empty*. **8** remain motionless or unchanged. **9** be likely to do something: *investors stood to lose heavily*. **10** adopt a particular attitude toward an issue. **11** take a particular role: *he stood security for the government's borrowings*.

– SYNONYMS **1 rise,** get to one's feet, get up, pick one's up. **2** *today a house stands on the site* **be situated,** be located, be positioned, be sited. **3** *he stood the book on the shelf* **put,** set, erect, place, position, prop, install, arrange; informal park. **4** *my decision stands* **remain in force,** remain in operation, hold, hold good, apply, be the case, exist, prevail. **5** *her heart could not stand the strain* **withstand,** endure, bear, put up with, take, cope with, handle, sustain, resist, stand up to. **6** *I can't stand arrogance* **put up with,** endure, tolerate, accept, take, abide, stand for, support, countenance; formal brook.
– ANTONYMS sit, lie down.

▸ **noun 1** an attitude toward a particular issue: *the party's tough stand in immigration*. **2** a determined effort to hold one's ground or resist something. **3** a rack, base, or item of furniture for holding or displaying something. **4** a small stall from which goods are sold or displayed. **5** a large structure for spectators to sit or stand in at different levels. **6** a raised platform for a band, orchestra, or speaker. **7** (**the stand**) a witness box in a court of law. **8** a stopping of movement or progress. **9** a place where vehicles wait for passengers. **10** a group of trees of the same kind.

– SYNONYMS **1 attitude,** stance, opinion, standpoint, position, approach, policy, line. **2 opposition,** resistance. **3 base,** support, platform, stage, dais, rest, plinth, tripod, rack, trivet. **4 stall,** counter, booth, kiosk.

– PHRASES **stand by 1** watch something bad without becoming involved. **2** support someone or keep a promise. **3** be ready to take action if required. **stand down 1** (also **stand aside**) resign from or leave a job or office. **2** relax after a state of readiness. **stand for 1** be an abbreviation of or symbol for. **2** put up with; tolerate. **stand in** take someone's place; deputize. **stand on** be very concerned to follow correct behavior: *one doesn't stand on rights when driving in Japan*. **stand on one's own (two) feet** be or become independent. **stand out 1** project or be easily noticeable. **2** be clearly better. **stand to** Military stand ready for an attack. **stand trial** be tried in a court of law. **stand someone up** informal fail to keep a date with someone. **stand up for** speak or act in support of. **stand up to 1** resist someone in a spirited way. **2** resist the harmful effects of.

– ORIGIN Old English.

stand·a·lone /ˈstandəˌlōn/ ▸ **adjective** (of computer hardware or software) able to operate independently of other hardware or software.

stand·ard /ˈstandərd/ ▸ **noun 1** a level of quality or achievement: *the restaurant offers a high standard of service*. **2** a required or accepted level of quality or achievement. **3** something used as a measure in order to make comparisons. **4** (**standards**) principles of morally acceptable behavior. **5** a military or ceremonial flag. **6** a popular tune or song that has become well established. **7** (usu. before another noun) a shrub grafted on an upright stem and trained to grow in the shape of a tree: *a standard rose*.

– SYNONYMS **1 quality,** level, caliber, merit, excellence. **2 guideline,** norm, yardstick, benchmark, gauge, measure, criterion, guide, touchstone, model, pattern. **3 principle,** ideal; (**standards**) morals, code of behavior, ethics. **4 flag,** banner, ensign, color(s).

▸ **adjective 1** used or accepted as normal or average. **2** (of a size, measure, etc.) regularly used or produced. **3** (of a work, writer, etc.) viewed as authoritative and so widely read.

– SYNONYMS **1 normal,** usual, average, typical, stock, common, ordinary, customary, conventional, established. **2 definitive,** classic, recognized, accepted, approved, authoritative.
– ANTONYMS unusual, special.

– DERIVATIVES **stand·ard·ly** adverb.

– ORIGIN Old French *estendart*.

WORD TOOLKIT

See **TYPICAL**.

stand·ard-bear·er ▸ **noun 1** a leading figure in a cause or movement. **2** a soldier carrying the flag of a unit, regiment, or army.

stand·ard·ize /ˈstandərˌdīz/ ▸ **verb** make things of the same type have the same features or qualities.

– DERIVATIVES **stand·ard·i·za·tion** /ˌstandərdiˈzāSHən/ noun.

stand·ard of liv·ing ▸ **noun** the amount of money and level of comfort available to a person or community.

stand·ard time ▸ **noun** a uniform time for places in approximately the same longitude.

stand·by /ˈstan(d)ˌbī/ ▸ **noun** (pl. **standbys**) **1** readiness for duty or immediate action. **2** a person or thing ready to be used in an emergency. ▸ **adjective** (of tickets for a journey or performance) sold only at the last minute if still available.

stand·ee /stanˈdē/ ▸ **noun** a person who is standing rather than seated.

stand-in ▸ **noun** a person who stands in or deputizes for another.

stand·ing /ˈstandiNG/ ▸ **noun 1** the position, status, or reputation of someone or something. **2** the length of time that something has existed: *a problem of long standing*.

– SYNONYMS **1 status,** ranking, position, reputation, stature. **2 prestige,** rank, eminence, seniority, repute, stature, esteem, importance, account.

▸ **adjective 1** remaining in force or use: *a standing*

invitation. **2** (of a jump or start of a race) performed from rest or an upright position. **3** (of water) stagnant or still.
– PHRASES **leave someone/thing standing** informal be much better or faster than someone or something.

stand·ing joke ▶ **noun** something that regularly causes amusement.

stand·ing or·der ▶ **noun 1** an order placed on a regular basis with a retailer. **2** an order or ruling that governs the procedures of a society, council, etc. **3** a military order or ruling that is retained even under changing circumstances.

stand·ing o·va·tion ▶ **noun** a period of prolonged applause during which the audience rise to their feet.

stand·ing stone ▶ **noun** another term for **MENHIR**.

stand·off /ˈstand,ôf, -,äf/ ▶ **noun** a situation in a dispute in which no agreement can be reached.

stand·off·ish /,standˈôfish, -ˈäfish/ ▶ **adjective** informal cold and unfriendly.

stand·out /ˈstand,out/ ▶ **noun** informal an outstanding person or thing.

stand·pipe /ˈstan(d),pīp/ ▶ **noun** a vertical pipe extending from a water supply, connecting a temporary tap to the mains.

stand·point /ˈstan(d),point/ ▶ **noun 1** an attitude toward a particular issue. **2** the position from which a person can view a scene or an object.

stand·still /ˈstan(d),stil/ ▶ **noun** a situation without movement or activity.

stand-up ▶ **adjective 1** (of comedy or a comedian) performed or performing by telling jokes to an audience. **2** brave and fiercely loyal: *a stand-up guy.* **3** designed to stay upright or erect: *a stand-up collar.* **4** involving or used by people standing up.

stank /stangk/ past of **STINK**.

stan·za /ˈstanzə/ ▶ **noun** a group of lines forming the basic recurring unit in a poem; a verse.
– ORIGIN Italian, 'standing place, stanza.'

staph·y·lo·coc·cus /,staf(ə)lōˈkäkəs/ ▶ **noun** (pl. **staphylococci** /-ˈkäk,sī, -,sē/) a bacterium of a group including many kinds that cause pus to be formed.
– ORIGIN from Greek *staphulē* 'bunch of grapes' + *kokkos* 'berry.'

sta·ple[1] /ˈstāpəl/ ▶ **noun 1** a small U-shaped piece of wire used to fasten papers together. **2** a small U-shaped metal bar with pointed ends, driven into wood to hold things such as wires in place. ▶ **verb** secure something with a staple or staples.
– ORIGIN Old English, 'pillar.'

staple[2] ▶ **noun 1** a main item of trade or production. **2** a main or important element of something. **3** the fiber of cotton or wool considered in terms of its length and fineness. ▶ **adjective** main or important: *a staple food.*

– SYNONYMS **main,** principal, chief, major, primary, leading, foremost, first, most important, predominant, dominant, basic, prime; informal number-one.

– ORIGIN from German or Dutch *stapel* 'pillar, emporium.'

sta·pler /ˈstāp(ə)lər/ ▶ **noun** a device for fastening papers together with staples.

star /stär/ ▶ **noun 1** a huge mass of burning gas that is visible as a glowing point in the night sky. **2** a shape with five or six points representing a star, often used to indicate a category of excellence. **3** a famous or talented entertainer or athlete: *a pop star.* **4** an outstanding person or thing in a group: *a rising star in the party* | (as adjective) *Ellen was a star student.* **5** Astrology a planet, constellation, etc., considered to influence one's fortunes or personality: *his destiny was written in the stars.*

– SYNONYMS **1 heavenly body,** celestial body. **2 principal,** leading lady/man, lead, hero, heroine. **3 celebrity,** superstar, famous name, household name, leading light, VIP, personality, luminary; informal celeb, big shot, megastar. **4** (as adj.) *a star pupil* **brilliant,** talented, gifted, able, exceptional, outstanding, bright, clever, masterly, consummate, precocious, prodigious. **5** (as adj.) *the star attraction* **top,** leading, greatest, foremost, major, preeminent.

▶ **verb** (**stars, starring, starred**) **1** (of a movie, play, etc.) have someone as a leading performer. **2** (of a performer) have a leading role in a movie, play, etc. **3** mark, decorate, or cover something with star-shaped marks or objects.
– PHRASES **see stars** seem to see flashes of light as a result of a blow on the head.
– ORIGIN Old English.

WORD LINKS

astral, **stellar** *relating to stars*
astronomy *study of stars*

star an·ise ▶ **noun** a small star-shaped fruit with an anise flavor, used in Asian cooking.

star·board /ˈstär,bôrd/ ▶ **noun** the side of a ship or aircraft on the right when one is facing forward. The opposite of **PORT**[3].
– ORIGIN Old English, 'rudder side,' because early sailing vessels were steered with a paddle on the right side.

star·burst /ˈstär,bərst/ ▶ **noun 1** a pattern of lines or rays radiating from a central point. **2** a period of intense activity in a galaxy involving the formation of stars.

starch /stärch/ ▶ **noun 1** a carbohydrate that is obtained chiefly from cereals and potatoes and is an important constituent of the human diet. **2** powder or spray made from starch, used to stiffen fabric. ▶ **verb** stiffen fabric with starch.
– ORIGIN from Old English, 'stiffened.'

starch·y /ˈstärchē/ ▶ **adjective** (**starchier, starchiest**) **1** (of food) containing a lot of starch. **2** informal (of a person) stiff and formal in manner or behavior.
– DERIVATIVES **starch·i·ly** adverb **starch·i·ness** noun.

star-crossed ▶ **adjective** literary fated to be unlucky.

star·dom /ˈstärdəm/ ▶ **noun** the state or status of being a famous or talented entertainer or athlete.

stare /ste(ə)r/ ▶ **verb 1** look fixedly at someone or something with the eyes wide open. **2** (**stare someone out**) look fixedly at someone until they feel forced to look away.

– SYNONYMS **gaze,** gape, goggle, glare, ogle, peer; informal gawk.

▶ **noun** an act of staring.
– DERIVATIVES **star·er** noun.
– PHRASES **be staring someone in the face** be obvious.
– ORIGIN Old English.

star·fish /ˈstärˌfisʜ/ ▶ **noun** (pl. same or **starfishes**) a sea creature having a flattened body with five or more arms.

star·fruit /ˈstärˌfro͞ot/ ▶ **noun** another term for CARAMBOLA.

star·gaz·er /ˈstärˌgāzər/ ▶ **noun** informal an astronomer or astrologer.

stark /stärk/ ▶ **adjective 1** severe or bare in appearance. **2** unpleasantly or sharply clear. **3** complete; sheer: *stark terror*.

– SYNONYMS **1 sharp,** sharply defined, crisp, distinct, clear, clear-cut. **2 desolate,** bare, barren, empty, bleak, dreary, depressing, grim.
– ANTONYMS indistinct, ornate.

– DERIVATIVES **stark·ly** adverb **stark·ness** noun.
– PHRASES **stark naked** completely naked. **stark raving mad** informal completely mad.
– ORIGIN Old English, 'unyielding, severe.'

stark·ers /ˈstärkərz/ ▶ **adjective** Brit. informal completely naked.

star·let /ˈstärlit/ ▶ **noun** informal a promising young actress or performer.

star·light /ˈstärˌlīt/ ▶ **noun** light coming from the stars.
– DERIVATIVES **star·lit** /ˈstärˌlit/ adjective.

star·ling /ˈstärlɪɴɢ/ ▶ **noun** a songbird with dark shiny plumage.
– ORIGIN Old English.

Star of Da·vid /ˈdāvid/ ▶ **noun** a six-pointed figure consisting of two interlaced equilateral triangles, used as a Jewish and Israeli symbol.

star route ▶ **noun** a postal delivery route served by a private contractor.

star·ry /ˈstärē/ ▶ **adjective** (**starrier, starriest**) **1** full of or lit by stars. **2** informal relating to stars in entertainment.

star·ry-eyed ▶ **adjective** full of unrealistic hopes and dreams about someone or something.

Stars and Bars ▶ **plural noun** (treated as sing.) historical the flag of the Confederate States of America.

Stars and Stripes ▶ **plural noun** (treated as sing.) the national flag of the US.

star·ship /ˈstärˌsʜip/ ▶ **noun** (in science fiction) a large manned spaceship for travel between the stars.

star sign ▶ **noun** a sign of the zodiac.

star-span·gled ▶ **adjective** informal impressively successful.

star·struck ▶ **adjective** fascinated and very impressed by famous people.

star-stud·ded ▶ **adjective** featuring a number of famous people.

START /stärt/ ▶ **abbreviation** Strategic Arms Reduction Talks.

start /stärt/ ▶ **verb 1** begin to do, be, happen, or engage in: *she started talking to him*. **2** begin to operate or work. **3** make something happen or operate. **4** begin to move or travel. **5** jump or jerk from surprise.

– SYNONYMS **1 begin,** commence, get under way, get going, go ahead, make a start; informal kick off, get the ball rolling, get the show on the road. **2 come into being,** begin, arise, originate, develop. **3 establish,** set up, found, create, bring into being, institute, initiate, inaugurate, introduce, open, launch. **4 activate,** switch/turn on, start up, fire up, boot up. **5 flinch,** jerk, jump, twitch, wince.
– ANTONYMS end, finish, stop.

▶ **noun 1** the point at which something begins. **2** an act of beginning. **3** an advantage consisting in having set out in a race or on a journey before one's rivals or opponents. **4** a sudden movement of surprise.

– SYNONYMS **1 beginning,** commencement, inception, onset, inauguration, dawn, birth, emergence; informal kickoff. **2 lead,** head start, advantage. **3 jerk,** twitch, spasm, jump.
– ANTONYMS end.

– PHRASES **for a start** in the first place. **start at** cost at least a specified amount. **start out** (or **up**) begin a venture or undertaking. **to start with** as the first thing to be taken into account.
– ORIGIN Old English, 'to caper, leap.'

start·er /ˈstärtər/ ▶ **noun 1** a person or thing that starts. **2** chiefly Brit. the first course of a meal. **3** an automatic device for starting a machine. **4** a competitor taking part in a race or game at the start. **5** a topic or question with which to start a discussion or course of study.
– PHRASES **for starters** informal first of all. **under starter's orders** waiting for the signal to start a race.

start·er home ▶ **noun** a small house or apartment designed for people buying their first home.

start·ing block ▶ **noun** a block against which runners brace their feet at the start of a race.

start·ing gate ▶ **noun** a barrier raised at the start of a horse race to ensure that all the competitors start at the same time.

start·ing price ▶ **noun** the final odds at the start of a horse race.

star·tle /ˈstärtl/ ▶ **verb** make someone feel sudden shock or alarm.

– SYNONYMS **surprise,** frighten, scare, alarm, shock, give someone a fright, make someone jump.

– DERIVATIVES **star·tled** adjective.
– ORIGIN Old English, 'kick, struggle.'

star·tling /ˈstärtl-ɪɴɢ/ ▶ **adjective** very surprising or remarkable.

– SYNONYMS **surprising,** astonishing, amazing, unexpected, unforeseen, shocking, stunning; frightening, alarming, scary.
– ANTONYMS predictable, ordinary.

– DERIVATIVES **star·tling·ly** adverb.

start·up ▶ **noun 1** the action of starting something. **2** a newly established business.

starve /stärv/ ▶ **verb 1** suffer or die from hunger. **2** make someone starve by preventing them from eating. **3** (**be starving** or **starved**) informal feel very hungry. **4** (**be starved of**) be deprived of: *the arts are being starved of funds*.

– SYNONYMS (as adj. **starving**) *the world's starving children* **hungry,** undernourished, malnourished, starved; famished, ravenous.
– ANTONYMS full.

– DERIVATIVES **star·va·tion** /-ˈvāsʜən/ noun.
– ORIGIN Old English, 'to die.'

stash /stasʜ/ informal ▶ **verb** store something safely in a secret place.

– SYNONYMS **store,** stow, pack, load, cache, hide, conceal, secrete, hoard, save, stockpile.

▶ **noun** a secret store of something.

– SYNONYMS **cache,** hoard, stock, stockpile, store, supply, reserve.

– ORIGIN unknown.

sta·sis /ˈstāsis, ˈsta-/ ▶ **noun 1** formal or technical a period or state when there is no change or development. **2** Medicine a stopping of the normal flow of a body fluid.
– ORIGIN Greek, 'standing, stoppage.'

state /stāt/ ▶ **noun 1** the condition of someone or something at a particular time. **2** a nation or territory considered as an organized political community under one government. **3** a community or area forming part of a federal republic. **4** (**the States**) the United States of America. **5** the government of a country. **6** the grand ceremonial procedures associated with monarchy or government: *he was buried in state*. **7** (**a state**) informal an agitated, untidy, or dirty condition.

– SYNONYMS **1 condition,** shape, position, situation, circumstances, state of affairs, predicament, plight. **2 country,** nation, land, kingdom, realm, power, republic. **3 government,** administration, parliament, regime. **4 state of anxiety,** panic, fluster; informal flap, tizzy.

▶ **verb** express something definitely or clearly in speech or writing.

– SYNONYMS **express,** voice, utter, put into words, declare, announce, make known, put across/over, communicate, air.

– DERIVATIVES **state·hood** /ˈstātˌho͝od/ noun.
– PHRASES **state of affairs** a situation. **state-of-the-art** using the newest ideas and most up-to-date features. **state of emergency** a situation of national danger or disaster in which a government suspends normal constitutional procedures. **state of grace** a state of being free from sin.
– ORIGIN partly a shortening of **ESTATE**, partly from Latin *status* 'standing.'

state·craft /ˈstātˌkraft/ ▶ **noun** the skillful management of state affairs.

State De·part·ment ▶ **noun** the department of foreign affairs.

state house (also **statehouse**) ▶ **noun** the building where a state legislature meets.

state·less /ˈstātlis/ ▶ **adjective** not recognized as a citizen of any country.

state·ly /ˈstātlē/ ▶ **adjective** (**statelier, stateliest**) dignified, grand, or impressive.

– SYNONYMS **dignified,** majestic, ceremonious, courtly, imposing, solemn, regal, grand.
– ANTONYMS undignified.

– DERIVATIVES **state·li·ness** noun.

state·ment /ˈstātmənt/ ▶ **noun 1** a definite or clear expression of something in speech or writing. **2** a formal account of facts or events, especially one given to the police or in court. **3** a document setting out items of debit and credit between a bank or other organization and a customer.

– SYNONYMS **declaration,** expression, assertion, affirmation, announcement, utterance, communication, bulletin, communiqué.

state·room /ˈstātˌro͞om, -ˌro͝om/ ▶ **noun 1** a large room in a palace or public building, for use on formal occasions. **2** a private room on a ship.

state school ▶ **noun** another term for **STATE UNIVERSITY**.

state's ev·i·dence ▶ **noun** Law evidence for the prosecution given by a participant in or accomplice to the crime being tried.

state·side /ˈstātˌsīd/ ▶ **adjective & adverb** informal relating to, in, or toward the US.

states·man /ˈstātsmən/ (or **stateswoman** /ˈstātsˌwo͝omən/) ▶ **noun** (pl. **statesmen** or **stateswomen**) an experienced and respected political leader.
– DERIVATIVES **states·man·like** /-ˌlīk/ adjective **states·man·ship** /-ˌsʜip/ noun.

states' rights ▶ **plural noun** the rights and powers held by individual US states rather than by the federal government.

state u·ni·ver·si·ty ▶ **noun** a university managed by the authorities of a particular US state.

state·wide /ˈstātˈwīd/ ▶ **adjective & adverb** extending throughout a particular US state.

stat·ic /ˈstatik/ ▶ **adjective 1** not moving, changing, or active: *they believed in a static social order*. **2** Physics concerned with bodies at rest or forces in equilibrium. Often contrasted with **DYNAMIC**. **3** (of an electric charge) acquired by objects that cannot conduct a current.

– SYNONYMS **1 unchanged,** fixed, stable, steady, unchanging, unvarying, constant. **2 stationary,** motionless, immobile, unmoving, still, at a standstill.
– ANTONYMS variable, dynamic.

▶ **noun 1** static electricity. **2** crackling or hissing on a telephone, radio, etc.
– DERIVATIVES **stat·i·cal·ly** /-ik(ə)lē/ adverb.
– ORIGIN Greek *statikos* 'causing to stand.'

stat·ice /ˈstatisē, ˈstatis/ ▶ **noun** a plant with small pink or lilac funnel-shaped flowers, growing mainly in coastal areas.
– ORIGIN Latin.

stat·ic e·lec·tric·i·ty ▶ **noun** stationary electric charge produced by friction, causing sparks or crackling or the attraction of dust or hair.

stat·ics /ˈstatiks/ ▶ **plural noun** (usu. treated as sing.) the branch of mechanics concerned with bodies at rest and forces in equilibrium.

stat·in /ˈstatn/ ▶ **noun** any of a group of drugs that act to reduce levels of cholesterol in the blood.

sta·tion /ˈstāsʜən/ ▶ **noun 1** a place where passenger trains stop on a railroad line, typically with platforms and buildings. **2** a place where a particular activity or service is based: *a radar station*. **3** a broadcasting company. **4** the place where someone or something stands or is placed for a particular purpose or duty. **5** a person's social rank or position. **6** Austral./NZ a large sheep or cattle farm.

– SYNONYMS **1 establishment,** base, camp, post, depot, mission, site, facility, installation. **2 office,** depot, base, headquarters. **3 channel,** wavelength.

▶ **verb** put in or send to a particular place: *troops were stationed in the town*.

– SYNONYMS **base,** post, establish, deploy, garrison.

– ORIGIN Latin.

sta·tion·ar·y /ˈstāsʜəˌnerē/ ▶ **adjective 1** not moving. **2** not changing in quantity or condition.

– SYNONYMS **static,** parked, motionless, immobile, still, stock-still, at a standstill, at rest.
– ANTONYMS moving.

USAGE

Do not confuse **stationary** and **stationery**: **stationary** is an adjective meaning 'not moving or changing' (*the truck crashed into a stationary car*), while **stationery** is a noun meaning 'paper and other writing materials.'

sta·tion break ▸ **noun** a pause between broadcast programs for an announcement of the identity of the station transmitting them.

sta·tion·er /ˈstāsh(ə)nər/ ▸ **noun** a person who sells stationery.
– ORIGIN Latin *stationarius* 'tradesman at a fixed location.'

sta·tion·er·y /ˈstāshəˌnerē/ ▸ **noun** paper and other materials needed for writing.

sta·tion·mas·ter /ˈstāshənˌmastər/ ▸ **noun** a person in charge of a railroad station.

Sta·tion of the Cross ▸ **noun** each of a series of fourteen pictures representing incidents during Jesus's progress from Pilate's house to his entombment.

sta·tion wag·on ▸ **noun** a car that has a large carrying area behind the seats and an extra door at the rear.

stat·ism /ˈstātˌizəm/ ▸ **noun** a political system in which the government has a great deal of central control over social and economic affairs.
– DERIVATIVES **stat·ist** noun & adjective.

sta·tis·tic /stəˈtistik/ ▸ **noun** a fact or piece of data obtained from a study of a large quantity of numerical information.
– ORIGIN German *Statistik*.

sta·tis·ti·cal /stəˈtistikəl/ ▸ **adjective** relating to statistics.
– DERIVATIVES **sta·tis·ti·cal·ly** adverb.

sta·tis·tics /stəˈtistiks/ ▸ **plural noun** (treated as sing.) the collection and analysis of large quantities of numerical information.
– DERIVATIVES **stat·is·ti·cian** /ˌstatiˈstishən/ noun.

stats /stats/ ▸ **plural noun** informal statistics.

stat·u·ar·y /ˈstachoo͞ˌerē/ ▸ **noun** statues considered as a group.

stat·ue /ˈstachoo͞/ ▸ **noun** a carved or cast figure of a person or animal, especially one that is life-size or larger.
– ORIGIN Latin *statua*.

stat·u·esque /ˌstachoo͞ˈesk/ ▸ **adjective** (of a woman) attractively tall, graceful, and dignified.

stat·u·ette /ˌstachoo͞ˈet/ ▸ **noun** a small statue.

stat·ure /ˈstachər/ ▸ **noun 1** a person's natural height when standing. **2** the importance or reputation gained by a person as a result of their ability or achievements: *an architect of international stature*.

– SYNONYMS **1 height,** size, build. **2 reputation,** repute, standing, status, position, prestige, distinction, eminence, prominence, importance.

– ORIGIN Latin *statura*.

sta·tus /ˈstātəs, ˈstatəs/ ▸ **noun 1** a person's social or professional standing in relation to other people. **2** high rank or social standing. **3** the situation at a particular time during a process. **4** the official classification given to someone or something.

– SYNONYMS **1 standing,** rank, position, level, place. **2 prestige,** kudos, cachet, standing, stature, esteem, image, importance, authority, fame.

– ORIGIN Latin, 'standing.'

sta·tus quo /ˈstātəs ˈkwō, ˈstatəs/ ▸ **noun** the existing situation.
– ORIGIN Latin, 'the state in which.'

sta·tus sym·bol ▸ **noun** a possession seen as an indication of a person's wealth or high social or professional status.

stat·ute /ˈstachoo͞t/ ▸ **noun 1** a written law passed by a parliament or other legislative assembly. **2** a rule of an organization or institution.

– SYNONYMS **law,** regulation, act, bill, decree, edict, rule, ruling, resolution, dictum, command, order, directive, bylaw; formal ordinance.

– ORIGIN Latin *statutum* 'thing set up.'

stat·ute book ▸ **noun** (**the statute book**) the whole of a nation's laws.

stat·ute law ▸ **noun** all the written laws of a legislature, country, etc., considered as a group.

stat·ute of lim·i·ta·tions ▸ **noun** a law that limits the period in which certain kinds of actions can be brought.

stat·u·to·ry /ˈstachəˌtôrē/ ▸ **adjective 1** required, permitted, or enacted by law. **2** having come to be required or expected as a result of being done regularly: *the statutory Christmas phone call to his mother*.
– DERIVATIVES **stat·u·to·ri·ly** /-ˌtôrəlē/ adverb.

stat·u·to·ry rape ▸ **noun** Law sexual intercourse with a minor.

staunch[1] /stônch, stänch/ ▸ **adjective** very loyal and committed.

– SYNONYMS **stalwart,** loyal, faithful, committed, devoted, dedicated, reliable.
– ANTONYMS disloyal, unfaithful.

– DERIVATIVES **staunch·ly** adverb.
– ORIGIN Old French *estanche* 'watertight.'

WORD TOOLKIT

staunch ...	resolute ...	determined ...
supporter	refusal	effort
support	determination	resistance
opposition	declaration	attempt
Republican	conviction	stride

staunch[2] ▸ **verb** British variant spelling of STANCH.
– ORIGIN Old French *estanchier*.

stave /stāv/ ▸ **noun 1** any of the lengths of wood fixed side by side to make a barrel, bucket, etc. **2** a strong stick, post, or pole. **3** (also **staff**) Music a set of five parallel lines on or between any of which a note is written to indicate its pitch. **4** a verse or stanza of a poem. ▸ **verb 1** (past and past part. **staved** or **stove** /stōv/) (**stave something in**) break something by forcing it inward or piercing it roughly. **2** (past and past part. **staved**) (**stave something off**) prevent or delay something undesirable: *emergency measures were introduced to stave off a crisis*.
– ORIGIN from *staves*, former plural of STAFF.

stay[1] /stā/ ▸ **verb 1** remain in the same place. **2** remain in a particular state or position: *inflation will stay down*. **3** live somewhere temporarily as a visitor or guest.

4 stop, delay, or prevent something.

– SYNONYMS 1 *he stayed where he was* **remain (behind),** wait, linger, stick, be left, hold on, hang on; informal hang around; old use tarry. 2 *they won't stay hidden* **continue (to be),** remain, keep, carry on being. 3 *our aunt is staying with us* **visit,** stop (off/over), vacation, lodge.
– ANTONYMS leave.

▶ **noun 1** a period of staying somewhere. **2** a suspension or postponement of judicial or legal proceedings: *a stay of execution*. **3** (**stays**) historical a corset made of two pieces laced together and stiffened by strips of whalebone.

– SYNONYMS **visit,** stop, stopover, break, vacation; literary sojourn.

– DERIVATIVES **stay·er** noun.
– PHRASES **stay the course** (or **distance**) **1** keep going to the end of a race or contest. **2** continue with a difficult task or activity to the end. **stay on** continue to study, work, or be somewhere after others have left. **stay over** stay for the night as a visitor or guest. **stay put** remain somewhere without moving.
– ORIGIN Old French *ester*.

stay[2] ▶ **noun 1** a large rope, wire, or rod used to support a ship's mast or other upright pole. **2** a supporting wire or cable on an aircraft.
– ORIGIN Old English.

stay·ing pow·er ▶ **noun** endurance or stamina.

stay·sail /ˈstāsəl, -ˌsāl/ ▶ **noun** a triangular sail fastened on a stay.

stead /sted/ ▶ **noun** (in phrase **in someone's/something's stead**) instead of someone or something: *she was appointed in his stead*.
– PHRASES **stand someone in good stead** be useful to someone over time or in the future.
– ORIGIN Old English.

stead·fast /ˈstedˌfast/ ▶ **adjective** completely unwavering in one's attitudes or aims.
– DERIVATIVES **stead·fast·ly** adverb **stead·fast·ness** noun.
– ORIGIN Old English, 'standing firm.'

stead·y /ˈstedē/ ▶ **adjective** (**steadier, steadiest**) **1** firmly fixed, supported, or balanced. **2** not faltering or wavering: *a steady gaze*. **3** sensible and reliable. **4** regular, even, and continuous in development, frequency, or strength: *a steady decline in the national birth rate*.

– SYNONYMS **1 stable,** firm, fixed, secure. **2 still,** motionless, static, stationary, unmoving. **3** *a steady gaze* **fixed,** intent, unwavering, unfaltering. **4** *steady breathing* **constant,** consistent, regular, even, rhythmic. **5 continuous,** continual, unceasing, ceaseless, perpetual, unremitting, endless. **6 regular,** settled, firm, committed, long-term.
– ANTONYMS unstable, shaky, fluctuating.

▶ **verb** (**steadies, steadying, steadied**) make or become steady.

– SYNONYMS **1 stabilize,** hold steady, brace, support, balance, rest. **2 calm,** soothe, quiet, compose, settle, subdue, quell.

▶ **exclamation** (also **steady on!**) a warning to keep calm or take care.
– DERIVATIVES **stead·i·ly** adverb **stead·i·ness** noun.
– PHRASES **go steady** informal have a regular romantic or sexual relationship with someone.
– ORIGIN from STEAD.

steak /stāk/ ▶ **noun 1** high-quality beef from the hindquarters of the animal, cut into thick slices for broiling or frying. **2** a thick slice of other meat or fish. **3** poorer-quality beef for braising or stewing.
– ORIGIN Old Norse.

steak·house /ˈstākˌhous/ ▶ **noun** a restaurant that specializes in serving steaks.

steak tar·tare /tä(r)ˈtär/ ▶ **noun** a dish consisting of raw ground steak mixed with raw egg.

steal /stēl/ ▶ **verb** (past **stole** /stōl/; past part. **stolen** /ˈstōlən/) **1** take something without permission or legal right and without intending to return it. **2** move somewhere quietly or surreptitiously.

– SYNONYMS **1 take,** thieve, help oneself to, pilfer, embezzle; informal swipe, lift, heist, filch. **2 plagiarize,** copy, pirate; informal rip off, lift, crib. **3 creep,** sneak, steal away, slink, slip, glide, tiptoe, slope.

▶ **noun** informal a bargain.
– DERIVATIVES **steal·er** noun.
– PHRASES **steal a look** (or **glance**) take a quick and surreptitious look at someone or something. **steal a march on** gain an advantage over someone by acting before they do. **steal the show** attract the most attention and praise. **steal someone's thunder** win the praise or attention expected by someone else by acting or speaking before them.
– ORIGIN Old English.

WORD LINKS

kleptomania *compulsion to steal*

stealth /stelTH/ ▶ **noun** cautious and surreptitious action or movement.

– SYNONYMS **furtiveness,** secretiveness, secrecy, surreptitiousness.

▶ **adjective** (of aircraft) designed to be difficult to detect by radar or sonar: *a stealth bomber*.
– ORIGIN first in the sense 'theft': probably related to STEAL.

stealth tax ▶ **noun** a tax charged in such a way that it is not noticed as a tax.

stealth·y /ˈstelTHē/ ▶ **adjective** (**stealthier, stealthiest**) cautious and surreptitious.

– SYNONYMS **furtive,** secretive, secret, surreptitious, sneaky, sly.
– ANTONYMS open.

– DERIVATIVES **stealth·i·ly** adverb **stealth·i·ness** noun.

steam /stēm/ ▶ **noun 1** the hot vapor into which water is converted when heated, which condenses in the air into a mist of minute water droplets. **2** power for machines produced by steam under pressure. **3** energy or force of movement; momentum: *the dispute gathered steam*.
▶ **verb 1** give off or produce steam. **2** (**steam up**) mist over with steam. **3** cook food by heating it in steam from boiling water. **4** clean or treat something with steam. **5** (of a ship or train) travel somewhere under steam power. **6** informal move somewhere rapidly or forcefully. **7** (**be/get steamed up**) informal be or become very agitated or angry.
– PHRASES **get up** (or **pick up**) **steam 1** generate enough pressure to drive a steam engine. **2** (of an activity, project, etc.) gradually gain momentum. **let off steam** informal get rid of pent-up energy or strong emotion. **run out of steam** informal lose momentum or enthusiasm. **under one's own steam** without help from other people.
– ORIGIN Old English.

steam bath ▶ noun a room filled with hot steam for cleaning and refreshing the body.

steam·boat /ˈstēmˌbōt/ ▶ noun a boat propelled by a steam engine, especially a paddle-wheel craft of a type used on rivers in the 19th century.

steam en·gine ▶ noun **1** an engine that uses the expansion or rapid condensation of steam to generate power. **2** a steam locomotive.

steam·er /ˈstēmər/ ▶ noun **1** a ship or boat powered by steam. **2** a type of saucepan in which food can be steamed.

steam i·ron ▶ noun an electric iron that gives off steam from holes in its flat surface.

steam·roll·er /ˈstēmˌrōlər/ ▶ noun a heavy, slow-moving vehicle with a roller, used to flatten the surfaces of roads during construction. ▶ verb (also **steamroll** /ˈstēmˌrōl/) **1** force someone into doing or accepting something. **2** (of a government or other authority) forcibly pass a law by limiting debate or overriding opposition.

steam·ship /ˈstēmˌSHip/ ▶ noun a ship that is powered by a steam engine.

steam·y /ˈstēmē/ ▶ adjective (**steamier, steamiest**) **1** producing, filled with, or clouded with steam. **2** hot and humid. **3** informal involving passionate sexual activity.

– SYNONYMS **1 humid,** muggy, sticky, moist, damp, clammy, sultry, sweaty, steaming. **2** *a steamy love scene* **erotic,** sexually arousing, sexually stimulating, titillating, suggestive.

– DERIVATIVES **steam·i·ly** adverb **steam·i·ness** noun.

ste·ar·ic ac·id /stēˈarik, ˈsti(ə)r-/ ▶ noun a solid saturated fatty acid obtained from animal or vegetable fats.
– ORIGIN from Greek *stear* 'tallow.'

ste·a·tite /ˈstēəˌtīt/ ▶ noun the mineral talc occurring especially as soapstone.
– ORIGIN Greek *steatītēs*.

steed /stēd/ ▶ noun old use or literary a horse.
– ORIGIN Old English.

steel /stēl/ ▶ noun **1** a hard, strong gray or bluish-gray alloy of iron with carbon and usually other elements, used as a structural material and in manufacturing. **2** strength and determination: *nerves of steel*. ▶ verb mentally prepare oneself to do or face something difficult.
– ORIGIN Old English.

steel band ▶ noun a band that plays music on steel drums.

steel drum (also **steel pan**) ▶ noun a percussion instrument made out of an oil drum with one end beaten down and divided into sections to give different notes.

steel·head /ˈstēlˌhed/ (also **steelhead trout**) ▶ noun a rainbow trout of a large migratory variety.

steel wool ▶ noun fine strands of steel matted together into a mass, used for polishing or cleaning hard surfaces.

steel·work /ˈstēlˌwərk/ ▶ noun articles made of steel.

steel·works /ˈstēlˌwərks/ ▶ plural noun (usu. treated as sing.) a factory where steel is manufactured.

steel·y /ˈstēlē/ ▶ adjective (**steelier, steeliest**) **1** resembling steel in color, brightness, or strength. **2** coldly determined.

– SYNONYMS **1** *his steely gaze* **piercing,** penetrating; merciless, ruthless, pitiless, severe, unrelenting, unpitying, unforgiving; literary adamantine. **2** *steely determination* **resolute,** firm, steadfast, unflinching, unswerving, unfaltering, untiring, unwavering, single-minded, ruthless, iron, grim, gritty.
– ANTONYMS half-hearted.

– DERIVATIVES **steel·i·ness** noun.

steel·yard /ˈstēlˌyärd/ ▶ noun a weighing device that has a short arm taking the item to be weighed and a long graduated arm along which a weight is moved until it balances.
– ORIGIN from **STEEL** + **YARD**[1] in the former sense 'rod, measuring stick.'

steep[1] /stēp/ ▶ adjective **1** rising or falling sharply; almost perpendicular. **2** (of a rise or fall in an amount) very large or rapid. **3** informal (of a price or demand) not reasonable; excessive.

– SYNONYMS **1 sheer,** precipitous, abrupt, sharp, perpendicular, vertical. **2** *a steep increase* **sharp,** sudden, dramatic, precipitate.
– ANTONYMS gentle, gradual.

▶ noun chiefly literary a steep mountain slope.
– DERIVATIVES **steep·ly** adverb **steep·ness** noun.
– ORIGIN Old English, 'extending to a great height.'

steep[2] ▶ verb **1** soak something in water or other liquid. **2** (**be steeped in**) be filled with a particular quality.

– SYNONYMS (**be steeped in**) *a castle steeped in history* **imbued with,** filled with, permeated with, suffused with, soaked in, pervaded by.

– ORIGIN Germanic.

steep·en /ˈstēpən/ ▶ verb become or make steeper.

stee·ple /ˈstēpəl/ ▶ noun **1** a church tower and spire. **2** a spire on the top of a church tower or roof. ▶ verb place the fingers or hands together so that they form an upward-pointing V-shape.
– ORIGIN Old English.

stee·ple·chase /ˈstēpəlˌCHās/ ▶ noun **1** a horse race run on a racetrack that has ditches and hedges as jumps. **2** a running race in which runners must clear hurdles and water jumps.
– DERIVATIVES **stee·ple·chas·er** noun **stee·ple·chas·ing** noun.
– ORIGIN so named because the race was originally run across country, with a steeple marking the finishing point.

stee·ple·jack /ˈstēpəlˌjak/ ▶ noun a person who climbs tall structures such as chimneys and steeples in order to carry out repairs.

steer[1] /sti(ə)r/ ▶ verb **1** guide or control the movement of a vehicle, ship, or aircraft. **2** direct or guide: *he steered her to a chair*.

– SYNONYMS **guide,** direct, maneuver, drive, pilot, navigate.

▶ noun informal a piece of advice or information.
– DERIVATIVES **steer·a·ble** adjective **steer·er** noun.
– PHRASES **steer clear of** take care to avoid.
– ORIGIN Old English.

steer[2] ▶ noun a bullock.
– ORIGIN Old English.

steer·age /ˈsti(ə)rij/ ▶ noun **1** historical the cheapest accommodations in a ship. **2** old use or literary the action of steering a boat.

steer·ing /ˈsti(ə)riNG/ ▸ **noun** the mechanism in a vehicle, ship, or aircraft that allows it to be steered.

steer·ing col·umn ▸ **noun** a shaft that connects the steering wheel of a vehicle to the rest of the steering mechanism.

steer·ing com·mit·tee (also **steering group**) ▸ **noun** a committee that decides on the priorities or order of business of an organization.

steer·ing wheel ▸ **noun** a wheel that a driver turns in order to steer a vehicle.

steers·man /ˈsti(ə)rzmən/ ▸ **noun** (pl. **steersmen**) a person who steers a boat or ship.

steg·o·saur /ˈstegəˌsôr/ (also **stegosaurus** /ˌstegəˈsôrəs/) ▸ **noun** a plant-eating dinosaur with a double row of large bony plates along the back.
– ORIGIN from Greek *stegē* 'covering' + *sauros* 'lizard.'

stein /stīn/ ▸ **noun** a large earthenware beer mug.
– ORIGIN German, 'stone.'

ste·la /ˈstēlə/ (also **stele** /stēl/) ▸ **noun** (pl. **stelae** /-ˌlē/) Archaeology an upright stone slab or column with an inscription or design.
– ORIGIN Greek.

stel·lar /ˈstelər/ ▸ **adjective 1** relating to a star or stars. **2** informal featuring or having the quality of a star performer. **3** informal excellent; outstanding.
– ORIGIN from Latin *stella* 'star.'

stem[1] /stem/ ▸ **noun 1** the main body or stalk of a plant or shrub. **2** the stalk supporting a fruit, flower, or leaf. **3** a long, thin supporting or main section of something, such as that of a wine glass or tobacco pipe. **4** a vertical stroke in a letter or musical note. **5** Grammar the root or main part of a word, to which other elements are added. **6** the main upright timber or metal piece at the bow of a ship.

– SYNONYMS **stalk,** shoot, trunk.

▸ **verb** (**stems, stemming, stemmed**) (**stem from**) come from or be caused by: *depression stemming from domestic difficulties.*

– SYNONYMS **come from,** arise from, originate from, have its origins in, spring from, derive from.

– PHRASES **from stem to stern** from one end to the other, especially of a ship.
– ORIGIN Old English.

stem[2] ▸ **verb** (**stems, stemming, stemmed**) stop or restrict the flow or progress of something.

– SYNONYMS **stop,** stanch, halt, check, curb.

– ORIGIN Old Norse.

stem cell ▸ **noun** an undifferentiated cell within an organism that can divide to produce more cells of the same kind or develop into a specialized cell.

stem·ware /ˈstemˌwe(ə)r/ ▸ **noun** goblets and stemmed drinking glasses regarded collectively.

stench /stenCH/ ▸ **noun** a strong and very unpleasant smell.

– SYNONYMS **stink,** reek; informal funk; literary miasma.

– ORIGIN Old English.

sten·cil /ˈstensəl/ ▸ **noun** a thin sheet of card, plastic, or metal with a pattern or letters cut out of it, used to produce a design on the surface below by applying ink or paint through the holes. ▸ **verb** (**stencils, stenciling, stenciled**) decorate something with a stencil.
– ORIGIN from Old French *estanceler* 'decorate brightly.'

ste·nog·ra·pher /stəˈnägrəfər/ ▸ **noun** a shorthand typist.
– ORIGIN from Greek *stenos* 'narrow.'

stent /stent/ ▸ **noun** Medicine **1** a tubular support placed temporarily inside a blood vessel, canal, or duct to aid healing or relieve an obstruction. **2** an impression or cast of a part or body cavity, used to maintain pressure so as to promote healing, especially of a skin graft.
– ORIGIN from the name of the English dentist Charles T. *Stent.*

sten·to·ri·an /stenˈtôrēən/ ▸ **adjective** (of a person's voice) loud and powerful.
– ORIGIN from *Stentor*, a herald in the Trojan War.

step /step/ ▸ **noun 1** an act of lifting and putting down the foot or alternate feet, as in walking. **2** the distance covered by a step. **3** a flat surface on which to place one's foot when moving from one level to another. **4** a measure or action taken to deal with or achieve something. **5** a position or grade in a scale or series. **6** a block fixed to a boat's keel to take the base of a mast or other fitting.

– SYNONYMS **1 pace,** stride, footstep, footfall, tread, tramp. **2 stair,** tread; (**steps**) stairs, staircase, flight of stairs. **3** *resigning is a very serious step* **action,** act, course of action, measure, move, operation, procedure. **4** *a significant step toward a cease-fire* **advance,** development, move, movement, breakthrough. **5** *the first step on the managerial ladder* **stage,** level, grade, rank, degree, phase.

▸ **verb** (**steps, stepping, stepped**) lift and put down one's foot or alternate feet.

– SYNONYMS **walk,** move, tread, pace, stride.

– PHRASES **in** (or **out of**) **step 1** walking, marching, or dancing in the same (or a different) rhythm and pace as other people. **2** conforming (or not conforming) to what other people are doing or thinking. **mind** (or **watch**) **one's step** walk or act carefully. **step down** (or **aside**) withdraw or resign from a position or job. **step forward** offer one's help or services. **step in 1** become involved in a difficult situation, especially in order to help. **2** act as a substitute for someone. **step on it** informal go faster. **step out of line** behave inappropriately or disobediently. **step something up** increase the amount, speed, or strength of something.
– ORIGIN Old English.

step- ▸ **combining form** referring to a relationship resulting from a remarriage: *stepmother.*
– ORIGIN Old English.

step aer·o·bics ▸ **plural noun** a type of aerobics that involves stepping up onto and down from a portable block.

step·broth·er /ˈstepˌbrəT͟Hər/ ▸ **noun** a son of one's stepparent by a marriage other than that with one's own father or mother.

step·child /ˈstepˌCHīld/ ▸ **noun** (pl. **stepchildren**) a child of one's husband or wife by a previous marriage.

step·daugh·ter /ˈstepˌdôtər, ˈstepˌdätər/ ▸ **noun** a daughter of one's husband or wife by a previous marriage.

step·fa·ther /ˈstepˌfäT͟Hər/ ▸ **noun** a man who is married to one's mother after the divorce of one's parents or the death of one's father.

steph·a·no·tis /ˌstefəˈnōtis/ ▸ **noun** a climbing plant with fragrant waxy white flowers.
– ORIGIN Greek, 'fit for a wreath.'

step·lad·der /ˈstepˌladər/ ▶ **noun** a short folding ladder with flat steps and a small platform.

step·moth·er /ˈstepˌməT͟Hər/ ▶ **noun** a woman who is married to one's father after the divorce of one's parents or the death of one's mother.

step·par·ent /ˈste(p)ˌparənt, -ˌpe(ə)r-/ ▶ **noun** a stepfather or stepmother.

steppe /step/ ▶ **noun** a large area of flat grassland without trees in SE Europe or Siberia.
– ORIGIN Russian *step'*.

step·ping·stone /ˈstepiNGˌstōn/ ▶ **noun 1** a raised stone on which to step when crossing a stream or muddy area. **2** an action that helps someone make progress toward a goal.

step·sis·ter /ˈstepˌsistər/ ▶ **noun** a daughter of one's stepparent by a marriage other than that with one's own father or mother.

step·son /ˈstepˌsən/ ▶ **noun** a son of one's husband or wife by a previous marriage.

step·wise /ˈstepˌwīz/ ▶ **adverb & adjective 1** in a series of distinct stages; not continuously: *the concentrations tend to decrease stepwise.* **2** Music (of melodic motion) moving by adjacent scale steps rather than leaps.

ster·e·o /ˈsterē-ō, ˈsti(ə)r-/ ▶ **noun** (pl. **stereos**) **1** sound that is directed through two or more speakers so that it seems to surround the listener and come from more than one source. **2** a CD player, record player, etc., that has two or more speakers and produces this type of sound. ▶ **adjective** relating to or producing this type of sound.

ster·e·o·phon·ic /ˌsterēəˈfänik, ˌsti(ə)r-/ ▶ **adjective** full form of **STEREO**.
– ORIGIN from Greek *stereos* 'solid.'

ster·e·o·scope /ˈsterēəˌskōp, ˈsti(ə)r-/ ▶ **noun** a device by which two photographs of the same object taken at slightly different angles are viewed together, creating a three-dimensional impression.

ster·e·o·scop·ic /ˌsterēəˈskäpik, ˌsti(ə)r-/ ▶ **noun 1** able to see objects as three-dimensional forms. **2** relating to a stereoscope.

ster·e·o·type /ˈsterēəˌtīp, ˈsti(ə)r-/ ▶ **noun** a widely held but oversimplified idea of the typical characteristics of a person or thing.

– SYNONYMS **conventional idea,** standard image, cliché, formula.

▶ **verb** view or represent someone or something as a stereotype.

– SYNONYMS **typecast,** pigeonhole, conventionalize, categorize, label, tag.

ster·e·o·typ·i·cal /ˌsterēəˈtipikəl/ ▶ **adjective** relating to or resembling a stereotype: *stereotypical images of femininity.*
– DERIVATIVES **ster·e·o·typ·i·cal·ly** adverb.

ster·ile /ˈsterəl/ ▶ **adjective 1** not able to produce children, young, crops, or fruit. **2** free from bacteria or other living microorganisms. **3** lacking imagination, creativity, or excitement.

– SYNONYMS **1 unproductive,** infertile, unfruitful, barren. **2 hygienic,** clean, pure, uncontaminated, sterilized, disinfected, germ-free, antiseptic.
– ANTONYMS fertile.

– DERIVATIVES **ste·ril·i·ty** /stəˈrilitē/ noun.
– ORIGIN Latin *sterilis*.

CHOOSE THE RIGHT WORD

See **SANITARY**.

ster·i·lize /ˈsterəˌlīz/ ▶ **verb 1** make something free from bacteria. **2** make a person or animal unable to produce offspring by removing or blocking the sex organs.

– SYNONYMS **1 disinfect,** fumigate, decontaminate, sanitize, clean, cleanse, purify. **2 neuter,** castrate, spay, alter, geld.
– ANTONYMS contaminate.

– DERIVATIVES **ster·i·li·za·tion** /ˌsterəl(ə)ˈzāSHən/ noun.

ster·ling /ˈstərliNG/ ▶ **noun 1** an item or set of items, especially flatware, made of sterling silver: *get out the sterling for dinner.* **2** British money. ▶ **adjective 1** made of sterling silver. **2** excellent; of great value: *they do sterling work for charity.*
– ORIGIN probably from Old English *steorra* 'star' (because some early Norman pennies bore a small star).

ster·ling sil·ver ▶ **noun** silver of at least 92¼ percent purity.

stern[1] /stərn/ ▶ **adjective 1** serious and strict. **2** severe; demanding: *the team are facing a stern test.*

– SYNONYMS **1 unsmiling,** frowning, serious, severe, forbidding, grim, unfriendly, austere, dour. **2 strict,** severe, stringent, harsh, drastic, hard, tough, extreme, draconian.
– ANTONYMS genial, lax.

– DERIVATIVES **stern·ly** adverb **stern·ness** noun.
– ORIGIN Old English.

CHOOSE THE RIGHT WORD

See **SEVERE**.

stern[2] ▶ **noun** the rearmost part of a ship or boat.
– ORIGIN probably from an Old Norse word meaning 'steering.'

ster·num /ˈstərnəm/ ▶ **noun** (pl. **sternums** or **sterna** /-nə/) the breastbone.
– ORIGIN Greek *sternon* 'chest.'

ste·roid /ˈsterˌoid, ˈsti(ə)r-/ ▶ **noun 1** any of a large class of organic compounds that includes certain hormones and vitamins. **2** an anabolic steroid.
– DERIVATIVES **ste·roi·dal** /steˈroidl, sti-/ adjective.
– ORIGIN from **STEROL**.

ste·rol /ˈsterôl, -äl, ˈsti(ə)r-/ ▶ **noun** Biochemistry any of a group of naturally occurring unsaturated steroid alcohols, such as cholesterol.
– ORIGIN from the ending of words such as **CHOLESTEROL**.

ster·to·rous /ˈstərtərəs/ ▶ **adjective** (of breathing) noisy and labored.
– DERIVATIVES **ster·to·rous·ly** adverb.
– ORIGIN from Latin *stertere* 'to snore.'

stet /stet/ ▶ **verb** let it stand (used as an instruction on a printed proof to ignore a correction).
– ORIGIN Latin.

steth·o·scope /ˈsteTHəˌskōp/ ▶ **noun** a medical instrument for listening to the action of someone's heart or breathing, having a small disk that is placed against the chest and two tubes connected to earpieces.
– ORIGIN from Greek *stēthos* 'breast' + *skopein* 'look at.'

Stet·son /ˈstetsən/ ▶ **noun** trademark a hat with a high crown and a very wide brim, traditionally worn by cowboys in the US.

– ORIGIN named after the American hat manufacturer John B. *Stetson*.

ste·ve·dore /ˈstēvəˌdôr/ ▸ **noun** a person employed at a dock to load and unload ships.
– ORIGIN Spanish *estivador*.

ste·vi·a /ˈstēvēə, ˈstev-/ ▸ **noun** a composite herb native to South America whose leaves are the source of a noncaloric sweetener.
– ORIGIN from the name of the 16th-century Spanish botanist Pedro Jaime *Esteve*.

stew /st(y)o͞o/ ▸ **noun 1** a dish of meat and vegetables cooked slowly in liquid in a closed dish. **2** informal a state of anxiety or agitation. ▸ **verb 1** cook food slowly in liquid in a closed dish. **2** informal be in a heated or stuffy atmosphere. **3** informal be anxious or agitated.
– PHRASES **stew in one's own juices** informal be left to suffer the consequences of one's own actions.
– ORIGIN Old French *estuve*.

stew·ard /ˈst(y)o͞oərd/ ▸ **noun 1** a person who looks after the passengers on a ship or aircraft. **2** an official who supervises arrangements at a large public event. **3** a person employed to manage a large house or estate. **4** a person responsible for supplies of food to a college, club, etc. ▸ **verb** act as a steward of something.
– DERIVATIVES **stew·ard·ship** /-ˌsHip/ noun.
– ORIGIN Old English.

stew·ard·ess /ˈst(y)o͞oərdis/ ▸ **noun** a woman who looks after the passengers on a ship or aircraft.

stick¹ /stik/ ▸ **noun 1** a thin piece of wood that has fallen or been cut off a tree. **2** a piece of trimmed wood used for support in walking or as a weapon. **3** (in hockey, polo, etc.) a long, thin implement used to hit or direct the puck or ball. **4** a long, thin object or piece: *a stick of dynamite*. **5** **(the sticks)** informal, derogatory country areas far from towns or cities.

> – SYNONYMS **1 branch,** twig, switch. **2 walking stick,** cane, staff, crutch. **3 post,** pole, cane, stake, rod.

– ORIGIN Old English.

stick² ▸ **verb** (past and past part. **stuck** /stək/) **1** **(stick something in/into/through)** insert or push a pointed object into or through something. **2** **(stick in/into/through)** (of a pointed object) be or remain fixed with its point embedded in something. **3** fasten or become fastened to something. **4** be or become fixed in a particular position or unable to move or be moved. **5** protrude or extend in a particular direction. **6** **(be stuck)** be unable to continue with a task or find the answer or solution. **7** informal put something somewhere in a quick or careless way.

> – SYNONYMS **1** **(stick something in/into/through)** *he stuck his fork into the sausage* **thrust,** push, insert, jab, poke, dig, plunge. **2** **(stick in/into/through)** *the bristles stuck into her skin* **pierce,** penetrate, puncture, prick, stab. **3** *the cup stuck to its saucer* **adhere,** cling. **4** *stick the stamp there* **attach,** fasten, affix, fix, paste, glue, gum, tape. **5** *the wheels stuck in the mud* **jam,** get jammed, catch, get caught, get trapped. **6** **(stick out)** *his front teeth stick out* **protrude,** jut (out), project, stand out, extend, poke out, bulge. **7** **(be stuck)** *if you get stuck, leave a blank* **baffled,** beaten, at a loss; informal stumped.

– PHRASES **be stuck on** informal be infatuated with. **be stuck with** informal be unable to get rid of or escape from. **stick around** informal remain in or near a place. **stick at** informal persevere with something. **stick by** continue to support or be loyal to someone. **stick in one's throat** (or **craw**) be difficult or impossible to accept. **stick it out** informal put up with or persevere with something difficult or unpleasant. **stick one's neck out** informal risk criticism or anger by acting or speaking boldly. **stick out** be extremely noticeable. **stick to** continue doing or using something rather than changing to something else: *I'll stick to tap water*. **stick together** informal (of two or more people) support and remain loyal to each other. **stick up for** support or defend a person or cause.
– ORIGIN Old English.

stick·ball /ˈstikˌbôl/ ▸ **noun** an informal game resembling baseball, played with a stick and a (usually rubber) ball.

stick·er /ˈstikər/ ▸ **noun** a sticky label or notice.

stick·er price ▸ **noun** the advertised retail price of an item, especially the price listed on a sticker attached to the window of a new automobile.

stick·er shock ▸ **noun** informal shock or dismay experienced by the potential buyers of a particular product on discovering its high or increased price.

stick·ing point ▸ **noun** an obstacle that prevents progress toward an agreement or goal.

stick in·sect ▸ **noun** another term for WALKING STICK (sense 2).

stick-in-the-mud ▸ **noun** informal a person who is unwilling to try anything new or exciting.

stick·le·back /ˈstikəlˌbak/ ▸ **noun** a small freshwater or coastal fish with sharp spines along its back.
– ORIGIN from Old English words meaning 'thorn, sting' + 'back.'

stick·ler /ˈstik(ə)lər/ ▸ **noun** a person who insists on a certain quality or type of behavior: *Susan was a stickler for punctuality*.
– ORIGIN from Old English, 'set in order.'

stick shift ▸ **noun** a gear lever or manual gearbox.

stick·up /ˈstikˌəp/ ▸ **noun** informal an armed robbery in which a gun is used to threaten people.

stick·y /ˈstikē/ ▸ **adjective** (**stickier, stickiest**) **1** tending or designed to stick to things on contact; adhesive. **2** (of a substance) like glue in texture. **3** (of the weather) hot and humid; muggy. **4** informal difficult or awkward: *the relationship is going through a sticky patch*.

> – SYNONYMS **1 adhesive,** self-adhesive, gummed. **2 tacky,** gluey, gummy, treacly, glutinous, viscous; informal gooey. **3 humid,** muggy, close, sultry, steamy, sweaty, sweltering, oppressive. **4 awkward,** difficult, tricky, ticklish, delicate, embarrassing, sensitive; informal hairy.
> – ANTONYMS dry, fresh, cool.

▸ **noun** (pl. **stickies**) a piece of paper with an adhesive strip on one side, used for leaving notes.
– DERIVATIVES **stick·i·ly** adverb **stick·i·ness** noun.

stiff /stif/ ▸ **adjective 1** not easily bent; rigid. **2** not moving freely; difficult to turn or operate. **3** unable to move easily and without pain. **4** (of a person or their manner) not relaxed or friendly. **5** severe or difficult: *the company faces stiff competition for the contracts*. **6** (of an alcoholic drink) strong. **7** (—— **stiff**) informal having a particular unpleasant feeling to an extreme extent: *scared stiff*.

> – SYNONYMS **1 rigid,** hard, firm, inelastic, unyielding, brittle. **2 thick,** firm, viscous, semisolid. **3 aching,** achy, painful, arthritic; informal creaky. **4 formal,** reserved, wooden, forced, strained, stilted; informal starchy, uptight. **5** *stiff penalties* **harsh,** severe, heavy, stringent, drastic, draconian. **6** *they put*

up a *stiff resistance* **vigorous,** determined, strong, spirited, resolute, tenacious, dogged, stubborn. **7 difficult,** hard, arduous, tough, strenuous, laborious, exacting, tiring, demanding. **8 strong,** potent, alcoholic.
– ANTONYMS flexible, soft, limp.

▶ **noun** informal a dead body.
– DERIVATIVES **stiff·ly** adverb **stiff·ness** noun.
– PHRASES **stiff upper lip** the tendency to endure difficulty without complaining or showing one's feelings.
– ORIGIN Old English.

stiff·en /'stifən/ ▶ **verb 1** make or become stiff. **2** make or become stronger.
– DERIVATIVES **stiff·en·er** noun.

stiff-necked ▶ **adjective** proud and stubborn.

sti·fle[1] /'stīfəl/ ▶ **verb 1** prevent someone from breathing freely. **2** smother or suppress: *she stifled a giggle*.

– SYNONYMS **1 smother,** check, restrain, keep back, hold back, hold in, withhold, choke back, muffle, suppress, curb. **2 suppress,** quash, quell, put an end to, put down, stop, extinguish, stamp out, crush, subdue, repress. **3 suffocate,** smother, asphyxiate, choke.

– ORIGIN perhaps from Old French *estouffer*.

stifle[2] ▶ **noun** a joint in the legs of horses and other animals, equivalent to the knee in humans.
– ORIGIN unknown.

sti·fling /'stīf(ə)liNG/ ▶ **adjective** unpleasantly hot and stuffy.

– SYNONYMS **airless,** suffocating, oppressive; sweltering; humid, close, muggy; informal boiling.
– ANTONYMS fresh, airy, cold.

– DERIVATIVES **sti·fling·ly** adverb.

stig·ma /'stigmə/ ▶ **noun** (pl. **stigmas** or in sense 2 **stigmata** /stig'mätə, 'stigmətə/) **1** a mark or sign of disgrace. **2** (**stigmata**) (in Christian tradition) marks on a person's body corresponding to those left on Jesus's body by the Crucifixion. **3** the part of a plant's pistil that receives the pollen during pollination.

– SYNONYMS **shame,** disgrace, dishonor, ignominy, humiliation, stain, taint.
– ANTONYMS honor.

– ORIGIN Greek, 'a mark made by a pointed instrument, a dot.'

stig·mat·ic /stig'matik/ ▶ **adjective** relating to a stigma or stigmas. ▶ **noun** a person with stigmata.

stig·ma·tize /'stigmə,tīz/ ▶ **verb** regard or treat someone or something as worthy of disgrace or great disapproval.

– SYNONYMS **condemn,** denounce, brand, label, mark.

– DERIVATIVES **stig·ma·ti·za·tion** /,stigməti'zāsHən/ noun.

stile /stīl/ ▶ **noun** an arrangement of steps set into a fence or wall that allows people to climb over.
– ORIGIN Old English.

sti·let·to /stə'letō/ ▶ **noun** (pl. **stilettos**) **1** (also **stiletto heel**) a thin, high tapering heel on a woman's shoe. **2** a short dagger with a tapering blade.
– ORIGIN Italian, 'little dagger.'

still[1] /stil/ ▶ **adjective 1** not moving. **2** (of air or water) not disturbed by wind, sound, or currents.

– SYNONYMS **1 motionless,** unmoving, stock-still, immobile, rooted to the spot, transfixed, static, stationary. **2 quiet,** silent, calm, peaceful, serene, windless, noiseless, undisturbed, flat, smooth, like a millpond.
– ANTONYMS moving, noisy.

▶ **noun 1** a state of deep and quiet calm. **2** a photograph or a single shot from a movie.
▶ **adverb 1** even now or at a particular time.
2 nevertheless. **3** even: *better still*.

– SYNONYMS **1 even now,** yet. **2 nevertheless,** nonetheless, all the same, even so, but, however, despite that, in spite of that.

▶ **verb** make or become still.

– SYNONYMS **quiet,** silence, hush, calm, settle, pacify, quieten, subdue.

– DERIVATIVES **still·ness** noun.
– ORIGIN Old English.

still[2] ▶ **noun** a piece of equipment for distilling alcoholic drinks such as whiskey.
– ORIGIN from **DISTILL**.

still·birth /'stil,bərTH/ ▶ **noun** the birth of a baby that has died in the uterus.

still·born /'stil,bôrn/ ▶ **adjective 1** (of a baby) born dead. **2** (of a proposal or plan) having failed to develop or succeed.

still life ▶ **noun** (pl. **still lifes**) a painting or drawing of an arrangement of objects such as flowers or fruit.

stilt /stilt/ ▶ **noun 1** either of a pair of upright poles with supports for the feet enabling the user to walk raised above the ground. **2** each of a set of posts supporting a building. **3** a wading bird with very long, slender legs.
– ORIGIN Germanic.

stilt·ed /'stiltid/ ▶ **adjective** (of speech or writing) not natural, relaxed, or flowing easily.
– DERIVATIVES **stilt·ed·ly** adverb **stilt·ed·ness** noun.

Stil·ton /'stiltn/ ▶ **noun** trademark a kind of strong, rich blue cheese.
– ORIGIN so named because it was formerly sold in *Stilton*, Cambridgeshire.

stim·u·lant /'stimyələnt/ ▶ **noun 1** a substance that acts to increase levels of physiological or nervous activity in the body. **2** something that increases activity, interest, or enthusiasm. ▶ **adjective** acting as a stimulant.

stim·u·late /'stimyə,lāt/ ▶ **verb 1** help something to develop or become more active: *policies designed to stimulate economic growth*. **2** encourage or arouse interest or enthusiasm in someone. **3** raise levels of physiological or nervous activity in the body.

– SYNONYMS **encourage,** prompt, motivate, trigger, spark, spur on, galvanize, fire, inspire, excite, light a fire under.
– ANTONYMS discourage.

– DERIVATIVES **stim·u·la·tion** /,stimyə'lāsHən/ noun **stim·u·la·tor** /-,lātər/ noun **stim·u·la·to·ry** /-lə,tôrē/ adjective.
– ORIGIN Latin *stimulare* 'urge, goad.'

stim·u·lat·ing /'stimyə,lātiNG/ ▶ **adjective** encouraging or arousing interest or enthusiasm: *a stimulating lecture*.

– SYNONYMS **thought-provoking,** interesting, inspiring, inspirational, lively, exciting, provocative.
– ANTONYMS uninspiring, boring.

stim·u·lus /'stimyələs/ ▶ **noun** (pl. **stimuli** /-,lī/) **1** something that causes a specific reaction in an organ or tissue of the body. **2** something that encourages activity, interest, or enthusiasm.

– SYNONYMS **motivation,** encouragement, impetus, prompt, spur, inducement, incentive, inspiration, fillip; informal shot in the arm.
– ANTONYMS deterrent.

– ORIGIN Latin, 'goad, incentive.'

sting /stiNG/ ▶ **noun 1** a small sharp-pointed organ of an insect, capable of inflicting a painful wound by injecting poison. **2** any of a number of minute hairs on certain plants, causing inflammation if touched. **3** a wound from a sting. **4** a sharp tingling sensation or hurtful effect. **5** informal a carefully planned undercover operation.

– SYNONYMS **1 prick,** wound, injury. **2 pain,** pricking, smarting, soreness, hurt, irritation.

▶ **verb** (past and past part. **stung**) **1** wound someone or something with a sting. **2** produce a stinging sensation. **3** make someone feel angry or upset. **4** (**sting someone into**) provoke someone to do something by causing annoyance or offense. **5** informal swindle or overcharge someone.

– SYNONYMS **1 prick,** wound. **2 smart,** burn, hurt, be irritated, be sore. **3** *the criticism stung her* **upset,** wound, hurt, distress, pain, mortify.

– ORIGIN Old English.

sting·er /'stiNGər/ ▶ **noun 1** the part of an insect or animal that holds a sting. **2** an insect or animal that stings, such as a bee or jellyfish. **3** informal a painful blow: *he suffered a stinger on his right shoulder.* **4** a cocktail including crème de menthe and brandy.

sting·ing net·tle ▶ **noun** a nettle covered in stinging hairs.

sting·ray /'stiNG,rā/ ▶ **noun** a ray (fish) with a long poisonous serrated spine at the base of the tail.

stin·gy /'stinjē/ ▶ **adjective** (**stingier, stingiest**) informal not generous.

– SYNONYMS **mean,** miserly, close-fisted, parsimonious, niggardly, penny-pinching; informal cheap, tight-fisted, tight, mingy.
– ANTONYMS generous, liberal.

– DERIVATIVES **stin·gi·ly** adverb **stin·gi·ness** noun.
– ORIGIN perhaps a dialect variant of **STING**.

stink /stiNGk/ ▶ **verb** (past **stank** /staNGk/ or **stunk** /stəNGk/; past part. **stunk**) **1** have a strong, unpleasant smell. **2** informal seem very bad, unpleasant, or dishonest.

– SYNONYMS **reek,** smell.

▶ **noun 1** a strong, unpleasant smell; **2** informal a commotion or fuss.

– SYNONYMS **stench,** smell, reek; informal funk.

– ORIGIN Old English.

stink bomb ▶ **noun** a small container that when broken releases a substance with a very unpleasant smell.

stink·er /'stiNGkər/ ▶ **noun** informal a very unpleasant person or thing.

stink·horn /'stiNGk,hôrn/ ▶ **noun** a fungus with a rounded head that turns into a foul-smelling slimy substance containing the spores.

stink·ing /'stiNGkiNG/ ▶ **adjective 1** smelling very unpleasant. **2** informal very bad or unpleasant. ▶ **adverb** informal extremely: *stinking rich.*

stink·y /'stiNGkē/ ▶ **adjective** (**stinkier, stinkiest**) informal having a strong, unpleasant smell.

stint /stint/ ▶ **verb** (also **stint on**) be very economical or stingy about spending or providing something: *he doesn't stint on wining and dining.* ▶ **noun 1** a period of work: *his career included a stint as a musician.* **2** limited supply or effort.

– SYNONYMS **spell,** stretch, turn, session, term, time, shift, tour of duty.

– ORIGIN Old English, 'make blunt.'

sti·pend /'stī,pend, -pənd/ ▶ **noun** a fixed regular sum paid as a salary or allowance to a clergyman, teacher, or public official.
– ORIGIN Latin *stipendium.*

sti·pen·di·ar·y /stī'pendē,erē/ ▶ **adjective 1** receiving a stipend; working for pay rather than voluntarily. **2** relating to a stipend.

stip·ple /'stipəl/ ▶ **verb 1** mark a surface with numerous small dots or specks. **2** produce a decorative effect on paint or other material by roughening its surface when wet.
– ORIGIN Dutch *stippelen* 'to prick.'

stip·u·late /'stipyə,lāt/ ▶ **verb** demand or specify something as part of a bargain or agreement.

– SYNONYMS **specify,** set out, lay down, demand, require, insist on.

– DERIVATIVES **stip·u·la·tion** /,stipyə'lāSHən/ noun.
– ORIGIN Latin *stipulari* 'demand as a formal promise.'

stir[1] /stər/ ▶ **verb** (**stirs, stirring, stirred**) **1** move an implement around and around in a liquid or soft substance to mix it thoroughly. **2** move slightly or begin to be active. **3** wake up or get out of bed. **4** (often **stir someone up**) arouse a strong feeling in someone.

– SYNONYMS **1 mix,** blend, beat, whip, whisk, fold in, muddle. **2 disturb,** rustle, shake, move, agitate. **3 move,** get up, get out of bed, rise, rouse oneself, bestir oneself. **4** *the war stirred him to action* **spur,** drive, rouse, prompt, propel, motivate, encourage, urge, impel, provoke, goad.

▶ **noun 1** an act of stirring. **2** a disturbance or commotion: *the event caused quite a stir.*

– SYNONYMS **commotion,** disturbance, fuss, excitement, sensation; informal to-do, hoo-ha.

– DERIVATIVES **stir·rer** noun.
– ORIGIN Old English.

stir[2] ▶ **noun** informal prison.
– ORIGIN perhaps from Romany *sturbin* 'jail.'

stir-cra·zy ▶ **adjective** informal psychologically disturbed as a result of being imprisoned.

stir-fry ▶ **verb** fry food rapidly over a high heat while stirring it briskly.

stir·ring /'stəriNG/ ▶ **adjective** causing great excitement or strong emotion.

– SYNONYMS **exciting,** thrilling, rousing, stimulating, moving, inspiring, heady.
– ANTONYMS boring, pedestrian.

▶ **noun** a first sign of activity, movement, or emotion.

stir·rup /'stərəp, 'stə-rəp, 'stir-/ ▶ **noun 1** each of a pair of metal loops attached at either side of a horse's saddle to support the rider's foot. **2** a pair of metal supports for the ankles used during gynecological examinations.
– ORIGIN Old English.

stitch /stiCH/ ▶ **noun 1** a loop of thread or yarn made by a single pass of the needle in sewing, knitting, or crocheting. **2** a method of sewing, knitting, or

crocheting producing a particular pattern. **3** informal the smallest item of clothing: *a voluptuous woman without a stitch on*. **4** a sudden sharp pain in the side of the body, caused by vigorous exercise. ▸ **verb** make or mend something with stitches.
– DERIVATIVES **stitch·er** noun **stitch·ing** noun.
– PHRASES **in stitches** informal laughing uncontrollably.
– ORIGIN Old English.

stoat /stōt/ ▸ **noun** a small mammal of the weasel family, with chestnut fur (white in northern animals in winter), white underparts, and a black-tipped tail.
– ORIGIN unknown.

sto·chas·tic /stəˈkastik/ ▸ **adjective** technical not precisely predictable; random or affected by chance.
– ORIGIN Greek *stokhastikos*.

stock /stäk/ ▸ **noun 1** a supply of goods or materials available for sale or use. **2** farm animals bred and kept for their meat or milk; livestock. **3** the capital of a company raised through the selling of shares. **4** (**stocks**) a portion of a company's stock held by an individual or group as an investment. **5** water in which bones, meat, fish, or vegetables have been slowly simmered. **6** a person's ancestry. **7** a breed, variety, or population of an animal or plant. **8** the trunk or woody stem of a tree or shrub. **9** a plant with sweet-smelling white, pink, or lilac flowers. **10** (**the stocks**) (treated as sing. or pl.) historical a wooden structure with holes for securing a person's feet and hands, in which criminals were locked as a public punishment. **11** the part of a rifle or other gun to which the barrel and firing mechanism are attached, held against the shoulder when firing. **12** a band of material worn around the neck.

– SYNONYMS **1 merchandise,** goods, wares. **2 store,** supply, stockpile, reserve, hoard, cache, bank. **3 animals,** livestock, beasts, flocks, herds. **4 descent,** ancestry, origin(s), lineage, birth, extraction, family, blood, pedigree.

▸ **adjective 1** (of a product) usually kept in stock and so regularly available for sale. **2** (of a phrase or expression) used too regularly: *a stock response*. **3** referring to a conventional character type that recurs in a particular genre of literature, theater, or movies.

– SYNONYMS **usual,** routine, predictable, set, standard, staple, customary, familiar, conventional, traditional, stereotyped, clichéd, hackneyed, unoriginal, formulaic.
– ANTONYMS unusual, original.

▸ **verb 1** have or keep a supply of a product. **2** (also **stock something up**) fill something with a supply of goods. **3** (**stock up**) obtain supplies of something for future use.

– SYNONYMS **sell,** carry, keep (in stock), offer, supply, provide, furnish.

– PHRASES **in** (or **out of**) **stock** available (or unavailable) for immediate sale or use. **take stock** make an overall assessment of a particular situation.
– ORIGIN Old English, 'trunk, post.'

stock·ade /stäˈkād/ ▸ **noun 1** a barrier or enclosure formed from upright wooden posts. **2** a military prison.
– ORIGIN former French *estocade*.

stock·breed·er /ˈstäk,brēdər/ ▸ **noun** a farmer who breeds livestock.

stock·brok·er /ˈstäk,brōkər/ ▸ **noun** a person who buys and sells stocks and shares on behalf of clients.
– DERIVATIVES **stock·brok·ing** noun.

stock car ▸ **noun** an ordinary car that has been strengthened for use in a race in which the competing cars collide with each other.

stock com·pa·ny ▸ **noun** a repertory company that is largely based in one theater.

stock cube ▸ **noun** a cube of dried meat, vegetable, or fish stock for use in cooking.

stock ex·change ▸ **noun** a market in which stocks and shares are bought and sold.

stock·hold·er /ˈstäk,hōldər/ ▸ **noun** an owner of shares in a company.

stock·i·nette /,stäkəˈnet/ ▸ **noun** a soft, loosely knitted stretchy fabric.
– ORIGIN probably an alteration of *stocking-net*.

stock·ing /ˈstäkiNG/ ▸ **noun 1** either of a pair of separate close-fitting nylon garments covering the foot and leg, worn by women. **2** a long sock worn by men. **3** a long sock or sock-shaped receptacle hung up by children on Christmas Eve to be filled with presents. **4** a white marking of the lower part of a horse's leg.
– DERIVATIVES **stock·inged** adjective.
– PHRASES **in one's stocking feet** without shoes.
– ORIGIN from *stock* in the dialect sense 'stocking.'

stock·ing cap ▸ **noun** a knitted hat with a long tapered end that hangs down.

stock·ing stitch ▸ **noun** a knitting stitch consisting of alternate rows of plain and purl stitch.

stock·ing stuff·er ▸ **noun** a small present suitable for putting in a Christmas stocking.

stock-in-trade ▸ **noun** the typical subject or item a person, company, or profession uses or deals in.

stock·man /ˈstäkmən, -,man/ ▸ **noun** (pl. **stockmen**) **1** a person who looks after livestock. **2** an owner of livestock.

stock mar·ket ▸ **noun** a stock exchange.

stock op·tion ▸ **noun** an option for an employee to buy stock in their company at a discount or at a stated fixed price.

stock·pile /ˈstäk,pīl/ ▸ **noun** a large supply of goods or materials that has been gathered together.

– SYNONYMS **stock,** store, supply, collection, reserve, hoard, cache; informal stash.

▸ **verb** gather together and keep a large supply of goods or materials.

– SYNONYMS **store up,** amass, accumulate, store (up), stock up on, hoard, cache, collect, lay in, put away, put/set aside, put by, stow away, save; informal salt away, stash away.

stock·pot /ˈstäk,pät/ ▸ **noun** a pot in which stock is prepared by long, slow cooking.

stock·room /ˈstäk,ro͞om, -,ro͝om/ ▸ **noun** a room in which stocks of goods or materials are stored.

stock split ▸ **noun** an issue of new shares in a company to existing shareholders in proportion to their current holdings.

stock-still ▸ **adverb** without any movement; completely still.

stock swap ▸ **noun 1** acquisition of a company in which payment consists of stock in the buying company. **2** a means of exercising stock options in which shares already owned are traded for a greater number of shares at the exercise price.

stock·tak·ing /'stäk,tākiNG/ ▶ **noun** the action or process of recording the amount of stock held by a business.
– DERIVATIVES **stock·take** noun & verb.

stock·y /'stäkē/ ▶ **adjective** (**stockier, stockiest**) (especially of a person) short and sturdy.

> – SYNONYMS **thickset,** sturdy, heavily built, chunky, burly, strapping, brawny, solid, heavy, hefty, beefy.
> – ANTONYMS slender.

– DERIVATIVES **stock·i·ly** adverb **stock·i·ness** noun.

stock·yard /'stäk,yärd/ ▶ **noun** a large yard containing pens and sheds in which livestock is kept.

stodg·y /'stäjē/ ▶ **adjective 1** (of food) heavy and filling. **2** rather serious and dull.
– DERIVATIVES **stodg·i·ness** noun.

sto·gie /'stōgē/ (also **stogy**) ▶ **noun** (pl. **stogies**) a long, thin, inexpensive cigar.
– ORIGIN (originally as *stoga*): short for *Conestoga.*

sto·ic /'stō-ik/ ▶ **noun 1** a stoical person. **2** (**Stoic**) a member of the ancient philosophical school of Stoicism.
▶ **adjective 1** stoical. **2** (**Stoic**) relating to the Stoics or Stoicism.
– ORIGIN Greek *stōïkos.*

sto·i·cal /'stō-ikəl/ ▶ **adjective** enduring pain and hardship without showing one's feelings or complaining.

> – SYNONYMS **long-suffering,** uncomplaining, patient, forbearing, accepting, tolerant, resigned, phlegmatic, philosophical.
> – ANTONYMS complaining, intolerant.

– DERIVATIVES **sto·i·cal·ly** /-ik(ə)lē/ adverb.

sto·i·cism /'stō-i,sizəm/ ▶ **noun 1** stoical behavior. **2** (**Stoicism**) an ancient Greek school of philosophy that taught that it is wise to remain indifferent to changes of fortune and to pleasure and pain.

stoke /stōk/ ▶ **verb 1** add coal to a fire, furnace, etc. **2** encourage or stir up a strong emotion. **3** (**stoke up**) informal eat a large quantity of food to give oneself energy.

stok·er /'stōkər/ ▶ **noun** a person who tends the furnace on a steamship or steam train.
– ORIGIN Dutch.

stole[1] /stōl/ ▶ **noun 1** a woman's long scarf or shawl, worn loosely over the shoulders. **2** a priest's garment worn over the shoulders.
– ORIGIN Greek, 'clothing.'

stole[2] past of **STEAL**.

sto·len /'stōlən/ past participle of **STEAL**.

stol·id /'stälid/ ▶ **adjective** calm, dependable, and showing little emotion or reaction.
– DERIVATIVES **sto·lid·i·ty** /stə'liditē/ noun **stol·id·ly** adverb.
– ORIGIN Latin *stolidus,* perhaps related to *stultus* 'foolish.'

stol·len /'stōlən, 'SHtô-/ ▶ **noun** a rich German fruit and nut cake.
– ORIGIN German.

sto·ma /'stōmə/ ▶ **noun** (pl. **stomas** or **stomata** /-mətə, ,stō'mätə/) technical **1** a minute pore in the leaf or stem of a plant, allowing gases to move in and out. **2** a small mouthlike opening in some invertebrate animals. **3** an artificial opening made into a hollow organ, especially the gut.
– ORIGIN Greek, 'mouth.'

stom·ach /'stəmək/ ▶ **noun 1** the organ of the body in which the first part of digestion occurs. **2** the abdominal area of the body; the belly. **3** an appetite or desire for something: *they had no stomach for a fight.*

> – SYNONYMS **1 abdomen,** middle, belly, gut, paunch; informal tummy, insides, pot, spare tire. **2 appetite,** taste, inclination, desire, wish.

▶ **verb 1** consume food or drink without feeling or being sick: *he cannot stomach milk.* **2** endure or accept: *what I won't stomach is thieving.*

> – SYNONYMS **tolerate,** put up with, take, stand, endure, bear; informal hack, abide.

– PHRASES **a strong stomach** an ability to see or do unpleasant things without feeling sick or squeamish.
– ORIGIN Greek *stomakhos* 'gullet.'

> **WORD LINKS**
>
> **gastric** *relating to the stomach*

stom·ach·ache /'stəmək,āk/ ▶ **noun** a pain in a person's belly.

sto·mach pump ▶ **noun** a syringe attached to a long tube, used for extracting the contents of a person's stomach (for example, if they have swallowed poison).

sto·ma·ta /'stōmətə, stō'mätə/ plural of **STOMA**.

stomp /stämp, stômp/ ▶ **verb** tread or stamp heavily and noisily.
– ORIGIN variant of **STAMP**.

stomp·ing ground (chiefly Brit. also **stamping ground**) ▶ **noun** a place that a person regularly visits or spends time at.

stone /stōn/ ▶ **noun 1** the hard, solid nonmetallic mineral matter that rock is made of. **2** a small piece of stone found on the ground. **3** a piece of stone shaped as a memorial or to mark out a boundary. **4** a gem or jewel. **5** a hard seed in certain fruits. **6** (pl. same) Brit. a unit of weight equal to 14 lb (6.35 kg). **7** a whitish or brownish-gray color.

> – SYNONYMS **1 rock,** pebble, boulder. **2 gem,** gemstone, jewel; informal rock, sparkler. **3 kernel,** seed, pip, pit.

▶ **verb 1** throw stones at someone. **2** remove the stone from a fruit.
▶ **adverb** extremely or totally: *stone cold.*
– PHRASES **leave no stone unturned** try everything possible in order to achieve something. **a stone's throw** a short distance.
– ORIGIN Old English.

> **WORD LINKS**
>
> **lapidary** *relating to stone*

Stone Age ▶ **noun** a prehistoric period that came before the Bronze Age, when weapons and tools were made of stone.

stone-broke ▶ **adjective** informal having no money at all.

stone cir·cle ▶ **noun** a prehistoric monument consisting of stones arranged in a circle.

stone·crop /'stōn,kräp/ ▶ **noun** a plant with star-shaped yellow or white flowers that grows among rocks or on walls.

stoned /stōnd/ ▶ **adjective** informal strongly affected by drugs or alcohol.

stone-faced ▶ **adjective** informal revealing no emotions through the expressions of the face.

stone·ground /ˈstōnˈground/ ▶ **adjective** (of flour) ground with millstones.

stone·ma·son /ˈstōnˌmāsən/ ▶ **noun** a person who cuts, prepares, and builds with stone.

stone·wall /ˈstōnˌwôl/ ▶ **verb** delay or block a person or process by refusing to answer questions or by giving evasive replies.

stone·ware /ˈstōnˌwe(ə)r/ ▶ **noun** a type of hard and impermeable pottery.

stone·washed /ˈstōnˌwôsʜt, -ˌwäsʜt/ (also **stonewash**) ▶ **adjective** (of a garment or fabric) washed with small stones to produce a worn or faded appearance.

stone·work /ˈstōnˌwərk/ ▶ **noun** the parts of a building that are made of stone.

ston·y /ˈstōnē/ ▶ **adjective** (**stonier, stoniest**) **1** full of stones. **2** made of or resembling stone. **3** cold and unfeeling: *a stony glare*.

– SYNONYMS **1 rocky,** pebbly, gravelly, shingly, rough. **2** *a stony stare* **unfriendly,** hostile, unfeeling, uncaring, unsympathetic, indifferent, hard, flinty, steely, stern, severe, expressionless, blank, poker-faced.
– ANTONYMS smooth, friendly, sympathetic.

– DERIVATIVES **ston·i·ly** adverb.
– PHRASES **fall on stony ground** (of words or a suggestion) be ignored or badly received. [with reference to the parable of the sower in the Gospel of Matthew.]

stood /sto͝od/ past and past participle of **STAND**.

stooge /sto͞oj/ ▶ **noun** informal **1** derogatory a less important person used by another to do routine or unpleasant work. **2** a performer whose act involves being the butt of a comedian's jokes.

– SYNONYMS **underling,** minion, lackey, henchman, subordinate, puppet, pawn, cat's paw; informal sidekick.

– ORIGIN unknown.

stool /sto͞ol/ ▶ **noun 1** a seat without a back or arms. **2** chiefly Medicine a piece of feces.
– ORIGIN Old English.

stool·ie /ˈsto͞olē/ ▶ **noun** informal short for **STOOL PIGEON**.

stool pi·geon ▶ **noun** informal a police informer.
– ORIGIN from the former use of a pigeon fixed to a stool as a decoy.

stoop[1] /sto͞op/ ▶ **verb 1** bend the head or body forward and downward. **2** have the head and shoulders permanently bent forward. **3** lower one's moral standards to do something wrong: *Craig wouldn't stoop to thieving*.

– SYNONYMS **bend,** lean, crouch, bow, duck.

▶ **noun** a stooping posture.
– ORIGIN Old English.

stoop[2] ▶ **noun** a porch with steps in front of a building.
– ORIGIN Dutch *stoep*.

stop /stäp/ ▶ **verb** (**stops, stopping, stopped**) **1** come or bring to an end. **2** prevent something from happening, moving, or operating. **3** prevent someone from doing something. **4** no longer move or operate: *my watch has stopped*. **5** (of a bus or train) call at a particular place to pick up or set down passengers. **6** block or close up a hole or leak. **7** withhold or deduct: *they stopped the strikers' wages*. **8** ask a bank to withhold payment on a check. **9** obtain the required pitch from the string of a musical instrument by pressing at the appropriate point with the finger.

– SYNONYMS **1 end,** halt, finish, terminate, wind up, bring to a stop/halt, discontinue, cut short, interrupt, nip in the bud, shut down. **2** *he stopped smoking* **cease,** refrain from, discontinue, desist from, break off, give up, abandon, cut out; informal quit, pack in. **3 pull up,** draw up, come to a stop/halt, come to (a) rest, pull in/over. **4** *the music stopped* **come to an end,** draw to a close, end, cease, halt, finish, be over, conclude. **5 prevent,** obstruct, impede, block, bar, preclude, dissuade from.
– ANTONYMS start, begin, continue.

▶ **noun 1** an act of stopping. **2** a place where a bus or train regularly stops. **3** an object or part of a mechanism that prevents movement. **4** a set of organ pipes of a particular tone and range of pitch. **5** a knob that controls such a set of organ pipes.

– SYNONYMS **1 halt,** end, finish, cessation, close, conclusion, termination, standstill. **2 break,** stopover, stop-off, stay, visit; literary sojourn. **3 stopping place,** station, halt.

– PHRASES **pull out all the stops** make a very great effort to achieve something. [with reference to the stops of an organ.] **stop off** (or **over**) pay a short visit to a place on the way to somewhere else.
– ORIGIN Old English.

stop-and-go ▶ **adjective** having progress marked by alternate stopping and restarting: *stop-and-go driving*.

stop·cock /ˈstäpˌkäk/ ▶ **noun** an externally operated valve regulating the flow of a liquid or gas through a pipe.

stop·gap /ˈstäpˌgap/ ▶ **noun** a temporary solution or substitute.

stop·light /ˈstäpˌlīt/ ▶ **noun 1** another term for **TRAFFIC LIGHT**. **2** a red traffic light.

stop-mo·tion ▶ **noun** a technique of film animation in which the camera is repeatedly stopped and started to give the impression of movement.

stop-off ▶ **noun** another term for **STOPOVER**.

stop·o·ver /ˈstäpˌōvər/ ▶ **noun** a break in a journey.

stop·page /ˈstäpij/ ▶ **noun 1** an instance of stopping. **2** an instance of industrial action. **3** a blockage.

stop·per /ˈstäpər/ ▶ **noun 1** a plug for sealing a container. **2** a person or thing that stops something: *a conversation stopper*. ▶ **verb** seal a container with a stopper.

stop·watch /ˈstäpˌwäcʜ/ ▶ **noun** a special watch with buttons that start and stop the display, used to time races.

stor·age /ˈstôrij/ ▶ **noun 1** the action of storing something. **2** space available for storing: *we put most of the furniture into storage*.

stor·age heat·er ▶ **noun** Brit. an electric heater that stores up heat during the night and releases it during the day.

store /stôr/ ▶ **noun 1** a retail establishment selling different types of goods. **2** a quantity or supply of something kept for use as needed. **3** a place where things are kept for future use or sale: *a grain store*. **4** (**stores**) supplies of equipment and food kept for use by members of an army, navy, or other institution. **5** a computer memory.

– SYNONYMS **1 stock,** supply, stockpile, hoard, cache, reserve, bank, pool; informal stash. **2 storeroom,** storehouse, repository, stockroom, depot, depository, warehouse. **3** *ship's stores* **supplies,** provisions, stocks, food, rations, materials, equipment, hardware. **4 shop,** market, grocery store, emporium, (retail) outlet, mart, boutique, department store, supermarket, superstore, megastore.

▶ **verb 1** keep for future use: *a small room used for storing furniture.* **2** enter or keep information in the memory of a computer. **3** (**store something up**) fail to deal with something, especially when this results in future problems.

– SYNONYMS **keep,** stockpile, stock up with, lay in, set aside, put aside, put away/by, save, collect, accumulate, amass, hoard; informal squirrel away, salt away, stash.
– ANTONYMS use, discard.

– PHRASES **in store** about to happen. **set store by** consider to be of a particular level of importance: *he set great store by teamwork.*
– ORIGIN Old French *estore.*

store brand ▶ **noun** a product manufactured specially for a retailer and bearing the retailer's name.

store·front /'stôr,frənt/ ▶ **noun 1** the part of a store that faces the street. **2** a commercial establishment, such as a store or restaurant, occupying space facing the street on the ground floor of a building.

store·house /'stôr,hous/ ▶ **noun 1** a building used for storing goods. **2** a thing that contains a large store of something: *the CD is an interactive storehouse of garden information.*

– SYNONYMS **warehouse,** depository, repository, store, storeroom, depot.

store·keep·er /'stôr,kēpər/ ▶ **noun 1** a person who owns or runs a store. **2** a person responsible for stored goods.

store·room /'stôr,ro͞om, -,ro͝om/ ▶ **noun** a room in which items are stored.

sto·rey /'stôrē/ ▶ **noun** Brit. variant spelling of **STORY[2]**.

sto·ried /'stôrēd/ ▶ **adjective** literary celebrated in or associated with stories or legends.

stork /stôrk/ ▶ **noun** a tall long-legged bird with a long heavy bill and white and black plumage.
– ORIGIN Old English.

storm /stôrm/ ▶ **noun 1** a violent disturbance of the atmosphere with strong winds and rain, and often thunder, lightning, or snow. **2** an uproar or controversy. **3** an intense outburst of a specified feeling or reaction: *the comedy attracted a storm of criticism.*

– SYNONYMS **1 tempest,** squall, gale, hurricane, tornado, cyclone, typhoon, thunderstorm, rainstorm, monsoon, hailstorm, snowstorm, blizzard. **2 uproar,** outcry, fuss, furor, ruckus, rumpus, trouble; informal to-do, hoo-ha, ruction(s), stink.

▶ **verb 1** move angrily or forcefully: *he stormed out of the house.* **2** (of troops) suddenly attack and capture a place. **3** shout angrily.

– SYNONYMS **1 stride,** march, stomp, stamp, stalk, flounce, fling. **2 attack,** charge, rush, swoop on.

– PHRASES **take something by storm 1** capture a place by a sudden attack. **2** have great and rapid success in a place.
– ORIGIN Old English.

CHOOSE THE RIGHT WORD

See **ATTACK**.

storm cloud ▶ **noun 1** a large dark rain cloud. **2** (**storm clouds**) a sign of problems or trouble to come: *storm clouds are looming over the PC market.*

storm door (or **storm window**) ▶ **noun** an additional outer door (or window) for protection in bad weather.

storm pet·rel ▶ **noun** a small petrel (bird) with blackish plumage, formerly believed to be a sign of bad weather to come.

storm sew·er (also **storm drain**) ▶ **noun** a sewer built to carry away excess water in times of heavy rain.

storm troops ▶ **plural noun** another term for **SHOCK TROOPS**.
– DERIVATIVES **storm troop·er** noun.

storm win·dow ▶ **noun** a window fixed outside a normal window for protection and insulation in bad weather or winter.

storm·y /'stôrmē/ ▶ **adjective** (**stormier, stormiest**) **1** affected by a storm. **2** full of angry or violent outbursts of feeling.

– SYNONYMS **1 blustery,** squally, windy, gusty, blowy, thundery, wild, violent, rough, foul. **2 angry,** heated, fierce, furious, passionate, acrimonious.
– ANTONYMS calm, peaceful.

– DERIVATIVES **storm·i·ly** adverb **storm·i·ness** noun.

sto·ry[1] /'stôrē/ ▶ **noun** (pl. **stories**) **1** an account of imaginary or real people and events told for entertainment. **2** a description of past events, experiences, etc.: *he issued a dossier giving his side of the story.* **3** an item of news. **4** a plot or storyline. **5** informal a lie.

– SYNONYMS **1 tale,** narrative, account, history, anecdote, saga; informal yarn. **2 news,** report, item, article, feature, piece. **3 rumor,** whisper, allegation, speculation, gossip. **4 plot,** storyline, scenario.

– ORIGIN Old French *estorie.*

sto·ry[2] (Brit. **storey**) ▶ **noun** (pl. **stories** or **storeys**) a floor or level of a building.
– ORIGIN from Latin *historia* 'history': perhaps first referring to a row of painted windows or sculptures on a building, representing a historical subject.

sto·ry·board /'stôrē,bôrd/ ▶ **noun** a sequence of drawings representing the shots planned for a movie or television production.

sto·ry·book /'stôrē,bo͝ok/ ▶ **noun** a book containing a story or stories for children. ▶ **adjective** perfect, as things typically are in children's stories: *a storybook romance.*

sto·ry·line /'stôrē,līn/ ▶ **noun** the plot of a novel, play, movie, etc.

sto·ry·tell·er /'stôrē,telər/ ▶ **noun** a person who tells stories.
– DERIVATIVES **sto·ry·tell·ing** noun.

stoup /sto͞op/ ▶ **noun** a basin for holy water in a church.
– ORIGIN Old Norse.

stout /stout/ ▶ **adjective 1** rather fat or heavily built. **2** (of an object) sturdy and thick. **3** brave and determined: *he put up a stout defense.*

– SYNONYMS **1 fat,** big, plump, portly, rotund, dumpy, corpulent, thickset, burly, bulky; informal tubby, pudgy, zaftig, corn-fed. **2 strong,** sturdy, solid, robust, tough, durable, hard-wearing. **3 determined,** vigorous, forceful, spirited, committed, brave, fearless, valiant, gallant, bold, plucky; informal gutsy.
– ANTONYMS thin, flimsy.

▶ **noun** a kind of strong, dark beer brewed with roasted malt or barley.
– DERIVATIVES **stout·ly** adverb **stout·ness** noun.
– ORIGIN Old French.

stout·heart·ed /ˈstoutˈhärtid/ ▶ **adjective** courageous or determined.

stove[1] /stōv/ ▶ **noun** a piece of equipment for cooking or heating that operates by burning fuel or using electricity.
– ORIGIN Dutch or German.

stove[2] past and past participle of **STAVE**.

stove·pipe /ˈstōvˌpīp/ ▶ **noun** a pipe taking the smoke and gases from a stove up through a roof or to a chimney.

stove·pipe hat ▶ **noun** a type of tall top hat.

stow /stō/ ▶ **verb 1** pack or store an object tidily in a particular place. **2** (**stow away**) hide oneself on a ship, aircraft, etc., so as to travel secretly or without paying.
– DERIVATIVES **stow·age** /ˈstōij/ noun.
– ORIGIN from **BESTOW**.

stow·a·way /ˈstōəˌwā/ ▶ **noun** a person who stows away on a ship, aircraft, etc.

stra·bis·mus /strəˈbizməs/ ▶ **noun** Medicine the condition of having a squint.
– ORIGIN Greek *strabismos*.

strad·dle /ˈstradl/ ▶ **verb 1** sit or stand with one leg on either side of something or someone. **2** extend across both sides of: *the plain straddles the border between Alaska and the Yukon*.
– ORIGIN from dialect *striddling* 'astride.'

Strad·i·var·i·us /ˌstradəˈve(ə)rēəs/ ▶ **noun** a violin or other stringed instrument made by the Italian violin-maker Antonio Stradivari or his followers.

strafe /strāf/ ▶ **verb** attack something with machine-gun fire or bombs from low-flying aircraft.
– ORIGIN from the German First World War catchphrase *Gott strafe England* 'may God punish England.'

strag·gle /ˈstragəl/ ▶ **verb 1** trail slowly behind the person or people in front. **2** grow or spread out in an irregular, untidy way. ▶ **noun** an irregular and untidy group.
– DERIVATIVES **strag·gler** /ˈstrag(ə)lər/ noun **strag·gly** /ˈstrag(ə)lē/ adjective.
– ORIGIN perhaps from dialect *strake* 'go.'

straight /strāt/ ▶ **adjective 1** extending uniformly in one direction only; without a curve or bend. **2** properly positioned so as to be level, upright, or symmetrical. **3** in proper order or condition: *it'll take a long time to get the place straight*. **4** honest and direct. **5** in continuous succession: *his fourth straight win*. **6** (of an alcoholic drink) undiluted. **7** informal conventional or respectable. **8** informal heterosexual. **9** (of drama) serious as opposed to comic or musical.

– SYNONYMS **1 direct,** linear, unswerving, undeviating. **2 level,** even, in line, aligned, square, vertical, upright, perpendicular, horizontal. **3 in order,** tidy, neat, shipshape, spick and span, orderly, organized, arranged, sorted out, straightened out. **4 honest,** direct, frank, candid, truthful, sincere, forthright, straightforward, plain-spoken, blunt, unambiguous; informal upfront. **5 undiluted,** neat, pure; informal straight up.
– ANTONYMS winding, crooked.

▶ **adverb 1** in a straight line or in a straight way. **2** without delay or diversion. **3** clearly and logically: *I'm so tired I can't think straight*.

– SYNONYMS **1 right,** directly, squarely, full; informal smack, smack dab, (slam) bang. **2 frankly,** directly, candidly, honestly, forthrightly, plainly, point-blank, bluntly, flatly; informal straight up. **3 logically,** rationally, clearly, lucidly, coherently, cogently.

▶ **noun 1** the straight part of something. **2** informal a conventional person. **3** informal a heterosexual person.
– DERIVATIVES **straight·ly** adverb **straight·ness** noun.
– PHRASES **go straight** live an honest life after being a criminal. **the straight and narrow** the honest and morally acceptable way of living. **straight off** (or **out**) informal without hesitating.
– ORIGIN former past participle of **STRETCH**.

USAGE

Do not confuse **straight** with **strait**. **Straight** means 'without a curve or bend' (*a long, straight road*), whereas **strait** means 'a narrow passage of water' (*the Straits of Gibraltar*) or 'trouble or difficulty' (*the economy is in dire straits*).

straight·a·way /ˈstrātəˌwā/ ▶ **adverb** immediately.

– SYNONYMS **at once,** right away, (right) now, this/that (very) minute, this/that instant, immediately, instantly, directly, forthwith, in short order, then and there, here and now; informal straight off, pronto, lickety-split.

▶ **adjective** extending or moving in a straight line.
▶ **noun** a straight section of a road or racetrack.

straight·edge /ˈstrātˌej/ ▶ **noun** a bar with one edge accurately straight, used for testing straightness.

straight·en /ˈstrātn/ ▶ **verb 1** make or become straight. **2** stand or sit up straight after bending.

– SYNONYMS **1 put straight,** adjust, put in order, arrange, rearrange, tidy, neaten. **2** *we must **straighten** things **out** with him* **put right,** sort out, clear up, settle, resolve, rectify, remedy; informal patch up.

straight-faced ▶ **adjective** having a blank or serious facial expression.
– DERIVATIVES **straight face** noun.

straight·for·ward /ˌstrātˈfôrwərd/ ▶ **adjective 1** easy to do or understand. **2** honest and open.

– SYNONYMS **1 uncomplicated,** easy, simple, elementary, undemanding. **2 honest,** frank, candid, open, truthful, sincere, on the level, forthright, plain-speaking, direct; informal on the up and up, upfront.
– ANTONYMS complicated, devious.

– DERIVATIVES **straight·for·ward·ly** adverb **straight·for·ward·ness** noun.

straight·jack·et ▶ **noun** variant spelling of **STRAITJACKET**.

straight-laced ▶ **adjective** variant spelling of **STRAIT-LACED**.

straight man ▶ **noun** a person in a show whose role is to provide a comedian with opportunities to make jokes.

straight-up ▶ **adjective** informal honest; trustworthy.

strain[1] /strān/ ▶ **verb 1** force a part of one's body or oneself to make an unusually great effort. **2** injure a limb, muscle, or organ by making it work too hard. **3** make severe or excessive demands on: *he strained her tolerance to the limit.* **4** pull or push forcibly at something. **5** pour a mainly liquid substance through a sieve or similar device to separate out any solid matter.

– SYNONYMS **1 overtax,** overwork, overextend, overreach, overdo it, exhaust, wear out; informal knock oneself out. **2 injure,** damage, pull, wrench, twist, sprain. **3 sieve,** sift, filter, screen.

▶ **noun 1** a force tending to pull or stretch something to an extreme degree. **2** an injury caused by straining a muscle, limb, etc. **3** a severe demand on strength or resources: *the large order is already putting a strain on the airline.* **4** a state of tension or exhaustion caused by severe demands on a person's strength or resources. **5** the sound of a piece of music as it is played.

– SYNONYMS **1 tension,** tightness, tautness. **2 injury,** sprain, wrench, twist. **3 pressure,** demands, burdens, stress; informal hassle. **4 stress,** (nervous) tension, exhaustion, fatigue, pressure, overwork.

– ORIGIN Old French *estreindre.*

strain[2] ▶ **noun 1** a distinct breed or variety of an animal, plant, or other organism. **2** a tendency in a person's character. **3** a type or kind of something: *the Tibetan strain of Buddhism.*

– SYNONYMS **variety,** kind, type, sort, breed, genus.

– ORIGIN Old English, 'acquisition, gain.'

strained /strānd/ ▶ **adjective 1** tense, tired, or uneasy. **2** produced by deliberate effort; artificial or forced: *a strained conversation.*

– SYNONYMS **1 awkward,** tense, uneasy, uncomfortable, edgy, difficult, troubled. **2 forced,** unnatural, artificial, insincere, false, affected, put-on.

strain·er /'strānər/ ▶ **noun** a device for straining liquids, having holes punched in it or made of wire mesh.

strait /strāt/ ▶ **noun 1** (also **straits**) a narrow passage of water connecting two seas or other large areas of water. **2** (**straits**) a situation of trouble or difficulty: *the economy is in dire straits.*

– SYNONYMS **1 channel,** sound, narrows, stretch of water. **2** (**straits**) **difficulty,** trouble, crisis, mess, predicament, plight; informal hot water, jam, hole, fix, scrape.

– ORIGIN Old French *estreit* 'tight, narrow.'

USAGE

On the confusion of **strait** and **straight**, see the note at **STRAIGHT**.

strait·ened /'strātnd/ ▶ **adjective** restricted because of poverty: *they lived in straitened circumstances.*

– SYNONYMS **impoverished,** poverty-stricken, poor, destitute, penniless, dirt poor, in penury, impecunious, unable to make ends meet, in reduced circumstances.

strait·jack·et /'strāt,jakət/ (also **straightjacket**) ▶ **noun 1** a strong garment with long sleeves that can be tied together to confine the arms of a violent prisoner or mental patient. **2** something that severely restricts freedom of action or development.

strait-laced (also **straight-laced**) ▶ **adjective** having very strict moral attitudes.

– SYNONYMS **prim (and proper),** prudish, puritanical, prissy, conservative, old-fashioned, stuffy, staid; informal starchy, square, fuddy-duddy.
– ANTONYMS broad-minded.

strand[1] /strand/ ▶ **verb 1** drive or leave a boat, person, or sea creature aground on a shore. **2** leave something without the means to move from a place: *the trucks are stranded in France.* ▶ **noun** literary or Irish the shore of a sea, lake, or large river.

– ORIGIN Old English.

strand[2] ▶ **noun 1** a single thin length of thread, wire, etc. **2** a single hair or thin lock of hair. **3** a part of a complex whole: *the two main strands of feminism.*

– SYNONYMS **thread,** filament, fiber, length.

– ORIGIN unknown.

strand·ed /'strandid/ ▶ **adjective 1** driven ashore or run aground. **2** abandoned and unable to leave a place.

– SYNONYMS **1** *a stranded ship* **shipwrecked,** wrecked, marooned, grounded, aground, beached. **2** *she was stranded in a strange city* **helpless,** abandoned, forsaken, left high and dry, left in the lurch.

strange /strānj/ ▶ **adjective 1** unusual or surprising and often difficult to understand. **2** not previously visited, seen, or encountered; unfamiliar: *finding ATMs in a strange city can be a problem.*

– SYNONYMS **1 unusual,** odd, curious, peculiar, funny, queer, bizarre, weird, uncanny, surprising, unexpected, anomalous, atypical; informal fishy. **2 unfamiliar,** unknown, new, novel.
– ANTONYMS ordinary, familiar.

– DERIVATIVES **strange·ly** adverb **strange·ness** noun.
– ORIGIN Old French *estrange.*

stran·ger /'strānjər/ ▶ **noun 1** a person one does not know. **2** a person who does not know, or is not known in, a particular place.

– SYNONYMS **newcomer,** new arrival, visitor, guest, outsider, foreigner.

– PHRASES **be no (**or **a) stranger to** be familiar (or not familiar) with a feeling or situation.

stran·gle /'straNGgəl/ ▶ **verb 1** kill or injure someone by squeezing their neck. **2** prevent from happening or developing: *industry is being strangled by high diesel taxes.*

– SYNONYMS **throttle,** choke, garrote, asphyxiate.

– DERIVATIVES **stran·gler** /'straNGg(ə)lər/ noun.
– ORIGIN Old French *estrangler.*

stran·gle·hold /'straNGgəl,hōld/ ▶ **noun 1** a grip around a person's neck that deprives them of oxygen and so can kill them. **2** complete control over something.

stran·gu·late /'straNGgyə,lāt/ ▶ **verb** (usu. as adj. **strangulated**) Medicine squeeze a part of the body so tightly that blood cannot circulate through it.
– ORIGIN Latin *strangulare* 'choke.'

stran·gu·la·tion /,straNGgyə'lāsHən/ ▶ **noun 1** the action of strangling someone or the state of being strangled. **2** a medical condition in which a part of the body is squeezed so tightly that blood cannot circulate through it.

strap /strap/ ▶ **noun 1** a strip of flexible material used for fastening, securing, carrying, or holding onto someone or something. **2** (**the strap**) punishment by beating with a leather strap.

– SYNONYMS **belt,** tie, band, thong.

▶ **verb** (**straps, strapping, strapped**) **1** fasten or secure someone or something with a strap. **2** beat someone with a leather strap. **3** (as adj. **strapped**) informal short of money: *I'm constantly strapped for cash.*

– SYNONYMS **tie,** lash, secure, fasten, bind, make fast, truss.

– DERIVATIVES **strap·less** adjective **strap·py** adjective.
– ORIGIN dialect form of STROP.

strap·hang·er /'strap,haNGər/ ▶ **noun** informal **1** a standing passenger in a bus or train. **2** a person who commutes to work by public transportation.

strap·ping[1] /'strapiNG/ ▶ **adjective** (of a person) big and strong.

– SYNONYMS **big,** strong, well built, brawny, burly, muscular; informal beefy.

strap·ping[2] ▶ **noun 1** adhesive plaster for strapping injuries. **2** strips of flexible material or metal used to fasten or strengthen something.

stra·ta /'strātə, 'stratə/ plural of STRATUM.

strat·a·gem /'stratəjəm/ ▶ **noun** a plan or scheme intended to outwit an opponent.

– SYNONYMS **plan,** scheme, tactic, maneuver, ploy, device, trick, ruse, plot, machination, dodge; subterfuge, artifice.

– ORIGIN Greek *stratēgēma.*

stra·te·gic /strə'tējik/ ▶ **adjective 1** forming part of a long-term plan to achieve a specific purpose. **2** relating to the gaining of long-term military advantage. **3** (of weapons) intended to be fired at enemy industrial areas and communication centers rather than used in a battle. Often contrasted with TACTICAL.

– SYNONYMS **planned,** calculated, deliberate, tactical, judicious, prudent, shrewd.

– DERIVATIVES **stra·te·gi·cal·ly** /-ik(ə)lē/ adverb.

strat·e·gy /'stratəjē/ ▶ **noun** (pl. **strategies**) **1** a plan designed to achieve a particular long-term aim. **2** the art of planning and directing military activity in a war or battle. Often contrasted with TACTICS (see TACTIC).

– SYNONYMS **plan,** grand design, game plan, policy, program, scheme, tactic.

– DERIVATIVES **strat·e·gist** noun.
– ORIGIN Greek *stratēgia* 'generalship.'

strat·i·fy /'stratə,fī/ ▶ **verb** (**stratifies, stratifying, stratified**) (usu. as adj. **stratified**) **1** form or arrange something into strata, layers, or levels. **2** arrange or classify someone or something.
– DERIVATIVES **strat·i·fi·ca·tion** /,stratəfi'kāSHən/ noun.

stra·tig·ra·phy /strə'tigrəfē/ ▶ **noun** the branch of geology concerned with the order and relative dating of rock strata.
– DERIVATIVES **strat·i·graph·ic** /,stratə'grafik/ adjective **strat·i·graph·i·cal** /,stratə'grafikəl/ adjective.

stra·to·cu·mu·lus /,stratō'kyo͞omyələs, ,strā-/ ▶ **noun** cloud forming a low layer of clumped or broken gray masses.

strat·o·sphere /'stratə,sfi(ə)r/ ▶ **noun 1** the layer of the earth's atmosphere above the troposphere and below the mesosphere. **2** informal the very highest levels of something.
– DERIVATIVES **strat·o·spher·ic** /,stratə'sfi(ə)rik, -'sferik/ adjective.

stra·tum /'strātəm, 'stra-/ ▶ **noun** (pl. **strata** /'strātə, 'stra-/) **1** a layer or a series of layers of rock. **2** a thin layer within any structure. **3** a level or class of society.
– DERIVATIVES **stra·tal** adjective.
– ORIGIN Latin, 'something spread or laid down.'

USAGE

Remember that, as in Latin, the singular form in English is **stratum** and the plural is **strata**: it is incorrect to create the form **stratas** as the plural.

stra·tus /'strātəs, 'stra-/ ▶ **noun** cloud forming a continuous horizontal gray sheet, often with rain or snow.
– ORIGIN Latin, 'strewn.'

straw /strô/ ▶ **noun 1** dried stalks of grain, used as fodder or bedding for animals and for thatching, packing, or weaving. **2** a single dried stalk of grain. **3** a thin hollow tube of paper or plastic for sucking drink from a container. **4** a pale yellow color.
– PHRASES **grasp** (or **clutch**) **at straws** turn in desperation to something that is unlikely to be helpful. [from the proverb *a drowning man will clutch at a straw.*] **draw the short straw** be chosen to perform an unpleasant task. **the last** (or **final**) **straw** a further minor difficulty that comes after a series of difficulties and makes a situation unbearable. [from the proverb *the last straw breaks the (laden) camel's back.*]
– ORIGIN Old English.

straw·ber·ry /'strô,berē, -b(ə)rē/ ▶ **noun** (pl. **strawberries**) a sweet soft red fruit with many seeds on the surface.

straw·ber·ry blond (also **strawberry blonde**) ▶ **adjective** (of hair) light reddish-blond in color. ▶ **noun** a person with strawberry blond hair.

straw poll (also **straw vote**) ▶ **noun** an unofficial test of opinion.

straw pur·chase ▶ **noun** a crime in which a person who is not allowed to buy a gun for themselves induces another person to buy it.

stray /strā/ ▶ **verb 1** move away aimlessly from a group or from the right course or place: *the child had strayed from home and was lost in the desert.* **2** (of the eyes or a hand) move idly in a particular direction. **3** dated be unfaithful to a husband, wife, or lover.

– SYNONYMS **1 wander off,** go astray, get separated, get lost, drift away. **2 digress,** deviate, wander, get sidetracked, go off on a tangent, get off the subject.

▶ **adjective 1** not in the right place; separated from a group. **2** (of a domestic animal) having no home or having wandered away from home.

– SYNONYMS **1 homeless,** lost, abandoned, feral. **2** *a stray bullet* **random,** chance, freak, unexpected, isolated.

▶ **noun** a stray person or thing, especially a domestic animal.
– ORIGIN Old French *estrayer.*

streak /strēk/ ▶ **noun 1** a long, thin mark. **2** an element of a particular kind in someone's character: *Lucy had a ruthless streak.* **3** a spell of successes or failures: *he hit a winning streak.*

– SYNONYMS **1 band,** line, strip, stripe, vein, slash, ray, smear. **2 element,** vein, strain, touch. **3 period,** spell, stretch, run; informal patch.

▶ **verb 1** mark something with streaks. **2** move very fast. **3** informal run naked in a public place so as to cause shock or amusement.

– SYNONYMS **1 stripe,** band, fleck, smear, mark. **2 race,** speed, flash, shoot, dash, rush, hurtle, whiz, zoom, career, fly; informal belt, tear, zip, whip, barrel.

– DERIVATIVES **streak·er** noun **streak·ing** noun.
– ORIGIN Old English.

streak·y /'strēkē/ ▶ **adjective** (**streakier, streakiest**) having streaks.
– DERIVATIVES **streak·i·ly** adverb **streak·i·ness** noun.

stream /strēm/ ▶ **noun 1** a small, narrow river. **2** a continuous flow of liquid, air, gas, people, etc.

– SYNONYMS **1 brook,** rivulet, tributary, creek. **2 jet,** flow, rush, gush, surge, torrent, flood, cascade. **3 succession,** series, string.

▶ **verb 1** run or move in a continuous flow. **2** run with tears, sweat, or other liquid: *I woke up in the night, streaming with sweat.* **3** float at full extent in the wind.

– SYNONYMS **1 flow,** pour, course, run, gush, surge, flood, cascade, spill. **2 pour,** surge, flood, swarm, pile, crowd.

– PHRASES **on stream** in or into production or operation.
– ORIGIN Old English.

stream·er /'strēmər/ ▶ **noun** a long, narrow strip of material used as a decoration or flag.

stream·ing /'strēmiNG/ ▶ **adjective** (of a cold) accompanied by running of the nose and eyes. ▶ **noun** a method of relaying data (especially video and audio material) over a computer network as a steady continuous stream.

stream·line /'strēm,līn/ ▶ **verb 1** (usu. as adj. **streamlined**) design or form in a way that presents very little resistance to a flow of air or water. **2** make an organization or system more efficient by employing faster or simpler working methods.

– SYNONYMS **1** (as adj. **streamlined**) *a streamlined train* **aerodynamic,** smooth, sleek, elegant. **2** (as adj. **streamlined**) *a streamlined organization* **efficient,** smooth-running, well run, well oiled, slick.

stream of con·scious·ness ▶ **noun** a literary style that records the continuous flow of thoughts and reactions in the mind of a character.

street /strēt/ ▶ **noun** a public road in a city, town, or village.

– SYNONYMS **road,** highway, thoroughfare, avenue, drive, boulevard, lane.

▶ **adjective 1** relating to fashionable young people living in cities and towns: *street style.* **2** homeless: *street children.*

– PHRASES **on the streets 1** homeless. **2** working as a prostitute.
– ORIGIN from Latin *strāta via* 'paved way.'

street·car /'strēt,kär/ ▶ **noun** a trolley car.

street·light /'strēt,līt/ (also **streetlamp**) ▶ **noun** a light illuminating a road, typically mounted on a tall pole.

street-smart ▶ **adjective** another term for STREETWISE. ▶ **noun** (**street smarts**) the skills and knowledge necessary for dealing with the difficulties of modern city life.

street val·ue ▶ **noun** the price for which something that is illegal or has been illegally obtained, especially drugs, can be sold.

street·walk·er /'strēt,wôkər/ ▶ **noun** a prostitute who seeks clients in the street.

street·wise /'strēt,wīz/ ▶ **adjective** informal having the skills and knowledge necessary for dealing with the difficulties of modern city life.

strength /streNG(k)TH, strenTH/ ▶ **noun 1** the quality or state of being strong or powerful. **2** a good or valuable quality. **3** the number of people making up a group. **4** the number of people that makes a group complete: *we are now 30 staff below strength.*

– SYNONYMS **1 power,** muscle, might, brawn, muscularity, robustness, sturdiness, vigor, stamina. **2 fortitude,** resilience, spirit, backbone, courage, bravery, pluck, grit; informal guts. **3** *strength of feeling* **intensity,** vehemence, force, depth. **4** *the strength of their argument* **force,** weight, power, persuasiveness, soundness, cogency, validity. **5 strong point,** advantage, asset, forte, aptitude, talent, skill, specialty.
– ANTONYMS weakness.

– PHRASES **in strength** in large numbers. **on the strength of** on the basis of. **tower** (or **pillar**) **of strength** a person who can be relied on to support and comfort others.
– ORIGIN Old English.

strength·en /'streNG(k)THən, 'stren-/ ▶ **verb** make or become stronger.

– SYNONYMS **1 make strong,** make stronger, build up, harden, toughen. **2 grow strong,** grow stronger, gain strength, intensify, pick up. **3 reinforce,** support, back up, bolster, authenticate, confirm, substantiate, corroborate.
– ANTONYMS weaken.

– DERIVATIVES **strength·en·er** noun.

stren·u·ous /'strenyōōəs/ ▶ **adjective** requiring or using great effort or exertion.

– SYNONYMS **1 difficult,** arduous, hard, tough, taxing, demanding, exacting, exhausting, tiring, grueling, back-breaking. **2 vigorous,** energetic, forceful, strong, spirited, intense, determined, resolute, dogged.
– ANTONYMS easy, half-hearted.

– DERIVATIVES **stren·u·ous·ly** adverb **stren·u·ous·ness** noun.
– ORIGIN Latin *strenuus* 'brisk.'

strep /strep/ ▶ **noun** informal short for STREPTOCOCCUS.

strep·to·coc·cus /,streptə'käkəs/ ▶ **noun** (pl. **streptococci** /-'käksī, -sē/) a bacterium of a large genus including those causing scarlet fever, pneumonia, and tooth decay.
– DERIVATIVES **strep·to·coc·cal** /-'käkəl/ adjective.
– ORIGIN from Greek *streptos* 'twisted.'

strep·to·my·cin /,streptə'mīsin/ ▶ **noun** an antibiotic used against tuberculosis.
– ORIGIN from Greek *streptos* 'twisted' + *mukēs* 'fungus.'

stress /stres/ ▶ **noun 1** pressure or tension exerted on an object. **2** a state of mental or emotional strain. **3** particular emphasis or importance. **4** emphasis given to a syllable or word in speech.

– SYNONYMS **1 strain,** pressure, (nervous) tension, worry, anxiety, trouble, difficulty; informal hassle. **2 emphasis,** importance, weight, accent, accentuation.

▶ **verb 1** emphasize a point, statement, etc., when

speaking or writing. **2** give emphasis to a syllable or word when pronouncing it. **3** subject to strain, tension, or pressure: *this type of workout does stress the knee joints.*

– SYNONYMS **1 emphasize,** draw attention to, underline, underscore, point up, highlight, accentuate. **2 overstretch,** overtax, pressurize, pressure, push to the limit, worry, harass; informal hassle.
– ANTONYMS play down.

– ORIGIN from **DISTRESS**, or partly from Old French *estresse* 'narrowness, oppression.'

stress·ful /ˈstresfəl/ ▸ **adjective** causing mental or emotional stress.

– SYNONYMS **demanding,** trying, taxing, difficult, hard, tough, fraught, traumatic, tense, frustrating.
– ANTONYMS relaxing.

stretch /strecʜ/ ▸ **verb 1** (of something soft or elastic) be made or be able to be made longer or wider without tearing or breaking. **2** pull something tightly from one point to another. **3** extend the body or a part of the body to its full length. **4** extend over an area or period of time: *the beach stretches for over four miles.* **5** last longer than expected. **6** (of finances or resources) be enough for a particular purpose. **7** make demands on: *directors churned out pictures that failed to stretch the imagination.*

– SYNONYMS **1 expand,** give, be elastic, be stretchy, be tensile. **2 pull (out),** draw out, extend, lengthen, elongate, expand. **3 bend,** strain, distort, exaggerate, embellish. **4** *she **stretched out** her arm* **reach out,** hold out, extend, straighten (out). **5** *I **stretched out** on the sofa* **lie down,** recline, lean back, sprawl, lounge, loll. **6 extend,** spread, continue, go on.
– ANTONYMS shorten, contract.

▸ **noun 1** a continuous area or period of time: *a treacherous stretch of road.* **2** an act of stretching. **3** the capacity to stretch or be stretched; elasticity. **4** the fact or state of being stretched. **5** informal a period of time spent in prison.

– SYNONYMS **1 expanse,** area, tract, belt, sweep, extent. **2 period,** time, spell, run, stint, session, shift.

▸ **adjective** informal (of a car) much longer than usual and seating more people: *a stretch limo.*
– DERIVATIVES **stretch·y** adjective (**stretchier, stretchiest**).
– PHRASES **at full stretch** using the maximum amount of one's resources or energy. **at a stretch 1** in one continuous period. **2** just possible but with difficulty. **stretch one's legs** go for a short walk. **stretch a point** allow or do something not usually acceptable.
– ORIGIN Old English.

stretch·er /ˈstrecʜər/ ▸ **noun 1** a framework of two poles with a long piece of canvas slung between them, used for carrying sick, injured, or dead people. **2** a brick or stone laid with its long side along the face of a wall. ▸ **verb** carry someone on a stretcher.

stretch marks ▸ **plural noun** marks on the skin, especially on the abdomen, caused by stretching of the skin from obesity or during pregnancy.

strew /stro͞o/ ▸ **verb** (past part. **strewn** or **strewed**) **1** scatter things untidily over a surface or area. **2** (**be strewn with**) be covered with untidily scattered things.
– ORIGIN Old English.

stri·a /ˈstrīə/ ▸ **noun** (pl. **striae** /ˈstrī-ē/) technical a line, ridge, or groove, especially one of a number of similar parallel features.
– ORIGIN Latin, 'furrow.'

striated /ˈstrī,ātid/ ▸ **adjective** technical **1** marked with a series of ridges or grooves. **2** striped or streaked.
– DERIVATIVES **stri·a·tion** /strīˈāsʜən/ noun.

strick·en /ˈstrikən/ past participle of **STRIKE** ▸ **adjective 1** seriously affected by something unpleasant. **2** (of a face or look) showing great distress.

strict /strikt/ ▸ **adjective 1** demanding that rules about behavior are obeyed. **2** (of a rule) that must be obeyed exactly. **3** (of a person) following rules or beliefs exactly. **4** very exact and clearly defined: *the characters are not soldiers in the strict sense of the word.*

– SYNONYMS **1 precise,** exact, literal, faithful, accurate, careful, scrupulous, meticulous, punctilious. **2 stringent,** rigorous, severe, harsh, hard, stern, rigid, tough, uncompromising, authoritarian, firm. **3** *in strict confidence* **absolute,** utter, complete, total.
– ANTONYMS loose, liberal.

– DERIVATIVES **strict·ly** adverb **strict·ness** noun.
– ORIGIN Latin *strictus* 'tightened.'

CHOOSE THE RIGHT WORD

See **SEVERE**.

stric·ture /ˈstrikcʜər/ ▸ **noun 1** a rule restricting behavior or action. **2** a sternly critical remark. **3** Medicine abnormal narrowing of a passage or duct in the body: *a colonic stricture.*

stride /strīd/ ▸ **verb** (past **strode** /strōd/; past part. **stridden** /ˈstridn/) walk with long, decisive steps.

– SYNONYMS **march,** pace, step.

▸ **noun 1** a long, decisive step. **2** the length of a step in running or walking. **3** a step made toward an aim: *the company has made huge strides in product quality.* **4** (**one's stride**) a good or regular rate of progress, especially after a slow start.

– SYNONYMS **step,** pace.

– PHRASES **take something in one's stride** deal calmly with something difficult.
– ORIGIN Old English.

stri·dent /ˈstrīdnt/ ▸ **adjective 1** loud and harsh. **2** presenting a point of view in an excessively forceful way.

– SYNONYMS **harsh,** raucous, rough, grating, jarring, loud, shrill, screeching, piercing, ear-piercing.
– ANTONYMS soft.

– DERIVATIVES **stri·den·cy** noun **stri·dent·ly** adverb.
– ORIGIN from Latin *stridere* 'creak.'

strid·u·late /ˈstrijə,lāt/ ▸ **verb** (of a grasshopper or similar insect) make a shrill sound by rubbing the legs, wings, or other parts of the body together.
– DERIVATIVES **strid·u·la·tion** /,strijəˈlāsʜən/ noun.
– ORIGIN from Latin *stridulus* 'creaking.'

strife /strīf/ ▸ **noun** angry or bitter disagreement; conflict.

– SYNONYMS **conflict,** friction, discord, disagreement, dissension, dispute, argument, quarreling.
– ANTONYMS peace.

– ORIGIN Old French *estrif.*

strike /strīk/ ▸ **verb** (past and past part. **struck** /strək/) **1** deliver a hard blow to someone or something. **2** come forcefully into contact with someone or something. **3** (in sports) hit or kick a ball. **4** (of a disaster, disease, etc.) occur suddenly and have harmful effects on: *a major earthquake struck the island.* **5** attack someone or something suddenly. **6** (**strike something into**) cause a strong emotion in someone. **7** cause to become suddenly: *he was struck dumb.* **8** suddenly come into the mind of someone. **9** (**be struck by/with**) find particularly interesting or impressive: *she was struck by the beauty of the scene.* **10** light a match by rubbing it against a rough surface. **11** (of employees) refuse to work as a form of organized protest. **12** go somewhere vigorously or purposefully: *those who could swim struck out for the bank.* **13** (**strike out**) start out on a new or independent course. **14** reach an agreement or compromise. **15** cross something out with a pen. **16** (**strike someone off**) officially remove someone from membership of a professional group. **17** (of a clock) indicate the time by sounding a chime or stroke. **18** make a coin or medal by stamping metal. **19** discover gold, minerals, or oil by drilling or mining. **20** take down a tent or camp.

– SYNONYMS **1 hit,** slap, smack, thump, punch, beat, bang; informal clout, wallop, belt, whack, thwack, bash, clobber, bop. **2 crash into,** collide with, hit, run into, bump into, smash into, impact. **3 occur to,** come to (mind), dawn on someone, hit, spring to mind, enter one's head. **4** *you* ***strike*** *me as intelligent* **seem to,** appear to, give someone the impression of being. **5 take industrial action,** go on strike, walk out.

▶ **noun 1** an act of striking by employees. **2** a refusal to do something, as a form of organized protest: *a rent strike.* **3** a sudden attack. **4** (in sports) an act of striking a ball. **5** an act of striking gold, minerals, or oil.

– SYNONYMS **1 industrial action,** walkout. **2 attack,** assault, bombing.

– PHRASES **strike an attitude** (or **pose**) hold one's body in a particular position to create an impression. **strike up** begin to play a piece of music. **strike something up** begin a friendship or conversation with someone. **strike while the iron is hot** make use of an opportunity immediately.

– ORIGIN Old English, 'go, flow' and 'rub lightly.'

strike·break·er /'strīk,brākər/ ▶ **noun** a person who works or is employed in place of others who are on strike.

strike·out /'strīk,out/ ▶ **noun** Baseball an out called when a batter accumulates three strikes. ▶ **adjective** Computing (of text) having a horizontal line through the middle; crossed out.

strik·er /'strīkər/ ▶ **noun 1** an employee on strike. **2** (chiefly in soccer) a forward or attacker.

strike zone ▶ **noun** Baseball an area over home plate through which the ball must be pitched in order for a strike to be called.

strik·ing /'strīkiNG/ ▶ **adjective 1** attracting attention; noticeable. **2** very attractive.

– SYNONYMS **1 noticeable,** obvious, conspicuous, visible, distinct, marked, unmistakable, strong, remarkable. **2 impressive,** imposing, magnificent, spectacular, breathtaking, marvelous, wonderful, stunning, sensational, dramatic.
– ANTONYMS unremarkable.

– DERIVATIVES **strik·ing·ly** adverb.

string /striNG/ ▶ **noun 1** material consisting of threads twisted together to form a thin length. **2** a sequence of similar items or events. **3** a piece of string. **4** a length of catgut or wire on a musical instrument, producing a note by vibration. **5** (**strings**) the stringed instruments in an orchestra. **6** a piece of nylon or similar material interwoven with others to form the head of a sports racket. **7** a set of things tied or threaded together on a thin cord. **8** Computing a sequence of characters or other data. **9** a G-string or thong.

– SYNONYMS **1 twine,** cord, yarn, thread. **2** *a string of convictions* **series,** succession, chain, sequence, run, streak. **3** *a string of wagons* **line,** procession, queue, file, column, convoy, train, cavalcade.

▶ **verb** (past and past part. **strung** /strəNG/) **1** hang or thread things on a string. **2** (**be strung** or **be strung out**) be arranged in a long line. **3** fit a string or strings to a musical instrument, a racket, or a bow.

– SYNONYMS **hang,** suspend, sling, stretch, run, thread, loop, festoon.

– DERIVATIVES **stringed** adjective.

– PHRASES **be strung out** informal **1** be tense or nervous. **2** be under the influence of alcohol or drugs. **no strings attached** informal there are no special conditions. **string someone along** informal mislead someone deliberately over a period of time. **string someone up** kill someone by hanging.

– ORIGIN Old English.

string bass /bās/ ▶ **noun** (especially among jazz musicians) a double bass.

string bean ▶ **noun** any of various beans eaten in their fibrous pods; a runner bean.

strin·gent /'strinjənt/ ▶ **adjective** (of regulations or requirements) very strict; that must be obeyed.

– SYNONYMS **strict,** firm, rigid, rigorous, severe, harsh, tough, tight, exacting, demanding.
– ANTONYMS lax.

– DERIVATIVES **strin·gen·cy** noun **strin·gent·ly** adverb.

– ORIGIN from Latin *stringere* 'draw tight.'

string·er /'striNGər/ ▶ **noun 1** informal a journalist who is not on the regular staff of a newspaper, but who reports part-time on a particular place. **2** a structural piece running lengthwise in a framework, especially that of a ship or aircraft.

string quar·tet ▶ **noun 1** a chamber music group consisting of a first and second violin, viola, and cello. **2** a composition for a string quartet.

string·y /'striNGē/ ▶ **adjective** (**stringier, stringiest**) **1** long and thin. **2** (of food) containing chewy fibers.

– SYNONYMS **1** *stringy hair* **straggly,** lank, thin. **2** *stringy meat* **fibrous,** gristly, sinewy, chewy, tough.

strip[1] /strip/ ▶ **verb** (**strips, stripping, stripped**) **1** remove all coverings or clothes from someone or something. **2** take off one's clothes. **3** remove all the contents from a room, vehicle, etc. **4** (**strip someone of**) deprive someone of rank, power, or property. **5** remove paint or varnish from a surface. **6** sell off a company's assets for profit.

– SYNONYMS **1 undress,** strip off, take one's clothes off, disrobe. **2 dismantle,** disassemble, take to bits/pieces, take apart. **3 empty,** clear, clean out, plunder, rob, burgle, loot, pillage, ransack, sack.

▶ **noun** an act of undressing.

– ORIGIN Germanic.

strip[2] ▶ **noun 1** a long, narrow piece of cloth, paper, or other material. **2** a long, narrow area of land. **3** a main road lined with stores and other facilities.

– SYNONYMS **(narrow) piece,** band, belt, ribbon, slip, shred, stretch.

– ORIGIN German *strippe* 'strap, thong.'

stripe /strīp/ ▶ **noun 1** a long narrow band of a different color or texture from its surroundings. **2** a chevron on a uniform, showing military rank. **3** a type or category.

– SYNONYMS **line,** band, strip, belt, bar, streak, vein, flash; technical stria, striation.

▶ **verb** mark someone or something with stripes.
– DERIVATIVES **striped** adjective **strip·y** (also **stripey**) adjective.
– ORIGIN perhaps from Dutch or German.

striped bass /bas/ ▶ **noun** a large migrating bass of North American coastal waters, with dark horizontal stripes along the upper sides.

strip·ling /ˈstripliNG/ ▶ **noun** old use or humorous a young man.
– ORIGIN probably from STRIP[2] (from the idea of 'narrowness', i.e. slimness).

strip mine ▶ **noun** an open-pit mine. ▶ **verb** (**strip-mine**) obtain ore or coal by open-pit mining.

stripped-down ▶ **adjective 1** reduced to essentials: *a stripped-down funding bill.* **2** (of a machine, motor vehicle, etc.) having had all internal parts removed; dismantled.

strip·per /ˈstripər/ ▶ **noun 1** a striptease performer. **2** a device or substance for stripping paint, varnish, etc.

strip-search ▶ **verb** search someone for concealed drugs, weapons, or other items, by stripping off their clothes.

strip·tease /ˈstrip,tēz/ ▶ **noun** a form of entertainment in which a performer gradually undresses to music in a sexually exciting way.

strive /strīv/ ▶ **verb** (past **strove** /strōv/ or **strived**; past part. **striven** /strivən/ or **strived**) make great efforts, especially to achieve or prevent something: *the charity strives to keep costs low.*

– SYNONYMS **try (hard),** attempt, endeavor, aim, make an effort, exert oneself, struggle, do one's best, do all one can, do one's utmost, labor, work, toil, strain; informal go all out, give it one's best shot.

– DERIVATIVES **striv·er** noun.
– ORIGIN Old French *estriver.*

strobe /strōb/ ▶ **noun** a stroboscope. ▶ **verb** flash at rapid intervals.

stro·bo·scope /ˈstrōbə,skōp/ ▶ **noun** an instrument that shines a bright light at rapid intervals so that a moving person or object appears stationary.
– DERIVATIVES **stro·bo·scop·ic** /,strōbəˈskäpik/ adjective.
– ORIGIN from Greek *strobos* 'whirling.'

strode /strōd/ past of STRIDE.

stro·ga·noff /ˈstrôgə,nôf, ˈstrō-/ ▶ **noun** a dish in which the main ingredient, typically beef, is cooked in a sour cream sauce.
– ORIGIN named after the Russian diplomat Count Pavel *Stroganov.*

stroke /strōk/ ▶ **noun 1** an act of hitting. **2** a mark made by drawing a pen, pencil, or paintbrush once across paper or canvas. **3** a line forming part of a written or printed character. **4** a short diagonal line separating characters or figures. **5** a sudden disabling attack or loss of consciousness caused by an interruption in the flow of blood to the brain. **6** a sound made by a striking clock. **7** an act of stroking with the hand. **8** one of a series of repeated movements, especially in swimming or rowing. **9** a style of moving the arms and legs in swimming. **10** the way in which the oar is moved in rowing. **11** Golf an act of hitting the ball with a club, as a unit of scoring.

– SYNONYMS **1 blow,** hit, slap, smack, thump, punch. **2 movement,** action, motion. **3 mark,** line. **4 thrombosis,** embolism, seizure; dated apoplexy.

▶ **verb** gently move one's hand over someone or something.

– SYNONYMS **caress,** fondle, pat, pet, touch, rub, massage, soothe.

– DERIVATIVES **strok·er** noun.
– PHRASES **stroke of genius** an outstandingly original idea. **stroke of luck** a lucky and unexpected event.
– ORIGIN Old English.

stroke play ▶ **noun** golf in which the score is reckoned by counting the number of strokes taken overall. Compare with MATCH PLAY.

stroll /strōl/ ▶ **verb 1** walk in a leisurely way. **2** informal in sports, achieve a victory easily.

– SYNONYMS **saunter,** amble, wander, meander, ramble, promenade, walk; informal mosey.

▶ **noun 1** a short leisurely walk. **2** informal a victory that is easily achieved.

– SYNONYMS **saunter,** amble, wander, walk, promenade; informal mosey.

– ORIGIN probably from German *strollen.*

stroll·er /ˈstrōlər/ ▶ **noun** a folding chair on wheels, in which a young child can be pushed along.

strong /strôNG, sträNG/ ▶ **adjective** (**stronger, strongest**) **1** physically powerful. **2** done with or exerting great force: *a strong current.* **3** able to withstand great force or pressure. **4** secure, stable, or firmly established. **5** great in power, influence, or ability: *a strong leader.* **6** (of something smelled, tasted, etc.) very intense. **7** (of language) forceful and using swear words. **8** (of a solution or drink) containing a large proportion of a substance. **9** used after a number to indicate the size of a group: *a crowd several thousands strong.* **10** (of verbs) forming the past tense and past participle by a change of vowel within the stem rather than by adding an ending or suffix (e.g., *swim, swam, swum*).

– SYNONYMS **1 powerful,** sturdy, robust, athletic, fit, tough, rugged, strapping, well built, muscular, brawny, lusty, healthy. **2 forceful,** determined, spirited, assertive, self-assertive, tough, formidable, strong-minded, redoubtable; informal gutsy, feisty. **3 secure,** solid, well built, durable, hard-wearing, heavy-duty, tough, sturdy, well made, long-lasting. **4** *a strong supporter* **keen,** passionate, fervent, zealous, enthusiastic, eager, dedicated, loyal. **5** *strong feelings* **intense,** vehement, passionate, ardent, fervent, deep-seated. **6 forceful,** compelling, powerful, convincing, persuasive, sound, valid, cogent, well founded. **7 intense,** bright, brilliant, vivid, vibrant, dazzling, glaring. **8 highly flavored,** mature, ripe, piquant, tangy, spicy. **9 concentrated,** undiluted. **10 alcoholic,** intoxicating, hard, stiff.
– ANTONYMS weak, gentle, mild.

– DERIVATIVES **strong·ly** adverb.
– PHRASES **going strong** informal continuing to be healthy, vigorous, or successful. **strong on 1** good at. **2** possessing large quantities of. **one's strong point** (or **suit**) something one is very good at.
– ORIGIN Old English, related to STRING.

strong-arm ▶ **adjective** using force or violence. ▶ **verb** use force or violence against someone.

strong·box /ˈstrôNG,bäks/ ▶ **noun** a small lockable metal box in which valuables may be kept.

strong·hold /ˈstrôNG,hōld/ ▶ **noun** **1** a place of strong support for a cause or political party. **2** a place that has been fortified against attack.

– SYNONYMS **1 fortress,** fort, castle, citadel, garrison. **2** *a Republican stronghold* **bastion,** center, hotbed.

strong·man /ˈstrôNG,man/ ▶ **noun** (pl. **strongmen**) **1** a very strong man, especially one who performs feats of strength for entertainment. **2** a leader who rules by force or violence.

strong·room /ˈstrôNG,ro͞om, -,ro͝om/ ▶ **noun** a room, typically one in a bank, designed to protect valuable items against fire and theft.

strong suit ▶ **noun** **1** (in bridge) a holding of a number of high cards of one suit in a hand. **2** a desirable quality that is particularly prominent in someone's character or an activity at which they excel.

stron·ti·um /ˈstränCHēəm, -tēəm/ ▶ **noun** a soft silver-white metallic chemical element.
– ORIGIN from *Strontian* in Scotland.

strop /sträp/ ▶ **noun** a strip of leather for sharpening razors. ▶ **verb** (**strops, stropping, stropped**) sharpen a razor on or with a strop.
– ORIGIN probably from Latin *stroppus* 'thong.'

strove /strōv/ past of STRIVE.

struck /strək/ past and past participle of STRIKE.

struc·tur·al /ˈstrəkCHərəl/ ▶ **adjective** relating to or forming part of a structure.
– DERIVATIVES **struc·tur·al·ly** adverb.

struc·tur·al·ism /ˈstrəkCHərə,lizəm/ ▶ **noun** a theory that pieces of writing, languages, and social systems should be seen as a structure whose various parts have meaning only when considered in relation to each other.
– DERIVATIVES **struc·tur·al·ist** noun & adjective.

struc·ture /ˈstrəkCHər/ ▶ **noun** **1** the arrangement of and relations between the parts of something complex: *changes to the company's organizational structure.* **2** a building or other object constructed from several parts. **3** the quality of being well organized.

– SYNONYMS **1 building,** edifice, construction, erection. **2 construction,** organization, system, arrangement, framework, form, formation, shape, composition, anatomy, makeup.

▶ **verb** organize or arrange something according to a plan or system.

– SYNONYMS **arrange,** organize, design, shape, construct, build.

– ORIGIN Latin *structura.*

stru·del /ˈstro͞odl/ ▶ **noun** a dessert of thin pastry rolled up around a fruit filling and baked.
– ORIGIN German, 'whirlpool.'

strug·gle /ˈstrəgəl/ ▶ **verb** **1** make forceful efforts to get free. **2** try hard to do something under difficult circumstances. **3** make one's way with difficulty.

– SYNONYMS **1 strive,** try hard, endeavor, make every effort, exert oneself, do one's best, do one's utmost. **2 fight,** battle, grapple, wrestle, scuffle.

▶ **noun** **1** an act of struggling. **2** a conflict or contest: *a power struggle for the leadership.* **3** a very difficult task.

– SYNONYMS **1 striving,** endeavor, effort, exertion, campaign, battle, drive, push. **2 fight,** scuffle, brawl, tussle, fracas; informal set-to. **3** *a power struggle* **contest,** competition, fight, clash, rivalry, friction, feuding, conflict.

– DERIVATIVES **strug·gler** /ˈstrəg(ə)lər/ noun.
– ORIGIN uncertain.

strum /strəm/ ▶ **verb** (**strums, strumming, strummed**) play a guitar or similar instrument by sweeping the thumb or a plectrum up or down the strings.
– ORIGIN imitating the sound.

strum·pet /ˈstrəmpət/ ▶ **noun** old use or humorous a woman who has many sexual partners.
– ORIGIN unknown.

strung /strəNG/ past and past participle of STRING.

strut /strət/ ▶ **noun** **1** a bar used to support or strengthen a structure. **2** an arrogant or very confident walk. ▶ **verb** (**struts, strutting, strutted**) **1** walk in an arrogant or very confident way, with one's back straight and head up. **2** brace something with a strut or struts.

– SYNONYMS **swagger,** prance, parade, stride, sweep, flounce; informal sashay.

– ORIGIN from Old English, 'protrude stiffly.'

strych·nine /ˈstrik,nīn, -,nēn/ ▶ **noun** a bitter and highly poisonous substance obtained from the seeds of nux vomica (an Asian tree).
– ORIGIN from Greek *strukhnos*, referring to a kind of nightshade.

Stu·art /ˈst(y)o͞oərt/ (also **Stewart** pronunc. same) ▶ **adjective** belonging or relating to the royal family ruling Scotland 1371–1714 and Britain 1603–1714 (interrupted by the Commonwealth 1649–60). ▶ **noun** a member of the Stuart family.

stub /stəb/ ▶ **noun** **1** the remnant of a pencil, cigarette, or similar-shaped object after use. **2** a shortened or unusually short thing. **3** the counterfoil of a check, ticket, or other document. ▶ **verb** (**stubs, stubbing, stubbed**) **1** accidentally hit one's toe against something. **2** (often **stub something out**) put a cigarette out by pressing the lighted end against something.
– ORIGIN Old English, 'stump of a tree.'

stub·ble /ˈstəbəl/ ▶ **noun** **1** short, stiff hairs growing on a man's face when he has not shaved for a while. **2** the cut stalks of cereal plants left in the ground after harvesting.
– DERIVATIVES **stub·bly** adjective.
– ORIGIN Old French *stuble.*

stub·born /ˈstəbərn/ ▶ **adjective** **1** determined not to change one's attitude or position. **2** difficult to move, remove, or cure: *a stubborn stain.*

– SYNONYMS **1 obstinate,** headstrong, willful, strong-willed, pigheaded, mulish, inflexible, uncompromising, unbending, unyielding, obdurate, intractable, recalcitrant; informal stiff-necked. **2 indelible,** permanent, persistent, tenacious, resistant.

– DERIVATIVES **stub·born·ly** adverb **stub·born·ness** noun.
– ORIGIN unknown.

CHOOSE THE RIGHT WORD

stubborn, dogged, intractable, obdurate, obstinate, pertinacious, perverse

If you're the kind of person who takes a stand and then refuses to back down, your friends might say you have a **stubborn** disposition, a word that implies an innate resistance to any attempt to change one's purpose, course, or opinion. People who are *stubborn* by nature exhibit this kind of behavior in most situations, but they might be **obstinate** in a particular instance (*a stubborn child, he was obstinate in his refusal to eat vegetables*). *Obstinate* implies sticking persistently to an opinion, purpose, or course of action, especially in the face of persuasion or attack. While *obstinate* is usually a negative term, **dogged** can be either positive or negative, implying both tenacious, often sullen, persistence (*dogged pursuit of a college degree, even though he knew he would end up in the family business*) and great determination (*dogged loyalty to a cause*). **Obdurate** usually connotes a stubborn resistance marked by harshness and lack of feeling (*obdurate in ignoring their pleas*), while **intractable** means stubborn in a headstrong sense and difficult for others to control or manage (*intractable pain*). No matter how stubborn you are, you probably don't want to be called **pertinacious**, which implies persistence to the point of being annoying or unreasonable (*a pertinacious panhandler*).

stub·by /ˈstəbē/ ▸ **adjective** (**stubbier, stubbiest**) short and thick.

stuc·co /ˈstəkō/ ▸ **noun** fine plaster used for coating wall surfaces or molding into architectural decorations.
– DERIVATIVES **stuc·coed** adjective.
– ORIGIN Italian.

stuck /stək/ past participle of STICK[2].

stuck-up ▸ **adjective** informal unfriendly toward others because one believes that one is superior to them.

stud[1] /stəd/ ▸ **noun 1** a large-headed piece of metal that pierces and projects from a surface, especially for decoration. **2** a small piece of jewelry that is pushed through a pierced ear or nostril. **3** a device consisting of two buttons joined with a bar, used to fasten a collar to a shirt. ▸ **verb** (**studs, studding, studded**) **1** decorate something with studs or similar small objects. **2** cover or scatter with many small things: *the sky was studded with stars.*
– DERIVATIVES **stud·ding** noun.
– ORIGIN Old English, 'post, upright prop.'

stud[2] ▸ **noun 1** an establishment where horses or other domesticated animals are kept for breeding. **2** (also **stud horse**) a stallion. **3** informal a man who has many sexual partners or is considered sexually desirable.
– ORIGIN Old English.

stu·dent /ˈst(y)o͞odnt/ ▸ **noun 1** a person studying at a school or college. **2** a person who takes a particular interest in a subject.

– SYNONYMS **1 scholar,** pupil, schoolchild, schoolboy, schoolgirl; freshman, sophomore, junior, senior, undergraduate. **2 trainee,** apprentice, probationer, novice, learner.

▸ **adjective** referring to a person who is studying to enter a particular profession: *a student nurse.*
– ORIGIN from Latin *studere* 'apply oneself to.'

stu·di·o /ˈst(y)o͞odēˌō/ ▸ **noun** (pl. **studios**) **1** a room from which television or radio programs are broadcast, or in which they are recorded. **2** a place where film or sound recordings are made. **3** a room where an artist works or where dancers practice.

– SYNONYMS **workshop,** workroom, atelier; recording studio.

– ORIGIN Italian.

stu·di·o a·part·ment ▸ **noun** an apartment containing one main room.

stu·di·ous /ˈst(y)o͞odēəs/ ▸ **adjective 1** spending a lot of time studying or reading. **2** done deliberately or with great care.

– SYNONYMS **scholarly,** academic, bookish, intellectual, erudite, learned, donnish; informal **brainy.**

– DERIVATIVES **stu·di·ous·ly** adverb **stu·di·ous·ness** noun.

stud·ly /ˈstədlē/ ▸ **adjective** (**studlier, studliest**) informal (of a man) sexually attractive in a strongly masculine way.
– ORIGIN from STUD[2].

stud·y /ˈstədē/ ▸ **noun** (pl. **studies**) **1** the activity of learning or gaining knowledge, typically by reading or research. **2** a detailed investigation and analysis of a subject or situation: *a recent study of army recruits.* **3** a room for reading, writing, or academic work. **4** a drawing or painting done for practice or before creating a larger picture. **5** a piece of music designed to develop a player's technical skill.

– SYNONYMS **1 learning,** education, schooling, scholarship, tuition, research. **2 investigation,** inquiry, research, examination, analysis, review, survey. **3 office,** workroom, studio.

▸ **verb** (**studies, studying, studied**) **1** gain knowledge of a subject. **2** investigate and analyze a subject or situation in detail. **3** concentrate on gaining knowledge. **4** look at closely: *she bent her head to study the plans.* **5** (as adj. **studied**) done deliberately and carefully: *she takes a studied approach to her work.*

– SYNONYMS **1 work,** review; informal cram. **2 learn,** read up on, be taught. **3 investigate,** research, inquire into, look into, examine, analyze, survey. **4 scrutinize,** examine, inspect, consider, regard, look at, observe, watch, survey.

– PHRASES **a study in** a good example of a quality or emotion.
– ORIGIN Latin *studium* 'zeal, painstaking application.'

stuff /stəf/ ▸ **noun 1** substance, things, or activities that one does not know the name of or that one does not need to specify. **2** basic characteristics: *Helen was made of sterner stuff.* **3** (**one's stuff**) informal the things that one has knowledge of or experience in.

– SYNONYMS **1 material,** substance, fabric, matter. **2 items,** articles, objects, goods, belongings, possessions, effects, paraphernalia; informal gear, things, bits and pieces, odds and ends.

▸ **verb 1** fill a container or space tightly or hastily with something. **2** fill out the skin of a dead animal or bird with material to restore its original shape and appearance. **3** fill the inside of an item of food with a savory or sweet mixture. **4** (**be stuffed up**) informal have one's nose blocked up with mucus as the result of a cold. **5** (**stuff oneself**) informal eat greedily.

– SYNONYMS **1 fill,** pack, pad, upholster. **2 shove,** thrust, push, ram, cram, squeeze, force, jam, pack, pile.

– ORIGIN Old French *estoffe* 'material, furniture.'

stuffed shirt ▸ **noun** informal a pompous or conventional person.

stuff·ing /ˈstəfiNG/ ▸ **noun 1** a mixture used to stuff poultry or meat before cooking. **2** padding used to stuff cushions, furniture, or soft toys.

– SYNONYMS **padding,** wadding, filling, packing.

– PHRASES **knock the stuffing out of** informal severely damage someone's confidence or strength.

stuff·y /ˈstəfē/ ▸ **adjective** (**stuffier, stuffiest**) **1** lacking fresh air or ventilation. **2** conventional and narrow-minded. **3** (of a person's nose) blocked up.

– SYNONYMS **1 airless,** close, musty, stale, unventilated. **2 staid,** sedate, sober, priggish, strait-

laced, conformist, conservative, old-fashioned; informal straight, starchy, square, fuddy-duddy.
– ANTONYMS airy.

– DERIVATIVES **stuff·i·ly** adverb **stuff·i·ness** noun.

stul·ti·fy /'stəltəˌfī/ ▶ verb (**stultifies, stultifying, stultified**) (usu. as adj. **stultifying**) make someone feel bored or drained of energy.
– DERIVATIVES **stul·ti·fi·ca·tion** /ˌstəltəfi'kāsʜən/ noun **stul·ti·fy·ing·ly** adverb.
– ORIGIN Latin *stultificare.*

stum·ble /'stəmbəl/ ▶ verb **1** trip and briefly lose one's balance. **2** walk unsteadily. **3** (**stumble across/on/upon**) find someone or something by chance. **4** make a mistake or mistakes in speaking.

– SYNONYMS **1 trip,** lose one's balance, lose one's footing, slip. **2 stagger,** totter, blunder, hobble. **3** (**stumble across/on**) **find,** chance on, happen on, light on, come across/upon, discover, unearth, uncover; informal dig up.

▶ noun an act of stumbling.
– ORIGIN Old Norse.

stum·bling block ▶ noun an obstacle.

stump /stəmp/ ▶ noun **1** the part of a tree trunk left projecting from the ground after the rest has fallen or been cut down. **2** a part of something that remains after the rest has been cut off or worn away. ▶ verb **1** informal baffle someone. **2** walk stiffly and noisily.

– SYNONYMS **baffle,** perplex, puzzle, confound, defeat, put at a loss; informal flummox, throw, floor.

– ORIGIN German *stumpe* or Dutch *stomp.*

stump·er /'stəmpər/ ▶ noun informal a puzzling question.

stump·y /'stəmpē/ ▶ adjective short and thick; squat.

stun /stən/ ▶ verb (**stuns, stunning, stunned**) **1** make a person or animal unconscious or dazed by hitting them on the head. **2** astonish or shock someone so that they are temporarily unable to react.

– SYNONYMS **1 daze,** stupefy, knock out, lay out. **2 astound,** amaze, astonish, dumbfound, stupefy, stagger, shock, take aback; informal flabbergast, knock sideways.

– ORIGIN Old French *estoner* 'astonish.'

stung /stəɴɢ/ past and past participle of **STING**.

stun gun ▶ noun a device that makes an attacker unable to move, typically by giving them a nonfatal electric shock.

stunk /stəɴɢk/ past and past participle of **STINK**.

stun·ner /'stənər/ ▶ noun informal a strikingly beautiful or impressive person or thing.

stun·ning /'stəniɴɢ/ ▶ adjective very impressive or attractive.

– SYNONYMS **beautiful,** lovely, glorious, wonderful, marvelous, magnificent, superb, sublime, spectacular, fine, delightful; informal fantastic, terrific, tremendous, sensational, heavenly, divine, gorgeous, fabulous, awesome.
– ANTONYMS ordinary.

– DERIVATIVES **stun·ning·ly** adverb.

stunt[1] /stənt/ ▶ verb (often as adj. **stunted**) slow down the growth or development of someone or something.

– SYNONYMS (as adj. **stunted**) *a stunted geranium* **small,** undersized, underdeveloped, diminutive.

– ORIGIN Germanic.

stunt[2] ▶ noun **1** an action displaying spectacular skill and daring. **2** something unusual done to attract attention: *a publicity stunt.*

– SYNONYMS **feat,** exploit, trick.

– ORIGIN unknown.

stunt·man /'stəntˌman/ (or **stuntwoman** /'stəntˌwo͝omən/) ▶ noun (pl. **stuntmen** or **stuntwomen**) a person who takes an actor's place in performing dangerous stunts.

stu·pa /'sto͞opə/ ▶ noun a Buddhist shrine in the form of a dome-shaped building.
– ORIGIN Sanskrit.

stu·pe·fy /'st(y)o͞opəˌfī/ ▶ verb (**stupefies, stupefying, stupefied**) **1** make someone unable to think or feel properly. **2** astonish and shock someone.

– SYNONYMS **1 drug,** sedate, tranquilize, intoxicate, inebriate. **2** *his reply stupefied us* **shock,** stun, astound, dumbfound, overwhelm, stagger, amaze, astonish, take someone's breath away; informal flabbergast, knock sideways, knock for a loop, bowl over, floor.

– DERIVATIVES **stu·pe·fac·tion** /ˌst(y)o͞opə'faksʜən/ noun.
– ORIGIN Latin *stupefacere.*

stu·pen·dous /st(y)o͞o'pendəs/ ▶ adjective very impressive.

– SYNONYMS **amazing,** astounding, astonishing, extraordinary, remarkable, phenomenal, staggering, breathtaking; informal fantastic, mind-boggling, awesome; literary wondrous.
– ANTONYMS ordinary.

– DERIVATIVES **stu·pen·dous·ly** adverb.
– ORIGIN Latin *stupendus* 'to be wondered at.'

stu·pid /'st(y)o͞opid/ ▶ adjective (**stupider, stupidest**) **1** lacking intelligence or common sense. **2** informal used to express annoyance or boredom: *your stupid paintings!* **3** dazed and unable to think clearly.

– SYNONYMS **1 unintelligent,** dense, obtuse, foolish, idiotic, slow, simpleminded, brainless, mindless; informal thick, dim, dumb, dopey, daft, moronic, cretinous. **2 foolish,** silly, senseless, idiotic, ill-advised, ill-considered, unwise, nonsensical, ludicrous, ridiculous, laughable, fatuous, asinine, lunatic; informal crazy, half-baked, cockeyed, harebrained, crackbrained.
– ANTONYMS intelligent, sensible.

– DERIVATIVES **stu·pid·i·ty** /st(y)o͞o'piditē/ noun **stu·pid·ly** adverb.
– ORIGIN Latin *stupidus.*

CHOOSE THE RIGHT WORD

stupid, asinine, dense, dull, dumb, obtuse, slow, unintelligent

If you want to impugn someone's intelligence, the options are almost limitless. You can call the person **stupid**, a term that implies a sluggish, slow-witted lack of intelligence. **Asinine** is a harsher word, implying asslike or foolish behavior rather than slow-wittedness (*a woman her age looked asinine in a miniskirt*). Calling someone **dumb** is risky, because it is not only an informal word (*you dumb bunny!*), but because it also means mute and is associated with the offensive expression "deaf and dumb," used to describe people who cannot hear or speak. **Dense** implies an inability to understand even simple facts or instructions (*too dense to get the joke*), while **dull** suggests a sluggishness of mind unrelieved by any hint of quickness, brightness, or liveliness (*a dull stare*). **Slow** also implies a lack of quickness in comprehension or reaction and is often used as a euphemistic substitute for *stupid* (*he was a little slow intellectually*). **Obtuse** is a more formal word for slow-wittedness, but with a strong undercurrent of scorn (*it almost seemed as though he were being deliberately obtuse*). You can't go wrong with a word like **unintelligent**, which is probably the most objective term for low mental ability and the least likely to provoke an angry response (*unintelligent answers to the teacher's questions*).

stu·por /ˈst(y)o͞opər/ ▶ **noun** a state of being dazed or nearly unconscious.

– SYNONYMS **daze,** torpor, insensibility, oblivion.

– DERIVATIVES **stu·por·ous** /-rəs/ adjective.
– ORIGIN Latin.

stur·dy /ˈstərdē/ ▶ **adjective** (**sturdier, sturdiest**) **1** strongly and solidly built or made. **2** confident and determined: *the townspeople have a sturdy independence.*

– SYNONYMS **1 strapping,** well built, muscular, strong, hefty, brawny, powerful, solid, burly; informal beefy. **2 robust,** strong, well built, solid, stout, tough, durable, long-lasting, hard-wearing.
– ANTONYMS feeble.

– DERIVATIVES **stur·di·ly** adverb **stur·di·ness** noun.
– ORIGIN Old French *esturdi* 'stunned, dazed.'

WORD TOOLKIT

See **BURLY**.

stur·geon /ˈstərjən/ ▶ **noun** a very large river or sea fish with bony plates on the body, from whose roe caviar is made.
– ORIGIN Old French.

Sturm und Drang /ˈsʜto͝orm o͝on(t) ˈdräɴɢ/ ▶ **noun 1** an 18th-century German literary and artistic movement characterized by the expression of emotional unrest. **2** a state or situation of emotional upheaval or stress: *the Sturm und Drang of adolescence.*
– ORIGIN German, 'storm and stress.'

stut·ter /ˈstətər/ ▶ **verb 1** have difficulty speaking as a result of the involuntary repetition of the first sounds of a word. **2** (of a machine or gun) produce a series of short, sharp sounds.

– SYNONYMS **stammer,** stumble, falter, hesitate.

▶ **noun** a tendency to stutter while speaking.
– DERIVATIVES **stut·ter·er** noun.
– ORIGIN Germanic.

sty[1] /stī/ ▶ **noun** (pl. **sties**) a pigsty.
– ORIGIN Old English.

sty[2] (also **stye**) ▶ **noun** (pl. **sties** or **styes**) an inflamed swelling on the edge of an eyelid.
– ORIGIN from an Old English word meaning 'riser' + **EYE**.

Styg·i·an /ˈstijēən/ ▶ **adjective** literary very dark.
– ORIGIN from the *Styx*, an underworld river in Greek mythology.

style /stīl/ ▶ **noun 1** a way of doing something. **2** a distinctive appearance, design, or arrangement: *new styles in jewelry.* **3** a way of painting, writing, etc., characteristic of a particular period, person, or movement. **4** elegance and sophistication. **5** an official or legal title. **6** a narrow extension of a plant's ovary, bearing the stigma.

– SYNONYMS **1 manner,** way, technique, method, methodology, approach, system, mode. **2 flair,** elegance, stylishness, chic, taste, grace, poise, polish, sophistication, suavity, urbanity; informal class. **3 kind,** type, variety, sort, design, pattern, genre. **4 fashion,** trend, vogue, mode.

▶ **verb 1** design, make, or arrange in a particular form: *he styled my hair differently this time.* **2** give a particular name, description, or title to someone or something.

– SYNONYMS **design,** fashion, tailor, cut.

– DERIVATIVES **style·less** /ˈstīl(l)is/ adjective **styl·er** noun.
– ORIGIN Latin *stilus* 'stylus, stake, style.'

sty·li /ˈstīlī/ plural of **STYLUS**.

styl·ish /ˈstīlisʜ/ ▶ **adjective 1** having or showing a good sense of style. **2** fashionably elegant.

– SYNONYMS **fashionable,** modern, up to date, modish, smart, sophisticated, elegant, chic, dapper, dashing; informal trendy, natty, kicky, tony.
– ANTONYMS unfashionable.

– DERIVATIVES **styl·ish·ly** adverb **styl·ish·ness** noun.

WORD TOOLKIT

See **GRACIOUS**.

styl·ist /ˈstīlist/ ▶ **noun 1** a person who cuts hair or designs fashionable clothes. **2** a person whose job is to arrange and coordinate food, clothes, etc., in an attractive way in photographs, movies, etc.

styl·is·tic /stīˈlistik/ ▶ **adjective** relating to style, especially literary style.
– DERIVATIVES **styl·is·ti·cal·ly** /-ik(ə)lē/ adverb.

styl·is·tics /stīˈlistiks/ ▶ **plural noun** (treated as sing.) the study of the literary styles of particular writers or types of literature.

styl·ized /ˈstīˌlīzd/ ▶ **adjective** represented or treated in a nonrealistic style.
– DERIVATIVES **styl·i·za·tion** /ˌstīliˈzāsʜən/ noun.

sty·lus /ˈstīləs/ ▶ **noun** (pl. **styli** /-ˌlī/) **1** a pointed implement used for scratching or tracing letters or engraving. **2** a penlike device used to input handwriting directly into a computer. **3** a hard point following a groove in a phonograph record and transmitting the recorded sound for reproduction.
– ORIGIN Latin *stilus*.

sty·mie /ˈstīmē/ ▶ **verb** (**stymies, stymying** or **stymieing, stymied**) informal prevent or hinder the progress of someone or something.
– ORIGIN unknown.

styp·tic /ˈstiptik/ ▶ **adjective** able to stop bleeding. ▶ **noun** a substance that stops bleeding.
– ORIGIN Greek *stuptikos*.

sty·rene /ˈstīˌrēn/ ▶ **noun** Chemistry an unsaturated liquid hydrocarbon obtained as a petroleum byproduct and used to make plastics.
– ORIGIN from *styrax*, a resin obtained from a tree.

sty·ro·foam /ˈstīrəˌfōm/ ▶ **noun** trademark a kind of expanded polystyrene, used for making food containers.
– ORIGIN from **POLYSTYRENE** + **FOAM**.

sua·sion /ˈswāzʜən/ ▶ **noun** formal persuasion as opposed to force.
– ORIGIN Latin.

suave /swäv/ ▶ **adjective** (**suaver, suavest**) (of a man) charming, confident, and elegant.

– SYNONYMS **charming,** sophisticated, debonair, urbane, smooth, polished, refined, poised, self-

possessed, gallant.
– ANTONYMS unsophisticated.

– DERIVATIVES **suave·ly** adverb **suave·ness** noun **suav·i·ty** /-itē/ noun (pl. **suavities**).
– ORIGIN Latin *suavis* 'agreeable.'

CHOOSE THE RIGHT WORD

See **URBANE**.

sub /səb/ informal ▶ **noun 1** a submarine. **2** a substitute, especially for a teacher in a school or for a player on a sports team. **3** a submarine sandwich. ▶ **verb (subs, subbing, subbed)** act as a substitute.

sub- ▶ **prefix 1** under: *submarine*. **2** lower in rank or importance: *subaltern*. **3** below; less than: *subzero*. **4** subsequent or secondary: *subdivision*.
– ORIGIN from Latin *sub* 'under, close to.'

sub·al·tern /səb'ôltərn/ ▶ **noun** an officer in the British army below the rank of captain.
– ORIGIN from Latin *sub-* 'next below' + *alternus* 'every other.'

sub·a·quat·ic /ˌsəbə'kwätik, -'kwa-/ ▶ **adjective** underwater: *subaquatic life forms*.

sub·a·que·ous /səb'ākwēəs, -'ak-/ ▶ **adjective** existing, formed, or taking place under water.

sub·arc·tic /ˌsəb'ärktik, -'ärtik/ ▶ **adjective** relating to the region immediately south of the Arctic Circle.

sub·as·sem·bly /ˌsəbə'semblē/ ▶ **noun** (pl. **subassemblies**) a unit assembled separately but designed to be incorporated with other units into a larger manufactured product.

sub·a·tom·ic /ˌsəbə'tämik/ ▶ **adjective** smaller than or occurring within an atom.

sub·a·tom·ic par·ti·cle ▶ **noun** a particle smaller than an atom (for example, a neutron) or a cluster of such particles. Compare with **ELEMENTARY PARTICLE**.

sub·cat·e·go·ry /'səbˌkatəˌgôrē/ ▶ **noun** (pl. **subcategories**) a secondary or less important category.

sub·com·mit·tee /'səbkəˌmitē/ ▶ **noun** a committee consisting of some members of a larger committee, formed in order to study a subject in more detail.

sub·com·pact /səb'kämpakt/ ▶ **noun** a motor vehicle that is smaller than a compact.

sub·con·scious /səb'känsHəs/ ▶ **adjective** relating to the part of the mind of which one is not fully aware but which influences one's actions and feelings.

– SYNONYMS **unconscious,** latent, suppressed, repressed, subliminal, dormant, underlying, innermost.

▶ **noun (one's/the subconscious)** this part of the mind.

– SYNONYMS **(unconscious) mind,** imagination, inner(most) self, psyche.

– DERIVATIVES **sub·con·scious·ly** adverb **sub·con·scious·ness** noun.

sub·con·ti·nent /ˌsəb'käntənənt/ ▶ **noun** a large part of a continent considered as a particular area, such as North America.
– DERIVATIVES **sub·con·ti·nen·tal** /-ˌkäntə'nen(t)l/ adjective.

sub·con·tract ▶ **verb** /səb'käntrakt, ˌsəbkən'trakt/ employ a firm or person outside one's company to do work as part of a larger project. ▶ **noun** /səb'käntrakt/ a contract to do work for another company as part of a larger project.
– DERIVATIVES **sub·con·trac·tor** noun.

sub·cul·ture /'səbˌkəlCHər/ ▶ **noun** a distinct group within a society or class, having beliefs or interests that are different from those of the larger group.
– DERIVATIVES **sub·cul·tur·al** adjective.

sub·cu·ta·ne·ous /ˌsəbkyōō'tānēəs/ ▶ **adjective** situated or applied under the skin.
– DERIVATIVES **sub·cu·ta·ne·ous·ly** adverb.

sub·di·vide /'səbdəˌvīd/ ▶ **verb** divide into smaller parts something that has already been divided.

sub·di·vi·sion /'səbdəˌvizHən/ ▶ **noun 1** the action of subdividing something. **2** a secondary or less important division.

sub·duc·tion /səb'dəksHən/ ▶ **noun** Geology the sideways and downward movement of the edge of a plate of the earth's crust into the mantle beneath another plate.
– ORIGIN Latin, from *subducere* 'drawn from below.'

sub·due /səb'd(y)ōō/ ▶ **verb (subdues, subduing, subdued) 1** overcome, quiet, or bring under control: *she managed to subdue an instinct to applaud*. **2** bring a country under control by force.

– SYNONYMS **conquer,** defeat, vanquish, overcome, overwhelm, crush, beat, subjugate, suppress.

– ORIGIN Latin *subducere* 'draw from below.'

sub·dued /ˌsəb'd(y)ōōd/ ▶ **adjective 1** quiet and rather thoughtful or depressed. **2** (of color or lighting) soft; muted.

– SYNONYMS **1 somber,** downcast, sad, dejected, depressed, gloomy, despondent. **2 hushed,** muted, quiet, low, soft, faint, muffled, subtle, indistinct, dim, unobtrusive.
– ANTONYMS cheerful, loud, bright.

sub·fam·i·ly /'səbˌfam(ə)lē/ ▶ **noun** (pl. **subfamilies**) a subdivision of a group, especially the taxonomic category that ranks below family and above tribe or genus.

sub·group /'səbˌgrōōp/ ▶ **noun** a small group that is part of a larger one.

sub·head·ing /'səbˌhedinG/ (also **subhead**) ▶ **noun** a heading given to a section within a larger piece of writing.

sub·hu·man /səb'(h)yōōmən/ ▶ **adjective** not having the normal qualities of a human being, especially so as to be lacking in intelligence. ▶ **noun** a subhuman creature or person.

subj. ▶ **abbreviation 1** subject. **2** subjective. **3** subjectively. **4** subjunctive.

sub·ject ▶ **noun** /'səbjəkt/ **1** a person or thing that is being discussed, studied, or dealt with. **2** a branch of knowledge studied or taught in a school, college, etc. **3** a member of a country or state other than its ruler. **4** Grammar the word or words in a sentence that name who or what performs the action of the verb.

– SYNONYMS **1** *the subject of this chapter* **theme,** subject matter, topic, issue, thesis, question, concern. **2** *popular university subjects* **branch of study,** discipline, field. **3** *Her Majesty's subjects* **citizen,** national, resident, taxpayer, voter.

▶ **adjective** /'səbjəkt/ **(subject to) 1** dependent or conditional on: *the merger is subject to shareholders' approval*. **2** likely or having a tendency to be affected by something unpleasant or unwelcome: *he was subject to* *bouts of depression*. **3** under someone's or something's control or authority.

– SYNONYMS **conditional on,** contingent on, dependent on.

▶ **adverb** /ˈsəbjəkt/ (**subject to**) if certain conditions are fulfilled.

▶ **verb** /səbˈjekt/ (usu. **subject someone/thing to**) **1** make someone or something undergo an unpleasant experience. **2** bring a person or country under one's control or authority.

– SYNONYMS *they were* ***subjected to*** *violence* **expose to,** submit to, treat with, put through.

– DERIVATIVES **sub·jec·tion** /səbˈjekSHən/ noun.
– ORIGIN from Latin *subicere* 'bring under.'

sub·jec·tive /səbˈjektiv/ ▶ **adjective 1** based on or influenced by personal feelings, tastes, or opinions. **2** Grammar relating to a case of nouns and pronouns used for the subject of a sentence.

– SYNONYMS **personal,** individual, emotional, biased, intuitive.
– ANTONYMS objective.

– DERIVATIVES **sub·jec·tive·ly** adverb **sub·jec·tiv·i·ty** /ˌsəbjekˈtivitē/ noun.

sub·ject mat·ter ▶ **noun** the thing dealt with or represented in a book, speech, work of art, etc.

sub ju·di·ce /ˌso͝ob ˈyo͞odiˌkā, ˌsəb ˈjo͞odiˌsē/ ▶ **adjective** being considered by a court of law.
– ORIGIN Latin, 'under a judge.'

sub·ju·gate /ˈsəbjəˌgāt/ ▶ **verb** conquer or gain control of someone or something.

– SYNONYMS **conquer,** vanquish, defeat, crush, quash, bring someone to their knees, enslave, subdue, suppress.
– ANTONYMS liberate.

– DERIVATIVES **sub·ju·ga·tion** /ˌsəbjəˈgāSHən/ noun.
– ORIGIN Latin *subjugare* 'bring under a yoke.'

sub·junc·tive /səbˈjəNG(k)tiv/ Grammar ▶ **adjective** (of a form of a verb) expressing what is imagined or wished or possible. ▶ **noun** a subjunctive form of a verb.
– ORIGIN Latin *subjunctivus*.

USAGE

The **subjunctive** form of a verb is used to express what is imagined, wished, or possible. It is usually the same as the ordinary (**indicative**) form of the verb except in the third person singular (*he*, *she*, or *it*), where the normal **-s** ending is omitted. For example, you should say *face* rather than *faces* in the sentence *the report recommends that he face the tribunal*. The subjunctive is also different from the indicative when using the verb 'to be'; for example, you should say *I were* rather than *I was* in the sentence *I wouldn't try it if I were you*. See also **LEST**.

sub·lease ▶ **noun** /ˈsəbˌlēs/ a lease of a property by a tenant to a subtenant. ▶ **verb** /ˈsəbˈlēs/ another term for **SUBLET**.

sub·let /ˈsəbˈlet/ ▶ **verb** (**sublets, subletting, sublet**) let a property or part of a property that one is already renting to someone else.

sub·li·mate /ˈsəbləˌmāt/ ▶ **verb 1** direct an instinctive impulse, especially sexual energy, into a more socially acceptable activity. **2** transform something into a purer or idealized form. **3** Chemistry another term for **SUBLIME**.
– DERIVATIVES **sub·li·ma·tion** /ˌsəbləˈmāSHən/ noun.
– ORIGIN Latin *sublimare* 'raise up.'

sub·lime /səˈblīm/ ▶ **adjective** (**sublimer, sublimest**) **1** of such excellence or beauty as to inspire great admiration or awe. **2** extreme: *the sublime confidence of youth*.

– SYNONYMS **1** *sublime music* **exalted,** elevated, noble, lofty, awe-inspiring, majestic, magnificent, glorious, superb, wonderful, marvelous, splendid; informal fantastic, fabulous, terrific, heavenly, divine, out of this world. **2** *the sublime confidence of youth* **supreme,** total, complete, utter, consummate.

▶ **verb** Chemistry (with reference to a solid substance) change directly into vapor when heated, typically forming a solid deposit again on cooling.
– DERIVATIVES **sub·lime·ly** adverb **sub·lim·i·ty** /səˈblimitē/ noun.
– ORIGIN Latin *sublimis*.

sub·lim·i·nal /səˈblimənl/ ▶ **adjective** (of a stimulus or mental process) affecting someone's mind without their being aware of it.
– DERIVATIVES **sub·lim·i·nal·ly** adverb.
– ORIGIN from **SUB-** + Latin *limen* 'threshold.'

sub·ma·chine gun /ˌsəbməˈSHēn/ ▶ **noun** a hand-held lightweight machine gun.

sub·ma·rine /ˌsəbməˈrēn, ˈsəbməˌrēn/ ▶ **noun** a streamlined warship designed to operate under the surface of the sea for long periods. ▶ **adjective** existing, happening, done, or used under the surface of the sea.
– DERIVATIVES **sub·ma·rin·er** /səbˈmarənər, -məˈrēnər/ noun.

sub·ma·rine sand·wich ▶ **noun** a sandwich made of a long roll typically filled with meat, cheese, and vegetables such as lettuce, tomato, and onions.

sub·merge /səbˈmərj/ ▶ **verb 1** push or hold someone or something under water. **2** go down below the surface of water. **3** completely cover or hide something.

– SYNONYMS **1 go under (water),** dive, sink, plunge, plummet. **2 immerse,** dip, plunge, duck, dunk. **3** *the farmland was submerged* **flood,** deluge, swamp, overwhelm, inundate.

– DERIVATIVES **sub·mer·gence** noun.
– ORIGIN Latin *submergere*.

sub·merse /səbˈmərs/ ▶ **verb** technical submerge something.

sub·mers·i·ble /səbˈmərsəbəl/ ▶ **adjective** designed to operate under water. ▶ **noun** a small boat or craft that is submersible.

sub·mer·sion /səbˈmərZHən, -SHən/ ▶ **noun** the action of submerging or the state of being submerged.

sub·mi·cro·scop·ic /ˌsəbmīkrəˈskäpik/ ▶ **adjective** too small to be seen by an ordinary microscope.

sub·mis·sion /səbˈmiSHən/ ▶ **noun 1** the action of submitting something. **2** a proposal or application submitted for consideration.

– SYNONYMS **1 yielding,** capitulation, surrender, resignation, acceptance, consent, compliance, acquiescence, obedience, subjection, subservience, servility. **2 proposal,** suggestion, proposition, tender, presentation. **3 argument,** assertion, contention, statement, claim, allegation.
– ANTONYMS defiance.

sub·mis·sive /səbˈmisiv/ ▶ **adjective** meekly obedient or passive.

– SYNONYMS **compliant,** yielding, acquiescent, passive, obedient, dutiful, docile, pliant, tractable, biddable, malleable, meek, unassertive; informal under someone's thumb.

– DERIVATIVES **sub·mis·sive·ly** adverb **sub·mis·sive·ness** noun.

sub·mit /səb'mit/ ▶ **verb** (**submits, submitting, submitted**) **1** accept or give in to someone's or something's authority, control, or greater strength. **2** present a proposal or application to a person or group of people for consideration or assessment. **3** subject someone or something to a particular process or treatment. **4** (especially in the context of a court of law) suggest or argue.

> – SYNONYMS **1 yield,** give in/way, back down, cave in, capitulate, surrender, acquiesce. **2** *he refused to **submit to** their authority* **be governed by,** abide by, comply with, accept, be subject to, agree to, consent to, conform to. **3 put forward,** present, offer, tender, propose, suggest, enter, put in, send in. **4 contend,** assert, argue, state, claim, allege.
> – ANTONYMS resist.

– ORIGIN Latin *submittere.*

sub·nor·mal /səb'nôrməl/ ▶ **adjective** not meeting standards or reaching a level regarded as normal or usual.
– DERIVATIVES **sub·nor·mal·i·ty** /ˌsəbnôr'malitē/ noun.

sub·op·ti·mal /səb'äptəməl/ ▶ **adjective** technical of less than the highest standard or quality.

sub·or·der /'səbˌôrdər/ ▶ **noun** Biology a taxonomic category that ranks below order and above family.

sub·or·di·nate ▶ **adjective** /sə'bôrdnit/ **1** lower in rank or position. **2** less important.

> – SYNONYMS **inferior,** junior, lower-ranking, lower, supporting.

▶ **noun** /sə'bôrdnit/ a person under the authority or control of someone else.

> – SYNONYMS **junior,** assistant, second (in command), number two, deputy, aide, underling, minion.
> – ANTONYMS superior, senior.

▶ **verb** /-ˌāt/ treat or regard as less important: *economic reforms should be subordinated to financial constraints.*
– DERIVATIVES **sub·or·di·na·tion** /-ˌbôrdn'āsʜən/ noun.
– ORIGIN Latin *subordinatus* 'placed in a lower rank.'

sub·or·di·nate clause ▶ **noun** a clause that forms part of and is dependent on a main clause (e.g., *when it rang* in *she answered the phone when it rang*).

sub·orn /sə'bôrn/ ▶ **verb** persuade or bribe someone to commit an unlawful act such as perjury.
– ORIGIN Latin *subornare* 'incite secretly.'

sub·plot /'səbˌplät/ ▶ **noun** a plot in a play, novel, etc., that is secondary to the main plot.

sub·poe·na /sə'pēnə/ ▶ **noun** a written order instructing a person to attend a court of law. ▶ **verb** (**subpoenas, subpoenaing, subpoenaed** or **subpoena'd**) summon someone with a subpoena.
– ORIGIN from Latin *sub poena* 'under penalty' (the first words of the order).

sub·prime /'səbˌprīm/ ▶ **adjective** referring to credit or loan arrangements for borrowers with a poor credit history, incurring higher than usual risk and so involving high rates of interest.

sub·ro·ga·tion /ˌsəbrə'gāsʜən/ ▶ **noun** Law the substitution of one person or group by another in respect of a debt or insurance claim, accompanied by the transfer of any associated rights and duties.
– ORIGIN from Latin *subrogare* 'choose as substitute.'

sub ro·sa /ˌsəb 'rōzə/ ▶ **adjective & adverb** formal happening or done in secret.
– ORIGIN Latin, 'under the rose' (the rose being an emblem of secrecy).

sub·rou·tine /'səbroōˌtēn/ ▶ **noun** Computing a set of instructions designed to perform a frequently used operation within a program.

sub-Sa·har·an ▶ **adjective** from or forming part of the African regions south of the Sahara Desert.

sub·scribe /səb'skrīb/ ▶ **verb 1** (often **subscribe to**) arrange to receive something, especially a magazine, on a regular basis by paying in advance. **2** (**subscribe to**) express agreement with an idea or proposal. **3** (**subscribe to**) contribute a sum of money to a project or cause on a regular basis. **4** apply to take part in: *the course is fully subscribed.* **5** apply to buy shares in a company.

> – SYNONYMS **1** *we **subscribe to** several news magazines* **pay a subscription for,** have a subscription to, take, buy regularly. **2** (**subscribe to**) *I can't subscribe to that theory* **support,** endorse, agree with, accept, go along with.

– DERIVATIVES **sub·scrib·er** noun.
– ORIGIN Latin *subscribere* 'write below.'

sub·script /'səbˌskript/ ▶ **adjective** (of a letter, figure, or symbol) written or printed below the line.

sub·scrip·tion /səb'skripsʜən/ ▶ **noun 1** an advance payment made in order to receive or take part in something, or as a donation. **2** the action or fact of subscribing.

> – SYNONYMS **membership fee,** dues, annual payment, charge.

sub·sec·tion /'səbˌseksʜən/ ▶ **noun** a division of a section.

sub·sense /'səbˌsens/ ▶ **noun** a related but less important sense of a word defined in a dictionary.

sub·se·quent /'səbsəkwənt/ ▶ **adjective** coming after something in time.

> – SYNONYMS **following,** ensuing, succeeding, later, future, coming, to come, next.
> – ANTONYMS previous.

– DERIVATIVES **sub·se·quent·ly** adverb.
– ORIGIN from Latin *subsequi* 'follow after.'

sub·ser·vi·ent /səb'sərvēənt/ ▶ **adjective 1** too willing to obey other people. **2** less important.

> – SYNONYMS **1 submissive,** deferential, compliant, obedient, dutiful, docile, passive, subdued, downtrodden; informal under someone's thumb. **2** *individual rights are subservient to the interests of the state* **subordinate,** secondary, subsidiary.
> – ANTONYMS independent.

– DERIVATIVES **sub·ser·vi·ence** noun.
– ORIGIN Latin, 'complying with.'

CHOOSE THE RIGHT WORD

See **OBSEQUIOUS**.

sub·set /'səbˌset/ ▶ **noun 1** a part of a larger group of related things. **2** Mathematics a set of which all the elements are contained in another set.

sub·side /səb'sīd/ ▶ **verb 1** become less intense, violent, or severe. **2** (of water) go down to a lower or the normal level. **3** (of a building) sink lower into the ground. **4** (of the ground) cave in; sink. **5** (**subside into**) give way to a strong feeling.

– SYNONYMS **1 abate,** let up, quiet down, calm, slacken (off), ease (up), relent, die down, diminish, decline. **2 recede,** ebb, fall, go down, get lower. **3 sink,** settle, cave in, collapse, give way.
– ANTONYMS intensify, rise.

– ORIGIN Latin *subsidere.*

sub·sid·ence /səb'sīdns, 'səbsidns/ ▶ **noun** the gradual caving in or sinking of an area of land.

sub·sid·i·a·ri·ty /səbˌsidē'aritē/ ▶ **noun** (in politics) the principle that a central authority should carry out only those tasks that cannot be carried out at a more local level.

sub·sid·i·ar·y /səb'sidēˌerē/ ▶ **adjective 1** related but less important. **2** (of a company) controlled by a holding or parent company.

– SYNONYMS **subordinate,** secondary, subservient, supplementary, peripheral, auxiliary.
– ANTONYMS principal.

▶ **noun** (pl. **subsidiaries**) a subsidiary company.

– SYNONYMS **branch,** division, subdivision, derivative, offshoot.

– ORIGIN Latin *subsidiarius.*

sub·si·dize /'səbsəˌdīz/ ▶ **verb 1** support an organization or activity financially. **2** pay part of the cost of producing something to help keep the price low.

– SYNONYMS **finance,** fund, support, contribute to, give money to, underwrite, sponsor; informal shell out for, bankroll.

– DERIVATIVES **sub·si·di·za·tion** /ˌsəbsədi'zāshən/ noun.

sub·si·dy /'səbsidē/ ▶ **noun** (pl. **subsidies**) **1** a sum of money given to an industry or business from public funds to help keep the price of a product or service low. **2** a sum of money granted to support an activity or undertaking that is held to be in the public interest. **3** a grant or contribution of money.

– SYNONYMS **finance,** funding, backing, support, grant, sponsorship, allowance, contribution, handout.

– ORIGIN Latin *subsidium* 'assistance.'

sub·sist /səb'sist/ ▶ **verb 1** manage to stay alive, especially with limited resources. **2** chiefly Law remain in force or effect.

– SYNONYMS **survive,** live, stay alive, exist, eke out an existence/living, support oneself, manage, get along/by, make ends meet.

– ORIGIN Latin *subsistere* 'stand firm.'

sub·sist·ence /səb'sistəns/ ▶ **noun** the action or fact of subsisting. ▶ **adjective** referring to production at a level that is only enough for one's own use, without any surplus for trade: *subsistence agriculture.*

sub·sist·ence lev·el (also **subsistence wage**) ▶ **noun** a standard of living (or wage) that provides only the basic necessities of life.

sub·soil /'səbˌsoil/ ▶ **noun** the soil lying immediately under the surface soil.

sub·son·ic /ˌsəb'sänik/ ▶ **adjective** relating to or flying at a speed or speeds less than that of sound.

sub·spe·cies /'səbˌspēshēz, -sēz/ ▶ **noun** (pl. same) Biology a subdivision of a species.

subst. ▶ **abbreviation 1** substantive. **2** substantively. **3** substitute.

sub·stance /'səbstəns/ ▶ **noun 1** a type of solid, liquid, or gas that has particular properties. **2** the real physical matter of which a person or thing consists. **3** solid basis in reality or fact: *the claim has no substance.* **4** the most important or essential part or meaning. **5** the quality of being important or significant: *nothing of substance was achieved.* **6** the subject matter of a piece of writing or work of art. **7** an intoxicating or narcotic drug, especially an illegal one.

– SYNONYMS **1 material,** compound, matter, stuff. **2 significance,** importance, import, validity, foundation. **3 content,** subject matter, theme, message, essence. **4 wealth,** fortune, riches, affluence, prosperity, money, means.

– PHRASES **in substance** with regard to the fundamental points; essentially.
– ORIGIN Latin *substantia* 'being, essence.'

sub·stand·ard /səb'standərd/ ▶ **adjective** below the usual or required standard.

– SYNONYMS **inferior,** second-rate, poor, below par, imperfect, faulty, defective, shoddy, shabby, unsound, unsatisfactory; informal tenth-rate, crummy, lousy.

sub·stan·tial /səb'stanchəl/ ▶ **adjective 1** of great importance, size, or value. **2** strongly built or made. **3** concerning the essential points of something: *there was substantial agreement on changing policies.* **4** real and tangible rather than imaginary.

– SYNONYMS **1 considerable,** real, significant, important, major, valuable, useful, sizable, appreciable. **2 sturdy,** solid, stout, strong, well built, durable, long-lasting, hard-wearing.
– ANTONYMS insubstantial.

– DERIVATIVES **sub·stan·ti·al·i·ty** /-ˌstanchē'alitē/ noun.

sub·stan·tial·ly /səb'stanchəlē/ ▶ **adverb 1** to a great extent. **2** for the most part; mainly: *things will remain substantially the same.*

sub·stan·ti·ate /səb'stanchēˌāt/ ▶ **verb** provide evidence to prove that something is true.

– SYNONYMS **prove,** show to be true, support, justify, vindicate, validate, corroborate, verify, authenticate, confirm.
– ANTONYMS disprove.

– DERIVATIVES **sub·stan·ti·a·tion** /-ˌstanchē'āshən/ noun.
– ORIGIN Latin *substantiare* 'give substance.'

sub·stan·tive /'səbstəntiv/ ▶ **adjective** important or meaningful. ▶ **noun** Grammar, dated a noun.
– DERIVATIVES **sub·stan·tive·ly** adverb.

sub·sta·tion /'səbˌstāshən/ ▶ **noun 1** a set of equipment reducing the high voltage of electrical power transmission to that suitable for supply to consumers. **2** a small police station or fire station.

sub·sti·tute /'səbstiˌt(y)o͞ot/ ▶ **noun 1** a person or thing acting or used in place of another. **2** an athlete who may replace another after a match has begun.

– SYNONYMS **replacement,** deputy, relief, proxy, reserve, surrogate, cover, stand-in, understudy; informal sub.

▶ **verb 1** use one person or thing instead of another. **2** replace one person or thing with another. **3** replace an athlete with a substitute during a match.

– SYNONYMS **1 exchange,** swap, use instead of, use as an alternative to, use in place of, replace with. **2** *I found someone to* ***substitute for*** *me* **deputize**

for, stand in for, cover for, fill in for, take over from.

– DERIVATIVES **sub·sti·tut·a·ble** adjective **sub·sti·tu·tion** /ˌsəbstiˈt(y)o͞oSHən/ noun.
– ORIGIN Latin *substituere* 'put in place of.'

USAGE

Traditionally, **substitute** is followed by **for** and means 'use one person or thing instead of another,' as in *she substituted the fake vase for the real one*. It may also be used with **with** or **by** to mean 'replace something with something else,' as in *she substituted the real vase with the fake one*. This can be confusing, since the two sentences shown above mean the same thing, yet the object of the verb and the object of the preposition have swapped positions. Despite the potential confusion, the second, newer use is acceptable, although still disapproved of by some people.

sub·strate /ˈsəbˌstrāt/ ▶ **noun 1** the surface or material on which an organism lives, grows, or feeds. **2** the substance on which an enzyme acts.
– ORIGIN from **SUBSTRATUM**.

sub·stra·tum /ˈsəbˌstrātəm, -ˌstra-/ ▶ **noun** (pl. **substrata** /ˈsəbˌstrātə, -ˌstra-/) **1** an underlying layer or substance, in particular a layer of rock or soil beneath the surface of the ground. **2** a foundation or basis.

sub·struc·ture /ˈsəbˌstrəkCHər/ ▶ **noun** an underlying or supporting structure.

sub·sume /səbˈso͞om/ ▶ **verb** include something in a larger category or group.
– ORIGIN Latin *subsumere*.

sub·ten·ant /səbˈtenənt/ ▶ **noun** a person who rents property from a tenant.

sub·tend /səbˈtend/ ▶ **verb** Geometry (of a line, arc, etc.) form an angle at a particular point when straight lines from its extremities meet.
– ORIGIN Latin *subtendere*.

sub·ter·fuge /ˈsəbtərˌfyo͞oj/ ▶ **noun** secret or dishonest actions used in order to achieve an aim.

– SYNONYMS **1 trickery,** intrigue, deviousness, deceit, deception, dishonesty, cheating, duplicity, guile, cunning, craftiness, chicanery, pretense, fraud, fraudulence. **2** *a disreputable subterfuge* **trick,** hoax, ruse, wile, ploy, stratagem, artifice, dodge, bluff, pretense, deception; informal con, scam.

– ORIGIN from Latin *subterfugere* 'escape secretly.'

sub·ter·ra·ne·an /ˌsəbtəˈrānēən/ ▶ **adjective** existing or happening under the earth's surface.
– DERIVATIVES **sub·ter·ra·ne·ous** adjective.
– ORIGIN Latin *subterraneus*, from *terra* 'earth.'

sub·text /ˈsəbˌtekst/ ▶ **noun** an underlying theme in a speech or piece of writing.

sub·ti·tle /ˈsəbˌtītl/ ▶ **noun 1** (**subtitles**) captions displayed at the bottom of a movie or television screen that translate the dialogue. **2** a secondary title of a published work. ▶ **verb** provide something with a subtitle or subtitles.

sub·tle /ˈsətl/ ▶ **adjective** (**subtler, subtlest**) **1** so delicate or precise that it is difficult to analyze or describe: *a subtle distinction*. **2** cleverly achieving an effect in a way that is not immediately obvious: *subtle lighting*. **3** making use of clever and indirect methods to achieve something. **4** able to make fine distinctions: *a subtle mind*.

– SYNONYMS **1 understated,** muted, subdued, delicate, soft, low-key, toned-down. **2 gentle,** slight, gradual. **3** *a subtle distinction* **fine,** fine-drawn, nice, tenuous.
– ANTONYMS gaudy, crude.

– DERIVATIVES **sub·tle·ty** /ˈsətltē/ noun (pl. **subtleties**) **sub·tly** adverb.
– ORIGIN Latin *subtilis*.

sub·to·tal /ˈsəbˌtōtl/ ▶ **noun** the total of one set within a larger group of figures to be added.

sub·tract /səbˈtrakt/ ▶ **verb** take one number or amount away from another to calculate the difference between them.
– DERIVATIVES **sub·trac·tion** /səbˈtrakSHən/ noun **sub·trac·tive** /-tiv/ adjective.
– ORIGIN Latin *subtrahere* 'draw away.'

sub·trop·i·cal /səbˈträpikəl/ ▶ **adjective** relating to the regions of the world that are near or next to the tropics.
– DERIVATIVES **sub·trop·ics** /səbˈträpiks/ plural noun.

sub·u·nit /ˈsəbˌyo͞onit/ ▶ **noun** a distinct component of something.

sub·urb /ˈsəbərb/ ▶ **noun** a residential district on the outskirts of a city.
– ORIGIN from Latin *sub-* 'near to' + *urbs* 'city.'

sub·ur·ban /səˈbərbən/ ▶ **adjective 1** relating to or like a suburb. **2** boringly conventional.

– SYNONYMS **1 residential,** commuter, dormitory. **2 dull,** boring, uninteresting, conventional, ordinary, unsophisticated, provincial, parochial, bourgeois, middle-class.

– DERIVATIVES **sub·ur·ban·ize** /səˈbərbəˌnīz/ verb.

sub·ur·ban·ite /səˈbərbəˌnīt/ ▶ **noun** a person who lives in a suburb.

sub·ur·bi·a /səˈbərbēə/ ▶ **noun** suburbs and the way of life of the people who live in them.

sub·ven·tion /səbˈvenCHən/ ▶ **noun** a grant of money, especially from a government.
– ORIGIN Latin, from *subvenire* 'assist.'

sub·ver·sive /səbˈvərsiv/ ▶ **adjective** trying or intended to damage or weaken the power of an established system or institution.

– SYNONYMS **disruptive,** troublemaking, insurrectionary, seditious, dissident.

▶ **noun** a subversive person.

– SYNONYMS **troublemaker,** dissident, agitator, renegade.

– DERIVATIVES **sub·ver·sive·ly** adverb **sub·ver·sive·ness** noun.

sub·vert /səbˈvərt/ ▶ **verb** damage or weaken the power of an established system or institution.
– DERIVATIVES **sub·ver·sion** /-ˈvərZHən, -SHən/ noun **sub·vert·er** noun.
– ORIGIN Latin *subvertere*.

sub·way /ˈsəbˌwā/ ▶ **noun 1** an underground electric railroad. **2** Brit. a tunnel under a road for pedestrians to use.

sub·woof·er /ˈsəbˌwo͝ofər/ ▶ **noun** a part of a loudspeaker designed to reproduce very low bass frequencies.

sub·ze·ro /ˌsəbˈzi(ə)rō/ ▶ **adjective** (of temperature) lower than zero; (on the Celsius scale) below freezing.

suc·ceed /səkˈsēd/ ▶ **verb 1** achieve an aim or purpose. **2** gain fame, wealth, or social status. **3** take over a position or title from someone else. **4** become the new rightful holder of a position or title: *James I succeeded to the throne in 1603.* **5** come after and take the place of: *her embarrassment was succeeded by fear.*

– SYNONYMS **1 triumph,** achieve success, be successful, do well, flourish, thrive; informal make it, make the grade. **2 be successful,** turn out well, work (out), be effective; informal come off, pay off. **3 replace,** take over from, follow, supersede.
– ANTONYMS fail, precede.

– ORIGIN Latin *succedere* 'come close after.'

suc·cess /sək'ses/ ▸ **noun 1** the achievement of an aim or purpose. **2** the gaining of fame, wealth, or social status. **3** a person or thing that achieves success.

– SYNONYMS **1 victory,** triumph. **2 prosperity,** affluence, wealth, riches, opulence. **3 best-seller,** sellout, winner, triumph; informal hit, smash, sensation.
– ANTONYMS failure.

– ORIGIN Latin *successus*.

suc·cess·ful /sək'sesfəl/ ▸ **adjective 1** having achieved an aim or purpose. **2** having achieved fame, wealth, or social status.

– SYNONYMS **1 prosperous,** affluent, wealthy, rich, famous, eminent, top, respected. **2 flourishing,** thriving, booming, buoyant, profitable, moneymaking, lucrative.

– DERIVATIVES **suc·cess·ful·ly** adverb.

suc·ces·sion /sək'sesHən/ ▸ **noun 1** a number of people or things following one after the other. **2** the action or right of inheriting a position or title.

– SYNONYMS **sequence,** series, progression, chain, string, train, line, run.

– PHRASES **in quick succession** following one another at short intervals. **in succession** following one after the other without interruption.

suc·ces·sive /sək'sesiv/ ▸ **adjective** following one another or following others.

– SYNONYMS **consecutive,** in a row, sequential, in succession, running.

– DERIVATIVES **suc·ces·sive·ly** adverb.

suc·ces·sor /sək'sesər/ ▸ **noun** a person or thing that succeeds another.

suc·cess sto·ry ▸ **noun** informal a successful person or thing.

suc·cinct /sə(k)'siNG(k)t/ ▸ **adjective** expressed clearly and in few words.

– SYNONYMS **concise,** short (and sweet), brief, compact, condensed, crisp, laconic, terse, to the point, pithy.
– ANTONYMS verbose.

– DERIVATIVES **suc·cinct·ly** adverb **suc·cinct·ness** noun.
– ORIGIN from Latin *succingere* 'tuck up.'

suc·cor /'səkər/ (Brit. **succour**) ▸ **noun** help given to someone who is suffering or in difficulty.

– SYNONYMS **aid,** help, a helping hand, assistance, comfort, ease, relief, support.

▸ **verb** help someone who is suffering or in difficulty.
– ORIGIN Latin *succursus*, from *succurrere* 'run to the help of.'

suc·co·tash /'səkə,tasH/ ▸ **noun** a dish of corn and lima beans cooked together.
– ORIGIN from an American Indian language.

suc·cu·bus /'səkyəbəs/ ▸ **noun** (pl. **succubi** /-,bī/) a female demon believed to have sex with sleeping men.
– ORIGIN Latin, 'prostitute.'

suc·cu·lent /'səkyələnt/ ▸ **adjective 1** (of food) tender, juicy, and tasty. **2** (of a plant) having thick fleshy leaves or stems adapted to storing water.

– SYNONYMS **juicy,** moist, luscious, soft, tender, choice, mouthwatering, appetizing, flavorsome, tasty, delicious; informal scrumptious.
– ANTONYMS dry.

▸ **noun** a succulent plant.
– DERIVATIVES **suc·cu·lence** noun **suc·cu·lent·ly** adverb.
– ORIGIN Latin *succulentus*, from *succus* 'juice.'

WORD TOOLKIT

See **RIPE**.

suc·cumb /sə'kəm/ ▸ **verb 1** give in to pressure, temptation, etc. **2** die from the effect of a disease or injury.

– SYNONYMS **yield,** give in/way, submit, surrender, capitulate, cave in, fall victim.
– ANTONYMS resist.

– ORIGIN Latin *succumbere*.

such /səCH/ ▸ **determiner, predeterminer, & pronoun 1** of the type previously mentioned. **2** (**such —— as/that**) of the type about to be mentioned: *there's no such thing as a free lunch.* **3** to so high a degree; so great.
– PHRASES **as such** in the exact sense of the word. **such-and-such** an unspecified person or thing. **such as 1** for example. **2** of a kind that; like.
– ORIGIN Old English, related to **SO**[1] and **ALIKE**.

such·like /'səCH,līk/ ▸ **pronoun** things of the type mentioned. ▸ **determiner** of the type mentioned.

suck /sək/ ▸ **verb 1** draw liquid or air into the mouth by tightening the lip muscles and breathing in. **2** hold something in the mouth and draw at it by tightening the lip and cheek muscles. **3** pull forcefully: *he was sucked under the surface of the river.* **4** (**suck someone in/into**) involve someone in a situation or activity, especially against their will. **5** (**suck up to**) informal try to please someone in authority in order to gain advantage for oneself. **6** informal be very bad or unpleasant.

– SYNONYMS **sip,** sup, slurp, drink, siphon.

▸ **noun** an act or sound of sucking.
– ORIGIN Old English, related to **SOAK**.

suck·er /'səkər/ ▸ **noun 1** a rubber cup that sticks to a surface by suction. **2** a flat or concave organ that enables an animal to cling to a surface by suction. **3** informal a gullible person. **4** (**a sucker for**) informal a person who is especially influenced by or fond of a particular thing: *I was a sucker for flattery.* **5** a shoot springing from the base of a tree or other plant, especially one coming from the root at some distance from the trunk.

suck·er punch informal ▸ **noun** an unexpected punch or blow. ▸ **verb** (**sucker-punch**) punch or hit someone unexpectedly.

suck·le /'səkəl/ ▸ **verb** (with reference to a baby or young animal) feed from the breast or udder.

suck·ling /'səkliNG/ ▸ **noun** a baby or young animal that is still feeding on its mother's milk.

su·crose /'so͞o,krōs/ ▸ **noun** a compound that is the chief component of cane or beet sugar.
– ORIGIN from French *sucre* 'sugar.'

suc·tion /ˈsəksʜən/ ▶ **noun** the process of removing air or liquid from a space or container, creating a partial vacuum that causes something else to be sucked in or that causes surfaces to stick together. ▶ **verb** remove something using suction.
– ORIGIN Latin, from *sugere* 'to suck.'

Su·da·nese /ˌso͞odnˈēz, -ˈēs/ ▶ **noun** a person from Sudan. ▶ **adjective** relating to Sudan.

sud·den /ˈsədn/ ▶ **adjective** happening or done quickly and unexpectedly.

– SYNONYMS **unexpected,** unforeseen, immediate, instantaneous, instant, precipitous, abrupt, rapid, swift, quick.

– DERIVATIVES **sud·den·ness** noun.
– PHRASES **(all) of a sudden** suddenly.
– ORIGIN Old French *sudein.*

sud·den death ▶ **noun** a means of deciding the winner in a tied match, in which play continues and the winner is the first side or player to score.

sud·den in·fant death syn·drome ▶ **noun** technical term for **CRIB DEATH**.

sud·den·ly /ˈsədn-lē/ ▶ **adverb** quickly and unexpectedly.

– SYNONYMS **all of a sudden,** all at once, abruptly, swiftly, quickly, unexpectedly, without warning, out of the blue.
– ANTONYMS gradually.

su·do·ku /so͞oˈdōko͞o/ ▶ **noun** a puzzle in which one must fill a grid of nine squares by nine squares (subdivided into nine regions of three by three squares) with the numbers one to nine, in such a way that no number is repeated in any horizontal line, vertical line, or three-by-three subdivision.
– ORIGIN Japanese.

Su·dra /ˈso͞oˌdrə/ ▶ **noun** a member of the worker caste, lowest of the four Hindu castes.
– ORIGIN Sanskrit.

suds /sədz/ ▶ **plural noun** froth made from soap and water.

– SYNONYMS **lather,** foam, froth, bubbles, soap.

– DERIVATIVES **suds·y** adjective.
– ORIGIN probably related to **SEETHE**.

sue /so͞o/ ▶ **verb (sues, suing, sued) 1** take legal action against a person, institution, etc., typically in order to get compensation for something. **2 (sue for)** formal appeal formally to a person for: *the rebels were forced to sue for peace.*

– SYNONYMS **take legal action,** go to court, take to court, litigate.

– ORIGIN Old French *suer.*

suede /swād/ ▶ **noun** leather with the flesh side rubbed to make a velvety nap.
– ORIGIN from French *gants de Suède* 'gloves of Sweden.'

su·et /ˈso͞oit/ ▶ **noun** the hard white fat on the kidneys of cattle, sheep, and other animals, used as a shortening in pastry, etc., and as a food for wild birds.
– DERIVATIVES **su·et·y** adjective.
– ORIGIN Old French.

suf·fer /ˈsəfər/ ▶ **verb 1** experience or be subjected to something bad or unpleasant. **2 (suffer from)** be affected by or subject to an illness or condition. **3** become or appear worse in quality: *his relationship with her did suffer.* **4** old use tolerate someone or something. **5** old use allow someone to do something.

– SYNONYMS **1** *I hate to see him suffer* **hurt,** ache, be in pain, be in distress, be upset, be miserable. **2** *Brazil suffered a humiliating defeat* **undergo,** experience, be subjected to, receive, sustain, endure, face, meet with. **3 (suffer from)** *he suffers from asthma* **be afflicted by,** be affected by, be troubled with, have.

– DERIVATIVES **suf·fer·er** noun.
– ORIGIN Latin *sufferre.*

suf·fer·ance /ˈsəf(ə)rəns/ ▶ **noun** lack of objection rather than genuine approval; toleration.

suf·fer·ing /ˈsəfəriɴɢ/ ▶ **noun** pain or distress.

– SYNONYMS *the suffering of these refugees defied description* **hardship,** distress, misery, adversity, pain, agony, anguish, trauma, torment, torture, hurt, affliction.
– ANTONYMS pleasure, joy.

suf·fice /səˈfīs/ ▶ **verb** be enough or adequate: *a quick look should suffice.*
– PHRASES **suffice (it) to say** used to indicate that one is withholding details in order to be brief or discreet.
– ORIGIN Latin *sufficere.*

suf·fi·cien·cy /səˈfisʜənsē/ ▶ **noun** (pl. **sufficiencies**) **1** the condition or quality of being sufficient. **2** an adequate amount, especially of something essential.

suf·fi·cient /səˈfisʜənt/ ▶ **adjective & determiner** enough; adequate.

– SYNONYMS **enough,** adequate, plenty of, ample.
– ANTONYMS inadequate.

– DERIVATIVES **suf·fi·cient·ly** adverb.

suf·fix /ˈsəfiks/ ▶ **noun** a letter or group of letters added at the end of a word to form another word (e.g., *-ation*).

suf·fo·cate /ˈsəfəˌkāt/ ▶ **verb 1** die or cause to die from lack of air or inability to breathe. **2** have or cause to have difficulty in breathing.
– DERIVATIVES **suf·fo·ca·tion** /ˌsəfəˈkāsʜən/ noun.
– ORIGIN Latin *suffocare* 'stifle.'

suf·fra·gan /ˈsəfrəgən/ (also **suffragan bishop**) ▶ **noun** a bishop appointed to help the bishop in charge of a diocese.
– ORIGIN Latin *suffraganeus* 'assistant.'

suf·frage /ˈsəfrij/ ▶ **noun** the right to vote in political elections.
– ORIGIN Latin *suffragium.*

suf·fra·gette /ˌsəfrəˈjet/ ▶ **noun** historical a woman who campaigned for women to be given the right to vote in political elections.

suf·fra·gist /ˈsəfrəjist/ ▶ **noun** historical a person in favor of women being given the right to vote in political elections.

suf·fuse /səˈfyo͞oz/ ▶ **verb** gradually spread through or over: *her cheeks were suffused with color.*

– SYNONYMS **permeate,** spread over, cover, bathe, pervade, wash, saturate, imbue.

– DERIVATIVES **suf·fu·sion** /səˈfyo͞ozʜən/ noun.
– ORIGIN Latin *suffundere* 'pour into.'

Su·fi /ˈso͞ofē/ ▶ **noun** (pl. **Sufis**) a member of a mystic Muslim group.
– DERIVATIVES **Su·fism** /ˈso͞oˌfizəm/ noun.
– ORIGIN Arabic.

sug·ar /ˈsʜo͝ogər/ ▶ **noun 1** a sweet crystalline substance obtained especially from sugarcane and sugar beet.

2 any of the class of soluble crystalline sweet-tasting carbohydrates found in plant and animal tissue, including sucrose and glucose. ▶ **verb** sweeten, sprinkle, or coat something with sugar.
– DERIVATIVES **sug·ar·less** adjective.
– PHRASES **sugar the pill** see **PILL**.
– ORIGIN Old French *sukere*, from Arabic.

sug·ar beet ▶ **noun** a type of beet (plant) from which sugar is extracted.

sug·ar·cane /ˈSHo͝ogər,kān/ ▶ **noun** a tropical grass with tall thick stems from which sugar is extracted.

sug·ar·coat·ed /ˈSHo͝ogər,kōtid/ ▶ **adjective** superficially attractive or acceptable.

sug·ar dad·dy ▶ **noun** informal a rich older man who lavishes gifts on a much younger woman.

sug·ar ma·ple ▶ **noun** a North American maple, which yields the sap from which maple sugar and maple syrup are made.

sug·ar·plum /ˈSHo͝ogər,pləm/ ▶ **noun** a small round candy of flavored boiled sugar.

sug·ar snap (also **sugar snap pea**) ▶ **noun** a type of snow pea with thick, rounded pods.

sug·ar·y /ˈSHo͝ogərē/ ▶ **adjective 1** containing much sugar. **2** coated in sugar. **3** too sentimental.

sug·gest /sə(g)ˈjest/ ▶ **verb 1** put an idea or plan forward for consideration. **2** make someone think that something exists or is the case: *evidence suggests that he died soon after 1190.* **3** say or express indirectly: *are you suggesting that I should ignore her?* **4** (**suggest itself**) (of an idea) come into one's mind.

> – SYNONYMS **1 propose,** put forward, recommend, advocate, advise. **2 indicate,** lead someone to the belief, give the impression, demonstrate, show. **3 hint,** insinuate, imply, intimate.

– ORIGIN Latin *suggerere* 'suggest, prompt.'

sug·gest·i·ble /sə(g)ˈjestəbəl/ ▶ **adjective** quick to accept other people's ideas or suggestions; easily influenced.
– DERIVATIVES **sug·gest·i·bil·i·ty** /sə(g),jestəˈbilitē/ noun.

sug·ges·tion /sə(g)ˈjesCHən/ ▶ **noun 1** an idea or plan put forward for consideration. **2** something that implies or indicates a certain fact or situation: *there is no suggestion that she was involved in wrongdoing.* **3** a slight trace or indication: *a suggestion of a smile.* **4** Psychology the process by which a person is led to accept an idea or belief uncritically, especially as a technique in hypnosis.

> – SYNONYMS **1 proposal,** proposition, recommendation, advice, counsel, hint, tip, clue, idea. **2 hint,** trace, touch, suspicion, ghost, semblance, shadow, glimmer. **3 insinuation,** hint, implication.

sug·ges·tive /sə(g)ˈjestiv/ ▶ **adjective 1** bringing ideas, images, etc., to mind: *flavors suggestive of coffee and blackberry.* **2** (of a remark, joke, etc.) hinting at sexual matters; mildly indecent.

> – SYNONYMS **1 redolent,** evocative, reminiscent, characteristic, indicative, typical. **2 provocative,** titillating, sexual, sexy, risqué, **indecent,** indelicate, improper, unseemly, smutty, dirty.

– DERIVATIVES **sug·ges·tive·ly** adverb **sug·ges·tive·ness** noun.

su·i·cid·al /,so͞oiˈsīdl/ ▶ **adjective 1** deeply unhappy or depressed and likely to commit suicide. **2** likely to have a disastrously damaging effect on oneself or one's interests: *a suicidal career move.*
– DERIVATIVES **su·i·cid·al·ly** adverb.

su·i·cide /ˈso͞oi,sīd/ ▶ **noun 1** the action of killing oneself deliberately. **2** a person who commits suicide. **3** a course of action that is likely to be very damaging to one's career, position in society, etc. ▶ **adjective** referring to a military operation carried out by people who do not expect to survive it: *a suicide bomber.*
– ORIGIN from Latin *sui* 'of oneself' + *caedere* 'kill.'

su·i·cide pact ▶ **noun** an agreement between two or more people to commit suicide together.

su·i ge·ne·ris /,so͞o,ī ˈjenərəs, ,so͞oē/ ▶ **adjective** unique.
– ORIGIN Latin, 'of its own kind.'

suit /so͞ot/ ▶ **noun 1** a set of outer clothes made of the same fabric and designed to be worn together, consisting of a jacket and pants or a jacket and a skirt. **2** a set of clothes for a particular activity. **3** any of the sets into which a deck of playing cards is divided (spades, hearts, diamonds, and clubs). **4** a lawsuit. **5** informal a high-ranking business executive. **6** the process of trying to win a woman's affection with a view to marriage.

> – SYNONYMS **1 outfit,** ensemble. **2 legal action,** lawsuit, (court) case, action, (legal/judicial) proceedings, litigation.

▶ **verb 1** be convenient for or acceptable to: *what time would suit you?* **2** (of clothes, colors, etc.) go well with or be right for someone's features or figure. **3** (**suit oneself**) do exactly as one wants. **4** (as adj. **suited**) right or appropriate for a particular person, purpose, or situation: *washable wallpaper ideally suited to bathrooms and kitchens.*

> – SYNONYMS **1 look attractive on,** look good on, become, flatter. **2 be convenient for,** be acceptable to, be suitable for, meet the requirements of; informal fit. **3** *recipes* ***suited to*** *students* **be appropriate for,** tailor to/for, fashion for, adjust to/for, adapt to/for, modify to/for, fit for, gear to, design for.

– ORIGIN Old French *siwte*.

suit·a·ble /ˈso͞otəbəl/ ▶ **adjective** right or appropriate for a particular person, purpose, or situation.

> – SYNONYMS **1 acceptable,** satisfactory, convenient. **2 appropriate,** apposite, apt, fitting, fit, suited, tailor-made, in keeping, ideal; informal right up someone's alley. **3 proper,** right, seemly, decent, appropriate, fitting, correct, due.
> – ANTONYMS unsuitable.

– DERIVATIVES **suit·a·bil·i·ty** /,so͞otəˈbilitē/ noun **suit·a·bly** /-blē/ adverb.

suit·case /ˈso͞ot,kās/ ▶ **noun** a case with a handle and a hinged lid, used for carrying clothes and other personal possessions.

suite /swēt/ ▶ **noun 1** a set of rooms for one person's or family's use or for a particular purpose. **2** a set of furniture of the same design. **3** a set of pieces of instrumental music to be played in succession. **4** a set of pieces from an opera or musical arranged as one instrumental work.

> – SYNONYMS **apartment,** flat, rooms.

– ORIGIN French.

suit·or /ˈso͞otər/ ▶ **noun** a man who wishes to marry a particular woman.

sul·fa drugs /ˈsəlfə/ (chiefly Brit. also **sulpha drugs**) ▶ **plural noun** the sulfonamide family of drugs.

– ORIGIN abbreviation.

sul·fate /ˈsəlˌfāt/ (Brit. **sulphate**) ▶ **noun** Chemistry a salt or ester of sulfuric acid.

sul·fide /ˈsəlˌfīd/ (Brit. **sulphide**) ▶ **noun** Chemistry a compound of sulfur with another element or group.

sul·fon·a·mide /səlˈfänəˌmīd/ (Brit. **sulphonamide**) ▶ **noun** any of a class of sulfur-containing drugs that are able to prevent the multiplication of certain bacteria.

sul·fur /ˈsəlfər/ (Brit. **sulphur**) ▶ **noun** a nonmetallic chemical element that easily catches fire, typically occurring as yellow crystals.
– ORIGIN Latin *sulfur, sulphur*.

sul·fur di·ox·ide ▶ **noun** a colorless strong-smelling poisonous gas formed by burning sulfur.

sul·fu·ric /səlˈfyo͞orik/ ▶ **adjective** containing sulfur or sulfuric acid.

sul·fu·ric a·cid ▶ **noun** a strong corrosive acid made by oxidizing solutions of sulfur dioxide.

sul·fur·ous /ˈsəlfərəs/ ▶ **adjective** containing or obtained from sulfur.

sulk /səlk/ ▶ **verb** be silent, bad-tempered, and resentful as a result of annoyance or disappointment.

– SYNONYMS **mope,** brood, be in a bad mood, be in a huff.

▶ **noun** a period of sulking.

– SYNONYMS **(bad) mood,** fit of pique, pet, huff.

sulk·y /ˈsəlkē/ ▶ **adjective** (**sulkier, sulkiest**) silent, bad-tempered, and resentful.

– SYNONYMS **sullen,** surly, petulant, disgruntled, put out, bad-tempered, grumpy, moody.
– ANTONYMS cheerful.

– DERIVATIVES **sulk·i·ly** adverb **sulk·i·ness** noun.
– ORIGIN perhaps from former *sulke* 'hard to dispose of.'

sul·len /ˈsələn/ ▶ **adjective** bad-tempered and sulky.

– SYNONYMS **surly,** sulky, morose, resentful, moody, grumpy, bad-tempered, unsociable, uncommunicative, unresponsive.
– ANTONYMS cheerful.

– DERIVATIVES **sul·len·ly** adverb **sul·len·ness** noun.
– ORIGIN Old French *sulein*.

sul·ly /ˈsəlē/ ▶ **verb** (**sullies, sullying, sullied**) literary **1** damage someone's or something's purity or reputation. **2** make something dirty.

– SYNONYMS **taint,** defile, soil, tarnish, stain, blemish, pollute, spoil, mar; literary besmirch.

– ORIGIN perhaps from French *souiller* 'to soil.'

sul·pha drugs ▶ **plural noun** British spelling of **SULFA DRUGS**.

sul·phate ▶ **plural noun** British spelling of **SULFATE**.

sul·phide ▶ **plural noun** British spelling of **SULFIDE**.

sul·phon·a·mide ▶ **plural noun** British spelling of **SULFONAMIDE**.

sul·phur, etc. ▶ **noun** British spelling of **SULFUR**, etc.

sul·tan /ˈsəltn/ ▶ **noun** the title given to a ruler in some Muslim countries.
– ORIGIN Arabic, 'power, ruler.'

sul·tan·a /səlˈtanə/ ▶ **noun 1** a small light brown seedless raisin; a golden raisin. **2** a wife of a sultan.
– ORIGIN Italian, feminine of *sultano* 'sultan.'

sul·tan·ate /ˈsəltnˌāt/ ▶ **noun 1** the rank or position of a sultan. **2** the territory ruled by a sultan.

sul·try /ˈsəltrē/ ▶ **adjective** (**sultrier, sultriest**) **1** (of the weather) hot and humid. **2** displaying or suggesting sexual passion.

– SYNONYMS **1 humid,** close, airless, stifling, oppressive, muggy, sticky, sweltering, hot, tropical, heavy; informal boiling, roasting. **2 passionate,** sensual, sexy, seductive.
– ANTONYMS refreshing.

– ORIGIN from former *sulter* 'swelter.'

sum /səm/ ▶ **noun 1** a particular amount of money. **2** (also **sum total**) the total amount resulting from the addition of two or more numbers or amounts. **3** an arithmetical calculation.

– SYNONYMS **1 amount,** quantity, price, charge, fee, cost. **2 total,** sum total, grand total, tally, aggregate. **3 calculation,** problem.

▶ **verb** (**sums, summing, summed**) (**sum someone/thing up**) **1** (**sum something up** or **sum up**) summarize something briefly. **2** concisely describe someone's or something's nature or character. **3** Law (of a judge) review the evidence at the end of a case, and direct the jury about points of law.

– SYNONYMS *he summed up his reasons* **summarize,** make/give a summary of, encapsulate, put in a nutshell, précis, outline, recapitulate, review, recap.

– PHRASES **in sum** to sum up.
– ORIGIN Latin *summa* 'main part, sum total.'

su·mac /ˈso͞omak, ˈsho͞o-/ (also **sumach**) ▶ **noun** a shrub or small tree with clusters of fruits that are ground and used as a spice in Middle Eastern cooking.
– ORIGIN Arabic.

Su·ma·tran /səˈmätrən/ ▶ **noun** a person from the Indonesian island of Sumatra. ▶ **adjective** relating to Sumatra.

Su·me·ri·an /səˈmerēən, -ˈmiər-/ ▶ **adjective** relating to Sumer, an ancient region of what is now Iraq. ▶ **noun** a person from Sumer.

sum·mar·i·ly /səˈme(ə)rəlē, ˈsəmərəlē/ immediately; without delay: *accused of treason, he was summarily executed.*

– SYNONYMS **immediately,** instantly, right away, straightaway, at once, on the spot, speedily, swiftly, rapidly, without delay, promptly, arbitrarily, without formality, peremptorily.

sum·ma·rize /ˈsəməˌrīz/ ▶ **verb** give a brief statement of the main points of something.

– SYNONYMS **sum up,** abridge, condense, outline, put in a nutshell, précis.

sum·ma·ry /ˈsəmərē/ ▶ **noun** (pl. **summaries**) a brief statement of the main points of something.

– SYNONYMS **synopsis,** précis, résumé, abstract, outline, rundown, summing-up, overview.

▶ **adjective 1** not including unnecessary details or formalities. **2** (of a legal process or judgment) done or made without the normal legal formalities.
– ORIGIN Latin *summarius*.

USAGE

Do not confuse **summary** and **summery**. A **summary** is a brief statement of the main points of something (*a summary of today's news*), whereas **summery** is an adjective meaning 'typical of or suitable for summer' (*summery weather*).

sum·ma·tion /sə'māsʜən/ ▶ **noun 1** the process of adding things together. **2** the action of summing something up. **3** a summary.

sum·mer /'səmər/ ▶ **noun** the season after spring and before autumn, when the weather is warmest. ▶ **verb** spend the summer in a particular place.
– DERIVATIVES **sum·mer·y** adjective.
– ORIGIN Old English.

sum·mer·house /'səmər,hous/ ▶ **noun 1** a house or cottage used as a second residence during the summer months. **2** a small building in a garden or park, used for sitting in during the summer months.

sum·mer school ▶ **noun** courses held during school summer vacations.

sum·mer squash ▶ **noun** a squash that is eaten before the seeds and rind have hardened.

sum·mer·time /'səmər,tīm/ ▶ **noun** the season or period of summer.

sum·ming-up ▶ **noun 1** a summary. **2** a judge's review of evidence at the end of a case, with a direction to the jury about points of law.

sum·mit /'səmit/ ▶ **noun 1** the highest point of a hill or mountain. **2** the highest possible level of achievement. **3** a meeting between heads of government.

– SYNONYMS **1 (mountain) top,** peak, crest, crown, apex, tip, cap, hilltop. **2 meeting,** conference, talk(s).
– ANTONYMS base.

– ORIGIN Old French *somete*.

sum·mon /'səmən/ ▶ **verb 1** instruct someone to be present. **2** order someone to appear in a court of law. **3** urgently ask for help. **4** call people to attend a meeting. **5** produce a quality or reaction from within oneself by making an effort: *she managed to summon up a smile*.

– SYNONYMS **1 send for,** call for, request the presence of, ask, invite. **2 convene,** call, assemble, rally, muster, gather together. **3 summons,** subpoena.

– ORIGIN Latin *summonere* 'give a hint.'

sum·mons /'səmənz/ ▶ **noun** (pl. **summonses**) **1** an order to appear in a court of law. **2** an act of instructing someone to be present.

– SYNONYMS **writ,** subpoena, warrant, court order.

▶ **verb** chiefly Law serve someone with a summons.

– SYNONYMS **serve with a summons,** summon, subpoena.

su·mo /'sōōmō/ ▶ **noun** Japanese wrestling in which a wrestler must not go outside a circle or touch the ground with any part of his body except the soles of his feet.
– ORIGIN Japanese.

sump /səmp/ ▶ **noun 1** the base of an internal-combustion engine, which serves as a reservoir of oil for the lubrication system. **2** a hollow in the floor of a mine or cave in which water collects. **3** a cesspool.
– ORIGIN from Dutch or German *sump* 'marsh.'

sump·tu·ous /'səm(p)cʜōōəs/ ▶ **adjective** splendid and expensive-looking.

– SYNONYMS **lavish,** luxurious, opulent, magnificent, resplendent, gorgeous, splendid; informal plush, swish.
– ANTONYMS plain.

– DERIVATIVES **sump·tu·ous·ly** adverb **sump·tu·ous·ness** noun.
– ORIGIN Latin *sumptuosus*, from *sumptus* 'cost.'

sum to·tal ▶ **noun** another term for **SUM** (sense 2 of the noun).

sun /sən/ ▶ **noun 1** (also **Sun**) the star around which the earth orbits. **2** any similar star, with or without planets. **3** the light or warmth received from the sun.

– SYNONYMS **sunshine,** sunlight, daylight, light, warmth.

▶ **verb** (**suns, sunning, sunned**) (**sun oneself**) sit or lie in the sun.
– DERIVATIVES **sun·less** adjective.
– PHRASES **under the sun** in existence.
– ORIGIN Old English.

WORD LINKS

solar *relating to the sun*

sun-baked ▶ **adjective** exposed to the heat of the sun.

sun·bathe /'sən,bāᴛʜ/ ▶ **verb** sit or lie in the sun to get a suntan.
– DERIVATIVES **sun·bath·er** noun.

sun·beam /'sən,bēm/ ▶ **noun** a ray of sunlight.

sun·belt /'sən,belt/ ▶ **noun** a strip of territory receiving a high amount of sunshine, especially the southern US from California to Florida.

sun·block /'sən,bläk/ ▶ **noun** a cream or lotion for protecting the skin from sunburn.

sun·burn /'sən,bərn/ ▶ **noun** inflammation of the skin caused by too much exposure to the ultraviolet rays of the sun.
– DERIVATIVES **sun·burned** (or **sunburnt**) adjective.

sun·burst /'sən,bərst/ ▶ **noun 1** a design or ornament representing the sun and its rays. **2** a sudden brief appearance of the full sun from behind clouds.

sun·cream /'sən,krēm/ ▶ **noun** a cream rubbed onto the skin to protect it from sunburn.

sun·dae /'sən,dā/ ▶ **noun** a dish of ice cream with added ingredients such as fruit, nuts, and syrup.
– ORIGIN perhaps from **SUNDAY**, either because the dish was made with ice cream left over from Sunday, or because it was sold only on Sundays.

Sun·day /'səndā, -dē/ ▶ **noun** the day of the week before Monday and following Saturday, observed by most Christians as a day of religious worship.
– ORIGIN Old English, 'day of the sun.'

Sun·day best ▶ **noun** a person's best clothes.

Sun·day school ▶ **noun** a class held on Sundays to teach children about Christianity or Judaism.

sun deck ▶ **noun 1** the deck of a yacht or cruise ship that is open to the sky. **2** a terrace or balcony positioned to catch the sun.

sun·der /'səndər/ ▶ **verb** literary **1** split something apart. **2** break the connection or relationship between two or more people or things.
– ORIGIN Old English.

sun·dew /'sən,d(y)ōō/ ▶ **noun** a small carnivorous plant found in boggy places, with leaves bearing sticky hairs for trapping insects.

sun·di·al /ˈsənˌdīl/ ▶ **noun** a device used for telling the time, consisting of a pointer that casts a shadow on a surface marked with hours like a clock.

sun·down /ˈsənˌdoun/ ▶ **noun** sunset.

sun·dress /ˈsənˌdres/ ▶ **noun** a light, loose sleeveless dress.

sun-dried ▶ **adjective** dried in the sun, as opposed to by artificial heat.

sun·dry /ˈsəndrē/ ▶ **adjective** of various kinds.

– SYNONYMS **various,** varied, miscellaneous, assorted, mixed, diverse, diversified, several, numerous, many, manifold, multifarious, multitudinous; literary divers.

▶ **plural noun** (**sundries**) various items not important enough to be mentioned individually.
– ORIGIN Old English, 'distinct, separate.'

WORD TOOLKIT

See **DIVERSE**.

sun·fish /ˈsənˌfisʜ/ ▶ **noun** (pl. same or **sunfishes**) a large sea fish with tall fins near the rear of the body.

sun·flow·er /ˈsənˌflou(-ə)r/ ▶ **noun** a tall plant bearing very large yellow flowers with edible seeds from which an oil used in cooking, margarine, etc., is extracted.

sung /səɴɢ/ past participle of **SING**.

sun·glass·es /ˈsənˌglasiz/ ▶ **plural noun** glasses tinted to protect the eyes from sunlight or glare.

sunk /səɴɢk/ past participle of **SINK**[1].

sunk·en /ˈsəɴɢkən/ ▶ **adjective 1** having sunk. **2** at a lower level than the surrounding area. **3** (of a person's cheeks or eyes) hollow or appearing set back into the face as a result of age, disease, etc.
– ORIGIN past participle of **SINK**[1].

sun-kissed ▶ **adjective** made warm or brown by the sun.

sun·lamp /ˈsənˌlamp/ ▶ **noun** a lamp giving off ultraviolet rays, used chiefly to produce an artificial suntan.

sun·light /ˈsənˌlīt/ ▶ **noun** light from the sun.
– DERIVATIVES **sun·lit** /ˈsənˌlit/ adjective.

Sun·na /ˈso͝onə, ˈsənə/ ▶ **noun** the traditional part of Muslim law based on Muhammad's words or acts, accepted as authoritative by Muslims.
– ORIGIN Arabic, 'form, way, rule.'

Sun·ni /ˈso͝onē/ ▶ **noun** (pl. same or **Sunnis**) **1** one of the two main branches of Islam, the other being Shia. **2** a Muslim who follows the Sunni branch of Islam.
– ORIGIN Arabic, 'custom, standard rule.'

sun·ny /ˈsənē/ ▶ **adjective** (**sunnier, sunniest**) **1** bright with or receiving much sunlight. **2** cheerful.

– SYNONYMS **1 bright,** sunlit, clear, fine, cloudless. **2 cheerful,** cheery, happy, bright, merry, bubbly, jolly, good-natured, good-tempered, optimistic, upbeat.
– ANTONYMS dull, cloudy.

sun·ny side ▶ **noun 1** the side of something that receives the sun for longest. **2** the more cheerful or pleasant aspect of something.
– PHRASES **sunny side up** (of an egg) fried on one side only.

sun·rise /ˈsənˌrīz/ ▶ **noun 1** the time in the morning when the sun rises. **2** the colors and light visible in the sky at sunrise.

– SYNONYMS **dawn,** crack of dawn, daybreak, sunup, break of day, first light, early morning.

sun·roof /ˈsənˌro͞of, -ˌro͝of/ ▶ **noun** a panel in the roof of a car that can be opened for extra ventilation.

sun·screen /ˈsənˌskrēn/ ▶ **noun** a cream or lotion rubbed onto the skin to protect it from the sun.

sun·set /ˈsənˌset/ ▶ **noun 1** the time in the evening when the sun sets. **2** the colors and light visible in the sky at sunset.

– SYNONYMS **sundown,** nightfall, twilight, dusk, evening.

sun·shade /ˈsənˌsʜād/ ▶ **noun** a parasol, awning, or other device giving protection from the sun.

sun·shine /ˈsənˌsʜīn/ ▶ **noun** sunlight unbroken by cloud.
– DERIVATIVES **sun·shin·y** adjective.

sun·spot /ˈsənˌspät/ ▶ **noun** a temporary darker and cooler patch on the sun's surface.

sun·stroke /ˈsənˌstrōk/ ▶ **noun** heatstroke caused by spending too much time exposed to hot sunlight.

sun·tan /ˈsənˌtan/ ▶ **noun** a golden-brown coloring of the skin caused by spending time in the sun.
– DERIVATIVES **sun·tanned** adjective.

sun·up /ˈsənˌəp/ ▶ **noun** sunrise.

sup /səp/ ▶ **verb** (**sups, supping, supped**) dated eat supper.
– ORIGIN Old French *super*.

su·per /ˈso͞opər/ ▶ **adjective** informal excellent.

– SYNONYMS **excellent,** superb, superlative, first-class, outstanding, marvelous, magnificent, wonderful, splendid, glorious; informal great, fantastic, fabulous, terrific, ace, divine, wicked, cool; Brit. informal smashing, brilliant.
– ANTONYMS rotten.

super- ▶ **combining form 1** above; over; beyond: *superstructure*. **2** to a great or extreme degree: *superabundant*. **3** extra large of its kind: *superpower*.
– ORIGIN from Latin *super* 'above, beyond.'

su·per·a·bun·dant /ˌso͞opərəˈbəndənt/ ▶ **adjective** formal occurring in very large quantities.
– DERIVATIVES **su·per·a·bun·dance** noun.

su·per·an·nu·a·ted /ˌso͞opərˈanyo͞oˌātid/ ▶ **adjective 1** (of an employee) discharged from a job with a pension. **2** too old to be effective or useful.
– ORIGIN from Latin *super-* 'over' + *annus* 'year.'

su·per·an·nu·a·tion /ˌso͞opərˌanyo͞oˈāsʜən/ ▶ **noun** regular payment made into a fund by an employee toward a future pension.

su·perb /so͞oˈpərb, sə-/ ▶ **adjective** extremely good or impressive.

– SYNONYMS **excellent,** first-class, outstanding, marvelous, wonderful, splendid, admirable, fine, exceptional, glorious; informal great, fantastic, fabulous, terrific, super, awesome, ace; Brit. informal brilliant, smashing.
– ANTONYMS poor, unimpressive.

– DERIVATIVES **su·perb·ly** adverb.
– ORIGIN Latin *superbus* 'proud, magnificent.'

su·per·bike /ˈso͞opərˌbīk/ ▶ **noun** a high-performance motorcycle.

su·per·bug /'so͞opər,bəg/ ▶ **noun** informal a bacterium, insect, etc., that has become resistant to antibiotics or pesticides.

su·per·car /'so͞opər,kär/ ▶ **noun** a high-performance sports car.

su·per·cen·ter /'so͞opər,sentər/ ▶ **noun** a superstore.

su·per·charge /'so͞opər,CHärj/ ▶ **verb** (usu. as adj. **supercharged**) **1** provide an engine with a supercharger. **2** give extra power, energy, or intensity to: *a supercharged collection of dance tracks.*

su·per·charg·er /'so͞opər,CHärjər/ ▶ **noun** a device that increases the efficiency of an internal-combustion engine by raising the pressure of the fuel-air mixture supplied to it.

su·per·cil·i·ous /,so͞opər'silēəs/ ▶ **adjective** behaving as though one thinks one is superior to other people.

– SYNONYMS **arrogant,** haughty, conceited, disdainful, overbearing, pompous, condescending, superior, patronizing, imperious, proud, snobbish, smug, scornful, sneering; informal high and mighty, snooty, stuck-up.

– DERIVATIVES **su·per·cil·i·ous·ly** adverb **su·per·cil·i·ous·ness** noun.
– ORIGIN Latin *superciliosus* 'haughty.'

su·per·com·put·er /'so͞opərkəm,pyo͞otər/ ▶ **noun** a particularly powerful mainframe computer.

su·per·con·duc·tiv·i·ty /,so͞opər,kän,dək'tivitē/ ▶ **noun** Physics the property of zero electrical resistance in some substances at very low temperatures.
– DERIVATIVES **su·per·con·duct·ing** /-kən'dəktiNG/ adjective **su·per·con·duc·tor** /'so͞opərkən,dəktər/ noun.

su·per·con·ti·nent /'so͞opər,käntn-ənt/ ▶ **noun** a huge landmass believed to have divided in the geological past to form some of the present continents.

su·per·cool /,so͞opər'ko͞ol/ ▶ **verb** Chemistry cool a liquid below its freezing point without solidification or crystallization.

su·per·crit·i·cal /,so͞opər'kritikəl/ ▶ **adjective** Physics greater than or above a critical threshold such as critical mass or temperature.

su·per-du·per /'so͞opər 'do͞opər/ ▶ **adjective** humorous **1** very good; marvelous. **2** tremendous or colossal in size or degree.

su·per·e·go /,so͞opər'ēgō/ ▶ **noun** (pl. **superegos**) the part of the mind that acts as a conscience, reflecting social standards that have been learned. Compare with **EGO** and **ID**.

su·per·e·rog·a·to·ry /,so͞opərə'rägə,tôrē/ ▶ **adjective** more than what is needed or required; superfluous.
– ORIGIN Latin, from *supererogare* 'pay in addition.'

su·per·fam·i·ly /'so͞opər,fam(ə)lē/ ▶ **noun** (pl. **superfamilies**) Biology a taxonomic category that ranks above family and below order.

su·per·fi·cial /,so͞opər'fiSHəl/ ▶ **adjective 1** existing or happening at or on the surface. **2** appearing to exist or be true until examined more closely: *the resemblance is superficial.* **3** not thorough: *a superficial knowledge of the system.* **4** lacking depth of character or understanding; not concerned with serious matters.

– SYNONYMS **1 surface,** exterior, external, outer, slight. **2 cursory,** perfunctory, casual, sketchy, desultory, token, slapdash, offhand, rushed, hasty, hurried. **3 apparent,** seeming, outward, ostensible, cosmetic, slight. **4 facile,** shallow, flippant, empty-headed, trivial, frivolous, silly, inane.
– ANTONYMS deep, thorough.

– DERIVATIVES **su·per·fi·ci·al·i·ty** /-,fiSHē'alitē/ noun (pl. **superficialities**) **su·per·fi·cial·ly** adverb.
– ORIGIN Latin *superficialis.*

su·per·flu·ous /so͞o'pərfləwəs/ ▶ **adjective** more than is needed; unnecessary.

– SYNONYMS **surplus,** redundant, unneeded, unnecessary, excess, extra, (to) spare, remaining, unused, left over, waste.
– ANTONYMS necessary.

– DERIVATIVES **su·per·flu·i·ty** noun (pl. **superfluities**) **su·per·flu·ous·ly** adverb.
– ORIGIN Latin *superfluus.*

su·per·food /'so͞opər,fo͞od/ ▶ **noun** a food considered especially nutritious or otherwise beneficial to health and well-being.

su·per·glue /'so͞opər,glo͞o/ ▶ **noun** a very strong quick-setting glue.

su·per·heat /,so͞opər'hēt/ ▶ **verb** Physics **1** heat a liquid under pressure above its boiling point without vaporization. **2** heat steam or other vapor above the temperature of the liquid from which it was formed.

su·per·he·ro /'so͞opər,hirō/ ▶ **noun** (pl. **superheroes**) a fictional hero with superhuman powers.

su·per·high·way /'so͞opər,hīwā, ,so͞opər'hī,wā/ ▶ **noun** an expressway.

su·per·hu·man /,so͞opər'(h)yo͞omən/ ▶ **adjective** having or showing exceptional ability or powers.

– SYNONYMS **extraordinary,** phenomenal, prodigious, stupendous, exceptional, immense, heroic, Herculean.

– DERIVATIVES **su·per·hu·man·ly** adverb.

su·per·im·pose /,so͞opərim'pōz/ ▶ **verb** place or lay one thing over another.
– DERIVATIVES **su·per·im·po·si·tion** /-,impə'ziSHən/ noun.

su·per·in·tend /,so͞opərin'tend/ ▶ **verb** manage or oversee an activity, organization, etc.
– DERIVATIVES **su·per·in·tend·ence** noun.

su·per·in·tend·ent /,so͞opərin'tendənt/ ▶ **noun 1** a person who supervises or is in charge of an activity, organization, etc. **2** the head custodian of a building. **3** (in the UK) a police officer ranking above chief inspector. **4** (in the US) the chief of a police department.

– SYNONYMS **manager,** director, administrator, supervisor, overseer, controller, chief, head, governor; informal boss.

– ORIGIN from Latin *superintendere.*

su·pe·ri·or /sə'pi(ə)rēər/ ▶ **adjective 1** higher in status, quality, or power. **2** of a high standard or quality. **3** having or showing a belief that one is better than other people: *he had a rather superior manner.* **4** (of a letter, figure, or symbol) written or printed above the line. **5** chiefly Anatomy higher in position.

– SYNONYMS **1 senior,** higher-ranking, higher. **2 better,** finer, higher quality, top-quality, choice, select, prime, excellent. **3 condescending,** supercilious, patronizing, haughty, disdainful, lordly, snobbish; informal high and mighty, snooty.
– ANTONYMS junior, inferior.

▶ **noun 1** a person of higher rank. **2** the head of a monastery or other religious institution.

– SYNONYMS **manager,** chief, supervisor, senior, controller, foreman; informal boss.
– ANTONYMS subordinate.

– ORIGIN Latin, 'higher.'

su·pe·ri·or·i·ty /səˌpi(ə)rēˈôritē, -ˈäritē/ ▸ **noun** the state of being superior.

– SYNONYMS **supremacy,** advantage, lead, dominance, primacy, ascendancy, eminence.

su·per·la·tive /səˈpərlətiv/ ▸ **adjective 1** of the highest quality or degree. **2** Grammar (of an adjective or adverb) expressing the highest degree of a quality (e.g., *bravest, most fiercely*). Contrasted with **POSITIVE** and **COMPARATIVE.** ▸ **noun** an exaggerated expression of praise.
– DERIVATIVES **su·per·la·tive·ly** adverb.
– ORIGIN Latin *superlativus.*

su·per·man /ˈso͞opərˌman/ (or **superwoman** /ˈso͞opərˌwo͝omən/) ▸ **noun** (pl. **supermen** or **superwomen**) informal a person with exceptional physical or mental abilities.

su·per·mar·ket /ˈso͞opərˌmärkit/ ▸ **noun** a large self-service store selling foods and household goods.

su·per·max /ˈso͞opərˌmaks/ ▸ **noun** an extremely high-security prison or part of a prison, intended for particularly dangerous prisoners. ▸ **adjective** (of a prison) having extremely high-security features or facilities: *12 percent of prisoners live in supermax units.*

su·per·mod·el /ˈso͞opərˌmädl/ ▸ **noun** a very successful and famous fashion model.

su·per·nat·u·ral /ˌso͞opərˈnacH(ə)rəl/ ▸ **adjective** referring or relating to events, forces, or powers that cannot be explained by science or the laws of nature.

– SYNONYMS **1 paranormal,** psychic, magic, magical, occult, mystic, mystical. **2 ghostly,** phantom, spectral, other-worldly, unearthly.

▸ **noun** (**the supernatural**) supernatural events, forces, or powers.
– DERIVATIVES **su·per·nat·u·ral·ly** adverb.

su·per·no·va /ˈso͞opərˌnōvə/ ▸ **noun** (pl. **supernovae** /-ˌnōvē/ or **supernovas**) a star that undergoes an explosion, becoming suddenly very much brighter.

su·per·nu·mer·ar·y /ˌso͞opərˈn(y)o͞oməˌrerē/ ▸ **adjective 1** more than is normally needed; extra. **2** not belonging to a regular staff but employed for extra work. ▸ **noun** (pl. **supernumeraries**) an extra person or thing.
– ORIGIN Latin *supernumerarius* 'soldier added to a legion after it is complete.'

su·per·or·di·nate /ˌso͞opərˈôrdn-ət/ ▸ **noun** a thing that represents a higher order or category within a system of classification.

su·per·pose /ˌso͞opərˈpōz/ ▸ **verb** place something on or above something else.
– DERIVATIVES **su·per·po·si·tion** /-pəˈzisHən/ noun.
– ORIGIN French *superposer.*

su·per·pow·er /ˈso͞opərˌpouər/ ▸ **noun** a very powerful and influential nation.

su·per·script /ˈso͞opərˌskript/ ▸ **adjective** (of a letter, figure, or symbol) written or printed above the line.

su·per·sede /ˌso͞opərˈsēd/ ▸ **verb** take the place of someone or something previously in authority or use.

– SYNONYMS **replace,** take the place of, take over from, succeed, supplant.

– ORIGIN Latin *supersedere* 'be superior to.'

USAGE

The ending of **supersede** is spelled **-sede**, not *-cede;* it is the only verb that has this ending.

CHOOSE THE RIGHT WORD

See **REPLACE**.

su·per·size /ˈso͞opərˌsīz/ ▸ **verb** produce or serve (something) in a larger size: *click here to supersize the picture.* ▸ **adjective** larger than normal.

su·per·son·ic /ˌso͞opərˈsänik/ ▸ **adjective** involving or referring to a speed greater than that of sound.
– DERIVATIVES **su·per·son·i·cal·ly** /-ik(ə)lē/ adverb.

su·per·star /ˈso͞opərˌstär/ ▸ **noun** an extremely famous and successful performer or athlete.
– DERIVATIVES **su·per·star·dom** /-dəm/ noun.

su·per·state /ˈso͞opərˌstāt/ ▸ **noun** a large and powerful state formed from a federation or union of several nations.

su·per·sti·tion /ˌso͞opərˈstisHən/ ▸ **noun 1** irrational belief in supernatural events. **2** a widely held but irrational belief that certain objects, actions, or events bring good or bad luck.
– ORIGIN Latin.

su·per·sti·tious /ˌso͞opərˈstisHəs/ ▸ **adjective** believing in the supernatural and its influence in bringing good or bad luck.
– DERIVATIVES **su·per·sti·tious·ly** adverb.

su·per·store /ˈso͞opərˌstôr/ ▸ **noun** a retail store with more than the average amount of space and variety of stock.

su·per·struc·ture /ˈso͞opərˌstrəkcHər/ ▸ **noun 1** a structure built on top of something else. **2** the part of a building above its foundations. **3** the parts of a ship, other than masts and rigging, above its hull and main deck.

su·per·tank·er /ˈso͞opərˌtaNGkər/ ▸ **noun** a very large oil tanker.

su·per·vene /ˌso͞opərˈvēn/ ▸ **verb** happen so as to interrupt or change an existing situation.
– DERIVATIVES **su·per·ven·ient** /-ˈvēnyənt/ adjective **su·per·ven·tion** /-ˈvencHən/ noun.
– ORIGIN Latin *supervenire* 'come in addition.'

su·per·vil·lain /ˈso͞opərˌvilən/ ▸ **noun** a very wicked fictional character, especially one with superhuman powers.

su·per·vise /ˈso͞opərˌvīz/ ▸ **verb** observe and direct the performance of a task or the work of a person.

– SYNONYMS **oversee,** be in charge of, superintend, preside over, direct, manage, run, look after, be responsible for, govern, keep an eye on, observe, monitor, mind.

– DERIVATIVES **su·per·vi·sion** /ˌso͞opərˈvizHən/ noun **su·per·vi·so·ry** /ˌso͞opərˈvīzərē/ adjective.
– ORIGIN Latin *supervidere* 'survey, supervise.'

su·per·vi·sor /ˈso͞opərˌvīzər/ ▸ **noun** a person who supervises.

– SYNONYMS *the supervisor of sector B* **manager,** director, overseer, controller, superintendent, governor, chief, head, foreman; informal boss.

su·pi·nate /ˈsōōpəˌnāt/ ▶ **verb** technical **1** put or hold (a hand, foot, or limb) with the palm or sole turned upward. Compare with **PRONATE. 2** walk or run with most of the weight on the inside of the feet.
– DERIVATIVES **su·pi·na·tion** /ˌsōōpəˈnāsʜən/ noun.
– ORIGIN Latin *supinare* 'lay backward.'

su·pi·na·tor /ˈsōōpəˌnātər/ ▶ **noun 1** a muscle whose contraction produces or assists in the supination of a limb or part of a limb. **2** any of several specific muscles in the forearm. **3** one who supinates when walking or running.

su·pine /ˈsōōˌpīn/ ▶ **adjective 1** lying face upward. **2** failing to act as a result of laziness or weakness.

– SYNONYMS **1 flat on one's back,** face up, flat, stretched out. **2** *a supine media* **weak,** spineless, docile, acquiescent, submissive, passive.
– ANTONYMS prostrate, strong.

– DERIVATIVES **su·pine·ly** adverb **su·pine·ness** noun.
– ORIGIN Latin *supinus* 'bent backward.'

sup·per /ˈsəpər/ ▶ **noun** a light or informal evening meal.
– PHRASES **sing for one's supper** provide a service in return for a benefit.
– ORIGIN from Old French *super* 'to sup.'

sup·plant /səˈplant/ ▶ **verb** take the place of: *another technology might supplant the CD.*

– SYNONYMS **1 replace,** supersede, displace, take over from. **2 oust,** usurp, overthrow, remove, topple, unseat, depose, dethrone, succeed.

– DERIVATIVES **sup·plant·er** noun.
– ORIGIN Latin *supplantare* 'trip up.'

CHOOSE THE RIGHT WORD

See note at **REPLACE**.

sup·ple /ˈsəpəl/ ▶ **adjective** (**suppler**, **supplest**) able to bend or move easily; flexible.

– SYNONYMS **1 lithe,** lissom, willowy, flexible, agile, acrobatic, nimble. **2 pliable,** flexible, soft, bendy, workable, stretchy, springy.
– ANTONYMS stiff, rigid.

– DERIVATIVES **sup·ple·ness** noun.
– ORIGIN Latin *supplex* 'submissive.'

CHOOSE THE RIGHT WORD

See **FLEXIBLE**.

sup·ple·ment /ˈsəpləmənt/ ▶ **noun 1** a thing added to something else to improve or complete it. **2** a separate section added to a newspaper or magazine. **3** an additional charge payable for an extra service or facility.

– SYNONYMS **1 extra,** add-on, accessory, adjunct. **2 surcharge,** addition, increase, increment. **3 appendix,** addendum, postscript, addition, coda. **4 pullout,** insert.

▶ **verb** add an extra element or amount to something.

– SYNONYMS **add to,** augment, increase, boost, swell, amplify, enlarge, top up.

– DERIVATIVES **sup·ple·men·tal** /ˌsəpləˈmentl/ adjective **sup·ple·men·ta·tion** /ˌsəpləˌmenˈtāsʜən/ noun.
– ORIGIN Latin *supplementum*.

sup·ple·men·ta·ry /ˌsəpləˈmentərē/ ▶ **adjective** provided in addition to something so as to complete or improve it: *supplementary information.*

– SYNONYMS **additional,** supplemental, extra, more, further, add-on, subsidiary, auxiliary, ancillary.

sup·pli·ant /ˈsəplēənt/ ▶ **noun** a person who makes a humble request.

sup·pli·cate /ˈsəpliˌkāt/ ▶ **verb** humbly ask or beg for something.
– DERIVATIVES **sup·pli·cant** /-kənt/ noun **sup·pli·ca·tion** /ˌsəpliˈkāsʜən/ noun **sup·pli·ca·to·ry** /-kəˌtôrē/ adjective.
– ORIGIN Latin *supplicare* 'implore.'

sup·ply /səˈplī/ ▶ **verb** (**supplies, supplying, supplied**) make something needed available to someone; provide someone with something.

– SYNONYMS **1 provide,** give, furnish, equip, contribute, donate, grant, confer, dispense. **2** *windmills supply their power needs* **satisfy,** meet, fulfill, cater for.

▶ **noun** (pl. **supplies**) **1** a stock or amount of something supplied or available. **2** the action of supplying something. **3** (**supplies**) provisions and equipment necessary for an army or expedition.

– SYNONYMS **1 stock,** store, reserve, reservoir, stockpile, hoard, cache, fund, bank. **2** (**supplies**) **provisions,** stores, rations, food, necessities.

▶ **adjective** acting as a temporary substitute for another: *a supply teacher.*
– DERIVATIVES **sup·pli·er** noun.
– PHRASES **supply and demand** the amount of goods or services available and the desire of buyers for them, considered as factors deciding their price.
– ORIGIN Latin *supplere* 'fill up.'

sup·ply-side ▶ **adjective** Economics (of a policy) designed to increase output and employment by reducing taxation.

sup·port /səˈpôrt/ ▶ **verb 1** bear all or part of the weight of someone or something. **2** give help, encouragement, or approval to. **3** confirm the truth of; back up. **4** provide someone with a home and the necessities of life. **5** provide enough food and water for life to exist. **6** (of a pop or rock group or performer) appear before the main act at a concert. **7** (as adj. **supporting**) of secondary importance to the leading roles in a play, movie, etc.

– SYNONYMS **1** *a roof supported by pillars* **hold up,** bear, carry, prop up, keep up, brace, shore up, underpin, buttress, reinforce. **2** *the money supports charitable projects* **help,** aid, assist, contribute to, back, subsidize, fund, finance; informal bankroll. **3** *many famous women have supported her cause* **back,** champion, favor, be in favor of, advocate, encourage, promote, endorse, espouse. **4** *she supported him to the end* **stand by,** defend, back, stand/stick up for, take someone's side, side with. **5** *the studies support our findings* **back up,** substantiate, bear out, corroborate, confirm, verify. **6** *he struggled to support his family* **provide for,** maintain, sustain, keep, take care of, look after.
– ANTONYMS contradict, oppose.

▶ **noun 1** a person or thing that supports someone or something. **2** the action of supporting or the state of being supported. **3** help, encouragement, or approval: *her loyal support of her husband.*

– SYNONYMS **1 pillar,** post, prop, upright, brace, buttress, foundation, underpinning. **2 encouragement,** friendship, backing, endorsement, help, assistance, comfort. **3 contributions,** donations, money, subsidy, funding, funds, finance, capital.

– DERIVATIVES **sup·port·a·ble** adjective.

– ORIGIN Latin *supportare*.

sup·port·er /sə'pôrtər/ ▶ noun a person who supports a political party, etc.

– SYNONYMS **1 advocate,** backer, adherent, promoter, champion, defender, upholder, campaigner. **2 contributor,** donor, benefactor, sponsor, backer, patron, subscriber, well-wisher. **3 fan,** follower, enthusiast, devotee, admirer.

sup·port·ive /sə'pôrtiv/ ▶ adjective providing encouragement or emotional help.

– SYNONYMS **encouraging,** caring, sympathetic, reassuring, understanding, concerned, helpful.

– DERIVATIVES **sup·port·ive·ly** adverb **sup·port·ive·ness** noun.

sup·pose /sə'pōz/ ▶ verb **1** think that something is true or probable, but without proof. **2** (of a theory or argument) assume or require that something is the case as a necessary condition: *the procedure supposes that a will has already been proved.* **3** (**be supposed to do**) be required or expected to do something.

– SYNONYMS **1 assume,** presume, surmise, expect, imagine, dare say, take it, take as read, suspect, guess, conjecture. **2 hypothesize,** postulate, posit.

– ORIGIN Latin *supponere*.

sup·posed /sə'pōzd, sə'pōzid/ ▶ adjective thought to be true or probable, but without proof: *people admire their supposed industriousness.*

– SYNONYMS **alleged,** reputed, rumored, claimed, purported.

sup·pos·ed·ly /sə'pōzidlē/ ▶ adverb according to what is generally believed.

sup·po·si·tion /ˌsəpə'zisHən/ ▶ noun a belief held without proof or certain knowledge; an assumption or hypothesis.

– SYNONYMS **belief,** conjecture, speculation, assumption, presumption, inference, theory, hypothesis, feeling, idea, notion, guesswork.

sup·pos·i·to·ry /sə'päzəˌtôrē/ ▶ noun (pl. **suppositories**) a small piece of a medicinal substance that dissolves after being placed in the rectum or vagina.

– ORIGIN Latin *suppositorium* 'thing placed underneath.'

sup·press /sə'pres/ ▶ verb **1** forcibly put an end to an activity that threatens an established authority. **2** prevent from acting or developing: *the immune system is suppressed with powerful drugs.* **3** prevent something from being published. **4** consciously avoid thinking of an unpleasant idea or memory.

– SYNONYMS **1 subdue,** crush, quell, quash, squash, stamp out, crack down on, clamp down on, put an end to. **2 restrain,** repress, hold back, control, stifle, smother, check, keep in check, curb, contain, bottle up. **3 censor,** keep secret, conceal, hide, hush up, gag, withhold, cover up, stifle.
– ANTONYMS encourage, reveal.

– DERIVATIVES **sup·pres·sion** /sə'presHən/ noun **sup·pres·sive** adjective **sup·pres·sor** noun.
– ORIGIN Latin *supprimere* 'press down.'

sup·pres·sant /sə'presənt/ ▶ noun a drug or other substance that prevents a bodily function from working.

sup·pu·rate /'səpyəˌrāt/ ▶ verb (of a wound, ulcer, etc.) form or discharge pus.
– DERIVATIVES **sup·pu·ra·tion** /ˌsəpyə'rāsHən/ noun **sup·pu·ra·tive** /-ˌrātiv/ adjective.
– ORIGIN from Latin *sub-* 'below' + *pus* 'pus.'

su·pra /'so͞oprə/ ▶ adverb formal used in academic or legal texts to refer to someone or something mentioned above or earlier.
– ORIGIN Latin.

su·pra·na·tion·al /ˌso͞oprə'nasHənl/ ▶ adjective having power or influence that goes beyond national boundaries or governments.
– ORIGIN from Latin *supra* 'above, beyond.'

su·prem·a·cist /sə'preməsist, so͞o-/ ▶ noun a person who believes that a particular group, especially a racial group, is superior to all others. ▶ adjective relating to the belief that a particular group is superior to all others.
– DERIVATIVES **su·prem·a·cism** /sə'preməˌsizəm, so͞o-/ noun.

su·prem·a·cy /sə'preməsē, so͞o-/ ▶ noun the state of being superior to all others in authority, power, or status.

– SYNONYMS **control,** power, rule, sovereignty, dominance, superiority, predominance, primacy, dominion, authority, mastery, ascendancy.

su·preme /sə'prēm, so͞o-/ ▶ adjective **1** highest in authority, rank, or importance. **2** very great or greatest: *the chapel is a supreme example of medieval architecture.*

– SYNONYMS **1 highest,** chief, head, top, foremost, principal, superior, premier, first, prime. **2 extraordinary,** remarkable, phenomenal, exceptional, outstanding, incomparable, unparalleled. **3** *the supreme sacrifice* **ultimate,** greatest, highest, extreme, final, last.
– ANTONYMS subordinate.

▶ noun (also **suprême**) a rich cream sauce or a dish served in a cream sauce.
– DERIVATIVES **su·preme·ly** adverb.
– ORIGIN Latin *supremus* 'highest.'

su·preme court ▶ noun the highest court of law in a country or state.

su·pre·mo /sə'prēˌmō, so͞o-/ ▶ noun (pl. **supremos**) Brit. informal **1** a person in charge of an organization. **2** a person with great skill in a particular area: *a marketing supremo.*
– ORIGIN Spanish, 'supreme.'

Supt. ▶ abbreviation Superintendent.

sur- ▶ prefix equivalent to SUPER-.
– ORIGIN French.

su·ra /'so͝orə/ (also **surah**) ▶ noun a chapter or section of the Koran.
– ORIGIN from Arabic *sūra*.

sur·cease /sər'sēs/ ▶ noun **1** the ending or stopping of something. **2** relief from something unpleasant.
– ORIGIN from Old French *surseoir* 'refrain, delay.'

sur·charge /'sərˌcHärj/ ▶ noun an additional charge or payment. ▶ verb make someone pay an additional charge.

surd /sərd/ ▶ noun Mathematics a number that cannot be expressed as a ratio of two whole numbers.
– ORIGIN from Latin *surdus* 'deaf, mute.'

sure /sHo͝or/ ▶ adjective **1** completely confident that one is right. **2** (**sure of/to do**) certain to receive, get, or do: *the menu is sure to please everyone.* **3** undoubtedly true; completely reliable. **4** steady and confident.

– SYNONYMS **1 certain,** positive, convinced, confident, definite, satisfied, persuaded, assured, free from doubt. **2 guaranteed,** unfailing, infallible,

unerring, foolproof, certain, reliable, dependable, trustworthy, trusty; informal sure-fire.
– ANTONYMS uncertain, unlikely.

▶ **adverb** informal certainly.
– DERIVATIVES **sure·ness** noun.
– PHRASES **be sure to do** do not fail to do. **for sure** informal without doubt. **make sure** confirm or ensure that something is the case or is done. **to be sure** certainly; it must be admitted.
– ORIGIN Old French *sur*.

sure-fire ▶ **adjective** informal certain to succeed.

sure-foot·ed ▶ **adjective 1** unlikely to stumble or slip. **2** confident and competent.

sure·ly /'sʜo͝orlē/ ▶ **adverb 1** it must be true that. **2** without doubt; certainly. **3** in a confident way. **4** informal of course.

sur·e·ty /'sʜo͝oritē/ ▶ **noun** (pl. **sureties**) **1** a person who accepts responsibility if another person fails to pay a debt, appear in court, etc. **2** money given as a guarantee that someone will do something. **3** the state of being sure or certain of something.

surf /sərf/ ▶ **noun** waves that break and form foam on a seashore or reef. ▶ **verb 1** stand or lie on a surfboard and ride on the crest of a wave toward the shore. **2** move from site to site on the Internet. **3** channel-surf.
– DERIVATIVES **surf·er** noun **surf·ing** noun.
– ORIGIN unknown.

sur·face /'sərfis/ ▶ **noun 1** the outside part or uppermost layer of something. **2** the upper limit of a body of liquid. **3** the outward appearance of someone or something as distinct from less obvious aspects: *Tom was a womanizer, but on the surface he remained respectable*.

– SYNONYMS **1 outside,** exterior, top, side, finish. **2 outward appearance,** facade, veneer.
– ANTONYMS inside, interior.

▶ **adjective 1** relating to or occurring on the surface. **2** (of transportation) by sea or overland rather than by air. **3** outward or superficial: *surface politeness*.
▶ **verb 1** rise or come up to the surface. **2** become apparent: *the row first surfaced two years ago*. **3** provide something, especially a road, with a particular surface. **4** informal appear after having been asleep.

– SYNONYMS **1 come to the surface,** come up, rise. **2 emerge,** arise, appear, come to light, crop up, materialize, spring up.

– ORIGIN French.

sur·face ten·sion ▶ **noun** the tension of the surface film of a liquid, which tends to minimize surface area.

sur·fac·tant /sər'faktənt/ ▶ **noun** a substance, such as a detergent, that is added to a liquid to increase its spreading or wetting properties by reducing its surface tension.
– ORIGIN from *surface-active*.

surf·board /'sərf,bôrd/ ▶ **noun** a long, narrow board used in surfing.

sur·feit /'sərfət/ ▶ **noun 1** an excessive amount of something. **2** old use an illness caused by excessive eating or drinking.

– SYNONYMS **excess,** surplus, too much, abundance, oversupply, superabundance, superfluity, glut.
– ANTONYMS lack.

▶ **verb** (**surfeits, surfeiting, surfeited**) make someone want no more of something as a result of having consumed or done it to excess: *I am surfeited with shopping*.
– ORIGIN Old French.

surge /sərj/ ▶ **noun 1** a sudden powerful forward or upward movement. **2** a sudden large temporary increase. **3** a powerful rush of an emotion.

– SYNONYMS **1 gush,** rush, outpouring, stream, flow. **2** *a surge in demand* **increase,** rise, growth, upswing, upsurge, escalation, leap.

▶ **verb 1** move suddenly and powerfully forward or upward. **2** increase suddenly and powerfully: *shares surged to a record high*.

– SYNONYMS **1 gush,** rush, stream, flow, burst, pour, cascade, spill, sweep, roll. **2 increase,** rise, grow, leap.

– ORIGIN from Latin *surgere* 'to rise.'

sur·geon /'sərjən/ ▶ **noun** a medical practitioner qualified to practice surgery.
– ORIGIN Old French *serurgien*.

sur·geon gen·er·al ▶ **noun** (pl. **surgeons general**) the head of a public health service or of an armed forces medical service.

sur·ger·y /'sərjərē/ ▶ **noun** (pl. **surgeries**) **1** the medical treatment of injuries or disorders by cutting open the body and removing or repairing parts. **2** Brit. a place where a doctor or nurse treats or advises patients.

sur·gi·cal /'sərjikəl/ ▶ **adjective 1** relating to or used in surgery. **2** worn to correct or relieve an injury, illness, or deformity. **3** done with great precision: *surgical bombing*.
– DERIVATIVES **sur·gi·cal·ly** /-ik(ə)lē/ adverb.

Su·ri·na·mese /,so͝orənə'mēz, -'mēs/ ▶ **adjective** relating to Suriname, a country on the NE coast of South America.

sur·ly /'sərlē/ ▶ **adjective** (**surlier, surliest**) bad-tempered and unfriendly.

– SYNONYMS **sullen,** sulky, moody, morose, unfriendly, unpleasant, scowling, unsmiling, bad-tempered, grumpy, gruff, churlish, ill-humored.
– ANTONYMS friendly.

– DERIVATIVES **sur·li·ly** /-ləlē/ adverb **sur·li·ness** noun.
– ORIGIN from former *sirly* 'haughty,' from **SIR**.

CHOOSE THE RIGHT WORD

See **BRUSQUE**.

sur·mise /sər'mīz/ ▶ **verb** believe something to be true without having evidence.

– SYNONYMS **guess,** conjecture, suspect, deduce, infer, conclude, theorize, speculate, assume, presume, suppose, understand, gather.

▶ **noun** a belief that something is true without having evidence to confirm it.
– ORIGIN from Old French, 'accused.'

sur·mount /sər'mount/ ▶ **verb 1** overcome a difficulty or obstacle. **2** stand or be placed on top of something.

– SYNONYMS **overcome,** prevail over, triumph over, beat, vanquish, conquer, get the better of.

– DERIVATIVES **sur·mount·a·ble** adjective.

sur·name /'sər,nām/ ▶ **noun** an inherited name shared by members of a family, as distinct from a personal name.

sur·pass /sər'pas/ ▶ **verb 1** be greater or better than: *demand for the college's Latin courses has surpassed expectations*. **2** (as adj. **surpassing**) old use or literary outstanding; very great.

– SYNONYMS **excel,** exceed, transcend, outdo, outshine, outstrip, outclass, eclipse, improve on, top, trump, cap, beat, better, outperform.

– DERIVATIVES **sur·pass·a·ble** adjective.

sur·plice /ˈsərplis/ ▶ **noun** a loose white garment worn over a cassock by Christian clergy and members of church choirs.
– ORIGIN Old French *sourpelis*.

sur·plus /ˈsərpləs/ ▶ **noun 1** an amount left over when requirements have been met. **2** the amount by which the amount of money received is greater than the amount of money spent over a specific period.

– SYNONYMS **excess,** surfeit, superfluity, oversupply, glut, remainder, residue, remains, leftovers.
– ANTONYMS dearth.

▶ **adjective** more than what is needed or used; extra.

– SYNONYMS **excess,** leftover, unused, remaining, extra, additional, spare, superfluous, redundant, unwanted, unneeded, dispensable.
– ANTONYMS insufficient.

– ORIGIN from Latin *super-* 'in addition' + *plus* 'more.'

sur·prise /sə(r)ˈprīz/ ▶ **noun 1** a feeling of mild astonishment or shock caused by something unexpected. **2** an unexpected or astonishing thing.

– SYNONYMS **1 astonishment,** amazement, wonder, bewilderment, disbelief. **2 shock,** bolt from the blue, bombshell, revelation, rude awakening, eye-opener.

▶ **verb 1** make someone feel mild astonishment or shock. **2** capture, attack, or discover suddenly and unexpectedly: *he surprised a gang stealing scrap metal.*

– SYNONYMS **1 astonish,** amaze, startle, astound, stun, stagger, shock, take aback; informal bowl over, knock for a loop, floor, flabbergast. **2 take by surprise,** catch unawares, catch off guard, catch red-handed.

– PHRASES **take someone by surprise** happen when someone is not prepared. **take someone/thing by surprise** attack or capture someone or something unexpectedly.
– ORIGIN Old French.

sur·prised /sə(r)ˈprīzd/ ▶ **adjective** feeling mild astonishment or shock.

– SYNONYMS **astonished,** amazed, astounded, startled, stunned, staggered, nonplussed, shocked, taken aback, dumbfounded, speechless, thunderstruck; informal bowled over, flabbergasted.

sur·pris·ing /sə(r)ˈprīziNG/ ▶ **adjective** causing mild astonishment or shock.

– SYNONYMS **unexpected,** unforeseen, astonishing, amazing, startling, astounding, staggering, incredible, extraordinary.

– DERIVATIVES **sur·pris·ing·ly** adverb.

sur·re·al /səˈrēəl/ ▶ **adjective** having ideas or images mixed together in a strange way; like a dream: *a surreal road movie.*
– DERIVATIVES **sur·re·al·ly** adverb.

sur·re·al·ism /səˈrēəˌlizəm/ ▶ **noun** a 20th-century movement in art and literature in which images or events are combined in a strange or irrational way.
– DERIVATIVES **sur·re·al·ist** noun & adjective **sur·re·al·is·tic** /səˌrēəˈlistik/ adjective.

sur·ren·der /səˈrendər/ ▶ **verb 1** stop resisting an opponent and put oneself under their control. **2** give up a person, right, or possession when demanded to do so. **3** (**surrender to**) give in completely to a powerful emotion or influence. **4** cancel a life insurance policy and receive back a proportion of the premiums paid.

– SYNONYMS **1 give up,** give oneself up, give in, cave in, capitulate, concede (defeat), submit, lay down one's arms/weapons. **2 give up,** relinquish, renounce, cede, abdicate, forfeit, sacrifice, hand over, turn over, yield.
– ANTONYMS resist.

▶ **noun** the action or an act of surrendering: *the final surrender of Germany on May 8, 1945.*

– SYNONYMS **1 capitulation,** submission, yielding. **2 relinquishing,** renunciation, abdication, resignation.

– ORIGIN Old French *surrendre*.

CHOOSE THE RIGHT WORD

See **RELINQUISH**.

sur·rep·ti·tious /ˌsərəpˈtisHəs/ ▶ **adjective** done secretly.

– SYNONYMS **secret,** secretive, stealthy, clandestine, sneaky, sly, furtive, covert.
– ANTONYMS blatant.

– DERIVATIVES **sur·rep·ti·tious·ly** adverb.
– ORIGIN Latin *surreptitius* 'obtained secretly.'

sur·ro·gate /ˈsərəgit, -ˌgāt/ ▶ **noun** a substitute, especially a person who stands in for another in a role or office.
– DERIVATIVES **sur·ro·ga·cy** /ˈsərəgəsē/ noun.
– ORIGIN from Latin *surrogare* 'elect as a substitute.'

sur·ro·gate moth·er ▶ **noun** a woman who bears a child on behalf of another woman, either from her own egg or from having a fertilized egg from the other woman implanted in her uterus.

sur·round /səˈround/ ▶ **verb 1** be all around or encircle someone or something: *we were surrounded by cops* | (as adj. **surrounding**) *tenants in the surrounding buildings were evacuated as a precaution.* **2** be associated with: *the killings were surrounded by controversy.*

– SYNONYMS **1 encircle,** enclose, encompass, ring, hem in, confine, cut off, besiege, trap. **2** (as adj. **surrounding**) **neighboring,** enclosing, nearby, near, local, adjoining, adjacent.

▶ **noun 1** a border or edging. **2** (**surrounds**) the area around something; surroundings.
– ORIGIN Latin *superundare* 'to overflow.'

sur·round·ings /səˈroundiNGz/ ▶ **plural noun** the area or conditions around a person or thing: *a school in rural surroundings.*

– SYNONYMS **environment,** setting, background, backdrop, vicinity, locality, habitat.

sur·tax /ˈsərˌtaks/ ▶ **noun** an additional tax on something already taxed, especially a higher rate of tax on incomes above a certain level.

surtitle /ˈsərˌtītl/ ▶ **noun** a caption projected on a screen above the stage in an opera, translating the words being sung. ▶ **verb** provide with surtitles.

sur·veil·lance /sərˈvāləns/ ▶ **noun** close observation, especially of a suspected spy or criminal.

– SYNONYMS **observation,** scrutiny, watch, view, inspection, supervision, spying, espionage.

– ORIGIN French.

sur·vey ▸ **verb** /sərˈvā, ˈsərˌvā/ **1** look carefully and thoroughly at someone or something. **2** examine and record the features of an area of land to produce a map or description. **3** question a group of people to investigate their opinions.

– SYNONYMS **1 look at,** look over, view, contemplate, regard, gaze at, stare at, eye, scrutinize, examine, inspect, scan, study, assess, appraise, take stock of; informal size up. **2 interview,** question, canvass, poll, investigate, research.

▸ **noun** /ˈsərˌvā/ **1** a general view, examination, or description. **2** an investigation of the opinions or experience of a group of people, based on a series of questions. **3** an act of surveying an area of land. **4** a map or report obtained by surveying.

– SYNONYMS **1 study,** review, overview, examination, inspection, assessment, appraisal. **2 poll,** enquiry, investigation, study, probe, questionnaire, census, research.

– ORIGIN Old French *surveier*.

sur·vey·or /sərˈvāər/ ▸ **noun** a person who surveys land as a profession.

sur·viv·al /sərˈvīvəl/ ▸ **noun 1** the state or fact of surviving: *the animal's chances of survival were low.* **2** an object or practice that has survived from an earlier time.
– PHRASES **survival of the fittest** the principle that only the people or things that are best adapted to their situation or environment will continue to exist.

sur·viv·al·ist /sərˈvīvəlist/ ▸ **noun** a person who practices outdoor survival skills as a sport or hobby.
– DERIVATIVES **sur·viv·al·ism** /sərˈvīvəˌlizəm/ noun.

sur·viv·al kit ▸ **noun 1** a pack of emergency equipment, including food, medical supplies, and tools. **2** a collection of items to help someone in a particular situation: *a substitute teacher survival kit.*

sur·vive /sərˈvīv/ ▸ **verb 1** continue to live or exist. **2** continue to live in spite of an accident or ordeal. **3** remain alive after the death of someone.

– SYNONYMS **1 remain alive,** live, sustain oneself, pull through, hold out, make it. **2 continue,** remain, persist, endure, live on, persevere, abide, go on, carry on. **3 outlive,** outlast, remain alive after.

– DERIVATIVES **sur·viv·a·bil·i·ty** /sərˌvīvəˈbilətē/ noun **sur·viv·a·ble** /sərˈvīvəbəl/ adjective.
– ORIGIN Old French *sourvivre*.

sur·vi·vor /sərˈvīvər/ ▸ **noun** a person who survives, especially one who remains alive after an accident or ordeal.

sus·cep·ti·bil·i·ty /səˌseptəˈbilitē/ ▸ **noun** (pl. **susceptibilities**) **1** the state of being easily harmed or influenced. **2** (**susceptibilities**) a person's sensitive feelings.

sus·cep·ti·ble /səˈseptəbəl/ ▸ **adjective 1** likely to be influenced or harmed by a particular thing. **2** easily influenced by feelings or emotions. **3** (**susceptible of**) capable of something.

– SYNONYMS **1** *patients with liver disease may be **susceptible to** infection* **liable to,** prone to, subject to, inclined to, predisposed to, open to, vulnerable to, an easy target for. **2 impressionable,** credulous, gullible, innocent, ingenuous, naive, easily led, defenseless, vulnerable.
– ANTONYMS immune, resistant.

– DERIVATIVES **sus·cep·ti·bly** /-blē/ adverb.
– ORIGIN Latin *susceptibilis*.

su·shi /ˈso͞oshē/ ▸ **noun** a Japanese dish consisting of small balls or rolls of cold rice with vegetables, egg, or raw seafood.
– ORIGIN Japanese.

sus·pect ▸ **verb** /səˈspekt/ **1** believe to be probable or possible: *if you suspect a problem with the thermostat, call a repair technician.* **2** believe that someone is guilty of a crime or offense, without definite proof. **3** doubt that something is genuine or true.

– SYNONYMS **1 have a suspicion,** have a feeling, feel, be inclined to think, fancy, reckon, guess, conjecture, surmise, have a hunch, fear. **2 doubt,** distrust, mistrust, have misgivings about, have qualms about, be suspicious of, be skeptical about.

▸ **noun** /ˈsəsˌpekt/ a person suspected of a crime or offense.
▸ **adjective** /ˈsəsˌpekt/ possibly dangerous or false.

– SYNONYMS **suspicious,** dubious, doubtful, untrustworthy; informal fishy, funny.

– ORIGIN Latin *suspicere* 'mistrust.'

sus·pend /səˈspend/ ▸ **verb 1** stop something temporarily. **2** temporarily bar someone from a job or from attending school, as a punishment or during investigation. **3** postpone or delay an action, event, or judgment. **4** (as adj. **suspended**) Law (of a sentence) not enforced as long as no further offense is committed within a specified period. **5** hang from somewhere. **6** (**be suspended**) technical (of particles) be dispersed throughout a fluid.

– SYNONYMS **1 adjourn,** table, interrupt, break off, cut short, discontinue. **2 exclude,** debar, remove, expel, eject, rusticate. **3 hang,** sling, string, swing, dangle.

– ORIGIN Latin *suspendere*.

CHOOSE THE RIGHT WORD

See **POSTPONE**.

sus·pend·ed an·i·ma·tion ▸ **noun** a state in which most of the functions of an animal or plant stop for a time, without death.

su·spend·ed ceil·ing ▸ **noun** a ceiling with a space between it and the floor above from which it hangs.

sus·pend·ers /səˈspendərz/ ▸ **plural noun** a pair of straps passing over the shoulders and fastening to the top of a pair of pants to hold them up.

sus·pense /səˈspens/ ▸ **noun** a state or feeling of excited or anxious uncertainty about what may happen.

– SYNONYMS **tension,** uncertainty, doubt, anticipation, excitement, anxiety, strain.

– DERIVATIVES **sus·pense·ful** /-fəl/ adjective.
– ORIGIN Old French *suspens* 'abeyance.'

sus·pen·sion /səˈspenshən/ ▸ **noun 1** the action of suspending or the state of being suspended. **2** the temporary barring of someone from a job or from school, especially as a punishment. **3** the system of springs and shock absorbers that supports a vehicle on its wheels. **4** technical a mixture in which particles are dispersed throughout a fluid.

sus·pen·sion bridge ▸ **noun** a bridge in which the deck is suspended from cables running between towers.

sus·pi·cion /səˈspishən/ ▸ **noun 1** a feeling or thought that something is true or probable: *she had a suspicion that he was laughing at her.* **2** a feeling or belief that someone has done something wrong. **3** distrust of someone or something. **4** a very slight trace: *a suspicion of a smile*.

– SYNONYMS **1 intuition,** feeling, impression, inkling, hunch, fancy, notion, idea, theory, premonition; informal gut feeling. **2 misgiving,** doubt, qualm(s), reservation, hesitation, skepticism.
– ANTONYMS trust.

– PHRASES **above suspicion** too good or honest to be thought capable of wrongdoing. **under suspicion** suspected of wrongdoing.
– ORIGIN Old French *suspeciun*.

sus·pi·cious /sə'spisHəs/ ▶ **adjective 1** having a feeling that someone has done something wrong. **2** (also **suspicious of**) not able to trust someone or something. **3** seeming to be dishonest or dangerous: *a suspicious package*.

– SYNONYMS **1 doubtful,** unsure, dubious, wary, chary, skeptical, mistrustful. **2 suspect,** dubious, unsavory, disreputable; informal shifty, shady. **3** *suspicious circumstances* **strange,** odd, questionable, irregular, funny, doubtful, mysterious; informal fishy.
– ANTONYMS trusting, innocent.

– DERIVATIVES **sus·pi·cious·ly** adverb **sus·pi·cious·ness** noun.

suss /səs/ ▶ **verb (susses, sussing, sussed)** chiefly Brit. informal (often **suss someone/thing out**) realize or understand the true nature of someone or something.
– ORIGIN from SUSPECT.

sus·tain /sə'stān/ ▶ **verb 1** support someone physically or mentally. **2** cause to continue for some time: *he cannot sustain a normal conversation*. **3** suffer something unpleasant. **4** decide that a claim is valid. **5** bear the weight of an object.

– SYNONYMS **1 comfort,** help, assist, encourage, support, give strength to, buoy up. **2 continue,** carry on, keep up, keep alive, maintain, preserve. **3 nourish,** feed, nurture, keep alive. **4 suffer,** experience, undergo, receive. **5 confirm,** corroborate, substantiate, bear out, prove, authenticate, back up, uphold.

– DERIVATIVES **sus·tain·er** noun **sus·tain·ment** noun.
– ORIGIN Latin *sustinere*.

sus·tain·a·ble /sə'stānəbəl/ ▶ **adjective 1** able to be sustained or continued. **2** (of industry, development, or agriculture) not making excessive use of natural resources.
– DERIVATIVES **sus·tain·a·bil·i·ty** /sə,stānə'bilitē/ noun **sus·tain·a·bly** /-blē/ adverb.

sus·tained /sə'stānd/ ▶ **adjective** continuing for some time: *several years of sustained economic growth*.

– SYNONYMS **continuous,** ongoing, steady, continual, constant, prolonged, persistent, nonstop, perpetual, relentless.
– ANTONYMS sporadic.

sus·te·nance /'səstənəns/ ▶ **noun 1** food and drink as needed to keep someone alive. **2** the process of making something continue.

– SYNONYMS **nourishment,** food, nutrition, provisions, rations; informal grub, chow, vittles; literary viands; dated victuals.

su·tra /'sōōtrə/ ▶ **noun 1** a rule or saying in Sanskrit literature, or a set of these on grammar or Hindu law or philosophy. **2** a Buddhist or Jainist scripture.
– ORIGIN Sanskrit, 'thread, rule.'

sut·tee /sə'tē, 'sə,tē/ ▶ **noun** variant spelling of SATI.

su·ture /'sōōcHər/ ▶ **noun 1** a stitch or stitches holding together the edges of a wound or surgical cut. **2** a thread or wire used for stitching a wound or cut. ▶ **verb** stitch up a wound or cut with a suture.
– ORIGIN Latin *sutura*.

SUV ▶ **abbreviation** sport utility vehicle.

su·ze·rain·ty /'sōōzərəntē, 'sōōzə,rāntē/ ▶ **noun** the right of one country to rule over another country that has its own ruler but is not fully independent.
– DERIVATIVES **su·ze·rain** /'sōōzərən, 'sōōzə,rān/ noun.
– ORIGIN French.

s.v. ▶ **abbreviation** (in references in written works) under the word or heading given.
– ORIGIN from Latin *sub voce* or *sub verbo* 'under the word or voice.'

svelte /svelt, sfelt/ ▶ **adjective** slender and elegant.
– ORIGIN Italian *svelto*.

Sven·ga·li /sven'gälē, sfen-/ ▶ **noun** a person who exercises a controlling influence on another, especially for a sinister purpose.
– ORIGIN from *Svengali*, a musician in George Du Maurier's novel *Trilby*.

SW ▶ **abbreviation 1** southwest. **2** southwestern.

swab /swäb/ ▶ **noun 1** an absorbent pad used for cleaning wounds or taking a sample from the body for testing. **2** a sample taken with a swab. ▶ **verb (swabs, swabbing, swabbed) 1** clean a wound with an absorbent pad. **2** wash a floor or ship's deck with a mop or cloth.
– ORIGIN Dutch *zwabber* 'sailor who cleans a ship's deck.'

swad·dle /'swädl/ ▶ **verb** wrap someone in clothes or cloth.
– ORIGIN from SWATHE.

swad·dling clothes /'swädliNG/ ▶ **plural noun** strips of cloth formerly wrapped around a newborn baby to calm it.

swag /swag/ ▶ **noun 1** a decorative garland of flowers, fruit, and greenery. **2** a curtain or piece of fabric fastened to hang in a drooping curve. **3** informal money or goods taken by a thief or burglar. ▶ **verb (swags, swagging, swagged)** arrange fabric so as to hang in a drooping curve.
– ORIGIN probably Scandinavian.

swag·ger /'swagər/ ▶ **verb** walk or behave in a very confident or arrogant way.

– SYNONYMS **strut,** parade, stride, prance; informal sashay.

▶ **noun** a very confident or arrogant way of walking.
▶ **adjective** (of a coat or jacket) cut with a loose flare from the shoulders.
– ORIGIN probably from SWAG.

swag·ger stick ▶ **noun** a short cane carried by a military officer.

Swa·hi·li /swä'hēlē/ ▶ **noun** (pl. same) **1** a Bantu language widely spoken in East Africa. **2** a member of a people of Zanzibar and nearby coastal regions.
– ORIGIN from an Arabic word meaning 'coasts.'

swain /swān/ ▶ **noun 1** literary a young male lover. **2** old use a country youth.
– ORIGIN Old Norse, 'lad.'

swal·low[1] /'swälō/ ▶ **verb 1** pass food, drink, or saliva down the throat. **2** take in or cover completely: *the dark mist swallowed her up*. **3** use the throat muscles as if swallowing, especially because of nervousness. **4** completely use up money or resources. **5** put up with unfair treatment. **6** believe something untrue without question. **7** hide a feeling: *he swallowed his pride.*

– SYNONYMS **eat,** drink, gulp down, consume, devour, put away, quaff, slug; informal swig, swill, down, scarf (down).

▶ **noun** an act of swallowing.
– DERIVATIVES **swal·low·er** noun.
– ORIGIN Old English.

swallow² ▶ **noun** a swift-flying migratory songbird with a forked tail.
– ORIGIN Old English.

swal·low·tail /ˈswälō,tāl/ ▶ **noun** a large brightly colored butterfly with tail-like projections on the hind wings.

swam /swam/ past of **SWIM**.

swa·mi /ˈswämē/ ▶ **noun** (pl. **swamis**) a male Hindu religious teacher.
– ORIGIN Hindi, 'master, prince.'

swamp /swämp/ ▶ **noun** a bog or marsh.

– SYNONYMS **marsh,** bog, fen, quagmire, morass.

▶ **verb 1** overwhelm or flood something with water. **2** overwhelm with too much of something; inundate: *the country was swamped with goods from abroad.*

– SYNONYMS **1 flood,** inundate, deluge, fill. **2** *fans swamped her message board* **overwhelm,** engulf, snow under, overload, inundate, deluge.

– DERIVATIVES **swamp·y** adjective.
– ORIGIN probably from a Germanic word meaning 'sponge' or 'fungus.'

swamp·land /ˈswämp,land/ ▶ **noun** (also **swamplands**) land consisting of swamps.

swan /swän/ ▶ **noun** a large white waterbird with a long flexible neck and webbed feet. ▶ **verb** (**swans, swanning, swanned**) Brit. informal go around enjoying yourself in a way that makes other people jealous or annoyed.
– ORIGIN Old English.

swan dive ▶ **noun** a dive performed with the arms outspread until close to the water.

swank /swaNGk/ informal ▶ **verb** try to impress others with one's wealth, knowledge, or achievements. ▶ **noun** behavior or talk intended to impress others.
– ORIGIN unknown.

swank·y /ˈswaNGkē/ ▶ **adjective** (**swankier, swankiest**) informal **1** stylishly luxurious and expensive. **2** inclined to show off.

swans·down /ˈswänz,doun/ ▶ **noun** the fine soft feathers of a swan, used for trimmings and powder puffs.

swan·song /ˈswän,sôNG/ ▶ **noun** the final performance or activity of a person's career.
– ORIGIN suggested by German *Schwanengesang*, referring to a mythical song sung by a dying swan.

swap /swäp/ (also Brit. **swop** pronunc. same) ▶ **verb** (**swaps, swapping, swapped**) exchange or substitute one thing or person for another.

– SYNONYMS **exchange,** trade, barter, switch, change, replace.

▶ **noun** an act of exchanging one thing or person for another.
– ORIGIN uncertain.

swap meet ▶ **noun 1** a gathering at which people trade or exchange items of common interest: *a computer swap meet.* **2** a flea market.

sward /swôrd/ ▶ **noun** literary an expanse of short grass.
– ORIGIN Old English, 'skin.'

swarm /swôrm/ ▶ **noun 1** a large group of insects flying closely together. **2** a large number of honeybees that leave a hive with a queen in order to establish a new colony. **3** a large group of people or things.

– SYNONYMS **1 hive,** flock. **2 crowd,** horde, mob, throng, mass, army, herd, pack.

▶ **verb 1** move in or form a swarm. **2** (**swarm with**) be crowded or overrun with: *the place was swarming with police.* **3** (**swarm up**) climb rapidly by gripping something with one's hands and feet.

– SYNONYMS **flock,** crowd, throng, surge, stream.

– ORIGIN Old English.

swarth·y /ˈswôrTHē/ ▶ **adjective** (**swarthier, swarthiest**) having a dark complexion.

– SYNONYMS **dark-skinned,** olive-skinned, dusky, tanned.
– ANTONYMS pale.

– DERIVATIVES **swarth·i·ness** noun.
– ORIGIN Old English.

swash·buck·ling /ˈswôsH,bəkliNG, ˈswäsH-/ ▶ **adjective** engaging in or showing daring and romantic adventures: *he made eight swashbuckling films.*
– DERIVATIVES **swash·buck·ler** /ˈswôsH,bəklər, ˈswäsH-/ noun.

swas·ti·ka /ˈswästikə/ ▶ **noun** an ancient symbol in the form of an equal-armed cross with each arm continued at a right angle, used (in clockwise form) as the emblem of the German Nazi party.
– ORIGIN from a Sanskrit word meaning 'well-being.'

swat /swät/ ▶ **verb** (**swats, swatting, swatted**) hit someone or something with a sharp blow from a flat object.
– ORIGIN northern English and US form of **SQUAT**.

swatch /swäcH/ ▶ **noun 1** a piece of fabric used as a sample. **2** a number of fabric samples bound together.
– ORIGIN unknown.

swath /swäTH, swôTH/ (also **swathe** /swäTH, swāTH/) ▶ **noun** (pl. **swaths** /swäTHs, swôTHs/ or **swathes** /swäTHz, swāTHz/) **1** a broad strip or area: *vast swathes of countryside.* **2** a row or line of grass, wheat, etc., as it falls when mown or reaped.
– ORIGIN Old English, 'track, trace.'

swathe /swäTH, swāTH/ ▶ **verb** wrap someone or something in several layers of fabric.

– SYNONYMS **wrap,** envelop, bandage, cover, shroud, drape, wind, enfold.

▶ **noun** a strip of material in which something is wrapped.
– ORIGIN Old English.

SWAT team /swät/ ▶ **noun** a group of police marksmen who specialize in high-risk tasks such as hostage rescue.
– ORIGIN from the initial letters of *Special Weapons and Tactics*.

sway /swā/ ▶ **verb 1** move slowly and rhythmically backward and forward or from side to side. **2** make someone change their opinion.

– SYNONYMS **1 swing,** shake, undulate, move to and fro. **2 stagger,** wobble, rock, lurch, reel, roll. **3 influence,** affect, manipulate, bend, mold.

▶ **noun 1** a swaying movement. **2** power, influence, or control: *he fell under the sway of a revolutionary scientist.*

– SYNONYMS **1 swing,** roll, shake, undulation. **2 power,** rule, government, sovereignty, dominion, control, jurisdiction, authority.

– PHRASES **hold sway** have great power or influence.
– ORIGIN perhaps from German *swājen* 'be blown to and fro.'

CHOOSE THE RIGHT WORD

See **JURISDICTION**.

swear /swe(ə)r/ ▶ **verb** (past **swore**; past part. **sworn**) **1** state or promise something solemnly or on oath. **2** make someone promise to do something: *I am sworn to secrecy.* **3** use offensive or obscene language.

– SYNONYMS **1 promise,** vow, pledge, give one's word, undertake, guarantee. **2 insist,** declare, proclaim, assert, maintain, emphasize, stress. **3 curse,** blaspheme, use bad language; informal cuss.

– DERIVATIVES **swear·er** noun.
– PHRASES **swear by** informal be certain that something is very good or useful. **swear someone in** admit someone to a new post or job by making them take a formal oath. **swear off** informal promise to stop doing or to give up something. **swear to** say that something is definitely the case.
– ORIGIN Old English.

swear word ▶ **noun** an offensive or obscene word.

sweat /swet/ ▶ **noun 1** moisture given out through the pores of the skin, especially in reaction to heat, physical effort, or anxiety. **2** informal hard work. **3** informal a state of anxiety or distress. ▶ **verb** (past and past part. **sweated** or **sweat**) **1** produce sweat. **2** make a great deal of effort: *I've sweated over this for six months.* **3** be very anxious. **4** (of a substance) give off moisture. **5** cook chopped vegetables slowly in a pan with a small amount of fat.

– SYNONYMS **1 perspire,** drip with sweat. **2 work,** labor, toil, slave, work one's fingers to the bone.

– PHRASES **break a sweat** informal make a great physical effort. **no sweat** informal all right; no problem. **sweat blood** informal make a very great effort. **sweat bullets** informal be extremely anxious or nervous.
– ORIGIN Old English.

WORD LINKS

sudorific *causing sweating*

sweat·band /ˈswet,band/ ▶ **noun** a band of absorbent material worn to soak up sweat.

sweat·er /ˈswetər/ ▶ **noun** a knitted garment worn over the upper body, typically with long sleeves.

sweat gland ▶ **noun** a small gland that secretes sweat, situated in the dermis of the skin.

sweat·pants /ˈswet,pants/ ▶ **plural noun** loose, warm trousers with an elastic or drawstring waist, worn for exercise or leisure.

sweat·shirt /ˈswet,sʜərt/ ▶ **noun** a loose, heavy, collarless shirt, typically made of cotton and worn for exercise or leisure.

sweat·shop /ˈswet,sʜäp/ ▶ **noun** a factory or workshop employing workers for long hours in poor conditions.

sweat·suit /ˈswet,so͞ot/ ▶ **noun** an outfit consisting of a sweatshirt and sweatpants, worn when exercising or as leisurewear.

sweat·y /ˈswetē/ ▶ **adjective** (**sweatier, sweatiest**) soaked in or causing sweat.

– SYNONYMS **perspiring,** sweating, clammy, sticky, moist, damp.

– DERIVATIVES **sweat·i·ly** adverb **sweat·i·ness** noun.

Swede /swēd/ ▶ **noun** a person from Sweden.

Swed·ish /ˈswēdisʜ/ ▶ **noun** the Scandinavian language of Sweden. ▶ **adjective** relating to Sweden.

sweep /swēp/ ▶ **verb** (past and past part. **swept** /swept/) **1** clean an area by brushing away dirt or litter. **2** move forcefully: *I was swept along by the crowd.* **3** move swiftly and smoothly. **4** affect swiftly and widely: *violence swept the country.* **5** (**sweep something away/aside**) remove or abolish something quickly and suddenly. **6** search an area. **7** extend continuously in an arc or curve: *forests swept down the hillsides.*

– SYNONYMS **brush,** clean (up), clear (up).

▶ **noun 1** an act of sweeping. **2** a long, swift curving movement. **3** a long curved stretch of road, river, etc. **4** the range or scope of something: *the whole sweep of the history of the USA.* **5** a chimney sweep. **6** informal a sweepstake.
– PHRASES **sweep the board** win every event or prize in a contest.
– ORIGIN Old English.

CHOOSE THE RIGHT WORD

See **RANGE**.

sweep·er /ˈswēpər/ ▶ **noun 1** a person or device that cleans by sweeping. **2** Soccer a player stationed behind the other defenders, free to defend at any point across the field.

sweep·ing /ˈswēpiɴɢ/ ▶ **adjective 1** extending or performed in a long, continuous curve. **2** wide in range or effect. **3** (of a statement) too general.

– SYNONYMS **1 extensive,** wide-ranging, broad, comprehensive, far-reaching, thorough, radical. **2 wholesale,** blanket, general, unqualified, indiscriminate, oversimplified.
– ANTONYMS limited.

▶ **noun** (**sweepings**) dirt or refuse collected by sweeping.
– DERIVATIVES **sweep·ing·ly** adverb.

sweep·stakes /ˈswēp,stāks/ (also **sweepstake**) ▶ **noun** a form of gambling in which the winner receives all the money bet by the other participants.

sweet /swēt/ ▶ **adjective 1** having the pleasant taste of sugar or honey. **2** having a pleasant smell; fragrant. **3** kind or thoughtful. **4** charming and endearing. **5** pleasant or satisfying: *the sweet life.* **6** working or done smoothly or easily: *the sweet handling of this motorcycle.* **7** (of air, water, etc.) fresh and pure. **8** (**sweet on**) informal, dated in love with someone.

– SYNONYMS **1 sugary,** sweetened, sugared, honeyed, syrupy; sickly, cloying. **2 fragrant,** aromatic, perfumed. **3** *she has a sweet nature* **likable,** appealing, engaging, amiable, pleasant, agreeable, kind, nice, thoughtful, considerate, delightful, lovely. **4** *she looks quite sweet* **cute,** lovable, adorable, endearing, charming, winsome.
– ANTONYMS sour, savory, disagreeable.

▶ **noun 1** (**sweets**) sweet foods, collectively. **2** Brit. a small piece of candy. **3** Brit. a dessert.

– SYNONYMS (**sweets**) **desserts,** treats, cakes, cookies, pastries.

– DERIVATIVES **sweet·ish** adjective **sweet·ly** adverb.
– ORIGIN Old English.

sweet-and-sour ▶ **adjective** cooked with sugar and either vinegar or lemon.

sweet·bread /ˈswētˌbred/ ▶ **noun** the thymus gland or pancreas of an animal, used for food.

sweet corn ▶ **noun** a variety of corn with sweet kernels that are eaten as a vegetable.

sweet·en /ˈswētn/ ▶ **verb** **1** make or become sweet or sweeter. **2** make something more acceptable. **3** (**sweeten someone up**) informal be pleasant to someone in order to make them agree to something, help, etc.

> – SYNONYMS **1 make sweet,** add sugar to, sugar. **2 mollify,** placate, soothe, soften up, pacify, appease, win over.

sweet·en·er /ˈswētn-ər, ˈswētnər/ ▶ **noun** **1** a substance used to sweeten food or drink. **2** informal a bribe.

sweet·heart /ˈswētˌhärt/ ▶ **noun** a person who is loved by someone.

> – SYNONYMS **lover,** love, girlfriend, boyfriend, beloved, beau; informal steady, squeeze; literary swain.

▶ **adjective** informal agreed privately by two sides in their own interests at others' expense: *a sweetheart deal.*

sweet·ie /ˈswētē/ ▶ **noun** informal used as a term of affection.

sweet·meat /ˈswētˌmēt/ ▶ **noun** old use a candy or item of sweet food.

sweet·ness /ˈswētnis/ ▶ **noun** the quality of being sweet.
– PHRASES **sweetness and light** pleasantness or harmony.

sweet pea ▶ **noun** a climbing plant of the pea family with colorful fragrant flowers.

sweet pep·per ▶ **noun** a variety of pepper with a mild or sweet flavor.

sweet po·ta·to ▶ **noun** the edible tuber of a tropical climbing plant, with pinkish-orange flesh.

sweet-talk ▶ **verb** informal use charm or flattery to persuade someone to do something.

sweet tooth ▶ **noun** (pl. **sweet tooths**) a great liking for sweet foods.

sweet wil·liam ▶ **noun** a fragrant plant with clusters of vivid red, pink, or white flowers.

swell /swel/ ▶ **verb** (past part. **swollen** /ˈswōlən/ or **swelled**) **1** become larger or rounder in size. **2** increase in intensity, amount, or volume: *the low murmur swelled to a roar.*

> – SYNONYMS **1** *her lip **swelled up*** **expand,** bulge, distend, inflate, dilate, bloat, blow up, puff up, balloon, fatten, fill out. **2** (as adj. **swollen**) **distended,** bulging, inflated, dilated, bloated, puffed up, puffy, tumescent, inflamed. **3** *the population swelled* **grow,** enlarge, increase, expand, rise, escalate, multiply, proliferate, snowball, mushroom.
> – ANTONYMS shrink, decrease.

▶ **noun** **1** a full or gently rounded form. **2** a gradual increase in sound, amount, or intensity. **3** a slow, regular movement of the sea in rolling waves that do not break. **4** informal, dated a fashionable upper-class person.
▶ **adjective** informal, dated excellent; very good.
– ORIGIN Old English.

swell·ing /ˈsweliNG/ ▶ **noun** a place on the body that has swollen as a result of illness or an injury.

> – SYNONYMS **bump,** lump, bulge, protuberance, protrusion, distension.

swel·ter /ˈsweltər/ ▶ **verb** be uncomfortably hot.
– ORIGIN Germanic.

swel·ter·ing /ˈsweltəriNG/ ▶ **adjective** uncomfortably hot.

> – SYNONYMS **hot,** stifling, humid, sultry, sticky, muggy, close, stuffy, tropical, torrid, searing, blistering; informal boiling (hot), baking, roasting, sizzling.
> – ANTONYMS freezing.

swept /swept/ past and past participle of **SWEEP** ▶ **adjective** (also **swept back**) (of an aircraft's wings) directed backward from the fuselage.

swerve /swərv/ ▶ **verb** abruptly depart from a straight course.

> – SYNONYMS **veer,** deviate, diverge, weave, zigzag, change direction; Sailing tack.

▶ **noun** an abrupt change of course.
– ORIGIN Old English, 'leave, turn aside.'

swift /swift/ ▶ **adjective** **1** happening quickly or promptly. **2** moving or capable of moving at high speed.

> – SYNONYMS **fast,** rapid, quick, speedy, expeditious, prompt, brisk, immediate, instant, hasty, hurried, sudden, abrupt.
> – ANTONYMS slow, leisurely.

▶ **noun** a fast-flying bird with long, slender wings, spending most of its life flying.
– DERIVATIVES **swift·ly** adverb **swift·ness** noun.
– ORIGIN from an Old English word meaning 'move in a course, sweep.'

swig /swig/ informal ▶ **verb** (**swigs, swigging, swigged**) drink something in large gulps. ▶ **noun** a large gulp of a drink.
– ORIGIN unknown.

swill /swil/ ▶ **verb** informal drink something in large quantities. ▶ **noun** waste food mixed with water for feeding to pigs.
– ORIGIN Old English.

swim /swim/ ▶ **verb** (**swims, swimming, swam** /swam/; past part. **swum** /swəm/) **1** propel oneself through water by moving the arms and legs. **2** be immersed in or covered with liquid. **3** experience a dizzily confusing feeling. ▶ **noun** an act or period of swimming.
– DERIVATIVES **swim·mer** noun.
– PHRASES **in the swim** involved in or aware of current events.
– ORIGIN Old English.

swim·ming·ly /ˈswimiNGlē/ ▶ **adverb** informal smoothly and satisfactorily.

swim·ming pool ▶ **noun** an artificial pool for swimming in.

swim·suit /ˈswimˌso͞ot/ ▶ **noun** a garment worn for swimming.

swim trunks (also **swimming trunks**) ▶ **plural noun** shorts worn by men for swimming.

swim·wear /ˈswimˌwe(ə)r/ ▶ **noun** clothing worn for swimming.

swin·dle /ˈswindl/ ▶ **verb** use deception to obtain money or possessions from someone.

> – SYNONYMS **defraud,** cheat, trick, dupe, deceive, fool, hoax, hoodwink, bamboozle; informal fleece, do,

con, stiff, rip off, take for a ride, pull a fast one on, put one over on.

▶ **noun** a scheme or act designed to obtain money dishonestly.

– SYNONYMS **fraud,** trick, deception, cheat, racket; informal con, con job, rip-off.

– ORIGIN German *schwindeln* 'be giddy, tell lies.'

swin·dler /ˈswindlər/ ▶ **noun** a person who uses deception to obtain money or possessions from someone.

– SYNONYMS **fraudster,** fraud, (confidence) trickster, cheat, rogue, charlatan, impostor, hoaxer; informal con man, shark, hustler, phony, crook.

swine /swīn/ ▶ **noun 1** (pl. same) a pig. **2** (pl. same or **swines**) informal an unpleasant person.
– DERIVATIVES **swin·ish** adjective.
– ORIGIN Old English.

swine fe·ver ▶ **noun** an intestinal disease of pigs, caused by a virus.

swine·herd /ˈswīnˌhərd/ ▶ **noun** chiefly historical a person who tends pigs.

swing /swiNG/ ▶ **verb** (past and past part. **swung** /swəNG/) **1** move back and forth or from side to side while hanging from a fixed point. **2** move by grasping a support and leaping. **3** move in a smooth, curving line: *the cab swung into the car park*. **4** (**swing at**) attempt to punch someone. **5** shift from one opinion, mood, or situation to another: *opinion swung in the senator's favor*. **6** have a decisive influence on a vote or decision. **7** informal succeed in bringing something about. **8** informal swap sexual partners or engage in group sex. **9** informal be lively, exciting, or fashionable.

– SYNONYMS **1 sway,** move back and forth, oscillate, wave, rock, swivel, pivot, turn, rotate. **2 brandish,** wave, flourish, wield. **3 curve,** bend, veer, turn, bear, wind, twist, deviate, slew. **4 change,** fluctuate, waver, seesaw.

▶ **noun 1** a seat hanging from ropes or chains, on which someone can sit and swing. **2** an act of swinging. **3** a clear change in public opinion, especially in an election. **4** a style of jazz or dance music with an easy flowing rhythm.

– SYNONYMS **1 oscillation,** sway, wave. **2 change,** move, turnaround, turnabout, reversal, fluctuation, variation.

– DERIVATIVES **swing·er** noun **swing·y** adjective.
– PHRASES **get into the swing of things** informal become used to an activity. **in full swing** at the height of activity.
– ORIGIN Old English, 'beat, whip, rush.'

swing bridge ▶ **noun** a bridge that can be swung to one side to allow ships to pass.

swing·ing /ˈswiNGiNG/ ▶ **adjective** informal **1** lively, exciting, and fashionable. **2** sexually liberated.

swing·ing door ▶ **noun** a door that can be opened in either direction and is closed by a spring device when released.

swipe /swīp/ informal ▶ **verb 1** hit or try to hit someone or something with a swinging blow. **2** steal something. **3** pass a swipe card through an electronic reader. ▶ **noun 1** a sweeping blow. **2** an act of criticizing someone or something.
– ORIGIN perhaps from **SWEEP**.

swipe card ▶ **noun** a plastic card carrying coded information that is read when the card is slid through an electronic device.

swirl /swərl/ ▶ **verb** move in a twisting or spiraling pattern.

– SYNONYMS **whirl,** eddy, billow, spiral, twist, twirl, circulate, revolve, spin.

▶ **noun** a swirling movement or pattern.
– DERIVATIVES **swirl·y** adjective.
– ORIGIN perhaps German or Dutch.

swish /swiSH/ ▶ **verb** move with a soft rushing sound. ▶ **noun** a soft rushing sound or movement. ▶ **adjective** Brit. informal impressively smart and fashionable.
– DERIVATIVES **swish·y** adjective.
– ORIGIN imitating the sound.

Swiss /swis/ ▶ **adjective** relating to Switzerland or its people. ▶ **noun** (pl. same) a person from Switzerland.

Swiss chard ▶ **noun** see **CHARD**.

Swiss cheese ▶ **noun 1** cheese of a style originating in Switzerland, typically containing large holes. **2** used figuratively to refer to something that is full of holes, gaps, or defects.

switch /swiCH/ ▶ **noun 1** a device for making and breaking an electrical connection. **2** a change from one thing to another. **3** a slender, flexible shoot cut from a tree. **4** a set of points on a railroad track.

– SYNONYMS **1 button,** lever, control. **2 change,** move, shift, transition, transformation, reversal, turnaround, U-turn, changeover, transfer, conversion.

▶ **verb 1** change from one thing to another: *she worked as a librarian and then switched to teaching*. **2** exchange one thing for another. **3** (**switch something off/on**) turn an electrical device off or on. **4** (**switch off**) informal cease to pay attention.

– SYNONYMS **1 change,** shift. **2 exchange,** swap, interchange, change around, rotate.

– DERIVATIVES **switch·a·ble** adjective **switch·er** noun.
– ORIGIN probably German.

switch·back /ˈswiCHˌbak/ ▶ **noun 1** a 180° bend in a road or path, especially one leading up the side of a mountain; a hairpin turn. **2** Brit. a road with alternate sharp ascents and descents.

switch·blade /ˈswiCHˌblād/ ▶ **noun** a knife with a blade that springs out from the handle when a button is pressed.

switch·board /ˈswiCHˌbôrd/ ▶ **noun** a device for routing telephone calls within an organization.

switch-hit·ter ▶ **noun 1** Baseball a batter who can hit from either side of home plate. **2** informal a bisexual.

switch·yard /ˈswiCHˌyärd/ ▶ **noun** a large railroad yard in which freight cars are organized into trains.

swiv·el /ˈswivəl/ ▶ **verb** (**swivels, swiveling, swiveled**) turn around, or around a central point. ▶ **noun** a connecting device between two parts enabling one to revolve without turning the other.
– ORIGIN Old English, 'move along a course, sweep.'

swiz·zle stick /ˈswizəl/ ▶ **noun** a stick used for frothing up or taking the fizz out of drinks.
– ORIGIN unknown.

swol·len /ˈswōlən/ past participle of **SWELL**.

WORD TOOLKIT

See **PUFFY**.

swoon /swo͞on/ literary ▶ **verb** faint, especially from extreme emotion. ▶ **noun** an instance of fainting.
– ORIGIN Old English, 'overcome.'

swoop /swo͞op/ ▶ **verb 1** move rapidly downward through the air. **2** carry out a sudden raid.

– SYNONYMS **dive,** descend, pounce, sweep down, plunge, drop down.

▶ **noun** a swooping or snatching movement or action.
– PHRASES **at** (or **in**) **one fell swoop** see FELL[3].
– ORIGIN perhaps from SWEEP.

swoosh /swo͝osн, swo͞osн/ ▶ **noun 1** the sound produced by a sudden rush of air or liquid. **2** an emblem or design representing a flash or stripe of color. ▶ **verb** move with a rushing sound.
– ORIGIN imitating the sound.

swop /swäp/ ▶ **verb & noun** British variant spelling of SWAP.

sword /sôrd/ ▶ **noun 1** a weapon with a long metal blade and a handle, used for thrusting or striking. **2** (**the sword**) literary military power; violence.

– SYNONYMS **blade,** foil, épée, cutlass, rapier, saber, scimitar.

– PHRASES **put someone to the sword** kill someone, especially in war.
– ORIGIN Old English.

sword·fish /'sôrd,fisн/ ▶ **noun** (pl. same or **swordfishes**) a large sea fish with a long swordlike snout.

sword of Dam·o·cles /'daməˌklēz/ ▶ **noun** something bad that threatens to happen at any time.
– ORIGIN with reference to *Damocles*, a courtier who praised the happiness of the ancient Greek ruler Dionysius I so much that the king made him sit under a sword suspended by a single hair, to show him how insecure this happiness was.

sword·play /'sôrd,plā/ ▶ **noun** fencing with swords or foils.

swords·man /'sôrdzmən/ ▶ **noun** (pl. **swordsmen**) a man who fights with a sword.
– DERIVATIVES **swords·man·ship** /-ˌsнip/ noun.

swore /swôr/ past of SWEAR.

sworn /swôrn/ past participle of SWEAR ▶ **adjective 1** given under oath. **2** determined to remain the specified thing: *sworn enemies.*

swum /swəm/ past participle of SWIM.

swung /swəNG/ past and past participle of SWING.

syb·a·rite /'sibəˌrīt/ ▶ **noun** a person who is very fond of luxury and pleasure.
– DERIVATIVES **syb·a·rit·ic** /ˌsibə'ritik/ adjective.
– ORIGIN first referring to an inhabitant of *Sybaris*, an ancient Greek city in Italy.

syc·a·more /'sikəˌmôr/ ▶ **noun 1** an American plane tree. **2** a large maple tree native to central and southern Europe.
– ORIGIN Greek *sukomoros.*

syc·o·phant /'sikəfənt, -ˌfant/ ▶ **noun** a person who flatters someone important in order to try to gain favor with them.

– SYNONYMS **toady,** flatterer; informal bootlicker, yes-man.

– DERIVATIVES **syc·o·phan·cy** /-fənsē, -ˌfansē/ noun.
– ORIGIN Greek *sukophantēs* 'informer.'

syc·o·phan·tic /ˌsikə'fantik/ ▶ **adjective** flattering and obsequious.

– SYNONYMS **obsequious,** servile, subservient, groveling, toadying, fawning, flattering, ingratiating, unctuous; informal smarmy, bootlicking.

Sy·den·ham's cho·rea /'sidnəmz kô'rēə/ ▶ **noun** a form of chorea (disorder of the nervous system) chiefly affecting children and associated with rheumatic fever.
– ORIGIN named after the English physician Thomas *Sydenham.*

syl·la·bar·y /'siləˌberē/ ▶ **noun** (pl. **syllabaries**) a set of written characters representing syllables and (in some languages or stages of writing) serving the purpose of an alphabet.

syl·lab·ic /sə'labik/ ▶ **adjective 1** relating to or based on syllables. **2** (of a consonant) that forms a whole syllable, such as the *l* in *bottle.*
– DERIVATIVES **syl·lab·i·cal·ly** /-ik(ə)lē/ adverb.

syl·lab·i·fy /sə'labəˌfī/ ▶ **verb** (**syllabifies, syllabifying, syllabified**) divide words into syllables.
– DERIVATIVES **syl·lab·i·fi·ca·tion** /səˌlabəfi'kāsнən/ noun.

syl·la·ble /'siləbəl/ ▶ **noun** a unit of pronunciation having one vowel sound and forming all or part of a word (e.g., *butter* has two syllables).
– ORIGIN Greek *sullabē.*

syl·la·bub /'siləˌbəb/ ▶ **noun** a whipped cream dessert, typically flavored with white wine or sherry.
– ORIGIN unknown.

syl·la·bus /'siləbəs/ ▶ **noun** (pl. **syllabuses** or **syllabi** /-ˌbī/) the subjects covered in a course of study or teaching.
– ORIGIN Latin.

syl·lo·gism /'siləˌjizəm/ ▶ **noun** a form of reasoning in which a conclusion is drawn from two propositions (premises) (e.g., *all dogs are animals; all animals have four legs; therefore all dogs have four legs*).
– DERIVATIVES **syl·lo·gis·tic** /ˌsilə'jistik/ adjective.
– ORIGIN Greek *sullogismos.*

sylph /silf/ ▶ **noun 1** an imaginary spirit of the air. **2** a slender woman or girl.
– DERIVATIVES **sylph·like** /'silf,līk/ adjective.
– ORIGIN Latin *sylphes* (plural).

syl·van /'silvən/ ▶ **adjective** chiefly literary consisting of or relating to woods; wooded.
– ORIGIN from Latin *silva* 'a wood.'

sym. ▶ **abbreviation 1** symbol. **2** Chemistry symmetrical. **3** symphony. **4** symptom.

sym·bi·ont /'simbēˌänt, -bī-/ ▶ **noun** Biology either of two organisms that live in symbiosis with one another.
– ORIGIN from Greek *sumbiōn* 'living together.'

sym·bi·o·sis /ˌsimbē'ōsis, -bī-/ ▶ **noun** (pl. **symbioses** /-ˌsēz/) **1** Biology a situation in which two different organisms live with and are dependent on each other, to the advantage of both. **2** a relationship between different people or groups that is beneficial to both: *his dances celebrate the symbiosis of music and dance.*
– DERIVATIVES **sym·bi·ot·ic** /-'ätik/ adjective.
– ORIGIN Greek *sumbiōsis.*

sym·bol /'simbəl/ ▶ **noun 1** a thing or person that represents or stands for something else: *the limousine was a symbol of his wealth.* **2** a sign, letter, or mark that has a fixed meaning, especially in music, science, or mathematics.

– SYNONYMS **1 representation,** token, sign, emblem, figure, image, metaphor, allegory. **2 sign,** character, mark, letter. **3 logo,** emblem, badge, stamp, trademark, crest, insignia, coat of arms, seal, device, monogram, hallmark, motif.

– ORIGIN Greek *sumbolon* 'mark, token.'

CHOOSE THE RIGHT WORD

See **EMBLEM**.

sym·bol·ic /sim'bälik/ ▸ **adjective 1** acting as a symbol: *a repeating design symbolic of eternity.* **2** involving the use of symbols or symbolism.

– SYNONYMS **1 emblematic,** representative, typical, characteristic, symptomatic. **2 figurative,** metaphorical, allegorical.
– ANTONYMS literal.

– DERIVATIVES **sym·bol·i·cal·ly** /-ik(ə)lē/ adverb.

sym·bol·ism /'simbə,lizəm/ ▸ **noun 1** the use of symbols to represent ideas or qualities. **2** (**Symbolism**) an artistic and poetic movement or style using symbolic images and indirect suggestion to express mystical ideas, emotions, and states of mind.
– DERIVATIVES **sym·bol·ist** noun & adjective.

sym·bol·ize /'simbə,līz/ ▸ **verb 1** be a symbol of: *the ceremonial dagger symbolizes justice.* **2** represent something by means of symbols.

– SYNONYMS **represent,** stand for, be a sign of, denote, signify, mean, indicate, convey, express, embody, epitomize, encapsulate, personify.

– DERIVATIVES **sym·bol·i·za·tion** /,simbəli'zāsʜən/ noun.

sym·bol·o·gy /sim'bäləjē/ ▸ **noun 1** the study or use of symbols. **2** symbols as a whole.

sym·met·ri·cal /sə'metrikəl/ ▸ **adjective** made up of exactly similar parts facing each other or around an axis; showing symmetry.

– SYNONYMS **regular,** uniform, consistent, even, equal, balanced, proportional.

– DERIVATIVES **sym·met·ric** adjective **sym·met·ri·cal·ly** /-ik(ə)lē/ adverb.

sym·me·try /'simitrē/ ▸ **noun** (pl. **symmetries**) **1** the quality of being made up of exactly similar parts facing each other or around an axis. **2** the quality of being the same or very similar: *the political symmetry between the two debates.* **3** correct or pleasing proportion of the parts of something.
– ORIGIN Latin *symmetria.*

sym·pa·thet·ic /,simpə'ᴛʜetik/ ▸ **adjective 1** feeling or expressing kindness or understanding toward someone. **2** showing that one approves of an idea or action: *many people are sympathetic to the idea of globalization.* **3** pleasing or likable. **4** referring to the part of the nervous system supplying the internal organs, blood vessels, and glands.

– SYNONYMS **1 compassionate,** caring, concerned, understanding, sensitive, supportive, empathetic, kind-hearted, warmhearted. **2 likable,** pleasant, agreeable, congenial, companionable.
– ANTONYMS unsympathetic.

– DERIVATIVES **sym·pa·thet·i·cal·ly** /-ik(ə)lē/ adverb.

sym·pa·thize /'simpə,ᴛʜīz/ ▸ **verb 1** feel or express sympathy. **2** support an opinion or political movement.

– SYNONYMS **commiserate,** show concern, offer condolences; (**sympathize with**) pity, feel sorry for, feel for, identify with, understand, relate to.

– DERIVATIVES **sym·pa·thiz·er** noun.

sym·pa·thy /'simpəᴛʜē/ ▸ **noun** (pl. **sympathies**) **1** the feeling of being sorry for someone who is unhappy or in difficulty: *they had great sympathy for the flood victims.* **2** support for or approval of an idea, cause, etc. **3** understanding between people who have similar views or interests.

– SYNONYMS **compassion,** care, concern, commiseration, pity, condolence.
– ANTONYMS indifference.

– PHRASES **in sympathy 1** relating harmoniously to something else; in keeping. **2** happening in a way that corresponds to something else.
– ORIGIN Greek *sumpatheia.*

USAGE

On the difference between **sympathy** and **empathy**, see the note at **EMPATHY**.

sym·phon·ic /sim'fänik/ ▸ **adjective** relating to or having the form of a symphony.

sym·pho·ny /'simfənē/ ▸ **noun** (pl. **symphonies**) an elaborate musical composition for full orchestra, typically in four movements.
– ORIGIN Greek *sumphōnia.*

sym·pho·ny or·ches·tra ▸ **noun** a large classical orchestra, including string, woodwind, brass, and percussion instruments.

sym·po·si·um /sim'pōzēəm/ ▸ **noun** (pl. **symposia** /-zēə/ or **symposiums**) **1** a conference to discuss a particular academic or specialist subject. **2** a collection of related papers by a number of contributors.
– ORIGIN Greek *sumposion.*

symp·tom /'sim(p)təm/ ▸ **noun 1** a change in the body or mind that is the sign of a disease. **2** an indication of an undesirable situation.

– SYNONYMS **indication,** indicator, manifestation, sign, mark, feature, trait, clue, hint, warning, evidence, proof.

– ORIGIN Greek *sumptōma* 'chance, symptom.'

CHOOSE THE RIGHT WORD

See **SIGN**.

symp·to·mat·ic /,sim(p)tə'matik/ ▸ **adjective** acting as a symptom or sign of something: *these difficulties are symptomatic of fundamental problems.*

– SYNONYMS **indicative,** characteristic, suggestive, typical, representative, symbolic.

– DERIVATIVES **symp·to·mat·i·cal·ly** /-ik(ə)lē/ adverb.

syn·a·gogue /'sinə,gäg/ ▸ **noun** a building where Jewish people meet for religious worship and instruction.
– ORIGIN Greek *sunagōgē* 'meeting.'

syn·apse /'sin,aps/ ▸ **noun** a gap between two nerve cells, across which impulses are conducted.
– DERIVATIVES **syn·ap·tic** /sə'naptik/ adjective.
– ORIGIN Greek *sunapsis.*

sync /siɴɢk/ (also **synch** pronunc. same) informal ▸ **noun** synchronization. ▸ **verb** synchronize something with something else.

– PHRASES **in** (or **out of**) **sync** working well (or badly) together.

syn·chro·mesh /ˈsiNGkrō,mesH/ ▶ **noun** a system of gear changing in which the gearwheels are made to revolve at the same speed during engagement.
– ORIGIN from *synchronized mesh*.

syn·chron·ic /siNGˈkränik/ ▶ **adjective** concerned with something, especially a language, as it exists at one point in time: *synchronic narratives*. Often contrasted with **DIACHRONIC**.

syn·chro·nic·i·ty /,siNGkrəˈnisitē/ ▶ **noun** the occurrence of events at the same time, which appear to be related but have no obvious connection.

syn·chro·nize /ˈsiNGkrə,nīz/ ▶ **verb** cause to occur or operate at the same time or rate: *synchronize your hand gestures with your main points*.
– DERIVATIVES **syn·chro·ni·za·tion** /,siNGkrənəˈzāsHən/ noun **syn·chro·niz·er** noun.

syn·chro·nized swim·ming ▶ **noun** a sport in which teams of swimmers perform coordinated movements in time to music.

syn·chro·nous /ˈsiNGkrənəs/ ▶ **adjective** existing or occurring at the same time.
– DERIVATIVES **syn·chro·nous·ly** adverb.
– ORIGIN Greek *sunkhronos*.

syn·chro·ny /ˈsiNGkrənē/ ▶ **noun** the state of operating or developing at the same time or rate as something else.

syn·cline /ˈsin,klīn/ ▶ **noun** a ridge or fold of rock in which the strata slope upward from the axis. Compare with **ANTICLINE**.
– ORIGIN from Greek *sun* 'with' + *klinein* 'to lean.'

syn·co·pat·ed /ˈsiNGkə,pātid/ ▶ **adjective** (of music or a rhythm) having the beats or accents altered so that strong beats become weak and vice versa.
– DERIVATIVES **syn·co·pa·tion** /,siNGkəˈpāsHən/ noun.
– ORIGIN from **SYNCOPE**.

syn·co·pe /ˈsiNGkəpē/ ▶ **noun 1** Medicine fainting caused by low blood pressure. **2** Grammar the omission of sounds or letters from within a word, for example when *library* is pronounced /ˈlī,brē/.
– ORIGIN Greek *sunkopē*.

syn·cre·tism /ˈsiNGkrə,tizəm/ ▶ **noun** the combining of different religions, cultures, or schools of thought.
– DERIVATIVES **syn·cret·ic** /siNGˈkretik/ adjective **syn·cre·tist** noun & adjective **syn·cre·tis·tic** /,siNGkrəˈtistik/ adjective.
– ORIGIN from Greek *sunkrētizein* 'unite against a third party.'

syn·cre·tize /ˈsiNGkri,tīz/ ▶ **verb** attempt to combine differing religious beliefs, cultures, or schools of thought.
– DERIVATIVES **syn·cre·ti·za·tion** /,siNGkritəˈzāsHən/ noun.

syn·di·cal·ism /ˈsindəkə,lizəm/ ▶ **noun** a movement that believes in transferring the ownership and control of industry and business to workers' unions.
– DERIVATIVES **syn·di·cal·ist** noun & adjective.

syn·di·cate ▶ **noun** /ˈsindikit/ **1** a group of people or organizations that combine to promote a common interest. **2** an agency that supplies items to a number of news media at the same time. **3** (**the syndicate**) organized crime. ▶ **verb** /ˈsindi,kāt/ **1** publish or broadcast material in a number of news media at the same time. **2** control or manage something by a syndicate.
– DERIVATIVES **syn·di·ca·tion** /,sindiˈkāsHən/ noun.

syn·drome /ˈsin,drōm/ ▶ **noun 1** a group of medical symptoms that consistently occur together. **2** a set of opinions or behavior that is typical of a particular group of people.
– ORIGIN Greek *sundromē*.

syn·ec·do·che /siˈnekdəkē/ ▶ **noun** a figure of speech in which a part is made to represent the whole or vice versa, as in *England lost by six wickets* (meaning 'the English cricket team').
– ORIGIN Greek *sunekdokhē*.

syn·er·gy /ˈsinərjē/ (also **synergism** /-,jizəm/) ▶ **noun** cooperation of two or more people or things to produce a combined effect that is greater than the sum of their separate effects: *the synergy between artist and record company*.
– DERIVATIVES **syn·er·get·ic** /,sinərˈjetik/ adjective.
– ORIGIN from Greek *sunergos* 'working together.'

syn·od /ˈsinəd/ ▶ **noun** an official meeting of the ministers and other members of a Christian Church.
– DERIVATIVES **syn·od·al** /ˈsinədl/ adjective **syn·od·i·cal** /səˈnädikəl/ adjective.
– ORIGIN Greek *sunodos* 'meeting.'

syn·o·nym /ˈsinə,nim/ ▶ **noun** a word or phrase that means the same as another word or phrase in the same language.
– DERIVATIVES **syn·on·y·my** /səˈnänəmē/ noun.
– ORIGIN Greek *sunōnumon*.

syn·on·y·mous /səˈnänəməs/ ▶ **adjective 1** (of a word or phrase) having the same meaning as another word or phrase in the same language. **2** closely associated with something: *his name was synonymous with victory*.
– DERIVATIVES **syn·on·y·mous·ly** adverb.

syn·op·sis /səˈnäpsis/ ▶ **noun** (pl. **synopses** /-,sēz/) a brief summary or outline.

– SYNONYMS **summary,** précis, abstract, outline, rundown, roundup, abridgment.

– ORIGIN from Greek *sun-* 'together' + *opsis* 'seeing.'

syn·op·tic /səˈnäptik/ ▶ **adjective 1** relating to a synopsis. **2** (**Synoptic**) referring to the Gospels of Matthew, Mark, and Luke, which describe events from a similar point of view, as contrasted with that of John.

syn·o·vi·al /səˈnōvēəl/ ▶ **adjective** relating to a type of joint in the body that is enclosed in a flexible membrane containing a lubricating fluid.
– ORIGIN from Latin *synovia*.

syn·tax /ˈsin,taks/ ▶ **noun 1** the arrangement of words and phrases to create well-formed sentences. **2** a set of rules for the formation of sentences.
– DERIVATIVES **syn·tac·tic** /sinˈtaktik/ adjective **syn·tac·ti·cal** /sinˈtaktikəl/ adjective **syn·tac·ti·cal·ly** /-ik(ə)lē/ adverb.
– ORIGIN Greek *suntaxis*.

synth /sinTH/ ▶ **noun** informal a synthesizer.
– DERIVATIVES **synth·y** adjective.

syn·the·sis /ˈsinTHəsis/ ▶ **noun** (pl. **syntheses** /-,sēz/) **1** the combination of parts to form a connected whole. **2** the production of chemical compounds by reaction from simpler materials.

– SYNONYMS **combination,** union, amalgam, blend, mixture, compound, fusion, composite, alloy.

– DERIVATIVES **syn·the·sist** noun.
– ORIGIN Greek *sunthesis*.

syn·the·size /ˈsinTHi,sīz/ ▶ **verb 1** combine things into a connected whole. **2** make something by chemical synthesis. **3** produce sound electronically.

syn·the·siz·er /'sinTHə,sīzər/ ▸ **noun** an electronic musical instrument that produces sounds by generating and combining signals of different frequencies.

syn·thet·ic /sin'THetik/ ▸ **adjective 1** made by chemical synthesis, especially to imitate a natural product: *synthetic rubber*. **2** not genuine; insincere.

– SYNONYMS **artificial,** fake, imitation, mock, simulated, man-made, manufactured; informal pretend.
– ANTONYMS natural.

▸ **noun** a synthetic substance.
– DERIVATIVES **syn·thet·i·cal·ly** /-ik(ə)lē/ adverb.

WORD TOOLKIT

See **ARTIFICIAL**.

syph·i·lis /'sifəlis/ ▸ **noun** a serious sexually transmitted disease spread by bacteria.
– DERIVATIVES **syph·i·lit·ic** /,sifə'litik/ adjective & noun.
– ORIGIN from *Syphilus*, the subject of a Latin poem who was the supposed first sufferer of the disease.

syphon ▸ **noun & verb** variant spelling of **SIPHON**.

Syr·i·an /'si(ə)rēən/ ▸ **noun** a person from Syria. ▸ **adjective** relating to Syria.

sy·ringe /sə'rinj, 'sirinj/ ▸ **noun** a tube with a nozzle and piston for sucking in and forcing out liquid in a thin stream, often one fitted with a hollow needle for injecting drugs or withdrawing bodily fluids. ▸ **verb** (**syringes, syringing, syringed**) spray liquid into or over something with a syringe.
– ORIGIN Latin *syringa*.

syr·up /'sirəp, 'sər-/ ▸ **noun 1** a thick sweet liquid made by dissolving sugar in boiling water. **2** a thick sweet liquid containing medicine or used as a drink.
– ORIGIN Arabic, 'beverage.'

syr·up·y /'sirəpē, 'sər-/ ▸ **adjective 1** thick or sweet, like syrup. **2** excessively sentimental.

sys·tem /'sistəm/ ▸ **noun 1** a set of things working together as a mechanism or network: *the railroad system*. **2** an organized scheme or method by which something is done. **3** (**the system**) the rules or people that control a country or society, especially when regarded as restrictive or unfair. **4** a person's body. **5** the state of being well organized. **6** Computing a group of related hardware units or programs or both. **7** Geology a major range of rock strata that corresponds to a period in time: *the Devonian system*.

– SYNONYMS **1 structure,** organization, arrangement, order, network; informal setup. **2 method,** methodology, modus operandi, technique, procedure, means, way, scheme, plan, policy, program, formula, routine. **3** (**the system**) **the establishment,** the administration, the authorities, the powers that be, bureaucracy, officialdom.

– ORIGIN Greek *sustēma*.

sys·tem·at·ic /,sistə'matik/ ▸ **adjective** done or acting according to a system; methodical.

– SYNONYMS **structured,** methodical, organized, orderly, planned, regular, routine, standardized, standard, logical, coherent, consistent.
– ANTONYMS disorganized.

– DERIVATIVES **sys·tem·at·i·cal·ly** /-ik(ə)lē/ adverb **sys·tem·a·tist** /'sistəmə,tist/ noun.

sys·tem·at·ics /,sistə'matiks/ ▸ **plural noun** (treated as sing.) the branch of biology that deals with classification and nomenclature; taxonomy.

sys·tem·a·tize /'sistəmə,tīz/ ▸ **verb** arrange things according to an organized system.
– DERIVATIVES **sys·tem·a·ti·za·tion** /,sistəməti'zāSHən/ noun.

sys·tem·ic /sə'stemik/ ▸ **adjective 1** relating to a system as a whole. **2** (of an insecticide or fungicide) entering the plant via the roots or shoots and passing through the tissues.
– DERIVATIVES **sys·tem·i·cal·ly** /-ik(ə)lē/ adverb.

sys·tems an·a·lyst /'sistəmz/ ▸ **noun** a person who analyzes a complex process or operation in order to improve its efficiency.
– DERIVATIVES **sys·tems a·nal·y·sis** noun.

sys·to·le /'sistəlē/ ▸ **noun** the phase of the heartbeat when the heart muscle contracts and pumps blood into the arteries. Often contrasted with **DIASTOLE**.
– DERIVATIVES **sys·tol·ic** /si'stälik/ adjective.
– ORIGIN Greek *sustolē*.

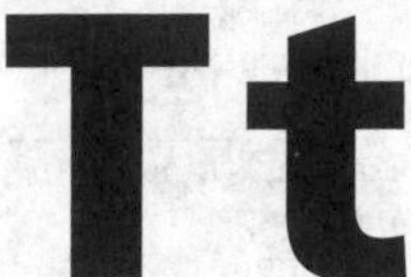

T[1] (also **t**) ▶ **noun** (pl. **Ts** or **T's**) the twentieth letter of the alphabet.
– PHRASES **to a T** informal to perfection; exactly.

T[2] ▶ **abbreviation 1** tera- (10^{12}). **2** tesla. **3** tablespoon(s); tablespoonful(s).

t ▶ **abbreviation 1** ton(s). **2** teaspoon(s); teaspoonful(s).

TA ▶ **abbreviation** teaching assistant; a graduate student who assists a college professor.

Ta /tä/ ▶ **symbol** the chemical element tantalum.

ta /tä/ ▶ **exclamation** Brit. informal thank you.
– ORIGIN a child's word.

tab[1] /tab/ ▶ **noun 1** a small flap or strip of material attached to something, used to give information or to hold it, fasten it, etc. **2** informal a tally of items ordered in a bar or restaurant. **3** informal a restaurant or bar bill. **4** a ring on a can that is pulled to open it. ▶ **verb** (**tabs, tabbing, tabbed**) mark something with a tab.
– PHRASES **keep tabs on someone** informal monitor someone's activities. **pick up the tab** informal pay for something.
– ORIGIN perhaps from **TAG**[1].

tab[2] ▶ **noun** short for **TABULATOR**. ▶ **verb** (**tabs, tabbing, tabbed**) short for **TABULATE**.

tab[3] ▶ **noun** informal a tablet, especially one containing an illegal drug.

Ta·bas·co /tə'baskō/ ▶ **noun** trademark a very hot sauce made from a type of pepper.
– ORIGIN named after the state of *Tabasco* in Mexico.

tab·bou·leh /tə'bo͞olē/ ▶ **noun** a Middle Eastern salad of cracked wheat mixed with finely chopped tomatoes, onions, parsley, etc.
– ORIGIN Arabic.

tab·by /'tabē/ ▶ **noun** (pl. **tabbies**) a gray or brownish cat with dark stripes.
– ORIGIN French *tabis* 'striped silk taffeta.'

tab·er·nac·le /'tabər,nakəl/ ▶ **noun 1** a place of worship used by some Protestants or Mormons. **2** (in a Roman Catholic church) a box or cabinet in which the bread consecrated for Holy Communion may be placed. **3** (in the Bible) a tent used by the Israelites to house the Ark of the Covenant during the Exodus.
– ORIGIN Latin *tabernaculum* 'tent.'

ta·bla /'täblə/ ▶ **noun** a pair of small hand drums fixed together, used in Indian music.
– ORIGIN Arabic.

tab·la·ture /'tabləCHər, -,CHo͝or/ ▶ **noun** a form of musical notation indicating fingering rather than the pitch of notes.
– ORIGIN French.

ta·ble /'tābəl/ ▶ **noun 1** a piece of furniture with a flat top supported by legs, for eating, writing, or working at. **2** a set of facts or figures displayed in rows or columns. **3** (**tables**) multiplication tables. **4** food provided in a restaurant or household: *food includes a lunchtime buffet table.*

– SYNONYMS **chart,** diagram, figure, graphic, graph, plan, list.

▶ **verb 1** postpone consideration of: *we'll table this discussion until next week.* **2** Brit. formally present something for discussion at a meeting.
– PHRASES **on the table** available for discussion. **turn the tables** turn a situation of disadvantage to oneself into one of advantage.
– ORIGIN Latin *tabula* 'plank, tablet, list.'

tab·leau /,ta'blō/ ▶ **noun** (pl. **tableaux** or **tableaus** /,ta'blōz/) a group of models or motionless figures representing a scene from a story or from history.
– ORIGIN French, 'picture.'

tab·leau vi·vant /tä'blō vē'väN, -'vänt/ ▶ **noun** (pl. **tableaux vivants** pronunc. same) a silent and motionless group of people arranged to represent a scene.
– ORIGIN French, 'living picture.'

ta·ble·cloth /'tābəl,klôTH, -,kläTH/ ▶ **noun** a cloth spread over a table, especially during meals.

ta·ble d'hôte /,täbəl 'dōt, ,täblə, ,tabəl/ ▶ **noun** a restaurant menu or meal offered at a fixed price and with limited choices.
– ORIGIN French, 'host's table.'

ta·ble·land /'tābəl,(l)and/ ▶ **noun** a broad, high, level region; a plateau.

ta·ble man·ners ▶ **plural noun** behavior that is considered polite while eating at a table.

ta·ble salt ▶ **noun** see **SALT**.

ta·ble·spoon /'tābəl,spo͞on/ ▶ **noun 1** a large spoon for serving food. **2** the amount held by a tablespoon, equivalent to 3 teaspoons, ½ fluid ounce, or 15 milliliters.
– DERIVATIVES **ta·ble·spoon·ful** noun.

tab·let /'tablit/ ▶ **noun 1** a slab of stone, clay, or wood on which an inscription is written. **2** a writing pad. **3** a pill.

– SYNONYMS **1 slab,** stone, panel, plaque, plate, sign. **2 pill,** capsule, lozenge, pastille, drop. **3 bar,** cake, slab, brick, block.

– ORIGIN Latin *tabula* 'plank, tablet, list.'

ta·ble ten·nis ▶ **noun** an indoor game played with small bats and a small hollow ball hit across a table divided by a net.

ta·ble·top /'tābəl,täp/ ▶ **noun** the horizontal top part of a table.

ta·ble·ware /'tābəl,wer/ ▶ **noun** dishes, utensils, and glassware used for serving and eating meals.

ta·ble wine ▶ **noun** wine of moderate quality considered suitable for drinking with a meal.

tab·loid /'tab,loid/ ▶ **noun** a newspaper having pages half the size of those of a broadsheet, written in a popular style and typically dominated by sensational stories.
– DERIVATIVES **tab·loid·i·za·tion** /,tabloidə'zāsʜən/ noun.
– ORIGIN first referring to a tablet of medicine: the current sense reflects the idea of information being presented in a form that is concentrated and easily digested.

ta·boo /tə'bo͞o, ta-/ ▶ **noun** (pl. **taboos**) a social or religious custom placing a ban or restriction on a particular thing or person.

– SYNONYMS **prohibition,** proscription, veto, ban, interdict.

▶ **adjective** banned or restricted by social custom: *sex was a taboo subject.*

– SYNONYMS **forbidden,** prohibited, vetoed, banned, proscribed, outlawed, off limits, beyond the pale, unmentionable, unspeakable; informal no go.
– ANTONYMS acceptable.

▶ **verb** (**taboos, tabooing, tabooed**) put a ban or taboo on someone or something.
– ORIGIN from Tongan, 'set apart, forbidden.'

ta·bor /'tābər/ ▶ **noun** historical a small drum, especially one played at the same time as a simple pipe.
– ORIGIN Old French *tabour.*

tab·u·lar /'tabyələr/ ▶ **adjective 1** (of data) consisting of or presented in columns or tables. **2** broad and flat, like the top of a table.
– ORIGIN Latin *tabularis.*

ta·bu·la ra·sa /'täbyo͝olə 'räsə, 'räzə/ ▶ **noun 1** an absence of preconceived ideas. **2** a person's mind, especially at birth, regarded as being empty of ideas.
– ORIGIN Latin, 'scraped tablet,' i.e., a tablet with the writing erased.

tab·u·late /'tabyə,lāt/ ▶ **verb** arrange data in columns or tables.
– DERIVATIVES **tab·u·la·tion** /,tabyə'lāsʜən/ noun.

tab·u·la·tor /'tabyəlātər/ ▶ **noun** a facility in a word-processing program, or a device on a typewriter, for advancing to set positions when producing tables of data.

tach /tak/ ▶ **noun** informal short for **TACHOMETER**.

ta·chom·e·ter /ta'kämitər, tə-/ ▶ **noun** an instrument that measures the working speed of an engine, typically in revolutions per minute.

tach·y·car·di·a /,taki'kärdēə/ ▶ **noun** an abnormally rapid heart rate.
– ORIGIN from Greek *takhus* 'swift' + *kardia* 'heart.'

tac·it /'tasit/ ▶ **adjective** understood or suggested without being stated: *your silence may be taken to mean tacit agreement.*

– SYNONYMS **implicit,** understood, implied, inferred, hinted, suggested, unspoken, unstated, unsaid, unexpressed, unvoiced, taken for granted, taken as read.
– ANTONYMS explicit.

– DERIVATIVES **tac·it·ly** adverb.
– ORIGIN Latin *tacitus* 'silent.'

tac·i·turn /'tasi,tərn/ ▶ **adjective** saying little; uncommunicative.

– SYNONYMS **untalkative,** uncommunicative, reticent, unforthcoming, quiet, secretive, tight-lipped, close-mouthed; silent, mute, dumb, inarticulate.
– ANTONYMS talkative.

– DERIVATIVES **tac·i·tur·ni·ty** /,tasi'tərnitē/ noun **tac·i·turn·ly** adverb.
– ORIGIN Latin *taciturnus.*

tack[1] /tak/ ▶ **noun 1** a small broad-headed nail. **2** a thumbtack. **3** a course of action: *the board changed tack and recommended that shareholders accept a takeover.* **4** a long stitch used to fasten fabrics together temporarily. **5** a sailboat's course relative to the direction of the wind: *the ketch swung to the opposite tack.*

– SYNONYMS **pin,** nail, staple, rivet.

▶ **verb 1** fasten or fix something with tacks. **2** (**tack something on**) add something to something that already exists. **3** change the direction of a sailboat so that the wind blows into the sails from the opposite side.

– SYNONYMS **1 pin,** nail, staple, fix, fasten, attach, secure. **2** (**tack something on**) **add,** append, attach, join on, tag on.

– ORIGIN probably from Old French *tache* 'clasp, large nail.'

tack[2] ▶ **noun** equipment used in horse riding, including the saddle and bridle.
– ORIGIN from **TACKLE**.

tack·le /'takəl/ ▶ **verb 1** make a determined effort to deal with a problem or difficult task: *police launched an initiative to tackle rising crime.* **2** begin to discuss a difficult issue with someone. **3** (in football) seize and stop or throw down an opposing player. **4** (in soccer, rugby, etc.) try to take the ball from or prevent the movement of an opponent.

– SYNONYMS **1 deal with,** take care of, attend to, see to, handle, manage, get to grips with, address. **2 confront,** face up to, take on, challenge, attack, grab, struggle with, intercept, block, stop, bring down, floor, fell; informal have a go at.

▶ **noun 1** the equipment required for a task or sport. **2** a mechanism consisting of ropes, pulley blocks, and hooks for lifting heavy objects. **3** (in sports) an act of tackling an opponent. **4** the rigging and pulleys used to work a boat's sails.

– SYNONYMS **1 equipment,** apparatus, kit, implements, paraphernalia; informal gear, clobber. **2 interception,** challenge, block, attack.

– DERIVATIVES **tack·ler** /'tak(ə)lər/ noun.
– ORIGIN probably from German *taken* 'lay hold of.'

tack·y[1] /'takē/ ▶ **adjective** (**tackier, tackiest**) (of glue, paint, etc.) slightly sticky because not fully dry.

– SYNONYMS **sticky,** wet, gluey, viscous, gummy; informal gooey.

– DERIVATIVES **tack·i·ness** noun.

tack·y[2] ▶ **adjective** (**tackier, tackiest**) informal showing poor taste and quality.

– SYNONYMS **tawdry,** tasteless, kitsch, vulgar, crude, garish, gaudy, trashy, cheap; informal cheesy.
– ANTONYMS tasteful.

– DERIVATIVES **tack·i·ness** noun.
– ORIGIN unknown.

ta·co /'täkō/ ▶ **noun** (pl. **tacos**) a Mexican dish consisting of a folded tortilla filled with seasoned meat or beans.
– ORIGIN Spanish, 'plug, wad.'

tact /takt/ ▶ **noun** sensitivity and skill in dealing with others or with difficult issues.

– SYNONYMS **diplomacy,** sensitivity, understanding, thoughtfulness, consideration, delicacy, discretion, prudence, judiciousness, subtlety; informal savvy.

– ORIGIN Latin *tactus* 'touch, sense of touch.'

tact·ful /'tak(t)fəl/ ▶ **adjective** having or showing skill and sensitivity in dealing with others or with difficult issues.

– SYNONYMS **diplomatic,** discreet, considerate, sensitive, understanding, thoughtful, delicate, judicious, subtle.

– DERIVATIVES **tact·ful·ly** adverb **tact·ful·ness** noun.

tac·tic /'taktik/ ▶ **noun 1** an action or plan that is intended to achieve a specific result. **2** (**tactics**) the art of directing and organizing the movement of armed forces and equipment during a war. Often contrasted with **STRATEGY**.

– SYNONYMS **1 scheme,** plan, maneuver, method, trick, ploy. **2** (**tactics**) **strategy,** policy, campaign, game plan, planning, maneuvers, logistics.

– DERIVATIVES **tac·ti·cian** /tak'tisʜən/ noun.
– ORIGIN from Greek *taktikē tekhnē* 'art of tactics.'

tac·ti·cal /'taktikəl/ ▶ **adjective 1** done or planned to achieve a particular result. **2** (of weapons) for use in direct support of military or naval operations. Often contrasted with **STRATEGIC**. **3** relating to military tactics.

– SYNONYMS **calculated,** planned, strategic, prudent, politic, diplomatic, judicious, shrewd.

– DERIVATIVES **tac·ti·cal·ly** adverb.

tac·tile /'taktl, 'tak,tīl/ ▶ **adjective 1** relating to the sense of touch. **2** liking to touch others in a friendly or sympathetic way.
– DERIVATIVES **tac·til·i·ty** /tak'tilitē/ noun.
– ORIGIN Latin *tactilis*.

tact·less /'taktləs/ ▶ **adjective** thoughtless and insensitive.

– SYNONYMS **insensitive,** inconsiderate, thoughtless, indelicate, undiplomatic, indiscreet, unsubtle, inept, gauche, blunt.

– DERIVATIVES **tact·less·ly** adverb **tact·less·ness** noun.

tad /tad/ informal ▶ **adverb** (**a tad**) to a minor extent; rather. ▶ **noun** a small amount of something.
– ORIGIN perhaps from **TADPOLE**.

tad·pole /'tad,pōl/ ▶ **noun** the larva of an amphibian such as a frog or toad, at the stage when it lives in water and has gills and a tail.
– ORIGIN from an Old English word meaning 'toad' + **POLL**.

tae-bo /'tī 'bō/ ▶ **noun** trademark an exercise system combining elements of aerobics and kick-boxing.
– ORIGIN from Korean *tae* 'leg' + *bo*, short for *boxing*.

tae kwon do /'tī 'kwän 'dō/ ▶ **noun** a modern Korean martial art similar to karate.
– ORIGIN Korean, 'art of hand and foot fighting.'

taf·fe·ta /'tafitə/ ▶ **noun** a fine shiny silk or similar synthetic fabric.
– ORIGIN Latin.

taf·fy /'tafē/ ▶ **noun** (pl. **taffies**) **1** a candy similar to toffee, made from sugar or molasses, boiled with butter and pulled until glossy. **2** dated, informal insincere flattery.
– ORIGIN earlier form of **TOFFEE**.

tag¹ /tag/ ▶ **noun 1** a label used to identify something or to give other information about it. **2** an electronic device attached to someone to monitor their movements. **3** a nickname or description by which someone or something is widely known. **4** a nickname or other identifying mark written as the signature of a graffiti artist. **5** a frequently repeated quotation or phrase. **6** Computing a character or set of characters attached to an item of data in order to identify it.

– SYNONYMS **label,** ticket, badge, mark, tab, sticker, docket.

▶ **verb** (**tags, tagging, tagged**) **1** attach a tag or label to someone or something. **2** (**tag something on**) add something to the end of something else as an afterthought. **3** (**tag along**) accompany someone without being invited. **4** (of a graffiti artist) write a tag or nickname on a surface.

– SYNONYMS **label,** mark, ticket, identify, flag, indicate.

– ORIGIN unknown.

tag² ▶ **noun** a children's game in which one player chases the rest, and anyone who is caught then becomes the person doing the chasing.

Ta·ga·log /tə'gäləg, -lôg/ ▶ **noun 1** a member of a people from the Philippine Islands. **2** the language of the Tagalogs, the basis of Filipino.
– ORIGIN from the Tagalog words for 'native' + 'river.'

ta·gli·a·tel·le /,tälyə'telē/ ▶ **plural noun** pasta in narrow ribbons.
– ORIGIN Italian.

tag line ▶ **noun** informal a catchphrase, slogan, or punchline.

ta·hi·ni /tə'hēnē/ ▶ **noun** a Middle Eastern paste or spread made from ground sesame seeds.
– ORIGIN modern Greek *takhini*.

Ta·hi·tian /tə'hēsʜən/ ▶ **noun 1** a person from Tahiti. **2** the language of Tahiti. ▶ **adjective** relating to Tahiti.

t'ai chi /'tī 'cʜē, 'jē/ (also **t'ai chi ch'uan** /'tī ,cʜē 'cʜwän, ,jē/) ▶ **noun** a Chinese martial art and system of exercises, consisting of sequences of very slow controlled movements.
– ORIGIN Chinese, 'great ultimate boxing.'

tai·ga /'tīgə/ ▶ **noun** swampy coniferous forest of high northern latitudes, especially that between the tundra and steppes of Siberia.
– ORIGIN Mongolian.

tail¹ /tāl/ ▶ **noun 1** the part at the rear of an animal that sticks out from the rest of the body. **2** something that resembles an animal's tail in shape or position. **3** the rear part of an aircraft, with the horizontal stabilizer and rudder. **4** the final, more distant, or weaker part: *the tail of a hurricane*. **5** (**tails**) the side of a coin without the image of a head on it. **6** (**tails**) informal a tailcoat, or a man's formal evening suit with such a coat. **7** informal a person secretly following another to observe their movements.

– SYNONYMS **rear,** end, back, extremity, bottom.
– ANTONYMS head, front.

▶ **verb 1** informal secretly follow and observe someone. **2** (**tail off/away**) gradually become smaller or weaker.

– SYNONYMS **follow,** shadow, stalk, trail, track, keep under surveillance.

– DERIVATIVES **tail·less** adjective.
– PHRASES **on someone's tail** informal following someone closely. **with one's tail between one's legs** informal feeling dejected or humiliated.
– ORIGIN Old English.

USAGE

Do not confuse **tail** with **tale**. **Tail** means *the rear or end part of an animal or thing (the dog wagged its tail)*, whereas **tale** means *a story (a fairy tale)*.

tail² ▶ **noun** Law, chiefly historical limitation of ownership of an estate or title to a person and their direct descendants.
– ORIGIN Old French *taille* 'notch, tax.'

tail·coat /'tāl,kōt/ ▶ **noun** a man's formal coat, with a long skirt divided at the back into tails and cut away in front.

tail end ▶ **noun** the last or rear part of something.

tail fin ▶ **noun 1** a fin at the rear of a fish's body. **2** a projecting vertical surface on the tail of an aircraft, providing stability. **3** an upswept projection on each rear corner of a car, popular in the 1950s.

tail·gate /'tāl,gāt/ ▶ **noun 1** a hinged flap at the back of a truck. **2** the door at the back of a station wagon or hatchback. ▶ **verb** informal **1** drive too closely behind another vehicle. **2** eat a meal served from the back of a parked vehicle.
– DERIVATIVES **tail·gat·er** noun.

tail·light ▶ **noun** a red light at the rear of a vehicle.

tai·lor /'tālər/ ▶ **noun** a person whose occupation is making men's clothing for individual customers.

– SYNONYMS **outfitter,** couturier, costumier, dressmaker, fashion designer.

▶ **verb 1** make clothes to fit individual customers. **2** make or adapt for a particular purpose or person: *the database has been tailored to meet the needs of the restaurant industry.*

– SYNONYMS **customize,** adapt, adjust, modify, change, convert, alter, mold, gear, fit, shape, tune.

– ORIGIN Old French *taillour* 'cutter.'

WORD LINKS

sartorial *relating to tailoring*

tai·lored /'tālərd/ ▶ **adjective** (of clothes) smart, fitted, and well cut.

tai·lor·ing /'tāləriNG/ ▶ **noun 1** the activity or occupation of a tailor. **2** the style or cut of an item of clothing.

tai·lor-made ▶ **adjective 1** made or adapted for a particular purpose or person. **2** (of clothes) made by a tailor for a particular customer.

tail·piece /'tāl,pēs/ ▶ **noun 1** the final or end part of something. **2** a part added to the end of a piece of writing. **3** a small decorative design at the foot of a page or the end of a chapter or book.

tail·pipe /'tāl,pīp/ ▶ **noun** the rear section of the exhaust pipe of a motor vehicle.

tail·spin /'tāl,spin/ ▶ **noun** a fast revolving motion made by a rapidly descending aircraft.

tail·wind /'tāl,wind/ ▶ **noun** a wind blowing in the direction that a vehicle or aircraft is traveling in.

taint /tānt/ ▶ **verb 1** affect with an undesirable quality: *his reputation was tainted by scandal.* **2** contaminate or pollute something.

– SYNONYMS **1 contaminate,** pollute, adulterate, infect, blight, spoil, soil, ruin. **2 tarnish,** sully, blacken, stain, blot, damage.

▶ **noun** a trace of an undesirable quality or substance.
– ORIGIN from Old French *teint* 'tinged.'

Tai·wan·ese /,tīwə'nēz, -wä-, -'nēs/ ▶ **noun** (pl. same) a person from Taiwan. ▶ **adjective** relating to Taiwan.

Ta·jik /tä'jik/ (also **Tadzhik**) ▶ **noun 1** a member of a mainly Muslim people inhabiting Tajikistan and parts of neighboring countries. **2** a person from the republic of Tajikistan.

take /tāk/ ▶ **verb** (past **took** /to͝ok/; past part. **taken** /'tākən/) **1** reach for and hold something. **2** remove someone or something from a place. **3** subtract something from something else. **4** occupy a place or position. **5** perform an action or undertake a task. **6** carry or bring someone or something with one. **7** use something as a route or a means of transport. **8** tolerate or endure. **9** bring into a particular state: *the invasion took Europe to the brink of war.* **10** accept or receive someone or something. **11** require or use up: *the journey took four hours in all.* **12** experience or be affected by something. **13** consume something as food, drink, medicine, or drugs. **14** acquire or assume a position, state, or form. **15** act on an opportunity. **16** hold or accommodate: *the hotel takes just twenty guests.* **17** view or deal with in a specified way: *he took it as an insult.* **18** gain possession of something by force. **19** study a subject. **20** submit answers to an exam or test. **21** make a photograph with a camera.

– SYNONYMS **1** *she took his hand* **grasp,** get hold of, grip, clasp, clutch, grab. **2** *he took an envelope from his pocket* **remove,** pull, draw, withdraw, extract, fish. **3** *many prisoners were taken* **capture,** seize, catch, arrest, apprehend, take into custody, carry off, abduct. **4** *someone's taken my car* **steal,** remove, appropriate, make off with, pilfer, purloin; informal filch, swipe. **5** *take four from the total* **subtract,** deduct, remove, discount; informal knock off, minus. **6** *all the seats had been taken* **occupy,** use, utilize, fill, hold, reserve, engage. **7** *he took notes* **write,** note (down), jot (down), scribble, scrawl, record, register, document, minute. **8** *I took the package to Wilmington* **bring,** carry, bear, transport, convey, move, transfer, ferry; informal cart, tote. **9** *the police took her home* **escort,** accompany, help, assist, show, lead, guide, see, usher, convey. **10** *he took the train* **travel on/by,** journey on, go via, use. **11** *I can't take much more* **endure,** bear, tolerate, stand, put up with, abide, stomach, accept, allow, countenance, support, shoulder; formal brook.
– ANTONYMS give, add.

▶ **noun 1** a sequence of sound or part of a movie filmed or recorded continuously. **2** a particular version of or approach to something: *his whimsical take on life.* **3** an amount gained or acquired from one source or in one session.
– DERIVATIVES **tak·er** noun.
– PHRASES **be on the take** informal take bribes. **take after** resemble a parent or ancestor. **take something back** withdraw a statement. **take five** informal have a short break. **take someone in** cheat or deceive someone. **take something in 1** make an item of clothing tighter by altering its seams. **2** include or understand something. **take someone in hand** undertake to control or reform someone. **take something in hand** start dealing with a task. **take it out of** exhaust someone. **take off 1** become airborne. **2** leave hastily. **take someone off** imitate someone. **take something off** remove clothing. **take someone on** engage an employee. **take something on 1** undertake a task. **2** begin to have a particular meaning or quality. **take something out on** relieve one's frustration or anger by mistreating someone. **take**

over assume control of or responsibility for something. **take one's time** not hurry. **take to 1** get into the habit of. **2** form a liking or develop an ability for. **3** go to a place to escape danger. **take something up 1** become interested in a pursuit. **2** occupy time, space, or attention. **3** pursue a matter further. **take someone up on** accept an offer or challenge from someone. **take up with** begin to associate with someone.
– ORIGIN Old Norse.

take·a·way /ˈtākəˌwā/ ▸ **noun** Brit. takeout.

take·down /ˈtākˌdoun/ ▸ **noun 1** a wrestling maneuver in which an opponent is swiftly brought to the mat from a standing position. **2** informal a police raid or arrest. **3** (as adj.) denoting a firearm with the capacity to have the barrel and magazine detached from the stock.

take-home pay ▸ **noun** the pay received by an employee after tax and insurance have been deducted.

take·off /ˈtākˌôf, -ˌäf/ ▸ **noun 1** an act of becoming airborne. **2** informal an act of imitating someone or something.

take·out /ˈtākˌout/ ▸ **noun** a meal of prepared food purchased from a restaurant, deli, etc., and eaten elsewhere.

take·o·ver /ˈtākˌōvər/ ▸ **noun** an act of taking control of something such as a company from someone else.

> – SYNONYMS **buyout,** purchase, acquisition, amalgamation, merger.

take-up ▸ **noun 1** a device for taking up slack or excess: (as adj.) *a take-up reel.* **2** chiefly Brit. the acceptance of something offered: *practices that discourage take-up of legal advice.*

tak·ing /ˈtākiNG/ ▸ **noun** (**takings**) the amount of money earned by a business from the sale of goods or services.

> – SYNONYMS **proceeds,** returns, receipts, earnings, winnings, pickings, spoils, profit, gain, income, revenue.

▸ **adjective** dated pleasant and charming.
– PHRASES **for the taking** available to take advantage of.

talc /talk/ ▸ **noun 1** talcum powder. **2** a soft mineral that is a form of magnesium silicate.

tal·cum pow·der /ˈtalkəm/ ▸ **noun** the mineral talc in powdered form used on the skin to make it feel smooth and dry.
– ORIGIN Latin, from Persian.

tale /tāl/ ▸ **noun 1** a fictional or true story. **2** a lie.

> – SYNONYMS **story,** narrative, anecdote, account, history, legend, fable, myth, saga; informal yarn.

– ORIGIN Old English, 'telling, something told.'

> **USAGE**
>
> On the confusion of **tale** and **tail**, see the note at **TAIL**[1].

ta·leg·gio /təˈlejē-ō/ ▸ **noun** a soft Italian cheese made from cow's milk.
– ORIGIN named after the *Taleggio* valley in Lombardy.

tal·ent /ˈtalənt/ ▸ **noun 1** natural ability or skill. **2** people possessing natural ability or skill. **3** an ancient weight and unit of currency. **4** chiefly Brit. informal people regarded in terms of their sexual attractiveness or availability.

> – SYNONYMS **flair,** aptitude, facility, gift, knack, technique, bent, ability, forte, genius, brilliance.

– DERIVATIVES **tal·ent·less** adjective.
– ORIGIN Greek *talanton* 'weight, sum of money': sense 1 derives from the parable of the talents (Gospel of Matthew, chapter 25).

tal·ent·ed /ˈtaləntid/ ▸ **adjective** having a natural ability or skill for something.

> – SYNONYMS *a talented sculptor* **gifted,** skillful, accomplished, brilliant, expert, consummate, able, proficient; informal ace.
> – ANTONYMS inept.

tal·ent scout ▸ **noun** a person whose job is searching for talented performers, especially in sports and entertainment.

tal·is·man /ˈtalismən, -iz-/ ▸ **noun** (pl. **talismans**) an object thought to have magic powers and to bring good luck.
– DERIVATIVES **tal·is·man·ic** /ˌtalizˈmanik/ adjective.
– ORIGIN Arabic.

talk /tôk/ ▸ **verb 1** speak in order to give information or express ideas or feelings. **2** be able to speak. **3** (**talk something over/through**) discuss something thoroughly. **4** (**talk back**) reply in a defiant or insolent way. **5** (**talk down to**) speak to someone in a way that suggests one feels superior to them. **6** (**talk someone around/round**) persuade someone to accept or agree to something. **7** (**talk someone into/out of**) convince someone to do or not to do something. **8** reveal secret or private information.

> – SYNONYMS **1 speak,** chat, chatter, gossip, jabber, prattle; informal yak. **2** *they were able to talk in peace* **converse,** communicate, speak (to one another), confer, consult, negotiate, parley; informal have a confab.

▸ **noun 1** conversation or discussion. **2** rumor, gossip, or speculation: *there's talk of a conspiracy.* **3** (**talks**) formal discussions or negotiations. **4** a speech or lecture.

> – SYNONYMS **1 conversation,** chat, discussion, tête-à-tête, heart-to-heart, dialogue; informal confab, gossip. **2 chatter,** gossip, prattle, jabbering; informal yak. **3** (**talks**) **negotiations,** discussions, conference, summit, meeting, consultation, dialogue. **4 lecture,** speech, address, discourse, oration, presentation, report, sermon.

– DERIVATIVES **talk·er** noun.
– PHRASES **you should talk** informal used to tell someone that the criticism they are making applies equally well to them. **now you're talking** informal expressing enthusiastic agreement or approval. **talk the talk** informal speak in a way intended to convince or impress someone.
– ORIGIN from **TALE** or **TELL**.

talk·a·tive /ˈtôkətiv/ ▸ **adjective** fond of talking.

> – SYNONYMS **chatty,** garrulous, loquacious, voluble, communicative; informal mouthy.
> – ANTONYMS taciturn.

– DERIVATIVES **talk·a·tive·ly** adverb **talk·a·tive·ness** noun.

> **WORD TOOLKIT**
>
> | **talkative ...** | **voluble ...** | **garrulous ...** |
> |---|---|---|
> | mood | critics | old fool |
> | nature | crowd | crows |
> | child | public | big shot |
> | fellow | actress | crone |
> | parrot | fans | geezer |

talk·ie /ˈtôkē/ ▸ **noun** informal a movie with a soundtrack, as distinct from a silent movie.

talk·ing book ▸ **noun** a recorded reading of a book.

talk·ing head ▸ **noun** informal a commentator or reporter on television who speaks to the camera and is viewed in closeup.

talk·ing point ▸ **noun** a topic that causes discussion or argument.

talk·ing-to ▸ **noun** informal a sharp reprimand.

talk ra·di·o ▸ **noun** a type of radio program in which topical issues are discussed by the host and by listeners who phone in.

talk show ▸ **noun** a television or radio program in which celebrities or other guests talk informally to a host.

talk·time /'tôk,tīm/ ▸ **noun** the time during which a cell phone is in use to handle calls, especially as a measure of the duration of the battery.

tall /tôl/ ▸ **adjective 1** of great or more than average height. **2** measuring a specified distance from top to bottom.

– SYNONYMS **1** *a tall man* **big,** large, huge, giant, lanky, gangling. **2** *tall buildings* **high,** big, lofty, towering, sky-high, gigantic, colossal.
– ANTONYMS short, low.

– DERIVATIVES **tall·ish** adjective **tall·ness** noun.
– PHRASES **a tall order** an unreasonable or difficult demand. **a tall story** (or **tale**) an account that is difficult to believe and seems unlikely to be true.
– ORIGIN probably from Old English, 'swift, prompt.'

tall·boy /'tôl,boi/ ▸ **noun** a tall chest of drawers in two sections, one standing on the other.

tal·low /'talō/ ▸ **noun** a hard substance made from animal fat, used (especially in the past) in making candles and soap.
– DERIVATIVES **tal·low·y** adjective.
– ORIGIN perhaps from German.

tall ship ▸ **noun** a sailing ship with a high mast or masts.

tal·ly /'talē/ ▸ **noun** (pl. **tallies**) **1** a current score or amount. **2** a record of a score or amount. **3** (also **tally stick**) historical a piece of wood marked with notches as a record of the items in an account.

– SYNONYMS **running total,** count, record, reckoning, register, account, roll.

▸ **verb** (**tallies, tallying, tallied**) **1** agree or correspond: *this account does not tally with accounts from local people.* **2** calculate the total number of something.

– SYNONYMS **correspond,** agree, accord, concur, coincide, match, fit, be consistent, conform, equate, parallel; informal square.
– ANTONYMS disagree.

– ORIGIN Old French *tallie.*

tal·ly-ho ▸ **exclamation** a huntsman's cry to the hounds on sighting a fox.
– ORIGIN probably from French *taïaut.*

Tal·mud /'täl,mo͝od, 'talməd/ ▸ **noun** a collection of ancient writings on Jewish civil and ceremonial law and legend.
– DERIVATIVES **Tal·mud·ic** /tal'm(y)o͞odik, -'mo͝odik/ adjective **Tal·mud·ist** /'tälmo͝odist, 'talməd-/ noun.
– ORIGIN Hebrew, 'instruction.'

tal·on /'talən/ ▸ **noun** a claw of a bird of prey.
– DERIVATIVES **tal·oned** adjective.
– ORIGIN Old French, 'heel.'

ta·lus[1] /'tāləs/ ▸ **noun** (pl. **tali** /'tālī/) the bone in the ankle that forms a movable joint with the shinbone.
– ORIGIN Latin, 'ankle, heel.'

talus[2] ▸ **noun** (pl. **taluses**) a sloping mass of rock fragments at the foot of a cliff.
– ORIGIN French.

tam /tam/ ▸ **noun** a tam-o'-shanter.

ta·ma·le /tə'mälē/ ▸ **noun** a Mexican dish of seasoned meat wrapped in cornmeal dough and steamed or baked in corn husks.
– ORIGIN Mexican Spanish *tamal,* from Nahuatl.

tam·a·rack /'tamə,rak/ ▸ **noun** a slender North American larch.
– ORIGIN Canadian French.

ta·ma·ril·lo /,tamə'rilō, -'rē-ō/ ▸ **noun** (pl. **tamarillos**) the red egg-shaped fruit of a tropical South American plant.
– ORIGIN an invented name.

tam·a·rin /'tamərin, -,ran/ ▸ **noun** a small monkey native to forests in South America.
– ORIGIN Carib.

tam·a·rind /'tamə,rind/ ▸ **noun** sticky brown acidic pulp from the pod of a tropical African tree, used in Asian cooking.
– ORIGIN Arabic, 'Indian date.'

tam·a·risk /'tamə,risk/ ▸ **noun** a shrub or small tree with tiny scalelike leaves on slender branches.
– ORIGIN Latin *tamarix.*

tam·bour /'tam,bo͝or/ ▸ **noun 1** historical a small drum. **2** a circular frame for holding fabric taut while it is being embroidered.
– ORIGIN French, 'drum.'

tam·bou·rine /,tambə'rēn/ ▸ **noun** a percussion instrument resembling a shallow drum with metal disks around the edge, played by being shaken or hit with the hand.
– ORIGIN French *tambourin* 'small tambour.'

tame /tām/ ▸ **adjective 1** (of an animal) not dangerous or frightened of people. **2** not exciting or adventurous: *Saturday night TV is a pretty tame affair.* **3** informal (of a person) willing to cooperate.

– SYNONYMS **1 domesticated,** docile, trained, gentle, mild, pet. **2 unexciting,** uninteresting, uninspiring, uninspired, dull, bland, flat, pedestrian, humdrum, boring.
– ANTONYMS wild.

▸ **verb 1** make an animal tame. **2** control or make less powerful: *the battle to tame inflation.*

– SYNONYMS **1 domesticate,** break in, train. **2** *she learned to tame her emotions* **subdue,** curb, control, calm, master, moderate, discipline, overcome.

– DERIVATIVES **tame·ly** adverb **tame·ness** noun **tam·er** noun.
– ORIGIN Old English.

Tam·il /'taməl/ ▸ **noun 1** a member of a people living in parts of South India and Sri Lanka. **2** the language of the Tamils.
– ORIGIN Tamil.

tam-o'-shan·ter /'tam ə ,SHantər/ ▸ **noun** a round Scottish cap with a pompom in the center.
– ORIGIN named after the hero of Robert Burns's poem *Tam o' Shanter.*

ta·mox·i·fen /tə'mäksəfən/ ▸ **noun** a synthetic drug used to treat breast cancer and infertility in women.
– ORIGIN from the drug's chemical name.

tamp /tamp/ ▶ **verb** firmly ram or pack a substance down or into something.
– ORIGIN probably from French *tampon* 'tampon, plug.'

tam·per /'tampər/ ▶ **verb** (**tamper with**) interfere with something without permission or so as to cause damage.

> – SYNONYMS **interfere,** meddle, monkey around, tinker, fiddle; informal mess around/about.

– DERIVATIVES **tam·per·er** noun.
– ORIGIN from **TEMPER**.

tam·pon /'tam,pän/ ▶ **noun** a plug of soft material put into the vagina to absorb blood during a woman's period.
– ORIGIN French.

tan¹ /tan/ ▶ **noun 1** a golden-brown shade of skin developed by pale-skinned people after being in the sun. **2** a yellowish-brown color. ▶ **verb** (**tans, tanning, tanned**) **1** become golden brown after being in the sun. **2** convert animal skin into leather. **3** informal, dated beat someone as a punishment.
– DERIVATIVES **tan·ner** noun.
– ORIGIN Old English.

tan² ▶ **abbreviation** tangent.

tan·a·ger /'tanəjər/ ▶ **noun** a brightly colored American songbird.
– ORIGIN Tupi.

tan·dem /'tandəm/ ▶ **noun** a bicycle with seats and pedals for two riders, one behind the other.
– PHRASES **in tandem** together or at the same time.
– ORIGIN from Latin, 'at length.'

tan·door /tan'do͝or, tän-/ ▶ **noun** a clay oven of a type used originally in northern India and Pakistan.
– ORIGIN Arabic.

tan·door·i /tan'do͝orē, tän-/ ▶ **adjective** (of Indian food) cooked in a tandoor.

tang /taNG/ ▶ **noun 1** a strong taste, flavor, or smell. **2** the projection on the blade of a knife or other tool by which the blade is held firmly in the handle.
– ORIGIN Old Norse, 'point, tang of a knife.'

tan·gent /'tanjənt/ ▶ **noun 1** a straight line or plane that touches a curve or curved surface at a point, but if extended does not cross it at that point. **2** Mathematics the ratio of the sides (other than the hypotenuse) opposite and adjacent to an angle in a right triangle. **3** a completely different line of thought or action: *her mind went off on a tangent.*
– DERIVATIVES **tan·gen·cy** noun.
– ORIGIN from Latin *tangere* 'to touch.'

tan·gen·tial /tan'jenCHəl/ ▶ **adjective 1** only slightly connected or relevant: *such concoctions have only a tangential relationship with food as eaten in India.* **2** relating to or along a tangent.
– DERIVATIVES **tan·gen·tial·ly** adverb.

tan·ge·rine /,tanjə'rēn/ ▶ **noun 1** a small citrus fruit with a loose orange-red skin. **2** a deep orange-red color.
– ORIGIN from *Tanger*, the former name of *Tangier* in Morocco.

tan·gi·ble /'tanjəbəl/ ▶ **adjective 1** able to be perceived by touch. **2** clear and definite; real: *I was seeing tangible benefits from working out.*

> – SYNONYMS **real,** actual, physical, solid, palpable, material, substantial, concrete, visible, definite, perceptible, discernible.
> – ANTONYMS abstract, theoretical.

– DERIVATIVES **tan·gi·bil·i·ty** /,tanjə'bilitē/ noun **tan·gi·bly** /-blē/ adverb.
– ORIGIN Latin *tangibilis.*

tan·gle /'taNGgəl/ ▶ **verb 1** twist strands together into a confused mass. **2** (**tangle with**) informal become involved in a conflict with.

> – SYNONYMS **entangle,** snarl, catch, entwine, twist, knot, mat.

▶ **noun 1** a confused mass of something twisted together. **2** a confused or complicated state.

> – SYNONYMS **1 snarl,** mass, knot, mesh. **2 muddle,** mix-up, confusion, jumble, shambles.

– DERIVATIVES **tan·gly** adjective.
– ORIGIN probably Scandinavian.

tan·go /'taNGgō/ ▶ **noun** (pl. **tangos**) **1** a Latin American ballroom dance characterized by marked rhythms and postures and abrupt pauses. **2** a piece of music in the style of a tango. ▶ **verb** (**tangoes, tangoing, tangoed**) dance the tango.
– ORIGIN Latin American Spanish.

tang·y /'taNGē/ ▶ **adjective** (**tangier, tangiest**) having a strong, sharp flavor or smell.

> – SYNONYMS **zesty,** sharp, tart, sour, bitter, piquant, spicy, tasty, flavorsome, pungent.
> – ANTONYMS bland.

– DERIVATIVES **tang·i·ness** noun.

tank /taNGk/ ▶ **noun 1** a large container or storage chamber for holding liquid or gas. **2** the container holding the fuel supply in a motor vehicle. **3** a container with transparent sides in which to keep fish. **4** a heavy armored fighting vehicle carrying guns and moving on a continuous metal track.

> – SYNONYMS **container,** receptacle, vat, cistern, repository, reservoir, basin.

▶ **verb** (**be/get tanked up**) informal drink heavily or become drunk.
– DERIVATIVES **tank·ful** /-,fo͝ol/ noun.
– ORIGIN perhaps from a word in Gujarati or Marathi (an Indian language) meaning 'underground cistern.'

tan·kard /'taNGkərd/ ▶ **noun** a tall beer mug with a handle and sometimes a hinged lid.
– ORIGIN perhaps from Dutch *tanckaert.*

tank·er /'taNGkər/ ▶ **noun** a ship, road vehicle, or aircraft for carrying liquids in bulk.

tank top ▶ **noun** a close-fitting sleeveless top.

tan·ner·y /'tanərē/ ▶ **noun** (pl. **tanneries**) a place where animal hides are tanned.

tan·nic ac·id /'tanik/ ▶ **noun** another term for **TANNIN**.

tan·nin /'tanin/ ▶ **noun** a bitter yellowish or brownish substance present in tea, grapes, and the bark of some trees.
– DERIVATIVES **tan·nic** adjective.
– ORIGIN French *tanin.*

tan·ning bed ▶ **noun** a piece of equipment for acquiring an artificial tan, consisting of two banks of sunlamps between which a person lies or stands.

tan·sy /'tanzē/ ▶ **noun** a plant with yellow flat-topped buttonlike flowerheads.
– ORIGIN Old French *tanesie.*

tan·ta·lize /'tantl,īz/ ▶ **verb** torment or tease someone by showing or promising them something that they cannot have.

> – SYNONYMS **tease,** torment, torture, tempt, entice, lure, beguile, excite, fascinate, titillate, intrigue.

– DERIVATIVES **tan·ta·li·za·tion** /ˌtantliˈzāsʜən/ noun **tan·ta·liz·ing** adjective.
– ORIGIN from *Tantalus* in Greek mythology, who was punished by being provided with fruit and water that moved away when he reached for them.

tan·ta·lum /ˈtantl-əm/ ▶ **noun** a hard silver-gray metallic chemical element.
– ORIGIN from *Tantalus* (see **TANTALIZE**), with reference to its frustrating insolubility in acids.

tan·ta·mount /ˈtantəˌmount/ ▶ **adjective** (**tantamount to**) equivalent in seriousness to: *the resignations were tantamount to an admission of guilt.*
– ORIGIN from Italian *tanto montare* 'amount to as much.'

tan·tra /ˈtəntrə, ˈtan-/ ▶ **noun 1** a Hindu or Buddhist written work dealing with mystical or magical practices. **2** the fact of following the principles of these works, involving mantras, meditation, yoga, and ritual.
– DERIVATIVES **tan·tric** /-trik/ adjective **tan·trism** /-ˌtrizəm/ noun.
– ORIGIN Sanskrit, 'loom, groundwork, doctrine.'

tan·trum /ˈtantrəm/ ▶ **noun** an uncontrolled outburst of anger and frustration.

– SYNONYMS **fit of temper,** fit of rage, outburst, pet, paroxysm, frenzy; informal hissy fit.

– ORIGIN unknown.

Tan·za·ni·an /ˌtanzəˈnēən/ ▶ **noun** a person from Tanzania, a country in East Africa. ▶ **adjective** relating to Tanzania.

Taoi·seach /ˈtēsʜək, -sʜəkʜ, ˈtʜē-/ ▶ **noun** the prime minister of the Republic of Ireland.
– ORIGIN Irish, 'chief, leader.'

Tao·ism /ˈdouˌizəm, ˈtou-/ ▶ **noun** a Chinese philosophy based on the belief that everything in the universe is connected and that a person should try to balance the opposing principles of yin and yang to reach a calm acceptance of life.
– DERIVATIVES **Tao·ist** noun & adjective.
– ORIGIN from Chinese, 'the right way.'

tap[1] /tap/ ▶ **noun 1** a device for controlling a flow of liquid or gas from a pipe or container. **2** a device connected to a telephone for listening secretly to conversations.

– SYNONYMS **faucet,** spigot, valve, stopcock.

▶ **verb** (**taps, tapping, tapped**) **1** make use of a resource or supply: *clients seeking to tap the agency's resources of expertise.* **2** connect a device to a telephone in order to listen to conversations secretly. **3** draw liquid through the tap or spout of a cask, barrel, etc. **4** draw sap from a tree by cutting into it. **5** informal obtain money or information from someone.

– SYNONYMS **1 draw on,** exploit, milk, mine, use, utilize, turn to account. **2 bug,** wiretap, monitor, eavesdrop on.

– DERIVATIVES **tap·pa·ble** adjective.
– PHRASES **on tap** informal freely available whenever needed.
– ORIGIN Old English, 'stopper for a cask.'

tap[2] ▶ **verb** (**taps, tapping, tapped**) **1** hit someone or something with a quick, light blow or blows. **2** strike something lightly and repeatedly against something else.

– SYNONYMS **knock,** rap, strike, beat, pat, drum.

▶ **noun 1** a quick, light blow. **2** a piece of metal attached to the toe and heel of a tap dancer's shoe. **3** tap dancing.
– DERIVATIVES **tap·per** noun.
– ORIGIN Old French *taper.*

ta·pas /ˈtäpəs/ ▶ **plural noun** small Spanish savory dishes, typically served with drinks at a bar.
– ORIGIN Spanish *tapa* 'cover, lid' (because the dishes were served on a dish balanced on the glass of a drink).

tap dance ▶ **noun** a dance performed wearing shoes fitted with metal taps, characterized by rhythmical tapping of the toes and heels.
– DERIVATIVES **tap danc·er** noun **tap-dancing** noun.

tape /tāp/ ▶ **noun 1** light, flexible material in a narrow strip, used to hold, fasten, or mark off something. **2** (also **adhesive tape**) a strip of paper or plastic coated with adhesive, used to stick things together. **3** a kind of tape with magnetic properties, used for recording sound, pictures, or computer data. **4** a cassette or reel containing magnetic tape.

– SYNONYMS **1 binding,** ribbon, string, braid, band. **2 cassette,** recording, video.

▶ **verb 1** record sound or pictures on magnetic tape. **2** fasten, attach, or mark off something with tape.

– SYNONYMS **1 bind,** stick, fix, fasten, secure, attach. **2 record,** tape-record, video.

– ORIGIN Old English.

tape deck ▶ **noun** a piece of equipment for playing audiotapes, especially as part of a stereo system.

tape meas·ure ▶ **noun** a strip of tape marked at regular intervals for measuring something.

ta·pe·nade /ˌtäpəˈnäd/ ▶ **noun** a Provençal savory paste or dip, made from black olives, capers, and anchovies.
– ORIGIN Provençal.

ta·per /ˈtāpər/ ▶ **verb 1** reduce in thickness toward one end. **2** (**taper off**) gradually lessen.

– SYNONYMS **1 narrow,** thin (out), come to a point, attenuate. **2** (**taper off**) **decrease,** lessen, dwindle, diminish, reduce, decline, die down, peter out, wane, ebb, slacken (off), fall off, let up, thin out.
– ANTONYMS thicken.

▶ **noun 1** a long, thin candle. **2** a wick coated with wax, or a long piece of paper or wood, used for lighting a lamp, candle, etc.
– ORIGIN Old English.

tape re·cord·er ▶ **noun** a device for recording sounds on magnetic tape and then reproducing them.
– DERIVATIVES **tape-re·cord** verb **tape re·cord·ing** noun.

tap·es·try /ˈtapistrē/ ▶ **noun** (pl. **tapestries**) a piece of thick fabric with pictures or designs woven or embroidered on it.
– DERIVATIVES **tap·es·tried** adjective.
– ORIGIN Old French *tapisserie.*

tape·worm /ˈtāpˌwərm/ ▶ **noun** a flatworm with a long ribbonlike body, the adult of which lives as a parasite in the intestines.

tap·i·o·ca /ˌtapēˈōkə/ ▶ **noun** a starchy substance in the form of hard white grains, obtained from cassava and used for puddings and other dishes.
– ORIGIN Tupi-Guarani, 'squeezed-out dregs.'

ta·pir /ˈtāpər/ ▶ **noun** a piglike mammal with a long flexible snout, native to tropical America and Malaysia.
– ORIGIN Tupi.

tap·pet /ˈtapit/ ▶ **noun** a moving part in a machine that transmits motion in a straight line between a cam and another part.
– ORIGIN from **TAP**[2].

tap·room /ˈtap,ro͞om, -,ro͝om/ ▶ **noun** a room in which beer is available on tap; a bar in a hotel or inn.

tap·root /ˈtap,ro͞ot, -,ro͝ot/ ▶ **noun** a tapering root growing straight downward and forming the center from which smaller roots spring.

tap wa·ter ▶ **noun** water from a piped supply; water from a faucet.

tar[1] /tär/ ▶ **noun 1** a dark, thick flammable liquid distilled from wood or coal, used in road-making and for preserving timber. **2** a similar substance formed by burning tobacco or other material. ▶ **verb** (**tars, tarring, tarred**) cover something with tar.
– PHRASES **tar and feather someone** smear someone with tar and then cover them with feathers as a punishment. **tar people with the same brush** consider certain people to have the same faults.
– ORIGIN Old English.

tar[2] ▶ **noun** informal, dated a sailor.
– ORIGIN perhaps short for **TARPAULIN**, formerly used as a nickname for a sailor.

ta·ra·ma·sa·la·ta (also **taramosalata**) /ˌtärəməsəˈlätə/ ▶ **noun** a dip made from the roe of cod or other fish, olive oil, and seasoning.
– ORIGIN from modern Greek *taramas* 'roe' + *salata* 'salad.'

tar·an·tel·la /ˌtarənˈtelə/ ▶ **noun** a rapid whirling dance originating in southern Italy.
– ORIGIN Italian.

ta·ran·tu·la /təˈrancнələ/ ▶ **noun 1** a very large hairy spider found chiefly in tropical and subtropical America. **2** a large black spider of southern Europe.
– ORIGIN Italian *tarantola*.

tar·boosh /tärˈbo͞osн/ ▶ **noun** a hat similar to a fez worn by Muslim men in some countries.
– ORIGIN Egyptian Arabic.

tar·dy /ˈtärdē/ ▶ **adjective** (**tardier, tardiest**) **1** late in happening. **2** slow to act or respond: *the law may be tardy in reacting to changing attitudes*.
– DERIVATIVES **tar·di·ly** adverb **tar·di·ness** noun.
– ORIGIN Latin *tardus* 'slow.'

tare[1] /te(ə)r/ ▶ **noun 1** a vetch (plant). **2** (in the Bible) a type of weed.
– ORIGIN unknown.

tare[2] ▶ **noun 1** the weight of a vehicle without its fuel or load. **2** an allowance made for the weight of the packaging in determining the net weight of goods.
– ORIGIN French, 'deficiency, tare.'

tar·get /ˈtärgit/ ▶ **noun 1** a person, object, or place selected as the aim of an attack. **2** a board marked with a series of circles sharing the same center, aimed at in archery or shooting. **3** a goal or result that one aims to achieve: *a sales target*.

– SYNONYMS **1 objective,** goal, aim, mark, end, plan, intention, aspiration, ambition. **2 victim,** butt, recipient, focus, object, subject.

▶ **verb** (**targets, targeting, targeted**) **1** select someone or something as an object of attention or attack. **2** aim or direct something.

– SYNONYMS **1 pick out,** single out, earmark, fix on, attack, aim at, fire at. **2** *a product targeted at women* **aim at,** direct at, level at, intend for, focus on.

– DERIVATIVES **tar·get·a·ble** adjective.
– PHRASES **on** (or **off**) **target** succeeding (or not succeeding) in hitting or achieving the thing aimed at.
– ORIGIN Old English, 'small round shield.'

tar·iff /ˈtarif/ ▶ **noun 1** a tax or duty to be paid on a particular class of imports or exports. **2** a list of the fixed prices charged by a business such as a hotel or restaurant. **3** Law a scale of sentences and damages for crimes and injuries of varying degrees of seriousness.

– SYNONYMS **1 tax,** duty, toll, excise, levy, charge, rate, fee. **2 price list,** menu.

▶ **verb** fix the price of something according to a tariff.
– ORIGIN Italian *tariffa*.

tar·mac /ˈtär,mak/ ▶ **noun 1** trademark material used for surfacing roads or other outdoor areas, consisting of broken stone mixed with tar. **2** (**the tarmac**) a runway or other area surfaced with tarmac. ▶ **verb** (**tarmacs, tarmacking, tarmacked**) surface an area with tarmac.
– ORIGIN from **TAR**[1] + **MACADAM**.

tarn /tärn/ ▶ **noun** a small mountain lake.
– ORIGIN Old Norse.

tar·na·tion /tärˈnāsнən/ ▶ **noun & exclamation** used as a euphemism for **DAMNATION**.

tar·nish /ˈtärnisн/ ▶ **verb 1** (of metal) become dull as a result of exposure to air or moisture. **2** cause harm or a loss of respect to: *they will make up negative stories to tarnish my image*.

– SYNONYMS **1 discolor,** rust, oxidize, corrode, stain, dull, blacken. **2 sully,** blacken, stain, blemish, ruin, disgrace, mar, damage, harm, drag through the mud.

▶ **noun** a film or stain formed on an exposed surface of a mineral or metal.

– SYNONYMS **discoloration,** oxidation, rust, verdigris.

– DERIVATIVES **tar·nish·a·ble** adjective.
– ORIGIN French *ternir*.

ta·ro /ˈtarō, ˈte(ə)rō/ ▶ **noun** the starchy corm of a tropical Asian plant, eaten as a vegetable.
– ORIGIN Polynesian.

ta·rot /ˈtarō, ˈte(ə)rō, təˈrō/ ▶ **noun** a set of special playing cards used for fortune-telling.
– ORIGIN French.

tarp /tärp/ ▶ **noun** informal a tarpaulin sheet or cover.

tar·pau·lin /tärˈpôlən, ˈtärpə-/ ▶ **noun 1** heavy-duty waterproof cloth. **2** a sheet of tarpaulin used as a covering.
– ORIGIN probably from **TAR**[1] + **PALL**[1] (the cloth was originally made of tarred canvas).

tar·pon /ˈtärpən/ ▶ **noun** a large tropical sea fish resembling a herring in appearance.
– ORIGIN probably from Dutch *tarpoen*.

tar·ra·gon /ˈtarə,gän, -gən/ ▶ **noun** a plant with narrow strong-tasting leaves, used as an herb in cooking.
– ORIGIN from Latin *tragonia* and *tarchon*.

tar·ry[1] /ˈtärē/ ▶ **adjective** relating to or covered with tar.
– DERIVATIVES **tar·ri·ness** noun.

tar·ry[2] /ˈtarē/ ▶ **verb** (**tarries, tarrying, tarried**) literary stay longer than intended.
– ORIGIN unknown.

tar·sal /ˈtärsəl/ ▶ **adjective** relating to the tarsus. ▶ **noun** a bone of the tarsus.

tar·si·er /ˈtärsēər/ ▶ **noun** a small tree-dwelling primate (mammal) with very large eyes, native to the islands of SE Asia.
– ORIGIN French.

tar·sus /ˈtärsəs/ ▶ **noun** (pl. **tarsi** /ˈtärsī, -sē/) the group of

small bones in the ankle and upper foot.
– ORIGIN Greek *tarsos* 'flat of the foot, the eyelid.'

tart[1] /tärt/ ▶ **noun** an open pastry case containing a sweet or savory filling.

– SYNONYMS **pastry,** flan, quiche, tartlet, vol-au-vent, pie.

– DERIVATIVES **tart·let** /-lit/ noun.
– ORIGIN Old French *tarte.*

tart[2] informal ▶ **noun 1** derogatory a woman who has many sexual partners. **2** a prostitute. ▶ **verb** informal, chiefly Brit. **1** (**tart oneself up**) make oneself look attractive with clothes or makeup. **2** (**tart something up**) improve the appearance of something.
– DERIVATIVES **tart·y** adjective (**tartier, tartiest**).
– ORIGIN probably from **SWEETHEART.**

tart[3] ▶ **adjective 1** sharp or acid in taste. **2** (of a remark or tone of voice) sharp or sarcastic.

– SYNONYMS **1 sour,** sharp, acidic, zesty, tangy, piquant. **2 scathing,** sharp, biting, cutting, sarcastic, hurtful, spiteful.
– ANTONYMS sweet, kind.

– DERIVATIVES **tart·ly** adverb **tart·ness** noun.
– ORIGIN Old English, 'harsh, severe.'

tar·tan /ˈtärtn/ ▶ **noun 1** a pattern of colored checks and intersecting lines, especially one associated with a particular Scottish clan. **2** a woolen cloth with a tartan pattern.
– ORIGIN perhaps from Old French *tertaine*, referring to a kind of cloth.

Tar·tar /ˈtärtər/ ▶ **noun 1** historical a member of a group of central Asian peoples who conquered much of Asia and eastern Europe in the early 13th century. **2** (**tartar**) a person who is fierce or difficult to deal with.
– ORIGIN alteration of **TATAR.**

tar·tar /ˈtärtər/ ▶ **noun 1** a hard deposit that forms on the teeth and contributes to their decay. **2** a deposit of impure cream of tartar formed during the fermentation of wine.
– ORIGIN Greek *tartaron.*

tar·tare /tärˈtär, ˈtärtər/ ▶ **adjective** (of fish or meat) served raw, seasoned and shaped into small cakes: *steak tartare.*
– ORIGIN French, 'Tartar.'

tar·tar·ic ac·id /tärˈtarik/ ▶ **noun** an organic acid found especially in unripe grapes and used in baking powders and as a food additive.
– ORIGIN from **TARTAR.**

tar·tar sauce (also **tartare sauce**) ▶ **noun** mayonnaise mixed with chopped onions, pickles, and capers, typically eaten with fish.

tar·tra·zine /ˈtärtrəˌzēn, -zin/ ▶ **noun** a bright yellow synthetic dye made from tartaric acid and used to color food, drugs, and cosmetics.

Tar·zan /ˈtärzan, -zən/ ▶ **noun** a very strong and agile man.
– ORIGIN named after a fictional character created by the American writer Edgar Rice Burroughs.

task /task/ ▶ **noun** a piece of work to be done.

– SYNONYMS **job,** duty, chore, charge, assignment, detail, mission, engagement, occupation, undertaking, exercise.

▶ **verb** (**task someone with**) give a task to someone.
– PHRASES **take someone to task** reprimand or criticize someone.
– ORIGIN Old French *tasche.*

task force ▶ **noun 1** an armed force organized for a special operation. **2** a group of people specially organized for a task.

task·mas·ter /ˈtaskˌmastər/ ▶ **noun** (fem. **taskmistress**) a person who makes someone work very hard.

Tas·ma·ni·an dev·il /tazˈmānēən, -ˈmānyən/ ▶ **noun** a heavily built aggressive marsupial with a large head, powerful jaws, and mainly black fur, found only on the Australian island of Tasmania.

tas·sel /ˈtasəl/ ▶ **noun 1** a tuft of hanging threads, knotted together at one end and used for decoration in soft furnishing and clothing. **2** the tufted head of some plants.
– DERIVATIVES **tas·seled** adjective.
– ORIGIN Old French, 'clasp.'

taste /tāst/ ▶ **noun 1** the sensation of flavor perceived in the mouth on contact with a substance. **2** the sense by which taste is perceived. **3** a small amount of food or drink taken as a sample. **4** a brief experience of something: *it was his first taste of artistic success.* **5** a person's liking for something. **6** the ability to judge what is of good quality or of a high artistic standard. **7** (**taste for**) a liking for or interest in something. **8** (often **in good** (or **bad**) **taste**) the quality of being (or not being) acceptable: *a joke in bad taste.*

– SYNONYMS **1 flavor,** savor, relish, tang. **2 mouthful,** morsel, drop, bit, sip, nip, touch, soupçon, dash. **3** *a taste for adventure* **liking,** love, fondness, fancy, desire, penchant, partiality, inclination, appetite, stomach, palate, thirst, hunger. **4** *his first taste of opera* **experience with,** impression of, exposure to, contact with, involvement with. **5 judgment,** discrimination, discernment, refinement, elegance, grace, style. **6 sensitivity,** decorum, propriety, etiquette, nicety, discretion.

▶ **verb 1** perceive the flavor of something. **2** have a specified flavor. **3** test the flavor of something by eating or drinking a small amount of it. **4** have a brief experience of: *the team has not yet tasted victory.*

– SYNONYMS **1** *I tasted the wine* **sample,** test, try, savor. **2** *he could taste blood* **perceive,** discern, make out, distinguish.

– PHRASES **a bad** (or **bitter**) **taste in someone's mouth** a feeling of distress or disgust following an experience. **to taste** according to one's personal liking.
– ORIGIN Old French *taster* 'touch, try, taste.'

WORD LINKS

gustatory *relating to the sense of taste*

taste bud ▶ **noun** any of the clusters of nerve endings on the tongue and in the lining of the mouth that provide the sense of taste.

taste·ful /ˈtāstfəl/ ▶ **adjective** showing good judgment as to quality, appearance, or appropriate behavior.

– SYNONYMS **stylish,** refined, cultured, elegant, smart, chic, exquisite.
– ANTONYMS tasteless.

– DERIVATIVES **taste·ful·ly** adverb **taste·ful·ness** noun.

taste·less /ˈtāstlis/ ▶ **adjective 1** lacking flavor. **2** lacking in judgment as to quality, appearance, or appropriate behavior.

– SYNONYMS **1 flavorless,** bland, insipid, unappetizing, watery, weak, thin. **2 vulgar,** crude, tawdry, garish, gaudy, loud, trashy, showy, ostentatious, cheap; informal flash, tacky, kitsch.

3 **crude,** indelicate, uncouth, crass, tactless, undiplomatic, indiscreet, inappropriate, offensive.
– ANTONYMS tasty, tasteful.

– DERIVATIVES **taste·less·ly** adverb **taste·less·ness** noun.

tast·er /ˈtāstər/ ▶ **noun** a person who tests food or drink by tasting it.

-tastic ▶ **combining form** informal forming adjectives referring to someone or something that is excellent in a particular respect: *poptastic*.
– ORIGIN from **FANTASTIC**.

tast·y /ˈtāstē/ ▶ **adjective** (**tastier, tastiest**) **1** (of food) having a pleasant, distinct flavor. **2** informal, chiefly Brit. attractive or appealing.

– SYNONYMS **delicious,** palatable, luscious, mouthwatering, delectable, appetizing, tempting; informal yummy, scrumptious.
– ANTONYMS bland.

– DERIVATIVES **tast·i·ly** adverb **tast·i·ness** noun.

ta·ta·mi /təˈtämē/ ▶ **noun** (pl. same or **tatamis**) a rush-covered straw mat forming a traditional Japanese floor covering.
– ORIGIN Japanese.

Ta·tar /ˈtätər/ ▶ **noun 1** a member of a Turkic people living in Tatarstan and other parts of Russia and Ukraine. **2** the Turkic language of this people.
– ORIGIN the Turkic name of a Tartar tribe.

ta·ter /ˈtātər/ ▶ **noun** informal a potato.
– ORIGIN from **POTATO**.

tat·tered /ˈtatərd/ ▶ **adjective 1** old and torn. **2** ruined; in tatters.

tat·ters /ˈtatərz/ ▶ **plural noun** irregularly torn pieces of cloth, paper, etc.
– PHRASES **in tatters** destroyed; ruined.
– ORIGIN Old Norse, 'rags.'

tat·ting /ˈtatiNG/ ▶ **noun 1** a kind of knotted lace made by hand with a small shuttle. **2** the process of making such lace.
– ORIGIN unknown.

tat·tle /ˈtatl/ ▶ **noun** gossip; casual talk. ▶ **verb** gossip about someone or something.
– DERIVATIVES **tat·tler** noun.
– ORIGIN Flemish *tatelen, tateren*.

tat·tle·tale /ˈtatlˌtāl/ ▶ **noun** a person who reports other people's wrongdoings or reveals their secrets.

tat·too[1] /taˈto͞o/ ▶ **noun** (pl. **tattoos**) a permanent design made on the skin by making small holes in it with a needle and filling them with colored ink. ▶ **verb** (**tattoos, tattooing, tattooed**) mark a person's skin in this way.
– DERIVATIVES **tat·too·er** noun **tat·too·ist** noun.
– ORIGIN Polynesian.

tat·too[2] ▶ **noun** (pl. **tattoos**) **1** an evening drum or bugle signal recalling soldiers to their quarters. **2** a rhythmic tapping or drumming.
– ORIGIN from Dutch *taptoe!* 'close the tap of the cask!'

tat·ty /ˈtatē/ ▶ **adjective** (**tattier, tattiest**) informal worn and shabby.
– DERIVATIVES **tat·ti·ly** adverb **tat·ti·ness** noun.
– ORIGIN from Old English, 'rag.'

taught /tôt/ past and past participle of **TEACH**.

taunt /tônt/ ▶ **noun** a remark made in order to anger, upset, or provoke someone.

– SYNONYMS **jeer,** jibe, sneer, insult, barb; informal dig, put-down; (**taunts**) teasing, provocation, goading, derision, mockery.

▶ **verb** provoke or upset someone with taunts.

– SYNONYMS **jeer at,** sneer at, scoff at, poke fun at, make fun of, get at, insult, tease, torment, ridicule, deride, mock, ride; informal rib, needle.

– DERIVATIVES **taunt·er** noun **taunt·ing** adjective **taunt·ingly** adverb.
– ORIGIN from French *tant pour tant* 'like for like, tit for tat.'

taupe /tōp/ ▶ **noun** a gray color tinged with brown.
– ORIGIN French, 'mole, moleskin.'

Tau·rus /ˈtôrəs/ ▶ **noun 1** a constellation and the second sign of the zodiac (the Bull), which the sun enters about April 21. **2** (**a Taurus**) a person born when the sun is in this sign.
– DERIVATIVES **Tau·re·an** /ˈtôrēən, tôˈrēən/ noun & adjective.
– ORIGIN Latin.

taut /tôt/ ▶ **adjective 1** stretched or pulled tight. **2** (of muscles or nerves) tense. **3** (of writing, music, etc.) concise and controlled.

– SYNONYMS **tight,** stretched, rigid, flexed, tensed.
– ANTONYMS slack.

– DERIVATIVES **taut·en** verb **taut·ly** adverb **taut·ness** noun.
– ORIGIN perhaps from **TOUGH**.

tau·tog /tôˈtôg, tôˈtäg/ ▶ **noun** a grayish-olive edible wrasse found off the Atlantic coast of North America.
– ORIGIN from Naragansett *tautauog*, plural of *taut*.

tau·tol·o·gy /tôˈtäləjē/ ▶ **noun** (pl. **tautologies**) the saying of the same thing over again in different words, considered as a fault of style (e.g., *they arrived one after the other in succession*).
– DERIVATIVES **tau·to·log·i·cal** /ˌtôtlˈäjikəl/ adjective **tau·to·log·i·cal·ly** /ˌtôtlˈäjik(ə)lē/ adverb **tau·tol·o·gist** /-jist/ noun **tau·tol·o·gize** /-jīz/ verb **tau·tol·o·gous** /-gəs/ adjective.
– ORIGIN from Greek *tauto-* 'same' + *logos* 'word, telling.'

tav·ern /ˈtavərn/ ▶ **noun** a bar, especially one that sells food.
– ORIGIN Latin *taberna* 'hut, tavern.'

ta·ver·na /təˈvərnə/ ▶ **noun** a small Greek restaurant.
– ORIGIN modern Greek.

taw·dry /ˈtôdrē/ ▶ **adjective** (**tawdrier, tawdriest**) **1** showy but cheap and of poor quality. **2** sleazy or unpleasant: *the tawdry business of politics*.

– SYNONYMS **gaudy,** flashy, showy, garish, loud, tasteless, vulgar, trashy, cheapjack, shoddy, shabby, gimcrack; informal rubbishy, tacky, kitsch.
– ANTONYMS tasteful.

– DERIVATIVES **taw·dri·ly** adverb **taw·dri·ness** noun.
– ORIGIN short for *tawdry lace*, from *St. Audrey's lace*, a fine silk lace or ribbon.

taw·ny /ˈtônē/ ▶ **adjective** (**tawnier, tawniest**) orange-brown or yellowish-brown in color.
– DERIVATIVES **taw·ni·ness** noun.
– ORIGIN Old French *tane*.

tax /taks/ ▶ **noun** money that must be paid to the government.

– SYNONYMS **duty,** excise, customs, dues, levy, tariff, toll, tithe, charge.

▶ **verb 1** put a tax on something, or make someone pay a tax. **2** pay tax on a vehicle. **3** make heavy demands on:

the ordeal would tax her strength. **4** accuse someone of wrongdoing.

– SYNONYMS **strain,** stretch, overburden, overload, overwhelm, try, wear out, exhaust, sap, drain, weary, weaken.

– DERIVATIVES **tax·a·ble** adjective.
– ORIGIN from Latin *taxare* 'to censure, charge.'

WORD LINKS
fiscal *relating to taxes*

tax·a /'taksə/ plural form of TAXON.

tax·a·tion /tak'sāsʜən/ ▶ **noun 1** the imposing of tax on someone or something. **2** money paid as tax.

tax a·void·ance ▶ **noun** the arrangement of one's financial affairs so as to pay only the minimum of tax that is legally required.

tax break ▶ **noun** informal a tax reduction or advantage allowed by the government.

tax-de·duct·i·ble ▶ **adjective** permitted to be deducted from income before the amount of tax to be paid is calculated.

tax e·va·sion ▶ **noun** the illegal nonpayment or underpayment of tax.

tax-ex·empt ▶ **adjective** not liable to tax.
– DERIVATIVES **tax ex·emp·tion** noun.

tax ha·ven ▶ **noun** a country or independent area where taxes are low.

tax·i /'taksē/ ▶ **noun** (pl. **taxis**) a motor vehicle licensed to carry passengers to the place of their choice in return for payment of a fare. ▶ **verb** (**taxies, taxiing** or **taxying, taxied**) (of an aircraft) move slowly along the ground before takeoff or after landing.
– ORIGIN abbreviation of *taxicab* or *taximeter cab* (see TAXIMETER).

tax·i·cab /'taksē,kab/ ▶ **noun** a taxi.

tax·i·der·my /'taksə,dərmē/ ▶ **noun** the art of preparing, stuffing, and mounting the skins of animals so that they appear lifelike.
– DERIVATIVES **tax·i·der·mic** /,taksə'dərmik/ adjective **tax·i·der·mist** /'taksə,dərmist/ noun.
– ORIGIN from Greek *taxis* 'arrangement' + *derma* 'skin.'

tax·i·me·ter /'taksē,mētər/ ▶ **noun** a device used in taxis that automatically records the distance traveled and the fare to be paid.
– ORIGIN French *taximètre*, from *taxe* 'tariff' + *mètre* 'meter.'

tax·ing /'taksiɴɢ/ ▶ **adjective** physically or mentally demanding.

– SYNONYMS **demanding,** exacting, challenging, burdensome, arduous, onerous, difficult, hard, tough, laborious, back-breaking, strenuous, rigorous, punishing; tiring, exhausting, enervating, wearing, stressful.
– ANTONYMS easy.

tax·i stand (Brit. **taxi rank**) ▶ **noun** a place where taxis park while waiting to be hired.

tax·i·way /'taksē,wā/ ▶ **noun** a route along which an aircraft taxies when moving to or from a runway.

tax·man /'taks,man/ ▶ **noun** (pl. **taxmen**) informal, chiefly Brit. an inspector or collector of taxes.

tax·on /'taksän/ ▶ **noun** (pl. **taxa** /'taksə/) Biology a taxonomic group of any rank, such as a species, family, or class.
– ORIGIN from TAXONOMY.

tax·on·o·my /tak'sänəmē/ ▶ **noun 1** the branch of science concerned with the classification of things, especially plants and animals. **2** a particular scheme of classification.
– DERIVATIVES **tax·o·nom·ic** /,taksə'nämik/ adjective **tax·on·o·mist** /-mist/ noun.
– ORIGIN from Greek *taxis* 'arrangement' + *-nomia* 'distribution.'

tax·pay·er /'taks,pāər/ ▶ **noun** a person who pays taxes.

tax re·turn ▶ **noun** a form on which a taxpayer makes a statement of their income and personal circumstances, used to assess how much tax they should pay.

tax shel·ter ▶ **noun** a financial arrangement made to avoid or minimize taxes.

tax year ▶ **noun** a period of twelve months used for calculating taxes.

TB ▶ **abbreviation** tubercle bacillus; tuberculosis.

Tb ▶ **symbol** the chemical element terbium.

TBA ▶ **abbreviation** to be announced (or arranged).

T-bar ▶ **noun 1** a beam or bar shaped like the letter T. **2** (also **T-bar lift**) a type of ski lift in the form of a series of inverted T-shaped bars for towing two skiers at a time uphill.

T-bone ▶ **noun** a large choice piece of loin steak containing a T-shaped bone.

tbsp. (also **Tbsp**) ▶ **abbreviation** (pl. same or **tbsps**) tablespoonful.

Tc ▶ **symbol** the chemical element technetium.

T-cell ▶ **noun** Physiology a lymphocyte of a type produced or processed by the thymus gland and actively participating in the immune response.

TCP/IP ▶ **abbreviation** trademark transmission control protocol/Internet protocol, used to govern the connection of computer systems to the Internet.

TD ▶ **abbreviation 1** Football touchdown. **2** technical drawing. **3** Treasury Department.

Te ▶ **symbol** the chemical element tellurium.

tea /tē/ ▶ **noun 1** a hot drink made by infusing the dried, crushed leaves of an evergreen Asian shrub (the tea plant) in boiling water. **2** the dried leaves used to make tea. **3** a drink made from the leaves, fruits, or flowers of other plants. **4** chiefly Brit. a light afternoon meal consisting of sandwiches, cakes, etc., with tea to drink.
– ORIGIN Chinese.

tea bag ▶ **noun** a small porous bag containing tea leaves, onto which boiling water is poured to make tea.

teach /tēcʜ/ ▶ **verb** (past and past part. **taught**) **1** give information about a particular subject to a class or student. **2** show someone how to do something. **3** make someone realize or understand something: *the experience taught me the real value of money.*

– SYNONYMS **educate,** instruct, school, tutor, inform, coach, train, drill.

– DERIVATIVES **teach·a·ble** adjective **teach·ing** noun.
– ORIGIN Old English, 'show, present, point out.'

WORD LINKS
educational *relating to teaching*

teach·er /ˈtēCHər/ ▸ **noun** a person who teaches in a school.

– SYNONYMS **educator,** instructor, schoolteacher, professor, tutor, governess, coach, trainer, lecturer, guide, mentor, guru; Brit. master, mistress, schoolmaster, schoolmistress, don; old use schoolmarm.

– DERIVATIVES **teach·er·ly** adjective.

tea co·zy ▸ **noun** a thick or padded cover placed over a teapot to keep the tea hot.

tea·cup /ˈtēˌkəp/ ▸ **noun** a cup from which tea is drunk.

teak /tēk/ ▸ **noun** hard wood used in shipbuilding and for making furniture, obtained from a tree native to India and SE Asia.
– ORIGIN Portuguese *teca*.

teal /tēl/ ▸ **noun** (pl. same or **teals**) **1** a small freshwater duck, typically with a bright blue-green patch on the wing plumage. **2** (also **teal blue**) a dark greenish-blue color.
– ORIGIN unknown.

team /tēm/ ▸ **noun 1** a group of players forming one side in a competitive game or sport. **2** two or more people working together. **3** two or more horses harnessed together to pull a vehicle.

– SYNONYMS **group,** squad, company, party, crew, troupe, band, side, lineup; informal bunch, gang.

▸ **verb 1** (**team up**) join with another person or group to do or achieve something. **2** (**team something with**) wear an item of clothing with another.

– SYNONYMS **1** (**team up**) **join (forces),** collaborate, work together, unite, combine, cooperate, link, ally, associate. **2** (**team something with**) *a pinstripe suit teamed with a white shirt* **match,** coordinate, complement, pair up.

– ORIGIN Old English.

USAGE

Do not confuse **team** with **teem**. **Team** means 'a group of people playing or working together' or 'join with another person or group to achieve something' (*she teamed up with other singers to form the group*), while **teem** means 'be full of something' (*every garden is teeming with wildlife*) or 'pour down' (*rain teemed down all morning*).

team·mate /ˈtē(m)ˌmāt/ ▸ **noun** a fellow member of a team.

team play·er ▸ **noun** a person who plays or works well as a member of a team.

team spir·it ▸ **noun** feelings of trust and cooperation among the members of a team.

team·ster /ˈtēmstər/ ▸ **noun 1** a truck driver. **2** a member of the International Brother of Teamsters (a major US labor union). **3** a driver of a team of animals.

team·work /ˈtēmˌwərk/ ▸ **noun** the effective action of a team of people working together.

tea·pot /ˈtēˌpät/ ▸ **noun** a pot with a handle, spout, and lid, in which tea is prepared.

tear[1] /te(ə)r/ ▸ **verb** (past **tore** /tôr/; past part. **torn** /tôrn/) **1** (often **tear something up**) pull something apart or into pieces. **2** rip a hole or split in something. **3** remove something by pulling it roughly or forcefully. **4** (**be torn**) be unable to choose between two options. **5** damage a muscle or ligament by overstretching it. **6** (**tear something down**) demolish or destroy something. **7** (**tear something apart**) destroy good relations between people. **8** (**tear oneself away**) leave despite a strong desire to stay. **9** informal move very quickly and in a reckless or excited way. **10** (**tear into**) attack someone verbally.

– SYNONYMS **1** *I tore up the letter* **rip,** split, slit, pull apart, pull to pieces, shred, rupture, sever. **2** (as adj. **torn**) *a torn shirt* **ripped,** rent, cut, slit, ragged, tattered. **3** *his flesh was torn* **lacerate,** cut (open), gash, slash, scratch, hack, pierce, stab. **4** *Gina tore the book from his hands* **snatch,** grab, seize, rip, wrench, wrest, pull, pluck; informal yank. **5** (**be torn**) *she was torn between the two options* **wavering,** vacillating, irresolute, dithering, uncertain, unsure, undecided, in two minds.

▸ **noun** a hole or split caused by tearing.

– SYNONYMS **rip,** hole, split, slash, slit, run, snag.

– DERIVATIVES **tear·a·ble** adjective.
– ORIGIN Old English.

tear[2] /ti(ə)r/ ▸ **noun** a drop of clear salty liquid produced by glands in a person's eye when they are crying or when the eye is irritated.
– DERIVATIVES **tear·y** adjective.
– PHRASES **in tears** crying.
– ORIGIN Old English.

tear·drop /ˈti(ə)rˌdräp/ ▸ **noun** a single tear. ▸ **adjective** shaped like a tear.

tear duct /ti(ə)r/ ▸ **noun** a passage through which tears pass from the glands that produce them to the eye, or from the eye to the nose.

tear·ful /ˈti(ə)rfəl/ ▸ **adjective 1** crying or about to cry. **2** causing tears; sad: *a tearful farewell.*

– SYNONYMS **1 close to tears,** emotional, upset, distressed, sad, unhappy, in tears, crying, weeping, sobbing, sniveling; informal weepy, blubbering; formal lachrymose. **2 emotional,** upsetting, distressing, sad, heartbreaking, sorrowful, poignant, moving, touching, tear-jerking.
– ANTONYMS cheerful.

– DERIVATIVES **tear·ful·ly** adverb **tear·ful·ness** noun.

tear gas /ti(ə)r/ ▸ **noun** gas that causes severe irritation to the eyes, used in warfare and riot control.

tear·jerk·er /ˈti(ə)rˌjərkər/ ▸ **noun** informal a story or movie intended to arouse feelings of sadness in an audience.

tea·room ▸ **noun** a small restaurant or cafe where tea and other light refreshments are served.

tea rose ▸ **noun** a garden rose having a delicate scent resembling that of tea.

tease /tēz/ ▸ **verb 1** make fun of someone in a playful way or in order to annoy or embarrass them. **2** tempt someone sexually, without intending to have sex with them. **3** (**tease something out**) find out something by searching through a mass of information. **4** gently pull or comb tangled wool, hair, etc., into separate strands. **5** comb hair in the reverse direction of its growth to make it look fuller.

– SYNONYMS **make fun of,** laugh at, deride, mock, ridicule, make a monkey (out) of, taunt, bait, goad, pick on; informal rag, pull someone's leg.

▸ **noun** informal **1** a person who teases. **2** an act of teasing someone.
– ORIGIN Old English, related to **TEASEL**.

tea·sel /ˈtēzəl/ (also **teazle** or **teazel**) ▸ **noun** a tall prickly plant with spiny purple flowerheads.
– ORIGIN Old English.

teas·er /ˈtēzər/ ▶ **noun** informal a tricky question or task.

tea set ▶ **noun** a set of dishes for serving tea.

tea·spoon /ˈtēˌspo͞on/ ▶ **noun 1** a small spoon used for adding sugar to and stirring hot drinks. **2** the amount held by a teaspoon, equivalent to ⅙ fluid ounce or 5 milliliters.
– DERIVATIVES **tea·spoon·ful** noun.

teat /tēt/ ▶ **noun** a nipple of the mammary gland of a female animal's body from which milk is sucked by the young.
– ORIGIN Old French *tete*.

tea·time /ˈtēˌtīm/ ▶ **noun** chiefly Brit. the time in the afternoon when tea is served.

tea tow·el ▶ **noun** chiefly Brit. a dish towel.

tea-tree oil ▶ **noun** an oil obtained from a species of tea tree, used in soaps and other products for its refreshing fragrance and antiseptic properties.

tech /tek/ ▶ **noun** informal **1** technology. **2** a technician. **3** Basketball a technical foul.

tech·ie /ˈtekē/ ▶ **noun** (pl. **techies**) informal a person who is an expert in technology, especially computing.

tech·ne·ti·um /tekˈnēsʜ(ē)əm/ ▶ **noun** an unstable radioactive metallic element made by high-energy collisions.
– ORIGIN from Greek *tekhnētos* 'artificial.'

tech·nic /ˈteknik/ ▶ **noun 1** technique. **2** (**technics**) (treated as sing. or pl.) technical terms, details, and methods.
– DERIVATIVES **tech·ni·cist** /-nisist/ noun.
– ORIGIN from Greek *tekhnē* 'art.'

tech·ni·cal /ˈteknikəl/ ▶ **adjective 1** relating to a particular subject, art, or craft, or its practical skills and techniques. **2** relating to the practical use of machinery and methods in science and industry. **3** requiring specialized knowledge in order to be understood. **4** according to a strict application or interpretation of the law or rules: *a technical violation of the treaty*. **5** Basketball a technical foul.

– SYNONYMS **1 practical,** scientific, technological, high-tech. **2 specialist,** specialized, scientific, complex, complicated, esoteric.

– DERIVATIVES **tech·ni·cal·ly** adverb.

tech·ni·cal foul ▶ **noun** Basketball a violation of certain rules of the game, not usually involving physical contact.

tech·ni·cal·i·ty /ˌtekniˈkalitē/ ▶ **noun** (pl. **technicalities**) **1** a small formal detail within a set of rules, as contrasted with the intent or purpose of the rules. **2** (**technicalities**) the details of how something works or is done: *the technicalities of police procedure*. **3** the use of technical terms or methods.

tech·ni·cal knock·out ▶ **noun** Boxing the ending of a fight by the referee because a contestant is judged to be unable to continue, the opponent being declared the winner.

tech·ni·cian /tekˈnisʜən/ ▶ **noun 1** a person employed to look after technical equipment or do practical work in a laboratory. **2** a person skilled in the technique of an art, science, craft, or sport.

Tech·ni·col·or /ˈtekniˌkələr/ ▶ **noun 1** trademark a process of producing motion pictures in color by using synchronized monochrome films, each of a different color, to produce a color print. **2** (**technicolor**) informal vivid color.

tech·nique /tekˈnēk/ ▶ **noun 1** a method or skill used for carrying out a particular task. **2** a person's level of skill in a particular field. **3** a skillful or efficient way of doing or achieving something.

– SYNONYMS **1 method,** approach, procedure, system, way, manner, means, strategy. **2 skill,** ability, proficiency, expertise, artistry, craftsmanship, adroitness, deftness, dexterity.

– ORIGIN French, from Greek *tekhnē* 'art.'

tech·no /ˈteknō/ ▶ **noun** a style of fast electronic dance music, with a strong beat and few or no vocals.
– ORIGIN abbreviation of **TECHNOLOGICAL** (see **TECHNOLOGY**).

tech·no·bab·ble /ˈteknōˌbabəl/ ▶ **noun** informal incomprehensible technical jargon.

tech·noc·ra·cy /tekˈnäkrəsē/ ▶ **noun** (pl. **technocracies**) a social or political system in which scientific or technical experts hold a great deal of power.
– DERIVATIVES **tech·no·crat** /ˈteknəˌkrat/ noun **tech·no·crat·ic** /ˌteknəˈkratik/ adjective.

tech·nol·o·gy /tekˈnäləjē/ ▶ **noun** (pl. **technologies**) **1** the application of scientific knowledge for practical purposes. **2** machinery and equipment developed from such scientific knowledge. **3** the branch of knowledge concerned with applied sciences.
– DERIVATIVES **tech·no·log·i·cal** /ˌteknəˈläjikəl/ adjective **tech·no·log·i·cal·ly** /-ik(ə)lē/ adverb **tech·nol·o·gist** noun.
– ORIGIN Greek *tekhnologia* 'systematic treatment.'

tech·nol·o·gy trans·fer ▶ **noun** the transfer of new technology from the originator to a secondary user, especially from developed to underdeveloped countries.

tech·no·phile /ˈteknəˌfīl/ ▶ **noun** a person who is enthusiastic about new technology.
– DERIVATIVES **tech·no·phil·i·a** /ˌteknəˈfilēə/ noun **tech·no·phil·ic** /ˌteknəˈfilik/ adjective.

tech·no·phobe /ˈteknəˌfōb/ ▶ **noun** a person who dislikes or fears new technology.
– DERIVATIVES **tech·no·pho·bi·a** /ˌteknəˈfōbēə/ noun **tech·no·pho·bic** /ˌteknəˈfōbik/ adjective.

tech·no·speak /ˈteknəˌspēk/ ▶ **noun** another term for **TECHNOBABBLE**.

tec·ton·ic /tekˈtänik/ ▶ **adjective 1** Geology relating to the structure of the earth's crust and the large-scale processes that take place within it. **2** relating to building or construction. **3** (of an event, especially a change) very significant or considerable.
– DERIVATIVES **tec·ton·i·cal·ly** /-ik(ə)lē/ adverb.
– ORIGIN from Greek *tektōn* 'carpenter, builder.'

tec·ton·ics /tekˈtäniks/ ▶ **plural noun** (treated as sing. or pl.) Geology large-scale processes affecting the structure of the earth's crust.

ted·dy /ˈtedē/ ▶ **noun** (pl. **teddies**) **1** (also **teddy bear**) a soft toy bear. **2** a woman's all-in-one undergarment.
– ORIGIN from *Teddy*, informal form of the man's name *Theodore*: in sense 1 referring to the US president *Theodore* Roosevelt, an enthusiastic bear hunter.

Te De·um /tā ˈdāəm, tē ˈdēəm/ ▶ **noun** a Christian hymn beginning *Te Deum laudamus*, 'We praise Thee, O God,' sung at matins or on special occasions such as a thanksgiving.
– ORIGIN Latin.

te·di·ous /ˈtēdēəs/ ▶ **adjective** too long or slow; dull.

– SYNONYMS **boring,** dull, monotonous, repetitive, unrelieved, unvaried, uneventful, lifeless,

uninteresting, unexciting, uninspiring, lackluster, dreary, soul-destroying; informal deadly, dullsville.
– ANTONYMS exciting.

– DERIVATIVES **te·di·ous·ly** adverb **te·di·ous·ness** noun.
– ORIGIN from Latin *taedium* 'tedium.'

WORD TOOLKIT

See **INSIPID**.

te·di·um /'tēdēəm/ ▶ **noun** the state of being tedious.

– SYNONYMS **monotony,** boredom, ennui, uniformity, routine, dreariness, dryness, banality, vapidity, insipidity.
– ANTONYMS variety.

tee[1] /tē/ ▶ **noun 1** a cleared space on a golf course, from which the ball is struck at the beginning of play for each hole. **2** a small peg placed in the ground to support a golf ball before it is struck from a tee. **3** a mark aimed at in lawn bowling, quoits, curling, etc. ▶ **verb** (**tees, teeing, teed**) Golf **1** (**tee up**) place the ball on a tee ready to make the first stroke of the round or hole. **2** (**tee off**) begin a round or hole by playing the ball from a tee. **3** (**tee someone off**) informal make someone angry or annoyed.
– ORIGIN unknown.

tee[2] ▶ **noun** informal a T-shirt.

tee-hee /ˌtē 'hē/ ▶ **noun** a giggle or laugh.
– ORIGIN imitating the sound.

teem[1] /tēm/ ▶ **verb** (**teem with**) be full of or swarming with.

– SYNONYMS *the pond was **teeming with** fish* **be full of,** be alive with, be brimming with, abound in, be swarming with; be packed with, be crawling with, be overrun by, bristle with, seethe with, be thick with; informal be jam-packed with, be chock-full of.

– ORIGIN Old English, 'give birth to.'

USAGE

On the confusion of **teem** and **team**, see the note at **TEAM**.

teem[2] ▶ **verb** (of rain) pour down; fall heavily.
– ORIGIN Old Norse, 'to empty.'

teen /tēn/ informal ▶ **adjective** relating to teenagers. ▶ **noun** a teenager.

-teen ▶ **suffix** forming the names of numerals from 13 to 19.
– ORIGIN Old English.

teen·age /'tēnˌāj/ ▶ **adjective** relating to a teenager or teenagers.
– DERIVATIVES **teen·aged** adjective.

teen·ag·er /'tēnˌājər/ ▶ **noun** a person aged between 13 and 19 years.

– SYNONYMS **adolescent,** youth, young person, minor, juvenile; informal teen.

teens /tēnz/ ▶ **plural noun** the years of a person's age from 13 to 19.

teen·sy /'tēnsē/ ▶ **adjective** (**teensier, teensiest**) informal very tiny.
– ORIGIN probably from **TEENY**.

tee·ny /'tēnē/ ▶ **adjective** (**teenier, teeniest**) informal tiny.
– ORIGIN variant of **TINY**.

tee·ny·bop·per ▶ **noun** informal a young teenager who follows the latest fashions in clothes and pop music.

tee·ny-wee·ny /'tēnē 'wēnē/ (also **teensy-weensy**) ▶ **adjective** informal very tiny.

tee·pee ▶ **noun** variant spelling of **TEPEE**.

tee shirt ▶ **noun** variant spelling of **T-SHIRT**.

tee·ter /'tētər/ ▶ **verb 1** move or balance unsteadily. **2** be unable to decide between different options.

– SYNONYMS **1 totter,** wobble, toddle, sway, stagger, stumble, reel, lurch, pitch. **2** *the situation teetered between tragedy and farce* **seesaw,** veer, fluctuate, oscillate, swing, alternate, waver.

– ORIGIN Old Norse, 'shake, shiver.'

teeth /tēTH/ plural of **TOOTH**.

teethe /tē<u>TH</u>/ ▶ **verb** (of a baby) develop its first teeth.

teeth·ing ring /'tē<u>TH</u>iNG/ ▶ **noun** a small ring for a baby to bite on while teething.

tee·to·tal /'tēˌtōtl/ ▶ **adjective** choosing never to drink alcohol.

– SYNONYMS **abstinent,** abstemious, sober, dry; informal on the wagon.

– DERIVATIVES **tee·to·tal·ism** /-ˌizəm/ noun **tee·to·tal·er** noun.
– ORIGIN from **TOTAL** (referring to total abstinence from all alcohol).

Tef·lon /'tefˌlän/ ▶ **noun** trademark a tough synthetic resin used to make seals and bearings and to coat nonstick cooking utensils.

tel·co /'telkō/ ▶ **noun** (pl. **telcos**) a telecommunications company.

tele- ▶ **combining form 1** to or at a distance: *telecommunication*. **2** relating to television: *telegenic*. **3** done by means of the telephone: *telemarketing*.
– ORIGIN Greek, 'far off.'

tel·e·cast /'teləˌkast/ ▶ **noun** a television broadcast. ▶ **verb** broadcast a program by television.
– DERIVATIVES **tel·e·cast·er** noun.

tel·e·com /'teləˌkäm/ (Brit. also **telecoms**) ▶ **plural noun** (treated as sing.) telecommunications.

tel·e·com·mu·ni·ca·tion /ˌteləkəˌmyo͞oni'kāSHən/ ▶ **noun 1** long-distance communication by means of cable, telephone, broadcasting, satellite, etc. **2** (**telecommunications**) (treated as sing.) the technology concerned with this.

tel·e·com·mut·ing /ˌteləkə'myo͞otiNG/ ▶ **noun** the practice of working from home, communicating with a central workplace by telephone, email, and fax.
– DERIVATIVES **tel·e·com·mute** verb **tel·e·com·mut·er** noun.

tel·e·coms /'teləˌkämz/ (also **telecomms**) ▶ **plural noun** (treated as sing.) telecommunications.

tel·e·con·fer·ence /'teləˌkänf(ə)rəns/ ▶ **noun** a conference in which participants in different locations are linked by telecommunication devices.
– DERIVATIVES **tel·e·con·fer·enc·ing** noun.

tel·e·e·van·ge·list ▶ **noun** variant of **TELEVANGELIST**.

tel·e·gen·ic /ˌtelə'jenik/ ▶ **adjective** having an appearance or manner that is attractive on television.

tel·e·gram /'teləˌgram/ ▶ **noun** a message sent by telegraph and delivered in written or printed form.

tel·e·graph /'teləˌgraf/ ▶ **noun** a system or device for transmitting messages from a distance along a wire,

especially one creating signals by making and breaking an electrical connection. ▸ **verb 1** send a message to someone by telegraph. **2** convey a message by one's facial expression or body language.
– DERIVATIVES **te·leg·ra·pher** /tə'legrəfər/ noun **tel·e·graph·ic** /ˌtelə'grafik/ adjective **te·leg·ra·phist** /tə'legrəfist/ noun **te·leg·ra·phy** /tə'legrəfē/ noun.

tel·e·ki·ne·sis /ˌteləki'nēsis/ ▸ **noun** the supposed ability to move objects at a distance by mental power or other nonphysical means.
– DERIVATIVES **tel·e·ki·net·ic** /-'netik/ adjective.
– ORIGIN from Greek *kinēsis* 'motion.'

tel·e·mark /'teləˌmärk/ Skiing ▸ **noun** a turn in downhill skiing or a landing style in ski jumping with one ski advanced and the knees bent. ▸ **verb** perform such a turn while skiing.
– ORIGIN named after *Telemark*, a district in Norway, where it originated.

tel·e·mar·ket·ing /ˌtelə'märkitiNG/ ▸ **noun** the marketing of goods or services by telephoning potential customers.
– DERIVATIVES **tel·e·mar·ket·er** noun.

tel·e·mat·ics /ˌtelə'matiks/ ▸ **plural noun** (treated as sing.) the branch of information technology that deals with the long-distance transmission of computerized information.
– DERIVATIVES **tel·e·mat·ic** adjective.
– ORIGIN blend of **TELECOMMUNICATION** and **INFORMATICS**.

tel·e·med·i·cine /'teləˌmedisin/ ▸ **noun** the diagnosis and treatment of patients at a distance by means of telecommunications technology.

te·lem·e·ter /tə'lemitər, 'teləˌmētər/ ▸ **noun** a piece of equipment for recording the readings of an instrument and transmitting them by radio.
– DERIVATIVES **tel·e·met·ric** /ˌtelə'metrik/ adjective **te·lem·e·try** /tə'lemitrē/ noun.

tel·e·ol·o·gy /ˌtelē'äləjē, ˌtēlē-/ ▸ **noun** (pl. **teleologies**) **1** the philosophical theory that all natural phenomena can be explained with reference to their purpose. **2** the theological doctrine that there is evidence of design and purpose in the natural world.
– DERIVATIVES **tel·e·o·log·i·cal** /-ə'läjikəl/ adjective.
– ORIGIN from Greek *telos* 'end' + *logos* 'account, reason.'

te·lep·a·thy /tə'lepəTHē/ ▸ **noun** the supposed communication of thoughts or ideas without using speech, writing, or any other normal method.
– DERIVATIVES **tel·e·path** /'teləpaTH/ noun **tel·e·path·ic** /ˌtelə'paTHik/ adjective.

tel·e·phone /'teləˌfōn/ ▸ **noun 1** a system for transmitting voices over a distance using wire or radio, by converting sound vibrations to electrical signals. **2** a piece of equipment used as part of such a system, typically having a handset with a transmitting microphone and a set of numbered buttons by which a connection can be made to another such piece of equipment.

– SYNONYMS **phone,** handset, receiver, cellular phone, cell phone, cordless phone; informal blower, horn.

▸ **verb** contact someone by telephone.

– SYNONYMS **phone,** call, dial; informal call up, give someone a ring/buzz, get someone on the horn.

– DERIVATIVES **tel·e·phon·ic** adjective **tel·e·phon·i·cal·ly** adverb.

tel·e·phone booth ▸ **noun** a public booth or enclosure in which a pay phone is situated.

tel·e·phone di·rec·to·ry ▸ **noun** a book listing the names, addresses, and telephone numbers of the people and businesses in a particular area.

tel·e·phone ex·change ▸ **noun** a set of equipment that connects telephone lines during a call.

tel·e·phone num·ber ▸ **noun** a number given to a particular telephone and used in making connections to it.

tel·e·phone pole ▸ **noun** a tall pole used to carry telephone wires and other utility lines above the ground.

te·leph·o·nist /'teləˌfōnist, tə'lefə-/ ▸ **noun** Brit. a switchboard operator.

te·leph·o·ny /tə'lefənē, 'teləˌfōnē/ ▸ **noun** the working or use of telephones.

tel·e·pho·to lens /'teləˌfōtō/ ▸ **noun** a lens with a longer focal length than standard, producing a magnified image of a distant object.

tel·e·port /'teləˌpôrt/ ▸ **noun** a center providing connections between different forms of telecommunications, especially one that links satellites to ground-based communications. ▸ **verb** (especially in science fiction) transport or be transported across space and time instantly.
– DERIVATIVES **tel·e·por·ta·tion** /ˌteləˌpôr'tāSHən/ noun.
– ORIGIN from **TELE-** + a shortened form of *transportation.*

tel·e·pres·ence /'teləˌprezəns/ ▸ **noun** the use of virtual reality technology, especially for the remote control of machinery or to produce the impression of being in another location.

tel·e·print·er /'teləˌprin(t)ər/ ▸ **noun** Brit. a device for transmitting telegraph messages as they are keyed, and for printing messages received.

tel·e·prompt·er /'teləˌpräm(p)tər/ (also **TelePrompTer**) ▸ **noun** trademark a device used in television to project a speaker's script out of sight of the audience.

tel·e·sales /'teləˌsālz/ ▸ **plural noun** chiefly Brit. the selling of goods or services over the telephone.

tel·e·scope /'teləˌskōp/ ▸ **noun** an optical instrument designed to make distant objects appear nearer, containing an arrangement of lenses, or of curved mirrors and lenses, by which rays of light are collected and focused and the resulting image magnified. ▸ **verb 1** (of an object made of several tubular parts fitting into each other) slide into itself so as to become smaller. **2** condense or combine so as to occupy less space or time: *at sea the years are telescoped into hours.*
– DERIVATIVES **tel·e·scop·ic** /ˌtelə'skäpik/ adjective **tel·e·scop·i·cal·ly** /-ik(ə)lē/ adverb.

tel·e·sur·ger·y /'teləˌsərjərē/ ▸ **noun** surgery performed by a doctor considerably distant from the patient, using medical robotics and multimedia image communication.
– DERIVATIVES **tel·e·sur·geon** /'teləˌsərjən/ noun.

tel·e·text /'teləˌtekst/ ▸ **noun** a news and information service transmitted to televisions with appropriate receivers.

tel·e·thon /'teləˌTHän/ ▸ **noun** a long television program broadcast to raise money for a charity.
– ORIGIN from **TELE-** + *-thon* on the pattern of *marathon.*

tel·e·type /'teləˌtīp/ ▸ **noun** trademark a kind of teleprinter.

tel·e·van·ge·list /ˌtelə'vanjəlist/ (also **tele-evangelist**) ▶ **noun** an evangelical preacher who appears regularly on television.

tel·e·vise /'teləˌvīz/ ▶ **verb** broadcast something on television.

tel·e·vi·sion /'teləˌvizʜən/ ▶ **noun 1** a system for converting visual images (with sound) into electrical signals, transmitting them by radio or other means, and displaying them electronically on a screen. **2** (also **television set**) a device with a screen for receiving television signals. **3** the process or business of broadcasting programs on television.

> – SYNONYMS **TV**; informal the small screen, the tube; humorous the idiot box.

tel·e·vis·u·al /ˌtelə'vizʜo͞oəl/ ▶ **adjective** relating to or suitable for television.
– DERIVATIVES **tel·e·vi·su·al·ly** adverb.

tel·e·work·ing /'teləˌwərkiɴɢ/ ▶ **noun** another term for **TELECOMMUTING**.
– DERIVATIVES **tel·e·work·er** noun.

tel·ex /'teleks/ ▶ **noun 1** an international system of telegraphy in which printed messages are transmitted and received by teleprinters. **2** a machine used for this. **3** a message sent by telex. ▶ **verb** send a message to someone by telex.
– ORIGIN blend of **TELEPRINTER** and **EXCHANGE**.

tell /tel/ ▶ **verb** (past and past part. **told** /tōld/) **1** communicate information to someone. **2** order or advise someone to do something. **3** express something in words: *tell me the story again*. **4** (**tell someone off**) informal reprimand someone. **5** establish that something is the case: *you can tell they're in love*. **6** be able to recognize a difference. **7** (of an experience or period of time) have a noticeable effect on someone. **8** (**tell on**) informal inform someone about a person's wrongdoings.

> – SYNONYMS **1** *why didn't you tell me?* **inform,** notify, let know, make aware, acquaint with, advise, put in the picture, brief, fill in, alert, warn; informal clue in. **2** *she told the story slowly* **relate,** recount, narrate, report, recite, describe, sketch. **3 instruct,** order, command, direct, charge, enjoin, call on, require. **4** *it was hard to tell what he meant* **ascertain,** determine, work out, make out, deduce, discern, perceive, see, identify, recognize, understand, comprehend; informal figure out. **5** *he couldn't tell one from the other* **distinguish,** differentiate, discriminate. **6** *the strain began to* **tell on** *him* **take its toll on,** leave its mark on, affect.

– PHRASES **tell tales** gossip about another person's secrets or wrongdoings. **tell time** (or **tell the time**) be able to read the time from the face of a clock or watch.
– ORIGIN Old English, 'relate, count.'

tell·er /'telər/ ▶ **noun 1** a person who deals with customers' transactions in a bank. **2** a person who tells something. **3** a person appointed to count votes.

tell·ing /'teliɴɢ/ ▶ **adjective** having a striking or revealing effect; significant.

> – SYNONYMS **revealing,** significant, weighty, important, meaningful, influential, striking, potent, powerful, compelling.
> – ANTONYMS insignificant.

– DERIVATIVES **tell·ing·ly** adverb.

tell·ing-off ▶ **noun** (pl. **tellings-off**) Brit. informal a reprimand.

tell·tale /'telˌtāl/ ▶ **adjective** revealing something: *the telltale signs of a woman in love*. ▶ **noun** Brit. a tattletale.

tel·lu·ric /tə'lo͝orik/ ▶ **adjective 1** relating to the earth as a planet. **2** relating to the soil.
– ORIGIN from Latin *tellus* 'earth.'

tel·lu·ri·um /tə'lo͝orēəm/ ▶ **noun** a silvery-white crystalline nonmetallic element with semiconducting properties.
– ORIGIN from Latin *tellus* 'earth.'

tel·ly /'telē/ ▶ **noun** (pl. **tellies**) Brit. informal term for **TELEVISION**.

tel·net /'telˌnet/ ▶ **noun** Computing a network protocol or program that allows a user on one computer to log in to another computer that is part of the same network.

tel·o·mere /'tēləˌmi(ə)r, 'telə-/ ▶ **noun** Genetics a compound structure at the end of a chromosome.
– DERIVATIVES **tel·o·mer·ic** /ˌtēlə'merik, ˌtelə-/ adjective.
– ORIGIN from Greek *telos* 'end' + *meros* 'part.'

te·maz·e·pam /tə'mazəˌpam/ ▶ **noun** a sedative drug.

te·mer·i·ty /tə'meritē/ ▶ **noun** excessively confident or bold behavior.

> – SYNONYMS **audacity,** nerve, effrontery, impudence, impertinence, cheek, gall, presumption; daring; informal face, front, brass, chutzpah.

– ORIGIN Latin *temeritas*.

temp /temp/ informal ▶ **noun** a person working in an office who is employed on a temporary basis. ▶ **verb** work as a temp.

temp. ▶ **abbreviation** temperature.

tem·peh /'tempā/ ▶ **noun** an Indonesian dish consisting of deep-fried fermented soybeans.
– ORIGIN Indonesian.

tem·per /'tempər/ ▶ **noun 1** a person's state of mind in terms of their being angry or calm. **2** a tendency to become angry easily. **3** an angry state of mind. **4** the degree of hardness and elasticity in steel or another metal.

> – SYNONYMS **1** *she struggled to keep her temper* **composure,** self-control, self-possession, calm, good humor; informal cool. **2** *a display of temper* **anger,** fury, rage, annoyance, irritation, pique, petulance. **3** *he walked out in a temper* **rage,** fury, fit of pique, tantrum, bad mood, pet, sulk, huff; informal hissy fit.

▶ **verb 1** balance or modify something so as to make it less extreme: *their idealism is tempered with realism*. **2** improve the hardness and elasticity of a metal by reheating and then cooling it.

> – SYNONYMS **moderate,** modify, modulate, mitigate, alleviate, reduce, weaken, lighten, soften.

– PHRASES **keep** (or **lose**) **one's temper** manage (or fail to manage) to control one's anger.
– ORIGIN Latin *temperare* 'mingle, restrain oneself.'

> **CHOOSE THE RIGHT WORD**
>
> See **ALLEVIATE**.

tem·per·a /'tempərə, tem'po͝orə/ ▶ **noun** a method of painting that uses powdered colors mixed with egg yolk.
– ORIGIN from Italian *pingere a tempera* 'paint in distemper.'

tem·per·a·ment /'temp(ə)rəmənt/ ▶ **noun** a person's nature in terms of the effect it has on their behavior.

– SYNONYMS **character,** nature, disposition, personality, makeup, constitution, temper.

– ORIGIN Latin *temperamentum* 'correct mixture.'

tem·per·a·men·tal /ˌtemp(ə)rəˈmentl/ ▶ **adjective** **1** liable to unreasonable changes of mood. **2** relating to or caused by a person's temperament.

– SYNONYMS **volatile,** excitable, emotional, unpredictable, hotheaded, quick-tempered, impatient, touchy, moody, sensitive, highly strung.
– ANTONYMS placid.

– DERIVATIVES **tem·per·a·men·tal·ly** adverb.

tem·per·ance /ˈtemp(ə)rəns/ ▶ **noun** the practice of never drinking alcohol.
– ORIGIN Old French *temperaunce.*

CHOOSE THE RIGHT WORD

See **ABSTINENCE**.

tem·per·ate /ˈtemp(ə)rət/ ▶ **adjective** **1** (of a region or climate) having mild temperatures. **2** showing moderation or self-restraint.

– SYNONYMS **1** *temperate climates* **mild,** clement, benign, gentle, balmy. **2 self-restrained,** moderate, self-controlled, disciplined; abstemious, self-denying; teetotal, abstinent.
– ANTONYMS extreme.

– ORIGIN Latin *temperatus.*

tem·per·ate zone ▶ **noun** each of the two regions of the earth between the Arctic Circle and the Tropic of Cancer and the Antarctic Circle and the Tropic of Capricorn.

tem·per·a·ture /ˈtemp(ə)rəCHər, -ˌCHo͝or/ ▶ **noun** **1** the degree or intensity of heat present in a place, substance, or object. **2** a body temperature above normal. **3** the degree of excitement or tension in a situation or discussion: *the temperature of the debate lowered.*
– ORIGIN Latin *temperatura* 'the state of being mixed.'

tem·pest /ˈtempist/ ▶ **noun** a violent windy storm.
– PHRASES **a tempest in a teapot** great anger or excitement about a trivial matter.
– ORIGIN Latin *tempestas* 'season, weather, storm.'

tem·pes·tu·ous /temˈpesCHo͞oəs/ ▶ **adjective** **1** very stormy. **2** full of strong and changeable emotions: *a tempestuous relationship.*

– SYNONYMS **turbulent,** wild, stormy, violent, emotional, passionate, impassioned, fiery, intense, uncontrolled, unrestrained.
– ANTONYMS calm.

– DERIVATIVES **tem·pes·tu·ous·ly** adverb **tem·pes·tu·ous·ness** noun.

tem·pi /ˈtempē/ plural of **TEMPO**.

Tem·plar /ˈtemplər/ ▶ **noun** historical a member of the Knights Templar, a powerful religious and military order.
– ORIGIN Latin *templarius,* from *templum* (see **TEMPLE**[1]).

tem·plate /ˈtemplət/ ▶ **noun** **1** a shaped piece of rigid material used as a pattern for processes such as cutting out, shaping, or drilling. **2** something that acts as a model or example for others to copy.
– ORIGIN probably from *temple* 'a device in a loom for keeping the cloth stretched.'

tem·ple[1] /ˈtempəl/ ▶ **noun** **1** a building used for the worship of a god or gods. **2** (**the Temple**) either of two ancient religious buildings of the Jews in Jerusalem.

– SYNONYMS **house/place of worship,** shrine, sanctuary, church, cathedral, mosque, synagogue, house of prayer.

– ORIGIN Latin *templum* 'open or consecrated space.'

tem·ple[2] ▶ **noun** the flat part of either side of the head between the forehead and the ear.
– ORIGIN Old French.

tem·po /ˈtempō/ ▶ **noun** (pl. **tempos** or **tempi** /-pē/) **1** the speed at which a passage of music is played. **2** the pace of an activity or process.
– ORIGIN Italian, from Latin *tempus* 'time.'

tem·po·ral[1] /ˈtemp(ə)rəl/ ▶ **adjective** **1** relating to time. **2** relating to the physical world rather than to spiritual matters.
– DERIVATIVES **tem·po·ral·ly** adverb.
– ORIGIN Latin *temporalis,* from *tempus* 'time.'

tem·po·ral[2] ▶ **adjective** relating to or situated in the temples of the head.

tem·po·ral bone ▶ **noun** either of a pair of bones that form part of the side of the skull on each side and enclose the middle and inner ear.

tem·po·ral lobe ▶ **noun** each of the paired lobes of the brain lying beneath the temples, including areas concerned with the understanding of speech.

tem·po·rar·i·ly /ˌtempəˈre(ə)rəlē, ˈtempəˌrer-/ ▶ **adverb** for a short or limited time.

– SYNONYMS **1** *the girl was temporarily placed with a foster family* **for the time being,** for the moment, for now, for the present, provisionally, pro tem, in the interim. **2** *he was temporarily blinded by the light* **briefly,** for a short time, momentarily, fleetingly.
– ANTONYMS permanently.

tem·po·rar·y /ˈtempəˌrerē/ ▶ **adjective** lasting for only a short or limited time.

– SYNONYMS **1 provisional,** short-term, interim, makeshift, stopgap, acting, fill-in, stand-in, caretaker. **2 brief,** short-lived, momentary, fleeting, passing, ephemeral.
– ANTONYMS permanent, lasting.

– DERIVATIVES **tem·po·rar·i·ness** noun.
– ORIGIN Latin *temporarius,* from *tempus* 'time.'

CHOOSE THE RIGHT WORD

temporary, ephemeral, evanescent, fleeting, transient, transitory

Things that don't last long are called **temporary**, which emphasizes a measurable but limited duration (*a temporary appointment as chief of staff*). Something that is **fleeting** passes almost instantaneously and cannot be caught or held (*a fleeting thought; a fleeting glimpse*). **Transient** also applies to something that lasts or stays only a short time (*transient house guests*), while **transitory** refers to something that is destined to pass away or come to an end (*the transitory pleasure of eating*). **Evanescent** and **ephemeral** describe what is even more short-lived. *Ephemeral* literally means lasting for only a single day, but is often used to describe anything that is slight and perishable (*his fame was ephemeral*). *Evanescent* is a more lyrical word for whatever vanishes almost as soon as it appears. In other words, a job might be *temporary*, an emotion *fleeting*, a visitor *transient*, a woman's beauty *transitory*, and glory *ephemeral*, but the flash of a bird's wing across the sky would have to be called *evanescent*.

tem·po·rize /'tempəˌrīz/ ▶ **verb** be evasive or delay making a decision in order to gain time.
– ORIGIN French *temporiser* 'bide one's time.'

tempt /tem(p)t/ ▶ **verb 1** try to persuade someone to do something appealing but wrong or unwise. **2** (**be tempted to do**) have an urge or inclination to do something: *I was tempted to look at my watch.* **3** entice or attract: *programs designed to tempt young people into engineering.*

– SYNONYMS **entice,** persuade, convince, inveigle, induce, cajole, coax, lure, attract, appeal to, tantalize, whet the appetite of, seduce; informal sweet-talk.
– ANTONYMS discourage, deter.

– DERIVATIVES **tempt·er** noun.
– PHRASES **tempt fate** (or **providence**) do something risky or dangerous.
– ORIGIN Latin *temptare* 'to handle, test, try.'

CHOOSE THE RIGHT WORD

tempt, allure, beguile, entice, inveigle, lure, seduce

When we are under the influence of a powerful attraction, particularly to something that is wrong or unwise, we are **tempted**. **Entice** implies that a crafty or skillful person has attracted us by offering a reward or pleasure (*she was enticed into joining the group by a personal plea from its handsome leader*), while **inveigle** suggests that we are enticed through the use of deception or cajolery (*inveigled into supporting the plan*). If someone **lures** us, it suggests that we have been tempted or influenced for fraudulent or destructive purposes or attracted to something harmful or evil (*lured by gang members*). **Allure** may also suggest that we have been deliberately tempted against our will, but the connotations here are often sexual (*allured by her dark green eyes*). **Seduce** carries heavy sexual connotations (*seduced by an older woman*), although it can simply mean prompted to action against our will (*seduced by a clever sales pitch*). While **beguile** at one time referred exclusively to the use of deception to lead someone astray, nowadays it can also refer to the use of subtle devices to lead someone on (*a local festival designed to beguile the tourists*).

temp·ta·tion /tem(p)'tāsʜən/ ▶ **noun 1** the action of tempting or the state of being tempted. **2** a tempting thing.

– SYNONYMS **1 desire,** urge, itch, impulse, inclination. **2 lure,** allure, enticement, attraction, draw, pull.

tempt·ing /'tem(p)tiɴɢ/ ▶ **adjective** appealing, even if wrong or unwise: *a tempting financial offer.*

– SYNONYMS **enticing,** alluring, attractive, appealing, inviting, seductive, beguiling, fascinating, mouthwatering.
– ANTONYMS uninviting.

tempt·ress /'tem(p)tris/ ▶ **noun** a sexually attractive woman who sets out to make a man desire her.

– SYNONYMS **seductress,** siren, femme fatale; informal vamp.

tem·pu·ra /'tempərə, tem'pŏŏrə/ ▶ **noun** a Japanese dish of fish, shellfish, or vegetables, fried in batter.
– ORIGIN Japanese.

ten /ten/ ▶ **cardinal number** one more than nine; 10. (Roman numeral: **x** or **X**.)
– DERIVATIVES **ten·fold** /'tenˌfōld/ adjective & adverb.
– PHRASES **ten out of ten** referring to an excellent performance. **ten to one** very probably.
– ORIGIN Old English.

ten·a·ble /'tenəbəl/ ▶ **adjective 1** able to be defended against attack or objection. **2** (of a post, grant, etc.) able to be held or used for a particular period: *a scholarship tenable for three years.*

– SYNONYMS **defensible,** justifiable, supportable, sustainable, arguable, able to hold water, reasonable, rational, sound, viable, plausible, credible, believable, conceivable.
– ANTONYMS untenable.

– ORIGIN French, from Latin *tenere* 'to hold.'

te·na·cious /tə'nāsʜəs/ ▶ **adjective 1** holding firmly to something. **2** continuing to exist or do something for longer than might be expected: *a tenacious belief.*

– SYNONYMS **persevering,** persistent, determined, dogged, strong-willed, indefatigable, tireless, resolute, patient, purposeful, unflagging, staunch, steadfast, untiring, unwavering, unswerving, unshakable; formal pertinacious.

– DERIVATIVES **te·na·cious·ly** adverb **te·nac·i·ty** /-'nasitē/ noun.
– ORIGIN from Latin *tenere* 'to hold.'

ten·an·cy /'tenənsē/ ▶ **noun** (pl. **tenancies**) the possession or occupation of land or property as a tenant.

ten·ant /'tenənt/ ▶ **noun 1** a person who rents land or property from a landlord. **2** Law a person privately owning land or property.

– SYNONYMS **occupant,** resident, inhabitant, leaseholder, lessee, lodger.

▶ **verb** occupy property as a tenant.
– ORIGIN Old French, 'holding.'

ten·ant farm·er ▶ **noun** a person who farms rented land.

tench /tenʜ/ ▶ **noun** (pl. same) a freshwater fish of the carp family.
– ORIGIN Old French *tenche.*

Ten Com·mand·ments ▶ **plural noun** (in the Bible) the rules of conduct given by God to Moses on Mount Sinai.

tend[1] /tend/ ▶ **verb 1** frequently behave in a particular way or have a certain characteristic: *men tend to marry younger women.* **2** go or move in a particular direction.

– SYNONYMS **be inclined,** be apt, be disposed, be prone, be liable, be likely, have a tendency.

– ORIGIN Latin *tendere* 'stretch, tend.'

tend[2] ▶ **verb** care for or look after: *ambulance crews were tending to the injured.*

– SYNONYMS *who will **tend to** the children?* **look after,** take care of, minister to, attend to, see to, watch over, keep an eye on, mind, protect, guard.
– ANTONYMS neglect.

– ORIGIN from **ATTEND**.

ten·den·cy /'tendənsē/ ▶ **noun** (pl. **tendencies**) **1** an inclination toward a particular characteristic or type of behavior. **2** a group within a larger political party or movement.

– SYNONYMS **inclination,** propensity, proclivity, proneness, aptness, likelihood, bent, leaning, liability.

ten·den·tious /ten'densʜəs/ ▶ **adjective** expressing a strong opinion, especially a controversial one.

– DERIVATIVES **ten·den·tious·ly** adverb **ten·den·tious·ness** noun.
– ORIGIN suggested by German *tendenziös*.

ten·der[1] /ˈtendər/ ▶ **adjective** (**tenderer, tenderest**) **1** gentle and kind. **2** (of food) easy to cut or chew. **3** (of a part of the body) painful to the touch. **4** young and vulnerable. **5** (of a plant) easily damaged by severe weather.

– SYNONYMS **1** *a gentle, tender man* **caring,** kind, kind-hearted, softhearted, compassionate, sympathetic, warm, gentle, mild, benevolent. **2** *a tender kiss* **affectionate,** fond, loving, romantic, emotional; informal lovey-dovey. **3** *simmer until the meat is tender* **soft,** succulent, juicy, melt-in-one's-mouth. **4** *her ankle was swollen and tender* **sore,** sensitive, inflamed, raw, painful, hurting, aching, throbbing. **5** *he started sailing at the tender age of ten* **young,** youthful, impressionable, inexperienced; informal wet behind the ears.
– ANTONYMS hard-hearted, callous, tough.

– DERIVATIVES **ten·der·ly** adverb **ten·der·ness** noun.
– ORIGIN Old French *tendre*.

ten·der[2] ▶ **verb 1** offer or present something formally: *he tendered his resignation.* **2** make a formal written offer to carry out work, supply goods, etc., for a stated fixed price. **3** give money as payment for something.

– SYNONYMS **offer,** proffer, put forward, present, propose, suggest, advance, submit, hand in.

▶ **noun** a formal offer to carry out work, supply goods, etc. for a stated fixed price.

– SYNONYMS **bid,** offer, quotation, quote, estimate, price.

– DERIVATIVES **ten·der·er** noun.
– PHRASES **put something out to tender** ask for offers to carry out work, supply goods, etc. to be submitted.
– ORIGIN Latin *tendere* 'stretch, hold out.'

ten·der[3] ▶ **noun 1** a boat used to ferry people and supplies to and from a ship. **2** a railroad car attached to a steam locomotive, carrying fuel and water.
– ORIGIN from **TEND**[2] or **ATTEND**.

ten·der·foot /ˈtendərˌfo͝ot/ ▶ **noun** (pl. **tenderfoots** or **tenderfeet**) a person who is new to and lacks experience in an activity or situation.

ten·der·heart·ed /ˈtendərˈhärtid/ ▶ **adjective** having a kind, gentle, or sentimental nature.

ten·der·ize /ˈtendəˌrīz/ ▶ **verb** make meat more tender by beating it or cooking it slowly.
– DERIVATIVES **ten·der·iz·er** noun.

ten·der·loin /ˈtendərˌloin/ ▶ **noun** the tenderest part of a loin of beef, pork, etc., taken from under the short ribs in the hindquarters.

ten·di·ni·tis /ˌtendəˈnītis/ (also **tendonitis**) ▶ **noun** inflammation of a tendon.

ten·don /ˈtendən/ ▶ **noun 1** a band of strong fibrous tissue that attaches a muscle to a bone. **2** the hamstring of a four-legged mammal.
– ORIGIN Greek *tenōn* 'sinew.'

ten·dril /ˈtendrəl/ ▶ **noun 1** a slender threadlike part of a climbing plant, which stretches out and twines around any suitable support. **2** a slender ringlet of hair.
– ORIGIN probably from Old French *tendron* 'young shoot.'

ten·e·brous /ˈtenəbrəs/ ▶ **adjective** literary dark; shadowy.
– ORIGIN Latin *tenebrosus*.

ten·e·ment /ˈtenəmənt/ ▶ **noun 1** (also **tenement house**) a large house divided into several separate apartments. **2** a room or set of rooms forming a separate home within a house or apartment block.
– ORIGIN Latin *tenementum*.

ten·et /ˈtenit/ ▶ **noun** one of the principles or beliefs of a religion, philosophy, etc.

– SYNONYMS **principle,** belief, doctrine, precept, creed, credo, article of faith, dogma, canon; theory, thesis, conviction, idea, view, opinion, position, hypothesis, postulation; (**tenets**) ideology, code of belief, teaching(s).

– ORIGIN Latin, 'he holds.'

ten-gal·lon hat ▶ **noun** a large, broad-brimmed hat, traditionally worn by cowboys.

ten·ner /ˈtenər/ ▶ **noun** Brit. informal a ten-pound note.

ten·nis /ˈtenis/ ▶ **noun** a game for two or four players, who use rackets to strike a ball over a net stretched across a grass or clay court.
– ORIGIN apparently from Old French *tenez* 'take, receive' (called by the server in the game of real tennis).

ten·nis el·bow ▶ **noun** inflammation of the tendons of the elbow caused by overuse of the forearm muscles.

ten·nis shoe ▶ **noun** a light canvas or leather soft-soled shoe suitable for tennis or casual wear.

ten·on /ˈtenən/ ▶ **noun** a projecting piece of wood made to fit into a mortise in another piece of wood.
– ORIGIN French.

ten·or[1] /ˈtenər/ ▶ **noun** a singing voice between baritone and alto or countertenor, the highest of the ordinary adult male range. ▶ **adjective** referring to an instrument of the second or third lowest pitch in its family: *a tenor sax.*
– ORIGIN from Latin *tenere* 'to hold' (because the tenor part 'held' the melody).

ten·or[2] ▶ **noun** the general meaning or nature of something.

– SYNONYMS **1** *the general tenor of his speech* **sense,** meaning, theme, drift, thread, import, purport, intent, intention, burden, thrust, significance, message; gist, essence, substance, spirit. **2** *the even tenor of village life* **course,** direction, movement, drift, current, trend.

– ORIGIN Latin *tenor* 'course.'

ten·o·syn·o·vi·tis /ˌtenōˌsinəˈvītis/ ▶ **noun** inflammation and swelling of a tendon, especially in the wrist, often caused by repetitive movements such as those made when typing.
– ORIGIN from Greek *tenōn* 'tendon' + *synovitis* 'inflammation of a synovial membrane.'

ten·pin bowl·ing ▶ **noun** a game in which ten wooden pins are set up at the end of a track and knocked down by rolling a hard, heavy ball at them.

TENS /tenz/ ▶ **abbreviation** transcutaneous electrical nerve stimulation, a technique for relieving pain by applying electrodes to the skin.

tense[1] /tens/ ▶ **adjective 1** feeling, causing, or showing anxiety and nervousness. **2** (especially of a muscle) stretched tight or rigid.

– SYNONYMS **1 anxious,** nervous, on edge, edgy, strained, stressed, ill at ease, uneasy, restless, worked up, keyed up, overwrought, jumpy; informal a bundle of nerves, jittery, twitchy, uptight. **2 nerve-

racking, stressful, anxious, worrying, fraught, strained, nail-biting. **3 taut,** tight, rigid, stretched, strained, stiff.
– ANTONYMS relaxed, calm.

▶ **verb** make or become tense.

– SYNONYMS **tighten,** tauten, flex, contract, brace, stiffen.
– ANTONYMS relax.

– DERIVATIVES **tense·ly** adverb **tense·ness** noun.
– ORIGIN Latin *tensus*, from *tendere* 'stretch.'

WORD TOOLKIT

See **APPREHENSIVE**.

tense² ▶ **noun** Grammar a set of forms taken by a verb to indicate the time or completeness of the action.
– ORIGIN Latin *tempus* 'time.'

ten·sile /'tensəl, -ˌsīl/ ▶ **adjective 1** relating to tension or being stretched. **2** capable of being drawn out or stretched.

ten·sile strength ▶ **noun** the resistance of a material to breaking when being stretched.

ten·sion /'tensʜən/ ▶ **noun 1** a situation in which there is conflict or distrust because of differing views, aims, or needs: *months of tension between the military and the government.* **2** a feeling of anxiety and mental pressure. **3** the state of being stretched tight. **4** the degree of stitch tightness in knitting and machine sewing. **5** voltage of a particular magnitude: *high tension.*

– SYNONYMS **1 tightness,** tautness, rigidity, pull. **2 strain,** stress, anxiety, pressure, worry, nervousness, jumpiness, edginess, restlessness, suspense, uncertainty. **3 strained relations,** strain, ill feeling, friction, antagonism, antipathy, hostility.

– DERIVATIVES **ten·sion·al** adjective.

tent /tent/ ▶ **noun** a portable shelter made of cloth, supported by one or more poles and stretched tight by cords attached to pegs driven into the ground.
– ORIGIN Old French *tente.*

ten·ta·cle /'tentəkəl/ ▶ **noun** a long, thin flexible part extending from the body of an animal, used for feeling or holding things, or for moving about.
– DERIVATIVES **ten·ta·cled** adjective **ten·tac·u·lar** /ten'takyələr/ adjective.
– ORIGIN Latin *tentaculum.*

ten·ta·tive /'tentətiv/ ▶ **adjective 1** done without confidence; hesitant: *a few tentative steps.* **2** not certain or fixed; provisional: *a tentative arrangement.*

– SYNONYMS **1** *a tentative arrangement* **provisional,** unconfirmed, preliminary, exploratory, experimental. **2** *a few tentative steps* **hesitant,** uncertain, cautious, timid, hesitating, faltering, shaky, unsteady, halting.
– ANTONYMS definite, confident.

– DERIVATIVES **ten·ta·tive·ly** adverb **ten·ta·tive·ness** noun.
– ORIGIN Latin *tentativus.*

tent cat·er·pil·lar ▶ **noun** a moth caterpillar that lives in groups inside communal silken webs in a tree, which it often defoliates.

ten·ter·hook /'tentərˌhŏŏk/ ▶ **noun** (in phrase **on tenterhooks**) in a state of nervous suspense.
– ORIGIN first meaning a hook used to fasten cloth on a *tenter*, a framework on which fabric was held taut during manufacture.

tenth /tenᴛʜ/ ▶ **ordinal number 1** that is number ten in a sequence; 10th. **2** (**a tenth/one tenth**) each of ten equal parts into which something is divided. **3** a musical interval spanning an octave and a third in a scale.
– DERIVATIVES **tenth·ly** adverb.

tent stitch ▶ **noun** a series of parallel diagonal stitches.

ten·u·ous /'tenyōōəs/ ▶ **adjective 1** very slight or weak: *a sick woman with only a tenuous grasp of reality.* **2** very slender or fine.

– SYNONYMS **slight,** insubstantial, flimsy, weak, doubtful, dubious, questionable, suspect, vague, nebulous, hazy.
– ANTONYMS convincing.

– DERIVATIVES **ten·u·ous·ly** adverb **ten·u·ous·ness** noun.
– ORIGIN Latin *tenuis* 'thin.'

ten·ure /'tenyər, -yŏŏr/ ▶ **noun 1** the conditions under which land or buildings are held or occupied. **2** the holding of a job or position. **3** guaranteed permanent employment, especially in a teaching post at a college or university.
– PHRASES **security of tenure** the right of a tenant of property to occupy it after the lease expires (unless a court should order otherwise).
– ORIGIN Old French, from Latin *tenere* 'to hold.'

ten·ured /'tenyərd, -yŏŏrd/ ▶ **adjective** (especially of a professor) having a permanent post.

te·pee /'tēˌpē/ (also **teepee** or **tipi**) ▶ **noun** a cone-shaped tent made of skins or cloth on a frame of poles, as used by American Indians.
– ORIGIN Sioux, 'dwelling.'

tep·id /'tepid/ ▶ **adjective 1** (especially of a liquid) lukewarm. **2** unenthusiastic: *a tepid response.*

– SYNONYMS **1 lukewarm,** warmish. **2 unenthusiastic,** apathetic, half-hearted, indifferent, cool, lukewarm, uninterested.

– DERIVATIVES **te·pid·i·ty** /tə'piditē/ noun **tep·id·ly** adverb.
– ORIGIN Latin *tepidus*, from *tepere* 'be warm.'

te·qui·la /tə'kēlə/ ▶ **noun** a Mexican alcoholic spirit made from the agave plant.
– ORIGIN named after the town of *Tequila* in Mexico.

te·qui·la sun·rise ▶ **noun** a cocktail of tequila, orange juice, and grenadine.

ter- ▶ **combining form** three; having three: *tercentenary.*
– ORIGIN Latin *ter* 'thrice.'

tera- ▶ **combining form 1** referring to a factor of one million million (10^{12}): *terawatt.* **2** Computing referring to a factor of 2^{40}: *terabyte.*
– ORIGIN from Greek *teras* 'monster.'

ter·a·byte /'terəˌbīt/ ▶ **noun** a unit of information stored in a computer equal to one million million (10^{12}) or (strictly) 2^{40} bytes.

ter·a·flop /'terəˌfläp/ ▶ **noun** a unit of computing speed equal to one million million floating-point operations per second.

te·rat·o·gen /te'ratəjən, -ˌjen, 'terətəjən/ ▶ **noun** a substance or factor that causes abnormalities to develop in an embryo.
– DERIVATIVES **te·rat·o·gen·ic** /təˌratə'jenik, ˌterətə-/ adjective.
– ORIGIN from Greek *teras* 'monster.'

ter·bi·um /'tərbēəm/ ▶ **noun** a silvery-white metallic chemical element.
– ORIGIN from *Ytterby*, a Swedish quarry where it was first found.

ter·cen·ten·ni·al /ˌtərsenˈtenēəl/ ▶ **noun** (pl. **tercentennials**) a three-hundredth anniversary.

ter·gi·ver·sa·tion /ˌtərjivərˈsāsʜən/ ▶ **noun** the use of language that is evasive or ambiguous.
– DERIVATIVES **ter·gi·ver·sate** /tərˈjivərˌsāt, ˈtərjivər-/ verb.
– ORIGIN from Latin *tergiversari* 'turn one's back.'

ter·i·ya·ki /ˌterēˈyäkē/ ▶ **noun** a Japanese dish of fish or meat marinated in soy sauce and broiled.
– ORIGIN Japanese.

term /tərm/ ▶ **noun 1** a word or phrase used to describe a thing or to express an idea. **2** (**terms**) language used on a particular occasion: *a protest in the strongest possible terms.* **3** (**terms**) requirements or conditions laid down or agreed. **4** (**terms**) relations between people: *we're on good terms.* **5** each of the periods in the year during which teaching is given in a school or college or during which a court of law holds sessions. **6** a period for which something lasts or is intended to last. **7** (also **full term**) the completion of a normal length of pregnancy. **8** Mathematics each of the quantities in a ratio, series, or mathematical expression. **9** Logic a word or words that may be the subject or predicate of a proposition.

– SYNONYMS **1 word,** expression, phrase, name, title, designation, label, description. **2** *the terms of the contract* **condition,** stipulation, specification, provision, proviso, restriction, qualification. **3 period,** length of time, spell, stint, duration, stretch, run, session.

▶ **verb** call by a particular word or phrase: *these are termed "reactive" treatments.*

– SYNONYMS **call,** name, entitle, title, style, designate, describe as, dub, label, tag.

– PHRASES **come to terms with** become able to accept or deal with something. **in terms of** (or **in —— terms**) with regard to a particular aspect of something: *there are benefits to be gained in terms of cost.* **the —— term** a period that is a specified way into the future: *in the long term.* **on —— terms** in a specified relation or on a specified footing: *we are once again on speaking terms.*
– ORIGIN Latin *terminus* 'end, limit.'

ter·ma·gant /ˈtərməgənt/ ▶ **noun** a bad-tempered or overbearing woman.
– ORIGIN Italian *Trivagante* 'thrice-wandering,' referring to a violent imaginary god or goddess often appearing in medieval morality plays.

ter·mi·na·ble /ˈtərmənəbəl/ ▶ **adjective 1** able to be terminated. **2** coming to an end after a certain time.

ter·mi·nal /ˈtərmənl/ ▶ **adjective 1** relating to, forming, or situated at the end. **2** (of a disease) predicted to lead to a person's death. **3** informal extreme and usually beyond cure or alteration: *an industry in terminal decline.*

– SYNONYMS **1 incurable,** untreatable, inoperable, fatal, lethal, mortal, deadly. **2 final,** last, concluding, closing, end.

▶ **noun 1** the station at the end of a railroad or other transport route. **2** a departure and arrival building for passengers at an airport. **3** a point of connection for closing an electric circuit. **4** a piece of equipment, usually consisting of a keyboard and a screen, that is connected to a central computer system. **5** a place where oil or gas is stored at the end of a pipeline or at a port.

– SYNONYMS **1 station,** last stop, end of the line, depot, terminus. **2 workstation,** VDU, visual display unit.

– DERIVATIVES **ter·mi·nal·ly** adverb.
– ORIGIN from Latin *terminus* 'end, boundary.'

ter·mi·nal ve·loc·i·ty ▶ **noun** Physics the constant speed that a freely falling object reaches when the resistance of the medium through which it is falling prevents it from moving any faster.

ter·mi·nate /ˈtərməˌnāt/ ▶ **verb 1** bring something to an end. **2** end a pregnancy at an early stage by a medical procedure. **3** (of a train or bus service) end its journey. **4** (**terminate in**) (of a thing) have its end at a particular place or in a particular form: *the cord terminates in a five-pin plug.*

– SYNONYMS **bring to an end,** end, bring to a close, close, conclude, finish, stop, wind up, discontinue, cease, cut short, abort, ax; informal pull the plug on.
– ANTONYMS begin.

– DERIVATIVES **ter·mi·na·tion** /ˌtərməˈnāsʜən/ noun **ter·mi·na·tor** /ˈtərməˌnātər/ noun.

ter·mi·nol·o·gy /ˌtərməˈnäləjē/ ▶ **noun** (pl. **terminologies**) the set of terms used in a particular subject, profession, etc.

– SYNONYMS **phraseology,** terms, expressions, words, language, parlance, vocabulary, nomenclature, usage, idiom, jargon; informal lingo.

– DERIVATIVES **ter·mi·no·log·i·cal** /-nəˈläjikəl/ adjective.

ter·mi·nus /ˈtərmənəs/ ▶ **noun** (pl. **termini** /-nī/ or **terminuses**) chiefly Brit. a railroad or bus terminal.
– ORIGIN Latin, 'end, limit, boundary.'

ter·mite /ˈtərˌmīt/ ▶ **noun** a small, soft-bodied insect that feeds on wood and lives in colonies in large nests of earth.
– ORIGIN Latin *termes* 'woodworm.'

term life in·sur·ance ▶ **noun** life insurance that pays a benefit in the event of the death of the insured during a specified term. Compare with **WHOLE LIFE INSURANCE**.

term pa·per ▶ **noun** a student's lengthy essay on a subject drawn from the work done during a school or college term.

tern /tərn/ ▶ **noun** a seabird resembling a gull, with long pointed wings and a forked tail.
– ORIGIN Scandinavian.

ter·na·ry /ˈtərnərē/ ▶ **adjective 1** composed of three parts. **2** Mathematics using three as a base.
– ORIGIN Latin *ternarius,* from *terni* 'three at once.'

ter·pene /ˈtərˌpēn/ ▶ **noun** Chemistry any of a large group of unsaturated hydrocarbons found in the essential oils of conifers and other plants.
– ORIGIN from German *Terpentin* 'turpentine.'

terp·si·cho·re·an /ˌtərpsikəˈrēən, -ˈkôrēən/ ▶ **adjective** formal or humorous relating to dancing.
– ORIGIN from *Terpsichore,* the ancient Greek and Roman Muse of dance.

terr. ▶ **abbreviation 1** territory. **2** territorial. **3** terrace.

ter·race /ˈteris/ ▶ **noun 1** a level paved area next to a building; a patio. **2** each of a series of flat areas on a slope, used for growing crops. **3** Brit. a block of row houses. ▶ **verb** make sloping land into terraces.
– DERIVATIVES **ter·rac·ing** noun.
– ORIGIN Old French, 'rubble, platform,' from Latin *terra* 'earth.'

ter·raced /ˈterist/ ▶ **adjective** (of land) having been formed into terraces.

ter·ra cot·ta /ˈterə ˈkätə/ ▶ **noun 1** brownish-red earthenware that has not been glazed, used as a decorative building material and in modeling. **2** a

strong brownish-red color.
– ORIGIN from Italian *terra cotta* 'baked earth.'

ter·ra fir·ma /'terə 'fərmə/ ▶ **noun** dry land; the ground.
– ORIGIN Latin, 'firm land.'

ter·rain /tə'rān/ ▶ **noun** a stretch of land, especially seen in terms of its physical features: *mountainous terrain.*

– SYNONYMS **land,** ground, territory, topography, landscape, countryside, country.

– ORIGIN French.

ter·ra in·cog·ni·ta /'terə ˌinkäg'nētə, in'kägnitə/ ▶ **noun** unknown territory.
– ORIGIN Latin, 'unknown land.'

ter·ra·pin /'terəˌpin/ ▶ **noun 1** a small edible turtle with lozenge-shaped markings on its shell, found in coastal marshes of the eastern US. **2** a small freshwater turtle.
– ORIGIN Algonquian.

ter·rar·i·um /tə're(ə)rēəm/ ▶ **noun** (pl. **terrariums** or **terraria** /-'re(ə)rēə/) **1** a glass-fronted case in which to keep small reptiles or amphibians. **2** a sealed transparent globe or similar container in which plants are grown.
– ORIGIN from Latin *terra* 'earth,' on the pattern of *aquarium.*

ter·raz·zo /tə'räzō, tə'rätsō/ ▶ **noun** flooring material consisting of chips of marble or granite set in concrete and polished smooth.
– ORIGIN Italian, 'terrace.'

ter·res·tri·al /tə'restrēəl, -'resCHəl/ ▶ **adjective 1** relating to the earth or dry land. **2** (of an animal or plant) living on or in the ground. **3** (of television broadcasting) using ground-based equipment rather than a satellite.

– SYNONYMS **earthly,** worldly, mundane, earthbound.

– DERIVATIVES **ter·res·tri·al·ly** adverb.
– ORIGIN from Latin *terra* 'earth.'

ter·ri·ble /'terəbəl/ ▶ **adjective 1** extremely bad, serious, or unpleasant. **2** troubled, guilty, or unwell: *I felt terrible about forgetting her name.* **3** causing terror.

– SYNONYMS **1** *a terrible crime* **dreadful,** awful, appalling, horrific, horrible, horrendous, atrocious, monstrous, sickening, heinous, vile, gruesome, unspeakable. **2** *terrible pain* **severe,** extreme, intense, excruciating, agonizing, unbearable. **3** *a terrible movie* **very bad,** dreadful, awful, frightful, atrocious, execrable; informal pathetic, pitiful, useless, lousy, appalling.
– ANTONYMS minor, slight, excellent.

– ORIGIN Latin *terribilis,* from *terrere* 'frighten.'

ter·ri·bly /'terəblē/ ▶ **adverb 1** extremely. **2** very badly.

ter·ri·er /'terēər/ ▶ **noun** a small breed of dog originally used for hunting animals that live underground.
– ORIGIN from Old French *chien terrier* 'earth dog.'

ter·rif·ic /tə'rifik/ ▶ **adjective 1** of great size, amount, or strength. **2** informal excellent.

– SYNONYMS **1 tremendous,** huge, massive, gigantic, colossal, mighty, considerable; informal mega, whopping, ginormous. **2 marvelous,** wonderful, sensational, outstanding, superb, excellent, first-rate, dazzling, out of this world, breathtaking; informal great, fantastic, fabulous, super, wicked, awesome; Brit. informal brilliant.

– DERIVATIVES **ter·rif·i·cal·ly** /-ik(ə)lē/ adverb.
– ORIGIN Latin *terrificus,* from *terrere* 'frighten.'

ter·ri·fy /'terəˌfī/ ▶ **verb** (**terrifies, terrifying, terrified**) make someone feel terror.

– SYNONYMS **frighten,** horrify, petrify, scare, strike terror into, paralyze, transfix.

– DERIVATIVES **ter·ri·fy·ing** adjective.

ter·rine /tə'rēn/ ▶ **noun 1** a mixture of chopped meat, fish, or vegetables pressed into a container and served cold. **2** an earthenware container for such a dish.
– ORIGIN French, 'large earthenware pot.'

ter·ri·to·ri·al /ˌteri'tôrēəl/ ▶ **adjective 1** relating to the ownership of an area of land or sea: *a territorial dispute.* **2** (of an animal) having and defending a territory. ▶ **noun** (**Territorial**) (in the UK) a member of the Territorial Army.
– DERIVATIVES **ter·ri·to·ri·al·i·ty** /-ˌtôrē'alitē/ noun **ter·ri·to·ri·al·ly** adverb.

ter·ri·to·ri·al wa·ters ▶ **plural noun** the part of the sea legally under the control of a state or country, especially those within a stated distance from its coast.

ter·ri·to·ry /'terəˌtôrē/ ▶ **noun** (pl. **territories**) **1** an area under the control of a ruler or country. **2** an organized division of a country not having the full rights of a state. **3** an area defended by an animal against others of the same sex or species. **4** an area of land of a particular type: *a campaign in mountainous territory.* **5** an area in which a person has particular rights, responsibilities, experience, or knowledge: *the Oscars are familiar territory for this actor.*

– SYNONYMS **1 region,** area, enclave, country, state, land, dependency, colony, dominion. **2** *mountainous territory* **terrain,** land, ground, countryside.

– ORIGIN Latin *territorium.*

ter·roir /ter'wär/ ▶ **noun** the complete natural environment in which a particular wine is produced, including factors such as the soil and climate.
– ORIGIN French.

ter·ror /'terər/ ▶ **noun 1** extreme fear. **2** a cause of terror. **3** the use or threat of violence to cause extreme fear: *a campaign of terror.* **4** informal a person who is annoying or difficult to control.

– SYNONYMS **fear,** dread, horror, fright, alarm, panic, shock.

– ORIGIN Latin, from *terrere* 'frighten.'

ter·ror·ism /'terəˌrizəm/ ▶ **noun** the unofficial or unauthorized use of violence and intimidation in the attempt to achieve political aims.
– DERIVATIVES **ter·ror·ist** noun & adjective.

ter·ror·ize /'terəˌrīz/ ▶ **verb** threaten and frighten someone over a period of time.

– SYNONYMS **persecute,** victimize, torment, tyrannize, intimidate, menace, threaten, bully, browbeat, scare, frighten, terrify, petrify.

ter·ry /'terē/ ▶ **noun** (pl. **terries**) fabric with raised loops of thread on both sides, used for towels.
– ORIGIN unknown.

terse /tərs/ ▶ **adjective** (**terser, tersest**) using few words; abrupt.

– SYNONYMS **brief,** short, to the point, concise, succinct, crisp, pithy, incisive, laconic, elliptical, brusque, abrupt, curt, clipped, blunt.
– ANTONYMS long-winded, polite.

– DERIVATIVES **terse·ly** adverb **terse·ness** noun.
– ORIGIN Latin *tersus* 'wiped, polished.'

ter·ti·ar·y /'tərsHē,erē, -sHərē/ ▸ **adjective 1** third in order or level. **2** (of medical treatment) provided at a specialist institution. **3** (**Tertiary**) Geology relating to the first period of the Cenozoic era, about 65 to 1.64 million years ago.
– ORIGIN Latin *tertiarius* 'of the third part.'

TESL /'tesəl/ ▸ **abbreviation** teaching of English as a second language.

tes·la /'teslə/ ▸ **noun** Physics the SI unit of magnetic flux density.
– ORIGIN named after the American electrical engineer Nikola *Tesla*.

TESOL /'te,säl, -,sôl, 'tesəl/ ▸ **abbreviation** teaching of English to speakers of other languages.

tes·sel·lat·ed /'tesə,lātid/ ▸ **adjective** (of a floor) decorated with mosaics.
– DERIVATIVES **tes·sel·la·tion** /,tesə'lāsHən/ noun.
– ORIGIN from Latin *tessellare* 'decorate with mosaics.'

tes·ser·a /'tesərə/ ▸ **noun** (pl. **tesserae** /'tesərē/) a small tile or block of stone used in a mosaic.
– ORIGIN Greek.

tes·si·tu·ra /,tesi'to͝orə/ ▸ **noun** the range within which most musical notes of a vocal part fall.
– ORIGIN Italian, 'texture.'

test[1] /test/ ▸ **noun 1** a procedure intended to establish the quality, performance, or reliability of something. **2** a short examination of a person's skill or knowledge. **3** a means of testing something. **4** a difficult situation that reveals the strength or quality of someone or something: *this is the first serious test of the peace agreement.* **5** an examination of part of the body or a body fluid for medical purposes. **6** Chemistry a procedure for identifying a substance or revealing whether it is present.

– SYNONYMS **1 trial,** experiment, check, examination, assessment, evaluation, appraisal, investigation. **2 exam,** examination, quiz, questionnaire.

▸ **verb 1** make someone or something undergo a test. **2** touch or taste something before taking further action. **3** severely try a person's endurance or patience.

– SYNONYMS **try out,** put through its paces, experiment with, check, examine, assess, evaluate, appraise, investigate, sample; informal run it up the flagpole (and see who salutes).

– DERIVATIVES **test·a·ble** adjective.
– PHRASES **test the water** find out people's feelings or opinions before taking further action.
– ORIGIN Latin *testum* 'earthen pot.'

test[2] ▸ **noun** Zoology the shell or tough outer covering of some invertebrates and protozoans.
– ORIGIN Latin *testa* 'tile, jug, shell.'

tes·ta /'testə/ ▸ **noun** (pl. **testae** /-tē/) Botany the protective outer covering of a seed.
– ORIGIN Latin, 'tile, shell.'

tes·ta·ment /'testəmənt/ ▸ **noun 1** a person's will. **2** evidence of a fact, event, or quality: *the show's success is a testament to her talent.* **3** (**Testament**) a division of the Bible (see **OLD TESTAMENT**, **NEW TESTAMENT**).
– ORIGIN Latin *testamentum* 'a will.'

tes·ta·men·ta·ry /,testə'men(t)ərē/ ▸ **adjective** relating to a will.

tes·tate /'tes,tāt/ ▸ **adjective** having made a valid will before dying.
– ORIGIN Latin *testatus* 'testified, witnessed.'

tes·ta·tor /'testātər/ ▸ **noun** (fem. **testatrix** /te'stātriks/) a person who has made a will or given a legacy.
– ORIGIN Latin.

test bed ▸ **noun** a piece of equipment for testing new devices.

test case ▸ **noun** a legal case whose result is used as an example when decisions are being made on similar cases in the future.

test-drive ▸ **verb** drive a motor vehicle to judge its performance and other qualities.

test·er[1] /'testər/ ▸ **noun 1** a person or device that tests something. **2** a sample of a product allowing customers to try it before buying.

tes·ter[2] ▸ **noun** a canopy over a four-poster bed.
– ORIGIN Latin *testerium*.

tes·tes /'testēz/ plural form of **TESTIS**.

test flight ▸ **noun** a flight during which the performance of an aircraft or its equipment is tested.
– DERIVATIVES **test-fly** verb.

tes·ti·cle /'testikəl/ ▸ **noun** either of the two oval organs that produce sperm in male mammals, enclosed in the scrotum behind the penis.
– DERIVATIVES **tes·tic·u·lar** /te'stikyələr/ adjective.
– ORIGIN Latin *testiculus*.

tes·ti·fy /'testə,fī/ ▸ **verb** (**testifies, testifying, testified**) **1** give evidence as a witness in a court of law. **2** (**testify to**) be evidence or proof of: *luxurious villas testify to the wealth here.*

– SYNONYMS **swear,** attest, give evidence, state on oath, declare, assert, affirm.

– ORIGIN Latin *testificari*.

tes·ti·mo·ni·al /,testə'mōnēəl/ ▸ **noun 1** a formal statement of a person's character and qualifications. **2** a public tribute to someone. **3** (in sports) a game or event held in honor of a player, who receives part of the income generated.

– SYNONYMS **reference,** (letter of) recommendation, commendation.

tes·ti·mo·ny /'testə,mōnē/ ▸ **noun** (pl. **testimonies**) **1** a formal statement, especially one given in a court of law. **2** (**testimony to**) evidence or proof of something.

– SYNONYMS **evidence,** sworn statement, attestation, affidavit, statement, declaration, assertion.

– ORIGIN Latin *testimonium*.

tes·tis /'testis/ ▸ **noun** (pl. **testes** /-,tēz/) an organ that produces sperm.
– ORIGIN Latin, 'witness.'

tes·tos·ter·one /te'stästə,rōn/ ▸ **noun** a steroid hormone that stimulates the development of male secondary sexual characteristics.
– ORIGIN from **TESTIS**.

test pi·lot ▸ **noun** a pilot who flies new or modified aircraft to test their performance.

test tube ▸ **noun** a thin glass tube closed at one end, used to hold material for laboratory testing or experiments.

test-tube ba·by ▸ **noun** informal a baby conceived by in vitro fertilization.

tes·ty /'testē/ ▸ **adjective** (**testier, testiest**) easily irritated; irritable.
– DERIVATIVES **tes·ti·ly** adverb **tes·ti·ness** noun.
– ORIGIN first meaning 'headstrong': from Old French *teste* 'head.'

tet·a·nus /ˈtetn-əs/ ▶ **noun** a disease causing the muscles to stiffen and go into spasms, spread by bacteria.
– DERIVATIVES **te·tan·ic** /teˈtanik/ adjective.
– ORIGIN Greek *tetanos* 'muscular spasm.'

tetch·y /ˈtecHē/ ▶ **adjective** (**tetchier, tetchiest**) bad-tempered and irritable.
– DERIVATIVES **tetch·i·ly** adverb **tetch·i·ness** noun.
– ORIGIN probably from Old French *teche* 'blotch, fault.'

tête-à-tête /ˈtāt ə ˈtāt, ˈtet ə ˈtet/ ▶ **noun** (pl. same or **tête-à-têtes** pronunc. same) a private conversation between two people.
– ORIGIN French, 'head-to-head.'

> **CHOOSE THE RIGHT WORD**
>
> See **CONVERSATION**.

teth·er /ˈteTHər/ ▶ **verb** tie an animal with a rope or chain so as to restrict its movement.

> – SYNONYMS **tie (up),** hitch, rope, chain; fasten, secure.
> – ANTONYMS unleash.

▶ **noun** a rope or chain used to tether an animal.

> – SYNONYMS **rope,** chain, cord, lead, leash; restraint; halter.

– ORIGIN Old Norse.

tetra- (also **tetr-** before a vowel) ▶ **combining form** four; having four: *tetrahedron.*
– ORIGIN from Greek *tettares* 'four.'

tet·ra·cy·cline /ˌtetrəˈsīˌklēn, -klin/ ▶ **noun** Medicine any of a large group of antibiotics with a molecular structure containing four rings.

tet·rad /ˈteˌtrad/ ▶ **noun** technical a group or set of four.
– ORIGIN Greek *tetras.*

tet·ra·he·dron /ˌtetrəˈhēdrən/ ▶ **noun** (pl. **tetrahedra** /-drə/ or **tetrahedrons**) a solid having four plane triangular faces.
– DERIVATIVES **tet·ra·he·dral** /-drəl/ adjective.

te·tral·o·gy /teˈträləjē/ ▶ **noun** (pl. **tetralogies**) a group of four related books, operas, plays, etc.

te·tram·e·ter /teˈtramitər/ ▶ **noun** a line of verse made up of four metrical feet.

tet·ra·pod /ˈtetrəˌpäd/ ▶ **noun** an animal of a group that includes all vertebrates apart from fish.
– ORIGIN from Greek *tetrapous* 'four-footed.'

Teu·ton /ˈt(y)o͞otn/ ▶ **noun 1** a member of an ancient Germanic people who lived in Jutland. **2** often derogatory a German.
– ORIGIN from Latin *Teutones* (plural).

Teu·ton·ic /t(y)o͞oˈtänik/ ▶ **adjective 1** informal, often derogatory displaying qualities regarded as typical of Germans. **2** relating to the Teutons.

Tex·as hold 'em /ˈhōldəm/ ▶ **noun** a form of poker in which each player is dealt two cards face down and combines these with any of five community cards to make the best available five-card hand.

Tex-Mex /ˈteks ˈmeks/ ▶ **adjective** (especially of food or music) having a blend of Mexican and southern American features. ▶ **noun** Tex-Mex music or food.

text /tekst/ ▶ **noun 1** a book or other written or printed work. **2** the main body of a written work as distinct from appendices, illustrations, etc. **3** written or printed words or computer data. **4** a written work chosen as a subject of study. **5** a passage from the Bible, especially as the subject of a sermon. **6** a text message.

> – SYNONYMS **1 book,** work, textbook. **2** *the pictures relate well to the text* **words,** content, body, wording, script, copy.

▶ **verb** send a text message to someone.
– DERIVATIVES **text·er** noun **text·ing** noun.
– ORIGIN Latin *textus* 'tissue, literary style.'

text·book /ˈteks(t)ˌbo͝ok/ ▶ **noun** a book used as a standard work for the study of a subject. ▶ **adjective** done in exactly the recommended way: *a textbook example of damage control.*

text ed·i·tor ▶ **noun** Computing a system or program that allows a user to edit text.

tex·tile /ˈtekˌstīl/ ▶ **noun** a type of cloth or woven fabric. ▶ **adjective** relating to fabric or weaving.
– ORIGIN Latin *textilis.*

text mes·sage ▶ **noun** an electronic message sent and received by cell phone.
– DERIVATIVES **text mes·sag·ing** noun.

tex·tu·al /ˈteksCHo͞oəl/ ▶ **adjective** relating to a text or texts.
– DERIVATIVES **tex·tu·al·ly** adverb.

tex·tu·al·i·ty /ˌteksCHo͞oˈalitē/ ▶ **noun** the quality or use of language that is typical of written works as distinct from spoken usage.

tex·ture /ˈteksCHər/ ▶ **noun 1** the feel, appearance, or consistency of a surface, substance, or fabric. **2** the quality created by the combination of elements in a work of music or literature: *a closely knit symphonic texture.*

> – SYNONYMS **feel,** touch, appearance, finish, surface, grain, consistency.

▶ **verb** give a rough or raised texture to a surface.
– DERIVATIVES **tex·tur·al** adjective.
– ORIGIN Latin *textura* 'weaving.'

tex·tur·ize /ˈteksCHəˌrīz/ ▶ **verb** give a particular texture to something.

TFT ▶ **abbreviation** thin-film transistor, used to make flat color display screens.

TGV ▶ **noun** a French high-speed passenger train.
– ORIGIN abbreviation of French *train à grande vitesse.*

Th ▶ **symbol** the chemical element thorium.

Thai /tī/ ▶ **noun** (pl. same or **Thais**) **1** a person from Thailand. **2** the official language of Thailand.
– ORIGIN Thai, 'free.'

thal·a·mus /ˈTHaləməs/ ▶ **noun** (pl. **thalami** /-ˌmī/) each of two masses of gray matter in the front part of the brain, relaying sensory information to other parts of the brain.
– ORIGIN Greek *thalamos.*

tha·las·so·ther·a·py /THəˌlasōˈTHerəpē, ˌTHalәsō-/ ▶ **noun** the use of seawater in cosmetic and health treatment.
– ORIGIN from Greek *thalassa* 'sea.'

tha·lid·o·mide /THəˈlidəˌmīd/ ▶ **noun** a drug formerly used as a sedative, but found to cause malformation of the fetus when taken in early pregnancy.

thal·li·um /ˈTHalēəm/ ▶ **noun** a soft silvery-white metallic chemical element whose compounds are very poisonous.
– ORIGIN from Greek *thallos* 'green shoot.'

thal·lus /ˈTHaləs/ ▶ **noun** (pl. **thalli** /ˈTHalī/) a plant body that lacks true roots and a vascular system, typical of algae, fungi, and lichens.
– ORIGIN from Greek *thallos* 'green shoot.'

than /THan, THən/ ▸ **conjunction & preposition 1** used to introduce the second part of a comparison: *he was smaller than his son.* **2** used to introduce an exception or contrast: *insects other than bees.* **3** used in expressions indicating one thing happening immediately after another: *no sooner were we seated than we had to move.*
– ORIGIN Old English.

> **USAGE**
> For an explanation of whether to use **I** and **we** or **me** and **us** after **than**, see the note at **PERSONAL PRONOUN**.

than·a·tol·o·gy /ˌTHanəˈtäləjē/ ▸ **noun** the scientific study of death and practices associated with it.
– ORIGIN from Greek *thanatos* 'death.'

thank /THaNGk/ ▸ **verb 1** express gratitude to someone. **2** ironic blame or hold responsible: *you have only yourself to thank.*

> – SYNONYMS **express one's gratitude to,** say thank you to, show one's appreciation to.

– PHRASES **thank goodness** (or **God** or **heavens**) an expression of relief. **thank you** a polite expression of gratitude.
– ORIGIN Old English.

thank·ful /ˈTHaNGkfəl/ ▸ **adjective 1** pleased and relieved. **2** expressing gratitude.

> – SYNONYMS **grateful,** relieved, pleased, glad.

– DERIVATIVES **thank·ful·ness** noun.

thank·ful·ly /ˈTHaNGkfəlē/ ▸ **adverb 1** in a thankful way. **2** luckily; fortunately.

> **USAGE**
> The traditional sense of **thankfully** is 'in a thankful way' (*she accepted the offer thankfully*). The newer use, meaning 'luckily; fortunately' (*thankfully, we didn't have to wait*) is now by far the most common, although some people think that it is incorrect.

thank·less /ˈTHaNGklis/ ▸ **adjective 1** (of a job or task) unpleasant and unlikely to be appreciated by others. **2** not showing or feeling gratitude.

> – SYNONYMS **unenviable,** difficult, unpleasant, unrewarding, unappreciated, unrecognized, unacknowledged.
> – ANTONYMS rewarding.

thanks /THaNGks/ ▸ **plural noun 1** an expression of gratitude. **2** thank you.

> – SYNONYMS **gratitude,** appreciation, acknowledgment, recognition, credit.

– PHRASES **no thanks to** despite the unhelpfulness of. **thanks to** due to.
– ORIGIN Old English.

thanks·giv·ing /ˌTHaNGksˈgiviNG/ ▸ **noun 1** the expression of gratitude to God. **2** (**Thanksgiving**) an annual national holiday in the US held on the fourth Thursday in November, commemorating the Pilgrims' harvest festival in 1621; a similar holiday in Canada held on the second Monday in October.

that /THat, THət/ ▸ **pronoun & determiner 1** (pl. **those**) used to refer to a person or thing seen or heard by the speaker or already mentioned or known. **2** (pl. **those**) referring to the more distant of two things near to the speaker. **3** (pl. **those**) used in singling out someone or something with a particular feature. **4** (as pronoun) (pl. **that**) used instead of which, who, when, etc., to introduce a clause that defines or identifies something: *the woman that owns the place.* ▸ **adverb 1** to such a degree. **2** informal very: *he wasn't that far away.* ▸ **conjunction 1** introducing a subordinate clause (one that depends on a main clause): *she said that she'd be late.* **2** literary expressing a wish or regret.
– PHRASES **that is** (or **that is to say**) a set expression introducing or following an explanation. **that said** even so. **that's that** there is nothing more to do or say about the matter.
– ORIGIN Old English.

> **USAGE**
> When is it right to use **that** and when should you use **which**? The general rule is that when introducing clauses that define or identify something, **that** is the preferred relative pronoun: *a book that aims to simplify scientific language*. You should use **which**, but never **that**, to introduce a clause preceded by a comma and giving additional information: *the book, which costs $15, has sold over a million copies* (not *the book, that costs $15, has sold over a million copies*).

thatch /THaCH/ ▸ **noun 1** a roof covering of straw, reeds, or similar material. **2** informal a person's hair. ▸ **verb** cover a roof or building with thatch.
– DERIVATIVES **thatch·er** noun.
– ORIGIN Old English, 'cover.'

thaw /THô/ ▸ **verb 1** become or make liquid or soft after being frozen. **2** (**it thaws, it is thawing, it thawed**) the weather becomes warmer and causes snow and ice to melt. **3** (of a part of the body) become warm enough to stop feeling numb. **4** make or become friendlier.

> – SYNONYMS **melt,** unfreeze, defrost, soften, liquefy.
> – ANTONYMS freeze.

▸ **noun 1** a period of warmer weather that thaws ice and snow. **2** an improvement in relations or an increase in friendliness.
– ORIGIN Old English.

the /THē, THə/ ▸ **determiner 1** used to refer to one or more people or things already mentioned or easily understood; the definite article. **2** used to refer to someone or something that is unique: *the sun.* **3** used to refer to something in a general rather than a specific way: *he plays the violin.* **4** used to explain which person or thing is being referred to: *the house at the end of our street.* **5** enough of: *I don't have the money to buy a house.*
– ORIGIN Old English.

the·a·ter /ˈTHēətər/ (also **theatre**) ▸ **noun 1** a building in which plays and other dramatic performances are given. **2** the writing and production of plays. **3** a play considered in terms of its dramatic quality: *this is intense, moving theater.* **4** (also **lecture theater**) a room for lectures with seats in tiers. **5** Brit. an operating room. **6** the area in which something happens: *a new theater of war has opened up.*

> – SYNONYMS **1 playhouse,** auditorium, amphitheater; movie theater, movie house, cineplex, multiplex; Brit. cinema. **2 acting,** the stage, drama, dramaturgy, show business; informal showbiz. **3** *a lecture theater* **hall,** room, auditorium.

– ORIGIN Greek *theatron.*

the·at·ri·cal /THēˈatrikəl/ ▸ **adjective 1** relating to acting, actors, or the theater. **2** exaggerated and excessively dramatic: *he looked over his shoulder with theatrical caution.*

– SYNONYMS **1 stage,** dramatic, thespian, show-business; informal showbiz. **2 exaggerated,** ostentatious, stagy, melodramatic, showy, affected, overdone; informal hammy.

▶ **noun 1** (**theatricals**) theatrical performances or behavior. **2** a professional actor or actress.
– DERIVATIVES **the·at·ri·cal·i·ty** /-ˌatriˈkalitē/ noun **the·at·ri·cal·ly** /-ik(ə)lē/ adverb.

the·at·rics /THēˈatriks/ ▶ **plural noun** theatrical performances or behavior; theatricals.

thee /T͟Hē/ ▶ **pronoun** old use or dialect you (as the singular object of a verb or preposition).
– ORIGIN Old English.

theft /THeft/ ▶ **noun** the action or crime of stealing.

– SYNONYMS **robbery,** stealing, larceny, shoplifting, burglary, embezzlement, raid, holdup; informal heist.

– ORIGIN Old English.

their /T͟He(ə)r/ ▶ **possessive determiner 1** belonging to or associated with the people or things previously mentioned or easily identified. **2** belonging to or associated with a person whose sex is not specified (used in place of either 'his' or 'his or her'). **3** (**Their**) used in titles.
– ORIGIN Old Norse.

USAGE

Do not confuse **their**, **there**, and **they're**. **Their** means 'belonging to them' (*I went around to their house*), while **there** means 'in, at, or to that place' (*it will take an hour to get there*), and **they're** is short for 'they are' (*they're going to be late*).

On the use of **their** in the singular to mean 'his or her,' see the note at **THEY**.

theirs /T͟He(ə)rz/ ▶ **possessive pronoun** used to refer to something belonging to or associated with two or more people or things previously mentioned.

USAGE

There is no apostrophe: the spelling should be **theirs** not *their's*.

the·ism /ˈTHēˌizəm/ ▶ **noun** belief in the existence of a god or gods, specifically of a creator who intervenes in the universe. Compare with **DEISM**.
– DERIVATIVES **the·ist** noun **the·is·tic** /THēˈistik/ adjective.
– ORIGIN from Greek *theos* 'god.'

them /T͟Hem, T͟Həm/ ▶ **pronoun** (third person pl.) **1** used as the object of a verb or preposition to refer to two or more people or things previously mentioned or easily identified. **2** referring to a person whose sex is not specified (used in place of either 'him' or 'him or her').
– ORIGIN Old Norse.

USAGE

For an explanation of the use of **them** in the singular to mean 'his or her,' see the note at **THEY**.

the·mat·ic /THiˈmatik/ ▶ **adjective** arranged according to subject or relating to a subject.
– DERIVATIVES **the·mat·i·cal·ly** /-ik(ə)lē/ adverb.

theme /THēm/ ▶ **noun 1** the subject of a talk, piece of writing, etc. **2** a prominent or frequently recurring melody or group of notes in a musical composition. **3** an idea that often recurs in a work of art or literature: *the theme of journeys is apparent throughout the book*. **4** (also **theme song** or **music**) a piece of music played at the beginning and end of a movie, television show, etc.

– SYNONYMS **1 subject,** topic, argument, idea, thrust, thread, motif, keynote. **2 melody,** tune, air, motif, leitmotif.

▶ **adjective** (of a restaurant, bar, or leisure venue) designed in the style of a particular country, historical period, etc.
▶ **verb** (often as adj. **themed**) give a particular setting or style to: *an American-themed restaurant*.
– ORIGIN Greek *thema* 'proposition.'

theme park ▶ **noun** a large amusement park based around a particular idea.

them·self /T͟Həmˈself, T͟Hem-/ ▶ **pronoun** (third person sing.) informal used instead of 'himself' or 'herself' to refer to a person whose sex is not specified.

USAGE

The standard reflexive pronoun (a word such as *myself* or *herself*) corresponding to **they** and **them** is **themselves**, as in *they can do it themselves*. The singular form **themself** has been used recently to correspond to the singular use of **they** when referring to a person whose sex is not specified (*helping someone to help themself*). However, **themself** is not good English, and you should use **themselves** instead.

them·selves /T͟Həmˈselvz, T͟Hem-/ ▶ **pronoun** (third person pl.) **1** used as the object of a verb or preposition to refer to a group of people or things previously mentioned as the subject of the clause. **2** they or them personally. **3** used instead of 'himself' or 'herself' to refer to a person whose sex is not specified.

then /T͟Hen/ ▶ **adverb 1** at that time. **2** after that; next. **3** also; in addition. **4** in that case; therefore.
– PHRASES **but then** (**again**) on the other hand. **then and there** immediately.
– ORIGIN Old English.

thence /T͟Hens/ (also **from thence**) ▶ **adverb** formal **1** from a place or source previously mentioned. **2** as a consequence.

thence·forth /T͟HensˈfôrTH/ (also **thenceforward**) ▶ **adverb** old use or literary from that time, place, or point onward.

the·oc·ra·cy /THēˈäkrəsē/ ▶ **noun** (pl. **theocracies**) a system of government in which priests rule in the name of God or a god.
– DERIVATIVES **the·o·crat·ic** /THēəˈkratik/ adjective.
– ORIGIN from Greek *theos* 'god.'

the·od·o·lite /THēˈädəˌlīt/ ▶ **noun** a surveying instrument with a rotating telescope for measuring horizontal and vertical angles.
– ORIGIN Latin *theodelitus*.

the·o·lo·gian /THēəˈlōjən/ ▶ **noun** a person expert in or studying theology.

the·ol·o·gy /THēˈäləjē/ ▶ **noun** (pl. **theologies**) **1** the study of God and religious belief. **2** a system of religious beliefs and theory.
– DERIVATIVES **the·o·log·i·cal** /THēəˈläjikəl/ adjective **the·o·log·i·cal·ly** /-ik(ə)lē/ adverb **the·ol·o·gist** noun.

the·o·rem /ˈTHēərəm, ˈTHi(ə)r-/ ▶ **noun 1** Physics & Mathematics a general proposition or rules that can be proved by reasoning. **2** Mathematics a rule expressed by symbols or formulae.
– ORIGIN Greek *theōrēma* 'speculation, proposition.'

the·o·ret·i·cal /THēə'retikəl/ (also **theoretic** /THēə'retik/) ▸ **adjective 1** concerned with the theory of a subject rather than its practical application. **2** based on theory rather than experience or practice: *the theoretical possibility of a chain reaction.*

– SYNONYMS **hypothetical,** speculative, academic, conjectural, suppositional, notional, unproven.
– ANTONYMS actual.

– DERIVATIVES **the·o·ret·i·cal·ly** /-ik(ə)lē/ adverb.

the·o·re·ti·cian /ˌTHēərə'tisHən, ˌTHi(ə)rə-/ ▸ **noun** a person who develops or studies the theory of a subject.

the·o·rize /'THēəˌrīz, 'THi(ə)rˌīz/ ▸ **verb** form a theory or theories about something.
– DERIVATIVES **the·o·rist** /'THēərist, 'THi(ə)r-/ noun **the·o·ri·za·tion** /ˌTHēərə'zāsHən, ˌTHi(ə)r-/ noun.

the·o·ry /'THēərē, 'THi(ə)rē/ ▸ **noun** (pl. **theories**) **1** a reasoned set of ideas that is intended to explain why something happens or exists. **2** an idea that explains or justifies something: *I have this theory that these guys were mean because they had silly names.* **3** a set of principles on which an activity is based: *a theory of education.*

– SYNONYMS **1 hypothesis,** thesis, conjecture, supposition, speculation, postulation, proposition, premise, opinion, view, belief, contention. **2** *modern economic theory* **ideas,** concepts, philosophy, ideology, thinking, principles.

– PHRASES **in theory** in a possible situation, but probably not in reality.
– ORIGIN Greek *theōria* 'contemplation, speculation.'

the·os·o·phy /THē'äsəfē/ ▸ **noun** a philosophy that believes that a person may achieve knowledge of God through such things as intuition, meditation, and prayer, especially the movement called the Theosophical Society.
– DERIVATIVES **the·o·soph·i·cal** /ˌTHēə'säfikəl/ adjective **the·os·o·phist** noun.
– ORIGIN from Greek *theosophos* 'wise concerning God.'

ther·a·peu·tic /ˌTHerə'pyo͞otik/ ▸ **adjective 1** relating to the healing of disease. **2** having a good effect on the body or mind.

– SYNONYMS **healing,** curative, remedial, medicinal, restorative, health-giving.

– DERIVATIVES **ther·a·peu·ti·cal·ly** /-ik(ə)lē/ adverb **ther·a·peu·tics** plural noun.

ther·a·pist /'THerəpist/ ▸ **noun** a person who provides therapy.

– SYNONYMS **psychologist,** psychotherapist, analyst, psychoanalyst, psychiatrist, counselor; informal shrink.

ther·a·py /'THerəpē/ ▸ **noun** (pl. **therapies**) **1** treatment intended to relieve or heal a physical disorder. **2** the treatment of mental or emotional problems by psychological means.

– SYNONYMS **1 treatment,** remedy, cure. **2** *he's currently in therapy* **psychotherapy,** psychoanalysis, counseling.

– ORIGIN Greek *therapeia* 'healing.'

Ther·a·va·da /ˌTHerə'vädə/ ▸ **noun** the more conservative of the two major traditions of Buddhism (the other being Mahayana), practiced mainly in Sri Lanka, Burma (Myanmar), Thailand, Cambodia, and Laos.
– ORIGIN Pali (an ancient language related to Sanskrit), 'doctrine of the elders.'

there /T͟He(ə)r/ ▸ **adverb 1** in, at, or to that place or position. **2** on that issue. **3** used in attracting attention to someone or something. **4** (usu. **there is/are**) used to indicate the fact or existence of something. ▸ **exclamation 1** used to focus attention. **2** used to comfort someone.
– PHRASES **so there** informal used to express defiance. **there and then** immediately.
– ORIGIN Old English.

USAGE

For an explanation of the difference between **there**, **their**, and **they're**, see the note at **THEIR**.

there·a·bouts /'T͟He(ə)rəˌbouts/ (also **thereabout**) ▸ **adverb** near that place, time, or figure.

there·af·ter /T͟He(ə)r'aftər/ ▸ **adverb** formal after that time.

there·at /T͟He(ə)r'at/ ▸ **adverb** old use or formal **1** at that place. **2** on account of or after that.

there·by /T͟He(ə)r'bī/ ▸ **adverb** by that means; as a result of that.

there·fore /'T͟He(ə)rˌfôr/ ▸ **adverb** for that reason; consequently.

– SYNONYMS **consequently,** because of that, for that reason, that being the case, so, as a result, hence, accordingly.

there·from /T͟He(ə)r'frəm/ ▸ **adverb** old use or formal from that or that place.

there·in /T͟He(ə)r'in/ ▸ **adverb** formal in that place, document, or respect.

ther·e·min /'THerəˌmin/ ▸ **noun** an electronic musical instrument in which the tone is generated by two high-frequency oscillators and the pitch controlled by the movement of the performer's hand toward and away from the circuit.
– ORIGIN named after its Russian inventor Lev *Theremin.*

there·of /T͟He(ə)r'əv/ ▸ **adverb** formal of the thing just mentioned; of that.

there·on /T͟He(ə)r'än, -'ôn/ ▸ **adverb** formal on or following from the thing just mentioned.

there's /T͟He(ə)rz/ ▸ **contraction 1** there is. **2** there has.

there·to /T͟He(ə)r'to͞o/ ▸ **adverb** formal to that or that place.

there·un·der /T͟He(ə)r'əndər/ ▸ **adverb** chiefly formal in accordance with the thing mentioned.

there·un·to /ˌT͟He(ə)rˌən'to͞o/ ▸ **adverb** old use or formal to that.

there·up·on /'T͟He(ə)rəˌpän/ ▸ **adverb** formal immediately or shortly after that.

there·with /T͟He(ə)r'wiT͟H, -'wiTH/ ▸ **adverb** old use or formal **1** with or in the thing mentioned. **2** soon or immediately after that.

therm /THərm/ ▸ **noun** a unit of heat, equivalent to 100,000 Btu or 1.055×10^8 joules.
– ORIGIN from Greek *thermē* 'heat.'

ther·mal /'THərməl/ ▸ **adjective 1** relating to heat. **2** (of an item of clothing) made of a fabric that provides good insulation to keep the body warm. ▸ **noun 1** an upward current of warm air, used by birds, gliders, and balloonists to gain height. **2** (**thermals**) thermal clothing, especially underwear.
– DERIVATIVES **ther·mal·ly** adverb.

ther·mal im·ag·ing ▸ **noun** the technique of using the heat given off by an object to produce an image of it or locate it.

ther·mal spring ▸ **noun** a spring of naturally hot water.

ther·mic /ˈTHərmik/ ▸ **adjective** relating to heat.

therm·i·on·ic /ˌTHərmīˈänik/ ▸ **adjective** relating to the emission of electrons from substances heated to very high temperatures.

ther·mi·on·ic valve ▸ **noun** Electronics a vacuum tube giving a flow of thermionic electrons in one direction, used in rectifying a current and in radio reception.

therm·is·tor /ˈTHərˌmistər/ ▸ **noun** an electrical resistor whose resistance is greatly reduced by heating, used for measurement and control.
– ORIGIN from *thermal resistor*.

ther·mo·cou·ple /ˈTHərmōˌkəpəl/ ▸ **noun** a device for measuring or sensing a temperature difference, consisting of two wires of different metals connected at two points, between which a voltage is developed in proportion to any temperature difference.

ther·mo·dy·nam·ics /ˌTHərmōdīˈnamiks/ ▸ **plural noun** (treated as sing.) the branch of science concerned with the relations between heat and other forms of energy involved in physical and chemical processes.
– DERIVATIVES **ther·mo·dy·nam·ic** adjective **ther·mo·dy·nam·i·cal·ly** /-ik(ə)lē/ adverb.

ther·mo·e·lec·tric /ˌTHərmō-iˈlektrik/ ▸ **adjective** producing electricity by a difference of temperatures.

ther·mo·gen·e·sis /ˌTHərmōˈjenəsis/ ▸ **noun** technical the production of bodily heat.
– DERIVATIVES **ther·mo·gen·ic** /-məˈjenik/ adjective.

ther·mog·ra·phy /THərˈmägrəfē/ ▸ **noun** a printing technique in which a resinous powder is dusted onto wet ink and fused by heating to produce a raised impression.
– DERIVATIVES **ther·mo·graph·ic** /ˌTHərməˈgrafik/ adjective.

ther·mom·e·ter /THərˈmämitər/ ▸ **noun** an instrument for measuring temperature, typically consisting of a glass tube marked with a temperature scale and containing mercury or alcohol, which expands when heated.

ther·mo·nu·cle·ar /ˌTHərmōˈn(y)ōōklēər, -kli(ə)r/ ▸ **adjective** relating to or using nuclear fusion reactions that occur at very high temperatures.

ther·mo·pile /ˈTHərməˌpīl/ ▸ **noun** a set of thermocouples arranged for measuring small quantities of radiant heat.

ther·mo·plas·tic /ˌTHərməˈplastik/ ▸ **adjective** (of a substance) becoming plastic when heated.

ther·mo·reg·u·la·tion /ˌTHərmōˌregyəˈlāSHən/ ▸ **noun** technical the regulation of bodily temperature.

ther·mos /ˈTHərməs/ (also **Thermos**) ▸ **noun** trademark a container that keeps a substance hot or cold by means of a double wall enclosing a vacuum.
– ORIGIN from Greek, 'hot.'

ther·mo·set·ting /ˈTHərmōˌsetiNG/ ▸ **adjective** (of a substance) setting permanently when heated.

ther·mo·sphere /ˈTHərmōˌsfir/ ▸ **noun** the upper region of the atmosphere above the mesosphere.

ther·mo·stat /ˈTHərməˌstat/ ▸ **noun** a device that automatically regulates temperature or activates a device at a set temperature.
– DERIVATIVES **ther·mo·stat·ic** /ˌTHərməˈstatik/ adjective **ther·mo·stat·i·cal·ly** /ˌTHərməˈstatik(ə)lē/ adverb.

the·sau·rus /THəˈsôrəs/ ▸ **noun** (pl. **thesauri** /-ˈsôrī/ or **thesauruses**) a book containing lists of words that have the same, similar, or a related meaning.
– ORIGIN Greek *thēsauros* 'storehouse, treasure.'

these /T͟Hēz/ plural of **THIS**.

the·sis /ˈTHēsis/ ▸ **noun** (pl. **theses** /-sēz/) **1** a statement or theory put forward to be supported or proved. **2** a long essay involving personal research, written as part of a university degree.

> – SYNONYMS **1 theory,** contention, argument, proposal, proposition, premise, assumption, supposition, hypothesis. **2 dissertation,** essay, paper, treatise, composition, theme (paper), study.

– ORIGIN Greek, 'placing, a proposition.'

thes·pi·an /ˈTHespēən/ ▸ **adjective** relating to drama and the theater. ▸ **noun** an actor or actress.
– ORIGIN from the ancient Greek dramatic poet *Thespis*.

they /T͟Hā/ ▸ **pronoun** (third person pl.) **1** used to refer to two or more people or things previously mentioned or easily identified. **2** people in general. **3** informal people in authority regarded as a whole. **4** used to refer to a person whose sex is not specified (in place of either 'he' or 'he or she').
– ORIGIN Old Norse.

> **USAGE**
>
> Many people now feel that the traditional use of **he** to refer to a person of either sex is old-fashioned and sexist, and the alternative, **he or she**, is rather clumsy. For these reasons, **they** (with its counterparts **them** or **their**) have become acceptable instead, as in *anyone can join if they are a resident* and *each to their own*.

they'd /T͟Hād/ ▸ **contraction 1** they had. **2** they would.

they'll /T͟Hāl/ ▸ **contraction 1** they will. **2** they shall.

they're /T͟He(ə)r/ ▸ **contraction** they are.

> **USAGE**
>
> For an explanation of the difference between **they're**, **their**, and **there**, see the note at **THEIR**.

they've /T͟Hāv/ ▸ **contraction** they have.

thi·a·mine /ˈTHīəmin, -mēn/ (also **thiamin** /-min/) ▸ **noun** vitamin B_1, found in unrefined cereals, beans, and liver, a deficiency of which causes beriberi.
– ORIGIN from Greek *theion* 'sulphur.'

thick /THik/ ▸ **adjective 1** with opposite sides or surfaces relatively far apart. **2** (of a garment or fabric) made of heavy material. **3** made up of a large number of things or people close together: *thick forest*. **4** (**thick with**) densely filled or covered with something. **5** (of the air or atmosphere) heavy, or difficult to see through. **6** (of a liquid or a semiliquid substance) relatively firm in consistency; not flowing freely. **7** informal of low intelligence; stupid. **8** (of a voice) hoarse or husky. **9** (of an accent) very marked and difficult to understand. **10** informal having a very close, friendly relationship.

> – SYNONYMS **1 broad,** wide, deep, stout, bulky, hefty, chunky, solid, plump. **2** *the station was thick with people* **crowded,** full, packed, teeming, seething, swarming, crawling, crammed, thronged, bursting at the seams, solid, overflowing; informal jam-packed, chock-a-block, stuffed; Austral./NZ informal chocker. **3 plentiful,** abundant, profuse, luxuriant, bushy, rich, riotous, exuberant, rank, rampant, dense; informal jungly. **4 semisolid,** firm, stiff, heavy, viscous,

gelatinous. **5** *thick fog* **dense,** heavy, opaque, impenetrable, soupy, murky.
– ANTONYMS thin, slender, sparse.

▶ **noun** (**the thick**) the middle or the busiest part: *in the thick of battle*.
– DERIVATIVES **thick·ly** adverb.
– PHRASES **thick and fast** rapidly and in great numbers. **(as) thick as thieves** informal very close or friendly. **through thick and thin** under all circumstances, no matter how difficult.
– ORIGIN Old English.

thick·en /ˈTHikən/ ▶ **verb** make or become thick or thicker.

– SYNONYMS **stiffen,** condense, solidify, set, gel, congeal, clot, coagulate.

– DERIVATIVES **thick·en·er** noun.
– PHRASES **the plot thickens** the situation is becoming more complicated and puzzling.

thick·en·ing /ˈTHikəniNG/ ▶ **noun 1** a thicker area or part. **2** a substance added to a liquid to make it thicker.

thick·et /ˈTHikit/ ▶ **noun** a dense group of bushes or trees.
– ORIGIN Old English.

thick·head·ed /ˈTHikˌhedid/ ▶ **noun** informal dull and stupid.

thick·ness /ˈTHiknis/ ▶ **noun 1** the distance through an object, as distinct from width or height. **2** the state or quality of being thick. **3** a layer of material. **4** a thicker part of something: *beams set into the thickness of the wall*.

thick·set /ˈTHikˌset/ ▶ **adjective** heavily or solidly built; stocky.

thief /THēf/ ▶ **noun** (pl. **thieves** /THēvz/) a person who steals another person's property.

– SYNONYMS **robber,** burglar, housebreaker, shoplifter, pickpocket, mugger, kleptomaniac; informal crook.

– ORIGIN Old English.

thieve /THēv/ ▶ **verb** be a thief; steal things.

– SYNONYMS **steal,** take, purloin, help oneself to, snatch, pilfer, embezzle, misappropriate; informal rob, swipe, nab, lift.

– DERIVATIVES **thiev·er·y** /ˈTHēv(ə)rē/ noun **thiev·ish** adjective.

thigh /THī/ ▶ **noun** the part of the leg between the hip and the knee.
– ORIGIN Old English.

thigh bone ▶ **noun** the femur.

thim·ble /ˈTHimbəl/ ▶ **noun** a small metal or plastic cap, worn to protect the finger and push the needle in sewing.
– ORIGIN Old English.

thim·ble·ful /ˈTHimbəlˌfo͝ol/ ▶ **noun** a small quantity of something.

thin /THin/ ▶ **adjective** (**thinner, thinnest**) **1** having opposite surfaces or sides close together. **2** (of a garment or fabric) made of light material. **3** having little flesh or fat on the body. **4** having few parts or members in relation to the area covered or filled: *a thin crowd*. **5** (especially of the air) not dense or heavy. **6** containing much liquid and not much solid substance. **7** (of a sound) faint and high-pitched. **8** lacking substance; weak and inadequate: *the evidence is rather thin*.

– SYNONYMS **1 narrow,** fine, attenuated. **2 lightweight,** light, fine, delicate, flimsy, diaphanous, gauzy, gossamer, sheer, filmy, transparent, see-through. **3 slim,** lean, slender, willowy, svelte, sylphlike, spare, slight, skinny, underweight, scrawny, scraggy, bony, gaunt, emaciated, skeletal, lanky, spindly, gangly; informal anorexic. **4 watery,** weak, runny, sloppy.
– ANTONYMS thick, broad, fat.

▶ **verb** (**thins, thinning, thinned**) **1** make or become less thick. **2** (often **thin something out**) remove some plants from a row or area to allow the others more room to grow.

– SYNONYMS **1 dilute,** water down, weaken. **2** *the crowds* ***thinned out*** **disperse,** dissipate, scatter.
– ANTONYMS thicken.

– DERIVATIVES **thin·ly** adverb **thin·ness** noun.
– PHRASES **into thin air** so as to become invisible or nonexistent.
– ORIGIN Old English.

WORD TOOLKIT

thin ...	lean ...	gaunt ...
layer	meat	face
line	body	figure
filament	muscle	appearance
slice	beef	features
coating	tissue	cheeks
crust	protein	eyes
blanket	physique	shadow

thine /T͟Hīn/ old use ▶ **possessive pronoun** yours. ▶ **possessive determiner** (before a vowel) your.
– ORIGIN Old English.

thing /THiNG/ ▶ **noun 1** an unspecified object, action, creature, etc. **2** an object as distinct from a living creature. **3** (**one's things**) a person's belongings or clothing. **4** (**things**) unspecified circumstances or matters: *how are things?* **5** (**the thing**) informal what is needed, acceptable, or fashionable. **6** (**one's thing**) informal one's special interest.

– SYNONYMS **1 object,** article, item, artifact, commodity; informal doodad, whatsit. **2** (**one's things**) *I'll come back tomorrow to collect my things* **belongings,** possessions, stuff, property, worldly goods, goods and chattels, effects, paraphernalia, bits and pieces, luggage, baggage; informal gear, junk. **3** (**things**) *his gardening things* **equipment,** apparatus, gear, kit, tackle, stuff, implements, tools, utensils, impedimenta, accoutrements.

– ORIGIN Old English (also in the senses 'meeting' and 'matter, concern').

thing·a·ma·jig /ˈTHiNGəməˌjig/ (also **thingamabob** /-ˌbäb/) ▶ **noun** a person or thing whose name one has forgotten, does not know, or does not wish to mention.

thing·y /ˈTHiNGē/ ▶ **noun** (pl. **thingies**) another term for **THINGAMAJIG**.

think /THiNGk/ ▶ **verb** (past and past part. **thought** /THôt/) **1** have a particular opinion, belief, or idea about someone or something. **2** use the mind to form connected ideas about someone or something. **3** (**think of**) call something to mind. **4** (**think of/about**) take someone or something into account or consideration. **5** (**think of/about**) consider the possibility or advantages of: *I was thinking of going home*. **6** (**think of**) have a particular opinion of: *she thought of him as a friend*.

– SYNONYMS **1** *I think he's gone home* **believe,** be of the opinion, be of the view, be under the impression, expect, imagine, anticipate, suppose, guess, fancy; informal reckon, figure. **2** *Jack thought for a moment* **ponder,** reflect, deliberate, consider, meditate, contemplate, muse, ruminate, brood; formal cogitate. **3** *she* ***thought of*** *all the visits she had made* **recall,** remember, recollect, call to mind, imagine, picture, visualize, envisage.

▶ **noun** an act of thinking.
– DERIVATIVES **think·a·ble** adjective.
– PHRASES **think better of** decide not to do something after reconsideration. **think nothing of** consider an activity others regard as odd, wrong, or difficult as easy or normal. **think something over** consider something carefully. **think something through** consider every aspect of something before acting. **think twice** consider a course of action carefully before going ahead with it. **think something up** informal invent something.
– ORIGIN Old English.

think·er /ˈTHiNGkər/ ▶ **noun** a person who thinks deeply and seriously.

– SYNONYMS **intellectual,** philosopher, scholar, sage, ideologist, theorist, intellect, mind; informal brain.

think·ing /ˈTHiNGkiNG/ ▶ **noun** a person's ideas or opinions.

– SYNONYMS **reasoning,** idea(s), theory, thoughts, philosophy, beliefs, opinion(s), view(s).

▶ **adjective** using thought or rational judgment; intelligent.

– SYNONYMS **intelligent,** sensible, reasonable, rational, logical, analytical, thoughtful.

– PHRASES **put on one's thinking cap** informal think carefully about a problem.

think tank ▶ **noun** a group of experts providing advice and ideas on specific political or economic problems.

thin·ner /ˈTHinər/ (also **thinners**) ▶ **noun** a solvent used to thin paint or other solutions.

thin·nings /ˈTHiniNGz/ ▶ **plural noun** seedlings, trees, or fruit that have been thinned out to improve the growth of those remaining.

third /THərd/ ▶ **ordinal number 1** that is number three in a sequence; 3rd. **2** (**a third/one third**) each of three equal parts into which something is divided. **3** a musical interval spanning three consecutive notes in a scale.
– DERIVATIVES **third·ly** adverb.
– ORIGIN Old English.

third class ▶ **noun 1** a set of people or things grouped together as the third best. **2** a cheap class of mail for advertising and other unsealed printed material. **3** chiefly historical the cheapest and least comfortable accommodations in a train or ship. ▶ **adjective & adverb** relating to the third class.

third cous·in ▶ **noun** see **COUSIN**.

third-de·gree ▶ **adjective 1** (of burns) being of the most severe kind, affecting tissue below the skin. **2** Law (of a crime, especially murder) in the least serious category. ▶ **noun** (**the third degree**) long and harsh questioning to obtain information or a confession.

third-gen·er·a·tion ▶ **adjective** (of a broadband digital telephone technology) that supports Internet connection and multimedia services.

third par·ty ▶ **noun** a person or group besides the two main ones involved in a situation or dispute. ▶ **adjective** Brit. (of insurance) covering damage or injury suffered by a person other than the person who is insured.

third per·son ▶ **noun 1** a third party. **2** see **PERSON** (sense 3).

third-rate ▶ **adjective** of very poor quality; inferior.

third read·ing ▶ **noun** a third presentation of a bill to a lawmaking assembly, in the US to consider it for the last time and in the UK to debate committee reports.

Third Reich /rīk, rīKH/ ▶ **noun** the Nazi regime in Germany, 1933–45.
– ORIGIN German *Reich* 'empire.'

Third World ▶ **noun** the developing countries of Asia, Africa, and Latin America.
– ORIGIN first used to distinguish the developing countries from the capitalist and Communist blocs.

thirst /THərst/ ▶ **noun 1** a feeling of needing or wanting to drink. **2** the state of not having enough water to stay alive. **3** (**thirst for**) a strong desire for something.

– SYNONYMS (**thirst for**) *a thirst for knowledge* **craving,** desire, longing, yearning, hunger, hankering, eagerness, lust, appetite; informal yen, itch.

▶ **verb 1** (**thirst for/after**) have a strong desire for: *an opponent thirsting for revenge.* **2** old use feel a need to drink.

– SYNONYMS (**thirst for/after**) *she thirsted for power* **crave,** want, covet, desire, hunger for, lust after, hanker after, wish for, long for.

– ORIGIN Old English.

thirst·y /ˈTHərstē/ ▶ **adjective** (**thirstier, thirstiest**) **1** feeling or causing a need to drink: *modeling is thirsty work.* **2** (**thirsty for**) having or showing a strong desire for something. **3** (of an engine or plant) consuming a lot of fuel or water.

– SYNONYMS **longing for a drink,** dry, dehydrated; informal parched, gasping.

– DERIVATIVES **thirst·i·ly** adverb **thirst·i·ness** noun.

thir·teen /ˌTHərˈtēn, ˈTHərˌtēn/ ▶ **cardinal number** one more than twelve; 13. (Roman numeral: **xiii** or **XIII**.)
– DERIVATIVES **thir·teenth** /ˌTHərˈtēnTH, ˈTHərˌtēnTH/ ordinal number.
– ORIGIN Old English.

Thir·teen Col·o·nies the British colonies that ratified the Declaration of Independence in 1776 and became founding states of the US.

thir·ty /ˈTHərtē/ ▶ **cardinal number** (pl. **thirties**) ten less than forty; 30. (Roman numeral: **xxx** or **XXX**.)
– DERIVATIVES **thir·ti·eth** /-iTH/ ordinal number.
– ORIGIN Old English.

thir·ty-eight ▶ **noun** a revolver of .38 caliber.

thir·ty-sec·ond note ▶ **noun** a musical note having the time value of half a sixteenth note, represented by a solid dot with a three-hooked stem.

this /T͟His/ ▶ **pronoun & determiner** (pl. **these** /T͟Hēz/) **1** used to identify a specific person or thing close at hand, just mentioned, or being indicated or experienced. **2** referring to the nearer of two things close to the speaker. **3** (as determiner) used with periods of time related to the present. ▶ **adverb** to the degree or extent indicated: *they can't handle a job this big.*
– ORIGIN Old English.

this·tle /ˈTHisəl/ ▶ **noun** a plant with a prickly stem and leaves and rounded heads of purple flowers.
– ORIGIN Old English.

this·tle·down /ˈTHisəlˌdoun/ ▶ **noun** the light fluffy down of thistle seeds, which enables them to be blown about in the wind.

thith·er /ˈTHiT͟Hər, ˈT͟Hi-/ ▶ **adverb** old use or literary to or toward that place.
– ORIGIN Old English.

tho /T͟Hō/ ▶ **conjunction & adverb** informal spelling of **THOUGH**.

thong /THÔNG, THäNG/ ▶ **noun 1** a narrow strip of leather or other material, used as a fastening or as the lash of a whip. **2** a pair of panties or skimpy bathing suit like a G-string. **3** a light sandal or flip-flop.
– ORIGIN Old English.

tho·rac·ic /THəˈrasik/ ▶ **adjective** relating to the thorax.

tho·rax /ˈTHôrˌaks/ ▶ **noun** (pl. **thoraces** /ˈTHôrəˌsēz/ or **thoraxes**) **1** the part of the body between the neck and the abdomen. **2** the middle section of the body of an insect, bearing the legs and wings.
– ORIGIN Greek.

tho·ri·um /ˈTHôrēəm/ ▶ **noun** a white radioactive metallic chemical element.
– ORIGIN named after *Thor*, the Scandinavian god of thunder.

thorn /THôrn/ ▶ **noun 1** a stiff, sharp-pointed woody projection on the stem or other part of a plant. **2** a thorny bush, shrub, or tree.

– SYNONYMS **prickle,** spike, barb, spine.

– PHRASES **a thorn in someone's side** (or **flesh**) a source of continual annoyance or trouble.
– ORIGIN Old English.

thorn·y /ˈTHôrnē/ ▶ **adjective** (**thornier, thorniest**) **1** having many thorns or thorn bushes. **2** causing difficulty or trouble: *the thorny issue of censorship*.

– SYNONYMS **1 prickly,** spiky, barbed, spiny, sharp. **2 problematic,** tricky, ticklish, delicate, controversial, awkward, difficult, knotty, tough, complicated, complex, involved, intricate, vexed; informal sticky.

thor·ough /ˈTHərō/ ▶ **adjective 1** complete with regard to every detail. **2** done with or showing great care and completeness. **3** absolute; utter: *he is a thorough nuisance*.

– SYNONYMS **1** *a thorough investigation* **rigorous,** in-depth, exhaustive, minute, detailed, close, meticulous, methodical, careful, complete, comprehensive. **2** *he's slow but thorough* **meticulous,** scrupulous, assiduous, conscientious, painstaking, punctilious, methodical, careful. **3 utter,** downright, absolute, complete, total, out-and-out, real, perfect, proper.
– ANTONYMS superficial, cursory.

– DERIVATIVES **thor·ough·ly** adverb **thor·ough·ness** noun.
– ORIGIN Old English, 'through.'

thor·ough·bred /ˈTHərəˌbred/ ▶ **adjective 1** (especially of a horse) of pure breed. **2** informal of outstanding quality. ▶ **noun** a thoroughbred animal.

thor·ough·fare /ˈTHərəˌfe(ə)r/ ▶ **noun** a road or path forming a route between two places.

thor·ough·go·ing /ˈTHərəˌgōiNG/ ▶ **adjective 1** involving or dealing with every detail or aspect. **2** complete; absolute.

those /T͟Hōz/ plural of **THAT**.

thou¹ /T͟Hou/ ▶ **pronoun** old use or dialect you (as the singular subject of a verb).
– ORIGIN Old English.

thou² /THou/ ▶ **noun** (pl. same or **thous**) **1** informal a thousand. **2** one thousandth of an inch.

though /T͟Hō/ ▶ **conjunction 1** despite the fact that; although. **2** however; but. ▶ **adverb** however: *he was able to write, though*.
– ORIGIN Old English.

thought¹ /THôt/ ▶ **noun 1** an idea or opinion produced by thinking, or that suddenly comes into the mind. **2** the process of thinking. **3** (**one's thoughts**) one's mind or attention. **4** careful consideration: *I haven't given much thought to sexism*. **5** (**thought of**) an intention, hope, or idea of: *they had no thought of surrender*. **6** the formation of opinions, especially as a system of ideas, or the opinions so formed: *traditions of Western thought*.

– SYNONYMS **1 idea,** notion, opinion, view, impression, feeling, theory. **2 thinking,** contemplation, musing, pondering, consideration, reflection, rumination, deliberation, meditation; formal cogitation. **3** *have you no thought for others?* **consideration,** understanding, regard, sensitivity, care, concern, compassion, sympathy.

– ORIGIN Old English.

thought² past and past participle of **THINK**.

thought·ful /ˈTHôtfəl/ ▶ **adjective 1** thinking deeply. **2** showing careful consideration. **3** considerate toward other people.

– SYNONYMS **1 pensive,** reflective, contemplative, musing, meditative, ruminative, introspective, philosophical, preoccupied, in a brown study. **2 considerate,** caring, attentive, understanding, sympathetic, solicitous, concerned, helpful, obliging, accommodating, kind, compassionate.
– ANTONYMS thoughtless.

– DERIVATIVES **thought·ful·ly** adverb **thought·ful·ness** noun.

thought·less /ˈTHôtləs/ ▶ **adjective 1** not considerate toward other people. **2** without considering the consequences: *to think a few minutes of thoughtless pleasure could end in this*.

– SYNONYMS **1 inconsiderate,** uncaring, insensitive, uncharitable, unkind, tactless, undiplomatic, indiscreet, careless. **2 unthinking,** heedless, careless, unmindful, absentminded, injudicious, ill-advised, ill-considered, imprudent, unwise, foolish, silly, stupid, reckless, rash, precipitate, negligent, neglectful, remiss.
– ANTONYMS thoughtful.

– DERIVATIVES **thought·less·ly** adverb **thought·less·ness** noun.

thought po·lice ▶ **noun** (treated as pl.) a group of people who aim to suppress ideas that depart from the way of thinking that they believe to be correct.

thought-pro·vok·ing ▶ **adjective** stimulating careful consideration or attention: *thought-provoking questions*.

thou·sand /ˈTHouzənd/ ▶ **cardinal number 1** (**a/one thousand**) the number equivalent to the product of a hundred and ten; 1,000. (Roman numeral: **m** or **M.**) **2** (**thousands**) informal an unspecified large number.
– PHRASES **bat a thousand** see **BAT¹**.
– DERIVATIVES **thou·sand·fold** /-ˌfōld/ adjective & adverb **thou·sandth** /ˈTHouzən(t)TH/ ordinal number.
– ORIGIN Old English.

Thou·sand Is·land dress·ing ▸ **noun** a dressing for salad or seafood consisting of mayonnaise with ketchup and chopped pickles.
– ORIGIN named after a large group of islands in the St. Lawrence River between the US and Canada.

thrall /THrôl/ ▸ **noun** the state of being in another's power: *she was in thrall to her husband.*
– DERIVATIVES **thral·dom** /-dəm/ (also **thralldom**) noun.
– ORIGIN Old Norse, 'slave.'

thrash /THrash/ ▸ **verb 1** beat someone or something repeatedly and violently with a stick or whip. **2** move in a violent or uncontrolled way: *he lay thrashing around in pain.* **3** informal defeat someone heavily. **4** (**thrash something out**) discuss an issue frankly and thoroughly so as to reach a decision.

– SYNONYMS **1 hit,** beat, strike, batter, thump, hammer, pound; informal belt. **2** *he was thrashing about in pain* **flail,** writhe, thresh, jerk, toss, twist, twitch.

▸ **noun 1** a violent or noisy movement. **2** (also **thrash metal**) a style of fast, loud, harsh-sounding rock music.
– ORIGIN Old English.

thrash·er[1] /ˈTHrasHər/ ▸ **noun** a person or thing that thrashes.

thrash·er[2] ▸ **noun** a thrushlike American songbird with mainly brown or gray plumage, a long tail, and a down-curved bill.
– ORIGIN perhaps from English dialect *thrusher, thresher* 'thrush.'

thread /THred/ ▸ **noun 1** a long, thin strand of cotton, nylon, or other fibers used in sewing or weaving. **2** a long, thin line or piece of something. **3** (also **screw thread**) a spiral ridge on the outside of a screw, bolt, etc., or on the inside of a cylindrical hole, to allow two parts to be screwed together. **4** a theme running through a situation or piece of writing. **5** (**threads**) informal clothes.

– SYNONYMS **1 cotton,** yarn, fiber, filament. **2 train of thought,** drift, direction, theme, tenor.

▸ **verb 1** pass a thread through the eye of a needle. **2** move or weave in and out of obstacles: *I threaded my way through the tables.* **3** (as adj. **threaded**) (of a hole, screw, etc.) having a screw thread.

– SYNONYMS **weave,** inch, squeeze, navigate, negotiate.

– DERIVATIVES **thread·er** noun **thread·y** adjective.
– ORIGIN Old English.

thread·bare /ˈTHred,ber/ ▸ **adjective 1** (of cloth, clothing, etc.) old, thin, and shabby. **2** lacking originality or freshness: *threadbare clichés.*

– SYNONYMS **worn,** old, holey, moth-eaten, mangy, ragged, frayed, tattered, decrepit, shabby, scruffy; informal tatty, the worse for wear.

thread·worm /ˈTHred,wərm/ ▸ **noun** a very thin worm that lives as a parasite in the intestines of humans and animals.

threat /THret/ ▸ **noun 1** a stated intention to harm someone, especially if they do not do what one wants. **2** a likely cause of damage or danger. **3** the possibility of trouble or danger: *their culture is under threat from logging and dams.*

– SYNONYMS **1 threatening remark,** warning, ultimatum. **2** *a possible threat to aircraft* **danger,** peril, hazard, menace, risk. **3** *the company faces the threat of liquidation* **possibility,** chance, probability, likelihood, risk.

– ORIGIN Old English, 'oppression.'

threat·en /ˈTHretn/ ▸ **verb 1** state that one intends to harm someone or cause trouble if one does not get what one wants. **2** put at risk: *a broken finger threatened his career.* **3** (of a situation or the weather) seem likely to produce an unwelcome result.

– SYNONYMS **1 menace,** intimidate, browbeat, bully, terrorize. **2 endanger,** jeopardize, imperil, put at risk. **3 herald,** bode, warn of, presage, foreshadow, indicate, point to, be a sign of, signal.

– DERIVATIVES **threat·en·ing** adjective.

three /THrē/ ▸ **cardinal number** one more than two; 3. (Roman numeral: iii or **III**.)
– DERIVATIVES **three·fold** /ˈTHrē,fōld/ adjective & adverb.
– ORIGIN Old English.

three-di·men·sion·al ▸ **adjective 1** having or appearing to have length, breadth, and depth. **2** lifelike or real.

3G ▸ **adjective** (of telephone technology) third-generation.

three-leg·ged race /ˈlegəd/ ▸ **noun** a race run by pairs of people, one member of each pair having their left leg tied to the right leg of the other.

three-piece ▸ **adjective 1** (of a set of furniture) consisting of a sofa and two armchairs. **2** (of a set of clothes) consisting of pants or a skirt with a vest and jacket.

three-quar·ter ▸ **noun** Rugby each of four players in a team positioned across the field behind the halfbacks.

three-ring cir·cus ▸ **noun** informal a confused or disorganized situation.

three·score /ˈTHrēˈskôr/ ▸ **cardinal number** literary sixty.

three·some /ˈTHrēsəm/ ▸ **noun** a group of three people.

three-way ▸ **adjective** involving three directions, processes, or participants: *a three-way race for the presidency.*

three-wheel·er ▸ **noun** a vehicle with three wheels, especially a child's tricycle.

thren·o·dy /ˈTHrenədē/ ▸ **noun** (pl. **threnodies**) a song, piece of music, or poem expressing grief or regret.
– ORIGIN Greek *thrēnōidia.*

thresh /THresH/ ▸ **verb 1** separate grains of cereals from the rest of the plant. **2** move violently; thrash.
– DERIVATIVES **thresh·er** noun.
– ORIGIN Old English.

thresh·old /ˈTHresH,(h)ōld/ ▸ **noun 1** a strip of wood or stone forming the bottom of a doorway. **2** a level or point at which something would begin or come into effect: *he was on the threshold of a dazzling career.*

– SYNONYMS **1 doorstep,** entrance, entry, gate, portal. **2 start,** beginning, commencement, brink, verge, dawn, inception, day one, opening, debut.

– ORIGIN Old English.

threw /THrōō/ past of **THROW**.

thrice /THrīs/ ▸ **adverb** old use or literary **1** three times. **2** extremely; very: *I was thrice blessed.*
– ORIGIN Old English.

thrift /THrift/ ▸ **noun 1** carefulness and economy in the use of money and other resources. **2** a plant that forms low-growing tufts of slender leaves with rounded pink

flowerheads, found on sea cliffs and mountains.
– ORIGIN from Old Norse, 'grasp.'

thrift·less /'THriftlis/ ▶ **adjective** spending money in an extravagant and wasteful way.

thrift shop (also **thrift store**) ▶ **noun** a store selling secondhand clothes and other household goods.

thrift·y /'THriftē/ ▶ **adjective** (**thriftier, thriftiest**) careful with money; economical.

– SYNONYMS **frugal,** economical, sparing, careful with money, provident, prudent, abstemious, parsimonious, penny-pinching.
– ANTONYMS extravagant.

– DERIVATIVES **thrift·i·ly** adverb.

CHOOSE THE RIGHT WORD

See **ECONOMICAL**.

thrill /THril/ ▶ **noun 1** a sudden feeling of excitement and pleasure. **2** an exciting or pleasurable experience. **3** a wave of emotion or sensation: *a thrill of excitement ran through her.*

– SYNONYMS **excitement,** stimulation, pleasure, tingle; informal buzz, kick, charge.
– ANTONYMS boredom.

▶ **verb 1** give someone a sudden feeling of excitement and pleasure. **2** (**thrill to**) experience something exciting.

– SYNONYMS **excite,** stimulate, arouse, rouse, inspire, delight, exhilarate, intoxicate, stir, electrify, move; informal give someone a buzz/kick/charge.
– ANTONYMS bore.

– ORIGIN from dialect *thirl* 'pierce, bore.'

thrill·er /'THrilər/ ▶ **noun** a novel, play, or movie with an exciting plot that involves crime or spying.

thrill·ing /'THriliNG/ ▶ **adjective** causing excitement and pleasure.

– SYNONYMS *a thrilling race* **exciting,** stimulating, stirring, action-packed, rip-roaring, gripping, electrifying, riveting, fascinating, dramatic, hair-raising.
– ANTONYMS boring.

thrips /THrips/ (also **thrip**) ▶ **noun** (pl. same) a minute black insect that sucks plant sap, noted for swarming on warm, still summer days.
– ORIGIN Greek, 'woodworm.'

thrive /THrīv/ ▶ **verb** (past **thrived** or **throve** /THrōv/; past part. **thrived** or **thriven** /'THrivən/) **1** grow or develop well or vigorously. **2** be successful; flourish: *she has managed to thrive in a fickle sport.*

– SYNONYMS **flourish,** prosper, burgeon, bloom, blossom, do well, advance, succeed, boom.
– ANTONYMS decline, wither.

– ORIGIN Old Norse, 'grasp.'

thriv·ing /'THrīviNG/ ▶ **adjective** flourishing and successful.

– SYNONYMS *real estate continues to be a thriving industry* **flourishing,** prospering, growing, developing, blooming, healthy, successful, booming, profitable; informal going strong.
– ANTONYMS declining.

thro' /THrōō/ ▶ **preposition, adverb, & adjective** literary or informal spelling of **THROUGH**.

throat /THrōt/ ▶ **noun 1** the passage that leads from the back of the mouth, through which food passes to the esophagus and air passes to the lungs. **2** the front part of the neck.
– PHRASES **be at each other's throats** quarrel or fight persistently. **force something down someone's throat** force something on a person's attention. **stick in one's throat** be unwelcome or difficult to accept.
– ORIGIN Old English.

throat·y /'THrōtē/ ▶ **adjective** (**throatier, throatiest**) (of a voice or other sound) deep and husky.
– DERIVATIVES **throat·i·ly** adverb **throat·i·ness** noun.

throb /THräb/ ▶ **verb** (**throbs, throbbing, throbbed**) **1** beat or sound with a strong, regular rhythm. **2** feel pain in a series of regular beats.

– SYNONYMS **pulsate,** beat, pulse, palpitate, pound, thud, thump, drum, vibrate, quiver.

▶ **noun** a strong, regular beat or sound.

– SYNONYMS **pulsation,** beat, pulse, palpitation, pounding, thudding, thumping, drumming, vibration, quivering.

– ORIGIN probably imitating the sound.

throes /THrōz/ ▶ **plural noun** intense or violent pain and struggle.
– PHRASES **in the throes of** in the middle of experiencing or doing something difficult.
– ORIGIN perhaps from an Old English word meaning 'calamity.'

throm·bo·sis /THräm'bōsis/ ▶ **noun** (pl. **thromboses** /-ˌsēz/) the formation of a blood clot in a blood vessel or the heart.
– DERIVATIVES **throm·bot·ic** /-'bätik/ adjective.
– ORIGIN Greek, 'curdling.'

throne /THrōn/ ▶ **noun 1** a ceremonial chair for a sovereign or bishop. **2** (**the throne**) the power or rank of a sovereign.
– ORIGIN Greek *thronos* 'elevated seat.'

throng /THrôNG, THräNG/ ▶ **noun** a large, densely packed crowd.

– SYNONYMS **crowd,** horde, mass, army, herd, flock, drove, swarm, sea, troupe, pack; informal bunch, gaggle, gang.

▶ **verb** gather somewhere in large numbers.

– SYNONYMS **1** *pavements thronged with tourists* **fill,** crowd, pack, cram, jam. **2** *visitors thronged around him* **flock,** crowd, cluster, mill, swarm, congregate, gather.

– ORIGIN Old English.

throt·tle /'THrätl/ ▶ **noun** a device controlling the flow of fuel or power to an engine. ▶ **verb 1** attack or kill someone by choking or strangling them. **2** control an engine or vehicle with a throttle.

– SYNONYMS **choke,** strangle, garrote.

– ORIGIN perhaps from **THROAT**.

through /THrōō/ ▶ **preposition & adverb 1** moving in one side and out of the other side of an opening or location. **2** so as to make a hole or passage in. **3** (prep.) expressing the location of something beyond an opening or an obstacle. **4** continuing in time toward: *she struggled through until payday.* **5** from beginning to end of an experience or activity. **6** so as to inspect all or part of: *he read the letter through carefully.* **7** by means of. **8** (adv.) so as to be connected by telephone. **9** expressing the extent of turning from one direction to another.

– SYNONYMS **1 by means of,** by way of, by dint of, via, using, thanks to, by virtue of, as a result of, as a consequence of, on account of, owing to. **2 throughout,** for the duration of, until/to the end of, all.

▶ **adjective 1** (of public transportation or a ticket) continuing or valid to the final destination. **2** (of traffic, roads, etc.) passing straight through a place. **3** having successfully passed to the next stage of a competition. **4** informal having finished an activity, relationship, etc.
– PHRASES **through and through** thoroughly or completely.
– ORIGIN Old English.

through·out /THrōō'out/ ▶ **preposition & adverb** all the way through.

– SYNONYMS **1 all over,** in every part of, everywhere in. **2 all through,** for the duration of, for the whole of, until the end of, all.

through·put /'THrōō,po͝ot/ ▶ **noun** the amount of material or items passing through a system or process.

through·way ▶ **noun** another spelling of **THRUWAY**.

throve /THrōv/ past of **THRIVE**.

throw /THrō/ ▶ **verb** (past **threw** /THrōō/; past part. **thrown** /THrōn/) **1** send something from one's hand through the air by a rapid movement of the arm and hand. **2** move or place quickly, hurriedly, or forcefully. **3** direct, or cast light, an expression, etc., in a particular direction. **4** disconcert or confuse someone. **5** send suddenly into a particular state: *the country was thrown into chaos*. **6** have a fit or tantrum. **7** hold a party. **8** make a clay pot, dish, etc., on a potter's wheel. **9** (of a horse) cause its rider to fall off. **10** project one's voice so that it appears to come from somewhere else. **11** informal lose a race or contest on purpose.

– SYNONYMS **1 hurl,** toss, fling, pitch, cast, lob, launch, bowl; informal chuck, heave, sling. **2** *he threw the door open* **push,** thrust, fling, bang. **3** *she threw a withering glance at him* **cast,** send, give off, emit, radiate, project. **4** *her question threw me* **disconcert,** unnerve, fluster, ruffle, put off, throw off balance, unsettle, confuse; informal rattle, faze.

▶ **noun 1** an act of throwing. **2** a light cover for furniture. **3** a light blanket, used especially when sitting. **4** (**a throw**) informal a single turn, round, or item: *on-the-spot portraits at $25 a throw.*

– SYNONYMS **lob,** toss, pitch, bowl.

– DERIVATIVES **throw·er** noun.
– PHRASES **throw something away 1** get rid of something useless or unwanted. **2** fail to make use of an opportunity or advantage. **throw one's hand in** withdraw; give up. **throw something in 1** include something extra with something that is being sold or offered. **2** interrupt a conversation with a casual remark. **throw in the towel 1** (in boxing) throw a towel into the ring as a sign of defeat. **2** admit defeat. **throw oneself into** start to do something in an enthusiastic way. **throw something open** make something generally accessible. **throw someone out** force someone to leave. **throw something out 1** get rid of something useless or unwanted. **2** (of a court, lawmaking body, etc.) dismiss or reject something. **throw someone over** abandon or reject a lover. **throw up** informal vomit.
– ORIGIN Old English, 'to twist, turn.'

throw·a·way /'THrōə,wā/ ▶ **adjective 1** intended to be thrown away after being used once or a few times. **2** (of a remark) said in a casual way.

throw·back /'THrō,bak/ ▶ **noun** a person or thing that resembles someone or something that existed in the past.

throw-in ▶ **noun** Soccer & Rugby the act of throwing the ball from the sideline to restart the game after the ball has gone out of play.

throw rug ▶ **noun** a small decorative rug designed to be placed with a casual effect and moved as required.

thru /THrōō/ ▶ **preposition, adverb, & adjective** informal spelling of **THROUGH**.

thrum /THrəm/ ▶ **verb** (**thrums, thrumming, thrummed**) **1** make a continuous rhythmic humming sound. **2** strum the strings of a musical instrument in a rhythmic way. ▶ **noun** a continuous rhythmic humming sound.
– ORIGIN imitating the sound.

thrush¹ /THrəSH/ ▶ **noun** a small or medium-sized songbird with a brown back and spotted breast.
– ORIGIN Old English.

thrush² ▶ **noun** infection of the mouth and throat or the genitals by a yeastlike fungus.
– ORIGIN uncertain.

thrust /THrəst/ ▶ **verb** (past and past part. **thrust**) **1** push suddenly or forcibly: *she thrust her hands into her pockets*. **2** make one's way forcibly. **3** (**thrust something on**) force someone to accept or deal with something. **4** extend or project: *the jetty thrust out into the water*.

– SYNONYMS **1 shove,** push, force, plunge, stick, drive, ram, lunge. **2** *fame had been thrust on him* **force,** foist, impose, inflict.

▶ **noun 1** a sudden or violent lunge or attack. **2** the main theme of a course of action or argument: *the thrust of the book is to guard young men from folly*. **3** the force produced by an engine to propel a jet or rocket.

– SYNONYMS **1 shove,** push, lunge, poke. **2 advance,** push, drive, attack, assault, onslaught, offensive. **3 force,** propulsion, power, impetus. **4 gist,** substance, drift, message, import, tenor.

– DERIVATIVES **thrust·er** noun.
– ORIGIN Old Norse.

thru·way /'THrōō,wā/ (also **throughway**) ▶ **noun** a major road or highway.

thud /THəd/ ▶ **noun** a dull, heavy sound. ▶ **verb** (**thuds, thudding, thudded**) move, fall, or hit something with a thud.
– ORIGIN probably from Old English, 'to thrust, push.'

thug /THəg/ ▶ **noun 1** a violent and aggressive man. **2** (**Thug**) historical a member of an organization of robbers and assassins in India.

– SYNONYMS **ruffian,** hooligan, bully, hoodlum, gangster, villain; informal tough, hood, goon, bruiser, heavy.

– DERIVATIVES **thug·ger·y** /THəgərē/ noun **thug·gish** adjective.
– ORIGIN Hindi, 'swindler, thief.'

thu·li·um /'TH(y)o͞olēəm/ ▶ **noun** a soft silvery-white metallic chemical element.
– ORIGIN Latin, from *Thule*, a country said in ancient times to be the northernmost part of the world.

thumb /THəm/ ▶ **noun** the short, thick first digit of the hand, set lower and apart from the other four. ▶ **verb 1** press, touch, or indicate something with the thumb. **2** turn over pages with the thumb. **3** (as adj. **thumbed**) (of a book's pages) worn or dirty by repeated handling.

4 request a free ride in a passing vehicle by signaling with the thumb; hitchhike.
– PHRASES **thumb one's nose at** informal show contempt for. **thumbs up** (or **down**) informal an indication of satisfaction or approval (or of rejection or failure). [with reference to the signal of approval or disapproval used by spectators at a Roman amphitheater (although the Romans used the symbols in reverse).] **under someone's thumb** completely under someone's influence.
– ORIGIN Old English.

thumb drive ▶ **noun** another term for **USB FLASH DRIVE.**

thumb in·dex ▶ **noun** a set of lettered notches cut down the side of a book to make it easier to find the required section.

thumb·nail /ˈTHəmˌnāl/ ▶ **noun** the nail of the thumb. ▶ **adjective** brief or concise: *a thumbnail sketch.*

thumb·print /ˈTHəmˌprint/ ▶ **noun 1** a mark made by the inner part of the top joint of the thumb. **2** an identifying characteristic.

thumb·screw /ˈTHəmˌskro͞o/ ▶ **noun** an instrument of torture that crushes the thumbs.

thumb·tack /ˈTHəmˌtak/ ▶ **noun** a short flat-headed pin for fastening paper to a surface.

thump /THəmp/ ▶ **verb 1** hit someone or something heavily with the fist or a blunt object. **2** put down or move forcefully or noisily: *he thumped the gun down on the counter.* **3** (of a person's heart or pulse) beat strongly. **4** informal defeat someone heavily.

> – SYNONYMS **1 hit,** beat, punch, strike, smack, batter, pummel; informal whack, wallop, slug, bash, clobber, clout. **2 throb,** pound, beat, thud, hammer.

▶ **noun** a heavy, dull blow or noise.
– DERIVATIVES **thump·er** noun.
– ORIGIN imitating the sound.

thump·ing /ˈTHəmpiNG/ ▶ **adjective** informal impressively large: *a thumping 64 percent majority.*

thun·der /ˈTHəndər/ ▶ **noun 1** a loud rumbling or crashing noise heard after a lightning flash due to the expansion of rapidly heated air. **2** a loud deep resounding noise.

> – SYNONYMS **rumble,** boom, roar, pounding, crash, reverberation.

▶ **verb 1** (**it thunders, it is thundering, it thundered**) produce thunder. **2** make or move with a loud deep noise. **3** speak loudly and angrily.

> – SYNONYMS **1 rumble,** boom, roar, pound, crash, resound, reverberate. **2** *"Answer me!" he thundered* **shout,** roar, bellow, bark.

– DERIVATIVES **thun·der·y** adjective.
– ORIGIN Old English.

thun·der·bolt /ˈTHəndərˌbōlt/ ▶ **noun** a flash of lightning with a crash of thunder at the same time.

thun·der·clap /ˈTHəndərˌklap/ ▶ **noun** a crash of thunder.

thun·der·cloud /ˈTHəndərˌkloud/ ▶ **noun** a cumulus cloud with a towering or spreading top, charged with electricity and producing thunder and lightning.

thun·der·head /ˈTHəndərˌhed/ ▶ **noun** a rounded, projecting head of a cumulus cloud, which is a sign of a thunderstorm.

thun·der·ing /ˈTHənd(ə)riNG/ ▶ **adjective** informal very great or impressive: *he's a thundering bore.*

thun·der·ous /ˈTHənd(ə)rəs/ ▶ **adjective 1** relating to or resembling thunder. **2** (of a person's expression or mood) very angry or menacing.
– DERIVATIVES **thun·der·ous·ly** adverb.

thun·der·show·er /ˈTHəndərˌSHou(-ə)r/ ▶ **noun** a brief rain shower accompanied by thunder and lightning.

thun·der·storm /ˈTHəndərˌstôrm/ ▶ **noun** a storm with thunder and lightning.

thun·der·struck /ˈTHəndərˌstrək/ ▶ **adjective** very surprised or shocked.

thunk¹ /THəNGk/ ▶ **noun & verb** informal term for **THUD.**

thunk² ▶ **verb** informal or humorous past and past participle of **THINK**: *who would've thunk it?*

thu·ri·ble /ˈTHo͝orəbəl/ ▶ **noun** a container in which incense is burned; a censer.
– ORIGIN Latin *thuribulum.*

Thurs·day /ˈTHərzdā, -dē/ ▶ **noun** the day of the week before Friday and following Wednesday.
– ORIGIN Old English, 'day of thunder' (named after *Thor,* the Germanic god of thunder).

thus /T͟Həs/ ▶ **adverb** literary or formal **1** as a result of this; therefore. **2** in this way. **3** to this point; so.
– ORIGIN Old English.

thwack /THwak/ ▶ **verb** hit someone or something with a sharp blow. ▶ **noun** a sharp blow.
– ORIGIN imitating the sound.

thwart /THwôrt/ ▶ **verb 1** prevent someone from accomplishing something. **2** prevent something from succeeding.

> – SYNONYMS **foil,** frustrate, forestall, stop, check, block, prevent, defeat, impede, obstruct, derail, snooker; informal stymie.
> – ANTONYMS help.

▶ **noun** a crosspiece forming a seat for a rower in a boat.
– ORIGIN from Old Norse, 'transverse.'

> **CHOOSE THE RIGHT WORD**
>
> **thwart, baffle, balk, foil, frustrate, inhibit**
>
> These verbs refer to the various ways in which we can outwit or overcome opposing forces. **Thwart** suggests using cleverness rather than force to bring about the defeat of an enemy or to block progress toward an objective (*thwart a rebellion; have one's goals thwarted by lack of education*). **Balk** also emphasizes setting up barriers (*a sudden reversal that balked their hopes for a speedy resolution*), but it is used more often as an intransitive verb meaning to stop at an obstacle and refuse to proceed (*he balked at appearing in front of the angry crowd*). To **baffle** is to cause defeat by bewildering or confusing (*the police were baffled by the lack of evidence*), while **foil** means to throw off course so as to discourage further effort (*her plan to arrive early was foiled by heavy traffic*). **Frustrate** implies rendering all attempts or efforts useless (*frustrated by the increasingly bad weather, they decided to work indoors*), while **inhibit** suggests forcing something into inaction (*to inhibit wage increases by raising corporate taxes*). Both *frustrate* and *inhibit* are used in a psychological context to suggest barriers that impede normal development or prevent the realization of natural desires (*he was both frustrated by her refusal to acknowledge his presence and inhibited by his own shyness*).

thy /T͟Hī/ (also **thine** /T͟Hīn/ before a vowel) ▶ **possessive determiner** old use or dialect belonging to you; your.
– ORIGIN Old English.

thyme /tīm/ ▶ **noun** a low-growing plant of the mint family, used as an herb in cooking.
– ORIGIN Greek *thumon.*

thy·mine /ˈTHīˌmēn, -min/ ▶ **noun** Biochemistry a compound that is one of the four constituent bases of nucleic acids.

thy·mol /ˈTHīˌmôl, -ˌmōl/ ▶ **noun** a white crystalline compound present in oil of thyme and used as a flavoring and preservative.
– ORIGIN from Greek *thumon* 'thyme.'

thy·mus /ˈTHīməs/ ▶ **noun** (pl. **thymi** /-mī/) a gland in the neck that produces white blood cells for the immune system.
– DERIVATIVES **thy·mic** /ˈTHīmik/ adjective.
– ORIGIN Greek *thumos.*

thy·roid /ˈTHīˌroid/ (also **thyroid gland**) ▶ **noun** a large gland in the neck that produces hormones regulating growth and development through the rate of metabolism.
– ORIGIN from Greek *khondros thureoeidēs* 'shield-shaped cartilage.'

thy·self /T͟Hīˈself/ ▶ **pronoun** (second person sing.) old use or dialect yourself.

Ti ▶ **symbol** the chemical element titanium.

ti /tē/ ▶ **noun** Music the seventh note of a major scale, coming after 'la'.
– ORIGIN alteration of former *si*, adopted to avoid having two notes (*sol* and *si*) beginning with the same letter.

ti·ar·a /tēˈärə, -ˈarə, -ˈe(ə)rə/ ▶ **noun 1** a semicircular jeweled ornamental band worn on the front of a woman's hair. **2** a crown with three tiers worn by a pope.
– ORIGIN Greek.

Ti·bet·an /təˈbetn/ ▶ **noun 1** a person from Tibet. **2** the language of Tibet. ▶ **adjective** relating to Tibet.

tib·i·a /ˈtibēə/ ▶ **noun** (pl. **tibiae** /ˈtibēˌē/ or **tibias**) the inner and typically larger of the two bones between the knee and the ankle, parallel with the fibula.
– DERIVATIVES **tib·i·al** adjective.
– ORIGIN Latin, 'shin bone.'

tic /tik/ ▶ **noun** a recurring spasm of the muscles, most often in the face.
– ORIGIN Italian *ticchio.*

tick[1] /tik/ ▶ **noun 1** a regular short, sharp sound, such as made by a clock. **2** Brit. informal a moment. **3** Brit. a check mark. ▶ **verb 1** make regular short, sharp sounds. **2** (**tick away/by/past**) (of time) pass. **3** chiefly Brit. mark something with a check mark. **4** (**tick over**) (of an engine) run slowly while the vehicle is not moving. **5** (**tick over**) work or operate slowly or at a minimum level. **6** (**tick someone off**) informal make someone annoyed or angry.
– PHRASES **what makes someone tick** informal what motivates someone.
– ORIGIN probably Germanic.

tick[2] ▶ **noun** a tiny creature related to the spiders, which attaches itself to the skin and sucks blood.
– ORIGIN Old English.

tick·er /ˈtikər/ ▶ **noun** informal **1** a person's heart. **2** informal a watch.

tick·er tape ▶ **noun** a paper strip on which messages are recorded in an electronic or telegraphic machine.

tick·et /ˈtikit/ ▶ **noun 1** a piece of paper or card giving the holder a right to be admitted to a place or event or to travel on public transportation. **2** an official notice of a parking or driving offense. **3** a label attached to an item in a store, giving its price, size, etc. **4** a set of policies supported by a party in an election: *he ran on a right-wing ticket.* **5** (**the ticket**) informal the desirable thing.

> – SYNONYMS **1 pass,** authorization, permit, token, coupon, voucher. **2 label,** tag, sticker, tab, slip, docket.

▶ **verb** (**tickets, ticketing, ticketed**) issue someone with a ticket.
– DERIVATIVES **tick·et·less** adjective.
– ORIGIN Old French *estiquet.*

tick·ing /ˈtikiNG/ ▶ **noun** a hard-wearing material used to cover pillows and mattresses.
– ORIGIN probably from Greek *thēkē* 'case.'

tick·le /ˈtikəl/ ▶ **verb 1** lightly touch someone in a way that causes them to itch, twitch, or laugh. **2** be appealing or amusing to: *I was tickled by the idea.*

> – SYNONYMS **1 stroke,** pet. **2 stimulate,** interest, appeal to, amuse, entertain, divert, please, delight.

▶ **noun** an act of tickling or the feeling of being tickled.
– DERIVATIVES **tick·ler** /ˈtik(ə)lər/ noun **tick·ly** /ˈtik(ə)lē/ adjective.
– PHRASES **be tickled pink** informal be very amused or pleased.
– ORIGIN perhaps from TICK[1], or from Scots and dialect *kittle* 'to tickle.'

tick·lish /ˈtik(ə)lisH/ ▶ **adjective 1** sensitive to being tickled. **2** (of a situation or problem) needing careful handling; tricky.

tic-tac-toe /ˈtik ˌtak ˈtō/ (also **tick-tack-toe**) ▶ **noun** a game in which each of two players tries to be the first to complete a row, column, or diagonal with either three O's or three X's on a nine-square grid.
– ORIGIN from *tick-tack*, used earlier to refer to games in which the pieces made clicking sounds.

tid·al /ˈtīdl/ ▶ **adjective** relating to or affected by tides.
– DERIVATIVES **tid·al·ly** adverb.

tid·al bore ▶ **noun** another term for BORE[3].

tid·al wave ▶ **noun 1** an exceptionally large ocean wave, especially one caused by an underwater earthquake or volcanic eruption. **2** an overwhelming or widespread occurrence of an activity, emotion, or reaction: *a tidal wave of patriotism swept the nation.*

tid·bit /ˈtidˌbit/ (Brit. **titbit** /ˈtitˌbit/) ▶ **noun 1** a small piece of tasty food. **2** a small item of very interesting information.
– ORIGIN from dialect *tid* 'tender' + BIT[1].

tid·dly /ˈtidlē/ ▶ **adjective** (**tiddlier, tiddliest**) Brit. informal slightly drunk.
– ORIGIN perhaps from former slang *tiddlywink*, referring to an unlicensed pub.

tid·dl·ywinks /ˈtidlēˌwiNGks/ ▶ **plural noun** (treated as sing.) a game in which small plastic counters are flicked into a central container, using a larger counter.
– ORIGIN unknown.

tide /tīd/ ▶ **noun 1** the alternate rising and falling of the sea due to the attraction of the moon and sun. **2** a powerful surge of feeling or trend of events: *the rising tide of urban violence.*

> – SYNONYMS **1 current,** flow, stream, ebb. **2** *the tide of history* **course,** movement, direction, trend, current, drift, run.

▶ **verb** (**tide someone over**) help someone through a difficult period.
– ORIGIN Old English, 'time, period, era.'

tide·line /ˈtīdˌlīn/ (also **tidemark** /ˈtīdˌmärk/) ▶ **noun** a line left or reached by the sea on a shore at the highest point of a tide.

tide·wa·ter /ˈtīdˌwôtər, -ˌwätər/ ▶ **noun** water brought or affected by tides.

ti·dings /ˈtīdiNGz/ ▶ **plural noun** literary news; information.
– ORIGIN Old English.

ti·dy /ˈtīdē/ ▶ **adjective** (**tidier, tidiest**) **1** arranged neatly and in order. **2** liking to keep oneself and one's possessions neat and in order. **3** informal (of a sum of money) considerable.

– SYNONYMS **1** *a tidy room* **neat,** orderly, in good order, well kept, in apple-pie order, shipshape, spick and span, spruce, uncluttered. **2** *a tidy person* **organized,** neat, methodical, meticulous, systematic.
– ANTONYMS untidy.

▶ **verb** (**tidies, tidying, tidied**) **1** (often **tidy someone/thing up**) make someone or something tidy. **2** (**tidy something away**) put away for the sake of tidiness.

– SYNONYMS **put in order,** clear up, sort out, straighten (up), clean up, spruce up, smarten up.

▶ **noun** (pl. **tidies**) a container for holding small objects.
– DERIVATIVES **ti·di·ly** adverb **ti·di·ness** noun.
– ORIGIN first meaning 'timely': from **TIDE**.

tie /tī/ ▶ **verb** (**ties, tying, tied**) **1** attach or fasten someone or something with string, cord, etc. **2** form a string, lace, etc., into a knot or bow. **3** restrict or limit to a particular situation or place: *he didn't want to be tied down by a full-time job.* **4** connect or link: *Canada's economy is closely tied to that of the US.* **5** achieve the same score or ranking as another competitor. **6** hold things together by a crosspiece or tie.

– SYNONYMS **1 bind,** tie up, tether, hitch, strap, truss, fetter, rope, make fast, moor, lash. **2 do up,** lace, knot. **3 restrict,** restrain, limit, tie down, constrain, cramp, hamper, handicap, hamstring, encumber, shackle. **4 link,** connect, couple, relate, join, marry. **5 draw,** be equal, be even.

▶ **noun** (pl. **ties**) **1** a thing that ties. **2** a necktie. **3** a result in a game or match in which two or more competitors are equal. **4** a rod or beam holding parts of a structure together. **5** Music a curved line above or below two notes of the same pitch indicating that they are to be played as one note.

– SYNONYMS **1 lace,** string, cord, fastening. **2 bond,** connection, link, relationship, attachment, affiliation. **3 restriction,** constraint, curb, limitation, restraint, hindrance, encumbrance, handicap, obligation, commitment. **4 draw,** dead heat.

– PHRASES **tie in** fit or be in harmony: *her ideas don't tie in with mine.* **tie someone up 1** restrict someone's movement by binding their limbs or tying them to something. **2** informal occupy someone so that they have no time for any other activity. **tie something up 1** settle something in a satisfactory way. **2** invest capital so that it is not immediately available for use.
– ORIGIN Old English.

tie-back ▶ **noun** a decorative strip of fabric or cord used for holding an open curtain back from the window.

tie·break·er /ˈtīˌbrākər/ (also **tiebreak** /ˈtīˌbrāk/) ▶ **noun** a means of deciding a winner from competitors who are equal at the end of a game or match.

tie-dye ▶ **verb** produce patterns on fabric by tying knots in it before it is dyed.

tie-in ▶ **noun 1** a connection or association. **2** a product produced to take commercial advantage of a related movie, book, etc.

tie·pin /ˈtīˌpin/ ▶ **noun** a tie tack.

tier /ti(ə)r/ ▶ **noun 1** one of a series of rows or levels placed one above and behind the other. **2** a level or grade within an organization or system.

– SYNONYMS **1 row,** rank, bank, line, layer, level. **2 grade,** gradation, echelon, rung on the ladder.

– DERIVATIVES **tiered** adjective.
– ORIGIN French *tire* 'sequence, order.'

tie tack ▶ **noun** an ornamental pin for holding a tie in place.

tie-up ▶ **noun** a link or connection.

TIFF /tif/ ▶ **abbreviation** Computing tagged image file format.

tiff /tif/ ▶ **noun** informal a trivial quarrel.
– ORIGIN probably dialect.

ti·ger /ˈtīgər/ ▶ **noun 1** a large member of the cat family with a yellow-brown coat striped with black, native to the forests of Asia. **2** (also **tiger economy**) a dynamic economy of an East Asian country such as Taiwan or South Korea.
– ORIGIN Greek *tigris.*

ti·ger cat ▶ **noun 1** a small forest cat that has a light brown coat with dark stripes and blotches, native to Central and South America. **2** a domestic cat with markings like a tiger's.

ti·ger·ish /ˈtīgəriSH/ ▶ **adjective** resembling a tiger, especially in being fierce.

ti·ger lil·y ▶ **noun** a tall Asian lily with orange flowers spotted with black or purple.

ti·ger moth ▶ **noun** a moth with boldly spotted and streaked wings.

ti·ger's eye (also **tiger eye**) ▶ **noun** a yellowish-brown semiprecious variety of quartz.

ti·ger shrimp ▶ **noun** a large edible shrimp marked with dark bands.

tight /tīt/ ▶ **adjective 1** fixed, closed, or fastened firmly. **2** (of clothes) close-fitting. **3** well sealed against something such as water or air. **4** (of a rope, fabric, or surface) stretched so as to leave no slack. **5** (of an area or space) allowing little room for maneuver: *a tight parking spot.* **6** (of people or things) closely packed together. **7** (of a community or other group) having a close relationship between its members. **8** (of a form of control) strictly imposed: *security was tight.* **9** (of money or time) limited. **10** (of a bend, turn, or angle) changing direction sharply. **11** informal not generous, especially with money; stingy. **12** informal drunk.

– SYNONYMS **1 firm,** secure, fast. **2 taut,** rigid, stiff, tense, stretched, strained, clenched. **3 close-fitting,** narrow, figure-hugging, skintight; informal sprayed on. **4** *a tight mass of fibers* **compact,** compressed, dense, solid. **5 small,** tiny, narrow, limited, restricted, confined, cramped, constricted. **6** *tight security* **strict,** rigorous, stringent, tough.
– ANTONYMS slack, loose.

▶ **adverb** very firmly, closely, or tensely.
– DERIVATIVES **tight·ly** adverb **tight·ness** noun.
– PHRASES **a tight ship** a strictly controlled organization or operation. **a tight corner** (or **spot**) a difficult situation.
– ORIGIN probably from Germanic.

CHOOSE THE RIGHT WORD

See **DRUNK**.

tight·en /ˈtītn/ ▶ **verb** make or become tight or tighter.

– SYNONYMS **1 stretch,** tauten, strain, stiffen, tense. **2 strengthen,** increase, make stricter.
– ANTONYMS loosen, slacken.

tight·fist·ed ▶ **adjective** informal not willing to spend or give much money; stingy.

tight-knit (also **tightly knit**) ▶ **adjective** (of a group of people) closely linked by strong relationships and shared interests.

tight-lipped ▶ **adjective** unwilling to reveal information or express emotion.

tight·rope /ˈtīt,rōp/ ▶ **noun** a rope or wire stretched high above the ground, on which acrobats balance.

tights /tīts/ ▶ **plural noun** a close-fitting garment made of stretchy material, covering the hips, legs, and feet.

tight·wad /ˈtīt,wäd/ ▶ **noun** informal a mean or miserly person.

ti·gress /ˈtīgris/ ▶ **noun** a female tiger.

tike ▶ **noun** variant spelling of **TYKE**.

tik·ka /ˈtikə, ˈtē-/ ▶ **noun** an Indian dish of pieces of meat or vegetables marinated in a spice mixture.
– ORIGIN Punjabi.

ti·la·pi·a /təˈläpēə/ ▶ **noun** an African freshwater fish, introduced in other parts of the world for food.
– ORIGIN Latin.

til·de /ˈtildə/ ▶ **noun** an accent (~) placed over Spanish *n* or Portuguese *a* or *o* to show that they should be pronounced in a particular way.
– ORIGIN Spanish.

tile /tīl/ ▶ **noun 1** a thin square or rectangular piece of baked clay, concrete, cork, etc., used for covering roofs, floors, or walls. **2** a thin, flat piece used in Scrabble, mah-jongg, and other games. ▶ **verb** cover a surface with tiles.
– DERIVATIVES **til·er** noun.
– ORIGIN Latin *tegula*.

til·ing /ˈtīliNG/ ▶ **noun 1** a surface covered by tiles. **2** the tiles used to cover a surface.

till[1] /til/ ▶ **preposition & conjunction** less formal way of saying **UNTIL**.
– ORIGIN Old English (not a shortened form of *until*).

USAGE

Although **till** and **until** have the same meaning, **till** is more informal and is used more often in speech than in writing. It is also more usual to use **until** at the beginning of a sentence.

till[2] ▶ **noun** a cash register or drawer for money in a store, bank, or restaurant.
– ORIGIN unknown.

till[3] ▶ **verb** prepare and cultivate land for crops.
– DERIVATIVES **till·a·ble** adjective **till·age** /ˈtilij/ noun.
– ORIGIN Old English, 'strive for, obtain by effort.'

till·er[1] /ˈtilər/ ▶ **noun** a horizontal bar fitted to the head of a boat's rudder post and used for steering.
– ORIGIN Old French *telier* 'weaver's beam, stock of a crossbow.'

till·er[2] ▶ **noun** an implement or machine for breaking up soil, such as a plow.

tilt /tilt/ ▶ **verb 1** move into a sloping position. **2** change in attitude or tendency: *the balance of power tilted toward the workers*. **3** (**tilt at**) historical (in jousting) thrust at someone with a lance or other weapon.

– SYNONYMS **slope,** tip, lean, list, bank, slant, incline, pitch, cant, angle.

▶ **noun 1** a sloping position or movement. **2** (**tilt at**) an attempt to win something. **3** a bias or tendency. **4** historical a joust.

– SYNONYMS **slope,** list, camber, gradient, grade, bank, slant, incline, pitch, cant, bevel, angle.

– DERIVATIVES **tilt·er** noun.
– PHRASES (**at**) **full tilt** with maximum speed or force. **tilt at windmills** attack imaginary enemies. [with reference to the story of Don Quixote, who tilted at windmills believing they were giants.]
– ORIGIN perhaps from an Old English word meaning 'unsteady.'

tilth /tilTH/ ▶ **noun** the condition of soil that has been prepared for growing crops.
– ORIGIN Old English.

tim·bale /ˈtimbəl, timˈbäl/ ▶ **noun** a dish of finely ground meat or fish cooked with other ingredients in a mold or a pastry shell.
– ORIGIN French, 'drum.'

tim·ber /ˈtimbər/ ▶ **noun 1** wood prepared for use in building and carpentry. **2** a wooden beam used in building.

– SYNONYMS **1 wood,** lumber. **2 beam,** spar, plank, batten, lath, board, joist, rafter.

– DERIVATIVES **tim·bered** adjective **tim·ber·ing** noun.
– ORIGIN Old English, 'a building,' also 'building material.'

tim·ber·land /ˈtimbər,land/ ▶ **noun** (also **timberlands**) land covered with forest suitable or managed for timber.

tim·ber·line /ˈtimbər,līn/ ▶ **noun** another term for **TREELINE**.

tim·ber wolf ▶ **noun** a wolf of a large variety found mainly in northern North America, with tawny-gray fur.

tim·bre /ˈtambər, ˈtäNbrə/ ▶ **noun 1** the quality of a musical sound or voice as distinct from its pitch and intensity. **2** distinctive quality or character: *the phrase had the right bureaucratic timbre*.

– SYNONYMS **tone,** sound, voice, color, tonality.

– ORIGIN French.

tim·brel /ˈtimbrəl/ ▶ **noun** old use a tambourine or similar instrument.
– ORIGIN perhaps from Old French and related to **TIMBRE**.

time /tīm/ ▶ **noun 1** the unlimited continued progress of existence and events in the past, present, and future, regarded as a whole. **2** a point of time as measured in hours and minutes past midnight or noon. **3** the right or appropriate moment to do something. **4** (**a time**) an indefinite period. **5** (also **times**) a particular point or period of time. **6** the length of time taken to complete an activity. **7** time as available or used: *a waste of time*. **8** (**one's time**) a period regarded as characteristic of a stage of one's life. **9** an instance of something happening or being done: *the nurse came in four times a day*. **10** (**times**) (following a number) expressing multiplication. **11** the rhythmic pattern or tempo of a piece of music. **12** the normal rate of pay for time spent working. **13** informal a prison sentence.

– SYNONYMS **1** *late at night was the best time to leave* **moment,** point (in time), occasion, instant, juncture, stage. **2** *he worked there for a time* **while,** spell, stretch, stint, interval, period, length of time, duration, phase. **3** *the time of the dinosaurs* **era,** age, epoch, eon, period, years, days.

▸ **verb 1** arrange a time for: *the first race is timed for 11:15.* **2** perform an action at a particular time. **3** measure the time taken by someone or something. **4** (**time something out**) (of a computer or a program) cancel an operation automatically because a set interval of time has passed.

– SYNONYMS **schedule,** arrange, set, organize, fix, book, line up, slate, timetable, plan.

– PHRASES **about time** used to say that something should have happened earlier. **at the same time** nevertheless. **at a time** separately in the specified groups or numbers: *he took the stairs two at a time.* **behind the times** not aware of or using the latest ideas or techniques. **for the time being** until some other arrangement is made. **have no time for** dislike or disapprove of someone or something. **in time 1** not late. **2** eventually. **3** in accordance with the appropriate musical rhythm or tempo. **keep good time 1** (of a clock or watch) record time accurately. **2** be punctual. **keep time** play or accompany music in time. **on time** punctual; punctually. **pass the time of day** exchange greetings or casual remarks. **time immemorial** a time in the past that is so long ago that people cannot remember it. **the time of one's life** a very enjoyable period or occasion. **time will tell** the truth about something will be established in the future.

– ORIGIN Old English.

WORD LINKS

chronological, **temporal** *relating to time*

time-and-mo·tion stud·y ▸ **noun** a study of the efficiency of a company's working methods.

time bomb ▸ **noun 1** a bomb designed to explode at a set time. **2** a situation that is likely to cause serious problems if action is not taken: *the treatment of refugees had become a political time bomb.*

time cap·sule ▸ **noun** a container holding a selection of objects chosen as being typical of the present time, buried for discovery in the future.

time·card /'tīm'kärd/ ▸ **noun** a card used to record an employee's starting and quitting times, usually stamped by a time clock.

time clock ▸ **noun** a clock with a device for recording employees' times of arrival and departure.

time-con·sum·ing ▸ **adjective** taking a lot of or too much time.

time frame ▸ **noun** a specified period of time.

time-hon·ored ▸ **adjective** (of a custom or tradition) respected or valued because it has existed for a long time.

time·keep·er /'tīm,kēpər/ ▸ **noun 1** a person who records the amount of time taken by a process or activity. **2** a person regarded in terms of how punctual they are. **3** a watch or clock regarded in terms of how accurate it is.

– DERIVATIVES **time·keep·ing** noun.

time lag ▸ **noun** see LAG[1].

time-lapse ▸ **adjective** (of a photographic technique) taking a sequence of frames at set intervals to record changes that take place slowly over time.

time·less /'tīmlis/ ▸ **adjective** not affected by the passage of time or changes in fashion.

– SYNONYMS **lasting,** enduring, classic, ageless, permanent, perennial, abiding, unchanging, unvarying, never-changing, eternal, everlasting.
– ANTONYMS ephemeral.

– DERIVATIVES **time·less·ly** adverb **time·less·ness** noun.

time·line /'tīm,līn/ (also **time line**) ▸ **noun** a graphic representation of the passage of time as a line.

time·ly /'tīmlē/ ▸ **adjective** done or occurring at a favorable or appropriate time.

– SYNONYMS **opportune,** well timed, convenient, appropriate, expedient, seasonable, propitious.
– ANTONYMS ill-timed.

– DERIVATIVES **time·li·ness** noun.

CHOOSE THE RIGHT WORD

timely, opportune, propitious, seasonable

Some people seem to have a knack for doing or saying the right thing at the right time. A **timely** act or remark is one that comes at a moment when it is of genuine value or service (*a timely interruption*), while an **opportune** one comes in the nick of time, as if by design, and exactly meets the needs of the occasion (*a storm came up at an opportune moment, squelching enthusiasm for the fight*). **Seasonable** applies to whatever is suited to the season of the year or fits in with the needs of the moment or the character of the occasion (*seasonable weather; a seasonable menu for a cold winter day*). **Propitious** means presenting favorable conditions. In other words, while a warm day in December might not be *seasonable*, it might very well be *propitious* for the sailor setting off on a round-the-world cruise.

time ma·chine ▸ **noun** (in science fiction) a machine capable of taking a person to the past or future.

time off ▸ **noun** time that is not occupied with one's usual work or studies.

time out ▸ **noun 1** time for rest or leisure. **2** (**timeout**) a brief break from play in a game or sport. **3** a temporary suspension of activities, especially as a punishment for a child who has misbehaved while playing with others.

time·piece /'tīm,pēs/ ▸ **noun** an instrument for measuring time; a clock or watch.

tim·er /'tīmər/ ▸ **noun 1** an automatic device for stopping or starting a machine at a preset time. **2** a person or device that records the amount of time taken by something. **3** indicating how many times someone has done something: *a first-timer.*

time·scale /'tīm,skāl/ ▸ **noun** the time allowed for or taken by a process or sequence of events.

time·share /'tīm,sʜe(ə)r/ ▸ **noun** an arrangement in which joint owners use a property as a vacation home at different specified times.

time sheet ▸ **noun** a piece of paper for recording the number of hours worked.

time sig·na·ture ▸ **noun** a sign in the form of two numbers at the start of a piece of music showing the number of beats in a bar.

time switch ▸ **noun** a switch that is automatically activated at a set time.

time·ta·ble /ˈtīmˌtābəl/ ▶ **noun** a list or plan of times at which events are scheduled to take place.

– SYNONYMS **schedule,** program, agenda, calendar, diary.

▶ **verb** schedule something to happen at a particular time.

time tri·al ▶ **noun** (in various sports) a test of a competitor's individual speed over a set distance.

time warp ▶ **noun** (especially in science fiction) a situation in which it is possible for people or things belonging to one period to move to another.

time·worn ▶ **adjective** damaged or made less interesting as a result of age or a great deal of use.

time zone ▶ **noun** see **ZONE** (sense 2 of the noun).

tim·id /ˈtimid/ ▶ **adjective** (**timider, timidest**) not brave or confident.

– SYNONYMS **fearful,** afraid, faint-hearted, timorous, nervous, scared, frightened, shy, diffident.
– ANTONYMS bold.

– DERIVATIVES **ti·mid·i·ty** /təˈmiditē/ noun **tim·id·ly** adverb **tim·id·ness** noun.
– ORIGIN Latin *timidus.*

tim·ing /ˈtīmiNG/ ▶ **noun 1** the quality of being able to judge the right time to do something: *a politician with an unerring sense of timing.* **2** a particular time when something happens.

tim·or·ous /ˈtimərəs/ ▶ **adjective** lacking in courage or confidence; nervous.
– DERIVATIVES **tim·or·ous·ly** adverb **tim·or·ous·ness** noun.
– ORIGIN Latin *timorosus.*

tim·pa·ni /ˈtimpənē/ (also **tympani**) ▶ **plural noun** kettledrums.
– DERIVATIVES **tim·pa·nist** noun.
– ORIGIN Italian.

tin /tin/ ▶ **noun 1** a silvery-white metallic chemical element. **2** an airtight container with a lid, made of tinplate or aluminum. **3** Brit. a tinplate or aluminum container for preserving food; a can. ▶ **verb** (**tins, tinning, tinned**) cover something with a thin layer of tin.
– ORIGIN Old English.

tin can ▶ **noun** a tinplate or aluminum container for preserving food, especially an empty one.

tinc·ture /ˈtiNGkCHər/ ▶ **noun 1** a medicine made by dissolving a drug in alcohol. **2** a slight trace of something. ▶ **verb** (**be tinctured**) be tinged with a slight trace of: *his affability was tinctured with faint sarcasm.*
– ORIGIN Latin *tinctura* 'dyeing.'

tin·der /ˈtindər/ ▶ **noun** dry, flammable material used for lighting a fire.
– ORIGIN Old English.

tin·der·box /ˈtindərˌbäks/ ▶ **noun 1** a situation that is likely to become dangerous: *some prisons are tinderboxes of violence.* **2** historical a box containing tinder, flint, a steel, and other items for lighting a fire.

tine /ˈtīn/ ▶ **noun** a prong or sharp point, especially of a fork.
– ORIGIN Old English.

tin·e·a /ˈtinēə/ ▶ **noun** technical term for **RINGWORM**.
– ORIGIN Latin, 'worm.'

tin·foil /ˈtinˌfoil/ ▶ **noun** metal foil used for covering or wrapping food.

ting /tiNG/ ▶ **noun** a sharp, clear ringing sound. ▶ **verb** make a sharp, clear ringing sound.
– ORIGIN imitating the sound.

tinge /tinj/ ▶ **verb** (**tinges, tinging** or **tingeing, tinged**) **1** color something slightly. **2** affect with a small amount of a quality: *a visit tinged with sadness.*

– SYNONYMS **tint,** color, stain, shade, wash.

▶ **noun** a slight trace of a color, feeling, or quality.

– SYNONYMS **1 tint,** color, shade, tone, hue. **2 trace,** note, touch, suggestion, hint, flavor, element, streak, suspicion, soupçon.

– ORIGIN Latin *tingere* 'to dip or color.'

tin·gle /ˈtiNGgəl/ ▶ **verb** experience a slight prickling or stinging sensation.

– SYNONYMS **prickle,** prick, sting, itch, tickle.

▶ **noun** a slight prickling or stinging sensation.

– SYNONYMS **prickle,** pricking, tingling, sting, itch, pins and needles.

– DERIVATIVES **tin·gly** /ˈtiNGg(ə)lē/ adjective.
– ORIGIN perhaps from **TINKLE**.

tin·horn /ˈtinˌhôrn/ informal ▶ **noun** a contemptible person, especially one pretending to have money, influence, or ability. ▶ **adjective** pretending to be more significant or influential than one really is; small-time: *tinhorn dictators who turn out to be military incompetents.*

tin·ker /ˈtiNGkər/ ▶ **noun 1** a traveling mender of pots, kettles, etc. **2** an act of tinkering with something. ▶ **verb** (**tinker with**) try to repair or improve something by making many small changes.

– SYNONYMS **fiddle,** play around, mess about/around, adjust, try to mend.

– DERIVATIVES **tin·ker·er** noun.
– ORIGIN unknown.

tin·kle /ˈtiNGkəl/ ▶ **verb** make a light, clear ringing sound. ▶ **noun** a light, clear ringing sound.
– DERIVATIVES **tin·kly** /-k(ə)lē/ adjective.
– ORIGIN imitating the sound.

tin·ni·tus /ˈtinitəs, tiˈnī-/ ▶ **noun** Medicine ringing or buzzing in the ears.
– ORIGIN Latin.

tin·ny /ˈtinē/ ▶ **adjective 1** having a thin, metallic sound. **2** made of thin or poor-quality metal. **3** having an unpleasantly metallic taste.
– DERIVATIVES **tin·ni·ly** adverb **tin·ni·ness** noun.

Tin Pan Al·ley ▶ **noun 1** a district in New York City where many songwriters, arrangers, and music publishers were formerly based. **2** the world of composers and publishers of popular music.

tin·plate /ˈtinˌplāt/ ▶ **noun** sheet steel or iron coated with tin.
– DERIVATIVES **tin·plat·ed** adjective.

tin·pot /ˈtinˌpät/ ▶ **adjective** informal not significant or effective: *a tinpot dictator.*

tin·sel /ˈtinsəl/ ▶ **noun 1** a form of decoration consisting of thin strips of shiny metal foil attached to a length of thread. **2** superficial attractiveness or glamour: *the phony tinsel of Hollywood.*
– DERIVATIVES **tin·seled** adjective **tin·sel·ly** adjective.
– ORIGIN Old French *estincele* 'spark.'

Tin·sel·town /ˈtinsəlˌtoun/ ▶ **noun** the glamorous but artificial world of Hollywood and its film industry.

tin·smith /ˈtinˌsmiTH/ ▶ **noun** a person who makes or repairs articles made of tin or tinplate.

tin·snips /'tin,snips/ ▶ **plural noun** a pair of clippers for cutting sheet metal.

tint /tint/ ▶ **noun 1** a shade of a color. **2** a dye for coloring the hair.

– SYNONYMS **1 shade,** color, tone, hue, tinge, cast, flush, blush. **2 dye,** colorant, coloring, wash.

▶ **verb 1** color slightly: *the clouds were tinted with crimson*. **2** dye the hair.

– SYNONYMS **dye,** color, tinge.

– ORIGIN Latin *tinctus* 'dyeing.'

tin·tin·nab·u·la·tion /,tintə,nabyə'lāsʜən/ ▶ **noun** a ringing or tinkling sound.
– ORIGIN from Latin *tintinnabulum* 'tinkling bell.'

ti·ny /'tīnē/ ▶ **adjective** (**tinier, tiniest**) very small.

– SYNONYMS **minute,** minuscule, microscopic, very small, mini, diminutive, miniature, baby, toy, dwarf; Scottish wee; informal teeny, teensy, teeny-weeny, teensy-weensy.
– ANTONYMS huge.

▶ **noun** (pl. **tinies**) informal a very young child.
– DERIVATIVES **ti·ni·ly** adverb **ti·ni·ness** noun.
– ORIGIN unknown.

CHOOSE THE RIGHT WORD

See **SMALL**.

tip[1] /tip/ ▶ **noun 1** the pointed or rounded end of something thin or tapering. **2** a small part fitted to the end of an object.

– SYNONYMS **1 point,** end, extremity, head, spike, prong, nib. **2 peak,** top, summit, apex, crown, crest, pinnacle.

▶ **verb** (**tips, tipping, tipped**) (usu. as adj. **tipped**) attach to or cover the tip of: *a tipped cigarette*.
– PHRASES **on the tip of one's tongue** almost but not quite spoken or coming to mind.
– ORIGIN Old Norse.

tip[2] ▶ **verb** (**tips, tipping, tipped**) **1** overbalance so as to fall or turn over. **2** be or put in a sloping position. **3** empty out the contents of a container by holding it at an angle. **4** hit or touch lightly: *his shot was tipped over the bar by Nixon*.

– SYNONYMS **1 overturn,** turn over, topple (over), fall (over), keel over, capsize, roll over. **2 lean,** tilt, list, slope, bank, slant, incline, pitch, cant. **3 pour,** empty, drain, dump, discharge, decant.

▶ **noun 1** Brit. a place where rubbish is left. **2** informal a dirty or untidy place.

– SYNONYMS **dump,** rubbish dump, landfill site.

– PHRASES **tip one's hat** raise or touch one's hat as a greeting or mark of respect.
– ORIGIN perhaps Scandinavian.

tip[3] ▶ **noun 1** a small extra sum of money given to someone to reward good service. **2** a piece of practical advice. **3** a piece of expert information about the likely winner of a race or contest.

– SYNONYMS **1 gratuity,** present, gift, reward, baksheesh. **2 piece of advice,** suggestion, word of advice, pointer, hint; informal wrinkle.

▶ **verb** (**tips, tipping, tipped**) **1** give a tip to someone as a reward for good service. **2** (**tip someone off**) informal give someone secret information.
– ORIGIN probably from **TIP**[1].

tipi ▶ **noun** variant spelling of **TEPEE**.

tip-off ▶ **noun** informal a piece of secret information.

tip·per /'tipər/ ▶ **noun** a person who leaves a tip of a specified amount: *a good tipper*.

tip·ple /'tipəl/ ▶ **verb** drink alcohol regularly. ▶ **noun** informal an alcoholic drink.
– DERIVATIVES **tip·pler** /'tip(ə)lər/ noun.
– ORIGIN unknown.

tip·py-toe /'tipē/ ▶ **verb** informal tiptoe.

tip·ster /'tipstər/ ▶ **noun** a person who gives tips as to the likely winner of a race or contest.

tip·sy /'tipsē/ ▶ **adjective** (**tipsier, tipsiest**) slightly drunk.
– DERIVATIVES **tip·si·ly** adverb **tip·si·ness** noun.
– ORIGIN from **TIP**[2].

CHOOSE THE RIGHT WORD

See **DRUNK**.

tip·toe /'tip,tō/ ▶ **verb** (**tiptoes, tiptoeing, tiptoed**) walk quietly and carefully with the heels raised and the weight on the balls of the feet.
– PHRASES **on tiptoe** (or **tiptoes**) with the heels raised and the weight on the balls of the feet.

tip-top ▶ **adjective** of the very best quality; excellent.

ti·rade /'tī,rād, ,tī'rād/ ▶ **noun** a long angry speech criticizing someone or something.

– SYNONYMS **diatribe,** harangue, rant, attack, polemic, broadside, fulmination, tongue-lashing; informal blast.

– ORIGIN French.

tir·a·mi·su /,tirəmē'sōō, -'mēsōō/ ▶ **noun** an Italian dessert consisting of layers of sponge cake soaked in coffee and brandy, with powdered chocolate and mascarpone cheese.
– ORIGIN from Italian *tira mi sù* 'pick me up.'

tire[1] /tīr/ ▶ **verb 1** make or become in need of rest or sleep. **2** make someone feel impatient or bored. **3** (**tire of**) become impatient or bored with: *she will stay with him until he tires of her*.

– SYNONYMS **1 get tired,** weaken, flag, droop. **2 fatigue,** tire out, exhaust, wear out, drain, weary, enervate; informal knock out, take it out of.

– ORIGIN Old English.

tire[2] /tī(ə)r/ (Brit. **tyre**) ▶ **noun** a rubber covering that is inflated or that surrounds an inflated inner tube, fitted around a wheel to form a soft contact with the road.
– ORIGIN probably a shortening of **ATTIRE**.

tired /tīrd/ ▶ **adjective 1** in need of sleep or rest; weary. **2** (**tired of**) bored with someone or something. **3** (of a statement or idea) boring or uninteresting because used too often.

– SYNONYMS **1 exhausted,** worn out, weary, fatigued, ready to drop, drained, enervated; informal beat, all in, done in, pooped, tuckered out. **2** *I'm* ***tired of*** *him* **fed up with,** weary of, bored with/by, sick (and tired) of; informal (fed) up to here with. **3 hackneyed,** overused, stale, clichéd, predictable, unimaginative, unoriginal, dull, boring; informal corny.
– ANTONYMS energetic, fresh.

– DERIVATIVES **tired·ly** adverb **tired·ness** noun.

tire iron ▶ **noun** a steel lever for removing tires from wheel rims.

tire·less /'tīrlis/ ▶ **adjective** having or showing great effort or energy.

– SYNONYMS **vigorous,** energetic, industrious, determined, enthusiastic, keen, zealous, spirited, dynamic, stout, untiring, unwearying, indefatigable, unflagging.
– ANTONYMS lazy.

– DERIVATIVES **tire·less·ly** adverb **tire·less·ness** noun.

tire·some /ˈtīrsəm/ ▶ **adjective** annoying or boring.

– SYNONYMS **1 wearisome,** laborious, wearing, tedious, boring, monotonous, dull, uninteresting, unexciting, humdrum, routine. **2 troublesome,** irksome, vexatious, irritating, annoying, exasperating, trying; informal aggravating, pesky.
– ANTONYMS interesting, pleasant.

– DERIVATIVES **tire·some·ly** adverb **tire·some·ness** noun.

tir·ing /ˈtīriNG/ ▶ **adjective** causing exhaustion: *it was very tiring work.*

– SYNONYMS **exhausting,** wearying, taxing, draining, hard, arduous, strenuous, onerous, grueling.

ʼtis ▶ **contraction** chiefly literary it is.

ti·sane /tiˈzan, -ˈzän/ ▶ **noun** an herbal tea.
– ORIGIN French.

tis·sue /ˈtisHo͞o/ ▶ **noun 1** any of the distinct types of material of which animals or plants are made, consisting of specialized cells. **2** tissue paper. **3** a paper handkerchief. **4** delicate gauzy fabric.
– DERIVATIVES **tis·su·ey** adjective.
– PHRASES **a tissue of lies** a story that is full of lies.
– ORIGIN from Old French *tissu* 'woven.'

tis·sue cul·ture ▶ **noun** Biology & Medicine the growing of cells from a living organism in an artificial medium outside the organism.

tis·sue pa·per ▶ **noun** very thin, soft paper.

tit[1] /tit/ ▶ **noun** a small insect-eating songbird; a titmouse.
– ORIGIN probably Scandinavian.

tit[2] ▶ **noun** vulgar slang a woman's breast.
– ORIGIN Old English, 'teat, nipple.'

tit[3] ▶ **noun** (in phrase **tit for tat**) a situation in which a person insults or hurts someone to retaliate for something they have done.
– ORIGIN from former *tip for tap*, from TIP[2].

Ti·tan /ˈtītn/ ▶ **noun 1** any of a family of giant gods in Greek mythology. **2** (**titan**) a very strong, intelligent, or important person.

ti·tan·ic /tīˈtanik/ ▶ **adjective** very strong, large, or powerful: *a titanic struggle for survival.*
– DERIVATIVES **ti·tan·i·cal·ly** /-ik(ə)lē/ adverb.

ti·ta·ni·um /tīˈtānēəm/ ▶ **noun** a hard silver-gray metal used in strong corrosion-resistant alloys.
– ORIGIN from TITAN.

tithe /tīTH/ ▶ **noun 1** one tenth of the amount people produced or earned in a year, formerly taken as a tax to support the Church. **2** (in certain religious denominations) a tenth of a person's income pledged to the Church. ▶ **verb** pay a tenth of one's income as a tithe.
– ORIGIN Old English, 'tenth.'

Ti·tian /ˈtisHən/ ▶ **adjective** (of hair) bright golden auburn.
– ORIGIN from the Italian painter *Titian*, with reference to the bright auburn hair portrayed in many of his works.

tit·il·late /ˈtitl,āt/ ▶ **verb** interest or excite someone, especially in a sexual way.
– DERIVATIVES **tit·il·la·tion** /,titlˈāsHən/ noun.
– ORIGIN Latin *titillare* 'to tickle.'

tit·il·lat·ing /ˈtitl,ātiNG/ ▶ **adjective** interesting or exciting, especially in a sexual way.

– SYNONYMS *a titillating rendition of "Baby, It's Cold Outside"* **arousing,** exciting, stimulating, sexy, thrilling, provocative, tantalizing, interesting, fascinating; suggestive, salacious, lurid.
– ANTONYMS boring.

tit·i·vate /ˈtitə,vāt/ ▶ **verb** informal make someone or something neater or more attractive.
– DERIVATIVES **tit·i·va·tion** /,titəˈvāsHən/ noun.
– ORIGIN perhaps from TIDY.

ti·tle /ˈtītl/ ▶ **noun 1** the name of a book, musical composition, or other work. **2** a name that describes someone's position or job. **3** a word, such as *Dr.*, *Mrs.*, or *Prince*, used before or instead of someone's name to indicate their rank, profession, or status. **4** the position of being the winner of a competition, especially of being the champion of a sports competition: *he won the world title.* **5** a caption or credit in a movie or television broadcast. **6** the legal right to own something, especially land or property.

– SYNONYMS **1 heading,** label, inscription, caption, subheading, legend. **2 name,** designation, form of address, rank, office, position; informal moniker, handle. **3** *an Olympic title* **championship,** crown, first place.

▶ **verb** give a title to someone or something.
– ORIGIN Latin *titulus* 'inscription, title.'

ti·tled /ˈtītld/ ▶ **adjective** having a title indicating nobility or rank.

ti·tle deed ▶ **noun** a legal document providing evidence of a person's right to own a property.

ti·tle role ▶ **noun** the role in a play, movie, or television show from which the work's title is taken.

tit·mouse /ˈtit,mous/ ▶ **noun** (pl. **titmice** /ˈtit,mīs/) another term for TIT[1].
– ORIGIN from TIT[1] + the former word *mose* 'titmouse.'

ti·trate /ˈtī,trāt/ ▶ **verb** Chemistry calculate the amount of a substance in a solution by measuring the volume of a standard reagent required to react with it.
– DERIVATIVES **ti·tra·tion** /,tīˈtrāsHən/ noun.
– ORIGIN from French *titre* 'fineness of alloyed gold or silver.'

tit·ter /ˈtitər/ ▶ **verb** give a short, quiet laugh. ▶ **noun** a short, quiet laugh.
– ORIGIN imitating the sound.

tit·tle /ˈtitl/ ▶ **noun** a tiny amount or part of something.
– ORIGIN Latin *titulus* 'title,' later 'small stroke, accent.'

tit·tle-tat·tle ▶ **noun** trivial talk; gossip. ▶ **verb** engage in gossip.
– ORIGIN from TATTLE.

tit·u·lar /ˈticHələr/ ▶ **adjective 1** holding a formal position or title without any real authority: *the queen is titular head of the Church of England.* **2** relating to a title.
– DERIVATIVES **tit·u·lar·ly** adverb.

tiz·zy /ˈtizē/ ▶ **noun** (pl. **tizzies**) informal a state of nervous excitement or agitation.
– ORIGIN unknown.

TKO ▶ **abbreviation** Boxing technical knockout.

Tl ▶ **symbol** the chemical element thallium.

TLC ▶ **abbreviation** informal tender loving care.

TM ▸ **abbreviation 1** trademark. **2** trademark Transcendental Meditation.

Tm ▸ **symbol** the chemical element thulium.

TN ▸ **abbreviation** Tennessee.

TNC ▸ **abbreviation** transnational corporation.

TNT ▸ **abbreviation** trinitrotoluene, a high explosive.

to /to͞o/ ▸ **preposition 1** in the direction of. **2** situated in the direction mentioned: *there are mountains to the north.* **3** so as to reach a particular state. **4** identifying the person or thing affected by an action: *you were unkind to her.* **5** indicating that people or things are related, linked, or attached. **6** (in telling the time) before the hour specified: *it's four minutes to six.* **7** indicating a rate of return: *the car only does ten miles to the gallon.* **8** introducing the second part of a comparison: *the club's nothing to what it once was.* ▸ **infinitive marker** used with the base form of a verb to indicate that the verb is in the infinitive. ▸ **adverb** so as to be closed or nearly closed: *he pulled the door to.*
– PHRASES **to and fro** in a constant movement backward and forward or from side to side.
– ORIGIN Old English.

USAGE

Do not confuse **to** with **too** or **two**. **To** mainly means 'in the direction of' (*the next train to London*), while **too** means 'excessively' (*she was driving too fast*) or 'in addition' (*is he coming too?*). **Two** is a number meaning 'one less than three' (*we met two years ago*).

toad /tōd/ ▸ **noun 1** a tailless amphibian with a short stout body and short legs. **2** a very unpleasant or disliked person.
– ORIGIN Old English.

toad·flax /'tōd,flaks/ ▸ **noun** a plant with yellow or purplish flowers that resemble those of the snapdragon.

toad·stool /'tōd,sto͞ol/ ▸ **noun** a fungus, typically in the form of a rounded cap on a stalk.

toad·y /'tōdē/ ▸ **noun** (pl. **toadies**) a person who behaves in an excessively respectful way toward another in order to gain their favor. ▸ **verb** (**toadies, toadying, toadied**) act in an excessively respectful way to gain someone's favor.
– ORIGIN probably from *toad-eater*, a charlatan's assistant who ate toads (regarded as poisonous) as a demonstration of the power of the charlatan's remedy.

toast /tōst/ ▸ **noun 1** sliced bread that has been browned by putting it close to a source of heat, such as a broiler or fire. **2** an act of raising glasses at a gathering and drinking together in honor of a person or thing. **3** a person who is respected or admired: *he was the toast of the baseball world.* ▸ **verb 1** make bread or other food brown by putting it under a broiler or close to another source of heat. **2** drink a toast to someone. **3** (of a DJ) accompany reggae music with improvised rhythmic speech.

– SYNONYMS **drink (to) the health of,** salute, honor, pay tribute to; old use pledge.

– PHRASES **be toast** informal be finished, defunct, or dead.
– ORIGIN from Old French *toster* 'to roast'; sense 2 came from the idea that the name of the lady whose health was being drunk flavored the drink like the pieces of spiced toast formerly placed in wine.

toast·er /'tōstər/ ▸ **noun** an electrical device for making toast.

toast·mas·ter /'tōs(t),mastər/ (or **toastmistress** /'tōs(t),mistris/) ▸ **noun** an official responsible for proposing toasts and making other formal announcements at a large social event.

toast·y /'tōstē/ ▸ **adjective 1** of or resembling toast. **2** comfortably warm.

to·bac·co /tə'bakō/ ▸ **noun** (pl. **tobaccos**) the dried nicotine-rich leaves of an American plant, used for smoking or chewing.
– ORIGIN Spanish *tabaco.*

to·bac·co·nist /tə'bakənist/ ▸ **noun** a merchant who sells cigarettes and tobacco.

to·bog·gan /tə'bägən/ ▸ **noun** a light, long, narrow sled used for sliding downhill over snow or ice. ▸ **verb** ride on a toboggan.
– ORIGIN Micmac.

toc·ca·ta /tə'kätə/ ▸ **noun** a musical composition for a keyboard instrument designed to display the performer's touch and technique.
– ORIGIN Italian, 'touched.'

to·coph·er·ol /tə'käfə,rôl, -,räl/ ▸ **noun** vitamin E.
– ORIGIN from Greek *tokos* 'offspring' + *pherein* 'to bear.'

toc·sin /'täksən/ ▸ **noun** old use an alarm bell or signal.
– ORIGIN Provençal *tocasenh.*

to·day /tə'dā/ ▸ **adverb 1** on or during this present day. **2** at the present period of time; nowadays. ▸ **noun 1** this present day. **2** the present period of time.
– ORIGIN Old English, 'on this day.'

tod·dle /'tädl/ ▸ **verb 1** (of a young child) move with short unsteady steps while learning to walk. **2** informal go somewhere in a casual or leisurely way.

– SYNONYMS **totter,** teeter, wobble, falter, waddle, stumble.

▸ **noun** an act of toddling.
– ORIGIN unknown.

tod·dler /'tädlər/ ▸ **noun** a young child who is just beginning to walk.

tod·dy /'tädē/ ▸ **noun** (pl. **toddies**) a drink made of liquor with hot water and sugar.
– ORIGIN Sanskrit, 'palmyra' (referring to a palm tree with a naturally alcoholic sap).

to-do /tə 'do͞o/ ▸ **noun** informal a commotion or fuss.
– ORIGIN from *much to do*, first meaning 'much needing to be done.'

toe /tō/ ▸ **noun 1** any of the five digits at the end of the foot. **2** the lower end or tip of something. ▸ **verb** (**toes, toeing, toed**) push or touch someone or something with the toes.
– DERIVATIVES **toe·less** adjective.
– PHRASES **make someone's toes curl** informal make someone feel very embarrassed. **on one's toes** ready and alert. **toe the line** obey authority.
– ORIGIN Old English.

USAGE

The phrase **toe the line**, which comes from the meaning 'stand with the tips of the toes exactly touching a line,' is often misinterpreted and wrongly spelled as *tow the line*.

toe·cap /'tō,kap/ ▸ **noun** a piece of steel or leather on the front part of a boot or shoe.

toe·hold /'tō,hōld/ ▸ **noun 1** a relatively minor position from which further progress may be made: *the initiative* *is helping companies to gain a toehold in the Gulf.* **2** (in climbing) a small foothold.

toe·nail /ˈtōˌnāl/ ▶ **noun** a nail on the upper surface of the tip of each toe.

toe-tap·ping ▶ **adjective** informal (of music) lively.

toff /täf/ ▶ **noun** Brit. informal, derogatory a rich upper-class person.
– ORIGIN perhaps from **TUFT**, referring to a gold tassel worn on the cap by titled undergraduates at Oxford and Cambridge.

tof·fee /ˈtôfē, ˈtäfē/ ▶ **noun** a kind of firm candy that softens when sucked or chewed, made by boiling together sugar and butter.
– ORIGIN unknown.

to·fu /ˈtōfo͞o/ ▶ **noun** a soft white substance made from mashed soybeans, used in Asian and vegetarian cooking.
– ORIGIN Chinese, 'rotten beans.'

tog /täg/ informal ▶ **noun** (**togs**) clothes. ▶ **verb** (**be togged up/out**) be fully dressed for a particular occasion or activity.
– ORIGIN probably from former criminals' slang *togeman* 'light cloak,' from Latin *toga* 'toga.'

to·ga /ˈtōgə/ ▶ **noun** a loose outer garment made of a single piece of cloth, worn by the citizens of ancient Rome.
– ORIGIN Latin.

to·geth·er /təˈgeT͟Hər/ ▶ **adverb** **1** with or near to another person or people. **2** so as to touch, combine, or be united. **3** regarded as a whole. **4** (of two people) married or in a sexual relationship. **5** at the same time. **6** without interruption.

> – SYNONYMS **1 with each other,** in conjunction, jointly, in cooperation, in collaboration, in partnership, in combination, in league, side by side; informal in cahoots. **2 simultaneously,** at the same time, at once, concurrently, as a group, in unison, in chorus.
> – ANTONYMS separately.

▶ **adjective** informal sensible, calm, or well organized.

> – SYNONYMS **levelheaded,** well adjusted, sensible, practical, realistic, mature, stable, full of common sense, well organized, efficient, methodical, self-confident, self-assured; informal unflappable.

– DERIVATIVES **to·geth·er·ness** noun.
– PHRASES **together with** as well as.
– ORIGIN Old English.

tog·gle /ˈtägəl/ ▶ **noun** **1** a narrow piece of wood or plastic attached to a coat or jacket, pushed through a loop to act as a fastener. **2** Computing a key or command that is used to alternate between one effect, feature, or state and another. ▶ **verb** Computing switch from one effect, feature, or state to another by using a toggle.
– ORIGIN unknown.

tog·gle switch ▶ **noun** an electric switch operated by means of a projecting lever that is moved up and down.

To·go·lese /ˌtōgōˈlēz, ˌtōgə-, -ˈlēs/ ▶ **noun** (pl. same) a person from Togo, a country in West Africa. ▶ **adjective** relating to Togo.

toil /toil/ ▶ **verb** **1** work very hard. **2** move along slowly and with difficulty.

> – SYNONYMS **1 work,** labor, slave, strive; informal slog, beaver. **2 struggle,** drag oneself, trudge, slog, plod; informal schlep.

▶ **noun** exhausting work.

> – SYNONYMS **hard work,** labor, exertion, slaving, drudgery, effort, 'blood, sweat, and tears'; informal elbow grease. old use travail.

– DERIVATIVES **toil·er** noun.
– ORIGIN Old French *toiler* 'strive, dispute.'

> **CHOOSE THE RIGHT WORD**
> See **LABOR**.

toile /twäl/ ▶ **noun** **1** an early version of a finished garment made up in cheap material so that the design can be tested. **2** a semitransparent fabric.
– ORIGIN French, 'cloth, web.'

toi·let /ˈtoilit/ ▶ **noun** **1** a large bowl for urinating or defecating into. **2** a bathroom.
– ORIGIN first referring to a cloth cover for a dressing table: from French *toilette* 'cloth, wrapper.'

toi·let pa·per ▶ **noun** paper in sheets or on a roll for wiping oneself clean after using a toilet.

toi·let·ries /ˈtoilitrēz/ ▶ **plural noun** articles used in washing and taking care of the body, such as soap and shampoo.

toi·lette /twäˈlet/ ▶ **noun** old-fashioned term for **TOILET** (sense 2).
– ORIGIN French (see **TOILET**).

toi·let-train ▶ **verb** teach a young child to use the toilet.

toi·let wa·ter ▶ **noun** a diluted form of perfume.

toil·some /ˈtoilsəm/ ▶ **adjective** old use or literary involving hard work or effort.

To·kay /tōˈkā/ ▶ **noun** a sweet aromatic wine, originally made near Tokaj in Hungary.

toke /tōk/ informal ▶ **noun** a draw on a cigarette or pipe, especially one containing marijuana. ▶ **verb** smoke cannabis or tobacco.
– ORIGIN unknown.

to·ken /ˈtōkən/ ▶ **noun** **1** a thing that represents a fact, quality, or feeling: *the gift of a plant is a token of love.* **2** a voucher that can be exchanged for goods or services. **3** a disk used to operate a machine or in exchange for certain goods or services.

> – SYNONYMS **1 symbol,** sign, emblem, badge, representation, indication, mark, expression, demonstration. **2 memento,** souvenir, keepsake, reminder. **3 voucher,** coupon, note.

▶ **adjective** **1** done for the sake of appearances: *cases like this often bring token fines.* **2** chosen by way of tokenism to represent a particular group.

> – SYNONYMS *token resistance* **symbolic,** nominal, perfunctory, slight, minimal, superficial.

– PHRASES **by the same token** in the same way or for the same reason.
– ORIGIN Old English.

> **CHOOSE THE RIGHT WORD**
> See **EMBLEM**, **SIGN**.

to·ken·ism /ˈtōkəˌnizəm/ ▶ **noun** the practice of doing something in a superficial way, so as to be seen to be obeying the law or satisfying a particular group of people.
– DERIVATIVES **to·ken·is·tic** /ˌtōkəˈnistik/ adjective.

told /tōld/ past and past participle of **TELL**.

tol·er·a·ble /'tälərəbəl/ ▸ **adjective 1** able to be tolerated or endured. **2** fairly good.

– SYNONYMS **1 bearable,** endurable, supportable, acceptable. **2 fairly good,** fair, passable, adequate, all right, acceptable, satisfactory, average, run-of-the-mill, mediocre, middling, ordinary, unexceptional; informal OK, so-so, no great shakes.
– ANTONYMS intolerable.

– DERIVATIVES **tol·er·a·bil·i·ty** /ˌtäl(ə)rə'bilitē/ noun **tol·er·a·bly** /-blē/ adverb.

tol·er·ance /'täl(ə)rəns/ ▸ **noun 1** the ability to accept things that one dislikes or disagrees with. **2** the ability to endure specified conditions or treatment: *the plant's tolerance to pests and herbicides.* **3** an allowable amount of variation of a measurement, especially in the dimensions of a machine or part.

– SYNONYMS **1 toleration,** acceptance, open-mindedness, broad-mindedness, forbearance, patience, charity, understanding, lenience. **2 endurance,** resilience, resistance, immunity.

tol·er·ant /'tälərənt/ ▸ **adjective 1** able to accept things that one dislikes or disagrees with. **2** able to endure specified conditions or treatment.

– SYNONYMS **open-minded,** forbearing, broad-minded, liberal, unprejudiced, unbiased, patient, long-suffering, understanding, charitable, lenient, easygoing, indulgent, permissive.

– DERIVATIVES **tol·er·ant·ly** adverb.

tol·er·ate /'täləˌrāt/ ▸ **verb 1** allow something that one dislikes or disagrees with to exist or continue: *the organization will not tolerate racism.* **2** patiently endure someone or something that is unpleasant or annoying. **3** be able to be exposed to a drug, toxin, etc., without a bad reaction.

– SYNONYMS **1** *we do not tolerate tardiness* **allow,** permit, condone, accept, swallow, countenance; formal brook. **2** *he couldn't tolerate her moods any longer* **endure,** put up with, bear, take, stand, support, stomach, abide.

– DERIVATIVES **tol·er·a·tion** /ˌtälə'rāsʜən/ noun.
– ORIGIN Latin *tolerare* 'endure.'

toll[1] /tōl/ ▸ **noun 1** a charge payable to use a bridge or road or for a long-distance telephone call. **2** the number of deaths or casualties arising from an accident, disaster, etc. **3** the cost or damage resulting from something.

– SYNONYMS **1 charge,** fee, payment, levy, tariff, tax. **2 number,** count, tally, total, sum. **3** *the toll on the environment has been high* **harm to,** damage to, injury to, detriment to, adverse effect on, cost to, loss to.

– PHRASES **take its toll** (or **take a heavy toll**) have a very harmful effect.
– ORIGIN Greek *telōnion* 'toll house.'

toll[2] ▸ **verb 1** (of a bell) sound with slow, even strokes. **2** (of a bell) ring to announce the time, a service, or a person's death.

– SYNONYMS **ring,** sound, clang, chime, strike, peal.

▸ **noun** a single ring of a bell.
– ORIGIN probably from dialect *toll* 'drag, pull.'

toll·booth /'tōlˌbo͞oᴛʜ/ ▸ **noun** a booth at which drivers must stop to pay a toll.

toll·gate /'tōlˌgāt/ ▸ **noun** a barrier across a road where a toll must be paid to pass through.

Tol·tec /'tōlˌtek, 'täl-/ ▸ **noun** a member of an American Indian people that flourished in Mexico before the Aztecs.
– DERIVATIVES **Tol·tec·an** /tōl'tekən, täl-/ adjective.
– ORIGIN Nahuatl, 'person from *Tula*' (a town and former Toltec site in Mexico).

tol·u·ene /'tälyo͞oˌēn/ ▸ **noun** a liquid hydrocarbon resembling benzene, present in coal tar and petroleum.
– ORIGIN from *tolu*, a substance obtained from a South American tree.

tom /täm/ ▸ **noun** the male of various animals, especially a domestic cat.
– ORIGIN from the man's name *Thomas*.

tom·a·hawk /'täməˌhôk/ ▸ **noun** a light ax formerly used as a tool or weapon by American Indians.
– ORIGIN from an Algonquian language.

to·ma·to /tə'mātō, -'mätō/ ▸ **noun** (pl. **tomatoes**) a glossy red or yellow edible fruit, eaten as a vegetable or in salads.
– ORIGIN Nahuatl.

tomb /to͞om/ ▸ **noun 1** a burial place consisting of a stone structure above ground or a large underground vault. **2** a monument to a dead person, erected over their burial place. **3** (**the tomb**) literary death.

– SYNONYMS **burial chamber,** vault, crypt, catacomb, sepulcher, mausoleum, grave.

– ORIGIN Greek *tumbos*.

WORD LINKS

sepulchral *relating to a tomb*

tom·boy /'tämˌboi/ ▸ **noun** a girl who enjoys rough, noisy activities traditionally associated with boys.
– DERIVATIVES **tom·boy·ish** adjective.

tomb·stone /'to͞omˌstōn/ ▸ **noun** a large, flat inscribed stone standing or laid over a grave.

tom·cat /'tämˌkat/ ▸ **noun** a male domestic cat.

Tom Col·lins /täm 'kälənz/ ▸ **noun** a cocktail made from gin mixed with soda water, sugar, and lemon or lime juice.
– ORIGIN probably named after a London bartender.

Tom, Dick, and Har·ry /'täm 'dik and 'harē/ ▸ **noun** ordinary people in general.

tome /tōm/ ▸ **noun** chiefly humorous a book, especially a large, serious one.
– ORIGIN Greek *tomos* 'roll of papyrus, volume.'

tom·fool·er·y /täm'fo͞ol(ə)rē/ ▸ **noun** silly behavior.

Tom·my /'tämē/ ▸ **noun** (pl. **Tommies**) informal a British private soldier.
– ORIGIN from a use of the name *Thomas Atkins* in examples of completed forms in the British army.

tom·my gun /'tämē/ ▸ **noun** informal a type of submachine gun.
– ORIGIN from *Thompson gun*, named after John T. *Thompson*, the American army officer who conceived it.

to·mog·ra·phy /tə'mägrəfē/ ▸ **noun** a technique for displaying a cross section through a human body or other solid object using X-rays or ultrasound.
– DERIVATIVES **to·mo·gram** /'tōməˌgram/ noun **to·mo·graph·ic** /ˌtōmə'grafik/ adjective.
– ORIGIN from Greek *tomos* 'slice, section.'

to·mor·row /tə'môrō, -'märō/ ▸ **adverb 1** on the day after today. **2** in the near future. ▸ **noun 1** the day after today. **2** the near future.

tom-tom ▶ **noun** a drum beaten with the hands, associated with North American Indian, African, or Eastern cultures.
– ORIGIN Hindi.

ton /tən/ ▶ **noun 1** (also **short ton**) a unit of weight equal to 2,000 lb avoirdupois (907.19 kg). **2** (also **long ton**) a unit of weight equal to 2,240 lb avoirdupois (1,016.05 kg). **3** a metric ton. **4** (also **displacement ton**) a unit of measurement of a ship's weight equal to 2,240 lb or 35 cubic feet (0.99 cubic meters). **5** (also **tons**) informal a large number or amount of something. ▶ **adverb** (**tons**) Brit. informal much; a great deal.
– ORIGIN variant of **TUN**.

ton·al /ˈtōnl/ ▶ **adjective 1** relating to tone. **2** (of music) written using conventional keys and harmony.
– DERIVATIVES **ton·al·ly** adverb.

to·nal·i·ty /tōˈnalitē/ ▶ **noun** (pl. **tonalities**) **1** the character of a piece of music as determined by the key in which it is played or the relationships between the notes of a scale or key. **2** the use of conventional keys and harmony as the basis of musical composition.

ton·do /ˈtändō/ ▶ **noun** (pl. **tondi** /-dē/) a circular painting.
– ORIGIN Italian, 'round object.'

tone /tōn/ ▶ **noun 1** a musical or vocal sound with reference to its pitch, quality, and strength: *they spoke in hushed tones.* **2** the sound of a person's voice, expressing a feeling or mood. **3** the general character of something: *trust her to lower the tone of the conversation.* **4** the particular quality of brightness or deepness of a shade of a color. **5** (also **whole tone**) a basic interval in classical Western music, equal to two semitones. **6** the normal level of firmness in a resting muscle.

> – SYNONYMS **1 sound,** timbre, voice, color, tonality, intonation, inflection, modulation. **2 mood,** air, feel, flavor, note, attitude, character, spirit, vein. **3 shade,** color, hue, tint, tinge.

▶ **verb 1** (**tone something down**) make something less harsh, extreme, or intense: *he toned down his criticisms.* **2** (often **tone something up**) make the body or a muscle stronger or firmer. **3** (**tone with**) match the color of something.

> – SYNONYMS (**tone something down**) **moderate,** modify, temper, soften, modulate, lighten, subdue.

– DERIVATIVES **tone·less** adjective.
– ORIGIN Greek *tonos* 'tension, tone.'

tone arm ▶ **noun** the movable arm supporting the pickup of a record player.

tone-deaf ▶ **adjective** unable to recognize differences of musical pitch accurately.

tone po·em ▶ **noun** a piece of orchestral music, typically in one movement, describing a subject taken from mythology, literature, history, etc.

ton·er /ˈtōnər/ ▶ **noun 1** a liquid applied to the skin to reduce oiliness and improve its condition. **2** a powder used in photocopiers. **3** a chemical solution used to change the tone of a photographic print.

tong /tôNG, täNG/ ▶ **noun** a Chinese association or secret society associated with organized crime.
– ORIGIN Chinese, 'meeting place.'

Ton·gan /ˈtäNGgən/ ▶ **noun 1** a person from Tonga, a group of islands in the South Pacific. **2** the Polynesian language spoken in Tonga. ▶ **adjective** relating to Tonga.

tongs /tôNGz, täNGz/ ▶ **plural noun** a tool with two movable arms that are joined at one end, used for picking up and holding things.
– ORIGIN Old English.

tongue /təNG/ ▶ **noun 1** the fleshy muscular organ in the mouth, used for tasting, licking, swallowing, and (in humans) producing speech. **2** the tongue of an animal as food. **3** a person's style or way of speaking: *his sharp tongue.* **4** a particular language. **5** a strip of leather or fabric under the laces in a shoe. **6** the clapper of a bell. **7** a long, low promontory of land. **8** a projecting strip on a wooden board that fits into a groove on another. **9** the vibrating reed of a musical instrument or organ pipe. ▶ **verb** (**tongues, tonguing, tongued**) **1** sound a note distinctly on a wind instrument by interrupting the air flow with the tongue. **2** lick something with the tongue.
– PHRASES **the gift of tongues** the power of speaking in unknown languages, believed by some Christians to be one of the gifts of the Holy Spirit. **have lost one's tongue** be silent, especially as a result of shock, shyness, etc. **hold one's tongue** dated remain silent. (**with**) **tongue in cheek** not seriously meaning what one is saying.
– ORIGIN Old English.

tongue and groove ▶ **noun** wooden planking in which adjacent boards are joined by means of interlocking ridges and grooves down their sides.

tongue de·pres·sor ▶ **noun** an instrument used by health practitioners to press down the tongue in order to allow inspection of the mouth or throat.

tongue-in-cheek ▶ **adjective & adverb** with ironic or flippant intent.

tongue-lash·ing ▶ **noun** a severe scolding.

tongue-tied ▶ **adjective** too shy or embarrassed to speak.

tongue-twist·er ▶ **noun** a sequence of words that are difficult to pronounce quickly and correctly.

ton·ic /ˈtänik/ ▶ **noun 1** a medicinal drink taken to make a person feel healthier or more energetic. **2** anything that makes a person feel better: *a vacation is just the tonic you need to shake off those midwinter blues.* **3** short for **TONIC WATER**. **4** the first note in a musical scale that, in conventional harmony, provides the keynote of a piece of music.

> – SYNONYMS **stimulant,** boost, restorative, refresher, fillip; informal shot in the arm, pick-me-up, bracer.

– ORIGIN Greek *tonikos* 'for stretching.'

ton·ic sol-fa /ˌsōl ˈfä/ ▶ **noun** a system of naming the notes of the scale used to teach singing, with do as the keynote of all major keys and la as the keynote of all minor keys.

ton·ic wa·ter ▶ **noun** a bitter carbonated soft drink made with quinine, used especially as a mixer with gin or other liquors.

to·night /təˈnīt/ ▶ **adverb** on the evening or night of the present day. ▶ **noun** the evening or night of the present day.

ton·nage /ˈtənij/ ▶ **noun 1** weight in tons. **2** the size or carrying capacity of a ship measured in tons.

tonne /tən/ ▶ **noun** another term for **METRIC TON**.
– ORIGIN French.

ton·sil /ˈtänsəl/ ▶ **noun** either of two small masses of tissue in the throat, one on each side of the root of the tongue.
– ORIGIN Latin *tonsillae* (plural).

ton·sil·lec·to·my /ˌtänsəˈlektəmē/ ▶ **noun** (pl.

tonsillectomies) a surgical operation to remove the tonsils.

ton·sil·li·tis /ˌtänsəˈlītis/ ▶ **noun** inflammation of the tonsils.

ton·so·ri·al /tänˈsôrēəl/ ▶ **adjective** chiefly humorous relating to hairdressing.
– ORIGIN Latin *tonsor* 'barber.'

ton·sure /ˈtänsʜər/ ▶ **noun** a circular area on a monk's or priest's head where the hair is shaved off.
– DERIVATIVES **ton·sured** adjective.
– ORIGIN Latin *tonsura*.

Ton·y /ˈtōnē/ ▶ **noun** (pl. **Tonys**) any of a number of awards given annually for outstanding achievement in the theater.
– ORIGIN from the nickname of the US actress and director Antoinette Perry.

ton·y /ˈtōnē/ ▶ **adjective** (**tonier, toniest**) informal fashionable, stylish, or high-class.
– ORIGIN from TONE.

too /to͞o/ ▶ **adverb 1** to a higher degree than is desirable, allowed, or possible. **2** in addition; also: *is he coming too?* **3** informal very: *you're too kind.*

– SYNONYMS **1 excessively,** overly, unduly, immoderately, inordinately, unreasonably, extremely, very. **2 also,** as well, in addition, into the bargain, besides, furthermore, moreover.

– PHRASES **none too ——** not very: *she was none too pleased.*
– ORIGIN Old English.

USAGE

On the confusion of **too** with **to** or **two**, see the note at TO.

took /to͝ok/ past of TAKE.

tool /to͞ol/ ▶ **noun 1** a piece of equipment, especially a hand-held one, used to carry out a particular function. **2** a thing used to help achieve something or perform a job: *a dictionary is an invaluable tool while you are learning a language.* **3** a person used or controlled by another.

– SYNONYMS **implement,** utensil, instrument, device, apparatus, gadget, appliance, machine, contrivance, contraption; informal gizmo.

▶ **verb 1** make a decorative design on a leather book cover by using a heated tool. **2** provide a factory with the equipment needed to do or make something. **3** informal drive around in a casual or leisurely way.
– ORIGIN Old English.

CHOOSE THE RIGHT WORD

tool, apparatus, appliance, implement, instrument, utensil

A wrench is a **tool**, meaning that it is a device held in and manipulated by the hand and used by a mechanic, plumber, carpenter, or other laborer to work, shape, move, or transform material (*he couldn't fix the drawer without the right tools*). An **implement** is a broader term referring to any tool or mechanical device used for a particular purpose (*agricultural implements*). A washing machine is an **appliance**, which refers to a mechanical or power-driven device, especially for household use (*the newly-married couple went shopping for appliances*). A **utensil** is a hand-held implement for domestic use (*eating utensils*), while an **instrument** is used for scientific or artistic purposes (*musical instrument; surgical instrument*). **Apparatus** refers to a collection of distinct instruments, tools, or other devices that are used in connection or combination with one another for a certain purpose (*the gym was open, but the exercise apparatus had not been set up*).

tool·bar /ˈto͞olˌbär/ ▶ **noun** Computing a strip of icons used to perform certain functions.

tool·box /ˈto͞olˌbäks/ ▶ **noun 1** a box or container for tools. **2** Computing the set of programs or functions accessible from a single menu.

tool kit ▶ **noun 1** a set of tools. **2** Computing a set of software tools.

tool·mak·er /ˈto͞olˌmākər/ ▶ **noun** a person who makes and repairs tools for use in a manufacturing process.

toot /to͞ot/ ▶ **noun 1** a short, sharp sound made by a horn, trumpet, or similar instrument. **2** informal a spell of carousing; a spree. **3** informal cocaine, or a snort of cocaine.
▶ **verb 1** make a short, sharp sound with a horn, trumpet, or similar instrument. **2** informal snort cocaine.
– ORIGIN perhaps from German *tüten*.

tooth /to͞oᴛʜ/ ▶ **noun** (pl. **teeth** /tēᴛʜ/) **1** each of a set of hard enamel-coated structures in the jaws, used for biting and chewing. **2** a projecting part, especially a cog on a gearwheel or a point on a saw or comb. **3** (**teeth**) genuine power or effectiveness: *the Charter would be fine if it had teeth.*

– SYNONYMS **fang,** tusk; informal gnasher.

– DERIVATIVES **toothed** adjective.
– PHRASES **armed to the teeth** having many weapons. **fight tooth and nail** fight very fiercely. **get one's teeth into** work energetically and enthusiastically on a particular task. **in the teeth of 1** directly against the wind. **2** in spite of opposition or difficulty.
– ORIGIN Old English.

WORD LINKS

dental *relating to teeth*

tooth·ache /ˈto͞oᴛʜˌāk/ ▶ **noun** pain in a tooth or teeth.

tooth·brush /ˈto͞oᴛʜˌbrəsʜ/ ▶ **noun** a small brush with a long handle, used for cleaning the teeth.

toothed whale ▶ **noun** any of the large group of predatory whales with teeth, including sperm whales, killer whales, and dolphins.

tooth fair·y ▶ **noun** a fairy said to take children's milk teeth after they fall out and leave a coin under their pillow.

tooth·less /ˈto͞oᴛʜlis/ ▶ **adjective 1** having no teeth. **2** lacking genuine power or effectiveness: *laws that are well intentioned but toothless.*

tooth·paste /ˈto͞oᴛʜˌpāst/ ▶ **noun** a paste used on a brush for cleaning the teeth.

tooth·pick /ˈto͞oᴛʜˌpik/ ▶ **noun** a short pointed piece of wood or plastic used for removing bits of food stuck between the teeth.

tooth·some /ˈto͞oᴛʜsəm/ ▶ **adjective 1** (of food) appetizing or tasty. **2** informal attractive; appealing.

tooth·y /ˈto͞oᴛʜē/ ▶ **adjective** (**toothier, toothiest**) having or showing numerous, large, or prominent teeth.
– DERIVATIVES **tooth·i·ly** adverb.

too·tle /ˈto͞otl/ ▶ **verb 1** casually make a series of sounds on a horn, trumpet, etc. **2** informal go or travel

in a leisurely way. ▶ **noun 1** an act or sound of tootling. **2** informal a leisurely journey.
– ORIGIN from **TOOT**.

toot·sie /ˈto͝otsē/ (also **tootsy**) ▶ **noun** (pl. **tootsies**) informal **1** a person's foot. **2** a young woman.
– ORIGIN from **FOOT**.

top¹ /täp/ ▶ **noun 1** the highest or uppermost point, part, or surface. **2** a thing placed on, fitted to, or covering the upper part of something. **3** (**the top**) the highest or most important rank, level, or position. **4** the utmost degree: *she shouted at the top of her voice*. **5** an item of clothing covering the upper part of the body. **6** (**tops**) informal a particularly good person or thing.

– SYNONYMS **1 summit,** peak, pinnacle, crest, crown, brow, head, tip, apex, apogee. **2 lid,** cap, cover, stopper, cork. **3** *he was at the top of his career* **height,** peak, pinnacle, zenith, culmination, climax, prime.
– ANTONYMS bottom, base.

▶ **adjective** highest in position, rank, or degree.

– SYNONYMS **1** *the top floor* **highest,** topmost, uppermost. **2** *the world's top scientists* **foremost,** chief, leading, principal, preeminent, greatest, best, finest, elite, premier, prime, superior, select, five-star, grade A. **3** *they are traveling at top speed* **maximum,** greatest, utmost.
– ANTONYMS lowest, minimum.

▶ **verb** (**tops, topping, topped**) **1** be more, better, or taller than. **2** be at the highest place or rank in. **3** provide something with a top or topping. **4** reach the top of a hill, slope, etc.

– SYNONYMS **1** *sales topped $500,000 last year* **exceed,** surpass, go beyond, better, beat, outstrip, outdo, outshine, eclipse, transcend. **2** *the album topped the charts for five weeks* **lead,** head, be at the top of. **3** *mousse topped with whipped cream* **cover,** cap, coat, finish, garnish.

▶ **adverb** (**tops**) informal at the most.
– DERIVATIVES **top·most** /ˈtäpˌmōst/ adjective.
– PHRASES **on top** in addition. **on top of 1** so as to cover. **2** very near to. **3** in command or control of. **4** in addition to. **on top of the world** informal very happy. **over the top 1** informal to an excessive or exaggerated degree. **2** chiefly historical over the parapet of a trench and into battle. **top something off** finish something in a memorable way. **top something out** put the highest structural feature on a building. **top something up** fill up a partly full container.
– ORIGIN Old English.

top² ▶ **noun** a toy with a rounded top and pointed base, that can be made to spin when turned around very quickly.
– ORIGIN Old English.

to·paz /ˈtōpaz/ ▶ **noun 1** a colorless, yellow, or pale blue precious stone. **2** a dark yellow color.
– ORIGIN Greek *topazos*.

top brass ▶ **noun** see **BRASS**.

top·coat /ˈtäpˌkōt/ ▶ **noun 1** an overcoat. **2** an outer coat of paint.

top dog ▶ **noun** informal a person who is successful or dominant in their field.

top-down ▶ **adjective 1** referring to a system in which actions and policies are initiated at the highest level; hierarchical. **2** proceeding from the general to the particular: *a top-down approach to research*.

top draw·er ▶ **adjective** informal of the highest quality or social class.

tope¹ /tōp/ ▶ **verb** old use or literary regularly drink too much alcohol.
– DERIVATIVES **top·er** noun.
– ORIGIN perhaps from former *top* 'overbalance.'

tope² ▶ **noun** a small shark found chiefly in coastal waters.
– ORIGIN perhaps Cornish.

top flight ▶ **noun** the highest rank or level.

top·gal·lant /täpˈgalənt, təˈgal-/ ▶ **noun 1** the section of a square-rigged sailing ship's mast immediately above the topmast. **2** a sail set on a topgallant mast.

top hat ▶ **noun** a man's formal black hat with a high cylindrical crown.

top-heav·y ▶ **adjective 1** too heavy at the top and therefore likely to fall over or be unstable. **2** (of an organization) having too many senior executives compared to the number of ordinary workers.

to·pi·ar·y /ˈtōpēˌerē/ ▶ **noun** (pl. **topiaries**) **1** the art of clipping bushes or trees into decorative shapes. **2** bushes or trees clipped into decorative shapes.
– ORIGIN Latin *topiarius* 'ornamental gardener.'

top·ic /ˈtäpik/ ▶ **noun** a subject of a piece of writing, speech, conversation, etc.

– SYNONYMS **subject,** theme, issue, matter, point, question, concern, argument, thesis.

– ORIGIN from Greek *ta topika* 'matters concerning commonplaces' (the title of a work by Aristotle).

top·i·cal /ˈtäpikəl/ ▶ **adjective 1** relating to or dealing with current affairs. **2** relating to a particular subject. **3** (of a medicine) applied to part of the body.

– SYNONYMS **current,** up to date, up to the minute, contemporary, recent, relevant, in the news.
– ANTONYMS out of date.

– DERIVATIVES **top·i·cal·i·ty** /ˌtäpəˈkalitē/ noun **top·i·cal·ly** /-ik(ə)lē/ adverb.

top·knot /ˈtäpˌnät/ ▶ **noun 1** a section of hair tied up on the top of the head. **2** a tuft or crest of hair or feathers on the head of an animal or bird.

top·less /ˈtäpləs/ ▶ **adjective** having the breasts uncovered.

top-lev·el ▶ **adjective** of the highest level of importance.

top·mast /ˈtäpˌmast, -məst/ ▶ **noun** the second section of a square-rigged sailing ship's mast, immediately above the lower mast.

top-notch ▶ **adjective** informal of the highest quality.

to·pog·ra·phy /təˈpägrəfē/ ▶ **noun** (pl. **topographies**) **1** the arrangement of the physical features of an area. **2** a detailed representation of the physical features of an area on a map.
– DERIVATIVES **to·pog·ra·pher** noun **top·o·graph·ic** /ˌtäpəˈgrafik/ adjective **top·o·graph·i·cal** /ˌtäpəˈgrafikəl/ adjective.
– ORIGIN from Greek *topos* 'place.'

to·poi /ˈtōpoi/ plural of **TOPOS**.

to·pol·o·gy /təˈpäləjē/ ▶ **noun** (pl. **topologies**) **1** Mathematics the study of geometrical properties and spatial relations that remain unaffected by smooth changes in shape or size of figures. **2** the way in which the parts of something are interrelated or arranged.
– DERIVATIVES **top·o·log·i·cal** /ˌtäpəˈläjikəl/ adjective.

top·o·nym /ˈtäpəˌnim/ ▸ **noun** a place name, especially one derived from a physical feature of the area.

top·os /ˈtōpōs/ ▸ **noun** (pl. **topoi** /-poi/) a traditional theme in literature.
– ORIGIN Greek, 'place.'

top·ping /ˈtäpiNG/ ▸ **noun** a layer of food poured or spread over another food. ▸ **adjective** Brit. informal,, dated excellent.

top·ple /ˈtäpəl/ ▸ **verb** **1** overbalance and fall over. **2** remove a government or leader from power.

> – SYNONYMS **1 fall,** tumble, tip, overbalance, overturn, keel over, lose one's balance. **2 knock over,** upset, push over, tip over, upend. **3 overthrow,** oust, unseat, overturn, bring down, defeat, get rid of, dislodge, eject.

– ORIGIN from TOP[1].

top round ▸ **noun** a cut of meat taken from an inner section of a round of beef.

top·sail /ˈtäpsəl, -ˌsāl/ ▸ **noun** **1** a sail set on a ship's topmast. **2** a sail set lengthwise, above the gaff.

top se·cret ▸ **adjective** of the highest secrecy.

top-shelf ▸ **adjective** of a high quality; excellent: *top-shelf vocal talent.*

top·side /ˈtäpˌsīd/ ▸ **noun** the upper part of a ship's side, above the waterline.

top·soil /ˈtäpˌsoil/ ▸ **noun** the top layer of soil.

top·spin /ˈtäpˌspin/ ▸ **noun** a fast forward spin given to a moving ball, often resulting in a curved path or a strong forward motion on rebounding.

top·sy-tur·vy /ˈtäpsē ˈtərvē/ ▸ **adjective & adverb** **1** upside down. **2** in a state of confusion.
– ORIGIN apparently from TOP[1] and former *terve* 'overturn.'

top-tier ▸ **adjective** of the highest level or quality: *Canada's top-tier athletes.*

top-up ▸ **noun** Brit. an additional or extra amount or portion that restores something to a former level.

toque /tōk/ ▸ **noun** **1** a woman's small hat, typically having a narrow, closely turned-up brim. **2** a tall white hat with a full crown, worn by chefs.
– ORIGIN French.

tor /tôr/ ▸ **noun** a steep hill or rocky peak.
– ORIGIN perhaps Celtic.

To·rah /ˈtōrə, ˈtô-, tôˈrä/ ▸ **noun** (in Judaism) the law of God as revealed to Moses and recorded in the Pentateuch.
– ORIGIN Hebrew, 'instruction, doctrine, law.'

torch /tôrCH/ ▸ **noun** **1** chiefly historical a piece of wood or cloth soaked in tallow and ignited. **2** British term for FLASHLIGHT (sense 1). **3** a valuable quality, principle, or cause that needs to be protected and maintained: *the torch of freedom.* ▸ **verb** informal set fire to something.
– PHRASES **carry a torch for** be in love with someone who does not return one's love.
– ORIGIN Latin *torqua, torques* 'necklace, wreath,' from *torquere* 'to twist.'

torch·light /ˈtôrCHˌlīt/ ▸ **noun** the light of a torch or torches.
– DERIVATIVES **torch·lit** /-lit/ adjective.

torch song ▸ **noun** a sad or sentimental romantic song.

tore /tôr/ past of TEAR[1].

tor·e·a·dor /ˈtôrēəˌdôr/ ▸ **noun** a bullfighter, especially one on horseback.
– ORIGIN Spanish, from *toro* 'bull.'

to·ri /ˈtôrī/ plural of TORUS.

tor·ment ▸ **noun** /ˈtôrment/ **1** great physical or mental suffering. **2** a cause of great suffering.

> – SYNONYMS **agony,** suffering, torture, pain, anguish, misery, distress, trauma.

▸ **verb** /tôrˈment/ **1** make someone suffer greatly. **2** annoy or tease a person or animal in a cruel or unkind way.

> – SYNONYMS **1 torture,** afflict, rack, harrow, plague, haunt, distress, agonize. **2 tease,** taunt, bait, provoke, harass, bother, persecute; informal needle.

– DERIVATIVES **tor·men·tor** /tôrˈmentər/ noun.
– ORIGIN Latin *tormentum* 'instrument of torture.'

torn /tôrn/ past participle of TEAR[1].

tor·na·do /tôrˈnādō/ ▸ **noun** (pl. **tornadoes** or **tornados**) a storm with violently rotating winds having the appearance of a funnel-shaped cloud.

> – SYNONYMS **whirlwind,** cyclone, storm; informal twister.

– ORIGIN perhaps from Spanish *tronada* 'thunderstorm.'

to·roi·dal /tôˈroidl/ ▸ **adjective** Geometry of or resembling a torus.

tor·pe·do /tôrˈpēdō/ ▸ **noun** (pl. **torpedoes**) a long, narrow self-propelled underwater missile designed to be fired from a ship, submarine, or an aircraft. ▸ **verb** (**torpedoes, torpedoing, torpedoed**) **1** attack a ship with a torpedo or torpedoes. **2** ruin a plan or project.
– ORIGIN first meaning an electric ray (fish): from Latin, 'numbness.'

tor·pe·do boat ▸ **noun** a small, fast, light warship armed with torpedoes.

tor·pid /ˈtôrpid/ ▸ **adjective** **1** mentally or physically inactive; lacking energy. **2** (of an animal) dormant, especially during hibernation.
– DERIVATIVES **tor·pid·i·ty** /tôrˈpiditē/ noun **tor·pid·ly** adverb.
– ORIGIN Latin *torpidus.*

tor·por /ˈtôrpər/ ▸ **noun** the state of being inactive and lacking in energy.
– ORIGIN Latin.

torque /tôrk/ ▸ **noun** a force that tends to cause rotation.
– ORIGIN from Latin *torquere* 'to twist.'

tor·rent /ˈtôrənt, ˈtär-/ ▸ **noun** **1** a strong and fast-moving stream of water or other liquid. **2** an overwhelming outpouring of something: *a torrent of abuse.*

> – SYNONYMS **1** *a torrent of water* **flood,** deluge, spate, cascade, rush. **2** *a torrent of abuse* **outburst,** outpouring, stream, flood, volley, barrage, tide.
> – ANTONYMS trickle.

– ORIGIN French.

tor·ren·tial /tôˈrenCHəl, tə-/ ▸ **adjective** (of rain) falling rapidly and heavily.
– DERIVATIVES **tor·ren·tial·ly** adverb.

tor·rid /ˈtôrəd, ˈtär-/ ▸ **adjective** **1** very hot and dry. **2** full of sexual passion.

> – SYNONYMS **1** *a torrid summer* **hot,** dry, scorching, searing, blazing, blistering, sweltering, burning; informal boiling, baking. **2** *a torrid affair* **passionate,** ardent, lustful, amorous; informal steamy, sizzling.
> – ANTONYMS cold.

– DERIVATIVES **tor·rid·ly** adverb.
– ORIGIN Latin *torridus*, from *torrere* 'scorch.'

tor·rid zone ▸ **noun** the hot central region of the earth bounded by the tropics of Cancer and Capricorn.

tor·sion /'tôrsHən/ ▸ **noun** the action of twisting or the state of being twisted, especially of one end of an object in relation to the other.
– DERIVATIVES **tor·sion·al** adjective.
– ORIGIN Latin, from *torquere* 'to twist.'

tor·sion bar ▸ **noun** a bar forming part of a vehicle suspension, twisting in response to the motion of the wheels and absorbing their vertical movement.

tor·so /'tôrsō/ ▸ **noun** (pl. **torsos**) **1** the trunk of the human body. **2** a statue of a torso.
– ORIGIN Italian, 'stalk, stump.'

tort /tôrt/ ▸ **noun** Law a wrongful act or a violation of a right (other than under contract) leading to legal liability.
– ORIGIN Latin *tortum* 'wrong, injustice.'

torte /tôrt, 'tôrtə/ ▸ **noun** a rich, sweet cake or tart.
– ORIGIN German.

tor·tel·li·ni /ˌtôrtl'ēnē/ ▸ **plural noun** small pieces of pasta stuffed with meat, cheese, vegetables, etc., and then rolled and formed into the shape of rings.
– ORIGIN Italian, from *tortello* 'small cake, fritter.'

tor·til·la /tôr'tē(y)ə/ ▸ **noun 1** (in Mexican cooking) a thin, flat corn pancake. **2** (in Spanish cooking) an omelet.
– ORIGIN Spanish, 'little cake.'

tor·toise /'tôrtəs/ ▸ **noun** a slow-moving land reptile with a scaly or leathery domed shell into which it can draw its head and legs.
– ORIGIN Latin *tortuca*.

tor·toise·shell /'tôrtə(s)ˌsHel/ ▸ **noun 1** the semitransparent mottled yellow and brown shell of certain turtles, used to make jewelry or ornaments. **2** a domestic cat with markings resembling tortoiseshell. **3** a butterfly with mottled orange, yellow, and black markings.

tor·tu·ous /'tôrcHo͞oəs/ ▸ **adjective 1** full of twists and turns. **2** extremely long and complicated: *a tortuous legal battle*.

> – SYNONYMS **1 twisting,** winding, zigzag, sinuous, snaky, meandering, serpentine. **2 convoluted,** complicated, complex, labyrinthine, involved, Byzantine, lengthy.
> – ANTONYMS straight.

– DERIVATIVES **tor·tu·os·i·ty** /ˌtôrcHo͞o'äsitē/ noun **tor·tu·ous·ly** adverb **tor·tu·ous·ness** noun.
– ORIGIN Latin *tortuosus*, from *torquere* 'to twist.'

tor·ture /'tôrcHər/ ▸ **noun 1** the action of causing someone severe pain as a punishment or a means of persuasion. **2** great suffering or anxiety.

> – SYNONYMS **1 abuse,** ill-treatment, mistreatment, maltreatment, persecution, cruelty, atrocity. **2 torment,** agony, suffering, pain, anguish, misery, distress, heartbreak, trauma.

▸ **verb** subject someone to torture.

> – SYNONYMS **1 abuse,** ill-treat, mistreat, maltreat, persecute. **2 torment,** rack, afflict, harrow, plague, distress, trouble.

– DERIVATIVES **tor·tur·er** noun.
– ORIGIN Latin *tortura* 'torment.'

tor·tur·ous /'tôrcHərəs/ ▸ **adjective** involving or causing pain or suffering.

to·rus /'tôrəs/ ▸ **noun** (pl. **tori** /'tôrī/ or **toruses**) **1** Geometry a surface or solid resembling a ring-shaped doughnut, formed by rotating a closed curve about a line that lies in the same plane but does not intersect it. **2** a ring-shaped object or chamber. **3** Architecture a large convex molding with a semicircular cross section.
– ORIGIN Latin, 'swelling, round molding.'

To·ry /'tôrē/ ▸ **noun** (pl. **Tories**) **1** a member or supporter of the British Conservative Party. **2** a member of the English political party that opposed the exclusion of James II from the succession and later gave rise to the Conservative Party.
– DERIVATIVES **To·ry·ism** /-ˌizəm/ noun.
– ORIGIN first referring to Irish peasants dispossessed by English settlers and living as robbers: probably from Irish *toraidhe* 'outlaw, highwayman.'

toss /tôs, täs/ ▸ **verb 1** throw something lightly or casually. **2** move from side to side or back and forth. **3** jerk one's head or hair sharply backward. **4** throw a coin into the air so as to make a decision, based on which side of the coin faces uppermost when it lands. **5** shake or turn food in a liquid to coat it lightly.

> – SYNONYMS **1 throw,** hurl, fling, sling, pitch, lob, launch; informal heave, chuck. **2** *he tossed a coin* **flip,** flick, spin. **3** *small boats tossing among the waves* **pitch,** lurch, rock, roll, plunge, reel, sway.

▸ **noun** an act of tossing something.
– PHRASES **toss something off 1** drink something rapidly or all at once. **2** produce something rapidly or without thought or effort.
– ORIGIN unknown.

toss-up ▸ **noun** informal **1** a situation in which any of two or more outcomes is equally possible. **2** the tossing of a coin to make a decision.

tos·ta·da /tō'städə/ (also **tostado** /-dō/) ▸ **noun** (pl. **tostadas** also **tostados**) a Mexican deep-fried tortilla topped with a mixture of beans, ground meat, and vegetables.
– ORIGIN Spanish, literally 'toasted.'

tot[1] /tät/ ▸ **noun 1** a very young child. **2** chiefly Brit. a small drink of liquor.
– ORIGIN unknown.

tot[2] ▸ **verb** (**tots, totting, totted**) (**tot something up**) chiefly Brit. **1** add up numbers or amounts. **2** accumulate something over time: *he totted up 180 League appearances*.
– ORIGIN from TOTAL or Latin *totum* 'the whole.'

to·tal /'tōtl/ ▸ **adjective 1** being the whole number or amount. **2** complete; absolute: *a total stranger*.

> – SYNONYMS **1 entire,** complete, whole, full, combined, aggregate, gross, overall. **2 utter,** complete, absolute, thorough, perfect, downright, out-and-out, outright, sheer, unmitigated, unqualified, unalloyed.
> – ANTONYMS partial.

▸ **noun** the whole number or amount of something.

> – SYNONYMS **sum,** aggregate, whole, entirety, totality.

▸ **verb** (**totals, totaling, totaled**) **1** amount to a total number: *debts totaling $6,000*. **2** find the total of. **3** informal damage something beyond repair.

> – SYNONYMS **1 add up to,** amount to, come to, run to, make. **2** *he* **totaled up** *his score* **add (up),** count, reckon, tot up, compute, work out.

– ORIGIN Latin *totalis*, from *totum* 'the whole.'

to·tal e·clipse ▸ **noun** an eclipse in which the whole of the disk of the sun or moon is obscured.

to·tal·i·tar·i·an /tōˌtaliˈte(ə)rēən/ ▸ **adjective** (of a system of government) consisting of only one leader or party that has complete power and control and permits no opposition.

– SYNONYMS **autocratic,** undemocratic, one-party, dictatorial, tyrannical, despotic, fascist, oppressive, authoritarian, absolutist.
– ANTONYMS democratic.

▸ **noun** a person in favor of a totalitarian system of government.
– DERIVATIVES **to·tal·i·tar·i·an·ism** /-ˌnizəm/ noun.

to·tal·i·ty /tōˈtalitē/ ▸ **noun 1** the whole of something. **2** the time during which the sun or moon is totally obscured during an eclipse.

to·tal·i·za·tor /ˈtōtl-iˌzātər/ (or **totalizer** /ˈtōtlˌīzər/) ▸ **noun 1** a device showing the number and amount of bets staked on a race. **2** another term for **TOTE[2]**.

to·tal·ly /ˈtōtl-ē/ ▸ **adverb** completely; absolutely.

– SYNONYMS **completely,** entirely, wholly, thoroughly, fully, utterly, absolutely, perfectly, unreservedly, unconditionally, downright.
– ANTONYMS partly.

to·tal re·call ▸ **noun** the ability to remember with clarity every detail of the events of one's life or of a particular event, object, or experience.

to·tal war ▸ **noun** a war that is unrestricted in terms of the weapons used, the territory or combatants involved, or the objectives pursued.

tote[1] /tōt/ ▸ **verb** informal carry something. ▸ **noun** informal a tote bag.
– ORIGIN probably dialect.

tote[2] ▸ **noun (the tote)** informal a system of betting based on the use of a totalizator, in which winnings are calculated according to the amount staked rather than odds offered.

tote bag ▸ **noun** a large bag for carrying a number of items.

to·tem /ˈtōtəm/ ▸ **noun** a natural object or animal believed by a particular society to have spiritual significance and adopted by it as an emblem.
– DERIVATIVES **to·tem·ic** /tōˈtemik/ adjective.
– ORIGIN Ojibwa, a North American Indian language.

to·tem pole ▸ **noun** a pole on which totems are hung or on which the images of totems are carved.

tot·ter /ˈtätər/ ▸ **verb 1** move in an unsteady way. **2** shake or rock as if about to collapse. **3** be insecure or on the point of failure. ▸ **noun** an unsteady walk.
– DERIVATIVES **tot·ter·y** adjective.
– ORIGIN Dutch *touteren* 'to swing.'

tou·can /ˈto͞oˌkan, -ˌkän/ ▸ **noun** a tropical American fruit-eating bird with a massive bill and brightly colored plumage.
– ORIGIN Tupi.

tou·ch /təch/ ▸ **verb 1** come into or be in contact with someone or something. **2** bring one's hand or another part of one's body into contact with someone or something. **3** handle in order to harm or interfere with: *I didn't touch any of her stuff.* **4** have an effect on someone or something. **5** produce feelings of affection, gratitude, or sympathy in: *she was touched by his loyalty.* **6** informal be comparable to in quality, skill, etc. **7** use or consume: *he barely touched the food on his plate.* **8** have any dealings with. **9** (as adj. **touched**) informal slightly mad.

– SYNONYMS **1 contact,** meet, brush, graze, come up against, be in contact with, border, abut. **2 feel,** pat, tap, stroke, fondle, caress, pet, handle. **3 handle,** hold, pick up, move, use, meddle with, fiddle with, interfere with, tamper with, disturb. **4 affect,** move, stir, make an impression on. **5** *no one can touch him at judo* **compare with,** be on a par with, equal, match, rival, measure up to, better, beat; informal hold a candle to.

▸ **noun 1** an act or way of touching. **2** a distinctive or skillful way of dealing with something: *a sure political touch.* **3** a small amount. **4** a distinctive detail or feature. **5** the ability to be aware of something through physical contact, especially with the fingers. **6** Soccer & Rugby the area beyond the sidelines, out of play.

– SYNONYMS **1 tap,** pat, contact, stroke, caress. **2 skill,** expertise, dexterity, deftness, adroitness, adeptness, ability, talent, flair, facility, proficiency, knack. **3 trace,** bit, suggestion, suspicion, hint, scintilla, tinge, dash, taste, spot, drop, dab, soupçon. **4** *the gas lights are a nice touch* **detail,** feature, point, element, addition.

– DERIVATIVES **touch·a·ble** adjective.
– PHRASES **in touch 1** in or into communication. **2** having up-to-date knowledge about a particular subject, situation, etc. **lose touch 1** no longer be in communication. **2** stop being aware of or informed about a particular subject, situation, etc. **out of touch** lacking awareness of or up-to-date knowledge about a particular subject, situation, etc. **touch down** (of an aircraft or spacecraft) land. **touch someone for** informal ask someone for money as a loan or gift. **touch something off 1** cause something to ignite or explode by touching it with a match. **2** make something happen suddenly: *the incident touched off a global banking crisis.* **touch on** deal briefly with a subject. **touch something up** make small improvements to something.
– ORIGIN Old French *tochier*.

WORD LINKS

tactile *relating to touch*

touch-and-go ▸ **adjective** (of an outcome) possible but very uncertain.

touch·back /ˈtəchˌbak/ ▸ **noun** Football a ball downed deliberately behind one's own goal line or kicked through one's end zone.

touch·down /ˈtəchˌdoun/ ▸ **noun 1** the moment at which an aircraft lands. **2** Football & Rugby an act of scoring by touching the ball down behind the opponents' goal line.

tou·ché /to͞oˈshā/ ▸ **exclamation 1** used to acknowledge a good or clever point made at one's expense. **2** (in fencing) used to acknowledge a hit by one's opponent.
– ORIGIN French, 'touched.'

touch foot·ball ▸ **noun** a form of football in which a ball carrier is downed by touching instead of tackling.

touch·ing /ˈtəching/ ▸ **adjective** arousing gratitude or sympathy; moving.

– SYNONYMS **moving,** affecting, heartwarming, emotional, emotive, poignant, sad, tear-jerking.

▸ **preposition** concerning.
– DERIVATIVES **touch·ing·ly** adverb.

touch·line /ˈtəchˌlīn/ ▸ **noun** Soccer & Rugby the boundary line on each side of the field.

touch·point /ˈtəch,point/ ▸ **noun 1** Commerce any point of contact between a buyer and a seller. **2** a condition or circumstance likely to precipitate a highly unfavorable outcome.

touch screen ▸ **noun** a display device that allows the user to interact with a computer by touching areas on the screen.

touch·stone /ˈtəch,stōn/ ▸ **noun 1** a standard or criterion by which something may be judged. **2** a piece of stone formerly used for testing alloys of gold by observing the color of the mark that they made on it.

touch-tone ▸ **adjective** (of a telephone) having buttons that produce different sounds when pushed, rather than a dial.

touch-type ▸ **verb** type without looking at the keys.

touch·y /ˈtəchē/ ▸ **adjective** (**touchier, touchiest**) **1** quick to take offense; oversensitive. **2** (of a situation or issue) requiring careful handling.

– SYNONYMS **1 sensitive,** oversensitive, hypersensitive, easily offended, thin-skinned, highly strung, tense, irritable, tetchy, testy, crotchety, peevish, querulous, bad-tempered, petulant; informal snappy, cranky. **2 delicate,** sensitive, tricky, ticklish, embarrassing, awkward, difficult, contentious, controversial.

– DERIVATIVES **touch·i·ly** adverb **touch·i·ness** noun.
– ORIGIN perhaps an alteration of **TETCHY**, influenced by **TOUCH**.

touch·y-feel·y /ˈfēlē/ ▸ **adjective** informal, often derogatory openly expressing affection or other emotions, especially through physical contact.

tough /təf/ ▸ **adjective 1** strong enough to withstand wear and tear. **2** able to endure hardship, difficulty, or pain. **3** involving difficulty or hardship: *the training has been quite tough.* **4** strict and uncompromising: *tough anti-smoking laws.* **5** (of a person) rough or violent. **6** used to express a lack of sympathy.

– SYNONYMS **1 durable,** strong, resilient, sturdy, rugged, solid, stout, robust, hard-wearing, long-lasting, heavy-duty, well built, made to last. **2 chewy,** leathery, gristly, stringy, fibrous. **3 strict,** stern, severe, stringent, rigorous, hard, firm, hard-hitting, uncompromising. **4** *the training was pretty tough* **difficult,** hard, strenuous, onerous, grueling, exacting, arduous, demanding, taxing, tiring, exhausting, punishing. **5** *tough questions* **difficult,** hard, knotty, thorny, tricky.
– ANTONYMS weak, lenient, easy.

▸ **noun** informal a rough and violent man.

– SYNONYMS **ruffian,** thug, hoodlum, hooligan, bully; informal heavy, bruiser.

– DERIVATIVES **tough·ness** noun.
– PHRASES **tough it out** informal endure a period of hardship or difficulty.
– ORIGIN Old English.

tough·en /ˈtəfən/ ▸ **verb** make or become tough.

– SYNONYMS **1 strengthen,** fortify, reinforce, harden, temper, anneal. **2** *measures to toughen up discipline* **make stricter,** make more severe, stiffen, tighten up.

tough love ▸ **noun** the practice of helping a person by adopting a strict attitude toward them or requiring them to take responsibility for their actions.

tough-mind·ed ▸ **adjective** realistic and unsentimental.

tou·pee /to͞oˈpā/ ▸ **noun** a small wig or artificial hairpiece worn to cover a bald spot.
– ORIGIN French, from Old French *toup* 'tuft.'

tour /to͝or/ ▸ **noun 1** a journey for pleasure in which several different places are visited. **2** a short trip made to view or inspect something. **3** a journey made by performers or a sports team, in which they perform or play in several different places. **4** (also **tour of duty**) a period of duty on military or diplomatic service.

– SYNONYMS **1 trip,** excursion, journey, expedition, jaunt, outing, trek. **2** *a tour of the factory* **visit,** inspection, walkabout.

▸ **verb** make a tour of an area.

– SYNONYMS **travel around,** visit, explore, vacation in, go around.

– ORIGIN Old French, 'turn.'

tour de force /ˈto͝or də ˈfôrs/ ▸ **noun** (pl. **tours de force** pronunc. same) a performance or achievement that has been accomplished with great skill.
– ORIGIN French, 'feat of strength.'

Tou·rette's syn·drome /to͞oˈrets/ ▸ **noun** a disorder of the nervous system characterized by involuntary muscle spasms and in some cases the compulsive utterance of obscene words.
– ORIGIN named after the French neurologist Gilles de la *Tourette.*

tour·ism /ˈto͝or,izəm/ ▸ **noun** the business of organizing and running vacations and visits to places of interest.

tour·ist /ˈto͝orist/ ▸ **noun** a person who travels for pleasure.

– SYNONYMS **sightseer,** traveler, vacationer, visitor, out-of-towner, backpacker, globetrotter, day tripper.
– ANTONYMS local.

– DERIVATIVES **tour·is·tic** /to͞oˈristik/ adjective.

tour·ist class ▸ **noun** the cheapest accommodations or seating in a ship, aircraft, or hotel.

tour·ist·y /ˈto͝oristē/ ▸ **adjective** informal, often derogatory appealing to or visited by many tourists.

tour·ma·line /ˈto͝orməlan, -,lēn/ ▸ **noun** a brittle gray or black mineral used as a gemstone and in electrical devices.
– ORIGIN Sinhalese, 'carnelian.'

tour·na·ment /ˈtərnəmənt, ˈto͝or-/ ▸ **noun 1** a series of contests between a number of competitors, competing for an overall prize. **2** a medieval sporting event in which knights jousted with blunted weapons for a prize.

– SYNONYMS **competition,** contest, championship, meeting, event.

– ORIGIN Old French *torneiement.*

tour·ne·dos /ˈto͝ornə,dō/ ▸ **noun** (pl. same) a small, round, thick piece of meat cut from a fillet of beef.
– ORIGIN French, from *tourner* 'to turn' + *dos* 'back.'

tour·ney /ˈtərnē, ˈto͝or-/ ▸ **noun** (pl. **tourneys**) a medieval joust.
– ORIGIN Old French *tornei.*

tour·ni·quet /ˈtərnikit, ˈto͝or-/ ▸ **noun** a cord or tight bandage that is tied around a limb to stop a wound from bleeding.
– ORIGIN French.

tour op·er·a·tor ▸ **noun** a travel agent specializing in package tours.

tou·sle /ˈtouzəl/ ▸ **verb** make a person's hair untidy.
– ORIGIN Germanic.

tout /tout/ ▸ **verb 1** attempt to sell something, typically by using a direct or persistent approach. **2** attempt to persuade people of the value or merit of someone or something: *she was touted as a potential prime minister.* **3** offer horse-racing tips for a share of the winnings. **4** British term for **SCALP** (sense 2 of the verb). ▸ **noun** a person who touts.
– ORIGIN Germanic.

tow[1] /tō/ ▸ **verb** use a vehicle or boat to pull another vehicle or boat along.

– SYNONYMS **pull,** haul, drag, draw, tug, lug.

▸ **noun** an act of towing a vehicle or boat.
– DERIVATIVES **tow·a·ble** adjective.
– PHRASES **in tow 1** (also **on tow**) being towed. **2** accompanying or following someone.
– ORIGIN Old English.

USAGE

On the confusion of **tow** and **toe**, see the note at **TOE**.

tow[2] ▸ **noun** short, coarse fibers of flax or hemp, used for making yarn.
– ORIGIN Old English.

to·ward /tôrd, t(ə)'wôrd/ (also **towards** /tôrdz, t(ə)'wôrdz/) ▸ **preposition 1** in the direction of. **2** getting nearer to a time or aim. **3** in relation to. **4** contributing to the cost of.
– ORIGIN Old English.

tow bar ▸ **noun** a bar fitted to the back of a vehicle, used in towing a trailer or camper.

tow·el /'toul/ ▸ **noun** a piece of thick absorbent cloth or paper used for drying. ▸ **verb** (**towels, toweling, toweled**) dry someone or something with a towel.
– ORIGIN Old French *toaille.*

tow·er /'tou(ə)r/ ▸ **noun 1** a tall, narrow building, either freestanding or forming part of a building such as a church or castle. **2** a tall structure that houses machinery, operators, etc. **3** a tall structure used as a container or for storage. ▸ **verb** rise to or reach a great height.

– SYNONYMS **soar,** rise, rear, overshadow, overhang, hang over, dominate.

– ORIGIN Old English.

tow·er·ing /'tou(-ə)riNG/ ▸ **adjective 1** very tall. **2** of very high quality: *a towering performance.* **3** very strong or intense: *a towering rage.*

tow·head /'tō,hed/ ▸ **noun** a person with very light blond hair.
– DERIVATIVES **tow·head·ed** adjective.

town /toun/ ▸ **noun 1** a settlement larger than a village and generally smaller than a city, with defined boundaries and local government. **2** the central part of a town or city, with its business or shopping area. **3** densely populated areas, especially as contrasted with the country or suburbs. **4** the permanent residents of a college town, as distinct from the students.

– SYNONYMS **municipality,** township, borough, village, hamlet; city, metropolis, conurbation.

– PHRASES **go to town** informal do something thoroughly or enthusiastically. **on the town** informal enjoying the nightlife of a city or town.
– ORIGIN Old English, 'homestead, village.'

town car ▸ **noun** a large, luxurious car; a limousine.

town clerk ▸ **noun** a public official in charge of the records of a town.

town coun·cil ▸ **noun** the elected governing body in a town or district.
– DERIVATIVES **town coun·ci·lor** noun.

town cri·er ▸ **noun** historical a person employed to make public announcements in the streets.

town hall ▸ **noun** a building housing local government offices.

town·house /'toun,hous/ ▸ **noun 1** a tall, narrow traditional row house, generally having three or more floors. **2** a house in a town or city owned by a person who owns another property in the country.

town·ie /'tounē/ ▸ **noun** informal **1** a person who lives in a town, especially as distinct from one who lives in the country. **2** a resident in a college town, rather than a college student.

town plan·ning ▸ **noun** the planning and control of the construction, growth, and development of a town or other urban area.
– DERIVATIVES **town plan·ner** noun.

town·scape /'toun,skāp/ ▸ **noun** a view or picture of a town or city.

towns·folk /'tounz,fōk/ ▸ **plural noun** another term for **TOWNSPEOPLE**.

town·ship /'toun,SHip/ ▸ **noun 1** a division of a county that has certain powers of local administration. **2** (in South Africa) a suburb or city occupied chiefly by black people, formerly officially designated for black occupation by apartheid laws.
– ORIGIN Old English.

towns·man /'tounzmən/ (or **townswoman** /'tounz,wo͝omən/) ▸ **noun** (pl. **townsmen** or **townswomen**) a person living in a particular town or city.

towns·peo·ple /'tounz,pēpəl/ (also **townsfolk** /'tounz,fōk/) ▸ **plural noun** the people living in a particular town or city.

tow·path /'tō,paTH/ ▸ **noun** a path beside a river or canal, originally used as a pathway for horses towing barges.

tow rope ▸ **noun** a rope, cable, etc., used in towing.

tow truck ▸ **noun** a truck used to tow or pick up disabled vehicles.

tox·e·mi·a /täk'sēmēə/ (Brit. **toxaemia**) ▸ **noun 1** blood poisoning by toxins from a local bacterial infection. **2** a condition in pregnancy characterized especially by high blood pressure; preeclampsia.
– ORIGIN from Latin *toxicum* 'poison.'

tox·ic /'täksik/ ▸ **adjective 1** poisonous. **2** relating to or caused by poison.

– SYNONYMS **poisonous,** dangerous, harmful, injurious, noxious, pernicious, deadly, lethal.
– ANTONYMS harmless.

– DERIVATIVES **tox·ic·i·ty** /täk'sisitē/ noun.
– ORIGIN from Latin *toxicum* 'poison.'

tox·i·cant /'täksikənt/ ▸ **noun** a toxic substance introduced into the environment, e.g., a pesticide.
– ORIGIN variant of **INTOXICANT**.

tox·i·col·o·gy /,täksi'käləjē/ ▸ **noun** the branch of science concerned with the nature, effects, and detection of poisons.
– DERIVATIVES **tox·i·co·log·i·cal** /,täksikə'läjikəl/ adjective **tox·i·col·o·gist** noun.

tox·ic shock syn·drome ▶ **noun** acute blood poisoning in women, typically caused by bacterial infection from a tampon that has been kept in the body for too long.

tox·in /'täksin/ ▶ **noun** a poison produced by a microorganism or other organism, to which the body reacts by producing antibodies.

tox·o·car·i·a·sis /ˌtäksəkə'rīəsis/ ▶ **noun** infection of a human with the larvae of a worm that is a parasite of dogs, cats, and other animals, causing illness and a risk of blindness.
– ORIGIN from *toxocara*, the name of the worm.

tox·o·plas·mo·sis /ˌtäksōplaz'mōsis/ ▶ **noun** a disease caused by a parasite, transmitted chiefly through undercooked meat, soil, or cat feces.
– ORIGIN from *toxoplasma*, the name of the parasite.

toy /toi/ ▶ **noun 1** an object for a child to play with. **2** a gadget or machine that provides amusement for an adult.

– SYNONYMS **plaything,** game.

▶ **adjective** (of a breed or variety of pet dog) very small in full-grown size.

– SYNONYMS **model,** imitation, replica, miniature.

▶ **verb** (**toy with**) **1** consider an idea casually or indecisively. **2** handle absentmindedly or nervously. **3** eat or drink something in an unenthusiastic way.

– SYNONYMS **1** *I was toying with the idea of writing a book* **think about,** consider, flirt with, entertain the possibility of; informal kick around. **2** *she was toying with a loose strand of hair* **fiddle with,** play with, fidget with, twiddle, finger.

– DERIVATIVES **toy·like** /-ˌlīk/ adjective.
– ORIGIN unknown.

toy boy ▶ **noun** Brit. informal a male lover who is much younger than his partner.

trace[1] /trās/ ▶ **verb 1** find someone or something by careful investigation. **2** find or describe the origin or development: *the book traces his flying career with the RAF.* **3** copy a drawing, map, or design by drawing over its lines on a piece of transparent paper placed on top of it. **4** draw a pattern or outline. **5** follow the course or position of something with one's eye, mind, or finger.

– SYNONYMS **1 track down,** find, discover, detect, unearth, turn up, hunt down, ferret out, run to ground. **2 draw,** outline, mark.

▶ **noun 1** a mark or other indication of the existence or passing of something: *the aircraft disappeared without a trace.* **2** a very small quantity. **3** a barely noticeable indication: *a trace of a smile touched his lips.* **4** a line or pattern on a paper or screen corresponding to something that is being recorded or measured. **5** a procedure to trace something, such as the place from which a telephone call was made.

– SYNONYMS **1 sign,** mark, indication, evidence, clue, vestige, remains, remnant. **2 bit,** touch, hint, suggestion, suspicion, shadow, dash, tinge; informal smidgen, tad.

– DERIVATIVES **trace·a·ble** adjective.
– ORIGIN Old French *tracier*.

CHOOSE THE RIGHT WORD

trace, remnant, track, trail, vestige

You can follow the **track** of a deer in the snow, the **trace** of a sleigh, or the **trail** of someone who has just cut down a Christmas tree and is dragging it back to the car. A *track* is a line or a series of marks left by the passage of something or someone; it often refers specifically to a line of footprints or a path worn into the ground by the feet (*to follow the track of a grizzly bear*). *Trace* may refer to a line or a rut made by someone or something that has been present or passed by; it may also refer to a mark serving as evidence that something has happened or been there (*traces of mud throughout the house; the telephoto shots have a trace of a camera shake*). *Trail* may refer to the track created by the passage of animals or people, or to the mark or marks left by something being dragged along a surface (*they followed the trail of the injured dog*). **Vestige** and **remnant** come closer in meaning to *trace*, as they refer to what remains after something has passed away. A *vestige* is always slight when compared to what it recalls (*the last vestiges of a great civilization*), while a *remnant* is a fragment or scrap of something (*all that remained of the historic tapestry after the fire was a few scorched remnants*).

trace[2] ▶ **noun** each of the two side straps, chains, or ropes by which a horse is attached to a vehicle that it is pulling.
– ORIGIN Old French *trais*.

trace el·e·ment ▶ **noun** a chemical element present or required only in minute amounts.

trace min·er·al ▶ **noun** a trace element required for nutrition.

trac·er /'trāsər/ ▶ **noun 1** a bullet or shell whose course is made visible by a trail of flames or smoke, used to assist in aiming. **2** a substance that is introduced into the body and whose subsequent progress can be followed from its color, radioactivity, or other distinctive property.

trac·er·y /'trāsərē/ ▶ **noun** (pl. **traceries**) **1** a decorative design of holes and outlines in stone, especially in the upper part of a window. **2** a delicate branching pattern.
– DERIVATIVES **trac·er·ied** adjective.

tra·che·a /'trākēə/ ▶ **noun** (pl. **tracheae** /-kēˌē/ or **tracheas**) the tube conveying air between the larynx and the lungs; the windpipe.
– DERIVATIVES **tra·che·al** adjective.
– ORIGIN from Greek *trakheia artēria* 'rough artery.'

tra·che·ot·o·my /ˌtrākē'ätəmē/ (also **tracheostomy** /-'ästəmē/) ▶ **noun** (pl. **tracheotomies**) a surgical cut in the windpipe, made to enable someone to breathe when the windpipe is blocked.

tra·cho·ma /trə'kōmə/ ▶ **noun** a contagious infection transmitted by a bacterium and causing inflammation of the inner surface of the eyelids.
– ORIGIN Greek *trakhōma* 'roughness.'

trac·ing /'trāsiNG/ ▶ **noun 1** a copy of a drawing, map, etc., made by tracing. **2** a faint or delicate mark or pattern.

track /trak/ ▶ **noun 1** a rough path or minor road. **2** a prepared course or circuit for racing. **3** a mark or line of marks left by a person, animal, or vehicle in passing. **4** a continuous line of rails on a railroad. **5** a section of a record, compact disc, or cassette tape containing one song or piece of music. **6** a strip or rail along which something such as a curtain may be moved. **7** a jointed metal band around the wheels of a heavy vehicle. **8** the transverse distance between a vehicle's wheels.

– SYNONYMS **1 path,** footpath, lane, trail, route, way. **2 course,** racecourse, racetrack, circuit, velodrome. **3** *the tracks of a fox* **traces,** marks, prints, footprints, trail, spoor. **4** *the train tracks* **rail,** line. **5 song,** recording, number, piece.

▸ **verb 1** follow the course or movements of: *he tracked the flight of two military aircraft.* **2** (**track someone/thing down**) find someone or something after a thorough or difficult search. **3** follow a particular course. **4** (of a movie or television camera) move in relation to the subject being filmed.

– SYNONYMS **1 follow,** trail, pursue, shadow, stalk; informal tail. **2** (**track someone/thing down**) **discover,** find, detect, hunt down, unearth, uncover, turn up, dig up, ferret out, run to ground.

– DERIVATIVES **track·er** noun **track·less** adjective.
– PHRASES **keep** (or **lose**) **track of** keep (or fail to keep) fully aware of or informed about. **make tracks** informal leave. **on the right** (or **wrong**) **track** following a course likely to result in success (or failure). **stop** (or **be stopped**) **in one's tracks** informal come (or be brought) to a sudden and complete halt. **the wrong side of the tracks** informal a poor or less prestigious part of town. [with reference to the railroad tracks of American towns, once serving as a line of demarcation between rich and poor areas.]
– ORIGIN Old French *trac.*

CHOOSE THE RIGHT WORD

See note at **TRACE**.

track and field ▸ **noun** athletic events that take place on a running track and a nearby field; track events and field events.

track·ball /ˈtrakˌbôl/ ▸ **noun** a small ball set in a holder that can be rotated by hand to move a cursor on a computer screen.

track·ing /ˈtrakiNG/ ▸ **noun 1** Electronics the maintenance of a constant difference in frequency between connected circuits or components. **2** the alignment of the wheels of a vehicle.

track rec·ord ▸ **noun** the past achievements or performance of a person, organization, or product.

track·suit /ˈtrakˌso͞ot/ ▸ **noun** a warm, loose-fitting outfit consisting of a sweatshirt or light jacket and pants with an elastic or drawstring waist.

track·way /ˈtrakˌwā/ ▸ **noun** a path formed by the repeated treading of people or animals.

tract[1] /trakt/ ▸ **noun 1** a large area of land. **2** a system of organs or tubes in the body that are connected and that have a particular purpose: *the digestive tract.*
– ORIGIN Latin *tractus* 'drawing, draft.'

tract[2] ▸ **noun** a pamphlet containing a short piece of writing on a political or religious topic.
– ORIGIN apparently an abbreviation of Latin *tractatus* 'treatise.'

trac·ta·ble /ˈtraktəbəl/ ▸ **adjective 1** easy to control or influence. **2** (of a situation or problem) easy to deal with.
– DERIVATIVES **trac·ta·bil·i·ty** /ˌtraktəˈbilitē/ noun.
– ORIGIN Latin *tractabilis.*

trac·tion /ˈtrakSHən/ ▸ **noun 1** the action of pulling a thing along a surface. **2** the power used for pulling. **3** the applying of a sustained pull on a limb or muscle, especially to maintain the position of a fractured bone or to correct a deformity. **4** the grip of a tire on a road or a wheel on a rail.
– ORIGIN Latin, from *trahere* 'to pull.'

trac·tor /ˈtraktər/ ▸ **noun** a powerful motor vehicle with large rear wheels, used chiefly on farms for pulling equipment and trailers.
– ORIGIN Latin, from *trahere* 'to pull.'

trac·tor-trai·ler ▸ **noun** a vehicle consisting of a tractor or cab with an engine and a separate, attached trailer in which goods can be transported.

trade /trād/ ▸ **noun 1** the buying and selling of goods or services. **2** a commercial activity of a particular kind: *the tourist trade.* **3** a job requiring manual skills and special training. **4** (**the trade**) (treated as sing. or pl.) the people engaged in a particular area of business. **5** a trade wind.

– SYNONYMS **1 dealing,** buying and selling, commerce, traffic, business. **2 occupation,** work, craft, job, career, profession, business, line (of work), métier.

▸ **verb 1** buy and sell goods or services; operate as a business or company. **2** buy or sell a particular item or product. **3** exchange something for something else, typically as a commercial transaction. **4** (**trade something in**) exchange a used article in part payment for another. **5** (**trade on**) take advantage of: *the government is trading on fears of inflation.*

– SYNONYMS **1 deal,** do business, bargain, negotiate, traffic, buy and sell, merchandise. **2** *I traded the car for a newer model* **swap,** exchange, barter.

– DERIVATIVES **trad·a·ble** (or **tradeable**) adjective.
– ORIGIN German, 'track.'

WORD LINKS

mercantile *relating to trade*

trade def·i·cit ▸ **noun** the amount by which the cost of a country's imports exceeds the value of its exports.

trad·ed op·tion ▸ **noun** an option on a stock exchange or futures exchange that can itself be bought and sold.

trade-in ▸ **noun** (usu. as adj.) a used article accepted by a retailer in partial payment for another: *the trade-in value of the car.*

trade jour·nal (also **trade magazine**) ▸ **noun** a periodical containing news and items of interest concerning a particular trade.

trade·mark /ˈtrādˌmärk/ ▸ **noun 1** a symbol, word, or words chosen to represent a company or product, legally registered or established by use. **2** a distinctive characteristic or object: *the murder had all the trademarks of a Mafia hit.*

trade name ▸ **noun 1** a name that has the status of a trademark. **2** a name by which something is known in a particular trade or profession.

trade-off ▸ **noun** a balance achieved between two desirable but conflicting features; a compromise.

trad·er /ˈtrādər/ ▸ **noun 1** a person who trades goods, currency, or shares. **2** a merchant ship.

– SYNONYMS **dealer,** merchant, buyer, seller, vendor, purveyor, supplier, trafficker.

trad·es·can·tia /ˌtradəˈskanCH(ē)ə, -tēə/ ▸ **noun** an American plant with triangular flowers.
– ORIGIN named in honor of the English botanist John *Tradescant.*

trade se·cret ▸ **noun** a secret device or technique used by a company in manufacturing its products.

trades·man /ˈtrādzmən/ ▸ **noun** (pl. **tradesmen**) a person engaged in trading or in a skilled profession.

trade sur·plus ▸ **noun** the amount by which the value of a country's exports exceeds the cost of its imports.

trade un·ion (Brit. also **trades union**) ▶ **noun** a labor union.

trade wind /wind/ ▶ **noun** a wind blowing steadily toward the equator from the northeast in the northern hemisphere or from the southeast in the southern hemisphere, especially at sea.
– ORIGIN from the former phrase *blow trade* 'blow steadily.'

trad·ing card ▶ **noun** each of a set of picture cards that are collected and traded.

trad·ing post ▶ **noun** a store or small settlement established for trading in a remote place.

tra·di·tion /trəˈdisʜən/ ▶ **noun 1** the passing on of customs or beliefs from generation to generation. **2** a long-established custom or belief passed on in this way. **3** an artistic or literary method or style established by an artist, writer, or movement, and subsequently followed by other people.

– SYNONYMS **custom,** practice, convention, ritual, observance, way, usage, habit, institution, unwritten law; formal praxis.

– ORIGIN Latin.

tra·di·tion·al /trəˈdisʜənl/ ▶ **adjective** relating to or following customs or beliefs that have been passed from generation to generation: *traditional Irish music.*

– SYNONYMS **customary,** long-established, time-honored, classic, wonted, accustomed, standard, regular, normal, conventional, habitual, ritual, age-old.

– DERIVATIVES **tra·di·tion·al·ly** adverb.

tra·di·tion·al·ism /trəˈdisʜənl,izəm/ ▶ **noun** the support of tradition, especially so as to resist change.
– DERIVATIVES **tra·di·tion·al·ist** noun & adjective.

tra·duce /trəˈd(y)o͞os/ ▶ **verb** say unpleasant or untrue things about someone.
– ORIGIN Latin *traducere* 'lead in front of others, expose to ridicule.'

traf·fic /ˈtrafik/ ▶ **noun 1** vehicles moving on public roads. **2** the movement of ships or aircraft. **3** the commercial transportation of goods or passengers. **4** the messages or signals sent through a communications system. **5** the action of trading in something illegal. ▶ **verb** (**traffics, trafficking, trafficked**) deal or trade in something illegal.
– DERIVATIVES **traf·fick·er** noun.
– ORIGIN from French *traffique,* Spanish *tráfico,* or Italian *traffico.*

traf·fic cir·cle ▶ **noun** a road junction at which traffic moves in one direction around a central island.

traf·fic is·land ▶ **noun** a small raised area in the middle of a road that provides a safe place for pedestrians to stand.

traf·fic jam ▶ **noun** a line or lines of traffic at or virtually at a standstill.

– SYNONYMS **bottleneck,** holdup, congestion, gridlock; informal snarl-up.

traf·fic light (also **traffic lights**) ▶ **noun** a set of automatically operated colored lights for controlling traffic.

tra·ge·di·an /trəˈjēdēən/ ▶ **noun 1** (fem. **tragedienne** /trə,jēdēˈen/) an actor who plays tragic roles. **2** a writer of tragedies.

trag·e·dy /ˈtrajidē/ ▶ **noun** (pl. **tragedies**) **1** an event causing great suffering and distress. **2** a serious play with an unhappy ending, especially one concerning the downfall of the main character.

– SYNONYMS **disaster,** calamity, catastrophe, cataclysm, misfortune, adversity.

– ORIGIN Greek *tragōidia.*

trag·ic /ˈtrajik/ ▶ **adjective 1** extremely distressing or sad. **2** relating to tragedy in a literary work.

– SYNONYMS **1 disastrous,** calamitous, catastrophic, cataclysmic, devastating, terrible, dreadful, awful, appalling, horrendous, fatal. **2 sad,** unhappy, pathetic, moving, distressing, painful, harrowing, heart-rending, sorry.
– ANTONYMS fortunate, happy.

– DERIVATIVES **trag·i·cal·ly** /-ik(ə)lē/ adverb.

trag·i·com·e·dy /,trajəˈkämidē/ ▶ **noun** (pl. **tragicomedies**) a play or novel containing elements of both comedy and tragedy.
– DERIVATIVES **trag·i·com·ic** /-ˈkämik/ adjective.

trail /trāl/ ▶ **noun 1** a mark or a series of signs left behind by the passage of someone or something. **2** a track or scent used in following someone or hunting an animal. **3** a beaten path through rough country. **4** a route planned or followed for a particular purpose: *the tourist trail.* **5** a long, thin part stretching behind or hanging down from something.

– SYNONYMS **1** *a trail of clues* **series,** string, chain, succession, sequence. **2 track,** spoor, path, scent, traces, marks, signs, prints, footprints. **3 path,** way, footpath, track, route.

▶ **verb 1** draw or be drawn along behind someone or something: *her robe trailed along the ground.* **2** follow someone's or something's trail. **3** walk or move slowly or wearily. **4** (**trail away/off**) (of a person's voice) fade gradually before stopping. **5** be losing to an opponent in a contest. **6** (of a plant) grow along the ground or so as to hang down. **7** give advance publicity to a movie, television show, etc., with a trailer.

– SYNONYMS **1 drag,** sweep, be drawn, dangle. **2** *roses trailed over the banks* **hang,** droop, fall, spill, cascade. **3 follow,** pursue, track, shadow, stalk, hunt; informal tail. **4 lose,** be down, be behind, lag behind.

– ORIGIN from Old French *traillier* 'to tow' or German *treilen* 'haul a boat.'

CHOOSE THE RIGHT WORD

See **TRACE**[1].

trail·blaz·er /ˈtrāl,blāzər/ ▶ **noun 1** a person who is the first to do something. **2** a person who makes a new track through wild country.
– DERIVATIVES **trail·blaz·ing** noun & adjective.

trail·er /ˈtrālər/ ▶ **noun 1** an unpowered vehicle towed by another. **2** the rear section of a tractor-trailer. **3** an extract from a movie or television show used for advance advertising. **4** (also **travel trailer**) a vehicle equipped for living in, designed to be towed by a car.

trail·er park (also **trailer court**) ▶ **noun 1** an area where trailers are parked and used for recreation or as permanent homes. **2** (as adj.) lacking refinement, taste, or quality: *her trailer-park bleached perm.*

trail·er trash ▶ **noun** offensive poor, lower-class white people, typically regarded as living in mobile homes.

trail·er truck ▶ **noun** a tractor-trailer.

trail·ing edge ▶ **noun** the rear edge of a moving object, especially an airfoil.

trail mix ▶ **noun** a mixture of dried fruit and nuts eaten as a snack.

train /trān/ ▶ **verb 1** teach a person or animal a particular skill or type of behavior through regular practice and instruction. **2** be taught in such a way: *he trained as a plumber.* **3** make or become physically fit through a course of exercise and diet. **4** (**train something on**) point something at: *he trained his gun on the side door.* **5** make a plant grow in a particular direction or shape.

– SYNONYMS **1 instruct,** teach, coach, tutor, school, educate, prime, drill, ground. **2 study,** learn, prepare, take instruction. **3 exercise,** work out, get into shape, practice. **4 aim,** point, direct, level, focus.

▶ **noun 1** a series of railroad cars moved as a unit by a locomotive or by integral motors. **2** a number of vehicles or load-carrying animals moving in a line. **3** a series of connected events or thoughts. **4** a long piece of trailing material attached to the back of a formal dress or robe. **5** a group of attendants accompanying an important person.

– SYNONYMS **chain,** string, series, set, sequence, succession, course.

– DERIVATIVES **train·a·ble** adjective **train·ing** noun **train·load** /ˈtrān,lōd/ noun.
– PHRASES **in train** in progress.
– ORIGIN from Old French *trahiner.*

train·ee /trāˈnē/ ▶ **noun** a person undergoing training for a particular job or profession.
– DERIVATIVES **train·ee·ship** /-,SHip/ noun.

train·er /ˈtrānər/ ▶ **noun 1** a person who trains people or animals. **2** (also **training shoe**) Brit. a soft shoe, suitable for sports or casual wear.

– SYNONYMS **coach,** instructor, teacher, tutor, handler.

train·ing wheels ▶ **noun** a pair of small supporting wheels fitted on a child's bicycle.

train·spot·ter /ˈtrān,spätər/ ▶ **noun** Brit. a person who collects locomotive numbers as a hobby.
– DERIVATIVES **train·spot·ting** noun.

traipse /trāps/ ▶ **verb** walk or move wearily or reluctantly. ▶ **noun** a boring or tiring walk.
– ORIGIN unknown.

trait /trāt/ ▶ **noun 1** a distinguishing quality or characteristic. **2** a genetically determined characteristic.

– SYNONYMS **characteristic,** attribute, feature, quality, habit, mannerism, idiosyncrasy, peculiarity.

– ORIGIN French.

trai·tor /ˈtrātər/ ▶ **noun** a person who betrays their country, a cause, etc.

– SYNONYMS **betrayer,** backstabber, double-crosser, renegade, Judas, Benedict Arnold, quisling, fifth columnist, turncoat, defector; informal snake in the grass.

– DERIVATIVES **trai·tor·ous** adjective.
– ORIGIN Old French *traitour.*

tra·jec·to·ry /trəˈjektərē/ ▶ **noun** (pl. **trajectories**) the path followed by a moving object under the action of given forces.
– ORIGIN Latin *trajectoria.*

tram /tram/ (also **tramcar** /ˈtram,kär/) ▶ **noun** Brit. a trolley car; a cable car.
– ORIGIN German and Dutch *trame* 'beam, barrow shaft'; the word formerly referred to a barrow or cart used in coal mines, later the tracks on which such carts ran.

tram·mel /ˈtraməl/ ▶ **verb** (**trammels, trammeling, trammeled**) restrict someone's freedom of action.
▶ **plural noun** (**trammels**) literary things that restrict someone's freedom of action.
– ORIGIN Old French *tramail.*

tramp /tramp/ ▶ **verb 1** walk heavily or noisily. **2** walk wearily or reluctantly over a long distance.

– SYNONYMS **trudge,** plod, stamp, trample, lumber, trek, walk, slog, hike; informal traipse, schlep.

▶ **noun 1** a homeless person who travels around and lives by begging or doing casual work. **2** the sound of heavy steps. **3** a long walk. **4** a cargo ship running between many different ports rather than sailing a fixed route. **5** informal a promiscuous woman.

– SYNONYMS **1 vagrant,** vagabond, homeless person, down-and-out, traveler, drifter, hobo; informal bum. **2 tread,** step, footstep, footfall. **3 trek,** walk, hike, slog, march, roam, ramble; informal schlep.

– DERIVATIVES **tramp·er** noun **tramp·y** adjective (informal).
– ORIGIN probably German.

tram·ple /ˈtrampəl/ ▶ **verb 1** tread on something and crush it. **2** (**trample on/over**) treat someone or something with disrespect or contempt: *a statesman ought not to trample on the opinions of his advisers.*

– SYNONYMS **tread,** stamp, walk, squash, crush, flatten.

– ORIGIN from TRAMP.

tram·po·line /ˈtrampə,lēn/ ▶ **noun** a strong fabric sheet connected by springs to a frame, used as a springboard and landing area in doing acrobatic or gymnastic exercises.
– DERIVATIVES **tram·po·lin·ing** noun.
– ORIGIN Italian *trampolino.*

tram·way /ˈtram,wā/ ▶ **noun** Brit. **1** a set of rails for a trolley car. **2** a trolley car system.

trance /trans/ ▶ **noun 1** a half-conscious state in which someone does not respond to external stimuli, typically as brought about by hypnosis. **2** a state in which someone is not paying attention to what is happening around them. **3** (also **trance music**) a type of electronic dance music characterized by hypnotic rhythms.

– SYNONYMS **daze,** stupor, hypnotic state, dream, reverie.

– ORIGIN from Old French *transir* 'depart, fall into a trance.'

tranche /tränSH/ ▶ **noun** any of the parts into which something, especially an amount of money or an issue of shares in a company, is divided.
– ORIGIN Old French, 'slice.'

tran·nie /ˈtranē/ (also **tranny**) ▶ **noun** (pl. **trannies**) informal **1** a transvestite. **2** a transmission in a motor vehicle.

tran·quil /ˈtraNGkwəl/ ▶ **adjective** free from disturbance; calm.

– SYNONYMS **peaceful,** calm, restful, quiet, still, serene, relaxing, undisturbed.
– ANTONYMS busy, excitable.

– DERIVATIVES **tran·quil·i·ty** /,traNGˈkwilitē/ noun **tran·quil·ly** adverb.
– ORIGIN Latin *tranquillus.*

WORD TOOLKIT

See SLEEPY.

tran·quil·ize /'traNGkwə,līz/ ▶ **verb** make a person or animal calm or unconscious, especially by giving them a sedative drug.

tran·quil·iz·er /'traNGkwə,līzər/ ▶ **noun** a drug taken to reduce tension or anxiety.

– SYNONYMS **sedative,** barbiturate, calmative, narcotic, opiate; informal downer.
– ANTONYMS stimulant.

trans- ▶ **prefix 1** across; beyond: *transcontinental.* **2** on or to the other side of: *transatlantic.* **3** into another state or place: *translate.*
– ORIGIN from Latin *trans* 'across.'

trans·act /tran'sakt, -'zakt/ ▶ **verb** do business with a person or organization.

trans·ac·tion /tran'saksHən, -'zak-/ ▶ **noun 1** an act of buying or selling something. **2** the action of carrying out business.

– SYNONYMS **deal,** bargain, agreement, undertaking, arrangement, negotiation, settlement.

– DERIVATIVES **trans·ac·tion·al** adjective.
– ORIGIN Latin.

trans·at·lan·tic /,transət'lantik, ,tranz-/ ▶ **adjective 1** crossing the Atlantic. **2** concerning countries on both sides of the Atlantic, typically Britain and the US. **3** relating to or situated on the other side of the Atlantic.

trans·ax·le /trans'aksəl, tranz-/ ▶ **noun** an integral driving axle and differential gear in a motor vehicle.

trans·ceiv·er /tran'sēvər/ ▶ **noun** a combined radio transmitter and receiver.

tran·scend /tran'send/ ▶ **verb 1** be or go beyond the range or limits of: *an issue transcending party politics.* **2** be better than a person or achievement.

– SYNONYMS **go beyond,** rise above, exceed, surpass, excel, outstrip.

– ORIGIN Latin *transcendere.*

tran·scend·ent /tran'sendənt/ ▶ **adjective 1** going beyond normal or physical human experience. **2** (of God) existing apart from and not limited by the physical universe.
– DERIVATIVES **tran·scend·ence** noun **tran·scend·ent·ly** adverb.

tran·scen·den·tal /,transen'dentl/ ▶ **adjective** relating to a spiritual area that is beyond human experience or knowledge.
– DERIVATIVES **tran·scen·den·tal·ly** adverb.

Tran·scen·den·tal Med·i·ta·tion ▶ **noun** trademark a technique for relaxation and promoting harmony by meditation and repetition of a mantra.

trans·con·ti·nen·tal /,transkäntə'nentl, ,tranz-/ ▶ **adjective** crossing or extending across a continent or continents.

tran·scribe /tran'skrīb/ ▶ **verb 1** put thoughts, speech, or data into written or printed form. **2** make a copy of something, especially in another alphabet or language. **3** arrange a piece of music for a different instrument or voice.
– DERIVATIVES **tran·scrib·er** noun.
– ORIGIN Latin *transcribere.*

tran·script /'tran,skript/ ▶ **noun** a written or printed version of material that was originally spoken or presented in another form.
– ORIGIN Latin *transcriptum.*

tran·scrip·tion /tran'skripsHən/ ▶ **noun 1** a written or printed version of something; a transcript. **2** the action of transcribing something. **3** a piece of music transcribed for a different instrument or voice.

trans·der·mal /trans'dərməl, tranz-/ ▶ **adjective** relating to the application of a medicine or drug through the skin, especially by means of an adhesive patch.

trans·duc·er /trans'd(y)o͞osər, tranz-/ ▶ **noun** a device that converts variations in a physical quantity (such as pressure or brightness) into an electrical signal, or vice versa.
– DERIVATIVES **trans·duc·tion** /-'dəksHən/ noun.
– ORIGIN from Latin *transducere* 'lead across.'

tran·sect /tran'sekt/ technical ▶ **verb** cut across or make a transverse section in something. ▶ **noun** a straight line or narrow cross section through an object or across the earth's surface, along which observations or measurements are made.
– DERIVATIVES **tran·sec·tion** /-'seksHən/ noun.
– ORIGIN from TRANS- + Latin *secare* 'divide by cutting.'

tran·sept /'tran,sept/ ▶ **noun** (in a cross-shaped church) either of the two parts extending at right angles from the nave.
– ORIGIN Latin *transeptum.*

tran·sex·u·al /tran'seksHo͞oəl/ ▶ **noun & adjective** variant spelling of TRANSSEXUAL.

trans-fat /'trans'fat/ ▶ **noun** an unsaturated fatty acid found especially in margarines and cooking oils.

trans·fer ▶ **verb** /trans'fər, 'transfər/ (**transfers, transferring, transferred**) **1** move from one place to another: *transfer the rice to a saucepan.* **2** move to another department, job, team, etc. **3** change to another place, route, or means of transportation during a journey. **4** officially pass property, or a right or responsibility, to another person. **5** (as adj. **transferred**) (of the sense of a word or phrase) changed by extension or metaphor.

– SYNONYMS **move,** take, bring, shift, convey, remove, carry, transport, relocate.

▶ **noun** /'transfər/ **1** an act of transferring someone or something. **2** a small colored picture or design on paper, which can be transferred to another surface by being pressed or heated.
– DERIVATIVES **trans·fer·a·ble** /trans'fərəbəl, 'transfərə-/ adjective **trans·fer·ee** /,transfə'rē/ noun **trans·fer·or** /trans'fərər, 'transfərər/ (chiefly Law) noun **trans·fer·ral** /trans'fərəl/ noun.
– ORIGIN Latin *transferre.*

trans·fer·ence /trans'fərəns, 'transfərəns/ ▶ **noun 1** the action of transferring something. **2** Psychoanalysis the redirection to a substitute, usually a therapist, of emotions originally felt in childhood.

trans·fig·u·ra·tion /trans,figyə'rāsHən/ ▶ **noun 1** a complete transformation into a more beautiful or spiritual state. **2** (**the Transfiguration**) Jesus's appearance in glory to three of his disciples (in the gospels of Matthew and Mark).

trans·fig·ure /trans'figyər/ ▶ **verb** (**be transfigured**) be transformed into something more beautiful or spiritual.
– ORIGIN Latin *transfigurare.*

trans·fix /trans'fiks/ ▶ **verb 1** make someone motionless with horror, wonder, or astonishment. **2** pierce someone or something with a sharp implement.

– SYNONYMS **1** *transfixed by the images* **mesmerize,** hypnotize, spellbind, bewitch, captivate, entrance, enthrall, fascinate, enrapture, grip, rivet. **2** *a mouse is transfixed by the owl's talons* **impale,** stab, spear, pierce, spike, skewer, gore, stick, run through.

– ORIGIN Latin *transfigere* 'pierce through.'

trans·form /trans'fôrm/ ▶ **verb 1** change or be changed in appearance, form, or nature: *expressways have transformed our lives.* **2** change the voltage of an electric current.

– SYNONYMS **change,** alter, convert, revolutionize, overhaul, reconstruct, rebuild, reorganize, rearrange, rework.

– DERIVATIVES **trans·form·a·tive** /-mətiv/ adjective.

trans·for·ma·tion /ˌtransfər'māsʜən/ ▶ **noun** a marked change in nature, form, or appearance.

– SYNONYMS **change,** alteration, conversion, metamorphosis, revolution, overhaul, reconstruction, rebuilding, reorganization, rearrangement, reworking.

– DERIVATIVES **trans·for·ma·tion·al** adjective.

trans·form·er /trans'fôrmər/ ▶ **noun** a device for changing the voltage of an alternating current.

trans·fu·sion /trans'fyo͞ozʜən/ ▶ **noun 1** the medical process of transferring blood or its components from one person or animal to another. **2** a transfer of something vital, especially money: *the country's economy will receive a transfusion of at least $1 billion.*

– DERIVATIVES **trans·fuse** /trans'fyo͞oz/ verb.

– ORIGIN from Latin *transfundere* 'pour from one container to another.'

trans·gen·der /tranz'jendər, trans-/ (also **transgendered**) ▶ **adjective** transsexual.

trans·gen·ic /trans'jenik, tranz-/ ▶ **adjective** containing genetic material into which DNA from a different organism has been artificially added.

– DERIVATIVES **trans·gene** /trans'jēn, tranz-/ noun **trans·gen·ics** plural noun.

trans·gress /trans'gres, tranz-/ ▶ **verb** go beyond the limits of what is morally, socially, or legally acceptable.

– DERIVATIVES **trans·gres·sive** adjective **trans·gres·sor** noun.

– ORIGIN Latin *transgredi* 'step across.'

trans·gres·sion /trans'gresʜən, tranz-/ ▶ **noun** the action or an act of transgressing.

– SYNONYMS **offense,** crime, sin, wrong, wrongdoing, misdemeanor, misdeed, lawbreaking; error, lapse; violation, defiance, disobedience, nonobservance; old use trespass.

CHOOSE THE RIGHT WORD

See **SIN**[1].

tran·ship ▶ **verb** variant spelling of **TRANSSHIP**.

trans·hu·mance /trans'(h)yo͞oməns, tranz-/ ▶ **noun** the action or practice of moving livestock seasonally from one grazing ground to another.

– DERIVATIVES **trans·hu·mant** adjective.

– ORIGIN from Latin *trans-* 'across' + *humus* 'ground.'

tran·sient /'transʜənt, -zʜənt, -zēənt/ ▶ **adjective 1** lasting only for a short time. **2** staying or working in a place for a short time only.

– SYNONYMS **transitory,** temporary, short-lived, short-term, ephemeral, impermanent, brief, short, momentary, fleeting, passing.
– ANTONYMS permanent.

▶ **noun** a person who stays or works in a place for a short time.

– DERIVATIVES **tran·sience** noun **tran·sien·cy** noun **tran·sient·ly** adverb.

– ORIGIN from Latin *transire* 'go across.'

CHOOSE THE RIGHT WORD

See **TEMPORARY**.

tran·sis·tor /tran'zistər/ ▶ **noun 1** a semiconductor device with three connections, able to amplify or rectify an electric current. **2** (also **transistor radio**) a portable radio using circuits containing transistors.

– DERIVATIVES **tran·sis·tor·ize** /tran'zistəˌrīz/ verb.

– ORIGIN from **TRANSFER** + **RESISTOR**.

tran·sit /'tranzit/ ▶ **noun 1** the carrying of people or things from one place to another. **2** an act of passing through or across a place. ▶ **verb** (**transits, transiting, transited**) pass across or through an area.

– ORIGIN Latin *transitus.*

tran·si·tion /tran'zisʜən, -'sisʜən/ ▶ **noun** the process or a period of changing from one state or condition to another: *the rituals marked the transition from boyhood to manhood.*

– SYNONYMS **change,** passage, move, transformation, conversion, metamorphosis, alteration, changeover, shift, switch.

tran·si·tion·al /tran'zisʜənl, -'sisʜənl/ ▶ **adjective** of, relating to, or characterized by transition; temporary.

– SYNONYMS **1** *a transitional period* **intermediate,** interim, changeover, changing, fluid, unsettled. **2** *a transitional government* **interim,** temporary, provisional, pro tem, acting, caretaker.

tran·si·tion met·al ▶ **noun** any of the set of metallic chemical elements occupying the central block in the periodic table, e.g., iron, manganese, chromium, and copper.

tran·si·tion se·ries ▶ **noun** Chemistry the set of transition metals in the periodic table.

tran·si·tive /'transitiv, 'tranz-/ ▶ **adjective** (of a verb) able to take a direct object, e.g., *saw* in *he saw the donkey.* The opposite of **INTRANSITIVE**.

– DERIVATIVES **tran·si·tive·ly** adverb **tran·si·tiv·i·ty** /ˌtransə'tivitē, -zə-/ noun.

– ORIGIN Latin *transitivus.*

tran·si·to·ry /'transiˌtôrē, 'tranzi-/ ▶ **adjective** lasting for a short time; not permanent.

– SYNONYMS **transient,** temporary, brief, short, short-lived, short-term, impermanent, ephemeral, momentary, fleeting, passing.
– ANTONYMS permanent.

– DERIVATIVES **tran·si·to·ri·ly** adverb **tran·si·to·ri·ness** noun.

– ORIGIN Latin *transitorius.*

CHOOSE THE RIGHT WORD

See **TEMPORARY**.

trans·late /trans'lāt, tranz-/ ▶ **verb 1** express the sense of words or writing in another language. **2** be expressed or be able to be expressed in another language. **3** (**translate

into) convert or be converted into another form: *they were unable to translate their concert success into record sales.*

– SYNONYMS **interpret,** convert, render, put, change, express, decipher, reword, decode, gloss, explain.

– DERIVATIVES **trans·lat·a·ble** adjective **trans·la·tor** noun.
– ORIGIN from Latin *translatus* 'carried across.'

trans·la·tion /trans'lāsʜən, tranz-/ ▶ noun **1** the action of translating something. **2** a word or written work that is translated into another language.

– SYNONYMS **interpretation,** rendition, conversion, change, alteration, adaptation.

trans·lit·er·ate /trans'litəˌrāt, tranz-/ ▶ verb write a letter or word using the closest corresponding letters of a different alphabet or language.
– DERIVATIVES **trans·lit·er·a·tion** /transˌlitə'rāsʜən, tranz-/ noun.
– ORIGIN from TRANS- + Latin *littera* 'letter.'

trans·lo·cate /trans'lōˌkāt, tranz-/ ▶ verb chiefly technical move from one place to another.
– DERIVATIVES **trans·lo·ca·tion** /transˌlō'kāsʜən, tranz-/ noun.

trans·lu·cent /trans'lo͞osnt, tranz-/ ▶ adjective allowing light to pass through partially; semitransparent.

– SYNONYMS **semitransparent,** pellucid, limpid, clear; diaphanous, gossamer, sheer.
– ANTONYMS opaque.

– DERIVATIVES **trans·lu·cence** noun **trans·lu·cen·cy** noun.
– ORIGIN from Latin *translucere* 'shine through.'

WORD TOOLKIT

See **DIAPHANOUS**.

trans·mi·gra·tion /ˌtransˌmī'grāsʜən, ˌtranz-/ ▶ noun (in some beliefs) the passing of a person's soul after their death into another body.

trans·mis·si·ble /tranz'misəbəl/ ▶ adjective (especially of a disease, virus, etc.) able to be transmitted.
– DERIVATIVES **trans·mis·si·bil·i·ty** /-ˌmisə'bilitē/ noun.

trans·mis·sion /trans'misʜən, tranz-/ ▶ noun **1** the action of passing something from one person or place to another. **2** a program or signal that is transmitted. **3** the mechanism by which power is transmitted from an engine to the axle in a motor vehicle.

– SYNONYMS **1 transfer,** communication, passing on, conveyance, dissemination, spread, circulation, relaying. **2 broadcasting,** televising, airing. **3 broadcast,** program, show.

trans·mit /tranz'mit, trans-/ ▶ verb (**transmits, transmitting, transmitted**) **1** pass from one place or person to another: *the disease is transmitted by mosquitoes.* **2** broadcast or send out an electrical signal or a radio or television program. **3** allow heat, light, or other energy to pass through a medium.

– SYNONYMS **1 transfer,** communicate, pass on, hand on, convey, impart, channel, carry, relay, dispatch, disseminate, spread, circulate. **2 broadcast,** send out, air, televise.

– DERIVATIVES **trans·mit·tal** noun.
– ORIGIN Latin *transmittere.*

trans·mit·ter /trans'mitər, tranz-/ ▶ noun a device used to produce and transmit electromagnetic waves carrying messages or signals, especially those of radio or television.

trans·mog·ri·fy /trans'mägrəˌfī, tranz-/ ▶ verb (**transmogrifies, transmogrifying, transmogrified**) chiefly humorous change into someone or something completely different: *alchemists strove to transmogrify base metals into gold.*
– DERIVATIVES **trans·mog·ri·fi·ca·tion** /-ˌmägrəfi'kāsʜən/ noun.
– ORIGIN unknown.

trans·mute /trans'myo͞ot, tranz-/ ▶ verb change in form, nature, or substance.
– DERIVATIVES **trans·mu·ta·tion** /ˌtransmyo͞o'tāsʜən, ˌtranz-/ noun.
– ORIGIN Latin *transmutare.*

trans·na·tion·al /trans'nasʜənl, tranz-/ ▶ adjective extending or operating across national boundaries. ▶ noun a multinational company.

trans·o·ce·an·ic /ˌtransōsʜē'anik, ˌtranz-/ ▶ adjective crossing an ocean.

tran·som /'transəm/ ▶ noun **1** the flat surface forming the stern of a boat. **2** a strengthening crossbar above a window or door.
– PHRASES **over the transom** informal offered or sent without prior agreement; unsolicited.
– ORIGIN Old French *traversin.*

tran·som win·dow ▶ noun a window set above the transom of a door or larger window; a fanlight.

tran·son·ic /tran'sänik/ ▶ adjective referring to speeds close to that of sound.

trans·par·en·cy /tran'sparənsē/ ▶ noun (pl. **transparencies**) **1** the condition of being transparent. **2** a positive transparent photograph printed on plastic or glass, and viewed using a slide projector.

trans·par·ent /tran'spe(ə)rənt, -'spar-/ ▶ adjective **1** allowing light to pass through so that objects behind can be distinctly seen. **2** obvious or evident: *the company's transparent attempt to woo back women customers.*

– SYNONYMS **1 clear,** translucent, limpid, crystal clear, crystalline, pellucid. **2 see-through,** sheer, filmy, gauzy, diaphanous. **3 obvious,** blatant, unambiguous, unequivocal, clear, plain, apparent, unmistakable, manifest, conspicuous, patent.
– ANTONYMS opaque, obscure.

– DERIVATIVES **trans·par·ent·ly** adverb.
– ORIGIN from Latin *transparere* 'shine through.'

WORD TOOLKIT

See **DIAPHANOUS**.

trans·per·son·al /trans'pərsənl, tranz-/ ▶ adjective relating to states of consciousness beyond the limits of personal identity.

tran·spire /tran'spī(ə)r/ ▶ verb **1** come to be known or prove to be the case. **2** happen; occur. **3** Botany (of a plant or leaf) give off water vapor through the stomata (tiny pores).
– DERIVATIVES **tran·spi·ra·tion** /-spə'rāsʜən/ noun.
– ORIGIN Latin *transpirare.*

USAGE

The standard sense of **transpire** is 'come to be known' (*it transpired that he had bought a house*). From this, a newer sense developed, meaning 'happen' (*I'm going to find out what transpired*). This sense, although very common, is sometimes criticized for being an unnecessarily long word used where **occur** or **happen** would do just as well.

CHOOSE THE RIGHT WORD

See **HAPPEN**.

trans·plant ▶ **verb** /trans'plant/ **1** transfer someone or something to another place or situation. **2** take living tissue or an organ and implant it in another part of the body or in another body. ▶ **noun** /'trans,plant/ **1** an operation in which an organ or tissue is transplanted. **2** a person or thing that has been transferred to another place or situation.
– DERIVATIVES **trans·plant·a·ble** /trans'plantəbəl/ adjective **trans·plan·ta·tion** /-,plan'tāsHən/ noun.
– ORIGIN Latin *transplantare*.

tran·spon·der /tran'spändər/ ▶ **noun** a device for receiving a radio signal and automatically transmitting a different signal.
– ORIGIN from **TRANSMIT** and **RESPOND**.

trans·port ▶ **verb** /trans'pôrt/ **1** carry people or goods from one place to another by means of a vehicle, aircraft, or ship. **2** (**be transported**) be overwhelmed with a strong emotion: *she was transported with pleasure*. **3** historical send a convict to a distant country as a punishment.

– SYNONYMS **convey,** carry, take, transfer, move, shift, send, deliver, bear, ship, ferry; informal cart.

▶ **noun** /'trans,pôrt/ **1** a system or means of transporting people or goods. **2** the action of transporting people or goods. **3** a large vehicle, ship, or aircraft for carrying troops or stores. **4** (**transports**) overwhelmingly strong emotions.

– SYNONYMS **conveyance,** carriage, delivery, shipping, freight, shipment, haulage.

– DERIVATIVES **trans·port·a·bil·i·ty** /,trans,pôrtə'bilitē/ noun **trans·port·a·ble** /trans'pôrtəbəl/ adjective.
– ORIGIN Latin *transportare* 'carry across.'

CHOOSE THE RIGHT WORD

See **RAPTURE**.

trans·por·ta·tion /,transpər'tāsHən/ ▶ **noun** **1** a system or means of transporting people or goods. **2** the action of transporting people or goods. **3** historical the action or practice of transporting convicts to a penal colony.

trans·port·er /trans'pôrtər/ ▶ **noun** a large vehicle used to carry heavy objects.

trans·pose /trans'pōz/ ▶ **verb** **1** cause two or more things to exchange places. **2** transfer to a different place or situation: *the play is transposed to America*. **3** write or play music in a different key from the original.
– DERIVATIVES **trans·pos·a·ble** adjective **trans·po·si·tion** /,transpə'zisHən/ noun.
– ORIGIN Old French *transposer*.

trans·sex·u·al /tran(s)'seksHo͞oəl/ (also **transexual** /tran'seksHo͞oəl/) ▶ **noun** a person born with the physical characteristics of one sex who emotionally and psychologically feels that they belong to the opposite sex. ▶ **adjective** relating to a transsexual person.
– DERIVATIVES **trans·sex·u·al·ism** /-,lizəm/ noun **trans·sex·u·al·i·ty** /-,seksHo͞o'alitē/ noun.

trans·ship /tran(s)'sHip/ (also **tranship**) ▶ **verb** transfer cargo from one ship or other form of transport to another.
– DERIVATIVES **trans·ship·ment** noun.

tran·sub·stan·ti·a·tion /,transəb,stancHē'āsHən/ ▶ **noun** (in Christian belief) the doctrine that when the bread and wine of Holy Communion have been consecrated they are converted into the body and blood of Jesus.
– ORIGIN from Latin *transubstantiare* 'to change in substance.'

trans·u·ran·ic /,transyə'ranik, tranz-/ ▶ **adjective** (of a chemical element) having a higher atomic number than uranium (92).

trans·verse /trans'vərs, tranz-/ ▶ **adjective** situated or extending across something.
– DERIVATIVES **trans·verse·ly** adverb.
– ORIGIN from Latin *transvertere* 'turn across.'

trans·ves·tite /trans'ves,tīt, tranz-/ ▶ **noun** a person, typically a man, who gains pleasure from dressing in clothes usually worn by the opposite sex.
– DERIVATIVES **trans·ves·tism** /-,tizəm/ noun.
– ORIGIN German *Transvestit*.

trap /trap/ ▶ **noun** **1** a device, pit, or enclosure designed to catch and hold animals. **2** an unpleasant situation from which it is difficult to escape. **3** a trick that causes someone to do something that they do not intend or that will harm them: *the police set a trap for two local gangs*. **4** a container or device used to collect a specified thing. **5** a curve in the waste pipe from a bath, basin, or toilet that is always full of liquid to prevent the upward passage of gases. **6** a light, two-wheeled carriage pulled by a horse or pony. **7** the compartment from which a greyhound is released at the start of a race. **8** a device for hurling an object such as a clay pigeon into the air. **9** informal a person's mouth.

– SYNONYMS **1 snare,** net, mesh, gin. **2 trick,** ploy, ruse, deception, subterfuge; informal setup.

▶ **verb** (**traps, trapping, trapped**) **1** catch or hold in a trap: *twenty workers were trapped by the flames*. **2** trick someone into doing something.

– SYNONYMS **1 snare,** entrap, capture, catch, ambush. **2 confine,** cut off, corner, shut in, pen in, hem in, imprison. **3 trick,** dupe, deceive, fool, hoodwink.

– ORIGIN Old English.

trap·door /'trap,dôr/ ▶ **noun** a hinged or removable panel in a floor, ceiling, or roof.

tra·peze /trə'pēz, tra-/ ▶ **noun** (also **flying trapeze**) a horizontal bar hanging by two ropes high above the ground, used by acrobats in a circus.
– ORIGIN Latin *trapezium*.

tra·pe·zi·um /trə'pēzēəm/ ▶ **noun** (pl. **trapezia** /-zēə/ or **trapeziums**) Geometry **1** a quadrilateral with no sides parallel. **2** British term for **TRAPEZOID** (sense 1).
– ORIGIN Latin.

tra·pe·zi·us /trə'pēzēəs/ ▶ **noun** (pl. **trapezii** /-zē,ī/) either of a pair of large triangular muscles extending over the back of the neck and shoulders and moving the head and shoulder blade.
– ORIGIN Latin.

trap·e·zoid /'trapi,zoid/ ▶ **noun** Geometry **1** a quadrilateral with one pair of sides parallel. **2** British term for **TRAPEZIUM** (sense 1).
– DERIVATIVES **trap·e·zoi·dal** /,trapi'zoidl/ adjective.

trap·per /'trapər/ ▶ **noun** a person who traps wild animals, especially for their fur.

trap·pings /'trapiNGz/ ▶ **plural noun** **1** the signs or objects associated with a particular situation or role: *I had the trappings of success*. **2** a horse's ornamental harness.
– ORIGIN Old French *drap* 'drape.'

Trap·pist /ˈtrapist/ ▶ **noun** a monk belonging to a branch of the Cistercian order of monks who speak only in certain situations.
– ORIGIN French *trappiste*, from *La Trappe* in Normandy, where the order was founded.

trash /trasн/ ▶ **noun 1** waste material; refuse. **2** poor-quality writing, art, etc. **3** a person or people regarded as being of very low social standing.

– SYNONYMS **1 rubbish,** garbage, refuse, waste, litter, junk. **2 nonsense,** rubbish, trivia, pulp fiction, pap; informal drivel.

▶ **verb** informal wreck or destroy something.
– ORIGIN unknown.

trash can ▶ **noun** a receptacle for trash; a garbage can.

trash talk informal ▶ **noun** insulting or boastful speech intended to intimidate or humiliate someone. ▶ **verb** (**trash-talk**) use insulting or boastful speech for such a purpose.
– DERIVATIVES **trash talk·er** noun.

trash·y /ˈtrasнē/ ▶ **adjective** (**trashier, trashiest**) of poor quality: *trashy movies.*
– DERIVATIVES **trash·i·ness** noun.

trat·to·ri·a /ˌträtəˈrēə/ ▶ **noun** an Italian restaurant.
– ORIGIN Italian.

trau·ma /ˈtroumə, ˈtrô-/ ▶ **noun** (pl. **traumas**) **1** a deeply distressing experience. **2** emotional shock following a stressful event. **3** Medicine physical injury.

– SYNONYMS **1 shock,** upheaval, distress, stress, strain, pain, anguish, suffering, upset, ordeal. **2 injury,** damage, wound.

– ORIGIN Greek, 'wound.'

trau·mat·ic /trəˈmatik, trou-, trô-/ ▶ **adjective** emotionally disturbing or distressing.

– SYNONYMS **disturbing,** shocking, distressing, upsetting, painful, agonizing, hurtful, stressful, devastating, harrowing.

– DERIVATIVES **trau·mat·i·cal·ly** /-ik(ə)lē/ adverb.

trau·ma·tize /ˈtrouməˌtīz, ˈtrô-/ ▶ **verb** cause someone to experience lasting shock as a result of a disturbing experience or injury.

tra·vail /trəˈvāl, ˈtravˌāl/ (also **travails**) ▶ **noun** literary a situation or experience that involves much hard work or difficulty: *the museum records the town's wartime travails.*
– ORIGIN Old French.

CHOOSE THE RIGHT WORD

See LABOR.

trav·el /ˈtravəl/ ▶ **verb** (**travels, traveling, traveled**) **1** go from one place to another, especially over a long distance. **2** go along a road or through a region. **3** move at a particular speed, in a particular direction, or over a particular distance: *light travels faster than sound.* **4** remain in good condition after a journey: *certain wines do not travel well.*

– SYNONYMS **journey,** tour, take a trip, voyage, go sightseeing, globetrot, backpack, trek.

▶ **noun 1** (**travels**) journeys, especially abroad. **2** the action of traveling. **3** the range or motion of a part of a machine.

– SYNONYMS (**travels**) **traveling,** journeys, expeditions, trips, tours, excursions, voyages, treks, wanderings, jaunts.

▶ **adjective** (of a device) small enough to be packed for use when traveling: *a travel iron.*
– ORIGIN from TRAVAIL.

trav·el a·gen·cy ▶ **noun** an agency that makes the necessary arrangements for travelers.
– DERIVATIVES **trav·el a·gent** noun.

trav·eled /ˈtravəld/ ▶ **adjective 1** having traveled to many places. **2** used by people traveling: *a well-traveled route.*

trav·el·er /ˈtrav(ə)lər/ (Brit. **traveller**) ▶ **noun** a person who is traveling or who often travels.

– SYNONYMS **tourist,** vacationer, out-of-towner, sightseer, day tripper, globetrotter, backpacker, passenger, commuter.

trav·el·er's check ▶ **noun** a check for a fixed amount that may be exchanged for cash or used to pay for things abroad.

trav·el·ing sales·man ▶ **noun** a representative of a firm who visits businesses to show samples and gain orders.

tra·vel kit ▶ **noun** a waterproof bag for holding toothpaste, soap, etc., when traveling.

trav·e·logue /ˈtravəˌlôg, -ˌläg/ ▶ **noun** a movie, book, or illustrated talk about a person's travels.

trav·el trail·er ▶ **noun** see TRAILER (sense 4).

trav·erse /trəˈvərs/ ▶ **verb 1** travel or extend across or through: *he traversed the forest.* **2** move something back and forth or sideways. ▶ **noun 1** an act of traversing something. **2** a part of a structure that extends or is fixed across something.
– DERIVATIVES **tra·vers·a·ble** adjective **tra·vers·al** noun.
– ORIGIN Latin *traversare.*

trav·er·tine /ˈtravərˌtēn, -tin/ ▶ **noun** white or light-colored rock deposited from mineral springs, used in building.
– ORIGIN Italian *travertino.*

trav·es·ty /ˈtravistē/ ▶ **noun** (pl. **travesties**) an absurd or distorted representation: *the trial was a travesty of justice.*

– SYNONYMS *a travesty of justice* **misrepresentation,** distortion, perversion, corruption, mockery, parody; farce, charade, pantomime, sham; informal apology for.

▶ **verb** (**travesties, travestying, travestied**) represent someone or something in an absurd or distorted way.
– ORIGIN from French *travestir* 'to disguise.'

CHOOSE THE RIGHT WORD

See CARICATURE.

tra·vois /trəˈvoi, ˈtravˌoi/ ▶ **noun** (pl. same) a V-shaped frame of poles pulled by a horse, formerly used by North American Indians to carry goods.
– ORIGIN French.

trawl /trôl/ ▶ **verb 1** search widely and thoroughly: *he trawled the bars of Athens for a drink.* **2** catch fish with a trawl net or seine. ▶ **noun 1** a thorough search. **2** (also **trawl net**) a large wide-mouthed fishing net dragged by a boat along the bottom of the sea or a lake.
– ORIGIN probably from Dutch *traghelen* 'to drag.'

trawl·er /ˈtrôlər/ ▶ **noun** a fishing boat used for trawling.
– DERIVATIVES **trawl·er·man** /ˈtrôlərˌmən/ noun (pl. **trawlermen**).

tray /trā/ ▶ **noun** a flat, shallow container with a raised rim, used for carrying things.
– ORIGIN Old English.

treach·er·ous /ˈtrecHərəs/ ▶ **adjective 1** not loyal or able to be trusted. **2** having hidden or unpredictable dangers: *treacherous currents.*

– SYNONYMS **1 traitorous,** disloyal, unfaithful, duplicitous, deceitful, false, backstabbing, double-crossing, two-faced, untrustworthy, unreliable, apostate, renegade. **2 dangerous,** hazardous, perilous, unsafe, precarious, risky; informal dicey, hairy.
– ANTONYMS loyal, faithful.

– DERIVATIVES **treach·er·ous·ly** adverb.
– ORIGIN Old French *trecherous.*

treach·er·y /ˈtrecHərē/ ▶ **noun** (pl. **treacheries**) behavior that involves betraying someone's trust.

trea·cle /ˈtrēkəl/ ▶ **noun 1** excessively sweet sentimentality or flattery. **2** Brit. molasses.
– DERIVATIVES **trea·cly** /ˈtrēk(ə)lē/ adjective.
– ORIGIN Greek *thēriakē* 'antidote against venom.'

tread /tred/ ▶ **verb** (past **trod** /träd//träd/; past part. **trodden** /ˈträdn/ or **trod**) **1** walk in a specified way. **2** press down or crush something with the feet. **3** walk on or along something.

– SYNONYMS **1 walk,** step, stride, pace, march, tramp, plod, stomp, trudge. **2 crush,** flatten, press down, squash, trample on, stamp on.

▶ **noun 1** a person's way of walking or the sound made by this: *I heard the heavy tread of Dad's boots.* **2** the top surface of a step or stair. **3** the part of a vehicle tire that grips the road. **4** the part of the sole of a shoe that rests on the ground.

– SYNONYMS **step,** footstep, footfall, tramp.

– PHRASES **tread carefully** (or **lightly** or **warily**) take action in a cautious or restrained way. **tread on someone's toes** offend someone by getting involved in something that is their responsibility. **tread water 1** stay in an upright position in deep water by moving the feet with a walking movement. **2** fail to make progress.
– ORIGIN Old English.

trea·dle /ˈtredl/ ▶ **noun** a lever worked by the foot to operate a machine.
– ORIGIN Old English, 'stair, step.'

tread·mill /ˈtred,mil/ ▶ **noun 1** a device used for exercise, consisting of a continuous moving belt on which to walk or run. **2** a job or situation that is tiring, boring, and difficult to escape from: *they were on a never-ending treadmill of duty.* **3** a large wheel turned by the weight of people or animals treading on steps fitted into it, formerly used to drive machinery.

trea·son /ˈtrēzən/ (also **high treason**) ▶ **noun** the crime of betraying one's country, especially by attempting to kill or overthrow the sovereign or government.

– SYNONYMS **treachery,** disloyalty, betrayal, sedition, subversion, mutiny, rebellion.

– DERIVATIVES **trea·son·a·ble** adjective **trea·son·ous** adjective.
– ORIGIN Old French *treisoun.*

treas·ure /ˈtrezHər/ ▶ **noun 1** a quantity of precious metals, gems, or other valuable objects. **2** a very valuable object. **3** informal a much loved or highly valued person.

– SYNONYMS **1 riches,** valuables, jewels, gems, gold, silver, precious metals, money, cash, wealth, fortune. **2 masterpiece,** gem, pearl, jewel.

▶ **verb 1** look after a valuable or valued item carefully. **2** value someone or something highly.

– SYNONYMS **cherish,** hold dear, prize, set great store by, value greatly.

– ORIGIN Old French *tresor.*

treas·ure hunt ▶ **noun** a game in which players search for hidden objects by following a trail of clues.

treas·ur·er /ˈtrezHərər/ ▶ **noun** a person appointed to manage the finances of a society, company, or other organization.

treas·ure trove ▶ **noun** a collection or store of valuable or pleasant things.
– ORIGIN from Old French *tresor trové* 'found treasure.'

treas·ur·y /ˈtrezHərē/ ▶ **noun** (pl. **treasuries**) **1** the funds or income of a country, state, institution, or society. **2** (**Treasury**) (in some countries) the government department responsible for the overall management of the economy. **3** a place where treasure is stored. **4** a collection of valuable or pleasant things.

– SYNONYMS **storehouse,** repository, treasure house, exchequer, fund, mine, bank, coffers, purse.

Treas·ur·y bill ▶ **noun** a government security that does not pay interest, but is issued at a price that is less than the value it can be redeemed at.

treat /trēt/ ▶ **verb 1** behave toward or deal with in a particular way: *he treated her with courtesy.* **2** give medical care or attention to a person, illness, etc. **3** apply a process or a substance to something. **4** present or discuss a subject. **5** (**treat someone to**) pay for someone's food, drink, or entertainment. **6** (**treat oneself**) do or have something very enjoyable.

– SYNONYMS **1 behave toward,** act toward, use, deal with, handle. **2** *police are treating the fires as arson* **regard,** consider, view, look on, think of, put down. **3 deal with,** tackle, handle, discuss, explore, investigate. **4 tend,** nurse, attend to, give medical attention to. **5 cure,** heal, remedy. **6** *he* ***treated*** *her* ***to*** *lunch* **buy,** take out for, give, pay for; informal foot the bill for, pick up the tab for. **7** *the crowd was* ***treated to*** *a superb display* **entertain with,** regale with, fete with.

▶ **noun 1** a surprise gift, event, etc., that gives great pleasure. **2** (**one's treat**) an act of paying for someone's food, drink, or entertainment.

– SYNONYMS **1 celebration,** entertainment, amusement, surprise. **2 present,** gift, tidbit, delicacy, luxury, indulgence, extravagance; informal goody. **3 pleasure,** delight, thrill, joy.

– DERIVATIVES **treat·a·ble** adjective **treat·er** noun.
– ORIGIN Old French *traitier.*

trea·tise /ˈtrētis/ ▶ **noun** a written work dealing formally and systematically with a subject.
– ORIGIN Old French *tretis.*

treat·ment /ˈtrētmənt/ ▶ **noun 1** a way of behaving toward someone or dealing with something. **2** medical care for an illness or injury. **3** the use of a substance or process to preserve or give particular properties to something: *the treatment of hazardous waste.* **4** the presentation or discussion of a subject.

– SYNONYMS **1 behavior,** conduct, handling, management, dealings. **2 medical care,** therapy, nursing, ministrations, medication, medicament, drugs. **3 discussion,** handling, investigation, exploration, consideration, study, analysis.

trea·ty /ˈtrētē/ ▶ **noun** (pl. **treaties**) a formal agreement between nations.

– SYNONYMS **agreement,** settlement, pact, deal, entente, concordat, accord, protocol, compact, convention; formal concord.

– ORIGIN Old French *traite*.

tre·ble[1] /'trebəl/ ▶ **adjective 1** consisting of three parts. **2** multiplied or occurring three times. ▶ **noun** a threefold quantity or thing. ▶ **pronoun** an amount that is three times as large as usual. ▶ **verb** make or become three times as large or as many.
– ORIGIN from Latin *triplus* 'triple.'

treble[2] ▶ **noun 1** a high-pitched voice, especially a boy's singing voice. **2** the high-frequency output of a radio or audio system.
– ORIGIN from TREBLE[1].

tre·ble clef ▶ **noun** Music a clef placing G above middle C on the second-lowest line of the stave.

tree /trē/ ▶ **noun 1** a woody perennial plant consisting of a trunk and branches, that can typically grow to a considerable height. **2** a branching structure.
– DERIVATIVES **tree·less** adjective.
– ORIGIN Old English.

WORD LINKS

arboreal *relating to trees*

tree·creep·er /'trē,krēpər/ ▶ **noun** a small brown songbird that creeps about on the trunks of trees to search for insects.

tree di·a·gram ▶ **noun** a diagram with a structure of branching connecting lines.

tree fern ▶ **noun** a large palmlike fern with a stem that resembles a tree trunk.

tree frog ▶ **noun** a tree-living frog that has long toes with adhesive disks and is typically small and brightly colored.

tree house ▶ **noun** a structure built in the branches of a tree for children to play in.

tree-hug·ger ▶ **noun** informal, derogatory an environmental campaigner.
– DERIVATIVES **tree-hug·ging** noun.
– ORIGIN with reference to the practice of embracing a tree to prevent it from being felled.

tree·line /'trē,līn/ ▶ **noun** the height on a mountain above which trees are unable to grow.

tree ring ▶ **noun** each of a number of rings in the cross section of a tree trunk, representing a single year's growth.

tree sur·geon ▶ **noun** a person who prunes and treats old or damaged trees in order to preserve them.
– DERIVATIVES **tree sur·ger·y** noun.

tree·top /'trē,täp/ ▶ **noun** the uppermost part of a tree.

tre·foil /'trē,foil, 'tref,oil/ ▶ **noun 1** a small plant with yellow flowers and cloverlike leaves. **2** an ornamental design in the form of three rounded arcs like a clover leaf, used typically in stone tracery.
– ORIGIN Latin *trifolium*.

trek /trek/ ▶ **noun** a long, difficult journey, especially one made on foot.

– SYNONYMS **journey,** trip, expedition, safari, hike, march, tramp, walk.

▶ **verb** (**treks, trekking, trekked**) go on a trek.
– DERIVATIVES **trek·ker** noun.
– ORIGIN from South African Dutch *trekken* 'to pull, travel.'

trel·lis /'trelis/ ▶ **noun** a framework of bars used as a support for climbing plants.
– DERIVATIVES **trel·lised** adjective.
– ORIGIN Old French *trelis*.

trem·ble /'trembəl/ ▶ **verb 1** shake uncontrollably as a result of fear, excitement, or weakness. **2** be very worried or frightened. **3** (of a thing) shake slightly.

– SYNONYMS **shake,** quiver, shudder, vibrate, wobble, rock, move, sway.

▶ **noun** a trembling feeling, movement, or sound.
– DERIVATIVES **trem·bly** /'tremb(ə)lē/ adjective (informal).
– ORIGIN Old French *trembler*.

CHOOSE THE RIGHT WORD

See **SHAKE**.

tre·men·dous /trə'mendəs/ ▶ **adjective 1** very great in amount, scale, or intensity. **2** informal very good or impressive.

– SYNONYMS **1 huge,** enormous, immense, colossal, massive, prodigious, stupendous; informal whopping, astronomical, ginormous. **2 excellent,** first-class, outstanding, marvelous, wonderful, splendid, superb, admirable; informal great, fantastic, fabulous, terrific, super, awesome, ace; Brit. informal brilliant, smashing.

– DERIVATIVES **tre·men·dous·ly** adverb.
– ORIGIN Latin *tremendus*.

trem·o·lo /'tremə,lō/ ▶ **noun** (pl. **tremolos**) a wavering effect in singing or created when playing some musical instruments.
– ORIGIN Italian.

trem·or /'tremər/ ▶ **noun 1** an uncontrollable quivering movement. **2** (also **earth tremor**) a slight earthquake. **3** a sudden feeling of fear or excitement.

– SYNONYMS **1** *the sudden tremor of her hands* **tremble,** shake, quiver, twitch, tic. **2** *a tremor of fear ran through her* **shiver,** frisson, spasm, thrill, tingle, stab, dart, shaft; wave, surge, rush, ripple. **3** *the epicenter of the tremor* **earthquake,** shock; informal quake.

– ORIGIN Latin.

trem·u·lous /'tremyələs/ ▶ **adjective 1** shaking or quivering slightly. **2** timid; nervous.
– DERIVATIVES **trem·u·lous·ly** adverb **trem·u·lous·ness** noun.
– ORIGIN Latin *tremulus*.

trench /trenCH/ ▶ **noun 1** a long, narrow ditch. **2** a long ditch dug by troops to provide shelter from enemy fire. **3** (also **ocean trench**) a long, narrow, deep depression in the ocean bed.

– SYNONYMS **ditch,** channel, trough, excavation, furrow, rut, conduit.

▶ **verb** dig a trench or trenches in the ground.
– ORIGIN Old French *trenche*.

trench·ant /'trenCHənt/ ▶ **adjective** (of speech or writing) expressed forcefully and clearly.

– SYNONYMS **incisive,** penetrating, sharp, keen, acute, shrewd, razor-sharp, rapierlike, piercing.
– ANTONYMS vague.

– DERIVATIVES **trench·an·cy** noun **trench·ant·ly** adverb.
– ORIGIN Old French, 'cutting.'

trench coat ▶ **noun** a double-breasted raincoat with a belt.

trench·er[1] /'trenCHər/ ▶ **noun** historical a wooden plate or platter.
– ORIGIN Old French *trenchour.*

trench·er[2] ▶ **noun** a machine used to dig trenches.

trench·er·man /'trenCHərmən/ ▶ **noun** (pl. **trenchermen**) humorous a person who eats heartily.

trench war·fare ▶ **noun** warfare in which opposing troops fight from trenches facing each other.

trend /trend/ ▶ **noun 1** a general direction in which something is developing or changing: *an upward trend in sales.* **2** a fashion.

– SYNONYMS **1 tendency,** movement, drift, swing, shift, course, current, direction, inclination, leaning. **2 fashion,** vogue, style, mode, craze, mania, rage; informal fad, thing.

▶ **verb** develop in a particular direction.
– ORIGIN Old English, 'revolve, rotate.'

trend·set·ter /'tren(d),setər/ ▶ **noun** a person who leads the way in fashion or ideas.
– DERIVATIVES **trend·set·ting** adjective.

trend·y /'trendē/ informal ▶ **adjective** (**trendier, trendiest**) very fashionable or up to date. ▶ **noun** (pl. **trendies**) a fashionable person.
– DERIVATIVES **trend·i·ly** adverb **trend·i·ness** noun.

tre·pan /trə'pan/ chiefly historical ▶ **noun** a saw used by surgeons for perforating the skull. ▶ **verb** (**trepans, trepanning, trepanned**) perforate a person's skull with a trepan.
– DERIVATIVES **trep·a·na·tion** /,trepə'nāSHən/ noun.
– ORIGIN from Greek *trupan* 'to bore.'

trep·i·da·tion /,trepi'dāSHən/ ▶ **noun** a feeling of fear or nervousness about something that may happen.
– ORIGIN Latin.

trep·i·da·tious /,trepi'dāSHəs/ ▶ **adjective** informal apprehensive or nervous.

tres·pass /'trespəs, -,pas/ ▶ **verb 1** enter someone's land or property without their permission. **2** (**trespass on**) take advantage of someone's good nature, help, etc. **3** (**trespass against**) old use commit an offense against a person or law.

– SYNONYMS **intrude,** encroach, invade, enter without permission.

▶ **noun 1** Law entry to a person's land or property without their permission. **2** old use a sin or other morally wrong act.
– DERIVATIVES **tres·pass·er** noun.
– ORIGIN Old French *trespasser* 'pass over, trespass.'

tress /tres/ ▶ **noun** a long lock of a woman's hair.
– ORIGIN Old French *tresse.*

tres·tle /'tresəl/ ▶ **noun** a framework consisting of a horizontal beam supported by two pairs of sloping legs, used in pairs to support a flat surface such as a table top.
– ORIGIN Old French *trestel.*

tres·tle ta·ble ▶ **noun** a table consisting of a board or boards laid on trestles.

tri- ▶ **combining form** three; having three: *triathlon.*
– ORIGIN from Latin *tres*, Greek *treis* 'three.'

tri·a·ble /'trīəbəl/ ▶ **adjective** (of an offense or case) liable to trial in a court of law.

tri·ac·e·tate /trī'asi,tāt/ ▶ **noun** a form of cellulose acetate used as a basis for synthetic fibers.

tri·ad /'trī,ad/ ▶ **noun 1** a group of three related people or things. **2** (also **Triad**) a Chinese secret society involved in organized crime.
– DERIVATIVES **tri·ad·ic** /trī'adik/ adjective.
– ORIGIN Greek *trias.*

tri·age /trē'äZH, 'trē,äZH/ ▶ **noun** (in a hospital or in war) the assessment of the seriousness of wounds or illnesses to decide the order in which a large number of patients should be treated. ▶ **verb** (**triages, triaging, triaged**) decide the order of treatment of patients.
– ORIGIN French.

tri·al /'trī(ə)l/ ▶ **noun 1** a formal examination of evidence in a court of law to decide if someone accused of a crime is guilty or not. **2** a test of performance, qualities, or suitability. **3** a sports match to test the ability of players eligible for selection to a team. **4** (**trials**) an event in which horses or dogs compete or perform. **5** a test of a person's endurance or patience.

– SYNONYMS **1 case,** lawsuit, hearing, tribunal, litigation, proceedings. **2 test,** experiment, pilot study, examination, check, assessment, audition, evaluation, appraisal; informal dry run. **3 trouble,** affliction, ordeal, tribulation, difficulty, problem, misfortune, mishap.

▶ **verb** (**trials, trialing, trialed**) test something to assess its suitability or performance.
– PHRASES **on trial 1** being tried in a court of law. **2** being tested for suitability or performance. **trial and error** the process of experimenting with various methods until one finds the most successful.
– ORIGIN Latin *triallum.*

tri·al·ist /'trīəlist/ (Brit. **triallist**) ▶ **noun** a person who participates in a sports trial.

tri·al run ▶ **noun** a preliminary test of a new system or product.

tri·an·gle /'trī,aNGgəl/ ▶ **noun 1** a plane figure with three straight sides and three angles. **2** a thing shaped like a triangle. **3** a musical instrument consisting of a steel rod bent into a triangle, played by hitting it with a rod. **4** an emotional relationship involving a couple and a third person with whom one of them is involved.
– ORIGIN Latin *triangulum.*

tri·an·gu·lar /trī'aNGgyələr/ ▶ **adjective 1** shaped like a triangle. **2** involving three people or groups.
– DERIVATIVES **tri·an·gu·lar·i·ty** /trī,aNGgyə'laritē/ noun **tri·an·gu·lar·ly** adverb.

tri·an·gu·late /trī'aNGgyə,lāt/ ▶ **verb** (in surveying) divide an area into triangles in order to determine the distances and relative positions of points.
– DERIVATIVES **tri·an·gu·la·tion** /,trī,aNGgyə'lāSHən/ noun.

Tri·as·sic /trī'asik/ ▶ **adjective** Geology relating to the earliest period of the Mesozoic era (about 245 to 208 million years ago), when the first dinosaurs, ammonites, and primitive mammals appeared.
– ORIGIN from Latin *trias* 'set of three,' because the strata are divisible into three groups.

tri·ath·lon /trī'aTHlən, -,län/ ▶ **noun** an athletic contest consisting of three different events, typically swimming, cycling, and long-distance running.
– DERIVATIVES **tri·ath·lete** /trī'aTH,lēt/ noun.
– ORIGIN from **TRI-**, on the pattern of *decathlon.*

trib·al /'trībəl/ ▶ **adjective** relating to or typical of a tribe or tribes.
– DERIVATIVES **trib·al·ly** adverb.

trib·al·ism /'trībə,lizəm/ ▶ **noun** behavior and attitudes that are based on a person's loyalty to a tribe or other

social group.
– DERIVATIVES **trib·al·ist** adjective.

tri-band ▶ **adjective** (of a cell phone) having three frequencies, enabling it to be used in different regions.

tribe /'trīb/ ▶ **noun 1** a social group in a traditional society consisting of linked families or communities with a common culture and dialect. **2** derogatory a group with a shared interest, profession, etc.: *a tribe of speechwriters*. **3** (**tribes**) informal large numbers of people. **4** a category in scientific classification that ranks above genus and below family.

> – SYNONYMS **ethnic group,** people, family, clan, race, dynasty, house, nation.

– ORIGIN Latin *tribus*.

> **USAGE**
>
> The word **tribe** can cause offense when used to refer to a community living within a traditional society today, and it is better in such cases to use alternative terms such as **community** or **people**. However, when talking about such communities in the past, it is perfectly acceptable to say **tribe**: *the area was inhabited by Slavic tribes.*

tribes·man /'trībzmən/ (or **tribeswoman** /'trībz,wo͝omən/) ▶ **noun** (pl. **tribesmen** or **tribeswomen**) a member of a tribe in a traditional society.

trib·u·la·tion /,tribyə'lāsʜən/ ▶ **noun** a cause or state of great trouble or distress: *the tribulations of work and family.*

> – SYNONYMS **1 trouble,** difficulty, problem, worry, anxiety, burden, cross to bear, ordeal, trial, adversity, hardship, tragedy, trauma; informal hassle. **2 suffering,** distress, trouble, misery, wretchedness, unhappiness, sadness, heartache, woe, grief, pain, anguish, agony.

– ORIGIN Latin.

tri·bu·nal /trī'byo͞onl, trə-/ ▶ **noun** a court of justice.

> – SYNONYMS **court,** board, panel, committee.

– ORIGIN Latin, 'raised platform provided for a magistrate's seat.'

trib·une /'tribyo͞on, tri'byo͞on/ ▶ **noun 1** (in ancient Rome) an official chosen by the ordinary people to protect their interests. **2** literary a champion of people's rights.
– ORIGIN Latin *tribunus* 'head of a tribe.'

trib·u·tar·y /'tribyə,terē/ ▶ **noun** (pl. **tributaries**) **1** a river or stream flowing into a larger river or lake. **2** historical a person or nation that pays money to another more powerful ruler or nation.
– ORIGIN Latin *tributarius*.

trib·ute /'tribyo͞ot/ ▶ **noun 1** an act, statement, or gift that is intended to show gratitude, respect, or admiration. **2** something that indicates the worth of something else: *his victory was a tribute to his persistence*. **3** historical payment made regularly by one nation or ruler to a more powerful one.

> – SYNONYMS **accolade,** praise, commendation, salute, testimonial, homage, congratulations, compliments, plaudits.
> – ANTONYMS criticism.

– ORIGIN Latin *tributum*.

trice /trīs/ ▶ **noun** (in phrase **in a trice**) in a moment; very quickly.
– ORIGIN first meaning 'a tug,' also 'an instant': from Dutch *trīsen* 'pull sharply.'

tri·cen·ten·ni·al /,trīsen'tenēəl/ ▶ **noun** the three-hundredth anniversary of a significant event. ▶ **adjective** relating to a three-hundredth anniversary: *the tricentennial year.*

tri·ceps /'trī,seps/ ▶ **noun** (pl. same) the large muscle at the back of the upper arm.
– ORIGIN Latin, 'three-headed' (because the muscle has three points of attachment).

tri·cer·a·tops /trī'serə,täps/ ▶ **noun** a large plant-eating dinosaur having a huge head with two large horns, a smaller horn on the snout, and a bony frill above the neck.
– ORIGIN from Greek *trikeratos* 'three-horned' + *ōps* 'face.'

trich·i·no·sis /,trikə'nōsis/ ▶ **noun** a disease caught from infected meat, especially pork, characterized by digestive disturbance, fever, and muscular rigidity.

tri·chol·o·gy /tri'käləjē/ ▶ **noun** the branch of medicine concerned with the hair and scalp.
– DERIVATIVES **trich·o·log·i·cal** /,trikə'läjikəl/ adjective **tri·chol·o·gist** noun.
– ORIGIN from Greek *thrix* 'hair.'

tri·chro·mat·ic /,trīkrō'matik/ ▶ **adjective 1** having or using three colors. **2** having normal color vision, which is sensitive to all three primary colors.
– DERIVATIVES **tri·chro·ma·tism** /-'krōmə,tizəm/ noun.

trick /trik/ ▶ **noun 1** an act or scheme intended to deceive or outwit someone. **2** a skillful act performed for entertainment. **3** an illusion: *there was nothing there—it had only been a trick of the light*. **4** a habit or mannerism: *he had an odd trick of blowing through his lips when he was listening*. **5** (in bridge, whist, etc.) a sequence of cards forming a single round of play.

> – SYNONYMS **1 stratagem,** ploy, ruse, scheme, device, maneuver, dodge, subterfuge, swindle, fraud; informal con, setup, scam, sting. **2 practical joke,** hoax, prank; informal leg-pulling, spoof, put-on. **3 knack,** skill, technique, secret, art.

▶ **verb 1** cunningly deceive or outwit someone. **2** (**trick someone into/out of**) deceive someone into doing or parting with something.

> – SYNONYMS **deceive,** delude, hoodwink, mislead, take in, dupe, fool, gull, cheat, defraud, swindle; informal con, sucker, diddle, take for a ride, pull a fast one on.

▶ **adjective** intended to trick or to create an illusion: *a trick question.*
– DERIVATIVES **trick·er** noun **trick·er·y** noun.
– PHRASES **do the trick** informal achieve the required result. **trick or treat** a children's custom of calling at houses in costume at Halloween with the threat of pranks if they are not given candy. **tricks of the trade** special clever techniques used in a profession or craft.
– ORIGIN Old French *triche*.

trick·le /'trikəl/ ▶ **verb 1** (of a liquid) flow in a small stream. **2** come or go slowly or gradually: *details began to trickle out*. **3** (**trickle down**) (of wealth) gradually spread from the richest to the poorest people in society.

> – SYNONYMS **dribble,** drip, ooze, leak, seep, spill, exude, percolate.
> – ANTONYMS pour, gush.

▶ **noun 1** a small flow of liquid. **2** a small group or number of people or things moving slowly.

> – SYNONYMS **dribble,** drip, thin stream, rivulet.

– ORIGIN imitating the sound.

trick·le-down ▸ **noun** the theory that the poorest people in society gradually benefit as a result of the increasing wealth of the richest.

trick·ster /'trikstər/ ▸ **noun** a person who cheats or deceives people.

trick·y /'trikē/ ▸ **adjective** (**trickier, trickiest**) **1** difficult or awkward to do or deal with: *he knew how to handle tricky media questions.* **2** deceitful or crafty.

> – SYNONYMS **1 difficult,** awkward, problematic, delicate, ticklish, sensitive; informal sticky. **2 cunning,** crafty, wily, devious, sly, scheming, calculating, deceitful.
> – ANTONYMS straightforward.

– DERIVATIVES **trick·i·ly** adverb **trick·i·ness** noun.

tri·col·or /'trī,kələr/ ▸ **noun** a flag with three bands of different colors, especially the French national flag with equal bands of blue, white, and red. ▸ **adjective** (also **tricolored**) having three colors.

tri·corn /'trī,kôrn/ (also **tricorne**) ▸ **noun** a hat with a brim turned up on three sides.
– ORIGIN Latin *tricornis.*

tri·cot /'trēkō/ ▸ **noun** a fine knitted fabric.
– ORIGIN French, 'knitting.'

tri·cus·pid /trī'kəspid/ ▸ **noun** a tooth with three cusps or points.
– ORIGIN from Latin *cuspis* 'sharp point.'

tri·cy·cle /'trīsikəl, -,sikəl/ ▸ **noun** a vehicle similar to a bicycle, but having three wheels, two at the back and one at the front.

tri·cy·clic /trī'sīklik, -'sik-/ ▸ **noun** any of a class of drugs used to treat depression.
– ORIGIN from the fact that the molecules of the drugs have three fused rings.

tri·dent /'trīdnt/ ▸ **noun** a three-pronged spear.
– ORIGIN Latin.

tried /trīd/ past and past participle of **TRY**.

tri·en·ni·al /trī'enēəl/ ▸ **adjective** lasting for or recurring every three years.
– DERIVATIVES **tri·en·ni·al·ly** adverb.

tri·er /tri(ə)r/ ▸ **noun** a person who always makes an effort, however unsuccessful they may be.

tri·fid /'trīfid/ ▸ **adjective** technical (of part of a plant or animal) divided into three parts by a deep cleft.
– ORIGIN Latin *trifidus.*

tri·fle /'trīfəl/ ▸ **noun 1** a thing of little value or importance. **2** a cold dessert of sponge cake and fruit covered with layers of custard, gelatin, and cream.

> – SYNONYMS **triviality,** thing of no consequence, bagatelle, inessential, nothing, technicality; (**trifles**) trivia, minutiae.

▸ **verb** (**trifle with**) treat without seriousness or respect: *he was not a man to be trifled with.*
– DERIVATIVES **tri·fler** noun.
– PHRASES **a trifle** slightly; rather.
– ORIGIN from Old French *truffler* 'mock, deceive.'

tri·fling /'trīf(ə)liNG/ ▸ **adjective** unimportant or trivial.

> – SYNONYMS **trivial,** unimportant, insignificant, inconsequential, petty, minor, of no account, incidental; informal piffling.
> – ANTONYMS important.

– DERIVATIVES **tri·fling·ly** adverb.

tri·fo·li·ate /trī'fōlē-it, -,āt/ ▸ **adjective** (of a compound leaf) having three small leaves.

trig /trig/ ▸ **noun** informal trigonometry.

trig·ger /'trigər/ ▸ **noun 1** a device that releases a spring or catch and so fires a gun or sets off a mechanism. **2** an event that causes something to happen. ▸ **verb 1** (also **trigger something off**) cause to happen: *house dust may trigger an asthma attack.* **2** cause a device to function.

> – SYNONYMS **start,** set off, initiate, spark, activate, touch off, provoke, precipitate, prompt, stir up, cause, give rise to, lead to, set in motion, bring about.

– ORIGIN Dutch *trekker.*

trig·ger-hap·py ▸ **adjective** apt to shoot someone or take other violent action on the slightest provocation.

tri·glyc·er·ide /trī'glisə,rīd/ ▸ **noun** a compound formed from glycerol and three fatty acid groups, e.g., the main constituents of natural fats and oils.

trig·o·nom·e·try /,trigə'nämitrē/ ▸ **noun** the branch of mathematics concerned with the relations of the sides and angles of triangles and with the functions of angles.
– DERIVATIVES **trig·o·no·met·ric** /-nə'metrik/ adjective **trig·o·no·met·ri·cal** /-nə'metrikəl/ adjective.
– ORIGIN from Greek *trigōnos* 'three-cornered.'

trike /trīk/ ▸ **noun** informal a tricycle.

tri·lat·er·al /trī'latərəl/ ▸ **adjective 1** shared by or involving three parties: *trilateral talks.* **2** Geometry on or with three sides.

tril·by /'trilbē/ ▸ **noun** (pl. **trilbies**) chiefly Brit. a soft felt hat with a narrow brim and indented crown.
– ORIGIN from the heroine of George du Maurier's novel *Trilby,* in the stage version of which such a hat was worn.

tri·lin·gual /trī'liNGgwəl/ ▸ **adjective 1** speaking three languages fluently. **2** written or carried out in three languages.
– DERIVATIVES **tri·lin·gual·ism** /-,lizəm/ noun.

trill /tril/ ▸ **noun** a quavering or warbling sound, especially a rapid alternation of notes. ▸ **verb** make a quavering or warbling sound.
– ORIGIN Italian *trillo.*

tril·lion /'trilyən/ ▸ **cardinal number** (pl. **trillions** or (with numeral or quantifying word) same) **1** a million million (1,000,000,000,000 or 10^{12}). **2** Brit. dated a million million million (1,000,000,000,000,000,000 or 10^{18}). **3** (**trillions**) informal a very large number or amount.
– DERIVATIVES **tril·lionth** /'trilyənTH/ ordinal number.

tri·lo·bite /'trīlə,bīt/ ▸ **noun** a fossil marine arthropod (invertebrate creature) with a rear part divided into three segments.
– ORIGIN from Greek *tri-* 'three' + *lobos* 'lobe.'

tril·o·gy /'triləjē/ ▸ **noun** (pl. **trilogies**) a group of three related novels, plays, or movies.

trim /trim/ ▸ **verb** (**trims, trimming, trimmed**) **1** cut away unwanted or irregular parts from something. **2** decorate something, especially along its edges. **3** reduce the size, amount, or number of: *the company aims to trim production costs.* **4** adjust a boat's sail to take advantage of the wind.

> – SYNONYMS **1 cut,** crop, bob, shorten, clip, snip, shear, dock, lop off, prune, shave, pare. **2 decorate,** adorn, ornament, embellish, edge, border, fringe.

▸ **noun 1** decoration, especially along the edges of

something. **2** an act of cutting something. **3** the upholstery or interior lining of a car. **4** the state of being in good order.

– SYNONYMS **1 decoration,** ornamentation, adornment, embellishment, border, edging, piping, fringe, frill. **2 cut,** clip, snip; haircut.

▶ **adjective** (**trimmer, trimmest**) **1** neat and smart. **2** slim and fit.

– SYNONYMS **1 neat,** tidy, orderly, uncluttered, well kept, well maintained, immaculate, spick and span, spruce, dapper. **2 slim,** slender, lean, sleek, willowy.
– ANTONYMS untidy.

– DERIVATIVES **trim·ly** adverb **trim·mer** noun **trim·ness** noun.
– PHRASES **in trim** slim and fit. **trim one's sails (to the wind)** make changes to suit one's new situation.
– ORIGIN Old English, 'make firm, arrange.'

tri·ma·ran /'trīmə,ran/ ▶ **noun** a sailboat or other boat with three hulls side by side.
– ORIGIN from **TRI-** + **CATAMARAN**.

tri·mes·ter /trī'mestər, 'trī,mes-/ ▶ **noun 1** a period of three months as a division of the duration of pregnancy. **2** each of the three terms in an academic year.
– ORIGIN Latin *trimestris*.

trim·ming /'trimiNG/ ▶ **noun 1** decoration, especially for clothing. **2** (**the trimmings**) the traditional accompaniments to something: *roast turkey with all the trimmings*. **3** (**trimmings**) small pieces trimmed off.

– SYNONYMS **1 decoration,** ornamentation, adornment, borders, edging, piping, fringes, frills. **2** (**the trimmings**) **accompaniments,** extras, frills, accessories, accoutrements, trappings, paraphernalia.

Trin·i·da·di·an /,trinə'dadēən, -'dādē-/ ▶ **noun** a person from Trinidad. ▶ **adjective** relating to Trinidad.

Trin·i·tar·i·an /,trinə'te(ə)rēən/ ▶ **adjective** relating to the Christian doctrine of the Trinity. ▶ **noun** a Christian who believes in the doctrine of the Trinity.
– DERIVATIVES **Trin·i·tar·i·an·ism** /-,nizəm/ noun.

trin·i·ty /'trinitē/ ▶ **noun** (pl. **trinities**) **1** (**the Trinity** or **the Holy Trinity**) (in Christian belief) the three persons (Father, Son, and Holy Spirit) that together make up God. **2** a group of three people or things.
– ORIGIN Latin *trinitas*.

trin·ket /'triNGkit/ ▶ **noun** a small ornament or item of jewelry that is of little value.
– ORIGIN unknown.

tri·o /'trē-ō/ ▶ **noun** (pl. **trios**) **1** a set or group of three. **2** a group of three musicians.

– SYNONYMS **threesome,** three, triumvirate, triad, troika, trinity, trilogy.

– ORIGIN Italian.

tri·ode /'trī,ōd/ ▶ **noun** a semiconductor device with three connections, typically allowing the flow of current in one direction only.
– ORIGIN from **TRI-** + **ELECTRODE**.

tri·ox·ide /trī'äk,sīd/ ▶ **noun** Chemistry an oxide containing three atoms of oxygen.

trip /trip/ ▶ **verb** (**trips, tripping, tripped**) **1** catch one's foot on something and stumble or fall. **2** (**trip up** or **trip someone up**) make or cause to make a mistake. **3** walk, run, or dance with quick light steps. **4** (of words) flow lightly and easily: *a name that trips off the tongue*. **5** activate a mechanism, especially by contact with a switch. **6** (of part of an electric circuit) disconnect automatically as a safety measure. **7** informal experience hallucinations as a result of taking a drug such as LSD.

– SYNONYMS **1 stumble,** lose one's footing, catch one's foot, slip, fall (down), tumble. **2 skip,** dance, prance, bound, spring, scamper.

▶ **noun 1** a journey or excursion. **2** an instance of tripping or falling. **3** informal a period of hallucinations caused by taking a drug. **4** informal a self-indulgent attitude or activity: *a power trip*. **5** a device that trips a mechanism or circuit.

– SYNONYMS **1 excursion,** outing, jaunt, vacation, break, visit, tour, journey, expedition, voyage, drive, run; informal spin. **2 stumble,** slip, fall, misstep.

– PHRASES **trip the light fantastic** humorous dance. [from 'Trip it as you go On the light fantastic toe' (Milton's *L'Allegro*).]
– ORIGIN Dutch *trippen* 'to skip, hop.'

CHOOSE THE RIGHT WORD

See **JOURNEY**.

tri·par·tite /trī'pär,tīt/ ▶ **adjective 1** consisting of three parts. **2** shared by or involving three parties.

tripe /trīp/ ▶ **noun 1** the first or second stomach of a cow or sheep used as food. **2** informal nonsense; rubbish.
– ORIGIN Old French, 'entrails of an animal.'

trip ham·mer ▶ **noun** a large, heavy hammer used in forging, which is raised and then allowed to drop on the metal being worked.

Tri·pit·a·ka /tri'pitəkə/ ▶ **noun** the sacred writings of Theravada Buddhism.
– ORIGIN from Sanskrit *tripitaka* 'the three baskets or collections.'

tri·plane /'trī,plān/ ▶ **noun** an early type of aircraft with three pairs of wings, one above the other.

tri·ple /'tripəl/ ▶ **adjective 1** consisting of or involving three things or people. **2** having three times the usual size, quality, or strength.

– SYNONYMS **threefold,** tripartite, three-way, three times, treble.

▶ **predeterminer** three times as much or as many.
▶ **noun** a thing that is three times as large as usual or is made up of three parts.
▶ **verb** make or become three times as much or as many.
– DERIVATIVES **trip·ly** /'triplē/ adverb.
– ORIGIN Old French.

tri·ple bond ▶ **noun** a chemical bond in which three pairs of electrons are shared between two atoms.

Trip·le Crown ▶ **noun** an award or honor for winning a group of three important events in a sport.

tri·ple jump ▶ **noun 1** an athletic event in which competitors attempt to jump as far as possible by performing a hop, a step, and a jump from a running start. **2** a jump in which a skater makes three full turns while in the air.

tri·ple play ▶ **noun** Baseball a defensive play in which three runners are put out.

tri·ple point ▶ **noun** Chemistry the temperature and pressure at which the solid, liquid, and vapor phases of a pure substance can coexist in equilibrium.

tri·plet /'triplit/ ▶ **noun 1** each of three children or animals born at the same birth. **2** a group of three equal musical notes to be performed in the time of two or four. **3** a set of three rhyming lines of verse.

tri·ple time ▶ **noun** musical time with three beats to the bar.

tri·plex /'tripleks, 'trī-/ ▶ **noun** a residential building divided into three apartments. ▶ **adjective** having three parts.
– ORIGIN Latin.

trip·li·cate ▶ **adjective** /'triplikit/ existing in three copies or examples. ▶ **verb** /-ˌkāt/ **1** make three copies of something. **2** multiply something by three.
– DERIVATIVES **trip·li·ca·tion** /ˌtriplə'kāsʜən/ noun **tri·plic·i·ty** /tri'plisitē/ noun.
– ORIGIN from Latin *triplicare* 'make three.'

tri·pod /'trīpäd/ ▶ **noun 1** a three-legged stand for supporting a camera or other piece of equipment. **2** old use a stool, table, or cauldron set on three legs.
– ORIGIN Greek.

trip·py /'tripē/ ▶ **adjective** (**trippier**, **trippiest**) informal resembling or causing the hallucinations experienced after taking a drug such as LSD: *trippy dance music.*

trip·tych /'triptik/ ▶ **noun 1** a picture or carving on three panels, typically hinged together vertically and used as an altarpiece. **2** a set of three related artistic, literary, or musical works.
– ORIGIN from **TRI-**, on the pattern of *diptych*.

trip·wire /'tripˌwīr/ ▶ **noun** a wire that is stretched close to the ground and activates a trap, explosion, or alarm when disturbed.

tri·reme /'trīˌrēm/ ▶ **noun** an ancient Greek or Roman warship with three banks of oars.
– ORIGIN Latin *triremis*.

tri·sect /trī'sekt/ ▶ **verb** divide something into three parts.
– DERIVATIVES **tri·sec·tion** /-'seksʜən/ noun.
– ORIGIN from **TRI-** + Latin *secare* 'divide, cut.'

tris·mus /'trizməs/ ▶ **noun** technical term for **LOCKJAW**.
– ORIGIN Greek *trismos* 'a scream, grinding.'

tris·tesse /trē'stes/ ▶ **noun** literary a state of melancholy sadness.
– ORIGIN French.

trite /trīt/ ▶ **adjective** (of a remark or idea) unoriginal and dull because of overuse.

> – SYNONYMS **banal,** hackneyed, clichéd, platitudinous, vapid, commonplace, stock, conventional, stereotyped, overused, overdone, overworked, timeworn, tired, stale, hoary, hack, unimaginative, unoriginal; informal old hat, corny, played out.
> – ANTONYMS original, imaginative.

– DERIVATIVES **trite·ly** adverb **trite·ness** noun.
– ORIGIN Latin *tritus* 'rubbed.'

trit·i·um /'tritēəm, 'trisʜ-/ ▶ **noun** Chemistry a radioactive isotope of hydrogen with a mass approximately three times that of the usual isotope.
– ORIGIN from Greek *tritos* 'third.'

trit·u·rate /'tricʜəˌrāt/ ▶ **verb** technical grind a substance to a fine powder.
– DERIVATIVES **trit·u·ra·tion** /ˌtricʜə'rāsʜən/ noun.
– ORIGIN from Latin *tritura* 'rubbing.'

tri·umph /'trīəmf/ ▶ **noun 1** a great victory or achievement. **2** joy or satisfaction resulting from a success or victory. **3** the state of being victorious or successful. **4** a highly successful example: *their marriage was a triumph of togetherness.* **5** a ceremonial procession of a victorious general into ancient Rome.

> – SYNONYMS **1 victory,** win, conquest, success, achievement. **2 jubilation,** exultation, elation, delight, joy, happiness, glee, pride, satisfaction.
> – ANTONYMS defeat, disappointment.

▶ **verb 1** achieve victory or success. **2** rejoice in a victory or success: *she stopped triumphing over Mary's failure.*

> – SYNONYMS **win,** succeed, come first, be victorious, carry the day, prevail.
> – ANTONYMS lose.

– DERIVATIVES **tri·um·phal** /trī'əmfəl/ adjective.
– ORIGIN Latin *triumphus*.

tri·um·phal·ism /trī'əmfəˌlizəm/ ▶ **noun** excessive rejoicing over one's own success or achievements.
– DERIVATIVES **tri·um·phal·ist** adjective & noun.

tri·um·phant /trī'əmfənt/ ▶ **adjective 1** having won a battle or contest; victorious. **2** joyful after a victory or achievement.

> – SYNONYMS **1 victorious,** successful, winning, conquering. **2 jubilant,** exultant, celebratory, elated, joyful, delighted, gleeful, proud.
> – ANTONYMS defeated, despondent.

– DERIVATIVES **tri·um·phant·ly** adverb.

tri·um·vir /trī'əmvər/ ▶ **noun** (in ancient Rome) each of three public officials jointly responsible for overseeing any of the administrative departments.
– ORIGIN Latin.

tri·um·vi·rate /trī'əmvərit, -ˌrāt/ ▶ **noun 1** a group of three powerful or important people or things. **2** (in ancient Rome) a group of three men holding power.

tri·une /'trīˌ(y)o͞on/ ▶ **adjective** (especially with reference to the Christian Trinity) consisting of three in one.
– ORIGIN from **TRI-** + Latin *unus* 'one.'

triv·et /'trivit/ ▶ **noun 1** a metal stand on which hot dishes are placed. **2** an iron tripod placed over a fire for a cooking pot or kettle to stand on.
– ORIGIN probably from Latin *tripes* 'three-legged.'

triv·i·a /'trivēə/ ▶ **plural noun** unimportant details or pieces of information.
– ORIGIN Latin, plural of *trivium* 'place where three roads meet.'

triv·i·al /'trivēəl/ ▶ **adjective** not very important or serious: *doctors can find it frustrating to be called out on trivial matters.*

> – SYNONYMS **unimportant,** insignificant, inconsequential, minor, of no account, of no importance, petty, trifling, negligible; informal piffling.
> – ANTONYMS important, significant.

– DERIVATIVES **triv·i·al·i·ty** /ˌtrivē'alitē/ noun (pl. **trivialities**) **triv·i·al·ly** adverb.
– ORIGIN first meaning 'belonging to the trivium' (an introductory course at a medieval university involving the study of grammar, rhetoric, and logic): from Latin *trivium*, literally 'place where three roads meet.'

triv·i·al·ize /'trivēəˌlīz/ ▶ **verb** make something seem less important or complex than it really is.
– DERIVATIVES **triv·i·al·i·za·tion** /ˌtrivēəli'zāsʜən/ noun.

tro·chee /'trōkē/ ▶ **noun** a foot (unit of poetic meter) consisting of one long or stressed syllable followed by one short or unstressed syllable.
– DERIVATIVES **tro·cha·ic** /trō'kā-ik/ adjective.
– ORIGIN from Greek *trokhaios pous* 'running foot.'

trod /träd/ past and past participle of **TREAD**.

trod·den /'trädn/ past participle of **TREAD**.

trog·lo·dyte /'träglə,dīt/ ▶ **noun 1** a person who lives in a cave. **2** a person who is ignorant or old-fashioned.
– DERIVATIVES **trog·lo·dyt·ic** /,träglə'ditik/ adjective.
– ORIGIN Greek *trōglodutēs*.

troi·ka /'troikə/ ▶ **noun 1** a Russian vehicle pulled by a team of three horses side by side. **2** a group of three political leaders or managers working together.
– ORIGIN Russian.

troil·ism /'troi,lizəm/ ▶ **noun** sexual activity involving three participants.
– ORIGIN perhaps from French *trois* 'three.'

Tro·jan /'trōjən/ ▶ **noun** an inhabitant of ancient Troy in the western peninsula of Asia. ▶ **adjective** relating to Troy.
– PHRASES **work like a Trojan** work very hard.

Tro·jan Horse ▶ **noun** something intended to weaken or defeat an enemy secretly.
– ORIGIN from the hollow wooden statue of a horse in which the ancient Greeks are said to have hidden themselves in order to enter Troy.

troll[1] /trōl/ ▶ **noun** (in folklore) an ugly giant or dwarf that lives in a cave.
– ORIGIN Old Norse and Swedish, 'witch.'

troll[2] ▶ **verb** fish by trailing a baited line along behind a boat.
– DERIVATIVES **troll·er** noun.
– ORIGIN uncertain.

trol·ley /'trälē/ ▶ **noun** (pl. **trolleys**) **1** a trolley car or trolleybus. **2** (also **trolley wheel**) a wheel attached to a pole, used for collecting current from an overhead electric wire to drive a trolley car. **3** a large metal basket or frame on wheels, used for transporting heavy or bulky items such as luggage. **4** Brit. a shopping cart. **5** a small table on wheels, used to convey food and drink.
– PHRASES **off one's trolley** informal mad; insane.
– ORIGIN perhaps from **TROLL**[2].

trol·ley bus /'trälē,bəs/ ▶ **noun** a bus powered by electricity obtained from overhead wires by means of a trolley wheel.

trol·ley car ▶ **noun** a passenger vehicle powered by electricity obtained from an overhead cable by means of a trolley wheel.

trol·lop /'träləp/ ▶ **noun** dated or humorous a woman who has many sexual partners.
– ORIGIN perhaps from former *trull* 'prostitute,' from German *Trulle*.

trom·bone /träm'bōn, trəm-/ ▶ **noun** a large brass wind instrument with a sliding tube that is moved to produce different notes.
– DERIVATIVES **trom·bon·ist** noun.
– ORIGIN French or Italian.

trompe l'œil /,trômp 'loi/ ▶ **noun** (pl. **trompe l'œils** pronunc. same) a painting or method of painting that creates the illusion of a three-dimensional object or space.
– ORIGIN French, 'deceives the eye.'

troop /trōōp/ ▶ **noun 1** (**troops**) soldiers or armed forces. **2** a group of people or animals of a particular kind. **3** a unit of an armored or cavalry division. **4** a unit of Girl or Boy Scouts organized under a troop leader.

– SYNONYMS **1 soldiers,** armed forces, army, soldiery, servicemen, servicewomen. **2** (**troops**) **group,** party, band, gang, body, company, troupe, crowd, squad, unit.

▶ **verb** come or go as a group: *the girls trooped in for dinner.*

– SYNONYMS **walk,** march, file, flock, crowd, throng, stream, swarm.

– ORIGIN Latin *troppus* 'flock.'

troop car·ri·er ▶ **noun** a large aircraft or armored vehicle designed for transporting troops.

troop·er /'trōōpər/ ▶ **noun 1** a state police officer. **2** a mounted police officer. **3** a private soldier in a cavalry or armored unit. **4** chiefly Brit. a ship for transporting troops.

troop·ship /'trōōp,sʜip/ ▶ **noun** a ship for transporting troops.

trope /trōp/ ▶ **noun** a figurative or metaphorical use of a word or expression.
– ORIGIN Greek *tropos* 'turn, way, trope.'

tro·phy /'trōfē/ ▶ **noun** (pl. **trophies**) **1** a cup or other decorative object awarded as a prize. **2** a souvenir of an achievement, such as a head of an animal killed when hunting.

– SYNONYMS **1 cup,** medal, prize, award. **2 souvenir,** memento, keepsake, spoils, booty.

– ORIGIN French *trophée*.

tro·phy wife ▶ **noun** informal, derogatory a young, attractive wife regarded as a status symbol for an older man.

trop·ic /'träpik/ ▶ **noun 1** the line of latitude 23°26′ north (**tropic of Cancer**) or south (**tropic of Capricorn**) of the equator. **2** (**the tropics**) the region between the tropics of Cancer and Capricorn. ▶ **adjective** relating to the tropics; tropical.
– ORIGIN Greek *tropikos*.

trop·i·cal /'träpəkəl/ ▶ **adjective 1** relating to the tropics. **2** very hot and humid.

– SYNONYMS **hot,** sweltering, humid, sultry, steamy, sticky, oppressive, stifling.
– ANTONYMS cold.

– DERIVATIVES **trop·i·cal·ly** adverb.

trop·i·cal storm ▶ **noun** a localized, very intense low-pressure wind system with winds just below that of hurricane force, forming over tropical oceans.

tro·pism /'trō,pizəm/ ▶ **noun** Biology the turning of all or part of an organism toward or away from an external stimulus such as light.
– ORIGIN from Greek *tropos* 'turning.'

trop·o·sphere /'träpə,sfi(ə)r, 'trō-/ ▶ **noun** the lowest region of the atmosphere, extending from the earth's surface to a height of about 6–10 km (the lower boundary of the stratosphere).
– DERIVATIVES **trop·o·spher·ic** /,träpə'sfi(ə)rik, -'sferik, ,trō-/ adjective.
– ORIGIN from Greek *tropos* 'turning.'

trop·po /'träpō/ ▶ **adverb** Music too much; excessively.
– ORIGIN Italian.

trot /trät/ ▶ **verb** (**trots, trotting, trotted**) **1** (of a horse) move at a pace faster than a walk, lifting each diagonal pair of legs alternately. **2** (of a person) run at a moderate pace with short steps. **3** (**trot something out**) informal produce an account that has been produced many times before.

– SYNONYMS **run,** jog, scuttle, scurry, bustle, scamper.

▶ **noun 1** a trotting pace. **2** an act of trotting. **3** (**the trots**) informal diarrhea.
– ORIGIN Latin *trottare*.

troth /trôTH, trōTH/ ▶ **noun** old use or formal faith or loyalty when pledged in a solemn agreement.
– PHRASES **pledge** (or **plight**) **one's troth** make a solemn promise, especially to marry someone.
– ORIGIN from **TRUTH**.

Trot·sky·ism /ˈträtskēˌizəm/ ▶ **noun** the political or economic principles of the Russian revolutionary Leon Trotsky, especially the theory that socialism should be established throughout the world by continuing revolution.
– DERIVATIVES **Trot·sky·ist** noun & adjective **Trot·sky·ite** /ˈträtskēˌīt/ noun & adjective (derogatory).

trot·ter /ˈträtər/ ▶ **noun 1** a horse bred or trained for the sport of trotting. **2** a pig's foot.

trot·ting /ˈträtiNG/ ▶ **noun** racing for horses pulling a two-wheeled vehicle and driver.

trou·ba·dour /ˈtro͞obəˌdôr, -ˌdo͝or/ ▶ **noun** (in medieval France) a performing poet who composed and sang in Provençal, especially on the theme of courtly love.
– ORIGIN French.

trou·ble /ˈtrəbəl/ ▶ **noun 1** difficulty or problems. **2** effort made to do something. **3** a cause of worry or inconvenience. **4** public unrest or disorder. **5** a situation in which a person is likely to be punished or blamed: *he's been in trouble with the police*.

– SYNONYMS **1** *you've caused enough trouble already* **difficulty,** problems, bother, inconvenience, worry, anxiety, distress, stress, agitation, harassment, unpleasantness; informal hassle. **2** *she poured out all her troubles* **problem,** misfortune, difficulty, trial, tribulation, woe, grief, heartache, misery, affliction, suffering. **3** *he's gone to a lot of trouble* **bother,** inconvenience, fuss, effort, exertion, work, labor. **4** *Rodney has been no trouble at all* **nuisance,** bother, inconvenience, irritation, problem, trial, pest; informal headache, pain, drag. **5** *you're too gullible, that's your trouble* **shortcoming,** weakness, failing, fault. **6** *a game marred by serious crowd trouble* **disturbance,** disorder, unrest, fighting, scuffle, breach of the peace.

▶ **verb 1** cause distress or inconvenience to someone. **2** (as adj. **troubled**) showing or experiencing problems or anxiety. **3** (**trouble about/over/with**) be anxious about someone or something. **4** (**trouble to do**) make the effort to do: *oh, don't trouble to answer*.

– SYNONYMS **1** *this matter had been troubling her for some time* **worry,** bother, concern, disturb, upset, agitate, distress, perturb, annoy, nag, prey on someone's mind; informal bug. **2** *I'm sorry to trouble you* **inconvenience,** bother, impose on, disturb, put out, disoblige; informal hassle. **3** *he was troubled by bouts of ill health* **afflict,** burden, suffer from, be cursed with. **4** (as adj. **troubled**) *Joanna looked troubled* **anxious,** worried, concerned, perturbed, disturbed, bothered, uneasy, unsettled, agitated; distressed, upset, dismayed. **5** (as adj. **troubled**) *troubled times* **difficult,** problematic, unsettled, hard, tough, stressful, dark.

– PHRASES **look for trouble** informal deliberately try to start an argument or fight.
– ORIGIN Old French *truble*.

trou·ble·mak·er /ˈtrəbəlˌmākər/ ▶ **noun** a person who often causes trouble, especially by encouraging others to defy people in authority.

– SYNONYMS **mischief-maker,** rabble-rouser, firebrand, agitator, agent provocateur, ringleader, incendiary; scandalmonger, gossipmonger, meddler.

trou·ble·shoot /ˈtrəbəlˌSHo͞ot/ ▶ **verb 1** analyze and solve problems for an organization. **2** trace and correct faults in a mechanical or electronic system.
– DERIVATIVES **trou·ble·shoot·er** noun.

trou·ble·some /ˈtrəbəlsəm/ ▶ **adjective** causing difficulty or annoyance.

– SYNONYMS **1 annoying,** irritating, exasperating, maddening, infuriating, bothersome, tiresome, nagging, difficult, awkward; informal pesky. **2 difficult,** awkward, uncooperative, rebellious, unmanageable, unruly, obstreperous, disruptive, disobedient, naughty, recalcitrant.

– DERIVATIVES **trou·ble·some·ness** noun.

trou·ble spot ▶ **noun** a place where difficulties or conflict regularly occur.

trough /trôf/ ▶ **noun 1** a long, narrow open container for animals to eat or drink out of. **2** a channel used to convey a liquid. **3** Meteorology a long, narrow region of low pressure. **4** a point of low activity or achievement: *peaks and troughs in demand*. **5** a hollow between two wave crests in the sea.
– ORIGIN Old English.

trounce /trouns/ ▶ **verb** defeat someone heavily in a contest.

– SYNONYMS *Turner scored a season-high 19 points when the UConn women trounced St. Joseph's 87–34* **defeat convincingly,** rout, crush, overwhelm; informal hammer, clobber, thrash, whip, drub, shellac, cream, skunk, pulverize, massacre, crucify, demolish, destroy, blow away, annihilate, make mincemeat of, wipe the floor with, walk all over, murder.

– ORIGIN unknown.

troupe /tro͞op/ ▶ **noun** a group of dancers, actors, or other entertainers who tour to different venues.
– ORIGIN French.

troup·er /ˈtro͞opər/ ▶ **noun 1** an entertainer with long experience. **2** a reliable and uncomplaining person.

trou·sers /ˈtrouzərz/ ▶ **plural noun** an outer garment covering the body from the waist to the ankles, with a separate part for each leg; pants. ▶ **adjective** (**trouser**) relating to trousers: *his trouser pocket*.
– DERIVATIVES **trou·sered** adjective.
– ORIGIN from Irish *triús* and Scottish Gaelic *triubhas*.

trous·seau /ˈtro͞oˌsō, ˌtro͞oˈsō/ ▶ **noun** (pl. **trousseaux** pronunc. same, or **trousseaus** /-sōz/) the clothes, linen, and other belongings collected by a bride for her marriage.
– ORIGIN French, 'small bundle.'

trout /trout/ ▶ **noun** (pl. same or **trouts**) an edible fish of the salmon family, found chiefly in fresh water.
– ORIGIN Old English.

trove /trōv/ ▶ **noun** a store of valuable or pleasant things.
– ORIGIN from **TREASURE TROVE**.

trow /trō/ ▶ **verb** old use think or believe something.
– ORIGIN Old English, 'to trust.'

trow·el /ˈtrouəl/ ▶ **noun 1** a small garden tool with a curved scoop for lifting plants or earth. **2** a small tool with a flat, pointed blade, used to apply and spread mortar or plaster. ▶ **verb** (**trowels, troweling, troweled**) apply or spread something with a trowel.
– ORIGIN Latin *truella*.

troy /troi/ (also **troy weight**) ▶ **noun** a system of weights used mainly for precious metals and gems, with a pound of 12 ounces or 5,760 grains. Compare with **AVOIRDUPOIS**.
– ORIGIN from a weight used at the fair of *Troyes* in France.

tru·ant /ˈtro͞oənt/ ▶ **noun** a student who stays away from school without permission or explanation. ▶ **adjective** wandering; straying. ▶ **verb** (also chiefly Brit. **play truant**) (of a student) stay away from school without permission or explanation.
– DERIVATIVES **tru·an·cy** noun.
– ORIGIN first referring to a person begging through choice rather than necessity: from Old French.

truce /tro͞os/ ▶ **noun** an agreement between enemies to stop fighting for a certain time.
– SYNONYMS **ceasefire,** armistice, cessation of hostilities, peace.
– ORIGIN Old English, 'belief, trust.'

truck[1] /trək/ ▶ **noun 1** a large road vehicle for carrying goods or troops. **2** Brit. an open railroad car. ▶ **verb** convey goods by truck.
– ORIGIN perhaps from **TRUCKLE** in the sense 'wheel, pulley.'

truck[2] ▶ **noun** (in phrase **have no truck with**) refuse to deal or be associated with.
– ORIGIN probably from Old French.

truck·er /ˈtrəkər/ ▶ **noun** a long-distance truck driver.

truck farm ▶ **noun** a place where vegetables and fruit are grown for sale.
– DERIVATIVES **truck farm·er** noun.

truck·le /ˈtrəkəl/ ▶ **verb** submit or behave obsequiously.

truck stop ▶ **noun** a large roadside service station and restaurant for truck drivers on interstate highways.

truc·u·lent /ˈtrəkyələnt/ ▶ **adjective** quick to argue or fight.
– SYNONYMS **defiant,** aggressive, antagonistic, belligerent, pugnacious, confrontational, obstreperous, argumentative, quarrelsome, uncooperative; bad-tempered, short-tempered, cross, snappish; informal feisty.
– ANTONYMS cooperative, amiable.
– DERIVATIVES **truc·u·lence** noun **truc·u·lent·ly** adverb.
– ORIGIN Latin *truculentus*.

trudge /trəj/ ▶ **verb** walk slowly and with heavy steps. ▶ **noun** a long and tiring walk.
– ORIGIN unknown.

true /tro͞o/ ▶ **adjective** (**truer, truest**) **1** in accordance with fact or reality. **2** rightly so called; genuine: *true love*. **3** real or actual: *she guessed my true intentions*. **4** accurate and exact. **5** (**true to**) in keeping with a standard or expectation: *true to his threats, he retaliated*. **6** loyal or faithful. **7** correctly positioned or aligned; upright or level.
– SYNONYMS **1 correct,** truthful, accurate, right, verifiable, the case; formal veracious. **2 genuine,** authentic, real, actual, bona fide, proper, legitimate; informal kosher. **3 sincere,** genuine, real, unfeigned, heartfelt. **4 loyal,** faithful, constant, devoted, trustworthy, reliable, dependable, staunch. **5** *a true reflection* **accurate,** faithful, telling it like it is, realistic, factual, lifelike.
– ANTONYMS false, untrue.
▶ **verb** (**trues, truing** or **trueing, trued**) bring something into the exact shape or position required.
– DERIVATIVES **true·ness** noun.
– PHRASES **come true** actually happen or become the case. **out of true** not in the correct or exact shape or alignment. **true to form** (or **type**) being or behaving as expected.
– ORIGIN Old English, 'steadfast, loyal.'

true-blue ▶ **adjective** very loyal or traditional.

true north ▶ **noun** north according to the earth's axis, not magnetic north.

truf·fle /ˈtrəfəl/ ▶ **noun 1** an underground fungus that resembles a rough-skinned potato, eaten as a delicacy. **2** a soft chocolate candy.
– ORIGIN a former French word.

tru·ism /ˈtro͞oˌizəm/ ▶ **noun** a statement that is obviously true and says nothing new or interesting.

tru·ly /ˈtro͞olē/ ▶ **adverb 1** in a truthful way. **2** genuinely or properly. **3** in actual fact; really. **4** absolutely or completely (used for emphasis): *a truly dreadful song*.
– PHRASES **yours truly 1** used as a formula for ending a letter. **2** humorous used to refer to oneself.

trump[1] /trəmp/ ▶ **noun 1** (in bridge, etc.) a playing card of the suit chosen to rank above the others, which can win a trick where a card of a different suit has been led. **2** (also **trump card**) a valuable resource that may be used, especially as a surprise, to gain an advantage. **3** informal, dated a helpful or admirable person. ▶ **verb 1** play a trump on a card of another suit. **2** beat by saying or doing something better: *this sequel trumps the original movie*. **3** (**trump something up**) invent a false accusation or excuse.
– ORIGIN from **TRIUMPH**.

trump[2] ▶ **noun** old use a trumpet or a sound made by one.
– ORIGIN Old French *trompe*.

trump·er·y /ˈtrəmpərē/ old use ▶ **noun** (pl. **trumperies**) things that are superficially attractive or appealing but have little real worth. ▶ **adjective** showy but worthless.
– ORIGIN Old French *tromperie*.

trum·pet /ˈtrəmpit/ ▶ **noun 1** a brass musical instrument with a flared end. **2** something shaped like a trumpet, especially the central part of a daffodil flower. **3** the loud cry of an elephant. ▶ **verb** (**trumpets, trumpeting, trumpeted**) **1** announce widely or enthusiastically: *researchers trumpeted a major medical breakthrough*. **2** (of an elephant) make its loud cry. **3** play a trumpet.
– SYNONYMS **proclaim,** announce, declare, noise abroad, shout from the rooftops.
– DERIVATIVES **trum·pet·er** noun.
– ORIGIN Old French *trompette*.

trun·cate /ˈtrəNGˌkāt/ ▶ **verb** shorten something by cutting off the top or the end.
– DERIVATIVES **trun·ca·tion** /ˌtrəNGˈkāSHən/ noun.
– ORIGIN Latin *truncare* 'maim.'

trun·cheon /ˈtrənCHən/ ▶ **noun** chiefly Brit. a short, thick stick carried as a weapon by a police officer.
– ORIGIN Old French *tronchon* 'stump.'

trun·dle /ˈtrəndl/ ▶ **verb** move or roll along slowly and heavily.
– ORIGIN from former or dialect *trendle* 'revolve.'

trun·dle bed ▶ **noun** a low bed on wheels that can be stored under a larger bed.

trunk /trəNGk/ ▶ **noun 1** (also **tree trunk**) the main woody stem of a tree. **2** a person's or animal's body apart from the limbs and head. **3** the long nose of an elephant. **4** a large box with a hinged lid for storing or transporting clothes and other articles. **5** the space at the back of a car for carrying luggage and other goods.

– SYNONYMS **1 stem,** bole, stock, stalk. **2 torso,** body. **3 proboscis,** nose, snout. **4 chest,** box, crate, coffer, case, portmanteau.

▶ **adjective** relating to the main routes of a transport or communication network: *a trunk road.*
– ORIGIN Latin *truncus.*

trunks /trəNGks/ ▶ **plural noun** men's shorts worn for swimming or boxing.

truss /trəs/ ▶ **noun 1** a padded belt worn to support a hernia. **2** a framework of rafters, posts, and struts that supports a roof, bridge, or other structure. **3** a compact cluster of flowers or fruit growing on one stalk. **4** a large projection of stone or timber, typically one supporting a cornice. ▶ **verb 1** tie someone up tightly. **2** tie up the wings and legs of a chicken or other bird before cooking. **3** support something with a truss or trusses.
– ORIGIN Old French *trusser* 'pack up, bind in.'

trust /trəst/ ▶ **noun 1** firm belief that someone or something is reliable, true, or able to do something: *the need to restore trust in the police.* **2** acceptance of the truth of a statement without evidence or investigation. **3** the state of being responsible for someone or something. **4** a legal arrangement whereby a person (a trustee) holds property as its nominal owner for the good of one or more other people. **5** an organization managed by trustees.

– SYNONYMS **confidence,** belief, faith, certainty, assurance, conviction, credence, reliance.

▶ **verb 1** firmly believe to be reliable, true, or able to do something: *they trusted their neighbors to protect them.* **2** (**trust someone with**) have the confidence to allow someone to have, use, or look after someone or something. **3** (**trust someone/thing to**) give someone or something to another person for safekeeping. **4** (**trust to**) rely on luck, fate, etc. **5** hope: *I trust that you are well.*

– SYNONYMS **1 have faith in,** have (every) confidence in, believe in, pin one's hopes/faith on. **2 rely on,** depend on, bank on, count on, be sure of. **3** *I trust we shall meet again* **hope,** expect, take it, assume, presume. **4 entrust,** consign, commit, give, hand over, turn over, assign.
– ANTONYMS distrust, mistrust.

– DERIVATIVES **trust·a·ble** adjective **trust·ed** adjective.
– ORIGIN from Old Norse, 'strong.'

trust com·pa·ny ▶ **noun** a company formed to act as a trustee or to deal with trusts.

trust·ee /trəˈstē/ ▶ **noun** a person given legal powers to hold and manage property in trust for the benefit of another person or people.
– DERIVATIVES **trust·ee·ship** noun.

trust·ful /ˈtrəs(t)fəl/ ▶ **adjective** having or showing total trust in someone.
– DERIVATIVES **trust·ful·ly** adverb **trust·ful·ness** noun.

trust fund ▶ **noun** a fund consisting of money or property that is held and managed for another person or people by a trust.

trust·ing /ˈtrəstiNG/ ▶ **adjective** tending to trust others; not suspicious.

– SYNONYMS **trustful,** unsuspecting, unquestioning, naive, innocent, childlike, ingenuous, wide-eyed, credulous, gullible, easily taken in.
– ANTONYMS distrustful, suspicious.

– DERIVATIVES **trust·ing·ly** adverb **trust·ing·ness** noun.

CHOOSE THE RIGHT WORD

See **GULLIBLE**.

trust·wor·thy /ˈtrəstˌwərT͟Hē/ ▶ **adjective** able to be relied on as honest and truthful.

– SYNONYMS **reliable,** dependable, honest, as good as one's word, above suspicion; informal on the level, on the up and up.
– ANTONYMS unreliable.

– DERIVATIVES **trust·wor·thi·ness** noun.

trust·y /ˈtrəstē/ ▶ **adjective** (**trustier, trustiest**) old use or humorous having been used or known for a long time and regarded as reliable: *my trusty old typewriter.*

– SYNONYMS **reliable,** dependable, trustworthy, unfailing; loyal, faithful, true, staunch, steadfast, constant.
– ANTONYMS unreliable.

truth /tro͞oTH/ ▶ **noun** (pl. **truths** /tro͞oT͟HZ, tro͞oTHS/) **1** the state of being true: *no one could doubt the truth of his claims.* **2** (also **the truth**) that which is true; actual facts. **3** a fact or belief that is accepted as true.

– SYNONYMS **1 accuracy,** correctness, authenticity, veracity, verity, truthfulness. **2 fact(s),** reality, real life, actuality.
– ANTONYMS lies, fiction, falsehood.

– PHRASES **in truth** really; in fact.
– ORIGIN Old English.

truth·ful /ˈtro͞oTHfəl/ ▶ **adjective 1** telling or expressing the truth; honest. **2** realistic; lifelike.

– SYNONYMS **true,** accurate, correct, factual, faithful, reliable.
– ANTONYMS deceitful, untrue.

– DERIVATIVES **truth·ful·ly** adverb **truth·ful·ness** noun.

try /trī/ ▶ **verb** (**tries, trying, tried**) **1** make an attempt or effort to do something. **2** (also **try something out**) test something new or different to see if it is suitable, effective, or pleasant. **3** attempt to open a door or window. **4** (**try something on**) put on an item of clothing to see if it fits or suits one. **5** make severe demands on: *Mary tried everyone's patience to the limit.* **6** put someone on trial. **7** investigate and decide a case or issue in a formal trial.

– SYNONYMS **1 attempt,** endeavor, make an effort, exert oneself, strive, do one's best, do one's utmost, aim, seek; informal have a go/shot/crack/stab, go all out. **2 test,** put to the test, sample, taste, inspect, investigate, examine, appraise, evaluate, assess; informal check out. **3** *she tried his patience* **tax,** strain, test, stretch, sap, drain, exhaust, wear out.

▶ **noun** (pl. **tries**) **1** an attempt to do something. **2** a test of something new or different.

– SYNONYMS **attempt,** effort, endeavor; informal go, shot, crack, stab.

– PHRASES **tried and true** (or **tested**) having proved effective or reliable before. **try one's hand at** attempt to do something for the first time.
– ORIGIN Old French *trier* 'sift.'

USAGE

The expressions **try to** and **try and** both mean the same thing, but it is better to use **try to** in writing (*we should try to help them* rather than *we should try and help them*).

try·ing /'trī-iNG/ ▶ adjective difficult or annoying.

– SYNONYMS 1 **stressful,** taxing, demanding, difficult, challenging, frustrating, tough, hard; informal hellish. 2 **annoying,** irritating, exasperating, maddening, infuriating, tiresome, troublesome, irksome, vexatious.

try·out /'trī,out/ ▶ noun a test of the potential of someone or something, especially in sports.

tryp·to·phan /'triptə,fan/ ▶ noun an amino acid that is a constituent of most proteins and is an essential nutrient in the diet of vertebrates.
– ORIGIN from *tryptic* 'relating to trypsin' (a digestive enzyme) + Greek *phainein* 'appear.'

try square ▶ noun an implement used to check and mark right angles in construction work.

tryst /trist/ literary ▶ noun a private, romantic meeting between lovers. ▶ verb meet privately with a lover.
– ORIGIN Latin *trista* 'an appointed place in hunting.'

tsar /zär/ (also **czar** or **tzar**) ▶ noun 1 an emperor of Russia before 1917. 2 a person with great authority or power in a particular area: *America's new drug tsar.*
– DERIVATIVES **tsar·ist** noun & adjective.
– ORIGIN Russian, representing Latin *Caesar.*

tsa·ri·na /zä'rēnə, (t)sä-/ (also **czarina** or **tzarina**) ▶ noun an empress of Russia before 1917.

tset·se /'(t)sētsē, '(t)set-/ (also **tsetse fly**) ▶ noun an African bloodsucking fly that transmits sleeping sickness and other diseases.
– ORIGIN from a southern African language.

T-shirt (also **tee shirt**) ▶ noun a short-sleeved casual top, having the shape of a T when spread out flat.

tsp. ▶ abbreviation (pl. same or **tsps.**) teaspoonful.

T-square ▶ noun a T-shaped instrument for drawing or testing right angles.

TSS ▶ abbreviation toxic shock syndrome.

tsu·na·mi /(t)sōō'nämē/ ▶ noun (pl. same or **tsunamis**) a tidal wave caused by an earthquake or other disturbance.
– ORIGIN Japanese, 'harbor wave.'

TT ▶ abbreviation Trust Territories.

TTL ▶ abbreviation 1 transistor transistor logic, a widely used technology for making integrated electronic circuits. 2 (of a camera focusing system) through-the-lens.

Tua·reg /'twä,reg/ ▶ noun (pl. same or **Tuaregs**) a member of a Berber people of the western and central Sahara.
– ORIGIN the name in Berber.

tub /təb/ ▶ noun 1 a low, wide, open container with a flat bottom. 2 a small plastic or cardboard container for food. 3 informal a bath. 4 informal a short, broad boat that is awkward to handle.
– ORIGIN probably German or Dutch.

tu·ba /'t(y)ōōbə/ ▶ noun a large low-pitched brass wind instrument.
– ORIGIN Latin, 'trumpet.'

tub·al /'t(y)ōōbəl/ ▶ adjective relating to or occurring in a tube, especially the Fallopian tubes.

tub·by /'təbē/ ▶ adjective (**tubbier, tubbiest**) informal (of a person) short and rather fat.
– DERIVATIVES **tub·bi·ness** noun.

tube /t(y)ōōb/ ▶ noun 1 a long, hollow cylinder for conveying or holding something. 2 a flexible metal or plastic container sealed at one end and having a cap at the other: *a tube of toothpaste.* 3 a hollow cylindrical organ or structure in an animal or plant. 4 Brit. trademark (**the Tube**) the underground railroad system in London. 5 a sealed container containing two electrodes between which an electric current can be made to flow. 6 a cathode ray tube, especially in a television set. 7 (**the tube**) informal television. ▶ verb (usu. as adj. **tubed**) provide something with a tube or tubes.
– PHRASES **go down the tube** (or **tubes**) informal be completely lost or wasted.
– ORIGIN Latin *tubus.*

tu·ber /'t(y)ōōbər/ ▶ noun 1 a thickened underground part of a stem or rhizome, e.g., that of the potato, bearing buds from which new plants grow. 2 a thickened fleshy root, e.g., of the dahlia.
– ORIGIN Latin, 'hump, swelling.'

tu·ber·cle /'t(y)ōōbərkəl/ ▶ noun 1 a small lump on a bone or on the surface of an animal or plant. 2 a small rounded swelling in the lungs or other tissues, characteristic of tuberculosis.
– ORIGIN Latin *tuberculum* 'small lump or swelling.'

tu·ber·cu·lar /t(y)ōō'bərkyələr/ ▶ adjective 1 relating to or affected with tuberculosis. 2 having or covered with tubercles.

tu·ber·cu·lin /t(y)ōō'bərkyəlin/ ▶ noun a sterile protein extract produced from cultures of tubercle bacillus, used to test for tuberculosis.

tu·ber·cu·lo·sis /tə,bərkyə'lōsis, t(y)ōō-/ ▶ noun an infectious disease transmitted by a bacterium, in which tubercles (small swellings) appear in the tissues, especially the lungs.

tu·ber·ose /'t(y)ōōbə,rōs, -,rōz/ ▶ noun a Mexican plant with heavily scented white waxy flowers and a bulblike base.

tu·ber·ous /'t(y)ōōbərəs/ ▶ adjective 1 (of a plant) resembling, forming, or having a tuber or tubers. 2 Medicine having rounded swellings.

tub·ing /'t(y)ōōbiNG/ ▶ noun a length or lengths of material in the form of tubes.

tu·bu·lar /'t(y)ōōbyələr/ ▶ adjective 1 long, round, and hollow like a tube. 2 made from a tube or tubes.

tu·bu·lar bells ▶ plural noun an orchestral instrument consisting of a row of hanging metal tubes struck with a mallet.

tu·bule /'t(y)ōō,byōōl/ ▶ noun a very small tube, especially in an animal or plant.
– ORIGIN Latin *tubulus.*

tuck /tək/ ▶ verb 1 push, fold, or turn under or between two surfaces: *he tucked his shirt into his trousers.* 2 (**tuck someone in/up**) settle someone in bed by pulling the edges of the bedclothes firmly under the mattress. 3 store or locate in a safe or hidden place: *a French restaurant tucked away in an arcade.* 4 (**tuck in/into**) informal eat food heartily. 5 make a flattened, stitched fold in a garment or material.

– SYNONYMS **push,** insert, slip, thrust, stuff, stick, cram.

▶ noun a flattened, stitched fold in a garment or material.
– ORIGIN Old English, 'punish, ill-treat.'

tuck·er /'təkər/ ▶ noun 1 historical a piece of lace or linen worn on a bodice or as an insert at the front of a low-cut dress: *wear your best bib and tucker.* 2 Austral./NZ informal

food. ▶ **verb** (**be tuckered out**) informal be exhausted or worn out.
– ORIGIN from TUCK.

Tu·dor /'t(y)o͞odər/ ▶ **adjective** **1** relating to the English royal family that held the throne from 1485 to 1603. **2** referring to the main architectural style of the Tudor period, characterized by half-timbering.
▶ **noun** a member of the Tudor family.

Tues·day /'t(y)o͞ozdā, -dē/ ▶ **noun** the day of the week before Wednesday and following Monday.
– ORIGIN Old English, named after the Germanic god *Tīw*.

tu·fa /'t(y)o͞ofə/ ▶ **noun** **1** a porous rock composed of calcium carbonate and formed as a deposit from mineral springs. **2** another term for TUFF.
– ORIGIN Italian.

tuff /təf/ ▶ **noun** a light, porous rock formed from volcanic ash.
– ORIGIN Latin *tofus*.

tuf·fet /'təfit/ ▶ **noun** **1** a tuft or clump. **2** a footstool or low seat.
– ORIGIN from TUFT.

tuft /təft/ ▶ **noun** a bunch of threads, grass, or hair, held or growing together at the base.
– DERIVATIVES **tuft·ed** adjective **tuft·y** adjective.
– ORIGIN probably from Old French *tofe*.

tug /təg/ ▶ **verb** (**tugs, tugging, tugged**) pull something hard or suddenly.

> – SYNONYMS **1** *he tugged at her sleeve* **pull,** pluck, tweak, twitch, jerk, catch hold of; informal yank. **2** **drag,** pull, lug, draw, haul, heave, tow, trail.

▶ **noun** **1** a hard or sudden pull. **2** (also **tugboat** /'təg,bōt/) a small, powerful boat for towing larger boats and ships.
– ORIGIN from TOW[1].

tug of war ▶ **noun** a contest in which two teams pull at opposite ends of a rope until one drags the other over a central line.

tu·i·tion /t(y)o͞o'isʜən/ ▶ **noun** **1** a sum of money charged for teaching or instruction by a school, college, or university. **2** teaching or instruction, especially of individuals or small groups.
– ORIGIN Latin.

tu·la·re·mi·a /,t(y)o͞olə'rēmēə/ (Brit. **tularaemia**) ▶ **noun** a severe bacterial disease of animals transmissible to humans, characterized by ulcers, fever, and loss of weight.
– ORIGIN from *Tulare*, the county in California where it was first observed.

tu·lip /'t(y)o͞oləp/ ▶ **noun** a spring-flowering plant with boldly colored cup-shaped flowers.
– ORIGIN Persian, 'turban' (from the shape of the flower).

tu·lip tree ▶ **noun** **1** a North American tree with large leaves and small tuliplike flowers. **2** informal a magnolia tree or shrub.

tulle /to͞ol/ ▶ **noun** a soft, fine net material, used for making veils and dresses.
– ORIGIN from *Tulle*, a town in SW France.

tum·ble /'təmbəl/ ▶ **verb** **1** fall suddenly, clumsily, or headlong. **2** move in an uncontrolled way. **3** decrease rapidly in amount or value. **4** rumple; disarrange. **5** (**tumble to**) informal suddenly realize something.

> – SYNONYMS **1** *he tumbled over* **fall over,** fall down, topple over, go head over heels, lose one's balance, take a spill, trip (up), stumble. **2** *housing prices tumbled* **plummet,** plunge, dive, nosedive, drop, slump, slide; informal crash.
> – ANTONYMS rise.

▶ **noun** **1** a sudden or clumsy fall. **2** an untidy or confused arrangement or state: *a tumble of untamed curls.* **3** an acrobatic feat such as a cartwheel.
– ORIGIN German *tummelen*.

tum·ble·down /'təmbəl,doun/ ▶ **adjective** (of a building) falling or fallen into ruin.

tum·bler /'təmblər/ ▶ **noun** **1** a drinking glass with straight sides and no handle or stem. **2** an acrobat. **3** a part of a lock that holds the bolt until lifted by a key. **4** an electrical switch worked by pushing a small sprung lever.
– ORIGIN sense 1 so called because such a glass formerly had a rounded bottom so that it could not be put down until emptied.

tum·ble·weed /'təmbəl,wēd/ ▶ **noun** a plant of dry regions that breaks off near the ground in late summer, forming light masses blown about by the wind.

tum·bril /'təmbrəl/ (also **tumbrel**) ▶ **noun** historical an open cart that tilted backward to empty out its load, especially one used to take prisoners to the guillotine during the French Revolution.
– ORIGIN Old French *tomberel*.

tu·mes·cent /t(y)o͞o'mesənt/ ▶ **adjective** swollen or becoming swollen.
– DERIVATIVES **tu·mes·cence** noun.
– ORIGIN from Latin *tumere* 'to swell.'

tu·mid /'t(y)o͞omid/ ▶ **adjective** **1** (of a part of the body) swollen. **2** (of language) pompous.
– ORIGIN Latin *tumidus*.

tum·my /'təmē/ ▶ **noun** (pl. **tummies**) informal a person's stomach or abdomen.
– ORIGIN a child's pronunciation of STOMACH.

tum·my but·ton ▶ **noun** informal a person's navel.

tu·mor /'t(y)o͞omər/ (Brit. **tumour**) ▶ **noun** a swelling of a part of the body caused by an abnormal growth of tissue.

> – SYNONYMS **cancer,** growth, lump, malignancy; Medicine carcinoma, sarcoma.

– DERIVATIVES **tu·mor·ous** adjective.
– ORIGIN Latin *tumor*.

> **WORD LINKS**
> **oncology** *branch of medicine concerning tumors*

tu·mult /'t(y)o͞o,məlt/ ▶ **noun** **1** a loud, confused noise, as caused by a large mass of people. **2** confusion or disorder.

> – SYNONYMS **1** **clamor,** din, noise, racket, uproar, commotion, ruckus, pandemonium, melee, frenzy; informal hullabaloo; Brit. informal row. **2** *years of political tumult* **turmoil,** confusion, disorder, disarray, unrest, chaos, turbulence, mayhem, havoc, upheaval.
> – ANTONYMS tranquility.

– ORIGIN Latin *tumultus*.

tu·mul·tu·ous /t(y)o͞o'məlcʜo͞oəs, tə-/ ▶ **adjective** **1** very loud or uproarious. **2** excited, confused, or disorderly.

> – SYNONYMS **1** *tumultuous applause* **loud,** deafening, thunderous, uproarious, noisy, clamorous,

vociferous. **2** *a tumultuous crowd* **disorderly,** unruly, rowdy, turbulent, boisterous, excited, agitated, restless, wild, riotous.
– ANTONYMS soft, orderly.

– DERIVATIVES **tu·mul·tu·ous·ly** adverb.

tu·mu·lus /ˈt(y)o͞omyə,ləs/ ▶ **noun** (pl. **tumuli** /-,lī/) an ancient burial mound.
– ORIGIN Latin.

tun /tən/ ▶ **noun** a large beer or wine cask.
– ORIGIN Latin *tunna.*

tu·na /ˈt(y)o͞onə/ ▶ **noun** (pl. same or **tunas**) a large edible fish of warm seas.
– ORIGIN Spanish *atún.*

tun·dra /ˈtəndrə/ ▶ **noun** a vast, flat, treeless Arctic region of Europe, Asia, and North America in which the subsoil is permanently frozen.
– ORIGIN Lappish (the language of the Lapps).

tune /t(y)o͞on/ ▶ **noun** a sequence of notes that forms a piece of music; a melody.
– SYNONYMS **melody,** air, strain, theme, song, jingle, ditty.

▶ **verb 1** (also **tune up**) adjust a musical instrument to the correct pitch. **2** adjust a radio or television to a particular frequency. **3** (**tune in**) watch or listen to a television or radio broadcast. **4** adjust an engine or balance mechanical parts so that they run smoothly and efficiently. **5** adjust or adapt to a purpose or situation: *the animals are finely tuned to life in the desert.*
– SYNONYMS **attune,** adapt, adjust, regulate.

– DERIVATIVES **tun·a·ble** (also **tuneable**) adjective.
– PHRASES **in** (or **out of**) **tune** in (or not in) the correct musical pitch. **to the tune of** informal amounting to or involving a particular sum of money.
– ORIGIN from **TONE**.

tune·ful /ˈt(y)o͞onfəl/ ▶ **adjective** having a pleasing tune; melodious.
– DERIVATIVES **tune·ful·ly** adverb **tune·ful·ness** noun.

tune·less /ˈt(y)o͞onləs/ ▶ **adjective** not pleasing to listen to.
– DERIVATIVES **tune·less·ly** adverb **tune·less·ness** noun.

tun·er /ˈt(y)o͞onər/ ▶ **noun 1** a person who tunes musical instruments, especially pianos. **2** an electronic device used for tuning. **3** an electronic device in a stereo system that receives radio signals and supplies them to an audio amplifier.

tune·smith /ˈt(y)o͞on,smiᴛʜ/ ▶ **noun** informal a composer of popular music or songs.

tung·sten /ˈtəɴɢstən/ ▶ **noun** a hard gray metallic element with a very high melting point, used to make electric light filaments.
– ORIGIN Swedish.

tung·sten car·bide ▶ **noun** a very hard gray compound used in making engineering dies, cutting and drilling tools, etc.

tu·nic /ˈt(y)o͞onik/ ▶ **noun 1** a loose sleeveless garment reaching to the thighs or knees. **2** a close-fitting short coat worn as part of a uniform.
– ORIGIN Latin *tunica.*

tu·ni·cate /ˈt(y)o͞oni,kāt/ ▶ **noun** Zoology a marine invertebrate with a rubbery or hard outer coat.
▶ **adjective** (usu. **tunicated**) Botany (of a plant bulb, such as an onion) having concentric layers.

tun·ing fork ▶ **noun** a two-pronged steel device used for tuning instruments, which vibrates when hit against a surface to give a note of specific pitch.

Tu·ni·sian /t(y)o͞oˈnēzʜən/ ▶ **noun** a person from Tunisia.
▶ **adjective** relating to Tunisia.

tun·nel /ˈtənl/ ▶ **noun** an underground passage, built through a hill or under a building or dug by a burrowing animal.
– SYNONYMS **underground passage,** underpass, subway, shaft, burrow, hole, warren, labyrinth.

▶ **verb** (**tunnels, tunneling, tunneled**) dig or force a passage underground or through something.
– SYNONYMS **dig,** burrow, mine, bore, drill.

– DERIVATIVES **tun·nel·er** noun.
– ORIGIN Old French *tonel* 'small cask.'

tun·nel vi·sion ▶ **noun 1** a condition in which a person cannot see things properly if they are not straight ahead. **2** informal the tendency to focus only on a single or limited aspect of a subject or situation.

tu·pe·lo /ˈt(y)o͞opə,lō/ ▶ **noun** (pl. **tupelos**) a North American or Asian tree of damp and swampy habitats that yields useful timber.
– ORIGIN from an American Indian language.

Tu·pi /ˈto͞opē, to͞oˈpē/ ▶ **noun** (pl. same or **Tupis**) **1** a member of a group of American Indian peoples of the Amazon valley. **2** any of the languages of the Tupi.
– DERIVATIVES **Tu·pi·an** adjective.
– ORIGIN a local name.

Tu·pi-Gua·ra·ni /to͞oˈpē ,gwärəˈnē/ ▶ **noun** a South American Indian language family whose main members are Guarani and the Tupian languages.

tup·pence /ˈtəpəns/ ▶ **noun** Brit. variant spelling of **TWOPENCE**.

Tup·per·ware /ˈtəpər,wer/ ▶ **noun** trademark a range of plastic containers used chiefly for storing food.
– ORIGIN from *Tupper,* the name of the American manufacturer, + **WARE**.

tur·ban /ˈtərbən/ ▶ **noun** a long length of material wound around a cap or the top of the head, worn especially by Muslim and Sikh men.
– DERIVATIVES **tur·baned** (also **turbanned**) adjective.
– ORIGIN Persian.

tur·bid /ˈtərbid/ ▶ **adjective 1** (of a liquid) cloudy or muddy; not clear. **2** confused or unclear in meaning.
– DERIVATIVES **tur·bid·i·ty** /tərˈbiditē/ noun.
– ORIGIN Latin *turbidus.*

tur·bine /ˈtər,bīn, -bin/ ▶ **noun** a machine for producing power in which a wheel or rotor is made to revolve by a fast-moving flow of water, steam, gas, or air.
– ORIGIN Latin *turbo* 'spinning top, whirl.'

tur·bo /ˈtərbō/ ▶ **noun** (pl. **turbos**) short for **TURBOCHARGER**.

tur·bo·charge /ˈtərbō,ᴄʜärj/ ▶ **verb** (often as adj. **turbocharged**) **1** equip an engine or vehicle with a turbocharger. **2** make more powerful, fast, or exciting: *turbocharged business growth.*

tur·bo·charg·er /ˈtərbō,ᴄʜärjər/ ▶ **noun** a supercharger driven by a turbine powered by the engine's exhaust gases.

tur·bo·fan /ˈtərbō,fan/ ▶ **noun** a jet engine in which a turbine-driven fan provides additional thrust.

tur·bo·jet /ˈtərbō,jet/ ▶ **noun** a jet engine in which the jet gases also operate a turbine-driven compressor for compressing the air drawn into the engine.

tur·bo·prop /'tərbō,präp/ ▶ **noun** a jet engine in which a turbine is used to drive a propeller.

tur·bot /'tərbət/ ▶ **noun** (pl. same or **turbots**) an edible flatfish of inshore waters, which has large bony swellings on the body.
– ORIGIN Scandinavian.

tur·bu·lence /'tərbyələns/ ▶ **noun 1** violent or unsteady movement of air or water, or of another fluid. **2** upheaval, conflict, or confusion: *Europe emerged from a long period of political turbulence.*

tur·bu·lent /'tərbyələnt/ ▶ **adjective 1** involving much conflict, upheaval, or confusion. **2** (of air or water) moving violently or unsteadily.

– SYNONYMS **tempestuous,** stormy, unstable, unsettled, tumultuous, chaotic, anarchic, lawless.
– ANTONYMS peaceful.

– DERIVATIVES **tur·bu·lent·ly** adverb.
– ORIGIN Latin *turbulentus* 'full of commotion.'

turd /tərd/ ▶ **noun** vulgar slang **1** a lump of excrement. **2** an unpleasant or disliked person.
– ORIGIN Old English.

tu·reen /t(y)ŏŏ'rēn/ ▶ **noun** a deep covered dish from which soup is served.
– ORIGIN French *terrine* 'large earthenware pot.'

turf /tərf/ ▶ **noun** (pl. **turfs** or **turves** /tərvz/) **1** grass and the surface layer of earth held together by its roots. **2** a piece of turf cut from the ground. **3** (**the turf**) horse racing or racetracks generally. **4** (**someone's turf**) informal a place or area of activity regarded as someone's personal territory or responsibility: *he did not like poachers on his turf.* ▶ **verb** cover ground with turf.
– ORIGIN Old English.

tur·gid /'tərjid/ ▶ **adjective 1** (of language or style) pompous and boring. **2** swollen or full: *a turgid river.*
– DERIVATIVES **tur·gid·i·ty** /tər'jiditē/ noun **tur·gid·ly** adverb.
– ORIGIN Latin *turgidus.*

Turk /tərk/ ▶ **noun 1** a person from Turkey. **2** a member of any of the ancient peoples who spoke Turkic languages.

tur·key /'tərkē/ ▶ **noun** (pl. **turkeys**) **1** a large game bird native to North America, that is bred for food. **2** informal something that is very unsuccessful or of very poor quality.
– PHRASES **talk turkey** informal talk frankly and openly.
– ORIGIN short for **TURKEYCOCK** or *turkeyhen*, first referring to the guineafowl (which was imported through Turkey), and then wrongly to the American bird.

tur·key·cock /'tərkē,käk/ ▶ **noun** a male turkey.

tur·key vul·ture ▶ **noun** a common American vulture with black plumage and a bare red head.

Tur·kic /'tərkik/ ▶ **adjective** referring to a large group of languages of western and central Asia, including Turkish, Kazakh, and Uzbek.

Turk·ish /'tərkisн/ ▶ **noun** the language of Turkey. ▶ **adjective** relating to Turkey or its language.

Turk·ish bath ▶ **noun 1** a cleansing treatment that involves sitting in a room filled with very hot air or steam, followed by washing and massage. **2** a building or room where a Turkish bath is available.

Turk·ish cof·fee ▶ **noun** very strong black coffee served with the fine grounds in it.

Turk·ish de·light ▶ **noun** a candy made of gelatin coated in powdered sugar.

tur·mer·ic /'tərmərik/ ▶ **noun** a bright yellow powder obtained from a plant of the ginger family, used as a spice in Asian cooking.
– ORIGIN perhaps from French *terre mérite* 'deserving earth.'

tur·moil /'tər,moil/ ▶ **noun** a state of great disturbance, confusion, or uncertainty.

– SYNONYMS **confusion,** upheaval, turbulence, tumult, disorder, disturbance, ferment, chaos, mayhem.
– ANTONYMS peace, order.

– ORIGIN unknown.

turn /tərn/ ▶ **verb 1** move in a circular direction around a central point. **2** move so as to face or go in a different direction. **3** change in nature, state, form, or color. **4** pass or reach a particular age or time. **5** (of milk) become sour. **6** (of the tide) change from flood to ebb or vice versa. **7** twist or sprain an ankle. **8** make a profit. **9** shape something on a lathe. **10** (usu. as adj. **turned**) give a pleasing form to: *finely turned phrases.*

– SYNONYMS **1** *the wheels were still turning* **go around,** revolve, rotate, spin, roll, circle, wheel, whirl, twirl, gyrate, swivel, pivot. **2** *I turned and headed back* **change direction,** change course, make a U-turn, turn around/about, wheel around. **3** *the path turned to right and left* **bend,** curve, wind, twist, meander, snake, zigzag. **4** *the drizzle* ***turned into*** *a downpour* **become,** develop into, turn out to be, be transformed into, change into, metamorphose into. **5** *he turned the house into apartments* **convert,** change, transform, make, adapt, modify. **6** *he turned pale* **become,** go, grow, get. **7** *I've just turned forty* **reach,** get to, become, hit. **8** **(go) sour,** curdle, become rancid, go bad, spoil.

▶ **noun 1** an act of turning. **2** a bend in a road, river, etc. **3** a place where a road meets or branches off another; a turning. **4** a time when a member of a group must or is allowed to do something: *it was her turn to speak.* **5** a time when one period of time ends and another begins: *the turn of the century.* **6** a change in a situation. **7** a brief feeling of illness: *a funny turn.* **8** a short performance, especially one of a number given by different performers. **9** a short walk or ride. **10** one round in a coil of rope or other material.

– SYNONYMS **1 rotation,** revolution, spin, whirl, twirl, gyration, swivel. **2 bend,** corner, junction, twist, dogleg, hairpin turn. **3 opportunity,** chance, say, stint, time, try; informal go, shot, stab, crack.

– DERIVATIVES **turn·er** noun.
– PHRASES **at every turn** on every occasion; continually. **be turned out** be dressed in the specified way. **by turns** alternately. **do someone a good turn** do something that is helpful for someone. **in turn** one after the other. **out of turn** at a time when it is inappropriate or not one's turn. **take turns** (or Brit. **take it in turns**) (of two or more people) do something alternately or one after the other. **to a turn** to exactly the right degree. **turn something around** make an organization successful after a period of poor performance. **turn someone away** refuse to allow someone to enter a place. **turn someone/thing down 1** reject something offered or proposed by someone. **2** reduce the volume or strength of sound, heat, etc., produced by a device by adjusting its controls. **turn in** informal go to bed in the evening. **turn someone/thing in** hand someone or something over to the authorities. **turn off** leave one road in order to join another. **turn someone off** informal make someone feel bored or disgusted. **turn something off** (or **on**)

stop (or start) the operation of something by means of a tap, switch, or button. **turn of mind** a particular way of thinking. **turn on** suddenly attack someone or something. **turn someone on** informal excite someone, especially sexually. **turn out 1** prove to be the case. **2** attend a meeting, go to vote, etc. **turn something out 1** switch off an electric light. **2** produce something. **3** empty something, especially one's pockets. **turn over** (of an engine) start or continue to run properly. **turn someone over** hand someone over to the custody or care of someone in authority. **turn something over 1** transfer control or management of something to someone else. **2** (of a business) have a turnover of a particular amount. **turn tail** informal turn around and run away. **turn to 1** start doing or becoming involved with something. **2** go to someone for help or information. **turn up 1** be found, especially by chance. **2** put in an appearance; arrive. **turn something up 1** increase the volume or strength of sound, heat, etc., produced by a device by adjusting its controls. **2** reveal or discover something.
– ORIGIN Latin *tornare*.

turn·a·bout /'tərnə,bout/ ▶ **noun** a sudden and complete change or reversal of opinion or of a situation.

turn·a·round /'tərnə,round/ ▶ **noun 1** an abrupt or unexpected change. **2** the process of completing a task, or the time needed to do this.

turn·coat /'tərn,kōt/ ▶ **noun** a person who deserts one party or cause in order to join an opposing one.

turn·down /'tərn,doun/ ▶ **noun 1** a rejection or refusal. **2** a decline; a downturn.

turn·ing /'tərniNG/ ▶ **noun 1** a place where a road branches off another. **2** the action or skill of using a lathe. **3** (**turnings**) shavings of wood resulting from turning wood on a lathe.

– SYNONYMS **junction,** turnoff, side road, exit; turnout.

turn·ing cir·cle ▶ **noun** the smallest circle in which a vehicle or boat can turn without reversing.

turn·ing point ▶ **noun** a time when a decisive change happens, especially one with good results.

– SYNONYMS **watershed,** critical moment, decisive moment, moment of truth, crossroads, crisis.

tur·nip /'tərnəp/ ▶ **noun** a round root vegetable with white or cream flesh.
– ORIGIN from an unknown first element + Scottish and Northern English *neep* 'a turnip.'

turn·key /'tərn,kē/ ▶ **noun** (pl. **turnkeys**) old use a jailer.

turn·off ▶ **noun** (also **turn-off**) **1** a junction at which a road branches off another. **2** informal a person or thing that makes one feel bored or disgusted.

turn-on ▶ **noun** informal a person or thing that makes one feel excited or sexually aroused.

turn·out /'tərn,out/ ▶ **noun** the number of people attending or taking part in an event, especially the number of people voting in an election.

– SYNONYMS **attendance,** audience, house, congregation, crowd, gate, gathering.

turn·o·ver /'tərn,ōvər/ ▶ **noun 1** the amount of money taken by a business in a particular period. **2** the rate at which employees leave a workforce and are replaced. **3** the rate at which goods are sold and replaced in a store. **4** a small pie made by folding a piece of pastry over on itself to enclose a filling.

– SYNONYMS **1 gross revenue,** income, yield, sales, business. **2** *staff turnover* **rate of replacement,** change, movement.

turn·pike /'tərn,pīk/ ▶ **noun 1** an expressway, especially one on which a toll is charged. **2** historical a tollgate. **3** historical a road on which a toll was collected.
– ORIGIN first referring to a spiked barrier fixed across a road as a defense against attack: from PIKE².

turn sig·nal ▶ **noun** a flashing light on a vehicle to show that it is about to change lanes or turn.

turn·stile /'tərn,stīl/ ▶ **noun** a mechanical gate with revolving horizontal arms that allow only one person at a time to pass through.

turn·stone /'tərn,stōn/ ▶ **noun** a small short-billed sandpiper noted for turning over stones to find small animals.

turn·ta·ble /'tərn,tābəl/ ▶ **noun 1** a circular revolving plate supporting a record as it is played. **2** a circular revolving platform for turning a railroad locomotive.

tur·pen·tine /'tərpən,tīn/ ▶ **noun 1** a substance produced by certain trees, distilled to make oil of turpentine. **2** (also **oil of turpentine**) a strong-smelling oil distilled from this substance, used in mixing and thinning paints and varnishes and for cleaning paintbrushes.
– ORIGIN Old French *terebentine*.

tur·pi·tude /'tərpi,t(y)o͞od/ ▶ **noun** formal wicked behavior or character: *acts of moral turpitude*.
– ORIGIN Latin *turpitudo*.

turps /tərps/ ▶ **noun** informal turpentine.

tur·quoise /'tər,k(w)oiz/ ▶ **noun 1** a greenish-blue or sky-blue semiprecious stone. **2** a greenish-blue color.
– ORIGIN Old French *turqueise* 'Turkish stone.'

tur·ret /'tərit/ ▶ **noun 1** a small tower at the corner of a building or wall, especially of a castle. **2** an armored tower, usually one that revolves, for a gun and gunners in a ship, aircraft, or tank.
– DERIVATIVES **tur·ret·ed** adjective.
– ORIGIN Old French *tourete* 'small tower.'

tur·tle /'tərtl/ ▶ **noun** a sea or freshwater reptile with a bony or leathery shell and flippers or webbed toes.
– PHRASES **turn turtle** (chiefly of a boat) turn upside down.
– ORIGIN probably from French *tortue* 'tortoise.'

tur·tle·dove ▶ **noun** a small dove with a soft purring call.
– ORIGIN from Latin *turtur*.

tur·tle·neck /'tərtl,nek/ ▶ **noun** a high, close-fitting, turned-over collar on a knit shirt, sweater, or similar garment.

turves /tərvz/ plural of TURF.

Tus·can /'təskən/ ▶ **adjective 1** relating to Tuscany in central Italy. **2** relating to a classical order of architecture resembling the Doric but lacking all decoration. ▶ **noun** a person from Tuscany.

tush¹ /təsH/ ▶ **exclamation** old use or humorous expressing disapproval, impatience, or dismissal.

tush² /to͝osH/ ▶ **noun** informal a person's buttocks.
– ORIGIN Yiddish.

tusk /təsk/ ▶ **noun** a long pointed tooth that protrudes from a closed mouth, as one of a pair in the elephant, walrus, or wild boar.
– DERIVATIVES **tusked** adjective.
– ORIGIN Old English.

tusk·er /ˈtəskər/ ▶ **noun** an elephant or wild boar with well-developed tusks.

tus·sle /ˈtəsəl/ ▶ **noun** a vigorous struggle or scuffle. ▶ **verb** take part in a tussle.
– ORIGIN perhaps from dialect *touse* 'handle roughly.'

tus·sock /ˈtəsək/ ▶ **noun** a dense clump or tuft of grass.
– DERIVATIVES **tus·sock·y** adjective.
– ORIGIN perhaps from dialect *tusk* 'tuft.'

tus·sore /ˈtəsôr/ ▶ **noun** a strong but coarse kind of silk.
– ORIGIN Hindi.

tu·tee /t(y)o͞oˈtē/ ▶ **noun** a student of a tutor.

tu·te·lage /ˈt(y)o͞otl-ij/ ▶ **noun 1** protection of or authority over someone or something: *the organizations remained under firm government tutelage*. **2** instruction; tuition.
– ORIGIN Latin *tutela* 'keeping.'

tu·te·lar·y /ˈt(y)o͞otlˌerē/ ▶ **adjective 1** acting as a protector, guardian, or patron. **2** relating to protection or a guardian.

tu·tor /ˈt(y)o͞otər/ ▶ **noun 1** a private teacher who teaches a single student or a very small group. **2** chiefly Brit. a college or university teacher responsible for the teaching and supervision of students assigned to them.

– SYNONYMS **teacher,** instructor, coach, educator, lecturer, trainer, mentor.

▶ **verb** act as a tutor to one student or a very small group.

– SYNONYMS **teach,** instruct, educate, school, coach, train, drill.

– ORIGIN Latin.

tu·to·ri·al /t(y)o͞oˈtôrēəl/ ▶ **noun 1** a period of instruction given by a tutor. **2** a book or computer program giving information about a subject or explaining how to do something. ▶ **adjective** relating to a tutor or tuition.

Tut·si /ˈto͝otsē/ ▶ **noun** (pl. same or **Tutsis**) a member of a people forming a minority of the population of Rwanda and Burundi.

tut·ti /ˈto͞otē/ ▶ **adverb & adjective** Music with all voices or instruments together.
– ORIGIN Italian.

tut·ti-frut·ti /ˈto͞otē ˈfro͞otē/ ▶ **noun** (pl. **tutti-fruttis**) a type of ice cream containing mixed fruits.
– ORIGIN Italian, 'all fruits.'

tu·tu /ˈto͞oˌto͞o/ ▶ **noun** a female ballet dancer's costume consisting of a bodice attached to a very short, stiff skirt made of many layers of fabric and projecting horizontally from the waist.
– ORIGIN French.

Tu·va·lu·an /to͞oˈvälo͞oən/ ▶ **noun** a person from Tuvalu, a country made up of a number of islands in the SW Pacific. ▶ **adjective** relating to Tuvalu.

tux /təks/ ▶ **noun** informal a tuxedo.

tux·e·do /təkˈsēdō/ ▶ **noun** (pl. **tuxedos** or **tuxedoes**) **1** a man's dinner jacket. **2** a formal evening suit including a dinner jacket.
– DERIVATIVES **tux·e·doed** adjective.
– ORIGIN from *Tuxedo* Park, the site of a country club in New York.

TV ▶ **abbreviation** television.

TVP ▶ **abbreviation** trademark textured vegetable protein, a protein obtained from soybeans and made to resemble ground meat.

twad·dle /ˈtwädl/ ▶ **noun** dated, informal trivial or foolish speech or writing; nonsense.
– ORIGIN unknown.

twain /twān/ ▶ **cardinal number** old-fashioned term for **TWO**.
– ORIGIN Old English.

twang /twaNG/ ▶ **noun 1** a strong ringing sound such as that made by the plucked string of a musical instrument. **2** a distinctive nasal way of speaking. ▶ **verb** make a twang.
– DERIVATIVES **twang·y** adjective.
– ORIGIN imitating the sound.

'twas ▶ **contraction** old use or literary it was.

twat /twät/ ▶ **noun** vulgar slang **1** a woman's genitals. **2** a stupid or unpleasant person. ▶ **verb** Brit. informal hit or punch someone.
– ORIGIN unknown.

tweak /twēk/ ▶ **verb 1** twist or pull something with a small sharp movement. **2** informal improve a mechanism or system by making fine adjustments. ▶ **noun 1** an act of tweaking. **2** informal a fine adjustment.
– DERIVATIVES **tweak·er** noun.
– ORIGIN probably from dialect *twick* 'pull sharply.'

tweed /twēd/ ▶ **noun 1** a rough woolen cloth flecked with mixed colors. **2** (**tweeds**) clothes made of tweed.
– ORIGIN from a Scots form of **TWILL**, influenced by association with the river *Tweed.*

tweed·y /ˈtwēdē/ ▶ **adjective** (**tweedier, tweediest**) **1** made of tweed cloth. **2** informal of a refined, traditional, upscale character.
– DERIVATIVES **tweed·i·ness** noun.

tween /twēn/ (also **tweenager** /ˈtwēnˌājər/) ▶ **noun** informal a child between the ages of about 10 and 14.

'tween ▶ **contraction** old use or literary between.

tweet /twēt/ ▶ **noun** the chirp of a small bird. ▶ **verb** make a chirping noise.
– ORIGIN imitating the sound.

tweet·er /ˈtwētər/ ▶ **noun** a loudspeaker designed to reproduce high frequencies.

tweeze /twēz/ ▶ **verb** pluck or pull something with tweezers.

tweez·ers /ˈtwēzərz/ ▶ **plural noun** (also **pair of tweezers**) a small instrument like a pair of pincers for plucking out hairs or embedded slivers and picking up small objects.
– ORIGIN from former *tweeze* 'case of surgical instruments.'

twelfth /twelfTH/ ▶ **ordinal number 1** that is number twelve in a sequence; 12th. **2** (**a twelfth/one twelfth**) each of twelve equal parts into which something is divided. **3** a musical interval spanning an octave and a fifth in a scale.
– DERIVATIVES **twelfth·ly** adverb.

Twelfth Night ▶ **noun 1** January 6, the Christian feast of the Epiphany. **2** the evening of January 5, formerly the twelfth and last day of Christmas festivities.

twelve /twelv/ ▶ **cardinal number** two more than ten; 12. (Roman numeral: **xii** or **XII.**)
– ORIGIN Old English.

twelve·month /ˈtwelvˌmənTH/ ▶ **noun** old use a year.

twelve-step ▶ **adjective** denoting or referring to a process of recovery from addiction by following a twelve-stage program, especially one modeled on that of

Alcoholics Anonymous. ▶ verb (often as n. **twelve-stepping**) (of an addict) undergo such a program.

twen·ty /ˈtwentē/ ▶ cardinal number (pl. **twenties**) ten less than thirty; 20. (Roman numeral: **xx** or **XX**.)
– DERIVATIVES **twen·ti·eth** /ˈtwentēiTH/ ordinal number.
– ORIGIN Old English.

24-7 (also **24/7**) ▶ adverb informal twenty-four hours a day, seven days a week; all the time.

twen·ty-one ▶ noun the card game blackjack.

twen·ty-twen·ty vi·sion (also **20/20 vision**) ▶ noun normal sharpness of vision.
– ORIGIN with reference to the fraction for normal visual sharpness in eyesight tests.

'twere ▶ contraction old use or literary it were.

twerp /twərp/ ▶ noun informal a silly or annoying person.
– ORIGIN unknown.

twice /twīs/ ▶ adverb **1** two times. **2** double in degree or quantity.
– ORIGIN Old English.

twid·dle /ˈtwidl/ ▶ verb play or fiddle with something in an aimless or nervous way. ▶ noun an act of twiddling.
– DERIVATIVES **twid·dler** noun **twid·dly** adjective.
– PHRASES **twiddle one's thumbs** have nothing to do.
– ORIGIN probably combining *twirl* or *twist* with *fiddle*.

twig /twig/ ▶ noun a slender woody shoot growing from a branch or stem of a tree or shrub.

– SYNONYMS **stick,** sprig, shoot, offshoot, stem, branchlet.

– DERIVATIVES **twigged** adjective **twig·gy** adjective.
– ORIGIN Old English.

twi·light /ˈtwīˌlīt/ ▶ noun **1** the soft glowing light from the sky when the sun is below the horizon. **2** a period or state of gradual decline: *he was in the twilight of his career.*

– SYNONYMS **1 dusk,** sunset, sundown, nightfall, evening, close of day. **2 half-light,** semidarkness, gloom.

▶ adjective mysterious, secret, or unreal: *the twilight world of drugs.*
– ORIGIN from an Old English base meaning 'two' + LIGHT[1].

WORD LINKS

crepuscular *resembling twilight*

twi·light zone ▶ noun **1** a conceptual area that is undefined, uncertain, or intermediate. **2** the lowest level of the ocean to which light can penetrate.

twi·lit /ˈtwīˌlit/ ▶ adjective dimly lit.

twill /twil/ ▶ noun a fabric so woven as to have a surface of diagonal parallel ridges.
– DERIVATIVES **twilled** adjective.
– ORIGIN from Old English, 'two.'

'twill ▶ contraction old use or literary it will.

twin /twin/ ▶ noun **1** one of two children or animals born at the same birth. **2** a thing that is exactly like another.

– SYNONYMS **duplicate,** double, carbon copy, likeness, mirror image, replica, lookalike, clone, match, pair; informal spitting image, dead ringer.

▶ adjective **1** forming or being one of a pair of twins or matching things: *the twin problems of economic failure and social decline.* **2** (of a bedroom) containing two single beds.

– SYNONYMS **1 matching,** identical, paired. **2 twofold,** double, dual, related, linked, connected, parallel, complementary.

▶ verb (**twins, twinning, twinned**) link or combine things as a pair.

– SYNONYMS **combine,** join, link, couple, pair.

– ORIGIN Old English.

twin bed ▶ noun a bed designed or suitable for one person; a single bed.

twine /twīn/ ▶ noun strong thread or string consisting of strands of hemp or cotton twisted together. ▶ verb wind something around something else.
– ORIGIN Old English, 'thread, linen.'

twinge /twinj/ ▶ noun **1** a sudden, sharp pain. **2** a brief, sharp pang of emotion.

– SYNONYMS **pain,** spasm, ache, throb, cramp, stitch, pang.

▶ verb (**twinges, twingeing** or **twinging, twinged**) suffer a sudden, sharp pain.
– ORIGIN Old English, 'pinch, wring.'

twin·kle /ˈtwiNGkəl/ ▶ verb **1** (of a star or light) shine with a gleam that changes constantly from bright to faint. **2** (of a person's eyes) sparkle with amusement or liveliness. **3** (of a person's feet) move lightly and rapidly.

– SYNONYMS **glitter,** sparkle, shine, glimmer, shimmer, glint, gleam, flicker, flash, wink.

▶ noun a twinkling sparkle or gleam.
– DERIVATIVES **twin·kly** /-k(ə)lē/ adjective.
– PHRASES **in the twinkling of an eye** in an instant.
– ORIGIN Old English.

twirl /twərl/ ▶ verb spin quickly and lightly around.

– SYNONYMS **1** *she twirled her parasol* **spin,** whirl, turn, gyrate, pivot, swivel, twist, revolve, rotate. **2** *she twirled her hair around her finger* **wind,** twist, coil, curl, wrap.

▶ noun **1** an act of twirling. **2** a spiral shape.

– SYNONYMS **pirouette,** spin, whirl, turn, twist, rotation, revolution, gyration.

– DERIVATIVES **twirl·er** noun **twirl·y** adjective.
– ORIGIN probably from former *trill* 'twiddle, spin.'

twist /twist/ ▶ verb **1** form something into a bent, curled, or distorted shape. **2** turn or bend around or into a different direction: *she twisted in her seat to look at the buildings.* **3** force out of the natural position by a twisting action: *he twisted his ankle.* **4** take or have a winding course. **5** deliberately distort the meaning of words. **6** (as adj. **twisted**) strange or abnormal in an unpleasant way; perverted. **7** dance the twist.

– SYNONYMS **1 crumple,** crush, buckle, mangle, warp, deform, distort, contort. **2 sprain,** wrench, turn, crick. **3** *twist the ribbon around a pencil* **wind,** twirl, coil, curl, wrap. **4** *the wires were twisted together* **intertwine,** interlace, weave, plait, braid, coil, wind. **5** *the road twisted and turned* **wind,** bend, curve, turn, meander, weave, zigzag, snake.

▶ noun **1** an act of twisting. **2** a thing with a spiral or curved shape. **3** a new or unexpected development or way of treating something: *the plot includes a clever twist.* **4** (**the twist**) a dance with a twisting movement of the body, popular in the 1960s. **5** a fine strong thread consisting of twisted fibers. **6** a carpet with a tightly curled pile.

– SYNONYMS **bend,** curve, turn, zigzag, dogleg.

– DERIVATIVES **twist·y** adjective.
– PHRASES **twist someone's arm** informal forcefully persuade someone to do something that they are reluctant to do.
– ORIGIN Old English.

twist·er /ˈtwistər/ ▸ **noun** a tornado.

twit[1] /twit/ ▸ **noun** informal, chiefly Brit. a foolish person.
– DERIVATIVES **twit·tish** adjective.
– ORIGIN perhaps from **TWIT**[2].

twit[2] ▸ **verb** (**twits, twitting, twitted**) informal tease someone good-humoredly.
– ORIGIN Old English, 'reproach with.'

twitch /twich/ ▸ **verb** make a short jerking movement.

– SYNONYMS **jerk,** convulse, have a spasm, quiver, tremble, shiver, shudder.

▸ **noun 1** a twitching movement. **2** a pang: *he felt a twitch of annoyance.*

– SYNONYMS **spasm,** convulsion, quiver, tremor, shiver, shudder, tic.

– ORIGIN Germanic.

twitch·y /ˈtwichē/ ▸ **adjective** (**twitchier, twitchiest**) informal nervous; anxious.

twit·ter /ˈtwitər/ ▸ **verb 1** (of a bird) make a series of short high sounds. **2** talk rapidly in a nervous or trivial way. ▸ **noun 1** a twittering sound. **2** informal an agitated or excited state.
– DERIVATIVES **twit·ter·y** adjective.
– ORIGIN imitating the sound.

'twixt ▸ **contraction** betwixt; between.

two /to͞o/ ▸ **cardinal number** one less than three; 2. (Roman numeral: **ii** or **II**.)
– DERIVATIVES **two·fold** /ˈto͞oˌfōld/ adjective & adverb.
– PHRASES **put two and two together** draw an obvious conclusion from the available evidence. **two by two** side by side in pairs. **two-horse race** a contest in which only two of the competitors are likely winners.
– ORIGIN Old English.

USAGE

For an explanation of the difference between **two, to,** and **too**, see the note at **TO**.

two-bit ▸ **adjective** informal unimportant, cheap, or worthless.

two-by-four ▸ **noun** a length of wood with a rectangular cross section approximately two inches by four inches.

two-di·men·sion·al ▸ **adjective 1** having or appearing to have length and breadth but no depth. **2** lacking depth; superficial: *two-dimensional bad guys.*

two-faced ▸ **adjective** insincere and deceitful.

two-fist·ed ▸ **adjective** strong, virile, and straightforward.

two-hand·ed ▸ **adjective & adverb** having, using, or requiring the use of two hands.

two·pence /ˈtəpəns/ (also **tuppence**) ▸ **noun** Brit. **1** the sum of two pence, especially before decimalization (1971). **2** informal anything at all: *he didn't care twopence for her.*

two-piece ▸ **adjective** consisting of two matching items.

two·some /ˈto͞osəm/ ▸ **noun** a set of two people or things.

two-step ▸ **noun** a dance with sliding steps in march or polka time.

two-stroke ▸ **adjective** (of an internal-combustion engine) having its power cycle completed in one up-and-down movement of the piston.

two-time ▸ **verb** informal be unfaithful to a lover or spouse.
– DERIVATIVES **two-tim·er** noun.

two-tone (also **two-toned**) ▸ **adjective** having two different shades or colors: *a two-tone jacket.*

'twould ▸ **contraction** old use it would.

two-way ▸ **adjective 1** involving movement or communication in opposite directions. **2** (of a switch) permitting a current to be switched on or off from either of two points.
– PHRASES **two-way street** a situation involving shared action or responsibility: *trust is a two-way street.*

two-way mir·ror ▸ **noun** a panel of glass that can be seen through from one side and is a mirror on the other.

twp. ▸ **abbreviation** township.

TX ▸ **abbreviation** Texas.

ty·coon /tīˈko͞on/ ▸ **noun** a wealthy, powerful person in business or industry.

– SYNONYMS **magnate,** mogul, businessman, captain of industry, industrialist, financier, entrepreneur; informal, derogatory fat cat.

– ORIGIN Japanese, 'great lord.'

ty·ing /ˈtī-iNG/ present participle of **TIE**.

tyke /tīk/ (also **tike**) ▸ **noun** informal a mischievous child.
– ORIGIN Old Norse, 'bitch.'

ty·lo·sin /ˈtīləˌsin/ ▸ **noun** an antibiotic that is fed to livestock as a growth promoter.

tym·pa·ni ▸ **plural noun** variant spelling of **TIMPANI**.

tym·pa·num /ˈtimpənəm/ ▸ **noun** (pl. **tympanums** or **tympana** /-nə/) **1** the eardrum. **2** Architecture a space enclosed between the lintel of a doorway and an arch over it, or the triangle enclosed by a classical pediment.
– DERIVATIVES **tym·pan·ic** /timˈpanik/ adjective.
– ORIGIN Greek *tumpanon* 'drum.'

type /tīp/ ▸ **noun 1** a category of people or things that share particular qualities or features. **2** informal a person of a specified character or nature: *sporty types in tracksuits.* **3** a person or thing that is a typical example of something: *she described his sayings as the type of modern wisdom.* **4** printed characters or letters. **5** pieces of metal with raised letters or characters on their upper surface, for use in letterpress printing.

– SYNONYMS **1 kind,** sort, variety, class, category, set, genre, species, order, breed, ilk. **2 print,** typeface, characters, lettering, font.

▸ **verb 1** write using a typewriter or computer. **2** Medicine determine the type to which a person or their blood or tissue belongs.
– DERIVATIVES **typ·ing** noun.
– ORIGIN Greek *tupos* 'impression, figure, type.'

CHOOSE THE RIGHT WORD

See **EMBLEM**.

type·cast /ˈtīpˌkast/ ▸ **verb** (past and past part. **typecast**) **1** repeatedly cast an actor in the same type of role because their appearance is appropriate or they are known for such roles. **2** regard as fitting a stereotype: *she didn't want to be typecast as an angst-ridden female rock musician.*

type·face /ˈtīpˌfās/ ▶ **noun** a particular design of printed letters or characters.

type·script /ˈtīpˌskript/ ▶ **noun** a typed copy of a written work.

type·set /ˈtīpˌset/ ▶ **verb** (**typesets, typesetting, typeset**) arrange or generate the data or type for written material to be printed.
– DERIVATIVES **type·set·ter** noun **type·set·ting** noun.

type·writ·er /ˈtīpˌrītər/ ▶ **noun** an electric, electronic, or manual machine with keys for producing characters similar to printed ones.
– DERIVATIVES **type·writ·ing** /-ˌrītiNG/ noun **type·writ·ten** /-ˌritn/ adjective.

ty·phoid /ˈtīˌfoid/ (also **typhoid fever**) ▶ **noun** an infectious fever caused by a bacterium, resulting in red spots on the chest and abdomen and severe irritation of the intestines.
– ORIGIN from TYPHUS.

ty·phoon /tīˈfo͞on/ ▶ **noun** a tropical storm with very high winds, occurring in the region of the Indian Ocean or the western Pacific Ocean.
– ORIGIN partly from Arabic, partly from a Chinese dialect word meaning 'big wind.'

ty·phus /ˈtīfəs/ ▶ **noun** an infectious disease caused by a bacterium, resulting in a purple rash, headaches, fever, and usually delirium.
– ORIGIN Greek *tuphos* 'smoke, stupor.'

typ·i·cal /ˈtipikəl/ ▶ **adjective 1** having the distinctive qualities of a particular type of person or thing: *a typical example of a small American town.* **2** behaving or happening in the expected or usual way: *a typical day began with breakfast at 7:30 a.m.*

– SYNONYMS **1 representative,** characteristic, classic, quintessential, archetypal. **2 normal,** average, ordinary, standard, regular, routine, run-of-the-mill, conventional, unremarkable.
– ANTONYMS unusual, exceptional.

– DERIVATIVES **typ·i·cal·i·ty** /ˌtipiˈkalitē/ noun **typ·i·cal·ly** adverb.

WORD TOOLKIT

typical ...	standard ...	common ...
example	practice	man
day	procedure	people
American	treatment	theme
fashion	method	sight
family	equipment	belief
male	protocol	complaint
teenager	reference	method
household	format	misconception
summer	size	mistake

typ·i·fy /ˈtipəˌfī/ ▶ **verb** (**typifies, typifying, typified**) be a typical example or feature of: *their furniture is typified by its functional design.*

– SYNONYMS **epitomize,** exemplify, characterize, embody, be representative of, personify, symbolize.

– DERIVATIVES **typ·i·fi·ca·tion** /ˌtipəfiˈkāSHən/ noun.

typ·ist /ˈtīpist/ ▶ **noun** a person skilled in typing and employed for this purpose.

ty·po /ˈtīpō/ ▶ **noun** (pl. **typos**) informal a small mistake in typed or printed writing.

ty·pog·ra·phy /tīˈpägrəfē/ ▶ **noun 1** the art or process of preparing material for printing, especially of designing how printed text will appear. **2** the style and appearance of printed matter.
– DERIVATIVES **ty·pog·ra·pher** noun **ty·po·graph·ic** /ˌtīpəˈgrafik/ adjective **ty·po·graph·i·cal** /ˌtīpəˈgrafikəl/ adjective.

ty·pol·o·gy /tīˈpäləjē/ ▶ **noun** (pl. **typologies**) a classification of things according to general type.
– DERIVATIVES **ty·po·log·i·cal** /ˌtīpəˈläjikəl/ adjective **ty·pol·o·gist** noun.

ty·ran·ni·cal /təˈranikəl/ ▶ **adjective** exercising power in a cruel and unfair way.
– DERIVATIVES **ty·ran·ni·cal·ly** adverb.

ty·ran·ni·cide /təˈraniˌsīd/ ▶ **noun 1** the killing of a tyrant. **2** the killer of a tyrant.
– DERIVATIVES **ty·ran·ni·cid·al** /təˌraniˈsīdl/ adjective.

tyr·an·nize /ˈtirəˌnīz/ ▶ **verb** rule or dominate someone in a cruel or oppressive way.

ty·ran·no·sau·rus /təˌranəˈsôrəs/ (also **tyrannosaurus rex** /reks/) ▶ **noun** a very large meat-eating dinosaur with powerful jaws and small clawlike front legs.
– ORIGIN from Greek *turannos* 'tyrant' + *sauros* 'lizard.'

tyr·an·ny /ˈtirənē/ ▶ **noun** (pl. **tyrannies**) **1** cruel and oppressive government or rule. **2** a nation under cruel and oppressive government. **3** cruel and unfair use of power or control: *a young man liberated from the tyranny of his father.*

– SYNONYMS **despotism,** absolute power, autocracy, dictatorship, totalitarianism, fascism, oppression, repression, subjugation, enslavement.

– DERIVATIVES **tyr·an·nous** adjective.

ty·rant /ˈtīrənt/ ▶ **noun 1** a cruel and oppressive ruler. **2** a person who uses their power in a cruel and unfair way.

– SYNONYMS **dictator,** despot, autocrat, authoritarian, oppressor, slave driver, martinet, bully.

– ORIGIN Greek *turannos.*

tyre, etc. ▶ **noun** British spelling of TIRE², etc.

ty·ro /ˈtīrō/ ▶ **noun** (pl. **tyros**) a beginner or novice.
– ORIGIN Latin, 'recruit.'

ty·ro·sine /ˈtīrəˌsēn/ ▶ **noun** an amino acid that is a constituent of most proteins and is important in the synthesis of some hormones.
– ORIGIN Greek *turos* 'cheese.'

tzar ▶ **noun** variant spelling of TSAR.

tza·ri·na ▶ **noun** variant spelling of TSARINA.

tza·tzi·ki /tsäˈtsēkē/ ▶ **noun** a Greek side dish of yogurt with cucumber, garlic, and often mint.
– ORIGIN modern Greek.

U[1] (also **u**) ▶ **noun** (pl. **Us** or **U's**) the twenty-first letter of the alphabet.

U[2] ▶ **symbol** the chemical element uranium.

UAE ▶ **abbreviation** United Arab Emirates.

UAV ▶ **abbreviation** unmanned aerial vehicle.

uber- /'o͞obər/ (also **über-** /'ʏbər/) ▶ **prefix** referring to an outstanding or supreme example of a person or thing: *an uberbabe.*
– ORIGIN German *über* 'over.'

Über·mensch /'o͞obər,mencн, 'ʏbər-/ ▶ **noun** the ideal superior man of the future who could rise above conventional Christian morality to create and impose his own values.
– ORIGIN German, 'superhuman person,' originally described by Nietzsche in *Thus Spake Zarathustra.*

u·biq·ui·tous /yo͞o'bikwətəs/ ▶ **adjective** present, appearing, or found everywhere: *ubiquitous coffee shops.*

– SYNONYMS **everywhere,** omnipresent, all over the place, all-pervasive, universal, worldwide, global.
– ANTONYMS rare.

– DERIVATIVES **u·biq·ui·tous·ly** adverb **u·biq·ui·tous·ness** noun **u·biq·ui·ty** noun.
– ORIGIN from Latin *ubique* 'everywhere.'

U-boat ▶ **noun** a German submarine of World War I or II.
– ORIGIN German *U-Boot*, abbreviation of *Unterseeboot* 'undersea boat.'

u.c. ▶ **abbreviation** upper case.

ud·der /'ədər/ ▶ **noun** the milk-producing gland of female cattle, sheep, goats, horses, etc., hanging near the hind legs as a baglike organ with two or more teats.
– ORIGIN Old English.

u·don /'o͞o,dän/ ▶ **noun** (in Japanese cooking) large noodles made from wheat flour.
– ORIGIN Japanese.

UFO ▶ **noun** (pl. **UFOs**) a mysterious object seen in the sky for which it is claimed no scientific explanation can be found, believed by some to be a vehicle carrying beings from outer space.
– DERIVATIVES **u·fol·o·gist** /yo͞o'fäləjist/ noun **u·fol·o·gy** /yo͞o'fäləjē/ noun.
– ORIGIN abbreviation of *unidentified flying object.*

U·gan·dan /yo͞o'gandən/ ▶ **noun** a person from Uganda. ▶ **adjective** relating to Uganda.

ugh /əg, əкн, o͝oкн/ ▶ **exclamation** informal used to express disgust or horror.
– ORIGIN imitative.

Ug·li fruit /'əglē/ ▶ **noun** (pl. same) trademark a mottled green and yellow citrus fruit that is a cross between a grapefruit and a tangerine.
– ORIGIN from **UGLY**.

ug·li·fy /'əglə,fī/ ▶ **verb** (**uglifies, uglifying, uglified**) make something ugly.

ug·ly /'əglē/ ▶ **adjective** (**uglier, ugliest**) **1** unpleasant or unattractive in appearance. **2** involving violence or other unpleasantness: *an ugly scene was averted.* **3** disturbing or disagreeable: *the whole ugly truth of slavery.*

– SYNONYMS **1 unattractive,** unsightly, ill-favored, hideous, plain, unprepossessing, horrible, ghastly, repellent, grotesque, homely. **2 unpleasant,** nasty, disagreeable, alarming, dangerous, perilous, threatening, menacing, hostile, ominous, sinister. **3 horrible,** despicable, reprehensible, nasty, appalling, objectionable, offensive, obnoxious, vile, dishonorable.
– ANTONYMS beautiful.

– DERIVATIVES **ug·li·ness** noun.
– ORIGIN from Old Norse, 'to be dreaded.'

ug·ly duck·ling ▶ **noun** a person who unexpectedly turns out to be beautiful or talented.
– ORIGIN from one of Hans Christian Andersen's fairy tales, in which the 'ugly duckling' is actually a young swan.

UHF ▶ **abbreviation** ultrahigh frequency.

uh-huh /ə 'hə, əɴ 'həɴ/ ▶ **exclamation** used to express agreement or as a noncommittal response to a question or remark.
– ORIGIN imitative.

UHT ▶ **abbreviation** ultrahigh temperature (a process used to extend the shelf life of certain foods, particularly milk).

uil·lean pipes /'ilən, 'ilyən/ ▶ **plural noun** Irish bagpipes played using bellows worked by the elbow.
– ORIGIN from Irish *píob uilleann* 'pipe of the elbow.'

UK ▶ **abbreviation** United Kingdom.

u·kase /yo͞o'kās, -'kāz/ ▶ **noun 1** historical a decree with the force of law, issued by the tsarist Russian government. **2** a dictatorial command.
– ORIGIN Russian *ukaz* 'ordinance, edict.'

uke /yo͞ok/ ▶ **noun** informal short for **UKULELE**.

U·krain·i·an /yo͞o'krānēən/ ▶ **noun 1** a person from Ukraine. **2** the language of Ukraine. ▶ **adjective** relating to Ukraine.

u·ku·le·le /,yo͞okə'lālē/ (also **ukelele**) ▶ **noun** a small four-stringed guitar of Hawaiian origin.
– ORIGIN Hawaiian, 'jumping flea.'

u·la·ma ▶ **noun** variant spelling of **ULEMA**.

ul·cer /'əlsər/ ▶ **noun** an open sore on an external or internal surface of the body, caused by a break in the skin or mucous membrane that fails to heal.
– DERIVATIVES **ul·cered** adjective **ul·cer·ous** adjective.
– ORIGIN Latin *ulcus.*

ul·cer·ate /ˈəlsəˌrāt/ ▶ verb develop into or become affected by an ulcer.
– DERIVATIVES **ul·cer·a·tion** /ˌəlsəˈrāsHən/ noun **ul·cer·a·tive** /-rətiv, -ˌrātiv/ adjective.

u·le·ma /ˈo͞oləˌmä/ (also **ulama**) ▶ noun **1** (treated as sing. or pl.) a group of Muslim scholars recognized as having specialist knowledge of Islamic sacred law and theology. **2** a member of an ulema.
– ORIGIN Arabic.

ul·lage /ˈəlij/ ▶ noun **1** the amount by which a container falls short of being full. **2** loss of liquid by evaporation or leakage.
– ORIGIN from Old French *euillier* 'fill up.'

ul·na /ˈəlnə/ ▶ noun (pl. **ulnae** /-ˌnē, -ˌnī/ or **ulnas**) the thinner and longer of the two bones in the human forearm.
– DERIVATIVES **ul·nar** adjective.
– ORIGIN Latin, related to former *ell*, a measure of length.

ul·ster /ˈəlstər/ ▶ noun a long, loose overcoat made of rough cloth, worn by men.
– ORIGIN from *Ulster* in Ireland, where it was originally sold.

Ul·ster·man /ˈəlstərmən/ (or **Ulsterwoman** /ˈəlstərˌwo͝omən/) ▶ noun (pl. **Ulstermen** or **Ulsterwomen**) a person from Northern Ireland or Ulster.

ul·te·ri·or /ˌəlˈti(ə)rēər/ ▶ adjective other than what is obvious or has been admitted: *she had some ulterior motive in coming.*

> – SYNONYMS **underlying,** undisclosed, undivulged, concealed, hidden, covert, secret, unapparent.
> – ANTONYMS overt.

– ORIGIN Latin, 'further, more distant.'

ul·ti·mate /ˈəltəmit/ ▶ adjective **1** being or happening at the end of a process; final. **2** being the best or most extreme example of its kind: *climbing Mount Everest is the ultimate challenge.* **3** basic or fundamental: *atoms are the ultimate constituents of anything that exists.*

> – SYNONYMS **1 eventual,** final, concluding, terminal, end. **2 best,** ideal, greatest, quintessential, supreme. **3 fundamental,** basic, primary, elementary, absolute, central, crucial, essential.

▶ noun (**the ultimate**) the best of its kind: *the scooter was the ultimate in continental chic.*
– DERIVATIVES **ul·ti·ma·cy** /-məsē/ noun.
– ORIGIN Latin *ultimatus*.

ul·ti·mate·ly /ˈəltəmitlē/ ▶ adverb **1** in the end; finally. **2** at the most basic level.

> – SYNONYMS **1** *the money will ultimately belong to us* **eventually,** in the end, in the long run, at length, finally, in time, one day. **2** *two ultimately contradictory reasons* **fundamentally,** basically, primarily, essentially, at heart, deep down.

ul·ti·ma·tum /ˌəltəˈmātəm, -ˈmät-/ ▶ noun (pl. **ultimatums** or **ultimata** /-ˈmātə, -ˈmätə/) a final warning that action will be taken against someone unless they agree to another party's demands.
– ORIGIN Latin, 'thing that has come to an end.'

ul·tra /ˈəltrə/ ▶ noun informal a person with extreme political or religious views.

ultra- ▶ prefix **1** to an extreme degree; very: *ultralight.* **2** beyond; on the other side of: *ultramarine.*
– ORIGIN Latin *ultra*.

ultra·high fre·quen·cy ▶ noun (in radio) a frequency of 300–3,000 megahertz.

ul·tra·light /ˌəltrəˈlīt, ˈəltrəˌlīt/ ▶ adjective very lightweight.

ul·tra·ma·rine /ˌəltrəməˈrēn/ ▶ noun a brilliant deep blue pigment and color.
– ORIGIN from Latin *ultramarinus* 'beyond the sea' (because the pigment was obtained from lapis lazuli, which was imported).

ul·tra·mon·tane /ˌəltrəˌmänˈtān, -ˈmänˌtān/ ▶ adjective **1** (in the Roman Catholic Church) believing that the pope should have supreme authority in matters of faith and discipline. **2** situated on the other side of the Alps from the speaker. ▶ noun a person who believes that the pope should have supreme authority.
– DERIVATIVES **ul·tra·mon·ta·nism** /-ˈmäntəˌnizəm/ noun.
– ORIGIN first referring to a representative of the Roman Catholic Church north of the Alps: from Latin *ultra* 'beyond' + *mons* 'mountain.'

ul·tra·son·ic /ˌəltrəˈsänik/ ▶ adjective involving sound waves with a frequency above the upper limit of human hearing.
– DERIVATIVES **ul·tra·son·i·cal·ly** /-ik(ə)lē/ adverb.

ul·tra·son·ics /ˌəltrəˈsäniks/ ▶ plural noun **1** (treated as sing.) the science and application of sound waves with a frequency above the upper limit of human hearing. **2** (treated as sing. or pl.) ultrasonic waves; ultrasound.

ul·tra·so·nog·ra·phy /ˌəltrəsəˈnägrəfē/ ▶ noun a medical technique that uses echoes of ultrasound pulses to show objects or areas of different density in the body.
– DERIVATIVES **ul·tra·son·o·graph·ic** /əltrəˌsänəˈgrafik, -ˌsōnə-/ adjective.

ul·tra·sound /ˈəltrəˌsound/ ▶ noun **1** sound or other vibrations having a frequency above the upper limit of human hearing, particularly as used in medical scans. **2** an ultrasound scan, especially one of a pregnant woman's fetus.

ul·tra·struc·ture /ˈəltrəˌstrəkCHər/ ▶ noun Biology a fine structure, especially within a cell, that is so small that it can be seen only with an electron microscope.
– DERIVATIVES **ul·tra·struc·tur·al** /-CHərəl/ adjective.

ul·tra·vi·o·let /ˌəltrəˈvī(ə)lət/ ▶ noun electromagnetic radiation having a wavelength just shorter than that of violet light but longer than that of X-rays. ▶ adjective referring to such radiation.

ul·tra vi·res /ˌəltrə ˈvīrēz/ ▶ adjective & adverb Law beyond the legal power or authority of a person or organization.
– ORIGIN Latin, 'beyond the powers.'

ul·u·late /ˈəlyəˌlāt, ˈyo͞ol-/ ▶ verb howl or wail, especially to express grief.
– DERIVATIVES **ul·u·la·tion** /ˌəlyəˈlāsHən, ˌyo͞ol-/ noun.
– ORIGIN Latin *ululare*.

um·bel /ˈəmbəl/ ▶ noun Botany a flower cluster in which stalks spring from a common center and form a flat or curved surface.
– ORIGIN Latin *umbella* 'sunshade.'

um·bel·lif·er /ˌəmˈbeləfər/ ▶ noun Botany a plant of the parsley family, having its flowers arranged in umbels.
– DERIVATIVES **um·bel·lif·er·ous** /-bəˈlif(ə)rəs/ adjective.

um·ber /ˈəmbər/ ▶ noun a natural pigment, normally dark yellowish-brown (**raw umber**) or dark brown when roasted (**burnt umber**).
– ORIGIN from French *terre d'ombre* 'earth of shadow.'

um·bil·i·cal /ˌəmˈbilikəl/ ▶ adjective **1** relating to the navel or the umbilical cord. **2** (of a relationship) very

close; inseparable: *the umbilical connection between land and people.*
– DERIVATIVES **um·bil·i·cal·ly** adverb.

um·bil·i·cal cord ▶ **noun** a flexible cordlike structure containing blood vessels, attaching a fetus to the placenta while it is in the uterus.

um·bil·i·cus /ˌəmˈbilikəs/ ▶ **noun** (pl. **umbilici** /-ˌkī, -ˌsī, -ˌkē/ or **umbilicuses**) the navel.
– ORIGIN Latin.

um·bra /ˈəmbrə/ ▶ **noun** (pl. **umbras** or **umbrae** /-ˌbrē, -ˌbrī/) the darkest inner part of a shadow, especially the dark central part of the shadow cast by the earth or the moon in an eclipse.
– DERIVATIVES **um·bral** adjective.
– ORIGIN Latin, 'shade.'

um·brage /ˈəmbrij/ ▶ **noun** (in phrase **take umbrage**) take offense or become annoyed.
– ORIGIN first meaning 'shade, shadowy outline,' later 'ground for suspicion': from Latin *umbra* 'shade.'

um·brel·la /ˌəmˈbrelə/ ▶ **noun 1** a device consisting of a circular fabric canopy on a folding metal frame supported by a central rod, used as protection against rain. **2** a thing that includes or contains a range of different parts or aspects: *the concepts embodied under the broad umbrella of personality disorder.* **3** a protecting force or influence. ▶ **adjective** including or involving different parts or aspects: *an umbrella organization.*
– ORIGIN Italian *ombrella.*

um·laut /ˈŏŏmˌlout/ ▶ **noun** a mark (¨) used over a vowel in German and some other languages to indicate how it should be pronounced.
– ORIGIN German.

um·ma /ˈŏŏmə/ (also **ummah**) ▶ **noun** the whole community of Muslims bound together by ties of religion.
– ORIGIN Arabic, 'people, community.'

ump /əmp/ ▶ **noun & verb** informal short for **UMPIRE**.

umph ▶ **noun** variant spelling of **OOMPH**.

um·pire /ˈəmˌpī(ə)r/ ▶ **noun 1** (in certain sports) an official who supervises a game to ensure that players keep to the rules and who settles disputes arising from the play. **2** a person chosen to settle a dispute.

> – SYNONYMS **referee,** judge, line judge, linesman, adjudicator, arbitrator, moderator; informal ref.

▶ **verb** act as an umpire of a game.
– ORIGIN from Old French *nonper* 'not equal.'

ump·teen /ˈəm(p)ˌtēn/ ▶ **cardinal number** informal very many.
– DERIVATIVES **ump·teenth** /-ˌtēnTH/ ordinal number.
– ORIGIN humorous formation.

UN ▶ **abbreviation** United Nations.

un-[1] ▶ **prefix 1** (added to adjectives, participles, and their derivatives) not; the reverse of: *unacceptable* | *unselfish.* **2** (added to nouns) a lack of: *untruth.*
– ORIGIN Old English.

> **USAGE**
>
> For an explanation of the difference between the prefixes (word beginnings) **un-** and **non-**, see the note at **NON-**.

un-[2] ▶ **prefix** added to verbs. **1** referring to the reversal or cancellation of an action or state: *unsettle.* **2** referring to deprivation, separation, or change to a lesser state: *unmask.* **3** referring to release: *unhand.*
– ORIGIN Old English.

'un ▶ **contraction** informal one.

un·a·bashed /ˌənəˈbasHt/ ▶ **adjective** not embarrassed or ashamed.

> – SYNONYMS **unashamed,** shameless, brazen, audacious, barefaced, blatant, flagrant, bold.
> – ANTONYMS sheepish.

– DERIVATIVES **un·a·bash·ed·ly** adverb.

un·a·bat·ed /ˌənəˈbātid/ ▶ **adjective** without any reduction in intensity or strength.

un·a·ble /ˌənˈābəl/ ▶ **adjective** lacking the skill, means, strength, or opportunity to do something.

> – SYNONYMS **incapable,** powerless, impotent, inadequate, incompetent, unqualified, unfit.

un·a·bridged /ˌənəˈbrijd/ ▶ **adjective** (of a novel, play, or other written work) not cut or shortened; complete.

un·ac·cent·ed /ənˈakˌsentid, ˌənakˈsen-/ ▶ **adjective** having no accent, stress, or emphasis.

un·ac·cept·a·ble /ˌənəkˈseptəbəl/ ▶ **adjective** not satisfactory or allowable.

> – SYNONYMS **unsatisfactory,** inadmissible, inappropriate, unsuitable, undesirable, unreasonable, insupportable, intolerable, objectionable, distasteful; informal out of order.
> – ANTONYMS satisfactory.

– DERIVATIVES **un·ac·cept·a·bil·i·ty** /-ˌseptəˈbilətē/ noun **un·ac·cept·a·bly** adverb.

un·ac·com·pa·nied /ˌənəˈkəmp(ə)nēd/ ▶ **adjective 1** having no companion or escort. **2** without instrumental accompaniment. **3** happening without something else occurring at the same time: *no happiness comes unaccompanied by sorrow.*

un·ac·count·a·ble /ˌənəˈkountəbəl/ ▶ **adjective 1** unable to be explained. **2** not responsible for the outcome of something or required to justify actions or decisions.
– DERIVATIVES **un·ac·count·a·bil·i·ty** /-ˌkountəˈbilətē/ noun **un·ac·count·a·bly** /-blē/ adverb.

un·ac·count·ed /ˌənəˈkountid/ ▶ **adjective** (**unaccounted for**) not taken into consideration or explained.

un·ac·cus·tomed /ˌənəˈkəstəmd/ ▶ **adjective 1** not usual or customary. **2** (**unaccustomed to**) not familiar with or used to something.
– DERIVATIVES **un·ac·cus·tomed·ly** adverb.

un·ac·knowl·edged /ˌənakˈnälijd/ ▶ **adjective 1** existing or having taken place but not accepted or admitted to. **2** (of a person or their work) deserving recognition but not receiving it.

un·ac·quaint·ed /ˌənəˈkwāntid/ ▶ **adjective 1** (**unacquainted with**) having no experience of or familiarity with something. **2** not having met before.

un·a·dorned /ˌənəˈdôrnd/ ▶ **adjective** not decorated; plain.

un·a·dul·ter·at·ed /ˌənəˈdəltəˌrātid/ ▶ **adjective 1** not mixed with any different or inferior substances. **2** complete; total: *pure, unadulterated happiness.*

un·ad·ven·tur·ous /ˌənadˈvencHərəs, ˌənəd-/ ▶ **adjective** not offering, involving, or eager for new or exciting things.
– DERIVATIVES **un·ad·ven·tur·ous·ly** adverb.

un·ad·vis·ed·ly /ˌənədˈvīzidlē/ ▶ **adverb** in an unwise or rash way.

un·aes·thet·ic /ˌənes'THetik/ (also **unesthetic**) ▶ **adjective** not visually pleasing; unattractive.

un·af·fect·ed /ˌənə'fektid/ ▶ **adjective 1** feeling or showing no effects. **2** (of a person) sincere and genuine.
– DERIVATIVES **un·af·fect·ed·ly** adverb.

un·af·fil·i·at·ed /ənə'filēˌātid/ ▶ **adjective** not officially attached to or connected with an organization.

un·af·ford·a·ble /ˌənə'fôrdəbəl/ ▶ **adjective** too expensive to be afforded by the average person.

un·a·fraid /ˌənə'frād/ ▶ **adjective** feeling no fear.

un·aid·ed /ˌən'ādid/ ▶ **adjective** needing or having no help.

un·a·ligned /ˌənə'līnd/ ▶ **adjective 1** not placed or arranged in a straight line or in correct relative positions. **2** not allied with or supporting an organization or cause.

un·a·like /ˌənə'līk/ ▶ **adjective** differing from each other; not similar.

un·al·loyed /ˌənə'loid/ ▶ **adjective 1** complete; total: *unalloyed delight*. **2** (of metal) not alloyed; pure.

un·al·ter·a·ble /ˌən'ôlt(ə)rəbəl/ ▶ **adjective** not able to be changed.
– DERIVATIVES **un·al·ter·a·bly** /-blē/ adverb.

un·al·tered /ˌən'ôltərd/ ▶ **adjective** remaining the same.

un·am·big·u·ous /ˌənam'bigyo͞oəs/ ▶ **adjective** not open to more than one interpretation; clear in meaning.
– DERIVATIVES **un·am·big·u·ous·ly** adverb.

un·am·bi·tious /ˌənam'bisHəs/ ▶ **adjective 1** not motivated by a strong desire to succeed. **2** (of a plan or piece of work) not involving anything new, exciting, or demanding.

un-A·mer·i·can /ˌənə'merikən/ ▶ **adjective 1** not American in nature. **2** US against the interests of the US and therefore treasonable.

u·nan·i·mous /yo͞o'nanəməs/ ▶ **adjective 1** (of people) fully in agreement. **2** (of an opinion, decision, or vote) held or carried by everyone involved.
– SYNONYMS **in agreement,** of one mind, in accord, united, undivided, with one voice.
– ANTONYMS split.
– DERIVATIVES **u·na·nim·i·ty** /ˌyo͞onə'nimətē/ noun **u·nan·i·mous·ly** adverb.
– ORIGIN Latin *unanimus*.

un·an·nounced /ˌənə'nounst/ ▶ **adjective** without warning or notice: *he often dropped in unannounced*.

un·an·swer·a·ble /ˌən'ans(ə)rəbəl/ ▶ **adjective 1** unable to be answered. **2** unable to be questioned or disagreed with: *an unanswerable case for investment*.

un·an·swered /ˌən'ansərd/ ▶ **adjective** not answered or responded to.

un·a·pol·o·get·ic /ˌənəˌpälə'jetik/ ▶ **adjective** not sorry for one's actions.
– DERIVATIVES **un·a·pol·o·get·i·cal·ly** /-ik(ə)lē/ adverb.

un·ap·peal·ing /ˌənə'pēliNG/ ▶ **adjective** not inviting or attractive.
– DERIVATIVES **un·ap·peal·ing·ly** adverb.

un·ap·pe·tiz·ing /ˌən'apəˌtīziNG/ ▶ **adjective** not inviting or attractive.
– SYNONYMS **unpalatable,** uninviting, unappealing, unpleasant, off-putting, distasteful, unsavory, insipid, flavorless; informal yucky, gross.
– ANTONYMS tempting.
– DERIVATIVES **un·ap·pe·tiz·ing·ly** adverb.

un·ap·pre·ci·at·ed /ˌənə'prēsHēˌātid/ ▶ **adjective** not fully understood, recognized, or valued.

un·ap·pre·ci·a·tive /ˌənə'prēsH(ē)ətiv/ ▶ **adjective** not fully understanding or recognizing something.

un·ap·proach·a·ble /ˌənə'prōCHəbəl/ ▶ **adjective** not welcoming or friendly.
– SYNONYMS **aloof,** distant, remote, detached, reserved, withdrawn, uncommunicative, unforthcoming, unfriendly, unsympathetic; cool, frosty, stiff; informal standoffish.
– ANTONYMS friendly.

un·ap·proved /ˌənə'pro͞ovd/ ▶ **adjective** not officially accepted or permitted.

un·ar·gu·a·ble /ˌən'ärgyo͞oəbəl/ ▶ **adjective** not open to disagreement; certain.
– DERIVATIVES **un·ar·gu·a·bly** /-blē/ adverb.

un·armed /ˌən'ärmd/ ▶ **adjective** not equipped with or carrying weapons.
– SYNONYMS **defenseless,** unprotected, unguarded.

un·a·shamed /ˌənə'sHāmd/ ▶ **adjective** feeling or showing no guilt or embarrassment.
– DERIVATIVES **un·a·sham·ed·ly** /-'sHāmidlē/ adverb.

un·asked /ˌən'as(k)t/ ▶ **adjective 1** (of a question) not asked. **2** without being invited or asked: *we'd never have entered the house unasked*.

un·as·sail·a·ble /ˌənə'sāləbəl/ ▶ **adjective** unable to be attacked, questioned, or defeated.
– DERIVATIVES **un·as·sail·a·bil·i·ty** /-ˌsālə'bilətē/ noun **un·as·sail·a·bly** /-blē/ adverb.

WORD TOOLKIT

See **INDOMITABLE**.

un·as·ser·tive /ˌənə'sərtiv/ ▶ **adjective** not having or showing a confident and forceful personality.

un·as·sist·ed /ˌənə'sistid/ ▶ **adjective** not helped by anyone or anything.

un·as·so·ci·at·ed /ˌənə'sōsHēˌātid, -'sōsē-/ ▶ **adjective** not connected or associated: *they perform music previously unassociated with the saxophone*.

un·as·sum·ing /ˌənə'so͞omiNG/ ▶ **adjective** not wanting to draw attention to oneself or one's abilities.
– SYNONYMS **modest,** self-effacing, humble, meek, reserved, diffident, unobtrusive, unostentatious, unpretentious, unaffected, natural.
– DERIVATIVES **un·as·sum·ing·ly** adverb.

un·at·tached /ˌənə'taCHt/ ▶ **adjective 1** not married or having an established lover. **2** not working for or belonging to a particular organization.

un·at·tain·a·ble /ˌənə'tānəbəl/ ▶ **adjective** not able to be reached or achieved.
– DERIVATIVES **un·at·tain·a·bly** /-blē/ adverb.

WORD TOOLKIT

See **IMPOSSIBLE**.

un·at·tend·ed /ˌənə'tendid/ ▶ **adjective** without the owner or a responsible person present; not being supervised or looked after.

un·at·trac·tive /ˌənəˈtraktiv/ ▶ **adjective** not pleasing, appealing, or inviting.
– DERIVATIVES **un·at·trac·tive·ly** adverb **un·at·trac·tive·ness** noun.

un·at·trib·ut·ed /ˌənəˈtribyətid/ ▶ **adjective** (of a quotation, story, or work of art) of unknown or unpublished origin.
– DERIVATIVES **un·at·trib·ut·a·ble** /-yətəbəl/ adjective.

un·au·thor·ized /ənˈôTHəˌrīzd/ ▶ **adjective** not having official permission or approval.

> – SYNONYMS **unofficial,** unsanctioned, unaccredited, unlicensed, unwarranted, unapproved, disallowed, prohibited, banned, forbidden, outlawed, illegal, illicit, proscribed.
> – ANTONYMS official.

un·a·vail·a·ble /ˌənəˈvāləbəl/ ▶ **adjective 1** not able to be used or obtained. **2** not free to do something: *he was unavailable for comment.*
– DERIVATIVES **un·a·vail·a·bil·i·ty** /ˌənəˌvāləˈbilitē/ noun.

un·a·vail·ing /ˌənəˈvāliNG/ ▶ **adjective** achieving little or nothing.
– DERIVATIVES **un·a·vail·ing·ly** adverb.

un·a·void·a·ble /ˌənəˈvoidəbəl/ ▶ **adjective** not able to be avoided or prevented; inevitable.
– DERIVATIVES **un·a·void·a·bil·i·ty** /-ˌvoidəˈbilətē/ noun **un·a·void·a·bly** /-blē/ adverb.

un·a·ware /ˌənəˈwe(ə)r/ ▶ **adjective** having no knowledge of a situation or fact.

> – SYNONYMS **ignorant,** oblivious, unconscious, unwitting, unsuspecting, uninformed, unenlightened, innocent; informal in the dark.
> – ANTONYMS aware.

– DERIVATIVES **un·a·ware·ness** noun.

un·a·wares /ˌənəˈwe(ə)rz/ (also **unaware**) ▶ **adverb** so as to surprise someone; unexpectedly: *modern life has caught that woman completely unawares.*

un·bal·ance /ˌənˈbaləns/ ▶ **verb 1** upset the balance or stability of: *judo unbalances an opponent before throwing him.* **2** (as adj. **unbalanced**) mentally or emotionally disturbed. **3** (as adj. **unbalanced**) not giving equal coverage or treatment to all aspects of something.

> – SYNONYMS **1** (as adj. **unbalanced**) **unstable,** mentally ill, deranged, demented, disturbed, unhinged, insane, mad; informal crazy, loopy, nuts, batty, bonkers. **2** (as adj. **unbalanced**) *an unbalanced article* **biased,** prejudiced, one-sided, partisan, inequitable, unfair.
> – ANTONYMS sane, unbiased.

un·bear·a·ble /ˌənˈbe(ə)rəbəl/ ▶ **adjective** not able to be endured or tolerated.

> – SYNONYMS **intolerable,** insufferable, insupportable, unendurable, unacceptable, unmanageable, overpowering; informal too much.
> – ANTONYMS tolerable.

– DERIVATIVES **un·bear·a·bly** /-blē/ adverb.

un·beat·a·ble /ˌənˈbētəbəl/ ▶ **adjective 1** not able to be bettered or beaten: *CDs at unbeatable prices.* **2** very good.
– DERIVATIVES **un·beat·a·bly** /-blē/ adverb.

un·beat·en /ˌənˈbētn/ ▶ **adjective** not defeated or bettered.

un·be·com·ing /ˌənbiˈkəmiNG/ ▶ **adjective 1** (especially of clothing) not flattering. **2** (of behavior) not appropriate or acceptable.
– DERIVATIVES **un·be·com·ing·ly** adverb.

un·be·known /ˌənbiˈnōn/ (also **unbeknownst** /-ˈnōnst/) ▶ **adjective** (**unbeknown to**) without the knowledge of someone.

un·be·lief /ˌənbəˈlēf/ ▶ **noun** lack of religious belief.

un·be·liev·a·ble /ˌənbəˈlēvəbəl/ ▶ **adjective 1** so extreme as to be difficult to believe; extraordinary: *the rent is unbelievable!* **2** not likely to be true.

> – SYNONYMS **incredible,** inconceivable, unthinkable, unimaginable, unconvincing, far-fetched, implausible, improbable; informal hard to swallow.

– DERIVATIVES **un·be·liev·a·bly** /-ˈlēvəblē/ adverb.

un·be·liev·er /ˌənbəˈlēvər/ ▶ **noun** a person who does not believe in God or a particular religion.

un·be·liev·ing /ˌənbəˈlēviNG/ ▶ **adjective** feeling or showing that one does not believe someone or something.

un·bend /ˌənˈbend/ ▶ **verb** (past and past part. **unbent**) **1** make or become straight. **2** become less formal or strict.

un·bend·ing /ˌənˈbendiNG/ ▶ **adjective** strict and unwilling to change one's views; inflexible.

> – SYNONYMS **uncompromising,** inflexible, unyielding, hard-line, tough, strict, firm, resolute, determined, unrelenting, inexorable, intransigent, immovable.

un·bi·ased /ˌənˈbīəst/ ▶ **adjective** showing no prejudice; impartial.

> – SYNONYMS **impartial,** unprejudiced, neutral, nonpartisan, disinterested, detached, dispassionate, objective, even-handed, fair.

> **WORD TOOLKIT**
>
> See **EQUITABLE**.

un·bid·den /ˌənˈbidn/ ▶ **adjective 1** without having been invited. **2** (of a thought or feeling) arising without conscious effort.

un·bleached /ˌənˈblēCHt/ ▶ **adjective** (especially of paper, cloth, or flour) not bleached.

un·blem·ished /ˌənˈblemisHt/ ▶ **adjective** not damaged or marked in any way.

un·blink·ing /ˌənˈbliNGkiNG/ ▶ **adjective** (of a description or look) direct, thorough, and honest: *an unblinking portrait of the man and the writer.*
– DERIVATIVES **un·blink·ing·ly** adverb.

un·block /ˌənˈbläk/ ▶ **verb** remove an obstruction from something.

un·blush·ing /ˌənˈbləsHiNG/ ▶ **adjective** not feeling or showing embarrassment or shame.
– DERIVATIVES **un·blush·ing·ly** adverb.

un·bolt /ˌənˈbōlt/ ▶ **verb** open a door or window by drawing back a bolt.

un·born /ˌənˈbôrn/ ▶ **adjective** (of a baby) not yet born.

> – SYNONYMS **expected,** embryonic, fetal, in utero.

un·bos·om /ˌənˈbo͝ozəm/ ▶ **verb** old use (**unbosom oneself**) reveal one's thoughts or secrets.

un·bound /ˌənˈbound/ ▶ **adjective 1** not restricted or tied up: *they were unbound by convention.* **2** (of printed pages) not bound together.

un·bound·ed /ˌən'boundid/ ▸ adjective having no limits.

un·bowed /ˌən'boud/ ▸ adjective not having given in to pressure or defeat.

un·break·a·ble /ˌən'brākəbəl/ ▸ adjective not liable to break or able to be broken.

– SYNONYMS **shatterproof,** indestructible, durable, toughened, laminated, sturdy, stout, hard-wearing, heavy-duty.
– ANTONYMS fragile.

un·breath·a·ble /ˌən'brēTHəbəl/ ▸ adjective (of air) not fit or pleasant to breathe.

un·bridge·a·ble /ˌən'brijəbəl/ ▸ adjective (of a gap or difference between people or opinions) not able to be closed or made less significant.

un·bri·dled /ˌən'brīdld/ ▸ adjective not controlled; unrestrained: *a night of unbridled passion.*

un·bro·ken /ˌən'brōkən/ ▸ adjective **1** not broken; intact. **2** not interrupted or disturbed. **3** (of a record) not beaten. **4** (of a horse) not broken in.

– SYNONYMS **1 undamaged,** unharmed, unscathed, untouched, sound, intact, whole. **2 uninterrupted,** continuous, endless, constant, unremitting, ongoing. **3 unbeaten,** undefeated, unsurpassed, unrivaled, unmatched, supreme.

un·buck·le /ˌən'bəkəl/ ▸ verb unfasten the buckle of a belt, shoe, etc.

un·built /ˌən'bilt/ ▸ adjective (of buildings or land) not yet built or built on.

un·bun·dle /ˌən'bəndl/ ▸ verb **1** market or charge for items or services separately rather than as part of a package. **2** split a company or conglomerate into its constituent businesses, especially before selling them off.

un·bur·den /ˌən'bərdn/ ▸ verb **1** (**unburden oneself**) talk to someone about a worry or problem, so that one feels less anxious. **2** (**be unburdened**) not be burdened or worried.

un·burned /ˌən'bərnd/ (also chiefly Brit. **unburnt** /ˌən'bərnt/) ▸ adjective not damaged or destroyed by fire.

un·but·ton /ˌən'bətn/ ▸ verb **1** unfasten the buttons of an item of clothing. **2** informal relax and become less inhibited.

un·called /ˌən'kôld/ ▸ adjective (**uncalled for**) not desirable, justified, or necessary: *we got a reprimand that was totally uncalled for.*

un·can·ny /ˌən'kanē/ ▸ adjective (**uncannier, uncanniest**) **1** strange or mysterious. **2** so accurate or intense as to be unsettling: *he bore an uncanny resemblance to the current prime minister.*

– SYNONYMS **1 eerie,** unnatural, unearthly, other-worldly, ghostly, strange, abnormal, weird; informal creepy, spooky. **2 striking,** remarkable, extraordinary, exceptional, incredible.

– DERIVATIVES **un·can·ni·ly** adverb.

un·cared /ˌən'ke(ə)rd/ ▸ adjective (**uncared for**) not looked after properly.

un·car·ing /ˌən'ke(ə)riNG/ ▸ adjective not sympathetic to or concerned about others.
– DERIVATIVES **un·car·ing·ly** adverb.

un·cas·trat·ed /ˌən'kastrātid/ ▸ adjective (of a male animal) not castrated.

un·ceas·ing /ˌən'sēsiNG/ ▸ adjective not stopping; continuous.
– DERIVATIVES **un·ceas·ing·ly** adverb.

un·cer·e·mo·ni·ous /ˌənserə'mōnēəs/ ▸ adjective lacking courtesy; rude or abrupt.
– DERIVATIVES **un·cer·e·mo·ni·ous·ly** adverb.

un·cer·tain /ˌən'sərtn/ ▸ adjective **1** not known, reliable, or definite: *an uncertain future.* **2** not completely confident or sure.

– SYNONYMS **1** *the effects are uncertain* **unknown,** debatable, open to question, in doubt, in the balance, up in the air, unpredictable, unforeseeable, undetermined; informal iffy. **2** *he was uncertain about the decision* **unsure,** doubtful, dubious, undecided, irresolute, hesitant, vacillating, vague, unclear, ambivalent, in two minds.
– ANTONYMS certain, sure.

– DERIVATIVES **un·cer·tain·ly** adverb.
– PHRASES **in no uncertain terms** clearly and forcefully.

un·cer·tain·ty /ˌən'sərtntē/ ▸ noun (pl. **uncertainties**) **1** the state of being uncertain. **2** something that is uncertain or makes one feel uncertain.

CHOOSE THE RIGHT WORD

uncertainty, doubt, dubiety, skepticism

If you're not sure about something, you're probably experiencing a degree of **uncertainty**, which is a general term covering everything from a mere lack of absolute certainty (*uncertainty about the time of the dinner party*) to an almost complete lack of knowledge that makes it impossible to do more than guess at the result or outcome (*uncertainty about the country's future*). **Doubt** implies both uncertainty and an inability to make a decision because the evidence is insufficient (*considerable doubt as to her innocence*). **Dubiety** comes closer in meaning to *uncertainty* than to *doubt*, because it stresses a lack of sureness rather than an inability to reach a decision; but unlike *uncertainty*, it connotes wavering or fluctuating between one conclusion and another (*no one could fail to notice the dubiety in his voice*). If you exhibit **skepticism**, you are not so much uncertain as unwilling to believe. It usually refers to an habitual state of mind or to a customary reaction (*she always listened to his excuses with skepticism*).

un·chal·lenge·a·ble /ˌən'CHalənjəbəl/ ▸ adjective not able to be questioned or opposed.

un·chal·lenged /ˌən'CHalənjd/ ▸ adjective **1** not questioned or opposed: *the report's findings did not go unchallenged.* **2** not called on to prove one's identity.

un·chal·leng·ing /ˌən'CHalənjiNG/ ▸ adjective not demanding or testing one's abilities.

un·change·a·ble /ˌən'CHānjəbəl/ ▸ adjective not liable to change or able to be altered.

un·changed /ˌən'CHānjd/ ▸ adjective not changed; unaltered.

un·chang·ing /ˌən'CHānjiNG/ ▸ adjective remaining the same.
– DERIVATIVES **un·chang·ing·ly** adverb.

un·char·ac·ter·is·tic /ˌənkariktə'ristik/ ▸ adjective not typical of a particular person or thing.
– DERIVATIVES **un·char·ac·ter·is·ti·cal·ly** /-ik(ə)lē/ adverb.

un·char·is·mat·ic /ˌənkariz'matik/ ▸ adjective lacking the charm that can inspire admiration in others.

un·char·i·ta·ble /ˌənˈCHaritəbəl/ ▶ adjective unkind or unsympathetic to others.
– DERIVATIVES **un·char·i·ta·bly** /-blē/ adverb.

un·chart·ed /ˌənˈCHärtid/ ▶ adjective (of an area of land or sea) not mapped or surveyed.

un·checked /ˌənˈCHekt/ ▶ adjective (of something undesirable) not controlled or restrained.

un·chiv·al·rous /ˌənˈSHivəlrəs/ ▶ adjective (of a man) discourteous, especially toward women.

un·chris·tian /ˌənˈkrisCHən/ ▶ adjective **1** not in accordance with the teachings of Christianity. **2** unkind or unfair: *she felt an unchristian hope that he stepped on a sea urchin.*

un·ci·al /ˈənsHəl, -sēəl/ ▶ adjective written in rounded separated letters similar to modern capital letters, as found in manuscripts of the 4th–8th centuries. ▶ noun an uncial letter or manuscript.
– ORIGIN from Latin *uncia* 'inch'; the connection is unclear.

un·cir·cum·cised /ˌənˈsərkəmˌsīzd/ ▶ adjective (of a boy or man) not circumcised.

un·civ·il /ˌənˈsivəl/ ▶ adjective not polite; discourteous.

un·civ·i·lized /ˌənˈsivəˌlīzd/ ▶ adjective **1** not having developed a modern culture or way of life. **2** not behaving in accordance with accepted moral or social standards.

> – SYNONYMS **uncouth,** coarse, rough, boorish, vulgar, philistine, uneducated, uncultured, benighted, unsophisticated, ill-bred, barbarian, primitive, savage.

un·clad /ˌənˈklad/ ▶ adjective not wearing any clothes; naked.

un·claimed /ˌənˈklāmd/ ▶ adjective not having been claimed.

un·clasp /ˌənˈklasp/ ▶ verb **1** unfasten a clasp or similar device. **2** release the grip of: *I unclasped her fingers from my hair.*

un·clas·si·fi·a·ble /ˌənˈklasəˌfīəbəl/ ▶ adjective not able to be put into a particular category.

un·clas·si·fied /ˌənˈklasəˌfīd/ ▶ adjective **1** not put into categories. **2** not officially classed as secret.

un·cle /ˈəNGkəl/ ▶ noun the brother of one's father or mother or the husband of one's aunt.
– ORIGIN Latin *avunculus* 'maternal uncle.'

un·clean /ˌənˈklēn/ ▶ adjective **1** not clean; dirty. **2** morally wrong. **3** (of food) regarded in a particular religion as impure and unfit to be eaten.

un·clean·li·ness /ˌənˈklenlēnis/ ▶ noun the state of being dirty.

un·clear /ˌənˈkli(ə)r/ ▶ adjective **1** difficult to see, hear, or understand. **2** confused or not certain about something: *we are unclear about how to classify this activity.*

> – SYNONYMS **uncertain,** unsure, unsettled, up in the air, in doubt, ambiguous, equivocal, indefinite, vague, mysterious, obscure, hazy, nebulous.
> – ANTONYMS clear, evident.

un·cleared /ˌənˈkli(ə)rd/ ▶ adjective **1** (of land) not cleared of vegetation. **2** (of a check) not having passed through a clearinghouse and been paid into a person's account.

un·clench /ˌənˈklenCH/ ▶ verb release a clenched part of the body.

Un·cle Sam /sam/ ▶ noun the US or its federal government, often shown as a man with a tall hat and a white beard.
– ORIGIN said to be an expansion of the letters US.

Un·cle Tom /täm/ ▶ noun derogatory a black man considered to be excessively obedient or servile to white people.
– ORIGIN the hero of H. B. Stowe's *Uncle Tom's Cabin.*

un·climbed /ˌənˈklīmd/ ▶ adjective (of a mountain or rock face) not previously climbed.
– DERIVATIVES **un·climb·a·ble** /-ˈklīməbəl/ adjective.

un·clip /ˌənˈklip/ ▶ verb (**unclips, unclipping, unclipped**) release something from being fastened or held with a clip.

un·clog /ˌənˈklôg, -ˈkläg/ ▶ verb (**unclogs, unclogging, unclogged**) remove a blockage from something.

un·clothed /ˌənˈklōT͟Hd/ ▶ adjective wearing no clothes; naked.

un·cloud·ed /ˌənˈkloudid/ ▶ adjective **1** (of the sky) not dark or overcast. **2** not troubled or spoiled by anything.

un·clut·tered /ˌənˈklətərd/ ▶ adjective not cluttered by too many objects or unnecessary items.

un·coil /ˌənˈkoil/ ▶ verb straighten from a coiled position.

un·col·ored /ˌənˈkələrd/ ▶ adjective **1** having no color. **2** not influenced: *her views were uncolored by her husband's.*

un·combed /ˌənˈkōmd/ ▶ adjective (of a person's hair) not combed.

un·com·fort·a·ble/ ˌənˈkəmfərtəbəl, -ˈkəmftərbəl/ ▶ adjective **1** causing slight physical discomfort. **2** uneasy or awkward: *an uncomfortable silence.*

> – SYNONYMS **1 painful,** awkward, lumpy, confining, cramped. **2 uneasy,** ill at ease, awkward, nervous, tense, edgy, restless, embarrassed, anxious; informal rattled, twitchy.
> – ANTONYMS comfortable, relaxed.

– DERIVATIVES **un·com·fort·a·bly** /-blē/ adverb.

un·com·mer·cial /ˌənkəˈmərSHəl/ ▶ adjective not making or intended to make a profit.

un·com·mon /ˌənˈkämən/ ▶ adjective **1** out of the ordinary; unusual. **2** remarkably great.

> – SYNONYMS **unusual,** abnormal, rare, atypical, exceptional, unconventional, unfamiliar, strange, extraordinary, peculiar, scarce, few and far between, isolated, infrequent.

– DERIVATIVES **un·com·mon·ly** adverb.

un·com·mu·ni·ca·tive /ˌənkəˈmyo͞onəkətiv, -ˌkātiv/ ▶ adjective unwilling to talk or give out information.

> – SYNONYMS **taciturn,** quiet, unforthcoming, reserved, reticent, laconic, tongue-tied, silent, tight-lipped; guarded, secretive, close, private; distant, remote, aloof, withdrawn; informal mum, standoffish.
> – ANTONYMS talkative.

un·com·pet·i·tive /ˌənkəmˈpetətiv/ ▶ adjective not cheaper or better than others and therefore not able to compete commercially.

un·com·plain·ing /ˌənkəmˈplāniNG/ ▶ adjective not complaining about an unpleasant situation.
– DERIVATIVES **un·com·plain·ing·ly** adverb.

un·com·pli·cat·ed /ˌənˈkämpləˌkātid/ ▶ **adjective** simple or straightforward.

– SYNONYMS **simple,** straightforward, clear, accessible, undemanding, unchallenging, unsophisticated, trouble-free, painless, effortless, easy, elementary, idiot-proof; informal a piece of cake, child's play, a cinch, a breeze.
– ANTONYMS complex.

un·com·pli·men·ta·ry /ˌənkämpləˈmentərē, -ˈmentrē/ ▶ **adjective** not expressing praise; rude or insulting.

un·com·pre·hend·ing /ˌənˌkämpriˈhendiNG/ ▶ **adjective** not able to understand something.
– DERIVATIVES **un·com·pre·hend·ing·ly** adverb.

un·com·pro·mis·ing /ˌənˈkämprəˌmīziNG/ ▶ **adjective** **1** unwilling to change one's mind or behavior; resolute. **2** harsh or relentless: *uncompromising club music.*

– SYNONYMS **inflexible,** unbending, unyielding, unshakable, resolute, rigid, hard-line, immovable, intractable, firm, determined, iron-willed, obstinate, stubborn, adamant, obdurate, intransigent, headstrong, pigheaded.
– ANTONYMS flexible.

– DERIVATIVES **un·com·pro·mis·ing·ly** adverb.

un·con·cealed /ˌənkənˈsēld/ ▶ **adjective** (especially of an emotion) not concealed; obvious.

un·con·cern /ˌənkənˈsərn/ ▶ **noun** a lack of worry or interest.

un·con·cerned /ˌənkənˈsərnd/ ▶ **adjective** not concerned or interested.
– DERIVATIVES **un·con·cern·ed·ly** /-ˈsərnədlē/ adverb.

un·con·di·tion·al /ˌənkənˈdisHənl, -ˈdisHnəl/ ▶ **adjective** not subject to any conditions or requirements.

– SYNONYMS **unquestioning,** unqualified, unreserved, unlimited, unrestricted, wholehearted, complete, total, entire, full, absolute, unequivocal.

– DERIVATIVES **un·con·di·tion·al·ly** adverb.

un·con·di·tioned /ˌənkənˈdisHənd/ ▶ **adjective** (of behavior) not formed or influenced by conditioning or learning; instinctive.

un·con·fi·dent /ˌənˈkänfədənt, -fəˌdent/ ▶ **adjective** not confident; shy or hesitant.

un·con·fined /ˌənkənˈfīnd/ ▶ **adjective** **1** not confined to a limited space. **2** (of joy or excitement) very great.

un·con·firmed /ˌənkənˈfərmd/ ▶ **adjective** not yet confirmed as true or valid.

un·con·gen·ial /ˌənkənˈjēnyəl/ ▶ **adjective** **1** not friendly or pleasant to be with. **2** not suitable for or encouraging something: *the atmosphere was uncongenial to good conversation.*

un·con·nect·ed /ˌənkəˈnektid/ ▶ **adjective** **1** not joined together or to something else. **2** not associated or linked in a sequence.

un·con·quer·a·ble /ˌənˈkäNGk(ə)rəbəl/ ▶ **adjective** not able to be conquered or overcome.

un·con·scion·a·ble /ˌənˈkänsH(ə)nəbəl/ ▶ **adjective** **1** not morally right. **2** excessive: *he takes an unconscionable time to get there.*
– DERIVATIVES **un·con·scion·a·bly** /-blē/ adverb.
– ORIGIN from former *conscionable* 'conscientious.'

un·con·scious /ˌənˈkänsHəs/ ▶ **adjective** **1** not awake and aware of and responding to one's surroundings. **2** done or existing without realizing. **3** (**unconscious of**) unaware of.

– SYNONYMS **1 knocked out,** senseless, comatose, inert, stunned; informal out cold, down for the count. **2 subconscious,** instinctive, involuntary, uncontrolled, subliminal; informal gut. **3 unaware,** oblivious, ignorant, in ignorance, heedless.
– ANTONYMS aware.

▶ **noun** (**the unconscious**) the part of the mind that cannot be accessed by the conscious mind but that affects behavior and emotions.
– DERIVATIVES **un·con·scious·ly** adverb **un·con·scious·ness** noun.

un·con·se·crat·ed /ˌənˈkänsiˌkrātid/ ▶ **adjective** not made or declared to be holy or sacred.

un·con·sid·ered /ˌənkənˈsidərd/ ▶ **adjective** **1** not thought about carefully. **2** not fully appreciated.

un·con·sti·tu·tion·al /ˌənˌkänstəˈt(y)o͞osHənl/ ▶ **adjective** not in accordance with the constitution of a country or the rules of an organization.
– DERIVATIVES **un·con·sti·tu·tion·al·ly** adverb.

un·con·strained /ˌənkənˈstrānd/ ▶ **adjective** not restricted or limited.

un·con·sum·mat·ed /ˌənˈkänsəˌmātid/ ▶ **adjective** (of a marriage or relationship) not having been consummated by having sex.

un·con·tain·a·ble /ˌənkənˈtānəbəl/ ▶ **adjective** (especially of an emotion) very strong.

un·con·tam·i·nat·ed /ˌənkənˈtaməˌnātid/ ▶ **adjective** not contaminated by something impure or harmful.

un·con·ten·tious /ˌənkənˈtencHəs/ ▶ **adjective** not causing or likely to cause disagreement or controversy.

un·con·test·ed /ˌənkənˈtestid/ ▶ **adjective** not contested or challenged.

un·con·trived /ˌənkənˈtrīvd/ ▶ **adjective** not appearing artificial.

un·con·trol·la·ble /ˌənkənˈtrōləbəl/ ▶ **adjective** not able to be controlled.

– SYNONYMS **unmanageable,** ungovernable, wild, unruly, disorderly, irrepressible, unstoppable, recalcitrant, undisciplined; violent, frenzied, furious, mad, hysterical, passionate; formal refractory.
– ANTONYMS compliant.

– DERIVATIVES **un·con·trol·la·bly** adverb.

un·con·trolled /ˌənkənˈtrōld/ ▶ **adjective** not controlled or restricted.

un·con·tro·ver·sial /ˌənˌkäntrəˈvərsHəl/ ▶ **adjective** not causing debate or conflicting opinions.
– DERIVATIVES **un·con·tro·ver·sial·ly** adverb.

un·con·ven·tion·al /ˌənkənˈvensHənl/ ▶ **adjective** not in accordance with what is generally done or believed: *his unconventional approach to life.*

– SYNONYMS **unusual,** irregular, unorthodox, unfamiliar, uncommon, unwonted, out of the ordinary, atypical, singular, alternative, different; new, novel, innovative, groundbreaking, pioneering, original, unprecedented; eccentric, idiosyncratic, quirky, odd, strange, bizarre, weird, outlandish, curious; extraordinary; nonconformist, bohemian, avant-garde; informal way out, far out, offbeat, wacky, madcap, zany, kooky.
– ANTONYMS orthodox.

– DERIVATIVES **un·con·ven·tion·al·i·ty** /-ˌvensHəˈnalətē/ noun **un·con·ven·tion·al·ly** adverb.

un·con·vinced /ˌənkənˈvinst/ ▶ **adjective** not certain that something is true or can be relied on.

un·con·vinc·ing /ˌənkənˈvinsiNG/ ▶ **adjective** failing to convince or impress.
– DERIVATIVES **un·con·vinc·ing·ly** adverb.

un·cooked /ˌənko͝okt/ ▶ **adjective** not cooked; raw.

un·cool /ˌənˈko͞ol/ ▶ **adjective** informal not fashionable or impressive.

un·co·op·er·a·tive /ˌənkōˈäp(ə)rətiv/ ▶ **adjective** unwilling to help others or do what they ask.

– SYNONYMS **unhelpful,** awkward, disobliging, recalcitrant, perverse, contrary, stubborn, willful, unyielding, unbending, inflexible, immovable, obstructive.
– ANTONYMS obliging.

un·co·or·di·nat·ed /ˌənkōˈôrdnˌātid/ ▶ **adjective** **1** badly organized. **2** (of a person or their movements) clumsy.

un·cork /ˌənˈkôrk/ ▶ **verb** pull the cork out of a bottle.

un·cor·rob·o·rat·ed /kəˈräbəˌrātid/ ▶ **adjective** not supported or confirmed by evidence.

un·count·a·ble /ˌənˈkountəbəl/ ▶ **adjective** too many to be counted.

un·count·ed /ˌənˈkountid/ ▶ **adjective** **1** not counted. **2** very numerous.

un·cou·ple /ˌənˈkəpəl/ ▶ **verb** disconnect something from something else.

un·couth /ˌənˈko͞oTH/ ▶ **adjective** lacking good manners or sophistication.

– SYNONYMS **uncivilized,** uncultured, rough, coarse, crude, loutish, boorish, rude, discourteous, disrespectful, bad-mannered, ill-bred.
– ANTONYMS civilized.

– ORIGIN Old English, 'unknown.'

un·cov·er /ˌənˈkəvər/ ▶ **verb** **1** remove a cover or covering from someone or something. **2** discover something previously secret or unknown.

– SYNONYMS **1 expose,** reveal, lay bare, unwrap, unveil, strip. **2 discover,** detect, come across, stumble on, chance on, find, turn up, unearth, dig up.

un·cov·ered /ˌənˈkəvərd/ ▶ **adjective** not covered by something.

un·crit·i·cal /ˌənˈkritikəl/ ▶ **adjective** not willing to criticize or judge someone or something.
– DERIVATIVES **un·crit·i·cal·ly** /-ik(ə)lē/ adverb.

un·cross /ˌənˈkrôs, -ˈkräs/ ▶ **verb** move something back from a crossed position.

un·crowd·ed /ˌənˈkroudid/ ▶ **adjective** (of a place) not crowded.

un·crowned /ˌənˈkround/ ▶ **adjective** not formally crowned as a monarch.

unc·tion /ˈəNG(k)SHən/ ▶ **noun** **1** formal the smearing of someone with oil or ointment as a religious ceremony. **2** excessive politeness or flattery.
– ORIGIN Latin.

unc·tu·ous /ˈəNG(k)CHo͞oəs/ ▶ **adjective** excessively flattering or friendly.

– DERIVATIVES **unc·tu·ous·ly** adverb **unc·tu·ous·ness** noun.

un·cul·ti·vat·ed /ˌənˈkəltəˌvātid/ ▶ **adjective** **1** (of land) not used for growing crops. **2** not highly educated.

un·cul·tured /ˌənˈkəlCHərd/ ▶ **adjective** not having good taste, manners, or education.

un·cured /ˌənˈkyo͝ord/ ▶ **adjective** (of food) not preserved by salting, drying, or smoking.

un·curl /ˌənˈkərl/ ▶ **verb** straighten from a curled position.

un·cut /ˌənˈkət/ ▶ **adjective** **1** not cut or shaped by cutting. **2** (of a written work, movie, or performance) left in its complete form; not censored or abridged.

un·dam·aged /ˌənˈdamijd/ ▶ **adjective** not harmed or damaged.

un·dat·ed /ˌənˈdātid/ ▶ **adjective** not provided or marked with a date.

un·daunt·ed /ˌənˈdôntid, -ˈdänt-/ ▶ **adjective** not discouraged by difficulty, danger, or disappointment.

un·de·ceive /ˌəndiˈsēv/ ▶ **verb** tell someone that an idea or belief is mistaken.

un·de·cid·ed /ˌəndiˈsīdid/ ▶ **adjective** **1** not having made a decision; uncertain. **2** not settled or resolved: *the ship's fate is still undecided.*
– DERIVATIVES **un·de·cid·ed·ly** adverb.

un·de·ci·pher·a·ble /ˌəndiˈsīf(ə)rəbəl/ ▶ **adjective** (of speech or writing) not able to be read or understood.

un·de·feat·ed /ˌəndiˈfētid/ ▶ **adjective** not defeated.

un·de·fend·ed /ˌəndiˈfendid/ ▶ **adjective** not defended.

un·de·fined /ˌəndiˈfīnd/ ▶ **adjective** not clear or defined.
– DERIVATIVES **un·de·fin·a·ble** adjective.

un·de·mand·ing /ˌəndəˈmandiNG, ˌəndēˈmandiNG/ ▶ **adjective** (especially of a task) not demanding.

un·dem·o·crat·ic /ˌəndeməˈkratik/ ▶ **adjective** not according to democratic principles.
– DERIVATIVES **un·dem·o·crat·i·cal·ly** /-ik(ə)lē/ adverb.

un·de·mon·stra·tive /ˌəndiˈmänstrətiv/ ▶ **adjective** not tending to express feelings openly.

un·de·ni·a·ble /ˌəndiˈnīəbəl/ ▶ **adjective** unable to be denied or questioned.

– SYNONYMS **indisputable,** indubitable, unquestionable, beyond doubt, undebatable, incontrovertible, irrefutable, unassailable; certain, sure, definite, positive, conclusive, self-evident, patent, unequivocal.
– ANTONYMS questionable.

– DERIVATIVES **un·de·ni·a·bly** /-blē/ adverb.

un·der /ˈəndər/ ▶ **preposition** **1** extending or directly below. **2** below or behind something covering or protecting. **3** at a lower level, layer, or grade than. **4** lower than a specified amount, rate, or norm. **5** expressing submission or control: *I was under his spell.* **6** as provided for by the rules of; in accordance with. **7** used to express grouping or classification. **8** undergoing a process.

– SYNONYMS **1 below,** beneath, underneath. **2 less than,** lower than, below. **3 subordinate to,** answerable to, responsible to, subject to, junior to, inferior to.
– ANTONYMS above, over.

▶ **adverb** **1** extending or directly below something.

2 affected by an anesthetic; unconscious.
– PHRASES **under way 1** having started and making progress. **2** (of a boat) moving through the water.
– ORIGIN Old English.

under- ▶ **prefix 1** below; beneath: *undercover*. **2** lower in status: *undersecretary*. **3** insufficiently; incompletely: *undernourished*.

un·der·a·chieve /ˌəndərəˈCHēv/ ▶ **verb** do less well than is expected.
– DERIVATIVES **un·der·a·chieve·ment** noun **un·der·a·chiev·er** noun.

un·der·age /ˌəndərˈāj/ ▶ **adjective** too young to take part legally in a particular activity.

un·der·arm /ˈəndərˌärm/ ▶ **adjective & adverb** (of a throw or stroke in sports) made with the arm or hand below shoulder level. ▶ **noun** a person's armpit.

un·der·bel·ly /ˈəndərˌbelē/ ▶ **noun** (pl. **underbellies**) **1** the soft underside or abdomen of an animal. **2** a hidden and unpleasant or criminal part of society.

un·der·bid /ˌəndərˈbid/ ▶ **verb** (**underbidding**; past and past part. **underbid**) (especially when trying to secure a contract) make a lower bid than someone else.

un·der·bite /ˈəndərˌbīt/ ▶ **noun** the projection of the lower teeth beyond the upper.

un·der·brush /ˈəndərˌbrəSH/ ▶ **noun** undergrowth in a forest.

un·der·car·riage /ˈəndərˌkarij/ ▶ **noun 1** a wheeled structure beneath an aircraft that supports the aircraft on the ground. **2** the supporting frame under the body of a vehicle.

un·der·charge /ˌəndərˈCHärj/ ▶ **verb** charge someone a price or amount that is too low.

un·der·class /ˈəndərˌklas/ ▶ **noun** the lowest social class in a country or community, consisting of the poor and unemployed.

un·der·clothes /ˈəndərˌklō(TH)z/ ▶ **plural noun** clothes worn under others next to the skin.
– DERIVATIVES **un·der·cloth·ing** noun.

un·der·coat /ˈəndərˌkōt/ ▶ **noun** a layer of paint applied after the primer and before the topcoat.

un·der·cook /ˌəndərˈko͝ok, ˈəndərˌko͝ok/ ▶ **verb** cook food for too short a time.

un·der·cov·er /ˌəndərˈkəvər/ ▶ **adjective & adverb** involving secret work for the purposes of investigation or spying.

> – SYNONYMS **secret,** covert, clandestine, underground, surreptitious, furtive, cloak-and-dagger, stealthy; informal hush-hush.
> – ANTONYMS overt.

un·der·croft /ˈəndərˌkrôft, -ˌkräft/ ▶ **noun** the crypt of a church.
– ORIGIN from the rare term *croft* 'crypt.'

un·der·cur·rent /ˈəndərˌkərənt/ ▶ **noun 1** a hidden or underlying feeling or influence: *I sensed an undercurrent of resentment among the other girls*. **2** a current of water below the surface, moving in a different direction from any surface current.

un·der·cut /ˌəndərˈkət/ ▶ **verb** (**undercutting**; past and past part. **undercut**) **1** offer goods or services at a lower price than a competitor. **2** weaken or undermine: *his authority was being undercut*. **3** cut or wear away the part below or under something.

un·der·de·vel·oped /ˌəndərdiˈveləpt/ ▶ **adjective 1** not fully developed. **2** (of a country or region) not economically advanced.
– DERIVATIVES **un·der·de·vel·op·ment** noun.

un·der·dog /ˈəndərˌdôg, -ˌdäg/ ▶ **noun** a competitor thought to have little chance of winning a fight or contest.

un·der·done /ˌəndərˈdən/ ▶ **adjective** (of food) not cooked for long enough.

un·der·dress /ˌəndərˈdres/ ▶ **verb** (**be underdressed**) be dressed too plainly or too informally for a particular occasion.

un·der·em·ployed /ˌəndərimˈploid/ ▶ **adjective** not having enough work, or not having work that makes full use of one's abilities.
– DERIVATIVES **un·der·em·ploy·ment** noun.

un·der·es·ti·mate /ˌəndərˈestəˌmāt/ ▶ **verb 1** estimate something to be smaller or less important than it really is. **2** regard someone as less capable than they really are.

> – SYNONYMS **underrate,** undervalue, miscalculate, misjudge, do an injustice to.
> – ANTONYMS overestimate.

▶ **noun** /-mit/ an estimate that is too low.
– DERIVATIVES **un·der·es·ti·ma·tion** /-ˌestəˈmāSHən/ noun.

un·der·ex·pose /ˌəndərikˈspōz/ ▶ **verb** expose photographic film for too short a time.
– DERIVATIVES **un·der·ex·po·sure** /-ˈspōZHər/ noun.

un·der·fed /ˌəndərˈfed/ ▶ **adjective** having had too little to eat.

un·der·foot /ˌəndərˈfo͝ot/ ▶ **adverb 1** under one's feet; on the ground. **2** constantly present and in one's way.

un·der·fund /ˌəndərˈfənd/ ▶ **verb** fail to provide an organization, project, etc., with enough funding.
– DERIVATIVES **un·der·fund·ing** noun.

un·der·gar·ment /ˈəndərˌgärmənt/ ▶ **noun** an item of underclothing.

un·der·glaze /ˈəndərˌglāz/ ▶ **noun** color or decoration applied to pottery before the glaze is applied.

un·der·go /ˌəndərˈgō/ ▶ **verb** (**undergoes**; past **underwent** /ˌəndərˈwent/; past part. **undergone** /ˌəndərˈgôn/) experience or be subjected to something unpleasant or difficult.

> – SYNONYMS **experience,** go through, submit to, face, be subjected to, receive, endure, brave, bear, withstand, weather.

– ORIGIN Old English, 'undermine.'

un·der·grad /ˈəndərˌgrad/ ▶ **noun** informal an undergraduate.

un·der·grad·u·ate /ˌəndərˈgrajəwit/ ▶ **noun** a student at a college or university who has not yet earned a bachelor's degree.

un·der·ground /ˌəndərˈground/ ▶ **adjective & adverb 1** beneath the surface of the ground. **2** in secrecy or hiding. **3** favoring alternative or experimental forms of lifestyle or artistic expression.

> – SYNONYMS **1 subterranean,** buried, sunken. **2 secret,** clandestine, surreptitious, covert, undercover, closet, cloak-and-dagger, resistance, subversive.

▶ **noun 1** a group or movement organized secretly to

work against an existing government. **2** Brit. a subway.

– SYNONYMS **metro**; N. Amer. subway; Brit. informal tube.

un·der·growth /ˈəndərˌgrōTH/ ▶ **noun** a dense growth of shrubs and other plants.

un·der·hand /ˈəndərˌhand/ ▶ **adjective 1** underarm. **2** (usu. **underhanded**) acting or done in a secret or dishonest way.

un·der·lay[1] ▶ **noun** /ˈəndərˌlā/ material laid under a carpet for protection or support. ▶ **verb** /ˌəndərˈlā/ (past and past part. **underlaid**) place something under something else, especially to support or raise it.

un·der·lay[2] /ˌəndərˈlā/ past tense of **UNDERLIE**.

un·der·lie /ˌəndərˈlī/ ▶ **verb** (**underlying**; past **underlay**; past part. **underlain**) lie or be situated under something.

un·der·line /ˈəndərˌlīn/ ▶ **verb 1** draw a line under a word or phrase to give emphasis. **2** emphasize: *he underlined the importance of spending on health and education.*

– SYNONYMS **1 underscore,** mark, point out, emphasize, highlight. **2 emphasize,** stress, highlight, accentuate, accent, focus on, spotlight.

▶ **noun** a line drawn under a word or phrase.

un·der·ling /ˈəndərliNG/ ▶ **noun** chiefly derogatory a person of lower rank or status.

un·der·lit /ˌəndərˈlit/ ▶ **adjective** not having enough light or lighting; dim.

un·der·ly·ing /ˌəndərˈlī-iNG/ ▶ **adjective** basic or fundamental: *the underlying aims of the research.*

– SYNONYMS **fundamental,** basic, primary, central, essential, principal, elementary, initial.

un·der·man /ˌəndərˈman/ ▶ **verb** (**undermans, undermanning, undermanned**) fail to provide an organization with enough workers.

un·der·mine /ˌəndərˈmīn, ˈəndərˌmīn/ ▶ **verb 1** damage or weaken: *an attempt to undermine the president's authority.* **2** wear away the base or foundation of a rock formation. **3** dig or excavate beneath a building or fortification so as to make it collapse.

– SYNONYMS **weaken,** diminish, reduce, impair, mar, spoil, ruin, damage, sap, shake, threaten, subvert, compromise, sabotage.
– ANTONYMS strengthen.

un·der·neath /ˌəndərˈnēTH/ ▶ **preposition & adverb 1** situated directly below. **2** so as to be partly or wholly concealed by. ▶ **noun** the part or side facing toward the ground.
– ORIGIN Old English.

un·der·nour·ished /ˌəndərˈnərisHt, -ˈnə-risht/ ▶ **adjective** not having enough food or the right type of food for good health.
– DERIVATIVES **un·der·nour·ish·ment** noun.

un·der·paid /ˌəndərˈpād/ past and past participle of **UNDERPAY**.

un·der·pants /ˈəndərˌpan(t)s/ ▶ **plural noun** an undergarment covering the lower part of the torso and having two holes for the legs.

un·der·part /ˈəndərˌpärt/ ▶ **noun** a lower part or portion.

un·der·pass /ˈəndərˌpas/ ▶ **noun** a road or pedestrian tunnel passing under another road or a railroad.

un·der·pay /ˌəndərˈpā/ ▶ **verb** (past and past part. **underpaid**) pay someone too little, or pay less than is due for something.

un·der·per·form /ˌəndərpərˈfôrm/ ▶ **verb** perform less well than expected.
– DERIVATIVES **un·der·per·for·mance** noun.

un·der·pin /ˌəndərˈpin/ ▶ **verb** (**underpins, underpinning, underpinned**) **1** support, justify, or form the basis for an argument, claim, etc. **2** support a structure from below by laying a solid foundation or replacing weak materials with stronger ones.

un·der·play /ˌəndərˈplā, ˈəndərˌplā/ ▶ **verb** represent something as being less important than it really is.

un·der·priv·i·leged /ˌəndərˈpriv(ə)lijd/ ▶ **adjective** not enjoying the same rights or standard of living as the majority of the population.

un·der·rate /ˌəndə(r)ˈrāt/ ▶ **verb** (often as adj. **underrated**) fail to recognize the quality, value, or importance of someone or something.

un·der·re·port /ˌəndə(r)riˈpôrt/ ▶ **verb** fail to report news or data fully.

un·der·rep·re·sent /ˌəndə(r)ˌrepriˈzent/ ▶ **verb** (**be underrepresented**) form a disproportionately small percentage: *women are underrepresented in the Senate.*

un·der·re·sourced /ˌəndə(r)ˈrēˌsôrst, -riˈsôrst/ ▶ **adjective** provided with insufficient resources.

un·der·score /ˈəndərˌskôr, ˌəndərˈskôr/ ▶ **verb & noun** another term for **UNDERLINE**.

un·der·sea /ˌəndərˈsē/ ▶ **adjective** relating to or situated below the sea or the surface of the sea.

un·der·sec·re·tar·y /ˌəndərˈsekriˌterē/ ▶ **noun** (pl. **undersecretaries**) **1** (in the US) the chief assistant to a member of the cabinet. **2** (in the UK) a junior minister or senior civil servant.

un·der·sell /ˌəndərˈsel/ ▶ **verb** (past and past part. **undersold**) **1** sell something at a lower price than a competitor. **2** fail to represent someone's or something's true quality or worth.

un·der·sexed /ˌəndərˈsekst/ ▶ **adjective** having unusually weak sexual desires.

un·der·shirt /ˈəndərˌsHərt/ ▶ **noun** an undergarment worn under a shirt.

un·der·shoot /ˌəndərˈsHo͞ot/ ▶ **verb** (past and past part. **undershot**) **1** (of an aircraft) land short of the runway. **2** fall short of a point or target.

un·der·shorts /ˈəndərˌsHôrts/ ▶ **plural noun** men's underpants.

un·der·side /ˈəndərˌsīd/ ▶ **noun** the bottom or lower side or surface of something.

un·der·signed /ˈəndərˌsīnd/ ▶ **noun** (**the undersigned**) formal the person or people who have signed the document in question.

un·der·sized /ˌəndərˈsīzd/ (also **undersize**) ▶ **adjective** smaller than the usual size.

un·der·skirt /ˈəndərˌskərt/ ▶ **noun** a petticoat.

un·der·sold /ˌəndərˈsōld/ past and past participle of **UNDERSELL**.

un·der·spend /ˌəndərˈspend/ ▶ **verb** (past and past part. **underspent**) spend too little or less than planned.

un·der·staffed /ˌəndər'staft/ ▶ **adjective** (of an organization) having too few members of staff to operate effectively.

un·der·stand /ˌəndər'stand/ ▶ **verb** (past and past part. **understood**) **1** know or realize the intended meaning of words, a language, or a speaker. **2** be aware of the significance, explanation, or cause of something: *he didn't understand why we were laughing.* **3** be sympathetically aware of: *I understand how you feel.* **4** interpret or view something in a particular way. **5** believe to be the case from information received: *I understand you're at art school.* **6** assume that something is present or is the case: *he liked to play the field, that was understood.*

– SYNONYMS **1 comprehend,** grasp, take in, see, apprehend, follow, make sense of, fathom; informal work out, figure out, make heads or tails of, get. **2 know,** realize, recognize, acknowledge, appreciate, be aware of, be conscious of. **3 believe,** gather, take it, hear (tell), notice, see, learn.

un·der·stand·a·ble /ˌəndər'standəbəl/ ▶ **adjective** **1** able to be understood. **2** to be expected; natural, reasonable, or forgivable.

– SYNONYMS **1 comprehensible,** intelligible, clear, plain, unambiguous, transparent, straightforward, explicit, coherent. **2 unsurprising,** expected, predictable, inevitable, reasonable, acceptable, logical, rational, normal, natural, justifiable, excusable, pardonable, forgivable.
– ANTONYMS incomprehensible.

– DERIVATIVES **un·der·stand·a·bly** /-blē/ adverb.

un·der·stand·ing /ˌəndər'standiNG/ ▶ **noun** **1** the ability to understand something. **2** the power of abstract thought; intellect. **3** a person's interpretation or judgment of a situation. **4** sympathetic awareness or tolerance. **5** an informal or unspoken agreement or arrangement.

– SYNONYMS **1 comprehension,** grasp, mastery, appreciation, knowledge, awareness, skill, expertise, proficiency; informal know-how. **2 intellect,** intelligence, brainpower, judgment, insight, intuition, acumen, sagacity, wisdom. **3 belief,** perception, view, conviction, feeling, opinion, intuition, impression. **4 sympathy,** compassion, pity, feeling, concern, consideration, kindness, sensitivity, decency, goodwill. **5 agreement,** arrangement, deal, bargain, settlement, pledge, pact.
– ANTONYMS ignorance.

▶ **adjective** sympathetically aware of other people's feelings.

– SYNONYMS **sympathetic,** compassionate, sensitive, considerate, kind, thoughtful, tolerant, patient, forbearing, lenient, forgiving.

– DERIVATIVES **un·der·stand·ing·ly** adverb.

un·der·state /ˌəndər'stāt/ ▶ **verb** describe or represent something as being smaller or less important than it really is.

– SYNONYMS **play down,** underrate, underplay, trivialize, minimize, diminish, downgrade, brush aside, gloss over.
– ANTONYMS exaggerate.

– DERIVATIVES **un·der·state·ment** noun.

un·der·stat·ed /ˌəndər'stātid/ ▶ **adjective** presented or expressed in a subtle and effective way.
– DERIVATIVES **un·der·stat·ed·ly** adverb.

un·der·steer /ˌəndər'sti(ə)r/ ▶ **verb** (of a motor vehicle) have a tendency to turn less sharply than is intended.

un·der·stood /ˌəndər'stŏŏd/ past and past participle of **UNDERSTAND**.

un·der·sto·ry /'əndərˌstôrē/ ▶ **noun** (pl. **understories**) Ecology a layer of vegetation beneath the top branches of the trees in a forest.

un·der·stud·y /'əndərˌstədē/ ▶ **noun** (pl. **understudies**) an actor who learns another's role in order to be able to act in their absence. ▶ **verb** (**understudies, understudying, understudied**) be an understudy for another actor.

un·der·take /ˌəndər'tāk/ ▶ **verb** (past **undertook** /ˌəndər'tŏŏk/; past part. **undertaken** /ˌəndər'tākn/) **1** make oneself responsible for carrying out a project, activity, etc.; take something on: *a firm of builders undertook the construction work.* **2** formally guarantee or promise to do something.

– SYNONYMS **1 set about,** embark on, go about, engage in, take on, be responsible for, get down to, tackle, attempt; informal have a go at. **2 promise,** pledge, vow, give one's word, swear, guarantee, contract, give an assurance, commit oneself.

un·der·tak·er /'əndərˌtākər/ ▶ **noun** a funeral director.

– SYNONYMS **funeral director,** mortician.

un·der·tak·ing /'əndərˌtākiNG, ˌəndər'tā-/ ▶ **noun** **1** a formal promise to do something. **2** a task or project that is taken on by someone. **3** the management of funerals as a profession.

– SYNONYMS **1 promise,** pledge, agreement, oath, covenant, vow, commitment, guarantee, assurance. **2 enterprise,** venture, project, campaign, scheme, plan, operation, endeavor, effort, task.

un·der·tone /'əndərˌtōn/ ▶ **noun** **1** a subdued or muted tone of sound or color. **2** an underlying quality or feeling.

un·der·tow /'əndərˌtō/ ▶ **noun** another term for **UNDERCURRENT**.

un·der·use ▶ **verb** /ˌəndər'yōōz/ fail to make enough use of something. ▶ **noun** /ˌəndər'yōōs/ insufficient use of something.
– DERIVATIVES **un·der·used** adjective.

un·der·u·ti·lize /ˌəndər'yōōtlˌīz/ ▶ **verb** underuse something.

un·der·val·ue /ˌəndər'valyōō/ ▶ **verb** (**undervalues, undervalued, undervaluing**) **1** fail to recognize someone's or something's importance or worth. **2** underestimate something's financial value.

un·der·wa·ter /ˌəndər'wôtər, -'wätər/ ▶ **adjective & adverb** situated or happening beneath the surface of the water.

– SYNONYMS **submerged,** sunken, undersea, submarine.

un·der·way /ˌəndər'wā/ ▶ **adjective** variant of **UNDER WAY** (see **UNDER**).

USAGE

The spelling **underway** is best avoided in formal writing: use **under way** instead.

un·der·wear /'əndərˌwer/ ▶ **noun** clothing worn under other clothes next to the skin.

– SYNONYMS **underclothes,** undergarments, underthings, lingerie; informal undies.

un·der·weight /ˈəndərˌwāt, ˌəndərˈwāt/ ▸ **adjective** below a weight considered normal or desirable.

un·der·went /ˌəndərˈwent/ past of **UNDERGO**.

un·der·whelm /ˌəndərˈ(h)welm/ ▸ **verb** humorous fail to impress or make a positive impact on someone.
– ORIGIN suggested by **OVERWHELM**.

un·der·wire /ˈəndərˌwīr/ ▸ **noun** a semicircular wire support stitched under each cup of a bra. ▸ **adjective** (of a bra) having such a wire.

un·der·world /ˈəndərˌwərld/ ▸ **noun 1** the world of criminals or of organized crime. **2** (in myths and legends) the home of the dead, imagined as being under the earth.

un·der·write /ˈəndə(r)ˌrīt, ˌəndə(r)ˈrīt/ ▸ **verb** (past **underwrote** /ˈəndə(r)ˌrōt, ˌəndə(r)ˈrōt/; past part. **underwritten** /ˈəndə(r)ˌritn, ˌəndə(r)ˈritn/) **1** sign and accept liability under an insurance policy. **2** undertake to finance or otherwise support or guarantee something.

– SYNONYMS **sponsor,** support, back, insure, indemnify, subsidize, pay for, finance, fund; informal bankroll.

– DERIVATIVES **un·der·writ·er** noun.

un·de·scend·ed /ˌəndiˈsendid/ ▸ **adjective** (of a testicle) remaining in the abdomen instead of descending normally into the scrotum.

un·de·served /ˌəndiˈzərvd/ ▸ **adjective** not deserved or earned.
– DERIVATIVES **un·de·serv·ed·ly** /-ˈzərvədlē/ adverb.

un·de·serv·ing /ˌəndiˈzərviNG/ ▸ **adjective** not deserving or worthy of something.

un·de·sir·a·ble /ˌəndiˈzīrəbəl/ ▸ **adjective** not wanted or desirable because harmful, offensive, or unpleasant.

– SYNONYMS **unpleasant,** disagreeable, nasty, unwelcome, unwanted, unfortunate.
– ANTONYMS pleasant.

▸ **noun** an unpleasant or offensive person.
– DERIVATIVES **un·de·sir·a·bil·i·ty** noun **un·de·sir·a·bly** /-blē/ adverb.

un·de·sired /ˌəndiˈzīrd/ ▸ **adjective** not wanted or desired.

un·de·tect·a·ble /ˌəndiˈtektəbəl/ ▸ **adjective** not able to be detected.

WORD TOOLKIT

See **INVISIBLE**.

un·de·tect·ed /ˌəndiˈtektid/ ▸ **adjective** not detected or discovered.

un·de·ter·mined /ˌəndiˈtərmənd/ ▸ **adjective** not firmly decided or settled.

un·de·terred /ˌəndiˈtərd/ ▸ **adjective** persevering despite setbacks.

un·de·vel·oped /ˌəndiˈveləpt/ ▸ **adjective** not having developed or been developed.

un·de·vi·at·ing /ˌənˈdēvēˌātiNG/ ▸ **adjective** showing no deviation; constant and steady.

un·di·ag·nosed /ˌəndīəgˈnōst/ ▸ **adjective** not diagnosed.

un·did /ˌənˈdid/ past of **UNDO**.

un·dies /ˈəndēz/ ▸ **plural noun** informal articles of underwear.

un·dif·fer·en·ti·at·ed /ˌənˌdifəˈrenCHēˌātid/ ▸ **adjective** not different or differentiated.

un·di·gest·ed /ˌəndəˈjestəd, -ˌdī-/ ▸ **adjective 1** (of food) not digested. **2** (of information) not having been properly understood or absorbed.

un·dig·ni·fied /ˌənˈdigniˌfīd/ ▸ **adjective** appearing foolish; lacking in dignity.

un·di·lut·ed /ˌəndiˈlo͞otid, -dī-/ ▸ **adjective 1** (of a liquid) not diluted. **2** (of a feeling or quality) not mixed or combined with any other: *pure, undiluted happiness.*

un·di·min·ished /ˌəndiˈminisHt/ ▸ **adjective** not reduced or lessened.

un·dimmed /ˌənˈdimd/ ▸ **adjective** not dimmed; still bright or intense.

un·dip·lo·mat·ic /ˌənˌdipləˈmatik/ ▸ **adjective** insensitive and tactless.
– DERIVATIVES **un·dip·lo·mat·i·cal·ly** /-ik(ə)lē/ adverb.

un·di·rect·ed /ˌəndəˈrektəd, -ˌdī-/ ▸ **adjective** lacking a proper plan or purpose.

un·dis·cern·ing /ˌəndiˈsərniNG/ ▸ **adjective** lacking judgment or taste.

un·dis·ci·plined /ˌənˈdisəplind/ ▸ **adjective** uncontrolled in behavior or manner.

un·dis·closed /ˌəndisˈklōzd/ ▸ **adjective** not revealed or made known.

un·dis·cov·ered /ˌəndisˈkəvərd/ ▸ **adjective** not discovered.

un·dis·crim·i·nat·ing /ˌəndisˈkriməˌnātiNG/ ▸ **adjective** lacking good judgment or taste.

un·dis·guised /ˌəndisˈgīzd/ ▸ **adjective** (of a feeling) not disguised or concealed; open.

un·dis·mayed /ˌəndisˈmād/ ▸ **adjective** not dismayed or discouraged by a setback.

un·dis·put·ed /ˌəndiˈspyo͞otid/ ▸ **adjective** not disputed or called into question.

un·dis·tin·guished /ˌəndiˈstiNGgwisHt/ ▸ **adjective** lacking distinction; not very good or impressive.

un·dis·turbed /ˌəndisˈtərbd/ ▸ **adjective** not disturbed.

un·di·vid·ed /ˌəndəˈvīdid/ ▸ **adjective 1** not divided, separated, or broken into parts. **2** devoted completely to one person or thing: *you have my undivided attention.*

– SYNONYMS **complete,** full, total, whole, entire, absolute, unqualified, unreserved, unmitigated, unbroken, consistent, thorough, exclusive, dedicated; focused, engrossed, absorbed, attentive, committed.

un·do /ˌənˈdo͞o/ ▸ **verb** (**undoes** /ˌənˈdəs/; past **undid** /ˌənˈdid/; past part. **undone** /ˌənˈdən/) **1** unfasten or loosen. **2** cancel or reverse the effects of (a previous action or measure). **3** formal cause the downfall or ruin of.

– SYNONYMS **1 unfasten,** unbutton, unhook, untie, unlace, unlock, unbolt, loosen, detach, free, open. **2 cancel,** reverse, overrule, overturn, repeal, rescind, countermand, revoke, annul, invalidate, negate. **3 ruin,** undermine, overturn, scotch, sabotage, spoil, impair, mar, destroy, wreck; informal blow.
– ANTONYMS fasten.

un·do·cu·ment·ed /ˌənˈdäkyəˌmentid/ ▸ **adjective** not recorded in or proved by documents.

un·do·ing /ˌənˈdo͞o-iNG/ ▶ **noun** a person's ruin or downfall.

un·done /ˌənˈdən/ ▶ **adjective 1** not tied or fastened. **2** not done or finished. **3** formal or humorous ruined by a disastrous setback.

un·doubt·ed /ˌənˈdoutid/ ▶ **adjective** not questioned or doubted by anyone.

un·doubt·ed·ly /ˌənˈdoutidlē/ ▶ **adverb** without doubt: *they are undoubtedly guilty.*

– SYNONYMS **doubtless,** indubitably, unquestionably, indisputably, undeniably, incontrovertibly, without (a) doubt, clearly.

un·dreamed /ˌənˈdrēmd/ (also **undreamt** /-ˈdremt/) ▶ **adjective** (**undreamed of**) not previously thought to be possible.

un·dress /ˌənˈdres/ ▶ **verb 1** (also **get undressed**) take off one's clothes. **2** take the clothes off someone else. ▶ **noun 1** the state of being naked or only partially clothed. **2** Military ordinary clothing or uniform, as opposed to full dress.

un·dressed /ˌənˈdrest/ ▶ **adjective 1** wearing no clothes; naked. **2** not treated, processed, or prepared for use. **3** (of food) not having a dressing.

un·drink·a·ble /ˌənˈdriNGkəbəl/ ▶ **adjective** not fit to be drunk because of impurity or poor quality.

un·due /ˌənˈd(y)o͞o/ ▶ **adjective** more than is reasonable or necessary; excessive.

– SYNONYMS **excessive,** immoderate, intemperate, inordinate, disproportionate, uncalled for, unnecessary, unwarranted, unjustified, unreasonable, inappropriate, unmerited, unsuitable, improper.
– ANTONYMS appropriate.

– DERIVATIVES **un·du·ly** adverb.

un·du·lant /ˈənjələnt, ˈəndyə-/ ▶ **adjective** undulating.

un·du·late /ˈənjəˌlāt, ˈəndyə-/ ▶ **verb 1** move with a smooth wavelike motion. **2** have a wavy form or outline.
– DERIVATIVES **un·du·la·tion** /ˌənjəˈlāSHən, ˌəndyə-/ noun **un·du·la·to·ry** /ˈənjələˌtôrē, ˈəndyə-/ adjective.
– ORIGIN from Latin *unda* 'a wave.'

un·dyed /ˌənˈdīd/ ▶ **adjective** (of fabric) not dyed; of its natural color.

un·dy·ing /ˌənˈdī-iNG/ ▶ **adjective** lasting forever.

un·earned /ˌənˈərnd/ ▶ **adjective** not earned or deserved.

un·earned in·come ▶ **noun** income from private means (such as investments) rather than from work.

un·earth /ˌənˈərTH/ ▶ **verb 1** find something in the ground by digging. **2** discover something by investigation or searching.

– SYNONYMS **1 dig up,** excavate, exhume, disinter, root out. **2** *I unearthed an interesting fact* **discover,** find, come across, hit on, bring to light, expose, turn up.

un·earth·ly /ˌənˈərTHlē/ ▶ **adjective 1** unnatural or mysterious. **2** informal unreasonably early or inconvenient: *an unearthly hour.*

un·ease /ˌənˈēz/ ▶ **noun** anxiety or discontent.

un·eas·y /ˌənˈēzē/ ▶ **adjective** (**uneasier, uneasiest**) **1** anxious or uncomfortable. **2** liable to change; not settled: *an uneasy truce.*

– SYNONYMS **1 worried,** anxious, troubled, disturbed, nervous, nervy, tense, edgy, on edge, apprehensive, fearful, uncomfortable, unsettled, ill at ease; informal jittery. **2** *an uneasy peace* **tense,** awkward, strained, fraught, precarious, unstable, insecure.
– ANTONYMS calm.

– DERIVATIVES **un·eas·i·ly** adverb **un·eas·i·ness** noun.

un·eat·a·ble /ˌənˈētəbəl/ ▶ **adjective** not fit to be eaten.

un·eat·en /ˌənˈētn/ ▶ **adjective** not eaten.

un·ec·o·nom·ic /ˌənˌekəˈnämik, -ˌēkə-/ ▶ **adjective** not profitable or making efficient use of resources.

un·ec·o·nom·i·cal /ˌənˌekəˈnämikəl, -ˌēkə-/ ▶ **adjective** wasteful of money or other resources; not economical.

un·ed·i·fy·ing /ˌənˈedəˌfī-iNG/ ▶ **adjective** arousing disapproval; distasteful or unpleasant.

un·ed·it·ed /ˌənˈeditid/ ▶ **adjective** (of material for publication or broadcasting) not edited.

un·ed·u·cat·ed /ˌənˈejəˌkātid/ ▶ **adjective** poorly educated.

un·e·lect·ed /ˌəniˈlektid/ ▶ **adjective** (of an official) not elected.

un·em·bar·rassed /ˌənemˈbarəst/ ▶ **adjective** not feeling or showing embarrassment.

un·e·mo·tion·al /ˌəniˈmōSHənl/ ▶ **adjective** not having or showing strong feelings.
– DERIVATIVES **un·e·mo·tion·al·ly** adverb.

un·em·ploy·a·ble /ˌənimˈploi-əbəl/ ▶ **adjective** not able or likely to get paid employment because of a lack of skills or qualifications.

un·em·ployed /ˌənimˈploid/ ▶ **adjective 1** without a paid job but available to work. **2** (of a thing) not in use.

– SYNONYMS **jobless,** out of work, laid off.

un·em·ploy·ment /ˌənimˈploimənt/ ▶ **noun 1** the state of being unemployed. **2** the number or proportion of unemployed people.

un·em·ploy·ment ben·e·fit ▶ **noun** payment made by a government or labor union to an unemployed person.

un·en·closed /ˌənenˈklōzd/ ▶ **adjective** (especially of land) not enclosed.

un·en·cum·bered /ˌənenˈkəmbərd/ ▶ **adjective** not burdened or prevented from moving or acting freely.

un·end·ing /ˌənˈendiNG/ ▶ **adjective** seeming to last or continue for ever.

CHOOSE THE RIGHT WORD

See **ETERNAL**.

un·en·dur·a·ble /ˌəninˈd(y)o͝orəbəl/ ▶ **adjective** not able to be tolerated or endured.

un·en·force·a·ble /ˌənenˈfôrsəbəl/ ▶ **adjective** (especially of a law) impossible to enforce.

un·en·light·ened /ˌənenˈlītnd/ ▶ **adjective** not enlightened in outlook.

un·en·ter·pris·ing /ˌənˈentərˌprīziNG/ ▶ **adjective** lacking initiative or resourcefulness.

un·en·thu·si·as·tic /ˌənenˌTHo͞ozēˈastik/ ▶ **adjective** not having or showing enthusiasm.
– DERIVATIVES **un·en·thu·si·as·ti·cal·ly** /-ik(ə)lē/ adverb.

WORD TOOLKIT

See **UNWILLING**.

un·en·vi·a·ble /ˌənˈenvēəbəl/ ▶ **adjective** difficult, undesirable, or unpleasant.

un·e·qual /ˌənˈēkwəl/ ▶ **adjective 1** not equal in quantity, size, or value. **2** not fair, evenly balanced, or having equal advantage. **3** (**unequal to**) not having the ability or resources to meet a challenge.
– DERIVATIVES **un·e·qual·ly** adverb.

un·e·qualed /ˌənˈēkwəld/ (Brit. **unequalled**) ▶ **adjective** better or greater than all others of the same kind.

un·e·quiv·o·cal /ˌəniˈkwivəkəl/ ▶ **adjective** leaving no doubt; completely clear in meaning.
– DERIVATIVES **un·e·quiv·o·cal·ly** /-ək(ə)lē/ adverb.

un·err·ing /ˌənˈəriNG, -ˈer-/ ▶ **adjective** always right or accurate.
– DERIVATIVES **un·err·ing·ly** adverb.

UNESCO /yo͞oˈneskō/ ▶ **abbreviation** United Nations Educational, Scientific, and Cultural Organization.

un·es·sen·tial /ˌənəˈsenCHəl/ ▶ **adjective** not essential or absolutely necessary.

un·eth·i·cal /ˌənˈeTHikəl/ ▶ **adjective** not morally correct or acceptable.
– DERIVATIVES **un·eth·i·cal·ly** /-ik(ə)lē/ adverb.

un·e·ven /ˌənˈēvən/ ▶ **adjective 1** not level or smooth. **2** not regular, consistent, or equal.

– SYNONYMS **1 bumpy,** rough, lumpy, stony, rocky, rutted. **2 irregular,** crooked, lopsided, askew, asymmetrical. **3 inconsistent,** variable, fluctuating, irregular, erratic, patchy, fitful.
– ANTONYMS flat, regular.

– DERIVATIVES **un·e·ven·ly** adverb **un·e·ven·ness** noun.

un·e·vent·ful /ˌəniˈventfəl/ ▶ **adjective** not marked by interesting or exciting events.
– DERIVATIVES **un·e·vent·ful·ly** adverb **un·e·vent·ful·ness** noun.

WORD TOOLKIT

See **INSIPID**.

un·ex·am·ined /ˌənigˈzamind/ ▶ **adjective** not investigated or examined.

un·ex·cep·tion·a·ble /ˌənikˈsepSH(ə)nəbəl/ ▶ **adjective** not open to objection, but not particularly new or exciting.

un·ex·cep·tion·al /ˌənikˈsepSHənl/ ▶ **adjective** not out of the ordinary; usual.
– DERIVATIVES **un·ex·cep·tion·al·ly** adverb.

un·ex·cit·ing /ˌənikˈsītiNG/ ▶ **adjective** not exciting; dull.

un·ex·pect·ed /ˌənikˈspektid/ ▶ **adjective** not expected or regarded as likely to happen.
– DERIVATIVES **un·ex·pect·ed·ly** adverb **un·ex·pect·ed·ness** noun.

un·ex·plained /ˌənikˈsplānd/ ▶ **adjective** not made clear or accounted for.
– DERIVATIVES **un·ex·plain·a·ble** adjective.

un·ex·plod·ed /ˌənikˈsplōdid/ ▶ **adjective** (of an explosive device) not having exploded.

un·ex·plored /ˌənikˈsplôrd/ ▶ **adjective** not explored, investigated, or evaluated.

un·ex·pressed /ˌənikˈsprest/ ▶ **adjective** (of a thought or feeling) not communicated or made known.

un·ex·pur·gat·ed /ˌənˈekspərˌgātid/ ▶ **adjective** (of a text) complete and containing all the original material; not censored.

un·fail·ing /ˌənˈfāliNG/ ▶ **adjective 1** without error. **2** reliable or constant.
– DERIVATIVES **un·fail·ing·ly** adverb.

un·fair /ˌənˈfe(ə)r/ ▶ **adjective** not based on or showing fairness.

– SYNONYMS **1 unjust,** prejudiced, biased, discriminatory, one-sided, unequal, uneven, unbalanced, partisan. **2 undeserved,** unmerited, unreasonable, unjustified; informal out of order. **3 unsporting,** dirty, underhanded/underhand, dishonorable, dishonest.
– ANTONYMS just, justified.

– DERIVATIVES **un·fair·ly** adverb **un·fair·ness** noun.

un·faith·ful /ˌənˈfāTHfəl/ ▶ **adjective 1** not faithful; disloyal. **2** having sex with a person other than one's husband, wife, or established partner.
– DERIVATIVES **un·faith·ful·ly** adverb **un·faith·ful·ness** noun.

WORD TOOLKIT

unfaithful ...	disloyal ...	seditious ...
wife/husband	subject	conspiracy
boyfriend/girlfriend	friend	act
lover	citizen	literature
partner	employee	ideas

un·fal·ter·ing /ˌənˈfôltəriNG/ ▶ **adjective** not faltering; steady or resolute.
– DERIVATIVES **un·fal·ter·ing·ly** adverb.

un·fa·mil·iar /ˌənfəˈmilyər/ ▶ **adjective 1** not known or recognized; uncharacteristic. **2** (**unfamiliar with**) not having knowledge or experience of something.
– DERIVATIVES **un·fa·mil·i·ar·i·ty** /-ˌmilēˈe(ə)ritē, -fəmilˈyer-/ noun.

WORD TOOLKIT

unfamiliar ...	novel ...	exotic ...
territory	idea	species
voice	approach	plants
surroundings	method	places
faces	solution	birds
situation	use	destinations
feeling	technique	fruit
language	technology	pets
landscape	insight	lands
streets	treatment	spices
sounds	theory	diseases

un·fash·ion·a·ble /ˌənˈfaSHənəbəl/ ▶ **adjective** not fashionable or popular.
– DERIVATIVES **un·fash·ion·a·bly** /-blē/ adverb.

un·fas·ten /ˌənˈfasən/ ▶ **verb** open the fastening of something.

– SYNONYMS **undo,** open, disconnect, untie, unbutton, unzip, loosen, free, unlock, unbolt.

un·fath·om·a·ble /ˌənˈfa<u>TH</u>əməbəl/ ▶ **adjective 1** too strange or difficult to be understood. **2** impossible to measure the depth or extent of.
– DERIVATIVES **un·fath·om·a·bly** /-blē/ adverb.

un·fa·vor·a·ble /ˌənˈfāv(ə)rəbəl/ (Brit. **unfavourable**) ▶ **adjective** **1** expressing lack of approval. **2** unlikely to lead to a successful outcome: *unfavorable economic conditions.*
– DERIVATIVES **un·fa·vor·a·bly** /-blē/ adverb.

un·fazed /ˌənˈfāzd/ ▶ **adjective** informal not disconcerted or worried by something unexpected.

un·fea·si·ble /ˌənˈfēzəbəl/ ▶ **adjective** inconvenient or impractical.
– DERIVATIVES **un·fea·si·bly** adverb.

un·feel·ing /ˌənˈfēliNG/ ▶ **adjective** unsympathetic, harsh, or callous.

– SYNONYMS **uncaring,** unsympathetic, unemotional, uncharitable; heartless, hard-hearted, harsh, austere, cold.
– ANTONYMS compassionate.

un·feigned /ˌənˈfānd/ ▶ **adjective** genuine; sincere.

un·fer·ment·ed /ˌənfərˈmentid/ ▶ **adjective** not fermented.

un·fer·ti·lized /ˌənˈfərtlˌīzd/ ▶ **adjective** not fertilized.

un·fet·tered /ˌənˈfetərd/ ▶ **adjective** unrestrained or uninhibited.

un·filled /ˌənˈfild/ ▶ **adjective** not filled; vacant or empty.

un·fin·ished /ˌənˈfinisHt/ ▶ **adjective** **1** not finished; incomplete. **2** not having been given an attractive surface appearance in manufacture.

un·fit /ˌənˈfit/ ▶ **adjective** **1** unsuitable or inadequate for something. **2** not in good physical condition.

– SYNONYMS **1** *a movie unfit for children* **unsuitable,** inappropriate, not designed. **2** *unfit for duty* **incapable of,** not up to, not equal to, unequipped for, inadequate for, unprepared for; informal not cut out for. **3 unhealthy,** out of condition/shape, debilitated.
– ANTONYMS suitable, healthy.

un·fit·ted /ˌənˈfitid/ ▶ **adjective** unfit for something.

un·fit·ting /ˌənˈfitiNG/ ▶ **adjective** unsuitable or unbecoming.

un·fixed /ˌənˈfikst/ ▶ **adjective** **1** unfastened; loose. **2** uncertain or variable.

un·flag·ging /ˌənˈflagiNG/ ▶ **adjective** not becoming tired or weak; remaining strong.
– DERIVATIVES **un·flag·ging·ly** adverb.

un·flap·pa·ble /ˌənˈflapəbəl/ ▶ **adjective** informal calm in a crisis.

un·flat·ter·ing /ˌənˈflatəriNG/ ▶ **adjective** not flattering.
– DERIVATIVES **un·flat·ter·ing·ly** adverb.

un·flinch·ing /ˌənˈflinCHiNG/ ▶ **adjective** not afraid or hesitant.
– DERIVATIVES **un·flinch·ing·ly** adverb.

un·fo·cused /ˌənˈfōkəst/ (also **unfocussed**) ▶ **adjective** **1** not focused; out of focus. **2** without a specific aim or direction.

un·fold /ˌənˈfōld/ ▶ **verb** **1** open or spread out from a folded position. **2** reveal or be revealed.

– SYNONYMS **1 open out,** spread out, flatten, straighten out, unroll, unfurl. **2 develop,** evolve, happen, take place, occur.

un·forced /ˌənˈfôrst/ ▶ **adjective** **1** produced naturally and without effort. **2** (of an action) not done as a result of pressure from another person.

un·fore·seen /ˌənfôrˈsēn, -fər-/ ▶ **adjective** not anticipated or predicted.
– DERIVATIVES **un·fore·see·a·ble** adjective.

un·for·get·ta·ble /ˌənfərˈgetəbəl/ ▶ **adjective** so enjoyable, impressive, etc., that it is impossible to forget.
– DERIVATIVES **un·for·get·ta·bly** /-blē/ adverb.

un·for·giv·a·ble /ˌənfərˈgivəbəl/ ▶ **adjective** so bad as to be unable to be forgiven or excused.
– DERIVATIVES **un·for·giv·a·bly** /-blē/ adverb.

un·for·giv·ing /ˌənfərˈgiviNG/ ▶ **adjective** **1** not willing to forgive or excuse faults. **2** (of conditions) harsh or hostile.

un·formed /ˌənˈfôrmd/ ▶ **adjective** **1** without a definite form. **2** not fully developed.

un·forth·com·ing /ˌənfôrTHˈkəmiNG/ ▶ **adjective** **1** not willing to reveal information. **2** not available when needed.

un·for·tu·nate /ˌənˈfôrCHənət/ ▶ **adjective** **1** having or marked by bad luck; unlucky. **2** regrettable or inappropriate: *an unfortunate remark.*

– SYNONYMS **1 unlucky,** hapless, ill-starred, star-crossed, wretched, poor, pitiful; informal down on one's luck. **2 unwelcome,** disadvantageous, unfavorable, unlucky, adverse, unpromising, inauspicious. **3 regrettable,** inappropriate, unsuitable, tactless, injudicious.
– ANTONYMS lucky.

▶ **noun** a person who suffers bad fortune.
– DERIVATIVES **un·for·tu·nate·ly** adverb.

un·found·ed /ˌənˈfoundid/ ▶ **adjective** having no basis in fact: *an unfounded rumor.*

un·freeze /ˌənˈfrēz/ ▶ **verb** (past **unfroze** /ˌənˈfrōz/; past part. **unfrozen** /ˌənˈfrōzən/) **1** thaw something frozen. **2** remove restrictions on the use of an asset.

un·friend·ly /ˌənˈfren(d)lē/ ▶ **adjective** (**unfriendlier, unfriendliest**) not friendly.

– SYNONYMS **hostile,** disagreeable, antagonistic, aggressive, unpleasant, surly, uncongenial, inhospitable, unneighborly, unwelcoming, unsociable, cool, cold, aloof, distant; informal standoffish.

– DERIVATIVES **un·friend·li·ness** noun.

un·frock /ˌənˈfräk/ ▶ **verb** another term for **DEFROCK**.

un·ful·filled /ˌənfo͝o(l)ˈfild/ ▶ **adjective** not fulfilled.
– DERIVATIVES **un·ful·fill·a·ble** adjective **un·ful·fill·ing** adjective.

un·fund·ed /ˌənˈfəndid/ ▶ **adjective** not receiving funds; not having a fund.

un·fun·ny /ˌənˈfənē/ ▶ **adjective** (**unfunnier, unfunniest**) (of something meant to be funny) not amusing.

un·furl /ˌənˈfərl/ ▶ **verb** spread out from a rolled or folded state.

un·fur·nished /ˌənˈfərnisHt/ ▶ **adjective** without furniture.

un·gain·ly /ˌənˈgānlē/ ▶ **adjective** clumsy or awkward.

– SYNONYMS **awkward,** clumsy, graceless, inelegant, gawky, gauche, uncoordinated.
– ANTONYMS graceful.

– DERIVATIVES **un·gain·li·ness** noun.
– ORIGIN from former *gainly* 'graceful,' from Old Norse.

un·gen·er·ous /ˌənˈjenərəs/ ▶ **adjective** not generous; stingy.

un·gen·tle·man·ly /ˌənˈjentlmənlē/ ▶ **adjective** (of a man's behavior) not well-mannered or pleasant.

un·glazed /ˌənˈglāzd/ ▶ **adjective** not glazed.

un·glued /ˌənˈglo͞od/ ▶ **adjective** not or no longer stuck.
– PHRASES **come unglued** informal **1** end in failure. **2** become confused or upset.

un·god·ly /ˌənˈgädlē/ ▶ **adjective 1** immoral or sinful. **2** informal unreasonably early or inconvenient: *telephone calls at ungodly hours.*
– DERIVATIVES **un·god·li·ness** noun.

un·gov·ern·a·ble /ˌənˈgəvərnəbəl/ ▶ **adjective** impossible to control or govern.

un·grace·ful /ˌənˈgrāsfəl/ ▶ **adjective** lacking in grace; clumsy.
– DERIVATIVES **un·grace·ful·ly** adverb.

un·gra·cious /ˌənˈgrāsнəs/ ▶ **adjective** not polite, kind, or pleasant.
– DERIVATIVES **un·gra·cious·ly** adverb.

un·gram·mat·i·cal /ˌəngrəˈmatikəl/ ▶ **adjective** not following grammatical rules.
– DERIVATIVES **un·gram·mat·i·cal·ly** /-ik(ə)lē/ adverb.

un·grate·ful /ˌənˈgrātfəl/ ▶ **adjective** not feeling or showing gratitude.
– DERIVATIVES **un·grate·ful·ly** adverb **un·grate·ful·ness** noun.

un·guard·ed /ˌənˈgärdid/ ▶ **adjective 1** without protection or a guard. **2** not well considered; careless: *an unguarded remark.*

un·guent /ˈənGgwənt/ ▶ **noun** a soft substance, especially a perfumed oil, used as ointment or for lubrication.
– ORIGIN Latin *unguentum.*

un·gu·late /ˈənGgyələt, -ˌlāt/ ▶ **noun** Zoology a mammal that has hoofs.
– ORIGIN from Latin *ungula* 'hoof.'

un·hand /ˌənˈhand/ ▶ **verb** old use or humorous release someone from one's grasp.

un·hap·py /ˌənˈhapē/ ▶ **adjective** (**unhappier, unhappiest**) **1** not happy. **2** not lucky; unfortunate.

> – SYNONYMS **1 sad,** miserable, sorrowful, dejected, despondent, disconsolate, morose, heartbroken, down, dispirited, downhearted, depressed, melancholy, mournful, gloomy, glum; informal down in the mouth, blue. **2** *unhappy with the service* **dissatisfied,** displeased, discontented, disappointed, disgruntled. **3 unfortunate,** unlucky, ill-starred, ill-fated, doomed; informal jinxed.
> – ANTONYMS happy, pleased.

– DERIVATIVES **un·hap·pi·ly** adverb **un·hap·pi·ness** noun.

un·harmed /ˌənˈhärmd/ ▶ **adjective** not harmed; uninjured.

UNHCR ▶ **abbreviation** United Nations High Commission for Refugees.

un·health·y /ˌənˈhelтнē/ ▶ **adjective** (**unhealthier, unhealthiest**) **1** not in good health. **2** likely to lead to illness or bad health: *an unhealthy diet.*

> – SYNONYMS **1 harmful,** detrimental, destructive, injurious, damaging, noxious, poisonous. **2 sick,** poorly, ill, unwell, unfit, ailing, weak, frail, infirm, washed out, rundown. **3 abnormal,** morbid, macabre, twisted, unwholesome, warped, depraved, unnatural; informal sick.

– DERIVATIVES **un·health·i·ly** adverb **un·health·i·ness** noun.

un·heard /ˌənˈhərd/ ▶ **adjective 1** not heard or listened to. **2** (**unheard of**) previously unknown.

un·heed·ed /ˌənˈhēdid/ ▶ **adjective** heard or noticed but ignored.

un·heed·ing /ˌənˈhēdiNG/ ▶ **adjective** not paying attention.

un·help·ful /ˌənˈhelpfəl/ ▶ **adjective** not helpful.
– DERIVATIVES **un·help·ful·ly** adverb **un·help·ful·ness** noun.

un·her·ald·ed /ˌənˈherəldid/ ▶ **adjective** not previously announced; without warning.

un·hes·i·tat·ing /ˌənˈheziˌtātiNG/ ▶ **adjective** without doubt or hesitation.
– DERIVATIVES **un·hes·i·tat·ing·ly** adverb.

un·hinge /ˌənˈhinj/ ▶ **verb** make someone mentally unbalanced.

un·his·tor·i·cal /ˌənhiˈstôrikəl, -ˈstär-/ ▶ **adjective** not in accordance with history or historical analysis.

un·ho·ly /ˌənˈhōlē/ ▶ **adjective** (**unholier, unholiest**) **1** sinful; wicked. **2** (of an alliance) unnatural and likely to be dangerous or harmful. **3** informal very bad: *an unholy row.*

un·hook /ˌənˈho͝ok/ ▶ **verb** unfasten or detach something held by a hook.

un·hoped /ˌənˈhōpt/ ▶ **adjective** (**unhoped for**) beyond one's hopes or expectations.

un·horse /ˌənˈhôrs/ ▶ **verb** make someone fall from a horse.

un·hur·ried /ˌənˈhərēd, -ˈhə-rēd/ ▶ **adjective** moving, acting, or taking place without haste or urgency.
– DERIVATIVES **un·hur·ried·ly** adverb.

un·hurt /ˌənˈhərt/ ▶ **adjective** not hurt or harmed.

un·hy·gi·en·ic /ˌənhīˈjēnik, ˌənhīˈjenik/ ▶ **adjective** not hygienic.

uni- ▶ **combining form** one; having or consisting of one: *unicycle.*
– ORIGIN from Latin *unus.*

U·ni·ate /ˈyo͞onēˌat, -it, -ˌāt/ (or **Uniat** /ˈyo͞onēˌat, -it/) ▶ **adjective** referring to any Christian community in eastern Europe or the Near East that acknowledges the supremacy of the pope but has its own liturgy.
– ORIGIN Russian *uniat.*

u·ni·cam·er·al /ˌyo͞onəˈkam(ə)rəl/ ▶ **adjective** (of a lawmaking assembly) having a single chamber.
– ORIGIN from Latin *camera* 'chamber.'

u·ni·cast /ˈyo͞oniˌkast/ ▶ **noun** transmission of a data package or an audiovisual signal to a single recipient.
– ORIGIN on the pattern of *broadcast.*

UNICEF /ˈyo͞onəˌsef/ ▶ **abbreviation** United Nations Children's Fund (originally United Nations International Children's Emergency Fund).

u·ni·cel·lu·lar /ˌyo͞onəˈselyələr/ ▶ **adjective** Biology consisting of a single cell.

u·ni·corn /ˈyo͞onəˌkôrn/ ▶ **noun** a mythical animal represented as a horse with a single straight horn

projecting from its forehead.
– ORIGIN Latin *unicornis*, from *cornu* 'horn.'

u·ni·cy·cle /'yo͞onə,sīkəl/ ▶ **noun** a cycle with a single wheel, chiefly used by acrobats.
– DERIVATIVES **u·ni·cy·clist** /-,sīklist/ noun.

un·i·den·ti·fi·a·ble /,ənī'dentə,fīəbəl/ ▶ **adjective** unable to be identified.

un·i·den·ti·fied /,ənī'dentə,fīəd/ ▶ **adjective** not recognized or identified.

un·id·i·o·mat·ic /,ən,idēə'matik/ ▶ **adjective** not using or containing expressions natural to a native speaker of a language.

u·ni·di·rec·tion·al /,yo͞onidi'reksʜənl/ ▶ **adjective** moving or operating in a single direction.

u·ni·fi·ca·tion /,yo͞onəfi'kāsʜən/ ▶ **noun** the process of being unified.

u·ni·form /'yo͞onə,fôrm/ ▶ **adjective** not varying in form or character; the same in all cases and at all times.

> – SYNONYMS **1 constant,** consistent, steady, invariable, unchanging, stable, static, regular, fixed, even. **2 identical,** matching, similar, equal, same, like, consistent.
> – ANTONYMS variable.

▶ **noun** the distinctive clothing worn by members of the same organization or by children attending certain schools.

> – SYNONYMS **costume,** outfit, suit, ensemble, livery, regalia; informal getup, rig, gear.

– DERIVATIVES **u·ni·formed** adjective **u·ni·form·i·ty** /,yo͞onə'fôrmətē/ noun **u·ni·form·ly** adverb.
– ORIGIN Latin *uniformis*.

u·ni·fy /'yo͞onə,fī/ ▶ **verb** (**unifies, unifying, unified**) make or become united or uniform.

> – SYNONYMS **unite,** combine, bring together, join, merge, fuse, amalgamate, coalesce, consolidate.
> – ANTONYMS separate.

– DERIVATIVES **u·ni·fi·er** noun.
– ORIGIN Latin *unificare*.

u·ni·lat·er·al /,yo͞onə'latərəl, -'latrəl/ ▶ **adjective** **1** performed by or affecting only one person, group, etc. **2** relating to or affecting only one side of an organ, the body, etc.
– DERIVATIVES **u·ni·lat·er·al·ism** /,yo͞onə'latərə,lizəm, -'latrə-/ noun **u·ni·lat·er·al·ist** noun & adjective **u·ni·lat·er·al·ly** adverb.

un·im·ag·i·na·ble /,ənə'maj(ə)nəbəl/ ▶ **adjective** impossible to imagine or understand.
– DERIVATIVES **un·im·ag·i·na·bly** /-blē/ adverb.

un·im·ag·i·na·tive /,ənə'maj(ə)nətiv/ ▶ **adjective** not using or displaying imagination; dull.
– DERIVATIVES **un·im·ag·i·na·tive·ly** adverb.

un·im·paired /,ənim'pe(ə)rd/ ▶ **adjective** not weakened or damaged.

un·im·peach·a·ble /,ənim'pēcʜəbəl/ ▶ **adjective** not able to be doubted, questioned, or criticized.
– DERIVATIVES **un·im·peach·a·bly** /-blē/ adverb.

un·im·ped·ed /,ənim'pēdid/ ▶ **adjective** not obstructed or hindered.

un·im·por·tant /,ənim'pôrtnt/ ▶ **adjective** lacking in importance.
– DERIVATIVES **un·im·por·tance** noun.

> **WORD TOOLKIT**
>
> See **MINOR**.

un·im·pressed /,ənim'prest/ ▶ **adjective** not impressed.

un·im·pres·sive /,ənim'presiv/ ▶ **adjective** not impressive.

un·im·proved /,ənim'pro͞ovd/ ▶ **adjective** (of land) not cleared or cultivated.

un·in·cor·po·rat·ed /,ənin'kôrpə,rātid, ,ənIɴɢ-/ ▶ **adjective** **1** not formed into a legal corporation. **2** not included as part of a whole.

un·in·form·a·tive /,ənin'fôrmətiv/ ▶ **adjective** not providing useful or interesting information.

un·in·formed /,ənin'fôrmd/ ▶ **adjective** lacking awareness or understanding of the facts.

> **WORD TOOLKIT**
>
> See **IGNORANT**.

un·in·hab·it·a·ble /,ənin'habətəbəl/ ▶ **adjective** not suitable for living in.

un·in·hab·it·ed /,ənin'habitid/ ▶ **adjective** without inhabitants.

un·in·hib·it·ed /,ənin'hibitid/ ▶ **adjective** expressing oneself or acting freely and naturally.
– DERIVATIVES **un·in·hib·it·ed·ly** adverb.

un·in·i·ti·at·ed /,ənə'nisʜē,ātid/ ▶ **adjective** without special knowledge or experience.

un·in·jured /,ən'injərd/ ▶ **adjective** not harmed or damaged.

un·in·spired /,ənin'spīrd/ ▶ **adjective** **1** not original or imaginative; dull. **2** not excited.

un·in·spir·ing /,ənin'spīrIɴɢ/ ▶ **adjective** not exciting or interesting.

un·in·stall /,ənin'stôl/ ▶ **verb** remove an application or file from a computer.
– DERIVATIVES **un·in·stall·er** noun.

un·in·sur·a·ble /,ənin'sʜo͝orəbəl/ ▶ **adjective** not eligible for insurance cover.

un·in·sured /,ənin'sʜo͝ord/ ▶ **adjective** not covered by insurance.

un·in·tel·li·gent /,ənin'teləjənt/ ▶ **adjective** lacking intelligence.

> **CHOOSE THE RIGHT WORD**
>
> See **STUPID**.

un·in·tel·li·gi·ble /,ənin'teləjəbəl/ ▶ **adjective** impossible to understand.
– DERIVATIVES **un·in·tel·li·gi·bil·i·ty** /-,teləjə'bilətē/ noun **un·in·tel·li·gi·bly** /-blē/ adverb.

un·in·tend·ed /,ənin'tendid/ ▶ **adjective** not planned or meant.

un·in·ten·tion·al /,ənin'tencʜənl/ ▶ **adjective** not done on purpose.
– DERIVATIVES **un·in·ten·tion·al·ly** adverb.

> **WORD TOOLKIT**
>
> See **SPONTANEOUS**.

un·in·ter·est·ed /ˌən'intristid, -'intəˌrestid/ ▸ **adjective** not interested or concerned.

> **USAGE**
>
> For an explanation of the meaning and use of **uninterested** and **disinterested**, see the note at **DISINTERESTED**.

un·in·ter·est·ing /ˌən'intristiNG, -'intəˌrestiNG/ ▸ **adjective** not interesting; dull.

> – SYNONYMS **boring,** dull, unexciting, tiresome, tedious, dreary, lifeless, humdrum, colorless, bland, insipid, banal, dry.
> – ANTONYMS exciting.

un·in·ter·rupt·ed /ˌənˌintə'rəptid/ ▸ **adjective** **1** continuous. **2** not obstructed: *an uninterrupted view*.
– DERIVATIVES **un·in·ter·rupt·ed·ly** adverb.

un·in·vit·ed /ˌənin'vītid/ ▸ **adjective** arriving or acting without invitation.

un·in·vit·ing /ˌənin'vītiNG/ ▸ **adjective** not attractive; unpleasant.

un·in·volved /ˌənin'välvd/ ▸ **adjective** not involved.

un·ion /'yo͞onyən/ ▸ **noun** **1** the action of uniting or the fact of being united: *he supported closer economic union with Europe*. **2** a labor union. **3** a society or association formed by people with a common interest or purpose. **4** (also **Union**) a political unit consisting of a number of states or provinces with the same central government. **5** (**the Union**) the northern states of the US in the American Civil War. **6** a state of harmony or agreement. **7** a marriage.

> – SYNONYMS **1 unification,** joining, merger, fusion, amalgamation, coalition, combination, synthesis, blend. **2 association,** league, guild, confederation, federation.
> – ANTONYMS separation.

– ORIGIN Latin, 'unity.'

un·ion·ist /'yo͞onyənist/ ▸ **noun** **1** a member of a labor union. **2** (**Unionist**) a person in favor of the union of Northern Ireland with Great Britain.
– DERIVATIVES **un·ion·ism** /-ˌnizəm/ noun.

un·ion·ize /'yo͞onyəˌnīz/ ▸ **verb** join or cause to join a labor union.
– DERIVATIVES **un·ion·i·za·tion** /ˌyo͞onyəni'zāSHən, -ˌnī'zā-/ noun.

Un·ion Jack (also **Union flag**) ▸ **noun** the national flag of the UK.

un·ion shop ▸ **noun** a place of work where employers may hire nonunion workers who must join a labor union within an agreed time.

un·ion suit ▸ **noun** dated a single undergarment combining shirt and pants.

u·ni·po·lar /ˌyo͞onə'pōlər/ ▸ **adjective** having or relating to a single pole or extremity.

u·nique /yo͞o'nēk/ ▸ **adjective** **1** being the only one of its kind; unlike anything else. **2** (**unique to**) belonging or connected to one particular person, group, or place. **3** very special or unusual.

> – SYNONYMS **1 distinctive,** individual, special, particular, specific, idiosyncratic, single, sole, lone, unrepeated, solitary, exclusive. **2 remarkable,** special, notable, unequaled, unparalleled, unmatched, unsurpassed, incomparable.
> – ANTONYMS common.

– DERIVATIVES **u·nique·ly** adverb **u·nique·ness** noun.
– ORIGIN French.

> **USAGE**
>
> Strictly speaking, since the main meaning of **unique** is 'being the only one of its kind,' it is impossible to use adverbs with it that modify its meaning, such as **really** or **quite**. However, **unique** has a less precise sense in addition to its main meaning: 'very special or unusual' (*a really unique opportunity*). Here, **unique** does not relate to an absolute state that cannot be modified, and so the use of **really** and similar adverbs is acceptable.

> **WORD TOOLKIT**
>
> See **EXCEPTIONAL**.

u·ni·sex /'yo͞onəˌseks/ ▸ **adjective** designed for both sexes.

u·ni·son /'yo͞onəsən, -zən/ ▸ **noun** **1** the fact of two or more things being said or happening at the same time. **2** a coincidence in pitch of musical sounds or notes.
– ORIGIN Latin *unisonus*, from *sonus* 'sound.'

u·nit /'yo͞onit/ ▸ **noun** **1** an individual thing or person that is complete in itself but that can also form part of a larger whole. **2** a device, part, or item of furniture with a particular function: *a sink unit*. **3** a self-contained or distinct section of a building or group of buildings. **4** a subdivision of a larger military grouping. **5** a standard quantity in terms of which other quantities may be expressed. **6** one as a number or quantity.

> – SYNONYMS **1 component,** part, section, segment, element, module, constituent, subdivision. **2 quantity,** measure, denomination. **3 group,** detachment, contingent, division, cell, faction, department, office, branch.

– DERIVATIVES **u·nit·ize** verb.
– ORIGIN from Latin *unus* 'one.'

u·ni·tard /'yo͞onəˌtärd/ ▸ **noun** a tight-fitting one-piece garment covering the whole body.
– ORIGIN from **UNI-** + **LEOTARD**.

U·ni·tar·i·an /ˌyo͞oni'te(ə)rēən/ ▸ **noun** a member of a Christian Church that believes in the unity of God and rejects the idea of the Trinity.
– DERIVATIVES **U·ni·tar·i·an·ism** /-ˌnizəm/ noun.
– ORIGIN Latin *unitarius*.

u·ni·tar·y /'yo͞oniˌterē/ ▸ **adjective** **1** forming a single entity or unit. **2** relating to a unit or units.

u·nite /yo͞o'nīt/ ▸ **verb** come or bring together for a common purpose or to form a whole: *councilors were united in their opposition to the plans*.

> – SYNONYMS **1 unify,** join, link, connect, combine, amalgamate, fuse, weld, bond, bring together. **2 join together,** join forces, combine, band together, ally, cooperate, collaborate, work together, team up. **3 merge,** mix, blend, mingle, combine.
> – ANTONYMS divide.

– DERIVATIVES **u·nit·ed** adjective **u·ni·tive** /'yo͞onətiv, yo͞o'nī-/ adjective.
– ORIGIN Latin *unire* 'join together,' from *unus* 'one.'

> **CHOOSE THE RIGHT WORD**
>
> See **JOIN**.

u·ni·ty /'yo͞onətē/ ▸ **noun** (pl. **unities**) **1** the state of being united or forming a whole. **2** a thing forming a complex whole. **3** Mathematics the number one.

– SYNONYMS **1 union,** unification, integration, amalgamation, coalition, federation, confederation. **2 harmony,** accord, cooperation, collaboration, agreement, consensus, solidarity. **3 oneness,** singleness, wholeness, uniformity, homogeneity.
– ANTONYMS disunity.

u·ni·ver·sal /ˌyo͞onəˈvərsəl/ ▶ **adjective** affecting or done by all people or things in the world or in a particular group; applicable to all cases: *the incidents caused universal concern.*

– SYNONYMS **general,** common, widespread, ubiquitous, comprehensive, global, worldwide, international.

– DERIVATIVES **u·ni·ver·sal·i·ty** /-vərˈsalətē/ noun.

u·ni·ver·sal·ist /ˌyo͞onəˈvərsəlist/ ▶ **noun** (in Christian belief) a person who believes that all humankind will eventually be saved.
– DERIVATIVES **u·ni·ver·sal·ism** /-ˌlizəm/ noun **u·ni·ver·sal·is·tic** /-ˌvərsəˈlistik/ adjective.

u·ni·ver·sal·ize /ˌyo͞onəˈvərsəˌlīz/ ▶ **verb** make something universal, or make something available for all.
– DERIVATIVES **u·ni·ver·sal·i·za·tion** /-ˌvərsəliˈzāsʜən/ noun.

u·ni·ver·sal joint ▶ **noun** a joint that can transmit rotary power by a shaft at any selected angle.

u·ni·ver·sal·ly /ˌyo͞onəˈvərsəlē/ ▶ **adverb** by everyone; in every case.

– SYNONYMS **always,** without exception, by everyone, in all cases, everywhere, worldwide, globally, internationally, commonly, generally.

U·ni·ver·sal Time (also **Universal Time Coordinated**) another term for **GREENWICH MEAN TIME**.

u·ni·verse /ˈyo͞onəˌvərs/ ▶ **noun 1** all existing matter and space considered as a whole; the cosmos. **2** a particular sphere of activity or experience.

– SYNONYMS **cosmos,** macrocosm, space, infinity, nature, all existence.

– ORIGIN Latin *universus* 'combined into one, whole.'

WORD LINKS

cosmic *relating to the universe*

u·ni·ver·si·ty /ˌyo͞onəˈvərsətē/ ▶ **noun** (pl. **universities**) a high-level educational institution in which students study for degrees and academic research is carried out.
– ORIGIN Latin *universitas* 'the whole.'

U·NIX /ˈyo͞oniks/ (also **Unix**) ▶ **noun** trademark a widely used multiuser computer operating system.

un·just /ˌənˈjəst/ ▶ **adjective** not just; unfair.
– DERIVATIVES **un·just·ly** adverb.

un·jus·ti·fi·a·ble /ˌənˈjəstəˌfīəbəl, -jəstəˈfī-/ ▶ **adjective** impossible to justify.
– DERIVATIVES **un·jus·ti·fi·a·bly** /-blē/ adverb.

un·jus·ti·fied /ˌənˈjəstəˌfīd/ ▶ **adjective** not justified.

un·kempt /ˌənˈkem(p)t/ ▶ **adjective** having an untidy or disheveled appearance.
– ORIGIN from former *kempt* 'combed.'

un·kind /ˌənˈkīnd/ ▶ **adjective** not sympathetic, caring, or kind.

– SYNONYMS **unpleasant,** disagreeable, nasty, mean, cruel, vicious, spiteful, malicious, callous, unsympathetic, uncharitable, harsh, hard-hearted, heartless, cold-hearted; informal bitchy, catty.

– DERIVATIVES **un·kind·ly** adverb **un·kind·ness** noun.

un·know·a·ble /ˌənˈnōəbəl/ ▶ **adjective** not able to be known.
– DERIVATIVES **un·know·a·bil·i·ty** /-ˌnōəˈbilətē/ noun.

un·know·ing /ˌənˈnō-iɴɢ/ ▶ **adjective** not knowing or aware. ▶ **noun** literary ignorance.
– DERIVATIVES **un·know·ing·ly** adverb.

un·known /ˌənˈnōn/ ▶ **adjective** not known or familiar.

– SYNONYMS **1 undisclosed,** unrevealed, secret, undetermined, undecided. **2 unexplored,** uncharted, unmapped, undiscovered, untraveled. **3 unidentified,** unnamed, anonymous, nameless. **4 obscure,** unfamiliar, unheard of, unsung, minor, undistinguished.
– ANTONYMS familiar.

▶ **noun** an unknown person or thing.
– PHRASES **unknown to** without someone's knowledge.

un·known quan·ti·ty ▶ **noun** a person or thing whose nature, value, or significance is not known.

Un·known Sol·dier ▶ **noun** an unidentified representative member of a country's armed forces killed in war, buried with special honors in a national memorial.

un·la·beled /ˌənˈlābəld/ (Brit. **unlabelled**) ▶ **adjective** without a label.

un·lace /ˌənˈlās/ ▶ **verb** undo the laces of a shoe or garment.

un·lad·en /ˌənˈlādn/ ▶ **adjective** not carrying a load.

un·la·dy·like /ˌənˈlādēˌlīk/ ▶ **adjective** not appropriate for or behaving like a well-bred woman.

un·la·ment·ed /ˌənləˈmentid/ ▶ **adjective** not mourned or regretted.

un·latch /ˌənˈlacʜ/ ▶ **verb** unfasten the latch of a door or gate.

un·law·ful /ˌənˈlôfəl/ ▶ **adjective** not conforming to or permitted by law or rules.
– DERIVATIVES **un·law·ful·ly** adverb **un·law·ful·ness** noun.

USAGE

For an explanation of the difference between **unlawful** and **illegal**, see the note at **ILLEGAL**.

un·lead·ed /ˌənˈledid/ ▶ **adjective** (of gasoline) without added lead.

un·learn /ˌənˈlərn/ ▶ **verb** (past and past part. **unlearned** or **unlearnt**) attempt to forget something that has been learned.

un·learn·ed[1] /ˌənˈlərnid/ ▶ **adjective** not well educated.

un·learn·ed[2] /ˌənˈlərnd/ (also **unlearnt** /ˌənˈlərnt/) ▶ **adjective** not having been learned.

un·leash /ˌənˈlēsʜ/ ▶ **verb 1** release an animal from a leash. **2** allow something strong or destructive to happen: *the US unleashed a full-scale military attack.*

un·leav·ened /ˌənˈlevənd/ ▶ **adjective** (of bread) made without yeast or other raising agent.

un·less /ənˈles, ˌən-/ ▶ **conjunction** except when; if not.
– ORIGIN from **ON** or **IN** + **LESS**.

un·let·tered /ˌənˈletərd/ ▶ **adjective** poorly educated or illiterate.

un·li·censed /ˌənˈlīsənst/ ▸ **adjective** not having an official license, especially for the sale of alcoholic drinks.

un·like /ˌənˈlīk/ ▸ **preposition 1** different from; not like. **2** in contrast to. **3** uncharacteristic of. ▸ **adjective** different from each other.
– DERIVATIVES **un·like·ness** noun.

> **USAGE**
>
> It is not good English to use **unlike** as a conjunction (a word connecting words or clauses of a sentence together), as in *she was behaving unlike she'd ever behaved before*. Use **as** with a negative instead: *she was behaving as she'd never behaved before*.

un·like·ly /ˌənˈlīklē/ ▸ **adjective** (**unlikelier, unlikeliest**) not likely to happen or be the case; improbable.

> – SYNONYMS **improbable,** doubtful, dubious, questionable, unconvincing, implausible, far-fetched, unrealistic, incredible, unbelievable, inconceivable.
> – ANTONYMS probable, likely.

– DERIVATIVES **un·like·li·hood** noun.

un·lim·it·ed /ˌənˈlimitid/ ▸ **adjective** not limited or restricted; infinite.

un·lined[1] /ˌənˈlīnd/ ▸ **adjective** not marked with lines or wrinkles.

un·lined[2] ▸ **adjective** without a lining.

un·list·ed /ˌənˈlistid/ ▸ **adjective** not included on a list, especially of telephone numbers or stock exchange prices.

un·lit /ˌənˈlit/ ▸ **adjective 1** not provided with lighting. **2** not having been lit.

un·liv·a·ble /ˌənˈlivəbəl/ ▸ **adjective** not able to be lived in; uninhabitable.

un·lived /ˌənˈlivd/ ▸ **adjective** (**unlived in**) not appearing to be inhabited.

un·load /ˌənˈlōd/ ▸ **verb 1** remove goods from a vehicle, ship, etc. **2** remove ammunition from a gun or film from a camera. **3** informal get rid of something.

> – SYNONYMS **unpack,** empty, clear, remove, offload.

un·lock /ˌənˈläk/ ▸ **verb 1** unfasten the lock of a door, container, etc., using a key. **2** make something previously inaccessible or unexploited available.

un·looked /ˌənˈlo͝okt/ ▸ **adjective** (**unlooked for**) unexpected; unforeseen.

un·loose /ˌənˈlo͞os/ ▸ **verb** undo or release something.

un·loos·en /ˌənˈlo͞osən/ ▸ **verb** another term for **UNLOOSE**.

un·loved /ˌənˈləvd/ ▸ **adjective** loved by no one.

un·love·ly /ˌənˈləvlē/ ▸ **adjective** not attractive; ugly.

un·luck·y /ˌənˈləkē/ ▸ **adjective** (**unluckier, unluckiest**) having, bringing, or resulting from bad luck.

> – SYNONYMS **1 unfortunate,** hapless, luckless, down on one's luck, unsuccessful, ill-fated, ill-starred, jinxed. **2 unfavorable,** inauspicious, unpropitious, ominous.
> – ANTONYMS lucky, fortunate.

– DERIVATIVES **un·luck·i·ly** adverb.

un·made /ˌənˈmād/ ▸ **adjective** (of a bed) not arranged tidily.

un·man /ˌənˈman/ ▸ **verb** (**unmans, unmanning, unmanned**) literary deprive a man of qualities traditionally associated with men, such as self-control or courage.

un·man·age·a·ble /ˌənˈmanijəbəl/ ▸ **adjective** difficult or impossible to manage or control.
– DERIVATIVES **un·man·age·a·bly** /-blē/ adverb.

un·man·ly /ˌənˈmanlē/ ▸ **adjective** not manly.

un·manned /ˌənˈmand/ ▸ **adjective** not having or needing a crew or staff.

un·man·ner·ly /ˌənˈmanərlē/ ▸ **adjective** not well mannered.

un·marked /ˌənˈmärkt/ ▸ **adjective 1** not marked. **2** not noticed.

un·mar·ried /ˌənˈmarēd/ ▸ **adjective** not married; single.

un·mask /ˌənˈmask/ ▸ **verb** reveal someone's or something's true character or nature.

un·matched /ˌənˈmaCHt/ ▸ **adjective** not matched or equaled.

un·men·tion·a·ble /ˌənˈmenCHənəbəl/ ▸ **adjective** too embarrassing or offensive to be spoken about.

un·mer·ci·ful /ˌənˈmərsəfəl/ ▸ **adjective** showing no mercy.
– DERIVATIVES **un·mer·ci·ful·ly** adverb.

un·mer·it·ed /ˌənˈmeritid/ ▸ **adjective** not deserved.

un·met /ˌənˈmet/ ▸ **adjective** (of a requirement) not achieved or fulfilled.

un·mind·ful /ˌənˈmīn(d)fəl/ ▸ **adjective** (**unmindful of**) not conscious or aware of something.

un·miss·a·ble /ˌənˈmisəbəl/ ▸ **adjective** that should not or cannot be missed.

un·mis·tak·a·ble /ˌənməˈstākəbəl/ (also **unmistakeable**) ▸ **adjective** not able to be mistaken for anything else.
– DERIVATIVES **un·mis·tak·a·bly** /-blē/ adverb.

un·mit·i·gat·ed /ˌənˈmitəˌgātid/ ▸ **adjective** absolute; complete: *an unmitigated disaster*.
– DERIVATIVES **un·mit·i·gat·ed·ly** adverb.

> **CHOOSE THE RIGHT WORD**
>
> See **SEVERE**.

un·mixed /ˌənˈmikst/ ▸ **adjective** not mixed.

un·mod·er·at·ed /ˌənˈmädəˌrātid/ ▸ **adjective** (of an Internet bulletin board or chat room) not monitored for inappropriate or offensive content.

un·moor /ˌənˈmo͝or/ ▸ **verb** release the moorings of a boat or ship.

un·mo·ti·vat·ed /ˌənˈmōtəˌvātid/ ▸ **adjective 1** not motivated or enthusiastic. **2** without apparent motive: *an unmotivated attack*.

un·moved /ˌənˈmo͞ovd/ ▸ **adjective 1** not affected by emotion or excitement. **2** not changed in purpose or position.

un·mov·ing /ˌənˈmo͞oviNG/ ▸ **adjective 1** not moving; staying still. **2** not evoking emotion or excitement.

un·mu·si·cal /ˌənˈmyo͞ozikəl/ ▸ **adjective 1** not pleasing to the ear. **2** not enjoying or skilled at playing music.

un·name·a·ble /ˌənˈnāməbəl/ (also **unnamable**) ▶ **adjective** unmentionable.

un·named /ˌənˈnāmd/ ▶ **adjective** not named.

un·nat·u·ral /ˌənˈnacʜ(ə)rəl/ ▶ **adjective 1** contrary to what is found in nature; abnormal or artificial. **2** different from what is normal or expected.

– SYNONYMS **1 abnormal,** unusual, uncommon, extraordinary, strange, unorthodox, exceptional, irregular, untypical. **2 artificial,** man-made, synthetic. **3 affected,** artificial, stilted, forced, false, fake, insincere, contrived, mannered, self-conscious; informal put on, phony.
– ANTONYMS natural.

– DERIVATIVES **un·nat·u·ral·ly** adverb **un·nat·u·ral·ness** noun.

un·nav·i·ga·ble /ˌənˈnavəgəbəl/ ▶ **adjective** not able to be sailed on by ships or boats.

un·nec·es·sar·y /ˌənˈnesəˌserē/ ▶ **adjective** not necessary, or more than is necessary.

– SYNONYMS **unneeded,** inessential, not required, uncalled for, unwarranted, dispensable, optional, extraneous, expendable, redundant.

– DERIVATIVES **un·nec·es·sar·i·ly** /-ˌnesəˈse(ə)rəlē/ adverb.

un·nerve /ˌənˈnərv/ ▶ **verb** make someone feel nervous or frightened.

– SYNONYMS **demoralize,** discourage, dishearten, dispirit, alarm, frighten, disconcert, perturb, upset, discomfit, take aback, unsettle, disquiet, fluster, shake, ruffle, throw off balance; informal rattle, faze, shake up, discombobulate.
– ANTONYMS hearten.

– DERIVATIVES **un·nerv·ing** adjective.

un·no·tice·a·ble /ˌənˈnōtisəbəl/ ▶ **adjective** not easily observed or noticed.

un·no·ticed /ˌənˈnōtist/ ▶ **adjective** not noticed.

un·num·bered /ˌənˈnəmbərd/ ▶ **adjective 1** not given a number. **2** not counted, or not able to be counted.

un·ob·served /ˌənəbˈzərvd/ ▶ **adjective** not observed; unseen.

un·ob·struct·ed /ˌənəbˈstrəktid, -äb-/ ▶ **adjective** not obstructed.

un·ob·tain·a·ble /ˌənəbˈtānəbəl/ ▶ **adjective** not able to be obtained.

un·ob·tru·sive /ˌənəbˈtro͞osiv/ ▶ **adjective** not conspicuous or attracting attention.
– DERIVATIVES **un·ob·tru·sive·ly** adverb **un·ob·tru·sive·ness** noun.

un·oc·cu·pied /ˌənˈäkyəˌpīd/ ▶ **adjective** not occupied.

un·of·fi·cial /ˌənəˈfisʜəl/ ▶ **adjective** not officially authorized or confirmed.
– DERIVATIVES **un·of·fi·cial·ly** adverb.

un·o·pened /ˌənˈōpənd/ ▶ **adjective** not opened.

un·op·posed /ˌənəˈpōzd/ ▶ **adjective** not opposed; unchallenged.

un·or·gan·ized /ˌənˈôrgəˌnīzd/ ▶ **adjective** not organized.

un·o·rig·i·nal /ˌənəˈrijənl/ ▶ **adjective** lacking originality.
– DERIVATIVES **un·o·rig·i·nal·i·ty** /-ˌrijəˈnalətē/ noun **un·o·rig·i·nal·ly** adverb.

un·or·tho·dox /ˌənˈôrтʜəˌdäks/ ▶ **adjective** different from what is usual, traditional, or accepted.
– DERIVATIVES **un·or·tho·dox·y** noun.

un·os·ten·ta·tious /ˌənästənˈtāsʜəs/ ▶ **adjective** not ostentatious or showy.
– DERIVATIVES **un·os·ten·ta·tious·ly** adverb.

un·pack /ˌənˈpak/ ▶ **verb 1** remove the contents of a suitcase, bag, container, etc. **2** separate something into its different elements in order to make it easier to understand.

un·paid /ˌənˈpād/ ▶ **adjective 1** (of a debt) not yet paid. **2** (of work or leave) done or taken without payment. **3** not receiving payment for work done.

un·paired /ˌənˈpe(ə)rd/ ▶ **adjective 1** not arranged in pairs. **2** not forming one of a pair.

un·pal·at·a·ble /ˌənˈpalətəbəl/ ▶ **adjective 1** not pleasant to taste. **2** difficult to put up with or accept.

un·par·al·leled /ˌənˈparəˌleld/ ▶ **adjective** having no parallel or equal; exceptional.

un·par·don·a·ble /ˌənˈpärdn-əbəl, -ˈpärdnə-/ ▶ **adjective** (of a fault or offense) unforgivable.
– DERIVATIVES **un·par·don·a·bly** /-blē/ adverb.

un·par·lia·men·ta·ry /ˌənˌpärləˈmentərē/ ▶ **adjective** (especially of language or procedures) against the rules of behavior of a parliament.

un·pas·teur·ized /ˌənˈpascʜəˌrīzd/ ▶ **adjective** not pasteurized.

un·pa·tri·ot·ic /ˌənˌpātrēˈätik/ ▶ **adjective** not patriotic.
– DERIVATIVES **un·pa·tri·ot·i·cal·ly** /-(ə)lē/ adverb.

un·paved /ˌənˈpāvd/ ▶ **adjective** not having a paved surface.

un·peo·pled /ˈənˈpēpəld/ ▶ **adjective** empty of people.

un·per·son /ˈənˈpərsən, -ˌpər-/ ▶ **noun** (pl. **unpersons**) a person whose name or existence is officially denied or ignored.

un·per·turbed /ˌənpərˈtərbd/ ▶ **adjective** not perturbed or worried.

un·pick /ˌənˈpik/ ▶ **verb 1** undo the stitches from a piece of sewing. **2** carefully analyze the different elements of something.

un·pin /ˌənˈpin/ ▶ **verb** (**unpins, unpinning, unpinned**) unfasten or detach something by removing a pin or pins.

un·pit·y·ing /ˌənˈpitē-iɴɢ/ ▶ **adjective** not feeling or showing pity.

un·placed /ˌənˈplāst/ ▶ **adjective** chiefly Horse Racing not one of the first three (sometimes four) to finish in a race.

un·planned /ˌənˈpland/ ▶ **adjective** not planned.

un·play·a·ble /ˌənˈplāəbəl/ ▶ **adjective 1** not able to be played or played on: *the field was unplayable*. **2** (of music) too difficult to perform.

un·pleas·ant /ˌənˈplezənt/ ▶ **adjective 1** not pleasant. **2** not friendly or kind.

– SYNONYMS **1** *an unpleasant situation* **disagreeable,** distressing, nasty, horrible, terrible, awful, dreadful, invidious, objectionable. **2** *an unpleasant man* **unlikable,** unlovable, disagreeable, bad-tempered, unfriendly, rude, impolite, obnoxious, nasty, spiteful, mean, objectionable, annoying, irritating. **3 unappetizing,** unpalatable, unsavory, unappealing, disgusting, revolting, nauseating, sickening.
– ANTONYMS pleasant, agreeable.

– DERIVATIVES **un·pleas·ant·ly** adverb.

un·pleas·ant·ness /ˌənˈplezəntnəs/ ▶ **noun 1** the state or quality of being unpleasant. **2** bad feeling or quarreling between people.

un·plowed /ˌənˈploud/ ▶ **adjective** (of land) not having been plowed.

un·plug /ˌənˈpləg/ ▶ **verb** (**unplugs, unplugging, unplugged**) **1** disconnect an electrical device by removing its plug from a socket. **2** remove an obstacle or blockage from something.

un·plugged /ˌənˈpləgd/ ▶ **adjective** trademark (of pop or rock music) performed or recorded with acoustic rather than electrically amplified instruments.

un·plumbed /ˌənˈpləmd/ ▶ **adjective 1** not provided with plumbing. **2** not fully explored or understood.
– DERIVATIVES **un·plumb·a·ble** adjective.

un·pol·ished /ˌənˈpälisʜt/ ▶ **adjective 1** not having a polished surface. **2** (of a performance or piece of work) not having been refined or perfected.

un·pop·u·lar /ˌənˈpäpyələr/ ▶ **adjective** not liked or popular.

– SYNONYMS **disliked,** friendless, unloved, unwelcome, avoided, ignored, rejected, shunned, out of favor.

– DERIVATIVES **un·pop·u·lar·i·ty** /-ˌpäpyəˈlaritē/ noun.

un·pop·u·lat·ed /ˌənˈpäpyəˌlātid/ ▶ **adjective** without inhabitants.

un·pow·ered /ˌənˈpou(-ə)rd/ ▶ **adjective** (of a vehicle, boat, etc.) not propelled by burning a fuel such as gasoline.

un·prac·ticed /ˌənˈpraktist/ (Brit. **unpractised**) ▶ **adjective** not trained or experienced.

un·prec·e·dent·ed /ˌənˈpresəˌdentid/ ▶ **adjective** never done or known before.
– DERIVATIVES **un·prec·e·dent·ed·ly** adverb.

un·pre·dict·a·ble /ˌənpriˈdiktəbəl/ ▶ **adjective 1** not able to be predicted. **2** changeable or unreliable.
– DERIVATIVES **un·pre·dict·a·bil·i·ty** /-ˌdiktəˈbilətē/ noun **un·pre·dict·a·bly** /-blē/ adverb.

un·prej·u·diced /ˌənˈprejədist/ ▶ **adjective** without prejudice; unbiased.

un·pre·med·i·tat·ed /ˌənpriˈmedəˌtātid, -prē-/ ▶ **adjective** not thought out or planned beforehand.

un·pre·pared /ˌənpriˈpe(ə)rd/ ▶ **adjective 1** not ready or able to deal with something. **2** not made ready for use.

un·pre·pos·ses·sing /ˌənˌprēpəˈzesiɴɢ/ ▶ **adjective** not attractive or appealing in appearance.

un·pres·sur·ized /ˌənˈpresʜəˌrīzd/ ▶ **adjective 1** (of a gas or its container) not having raised pressure that is produced or maintained artificially. **2** (of an aircraft cabin) not having normal atmospheric pressure maintained at a high altitude.

un·pre·ten·tious /ˌənpriˈtencʜəs/ ▶ **adjective** not pretentious; modest or unassuming.
– DERIVATIVES **un·pre·ten·tious·ly** adverb **un·pre·ten·tious·ness** noun.

un·prin·ci·pled /ˌənˈprinsəpəld/ ▶ **adjective** not acting in accordance with moral principles.

un·print·a·ble /ˌənˈprintəbəl/ ▶ **adjective** (of words, comments, or thoughts) too offensive or shocking to be published.

un·prob·lem·at·ic /ˌənˌpräbləˈmatik/ ▶ **adjective** not presenting a problem or difficulty.
– DERIVATIVES **un·prob·lem·at·i·cal·ly** /-ik(ə)lē/ adverb.

un·proc·essed /ˌənˈpräˌsest, -səst-, -ˈprō-/ ▶ **adjective** not processed.

un·pro·duc·tive /ˌənprəˈdəktiv/ ▶ **adjective 1** not producing or able to produce large amounts of goods, crops, etc. **2** not achieving much; not very useful.

un·pro·fes·sion·al /ˌənprəˈfesʜənl/ ▶ **adjective** not in accordance with the standards expected in a particular profession.
– DERIVATIVES **un·pro·fes·sion·al·ly** adverb.

un·prof·it·a·ble /ˌənˈpräfitəbəl/ ▶ **adjective 1** not making a profit. **2** not beneficial or useful.

un·prom·is·ing /ˌənˈpräməsiɴɢ/ ▶ **adjective** not giving hope of future success or good results.

un·prompt·ed /ˌənˈpräm(p)tid/ ▶ **adjective** said or done without being prompted by someone else.

un·pro·nounce·a·ble /ˌənprəˈnounsəbəl/ ▶ **adjective** too difficult to pronounce.

un·pro·tect·ed /ˌənprəˈtektid/ ▶ **adjective 1** not protected or kept safe from harm. **2** (of sex) performed without a condom.

un·prov·en /ˌənˈproōvən/ (also **unproved**) ▶ **adjective 1** not shown by evidence or argument to be true or to exist. **2** not tried and tested.

un·pro·voked /ˌənprəˈvōkt/ ▶ **adjective** (of an attack, crime, etc.) not directly provoked.

un·pub·lished /ˌənˈpəblisʜt/ ▶ **adjective 1** (of a work) not published. **2** (of an author) having no writings published.
– DERIVATIVES **un·pub·lish·a·ble** adjective.

un·pun·ished /ˌənˈpənisʜt/ ▶ **adjective** (of an offense or offender) not receiving any punishment or penalty.

un·put·down·a·ble /ˌənˌpo͝otˈdounəbəl/ ▶ **adjective** informal (of a book) so absorbing that one cannot stop reading it.

un·qual·i·fied /ˌənˈkwäləˌfīd/ ▶ **adjective 1** not having the necessary qualifications or requirements. **2** without limitation; total: *an unqualified success.*

un·quan·ti·fi·a·ble /ˌənˈkwäntəˌfīəbəl, -ˌkwäntəˈfī-/ ▶ **adjective** impossible to express or measure.

un·quench·a·ble /ˌənˈkwencʜəbəl/ ▶ **adjective** not able to be quenched or satisfied.

un·ques·tion·a·ble /ˌənˈkwescʜənəbəl/ ▶ **adjective** not able to be disputed or doubted.
– DERIVATIVES **un·ques·tion·a·bly** /-blē, -ˈkwesʜ-/ adverb.

un·ques·tioned /ˌənˈkwescʜənd/ ▶ **adjective 1** not disputed or doubted; certain. **2** accepted without question.
– DERIVATIVES **un·ques·tion·ing** adjective.

un·qui·et /ˌənˈkwīət/ ▶ **adjective 1** unable to be still; restless. **2** uneasy or anxious.

un·quote /ˌənˈkwōt, ˈənˌkwōt/ ▶ **verb** see **QUOTE**
—— **UNQUOTE** at **QUOTE**.

un·quot·ed /ˌənˈkwōtid/ ▶ **adjective** not quoted or listed on a stock exchange.

un·ranked /ˌənˈraɴɢkt/ ▶ **adjective** not having achieved or been given a rank or ranking.

un·rav·el /ˌənˈravəl/ ▶ **verb** (**unravels, unraveling, unraveled**) **1** undo twisted, knitted, or woven threads. **2** become undone. **3** investigate and solve a mystery or puzzle. **4** begin to fail or collapse: *the peace process began to unravel.*

– SYNONYMS **1 untangle,** disentangle, separate out, unwind, untwist. **2 solve,** resolve, clear up, puzzle out, get to the bottom of, explain, clarify; informal figure out.
– ANTONYMS entangle.

un·reach·a·ble /ˌənˈrēCHəbəl/ ▶ **adjective** unable to be reached or contacted.

un·re·ac·tive /ˌənrēˈaktiv/ ▶ **adjective** having little tendency to react chemically.

un·read /ˌənˈred/ ▶ **adjective** not having been read.

un·read·a·ble /ˌənˈrēdəbəl/ ▶ **adjective 1** not clear enough to read; illegible. **2** too dull or difficult to be worth reading.
– DERIVATIVES **un·read·a·bil·i·ty** /-ˌrēdəˈbilətē/ noun **un·read·a·bly** /-blē/ adverb.

un·read·y /ˌənˈredē/ ▶ **adjective** not ready or prepared.

un·re·al /ˌənˈrē(ə)l/ ▶ **adjective 1** imaginary or not seeming real. **2** unrealistic.

– SYNONYMS **imaginary,** fictitious, pretend, make-believe, made-up, dreamed-up, mock, false, illusory, mythical, fanciful, hypothetical, theoretical; informal phony.

– DERIVATIVES **un·re·al·i·ty** /-rēˈalətē/ noun.

un·re·al·is·tic /ˌənrēəˈlistik/ ▶ **adjective 1** not having a sensible idea of what can be achieved or expected. **2** not representing things in a realistic way.
– DERIVATIVES **un·re·al·is·ti·cal·ly** /-ik(ə)lē/ adverb.

un·re·al·ized /ˌənˈrēəˌlīzd/ ▶ **adjective 1** not achieved or created. **2** not converted into money: *unrealized property assets.*

un·rea·son /ˌənˈrēzən/ ▶ **noun** lack of reasonable thought; irrationality.
– DERIVATIVES **un·rea·soned** adjective.

un·rea·son·a·ble /ˌənˈrēz(ə)nəbəl/ ▶ **adjective 1** not guided by or based on good sense. **2** beyond the limits of what is acceptable or achievable.
– DERIVATIVES **un·rea·son·a·ble·ness** noun **un·rea·son·a·bly** /-blē/ adverb.

un·rea·son·ing /ˌənˈrēz(ə)niNG/ ▶ **adjective** not guided by or based on reason; illogical.

un·re·cep·tive /ˌənriˈseptiv/ ▶ **adjective** not receptive.

un·rec·og·niz·a·ble /ˌənˈrekəgˌnīzəbəl/ ▶ **adjective** not able to be recognized.
– DERIVATIVES **un·rec·og·niz·a·bly** /-blē/ adverb.

un·rec·og·nized /ˌənˈrekəgˌnīzd/ ▶ **adjective 1** not identified from previous encounters or knowledge. **2** not acknowledged as valid.

un·re·con·struct·ed /ˌənˌrēkənˈstrəktid/ ▶ **adjective** not reconciled or converted to the current political theory or movement.

un·re·cord·ed /ˌənriˈkôrdid/ ▶ **adjective** not recorded.

un·reel /ˌənˈrēl/ ▶ **verb 1** unwind something. **2** (of movie film) wind from one reel to another during projection.

un·re·fined /ˌənriˈfīnd/ ▶ **adjective 1** not processed to remove impurities. **2** not elegant or cultured.

un·re·gen·er·ate /ˌənriˈjenərət/ ▶ **adjective** not reforming or showing repentance; obstinately wrong or bad.

un·reg·is·tered /ˌənˈrejəstərd/ ▶ **adjective** not officially recognized and recorded.

un·reg·u·lat·ed /ˌənˈregyəˌlātid/ ▶ **adjective** not controlled or supervised by regulations or laws.

un·re·hearsed /ˌənriˈhərst/ ▶ **adjective** not rehearsed.

un·re·lat·ed /ˌənriˈlātid/ ▶ **adjective** not related.

un·re·leased /ˌənriˈlēst/ ▶ **adjective** (especially of a movie or recording) not released.

un·re·lent·ing /ˌənriˈlentiNG/ ▶ **adjective 1** not stopping or becoming weaker. **2** refusing to relent or give in.

– SYNONYMS **1** *the unrelenting heat* **continual,** constant, unremitting, unabating, unrelieved, incessant, unceasing, endless, persistent. **2** *an unrelenting opponent* **implacable,** inflexible, uncompromising, unyielding, unbending, determined, dogged, tireless, unswerving, unwavering.
– ANTONYMS intermittent.

– DERIVATIVES **un·re·lent·ing·ly** adverb.

un·re·li·a·ble /ˌənriˈlīəbəl/ ▶ **adjective** not able to be relied on.
– DERIVATIVES **un·re·li·a·bil·i·ty** /ˌənriˌlīəˈbilətē/ noun **un·re·li·a·bly** /-blē/ adverb.

un·re·lieved /ˌənriˈlēvd/ ▶ **adjective** lacking variation or change; monotonous.
– DERIVATIVES **un·re·liev·ed·ly** /-ˈlēvidlē/ adverb.

un·re·mark·a·ble /ˌənriˈmärkəbəl/ ▶ **adjective** not particularly interesting or surprising.

un·re·marked /ˌənriˈmärkt/ ▶ **adjective** not noticed or remarked on.

un·re·mit·ting /ˌənriˈmitiNG/ ▶ **adjective** never relaxing or slackening.
– DERIVATIVES **un·re·mit·ting·ly** adverb.

un·re·mu·ner·a·tive /ˌənriˈmyo͞onərətiv, -ˌrātiv/ ▶ **adjective** bringing little or no profit or income.

un·re·peat·a·ble /ˌənriˈpētəbəl/ ▶ **adjective 1** not able to be repeated. **2** too offensive or shocking to be said again.

un·re·pent·ant /ˌənriˈpentənt/ ▶ **adjective** showing no regret for one's wrongdoings.
– DERIVATIVES **un·re·pent·ant·ly** adverb.

un·re·port·ed /ˌənriˈpôrtəd/ ▶ **adjective** not reported.

un·rep·re·sent·a·tive /ˌənˌrepriˈzentətiv/ ▶ **adjective** not typical of a class or group.

un·re·quit·ed /ˌənriˈkwītid/ ▶ **adjective** (of love) not returned.

un·re·served /ˌənriˈzərvd/ ▶ **adjective 1** without reservations; complete. **2** frank and open. **3** not set apart for a particular purpose or booked in advance.
– DERIVATIVES **un·re·serv·ed·ly** adverb.

un·re·solved /ˌənriˈzälvd, -ˈzôlvd/ ▶ **adjective** (of a problem, dispute, etc.) not resolved.

un·re·spon·sive /ˌənriˈspänsiv/ ▶ **adjective** not responsive.
– DERIVATIVES **un·re·spon·sive·ness** noun.

un·rest /ˌənˈrest/ ▶ **noun** a state of rebellious dissatisfaction in a group of people: *years of industrial unrest.*

– SYNONYMS **disturbance,** trouble, turmoil, disruption, disorder, chaos, anarchy, dissatisfaction, dissent, strife, agitation, protest, rebellion, uprising, rioting.
– ANTONYMS peace.

un·re·strained /ˌənriˈstrānd/ ▶ **adjective** not restrained or restricted.
– DERIVATIVES **un·re·strain·ed·ly** /-ˈstrānidlē/ adverb.

un·re·strict·ed /ˌənriˈstriktid/ ▶ **adjective** not limited or restricted.

un·re·ward·ing /ˌənrəˈwôrdiNG/ ▶ **adjective** not rewarding or satisfying.

un·ripe /ˌənˈrīp/ ▶ **adjective** not ripe.

un·ri·valed /ˌənˈrīvəld/ (Brit. **unrivalled**) ▶ **adjective** greater or better than all others.

un·roll /ˌənˈrōl/ ▶ **verb** open or cause to open out from a rolled-up state.

un·ro·man·tic /ˌənrōˈmantik, ˌənrə-/ ▶ **adjective** not romantic.

un·ruf·fled /ˌənˈrəfəld/ ▶ **adjective 1** (of a person) calm and unperturbed. **2** not disordered or disturbed.

un·ru·ly /ˌənˈro͞olē/ ▶ **adjective** (**unrulier, unruliest**) disorderly and disruptive; difficult to control.

– SYNONYMS **disorderly,** rowdy, wild, unmanageable, uncontrollable, disobedient, disruptive, undisciplined, wayward, willful, headstrong, obstreperous, difficult, intractable, out of hand, recalcitrant; formal refractory.
– ANTONYMS disciplined.

– DERIVATIVES **un·ru·li·ness** noun.
– ORIGIN from former *ruly* 'disciplined, orderly,' from **RULE.**

WORD TOOLKIT

unruly ...	rebellious ...	defiant ...
child	spirit	stance
students	nature	look
passengers	teenager	message
mob	stage	tone
fans	colonies	gesture
customers	slaves	voice

un·sad·dle /ˌənˈsadl/ ▶ **verb** remove the saddle from a horse.

un·safe /ˌənˈsāf/ ▶ **adjective 1** not safe; dangerous. **2** Law (of a verdict or conviction) not based on reliable evidence and likely to constitute a miscarriage of justice. **3** (of sexual activity) in which people do not take precautions to protect themselves against sexually transmitted diseases such as AIDS.

– SYNONYMS **1 dangerous,** risky, hazardous, high-risk, treacherous, insecure, unsound, harmful, injurious, toxic. **2 unreliable,** open to doubt, questionable, doubtful, dubious, suspect; informal iffy.
– ANTONYMS safe.

un·said /ˌənˈsed/ past and past participle of **UNSAY** ▶ **adjective** not said or expressed.

un·sal·a·ble /ˌənˈsāləbəl/ (also **unsaleable**) ▶ **adjective** not able to be sold.

un·salt·ed /ˌənˈsôltid/ ▶ **adjective** without added salt.

un·san·i·tar·y /ˌənˈsaniˌterē/ ▶ **adjective** not hygienic.

un·sat·is·fac·to·ry /ˌənˌsatəsˈfakt(ə)rē/ ▶ **adjective 1** not good enough. **2** Law another term for **UNSAFE.**

– SYNONYMS **disappointing,** displeasing, inadequate, unacceptable, poor, bad, substandard, weak, mediocre, not up to par, defective, deficient; informal leaving a lot to be desired.

– DERIVATIVES **un·sat·is·fac·to·ri·ly** /-ˈfakt(ə)rəlē/ adverb.

un·sat·is·fied /ˌənˈsatisˌfīd/ ▶ **adjective** not satisfied.

un·sat·is·fy·ing /ˌənˈsatisˌfīiNG/ ▶ **adjective** not satisfying.

un·sat·u·rat·ed /ˌənˈsaCHəˌrātid/ ▶ **adjective** Chemistry (of fats) having double and triple bonds between carbon atoms in their molecules and as a consequence being more easily processed by the body.

un·sa·vor·y /ˌənˈsāv(ə)rē/ (Brit. **unsavoury**) ▶ **adjective** **1** unpleasant to taste, smell, or look at. **2** not morally respectable; disreputable.

un·say /ˌənˈsā/ ▶ **verb** (past and past part. **unsaid**) withdraw or retract a statement.

un·say·a·ble /ˌənˈsāəbəl/ ▶ **adjective** not able to be said, especially because considered too controversial or offensive.

un·scarred /ˌənˈskärd/ ▶ **adjective** not scarred or damaged.

un·scathed /ˌənˈskāT͟Hd/ ▶ **adjective** without suffering any injury, damage, or harm.

un·scent·ed /ˌənˈsentid/ ▶ **adjective** not scented.

un·sched·uled /ˌənˈskeˌjo͞old, -əld/ ▶ **adjective** not scheduled.

un·schooled /ˌənˈsko͞old/ ▶ **adjective 1** lacking schooling or training. **2** not affected; natural and spontaneous.

un·sci·en·tif·ic /ˌənˌsīənˈtifik/ ▶ **adjective** not in accordance with scientific principles or methods.
– DERIVATIVES **un·sci·en·tif·i·cal·ly** /-ik(ə)lē/ adverb.

un·scram·ble /ˌənˈskrambəl/ ▶ **verb** restore a scrambled broadcast, message, etc., to an intelligible or readable state.

un·screened /ˌənˈskrēnd/ ▶ **adjective 1** not subjected to testing or investigation by screening. **2** not shown or broadcast.

un·screw /ˌənˈskro͞o/ ▶ **verb** unfasten something by twisting it.

un·script·ed /ˌənˈskriptid/ ▶ **adjective** said or delivered without a prepared script; impromptu.

un·scru·pu·lous /ˌənˈskro͞opyələs/ ▶ **adjective** without moral principles; dishonest or unfair.

– SYNONYMS **dishonest,** deceitful, devious, underhanded/underhand, unethical, immoral, shameless, exploitative, corrupt, unprincipled, dishonorable, disreputable; informal crooked, shady.

– DERIVATIVES **un·scru·pu·lous·ly** adverb **un·scru·pu·lous·ness** noun.

un·seal /ˌənˈsēl/ ▶ **verb** remove or break the seal of something.

un·sealed /ˌənˈsēld/ ▶ **adjective** not sealed.

un·sea·son·a·ble /ˌənˈsēzənəbəl/ ▶ **adjective** (of weather) unusual for the time of year.
– DERIVATIVES **un·sea·son·a·bly** /-blē/ adverb.

un·sea·son·al /ˌənˈsēzənəl/ ▶ **adjective** (especially of weather) unusual or inappropriate for the time of year.

un·sea·soned /ˌənˈsēzənd/ ▸ **adjective** **1** (of food) not flavored with salt, pepper, or other spices. **2** (of lumber) not treated for building purposes. **3** (of firewood) not aged or dry; green.

un·seat /ˌənˈsēt/ ▸ **verb** **1** make someone fall from a saddle or seat. **2** remove a government or person in authority from power.

un·se·cured /ˌənsiˈkyo͝ord/ ▸ **adjective** **1** (of a loan) made without an asset given as security. **2** not made secure or safe.

un·seed·ed /ˌənˈsēdid/ ▸ **adjective** (of a competitor in a sports tournament) not seeded.

un·see·ing /ˌənˈsēiNG/ ▸ **adjective** with one's eyes open but without noticing or seeing anything.
– DERIVATIVES **un·see·ing·ly** adverb.

un·seem·ly /ˌənˈsēmlē/ ▸ **adjective** (of behavior or actions) not proper or appropriate.
– DERIVATIVES **un·seem·li·ness** noun.

un·seen /ˌənˈsēn/ ▸ **adjective** not seen or noticed.

un·self·con·scious /ˌənˌselfˈkänsHəs/ ▸ **adjective** not shy or embarrassed.
– DERIVATIVES **un·self·con·scious·ly** adverb **un·self·con·scious·ness** noun.

un·sel·fish /ˌənˈselfisH/ ▸ **adjective** not selfish.
– DERIVATIVES **un·self·ish·ly** adverb **un·self·ish·ness** noun.

WORD TOOLKIT

See **GENEROUS**.

un·sen·ti·men·tal /ˌənˌsentəˈmen(t)l/ ▸ **adjective** not displaying or influenced by sentimental feelings.
– DERIVATIVES **un·sen·ti·men·tal·ly** adverb.

un·se·ri·ous /ˌənˈsi(ə)rēəs/ ▸ **adjective** not serious; lighthearted.

un·ser·vice·a·ble /ˌənˈsərvəsəbəl/ ▸ **adjective** not in working order; unfit for use.

un·set·tle /ˌənˈsetl/ ▸ **verb** make anxious or uneasy; disturb: *the crisis has unsettled financial markets.*

– SYNONYMS **disturb,** disconcert, unnerve, upset, disquiet, perturb, alarm, dismay, trouble, bother, agitate, fluster, ruffle, shake (up), throw; informal rattle, faze.

– DERIVATIVES **un·set·tling** adjective.

un·set·tled /ˌənˈsetld/ ▸ **adjective** **1** changeable or likely to change: *unsettled weather.* **2** agitated; uneasy. **3** not yet resolved.

un·sex /ˌənˈseks/ ▸ **verb** deprive someone of their gender, sexuality, or the characteristic features of one or the other sex.

un·shack·le /ˌənˈsHakəl/ ▸ **verb** release someone from shackles or other restraints.

un·shak·a·ble /ˌənˈsHākəbəl/ (also **unshakeable**) ▸ **adjective** (of a belief, feeling, etc.) firm and unable to be changed or disputed.

un·shak·en /ˌənˈsHākən/ ▸ **adjective** not having changed or weakened: *their trust in him remains unshaken.*

un·shav·en /ˌənˈsHāvən/ ▸ **adjective** not having shaved or been shaved.

un·sheathe /ˌənˈsHēT͟H/ ▸ **verb** pull a knife or similar weapon out of a sheath.

un·shed /ˌənˈsHed/ ▸ **adjective** (of tears) welling in a person's eyes but not falling.

un·shelled /ˌənˈsHeld/ ▸ **adjective** not extracted from its shell.

un·ship /ˌənˈsHip/ ▸ **verb** (**unships, unshipping, unshipped**) **1** remove an oar, mast, or other object from a fixed or regular position. **2** unload cargo from a ship or boat.

un·shock·a·ble /ˌənˈsHäkəbəl/ ▸ **adjective** impossible to shock.

un·shorn /ˌənˈsHôrn/ ▸ **adjective** (of hair or wool) not cut or shorn.

un·sight·ed /ˌənˈsītid/ ▸ **adjective** **1** lacking the power of sight. **2** (especially in sports) prevented from having a clear view.

un·sight·ly /ˌənˈsītlē/ ▸ **adjective** unpleasant to look at; ugly.

– SYNONYMS **unattractive,** ugly, unprepossessing, hideous, horrible, repulsive, revolting, offensive, grotesque.
– ANTONYMS attractive.

– DERIVATIVES **un·sight·li·ness** noun.

un·signed /ˌənˈsīnd/ ▸ **adjective** **1** not identified or authorized by a person's signature. **2** (of a musician or athlete) not having signed a contract of employment.

un·sink·a·ble /ˌənˈsiNGkəbəl/ ▸ **adjective** unable to be sunk.

un·skilled /ˌənˈskild/ ▸ **adjective** not having or requiring special skill or training.

un·skill·ful /ˌənˈskilfəl/ (Brit. also **unskilful**) ▸ **adjective** not having or showing skill.
– DERIVATIVES **un·skill·ful·ly** adverb.

un·sling /ˌənˈsliNG/ ▸ **verb** (past and past part. **unslung**) remove something from the place where it has been slung or suspended.

un·smil·ing /ˌənˈsmīliNG/ ▸ **adjective** not smiling; serious or unfriendly.
– DERIVATIVES **un·smil·ing·ly** adverb.

un·so·cia·ble /ˌənˈsōsHəbəl/ ▸ **adjective** **1** not enjoying the company of other people. **2** not contributing to friendly relationships between people.

– SYNONYMS **unfriendly,** uncongenial, unneighborly, unapproachable, introverted, reserved, withdrawn, retiring, aloof, distant, remote, detached; informal standoffish.

un·so·cial /ˌənˈsōsHəl/ ▸ **adjective** antisocial.

un·sold /ˌənˈsōld/ ▸ **adjective** (of an item) not sold.

un·so·lic·it·ed /ˌənsəˈlisitid/ ▸ **adjective** not asked for.

un·solved /ˌənˈsälvd, -ˈsôlvd/ ▸ **adjective** not solved.

un·so·phis·ti·cat·ed /ˌənsəˈfistəˌkātid/ ▸ **adjective** **1** lacking experience or taste in matters of culture or fashion. **2** not complicated or highly developed; basic.

– SYNONYMS **1 unworldly,** naive, simple, innocent, green, immature, callow, inexperienced, childlike, artless, guileless, ingenuous, natural, unaffected, unassuming, unpretentious. **2** *unsophisticated software* **simple,** crude, basic, rudimentary, primitive, rough and ready.

CHOOSE THE RIGHT WORD

See **GULLIBLE**.

un·sort·ed /ˌənˈsôrtid/ ▸ **adjective** not sorted or arranged.

un·sound /ˌənˈsound/ ▸ **adjective 1** not safe or strong; in poor condition. **2** not based on reliable evidence or reasoning; unreliable or unacceptable.

– SYNONYMS **1** *structurally unsound* **rickety,** flimsy, wobbly, unstable, crumbling, damaged, rotten, ramshackle, insubstantial, unsafe, dangerous. **2** *unsound evidence* **untenable,** flawed, defective, faulty, ill-founded, flimsy, unreliable, questionable, dubious, tenuous, suspect, fallacious; informal iffy. **3** *of unsound mind* **disordered,** deranged, disturbed, demented, unstable, unbalanced, unhinged, insane; informal touched.
– ANTONYMS strong.

un·spar·ing /ˌənˈspe(ə)riNG/ ▸ **adjective** merciless; severe.
– DERIVATIVES **un·spar·ing·ly** adverb.

un·speak·a·ble /ˌənˈspēkəbəl/ ▸ **adjective 1** not able to be expressed in words. **2** too bad or horrific to express in words.
– DERIVATIVES **un·speak·a·bly** /-blē/ adverb.

un·spe·cif·ic /ˌənspəˈsifik/ ▸ **adjective** not specific; vague.

un·spec·i·fied /ˌənˈspesəˌfīd/ ▸ **adjective** not stated clearly or exactly.

un·spec·tac·u·lar /ˌənspekˈtakyələr, -spək-/ ▸ **adjective** not spectacular; unremarkable.

un·spoiled /ˌənˈspoild/ (Brit. also **unspoilt** /ˌənˈspoilt/) ▸ **adjective** not spoiled, in particular (of a place) largely unaffected by building or development.

un·spo·ken /ˌənˈspōkən/ ▸ **adjective** understood without being expressed in speech: *an unspoken agreement.*

– SYNONYMS **unstated,** unexpressed, unuttered, unsaid, unvoiced, unarticulated, undeclared, not spelled out; tacit, implicit, implied, understood.
– ANTONYMS explicit.

un·spool /ˌənˈspo͞ol/ ▸ **verb** unwind or be unwound from a spool.

un·sport·ing /ˌənˈspôrtiNG/ ▸ **adjective** not fair or sportsmanlike.
– DERIVATIVES **un·sport·ing·ly** adverb.

un·sports·man·like /ˌənˈspôrtsmənˌlīk/ ▸ **adjective** not behaving according to the spirit of fair play in a particular sport.

un·sprung /ˌənˈsprəNG/ ▸ **adjective** not provided with springs.

un·sta·ble /ˌənˈstābəl/ ▸ **adjective** (**unstabler, unstablest**) **1** likely to change or collapse; not stable. **2** prone to sudden changes of mood or mental health problems.

– SYNONYMS **1 unsteady,** rocky, wobbly, rickety, shaky, unsafe, insecure, precarious. **2 changeable,** volatile, variable, fluctuating, irregular, unpredictable, erratic. **3 unbalanced,** of unsound mind, mentally ill, deranged, demented, disturbed, unhinged.
– ANTONYMS steady, firm.

WORD TOOLKIT

See **VARIABLE**.

un·stained /ˌənˈstānd/ ▸ **adjective** not stained.

un·stat·ed /ˌənˈstātid/ ▸ **adjective** not stated or declared.

un·stead·y /ˌənˈstedē/ ▸ **adjective** (**unsteadier, unsteadiest**) **1** liable to fall or shake. **2** not regular or controlled.
– DERIVATIVES **un·stead·i·ly** adverb **un·stead·i·ness** noun.

un·stick /ˌənˈstik/ ▸ **verb** (past and past part. **unstuck** /ˌənˈstək/) separate a thing that is stuck to another.

un·stint·ing /ˌənˈstintiNG/ ▸ **adjective** given or giving without restraint.
– DERIVATIVES **un·stint·ed** adjective **un·stint·ing·ly** adverb.

un·stop·pa·ble /ˌənˈstäpəbəl/ ▸ **adjective** impossible to stop or prevent.
– DERIVATIVES **un·stop·pa·bly** /-blē/ adverb.

un·stop·per /ˌənˈstäpər/ ▸ **verb** remove the stopper from a container.

un·stressed /ˌənˈstrest/ ▸ **adjective** (of a syllable) not pronounced with stress.

un·string /ˌənˈstriNG/ ▸ **verb** (past and past part. **unstrung** /ˌənˈstrəNG/) **1** (usu. as adj. **unstrung**) unnerve or upset: *a mind unstrung by loneliness.* **2** remove or relax the string or strings of a bow or musical instrument.

un·struc·tured /ˌənˈstrəkCHərd/ ▸ **adjective** without formal organization or structure.

un·stuck /ˌənˈstək/ past and past participle of **UNSTICK**.
– PHRASES **come unstuck** informal fail.

un·stud·ied /ˌənˈstədēd/ ▸ **adjective** not forced or artificial; natural.

un·stuff·y /ˌənˈstəfē/ ▸ **adjective** friendly, informal, and approachable.

un·sub·scribe /ˌənsəbˈskrīb/ ▸ **verb** cancel a subscription, especially to an electronic mailing list.

un·sub·stan·tial /ˌənsəbˈstanCHəl/ ▸ **adjective** having little or no solidity, reality, or factual basis.

un·sub·stan·ti·at·ed /ˌənsəbˈstanCHēˌātid/ ▸ **adjective** not supported or proven by evidence.

un·sub·tle /ˌənˈsətl/ ▸ **adjective** not subtle; obvious.
– DERIVATIVES **un·sub·tly** adverb.

un·suc·cess·ful /ˌənsəkˈsesfəl/ ▸ **adjective** not successful.

– SYNONYMS **1 failed,** abortive, ineffective, fruitless, profitless, unproductive, vain, futile. **2 unprofitable,** loss-making.

– DERIVATIVES **un·suc·cess·ful·ly** adverb.

un·suit·a·ble /ˌənˈso͞otəbəl/ ▸ **adjective** not right or appropriate for a particular purpose or occasion.

– SYNONYMS **1 inappropriate,** ill-suited, inapposite, inapt, unacceptable, unfitting, incompatible, out of place, out of keeping, incongruous, unseemly. **2** *an unsuitable moment* **inopportune,** badly timed, unfortunate, difficult, infelicitous.
– ANTONYMS appropriate.

– DERIVATIVES **un·suit·a·bil·i·ty** /-ˌso͞otəˈbilətē/ noun **un·suit·a·bly** /-blē/ adverb.

un·suit·ed /ˌənˈso͞otid/ ▸ **adjective** lacking the right or necessary qualities for something: *he was totally unsuited for the job.*

un·sul·lied /ˌənˈsəlēd/ ▸ **adjective** not spoiled or made impure.

un·sung /ˌənˈsəNG/ ▸ **adjective** not celebrated or praised: *unsung heroes.*

un·su·per·vised /ˌənˈso͞opərˌvīzd/ ▸ **adjective** not done or acting under supervision.

un·sup·port·a·ble /ˌənsəˈpôrtəbəl/ ▶ **adjective** insupportable.

un·sup·port·ed /ˌənsəˈpôrtid/ ▶ **adjective 1** not supported. **2** not proven to be true by evidence or facts.

un·sure /ˌənˈSHŏŏr/ ▶ **adjective 1** lacking confidence. **2** not fixed or certain.

– SYNONYMS **1 undecided,** uncertain, irresolute, dithering, in two minds, in a quandary, dubious, doubtful, skeptical, unconvinced. **2 unconfident,** unassertive, insecure, hesitant, diffident, anxious, apprehensive.
– ANTONYMS sure, certain.

– DERIVATIVES **un·sure·ly** adverb **un·sure·ness** noun.

un·sur·faced /ˌənˈsərfist/ ▶ **adjective** (of a road or path) not provided with a hard-wearing upper layer.

un·sur·pass·a·ble /ˌənsərˈpasəbəl/ ▶ **adjective** not able to be bettered or exceeded.

un·sur·passed /ˌənsərˈpast/ ▶ **adjective** better or greater than any other.

un·sur·pris·ing /ˌənsə(r)ˈprīziNG/ ▶ **adjective** expected and so not causing surprise.
– DERIVATIVES **un·sur·pris·ing·ly** adverb.

un·sus·pect·ed /ˌənsəˈspektid/ ▶ **adjective 1** not known or thought to exist; not imagined as possible. **2** not regarded with suspicion.

un·sus·pect·ing /ˌənsəˈspektiNG/ ▶ **adjective** not aware of the presence of danger; feeling no suspicion.
– DERIVATIVES **un·sus·pect·ing·ly** adverb.

un·sus·tain·a·ble /ˌənsəˈstānəbəl/ ▶ **adjective 1** not able to be maintained at the current rate or level. **2** not able to be upheld or defended. **3** upsetting the ecological balance by depleting natural resources.
– DERIVATIVES **un·sus·tain·a·bly** /-blē/ adverb.

un·swayed /ˌənˈswād/ ▶ **adjective** not influenced or affected.

un·sweet·ened /ˌənˈswētnd/ ▶ **adjective** (of food or drink) without added sugar or other sweetener.

un·swerv·ing /ˌənˈswərviNG/ ▶ **adjective** not changing or becoming weaker.
– DERIVATIVES **un·swerv·ing·ly** adverb.

un·sym·met·ri·cal /ˌənsəˈmetrikəl/ ▶ **adjective** not symmetrical.

un·sym·pa·thet·ic /ˌənˌsimpəˈTHetik/ ▶ **adjective 1** not sympathetic. **2** not showing approval of an idea or action. **3** not likable.
– DERIVATIVES **un·sym·pa·thet·i·cal·ly** /-ik(ə)lē/ adverb.

un·sys·tem·at·ic /ˌənˌsistəˈmatik/ ▶ **adjective** not done or acting according to a fixed plan or system.
– DERIVATIVES **un·sys·tem·at·i·cal·ly** /-ik(ə)lē/ adverb.

un·taint·ed /ˌənˈtān(t)id/ ▶ **adjective** not contaminated or tainted.

un·tamed /ˌənˈtāmd/ ▶ **adjective** not tamed or controlled.
– DERIVATIVES **un·tame·a·ble** (also **untamable**) adjective.

un·tan·gle /ˌənˈtaNGgəl/ ▶ **verb 1** undo something that has become twisted or tangled. **2** make something complicated or confusing easier to understand or deal with.

– SYNONYMS **disentangle,** unravel, unsnarl, straighten out, untwist, unknot, sort out.

un·tapped /ˌənˈtapt/ ▶ **adjective** (of a resource) not yet exploited or used.

un·tar·nished /ˌənˈtärnisHt/ ▶ **adjective 1** (of metal) not tarnished. **2** not spoiled or ruined.

un·tast·ed /ˌənˈtāstid/ ▶ **adjective** (of food or drink) not sampled.

un·taught /ˌənˈtôt/ ▶ **adjective 1** not having been taught or educated. **2** not gained by teaching; natural or spontaneous.

un·ten·a·ble /ˌənˈtenəbəl/ ▶ **adjective** not able to be maintained or defended against attack or objection.

un·tend·ed /ˌənˈtendid/ ▶ **adjective** not cared for or looked after; neglected.

un·ten·ured /ˌənˈtenyərd/ ▶ **adjective** (of a college teacher or post) without tenure; not permanent.

Un·ter·mensch /ˈŏŏntərˌmencH/ ▶ **noun** (pl. **Untermenschen** /-ˌmencHən/) a person considered racially or socially inferior.
– ORIGIN German, 'underperson.'

un·test·ed /ˌənˈtestid/ ▶ **adjective** not subjected to testing; unproven.
– DERIVATIVES **un·test·a·ble** adjective.

un·think·a·ble /ˌənˈTHiNGkəbəl/ ▶ **adjective** too unlikely or undesirable to be considered a possibility.

– SYNONYMS **unimaginable,** inconceivable, unbelievable, incredible, implausible, out of the question, impossible, unconscionable, unreasonable.

– DERIVATIVES **un·think·a·bly** /-blē/ adverb.

un·think·ing /ˌənˈTHiNGkiNG/ ▶ **adjective** without proper consideration.
– DERIVATIVES **un·think·ing·ly** adverb.

un·thought /ˌənˈTHôt/ ▶ **adjective** (**unthought of**) not imagined or dreamed of.

un·threat·en·ing /ˌənˈTHretniNG/ ▶ **adjective** not threatening.

un·ti·dy /ˌənˈtīdē/ ▶ **adjective** (**untidier, untidiest**) **1** not arranged tidily. **2** (of a person) not keeping things tidy or well organized.

– SYNONYMS **1 disordered,** messy, disorganized, cluttered, in chaos, haywire, in disarray, disorderly, topsy-turvy, at sixes and sevens, jumbled; informal higgledy-piggledy. **2 scruffy,** disheveled, unkempt, messy, rumpled, bedraggled.
– ANTONYMS neat, tidy.

– DERIVATIVES **un·ti·di·ly** adverb **un·ti·di·ness** noun.

un·tie /ˌənˈtī/ ▶ **verb** (**unties, untying, untied**) undo or unfasten something tied.

un·til /ˌənˈtil, ən-/ ▶ **preposition & conjunction** up to the point in time or the event mentioned.
– ORIGIN from Old Norse *und* 'as far as' + TILL[1].

USAGE

For an explanation of the difference between **until** and **till**, see the note at TILL[1].

un·time·ly /ˌənˈtīmlē/ ▶ **adjective 1** happening or done at an unsuitable time; inappropriate. **2** (of a death or end) happening too soon or sooner than normal.
– DERIVATIVES **un·time·li·ness** noun.

un·tir·ing /ˌənˈtīriNG/ ▶ **adjective** continuing at the same rate without loss of energy.
– DERIVATIVES **un·tir·ing·ly** adverb.

un·ti·tled /ˌən'tītld/ ▸ adjective **1** (of a book or other work) having no title. **2** not having a title indicating high social or official rank.

un·to /'əntōō/ ▸ preposition **1** old-fashioned term for **TO**. **2** old-fashioned term for **UNTIL**.
– ORIGIN from **UNTIL**, with **TO** replacing **TILL**[1].

un·told /ˌən'tōld/ ▸ adjective **1** too much or too many to be counted: *thieves caused untold damage*. **2** not told or recounted.

un·touch·a·ble /ˌən'təCHəbəl/ ▸ adjective **1** not able to be touched or affected. **2** unable to be matched or rivaled. ▸ noun a member of the lowest caste in Hindu society.
– DERIVATIVES **un·touch·a·bil·i·ty** /-ˌtəCHə'bilitē/ noun.

> **USAGE**
>
> The use of the term **untouchable** to refer to a member of the lowest caste in Hindu society was declared illegal in the constitution of India in 1949 and of Pakistan in 1953. The official term today is **scheduled caste**.

un·touched /ˌən'təCHt/ ▸ adjective **1** not handled, used, or tasted. **2** not affected, changed, or damaged in any way.

un·to·ward /ˌən'tôrd, -t(ə)'wôrd/ ▸ adjective unexpected and inappropriate or unwelcome.

> – SYNONYMS **unexpected,** unforeseen, surprising, unusual, inappropriate, inconvenient, unwelcome, unfavorable, adverse, unfortunate, infelicitous.

un·trace·a·ble /ˌən'trāsəbəl/ ▸ adjective unable to be found or traced.

un·tracked /ˌən'trakt/ ▸ adjective (of land) without a path or tracks.

un·trained /ˌən'trānd/ ▸ adjective not having been trained in a particular skill.

un·tram·meled /ˌən'traməld/ (Brit. also **untrammelled**) ▸ adjective not restricted or hampered.

un·trans·lat·a·ble /ˌənˌtrans'lātəbəl, -ˌtranz-/ ▸ adjective not able to be translated.

un·treat·a·ble /ˌən'trētəbəl/ ▸ adjective for whom or which no medical care is available or possible.

un·treat·ed /ˌən'trētid/ ▸ adjective **1** not given medical care. **2** not treated by the use of a chemical, physical, or biological process, substance, etc.

un·tried /ˌən'trīd/ ▸ adjective not yet tested; inexperienced.

un·trod·den /ˌən'trädn/ ▸ adjective not having been walked on.

un·trou·bled /ˌən'trəbəld/ ▸ adjective not troubled.

un·true /ˌən'trōō/ ▸ adjective **1** false or incorrect. **2** not faithful or loyal.

> – SYNONYMS **false,** invented, made up, fabricated, concocted, trumped up, erroneous, wrong, incorrect, inaccurate.
> – ANTONYMS true, correct.

un·trust·wor·thy /ˌən'trəstˌwərT͟Hē/ ▸ adjective unable to be trusted.
– DERIVATIVES **un·trust·wor·thi·ness** noun.

un·truth /ˌən'trōōTH/ ▸ noun (pl. **untruths**) **1** a lie. **2** the quality of being false.

un·truth·ful /ˌən'trōōTHfəl/ ▸ adjective not truthful.
– DERIVATIVES **un·truth·ful·ly** adverb **un·truth·ful·ness** noun.

un·tucked /ˌən'təkt/ ▸ adjective with the edges or ends hanging loose; not tucked in.

un·tu·tored /ˌən't(y)ōōtərd/ ▸ adjective not formally taught or trained.

un·twist /ˌən'twist/ ▸ verb open something from a twisted position.

un·ty·ing /ˌən'tī-iNG/ present participle of **UNTIE**.

un·typ·i·cal /ˌən'tipikəl/ ▸ adjective unusual or uncharacteristic.
– DERIVATIVES **un·typ·i·cal·ly** /-ik(ə)lē/ adverb.

un·us·a·ble /ˌən'yōōzəbəl/ ▸ adjective not fit to be used.

un·used ▸ adjective **1** /ˌən'yōōzd/ not used. **2** /ˌən'yōōst/ (**unused to**) not accustomed to something.

un·u·su·al /ˌən'yōōZHōōəl/ ▸ adjective **1** not habitually or commonly done or occurring. **2** remarkable; exceptional.

> – SYNONYMS **1** *an unusual sight* **uncommon,** abnormal, atypical, unexpected, surprising, unfamiliar, different, strange, odd, curious, extraordinary, unorthodox, unconventional, peculiar, queer, unwonted; informal weird, offbeat. **2** *a man of unusual talent* **remarkable,** extraordinary, exceptional, particular, outstanding, notable, noteworthy, distinctive, striking, significant, special, unique, unparalleled, prodigious.
> – ANTONYMS common.

– DERIVATIVES **un·u·su·al·ly** adverb **un·u·su·al·ness** noun.

un·ut·ter·a·ble /ˌən'ətərəbəl/ ▸ adjective too great or awful to describe.
– DERIVATIVES **un·ut·ter·a·bly** /-blē/ adverb.

un·ut·tered /ˌən'ətərd/ ▸ adjective not spoken or expressed.

un·var·ied /ˌən've(ə)rēd/ ▸ adjective not varied.

un·var·nished /ˌən'värnisHt/ ▸ adjective **1** not varnished. **2** plain and straightforward: *the unvarnished truth*.

un·var·y·ing /ˌən've(ə)rē-iNG/ ▸ adjective not varying.
– DERIVATIVES **un·var·y·ing·ly** adverb.

un·veil /ˌən'vāl/ ▸ verb **1** show or announce publicly for the first time: *he unveiled plans to crack down on crime*. **2** remove a veil or covering from a new monument or work of art as part of a public ceremony. **3** remove a veil from someone's face.

un·ven·ti·lat·ed /ˌən'ventlˌātid/ ▸ adjective not ventilated.

un·ver·i·fi·a·ble /ˌən'verəˌfīəbəl, ˌənˌverə'fī-/ ▸ adjective unable to be verified.

un·ver·i·fied /ˌən'verəˌfīd/ ▸ adjective not verified.

un·versed /ˌən'vərst/ ▸ adjective (**unversed in**) not experienced or skilled in.

un·vi·a·ble /ˌən'vīəbəl/ ▸ adjective not capable of working successfully.

un·voiced /ˌən'voist/ ▸ adjective **1** not expressed in words. **2** (of a speech sound) produced without vibration of the vocal cords.

un·want·ed /ˌən'wäntid, ˌən'wōntid/ ▸ adjective not wanted.

un·war·rant·a·ble /ˌən'wôrəntəbəl, -'wär-/ ▸ adjective unjustifiable.
– DERIVATIVES **un·war·rant·a·bly** /-blē/ adverb.

un·war·rant·ed /ˌənˈwôrəntid, -ˈwär-/ ▸ **adjective** not warranted.

– SYNONYMS **1 unjustified,** indefensible, inexcusable, unforgivable, unpardonable, uncalled for, unnecessary, unjust, groundless. **2 unauthorized,** unsanctioned, unapproved, uncertified, unlicensed, illegal, unlawful, illicit, illegitimate, criminal, actionable.
– ANTONYMS justified.

un·war·y /ˌənˈwe(ə)rē/ ▸ **adjective** not cautious.
– DERIVATIVES **un·war·i·ly** adverb.

un·washed /ˌənˈwôsʜt, -ˈwäsʜt/ ▸ **adjective** not washed.
– PHRASES **the (great) unwashed** derogatory ordinary people; the masses.

un·watch·a·ble /ˌənˈwäcʜəbəl/ ▸ **adjective** too disturbing or boring to watch.

un·watched /ˌənˈwäcʜt/ ▸ **adjective** not watched.

un·wa·ver·ing /ˌənˈwāvəriɴɢ/ ▸ **adjective** not wavering; steady or resolute.
– DERIVATIVES **un·wa·ver·ing·ly** adverb.

un·weaned /ˌənˈwēnd/ ▸ **adjective** not weaned.

un·wea·ried /ˌənˈwi(ə)rēd/ ▸ **adjective** not wearied.

un·wea·ry·ing /ˌənˈwi(ə)rē-iɴɢ/ ▸ **adjective** never tiring or slackening.

un·wed /ˌənˈwed/ ▸ **adjective** not married.

un·wel·come /ˌənˈwelkəm/ ▸ **adjective** not welcome.

un·wel·com·ing /ˌənˈwelkəmiɴɢ/ ▸ **adjective** unfriendly or inhospitable.

un·well /ˌənˈwel/ ▸ **adjective** physically or mentally ill.

un·whole·some /ˌənˈhōlsəm/ ▸ **adjective** not wholesome.

un·wield·y /ˌənˈwēldē/ ▸ **adjective** (**unwieldier, unwieldiest**) hard to move or manage because of its size, shape, or weight.

– SYNONYMS **awkward,** unmanageable, unmaneuverable, cumbersome, clumsy, massive, heavy, hefty, bulky.

– DERIVATIVES **un·wield·i·ness** noun.
– ORIGIN from **WIELD**.

un·will·ing /ˌənˈwiliɴɢ/ ▸ **adjective** not willing.

– SYNONYMS **1 reluctant,** unenthusiastic, hesitant, resistant, grudging, involuntary, forced. **2** *he was unwilling to go* **disinclined,** reluctant, averse, loath, not in the mood; (**be unwilling to do something**) balk at, demur at, shy away from, flinch from, shrink from, have qualms about, have misgivings about, have reservations about.
– ANTONYMS willing.

– DERIVATIVES **un·will·ing·ly** adverb **un·will·ing·ness** noun.

WORD TOOLKIT

unwilling ...	unenthusiastic ...	hesitant ...
participant	applause	step
victim	reception	pause
addict	tone	knock
accomplice	response	approach

un·wind /ˌənˈwīnd/ ▸ **verb** (past and past part. **unwound**) **1** undo something that has been wound. **2** relax after a period of work or tension.

un·win·na·ble /ˌənˈwinəbəl/ ▸ **adjective** not winnable.

un·wis·dom /ˌənˈwizdəm/ ▸ **noun** foolishness.

un·wise /ˌənˈwīz/ ▸ **adjective** foolish.
– DERIVATIVES **un·wise·ly** adverb.

un·wit·ting /ˌənˈwitiɴɢ/ ▸ **adjective 1** not aware of the full facts. **2** unintentional.
– DERIVATIVES **un·wit·ting·ly** adverb.
– ORIGIN Old English, 'not knowing or realizing.'

un·wom·an·ly /ˌənˈwo͝omənlē/ ▸ **adjective** not womanly.

un·wont·ed /ˌənˈwôntid/ ▸ **adjective** not usual or expected.
– DERIVATIVES **un·wont·ed·ly** adverb.

un·work·a·ble /ˌənˈwərkəbəl/ ▸ **adjective** not able to be done successfully; impractical.

un·worked /ˌənˈwərkt/ ▸ **adjective** not cultivated, mined, or carved.

un·world·ly /ˌənˈwərldlē/ ▸ **adjective 1** not interested in money or other material things. **2** lacking experience of life. **3** not seeming to belong to this world.
– DERIVATIVES **un·world·li·ness** noun.

un·worn /ˌənˈwôrn/ ▸ **adjective 1** not worn or damaged from much use. **2** (of an item of clothing) never worn.

un·wor·ried /ˌənˈwərēd/ ▸ **adjective** not worried or anxious.

un·wor·thy /ˌənˈwər<u>th</u>ē/ ▸ **adjective** (**unworthier, unworthiest**) **1** not deserving respect or attention. **2** not appropriate to someone's good reputation or social position: *such a suggestion is unworthy of the gentleman.*
– DERIVATIVES **un·wor·thi·ly** adverb **un·wor·thi·ness** noun.

un·wound /ˌənˈwound/ past and past participle of **UNWIND**.

un·wound·ed /ˌənˈwo͞ondid/ ▸ **adjective** not wounded.

un·wrap /ˌənˈrap/ ▸ **verb** (**unwraps, unwrapping, unwrapped**) remove the wrapping from something.

un·wrin·kled /ˌənˈriɴɢkəld/ ▸ **adjective** not wrinkled.

un·writ·a·ble /ˌənˈrītəbəl/ ▸ **adjective** not able to be written.

un·writ·ten /ˌənˈritn/ ▸ **adjective 1** not recorded in writing. **2** (of a law, rule, agreement, etc.) generally accepted although not formally established.

un·yield·ing /ˌənˈyēldiɴɢ/ ▸ **adjective** not yielding or giving way.

– SYNONYMS **1** *unyielding spikes of cane* **stiff,** inflexible, unbending, inelastic, firm, hard, solid, tough. **2 resolute,** inflexible, uncompromising, unbending, unshakable, unwavering, immovable, intractable, intransigent, determined, dogged, obstinate, stubborn, tenacious, relentless, implacable, single-minded.

un·zip /ˌənˈzip/ ▸ **verb** (**unzips, unzipping, unzipped**) **1** unfasten the zipper of an item of clothing. **2** Computing expand a compressed file.

up /əp/ ▸ **adverb 1** toward a higher place or position. **2** to the place where someone is: *I crept up behind him.* **3** at or to a higher level or value. **4** so as to be formed, finished, or brought together: *the government set up an inquiry.* **5** out of bed. **6** in a publicly visible place. **7** (of the sun) visible in the sky. **8** toward the north. **9** into a happy mood. **10** winning by a specified margin: *the Mets were up by 5 in the fourth inning.* **11** Brit. toward or

in the capital or a major city. ▶ **preposition** **1** from a lower to a higher point of something. **2** from one end of a street or other area to another. ▶ **adjective** **1** directed or moving toward a higher place or position. **2** at an end. **3** (of the road) being repaired. **4** feeling cheerful. **5** (of a computer system) working properly. ▶ **verb** (**ups, upping, upped**) increase a level or amount. ▶ **noun** informal a period of success or happiness.
– PHRASES **be up on** be well informed about. **on the up and up** informal legitimate; honest and sincere. **something is up** informal something significant is happening. **up against 1** close to or touching. **2** informal confronted with. **up and down** in various places throughout. **up before** appearing for a hearing in the presence of a judge, magistrate, etc. **up for 1** available for. **2** being considered for. **3** due for. **4** (often **up for it**) informal ready to take part in something. **ups and downs** a mixture of both good and bad experiences. **up to 1** as far as a particular number, level, point, etc. **2** (also **up until**) until. **3** good enough for or capable of. **4** the duty or choice of. **5** informal occupied with. **what's up?** informal **1** what is going on? **2** what is the matter?
– ORIGIN Old English.

up- ▶ **prefix** **1** (added to verbs and their derivatives) upward: *upturned*. **2** (added to verbs and their derivatives) to a more recent time: *update*. **3** (added to nouns) referring to motion up: *uphill*. **4** (added to nouns) higher: *upland*.

up-and-com·ing ▶ **adjective** likely to become successful.
– DERIVATIVES **up-and-com·er** noun.

U·pan·i·shad /(y)o͝o'panəˌsʜad, o͞o'pəniˌsʜəd/ ▶ **noun** each of a series of Hindu sacred books explaining the philosophy introduced in the Vedas (the oldest Hindu scriptures).
– ORIGIN Sanskrit, 'sitting near (i.e., at the feet of a master).'

up·beat /'əpˌbēt/ ▶ **adjective** positive and cheerful or enthusiastic.

> – SYNONYMS **cheerful,** optimistic, cheery, positive, confident, hopeful, sanguine, bullish, buoyant.
> – ANTONYMS pessimistic.

▶ **noun** (in music) an unstressed beat coming before a stressed beat.

up·braid /ˌəp'brād/ ▶ **verb** criticize or scold someone.
– ORIGIN Old English, 'allege as a basis for censure.'

> **CHOOSE THE RIGHT WORD**
>
> See **SCOLD**.

up·bring·ing /'əpˌbriɴɢiɴɢ/ ▶ **noun** the way in which a child is cared for and taught how to behave while it is growing up.

> – SYNONYMS **childhood,** early life, formative years, teaching, instruction, rearing.

UPC ▶ **abbreviation** Universal Product Code; a more formal term for **BAR CODE**.

up·chuck /'əpˌcʜək/ informal ▶ **verb** vomit. ▶ **noun** matter vomited from the stomach.

up·com·ing /'əpˌkəmiɴɢ/ ▶ **adjective** about to happen; forthcoming.

up·coun·try /ˌəp'kəntrē, 'əpˌkəntrē/ ▶ **adverb & adjective** in or toward the inland areas of a country.

up·date ▶ **verb** /ˌəp'dāt, 'əpˌdāt/ **1** make something more modern. **2** give someone the latest information.

> – SYNONYMS **1 modernize,** upgrade, improve, overhaul. **2 brief,** bring up to date, inform, fill in, tell, notify, keep posted; informal clue in, put in the picture, bring/keep up to speed.

▶ **noun** /'əpˌdāt/ an act of updating or an updated version.
– DERIVATIVES **up·dat·a·ble** adjective.

up·draft /'əpˌdraft/ (Brit. **updraught**) ▶ **noun** an upward current or draft of air.

up·end /ˌəp'end/ ▶ **verb** set or turn something on its end or upside down.

up·field /ˌəp'fēld/ ▶ **adverb** Football another term for **DOWNFIELD**.

up·front /ˌəp'frənt/ informal ▶ **adverb** (usu. **up front**) **1** at the front; in front. **2** (of a payment) in advance. ▶ **adjective** **1** expressing one's thoughts and intentions openly; frank. **2** (of a payment) made in advance.

up·grade /'əpˌgrād, ˌəp'grād/ ▶ **verb** **1** raise to a higher standard, level, etc.: *the company will be upgrading its services*. **2** promote an employee.

> – SYNONYMS **improve,** modernize, update, reform.
> – ANTONYMS downgrade.

▶ **noun** an act of upgrading or an upgraded version.
– DERIVATIVES **up·grad·a·ble** (also **upgradeable**) adjective **up·grad·er** noun.

up·heav·al /ˌəp'hēvəl/ ▶ **noun** a violent or sudden change or disruption.

> – SYNONYMS **disturbance,** disruption, trouble, turbulence, disorder, confusion, turmoil.

up·hill /ˌəp'hil/ ▶ **adverb** toward the top of a slope. ▶ **adjective** **1** sloping upward. **2** difficult: *an uphill struggle*.

> – SYNONYMS **1 upward,** rising, ascending, climbing. **2 difficult,** hard, tough, demanding, arduous, taxing, exacting, stiff, grueling, onerous.
> – ANTONYMS downhill.

up·hold /ˌəp'hōld/ ▶ **verb** (past and past part. **upheld** /ˌəp'held/) **1** support something and ensure that it continues to exist: *it is the sheriff's duty to uphold the law*. **2** (of a court of law or official body) agree that a previous decision was correct or that a request is reasonable.

> – SYNONYMS **1 confirm,** endorse, sustain, approve, support, back (up). **2 maintain,** sustain, continue, preserve, protect, keep, hold to, keep alive, keep going.
> – ANTONYMS oppose.

– DERIVATIVES **up·hold·er** noun.

up·hol·ster /əp'hōlstər, ə'pōl-/ ▶ **verb** provide a sofa, chair, etc., with a soft, padded covering.
– DERIVATIVES **up·hol·ster·er** noun.
– ORIGIN from **UPHOLD** in the former sense 'keep in repair.'

up·hol·ster·y /əp'hōlst(ə)rē, ə'pōl-/ ▶ **noun** **1** the soft, padded covering on a sofa, chair, etc. **2** the art or practice of upholstering furniture.

up·keep /'əpˌkēp/ ▶ **noun** **1** the process of keeping something in good condition. **2** the cost of supporting a person or keeping something in good condition.

> – SYNONYMS **1 maintenance,** repair(s), servicing, care, preservation, conservation, running. **2 (financial) support,** maintenance, keep, subsistence, care.

up·land /ˈəplənd/ ▶ **noun** (also **uplands**) an area of high or hilly land.

up·lift /ˌəpˈlift/ ▶ **verb 1** (often as adj. **uplifting**) make more happy, spiritual, or moral. **2** lift something up. **3** (**be uplifted**) (of an island, mountain, etc.) be created by an upward movement of the earth's surface.

– SYNONYMS (as adj. **uplifting**) *tender and uplifting songs* **inspiring**, stirring, inspirational, rousing, moving, touching, affecting, cheering, heartening, encouraging.

▶ **noun 1** an act of lifting or raising something. **2** support from a bra or similar garment for a woman's bust. **3** a feeling of new happiness, hope, or spirituality.
– DERIVATIVES **up·lift·er** noun.

up·light·er /ˈəpˌlītər/ ▶ **noun** a lamp designed to throw light upward.
– DERIVATIVES **up·light·ing** noun.

up·link /ˈəpˌlinɢk/ ▶ **noun** a communications link to a satellite. ▶ **verb** send something by a communications link to a satellite.

up·load /ˈəpˌlōd, ˌəpˈlōd/ ▶ **verb** transfer data to a larger computer system. ▶ **noun** the action or process of transferring data to a larger computer system.

up·mar·ket /ˌəpˈmärkit, ˈəpˌmär-/ ▶ **adjective & adverb** expensive and of high quality; upscale.

up·on /əˈpän, əˈpôn/ ▶ **preposition** more formal term for **ON**.

up·per /ˈəpər/ ▶ **adjective 1** situated above another part. **2** higher in position or status. **3** situated on higher ground. **4** (in place names) situated to the north.

– SYNONYMS **1 higher,** superior, top. **2 senior,** superior, higher-level, higher-ranking, top.
– ANTONYMS lower.

▶ **noun 1** the part of a boot or shoe above the sole. **2** informal a stimulating drug, especially an amphetamine.
– PHRASES **have the upper hand** have an advantage or control.

up·per·case /ˈəpərˈkās/ ▶ **noun** capital letters.

up·per class ▶ **noun** (treated as sing. or pl.) the social group with the highest status, especially the aristocracy. ▶ **adjective** (**upper-class**) relating to the upper class: *our upper-class relations look down on us.*

– SYNONYMS **aristocratic,** noble, patrician, titled, blue-blooded, high-born, elite; informal upper-crust, top-drawer, posh.

up·per·class·man /ˌəpərˈklasmən/ ▶ **noun** (pl. **upperclassmen**) a junior or senior in high school or college.

up·per crust ▶ **noun** (**the upper crust**) informal the upper classes.

up·per·cut /ˈəpərˌkət/ ▶ **noun** a punch delivered with an upward motion and the arm bent.

up·per house (also **upper chamber**) ▶ **noun 1** one of two houses (often the smaller) in a bicameral legislature or parliament. **2** the Senate (of the US or of a US state). **3** (**the Upper House**) (in the UK) the House of Lords.

up·per·most /ˈəpərˌmōst/ ▶ **adjective** highest in place, rank, or importance. ▶ **adverb** at or to the uppermost position.

up·pi·ty /ˈəpətē/ ▶ **adjective** informal self-important; arrogant.
– ORIGIN from **UP**.

up·raise /ˌəpˈrāz/ ▶ **verb** raise something to a higher level.

up·rate /ˌəpˈrāt, ˈəpˌrāt/ ▶ **verb 1** increase the value of a payment. **2** improve the performance of something.

up·right /ˈəpˌrīt/ ▶ **adjective 1** vertical; erect. **2** greater in height than breadth. **3** strictly respectable or honest: *an upright member of the community.* **4** (of a piano) having vertical strings.

– SYNONYMS **1 vertical,** perpendicular, plumb, straight (up), erect, on end, on one's feet. **2 honest,** honorable, upstanding, respectable, high-minded, law-abiding, worthy, righteous, decent, good, virtuous, principled.
– ANTONYMS flat, horizontal.

▶ **adverb** in or into an upright position.
▶ **noun 1** a vertical post, structure, or line. **2** an upright piano.
– DERIVATIVES **up·right·ly** adverb **up·right·ness** noun.

up·ris·ing /ˈəpˌrīzinɢ/ ▶ **noun** a rebellion or revolt against an established ruler or government.

– SYNONYMS **rebellion,** revolt, insurrection, mutiny, revolution, insurgence, rioting, coup.

up·riv·er /ˈəpˈrivər/ ▶ **adverb & adjective** toward or situated at a point nearer the source of a river.

up·roar /ˈəpˌrôr/ ▶ **noun 1** a loud and emotional noise or disturbance. **2** a public expression of outrage.

– SYNONYMS **1 commotion,** disturbance, rumpus, disorder, confusion, chaos, tumult, mayhem, pandemonium, bedlam, noise, din, clamor, hubbub, racket; Brit. row; informal hullabaloo. **2 outcry,** furor, fuss, commotion, hue and cry, rumpus; informal stink.
– ANTONYMS calm.

– ORIGIN Dutch *uproer*.

up·roar·i·ous /ˌəpˈrôrēəs/ ▶ **adjective 1** very noisy or lively. **2** very funny.
– DERIVATIVES **up·roar·i·ous·ly** adverb **up·roar·i·ous·ness** noun.

up·root /ˌəpˈro͞ot, -ˈro͝ot/ ▶ **verb 1** pull a plant, tree, etc., out of the ground. **2** move someone from their home or usual surroundings.

up·rush /ˈəpˌrəsʜ/ ▶ **noun** a sudden surge or flow, especially of a feeling.

UPS ▶ **abbreviation** Computing uninterruptible power supply.

up·scale /ˌəpˈskāl, ˈəpˌskāl/ ▶ **adjective & adverb** expensive and of high quality or status.

up·set ▶ **verb** /ˌəpˈset/ (**upsets, upsetting, upset**) **1** make someone unhappy, disappointed, or worried. **2** knock something over. **3** disrupt or disturb: *antibiotics can upset the balance of bacteria in the bowel.*

– SYNONYMS **1 distress,** trouble, perturb, dismay, sadden, grieve, disturb, unsettle, disconcert, disquiet, worry, bother, agitate, fluster, throw, ruffle, unnerve, shake. **2 knock over,** overturn, upend, tip over, topple, spill. **3 disrupt,** interfere with, disturb, throw into confusion, mess up.
– ANTONYMS calm.

▶ **noun** /ˈəpset/ **1** an unexpected result or situation. **2** the state of being unhappy, disappointed, or worried.

– SYNONYMS **1 distress,** trouble, dismay, disquiet, worry, bother, agitation, hurt, grief. **2** *a stomach upset* **disorder,** complaint, ailment, illness, sickness; informal bug.

▶ adjective 1 /ˌəpˈset/ unhappy, disappointed, or worried. 2 /ˈəpset/ (of a person's stomach) having disturbed digestion.

– SYNONYMS **1 distressed,** troubled, perturbed, dismayed, disturbed, unsettled, disconcerted, worried, bothered, anxious, agitated, flustered, ruffled, unnerved, shaken, saddened, grieved; informal cut up, choked up. **2** *an upset stomach* **disturbed,** unsettled, queasy, bad, poor.
– ANTONYMS calm.

– DERIVATIVES **up·set·ting** adjective.

up·shot /ˈəpˌSHät/ ▶ noun the eventual outcome or conclusion of something.

up·side /ˈəpˌsīd/ ▶ noun the positive aspect of a situation.

up·side down ▶ adverb & adjective 1 with the upper part where the lower part should be. 2 in or into total disorder.

– SYNONYMS **1 upturned,** upended, wrong side up, overturned, inverted, capsized. **2 in disarray,** in disorder, jumbled up, in a muddle, untidy, disorganized, in chaos, in confusion, topsy-turvy, at sixes and sevens; informal higgledy-piggledy.

– ORIGIN from *up so down*, perhaps meaning 'up as if down.'

up·side-down cake ▶ noun a cake that is baked over a layer of fruit in syrup and turned out upside down for serving.

up·size /ˈəpˌsīz/ ▶ verb increase in size or complexity.

up·stage /ˌəpˈstāj/ ▶ verb 1 divert attention from someone else and toward oneself. 2 (of an actor) move toward the back of a stage to make another actor face away from the audience. ▶ adverb & adjective at or toward the back of a stage.

up·stairs /ˌəpˈste(ə)rz/ ▶ adverb on or to an upper floor. ▶ adjective situated on an upper floor. ▶ noun an upper floor.

up·stand·ing /ˌəpˈstandiNG, ˈəpˌstan-/ ▶ adjective respectable and honest.

up·start /ˈəpˌstärt/ ▶ noun derogatory a person who has suddenly become important and behaves arrogantly.

up·state /ˈəpˈstāt/ ▶ adjective & adverb in or to a part of a state remote from its large cities. ▶ noun an upstate area.

up·stream /ˌəpˈstrēm/ ▶ adverb & adjective situated or moving in the direction opposite to that in which a stream or river flows.

up·stroke /ˈəpˌstrōk/ ▶ noun an upward stroke.

up·surge /ˈəpˌsərj/ ▶ noun a sudden large increase: *an upsurge in cases of domestic violence.*

up·swept /ˈəpˌswept/ ▶ adjective (of the hair) brushed upward and off the face.

up·swing /ˈəpˌswiNG/ ▶ noun an increase or improvement; an upward trend.

up·sy-dai·sy /ˈəpsē ˌdāzē/ ▶ exclamation expressing encouragement to a child who has fallen or is being lifted.

up·take /ˈəpˌtāk/ ▶ noun the action of taking up or making use of something.
– PHRASES **be quick** (or **slow**) **on the uptake** informal be quick (or slow) to understand things.

up·tem·po /ˈəpˌtempō/ ▶ adjective & adverb Music played with a fast or increased tempo.

up·thrust /ˈəpˌTHrəst/ ▶ noun 1 something that has been thrust upward. 2 the upward movement of part of the earth's surface. ▶ verb thrust something upward.

up·tight /ˌəpˈtīt/ ▶ adjective informal 1 nervously tense or angry. 2 unable to express one's feelings; repressed.

up·time /ˈəpˌtīm/ ▶ noun time during which a machine, especially a computer, is in operation.

up to date ▶ adjective incorporating or aware of the latest developments and trends.

– SYNONYMS **1 modern,** contemporary, the latest, state-of-the-art, new, up-to-the-minute, advanced. **2 informed,** up to speed, in the picture, in touch, au fait, conversant, familiar, knowledgeable, acquainted.
– ANTONYMS out of date, old-fashioned.

up·town ▶ adjective & adverb /ˌəpˈtoun/ in or typical of the residential area of a town or city, especially an area of affluence. ▶ noun /ˈəpˌtoun/ an uptown area.

up·trend /ˈəpˌtrend/ ▶ noun an upward tendency, especially in economic matters.

up·turn /ˈəpˌtərn/ ▶ noun an improvement or upward trend.

up·turned /ˈəpˌtərnd, ˌəpˈtərnd/ ▶ adjective turned upward or upside down.

uPVC ▶ abbreviation unplasticized polyvinyl chloride, a rigid form of PVC used for pipework and window frames.

up·ward /ˈəpwərd/ ▶ adverb (also **upwards**) toward a higher point or level. ▶ adjective moving or leading toward a higher point or level.
– DERIVATIVES **up·ward·ly** adverb.
– PHRASES **upwards of** more than.

up·ward·ly mo·bile ▶ adjective moving to a higher social class; acquiring wealth and status.

up·well·ing /ˌəpˈweliNG/ ▶ noun an instance or amount of something rising or building up: *a strong upwelling of nationalism.*

up·wind /ˌəpˈwind/ ▶ adverb & adjective into the wind.

u·ra·ni·um /yo͝oˈrānēəm/ ▶ noun a dense radioactive metallic chemical element used as a fuel in nuclear reactors.
– ORIGIN from **URANUS**.

U·ran·us /ˈyo͝orənəs, yo͝oˈrā-/ ▶ noun a planet of the solar system, seventh in order from the sun.
– DERIVATIVES **U·ra·ni·an** /yo͝oˈrānēən/ adjective.

ur·ban /ˈərbən/ ▶ adjective 1 relating to a town or city. 2 (of popular culture, especially dance music) of black origin.

– SYNONYMS **town,** city, municipal, metropolitan, built-up, inner-city, suburban.
– ANTONYMS rural.

– DERIVATIVES **ur·ban·ism** /ˈərbəˌnizəm/ noun **ur·ban·ist** /ˈərbənist/ noun.
– ORIGIN Latin *urbanus*.

ur·bane /ˌərˈbān/ ▶ adjective (of a man) confident, courteous, and sophisticated.
– DERIVATIVES **ur·bane·ly** adverb.
– ORIGIN first meaning 'urban': from Latin *urbanus*.

> **CHOOSE THE RIGHT WORD**
>
> **urbane, cosmopolitan, genteel, sophisticated, suave**
>
> In his long career as a film star, Cary Grant was known for playing **urbane, sophisticated** roles. *Urbane* in this context suggests the social poise and polished manner of someone who is well-traveled and well-bred, while *sophisticated* means worldly-wise as opposed to naive (*a sophisticated young girl who had spent her childhood in Paris and London*). **Cosmopolitan** describes someone who is at home anywhere in the world and is free from provincial attitudes (*a cosmopolitan man who could charm women of all ages and nationalities*), while **suave** suggests the gracious social behavior of *urbane* combined with a certain glibness or superficial politeness (*she was taken in by his expensive clothes and suave manner*). At one time **genteel** meant well-bred or refined, but nowadays it has connotations of self-consciousness or pretentiousness (*too genteel to drink wine from a juice glass*).

ur·ban·ite /ˈərbəˌnīt/ ▶ **noun** informal a person who lives in a town or city.

ur·ban·i·ty /ˌərˈbanitē/ ▶ **noun** the quality of being confident, courteous, and sophisticated.

ur·ban·ize /ˈərbəˌnīz/ ▶ **verb 1** build towns and cities in a country area. **2** make someone used to living in a city rather than a country area.
– DERIVATIVES **ur·ban·i·za·tion** /ˌərbənəˈzāsʜən/ noun.

ur·ban leg·end (also **urban myth**) ▶ **noun** an entertaining story or piece of information of uncertain origin that is circulated as if it is true.

ur·chin /ˈərcʜin/ ▶ **noun 1** a poor child dressed in ragged clothes. **2** short for SEA URCHIN.
– ORIGIN Old French *herichon* 'hedgehog.'

Ur·du /ˈo͝ordo͞o, ˈər-/ ▶ **noun** a language closely related to Hindi, the official language of Pakistan and widely used in India.
– ORIGIN from Persian, 'language of the camp' (because it developed as a means of communication between the occupying Muslim armies and the people of Delhi in the 12th century).

u·re·a /yo͞oˈrēə/ ▶ **noun** a colorless crystalline compound that is excreted from the body in urine.
– ORIGIN Latin.

u·re·ter /ˈyo͝oritər, yo͝oˈrētər/ ▶ **noun** the duct by which urine passes from the kidney to the bladder.
– ORIGIN Greek *ourētēr*.

u·re·thane /ˈyo͝orəˌᴛʜān/ ▶ **noun** a synthetic crystalline compound used to make pesticides and fungicides.
– ORIGIN from UREA + ETHANE.

u·re·thra /yo͝oˈrēᴛʜrə/ ▶ **noun** the duct by which urine passes out of the body, and which in males also carries semen.
– DERIVATIVES **u·re·thral** adjective.
– ORIGIN Greek *ourēthra*.

u·re·thri·tis /ˌyo͝orəˈᴛʜrītis/ ▶ **noun** inflammation of the urethra.

urge /ərj/ ▶ **verb 1** try earnestly or persistently to persuade someone to do something. **2** strongly recommend something. **3** encourage to move more quickly or in a particular direction: *he urged his pony on*.

> – SYNONYMS **1 encourage,** exhort, press, entreat, implore, call on, appeal to, beg, plead with. **2 advise,** counsel, advocate, recommend.

▶ **noun** a strong desire or impulse.

> – SYNONYMS *his urge to travel* **desire,** wish, need, compulsion, longing, yearning, hankering, craving, hunger, thirst; informal yen, itch.

– ORIGIN Latin *urgere* 'press, drive.'

ur·gent /ˈərjənt/ ▶ **adjective 1** requiring immediate action or attention. **2** earnest and insistent: *an urgent whisper*.

> – SYNONYMS **pressing,** acute, dire, desperate, critical, serious, grave, intense, crying, burning, compelling, extreme, high-priority, life-and-death.

– DERIVATIVES **ur·gen·cy** noun **ur·gent·ly** adverb.

u·ric ac·id /ˈyo͝orik/ ▶ **noun** an insoluble compound that is the main substance excreted by birds, reptiles, and insects.
– ORIGIN French *urique*.

u·ri·nal /ˈyo͝orənl/ ▶ **noun** a bowl attached to the wall in a public toilet, into which men urinate.

u·ri·nar·y /ˈyo͝orəˌnerē/ ▶ **adjective 1** relating to urine. **2** referring to the organs, structures, and ducts in which urine is produced and passed from the body.

u·ri·nate /ˈyo͝orəˌnāt/ ▶ **verb** pass urine from the body.
– DERIVATIVES **u·ri·na·tion** /ˌyo͝orəˈnāsʜən/ noun.
– ORIGIN Latin *urinare*.

u·rine /ˈyo͝orən/ ▶ **noun** a yellowish fluid stored in the bladder and discharged through the urethra, consisting of excess water and waste substances removed from the blood by the kidneys.
– ORIGIN Latin *urina*.

URL ▶ **abbreviation** uniform (or universal) resource locator, the address of a World Wide Web page.

urn /ərn/ ▶ **noun 1** a tall, rounded vase with a stem and base, especially one for storing a cremated person's ashes. **2** a large metal container with a tap, in which tea or coffee is made and kept hot.
– ORIGIN Latin *urna*.

u·ro·gen·i·tal /ˌyo͝orōˈjenətl, ˌyo͝orə-/ ▶ **adjective** referring to both the urinary and genital organs.

u·rol·o·gy /yo͝oˈräləjē/ ▶ **noun** the branch of medicine concerned with the urinary system.
– DERIVATIVES **u·ro·log·i·cal** /ˌyo͝orəˈläjikəl/ adjective **u·rol·o·gist** noun.

ur·sine /ˈərˌsīn/ ▶ **adjective** relating to or resembling bears.
– ORIGIN Latin *ursinus*.

Ur·su·line /ˈərs(y)əlin, -ˌlīn, -ˌlēn/ ▶ **noun** a nun of an order founded in Italy for nursing the sick and teaching girls. ▶ **adjective** relating to the Ursulines.
– ORIGIN from St. *Ursula*, the founder's patron saint.

ur·ti·car·i·a /ˌərtiˈke(ə)rēə/ ▶ **noun** technical term for HIVES.
– ORIGIN from Latin *urtica* 'nettle.'

U·ru·guay·an /ˌ(y)o͝orəˈgwīən, -ˈgwā-/ ▶ **noun** a person from Uruguay. ▶ **adjective** relating to Uruguay.

US ▶ **abbreviation** United States.

us /əs/ ▶ **pronoun** (first person pl.) **1** used by a speaker to refer to himself or herself and one or more others as the object of a verb or preposition. **2** used after the verb 'to be' and after 'than' or 'as'. **3** informal me.
– ORIGIN Old English.

> **USAGE**
>
> For an explanation of whether to use **us** or **we** after **than**, see the note at PERSONAL PRONOUN.

USA ▶ **abbreviation** United States of America.

us·a·ble /ˈyo͞ozəbəl/ (also **useable**) ▶ **adjective** able to be used.
– DERIVATIVES **us·a·bil·i·ty** /ˌyo͞ozəˈbilətē/ noun.

USAF ▶ **abbreviation** United States Air Force.

us·age /ˈyo͞osij, -zij/ ▶ **noun** **1** the action of using something or the fact of being used: *a survey of water usage*. **2** the way in which words are normally and correctly used in a language.

– SYNONYMS **1** *energy usage* **consumption,** use. **2** *the usage of equipment* **use,** utilization, operation, manipulation, running, handling. **3** **language,** expression, phraseology, parlance, idiom.

USB ▶ **abbreviation** universal serial bus, a connector that enables any of a variety of peripheral devices to be plugged into a computer.

USB flash drive ▶ **noun** a small external flash drive that can be used with any computer with a USB port.

USDA ▶ **abbreviation** United States Department of Agriculture.

use ▶ **verb** /yo͞oz/ **1** take, hold, or employ something as a means of achieving a purpose. **2** take or consume an amount from an available supply. **3** (**use something up**) consume the whole of something. **4** treat someone in a particular way. **5** take advantage of or exploit someone. **6** /yo͞ost/ (**used to**) did repeatedly or existed in the past: *this road used to be a track*. **7** /yo͞ost/ (**be/get used to**) be or become familiar with someone or something through experience.

– SYNONYMS **1** **utilize,** employ, avail oneself of, work, operate, wield, ply, apply, put into service. **2** **exercise,** employ, bring into play, practice, apply. **3** **take advantage of,** exploit, manipulate, take liberties with, impose on, abuse, capitalize on, profit from, trade on, milk; informal cash in on, walk all over. **4** *we have used up our funds* **consume,** go through, exhaust, deplete, expend, spend.

▶ **noun** /yo͞os/ **1** the action of using something or the state of being used. **2** the ability or power to move or control something: *he lost the use of his legs*. **3** a purpose for or way in which something can be used. **4** the value or point of something: *what's the use of crying?*

– SYNONYMS **1** **utilization,** application, employment, operation, manipulation. **2** **exploitation,** manipulation, abuse. **3** *what is the use of that?* **advantage,** benefit, good, point, object, purpose, sense, reason, service, utility, help, gain, avail, profit, value, worth.

– PHRASES **make use of** use or benefit from.
– ORIGIN Old French *user*.

USAGE

Confusion can arise over whether to write **used to** or **use to**. It is correct to write **used to** except in negatives and questions: *we used to go to the cinema all the time*. However, in negatives and questions using the verb **do**, you should write **use to**: *I didn't use to like mushrooms*.

use·a·ble /ˈyo͞ozəbəl/ ▶ **adjective** variant spelling of **USABLE**.

use-by date ▶ **noun** a date marked on packaged food indicating the recommended date by which it should be eaten.

used /yo͞ozd/ ▶ **adjective** **1** secondhand: *a used car*. **2** having already been used.

– SYNONYMS **secondhand,** pre-owned, nearly new, old, worn, hand-me-down, castoff.

use·ful /ˈyo͞osfəl/ ▶ **adjective** able to be used for a practical purpose or in several ways.

– SYNONYMS **1** *a useful tool* **functional,** practical, handy, convenient, utilitarian, serviceable, of service; informal nifty. **2** *a useful experience* **beneficial,** advantageous, helpful, worthwhile, profitable, rewarding, productive, constructive, valuable, fruitful.
– ANTONYMS useless.

– DERIVATIVES **use·ful·ly** adverb **use·ful·ness** noun.

use·less /ˈyo͞osləs/ ▶ **adjective** **1** serving no purpose. **2** informal having little ability or skill.

– SYNONYMS **1** **futile,** pointless, to no avail, vain, to no purpose, unavailing, hopeless, ineffectual, fruitless, unprofitable, unproductive, abortive. **2** **incompetent,** inept, ineffective, incapable, inadequate, hopeless, bad.
– ANTONYMS useful, beneficial.

– DERIVATIVES **use·less·ly** adverb **use·less·ness** noun.

Use·net /ˈyo͞ozˌnet/ ▶ **noun** an Internet service consisting of thousands of newsgroups.

us·er /ˈyo͞ozər/ ▶ **noun** a person who uses or operates something.

us·er-friend·ly ▶ **adjective** easy to use or understand.
– DERIVATIVES **us·er-friend·li·ness** noun.

us·er in·ter·face ▶ **noun** the method or software by which users communicate with computers, typically involving a graphic display with clickable items or dialog boxes.

ush·er /ˈəsʜər/ ▶ **noun** **1** a person who shows people to their seats in a theater or church. **2** an official in a court of law who swears in jurors and witnesses and keeps order.

– SYNONYMS **guide,** attendant, escort.

▶ **verb** **1** show or guide someone somewhere. **2** (**usher something in**) cause or mark the start of something new: *when the first jet crossed the Atlantic it ushered in a new era*.

– SYNONYMS **escort,** accompany, take, show, see, lead, conduct, guide.

– ORIGIN Old French *usser* 'doorkeeper.'

ush·er·ette /ˌəsʜəˈret/ ▶ **noun** a woman who shows people to their seats in a theater.

USMC ▶ **abbreviation** United States Marine Corps.

USN ▶ **abbreviation** United States Navy.

USO ▶ **abbreviation** United Service Organizations.

USP ▶ **abbreviation** unique selling point (or proposition).

USPS ▶ **abbreviation** United States Postal Service.

USS ▶ **abbreviation** United States Ship.

USSR ▶ **abbreviation** historical Union of Soviet Socialist Republics.

u·su·al /ˈyo͞ozʜo͞oəl/ ▶ **adjective** happening or done most of the time or in most cases.

– SYNONYMS **normal,** customary, accustomed, wonted, habitual, routine, regular, standard, typical, established, set, stock, conventional, traditional,

expected, familiar.
– ANTONYMS exceptional.

▶ **noun** informal **1** the thing that happens or is done most of the time. **2** (**the/one's usual**) the drink someone regularly prefers.
– ORIGIN Latin *usualis*.

u·su·al·ly /ˈyo͞ozʜ(o͞o)əlē/ ▶ **adverb 1** in a way that is usual or normal. **2** generally speaking; as a rule.

– SYNONYMS **normally,** generally, habitually, customarily, routinely, typically, ordinarily, commonly, as a rule, in general, more often than not, mainly, mostly.

u·su·ri·ous /yo͞oˈzʜo͝orēəs/ ▶ **adjective** relating to the lending of money at unreasonably high rates of interest.

u·surp /yo͞oˈsərp, yo͞oˈzərp/ ▶ **verb** take over a person's position or power illegally or by force.
– DERIVATIVES **u·sur·pa·tion** /ˌyo͞osərˈpāsʜən/ noun **u·surp·er** noun.
– ORIGIN Latin *usurpare* 'seize for use.'

u·su·ry /ˈyo͞ozʜ(ə)rē/ ▶ **noun** the practice of lending money at unreasonably high rates of interest.
– DERIVATIVES **u·su·rer** noun.
– ORIGIN Latin *usura*.

UT ▶ **abbreviation** Utah.

u·ten·sil /yo͞oˈtensəl/ ▶ **noun** a tool or container, especially for household use.

– SYNONYMS **implement,** tool, instrument, device, apparatus, gadget, appliance, contrivance, contraption; informal gizmo.

– ORIGIN from Latin *utensilis* 'usable.'

CHOOSE THE RIGHT WORD

See **TOOL**.

u·ter·ine /ˈyo͞otərin, -ˌrīn/ ▶ **adjective** relating to the uterus.

u·ter·us /ˈyo͞otərəs/ ▶ **noun** (pl. **uteri** /ˈyo͞otəˌrī, -ˌrē/) the organ in the body of a woman or female mammal in which offspring develop before birth; the womb.
– ORIGIN Latin.

u·til·i·tar·i·an /yo͞oˌtiliˈte(ə)rēən/ ▶ **adjective 1** useful or practical rather than attractive. **2** relating to utilitarianism. ▶ **noun** a person who supports utilitarianism.

u·til·i·tar·i·an·ism /yo͞oˌtiləˈte(ə)rēəˌnizəm/ ▶ **noun** the belief that the right course of action is the one that will lead to the greatest happiness of the greatest number of people.

u·til·i·ty /yo͞oˈtilətē/ ▶ **noun** (pl. **utilities**) **1** the state of being useful, profitable, or beneficial: *the garden was treated as a combination of utility and beauty.* **2** an organization supplying electricity, gas, water, or sewerage to the public.

– SYNONYMS **usefulness,** use, benefit, value, advantage, help, practicality, effectiveness, service.

▶ **adjective** having several uses or functions.
– ORIGIN Latin *utilitas*.

u·til·i·ty knife ▶ **noun** a knife with a short, strong replaceable blade.

u·til·i·ty room ▶ **noun** a room in which a washing machine and other domestic equipment are kept.

u·til·i·ty ve·hi·cle (also **utility truck**) ▶ **noun** a truck with low sides, used for small loads.

u·ti·lize /ˈyo͞otlˌīz/ ▶ **verb** make practical and effective use of something.

– SYNONYMS **use,** employ, avail oneself of, press into service, bring into play, deploy, draw on, exploit.

– DERIVATIVES **u·ti·liz·a·ble** /ˌyo͞otlˈīzəbəl, ˈyo͞otlˌī-/ adjective **u·ti·li·za·tion** /ˌyo͞otl-əˈzāsʜən/ noun.
– ORIGIN French *utiliser*.

ut·most /ˈətˌmōst/ ▶ **adjective** most extreme; greatest.

– SYNONYMS **greatest,** highest, maximum, most, extreme, supreme, paramount.

▶ **noun** (**the utmost**) the greatest or most extreme extent or amount.
– ORIGIN Old English, 'outermost.'

WORD TOOLKIT

See **VITAL**.

U·to·pi·a /yo͞oˈtōpēə/ ▶ **noun** an imaginary place, society, or situation where everything is perfect.
– ORIGIN the title of a book by Sir Thomas More, from Greek *ou* 'not' + *topos* 'place.'

u·to·pi·an /yo͞oˈtōpēən/ ▶ **adjective** relating to or aiming for a situation in which everything is perfect. ▶ **noun** a person with idealistic views on reform.
– DERIVATIVES **u·to·pi·an·ism** /-ˌnizəm/ noun.

ut·ter[1] /ˈətər/ ▶ **adjective** complete; absolute: *I stared at him in utter amazement.*

– SYNONYMS **complete,** total, absolute, thorough, perfect, downright, out-and-out, outright, sheer, arrant, positive, prize, pure, unmitigated, unadulterated, unqualified, unalloyed.

– DERIVATIVES **ut·ter·ly** adverb.
– ORIGIN Old English, 'outer.'

utter[2] ▶ **verb 1** make a sound or say something. **2** Law put forged money into circulation.

– SYNONYMS **say,** speak, voice, mouth, express, articulate, pronounce, enunciate, emit, let out, give, produce.

– DERIVATIVES **ut·ter·a·ble** adjective **ut·ter·er** noun.
– ORIGIN Dutch *ūteren* 'speak, make known, give currency to coins.'

ut·ter·ance /ˈətərəns/ ▶ **noun 1** a word, statement, or sound uttered. **2** the action of uttering something.

– SYNONYMS **remark,** comment, statement, observation, declaration, pronouncement.

ut·ter·most /ˈətərˌmōst/ ▶ **adjective & noun** another term for **UTMOST**.

U-turn ▶ **noun 1** the turning of a vehicle in a U-shaped course so as to face the opposite way. **2** a complete change of policy or behavior: *the government is doing a U-turn on road building.*

UV ▶ **abbreviation** ultraviolet.

UVA ▶ **abbreviation** ultraviolet radiation of relatively long wavelengths.

UVB ▶ **abbreviation** ultraviolet radiation of relatively short wavelengths.

UVC ▶ **abbreviation** ultraviolet radiation of very short wavelengths, which does not penetrate the earth's ozone layer.

u·vu·la /ˈyo͞ovyələ/ ▶ **noun** (pl. **uvulae** /-ˌlē, -ˌlī/) a fleshy part of the soft palate that hangs above the throat.
– ORIGIN Latin, 'little grape.'

UWB ▶ **abbreviation** ultra wideband, a radio communications technology for the transmission of signals over a very broad range of frequencies.

ux·o·ri·al /ˌəkˈsôrēəl, əgˈzôr-/ ▶ **adjective** relating to a wife.

ux·o·ri·ous /ˌəkˈsôrēəs, ˌəgˈzôr-/ ▶ **adjective** (of a man) very or excessively fond of his wife.
– DERIVATIVES **ux·o·ri·ous·ness** noun.
– ORIGIN Latin *uxoriosus*.

Uz·bek /ˈo͝ozˌbek, ˈəz-, o͝ozˈbek/ ▶ **noun 1** a person from Uzbekistan. **2** a member of a people living mainly in Uzbekistan. **3** the language of Uzbekistan.
– ORIGIN Uzbek.

U·zi /ˈo͞ozē/ ▶ **noun** a type of submachine gun.
– ORIGIN from *Uziel* Gal, the Israeli army officer who designed it.

Vv

V¹ (also v) ▶ noun (pl. **Vs** or **V's**) **1** the twenty-second letter of the alphabet. **2** the Roman numeral for five.

V² ▶ abbreviation volt(s). ▶ symbol **1** the chemical element vanadium. **2** voltage or potential difference. **3** (in mathematical formulae) volume.

v. ▶ abbreviation **1** Grammar verb. **2** versus. **3** very. ▶ symbol (v) velocity.

VA ▶ abbreviation Virginia.

vac /vak/ ▶ noun informal a vacuum cleaner.

va·can·cy /'vākənsē/ ▶ noun (pl. **vacancies**) **1** a job or position that is available for someone to do. **2** an available room in a hotel, guest house, etc. **3** empty space. **4** lack of intelligence or interest: *her wide-eyed vacancy.*

– SYNONYMS **opening,** position, post, job, opportunity.

va·cant /'vākənt/ ▶ adjective **1** not occupied; empty. **2** (of a job or position) not filled. **3** showing no intelligence or interest.

– SYNONYMS **1 empty,** unoccupied, not in use, free, available, unfilled, uninhabited, untenanted; informal up for grabs. **2 blank,** expressionless, unresponsive, emotionless, impassive, vacuous, empty, glazed.
– ANTONYMS full, occupied.

– DERIVATIVES **va·cant·ly** adverb.

va·cate /'vā,kāt/ ▶ verb **1** go out of a place, leaving it empty. **2** give up a job or position.

– SYNONYMS **1 leave,** move out of, evacuate, quit, depart from. **2 resign from,** leave, stand down from, give up, bow out of, relinquish, retire from; informal quit.
– ANTONYMS occupy.

– ORIGIN Latin *vacare* 'leave empty.'

va·ca·tion /vā'kāsHən, və-/ ▶ noun **1** an extended period of leisure, especially away from home. **2** a fixed period of time off between terms in schools and courts. **3** the action of leaving a place or job.

– SYNONYMS **break,** time off, recess, leave, holiday, trip, tour.

▶ verb take a vacation, especially away from home.
– DERIVATIVES **va·ca·tion·er** noun **va·ca·tion·ist** noun.

vac·ci·nate /'vaksə,nāt/ ▶ verb treat a person or animal with a vaccine to produce immunity against a disease.
– DERIVATIVES **vac·ci·na·tion** /,vaksə'nāsHən/ noun.

vac·cine /vak'sēn/ ▶ noun a substance made from the microorganisms that cause a disease, injected into the body to make it produce antibodies and so provide immunity against that disease.
– ORIGIN Latin *vaccinus.*

vac·il·late /'vasə,lāt/ ▶ verb keep changing one's mind about something.
– DERIVATIVES **vac·il·la·tion** /,vasə'lāsHən/ noun.
– ORIGIN Latin *vacillare* 'sway.'

vac·u·ole /'vakyoo͞,ōl/ ▶ noun Biology a space inside a cell, enclosed by a membrane and typically containing fluid.
– ORIGIN from Latin *vacuus* 'empty.'

vac·u·ous /'vakyəwəs/ ▶ adjective showing a lack of thought or intelligence.

– SYNONYMS **silly,** inane, unintelligent, foolish, stupid, brainless, vapid, vacant, empty-headed; informal gormless, moronic, brain-dead.
– ANTONYMS intelligent.

– DERIVATIVES **va·cu·i·ty** /va'kyoo͞ətē, və-/ noun **vac·u·ous·ly** adverb **vac·u·ous·ness** noun.
– ORIGIN Latin *vacuus* 'empty.'

WORD TOOLKIT

See **FOOLISH**.

vac·u·um /'vak,yoo͞(ə)m, -yəm/ ▶ noun (pl. **vacuums** or **vacua** /-yoo͞ə/) **1** a space that is completely empty of matter. **2** a space from which the air has been completely or partly removed. **3** a gap left by the loss or departure of someone or something important. **4** (pl. **vacuums**) a vacuum cleaner. ▶ verb clean something with a vacuum cleaner.
– PHRASES **in a vacuum** without relation to someone or something else; in isolation.
– ORIGIN Latin.

vac·u·um clean·er ▶ noun an electrical device that collects dust and other particles by means of suction.

vac·u·um-pack ▶ verb seal a product in a pack or wrapping with the air removed.

vac·u·um tube ▶ noun a sealed glass tube containing a near vacuum that allows the free passage of electric current.

va·de me·cum /,vädē 'mäkəm, ,vādē 'mē-/ ▶ noun a handbook or guide that a person carries with them to refer to.
– ORIGIN Latin, 'go with me.'

vag·a·bond /'vagə,bänd/ ▶ noun a person who has no settled home or job; a vagrant.
– ORIGIN Latin *vagabundus.*

va·gar·y /'vāgərē/ ▶ noun (pl. **vagaries**) a change that cannot be predicted or explained: *the vagaries of the weather.*
– ORIGIN from Latin *vagari* 'wander.'

va·gi·na /və'jīnə/ ▶ noun the muscular tube leading from the external genitals to the cervix (neck of the uterus) in women and most female mammals.
– DERIVATIVES **vag·i·nal** adjective **va·g·i·nal·ly** adverb.
– ORIGIN Latin, 'sheath, scabbard.'

va·grant /'vāgrənt/ ▶ noun a person who has no settled home or job.

– SYNONYMS **tramp,** drifter, hobo, down-and-out, beggar, itinerant, wanderer; informal bum.

▶ **adjective** relating to or living as a vagrant; wandering.
– DERIVATIVES **va·gran·cy** noun.
– ORIGIN from Old French *vagarant* 'wandering about.'

vague /vāg/ ▶ **adjective 1** not clear, certain, or detailed: *vague promises of a better future.* **2** thinking or expressing oneself in an imprecise or unclear way.

– SYNONYMS **1 indistinct,** indefinite, indeterminate, unclear, ill-defined, hazy, fuzzy, misty, blurry, out of focus, shadowy, obscure. **2 imprecise,** rough, approximate, inexact, nonspecific, ambiguous, hazy, uncertain. **3 absentminded,** forgetful, dreamy, abstracted; informal with one's head in the clouds, not with it.
– ANTONYMS clear, definite.

– DERIVATIVES **vague·ness** noun.
– ORIGIN Latin *vagus* 'wandering, uncertain.'

WORD TOOLKIT

See **INCOMPLETE**.

vague·ly /'vāglē/ ▶ **adverb** in a vague way.

– SYNONYMS **1** *she looks vaguely familiar* **slightly,** a little, a bit, somewhat, rather, in a way, faintly, obscurely; informal sort of, kind of. **2** *he smiled vaguely* **absentmindedly,** abstractedly, vacantly.

vain /vān/ ▶ **adjective 1** having an excessively high opinion of oneself. **2** not producing the required result; unsuccessful.

– SYNONYMS **1** *he was vain about his looks* **conceited,** narcissistic, proud, arrogant, boastful, cocky, egotistical, immodest; informal bigheaded. **2** *a vain attempt* **futile,** useless, pointless, ineffective, unavailing, fruitless, unproductive, unsuccessful, failed, abortive.
– ANTONYMS modest, successful.

– DERIVATIVES **vain·ly** adverb.
– PHRASES **in vain** without success. **take someone's name in vain** use someone's name in a way that shows a lack of respect.
– ORIGIN Latin *vanus* 'empty, without substance.'

USAGE

Do not confuse **vain** with **vane** or **vein**. **Vain** means 'having an excessively high opinion of oneself' (*a vain woman with a touch of snobbery*) or 'unsuccessful' (*a vain attempt to tidy up*); **vane** means 'a broad blade forming part of a windmill, propeller, or turbine'; **vein** means 'a tube that carries blood around the body' or 'a particular way, style, or quality' (*he continued in a more serious vein*).

vain·glo·ry /'vān,glôrē, ,vān'glôrē/ ▶ **noun** literary excessive pride in oneself.
– DERIVATIVES **vain·glo·ri·ous** /,vān'glôrēəs/ adjective **vain·glo·ri·ous·ly** /,vān'glôrēəslē/ adverb.

Vais·ya /'vīsнyə, 'vīs-/ (also **Vaishya** pronunc. same) ▶ **noun** a member of the third of the four Hindu castes, comprising merchants and farmers.
– ORIGIN Sanskrit, 'peasant, laborer.'

val·ance /'valəns, 'vāləns/ ▶ **noun 1** a length of fabric screening the curtain fittings above a window. **2** Brit. a bedskirt.
– DERIVATIVES **val·anced** adjective.
– ORIGIN perhaps from Old French *avaler* 'lower, descend.'

vale /vāl/ ▶ **noun** literary (except in place names) a valley.
– PHRASES **vale of tears** the world as a place of trouble or sorrow.
– ORIGIN Latin *vallis*.

val·e·dic·tion /,valə'diksнən/ ▶ **noun 1** the action of saying goodbye. **2** a farewell speech or statement.
– ORIGIN from Latin *vale* 'goodbye' + *dicere* 'to say.'

val·e·dic·to·ri·an /,valə,dik'tôrēən/ ▶ **noun** a student, typically having the highest academic achievements of their class, who delivers the valedictory at a graduation ceremony.

val·e·dic·to·ry /,valə'dikt(ə)rē/ ▶ **adjective** related to saying goodbye. ▶ **noun** (pl. **valedictories**) a farewell speech.

va·lence /'vāləns/ (also **valency** /'vālənsē/) ▶ **noun** the combining power of a chemical element, as measured by the number of hydrogen atoms it can displace or combine with.
– ORIGIN Latin *valentia* 'power, competence.'

val·en·tine /'valən,tīn/ ▶ **noun 1** a card sent on St. Valentine's Day (February 14) to a person one loves or is attracted to. **2** a person to whom one sends such a card.

va·le·ri·an /və'li(ə)rēən/ ▶ **noun 1** a plant with clusters of small pink, red, or white flowers. **2** a sedative drug obtained from a valerian root.
– ORIGIN Latin *valeriana*.

val·et /va'lā, 'valā, 'valit/ ▶ **noun 1** a man's male attendant, responsible for looking after his clothes and other personal needs. **2** a person employed to clean or park cars. ▶ **verb** (**valets, valeting, valeted**) **1** clean a car as a professional service. **2** act as a valet to a man.
– ORIGIN French.

val·e·tu·di·nar·i·an /,valə,t(y)o͞odn'e(ə)rēən/ ▶ **noun** a person in poor health or who worries too much about their health.
– ORIGIN from Latin *valetudinarius* 'in ill health.'

Val·hal·la /val'halə, väl'hälə/ ▶ **noun** Scandinavian Mythology a palace in which heroes killed in battle feasted for eternity.
– ORIGIN Old Norse, 'hall of the slain.'

val·iant /'valyənt/ ▶ **adjective** showing courage or determination.

– SYNONYMS **brave,** courageous, plucky, intrepid, heroic, gallant, bold, fearless, daring, unflinching, unafraid, undaunted, doughty, indomitable, stouthearted; informal game, gutsy.
– ANTONYMS cowardly.

– DERIVATIVES **val·iant·ly** adverb.
– ORIGIN Old French *vailant*.

val·id /'valid/ ▶ **adjective 1** (of a reason, argument, etc.) based on what is true or logical. **2** officially acceptable or legally binding: *a valid passport*.

– SYNONYMS **1 well founded,** sound, reasonable, rational, logical, justifiable, defensible, cogent, credible, forceful. **2 legally binding,** lawful, official, in force, in effect.

– DERIVATIVES **va·lid·i·ty** /və'lidətē/ noun **val·id·ly** adverb.
– ORIGIN Latin *validus* 'strong.'

val·i·date /'valə,dāt/ ▶ **verb 1** check or prove that something is true or valid. **2** make or declare something to be officially acceptable or legally binding.

– SYNONYMS **ratify,** endorse, approve, agree to, accept, authorize, legalize, legitimize, warrant, license, certify, recognize.

– DERIVATIVES **val·i·da·tion** /ˌvalə'dāsʜən/ noun.

va·lise /və'lēs/ ▸ **noun** a small travel bag or suitcase.
– ORIGIN French.

Val·i·um /'valēəm/ ▸ **noun** trademark for **DIAZEPAM**.
– ORIGIN unknown.

Val·kyr·ie /val'ki(ə)rē, 'valkərē/ ▸ **noun** Scandinavian Mythology each of Odin's twelve handmaids who chose heroes killed in battle to take to Valhalla.
– ORIGIN Old Norse, 'chooser of the slain.'

val·ley /'valē/ ▸ **noun** (pl. **valleys**) a low area between hills or mountains, typically with a river or stream flowing through it.

– SYNONYMS **dale,** vale, glen, hollow, gully, gorge, ravine, canyon, rift.

– ORIGIN Latin *vallis*.

val·or /'valər/ (Brit. **valour**) ▸ **noun** great courage in the face of danger.

– SYNONYMS **bravery,** courage, pluck, nerve, daring, fearlessness, audacity, boldness, stoutheartedness, heroism; informal guts.
– ANTONYMS cowardice.

– DERIVATIVES **val·or·ous** adjective.
– ORIGIN Latin *valor*.

val·or·ize /'valəˌrīz/ ▸ **verb** give value or validity to: *the English valorize stupidity*.
– DERIVATIVES **val·or·i·za·tion** /ˌvalərə'zāsʜən/ noun.
– ORIGIN from French *valorisation*.

Val·po·li·cel·la /ˌvalˌpōlə'cʜelə, ˌväl-/ ▸ **noun** a red wine made in the Val Policella district of Italy.

val·u·a·ble /'valy(o͞o)əbəl/ ▸ **adjective 1** worth a great deal of money. **2** very useful or important.

– SYNONYMS **1 precious,** costly, high-priced, expensive, dear, priceless. **2 useful,** helpful, beneficial, advantageous, invaluable, productive, worthwhile, worthy, important.
– ANTONYMS worthless.

▸ **noun** (**valuables**) valuable items.

– SYNONYMS **precious items,** costly items, prized possessions, treasures.

– DERIVATIVES **val·u·a·bly** /-blē/ adverb.

val·u·a·tion /ˌvalyo͞o'āsʜən/ ▸ **noun** an estimate of how much something is worth, especially one carried out by a professional valuer.

val·ue /'valyo͞o/ ▸ **noun 1** the amount of money that something is worth. **2** the importance or worth of something: *he realized the value of education*. **3** (**values**) beliefs about what is right and wrong and what is important. **4** Mathematics the amount represented by a letter, symbol, or number. **5** the relative duration of the sound represented by a musical note.

– SYNONYMS **1 price,** cost, worth, market price. **2 worth,** usefulness, advantage, benefit, gain, profit, good, help. **3 (values) principles,** ethics, morals, standards, code of behavior.

▸ **verb** (**values, valuing, valued**) **1** estimate the value of something. **2** consider to be important or worthwhile: *she had come to value her privacy*.

– SYNONYMS **1 evaluate,** assess, estimate, appraise, price. **2 think highly of,** have a high opinion of, rate highly, esteem, set great store by, respect.
– ANTONYMS despise.

– DERIVATIVES **val·ue·less** adjective.
– ORIGIN Old French.

val·ue-add·ed tax ▸ **noun** a tax on the amount by which a product rises in value at each stage of its production or distribution.

val·ue judg·ment ▸ **noun** an assessment of something as good or bad based on personal opinions rather than facts.

valve /valv/ ▸ **noun 1** a device for controlling the flow of a liquid or gas through a pipe or duct. **2** a cylindrical mechanism used to vary the length of the tube in a brass musical instrument. **3** a structure in the heart or in a blood vessel that allows blood to flow in one direction only. **4** each of the two parts of the hinged shell of a bivalve mollusk such as an oyster or mussel.
– ORIGIN Latin *valva* 'leaf of a folding or double door.'

val·vu·lar /'valvyələr/ ▸ **adjective** relating to or having a valve or valves.

va·moose /va'mo͞os, və-/ ▸ **verb** informal leave somewhere hurriedly.
– ORIGIN from Spanish *vamos* 'let us go.'

vamp[1] /vamp/ ▸ **verb** (**vamp something up**) informal improve something by adding something more interesting. ▸ **noun** the upper front part of a boot or shoe.
– ORIGIN first referring to the foot of a stocking: from Old French *avant* 'before' + *pie* 'foot.'

vamp[2] informal ▸ **noun** a woman who uses her sexual attractiveness to seduce and control men. ▸ **verb** blatantly set out to attract a man.
– DERIVATIVES **vamp·ish** adjective **vamp·y** adjective.
– ORIGIN short for **VAMPIRE**.

vam·pire /'vamˌpī(ə)r/ ▸ **noun 1** (in folklore) a dead person supposed to leave their grave at night to drink the blood of living people. **2** (also **vampire bat**) a small bat that feeds on blood by piercing the skin with its teeth, found mainly in tropical America.
– DERIVATIVES **vam·pir·ic** /vam'pirik/ adjective **vam·pir·ism** /'vampīˌrizəm/ noun.
– ORIGIN Hungarian *vampir*.

van[1] /van/ ▸ **noun 1** a motor vehicle used for transporting goods or people. **2** Brit. a baggage or freight car on a train.
– ORIGIN shortening of **CARAVAN**.

van[2] ▸ **noun** (**the van**) **1** the leading part of an advancing group of people. **2** the forefront: *we have always been in the van of progress*.
– ORIGIN short for **VANGUARD**.

va·na·di·um /və'nādēəm/ ▸ **noun** a hard gray metallic chemical element, used to make alloy steels.
– ORIGIN from an Old Norse name of the Scandinavian goddess Freyja.

Van Al·len belt /'alən/ ▸ **noun** each of two regions of intense radiation partly surrounding the earth at heights of several thousand kilometers.
– ORIGIN named after the American physicist James A. Van Allen.

van·dal /'vandl/ ▸ **noun** a person who deliberately destroys or damages property.
– DERIVATIVES **van·dal·ism** /'vandlˌizəm/ noun.
– ORIGIN Latin *Vandalus*, referring to a Germanic people that plundered parts of Europe and North Africa in the 4th–5th centuries.

van·dal·ize /ˈvandlˌīz/ ▸ **verb** deliberately destroy or damage property.

Van·dyke /vanˈdīk/ (also **Vandyke beard**) ▸ **noun** a neat pointed beard.
– ORIGIN named after the Flemish painter Sir Anthony *Van Dyck*.

vane /vān/ ▸ **noun 1** a broad blade attached to a rotating axis or wheel that pushes or is pushed by wind or water, forming part of a windmill, propeller, or turbine. **2** a weathervane.
– ORIGIN Germanic.

> **USAGE**
>
> For an explanation of the difference between **vane**, **vain**, and **vein**, see the note at **VAIN**.

van·guard /ˈvanˌgärd/ ▸ **noun 1** a group of people leading the way in new developments or ideas. **2** the leading part of an advancing army or naval force.
– ORIGIN Old French *avantgarde*.

va·nil·la /vəˈnilə/ ▸ **noun** a substance obtained from the pods of a tropical orchid or produced artificially, used as a flavoring.
– ORIGIN Spanish *vainilla* 'pod.'

van·ish /ˈvanisн/ ▸ **verb 1** disappear from view suddenly and completely. **2** stop existing: *woodlands are vanishing*.

> – SYNONYMS **disappear,** be lost to sight, become invisible, recede from view, fade (away), evaporate, melt away, end, cease to exist.
> – ANTONYMS appear.

– DERIVATIVES **van·ish·ing** adjective & noun **van·ish·ing·ly** adverb.
– ORIGIN Old French *esvanir*.

van·ish·ing point ▸ **noun** the point in the distance at which receding parallel lines appear to meet.

van·i·ty /ˈvanətē/ ▸ **noun** (pl. **vanities**) **1** excessive pride in one's appearance or achievements. **2** the quality of being pointless or futile: *the vanity of human wishes*. **3** a vanity table.

> – SYNONYMS **conceit,** narcissism, self-love, self-admiration, egotism, pride, arrogance, boastfulness, cockiness; informal bigheadedness.
> – ANTONYMS modesty.

– ORIGIN Latin *vanitas*.

> **CHOOSE THE RIGHT WORD**
>
> See **PRIDE**.

van·i·ty case ▸ **noun** a small case fitted with a mirror and compartments for makeup.

van·i·ty ta·ble ▸ **noun** a dressing table.

van·i·ty u·nit ▸ **noun** a unit consisting of a washbasin set into a flat top with cupboards beneath.

van·quish /ˈvaNGkwisн/ ▸ **verb** literary defeat someone or something completely.
– DERIVATIVES **van·quish·er** noun.
– ORIGIN Old French *vainquir*.

van·tage /ˈvantij/ (also **vantage point**) ▸ **noun** a place or position giving a good view.
– ORIGIN Old French *avantage* 'advantage.'

vap·id /ˈvapid/ ▸ **adjective** not interesting or original: *vapid musical comedies*.
– DERIVATIVES **va·pid·i·ty** /vaˈpidətē/ noun **vap·id·ly** adverb.
– ORIGIN Latin *vapidus*.

va·por /ˈvāpər/ (Brit. **vapour**) ▸ **noun 1** a liquid or substance that is suspended in the air in a mass of tiny drops or particles. **2** Physics a gaseous substance that can be made into liquid by pressure alone. **3** (**the vapors**) dated a fit of faintness, nervousness, or depression.
– DERIVATIVES **va·por·ous** adjective.
– ORIGIN Latin *vapor* 'steam, heat.'

va·po·ret·to /ˌväpəˈretō, ˌvapə-/ ▸ **noun** (pl. **vaporetti** /-ˈretē/ or **vaporettos**) (in Venice) a canal boat used for public transportation.
– ORIGIN Italian.

va·por·ize /ˈvāpəˌrīz/ ▸ **verb** convert a substance into vapor.
– DERIVATIVES **va·por·i·za·tion** /ˌvāpərəˈzāsнən, -ˌrīˈzā-/ noun.

va·por·iz·er /ˈvāpəˌrīzər/ ▸ **noun** a device that is used to breathe in medicine in the form of a vapor.

va·por trail ▸ **noun** a trail of condensed water from an aircraft or rocket at high altitude, seen as a white streak against the sky.

va·pour, etc. /ˈvāpər/ ▸ **noun** British spelling of **VAPOR**, etc.

va·que·ro /väˈkerō/ ▸ **noun** (pl. **vaqueros**) (in Spanish-speaking parts of the US) a cowboy; a cattle driver.
– ORIGIN Spanish.

VAR ▸ **abbreviation** value-added reseller, a company that adds extra features to products it has bought before selling them to consumers.

var·i·a·ble /ˈve(ə)rēəbəl/ ▸ **adjective 1** often changing or likely to change; not consistent: *the photos are of variable quality*. **2** able to be changed or adapted. **3** Mathematics (of a quantity) able to take on different numerical values.

> – SYNONYMS **changeable,** shifting, fluctuating, irregular, inconstant, inconsistent, fluid, unstable; informal up and down.
> – ANTONYMS constant.

▸ **noun** a variable element, feature, or quantity.
– DERIVATIVES **var·i·a·bil·i·ty** /ˌve(ə)rēəˈbilitē/ noun **var·i·a·bly** /-blē/ adverb.

WORD TOOLKIT

variable ...	unstable ...	mercurial ...
rate	situation	nature
length	world	talent
speed	region	temperament
size	environment	personality
results	condition	moods
effects	economy	shifts
frequency	government	energy

var·i·ance /ˈve(ə)rēəns/ ▸ **noun** the amount by which something changes or is different from something else.
– PHRASES **at variance (with)** inconsistent with or opposing.

var·i·ant /ˈve(ə)rēənt/ ▸ **noun** a form or version that varies from other forms of the same thing or from a standard type.

> – SYNONYMS **1** *there are a number of variants of the same idea* **variation,** version, form, alternative, adaptation, alteration, modification. **2** (as adj.) *a variant spelling* **alternative,** other, different, divergent.

var·i·a·tion /ˌve(ə)rēˈāsʜən/ ▶ **noun** **1** a change or slight difference in condition, amount, or level: *regional variations in house prices.* **2** a different or distinct form or version. **3** a new but still recognizable version of a musical theme.

– SYNONYMS **1 difference,** dissimilarity, disparity, contrast, discrepancy, imbalance. **2** *there was little variation from the pattern* **deviation,** variance, divergence, departure, fluctuation, change, alteration, modification.

– DERIVATIVES **var·i·a·tion·al** adjective.

var·i·col·ored /ˈve(ə)riˌkələrd/ ▶ **adjective** consisting of several different colors.

var·i·cose /ˈvarəˌkōs/ ▶ **adjective** (of a vein, especially in the leg) swollen, twisted, and lengthened, as a result of poor circulation.
– ORIGIN Latin *varicosus.*

var·ied /ˈve(ə)rēd/ ▶ **adjective** involving a number of different types or elements: *a long and varied career.*

– SYNONYMS **diverse,** assorted, miscellaneous, mixed, sundry, wide-ranging, disparate, heterogeneous, motley.

var·i·e·gat·ed /ˈver(ē)əˌgātid/ ▶ **adjective** having irregular patches or streaks of different colors.
– DERIVATIVES **var·i·e·ga·tion** /ˌver(ē)iˈgāsʜən/ noun.
– ORIGIN from Latin *variegare* 'make varied.'

va·ri·e·tal /vəˈrīətl/ ▶ **adjective** **1** (of a wine or grape) made from or belonging to a single specified variety of grape. **2** relating to or forming a variety of plant or animal.

va·ri·e·ty /vəˈrīətē/ ▶ **noun** (pl. **varieties**) **1** the quality or state of being different or varied. **2** (**a variety of**) a range of things of the same general type that are different in character: *the center offers a variety of activities.* **3** a type: *fifty varieties of pasta.* **4** a form of entertainment consisting of a series of different acts, such as singing, dancing, and comedy. **5** Biology a subspecies or cultivar.

– SYNONYMS **1 diversity,** variation, diversification, change, difference. **2 assortment,** miscellany, range, array, collection, selection, mixture, medley. **3 sort,** kind, type, class, category, style, form, make, model, brand, strain, breed.
– ANTONYMS uniformity.

– ORIGIN Latin *varietas.*

var·i·ous /ˈve(ə)rēəs/ ▶ **adjective** different from one another; of different kinds or sorts.

– SYNONYMS **diverse,** different, differing, varied, assorted, mixed, sundry, miscellaneous, disparate, heterogeneous, motley.

▶ **determiner & pronoun** more than one; individual and separate.
– DERIVATIVES **var·i·ous·ly** adverb **var·i·ous·ness** noun.
– ORIGIN Latin *varius* 'changing, diverse.'

var·let /ˈvärlət/ ▶ **noun** **1** old use a rogue or rascal. **2** historical a male servant.
– ORIGIN Old French, from *valet* (see **VALET**).

var·mint /ˈvärmənt/ ▶ **noun** dated, informal or dialect a troublesome or mischievous person or wild animal.
– ORIGIN from **VERMIN**.

var·nish /ˈvärnisʜ/ ▶ **noun** resin dissolved in a liquid, applied to wood or metal to give a hard, clear, shiny surface when dry.

– SYNONYMS **lacquer,** shellac, japan, enamel, glaze.

▶ **verb** **1** apply varnish to something. **2** disguise or gloss over a fact.

– SYNONYMS **lacquer,** shellac, japan, enamel, glaze.

– ORIGIN Old French *vernis.*

var·si·ty /ˈvärsətē/ ▶ **noun** (pl. **varsities**) a sports team representing a school or college. ▶ **adjective** referring to a school's sports team, especially one made up of the school's more advanced players: *she made varsity basketball in her sophomore year.*
– ORIGIN shortening of **UNIVERSITY**.

var·y /ˈve(ə)rē/ ▶ **verb** (**varies, varying, varied**) **1** differ in size, degree, or nature from something else of the same general class: *the houses vary in price.* **2** change from one form or state to another. **3** modify something to make it less uniform: *he tried to vary his diet.*

– SYNONYMS **1 differ,** be dissimilar, disagree, be at variance. **2 fluctuate,** rise and fall, go up and down, change, alter, shift, swing.

– ORIGIN Latin *variare.*

vas /vas/ ▶ **noun** (pl. **vasa** /ˈvāsə, -zə/) a vessel or duct in the body.
– ORIGIN Latin.

vas·cu·lar /ˈvaskyələr/ ▶ **adjective** referring to the system of vessels for carrying blood or (in plants) sap, water, and nutrients.
– ORIGIN Latin *vascularis.*

vas de·fe·rens /ˌvas ˈdefərənz, -ˌrenz/ ▶ **noun** (pl. **vasa deferentia** /ˌvāsə ˌdefəˈrensʜ(ē)ə, ˌvāzə/) either of the ducts that convey sperm from the testicles to the urethra.
– ORIGIN from **VAS** + Latin *deferens* 'carrying away.'

vase /vās, vāz, väz/ ▶ **noun** a decorative container used as an ornament or for displaying cut flowers.
– ORIGIN French.

vas·ec·to·my /vəˈsektəmē, va-/ ▶ **noun** (pl. **vasectomies**) the surgical cutting and sealing of part of each vas deferens as a means of sterilization.

Vas·e·line /ˌvasəˈlēn, ˈvasəˌlēn/ ▶ **noun** trademark a type of petroleum jelly used as an ointment and lubricant.
– ORIGIN from German *Wasser* 'water' + Greek *elaion* 'oil.'

vas·sal /ˈvasəl/ ▶ **noun** **1** historical (in the feudal system) a man who promised to fight for a monarch or lord in return for holding a piece of land. **2** a country that is controlled by or dependent on another.
– DERIVATIVES **vas·sal·age** /-əlij/ noun.
– ORIGIN Latin *vassallus* 'retainer.'

vast /vast/ ▶ **adjective** of very great extent or quantity; huge.

– SYNONYMS **huge,** extensive, broad, wide, boundless, enormous, immense, great, massive, colossal, gigantic, mammoth, giant, mountainous; informal mega, whopping.
– ANTONYMS tiny.

– DERIVATIVES **vast·ly** adverb **vast·ness** noun.
– ORIGIN Latin *vastus* 'void, immense.'

VAT /vat/ ▶ **abbreviation** value added tax.

vat /vat/ ▶ **noun** a large container used to hold liquid.
– ORIGIN Germanic.

vat·ic /ˈvatik/ ▶ **adjective** literary predicting what will happen in the future.

– ORIGIN from Latin *vates* 'prophet.'

Vat·i·can /'vatikən/ ▶ **noun** the palace and official residence of the Pope in Rome.

vaude·ville /'vôd(ə),vil, -vəl/ ▶ **noun** a type of entertainment featuring a mixture of musical and comedy acts.
– DERIVATIVES **vaude·vil·lian** /,vôd(ə)'vilyən/ adjective & noun.
– ORIGIN French.

vault[1] /vôlt/ ▶ **noun 1** a large room used for storing things securely, especially in a bank. **2** a room under a church or in a graveyard, used for burials. **3** a roof or ceiling in the form of an arch or a series of arches.

– SYNONYMS **1 safe,** strongroom, repository, wall safe. **2 cellar,** basement, crypt, undercroft, catacomb, burial chamber.

– DERIVATIVES **vault·ed** adjective.
– ORIGIN Old French *voute*.

vault[2] ▶ **verb** jump over something in a single movement, supporting or pushing oneself with the hands or a pole.

– SYNONYMS **jump,** leap, spring, bound, clear.

▶ **noun** an act of vaulting.
– DERIVATIVES **vault·er** noun.
– ORIGIN Old French *volter* 'to gambol.'

vault·ing /'vôltiNG/ ▶ **noun** the arrangement of vaults in a roof or ceiling.

vault·ing horse ▶ **noun** a padded wooden block used for vaulting over in gymnastics.

vaunt /vônt, vänt/ ▶ **verb** (usu. as adj. **vaunted**) boast about or praise: *his vaunted gift for spotting talent.*

– SYNONYMS **boast about,** brag about, make much of, crow about, parade, flaunt; informal show off about; formal laud.

– DERIVATIVES **vaunt·ing** adjective.
– ORIGIN Latin *vantare*.

va-va-voom /,vä vä 'vo͞om/ informal ▶ **noun** the quality of being exciting, vigorous, or sexually attractive. ▶ **adjective** sexually attractive: *her va-va-voom figure.*
– ORIGIN representing the sound of a car engine being revved.

VC ▶ **abbreviation** Victoria Cross.

V-chip ▶ **noun** a computer chip installed in a television receiver that can be programmed to block violent or sexually explicit material.

VCR ▶ **abbreviation** videocassette recorder.

VD ▶ **abbreviation** venereal disease.

VDT ▶ **abbreviation** video display terminal.

've ▶ **abbreviation** informal have.

veal /vēl/ ▶ **noun** meat from a young calf.
– ORIGIN Old French *veel*.

vec·tor /'vektər/ ▶ **noun 1** Mathematics & Physics a quantity having direction as well as magnitude, especially as determining the position of one point in space relative to another. **2** an organism that transmits a disease or parasite from one animal or plant to another.
– DERIVATIVES **vec·to·ri·al** /vek'tôrēəl/ adjective.
– ORIGIN Latin, 'carrier.'

Ve·da /'vādə, 'vēdə/ ▶ **noun** (treated as sing. or pl.) the earliest Hindu sacred writings.
– DERIVATIVES **Ve·dic** adjective.
– ORIGIN Sanskrit, 'sacred knowledge.'

Ve·dan·ta /vā'däntə, və-/ ▶ **noun** a Hindu philosophy based on the doctrine of the Upanishads.
– DERIVATIVES **Ve·dan·tic** adjective **Ve·dan·tist** noun.
– ORIGIN Sanskrit, from words meaning 'sacred knowledge' and 'end.'

V-E Day ▶ **noun** the day (May 8) marking the Allied victory in Europe in 1945.
– ORIGIN short for *Victory in Europe*.

vee /vē/ ▶ **noun 1** the letter V. **2** a thing shaped like a V.

vee·jay /'vē,jā/ ▶ **noun** informal a VJ.
– ORIGIN from *VJ*, short for *video jockey*.

veer /vi(ə)r/ ▶ **verb 1** change direction suddenly. **2** suddenly change in opinion, subject, etc.: *the conversation veered away from theatrical things.* **3** (of the wind) change direction clockwise around the points of the compass.

– SYNONYMS **turn,** swerve, swing, weave, wheel, change direction, change course, deviate.

▶ **noun** a sudden change of direction.
– ORIGIN French *virer*.

veg /vej/ ▶ **noun** (pl. same) Brit. informal vegetables, or a vegetable.

veg·an /'vēgən, 'vejən/ ▶ **noun** a person who does not eat or use any animal products.
– DERIVATIVES **veg·an·ism** /'-ə,nizəm/ noun.
– ORIGIN from **VEGETARIAN**.

veg·e·ta·ble /'vejtəbəl, 'vejətə-/ ▶ **noun 1** a plant or part of a plant used as food. **2** informal, derogatory a person who is incapable of normal mental or physical activity as a result of brain damage.
– ORIGIN from Latin *vegetabilis* 'animating.'

veg·e·ta·ble oil ▶ **noun** an oil obtained from plants, e.g., olive oil or sunflower oil.

veg·e·tal /'vejətl/ ▶ **adjective** formal relating to plants.
– ORIGIN Latin *vegetalis*.

veg·e·tar·i·an /,veji'te(ə)rēən/ ▶ **noun** a person who does not eat meat, and who may also choose to eat no other animal products. ▶ **adjective** eating or including no meat or other animal products.
– DERIVATIVES **veg·e·tar·i·an·ism** /-,nizəm/ noun.

veg·e·tate /'vejə,tāt/ ▶ **verb** spend time in a dull and inactive way that involves little mental stimulation.
– ORIGIN Latin *vegetare* 'enliven.'

veg·e·ta·tion /,vejə'tāSHən/ ▶ **noun** plants in general.
– DERIVATIVES **veg·e·ta·tion·al** adjective.

veg·e·ta·tive /'vejə,tātiv/ ▶ **adjective 1** relating to vegetation or the growth of plants. **2** relating to reproduction or propagation by asexual means. **3** (of a person) alive but in a coma and showing no sign of brain activity or responsiveness.

veg·gie /'vejē/ ▶ **noun & adjective 1** another term for **VEGETABLE**. **2** informal, chiefly Brit. another term for **VEGETARIAN**.

veg·gie burg·er (also trademark **Vegeburger**) ▶ **noun** a patty resembling a hamburger but made with vegetables or soybeans instead of meat.

ve·he·ment /'vēəmənt/ ▶ **adjective** showing strong feeling; forceful or passionate.

– SYNONYMS **passionate,** forceful, ardent, impassioned, heated, spirited, urgent, fervent, fierce, strong, forcible, powerful, emphatic,

vigorous, intense, earnest, keen, enthusiastic, zealous.
– ANTONYMS mild.

– DERIVATIVES **ve·he·mence** noun **ve·he·ment·ly** adverb.
– ORIGIN Latin, 'impetuous, violent.'

ve·hi·cle /'vēəkəl, 'vēˌhikəl/ ▶ **noun 1** a thing used for transporting people or goods on land, such as a car or truck. **2** a means of expressing or achieving something: *she used paint as a vehicle for her ideas.* **3** a movie, television show, song, etc., intended to display the leading performer to the best advantage.

– SYNONYMS **1 means of transport,** transportation, conveyance; motor vehicle, automobile, car, truck. **2 channel,** medium, means, agent, instrument, mechanism, organ, apparatus.

– DERIVATIVES **ve·hic·u·lar** /vē'hikyələr/ adjective.
– ORIGIN Latin *vehiculum.*

WORD LINKS

automotive *relating to vehicles*

veil /vāl/ ▶ **noun 1** a piece of fine material worn to protect or hide the face. **2** a piece of fabric forming part of a nun's headdress, resting on the head and shoulders. **3** a thing that hides or disguises something: *an eerie veil of mist.*

– SYNONYMS **covering,** screen, curtain, mantle, cloak, mask, blanket, shroud, canopy, cloud, pall.

▶ **verb 1** cover someone or something with a veil. **2** cover or hide: *the country is still veiled in mystery.* **3** (as adj. **veiled**) not expressed directly or clearly: *a thinly veiled threat.*

– SYNONYMS **cover,** surround, swathe, enfold, envelop, conceal, hide, obscure, screen, shield, cloak, blanket, shroud.

– PHRASES **draw a veil over** avoid discussing or drawing attention to something embarrassing or unpleasant. **take the veil** become a nun.
– ORIGIN Latin *velum* 'sail, curtain, veil.'

vein /vān/ ▶ **noun 1** any of the tubes forming part of the circulation system by which blood is carried from all parts of the body toward the heart. **2** (in general use) a blood vessel. **3** a very thin rib running through a leaf. **4** (in insects) a hollow rib forming part of the supporting framework of a wing. **5** a streak of a different color in wood, marble, cheese, etc. **6** a fracture in rock containing a deposit of minerals or ore. **7** a particular way, style, or quality: *he did a number of engravings in a similar vein.* **8** a source of a quality: *a rich vein of satire.*

– SYNONYMS **1 blood vessel,** capillary. **2 layer,** seam, lode, stratum, deposit.

– DERIVATIVES **veined** adjective **vein·ing** noun **vein·y** adjective.
– ORIGIN Old French *veine.*

USAGE

For an explanation of the difference between **vein, vane,** and **vain,** see the note at **VAIN.**

WORD LINKS

vascular, venous *relating to veins*

ve·lar /'vēlər/ ▶ **adjective** (of a speech sound such as *k* and *g* in English) pronounced with the back of the tongue near the soft palate.
– ORIGIN from Latin *velum* 'sail, curtain, covering, veil.'

Vel·cro /'velkrō/ ▶ **noun** trademark a fastener consisting of two strips of fabric that stick to each other when pressed together. ▶ **verb** fasten or join something with Velcro.
– ORIGIN from French *velours croché* 'hooked velvet.'

veld /velt/ (also **veldt**) ▶ **noun** open, uncultivated country or grassland in southern Africa.
– ORIGIN Afrikaans, 'field.'

vel·lum /'veləm/ ▶ **noun 1** fine parchment made from the skin of a sheep, goat, or calf. **2** smooth cream-colored writing paper.
– ORIGIN Old French *velin.*

ve·loc·i·pede /və'läsəˌpēd/ ▶ **noun** historical an early form of bicycle propelled by working pedals on cranks fitted to the front axle.
– ORIGIN from Latin *velox* 'swift' + *pes* 'foot.'

ve·loc·i·rap·tor /və'läsəˌraptər/ ▶ **noun** a small meat-eating dinosaur with a large slashing claw on each foot.
– ORIGIN Latin.

ve·loc·i·ty /və'läsətē/ ▶ **noun** (pl. **velocities**) **1** technical the speed of something in a given direction. **2** (in general use) speed.

– SYNONYMS **speed,** pace, rate, tempo, rapidity.

– ORIGIN Latin *velocitas.*

ve·lo·drome /'veləˌdrōm, 'vēlə-/ ▶ **noun** a cycle-racing track with steeply banked curves.
– ORIGIN French.

ve·lour /və'lo͝or/ (also **velours**) ▶ **noun** a plush woven fabric resembling velvet.
– ORIGIN French *velours* 'velvet.'

ve·lou·té /vəlo͞o'tā/ ▶ **noun** a white sauce made from a roux of butter and flour with chicken, veal, or pork stock.
– ORIGIN French, 'velvety.'

vel·vet /'velvət/ ▶ **noun 1** a fabric of silk, cotton, or nylon with a thick short pile on one side. **2** soft downy skin that covers a deer's antler while it is growing.
– DERIVATIVES **vel·vet·y** adjective.
– ORIGIN Old French *veluotte.*

vel·vet·een /'velvəˌtēn, ˌvelvə'tēn/ ▶ **noun** a cotton fabric with a pile resembling velvet.

ve·na ca·va /ˌvēnə 'kāvə, 'kāvə/ ▶ **noun** (pl. **venae cavae** /'vēnē 'kävē, 'kāvē, 'vēnī 'kävī, 'kāvī/) each of two large veins carrying deoxygenated blood into the heart.
– ORIGIN Latin, 'hollow vein.'

ve·nal /'vēnl/ ▶ **adjective** prepared to do dishonest or immoral things in return for money.
– DERIVATIVES **ve·nal·i·ty** /vē'nalətē, və-/ noun.
– ORIGIN from Latin *venum* 'thing for sale.'

USAGE

For an explanation of the difference between **venal** and **venial,** see the note at **VENIAL.**

vend /vend/ ▶ **verb 1** offer small items for sale. **2** Law or formal sell something.
– ORIGIN Latin *vendere* 'sell.'

ven·det·ta /ven'detə/ ▶ **noun 1** a prolonged bitter quarrel with or campaign against someone. **2** a prolonged feud between families in which people are murdered in revenge for previous murders.
– ORIGIN Italian.

vend·ing ma·chine ▶ **noun** a machine that dispenses food, drinks, cigarettes, or other small articles when a coin or token is inserted.

ven·dor /ˈvendər, -ˌdôr/ (also **vender**) ▶ **noun 1** a person or company offering something for sale. **2** Law the person who is selling a property.

ve·neer /vəˈni(ə)r/ ▶ **noun 1** a thin decorative covering of fine wood applied to a coarser wood or other material. **2** an outer quality or attractive appearance that hides the true nature of someone or something: *the area's veneer of respectability has gone.*

– SYNONYMS **1 surface,** lamination, layer, overlay, facing, covering, finish, exterior. **2 facade,** front, show, outward display, appearance, impression, semblance, guise, mask, pretense, cover, camouflage.

▶ **verb** (usu. as adj. **veneered**) cover something with a veneer.
– DERIVATIVES **ve·neer·ing** noun.
– ORIGIN from German *furnieren.*

ven·er·a·ble /ˈvenərəbəl, ˈvenrə-/ ▶ **adjective 1** greatly respected because of age, wisdom, or character. **2** (in the Anglican Church) a title given to an archdeacon. **3** (in the Roman Catholic Church) a title given to a dead person who has gained a certain degree of sanctity but has not been fully beatified or canonized.

ven·er·ate /ˈvenəˌrāt/ ▶ **verb** regard someone or something with great respect.
– DERIVATIVES **ven·er·a·tion** /ˌvenəˈrāsʜən/ noun **ven·er·a·tor** noun.
– ORIGIN Latin *venerari* 'adore, revere.'

CHOOSE THE RIGHT WORD

See **REVERE**.

ve·ne·re·al /vəˈni(ə)rēəl/ ▶ **adjective 1** relating to sexually transmitted disease. **2** formal relating to sex or sexual desire.
– ORIGIN Latin *venereus.*

ve·ne·re·al dis·ease ▶ **noun** a disease that is caught by having sex with a person who is already infected.

ven·er·y[1] /ˈvenərē/ ▶ **noun** old use indulgence in sexual activity.
– ORIGIN Latin *veneria.*

ven·er·y[2] ▶ **noun** old use hunting.
– ORIGIN from Latin *venari* 'to hunt.'

Ve·ne·tian /vəˈnēsʜən/ ▶ **adjective** relating to Venice. ▶ **noun** a person from Venice.

ve·ne·tian blind ▶ **noun** a window blind consisting of horizontal slats that can be adjusted to control the amount of light that passes through.

Ven·e·zue·lan /ˌvenəz(ə)ˈwālən/ ▶ **noun** a person from Venezuela. ▶ **adjective** relating to Venezuela.

venge·ance /ˈvenjəns/ ▶ **noun** punishment or harm caused to someone in return for an injury or wrong: *he'd had a terrible life and was now taking vengeance on humanity.*

– SYNONYMS **revenge,** retribution, retaliation, requital, reprisal, an eye for an eye.
– ANTONYMS forgiveness.

– PHRASES **with a vengeance** with great intensity.
– ORIGIN Old French.

venge·ful /ˈvenjfəl/ ▶ **adjective** wanting to punish or harm someone in return for a wrong or injury.
– DERIVATIVES **venge·ful·ly** adverb **venge·ful·ness** noun.

CHOOSE THE RIGHT WORD

See **VINDICTIVE**.

ve·ni·al /ˈvēnēəl, ˈvēnyəl/ ▶ **adjective 1** (of a fault or offense) minor and able to be forgiven. **2** Christian Theology (of a sin) that does not deprive the soul of God's grace. Often contrasted with **MORTAL**.
– ORIGIN Latin *venialis.*

USAGE

Venal and **venial** are sometimes confused. **Venal** means 'prepared to do dishonest or immoral things in return for money' (*venal politicians*), whereas **venial** is used to refer to a sin or fault that is minor and able to be forgiven.

ven·i·son /ˈvenəsən, -zən/ ▶ **noun** meat from a deer.
– ORIGIN Old French *venesoun.*

Venn di·a·gram /ven/ ▶ **noun** a diagram representing mathematical or logical sets as circles, common elements of the sets being represented by overlapping sections of the circles.
– ORIGIN named after the English logician John *Venn.*

ven·om /ˈvenəm/ ▶ **noun 1** poisonous fluid produced by animals such as snakes and scorpions and typically injected by biting or stinging. **2** extreme hatred or bitterness: *her voice was full of venom.*
– ORIGIN Old French *venim.*

ven·om·ous /ˈvenəməs/ ▶ **adjective 1** (of an animal) producing or capable of injecting venom. **2** full of hate or bitterness.

– SYNONYMS **poisonous,** toxic, dangerous, deadly, lethal, fatal.
– ANTONYMS harmless.

– DERIVATIVES **ven·om·ous·ly** adverb.

CHOOSE THE RIGHT WORD

See **VINDICTIVE**.

ve·nous /ˈvēnəs/ ▶ **adjective** relating to a vein or the veins.

vent[1] /vent/ ▶ **noun** an opening that allows air, gas, or liquid to pass out of or into a confined space.

– SYNONYMS **outlet, inlet,** opening, aperture, hole, gap, orifice, space, duct, flue, shaft, well, passage, airway.

▶ **verb 1** express a strong emotion freely. **2** discharge air, gas, or liquid through an outlet.

– SYNONYMS **let out,** release, pour out, utter, express, air, voice.

– PHRASES **give vent to** express a strong emotion.
– ORIGIN from French *vent* 'wind' or *éventer* 'expose to air.'

vent[2] ▶ **noun** a slit in a garment, especially in the lower part of the seam at the back of a coat.
– ORIGIN Old French *fente* 'slit.'

ven·ti·late /ˈventəˌlāt/ ▶ **verb 1** cause air to enter and circulate freely in a room or building. **2** discuss an opinion or issue in public.

– SYNONYMS **air,** aerate, oxygenate, freshen, cool.

– DERIVATIVES **ven·ti·la·tion** /ˌventəˈlāsʜən/ noun.
– ORIGIN Latin *ventilare* 'blow, winnow.'

ven·ti·la·tor /ˈventəˌlātər/ ▶ **noun 1** a device or opening for ventilating a room or building. **2** a machine that pumps air in and out of a person's lungs to help them to breathe.
– DERIVATIVES **ven·ti·la·to·ry** /ˈventələˌtôrē/ adjective.

ven·tral /ˈventrəl/ ▶ **adjective** technical on or relating to the underside or abdomen. Compare with **DORSAL**.
– DERIVATIVES **ven·tral·ly** adverb.
– ORIGIN from Latin *venter* 'belly.'

ven·tri·cle /ˈventrəkəl/ ▶ **noun 1** each of the two larger and lower cavities of the heart. **2** each of four connected fluid-filled cavities in the brain.
– DERIVATIVES **ven·tric·u·lar** /venˈtrikyələr/ adjective.
– ORIGIN Latin *ventriculus.*

ven·tril·o·quist /venˈtriləˌkwist/ ▶ **noun** an entertainer who can make their voice seem to come from a dummy of a person or animal.
– DERIVATIVES **ven·tri·lo·qui·al** /ˌventrəˈlōkwēəl/ adjective **ven·tril·o·quism** /-ˌkwizəm/ noun **ven·tril·o·quy** /-kwē/ noun.
– ORIGIN from Latin *venter* 'belly' + *loqui* 'speak.'

ven·ture /ˈvenCHər/ ▶ **noun 1** a business enterprise involving considerable risk. **2** a risky or daring activity or undertaking.

> – SYNONYMS **enterprise,** undertaking, project, scheme, operation, endeavor, speculation.

▶ **verb 1** dare to do something dangerous or risky. **2** dare to say something that may be considered bold.

> – SYNONYMS **1 put forward,** advance, proffer, offer, air, suggest, volunteer, submit, propose. **2 dare,** be so bold as, presume, have the audacity, have the nerve, take the liberty.

– DERIVATIVES **ven·tur·er** noun.
– ORIGIN shortening of **ADVENTURE**.

ven·ture cap·i·tal ▶ **noun** capital invested in a business project in which there is a large element of risk.

ven·ture·some /ˈvenCHərsəm/ ▶ **adjective** willing to do something risky or difficult.

ven·ue /ˈvenˌyo͞o/ ▶ **noun** the place where an event or meeting is held.
– ORIGIN Old French, 'a coming.'

Ve·nus /ˈvēnəs/ ▶ **noun** a planet of the solar system, second in order from the sun and the brightest object in the sky after the sun and moon.
– DERIVATIVES **Ve·nu·si·an** /vəˈn(y)o͞osH(ē)ən, -ZHən, -sēən/ adjective & noun.

Ve·nus fly·trap /ˈflīˌtrap/ ▶ **noun** a plant with hinged leaves that spring shut on and digest insects that land on them.

ve·ra·cious /vəˈrāsHəs/ ▶ **adjective** formal speaking or representing the truth.
– ORIGIN from Latin *verus* 'true.'

ve·rac·i·ty /vəˈrasətē/ ▶ **noun 1** the quality of being true or accurate. **2** the quality of telling the truth: *he devised a test of the agent's veracity.*

ve·ran·da /vəˈrandə/ (also **verandah**) ▶ **noun** a roofed structure with an open front along the outside of a house, level with the ground floor.
– ORIGIN Portuguese *varanda* 'railing, balustrade.'

verb /vərb/ ▶ **noun** a word used to describe an action, state, or occurrence, such as *hear, become*, or *happen.*
– ORIGIN Latin *verbum* 'word, verb.'

ver·bal /ˈvərbəl/ ▶ **adjective 1** relating to or in the form of words. **2** spoken rather than written; oral. **3** relating to a verb.

> – SYNONYMS **oral,** spoken, word-of-mouth, stated, said, unwritten.

▶ **noun** a word or words functioning as a verb.
– DERIVATIVES **ver·bal·ly** adverb.

ver·bal·ism /ˈvərbəˌlizəm/ ▶ **noun** concentration on words rather than their meaning or content.

ver·bal·ize /ˈvərbəˌlīz/ ▶ **verb** express ideas or feelings in words.
– DERIVATIVES **ver·bal·i·za·tion** /ˌvərbələˈzāsHən, -ˌlīˈzā-/ noun.

ver·bal noun ▶ **noun** a noun formed from a verb, such as *smoking* in *smoking is forbidden.*

ver·ba·tim /vərˈbātəm/ ▶ **adverb & adjective** in exactly the same words as were used originally.
– ORIGIN Latin.

ver·be·na /vərˈbēnə/ ▶ **noun** a garden plant with bright showy flowers.
– ORIGIN Latin, 'sacred bough.'

ver·bi·age /ˈvərbē-ij/ ▶ **noun** excessively lengthy or technical speech or writing.
– ORIGIN French.

ver·bose /vərˈbōs/ ▶ **adjective** using more words than are needed.

> – SYNONYMS **wordy,** loquacious, garrulous, talkative, voluble, long-winded, lengthy, prolix, circumlocutory, rambling.
> – ANTONYMS succinct.

– DERIVATIVES **ver·bose·ly** adverb **ver·bos·i·ty** /-ˈbäsətē/ noun.
– ORIGIN Latin *verbosus.*

ver·bo·ten /fərˈbōtn, vər-/ ▶ **adjective** forbidden by an authority.
– ORIGIN German.

ver·dant /ˈvərdnt/ ▶ **adjective** green with grass or other lush vegetation.
– DERIVATIVES **ver·dan·cy** noun **ver·dant·ly** adverb.
– ORIGIN perhaps from Old French *verdeant.*

ver·dict /ˈvərdikt/ ▶ **noun 1** a formal decision made by a jury in a court of law as to whether a person is innocent or guilty of an offense. **2** an opinion or judgment made after testing or considering something.

> – SYNONYMS **judgment,** adjudication, decision, finding, ruling, sentence.

– ORIGIN Old French *verdit.*

ver·di·gris /ˈvərdəˌgrēs, -ˌgris, -ˌgrē/ ▶ **noun** a bright bluish-green substance formed on copper or brass by oxidation.
– ORIGIN from Old French *vert de Grece* 'green of Greece.'

ver·dure /ˈvərjər/ ▶ **noun** literary lush green vegetation.
– ORIGIN from Old French *verd* 'green.'

verge /vərj/ ▶ **noun 1** an edge or border. **2** a limit beyond which something will happen.

> – SYNONYMS **1 edge,** border, margin, side, brink, rim, lip, fringe, boundary, perimeter. **2** *I was on the verge of tears* **brink,** threshold, edge, point.

▶ **verb** (**verge on**) be very close to: *the speed at which they drove verged on lunacy.*

> – SYNONYMS **approach,** border on, be close/near to, resemble, be tantamount to, tend toward, approximate to.

– ORIGIN Old French.

CHOOSE THE RIGHT WORD

See **BORDER**.

verg·er /'vərjər/ ▶ **noun 1** an official in a church who acts as a caretaker and attendant. **2** an officer who carries a rod in front of a bishop or dean as a symbol of office.
– ORIGIN Old French.

ver·i·fy /'verə,fī/ ▶ **verb** (**verifies, verifying, verified**) **1** check that something is true or accurate. **2** confirm or show to be true or accurate: *our instrument readings verified his statement.*

– SYNONYMS **confirm,** prove, substantiate, corroborate, back up, bear out, justify, support, uphold, testify to, validate, authenticate.
– ANTONYMS refute.

– DERIVATIVES **ver·i·fi·a·ble** /'verə,fīəbəl, ,verə'fī-/ adjective **ver·i·fi·ca·tion** /,verəfi'kāsHən/ noun **ver·i·fi·er** noun.
– ORIGIN Latin *verificare.*

ver·i·ly /'verəlē/ ▶ **adverb** old use truly; certainly.
– ORIGIN from **VERY**.

ver·i·si·mil·i·tude /,verəsə'mili,t(y)o͞od/ ▶ **noun** the appearance of being true or real.
– ORIGIN Latin *verisimilitudo.*

ve·ris·mo /və'rizmō, ve-/ ▶ **noun** realism or authenticity, especially in opera, art, or movies.
– ORIGIN Italian.

ver·i·ta·ble /'vəritəbəl/ ▶ **adjective** rightly so called (used for emphasis): *a veritable army of backpackers.*
– DERIVATIVES **ver·i·ta·bly** /-blē/ adverb.

vé·ri·té /,veri'tā/ ▶ **noun** a genre of movies and television that emphasizes realism and naturalism.
– ORIGIN French, 'truth.'

ver·i·ty /'veritē/ ▶ **noun** (pl. **verities**) **1** a true principle or belief: *the eternal verities of history.* **2** literary the quality of being true; truth.
– ORIGIN Latin *veritas.*

ver·mi·cel·li /,vərmə'cHelē, -'selē/ ▶ **plural noun** pasta made in long thin threads.
– ORIGIN Italian, 'little worms.'

ver·mic·u·lite /vər'mikyə,līt/ ▶ **noun** a yellow or brown mineral used for insulation or for growing plants in.
– ORIGIN from Latin *vermiculari* 'be full of worms' (because on expansion due to heat, it shoots out forms resembling small worms).

ver·mi·form /'vərmə,fôrm/ ▶ **adjective** technical resembling or having the shape of a worm.

ver·mi·fuge /'vərmə,fyo͞oj/ ▶ **noun** a medicine used to destroy worms that live in or on the bodies of people or animals.

ver·mil·ion /vər'milyən/ ▶ **noun** a brilliant red pigment or color.
– ORIGIN Old French *vermeillon.*

ver·min /'vərmən/ ▶ **noun** (treated as pl.) **1** wild mammals and birds that are harmful to crops, farm animals, or game, or that carry disease. **2** worms or insects that live in or on the bodies of animals or people. **3** people who are very unpleasant or dangerous to society.
– DERIVATIVES **ver·min·ous** adjective.
– ORIGIN Old French.

ver·mouth /vər'mo͞otH/ ▶ **noun** a red or white wine flavored with herbs.
– ORIGIN French *vermout.*

ver·nac·u·lar /vər'nakyələr/ ▶ **noun 1** the language or dialect spoken by the ordinary people of a country or region. **2** informal the vocabulary used by people in a particular group or activity: *baseball vernacular.* ▶ **adjective 1** spoken as or using the language or dialect of the ordinary people. **2** (of architecture) concerned with simple, traditional structures such as houses and barns rather than large public buildings.
– ORIGIN from Latin *vernaculus* 'domestic, native.'

ver·nal /'vərnl/ ▶ **adjective** relating to the season of spring.
– ORIGIN Latin *vernalis.*

ver·nier /'vərnēər/ ▶ **noun** a small movable graduated scale for indicating fractions of the main scale on a measuring device.
– ORIGIN named after the French mathematician Pierre *Vernier.*

ve·ron·i·ca /və'ränəkə/ ▶ **noun** a plant with narrow pointed leaves and blue or purple flowers.
– ORIGIN from the woman's name *Veronica.*

ver·ru·ca /və'ro͞okə/ ▶ **noun** (pl. **verrucae** /-kē, -kī/ or **verrucas**) a contagious wart on the sole of the foot.
– ORIGIN Latin.

ver·sa·tile /'vərsətl/ ▶ **adjective 1** having many different uses. **2** having a range of different skills: *one of our most versatile composers.*

– SYNONYMS **1** *a versatile device* **adjustable,** adaptable, multipurpose, all-purpose. **2** *a versatile player* **adaptable,** flexible, all-around, multitalented, resourceful.

– DERIVATIVES **ver·sa·til·i·ty** /,vərsə'tilətē/ noun.
– ORIGIN Latin *versatilis.*

verse /vərs/ ▶ **noun 1** writing arranged with a regular rhythm, and often having a rhyme. **2** a group of lines that form a unit in a poem or song. **3** each of the short numbered divisions of a chapter in the Bible or other scripture.

– SYNONYMS **1 poetry,** lyrics. **2 poem,** lyric, rhyme, ditty, limerick. **3 stanza,** canto.

– ORIGIN Latin *versus* 'a turn of the plow, a line of writing.'

versed /vərst/ ▶ **adjective** (**versed in**) experienced or skilled in; knowledgeable about.
– ORIGIN Latin *versatus.*

ver·si·fy /'vərsə,fī/ ▶ **verb** (**versifies, versifying, versified**) turn writing or ideas into verse.
– DERIVATIVES **ver·si·fi·ca·tion** /,vərsəfi'kāsHən/ noun **ver·si·fi·er** noun.

ver·sion /'vərzHən/ ▶ **noun 1** a form of something that differs in some way from other forms of the same type of thing: *the car comes in two-door and four-door versions.* **2** an account of something told from a particular person's point of view.

– SYNONYMS **1 type,** sort, kind, form, equivalent, variety, variant, design, model, style. **2 account,** report, statement, description, record, story, rendering, interpretation, explanation, understanding, reading, impression, side. **3 edition,** translation, impression.

▶ **verb** create a new version of something.
– ORIGIN Latin, 'action of turning.'

ver·so /'vərsō/ ▶ **noun** (pl. **versos**) a left-hand page of an open book, or the back of a loose document. Contrasted with **RECTO**.
– ORIGIN from Latin *verso folio* 'on the turned leaf.'

ver·sus /ˈvərsəs, -səz/ ▸ **preposition 1** against: *Penn versus Princeton.* **2** as opposed to; in contrast to.
– ORIGIN Latin, 'toward.'

vert /vərt/ ▸ **noun** green, as a conventional heraldic color.
– ORIGIN Old French.

ver·te·bra /ˈvərtəbrə/ ▸ **noun** (pl. **vertebrae** /-ˌbrē, -ˌbrā/) each of the series of small bones forming the backbone.
– DERIVATIVES **ver·te·bral** /-brəl, vərˈtē-/ adjective.
– ORIGIN Latin.

ver·te·brate /ˈvərtəbrət, -ˌbrāt/ ▸ **noun** an animal having a backbone, including mammals, birds, reptiles, amphibians, and fish. ▸ **adjective** relating to vertebrates.

ver·tex /ˈvərˌteks/ ▸ **noun** (pl. **vertices** /-təˌsēz/ or **vertexes**) **1** the highest point; the top. **2** each angular point of a polygon, triangle, or other geometrical figure. **3** a meeting point of two lines that form an angle.
– ORIGIN Latin, 'whirlpool, top.'

ver·ti·cal /ˈvərtikəl/ ▸ **adjective** at right angles to a horizontal line or surface; having the top directly above the bottom.

– SYNONYMS **upright,** erect, perpendicular, plumb, on end, standing.
– ANTONYMS flat, horizontal.

▸ **noun 1** (**the vertical**) a vertical line or surface. **2** an upright structure.
– DERIVATIVES **ver·ti·cal·i·ty** /ˌvərtiˈkalətē/ noun **ver·ti·cal·ly** adverb.
– ORIGIN Latin *verticalis.*

ver·tig·i·nous /vərˈtijənəs/ ▸ **adjective 1** very high or steep. **2** relating to or affected by vertigo.
– DERIVATIVES **ver·tig·i·nous·ly** adverb.

ver·ti·go /ˈvərtəgō/ ▸ **noun** a feeling of dizziness caused by looking down from a great height or by disease affecting the inner ear.
– ORIGIN Latin, 'whirling.'

ver·vain /ˈvərˌvān/ ▸ **noun** a plant with small blue, white, or purple flowers, used in herbal medicine.
– ORIGIN Old French *verveine.*

verve /vərv/ ▸ **noun** vigor, spirit, and style: *he writes with his usual verve.*
– ORIGIN French, 'vigor.'

ver·vet mon·key /ˈvərvət/ ▸ **noun** a common African monkey with greenish-brown upper parts and a black face.
– ORIGIN French.

ver·y /ˈverē/ ▸ **adverb 1** in a high degree. **2** used to emphasize a description: *the very best quality.*

– SYNONYMS **extremely,** exceedingly, exceptionally, extraordinarily, tremendously, immensely, acutely, singularly, decidedly, highly, remarkably, really; informal real, awfully, terribly, seriously, mega, mighty, ultra.
– ANTONYMS slightly.

▸ **adjective 1** actual; precise. **2** used to emphasize an extreme point in time or space. **3** mere: *the very thought of drink made him feel sick.* **4** old use real; genuine.
– ORIGIN from Latin *verus* 'true.'

very high fre·quen·cy ▸ **noun** (in radio) a frequency of 30-300 megahertz.

Ver·y light /ˈverē, ˈvi(ə)rē/ ▸ **noun** a flare fired into the air from a pistol for signaling.
– ORIGIN named after the American naval officer Edward W. *Very.*

Ver·y Rev·er·end ▸ **adjective** a title given to a dean in the Anglican Church.

ve·si·cle /ˈvesikəl/ ▸ **noun 1** a small fluid-filled sac or cyst in an animal or plant. **2** a blister full of clear fluid.
– DERIVATIVES **ve·sic·u·lar** /vəˈsikyələr/ adjective.
– ORIGIN Latin *vesicula* 'small bladder.'

ves·pers /ˈvespərz/ ▸ **noun** a service of evening prayer, especially in the Western Christian Church.
– ORIGIN Latin *vesperas* 'evensong.'

ves·sel /ˈvesəl/ ▸ **noun 1** a ship or large boat. **2** a bowl, cup, or other container for liquids. **3** a tube or duct that carries a fluid within the body, or within a plant. **4** a person or thing that conveys or embodies a quality or feeling: *the written word is a safer vessel for love than the spoken word.*

– SYNONYMS **1 boat,** ship, craft. **2 container,** receptacle, basin, bowl, pan, pot, jug.

– ORIGIN Old French *vessele.*

vest /vest/ ▸ **noun 1** a close-fitting, sleeveless waist-length garment typically having no collar and with buttons down the front. **2** a sleeveless garment worn for a particular purpose: *a bulletproof vest.* **3** Brit. a sleeveless undergarment worn on the upper part of the body. ▸ **verb 1** (**vest something in**) give power, property, etc., to someone. **2** give someone the legal right to power, property, etc.: *the court was vested with extensive powers.*
– ORIGIN Latin *vestis* 'garment.'

ves·tal /ˈvestl/ ▸ **adjective** literary chaste; pure. ▸ **noun** a Vestal Virgin.
– ORIGIN from the name of the Roman goddess *Vesta.*

Ves·tal Vir·gin ▸ **noun** (in ancient Rome) a virgin dedicated to the goddess Vesta and vowed to chastity.

vest·ed in·ter·est ▸ **noun 1** a personal reason for wanting something to happen, especially because one expects to gain advantage from it. **2** a person or group having such a reason. **3** Law an interest (usually in land or money held in trust) recognized as belonging to a particular person.

ves·ti·bule /ˈvestəˌbyo͞ol/ ▸ **noun 1** a room or hall just inside the outer door of a building. **2** Anatomy a chamber or channel opening into another.
– DERIVATIVES **ves·tib·u·lar** /veˈstibyələr, və-/ adjective (Anatomy).
– ORIGIN Latin *vestibulum* 'entrance court.'

ves·tige /ˈvestij/ ▸ **noun 1** a remaining trace of something that once existed: *the last vestiges of true wilderness.* **2** the smallest amount.

– SYNONYMS **remnant,** fragment, relic, echo, trace, mark, legacy, reminder.

– ORIGIN Latin *vestigium* 'footprint.'

CHOOSE THE RIGHT WORD

See **TRACE**[1].

ves·tig·i·al /veˈstij(ē)əl/ ▸ **adjective** remaining as the last small part of something: *he felt a vestigial flicker of anger from last night.*
– DERIVATIVES **ves·tig·i·al·ly** adverb.

vest·ment /ˈves(t)mənt/ ▸ **noun 1** a robe worn by the clergy or members of the choir during church services. **2** old use a robe worn on ceremonial occasions.
– ORIGIN Latin *vestimentum.*

ves·try /ˈvestrē/ ▸ **noun** (pl. **vestries**) a room in or attached to a church, used as an office and for changing into

ceremonial robes.
– ORIGIN Latin *vestiarium*.

vet[1] /vet/ ▸ **noun** informal a veterinarian. ▸ **verb** (**vets, vetting, vetted**) **1** check or examine something very carefully. **2** investigate a person's background in order to ensure that they are suitable for a job requiring secrecy, loyalty, or trustworthiness.

– SYNONYMS **check up on,** screen, investigate, examine, scrutinize, inspect, look over, assess, evaluate, appraise; informal check out.

vet[2] ▸ **noun** informal a veteran.

vetch /veCH/ ▸ **noun** a plant with purple, pink, or yellow flowers, grown for silage or fodder.
– ORIGIN Old French *veche*.

vet·er·an /'vetərən, 'vetrən/ ▸ **noun 1** a person who has had long experience in a particular field. **2** a person who used to serve in the armed forces.

– SYNONYMS **1** *a veteran of 16 political campaigns* **old hand,** past master, doyen, doyenne; informal vet, old-timer. **2** (as adj.) *a veteran diplomat* **long-serving,** seasoned, old, hardened, practiced, experienced; informal battle-scarred.
– ANTONYMS novice.

– ORIGIN Latin *veteranus*.

Vet·er·ans Day ▸ **noun** a US holiday held on November 11 to commemorate military veterans.

vet·er·i·nar·i·an /ˌvet(ə)rə'ne(ə)rēən/ ▸ **noun** a person qualified to treat diseased or injured animals.

vet·er·i·nar·y /'vet(ə)rəˌnerē/ ▸ **adjective** relating to the treatment of diseases and injuries in animals.
– ORIGIN Latin *veterinarius*.

vet·er·i·nar·y sur·geon ▸ **noun** British term for **VETERINARIAN**.

vet·i·ver /'vetəvər/ ▸ **noun** a fragrant extract or essential oil obtained from the root of an Indian grass, used in perfumery and aromatherapy.
– ORIGIN Tamil, 'root.'

ve·to /'vētō/ ▸ **noun** (pl. **vetoes**) **1** a right to reject a decision or proposal made by a lawmaking body. **2** any refusal to allow something.

– SYNONYMS **rejection,** dismissal, prohibition, proscription, embargo, ban, interdict.

▸ **verb** (**vetoes, vetoing, vetoed**) **1** use a veto against a decision or proposal of a lawmaking body. **2** refuse to allow: *I vetoed the idea of a vacation.*

– SYNONYMS **reject,** turn down, throw out, dismiss, prohibit, forbid, proscribe, disallow, embargo, ban, rule out; informal kill, give the thumbs down to.
– ANTONYMS approve.

– ORIGIN from Latin, 'I forbid.'

vex /veks/ ▸ **verb** make someone annoyed or worried.
– DERIVATIVES **vex·a·tion** /vek'sāSHən/ noun.
– ORIGIN Latin *vexare* 'shake, disturb.'

vex·a·tious /vek'sāSHəs/ ▸ **adjective 1** causing annoyance or worry. **2** Law referring to an action or the bringer of an action that is brought without sufficient grounds for winning, purely to cause annoyance to the defendant.

vexed /vekst/ ▸ **adjective 1** (of an issue) difficult to resolve and causing much debate: *the vexed question of Europe.* **2** annoyed or worried.

VGA ▸ **abbreviation** videographics array, a standard for defining color display screens for computers.

vgc ▸ **abbreviation** very good condition.

VHF ▸ **abbreviation** very high frequency.

VHS ▸ **abbreviation** trademark video home system (as used by home video recorders).

VI ▸ **abbreviation** Virgin Islands.

via /'vīə, 'vēə/ ▸ **preposition 1** traveling through a place en route to a destination. **2** by way of; through. **3** by means of.
– ORIGIN from Latin, 'way, road.'

vi·a·ble /'vīəbəl/ ▸ **adjective 1** capable of working successfully: *the belief that there are no viable alternatives to formal schooling.* **2** (of a plant, animal, or cell) capable of surviving or living successfully.

– SYNONYMS **feasible,** workable, practicable, practical, realistic, achievable, attainable; informal doable.
– ANTONYMS impracticable.

– DERIVATIVES **vi·a·bil·i·ty** /ˌvīə'bilətē/ noun **vi·a·bly** /-blē/ adverb.
– ORIGIN French.

vi·a·duct /'vīəˌdəkt/ ▸ **noun** a long bridgelike structure carrying a road or railroad across a valley or other low ground.
– ORIGIN from Latin *via* 'way' + *ducere* 'to lead.'

Vi·ag·ra /vī'agrə/ ▸ **noun** trademark a drug used to treat impotence in men.
– ORIGIN unknown.

vi·al /'vī(ə)l/ ▸ **noun** a small container used especially for holding liquid medicines.
– ORIGIN from **PHIAL**.

vi·ands /'vīəndz/ ▸ **plural noun** old use food.
– ORIGIN Old French *viande*.

vi·at·i·cum /vī'atikəm, vē-/ ▸ **noun** (pl. **viatica** /-kə/) (in the Christian Church) the Eucharist as given to a person who is dying or in danger of death.
– ORIGIN Latin.

vibe /vīb/ ▸ **noun** informal **1** (usu. **vibes**) the atmosphere of a place or a mood felt among a group of people: *a bar with good vibes.* **2** (**vibes**) short for **VIBRAPHONE**.

vi·brant /'vībrənt/ ▸ **adjective 1** full of energy and enthusiasm. **2** (of sound) strong or resonant. **3** (of color) bright or bold.

– SYNONYMS **1 spirited,** lively, energetic, vigorous, dynamic, passionate, fiery; informal feisty. **2 vivid,** bright, striking, brilliant, glowing, strong, rich.
– ANTONYMS lifeless, pale.

– DERIVATIVES **vi·bran·cy** noun **vi·brant·ly** adverb.
– ORIGIN from Latin *vibrare* 'shake to and fro.'

vi·bra·phone /'vībrəˌfōn/ ▸ **noun** a musical percussion instrument with a double row of metal bars that are hit by the player, each above a resonator with lids that open and close electrically, giving a vibrato effect.
– DERIVATIVES **vi·bra·phon·ist** /-ˌfōnist/ noun.

vi·brate /'vīˌbrāt/ ▸ **verb 1** move with small movements rapidly to and fro. **2** (of a sound) resonate.

– SYNONYMS **shake,** tremble, shiver, quiver, shudder, throb, pulsate.

– DERIVATIVES **vi·bra·to·ry** /'vībrəˌtôrē/ adjective.
– ORIGIN Latin *vibrare* 'move to and fro.'

vi·bra·tion /vī'brāSHən/ ▸ **noun 1** an instance or the state of vibrating. **2** (**vibrations**) informal the atmosphere of a place or a mood felt among a group of people.
– DERIVATIVES **vi·bra·tion·al** adjective.

vi·bra·to /və'brätō, vī-/ ▸ **noun** a rapid, slight variation in pitch in singing or playing some musical instruments, producing a stronger or richer tone.
– ORIGIN Italian.

vi·bra·tor /'vīˌbrātər/ ▸ **noun** a device that vibrates, used for massage or sexual stimulation.

vi·bur·num /vī'bərnəm/ ▸ **noun** a shrub or small tree with clusters of small white flowers.
– ORIGIN Latin, 'wayfaring tree.'

vic·ar /'vikər/ ▸ **noun 1** (in the Church of England) a priest in charge of a parish. **2** (in other Anglican Churches) a member of the clergy deputizing for another. **3** (in the Roman Catholic Church) a representative or deputy of a bishop.
– ORIGIN Latin *vicarius* 'substitute.'

vic·ar·age /'vikərij/ ▸ **noun** the house of a vicar.

vic·ar gen·er·al ▸ **noun** (pl. **vicars general**) an official serving as a deputy or representative of a bishop or archbishop.

vi·car·i·ous /vī'kerēəs, vi-/ ▸ **adjective 1** experienced in the imagination after watching or reading about another person's actions or feelings: *vicarious excitement.* **2** done by one person as a substitute for another.
– DERIVATIVES **vi·car·i·ous·ly** adverb.
– ORIGIN from Latin *vicarius* 'substitute.'

vice[1] /vīs/ ▸ **noun 1** immoral or wicked behavior. **2** criminal activities involving prostitution, pornography, or drugs. **3** an immoral or bad quality in a person's character. **4** a bad habit.

– SYNONYMS **1 immorality,** wrongdoing, wickedness, evil, iniquity, villainy, corruption, misconduct, sin, depravity. **2 fault,** failing, flaw, defect, shortcoming, weakness, deficiency, foible, frailty.
– ANTONYMS virtue.

– ORIGIN Old French.

CHOOSE THE RIGHT WORD

See **SIN[1]**.

vice[2] ▸ **noun** British spelling of **VISE**.

vice- ▸ **combining form** (often without hyphen) next in rank to and able to deputize for: *vice president.*
– ORIGIN from Latin *vice* 'in place of.'

vice ad·mi·ral ▸ **noun** a high rank of naval officer, above rear admiral and below admiral.

vice chan·cel·lor ▸ **noun** a deputy chancellor, such as one in a British university who is in charge of its administration.

vice pres·i·dent ▸ **noun** an official or executive who serves as a deputy to a president.

vice·re·gal /ˌvīs'rēgəl/ ▸ **adjective** relating to a viceroy.

vice·roy /'vīsˌroi/ ▸ **noun** a person who governs a colony on behalf of a sovereign.
– ORIGIN from former French.

vice squad ▸ **noun** a department of a police force that enforces laws against prostitution, drug abuse, illegal gambling, etc.

vice ver·sa /'vīs 'vərsə, 'vīsə/ ▸ **adverb** reversing the order of the items just mentioned.
– ORIGIN Latin, 'in-turned position.'

vi·chys·soise /ˌvēshē'swäz, ˌvishē-, 'vēshēˌswäz, 'vishē-/ ▸ **noun** a soup made with potatoes, leeks, and cream and typically served chilled.
– ORIGIN French, 'of *Vichy*' (a town in France).

vi·cin·i·ty /və'sinətē/ ▸ **noun** (pl. **vicinities**) the area near or surrounding a place.
– PHRASES **in the vicinity of** in the region of a price or amount.
– ORIGIN Latin *vicinitas.*

vi·cious /'vishəs/ ▸ **adjective 1** cruel or violent. **2** full of hatred or anger: *a vicious campaign to discredit him.* **3** very severe or serious: *a vicious stomach bug.* **4** (of an animal) wild and dangerous.

– SYNONYMS **1 brutal,** ferocious, savage, violent, ruthless, merciless, heartless, callous, cruel, cold-blooded, inhuman, barbaric, bloodthirsty. **2 malicious,** spiteful, vindictive, venomous, cruel, bitter, acrimonious, hostile, nasty; informal catty.
– ANTONYMS gentle.

– DERIVATIVES **vi·cious·ly** adverb **vi·cious·ness** noun.
– ORIGIN Latin *vitiosus* 'full of faults, immoral.'

vi·cious cir·cle ▸ **noun** a situation in which one problem leads to another, which then makes the first one worse.

vi·cis·si·tudes /və'sisəˌt(y)o͞odz/ ▸ **plural noun** changes of circumstances or fortune.
– ORIGIN Latin *vicissitudo.*

vi·comte /vē'kônt/ ▸ **noun** (pl. **vicomtes** pronunc. same) a French nobleman corresponding in rank to a viscount.
– ORIGIN French.

vic·tim /'viktəm/ ▸ **noun 1** a person harmed or killed as a result of a crime or accident. **2** a person who has been tricked. **3** an animal or person killed as a religious sacrifice.

– SYNONYMS **sufferer,** injured party, casualty, fatality, loss, survivor.

– DERIVATIVES **vic·tim·hood** /-ˌho͝od/ noun.
– PHRASES **fall victim to** be hurt, killed, or destroyed by someone or something.
– ORIGIN Latin *victima.*

vic·tim·ize /'viktəˌmīz/ ▸ **verb** single someone out for cruel or unfair treatment.

– SYNONYMS **persecute,** pick on, bully, abuse, discriminate against, exploit, take advantage of; informal have it in for.

– DERIVATIVES **vic·tim·i·za·tion** /ˌviktəmə'zāshən/ noun **vic·tim·iz·er** noun.

vic·tim·less /'viktəmləs/ ▸ **adjective** (of a crime) in which there is no injured party.

vic·tim·ol·o·gy /ˌviktə'mäləjē/ ▸ **noun** (pl. **victimologies**) the study of the victims of crime and the psychological effects on them.

vic·tor /'viktər/ ▸ **noun** a person who defeats an opponent in a battle, game, or competition.
– ORIGIN Latin.

Vic·to·ri·an /vik'tôrēən/ ▸ **adjective 1** relating to the reign of Queen Victoria (1837–1901). **2** relating to the attitudes associated with the Victorian period, especially those of prudishness and strict morality. ▸ **noun** a person who lived during the Victorian period.
– DERIVATIVES **Vic·to·ri·an·ism** /-ˌnizəm/ noun.

Vic·to·ri·an·a /vikˌtôrē'anə, -'änə/ ▸ **plural noun** articles, especially collectors' items, from the Victorian period.

vic·to·ri·ous /vik'tôrēəs/ ▸ **adjective 1** having won a victory. **2** relating to a victory; triumphant: *a victorious glance.*

– SYNONYMS **triumphant,** conquering, vanquishing, winning, champion, successful.
– ANTONYMS unsuccessful.

– DERIVATIVES **vic·to·ri·ous·ly** adverb.

vic·to·ry /ˈvikt(ə)rē/ ▶ **noun** (pl. **victories**) an act of defeating an opponent in a battle, game, or other competition.

– SYNONYMS **success,** triumph, conquest, win, coup; informal walkover.
– ANTONYMS defeat, loss.

– ORIGIN Latin *victoria*.

vict·ual /ˈvitl/ dated ▶ **noun** (**victuals**) food or provisions. ▶ **verb** (**victuals, victualing, victualed**) provide someone or something with food or other stores.
– ORIGIN Latin *victualis*.

vi·cu·ña /vīˈk(y)o͞onə və-, və-, ˈko͞onyə/ ▶ **noun 1** a wild relative of the llama, having fine silky wool. **2** cloth made from the wool of the vicuña.
– ORIGIN Quechua.

vid /vid/ ▶ **noun** informal short for **VIDEO**.

vi·de /ˈvēdē, ˈvē,dā, ˈvīdē/ ▶ **verb** see (used as an instruction in a written work to refer the reader elsewhere).
– ORIGIN Latin.

vid·e·o /ˈvidē,ō/ ▶ **noun** (pl. **videos**) **1** a system of recording, reproducing, or broadcasting moving images using magnetic tape. **2** a movie or other recording on magnetic tape. **3** a cassette of videotape. ▶ **verb** (**videoes, videoing, videoed**) film an event or make a video recording of a television program.
– ORIGIN from Latin *videre* 'to see.'

vid·e·o ar·cade ▶ **noun** an indoor area containing coin-operated video games.

vid·e·o·con·fer·ence /ˈvidēō,känf(ə)rəns, -,känf(ə)rns/ ▶ **noun** an arrangement in which television sets linked to telephone lines are used to enable a group of people to talk to and see each other.
– DERIVATIVES **vid·e·o·con·fer·enc·ing** noun.

vid·e·o·disc /ˈvidēō,disk/ (also **videodisk**) ▶ **noun** a CD-ROM or other disk used to store images.

vid·e·o dis·play ter·min·al ▶ **noun** a device for displaying information from a computer on a screen, typically a monitor.

vid·e·o game ▶ **noun** a computer game played on a television or other display screen.

vid·e·og·ra·phy /,vidēˈägrəfē/ ▶ **noun** the process or art of making video films.
– DERIVATIVES **vid·e·og·ra·pher** noun.

video jockey ▶ **noun** full form of **VJ**.

vid·e·o-on-de·mand ▶ **noun** a system in which viewers choose their own filmed entertainment, by means of a PC or interactive TV system.

vid·e·o·phile /ˈvidēə,fīl/ ▶ **noun** a person who is very enthusiastic about video recordings or technology.

vid·e·o·phone /ˈvidēō,fōn/ ▶ **noun** a telephone device that transmits and receives images as well as sound.

vid·e·o re·cord·er ▶ **noun** a machine linked to a television set, used for recording programs and playing videotapes.

vid·e·o·tape /ˈvidēō,tāp/ ▶ **noun 1** magnetic tape for recording and reproducing images and sound. **2** a cassette on which this magnetic tape is held. ▶ **verb** record or film something on videotape.

vie /vī/ ▶ **verb** (**vies, vying, vied**) compete eagerly with others in order to do or achieve something: *companies vying for a slice of the market*.

– SYNONYMS **compete,** contend, struggle, fight, battle, jockey.

– ORIGIN probably from former *envy*, from Latin *invitare* 'challenge.'

Vi·en·nese /,vēəˈnēz, -ˈnēs/ ▶ **noun** (pl. same) a person from Vienna. ▶ **adjective** relating to Vienna.

Vi·et·nam·ese /vē,etnəˈmēz, ,vyet-, ,vēət-, -ˈmēs/ ▶ **noun** (pl. same) **1** a person from Vietnam. **2** the language of Vietnam. ▶ **adjective** relating to Vietnam.

view /vyo͞o/ ▶ **noun 1** the ability to see something or to be seen from a particular position: *the mountains came into view*. **2** something seen from a particular position, especially beautiful scenery. **3** an attitude or opinion: *strong political views*. **4** an inspection of things for sale by prospective buyers.

– SYNONYMS **1 outlook,** prospect, panorama, vista, scene, scenery, landscape. **2 opinion,** viewpoint, belief, judgment, thinking, notion, idea, conviction, persuasion, attitude, feeling, sentiment. **3** *the church came into view* **sight,** perspective, vision, visibility.

▶ **verb 1** look at or inspect someone or something. **2** regard in a particular way: *he viewed beggars as potential thieves*. **3** inspect a house or other property with the prospect of buying or renting it. **4** watch something on television.

– SYNONYMS **1 look at,** observe, eye, gaze at, contemplate, regard, scan, survey, inspect, scrutinize; informal check out, eyeball. **2 consider,** regard, look on, see, perceive, judge, deem, reckon.

– DERIVATIVES **view·a·ble** adjective.
– PHRASES **in full view** clearly visible. **in view** able to be seen; visible. **in view of** because or as a result of. **with a view to** with the aim or intention of.
– ORIGIN Old French *vieue*.

CHOOSE THE RIGHT WORD

See **OPINION**.

view·er /ˈvyo͞oər/ ▶ **noun 1** a person who views something. **2** a device for looking at film transparencies or similar photographic images.

– SYNONYMS **watcher,** spectator, onlooker, observer; (**viewers**) audience, crowd.

view·er·ship /ˈvyo͞oər,ship/ ▶ **noun** (treated as sing. or pl.) the audience for a particular television program or channel.

view·find·er /ˈvyo͞o,fīndər/ ▶ **noun** a device on a camera that the user looks through in order to see what will appear in the photograph.

view·point /ˈvyo͞o,point/ ▶ **noun 1** a point of view; an opinion. **2** a position giving a good view.

view·screen /ˈvyo͞o,skrēn/ ▶ **noun** the screen on a television, computer, or similar device on which images and information are displayed.

vig·il /ˈvijəl/ ▶ **noun 1** a period of staying awake to keep watch or pray. **2** a stationary, peaceful demonstration in support of a cause.
– ORIGIN from Latin, 'awake.'

vig·i·lant /'vijələnt/ ▶ **adjective** keeping careful watch for possible danger or difficulties.

– SYNONYMS **watchful,** observant, attentive, alert, eagle-eyed, on the lookout, on one's guard; informal beady-eyed.
– ANTONYMS inattentive.

– DERIVATIVES **vig·i·lance** noun **vig·i·lant·ly** adverb.
– ORIGIN from Latin *vigilare* 'keep awake.'

vig·i·lan·te /ˌvijə'lantē/ ▶ **noun** a member of a group of people who take it on themselves to prevent crime or punish offenders without legal authority.
– DERIVATIVES **vig·i·lan·tism** /-ˌtizəm/ noun.
– ORIGIN from Spanish, 'vigilant.'

vig·ne·ron /ˌvēnyə'rôn, -'rōn/ ▶ **noun** a person who grows grapes for winemaking.
– ORIGIN French.

vi·gnette /vin'yet/ ▶ **noun 1** a brief, vivid description or episode. **2** a small illustration or portrait photograph that fades into its background without a definite border.
– ORIGIN French.

vig·or /'vigər/ (Brit. **vigour**) ▶ **noun 1** physical strength and good health. **2** effort, energy, and enthusiasm.

– SYNONYMS **health,** strength, robustness, energy, life, vitality, spirit, passion, determination, dynamism, drive; informal oomph, get-up-and-go.
– ANTONYMS lethargy.

– ORIGIN Latin *vigor*.

vig·or·ous /'vig(ə)rəs/ ▶ **adjective 1** strong, healthy, and full of energy. **2** involving effort, energy, or determination: *a vigorous election campaign*. **3** (of language) forceful.

– SYNONYMS **1 robust,** healthy, hale and hearty, strong, sturdy, fit, hardy, tough, energetic, lively, active. **2 strenuous,** powerful, forceful, spirited, determined, aggressive, passionate; informal feisty.
– ANTONYMS weak, feeble.

– DERIVATIVES **vig·or·ous·ness** noun.

vig·or·ous·ly /'vig(ə)rəslē/ ▶ **adverb** with vigor.

– SYNONYMS **strenuously,** strongly, powerfully, forcefully, energetically, heartily, all out, fiercely, hard; informal like mad.

Vi·king /'vīkiNG/ ▶ **noun** a member of the Scandinavian seafaring people who raided and settled in parts of Britain and elsewhere in NW Europe between the 8th and 11th centuries.
– ORIGIN Old Norse.

vile /vīl/ ▶ **adjective 1** very unpleasant. **2** morally bad; wicked.

– SYNONYMS **foul,** nasty, unpleasant, bad, horrid, repulsive, disgusting, hateful, nauseating; informal gross.
– ANTONYMS pleasant.

– DERIVATIVES **vile·ly** adverb **vile·ness** noun.
– ORIGIN Latin *vilis* 'cheap, base.'

vil·i·fy /'viləˌfī/ ▶ **verb** (**vilifies, vilifying, vilified**) speak or write about someone in a very abusive way.
– DERIVATIVES **vil·i·fi·ca·tion** /ˌviləfi'kāSHən/ noun.
– ORIGIN Latin *vilificare*.

vil·la /'vilə/ ▶ **noun 1** a rented vacation home, especially abroad. **2** (especially in continental Europe) a large country house in its own grounds. **3** (in Roman times) a large country house consisting of buildings arranged around a courtyard.
– ORIGIN Latin.

vil·lage /'vilij/ ▶ **noun 1** a community in a country area that is smaller than a town. **2** a self-contained district or community within a town or city.
– DERIVATIVES **vil·lag·er** noun.
– ORIGIN Old French.

vil·lain /'vilən/ ▶ **noun 1** a wicked person or a person guilty of a crime. **2** a bad character in a novel, play, movie, etc., whose evil actions are important to the plot.

– SYNONYMS **criminal,** lawbreaker, offender, felon, miscreant, wrongdoer, rogue, scoundrel, reprobate; informal crook, bad guy.

– DERIVATIVES **vil·lain·ous** adjective **vil·lain·y** noun (pl. **villainies**).
– ORIGIN first meaning 'an unsophisticated country person': from Old French *vilein*.

vil·la·nelle /ˌvilə'nel/ ▶ **noun** a poem of nineteen lines, with only two rhymes throughout, and some lines repeated.
– ORIGIN French.

vil·lein /'vilən, -ˌān/ ▶ **noun** (in medieval England) a poor man who had to work for a lord in return for a small piece of land on which to grow food.
– ORIGIN from **VILLAIN**.

vil·lus /'viləs/ ▶ **noun** (pl. **villi** /'vilī, 'vilē/) any of many tiny fingerlike growths of tissue on some membranes of the body, especially the small intestine.
– DERIVATIVES **vil·lous** /'viləs/ adjective.
– ORIGIN Latin, 'shaggy hair.'

vim /vim/ ▶ **noun** informal energy; enthusiasm.
– ORIGIN perhaps from Latin *vis* 'energy.'

VIN /vin/ ▶ **abbreviation** vehicle identification number.

vin·ai·grette /ˌvinə'gret/ ▶ **noun** a salad dressing of oil, wine vinegar, and seasoning.
– ORIGIN French.

vin·di·cate /'vindəˌkāt/ ▶ **verb 1** clear someone of blame or suspicion. **2** show to be right or justified: *more sober views were vindicated by events*.

– SYNONYMS **1 acquit,** clear, absolve, exonerate; informal let off. **2 justify,** warrant, substantiate, confirm, corroborate, prove, defend, support, back, endorse.
– ANTONYMS incriminate.

– DERIVATIVES **vin·di·ca·tion** /ˌvində'kāSHən/ noun.
– ORIGIN Latin *vindicare* 'claim, avenge.'

CHOOSE THE RIGHT WORD

See **ABSOLVE**.

vin·dic·tive /vin'diktiv/ ▶ **adjective** having or showing a strong or spiteful desire for revenge.

– SYNONYMS **vengeful,** unforgiving, resentful, acrimonious, bitter; spiteful, mean, rancorous, venomous, malicious, malevolent, nasty, cruel.
– ANTONYMS forgiving.

– DERIVATIVES **vin·dic·tive·ly** adverb **vin·dic·tive·ness** noun.
– ORIGIN from Latin *vindicta* 'vengeance.'

CHOOSE THE RIGHT WORD

vindictive, rancorous, spiteful, vengeful, venomous

Someone who is motivated by a desire to get even might be described as **vindictive**, a word that suggests harboring grudges for imagined wrongs (*a vindictive person who* *had alienated friends and neighbors alike*). **Spiteful** is a stronger term, implying a bitter or vicious vindictiveness (*a spiteful child who broke the toy she had been forced to share*). **Vengeful** implies a strong urge to actually seek vengeance (*she was vengeful after losing her husband in a hit-and-run accident*). Someone who is **rancorous** suffers from a deep-seated and lasting bitterness, although it does not imply a desire to hurt or to be vindictive (*his rancorous nature made him difficult to befriend*). **Venomous** takes its meaning from "venom" referring to someone or something of a spiteful, malignant nature and suggesting a poisonous sting (*a critic's venomous attack on the author's first novel*).

vine /vīn/ ▶ **noun 1** a climbing plant with a woody stem, especially one that produces grapes. **2** the slender stem of a climbing plant.
– ORIGIN Latin *vinea* 'vineyard, vine.'

vin·e·gar /'vinəgər/ ▶ **noun 1** a sour liquid made from wine, beer, or cider, used as a seasoning or for pickling. **2** bitterness or spitefulness: *she was bossy and full of vinegar*.
– DERIVATIVES **vin·e·gar·y** adjective.
– ORIGIN from Old French *vyn egre* 'sour wine.'

vine·yard /'vinyərd/ ▶ **noun** a plantation of grapevines, producing grapes used in winemaking.

vingt-et-un /ˌvant ā 'ən, ˌvan tā 'œn/ ▶ **noun** the card game blackjack or twenty-one.
– ORIGIN French, 'twenty-one.'

vi·nho ver·de /'vinyō 'vərdē, 'vēnyo͞o 'verdə/ ▶ **noun** a young Portuguese wine, not allowed to mature.
– ORIGIN Portuguese, 'green wine.'

vin·i·cul·ture /'vinəˌkəlchər/ ▶ **noun** the growing of grapevines for winemaking.

vin·i·fi·ca·tion /ˌvinəfi'kāshən/ ▶ **noun** the conversion of grape juice or other vegetable extract into wine by fermentation.

vi·no /'vēnō/ ▶ **noun** (pl. **vinos**) informal wine.
– ORIGIN Spanish and Italian, 'wine.'

vi·nous /'vīnəs/ ▶ **adjective** of, resembling, or associated with wine.

vin·tage /'vintij/ ▶ **noun 1** the year or place in which wine was produced. **2** a wine of high quality made from the crop of a single specified district in a good year. **3** the harvesting of grapes for winemaking. **4** the grapes or wine of a particular season. **5** the time that something was produced: *rifles of various vintages*.
▶ **adjective 1** referring to high-quality vintage wine. **2** (of something from the past) of high quality.

– SYNONYMS **1 high-quality,** quality, choice, select, superior. **2 classic,** ageless, timeless, old, antique, historic.

– ORIGIN Old French *vendange*.

vint·ner /'vintnər/ ▶ **noun** a wine merchant.
– ORIGIN Old French *vinetier*.

vi·nyl /'vīnl/ ▶ **noun 1** a type of strong plastic, used in making floor coverings, paint, and phonograph records. **2** Chemistry the unsaturated hydrocarbon radical $-CH{=}CH_2$, derived from ethylene.
– ORIGIN from Latin *vinum* 'wine' (suggested by the relationship of ethylene to ethyl alcohol).

vi·ol /'vīəl/ ▶ **noun** a musical instrument of the Renaissance and baroque periods, resembling a violin but with six strings and held vertically.
– ORIGIN Provençal *viola*.

vi·o·la¹ /vē'ōlə/ ▶ **noun** an instrument of the violin family, larger than the violin and tuned a fifth lower.
– ORIGIN Italian and Spanish.

vi·o·la² /vī'ōlə, vē-, 'vīələ/ ▶ **noun** a plant of a genus that includes pansies and violets.
– ORIGIN Latin, 'violet.'

vi·o·la da gam·ba /vē'ōlə də 'gämbə, 'gam-/ ▶ **noun** a viol, specifically a bass viol (corresponding to the modern cello).
– ORIGIN Italian, 'viol for the leg.'

vi·o·late /'vīəˌlāt/ ▶ **verb 1** fail to obey a rule, law, or formal agreement. **2** fail to respect a person's privacy or rights. **3** treat something sacred with disrespect. **4** chiefly literary rape someone.

– SYNONYMS **1 contravene,** breach, infringe, break, transgress, disobey, defy, flout, disregard, ignore. **2 desecrate,** profane, defile, degrade, debase, damage, vandalize, deface, destroy.
– ANTONYMS respect.

– DERIVATIVES **vi·o·la·tor** noun.
– ORIGIN Latin *violare* 'treat violently.'

vi·o·la·tion /ˌvīə'lāshən/ ▶ **noun** the action of violating someone or something.

– SYNONYMS *a flagrant violation of human rights* **contravention,** breach, infringement, transgression, defiance, flouting, disregard.

vi·o·lence /'vī(ə)ləns/ ▶ **noun 1** behavior involving physical force intended to hurt, damage, or kill. **2** the power of a destructive natural force. **3** strength of emotion: *the violence of her feelings*.

– SYNONYMS **1 brutality,** savagery, cruelty, barbarity. **2 force,** power, strength, might, ferocity, intensity, vehemence.

vi·o·lent /'vī(ə)lənt/ ▶ **adjective 1** using or involving violence. **2** very intense or powerful: *violent dislike*.

– SYNONYMS **1 brutal,** vicious, savage, rough, aggressive, threatening, fierce, ferocious, bloodthirsty. **2 powerful,** forceful, hard, sharp, smart, strong, vigorous, mighty, hefty. **3 intense,** extreme, strong, powerful, fierce, unbridled, uncontrollable, ungovernable, consuming, passionate.
– ANTONYMS gentle, mild.

– DERIVATIVES **vi·o·lent·ly** adverb.
– ORIGIN Latin, 'vehement, violent.'

vi·o·let /'vī(ə)lət/ ▶ **noun 1** a small plant with purple, blue, or white five-petaled flowers. **2** a bluish-purple color.
– ORIGIN Old French *violette*.

vi·o·lin /ˌvīə'lin/ ▶ **noun** a musical instrument having four strings and a body narrowed at the middle, played with a bow.
– DERIVATIVES **vi·o·lin·ist** noun.
– ORIGIN Italian *violino* 'small viola.'

vi·o·list /vē'ōlist/ ▶ **noun** a viola player.

vi·o·lon·cel·lo /ˌvīələn'chelō, ˌvē-/ ▶ **noun** formal term for **CELLO**.
– ORIGIN Italian.

VIP ▶ **noun** a very important person.

vi·per /'vīpər/ ▶ **noun 1** a poisonous snake with large fangs and a body with dark patterns on a lighter

background. **2** a spiteful or treacherous person.
– DERIVATIVES **vi·per·ish** adjective **vi·per·ous** adjective.
– ORIGIN Latin *vipera*.

vi·ra·go /və'rägō, -'rā-/ ▸ **noun** (pl. **viragos** or **viragoes**) a domineering, violent, or bad-tempered woman.
– ORIGIN from Latin, 'heroic woman, female warrior.'

vi·ral /'vīrəl/ ▸ **adjective** relating to or caused by a virus or viruses.
– DERIVATIVES **vi·ral·ly** adverb.

vi·ral mar·ket·ing ▸ **noun** a marketing technique whereby information about a product is passed electronically from one Internet user to another.

vi·re·mi·a /vī'rēmēə/ (Brit. also **viraemia**) ▸ **noun** Medicine the presence of viruses in the blood.
– ORIGIN from VIRUS.

vir·e·o /'virē,ō/ ▸ **noun** (pl. **vireos**) a small American songbird, typically green or gray with yellow or white underparts.
– ORIGIN Latin, referring to a finch with green or greenish plumage.

vir·gin /'vərjən/ ▸ **noun 1** a person who has never had sexual intercourse. **2** (**the Virgin**) the Virgin Mary, the mother of Jesus. **3** a person who is inexperienced in a particular activity: *a political virgin*. ▸ **adjective 1** having had no sexual experience. **2** not yet used or exploited: *virgin forest*. **3** (of olive oil) made from the first pressing of olives.
– ORIGIN Latin *virgo*.

vir·gin·al /'vərjənl/ ▸ **adjective** relating to or appropriate for a virgin: *virginal white*.

vir·gin·als /'vərjənlz/ ▸ **plural noun** a type of small harpsichord popular in the 16th and 17th centuries.

Vir·gin Birth ▸ **noun** the Christian doctrine of Jesus's birth from a mother, Mary, who was a virgin.

Vir·gin·ia creep·er /vər'jinyə/ ▸ **noun** a North American climbing plant, grown for its red autumn foliage.

vir·gin·i·ty /vər'jinətē/ ▸ **noun 1** the state of never having had sexual intercourse. **2** the state of being inexperienced in a particular activity.

Vir·go /'vərgō/ ▸ **noun 1** a constellation and the sixth sign of the zodiac (the Virgin), which the sun enters about August 23. **2** (**a Virgo**) a person born when the sun is in this sign.
– DERIVATIVES **Vir·go·an** /-gōən/ noun & adjective.
– ORIGIN Latin.

vir·i·des·cent /,virə'desənt/ ▸ **adjective** literary greenish or becoming green.
– DERIVATIVES **vir·i·des·cence** noun.
– ORIGIN from Latin *viridescere* 'become green.'

vi·rid·i·an /və'ridēən/ ▸ **noun** a bluish-green pigment or color.
– ORIGIN from Latin *viridis* 'green.'

vir·ile /'virəl/ ▸ **adjective 1** (of a man) strong, energetic, and having a strong sex drive. **2** vigorous or powerful: *virile guitar bursts*.

> – SYNONYMS **manly**, masculine, male; strong, tough, vigorous, robust, muscly, brawny; red-blooded, fertile; informal macho, butch.
> – ANTONYMS effeminate.

– DERIVATIVES **vi·ril·i·ty** /və'rilitē/ noun.
– ORIGIN Latin *virilis*.

vi·rol·o·gy /vī'räləjē/ ▸ **noun** the branch of science concerned with the study of viruses.
– DERIVATIVES **vi·ro·log·i·cal** /,vīrə'läjikəl/ adjective **vi·rol·o·gist** noun.

vir·tu·al /'vərCHōōəl/ ▸ **adjective 1** almost or nearly the thing described, but not completely: *the virtual absence of border controls*. **2** not existing in reality but made by computer software to appear to do so.

> – SYNONYMS **effective**, near (enough), essential, practical, to all intents and purposes, in all but name, implied, unacknowledged.

– DERIVATIVES **vir·tu·al·i·ty** /,vərCHōō'alitē/ noun.
– ORIGIN Latin *virtualis*.

vir·tu·al·ize /'vərCHōōə,līz/ ▸ **verb** convert something to a computer-generated version of reality.
– DERIVATIVES **vir·tu·al·i·za·tion** /,vərCHōōələ'zāSHən/ noun.

vir·tu·al·ly /'vərCHə(wə)lē/ ▸ **adverb 1** nearly; almost. **2** Computing by means of virtual reality techniques.

> – SYNONYMS **effectively**, all but, more or less, practically, almost, nearly, close to, verging on, just about, as good as, essentially, to all intents and purposes.

vir·tu·al mem·o·ry (also **virtual storage**) ▸ **noun** Computing memory that appears to exist as main storage although most of it is supported by data held in secondary storage.

vir·tu·al re·al·i·ty ▸ **noun** a system in which images that look like real, three-dimensional objects are created by computer.

vir·tue /'vərCHōō/ ▸ **noun 1** behavior showing high moral standards. **2** a good or desirable personal quality. **3** a good or useful quality of a thing: *the virtues of village life*. **4** old use virginity or chastity.

> – SYNONYMS **1 goodness**, righteousness, morality, integrity, dignity, rectitude, honor, probity. **2 good point**, good quality, strong point, asset, forte, attribute, strength, merit, advantage, benefit; informal plus.
> – ANTONYMS vice.

– PHRASES **by virtue of** as a result of.
– ORIGIN Latin *virtus* 'valor, merit, moral perfection.'

vir·tu·o·so /,vərCHōō'ōsō/ ▸ **noun** (pl. **virtuosi** /-sē/ or **virtuosos**) a person highly skilled in music or another artistic activity.
– DERIVATIVES **vir·tu·os·ic** /-'äsik, -'ōsik/ adjective **vir·tu·os·i·ty** /-'äsitē/ noun.
– ORIGIN from Italian, 'learned, skillful.'

vir·tu·ous /'vərCHəwəs/ ▸ **adjective 1** having or showing high moral standards. **2** old use (especially of a woman) chaste.

> – SYNONYMS **righteous**, good, moral, ethical, upright, upstanding, high-minded, principled, exemplary; irreproachable, honest, honorable, reputable, decent, respectable, worthy; pure, whiter than white, saintly, angelic; informal squeaky clean.

– DERIVATIVES **vir·tu·ous·ly** adverb **vir·tu·ous·ness** noun.

vir·tu·ous cir·cle ▸ **noun** a situation in which one event leads to another, each one increasing the beneficial effect of the next.

vir·u·lent /'vir(y)ələnt/ ▸ **adjective 1** (of a disease or poison) having a very severe or harmful effect. **2** (of a virus) highly infective. **3** bitterly hostile: *a virulent attack on liberalism*.

– DERIVATIVES **vir·u·lence** noun **vir·u·lent·ly** adverb.
– ORIGIN first describing a poisoned wound: from Latin *virulentus*.

vi·rus /'vīrəs/ ▶ **noun 1** a submicroscopic particle, typically consisting of nucleic acid coated in protein, that can cause infection or disease and can only multiply within the cells of a host organism. **2** an infection or disease caused by a virus. **3** (also **computer virus**) a piece of code introduced secretly into a computer system in order to damage or destroy data.
– ORIGIN Latin, 'slimy liquid, poison.'

vi·sa /'vēzə/ ▶ **noun** a stamp or note on a passport indicating that the holder is allowed to enter, leave, or stay for a specified time in a country.
– ORIGIN Latin.

vis·age /'vizij/ ▶ **noun** literary a person's facial features or expression.
– DERIVATIVES **vis·aged** adjective.
– ORIGIN Old French.

vis-à-vis /'vēz ə 'vē/ ▶ **preposition** in relation to.
– ORIGIN French, 'face to face.'

vis·cer·a /'visərə/ ▶ **plural noun** the internal organs of the body, especially those in the abdomen.
– ORIGIN Latin, plural of *viscus*.

vis·cer·al /'vis(ə)rəl/ ▶ **adjective 1** relating to the body's internal organs. **2** (of a feeling) deep and instinctive rather than rational: *the voters' visceral fear of change*.
– DERIVATIVES **vis·cer·al·ly** adverb.

vis·cid /'visid/ ▶ **adjective** sticky in consistency.
– ORIGIN Latin *viscidus*.

vis·cose /'vis,kōs, -,kōz/ ▶ **noun** rayon fabric or fiber made from treating cellulose with certain chemicals.
– ORIGIN from Latin *viscus* 'birdlime.'

vis·cos·i·ty /,vi'skäsitē/ ▶ **noun** (pl. **viscosities**) the state of being thick, sticky, and semifluid in consistency.

vis·count /'vī,kount/ ▶ **noun** a British nobleman ranking above a baron and below an earl.
– ORIGIN Latin *vicecomes*.

vis·count·ess /'vī,kountəs/ ▶ **noun** the wife or widow of a viscount, or a woman holding the rank of viscount in her own right.

vis·cous /'viskəs/ ▶ **adjective** having a thick, sticky consistency between solid and liquid.
– ORIGIN Latin *viscosus*.

vise /vīs/ (Brit. **vice**) ▶ **noun** a metal tool with movable jaws that are used to hold an object firmly in place while work is done on it.
– ORIGIN Old French *vis*.

vis·i·bil·i·ty /,vizə'bilitē/ ▶ **noun 1** the state of being able to see or be seen. **2** the distance that a person can see, depending on light and weather conditions.

vis·i·ble /'vizəbəl/ ▶ **adjective 1** able to be seen. **2** able to be noticed; prominent: *a more visible police presence could be the norm*. **3** (of light) within the range of wavelengths to which the eye is sensitive.

> – SYNONYMS **observable,** perceptible, noticeable, detectable, discernible, in sight, in view, on display, evident, apparent, manifest, plain.

– DERIVATIVES **vis·i·bly** /-blē/ adverb.
– ORIGIN Latin *visibilis*.

Vis·i·goth /'vizə,gäTH/ ▶ **noun** a member of the branch of the Goths who invaded the Roman Empire between the 3rd and 5th centuries AD.
– ORIGIN Latin *Visigothus*, perhaps meaning 'West Goth.'

vi·sion /'viZHən/ ▶ **noun 1** the ability to see. **2** the ability to think about the future with imagination or wisdom: *the organization has lost its vision and direction*. **3** an experience of imagining something, or of seeing someone or something in a dream or trance. **4** the images seen on a television screen. **5** a very beautiful person or sight.

> – SYNONYMS **1 eyesight,** sight, observation, eyes, view, perspective. **2 imagination,** creativity, inventiveness, inspiration, intuition, perception, insight. **3 apparition,** specter, phantom, ghost, wraith, manifestation, hallucination, illusion, mirage. **4 dream,** reverie, plan, hope, fantasy, pipe dream.

– ORIGIN Latin.

> **WORD LINKS**
>
> **visual**, **optic** *relating to vision*

vi·sion·ar·y /'viZHə,nerē/ ▶ **adjective 1** thinking about the future with imagination or wisdom. **2** relating to supernatural or dreamlike visions. ▶ **noun** (pl. **visionaries**) a person with imaginative and original ideas about the future.

> **WORD TOOLKIT**
>
> See **QUIXOTIC**.

vis·it /'vizit/ ▶ **verb** (**visits, visiting, visited**) **1** go to see a person or place for a period of time. **2** go to see someone for a particular purpose, such as to receive advice: *I visited my doctor for a checkup*. **3** access and view a website or web page. **4** (as adj. **visiting**) (of an academic) working for a fixed period of time at another college or university. **5** literary cause something harmful or unpleasant to affect someone: *they were visited with an epidemic*. **6** (usu. **visit with**) informal chat with someone.

> – SYNONYMS **call on,** go to see, look in on, stay with, stop by, drop by; informal pop/drop in on, look up.

▶ **noun 1** an act of going to see a person or place. **2** a temporary stay at a place.

> – SYNONYMS **(social) call,** stay, stopover, trip, vacation; literary sojourn.

– ORIGIN Latin *visitare* 'go to see.'

vis·it·a·tion /,vizə'tāSHən/ ▶ **noun 1** an official or formal visit. **2** the appearance of a god or goddess or a supernatural being. **3** a disaster or difficulty regarded as a punishment from God: *a visitation of the plague*. **4** (**the Visitation**) the visit of the Virgin Mary to Elizabeth described in the Gospel of Luke, chapter 1.

vis·i·tor /'vizitər/ ▶ **noun 1** a person visiting a person or place. **2** a bird that migrates to a particular area for only part of the year.

> – SYNONYMS **guest,** caller, company; tourist, traveler, day tripper, vacationer, sightseer.

vi·sor /'vīzər/ (also **vizor**) ▶ **noun 1** a movable part of a helmet that can be pulled down to cover the face. **2** a screen for protecting the eyes from unwanted light. **3** a stiff peak at the front of a cap.
– DERIVATIVES **vi·sored** adjective.
– ORIGIN Old French *viser*.

VISTA /'vistə/ ▶ **abbreviation** Volunteers in Service to America.

vis·ta /ˈvistə/ ▶ **noun 1** a pleasing view. **2** an imagined future event or situation: *vistas of freedom seemed to open ahead of him.*

– SYNONYMS **view,** scene, prospect, panorama, sight, scenery, landscape.

– ORIGIN Italian, 'view.'

vis·u·al /ˈvizHo͞oəl/ ▶ **adjective** relating to seeing or sight.

– SYNONYMS **1 optical,** ocular. **2 visible,** observable, perceptible, discernible.

▶ **noun** a picture, piece of film, or display used to illustrate or accompany something.

– DERIVATIVES **vis·u·al·ly** adverb.

– ORIGIN Latin *visualis.*

vis·u·al·ize /ˈvizH(ə)wəˌlīz/ ▶ **verb** form an image of someone or something in the mind.

– SYNONYMS **envisage,** conjure up, picture, call to mind, see, imagine, dream up.

– DERIVATIVES **vis·u·al·i·za·tion** /ˌvizH(ə)wələˈzāsHən/ noun **vis·u·al·iz·er** noun.

vi·tal /ˈvītl/ ▶ **adjective 1** absolutely necessary; essential. **2** essential for life: *the vital organs.* **3** full of energy; lively.

– SYNONYMS **1 essential,** critical, crucial, indispensable, all-important, imperative, mandatory, high-priority, key, life-and-death. **2 lively,** energetic, active, sprightly, spirited, vivacious, exuberant, dynamic, vigorous; informal full of beans.
– ANTONYMS unimportant.

▶ **noun** (**vitals**) the body's important internal organs.

– DERIVATIVES **vi·tal·ly** adverb.

– ORIGIN Latin *vitalis.*

WORD TOOLKIT

vital ...	crucial ...	utmost ...
information	role	importance
service	part	respect
work	question	care
ingredient	factor	concern
support	moment	caution
resources	step	attention
funds	stage	urgency
equipment	evidence	secrecy

vi·tal force ▶ **noun** the energy or spirit that gives life to living creatures.

vi·tal·ism /ˈvītlˌizəm/ ▶ **noun** the theory that life is dependent on a force or principle distinct from purely chemical or physical forces.

– DERIVATIVES **vi·tal·ist** noun & adjective **vi·tal·is·tic** /ˌvītlˈistik/ adjective.

vi·tal·i·ty /vīˈtalitē/ ▶ **noun** the state of being full of energy; liveliness.

– SYNONYMS **life,** energy, spirit, vivacity, exuberance, dynamism, vigor, passion, drive; informal get-up-and-go.

vi·tal·ize /ˈvītlˌīz/ ▶ **verb** give strength and energy to: *the drink is claimed to vitalize the body and mind.*

vi·tal signs ▶ **plural noun** clinical measurements, specifically pulse rate, temperature, blood pressure, and rate of breathing, that indicate the state of a patient's essential body functions.

vi·tal sta·tis·tics ▶ **plural noun 1** statistics relating to the population, such as the number of births, marriages, and deaths. **2** informal the measurements of a woman's bust, waist, and hips.

vi·ta·min /ˈvītəmən/ ▶ **noun** any of a group of organic compounds that are present in many foods and are essential for normal nutrition.

– ORIGIN from Latin *vita* 'life' + **AMINE**, because vitamins were originally thought to contain an amino acid.

vi·ta·min A ▶ **noun** retinol, a compound that is essential for growth and vision in dim light and is found in vegetables, egg yolk, and fish-liver oil.

vi·ta·min B ▶ **noun** any of a group of substances essential for the working of certain enzymes in the body, including thiamine (**vitamin B_1**), riboflavin (**vitamin B_2**), pyridoxine (**vitamin B_6**), and cyanocobalamin (**vitamin B_{12}**).

vi·ta·min C ▶ **noun** ascorbic acid, a compound found in citrus fruits and green vegetables, essential in maintaining healthy connective tissue.

vi·ta·min D ▶ **noun** any of a group of compounds found in liver and fish oils, essential for the absorption of calcium and including calciferol (**vitamin D_2**) and cholecalciferol (**vitamin D_3**).

vi·ta·min E ▶ **noun** tocopherol, a compound found in wheat-germ oil, egg yolk, and leafy vegetables and important in stabilizing cell membranes.

vi·ta·min K ▶ **noun** any of a group of compounds found mainly in green leaves and essential for the blood-clotting process, including phylloquinone (**vitamin K_1**) and menaquinone (**vitamin K_2**).

vi·ti·ate /ˈvisHēˌāt/ ▶ **verb** formal **1** make something less good or effective. **2** destroy or reduce the legal validity of something.

– ORIGIN Latin *vitiare* 'impair.'

vit·i·cul·ture /ˈvitiˌkəlCHər/ ▶ **noun 1** the cultivation of grapevines. **2** the study of grape cultivation.

– DERIVATIVES **vit·i·cul·tur·al** /ˌvitiˈkəlCHərəl/ adjective **vit·i·cul·tur·ist** /-rist/ noun.

– ORIGIN from Latin *vitis* 'vine.'

vit·i·li·go /ˌvītlˈīgō, -ˈēgō/ ▶ **noun** a medical condition in which the pigment is lost from areas of the skin, causing whitish patches.

– ORIGIN Latin.

vit·re·ous /ˈvitrēəs/ ▶ **adjective 1** resembling glass in appearance. **2** (of a substance) containing glass.

– ORIGIN Latin *vitreus.*

vit·re·ous hu·mor ▶ **noun** the transparent jellylike tissue filling the eyeball behind the lens.

vit·ri·fy /ˈvitrəˌfī/ ▶ **verb** (**vitrifies, vitrifying, vitrified**) convert something into glass or a glasslike substance by exposure to heat.

– DERIVATIVES **vit·ri·fi·ca·tion** /ˌvitrəfiˈkāsHən/ noun.

– ORIGIN from Latin *vitrum* 'glass.'

vit·ri·ol /ˈvitrēəl, -ˌôl/ ▶ **noun 1** extreme bitterness or malice: *a website where waiters vent their vitriol.* **2** old use sulfuric acid.

– ORIGIN first referring to the sulfate of various metals: from Latin *vitriolum.*

vit·ri·ol·ic /ˌvitrēˈälik/ ▶ **adjective** filled with bitterness or malice: *a vitriolic attack on working mothers.*

– DERIVATIVES **vit·ri·ol·ic·al·ly** /-ik(ə)lē/ adverb.

vi·tu·per·a·tion /vəˌt(y)o͞opəˈrāsHən, vī-/ ▶ **noun** bitter and abusive language.

– DERIVATIVES **vi·tu·per·a·tive** /və'tʼ(y)o͞opəˌrātiv, vī-, -p(ə)rətiv/ adjective.
– ORIGIN Latin.

CHOOSE THE RIGHT WORD

See **SCOLD**.

vi·va /'vēvə/ ▸ **exclamation** long live! (used to express praise or support).
– ORIGIN Italian.

vi·va·ce /vē'väˌCHā, -CHē/ ▸ **adverb & adjective** Music in a lively and brisk way.
– ORIGIN Italian.

vi·va·cious /və'vāSHəs, vī-/ ▸ **adjective** (especially of a woman) attractive and lively.

– SYNONYMS **lively,** spirited, bubbly, ebullient, buoyant, merry, happy, jolly, full of fun, cheery, perky, sunny, breezy, enthusiastic, vibrant, dynamic; informal peppy, bouncy, upbeat, chirpy.
– ANTONYMS dull.

– DERIVATIVES **vi·va·cious·ly** adverb **vi·vac·i·ty** /və'vasitē, vī-/ noun.
– ORIGIN from Latin *vivax* 'lively, vigorous.'

vi·var·i·um /vī've(ə)rēəm/ ▸ **noun** (pl. **vivaria** /-'ve(ə)rēə/) an enclosure or structure used for keeping animals in conditions similar to their natural environment for study or as pets.
– ORIGIN Latin, 'warren, fish pond.'

vi·va vo·ce /ˌvēvə 'vōCHā, ˌvīvə 'vōsē/ ▸ **adjective** (especially of an examination) oral rather than written. ▸ **adverb** orally rather than in writing.
– ORIGIN Latin, literally 'with the living voice.'

viv·id /'vivid/ ▸ **adjective 1** producing powerful feelings or strong, clear images in the mind: *a vivid description*. **2** (of a color) very deep or bright.

– SYNONYMS **1 graphic,** realistic, lifelike, faithful, authentic, striking, evocative, arresting, colorful, dramatic, memorable, powerful, stirring, moving, haunting. **2 bright,** colorful, brilliant, radiant, vibrant, strong, bold, deep, intense, rich, warm.
– ANTONYMS dull, vague.

– DERIVATIVES **viv·id·ly** adverb **viv·id·ness** noun.
– ORIGIN Latin *vividus* 'lively, vigorous.'

WORD TOOLKIT

See **GRAPHIC**.

viv·i·fy /'vivəˌfī/ ▸ **verb** (**vivifies, vivifying, vivified**) make someone or something more lively or interesting.
– DERIVATIVES **viv·i·fi·ca·tion** /ˌvivəfi'kāSHən/ noun.
– ORIGIN Latin *vivificare*.

vi·vip·a·rous /vī'vip(ə)rəs, vi-/ ▸ **adjective** (of an animal) giving birth to live young that have developed inside the body of the parent. Compare with **OVIPAROUS**.
– DERIVATIVES **viv·i·par·i·ty** /ˌvivə'paritē, ˌvīvə-/ noun.
– ORIGIN Latin *viviparus*.

viv·i·sec·tion /ˌvivə'sekSHən/ ▸ **noun** the practice of operating on live animals for scientific research (used by people opposed to such work).
– DERIVATIVES **viv·i·sec·tion·ist** noun & adjective **viv·i·sec·tor** /'vivəˌsektər, ˌvivə'sektər/ noun.
– ORIGIN from Latin *vivus* 'living,' on the pattern of *dissection*.

vix·en /'viksən/ ▸ **noun 1** a female fox. **2** a spirited or quarrelsome woman.
– DERIVATIVES **vix·en·ish** adjective.
– ORIGIN perhaps from an Old English word meaning 'of a fox.'

viz. /viz/ ▸ **adverb** namely; in other words.
– ORIGIN short for Latin *videlicet* in the same sense.

vi·zier /və'zi(ə)r/ ▸ **noun** historical a high-ranking official in some Muslim countries.
– ORIGIN Arabic, 'caliph's chief counselor.'

vi·zor ▸ **noun** variant spelling of **VISOR**.

vizs·la /'vizHlə, 'vēzlə/ ▸ **noun** a breed of golden-brown pointer (dog) with large drooping ears.
– ORIGIN named after the town of *Vizsla* in Hungary.

VJ /'vēˌjā/ ▸ **noun** a person who introduces and plays popular music videos; a video jockey. ▸ **verb** (**VJ's, VJ'ing, VJ'd**) perform as a VJ.

V-J Day ▸ **noun** the day (August 15) in 1945 on which Japan ceased fighting in World War II, or the day (September 2) when Japan formally surrendered.
– ORIGIN short for *Victory over Japan*.

VLF ▸ **abbreviation** very low frequency (referring to radio waves of frequency 3–30 kilohertz and wavelength 10–100 kilometers).

VLSI ▸ **abbreviation** Electronics very large-scale integration, the process of integrating hundreds of thousands of components on a single silicon chip.

V-neck ▸ **noun** a neckline having straight sides meeting at a point to form a V-shape.
– DERIVATIVES **V-necked** adjective.

vo·cab·u·lar·y /vō'kabyəˌlerē, və-/ ▸ **noun** (pl. **vocabularies**) **1** all the words used in a particular language or area of activity: *business vocabulary*. **2** all the words known to an individual person. **3** a list of words and their meanings, accompanying a piece of foreign or specialist writing. **4** a range of artistic or stylistic forms or techniques: *his command of the vocabulary of classical ballet*.
– ORIGIN Latin *vocabularius*.

vo·cal /'vōkəl/ ▸ **adjective 1** relating to the human voice. **2** expressing opinions or feelings freely or loudly. **3** (of music) consisting of or including singing.

– SYNONYMS **1 spoken,** said, voiced, uttered, articulated, oral. **2 vociferous,** outspoken, forthright, plain-spoken, blunt, frank, candid, passionate, vehement, vigorous.

▸ **noun** (also **vocals**) a part of a piece of music that is sung.
– DERIVATIVES **vo·cal·ly** adverb.
– ORIGIN Latin *vocalis*.

vo·cal cords (also **vocal folds**) ▸ **plural noun** the folds of the lining of the larynx whose edges vibrate in the airstream to produce the voice.

vo·cal·ic /vō'kalik, və-/ ▸ **adjective** Phonetics relating to or consisting of a vowel or vowels.

vo·cal·ist /'vōkəlist/ ▸ **noun** a singer, especially in jazz or popular music.

vo·cal·ize /'vōkəˌlīz/ ▸ **verb 1** make a sound or say a word. **2** express something with words. **3** sing with several notes to one vowel.
– DERIVATIVES **vo·cal·i·za·tion** /ˌvōkələ'zāSHən/ noun.

vo·ca·tion /vō'kāSHən/ ▸ **noun 1** a person's career or main occupation. **2** a profession. **3** a strong belief that one ought to pursue a particular career or occupation.

– SYNONYMS **calling,** life's work, mission, purpose, profession, occupation, career, job, employment, trade, craft, line (of work).

– ORIGIN Latin.

vo·ca·tion·al /vō'kāshənl/ ▶ **adjective** relating to a particular occupation and its skills or knowledge.
– DERIVATIVES **vo·ca·tion·al·ly** adverb.

voc·a·tive /'väkətiv/ ▶ **noun** the grammatical case used in addressing a person or thing.
– ORIGIN Latin *vocativus*.

vo·cif·er·ous /və'sifərəs, vō-/ ▶ **adjective** expressing opinions in a loud and forceful way: *he was a vociferous opponent of the takeover*.
– DERIVATIVES **vo·cif·er·ous·ly** adverb **vo·cif·er·ous·ness** noun.
– ORIGIN from Latin *vociferari* 'exclaim.'

vo·cod·er /'vō,kōdər/ ▶ **noun** an electronic synthesizer that produces sounds from an analysis of speech input.
– ORIGIN from **VOICE** + **CODE**.

VOD ▶ **abbreviation** video-on-demand.

vod·ka /'vädkə/ ▶ **noun** a clear, originally Russian alcoholic spirit made from rye, wheat, or potatoes.
– ORIGIN Russian, 'little water.'

vogue /vōg/ ▶ **noun** the fashion or style current at a particular time.

– SYNONYMS **fashion,** trend, fad, fancy, craze, rage, enthusiasm, passion.

– DERIVATIVES **vogu·ish** adjective.
– ORIGIN French.

voice /vois/ ▶ **noun 1** the sound produced in a person's larynx and uttered through the mouth, as speech or song. **2** the ability to speak or sing: *I've lost my voice*. **3** the range of pitch or type of tone with which a person sings, e.g., soprano. **4** a vocal part in a musical composition. **5** an opinion or the right to express an opinion: *giving the people a voice in decision-making*. **6** Grammar a form of a verb showing the relation of the subject to the action: *the passive voice*.

– SYNONYMS **opinion,** view, feeling, wish, desire, vote.

▶ **verb 1** express something in words. **2** (as adj. **voiced**) Phonetics (of a speech sound) produced with vibration of the vocal cords (e.g., *b*, *d*, *v*).

– SYNONYMS **express,** communicate, declare, state, vent, utter, say, speak, articulate, air; informal come out with.

– ORIGIN Latin *vox*.

WORD LINKS

vocal *relating to the human voice*

voice box ▶ **noun** the larynx.

voice·less /'voislis/ ▶ **adjective 1** lacking a voice; speechless. **2** Phonetics (of a speech sound) produced without vibration of the vocal cords (e.g., *f*, *k*, *p*).

voice·mail /'vois,māl/ ▶ **noun** a centralized electronic system that can store messages from telephone callers.

voice-o·ver ▶ **noun** a piece of narration in a movie or television broadcast that is spoken by a person who is not seen on the screen.

voice·print /'vois,print/ ▶ **noun** a visual record of a person's speech, analyzed with respect to frequency, duration, and amplitude, used for identification.

void /void/ ▶ **adjective 1** (especially of a contract or agreement) not valid or legally binding. **2** (**void of**) free from; lacking: *the tundra is seemingly void of life*. **3** completely empty.

– SYNONYMS **1 invalid,** null (and void), ineffective, worthless. **2 empty,** vacant, blank, bare, clear, free.
– ANTONYMS full, valid.

▶ **noun** a completely empty space.

– SYNONYMS **vacuum,** emptiness, nothingness, blankness, (empty) space, gap, cavity, chasm, gulf.

▶ **verb 1** declare that something is not valid or legally binding. **2** discharge or drain away water, gases, waste matter, etc.
– DERIVATIVES **void·a·ble** adjective.
– ORIGIN Old French *vuide*.

voi·la /vwä'lä/ ▶ **exclamation** there it is; there you are.
– ORIGIN French *voilà*.

voile /voil/ ▶ **noun** a thin, semitransparent fabric of cotton, wool, or silk.
– ORIGIN French, 'veil.'

VOIP ▶ **abbreviation** voice over Internet protocol, a technology for making telephone calls over the Internet in which speech sounds are converted into binary data.

vol·a·tile /'välətl/ ▶ **adjective 1** liable to change rapidly and unpredictably, especially for the worse: *volatile currency markets*. **2** (of a substance) easily evaporated at normal temperatures.

– SYNONYMS **1 unpredictable,** temperamental, capricious, fickle, impulsive, emotional, excitable, turbulent, erratic, unstable. **2** *a volatile situation* **tense,** strained, fraught, uneasy, uncomfortable, charged, explosive, inflammatory, turbulent.
– ANTONYMS stable.

▶ **noun** a substance that is easily evaporated at normal temperatures.
– DERIVATIVES **vol·a·til·i·ty** /,välə'tilitē/ noun **vol·a·til·ize** /'välətl,īz/ verb.
– ORIGIN from Latin *volare* 'to fly.'

vol·a·tile oil ▶ **noun** another term for **ESSENTIAL OIL**.

vol-au-vent /,vôl ō 'vän/ ▶ **noun** a small round case of puff pastry filled with a savory mixture.
– ORIGIN French, 'flight in the wind.'

vol·can·ic /väl'kanik, vôl-/ ▶ **adjective 1** relating to or produced by a volcano or volcanoes. **2** (of a feeling or emotion) very intense and liable to burst out suddenly.
– DERIVATIVES **vol·can·i·cal·ly** /-ik(ə)lē/ adverb.

vol·can·ic glass ▶ **noun** obsidian (a volcanic rock).

vol·can·ism /'välkə,nizəm, 'vôl-/ (also **vulcanism** /'vəlkə,nizəm/) ▶ **noun** volcanic activity or phenomena.

vol·ca·no /väl'kānō, vôl-/ ▶ **noun** (pl. **volcanoes** or **volcanos**) a mountain having a crater or opening through which lava, rocks, hot vapor, and gas are or have been forced from the earth's crust.
– ORIGIN from Latin *Volcanus* 'Vulcan,' the Roman god of fire.

vol·can·ol·o·gy /,välkə'näləjē, ,vôl-/ (also **vulcanology**) ▶ **noun** the scientific study of volcanoes.
– DERIVATIVES **vol·can·ol·o·gist** /-jist/ noun.

vole /vōl/ ▶ **noun** a small mouselike rodent with a rounded muzzle.
– ORIGIN from Norwegian *vollmus* 'field mouse.'

vo·li·tion /və'lisʜən, vō-/ ▶ **noun** a person's power to choose freely and make their own decisions: *he left college of his own volition.*
– DERIVATIVES **vo·li·tion·al** adjective.
– ORIGIN Latin.

vol·ley /'välē/ ▶ **noun** (pl. **volleys**) **1** a number of bullets or other missiles fired at one time. **2** a series of questions, insults, etc., directed at someone rapidly one after the other. **3** (in sports) a strike or kick of the ball made before it touches the ground.

– SYNONYMS **barrage,** cannonade, battery, bombardment, salvo, burst, storm, hail, shower, deluge, torrent.

▶ **verb** (**volleys, volleying, volleyed**) (in sports) hit or kick the ball before it touches the ground.
– DERIVATIVES **vol·ley·er** noun.
– ORIGIN French *volée.*

vol·ley·ball /'välē,bôl/ ▶ **noun** a team game in which a ball is hit by hand over a net and points are scored if the ball touches the ground on the opponent's side of the court.

volt /vōlt/ ▶ **noun** the SI unit of electromotive force, the difference of potential that would carry one ampere of current against a resistance of one ohm.
– ORIGIN named after the Italian physicist Alessandro *Volta.*

volt·age /'vōltij/ ▶ **noun** an electromotive force or potential difference expressed in volts.

vol·ta·ic /väl'tā-ik, vōl-, vôl-/ ▶ **adjective** referring to electricity produced by chemical action in a battery.

volte-face /,vält(ə) 'fäs, ,vōlt(ə), ,vôlt(ə)/ ▶ **noun 1** an abrupt and complete reversal of attitude or policy. **2** an act of turning around so as to face in the opposite direction.
– ORIGIN French.

volt·me·ter /'vōlt,mētər/ ▶ **noun** an instrument for measuring electric potential in volts.

vol·u·ble /'välyəbəl/ ▶ **adjective 1** speaking easily and at length. **2** expressed in many words: *voluble descriptions of horses.*
– DERIVATIVES **vol·u·bil·i·ty** /,välyə'bilətē/ noun **vol·u·bly** adverb.
– ORIGIN from Latin *volvere* 'to roll.'

WORD TOOLKIT

See **TALKATIVE**.

vol·ume /'välyəm, -,yo͞om/ ▶ **noun 1** the amount of space occupied by a substance or object or enclosed within a container. **2** the amount or quantity of something: *the growing volume of traffic.* **3** degree of loudness. **4** a book, especially one forming part of a larger work or series. **5** a consecutive sequence of issues of a periodical. **6** fullness or thickness of the hair.

– SYNONYMS **1 capacity,** mass, bulk, extent, size, dimensions. **2 quantity,** amount, mass, bulk, measure. **3 loudness,** sound, amplification. **4 book,** publication, tome, work, title.

– ORIGIN first referring to a roll of parchment with writing on: from Latin *volumen* 'a roll.'

vol·u·met·ric /,välyə'metrik/ ▶ **adjective** relating to the measurement of volume.
– DERIVATIVES **vol·u·met·ri·cal·ly** /-trik(ə)lē/ adverb.

vo·lu·mi·nous /və'lo͞omənəs/ ▶ **adjective 1** (of clothing) loose and full. **2** (of writing) very lengthy and detailed.
– DERIVATIVES **vo·lu·mi·nous·ly** adverb.
– ORIGIN partly from Latin *voluminosus* 'having many coils,' partly from Latin *volumen* 'a roll.'

vol·u·mize /'välyə,mīz, -yo͞o-/ ▶ **verb** give volume or body to hair.

vol·un·tar·i·ly /,välən'te(ə)rəlē, 'välən,ter-/ ▶ **adverb** of one's own free will: *they agreed to leave the country voluntarily.*

– SYNONYMS **of one's own free will,** of one's own volition, by choice, by preference, spontaneously, willingly, readily, freely.

vol·un·ta·rism /'väləntə,rizəm/ ▶ **noun** the principle of relying on voluntary action or participation.
– DERIVATIVES **vol·un·ta·rist** noun & adjective.

vol·un·tar·y /'välən,terē/ ▶ **adjective 1** done or acting of one's own free will: *a voluntary code of practice.* **2** willingly working or done without payment. **3** (of an action or part of the body) under the conscious control of the brain.

– SYNONYMS **1 optional,** discretionary, at one's discretion, elective, noncompulsory. **2 unpaid,** unsalaried, for free, honorary.
– ANTONYMS compulsory.

▶ **noun** (pl. **voluntaries**) an organ solo played before, during, or after a church service.
– ORIGIN Latin *voluntarius.*

vol·un·teer /,välən'tir/ ▶ **noun 1** a person who freely offers to do something. **2** a person who willingly works for an organization without being paid. **3** a person who freely joins the armed forces. ▶ **verb 1** freely offer to do something. **2** say or suggest something without being asked. **3** suggest someone for a task or activity without consulting them first.

– SYNONYMS **1 offer one's services,** present oneself, make oneself available, come forward. **2 offer,** tender, proffer, put forward, put up, venture.

– ORIGIN from French *volontaire* 'voluntary.'

vo·lup·tu·ar·y /və'ləpcʜo͞o,erē/ ▶ **noun** (pl. **voluptuaries**) a person who enjoys sensual or sexual pleasure very much.
– ORIGIN Latin *voluptuarius.*

vo·lup·tu·ous /və'ləpcʜəwəs/ ▶ **adjective 1** (of a woman) having a full, sexually attractive body. **2** giving sensual pleasure: *voluptuous fabrics.*
– DERIVATIVES **vo·lup·tu·ous·ly** adverb **vo·lup·tu·ous·ness** noun.
– ORIGIN Latin *voluptuosus.*

vo·lute /və'lo͞ot/ ▶ **noun** a decorative scroll shape typically found at the tops of columns in Ionic architecture.
– ORIGIN Latin *voluta.*

vom·it /'vämət/ ▶ **verb** (**vomits, vomiting, vomited**) **1** bring up food and other matter from the stomach through the mouth. **2** send out in an uncontrolled flow: *the machine vomited sheet after sheet of paper.*

– SYNONYMS **be sick,** spew, heave, retch, gag; informal throw up, puke, barf.

▶ **noun** food and other matter vomited from the stomach.
– ORIGIN Latin *vomere* 'to vomit.'

voo·doo /'vo͞o,do͞o/ ▶ **noun** a religious cult of African origin practiced chiefly in the Caribbean, involving sorcery, possession by spirits, and elements of Roman Catholic ritual.
– ORIGIN from Kwa (a Niger–Congo language).

vo·ra·cious /və'rāshəs/ ▶ **adjective 1** wanting or eating great quantities of food. **2** doing something eagerly and enthusiastically: *his voracious reading of literature.*
– DERIVATIVES **vo·ra·cious·ly** adverb **vo·rac·i·ty** /-'rasitē/ noun.
– ORIGIN from Latin *vorare* 'devour.'

-vorous ▶ **combining form** feeding on a specified food: *carnivorous.*
– DERIVATIVES **-vore** combining form.
– ORIGIN Latin *-vorus.*

vor·tex /'vôr,teks/ ▶ **noun** (pl. **vortexes** or **vortices** /-tə,sēz/) **1** a whirling mass of water or air. **2** a powerful feeling, force, or situation that is difficult to avoid or escape from: *the country could be drawn into the vortex of world politics.*
– DERIVATIVES **vor·ti·cal** /'vôrtikəl/ adjective **vor·tic·i·ty** /vôr'tisitē/ noun.
– ORIGIN Latin, 'eddy.'

vo·ta·ry /'vōtərē/ ▶ **noun** (pl. **votaries**) **1** a person who has taken vows to dedicate their life to God or religious service. **2** a devoted follower or supporter: *a votary of the arts.*
– ORIGIN from Latin *vovere* 'vow.'

vote /vōt/ ▶ **noun 1** a formal indication of a choice between two or more candidates or courses of action. **2** (**the vote**) the right to participate in an election. **3** (**the vote**) a particular group of voters or the votes cast by them: *the green vote.*

– SYNONYMS **1 ballot,** poll, election, referendum, plebiscite, show of hands. **2** (**the vote**) **suffrage,** franchise, voting rights.

▶ **verb 1** give or register a vote. **2** grant or permit something by vote. **3** informal suggest something: *I vote we have one more game.*
– DERIVATIVES **vot·er** noun.
– PHRASES **vote of (no) confidence** a vote showing that a majority continues to support (or no longer supports) the policy of a leader or governing body. **vote with one's feet** informal express an opinion by leaving voluntarily: *overtaxed Africans could vote with their feet, leaving to find farmland elsewhere.*
– ORIGIN Latin *votum* 'a vow, wish.'

WORD LINKS

psephology *study of trends in voting*

vo·tive /'vōtiv/ ▶ **adjective** offered to God or a god as a sign of gratitude. ▶ **noun** (also **votive candle**) any candle used as such an offering, or a short, thick candle used especially for decorative purposes.
– ORIGIN Latin *votivus.*

vouch /vouch/ ▶ **verb** (**vouch for**) **1** confirm that something is true or accurate. **2** say that someone is who they claim to be or that they are reliable or honest.
– ORIGIN Old French *voucher* 'summon.'

vouch·er /'vouchər/ ▶ **noun** a piece of paper that entitles the holder to a discount, or that may be exchanged for goods or services.

– SYNONYMS **coupon,** token, ticket, pass, chit, slip, stub.

vouch·safe /vouch'sāf, 'vouch,sāf/ ▶ **verb** give or reveal in a gracious or superior way: *you'd never vouchsafed that interesting fact before.*
– ORIGIN first as *vouch* something *safe* on someone, i.e., 'guarantee that something is granted to someone.'

vow /vou/ ▶ **noun** a solemn promise.

– SYNONYMS **promise,** pledge, oath, bond, covenant, commitment, word (of honor).

▶ **verb** solemnly promise to do something.

– SYNONYMS **promise,** pledge, swear, undertake, make a commitment, give one's word, guarantee.

– ORIGIN Old French *vou.*

vow·el /'vou(ə)l/ ▶ **noun 1** a speech sound in which the mouth is open and the tongue is not touching the top of the mouth, the teeth, or the lips. **2** a letter representing such a sound, such as *a, e, i, o, u.*
– ORIGIN Old French *vouel.*

vox pop·u·li /'väks 'päpyə,lī, -,lē/ ▶ **noun** popular opinion as represented by informal comments from members of the public.
– ORIGIN Latin, 'the people's voice.'

voy·age /'voi-ij/ ▶ **noun** a long journey by sea or in space.

– SYNONYMS **journey,** trip, cruise, passage, sail, crossing, expedition, odyssey.

▶ **verb** go on a voyage.
– DERIVATIVES **voy·ag·er** noun.
– ORIGIN Old French *voiage.*

CHOOSE THE RIGHT WORD

See **JOURNEY**.

vo·yeur /voi'yər, vwä-/ ▶ **noun 1** a person who gains sexual pleasure from watching others when they are naked or taking part in sexual activity. **2** a person who enjoys seeing the pain or distress of others.
– DERIVATIVES **vo·yeur·ism** /'voiyə,rizəm, voi'yər,izəm, vwä'yər-/ noun **voy·eur·is·tic** /,voiyə'ristik, ,vwäyə-/ adjective **voy·eur·is·ti·cal·ly** adverb.
– ORIGIN French.

VP ▶ **abbreviation** vice president.

VPN ▶ **abbreviation** virtual private network.

VR ▶ **abbreviation** virtual reality.

VRML ▶ **abbreviation** Computing virtual reality modeling language.

vs. ▶ **abbreviation** versus.

V-sign ▶ **noun 1** a gesture symbolizing victory, made by holding up the hand with the palm facing outward and making a V-shape with the first two fingers. **2** Brit. a similar V-shape gesture, but meant to be rude, made by having the palm face inward.

VSOP ▶ **abbreviation** Very Special Old Pale, a kind of brandy.

VT ▶ **abbreviation** Vermont.

VTOL /'vē,täl, -,tôl/ ▶ **abbreviation** vertical takeoff and landing.

vul·can·ism /'vəlkə,nizəm/ ▶ **noun** variant spelling of **VOLCANISM**.

vul·can·ite /'vəlkə,nīt/ ▶ **noun** hard black vulcanized rubber.
– ORIGIN from *Vulcan,* the Roman god of fire.

vul·can·ize /'vəlkə,nīz/ ▶ **verb** harden rubber by treating it with sulfur at a high temperature.
– DERIVATIVES **vul·can·i·za·tion** /,vəlkənə'zāshən/ noun.

vul·can·ol·o·gy /,vəlkə'näləjē/ ▶ **noun** variant spelling of **VOLCANOLOGY**.

vul·gar /ˈvəlgər/ ▶ **adjective** **1** lacking sophistication or good taste: *a vulgar striped suit.* **2** referring to sex or bodily functions in a rude way. **3** dated relating to or typical of ordinary people.

– SYNONYMS **1** *vulgar decor* **tasteless,** crass, tawdry, ostentatious, flamboyant, showy, gaudy, garish; informal flashy, tacky. **2** *vulgar online videos* **obscene,** smutty, indecent, crude, dirty, filthy, naughty, coarse, risqué; informal blue. **3** **impolite,** ill-mannered, boorish, uncouth, unsophisticated, unrefined.
– ANTONYMS tasteful.

– DERIVATIVES **vul·gar·i·ty** /ˌvəlˈgaritē/ noun (pl. **vulgarities**) **vul·gar·ly** adverb.
– ORIGIN Latin *vulgaris.*

vul·gar frac·tion ▶ **noun** British term for **COMMON FRACTION.**

vul·gar·i·an /ˌvəlˈge(ə)rēən/ ▶ **noun** a person who lacks good taste and sophistication, especially one who is wealthy.

vul·gar·ism /ˈvəlgəˌrizəm/ ▶ **noun** a word or expression that refers to sex or bodily functions in a rude way.

vul·gar·ize /ˈvəlgəˌrīz/ ▶ **verb** spoil something by making it ordinary or less refined.
– DERIVATIVES **vul·gar·i·za·tion** /ˌvəlgərəˈzāsʜən/ noun.

vul·gar Lat·in ▶ **noun** informal Latin of classical times.

Vul·gate /ˈvəlˌgāt, -gət/ ▶ **noun** the main Latin version of the Bible, prepared in the 4th century and later revised and adopted as the official version for the Roman Catholic Church.
– ORIGIN from Latin *vulgata editio* 'edition prepared for the public.'

vul·ner·a·ble /ˈvəln(ə)rəbəl/ ▶ **adjective** exposed to the possibility of being attacked or harmed: *maneuver your opponent into a vulnerable position.*

– SYNONYMS **1** **in danger,** in peril, in jeopardy, at risk, unprotected, undefended, unguarded, open to attack, exposed, defenseless, an easy target. **2** **helpless,** weak, sensitive, thin-skinned.
– ANTONYMS invulnerable.

– DERIVATIVES **vul·ner·a·bil·i·ty** /ˌvəln(ə)rəˈbilitē/ noun (pl. **vulnerabilities**) **vul·ner·a·bly** /-blē/ adverb.
– ORIGIN Latin *vulnerabilis.*

vul·pine /ˈvəlˌpīn/ ▶ **adjective** relating to or resembling a fox or foxes.
– ORIGIN Latin *vulpinus.*

vul·ture /ˈvəlcʜər/ ▶ **noun** **1** a large bird of prey without feathers on the head and neck, that feeds on dead animals. **2** a person who tries to benefit from the difficulties of others.
– ORIGIN Latin *vulturius.*

vul·va /ˈvəlvə/ ▶ **noun** the female external genitals.
– DERIVATIVES **vul·val** adjective.
– ORIGIN Latin, 'womb.'

vy·ing /ˈvī-ɪɴɢ/ present participle of **VIE.**

Ww

W[1] (also **w**) ▶ **noun** (pl. **Ws** or **W's**) the twenty-third letter of the alphabet.

W[2] ▶ **abbreviation 1** watt(s). **2** West or Western. **3** (in tables of sports results) won. ▶ **symbol** the chemical element tungsten.

w (also **w/**) ▶ **abbreviation** with.

WA ▶ **abbreviation** Washington (State).

WAC /wak/ ▶ **abbreviation** Women's Army Corps.

wack·o /ˈwakō/ (also **whacko**) informal ▶ **adjective** mad; insane. ▶ **noun** (pl. **wackos** or **wackoes**) a crazy person.

wack·y /ˈwakē/ (also **whacky**) ▶ **adjective** (**wackier**, **wackiest**) informal funny or amusing in a slightly odd way.
– DERIVATIVES **wack·i·ly** adverb **wack·i·ness** noun.
– ORIGIN from **WHACK**.

wad /wäd/ ▶ **noun 1** a lump or bundle of a soft material, used for padding, stuffing, or wiping. **2** a bundle or roll of paper or banknotes. ▶ **verb** (**wads**, **wadding**, **wadded**) **1** compress a soft material into a wad. **2** line or fill something with soft material.
– DERIVATIVES **wad·ding** noun.
– ORIGIN perhaps from Dutch *watten*, French *ouate* 'padding, absorbent cotton.'

wad·dle /ˈwädl/ ▶ **verb** walk with short steps and a clumsy swaying motion.

– SYNONYMS **toddle,** totter, wobble, shuffle.

▶ **noun** a waddling way of walking.
– ORIGIN perhaps from **WADE**.

wade /wād/ ▶ **verb 1** walk through water or mud. **2** (**wade through**) read or deal with something that is boring and takes a long time. **3** (**wade in/into**) informal attack or intervene in a forceful way: *he waded into the debate, calling for the policy to be scrapped.* ▶ **noun** an act of wading.
– ORIGIN Old English, 'move onward,' also 'penetrate.'

wad·er /ˈwādər/ ▶ **noun 1** a long-legged bird that feeds in shallow water, such as a sandpiper. **2** (**waders**) high waterproof boots, used by anglers.

wa·di /ˈwädē/ ▶ **noun** (pl. **wadis**) (in Arabic-speaking countries) a valley, ravine, or channel that is dry except in the rainy season.
– ORIGIN Arabic.

wad·ing pool ▶ **noun** a shallow artificial pool for children to paddle in.

wa·fer /ˈwāfər/ ▶ **noun 1** a very thin, light, crisp cookie or cracker. **2** a thin disk of unleavened bread used in the Christian service of Holy Communion. **3** a very thin slice of a semiconductor crystal used in solid-state electric circuits.
– ORIGIN Old French *gaufre* 'honeycomb.'

wa·fer-thin ▶ **adjective & adverb** very thin or thinly.

waf·fle[1] /ˈwäfəl, ˈwô-/ informal ▶ **verb** speak or write at length in a vague or trivial way. ▶ **noun** lengthy but vague or trivial talk or writing.
– DERIVATIVES **waf·fler** noun **waf·fly** adjective.
– ORIGIN from dialect *waff* 'yelp.'

waf·fle[2] ▶ **noun** a small crisp batter cake with a squared pattern on both sides, eaten hot with butter or syrup.
– ORIGIN Dutch *wafel*.

waf·fle i·ron ▶ **noun** a utensil used for baking waffles.

waft /wäft, waft/ ▶ **verb 1** move easily or gently through the air. **2** move along with a gliding motion: *models wafted down the catwalk in filmy skirts.* ▶ **noun 1** a scent carried in the air. **2** a gentle movement of air.
– ORIGIN from German or Dutch *wachten* 'to guard.'

wag[1] /wag/ ▶ **verb** (**wags**, **wagging**, **wagged**) move rapidly to and fro.

– SYNONYMS **1 swing,** swish, switch, sway, shake; informal waggle. **2 shake,** wave, wiggle, flourish, brandish.

▶ **noun** a wagging movement.
– ORIGIN Old English, 'to sway.'

wag[2] ▶ **noun** dated informal a person who likes making jokes.
– ORIGIN probably from former *waghalter* 'person likely to be hanged.'

wage /wāj/ ▶ **noun** (also **wages**) **1** a fixed regular payment for work, typically paid daily or weekly. **2** the result or effect of doing something wrong or unwise: *disasters are the wages of sin.*

– SYNONYMS **pay,** salary, stipend, fee, remuneration, income, earnings.

▶ **verb** carry on a war or campaign.

– SYNONYMS **engage in,** carry on, conduct, execute, pursue, prosecute, proceed with.

– DERIVATIVES **waged** adjective.
– ORIGIN Old French.

wa·ger /ˈwājər/ ▶ **noun & verb** more formal term for **BET**.
– ORIGIN from Old French, 'to wage.'

wag·gish /ˈwagisʜ/ ▶ **adjective** informal humorous in a playful way.
– DERIVATIVES **wag·gish·ly** adverb.

wag·gle /ˈwagəl/ ▶ **verb** move with short quick movements from side to side or up and down. ▶ **noun** an act of waggling.
– DERIVATIVES **wag·gler** noun **wag·gly** adjective.
– ORIGIN from **WAG**[1].

Wag·ne·ri·an /vägˈne(ə)rēən/ ▶ **adjective** relating to or typical of the German composer Richard Wagner or his work.

wag·on /ˈwagən/ (Brit. also **waggon**) ▶ **noun 1** a vehicle, especially a horse-drawn one, for transporting goods. **2** a wheeled cart or stall used by a food vendor. **3** Brit. a car on a freight train.
– DERIVATIVES **wag·on·er** noun **wag·on·load** noun.
– PHRASES **on** (or **off**) **the wagon** informal not drinking (or

drinking) alcohol.
– ORIGIN Dutch *wagen*.

wag·on-lit /ˈvägôɴ ˈlē/ ▶ **noun** (pl. **wagons-lits** pronunc. same) a sleeping car on a train in continental Europe.
– ORIGIN from French *wagon* 'railroad coach' + *lit* 'bed.'

wag·tail /ˈwagˌtāl/ ▶ **noun** a slender songbird with a long tail that wags up and down.

wah-wah /ˈwä ˈwä/ ▶ **noun** a musical effect achieved on an electric guitar by use of a pedal and on brass instruments by alternately applying and removing a mute.
– ORIGIN imitating the sound.

waif /wāf/ ▶ **noun 1** a homeless and helpless person, especially a child. **2** a person who appears thin or pale.
– DERIVATIVES **waif·ish** adjective **waif·like** adjective.
– ORIGIN first referring to an unclaimed piece of property: from Old French *gaif*.

wail /wāl/ ▶ **noun 1** a long high-pitched cry of pain, grief, or anger. **2** a long high-pitched sound.

– SYNONYMS **howl,** bawl, yowl, cry, moan, groan.

▶ **verb** make a long high-pitched cry or sound.

– SYNONYMS **howl,** weep, cry, yowl, bawl, whimper, moan, groan.

– DERIVATIVES **wail·er** noun.
– ORIGIN Old Norse.

wain /wān/ ▶ **noun** old use a wagon or cart.
– ORIGIN Old English.

wain·scot /ˈwānskət, -ˌskät, -skōt/ (also **wainscoting** or **wainscotting**) ▶ **noun** an area of wooden paneling on the lower part of the walls of a room.
– DERIVATIVES **wain·scot·ed** (also **wainscotted**) adjective.
– ORIGIN German *wagenschot*.

waist /wāst/ ▶ **noun 1** the part of the body below the ribs and above the hips. **2** a narrow part in the middle of something such as a violin.
– DERIVATIVES **waist·ed** adjective.
– ORIGIN probably from an Old English word related to **WAX[2]**.

waist·band /ˈwās(t)ˌband/ ▶ **noun** a strip of cloth forming the waist of a skirt or a pair of pants.

waist·coat /ˈwās(t)ˌkōt, ˈweskət/ ▶ **noun** Brit. a vest, especially one worn by men over a shirt and under a jacket.

waist·line /ˈwās(t)ˌlīn/ ▶ **noun 1** the measurement around a person's body at the waist. **2** the shaping and position of the waist of an item of clothing.

wait /wāt/ ▶ **verb 1** stay in a particular place or delay action until a particular time or event. **2** be delayed or postponed: *he needs a shirt but that can wait.* **3** (**wait on**) act as an attendant to. **4** serve food and drink to people at a meal or in a restaurant.

– SYNONYMS **1** *we waited in the airport* **stay (put),** remain, rest, stop, linger, loiter; informal stick around; old use tarry. **2** *she had to wait until her bags arrived* **stand by,** hold back, bide one's time, mark time, kill time, waste time, twiddle one's thumbs; informal hold on, hang around, sit tight.

▶ **noun** a period of waiting.

– SYNONYMS **delay,** holdup, interval, interlude, pause, break, suspension, stoppage, halt, interruption, lull, gap.

– PHRASES **in wait** watching for someone and preparing to attack them.
– ORIGIN Old French *waitier*.

wait·er /ˈwātər/ (or **waitress** /ˈwātris/) ▶ **noun** a person whose job is to serve customers at their tables in a restaurant.

– SYNONYMS **server,** waitperson, steward, stewardess, attendant, butler, servant.

wait·ing game ▶ **noun** a tactic in which one refrains from action in order to act more effectively later on: *policemen were playing a waiting game outside a country cottage.*

wait·ing list ▶ **noun** a list of people waiting for something that is not immediately available.

wait·ing room ▶ **noun** a room for people who are waiting, for example to see a doctor or to catch a train.

wait·per·son /ˈwātˌpərsən/ ▶ **noun** a waiter or waitress.

waive /wāv/ ▶ **verb** choose not to insist on or demand a right or claim.

– SYNONYMS **1 give up,** abandon, renounce, relinquish, surrender, sacrifice, turn down. **2 disregard,** ignore, overlook, set aside, forgo.

– ORIGIN Old French *gaiver* 'allow to become a waif, abandon.'

USAGE

Waive is sometimes confused with **wave**. **Waive** means 'choose not to insist on or demand a right or claim' (*he waived all rights to the money*), whereas the much more common word **wave** means 'move to and fro' (*the flag waved in the wind*).

CHOOSE THE RIGHT WORD

See **RELINQUISH**.

waiv·er /ˈwāvər/ ▶ **noun 1** an act of not insisting on a right or claim. **2** a document recording this.

wake[1] /wāk/ ▶ **verb** (past **woke** /wōk/ or **waked**; past part. **woken** /ˈwōkən/ or **waked**) **1** (often **wake up**) stop or cause someone to stop sleeping. **2** bring to life; stir: *his voice wakes desire in others.* **3** (**wake up to**) realize or become alert to something.

– SYNONYMS **awake,** waken, wake up, stir, come to, come round, rouse.

▶ **noun 1** (especially in Irish tradition) a party held after a funeral. **2** a watch held beside the body of someone who has died.

– SYNONYMS **vigil,** watch, funeral.

– ORIGIN Old English.

wake[2] ▶ **noun** a trail of disturbed water or air left by the passage of a ship or aircraft.

– SYNONYMS **backwash,** slipstream, trail, path, track.

– PHRASES **in the wake of** following as a result of.
– ORIGIN probably from an Old Norse word meaning 'opening in ice' (as made by a ship).

wake·board·ing /ˈwākˌbôrdiɴg/ ▶ **noun** the sport of riding on a short, wide board resembling a surfboard while being towed behind a motorboat.
– DERIVATIVES **wake·board** noun **wake·board·er** noun.

wake·ful /ˈwākfəl/ ▶ **adjective 1** unable or not needing to sleep. **2** alert and aware of possible danger.
– DERIVATIVES **wake·ful·ness** noun.

wak·en /ˈwākən/ ▶ **verb** wake someone from sleep.
– ORIGIN Old English, 'be aroused.'

wake-up call ▶ noun something that alerts people to an unsatisfactory situation.

Wal·dorf sal·ad /ˈwôlˌdôrf/ ▶ noun a salad made from apples, walnuts, celery, and mayonnaise.
– ORIGIN named after the *Waldorf*-Astoria Hotel in New York, where it was first served.

wale /wāl/ ▶ noun **1** a ridge on a textured fabric such as corduroy. **2** a horizontal wooden strip fitted to strengthen a boat's side.
– ORIGIN Old English, 'stripe, weal.'

walk /wôk/ ▶ verb **1** move on foot at a regular and fairly slow pace. **2** travel over a route or area on foot. **3** accompany or guide someone on foot. **4** take a dog out for exercise. **5** Baseball be awarded first base after not swinging at four balls pitched outside the strike zone. **6** Baseball allow or enable a batter to walk. **7** informal be released from suspicion or from a charge.

– SYNONYMS **1 stroll,** saunter, amble, trudge, plod, hike, tramp, trek, march, stride, troop, wander, ramble, promenade, traipse; informal mosey, hoof it. **2 accompany,** escort, guide, show, see, take, usher.

▶ noun **1** a journey on foot. **2** an unhurried rate of movement on foot. **3** a route or path for walking. **4** a person's way of walking. **5** Baseball an instance of being awarded (or allowing a batter to reach) first base after not swinging at four balls pitched outside the strike zone.

– SYNONYMS **1 ramble,** hike, tramp, march, stroll, promenade, constitutional, turn. **2 gait,** step, stride, tread. **3 path,** pathway, footpath, track, walkway, promenade, footway, pavement, trail, towpath.

– DERIVATIVES **walk·a·ble** adjective.
– PHRASES **walk it** informal achieve a victory easily. **walk off** (or **away**) **with** informal **1** steal something. **2** win something. **walk of life** the position within society that someone holds. **walk out** leave suddenly or angrily. **walk over** informal **1** treat someone thoughtlessly or unfairly. **2** defeat someone easily.
– ORIGIN Old English, 'roll, toss,' also 'wander.'

walk·a·bout /ˈwôkəˌbout/ ▶ noun **1** chiefly Brit. an informal stroll among a crowd conducted by an important visitor. **2** a journey (originally on foot) undertaken by an Australian Aboriginal in order to live in the traditional way.

walk·er /ˈwôkər/ ▶ noun **1** a person who walks, especially for exercise or enjoyment. **2** a frame used by disabled or infirm people for support while walking.

– SYNONYMS **pedestrian,** hiker, stroller, rambler, trekker.

walk·ie-talk·ie /ˈwôkē ˈtôkē/ ▶ noun a portable two-way radio.

walk-in ▶ adjective (of a storage area) large enough to walk into.

walk·ing pa·pers ▶ plural noun informal notice of dismissal from a job: *the reporter has been given his walking papers.*

walk·ing stick ▶ noun **1** a stick with a curved handle used for support when walking. **2** (also **walkingstick**) a long, slender, slow-moving insect that resembles a twig.

Walk·man /ˈwôkmən, -ˌman/ ▶ noun (pl. **Walkmans** or **Walkmen**) trademark a type of personal stereo.

walk-on ▶ adjective (of a part in a play or movie) small and not involving any speaking.

walk·out /ˈwôkˌout/ ▶ noun a sudden angry departure, especially as a protest or strike.

walk·o·ver /ˈwôkˌōvər/ ▶ noun an easy victory.

walk-up ▶ adjective **1** (of a building) allowing access to the upper floors by stairs only; having no elevator. **2** easily accessible to pedestrians: *a walk-up food stand.* ▶ noun a building allowing access to the upper floors by stairs only.

walk·way /ˈwôkˌwā/ ▶ noun a raised passageway in a building, or a wide path outdoors.

wall /wôl/ ▶ noun **1** a continuous upright structure forming the side of a building or room or enclosing or dividing an area of land. **2** a barrier or obstacle to progress: *police met a wall of silence from witnesses.* **3** Soccer a line of defenders forming a barrier against a free kick taken near the penalty area. **4** the outer layer or lining of a bodily organ or cavity.

– SYNONYMS **fortification,** rampart, barricade, bulwark, partition.

▶ verb **1** enclose an area within walls. **2** (**wall something up**) block or seal a place with a wall. **3** (**wall someone/thing in/up**) surround or imprison someone or something with a wall or barrier.
– DERIVATIVES **wall·ing** noun.
– PHRASES **drive someone** (or **go**) **up the wall** informal make someone (or become) very irritated. **go to the wall** informal (of a business) fail. **off the wall** informal eccentric or unconventional. **wall-to-wall 1** (of a carpet) fitted to cover an entire floor. **2** informal very numerous or plentiful.
– ORIGIN Latin *vallum* 'rampart.'

wal·la·by /ˈwäləbē/ ▶ noun (pl. **wallabies**) an Australasian marsupial resembling a small kangaroo.
– ORIGIN Dharuk (an Aboriginal language).

wal·lah /ˈwälə/ ▶ noun Indian or informal a person of a specified kind or having a specified role: *an office wallah.*
– ORIGIN from a Hindi word ending meaning 'doer' (often taken to mean 'fellow').

wall·board /ˈwôlˌbôrd/ ▶ noun a type of board used for covering walls and ceilings.

wall·cov·er·ing /ˈwôlˌkəv(ə)riNG/ ▶ noun material such as wallpaper used as a decorative covering for interior walls.

wal·let /ˈwälit, ˈwô-/ ▶ noun **1** a pocket-sized, flat, folding holder for money and plastic cards. **2** old use a bag for holding provisions when traveling.

– SYNONYMS **purse,** billfold, case, pouch, pocketbook.

– ORIGIN probably from Germanic.

wall·eye /ˈwôlˌī/ ▶ noun **1** an eye with a streaked or opaque white iris. **2** an eye directed abnormally outward. **3** a predatory freshwater fish with large, opaque silvery eyes.
– DERIVATIVES **wall·eyed** adjective.

wall·flow·er /ˈwôlˌflou(-ə)r/ ▶ noun **1** a plant with fragrant flowers that bloom in early spring. **2** informal a girl who does not have a man to dance with at a dance or party.

Wal·loon /wäˈlo͞on/ ▶ noun **1** a member of a people who speak a French dialect and live in southern and eastern Belgium and neighboring parts of France. **2** the French dialect spoken by the Walloons.
– ORIGIN French *Wallon.*

wal·lop /ˈwäləp/ informal ▶ **verb** (**wallops, walloping, walloped**) **1** hit someone or something very hard. **2** heavily defeat an opponent. **3** (as adj. **walloping**) very large or great: *walloping energy bills.* ▶ **noun** a heavy blow or punch.
– ORIGIN Old French *waloper* 'to gallop.'

wal·low /ˈwälō/ ▶ **verb 1** roll around or lie in mud or shallow water. **2** (of a boat or aircraft) roll from side to side. **3** (**wallow in**) enjoy something without restraint: *he wallowed in self-pity.*

– SYNONYMS **1 roll,** loll about, lie around, splash about. **2 luxuriate,** bask, take pleasure, take satisfaction, indulge (oneself), delight, revel, glory.

▶ **noun 1** an act of wallowing. **2** an area of mud or shallow water where mammals go to wallow.
– ORIGIN Old English.

wall·pa·per /ˈwôlˌpāpər/ ▶ **noun 1** paper pasted in strips over the walls of a room to provide a decorative or textured surface. **2** an optional background pattern or picture on a computer or cell phone screen. ▶ **verb** apply wallpaper to a wall or room.

wal·nut /ˈwôlˌnət/ ▶ **noun 1** an edible wrinkled nut with a hard round shell. **2** the tree that produces walnuts, a source of valuable ornamental wood.
– ORIGIN Old English, 'foreign nut.'

wal·rus /ˈwôlrəs, ˈwä-/ ▶ **noun** a large sea mammal with two large downward-pointing tusks, found in the Arctic Ocean.
– ORIGIN probably Dutch.

wal·rus mus·tache ▶ **noun** a long, thick, drooping mustache.

waltz /wôlts/ ▶ **noun** a dance in triple time performed by a couple, who turn around and around as they progress around the dance floor. ▶ **verb 1** dance a waltz. **2** move or behave in a casual or inconsiderate way: *she waltzed in and took all the credit.*
– DERIVATIVES **waltz·er** noun.
– ORIGIN German *Walzer*.

wam·pum /ˈwämpəm/ ▶ **noun** historical a string of small cylindrical beads made by North American Indians from shells, worn as a decorative belt or used as money.
– ORIGIN Algonquian.

WAN /wan/ ▶ **abbreviation** Computing wide area network.

wan /wän/ ▶ **adjective 1** (of a person) pale and appearing ill or exhausted. **2** (of light) pale; weak. **3** (of a smile) lacking enthusiasm; strained.

– SYNONYMS **pale,** ashen, white, gray, anemic, colorless, waxen, pasty, peaked, sickly, washed out, ghostly.

– DERIVATIVES **wan·ly** adverb.
– ORIGIN Old English, 'dark, black.'

wand /wänd/ ▶ **noun 1** a rod used in casting magic spells or performing conjuring tricks. **2** a staff or rod held as a symbol of office. **3** a hand-held electronic device passed over a bar code to read the data.
– ORIGIN Old Norse.

wan·der /ˈwändər/ ▶ **verb 1** walk or move in a leisurely, casual, or aimless way. **2** move slowly away from a fixed point or place: *my attention had wandered.*

– SYNONYMS **1 stroll,** amble, saunter, walk, ramble, meander, roam, range, drift; informal traipse, mosey. **2 stray,** depart, diverge, deviate, digress, drift, get sidetracked.

▶ **noun** an act or spell of wandering.
– DERIVATIVES **wan·der·er** noun **wan·der·ings** plural noun.
– ORIGIN Old English.

wan·der·lust /ˈwändərˌləst/ ▶ **noun** a strong desire to travel.
– ORIGIN German.

wane /wān/ ▶ **verb 1** (of the moon) appear to become smaller each day as a result of having a decreasing area of its surface illuminated by the sun. **2** decrease in strength or extent: *confidence in the dollar waned.*

– SYNONYMS **decline,** diminish, decrease, dwindle, shrink, tail off, ebb, fade, lessen, peter out, fall off, recede, slump, weaken, wither, evaporate, die out.
– ANTONYMS grow.

– PHRASES **on the wane** becoming smaller, or less important or common.
– ORIGIN Old English, 'lessen.'

wan·gle /ˈwaNGgəl/ informal ▶ **verb** obtain something desired by persuasion or cunning.
– DERIVATIVES **wan·gler** noun.
– ORIGIN unknown.

wank /waNGk/ Brit. vulgar slang ▶ **verb** (also **wank off**) masturbate. ▶ **noun** an act of masturbating.
– ORIGIN unknown.

wank·er /ˈwaNGkər/ ▶ **noun** Brit. vulgar slang a stupid or disliked person.

wan·na /ˈwônə, ˈwä-/ ▶ **contraction** informal want to; want a.

wan·na·be /ˈwänəbē, ˈwô-/ ▶ **noun** informal, derogatory a person who wants to be like someone famous.

want /wänt, wônt/ ▶ **verb 1** feel a need or desire to have or do something. **2** (**be wanted**) (of a suspected criminal) be sought by the police. **3** informal should or need to do something: *you don't want to believe all you hear.* **4** (often **want for**) literary lack something desirable or essential. **5** desire someone sexually. **6** informal, chiefly Brit. (of a thing) need something to be done: *the wheel wants greasing.*

– SYNONYMS **desire,** wish for, hope for, fancy, care for, like, long for, yearn for, crave, hanker after, hunger for, thirst for, cry out for, covet; informal have a yen for, be dying for.

▶ **noun 1** a lack or shortage of something. **2** lack of essentials; poverty. **3** a desire.

– SYNONYMS **1 lack,** absence, nonexistence, dearth, deficiency, inadequacy, insufficiency, paucity, shortage, scarcity. **2 need,** austerity, privation, deprivation, poverty, destitution. **3** *her wants would be taken care of* **wish,** desire, demand, longing, fancy, craving, need, requirement; informal yen.

– ORIGIN Old Norse, 'be lacking.'

want ad ▶ **noun** informal a classified advertisement, typically placed by someone wanting to hire a worker or to buy or sell an item.

want·ing /ˈwäntiNG, wônt-/ ▶ **adjective 1** lacking in something required or desired. **2** not good enough; unsatisfactory: *workers who are found wanting face dismissal.*

– SYNONYMS **deficient**, inadequate, lacking, insufficient, imperfect, flawed, unsound, substandard, inferior, second-rate.

wan·ton /ˈwäntn/ ▶ **adjective 1** (of a cruel or violent action) deliberate and unprovoked. **2** (especially of a woman) having many sexual partners.

– SYNONYMS **deliberate,** willful, malicious, gratuitous, unprovoked, motiveless, arbitrary, unjustifiable, senseless.

▶ **noun** old use a woman who has many sexual partners.
– DERIVATIVES **wan·ton·ly** adverb **wan·ton·ness** noun.
– ORIGIN first meaning 'rebellious': from former *wan-* 'badly' + an Old English word meaning 'trained.'

WAP /wap/ ▶ **abbreviation** Wireless Application Protocol, a means of enabling a cell phone to browse the Internet and display data.

wap·i·ti /ˈwäpitē/ ▶ **noun** (pl. **wapitis**) another term for **ELK**.
– ORIGIN Shawnee, 'white rump.'

war /wôr/ ▶ **noun 1** a state of armed conflict between different nations, states, or groups. **2** a state of hostility or intense competition between groups. **3** a campaign against something undesirable: *a war on drugs.*

– SYNONYMS **1 conflict,** warfare, combat, fighting, action, bloodshed, fight, campaign, hostilities. **2 campaign,** crusade, battle, fight, struggle.
– ANTONYMS peace.

▶ **verb** (**wars, warring, warred**) take part in a war.

– SYNONYMS **fight,** battle, combat, wage war, take up arms, feud, quarrel, struggle, contend, wrangle, cross swords.

– ORIGIN from Old French *guerre.*

WORD LINKS

martial *relating to war*
belligerent *engaged in a war*

War. ▶ **abbreviation** Warwickshire.

war·ble /ˈwôrbəl/ ▶ **verb 1** (of a bird) sing with a succession of constantly changing notes. **2** (of a person) sing in a trilling or quavering voice. ▶ **noun** a warbling sound.
– ORIGIN Old French *werbler.*

war·ble fly ▶ **noun** a large fly that lays its eggs on cattle, horses, and other mammals, the larvae of which form a swelling or abscess beneath the skin.
– ORIGIN uncertain.

war·bler /ˈwôrb(ə)lər/ ▶ **noun** a small songbird with a warbling song, typically living in trees and bushes.

war chest ▶ **noun** a reserve of funds used for fighting a war.

war crime ▶ **noun** an act carried out during a war that violates accepted international rules of war.

ward /wôrd/ ▶ **noun 1** a room or division in a hospital for one or more patients. **2** an administrative division of a city or borough that is represented by a councilor or councilors. **3** a child or young person under the care and control of a guardian appointed by their parents or a court. **4** any of the ridges or bars inside a lock that prevent the turning of any key without corresponding grooves.

– SYNONYMS **1 room,** department, unit, area. **2 district,** constituency, division, quarter, zone, parish. **3 dependant,** charge, protégé.

▶ **verb** (**ward someone/thing off**) prevent someone or something from harming or affecting one.
– DERIVATIVES **ward·ship** noun.
– ORIGIN Old English, 'keep safe, guard.'

-ward (also **-wards**) ▶ **suffix 1** (usu. **-wards**) (forming adverbs) toward the specified place or direction: *homewards.* **2** (usu. **-ward**) (forming adjectives) turned or tending toward: *upward.*
– ORIGIN Old English.

war·den /ˈwôrdn/ ▶ **noun 1** a person responsible for supervising a particular place or procedure. **2** the head official in charge of a prison. **3** Brit. the head of certain schools, colleges, or other institutions.

– SYNONYMS **1 superintendent,** caretaker, porter, steward, custodian, watchman, concierge, doorman, commissionaire. **2 guard,** prison officer, jailer, warder, keeper; informal screw.

– DERIVATIVES **war·den·ship** noun.
– ORIGIN Old French *wardein, guarden* 'guardian.'

ward·er /ˈwôrdər/ ▶ **noun** (fem. **wardress**) chiefly Brit. a prison guard.
– ORIGIN from Old French *warder* 'to guard.'

ward·robe /ˈwôrˌdrōb/ ▶ **noun 1** a large, tall cabinet for hanging clothes in. **2** a person's entire collection of clothes. **3** the costume department or costumes of a theater or movie company.
– ORIGIN Old French *warderobe, garderobe* 'private chamber.'

ward·room /ˈwôrdˌro͞om, -ˌro͝om/ ▶ **noun** a room on board a warship in which commissioned officers eat and relax.

-wards ▶ **suffix** variant spelling of **-WARD**.

ware /we(ə)r/ ▶ **noun 1** (**wares**) articles offered for sale. **2** pottery of a specified type: *porcelain ware.* **3** manufactured articles of a specified type.

– SYNONYMS (**wares**) **goods,** merchandise, products, produce, stock, commodities.

– ORIGIN Old English, 'commodities.'

ware·house /ˈwe(ə)rˌhous/ ▶ **noun 1** a large building where raw materials or manufactured goods are stored. **2** a large wholesale or retail store.

– SYNONYMS **storeroom,** depot, depository, stockroom; informal lockup.

▶ **verb** /-ˌhous, -ˌhouz/ store goods in a warehouse.

war·fare /ˈwôrˌfe(ə)r/ ▶ **noun** the activities involved in fighting a war.

– SYNONYMS **fighting,** war, combat, conflict, action, hostilities.

war·fa·rin /ˈwôrfərin/ ▶ **noun** a compound used as a rat poison and as a drug to prevent blood clotting.
– ORIGIN from the initial letters of *Wisconsin Alumni Research Foundation* + *-arin.*

war game ▶ **noun 1** a military exercise to test or improve tactical skill. **2** a mock military conflict carried out as a game or sport.

war·head /ˈwôrˌhed/ ▶ **noun** the explosive head of a missile, torpedo, or similar weapon.

war·horse /ˈwôrˌhôrs/ ▶ **noun** informal a veteran soldier, politician, etc., who has participated in many campaigns or contests.

war·like /ˈwôrˌlīk/ ▶ **adjective 1** tending to wage war; hostile. **2** relating to or prepared for war.

war·lock /ˈwôrˌläk/ ▶ **noun** a man who practices witchcraft.
– ORIGIN Old English, 'traitor, scoundrel, monster,' also 'the Devil.'

war·lord /ˈwôrˌlôrd/ ▶ **noun** a military commander, especially one who has complete control of a region.
– DERIVATIVES **war·lord·ism** noun.

warm /wôrm/ ▶ **adjective 1** of or at a fairly high temperature. **2** (of clothes or coverings) made of a material that helps the body to retain heat. **3** enthusiastic, affectionate, or kind. **4** (of a color) containing red, yellow, or orange tones. **5** (of a scent or trail) fresh and easy to follow. **6** close to finding or guessing something.

> – SYNONYMS **1** *a warm kitchen* **hot,** cozy, snug. **2** *a warm day* **balmy,** summery, sultry, hot, mild, temperate. **3** *warm water* **tepid,** lukewarm, heated. **4** *a warm sweater* **thick,** chunky, thermal, woolly. **5** *a warm welcome* **friendly,** cordial, amiable, genial, kind, pleasant, fond, welcoming, hospitable, hearty.
> – ANTONYMS cold, chilly.

▶ **verb 1** make or become warm. **2** (**warm to/toward**) become more interested in or enthusiastic about someone or something.
▶ **noun 1** (**the warm**) a warm place or area. **2** an act of warming.
– DERIVATIVES **warm·er** noun **warm·ly** adverb **warm·ness** noun.
– PHRASES **warm up 1** prepare for exercise by doing gentle stretches and exercises. **2** (of an engine or electrical device) reach a temperature high enough to operate efficiently. **warm something up** entertain an audience to make them more enthusiastic before the arrival of the main act.
– ORIGIN Old English.

warm-blood·ed ▶ **adjective 1** (of animals, chiefly mammals and birds) maintaining a constant body temperature by their metabolism. **2** passionate or spirited.

warmheart·ed /ˈwôrmˈhärtəd/ ▶ **adjective** sympathetic and kind.

war·mon·ger /ˈwôrˌməNGgər, -ˌmäNG-/ ▶ **noun** a person who tries to bring about war.

warmth /wôrmTH/ ▶ **noun 1** the quality, state, or feeling of being warm. **2** enthusiasm, affection, or kindness. **3** intensity of emotion.

> – SYNONYMS **1 heat,** coziness, snugness. **2 friendliness,** amiability, geniality, cordiality, kindness, tenderness, fondness.

warm-up ▶ **noun 1** a period or act of preparation for exercise. **2** a period before a stage performance in which the audience is entertained.

warn /wôrn/ ▶ **verb 1** inform someone about a possible danger or problem. **2** advise someone not to do something wrong or foolish. **3** (**warn someone off**) order someone to keep away or to refrain from doing something.

> – SYNONYMS **1 inform,** notify, tell, alert, apprise, make someone aware, remind; informal tip off. **2 advise,** exhort, urge, counsel, caution.

– ORIGIN Old English.

warn·ing /ˈwôrniNG/ ▶ **noun 1** a statement or event that indicates a possible danger or problem. **2** advice against doing something wrong or foolish. **3** advance notice: *he arrived without warning.*

> – SYNONYMS **1 (advance) notice,** alert, hint, signal, sign, alarm; informal tip-off. **2 caution,** notification, information, exhortation, advice. **3 omen,** premonition, foreboding, prophecy, prediction, forecast, token, portent, signal, sign. **4** *his sentence is a warning to other drunk drivers* **example,** deterrent, lesson, caution, message, moral. **5 reprimand,** caution, remonstrance, admonition, censure; informal dressing-down, talking-to, telling-off.

– DERIVATIVES **warn·ing·ly** adverb.

warp /wôrp/ ▶ **verb 1** make or become bent or twisted as a result of heat or dampness. **2** make abnormal or strange; distort: *his hatred has warped his judgment.*

> – SYNONYMS **1 buckle,** twist, bend, distort, deform, curve, bow, contort. **2 corrupt,** twist, pervert, deprave.

▶ **noun 1** a distortion or twist in shape. **2** (in weaving) the lengthwise threads on a loom over and under which the weft threads are passed to make cloth.
– ORIGIN Old English.

war·paint /ˈwôrˌpānt/ ▶ **noun 1** paint traditionally used to decorate the face and body before battle, especially by North American Indians. **2** informal or humorous elaborate or excessive makeup.

war·path /ˈwôrˌpaTH/ ▶ **noun** (in phrase **on the warpath**) in an angry or aggressive state.
– ORIGIN with reference to American Indians heading toward a battle.

war·plane /ˈwôrˌplān/ ▶ **noun** an aircraft designed and equipped to take part in air combat or to drop bombs.

war·rant /ˈwôrənt, ˈwä-/ ▶ **noun 1** an official authorization giving the police or another body the power to make an arrest, search somewhere, etc. **2** a document entitling the holder to receive goods, money, or services. **3** justification or authority: *there is no warrant for this assumption.* **4** an official certificate of appointment issued to an officer of lower rank than a commissioned officer.

> – SYNONYMS **1 authorization,** order, writ, mandate, license, permit, summons. **2 voucher,** chit, slip, ticket, coupon, pass.

▶ **verb 1** make necessary or justify a course of action. **2** officially state or guarantee something.

> – SYNONYMS **1 justify,** deserve, vindicate, call for, sanction, permit, authorize, excuse, account for, legitimize, support, license, merit, qualify for, rate. **2 guarantee,** promise, affirm, swear, vouch, vow, pledge, undertake, declare, testify.

– DERIVATIVES **war·rant·a·ble** adjective.
– PHRASES **I** (or **I'll**) **warrant** dated no doubt.
– ORIGIN first meaning 'protector' and 'protect from danger': from Old French *guarant, guarantir.*

war·rant of·fi·cer ▶ **noun** a rank of officer in the US armed forces below the commissioned officers and above the noncommissioned officers.

war·ran·ty /ˈwôrəntē, ˈwä-/ ▶ **noun** (pl. **warranties**) **1** a written guarantee promising to repair or replace an article if necessary within a specified period. **2** a guarantee by a person who is insured that certain statements are true or that certain conditions shall be fulfilled, the breach of which will make the policy invalid.

> – SYNONYMS **guarantee,** assurance, promise, commitment, undertaking, pledge, agreement, covenant.

war·ran·ty deed ▶ **noun** Law a deed that guarantees a clear title to the buyer of a property.

war·ren /ˈwôrən, ˈwä-/ ▶ **noun 1** a network of interconnecting rabbit burrows. **2** a complex network of paths or passages.
– ORIGIN Old French *garenne* 'game park.'

war·ri·or /ˈwôrēər/ ▶ **noun** (especially in the past) a brave or experienced soldier or fighter.

– SYNONYMS **fighter,** soldier, serviceman, combatant.

– ORIGIN Old French *werreior, guerreior.*

war·ship /ˈwôr,SHip/ ▶ **noun** a ship equipped with weapons and designed to take part in warfare at sea.

wart /wôrt/ ▶ **noun 1** a small, hard, growth on the skin, caused by a virus. **2** any rounded lump or growth on the skin of an animal or the surface of a plant.
– DERIVATIVES **wart·y** adjective.
– PHRASES **warts and all** informal including faults or unattractive qualities.
– ORIGIN Old English.

wart·hog /ˈwôrt,häg/ ▶ **noun** an African wild pig with a large head, warty lumps on the face, and curved tusks.

war·time /ˈwôr,tīm/ ▶ **noun** a period during which a war is taking place.

war-torn ▶ **adjective** (of a place) racked or devastated by war.

war·y /ˈwe(ə)rē/ ▶ **adjective** (**warier, wariest**) (often **wary of**) cautious about possible dangers or problems.

– SYNONYMS **1 cautious,** careful, circumspect, on one's guard, chary, alert, on the lookout, attentive, heedful, watchful, vigilant, observant. **2** *we are wary of strangers* **suspicious,** chary, leery, careful, distrustful.
– ANTONYMS inattentive, trustful.

– DERIVATIVES **war·i·ly** adverb **war·i·ness** noun.
– ORIGIN from Old English, 'be on one's guard.'

WORD TOOLKIT

wary ...	**watchful ...**	**circumspect ...**
investor	eye	approach
consumer	gaze	manner
rabbit	supervision	dissimulation
owners	parents	lawyer

was /wəz/ first and third person singular past of **BE**.

wa·sa·bi /wəˈsäbē/ ▶ **noun** an edible Japanese plant with a thick green root that tastes like strong horseradish.
– ORIGIN Japanese.

wash /wäSH, wôSH/ ▶ **verb 1** clean someone or something with water and, typically, soap or detergent. **2** (of flowing water) carry or move. **3** be carried by flowing water. **4** informal seem convincing or genuine: *excuses just don't wash with us.* **5** brush something with a thin coat of dilute paint or ink.

– SYNONYMS **1 clean oneself,** bathe, shower. **2 clean,** cleanse, scrub, wipe, shampoo, launder, lather, douse, swab, disinfect. **3** *she washed off the blood* **remove,** expunge, eradicate, sponge off, scrub off, wipe off, rinse off. **4** *waves washed against the hull* **splash,** lap, break, beat, surge, ripple, roll. **5** *the wreckage was washed downriver* **sweep,** carry, convey, transport.

▶ **noun 1** an act of washing or an instance of being washed. **2** a quantity of clothes needing to be or just having been washed. **3** the water or air disturbed by a moving boat or aircraft. **4** a medicinal or cleansing liquid: *antiseptic skin wash.* **5** a thin coating of paint or metal. **6** silt or gravel carried by water and deposited as sediment.

– SYNONYMS **1 laundry,** washing. **2 backwash,** wake, trail, path.

– DERIVATIVES **wash·a·ble** adjective.
– PHRASES **be washed out** be postponed or canceled because of rain. **come out in the wash** informal be resolved eventually. **wash one's dirty linen in public** informal discuss one's personal affairs in public. **wash one's hands of** take no further responsibility for. [with reference to Pontius Pilate washing his hands after the condemnation of Christ (Gospel of Matthew, chapter 27).] **wash over** occur all around without greatly affecting: *she allowed the conversation to wash over her.* **wash up** clean oneself, especially one's hands: *nobody eats until everyone washes up.*
– ORIGIN Old English.

wash·ba·sin /ˈwäSH,bāsən, ˈwôSH-/ ▶ **noun** a basin used for washing the hands and face.

wash·board /ˈwäSH,bôrd, ˈwôSH-/ ▶ **noun 1** a ridged or corrugated board against which clothes are scrubbed during washing. **2** a similar board played as a percussion instrument by scraping. ▶ **adjective** (of a person's stomach) lean and with well-defined muscles.

wash·cloth /ˈwäSH,klôTH, ˈwôSH-/ ▶ **noun** a small cloth of toweling for washing oneself with.

washed-out ▶ **adjective 1** faded by repeated washing. **2** pale and tired.

washed-up ▶ **adjective** informal no longer effective or successful.

wash·er /ˈwäSHər, ˈwôSH-/ ▶ **noun 1** a person or device that washes. **2** a small flat ring fixed between a nut and bolt to spread the pressure or between two joining surfaces to prevent leakage.

wash·er·wom·an /ˈwäSHər,wo͝omən, ˈwôSH-/ ▶ **noun** (pl. **washerwomen**) a woman whose occupation is washing clothes.

wash·ing /ˈwäSHiNG, ˈwôSH-/ ▶ **noun** a quantity of clothes, bed linen, etc., that is to be washed or has just been washed.

wash·ing ma·chine ▶ **noun** a machine for washing clothes, bed linen, etc.

wash·ing so·da ▶ **noun** sodium carbonate, used dissolved in water for washing and cleaning.

wash·out /ˈwäSH,out, ˈwôSH-/ ▶ **noun** informal a disappointing failure.

wash·room /ˈwäSH,ro͞om, ˈwôSH-, -,ro͝om/ ▶ **noun** a room with washing and toilet facilities.

wash·stand /ˈwäSH,stand, ˈwôSH-/ ▶ **noun** chiefly historical a piece of furniture designed to hold a jug, bowl, or basin for washing the hands and face.

wash·tub /ˈwäSH,təb, ˈwôSH-/ ▶ **noun** a large metal tub for washing laundry.

wash·y /ˈwäSHē, ˈwôSHē/ ▶ **adjective** (**washier, washiest**) **1** (of color) pale: *it's a washy sort of brown.* **2** thinly or unevenly colored, as if by watery paint: *a washy band of pale blue floats above.*

was·n't /ˈwəzənt/ ▶ **contraction** was not.

Wasp /wäsp/ (also **WASP**) ▶ **noun** an upper-class or middle-class American white Protestant, regarded as a member of the most powerful social group.
– ORIGIN from *white Anglo-Saxon Protestant.*

wasp /wäsp/ ▶ **noun** a stinging winged insect that typically nests in complex colonies and has a black and yellow-striped body.
– ORIGIN Old English.

wasp·ie /ˈwäspē/ ▶ **noun** (pl. **waspies**) a woman's corset or belt designed to emphasize a slender waist.

wasp·ish /ˈwäspisн/ ▶ **adjective** sharply irritable.
– DERIVATIVES **wasp·ish·ly** adverb **wasp·ish·ness** noun.

wasp-waist·ed ▶ **adjective** having a very narrow waist.

was·sail /ˈwäsəl, -ˌsāl/ old use ▶ **noun 1** spiced ale or mulled wine drunk during celebrations for Twelfth Night and Christmas Eve. **2** lively festivities involving the drinking of much alcohol. ▶ **verb 1** celebrate with much alcohol. **2** go from house to house at Christmas, singing carols.
– ORIGIN Old Norse, 'be in good health!'

wast /wəst, wäst/ old use or dialect second person singular past of **BE**.

wast·age /ˈwāstij/ ▶ **noun 1** the action of wasting something. **2** an amount wasted.

waste /wāst/ ▶ **verb 1** use more of something than is necessary or useful. **2** fail to make good use of: *we're wasted in this job.* **3** (**be wasted on**) not be appreciated by someone. **4** gradually become weaker and thinner: *she was wasting away from tuberculosis.* **5** informal kill someone. **6** (as adj. **wasted**) informal under the influence of alcohol or illegal drugs.

> – SYNONYMS **1 squander,** misspend, misuse, fritter away, throw away, lavish, dissipate; informal blow, splurge. **2 grow weak,** grow thin, shrink, wilt, fade, deteriorate, decline.
> – ANTONYMS conserve.

▶ **adjective 1** removed or discarded as no longer useful or required. **2** (of an area of land) not used, cultivated, or built on.

> – SYNONYMS **1 unwanted,** excess, superfluous, left over, scrap, unusable, unprofitable. **2 uncultivated,** barren, desert, arid, bare, desolate.

▶ **noun 1** an act or instance of wasting something: *it's a waste of time trying to find him.* **2** unusable or unwanted material or byproducts. **3** (usu. **wastes**) a large area of barren, uninhabited land.

> – SYNONYMS **1 misuse,** misapplication, abuse, extravagance, lavishness. **2 refuse,** garbage, trash, rubbish, litter, debris, junk, sewage, effluent. **3** (usu. **wastes**) **desert,** wasteland, wilderness, emptiness, wilds.

– PHRASES **go to waste** be wasted. **lay waste (to)** completely destroy a place.
– ORIGIN Old French.

waste·bas·ket /ˈwāstˌbaskit/ (also **wastepaper basket**) ▶ **noun** a receptacle for small quantities of rubbish.

waste·ful /ˈwāstfəl/ ▶ **adjective** using or using up something carelessly or extravagantly.

> – SYNONYMS **prodigal,** profligate, uneconomical, extravagant, lavish, excessive, imprudent, improvident, spendthrift.
> – ANTONYMS frugal.

– DERIVATIVES **waste·ful·ly** adverb **waste·ful·ness** noun.

waste·land /ˈwāstˌland/ ▶ **noun 1** a barren or empty area of land. **2** a situation, time, or place lacking in culture, spirituality, or intellectual activity: *the mid 1970s are now seen as a cultural wasteland.*

wast·er /ˈwāstər/ ▶ **noun 1** a wasteful person or thing. **2** informal a person who does little or nothing of value.

wast·rel /ˈwāstrəl/ ▶ **noun** literary a lazy person who spends their time and money in a careless way.
– ORIGIN from **WASTE.**

wat /wät/ ▶ **noun** (in SE Asia) a Buddhist monastery or temple.
– ORIGIN Thai.

watch /wäcн/ ▶ **verb 1** look at someone or something with attention or interest. **2** keep someone or something under careful observation. **3** treat with caution or control: *watch what you say!* **4** (**watch for**) look out for. **5** (**watch out**) be careful.

> – SYNONYMS **1 observe,** view, look at, eye, gaze at, peer at, contemplate, inspect, scrutinize, scan; informal check out, get a load of, eyeball. **2 spy on,** keep in sight, keep under surveillance, track, monitor, tail; informal keep tabs on, stake out. **3 guard,** mind, protect, look after, keep an eye on, take care of, shield, defend.
> – ANTONYMS ignore.

▶ **noun 1** a small timepiece usually worn on a strap on the wrist. **2** an act or instance of watching. **3** a period of keeping alert for danger or trouble during the night. **4** a fixed period of duty on a ship, usually lasting four hours. **5** a shift worked by firefighters or police officers. **6** (also **night watch**) historical a watchman or watchmen who patrolled the streets of a town at night.

> – SYNONYMS **1 wristwatch,** timepiece, chronometer. **2 guard,** vigil, lookout, observation, surveillance.

– DERIVATIVES **watch·er** noun.
– PHRASES **keep watch** stay on the lookout for danger or trouble. **watch one's back** protect oneself against unexpected danger.
– ORIGIN Old English.

watch·a·ble /ˈwäcнəbəl/ ▶ **adjective** (of a movie or television program) fairly enjoyable to watch.

watch·dog /ˈwäcнˌdôg/ ▶ **noun 1** a dog kept to guard private property. **2** a person or group that monitors the practices of companies providing a particular service.

> – SYNONYMS **ombudsman,** monitor, scrutineer, inspector, supervisor.

watch·ful /ˈwäcнfəl/ ▶ **adjective** alert to possible difficulty or danger.

> – SYNONYMS **observant,** alert, vigilant, attentive, aware, sharp-eyed, eagle-eyed, on the lookout, wary, cautious, careful.

– DERIVATIVES **watch·ful·ly** adverb **watch·ful·ness** noun.

> **WORD TOOLKIT**
>
> See **WARY**.

watch·mak·er /ˈwäcнˌmākər/ ▶ **noun** a person who makes and repairs watches and clocks.
– DERIVATIVES **watch·mak·ing** noun.

watch·man /ˈwäcнmən/ ▶ **noun** (pl. **watchmen**) a man employed to look after an empty building, especially at night.

watch·tow·er /ˈwäcнˌtou(-ə)r/ ▶ **noun** a tower built to create a high observation point.

watch·word /ˈwäcнˌwərd/ ▶ **noun** a word or phrase expressing the central aim or belief of a person or group.

wa·ter /ˈwôtər, ˈwä-/ ▶ noun **1** the liquid that forms the seas, lakes, rivers, and rain and is the basis of the fluids of living organisms. **2** (**waters**) an area of sea under the legal authority of a particular country. **3** (**the waters**) the water of a mineral spring used for medicinal purposes. **4** (**waters**) the fluid surrounding a fetus in the uterus, especially as passed from a woman's body shortly before she gives birth. **5** the quality of transparency and brilliance shown by a diamond or other gem. ▶ verb **1** pour water over a plant or an area of ground. **2** (of the eyes or mouth) produce tears or saliva: *the smell of bacon made my mouth water.* **3** dilute a drink with water. **4** (**water something down**) make something less forceful or controversial by changing or leaving out certain details. **5** give a drink of water to an animal. **6** (of a river) flow through an area.

– SYNONYMS **1 sprinkle,** moisten, dampen, wet, spray, splash, hose, douse. **2 salivate,** become wet, moisten. **3 dilute,** thin (out), weaken, adulterate. **4** (**water something down**) **tone down,** temper, mitigate, moderate, soften, tame.

– DERIVATIVES **wa·ter·less** adjective.

– PHRASES **hold water** (of a theory) seem valid or reasonable. **pass water** euphemistic urinate. **of the first water** of the highest degree: *she was a bore of the first water.* [first referring to a gem of the greatest brilliance and transparency.] **under water** submerged; flooded. **water on the brain** informal hydrocephalus. **water under the bridge** past events that are over and done with.

– ORIGIN Old English.

WORD LINKS

aquatic, **aqueous** *relating to water*

wa·ter-based ▶ adjective (of a substance or solution) using or having water as a medium or main ingredient.

wa·ter·bed /ˈwôtərˌbed, ˈwä-/ ▶ noun a bed with a water-filled rubber or plastic mattress.

wa·ter·bird /ˈwôtərˌbərd, ˈwä-/ ▶ noun a bird that lives on or near water.

wa·ter birth ▶ noun a birth in which the mother spends the final stages of labor in a birthing pool.

wa·ter boat·man ▶ noun a bug that lives in water and swims on its back using its back legs as oars.

wa·ter·borne ▶ noun **1** (of a vehicle or goods) conveyed by, traveling on, or involving travel or transportation on water. **2** (of a disease) communicated or propagated by contaminated water.

wa·ter buf·fa·lo ▶ noun a large black Asian buffalo with heavy swept-back horns, used for carrying heavy loads.

wa·ter can·non ▶ noun a device that sends out a powerful jet of water, used to disperse a crowd.

wa·ter chest·nut ▶ noun the crisp, white-fleshed tuber of a tropical plant, used in oriental cooking.

wa·ter clos·et ▶ noun dated a flush toilet.

wa·ter·col·or /ˈwôtərˌkələr, ˈwä-/ (Brit. **watercolour**) ▶ noun **1** artists' paint that is thinned with water rather than oil. **2** a picture painted with watercolors. **3** the art of painting with watercolors.

– DERIVATIVES **wa·ter·col·or·ist** noun.

wa·ter cool·er ▶ noun **1** a dispenser of cooled drinking water. **2** (as adj.) informal denoting the type of informal conversation among office workers that takes place around a water cooler: *a water-cooler chat about the president.*

wa·ter·course /ˈwôtərˌkôrs, ˈwä-/ ▶ noun a brook, stream, or artificially constructed water channel.

wa·ter crack·er ▶ noun a thin, crisp unsweetened cracker made from flour and water.

wa·ter·craft /ˈwôtərˌkraft, ˈwä-/ ▶ noun (pl. same) **1** a boat or other vessel. **2** skill in sailing and other activities that take place on water.

wa·ter·cress /ˈwôtərˌkres, ˈwä-/ ▶ noun a cress that grows in running water and whose strong-tasting leaves are used in salad.

wa·ter·fall /ˈwôtərˌfôl, ˈwä-/ ▶ noun a stream of water falling from a height, formed when a river or stream flows over a precipice or steep slope.

– SYNONYMS **falls,** cascade, cataract, rapids.

wa·ter fea·ture ▶ noun a pond or fountain in a garden.

wa·ter·fowl /ˈwôtərˌfoul, ˈwä-/ ▶ plural noun ducks, geese, or other large waterbirds.

wa·ter·front /ˈwôtərˌfrənt, ˈwä-/ ▶ noun a part of a town or city alongside a body of water.

wa·ter·hole /ˈwôtərˌhōl, ˈwä-/ ▶ noun a hollow in which water collects, typically one at which animals drink.

wa·ter·ing can ▶ noun a portable water container with a long spout and a detachable perforated cap, used for watering plants.

wa·ter·ing hole ▶ noun **1** a waterhole from which animals regularly drink. **2** informal a tavern or bar.

wa·ter·ing place ▶ noun **1** a watering hole. **2** a spa or seaside resort.

wa·ter lev·el ▶ noun the height reached by the water in a river, tank, etc.

wa·ter li·ly ▶ noun a plant that grows in water, with large round floating leaves and large cup-shaped flowers.

wa·ter·line /ˈwôtərˌlīn, ˈwä-/ ▶ noun **1** the level normally reached by the water on the side of a ship. **2** a line on a shore, riverbank, etc., marking the level reached by the sea or a river.

wa·ter·logged /ˈwôtərˌlôgd, ˈwä-/ ▶ adjective saturated with or full of water.

– ORIGIN from former *waterlog* 'make a ship unmanageable by flooding.'

Wa·ter·loo /ˈwôtərˌlo͞o, ˈwä-, ˌwôtərˈlo͞o, ˌwä-/ ▶ noun (usu. in phrase **meet one's Waterloo**) a decisive defeat or failure.

– ORIGIN from *Waterloo*, a village in what is now Belgium, site of a battle in which Napoleon was finally defeated.

wa·ter main ▶ noun the main pipe in a water supply system.

wa·ter·man /ˈwôtərmən, ˈwä-/ ▶ noun (pl. **watermen**) a person who provides transport by boat.

wa·ter·mark /ˈwôtərˌmärk, ˈwä-/ ▶ noun a faint design made in some paper that is visible when held against the light, identifying the maker. ▶ verb mark paper with a watermark.

wa·ter mead·ow ▶ noun a meadow that is periodically flooded by a stream or river.

wa·ter·mel·on /ˈwôtərˌmelən, ˈwä-/ ▸ noun a large melonlike fruit with smooth green skin, red pulp, and watery juice.

wa·ter·mill /ˈwôtərˌmil, ˈwä-/ ▸ noun a mill worked by a waterwheel.

wa·ter pis·tol ▸ noun a toy pistol that shoots a jet of water.

wa·ter po·lo ▸ noun a seven-a-side game played by swimmers in a pool, with a ball like a volleyball that the players try to throw into their opponents' net.

wa·ter·proof /ˈwôtərˌpro͞of, ˈwä-/ ▸ adjective preventing water from passing through. ▸ noun Brit. a waterproof garment. ▸ verb make something waterproof.

wa·ter rat ▸ noun a large ratlike rodent that lives both on land and in water.

wa·ter-re·sis·tant ▸ adjective partially able to prevent water from passing through.

wa·ter·shed /ˈwôtərˌsʜed, ˈwä-/ ▸ noun **1** an area or ridge of land that separates waters flowing to different rivers, basins, or seas. **2** a turning point in a situation: *the band's success produced a watershed in popular music.*
– ORIGIN from **WATER** + *shed* in the sense 'ridge of high ground' (related to **SHED**[2]).

wa·ter·side /ˈwôtərˌsīd, ˈwä-/ ▸ noun the area next to a sea, lake, or river.

wa·ter·ski /ˈwôtərˌskē, ˈwä-/ ▸ noun (pl. **waterskis**) each of a pair of skis enabling the wearer to skim the surface of the water when towed by a motorboat. ▸ verb (**waterskis, waterskiing, waterskied**) travel on waterskis.
– DERIVATIVES **wa·ter·ski·er** noun.

wa·ter snake ▸ noun a harmless snake that spends part of its time in fresh water.

wa·ter·spout /ˈwôtərˌspout, ˈwä-/ ▸ noun a funnel-shaped column of water and spray formed by a whirlwind occurring over the sea.

wa·ter ta·ble ▸ noun the level below which the ground is saturated with water.

wa·ter·tight /ˈwôtərˌtīt, ˈwä-/ ▸ adjective **1** closely sealed, fastened, or fitted so as to prevent the passage of water. **2** (of an argument or account) unable to be disputed or questioned.

> – SYNONYMS **1 impermeable,** impervious, (hermetically) sealed, waterproof. **2 indisputable,** unquestionable, incontrovertible, irrefutable, unassailable, foolproof, sound, flawless, conclusive.
> – ANTONYMS leaky.

wa·ter tow·er ▸ noun a tower supporting a water tank at a height to create enough pressure to distribute the water through a system of pipes.

wa·ter·way /ˈwôtərˌwā, ˈwä-/ ▸ noun a river, canal, or other route for travel by water.

wa·ter·weed /ˈwôtərˌwēd, ˈwä-/ ▸ noun vegetation growing in water.

wa·ter·wheel /ˈwôtərˌ(h)wēl, ˈwä-/ ▸ noun a large wheel driven by flowing water, used to work machinery or to raise water to a higher level.

wa·ter wings ▸ plural noun inflated floats fixed to the arms of someone learning to swim.

wa·ter witch ▸ noun a person who searches for underground water with a divining rod; a dowser.

wa·ter·works /ˈwôtərˌwərks, ˈwä-/ ▸ plural noun (treated as sing.) an establishment for managing a water supply.
– PHRASES **turn on the waterworks** informal start crying.

wa·ter·y /ˈwôtərē, ˈwä-/ ▸ adjective **1** consisting of, containing, or resembling water. **2** (of food or drink) thin or tasteless as a result of containing too much water. **3** weak or pale: *watery sunlight.*

> **WORD TOOLKIT**
>
> See **RUNNY**.

watt /wät/ ▸ noun the SI unit of power, equivalent to one joule per second and corresponding to the rate of energy in an electric circuit where the potential difference is one volt and the current one ampere.
– ORIGIN named after the Scottish engineer James *Watt.*

watt·age /ˈwätij/ ▸ noun an amount of electrical power expressed in watts.

wat·tle[1] /ˈwätl/ ▸ noun **1** a material for making fences, walls, etc., consisting of rods interlaced with twigs or branches. **2** an Australian acacia tree with long flexible branches.
– ORIGIN Old English.

wat·tle[2] ▸ noun a fleshy lobe hanging from the head or neck of the turkey and some other birds.
– ORIGIN unknown.

wat·tle and daub ▸ noun a material formerly used in building walls, consisting of wattle covered with mud or clay.

Wa·tu·si /wäˈto͞osē/ ▸ noun **1** an energetic dance popular in the 1960s. **2** (treated as pl.) the Tutsi people as a group (now dated in English use).
– ORIGIN a local name.

wave /wāv/ ▸ verb **1** move one's hand to and fro in greeting or as a signal. **2** move something held in one's hand to and fro. **3** move or sway to and fro while remaining fixed to one point. **4** style hair so that it curls slightly.

> – SYNONYMS **1** *the waiter waved them closer* **gesture,** signal, beckon, motion. **2** *he waved his flag in triumph* **flap,** wag, shake, swish, swing, brandish, flourish, wield. **3** *the flag waved in the wind* **ripple,** flutter, undulate, stir, flap, sway, shake, quiver.

▸ noun **1** a ridge of water moving along the surface of the sea or arching and breaking on the shore. **2** a sudden occurrence of or increase in a phenomenon or emotion. **3** a gesture or signal made by waving one's hand. **4** a slightly curling lock of hair. **5** Physics a periodic disturbance of the particles of a substance without overall movement of the particles, as in the transmission of sound, light, heat, etc.

> – SYNONYMS **1 breaker,** roller, comber, boomer, ripple; (**waves**) swell, surf. **2** *a wave of planning applications* **spate,** surge, rush, flow, flood, stream, torrent, tide. **3 signal,** sign, motion, gesture.

– PHRASES **make waves** informal **1** create a significant impression. **2** cause trouble.
– ORIGIN Old English.

> **USAGE**
>
> For an explanation of the confusion between **wave** and **waive**, see the note at **WAIVE**.

wave·band /ˈwāvˌband/ ▸ noun a range of wavelengths between two given limits, used in radio transmission.

wave·form /ˈwāvˌfôrm/ ▶ **noun** Physics a curve showing the shape of a wave at a given time.

wave·length /ˈwāvˌleNG(k)TH/ ▶ **noun 1** Physics the distance between successive crests of a wave of sound, light, radio waves, etc. **2** a person's way of thinking when communicated to another: *we weren't on the same wavelength.*

wave·let /ˈwāvlit/ ▶ **noun** a small wave.

wa·ver /ˈwāvər/ ▶ **verb 1** move quiveringly; flicker. **2** begin to weaken; falter: *his love for her had never wavered.* **3** be undecided between two opinions or courses of action.

> – SYNONYMS **1** *the candlelight wavered* **flicker,** quiver. **2** *his voice wavered* **falter,** wobble, tremble, quaver. **3** **hesitate,** dither, be irresolute, be undecided, vacillate, blow hot and cold, hem and haw; informal shilly-shally, sit on the fence.

– DERIVATIVES **wa·ver·er** noun **wa·ver·y** adjective.
– ORIGIN Old Norse, 'flicker.'

WAV file /wāv/ ▶ **noun** Computing a format for storing audio files that produces CD-quality audio.

wav·y /ˈwāvē/ ▶ **adjective** (**wavier, waviest**) having or consisting of a series of wavelike curves.
– DERIVATIVES **wav·i·ness** noun.

wax[1] /waks/ ▶ **noun 1** a soft solid oily substance that melts easily, used for making candles or polishes. **2** a substance produced by bees to make honeycombs; beeswax. ▶ **verb 1** polish or treat something with wax. **2** remove hair from a part of the body by applying melted wax and then peeling it off with the hairs.
– DERIVATIVES **wax·er** noun.
– ORIGIN Old English.

wax[2] ▶ **verb 1** (of the moon) gradually have a larger part of its visible surface lit up, so that it appears to increase in size. **2** literary become larger or stronger. **3** speak or write in a particular way: *they waxed lyrical about the old days.*
– ORIGIN Old English.

waxed pa·per (also **wax paper**) ▶ **noun** paper treated with wax to make it waterproof or greaseproof.

wax·en /ˈwaksən/ ▶ **adjective 1** having a smooth, pale, semitransparent surface like that of wax. **2** old use or literary made of wax.

wax·wing /ˈwaksˌwiNG/ ▶ **noun** a crested songbird, mainly pinkish-brown and with bright red tips to some wing feathers.

wax·work /ˈwaksˌwərk/ ▶ **noun 1** a lifelike dummy modeled in wax. **2** (**waxworks**) (treated as sing.) an exhibition of waxworks.

wax·y /ˈwaksē/ ▶ **adjective** (**waxier, waxiest**) resembling wax in consistency or appearance.
– DERIVATIVES **wax·i·ness** noun.

way /wā/ ▶ **noun 1** a method, style, or manner of doing something. **2** the typical manner in which someone behaves or in which something happens. **3** a route or means taken in order to reach, enter, or leave a place. **4** the route along which someone or something is traveling or would travel if unobstructed. **5** a specified direction. **6** the distance in space or time between two points. **7** a particular aspect. **8** a specified condition or state. **9** a road, track, path, or street. **10** informal a particular area: *they live somewhere around your way.* **11** (**ways**) parts into which something divides or is divided. **12** forward motion or momentum of a ship or boat through water.

> – SYNONYMS **1** *a way of reducing the damage* **method,** process, procedure, technique, system, plan, strategy, scheme, means, mechanism, approach. **2** *it was not his way to wait for things to happen* **manner,** style, fashion, mode. **3** *I've changed my ways* **practice,** wont, habit, custom, convention, routine, trait, attribute, peculiarity, idiosyncrasy, conduct, behavior. **4** *he blocked her way* **route,** course, direction, track, path, access, gate, exit, entrance, door. **5** *we just missed a car coming the other way* **direction,** bearing, course, orientation, line, tack. **6** *a short way downstream* **distance,** length, stretch, journey. **7** *April is a long way away* **time,** stretch, term, span, duration. **8** *in some ways, he may be better off* **respect,** regard, aspect, facet, sense, detail, point, particular. **9** *the country is in a bad way* **state,** condition, situation, circumstances, position, predicament, plight; informal shape.

▶ **adverb** informal at or to a considerable distance or extent.
– PHRASES **by the way** incidentally. **by way of 1** so as to pass through or across; via. **2** as a form of. **3** by means of. **come one's way** happen or become available to one. **get** (or **have**) **one's** (**own**) **way** get or do what one wants in spite of opposition. **give way 1** yield to someone or something. **2** collapse or break under pressure. **3** (**give way to**) be replaced or superseded by. **go one's way 1** (of events, circumstances, etc.) be favorable to one. **2** leave. **have a way with** have a particular talent for dealing with or ability in. **have one's way with** old use or humorous have sex with. **in a way** (or **in some ways** or **in one way**) to a certain extent. **lead the way 1** go first along a route. **2** be the first to do something. **one way and another** (or **one way or the other**) **1** taking most considerations into account. **2** by some means. **on the** (or **one's** or **its**) **way** about to arrive or happen. **on the** (or **one's** or **its**) **way out** informal going out of fashion or favor. **the other way around** (or **round**) **1** in the opposite position or direction. **2** the opposite of what is expected or supposed. **out of the way 1** (of a place) remote. **2** dealt with or finished. **3** no longer an obstacle to someone's plans. **4** unusual or exceptional. **ways and means** the methods and resources for achieving something, especially raising revenue.
– ORIGIN Old English.

way·bill /ˈwāˌbil/ ▶ **noun** a list of passengers or goods being carried on a vehicle.

way·far·er /ˈwāˌfe(ə)rər/ ▶ **noun** literary a person who travels on foot.
– DERIVATIVES **way·far·ing** noun & adjective.

way·lay /ˈwāˌlā/ ▶ **verb** (past and past part. **waylaid**) **1** intercept someone in order to attack them. **2** stop someone and keep them in conversation.

> – SYNONYMS **1** **ambush,** hold up, attack, pounce on. **2** **accost,** detain, intercept; informal buttonhole.

way·mark /ˈwāˌmärk/ ▶ **noun** (also **waymarker**) a sign forming one of a series used to mark out a footpath or similar route.

way-out ▶ **adjective** informal very unconventional or experimental.

-ways ▶ **suffix** forming adjectives and adverbs of direction or manner: *lengthways.*

way·side /ˈwāˌsīd/ ▶ **noun** the edge of a road.
– PHRASES **fall by the wayside** fail to continue with an undertaking. [with reference to the Gospel of Luke, chapter 8.]

way sta·tion ▸ **noun** a stopping place on a journey.

way·ward /ˈwāwərd/ ▸ **adjective** difficult to control because of unpredictable or willful behavior.

– SYNONYMS **willful,** headstrong, stubborn, obstinate, perverse, contrary, disobedient, undisciplined, rebellious, defiant, recalcitrant, unruly, wild; formal refractory.

– DERIVATIVES **way·ward·ly** adverb **way·ward·ness** noun.
– ORIGIN shortening of former *awayward* 'turned away.'

Wb ▸ **abbreviation** weber(s).

WBA ▸ **abbreviation** World Boxing Association.

WBC ▸ **abbreviation** World Boxing Council.

WC ▸ **abbreviation** Brit. water closet.

we /wē/ ▸ **pronoun** (first person pl.) **1** used by a speaker to refer to himself or herself and one or more other people considered together. **2** people in general. **3** used in formal situations for or by a royal person, or by a writer, to refer to himself or herself. **4** you (used in a superior way).
– ORIGIN Old English.

USAGE

On whether to use **we** or **us** following **than**, see the note at **PERSONAL PRONOUN**.

weak /wēk/ ▸ **adjective 1** lacking physical strength and energy. **2** liable to break or give way under pressure. **3** not secure, stable, or firmly established: *a weak economy.* **4** lacking power, influence, or ability. **5** lacking intensity: *a weak light from a single streetlamp.* **6** (of a liquid or solution) heavily diluted. **7** not convincing or forceful: *a weak plot.* **8** (of verbs) forming the past tense and past participle by adding a suffix (in English, typically *-ed*).

– SYNONYMS **1 feeble,** frail, delicate, fragile, infirm, ailing, debilitated, decrepit, exhausted, enervated. **2 inadequate,** poor, defective, faulty, deficient, imperfect, substandard. **3 unconvincing,** tenuous, implausible, unsatisfactory, poor, inadequate, lame, feeble, flimsy, hollow; informal pathetic. **4** *a weak bridge* **fragile,** rickety, insubstantial, wobbly, unstable, ramshackle, jerry-built, shoddy. **5 spineless,** craven, cowardly, timid, irresolute, indecisive, ineffectual, meek, tame, soft, faint-hearted; informal yellow, gutless. **6** *a weak voice* **indistinct,** muffled, muted, hushed, faint, low. **7 watery,** dilute, diluted, watered down, thin, tasteless.
– ANTONYMS strong.

– PHRASES **the weaker sex** (treated as sing. or pl.) dated women regarded as a group.
– ORIGIN Old English.

WORD TOOLKIT

weak ...	feeble ...	frail ...
link	attempt	body
signal	excuse	patient
support	effort	voice
dollar	response	frame
economy	protest	creature
market	apology	child
tea	explanation	grandparents

weak·en /ˈwēkən/ ▸ **verb** make or become weak.

– SYNONYMS **1 enfeeble,** debilitate, incapacitate, sap, tire, exhaust. **2 decrease,** dwindle, diminish, wane, ebb, subside, peter out, fizzle out, tail off, decline, falter. **3 impair,** undermine, compromise, lessen.
– ANTONYMS strengthen, bolster.

weak-kneed ▸ **adjective** lacking determination or courage.

weak·ling /ˈwēkliNG/ ▸ **noun** a weak person or animal.

– SYNONYMS **milksop,** namby-pamby, pushover; informal wimp, sissy, wuss, doormat.

weak·ly /ˈwēklē/ ▸ **adverb** in a weak way. ▸ **adjective** (**weaklier, weakliest**) weak or sickly.

weak·ness /ˈwēknis/ ▸ **noun 1** the state of being weak. **2** a disadvantage or fault. **3** a person or thing that one cannot resist or likes too much. **4** (**weakness for**) a liking for something that is hard to resist: *his weakness for shrimp cocktails.*

– SYNONYMS **1 frailty,** feebleness, fragility, delicacy, debility, incapacity, decrepitude. **2 fault,** flaw, defect, deficiency, failing, shortcoming, imperfection, Achilles heel. **3 fondness,** liking, partiality, love, penchant, predilection, inclination, taste; enthusiasm, appetite. **4 timidity,** cravenness, cowardliness, indecision, irresolution, ineffectuality, ineffectiveness, impotence.

weal[1] /wēl/ (also chiefly Medicine **wheal**) ▸ **noun** a red, swollen mark left on flesh by a blow or pressure.
– ORIGIN from **WALE**.

weal[2] ▸ **noun** formal that which is best for someone or something: *guardians of the public weal.*
– ORIGIN Old English, 'wealth, well-being.'

wealth /welTH/ ▸ **noun 1** a large amount of money, property, or valuable possessions. **2** the state of being rich. **3** a large amount of a resource or desirable thing: *a wealth of information.*

– SYNONYMS **1 affluence,** prosperity, riches, means, fortune, money, cash, capital, treasure, finance; informal wherewithal, dough, bread. **2 abundance,** profusion, plethora, mine, store; informal lot, load, mountain, stack, ton.
– ANTONYMS poverty, dearth.

– ORIGIN from **WELL**[1] or **WEAL**[2].

wealth·y /ˈwelTHē/ ▸ **adjective** (**wealthier, wealthiest**) having a great deal of money, resources, or assets; rich.

– SYNONYMS **rich,** affluent, moneyed, well off, well-to-do, prosperous; informal well heeled, rolling in it, made of money, loaded, flush.
– ANTONYMS poor.

wean /wēn/ ▸ **verb 1** make a young mammal used to food other than its mother's milk. **2** (often **wean someone off**) make someone give up a habit or addiction. **3** (**be weaned on**) be strongly influenced by something from an early age: *a generation weaned on television.*
– ORIGIN Old English.

wean·ling /ˈwēnliNG/ ▸ **noun** a newly weaned animal.

weap·on /ˈwepən/ ▸ **noun 1** a thing designed or used to cause physical harm or damage. **2** a means of gaining an advantage or attacking someone or something: *the drug is a powerful new weapon to treat cancer.*
– DERIVATIVES **weap·on·ry** noun.
– ORIGIN Old English.

weap·on·ize ▸ **verb** convert to use as a weapon.

weap·on of mass de·struc·tion ▸ noun a nuclear, biological, or chemical weapon able to cause widespread destruction and loss of life.

wear /we(ə)r/ ▸ verb (past **wore** /wôr/; past part. **worn** /wôrn/) **1** have something on one's body as clothing, decoration, or protection. **2** display a particular facial expression. **3** damage or destroy something by friction or continued use. **4** withstand continued use to a specified degree. **5** (**wear off**) become less effective or intense. **6** (**wear someone out**) exhaust someone. **7** (**wear out**) be used until no longer in good working order. **8** (as adj. **wearing**) mentally or physically tiring. **9** (**wear someone down**) overcome someone by persistence. **10** (**wear on**) (of time) pass in a slow or boring way.

– SYNONYMS **1 be dressed in,** be clothed in, have on, sport. **2** *Barbara wore a smile* **bear,** show, display, exhibit, give, put on, assume. **3** *the bricks have been worn down* **erode,** abrade, rub away, grind away, wash away, crumble (away), eat away (at). **4** *the tires are wearing well* **last,** endure, hold up, bear up. **5** (**wear off**) *the drug's effects were wearing off* **fade,** diminish, lessen, dwindle, decrease, wane, peter out, fizzle out, pall, disappear, vanish. **6** (**wear someone out**) **tire out,** fatigue, weary, exhaust, drain, sap, enervate; informal poop out, do in. **7** (**wear out**) *the fabric will eventually wear out* **deteriorate,** become worn, fray, become threadbare. **8** (as adj. **wearing**) **tiring,** exhausting, wearying, fatiguing, enervating, draining, sapping, demanding, exacting, taxing, grueling, punishing.

▸ noun **1** clothing suitable for a particular purpose or of a particular type: *evening wear.* **2** damage caused by continuous use. **3** the capacity for resisting continuous use without damage. **4** the wearing of something on the body: *tops for wear in the evening.*

– SYNONYMS **1 clothes,** garments, dress, attire, garb, wardrobe; informal getup, gear, togs. **2 damage,** friction, abrasion, erosion. **3 use,** service, value; informal mileage.

– DERIVATIVES **wear·a·ble** adjective **wear·er** noun.
– PHRASES **wear thin** be gradually used up or become less acceptable.
– ORIGIN Old English.

wear·i·some /ˈwi(ə)rēsəm/ ▸ adjective making one feel tired or bored.

wear·y /ˈwi(ə)rē/ ▸ adjective (**wearier, weariest**) **1** feeling or showing tiredness. **2** causing tiredness. **3** reluctant to experience any more of: *he was weary of constant arguments.*

– SYNONYMS **1 tired,** worn out, exhausted, fatigued, sapped, spent, drained; informal done in, ready to drop, bushed, pooped. **2 tiring,** exhausting, fatiguing, enervating, draining, sapping, demanding, taxing, arduous, grueling.
– ANTONYMS energetic.

▸ verb (**wearies, wearying, wearied**) **1** make someone weary. **2** (**weary of**) grow tired of someone or something.
– DERIVATIVES **wea·ri·ly** adverb **wea·ri·ness** noun.
– ORIGIN Old English.

wea·sel /ˈwēzəl/ ▸ noun **1** a small slender meat-eating mammal related to the stoat. **2** informal a deceitful or treacherous person. ▸ verb (**weasels, weaseling, weaseled**) achieve something by cunning or deceit: *somehow he weaseled her into going.*
– DERIVATIVES **wea·sel·ly** adjective.
– PHRASES **weasel words** words or statements that are deliberately confusing or misleading.
– ORIGIN Old English.

weath·er /ˈweT͟Hər/ ▸ noun the state of the atmosphere at a place and time as regards temperature, wind, rain, etc.

– SYNONYMS **conditions,** climate, elements, forecast, outlook.

▸ adjective referring to the side from which the wind is blowing; windward. Contrasted with **LEE**.
▸ verb **1** wear away or change in form or appearance by long exposure to the weather: *his face was weathered and pockmarked.* **2** come safely through a difficult or dangerous situation.

– SYNONYMS **survive,** come through, ride out, pull through, withstand, endure, rise above; informal stick out.

– PHRASES **keep a weather eye on** be watchful for developments. **make heavy weather of** informal have unnecessary difficulty in dealing with a task or problem. [from *make good* or *bad weather of it,* referring to a ship in a storm.] **under the weather** informal slightly unwell or depressed.
– ORIGIN Old English.

weath·er bal·loon ▸ noun a balloon equipped with meteorological apparatus that is sent up into the atmosphere to provide information about the weather.

weath·er-beat·en ▸ adjective damaged, worn, or tanned by exposure to the weather.

weath·er·cock /ˈweT͟Hərˌkäk/ ▸ noun a weathervane in the form of a rooster.

weath·er·man /ˈweT͟Hərˌman/ (or **weatherwoman**) ▸ noun (pl. **weathermen** or **weatherwomen**) a person who broadcasts a description and forecast of weather conditions.

weath·er·proof /ˈweT͟Hərˌpro͞of/ ▸ adjective resistant to the effects of bad weather. ▸ verb make something weatherproof.

weath·er sta·tion ▸ noun an observation post where weather conditions are observed and recorded.

weath·er·strip /ˈweT͟Hərˌstrip/ ▸ noun a strip of rubber, metal, etc., used to seal the edges of a door or window against rain and wind. ▸ verb (**weatherstrips, weatherstripped, weatherstripping**) apply such a strip to (a door or window).

weath·er·vane /ˈweT͟Hərˌvān/ ▸ noun a revolving pointer that shows the direction of the wind.

weave[1] /wēv/ ▸ verb (past **wove** /wōv/; past part. **woven** /ˈwōvən/ or **wove**) **1** make fabric by interlacing long threads passing in one direction with others at a right angle to them. **2** make basketwork or a wreath by interlacing rods or flowers. **3** make (a complex story or pattern) from a number of interconnected elements: *he weaves colorful plots.* **4** (**weave something into**) make facts, events, and other elements into a story: *interpretative comments are woven into the narrative.*

– SYNONYMS **1 entwine,** lace, twist, knit, braid, plait. **2 invent,** make up, fabricate, construct, create, spin.

▸ noun a particular way in which fabric is woven: *cloth of a very fine weave.*
– ORIGIN Old English.

weave[2] ▸ verb move from side to side to get around obstructions.

– SYNONYMS *he had to weave his way through the crowds* **thread,** wind, wend, dodge, zigzag.

– ORIGIN probably from an Old Norse word meaning 'to wave, brandish.'

weav·er /'wēvər/ ▶ **noun 1** a person who weaves fabric. **2** (also **weaver bird**) a songbird of tropical Africa and Asia that builds elaborately woven nests.

web /web/ ▶ **noun 1** a network of fine threads made by a spider to catch its prey. **2** a complex system of interconnected elements: *the story's web of lies.* **3** (**the Web**) the World Wide Web. **4** a membrane between the toes of a swimming bird or other animal that lives in water.

– SYNONYMS **1 mesh,** net, lattice, lacework, gauze, gossamer. **2 network,** nexus, complex, tangle, chain.

– ORIGIN Old English, 'woven fabric.'

webbed /webd/ ▶ **adjective** (of an animal's feet) having the toes connected by a web.

web·bing /'webiNG/ ▶ **noun** strong, closely woven fabric used for making straps and belts and for supporting the seats of upholstered chairs.

web·cam /'web,kam/ ▶ **noun** trademark a video camera connected to a computer, so that its images may be viewed by Internet users.

web·cast /'web,kast/ ▶ **noun** a live video broadcast of an event transmitted across the Internet.

we·ber /'webər/ ▶ **noun** the SI unit of magnetic flux, sufficient to cause an electromotive force of one volt in a circuit of one turn when generated or removed in one second.

– ORIGIN named after the German physicist Wilhelm Eduard *Weber.*

web-foot·ed ▶ **adjective** having webbed feet.

web host·ing ▶ **noun** the activity or business of providing storage space and access for websites.

web·link /'webliNGk/ ▶ **noun 1** another term for **HYPERLINK**. **2** a printed address of a website in a book, newspaper, etc.

web·log /'web,lôg, -,läg/ ▶ **noun** full form of **BLOG**.

web·mas·ter /'web,mastər/ ▶ **noun** a person who is responsible for a particular server on the Internet.

web page ▶ **noun** a hypertext document that can be accessed via the Internet.

web·site /'web,sīt/ ▶ **noun** a location connected to the Internet that maintains one or more web pages.

web·zine /'web,zēn/ ▶ **noun** a magazine published on the Internet.

wed /wed/ ▶ **verb** (**weds, wedding**; past and past part. **wedded** or **wed**) **1** formal or literary marry or get married. **2** formal or literary give or join someone in marriage. **3** (as adj. **wedded**) relating to marriage. **4** (**be wedded to**) be entirely devoted to an activity, belief, etc. **5** combine two desirable factors or qualities.

– SYNONYMS **1** (as adj. **wedded**) *wedded bliss* **married,** matrimonial, marital, conjugal, nuptial. **2** (**be wedded to**) *he is wedded to his work* **dedicated,** devoted, attached, fixated.

– ORIGIN Old English.

we'd /wēd/ ▶ **contraction 1** we had. **2** we should or we would.

wed·ding /'wediNG/ ▶ **noun** a marriage ceremony.

– SYNONYMS **marriage (service),** nuptials, union.

wed·ding band ▶ **noun** a wedding ring.

wed·ding cake ▶ **noun** a rich iced cake, typically in multiple tiers, served at a wedding reception.

wed·ding march ▶ **noun** a piece of march music played at the entrance of the bride or the exit of the couple at a wedding.

wed·ding ring ▶ **noun** a ring worn by a married person, given to them by their spouse at their wedding.

wedge /wej/ ▶ **noun 1** a piece of wood, metal, etc., with a thick end that tapers to a thin edge, that is driven between two objects or parts of an object to secure or separate them. **2** a wedge-shaped thing or piece. **3** a golf club with a low, angled face for hitting the ball as high as possible into the air. **4** a shoe with a fairly high heel forming a solid block with the sole.

– SYNONYMS **triangle,** segment, slice, section, chunk, lump, slab, hunk, block, piece.

▶ **verb 1** fix something in position with a wedge. **2** force into a narrow space: *she wedged her carryall between two bags.*

– SYNONYMS **squeeze,** cram, jam, ram, force, push, shove; informal **stuff.**

– PHRASES **drive a wedge between** cause a disagreement or hostility between. **the thin end of the wedge** informal an action unimportant in itself but which is likely to lead to more serious developments.

– ORIGIN Old English.

wedge is·sue ▶ **noun** a divisive political issue, especially one raised by a candidate for office in hopes of attracting or alienating an opponent's supporters.

wedg·ie /'wejē/ ▶ **noun** informal **1** a shoe with a wedged heel. **2** an act of pulling up the material of someone's underpants tightly between their buttocks as a practical joke.

Wedg·wood /'wej,wo͝od/ ▶ **noun** trademark a type of pottery made by the English potter Josiah Wedgwood and his successors, especially a kind of powder-blue stoneware with white embossed cameos.

wed·lock /'wed,läk/ ▶ **noun** formal the state of being married.

– PHRASES **born in** (or **out of**) **wedlock** born of married (or unmarried) parents.

– ORIGIN Old English, 'marriage vow.'

Wednes·day /'wenzdā, -dē/ ▶ **noun** the day of the week before Thursday and following Tuesday.

– ORIGIN Old English, named after the Germanic god *Odin.*

wee /wē/ ▶ **adjective** (**weer, weest**) chiefly Scottish little.

– ORIGIN Old English.

weed /wēd/ ▶ **noun 1** a wild plant growing where it is not wanted, especially among crops or garden plants. **2** informal marijuana. **3** (**the weed**) informal tobacco. **4** informal a thin and leggy person. ▶ **verb 1** remove weeds from an area of ground. **2** (**weed someone/thing out**) remove inferior or unwanted items or members from a group or collection.

– ORIGIN Old English.

weed·kill·er /'wēd,kilər/ ▶ **noun** a substance used to destroy weeds.

weed whack·er ▶ **noun** an electrically powered grass trimmer with a nylon cutting cord which rotates rapidly on a spindle.

weed·y /ˈwēdē/ ▶ **adjective** (**weedier, weediest**) **1** containing or covered with many weeds. **2** informal (of a person) thin and leggy.

wee hours ▶ **plural noun** (**the wee hours**) the early hours of the morning after midnight.

week /wēk/ ▶ **noun 1** a period of seven days. **2** the period of seven days generally reckoned from and to midnight on Saturday night. **3** the five days from Monday to Friday, or the time spent working during this period.
– ORIGIN Old English.

week·day /ˈwēkˌdā/ ▶ **noun** a day of the week other than Saturday or Sunday.

week·end /ˈwēkˌend/ ▶ **noun** Saturday and Sunday. ▶ **verb** informal spend a weekend somewhere.

week·end·er /ˈwēkˌendər/ ▶ **noun** a person who spends weekends away from their main home.

week·ly /ˈwēklē/ ▶ **adjective 1** done, produced, or happening once a week. **2** calculated in terms of a week: *weekly income*. ▶ **adverb** once a week. ▶ **noun** (pl. **weeklies**) a newspaper or periodical issued every week.

wee·nie /ˈwēnē/ ▶ **noun 1** another term for **WIENER** (sense 1). **2** vulgar slang a man's penis. **3** informal a weak, socially inept, or boringly studious person.

weep /wēp/ ▶ **verb** (past and past part. **wept**) **1** shed tears. **2** discharge liquid. **3** (as adj. **weeping**) used in names of trees and shrubs with drooping branches, e.g., **weeping willow**.

– SYNONYMS **cry,** shed tears, sob, snivel, whimper, wail, bawl, keen; informal boohoo, blubber.

▶ **noun** a fit or spell of shedding tears.
– DERIVATIVES **weep·er** noun.
– ORIGIN Old English.

weep·ie /ˈwēpē/ (also **weepy**) ▶ **noun** (pl. **weepies**) informal a sentimental or emotional movie, novel, or song.

weep·y /ˈwēpē/ ▶ **adjective** (**weepier, weepiest**) informal **1** inclined to weep; tearful. **2** sentimental: *a weepy TV movie*.
– DERIVATIVES **weep·i·ly** adverb **weep·i·ness** noun.

wee·vil /ˈwēvəl/ ▶ **noun** a small beetle with a long snout, several kinds of which are pests of crops or stored foodstuffs.
– ORIGIN Old English.

weft /weft/ ▶ **noun** (in weaving) the crosswise threads that are passed over and under the warp threads on a loom to make cloth.
– ORIGIN Old English.

Wehr·macht /ˈverˌmäkt, -ˌmäkʜt/ ▶ **noun** the German armed forces from 1921 to 1945.
– ORIGIN German, 'defensive force.'

weigh /wā/ ▶ **verb 1** find out how heavy someone or something is. **2** have a specified weight. **3** (**weigh something out**) measure and take out a portion of a particular weight. **4** (**weigh someone down**) make someone feel stressed or anxious. **5** (**weigh on**) be depressing or worrying to someone. **6** (**weigh in**) (of a boxer or jockey) be officially weighed before or after a contest. **7** (often **weigh something up**) assess the nature or importance of something. **8** (often **weigh against**) influence a decision or action: *the evidence weighed heavily against him*. **9** (**weigh in**) informal make a forceful contribution to a competition or argument. **10** (**weigh into**) join in or attack forcefully or enthusiastically: *he weighed into the companies for their high costs*.

– SYNONYMS **1 measure the weight of,** put on the scale(s). **2 have a weight of,** tip the scales at. **3** *he weighed the possibilities* **consider,** contemplate, think about, mull over, chew over, reflect on, ruminate about, muse on, assess, examine, review, explore, take stock of. **4** *they need to weigh benefit against risk* **balance,** evaluate, compare, juxtapose, contrast.

– PHRASES **weigh anchor** (of a boat) take up the anchor when ready to sail.
– ORIGIN Old English.

weigh·bridge /ˈwāˌbrij/ ▶ **noun** a machine for weighing vehicles, set into the ground to be driven onto.

weigh-in ▶ **noun** an official weighing, e.g., of boxers before a fight.

weigh sta·tion ▶ **noun** a roadside station where commercial vehicles can be required to stop and be inspected.

weight /wāt/ ▶ **noun 1** the amount that someone or something weighs. **2** the quality of being heavy. **3** a heavy object. **4** a unit or system of units used for expressing how much something weighs. **5** a piece of metal known to weigh a definite amount and used on scales to find out how heavy something is. **6** (**weights**) heavy blocks or disks used in weightlifting or weight training. **7** the ability to influence decisions or actions: *their recommendation will carry great weight*. **8** the importance attached to something. **9** a feeling of pressure or worry: *that'll be a weight off my mind*. **10** the surface density of cloth, used as a measure of its quality. **11** Physics the force exerted on the mass of a body by a gravitational field.

– SYNONYMS **1 mass,** heaviness, load, burden. **2 influence,** force, leverage, sway, pull, power, authority; informal clout. **3 burden,** load, millstone, trouble, worry. **4** *the weight of the evidence is against him* **most,** bulk, majority, preponderance, body, lion's share.

▶ **verb 1** make something heavier or keep something in place with a weight. **2** attach importance or value to: *reading and writing should be weighted equally in the assessment*. **3** (**be weighted**) be planned or arranged so as to give one party an advantage.
– PHRASES **be worth one's weight in gold** be very useful or helpful. **throw one's weight around** informal assert oneself in an unpleasant way.
– ORIGIN Old English.

weight·ing /ˈwātiɴɢ/ ▶ **noun** allowance or adjustment made to take account of special circumstances.

weight·less /ˈwātlis/ ▶ **adjective** (of a body) not apparently acted on by gravity.
– DERIVATIVES **weight·less·ly** adverb **weight·less·ness** noun.

weight·lift·ing /ˈwātˌliftiɴɢ/ ▶ **noun** the sport or activity of lifting barbells or other heavy weights.
– DERIVATIVES **weight·lift·er** noun.

weight train·ing ▶ **noun** physical training that involves lifting weights.

weight-watch·er ▶ **noun** a person who is on a diet in order to lose weight.

weight·y /ˈwātē/ ▶ **adjective** (**weightier, weightiest**) **1** weighing a great deal; heavy. **2** very serious and important.

– DERIVATIVES **weight·i·ly** adverb **weight·i·ness** noun.

Weil's dis·ease /vīlz/ ▶ **noun** an infectious disease caused by a bacterium and transmitted by rats via contaminated water.
– ORIGIN named after the German physician H. Adolf *Weil*.

Wei·mar·an·er /ˈwīmə,ränər, ˈvī-/ ▶ **noun** a thin-coated gray breed of pointer used as a gun dog.
– ORIGIN from *Weimar* in Germany, where the breed was developed.

weir /wi(ə)r/ ▶ **noun 1** a low dam built across a river to raise the level of water upstream or control its flow. **2** an enclosure of stakes set in a stream as a trap for fish.
– ORIGIN Old English.

weird /wi(ə)rd/ ▶ **adjective 1** informal very strange or unusual: *he's a weird little guy.* **2** mysterious or strange in a frightening way.

> – SYNONYMS **1 bizarre,** odd, curious, strange, quirky, outlandish, eccentric, unconventional, unorthodox, idiosyncratic, surreal, crazy, absurd, grotesque, peculiar; informal wacky, wacko, freaky. **2 uncanny,** eerie, unnatural, supernatural, unearthly, other-worldly, ghostly, mysterious, strange, abnormal, unusual; informal creepy, spooky, freaky.
> – ANTONYMS normal, conventional.

– DERIVATIVES **weird·ly** adverb **weird·ness** noun.
– ORIGIN Old English, 'destiny, fate.'

weird·o /ˈwi(ə)rdō/ ▶ **noun** (pl. **weirdos**) informal a strange or eccentric person.

welch ▶ **verb** variant spelling of **WELSH**.

wel·come /ˈwelkəm/ ▶ **noun 1** an instance or way of greeting someone. **2** a pleased or approving reaction.

> – SYNONYMS **greeting,** salutation, reception, hospitality, the red carpet.

▶ **exclamation** used to greet someone in a glad or friendly way.
▶ **verb 1** greet someone who is arriving in a polite or friendly way. **2** be glad to receive or hear of: *the decision was widely welcomed.*

> – SYNONYMS **1 greet,** salute, receive, meet, usher in. **2 be pleased by,** be glad about, approve of, applaud, appreciate, embrace.
> – ANTONYMS resent.

▶ **adjective 1** (of a guest or new arrival) gladly received. **2** very pleasing because much needed or desired. **3** allowed or invited to do a particular thing: *you are welcome to join in.* **4** (**welcome to**) used to indicate relief at giving up something to another: *the job is all yours and you're welcome to it!*

> – SYNONYMS **pleasing,** good, agreeable, encouraging, gratifying, heartening, promising, favorable, pleasant.

– DERIVATIVES **wel·com·er** noun.
– ORIGIN Old English, 'a person whose coming is pleasing.'

weld /weld/ ▶ **verb 1** join metal parts together by heating the surfaces to the point of melting and pressing or hammering them together. **2** make an article by welding. **3** unite into a strong and effective whole: *they welded diverse ethnic groups into a single political system.*

> – SYNONYMS **fuse,** bond, stick, join, attach, seal, splice, melt, solder.

▶ **noun** a welded joint.
– DERIVATIVES **weld·er** noun.
– ORIGIN from **WELL²** in the former sense 'melt or weld heated metal.'

wel·fare /ˈwel,fe(ə)r/ ▶ **noun 1** the health, happiness, and fortunes of a person or group. **2** organized practical or financial help provided, typically by the government, to help people in need.

> – SYNONYMS **1 well-being,** health, comfort, security, safety, protection, success, interest, good. **2 social security,** benefit, public assistance, pension, credit, support, sick pay, unemployment benefit; informal the dole.

– ORIGIN from **WELL¹** + **FARE**.

wel·fare state ▶ **noun** a system under which the government protects the health and well-being of its citizens by providing grants, pensions, and other benefits.

wel·far·ism /ˈwelfe(ə),rizəm/ ▶ **noun** the principles or policies associated with a welfare state.
– DERIVATIVES **wel·far·ist** noun & adjective.

wel·kin /ˈwelkin/ ▶ **noun** literary the sky or heaven.
– ORIGIN Old English, 'cloud, sky.'

well¹ /wel/ ▶ **adverb** (**better** /ˈbetər/, **best** /best/) **1** in a good or satisfactory way. **2** in a favorable or approving way. **3** in a thorough way: *add the mustard and mix well.* **4** to a great extent or degree; very much. **5** in prosperity or comfort. **6** Brit. informal very; extremely: *he was well out of order.* **7** very probably. **8** without difficulty. **9** with good reason: *what, you may well ask, are they doing here?* **10** old use at a good time; luckily: *hail fellow, well met.*

> – SYNONYMS **1** *he behaves well* **satisfactorily,** nicely, correctly, properly, fittingly, suitably, appropriately. **2** *he plays the piano well* **skillfully,** ably, competently, proficiently, adeptly, deftly, expertly, excellently. **3** *they speak well of him* **admiringly,** highly, approvingly, favorably, appreciatively, warmly, enthusiastically, in glowing terms.
> – ANTONYMS badly.

▶ **adjective** (**better, best**) **1** in good health. **2** in a satisfactory state or position. **3** sensible; advisable.

> – SYNONYMS **1** *she was completely well again* **healthy,** fine, fit, robust, strong, vigorous, blooming, thriving, in fine fettle; informal in the pink. **2** *all is not well* **satisfactory,** all right, fine, in order, as it should be, acceptable; informal OK, okay, hunky-dory.
> – ANTONYMS unwell, unsatisfactory.

▶ **exclamation** used to express surprise, anger, resignation, etc., or when pausing in speech.
– PHRASES **as well** in addition; too. **as well** (or **just as well**) **1** with equal reason or an equally good result. **2** sensible, appropriate, or desirable. **be well up on** know a great deal about something. **leave** (or **let**) **well enough alone** refrain from interfering with or trying to improve something. **well and truly** completely.
– ORIGIN Old English.

> **USAGE**
>
> As an adverb, **well** is often used with a past participle (such as *known* or *dressed*) to form compound adjectives: **well known, well dressed**, and so on. Such adjectives should be written without a hyphen when they are used immediately after a verb (*she is well known as a writer*) but with a hyphen when they come before a noun (*a well-known writer*).

well² ▶ **noun 1** a shaft sunk into the ground to obtain water, oil, or gas. **2** a hollow made to hold liquid. **3** a plentiful source or supply: *a deep well of sympathy.* **4** an enclosed space in the middle of a building, giving room for stairs or an elevator or allowing in light or air.

– SYNONYMS **borehole,** spring, waterhole, shaft.

▶ **verb** (often **well up**) **1** (of a liquid) rise up to the surface and spill or be about to spill. **2** (of an emotion) arise and become more intense.

– SYNONYMS **flow,** spill, stream, gush, roll, cascade, flood, spout, burst, issue.

– ORIGIN Old English.

we'll /wēl/ ▶ **contraction** we will; we shall.

well-ad·vised ▶ **adjective** sensible; wise.

well-ap·point·ed ▶ **adjective** (of a building or room) having a high standard of equipment or furnishing.

well-bal·anced ▶ **adjective** mentally and emotionally stable.

well-be·ing ▶ **noun** the state of being comfortable, healthy, or happy.

well-bred ▶ **adjective** polite and well brought up.

well-built ▶ **adjective** (of a person) strong and sturdy.

– SYNONYMS **sturdy,** strapping, brawny, burly, hefty, muscular, strong, rugged; informal hunky, beefy.
– ANTONYMS puny.

well-dis·posed ▶ **adjective** having a positive, sympathetic, or friendly attitude.

well-done ▶ **adjective** **1** carried out successfully or satisfactorily. **2** (of food) thoroughly cooked. ▶ **exclamation** (**well done**) used to express congratulation or approval.

well-en·dowed ▶ **adjective** **1** having plentiful supplies of a resource. **2** (of a woman) having large breasts.

well-found·ed ▶ **adjective** based on good evidence or reasons.

well·head /ˈwelˌhed/ ▶ **noun** **1** the place where a spring comes out of the ground. **2** the structure over an oil or gas well.

well-heeled ▶ **adjective** informal rich; wealthy.

wel·ling·ton /ˈweliNGtən/ (also **wellington boot**) ▶ **noun** Brit. a knee-length waterproof rubber or plastic boot.
– ORIGIN named after the British soldier and prime minister the 1st Duke of *Wellington.*

well-known ▶ **adjective** known widely or thoroughly.

– SYNONYMS **1** *well-known principles* **familiar,** popular, common, everyday, established. **2** *a well-known family of architects* **famous,** famed, prominent, notable, renowned, distinguished, eminent, illustrious, acclaimed.
– ANTONYMS unknown.

well-mean·ing (also **well-meant**) ▶ **adjective** having good intentions but not necessarily the desired effect.

well-nigh ▶ **adverb** almost.

well-off ▶ **adjective** **1** rich; wealthy. **2** in a favorable situation.

well-oiled ▶ **adjective** **1** operating smoothly. **2** informal drunk.

well-pre·served ▶ **adjective** (of an old person) showing little sign of aging.

well-read ▶ **adjective** very knowledgeable as a result of reading widely.

well-round·ed ▶ **adjective** **1** (of a person) having a pleasingly curved or plump shape. **2** having a mature personality and varied interests: *a well-rounded student.*

well-spo·ken ▶ **adjective** speaking in an educated and refined way.

well·spring /ˈwelˌspriNG/ ▶ **noun** literary **1** a plentiful source of something: *a wellspring of creativity.* **2** the place where a spring comes out of the ground.

well-to-do ▶ **adjective** wealthy; prosperous.

well-trav·eled ▶ **adjective** **1** (of a person) having traveled widely. **2** (of a route) much used by travelers.

well-tried ▶ **adjective** having been used often and therefore known to be reliable.

well-trod·den ▶ **adjective** (of a route) much used by travelers.

well-turned ▶ **adjective** **1** (of a phrase or compliment) elegantly expressed. **2** (of a woman's ankle or leg) attractively shaped.

well-wish·er ▶ **noun** a person who feels or expresses a desire that someone else finds happiness or success.

well-worn ▶ **adjective** **1** showing signs of extensive use or wear. **2** (of a phrase or idea) used or repeated so often that it is no longer interesting or original.

Welsh /welsH/ ▶ **noun** the language of Wales.
▶ **adjective** relating to Wales.
– DERIVATIVES **Welsh·man** noun (pl. **Welshmen**) **Welsh·ness** noun **Welsh·wom·an** noun (pl. **Welshwomen**).

welsh /welsH/ (also **welch**) ▶ **verb** (**welsh on**) fail to pay a debt or fulfill an obligation.
– ORIGIN unknown.

Welsh rare·bit (also **Welsh rabbit**) ▶ **noun** another term for **RAREBIT**.

welt /welt/ ▶ **noun** **1** a ribbed, reinforced, or decorative border on an item of clothing. **2** a weal. **3** a leather rim around the edge of the upper of a shoe, to which the sole is attached.
– ORIGIN unknown.

Welt·an·schau·ung /ˈveltˌänˌsHouəNG/ ▶ **noun** (pl. **Weltanschauungen** /-sHouəNGən/) a particular philosophy or view of life.
– ORIGIN German.

wel·ter /ˈweltər/ ▶ **noun** a large confused or disorganized mass or quantity: *a welter of new regulations.*
– ORIGIN from Dutch or German *welteren* 'writhe, wallow.'

wel·ter·weight /ˈweltərˌwāt/ ▶ **noun** a weight in boxing and other sports between lightweight and middleweight.
– ORIGIN unknown.

wen /wen/ ▶ **noun** a boil or other swelling or growth on the skin.
– ORIGIN Old English.

wench /wencH/ ▶ **noun** old use or humorous a girl or young woman.
– ORIGIN from former *wenchel* 'child, servant, prostitute.'

wend /wend/ ▶ **verb** (**wend one's way**) go slowly or by an indirect route.
– ORIGIN Old English, 'to turn, depart.'

Wens·ley·dale /ˈwenzlē,dāl/ ▸ **noun** a type of white cheese with a crumbly texture.
– ORIGIN named after *Wensleydale* in Yorkshire.

went /went/ past of **GO**[1].

wept /wept/ past and past participle of **WEEP**.

were /wər/ second person singular past, plural past, and past subjunctive of **BE**.

we're /wi(ə)r/ ▸ **contraction** we are.

weren't /wər(ə)nt/ ▸ **contraction** were not.

were·wolf /ˈwe(ə)r,wo͝olf/ ▸ **noun** (pl. **werewolves**) (in folklore) a person who periodically changes into a wolf, typically when there is a full moon.
– ORIGIN Old English.

wert /wərt/ old-fashioned second person singular past of **BE**.

Wes·ley·an /ˈwezlēən, ˈwes-/ ▸ **adjective** relating to the teachings of the English preacher John Wesley or the main branch of the Methodist Church, which he founded. ▸ **noun** a follower of Wesley or of the main Methodist tradition.

west /west/ ▸ **noun 1** the direction in which the sun sets at the equinoxes, on the left-hand side of a person facing north. **2** the western part of a place. **3** (**the West**) Europe and North America seen in contrast to other civilizations. **4** (**the West**) historical the non-Communist countries of Europe and North America. **5** (**the West**) historical America's western frontier, especially during the 19th century. ▸ **adjective 1** lying toward, near, or facing the west. **2** (of a wind) blowing from the west. ▸ **adverb** to or toward the west.
– DERIVATIVES **west·bound** /ˈwest,bound/ adjective & adverb.
– ORIGIN Old English.

west·er·ly /ˈwestərlē/ ▸ **adjective & adverb 1** facing or moving toward the west. **2** (of a wind) blowing from the west. ▸ **noun** (pl. **westerlies**) a wind blowing from the west.

west·ern /ˈwestərn/ ▸ **adjective 1** situated in, directed toward, or facing the west. **2** (usu. **Western**) coming from or typical of the West, in particular Europe and North America. ▸ **noun** a movie or novel about cowboys in western North America.
– DERIVATIVES **west·ern·most** /-,mōst/ adjective.

West·ern Church ▸ **noun** the part of the Christian Church originating in the Western Roman Empire, including the Roman Catholic, Anglican, Lutheran, and Reformed Churches.

West·ern·er /ˈwestərnər/ ▸ **noun** a person from the west, especially from western Europe or North America.

west·ern·ize /ˈwestər,nīz/ ▸ **verb** bring a country, system, etc., under the influence of the cultural, economic, or political systems of Europe and North America.
– DERIVATIVES **west·ern·i·za·tion** /,westərniˈzāsʜən/ noun **west·ern·iz·er** noun.

West In·di·an ▸ **noun** a person from the West Indies, or a person of West Indian descent. ▸ **adjective** relating to the West Indies.

west-north·west ▸ **noun** the direction midway between west and northwest.

west-south·west ▸ **noun** the direction midway between west and southwest.

west·ward /ˈwestwərd/ ▸ **adjective** toward the west. ▸ **adverb** (also **westwards**) in a westerly direction.

wet /wet/ ▸ **adjective** (**wetter, wettest**) **1** covered or saturated with liquid. **2** (of the weather) rainy. **3** (of paint, ink, etc.) not yet having dried or hardened. **4** (of a process) involving the use of water or liquid. **5** informal (of an area) allowing the free sale of alcoholic drink.

> – SYNONYMS **1 damp,** moist, soaked, drenched, saturated, sopping, dripping, soggy, waterlogged. **2 rainy,** pouring, teeming, showery, drizzly. **3 sticky,** tacky.

▸ **verb** (**wets, wetting;** past and past part. **wet** or **wetted**) **1** cover or touch someone or something with liquid. **2** urinate in or on something. **3** (**wet oneself**) urinate without intending to.

> – SYNONYMS **dampen,** moisten, sprinkle, spray, splash, soak, saturate, flood, douse, drench.
> – ANTONYMS dry.

▸ **noun 1** (**the wet**) rainy weather. **2** liquid that makes something damp.
– DERIVATIVES **wet·ly** adverb **wet·ness** noun.
– PHRASES **all wet** informal completely wrong. **wet behind the ears** informal lacking experience; immature. **wet one's whistle** informal have a drink.
– ORIGIN Old English.

WORD TOOLKIT

wet ...	damp ...	moist ...
weather	cloth	eyes
grass	basement	skin
sand	cave	towelette
snow	climate	gauze
dog	walls	breath

wet·back /ˈwet,bak/ ▸ **noun** informal, derogatory a Mexican living in the US, especially one who is an illegal immigrant.
– ORIGIN so named from the practice of swimming the Rio Grande to reach the US.

wet blan·ket ▸ **noun** informal a person who spoils other people's enjoyment by being disapproving or unenthusiastic.

wet dream ▸ **noun** an erotic dream that causes a man to involuntarily ejaculate semen.

wet fly ▸ **noun** an artificial fishing fly designed to sink below the surface of the water.

weth·er /ˈwe<u>TH</u>ər/ ▸ **noun** a castrated ram.
– ORIGIN Old English.

wet·land /ˈwet,land, -lənd/ ▸ **noun** (also **wetlands**) swampy or marshy land.

wet nurse ▸ **noun** chiefly historical a woman employed to breastfeed another woman's child. ▸ **verb** (**wet-nurse**) **1** act as a wet nurse to. **2** informal look after someone as if they were a helpless infant: *I have no intention of wet-nursing you prima donnas.*

wet·suit /ˈwet,so͞ot/ ▸ **noun** a close-fitting rubber garment covering the entire body, worn for warmth in water sports or diving.

we've /wēv/ ▸ **contraction** we have.

whack /(h)wak/ informal ▸ **verb 1** strike someone or something forcefully with a sharp blow. **2** put something somewhere roughly or carelessly. **3** defeat an opponent heavily. ▸ **noun 1** a sharp or resounding blow. **2** a try or attempt.
– PHRASES **out of whack** not working correctly. **top** (or **full**) **whack** chiefly Brit. the maximum price or rate.
– ORIGIN imitating the sound.

whack·o ▸ adjective & noun (pl. **whackos**) variant spelling of WACKO.

whack·y ▸ adjective variant spelling of WACKY.

whale[1] /(h)wāl/ ▸ noun (pl. same or **whales**) a very large sea mammal with a horizontal tail fin and a blowhole on top of the head for breathing.
– PHRASES **a whale of a ——** informal an extremely good example of something. **have a whale of a time** informal enjoy oneself very much.
– ORIGIN Old English.

whale[2] ▸ verb informal beat; hit.
– ORIGIN variant of WALE.

whale·bone /'(h)wāl,bōn/ ▸ noun **1** a horny substance that grows in a series of thin parallel plates in the upper jaw of some whales and is used by them to strain plankton from the seawater. **2** strips of this substance, formerly used to stiffen corsets.

whal·er /'(h)wālər/ ▸ noun **1** a ship used for hunting whales. **2** a sailor whose job is to hunt whales.

whal·ing /'(h)wāliNG/ ▸ noun the practice or industry of hunting and killing whales for their oil, meat, or whalebone.

wham /(h)wam/ informal ▸ exclamation used to express the sound of a forceful impact or the idea of a sudden and dramatic event. ▸ verb (**whams, whamming, whammed**) strike something forcefully.

wham·my /'(h)wamē/ ▸ noun (pl. **whammies**) informal **1** an event with a powerful and unpleasant effect; a blow. **2** an evil or unlucky influence; a curse: *I think that guy put the whammy on me.*

whap /(h)wap/ ▸ verb (**whaps, whapping, whapped**) & noun variant spelling of WHOP.

wharf /(h)wôrf/ ▸ noun (pl. **wharves** /(h)wôrvz/ or **wharfs**) a level quayside area to which a ship may be moored to load and unload.

– SYNONYMS **quay,** pier, dock, berth, landing, jetty, harbor, dockyard.

– ORIGIN Old English.

what /(h)wət, (h)wät/ ▸ pronoun & determiner **1** asking for information specifying something. **2** (as pronoun) asking for repetition of something not heard or confirmation of something not understood. **3** (as pronoun) the thing or things that. **4** no matter what; whatever. **5** used to emphasize something surprising or remarkable. ▸ adverb to what extent?
– PHRASES **give someone what for** informal punish or scold someone severely. **what for?** informal for what reason? **what's what** informal what is useful or important. **what with** because of.
– ORIGIN Old English.

what·cha·ma·call·it /'(h)wəCHəmə,kôlit, '(h)wä-/ ▸ noun informal a person or thing whose name one has forgotten, does not know, or does not wish to mention.

what·ev·er /(h)wət'evər, ˌ(h)wät-/ ▸ pronoun & determiner used to emphasize a lack of restriction in referring to any thing; no matter what. ▸ pronoun used for emphasis instead of 'what' in questions. ▸ adverb **1** at all; of any kind. **2** informal no matter what happens.

what·not /'(h)wət,nät, '(h)wät-/ ▸ noun informal used to refer to an unidentified item or items having something in common with items already named.

whats·it /'(h)wətsit, '(h)wät-/ ▸ noun informal a person or thing whose name one cannot remember, does not know, or does not wish to specify.

what·so·ev·er /ˌ(h)wətsō'evər, ˌ(h)wät-/ ▸ adverb at all. ▸ determiner & pronoun old use whatever.

wheal /(h)wēl/ ▸ noun variant spelling of WEAL[1].

wheat /(h)wēt/ ▸ noun a cereal widely grown in temperate countries, the grain of which is ground to make flour.
– ORIGIN Old English, related to WHITE.

wheat·ear /'(h)wēt,ir/ ▸ noun a songbird with black and gray, buff, or white plumage and a white rump.
– ORIGIN apparently from WHITE + ARSE.

wheat·en /'(h)wētn/ ▸ adjective made of wheat.

wheat germ ▸ noun a nutritious foodstuff consisting of the center parts of grains of wheat.

wheat·grass /'(h)wēt,gras/ ▸ noun a relative of couch grass that is cultivated for its nutritional benefits.

whee·dle /'(h)wēdl/ ▸ verb use endearments or flattery to persuade someone to do something.
– ORIGIN perhaps from German *wedeln* 'cringe, fawn.'

wheel /(h)wēl/ ▸ noun **1** a circular object that revolves on an axle, fixed below a vehicle to enable it to move along or forming part of a machine. **2** something resembling a wheel or having a wheel as its essential part. **3** (**the wheel**) a steering wheel. **4** (**wheels**) informal a car. **5** a turn or rotation. **6** a recurring cycle of events: *he attempted to stop the wheel of history.* ▸ verb **1** push or pull something with wheels. **2** carry or convey on something with wheels: *she was wheeled into the operating room.* **3** fly or turn in a wide circle or curve. **4** turn around quickly to face another way. **5** (**wheel something out**) informal resort to something that has been frequently seen or heard before.

– SYNONYMS **1 push,** trundle, roll. **2** *gulls wheeled overhead* **turn,** go around, circle, orbit.

– PHRASES **wheel and deal** take part in commercial or political scheming. **the wheel of Fortune** the wheel that the goddess Fortune is represented as turning as a symbol of random luck or change. **wheels within wheels** secret or indirect influences affecting a complex situation.
– ORIGIN Old English.

wheel·bar·row /'(h)wēl,barō/ ▸ noun a small cart with a single wheel at the front and two supporting legs and two handles at the rear, used for carrying loads in building or gardening.

wheel·base /'(h)wēl,bās/ ▸ noun the distance between the front and rear axles of a vehicle.

wheel·chair /'(h)wēl,CHe(ə)r/ ▸ noun a chair on wheels for use by a person who cannot walk as the result of an illness, accident, etc.

wheel·er /'(h)wēlər/ ▸ noun (in combination) a vehicle having a specified number of wheels: *a three-wheeler.*

wheel·er-deal·er (also **wheeler and dealer**) ▸ noun a person who takes part in commercial or political scheming.
– DERIVATIVES **wheel·er-deal·ing** noun.

wheel·house /'(h)wēl,hous/ ▸ noun a shelter for the person at the wheel of a boat or ship.

wheel·ie /'(h)wēlē/ ▸ noun informal a maneuver in which a bicycle or motorcycle is ridden for a short distance with the front wheel raised off the ground.

wheel·spin /'(h)wēl,spin/ ▶ **noun** the rotation of a vehicle's wheels without movement of the vehicle forward or backward.

wheel·wright /'(h)wēl,rīt/ ▶ **noun** chiefly historical a person who makes or repairs wooden wheels.

wheeze /(h)wēz/ ▶ **verb 1** breathe with a whistling or rattling sound in the chest, as a result of a blockage in the air passages. **2** (of a device) make an irregular rattling or spluttering sound.

– SYNONYMS **gasp,** whistle, hiss, rasp, croak, pant, cough.

▶ **noun** a sound of a person wheezing.
– DERIVATIVES **wheez·i·ly** adverb **wheez·i·ness** noun **wheez·y** adjective.
– ORIGIN probably from an Old Norse word meaning 'to hiss.'

whelk /(h)welk/ ▶ **noun** a large edible marine snail with a spiral shell that tapers into a long tubelike extension.
– ORIGIN Old English.

whelp /(h)welp/ ▶ **noun** chiefly old use **1** a puppy. **2** derogatory a boy or young man. ▶ **verb** give birth to a puppy.
– ORIGIN Old English.

when /(h)wen/ ▶ **adverb 1** at what time? **2** how soon? **3** in what circumstances? **4** at which time or in which situation. ▶ **conjunction 1** at or during the time that. **2** at any time that; whenever. **3** after which; and just then. **4** in view of the fact that. **5** although; whereas.
– ORIGIN Old English.

whence /(h)wens/ (also **from whence**) ▶ **adverb** formal or old use **1** from what place or source? **2** from which; from where. **3** to the place from which. **4** as a consequence of which.

when·ev·er /(h)wən'evər/ ▶ **conjunction 1** at whatever time; on whatever occasion. **2** every time that. ▶ **adverb** used for emphasis instead of 'when' in questions.

when·so·ev·er /,(h)wensō'evər/ ▶ **conjunction & adverb** formal word for **WHENEVER**.

where /(h)we(ə)r/ ▶ **adverb 1** in or to what place or position? **2** in what direction or respect? **3** at, in, or to which. **4** the place or situation in which. **5** in or to a place or situation in which.
– ORIGIN Old English.

where·a·bouts /'(h)we(ə)rə,bouts/ ▶ **adverb** where or approximately where? ▶ **noun** (treated as sing. or pl.) the place where someone or something is.

– SYNONYMS **location,** position, site, situation, spot, point, home, address, neighborhood.

where·af·ter /(h)we(ə)r'aftər/ ▶ **adverb** formal after which.

where·as /(h)we(ə)r'az/ ▶ **conjunction 1** in contrast or comparison with the fact that. **2** taking into consideration the fact that.

where·at /(h)we(ə)r'at/ ▶ **adverb & conjunction** old use or formal at which.

where·by /(h)we(ə)r'bī/ ▶ **adverb** by which.

where·fore /'(h)we(ə)r,fôr/ old use ▶ **adverb** for what reason? ▶ **adverb & conjunction** as a result of which.

where·from /,(h)we(ə)r'frəm/ ▶ **adverb** old use from which or from where.

where·in /(h)we(ə)r'in/ ▶ **adverb** formal **1** in which. **2** in what place or respect?

where·of /(h)we'räv, -'əv/ ▶ **adverb** formal of what or which.

where·on /(h)we(ə)r'än, -'ôn/ ▶ **adverb** old use on which.

where·so·ev·er /,(h)we(ə)rsō'evər/ ▶ **adverb & conjunction** formal word for **WHEREVER**.

where·to /(h)we(ə)r'to͞o/ ▶ **adverb** old use or formal to which.

where·up·on /,(h)we(ə)rə'pän, -'pôn/ ▶ **conjunction** immediately after which.

wher·ev·er /(h)we(ə)r'evər/ ▶ **adverb 1** in or to whatever place. **2** used for emphasis instead of 'where' in questions. ▶ **conjunction** in every case when.

where·with /(h)we(ə)r'wiᴛʜ, -'wiᴛʜ/ ▶ **adverb** formal or old use with or by which.

where·with·al /'(h)we(ə)rwiᴛʜ,ôl, -wiᴛʜ-/ ▶ **noun** the money or other resources needed for a particular purpose.

wher·ry /'(h)werē/ ▶ **noun** (pl. **wherries**) **1** a light rowboat used chiefly for carrying passengers. **2** Brit. a large, light barge.
– ORIGIN unknown.

whet /(h)wet/ ▶ **verb** (**whets, whetting, whetted**) **1** sharpen the blade of a tool or weapon. **2** arouse or stimulate someone's desire, interest, or appetite.
– ORIGIN Old English.

wheth·er /'(h)weᴛʜər/ ▶ **conjunction 1** expressing a doubt or choice between alternatives. **2** expressing an inquiry or investigation. **3** indicating that a statement applies whichever of the alternatives mentioned is the case.
– ORIGIN Old English.

USAGE

For an explanation of the use of **whether** and **if**, see the note at **IF**.

whet·stone /'(h)wet,stōn/ ▶ **noun** a fine-grained stone used to sharpen cutting tools.

whey /(h)wā/ ▶ **noun** the watery part of milk that remains after curds have formed.
– ORIGIN Old English.

whey-faced ▶ **adjective** (of a person) pale.

which /(h)wiᴄʜ/ ▶ **pronoun & determiner 1** asking for information specifying one or more people or things from a definite set. **2** used to refer to something previously mentioned when introducing a clause giving further information.
– ORIGIN Old English.

USAGE

For an explanation of the difference in use between **which** and **that**, see the note at **THAT**.

which·ev·er /,(h)wiᴄʜ'evər/ ▶ **determiner & pronoun 1** used to emphasize a lack of restriction in selecting one of a definite set of alternatives. **2** regardless of which.

whick·er /'(h)wikər/ ▶ **verb** (of a horse) give a soft breathy whinny. ▶ **noun** a sound of this type.
– ORIGIN imitating the sound.

whiff /(h)wif/ ▶ **noun 1** a smell that is smelled only briefly or faintly. **2** a trace or hint of something bad or exciting: *a whiff of danger*. **3** a puff or breath of air or smoke. ▶ **verb** get a brief or faint smell of something.
– ORIGIN imitating the sound of sniffing.

whif·fle /'(h)wifəl/ ▶ **verb 1** blow or move lightly. **2** make a soft sound. ▶ **noun** a slight movement of air.

Whig /(h)wig/ ▸ **noun 1** a member of a British political party that was succeeded in the 19th century by the Liberal Party. **2** an American colonist who supported the American Revolution. **3** a member of an American political party in the 19th century that was succeeded by the Republican Party.
– DERIVATIVES **Whig·gish** adjective **Whig·gism** noun.
– ORIGIN probably a shortening of Scots *whiggamore*, the nickname of 17th-century Scottish rebels, from *whig* 'to drive' + **MARE**[1].

while /(h)wīl/ ▸ **noun 1** (**a while**) a period of time. **2** (**a while**) for some time. **3** (**the while**) at the same time; meanwhile. **4** (**the while**) literary during the time that.

> – SYNONYMS *we chatted for a while* **time,** spell, stretch, stint, span, interval, period.

▸ **conjunction 1** at the same time as. **2** whereas (indicating a contrast). **3** although.
▸ **adverb** during which.
▸ **verb** (**while something away**) pass time in a leisurely way.

> – SYNONYMS *tennis helped to **while away** the time* **pass,** spend, occupy, use up, kill.

– PHRASES **worth while** (or **worth one's while**) worth the time or effort spent.
– ORIGIN Old English.

whilst /(h)wīlst/ ▸ **conjunction & adverb** chiefly Brit. while.

whim /(h)wim/ ▸ **noun** a sudden desire or change of mind.

> – SYNONYMS **impulse,** urge, notion, fancy, inclination, caprice, vagary.

– ORIGIN unknown.

whim·brel /ˈ(h)wimbrəl/ ▸ **noun** a small curlew with a striped crown and a trilling call.
– ORIGIN perhaps from **WHIMPER** (imitating the bird's call).

whim·per /ˈ(h)wimpər/ ▸ **verb** make a series of low, feeble sounds expressing fear, pain, or discontent.

> – SYNONYMS **whine,** cry, sob, moan, snivel, wail, groan.

▸ **noun** a whimpering sound.
– ORIGIN imitating the sound.

whim·si·cal /ˈ(h)wimzikəl/ ▸ **adjective 1** playfully unusual or fanciful: *a whimsical sense of humor.* **2** showing sudden changes of behavior.

> – SYNONYMS **fanciful,** playful, mischievous, waggish, quaint, curious, droll, eccentric, quirky, idiosyncratic, unconventional.

– DERIVATIVES **whim·si·cal·i·ty** noun **whim·si·cal·ly** adverb.

whim·sy /ˈ(h)wimzē/ (also **whimsey**) ▸ **noun** (pl. **whimsies** or **whimseys**) **1** playfully unusual or fanciful behavior or humor. **2** a fanciful or odd thing. **3** a whim.
– ORIGIN probably from former *whim-wham* 'trinket, whim.'

whine /(h)wīn/ ▸ **verb 1** give or make a long, high-pitched complaining cry. **2** (especially of a machine) make a long, high-pitched unpleasant sound. **3** complain in a petulant way.

> – SYNONYMS **1 wail,** whimper, cry, mewl, moan, howl, yowl. **2 complain,** grouse, grouch, grumble, moan, carp; informal gripe, bellyache, whinge.

▸ **noun 1** a whining cry or sound. **2** a petulant complaint.
– DERIVATIVES **whin·er** noun **whin·y** (also **whiney**) adjective.
– ORIGIN Old English, 'whistle through the air.'

whinge /(h)winj/ Brit. informal ▸ **verb** (**whinges, whingeing, whinged**) complain persistently and peevishly. ▸ **noun** an act of whingeing.
– DERIVATIVES **whing·er** noun.
– ORIGIN Old English.

whin·ny /ˈ(h)winē/ ▸ **noun** (pl. **whinnies**) a gentle, high-pitched neigh. ▸ **verb** (**whinnies, whinnying, whinnied**) (of a horse) make such a sound.
– ORIGIN imitating the sound.

whip /(h)wip/ ▸ **noun 1** a strip of leather or length of cord fastened to a handle, used for beating a person or urging on an animal. **2** an official of a political party appointed to maintain discipline among its members in Congress or Parliament, especially to ensure attendance and voting. **3** a dessert made from cream or eggs beaten into a light fluffy mass.

> – SYNONYMS **lash,** scourge, strap, belt.

▸ **verb** (**whips, whipping, whipped**) **1** beat a person or animal with a whip. **2** (of a flexible object or rain or wind) strike or beat violently: *the wind whipped their faces.* **3** move or take something out fast or suddenly. **4** beat cream, eggs, etc., into a froth.

> – SYNONYMS **1 flog,** lash, flagellate, cane, belt, thrash, beat; informal tan someone's hide. **2 whisk,** beat. **3 rouse,** stir up, excite, galvanize, electrify, stimulate, inspire, fire up, inflame, provoke.

– DERIVATIVES **whip·per** noun **whip·ping** noun.
– PHRASES **the whip hand** a position of power or control. **whip someone/thing up 1** make or prepare something very quickly. **2** deliberately excite or provoke someone. **3** stimulate a particular feeling in someone.
– ORIGIN probably from German and Dutch *wippen* 'swing, leap, dance.'

whip·cord /ˈ(h)wipˌkôrd/ ▸ **noun 1** thin, tough, tightly twisted cord used for making the flexible end part of whips. **2** a closely woven ribbed fabric.

whip·lash /ˈ(h)wipˌlasʜ/ ▸ **noun 1** the lashing action of a whip. **2** injury caused by a severe jerk to the head.

whip·per·snap·per /ˈ(h)wipərˌsnapər/ ▸ **noun** dated informal a young and inexperienced person who is disrespectful or overconfident.
– ORIGIN perhaps representing *whipsnapper*, expressing noise and unimportance.

whip·pet /ˈ(h)wipit/ ▸ **noun** a small slender breed of dog used in racing.
– ORIGIN partly from former *whippet* 'move briskly.'

whip·ping boy ▸ **noun** a person who is blamed or punished for other people's faults or mistakes.
– ORIGIN first referring to a boy educated with a young prince and punished instead of him.

whip·poor·will /ˈ(h)wipərˌwil/ ▸ **noun** a North and Central American nightjar with a distinctive call.
– ORIGIN imitating its call.

whip·py /ˈ(h)wipē/ ▸ **adjective** flexible; springy.

whip·saw /ˈ(h)wipˌsô/ ▸ **noun** a saw with a narrow blade and a handle at both ends. ▸ **verb** (past part. **whipsawn** or **whipsawed**) **1** cut something with a whipsaw. **2** informal subject someone or something to two difficult situations or opposing pressures at the same time.

whir /(h)wər/ (also **whirr**) ▸ **verb** (**whirrs, whirring, whirred**) (of something rapidly rotating or moving to and fro) make a low, continuous, regular sound.
▸ **noun** a whirring sound.
– ORIGIN probably Scandinavian.

whirl /(h)wərl/ ▶ **verb 1** move rapidly around and around. **2** (of the head or mind) seem to spin around.

– SYNONYMS **rotate,** circle, wheel, turn, revolve, orbit, spin, twirl, pirouette, gyrate.

▶ **noun 1** a rapid movement around and around. **2** frantic activity: *the mad social whirl.*
– PHRASES **give something a whirl** informal give something a try. **in a whirl** in a state of confusion.
– ORIGIN probably from an Old Norse word meaning 'turn about.'

whirl·i·gig /ˈ(h)wərlē,gig/ ▶ **noun 1** an object, especially a toy, that spins around, e.g., a top or pinwheel. **2** a process or activity characterized by constant change or hectic activity. **3** chiefly Brit. another term for **MERRY-GO-ROUND**. **4** (also **whirligig beetle**) a small black water beetle that typically swims rapidly in circles on the surface.
– ORIGIN from **WHIRL** + former *gig* 'toy for whipping.'

whirl·pool /ˈ(h)wərl,po͞ol/ ▶ **noun 1** a quickly rotating mass of water in a river that may draw floating objects toward its center. **2** (also **whirlpool bath**) a heated pool in which hot bubbling water is continuously circulated.

– SYNONYMS **eddy,** vortex, maelstrom.

whirl·wind /ˈ(h)wərl,wind/ ▶ **noun 1** a column of air moving rapidly around and around in a cylindrical or funnel shape. **2** a situation in which many things happen very quickly: *a whirlwind of activity.*

– SYNONYMS **tornado,** hurricane, typhoon, cyclone, vortex; informal twister.

▶ **adjective** happening very quickly or suddenly: *a whirlwind romance.*

– SYNONYMS **rapid,** lightning, headlong, impulsive, breakneck, meteoric, sudden, swift, fast, quick, speedy.

whisk /(h)wisk/ ▶ **verb 1** move or take suddenly and quickly: *he whisked her off to Paris.* **2** beat a substance with a light, rapid movement.

– SYNONYMS **1 speed,** hurry, rush, sweep, hurtle, shoot. **2 pull,** snatch, pluck, tug, jerk; informal whip, yank. **3 whip,** beat, mix.

▶ **noun 1** a utensil for whisking eggs or cream. **2** (also **whisk broom**) a small, stiff, short-handled broom used especially to brush clothing or upholstery. **3** a bunch of grass, twigs, or bristles for flicking away dust or flies. **4** a brief, rapid action or movement.

– SYNONYMS **beater,** mixer, blender.

– ORIGIN Scandinavian.

whisk broom ▶ **noun** a small, stiff broom used especially to brush clothing.

whis·ker /ˈ(h)wiskər/ ▶ **noun 1** a long hair or bristle growing from the face or snout of an animal. **2** (**whiskers**) the hair growing on a man's face. **3** (**a whisker**) informal a very small amount.
– DERIVATIVES **whis·kered** adjective **whis·ker·y** adjective.
– ORIGIN from **WHISK**.

whis·key /ˈ(h)wiskē/ (also chiefly Brit. **whisky**) ▶ **noun** (pl. **whiskeys, whiskies**) a liquor distilled from malted grain, especially barley or rye.
– ORIGIN from Irish and Scottish Gaelic *uisge beatha* 'water of life.'

whis·per /ˈ(h)wispər/ ▶ **verb 1** speak very softly. **2** literary rustle or murmur softly.

– SYNONYMS **murmur,** mutter, mumble, speak softly, breathe, say sotto voce.

▶ **noun 1** a whispered word or phrase, or a whispering tone of voice. **2** literary a soft rustling or murmuring sound. **3** a rumor or piece of gossip. **4** a slight trace.

– SYNONYMS **1 murmur,** mutter, mumble, low voice, undertone. **2 rumor,** story, report, gossip, speculation, suggestion, hint; informal buzz.
– ANTONYMS shout.

– DERIVATIVES **whis·per·er** noun **whis·per·y** adjective.
– ORIGIN Old English.

whis·per·ing cam·paign ▶ **noun** an attempt to damage someone's reputation by systematically circulating a rumor about them.

whist /(h)wist/ ▶ **noun** a card game in which points are scored according to the number of tricks won.
– ORIGIN earlier as *whisk*: perhaps from **WHISK** (with reference to whisking away the tricks).

whis·tle /ˈ(h)wisəl/ ▶ **noun 1** a clear, high-pitched sound made by forcing breath through pursed lips, or between one's teeth. **2** any similar high-pitched sound. **3** an instrument used to produce a whistling sound.

▶ **verb 1** produce a whistle: *the crowd cheered and whistled.* **2** produce a tune by whistling. **3** blow a whistle. **4** move rapidly through the air or a narrow opening with a whistling sound. **5** (**whistle for**) wish for or expect something in vain.
– DERIVATIVES **whis·tler** noun.
– PHRASES **blow the whistle on** informal bring an illicit activity to an end by informing on the person responsible. **(as) clean as a whistle** extremely clean or clear. **whistle in the dark** pretend to be unafraid.
– ORIGIN Old English.

whis·tle-blow·er ▶ **noun** informal a person who informs on someone engaged in an illicit activity.

whis·tle-stop ▶ **adjective** very fast and with only brief pauses.

whit /(h)wit/ ▶ **noun** a very small part or amount.
– PHRASES **not a whit** not at all.
– ORIGIN apparently from an Old English word meaning 'creature, small amount.'

white /(h)wīt/ ▶ **adjective 1** of the color of milk or fresh snow. **2** very pale. **3** relating to the human group having light-colored skin. **4** (of food such as bread or rice) light in color through having been refined. **5** (of wine) made from white grapes, or dark grapes with the skins removed, and having a yellowish color. **6** morally or spiritually pure. **7** Brit. (of coffee or tea) served with milk or cream.

– SYNONYMS **pale,** pallid, wan, ashen, chalky, pasty, peaked, washed out, ghostly, deathly.

▶ **noun 1** white color. **2** (also **whites**) white clothes or material. **3** the visible pale part of the eyeball around the iris. **4** the outer part that surrounds the yolk of an egg; the albumen. **5** a member of a light-skinned people. **6** a white or cream butterfly.

▶ **verb** (**white something out**) cover a mistake with white correction fluid.
– DERIVATIVES **white·ly** adverb **white·ness** noun **whit·ish** adjective.
– PHRASES **bleed someone/thing white** drain someone or something of wealth or resources. **whited sepulcher** literary a hypocrite. [with biblical reference to the Gospel of Matthew, chapter 23.]
– ORIGIN Old English, related to **WHEAT**.

white ant ▶ **noun** another term for **TERMITE**.

white·bait /ˈ(h)wīt,bāt/ ▶ **noun** the small silvery-white young of herrings, sprats, and similar sea fish as food.

white·beam /ˈ(h)wīt͵bēm/ ▸ **noun** a tree related to the rowan, with red berries and hairy oval leaves that are white underneath.

white belt ▸ **noun** a white belt worn by a beginner in judo or karate.

white blood cell ▸ **noun** less technical term for LEUKOCYTE.

white·board /ˈ(h)wīt͵bôrd/ ▸ **noun** a wipeable board with a white surface used for teaching or presentations.

white-bread ▸ **adjective** informal bland and unchallenging in a way thought characteristic of the white middle classes.

white·cap /ˈ(h)wīt͵kap/ ▸ **noun** a small wave with a foamy white crest.

white cell ▸ **noun** less technical term for LEUKOCYTE.

white Christ·mas ▸ **noun** a Christmas during which there is snow on the ground.

white-col·lar ▸ **adjective** relating to the work done or people who work in an office or other professional environment.

white dwarf ▸ **noun** Astronomy a small, very dense star.

white el·e·phant ▸ **noun** a possession that is useless or unwanted, especially one that is expensive to maintain.
– ORIGIN from the story that the kings of Siam (now Thailand) gave such animals to courtiers they disliked, in order to ruin the recipient by the great cost involved in maintaining the animal.

white·fish /ˈ(h)wīt͵fisʜ/ ▸ **noun** (pl. same or **whitefishes**) a mainly freshwater fish of the salmon family, widely used as food.

white flag ▸ **noun** a white flag or cloth used as a symbol of surrender, truce, or a wish to negotiate.

white·fly /ˈ(h)wīt͵flī/ ▸ **noun** (pl. **whiteflies**) a minute winged bug covered with powdery white wax, damaging plants by feeding on sap and coating them with honeydew.

white gold ▸ **noun** a silver-colored alloy of gold with another metal.

white goods ▸ **plural noun** large domestic electrical goods such as refrigerators and washing machines. Compare with BROWN GOODS.

white·head /ˈ(h)wīt͵(h)ed/ ▸ **noun** informal a pale or white-topped pustule on the skin.

white heat ▸ **noun** the temperature or state of something that is so hot that it gives out white light.

white hope (also **great white hope**) ▸ **noun** a person expected to bring much success to a team or organization.
– ORIGIN first referring to a white boxer believed capable of beating the first black world heavyweight champion.

white hors·es ▸ **plural noun** white-crested waves at sea.

white-hot ▸ **adjective** so hot as to glow white.

white knight ▸ **noun** a person or thing that comes to someone's aid.

white-knuck·le ▸ **adjective** causing fear or nervous excitement.
– ORIGIN with reference to the effect caused by gripping tightly to steady oneself on a fairground ride.

white lie ▸ **noun** a harmless lie told to avoid hurting someone's feelings.

white light ▸ **noun** apparently colorless light containing all the wavelengths of the visible spectrum at equal intensity (such as ordinary daylight).

white mag·ic ▸ **noun** magic used only for good purposes.

white meat ▸ **noun** pale meat such as the breast meat of chicken or turkey.

whit·en /ˈ(h)wītn/ ▸ **verb** make or become white.
– DERIVATIVES **whit·en·er** noun.

white noise ▸ **noun** noise containing many frequencies with equal intensities.

white·out /ˈ(h)wīt͵out/ ▸ **noun 1** a dense blizzard. **2** a weather condition in which the features and horizon of snow-covered country are indistinguishable.

white pa·per ▸ **noun** an official report giving information or proposals on a particular issue.

White Rus·sian ▸ **noun 1** dated a person from Belarus (formerly Belorussia) in eastern Europe. **2** an opponent of the Bolsheviks during the Russian Civil War. **3** a cocktail made from vodka, coffee liquor, and cream or milk. ▸ **adjective** relating to White Russians.

white sale ▸ **noun** a store's sale of household linens.

white sauce ▸ **noun** a sauce consisting of flour blended and cooked with butter and milk or stock.

white slave ▸ **noun** dated a white girl or woman tricked or forced into prostitution in a foreign country.

white spir·it ▸ **noun** Brit. a colorless liquid distilled from petroleum, used as a paint thinner and solvent.

white su·prem·a·cy ▸ **noun** the belief that white people are superior to those of all other races.
– DERIVATIVES **white su·prem·a·cist** noun & adjective.

white tie ▸ **noun 1** a white bow tie worn by men as part of full evening dress. **2** a man's full evening dress. ▸ **adjective** (of an event) requiring full evening dress to be worn.

white trash ▸ **noun** derogatory poor white people.

white·wash /ˈ(h)wīt͵wäsʜ, -͵wôsʜ/ ▸ **noun 1** a solution of lime or chalk and water, used for painting walls white. **2** a deliberate concealment of someone's mistakes or faults. **3** informal a victory by the same side in every game of a series. ▸ **verb 1** paint something with whitewash. **2** conceal unpleasant or incriminating facts about: *the editor and his newspaper have whitewashed the past.* **3** informal defeat an opposing side with a whitewash.

whitewa·ter /(h)wītˈwôtər, -ˈwä-/ ▸ **noun** a fast shallow stretch of water in a river.

white wed·ding ▸ **noun** Brit. a traditional wedding at which the bride wears a formal white dress.

white witch ▸ **noun** a person who uses witchcraft to help other people.

whit·ey /ˈ(h)wītē/ ▸ **noun** (pl. **whiteys**) informal, derogatory a white person.

whith·er /ˈ(h)wiᴛʜər/ old use or literary ▸ **adverb 1** to what place or state? **2** what is the likely future of? **3** to which (with reference to a place). **4** to whatever place.
– ORIGIN Old English.

whit·ing¹ /ˈ(h)wītiɴɢ/ ▸ **noun** (pl. same) a slender-bodied sea fish with edible white flesh.
– ORIGIN Dutch *wijting*.

whit·ing² ▸ **noun** ground chalk used for purposes such as whitewashing and cleaning metal plate.

whit·low /ˈ(h)witˌlō/ ▶ **noun** an abscess in the soft tissue near a fingernail or toenail.
– ORIGIN apparently from **WHITE** + **FLAW**.

Whit·sun·day ▶ **noun** another term for **PENTECOST** (sense 1).
– ORIGIN Old English, 'white Sunday,' probably with reference to the white robes worn by the newly baptized at Pentecost.

whit·tle /ˈ(h)witl/ ▶ **verb 1** form a piece of wood into an object by repeatedly cutting small slices from it. **2** (**whittle something away/down**) reduce something by degrees.
– ORIGIN from dialect *whittle* 'knife,' from an Old English word meaning 'cut, cut off.'

whiz /(h)wiz/ (also **whizz**) ▶ **verb** (**whizzes, whizzing, whizzed**) **1** move quickly through the air with a whistling sound. **2** move or go fast. **3** (**whiz through**) do or deal with something quickly. ▶ **noun 1** a whizzing sound. **2** informal a fast movement or brief journey. **3** (also **wiz**) informal a person who is extremely clever at something.
– DERIVATIVES **whiz·zy** adjective.
– ORIGIN imitating the sound.

whiz kid ▶ **noun** informal a young person who is very successful or highly skilled.

WHO ▶ **abbreviation** World Health Organization.

who /ho͞o/ ▶ **pronoun 1** what or which person or people? **2** introducing a clause giving further information about a person or people previously mentioned.
– ORIGIN Old English.

> **USAGE**
>
> According to formal grammar, **who** is used as the subject of a verb (*who decided this?*) and **whom** is used as the object of a verb or preposition (*to whom do you wish to speak?*). However, in modern English **who** is often used instead of **whom**, as in *who should we support?* and most people consider this to be acceptable.

whoa /wō/ ▶ **exclamation** used as a command to a horse to stop or slow down.

who'd /ho͞od/ ▶ **contraction 1** who had. **2** who would.

who·dun·it /ho͞oˈdənit/ (Brit. **whodunnit**) ▶ **noun** informal a story or play about a murder in which the identity of the murderer is not revealed until the end.

who·ev·er /ho͞oˈevər/ ▶ **pronoun 1** the person or people who; any person who. **2** regardless of who. **3** used for emphasis instead of 'who' in questions.

whole /hōl/ ▶ **adjective 1** complete; entire. **2** in an unbroken or undamaged state. **3** emphasizing a large extent or number: *a whole range of issues.*

> – SYNONYMS **1 entire,** complete, full, unabridged, uncut. **2 intact,** in one piece, unbroken, undamaged, flawless, unmarked, perfect.
> – ANTONYMS incomplete.

▶ **noun 1** a thing that is complete in itself. **2** (**the whole**) all of something.

> – SYNONYMS **1 entity,** unit, body, ensemble. **2** *the whole of the year* **all,** every part, the lot, the sum.

▶ **adverb** informal entirely; wholly: *a whole new meaning.*
– DERIVATIVES **whole·ness** noun.
– PHRASES **as a whole** as a single unit; in general. **on the whole** taking everything into account; in general. **the whole nine yards** informal everything possible or available.
– ORIGIN Old English.

whole·heart·ed /ˈhōlˈhärtid/ ▶ **adjective** completely sincere and committed.

> – SYNONYMS **unqualified,** unreserved, unconditional, complete, full, total, absolute.
> – ANTONYMS half-hearted.

– DERIVATIVES **whole·heart·ed·ly** adverb.

whole life in·sur·ance ▶ **noun** life insurance that pays a benefit on the death of the insured and also accumulates a cash value. Compare with **TERM LIFE INSURANCE**.

whole note ▶ **noun** a musical note having the time value of two half notes or four quarter notes, represented by a ring with no stem.

whole num·ber ▶ **noun** a number without fractions; an integer.

whole·sale /ˈhōlˌsāl/ ▶ **noun** the selling of goods in large quantities to be sold to the public by others. ▶ **adverb 1** being sold in such a way. **2** as a whole and in an indiscriminate way. ▶ **adjective** done on a large scale; extensive.

> – SYNONYMS **extensive,** widespread, large-scale, wide-ranging, comprehensive, total, mass, indiscriminate, sweeping.
> – ANTONYMS partial.

▶ **verb** sell goods wholesale.
– DERIVATIVES **whole·sal·er** noun.

whole·some /ˈhōlsəm/ ▶ **adjective 1** good for health and physical well-being. **2** morally good or beneficial.

> – SYNONYMS **1 healthy,** health-giving, good, nutritious, nourishing, natural, organic. **2 moral,** ethical, good, clean, virtuous, pure, innocent, chaste, uplifting, edifying.

– DERIVATIVES **whole·some·ly** adverb **whole·some·ness** noun.

whole step ▶ **noun** Music an interval of a (whole) tone.

whole wheat ▶ **noun** whole grains of wheat including the husk.

whol·ly /ˈhōl(l)ē/ ▶ **adverb** entirely; fully.

> – SYNONYMS **completely,** totally, absolutely, entirely, fully, thoroughly, utterly, downright, in every respect; informal one hundred percent.

whom /ho͞om/ ▶ **pronoun** used instead of 'who' as the object of a verb or preposition.

> **USAGE**
>
> For an explanation of the use of **who** and **whom**, see the note at **WHO**.

whom·ev·er /ho͞omˈevər/ ▶ **pronoun** formal used instead of 'whoever' as the object of a verb or preposition.

whomp /(h)wämp, (h)wômp/ informal ▶ **verb** strike someone or something heavily. ▶ **noun** a thump.
– ORIGIN imitating the sound.

whom·so·ev·er /ˌho͞omsōˈevər/ ▶ **relative pronoun** formal used instead of 'whosoever' as the object of a verb or preposition.

whoop /(h)wo͞op, ho͞op/ ▶ **noun** a loud cry of joy or excitement. ▶ **verb** give or make a whoop.
– PHRASES **whoop it up** informal enjoy oneself or celebrate enthusiastically.
– ORIGIN probably imitating the sound.

whoop·ee /ˈ(h)wo͝opē, ˈ(h)wo͞oˈpē/ ▶ **exclamation** informal expressing wild excitement or joy.
– PHRASES **make whoopee 1** celebrate wildly. **2** have sex.

whoop·ee cush·ion /ˈwo͝opē/ ▶ **noun** a rubber cushion that makes a sound like the breaking of wind when someone sits on it.

whoop·er swan /ˈ(h)wo͞opər, ˈho͞opər/ ▶ **noun** a large swan with a black and yellow bill and a loud trumpeting call, breeding in northern Eurasia and Greenland.

whoop·ing cough ▶ **noun** a contagious bacterial disease chiefly affecting children, characterized by convulsive coughs followed by a rasping indrawn breath.

whoop·ing crane ▶ **noun** a large mainly white crane with a trumpeting call.

whoops /wo͝ops, wo͞ops/ (also **whoops-a-daisy** /wo͝ops ə ˌdāzē, wo͞ops ə ˌdāzē/) ▶ **exclamation** informal another term for **OOPS**.
– ORIGIN probably from **UPSY-DAISY**.

whoosh /(h)wo͞osʜ, (h)wo͝osʜ/ (also **woosh**) ▶ **verb** move quickly or suddenly and with a rushing sound. ▶ **noun** a whooshing movement.
– ORIGIN imitating the sound.

whop /(h)wäp/ (also **whap**) informal ▶ **verb** (**whops, whopping, whopped**) hit someone or something hard. ▶ **noun** a heavy blow or its sound.
– ORIGIN from dialect *wap* 'strike.'

whop·per /ˈ(h)wäpər/ ▶ **noun** informal **1** a very large thing. **2** a complete or blatant lie.

whop·ping /ˈ(h)wäpiɴɢ/ ▶ **adjective** informal extremely large.

whore /hôr/ derogatory ▶ **noun 1** a prostitute. **2** a woman who has many sexual partners.
– DERIVATIVES **whor·ish** adjective.
– ORIGIN Old English.

whore·house /ˈhôrˌhous/ ▶ **noun** informal a brothel.

whorl /(h)wôrl/ ▶ **noun 1** each of the turns in the spiral shell of a mollusk. **2** a set of leaves, flowers, or branches springing from a stem at the same level and encircling it. **3** a complete circle in a fingerprint.
– DERIVATIVES **whorled** adjective.
– ORIGIN apparently from **WHIRL**.

who's /ho͞oz/ ▶ **contraction 1** who is. **2** who has.

USAGE

Do not confuse **who's** with **whose**. **Who's** is short for **who is** or **who has**, as in *he has a son who's a doctor*, or *who's locked the door?*, while **whose** means 'belonging to or associated with which person' or 'of whom or which,' as in *whose coat is this?* or *a man whose opinion I respect*.

whose /ho͞oz/ ▶ **possessive determiner & pronoun 1** belonging to or associated with which person. **2** (as possessive determiner) of whom or which.
– ORIGIN Old English.

whos·ev·er /ˌho͞ozˈevər/ ▶ **relative pronoun & determiner** belonging to or associated with whichever person; whoever's.

who·so·ev·er /ˌho͞osōˈevər/ ▶ **pronoun** formal term for **WHOEVER**.

whup /(h)wo͝op/ ▶ **verb** (**whups, whupping, whupped**) informal thrash someone or something.
– ORIGIN variant of **WHIP**.

why /(h)wī/ ▶ **adverb 1** for what reason or purpose? **2** on account of which; the reason for which. ▶ **exclamation** expressing surprise or indignation, or used for emphasis. ▶ **noun** (pl. **whys**) a reason or explanation.
– ORIGIN Old English.

WI ▶ **abbreviation 1** West Indies. **2** Wisconsin.

Wic·ca /ˈwikə/ ▶ **noun** the religious cult of modern witchcraft.
– DERIVATIVES **Wic·can** adjective & noun.
– ORIGIN Old English, 'witch.'

wick /wik/ ▶ **noun** a strip of porous material up which liquid fuel is drawn to the flame in a candle, lamp, or lighter. ▶ **verb** (usu. as adj. **wicking**) absorb or draw off liquid.
– PHRASES **get on someone's wick** Brit. informal annoy someone.
– ORIGIN Old English.

wick·ed /ˈwikid/ ▶ **adjective** (**wickeder, wickedest**) **1** evil or morally wrong. **2** playfully mischievous. **3** informal excellent; very good.

– SYNONYMS **1 evil,** sinful, immoral, wrong, bad, iniquitous, corrupt, base, vile, villainous, criminal, nefarious; informal crooked. **2 mischievous,** playful, naughty, impish, roguish, puckish, cheeky.
– ANTONYMS virtuous.

– DERIVATIVES **wick·ed·ly** adverb **wick·ed·ness** noun.
– ORIGIN probably from **WICCA**.

wick·er /ˈwikər/ ▶ **noun** flexible twigs, typically of willow, plaited or woven to make items such as furniture and baskets.
– DERIVATIVES **wick·er·work** /ˈwikərˌwərk/ noun.
– ORIGIN Scandinavian.

wick·et /ˈwikit/ ▶ **noun 1** a small door or gate, especially one beside or in a larger one. **2** one of the wire hoops on a croquet course. **3** Cricket each of the sets of three stumps with two bails across the top at either end of the pitch, defended by a batsman.
– ORIGIN Old French *wiket*.

wide /wīd/ ▶ **adjective** (**wider, widest**) **1** of great or more than average width. **2** extending a specified distance from side to side. **3** open to the full extent. **4** including a great variety of people or things. **5** spread among a large number or over a large area. **6** (in combination) extending over the whole of: *industry-wide*. **7** at a great or specified distance from a point or target.

– SYNONYMS **1 broad,** extensive, spacious, vast, spread out. **2 comprehensive,** ample, broad, extensive, wide-ranging, large, exhaustive, all-inclusive, expansive, all-embracing, encyclopedic, catholic. **3 off target,** off the mark, inaccurate.
– ANTONYMS narrow.

▶ **adverb 1** to the full extent. **2** far from a particular point or target. **3** (in field sports) at or near the side of the field.

▶ **noun** (also **wide ball**) Cricket a ball that is judged to be too wide of the stumps for the batsman to play.
– DERIVATIVES **wide·ly** adverb **wide·ness** noun.
– PHRASES **wide awake** fully awake. **wide of the mark** inaccurate.
– ORIGIN Old English.

wide-an·gle ▶ **adjective** (of a lens) having a short focal length and so covering a wider view than a standard lens.

wide ar·e·a net·work ▸ **noun** a computer network in which the computers connected may be far apart, generally having a radius of more than half a mile.

wide-eyed ▸ **adjective 1** having one's eyes wide open in amazement. **2** inexperienced; innocent.

wid·en /ˈwīdn/ ▸ **verb** make or become wider.

– SYNONYMS **broaden,** open up/out, expand, extend, enlarge.

wide-rang·ing ▸ **adjective** covering an extensive range of subjects or issues.

wide·screen /ˈwīdˌskrēn/ ▸ **noun** (often as adj.) a movie or television screen presenting a wide field of vision in relation to height: *widescreen TV*.

wide·spread /ˈwīdˈspred/ ▸ **adjective** spread among a large number or over a large area.

– SYNONYMS **general,** extensive, universal, common, global, worldwide, omnipresent, ubiquitous, across the board, predominant, prevalent, rife, broad.
– ANTONYMS limited.

widg·eon ▸ **noun** variant spelling of **WIGEON**.

widg·et /ˈwijit/ ▸ **noun** informal a small gadget or mechanical device.
– ORIGIN perhaps an alteration of **GADGET**.

wid·ow /ˈwidō/ ▸ **noun 1** a woman whose husband has died and who has not married again. **2** humorous a woman whose husband is often away taking part in a particular sport or activity: *a golf widow*. ▸ **verb** (**be widowed**) become a widow or widower.
– ORIGIN Old English.

wid·ow·er /ˈwidō-ər/ ▸ **noun** a man whose wife has died and who has not married again.

wid·ow·hood /ˈwidōˌho͝od/ ▸ **noun** the state or period of being a widow or widower.

wid·ow's mite ▸ **noun** a small monetary contribution from someone who is poor.
– ORIGIN with biblical allusion to the Gospel of Mark, chapter 12.

wid·ow's peak ▸ **noun** a V-shaped growth of hair toward the center of the forehead.

wid·ow's weeds ▸ **plural noun** black clothes worn by a widow in mourning.
– ORIGIN *weeds* is used in the former sense 'garments' and is from Old English.

width /widTH, witTH/ ▸ **noun 1** the measurement or extent of something from side to side. **2** a piece of something at its full extent from side to side. **3** wide range or extent.

– SYNONYMS **breadth,** thickness, span, diameter, girth.

width·wise /ˈwidTHˌwīz, ˈwitTH-/ (also **widthways** /ˈwidTHˌwāz, ˈwitTH-/) ▸ **adverb** in a direction parallel with a thing's width.

wield /wēld/ ▸ **verb 1** hold and use a weapon or tool. **2** have and be able to use power or influence.

– SYNONYMS **1 brandish,** flourish, wave, swing, use, employ, handle. **2** *he wields enormous power* **exercise,** exert, hold, maintain, command, control.

– DERIVATIVES **wield·er** noun.
– ORIGIN Old English, 'govern, subdue, direct.'

wie·ner /ˈwēnər/ ▸ **noun 1** a frankfurter or similar sausage. **2** another term for **WEENIE** (sense 3).

Wie·ner schnit·zel /ˈvēnər ˌsHnitsəl/ ▸ **noun** a thin slice of veal that is breaded and fried.
– ORIGIN German, 'Vienna cutlet.'

wife /wīf/ ▸ **noun** (pl. **wives** /wīvz/) **1** a married woman in relation to her husband. **2** old use a woman.

– SYNONYMS **spouse,** partner, mate, consort, bride; informal better half, missus.

– DERIVATIVES **wife·ly** adjective.
– ORIGIN Old English, 'woman.'

WORD LINKS

uxorious *very fond of one's wife*

Wi-Fi /ˈwī ˈfī/ ▸ **abbreviation** Wireless Fidelity, a set of technical standards for transmitting data over wireless networks.

wig /wig/ ▸ **noun** a covering for the head made of real or artificial hair.
– ORIGIN shortening of **PERIWIG**.

wig·eon /ˈwijən/ (also **widgeon**) ▸ **noun** a duck with reddish-brown and gray plumage, the male having a whistling call.
– ORIGIN perhaps suggested by **PIGEON**.

wig·gle /ˈwigəl/ ▸ **verb** move with short movements up and down or from side to side. ▸ **noun** a wiggling movement.
– DERIVATIVES **wig·gler** noun **wig·gly** adjective.
– ORIGIN German and Dutch *wiggelen*.

wig·wam /ˈwigˌwäm/ ▸ **noun** a dome-shaped or conical dwelling made by fastening mats, skins, or bark over a framework of poles (as used formerly by some North American Indian peoples).
– ORIGIN Algonquian, 'their house.'

wi·ki /ˈwikē/ ▸ **noun** a website that allows its users to edit its content and structure.
– ORIGIN coined by programmer Ward Cunningham, from Hawaiian *wiki-wiki* 'quick-quick.'

wild /wīld/ ▸ **adjective 1** (of animals or plants) living or growing in the natural environment; not domesticated or cultivated. **2** (of scenery or a region) not inhabited in or changed by people. **3** lacking discipline or control. **4** not civilized; primitive. **5** not based on reason or evidence. **6** (of looks, appearance, etc.) showing strong emotion. **7** informal very enthusiastic or excited. **8** informal very angry.

– SYNONYMS **1 untamed,** undomesticated, feral, fierce, ferocious, savage. **2 uncultivated,** native, indigenous. **3 uninhabited,** unpopulated, uncultivated, rugged, rough, inhospitable, desolate, barren. **4 stormy,** squally, tempestuous, turbulent, blustery. **5 uncontrolled,** unrestrained, undisciplined, unruly, rowdy, disorderly, riotous, out of control, unbridled. **6** *a wild scheme* **foolish,** ridiculous, ludicrous, stupid, foolhardy, idiotic, madcap, absurd, silly, impractical, impracticable, unworkable; informal crazy, crackpot. **7** *a wild guess* **random,** arbitrary, haphazard, uninformed.
– ANTONYMS tame, cultivated, calm, disciplined.

▸ **noun 1** (**the wild**) a natural state. **2** (also **the wilds**) a remote area with few or no inhabitants.
– DERIVATIVES **wild·ly** adverb **wild·ness** noun.
– PHRASES **run wild** grow or behave in an uncontrolled way.
– ORIGIN Old English.

wild card ▸ **noun 1** a playing card that can have any value, suit, color, or other property in a game according to the choice of the player holding it. **2** a person or thing whose qualities are uncertain. **3** Computing a character that will match any character or sequence of characters in a search. **4** an opportunity to enter a sports competition without taking part in qualifying matches or being ranked at a particular level.

wild·cat /'wīld,kat/ ▶ **noun 1** a small Eurasian and African cat, typically gray with black markings and a bushy tail, believed to be the ancestor of the domestic cat. **2** any of various North American cats, especially the bobcat. **3** an exploratory oil well. ▶ **adjective** (of a strike) sudden and unofficial.

wil·de·beest /'wildə,bēst/ ▶ **noun** (pl. same or **wildebeests**) another term for **GNU**.
– ORIGIN Afrikaans, 'wild beast.'

wil·der·ness /'wildərnis/ ▶ **noun 1** a wild, uninhabited, and inhospitable region. **2** a state of being out of political favor or office.

– SYNONYMS **wilds,** desert, wasteland.

– ORIGIN Old English, 'land inhabited only by wild animals'; related to **DEER**.

wild·fire /'wīld,fīr/ ▶ **noun** (in phrase **spread like wildfire**) spread with great speed.
– ORIGIN from *wildfire*, a highly flammable liquid formerly used in warfare.

wild·flow·er /'wīld,flou(-ə)r/ ▶ **noun** a flower of an uncultivated variety that grows freely without human intervention.

wild·fowl /'wīld,foul/ ▶ **plural noun** birds that are hunted as game, especially waterbirds.

wild goose chase ▶ **noun** a hopeless search for or pursuit of something that is impossible to find or does not exist.

wild·life /'wīld,līf/ ▶ **noun** the native animals of a region.

wild rice ▶ **noun** a tall American grass with edible grains, related to rice and growing on wet land.

Wild West the western US during its lawless early history.

wiles /wīlz/ ▶ **plural noun** cunning stratagems used by someone in order to get what they want.

– SYNONYMS **tricks,** ruses, ploys, schemes, dodges, maneuvers, subterfuges, guile, artfulness, cunning.

– ORIGIN perhaps related to an Old Norse word meaning 'craft.'

will[1] /wil/ ▶ **modal verb** (3rd sing. present **will**; past **would**) **1** expressing the future tense. **2** expressing a strong intention or assertion about the future. **3** expressing inevitable events. **4** expressing a request. **5** expressing desire, consent, or willingness. **6** expressing facts about ability or capacity. **7** expressing habitual behavior. **8** expressing probability or expectation about something in the present.
– ORIGIN Old English.

USAGE

For an explanation of the difference between **will** and **shall**, see the note at **SHALL**.

will[2] ▶ **noun 1** a person's power to decide on something and take action. **2** (also **willpower**) control or restraint deliberately exerted by a person: *a stupendous effort of will.* **3** a person's desire or intention in a particular situation: *the will to live.* **4** a legal document containing instructions about what should be done with a person's money and property after their death.

– SYNONYMS **1 determination,** strength of character, resolve, single-mindedness, drive, commitment, dedication, doggedness, tenacity, staying power. **2** *they stayed against their will* **desire,** wish, preference, inclination, intention. **3** *it was God's will* **wish,** desire, decision, choice, decree, command.

▶ **verb 1** intend or desire to happen. **2** bring about by the exercise of mental powers. **3** bequeath in one's will.

– SYNONYMS **1** *do what you will* **want,** wish, please, see fit, think best/fit, like, choose, prefer. **2** *God willed it* **decree,** order, ordain, command. **3** *she willed the money to her husband* **bequeath,** leave, hand down, pass on, settle on; Law devise.

– PHRASES **at will** at whatever time or in whatever way one pleases. **where there's a will there's a way** proverb determination will overcome any obstacle. **with a will** energetically and resolutely.
– ORIGIN Old English; related to **WILL**[1] and **WELL**[1].

will·ful /'wilfəl/ (Brit. **wilful**) ▶ **adjective 1** (of a bad or harmful act) deliberate. **2** stubborn and determined.

– SYNONYMS **1 deliberate,** intentional, premeditated, planned, conscious, calculated. **2 headstrong,** strong-willed, obstinate, stubborn, pig-headed, recalcitrant.
– ANTONYMS accidental.

– DERIVATIVES **will·ful·ly** adverb **will·ful·ness** noun.

wil·lie ▶ **noun** variant spelling of **WILLY**.

wil·lies /'wilēz/ ▶ **plural noun** (**the willies**) informal a strong feeling of nervousness or uneasiness.
– ORIGIN unknown.

will·ing /'wiliNG/ ▶ **adjective 1** ready, eager, or prepared to do something. **2** given or done readily.

– SYNONYMS **1 ready,** prepared, disposed, inclined, minded, happy, glad, pleased, agreeable, amenable; informal game. **2 readily given,** ungrudging.
– ANTONYMS reluctant.

will·ing·ly /'wiliNGlē/ ▶ **adverb** of one's own free will.

– SYNONYMS *I willingly agreed to make a donation* **voluntarily,** of one's own free will, of one's own accord, readily, without reluctance, ungrudgingly, cheerfully, happily, gladly, with pleasure.
– ANTONYMS reluctantly.

will·ing·ness /'wiliNGnis/ ▶ **noun** the state of being ready, eager, or prepared to do something: *we appreciate your willingness to help.*

– SYNONYMS **readiness,** inclination, will, wish, desire.
– ANTONYMS reluctance.

will-o'-the-wisp /'wil ə THə 'wisp/ ▶ **noun 1** a person or thing that is difficult or impossible to reach or catch. **2** a dim, flickering light seen hovering or floating at night on marshy ground, thought to result from the combustion of natural gases.
– ORIGIN originally as *Will with the wisp*, the sense of *wisp* being 'handful of lighted hay.'

wil·low /'wilō/ ▶ **noun** a tree or shrub that typically grows near water, has narrow leaves and flexible branches, and bears catkins.
– ORIGIN Old English.

wil·low herb ▶ **noun** a plant with long narrow leaves and pink or pale purple flowers.

wil·low·ware /ˈwilōˌwe(ə)r/ ▸ **noun** blue and white pottery with a design featuring a Chinese scene typically including a willow tree and figures on a bridge.

wil·low·y /ˈwilōē/ ▸ **adjective 1** (of a person) tall, slim, and graceful. **2** bordered, shaded, or covered by willows.

will·pow·er /ˈwilˌpou(ə)r/ ▸ **noun** see **WILL²** (sense 2 of the noun).

wil·ly /ˈwilē/ (also **willie**) ▸ **noun** (pl. **willies**) Brit. informal a penis.
– ORIGIN familiar form of the man's name *William*.

wil·ly-nil·ly /ˈwilē ˈnilē/ ▸ **adverb 1** whether one likes it or not. **2** without direction or planning; haphazardly.
– ORIGIN later spelling of *will I, nill I* 'I am willing, I am unwilling.'

wilt¹ /wilt/ ▸ **verb 1** (of a plant) become limp through heat, loss of water, or disease; droop. **2** (of a person) become tired and weak.

> – SYNONYMS **1 droop,** sag, become limp, flop. **2 languish,** flag, droop, become listless, fade.
> – ANTONYMS flourish.

▸ **noun** any of a number of plant diseases that cause foliage to wilt.
– ORIGIN perhaps from dialect *welk* 'lose freshness,' from German.

wilt² old-fashioned second person singular of **WILL¹**.

wil·y /ˈwīlē/ ▸ **adjective** (**wilier, wiliest**) using cunning or crafty methods to gain an advantage.

> – SYNONYMS **shrewd,** clever, sharp, astute, canny, smart, crafty, cunning, artful, sly, scheming, calculating, devious; informal foxy.
> – ANTONYMS naive.

– DERIVATIVES **wil·i·ness** noun.

wimp /wimp/ informal ▸ **noun** a weak and cowardly person. ▸ **verb** (**wimp out**) fail to do something as a result of fear or lack of confidence.
– DERIVATIVES **wimp·ish** adjective **wimp·y** adjective.
– ORIGIN perhaps from **WHIMPER**.

wim·ple /ˈwimpəl/ ▸ **noun** a cloth headdress covering the head, neck, and sides of the face, formerly worn by women and still by some nuns.
– ORIGIN Old English.

win /win/ ▸ **verb** (**winning**; past and past part. **won**) **1** be successful or victorious in a contest or conflict. **2** gain as a result of success in a contest, conflict, etc.: *you could win a trip to Australia*. **3** gain someone's attention, support, or love. **4** (**win someone over**) gain someone's support or favor. **5** (**win out/through**) manage to succeed or achieve something by effort.

> – SYNONYMS **1 come first,** be victorious, carry/win the day, come out on top, succeed, triumph, prevail. **2 earn,** gain, secure, collect, pick up, walk away/off with, carry off; informal land, net, bag, scoop.
> – ANTONYMS lose.

▸ **noun** a victory in a game or contest.

> – SYNONYMS **victory,** triumph, conquest.
> – ANTONYMS defeat.

– DERIVATIVES **win·less** adjective **win·na·ble** adjective.
– PHRASES **win the day** be victorious.
– ORIGIN Old English, 'strive, contend,' also 'subdue and take possession of, acquire.'

wince /wins/ ▸ **verb** give a slight involuntary grimace or flinch due to pain or distress.

> – SYNONYMS **grimace,** pull a face, flinch, blench, start.

▸ **noun** an instance of wincing.
– ORIGIN Old French *guenchir* 'turn aside.'

> **CHOOSE THE RIGHT WORD**
>
> **wince, cower, cringe, flinch, recoil**
>
> The same individual might **wince** when receiving a flu shot, **flinch** from a difficult task, and **cower** in fear at the approach of a tornado. All of these verbs mean to draw back in alarm, disgust, faintheartedness, or servility, but there are subtle differences among them. To *wince* is to make a slight recoiling movement, often an involuntary contraction of the facial features, in response to pain or discomfort (*to wince when a singer misses a high note*), while *flinch* may imply a similar drawing-back motion or, more abstractly, a reluctance or avoidance (*to tackle the job without flinching*). *Cower* and **cringe** both refer to stooped postures, although *cower* is usually associated with fearful trembling (*he cowered in the doorway*) while *cringe* is usually linked to servile, cowardly, or fawning behavior (*she cringed before her father's authority*). More than any of the other verbs here, **recoil** suggests a physical movement away from something (*recoil at the sight of a poisonous snake*), although that movement may also be psychological (*recoil at the very thought of a family reunion*).

winch /winCH/ ▸ **noun 1** a hauling or lifting device consisting of a rope or chain winding around a horizontal rotating drum, turned by a crank or by motor. **2** the crank of a wheel or axle. ▸ **verb** hoist or haul something with a winch.
– ORIGIN Old English, 'reel, pulley.'

wind¹ /wind/ ▸ **noun 1** the natural movement of the air, especially in the form of a current blowing from a particular direction. **2** breath as needed in physical exertion, speech, playing an instrument, etc. **3** air swallowed while eating or gas generated in the stomach and intestines by digestion. **4** meaningless talk. **5** (also **winds**) (treated as sing. or pl.) wind or woodwind instruments forming a band or section of an orchestra.

> – SYNONYMS **1 breeze,** current of air, gale, hurricane, gust, draft; informal blow; literary zephyr. **2 breath**; informal puff.

▸ **verb** make someone unable to breathe easily for a short time.
– DERIVATIVES **wind·less** adjective.
– PHRASES **get wind of** informal hear about something secret or private. **put the wind up** Brit. informal alarm or frighten someone. **sail close to** (or **near**) **the wind** informal come close to being indecent, dishonest, or disastrous. **take the wind out of someone's sails** frustrate someone by doing or saying something they were not expecting.
– ORIGIN Old English.

wind² /wīnd/ ▸ **verb** (past and past part. **wound** /wound/) **1** move in or take a twisting or spiral course. **2** pass something around a thing or person so as to encircle or enfold them. **3** (of something long) twist or be twisted around itself or a core. **4** make a clockwork device operate by turning a key or handle. **5** turn a key or handle repeatedly. **6** move audiotape, videotape, or film back or forward to a desired point. **7** hoist or pull something with a winch, windlass, etc.

> – SYNONYMS **1 twist (and turn),** bend, curve, loop, zigzag, weave, snake. **2 wrap,** furl, entwine, lace. **3 coil,** roll, twist, twine.

▸ **noun** a single turn made when winding.
– DERIVATIVES **wind·er** noun.
– PHRASES **wind down 1** (of a clockwork mechanism)

gradually lose power. **2** (also **wind something down**) draw or bring something gradually to a close. **3** informal relax after stress or excitement. **wind up** informal end up in a particular state, situation, or place. **wind someone up 1** make someone agitated or excited: *the kids are too wound up to sleep*. **2** Brit. informal tease or irritate someone. **wind something up** gradually bring something to an end.
– ORIGIN Old English, 'go rapidly,' 'twine.'

wind·bag /ˈwindˌbag/ ▶ **noun** informal a person who talks a lot but says little of any value.

wind·break /ˈwindˌbrāk/ ▶ **noun** a row of trees, wall, or screen that provides shelter from the wind.

wind·break·er /ˈwindˌbrākər/ ▶ **noun** trademark a wind-resistant jacket with a close-fitting neck, waistband, and cuffs.

wind·chill /ˈwin(d)ˌCHil/ ▶ **noun** the cooling effect of wind on a surface.

wind chimes /wind/ ▶ **plural noun** pieces of glass, metal rods, or similar items, hung near a door or window so as to strike each other and make a ringing sound in the breeze.

wind·fall /ˈwindˌfôl/ ▶ **noun 1** a large amount of money that is received unexpectedly. **2** an apple or other fruit blown from a tree by the wind.

– SYNONYMS **bonanza,** jackpot, pennies from heaven, godsend.

wind farm /wind/ ▶ **noun** an area containing a group of energy-producing windmills or wind turbines.

wind·ing /ˈwīndiNG/ ▶ **adjective** having a twisting or spiral course.

– SYNONYMS *the winding country roads* **twisting and turning,** meandering, twisty, bending, curving, zigzag, serpentine, sinuous, snaking.
– ANTONYMS straight.

▶ **noun 1** a twisting movement or course. **2** a thing that winds or is wound around something.

– SYNONYMS *the windings of the stream* **twist,** turn, turning, bend, loop, curve, zigzag, meander.

WORD TOOLKIT

See **SERPENTINE**.

wind·ing sheet /ˈwīndiNG/ ▶ **noun** a sheet in which a dead body is wrapped for burial; a shroud.

wind in·stru·ment /wind/ ▶ **noun 1** a musical instrument in which sound is produced by the vibration of air, typically by the player blowing into the instrument. **2** a woodwind instrument as distinct from a brass instrument.

wind·jam·mer /ˈwindˌjamər/ ▶ **noun** historical a merchant sailing ship.

wind·lass /ˈwindləs/ ▶ **noun** a winch, especially one on a ship or in a harbor.
– ORIGIN probably from an Old Norse word meaning 'winding pole.'

wind·mill /ˈwindˌmil/ ▶ **noun** a building with sails or vanes that turn in the wind and produce power to grind grain, generate electricity, or draw water. ▶ **verb** move one's arms in a way that suggests the movement of a windmill's sails.

win·dow /ˈwindō/ ▶ **noun 1** an opening in a wall or roof of a building, or in a vehicle, fitted with glass in a frame to let in light or air and allow people to see out. **2** an opening through which customers are served in a bank, ticket office, etc. **3** a framed area on a computer screen for viewing information. **4** a transparent panel in an envelope to show an address. **5** an interval or opportunity for action.
– DERIVATIVES **win·dow·less** adjective.
– ORIGIN Old Norse, from words meaning 'wind' + 'eye.'

win·dow box ▶ **noun** a long narrow box in which flowers and other plants are grown on an outside windowsill.

win·dow dress·ing ▶ **noun 1** the arrangement of a display in a store window. **2** the presentation of something in a superficially attractive way to give a good impression.

win·dow frame ▶ **noun** a frame holding the glass of a window.

win·dow ledge ▶ **noun** a windowsill.

win·dow·pane /ˈwindōˌpān/ ▶ **noun** a pane of glass in a window.

win·dow seat ▶ **noun 1** a seat below a window, especially one in a bay or alcove. **2** a seat next to a window in an aircraft or train.

win·dow-shop ▶ **verb** look at the goods displayed in store windows, especially without intending to buy.
– DERIVATIVES **win·dow-shop·per** noun.

win·dow·sill /ˈwindōˌsil/ ▶ **noun** a ledge or sill forming the bottom part of a window.

wind·pipe /ˈwindˌpīp/ ▶ **noun** the air passage from the throat to the lungs; the trachea.

wind·proof /ˈwindˌpro͞of/ ▶ **adjective** (of an item of clothing or fabric) giving protection from the wind.

wind·screen /ˈwindˌskrēn/ ▶ **noun** Brit. a windshield.

wind·shield /ˈwin(d)ˌSHēld/ ▶ **noun** a window at the front of a motor vehicle.

wind·shield wip·er ▶ **noun** a device consisting of a rubber blade on an arm that moves in an arc, for keeping a windshield clear of rain and snow.

wind·sock /ˈwindˌsäk/ ▶ **noun** a light, flexible cylinder or cone mounted on a mast to show the direction and strength of the wind, especially at an airfield.

wind·storm /ˈwindˌstôrm/ ▶ **noun** a storm with very strong wind but little or no rain or snow; a gale.

wind·surf·ing /ˈwindˌsərfiNG/ ▶ **noun** the sport of riding on a sailboard on water.
– DERIVATIVES **wind·surf** verb **wind·surf·er** noun.

wind·swept /ˈwindˌswept/ ▶ **adjective 1** (of a place) exposed to strong winds. **2** (of a person's hair or appearance) untidy after being in the wind.

wind tun·nel /wind/ ▶ **noun** a tunnel-like device for producing an airstream, in order to investigate flow or the effect of wind on an aircraft or other object.

wind·up /ˈwīndˌəp/ ▶ **noun 1** an act of bringing something to an end. **2** Baseball a pitching position in which one step is taken back or to either side, followed by one step forward during delivery of the ball.

wind·ward /ˈwindwərd/ ▶ **adjective & adverb** facing the wind or on the side facing the wind. Contrasted with **LEEWARD**. ▶ **noun** the side from which the wind is blowing.

wind·y[1] /ˈwindē/ ▶ **adjective** (**windier, windiest**) **1** marked by or exposed to strong winds: *a windy day.* **2** informal (of speaking or writing) using many words that sound impressive but mean little.

– SYNONYMS **breezy,** blowy, fresh, blustery, gusty, wild, stormy, squally.
– ANTONYMS still.

– DERIVATIVES **wind·i·ly** adverb **wind·i·ness** noun.

wind·y[2] /ˈwīndē/ ▶ **adjective** following a winding course.

wine /wīn/ ▶ **noun** **1** an alcoholic drink made from fermented grape juice. **2** a fermented alcoholic drink made from other fruits or plants.
– DERIVATIVES **wine·y** (also **winy**) adjective.
– PHRASES **wine and dine someone** entertain someone with drinks and a meal.
– ORIGIN Old English.

wine cel·lar ▶ **noun** **1** a cellar for storing wine. **2** a stock of wine.

wine·glass ▶ **noun** a glass with a stem and foot, used for drinking wine.

wine·grow·er /ˈwīnˌgrōər/ ▶ **noun** a grower of grapes for wine.

wine list ▶ **noun** a list of the wines available in a restaurant.

wine·mak·er /ˈwīnˌmākər/ ▶ **noun** a producer of wine.
– DERIVATIVES **wine·mak·ing** noun.

win·er·y /ˈwīnərē/ ▶ **noun** (pl. **wineries**) a place where wine is made.

wine·skin /ˈwīnˌskin/ ▶ **noun** an animal skin sewn up and used to hold wine.

wine tast·ing ▶ **noun** an occasion when wine is tasted in order to assess its quality.

wine vin·e·gar ▶ **noun** vinegar made from wine rather than malt.

wing /wiNG/ ▶ **noun** **1** a modified forelimb or other part enabling a bird, bat, or insect to fly. **2** a rigid horizontal structure projecting from both sides of an aircraft and supporting it in the air. **3** a part of a large building, especially one that projects from the main part. **4** a group within an organization having particular views or a particular function: *the militant wing of a religious group.* **5** (**the wings**) the sides of a theater stage out of view of the audience. **6** the part of a soccer, rugby, or hockey field close to the sidelines. **7** (also **wing forward**) an attacking player positioned near the sidelines.

– SYNONYMS **1 part,** section, side, annex, extension. **2 faction,** camp, caucus, arm, branch, group, section, set.

▶ **verb** **1** fly, or move quickly as if flying: *the prize will be winging its way to you soon.* **2** shoot a person or bird so as to wound in the arm or wing. **3** (**wing it**) informal speak or act without preparation.

– SYNONYMS **1 fly,** glide, soar. **2 wound,** graze, hit.

– DERIVATIVES **winged** adjective **wing·less** adjective.
– PHRASES **in the wings** ready for use or action at the appropriate time. **on the wing** (of a bird or insect) in flight. **on a wing and a prayer** with only a small chance of success. **spread one's wings** extend one's activities and interests. **take wing** fly away. **under one's wing** in or into one's protective care.
– ORIGIN Old Norse.

wing·beat /ˈwiNGˌbēt/ (also **wingstroke** /ˈwiNGˌstrōk/) ▶ **noun** one complete set of movements of a wing in flying.

wing chair ▶ **noun** an armchair with side pieces projecting forward from a high back.

wing col·lar ▶ **noun** a high stiff shirt collar with turned-down corners.

wing·er /ˈwiNGər/ ▶ **noun** **1** an attacking player on the wing in soccer, hockey, etc. **2** (in combination) a member of a specified political wing: *a religious right-winger.*

wing mir·ror ▶ **noun** a mirror projecting from the side of a vehicle; a side-view mirror.

wing nut ▶ **noun** a nut with a pair of projections for the fingers to turn it on a screw.

wing·span /ˈwiNGˌspan/ (also **wingspread** /-ˌspred/) ▶ **noun** the maximum extent from tip to tip of the wings of an aircraft, bird, etc.

wing tip ▶ **noun** a shoe with a toe cap having a backward extending point and curving sides.

wink /wiNGk/ ▶ **verb** **1** close and open one eye quickly as a signal of affection or greeting or to convey a message. **2** shine or flash on and off.

– SYNONYMS **1 blink,** flutter, bat. **2 sparkle,** twinkle, flash, glitter, gleam, shine, scintillate.

▶ **noun** an act of winking.
– DERIVATIVES **wink·er** noun.
– PHRASES **as easy as winking** informal very easy or easily. **in the wink of an eye** (or **in a wink**) very quickly. **not sleep a wink** (or **not get a wink of sleep**) not sleep at all.
– ORIGIN Old English.

win·kle /ˈwiNGkəl/ ▶ **noun** a small edible sea snail with a spiral shell. ▶ **verb** (**winkle something out**) chiefly Brit. extract or obtain something with difficulty.
– ORIGIN shortening of **PERIWINKLE**[2].

win·ner /ˈwinər/ ▶ **noun** **1** a person or thing that wins something. **2** informal a thing that is a success or is likely to be successful.

– SYNONYMS **victor,** champion, conqueror, medalist; informal champ, top dog.
– ANTONYMS loser.

win·ning /ˈwiniNG/ ▶ **adjective** **1** gaining, resulting in, or relating to victory. **2** attractive; endearing.

– SYNONYMS **1 victorious,** successful, triumphant, undefeated, conquering, first, top. **2 engaging,** charming, appealing, endearing, sweet, cute, winsome, attractive, prepossessing, fetching, disarming, captivating.

▶ **noun** (**winnings**) money won, especially by gambling.

– SYNONYMS **prize money,** gains, booty, spoils, proceeds, profits, takings, purse.

– DERIVATIVES **win·ning·ly** adverb.

win·ning post ▶ **noun** a post marking the end of a race.

win·now /ˈwinō/ ▶ **verb** **1** reduce people or things from a group until only the best ones are left: *we had to winnow out the losers.* **2** blow air through grain in order to remove the chaff.
– ORIGIN Old English.

win·o /ˈwīnō/ ▶ **noun** (pl. **winos**) informal a person who drinks excessive amounts of cheap wine or other alcohol, especially one who is homeless.

win·some /ˈwinsəm/ ▶ **adjective** attractive or appealing in a fresh or innocent way.

– DERIVATIVES **win·some·ly** adverb **win·some·ness** noun.
– ORIGIN from an Old English word meaning 'joy.'

win·ter /'wintər/ ▶ **noun** the coldest season of the year, after autumn and before spring. ▶ **verb** spend the winter in a particular place. ▶ **adjective** (of crops) sown in autumn for harvesting the following year.
– ORIGIN Old English.

win·ter·green /'wintər,grēn/ ▶ **noun 1** a North American shrub whose leaves produce oil. **2** (also **oil of wintergreen**) a pungent oil obtained from wintergreen or from birch bark, used as a medicine or flavoring.

win·ter·ize /'wintə,rīz/ ▶ **verb** adapt or prepare something for use in cold weather.

Win·ter O·lym·pics ▶ **plural noun** an international contest of winter sports held every four years at a two-year interval from the Summer Olympic Games.

win·ter sports ▶ **plural noun** sports performed on snow or ice.

win·ter·time /'wintər,tīm/ ▶ **noun** the season or period of winter.

win·try /'wintrē/ (also **wintery** /'wint(ə)rē/) ▶ **adjective** (**wintrier, wintriest**) typical of winter, especially in being very cold or bleak.

> – SYNONYMS **bleak,** cold, chilly, frosty, freezing, icy, snowy, arctic, glacial, bitter, raw; informal nippy.
> – ANTONYMS warm.

win-win ▶ **adjective** (of a situation) in which each party benefits.

wipe /wīp/ ▶ **verb 1** clean or dry something by rubbing with a cloth or the hand. **2** remove dirt or moisture with a cloth or the hand. **3** erase data from a tape, computer, etc.

> – SYNONYMS **1 rub,** mop, sponge, swab, clean, dry, polish. **2** *he wiped off the marks* **rub off,** clean off, remove, erase, efface.

▶ **noun 1** an act of wiping. **2** an absorbent disposable cleaning cloth.
– DERIVATIVES **wipe·a·ble** adjective **wip·er** noun.
– PHRASES **wipe the floor with** informal defeat someone completely. **wipe something off** subtract an amount from a value or debt. **wipe someone out 1** kill a large number of people. **2** (**be wiped out**) informal be exhausted or intoxicated. **wipe something out** remove or eliminate something. **wipe the slate clean** make a fresh start.
– ORIGIN Old English.

wipe·out /'wīp,out/ ▶ **noun** informal **1** an instance of complete destruction or failure. **2** a fall while surfing or skiing.

wire /wīr/ ▶ **noun 1** metal drawn out into a thin flexible strand or rod. **2** a length or quantity of wire used for fencing, to carry an electric current, etc. **3** a concealed electronic listening device. **4** informal a telegram.
▶ **verb 1** install electric circuits or wires in something. **2** provide, fasten, or reinforce something with wire. **3** informal send a telegram to someone.
– PHRASES **down to the wire** informal until the very last minute.
– ORIGIN Old English.

wire brush ▶ **noun** a brush with tough wire bristles for cleaning hard surfaces.

wired /wīrd/ ▶ **adjective** informal **1** making use of computers and information technology to transfer or receive information. **2** nervous, tense, or edgy. **3** under the influence of drugs or alcohol.

wire-haired ▶ **adjective** (especially of a dog breed) having wiry hair.

wire·less /'wīrlis/ ▶ **adjective** using radio, microwaves, etc. (as opposed to wires) to transmit signals. ▶ **noun** dated, chiefly Brit. **1** a radio. **2** broadcasting or telegraphy using radio signals.
– DERIVATIVES **wire·less·ly** adverb.

wire·less hot spot ▶ **noun** see **HOT SPOT** (sense 3).

wire serv·ice ▶ **noun** a news agency that supplies news stories to its subscribers, e.g., newspapers and radio and television stations.

wire·tap·ping /'wīr,tapiNG/ ▶ **noun** the practice of tapping a telephone line to monitor conversations secretly.

wire·worm /'wīr,wərm/ ▶ **noun** the wormlike larva of a kind of beetle, which feeds on roots and can cause damage to crops.

wir·ing /'wīriNG/ ▶ **noun** a system of wires providing electric circuits for a device or building.

wir·y /'wī(ə)rē/ ▶ **adjective** (**wirier, wiriest**) **1** resembling wire in form and texture. **2** lean, tough, and sinewy: *a small, wiry woman.*

> – SYNONYMS **1** *wiry hair* **coarse,** rough, strong. **2** *a wiry man* **sinewy,** tough, athletic, strong; lean, spare, thin, skinny.
> – ANTONYMS flabby, smooth.

wis·dom /'wizdəm/ ▶ **noun 1** the quality of having experience, knowledge, and good judgment. **2** the body of knowledge and experience that develops within a particular society or period: *old Yankee wisdom.*

> – SYNONYMS **1 understanding,** intelligence, sagacity, sense, common sense, shrewdness, astuteness, judgment, prudence, circumspection, logic, rationale, soundness, advisability. **2 knowledge,** learning, erudition, scholarship, philosophy, lore.
> – ANTONYMS folly.

> **CHOOSE THE RIGHT WORD**
>
> See **KNOWLEDGE**.

wis·dom tooth ▶ **noun** each of the four molars at the back of the mouth that usually appear at about the age of eighteen.

wise[1] /wīz/ ▶ **adjective 1** having or showing experience, knowledge, and good judgment. **2** (**wise to**) informal aware of.

> – SYNONYMS **sage,** sagacious, intelligent, clever, learned, knowledgeable, enlightened, astute, smart, shrewd, sharp-witted, canny, knowing, sensible, prudent, discerning, perceptive.
> – ANTONYMS foolish.

▶ **verb** (**wise up**) informal become aware of or informed about something.
– DERIVATIVES **wise·ly** adverb.
– PHRASES **be none** (or **not any**) **the wiser** not understand something, even though it has been explained.
– ORIGIN Old English.

wise[2] ▶ **noun** old use the way or extent of something.
– ORIGIN Old English.

-wise ▶ **suffix 1** forming adjectives and adverbs of manner or respect: *clockwise.* **2** informal concerning: *security-wise.*

wise·a·cre /ˈwīzˌākər/ ▶ **noun** a person who pretends to be wise or knowledgeable.
– ORIGIN Dutch *wijsseggher* 'soothsayer.'

wise·crack /ˈwīzˌkrak/ informal ▶ **noun** a witty remark or joke. ▶ **verb** make a wisecrack.
– DERIVATIVES **wise·crack·er** noun.

wise guy ▶ **noun** informal a person who makes sarcastic or sassy remarks to demonstrate their cleverness.

wish /wisн/ ▶ **verb 1** desire something that cannot or probably will not happen. **2** want to do something. **3** want someone to do something or something to be done. **4** express a hope that someone has happiness or success. **5** (**wish someone/thing on**) hope that someone has to deal with someone or something unpleasant.

– SYNONYMS **1** *I wished for power* **desire,** want, hope for, covet, dream of, long for, yearn for, crave, hunger for, aspire to, set one's heart on, seek, fancy, hanker after; informal have a yen for. **2** *they can do as they wish* **want,** desire, feel inclined, feel like, care, choose, please, think fit.

▶ **noun 1** a desire or hope. **2** (**wishes**) an expression of a hope for someone's happiness, success, or welfare. **3** a thing wished for.

– SYNONYMS **1** *a wish for a more leisurely life* **desire,** longing, yearning, whim, craving, hunger, hope, aspiration, aim, ambition, dream; informal hankering, yen. **2** *her parents' wishes* **request,** requirement, bidding, instruction, direction, demand, order, command, want, desire, will.

– ORIGIN Old English.

wish·bone /ˈwisнˌbōn/ ▶ **noun** a forked bone between the neck and breast of a cooked chicken or similar bird that, when broken by two people, entitles the holder of the longer portion to make a wish.

wish·ful /ˈwisнfəl/ ▶ **adjective 1** having or expressing a wish for something to happen. **2** based on impractical wishes rather than facts: *without resources the proposals were merely wishful thinking.*
– DERIVATIVES **wish·ful·ly** adverb.

wish·ful·fill·ment ▶ **noun** the satisfying of wishes in dreams or fantasies.

wish·ing well ▶ **noun** a well into which one drops a coin and makes a wish.

wish·y-wash·y /ˈwisнē ˈwäsнē, -ˈwôsнē/ ▶ **adjective** not firm or forceful; feeble: *wishy-washy liberalism.*

wisp /wisp/ ▶ **noun** a small thin bunch, strand, or amount of something.
– DERIVATIVES **wisp·y** adjective.
– ORIGIN uncertain.

wist /wist/ past and past participle of **WIT²**.

wis·te·ri·a /wiˈsti(ə)rēə/ (also **wistaria** /-ˈste(ə)r-/) ▶ **noun** a climbing shrub with hanging clusters of pale bluish-lilac flowers.
– ORIGIN named after the American anatomist Caspar *Wistar* (or *Wister*).

wist·ful /ˈwistfəl/ ▶ **adjective** having or showing a feeling of vague or regretful longing.

– SYNONYMS **nostalgic,** yearning, longing, forlorn, melancholy, sad, mournful, pensive, reflective, contemplative.

– DERIVATIVES **wist·ful·ly** adverb **wist·ful·ness** noun.
– ORIGIN probably from former *wistly* 'intently,' influenced by **WISHFUL**.

WORD TOOLKIT

wistful ...	plaintive ...	pensive ...
glance	cry	mood
memory	plea	state
lyrics	question	frown
sigh	refrain	look
nostalgia	call	silence
longing	letter	moment

wit¹ /wit/ ▶ **noun 1** (also **wits**) the capacity to think inventively and understand quickly; keen intelligence: *he needed all his wits to find the way back.* **2** a natural talent for using words and ideas in a quick, clever, and amusing way. **3** a witty person.

– SYNONYMS **1 intelligence,** shrewdness, astuteness, cleverness, canniness, sense, judgment, acumen, insight, brains, mind; informal nous. **2 wittiness,** humor, drollery, repartee, badinage, banter, wordplay, jokes, witticisms, quips, puns. **3 comedian,** humorist, comic, joker; informal wag.

– DERIVATIVES **wit·ted** adjective.
– PHRASES **be at one's wits' end** be so worried that one does not know what to do. **have** (or **keep**) **one's wits about one** be constantly alert. **live by one's wits** earn money by clever and sometimes dishonest means.
– ORIGIN Old English.

wit² ▶ **verb** (**wot, witting, wist**) old use know someone or something.
– PHRASES **to wit** that is to say.
– ORIGIN Old English.

witch /wicн/ ▶ **noun 1** a woman thought to have evil magic powers. **2** a person who follows or practices modern witchcraft. **3** informal an ugly or disliked old woman.

– SYNONYMS **sorceress,** enchantress, hex.

– DERIVATIVES **witch·y** adjective.
– ORIGIN Old English.

witch·craft /ˈwicнˌkraft/ ▶ **noun** the practice of magic, especially the use of spells and the calling up of evil spirits. See also **WICCA**.

– SYNONYMS **sorcery,** (black) magic, wizardry, spells, incantations, necromancy, Wicca.

witch doc·tor ▶ **noun** (among tribal peoples) a person believed to have magic powers of healing, seeing the future, etc.

witch·er·y /ˈwicнərē/ ▶ **noun 1** the practice of magic. **2** bewitching quality or power.

witch ha·zel ▶ **noun** a cleansing and medicinal astringent made from the bark and leaves of a shrub.
– ORIGIN *witch* is a variant spelling of *wych*, used in names of trees with flexible branches.

witch-hunt ▶ **noun** a campaign directed against a person or group whose views are considered to be unacceptable or a threat to society.

witch·ing hour ▶ **noun** midnight, regarded as the time when witches are supposedly active.
– ORIGIN with reference to *the witching time of night* from Shakespeare's *Hamlet* (III. ii. 377).

with /wiт͟н, wiтн/ ▶ **preposition 1** accompanied by. **2** possessing; having. **3** indicating the instrument used to perform an action or the material used for a purpose:

cut the fish with a knife. **4** in relation to. **5** in opposition to or competition with. **6** indicating the way or attitude in which a person does something. **7** indicating responsibility: *leave it with me*. **8** in the same direction as. **9** affected by a particular fact or condition. **10** employed by. **11** using the services of. **12** indicating separation or removal from something: *their jobs were dispensed with*.

– PHRASES **be with someone** informal follow someone's meaning. **with it** informal **1** up to date or fashionable. **2** alert and able to understand.

– ORIGIN Old English.

with·al /wiT͟H'ôl, wiTH-/ ▸ **adverb** old use in addition.

with·draw /wiT͟H'drô, wiTH-/ ▸ **verb** (past **withdrew** /-'dro͞o/; past part. **withdrawn**) **1** remove or take away something. **2** leave or cause to leave a place. **3** stop taking part in an activity or being a member of a team or organization. **4** discontinue something previously given or provided: *the party withdrew its support for the government*. **5** take back a statement. **6** take money out of an account. **7** go away to another place in order to be private or quiet. **8** stop taking an addictive drug.

– SYNONYMS **1 remove,** extract, pull out, take out, take back. **2 abolish,** cancel, lift, set aside, end, stop, remove, reverse, revoke, rescind, repeal, annul. **3 retract,** take back, go back on, recant, repudiate, renounce, back down, climb down, backtrack, back-pedal, do a U-turn, eat one's words. **4 retreat,** pull out of, evacuate, quit, leave. **5 retire,** retreat, adjourn, decamp, leave, depart, absent oneself; formal repair.

– ANTONYMS insert, enter.

with·draw·al /wiT͟H'drôl, wiTH-/ ▸ **noun 1** the action of withdrawing. **2** the process of giving up an addictive drug.

– SYNONYMS **1 removal,** abolition, cancellation, discontinuation, termination, elimination. **2 departure,** pullout, exit, exodus, evacuation, retreat.

with·drawn /wiT͟H'drôn, wiTH-/ past participle of WITHDRAW ▸ **adjective** very shy or reserved.

– SYNONYMS **introverted,** unsociable, inhibited, uncommunicative, unforthcoming, quiet, reticent, reserved, retiring, private, reclusive, distant, shy, timid.

– ANTONYMS outgoing.

with·er /'wiT͟Hər/ ▸ **verb 1** (of a plant) become dry and shriveled. **2** become shrunken or wrinkled from age or disease. **3** gradually die out: *support for the UN strategy withered away*. **4** (as adj. **withering**) showing scorn or contempt.

– SYNONYMS **1 shrivel (up),** dry up, wilt, droop, go limp, fade, perish. **2 waste (away),** shrivel (up), shrink, atrophy. **3 diminish,** dwindle, shrink, lessen, fade, wane, evaporate, disappear. **4** (as adj. **withering**) **scornful,** contemptuous, scathing, stinging.

– ANTONYMS thrive.

– DERIVATIVES **with·er·ing·ly** adverb.

– ORIGIN probably a variant of WEATHER.

with·ers /'wiT͟Hərz/ ▸ **plural noun** the highest part of a horse's back, lying at the base of the neck above the shoulders.

– ORIGIN probably from former *widersome*.

with·hold /wiTH'hōld, wiT͟H-/ ▸ **verb** (past and past part. **withheld** /wiTH'held, wiT͟H-/) **1** refuse to give someone something that they want or is due to them. **2** suppress or restrain an emotion or reaction.

– SYNONYMS **1 hold back,** keep back, refuse to give, retain, hold on to, hide, conceal, keep secret; informal sit on. **2 suppress,** repress, hold back, fight back, choke back, control, check, restrain, contain.

– ANTONYMS release.

– DERIVATIVES **with·hold·er** noun.

with·in /wiT͟H'in, wi'TH-/ ▸ **preposition 1** inside. **2** inside the range or bounds of: *we were within sight of the finish*. **3** occurring inside a particular period of time. **4** not further off than (used with distances). ▸ **adverb 1** inside; indoors. **2** internally or inwardly.

with·out /wiT͟H'out, wiTH-/ ▸ **preposition 1** not accompanied by or having the use of. **2** in circumstances in which the action mentioned does not happen. ▸ **adverb** old use outside.

with·stand /wiTH'stand, wiT͟H-/ ▸ **verb** (past and past part. **withstood** /wiTH'sto͝od, wiT͟H-/) **1** remain undamaged or unaffected by something. **2** offer strong resistance to: *the city withstood the eastern invaders*.

– SYNONYMS **resist,** weather, survive, endure, cope with, stand, tolerate, bear, defy, brave, hold out against.

with·y /'wiT͟Hē, 'wiTHē/ ▸ **noun** (pl. **withies**) a tough flexible willow branch, used for tying things or making baskets.

– ORIGIN Old English.

wit·less /'witlis/ ▸ **adjective** foolish; stupid.

– DERIVATIVES **wit·less·ly** adverb **wit·less·ness** noun.

wit·ness /'witnis/ ▸ **noun 1** a person who sees an event take place. **2** a person giving sworn evidence to a court of law or the police. **3** a person who is present at the signing of a document and signs it themselves to confirm this. **4** (**witness to**) evidence or proof of: *the memorial service was witness to his wide circle of interests*. **5** open expression of a person's religious faith through words or actions.

– SYNONYMS **observer,** onlooker, eyewitness, spectator, viewer, watcher, bystander, passerby.

▸ **verb 1** be a witness to an event. **2** be the place or period in which an event takes place: *the 1960s witnessed a drop in churchgoing*.

– SYNONYMS **1 see,** observe, watch, view, notice, spot, be present at, attend. **2 countersign,** sign, endorse, validate.

– ORIGIN Old English.

wit·ness stand (Brit. **witness box**) ▸ **noun** the place in a court of law from where a witness gives evidence.

wit·ti·cism /'witi,sizəm/ ▸ **noun** a witty remark.

wit·ting /'witiNG/ ▸ **adjective 1** deliberate; on purpose. **2** aware of the full facts.

– DERIVATIVES **wit·ting·ly** adverb.

– ORIGIN from WIT[2].

wit·ty /'witē/ ▸ **adjective** (**wittier, wittiest**) showing or having the ability to say clever and amusing things.

– SYNONYMS **humorous,** amusing, droll, funny, comic, jocular, sparkling, scintillating, entertaining, clever, quick-witted.

– DERIVATIVES **wit·ti·ly** adverb **wit·ti·ness** noun.

WORD TOOLKIT

witty ...	clever ...	droll ...
banter	idea	sense
dialogue	use	wit
repartee	ways	comedy
lyrics	strategy	voice
comeback	ploy	delivery
commentary	wordplay	manner
one-liner	twist	humor

wives /wīvz/ plural of **WIFE**.

wiz /wiz/ ▸ **noun** variant spelling of **WHIZ** (sense 3 of the noun).

wiz·ard /ˈwizərd/ ▸ **noun** **1** a man who has magical powers, especially in legends and fairy tales. **2** a person who is very skilled in a particular area or activity: *a financial wizard.* **3** a computer software tool that automatically guides a user through a process.

– SYNONYMS **1 sorcerer,** warlock, magus, (black) magician, enchanter. **2 genius,** expert, master, virtuoso, maestro, marvel; informal hotshot, whiz/wiz, whiz kid, maven; Brit. informal dab hand.

– DERIVATIVES **wiz·ard·ly** adjective.
– ORIGIN first meaning 'philosopher, wise man': from **WISE**[1].

wiz·ard·ry /ˈwizərdrē/ ▸ **noun** **1** the art or practice of magic. **2** great skill in a particular area or activity.

wiz·ened /ˈwizənd, ˈwē-/ ▸ **adjective** shriveled or wrinkled with age.
– ORIGIN from former *wizen* 'shrivel,' from Old English.

WLAN /ˈdəbəlyo͞o ˌlan/ ▸ **abbreviation** Computing wireless local area network.

WMD ▸ **abbreviation** weapon (or weapons) of mass destruction.

WNW ▸ **abbreviation** west-northwest.

WO ▸ **abbreviation** Warrant Officer.

woad /wōd/ ▸ **noun** a plant whose leaves were formerly used to make blue dye.
– ORIGIN Old English.

wob·ble /ˈwäbəl/ ▸ **verb** **1** move unsteadily from side to side. **2** (of the voice) tremble. **3** waver between different courses of action: *the president wobbled on Bosnia.*

– SYNONYMS **1 rock,** sway, seesaw, teeter, jiggle, shake. **2 teeter,** totter, stagger, lurch, waddle. **3** *her voice wobbled* **tremble,** shake, quiver, quaver, waver.

▸ **noun** a wobbling movement or sound.
– DERIVATIVES **wob·bler** noun.
– ORIGIN Germanic.

wob·bly /ˈwäb(ə)lē/ ▸ **adjective** (**wobblier, wobbliest**) **1** tending to wobble. **2** weak and unsteady from illness, tiredness, or anxiety. **3** uncertain or insecure: *the evening got off to a wobbly start.*

– SYNONYMS **1 unsteady,** unstable, shaky, rocky, rickety, unsafe, precarious; informal wonky. **2 shaky,** quivery, weak, unsteady; informal like jelly.
– ANTONYMS stable.

▸ **noun** Brit. informal a fit of temper or panic.
– DERIVATIVES **wob·bli·ness** noun.

woe /wō/ ▸ **noun** literary **1** great sorrow or distress. **2** (**woes**) troubles or problems.

– SYNONYMS **1 misery,** sorrow, distress, sadness, unhappiness, heartache, heartbreak, despair, adversity, misfortune, disaster, suffering, hardship. **2** *financial woes* **trouble,** difficulty, problem, trial, tribulation, misfortune, setback, reverse.
– ANTONYMS joy.

– PHRASES **woe betide someone** a person will be in trouble if they do a specified thing.
– ORIGIN Old English.

woe·be·gone /ˈwōbiˌgôn, -ˌgän/ ▸ **adjective** looking sad or miserable.
– ORIGIN from **WOE** + former *begone* 'surrounded.'

woe·ful /ˈwōfəl/ ▸ **adjective** **1** very sad or miserable. **2** shockingly bad: *the woeful state of public education.*

– SYNONYMS **1 sad,** unhappy, sorrowful, miserable, gloomy, doleful, plaintive, wretched. **2 dreadful,** awful, terrible, atrocious, disgraceful, deplorable, hopeless, lamentable; informal rotten, appalling, pathetic, pitiful, lousy, abysmal, dire.
– ANTONYMS cheerful, excellent.

– DERIVATIVES **woe·ful·ly** adverb.

wok /wäk/ ▸ **noun** a bowl-shaped frying pan used in Chinese cooking.
– ORIGIN Chinese.

woke /wōk/ past of **WAKE**[1].

wok·en /ˈwōkən/ past participle of **WAKE**[1].

wold /wōld/ ▸ **noun** (especially in British place names) a piece of high, open, uncultivated land.
– ORIGIN Old English.

wolf /wo͝olf/ ▸ **noun** (pl. **wolves** /wo͝olvz/) **1** a wild animal of the dog family, that lives and hunts in packs. **2** informal a man who seduces many women. ▸ **verb** (usu. **wolf something down**) eat food quickly and greedily.
– DERIVATIVES **wolf·ish** adjective.
– PHRASES **cry wolf** raise repeated false alarms, so that a real cry for help is ignored. [with reference to the fable of the shepherd boy who tricked people with false cries of 'Wolf!'.] **keep the wolf from the door** have enough money to be able to buy food. **throw someone to the wolves** sacrifice someone in order to avoid trouble for oneself. **a wolf in sheep's clothing** a person who appears friendly but is really hostile. [with reference to the Book of Matthew, chapter 7.]
– ORIGIN Old English.

wolf·hound /ˈwo͝olfˌhound/ ▸ **noun** a dog of a large breed originally used to hunt wolves.

wolf·ram /ˈwo͝olfrəm/ ▸ **noun** tungsten or its ore.
– ORIGIN German.

wolf whis·tle ▸ **noun** a whistle with a rising and falling pitch, used to express sexual attraction or admiration. ▸ **verb** (**wolf-whistle**) whistle at someone in this way.

wol·ver·ine /ˌwo͝olvəˈrēn, ˈwo͝olvəˌrēn/ ▸ **noun** a heavily built short-legged mammal with a long brown coat and a bushy tail, native to northern tundra and forests.
– ORIGIN from *wolv-*, plural stem of **WOLF**.

wolves /wo͝olvz/ plural of **WOLF**.

wom·an /ˈwo͝omən/ ▸ **noun** (pl. **women**) **1** an adult human female. **2** a female worker or employee. **3** a wife or lover.

– SYNONYMS **lady,** female; Scottish lass; Irish colleen; informal chick, sister, dame, broad; Austral. informal sheila; literary damsel.

– PHRASES **the little woman** a condescending way of

referring to one's wife.
– ORIGIN from the Old English words for **WIFE** and **MAN**.

> **WORD LINKS**
> **female, feminine** *relating to women*
> **gynecology** *branch of medicine concerning women*
> **misogyny** *hatred of women*

wom·an·hood /ˈwo͝omənˌho͝od/ ▸ **noun 1** the state or period of being a woman. **2** women as a group. **3** the qualities associated with women, such as femininity.

wom·an·ish /ˈwo͝omənisн/ ▸ **adjective** derogatory **1** suitable for or typical of a woman: *womanish indecision*. **2** (of a man) effeminate.

wom·an·ize /ˈwo͝oməˌnīz/ ▸ **verb** (usu. as n. **womanizing**) (of a man) have many casual sexual relationships with women.
– DERIVATIVES **wom·an·iz·er** noun.

wom·an·kind /ˈwo͝omənˌkīnd/ ▸ **noun** women as a group.

wom·an·ly /ˈwo͝omənlē/ ▸ **adjective 1** relating to or having the characteristics of a woman or women. **2** (of a girl's or woman's body) fully developed and curvaceous.

> – SYNONYMS **1** *womanly virtues* **feminine,** female. **2** *her womanly figure* **voluptuous,** curvaceous, shapely, ample, buxom, full-figured; informal curvy, busty.
> – ANTONYMS manly, boyish.

– DERIVATIVES **wom·an·li·ness** noun.

womb /wo͞om/ ▸ **noun** the uterus.
– ORIGIN Old English.

wom·bat /ˈwämˌbat/ ▸ **noun** a burrowing Australian marsupial that resembles a small bear with short legs.
– ORIGIN from an extinct Aboriginal language.

wom·en /ˈwimin/ plural of **WOMAN**.

wom·en·folk /ˈwiminˌfōk/ ▸ **plural noun** the women of a family or community considered as a group.

wom·en's lib·er·a·tion (also informal **women's lib**) ▸ **noun** a movement supporting the freedom of women to have the same rights, status, and treatment as men (now usually replaced by the term *feminism*).

wom·ens·wear /ˈwiminzˌwe(ə)r/ ▸ **noun** clothing for women.

won[1] /wən/ past and past participle of **WIN**.

won[2] /wän/ ▸ **noun** (pl. same) the basic unit of money of North and South Korea.
– ORIGIN Korean.

won·der /ˈwəndər/ ▸ **verb 1** desire to know something. **2** feel doubt: *I wondered about the validity of his comments*. **3** feel amazement and admiration.

> – SYNONYMS **1** *I wonder what she is thinking* **ponder (over),** think about, meditate on, reflect on, muse on, speculate about, be curious about. **2** *they wondered at the spectacle* **marvel,** be amazed, be astonished, stand in awe, be dumbfounded; informal be flabbergasted.

▸ **noun 1** a feeling of surprise and admiration caused by something beautiful, unexpected, or unfamiliar. **2** a cause of wonder: *the wonders of a coral reef*.

> – SYNONYMS **1 awe,** admiration, fascination, surprise, astonishment, amazement. **2** *the wonders of nature* **marvel,** miracle, phenomenon, sensation, spectacle, beauty, curiosity.

▸ **adjective** having remarkable qualities or abilities: *a wonder drug*.
– DERIVATIVES **won·der·er** noun.
– PHRASES **no** (or **little** or **small**) **wonder** it is not surprising. **wonders will never cease** often ironic an exclamation of surprise and pleasure. **work** (or **do**) **wonders** have a very beneficial effect.
– ORIGIN Old English.

won·der·ful /ˈwəndərfəl/ ▸ **adjective** very good, pleasant, or remarkable.

> – SYNONYMS **marvelous,** magnificent, superb, glorious, sublime, lovely, delightful; informal super, great, fantastic, terrific, tremendous, sensational, fabulous, awesome, neat, magic, wicked, peachy, dandy; Brit. informal smashing, brilliant.

– DERIVATIVES **won·der·ful·ly** adverb **won·der·ful·ness** noun.

won·der·land /ˈwəndərˌland/ ▸ **noun** a place full of wonderful things.

won·der·ment /ˈwəndərmənt/ ▸ **noun** a state of awed admiration or respect.

won·drous /ˈwəndrəs/ ▸ **adjective** literary causing amazement and admiration. ▸ **adverb** old use wonderfully; remarkably.
– DERIVATIVES **won·drous·ly** adverb.

wonk /wänɢk/ (also **policy wonk**) ▸ **noun** informal, derogatory a person who takes an excessive interest in minor details of political policy.
– ORIGIN unknown.

won·ky /ˈwänɢkē/ ▸ **adjective** (**wonkier, wonkiest**) informal **1** unsteady or faulty. **2** not straight; crooked.
– DERIVATIVES **won·ki·ly** adverb **won·ki·ness** noun.
– ORIGIN unknown.

wont /wônt, wōnt/ ▸ **noun** (**one's wont**) formal one's usual behavior. ▸ **adjective** (**wont to**) literary in the habit of doing something; accustomed.
– ORIGIN Old English.

won't /wōnt/ ▸ **contraction** will not.

wont·ed /ˈwôntid, ˈwōn-/ ▸ **adjective** literary usual; normal.

won·ton /ˈwänˌtän/ ▸ **noun** (in Chinese cooking) a small round dumpling with a savory filling, typically served in soup.
– ORIGIN Chinese.

woo /wo͞o/ ▸ **verb** (**woos, wooing, wooed**) **1** try to gain a woman's love. **2** try to gain the support or custom of: *the store decided to woo customers with parking*.

> – SYNONYMS **1 romantically pursue,** pursue, chase (after); dated court, pay court to, romance, seek the hand of. **2 seek,** pursue, curry favor with, try to win, try to attract, try to cultivate. **3 entice,** tempt, coax, persuade, wheedle, seduce; informal sweet-talk.

– DERIVATIVES **woo·er** noun.
– ORIGIN Old English.

wood /wo͝od/ ▸ **noun 1** the hard fibrous material forming the trunk or branches of a tree or shrub, used for fuel or lumber. **2** (also **woods**) a small forest. **3** (**the wood**) wooden barrels used for storing alcoholic drinks. **4** a golf club with a wooden or other head that is relatively broad from face to back.

> – SYNONYMS **1 lumber,** timber, logs, planks, boards. **2 forest,** woodland, trees, copse, coppice, grove.

– PHRASES **be unable to see the wood for the trees** fail to grasp the main issue because of overattention to details. **out of the woods** out of difficulty. **knock on wood** said

to prevent a confident statement from bringing bad luck, often accompanied by the old custom of knocking on or touching something wooden to prevent such bad luck.
– ORIGIN Old English.

WORD LINKS

ligneous *relating to wood*

wood·bine /ˈwo͝od,bīn/ ▶ **noun 1** another term for **VIRGINIA CREEPER**. **2** Brit. the common honeysuckle.

wood·block /ˈwo͝od,bläk/ ▶ **noun** a block of wood from which woodcut prints are made.

wood·carv·ing /ˈwo͝od,kärviNG/ ▶ **noun 1** the action or skill of carving wood. **2** a carved wooden object.
– DERIVATIVES **wood·carv·er** noun.

wood·chip /ˈwo͝od,CHip/ ▶ **noun** chiefly Brit. wallpaper with small chips of wood embedded in it to give a grainy surface texture.

wood·chuck /ˈwo͝od,CHək/ ▶ **noun** a North American marmot (burrowing rodent) with a heavy body and short legs.
– ORIGIN from an American Indian name (by association with **WOOD**).

wood·cock /ˈwo͝od,käk/ ▶ **noun** (pl. same) a long-billed woodland bird of the sandpiper family, with brown plumage.

wood·cut /ˈwo͝od,kət/ ▶ **noun** a print of a type made from a design cut in relief in a block of wood.

wood·cut·ter /ˈwo͝od,kətər/ ▶ **noun** a person who cuts down trees for wood.

wood·ed /ˈwo͝odid/ ▶ **adjective** (of land) covered with woods.

– SYNONYMS **forested,** afforested, tree-covered; literary sylvan.

wood·en /ˈwo͝odn/ ▶ **adjective 1** made of or resembling wood. **2** stiff and awkward in speech or behavior.

– SYNONYMS **1 wood,** timber. **2 stilted,** stiff, unnatural, awkward, flat, clumsy, graceless, inelegant. **3 expressionless,** impassive, poker-faced, emotionless, blank, vacant, unresponsive, lifeless.

– DERIVATIVES **wood·en·ly** adverb **wood·en·ness** noun.

wood·grain /ˈwo͝od,grān/ ▶ **adjective** (of a surface or finish) imitating the grain pattern of wood.

wood·land /ˈwo͝odlənd/ ▶ **noun** (also **woodlands**) land covered with trees.

wood·louse /ˈwo͝od,lous/ ▶ **noun** (pl. **woodlice**) a small insectlike creature with a gray segmented body that it is able to roll into a ball.

wood·peck·er /ˈwo͝od,pekər/ ▶ **noun** a bird with a strong bill and a stiff tail, typically pecking at tree trunks to find insects.

wood pulp ▶ **noun** wood fiber reduced chemically or mechanically to pulp and used in the manufacture of paper.

wood·ruff /ˈwo͝od,rəf/ (also **sweet woodruff**) ▶ **noun** a white-flowered plant with sweet-scented leaves used to flavor drinks and in perfumery.
– ORIGIN Old English.

wood·shed /ˈwo͝od,SHed/ ▶ **noun** a shed where wood for fuel is stored. ▶ **verb** informal practice a musical instrument.

woods·man /ˈwo͝odzmən/ ▶ **noun** (pl. **woodsmen**) a forester, hunter, or woodcutter.

woods·y /ˈwo͝odzē/ ▶ **adjective** (**woodsier, woodsiest**) relating to or characteristic of wood or woodlands.

wood·turn·ing /ˈwo͝od,tərniNG/ ▶ **noun** the activity of shaping wood with a lathe.
– DERIVATIVES **wood·turn·er** noun.

wood·wind /ˈwo͝od,wind/ ▶ **noun** (treated as sing. or pl.) wind instruments other than brass instruments forming a section of an orchestra, including flutes, oboes, and clarinets.

wood·work /ˈwo͝od,wərk/ ▶ **noun 1** the wooden parts of a room, building, or other structure. **2** Brit. woodworking.
– DERIVATIVES **wood·work·er** noun.
– PHRASES **come out of the woodwork** (of a disliked person or thing) suddenly appear, especially to take advantage of a situation.

wood·work·ing /ˈwo͝od,wərkiNG/ ▶ **noun** the activity or skill of making things from wood.

wood·worm /ˈwo͝od,wərm/ ▶ **noun 1** the wood-boring larva of a kind of small brown beetle. **2** the damaged condition of wood resulting from infestation with woodworm.

wood·y /ˈwo͝odē/ ▶ **adjective** (**woodier, woodiest**) **1** covered with trees. **2** made of or resembling wood.
– DERIVATIVES **wood·i·ness** noun.

woof[1] /wo͝of/ ▶ **noun** the barking sound made by a dog. ▶ **verb** (of a dog) bark.
– ORIGIN imitating the sound.

woof[2] ▶ **noun** another term for **WEFT**.
– ORIGIN Old English.

woof·er /ˈwo͝ofər/ ▶ **noun** a loudspeaker designed to reproduce low frequencies.

wool /wo͝ol/ ▶ **noun 1** the fine soft hair forming the coat of a sheep, goat, or similar animal, especially when shorn and made into cloth or yarn. **2** a metal or mineral made into a mass of fine fibers.

– SYNONYMS **fleece,** hair, coat.

– PHRASES **pull the wool over someone's eyes** deceive someone.
– ORIGIN Old English.

wool·en /ˈwo͝olən/ (Brit. **woollen**) ▶ **adjective 1** made of wool. **2** relating to the production of wool. ▶ **noun** (**woolens**) woolen clothes.

wool-gath·er·ing ▶ **noun** aimless thought or daydreaming.

wool·ly /ˈwo͝olē/ ▶ **adjective** (**woollier, woolliest**) **1** made of wool. **2** (of an animal or plant) covered with wool or hair resembling wool. **3** resembling wool in texture or appearance. **4** confused or unclear: *woolly thinking*.

– SYNONYMS **1 woolen,** wool. **2 fleecy,** shaggy, hairy, fluffy. **3 vague,** ill-defined, hazy, unclear, fuzzy, indefinite, confused, muddled.

▶ **noun** (pl. **woollies**) informal chiefly Brit. a woolen sweater or cardigan.
– DERIVATIVES **wool·li·ness** noun.

woosh ▶ **verb & noun** variant spelling of **WHOOSH**.

wooz·y /ˈwo͞ozē/ ▶ **adjective** (**woozier, wooziest**) informal unsteady, dizzy, or dazed.
– DERIVATIVES **wooz·i·ly** adverb **wooz·i·ness** noun.
– ORIGIN unknown.

wop /wäp/ ▶ **noun** informal, offensive an Italian or other southern European.
– ORIGIN perhaps from Italian *guappo* 'bold, showy.'

Worces·ter·shire sauce /ˈwo͝ostərˌsHi(ə)r, -sHər/ ▶ **noun** a tangy sauce containing soy sauce and vinegar, first made in Worcester in England.

word /wərd/ ▶ **noun 1** a single unit of language that has meaning and is used with others to form sentences. **2** a remark or statement. **3** (**a word**) even the smallest amount of something spoken or written: *don't believe a word.* **4** (**words**) angry talk. **5** (**the word**) a command or signal: *someone gave me the word to start playing.* **6** (**one's word**) a person's version of the truth. **7** (**one's word**) a promise. **8** news or information.

– SYNONYMS **1 term,** name, expression, designation. **2 remark,** comment, observation, statement, utterance. **3 script,** lines, lyrics, libretto. **4** *I give you my word* **promise,** assurance, guarantee, undertaking, pledge, vow, oath, bond. **5 talk,** conversation, chat, tête-à-tête, heart-to-heart, one-to-one, discussion; informal confab. **6** *there's no word from the hospital* **news,** information, communication, intelligence, message, report, communiqué, dispatch, bulletin; literary tidings.

▶ **verb** express something in particular words.

– SYNONYMS **phrase,** express, put, couch, frame, formulate, style.

– DERIVATIVES **word·less** adjective.
– PHRASES **have a word** speak briefly to someone. **in so many words** precisely in the way mentioned. **in a word** briefly. **a man** (or **woman**) **of his** (or **her**) **word** a person who keeps their promises. **on** (or **upon**) **my word** an exclamation of surprise or emphasis. **take someone at their word** assume that a person is speaking honestly or sincerely. **take the words out of someone's mouth** say what someone else was about to say. **take someone's word** (**for it**) believe what someone says or writes without checking for oneself. **word for word** in exactly the same or, when translated, exactly equivalent words. **word of honor** a solemn promise. **word of mouth** speech as a means of conveying information.
– ORIGIN Old English.

WORD LINKS

verbal, **lexical** *relating to words*

word class ▶ **noun** a part of speech.

word·ing /ˈwərdiNG/ ▶ **noun** the way in which something is expressed in words.

– SYNONYMS **phrasing,** phraseology, language, words, expression, terminology.

word-per·fect /ˈpərfəkt/ ▶ **adjective** (of an actor or speaker) knowing one's part or speech by heart.

word·play /ˈwərdˌplā/ ▶ **noun** the witty use of words and their meanings, especially in puns.

word proc·es·sor ▶ **noun** a computer or program for creating, editing, storing, and printing a document.
– DERIVATIVES **word proc·ess·ing** noun.

word·smith /ˈwərdˌsmiTH/ ▶ **noun** a skilled user of words.

word·y /ˈwərdē/ ▶ **adjective** (**wordier, wordiest**) using or expressed in too many words.

– SYNONYMS **long-winded,** verbose, lengthy, rambling, garrulous, voluble; informal windy.
– ANTONYMS succinct.

– DERIVATIVES **word·i·ly** adverb **word·i·ness** noun.

wore /wôr/ past of **WEAR**.

work /wərk/ ▶ **noun 1** activity involving mental or physical effort done in order to achieve a result. **2** the activity or job that a person does to earn money. **3** a task or tasks to be done. **4** a thing or things done or made; the result of an action: *her work hangs in the Wadsworth Atheneum.* **5** (**works**) (treated as sing., often in combination) a place where industrial or manufacturing processes are carried out: *they're hiring at the steel works.* **6** (**works**) the mechanism of a machine. **7** a defensive military structure. **8** Physics the exertion of force overcoming resistance or producing molecular change. **9** (**the works**) informal everything needed, wanted, or expected.

– SYNONYMS **1 labor,** toil, drudgery, exertion, effort, industry; informal grind, sweat. old use travail. **2 employment,** job, post, position, situation, occupation, profession, career, vocation, calling. **3 tasks,** jobs, duties, assignments, projects, chores. **4 composition,** piece, creation, opus; (**works**) oeuvre, canon.
– ANTONYMS leisure.

▶ **verb** (past and past part. **worked** or old use **wrought** /rôt/) **1** do work, especially as a job. **2** make someone do work. **3** (of a machine or system) function properly or effectively. **4** operate a machine. **5** have the desired result. **6** bring a material or mixture to a desired shape or consistency. **7** move gradually or with difficulty: *they worked their way up the steep hill.* **8** produce an article or design using a specified material or sewing stitch. **9** cultivate land or extract materials from a mine or quarry. **10** bring into a specified emotional state: *he'd worked himself into a rage.*

– SYNONYMS **1 labor,** toil, exert oneself, slave (away); informal slog (away), beaver away. **2 be employed,** have a job, earn one's living, do business. **3 function,** go, run, operate. **4 operate,** use, handle, control, run, manipulate. **5** *her plan worked admirably* **succeed,** turn out well, go as planned, get results, be effective; informal come off, pay off, do the trick.
– ANTONYMS rest, fail.

– DERIVATIVES **work·less** adjective.
– PHRASES **get worked up** become excited, angry, or stressed. **have one's work cut out (for one)** be faced with a hard or lengthy task. **in the works** being planned or produced. **work something in** try to include something. **work something off** get rid of something through physical effort. **work out 1** develop in a good or specified way. **2** engage in vigorous physical exercise. **work something out 1** solve a sum or calculate an amount. **2** plan something in detail. **work to rule** chiefly Brit. follow official working rules and hours exactly in order to reduce output and efficiency, as a form of industrial action. **work up to** proceed gradually toward something more advanced. **work something up** develop something gradually.
– ORIGIN Old English.

CHOOSE THE RIGHT WORD

See **LABOR**.

work·a·ble /ˈwərkəbəl/ ▶ **adjective 1** able to be shaped, manipulated, or dug. **2** capable of producing the desired result: *a workable peace settlement.*
– DERIVATIVES **work·a·bil·i·ty** /ˌwərkəˈbilitē/ noun **work·a·bly** adverb.

work·a·day /ˈwərkəˌdā/ ▶ **adjective** not special or interesting; ordinary.

work·a·hol·ic /ˌwərkəˈhôlik, -ˈhälik/ ▶ **noun** informal a person who works very hard and finds it difficult to stop working.
– DERIVATIVES **work·a·hol·ism** /ˈwərkəˌhôlizəm, -ˌhäl-/ noun.

work·a·round /ˈwərkəˌround/ ▶ **noun** a method for overcoming a problem in a computer program or system.

work·bench /ˈwərkˌbenCH/ ▶ **noun** a bench at which carpentry or other mechanical or practical work is done.

work·book /ˈwərkˌbo͝ok/ ▶ **noun** a student's book containing instruction and exercises.

work·day /ˈwərkˌdā/ ▶ **noun** a day on which a person works.

work·er /ˈwərkər/ ▶ **noun 1** a person who works. **2** a person who achieves a specified thing: *a miracle-worker*. **3** a neuter or undeveloped female bee, wasp, ant, etc., large numbers of which perform the basic work of a colony.

– SYNONYMS **employee,** member of staff, workman, laborer, hand, operator, operative, agent, wage-earner, breadwinner, proletarian.

work eth·ic ▶ **noun** the belief that it is a person's moral duty to work hard.

work·flow /ˈwərkˌflō/ ▶ **noun** the sequence of processes through which a piece of work passes from start to finish.

work·force /ˈwərkˌfôrs/ ▶ **noun** (treated as sing. or pl.) the people engaged in or available for work in a particular area, organization, or industry.

work·horse /ˈwərkˌhôrs/ ▶ **noun** a person or machine that works hard and reliably over a long period.

work·house /ˈwərkˌhous/ ▶ **noun** historical (in the UK) a public institution in which poor people received food and lodging in return for work.

work·ing /ˈwərkiNG/ ▶ **adjective 1** having paid employment. **2** doing manual work. **3** functioning or able to function. **4** used as the basis for work or discussion and likely to be changed later: *a working title*. ▶ **noun 1** a mine or a part of a mine from which minerals are being extracted. **2** (**workings**) the way in which a machine, organization, or system operates. **3** (**workings**) a record of the calculations made in solving a mathematical problem.

work·ing cap·i·tal ▶ **noun** the capital of a business that is used in its day-to-day trading operations.

work·ing class ▶ **noun** the social group consisting largely of people who do manual or industrial work. ▶ **adjective** relating to the working class.

work·load /ˈwərkˌlōd/ ▶ **noun** the amount of work to be done by someone or something.

work·man /ˈwərkmən/ ▶ **noun** (pl. **workmen**) **1** a person employed to do manual work. **2** a person who works in a specified way: *he's a good workman*.

work·man·like /ˈwərkmənˌlīk/ ▶ **adjective** showing efficient skill.

work·man·ship /ˈwərkmənˌSHip/ ▶ **noun** the degree of skill with which a product is made or a job done.

work·mate /ˈwərkˌmāt/ ▶ **noun** chiefly Brit. a person with whom one works; a colleague.

work of art ▶ **noun** a creative product with strong imaginative or artistic appeal.

work·out /ˈwərkˌout/ ▶ **noun** a session of vigorous physical exercise.

work per·mit ▶ **noun** an official document giving a foreigner permission to take a job in a country.

work·piece /ˈwərkˌpēs/ ▶ **noun** an object being worked on with a tool or machine.

work·place /ˈwərkˌplās/ ▶ **noun** a place where people work.

work·room /ˈwərkˌro͞om, -ˌro͝om/ ▶ **noun** a room for working in.

work·sheet /ˈwərkˌSHēt/ ▶ **noun 1** a paper listing questions or tasks for students. **2** a paper recording work done or in progress.

work·shop /ˈwərkˌSHäp/ ▶ **noun 1** a room or building in which goods are made or repaired. **2** a meeting for discussion and activity on a particular subject or project.

– SYNONYMS **1 workroom,** studio, factory, works, plant, industrial unit. **2 study group,** discussion group, seminar, forum, class.

work-shy ▶ **adjective** unwilling to work.

work·space /ˈwərkˌspās/ ▶ **noun 1** space in which a person or people can work. **2** Computing a memory storage facility for temporary use.

work·sta·tion /ˈwərkˌstāSHən/ ▶ **noun** a desktop computer terminal, typically one that is part of a network.

work sur·face ▶ **noun** another term for **COUNTERTOP**.

work·week /ˈwərkˌwēk/ ▶ **noun** the total number of hours or days worked in a week.

world /wərld/ ▶ **noun 1** (**the world**) the earth with all its countries and peoples. **2** a region or group of countries: *the English-speaking world*. **3** all that belongs to a particular period or area of activity: *the theater world*. **4** (**one's world**) a person's life and activities. **5** (**the world**) secular or material matters as opposed to spiritual or religious ones. **6** a planet. **7** (**a/the world of**) a very large amount of: *that makes a world of difference*.

– SYNONYMS **1 earth,** globe, planet, sphere. **2** *she would show **the world** that she was strong* **everyone,** people, mankind, humankind, humanity, the public, all and sundry. **3 sphere,** society, circle, arena, milieu, province, domain, preserve, realm, field.

– PHRASES **the best of both** (or **all possible**) **worlds** the benefits of widely differing situations, enjoyed at the same time. **man** (or **woman**) **of the world** a person with a great deal of experience of life and who is not easily shocked. **out of this world** informal very enjoyable or impressive.
– ORIGIN Old English.

world-beat·er ▶ **noun** a person or thing that is better than all others in its field.
– DERIVATIVES **world-beat·ing** adjective.

world-class ▶ **adjective** relating to or among the best in the world.

World Cup ▶ **noun** a competition between teams from many countries in a sport, in particular a soccer tournament held every four years.

world Eng·lish ▸ noun the English language including all of its regional varieties, such as North American, Australian, and South African English.

world-fa·mous ▸ adjective known throughout the world.

world·ly /ˈwərldlē/ ▸ adjective (**worldlier, worldliest**) **1** relating to material things rather than spiritual ones: *he gave up his worldly goods and left in search of enlightenment.* **2** having experience of life; sophisticated.

– SYNONYMS **1 earthly,** terrestrial, temporal, mundane, mortal, human, material, physical. **2 sophisticated,** experienced, worldly-wise, knowledgeable, knowing, enlightened, mature, seasoned, cosmopolitan, urbane, cultured.
– ANTONYMS spiritual, naive.

– DERIVATIVES **world·li·ness** noun.

world·ly-wise ▸ adjective having enough experience of life not to be easily shocked or cheated.

world mu·sic ▸ noun traditional music from the developing world, sometimes incorporating elements of Western popular music.

world or·der ▸ noun a system established internationally for preserving global political stability.

world pow·er ▸ noun a country that has significant influence in international affairs.

world-rank·ing ▸ adjective among the best in the world.

World Se·ries the championship for North American major league baseball, played between the champions of the American League and the National League.

world-shak·ing ▸ adjective very important.

world·view /ˈwərldˌvyo͞o/ ▸ noun a particular philosophy of life or conception of the world.

world war ▸ noun a war involving many large nations in different parts of the world, especially the wars of 1914–18 and 1939–45.

world-wea·ry ▸ adjective bored with or cynical about life.

world·wide /ˈwərldˈwīd/ ▸ adjective extending or applicable throughout the world.

– SYNONYMS **global,** international, intercontinental, universal, ubiquitous.
– ANTONYMS local.

▸ adverb throughout the world.

World Wide Web ▸ noun an extensive information system on the Internet providing facilities for documents to be connected to other documents by hypertext links.

WORM /wərm/ ▸ abbreviation Computing write-once read-many.

worm /wərm/ ▸ noun **1** an earthworm or other creeping or burrowing invertebrate animal with a long, thin, soft body and no limbs. **2** (**worms**) parasites that live in the intestines. **3** a maggot regarded as eating dead bodies buried in the ground: *food for worms.* **4** informal a weak or disliked person. ▸ verb **1** (**worm one's way**) move by crawling or wriggling. **2** (**worm one's way into**) gradually move into a situation in order to gain an advantage. **3** (**worm something out of**) obtain information from someone by continual questions or cunning.
– ORIGIN Old English.

worm cast ▸ noun a coiled mass of soil, mud, or sand thrown up at the surface by a burrowing worm.

worm-eat·en ▸ adjective (of wood) full of holes made by woodworm.

worm gear ▸ noun a mechanical arrangement consisting of a toothed wheel worked by a short revolving cylinder (worm) bearing a screw thread.

worm·hole /ˈwərmˌhōl/ ▸ noun **1** a hole made by a burrowing insect larva or worm in wood, fruit, etc. **2** Physics a hypothetical shortcut through space and time.

worm·wheel /ˈwərmˌ(h)wēl/ ▸ noun the wheel of a worm gear.

worm·wood /ˈwərmˌwo͝od/ ▸ noun a woody shrub with a bitter taste, used as an ingredient of vermouth and absinthe and in medicine.
– ORIGIN Old English.

worm·y /ˈwərmē/ ▸ adjective (**wormier, wormiest**) worm-eaten or full of worms.

worn /wôrn/ past participle of **WEAR** ▸ adjective **1** damaged by wear. **2** very tired.

– SYNONYMS **shabby,** worn out, threadbare, in tatters, falling to pieces, ragged, frayed, moth-eaten, scruffy, having seen better days.
– ANTONYMS new, smart.

worn out ▸ adjective **1** exhausted. **2** so damaged by wear as to be no longer usable.

wor·ried /ˈwərēd/ ▸ adjective feeling, showing, or expressing anxiety.

– SYNONYMS **anxious,** troubled, bothered, concerned, uneasy, fretful, agitated, nervous, edgy, tense, apprehensive, fearful, afraid, frightened; informal in a stew, in a tizzy, in a sweat, a bundle of nerves.
– ANTONYMS carefree.

– DERIVATIVES **wor·ried·ly** adverb.

wor·ri·some /ˈwərēˌsəm/ ▸ adjective causing anxiety or concern.

wor·ry /ˈwərē/ ▸ verb (**worries, worrying, worried**) **1** feel or cause to feel troubled over actual or possible difficulties: *you worry about your children when they stay out late.* **2** annoy or disturb someone. **3** (of a dog) tear at or pull something with the teeth. **4** (of a dog) chase and attack sheep or other livestock. **5** (**worry at**) pull at or fiddle with repeatedly: *he began to worry at the knot in the cord.*

– SYNONYMS **1 be anxious,** be concerned, fret, agonize, brood, panic, lose sleep, get worked up; informal get in a tizzy, get in a state. **2 trouble,** bother, make anxious, disturb, distress, upset, concern, unsettle, perturb, scare, prey on someone's mind; informal bug, get to.

▸ noun (pl. **worries**) **1** the state of being troubled about actual or possible difficulties. **2** a source of anxiety.

– SYNONYMS **1 anxiety,** distress, concern, unease, disquiet, nerves, agitation, edginess, tension, apprehension, fear, misgiving. **2 problem,** cause for concern, nuisance, pest, trial, trouble, bane, bugbear; informal pain, headache, hassle.

– DERIVATIVES **wor·ri·er** noun **wor·ry·ing** adjective.
– PHRASES **no worries** informal, chiefly Austral. all right; fine.
– ORIGIN Old English, 'strangle.'

wor·ry beads ▸ plural noun a string of beads that a person fingers so as to stay calm and relaxed.

wor·ry·wart /ˈwərē,wôrt/ ▸ **noun** informal a person who tends to dwell unduly on difficulty or troubles.

worse /wərs/ ▸ **adjective 1** less good, satisfactory, or pleasing. **2** more serious or severe. **3** more ill or unhappy. ▸ **adverb 1** less well. **2** more seriously or severely. ▸ **noun** a worse event or situation.
– PHRASES **none the worse for** not affected badly or harmed by. **the worse for wear** informal **1** in a poor condition; worn. **2** feeling rather drunk. **worse off** less fortunate or wealthy.
– ORIGIN Old English.

wors·en /ˈwərsən/ ▸ **verb** make or become worse.

– SYNONYMS **1 aggravate,** add to, intensify, increase, compound, magnify, heighten, inflame, exacerbate. **2 deteriorate,** degenerate, decline; informal go downhill.
– ANTONYMS improve.

wor·ship /ˈwərsHəp/ ▸ **noun 1** the practice of showing deep respect for and praying to a god or goddess. **2** religious rites and ceremonies. **3** great admiration or respect for someone.

– SYNONYMS **1 reverence,** veneration, adoration, glorification, exaltation, devotion, praise, thanksgiving, homage, honor. **2 service,** rite, prayer, praise, devotion, observance.

▸ **verb** (**worships, worshiping, worshiped**) **1** offer praise and prayers to a god or goddess. **2** feel great admiration or respect for someone.

– SYNONYMS **1 revere,** pray to, pay homage to, honor, adore, venerate, praise, glorify, exalt. **2 love,** cherish, treasure, hold dear, esteem, adulate, idolize, deify, hero-worship, lionize; informal put on a pedestal.

– DERIVATIVES **wor·ship·er** noun.
– ORIGIN Old English, 'worthiness, acknowledgment of worth.'

CHOOSE THE RIGHT WORD

See **REVERE**.

wor·ship·ful /ˈwərsHəpfəl/ ▸ **adjective** feeling or showing great respect and admiration.

worst /wərst/ ▸ **adjective** most bad, severe, or serious. ▸ **adverb 1** most severely or seriously. **2** least well. ▸ **noun** the worst part, event, or situation. ▸ **verb** defeat or get the better of someone.
– PHRASES **at worst** in the worst possible case. **do one's worst** do as much damage as one can. **if worst comes to worst** if the most serious or difficult situation arises.
– ORIGIN Old English.

wor·sted /ˈwo͝ostid, ˈwərstid/ ▸ **noun** smooth and close-textured woolen fabric made from a fine yarn.
– ORIGIN from *Worstead*, a parish in Norfolk, England.

wort /wərt, wôrt/ ▸ **noun** a sweet solution made from soaking ground malt or other grain before fermentation, used to produce beer.
– ORIGIN Old English.

worth /wərTH/ ▸ **adjective 1** equivalent in value to the sum or item specified. **2** deserving to be treated or regarded in the way specified: *the museum is worth a visit.* **3** having income or property amounting to a specified sum. ▸ **noun 1** the value or merit of someone or something. **2** an amount of a commodity equivalent to a specified sum of money: *a million dollars' worth of damage.*

– SYNONYMS **1 value,** price, cost, valuation, estimate. **2 benefit,** good, advantage, use, value, virtue, desirability, sense.

– PHRASES **for all one is worth** informal as energetically or enthusiastically as one can.
– ORIGIN Old English.

worth·less /ˈwərTHlis/ ▸ **adjective 1** having no real value or use. **2** having no good qualities.

– SYNONYMS **1 valueless,** of no value; informal trashy. **2 useless,** pointless, meaningless, senseless, inconsequential, ineffective, ineffectual, fruitless, unproductive, unavailing, valueless. **3 good-for-nothing,** ne'er-do-well, useless, despicable, contemptible, degenerate; informal no-good, lousy.
– ANTONYMS valuable, useful.

– DERIVATIVES **worth·less·ly** adverb **worth·less·ness** noun.

worth·while /ˈwərTH'(h)wīl/ ▸ **adjective** worth the time, money, or effort spent.

– SYNONYMS **valuable,** useful, of service, beneficial, rewarding, advantageous, positive, helpful, profitable, gainful, fruitful, productive, constructive, effective.

wor·thy /ˈwərT͟Hē/ ▸ **adjective** (**worthier, worthiest**) **1** deserving or good enough: *issues worthy of further consideration.* **2** deserving effort, attention, or respect. **3** well meaning but rather dull or unimaginative.

– SYNONYMS **good,** righteous, virtuous, moral, ethical, upright, respectable, upstanding, high-minded, principled, reputable, decent.
– ANTONYMS disreputable.

▸ **noun** (pl. **worthies**) often humorous a person important in a particular sphere: *local worthies.*

– SYNONYMS **dignitary,** personage, grandee, VIP, notable, pillar of society, luminary, leading light; informal bigwig.

– DERIVATIVES **wor·thi·ly** adverb **wor·thi·ness** noun.

-worthy ▸ **combining form 1** deserving of a specified thing: *newsworthy.* **2** suitable for a specified thing: *roadworthy.*

wot /wät/ singular present of **WIT**[2].

would /wo͝od/ ▸ **modal verb** (3rd sing. present **would**) **1** past of **WILL**[1], in various senses. **2** (expressing the conditional mood) indicating the result of an imagined event. **3** expressing a desire or inclination. **4** expressing a polite request. **5** expressing an opinion or assumption: *I would have to agree.* **6** literary expressing a wish or regret: *would that he had lived to finish it.*

USAGE

For an explanation of the difference between **would** and **should**, see the note at **SHOULD**.

would-be ▸ **adjective** often derogatory desiring or hoping to be a specified type of person: *a would-be actress.*

– SYNONYMS **aspiring,** budding, promising, prospective, potential, hopeful, keen, eager, ambitious; informal wannabe.

would·n't /ˈwo͝odnt/ ▸ **contraction** would not.

wouldst /wo͝odst/ old-fashioned second person singular of **WOULD**.

wound[1] /wo͞ond/ ▸ **noun 1** an injury to the body caused by a cut, blow, or other impact. **2** mental pain caused to someone: *what I'm saying might open up old wounds.*

– SYNONYMS **1 injury,** cut, gash, laceration, graze, scratch, abrasion, puncture, lesion; Medicine trauma. **2 insult,** blow, slight, offense, affront, hurt, damage, injury.

▶ **verb 1** injure a person or part of the body. **2** hurt someone's feelings.

– SYNONYMS **1 injure,** hurt, harm, lacerate, cut, graze, gash, stab, slash. **2** *her words wounded him* **hurt,** offend, affront, distress, grieve, pain.

– ORIGIN Old English.

wound² /wound/ past and past participle of **WIND²**.

wove /wōv/ past of **WEAVE¹**.

wo·ven /'wōvən/ past participle of **WEAVE¹**.

wow¹ /wou/ informal ▶ **exclamation** (also **wowee** /'woueē, 'wou'(w)ē/) expressing astonishment or admiration. ▶ **verb** impress and excite someone greatly. ▶ **noun** a sensational success.

wow² ▶ **noun** Electronics slow pitch variation in sound reproduction, perceptible in long notes. Compare with **FLUTTER** (sense 3 of the noun).
– ORIGIN imitating the sound.

WP ▶ **abbreviation** word processing or word processor.

wpm ▶ **abbreviation** words per minute (used after a number to indicate typing speed).

wrack¹ /rak/ ▶ **verb** variant spelling of **RACK¹**.

USAGE

For an explanation of the difference between **wrack** and **rack**, see the note at **RACK¹**.

wrack² ▶ **noun** a coarse brown seaweed that grows on the shoreline.
– ORIGIN probably from Dutch *wrak* 'shipwreck.'

wraith /rāTH/ ▶ **noun** a ghost or ghostly image of someone, especially one seen shortly before or after a person's death.
– DERIVATIVES **wraith·like** adjective.
– ORIGIN unknown.

wran·gle /'raNGgəl/ ▶ **noun** a long and complicated dispute or argument. ▶ **verb 1** have a long and complicated dispute or argument. **2** round up or take charge of livestock.
– DERIVATIVES **wran·gler** noun.
– ORIGIN perhaps from German *wrangen* 'to struggle.'

wrap /rap/ ▶ **verb** (**wraps, wrapping, wrapped**) **1** cover or enclose someone or something in paper or soft material. **2** encircle or wind around: *he wrapped an arm around her waist.* **3** (in word processing, etc.) cause a word or words to be carried over to a new line automatically. **4** informal finish filming or recording.

– SYNONYMS **1 enclose,** enfold, envelop, encase, cover, fold, wind, swathe, bundle, swaddle. **2 pack,** package, parcel up, bundle (up), gift-wrap.

▶ **noun 1** a loose outer garment or piece of material. **2** paper or material used for wrapping. **3** a tortilla wrapped around a filling, eaten as a sandwich. **4** informal the end of a session of filming or recording.

– SYNONYMS **shawl,** stole, cloak, cape, mantle, scarf.

– DERIVATIVES **wrap·ping** noun.
– PHRASES **be wrapped up in** be so involved in something that one does not notice other people or things. **under wraps** kept secret. **wrap up** (also **wrap someone up**) put on or dress someone in warm clothes. **wrap something up** end a discussion or complete a deal.
– ORIGIN unknown.

wrap·a·round ▶ **adjective 1** curving or extending around at the sides. **2** (of a skirt, dress, etc.) having one part overlapping another and fastened loosely.

wrap·per /'rapər/ ▶ **noun** a piece of paper or other material used for wrapping something.

wrasse /ras/ ▶ **noun** (pl. same or **wrasses**) a brightly colored sea fish with thick lips and strong teeth.
– ORIGIN Cornish *wrah*.

wrath /raTH/ ▶ **noun** extreme anger.

– SYNONYMS **anger,** rage, temper, fury, outrage, spleen, resentment, (high) dudgeon, indignation; literary ire.
– ANTONYMS happiness.

– ORIGIN Old English.

wrath·ful /'raTHfəl/ ▶ **adjective** literary full of or showing great anger.
– DERIVATIVES **wrath·ful·ly** adverb.

wreak /rēk/ ▶ **verb 1** cause a great amount of damage or harm. **2** take revenge on someone.
– ORIGIN Old English, 'drive (out), avenge.'

USAGE

The past tense of **wreak** is **wreaked**, as in *rainstorms wreaked havoc yesterday*, not **wrought**. **Wrought** is in fact an old-fashioned past tense of **work**.

wreath /rēTH/ ▶ **noun** (pl. **wreaths** /rēT͟HZ, rēTHS/) **1** an arrangement of flowers, leaves, or stems fastened in a ring and used for decoration or for placing on a grave. **2** a curl or ring of smoke or cloud.

– SYNONYMS **garland,** circlet, chaplet, crown, festoon, lei, ring, loop, circle.

– ORIGIN Old English, related to **WRITHE**.

wreathe /rēT͟H/ ▶ **verb 1** envelop, surround, or encircle: *the mountain was wreathed in mist.* **2** (of smoke) move with a curling motion.

– SYNONYMS **1 festoon,** garland, drape, cover, deck, decorate, ornament, adorn. **2 spiral,** coil, loop, wind, curl, twist, snake.

– ORIGIN from **WRITHE**.

wreck /rek/ ▶ **noun 1** the destruction of a ship at sea; a shipwreck. **2** a ship destroyed at sea. **3** a building, vehicle, etc., that has been destroyed or badly damaged. **4** a person in a very bad physical or mental state. **5** a road or rail crash.

– SYNONYMS **1 shipwreck,** sunken ship, hull. **2 wreckage,** debris, ruins, remains, burned-out shell.

▶ **verb 1** cause a ship to sink or break up. **2** destroy or severely damage a structure or vehicle. **3** spoil completely: *the injury wrecked his chances.*

– SYNONYMS **1 destroy,** break, demolish, crash, smash up, write off; informal trash, total. **2 ruin,** spoil, disrupt, undo, put a stop to, frustrate, blight, crush, dash, destroy, scotch, shatter, devastate, sabotage; informal mess up, screw up, put paid to, stymie.

– ORIGIN Old French *wrec*, from Old Norse.

wreck·age /'rekij/ ▶ **noun** the remains of something that has been badly damaged or destroyed.

wrecked /rekt/ ▶ **adjective** informal **1** exhausted. **2** under the influence of drugs or alcohol: *she got wrecked on the champagne.*

wreck·er /ˈrekər/ ▶ **noun 1** a person or thing that wrecks something. **2** a person who breaks up damaged vehicles to obtain usable spares or scrap. **3** a tow truck.

wren /ren/ ▶ **noun** a very small short-winged songbird with a cocked tail.
– ORIGIN Old English.

wrench /renCH/ ▶ **verb 1** pull or twist suddenly and violently: *he wrenched the gun from my hand.* **2** injure a part of the body as a result of a sudden twisting movement.

– SYNONYMS **1 tug,** pull, jerk, wrest, heave, twist, force, pry, prize; informal yank. **2 sprain,** twist, turn, strain, crick.

▶ **noun 1** a sudden violent twist or pull. **2** a feeling of acute sadness and distress caused by leaving a person or place. **3** an adjustable tool used for gripping and turning nuts or bolts.
– ORIGIN Old English.

wrest /rest/ ▶ **verb 1** take power or control from someone after a struggle. **2** forcibly pull something from a person's grasp.
– ORIGIN Old English, 'twist, tighten.'

wres·tle /ˈresəl/ ▶ **verb 1** take part in a fight or contest that involves close grappling with one's opponent. **2** struggle with a difficulty or problem. **3** move or manipulate with difficulty: *she wrestled the keys out of the ignition.*

– SYNONYMS **grapple,** fight, struggle, scuffle, tussle, brawl; informal scrap.

▶ **noun 1** a wrestling bout or contest. **2** a hard struggle.
– DERIVATIVES **wres·tler** noun **wres·tling** noun.
– ORIGIN Old English.

wretch /reCH/ ▶ **noun 1** an unfortunate person. **2** informal a disliked or unpleasant person.
– ORIGIN Old English.

wretch·ed /ˈreCHid/ ▶ **adjective (wretcheder, wretchedest) 1** in a very unhappy or unfortunate state; miserable. **2** very bad or unpleasant: *the wretched conditions of the slums.* **3** used to express anger or annoyance: *she disliked the wretched man intensely.*

– SYNONYMS **1 miserable,** unhappy, sad, heartbroken, grief-stricken, distressed, desolate, devastated, disconsolate, downcast, dejected, depressed, melancholy, forlorn. **2 harsh,** hard, grim, difficult, poor, pitiful, piteous, pathetic, tragic, miserable, bleak, cheerless, hopeless, sorry, sordid; informal crummy.
– ANTONYMS cheerful, comfortable.

– DERIVATIVES **wretch·ed·ly** adverb **wretch·ed·ness** noun.

wrig·gle /ˈrigəl/ ▶ **verb 1** twist and turn with quick short movements. **2 (wriggle out of)** manage to avoid doing something that one ought to do.

– SYNONYMS **1 squirm,** writhe, wiggle, thresh, flounder, flail, twitch, twist and turn, snake, worm. **2 (wriggle out of) avoid,** shirk, dodge, evade, sidestep, escape; informal duck.

▶ **noun** a wriggling movement.
– DERIVATIVES **wrig·gler** noun **wrig·gly** adjective.
– ORIGIN German *wriggelen.*

wright /rīt/ ▶ **noun** old use a maker or builder.
– ORIGIN Old English.

wring /riNG/ ▶ **verb** (past and past part. **wrung** /rəNG/) **1** squeeze and twist something to force liquid from it. **2** twist and break an animal's neck. **3** squeeze someone's hand tightly. **4 (wring something from/out of)** obtain something with difficulty or effort.
– PHRASES **wring one's hands** clasp and twist one's hands together as a gesture of distress or despair.
– ORIGIN Old English.

wring·er /ˈriNGər/ ▶ **noun** a device for wringing water from wet clothes or other objects.
– PHRASES **put someone through the wringer** informal subject someone to a very stressful experience, especially a severe interrogation.

wring·ing /ˈriNGiNG/ ▶ **adjective** extremely wet; soaked.

wrin·kle /ˈriNGkəl/ ▶ **noun 1** a slight line or fold, especially in fabric or the skin of the face. **2** informal a minor difficulty.

– SYNONYMS **crease,** fold, pucker, line, crinkle, furrow, ridge, groove; informal crow's feet, laugh line.

▶ **verb** make or become wrinkled.

– SYNONYMS **crease,** pucker, gather, crinkle, crumple, rumple, ruck up, scrunch up.

– DERIVATIVES **wrin·kled** adjective.
– ORIGIN possibly from an Old English word meaning 'sinuous.'

wrin·kly /ˈriNGk(ə)lē/ ▶ **adjective (wrinklier, wrinkliest)** having many wrinkles.

wrist /rist/ ▶ **noun** the joint connecting the hand with the forearm.
– ORIGIN Old English.

wrist·band /ˈristˌband/ ▶ **noun** a band worn around the wrist, especially for identity purposes or to soak up sweat when playing sports.

wrist·watch /ˈristˌwäCH/ ▶ **noun** a watch worn on a strap around the wrist.

writ[1] /rit/ ▶ **noun** an official document issued in the name of a court or other legal authority, ordering a person to do or not to do something.
– ORIGIN Old English.

writ[2] ▶ **verb** old-fashioned past participle of **WRITE**.
– PHRASES **writ large** in an obvious or exaggerated form.

write /rīt/ ▶ **verb** (past **wrote**; past part. **written**) **1** mark letters, words, or other symbols on a surface, with a pen, pencil, or similar implement. **2** compose and send a letter to someone. **3** compose a book or other written work. **4** compose a musical work. **5** fill out or complete a check or similar document. **6** Computing enter data into a specified storage medium or location.

– SYNONYMS **1 put in writing,** put down, jot down, note (down), take down, record, inscribe, sign, scribble, scrawl, pen, pencil. **2 compose,** draft, think up, formulate, compile, pen, dash off, produce. **3 correspond,** communicate, get in touch, keep in contact; informal drop someone a line.

– DERIVATIVES **writ·a·ble** adjective (chiefly Computing).
– PHRASES **be written all over one's face** informal be obvious from one's expression. **write someone/thing off 1** dismiss someone or something as insignificant. **2** cancel a bad debt or acknowledge that an asset will not be recovered.
– ORIGIN Old English.

write-off ▶ **noun 1** a worthless or ineffectual person or thing. **2** Finance a bad debt that is taken as a loss or an asset that will not be recovered.

writ·er /ˈrītər/ ▶ **noun 1** a person who has written a particular work, or who writes books or articles as an occupation. **2** Computing a device that writes data to a storage medium.

– SYNONYMS **author,** wordsmith; informal scribbler, scribe, pen-pusher, hack.

writ·er·ly /ˈrītərlē/ ▸ **adjective 1** relating to or characteristic of a professional author. **2** deliberately literary in style.

writ·er's block ▸ **noun** the condition of being unable to think of what to write or how to proceed with writing.

writ·er's cramp ▸ **noun** pain or stiffness in the hand caused by writing for a long time.

write-up ▸ **noun** a newspaper review of a recent book, performance, product, etc.

writhe /rīTH/ ▸ **verb** twist or squirm in pain or distress.

– SYNONYMS **squirm,** wriggle, thrash, flail, toss, twist.

– ORIGIN Old English, 'make into coils, plait.'

writ·ing /ˈrītiNG/ ▸ **noun 1** the activity or skill of writing. **2** written work. **3** (**writings**) books or other written works by a particular author or on a particular subject. **4** a sequence of letters or symbols forming words.

– SYNONYMS **1 handwriting,** hand, script, calligraphy, lettering, print, printing; informal scribble, scrawl. **2 written work,** compositions, books, publications, papers, articles, essays, oeuvre.

– PHRASES **the writing** (or **handwriting**) **is on the wall** see **HANDWRITING**.

WORD LINKS

graphology *study of handwriting*

writ·ten /ˈritn/ past participle of **WRITE**.

wrong /rôNG/ ▸ **adjective 1** not correct or true; mistaken or in error. **2** unjust, dishonest, or immoral. **3** in a bad or abnormal condition: *something's wrong with the car.*

– SYNONYMS **1 incorrect,** mistaken, erroneous, inaccurate, wide of the mark, inexact, imprecise; informal off beam, out. **2 inappropriate,** unsuitable, ill-advised, ill-considered, ill-judged, unwise, infelicitous; informal out of order. **3 bad,** dishonest, illegal, unlawful, illicit, criminal, corrupt, unethical, unjust, immoral, wicked, sinful, iniquitous, nefarious, reprehensible; informal crooked. **4 amiss,** awry, out of order, not right, defective, faulty.
– ANTONYMS right, correct.

▸ **adverb 1** in a mistaken or undesirable way or direction. **2** with an incorrect result.

– SYNONYMS **incorrectly,** wrongly, inaccurately, erroneously, mistakenly.

▸ **noun** an unjust, dishonest, or immoral action.

– SYNONYMS **1 immorality,** sin, wickedness, evil, illegality, unlawfulness, crime, corruption, villainy, dishonesty, injustice, misconduct, transgression. **2 misdeed,** offense, injury, crime, transgression, sin, injustice, outrage, atrocity.
– ANTONYMS right.

▸ **verb 1** act unjustly or dishonestly toward someone. **2** mistakenly attribute bad motives to someone.

– SYNONYMS **mistreat,** ill-use, ill-treat, do an injustice to, abuse, harm, hurt, injure.

– DERIVATIVES **wrong·ly** adverb **wrong·ness** noun.
– PHRASES **get hold of the wrong end of the stick** Brit. misunderstand something. **in the wrong** responsible for a mistake or offense. **on the wrong side of 1** out of favor with. **2** somewhat more than a particular age.
– ORIGIN Old Norse, 'awry, unjust.'

wrong·do·er /ˈrôNG,do͞oər/ ▸ **noun** a person who behaves in an illegal or dishonest way.

– SYNONYMS **offender,** lawbreaker, criminal, felon, delinquent, villain, culprit, evildoer, sinner, transgressor, malefactor, miscreant, rogue, scoundrel; informal crook.

wrong·do·ing /ˈrôNG,do͞oiNG/ ▸ **noun** illegal or dishonest behavior.

wrong·ful /ˈrôNGfəl/ ▸ **adjective** not fair, just, or legal.
– DERIVATIVES **wrong·ful·ly** adverb.

wrong·head·ed /ˈrôNG,hedid/ ▸ **adjective** having or showing bad judgment; misguided.

wrote /rōt/ past tense of **WRITE**.

wroth /rôTH/ ▸ **adjective** old use angry.
– ORIGIN Old English.

wrought /rôt/ ▸ **adjective 1** (of metals) beaten out or shaped by hammering. **2** (in combination) made or fashioned in the specified way: *well-wrought.* **3** (**wrought up**) upset and anxious.
– ORIGIN old-fashioned past and past participle of **WORK**.

wrought i·ron ▸ **noun** a tough malleable form of iron suitable for forging or rolling rather than casting.

wrung /rəNG/ past and past participle of **WRING**.

wry /rī/ ▸ **adjective** (**wryer, wryest** or **wrier, wriest**) **1** using or expressing dry, especially mocking, humor. **2** (of a person's face) twisted into an expression of disgust, disappointment, or annoyance. **3** bending or twisted to one side.

– SYNONYMS **1** *his wry humor* **ironic,** sardonic, satirical, mocking, sarcastic; dry, droll, witty, humorous. **2** *a wry expression* **unimpressed,** displeased, annoyed, irritated, irked, vexed, piqued, disgruntled, dissatisfied; informal peeved.

– DERIVATIVES **wry·ly** adverb **wry·ness** noun.
– ORIGIN from an Old English word meaning 'tend, incline,' later 'swerve, contort.'

WSW ▸ **abbreviation** west-southwest.

wt ▸ **abbreviation** weight.

WTO ▸ **abbreviation** World Trade Organization.

wun·der·kind /ˈwo͝ondər,kind/ ▸ **noun** (pl. **wunderkinds** or **wunderkinder**) a person who achieves great success at a relatively young age.
– ORIGIN German, from *Wunder* 'wonder' + *Kind* 'child.'

Wur·litz·er /ˈwərlitsər/ ▸ **noun** trademark a large pipe organ or electric organ.
– ORIGIN named after the American instrument-maker Rudolf *Wurlitzer*.

wuss /wo͝os/ ▸ **noun** informal a weak or ineffectual person.
– ORIGIN unknown.

WV ▸ **abbreviation** West Virginia.

WWF ▸ **abbreviation 1** World Wildlife Fund. **2** World Wrestling Federation.

WWI ▸ **abbreviation** World War I.

WWII ▸ **abbreviation** World War II.

WWW ▶ **abbreviation** World Wide Web.

WY ▶ **abbreviation** Wyoming.

WYSIWYG /'wizē,wig/ ▶ **adjective** Computing referring to the display of text on-screen in a form exactly corresponding to its appearance on a printout.
– ORIGIN from the initial letters of *what you see is what you get*.

wy·vern /'wīvərn/ ▶ **noun** Heraldry a winged two-legged dragon with a barbed tail.
– ORIGIN first referring to a viper: from Old French *wivre*.

X[1] (also **x**) ▶ **noun** (pl. **Xs** or **X's**) **1** the twenty-fourth letter of the alphabet. **2** referring to an unknown or unspecified person or thing. **3** (usu. *x*) the first unknown quantity in an algebraic expression. **4** (usu. *x*) referring to the main or horizontal axis in a system of coordinates. **5** a cross-shaped written symbol, used to indicate a wrong answer or to symbolize a kiss. **6** the Roman numeral for ten.

X[2] ▶ **symbol** movies classified as suitable for adults only (replaced in 1990 by *NC–17*).

X chro·mo·some ▶ **noun** (in humans and other mammals) a sex chromosome, two of which are normally present in female cells (known as XX) and only one in male cells (known as XY). Compare with **Y CHROMOSOME**.

Xe ▶ **symbol** the chemical element xenon.

xe·bec /ˈzēˌbek/ ▶ **noun** historical a small three-masted Mediterranean sailing ship.
– ORIGIN Arabic.

xe·non /ˈzēˌnän, ˈzenˌän/ ▶ **noun** an inert gaseous chemical element, present in trace amounts in the air and used in some kinds of electric light.
– ORIGIN from Greek *xenos* 'strange.'

xen·o·pho·bi·a /ˌzēnəˈfōbēə, ˌzenə-/ ▶ **noun** intense or irrational dislike or fear of people from other countries.
– DERIVATIVES **xen·o·phobe** /ˈzēnəˌfōb, ˈzenə-/ noun **xen·o·pho·bic** adjective.
– ORIGIN from Greek *xenos* 'stranger.'

xen·o·trans·plan·ta·tion /ˌzenəˌtransplanˈtāsʜən, ˌzēnə-/ ▶ **noun** the process of grafting or transplanting organs or tissues between members of different species.
– DERIVATIVES **xen·o·trans·plant** /-ˈtransˌplant/ noun.
– ORIGIN from Greek *xenos* 'strange.'

X·er /ˈeksər/ ▶ **noun** a Generation Xer.

xe·ri·scape /ˈzi(ə)rəˌskāp, ˈzerə-/ ▶ **noun 1** a style of landscape design needing little or no water or maintenance, used in arid regions. **2** a garden or landscape created in such a style. ▶ **verb** landscape an area in such a style.

xe·rog·ra·phy /ziˈrägrəfē/ ▶ **noun** a dry copying process in which powder sticks to parts of a surface remaining electrically charged after being exposed to light from an image of the document to be copied.
– DERIVATIVES **xe·ro·graph·ic** /ˌzi(ə)rəˈgrafik/ adjective.
– ORIGIN from Greek *xēros* 'dry.'

Xer·ox /ˈzi(ə)rˌäks/ ▶ **noun** trademark **1** a xerographic copying process. **2** a copy made using such a process. ▶ **verb** (**xerox**) copy a document using xerography.
– ORIGIN based on **XEROGRAPHY**.

Xho·sa /ˈkōsə, ˈkô-, ˈᴋʜō-, ˈᴋʜô-/ ▶ **noun** (pl. same or **Xhosas**) **1** a member of a South African people traditionally living in the Eastern Cape Province. **2** the Bantu language of the Xhosa.
– ORIGIN Xhosa.

XHTML ▶ **abbreviation** Computing Extensible Hypertext Markup Language.

XL ▶ **abbreviation** extra large (as a clothes size).

Xmas /ˈkrisməs, ˈeksməs/ ▶ **noun** informal Christmas.
– ORIGIN *X* representing the initial Greek character of Greek *Khristos* 'Christ.'

XML ▶ **abbreviation** Extensible Markup Language.

X-rat·ed /ˈeks ˌrātid/ ▶ **adjective 1** pornographic or indecent. **2** (formerly) referring to a movie given an X classification.

X-ray /ˈeks ˌrā/ ▶ **noun 1** an electromagnetic wave of very short wavelength, able to pass through many materials opaque to light and so make it possible to see into or through them. **2** an image of the internal structure of an object produced by passing X-rays through it. ▶ **verb** photograph or examine something or someone with X-rays.
– ORIGIN from *X-* (because, when discovered in 1895, the nature of the rays was unknown).

xy·lem /ˈzīləm/ ▶ **noun** the tissue in plants that carries water and dissolved nutrients upward from the root and also helps to form the woody element in the stem.
– ORIGIN from Greek *xulon* 'wood.'

xy·lene /ˈzīˌlēn/ ▶ **noun** a liquid hydrocarbon obtained by distilling wood, coal tar, or petroleum, used in fuels and solvents.
– ORIGIN from Greek *xulon* 'wood.'

xy·lo·phone /ˈzīləˌfōn/ ▶ **noun** a musical instrument played by striking a row of wooden bars of graduated length with small hammers.
– ORIGIN from Greek *xulon* 'wood.'

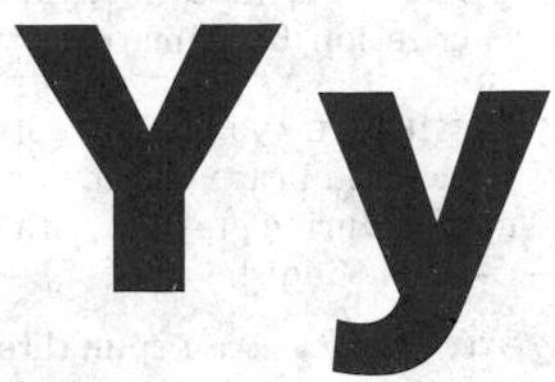

Y[1] (also **y**) ▶ **noun** (pl. **Ys** or **Y's**) **1** the twenty-fifth letter of the alphabet. **2** referring to an unknown or unspecified person or thing (coming second after 'x'). **3** (usu. *y*) the second unknown quantity in an algebraic expression. **4** (usu. *y*) referring to the secondary or vertical axis in a system of coordinates.

Y[2] ▶ **abbreviation** yen. ▶ **symbol** the chemical element yttrium.

y ▶ **abbreviation** year(s).

Y2K ▶ **abbreviation** year 2000 (with reference to the millennium bug).

yacht /yät/ ▶ **noun** **1** a medium-sized sailboat equipped for cruising or racing. **2** a powered boat or small ship equipped for cruising.
– DERIVATIVES **yacht·ing** noun.
– ORIGIN Dutch *jaghte*, from *jaghtschip* 'fast pirate ship.'

yachts·man /'yätsmən/ (or **yachtswoman**) ▶ **noun** (pl. **yachtsmen** or **yachtswomen**) a person who sails yachts.

yack /yak/ ▶ **noun & verb** variant spelling of **YAK**[2].

ya·hoo[1] /'yä,hōō, yä'hōō/ ▶ **noun** informal a rude, coarse, or violent person.
– ORIGIN the name of an imaginary people in Jonathan Swift's *Gulliver's Travels*.

ya·hoo[2] /yä'hōō/ ▶ **exclamation** expressing great joy or excitement.
– ORIGIN natural exclamation: first recorded in English in the 1970s.

Yah·weh /'yä,wā, -,we, -,vā/ ▶ **noun** a form of the Hebrew name of God used in the Bible.
– ORIGIN Hebrew.

yak[1] /yak/ ▶ **noun** a large ox with shaggy hair and large horns, used in Tibet to carry loads and for its milk, meat, and hide.
– ORIGIN Tibetan.

yak[2] (also **yack**) informal ▶ **verb** (**yaks, yakking, yakked**) talk at length about unimportant or boring subjects. ▶ **noun** a trivial or lengthy conversation.
– ORIGIN imitating the sound.

ya·ku·za /yä'kōōzə, 'yäkōō,zä/ ▶ **noun** (pl. same) (**the Yakuza**) a powerful Japanese criminal organization.
– ORIGIN Japanese, from the words for 'eight' + 'nine' + 'three,' referring to the worst hand in a gambling game.

Yale lock /yāl/ ▶ **noun** trademark a cylinder lock.
– ORIGIN named after the American locksmith Linus *Yale*, Jr.

y'all /yôl/ ▶ **contraction** you-all.

yam /yam/ ▶ **noun** **1** the edible starchy tuber of a tropical and subtropical climbing plant, eaten as a vegetable. **2** a sweet potato.
– ORIGIN from Portuguese *inhame* or former Spanish *iñame*.

yam·mer /'yamər/ informal ▶ **verb** **1** talk loudly and continuously. **2** make a loud, continuous noise. ▶ **noun** loud and continuous noise.
– ORIGIN Old English, 'to lament.'

yang /yaNG, yäNG/ ▶ **noun** (in Chinese philosophy) the active male principle of the universe. Contrasted with **YIN**.
– ORIGIN Chinese, 'male genitals,' 'sun,' 'positive.'

Yank /yaNGk/ ▶ **noun** informal short for **YANKEE**.

yank /yaNGk/ informal ▶ **verb** pull quickly and hard: *he yanked her to her feet.*

– SYNONYMS **jerk,** pull, tug, wrench.

▶ **noun** a sudden hard pull.
– ORIGIN unknown.

Yan·kee /'yaNGkē/ ▶ **noun** informal **1** often derogatory an American. **2** a person from New England or one of the US northern states. **3** historical a Union soldier in the Civil War. **4** a bet on four or more horses to win (or be placed) in different races.
– ORIGIN perhaps from Dutch *Janke*, from *Jan* 'John.'

yap /yap/ ▶ **verb** (**yaps, yapping, yapped**) **1** give a sharp, shrill bark. **2** informal talk at length in an irritating way. ▶ **noun** a sharp, shrill bark.
– DERIVATIVES **yap·py** adjective (informal).
– ORIGIN imitating the sound.

yard[1] /yärd/ ▶ **noun** **1** a unit of length equal to 3 feet (0.9144 meter). **2** a square or cubic yard, especially of sand or other building materials. **3** a long pole slung across a ship's mast for a sail to hang from.
– PHRASES **by the yard** in large numbers or quantities.
– ORIGIN Old English.

yard[2] ▶ **noun** **1** a piece of ground adjoining a building or house. **2** an area of land used for a particular purpose or business: *they're out in the yard loading lumber.*
– ORIGIN Old English, 'building, home, region.'

yard·age /'yärdij/ ▶ **noun** a distance or length measured in yards.

yard·arm /'yärd,ärm/ ▶ **noun** either end of the yard (long pole) slung across a ship's mast for a sail to hang from.

yard·bird /'yärd,bərd/ ▶ **noun** informal **1** a new military recruit, especially one given menial jobs to do. **2** a convict.
– ORIGIN perhaps suggested by **JAILBIRD**.

yard·man /'yärd,man/ ▶ **noun** (pl. **yardmen**) **1** a person working in a railroad or lumberyard. **2** a person who does various outdoor jobs.

yard sale ▶ **noun** a sale of miscellaneous secondhand items held on the grounds of the seller's home.

yard·stick /'yärd,stik/ ▶ **noun** **1** a standard used for judging the value or success of something: *test scores are not the only yardstick of a school's performance.* **2** a measuring rod a yard long.

– SYNONYMS **standard,** measure, gauge, scale, guide, guideline, indicator, test, touchstone, barometer, criterion, benchmark.

yar·mul·ke /ˈyämə(l)kə, ˈyärmə(l)kə/ (also **yarmulka**) ▶ **noun** a skullcap worn in public by Orthodox Jewish men or during prayer by other Jewish men.
– ORIGIN Yiddish.

yarn /yärn/ ▶ **noun 1** spun thread used for knitting, weaving, or sewing. **2** informal a long or rambling story.

– SYNONYMS **thread,** cotton, wool, fiber, filament.

– ORIGIN Old English.

yar·row /ˈyarō/ ▶ **noun** a plant with feathery leaves and heads of small white or pale pink flowers, used in herbal medicine.
– ORIGIN Old English.

yash·mak /yäsʜˈmäk, ˈyasʜˌmak/ ▶ **noun** a veil concealing all of the face except the eyes, worn by some Muslim women in public.
– ORIGIN Turkish.

yat·ter /ˈyatər/ informal ▶ **verb** talk continuously; chatter.
▶ **noun** continuous talk.
– ORIGIN imitating the sound.

yaw /yô/ ▶ **verb** (of a moving ship or aircraft) turn to one side or from side to side. ▶ **noun** yawing movement of a ship or aircraft.
– ORIGIN unknown.

yawl /yôl/ ▶ **noun** a kind of two-masted sailboat.
– ORIGIN from German *jolle* or Dutch *jol.*

yawn /yôn/ ▶ **verb 1** involuntarily open one's mouth wide and inhale deeply due to tiredness or boredom. **2** (often as adj. **yawning**) wide open: *a yawning chasm.*

– SYNONYMS (as adj. **yawning**) **gaping,** wide, cavernous, deep, huge, vast.

▶ **noun 1** an act of yawning. **2** informal a boring or tedious thing or event.
– ORIGIN Old English.

yawp /yôp/ ▶ **noun** a harsh or hoarse cry or yelp.
▶ **verb** shout or exclaim hoarsely.
– ORIGIN imitating the sound.

yaws /yôz/ ▶ **plural noun** (treated as sing.) a contagious tropical disease caused by a bacterium that enters cuts on the skin and causes small lesions that may develop into deep ulcers.
– ORIGIN probably from Carib.

Yb ▶ **symbol** the chemical element ytterbium.

Y chro·mo·some ▶ **noun** (in humans and other mammals) a sex chromosome that is normally present only in male cells, which are known as XY. Compare with **X CHROMOSOME.**

yd. ▶ **abbreviation** yard (measure).

ye[1] /yē/ ▶ **pronoun** (second person pl.) old use or dialect plural of **THOU**[1].
– ORIGIN Old English.

ye[2] ▶ **determiner** mock old-fashioned term for **THE.**
– ORIGIN from a misunderstanding of the Old English letter þ (now written *th*), which could be written as y, so that *the* could be written *ye*; it was never, however, pronounced as 'ye'

yea /yā/ old use or formal ▶ **adverb** yes. ▶ **noun** an answer indicating agreement.
– ORIGIN Old English.

yeah /ˈye(ə), ˈya(ə)/ (also **yeh** /ye/) ▶ **exclamation & noun** informal variant of **YES.**

year /yi(ə)r/ ▶ **noun 1** the time taken by the earth to make one complete orbit around the sun. **2** (also **calendar year**) the period of 365 days (or 366 days in leap years) starting from the first of January. **3** a period of the same length as this starting at a different point. **4** a similar period used for reckoning time according to other calendars. **5** (**one's years**) one's age or time of life. **6** (**years**) informal a very long time. **7** a set of students of similar ages who enter and leave a school or college at the same time: *we were in the same year at Choate.*
– PHRASES **year in, year out** continuously or repeatedly over a period of years.
– ORIGIN Old English.

year·book /ˈyi(ə)rˌbo͝ok/ ▶ **noun 1** an annual publication of the graduating class in a school or college, giving photographs of students and details of school activities in the previous year. **2** an annual publication giving details of events of the previous year, especially those connected with a particular area of activity.

year·ling /ˈyi(ə)rliɴɢ/ ▶ **noun 1** an animal of a year old, or in its second year. **2** a racehorse in the calendar year after the year in which it was born. ▶ **adjective** having lived for a year.

year·long ▶ **adjective** lasting for or throughout a year.

year·ly /ˈyi(ə)rlē/ ▶ **adjective & adverb** happening or produced once a year or every year.

– SYNONYMS **annually,** once a year, per annum, each/every year.

yearn /yərn/ ▶ **verb** have a strong feeling of loss and longing for something.

– SYNONYMS **long,** pine, crave, desire, want, wish, hanker, covet, hunger, thirst, ache; informal itch.

– DERIVATIVES **yearn·ing** noun & adjective.
– ORIGIN Old English.

year-on-year ▶ **adjective** (of figures, prices, etc.) as compared with the corresponding ones from a year earlier.

year-round ▶ **adjective** happening or continuing throughout the year.

yeast /yēst/ ▶ **noun 1** a microscopic single-celled fungus capable of converting sugar into alcohol and carbon dioxide. **2** a grayish-yellow preparation of the yeast fungus, used to make bread dough rise and to ferment beer, wine, etc. **3** Biology any single-celled fungus that reproduces by budding or dividing in two.
– DERIVATIVES **yeast·y** adjective.
– ORIGIN Old English.

yell /yel/ ▶ **noun** a loud, sharp cry. ▶ **verb** shout loudly.

– SYNONYMS **shout,** cry out, howl, wail, scream, shriek, screech, yelp, squeal, roar, bawl; informal holler.

– ORIGIN Old English.

yel·low /ˈyelō/ ▶ **adjective 1** of the color of egg yolks or ripe lemons. **2** offensive having a yellowish or olive skin (as used to describe Chinese or Japanese people). **3** informal cowardly.

– SYNONYMS golden, gold, blond/blonde, fair, flaxen, lemon, primrose, mustard.

▶ **noun** yellow color.
▶ **verb** (of paper, fabric, paint, etc.) become slightly yellow, especially with age.

– DERIVATIVES **yel·low·ish** adjective **yel·low·ness** noun **yel·low·y** adjective.
– ORIGIN Old English.

yel·low-bel·ly ▶ **noun** informal a coward.
– DERIVATIVES **yel·low-bel·lied** adjective.

yel·low card ▶ **noun** (especially in soccer) a yellow card shown by the referee to a player being cautioned.

yel·low fe·ver ▶ **noun** a tropical disease caused by a virus transmitted by mosquitoes, causing fever and jaundice and often fatal.

yel·low·fin /ˈyelō,fin/ (also **yellowfin tuna**) ▶ **noun** a tuna with yellow anal and dorsal fins that is an important food fish.

yel·low jack·et ▶ **noun** informal a wasp or hornet with bright yellow markings.

yel·low jer·sey ▶ **noun** (in a cycling race involving stages) a yellow jersey worn each day by the rider who is ahead on time over the whole race, and presented to the rider with the shortest overall time at the finish of the race.

yel·low jour·nal·ism ▶ **noun** journalism using sensationalism and crude exaggeration.
– DERIVATIVES **yel·low jour·nal·ist** noun.

Yel·low Pag·es (also **yellow pages**) ▶ **plural noun** trademark (in the UK) a telephone directory printed on yellow paper and listing businesses and other organizations according to the goods or services they offer.

yelp /yelp/ ▶ **noun** a short, sharp cry. ▶ **verb** make a yelp or yelps.
– ORIGIN from Old English, 'to boast.'

Yem·e·ni /ˈyemənē/ ▶ **noun** a person from Yemen. ▶ **adjective** relating to Yemen.

Yem·en·ite /ˈyemə,nīt/ ▶ **noun & adjective** another term for **YEMENI**.

yen¹ /yen/ ▶ **noun** (pl. same) the basic unit of money of Japan.
– ORIGIN from Japanese, 'round.'

yen² ▶ **noun** a strong desire to do or have something.
– ORIGIN first meaning 'a craving for a drug': from Chinese.

yeo·man /ˈyōmən/ ▶ **noun** (pl. **yeomen**) historical **1** a man owning a house and a small area of farming land. **2** a servant in a royal or noble household.
– ORIGIN probably from **YOUNG** + **MAN**.

Yeo·man of the Guard ▶ **noun** a member of the British monarch's bodyguard (now having only ceremonial duties).

yep /yep/ (also **yup**) ▶ **exclamation & noun** nonstandard variant of **YES**, representing informal pronunciation.

yer·ba ma·té /ˈyerbə ˈmä,tā, ˈyər-/ ▶ **noun** another term for **MATÉ**.

yes /yes/ ▶ **exclamation 1** used to confirm, agree to, or accept something. **2** used to reply to someone who is trying to attract one's attention. **3** used to express delight.

> – SYNONYMS **certainly,** very well, of course, by all means, sure, all right, absolutely, indeed, affirmative, agreed, roger; old use or dialect aye; informal yeah, yep.
> – ANTONYMS no.

▶ **noun** (pl. **yeses** or **yesses**) an answer or vote in favor of something.
– ORIGIN Old English.

ye·shi·va /yəˈsнēvə/ ▶ **noun** an Orthodox Jewish college or seminary.

yes-man ▶ **noun** informal a person who always agrees with people in authority.

yes·ter·day /ˈyestər,dā, -dē/ ▶ **adverb** on the day before today. ▶ **noun 1** the day before today. **2** the recent past.
– ORIGIN Old English.

yes·ter·year /ˈyestər,yir/ ▶ **noun** literary last year or the recent past.

yet /yet/ ▶ **adverb 1** up until now or then. **2** as soon as the present or a specified time: *wait, don't go yet.* **3** from now into the future for a specified length of time. **4** referring to something that will or may happen in the future. **5** still; even (used for emphasis): *yet another diet book.* **6** in spite of that. ▶ **conjunction** but at the same time.
– ORIGIN Old English.

yet·i /ˈyetē, ˈyātē/ ▶ **noun** a large hairy manlike creature said to live in the highest part of the Himalayas.
– ORIGIN Tibetan, 'little manlike animal.'

yew /yo͞o/ ▶ **noun** a coniferous tree with poisonous red fruit and springy wood.
– ORIGIN Old English.

Yid·dish /ˈyidisн/ ▶ **noun** a language used by Jews in or from central and eastern Europe, originally a German dialect with words from Hebrew and several modern languages. ▶ **adjective** relating to Yiddish.
– DERIVATIVES **Yid·dish·er** noun.
– ORIGIN from Yiddish *yidish daytsh* 'Jewish German.'

yield /yēld/ ▶ **verb 1** produce or provide a natural or industrial product. **2** produce a result, gain, or financial return. **3** give way to demands or pressure. **4** give up possession of: *residents vowed they will yield no more ground to increasing traffic.* **5** (of a mass or structure) give way under force or pressure.

> – SYNONYMS **1 produce,** bear, give, provide, afford, return, bring in, earn, realize, generate, deliver, pay out. **2 surrender,** capitulate, submit, admit defeat, back down, give in, cave in, raise the white flag, throw in the towel, give up the struggle.
> – ANTONYMS withhold, resist.

▶ **noun** an amount or result produced: *the milk yield was poor.*

> – SYNONYMS **profit,** gain, return, dividend, earnings.

– DERIVATIVES **yield·er** noun.
– ORIGIN Old English, 'pay, repay.'

> **CHOOSE THE RIGHT WORD**
>
> See **RELINQUISH**.

yin /yin/ ▶ **noun** (in Chinese philosophy) the passive female principle of the universe. Contrasted with **YANG**.
– ORIGIN Chinese, 'feminine,' 'moon,' 'shade.'

yip·pee /ˈyipē, ,yipˈē/ ▶ **exclamation** expressing excitement or delight.

y·lang-y·lang /ˈē,länɢ ˈē,länɢ/ ▶ **noun** a sweet-scented essential oil obtained from the flowers of a tropical tree, used in perfume and in aromatherapy.
– ORIGIN Tagalog.

YMCA ▶ **abbreviation** Young Men's Christian Association.

yo /yō/ ▶ **exclamation** informal used to greet someone, attract their attention, or express excitement.

yo·del /'yōdl/ ▸ verb (**yodels, yodeling, yodeled**) call or sing in a style that alternates rapidly between a normal voice and a very high one. ▸ noun a song or call of this type.
– DERIVATIVES **yo·del·er** noun.
– ORIGIN German *jodeln*.

yo·ga /'yōgə/ ▸ noun a Hindu spiritual discipline, a part of which, including breath control, simple meditation, and the holding of specific body positions, is widely practiced for health and relaxation.
– DERIVATIVES **yo·gic** adjective.
– ORIGIN Sanskrit, 'union.'

yo·gi /'yōgē/ ▸ noun (pl. **yogis**) a person who is skilled in yoga.
– ORIGIN Sanskrit.

yo·gurt /'yōgərt/ (also **yoghurt** or **yoghourt**) ▸ noun a thick liquid food prepared from milk that has been fermented by adding bacteria to it.
– ORIGIN Turkish.

yoke /yōk/ ▸ noun **1** a piece of wood fastened over the necks of two animals and attached to a plow or cart in order for them to pull it. **2** something that restricts freedom or is difficult to bear: *the yoke of imperialism*. **3** a part of an item of clothing that fits over the shoulders and to which the main part of the garment is attached. **4** (pl. same or **yokes**) a pair of animals joined together with a yoke. **5** a frame fitting over a person's neck and shoulders, used for carrying buckets or baskets. ▸ verb **1** join together or attach with a yoke. **2** bring people or things into a close relationship: *we are yoked to the fates of others*.
– ORIGIN Old English.

yo·kel /'yōkəl/ ▸ noun an unsophisticated country person.

> – SYNONYMS **rustic,** bumpkin, peasant, provincial; informal hayseed, hillbilly, hick.

– ORIGIN perhaps from dialect *yokel* 'green woodpecker.'

yolk /yōk/ ▸ noun the yellow inner part of a bird's egg, which is rich in protein and fat and nourishes the developing embryo.
– DERIVATIVES **yolked** adjective **yolk·y** adjective.
– ORIGIN Old English.

Yom Kip·pur /'yôm ki'po͝or, 'yōm, 'yäm, 'kipər/ ▸ noun the most solemn religious fast of the Jewish year, the last of the ten days of penitence that begin with Rosh Hashana (the Jewish New Year).
– ORIGIN Hebrew, 'day of atonement.'

yon /yän/ literary or dialect ▸ determiner & adverb yonder; that. ▸ pronoun that person or thing over there.
– ORIGIN Old English.

yon·der /'yändər/ old use or dialect ▸ adverb over there. ▸ determiner that or those (referring to something situated at a distance).

yo·ni /'yōnē/ ▸ noun (pl. **yonis**) Hinduism the vulva, regarded as a symbol of divine reproductive energy and represented by a circular stone.
– ORIGIN Sanskrit, 'source, womb, female genitals.'

yoo-hoo /'yo͞o ˌho͞o/ ▸ exclamation a call used to attract attention: *Yoo-hoo!—Is anyone there?* ▸ verb make such a call.

yore /yôr/ ▸ noun (in phrase **of yore**) literary of former times or long ago.
– ORIGIN Old English.

York·shire pud·ding ▸ noun a baked batter pudding typically eaten with roast beef.

York·shire ter·ri·er ▸ noun a small long-haired blue-gray and tan breed of terrier.

Yo·ru·ba /'yôrəbə/ ▸ noun (pl. same or **Yorubas**) **1** a member of an African people of SW Nigeria and Benin. **2** the language of the Yoruba.
– ORIGIN the name in Yoruba.

you /yo͞o/ ▸ pronoun (second person sing. or pl.) **1** used to refer to the person or people that the speaker is addressing. **2** used to refer to the person being addressed together with other people of the same type: *you Canadians*. **3** used to refer to any person in general.
– ORIGIN Old English.

you-all /'yo͞o ˌôl, yôl/ (also **y'all**) ▸ pronoun Southern US you (used to refer to more than one person).

you'd /yo͞od/ ▸ contraction **1** you had. **2** you would.

you'll /yo͞ol/ ▸ contraction you will; you shall.

young /yəNG/ ▸ adjective (**younger, youngest**) **1** having lived or existed for only a short time. **2** relating to or typical of young people.

> – SYNONYMS **1 youthful,** juvenile, junior, adolescent, teenage, in one's salad days. **2** *a young industry* **new,** fledgling, developing, budding, in its infancy, emerging, in the making. **3 immature,** childish, inexperienced, naive, green, wet behind the ears.
> – ANTONYMS old, mature.

▸ noun (treated as pl.) young children or animals; offspring.

> – SYNONYMS **offspring,** progeny, family, babies, litter, brood.

– DERIVATIVES **young·ish** adjective.
– ORIGIN Old English.

young gun ▸ noun informal an energetic and confident young man.

young·ster /'yəNGstər/ ▸ noun a child or young person.

> – SYNONYMS **child,** teenager, adolescent, youth, juvenile, minor, junior, boy, girl; Scottish lass, lassie; informal teen, kid, lad, whippersnapper.

Young Turk ▸ noun a young person eager for complete social or political change.
– ORIGIN with reference to a revolutionary party active in the Ottoman Empire in the late 19th and early 20th centuries.

your /yôr, yo͝or/ ▸ possessive determiner **1** belonging to or associated with the person or people that the speaker is addressing. **2** belonging to or associated with any person in general. **3** (**Your**) used when addressing the holder of certain titles.
– ORIGIN Old English.

> **USAGE**
>
> Do not confuse the possessive **your** meaning 'belonging to you' (*let me talk to your daughter*) with the form **you're**, which is short for **you are** (*you're a good cook*).

you're /yo͝or, yôr/ ▸ contraction you are.

yours /yôrz, yo͝orz/ ▸ possessive pronoun used to refer to something belonging to or associated with the person or people that the speaker is addressing.

> **USAGE**
>
> There is no apostrophe: the spelling should be **yours** not *your's*.

your·self /yər'self, yôr-, yo͝or-/ ▸ pronoun (second person sing.) (pl. **yourselves**) **1** used as the object of a verb or preposition when this is the same as the subject of the clause and the subject is the person or people being addressed. **2** (emphatic) you personally.

youth /yo͞oTH/ ▸ **noun** (pl. **youths**) **1** the period between childhood and adult age. **2** a young man. **3** the state or quality of being young, energetic, or immature: *men are attracted to youth and beauty.* **4** (treated as sing. or pl.) young people.

– SYNONYMS **1 early years,** teens, adolescence, boyhood, girlhood, childhood, minority. **2 young man,** boy, juvenile, teenager, adolescent, junior, minor; informal lad, kid.

– ORIGIN Old English.

youth cen·ter ▸ **noun** a place or organization providing leisure activities for young people.

youth·ful /ˈyo͞oTHfəl/ ▸ **adjective 1** young or seeming young. **2** typical of young people; energetic, fresh, or immature.

– SYNONYMS **young,** boyish, girlish, fresh-faced, young-looking, spry, sprightly, vigorous, active.
– ANTONYMS elderly.

– DERIVATIVES **youth·ful·ly** adverb **youth·ful·ness** noun.

WORD TOOLKIT

youthful ...	immature ...	juvenile ...
exuberance	cell	delinquent
enthusiasm	tissue	offender
indiscretion	seed	court
appearance	fruit	crime
passion	leaf	nuisance
idealism	stage	diabetes
innocence	male	arthritis

youth hos·tel ▸ **noun** a place providing inexpensive accommodations, aimed mainly at young people on vacation.
– DERIVATIVES **youth-hos·tel·ing** noun.

you've /yo͞ov/ ▸ **contraction** you have.

yowl /youl/ ▸ **noun** a loud wailing cry of pain or distress. ▸ **verb** make a loud wailing cry.
– ORIGIN imitating the sound.

yo-yo /ˈyō ˌyō/ ▸ **noun** (pl. **yo-yos**) trademark (in the UK) a toy consisting of a pair of joined disks with a deep groove between them in which string is attached and wound, which can be spun down and up by its weight as the string unwinds and rewinds. ▸ **verb** (**yo-yoes, yo-yoing, yo-yoed**) move up and down repeatedly; fluctuate: *the stock market has yo-yoed.*
– ORIGIN probably from a language of the Philippines.

YT ▸ **abbreviation** Yukon Territory.

yt·ter·bi·um /iˈtərbēəm/ ▸ **noun** a silvery-white metallic chemical element.
– ORIGIN from *Ytterby* in Sweden.

yt·tri·um /ˈitrēəm/ ▸ **noun** a grayish-white metallic chemical element.
– ORIGIN from *Ytterby* (see **YTTERBIUM**).

yu·an /yo͞oˈän/ ▸ **noun** (pl. same) the basic unit of money of China.
– ORIGIN from Chinese, 'round.'

yuc·ca /ˈyəkə/ ▸ **noun** a plant with swordlike leaves and white bell-shaped flowers, native to warm regions of the US and Mexico.
– ORIGIN Carib.

yuck /yək/ (also **yuk**) informal ▸ **exclamation** used to express disgust. ▸ **noun** something messy or disgusting.
– DERIVATIVES **yuck·y** (also **yukky**) adjective.
– ORIGIN imitating the sound.

Yu·go·slav /ˈyo͞ogōˌsläv, ˌyo͞ogōˈsläv, -gə-/ ▸ **noun** a person from any of the states of the former country of Yugoslavia.
– DERIVATIVES **Yu·go·sla·vi·an** noun & adjective.

Yule /yo͞ol/ (also **Yuletide**) ▸ **noun** old use Christmas.
– ORIGIN Old English or Old Norse.

yule log ▸ **noun 1** a large log traditionally burned in the hearth on Christmas Eve. **2** a log-shaped cake eaten at Christmas.

yum /yəm/ (also **yum-yum**) informal ▸ **exclamation** used to express pleasure at eating, or at the prospect of eating, a particular food. ▸ **adjective** (of food) delicious.
– ORIGIN imitative.

yum·my /ˈyəmē/ ▸ **adjective** (**yummier, yummiest**) informal very good to eat; delicious.

yup /yəp/ ▸ **exclamation & noun** variant form of **YEP**.

Yu·pik /ˈyo͞opik/ ▸ **noun** (pl. same or **Yupiks**) **1** a member of an Eskimo people of Siberia, the Aleutian Islands, and Alaska. **2** any of the languages of the Yupik.
– ORIGIN Alaskan Yupik, 'real person.'

yup·pie /ˈyəpē/ (also **yuppy**) ▸ **noun** (pl. **yuppies**) informal, derogatory a well-paid young middle-class professional working in a city.
– DERIVATIVES **yup·pie·dom** noun.
– ORIGIN partly from the initial letters of *young urban professional.*

yup·pie flu ▸ **noun** informal derogatory term for **CHRONIC FATIGUE SYNDROME**.

yup·pi·fy /ˈyəpəˌfī/ ▸ **verb** (**yuppifies, yuppifying, yuppified**) informal, derogatory make a place more upmarket or expensive, in keeping with the taste and lifestyle of yuppies.
– DERIVATIVES **yup·pi·fi·ca·tion** /ˌyəpəfiˈkāSHən/ noun.

yurt /yo͝ort, yərt/ ▸ **noun** a circular tent of felt or skins used by nomads in Mongolia, Siberia, and Turkey.
– ORIGIN Russian *yurta.*

YWCA ▸ **abbreviation** Young Women's Christian Association.

Zz

Z /zē/ (also **z**) ▶ **noun** (pl. **Zs** or **Z's**) **1** the twenty-sixth letter of the alphabet. **2** (usu. z) the third unknown quantity in an algebraic expression. **3** used in repeated form to represent buzzing or snoring.

za·ba·glio·ne /ˌzäbəl'yōnē/ ▶ **noun** an Italian dessert made of whipped egg yolks, sugar, and wine.
– ORIGIN Italian.

zag /zag/ ▶ **noun** a sharp change of direction in a zigzag course: *we traveled in a series of zigs and zags.* ▶ **verb** (**zagged, zagging**) make a sharp change of direction: *a long path zigged and zagged through the woods.*
– ORIGIN shortening of ZIGZAG.

Za·ir·e·an /zä'i(ə)rēən/ (also **Zairian**) ▶ **noun** a person from the Democratic Republic of Congo (known as Zaire from 1971 to 1997). ▶ **adjective** relating to Zaire.

Zam·bi·an /'zambēən/ ▶ **noun** a person from Zambia. ▶ **adjective** relating to Zambia.

za·ny /'zānē/ ▶ **adjective** (**zanier, zaniest**) amusingly unconventional and individual.

> – SYNONYMS **eccentric,** odd, unconventional, bizarre, weird, mad, crazy, comic, madcap, quirky, idiosyncratic; informal wacky, oddball, off the wall, daft, kooky.
> – ANTONYMS conventional.

– DERIVATIVES **za·ni·ly** adverb **za·ni·ness** noun.
– ORIGIN Italian *zani* or *zanni*, Venetian form of *Gianni, Giovanni* 'John,' a clown in traditional Italian comedy.

zap /zap/ informal ▶ **verb** (**zaps, zapping, zapped**) **1** destroy or get rid of: *it's vital to zap stress fast.* **2** move or do suddenly and rapidly. **3** use a remote control to change television channels, operate a DVD player, etc. **4** cook or warm food or a beverage in a microwave oven. ▶ **noun** a sudden burst of energy or sound.
– ORIGIN imitating the sound.

zap·per /'zapər/ ▶ **noun** informal **1** a remote control for a television, DVD player, etc. **2** an electronic device used for killing insects.

zap·py /'zapē/ ▶ **adjective** (**zappier, zappiest**) informal lively; energetic.

za·zen /ˌzä'zen/ ▶ **noun** Zen meditation.
– ORIGIN Japanese.

zeal /zēl/ ▶ **noun** great energy or enthusiasm for a cause or aim.

> – SYNONYMS **enthusiasm,** passion, ardor, fervor, fervency, fire, devotion, gusto, vigor, energy, vehemence, intensity, eagerness, fanaticism.
> – ANTONYMS apathy.

– ORIGIN Greek *zēlos*.

zeal·ot /'zelət/ ▶ **noun** a person who follows a religion, cause, or policy very strictly or enthusiastically.

> – SYNONYMS **fanatic,** enthusiast, extremist, radical, diehard, activist, militant.

– DERIVATIVES **zeal·ot·ry** noun.

zeal·ous /'zeləs/ ▶ **adjective** having or showing great enthusiasm or energy for a cause or aim.

> – SYNONYMS **ardent,** fervent, passionate, impassioned, enthusiastic, devoted, committed, dedicated, eager, keen, avid, vehement, intense, fierce, fanatical.
> – ANTONYMS apathetic.

– DERIVATIVES **zeal·ous·ly** adverb **zeal·ous·ness** noun.

WORD TOOLKIT

zealous ...	fervent ...	fanatical ...
fan	hope	devotion
pursuit	appeal	support
nationalism	imagination	groups
missionary	embrace	hatred

ze·bra /'zēbrə/ ▶ **noun** an African wild horse with black-and-white stripes and an erect mane.
– ORIGIN from Italian, Spanish, or Portuguese, first meaning 'wild ass.'

ze·bu /'zēˌb(y)o͞o/ ▶ **noun** a breed of domesticated ox with a humped back.
– ORIGIN French.

zed /zed/ ▶ **noun** Brit. the letter Z.
– ORIGIN from Greek *zēta*.

zee /zē/ ▶ **noun** the letter Z.
– ORIGIN variant of ZED.

zeit·geist /'tsītˌgīst, 'zīt-/ ▶ **noun** the characteristic spirit or mood of a particular period of history.
– ORIGIN German.

Zen /zen/ ▶ **noun** a Japanese school of Buddhism emphasizing the value of meditation and intuition.
– ORIGIN Japanese, 'meditation.'

ze·na·na /zə'nänə/ ▶ **noun** (in India and Iran) separate living quarters for women in a house.
– ORIGIN Persian and Urdu, 'woman.'

ze·nith /'zēniᴛʜ/ ▶ **noun** **1** the time at which someone or something is most powerful or successful: *the designer reached his zenith in the sixties.* **2** the point in the sky directly overhead. **3** the highest point in the sky reached by the sun or moon.

> – SYNONYMS **high point,** crowning point, height, top, acme, peak, pinnacle, apex, apogee, crown, crest, summit, culmination, climax.
> – ANTONYMS nadir.

– DERIVATIVES **ze·nith·al** adjective.
– ORIGIN from an Arabic phrase meaning 'path over the head.'

zeph·yr /'zefər/ ▶ **noun** literary a soft, gentle breeze.
– ORIGIN Greek *zephuros* 'god of the west wind, west wind.'

Zep·pe·lin /ˈzep(ə)lən/ ▶ **noun** a large German airship of the early 20th century.
– ORIGIN named after Ferdinand, Count von *Zeppelin*, German airship pioneer.

ze·ro /ˈzi(ə)rō, ˈzēˌrō/ ▶ **cardinal number** (pl. **zeros**) **1** the figure 0; naught. **2** a point on a scale or instrument from which a positive or negative quantity is calculated. **3** a temperature of 0°C (32°F), marking the freezing point of water. **4** the lowest possible amount or level: *I rated my chances as zero.*

– SYNONYMS **nothing,** nil, o, naught/nought; informal zilch, zip, nada, diddly-squat.

▶ **verb** (**zeroes, zeroing, zeroed**) **1** (**zero in on**) target or focus attention on: *drugs that zero in on diseased cells.* **2** adjust an instrument to zero. **3** set the sights of a gun for firing.
– ORIGIN Arabic, 'cipher.'

ze·ro hour ▶ **noun** the time at which a military or other operation is set to begin.

ze·ro-sum ▶ **adjective** (of a game or situation) in which whatever is gained by one side is lost by the other.

ze·ro tol·er·ance ▶ **noun** strict enforcement of the law regarding any form of antisocial behavior.

zest /zest/ ▶ **noun 1** great enthusiasm and energy: *her remarkable zest for life.* **2** the quality of being exciting or interesting. **3** the outer colored part of the peel of citrus fruit, used as flavoring.

– SYNONYMS **enthusiasm,** gusto, relish, appetite, eagerness, keenness, zeal, passion, energy, liveliness.

– DERIVATIVES **zest·ful** adjective **zest·y** adjective.
– ORIGIN French *zeste.*

zest·er /ˈzestər/ ▶ **noun** a kitchen utensil for scraping or peeling zest from citrus fruit.

zeug·ma /ˈzo͞ogmə/ ▶ **noun** a figure of speech in which a word applies to two others in different senses (e.g., *John and his driving license expired last week*).
– ORIGIN Greek.

zi·do·vu·dine /zīˈdävyəˌdēn, zə-, -ˈdō-/ ▶ **noun** an antiviral drug used to slow the growth of HIV infection in the body.

zig /zig/ ▶ **noun** a sharp change of direction in a zigzag course: *we traveled in a series of zigs and zags.* ▶ **verb** (**zigged, zigging**) make a sharp change of direction: *we zigged to the right.*
– ORIGIN shortening of **ZIGZAG**.

zig·gu·rat /ˈzigəˌrat/ ▶ **noun** (in ancient Mesopotamia, part of present-day Iraq) a tower in the shape of a tiered pyramid, often with a temple on top.
– ORIGIN from an ancient Semitic language.

zig·zag /ˈzigˌzag/ ▶ **noun** a line or course having sharp alternate right and left turns. ▶ **adjective & adverb** veering to right and left alternately. ▶ **verb** (**zigzags, zigzagging, zigzagged**) take a zigzag course.

– SYNONYMS **twist,** meander, snake, wind, weave, swerve.

– ORIGIN German *Zickzack.*

zilch /zilCH/ ▶ **pronoun** informal nothing.
– ORIGIN perhaps from a Mr. *Zilch*, a character in *Ballyhoo*, a 1930s magazine.

zil·lion /ˈzilyən/ ▶ **cardinal number** informal a very large number of people or things.
– DERIVATIVES **zil·lion·aire** noun **zil·lionth** ordinal number.
– ORIGIN from Z + **MILLION**.

Zim·bab·we·an /zimˈbäbwāən, -wēən/ ▶ **noun** a person from Zimbabwe. ▶ **adjective** relating to Zimbabwe.

zinc /ziNGk/ ▶ **noun** a silvery-white metallic chemical element that is used in making brass and for coating iron and steel as a protection against corrosion.
– ORIGIN German *Zink.*

zine /zēn/ (also **'zine**) ▶ **noun** informal **1** a magazine, especially a fanzine. **2** a webzine.

Zin·fan·del /ˈzinfənˌdel/ ▶ **noun** a variety of black wine grape grown in California, from which a red wine is made.
– ORIGIN unknown.

zing /ziNG/ informal ▶ **noun** energy, enthusiasm, or liveliness. ▶ **verb** move swiftly.
– DERIVATIVES **zing·y** adjective.
– ORIGIN imitating the sound.

zing·er /ˈziNGər/ ▶ **noun** informal **1** a striking or amusing remark. **2** an outstanding person or thing: *a zinger of a shot.*

zin·ni·a /ˈzinēə/ ▶ **noun** a plant of the daisy family with bright showy flowers.
– ORIGIN named after the German physician and botanist Johann G. *Zinn.*

Zi·on /ˈzīən/ (also **Sion** /ˈsīən/) ▶ **noun 1** the Jewish people or religion. **2** (in Christian thought) the heavenly city or kingdom of heaven.
– ORIGIN Hebrew, the name of the hill in Jerusalem on which the city of David was built.

Zi·on·ism /ˈzīəˌnizəm/ ▶ **noun** a movement for the development and protection of a Jewish nation in Israel.
– DERIVATIVES **Zi·on·ist** noun & adjective.

zip /zip/ ▶ **noun 1** informal energy or liveliness. **2** British term for **ZIPPER**.

– SYNONYMS **energy,** liveliness, vivacity, verve, zest; informal pep, zing, pizzazz.

▶ **verb** (**zips, zipping, zipped**) **1** fasten something with a zipper. **2** informal move at high speed. **3** Computing compress a file so that it takes up less space.

– SYNONYMS **hurry,** rush, dart, dash, speed, shoot, fly; informal tear, belt, zoom, whizz.

▶ **pronoun** informal nothing at all.
– ORIGIN imitating the sound.

zip code (also **ZIP code**) ▶ **noun** a five- or nine-digit postal code.
– ORIGIN from the initial letters of *zone improvement plan.*

zip file ▶ **noun** a computer file whose contents are compressed for storage or transmission.
– ORIGIN from the shareware program *WinZip*, a popular file compression utility.

zip·per /ˈzipər/ ▶ **noun** a fastener consisting of two flexible strips of metal or plastic with interlocking projections that are closed or opened by pulling a slide along them. ▶ **verb** fasten something with a zipper.

zip·py /ˈzipē/ ▶ **adjective** (**zippier, zippiest**) informal **1** bright, fresh, or lively. **2** fast or speedy.

zir·con /ˈzərˌkän/ ▶ **noun** a brown or semitransparent mineral, used as a gem and in industry.
– ORIGIN German *Zirkon.*

zir·co·ni·um /ˌzərˈkōnēəm/ ▶ **noun** a hard silver-gray metallic chemical element.

zit /zit/ ▶ **noun** informal a pimple on the skin.
– DERIVATIVES **zit·ty** adjective.
– ORIGIN unknown.

zith·er /ˈziTHər, ˈziTH-/ ▶ **noun** a musical instrument with numerous strings stretched across a flat soundbox, placed horizontally and played with the fingers and a plectrum.
– ORIGIN German.

zlo·ty /ˈzlôtē, ˈzlä-/ ▶ **noun** (pl. same, **zlotys**, or **zloties**) the basic unit of money of Poland.
– ORIGIN from Polish, 'golden.'

Zn ▶ **symbol** the chemical element zinc.

zo·di·ac /ˈzōdē,ak/ ▶ **noun** an area of the sky in which the sun, moon, and planets appear to lie, divided by astrologers into twelve equal divisions or signs.
– DERIVATIVES **zo·di·a·cal** /zōˈdīəkəl/ adjective.
– ORIGIN Greek *zōidiakos*.

zom·bie /ˈzämbē/ ▶ **noun 1** informal a person who seems to be barely aware of or interested in what is happening. **2** a corpse supposedly brought back to life by witchcraft.
– DERIVATIVES **zom·bi·fy** verb (**zombifies, zombifying, zombified**).
– ORIGIN West African.

zone /zōn/ ▶ **noun 1** an area that has a particular characteristic or use, or is subject to certain restrictions. **2** (also **time zone**) a range of longitudes where a common standard time is used.

– SYNONYMS **area,** sector, section, belt, stretch, region, territory, district, quarter, neighborhood.

▶ **verb** divide an area into zones.
– DERIVATIVES **zon·al** adjective.
– ORIGIN Greek, 'girdle.'

zonk /zäNGk, zôNGk/ ▶ **verb** informal **1** (**zonk out**) fall suddenly and heavily asleep. **2** hit someone or something heavily. **3** (as adj. **zonked**) under the influence of drugs or alcohol.
– ORIGIN imitating the sound.

zoo /zo͞o/ ▶ **noun 1** a place that keeps wild animals for study, conservation, or display to the public. **2** informal a confused or chaotic situation.
– ORIGIN short for *zoological garden*.

zo·o·ge·og·ra·phy /,zōəjēˈägrəfē/ ▶ **noun** the branch of zoology concerned with the geographical distribution of animals.
– DERIVATIVES **zo·o·ge·og·ra·pher** noun **zo·o·ge·o·graph·ic** /,zōə,jēəˈgrafik/ adjective **zo·o·ge·o·graph·i·cal** /,zōə,jēəˈgrafikəl/ adjective.

zo·oid /ˈzō,oid/ ▶ **noun** Zoology an individual member of a colony of invertebrate animals.

zoo·keep·er /ˈzo͞o,kēpər/ ▶ **noun** a person employed to look after the animals in a zoo.

zo·ol·o·gy /zōˈäləjē, zo͞o-/ ▶ **noun 1** the scientific study of animals. **2** the animal life of a particular region or period.
– DERIVATIVES **zo·o·log·i·cal** /,zōəˈläjikəl, ,zo͞oə-/ adjective **zo·o·log·i·cal·ly** /,zōəˈläjik(ə)lē, ,zo͞oə-/ adverb **zo·ol·o·gist** noun.
– ORIGIN from Greek *zōion* 'animal.'

zoom /zo͞om/ ▶ **verb 1** move or travel very quickly. **2** (of a camera) change smoothly from a long shot to a closeup or vice versa.

– SYNONYMS **hurry,** rush, dash, race, speed, sprint, career, shoot, hurtle, fly; informal tear, belt, whiz.

– ORIGIN imitating the sound.

zoom lens ▶ **noun** a lens allowing a camera to zoom by varying the distance between the center of the lens and its focus.

zo·o·mor·phic /,zōəˈmôrfik/ ▶ **adjective** having or representing animal forms or gods of animal form: *zoomorphic art*.
– ORIGIN from Greek *zōion* 'animal' + *morphē* 'form.'

zo·o·plank·ton /ˈzōə,plaNGktən/ ▶ **noun** Biology plankton consisting of small animals and the immature stages of larger animals.

zoot suit /zo͞ot/ ▶ **noun** a man's suit typically having a long loose jacket with padded shoulders and high-waisted tapering trousers, popular in the 1940s.
– ORIGIN from a rhyme on **SUIT**.

Zo·ro·as·tri·an·ism /,zôrōˈastrēə,nizəm/ ▶ **noun** a religion of ancient Persia based on the worship of a single god, founded by the prophet Zoroaster (also called Zarathustra) in Persia in the 6th century BC.
– DERIVATIVES **Zo·ro·as·tri·an** adjective & noun.

zouk /zo͞ok/ ▶ **noun** a style of popular music combining Caribbean and Western elements and having a fast heavy beat.
– ORIGIN from a word in a Creole language of Guadeloupe meaning 'to party.'

zounds /zoundz/ ▶ **exclamation** old use or humorous expressing surprise or indignation.
– ORIGIN from *God's wounds*.

Zr ▶ **symbol** the chemical element zirconium.

zuc·chi·ni /zo͞oˈkēnē/ ▶ **noun** (pl. same or **zucchinis**) a green variety of smooth-skinned summer squash.
– ORIGIN Italian 'little gourd.'

Zu·lu /ˈzo͞olo͞o/ ▶ **noun 1** a member of a South African people. **2** the Bantu language of the Zulus.

zy·de·co /ˈzīdə,kō/ ▶ **noun** a kind of black American dance music originally from Louisiana, typically featuring accordion and guitar.
– ORIGIN Louisiana Creole.

zy·gote /ˈzī,gōt/ ▶ **noun** Biology a cell resulting from the fusion of two gametes.
– DERIVATIVES **zy·got·ic** /zīˈgätik/ adjective.
– ORIGIN from Greek *zugōtos* 'yoked.'